Chilton's 1982 AUTOMOTIVE SERVICE MANUAL

Editor-in-Chief Paul A. Murphy, S.A.E.

Managing Editor John H. Weise, S.A.E. ☐ **Specifications Editor** Harry Eissler
Service Editors Arthur Birney, Mark F. Devlin, David Lee,
Robert McAnally, Larry A. Stovey

National Sales Manager Albert M. Kushnerick ☐ **Assistant** Jacquelyn T. Powers
Regional Managers Joseph Andrews, Jr., James O. Callahan

Production Manager Warren Owens
Assistant Production Manager Timothy Frelick ☐ **Production Assistant** Nancy A. Hassler
Mechanical Pasteup Dru Brown, Donna P. Fisher, Robin Miller, Margaret A. Stoner

OFFICERS: President William A. Barbour ☐ **Executive Vice President** James Miades
Vice President & General Manager John P. Kushnerick

CHILTON BOOK COMPANY Chilton Way, Radnor, Pa. 19089

Manufactured in USA © 1981 Chilton Book Company ISBN 0-8019-7127-6 Library of Congress Catalog Card No. 54-17274

1234567890 0987654321

HOW TO USE THIS MANUAL

For convenience, this Manual is divided into two main sections:

"A" Section: The Car Section is in the front of the manual and lists all American passenger cars from 1976 through 1982. A Vehicle Identification Number method of engine identification is listed in every Car Section, to thoroughly acquaint the mechanic with the Power-to-Car Model involved; engine identification being more important now than ever.

"B" Section: The Unit Repair Section is designed to guide the mechanic in Step-By-Step repair procedures of specific areas of the car. The treatment generally comprises unit reconditioning procedures. Specific component diagnosis and troubleshooting charts, as well as illustrated meter and test instrument hook-ups, are included. Illustrations, charts and tables put scientific diagnosis on an understandable basis.

SAFETY NOTICE

Proper service and repair procedures are vital to the safe, reliable operation of all motor vehicles, as well as the personal safety of those performing repairs. This manual outlines procedures for servicing and repairing vehicles using safe effective methods. The procedures contain many NOTES, CAUTIONS and WARNINGS which should be followed along with standard safety procedures to eliminate the possibility of personal injury or improper service which could damage the vehicle or compromise its safety.

It is important to note that repair procedures and techniques, tools and parts for servicing motor vehicles, as well as the skill and experience of the individual performing the work vary widely. It is not possible to anticipate all of the conceivable ways or conditions under which vehicles may be serviced, or to provide cautions as to all of the possible hazards that may result. Standard and accepted safety precautions and equipment should be used when handling toxic or flammable fluids, and safety goggles or other protection should be used during cutting, grinding, chiseling, prying, or any other process that can cause material removal or projectiles.

Some procedures require the use of tools specially designed for a specific purpose. Before substituting another tool or procedure, you must be completely satisfied that neither your personal safety, nor the performance of the vehicle will be endangered.

AMC PASSENGER CARS AND JEEP

INDEX

MODEL IDENTIFICATION

Passenger Cars

1978 AMX
W.B. **108**″ Length **183.6**″ Ship. Wgt. 6 Cyl. 2 Dr. 2047 Lbs.

1979 AMX
W.B. **96.0**″ Length **168.5**″ Ship. Wgt. 2 Dr. 2970 Lbs.

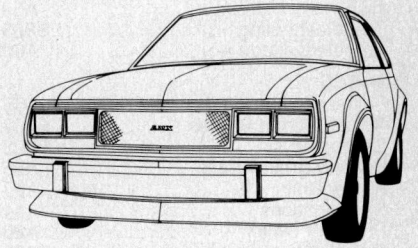

1980 AMX
W.B. **96**″. Length **168**″. Ship. Wgt. Approx. 2939 Lbs.

1978 CONCORD
W.B. **108**″ Length **183.6**″ Ship. Wgt. 6 Cyl. 2 Dr. 3047 Lbs.

1979 CONCORD
W.B. **108.0**″ Length **186.0**″ Ship. Wgt. 2 Dr. 2946 Lbs.

1980 CONCORD
W.B. **108**″. Length **186**″. Ship. Wgt. 2 Dr. Approx. 2710 Lbs.

1981-82 CONCORD
W.B. **108.0**″. Length **185.0**″. 6 Cyl. 2 Dr. Curb Wgt. 2756 Lbs.

1976 GREMLIN
W.B. **96**″. Length **170**″. Ship Wgt. 6 Cyls. 2 Dr. 2771 Lbs. 8 Cyl. 2 Dr. 3037 Lbs.

1977 GREMLIN
W.B. **96**″. Length **167**″. Width 71″. Ship. Wgt. 6 Cyl. 2 Dr. 2777 Lbs.

1978 GREMLIN

W.B. 96″ Length 166.56″ Ship. Wgt. 4 Cyl. 2 Dr. 2820 Lbs.

1976 HORNET

W.B. 108″. Length 186″. Ship. Wgt. 6 Cyl. 2 Dr. 2909 Lbs. 4 Dr. 2972 Lbs. S/W 3040 Lbs. H/B 2920 Lbs. 8 Cyl. 2 Dr. 3142 Lbs. 4 Dr. 3204 Lbs. S/W 3273 Lbs. H/B 3153 Lbs.

1977 HORNET

W.B. 108″. Length 186″. Width″. Ship. Wgt. V8 2 Dr. H/B 3192 Lbs.

1976 MATADOR

W.B. 118″, 2D 114″. Length 216″, 2D 210″. Ship. Wgt. 6 Cyl. 2 Dr. 3562 Lbs. 4 Dr. 3589 Lbs. 8 Cyl. 2 Dr. 3795 Lbs. 4 Dr. 3822 Lbs. S/W 4025 Lbs.

1977 MATADOR

W.B. 118″, Cpe. 114″. Length 216″, Cpe. 210″. Width 78″. Ship. Wgt. 6 Cyl. 2 Dr. 3118 Lbs.

1978 MATADOR

W.B. 114.0″ Length 209.9″ Ship. Wgt. 6 Cyl. 2 Dr. 3709 Lbs.

1976 PACER

W.B. 100″. Length 170″. Ship. Wgt. 6 Cyl. 3114 Lbs.

1977 PACER

W.B. 100″. Length 170″, S/W 174″. Width 77″. Ship. Wgt. 6 Cyl. 2 Dr. 3671 V8 2 Dr. 3878 Lbs.

1978 PACER

W.B. 100″ Length 172.1″ Ship. Wgt. 6 Cyl. 2 Dr. 3236 Lbs.

1979 PACER

W.B. 100.0″ Length 172.7″ Ship. Wgt. 2 Dr. H.B. 3204 Lbs.

1980 PACER

W.B. 100″. Length 172.7″. Ship. Wgt. Hatchback Approx. 3197 Lbs.

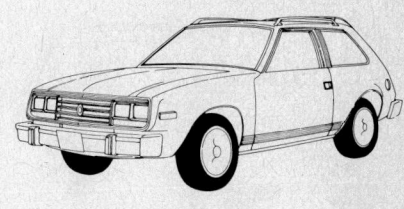

1979 SPIRIT

W.B. 96.0″ Length 166.8″ Ship. Wgt. 2 Dr. 2517 Lbs.

AMC PASSENGER CARS AND JEEP

1980 SPIRIT

W.B. 96″. Length 169″. Length 169″. Ship. Wgt. Liftback Approx. 2615 Lbs.

1981-82 SPIRIT

W.B. 96.0″. Length 167.0″. 4 Cyl. 2 Dr. Curb Wgt. 2621 Lbs.

1980 EAGLE

W.B. 109.3″. Length 186.2″. Ship. Wgt. 2 Dr. Approx. 3463 Lbs.

1981-82 EAGLE

W.B. 109.3″. Length 183.2″. 6 Cyl. 2 Dr. Ship. Wgt. 3274 Lbs.

Jeeps

1976 CHEROKEE

W.B. 198.7″ Length 183.5″ Ship. Wgt. 6 Cyl. 3918 Lbs.

1977 CHEROKEE

W.B. 108.7″ Length 183.5″ Ship. Wgt. 6 Cyl. 3971 Lbs.

1978 CHEROKEE

W.B. 108.7″ Length 183.5″ Ship. Wgt. 6 Cyl. 3975 Lbs.

1979 CHEROKEE

W.B. 108.7″. Length 183.5″. Ship. Wgt. 6 Cyl. 3975 Lbs.

1980 CHEROKEE

W.B. 108.7″. Length 183.5″. Ship. Wgt. Approx. 3975 Lbs.

1981-82 CHEROKEE

W.B. 108.7″. Length 183.5″. 6 Cyl. 2 Dr. Ship. Wgt. 3780 Lbs.

1978–80 CJ5

W.B. **83.5″** Length 138.4″ Ship. Wgt. 6 Cyl. 2610 Lbs.

1981-82 CJ5

W.B. **8315″**. Length 144.3″. 6 Cyl. Ship. Wgt. 2460 Lbs.

1978–80 CJ7

W.B. **93.5″** Length 147.9″ Ship. Wgt. 6 Cyl. 2655 Lbs.

1981-82 CJ7

W.B. **93.5″**. Length 153.2″. 6 Cyl. Ship. Wgt. 2505 Lbs.

1976 WAGONEER

W.B. **108.7″** Length 183.5″ Ship. Wgt. 6 Cyl. 4329 Lbs.

1977 WAGONEER

W.B. **108.7″** Length 183.5″ Ship. Wgt. 6 Cyl. 4345 Lbs.

1978 WAGONEER

W.B. **108.7″** Length 183.5″ Ship. Wgt. 6 Cyl. 4349 Lbs.

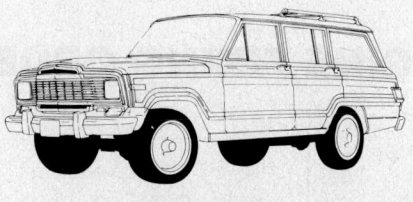

1979 WAGONEER

W.B. **108.7″** Length 183.5″ Ship. Wgt. 6 Cyl. 4359 Lbs.

1980 WAGONEER

W.B. **108.7″**. Length 183.5″. Ship. Wgt. 6 Cyl. Approx. 4357 Lbs.

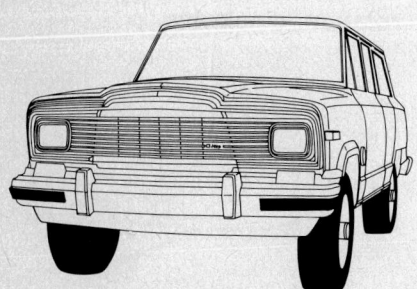

1981-82 WAGONEER

W.B. **108.7″**. Length 183.5″. 6 Cyl. 4 Dr. Ship. Wgt. 4180 Lbs.

FUSE IDENTIFICATION

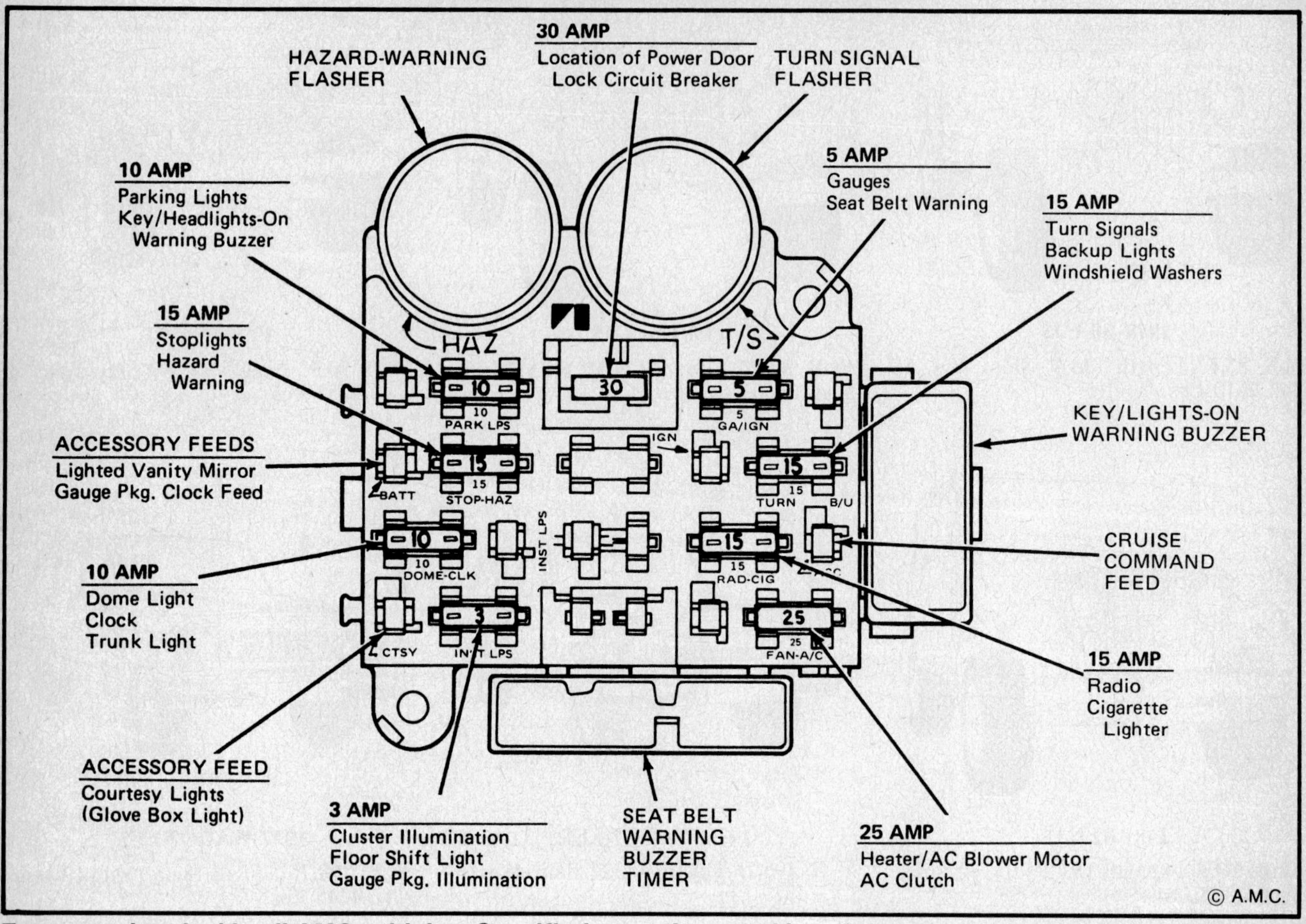

30 AMP
Location of Power Door Lock Circuit Breaker
HAZARD-WARNING FLASHER
TURN SIGNAL FLASHER
10 AMP
Parking Lights
Key/Headlights-On Warning Buzzer
5 AMP
Gauges
Seat Belt Warning
15 AMP
Turn Signals
Backup Lights
Windshield Washers
15 AMP
Stoplights
Hazard Warning
HAZ
T/S
10 PARK LPS
30
5 GA/IGN
KEY/LIGHTS-ON WARNING BUZZER
ACCESSORY FEEDS
Lighted Vanity Mirror
Gauge Pkg. Clock Feed
BATT
15 STOP-HAZ
IGN
15 TURN
B/U
INST LPS
10 DOME-CLK
15 RAD-CIG
CRUISE COMMAND FEED
10 AMP
Dome Light
Clock
Trunk Light
CTSY
3 INST LPS
25 FAN-A/C
15 AMP
Radio
Cigarette Lighter
ACCESSORY FEED
Courtesy Lights (Glove Box Light)
3 AMP
Cluster Illumination
Floor Shift Light
Gauge Pkg. Illumination
SEAT BELT WARNING BUZZER TIMER
25 AMP
Heater/AC Blower Motor
AC Clutch
© A.M.C.

Fuse panel typical in all AMC vehicles. Specific fuse ratings and locations vary from model to model and year to year

ENGINE FIRING ORDERS

7
5
3
1
8
6
4
2
RIO
5
TDC
5
AIO

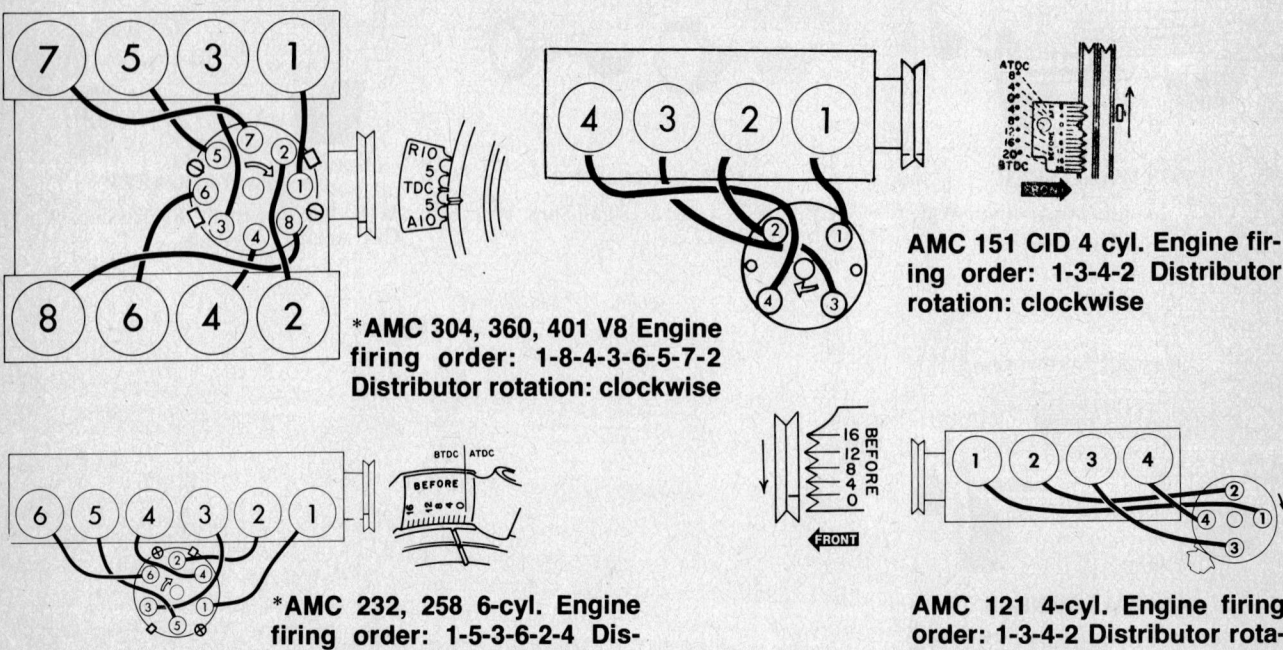

***AMC 304, 360, 401 V8 Engine firing order: 1-8-4-3-6-5-7-2 Distributor rotation: clockwise**

4
3
2
1
ATDC
BTDC
FRONT

AMC 151 CID 4 cyl. Engine firing order: 1-3-4-2 Distributor rotation: clockwise

6
5
4
3
2
1
BTDC
ATDC
BEFORE

***AMC 232, 258 6-cyl. Engine firing order: 1-5-3-6-2-4 Distributor rotation: clockwise**

16
12
8
4
0
BEFORE
FRONT
1
2
3
4

AMC 121 4-cyl. Engine firing order: 1-3-4-2 Distributor rotation: clockwise

VEHICLE IDENTIFICATION NUMBER (VIN)

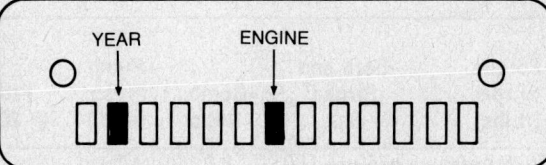

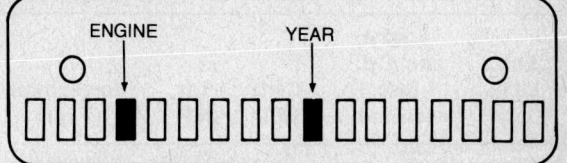

MODEL YEAR CODE		ENGINE CODE			
Code	Year	Code	Eng. Disp. (cu in)	Eng. Config.	Carb
6	1976	E	232/3.8L	L6	1V
		A	258,4.3L	L6	1V
		A	258,4.3L	L6	1V
		C	258,4.3L	L6	2V
		H	304,5.0L	V8	2V
		H	304,5.0L	V8	2V
		N	360,5.9L	V8	2V
		E	360,5.9L	V8	4V
7	1977	G	121,2.0L	L4	2V
		E	232,3.8L	L6	1V
		A	258,4.3L	L6	1V
		C	258,4.3L	L6	2V
		H	304,5.0L	V8	2V
		N	360,5.9L	V8	2V
8	1978	G	121,2.0L	L4	2V
		E	232,3.8L	L6	1V
		A	258,4.3L	L6	1V
		C	258,4.3L	L6	2V
		H	304,5.0L	V8	2V
		N	360,5.9L	V8	2V
9	1979	G	121,2.0L	L4	2V
		E	232,3.8L	L6	1V
		A	258,4.3L	L6	1V
		C	258,4.3L	L6	2V
		H	304,5.0L	V8	2V
		N	360,5.9L	V8	2V
A	1980	B	151,2.5L	L4	2V
		C	258,4.3L	L6	2V
		H	304,5.0L	V8	2V
		N	360,5.9L	V8	2V
B	1981	B	151,2.5L	L4	2V
		C	258,4.3L	L6	2V
		H	304,5.0L	V8	2V
		N	360,5.9L	V8	2V
C	1982	B	151,2.5L	L4	2V
		C	258,4.3L	L6	2V
		H	304,5.0L	V8	2V
		N	360,5.9L	V8	2V

AMC PASSENGER CARS AND JEEP

Year	Eng. V.I.N. Code	Engine No. Cyl. Disp. (cu. in.)	Carb BBL	Tax H.P.	Horsepower @ rpm	Torque @ rpm (ft lbs)	Bore and Stroke (in.)	Comp. Ratio	Fuel Pump Press. (p.s.i.)	Oil Pressure @ 2000 rpm
'76	E	6–232	1	33.75	90 @ 3050	170 @ 2000	3.750×3.500	8.0:1	4-5	46
	A	6–258	1	33.75	95 @ 3050	180 @ 2100	3.750×3.895	8.0:1	4-5	46
	C	6–258	2	33.75	120 @ 3400	200 @ 2000	3.750×3.895	8.0:1	4-5	46
	H	8–304	2	45.0	120 @ 3200	220 @ 2200	3.750×3.440	8.4:1	5-6½	46
	N	8–360	2	53.27	140 @ 3200	260 @ 1600	4.080×3.440	8.25:1	5-6½	46
	P	8–360	4	53.27	180 @ 3600	280 @ 2800	4.080×3.440	8.25:1	5-6½	46
	Z	8–401	4	55.51	215 @ 4200	320 @ 2800	4.165×3.680	8.25:1	5-6½	46
'77	G	4–121	2	18.5	80 @ 5000	105 @ 2800	3.410×3.320	8.2:1	4-6	28.5
	E	6–232	1	33.75	88 @ 3400	164 @ 1600	3.750×3.500	8.0:1	4-5	46
	A	6–258	1	33.75	98 @ 3200	193 @ 1600	3.750×3.895	8.0:1	4-5	46
	C	6–258	2	33.75	114 @ 3600	192 @ 2000	3.750×3.895	8.0:1	4-5	46
	H	8–304	2	45.0	121 @ 3450	219 @ 2000	3.750×3.440	8.4:1	5-6½	46
	N	8–360	2	53.27	129 @ 3700	245 @ 1600	4.080×3.440	8.25:1	5-6½	46
'78	G	4–121	2	18.5	80 @ 5000	105 @ 2800	3.410×3.320	8.2:1	4-6	28.5
	E	6–232	1	33.75	88 @ 3400	168 @ 1600	3.750×3.500	8.0:1	4-5	46
	A	6–258	1	33.75	100 @ 3400	193 @ 1600	3.750×3.895	8.0:1	4-5	46
	C	6–258	2	33.75	120 @ 3600	201 @ 1800	3.750×3.895	8.0:1	4-5	46
	H	8–304	2	45.0	130 @ 3200	238 @ 2000	3.750×3.440	8.4:1	5-6½	46
	N	8–360	2	53.27	140 @ 3350	278 @ 2000	4.080×3.440	8.25:1	5-6½	46
'79	G	4–121	2	18.5	80 @ 5000†	105 @ 2800†	3.410×3.320	8.2:1	4-6	28.5
	E	6–232	1	33.75	90 @ 3400†	168 @ 1600†	3.750×3.500	8.0:1	4-5	46
	A	6–258	1	33.75	100 @ 3400†	200 @ 1600†	3.750×3.895	8.0:1	4-5	46
	C	6–258	2	33.75	120 @ 3600†	201 @ 1800†	3.750×3.895	8.0:1	4-5	46
	H	8–304	2	45.00	130 @ 3200†	238 @ 2000†	3.750×3.440	8.4:1	5-6½	46
	N	8–360	2	53.27	140 @ 3350†	278 @ 2000	4.080×3.440	8.25:1	5-6½	46
'80	B	4–151 (2.5L)	2②	25.60	90 @ 4000†	134 @ 2400†	4.000×3.000	8.3:1	6½-8	39
	C	6–258 (4.2L)	2②	33.75	120 @ 3600†	201 @ 1800†	3.750×3.895	8.3:1	4-5	46
'81	B	4–151 (2.5L)	2②	25.60	90 @ 4000†	134 @ 2400†	4.000×3.000	8.2:1	6½-8	39
	C	6–258 (4.2L)	2②	33.75	120 @ 3600†	201 @ 1800†	3.750×3.895	8.3:1	4-5	46
'82	B	4–151 (2.5L)	2②	25.60	90 @ 4000†	134 @ 2400†	4.000×3.000	8.24:1	6½-8	39
	C	6–258 (4.2L)	2②	33.75	120 @ 3600†	201 @ 1800†	3.750×3.895	8.0:1	4-5	46

† Chilton Estimate
② Feedback carburetor

TUNE UP SPECIFICATIONS

PASSENGER CARS

Year	V.I.N. Code	No. Cyl Disp. (cu. in.)	Spark Plugs Orig. Type	Gap (in.)	Distributor	Timing①⑦ (deg. B.T.D.C.) Man. Trans.	Auto Trans.	Valves Intake Opens (deg. B.T.D.C.)	Idle Speed Manual Fed.	Manual Cal.	Auto (in drive) Fed.	Cal.
'76	E	6-232	N-12Y	.035	E.I.	8	8	12	850	850	550	700
	A	6-258	N-12Y	.035	E.I.	6	8	12	850	850	550	700
	H	6-258	N-12Y	.035	E.I.	6	8	12	850	850	550	700
	N	8-304	N-12Y	.035	E.I.	5	10(5)①	14¾	750	750	700	700
	P	8-360	N-12Y	.035	E.I.	—	10(5)①	14¾	—	—	700	700
	P	8-360	N-12Y	.035	E.I.	—	10(5)①	14¾	—	—	700	700
	Z	8-401	N-12Y	.035	E.I.	—	10(5)①	25½	—	—	700	700
'77	G	4-121	N-8L	.035	③	12	12(8)	41¾④	900	900	800	800
	E	6-232	N-12Y	.035	E.I.	8(10)	10	12	600	850	550	700
	A	6-258	N-12Y	.035	E.I.	6	8	12	600	600	550	700
	C	6-258	N-12Y	.035	E.I.	6	8	12	600	600	550	700
	H	8-304	N-12Y	.035	E.I.	—	10(5)①	14¾	—	—	600	700
	N	8-360	N-12Y	.035	E.I.	—	10(5)①	14¾	—	—	600	700
'78	G	4-121	N-8L	.035	③	12	12(8)①	41¾④	900	900	800	800
	E	6-232	N-13L	.035	E.I.	8	10	12	600	900	550	550
	A	6-258	N-13L	.035	E.I.	10(6)	10(8)①	12	600	850	550	700
	C	6-258	N-13L	.035	E.I.	6	8	14½	600	600	550	550
	H	8-304	N-12Y	.035	E.I.	—	10(5)①	14¾	—	—	600	700
	N	8-360	N-12Y	.035	E.I.	—	10	14¾	—	—	600	650
'79	G	4-121	N-8L	.035	③	12	12(8)①	25④	900	900	800	800
	E	6-232	N-13L	.035	E.I.	8	10	12	600	600	550	550
	A	6-258	N-13L	.035	E.I.	—	8	12	—	—	700	700
	C	6-258	N-13L	.035	E.I.	4	8	14½	700	700	600	600
	H	8-304	N-12Y	.035	E.I.	5	8	12	800	800	600	600
'80	B	4-151	R44TSX	.060	E.I.	10(6)	12(6)①	33	900	700	700	700
	C	6-258	②	.035	E.I.	6	14(6)①	9	700	700	600	600
'81	FED-B-EXC EAGLE	4.151	R44TSX	.060	E.I.	10° @ 800	12° @ 600	33	900	—	700	—
	FED-B-EAGLE	4.151	R44TSX	.060	E.I.	10° @ 800	12° @ 600	33	900	—	700	—
	CAL-B-EXC EAGLE	4.151	R44TSX	.060	E.I.	10° @ 900	12° @ 700	33	—	900	—	800
	CAL-B-EAGLE	4.151	R44TSX	.060	E.I.	10° @ 900	8° @ 700	33	—	900	—	800
	FED-C-EXC EAGLE	6.258	RFN14LY	.035	E.I.	6° @ 650	6° @ 550	9	500	—	650	—
	FED-C-EAGLE	6.258	RFN14LY	.035	E.I.	8° @ 650	8° @ 550	9	750	—	650	—
	CAL—C-EXC EAGLE	6.258	RFN14LY	.035	E.I.	10° @ 700	10° @ 550	9	—	750	—	650
	CAL-C-EAGLE	6.258	RFN14LY	.035	E.I.	4° @ 650	6° @ 550	9	—	650	—	550
'82	FED-B-EXC EAGLE	4.151	R44TSX	.060	E.I.	⑤	⑤	33	900	—	700	—
	FED-B-EAGLE	4.151	R44TSX	.060	E.I.	⑤	⑤	33	900	—	700	—
	CAL-B-EXC EAGLE	4.151	R44TSX	.060	E.I.	⑤	⑤	33	—	900	—	800
	CAL-B-EAGLE	4.151	R44TSX	.060	E.I.	⑤	⑤	33	—	900	—	800
	FED-C-EXC EAGLE	6.258	RFN14LY	.035	E.I.	⑤	⑤	9	500	—	650	—
	FED-C-EAGLE	6.258	RFN14LY	.035	E.I.	⑤	⑤	9	750	—	650	—
	CAL—C-EXC EAGLE	6.258	RFN14LY	.035	E.I.	⑤	⑤	9	—	750	—	650
	CAL-C-EAGLE	6.258	RFN14LY	.035	E.I.	⑤	⑤	9	—	650	—	550

—   Not applicable
Fed. = Federal
Cal. = California
E.I. = Electronic Ignition
①   Figure in parentheses is for California applications

②   All except Eagle use N14LY. Eagle uses N13L.
③   Set point gap at .018 in. and dwell at 47°.
④   Set valve clearance with engine warm to: Intake .006-.009 in., exhaust .016-.019 in.
⑤   See engine decal

⑥   Eagle except California 11°
⑦   With vacuum advance hose disconnected.
⑧   With idle soleniod active, if so equipped
⑥   Eagle except California 11°

AMC PASSENGER CARS AND JEEP

Year	Eng. V.I.N. Code	Engine No. Cyl. Disp. (cu. in.)	Carb BBL	Tax H.P.	Horsepower @ rpm	Torque @ rpm (ft lbs)	Bore and Stroke (in.)	Comp. Ratio	Fuel Pump Press. (p.s.i.)	Oil Pressure @ 2000 rpm
'76	E	6–232	1	33.75	90 @ 3050	170 @ 2000	3.750×3.500	8.0:1	4-5	46
	A	6–258	1	33.75	95 @ 3050	180 @ 2100	3.750×3.895	8.0:1	4-5	46
	C	6–258	2	33.75	120 @ 3400	200 @ 2000	3.750×3.895	8.4:1	5-6½	46
	H	8–304	2	45.0	120 @ 3200	220 @ 2200	3.750×3.440	8.25:1	5-6½	46
	N	8–360	2	53.27	140 @ 3200	260 @ 1600	4.080×3.440	8.25:1	5-6½	46
	P	8–360	4	53.27	180 @ 3600	280 @ 2800	4.080×3.440	8.25:1	5-6½	46
	Z	8–401	4	55.51	215 @ 4200	320 @ 2800	4.165×3.680	8.25:1	5-6½	46
'77	E	6–232	1	33.75	88 @ 3400	164 @ 1600	3.750×3.500	8.0:1	4-5	46
	A	6–258	1	33.75	98 @ 3200	193 @ 1600	3.750×3.895	8.0:1	4-5	46
	C	6–258	2	33.75	114 @ 3600	192 @ 2000	3.750×3.895	8.0:1	4-5	46
	H	8–304	2	45.0	121 @ 3450	219 @ 2000	3.750×3.440	8.4:1	5-6½	46
	N	8–360	2	53.27	129 @ 3700	245 @ 1600	4.080×3.440	8.25:1	5-6½	46
	P	8–360	4	53.27	180 @ 3600	280 @ 2800	4.080×3.440	8.25:1	5-6½	46
	Z	8–401	4	55.51	215 @ 4200	320 @ 2800	4.165×3.680	8.25:1	5-6½	46
'78	E	6–232	1	33.75	88 @ 3400	164 @ 1600	3.750×3.500	8.0:1	4-5	46
	A	6–258	1	33.75	98 @ 3200	193 @ 1600	3.750×3.895	8.0:1	4-5	46
	C	6–258	2	33.75	114 @ 3600	192 @ 2000	3.750×3.895	8.4:1	5-6½	46
	H	8–304	2	45.0	121 @ 3450	219 @ 2000	3.750×3.440	8.4:1	5-6½	46
	N	8–360	2	53.27	129 @ 3700	245 @ 1600	4.080×3.440	8.25:1	5-6½	46
	P	8–360	4	53.27	180 @ 3600†	251 @ 1600	4.080×3.440	8.25:1	5-6½	46
	Z	8–401	4	55.51	215 @ 4200	320 @ 2800	4.165×3.680	8.25:1	5-6½	46
'79	E	6–232	1	33.75	88 @ 3400†	164 @ 1600†	3.750 ×3.500	8.0:1	4-5	46
	A	6–258	1	33.75	98 @ 3200†	193 @ 1600†	3.750×3.895	8.0:1	4-5	46
	C	6–258	2	33.75	114 @ 3600†	192 @ 2000†	3.750×3.895	8.0:1	4-5	46
	H	8–304	2	45.0	121 @ 3450†	219 @ 2000†	3.750×3.440	8.4:1	5-6½	46
	N	8–360	2	53.27	129 @ 3700†	245 @ 1600†	4.080×3.440	8.25:1	5-6½	46
'80	B	4–451	2	25.60	90 @ 3400†	164 @ 1600†	4.000×3.000	8.3:1	6½-8	39
	C	6–258	2	33.75	114 @ 3600†	192 @ 2000†	3.750×3.895	8.3:1	4-5	46
	H	8–304	2	45.00	121 @ 3450†	219 @ 2000†	3.750×3.440	8.4:1	5-6½	46
	N	8–360	2	53.27	129 @ 3700†	245 @ 1600†	4.080×3.440	8.25:1	5-6½	46
'81	B	4-151	2	25.60	90 @ 3600†	164 @ 1600†	4.000×3.000	8.3:1	6½-8	39
	C	6-258	2	33.75	114 @ 3600†	192 @ 2000†	3.750×3.895	8.3:1	4-5	46
	H	8-304	2	45.00	121 @ 3450†	219 @ 2000†	3.750×3.440	8.4:1	5-6½	46
	N	8-360	2	53.27	129 @ 3700†	245 @ 1600†	4.080×3.440	8.25:1	5-6½	46
'82	B	4-151	2	25.60	90 @ 3600†	164 @ 1600†	4.000×3.000	8.24:1	6½-8	39
	C	6-258	2	33.75	114 @ 3600†	192 @ 2000†	3.750×3.895	8.0:1	4-5	46
	H	8-304	2	45.00	121 @ 3450†	219 @ 2000†	3.750×3.440	8.4:1	5-6½	46
	N	8-360	2	53.27	129 @ 3700†	245 @ 1600†	4.080×3.440	8.25:1	5-6½	46

† Chilton Estimate

TUNE UP SPECIFICATIONS   JEEP

Year	V.I.N. Code	No. Cyl Disp. (cu. in.)	Spark Plugs Orig. Type	Gap (in.)	Distributor	Timing① ⑦ (deg. B.T.D.C.) Man. Trans.	Auto Trans.	Valves Intake Opens (deg. B.T.D.C.)	Idle Speed Manual Fed.	Cal.	Auto (in drive) Fed.	Cal.
'76	E	6-232	N-12Y	.035	E.I.	8	8	12	850	850	550	700
	A	6-258	N-12Y	.035	E.I.	6	8	12	850	850	550	700
	C	6-258	N-12Y	.035	E.I.	6	8	12	850	850	550	700
	H	8-304	N-12Y	.035	E.I.	5	10(5)	14¾	750	750	700	700
	N	8-360	N-12Y	.035	E.I.	—	10(5)	14¾	—	—	700	700
	P	8-360	N-12Y	.035	E.I.	—	10(5)	14¾	—	—	700	700
	Z	8-401	N-12Y	.035	E.I.	—	10(5)	25½	—	—	700	700
'77	E	6-232	N-12Y	.035	E.I.	8(10)	10	12	600	600	550	700
	A	6-258	N-12Y	.035	E.I.	6	8	12	600	600	550	700
	C	6-258	N-12Y	.035	E.I.	6	8	12	600	600	550	700
	H	8-304	RN-12Y	.035	E.I.	5	10(5)	14¾	750	750	700	700
	N	8-360	RN-12Y	.035	E.I.	5	8	14¾	750	750	700	700
	P	8-360	RN-12Y	.035	E.I.	5	8	14¾	750	700	700	700
	Z	8-401	RN-12Y	.035	E.I.	—	8	25½	—	—	700	700
'78	E	6-232	N-13L	.035	E.I.	5③	—	12	850④	850④	—	—
	A	6-258	N-13L	.035	E.I.	3(8)③	8③	12	850④	850④	550	550
	C	6-258	N-13L	.035	E.I.	6	6	14½	650	650	550	550
	H	8-304	N-12Y	.035	E.I.	5	10(5)③	14¾	750	750	700	700
	N	8-360	N-12Y	.035	E.I.	5	8	14¾	750	750	700	700
	P	8-360	N-13Y	.035	E.I.	5	10	14¾	750	700	700	700
	Z	8-401	N-13Y	.035	E.I.	5	10	25½	750	700	700	700
'79	C	6-258	N-13L⑤	.035	E.I.	6	6	14½	700	700	600	600
	H	8-304	N-12Y⑥	.035	E.I.	6	6	14¾	700	700	600	600
	N	8-360	N-12Y⑥	.035	E.I.	6	6	14¾	800	800	600	600
'80	B	4-151	R44TSX	.060	E.I.	10	12(10)	33	1000	1000	650	650
	C	6-258	N13L⑤	.035	E.I.	8(4)	8(6)	14½	700	700	600	600
	H	8-304	N12Y⑥	.035	E.I.	8⑧	10	14¾	700	700	600	600
	N	8-360	N12Y⑥	.035	E.I.	10	10	14¾	750	700	700	700
'81	B	Y-151	R44TSX	.060	E.I.	10	12(10)	33	1000	1000	650	650
	C	6-258	N13L⑤	.035	E.I.	8(4)	8(6)	14½	700	700	600	600
	H	8-304	N12Y⑥	.035	E.I.	8⑧	10	14¾	700	700	600	600
	N	8-360	N12Y⑥	.035	E.I.	10	10	14¾	750	700	700	700
'82	B	Y-151	R44TSX	.060	E.I.	10	12(10)	33	1000	1000	650	650
	C	6-258	N13L⑤	.035	E.I.	8(4)	8(6)	14½	700	700	600	600
	H	8-304	N12Y⑥	.035	E.I.	8⑧	10	14¾	700	700	600	600
	N	8-360	N12Y⑥	.035	E.I.	10	10	14¾	750	700	700	700

NOTE: Should the information provided in this manual deviate from the specifications on the underhood tune-up label, the label specifications should be used, as they may reflect production changes.

NOTE: Spark plugs shown are original equipment. For other manufacturers' equivalent plugs, see Popular Replacement Spark Plug Tables.

—   Not applicable
Fed. =Federal
Cai. =California
E.I. =Electronic Ignition
①   Figure in parentheses is for California applications
③   Set high altitude engine at 10
④   Set high altitude engine at 600
⑤   Use RN 13L in high altitude applications, N14L manual transmission
⑥   Use RN 12Y in high altitude applications
⑦   See underhood specifications decal
⑧   Hilly torrain 12°B

AMC PASSENGER CARS AND JEEP

FLUID CAPACITIES—Coolant Lubricant   PASSENGER CARS

Year	ENGINE No. Cyl. Displacement (cu in.)	Eng. VIN Code	Engine Crankcase Add 1 Qt. For New Filter	TRANSMISSION (Pts to Refill After Draining) Manual 3-Speed	Manual 4-Speed	Automatic	Drive Axle (pts)	COOLING SYSTEM (qts) With Heater	With A/C	Rad. Cap Press. (lbs.)	Therm Open Temp.
'76	6-232	E	4	3.5①⑧	3.5	17	3②	11⑨	11.5⑩	12-15	195
	6-258	A	4	3.5①⑧	3.5	17	3	11⑨	11.5⑩	12-15	195
	8-304	H	4	3.5	—	17	4	16.0⑪	16.0⑪	12-15	195
	8-360	N,P	4	—	—	19	4	15.5⑪	15.5⑪	12-15	195
	8-401	Z	4	—	—	19	4	15.5⑪	15.5⑪	12-15	195
'77	4-121	G	3.5⑫	—	2.8	14.2	3.0	6.5	—	12-15	189
	6-232	E	4	3.5①⑧	3.5	17	3②	11⑨	11.5⑩	12-15	195
	6-258	A	4	3.5①⑧	3.5	17	3②	11⑨	11.5⑩	12-15	195
	6-258	C	4	3.5	—	17	4	16.0⑪	16.0⑪	12-15	195
	8-304	H	4	—	—	19	4	15.5⑪	15.5⑪	12-15	195
	8-360	N	4	—	—	19	4	15.5⑪	15.5⑪	12-15	195
'78	4-121	G	3.5⑫	—	2.4	14.2	3.0	6.5	—	12-15	189
	6-232	E	4	3.0	3.0	17	3.0	11⑬	14⑬	12-15	195
	6-258	A	4	3.0	3.0	17	3.0⑮	11⑬	14⑬	12-15	195
	6-258	C	4	3.0	3.0	17	3.0⑮	11⑬	14⑬	12-15	195
	8-304	H	4	—	—	17	4	15.5⑯⑭	15.5⑯⑭	12-15	195
'79	4-121	G	3.5⑫	—	2.4	14.2	3.0	6.5	—	12-15	189
	6-232	E	4	3.0	3.0	17	3.0	11⑬	14⑬	12-15	195
	6-258	A	4	3.0	3.0	17	3.0⑮	11⑪	14⑬	12-15	195
	6-258	C	4	3.0	3.0	17	3.0⑮	11⑬	14⑬	12-15	195
	8-304	H	4	—	—	17	4	15.5⑯	15.5⑯	12-15	195
	8-360	N	4	—	—	19	4	15.5⑯⑭	15.5⑯⑭	12-15	195
'80	4-151	B	3.0⑰	—	3.3	14.2	3.0	6.5	—	12-15	195
	6-258	C	4	3.0	3.3	17	3.0⑱	11⑬	14⑬	12-15	195
'81	4-151	B	3.0⑰	—	3.3	14.2	3.0	6.5	—	12-15	195
	6-258	C	4	3.0	3.3	17	3.0⑱	11⑬	14⑬	12-15	195
'82	4-151	B	3.0	—	3.3	14.2	3.0	6.5	—	15	195
	6-258	C	4	3.0	3.3	17.0	3.0⑱	11⑬	14⑬	15	195

① 4 pts with overdrive
② 8.875 ring gear—4 pts
③ Matador Coupe—18.5 qts; with coolant recovery system—20.5 qts; Hornet and Gremlin—16 qts.
④ Matador Coupe—17.5 qts, with coolant recovery system—19.5 qts.
⑤ 13.5 qts in Matador Coupe, 15.5 qts in Matador Coupe with coolant recovery system, 14.5 qts in Pacer
⑥ 16.5 qts in Matador Sedan and Wagon
⑦ 14.5 qts in Pacer
⑧ Gremlin & Hornet—2.5
⑨ 14.0 qts in Pacer
⑩ 13.5 qts in Matador Coupe
⑪ Add 2 qts in Matador Coupe or with coolant recovery system
⑫ Add ½ qt. for filter
⑬ Spirit, Gremlin & Concord only; 13.5 in Matador 2 dr. Coupe, 11.5 in all other Matadors, and 14 in all Pacers.
⑭ Add 2 qts. w/coolant recovery system on Matador Wagons
⑮ 4.0 pts. in Matadors
⑯ 18 qts. in Concord, 17.5 qts. in Matador Coupe.
⑰ With or without filter change
⑱ Eagle front axle 2.5 pts.

FLUID CAPACITIES—Coolant, Fuel, & Lubricant   JEEP

Engine No. Cyl. Displacement (cu in.)	Engine Crankcase Add 1 Qt For New Filter	TRANSMISSION (Pts to Refill After Draining)			Transfer Case (pts)	Front Axle (pts)	Rear Axle (pts)	Gasoline Tank Tank (gals)	Cooling System (qts) Heater Included
		Manual		Automatic①					
		3-Speed	4-Speed						
4–151	3	3	⑦	8.5	⑥	④	④	⑤	7.8
6–232	5	2.5③⑪	⑦	8.5	⑥	④	④	⑤	10½
6–258	5	2.5③⑪	⑦	8.5	⑥	④	④	⑤	10½
8–304	5⑩	2.75③⑪	⑦	8.5	⑥	④	④	⑤	13
8–360	4	2.75③⑪	⑦	8.5	⑥	④	④	⑤	14
8–401	4	—	⑦	8.5	⑥	④	④	⑤	14

— Not applicable
① 17 pts if converter is drained
③ 3 pts in CJ 1976–77; 2.7 pts in Cherokee and Wagoneer
④ Axles
  CJ front axle — 2.5 pints
  CJ rear axle — 4.8 pints
  Cherokee front axle — 3.0 pints
  Cherokee rear axle — 4.8 pints
  Wagoneer front axle — 3.0 pints
  Wagoneer rear axle — 4.8 pints
  J-10 Truck front axle — 3.0 pints

J-10 Truck rear axle — 4.8 pints
J-20 Truck front axle — 3.0
J-20 Truck rear axle — 6.0 pints
⑤ Gas Tanks (Approximate Capacity)
  CJ Models — 14.8 gallons
  Cherokee Models — 20.3 gallons
  Wagoneer Models — 20.3 gallons
  Truck Models — 19.0 gallons
⑥ Transfer Case
  Model 300 — 4.0 pints
  Model 208 — 6.0 pints
  Quadra-Trac — 4.0 pints

⑦ 4 Speed SR-4 — 3 pts
  4 Speed T-176 — 3.5 pts
  4 Speed T-18 — 6.5 pts
⑨ AMC rear—4.0 pts 1976–77 CJ only, 1978–80 CJ models—4.8
⑩ '78–'80 304,—4 qts.
⑪ '78–'80 all models—2.8 pts.
⑫ '78–'80 models with quadra-trac 4 pts, w/quadra trac and reduction unit 5 pts.

ENGINE TORQUE SPECIFICATIONS   PASSENGER CARS & JEEP

All readings in ft/lbs

Year	Engine	Cylinder Head Bolts	Rod Bearing Bolts	Main Bearing Bolts	Crankshaft Vibration Damper Bolt	Flywheel Crankshaft Bolt	MANIFOLD	
							Intake	Exhaust
ALL	4-121	①	41	②	③	65	18	18
ALL	4-151	85④	32	70	200	50	29	44
76-80	6-258	105	33-30	80	80⑤⑥	105	23	23
81-82	6-258	92	30	65	80⑤⑥	105	37	37
76-82	8 cyl.	110	33	100	90⑤⑧⑩	105	43	⑨

① Cold engine—65
  Warm engine—80
② Hex head—58
  Rear cap, socket head—47
③ Sprocket-to-crank-shaft—181
④ Use thread sealant
⑤ Lubricate threads when installing
⑥ Pulley-to-damper bolt—20
⑦ 304 & 360 CID engines—28
⑧ Pulley-to-damper bolt—23
⑨ ⅜ inch bolt—25
  5/16 inch bolt—15
⑩ 1976—80

Crankshaft pulley-to-sprocket—15

401 CID engine—38

WHEEL LUG TORQUE DATA

Year	Model	Torque ft/lbs
ALL	All Passenger Cars	75
ALL	CJ	65-90
ALL	Cherokee, Wagoneer	65-80

AMC PASSENGER CARS AND JEEP

CRANKSHAFT & CONNECTING ROD SPECIFICATIONS

PASSENGER CARS & JEEP

All measurements in inches

Year	Engine	CRANKSHAFT				CONNECTING ROD		
		Main Bearing Journal Dia.	Main Bearing Oil Clearance	Shaft End Play	Thrust On No.	Journal Diameter	Oil Clearance	Side Clearance
ALL	4-121	2.1581-2.1587	.00098-.00311	.0039-.0075	3	1.8882-1.8888	.0007-.0024	.002-.012
ALL	4-151	2.300	.0005-.0022	.0035-.0085	5	2.000	.0005-.0026	.006-.022
ALL	6 cyl.	2.4986-2.5001	.001-.003	.0015-.0065	3	2.0934-2.0955	.001-.0025①	.005-.014
ALL	8 cyl.	2.7474-2.7489②	.001-.003③	.003-.008	3	2.0934-2.0955④	.001-.003	.006-.018

① 1975—.001-.003
② Rear main—2.7464-2.7479
③ Rear main 1976-80—.002-.004, 1974-75—.001--003
④ 401 CID engine—2.2464-2.2485

DISC BRAKE SPECIFICATIONS

PASSENGER CARS & JEEP

All measurements given in inches

Year	Model	Caliper Type	Caliper Mount Bolt Torque (ft./lbs.)	Maximum Allowable Rotor Scoring	Disc Pad Minimum Thickness	Rotor Lateral Runout	Rotor Minimum Allowable Thickness	Rotor Thickness Variation
'76	All Passenger Cars	Sliding⑤	15⑥	0.009	②	0.003③	1.120	0.0005
	All Jeep	Floating①	35	0.015	②	0.005③	1.230④	0.0005
'77	All Passenger Cars	Sliding⑤	15⑥	0.009	②	0.003③	0.81	0.0005
	CJ	Sliding⑤	15⑥	0.009	②	0.005③	1.120	0.001
	Cherokee, Wagoneer	Floating①	35	0.015	②	0.005③	1.215	0.001
'78	All Passenger Cars	Sliding⑤	15⑥	0.009	②	0.003③	0.81	0.0005
	CJ	Sliding⑤	15⑥	0.009	②	0.005③	1.120	0.001
	Cherokee, Wagoneer	Floating①	35	0.015	②	0.005③	1.215	0.001
'79	All Passenger Cars	Sliding⑤	15⑥	0.009	②	0.003③	0.81	0.0005
	CJ	Sliding⑤	15⑥	0.009	②	0.005③	0.815	0.001
	Cherokee, Wagoneer	Floating①	35	0.015	②	0.005③	1.215	0.001
'80	All Passenger Cars	Sliding⑤	15⑥	0.009	②	0.003③	0.81	0.0005
	CJ	Sliding⑤	15⑥	0.009	②	0.005③	0.815	0.001
	Cherokee, Wagoneer	Floating①	35	0.015	②	0.005③	1.215	0.001
'81	All passenger cars	Sliding⑤	15⑥	0.009	②	0.003③	0.81	0.0005
	CJ	Sliding⑤	15⑥	0.009	②	0.005③	0.815	0.001
	Cherokee, Wagoneer, Eagle	Floating①	35	0.015	②	0.005③	1.215	0.001
'82	All passenger cars	Sliding⑤	15⑥	0.009	②	0.003③	0.81	0.0005
	CJ	Sliding⑤	15⑥	0.009	②	0.005③	0.815	0.001
	Cherokee, Wagoneer, Eagle	Floating①	35	0.015	②	0.005③	1.215	0.001

① Kelsey Hayes single piston
② Replace when lining is same thickness as metal shoe
③ Maximum rate of change should not exceed 0.001 in.
④ Discard at 1.215 in.
⑤ Bendix single piston
⑥ Caliper support key retaining screw

BRAKE SPECIFICATIONS   PASSENGER CARS AND JEEP

| Year | Model | MASTER CYLINDER BORE DIAMETER | | WHEEL CYLINDER BORE DIAMETER | | | BRAKE DISC OR DRUM DIAMETER | | |
| | | | | Front | | | Front | | |
		Disc	Drum	Disc	Drum	Rear	Disc	Drum	Rear
'76	Gremlin, Hornet—6 cyl.	1.00⑤	1.00	3.100	1.125	0.875③	10.75	9.0	9.0
	Gremlin, Hornet—8 cyl.	1.00⑤	1.00	3.100	1.187	0.875	10.75	10.0	10.0
	Matador	1.125⑤	—	3.100	—	0.875⑥	10.75	—	10.0
	Pacer	1.00⑤	1.00	3.100	1.0937	0.875	10.75	10.0	9.0
	CJ	—	1.00	—	1.125	0.9375	—	11.0	11.0
	Cherokee, Wagoneer	1.125	1.00	2.9375	1.125	0.9375	12.0	11.0	11.0
'77	Gremlin, Hornet—6 cyl.	1.00	—	2.60	—	0.812	10.82	—	10.0
	Gremlin, Hornet—8 cyl.	1.00	—	2.60	—	0.812	10.82	—	10.0
	Matador	1.125	—	3.10	—	0.875⑥	10.82	—	10.0
	Pacer	1.00	—	2.60	—	0.812	10.82	—	10.0
	CJ	1.00	1.00	2.9375	1.125	0.9375	12.0	11.0	11.0
	Cherokee, Wagoneer	1.125	—	2.9375	—	0.9375	12.0	—	11.0
'78	All except Matador	0.960	—	2.60	—	0.812⑦	10.80⑧	—	10.0
	Matador	1.125	—	3.10	—	0.875⑥	10.82	—	10.0
	CJ	1.00	—	3.10	—	0.875	11.70	—	11.0
	Cherokee, Wagoneer	1.125	—	2.9375	—	0.9375	12.0	—	11.0
'79	Spirit, Concord—4 cyl.	0.94	—	2.640	—	0.94	10.27	—	9.0⑩
	Concord, Pacer, Spirit—6 & 8 cyl.	0.94	—	2.640	—	0.81	10.80	—	10.0
	AMX	0.94	—	2.640	—	0.94	10.80	—	10.0
	CJ	1.00	—	2.6	—	0.875	11.70	—	10.0
	Cherokee, Wagoneer	1.125	—	2.937	—	0.937	12.0	—	11.0
'80	Spirit, Concord—4 cyl.	0.94	—	2.6	—	0.94	10.27	—	9.0⑩
	Concord, Pacer, Spirit—6 & 8 cyl.	0.94	—	2.6	—	0.81	10.80	—	10.0
	Eagle	0.94	—	2.6	—	0.94	10.80	—	10.0
	CJ	1.00	—	2.6	—	0.875	11.70	—	10.0
	Cherokee, Wagoneer	1.125	—	2.937	—	0.937	12.0	—	11.0
'81	Spirit, Concord—4cyl.	0.94	—	2.6	—	0.94	10.27	—	9.0⑩
	Concord, Spirit-6 cyl.	0.94	—	2.6	—	0.81	10.80⑪	—	9.0
	Eagle	0.94	—	2.6	—	0.94	11.02	—	10.0
	CJ	1.00	—	2.6	—	0.875	11.7	—	10.0
	Cherokee, Wagoneer	1.125	—	2.937	—	0.937	12.0	—	11.0
'82	Spirit, Concord—4cyl.	0.94	—	2.6	—	0.94	10.27	—	9.0⑩
	Concord, Spirit-6 cyl.	0.94	—	2.6	—	0.81	10.80⑪	—	9.0
	Eagle	0.94	—	2.6	—	0.94	11.02	—	10.0
	CJ	1.00	—	2.6	—	0.875	11.7	—	10.0
	Cherokee, Wagoneer	1.125	—	2.937	—	0.937	12.0	—	11.0

— Not Applicable
③ Hornet shown; Gremlin—0.812
⑤ Power assisted shown; non-power—1.0625
⑥ Sedan and Coupe shown; station wagon—0.9375
⑦ All models shown except: 4cyl. Gremlin—0.94
⑧ All models shown except: 8 cyl. AMX—10.30, 4 cyl. Gremlin—10.27
⑨ All models shown except: 4 cyl. Gremlin—9.0
⑩ Spirit shown; Concord—10.0
⑪ 4 cyl.—10.27

AMC PASSENGER CARS AND JEEP

VALVE SPECIFICATIONS PASSENGER CARS & JEEP

Year	Engine	SEAT ANGLE (deg.) In.	SEAT ANGLE (deg.) Ex.	FACE ANGLE (deg.) In.	FACE ANGLE (deg.) Ex.	Spring Test Pressure (lbs. @ ins.)	Spring Installed Height (ins.)	STEM-TO GUIDE CLEARANCE (ins.) In.	STEM-TO GUIDE CLEARANCE (ins.) Ex.	Stem Diameter (ins.)
ALL	4-121	45	45	45	45	①	1.70	.031	.039	②
ALL	4-151	46	46	45	45	150 @ 1.254	1.66③	.0010-.0027	④	.3418-.3425
ALL	6 cyl.	30	44.5	29	44	204 @ 1.382	1.786	.0010-.0030	.0010-.0030	.3715-.3725
ALL	8 cyl.	30	44.5	29	44	202 @ 1.411	1.786	.0010-.0030	.0010-.0030	.3715-.3725

① Intake outer spring—166 @ 1.30
   Intake inner spring—39 @ 1.09
   Exhaust outer spring—160 @ 1.32
   Exhaust inner spring—37 @ 1.11
② Intake—.3526-.3531
   Exhaust—.3522-.3528
③ Valve installed height—1.69
④ Top—.0010-.0027
   Bottom—.0020-.0037

DISTRIBUTOR SPECIFICATIONS PASSENGER CARS & JEEP

Year	Distributor Identifisction	CENTRIFUGAL ADVANCE Start Dist. Deg. @ Dist. RPM	CENTRIFUGAL ADVANCE Maximum Dist. Deg. @ Dist. RPM	Vacuum Control No.	VACUUM ADVANCE Start @ In. Hg.	VACUUM ADVANCE Maximum Dist. Deg. @ In. Hg.
'76	3227331	0-0.4 @ 500	5.25-7.25 @ 2200	—	5-7	7-9 @ 12.6
	3228263	0-2.8 @ 500	11-13 @ 2200	—	4-6	6.5-8.5 @ 12.7
	3228264	0-2.4 @ 500	13.5-15.5 @ 2200	—	5-7	6.5-8.5 @ 12.5
	3228265	0-2.7 @ 500	7.5-9.5 @ 2200	—	4-6	6.5-8.5 @ 12.7
	3228266	0-3.75 @ 500	10-12 @ 2200	—	4-6	6.5-8.5 @ 11.7-12.8
	3229719	0-1.5 @ 500	9-11 @ 2200	—	5-7	7-9 @ 12.6
'77	3227331	0-0.4 @ 500	5.25-7.25 @ 2200	—	5-7	7-9 @ 12.6
	3228263	0-2.8 @ 500	11-13 @ 2200	—	4-6	6.5-8.5 @ 12.7
	3228264	0-2.4 @ 500	13.5-15.5 @ 2200	—	5-7	6.5-8.5 @ 12.5
	3228265	0-2.7 @ 500	7.5-9.5 @ 2200	—	4-6	6.5-8.5 @ 12.7
	3228266	0-3.75 @ 500	10-12 @ 2200	—	4-6	6.5-8.5 @ 11.7-12.8
	3229719	0-1.5 @ 500	9-11 @ 2200	—	5-7	7-9 @ 12.6
'78	3230443	−.8-1.8 @ 475	10.8-13.2 @ 2200	—	1.5-5.5	6.8-9.5 @ 13.2
	3231340	−1-1.8 @ 475	13.5-16 @ 2200	—	2-6.5	6.8-9.3 @ 12.8
	3231341	−.9-1.9 @ 500	7-9.5 @ 2200	—	1.5-5.5	6.8-9.5 @ 13.2
	3231915	−1.2-1 @ 500	8-10.8 @ 2200	—	1.5-3.5	10.8-13.2 @ 11.5
	3232434	−1-1 @ 500	8-10.5 @ 2200	—	2.2-6.5	6.8-9.3 @ 13.5
	3233173	−1-2 @ 450	10.8-13.2 @ 2200	—	1.5-4	10.8-13.2 @ 13.0
	3233174	−.9-1.5 @ 475	7-9.5 @ 2200	—	1.5-4	10.8-13.2 @ 13.0
	3250163	0-3 @ 675	15-17 @ 2250	—	2-4	7-9 @ 11.0
'79	3231340	−1-1.5 @ 500	13-16 @ 2200	—	2-7	6.5-8.5 @ 12.5
	3231915	−1-0.5 @ 500	8-10.5 @ 2200	—	1.5-3.5	11.5-13.5 @ 11.5
	3232434	−1-0.5 @ 500	8-10 @ 2200	—	2-7	7-8.5 @ 13.5
	3233174	−1-0.5 @ 450	7-9 @ 2200	—	1.5-4	11-13 @ 12
	3233959	−1-0.5 @ 500	12-14.5 @ 2200	—	1.5-2	14.5-17.5 @ 12.5
	3234693	−1-0.5 @ 500	12-14 @ 2200	—	2-3.5	11.5-12 @ 12.5
	3250163	0-2 @ 750	15-17 @ 2200	—	2-4	7-8.5 @ 10
	3250497	−1-0.5 @ 500	8-11 @ 1700	—	2-4	15-17.5 @ 14

DISTRIBUTOR SPECIFICATIONS

Year	Distributor Identifisction	CENTRIFUGAL ADVANCE Start Dist. Deg. @ Dist. RPM	CENTRIFUGAL ADVANCE Maximum Dist. Deg. @ Dist. RPM	Vacuum Control No.	VACUUM ADVANCE Start @ In. Hg.	VACUUM ADVANCE Maximum Dist. Deg. @ In. Hg.
'80	110560	−0.5-0 @ 600①	6-10 @ 2400①	—	3-5	19-22② @ 9.5-10.5
	110561	−0.5-0 @ 600①	6-10 @ 2400①	—	3-5	13-16② @ 6-7
	3231340	−0.5-0.5 @ 600①	14-18 @ 2400①	—	2-6.5	13.5-19.5② @ 12-13
	3233174	−0.5-0.5 @ 700①	5-12 @ 2400①	—	1.5-4	21-25.5② @ 11.5-13
	3235141③	−1-1 @ 700①	5-10 @ 2400①	—	3-5	21.5-25.5② @ 15.5-16.5
	3235141④	−0.5-0.5 @ 700①	6-10 @ 2400①	—	3-5	20.5-26.5② @ 15.516.5
	3235141⑤	−1-1 @ 700①	6-10 @ 2400①	—	2.5-4.5	19-25② @ 19
	3235141⑥	−1-1 @ 800①	6-10 @ 2400①	—	3-5	21.5-25② @ 15.5-16.5
	3237198	−1-0.5 @ 800①	8-12 @ 2400①	—	3-5	20.5-25.5② @ 11-12.5
	3237199	−0.5-0.5 @ 800①	8-12 @ 2400①	—	2.5-4.5	29.5-34.5② @ 12-14
	3238428	−1-1 @ 900①	6-10 @ 2400①	—	2.5-4.5	18-25② @ 18
'81	1110595	−2.0 @ 1000	16 @ 2400	8133515	2.5-3.5	19-21 @ 10
	1110561	−2.0 @ 1200	16 @ 2500	8132515	3.5	16 @ 6
	1111393	−1.5 @ 1050	12-16 @ 2400	8131969	3.5	25 @ 15
	1110560	−2 @ 1000	16 @ 2500	8131968	4.8	25.2 @ 16
	3239833	−2.0 @ 1200	13 @ 2200			
	3235141	−1 @ 950	12.5 @ 2200			
	3239829	−1.0 @ 900	12.5 @ 2200			

① Engine r.p.m.
② Engine degrees
③ 6 cylinder automatic transmission 49-state
④ Jeep only
⑤ 6 cylinder manual transmission 50-state
⑥ 6 cylinder automatic transmission 50-state

ELECTRICAL SECTION

Starter solenoid ohmmeter check

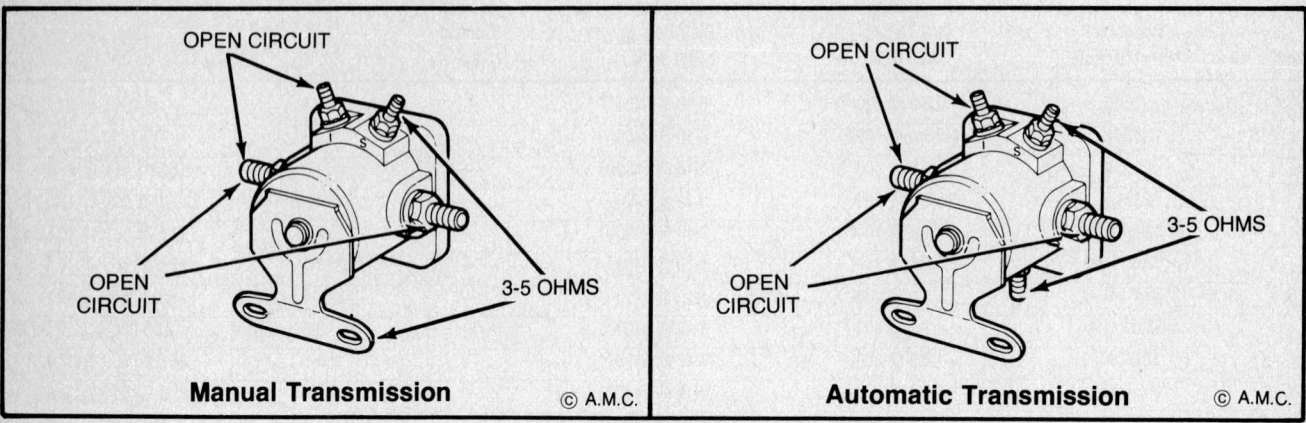

Manual Transmission © A.M.C.

Automatic Transmission © A.M.C.

Starter

- Disconnect electrical wiring, remove mounting bolts, and remove starter.

NOTE: Four cylinder engine solenoids are not interchangeable with six and eight cylinder solenoids.

Ignition Distributor R&R

- Remove distributor cap, electrical wiring and vacuum hose from distributor.
- Put alignment marks on rotor and distributor housing for installation reference.
- Remove hold-down clamp, and pull distributor up out of the engine block.
- Install the distributor in the correct position, and time engine to specifications.

NOTE: Some engines may be sensitive to the routing of the distributor sensor wires. If routed near the high-voltage coil wire or spark plug wires, the electromagnetic field surrounding the high-voltage wires could generate an occasional disruption of the ignition system operation.

Rotor position reference mark

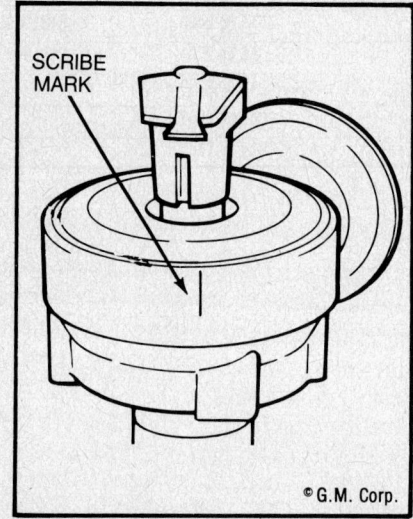

SCRIBE MARK

© G.M. Corp.

Make mark as shown for installation reference.

Ignition distributor

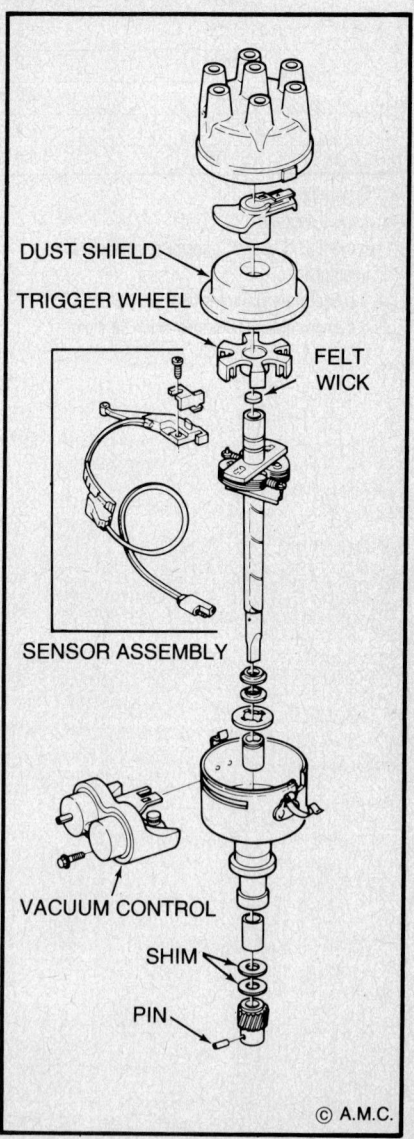

DUST SHIELD

TRIGGER WHEEL

FELT WICK

SENSOR ASSEMBLY

VACUUM CONTROL

SHIM

PIN

© A.M.C.

Ignition distributor used in six cylinder engine

Distributor mounting

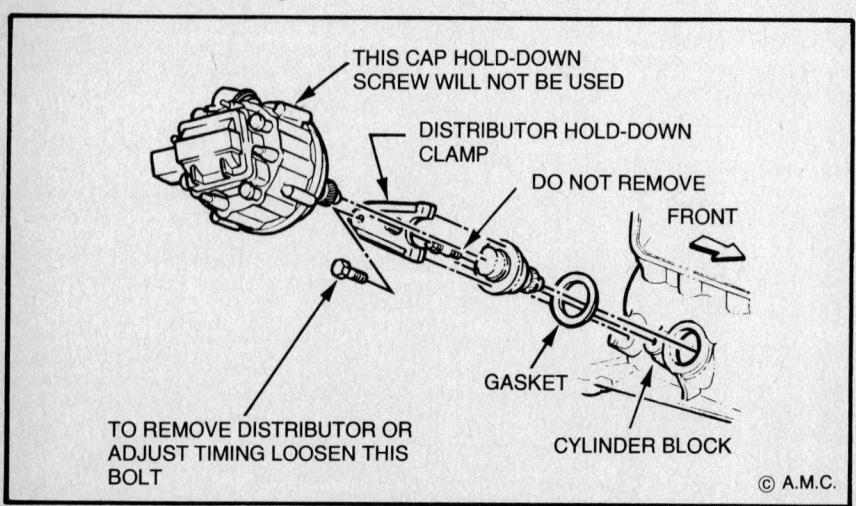

THIS CAP HOLD-DOWN SCREW WILL NOT BE USED

DISTRIBUTOR HOLD-DOWN CLAMP

DO NOT REMOVE

FRONT

GASKET

CYLINDER BLOCK

TO REMOVE DISTRIBUTOR OR ADJUST TIMING LOOSEN THIS BOLT

© A.M.C.

Distributor mounting in 151 CID, four cylinder engine

Ignition Lock

Column Mounted
- Remove steering wheel and lock plate, and pull turn signal switch assembly up out of the way.
- With cylinder in the "LOCK" position, depress retaining tab and pull lock cylinder out of housing.
- Before installing, turn lock cylinder to full counterclockwise position.
- Push sleeve into housing while rotating counterclockwise until cylinder mates with sector and retainer snaps into place.

Instrument Panel Mounted
- Press switch body toward instrument panel, and turn notched bezel counterclockwise. Separate lock and switch assembly from instrument panel and electrical connections.

Ignition Switch
- For instrument panel mounted switches, use "Ignition Lock" procedure.
- The ignition switch is mounted on the lower steering column and is connected to the key lock by a remote lock rod.
- With key in "OFF LOCK" position, remove mounting screws, rod and wiring.
- When installing, move slider to extreme left of switch pointing inward toward steering column. Put actuator rod in slider hole and install switch. On tilt wheel columns, remove lash by pushing downward on switch before tightening mounting screws.

Neutral Safety Switch

Except Four Wheel Drive
- The neutral safety switch is located on the left side of the automatic transmission. Fluid will drain from transmission when the switch is removed.

Ignition lock cylinder retaining tab

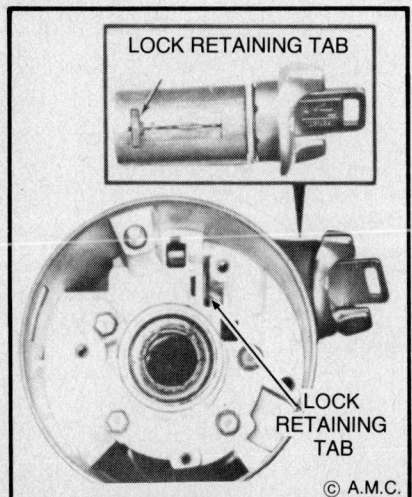

Insert a screwdriver into the retaining tab access slot and press to release lock cylinder.

Lock cylinder and sleeve

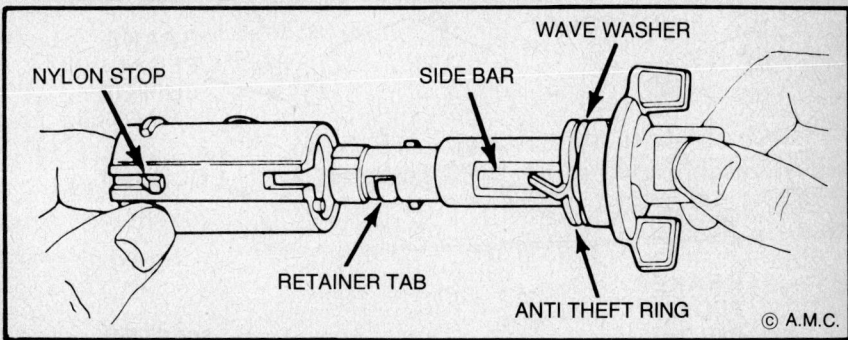

Steering column mounted ignition switch

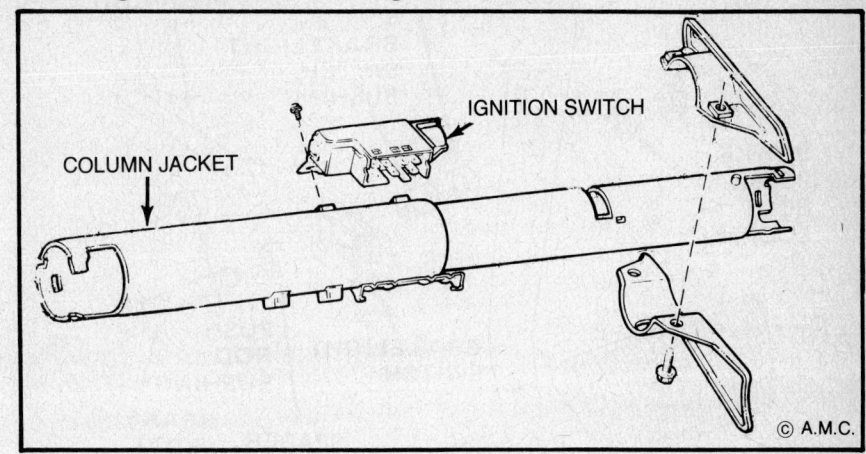

- Place sealant on the threads when installing.

Four Wheel Drive Vehicles
- The neutral safety switch is mounted on the lower steering column. Access to it may require removal of lower finish panel, air conditioning ducting, etc.

- The switch is adjusted by loosening its mounting screws and moving the switch until the vehicle will start only in "PARK" and "NEUTRAL" positions, and the backup lights operate only in "REVERSE."
- Be extremely careful not to strip the mounting screws when retightening.

Neutral start switch

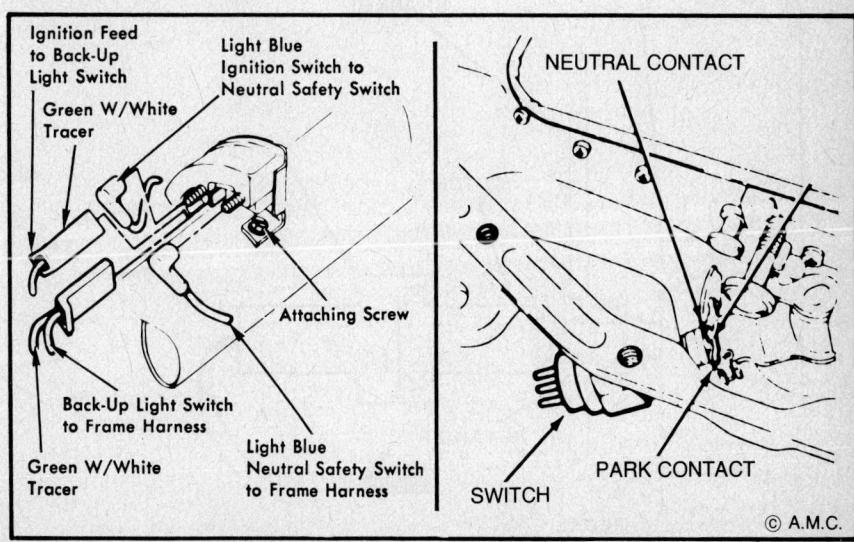

Typical steering column mounted back-up and neutral safety switch

Neutral start switch installed in automatic transmission

Brakelight switch mounting

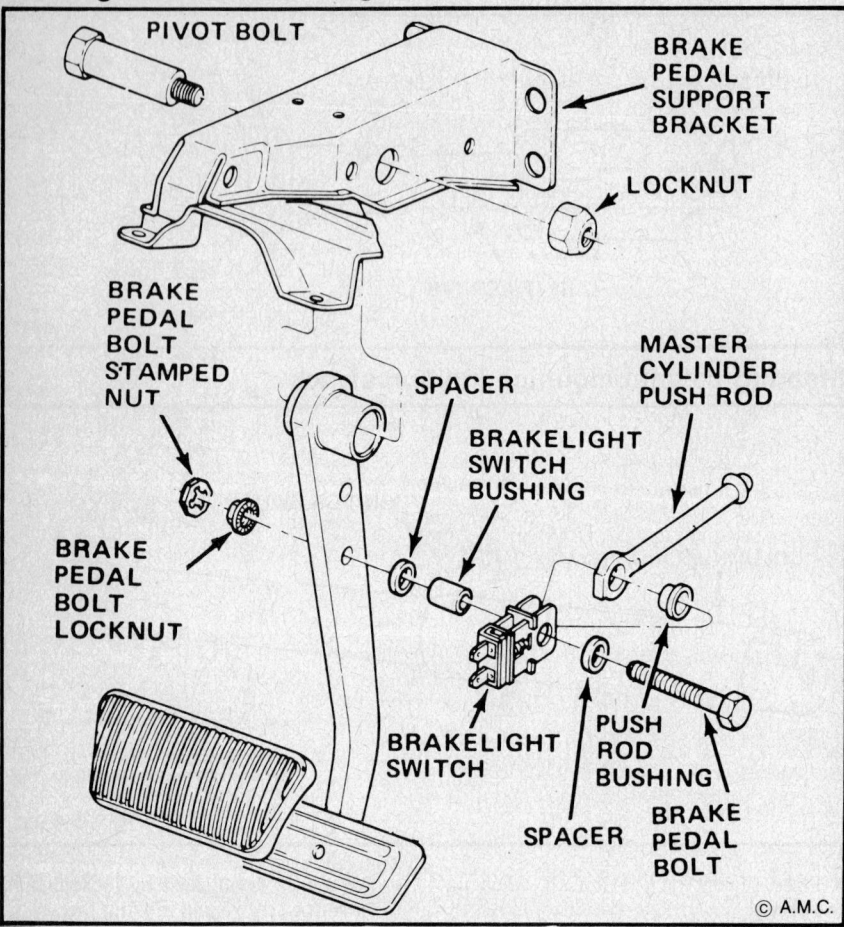

Used on two wheel drive passenger cars with power brakes. Use upper mounting hole with non-power brakes. New locknut and stamped nut must always be used when the switch is disconnected

Stop Light Switch

Except Four Wheel Drive

• The switch is mounted on the brake pedal and is not adjustable.

NOTE: Each time the brake pedal bolt is removed a new locknut and a new stamped nut *must* be used.

• Brakelights should illuminate at first ½ inch of pedal travel.
• The brake pedal has two mounting bolt holes. On cars with power brakes, install the bolt in the lower hole. On cars without power brakes, install the bolt in the upper hole.

Four Wheel Drive Vehicles

• On models equipped with a stoplight switch mounted to the pedal lever end of the master cylinder or power unit push rod, the switch is not adjustable.
• Adjustments can be made on models equipped with a stop light switch mounted to a flange attached to the brake pedal support bracket. The switch position should be adjusted to activate the brake lights at ⅜ to ⅝ inch of brake pedal travel.

Stoplight switch used in Cherokee and Wagoneer

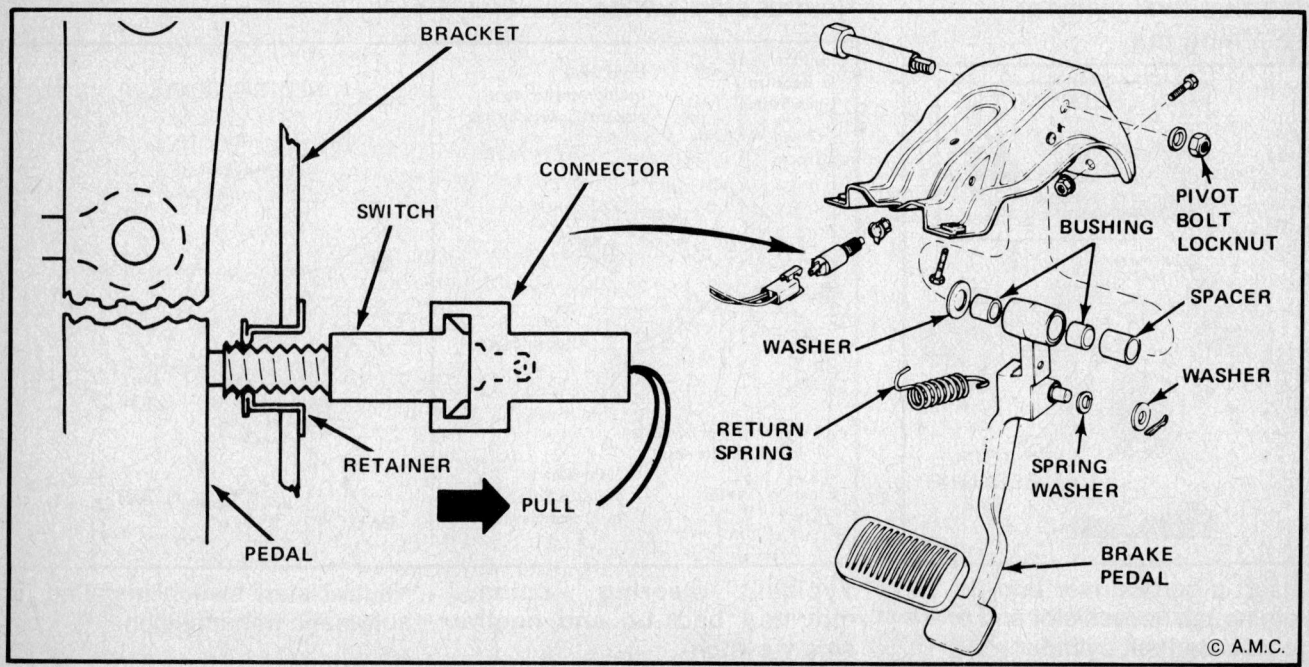

Sport steering wheel and horn switch components

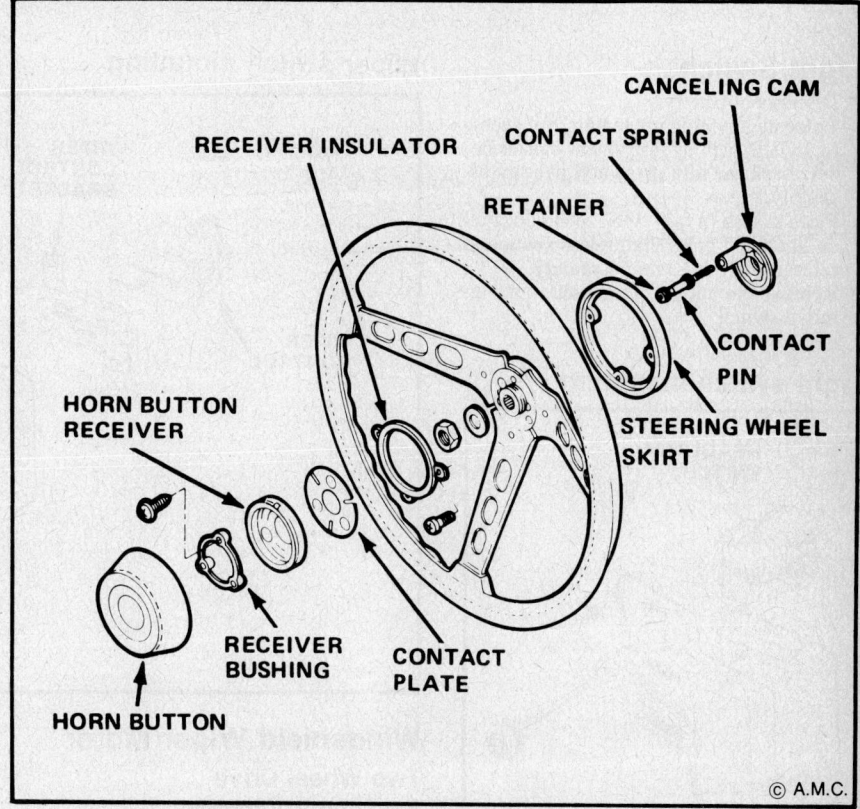

CANCELING CAM
CONTACT SPRING
RETAINER
RECEIVER INSULATOR
CONTACT PIN
STEERING WHEEL SKIRT
HORN BUTTON RECEIVER
RECEIVER BUSHING
HORN BUTTON
CONTACT PLATE

© A.M.C.

Horn Switch & Steering Wheel

- Disconnect battery.
- On steering wheels with center horn buttons, remove the button by first lifting it up and then pulling it out. On other types, remove the mounting screws at the back of the wheel, and pull the horn wire plastic retainer out of the turn signal cancelling cam, and remove the button.
- Use a steering wheel puller to remove the steering wheel.

CHILTON CAUTION: *Do not hammer on the end of shaft.*

Metric steering shaft identification

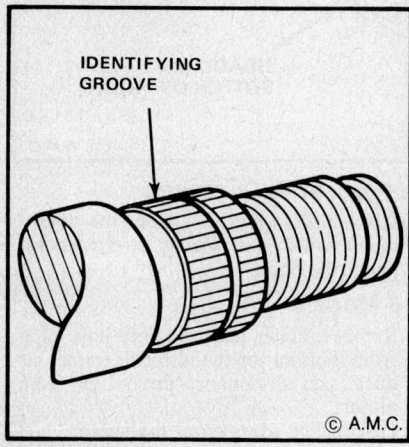

IDENTIFYING GROOVE

© A.M.C.

Do not use a non-metric nut on this type shaft

Turn Signal Switch

- Disconnect battery.
- Remove steering wheel, anti-theft cover, lock plate and turn signal cancelling cam.
- Place turn signal lever in right turn position, and remove the lever.
- Depress hazard warning light switch, and remove button by turning counterclockwise.
- Remove wire harness connector block. On column shift automatic transmission vehicles, use a stiff wire to depress the lock tab holding the shift quadrant light wire in the connector block.
- Remove switch screws, and pull the switch and wire harness out of the column.

Turn signal switch and attaching parts

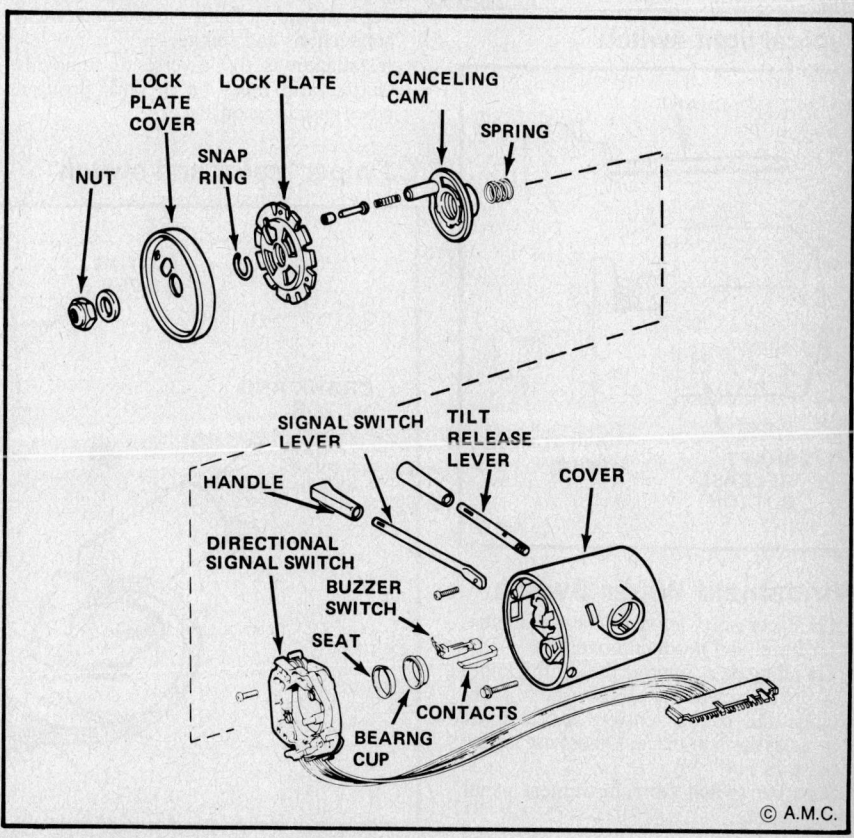

NUT
LOCK PLATE COVER
SNAP RING
LOCK PLATE
CANCELING CAM
SPRING
SIGNAL SWITCH LEVER
TILT RELEASE LEVER
HANDLE
COVER
DIRECTIONAL SIGNAL SWITCH
BUZZER SWITCH
SEAT
CONTACTS
BEARNG CUP

© A.M.C.

WIPER SECTION

Light Switch
- Disconnect battery.
- Relocate anything preventing full access to switch such as instrument cluster bezel, package tray or switch overlay assembly.
- Place switch in full "ON" position. Pull on knob and press shaft release button to release shaft and knob assembly.
- Remove mounting sleeve nut, and remove switch.

Light switch mounting

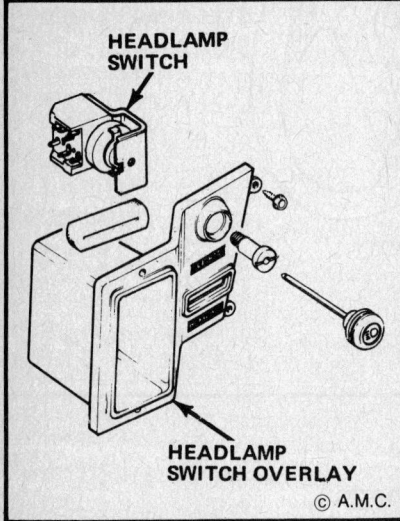

Typical light switch

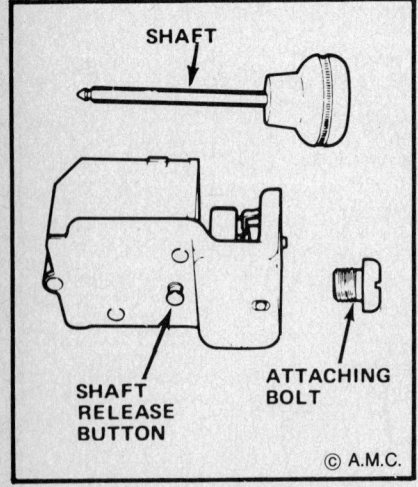

Windshield Wiper Switch
- On Pacer only, remove instrument cluster bezel and headlamp overlay.
- On all models, remove the control knob. A small screwdriver can be used to overcome the spring tension which holds most of them in place. Others use a slotted trim nut.
- Separate switch from instrument panel and wiring.

Wiper switch mounting

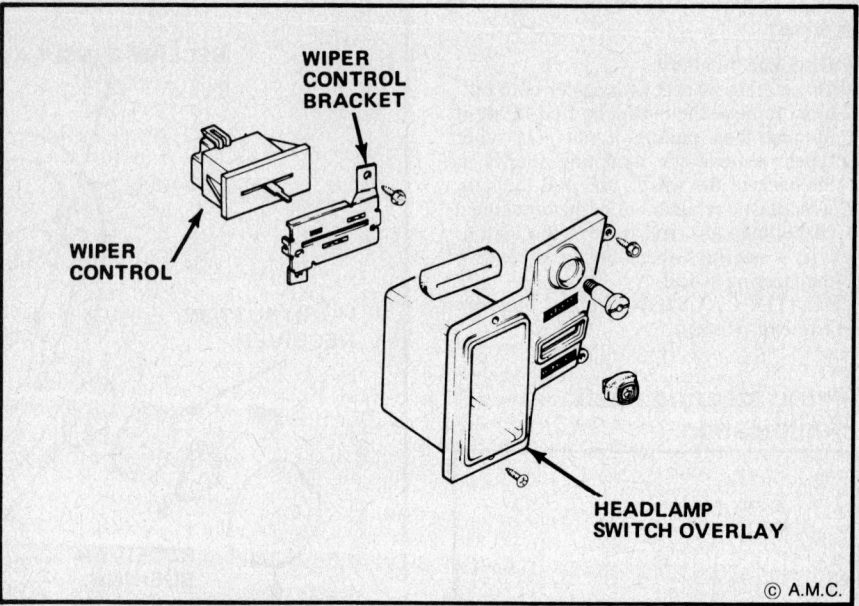

Windshield Wiper Motor
Two Wheel Drive
Passenger Vehicles
- On Pacer, move heater housing forward for access. On other models, remove wiper arms and if necessary, cowl screen.
- Separate motor from mounts, electrical connections and linkage.
- Installation is the reverse of removal. Output arm must be in park position when installing on Pacer.

Wagoneer & Cherokee
- Disconnect drive link under the instrument panel and wiring at the motor under the hood.

CJ Models
- Remove crash pad and left hole plug from bottom of windshield frame air duct, and disconnect drive link from motor.
- Disconnect wires from the switch, and remove motor.
- When installing, the motor cover must be sealed.

CJ wiper motor and switch

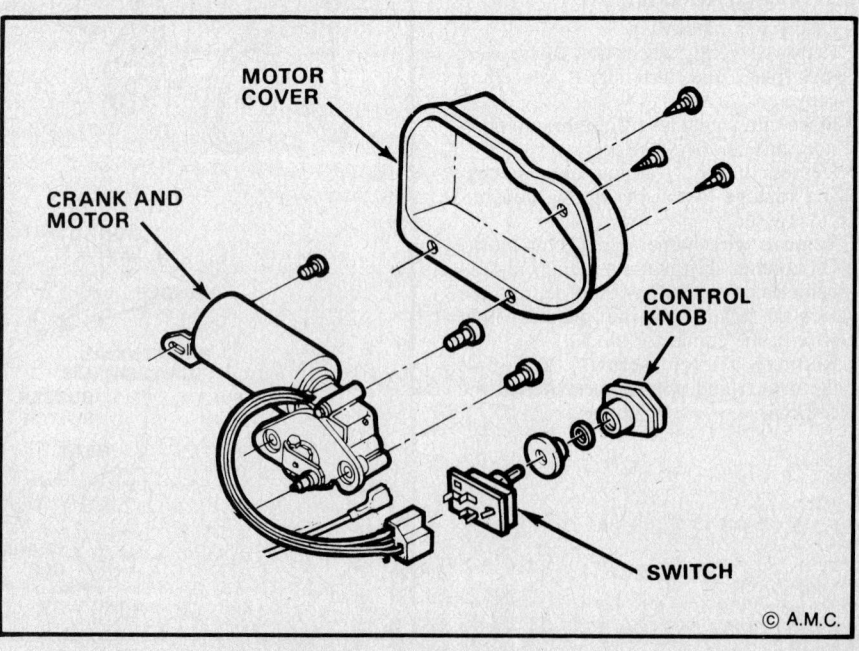

Windshield Wiper Linkage

Except Four Wheel Drive

- Remove wiper arms, and, if necessary, cowl screen.
- On Pacer and Matador Coupe, use Torx Bit Tool J-25359-02 to remove pivot shaft-to-cowl screws.
- On Concord, Gremlin, Hornet and Javelin, remove wiper motor.
- Disconnect linkage from motor and remove.
- Installation is the reverse of removal.

Four Wheel Drive Vehicles

- Remove wiper arms.
- Disconnect linkage at motor. On CJ models, remove access hole covers.
- In some cases it may be easier to remove individual links.

Windshield wiper system

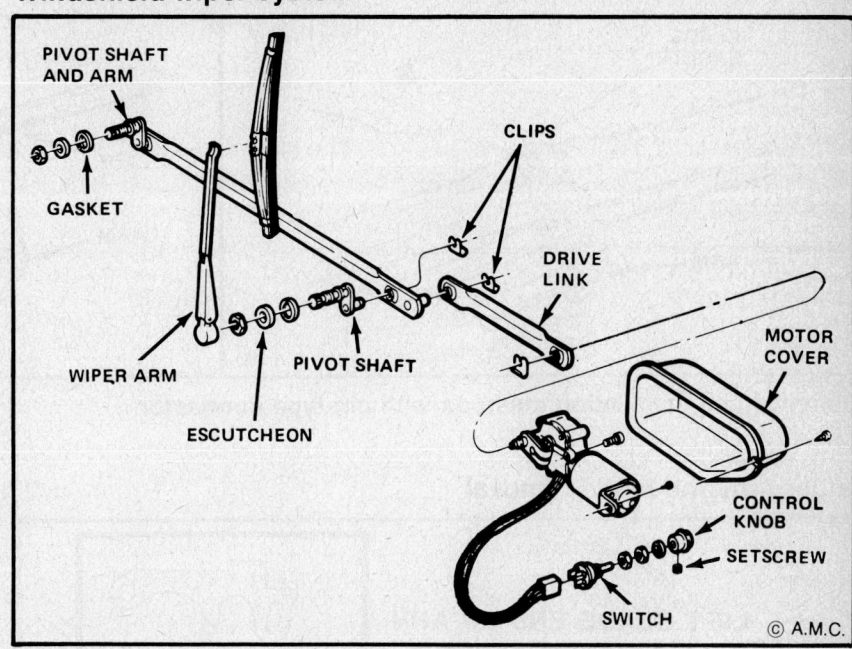

Windshield wiper components used in CJ models

Windshield wiper system

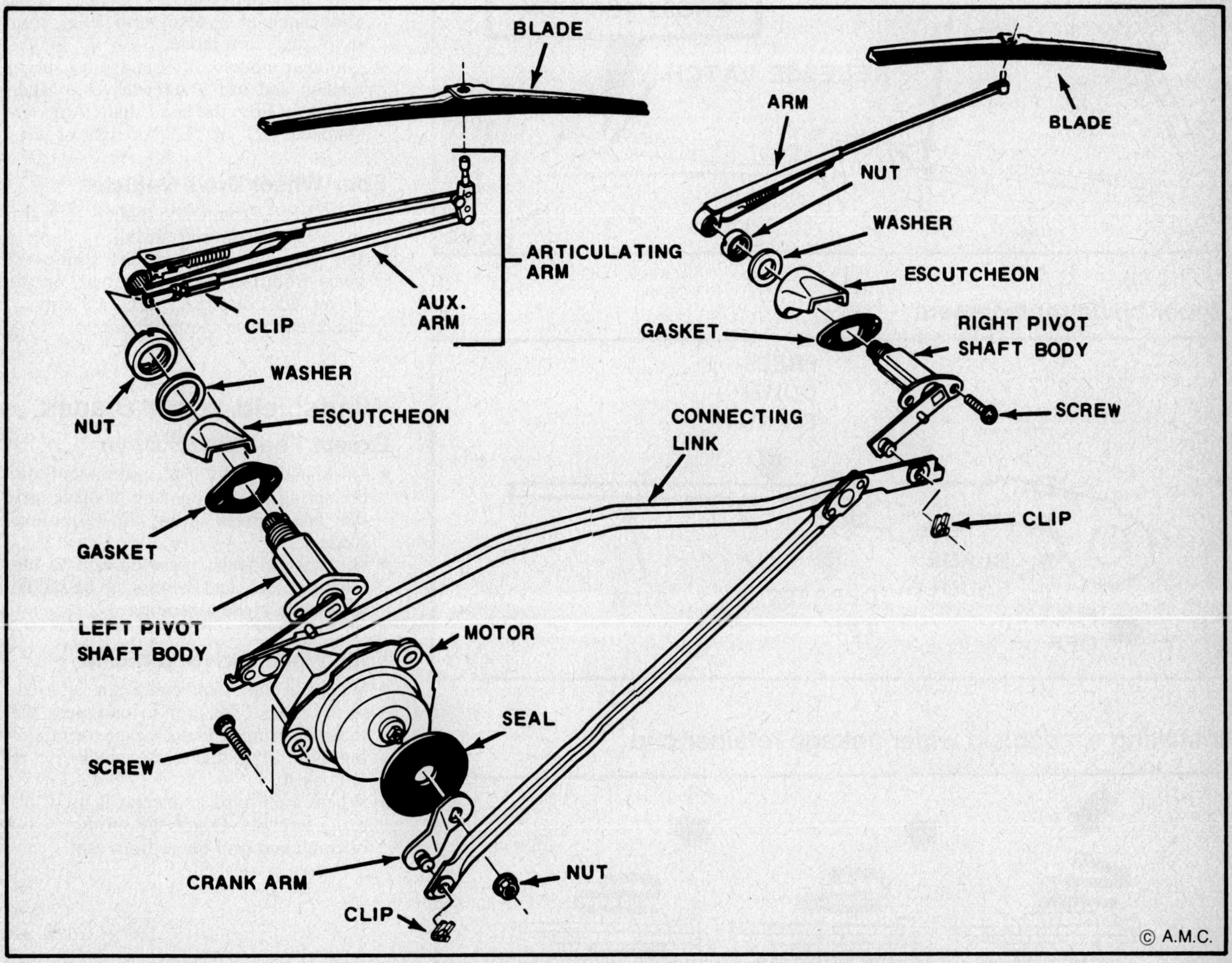

Windshield wiper components used typically in Cherokee and Wagoneer models

A23

AMC PASSENGER CARS AND JEEP

Wiper blade replacement

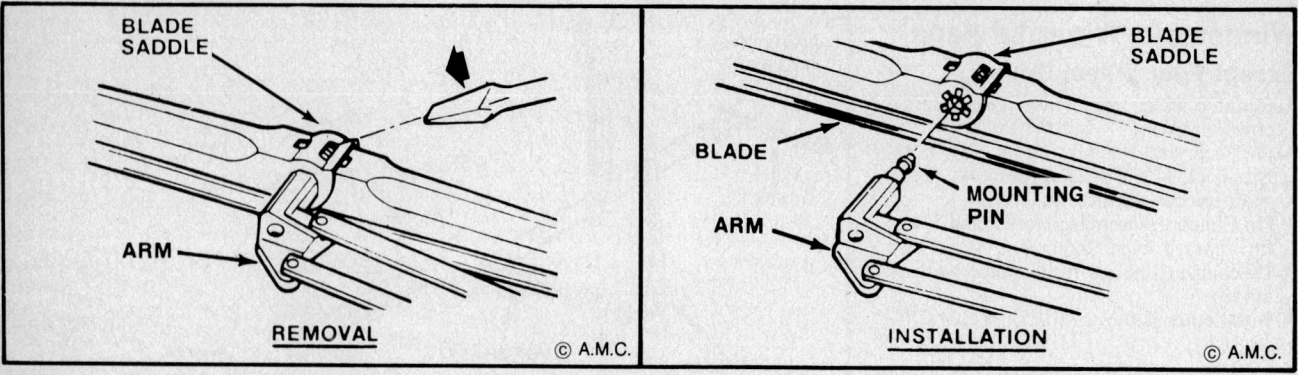

Removal and installation methods with pin-type connector

Wiper arm and blade removal

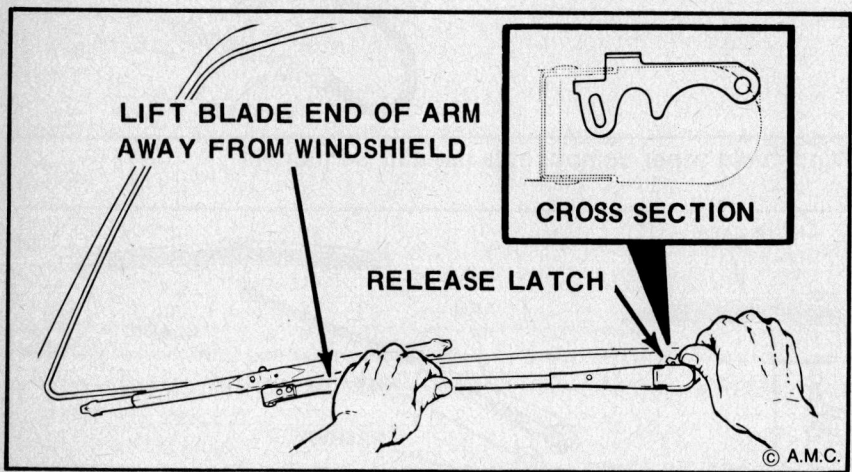

Wiper blade replacement

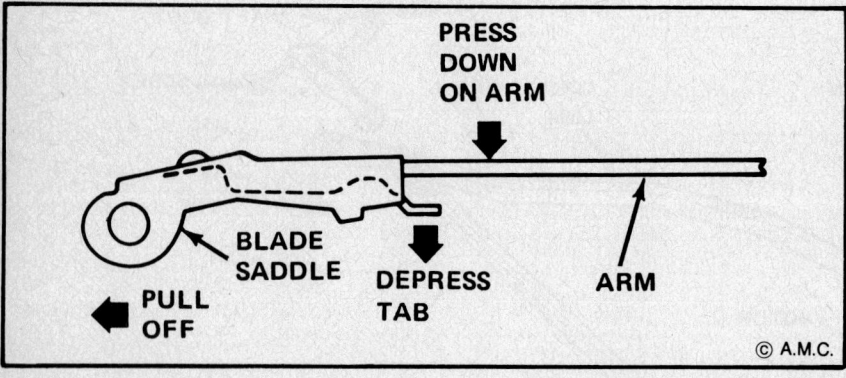

Windshield Wiper Arms
Except Four Wheel Drive
- On Pacer and Matador Coupe, move slide latch at base of arm away from pivot shaft to remove.
- On other models, lift arm against spring tension and use a screwdriver to slide cap away from the pivot shaft. Arms are stamped ''R'' or ''L'' for right or left.

Four Wheel Drive Vehicles
- On CJ and Commando models, pry arm off shaft. Press on to install.
- On other models, push the spring tab away from the pivot shaft, and, on the driver side, disengage auxiliary arm retainer clip from the pivot pin.

Windshield Wiper Blades
Except Four Wheel Drive
- On Matador and Pacer, insert a tool into the spring release opening of blade saddle, and depress spring clip to remove blade.
- On other models, press on arm to unlatch top stud, and depress tab on saddle to remove blade assembly.

Four Wheel Drive Vehicles
- Where a flat hook connector is used, push against the arm to compress the locking spring, and disengage the retaining pin. Pivot the blade clockwise to unhook it.
- Where a pin-type connector is used, insert a screwdriver into the spring release opening and pull blade from arm.

Installing windshield wiper linkage retainer clip

HEATER SECTION

Pacer temperature control unit

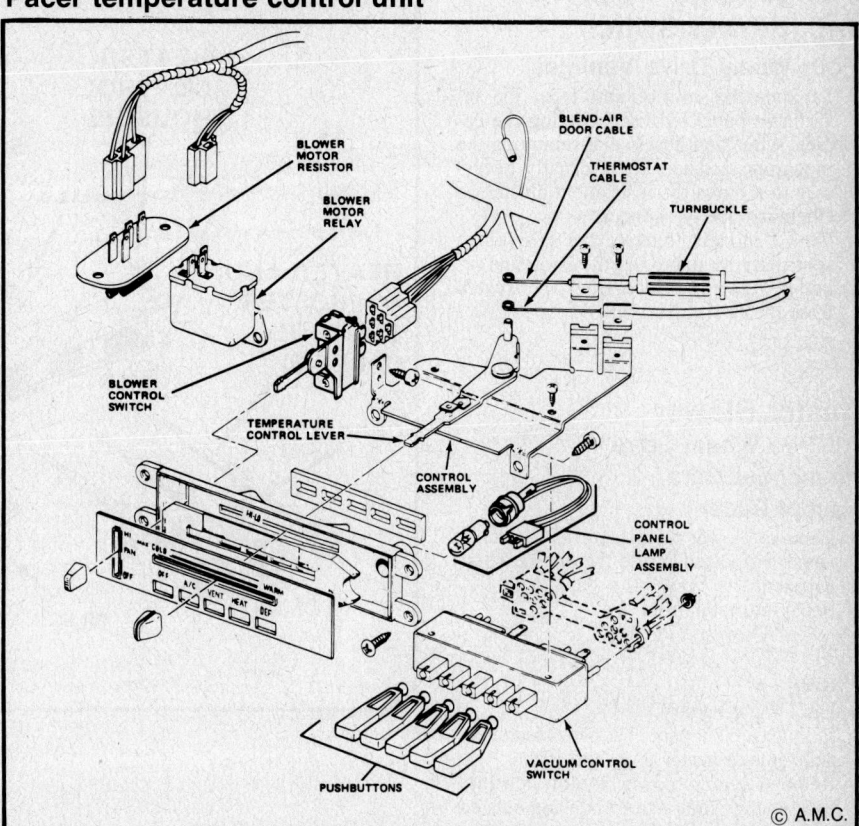

Radio

Except Four Wheel Drive

- Disconnect battery.
- On Javelin, remove entire crash pad.
- On Gremlin, Hornet and Concord, remove package tray, ash tray, etc. for access to radio. On air conditioned models, remove instrument panel center housing.
- On Matador and Ambassador, remove instrument cluster bezel.
- Loosen or remove mounting screws, knobs, etc., and remove radio from antenna, power and speaker connections.

Four Wheel Drive Vehicles

- On Wagoneer and Cherokee, remove the glove box liner, and remove radio through this opening.
- On all other models, remove radio from under instrument panel.

Hidden mounting nut

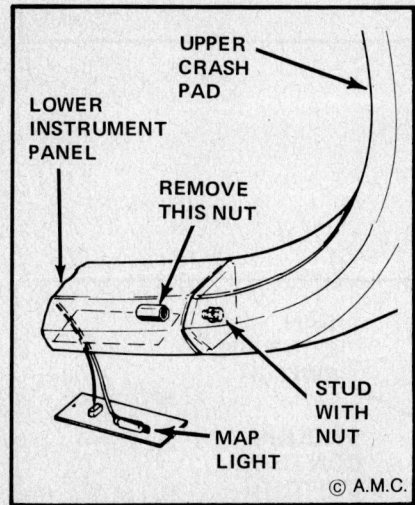

Access to Javelin crash pad hidden mounting nut is through map light compartment

Temperature Control Unit/Blower Switch

Except Four Wheel Drive

- Disconnect battery.
- Remove radio and instrument cluster bezel or center housing for access.
- Remove mounting screws, and separate unit from control cables, vacuum lines and electrical connections.

Temperature control unit typical in all except Pacer models

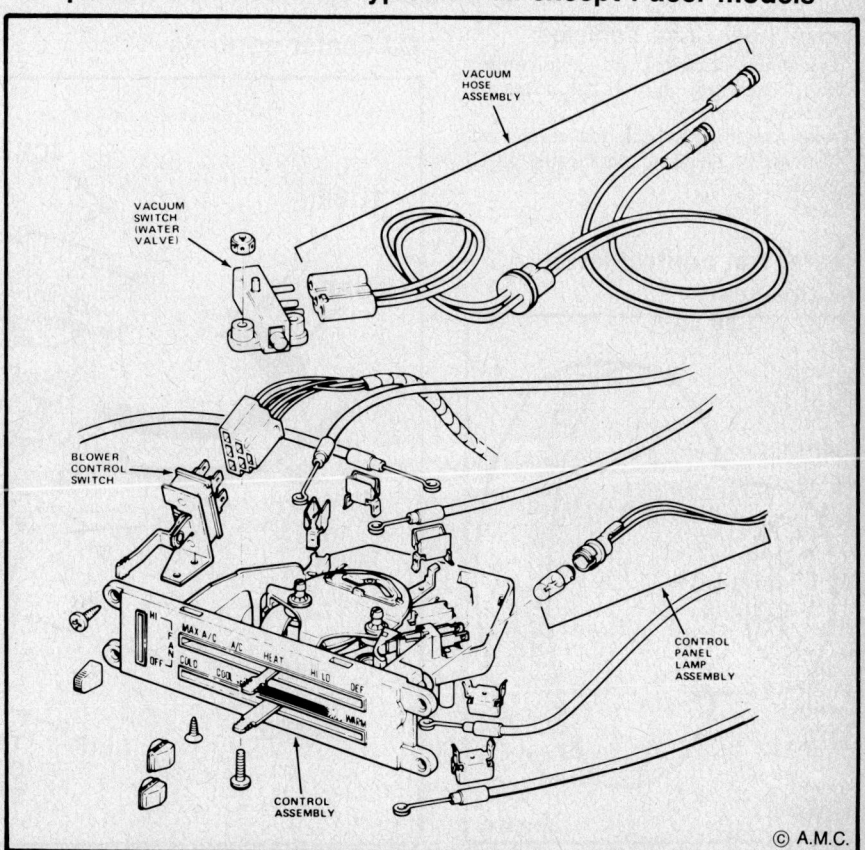

AMC PASSENGER CARS AND JEEP

Temperature Control Unit/Blower Switch

Four Wheel Drive Vehicles

- Separate the control unit from the instrument panel by disconnecting the cables, wires and hoses, and removing the mounting fasteners. It is usually necessary to remove the instrument cluster on Cherokee and Wagoneer.
- On CJ models, remove the fan switch separately by removing the knob and retaining nut, and separating the switch from the instrument panel.

Heater Blower

All Two Wheel Drive Passenger Cars Except Pacer

- Remove blower motor and fan assembly which is located inside the engine compartment.
- Separate motor from fan.

Pacer

- Disconnect battery.
- Pull instrument panel back for clearance, and remove heater core housing.
- Remove entire blower motor housing, and separate motor from housing outside of car.

Four Wheel Drive Vehicles

- Disconnect electrical and cable connections, and remove blower motor, fan and housing assembly.
- After installing, check for correct adjustment of blend air door cable on CJ models.

Heater fan control knob lock release

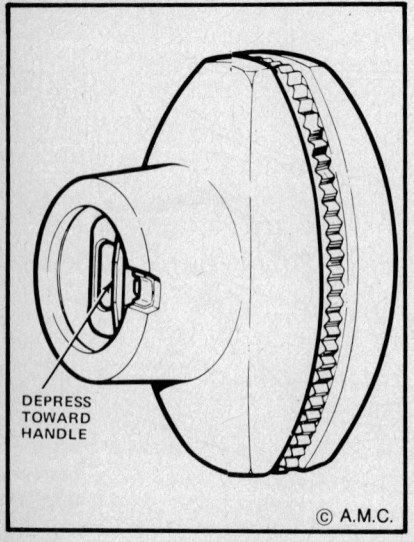

Heater/defroster control unit—Cherokee and Wagoneer

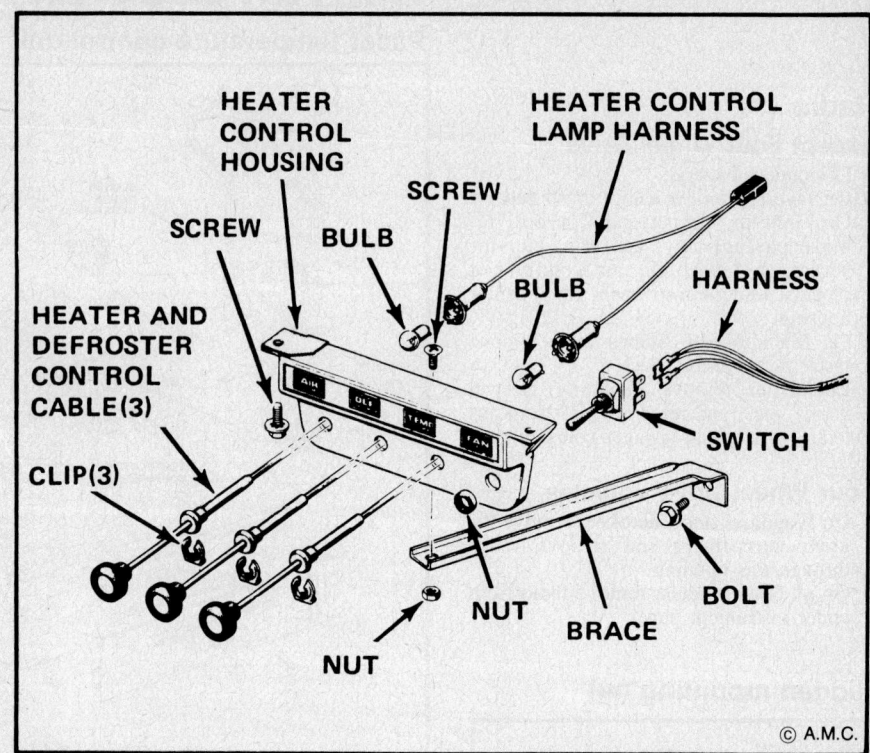

CJ heater controls

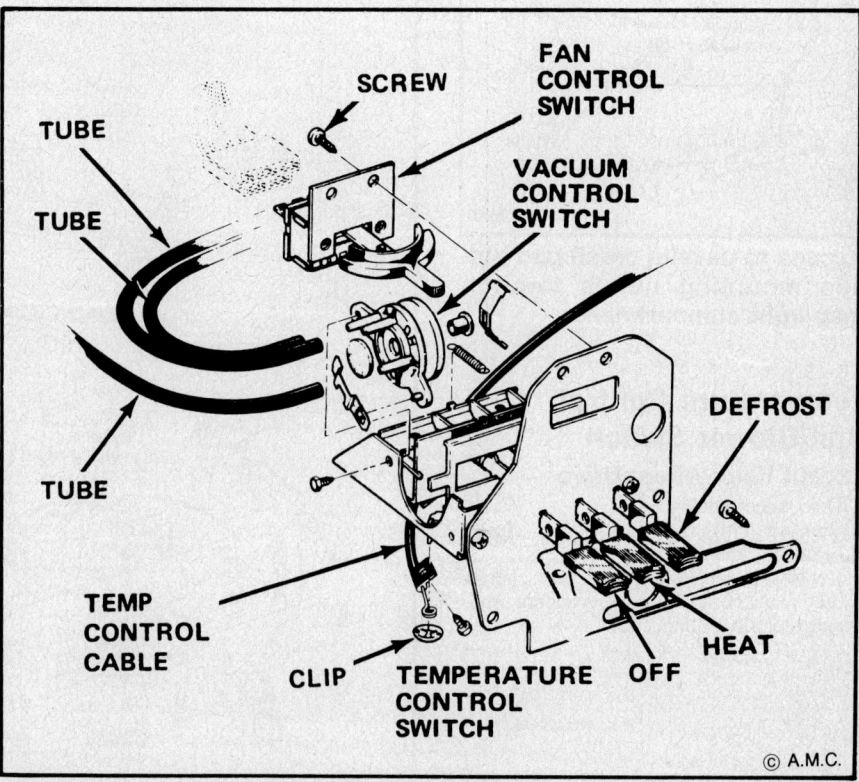

Heater blower fan mounting

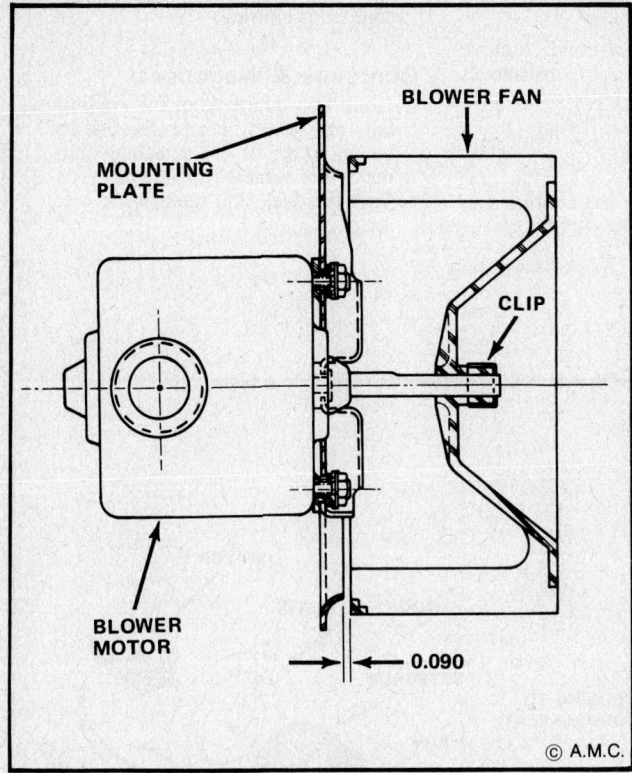

Heater blower fan mounting plate clearance in Pacer

Heater blower fan mounting

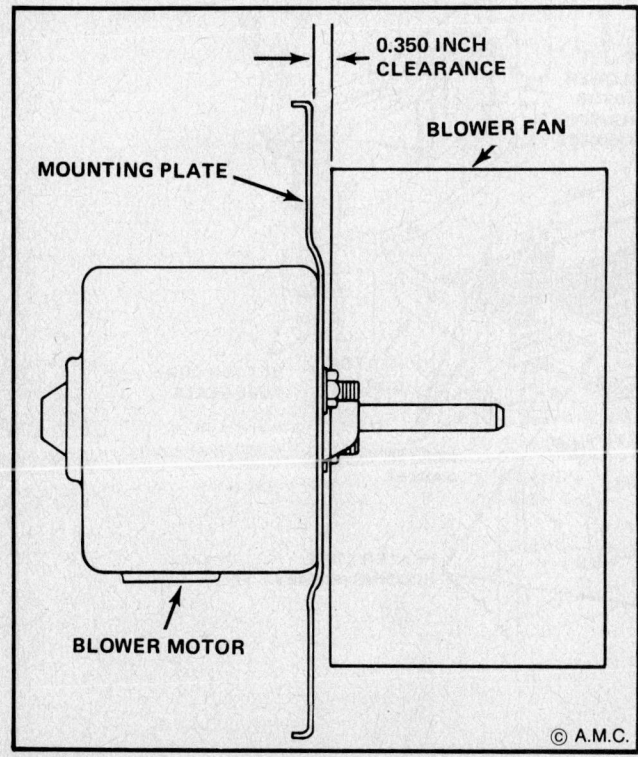

Heater blower fan mounting plate in two wheel drive passenger cars except Pacer

Blower fan retainer placement

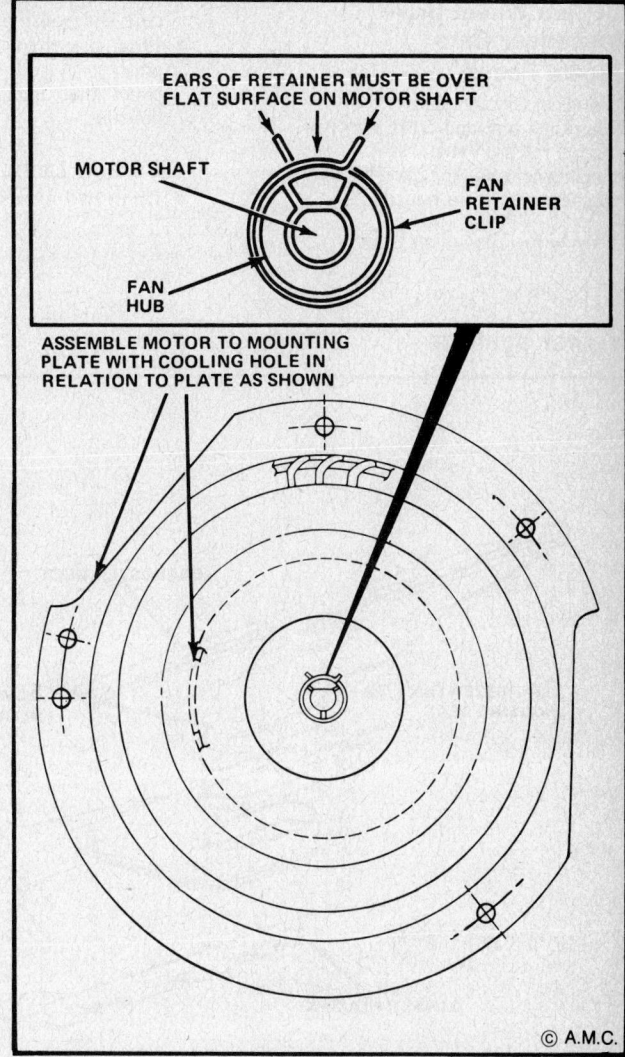

Typical blower motor, fan and mounting plate

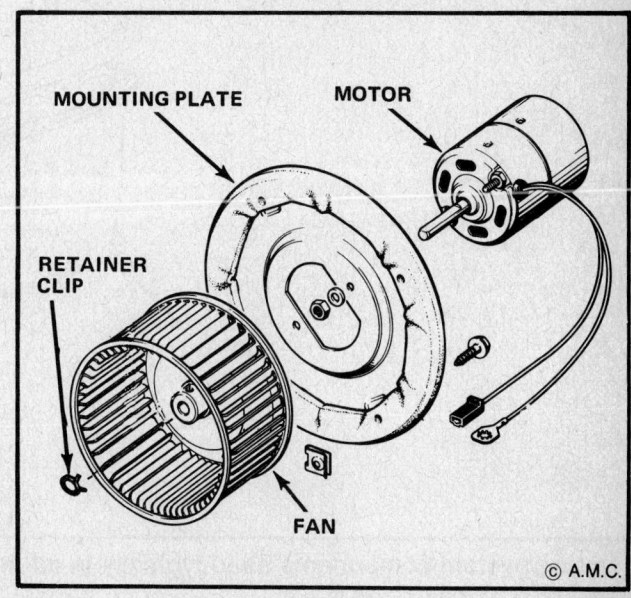

Heater Core
All Two Wheel Drive
Passenger Cars
Except Pacer

It is necessary to remove
- package tray and cowl trim pad
- hood release cable
- instrument panel center housing
- heater core from housing

Pacer
- From engine side of cowl, remove heater core and housing.
- From passenger side of cowl, remove crash pad and section of instrument panel that interferes with evaporator housing.

1976 and Later CJ
- Drain two quarts from the cooling sys-tem, and remove battery box, glove box and heater housing assembly. Separate core from housing.

Cherokee & Wagoneer
- Drain two quarts from the cooling sys-tem, and remove heater duct and core as a unit. Two of the attaching nuts are inside the vehicle.
- Split the duct, and remove the core.

Heater system

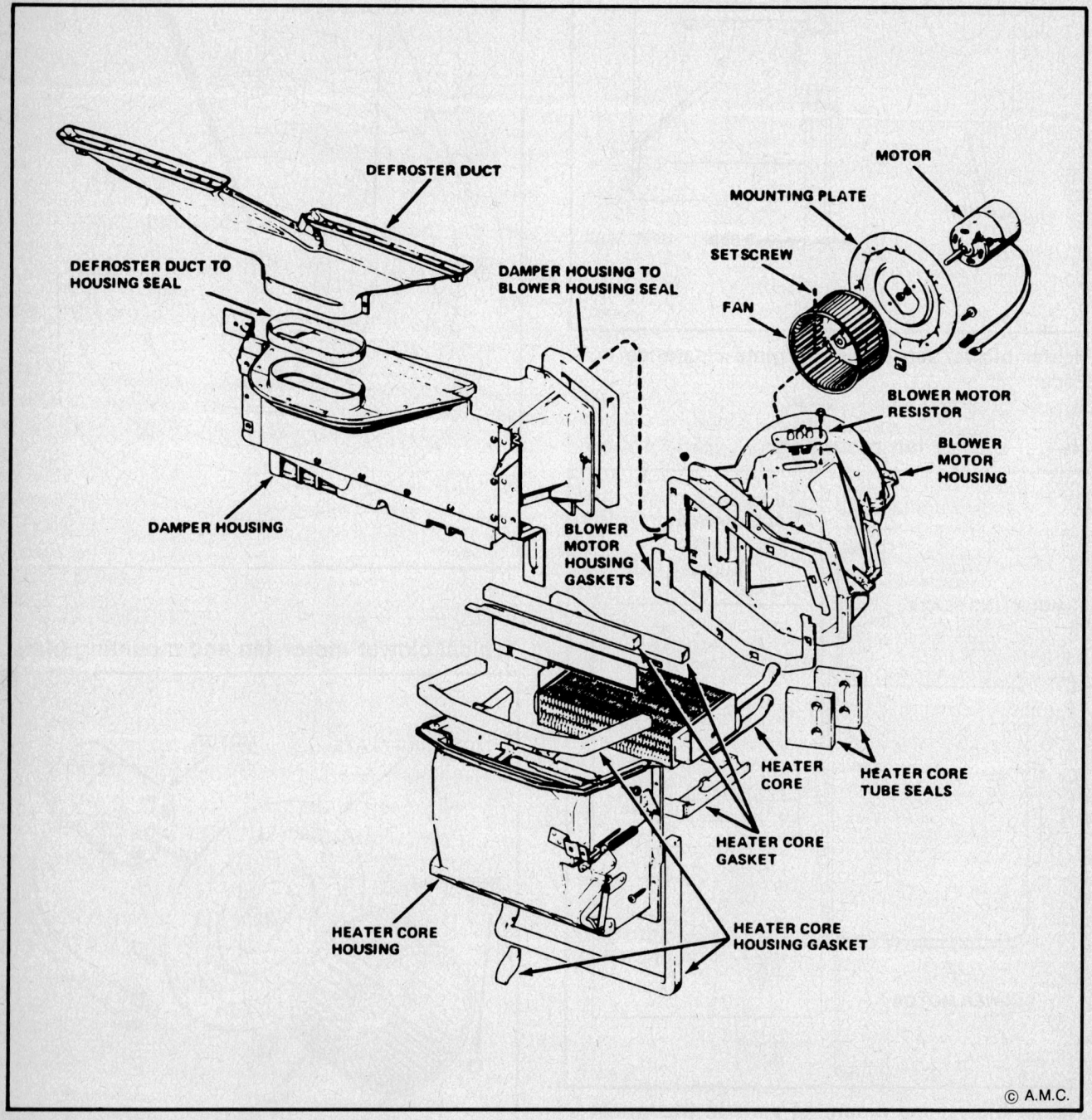

DEFROSTER DUCT

DEFROSTER DUCT TO HOUSING SEAL

DAMPER HOUSING TO BLOWER HOUSING SEAL

MOTOR

MOUNTING PLATE

SETSCREW

FAN

BLOWER MOTOR RESISTOR

BLOWER MOTOR HOUSING

DAMPER HOUSING

BLOWER MOTOR HOUSING GASKETS

HEATER CORE

HEATER CORE TUBE SEALS

HEATER CORE GASKET

HEATER CORE HOUSING

HEATER CORE HOUSING GASKET

© A.M.C.

Heating system components used typically in all models except Pacer

Pacer heater/air conditioner components

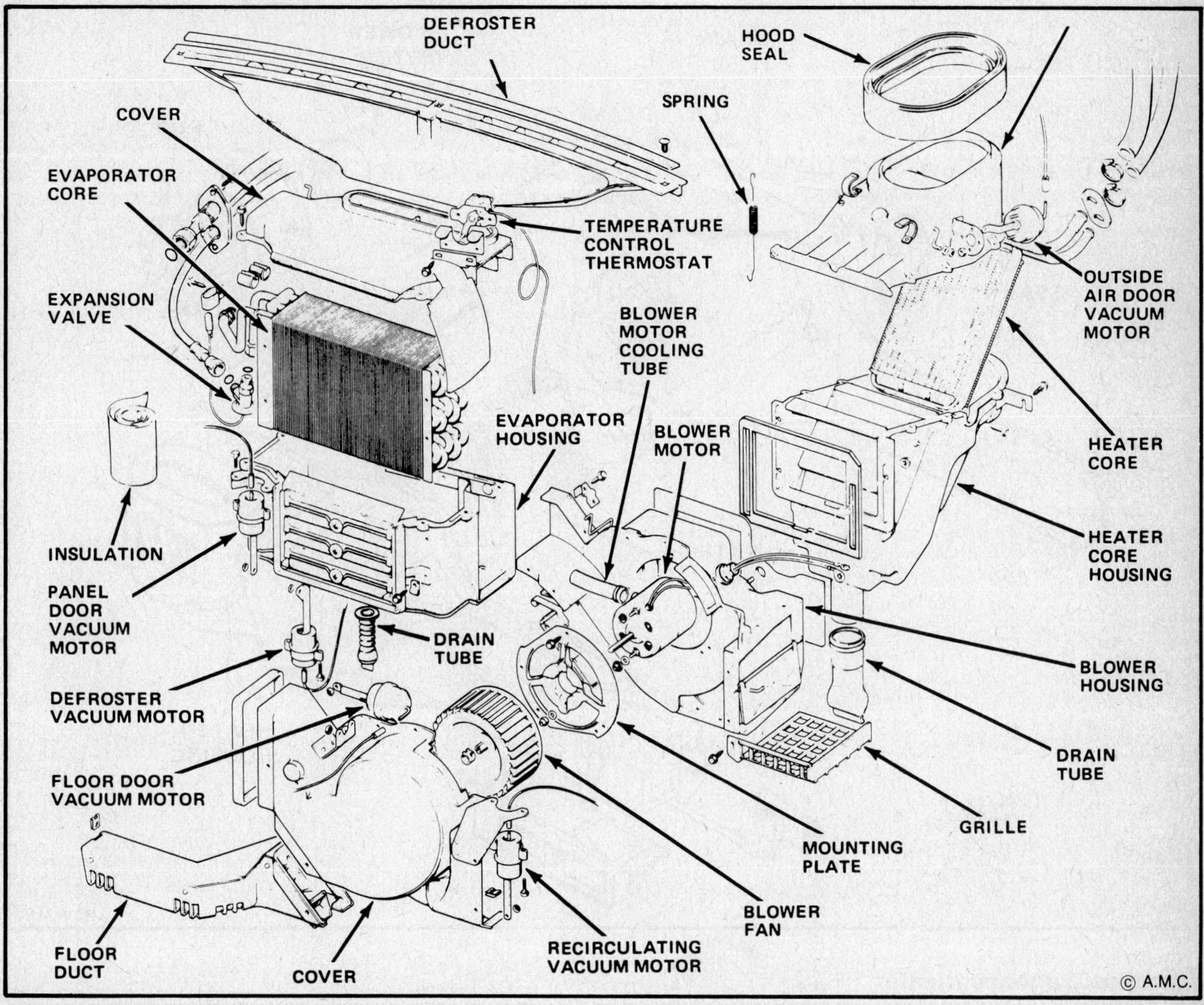

DEFROSTER
DUCT

HOOD
SEAL

COVER

SPRING

EVAPORATOR
CORE

TEMPERATURE
CONTROL
THERMOSTAT

EXPANSION
VALVE

BLOWER
MOTOR
COOLING
TUBE

OUTSIDE
AIR DOOR
VACUUM
MOTOR

EVAPORATOR
HOUSING

BLOWER
MOTOR

HEATER
CORE

INSULATION

HEATER
CORE
HOUSING

PANEL
DOOR
VACUUM
MOTOR

DRAIN
TUBE

DEFROSTER
VACUUM MOTOR

BLOWER
HOUSING

FLOOR DOOR
VACUUM MOTOR

DRAIN
TUBE

FLOOR
DUCT

COVER

RECIRCULATING
VACUUM MOTOR

BLOWER
FAN

MOUNTING
PLATE

GRILLE

© A.M.C.

CJ heater/defroster

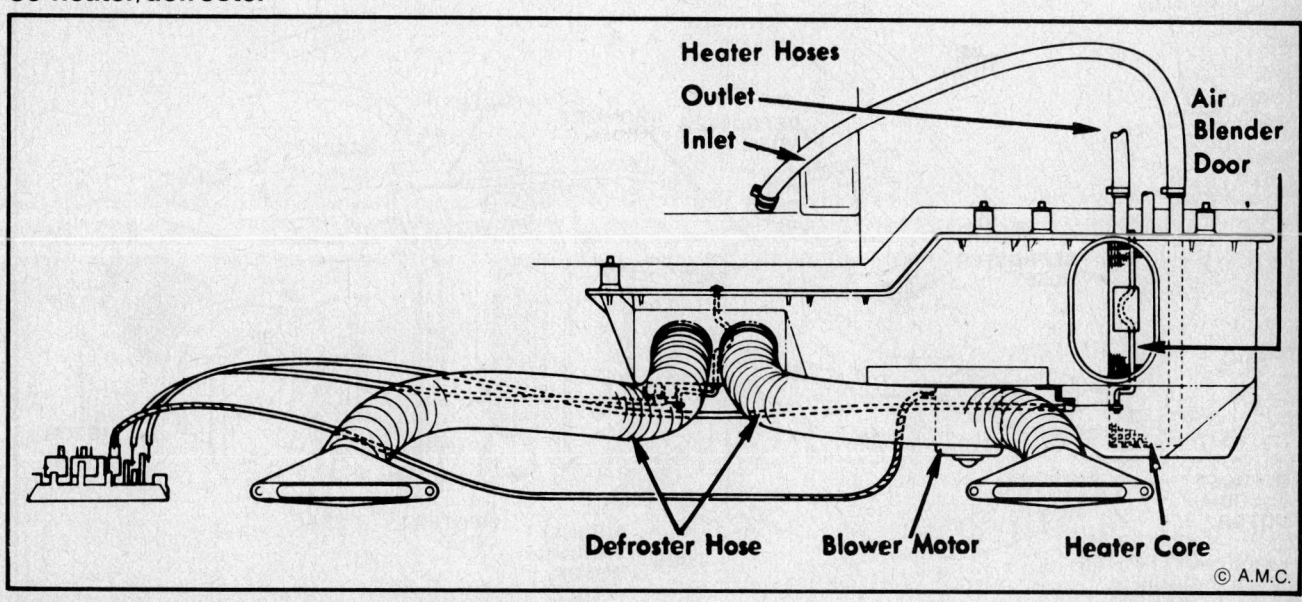

Heater Hoses

Outlet

Inlet

Air
Blender
Door

Defroster Hose

Blower Motor

Heater Core

© A.M.C.

1977 and earlier CJ heater and defroster system

AMC PASSENGER CARS AND JEEP

1978 and later CJ heater housing and components

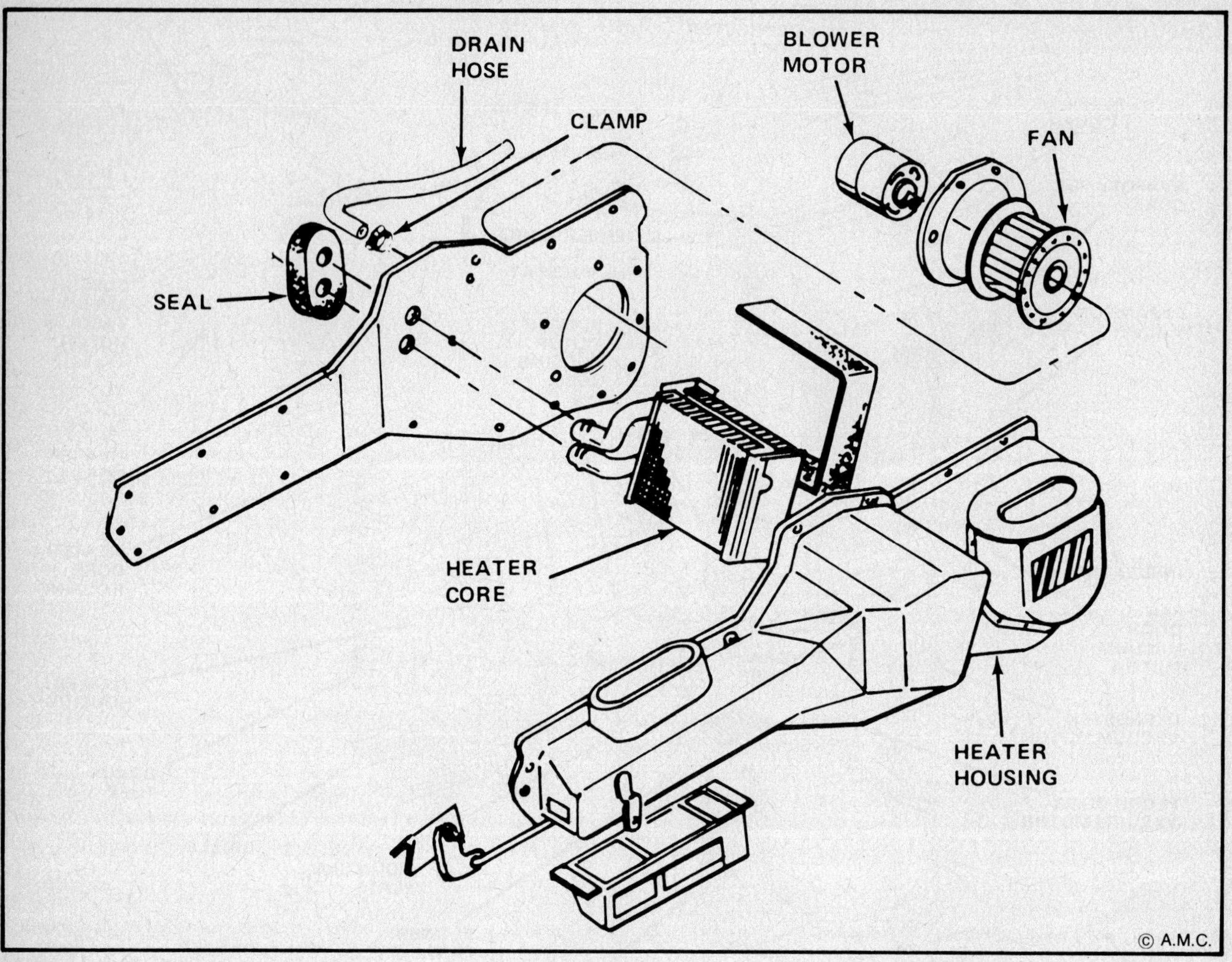

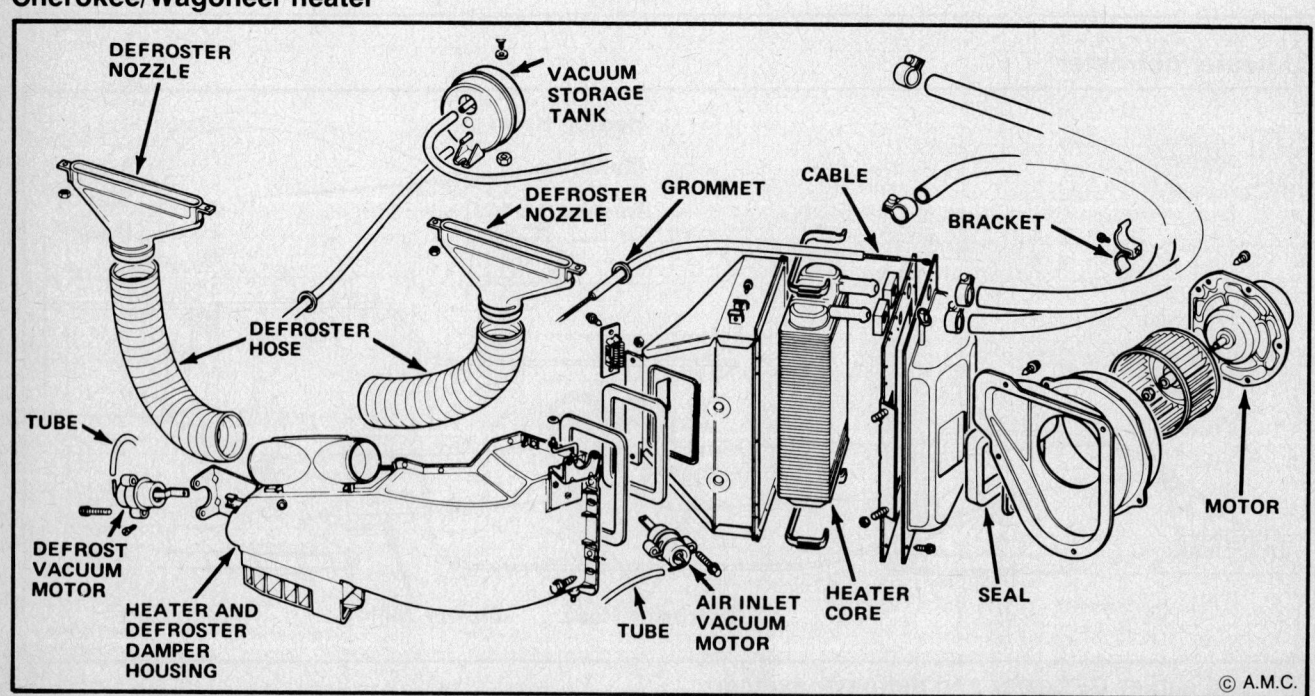

DRAIN HOSE

CLAMP

BLOWER MOTOR

FAN

SEAL

HEATER CORE

HEATER HOUSING

© A.M.C.

Cherokee/Wagoneer heater

DEFROSTER NOZZLE

VACUUM STORAGE TANK

DEFROSTER NOZZLE

GROMMET

CABLE

BRACKET

DEFROSTER HOSE

TUBE

DEFROST VACUUM MOTOR

HEATER AND DEFROSTER DAMPER HOUSING

TUBE

AIR INLET VACUUM MOTOR

HEATER CORE

SEAL

MOTOR

© A.M.C.

Wagoneer and Cherokee evaporator and air distribution

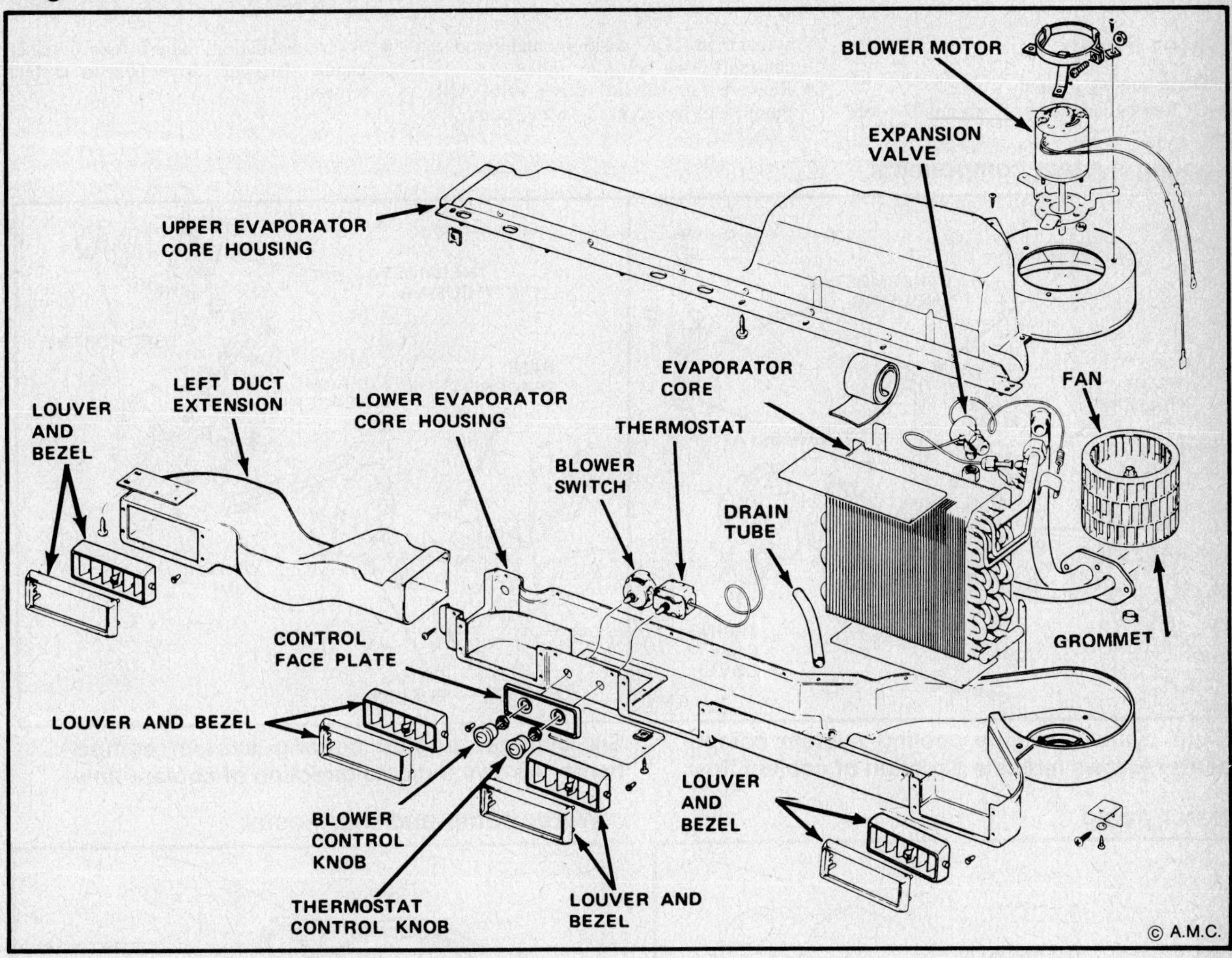

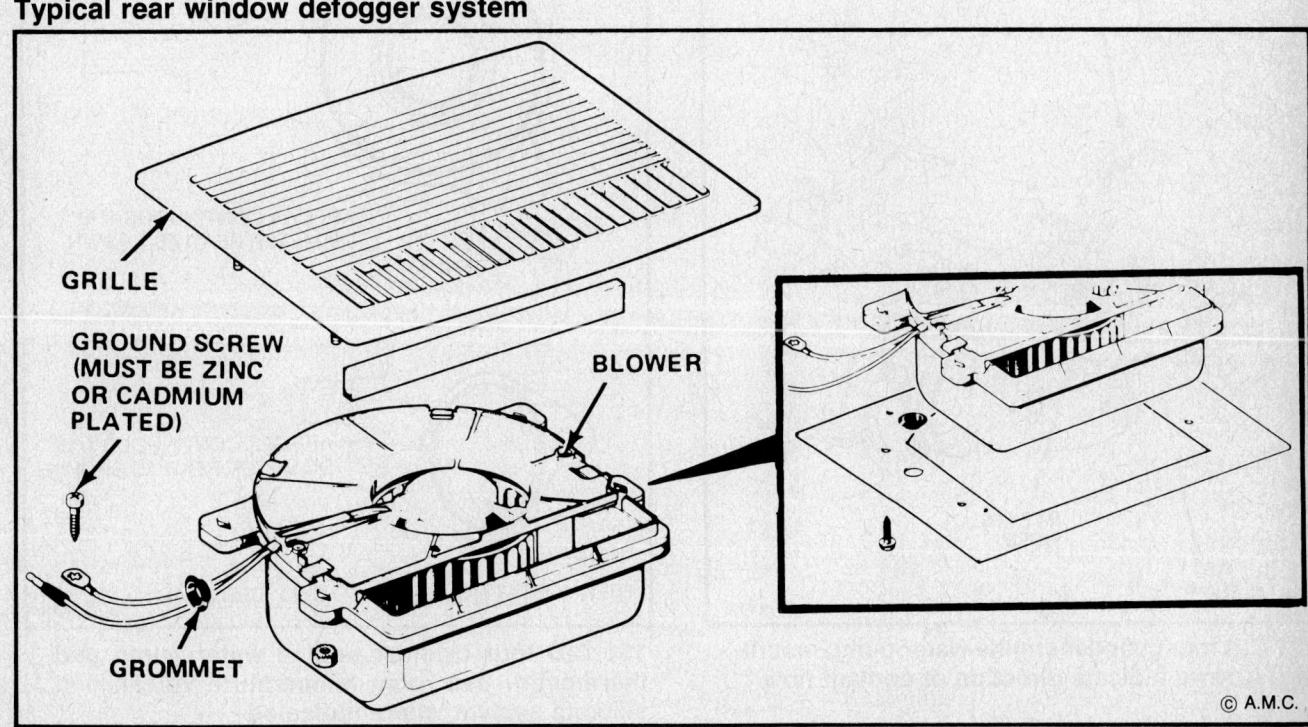

BLOWER MOTOR

EXPANSION VALVE

UPPER EVAPORATOR CORE HOUSING

EVAPORATOR CORE

FAN

LEFT DUCT EXTENSION

LOWER EVAPORATOR CORE HOUSING

THERMOSTAT

LOUVER AND BEZEL

BLOWER SWITCH

DRAIN TUBE

CONTROL FACE PLATE

GROMMET

LOUVER AND BEZEL

BLOWER CONTROL KNOB

LOUVER AND BEZEL

THERMOSTAT CONTROL KNOB

LOUVER AND BEZEL

© A.M.C.

Typical rear window defogger system

GRILLE

GROUND SCREW (MUST BE ZINC OR CADMIUM PLATED)

BLOWER

GROMMET

© A.M.C.

ENGINE SECTION

Water Pump

- Drain cooling system.
- On four cylinder engine, put number one cylinder in TDC position, and remove camshaft drive belt idler pulley.
- Remove fan shroud, drive belts AIR pump, etc. for access to water pump.
- After installation, adjust four cylinder engine camshaft drive belt to correct tension.

Cooling system components

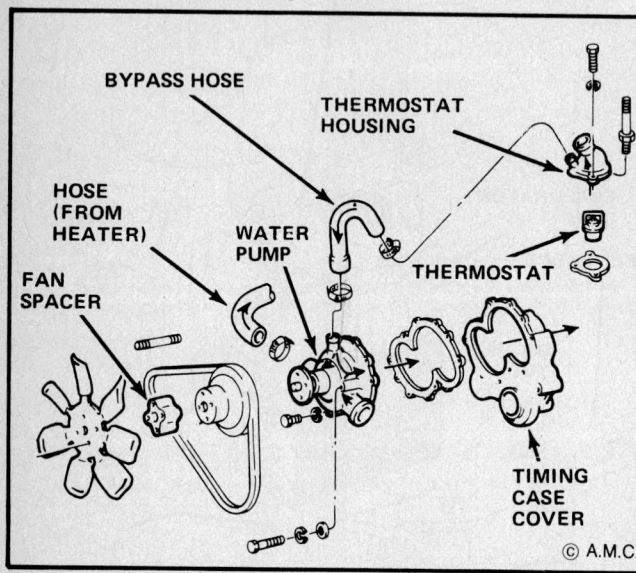

Eight cylinder engine cooling system components. Arrows indicate direction of coolant flow

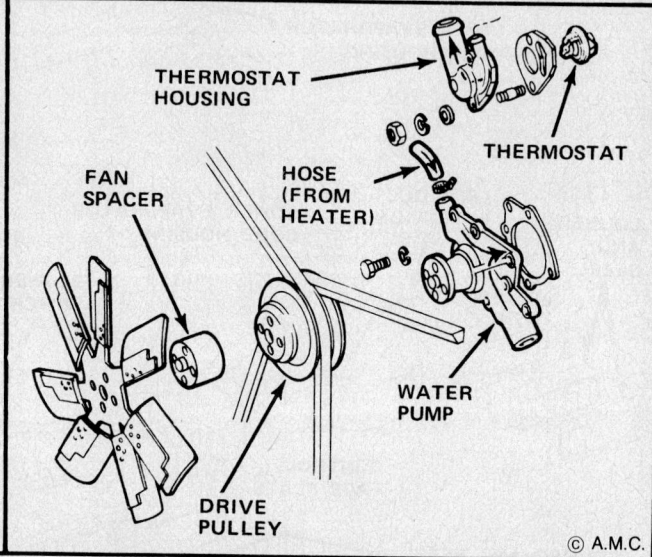

Six cylinder engine cooling system components. Arrows indicate direction of coolant flow

Water pump

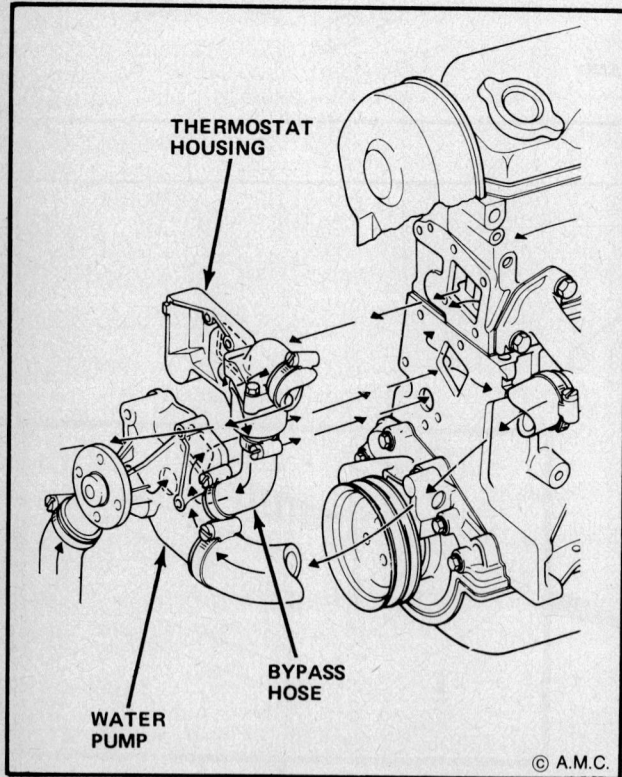

121 CID four cylinder engine water pump mounting. Arrows indicate direction of coolant flow

Water pump and thermostat

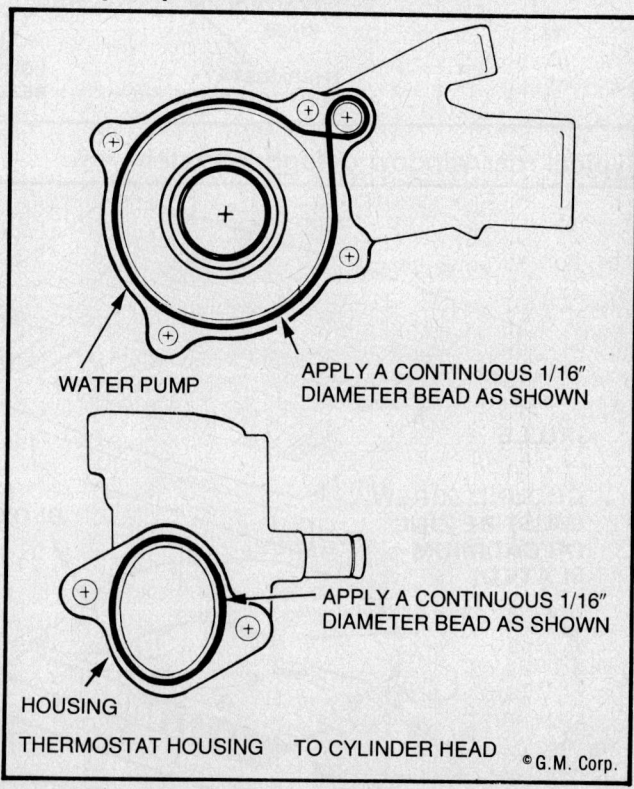

151 CID four cylinder engine water pump and thermostat. Use room temperature vulcanizing silicone sealant where indicated

Fuel pump operation

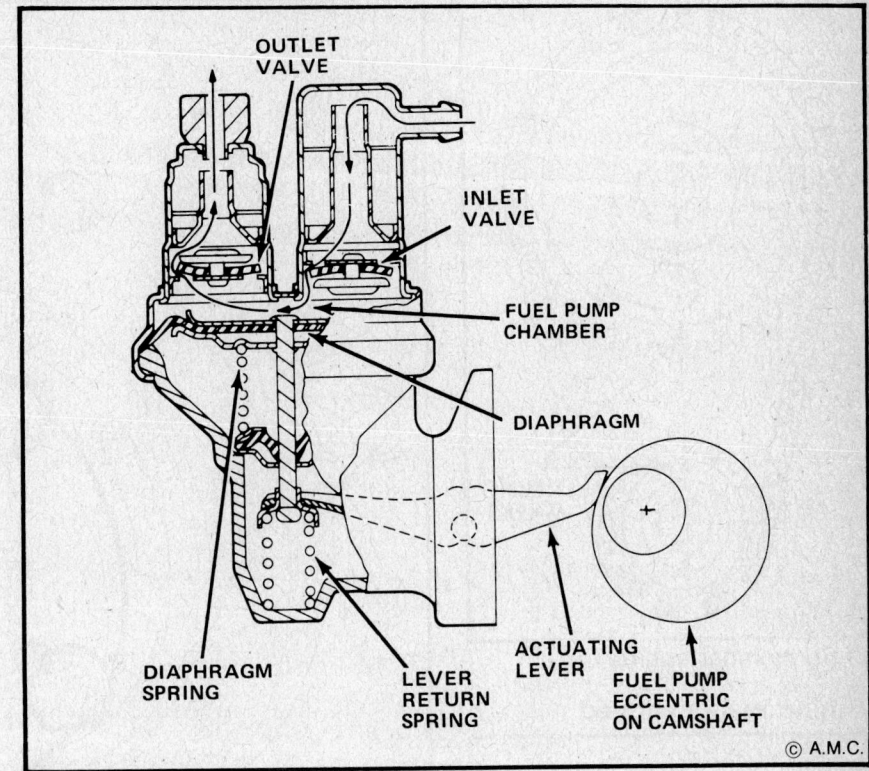

Typical fuel pump used on all except 121 CID four cylinder engine

Fuel Pump

- When installing on six or eight cylinder engine or the 151 CID four cylinder engine, crank the engine until the camshaft eccentric lobe is out of the way of the fuel pump rocker arm.
- When installing on a 121 CID four cylinder engine, be sure the pushrod is correctly positioned against the pump actuating lever.

Timing Chain

Six Cylinder Engines

NOTE: The front seal can be replaced without removing front cover.

- For access, remove drive belts, fan damper pulley and vibration damper.
- When removing front cover, cut off oil pan gasket end tabs flush with front face of block, and remove gasket tabs.
- Align timing marks, and remove both sprockets and chain as an assembly.
- When installing, use a new front cover oil seal and new pieces of oil pan gasket to replace those cut off when the cover was removed.
- An alignment tool must be used when installing front cover.

Eight Cylinder Engines

NOTE: The front cover must be removed to replace oil seal.

- Drain the cooling system.
- Remove drive belts, fan and hub, air conditioning compressor, power steering pump, alternator, fuel pump, distributor and vibration damper (puller required).
- With front cover off, remove oil slinger, distributor drive gear and fuel pump eccentric. Align timing marks, and remove sprockets and chain as an assembly.
- Replace front cover oil seal before installing.
- Cut off and replace used section of oil pan gasket.
- Install fuel pump eccentric with stamped word ''REAR'' facing camshaft sprocket.
- Lower dowel pin must be driven into place after front cover is installed.

Timing case cover alignment

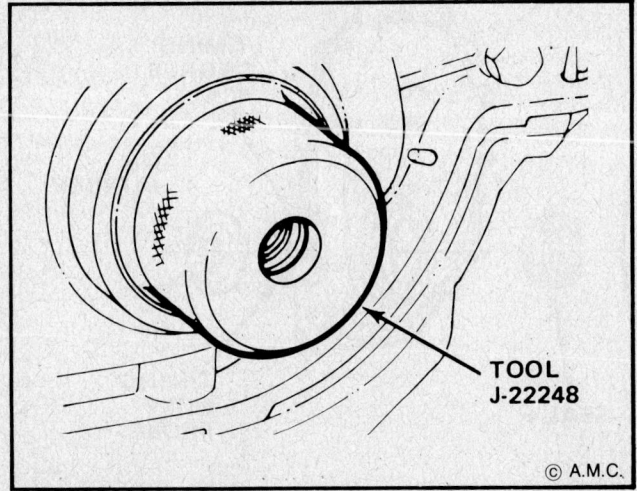

Six cylinder engine

Timing case cover oil seal installation

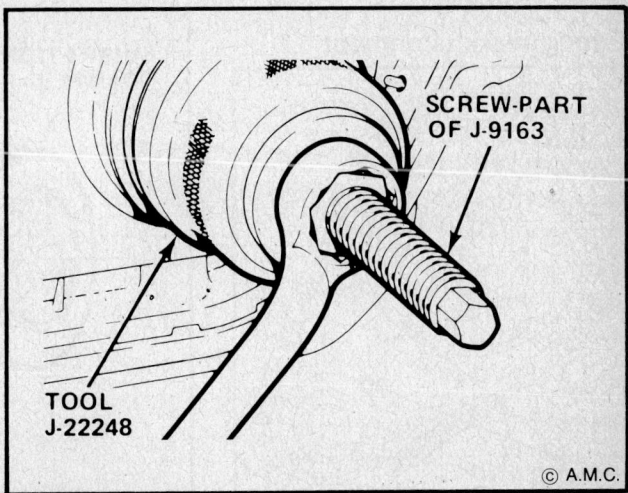

Installing timing case cover oil seal six cylinder engine

Timing mark alignment

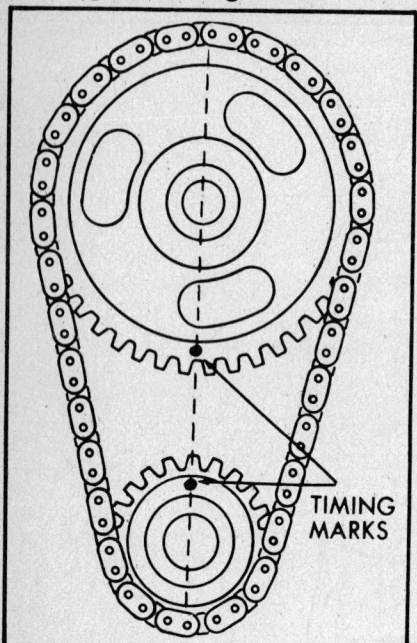

Eight cylinder engine

Timing marks aligned

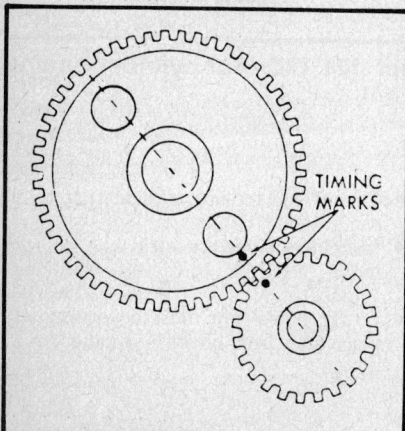

151 CID engine

Timing mark alignment

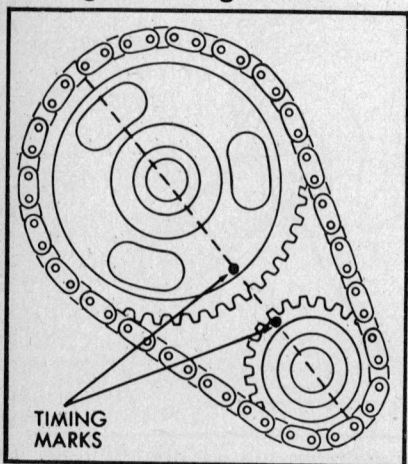

TIMING MARKS

Six cylinder engine

Vibration damper removal

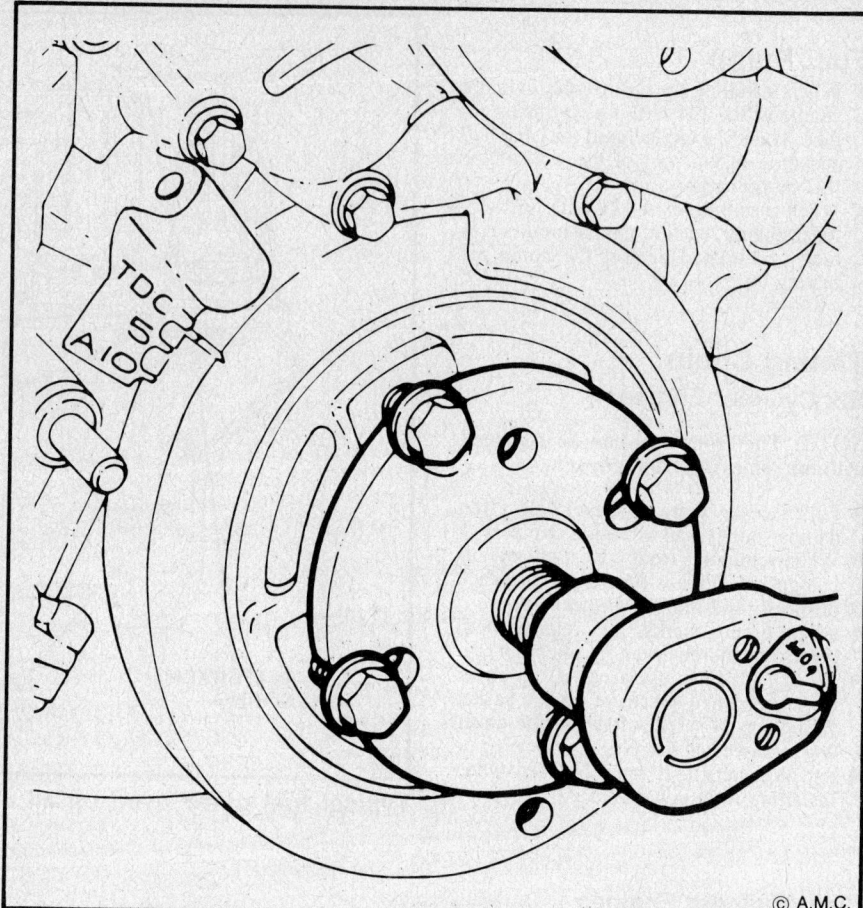

© A.M.C.

Eight cylinder engine

Six cylinder engine timing chain cover

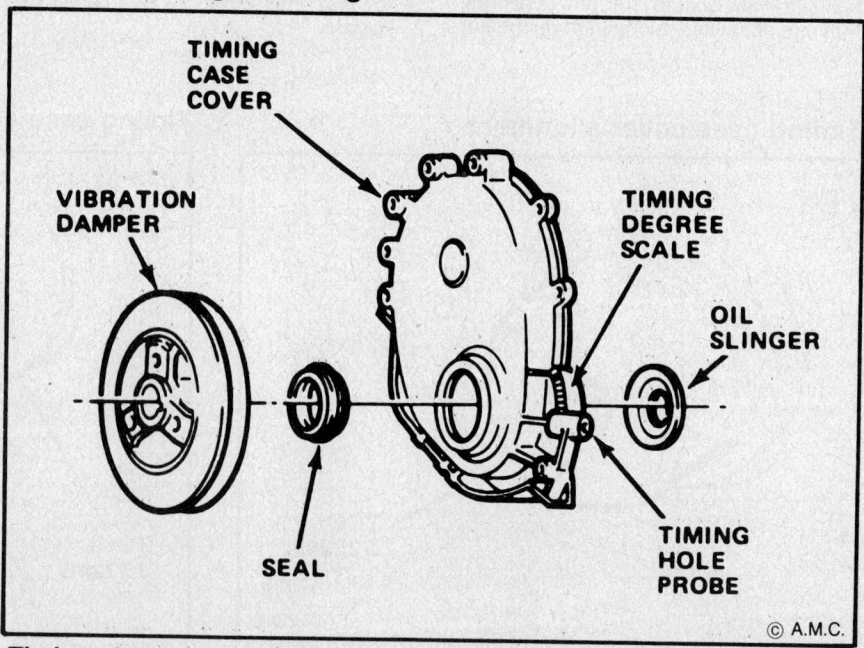

TIMING CASE COVER

VIBRATION DAMPER

TIMING DEGREE SCALE

OIL SLINGER

SEAL

TIMING HOLE PROBE

© A.M.C.

Timing chain cover used on six cylinder engine. Seal is replaced without removing cover

Six cylinder engine timing chain installation

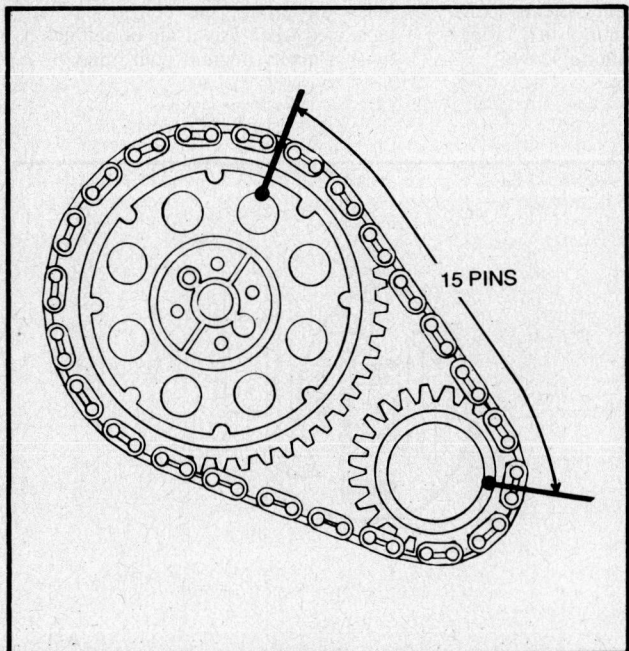

Eight cylinder engine timing chain installation

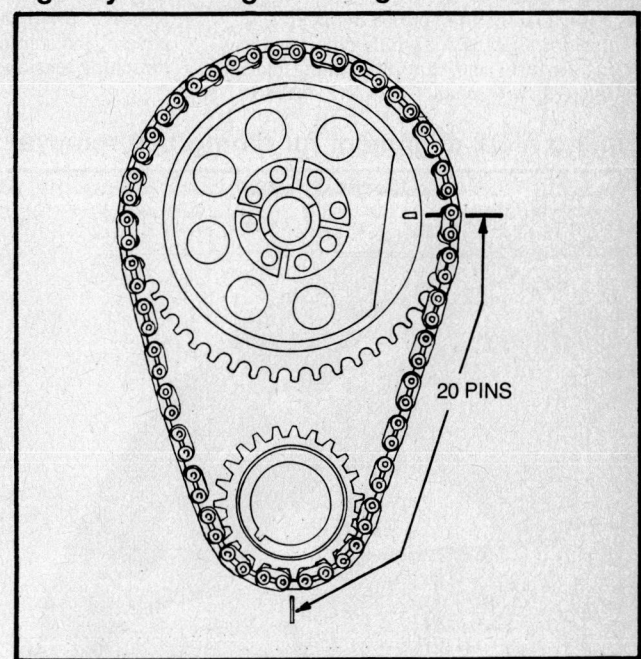

To verify correct installation, rotate crankshaft until camshaft sprocket timing mark is at about a one o'clock position. There must be 15 pins between the timing marks

To verify correct installation, rotate crankshaft until camshaft sprocket timing mark is at a three o'clock position. There must be 20 pins between the timing marks

Eight cylinder engine timing chain cover

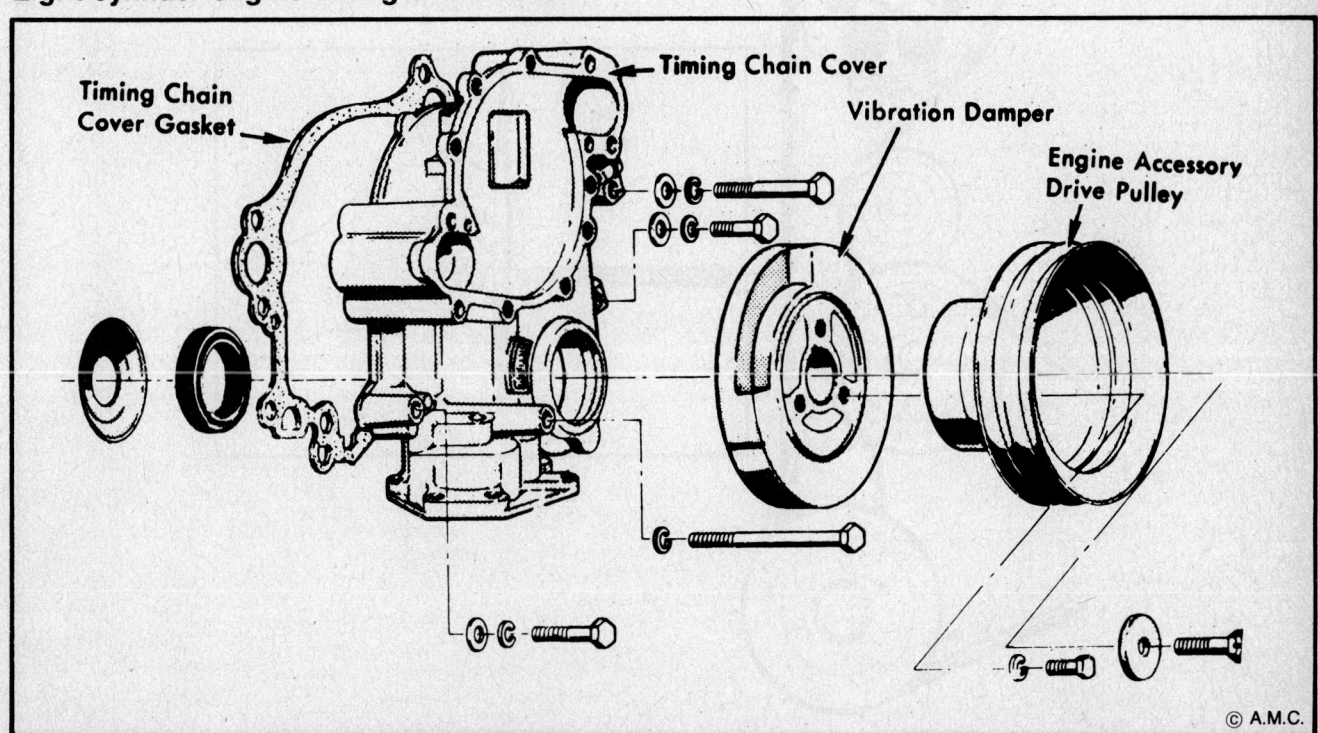

© A.M.C.

Cover must be removed to replace oil seal

Timing Belt

- Put engine in number one cylinder TDC position. (Crankshaft timing mark pointing to zero, and camshaft timing mark lined up with pointer on valve cover.)

- Remove drive belts and timing belt cover, and remove timing belt after loosening tensioner retaining screw.

- When installing, the belt is correctly tensioned when drive side of belt can be twisted ninety degrees with fingers.

Timing mark alignment for timing belt removal

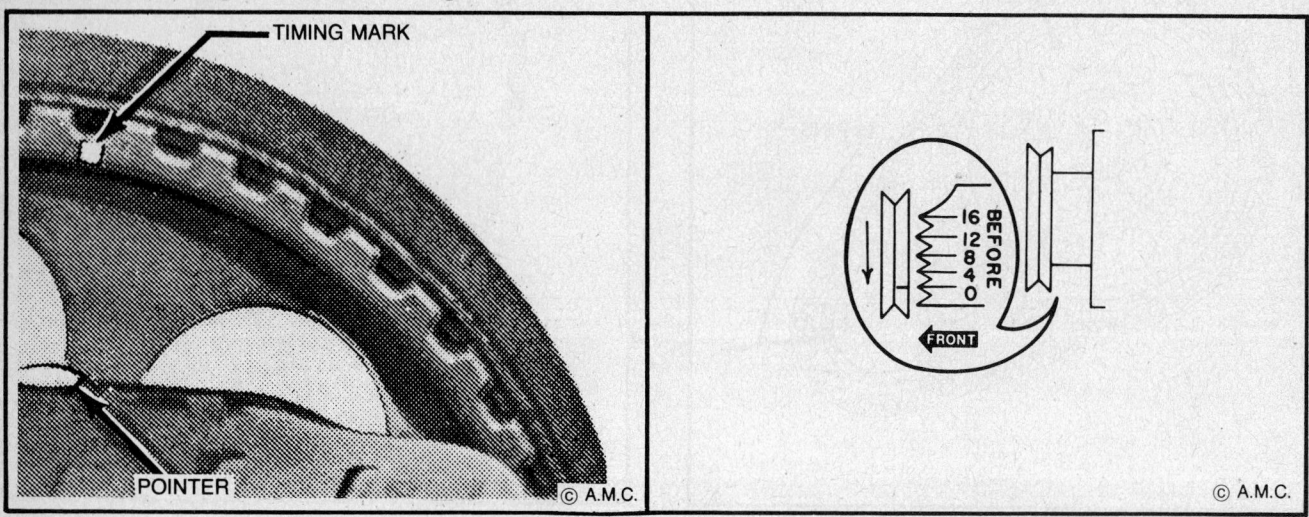

TIMING MARK

POINTER

© A.M.C.

BEFORE 16 12 8 4 0

FRONT

© A.M.C.

Align these marks before removing timing belt. Illustration on left is camshaft sprocket timing mark; on right crankshaft timing mark. Position number one cylinder at top dead center with these marks aligned when installing timing belt.

Timing belt installation

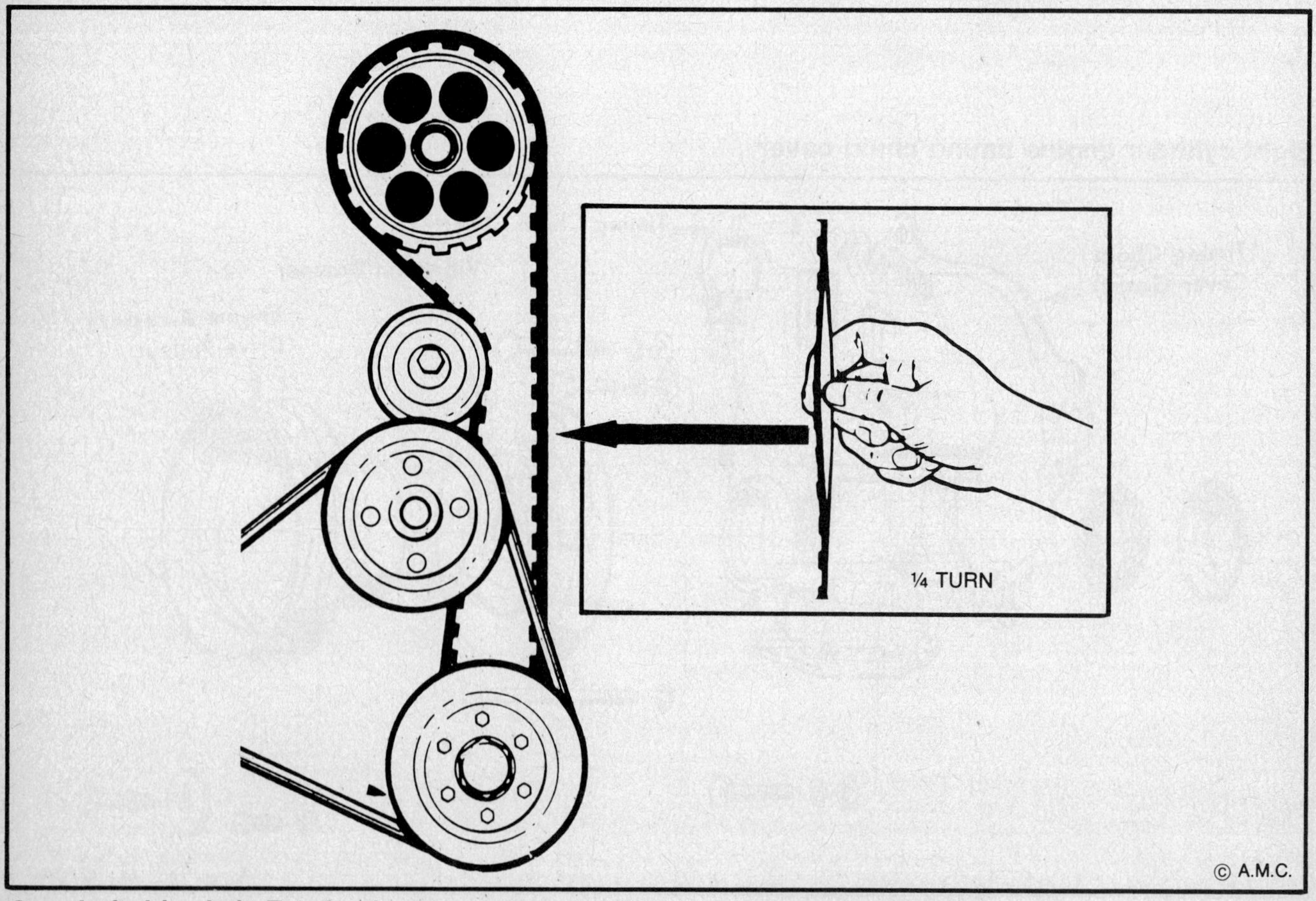

¼ TURN

© A.M.C.

Camshaft drive belt. Tension is correct when belt can be twisted ninety degrees

Forward mount—four cylinder engine

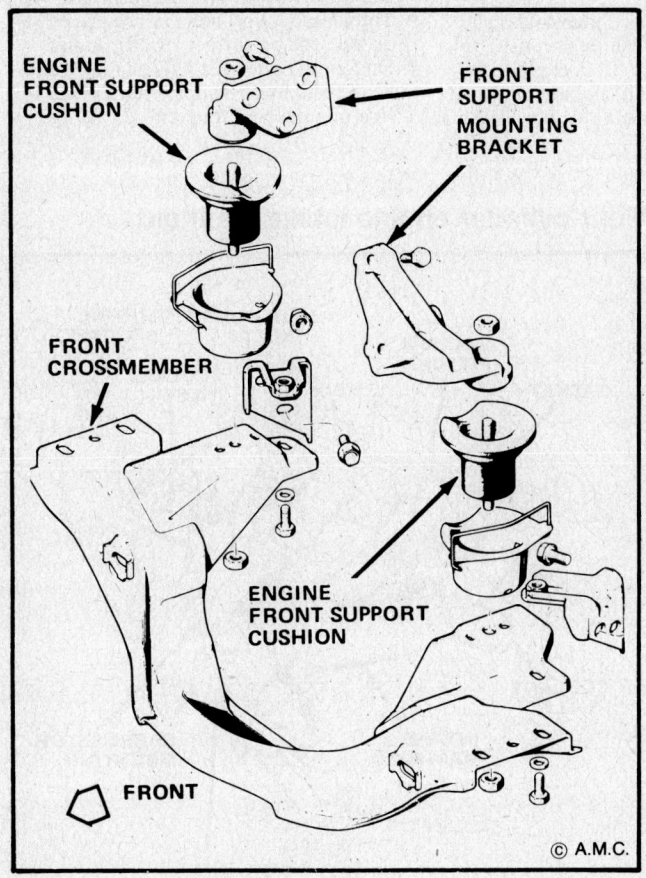

ENGINE FRONT SUPPORT CUSHION

FRONT SUPPORT MOUNTING BRACKET

FRONT CROSSMEMBER

ENGINE FRONT SUPPORT CUSHION

FRONT

© A.M.C.

Engine Mounts

- Engines are mounted at each side on the engine centerline and at the rear crossmember. To change a mount, support the engine in that area only.

Six cylinder engine forward mount

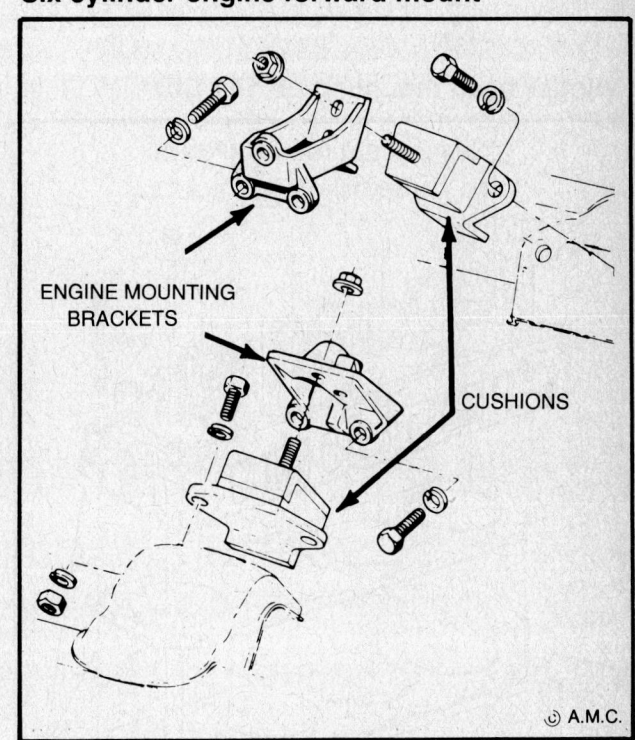

ENGINE MOUNTING BRACKETS

CUSHIONS

© A.M.C.

151 CID cross section

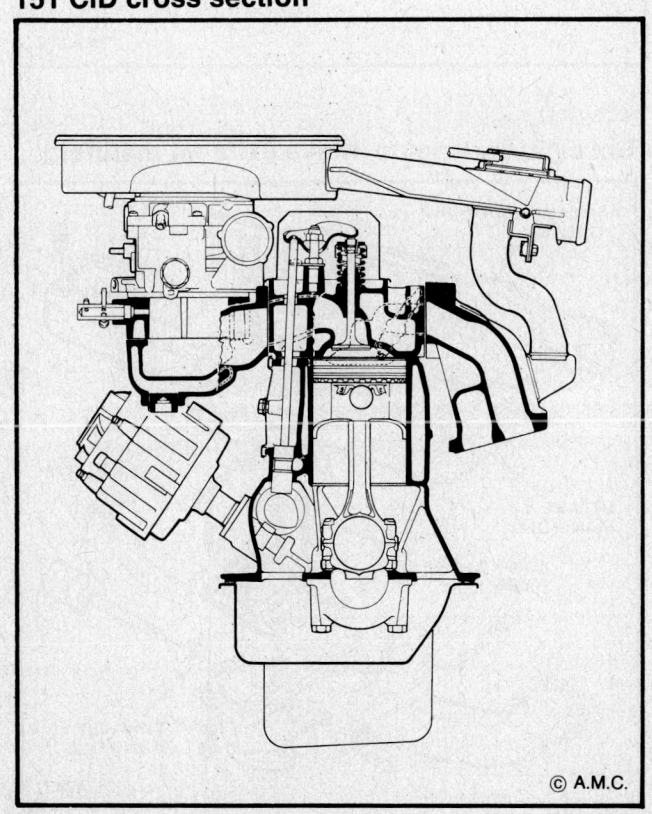

© A.M.C.

151 CID lubrication diagram

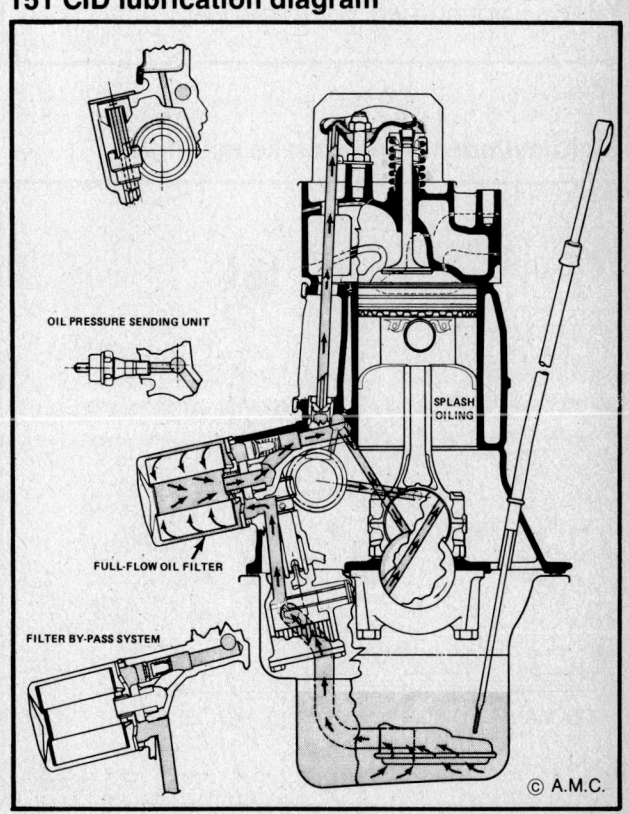

OIL PRESSURE SENDING UNIT

SPLASH OILING

FULL-FLOW OIL FILTER

FILTER BY-PASS SYSTEM

© A.M.C.

Cylinder Head

NOTE: On Pacer, park windshield wipers in center positions.

- Drain cooling system, and remove air cleaner, valve cover and any accessories attached to head.
- On six and eight cylinder engines and the 151 CID four cylinder engine, remove intake and exhaust manifolds, and remove rocker arms and push rods.
- On four cylinder 121 CID engine, the head is removed with carburetor, and intake and exhaust manifolds attached.
- When installing, replace rocker arms and push rods in original locations.
- Torque mounting bolts in prescribed sequence and to correct specifications.
- On four cylinder 121 CID engine, torque head bolts to 65 ft./lbs., run engine for five minutes and torque to 73 ft./lbs.

Cylinder head mounting on 151 CID

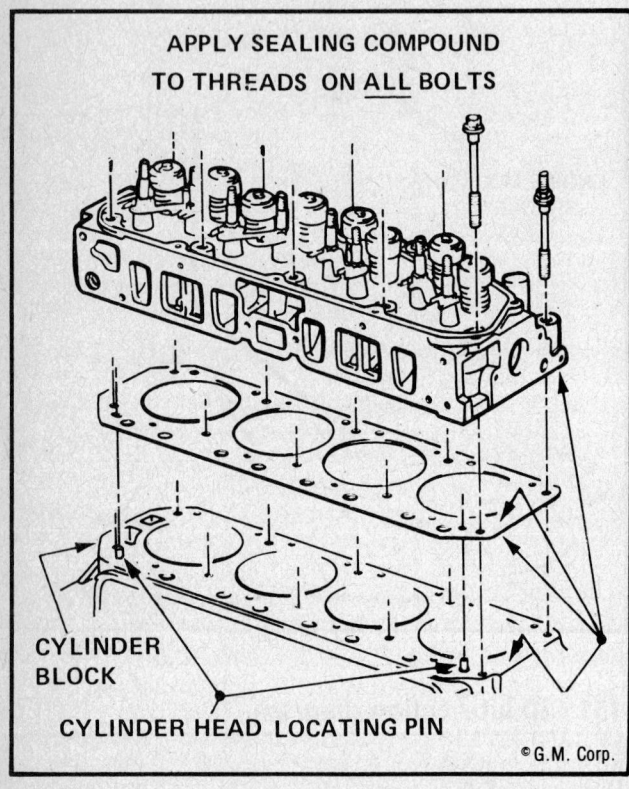

Four cylinder engine intake manifold

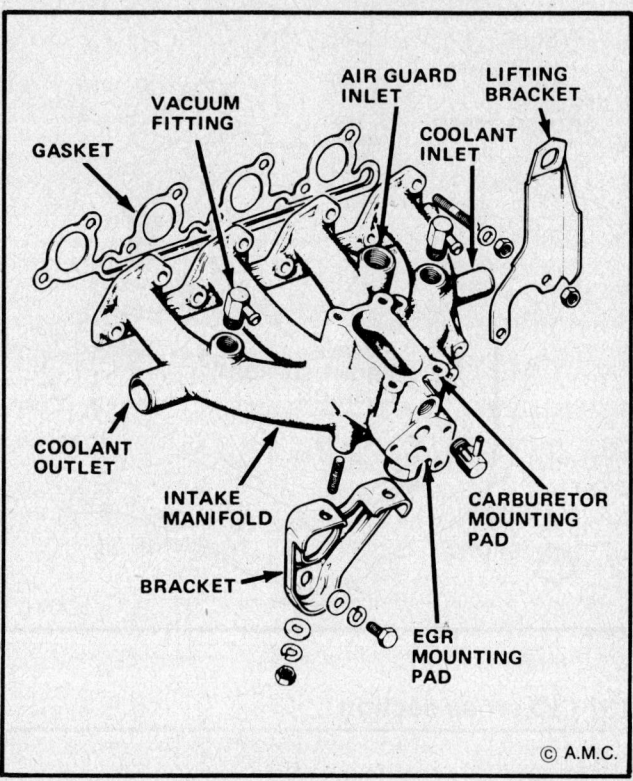

Eight cylinder engine intake manifold

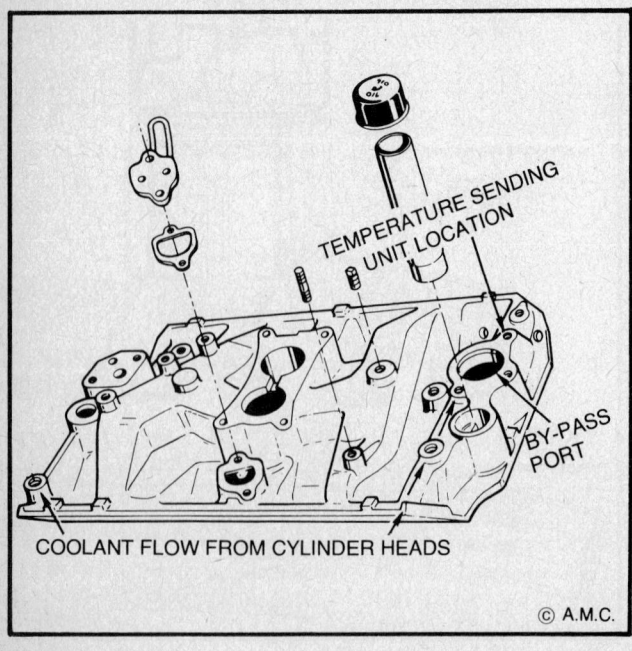

Six cylinder engine intake/exhaust manifold

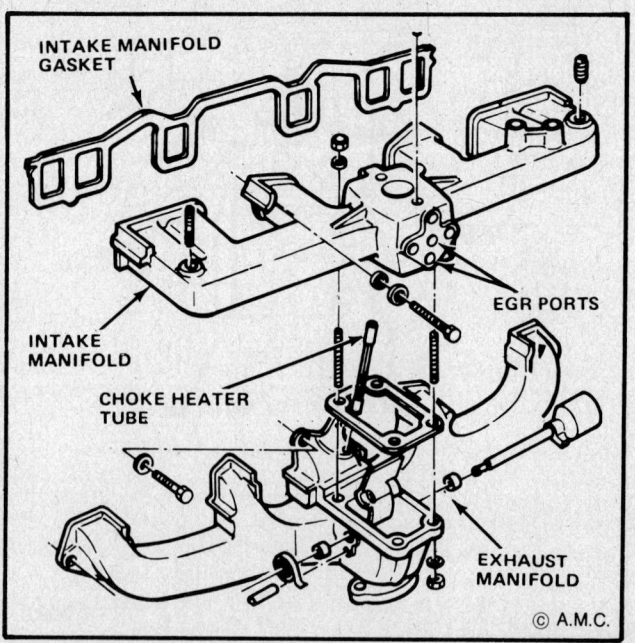

Intake manifold

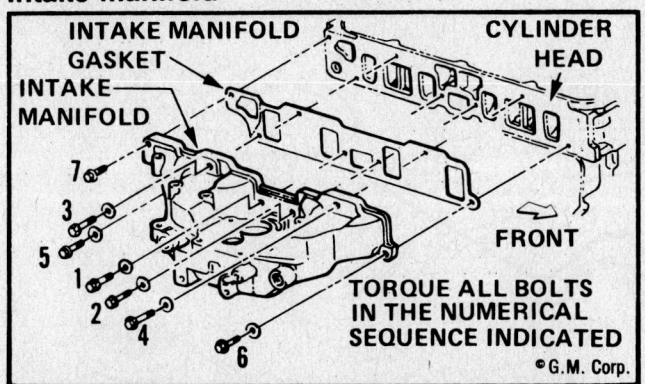

Intake manifold mount bolt torque sequence 151 CID four cylinder engine

Six cylinder engine cylinder head bolt torque sequence

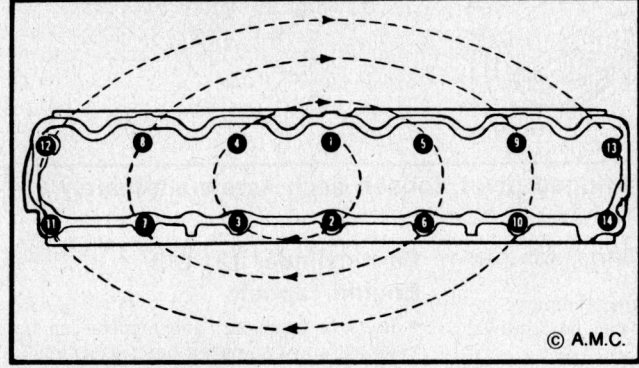

Exhaust manifold

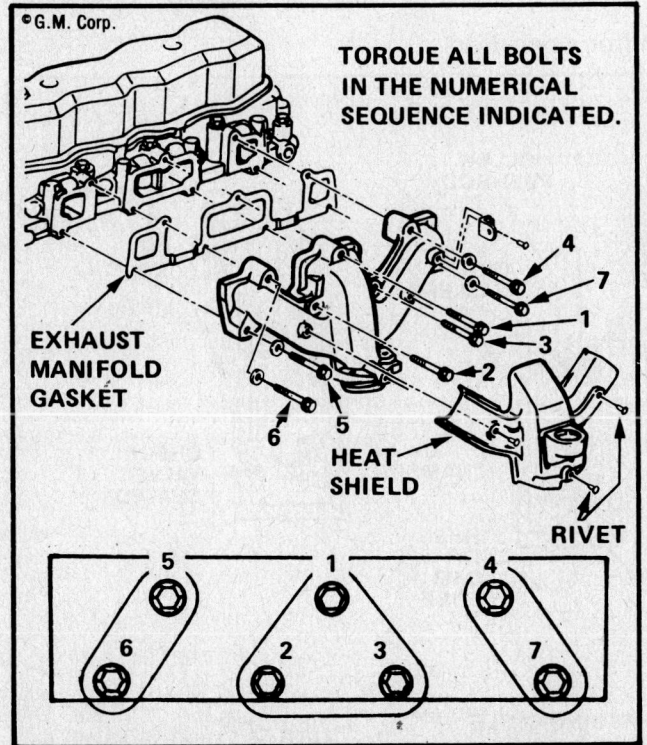

Exhaust manifold mounting and bolt torque sequence on 151 CID four cylinder engine

Four cylinder 121 CID engine cylinder head bolt torque sequence

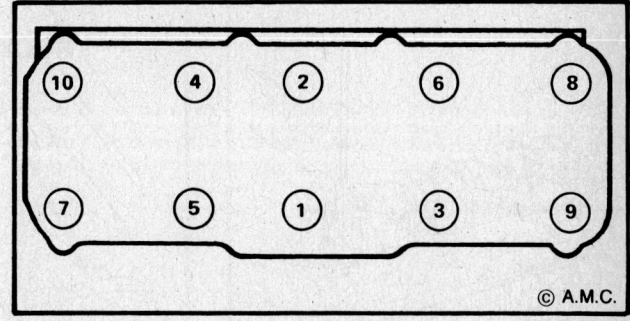

Eight cylinder engine cylinder head bolt torque sequence

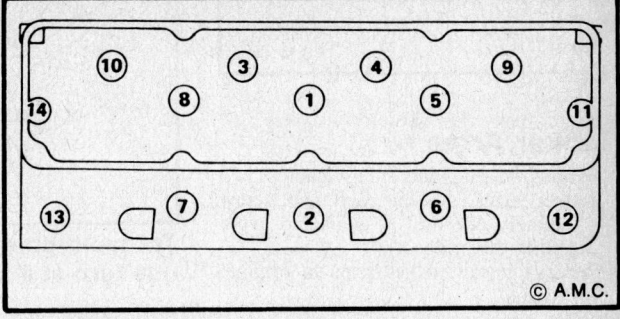

Cylinder head mount bolt torque sequence on 151 CID four cylinder engine

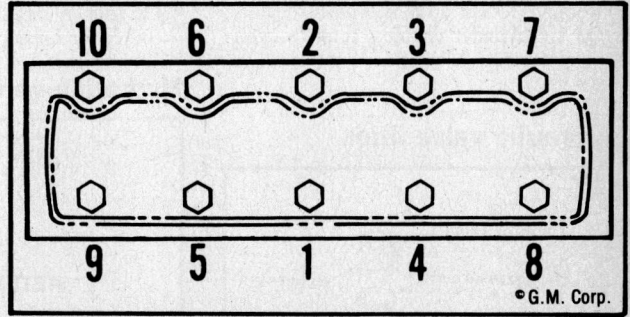

Six cylinder engine intake manifold bolt torque sequence

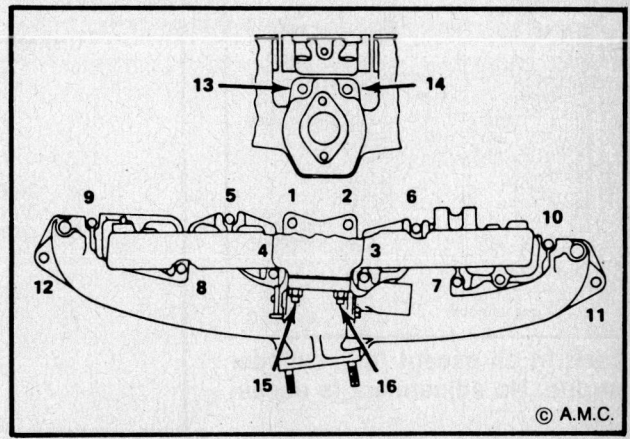

Valve train in 151 CID four cylinder engine

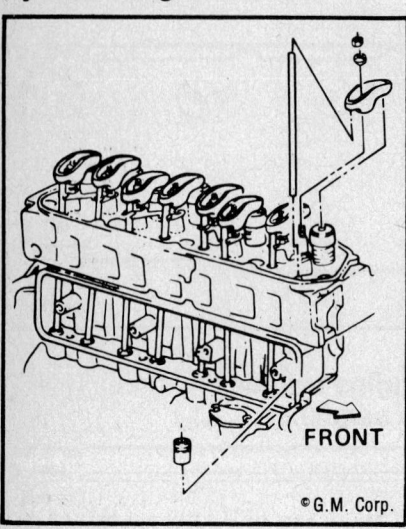

© G.M. Corp.

Eight cylinder engine rocker arm assembly

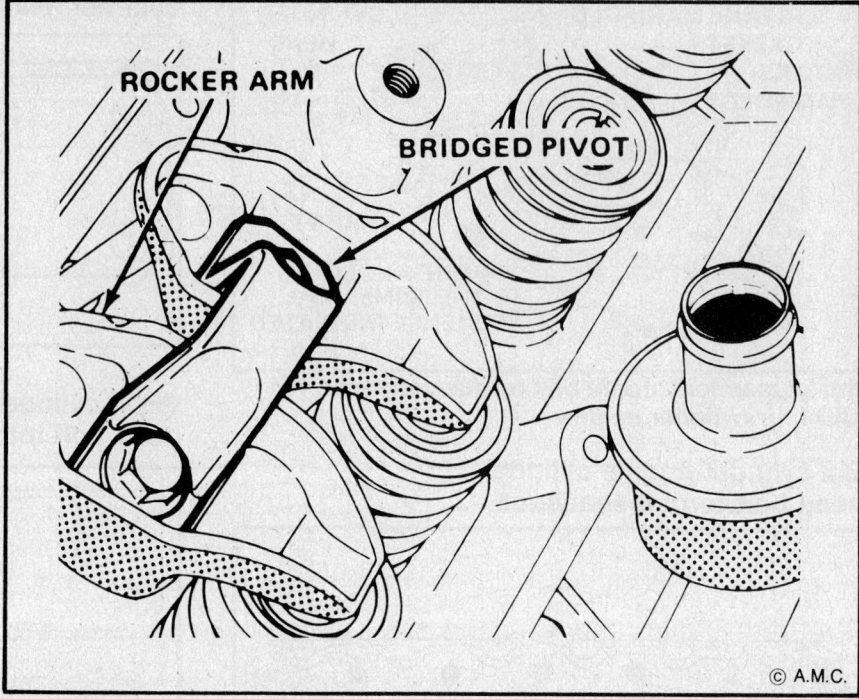

ROCKER ARM

BRIDGED PIVOT

© A.M.C.

To avoid cracking bridged pivot, loosen each screw alternately one turn at a time

Rocker Arms
- When bridged pivots are used across two rocker arms, loosen each cap screw alternately one turn at a time to avoid cracking the bridge.
- Always install rocker arms in original locations.

Valve Lifters

Six and Eight Cylinder and 151 CID Four Cylinder Engines
- Remove rocker arms and push rods.
- On six cylinder engines, remove cylin-

der head, and pull lifters with tool J-21884.
- On eight cylinder engines, remove intake manifold. Lifters can be removed without special tools.
- On four cylinder engines, remove push rod cover for access to lifters.

Four cylinder 121 CID Engine Tappets
- Remove camshaft, and tappets can be pulled upwards out of bores.
- After installing, adjust tappet clearance to correct specifications.

Hydraulic valve lifter operation

Hydraulic valve lifter

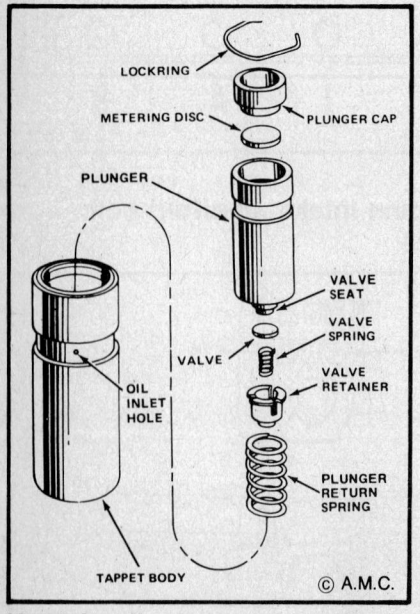

LOCKRING

METERING DISC

PLUNGER CAP

PLUNGER

VALVE SEAT

VALVE SPRING

VALVE

VALVE RETAINER

OIL INLET HOLE

PLUNGER RETURN SPRING

TAPPET BODY

© A.M.C.

Used in all except four cylinder engine. No adjustment is necessary

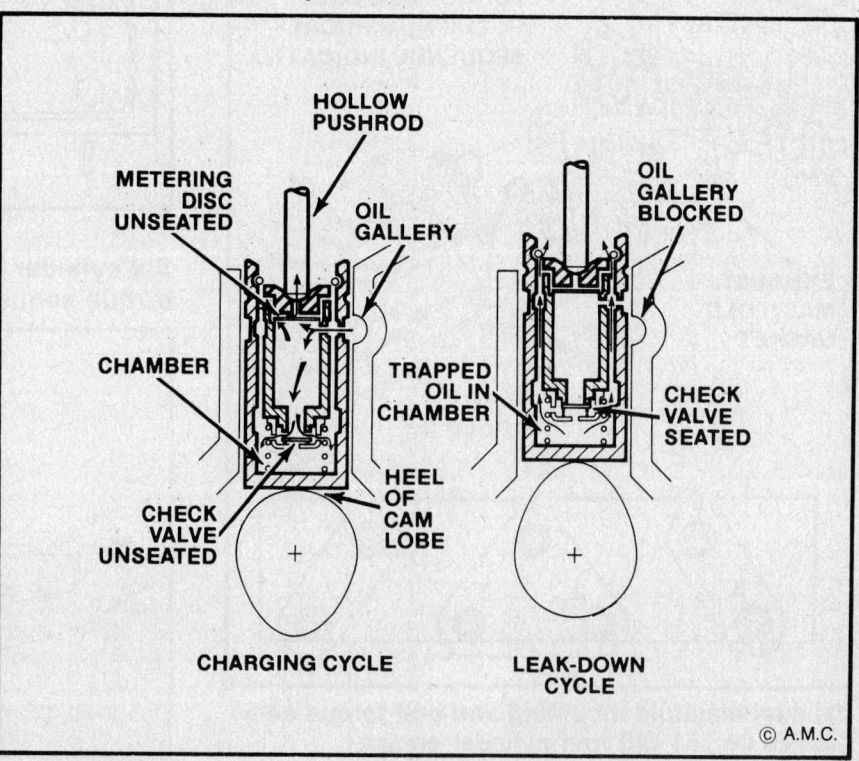

HOLLOW PUSHROD

METERING DISC UNSEATED

OIL GALLERY

OIL GALLERY BLOCKED

CHAMBER

TRAPPED OIL IN CHAMBER

CHECK VALVE SEATED

CHECK VALVE UNSEATED

HEEL OF CAM LOBE

CHARGING CYCLE

LEAK-DOWN CYCLE

© A.M.C.

121 CID four cylinder engine valve train

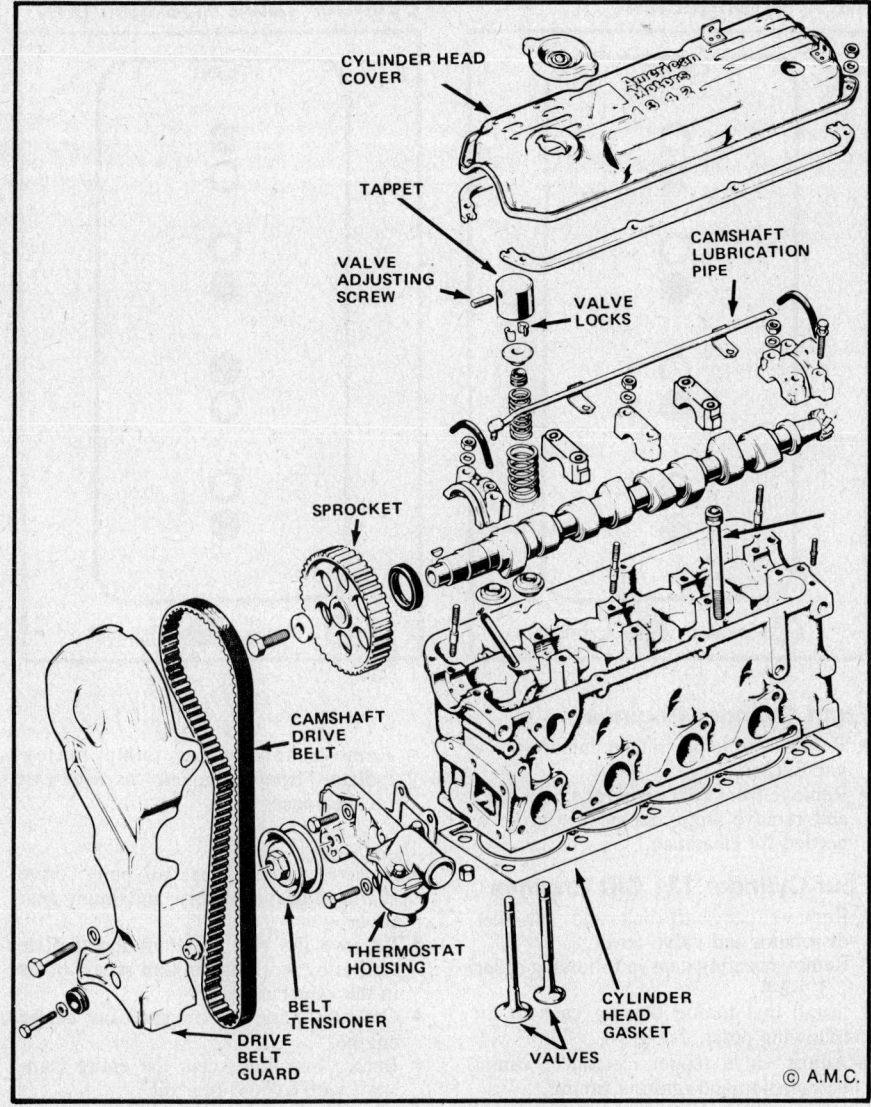

121 CID engine valve train

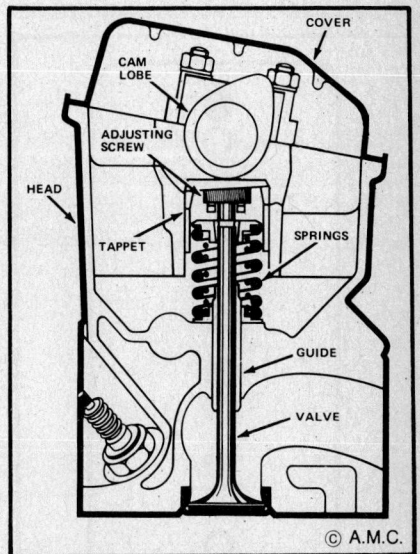

Valve Adjustment

Six & Eight Cylinder & 151 CID Four Cylinder Engines

- Hydraulic lifters are used, and are not adjustable.

Four Cylinder 121 CID Engine

- Place engine in number one cylinder TDC position, and check and adjust clearance for the following valves:
  - Intake . . . . Cylinders 1 & 2
  - Exhaust . . . Cylinders 1 & 3
- To adjust, use tool J-26810 to turn the adjusting screw. Each turn changes clearance by 0.05mm (0.002 in).
- Rotate engine 180 degrees, and repeat for remaining valves.
- After clearances are correct, the adjusting screws must be measured and changed if not within specifications.
- Tool J-26860 is used to make adjusting screw measurements.

Four cylinder 121 engine valve adjusting

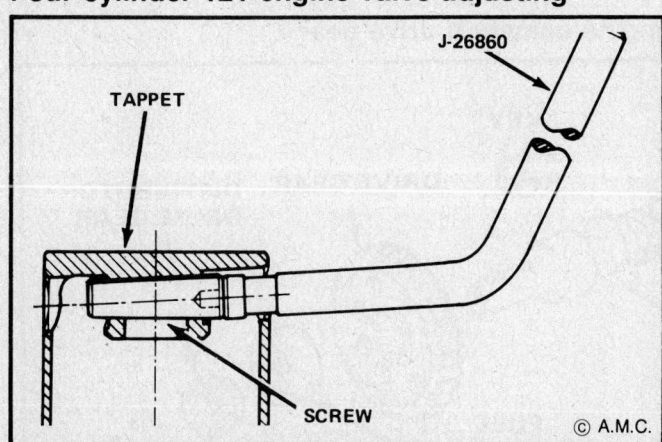

Four cylinder engine valve tappet adjusting screw position measurement. Adjusting screw must be replaced with a larger one if the screw must be turned in too far to obtain correct valve lash

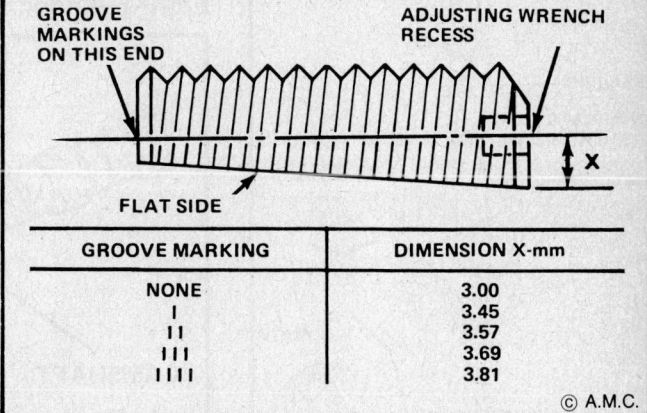

GROOVE MARKING	DIMENSION X-mm
NONE	3.00
I	3.45
II	3.57
III	3.69
IIII	3.81

Valve tappet adjusting screw selection

6 cylinder valve arrangement

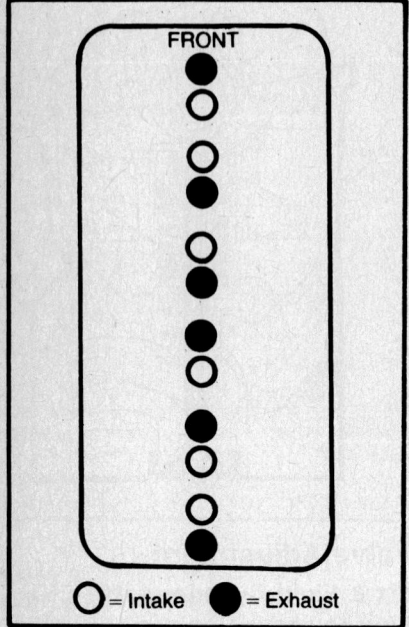

○ = Intake ● = Exhaust

Four cylinder 121 CID engine valve arrangement

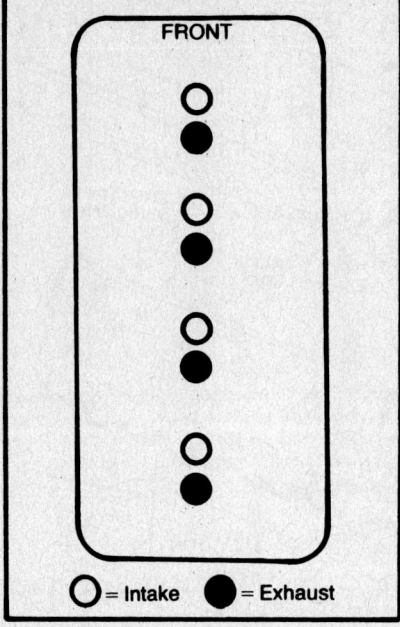

○ = Intake ● = Exhaust

Eight cylinder and 151 CID 4 cylinder valve arrangement

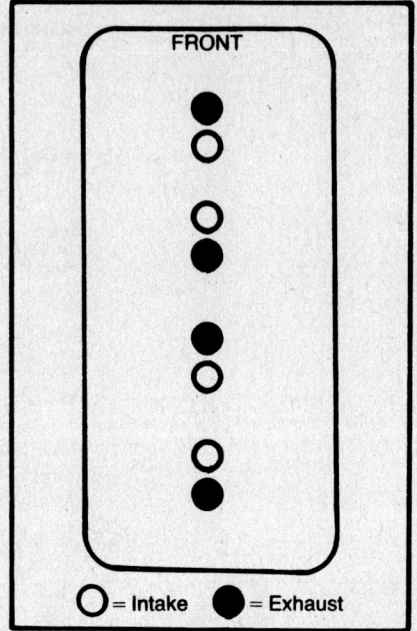

○ = Intake ● = Exhaust

Camshaft

Six Cylinder Engines

NOTE: Since Pacer engines must be raised, complete engine removal may be simpler in most cases.
- Remove radiator, grille and front bumper as required for clearance.
- Remove cylinder head, valve lifters, front cover and timing chain and sprockets (align timing marks before removing).
- Carefully slide camshaft out of engine.

Oil pump drive shaft in 151 CID four cylinder engines

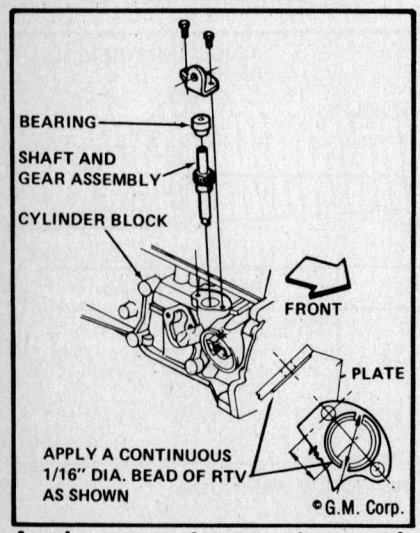

APPLY A CONTINUOUS 1/16" DIA. BEAD OF RTV AS SHOWN

© G.M. Corp.

Apply room temperature vulcanizing sealer to drive shaft retainer as shown

Eight Cylinder Engines
- Remove radiator, intake manifold and valve lifters.
- Remove front cover, timing chain, etc., and remove front bumper or grille as needed for clearance.

Four Cylinder 121 CID Engines
- Remove camshaft belt and sprocket, distributor and valve cover.
- Remove bearing caps in following order: 1-3-5-2-4.
- Install and torque bearing caps in the following order: 2-4-3-5-1.
- Adjust valve tappet clearance, timing belt tension and ignition timing.

- Remove fan, water pump pulley, radiator, front grille, etc. as necessary for clearance.

- Remove valve lifters, oil pump drive shaft and gear assembly, and timing gear cover.
- Remove the two camshaft thrust plate screws by working through access holes in the camshaft gear.
- Carefully slide the camshaft out of the engine.
- Before installing, coat the entire camshaft with hypoid gear oil.

Eight cylinder engine camshaft drive gear

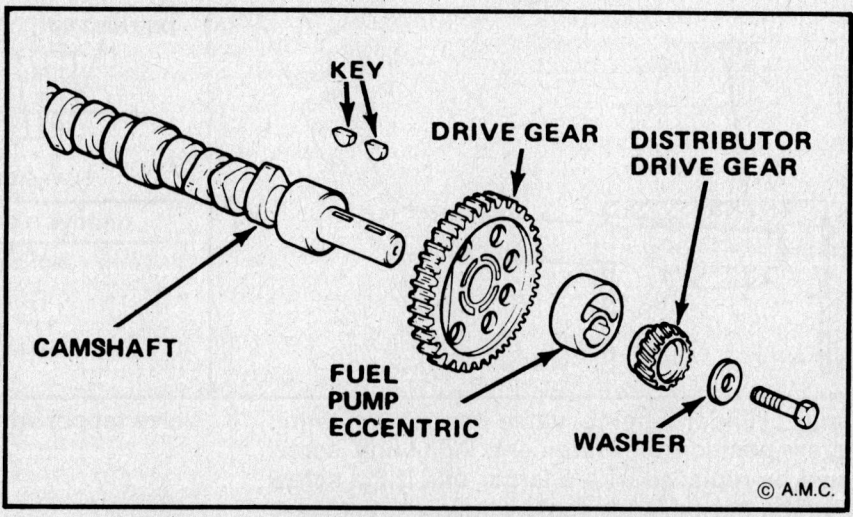

© A.M.C.

"Rear" stamped on fuel pump eccentric must face drive gear

Measuring crankshaft end play

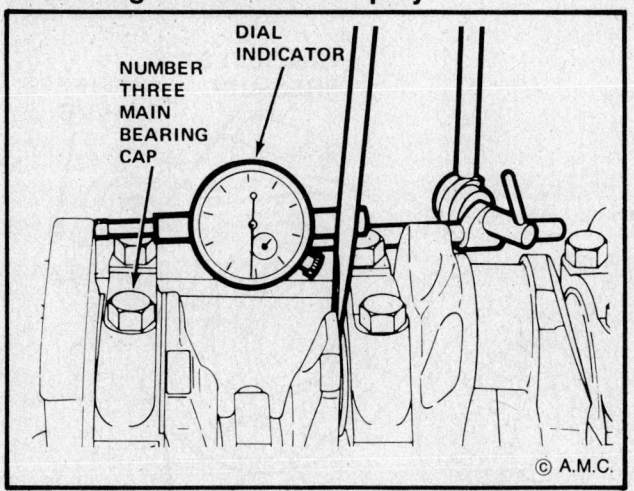

Pry shaft back and forth for total reading

Piston installation

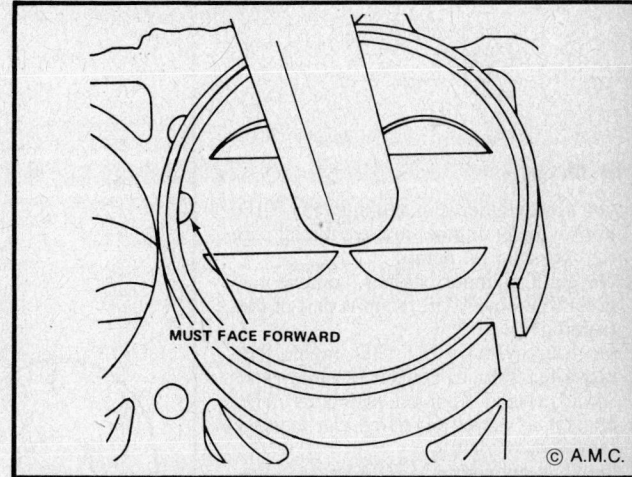

As shown the notch on the piston is toward the front of the engine when correctly installed

Correct piston installation 121 CID four cylinder engine

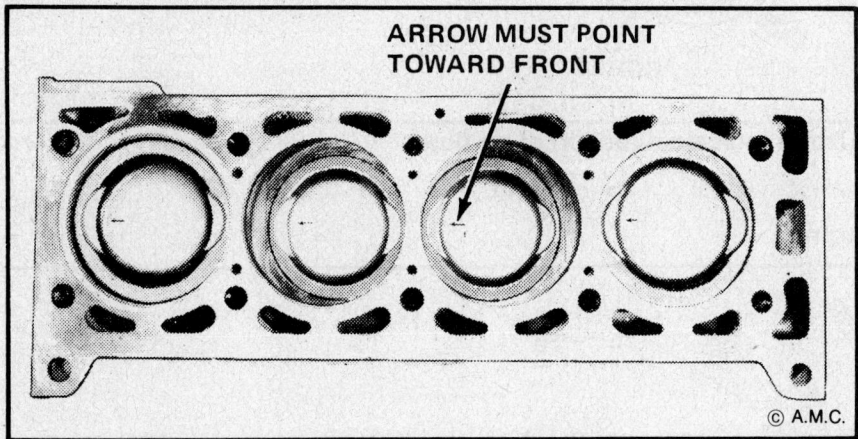

Pistons, Rods & Bearings

- Pistons are removed through the top on all engines.
- On four cylinder 121 CID engine, all four rods are a matched, balanced set and cannot be replaced individually.
- The gapless oil control ring on the four cylinder 121 CID engine requires no special installation tool. Compression ring gaps should be 180 degrees apart and not in line with piston pin.

Piston installation eight cylinder engines

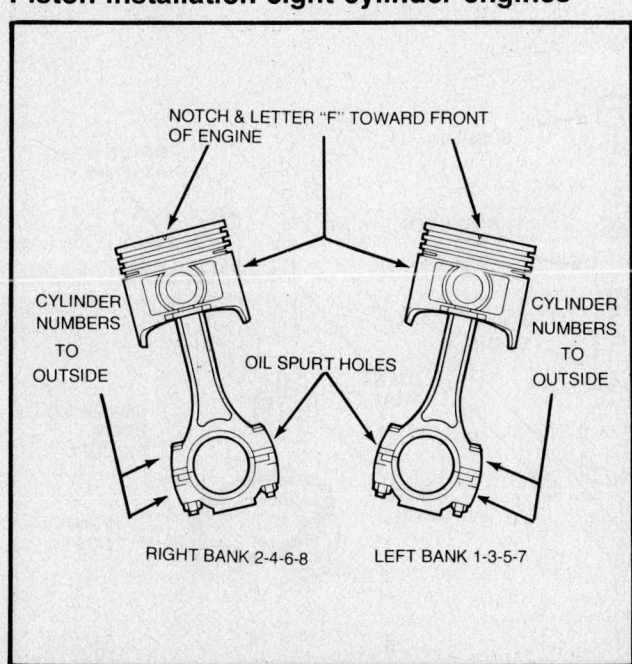

Piston installation six cylinder engines

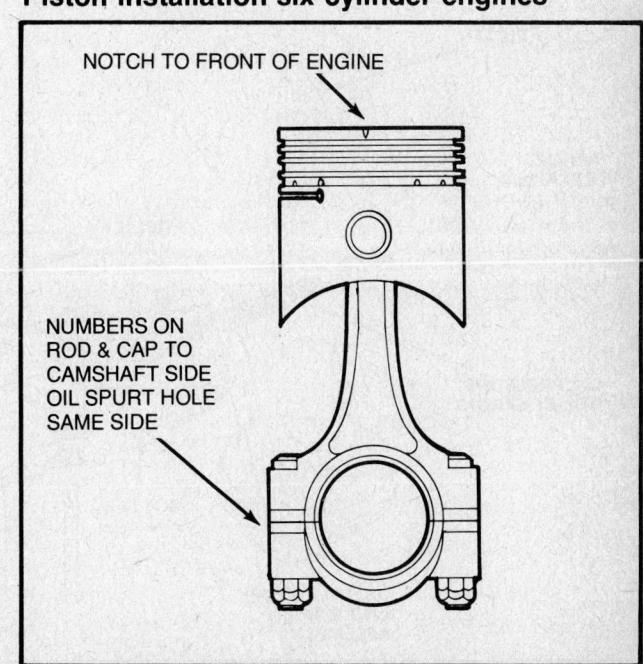

Four cylinder 121 CID engine oil pump

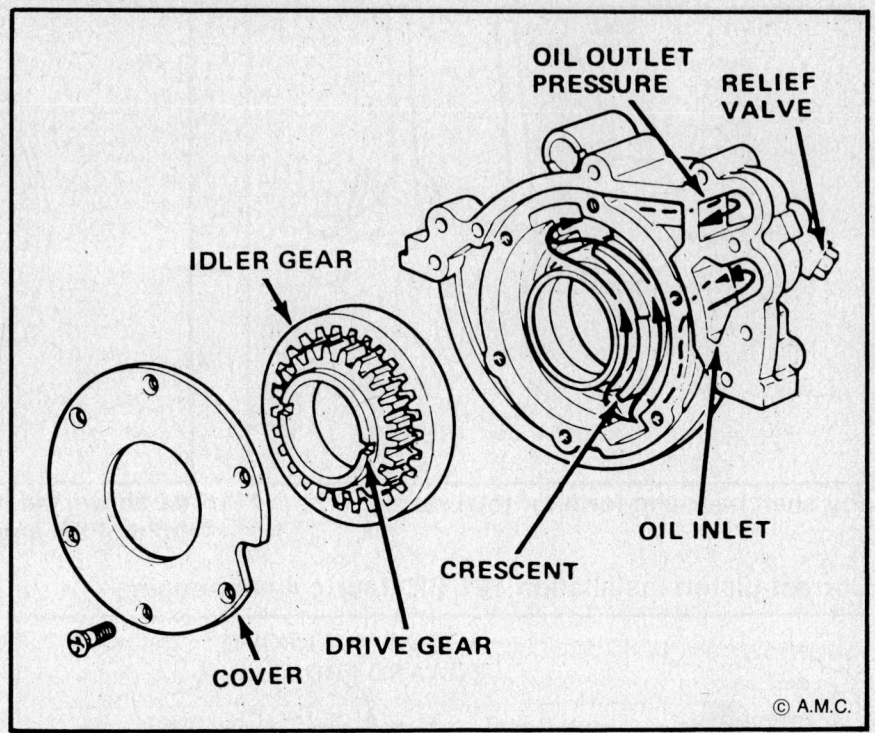

Oil Pump

- On six cylinder engines and 151 CID four cylinder engine, remove the oil pan for access to oil pump.
- On eight cylinder engines, remove engine front cover. Oil pump is part of the front cover.
- On four cylinder 121 CID engine, remove fan shroud, crankshaft pulley and sprocket, and front oil pan bolts. The crankshaft driven oil pump can then be removed.
- On four cylinder 121 CID engines, install new crankshaft oil seal.
- To insure oil pump priming, fill pump with petroleum jelly before installation.

Arrows indicate direction of oil flow

Oil pump and filter six cylinder engine

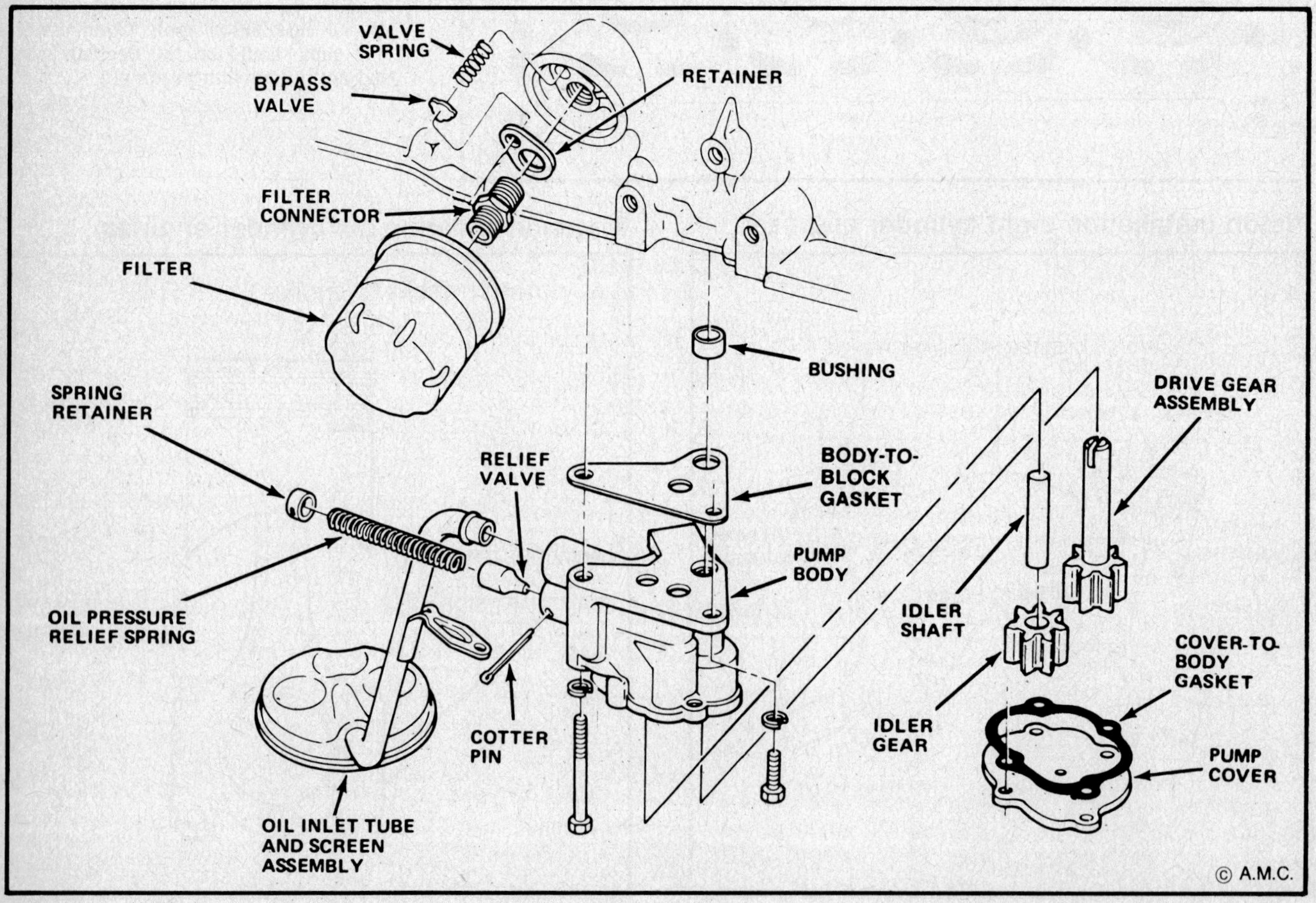

Lubrication schematic eight cylinder engine

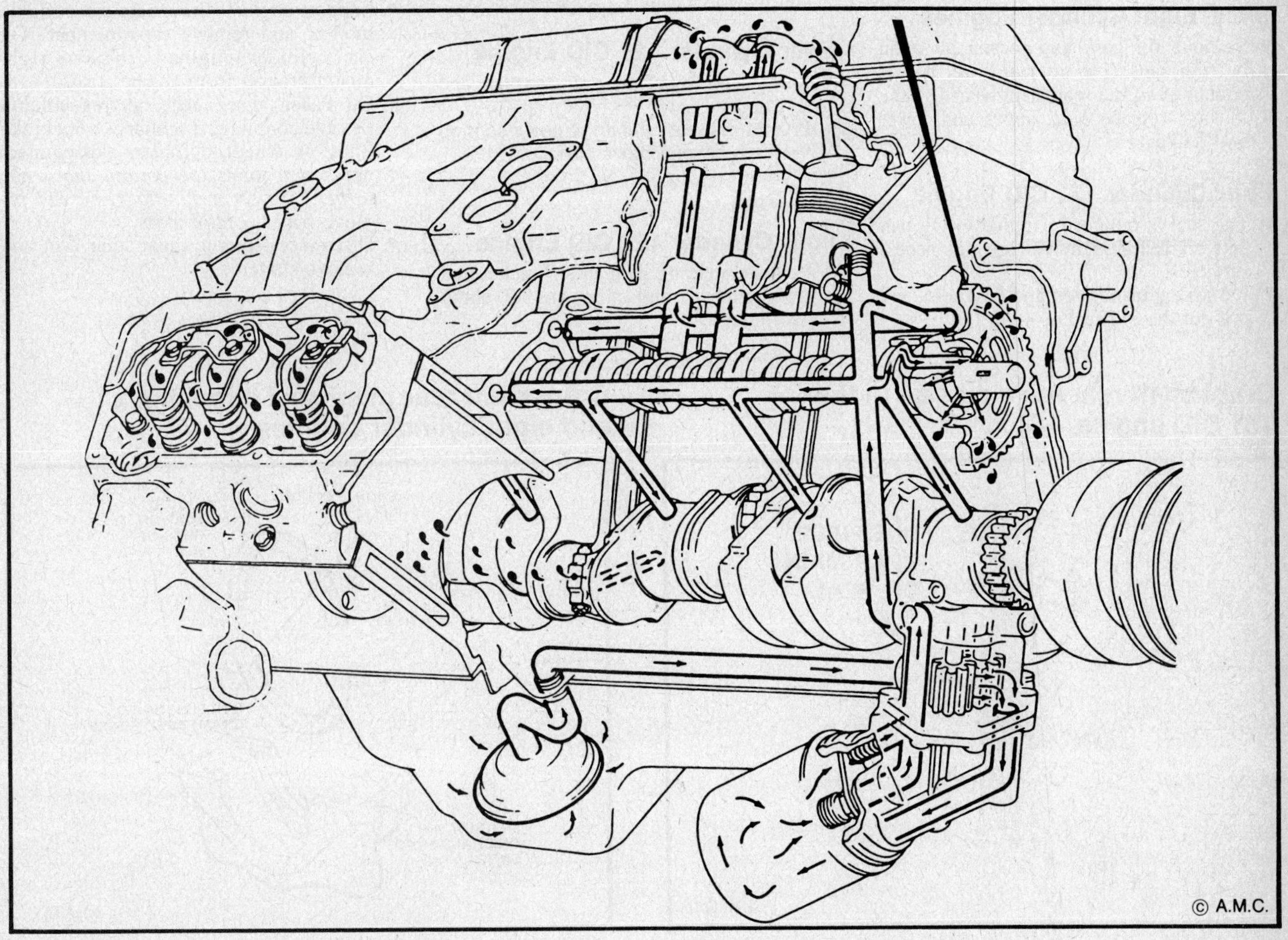

© A.M.C.

Oil pump and oil pan mounting in 151 CID four cylinder engine

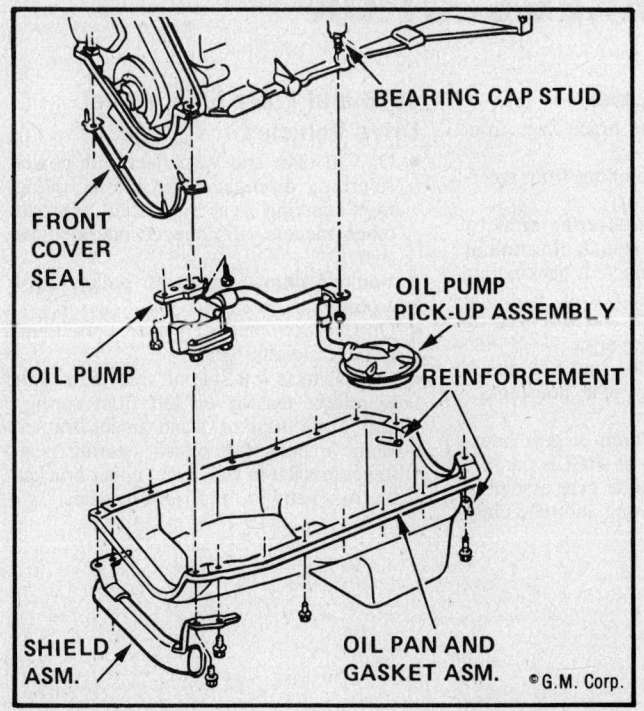

BEARING CAP STUD

FRONT COVER SEAL

OIL PUMP

OIL PUMP PICK-UP ASSEMBLY

REINFORCEMENT

SHIELD ASM.

OIL PAN AND GASKET ASM.

© G.M. Corp.

Oil pump eight cylinder engine

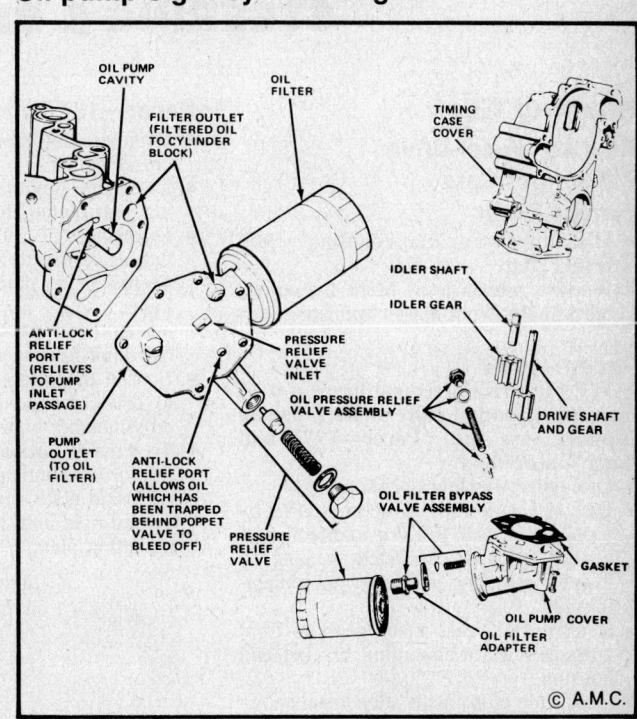

OIL PUMP CAVITY

FILTER OUTLET (FILTERED OIL TO CYLINDER BLOCK)

OIL FILTER

TIMING CASE COVER

IDLER SHAFT

IDLER GEAR

ANTI-LOCK RELIEF PORT (RELIEVES TO PUMP INLET PASSAGE)

PRESSURE RELIEF VALVE INLET

OIL PRESSURE RELIEF VALVE ASSEMBLY

DRIVE SHAFT AND GEAR

PUMP OUTLET (TO OIL FILTER)

ANTI-LOCK RELIEF PORT (ALLOWS OIL WHICH HAS BEEN TRAPPED BEHIND POPPET VALVE TO BLEED OFF)

PRESSURE RELIEF VALVE

OIL FILTER BYPASS VALVE ASSEMBLY

GASKET

OIL PUMP COVER

OIL FILTER ADAPTER

© A.M.C.

Crankshaft Rear Oil Seal

Six & Eight Cylinder Engines

- Remove oil pan, and loosen all main bearing caps. The oil seal lower half is contained in the rear main bearing cap.
- Always replace *both* upper and lower seal halves.

Four Cylinder 151 CID Engine

- The seal is mounted externally. Oil pan and crankshaft removal are not necessary.
- Remove transmission and flywheel, and pry out the old seal.

- Lubricate the new seal with engine oil and install by hand.

Four Cylinder 121 CID Engine

- Remove transmission, pressure plate and flywheel.
- Pry out old seal, and drive new one in to $1/32$ inch beyond block surface.

Oil Pan

Four Cylinder 121 CID Engine

- Remove steering gear idler bracket and crossmember, and raise engine about two inches.

Six & Eight Cylinder Engines

- Support engine, disconnect front engine mounts and remove crossmember. On six cylinder engines, remove right mount bracket from engine.
- On Pacer, disconnect steering column flexible coupling, disconnect front brake lines at wheel cylinders, disconnect upper ball joints (*be certain shock absorbers are securely attached*), and remove upper control arms.
- Disconnect steering gear idler arm and remove starter.

Crankshaft rear main oil seal in the 151 CID engine

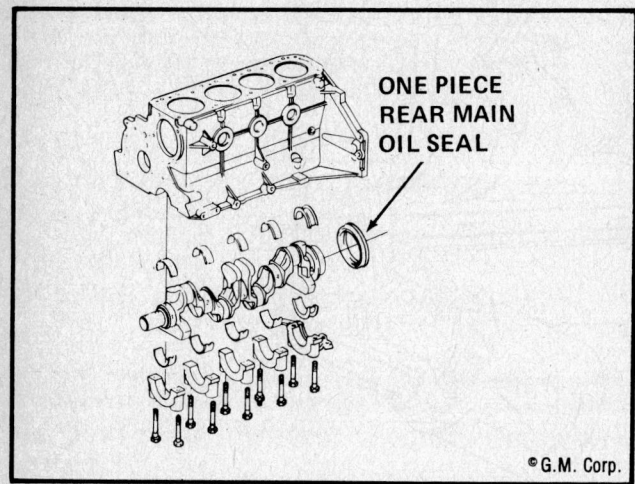

ONE PIECE REAR MAIN OIL SEAL

© G.M. Corp.

Crankshaft rear main seal used in six and eight cylinder engines

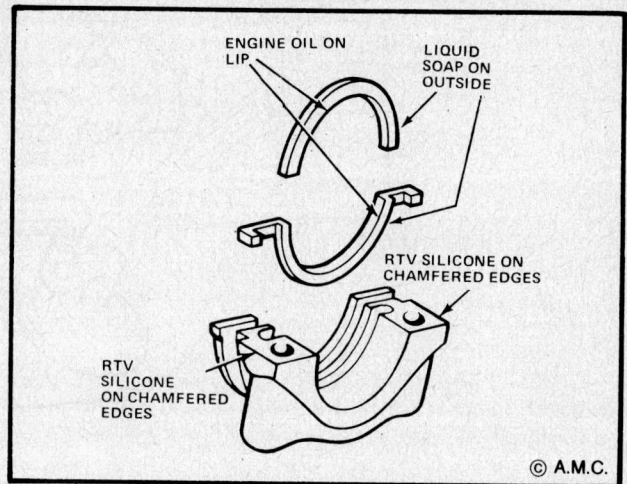

ENGINE OIL ON LIP

LIQUID SOAP ON OUTSIDE

RTV SILICONE ON CHAMFERED EDGES

RTV SILICONE ON CHAMFERED EDGES

© A.M.C.

STEERING & BRAKES SECTION

Steering Gear

All Two Wheel Drive Passenger Cars Except Pacer

- Disconnect flexible coupling, fluid hoses, etc.
- Remove pitman arm. Mark for correct reassembly if not master-splined.

Pacer—1976

NOTE: If a reinforcement brace is used between mounting plate and left engine support, use the "Pacer—1977 and Later" procedure.

- Disconnect flexible coupling.
- Disconnect tie rods at steering arms by turning wheels to full stop in direction of tie rod being disconnected, jacking up lower control arm and removing remaining nut.
- Remove bolts that attach gears to front crossmember at mounting bracket and housing.
- Check toe adjustment after installation.

Pacer—1977 and Later

- Remove reinforcement brace from front crossmember.
- Disengage flexible coupling from steering gear pinion shaft.
- Disconnect tie rods at steering arms by turning wheels to full stop in direction of tie rod being disconnected, jacking up lower control arm, removing retaining nut from tie rod end, and disengaging ball joint from steering arm.
- Loosen mounting bolts, and use punch to drive out steering gear housing-to-crossmember bolts.
- To remove, rotate bottom of gear housing forward until pinion shaft is parallel with skid plate, and slide gear assembly toward right until housing and tube clear mounting plate.

1976 and Later Four Wheel Drive Vehicles

- On Cherokee and Wagoneer with power steering, disengage flexible coupling from steering gear stub shaft. On all other models, disconnect intermediate shaft.
- Remove pitman arm with puller, Tool J-6632.
- On Cherokee and Wagoneer, unbolt and remove steering gear.
- On CJ, raise left side of vehicle enough to relieve tension on left front spring, and place support stand under frame. Remove bolts that attach steering gear lower bracket to frame and upper bracket to crossmember, and remove gear.

Pacer power steering gear

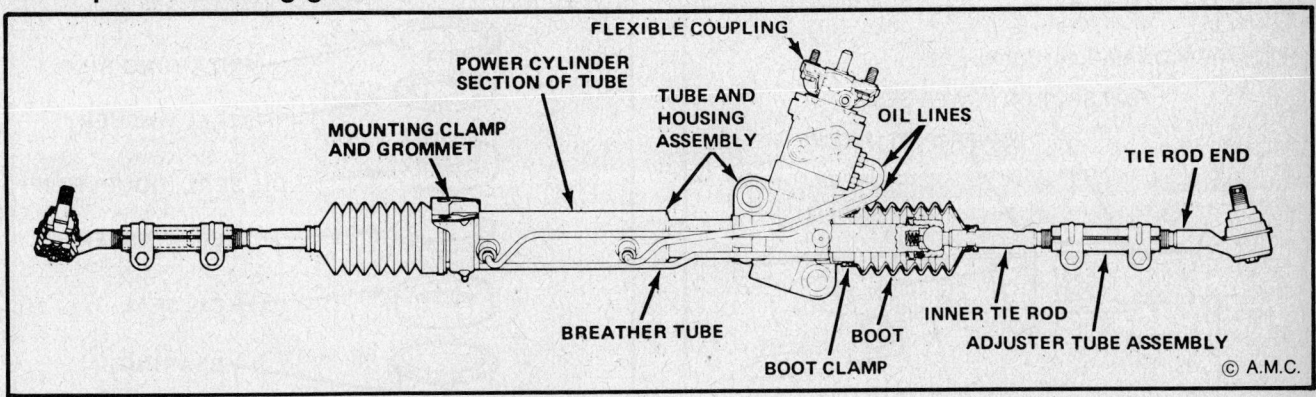

Cherokee and Wagoneer steering linkage

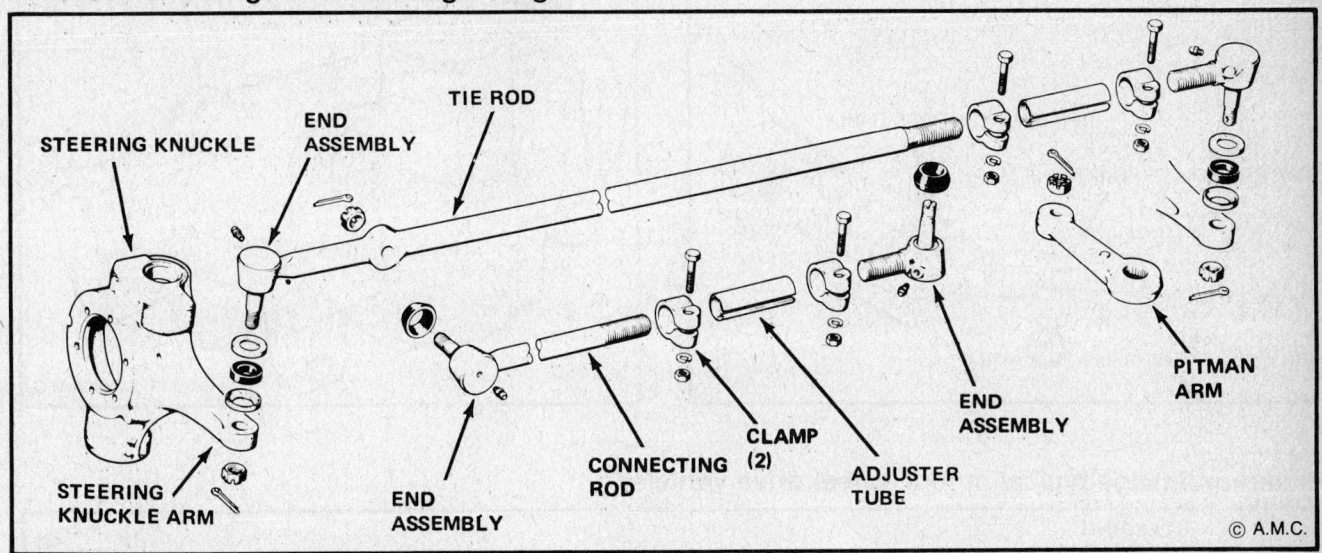

Steering linkage except Pacer

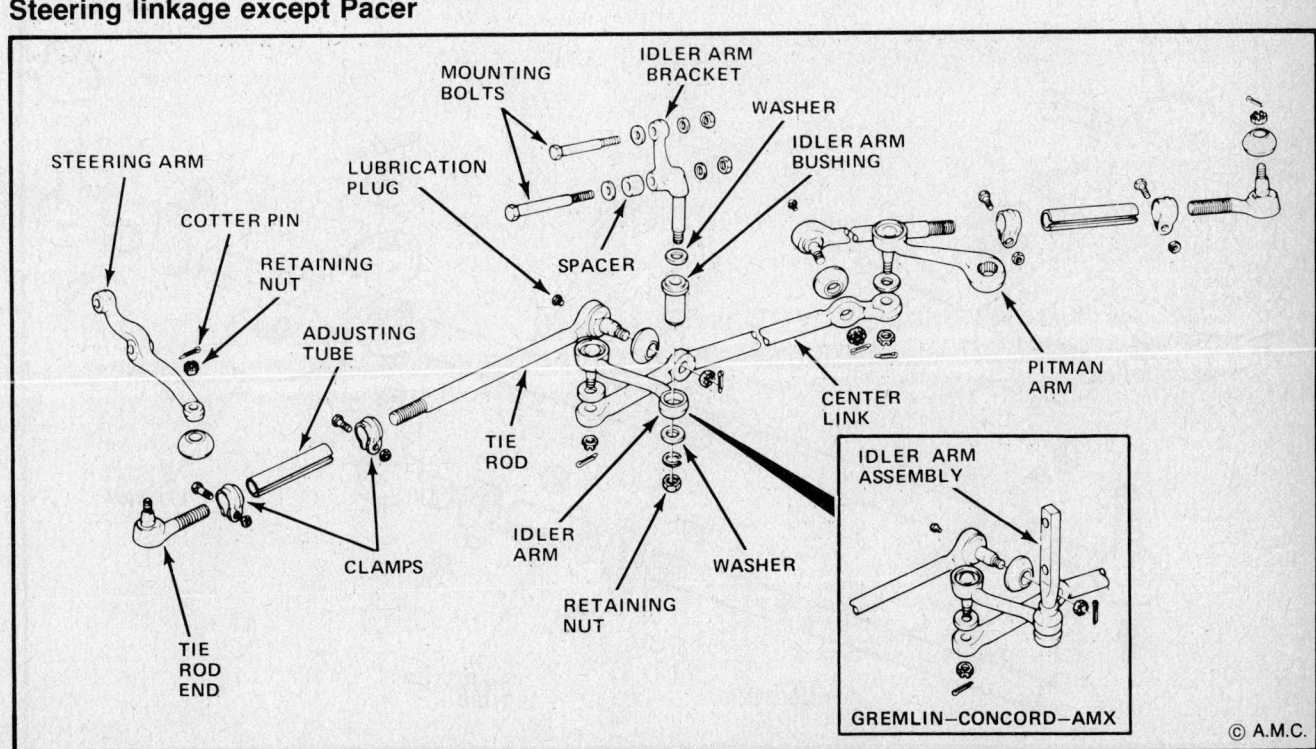

AMC PASSENGER CARS AND JEEP

Steering gear-to-steering wheel alignment

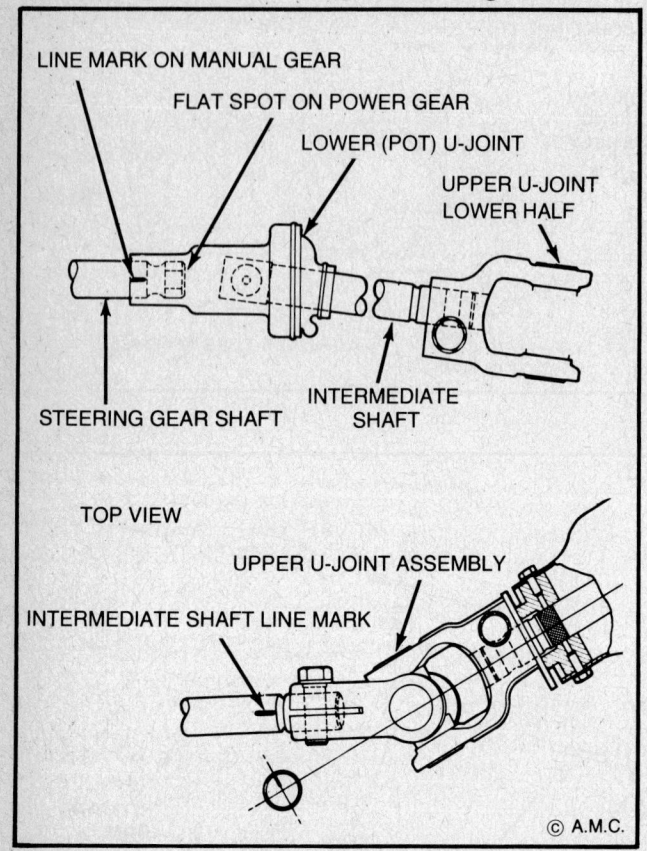

LINE MARK ON MANUAL GEAR

FLAT SPOT ON POWER GEAR

LOWER (POT) U-JOINT

UPPER U-JOINT LOWER HALF

STEERING GEAR SHAFT

INTERMEDIATE SHAFT

TOP VIEW

UPPER U-JOINT ASSEMBLY

INTERMEDIATE SHAFT LINE MARK

© A.M.C.

Pitman shaft bearing and seals

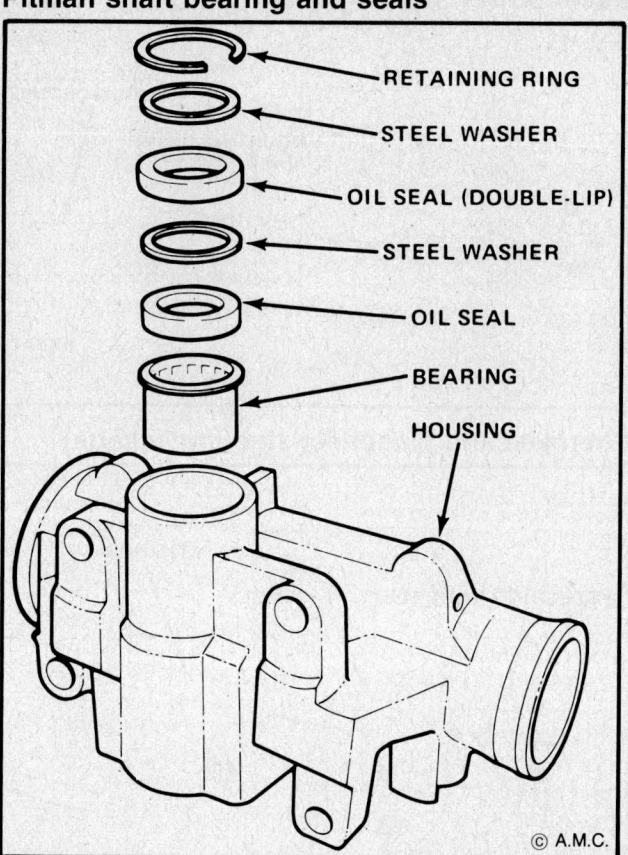

RETAINING RING

STEEL WASHER

OIL SEAL (DOUBLE-LIP)

STEEL WASHER

OIL SEAL

BEARING

HOUSING

© A.M.C.

Steering linkage typical in four wheel drive vehicles

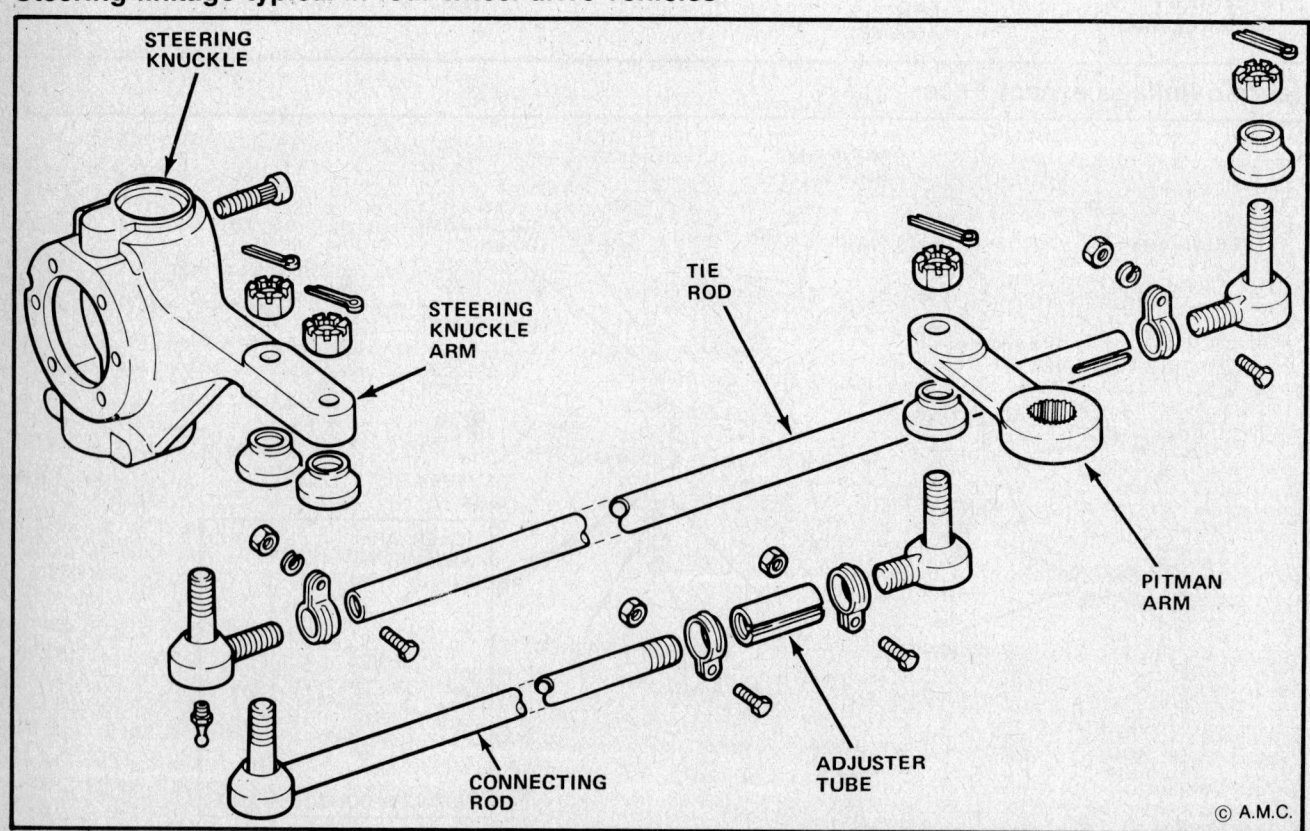

STEERING KNUCKLE

STEERING KNUCKLE ARM

TIE ROD

PITMAN ARM

CONNECTING ROD

ADJUSTER TUBE

© A.M.C.

Lock plate retainer

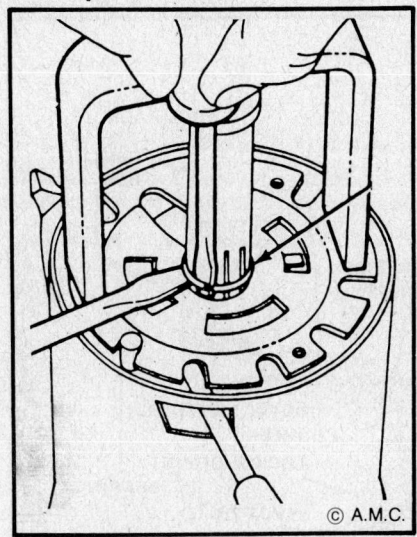

© A.M.C.

Metric steering shaft identification

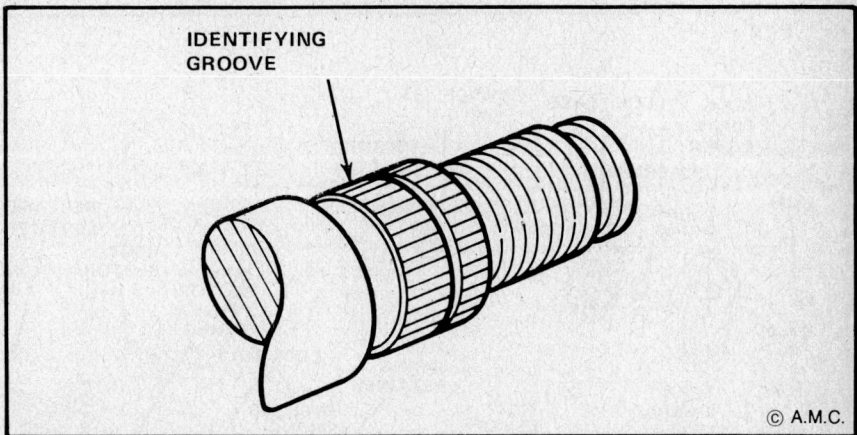

IDENTIFYING GROOVE

© A.M.C.

Starting in 1978, some models are equipped with steering shafts using metric steering wheel nut threads. American thread shafts have no identifying groove

Steering Column

NOTE: Handle the steering column very carefully. Rapping on the end of it or leaning on it could shear off the plastic inserts which allow the column to collapse in a crash.

NOTE: When installing steering columns, use only specified hardware. Over-length bolts could prevent the column from properly collapsing in a crash.

Two Wheel Drive
Passenger Vehicles

- Disconnect battery.
- Disconnect flexible coupling.
- Disconnect electrical wiring, shift linkages, etc.
- Remove toeboard bolts from dash panel and then bolts attaching mounting bracket to column.

1976 and Earlier Four Wheel Drive Vehicles

- Disconnect the battery, and disconnect the steering column electrical wiring under the instrument panel.
- On vehicles without power steering, scribe a line mark on steering shaft and upper steering shaft-to-lower shaft U-joint pinch bolt.
- On vehicles with power steering, disconnect the flexible coupling.
- Disconnect the shift linkage from the lever on column shift models.
- Disconnect column mounts and remove column.

1977 and Later Four Wheel Drive Vehicles

- Disconnect battery.

- Disconnect automatic transmission shift rod at steering column shift lever. On Cherokee and Wagoneer with power brakes, the linkage must be in the "1" range detent position for access to shift rod-to-shift lever retaining clip.
- Remove the steering column-to-intermediate shaft U-joint pinch bolt, but do not separate shaft and column until column is being removed.
- Remove air conditioning ducting and column-to-instrument panel bezel. Remove mounts to instrument panel, and remove upper and lower toe plates.
- Disconnect ignition wiring harness at switch. Disconnect black connector first, and when installing, connect white connector first. Disconnect speed control wiring.
- Remove steering column after carefully separating it from the intermediate shaft.

Steering system flexible coupling

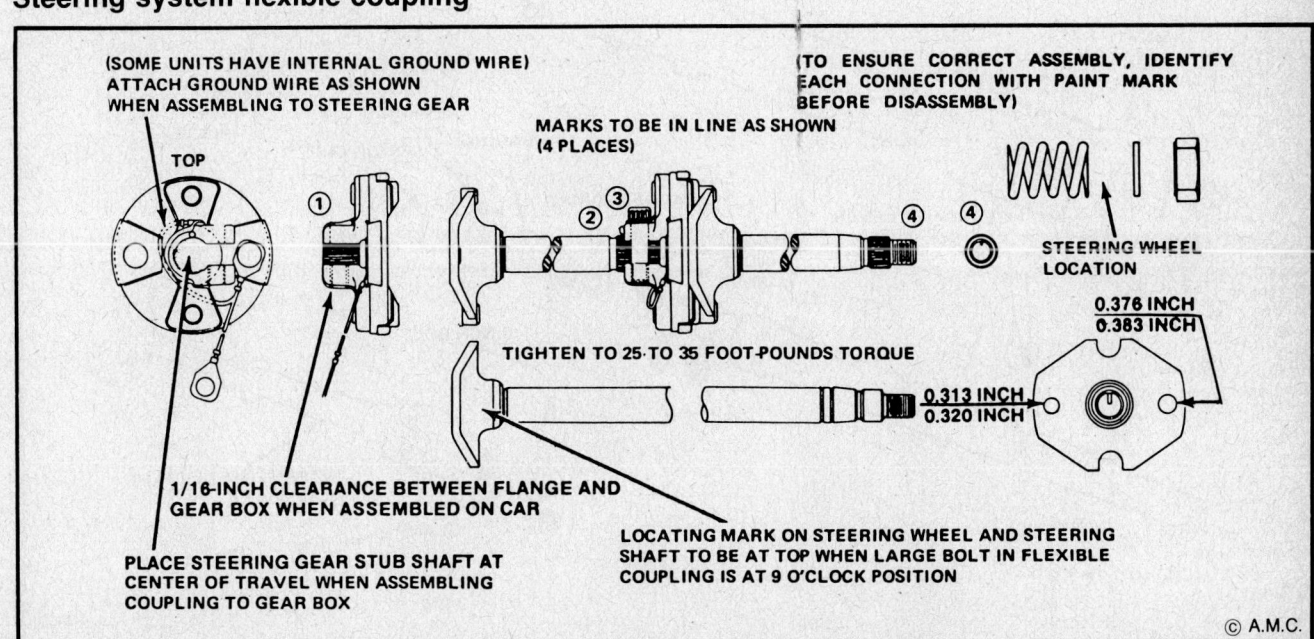

(SOME UNITS HAVE INTERNAL GROUND WIRE) ATTACH GROUND WIRE AS SHOWN WHEN ASSEMBLING TO STEERING GEAR

TOP

(TO ENSURE CORRECT ASSEMBLY, IDENTIFY EACH CONNECTION WITH PAINT MARK BEFORE DISASSEMBLY)

MARKS TO BE IN LINE AS SHOWN (4 PLACES)

STEERING WHEEL LOCATION

0.376 INCH
0.383 INCH

TIGHTEN TO 25 TO 35 FOOT-POUNDS TORQUE

0.313 INCH
0.320 INCH

1/16-INCH CLEARANCE BETWEEN FLANGE AND GEAR BOX WHEN ASSEMBLED ON CAR

PLACE STEERING GEAR STUB SHAFT AT CENTER OF TRAVEL WHEN ASSEMBLING COUPLING TO GEAR BOX

LOCATING MARK ON STEERING WHEEL AND STEERING SHAFT TO BE AT TOP WHEN LARGE BOLT IN FLEXIBLE COUPLING IS AT 9 O'CLOCK POSITION

© A.M.C.

Typical tilt steering column

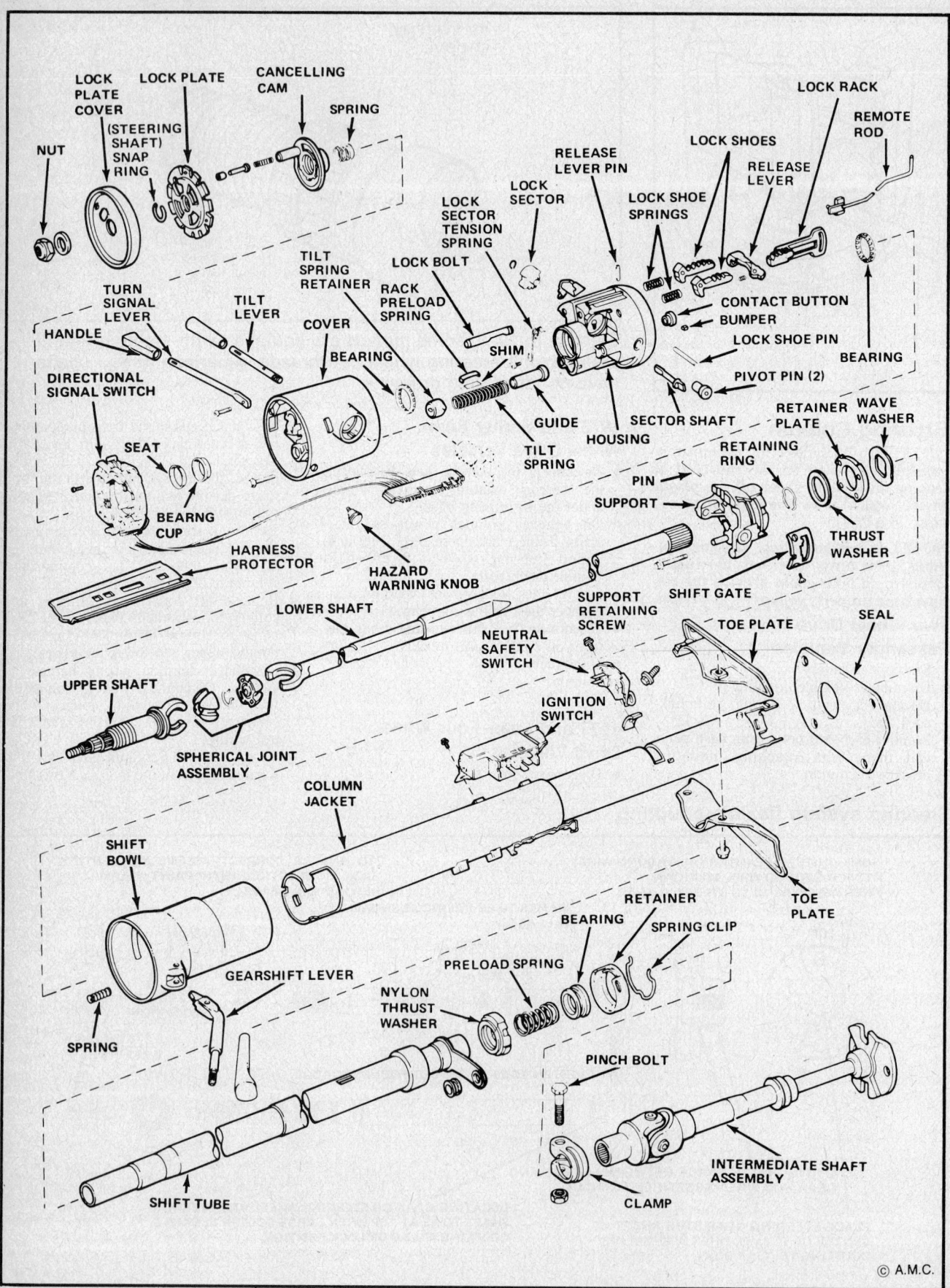

© A.M.C.

Steering column used with automatic transmission

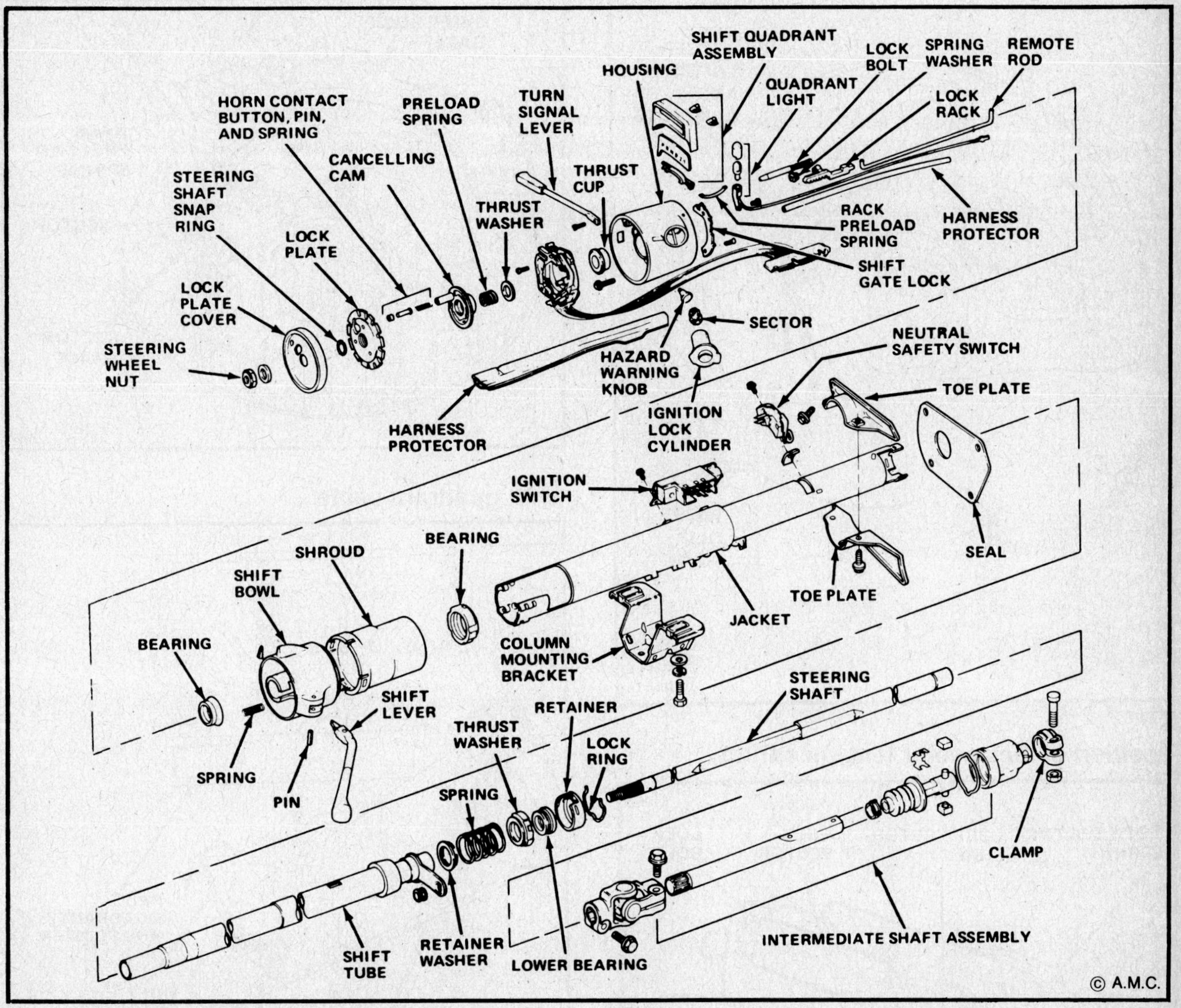

SHIFT QUADRANT ASSEMBLY

HOUSING

QUADRANT LIGHT

LOCK BOLT

SPRING WASHER

REMOTE ROD

LOCK RACK

HORN CONTACT BUTTON, PIN, AND SPRING

PRELOAD SPRING

TURN SIGNAL LEVER

CANCELLING CAM

THRUST CUP

STEERING SHAFT SNAP RING

THRUST WASHER

RACK PRELOAD SPRING

HARNESS PROTECTOR

LOCK PLATE

SHIFT GATE LOCK

LOCK PLATE COVER

STEERING WHEEL NUT

SECTOR

NEUTRAL SAFETY SWITCH

HAZARD WARNING KNOB

TOE PLATE

HARNESS PROTECTOR

IGNITION LOCK CYLINDER

IGNITION SWITCH

SEAL

BEARING

SHROUD

BEARING

TOE PLATE

JACKET

SHIFT BOWL

COLUMN MOUNTING BRACKET

BEARING

STEERING SHAFT

SHIFT LEVER

RETAINER

THRUST WASHER

LOCK RING

SPRING

PIN

SPRING

CLAMP

SHIFT TUBE

RETAINER WASHER

LOWER BEARING

INTERMEDIATE SHAFT ASSEMBLY

© A.M.C.

Steering column lower bearing assembly

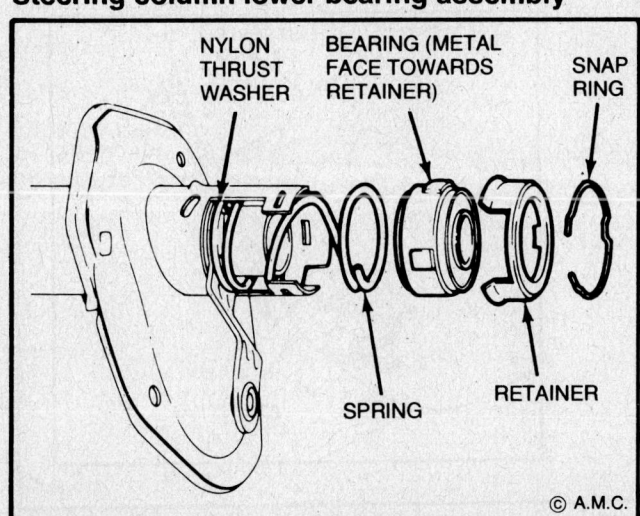

NYLON THRUST WASHER

BEARING (METAL FACE TOWARDS RETAINER)

SNAP RING

SPRING

RETAINER

© A.M.C.

Floor shift steering columns have no thrust washer or spring

Steering column mounting bracket

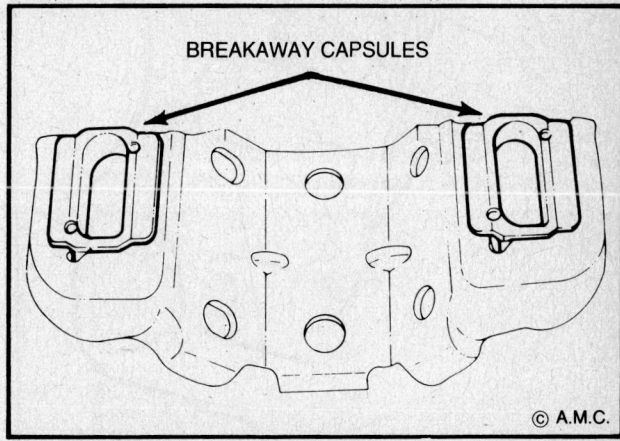

BREAKAWAY CAPSULES

© A.M.C.

The breakaway capsules are part of the energy absorption system which allows the steering column to compress in a collision. When the bracket is removed, store it separately to prevent damage to the capsules

AMC PASSENGER CARS AND JEEP

Removing buzzer switch and contacts

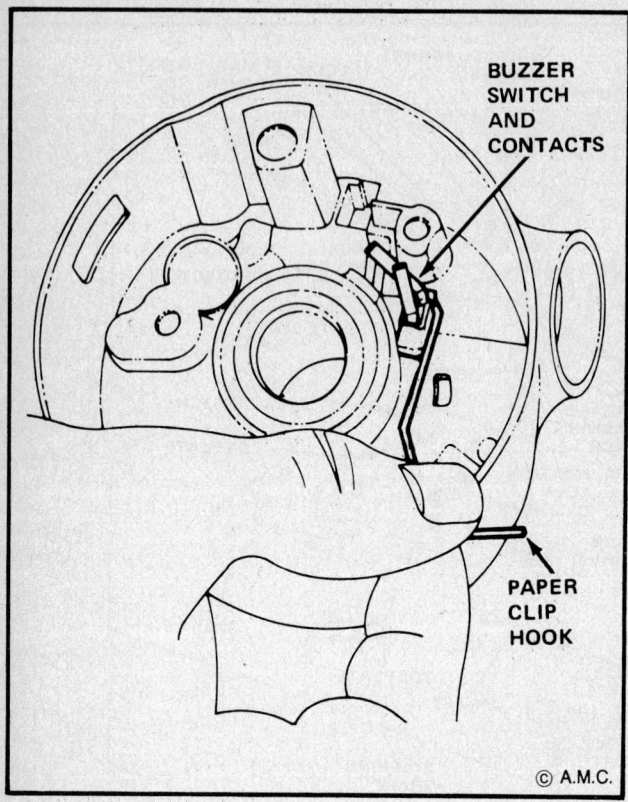

Removing rack preload spring

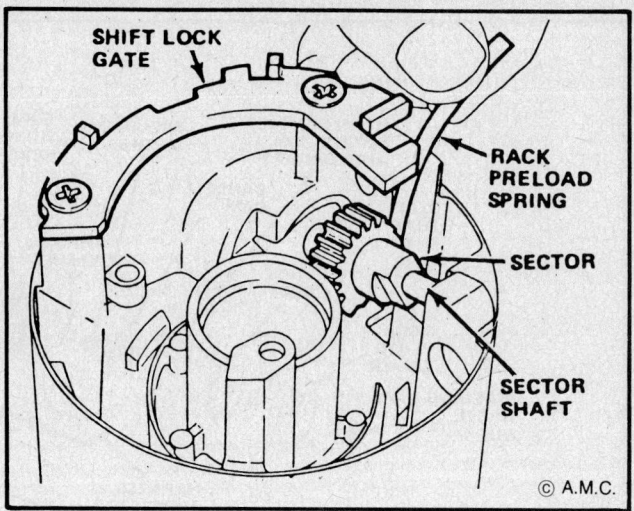

Position of lock sector tension spring

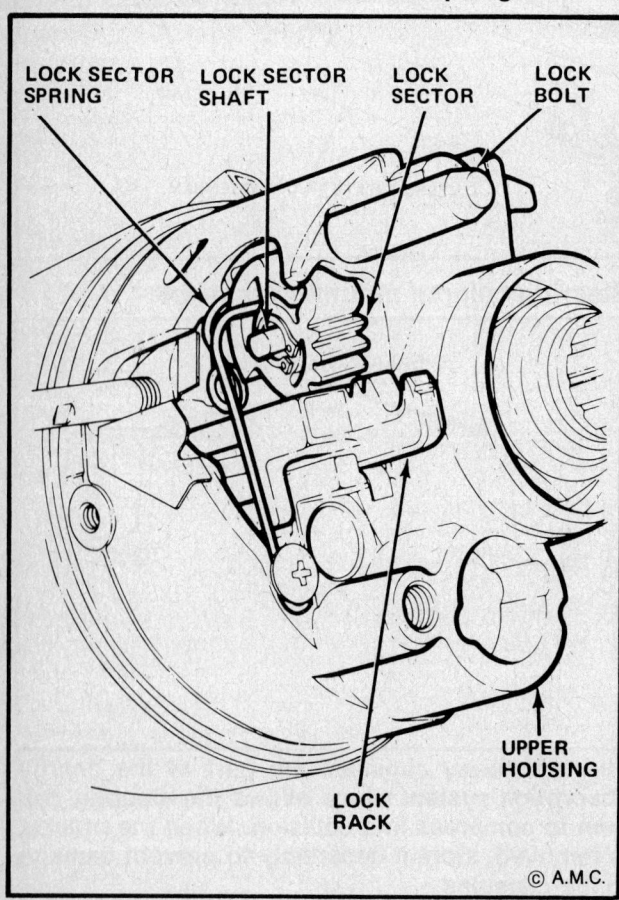

Shift quadrant cable

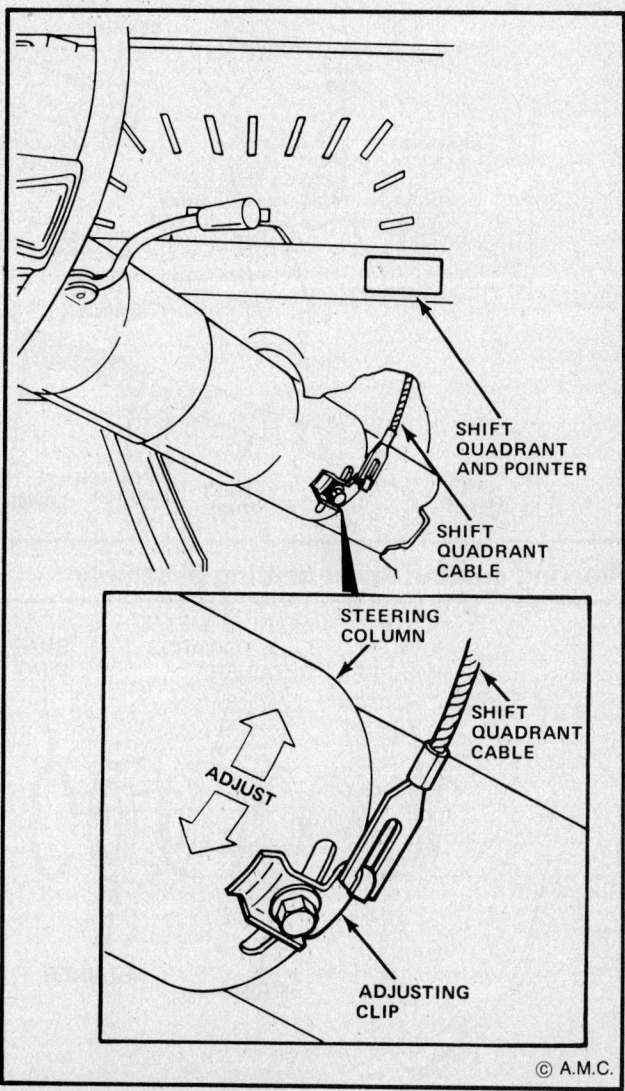

To adjust shift quadrant pointer, move clip up or down as necessary to center quadrant pointer on the neutral position

Power steering system

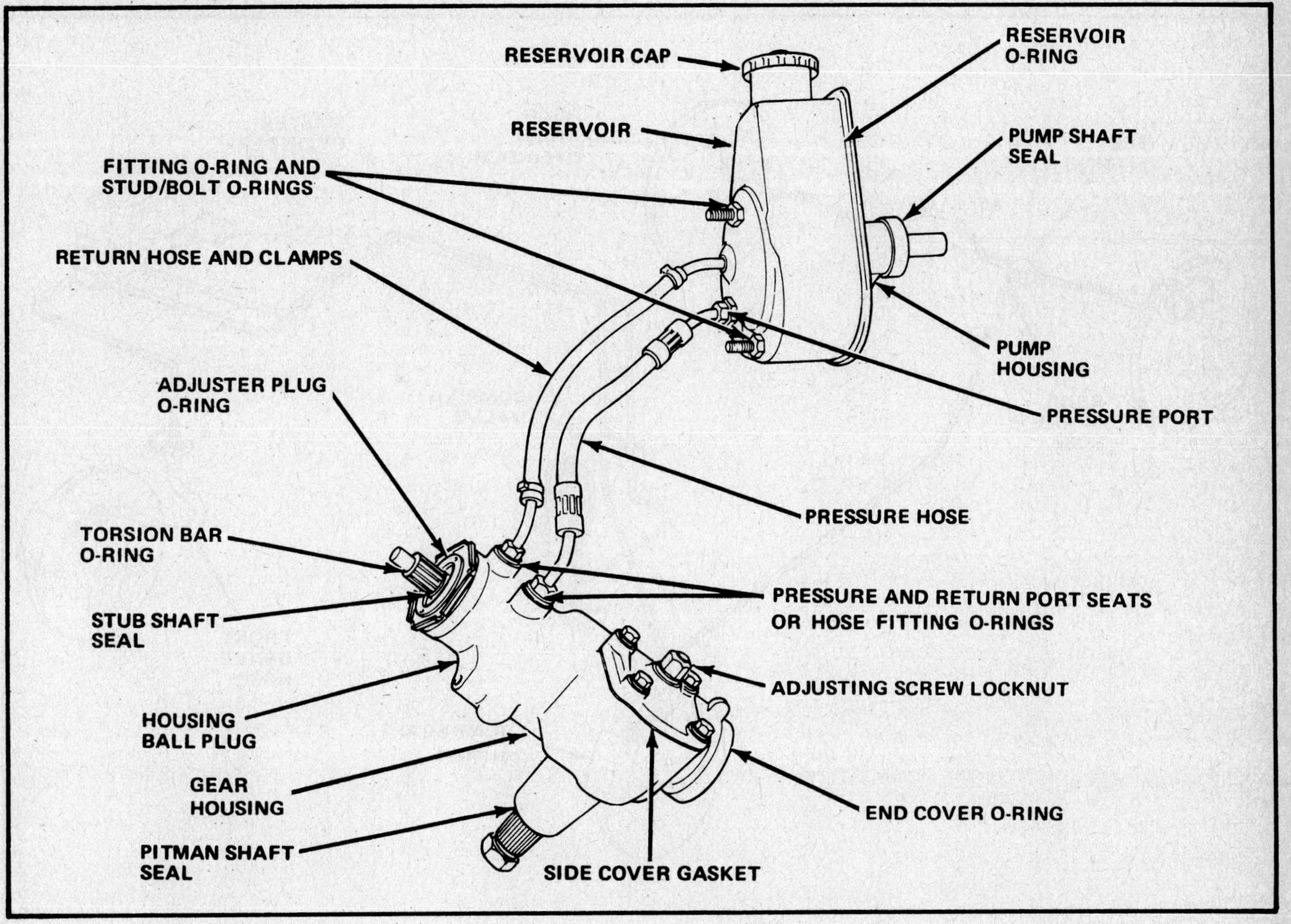

RESERVOIR CAP

RESERVOIR O-RING

RESERVOIR

PUMP SHAFT SEAL

FITTING O-RING AND STUD/BOLT O-RINGS

RETURN HOSE AND CLAMPS

PUMP HOUSING

PRESSURE PORT

ADJUSTER PLUG O-RING

PRESSURE HOSE

TORSION BAR O-RING

PRESSURE AND RETURN PORT SEATS OR HOSE FITTING O-RINGS

STUB SHAFT SEAL

ADJUSTING SCREW LOCKNUT

HOUSING BALL PLUG

GEAR HOUSING

END COVER O-RING

PITMAN SHAFT SEAL

SIDE COVER GASKET

Pump leak points

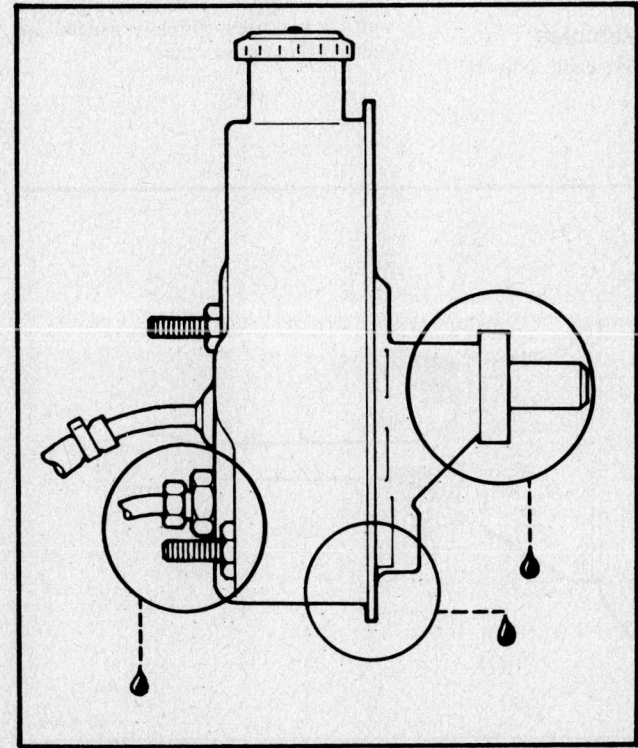

Pump shaft seal

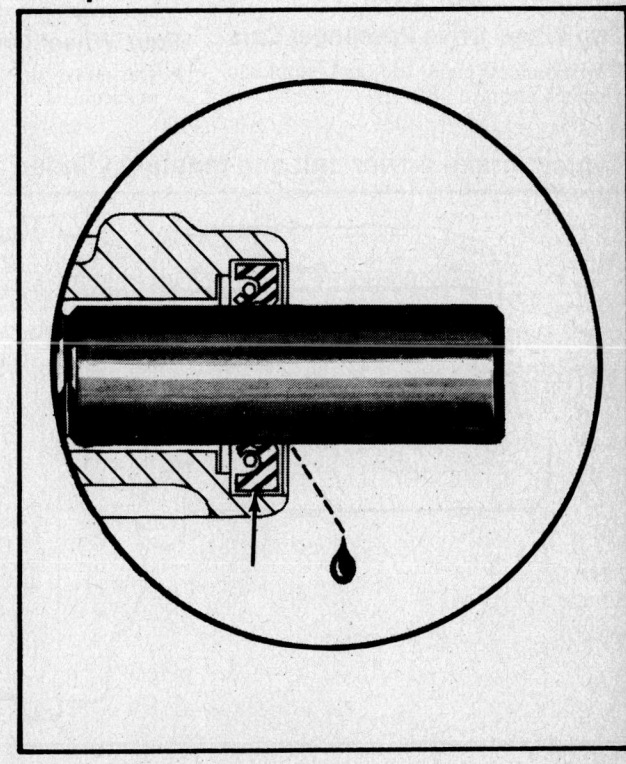

AMC PASSENGER CARS AND JEEP

Brake hydraulic system

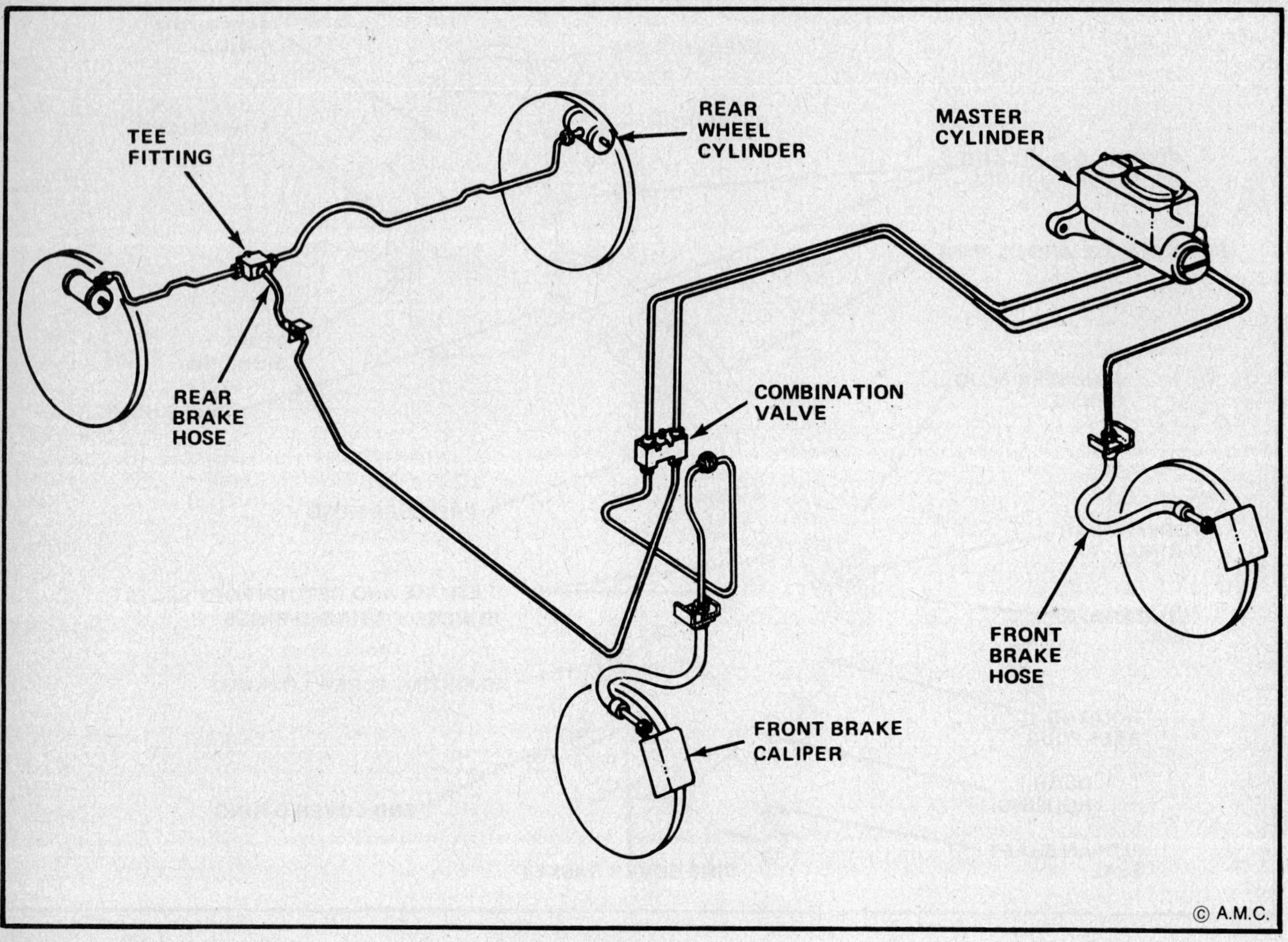

TEE FITTING

REAR WHEEL CYLINDER

MASTER CYLINDER

REAR BRAKE HOSE

COMBINATION VALVE

FRONT BRAKE HOSE

FRONT BRAKE CALIPER

© A.M.C.

Brake Power Unit

Two Wheel Drive Passenger Cars
- Disconnect push rod and stoplamp switch at brake pedal.

- Separate power unit and master cylinder, and unbolt power unit from firewall.

Four Wheel Drive Vehicles
- The power unit is serviceable only by replacement.

- When replacing a power unit, use the push rod supplied with the replacement unit. It has been correctly gauged and preset to that power unit.

Typical brake power unit and master cylinder

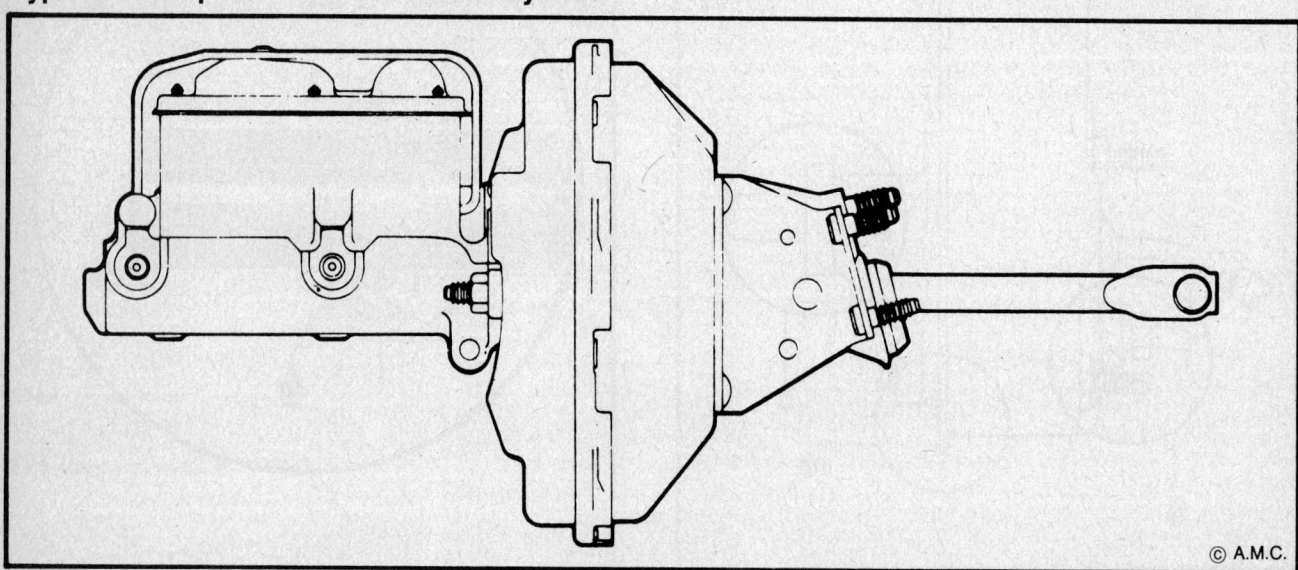

© A.M.C.

Parking Brake Cable R&R

Two Wheel Drive Passenger Cars Except Pacer
- Disconnect lever-to-equalizer cable and lever assembly attaching nuts and bolts.
- Remove clevis clips at end of cable and all hold-down clips, and remove cable.

Pacer
- Disconnect front cable at equalizer.
- Remove parking brake lever.

- Slide cable out of retaining clip on underside of floorpan and pull cable out.

Parking Brake Adjustment

Two Wheel Drive Passenger Cars
- Correctly adjust service brakes.
- On cars using a foot operated lever, set the lever on the first notch from the full-release position. On cars using a T-handle, set it in the fifth notch from full-release.

- Tighten cable at equalizer until rear wheels lock.
- Release lever, and check that there is no brake drag at wheels.

Four Wheel Drive Vehicles
- Correctly adjust service brakes.
- With parking brake fully released, loosen locknuts at equalizer, and tighten cables until slight drag is felt at the wheels. Loosen cables until wheels turn freely, and tighten equalizer locknuts.

Parking brake cable typical in two wheel drive passenger vehicles

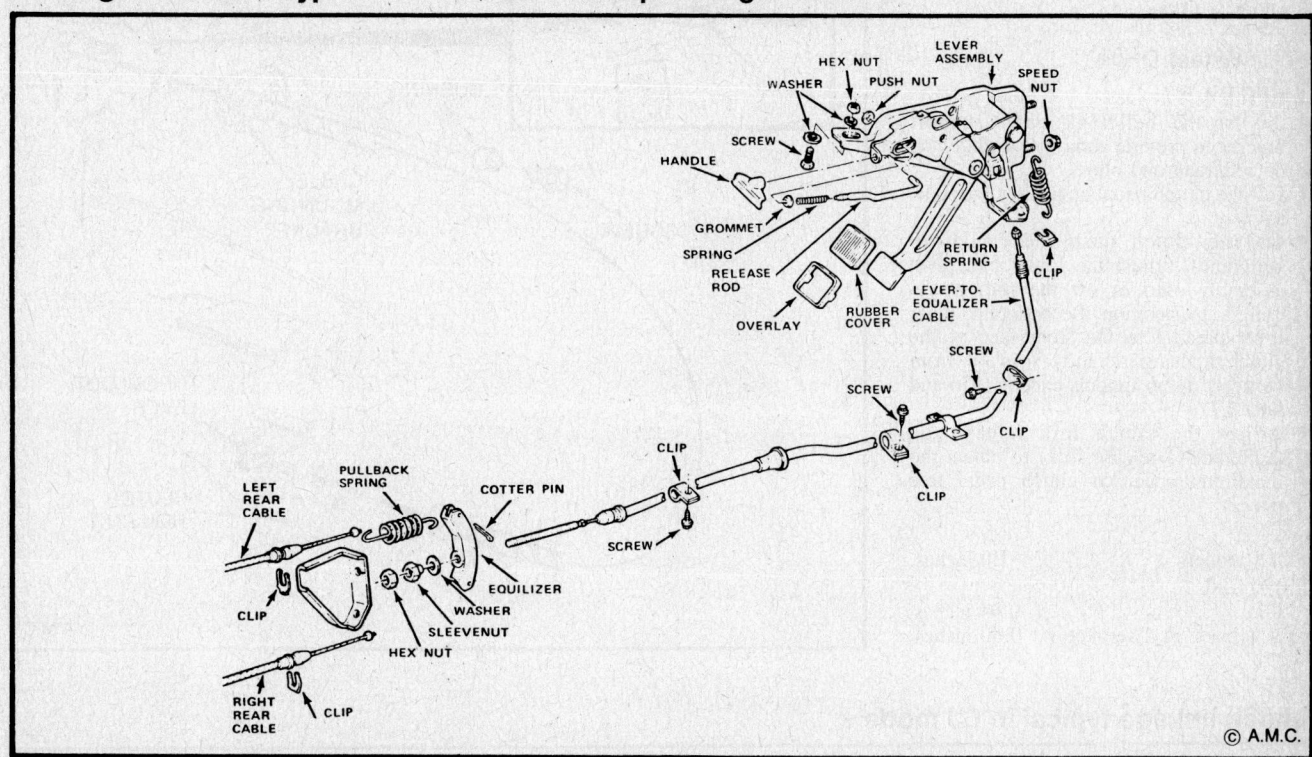

Parking brake cable typical in four wheel drive vehicles

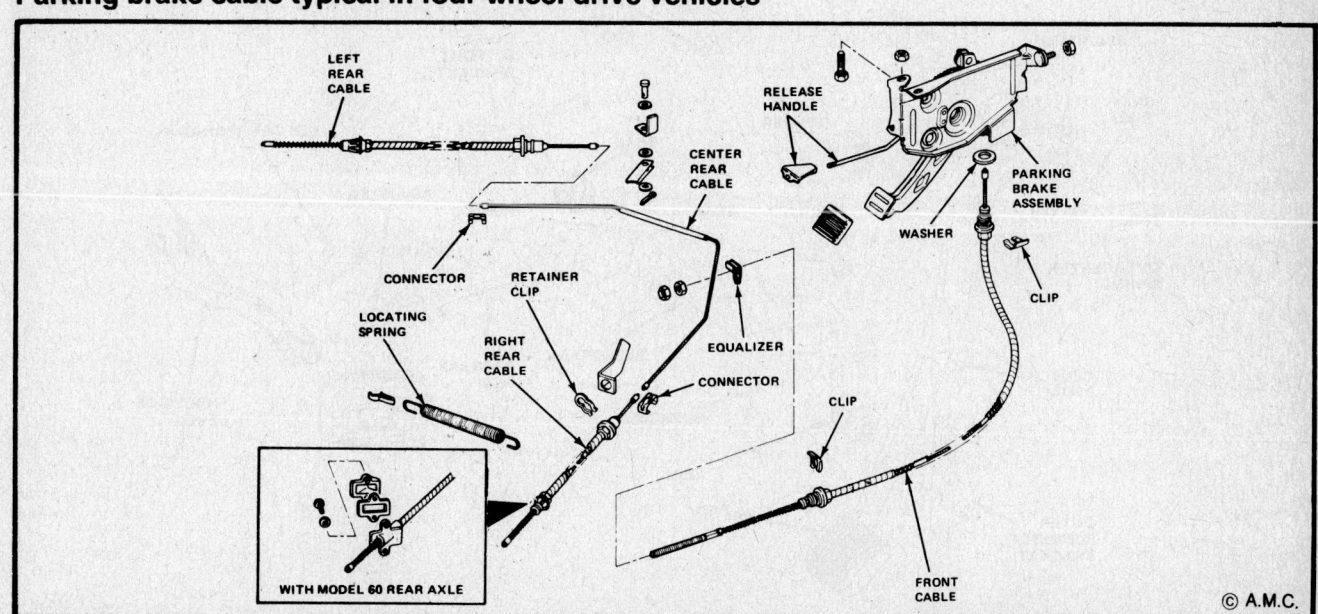

CLUTCH, TRANSMISSION, PROPELLER SHAFT & REAR AXLE SECTION

Clutch Adjustment

Two Wheel Drive Passenger Cars

- Preferred clutch pedal free play with six and eight cylinder engines is 1⅛ inch. Adjust at the bellcrank-to-throw-out lever rod.
- Preferred clutch pedal free play with four cylinder 121 CID engine is ⅝ inch. Adjust by increasing or decreasing clutch cable travel.

Four Wheel Drive Vehicles

- Adjust the bellcrank outer support bracket to provide about one-eighth inch of bellcrank end play.
- Lift the clutch pedal up against the pedal stop.
- On the clutch push rod (pedal-to-bellcrank), adjust the lower ball pivot assembly onto or off the rod, as required, to position the bellcrank inner lever parallel to the front face of the clutch housing (slightly forward from vertical) on all models except 1976 and later CJ.
- Adjust the clutch fork release rod (bellcrank-to-release fork) to obtain the maximum specified clutch pedal free play:

1976	
All models	1.0 inches.
1977-80	
CJ	0.94 inches.
Wagoneer & Cherokee	0.50 inches.

Clutch cable installation used with four cylinder 121 CID engines

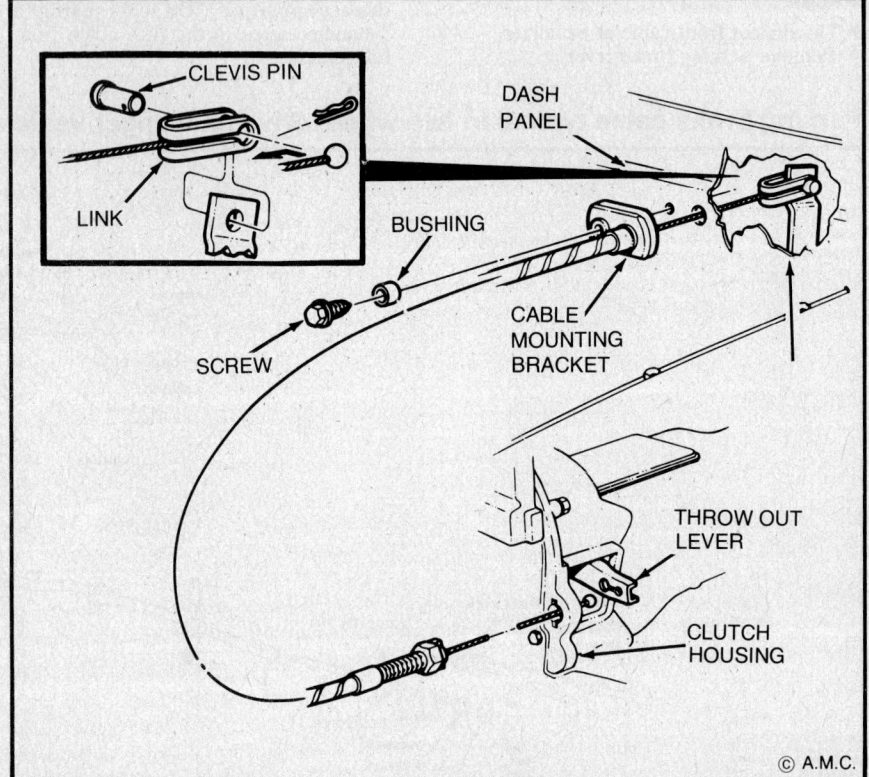

CLEVIS PIN
LINK
DASH PANEL
BUSHING
SCREW
CABLE MOUNTING BRACKET
THROW OUT LEVER
CLUTCH HOUSING
© A.M.C.

Clutch linkage typical in CJ models

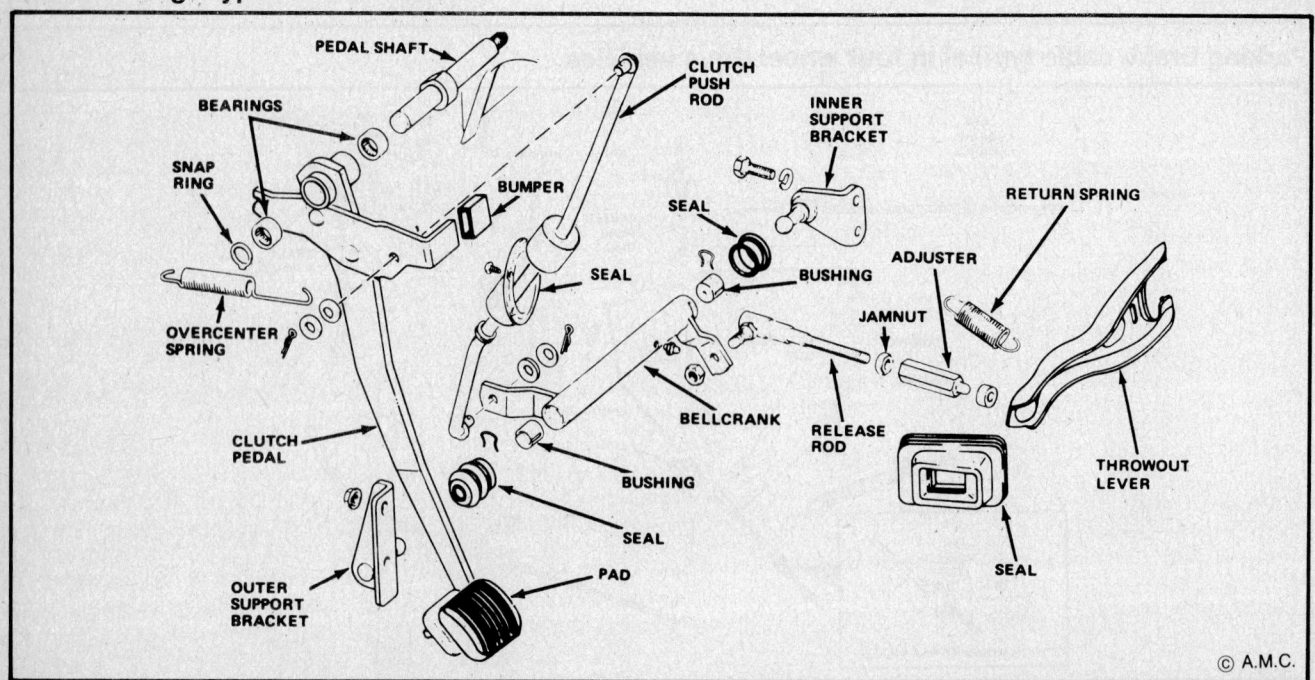

PEDAL SHAFT
CLUTCH PUSH ROD
INNER SUPPORT BRACKET
RETURN SPRING
BEARINGS
SNAP RING
BUMPER
SEAL
ADJUSTER
SEAL
BUSHING
JAMNUT
OVERCENTER SPRING
CLUTCH PEDAL
BELLCRANK
RELEASE ROD
THROWOUT LEVER
BUSHING
SEAL
SEAL
OUTER SUPPORT BRACKET
PAD
© A.M.C.

Cherokee clutch linkage

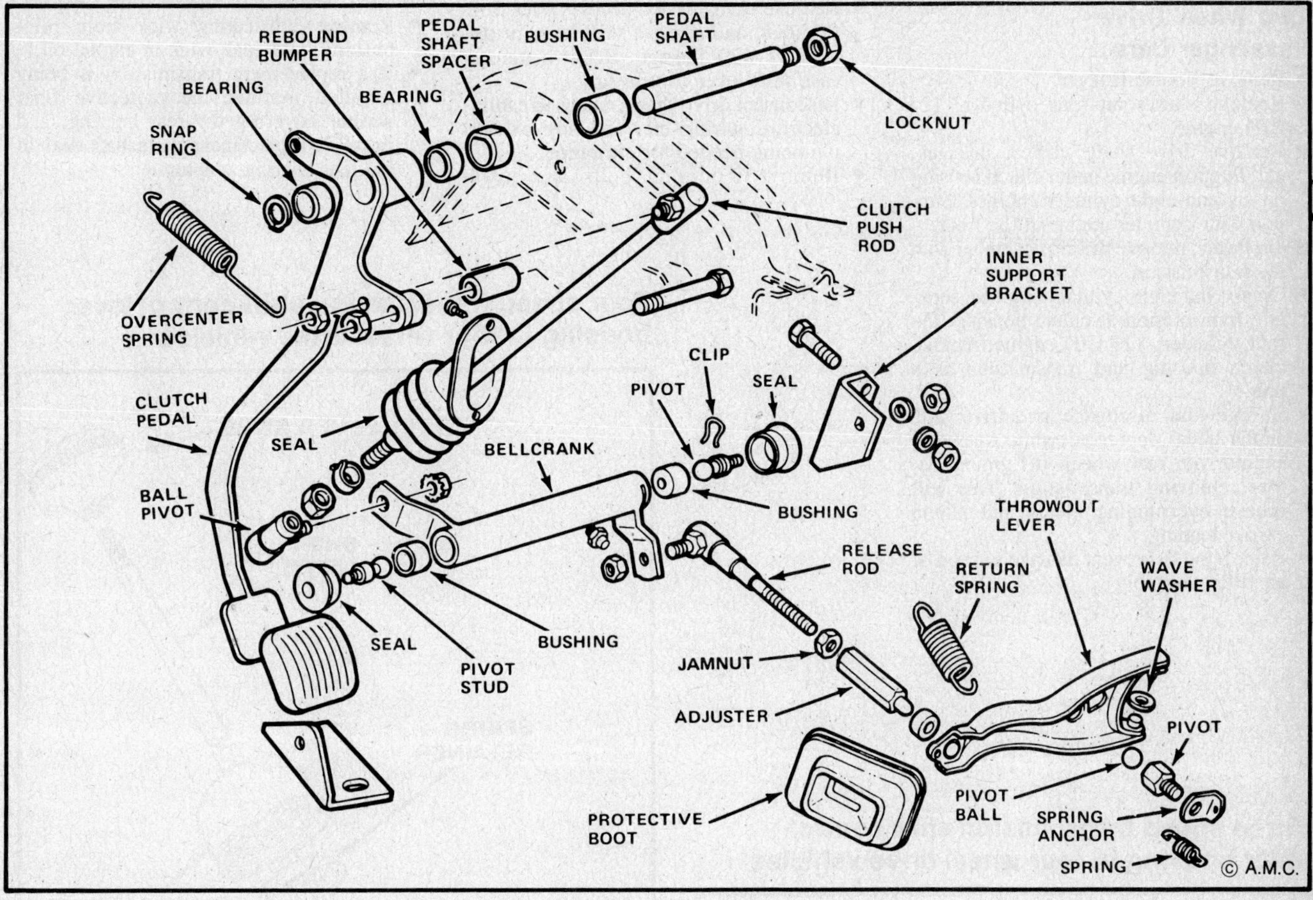

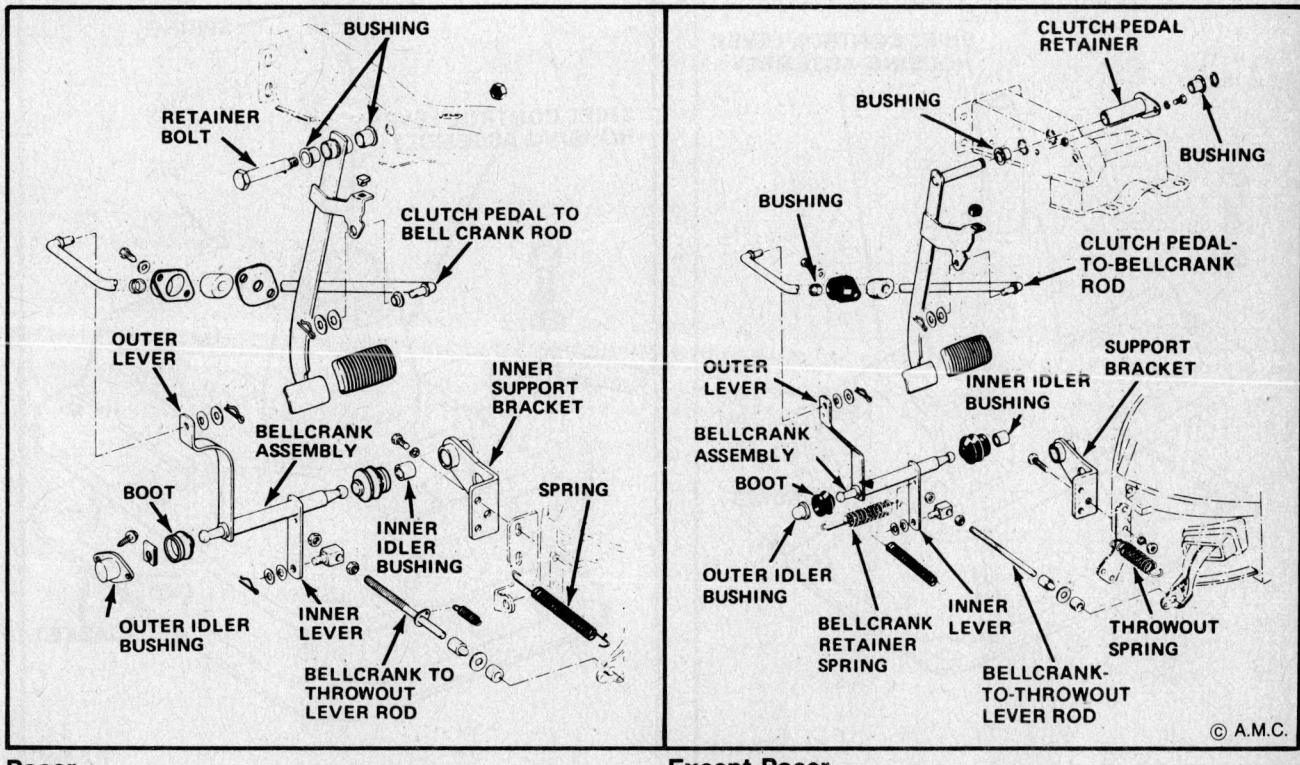

REBOUND BUMPER

PEDAL SHAFT SPACER

BUSHING

PEDAL SHAFT

BEARING

BEARING

LOCKNUT

SNAP RING

CLUTCH PUSH ROD

INNER SUPPORT BRACKET

OVERCENTER SPRING

CLUTCH PEDAL

CLIP

PIVOT

SEAL

SEAL

BELLCRANK

THROWOUT LEVER

BALL PIVOT

RETURN SPRING

WAVE WASHER

BUSHING

RELEASE ROD

SEAL

PIVOT STUD

BUSHING

JAMNUT

ADJUSTER

PIVOT

PIVOT BALL

SPRING ANCHOR

PROTECTIVE BOOT

SPRING

© A.M.C.

Clutch linkage

BUSHING

RETAINER BOLT

CLUTCH PEDAL TO BELL CRANK ROD

OUTER LEVER

INNER SUPPORT BRACKET

BOOT

BELLCRANK ASSEMBLY

SPRING

OUTER IDLER BUSHING

INNER LEVER

INNER IDLER BUSHING

BELLCRANK TO THROWOUT LEVER ROD

CLUTCH PEDAL RETAINER

BUSHING

BUSHING

BUSHING

CLUTCH PEDAL-TO-BELLCRANK ROD

OUTER LEVER

INNER IDLER BUSHING

SUPPORT BRACKET

BELLCRANK ASSEMBLY

BOOT

OUTER IDLER BUSHING

BELLCRANK RETAINER SPRING

INNER LEVER

THROWOUT SPRING

BELLCRANK-TO-THROWOUT LEVER ROD

© A.M.C.

Pacer

Except Pacer

Manual Transmission R&R

Two Wheel Drive
Passenger Cars

- Remove floorshift lever.
- Remove starter on four cylinder, 121 CID engine.
- Remove drive shaft, cables, linkages, etc. Support engine under clutch housing on six and eight cylinder engines. Support four cylinder engine at the front.
- On Pacer, remove the crossmember with the transmission.
- On six and eight cylinder engines, separate transmission at clutch housing. On four cylinder, 121 CID engine, remove clutch housing and transmission as a unit.
- Engage and disengage overdrive with clutch pedal depressed while operating engine with rear wheels off ground before removing transmission. This will relieve overrunning clutch and pinion carrier loading.
- Raise hood to prevent damage to hood or air filter assembly.

Four Wheel Drive Vehicles

- Remove transmission access cover from floorpan, and remove shift lever or disconnect shift linkage. Remove transfer case shift lever if necessary.
- Disconnect drive shafts, attached cables, electrical wiring etc. and any exhaust plumbing needed for clearance.
- Remove mounting bolts and lower transmission out of vehicle with crossmember and transfer case attached.
- Remove lubricating wick from pilot bushing, and soak wick in engine oil.
- If a replacement transmission is being installed, remove the protective fiber washer covering the rear bearing, and install a replacement mainshaft seal in the rear bearing adaptor.

Four speed transmission shift control lever housing in four wheel drive vehicles

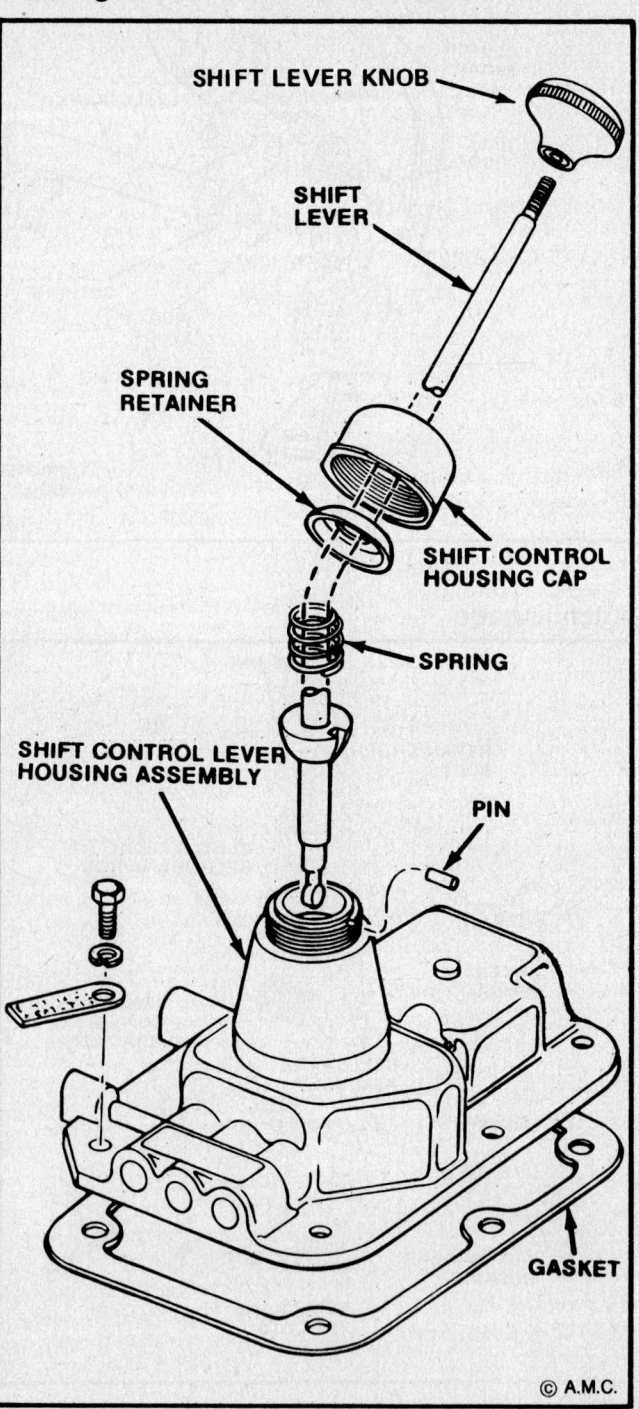

SHIFT LEVER KNOB

SHIFT LEVER

SPRING RETAINER

SHIFT CONTROL HOUSING CAP

SPRING

SHIFT CONTROL LEVER HOUSING ASSEMBLY

PIN

GASKET

© A.M.C.

Three speed transmission shift control lever housing in four wheel drive vehicles

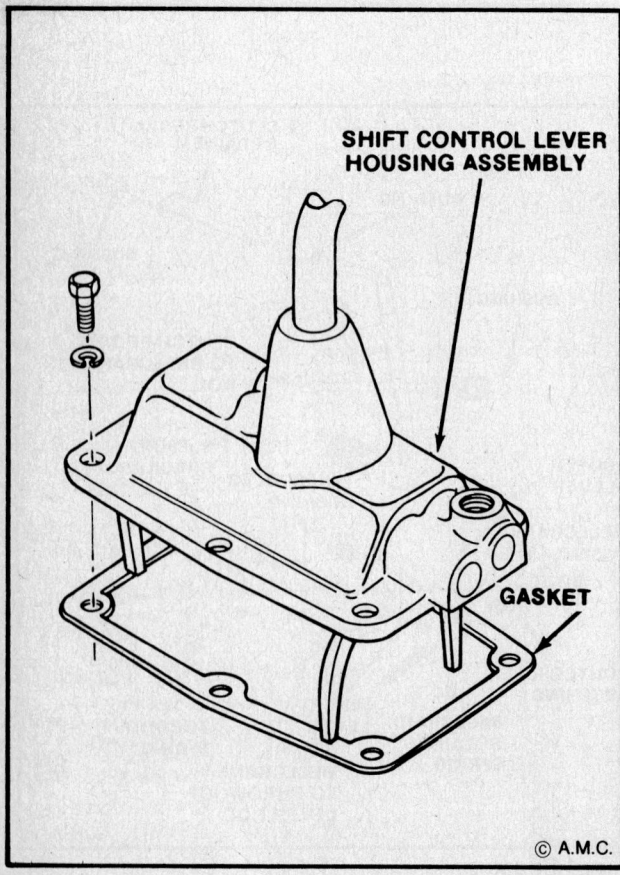

SHIFT CONTROL LEVER HOUSING ASSEMBLY

GASKET

© A.M.C.

Transmission overdrive attachment

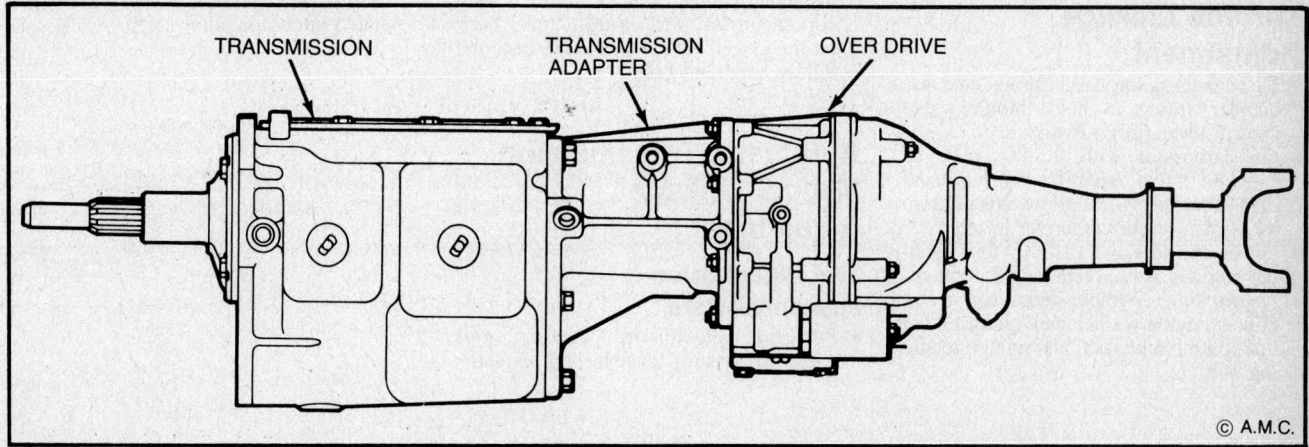

TRANSMISSION   TRANSMISSION ADAPTER   OVER DRIVE

© A.M.C.

When removing the overdrive unit separate the overdrive and transmission adaptor assembly from the transmission

Overdrive Unit

- Engage and disengage overdrive with clutch pedal depressed while operating engine with rear wheels off the ground before removing overdrive. This relieves overrunning clutch and pinion carrier loading.
- Remove by disconnecting all attachments and unbolting from transmission housing.
- Before installing overdrive unit, align overrunning clutch splines with transmission output shaft splines.

Automatic Transmission R&R

Two Wheel Drive
Passenger Cars

- Before raising car, disconnect fan shroud and upper mounting of transmission fill tube. Leave hood open to prevent damage to hood or air filter assembly.
- Drain torque converter, and remove fill tube and starter motor.
- Remove drive shaft, crossmember, cables, linkages, oil lines, etc.
- Put installation reference mark on converter and drive plate before removing attaching bolts.
- Disconnect all transmission mounts and lower transmission away from engine.
- After installing, check fluid level, and adjust manual and throttle linkages.

Four Wheel Drive
Vehicles

- Disconnect all attached shift linkages including transfer case and reduction unit.
- Disconnect drive shafts, attached cables, electrical wiring, vacuum hoses, dipstick holder, etc. Remove any exhaust plumbing needed for clearance.
- Remove starter.
- Remove parking brake cable if it passes through rear crossmember

- Remove rear crossmember after supporting transmission with a jack.
- Remove converter-to-flywheel bolts and converter housing-to-engine bolts. Lower transmission out of vehicle.

Manual Transmission Linkage Adjustment
Floor Shift

- With transmission in neutral, loosen second/third shift rod adjustment bolt. Align notch in that rod with notch in first/reverse shift rod, and tighten adjustment bolt.
- On cars with tilt-wheel steering columns, loosen steering column reverse lockup and trunnion. Put transmission in reverse and lock steering column. To do this it may be necessary to rotate the lower column shift lever upward. Tighten lower trunnion locknut until it contacts trunnion, and tighten upper locknut while holding trunnion centered

in column lever. Unlock column and shift transmission through all gears. Shift into reverse and lock column. Column must lock without binding.

Column Shift

- Disconnect shift rods from steering column levers, and put a 3/16 in. diameter rod through alignment holes in steering column shift levers. Put column gearshift lever in reverse, lock column, and put transmission first/reverse rod in reverse.
- Adjust column shift rod trunnion for free pin fit in transmission shifter lever and tighten trunnion locknuts.
- Unlock column and put gearshift lever in neutral with both transmission shift rods in neutral.
- Adjust second/third shift rod trunnion to obtain free pin fit in column levers. Tighten trunnion locknuts.
- Check that column will lock in reverse without binding.

Speedometer cable adapter except Pacer

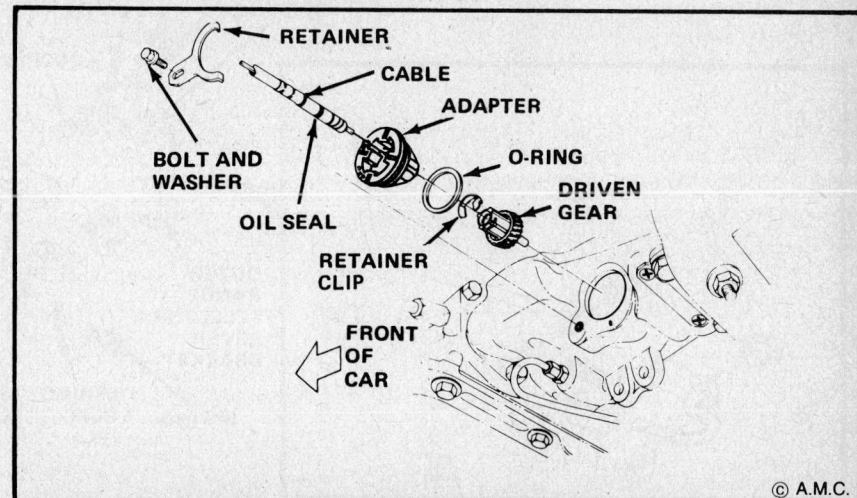

RETAINER

CABLE

ADAPTER

O-RING

DRIVEN GEAR

BOLT AND WASHER

OIL SEAL

RETAINER CLIP

FRONT OF CAR

© A.M.C.

Remove the adaptor when disconnecting speedometer cable. When installing, correctly index the adaptor in the position corresponding to the number of teeth on the pinion

Automatic Transmission Throttle Linkage Adjustment

- Disconnect control rod spring, and use another spring to hold throttle valve control lever fully forward.
- On carburetor with throttle operated solenoid valve, energize solenoid and open throttle ½ to allow solenoid to lock, then return carburetor to idle.
- On six cylinder and 121 CID four cylinder engines, loosen retaining bolt on adjusting link. Without removing spring clip and nylon washer, pull on the end of link to eliminate lash, and tighten retaining bolt.

- On eight cylinder engines, loosen adjusting link retainer bolt. Remove spring clip and nylon washer from link. Push on the end of link to eliminate lash and tighten retaining bolt.

Automatic Transmission Manual Linkage Adjustment

Two Wheel Drive Passenger Cars

- Put shift selector in ''PARK'' and transmission shift lever in park detent.

- Adjust for a free pin fit, and check for correct steering column lock and neutral start switch operation.

Automatic transmission manual linkage and neutral start switch typical in four wheel drive vehicles

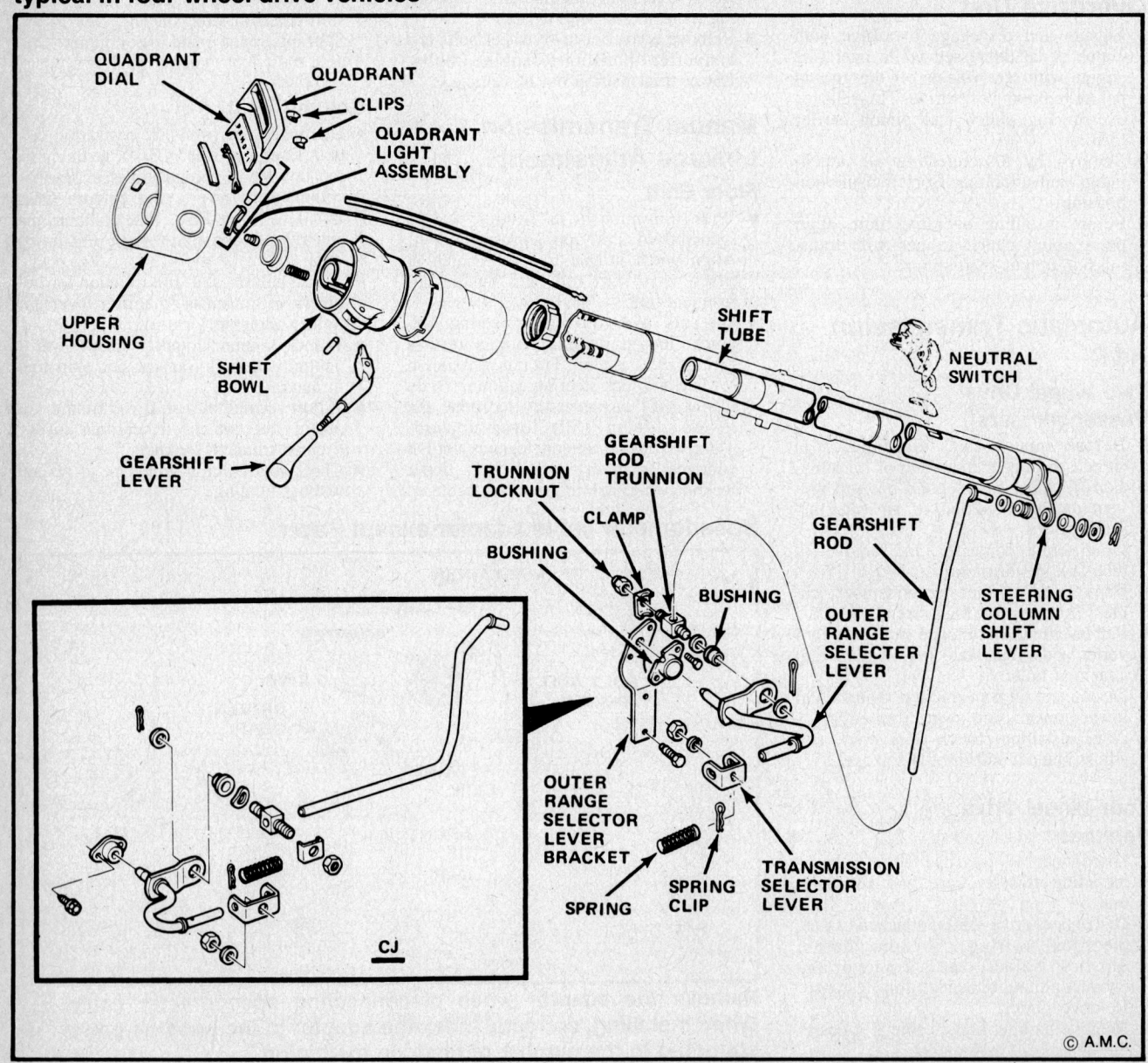

1976 and Later Four Wheel Drive Vehicles

- Place the column gearshift lever in Neutral position.
- Loosen locknut on gearshift rod trunnion just enough to permit movement of rod in the trunnion.
- Place the transmission outer range selector lever fully into the neutral detent position. Tighten trunnion locknut to 9 ft./lbs.

Pinion Oil Seal

Two Wheel Drive Passenger Cars

- Raise vehicle, and remove rear wheels and brake drums.
- With driveshaft disconnected, use an in./lb. torque wrench to measure torque required to turn the drive pinion. When installing new drive pinion nut, add five in./lb. to this for the correct torque.
- A new pinion nut *must* be used on installation. If desired torque is exceeded, a new collapsible pinion spacer must be installed and the drive pinion preload reset.
- Remove yoke with a puller, and if seal surface is grooved or heavily rusted replace the yoke.

Four Wheel Drive Front Axle

- Disconnect drive shaft from yoke.
- Remove pinion nut first, then remove yoke.
- Remove the old seal, and drive a new one into place.
- When installing the pinion nut, torque to 210 ft./lbs.

Four Wheel Drive Rear Axle
EXCEPT 1976 AND LATER CJ

- Disconnect drive shaft from yoke.
- Remove pinion nut first, then remove the yoke.
- Remove the old seal, and drive a new one into place.
- When installing the pinion nut, torque to 210 ft./lbs.

1976 AND LATER CJ

- Raise vehicle, and remove rear wheels and brake drums.
- With driveshaft disconnected, use an in./lb. torque wrench to measure torque required to turn the drive pinion. When installing the new drive pinion nut, add five in./lbs. to this for the correct torque.
- A new pinion nut *must* be used on installation. If desired torque is exceeded, a new collapsible pinion spacer must be installed and the drive pinion preload reset.
- Remove yoke with a puller, and if seal surface is grooved or heavily rusted replace the yoke.

Drive shafts in four wheel drive vehicles

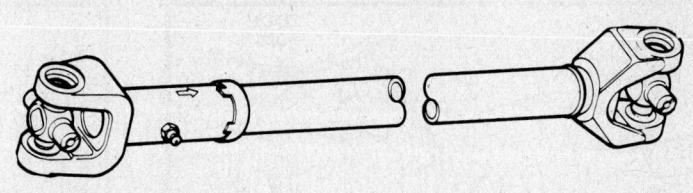

Front drive shaft used with manual transmission

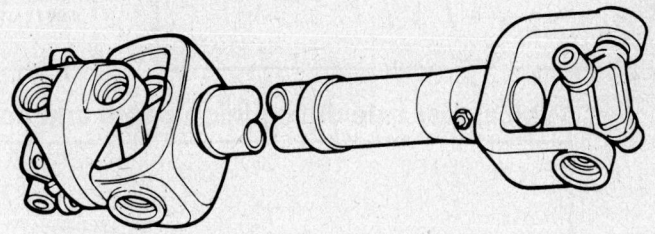

Rear drive shaft used with manual transmission

Rear drive shaft used with automatic transmission

© A.M.C.

Typical drive shaft used in two wheel drive passenger cars

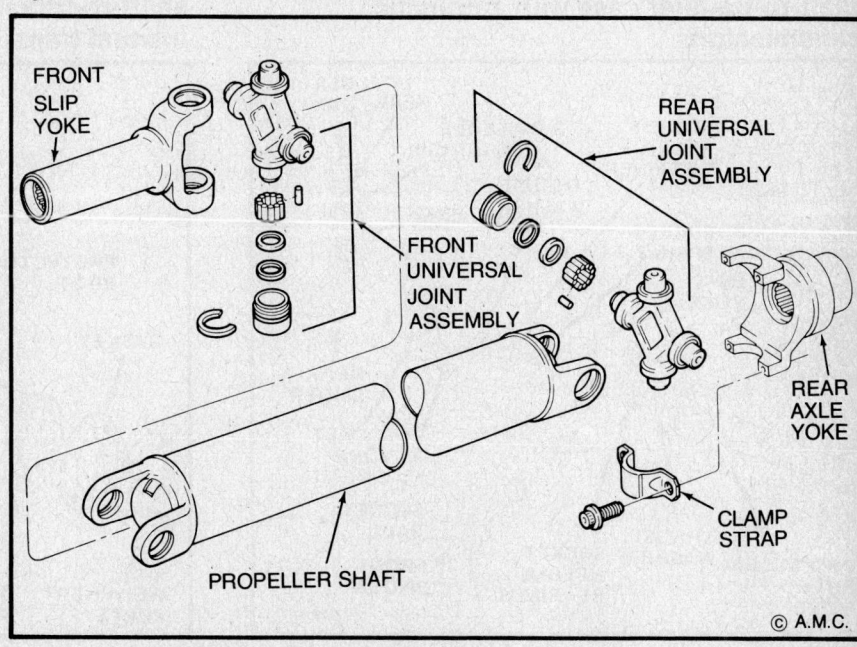

© A.M.C.

AMC PASSENGER CARS AND JEEP

Removing rear axle pinion nut in passenger cars and CJ models

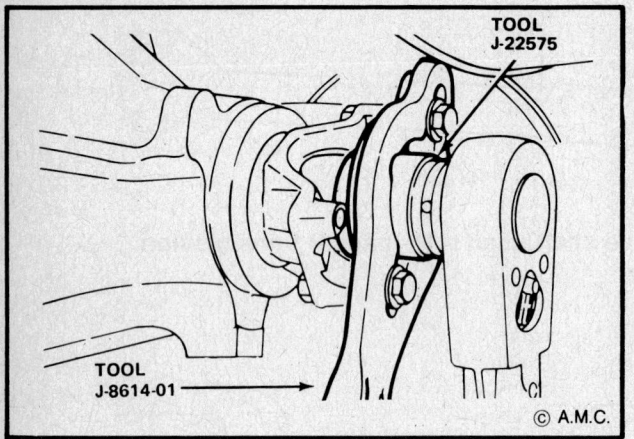

TOOL
J-22575

TOOL
J-8614-01

© A.M.C.

Removing rear axle yoke

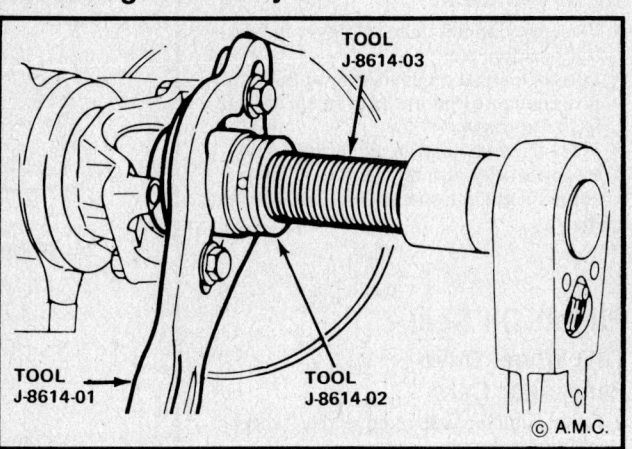

TOOL
J-8614-03

TOOL
J-8614-01

TOOL
J-8614-02

© A.M.C.

Typical rear axle drive pinion depth and collapsible spacer location

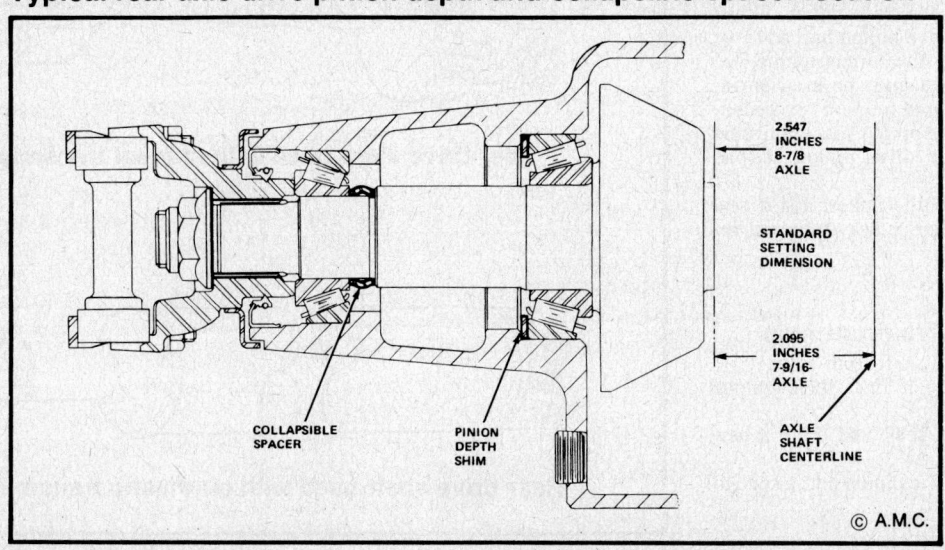

2.547
INCHES
8-7/8
AXLE

STANDARD
SETTING
DIMENSION

2.095
INCHES
7-9/16-
AXLE

AXLE
SHAFT
CENTERLINE

COLLAPSIBLE
SPACER

PINION
DEPTH
SHIM

© A.M.C.

Constant velocity joint used for front drive shaft-to-transfer case with automatic transmissions

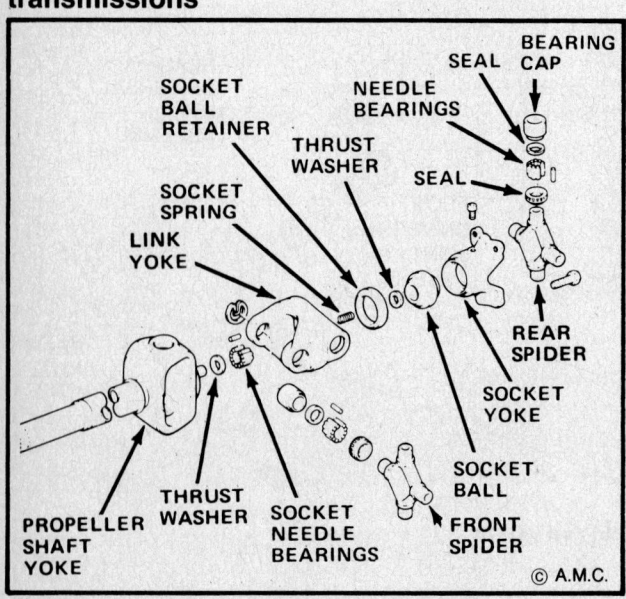

SOCKET
BALL
RETAINER

SEAL

NEEDLE
BEARINGS

BEARING
CAP

THRUST
WASHER

SEAL

SOCKET
SPRING

LINK
YOKE

REAR
SPIDER

SOCKET
YOKE

PROPELLER
SHAFT
YOKE

THRUST
WASHER

SOCKET
NEEDLE
BEARINGS

SOCKET
BALL

FRONT
SPIDER

© A.M.C.

Ball and trunnion u-joint used for rear drive shaft-to-transfer case on Cherokee with manual transmission

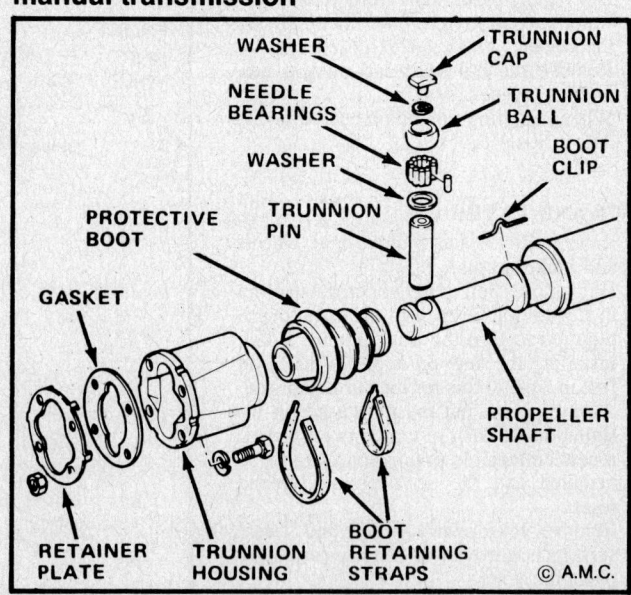

WASHER

TRUNNION
CAP

NEEDLE
BEARINGS

TRUNNION
BALL

WASHER

BOOT
CLIP

PROTECTIVE
BOOT

TRUNNION
PIN

GASKET

PROPELLER
SHAFT

RETAINER
PLATE

TRUNNION
HOUSING

BOOT
RETAINING
STRAPS

© A.M.C.

A62

Rear Axle Shaft and Bearing

Passenger Cars and CJ

- Remove axle shaft nut, and pull the axle hub with puller Tool J-25109-01.
- Remove brake backing plate and axle shaft oil seal and retainer.
- Pull axle shaft with puller Tool J-2498.
- The bearing is a press fit on the shaft.
- When a new axle shaft is installed a new hub must also be installed.

Cherokee and Wagoneer

- Remove the nuts attaching support plate and retainer to axle tube flange, and use a slide hammer to pull the axle shaft and bearing.
- Using a drill and chisel, cut the old bearing off the shaft. The new bearing must be pressed on.

Front Axle Shaft

CJ Models

- Remove brake caliper, rotor, splash shield, spindle, etc.
- Remove axle shaft and universal joint assembly.

Cherokee and Wagoneer

- Remove brake caliper and rotor, and remove spindle and shield.
- Remove axle shaft.

CJ and passenger cars rear axle shaft puller

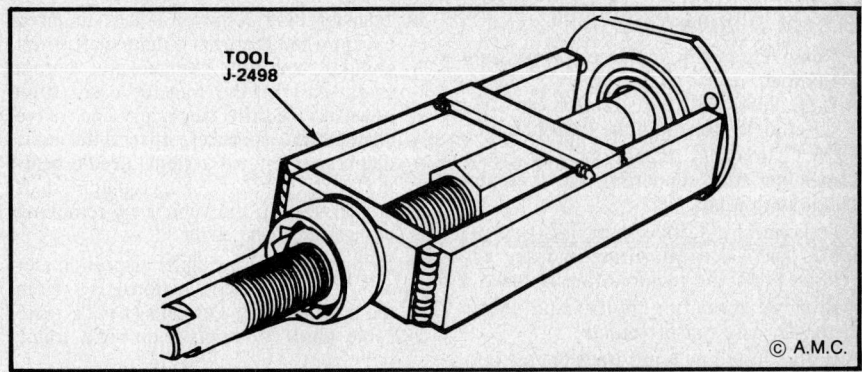

Front axle universal joint used in four wheel drive vehicles

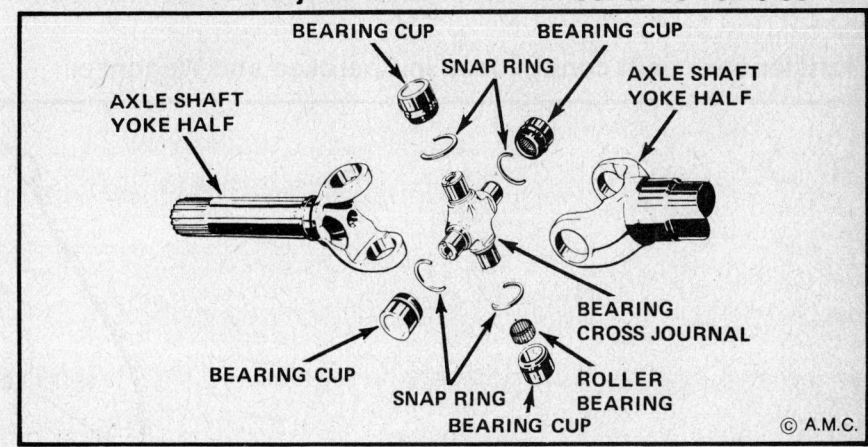

CJ and passenger cars typical rear axle

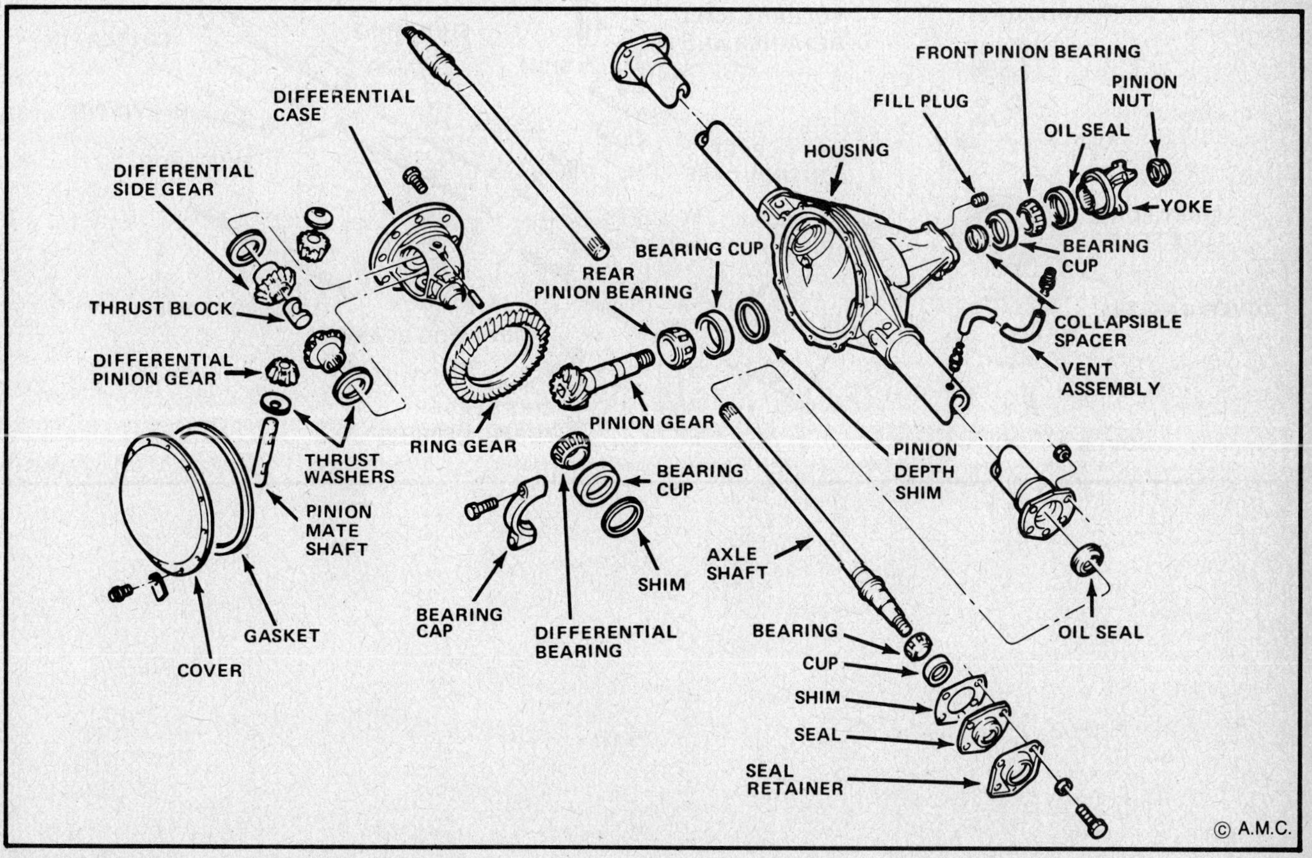

AMC PASSENGER CARS AND JEEP

Transfer Case

Except Quadra-Trac

- Remove transmission access cover from floorpan.
- Drain lubricant from transfer case. On CJ models also drain the transmission.
- On CJ models, remove the rear cross-member after supporting the transmission with a jack.
- Disconnect the drive shaft, attached cables and electrical wiring and any exhaust plumbing required for clearance.
- Remove mounting bolts, and lower transfer case out of vehicle.
- Before installing, shift transfer case into 4L position.

Quadra-Trac

- Transfer case removal is not required except when the front output shaft, front annular bearing, transmission output shaft seals or the transfer case (front housing) require service. The drive chain, drive sprocket, differential unit, diaphragm control system, needle bearing, thrust washer, or rear output shaft are serviced in the vehicle by removing the transfer case cover.
- Disconnect drive shafts, speedometer cable, electrical connections, etc. from the transfer case. Disconnect park brake cable guide from pivot on right frame rail.
- On CJ-7 models, place support stand under clutch housing and remove rear crossmember.
- Remove two transfer case-to-transmission bolts which enter from front side, and install 7/16-14 x 5 inch guide pin in upper hole.
- Remove two transfer case-to-transmission bolts which enter from rear, and install 7/16-14 x 5 inch guide pin in upper hole.
- Move transfer case assembly rearward until free of transmission output shaft and guide pins, and lower assembly out of vehicle.
- Use guide pins when installing, and do not install any mounting bolts until the transfer case is fully seated against the transmission.

Transfer case shift control used in Cherokee and Wagoneer

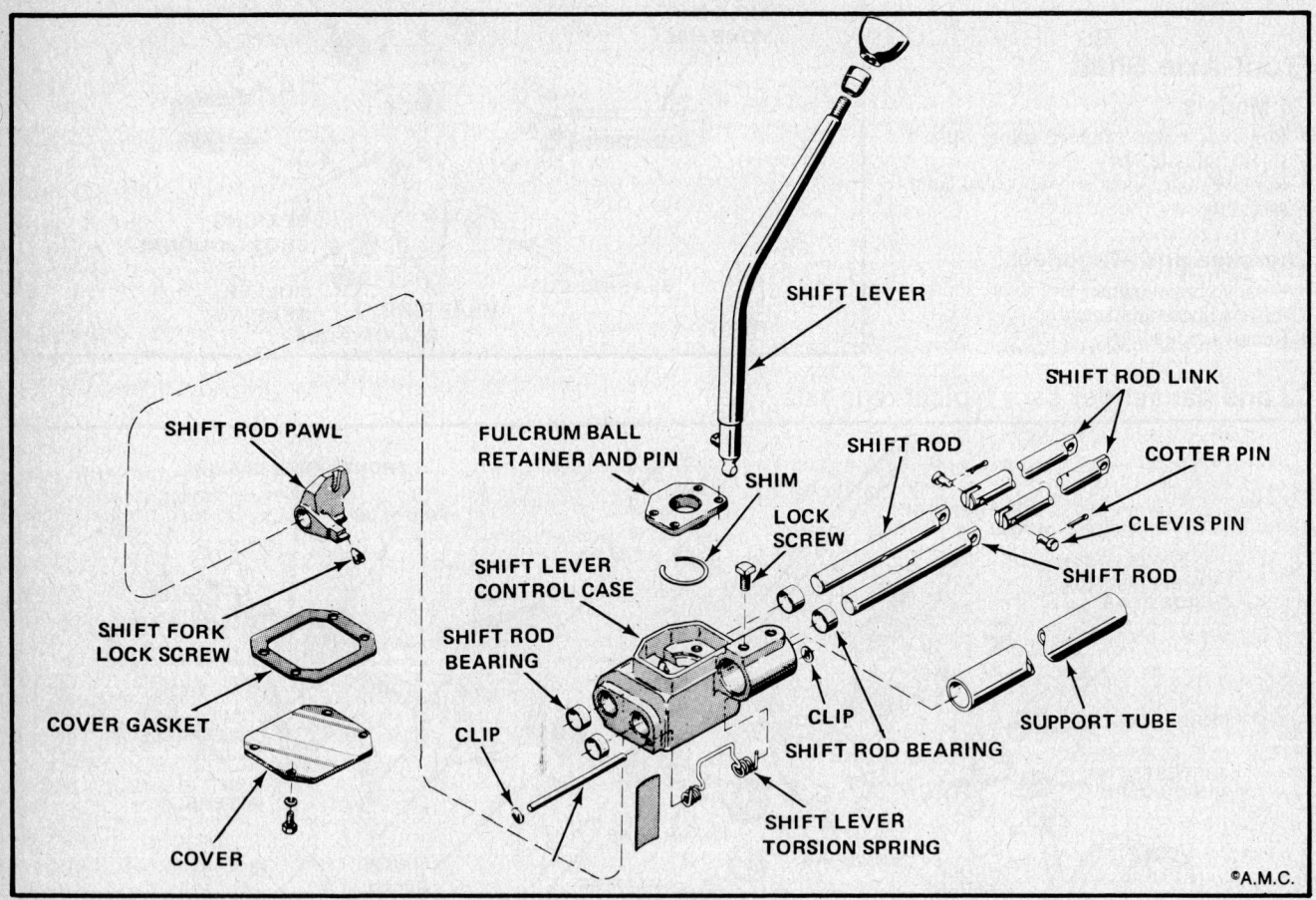

SHIFT LEVER

SHIFT ROD LINK

SHIFT ROD

COTTER PIN

CLEVIS PIN

SHIFT ROD

FULCRUM BALL
RETAINER AND PIN

SHIM

SHIFT ROD PAWL

LOCK
SCREW

SHIFT LEVER
CONTROL CASE

SHIFT FORK
LOCK SCREW

SHIFT ROD
BEARING

CLIP

SUPPORT TUBE

COVER GASKET

CLIP

CLIP

SHIFT ROD BEARING

SHIFT LEVER
TORSION SPRING

COVER

©A.M.C.

EAGLE AND JEEP

The heart of the American Motors Eagle four-wheel-drive Quadra-Trac system is the Model NP 119 single speed, full-time drive transfer case assembly with viscous torque biasing control. Operation of vehicles equipped with Model NP 119 is simple inasmuch as no transfer case controls are required.

POWER FLOW ARRANGEMENT

The power flow is direct through the inter-axle differential to the rear wheels. A driving chain is utilized to connect the front output of the differential to the front wheel driveshaft. With this arrangement the front wheel driving chain delivers only the load required by the front wheels.

INTER-AXLE DIFFERENTIAL

Operation of the vehicle in full-time four-wheel-drive on hard surfaces is made possible by the inter-axle differential. This differential is a durable assembly utilizing four pinions for maximum strength. The pinions are mounted on needle bearings for friction free action.

TRANSFER CASE SEALS

Three shaft seals are required for the transfer case assembly.
- Front input shaft—This seal is a poly-acrylic seal to withstand higher temperature due to proximity of the engine, transmission and catalytic converter.
- Front & Rear output shaft—Identical seals are used for the front and rear drive output shaft location. The seals have two lips. The inner lip is a nitrile sealing surface to seal the lubricant within the transfer case, the outer lip is heavily PTFE coated to seal dirt, slush, water and debris out of the assembly.

LUBRICATION

10 W 30 engine oil is specified for use in the assembly. A small volume of fluid is specified as adequate lubrication is achieved with minimum losses in churning action. The specified oil fill is three (3) pints.

Transfer case for four-wheel-drive Eagle

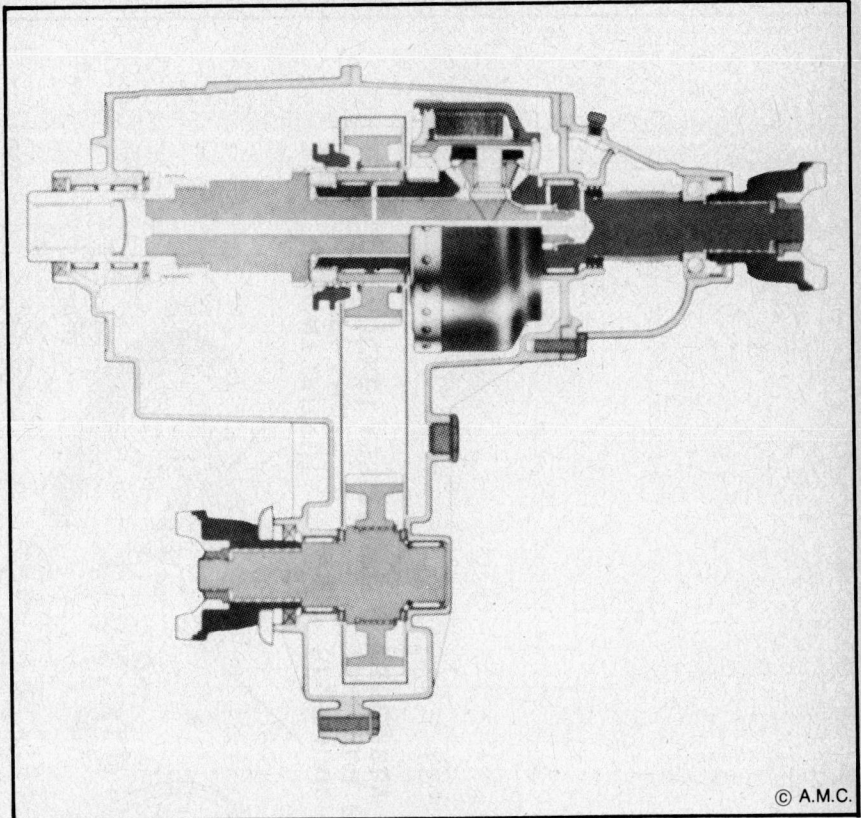

© A.M.C.

Eagle transfer case—front suspension

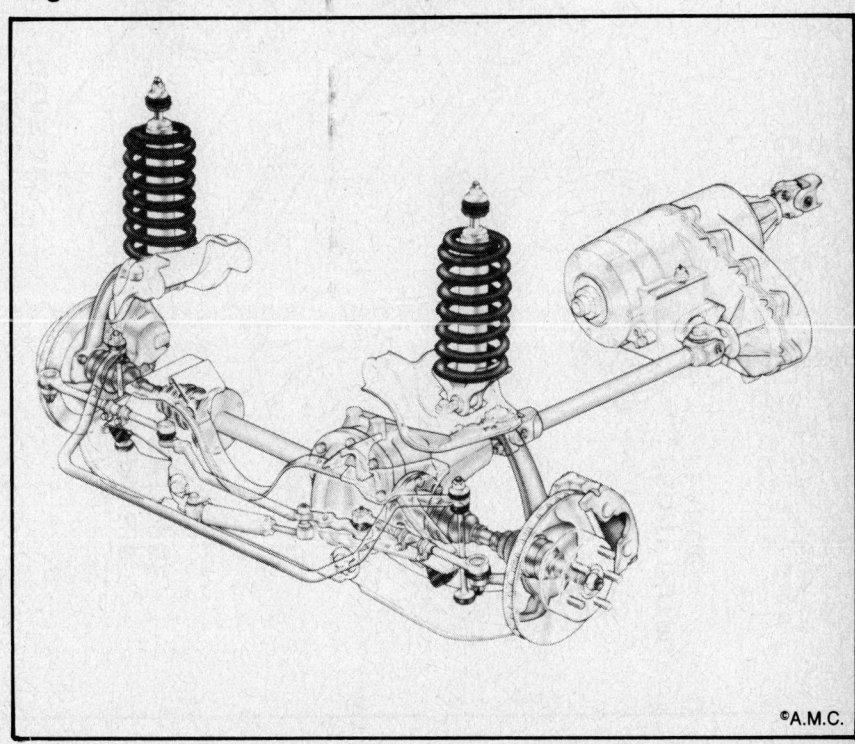

©A.M.C.

Jeep (new process) transfer case

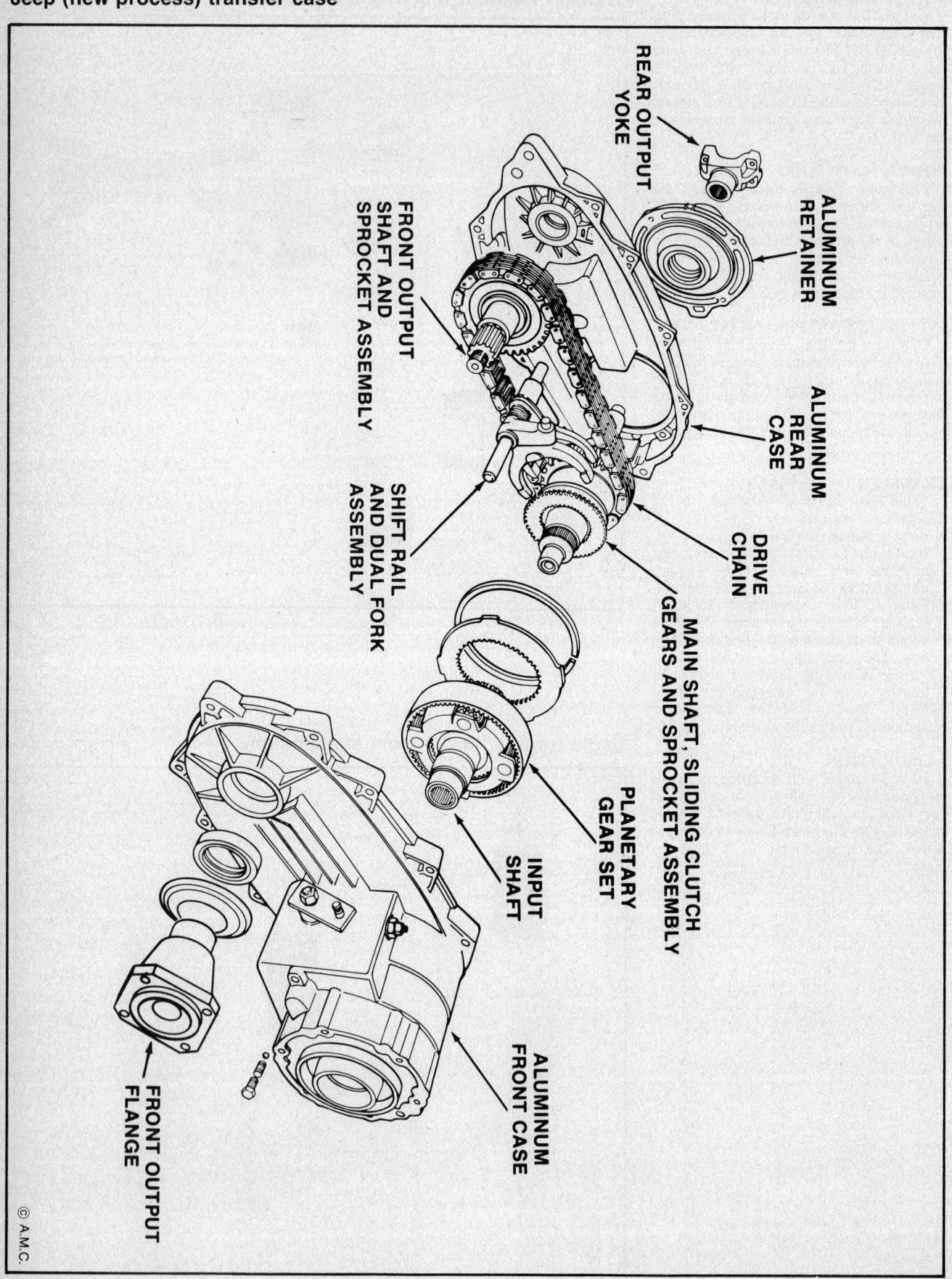

REAR OUTPUT YOKE

ALUMINUM RETAINER

FRONT OUTPUT SHAFT AND SPROCKET ASSEMBLY

ALUMINUM REAR CASE

DRIVE CHAIN

MAIN SHAFT, SLIDING CLUTCH GEARS AND SPROCKET ASSEMBLY

SHIFT RAIL AND DUAL FORK ASSEMBLY

INPUT SHAFT

PLANETARY GEAR SET

ALUMINUM FRONT CASE

FRONT OUTPUT FLANGE

© A.M.C.

INDEX

BUICK
EXCEPT CENTURY (FRONT WHEEL DRIVE), SKYHAWK & '80-'82 SKYLARK

MODEL IDENTIFICATION

1976 ELECTRA
W.B. **127″**. Length 234″. Ship. Wgt. V8 4 Dr. 4641 Lbs.

1977 ELECTRA
W.B. **119″**. Length 223″. Width 78″. Ship Wgt. V8 2 Dr. 5033 Lbs.

1978 ELECTRA
W.B. **118.9″** Length 222.1″ Ship. Wgt. 8 Cyl. 2 Dr. 3793 Lbs.

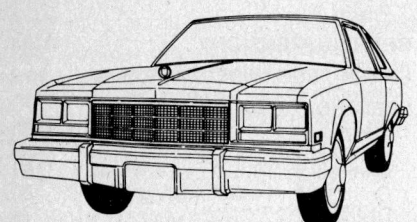

1979 ELECTRA
W.B. **118.9″** Length 222.1″ Ship. Wgt. 2 Dr. 3926 Lbs.

1980 ELECTRA
W.B. **118.9″**. Length 222.1″. Ship. Wgt. 2 Dr. Approx. 3776 Lbs.

1981-82 ELECTRA
W.B. **118.9″**. Length 220″. Ship Wgt. 6 Cyl. 4 Dr. 3722 Lbs.

1976 LESABRE
W.B. **124″**, Est. Wgn. **127″**. Length 227″, Est. Wgn. Ship. Wgt. V6 2 Dr. 4129 Lbs. V8 2 Dr. 4275 Lbs.

1977 LESABRE
W.B. **115.9″**. Length 219″, S/W 217″. Width 77″. Ship. Wgt. V8 2 Dr. 3765 Lbs.

1978 LESABRE
W.B. **115.9″** Length 218.2″ Ship. Wgt. 6 Cyl. 2 Dr. 3725 Lbs.

1979 LESABRE
W.B. **115.9″** Length 218.2″ Ship. Wgt. 2 Dr. 3684 Lbs.

1980 LESABRE
W.B. **115.9″**. Length 218.2″. Ship. Wgt. 2 Dr. Approx. 3534 Lbs.

1981-82 LESABRE
W.B. **115.9″**. Length 217.4″. Ship. Wgt. 6 Cyl. 4 Dr. 3493 Lbs.

1976 RIVIERA
W.B. **122″**. Length 223″. Ship. Wgt. V8 2 Dr. 4531 Lbs.

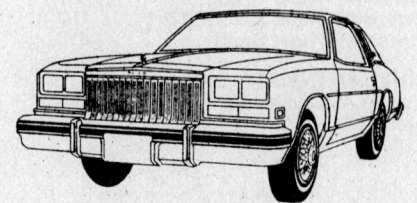

1977 RIVIERA
W.B. **116″**. Length 219″. Width 78″. Ship. Wgt. V8 2 Dr. 3788 Lbs.

1978 RIVIERA
W.B. **115.9″** Length 218.2″ Ship. Wgt. 8 Cyl. 2 Dr. 3868 Lbs.

1979 RIVIERA

W.B. 114.0″ Length 206.6″ Ship. Wgt. 2 Dr. 3862 Lbs.

1980 RIVIERA

W.B. 114″. Length 206.6″. Ship. Wgt. Approx. 3862 Lbs.

1981 RIVIERA

W.B. 114.0″. Length 206.6″. 6 Cyl. 2 Dr. Curb Wgt. 3850 Lbs.

1982 RIVERA

W.B. 114″. Length 206″. Ship Wgt. 3704 Lbs.

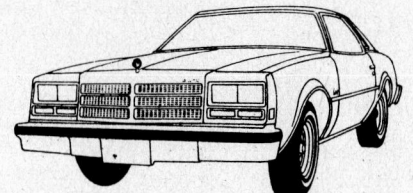

1976 CENTURY

W.B. Cpe 112″, Sed & S/W 116″. Length Ship. Wgt. V6 2 Dr. 3652 Lbs. V8 2 Dr. 3844 Lbs.

1977 CENTURY

W.B. Cpe 112″, Sed & S/W 116″. Length Cpe 210″, Sed 214″, S/W 219″. Width Cpe 77″, Sed & S/W 79″ Ship. Wgt. V6 2 Dr. 3520 Lbs. V8 2 Dr. 3648 Lbs.

1978 CENTURY

W.B. 108.1″ Length 195.6″ Ship. Wgt. 6 Cyl. 2 Dr. 2790 Lbs.

1979 CENTURY

W.B. 108.1″ Length 196.0″ Ship. Wgt. 2 Dr. 3130 Lbs.

1980 CENTURY

W.B. 108″. Length 196″. Ship. Wgt. 2 Dr. Approx. 3130 Lbs.

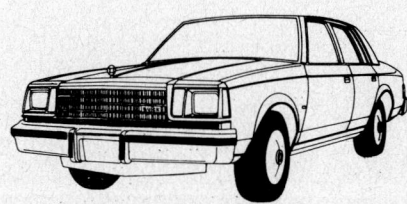

1981 Century

W.B. 108.1″. Length 196.0″. 6 Cyl. 4 Dr. Curb Wgt. 3236 Lbs.

1978 REGAL

W.B. 108.1″ Length 199.6″ Ship. Wgt. 6 Cyl. 2 Dr. 2806 Lbs.

1979 REGAL

W.B. 108.1″ Length 199.0″ Ship. Wgt. 2 Dr. 3133 Lbs.

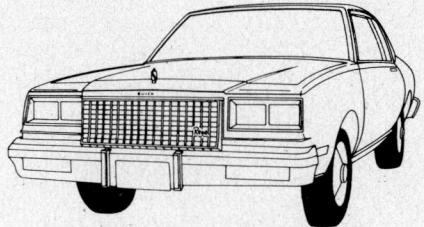

1980 REGAL

W.B. 108.1″. Length 199″. Ship. Wgt. 2 Dr. Approx. 3133 Lbs.

1981-82 REGAL

W.B. 108.1″. Length 200.6″. 6 Cyl. 2 Dr. Curb Wgt. 3281 Lbs.

1976 SKYLARK

W.B. 111″. Length 201″. Ship. Wgt. V6 2 Dr. 3316 Lbs. V8 2 Dr. 3526 Lbs.

1977 SKYLARK

W.B. 111". Length 201". Width 73". Ship. Wgt. V6 2 Dr. 3257 Lbs. V8 2 Dr. 3287 Lbs.

1978 SKYLARK

W.B. 111.0" Length 200.2" Ship. Wgt. 6 Cyl. 2 Dr. 3204 Lbs.

1979 SKYLARK

W.B. 111.0" Length 200.2" Ship Wgt. 2 Dr. 3212 Lbs.

BODY MODEL IDENTIFICATION

Body	Model
A 1976-81	Century
A 1976-82	Regal
A 1982	Front Drive①
B	LeSabre, Estate Wagon
C	Electra
H	Skyhawk①
X 1976-79	Skylark
X 1980-82	Skylark①

① Information on these models is covered in other chapters in this manual

VEHICLE IDENTIFICATION NUMBER (VIN)①

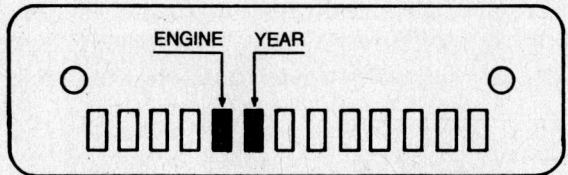

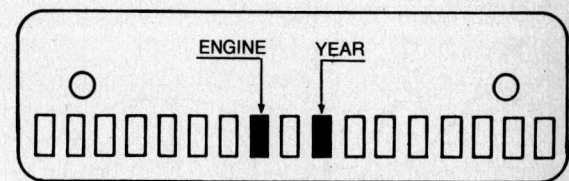

Code	ENGINE CODE Eng. Disp. (cu in)	ENGINE CODE Eng. Config.	ENGINE CODE Carb	ENGINE CODE Eng. Mfgr.	MODEL YEAR CODE Code	MODEL YEAR CODE Year
C	231	V-6	2v	Buick	6	1976
F	260	V-8	2v	Olds		
H	350	V-8	2v	Buick		
J	350	V-8	4v	Buick		
T	455	V-8	4v	Buick		
C	231	V-6	2v	Buick	7	1977
Y	301	V-8	2v	Pont		
U	305	V-8	2v	Chev		
H	350	V-8	2v	Buick		
J	350	V-8	4v	Buick		
L	350	V-8	4v	Chev		
R	350	V-8	4v	Olds		
K	403	V-8	4v	Olds		
A	231	V-6	2v	Buick	8	1978
2	231	V-6	2v	Buick		
C	196	V-6	2v	Buick		
G	231	V-6	2v	Buick		
3	231	V-6	4v	Buick		
H	305	V-8	4v	Chev		
K	403	V-8	4v	Olds		
L	350	V-8	4v	Chev		
X	350	V-8	4v	Buick		
U	305	V-8	2v	Chev		
R	350	V-8	4v	Olds		
Y	301	V-8	2v	Pont		
A	231	V-6	2v	Buick	9	1979
C	196	V-6	2v	Buick		
2	231	V-6	2v	Buick		
D	250	L-6	1v	Chev.		
3	231	V-6	4v	Buick		
G	305	V-8	2v	Chev.		
H	305	V-8	4v	Chev.		

Code	ENGINE CODE Eng. Disp. cu in	ENGINE CODE Eng. Config.	ENGINE CODE Carb	ENGINE CODE Eng. Mfgr.	MODEL YEAR CODE Code	MODEL YEAR CODE Year
J	267	V-8	2v	Chev.		
4	350	V-8	4v	Chev.		
8	350	V-8	4v	Chev.		
K	403	V-8	4v	Olds.		
L	350	V-8	4v	Chev.		
M	200	V-6	2v	Chev.		
R	350	V-8	4v	Olds.		
W	301	V-8	4v	Pont.		
X	350	V-8	4v	Buick		
Y	301	V-8	2v	Pont.		
A	231	V-6	2v	Buick	A	1980
3	231	V-6	4v	Buick		
4	252	V-6	4v	Buick		
W	301	V-8	4v	Pont.		
H	305	V-8	4v	Chev.		
X	350	V-8	4v	Buick		
N	350	V-8	Diesel	Olds		
R	350	V-8	4v	Olds		
A	231 3.8L	V-6	2V	Buick	1	1981
3	231 3.8L	V-6	4V	Buick		
4	252 4.1L	V-6	4V	Buick		
S	265 4.3L	V-8	2V	Pont		
W	301 4.9L	V-8	4V	Pont.		
Y	307 5.0L	V-8	4V	Olds		
N	350 5.7L	V-8	Diesel	Olds		
A	231 3.8L	V-6	2V	Buick	2	1982
3	231 3.8L	V-6	4V	Buick		
4	252 4.1L	V-6	4V	Buick		
Y	307 5.0L	V-8	4V	Olds		
V	263 4.3L	V-6	Diesel	Olds		
N	350 5.7L	V-8	Diesel	Olds		

ENGINE FIRING ORDER

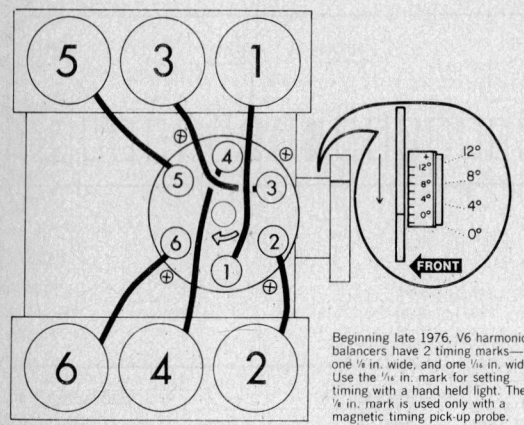

Beginning late 1976, V6 harmonic balancers have 2 timing marks—one ⅛ in. wide, and one ¹⁄₁₆ in. wide. Use the ¹⁄₁₆ in. mark for setting timing with a hand held light. The ⅛ in. mark is used only with a magnetic timing pick-up probe.

GM (Buick) 196, 231, 252 CID V6 Engine firing order: 1-6-5-4-3-2 Distributor rotation: clockwise

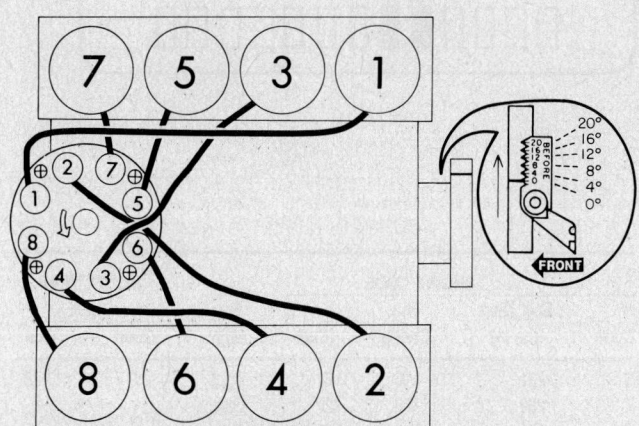

GM (Oldsmobile) 260, 307 V8 Engine firing order: 1-8-4-3-6-5-7-2 Distributor rotation: counterclockwise

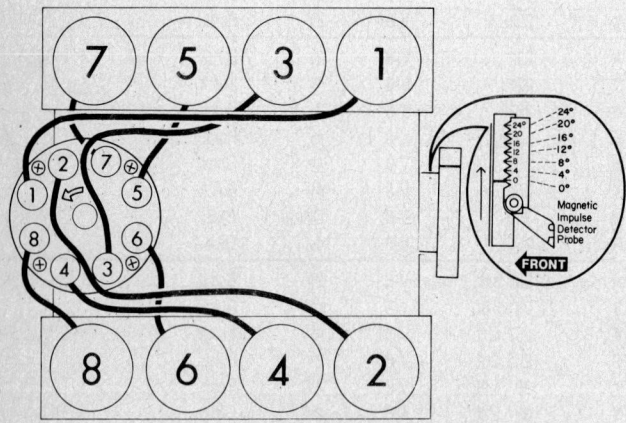

GM (Pontiac) 265, 301 V8 Engine firing order: 1-8-4-3-6-5-7-2 Distributor rotation: counterclockwise

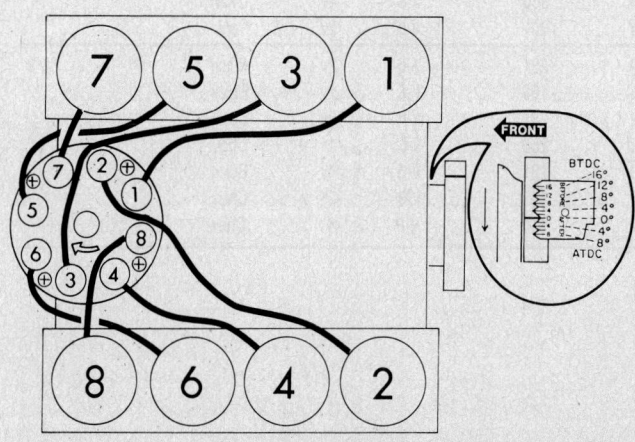

GM (Chevrolet) 267, 305, 350 CID V8 Engine firing order: 1-8-4-3-6-5-7-2 Distributor rotation: clockwise

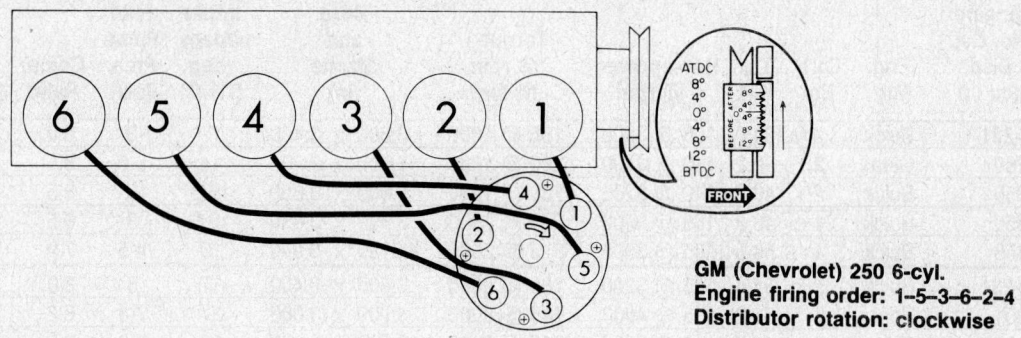

GM (Chevrolet) 250 6-cyl.
Engine firing order: 1-5-3-6-2-4
Distributor rotation: clockwise

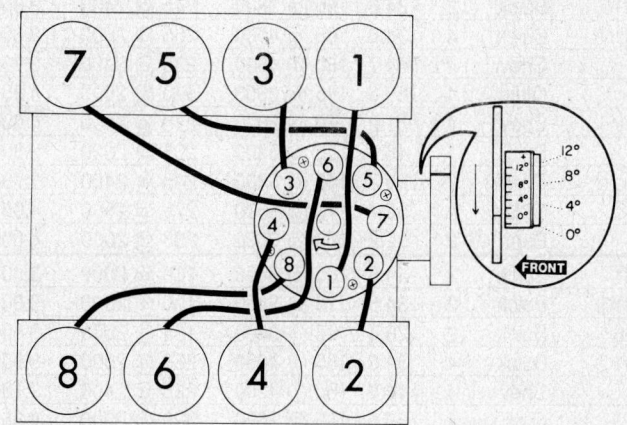

GM (Buick) 350, 455 V8
Engine firing order: 1-8-4-3-6-5-7-2
Distributor rotation: clockwise

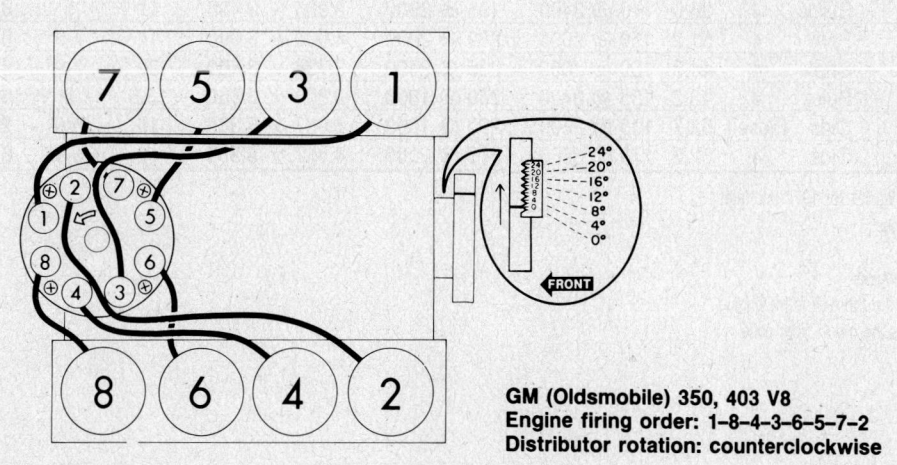

GM (Oldsmobile) 350, 403 V8
Engine firing order: 1-8-4-3-6-5-7-2
Distributor rotation: counterclockwise

BUICK
EXCEPT CENTURY (FRONT WHEEL DRIVE), SKYHAWK & '80-'82 SKYLARK

ENGINE SPECIFICATIONS

Yr.	Engine V.I.N. Code	Engine No. Cyl. Disp. (cu in)	Eng. Mfg.	Carb Bbl	Tax H.P.	Horsepower① @ rpm	Torque① @ rpm (ft lbs)	Bore and Stroke (in)	Valves Intake Opens (deg BTDC)	Fuel Pump Pres. (psi)	Comp. Ratio	Oil Pressure @ 2000 rpm
'76	C	V6-231	Buick	2	34.6	105 @ 3400	185 @ 2000	3.800 × 3.400	17	3	8.0	37
	F	8-260	Olds	2	39.2	110 @ 3400	210 @ 1600	3.500 × 3.385	14	5-6	8.5	35
	H	8-350	Buick	2	46.2	140 @ 3200	280 @ 1600	3.800 × 3.850	13.5	3	8.5	37
	J	8-350	Buick	4	46.2	155 @ 3400	280 @ 1800	3.800 × 3.850	13.5	3	8.5	37
	T	8-455	Buick	4	59.5	205 @ 3800	345 @ 2000	4.3125 × 3.900	10	4-5	7.9	40
'77	C	V6-231	Buick	2	34.6	105 @ 3200	185 @ 2000	3.800 × 3.400	17	3	8.0	37
	Y	8-301	Pont	2	51.2	135 @ 4000	245 @ 2000	4.000 × 3.000	27	7-8	8.2	35-40
	U	8-305	Chev	2	44.7	145 @ 3800	245 @ 2400	3.736 × 3.480	28	7-9	8.5	32-40
	H	8-350	Buick	2	46.2	140 @ 3200	280 @ 1400	3.800 × 3.850	13.5	3	8.5	37
	J	8-350	Buick	4	46.2	155 @ 3400	275 @ 1800	3.800 × 3.850	13.5	3	8.5	37
	L	8-350	Chev	4	51.2	170 @ 3800	270 @ 2400	4.000 × 3.480	28	7-9	8.5	32-40
	R	8-350	Olds	4	52.7	170 @ 3800	275 @ 2000	4.057 × 3.385	22	5-6	7.9	30-45
	K	8-403	Olds	4	60.6	185 @ 3600	320 @ 2200	4.351 × 3.385	13.5	5-6	7.9	30-45
'78	A	V6-231	Buick	2	34.6	105 @ 3400	185 @ 2000	3.800 × 3.400	17	3	8.0	37
	C	V6-196	Buick	2	29.4	95 @ 3800①	155 @ 2000	3.500 × 3.400	18	3	8.0	37
	G	V6-231②	Buick	2	34.6	150 @ 3800	245 @ 2400	3.800 × 3.400	17	5	8.0	37
	3	V6-231②	Buick	4	34.6	165 @ 4000	265 @ 2800	3.800 × 3.400	17	5	8.0	37
	H	8-305	Chev	4	44.7	160 @ 4000	235 @ 2400	3.736 × 3.480	28	7-9	8.4	32-40
	K	8-403	Olds	4	60.6	185 @ 3600	320 @ 2000	4.351 × 3.385	16	5-6	7.9	30-45
	L	8-350	Chev	4	51.2	170 @ 3800	270 @ 2400	4.000 × 3.480	28	7-9	8.2	32-40
	X	8-350	Buick	4	46.2	155 @ 3400	265 @ 2800	3.800 × 3.850	13.5	3	8.0	37
	U	8-305	Chev	2	44.7	145 @ 3800	245 @ 2400	3.736 × 3.480	28	7-9	8.4	32-40
	R	8-350	Olds	4	52.7	170 @ 3800	275 @ 2000	4.057 × 3.385	16	5-6	7.9	30-45
	Y	8-301	Pont	2	51.2	165 @ 3600	235 @ 2000	4.000 × 3.000	27	7-8	8.2	38-42
'79	A	V6-231	Buick	2	34.6	105 @ 3400	185 @ 2000	3.800 × 3.400	17	3	8.0	37
	2	V6-231③	Buick	2	34.6	110 @ 3400	190 @ 2000	3.800 × 3.400	—	3	8.0	37
	C	V6-196	Buick	2	29.4	95 @ 3800	155 @ 2000	3.500 × 3.400	18	3	8.0	37
	3	V6-231②	Buick	4	34.6	165 @ 4000	265 @ 2800	3.800 × 3.400	17	5	8.0	37
	H	8-305	Chev	4	44.7	160 @ 4000	235 @ 2400	3.736 × 3.480	28	7-9	8.5	32-40
	K	8-403	Olds	4	60.6	185 @ 3600	320 @ 2000	4.351 × 3.385	16	5-6	8.3	30-45
	L	8-350	Chev	4	51.2	170 @ 3800	270 @ 2400	4.000 × 3.480	28	7-9	8.5	32-40
	X	8-350	Buick	4	46.2	155 @ 3400	280 @ 1800	3.800 × 3.850	13.5	3	8.0	37
	G	8-305	Chev	2	44.7	145 @ 3800	245 @ 2400	3.736 × 3.480	28	7-9	8.5	32-40
	R	8-350	Olds	4	52.7	170 @ 3800	275 @ 2000	4.057 × 3.385	16	5-6	8.3	30-45
	Y	8-301	Pont	2	51.2	165 @ 3600	235 @ 2000	4.000 × 3.000	27	7-9	8.2	38-42
	W	8-301	Pont	4	51.2	150 @ 4000	239 @ 2000	4.000 × 3.000	14	7-9	8.2	38-42
'80	A	6-231	Buick	2	34.6	105 @ 3400	185 @ 2000	3.800 × 3.400	17	3	8.0	37
	3	6-231②	Buick	4	34.6	165 @ 4000	265 @ 2800	3.800 × 3.400	17	5	—	37
	4	6-252	Buick	4	36.0	110 @ 3400	195 @ 2000	3.965 × 3.400	17	5	8.0	37
	W	8-301	Pont	4	51.2	150 @ 4000	239 @ 2000	4.000 × 3.000	14	7-9	8.2	38-42
	H	8-305	Chev	4	44.7	160 @ 4000	235 @ 2400	3.736 × 3.480	28	7-9	8.5	32-40
	X	8-350	Buick	4	46.2	155 @ 3400	280 @ 1800	3.800 × 3.850	13.5	3	8.0	37
	N	8-350	Olds	Diesel	52.7	105 @ 3600	220 @ 1600	4.057 × 3.385	16	5-6	22.5	30-45
	R	8-350	Olds	4	52.7	170 @ 3800	275 @ 2000	4.057 × 3.385	16	5-6	8.3	30-45

① Horsepower and torque figures for 1977 and later years are Chilton estimates.

② Turbocharged

③ Electronic Fuel Control engine.

④ If a 17-digit VIN is used, the 8th digit is the engine code and the 10th digit is the model year code

N.A. Not available

TUNE-UP SPECIFICATIONS

Year	V.I.N. Code	No. Cyl Disp. (cu in)	SPARK PLUGS Orig. Type	Gap (in)	Dist.	IGNITION TIMING① (deg B.T.D.C. @ rpm) Man. Trans.	Auto Trans.	CARBURETION IDLE SPEED② (r.p.m.) Man. Trans.	Auto. Trans. Fed.	Cal.	Hi. Alt.
'76	C	6-231	R44SX	.060	E.I.	12	12	600/800	600	600	600
	F	8-260	R46SX	.080	E.I.	16 @ 1100	18 @ 1100⑤⑥	—	550/650	600/650	550/650
	H	8-350	R45TSX	.060	E.I.	—	12	—	600	600	600
	J	8-350	R45TSX	.060	E.I.	—	12	—	600	600	600
	T	8-455	R45TSX	.060	E.I.	—	12	—	600	600	600
'77	C	6-231	R46TSX	.060	E.I.	12 @ 600	12	500/800⑨	600	600	600
	Y	8-301	R46TSX	.060	E.I.	—	12	—	550/650	550/650	550/650
	U	8-305	R45TS	.045	E.I.	—	8	—	500/650	500/650	500/650
	H	8-350	R46TSX	.060	E.I.	—	12	—	600	600	600
	J	8-350	R46TSX	.060	E.I.	—	12 @ 600	—	550	550	550
	L	8-350	R45TS	.045	E.I.	—	8	—	500/650	500/650	600/650
	R	8-350	R46SZ	.060	E.I.	—	20 @ 1100⑦	—	550/650	550/650	600/650
	K	8-403	R46SZ	.060	E.I.	—	24 @ 1100⑧	—	550/650	550/650	600/650
'78	A	6-231	R46TSX	.060	E.I.	15 @ 800	15	600/800	600/670	600/670	600/670
	C	6-196	R46TSX	.060	E.I.	15 @ 800	15	600/800	600	—	—
	G	6-231	R46TSX	.060	E.I.	—	15 @ 650	—	650	—	—
	3	6-231	R46TSX	.060	E.I.	—	15 @ 650	—	650	—	650
	H	8-305	R45TS	.045	E.I.	—	4	—	500/600	—	—
	K	8-403	R46SZ	.060	E.I.	—	20 @ 1100	—	550/650	550/650	600/700
	L	8-350	R45TS	.045	E.I.	—	8	—	—	500/600	600/650
	X	8-350	R46TSX	.060	E.I.	—	15 @ 650	—	550	—	—
	U	8-305	R45TS	.045	E.I.	—	6⑩	—	—	500/650	600/700
	R	8-350	R46SZ	.060	E.I.	—	20 @ 1100	—	—	550/650	600/700
	Y	8-301	R46TSX	.060	E.I.	—	12	—	550/650	—	—
'79	A	6-231	R46TSX	.060	E.I.	15 @ 800	15 @ 600	600/800	550/670	600	600
	2	6-231	R46TSX	.060	E.I.	—	15	—	—	580/670	—
	C	6-196	R46TSX	.060	E.I.	15 @ 800	15 @ 600	600/800	550/670	—	—
	3	6-231	R46TSX	.060	E.I.	—	15 @ 650	—	650⑫	650⑫	650
	H	8-305	R45TS	.045	E.I.	—	⑪	—	—	500/600	600/650
	K	8-403	R46SZ	.060	E.I.	—	20 @ 1100	—	550/650	500/600	600/700
	R	8-350	R46SZ	.060	E.I.	—	20 @ 1100	—	—	550/650	600/700
	Y	8-301	R46TSX	.060	E.I.	—	12@650	—	500/650	—	—
	W	8-301	R45TSX	.060	E.I.	—	12@650	—	500/650	—	—
'80	A	6-231	R45TSX	.060	E.I.	15 @ 550	15 @ 550	600/800	500/670		500/620
	3	6-231	R45TS	.040	E.I.	—	15 @ 650	—	600/650		600/650
	4	6-252	R45TSX	.060	E.I.	—	15 @ 550	—	550/680	—	—
	W	8-301	R45TSX	.060	E.I.	—	12 @ 550	—	550/650	—	—
	H	8-305	R45TS	.035	D.I.	—	4 @ 550	—	—	—	550/650
	X	8-350	R45TSX	.060	E.I.	—	15 @ 550	—	550/670	—	—
	N	8-350	—	—	E.I.	—	7 @ 800	—	600	—	—
	R	8-350	R46SX	.080	E.I.	—	18 @ 1100④	—	550/600	—	550/650

NOTE: The underhood certification/specification decal is the authority for performance specifications affecting exhaust emissions. Use this manual's information only when that decal is not available.

FED —Federal
CAL —California HI. ALT.—High Altitude
— Not Applicable
① Time at curb idle speed unless otherwise indicated
② Set idle speed with automatic transmission in Drive; manual transmission in Neutral. Where two figures appear, the lower figure indicates idle speed with A/C solenoid deenergized
⑤ 14° at 1100 on all high altitude and California applications
⑥ 16° at 1100 with distributor no. 1103208
⑦ 18° at 1100 on California LeSabre, Riviera and Skylark
⑧ 20° at 1100 on all high altitude and California applications
⑨ 600/800 for California applications
⑩ 8° on high altitude applications
⑪ On California applications, set timing to 4° at 500 rpm. On high altitude applications, set timing to 8° at 600 rpm
⑫ 650 on Riviera
⑬ See underhood certification/specification decal
⑭ SEE DIESEL SECTION

BUICK
EXCEPT CENTURY (FRONT WHEEL DRIVE), SKYHAWK & '80-'82 SKYLARK

ENGINE SPECIFICATIONS

Yr.	Engine V.I.N. Code	Engine No. Cyl. Disp. (cu in)	Eng. Mfg.	Carb Bbl	Tax H.P.	Horsepower[1] @ rpm	Torque[1] @ rpm (ft lbs)	Bore and Stroke (in)	Valves Intake Opens (deg BTDC)	Fuel Pump Pres. (psi)	Comp. Ratio	Oil Pressure @ 2000 rpm
'81	A	6-231 3.8L	Buick	2	34.6	110 @ 3400	185 @ 2000	3.800 × 3.400	17	3	8.0	37
	3	6-321 3.8L	Buick	4	34.6	165 @ 4000	265 @ 2800	3.800 × 3.400	17	5	8.0	37
	4	6-252 4.1L	Buick	4	36.0	125 @ 3400	195 @ 2000	3.965 × 3.400	17	5	8.0	37
	S	8-265 4.3L	Pont	2	39.2	125 @ 3800	215 @ 2400	3.750 × 3.000	27	7-9	8.2	40
	W	8-301 5.0L	Pont	4	51.2	150 @ 4000	239 @ 2000	4.000 × 3.000	27	7-9	8.2	40
	Y	8-307 5.0L	Olds	4	46.2	148 @ 3800	250 @ 2400	3.800 × 3.385	—	5.5-6.5	8.5	30-45
	N	8-350 5.7L	Olds	Diesel	52.7	110 @ 3600	220 @ 1600	4.057 × 3.385	16	5-6	22.5	30-45
'82	A	V6-231 3.8L	Buick	2	34.6	105 @ 3400	185 @ 2000	3.800 × 3.400	17	3	8.0	35-40
	3	V6-321 3.8L	Buick	4	34.6	170 @ 3600	265 @ 2000	3.800 × 3.400	17	5	8.0	35-40
	4	V6-252 4.1L	Buick	4	36.0	125 @ 3400	195 @ 2000	3.965 × 3.400	17	5	8.0	35-40
	Y	8-307 5.0L	Olds	4	46.2	148 @ 4400	250 @ 2400	3.800 × 3.385	—	5-6	8.5	30-45
	V and T	V6-263 4.3L	Olds	Diesel	—	(See Diesel Section)						
	N	V8-350 5.7L	Olds	Diesel	—	(See Diesel Section)						
	N	8-350 5.7L	Olds	Diesel	52.7	110 @ 3600	220 @ 1600	4.057 × 3.385	16	5-6	22.5	30-45

① Horsepower and torque figures for 1977 and later
  years are Chilton estimates.
② Turbocharged
③ Electronic Fuel Control engine.
④ If a 17-digit VIN is used, the 8th digit is the engine
  code and the 10th digit is the model year code
N.A. Not available

BUICK—ALL MODELS EXCEPT SKYHAWK

WHEEL LUG TORQUE DATA

YEAR	MODEL	TORQUE ft./lb.
'76-'82	¾ nut	80
	¹³/₁₆ nut	100

TUNE-UP SPECIFICATIONS

Year	V.I.N. Code	No. Cyl Disp. (cu in)	SPARK PLUGS Orig. Type	Gap (in)	Dist.	IGNITION TIMING[1] (deg B.T.D.C. @ rpm) Man. Trans.	Auto Trans.	CARBURETION IDLE SPEED[2] (r.p.m.) Man. Trans.	Auto. Trans. Fed.	Cal.	Hi. Alt.
'81	A	6-231	R45TSX	.080	E.I.	15 @ 800N	15 @ 500P	800N	500D	500D	500D
	3	6-231	R45TS	.080	E.I.	15 @ 800N	15 @ 800	800	800	800	—
	4	6-252	R45TSX	.045	E.I.	—	15 @ 500P	—	550D	500D	—
	S	8-265	R45TSX	.060	E.I.	—	12 @ 600P	—	450D	450D	450D
	W	8-301	R45TSX	.060	E.I.	—	12 @ 600P	[13]		[13]	
	Y	8-307	R46TS	.080	E.I.	—	15 @ 1100P	[13]	500D	500D	—
	N	8-350	—	—	—	—	[13]	[13]		[13]	
	T	8-301	R45TSX	.060	E.I.		6 @ 700P	—	450D	450D	—
'82	A	6-231 3.8L	R45TSX	.080	E.I.	[13]	[13]	[13]	[13]	[13]	[13]
	3	6-231 3.8L	R45TS	.080	E.I.	[13]	[13]	[13]	[13]	[13]	[13]
	4	6-252 4.1L	R45TSX	.045	E.I.	[13]	[13]	[13]	[13]	[13]	[13]
	Y	V8-307 5.0L	R46TS	.080	E.I.	[13]	[13]	[13]	[13]	[13]	[13]
	V	V6-263 4.3L	DIESEL	—	—	[14]	[14]	[14]	[14]	[14]	[14]
	N	V8-350 5.7L	DIESEL	—	—	—	[14]	[14]	—	[13][14]	[13][14]

NOTE: The underhood certification/specification decal is the authority for performance specifications affecting exhaust emissions. Use this manual's information only when that decal is not available.

FED —Federal
CAL —California HI. ALT.—High Altitude
— Not Applicable
[1] Time at curb idle speed unless otherwise indicated
[2] Set idle speed with automatic transmission in Drive; manual transmission in Neutral. Where two figures appear, the lower figure indicates idle speed with A/C solenoid deenergized
[5] 14° at 1100 on all high altitude and California applications
[6] 16° at 1100 with distributor no. 1103208
[7] 18° at 1100 on California LeSabre, Riviera and Skylark
[8] 20° at 1100 on all high altitude and California applications
[9] 600/800 for California applications
[10] 8° on high altitude applications
[11] On California applications, set timing to 4° at 500 rpm. On high altitude applications, set timing to 8° at 600 rpm
[12] 650 on Riviera
[13] See underhood certification/specification decal
[14] SEE DIESEL SECTION

BUICK
EXCEPT CENTURY (FRONT WHEEL DRIVE), SKYHAWK & '80-'82 SKYLARK

VALVE SPECIFICATIONS

Year	Engine No. Cyl. Disp. (cu in.)	Seat Angle (deg)	Face Angle (deg)	Spring Test Pressure (lbs @ in.)	Spring Installed Height (in.)	STEM TO GUIDE CLEARANCE (in.) Intake	Exhaust	STEM DIAMETER (in.) Intake	Exhaust
'76	V6-231	45	45	164 @ 1.34 [1]	1 47/64	.0015-.0035	.0015-.0032	.3407	.3407
	6-250	46	45	186 @ 1.27	1 21/32	.0010-.0027	.0010-.0020	.3413	.3413
	8-260	45 [2]	46 [2]	187 @ 1.27	—	.0010-.0027	.0015-.0032	.3428	.3424
	8-350	45	45	180 @ 1.34 [3]	1 47/64	.0015-.0035	.0015-.0032	.3725	.3727
	8-455	45	45	177 @ 1.45	1 57/64	.0015-.0035	.0015-.0032	.3725	.3727
'77	V6-231	45	45	164 @ 1.34 [1]	1 47/64	.0015-.0035	.0015-.0032	.3407	.3407
	8-301	46	45	165 @ 1.29	1 21/32	.0010-.0027	.0010-.0027	.3422	.3422
	8-305	46	45	200 @ 1.25	1 45/64	.0010-.0037	.0010-.0037	.3414	.3414
	8-350	45	45	180 @ 1.34 [3]	1 47/64	.0015-.0035	.0015-.0032	.3725	.3727
	8-350(VIN-L)	46	45	200 @ 1.25	1 45/64	.0010-.0037	.0010-.0037	.3414	.3414
	8-350(VIN-R)	[6]	[7]	187 @ 1.27	1 43/64	.0010-.0027	.0015-.0032	.3429	.3427
	8-403	[6]	[7]	187 @ 1.27	1 43/64	.0010-.0027	.0015-.0032	.3429	.3427
'78	V6-196	45	45	168±6 @ 1.327	1.727	.0015-.0032	.0015-.0032	.3412	.3405
	V6-231	45	45	168±6 @ 1.327	1.727	.0015-.0032	.0015-.0032	.3412	.3405
	8-301	46	45	170 @ 1.26	1.69	.0017-.0020	.0017-.0020	.3400	.3400
	8-305	46	45	206 @ 1.25 [8]	1 23/32 [8]	.0010-.0037	.0010-.0037	.3414	.3414
	8-350 (VIN-L)	46	45	206 @ 1.25 [8]	1 23/32 [8]	.0010-.0037	.0010-.0037	.3414	.3414
	8-350 (VIN-X)	45	45	180±7 @ 1.340 [9]	1.727	.0015-.0035	.0015-.0032	.3730-.3720	.3730-.3723
	8-350 (VIN-R)	[6]	[7]	180-194 @ 1.270	1.670	.0010-.0027	.0015-.0032	.3425-.3432	.3420-.3427
	8-403	[6]	[7]	180-194 @ 1.270	1.670	.0010-.0027	.0015-.0032	.3425-.3432	.3420-.3427
'79	V6-196	45	45	164±5 @ 1.340 [10]	1.727	.0015-.0035	.0015-.0032	.3412-.3401	.3412-.3405
	V6-231	45	45	164±5 @ 1.340 [10]	1.727	.0015-.0035	.0015-.0032	.3412-.3401	.3412-.3405
	8-301	46	45	170 @ 1.26	1.69	.0017-.0020	.0017-.0020	.3400	.3400
	8-305	46	45	206 @ 1.25	1 23/32	.0010-.0037	.0010-.0037	.3414	.3414
	8-350 (VIN-L)	46	45	206 @ 1.25	1 23/32	.0010-.0037	.0010-.0037	.3414	.3414
	8-350 (VIN-X)	45	45	180±7 @ 1.340 [9]	1.727	.0015-.0035	.0015-.0032	.3730-.3720	.3730-.3723
	8-350 (VIN-R)	[6]	[7]	180-194 @ 1.270	1.670	.0010-.0027	.0015-.0032	.3432-.3425	.3427-.3420
	8-403	[6]	[7]	180-194 @ 1.270	1.670	.0010-.0027	.0015-.0032	.3432-.3425	.3427-.3420
'80	6-231	45	45	164±5 @ 1.340 [10]	1.727	.0015-.0035	.0015-.0032	.3412-.3401	.3412-.3405
	6-252	45	45	164±5 @ 1.340 [10]	1.727	.0015-.0035	.0015-.0032	3.412-3.401	3.412-3.405
	8-301	46	45	170 @ 1.26	1.69	.0017-.0020	.0017-.0020	.3400	.3400
	8-305	46	45	206 @ 1.25	1 23/32	.0010-.0037	.0010-.0037	.3414	.3414
	8-350 (X)	45	45	180±7 @ 1.340 [9]	1.727	.0015-.0035	.0015-.0032	.3730-.3720	.3730-.3723
	8-350 (N)	[6]	[7]	144-158 @ 1.300	1.670	.0010-.0027	.0015-.0032	.3432-.3425	.3427-.3420
	8-350 (R)	[6]	[7]	180-194 @ 1.270	1.670	.0010-.0027	.0015-.0032	.3432-.3425	.3427-.3420
'81	6-231 3.8L	45	45	164±5 @ 1.340 [10]	1.727	.0015-.0035	.0015-.0032	.3412-.3401	.3412-.3405
	6-252 4.1L	45	45	164±5 @ 1.340 [10]	1.727	.0015-.0035	.0015-.0032	.3412-.3401	.3412-.3405
	8-265, 301	46	45	170 @ 1.26	1.69	.0017-.0020	.0017-.0020	.3400	.3400
	8-307 5.0L	[6]	[7]	180-194 @ 1.270	1.670	.0010-.0027	.0015-.0032	.3425-.3432	.3420-.3427
	8-350 (N) 5.7L	[6]	[7]	144-158 @ 1.300	1.670	.0010-.0027	.0015-.0032	.3425-.3432	.3420-.3427
'82	6-231 3.8L	45	45	164±5 @ 1.340 [10]	1.727	.0015-.0035	.0015-.0032	.3412-.3401	.3412-.3405
	6-252 4.1L	45	45	164±5 @ 1.340 [10]	1.727	.0015-.0035	.0015-.0032	.3412-.3401	.3412-.3405
	8-307 5.0L	[6]	[7]	180-194 @ 1.270	1.670	.0010-.0027	.0015-.0032	.3425-.3432	.3420-.3427
	8-350 (N) 5.7L	[6]	[7]	144-158 @ 1.300	1.670	.0010-.0027	.0015-.0032	.3425-.3432	.3420-.3427
	V6-263 4.3L	Diesel		(See Diesel Section)					

[1] Intake shown. Exhaust—182 @ 1.34
[2] Intake shown. Exhaust—59 seat, 60 face
[3] Intake shown. Exhaust—175 @ 1.34
[4] Engines using small valves:
    Intake—45
    Exhaust—45
[5] Engines using small valves:
    Intake—44
    Exhaust—44

Engines using large valves:
Intake—30
Exhaust—45

[6] Intake—45, Exhaust—31
[7] Intake—44, Exhaust—30

Engines using large valves:
Intake—29
Exhaust—44

[8] Intake shown. Exhaust—194-206 @ 1.16, assembled height—1 19/32
[9] Intake shown. Exhaust—177±7 @ 1.450
[10] Intake shown. Exhaust—182±8 @ 1.340

DISTRIBUTOR SPECIFICATIONS

Year	Dist. Ident.	CENTRIFUGAL ADVANCE Start Crank. Deg. @ Eng. RPM	CENTRIFUGAL ADVANCE Finish Crank. Deg. @ Eng. RPM	VACUUM ADVANCE Start @ In. Hg.	VACUUM ADVANCE Finish Crank. Deg. @ In. Hg.
'76	6-231	0 @ 1550	18 @ 5000	5.3	25.5 @ 12.8
	8-260	0 @ 650	28 @ 4400	4.5	30 @ 11
	8-260①	0 @ 910	26 @ 4450	6	20 @ 14.75
	8-350	0 @ 1750	22 @ 5000	6.9	23.5 @ 14.3
	8-455	0 @ 1320	18 @ 5000	4.5	25.5 @ 14.1
	8-455①	0 @ 1320	18 @ 5000	4.5	19.5 @ 12
'77	1103239	0 @ 1200	20 @ 4400	—	②
	1103244	0 @ 1000	20 @ 3800	—	③
	1103246	0 @ 1200	22 @ 4200	4	18 @ 12
	1103248	0 @ 1200	20-24 @ 4200	3-5	8-12 @ 7-9
	1103252	0 @ 1000	20 @ 3800	4	18 @ 12
	1103259	0 @ 1000	19 @ 4000	6	24 @ 13
	1103260	0 @ 1000	13 @ 3600	6	24 @ 13
	1103264	0 @ 1000	13 @ 3600	5	16 @ 11
	1103266	0 @ 1000	19 @ 4000	5	16 @ 11
	1103272	0 @ 925	21 @ 3425	4	25 @ 12
	1103273	0 @ 1000	19 @ 3600	4	25 @ 12
	1110677	0 @ 1400	20 @ 3600	4	24 @ 11
	1110686	0 @ 1400	20 @ 3600	7	8 @ 9
	1110694	0 @ 1525	16-22 @ 5000	3-4	30 @ 20
'78	1110695	0 @ 1675	12-18 @ 3600	3-6	24 @ 10-13
	1110723	—	8-12 @ 4000	4-6	8 @ 5-7
	1110728	—	14-18 @ 3200	1-5	20 @ 4-8
	1110730	—	19-23 @ 4000	4-6	24 @ 7-10
	1110731	0 @ 1675	13-17 @ 3600	4-6	16 @ 7-9
	1110732	0 @ 1675	13-17 @ 3600	7-9	14 @ 11-13
	1110735	0 @ 900-1200	19-23 @ 4000	2-4	20 @ 11-13
	1110739	—	13-17 @ 3600	2-4	20 @ 11-13
	11103285	0 @ 1200	20-24 @ 4200	3-5	10 @ 7-9
	1103281	0 @ 1000	18-22 @ 3800	3-5	18 @ 11-13
	1103282	0 @ 1000	18-22 @ 3800	3-6	20 @ 9-12
	1103314	0 @ 825	19-23 @ 3400	3-5	25 @ 11-13
	1103322	0 @ 600	27-31 @ 4000	4-6	24 @ 12-14
	1103323	0 @ 1000	17-21 @ 4000	4-5	16 @ 10-12
	1103324	0 @ 600	21-25 @ 3600	4-6	24 @ 12-14
	1103325	0 @ 1000	13-15 @ 3600	4-5	16 @ 10-12
	1103342	0 @ 1900	15-19 @ 4400	5-7	24 @ 11-13
	1103346	0 @ 1000	17-21 @ 4000	4-6	24 @ 12-14
	1103347	0 @ 1000	13-17 @ 3600	4-6	24 @ 12-14
	1103353	0 @ 2200	22-24 @ 4500	3-6	20 @ 9-12
'79	1103281	—	18-22 @ 3800	3-6	18 @ 11-13
	1103314	—	18-24 @ 3400	3-5	26 @ 11-13
	1103322	—	26-32 @ 4000	4-6	24 @ 12-14

DISTRIBUTOR SPECIFICATIONS

Year	Dist. Ident.	CENTRIFUGAL ADVANCE Start Crank. Deg. @ Eng. RPM	CENTRIFUGAL ADVANCE Finish Crank. Deg. @ Eng. RPM	VACUUM ADVANCE Start @ In. Hg.	VACUUM ADVANCE Finish Crank. Deg. @ In. Hg.
'79	1103323	—	16-22 @ 4000	4-5	16 @ 10-12
	1103324	—	20-26 @ 3600	4-6	24 @ 12-14
	1103325	—	12-16 @ 3600	4-5	16 @ 10-12
	1103342	—	14-18 @ 4400	5-7	24 @ 11-13
	1103346	—	16-22 @ 4000	4-6	24 @ 12-14
	1103347	—	12-16 @ 3600	4-6	24 @ 12-14
	1103368	—	18-22 @ 3800	3-6	10 @ 7-9
	1103379	—	18-22 @ 3800	2-4	20 @ 6-9
	1103399	—	18-22 @ 4400	3-5	26 @ 11-13
	1103400	—	14-28 @ 4600	3-5	26 @ 10-13
	1110765	—	12-18 @ 4400	2-4	20 @ 11-13
	1110766	—	12-18 @ 3600	4-5	24 @ 10-12
	1110767	—	12-18 @ 3600	2-4	20 @ 11-13
	1110768	—	12-18 @ 3600	2-4	20 @ 11-13
	1110769	—	12-18 @ 3600	4-5	24 @ 10-12
	1110770	—	12-18 @ 3600	2-4	20 @ 8-10
	1110772	—	12-18 @ 3600	2-4	24 @ 9-11
	1110774	—	8-12 @ 4400	2-4	20 @ 11-13
	111-775	—	12-18 @ 3600	2-4	20 @ 8-10
	1110779	—	12-18 @ 3600	2-4	24 @ 8-11
'80	1103384	0-8 @ 1000	18-22 @ 4000	3-6	24 @ 10-13
	1103386	0-6 @ 1200	18-22 @ 3800	3-5	16 @ 6-8
	1103398	0-4 @ 1100	24-28 @ 4100		
	1103412	—	—		
	1103413	—	—		
	1103414	—	—		
	1103417	0-4 @ 2200	14-18 @ 4400	5-6	24 @ 12-14
	1103407	0-4 @ 1200	20-26 @ 4400	4-5	20 @ 10-11
	1103425	—			
	1103444	0-8 @ 1400	12-18 @ 2000	7-8	20 @ 13-15
	1103447	0-4 @ 2200	14-18 @ 4400		
	1103449	—			
	1103450	0-6 @ 1300	16-22 @ 3200	2-4	14 @ 6-7
	1110550	0-6 @ 1000	12-18 @ 4400	2-4	20 @ 10-13
	1110551	0-8 @ 1000	8-12 @ 4400	—	—
	1110554	0-4 @ 2000	12-18 @ 3600	2-4	24 @ 11-13
	1110571	0-6 @ 1000	12-18 @ 4400	2-4	20 @ 8-10
	1110572	0-8 @ 1000	8-12 @ 4400	—	—
	1110573	—	—		
	1110784	—	—		

① California application
② 0 @ 14, 7.5 @ 10
③ 0 @ 14, 10 @ 10

BUICK
EXCEPT CENTURY (FRONT WHEEL DRIVE), SKYHAWK & '80-'82 SKYLARK

TORQUE SPECIFICATIONS

Readings in ft/lbs (N•m)

Year	Engine No. Cyl. Disp. (cu in.)	Cylinder Head Bolts	Rod Bearing Bolts	Main Bearing Bolts	Crankshaft Bolts	Flywheel To Crankshaft Bolts	MANIFOLD Intake	MANIFOLD Exhaust
'76	6-231	80	40	115	200	60	45	25
	8-260	85	42	120	160	40	25	25
	8-350	80	40	115	175	60	45	25
	8-455	100	45	115	225	60	45	25
'77	6-231	80	40	100	175	60	45	25
	8-301	90	35	60④	160	95	40	35
	8-305	65	45	70	60	60	30	20
	8-350	80	40	100	175	60	45	25
	8-350 (VIN-L)	65	45	70	60	60	30	20
	8-350 (VIN-R)	130	42	80②	200-310	60③	40	25
	8-403	130	42	80②	200-310	60③	40	25
'78	6-196	80	40	100	225	60	45	25
	6-231	80	40	100	225	60	45	25
	8-301	90	35	60④	160	95	40	35
	8-305	65	45	70	60	60	30	20
	8-350 (L)	65	45	70	60	60	30	20
	8-350 (X)	80	40	100	225	60	45	25
	8-350 (R)	130⑤	42	80②	200-310	60③	40⑤	25
	8-403	130⑤	42	80②	200-310	60③	40⑤	25
'79	6-196	80	40	100	225	60	45	25
	6-231	80	40	100	225	60	45	25
	8-301	95	35	70④	160	95	40	35
	8-305	65	45	70	60	60	30	20
	8-350 (L)	65	45	70	60	60	30	20
	8-350 (X)	80	40	100	225	60	45	25
	8-350 (R)	130⑤	42	80②	255	60③	40⑤	25
	8-403	130⑤	42	80②	255	60③	40⑤	25
'80	6-231	80	40	100	225	60	45	25
	6-252	80	40	100	225	60	45	25
	8-301	95	35	70④	160	95	40	35
	8-305	65	45	70	60	60	30	20
	8-350 (X)	80	40	100	225	60	45	25
	8-350 (N)	130⑤	42	120	200-310	60	40⑤	25
	8-350 (R)	130⑤	42	80②	255	60③	40⑤	25
'81	6-231 (3.8L)	80 (108)	40 (54)	100 (136)	225 (306)	60 (81)	45 (61)	25 (34)
	6-252 (4.1L)	80 (108)	40 (54)	100 (136)	225 (306)	60 (81)	45 (61)	25 (34)
	8-265 (4.3L)	95 (109)	30 (41)⑥	70④ (95)	160 (217)	95 (109)	40 (54)	35 (47)
	8-301 (5.0L)	95 (109)	35 (48)	70④ (95)	160 (217)	95 (109)	40 (54)	35 (47)
	8-307 (5.0L)	130 (177)	42 (57)	80① (108)	200-310 (308)	60③ (81)	40 (54)	25 (34)
	8-350 (N) DIESEL	130⑤ (177)	42 (57)	120 (163)	200-310 (308)	60 (81)	40⑤ (54)	25 (34)
'82	6-231 (3.8L)	80 (108)	40 (54)	100 (136)	225 (306)	60 (81)	45 (61)	25 (34)
	6-252 (4.1L)	80 (108)	40 (54)	100 (136)	225 (306)	60 (81)	45 (61)	25 (34)
	8-307 (5.0L)	130 (177)	42 (57)	80① (108)	200-310 (308)	60③ (81)	40 (54)	25 (34)
	8-350 (N) DIESEL	130⑤ (177)	42 (57)	120 (163)	200-310 (308)	60 (81)	40⑤ (54)	25 (34)
	V6-263 (4.3L) DIESEL				See Diesel Section			

① No. 5—120 (136 N-M)   ④ Rear Main—100 (136 N-M)
② Rear Main—120   ⑤ Clean and dip bolts in engine oil before tightening
③ With manual transmission—90 (108 N-M)   ⑥ TURBO 28-(40 N-M)

BRAKE SPECIFICATIONS

All readings in inches

Year	Model	Master Cylinder Bore Diameter	CALIPER OR WHEEL CYLINDER		BRAKE DRUM/ROTOR Diameter		Rotor Runout	Rotor Allowable Minimum Machined Thickness	Rotor Thickness Variation Maximum
			Front	Rear	Front	Rear			
'76	Skylark	1⅛	2.9375	⅞	—	9.5	.004	.980	.0005
	Century, Regal	1⅛②	2.9375	15/16	—	11.0	.004	.980	.0005
	LeSabre, Riviera, Electra	1⅛	2.9375	1	—	11.0	.005	1.230	.0005
	Estate Wagon	1⅛	2.9375	1	—	12.0	.005	1.230	.0005
'77	Skylark	1⅛	2.9375	15/16	—	9.5	.004	.980	.0005
	Century, Regal	1⅛②	2.9375	15/16	—	11.0	.004	.980	.0005
	LeSabre,	1⅛	2.9375	⅞	—	9.5	.004	.980	.0005
	Electra, Riviera, Estate Wagon	1⅛	2.9375	15/16	—	11.0	.004	.980	.0005
'78	Skylark	1⅛	2.9375	15/16	—	9.5	.004	.980	.0005
	Century, Regal	.94③	2.43	¾	—	9.45	.004	.980	.0005
	LeSabre	1⅛	2.9375	⅞	—	9.5	.004	.980	.0005
	Electra, Riviera, Estate Wagon	1⅛	2.9375	15/16	—	11.0	.004	.980	.0005
'79	Skylark	1⅛①	2.9375	15/16	—	9.5	.005	.965	.0005
	Century, Regal	.94③	2.43	¾	—	9.45	.004	.965	.0005
	LeSabre, Riviera	1⅛	2.9375	⅞	—	9.5	.005	.965	.0005
	Electra, Estate Wagon	1⅛	2.9375	15/16	—	11.0	.005	.965	.0005
	Riviera	.945	2.50	¾	—	9.45	.005	.965	.0005
'80	Century, Regal	.94③	2.43	¾	—	9.45	.004	.965	.0005
	LeSabre	1⅛	2.9375	⅞	—	9.5	.005	.965	.0005
	Electra, Estate Wagon	1⅛	2.9375	15/16	—	11.0	.005	.965	.0005
	Riviera	.945	2.50	¾	—	9.45	.005	.965	.0005
'81	Century, Regal	.94③	2.43	¾	—	9.5	.004	.965	.0005
	LeSabre	1⅛	2.9375	⅞	—	9.5	.005	.965	.0005
	Electra, Estate Wagon	1⅛	2.9375	15/16	—	11.0	.005	.965	.0005
	Riviera	.945	2.50	¾	—	9.5	.005	.965	.0005
'82	Century, Regal	.94③	2.43	¾	—	9.5	.004	.965	.0005
	LeSabre	1⅛	2.9375	⅞	—	9.5	.005	.965	.0005
	Electra, Estate Wagon	1⅛	2.9375	15/16	—	11.0	.005	.965	.0005
	Riviera	.945	2.50	¾	—	9.5	.005	.965	.0005

— Not applicable
① Manual brake—1.0
② Manual brake—15/16
③ Manual brake—0.87

CRANKSHAFT & CONNECTING ROD SPECIFICATIONS

All measurements given in inches

| Year | Engine No. Cyl. Disp. (cu in) | Main Brg. Journal | CRANKSHAFT | | | | CONNECTING ROD | | |
			Main Brg. Journal Dia	Main Brg. Oil Clearance	Shaft End-Play	Thrust on No.	Journal Diameter	Oil Clearance	Side Clearance
'76-'77	V6-231		2.4995	.0004-.0015	.004-.008	2	2.0000	.0002-.0023	.006-.014
	8-301		3.000	.0002-.0020	.003-.009	4	2.2500	.0005-.0026	.006-.022
	8-305		2.4485	.002	.002-.006	5	2.199	.0013-.0035	.008-.014
	8-350		2.9995	.0004-.0015	.002-.006	3	2.0000	.0005-.0026	.006-.026
	8-350(VIN-L)		2.4485	.002	.002-.006	5	2.199	.0013-.0035	.008-.014
	8-350(VIN-R)		2.4990	.0005-.0021	.0035-.0135	3	2.1242	.0004-.0033	.006-.020
	8-403		2.4990	.0005-.0021	.0035-.0135	3	2.1242	.0004-.0033	.006-.020
'78	V6-196		2.4995	.0003-.0017	.004-.008	2	2.2487-2.2495	.0005-.0026	.006-.027
	V6-231		2.4995	.0003-.0017	.004-.008	2	2.2487-2.2495	.0005-.0026	.006-.027
	8-301		3.000	.0004-.0020	.006-.022	5	2.250	.0005-.0025	.006-.022
	8-305	1	2.4484-2.4493	.002 (max.)	.002-.006	5	2.099-2.100	.0035 (max.)	.008-.014
		2-4	2.4481-2.4490	.0035 (max.)	.004-.006				
		5	2.4479-2.4488	.0035 (max.)	.004-.006				
	8-350(VIN-L)	1	2.4484-2.4493	.002 (max.)	.002-.006	5	2.099-2.100	.0035 (max.)	.008-.014
		2-4	2.4481-2.4490	.0035 (max.)	.004-.006				
		5	2.4479-2.4488	.0035 (max.)	.004-.006				
	8-350(VIN-X)		3.0000	.0004-.0015	.003-.009	3	1.991-2.000	.0005-.0026	.006-.027
	8-350(VIN-R)	1	2.4988-2.4998	.005-.021	.0035-.0135	3	2.1238-2.1248	.0004-.0033	.006-.020
		2-4	2.4985-2.4995	.005-.021		.0035-.0135			
		5	2.4985-2.4995	.0015-.0031	.0035-.0135				
	8-403	1	2.4988-2.4998	.005-.021	.0035-.0135	3	2.1238-2.1248	.0004-.0033	.006-.020
		2-4	2.4985-2.4995	.005-.021	.0035-.0135				
		5	2.4985-2.4995	.0015-.0031					
'79	V6-196	ALL	2.4995	.0003-.0017	.004-.008	2	2.2487-2.2495	.0005-.0026	.006-.027
	V6-231	ALL	2.4995	.0003-.0017	.004-.008	2	2.2487-2.2495	.0005-.0026	.006-.027
	8-301	ALL	3.000	.0004-.0020	.006-.022	5	2.25	.0005-.0025	.006-.022
	8-305	1	2.4484-2.4493	.002 (max.)	.002-.006	5	2.099-2.100	.0035 (max.)	.008-.014
		2-4	2.4481-2.4490	.0035 (max.)					
		5	2.4479-2.4488	.0035 (max.)					
	8-350(VIN-L)	1	2.4484-2.4493	.002 (max.)	.002-.006	5	2.099-2.100	.0035 (max.)	.008-.014
		2-4	2.4481-2.4490	.0035 (max.)					
		5	2.4479-2.4488	.0035 (max.)					
	8-350(VIN-X)		3.0000	.0004-.0015	.003-.019	3	1.991-2.000	.0005-.0026	.006-.027
	8-350(VIN-R)	1	2.4988-2.4998	.005-.021	.0035-.0135	3	2.1238-2.1248	.0004-.0033	.006-.020
		2-4	2.4985-2.4995	.005-.021					
		5	2.4985-2.4995	.0015-.0031					
	8-403	1	2.4988-2.4998	.005-.021	.0035-.0135	3	2.1238-2.1248	.0004-.0033	.006-.020
		2-4	2.4985-2.4995	.005-.021					
		5	2.4985-2.4998	.0015-.0031					

CRANKSHAFT & CONNECTING ROD SPECIFICATIONS

All measurements given in inches

Year	Engine No. Cyl. Disp. (cu in)	Main Brg. Journal	CRANKSHAFT				CONNECTING ROD		
			Main Brg. Journal Dia	Main Brg. Oil Clearance	Shaft End-Play	Thrust on No.	Journal Diameter	Oil Clearance	Side Clearance
'80	6-231 (3.8L)	ALL	2.4995	.0003–.0018	.003–.009	2	2.2487–2.2495	.0005–.0026	.006–.023
	6-252 (4.1L)	ALL	2.4995	.0003–.0018	.003–.009	2	2.2487–2.2495	.0005–.0026	.006–.023
	8-301 (5.0L)	ALL	3.000	.0004–.0020	.006–.022	4	2.25	.0005–.0025	.006–.022
	8-305 (5.0L)	1	2.4484–2.4493	.002(max)	.002–.006	5	2.099–2.100	.0035(max)	.006–.014
		2–4	2.4481–2.4490	.0035(max)					
		5	2.4479–2.4488						
	8-350(X) (5.7L)		3.0000	.0004–.0015	.003–.009	3	1.991–2.000	.0005–.0026	.006–.023
	8-350(N) (5.7L)	1–4	2.993–3.0003	.0005–.0021	.0035–.0135	3	2.1238–2.1248	.0004–.0033	.006–.020
		5	2.9993–3.0003	.0015–.0031					
	8-350(R) (5.7L)	1	2.4988–2.4998	.005–.021	.0035–.0135	3	2.1238–2.1248	.0004–.0033	.006–.020
		2–4	2.4985–2.4995	.005–.021					
		5	2.4985–2.4995	.0015–.0031					
'81	6-231, 252 (3.8L)(4.1L)	ALL	2.4995	.0003–.0018	.003–.009	2	2.2487–2.2495	.0005–.0026	.006–.023
	8-265, 301	ALL	3.000	.0004–.0020	.006–.022	4	2.25	.0005–.0026	.006–.022
	8-307 (5.0L)	1	2.4988–2.4998	.0005–.0021	.0035–.0135	3	2.1238–2.1248	.0004–.0033	.006–.020
		2–4	2.4985–2.4995	.0005–.0021					
		5	2.4985–2.4995	.0015–.0031					
	8-350(N) (5.7L)	1–4	2.9993–3.0003	.0005–.0021	.0035–.0135	3	2.1238–2.1248	.0004–.0033	.006–.020
		5	2.9993–3.0003	.0015–.0035					
'82	6-231, 252 (3.8L)(4.1L)	ALL	2.4995	.0003–.0018	.003–.009	2	2.2487–2.2495	.0005–.0026	.006–.023
	8-307 (5.0L)	1	2.4988–2.4998	.0005–.0021	.0035–.0135	3	2.1238–2.1248	.0004–.0033	.006–.020
		2–4	2.4985–2.4995	.0005–.0021					
		5	2.4985–2.4995	.0015–.0031					
	8-350(N) DIESEL	1–4	2.9993–3.0003	.0005–.0021	.0035–.0135	3	2.1238–2.1248	.0004–.0033	.006–.020
		5	2.9993–3.0003	.0015–.0035					
	V-6-260 (4.3L)(v)DIESEL			(SEE DIESEL SECTION)					

① No. 1—.0010-.0015
No. 2, 3, 4—.0011-.0035
No. 5—.0017-.0035
② No. 1—.0008-.0020
No. 2, 3, 4—.0011-.0035
No. 5—.0017-.0035
③ No. 5—.0015-.0031

FLUID CAPACITIES—Coolant, Fuel & Lubricant   **CENTURION, ELECTRA, ESTATE WAGON, LESABRE, RIVIERA**

Year	Engine No. Cyl. Disp. (cu in)	Engine Crankcase (Add 1 Qt For New Filter)	TRANSMISSION (Pts to Refill After Draining) Manual 3-Speed	4-Speed	Automatic	Drive Axle (pts)	Gasoline Tank (gals)	Rad. Cap Press.	Therm. Temp.	COOLING SYSTEM (qts) With Heater	with A/C
'76	6-231	4	—	—	6	4.25	26	15	195	15.5	15.4
	8-350	4	—	—	6	4.25	26②	15	195	16.91④	17.22⑤
	8-455	4	—	—	7	5.5	26②	15	195	19.64	19.95⑥
'77	6-231	4	—	—	6	4.25	21	15	195	12	12
	8-301	5	—	—	⑦	4.3	21	15	195	20.2	20.2
	8-350	4	—	—	⑦	4.3	24.5	15	195	21.4	22
	8-403, 350(VIN-R)	4	—	—	⑦	4.3	21	15	195	17.9	17.9
'78	6-231	4	—	—	⑧	4.25	25.3⑨	15	195	12.9	12.9
	8-301	5	—	—	⑧	4.25	25.3⑨	15	195	20.9	20.9
	8-305	4	—	—	⑧	4.25	25.3⑨	15	195	16.6	16.7
	8-350 (VIN-X)	4	—	—	⑧	4.25	25.3⑨	15	195	14.1	14.1
	8-350 (VIN-R)	4	—	—	⑧	4.25	25.3⑨	15	195	14.6	14.5
	8-350 (VIN-L)	4	—	—	⑧	4.25	25.3⑨	15	195	16.6	16.7
	8-403	4	—	—	⑧	4.25	25.3⑨	15	195	15.7	16.6
'79	6-231	4	—	—	⑧	4.25	25.3⑨	15	195	13.7	13.7
	8-301	5	—	—	⑧	4.25	25.3⑨	15	195	21	21
	8-350 (VIN-X)	4	—	—	⑧	4.25	25.3⑨	15	195	14.6	14.5
	8-350 (VIN-R)	4	—	—	⑧	4.25	25.3⑨	15	195	14.6	14.5
	8-350 (VIN-L)	4	—	—	⑧	4.25	25.3⑨	15	195	15.7	16.4
	8-403	4	—	—	⑧	4.25	25.3⑨	15	195	15.7	16.6
'80	6-231	4	—	—	⑧	4.25	25⑨	15	195	13.7	13.7
	6-252	4	—	—	⑧	4.25	25⑨	15	195	⑩	⑩
	8-301	5	—	—	⑧	4.25	25⑨	15	195	21	21
	8-305	4	—	—	⑧	4.25	25⑨	15	195	15.7	15.6
	8-350 (VIN-X)	4	—	—	⑧	4.25	25⑨	15	195	14.6	14.5
	8-350 (VIN-N)	7.5	—	—	⑧	4.25	25⑨	15	195	18.0	17.9
	8-350 (VIN-R)	4	—	—	⑧	4.25	25⑨	15	195	14.6	14.5
'81	6-231 (3.8L)	4	—	—	⑧	4.25	25⑨	15	195	13.7	13.7
	6-252 (4.1L)	4	—	—	⑧	4.25	25⑨	15	195	⑩	⑩
	8-265 (4.3L)	5	—	—	⑧	4.25	25⑨	15	195	12.8	12.8
	8-301 (4.9L)	5	—	—	⑧	4.25	25⑨	15	195	21	21
	8-307 (5.0L)	4	—	—	⑧	4.25	25⑨	15	195	17.5	17.5
	8-350 (N) (5.7L)	7.5	—	—	⑧	4.25	25⑨	15	195	18.0	17.9
'82	6-231 (3.8L)	4	—	—	⑧	4.25	25⑨	15	195	13.7	13.7
	6-252 (4.1L)	4	—	—	⑧	4.25	25⑨	15	195	⑩	⑩
	8-307 (5.0L)	4	—	—	⑧	4.25	25⑨	15	195	17.5	17.5
	V6-263 (4.3L)	NA	—	—	⑧	4.25	25⑨	15	195	18.0	18.0
	8-350 (N) (5.7L)	7.5	—	—	⑧	4.25	25⑨	15	195	18.0	17.9

— Not Applicable

① LeSabre—6
② Estate Wagon—22
③ Heavy duty cooling system—20.2
④ 231 CID engine—15.3
⑤ Heavy duty cooling system—18.7
⑥ Heavy duty cooling system—21.45
⑦ THM 250—5, THM 350—8, THM 400—7.5

⑧ THM 200—7, THM 325—5, THM 350—6, THM 400—7
(plus enough to indicate correct level on dipstick)
⑨ LeSabre—21.0, Station Wagon—22.0, Riviera—20.7
⑩ Refer to underhood tune-up/certification decal

FLUID CAPACITIES—Coolant, Fuel & Lubricant

CENTURY, GRAN SPORT, LUXUS, REGAL, SPECIAL, SPORT WAGON

Year	Engine No. Cyl. Disp. (cu in)	Engine Crankcase (Add 1 Qt For New Filter)	TRANSMISSION (Pts to Refill After Draining) Manual 3-Speed	4-Speed	Automatic	Drive Axle (pts)	Fuel Tank (gals)	Rad. Cap Press.	Therm. Temp.	COOLING SYSTEM (qts) With Heater	with A/C
'76	6-231	4	3.5	—	6	4.25	22	15	195	15.3	15.3
	8-260	4	3.5	—	6	4.25	21	15	195	22.3	22.8
	8-350	4	—	—	6	4.25	22	15	195	16.8	17.1
	8-455	4	—	—	7	5.5	26	15	195	19.64	19.95
'77	6-231	4	3.5	—	②	4.3	22	15	195	14.5	14.5
	8-301	5	3.5	—	②	4.3	22	15	195	20.2	20.2
	8-305	4	3.5	—	②	4.3	22	15	195	17.3	17.3
	8-350	4	—	—	②	4.3	22	15	195	21.4	22.0
	8-350 (VIN-L)	4	—	—	②	4.3	22	15	195	15.7	15.7
	8-350 (VIN-R)	4	—	—	②	4.3	22	15	195	16.7	16.7
	8-403	4	—	—	②	4.3	22	15	195	17.9	17.9
'78	6-196	4	3.12	3.12	④	4.25	17.5③	15	195	13.1	13.2
	6-231	4	3.12	3.12	④	4.25	17.5③	15	195	13.1	13.2
	8-305	4	3.12	3.12	④	4.25	17.5③	15	195	19.2	18.9
	8-350	4	3.12	3.12	④	4.25	17.5③	15	195	19.2	18.9
'79	6-196	4	3.12	3.12	④	4.25	18.2	15	195	13.7	13.7
	6-231	4	3.12	3.12	④	4.25	18.2	15	195	13.7	13.7
	8-305	4	3.12	3.12	④	4.25	18.2	15	195	15.7	15.6
	8-350	4	3.12	3.12	④	4.25	18.2	15	195	15.7	16.4
'80	6-231	4	3.12	3.12	④	4.25	18.2	15	195	13.7	13.7
	6-252	⑤	3.12	3.12	④	4.25	18.2	15	195	⑤	⑤
	8-301	5	3.12	3.12	④	4.25	18.2	15	195	17.6	17.9
	8-305	4	3.12	3.12	④	4.25	18.2	15	195	15.7	15.6
	8-350 (VIN-X)	4	3.12	3.12	④	4.25	18.2	15	195	14.6	14.5
	8-350 (VIN-N)	7.5	3.12	3.12	④	4.25	18.2	15	195	18.0	17.9
	8-350 (VIN-R)	4	3.12	3.12	④	4.25	18.2	15	195	14.9	15.7
'81	6-231 (3.8L)	4	3.12	3.12	④	4.25	18.2	15	195	13.7	13.7
	6-252 (4.1L)	⑤	3.12	3.12	④	4.25	18.2	15	195	⑤	⑤
	8-265 (4.3L)	4	3.5	—	④	4.25	18.2	15	195	12.8	12.8
	8-301 (4.9L)	5	3.12	3.12	④	4.25	18.2	15	195	17.6	17.9
	8-307 (5.0L)	4	3.12	3.12	④	4.25	18.2	15	195	17.5	17.5
'82	6-231 (3.8L)	4	3.12	3.12	④	4.25	18.2	15	195	13.7	13.7
	6-252 (4.1L)	⑤	3.12	3.12	④	4.25	18.2	15	195	⑤	⑤
	8-307 (5.0L)	4	3.12	3.12	④	4.25	18.2	15	195	17.5	17.5
	V6-263 (4.3L)	NA	—	—	④	4.25	18.2	15	195	17.25	17.5
	V8-350 (5.0L)	7.5	—	—	④	4.25	18.2	15	195	17.5	17.5

— Not Applicable

② THM-200—6
THM-250—5
THM-350—8
THM-400—7.5

③ STA. WGN. 18.3 GAL.

④ THM 200—7, THM 325—5, THM 350—6, THM 400—7
(plus enough to indicate correct level on the dipstick)

⑤ Refer to underhood tune-up/certification decal

ELECTRICAL SECTION

Miniaturized fuse block

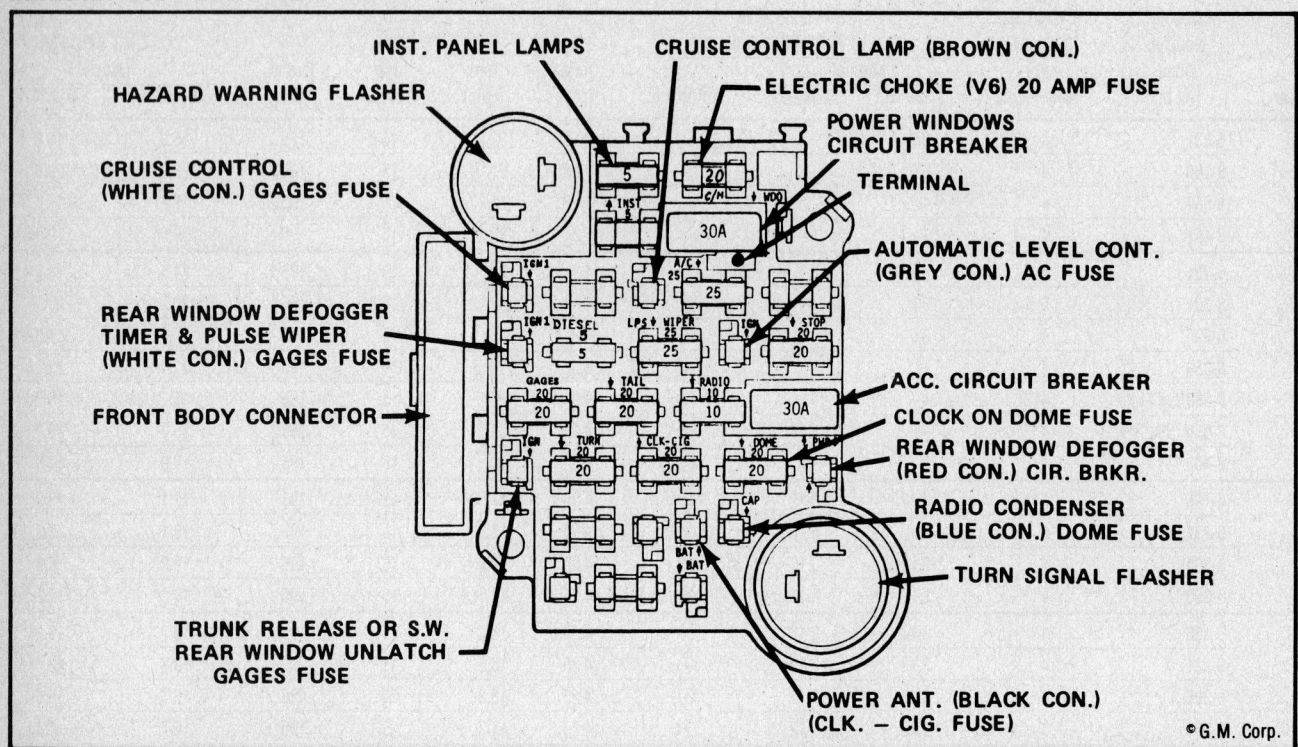

INST. PANEL LAMPS

CRUISE CONTROL LAMP (BROWN CON.)

HAZARD WARNING FLASHER

ELECTRIC CHOKE (V6) 20 AMP FUSE

POWER WINDOWS CIRCUIT BREAKER

CRUISE CONTROL (WHITE CON.) GAGES FUSE

TERMINAL

AUTOMATIC LEVEL CONT. (GREY CON.) AC FUSE

REAR WINDOW DEFOGGER TIMER & PULSE WIPER (WHITE CON.) GAGES FUSE

FRONT BODY CONNECTOR

ACC. CIRCUIT BREAKER

CLOCK ON DOME FUSE

REAR WINDOW DEFOGGER (RED CON.) CIR. BRKR.

RADIO CONDENSER (BLUE CON.) DOME FUSE

TURN SIGNAL FLASHER

TRUNK RELEASE OR S.W. REAR WINDOW UNLATCH GAGES FUSE

POWER ANT. (BLACK CON.) (CLK. – CIG. FUSE)

© G.M. Corp.

Optional connectors

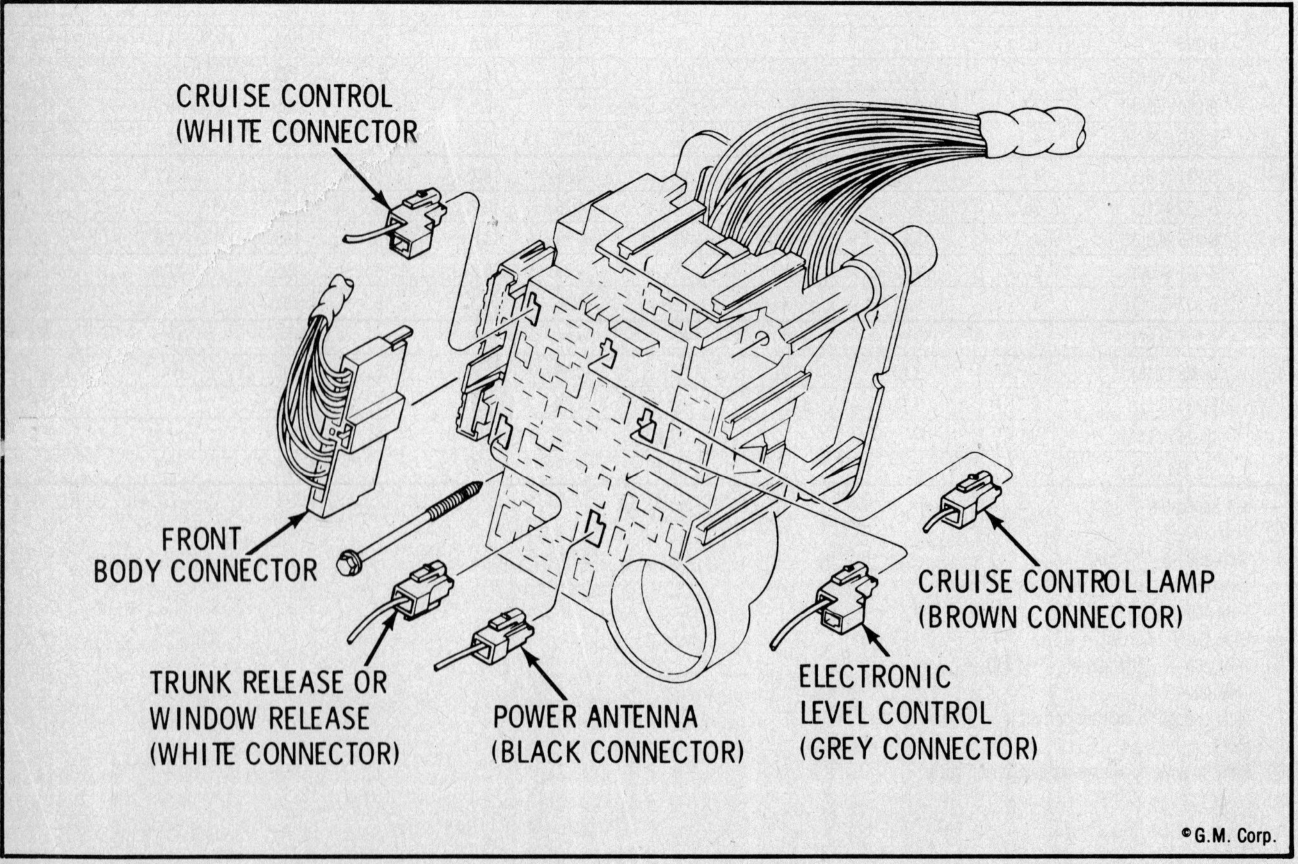

CRUISE CONTROL (WHITE CONNECTOR)

FRONT BODY CONNECTOR

TRUNK RELEASE OR WINDOW RELEASE (WHITE CONNECTOR)

POWER ANTENNA (BLACK CONNECTOR)

ELECTRONIC LEVEL CONTROL (GREY CONNECTOR)

CRUISE CONTROL LAMP (BROWN CONNECTOR)

© G.M. Corp.

Starter

- Disconnect electrical wiring, remove flywheel inspection cover and remove mounting bolts.
- If the original starter is being installed, put all the mounting pad shims back in their original locations. With a new starter, use shims to establish a clearance of 0.025-0.060 inch between the tip of one pinion tooth and the root between two flywheel teeth.

Starter Noise
Diagnostic Procedure

- If there is starter noise during cranking, remove 1-.015″ double shim or add single .015″ shim to outer bolt only.
- If there is a high pitched whine after engine fires, add .015″ double shims until noise disappears.

Miniaturized fuse

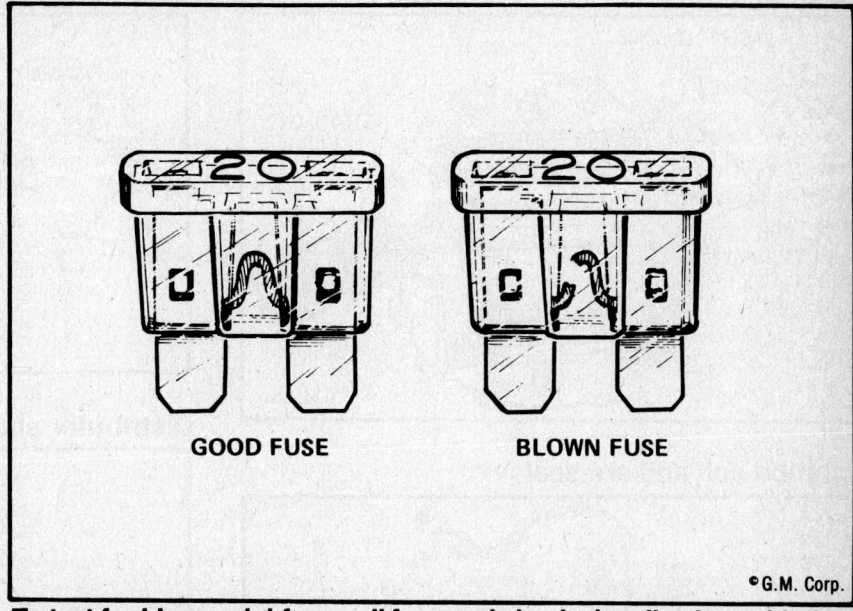

GOOD FUSE   BLOWN FUSE

© G.M. Corp.

To test for blown mini-fuse pull fuse and check visually, then with the circuit activated, use a test light across the points shown.

Starter mountings

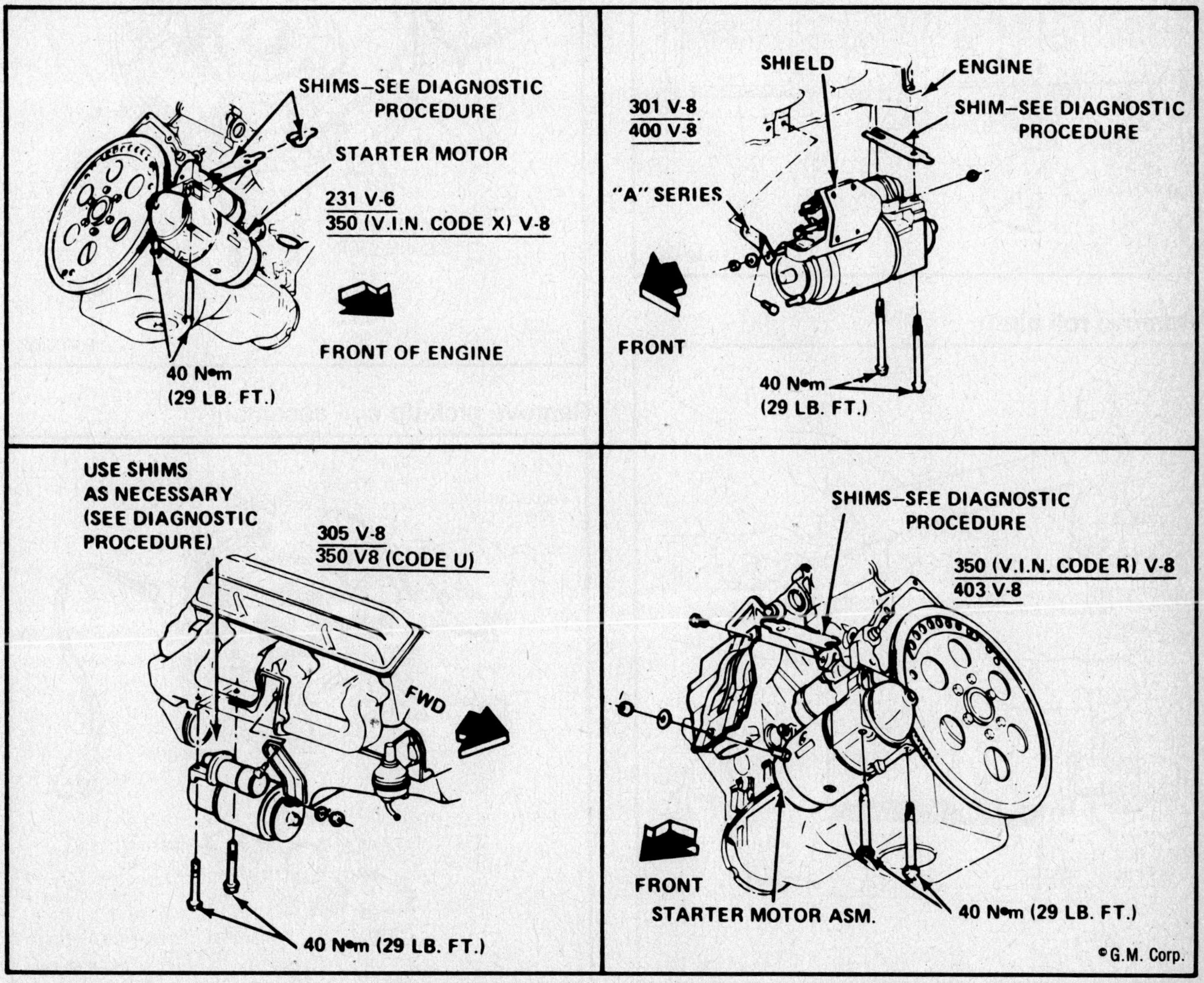

SHIMS—SEE DIAGNOSTIC PROCEDURE STARTER MOTOR 231 V-6 350 (V.I.N. CODE X) V-8 FRONT OF ENGINE 40 N•m (29 LB. FT.)	SHIELD ENGINE 301 V-8 400 V-8 SHIM—SEE DIAGNOSTIC PROCEDURE "A" SERIES FRONT 40 N•m (29 LB. FT.)
USE SHIMS AS NECESSARY (SEE DIAGNOSTIC PROCEDURE) 305 V-8 350 V8 (CODE U) FWD 40 N•m (29 LB. FT.)	SHIMS—SEE DIAGNOSTIC PROCEDURE 350 (V.I.N. CODE R) V-8 403 V-8 FRONT STARTER MOTOR ASM. 40 N•m (29 LB. FT.) © G.M. Corp.

BUICK
EXCEPT CENTURY (FRONT WHEEL DRIVE), SKYHAWK & '80-'82 SKYLARK

Ignition coil mounting

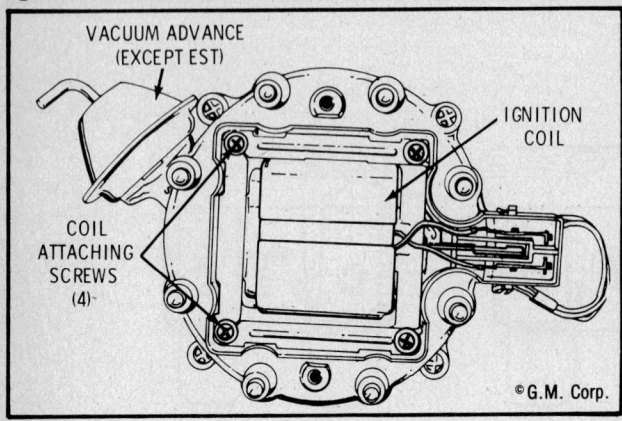

V-8 distributor (shaft removed)

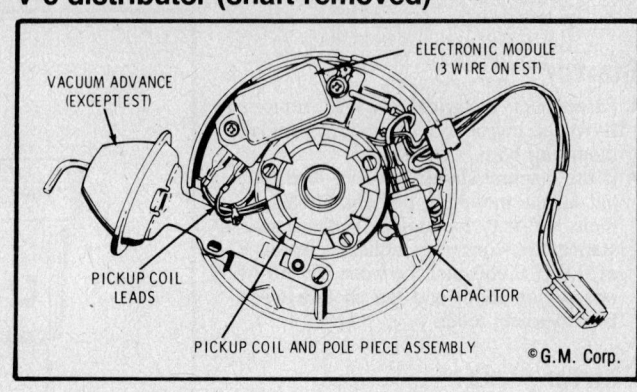

Ignition coil and arc seal

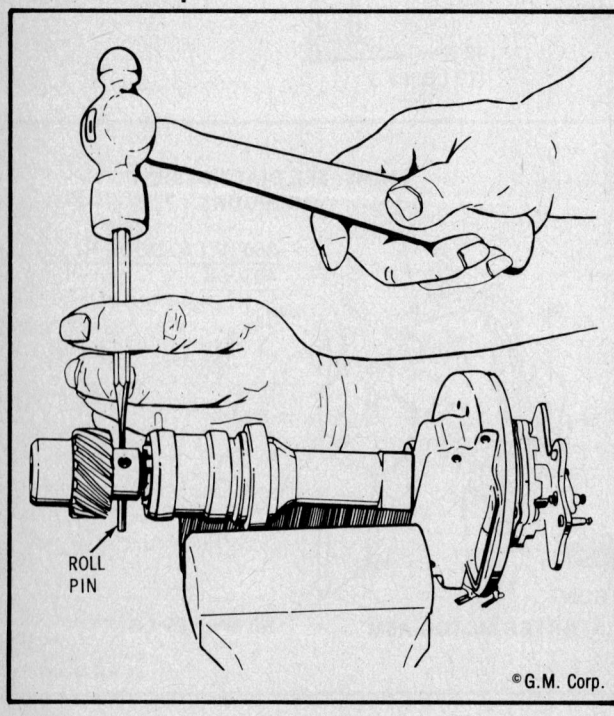

Distributor shaft removed

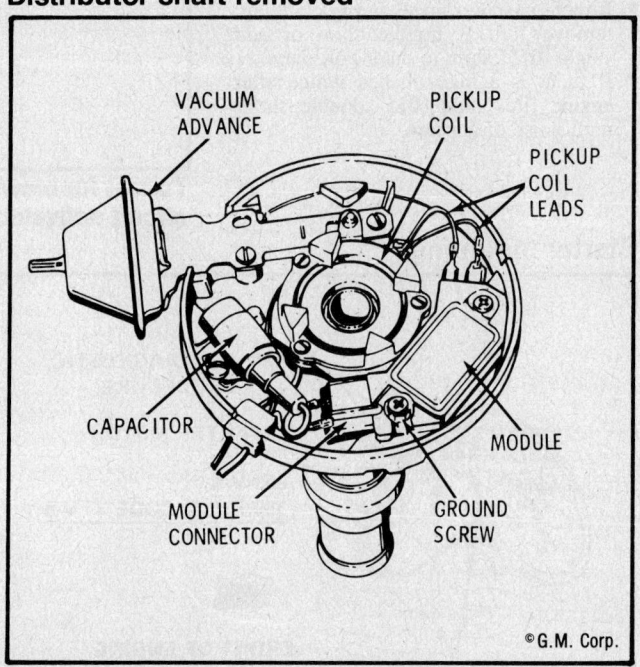

Remove roll pin

Remove pick-up coil assembly

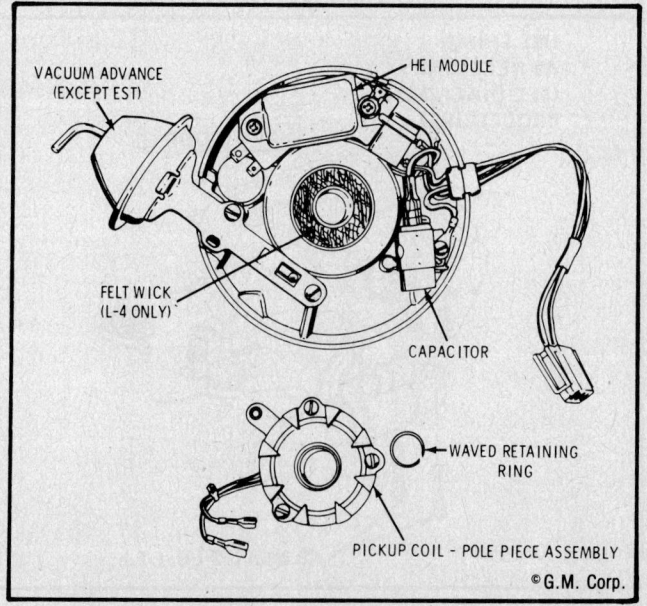

A88

Ignition Distributor

- Remove distributor cap, electrical wiring, vacuum hose, etc. from the distributor.
- Put alignment marks on rotor and distributor housing for installation reference.
- Remove the hold-down device, and pull the distributor up out of the engine.
- After installation, set ignition timing.

Ignition Lock

CHILTON CAUTION: *Disconnect the battery positive cable to insure against accidental deployment of the air cushion restraint system on cars so equipped.*

- Remove the steering wheel and lock plate, and pull the turn signal switch up out of the way.
- With key cylinder in LOCK position, depress retaining tab and pull lock cylinder out of housing.
- To install, turn the key fully clockwise to stop. Insert cylinder into housing until it bottoms, then turn key counterclockwise with slight inward pressure until drive section clicks into drive shaft.

Ignition Switch

CHILTON CAUTION: *Disconnect the battery positive cable to insure against*

Remove and install ignition lock

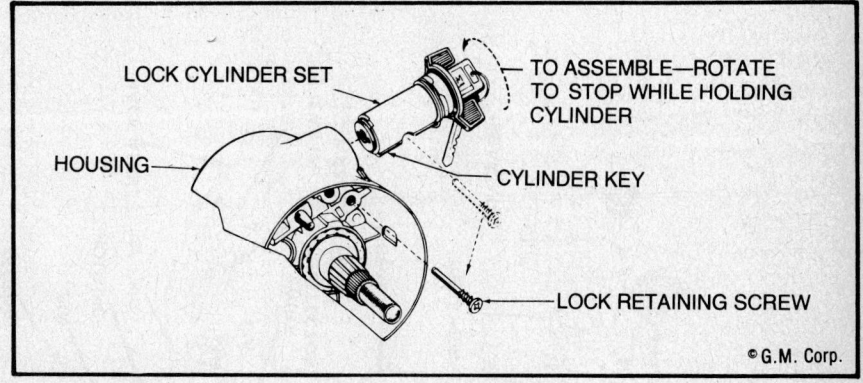

LOCK CYLINDER SET

HOUSING

TO ASSEMBLE—ROTATE TO STOP WHILE HOLDING CYLINDER

CYLINDER KEY

LOCK RETAINING SCREW

© G.M. Corp.

accidental deployment of the air cushion restraint system on cars so equipped.

- The ignition switch is mounted on the lower section of the steering column. The column must be lowered for switch replacement.
- Disconnect the shift indicator linkage and lower the steering column.
- Disconnect actuator rod and electrical connection.

Neutral Safety Switch

CHILTON CAUTION: *Disconnect the battery positive cable to insure against accidental deployment of the air cushion restraint system on cars so equipped.*

Automatic Transmission

- The switch is located on the lower section of the steering column. Vehicles with no switches utilize a mechanical lockout system located inside the column.

Manual Transmission

- The switch is located on the clutch pedal bracket, and allows the engine start circuit to activate only when the clutch pedal is depressed.

Steering column wiring connections showing neutral start switch and ignition switch

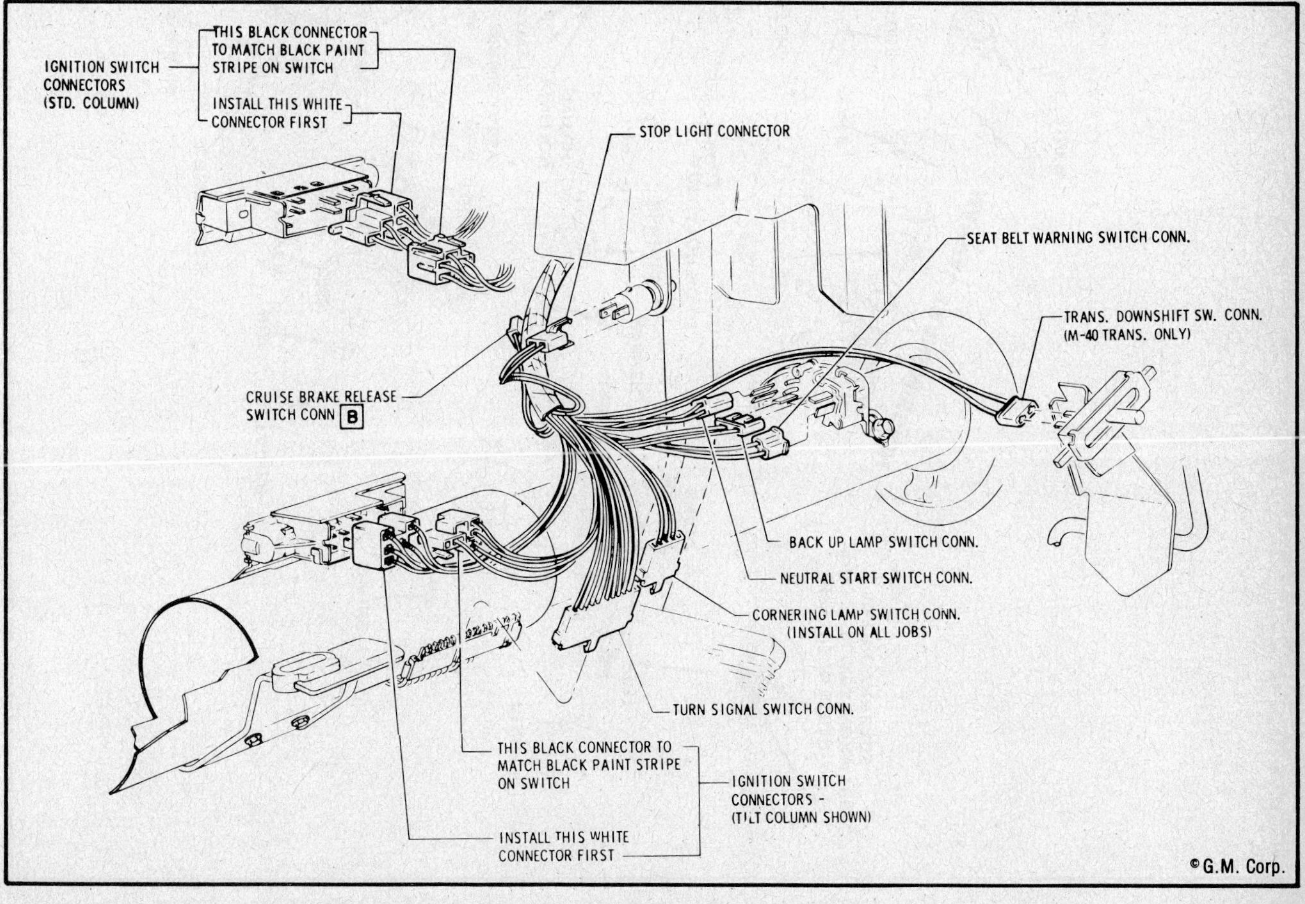

IGNITION SWITCH CONNECTORS (STD. COLUMN)

THIS BLACK CONNECTOR TO MATCH BLACK PAINT STRIPE ON SWITCH

INSTALL THIS WHITE CONNECTOR FIRST

STOP LIGHT CONNECTOR

SEAT BELT WARNING SWITCH CONN.

TRANS. DOWNSHIFT SW. CONN. (M-40 TRANS. ONLY)

CRUISE BRAKE RELEASE SWITCH CONN. B

BACK UP LAMP SWITCH CONN.

NEUTRAL START SWITCH CONN.

CORNERING LAMP SWITCH CONN. (INSTALL ON ALL JOBS)

TURN SIGNAL SWITCH CONN.

THIS BLACK CONNECTOR TO MATCH BLACK PAINT STRIPE ON SWITCH

IGNITION SWITCH CONNECTORS - (TILT COLUMN SHOWN)

INSTALL THIS WHITE CONNECTOR FIRST

© G.M. Corp.

A89

Buick regular column and electrical components

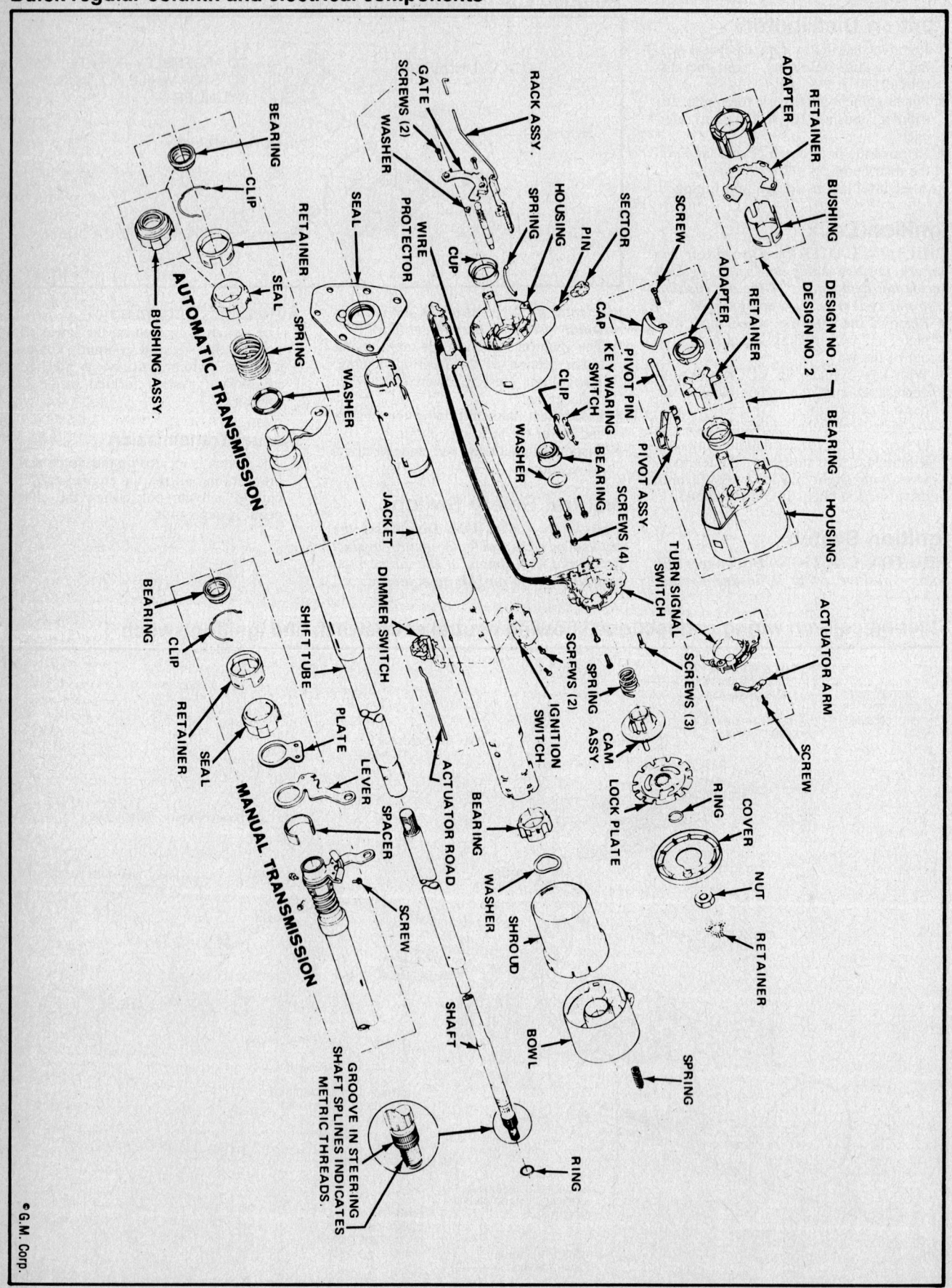

Back-up Light Switch Automatic Transmission

Installation (With AU4)

- Position shift lever in neutral gate notch.
- Assemble the switch to the column by inserting the switch carrier tang in the shift tube slot and fasten in position by assembling mounting screws to retainers.

NOTE: The switch is pinned in neutral position with plastic shear pin, no additional pinning is required for installation.

Reset Installation Procedure

- Position shift lever in neutral gate notch.
- Loosen attaching screws.
- Rotate switch on column and insert 2.34mm diameter gauge pin into neutral gauge hole.
- Tighten attaching screws.
- Remove 2.43mm diameter gauge pin.

Installation (Less AU4)

- Position shift lever in park gate notch.
- Assemble the switch to the column by inserting the switch carrier tang in the shift tube slot and fasten in position by assembling mounting screws to retainers.

Reset Installation Procedure

- Position shift lever in lock position.
- Loosen attaching screws.
- Rotate switch on column and insert 2.43mm diameter gauge pin into park gauge hole.
- Tighten attaching screws.
- Remove 2.43mm diameter gauge pin.

Back-up light switch automatic transmission

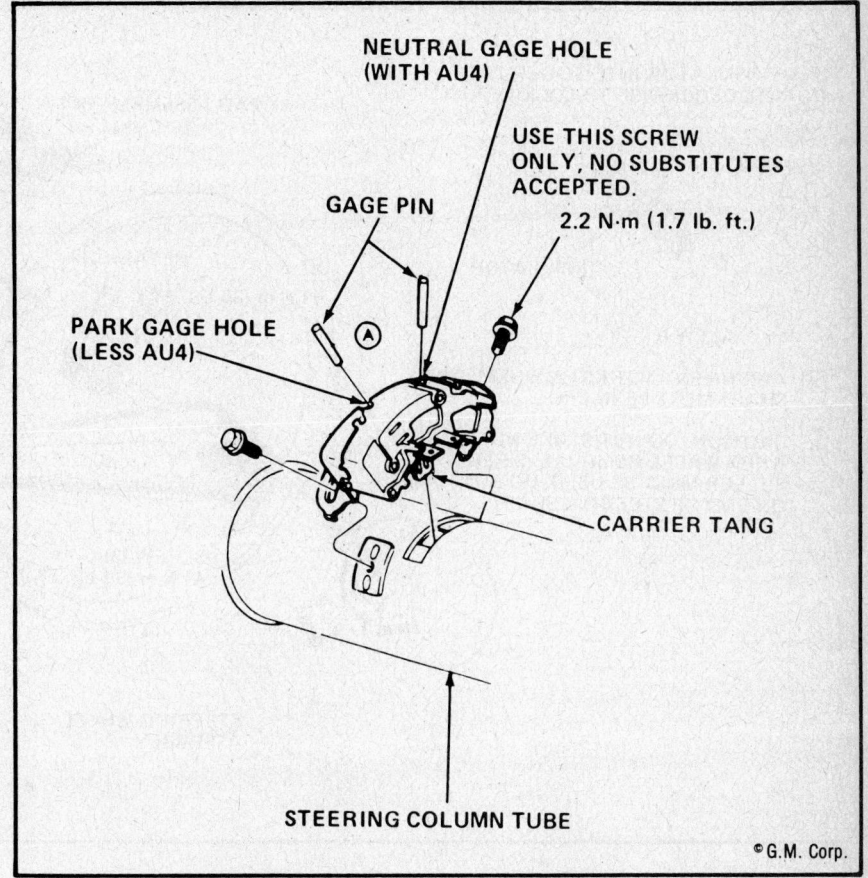

NEUTRAL GAGE HOLE (WITH AU4)

GAGE PIN

USE THIS SCREW ONLY, NO SUBSTITUTES ACCEPTED.
2.2 N·m (1.7 lb. ft.)

PARK GAGE HOLE (LESS AU4)

Ⓐ

CARRIER TANG

STEERING COLUMN TUBE

© G.M. Corp.

Back-up light switch manual transmission

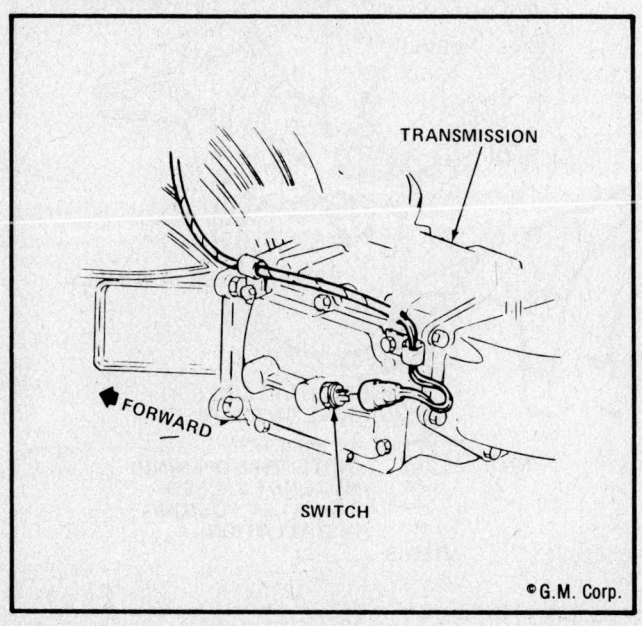

TRANSMISSION

FORWARD

SWITCH

© G.M. Corp.

Stoplight switch adjustment

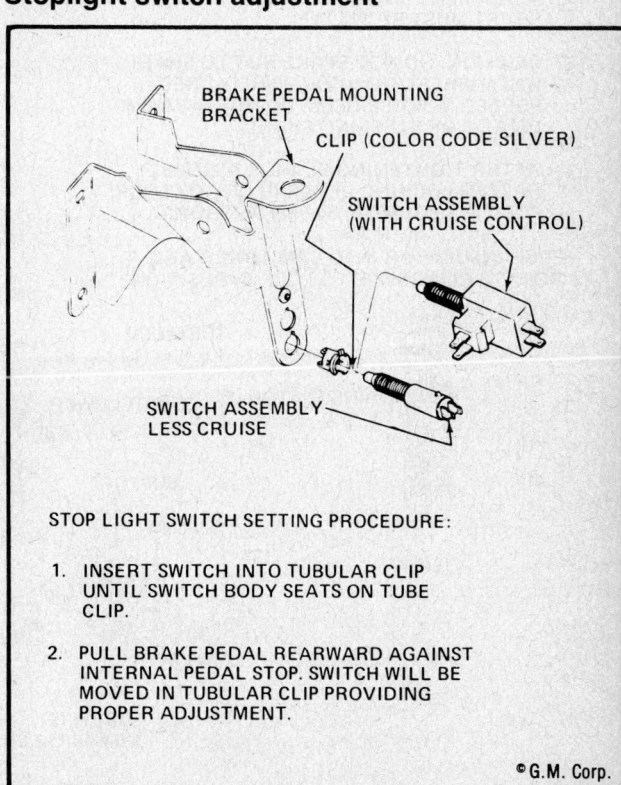

BRAKE PEDAL MOUNTING BRACKET

CLIP (COLOR CODE SILVER)

SWITCH ASSEMBLY (WITH CRUISE CONTROL)

SWITCH ASSEMBLY LESS CRUISE

STOP LIGHT SWITCH SETTING PROCEDURE:

1. INSERT SWITCH INTO TUBULAR CLIP UNTIL SWITCH BODY SEATS ON TUBE CLIP.

2. PULL BRAKE PEDAL REARWARD AGAINST INTERNAL PEDAL STOP. SWITCH WILL BE MOVED IN TUBULAR CLIP PROVIDING PROPER ADJUSTMENT.

© G.M. Corp.

BUICK
EXCEPT CENTURY (FRONT WHEEL DRIVE), SKYHAWK & '80-'82 SKYLARK

Standard steering wheel

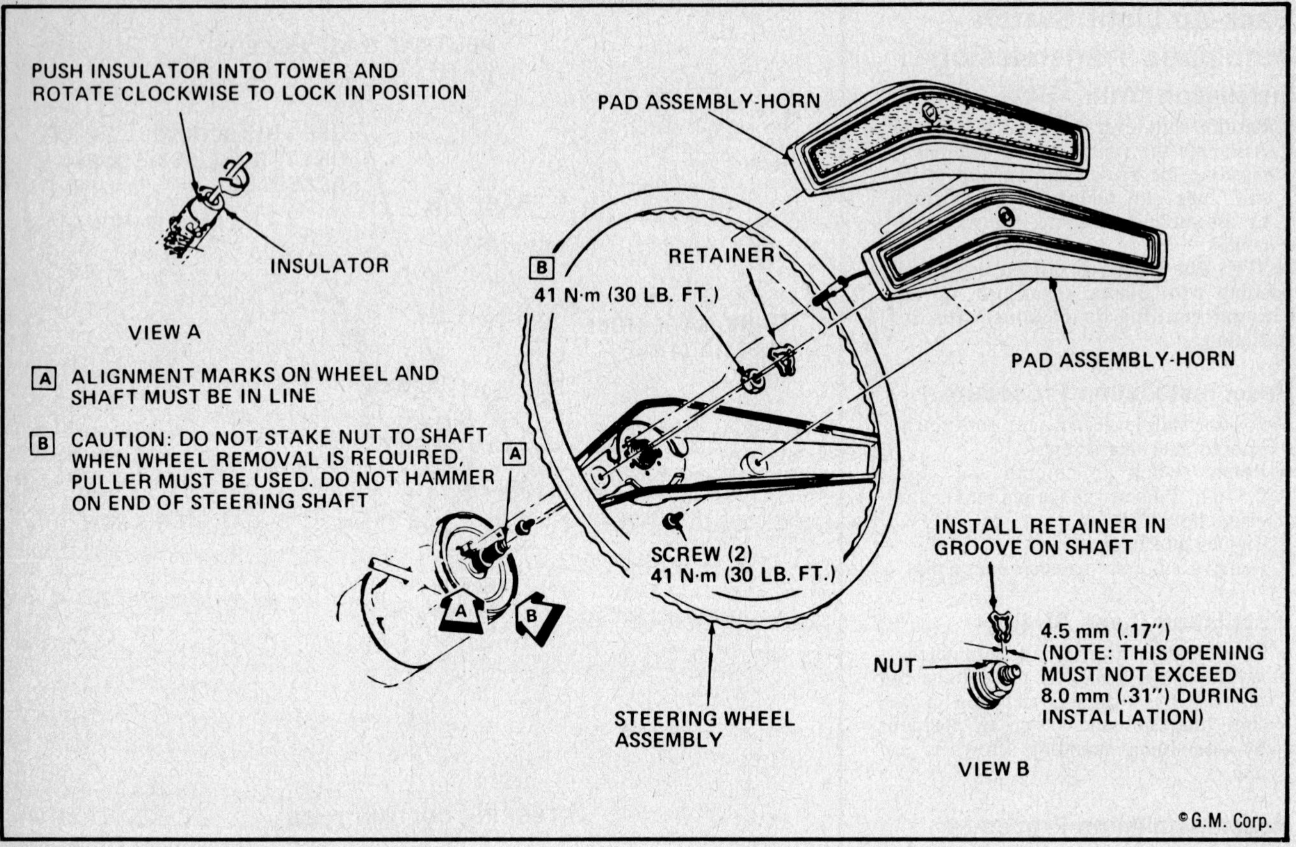

PUSH INSULATOR INTO TOWER AND ROTATE CLOCKWISE TO LOCK IN POSITION

INSULATOR

VIEW A

PAD ASSEMBLY-HORN

B RETAINER
41 N·m (30 LB. FT.)

PAD ASSEMBLY-HORN

A ALIGNMENT MARKS ON WHEEL AND SHAFT MUST BE IN LINE

B CAUTION: DO NOT STAKE NUT TO SHAFT WHEN WHEEL REMOVAL IS REQUIRED, PULLER MUST BE USED. DO NOT HAMMER ON END OF STEERING SHAFT

A B

SCREW (2)
41 N·m (30 LB. FT.)

STEERING WHEEL ASSEMBLY

INSTALL RETAINER IN GROOVE ON SHAFT

4.5 mm (.17")
(NOTE: THIS OPENING MUST NOT EXCEED 8.0 mm (.31") DURING INSTALLATION)

NUT

VIEW B

© G.M. Corp.

Tilt and telescoping steering wheel

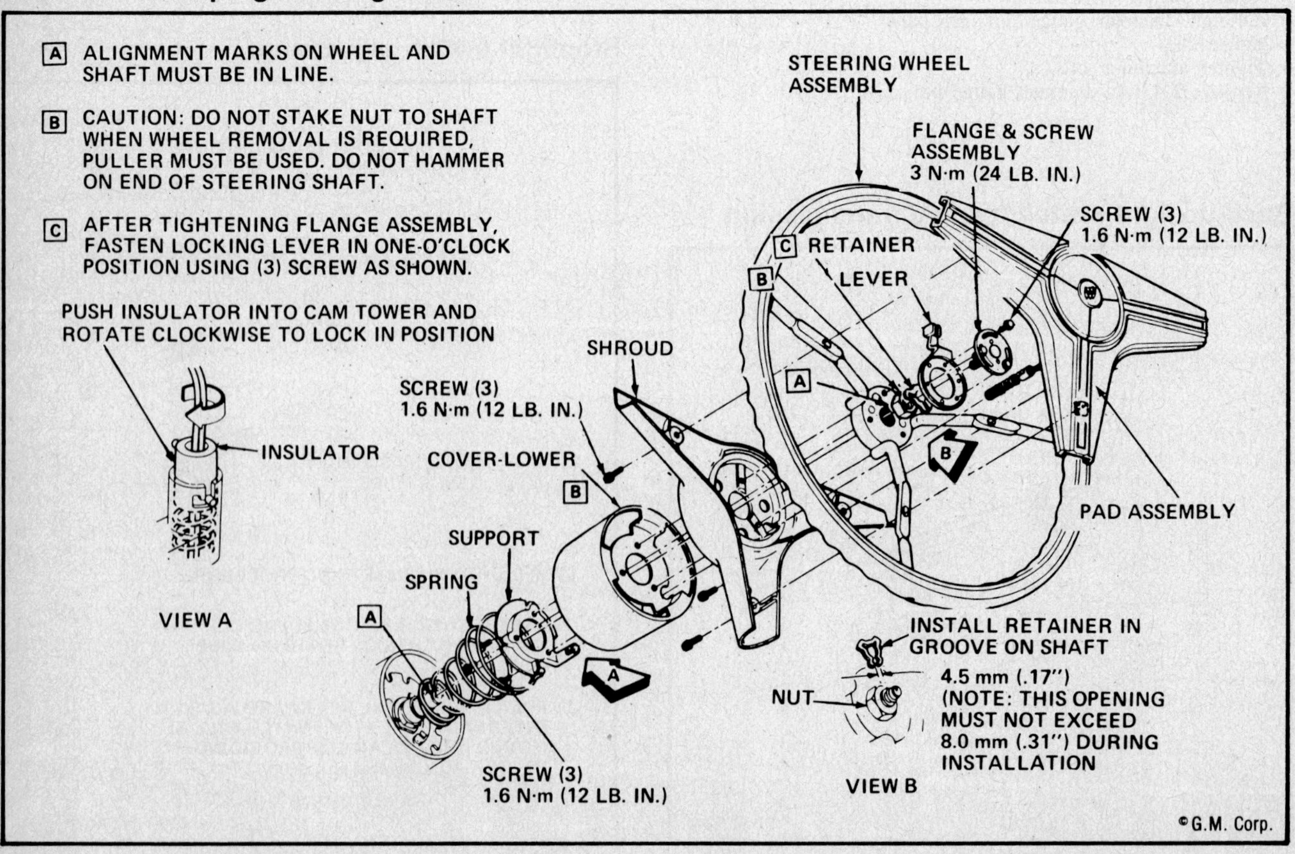

A ALIGNMENT MARKS ON WHEEL AND SHAFT MUST BE IN LINE.

B CAUTION: DO NOT STAKE NUT TO SHAFT WHEN WHEEL REMOVAL IS REQUIRED, PULLER MUST BE USED. DO NOT HAMMER ON END OF STEERING SHAFT.

C AFTER TIGHTENING FLANGE ASSEMBLY, FASTEN LOCKING LEVER IN ONE-O'CLOCK POSITION USING (3) SCREW AS SHOWN.

PUSH INSULATOR INTO CAM TOWER AND ROTATE CLOCKWISE TO LOCK IN POSITION

INSULATOR

VIEW A

SCREW (3)
1.6 N·m (12 LB. IN.)

COVER-LOWER

SUPPORT

SPRING

A

SCREW (3)
1.6 N·m (12 LB. IN.)

STEERING WHEEL ASSEMBLY

FLANGE & SCREW ASSEMBLY
3 N·m (24 LB. IN.)

SCREW (3)
1.6 N·m (12 LB. IN.)

C RETAINER

B LEVER

SHROUD

B

A

B

PAD ASSEMBLY

INSTALL RETAINER IN GROOVE ON SHAFT

4.5 mm (.17")
(NOTE: THIS OPENING MUST NOT EXCEED 8.0 mm (.31") DURING INSTALLATION

NUT

VIEW B

© G.M. Corp.

A92

Typical turn signal switch—tilt column

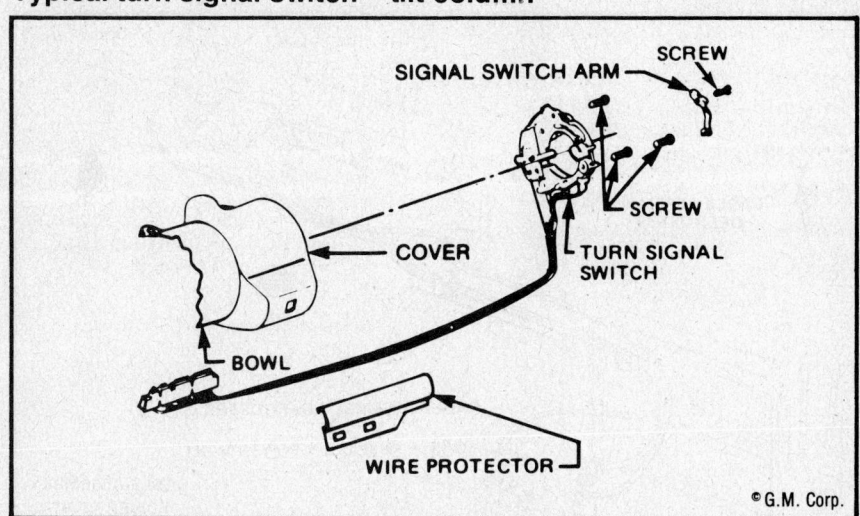

© G.M. Corp.

Turn signal wires

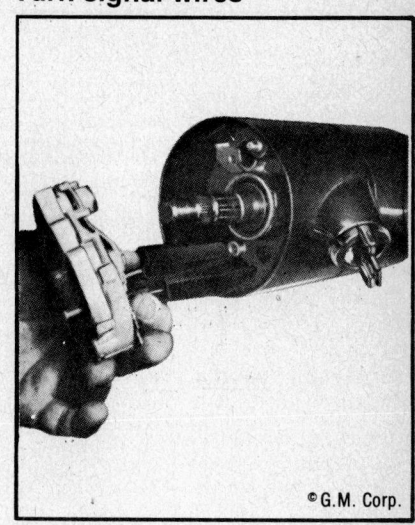

© G.M. Corp.

Turn Signal Switch

CHILTON CAUTION: Disconnect the battery positive cable to insure against accidental deployment of the air cushion restraint system on cars so equipped.

- Remove the steering wheel and lock plate cover. On tilt columns, remove the tilt lever and lower the column.
- Remove the lock plate, cancelling cam and spring, hazard warning switch, turn signal lever and switch mounting screws.
- Tape the wiring connector to prevent snagging, and pull the switch and wiring up out of the column.

Light Switch

- Relocate anything preventing access to the switch such as air conditioner ducting or trim panel.
- Place switch in full ON position. Pull on knob and press shaft release button to release shaft and knob assembly.
- Separate switch from mounting bracket.

Windshield Wiper Switch

- Relocate anything preventing access to the switch such as trim panel, light switch or air conditioner ducting.
- Separate switch from instrument panel and electrical wiring.

Windshield Wiper Motor

- Remove the cowl screen, and separate the motor from mounts, electrical connections, linkage, etc.
- Motor must be in "Park" position when assembling crank arm to drive link in vehicles using a round motor.

Windshield Wiper Linkage

- Remove the cowl vent screen and remove wiper arms.
- Separate linkage from motor and mounts

Steering column mounted headlight dimmer switch

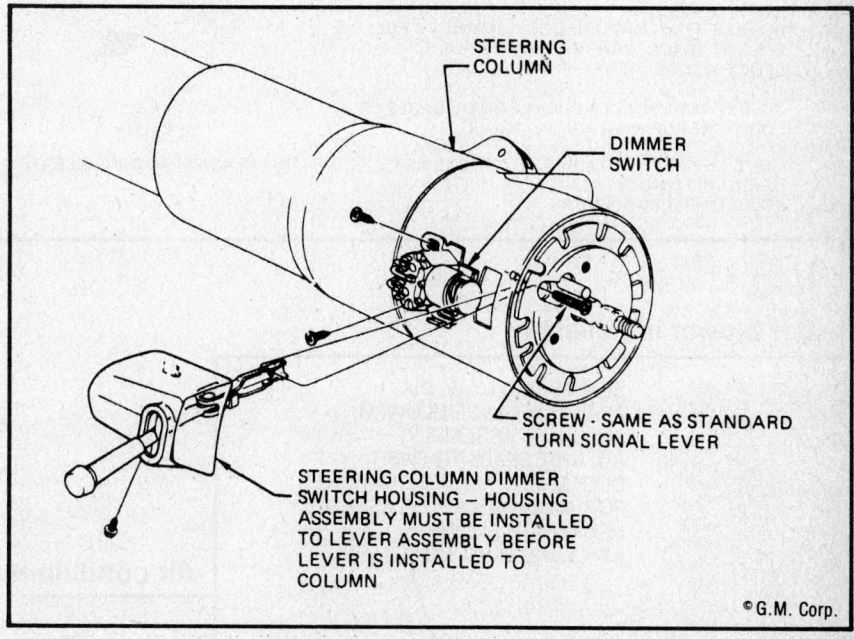

© G.M. Corp.

and guide it out through the cowl opening.

Windshield Wiper Arms

- On car using rectangular motor, place motor in "Park" position and pry arm off drive shaft.
- On car using a round motor, release whatever holding device is employed and lift arm off drive shaft.

Windshield Wiper Blades

- Trigger the release device and slide the blade off the wiper arm.
- Remove mounting screws, knobs, etc., and remove radio from antenna, power and speaker connections.

Radio

- Relocate anything preventing full access to radio such as air conditioner ducting, ash tray, instrument panel trim, etc.

Temperature Control Unit/Blower Switch

- Relocate anything preventing access to the control unit such as trim panel, radio, etc.
- Remove mounting screws, pull control unit out and separate it from control cables, vacuum lines and electrical connections.

Heater control cables

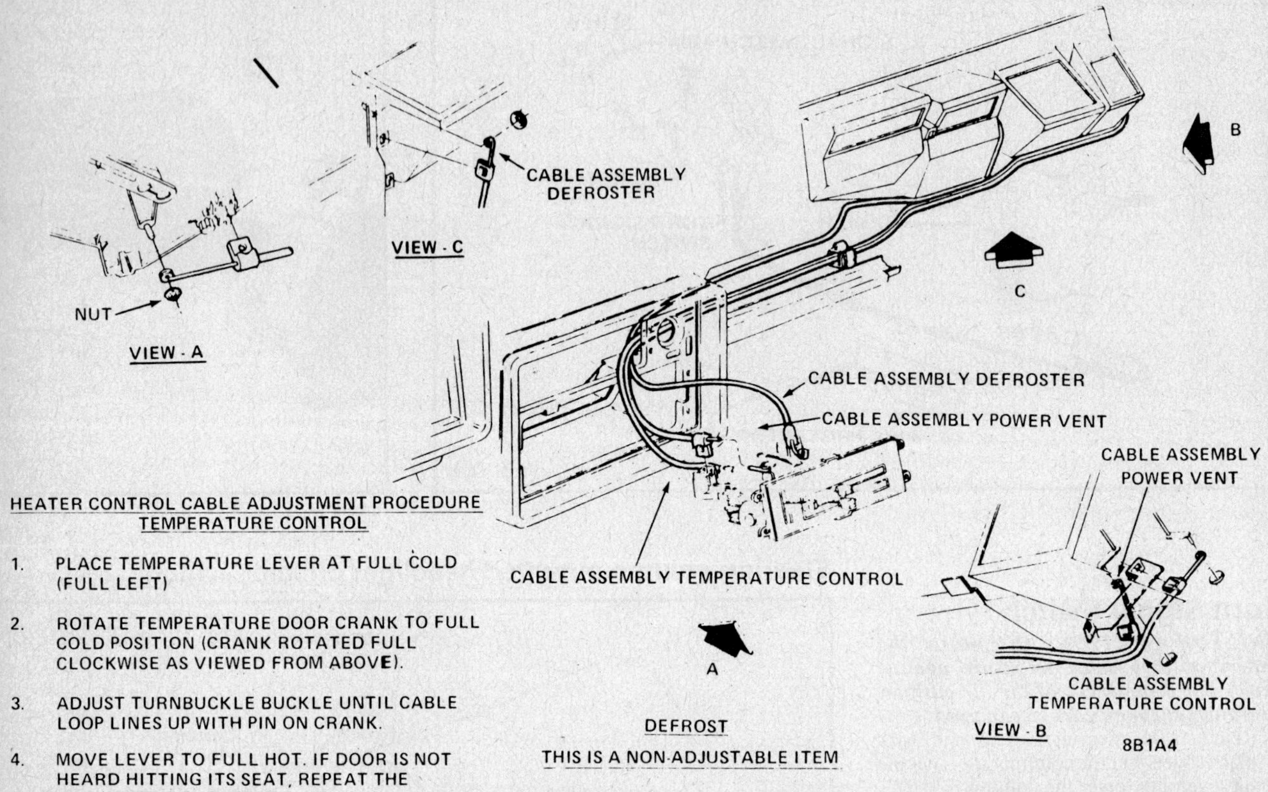

CABLE ASSEMBLY DEFROSTER

VIEW - C

NUT

VIEW - A

B

C

CABLE ASSEMBLY DEFROSTER

CABLE ASSEMBLY POWER VENT

CABLE ASSEMBLY POWER VENT

HEATER CONTROL CABLE ADJUSTMENT PROCEDURE
TEMPERATURE CONTROL

1. PLACE TEMPERATURE LEVER AT FULL COLD
    (FULL LEFT)

2. ROTATE TEMPERATURE DOOR CRANK TO FULL
    COLD POSITION (CRANK ROTATED FULL
    CLOCKWISE AS VIEWED FROM ABOVE).

3. ADJUST TURNBUCKLE BUCKLE UNTIL CABLE
    LOOP LINES UP WITH PIN ON CRANK.

4. MOVE LEVER TO FULL HOT. IF DOOR IS NOT
    HEARD HITTING ITS SEAT, REPEAT THE
    ADJUSTMENT PROCEDURE.

CABLE ASSEMBLY TEMPERATURE CONTROL

A

DEFROST
THIS IS A NON-ADJUSTABLE ITEM

CABLE ASSEMBLY
TEMPERATURE CONTROL

VIEW - B   8B1A4

© G.M. Corp.

Heater blower installation

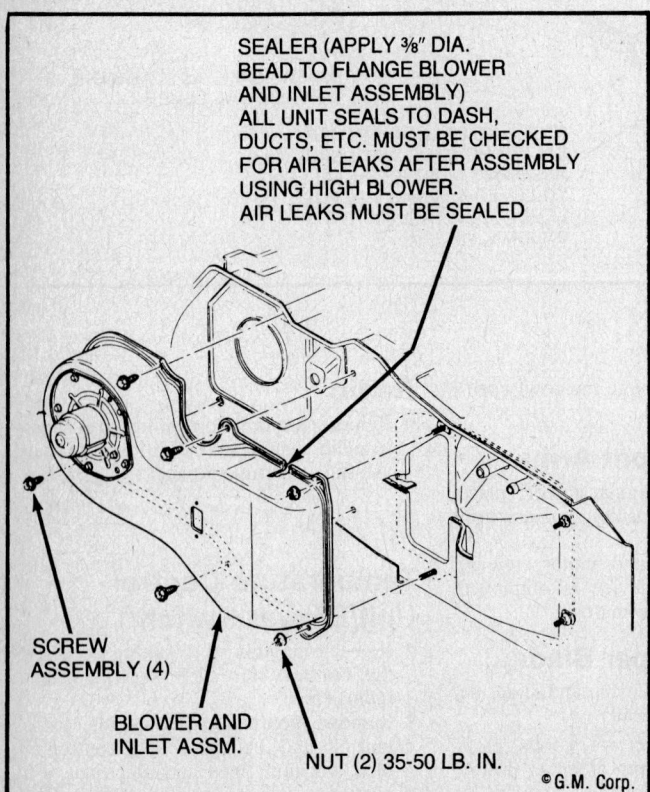

SEALER (APPLY ⅜" DIA.
BEAD TO FLANGE BLOWER
AND INLET ASSEMBLY)
ALL UNIT SEALS TO DASH,
DUCTS, ETC. MUST BE CHECKED
FOR AIR LEAKS AFTER ASSEMBLY
USING HIGH BLOWER.
AIR LEAKS MUST BE SEALED

SCREW
ASSEMBLY (4)

BLOWER AND
INLET ASSM.

NUT (2) 35-50 LB. IN.

© G.M. Corp.

Heater Blower

- Disconnect mounts and electrical connection, and remove blower and motor.
- On the Apollo and Skylark, remove all fender skirt attaching bolts except those attaching to radiator. Place a wooden block between the skirt and fender for blower removal clearance.
- Some Riviera models may require the hood hinge extension be removed for clearance.

Air conditioner control unit vacuum harness

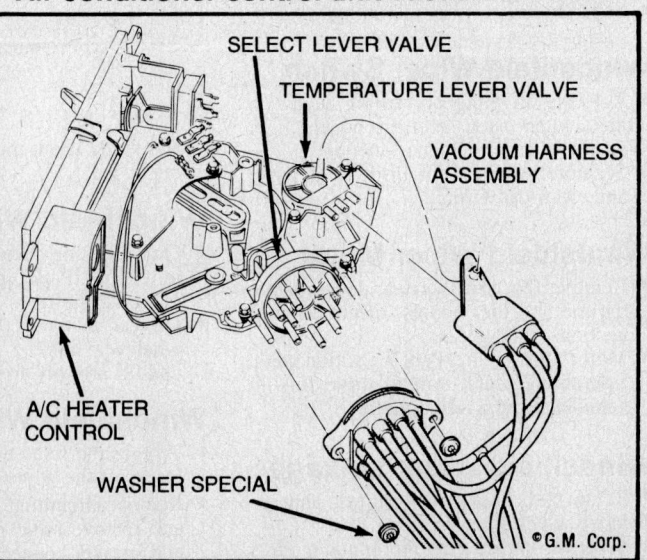

SELECT LEVER VALVE

TEMPERATURE LEVER VALVE

VACUUM HARNESS
ASSEMBLY

A/C HEATER
CONTROL

WASHER SPECIAL

© G.M. Corp.

Heater Core

- Drain the cooling system, disconnect heater hoses etc.
- Under the instrument panel, remove air conditioner ducting, and disconnect cables, vacuum lines and electrical leads from the heater assembly.
- Remove mounting nuts, and work heater assembly rearward and out of the car.
- Separate the heater and core.
- When installing, seal along mating surfaces between dash and heater.

Heater core and case assembly

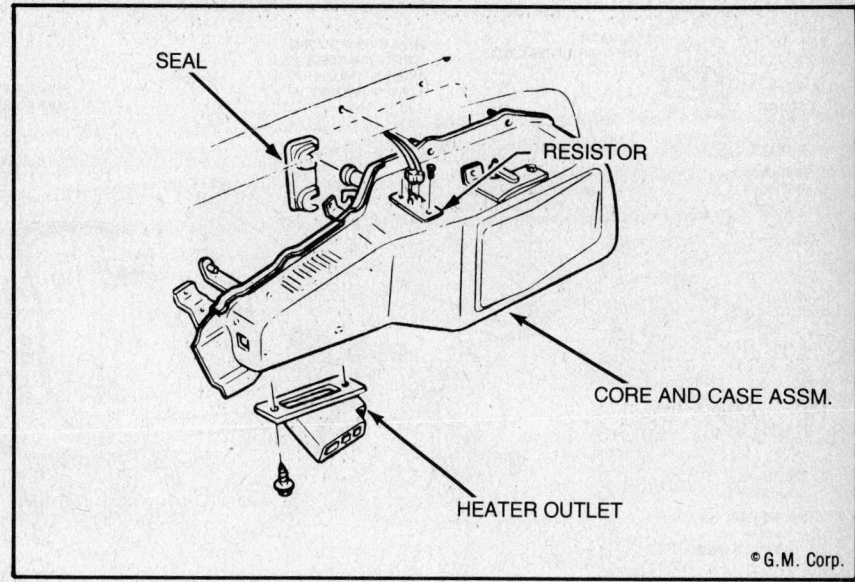

SEAL

RESISTOR

CORE AND CASE ASSM.

HEATER OUTLET

© G.M. Corp.

Air conditioner/heater core and case in compact car model

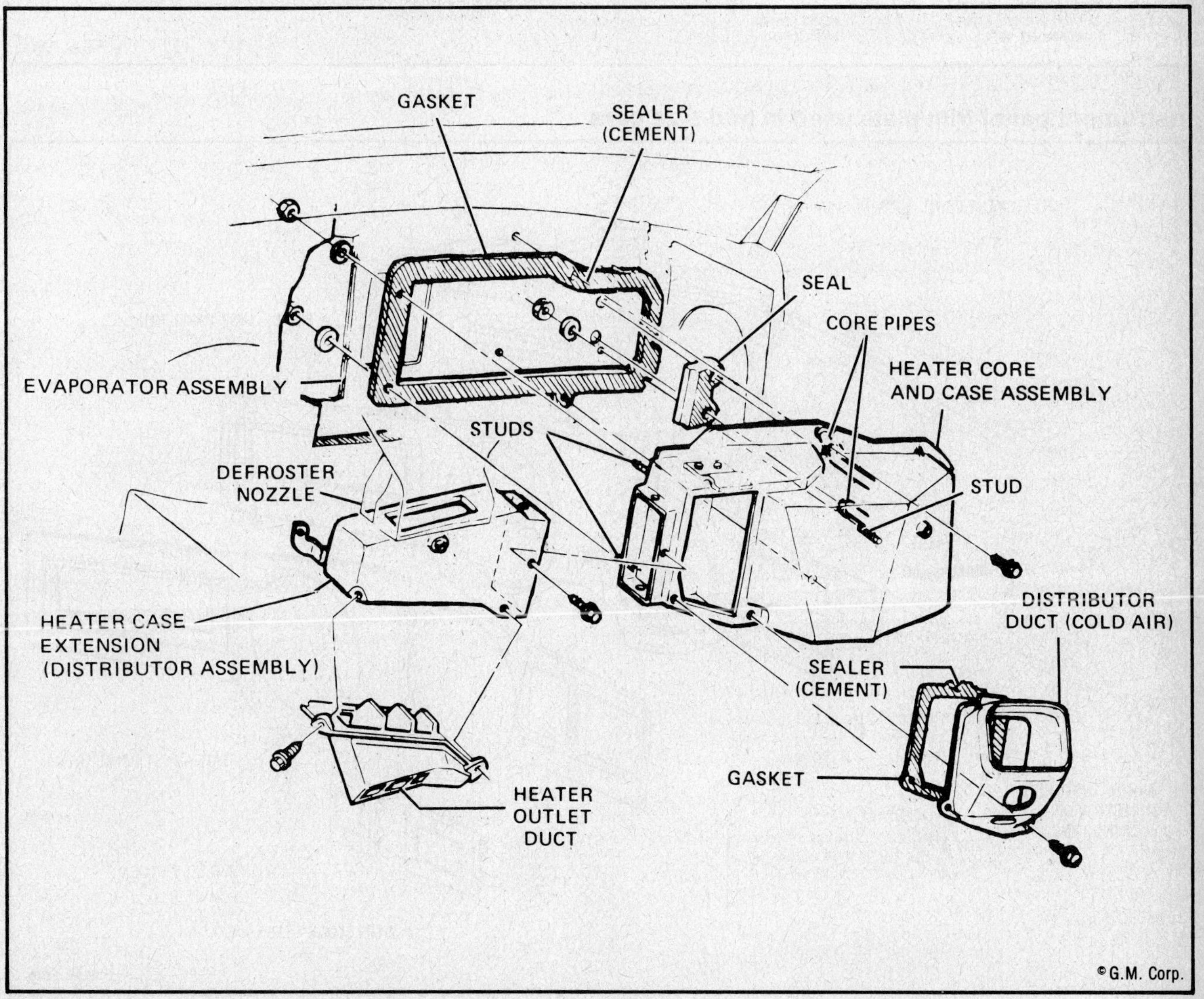

GASKET

SEALER (CEMENT)

SEAL

CORE PIPES

HEATER CORE AND CASE ASSEMBLY

EVAPORATOR ASSEMBLY

STUDS

STUD

DEFROSTER NOZZLE

DISTRIBUTOR DUCT (COLD AIR)

HEATER CASE EXTENSION (DISTRIBUTOR ASSEMBLY)

SEALER (CEMENT)

HEATER OUTLET DUCT

GASKET

© G.M. Corp.

BUICK
EXCEPT CENTURY (FRONT WHEEL DRIVE), SKYHAWK & '80-'82 SKYLARK

Instrument panel wire harness routing in full-size cars

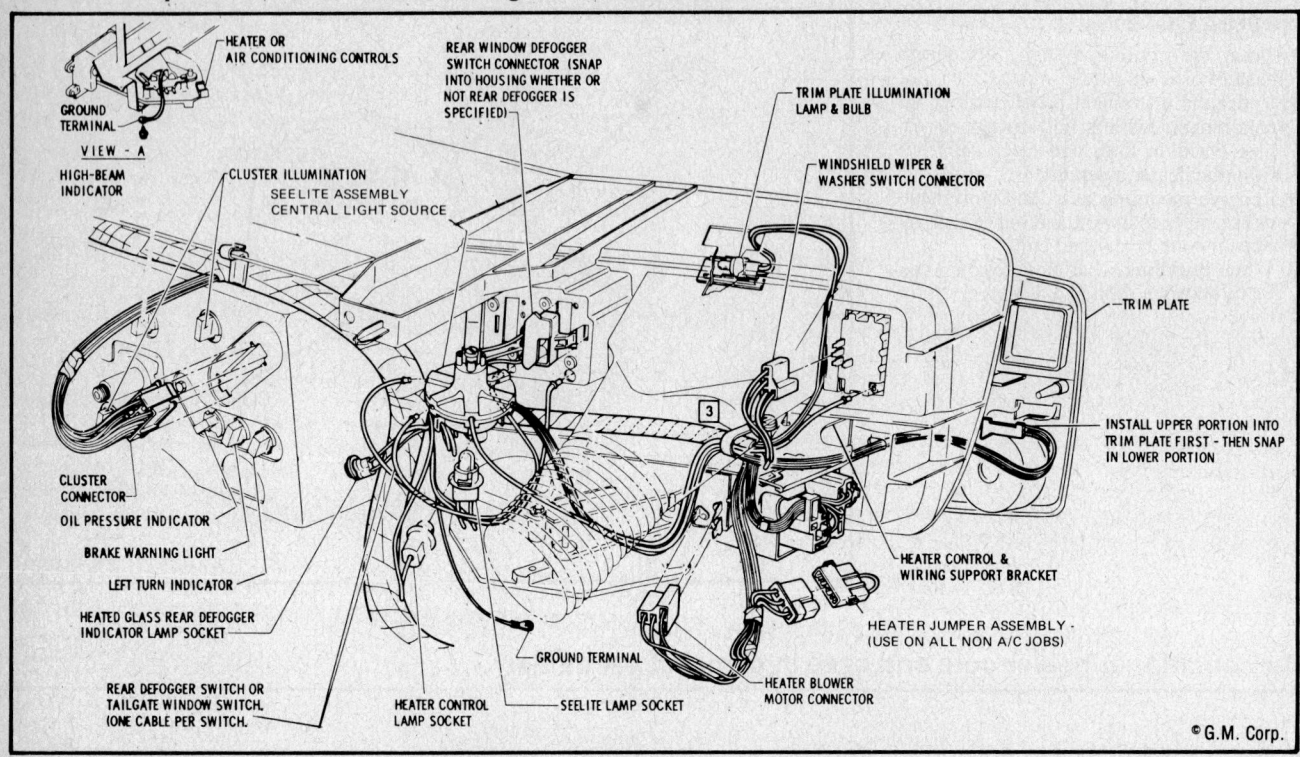

HEATER OR AIR CONDITIONING CONTROLS

GROUND TERMINAL

VIEW - A

HIGH-BEAM INDICATOR

CLUSTER ILLUMINATION
SEELITE ASSEMBLY CENTRAL LIGHT SOURCE

REAR WINDOW DEFOGGER SWITCH CONNECTOR (SNAP INTO HOUSING WHETHER OR NOT REAR DEFOGGER IS SPECIFIED)

TRIM PLATE ILLUMINATION LAMP & BULB

WINDSHIELD WIPER & WASHER SWITCH CONNECTOR

TRIM PLATE

INSTALL UPPER PORTION INTO TRIM PLATE FIRST - THEN SNAP IN LOWER PORTION

CLUSTER CONNECTOR

OIL PRESSURE INDICATOR

BRAKE WARNING LIGHT

LEFT TURN INDICATOR

HEATED GLASS REAR DEFOGGER INDICATOR LAMP SOCKET

REAR DEFOGGER SWITCH OR TAILGATE WINDOW SWITCH. (ONE CABLE PER SWITCH.

HEATER CONTROL LAMP SOCKET

SEELITE LAMP SOCKET

GROUND TERMINAL

HEATER BLOWER MOTOR CONNECTOR

HEATER CONTROL & WIRING SUPPORT BRACKET

HEATER JUMPER ASSEMBLY - (USE ON ALL NON A/C JOBS)

© G.M. Corp.

Instrument panel trim plate used in mid-size cars

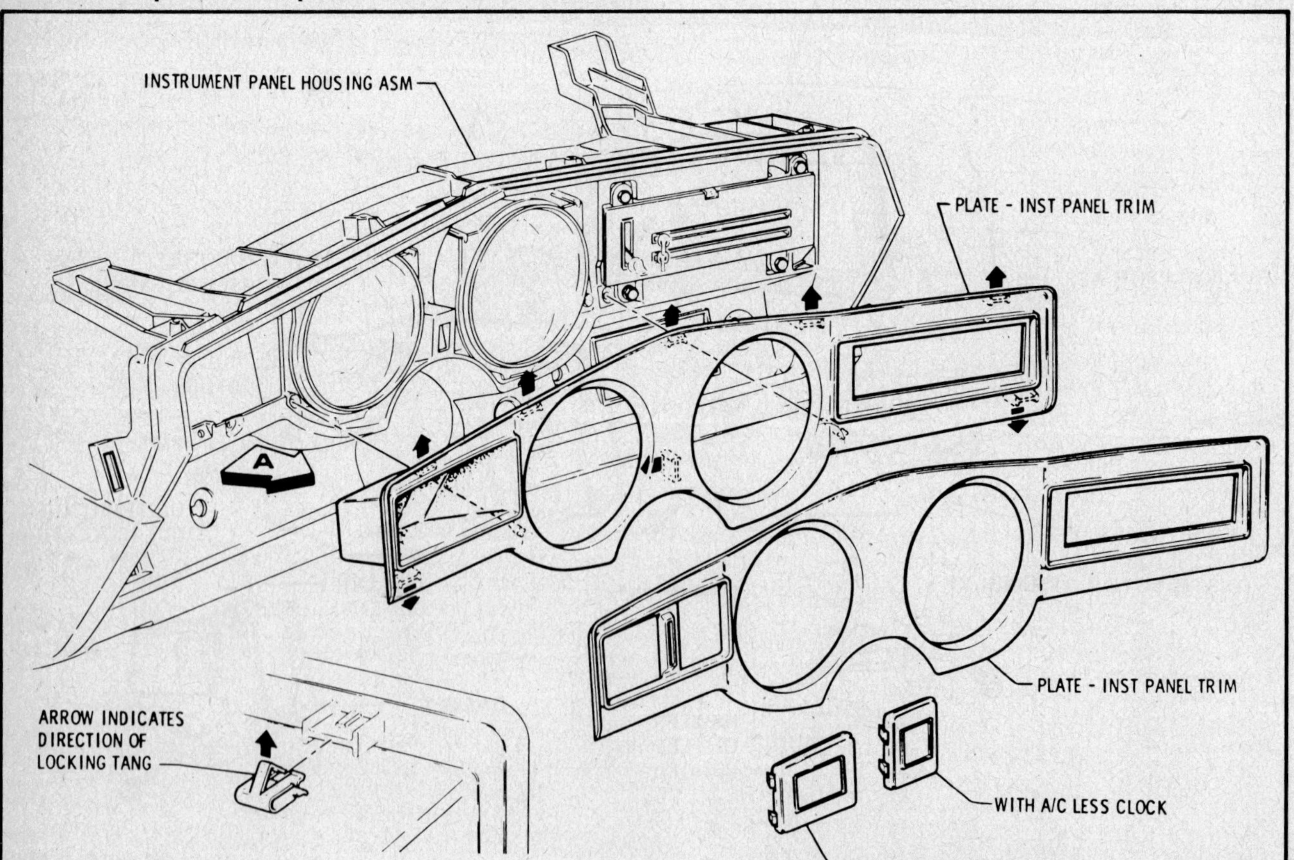

INSTRUMENT PANEL HOUSING ASM

PLATE - INST PANEL TRIM

PLATE - INST PANEL TRIM

ARROW INDICATES DIRECTION OF LOCKING TANG

WITH A/C LESS CLOCK

WITH CLOCK - LESS A/C

© G.M. Corp.

Instrument panel center full-size cars

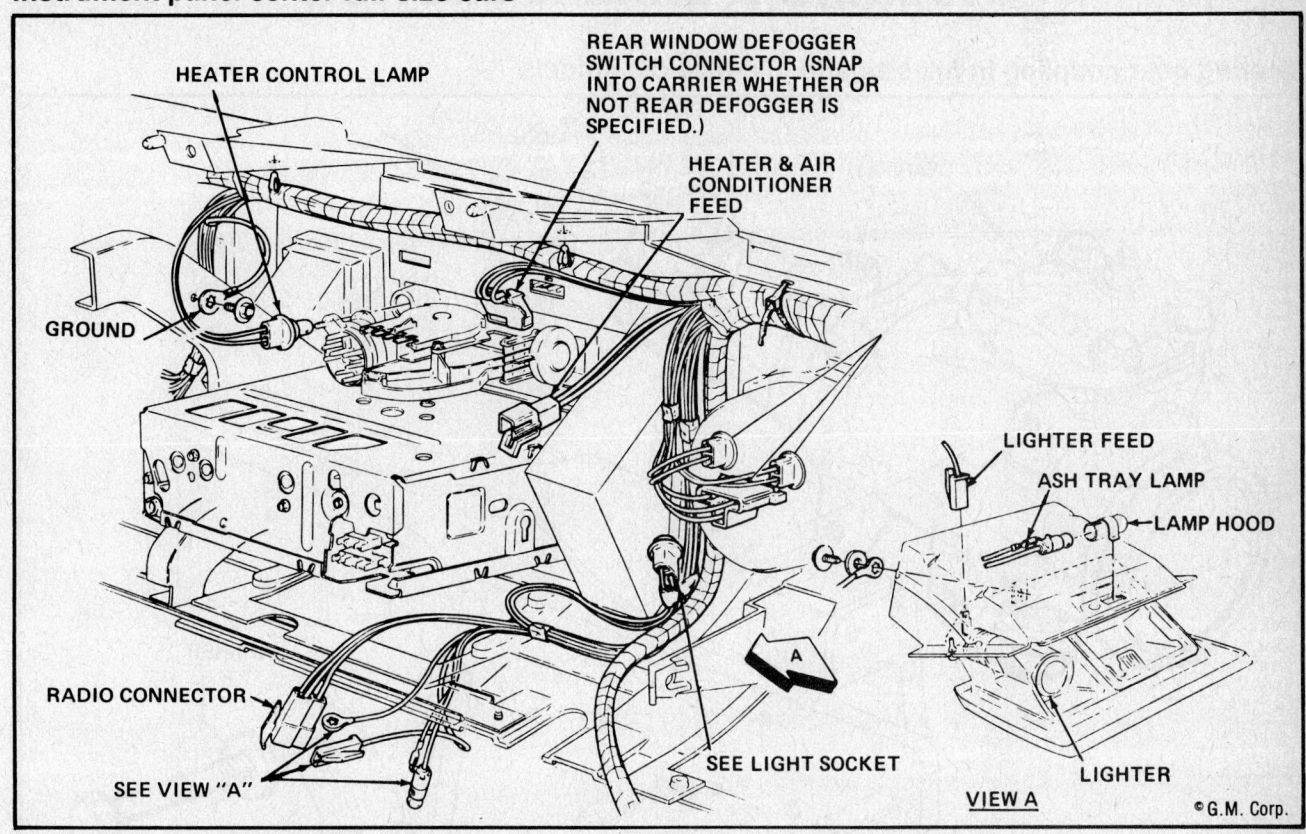

HEATER CONTROL LAMP

REAR WINDOW DEFOGGER SWITCH CONNECTOR (SNAP INTO CARRIER WHETHER OR NOT REAR DEFOGGER IS SPECIFIED.)

HEATER & AIR CONDITIONER FEED

GROUND

LIGHTER FEED

ASH TRAY LAMP

LAMP HOOD

RADIO CONNECTOR

SEE VIEW "A"

SEE LIGHT SOCKET

LIGHTER

VIEW A

© G.M. Corp.

Steering column harness in full-size cars

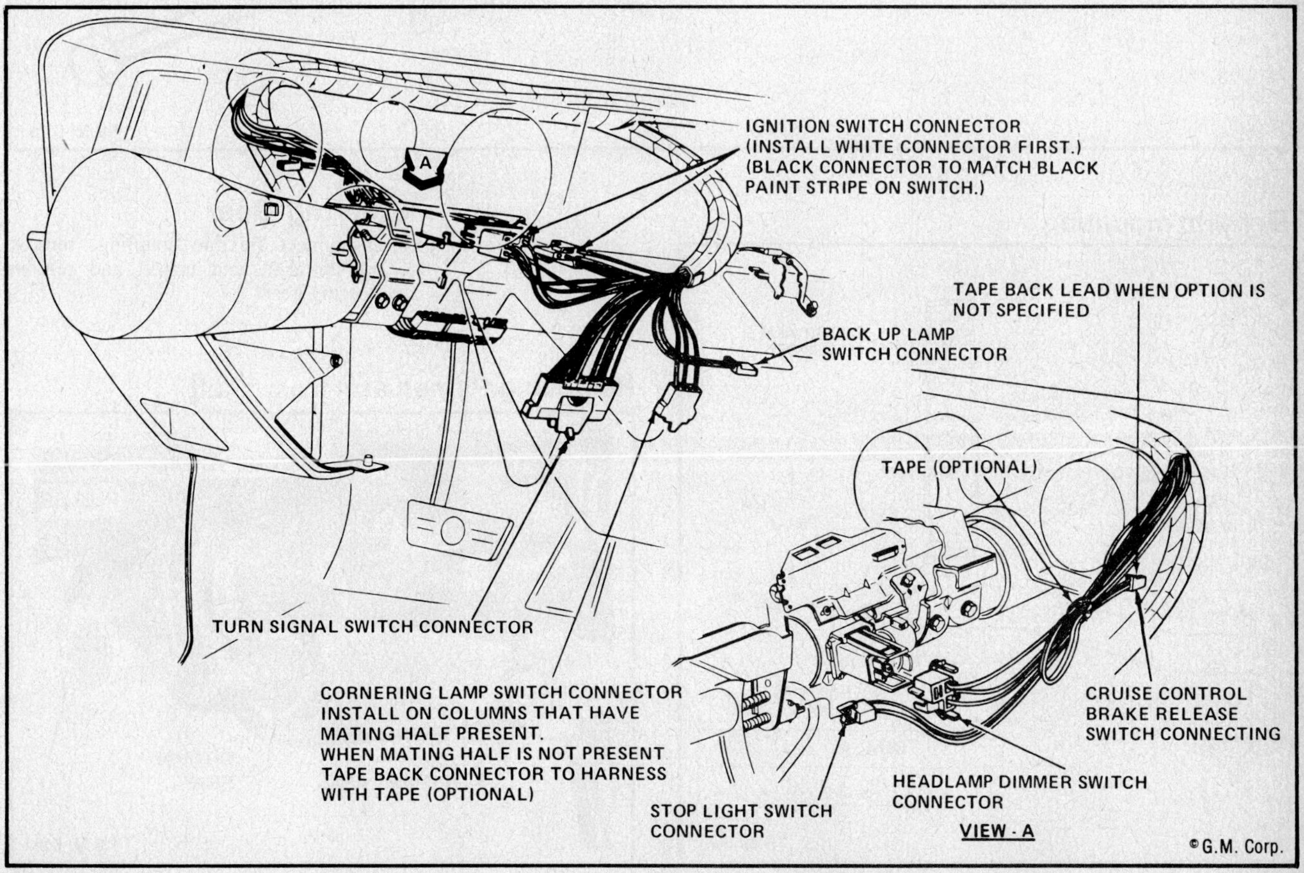

IGNITION SWITCH CONNECTOR (INSTALL WHITE CONNECTOR FIRST.) (BLACK CONNECTOR TO MATCH BLACK PAINT STRIPE ON SWITCH.)

TAPE BACK LEAD WHEN OPTION IS NOT SPECIFIED

BACK UP LAMP SWITCH CONNECTOR

TAPE (OPTIONAL)

TURN SIGNAL SWITCH CONNECTOR

CORNERING LAMP SWITCH CONNECTOR INSTALL ON COLUMNS THAT HAVE MATING HALF PRESENT. WHEN MATING HALF IS NOT PRESENT TAPE BACK CONNECTOR TO HARNESS WITH TAPE (OPTIONAL)

CRUISE CONTROL BRAKE RELEASE SWITCH CONNECTING

HEADLAMP DIMMER SWITCH CONNECTOR

STOP LIGHT SWITCH CONNECTOR

VIEW - A

© G.M. Corp.

STEERING & BRAKES SECTION

Steering gear coupling in full-size and mid-size car models

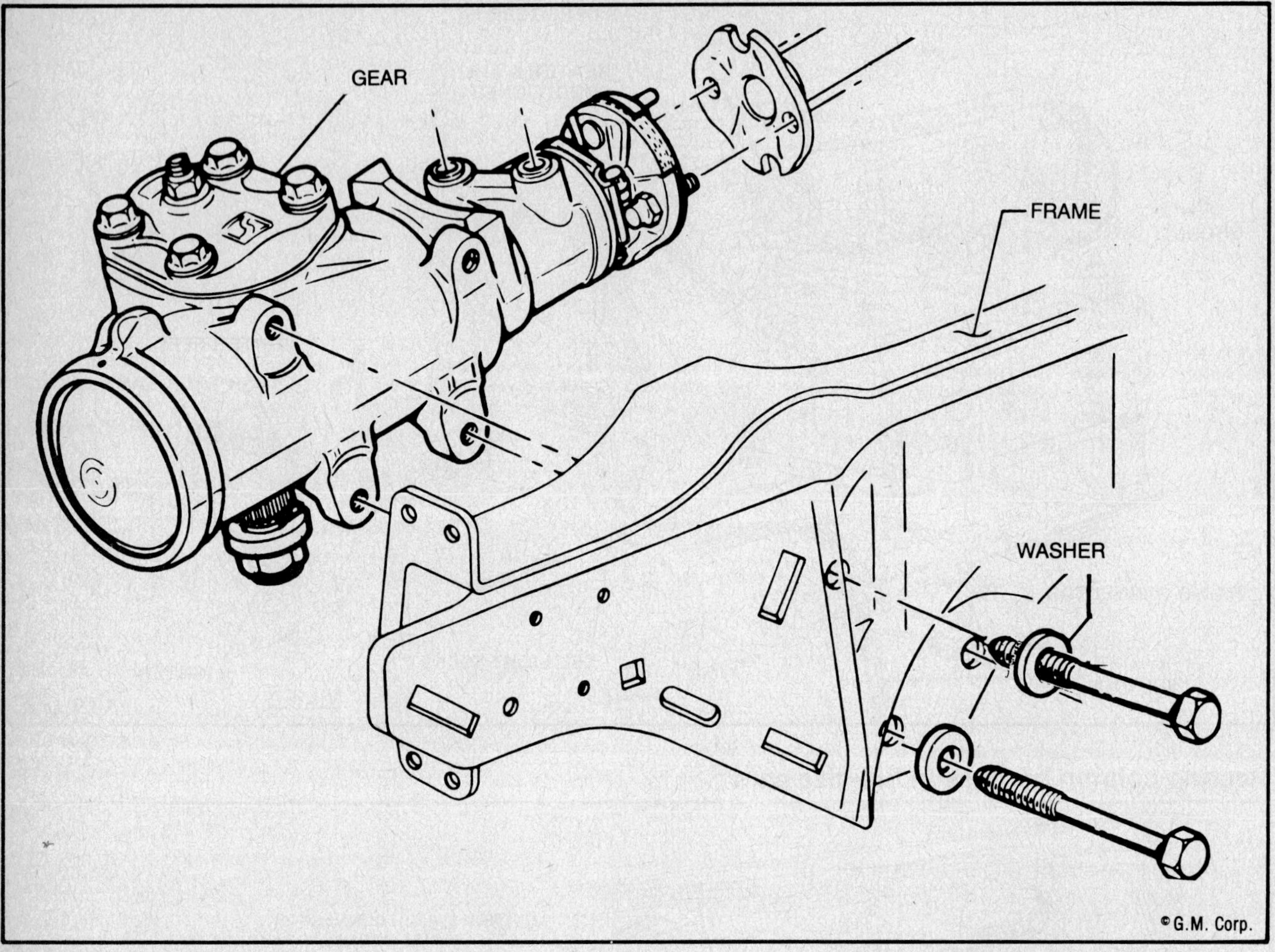

GEAR

FRAME

WASHER

© G.M. Corp.

Idler arm mounting

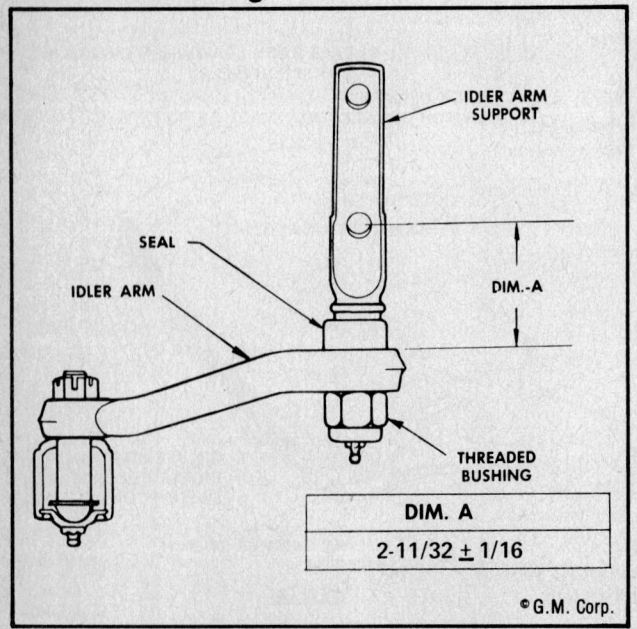

IDLER ARM SUPPORT

SEAL

IDLER ARM

DIM.-A

THREADED BUSHING

DIM. A
2-11/32 ± 1/16

© G.M. Corp.

Steering Gear
- Disconnect flexible coupling, remove pitman arm, and unbolt and remove steering gear.

Removing Pitman arm from shaft

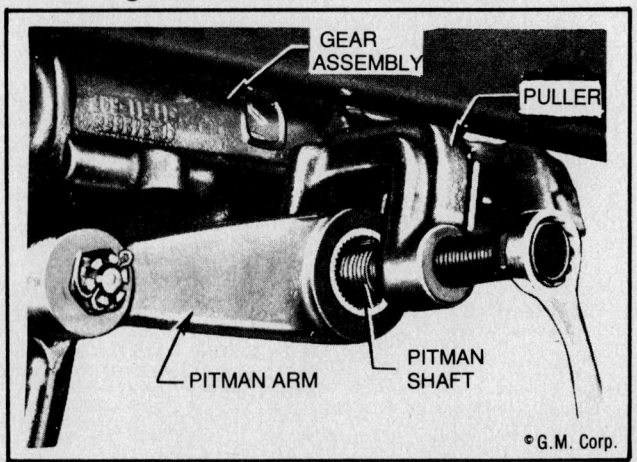

GEAR ASSEMBLY

PULLER

PITMAN ARM

PITMAN SHAFT

© G.M. Corp.

Steering Column

NOTE: Handle the steering column very carefully. Rapping on the end of it or leaning on it could shear off the inserts which allow the column to collapse in a crash.

- Disconnect battery.
- Disconnect flexible coupling.
- Remove cover and toe-pan attaching screws.
- If necessary, remove instrument panel lower trim panel.
- Disconnect shift linkages, wiring, etc.
- Remove column mounts, and lower column.
- When installing, check that flexible coupling alignment is correct.

NOTE: When installing use only the specified hardware. Over-length bolts could prevent the column from properly collapsing in a crash.

Steering column mounting (Century, Regal)

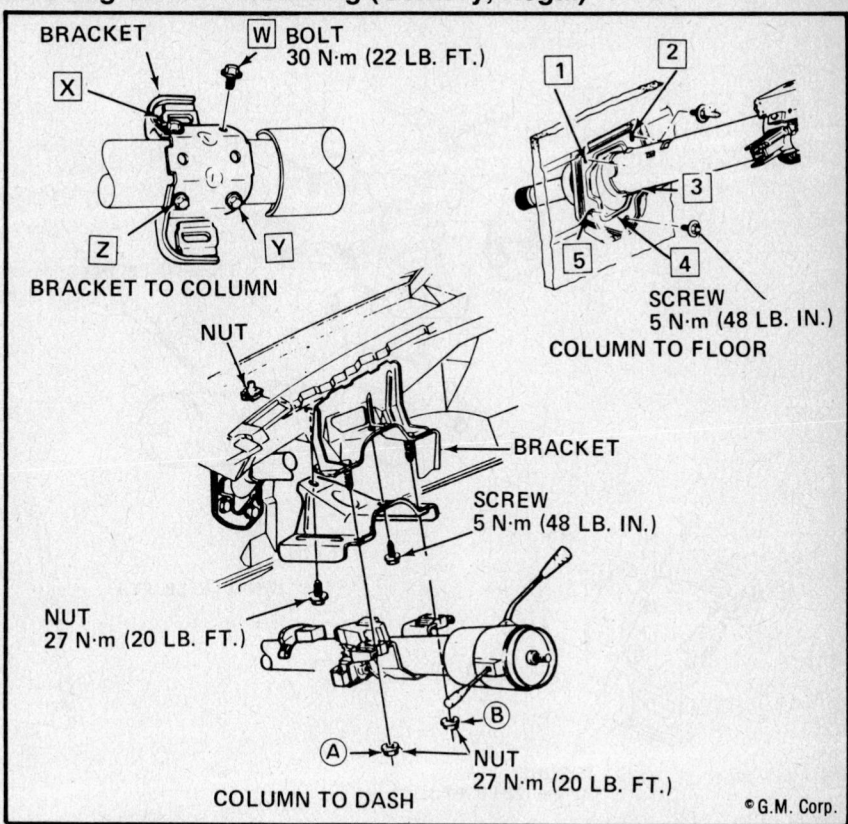

BRACKET
W BOLT
30 N·m (22 LB. FT.)
X
Z
Y
BRACKET TO COLUMN

1
2
3
5
4
SCREW
5 N·m (48 LB. IN.)
COLUMN TO FLOOR

NUT
BRACKET
SCREW
5 N·m (48 LB. IN.)
NUT
27 N·m (20 LB. FT.)
A
B
NUT
27 N·m (20 LB. FT.)
COLUMN TO DASH

© G.M. Corp.

Steering column mounting (rear drive Skylark)

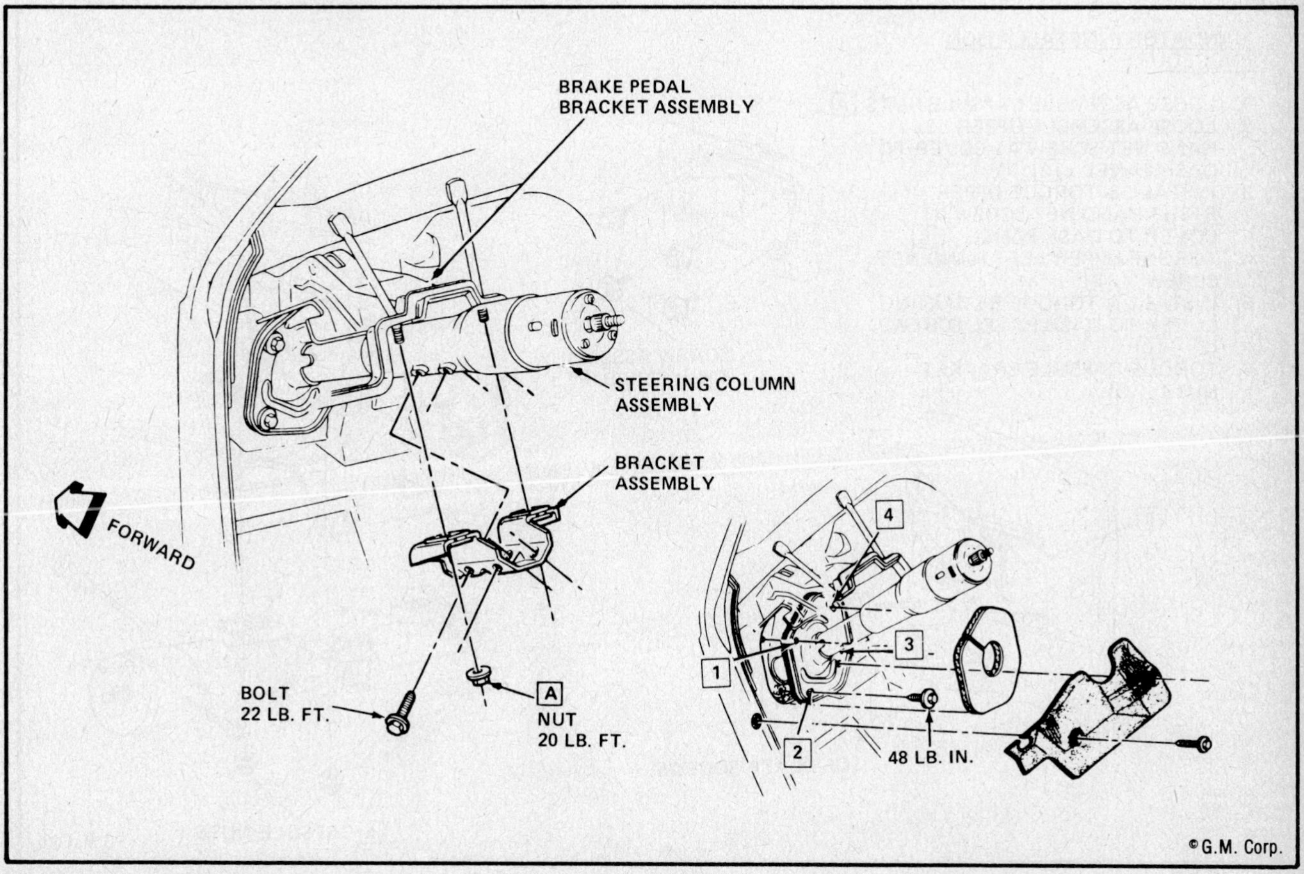

BRAKE PEDAL
BRACKET ASSEMBLY

STEERING COLUMN
ASSEMBLY

BRACKET
ASSEMBLY

FORWARD

BOLT
22 LB. FT.

A
NUT
20 LB. FT.

4
1
2
3
48 LB. IN.

© G.M. Corp.

BUICK
EXCEPT CENTURY (FRONT WHEEL DRIVE), SKYHAWK & '80-'82 SKYLARK

Steering column mounting (Electra, LaSabre)

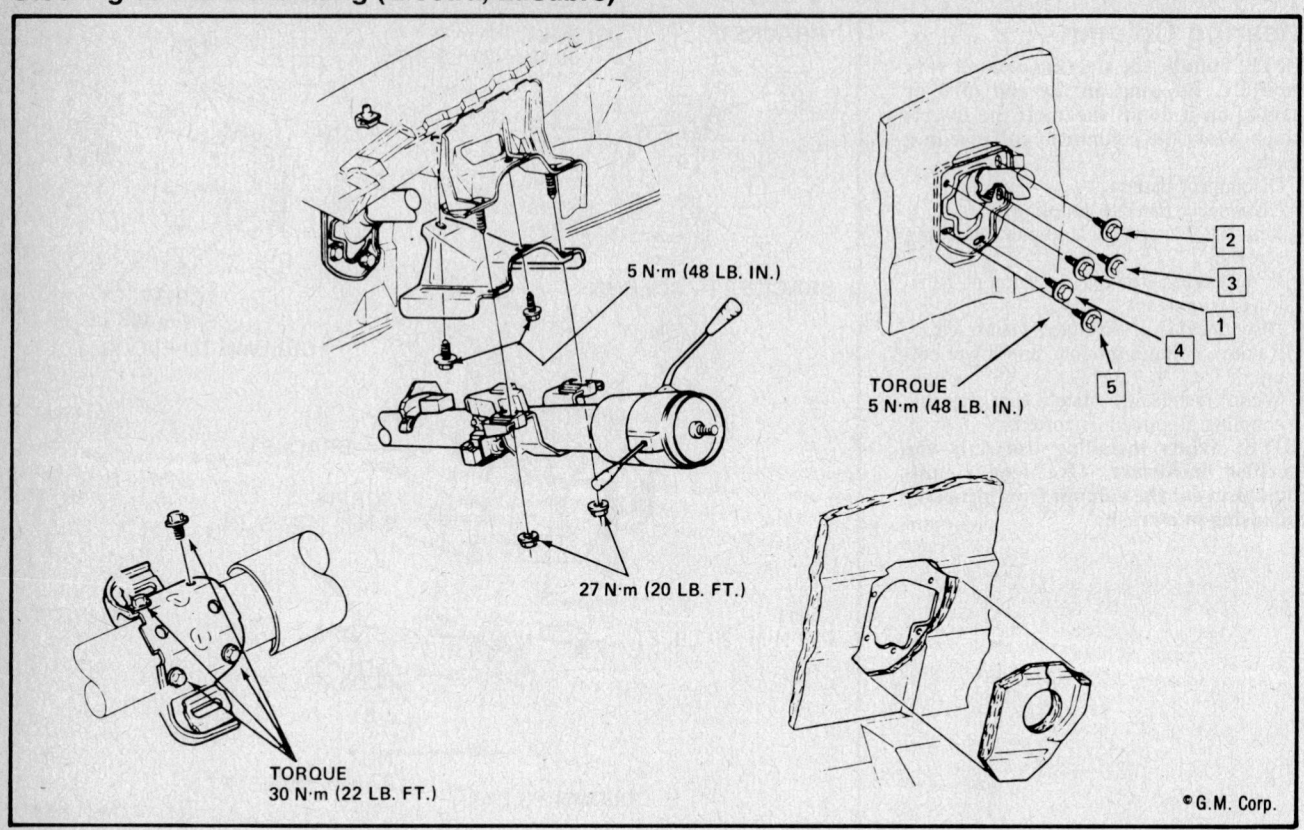

5 N·m (48 LB. IN.)

TORQUE
5 N·m (48 LB. IN.)

27 N·m (20 LB. FT.)

TORQUE
30 N·m (22 LB. FT.)

© G.M. Corp.

Steering column mounting (front drive cars)

MANDATORY INSTALLATION
PROCEDURE

1. LOOSE ASSEMBLE CAPSULE NUTS [A]
2. LOOSE ASSEMBLE UPPER LEFT
   HAND NET SCREW AT COVER TO
   DASH PANEL [B]
3. INSTALL & TORQUE UPPER
   RIGHT HAND NET SCREW AT
   COVER TO DASH PANEL [C]
4. TORQUE UPPER LEFT HAND NET
   SCREW [B]
5. INSTALL & TORQUE REMAINING
   COVER TO DASH PANEL SCREWS
   (2) [D]
6. TORQUE CAPSULE BRACKET
   NUTS [A]

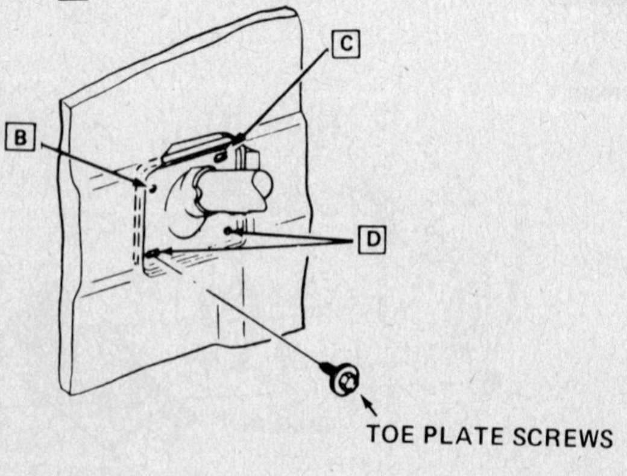

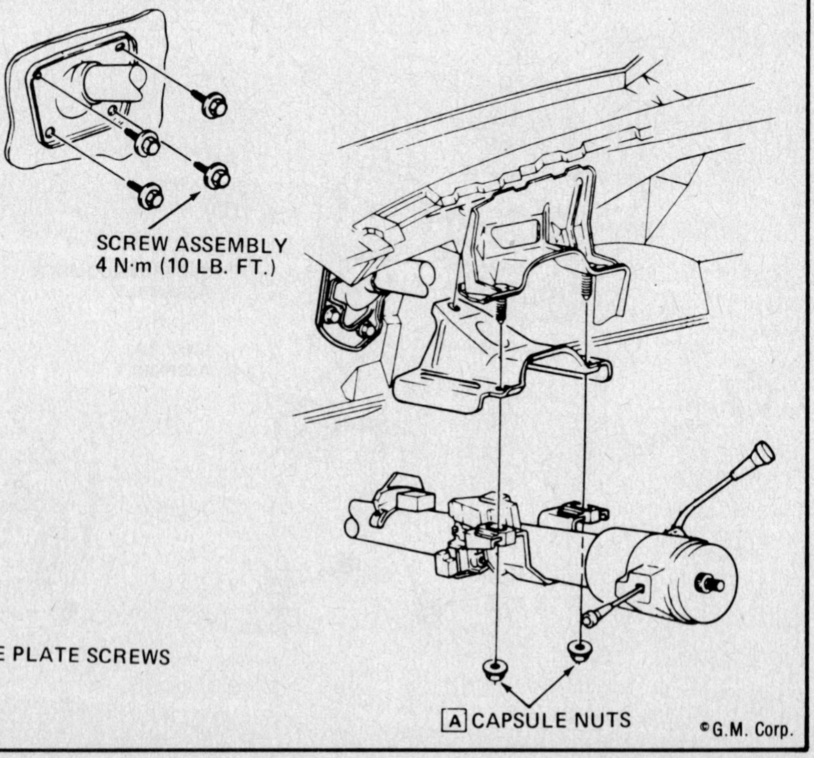

SCREW ASSEMBLY
4 N·m (10 LB. FT.)

TOE PLATE SCREWS

[A] CAPSULE NUTS

© G.M. Corp.

Regular column

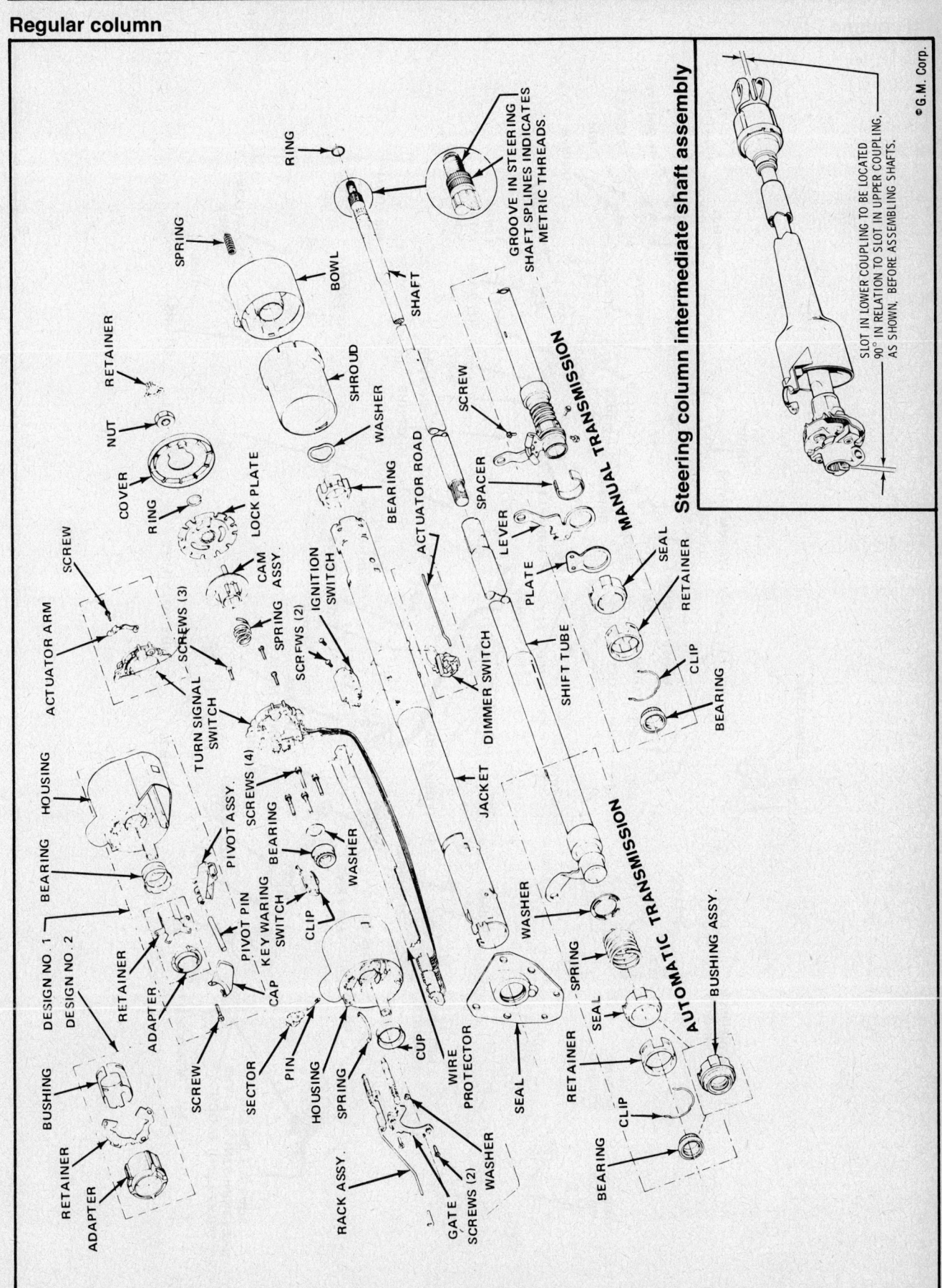

Steering column intermediate shaft assembly

SLOT IN LOWER COUPLING TO BE LOCATED 90° IN RELATION TO SLOT IN UPPER COUPLING, AS SHOWN, BEFORE ASSEMBLING SHAFTS.

© G.M. Corp.

Tilt column

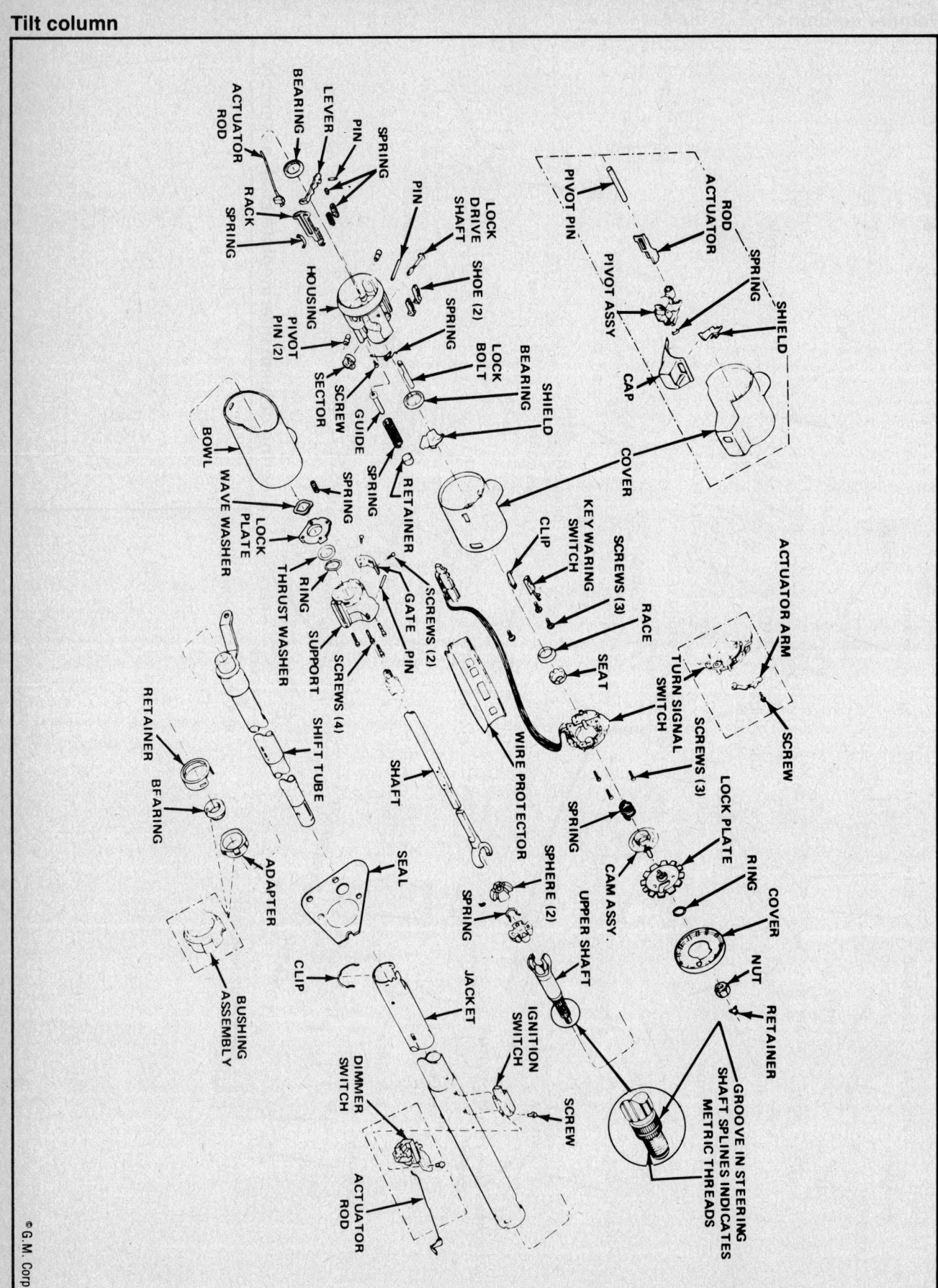

© G.M. Corp.

Typical brake mounting

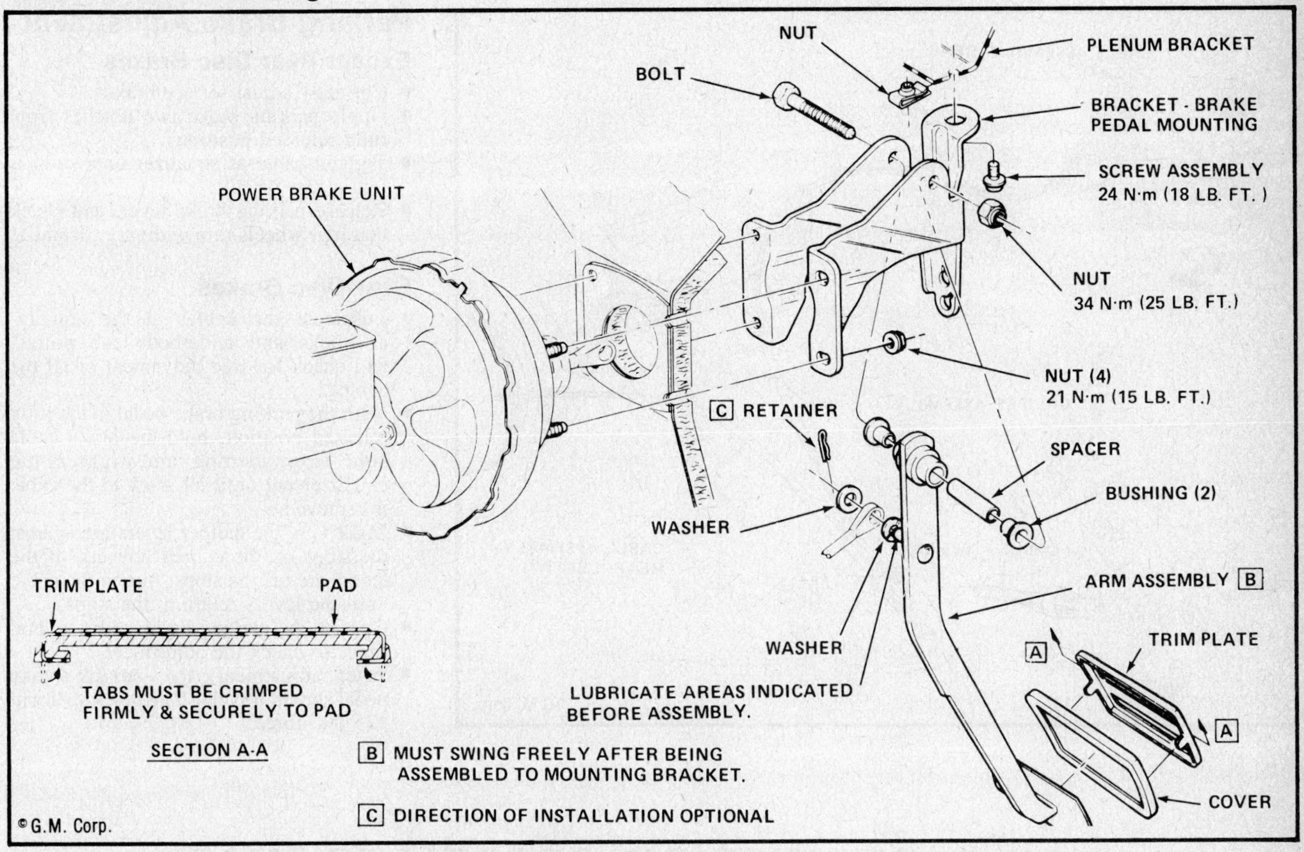

NUT

BOLT

PLENUM BRACKET

BRACKET - BRAKE PEDAL MOUNTING

SCREW ASSEMBLY
24 N·m (18 LB. FT.)

POWER BRAKE UNIT

NUT
34 N·m (25 LB. FT.)

NUT (4)
21 N·m (15 LB. FT.)

SPACER

BUSHING (2)

C RETAINER

WASHER

ARM ASSEMBLY B

TRIM PLATE   PAD

TRIM PLATE

WASHER

A

TABS MUST BE CRIMPED
FIRMLY & SECURELY TO PAD

LUBRICATE AREAS INDICATED
BEFORE ASSEMBLY.

A

SECTION A-A

B MUST SWING FREELY AFTER BEING
ASSEMBLED TO MOUNTING BRACKET.

COVER

© G.M. Corp.

C DIRECTION OF INSTALLATION OPTIONAL

Brake Power Unit R&R

- Separate power unit and master cylinder, and unbolt power unit from firewall.
- Disconnect the power brake push rod from the brake pedal.

Parking Brake Cable R&R

- Disconnect cables from equalizers.
- For front cable removal, remove the wheelhouse panel and disconnect cable from parking brake pedal assembly. Route new cable through in place of the old.

Typical parking brake

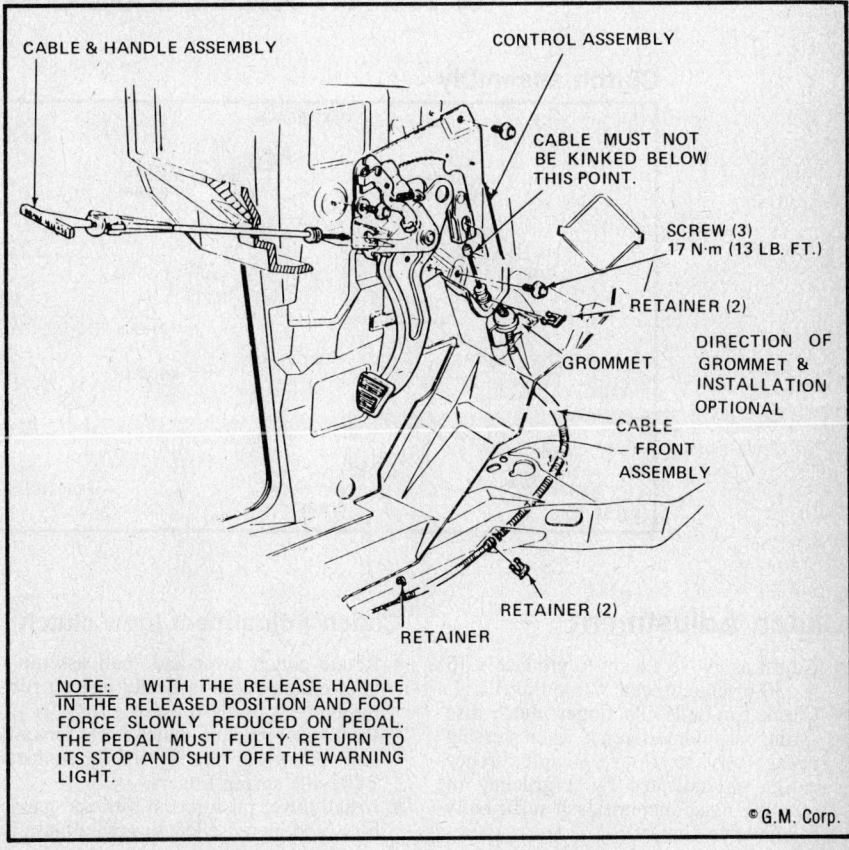

CABLE & HANDLE ASSEMBLY

CONTROL ASSEMBLY

CABLE MUST NOT
BE KINKED BELOW
THIS POINT.

SCREW (3)
17 N·m (13 LB. FT.)

RETAINER (2)

DIRECTION OF
GROMMET &
INSTALLATION
OPTIONAL

GROMMET

CABLE
- FRONT
ASSEMBLY

RETAINER (2)

RETAINER

NOTE: WITH THE RELEASE HANDLE
IN THE RELEASED POSITION AND FOOT
FORCE SLOWLY REDUCED ON PEDAL,
THE PEDAL MUST FULLY RETURN TO
ITS STOP AND SHUT OFF THE WARNING
LIGHT.

© G.M. Corp.

Parking brake cable used with rear disc brakes

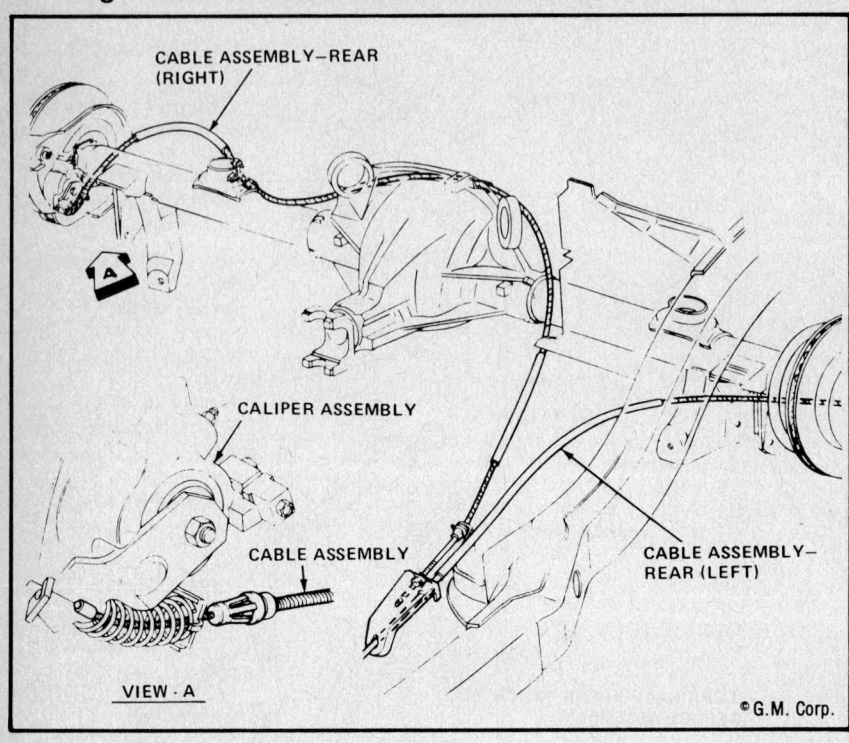

VIEW · A

© G.M. Corp.

Parking Brake Adjustment
Except Rear Disc Brakes
- Correctly adjust service brakes.
- Apply parking brake two notches from fully released position.
- Tighten cable at equalizer until drag is felt at rear wheels.
- Release parking brake lever, and check that rear wheels turn without resistance.

Rear Disc Brakes
- Lubricate the cables at the equalizer hooks and underbody rub points, and check for free movement of all the cables.
- With the parking brake pedal in the fully released position, hold the brake cable stud from turning and tighten the equalizer nut until all slack in the cable is removed.
- Make sure the caliper levers are against the stops on the caliper housing. If the levers are off the stops, loosen the cable until the levers return to the stops.
- Operate the parking brake pedal several times to check the adjustment.
- After adjustment, the parking brake pedal should travel 4-5 inches with about 125 lbs. force.

CLUTCH, TRANSMISSION, PROPELLER SHAFT & REAR AXLES SECTION

Clutch assembly

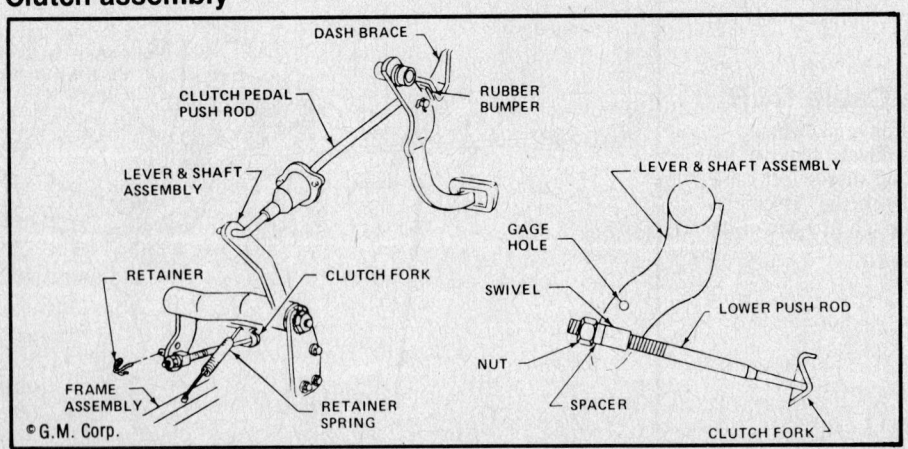

© G.M. Corp.

Clutch Adjustment
- Adjust as above except to produce 1.15 ± .30 of clutch pedal "free travel".
- Check for Belleville finger clutch disc spring pocket interference when pressing pedal fully to floor. If interference exists, as indicated by a grinding or scraping noise increase lash sufficiently to eliminate contact.

Clutch Adjustment (new clutch)
- Rotate clutch lever and shaft assembly until clutch pedal is firmly against rubber bumper on dash brace.
- Push outer end of clutch fork forward until throw-out bearing lightly contacts Belleville spring fingers.
- Install lower push rod in fork and gauge hole, and increase length until all lash is removed from system.
- Install swivel or rod in hole furthest from centerline of lever and shaft assembly and install retainer.
- Tighten lock nut and spacer against swivel.
- Install clutch fork retainer spring.
- Above procedure will produce 1.15 ± .30 of clutch pedal "free travel" when measured at the center of the pedal pad.

Manual Transmission R&R

- Remove, disconnect, or relocate the following:
  a. Speedometer gear
  b. Shift rods
  c. Propeller shaft
- Support rear of engine and remove the transmission crossmember.
- Remove the two upper mount bolts, and insert guide pins. Remove the lower bolts, and slide the transmission back and out.

4 speed floor shift linkage

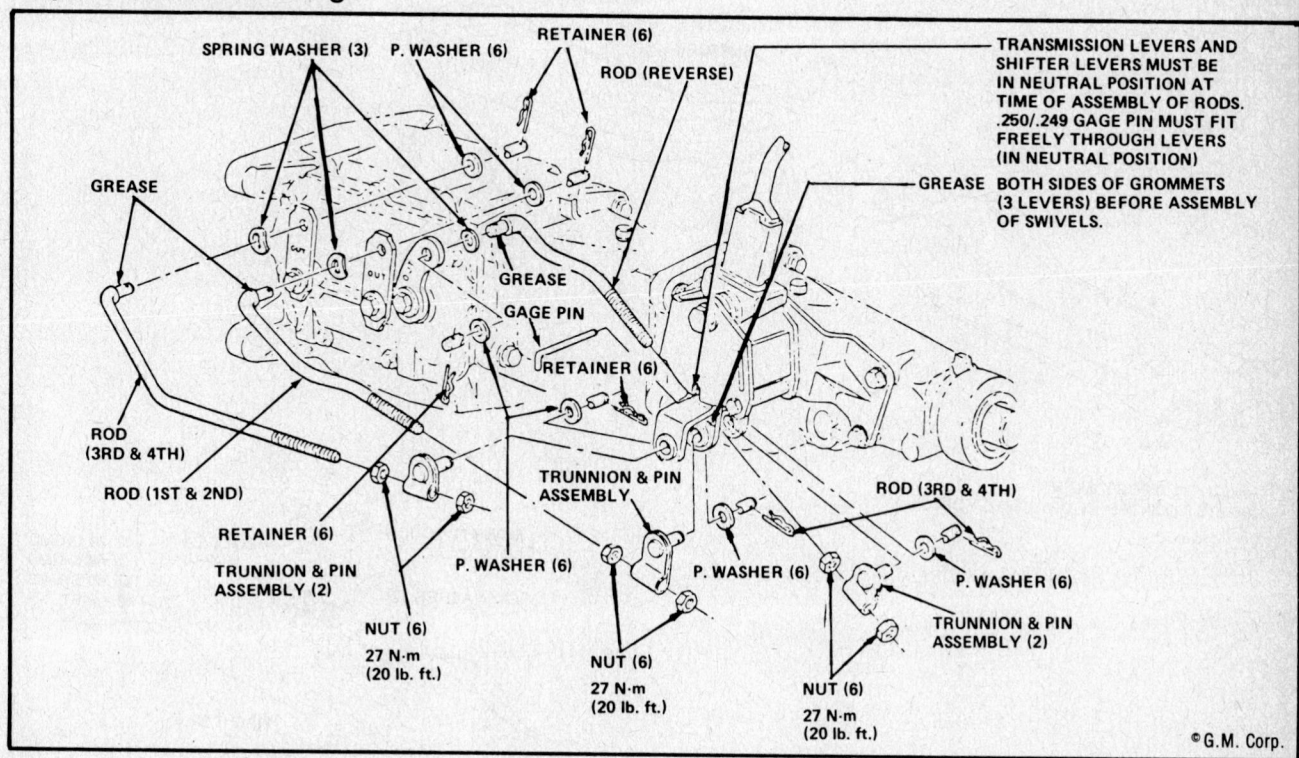

3 speed floor shift linkage

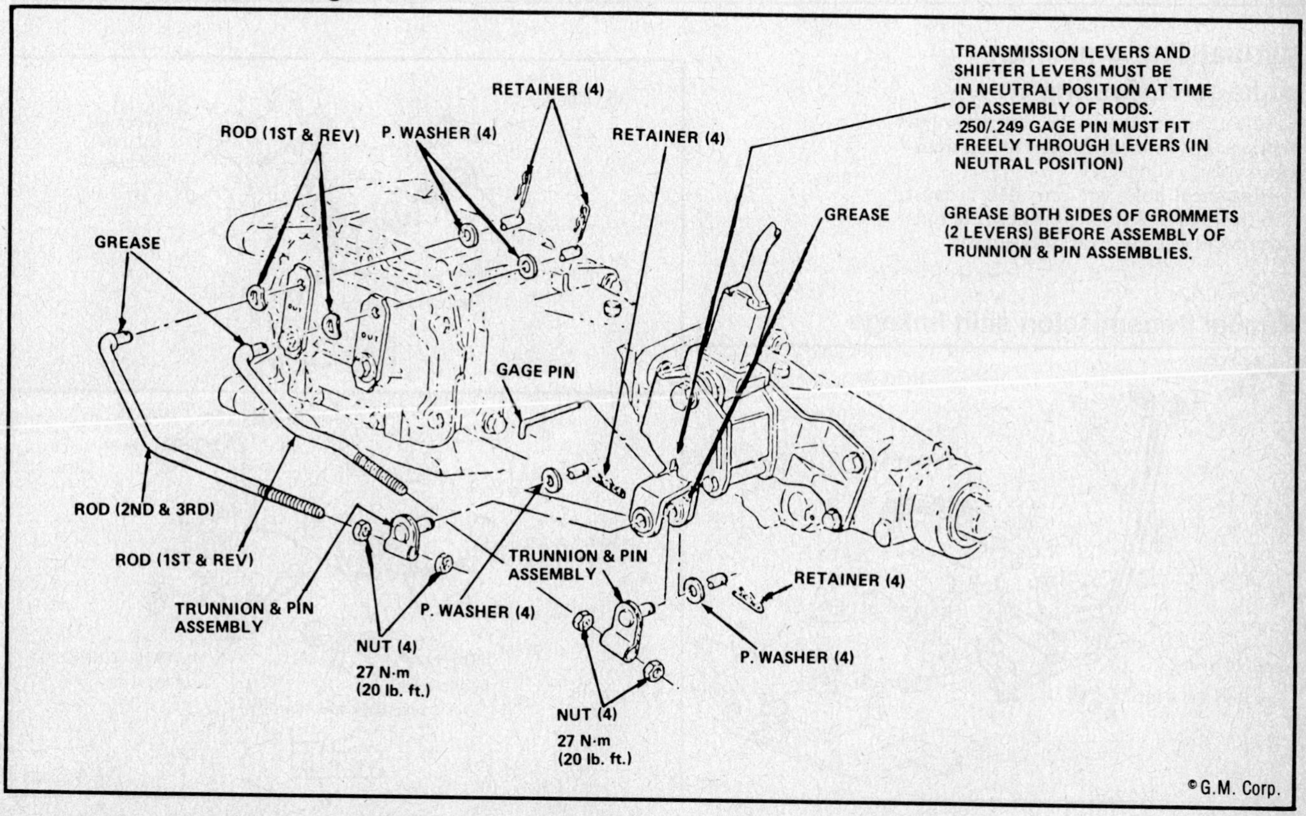

Transmission-to-crossmember support

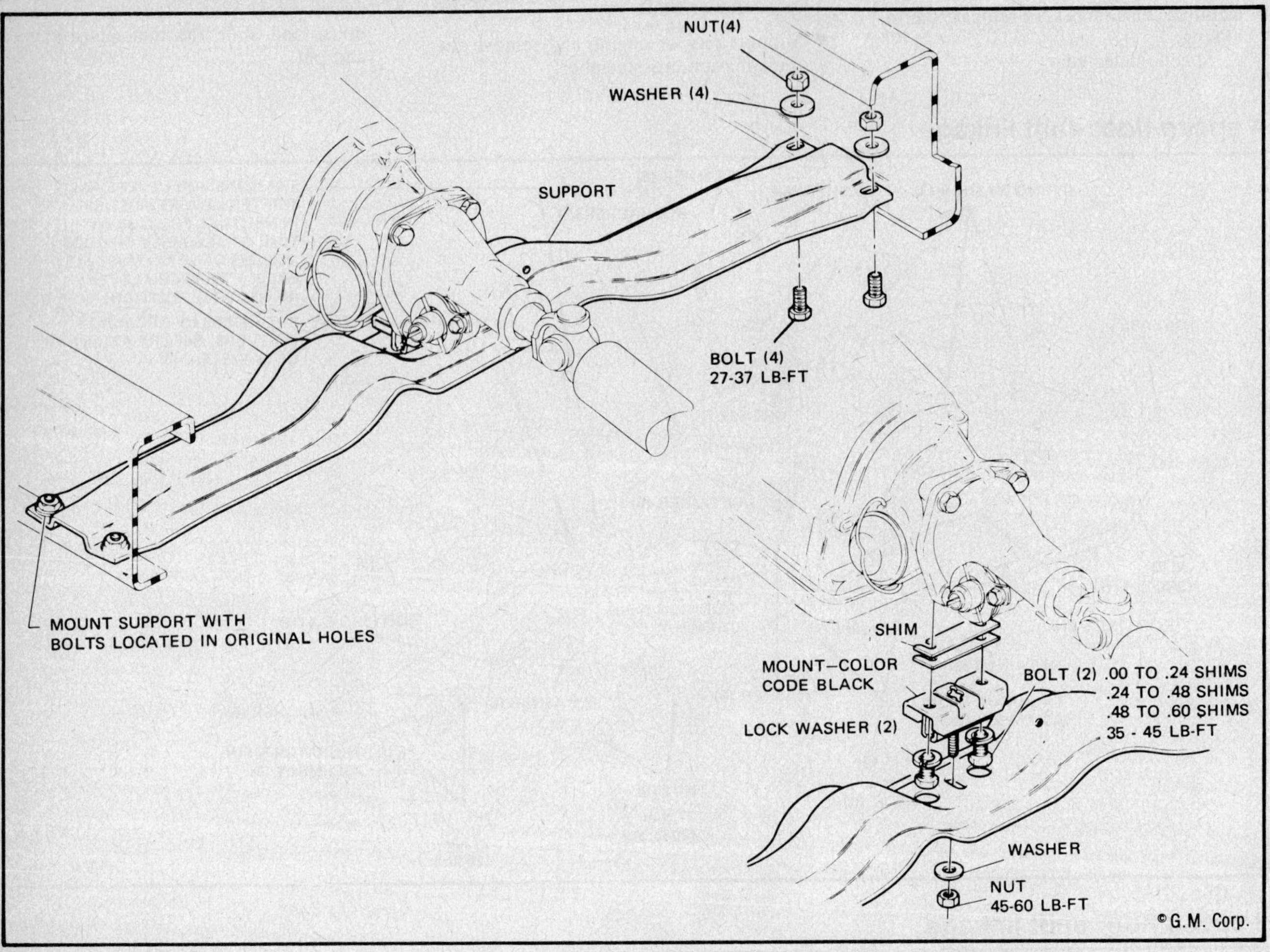

NUT(4)

WASHER (4)

SUPPORT

BOLT (4)
27-37 LB-FT

MOUNT SUPPORT WITH
BOLTS LOCATED IN ORIGINAL HOLES

SHIM

MOUNT—COLOR
CODE BLACK

LOCK WASHER (2)

BOLT (2) .00 TO .24 SHIMS
.24 TO .48 SHIMS
.48 TO .60 SHIMS
35 - 45 LB-FT

WASHER

NUT
45-60 LB-FT

© G.M. Corp.

Manual Transmission Linkage Adjustment

- Adjust the linkage so the shift lever positions correspond exactly to the transmission positions.
- Adjustment holes are provided in most shift assemblies through which drill rods can be placed for exact adjustment.

Manual transmission shift linkage

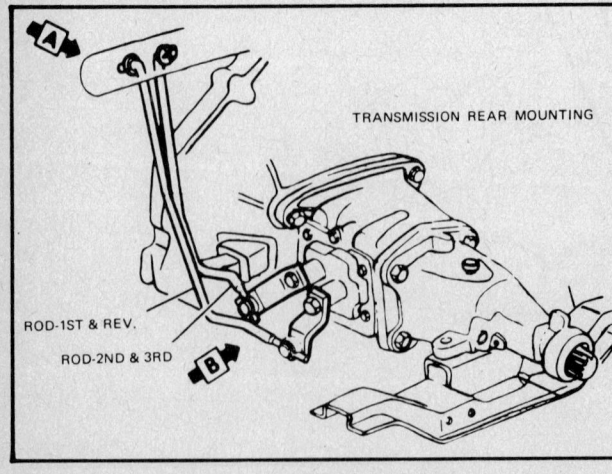

TRANSMISSION REAR MOUNTING

ROD-1ST & REV.

ROD-2ND & 3RD

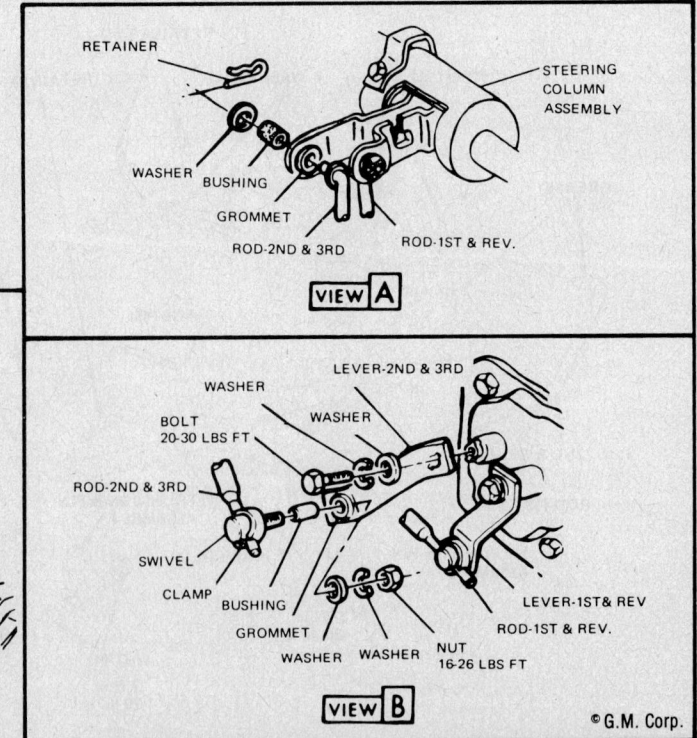

RETAINER

STEERING
COLUMN
ASSEMBLY

WASHER BUSHING

GROMMET

ROD-2ND & 3RD

ROD-1ST & REV.

VIEW A

LEVER-2ND & 3RD

WASHER

BOLT
20-30 LBS FT

WASHER

ROD-2ND & 3RD

SWIVEL

CLAMP

BUSHING

GROMMET

WASHER   WASHER

NUT
16-26 LBS FT

LEVER-1ST& REV

ROD-1ST & REV.

VIEW B

© G.M. Corp.

Automatic Transmission R&R

Except Front Wheel Drive Riviera

- Disconnect the battery.
- Disconnect detent cable (if so equipped) from accelator lever or carburetor.
- Remove, disconnect or relocate any of the following necessary for removal:
  a. Exhaust crossover pipe
  b. Drive shaft
  c. Oil cooler lines
  d. Transmission crossmember (support engine and transmission as needed)
  e. Speedometer cable
  f. Shift linkage
  g. Electrical connections
  h. Flywheel cover pan
- Mark flywheel and converter for installation reference.
- Remove mounting bolts, and slide transmission back and out of vehicle.

Front Wheel Drive Riviera

- Disconnect the battery, and remove, disconnect or relocate the following:
  a. Filter tube
  b. Speedometer cable
  c. Electrical and vacuum leads
  d. Oil cooler tubes
  e. Starter
  f. Converter cover plate
  g. Shift linkage
  h. Remove starter
- Remove mount bolts to separate transmission from engine and final drive, and remove transmission. Remove engine mounts, and pry engine back for clearance as necessary.
- Remove transmission and torque converter ASA assembly.

Typical automatic transmission rear drive cars

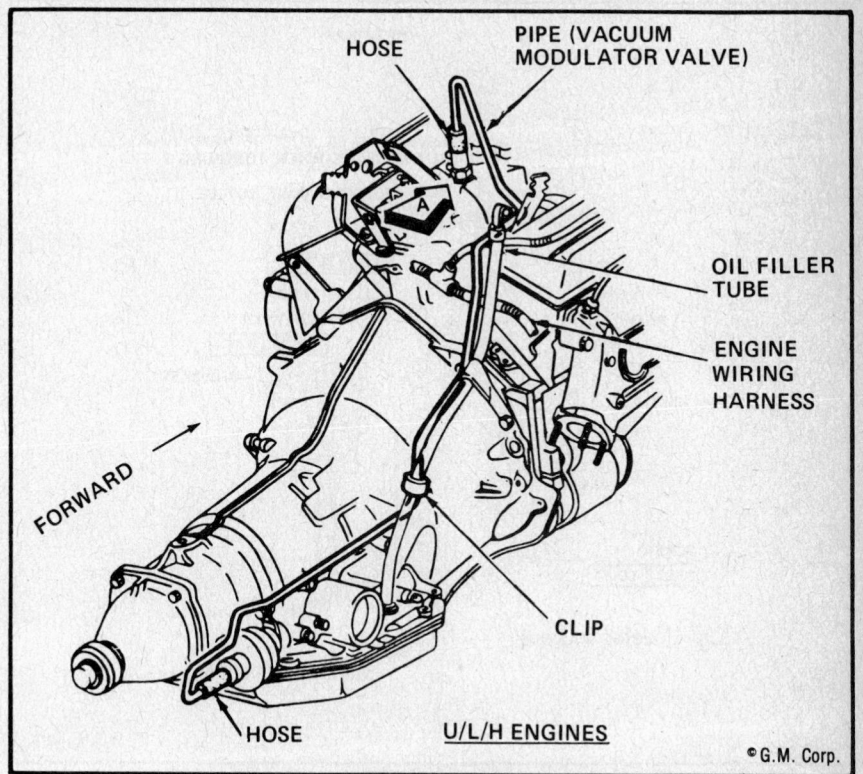

Remove torque converter as an assembly

325 automatic transmission

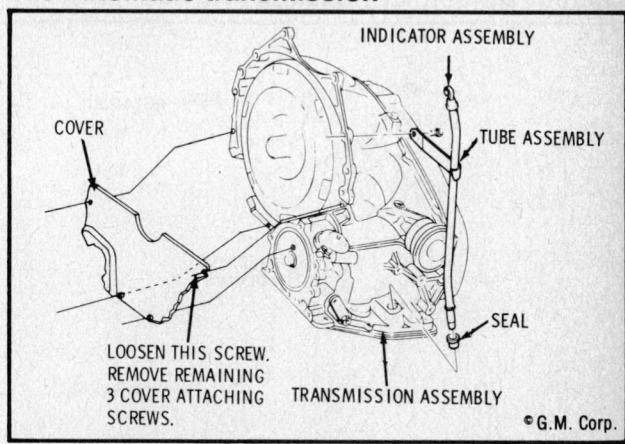

Final drive to transmission

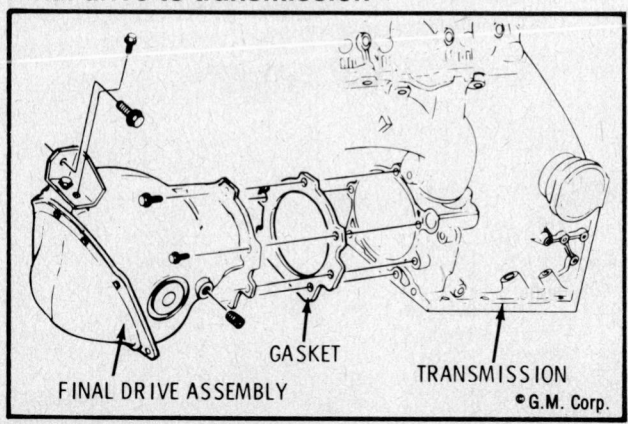

325 automatic transmission

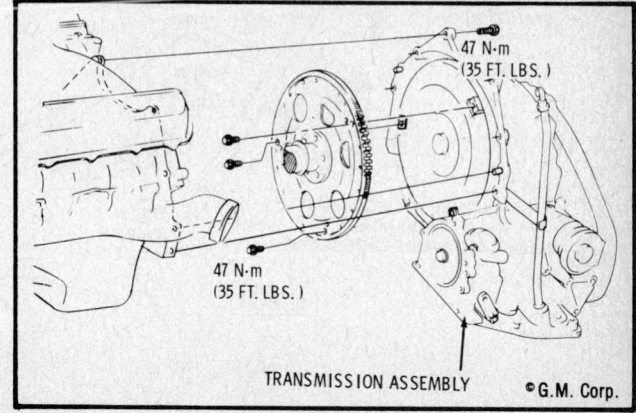

BUICK
EXCEPT CENTURY (FRONT WHEEL DRIVE), SKYHAWK & '80-'82 SKYLARK

Linkage adjustment Century, Regal, LaSabre

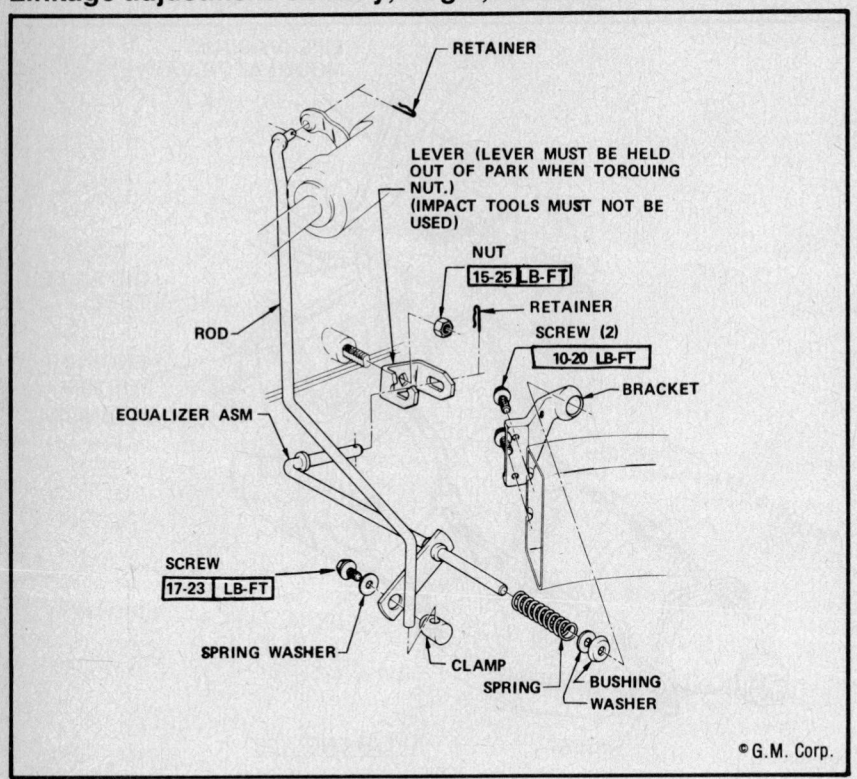

RETAINER

LEVER (LEVER MUST BE HELD OUT OF PARK WHEN TORQUING NUT.) (IMPACT TOOLS MUST NOT BE USED)

NUT 15-25 LB-FT

RETAINER

SCREW (2) 10-20 LB-FT

ROD

BRACKET

EQUALIZER ASM

SCREW 17-23 LB-FT

SPRING WASHER

CLAMP

SPRING

BUSHING

WASHER

© G.M. Corp.

Linkage Adjustment Procedure

- Steering column attachment to body must be complete and all body bolts must be secured before adjusting transmission control linkage.
- Set transmission lever in neutral detent.
- Assemble clamp, spring washer and screw to equalizer lever and control rod.
- Hold clamp flush against equalizer lever and finger tighten clamping screw against rod. No force should be exerted in either direction on the rod or equalizer lever while tightening the clamping screw.
- Tighten screw to specified torque.

Linkage adjustment Skylark

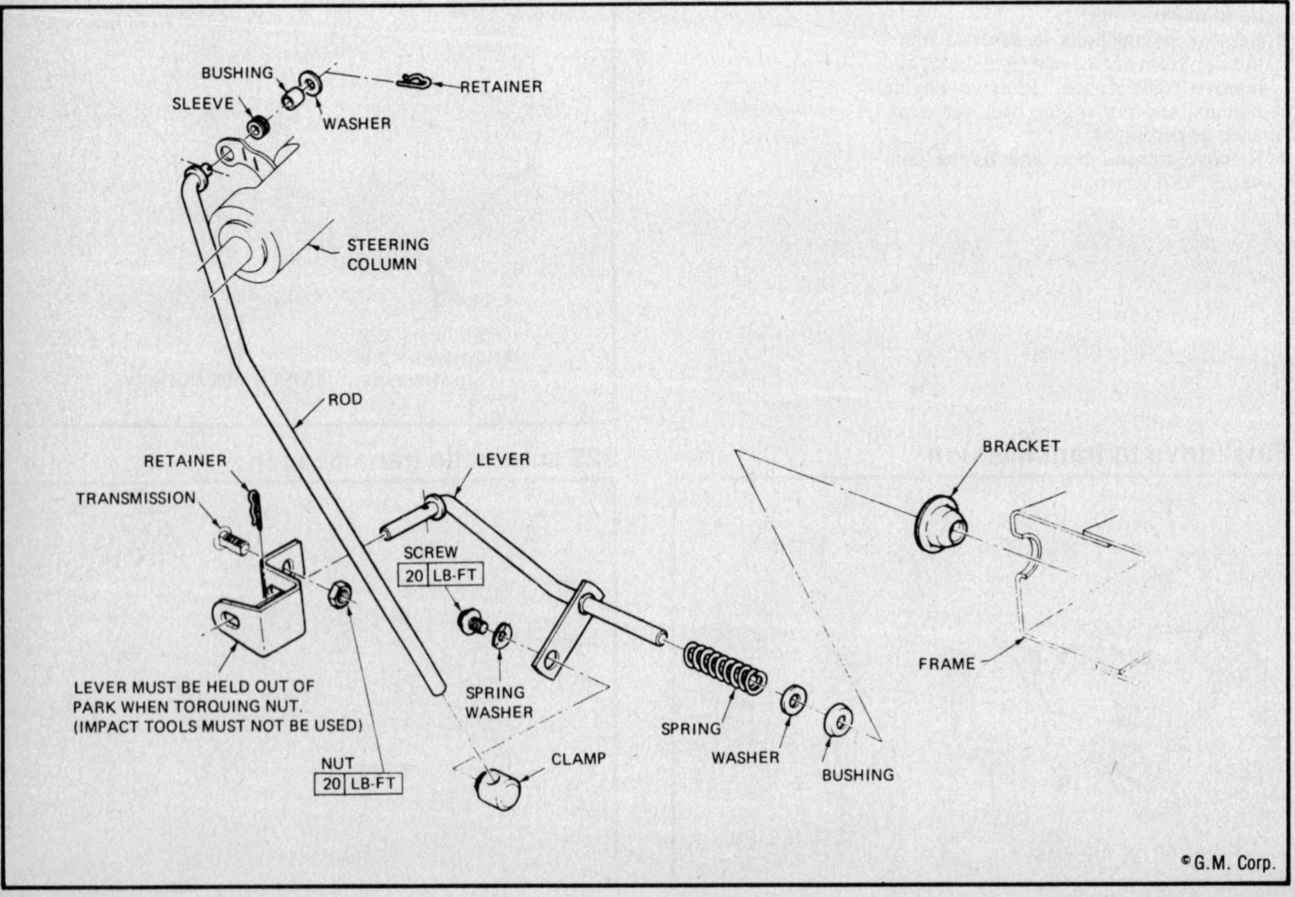

BUSHING

SLEEVE

WASHER

RETAINER

STEERING COLUMN

ROD

RETAINER

LEVER

TRANSMISSION

SCREW 20 LB-FT

BRACKET

FRAME

LEVER MUST BE HELD OUT OF PARK WHEN TORQUING NUT. (IMPACT TOOLS MUST NOT BE USED)

NUT 20 LB-FT

SPRING WASHER

CLAMP

SPRING

WASHER

BUSHING

© G.M. Corp.

Detent cable adjustment Skylark

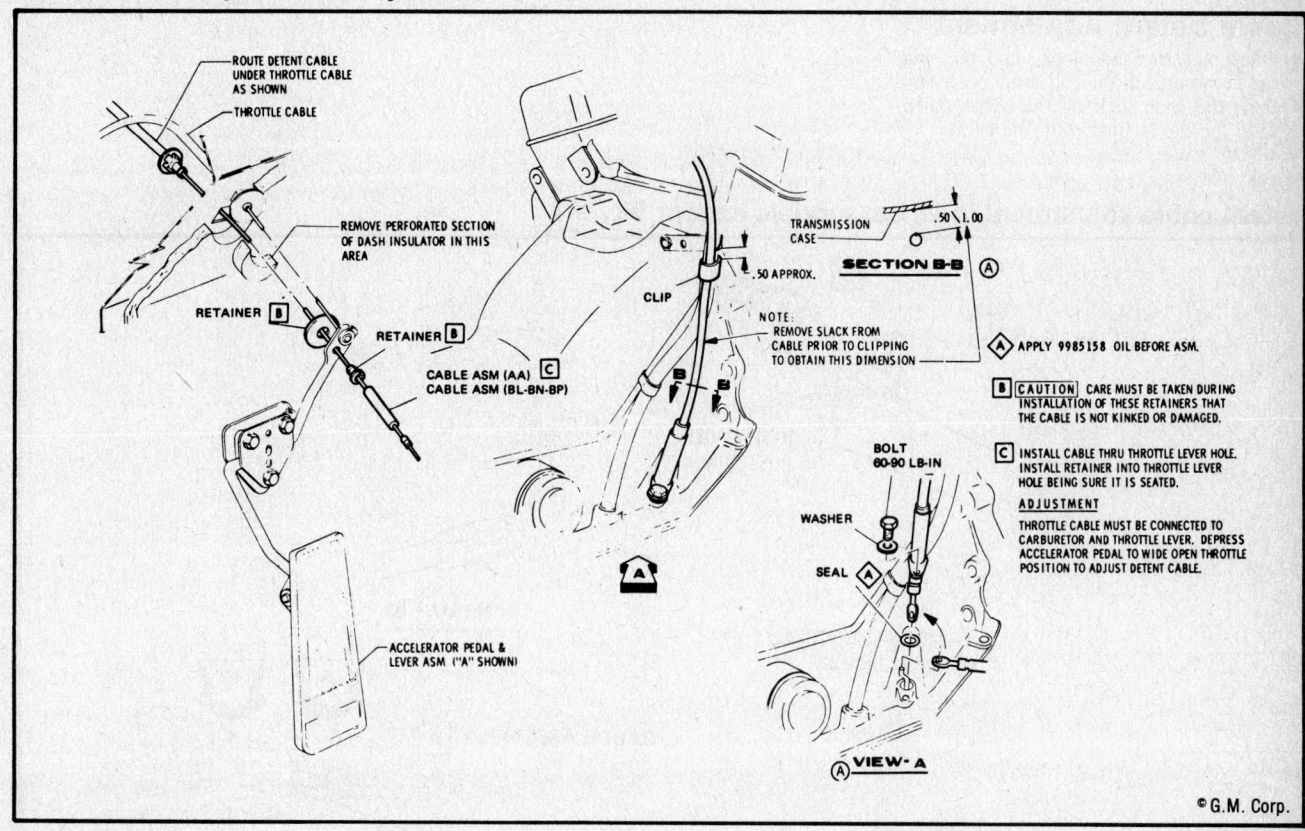

ROUTE DETENT CABLE UNDER THROTTLE CABLE AS SHOWN

THROTTLE CABLE

REMOVE PERFORATED SECTION OF DASH INSULATOR IN THIS AREA

RETAINER B

RETAINER B

CABLE ASM (AA) C
CABLE ASM (BL-BN-BP)

ACCELERATOR PEDAL & LEVER ASM ("A" SHOWN)

CLIP

TRANSMISSION CASE

.50 1.00

SECTION B-B A

.50 APPROX.

NOTE:
REMOVE SLACK FROM CABLE PRIOR TO CLIPPING TO OBTAIN THIS DIMENSION

A APPLY 9985158 OIL BEFORE ASM.

B CAUTION CARE MUST BE TAKEN DURING INSTALLATION OF THESE RETAINERS THAT THE CABLE IS NOT KINKED OR DAMAGED.

C INSTALL CABLE THRU THROTTLE LEVER HOLE. INSTALL RETAINER INTO THROTTLE LEVER HOLE BEING SURE IT IS SEATED.

ADJUSTMENT
THROTTLE CABLE MUST BE CONNECTED TO CARBURETOR AND THROTTLE LEVER. DEPRESS ACCELERATOR PEDAL TO WIDE OPEN THROTTLE POSITION TO ADJUST DETENT CABLE.

BOLT 80-90 LB-IN

WASHER

SEAL A

A VIEW-A

© G.M. Corp.

Linkage adjustment console shift

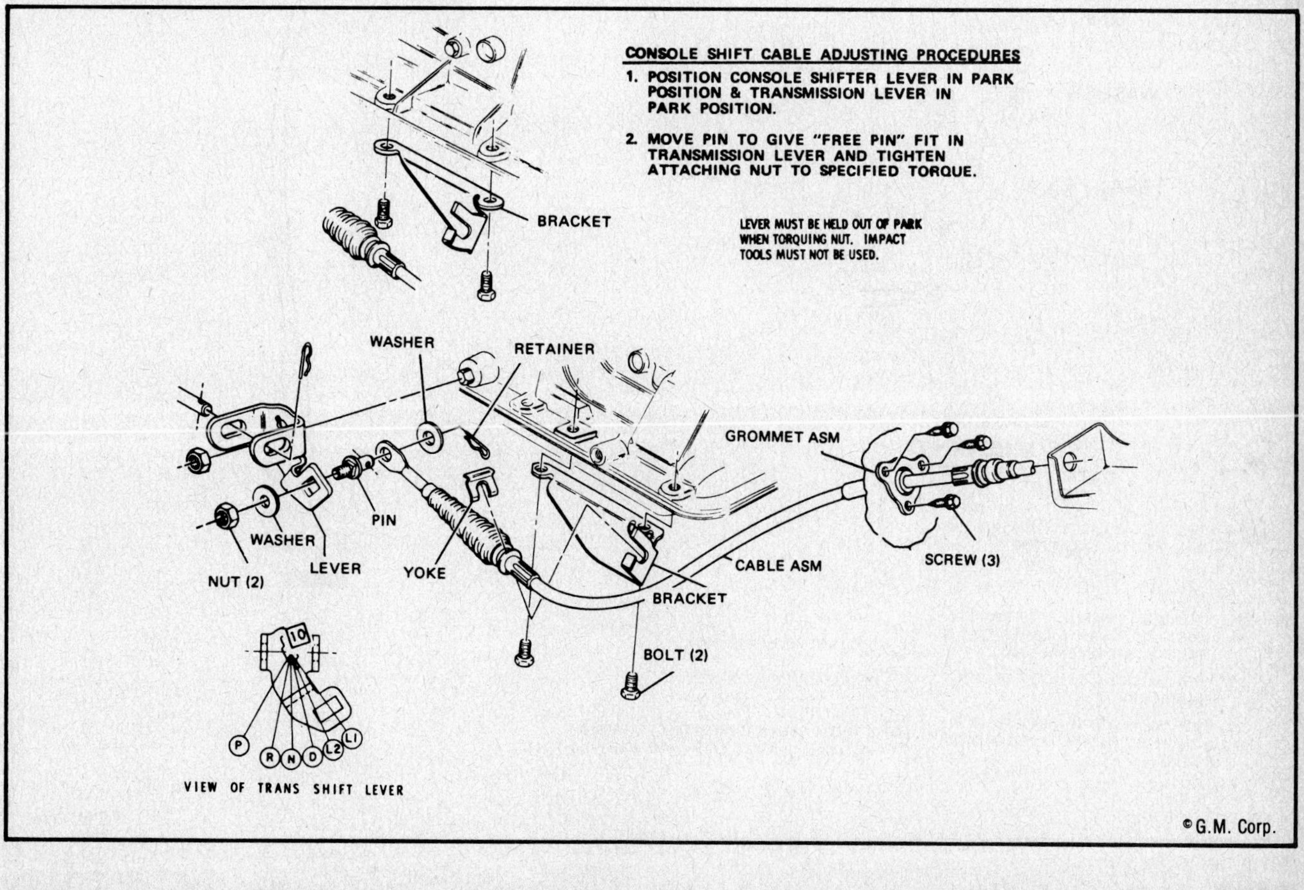

CONSOLE SHIFT CABLE ADJUSTING PROCEDURES

1. POSITION CONSOLE SHIFTER LEVER IN PARK POSITION & TRANSMISSION LEVER IN PARK POSITION.

2. MOVE PIN TO GIVE "FREE PIN" FIT IN TRANSMISSION LEVER AND TIGHTEN ATTACHING NUT TO SPECIFIED TORQUE.

LEVER MUST BE HELD OUT OF PARK WHEN TORQUING NUT. IMPACT TOOLS MUST NOT BE USED.

BRACKET

WASHER

RETAINER

GROMMET ASM

NUT (2)

WASHER

LEVER

PIN

YOKE

CABLE ASM

BRACKET

SCREW (3)

BOLT (2)

P R N D L2 L1

VIEW OF TRANS SHIFT LEVER

© G.M. Corp.

© G.M. Corp.

Automatic Transmission
Cable Detent Adjustment

- Disengage the snap lock, and position the carburetor in the full open position.
- Push the snap lock on the cable down until the top is flush with the cable.

Detent cable adjustment in all car models except Skylark

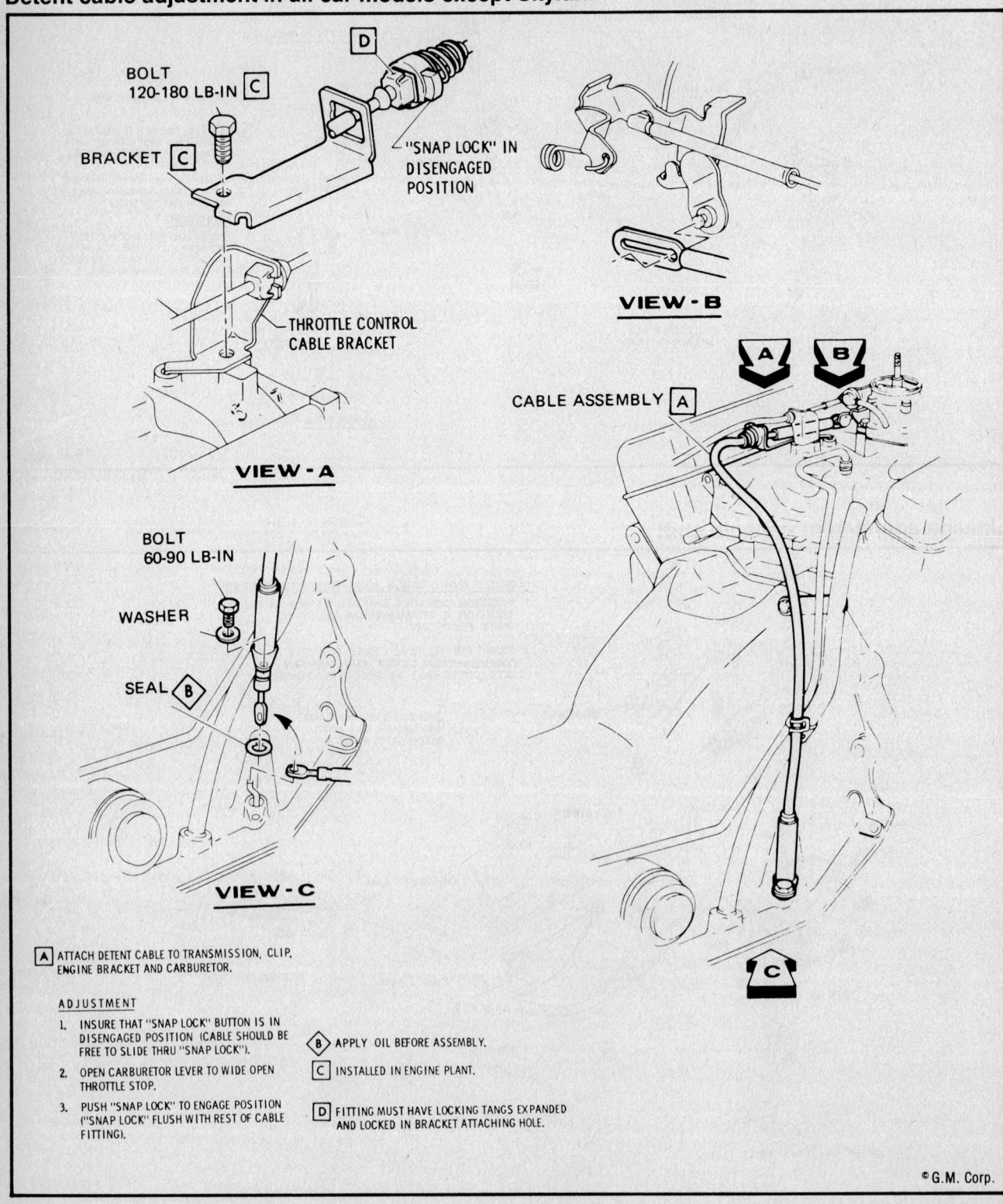

BOLT 120-180 LB-IN C

BRACKET C

D

"SNAP LOCK" IN DISENGAGED POSITION

THROTTLE CONTROL CABLE BRACKET

VIEW - A

VIEW - B

CABLE ASSEMBLY A

A   B

C

BOLT 60-90 LB-IN

WASHER

SEAL B

VIEW - C

A ATTACH DETENT CABLE TO TRANSMISSION, CLIP, ENGINE BRACKET AND CARBURETOR.

ADJUSTMENT

1. INSURE THAT "SNAP LOCK" BUTTON IS IN DISENGAGED POSITION (CABLE SHOULD BE FREE TO SLIDE THRU "SNAP LOCK").

2. OPEN CARBURETOR LEVER TO WIDE OPEN THROTTLE STOP.

3. PUSH "SNAP LOCK" TO ENGAGE POSITION ("SNAP LOCK" FLUSH WITH REST OF CABLE FITTING).

B APPLY OIL BEFORE ASSEMBLY.

C INSTALLED IN ENGINE PLANT.

D FITTING MUST HAVE LOCKING TANGS EXPANDED AND LOCKED IN BRACKET ATTACHING HOLE.

Pinion Oil Seal

- Scribe a line down the pinion stem, nut and flange, and count the number of exposed pinion stem threads. After replacing the seal, install these components in their exact original locations.

Axle identification

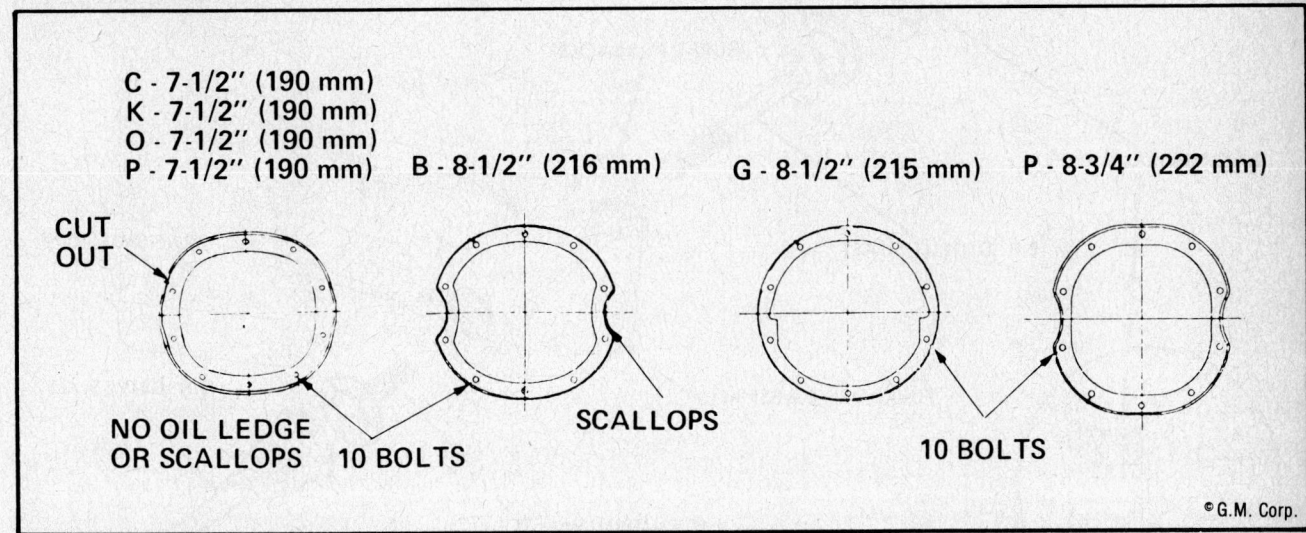

C - 7-1/2'' (190 mm)
K - 7-1/2'' (190 mm)
O - 7-1/2'' (190 mm)
P - 7-1/2'' (190 mm)   B - 8-1/2'' (216 mm)   G - 8-1/2'' (215 mm)   P - 8-3/4'' (222 mm)

CUT OUT

NO OIL LEDGE OR SCALLOPS   10 BOLTS   SCALLOPS   10 BOLTS

© G.M. Corp.

Final Drive Differential (Front Wheel Drive Riviera)

NOTE: The final drive differential is serviced by replacement only. Overhaul is never recommended.

- Disconnect the battery, and remove, disconnect or relocate the following:
  a. Transmission filter tube
  b. Transmission oil cooler lines
  c. Final drive support brace
  d. Right hand output shaft
  e. Steering or suspension linkage
- Remove the final drive-to-transmission mount bolts, and remove the final drive.

Transmission-to-engine attachment in front wheel drive Riviera

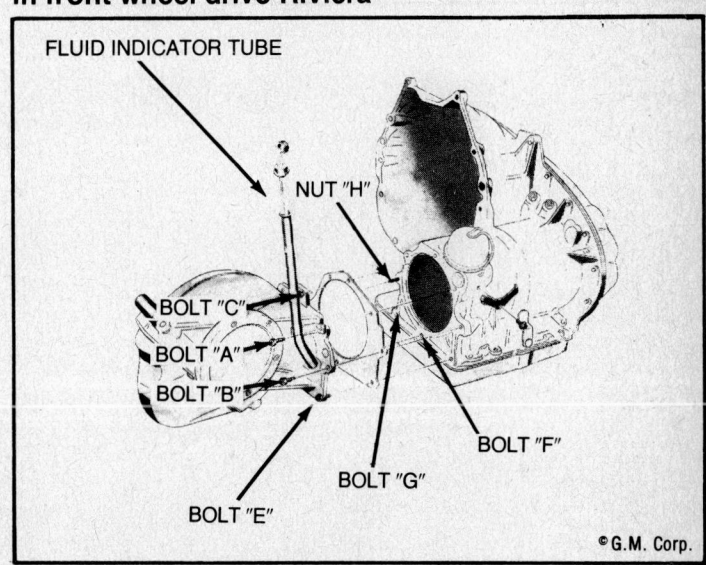

FLUID INDICATOR TUBE

NUT "H"

BOLT "C"

BOLT "A"

BOLT "B"

BOLT "F"

BOLT "G"

BOLT "E"

© G.M. Corp.

Final drive and attaching components Riviera

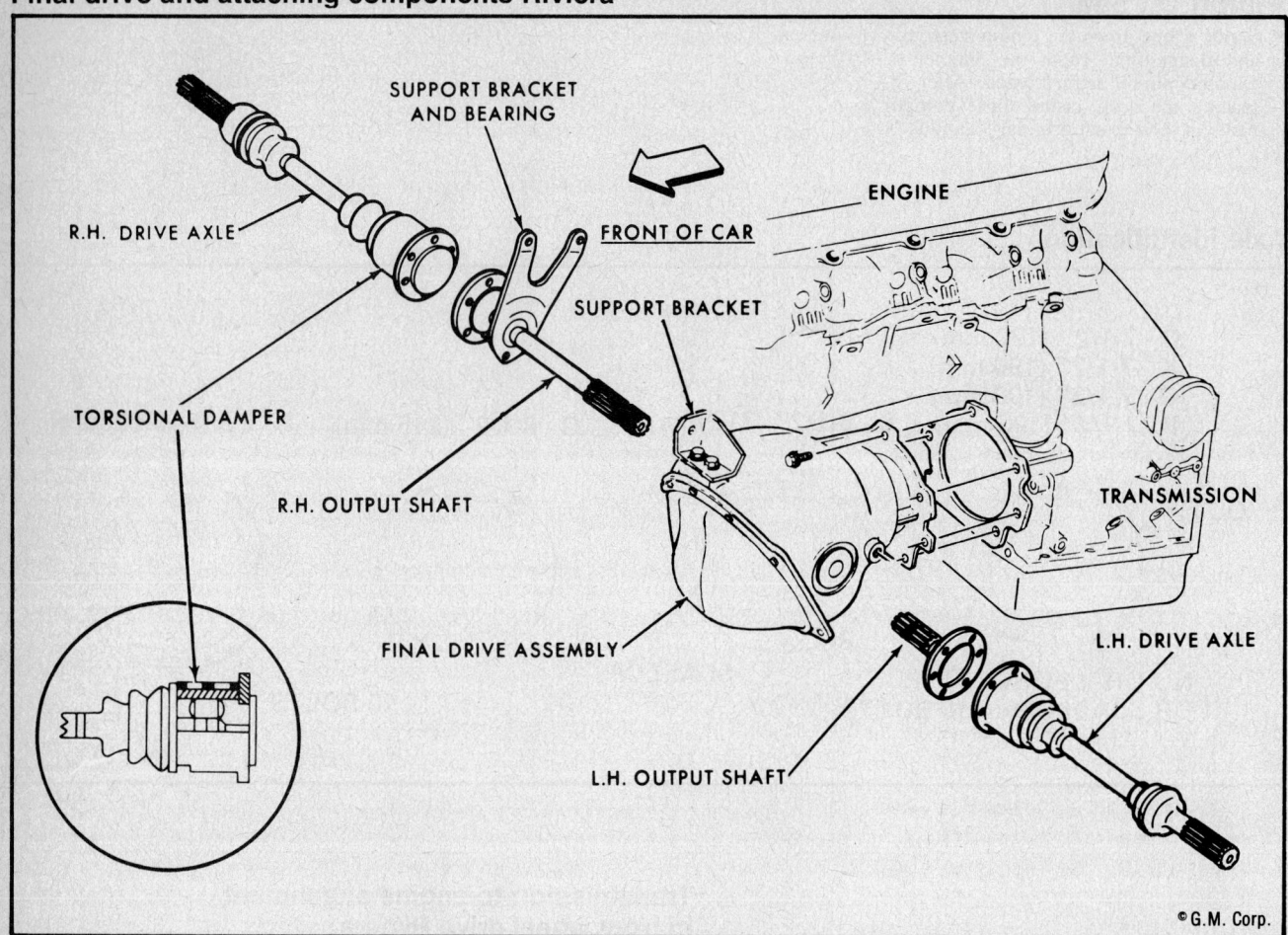

INDEX

CADILLAC
EXCEPT CIMARRON

MODEL IDENTIFICATION

1976 CADILLAC

W.B. **130″**, Broug. **133″**, "75" **151.5″**. Length 231″, Ship. Wgt. V8 4 Dr. 5083 Lbs.

1977 CADILLAC

W.B. **121.5″**, "75" **144.5″**. Length 222″, "75" 245″. Width 77″. Ship. Wgt. V8 4 Dr. 4222 Lbs.

1978 CADILLAC

W.B. **121.5″** Length 221.2″ Ship. Wgt. 8 Cyl. 2 Dr. 4,500 Lbs.

1979 CADILLAC

W.B. **121.5″** Length 221.2″ Ship. Wgt. 8 Cyl. 2 Dr. 4500 Lbs.

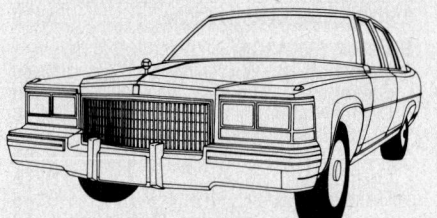

1980 CADILLAC

W.B. **121.5″**. Length 221.2″. Ship. Wgt. 2 Dr. Approx. 4183 Lbs.

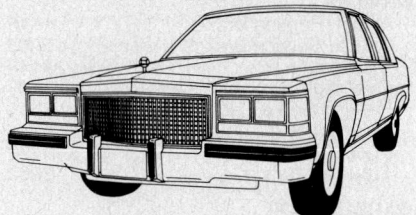

1981 FLEETWOOD

W.B. **121.5″**. Length 221.2″. 2 Dr. Ship. Wgt. 4160 Lbs.

1982 CADILLAC SEDAN DEVILLE

W.B. **121.4″**. Length 221.0″. 8 Cyl. 2 Dr. Curb Wgt. 4006 Lbs.

1976 ELDORADO

W.B. **126.3″**. Length. 225″ Ship. Wgt. V8 2 Dr. 5085

1977 ELDORADO

W.B. **126.3″**. Length 244″. Width″. Ship. Wgt. V8 2 Dr. 4955 Lbs.

1978 ELDORADO

W.B. **126.3″** Length 224.0″ Ship. Wgt. 8 Cyl. 2 Dr. 5,500 Lbs.

1979 ELDORADO

W.B. **113.9″** Length 204.0″ Ship. Wgt. 8 Cyl. 2 Dr. 3711 Lbs.

1980 ELDORADO

W.B. **113.9″**. Length 204″. Ship. Wgt. 2 Dr. Approx. 3914 Lbs.

1981 ELDORADO

W.B. **114″**. Length 204.0″. Ship. Wgt. 3908 Lbs.

1982 ELDORADO

W.B. **114.0″**. Length 204.5″. 8 Cyl. 2 Dr. Curb Wgt. 3733 Lbs.

1976 SEVILLE

W.B. **114.3″**, Length 204″. Width 72″. Ship. Wgt. V8 4 Dr. 4232 Lbs.

1977 SEVILLE

W.B. 114.3″. Length 204″. Width 72″. Ship. Wgt., V8 2 Dr. 4192 Lbs.

1978 SEVILLE

W.B. 114.3″ Length 204.0″ Ship. Wgt. 8 Cyl. 4 Dr. 4,500 Lbs.

1979 SEVILLE

W.B. 114.3″ Length 204.0″ Ship. Wgt. 8 Cyl. 4 Dr. 4360 Lbs.

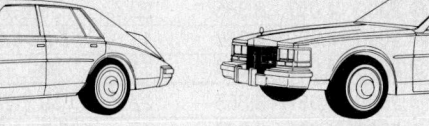

1980 SEVILLE

W.B. 114″. Length 205″. Ship. Wgt. Approx. 4185 Lbs.

1981 SEVILLE

W.B. 114″. Length 204.0″. 8 Cyl. Ship. Wgt. 4360 Lbs.

1982 SEVILLE

W.B. 114.0″. Length 204.8″. 8 Cyl. 2 Dr. Curb Wgt. 3814 Lbs.

VEHICLE IDENTIFICATION NUMBER (VIN)

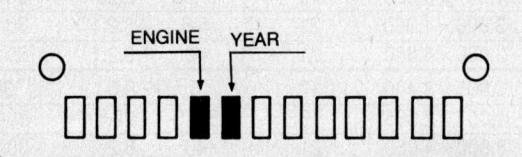

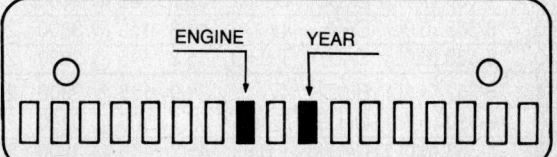

	ENGINE CODE				MODEL YEAR CODE	
Code	Eng. Disp. cu in	Eng. Config.	Carb	Eng. Mfgr.	Code	Year
R	350	V-8	E.F.I.	Olds.	6	1976
S	500	V-8	4V	Cad.		
S	500	V-8	E.F.I.	Cad.		
R	350	V-8	E.F.I.	Olds.	7	1977
S	425	V-8	4V	Cad.		
T	425	V-8	E.F.I.	Cad.		
N	350	V-8	Diesel	Olds.	8	1978
B	350	V-8	E.F.I.	Cad.		
S	425	V-8	4V	Cad.		
T	425	V-8	E.F.I.	Cad.		
N	350	V-8	Diesel	Olds.	9	1979
B	350	V-8	E.F.I.	Cad.		
S	425	V-8	4V	Cad.		
T	425	V-8	E.F.I.	Cad.		
4	252 (4.1L)	V-6	4V	Buick	A	1980
N	350 (5.7L)	V-8	Diesel	Olds.		
6	368 (6.0L)	V-8	4V	Cad.		
9	368 (6.0L)	V-8	T.B.F.I.	Cad.		
4	252 (4.1L)	V-6	4V	Buick	B	1981
N	350 (5.7L)	V-8	Diesel	Olds.		
6	368 (6.0L)	V-8	4V	Cad.		
9	368 (6.0L)	V-8	T.B.F.I.	Cad.		
8	250 (4.1L)	V-8	T.B.F.I	Cad.	1	1982
4	252 (4.1L)	V-6	4V	Buick		
N	350 (5.7L)	V-8	Diesel	Olds.		
6	368 (6.0L)	V-8	4V	Cad.		
9	368 (6.0L)	V-8	T.B.F.I.	Cad.		

① If a 17-digit VIN is used, the 8th digit is the engine code and the 10th digit is the model year code.

E.F.I. = Electronic Fuel Injection   T.B.F.I. = Throttle Body Fuel Injection

CADILLAC
EXCEPT CIMARRON

ENGINE SPECIFICATIONS
Engine Code, 5th character of the VIN number
Model Year Code, 6th character of the VIN number①

Yr.	Eng. V.I.N. Code	Engine No. Cyl. Disp. (cu in)	Eng. Mfgr.	Carb Bbl	Tax H.P.	Horsepower @ rpm	Torque @ rpm (ft lbs)	Bore and Stroke (in)	Valves Intake Opens (deg BTDC)	Fuel Pump Pres. (p.s.i.)	Comp. Ratio	Oil Pressure @ 2000 rpm
'76	R	8-350	OLDS.	E.F.I.	52.6	180 @ 4400	275 @ 2000	4.057×3.385	16	39±.78	8.25	30-45
	S	8-500	CAD.	4v	59.2	190 @ 3600	360 @ 2000	4.300×4.304	21	5.25-6.50	8.5	35
	S	8-500	CAD.	E.F.I.	59.2	215 @ 3600	400 @ 2000	4.300×4.304	21	39±.78	8.5	35
'77	R	8-350	OLDS.	E.F.I.	52.6	180 @ 4400	275 @ 2000	4.057×3.385	22	39±.78	8.25	30-45
	S	8-425	CAD.	4v	53.3	180 @ 4000	260 @ 2000	4.082×4.060	11	5.25-6.50	8.2	40-48
	T	8-425	CAD.	E.F.I.	53.3	195 @ 3800	260 @ 2000	4.082×4.060	11	39±.78	8.2	40-48
'78	B	8-350	OLDS.	E.F.I.	52.6	170 @ 4200	270 @ 2000	4.057×3.385	22	39±.78	8.0	30-45
	S	8-425	CAD.	4v	53.3	180 @ 4000	320 @ 2000	4.082×4.060	11	5.25-6.50	8.2	40-48
	T	8-425	CAD.	E.F.I.	53.3	195 @ 3800	320 @ 2400	4.082×4.060	11	39±.78	8.2	40-48
'79	S	8-425	CAD.	4v	53.3	180 @ 4000	320 @ 2000	4.082×4.060	21	5.25-6.50	8.2	40-48
	T	8-425	CAD.	E.F.I.	53.3	195 @ 3800	320 @ 2400	4.082×4.060	21	39±.78	8.2	40-48
	N	8-350	OLDS.	Diesel	52.7	125 @ 3600	225 @ 1600	4.057×3.385	16	5-6.5	22.5	30-45
'80	4	6-252 (4.1L)	BUICK	4v	36.0	110 @ 3400	195 @ 2000	3.965×3.400	17	5	8.0	37
	N	8-350 (5.7L)	OLDS.	Diesel	52.7	125 @ 3600	225 @ 1600	4.057×3.385	16	5-6.5	22.5	30-45
	6	8-368 (6.0L)	CAD.	4v	45.3	150 @ 3800	270 @ 1600	3.800×4.060	21	5-6	8.2:1	30-45
	9	8-368 (6.0L)	CAD.	T.B.F.I.	45.3	145 @ 3600	270 @ 1600	3.800×4.060	21	40	8.2:1	30-45
'81	4	6-252 (4.1L)	BUICK	4v	36.0	125 @ 3800	210 @ 2000	3.965×3.400	17	5	8.0	37
	N	8-350 (5.7L)	OLDS.	Diesel	52.7	105 @ 3200	200 @ 1600	4.057×3.385	16	5-6.5	22.5	30-45
	9	8-368 (6.0L)	CAD.	T.B.F.I.	45.3	140 @ 3800	265 @ 1400	3.800×4.060	21	40	8.2	30-45
'82	8	8-250 (4.1L)		T.B.F.I.	36.0	125 @ 4200	190 @ 2000	3.465×3.307	37	40	8.5:1	30-45
	4	6-252 (4.1L)	BUICK	4v	36.0	125 @ 3800	210 @ 2000	3.965×3.400	17	5	8.0:1	30-45
	N	8-350 (5.7L)	OLDS.	Diesel	52.7	105 @ 3200	200 @ 1600	4.057×3.385	16	5-6	22.5:1	30-45
	9	8-368 (6.0L)	CAD.	T.B.F.I.	51.2	140 @ 3800	265 @ 1400	3.800×4.060	21	40	8.2:1	30-45

E.F.I. = Electronic Fuel Injection
T.B.F.I. = Throttle Body Fuel Injection

ENGINE FIRING ORDER

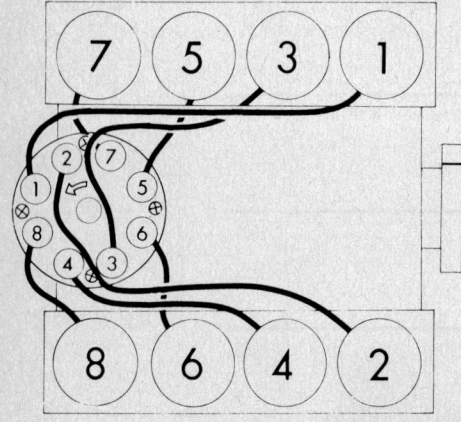

GM (Cadillac) 250 (4.1L) V8
Engine firing order: 1-8-4-3-6-5-7-2
Distributor rotation: counterclockwise

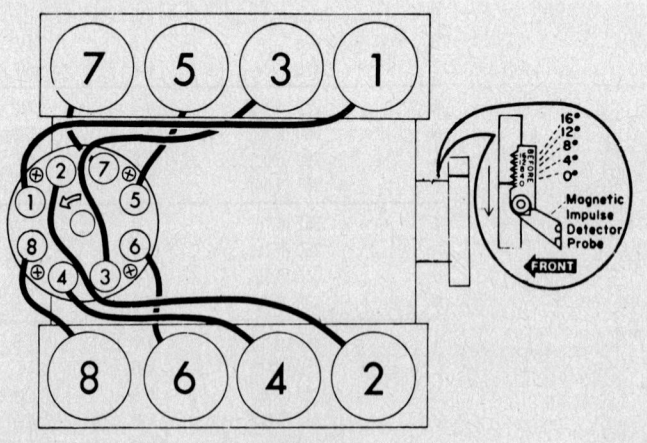

GM (Oldsmobile) 350 V8 w/EFI
Engine firing order: 1-8-4-3-6-5-7-2
Distributor rotation: counterclockwise

TUNE UP SPECIFICATIONS
Engine Code, 5th character of the VIN number
Model Year Code, 6th character of the VIN number⑥

Year	Eng. V.I.N. Code	Engine No. Cyl. Disp. (cu in)	SPARK PLUGS* Orig. Type	Gap (in)	Dist.	IGNITION TIMING (deg BTDC) Lo-Alt.	Calif.	CARBURETOR HOT IDLE (In Drive)③ Lo-Alt.	Calif.	Hi-Alt.
76	R	8-350	R-46SX	.080	E.I.	10	6	600	600	—
	S	8-500	R-45NSX	.060	E.I.	6	6	600	600	—
	S	8-500	R-45NSX	.060	E.I.	12	12	600	600	—
77	R	8-350	R-47SX	.060	E.I.	10 @ 600	8 @ 600	650	600	600
	S	8-425	R-45NSX	.060	E.I.	18 @ 1400	18 @ 1400	600	600	600
	T	8-425	R-45NSX	.060	E.I.	10 @ 1400	18 @ 1400	650	650	650
78	B	8-350	R-47SX	.060	E.I.	10 @ 600	8 @ 600	600	600	600
	S	8-425	R-45NSX	.060	E.I.	①	①	600	600	600
	T	8-425	R-45NSX	.060	E.I.	18 @ 1400	18 @ 1400	650	650	650
79	S	8-425	R-45NSX	.060	E.I.	23 @ 1600	23 @ 1600	600	600	600
	T	8-425	R-45NSX	.060	E.I.	18 @ 1400	18 @ 1400	600	600	600
	N	8-350	DIESEL	—	—	—	—	650	②	②
80	4	6-252	R-45TSX	.060	E.I.	15 @ 550	15 @ 550	550④	550④	②
	N	350	DIESEL	—	—	—	—	650	②	②
	6	368	R-45NSX	.060	E.I.	18	—	600	600	600
	9	368	R-45NSX	.060	E.I.	10⑤	—	600	600	600
81	4	6-252	R-45TSX	.060	E.S.T.⑥	15 @ 550	15 @ 550	550④	550④	②
	N	8-350	DIESEL	—	—	—	—	②	②	②
	9	8-368	R-45NSX	.060	E.S.T.⑥	10⑤	10⑤	⑦	⑦	⑦
82	8	8-250	R-45TSX	.060	E.S.T.⑥	10⑤	10⑤	⑦	⑦	⑦
	4	6-252	R-45TSX	.060	E.S.T.⑥	15 @ 550	15 @ 550	550④	550④	②
	N	8-350	DIESEL	—	—	—	—	②	②	②
	9	8-368	R-45NSX	.060	E.S.T.⑥	10⑤	10⑤	⑦	⑦	⑦

NOTE: Information listed on the emission control tune-up decal supercedes all published information as it may reflect production changes.

Eldorado—22° @ 1600; Brougham and DeVille w/4v—21°B @ 1600 rpm; federal and California Fleetwood w/4v—18°B @ 1600 rpm; federal and California high altitude Brougham, DeVille, and Fleetwood w/4v—23°B @ 1600 rpm

② See engine decal

③ Disconnect air leveling compressor hose at air cleaner and plug hose. Disconnect parking brake hose and plug. Air conditioner turned off.

④ With A/C, set solenoid screw to 680(D)

⑤ On Federal models, ground engine wiring harness test lead (green connector) set timing at less than 800 r.p.m. On California models, set timing at 600 r.p.m.

⑥ Electronic Spark Timing (EST) is controlled by an electronic control module. (ECM) The ECM receives its information from sensors that monitor a wide range of engine operating variables. Included are manifold absolute pressure, ambient barometric pressure, engine coolant temperature, air/fuel mixture temperature, engine speed, throttle position, exhaust gas oxygen and vehicle speed sensors. As the sensors supply data to the ECM, it computes spark timing and fuel delivery rate to maintain a desired mixture.

⑦ Electronic controlled idle, no adjustment.

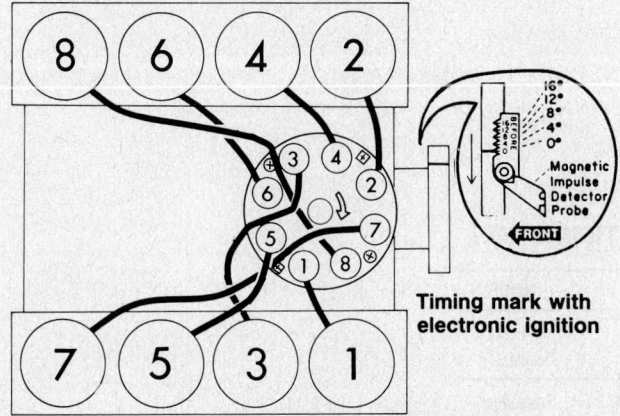

Timing mark with electronic ignition

GM (Cadillac) 368, 425, 500 V8
Engine firing order: 1-5-6-3-4-2-7-8
Distributor rotation: clockwise

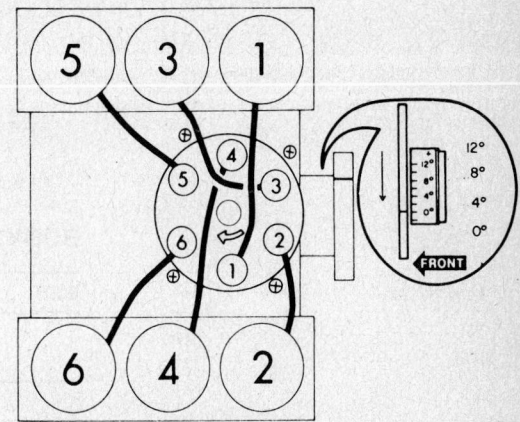

GM (Buick) 252 CID V6 Engine firing order: 1-6-5-4-3-2 Distributor rotation: clockwise

CADILLAC

EXCEPT CIMARRON

CRANKSHAFT & CONNECTING ROD SPECIFICATIONS

All measurements given in inches

Year	Engine No. Cyl. Disp. (cu in)	Eng. V.I.N Code	CRANKSHAFT Main Brg. Journal Dia	Main Brg. Oil Clearance	Shaft End Play	Thrust on No.	CONNECTING ROD Journal Diameter	Oil Clearance	Side Clearance
76	350	R	#1-2.4988-2.4998 #2-#5-2.4985-2.4995	#1-#4-.0005-.0021 #5-.0015-.0031	.004-.008	3	2.1238-2.1248	.0004-.0033	.006-.020
	500	S	3.250	.0001-.0026	.002-.012	3	2.5000	.0005-.0028	.008-.020
77	350	R	#1-2.4988-2.4998 #2-#5-2.4985-2.4995	#1-#4-.0005-.0021 #5-.0015-.0031	.0035-.0135	3	2.1238-2.1248	.0004-.0033	.006-.020
	425	S,T	3.250	.0001-.0026	.002-.012	3	2.5000	.0005-.0028	.008-.020
78	350	B	#1-2.4988-2.4998 #2-#5-2.4985-2.4995	#1-#4-.0005-.0021 #5-.0015-.0031	.0035-.0135	3	2.1238-2.1248	.0004-.0033	.006-.020
	350	N	2.9993-3.0003	#1-#4-.0005-.0021 #5-.0015-.0031	.0035-.0135	3	2.1238-2.1248	.0005-.0026	.006-.020
	425	S,T	3.250	.0001-.0026	.002-.012	3	2.500	.0005-.0028	.008-.020
79	350	B	#1-2.4988-2.4998 #2-#5-2.4985-2.4995	#1-4-.0005-.0021 #5-.0015-.0031	.0035-.0135	3	2.1238-2.1248	.0004-.0033	.006-.020
	350	N	2.9993-3.0003	#1-#4-.0005-.0021 #5-.0015-.0031	.0035-.0135	3	2.1238-2.1248	.0005-.0026	.006-.020
	425	S,T	3.250	.0001-.0026	.002-.012	3	2.500	.0005-.0028	.008-.020
80	6-252	4	2.4995	.0003-.0018	.003-.009	2	2.2487-2.2495	.0005-.0026	.006-.023
	350	8	#1-2.4988-2.4998 #2-5-2.4985-2.4995	#1-4-.0005-.0021 #5-.0015-.0031	.0035-.0135	3	1.877-1.887	.0004-.0033	.006-.020
	350	N	2.9993-3.0003	#1-#4-.0005-.0021 #5-.0015-.0031	.0035-.0135	3	1.877-1.887	.0005-.0026	.006-.020
	368	6-9	3.250	.0001-.0026	.002-.012	3	2.500	.0005-.0028	.008-.020
81	6-252	4	2.4995	.0003-.0018	.003-.009	2	2.2487-2.2495	.0005-.0026	.006-.023
	8-350 Diesel	N	2.9993-3.0003	#1-4-.0005-.0021 #5-.0015-.0031	.0035-.0135	3	1.877-1.887	.0005-.0026	.006-.020
	8-368	6-9	3.250	.0001-.0026	.002-.012	3	2.500	.0005-.0028	.008-.020
82	8-250	8	2.64	.0005-.0018	.0015	3	1.93	.0005-.0026	.008-.020
	368	6-9	3.250	.0001-.0026	.002-.012	3	2.500	.0005-.0028	.008-.020
	6-252	4	2.4995	.0003-.0018	.003-.009	2	2.2487-2.2495	.0005-.0026	.006-.023
	8-250 Diesel	N	2.9993-3.0003	#1-4-.0005-.0021 #5-.0015-.0031	.0035-.0135	3	1.877-1.887	.0005-.0026	.006-.020
	8-368	6-9	3.250	.0001-.0026	.002-.012	3	2.500	.0005-.0028	.008-.020

BODY MODEL IDENTIFICATION

BODY	MODEL
C	Fleetwood Deville
D	Passenger
K	Seville
E	Eldorado

VALVE SPECIFICATIONS

Year	Engine No. Cyl. Disp. (cu in.)	Eng. V.I.N. Code	Seat Angle (deg)	Face Angle (deg.)	Spring Test Pressure (lbs @ in)	Spring Installed Height (in.)	STEM TO GUIDE CLEARANCE (in.) Intake	Exhaust	STEM DIAMETER (in.) Intake	Exhaust
76	8-350	R	1-45 E-31	1-44 E-30	180-194 @ 1.270	1.670	.0010-.0027	.0015-.0032	.3425-.3432	.3420-.3427
	8-500	S	45	44	155-165 @ 1.496	1.946	.0010-.0027	.0010-.0027	.3413-.3420	.3413-.3420
77-78	8-350	B-R	1-45 E-31	E-44 I-30	180-194 @ 1.270	1.670	.0010-.0027	.0015-.0027	.3425-.3432	.3420-.3427
	8-350	N	I-45 E-31	I-44 E-30	144-158 @ 1.300	1.670	.0010-.0027	.0015-.0027	.3425-.3432	.3420-.3427
	8-425	S	45	44	155-165 @ 1.496	1.946	.0010-.0027	.0010-.0027	.3413-.3420	.3413-.3420
	8-425	T	45	44	155-165 @ 1.496	1.946	.0010-.0027	.0010-.0027	.3413-.3420	.3413-.3420
79	8-350	N	I-45 E-31	I-44 E-30	144-158 @ 1.300	1.670	.0010-.0027	.0015-.0027	.3425-.3432	.3420-.3427
	8-425	S	45	44	155-165 @ 1.496	1.946	.0010-.0027	.0010-.0027	.3413-.3420	.3413-.3420
	8-425	T	45	44	155-165 @ 1.496	1.946	.0010-.0027	.0010-.0027	.3413-.3420	.3413-.3420
80-81	6-252	4	45	45	159-169 @ 1.340	1.727	.0015-.0035	.0015-.0032	.3401-.3412	.3405-.3412
	8-350	N	I-45 E-31	I-44 E-30	144-158 @ 1.300	1.670	.0010-.0027	.0015-.0032	.3425-.3432	.3420-.3427
	368	6-9	45	44	155-165 @ 1.496	1.946	.0010-.0027	.0010-.0027	.3413-.3420	.3413-.3420
82	8-250	8	45	44	175-189 @ 1.280	N.A.	0.005	0.005	.3420-.3413	.3411-.3418
	6-252	4	45	45	159-169 @ 1.340	1.727	.0015-.0035	.0015-.0032	.3401-.3412	.3405-.3412
	8-350	N	I-45 E-31	I-44 E-30	144-158 @ 1.300	1.670	.0010-.0027	.0015-.0032	.3425-.3432	.3420-.3427
	368	6-9	45	44	155-165 @ 1.496	1.946	.0010-.0027	.0010-.0027	.3413-.3420	.3413-.3420

I = Intake Valve
E = Exhaust Valve

DISTRIBUTOR SPECIFICATIONS

Year	Distributor Identification①	CENTRIFUGAL ADVANCE Start Crank. Deg. @ Eng. RPM	Finish Crank. Deg. @ Eng. RPM	VACUUM ADVANCE Start @ In. Hg.	Finish Crank. Deg. @ In. Hg.
76	1112897	0 @ 400-900	16-20 @ 5000	5.5-6.5	21 @ 13
	1112924	0 @ 400-1050	12-16 @ 5000	4.5-5.5	29 @ 15
	1112931	0 @ 900	10.5 @ 5000	5	28 @ 15.5
	1112954	0 @ 400-900	16-20 @ 5000	4.5-5.5	29 @ 15
	1113202	0 @ 400-1050	16-20 @ 5000	5.5-6.5	21 @ 13
77	1103217	0 @ 700	17 @ 4000	5	28 @ 15.5
	1103219	0 @ 700	17 @ 4000	5	28 @ 15.5
	1103221	0 @ 900	21 @ 5000	7.5	24 @ 17.5
	1103222	0 @ 900	21 @ 5000	A-10 R-3	A-18 @ 18 R-8 @ 9
	1103297	0 @ 800	14 @ 5000	4	20 @ 12.6
	1103298	0 @ 800	14 @ 5000	5	20 @ 9.5

CADILLAC
EXCEPT CIMARRON

DISTRIBUTOR SPECIFICATIONS

Year	Distributor Identification①	CENTRIFUGAL ADVANCE		VACUUM ADVANCE	
		Start Crank. Deg. @ Eng. RPM	Finish Crank. Deg. @ Eng. RPM	Start @ In. Hg.	Finish Crank. Deg. @ In. Hg.
78	1103307(AB)	.5R-1.6 @ 900	20-22 @ 5000	9.5	17-19 @ 18.4
	1103331(AC)	.5-3.5 @ 900	13-19 @ 5000	3.5	27-29 @ 17.3
	1103332(AD)	.5-3.5 @ 900	13-19 @ 5000	3.5	19-21 @ 13.2
	1103334(AH)	.5-3.5 @ 900	14-19 @ 5000	4.4	27-29 @ 16.2
	1103335(AJ)	.5R-1.6 @ 900	12-16 @ 5000	3.5	19-21 @ 13.2
	1103345(AN)	.5-3.5 @ 900	13-19 @ 5000	3.5	15-17 @ 17.2
	1103348(AO)	.5R-1.6 @ 900	20-22 @ 5000	5.6	23-25 @ 12.5
	1103349(AP)	.5R-1.6 @ 900	20-22 @ 5000	5.6	27-29 @ 16.4
	1103352(AS)	.5-3.5 @ 900	13-19 @ 5000	5.6	9-11 @ 11.2
	1103389(AT)	.5-3.5 @ 900	13-19 @ 5000	3.5	27-29 @ 15.7
79	1103392	.25-0 @ 550	13-19 @ 4800	3.0	19-21 @ 14
	1103307	.047 @ 800	19.5-22 @ 6000	4.0	15-19 @ 17
	1103389	.25-.5 @ 600	14-19 @ 4000	4.0	27-29 @ 16
	1103393	.5-0 @ 800	19.5-22 @ 6000	5.625	22-25 @ 13
	1103394	.5-0 @ 800	19.5-22 @ 6000	5.625	27-29 @ 16
	1103395	.5-0 @ 550	11-19 @ 4800	8.4375	9-11 @ 12
	1103332	.125-0 @ 575	13-19 @ 4800	4.0	19-21 @ 13
	1103334	.25-0 @ 575	14-19 @ 5000	5.625	27-29 @ 16
	1103335	.25-0 @ 600	11-16 @ 5800	5.0	19-21 @ 13
80	1112891	0 @ 200	9 @ 2500	4½	14½ @ 13
	1112892	−¼-0 @ 330	10 @ 0000	5.5	9.5-10.5 @ 14
	1112954	−¼-0 @ 330	10 @ 3000	4.5	13.5-14.5 @ 16
	1112897	0 @ 200	10 @ 2500	5½	9½-10½ @ 13½
	1112924	0 @ 200	8 @ 2500	5	13½-14½ @ 16
	1112931	0 @ 200	22 @ 2500	5	13½-14½ @ 18
	1112932	0 @ 200	22 @ 2500	5	8½-9½ @ 18
	1112954	−¼-0 @ 330	10 @ 3000	4½	13½-14½ @ 16
	1113202	0 @ 200	9 @ 2500	4½	10½ @ 13

.5R = .5 Degrees Retarded
EFI = Electronic Fuel Injection
NA = not available
① For distributor specs on 252 V-6, see Buick section. On all other engines, timing advance is computer controlled.

Cylinder head bolt tightening sequence 250 CID V8 engine

Intake manifold bolt tightening sequence 250 CID V8 engine

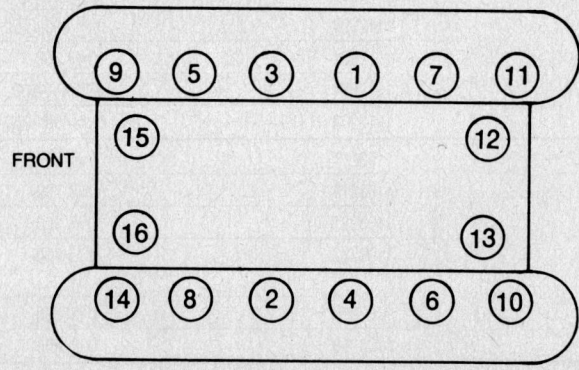

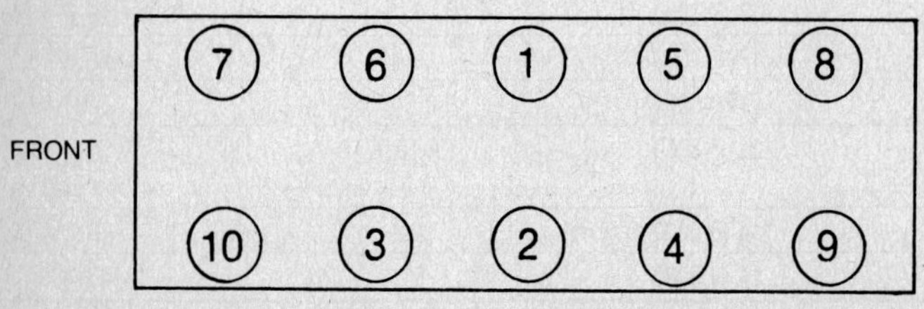

TORQUE SPECIFICATIONS

All readings in ft/lbs

Year	Engine No. Cyl. Disp. (cu in.)	Eng. V.I.N. Code	Cylinder Head Bolts	Rod Bearing Bolts	Main Bearing Bolts	Crankshaft Bolt	Flywheel To Crankshaft Bolts	MANIFOLD	
								Intake	Exhaust
76	350	R	85	42	80②	310③	60	40	25
	500	S	115	40	90	Press Fit①	75	30	35
77	350	R	85	42	80②	310③	60	40	25
	425	S,T	95⑤	40	90	Press Fit①	75	30	35⑥
78	350	B	130⑤	42	80②	310③	60	40⑤	25
	350	N	130⑤	42	120	200-310④	60	40⑤	25
	425	S,T	95⑤	40	90	Press Fit①	75	30	35⑥
79	350	B	130⑤	42	80②	310③ 310④	60	40⑤	25
	425	S,T	95⑤	40	90	Press Fit①	75	30	35⑥
80	252	T	80	40	100	225	60	45	25
	350	N	130⑤	42	120	200-310④	60	40⑤	25
	368	6,9	95⑤	40	90	Press Fit①	75	30	35⑥
81	252	4	80	40	100	225	60	45	25
	350	N	130⑤	42	120	200-310④	60	40⑤	25
	368	6,9	95⑤	40	90	Press Fit①	75	30	35⑥
82	250	8	⑦	22	85	225	75	⑧	18
	252	4	80	40	100	225	60	45	25
	350	N	130⑤	42	120	200-310④	60	40⑤	25
	368	6,9	95⑤	40	90	Press Fit①	75	30	35⑥

Note:—Some bolts and nuts are marked on the heads to indicate the grade of steel used. Do not use bolts of a lower grade than originally installed. The marks consist of lines: SAE 5-3 Lines; SAE 7-5 Lines; SAE 8-6 Lines

① Pulley to harmonic balancer screw—17 ft/lbs
② 120 ft./lbs., on no. 5 main bearing bolts
③ Balancer to crankshaft
④ Pulley to harmonic balancer screw—20 ft/lbs
⑤ Cleaned and lubricated
⑥ Long screw shown; short screw—12 ft/lbs
⑦ First pull 45 ft./lbs. (60 N•m)
　 Second pull 90 ft./lbs. (120 N•m)
⑧ '1-Tighten 1- 2- 3- 4 to 10-15 ft./lbs. (24.5-30 N•m)
　 '1-Tighten 5 thru 16 18-20 ft./lbs. (24.5-30 N•m)
　 '3-Retorque all to 18-22 ft./ibs. (24.5-30 (N•m)

CADILLAC
EXCEPT CIMARRON

BRAKE SPECIFICATIONS

Year	Model	Master Cylinder Bore Diameter	Caliper or Wheel Cylinder		Brake Drum/ Rotor* Diameter		Drum Maximum Machined Diameter	Rotor Runout	Rotor Allowable Minimum Machined Thickness	Rotor Thickness Variation Maximum
			Front	Rear	Front	Rear				
76	Seville	1.125	2 15/16	15/16	11.0	11.0	11.060	.005	.980	.0005
	All Exc. Eldorado and Seville	1.125	2 15/16	15/16①	11.74	12.0	12.060	.005	1.220	.0005
	Eldorado	1.125	2 15/16	2½	11.0	11.0	—	.008	1.190	.0005
77	Seville, Brougham	1.125	2 15/16	2½	11.74	11.14	—	F-.005 R-.0029	F-.980 R-.911	F-.0005 R-.0005
	DeVille	1.125	2 15/16	1	11.74	11.0	11.060	.005	.980	.0005
	Eldorado	1.125	2 15/16	2½	11.0	11.0	—	.008	1.190	.0005
	Limousine and Comm. Chassis									
	Chassis	1.125	2 15/16	15/16	11.74	12.0	12.060	.005	1.220	.0005
78	Seville, Brougham	1.125	2 15/16	2½	11.74	11.14	—	F-.005 R-.0029	F-.980 R-.911	F-.0005 R-.0005
	DeVille	1.125	2 15/16	1	11.74	11.0	11.060	.005	.980	.0005
	Eldorado	1.125	2 15/16	2½	11.0	11.0	—	.008	1.190	.0005
	Limousine and Comm.									
	Chassis	1.125	2 15/16	15/16	11.74	12.0	12.060	.005	1.220	.0005
79	Seville	1.125	2 15/16	2½	11.7	11.0	—	.005 R-.911	F-.980	.0005
	DeVille	1.125	2 15/16	2½①	11.7	11.0	11.060	.005	.980	.0005
	Eldorado	1.0	2½	2⅛	10.4	9.5	—	.005	1.036	.0005
	Comm. Chassis	1.125	2 15/16	2½	11.7	12.0	1.285	.005	1.220	.0005
80	Seville	1.0	2½	2⅛	10.4	9.5	—	.005	1.036	.0005
	DeVille	1.125	2 15/16	2½	11.7	11.0	11.060	.005	.980	.0005
	Eldorado	1.0	2½	2⅛	10.4	9.5	—	.005	1.036	.0005
	Comm. Chassis	1.125	2 15/16	2½	11.7	12.0	12.060	.005	1.220	.0005
81-82	Seville	1.0	2½	2⅛	16.4	9.5	—	.005	1.036	.0005
	DeVille	1.125	2 15/16	2½	11.74	11.0	11.060	.005	.980	.0005
	Eldorado	1.0	2½	2⅛	10.43	9.5	—	.005	1.036	.0005
	Comm. Chassis	1.125	2 15/16	2½	11.74	12.0	12.060	.005	1.220	.0005
82	Seville	1.0	2½	2⅛	11.74	9.5	—	.005	1.036	.0005
	DeVille	1.125	2 15/16	2½	11.74	11.0	11.060	.005	1.036	.0005
	Eldorado	1.0	2½	2⅛	10.43	9.5	—	.005	9.80	.0005
	Comm. Chassis	1.125	2 15/16	2½	11.74	12.0	12.060	.005	1.220	.0005

* Rotor Working Outer Diameter

F = Front

R = Rear

— Not Applicable

① Comm. chassis—1"

FLUID CAPACITIES—Coolant, Fuel & Lubricant

Year	Engine No. Cyl Displacement (Cu. In.)	Engine Crankcase (Add 1 Qt. For New Filter)	TRANSMISSION Automatic② (Pts. to Refill After Draining)	Drive Axle (pts)	Gasoline Tank (gals)	Rad. Cap. Pressure (lbs)	Thermo. Opening Temp.	Cooling System With A/C (qts)
SEVILLE								
76	350	4	8	4¼	21	15	180°	18.9
77	350	4	8	4¼	21	15	200°	17.2
78	350	4	9①	4¼	21	15	200°	17.2
79 EXC DIESEL	350	4	9①	4¼	21	15	180°	17.2
79 DIESEL	350	6	9.5	4¼	21	15	195°	20.1
80 DIESEL	350	6	6	3⅕	27.0	15	195°	18.4
80	368	4	8	3⅕	20.6	15	180°	20.3
81-82 DIESEL	350	6	6	3⅕	20.3	15	195°	18.4
EXC DIESEL	368	4	8	3⅕	20.3	15	180°	18.4
ELDORADO								
76	500	5	10	4	27½	15	180°	25.8
77	425	5	10	4	27½	15	180°	24.3
78	425	5	10	4	27½	15	195°	24.3
79 EXC DIESEL	425	5	10	3½	19.6	15	195°	14.9③
79 DIESEL	350	6	9.5	3⅔	22.4	15	195°	18.4
80 DIESEL	350	6	6	3⅕	27.0	15	195°	18.4
80	368	4	8	3⅕	20.6	15	180°	22.4
81 DIESEL	350	6	6	3⅕	20.3	15	195°	18.4
81	368	4	8	3⅕	20.3	15	180°	22.4
CADILLAC, EXCEPT SEVILLE AND ELDORADO								
76	500	4	8	4	27½	15	180°	23.0
77	425	4	8	4¼	24	15	195°	19.8
78	425	4	8	4¼	24	15	195°	19.8
79 EXC DIESEL	425	4	8	4¼	24	15	195°	20.8
79 DIESEL	350	6	9.5	4¼	25	15	195°	23.8
80 DIESEL	350	6	8	4¼	23.7	15	195°	23.7
80	368	4	6	4¼	20.3	15	180°	20.3
80	252	4	8	4¼	20.7	15	195°	13.0
81-82 DIESEL	350	6	8	4¼	25	15	195°	18.2
81-82	368	4	6	4¼	25	15	195°	21.4

—Not Applicable
① Diesel—6 pts
② Specifications Do Not Include Torque Converter
③ H.D. cooling—15.6 qts
④ 350 only: 368 22.4 qts.
⑤ THM 200C-4¼; THM 325-5; THM 400-4

CADILLAC
EXCEPT CIMARRON

FUSE IDENTIFICATION

Fuse block—all except Seville and Eldorado

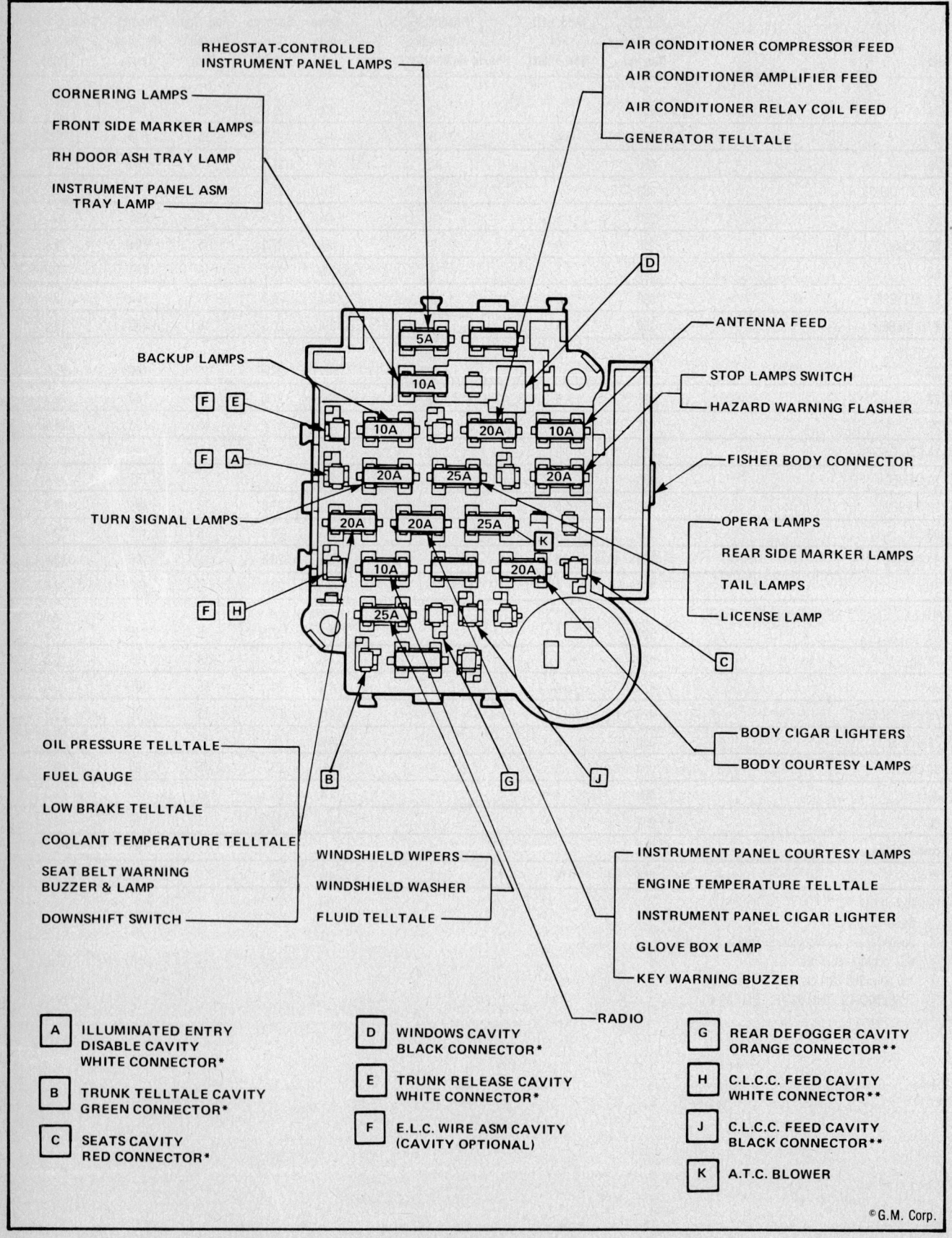

RHEOSTAT-CONTROLLED
INSTRUMENT PANEL LAMPS

AIR CONDITIONER COMPRESSOR FEED

AIR CONDITIONER AMPLIFIER FEED

AIR CONDITIONER RELAY COIL FEED

GENERATOR TELLTALE

CORNERING LAMPS

FRONT SIDE MARKER LAMPS

RH DOOR ASH TRAY LAMP

INSTRUMENT PANEL ASM
TRAY LAMP

BACKUP LAMPS

ANTENNA FEED

STOP LAMPS SWITCH

HAZARD WARNING FLASHER

FISHER BODY CONNECTOR

OPERA LAMPS

REAR SIDE MARKER LAMPS

TAIL LAMPS

LICENSE LAMP

TURN SIGNAL LAMPS

BODY CIGAR LIGHTERS

BODY COURTESY LAMPS

OIL PRESSURE TELLTALE

FUEL GAUGE

LOW BRAKE TELLTALE

COOLANT TEMPERATURE TELLTALE

SEAT BELT WARNING
BUZZER & LAMP

DOWNSHIFT SWITCH

WINDSHIELD WIPERS

WINDSHIELD WASHER

FLUID TELLTALE

INSTRUMENT PANEL COURTESY LAMPS

ENGINE TEMPERATURE TELLTALE

INSTRUMENT PANEL CIGAR LIGHTER

GLOVE BOX LAMP

KEY WARNING BUZZER

RADIO

Fuse values: 5A, 10A, 10A, 20A, 10A, 20A, 25A, 20A, 20A, 20A, 25A, 10A, 20A, 25A

A ILLUMINATED ENTRY DISABLE CAVITY WHITE CONNECTOR*	**D** WINDOWS CAVITY BLACK CONNECTOR*	**G** REAR DEFOGGER CAVITY ORANGE CONNECTOR**
B TRUNK TELLTALE CAVITY GREEN CONNECTOR*	**E** TRUNK RELEASE CAVITY WHITE CONNECTOR*	**H** C.L.C.C. FEED CAVITY WHITE CONNECTOR**
C SEATS CAVITY RED CONNECTOR*	**F** E.L.C. WIRE ASM CAVITY (CAVITY OPTIONAL)	**J** C.L.C.C. FEED CAVITY BLACK CONNECTOR**
		K A.T.C. BLOWER

© G.M. Corp.

Fuse block—Sevile and Eldorado

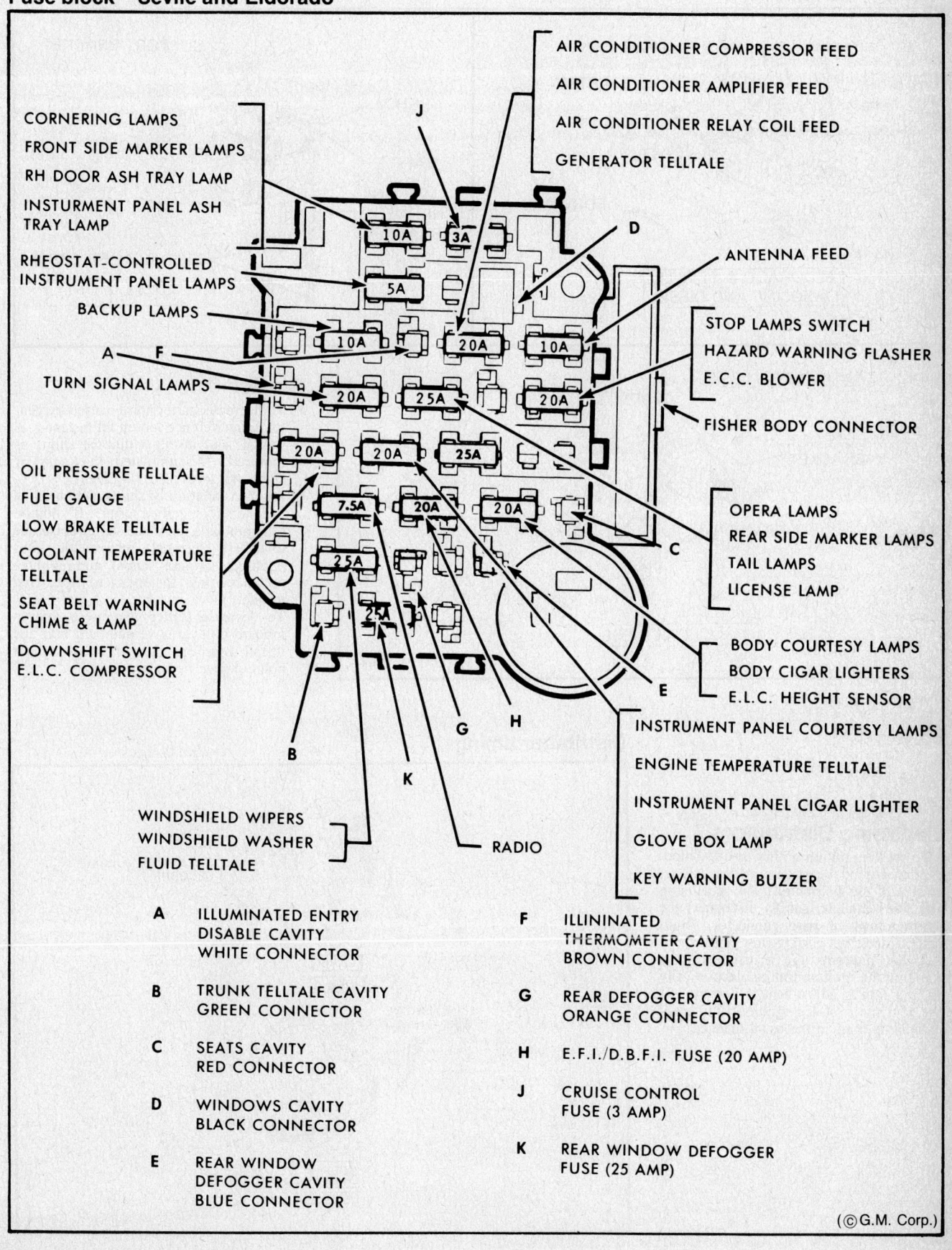

CORNERING LAMPS
FRONT SIDE MARKER LAMPS
RH DOOR ASH TRAY LAMP
INSTURMENT PANEL ASH TRAY LAMP

RHEOSTAT-CONTROLLED INSTRUMENT PANEL LAMPS

BACKUP LAMPS

A   F

TURN SIGNAL LAMPS

AIR CONDITIONER COMPRESSOR FEED
AIR CONDITIONER AMPLIFIER FEED
AIR CONDITIONER RELAY COIL FEED
GENERATOR TELLTALE

J

D

ANTENNA FEED

STOP LAMPS SWITCH
HAZARD WARNING FLASHER
E.C.C. BLOWER

FISHER BODY CONNECTOR

OIL PRESSURE TELLTALE
FUEL GAUGE
LOW BRAKE TELLTALE
COOLANT TEMPERATURE TELLTALE
SEAT BELT WARNING CHIME & LAMP
DOWNSHIFT SWITCH
E.L.C. COMPRESSOR

OPERA LAMPS
REAR SIDE MARKER LAMPS
TAIL LAMPS
LICENSE LAMP

C

BODY COURTESY LAMPS
BODY CIGAR LIGHTERS
E.L.C. HEIGHT SENSOR

E

INSTRUMENT PANEL COURTESY LAMPS
ENGINE TEMPERATURE TELLTALE
INSTRUMENT PANEL CIGAR LIGHTER
GLOVE BOX LAMP
KEY WARNING BUZZER

B

K

G   H

WINDSHIELD WIPERS
WINDSHIELD WASHER
FLUID TELLTALE

RADIO

10A 3A 5A 10A 20A 10A 20A 20A 25A 20A 20A 25A 7.5A 20A 20A 25A 25A

A	ILLUMINATED ENTRY DISABLE CAVITY WHITE CONNECTOR	**F**	ILLININATED THERMOMETER CAVITY BROWN CONNECTOR
B	TRUNK TELLTALE CAVITY GREEN CONNECTOR	**G**	REAR DEFOGGER CAVITY ORANGE CONNECTOR
C	SEATS CAVITY RED CONNECTOR	**H**	E.F.I./D.B.F.I. FUSE (20 AMP)
D	WINDOWS CAVITY BLACK CONNECTOR	**J**	CRUISE CONTROL FUSE (3 AMP)
E	REAR WINDOW DEFOGGER CAVITY BLUE CONNECTOR	**K**	REAR WINDOW DEFOGGER FUSE (25 AMP)

(©G.M. Corp.)

ELECTRICAL SECTION

Starter installation

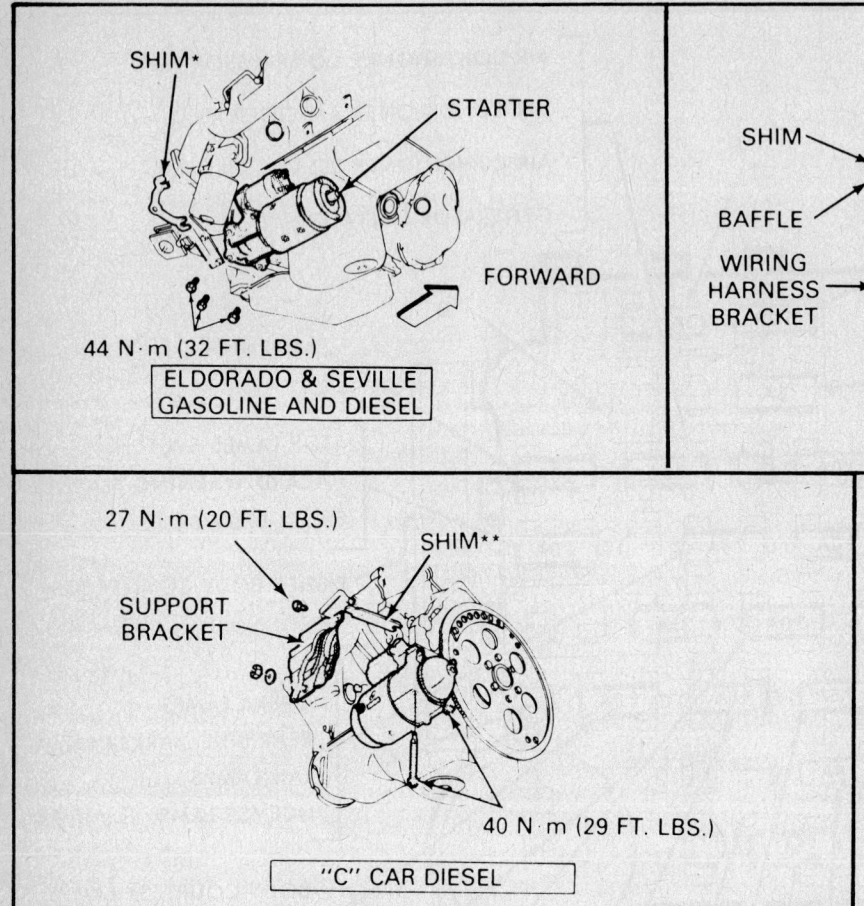

SHIM*

STARTER

FORWARD

44 N·m (32 FT. LBS.)

ELDORADO & SEVILLE
GASOLINE AND DIESEL

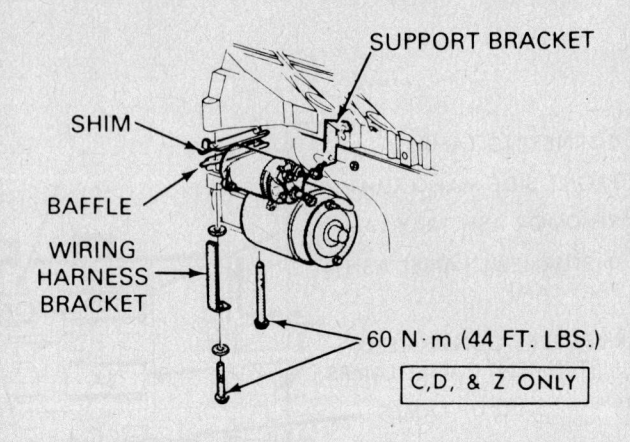

SUPPORT BRACKET

SHIM

BAFFLE

WIRING
HARNESS
BRACKET

60 N·m (44 FT. LBS.)

C, D, & Z ONLY

27 N·m (20 FT. LBS.)

SHIM**

SUPPORT
BRACKET

40 N·m (29 FT. LBS.)

"C" CAR DIESEL

(©G.M. Corp.)

Starter

- To decrease starter noise caused by gear tooth interference loosen all fasteners as shown, and install additional shims as required. (Accumulated thickness of shims not to exceed .047 inch).
- After installation of shims, retighten all fasteners to specified torque. If addition of shims fails to reduce starter noise due to excess clearance, remove all shims (including original shims), and retighten all mounting fasteners to specified torque.
- To decrease starter gear noise, loosen inboard bolt, remove outboard bolt and install shim (one shim max.). Retighten bolts to specified torque.

Distributor timing

Electronic Distributors

To set the ignition timing on 1980 models, first ground the green wire connector at the side of the distributor body. Beginning with 1981 models, simply disconnect the distributor green wire connector. (Both methods interrupt current flow to the module; this prevents the distributor from changing the ignition timing electronically while a timing adjustment is performed.) The remainder of the ignition timing adjustment is done in the usual manner.

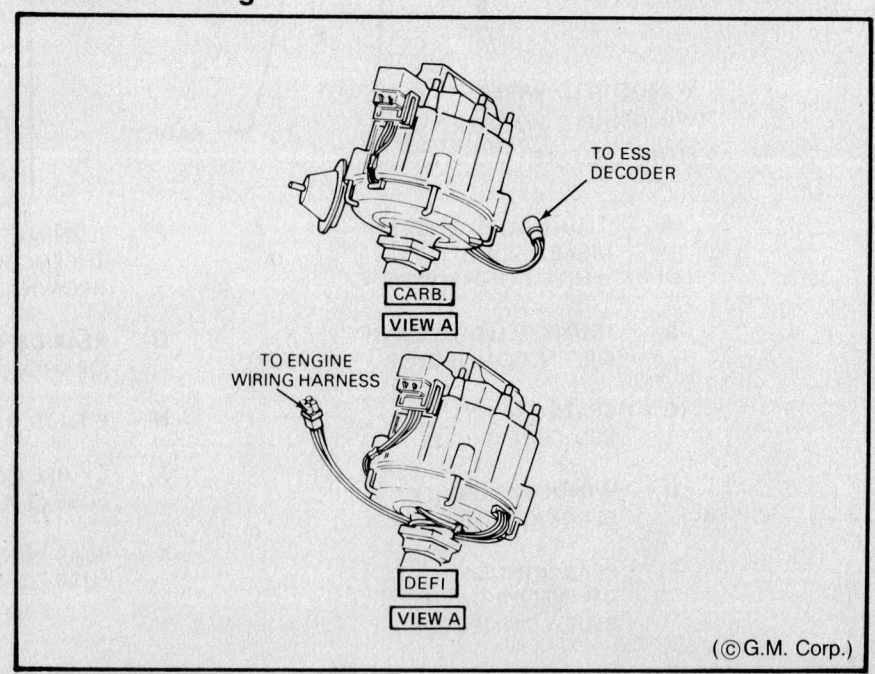

TO ESS
DECODER

CARB.

VIEW A

TO ENGINE
WIRING HARNESS

DEFI

VIEW A

(©G.M. Corp.)

Steering Column and Electrical Components

1. REMOVE AND INSTALL SHAFT LOCK AND/OR CANCELLING CAM

REMOVE

1. Disconnect negative battery cable.
2. Remove parts as shown.

INSTALL

1. Install parts as shown.
2. Connect negative battery cable.

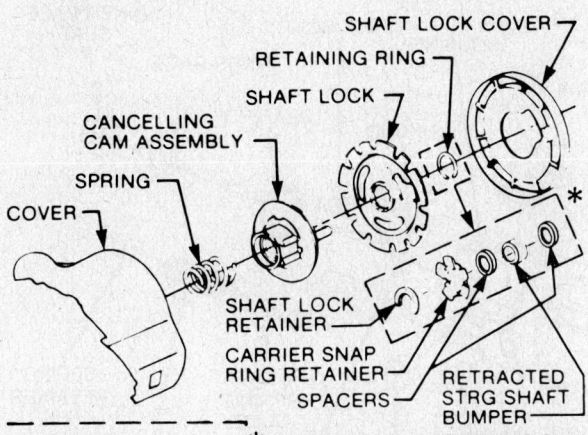

SHAFT LOCK COVER
RETAINING RING
SHAFT LOCK
CANCELLING CAM ASSEMBLY
SPRING
COVER
SHAFT LOCK RETAINER
CARRIER SNAP RING RETAINER
SPACERS
RETRACTED STRG SHAFT BUMPER
*

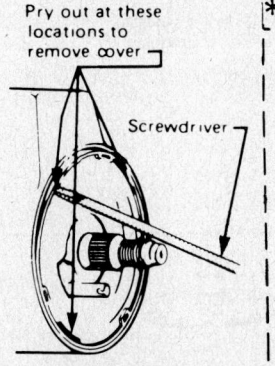

Pry out at these locations to remove cover
Screwdriver

REMOVE SHAFT LOCK COVER

*ON TELESCOPE STEERING ONLY

J-23653-4
J-23653
RETAINING RING

Tighten nut until tool slightly depresses shaft lock

REMOVE AND INSTALL RETAINING RING

2. REMOVE AND INSTALL TURN SIGNAL SWITCH

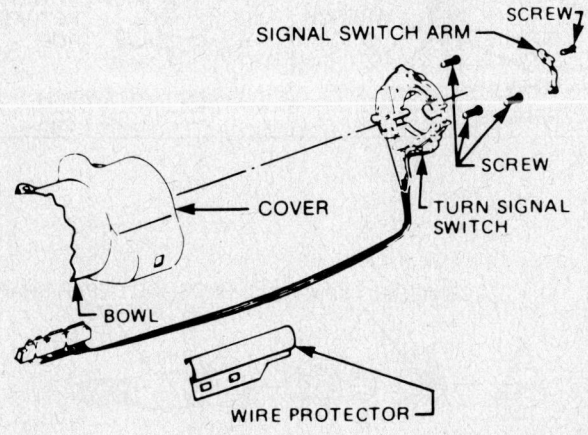

SIGNAL SWITCH ARM
SCREW
SCREW
COVER
TURN SIGNAL SWITCH
BOWL
WIRE PROTECTOR

3. REMOVE AND INSTALL IGNITION LOCK AND KEY WARNING BUZZER

REMOVE

1. Turn lock to "RUN" position and remove key warning buzzer.
2. Remove parts as shown.

To assemble, rotate to stop while holding cylinder.

INSTALL

1. Install lock cylinder.
2. Turn lock to "RUN" position and install key warning buzzer switch.

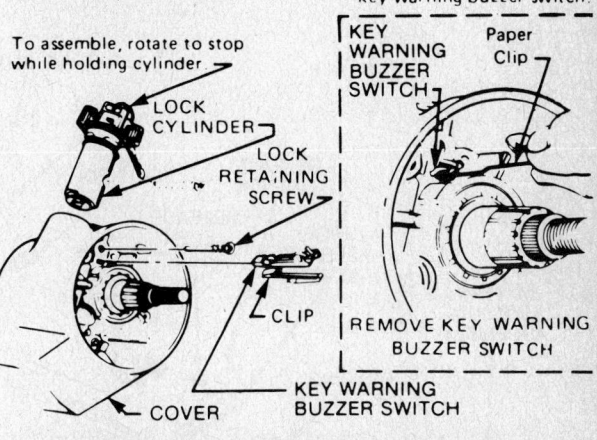

LOCK CYLINDER
LOCK RETAINING SCREW
CLIP
COVER
KEY WARNING BUZZER SWITCH

KEY WARNING BUZZER SWITCH
Paper Clip

REMOVE KEY WARNING BUZZER SWITCH

4. REMOVE AND INSTALL COVER AND WIPER SWITCH

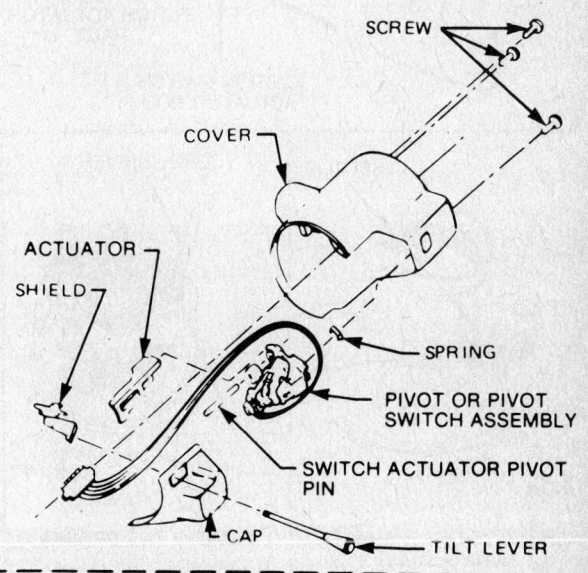

SCREW
COVER
ACTUATOR
SHIELD
SPRING
PIVOT OR PIVOT SWITCH ASSEMBLY
SWITCH ACTUATOR PIVOT PIN
CAP
TILT LEVER

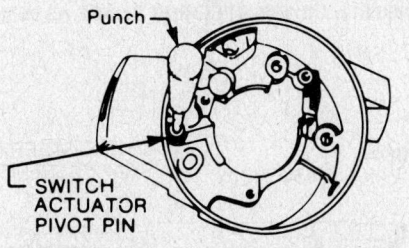

Punch
SWITCH ACTUATOR PIVOT PIN

REMOVE AND INSTALL PIVOT AND SWITCH ASSEMBLY

CADILLAC
EXCEPT CIMARRON

5. REMOVE AND INSTALL HOUSING

REMOVE
1. REINSTALL TILT LEVER AND PLACE COLUMN IN FULL "UP" POSITION.
2. REMOVE TILT SPRING AND PIVOT PINS.
3. REMOVE HOUSING BY PULLING UPWARD ON TILT LEVER AND PULL HOUSING UPWARD UNTIL IT STOPS. MOVE HOUSING TO THE RIGHT TO DISENGAGE RACK FROM ACTUATOR.
4. REMOVE TILT LEVER.
5. REMOVE PARTS AS SHOWN.

INSTALL
1. INSTALL PARTS AS SHOWN.
2. WHILE HOLDING UP ON TILT LEVER TO DISENGAGE LOCK SHOES INSTALL OVER STEERING SHAFT. MOVE RACK DOWNWARD AND HOLD. TIP HOUSING TO THE LEFT UNTIL RACK ENGAGES PIN ON ACTUATOR ROD. PUSH HOUSING DOWN UNTIL PIVOT PIN HOLES ARE IN ALIGNMENT.

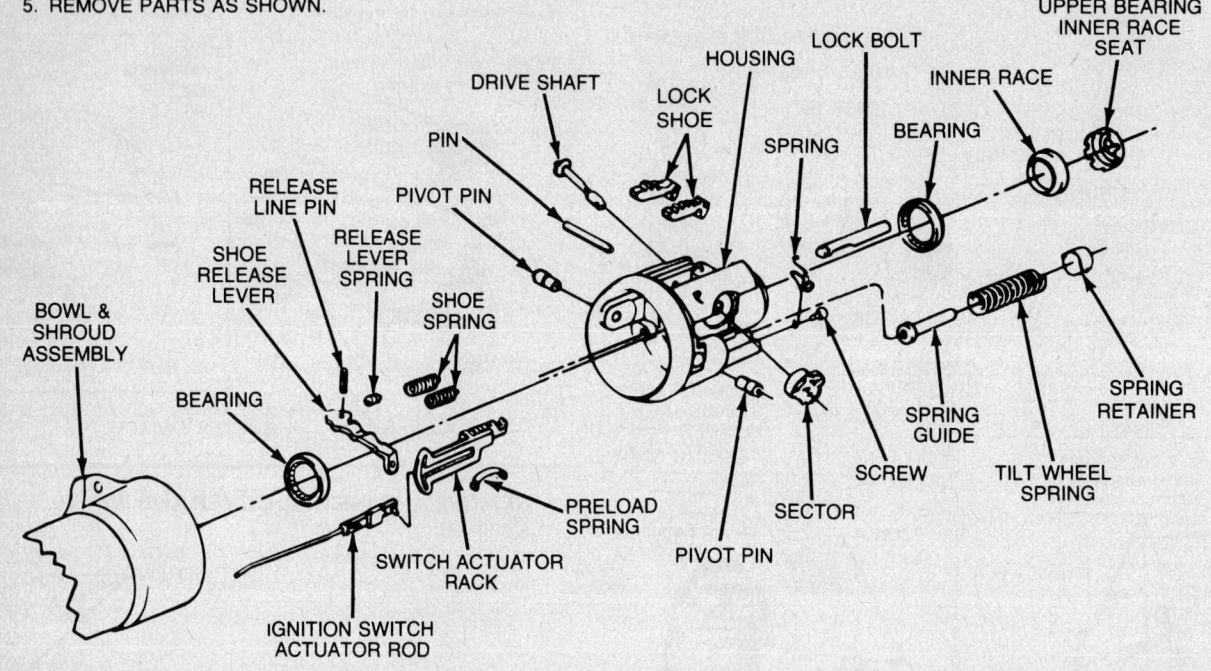

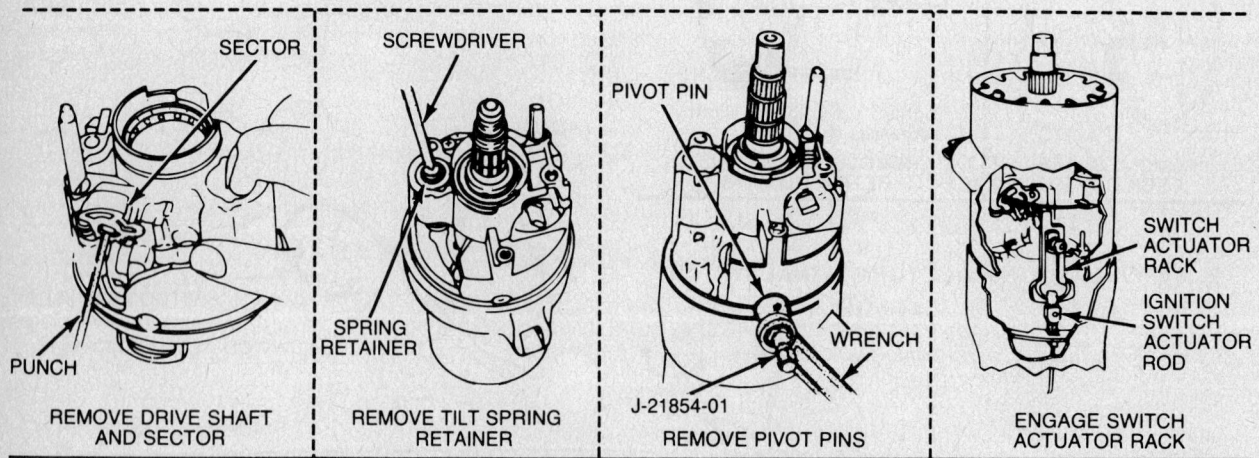

REMOVE DRIVE SHAFT AND SECTOR

REMOVE TILT SPRING RETAINER

J-21854-01
REMOVE PIVOT PINS

ENGAGE SWITCH ACTUATOR RACK

6. REMOVE AND INSTALL LOWER STEERING SHAFT ASSEMBLY

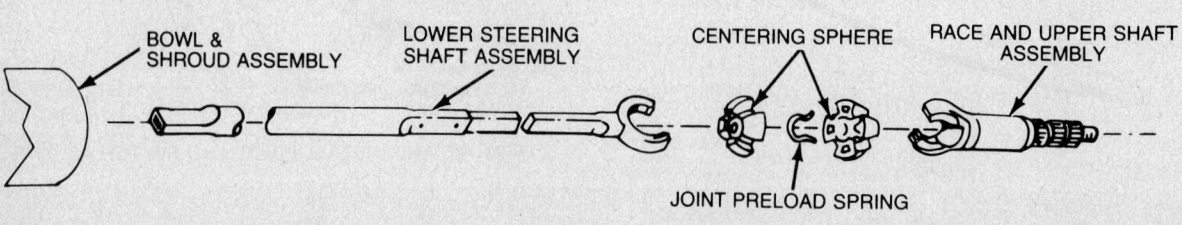

7. REMOVE AND INSTALL SHIFT TUBE, IGNITION AND DIMMER SWITCH ASSEMBLIES

REMOVE
1. REMOVE PARTS AS SHOWN.

INSTALL
1. INSTALL PARTS AS SHOWN.
2. POSITION ROD IN SLIDER HOLE AND INSTALL IGNITION SWITCH. INSTALL LOWER STUD AND TIGHTEN TO 4.0 N•m.
3. INSTALL DIMMER SWITCH AND DEPRESS SWITCH SLIGHTLY TO INSERT ³⁄₃₂" DRILL. FORCE SWITCH UP TO REMOVE LASH, THEN TIGHTEN SCREW, AND NUT TO 4.0 N•m.
4. PLACE SHIFTER IN NEUTRAL AND INSTALL SHIFT LEVER.

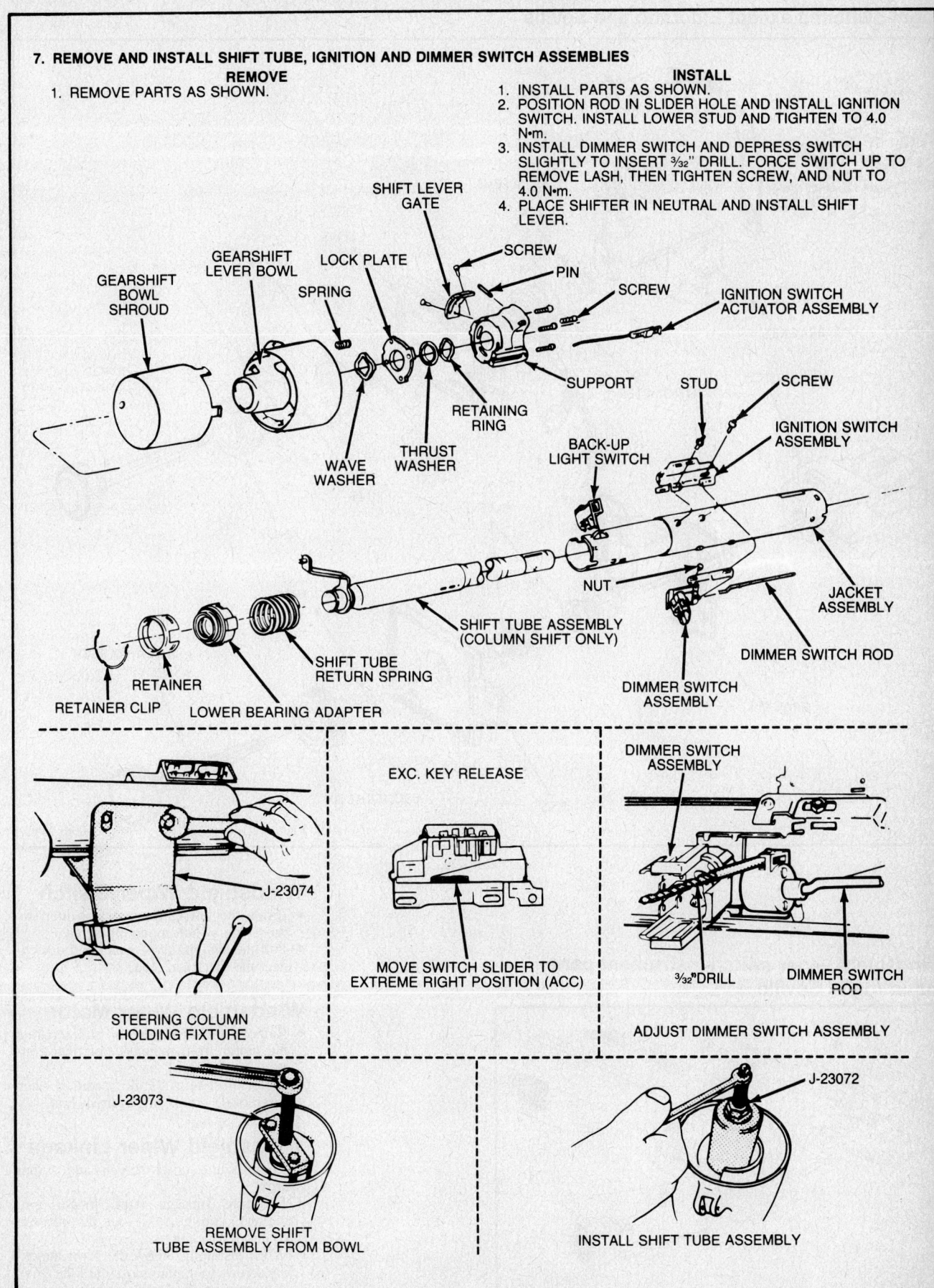

GEARSHIFT BOWL SHROUD

GEARSHIFT LEVER BOWL

LOCK PLATE

SPRING

SHIFT LEVER GATE

SCREW

PIN

SCREW

IGNITION SWITCH ACTUATOR ASSEMBLY

WAVE WASHER

THRUST WASHER

RETAINING RING

SUPPORT

BACK-UP LIGHT SWITCH

STUD

SCREW

IGNITION SWITCH ASSEMBLY

NUT

JACKET ASSEMBLY

DIMMER SWITCH ROD

DIMMER SWITCH ASSEMBLY

SHIFT TUBE ASSEMBLY (COLUMN SHIFT ONLY)

SHIFT TUBE RETURN SPRING

RETAINER

RETAINER CLIP

LOWER BEARING ADAPTER

J-23074

STEERING COLUMN HOLDING FIXTURE

EXC. KEY RELEASE

MOVE SWITCH SLIDER TO EXTREME RIGHT POSITION (ACC)

DIMMER SWITCH ASSEMBLY

³⁄₃₂" DRILL

DIMMER SWITCH ROD

ADJUST DIMMER SWITCH ASSEMBLY

J-23073

REMOVE SHIFT TUBE ASSEMBLY FROM BOWL

J-23072

INSTALL SHIFT TUBE ASSEMBLY

CADILLAC
EXCEPT CIMARRON

Light switches except Eldorado and Seville

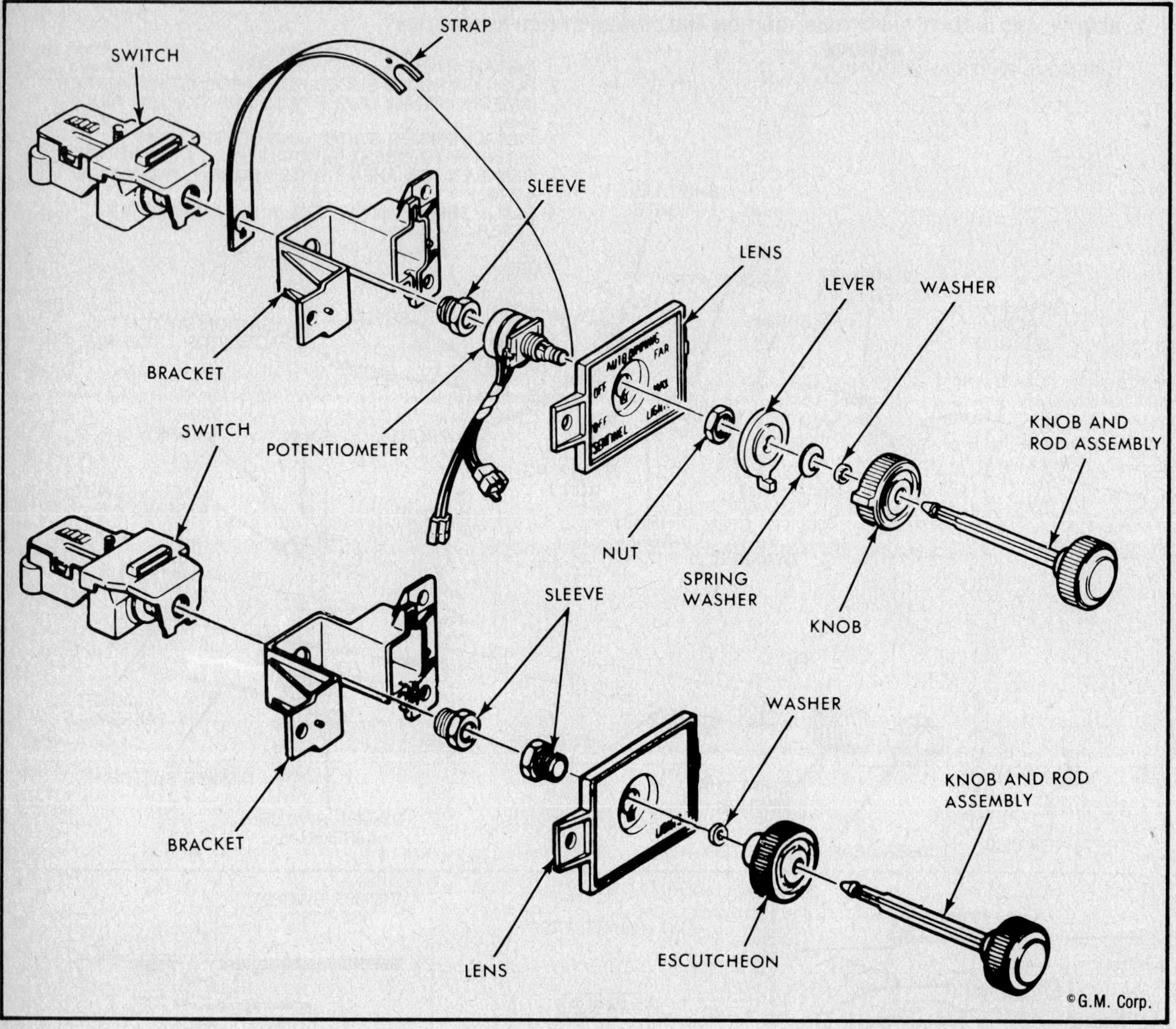

SWITCH

STRAP

SLEEVE

LENS

LEVER

WASHER

BRACKET

SWITCH

POTENTIOMETER

KNOB AND ROD ASSEMBLY

NUT

SPRING WASHER

KNOB

SLEEVE

WASHER

BRACKET

KNOB AND ROD ASSEMBLY

LENS

ESCUTCHEON

© G.M. Corp.

Windshield wiper switch instrument panel mounting in Seville

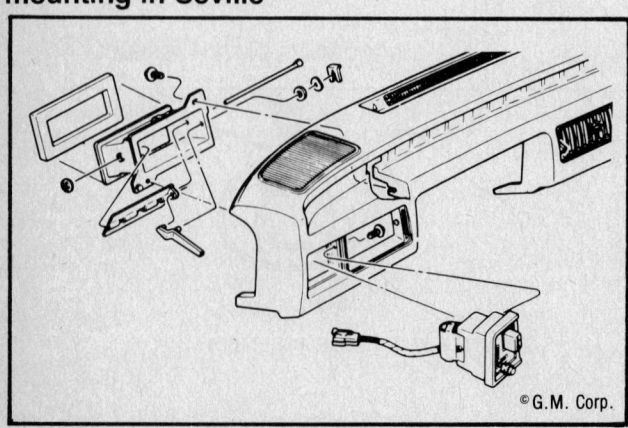

© G.M. Corp.

Windshield Wiper Switch
- Inside the left climate control duct, remove the switch mounting screw.
- Pull the switch out of panel and disconnect the electrical lead.

Windshield Wiper Motor
- Remove the cowl screen, and separate the motor from mounts, electrical connections, linkage, etc.
- Motor must be in "Park" position when assembling crank arm to drive link.

Windshield Wiper Linkage
- Remove the cowl screen and wiper arms.
- Separate linkage from motor and mounts, and guide it out the plenum chamber opening.
- When installing, allow the pivot attaching screws to remain loose until the drive links-to-crank arm screws are tightened.

Radio

- Relocate anything preventing full access to radio such as:
  a. Air conditioner ducting
  b. Ash tray
  c. Instrument panel trim
  d. EFI Control unit
- Remove radio mounts, control knobs, etc., and separate radio from antenna, power and speaker connections.

Climate Control Unit/Blower Switch

- Relocate anything preventing full access to the control unit such as lower steering column cover and cluster bezel.
- Remove control unit from supports, and separate it from control cables, vacuum lines and electrical connections.

Windshield wiper motor and linkage (except Eldorado and Seville)

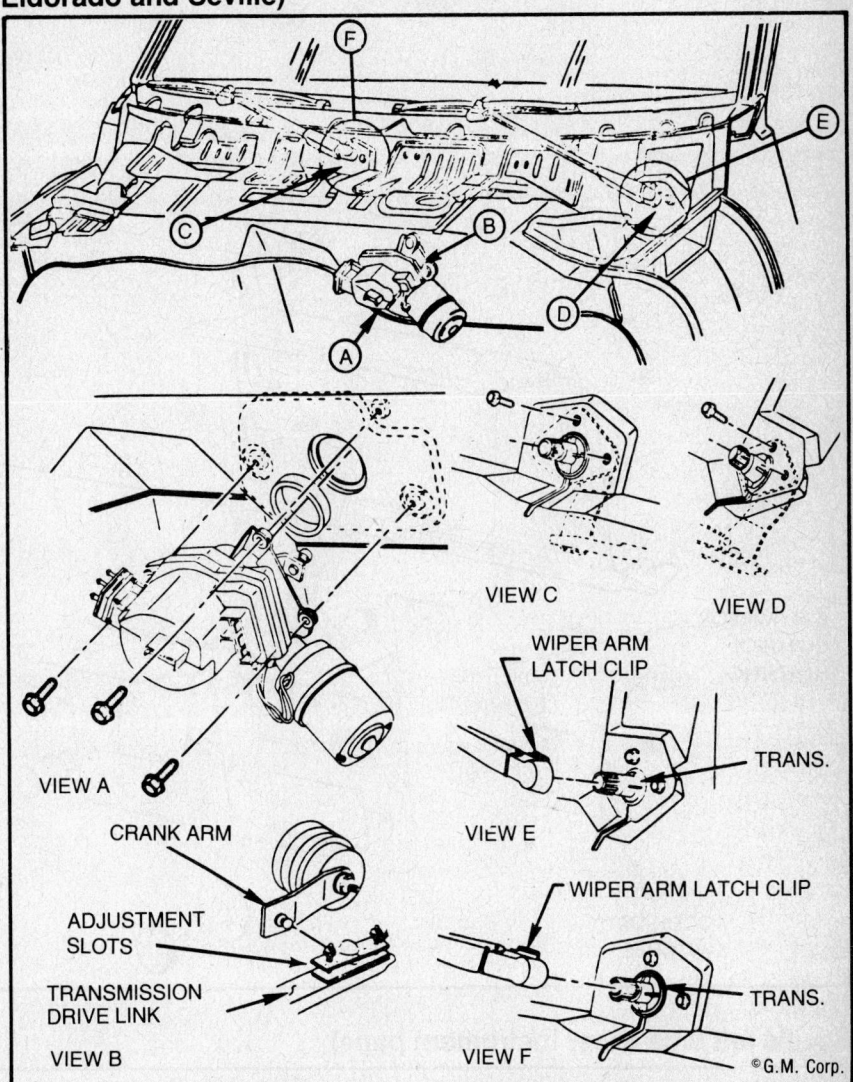

VIEW C

VIEW D

VIEW A

CRANK ARM

ADJUSTMENT SLOTS

TRANSMISSION DRIVE LINK

VIEW B

WIPER ARM LATCH CLIP

TRANS.

VIEW E

WIPER ARM LATCH CLIP

TRANS.

VIEW F

©G.M. Corp.

Radio mounting typical in Seville

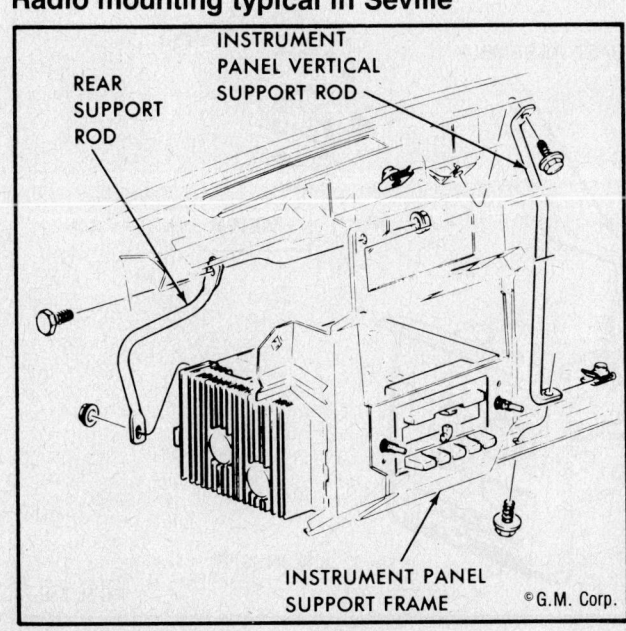

REAR SUPPORT ROD

INSTRUMENT PANEL VERTICAL SUPPORT ROD

INSTRUMENT PANEL SUPPORT FRAME

©G.M. Corp.

Air conditioner/heater temperature control unit

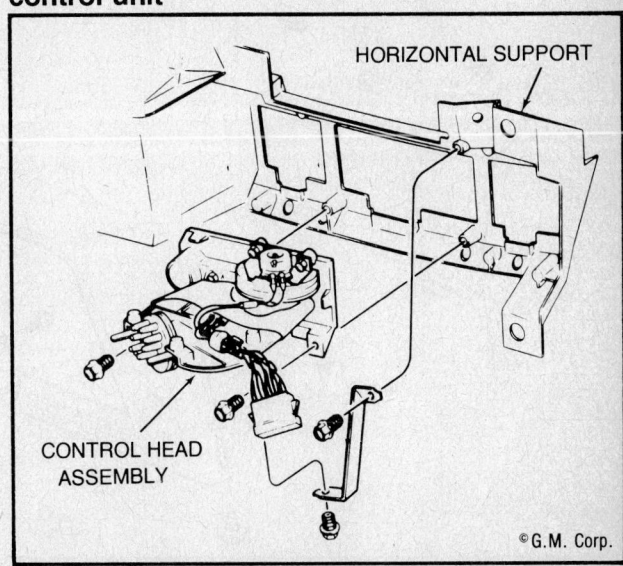

HORIZONTAL SUPPORT

CONTROL HEAD ASSEMBLY

©G.M. Corp.

CADILLAC
EXCEPT CIMARRON

Seville right side lower instrument panel

R.H. LOWER
INSTRUMENT
PANEL
COVER

R.H. MIRROR
CONTROL
HOUSING

R.H. INSERT
AND APPLIQUE

LAMP
SHIELD

VIEW A

ACCESSORY
SWITCHES

© G.M. Corp.

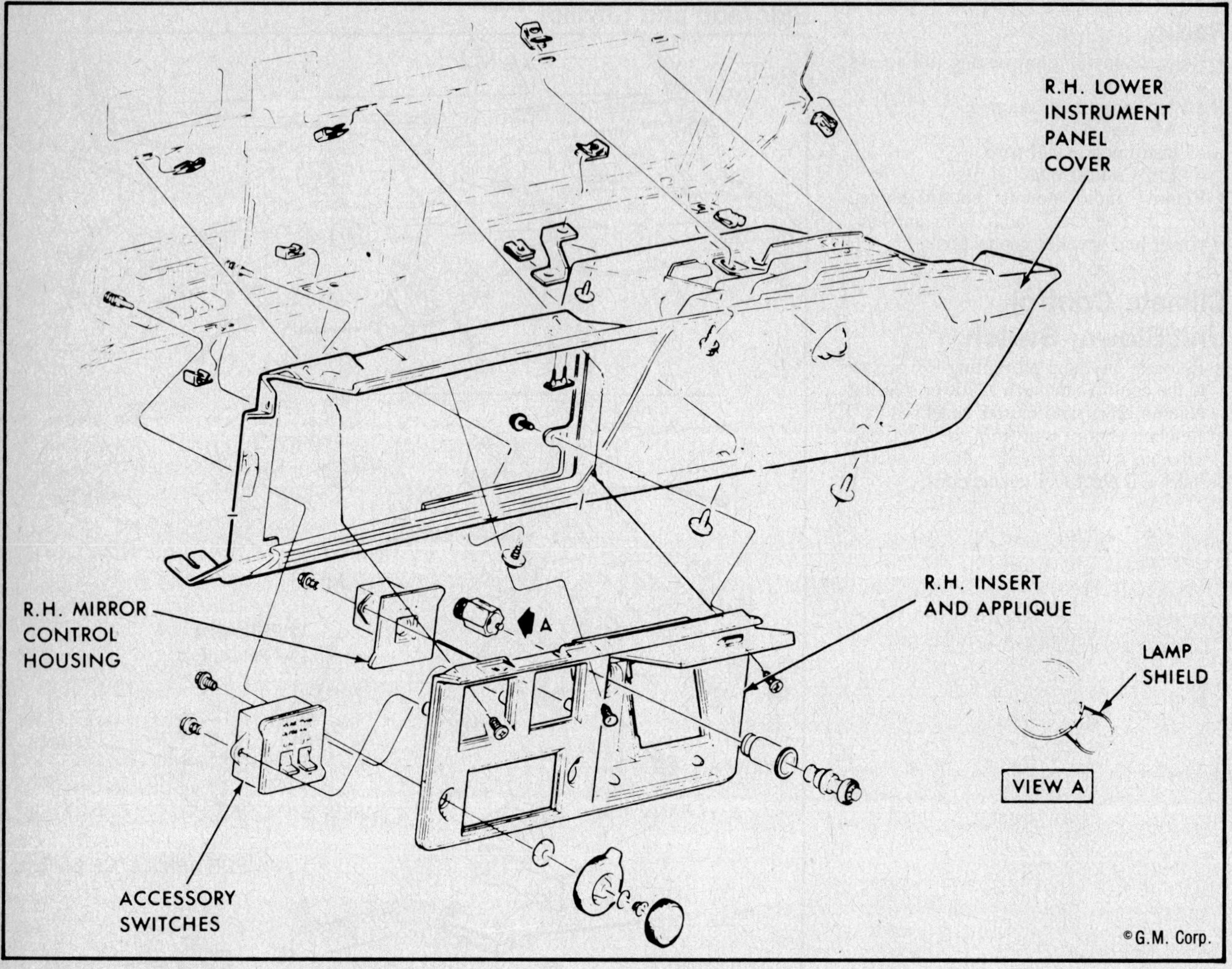

Seville left side lower instrument panel

BASE ASSEMBLY

VIEW A

L.H. INSERT

© G.M. Corp.

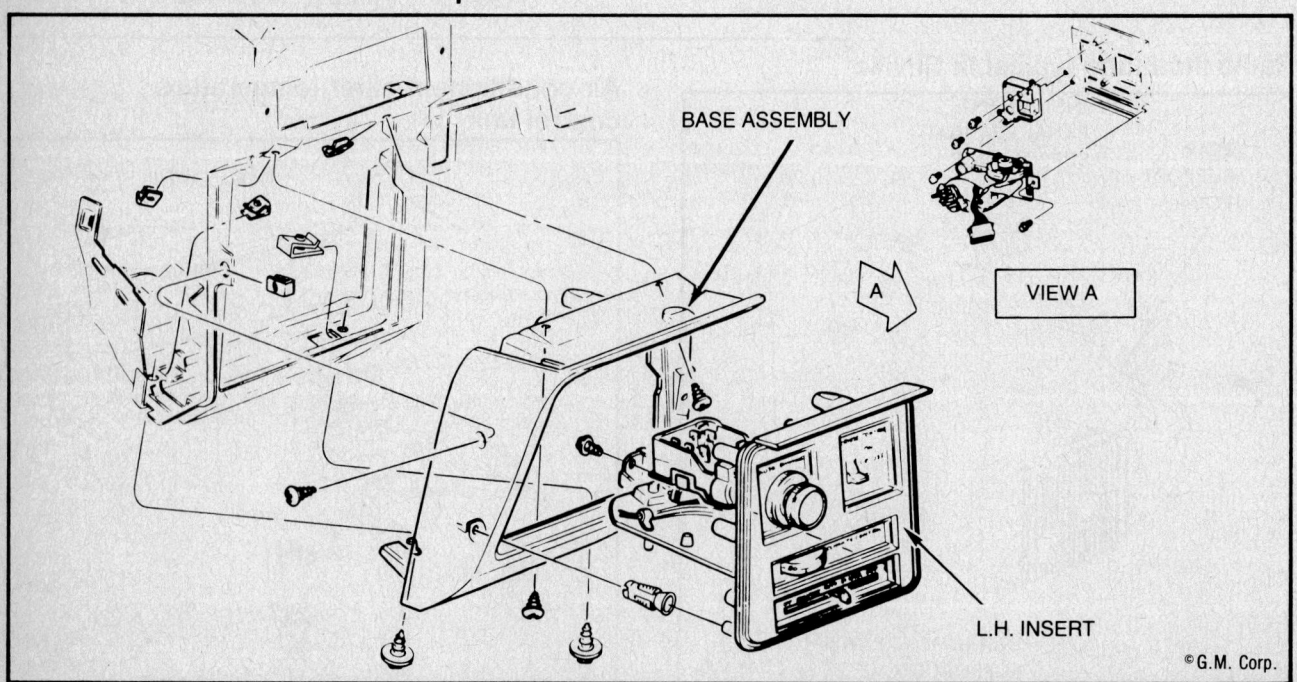

1977 and later Deville instrument cluster and attaching components

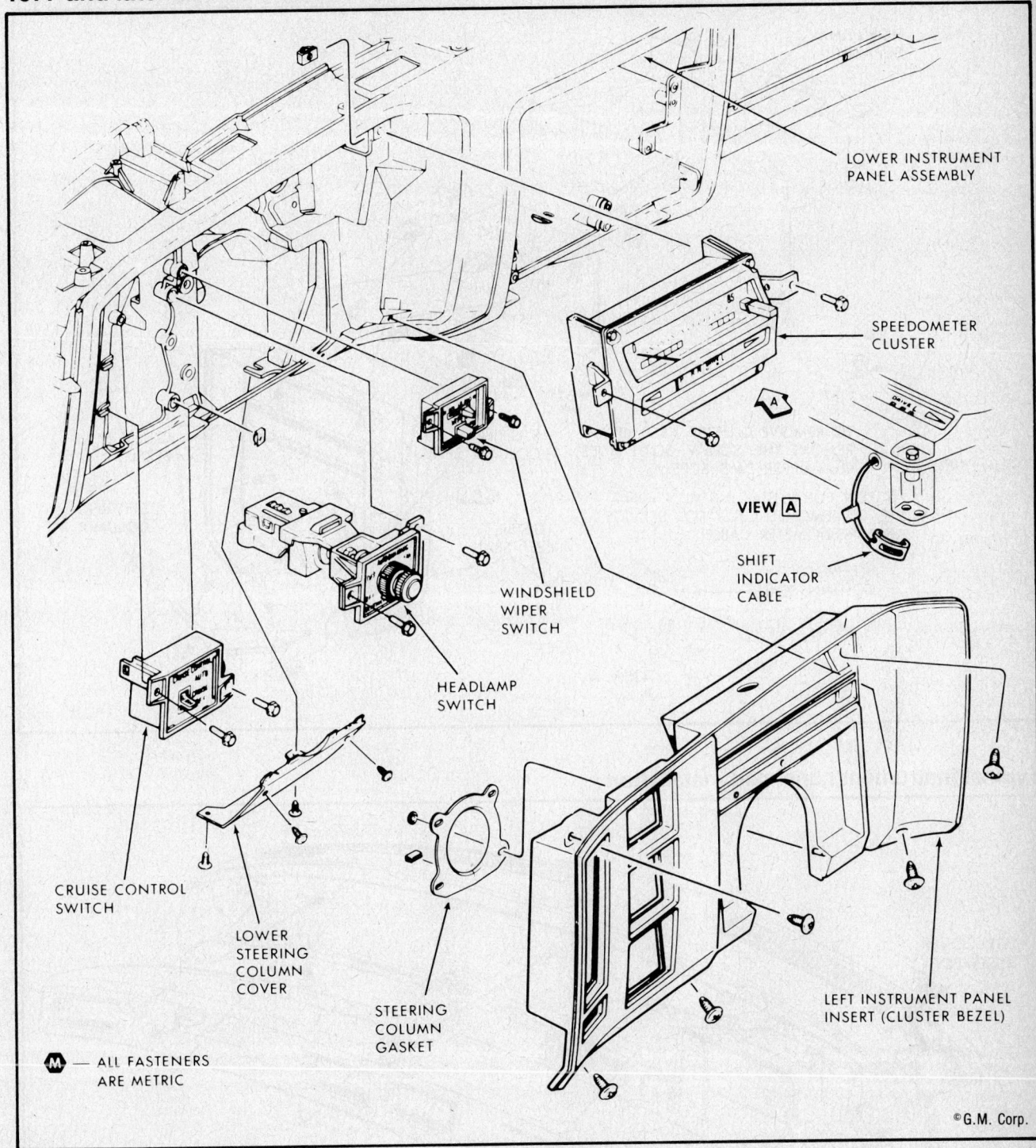

LOWER INSTRUMENT
PANEL ASSEMBLY

SPEEDOMETER
CLUSTER

VIEW Ⓐ

SHIFT
INDICATOR
CABLE

WINDSHIELD
WIPER
SWITCH

HEADLAMP
SWITCH

CRUISE CONTROL
SWITCH

LOWER
STEERING
COLUMN
COVER

STEERING
COLUMN
GASKET

LEFT INSTRUMENT PANEL
INSERT (CLUSTER BEZEL)

Ⓜ — ALL FASTENERS
ARE METRIC

© G.M. Corp.

Typical instrument panel cluster and bezel

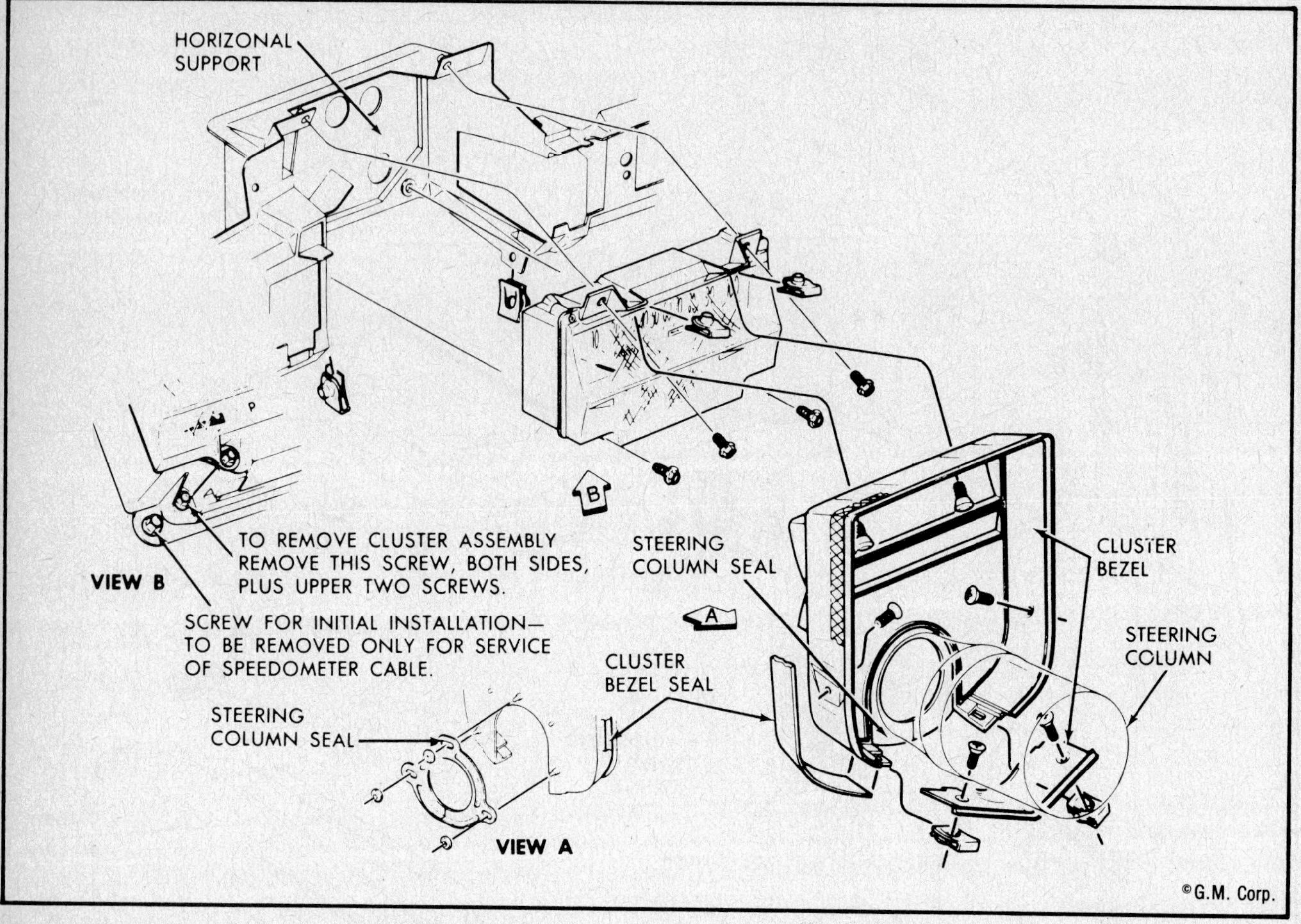

HORIZONAL SUPPORT

VIEW B

TO REMOVE CLUSTER ASSEMBLY
REMOVE THIS SCREW, BOTH SIDES,
PLUS UPPER TWO SCREWS.

SCREW FOR INITIAL INSTALLATION—
TO BE REMOVED ONLY FOR SERVICE
OF SPEEDOMETER CABLE.

STEERING
COLUMN SEAL

VIEW A

CLUSTER
BEZEL SEAL

STEERING
COLUMN SEAL

STEERING
COLUMN

CLUSTER
BEZEL

B

A

© G.M. Corp.

Typical instrument panel pad installation

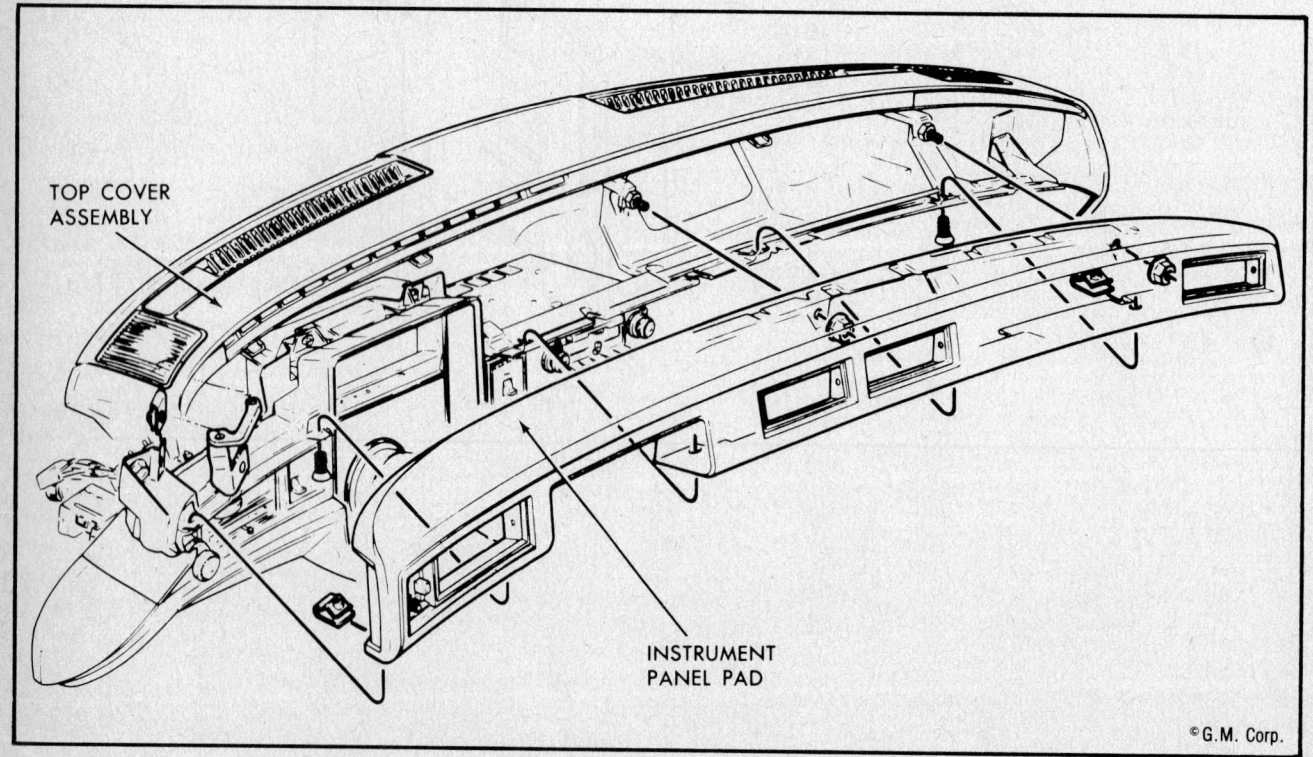

TOP COVER
ASSEMBLY

INSTRUMENT
PANEL PAD

© G.M. Corp.

Seville speedometer cluster, bezel and lower cover

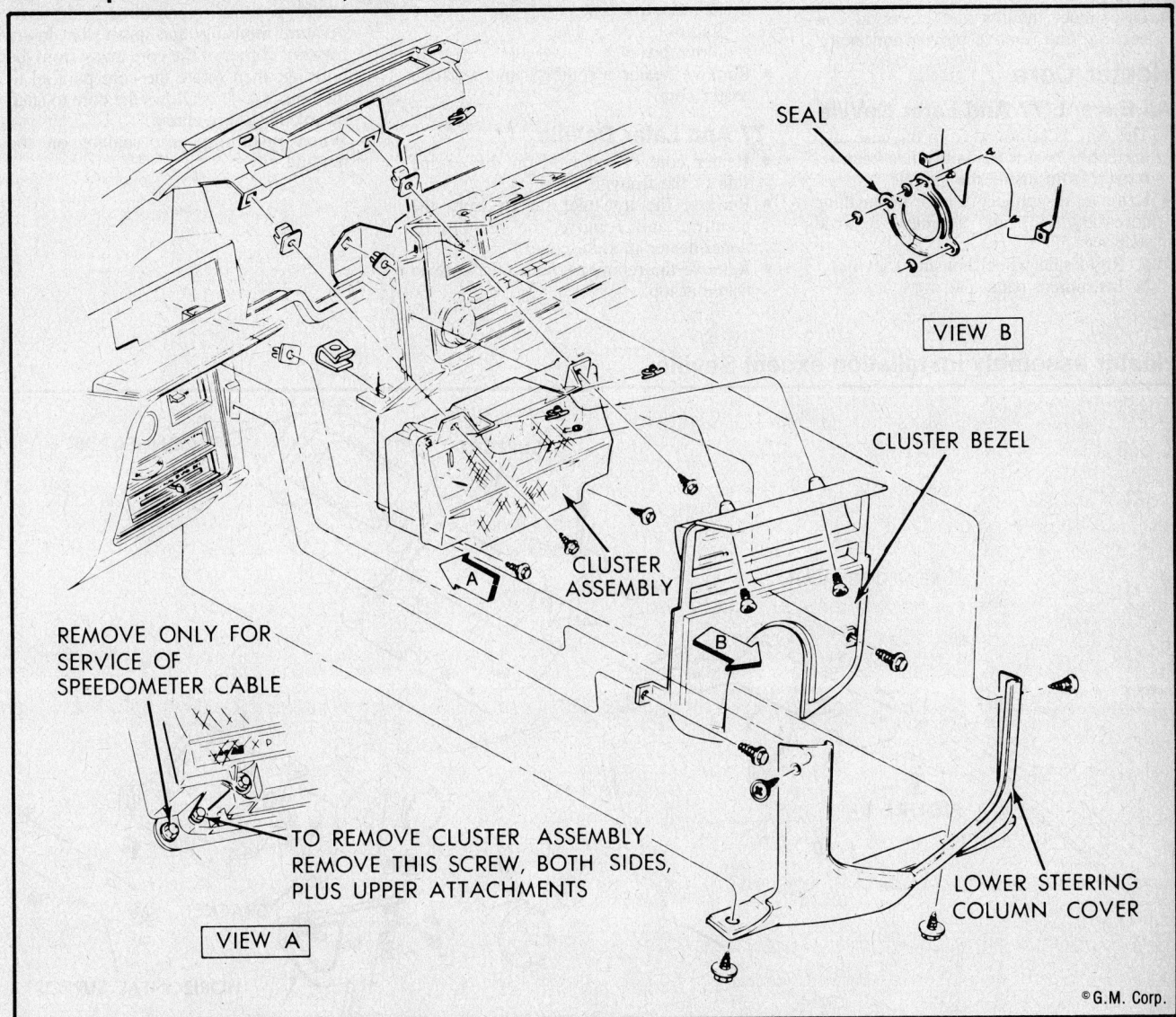

SEAL

VIEW B

CLUSTER BEZEL

CLUSTER ASSEMBLY

A

B

REMOVE ONLY FOR SERVICE OF SPEEDOMETER CABLE

TO REMOVE CLUSTER ASSEMBLY REMOVE THIS SCREW, BOTH SIDES, PLUS UPPER ATTACHMENTS

VIEW A

LOWER STEERING COLUMN COVER

© G.M. Corp.

Heater Blower

- Disconnect mounts and electrical connection, and remove blower and motor.

Heater Core

All Except '77 And Later DeVille

- The core is removed from the case after the entire heater assembly has been removed from inside the vehicle.
- Remove, disconnect or relocate anything necessary for heater assembly removal such as:
  a. Right side wheel housing (Seville)
  b. Instrument panel pad
  c. Air distribution ducting
  d. EFI Control unit
  e. Radio
  f. Glove box
- Remove heater assembly, and separate heater core.

'77 And Later DeVille

- Heater core is removed on the engine side of the firewall.
- Remove the air inlet screen from the plenum, and remove the air conditioner/heater module cover.
- Remove the retainer holding the core to frame at top.
- With the temperature door in the full "hot" position, reach through the temperature housing and push the lower forward corner of the core away from the housing; then rotate the core parallel to the housing. This allows the core to snap out of the lower clamp.
- When installing, use sealant on the module cover.

Heater assembly installation except Seville

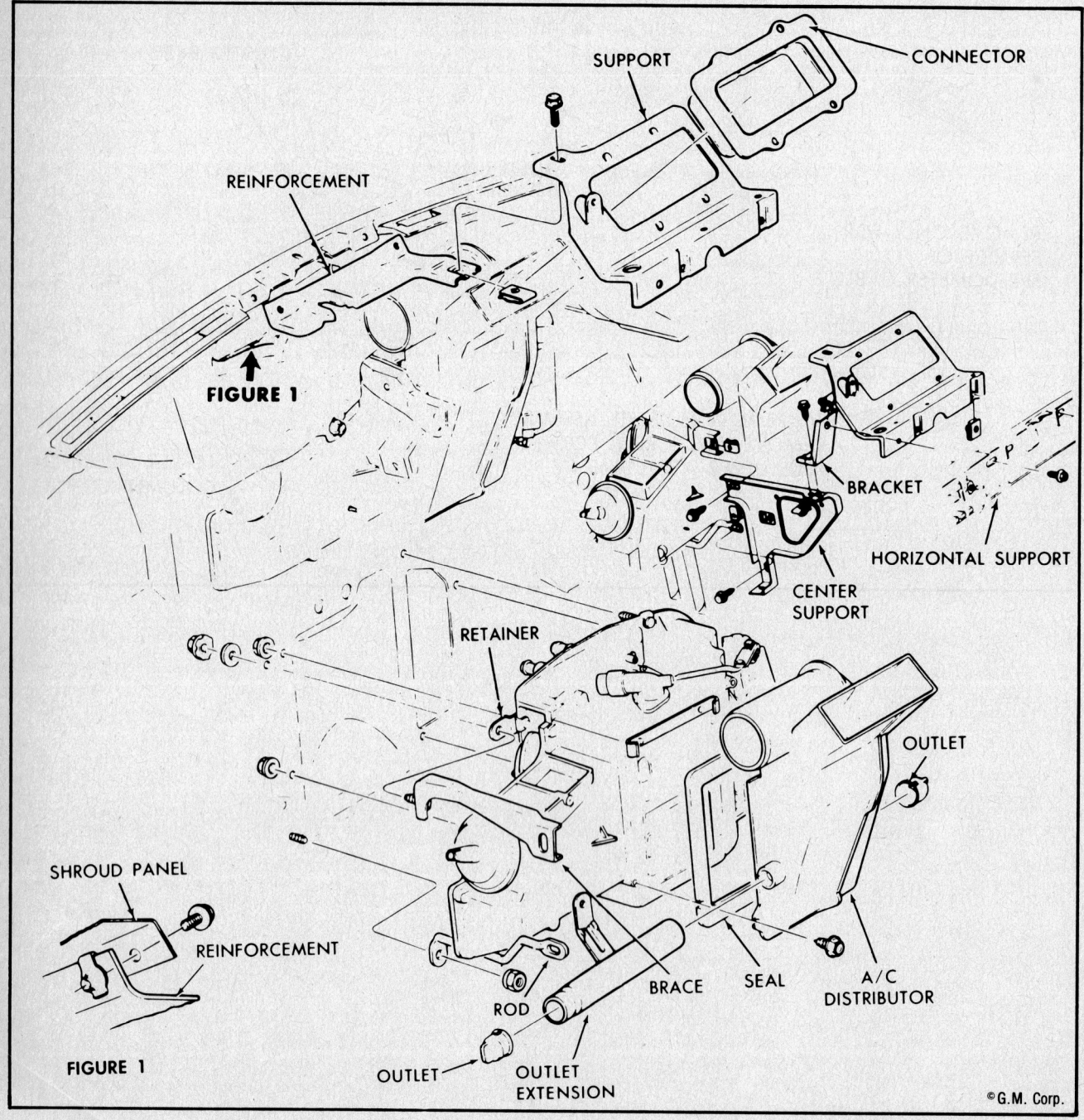

FIGURE 1

©G.M. Corp.

Seville heater case components

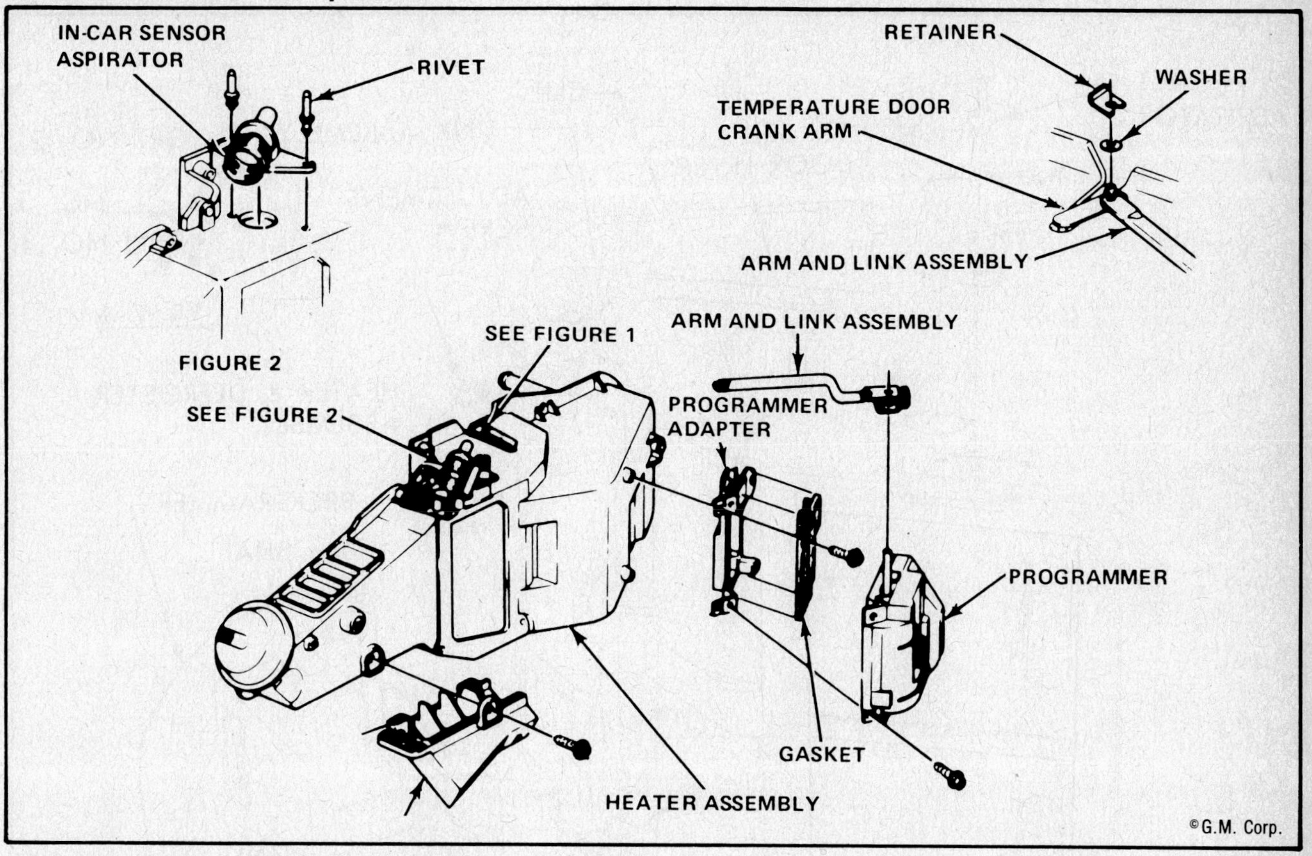

IN-CAR SENSOR ASPIRATOR

RIVET

RETAINER

WASHER

TEMPERATURE DOOR CRANK ARM

ARM AND LINK ASSEMBLY

ARM AND LINK ASSEMBLY

FIGURE 2

SEE FIGURE 1

SEE FIGURE 2

PROGRAMMER ADAPTER

PROGRAMMER

GASKET

HEATER ASSEMBLY

© G.M. Corp.

Heater assembly installed in Seville

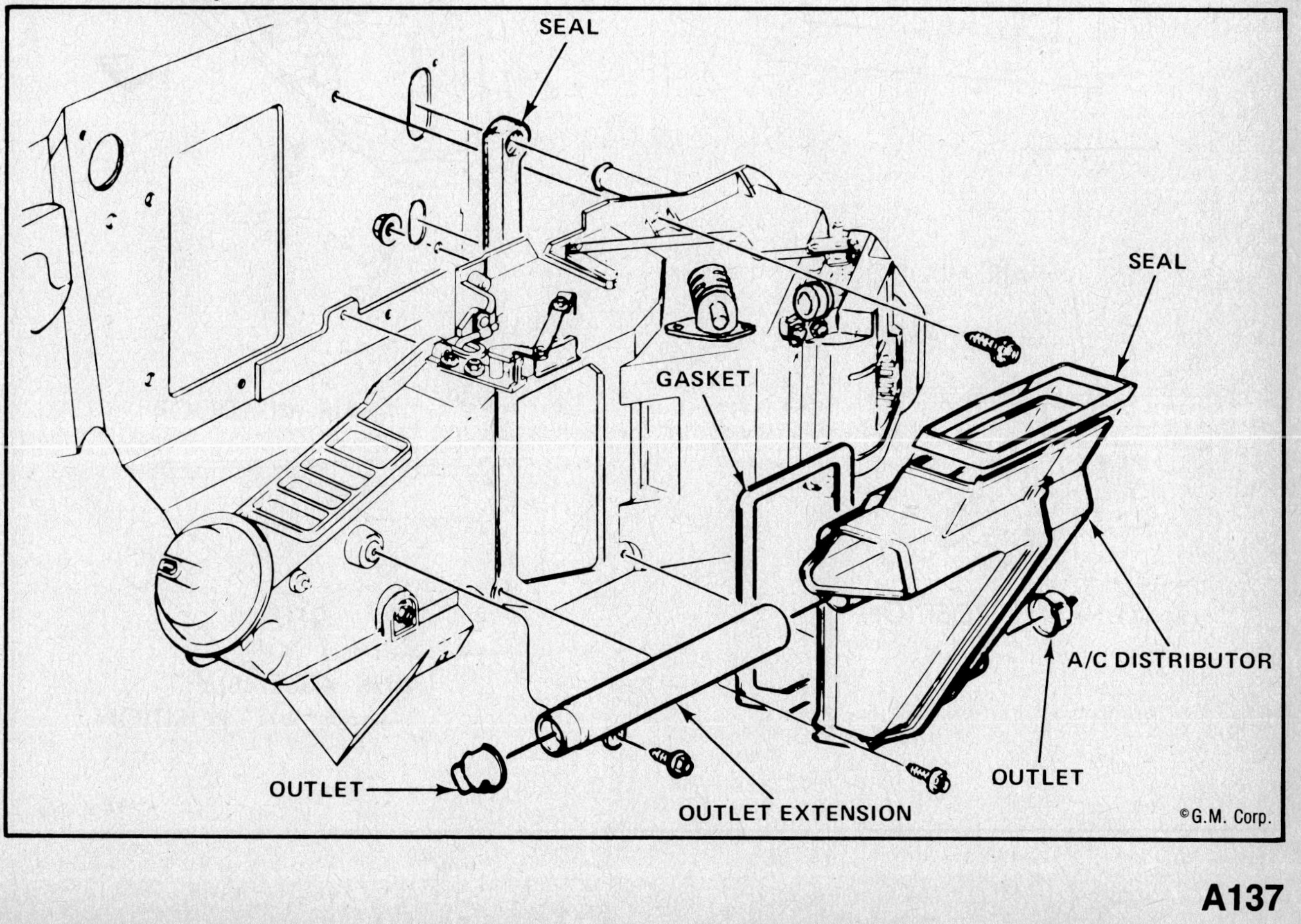

SEAL

SEAL

GASKET

A/C DISTRIBUTOR

OUTLET

OUTLET EXTENSION

OUTLET

© G.M. Corp.

Air conditioner programmer mounting and adjustment

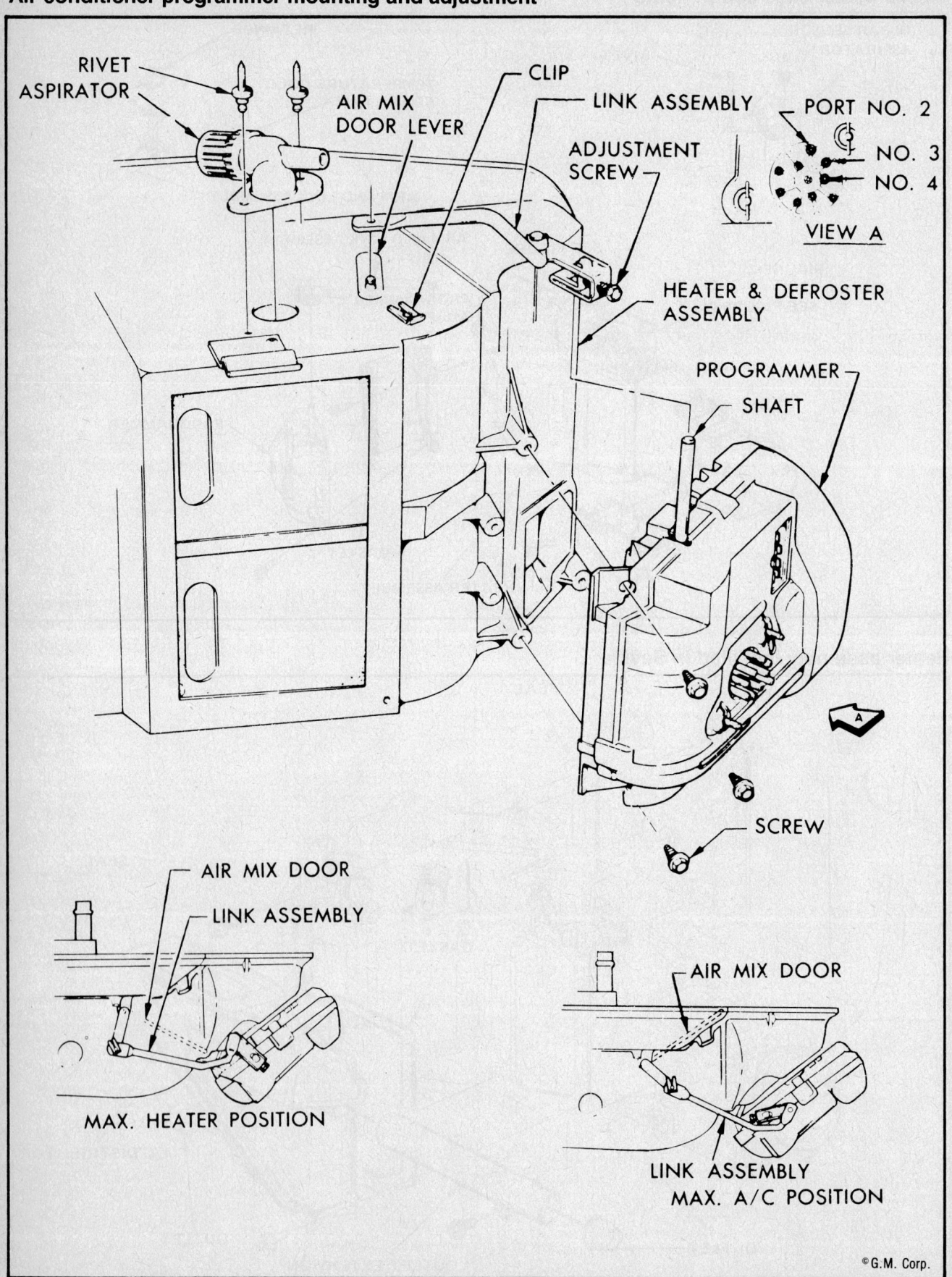

RIVET
ASPIRATOR
AIR MIX
DOOR LEVER
CLIP
LINK ASSEMBLY
ADJUSTMENT
SCREW
PORT NO. 2
NO. 3
NO. 4
VIEW A
HEATER & DEFROSTER
ASSEMBLY
PROGRAMMER
SHAFT
SCREW
A

AIR MIX DOOR
LINK ASSEMBLY
MAX. HEATER POSITION

AIR MIX DOOR
LINK ASSEMBLY
MAX. A/C POSITION

© G.M. Corp.

Vacuum hose routing

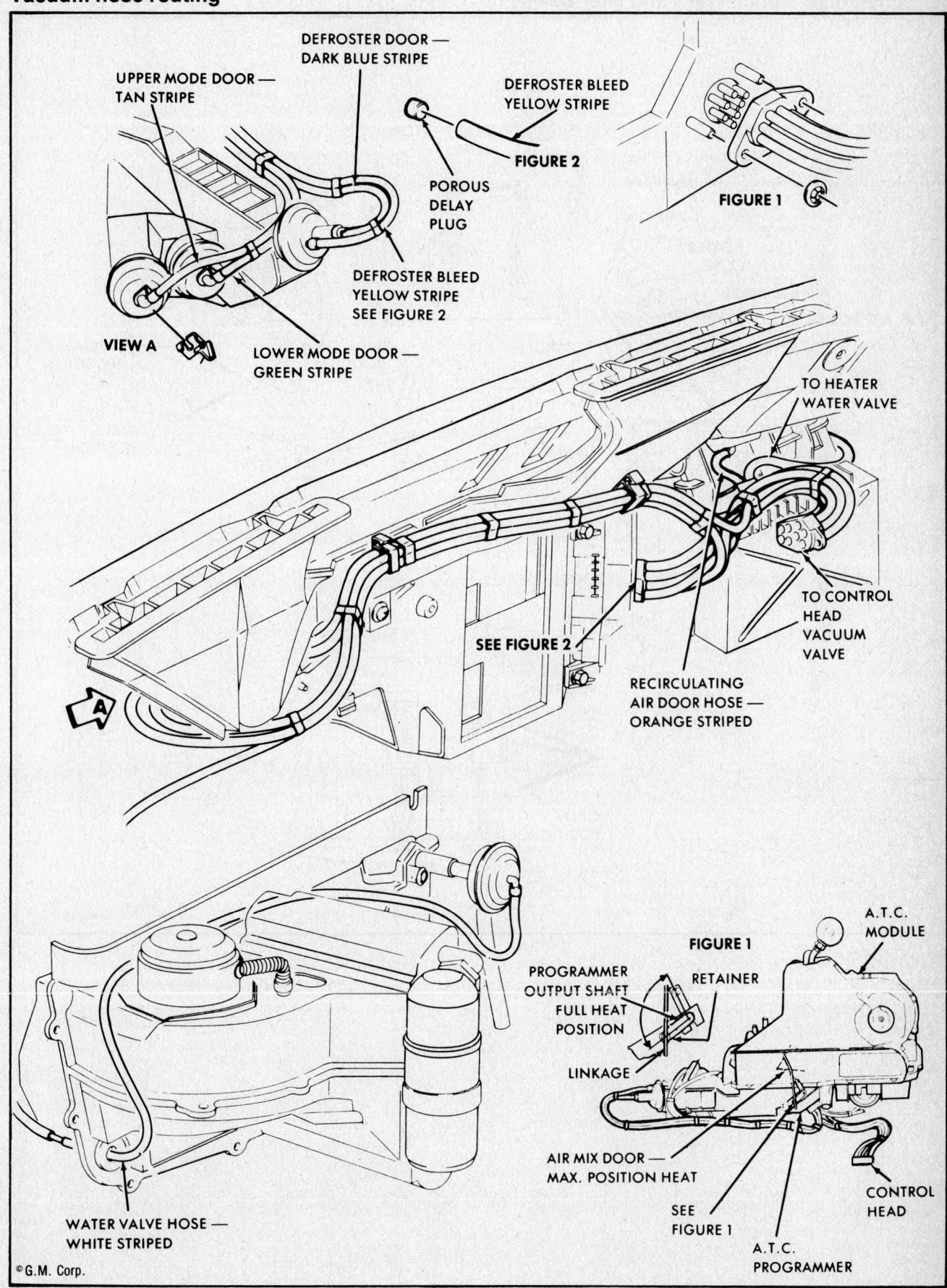

UPPER MODE DOOR —
TAN STRIPE

DEFROSTER DOOR —
DARK BLUE STRIPE

DEFROSTER BLEED
YELLOW STRIPE

FIGURE 2

POROUS
DELAY
PLUG

FIGURE 1

DEFROSTER BLEED
YELLOW STRIPE
SEE FIGURE 2

VIEW A

LOWER MODE DOOR —
GREEN STRIPE

TO HEATER
WATER VALVE

TO CONTROL
HEAD
VACUUM
VALVE

SEE FIGURE 2

RECIRCULATING
AIR DOOR HOSE —
ORANGE STRIPED

A

A.T.C.
MODULE

FIGURE 1

PROGRAMMER
OUTPUT SHAFT
FULL HEAT
POSITION

RETAINER

LINKAGE

AIR MIX DOOR —
MAX. POSITION HEAT

SEE
FIGURE 1

A.T.C.
PROGRAMMER

CONTROL
HEAD

WATER VALVE HOSE —
WHITE STRIPED

© G.M. Corp.

Air conditioner module-1977 and later Deville

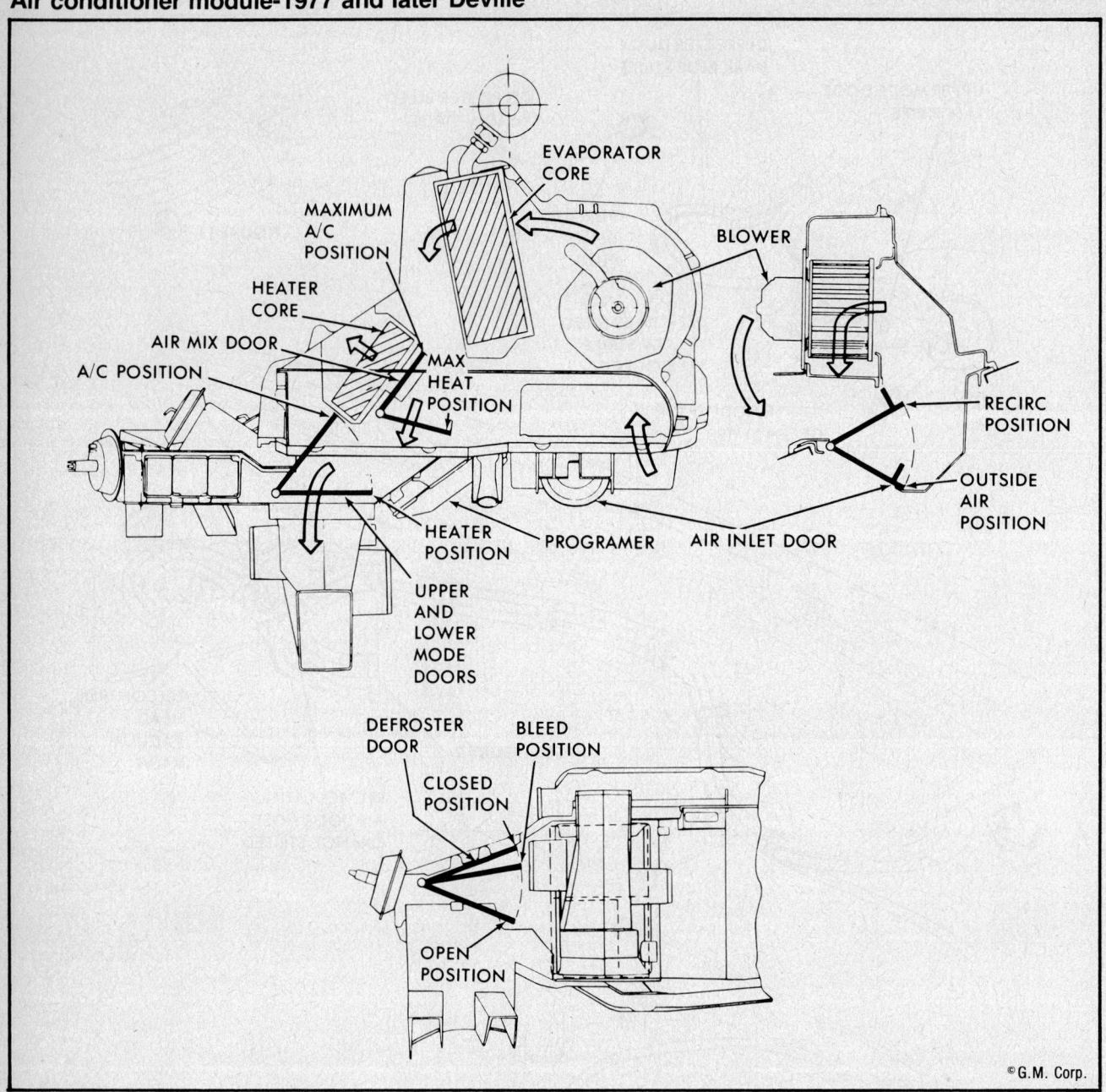

EVAPORATOR CORE

MAXIMUM A/C POSITION

BLOWER

HEATER CORE

AIR MIX DOOR

MAX HEAT POSITION

A/C POSITION

RECIRC POSITION

OUTSIDE AIR POSITION

HEATER POSITION

PROGRAMER

AIR INLET DOOR

UPPER AND LOWER MODE DOORS

DEFROSTER DOOR

BLEED POSITION

CLOSED POSITION

OPEN POSITION

© G.M. Corp.

Seville and Eldorado Heater/A/C Module

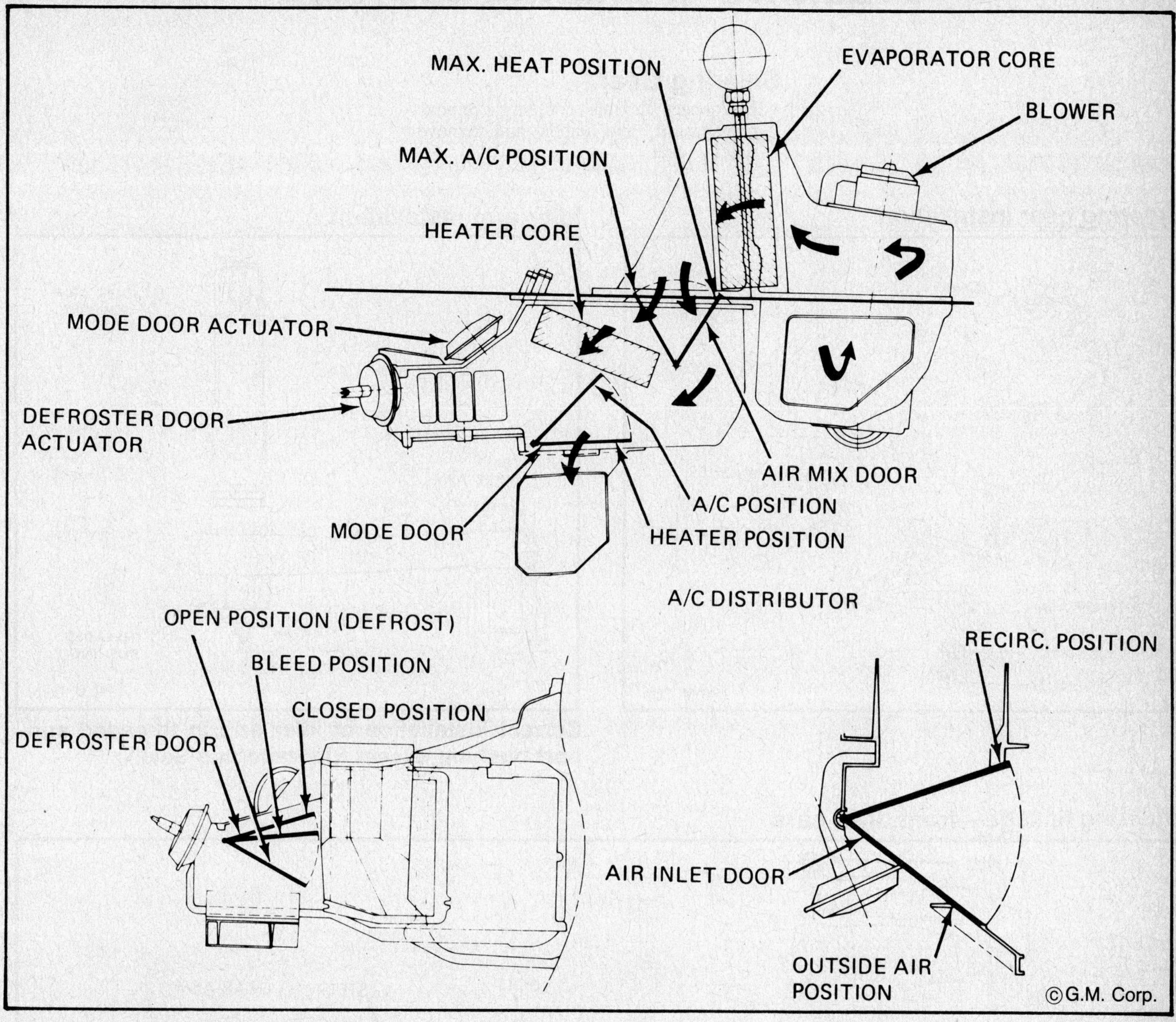

MAX. HEAT POSITION

EVAPORATOR CORE

BLOWER

MAX. A/C POSITION

HEATER CORE

MODE DOOR ACTUATOR

DEFROSTER DOOR ACTUATOR

AIR MIX DOOR

A/C POSITION

HEATER POSITION

MODE DOOR

A/C DISTRIBUTOR

OPEN POSITION (DEFROST)

BLEED POSITION

CLOSED POSITION

DEFROSTER DOOR

RECIRC. POSITION

AIR INLET DOOR

OUTSIDE AIR POSITION

©G.M. Corp.

Evaporator assembly—Seville and Eldorado

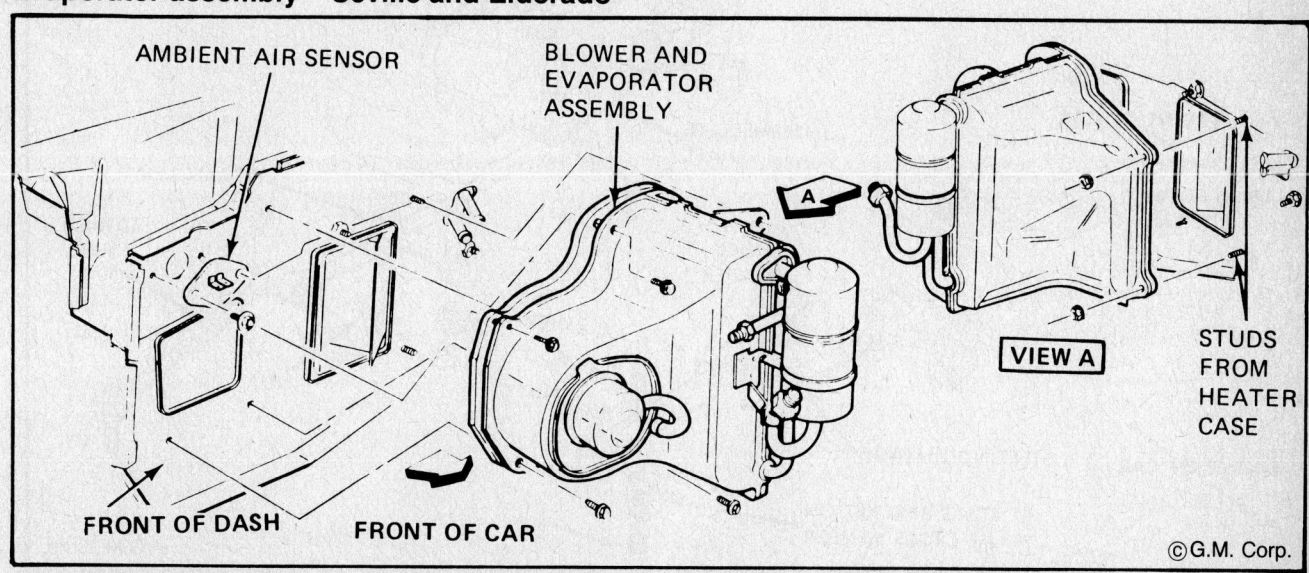

AMBIENT AIR SENSOR

BLOWER AND EVAPORATOR ASSEMBLY

VIEW A

STUDS FROM HEATER CASE

FRONT OF DASH

FRONT OF CAR

©G.M. Corp.

A141

STEERING & BRAKES SECTION

Steering Gear

- Disconnect flexible coupling, remove pitman arm, and unbolt and remove steering gear.

Steering gear installation

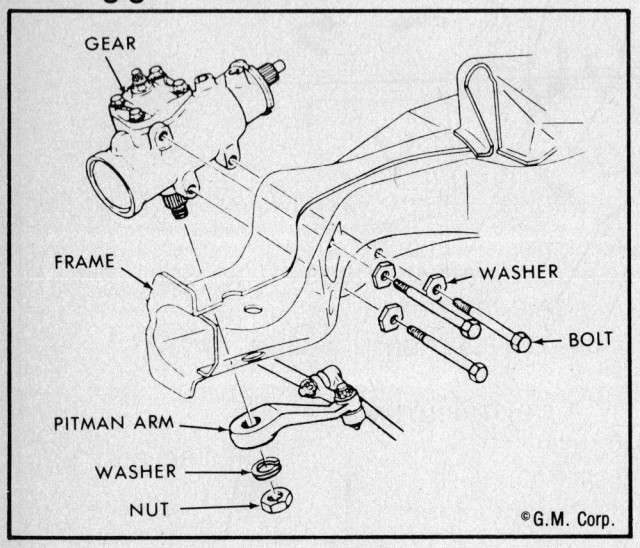

GEAR
FRAME
WASHER
BOLT
PITMAN ARM
WASHER
NUT
©G.M. Corp.

Idler arm installation

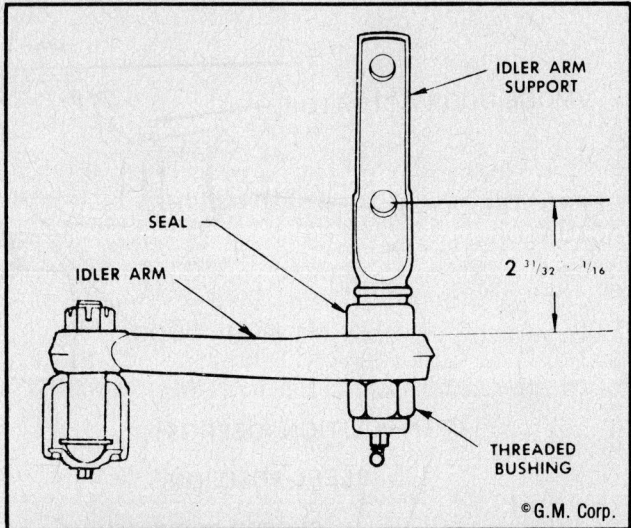

IDLER ARM SUPPORT
SEAL
IDLER ARM
2 31/32 ± 1/16
THREADED BUSHING
©G.M. Corp.

Correct installation of idler arm in threaded support bushing except Eldorado and Seville

Steering linkage—front drive cars

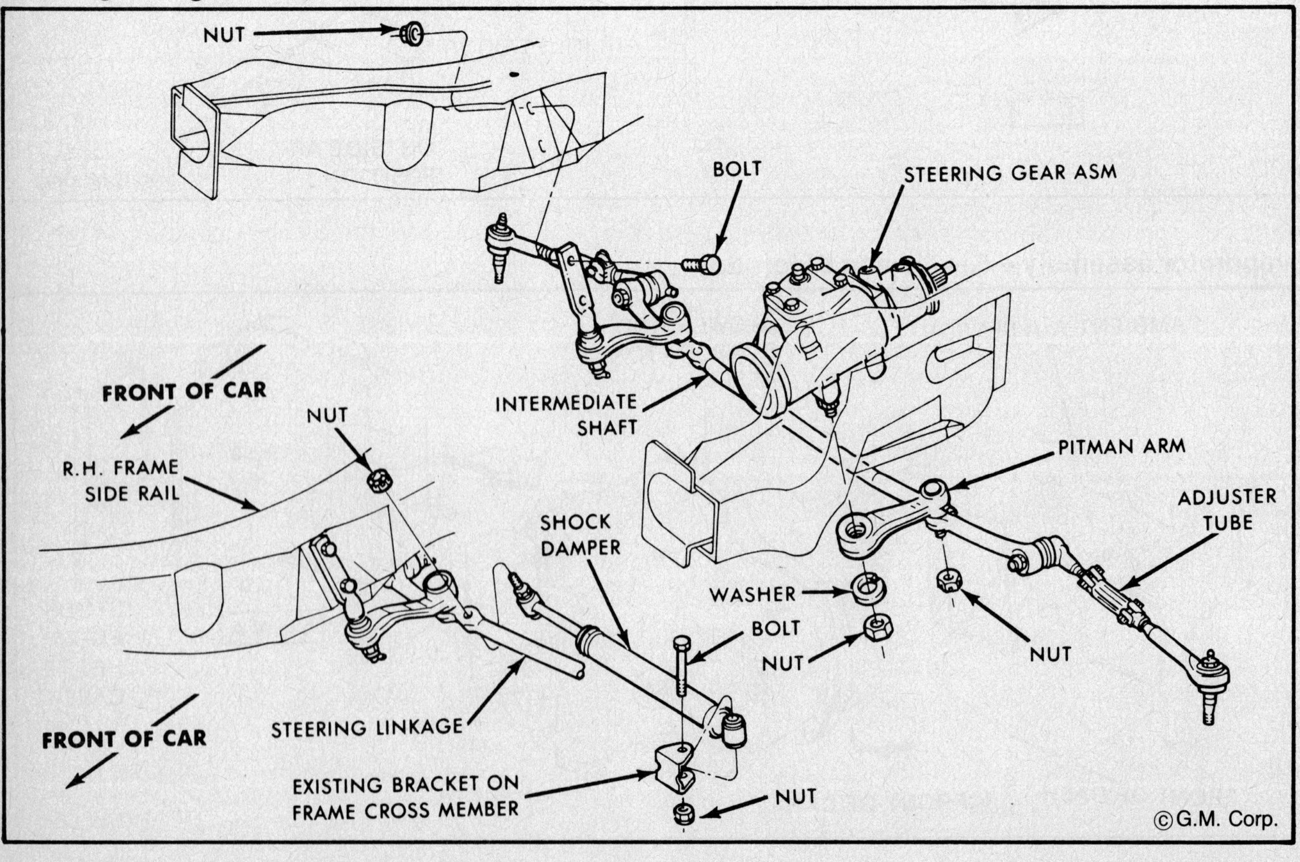

NUT
BOLT
STEERING GEAR ASM
FRONT OF CAR
NUT
INTERMEDIATE SHAFT
R.H. FRAME SIDE RAIL
PITMAN ARM
ADJUSTER TUBE
SHOCK DAMPER
WASHER
BOLT
NUT
NUT
STEERING LINKAGE
FRONT OF CAR
EXISTING BRACKET ON FRAME CROSS MEMBER
NUT
©G.M. Corp.

Tilt and telescope column

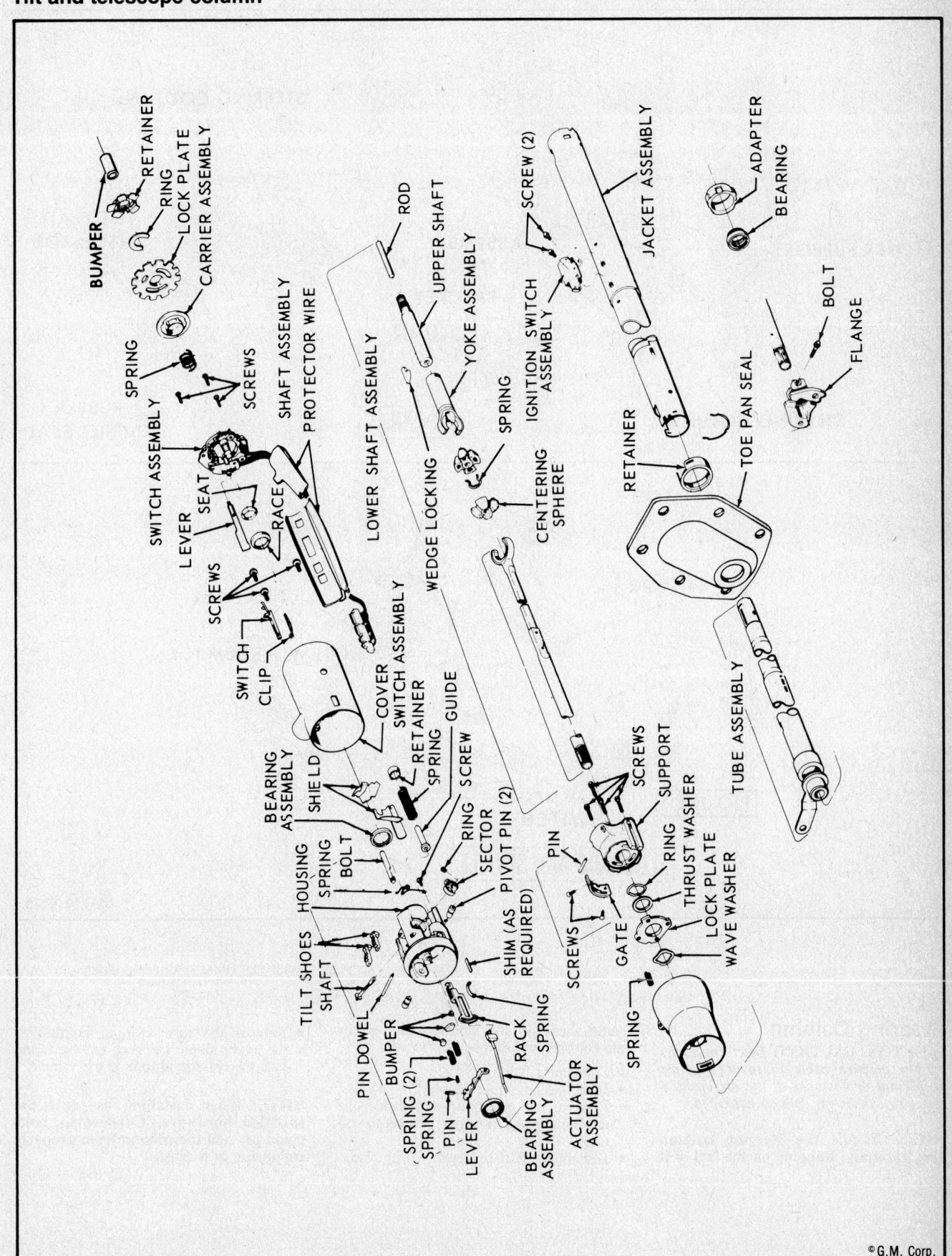

Steering column mounting

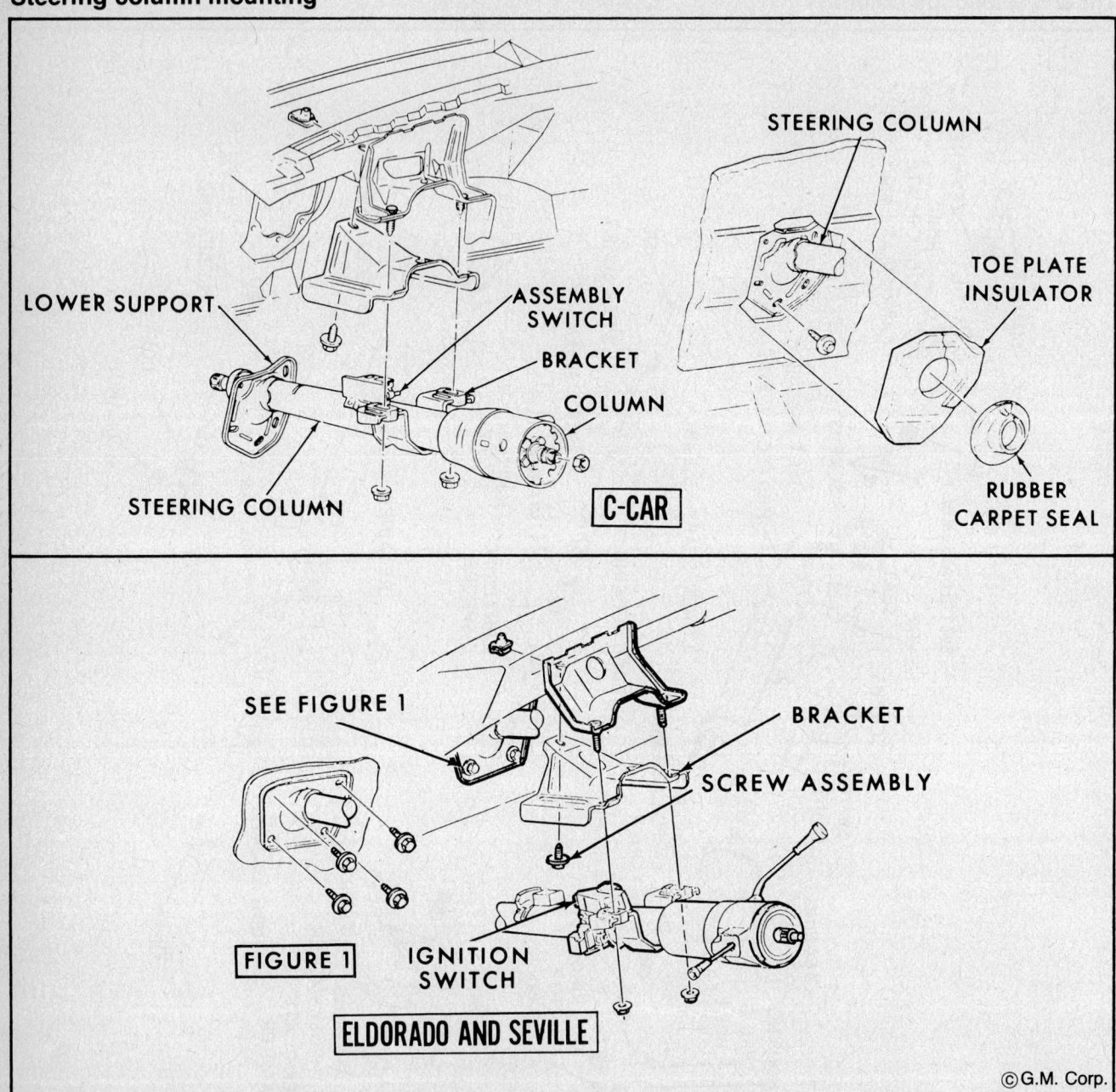

STEERING COLUMN

LOWER SUPPORT

ASSEMBLY SWITCH

BRACKET

COLUMN

STEERING COLUMN

C-CAR

TOE PLATE INSULATOR

RUBBER CARPET SEAL

SEE FIGURE 1

BRACKET

SCREW ASSEMBLY

FIGURE 1

IGNITION SWITCH

ELDORADO AND SEVILLE

©G.M. Corp.

Steering Column

CHILTON CAUTION: *Disconnect the battery positive cable to insure against accidental deployment of the air cushion restraint system on cars so equipped.*

NOTE: Handle the steering column very carefully. Rapping on the end of it could shear off the inserts which allow the column to collapse in a crash.

- Disconnect battery
- Disconnect flexible coupling.
- Remove toe pan bolts and then bolts attaching lower mounting bracket to column.
- Disconnect shift linkages, wiring, etc.

- Remove the upper column mount *after* the lower mount has been removed, and pull the column up out of the vehicle.

NOTE: When installing use only the specified hardware. Over-length bolts could prevent the column from properly collapsing in a crash.

Hydro-boost brake power unit

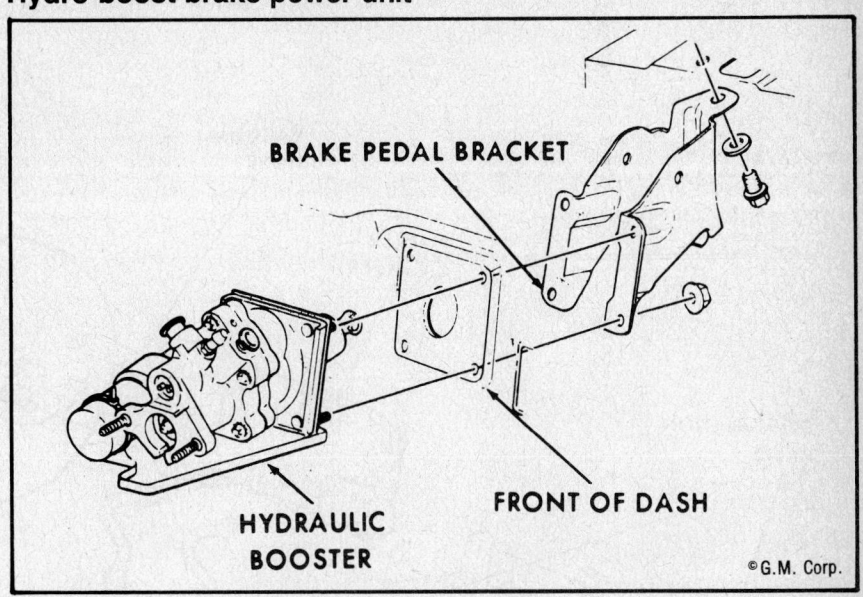

BRAKE PEDAL BRACKET

HYDRAULIC BOOSTER

FRONT OF DASH

© G.M. Corp.

Brake Power Unit R&R

Hydro-Boost
- Pump the brake pedal several times with the engine off to empty hydraulic fluid from the accumulator.
- Remove the master cylinder from the power unit.
- Remove booster hydraulic lines, booster pedal rod-to-brake pedal arm attachment and booster mount bolts.

Vacuum Boost
- Disconnect all master cylinder and power unit connections and remove them as an assembly.

Vacuum power brake unit mounting

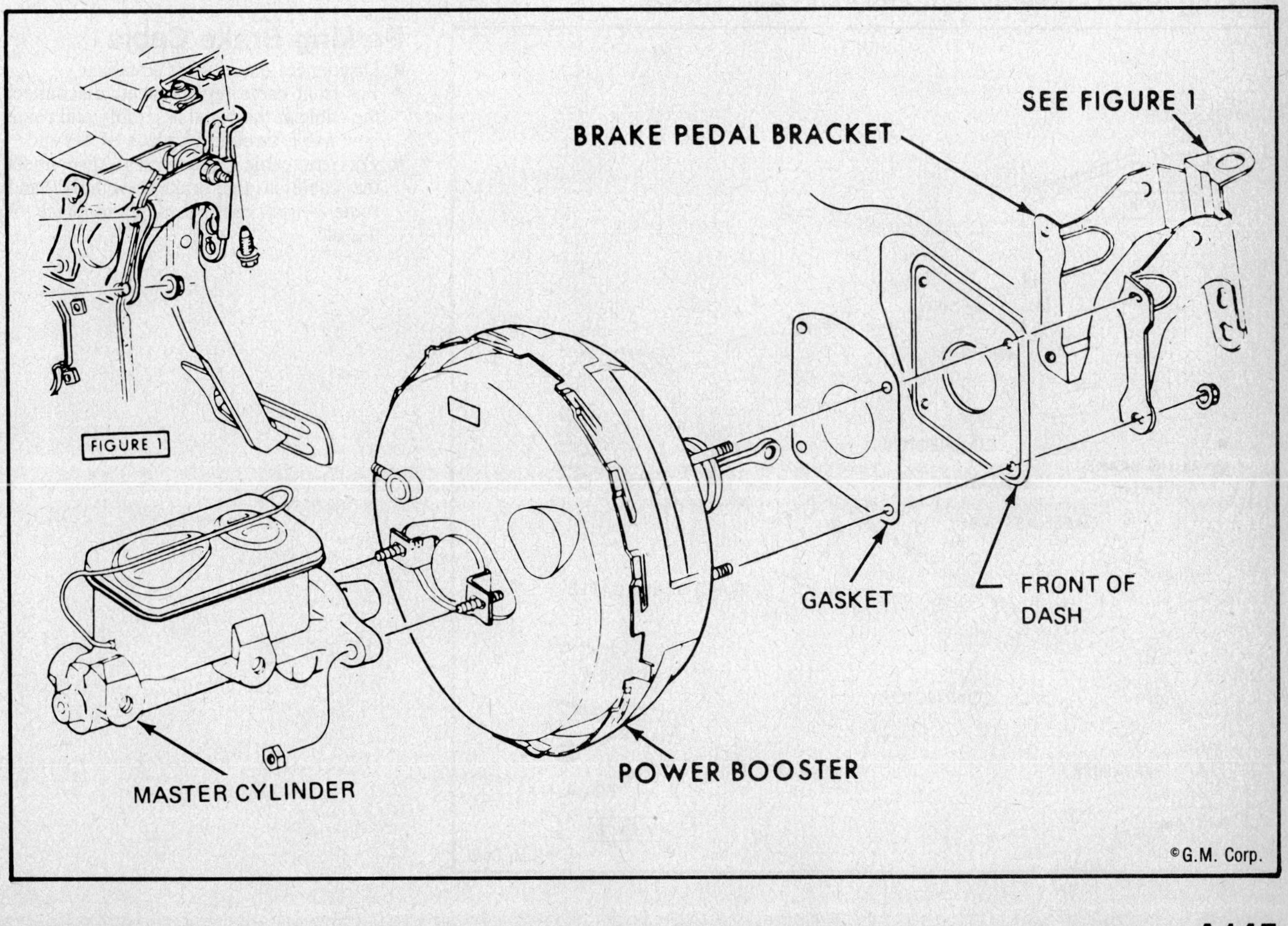

FIGURE 1

BRAKE PEDAL BRACKET

SEE FIGURE 1

GASKET

FRONT OF DASH

MASTER CYLINDER

POWER BOOSTER

© G.M. Corp.

Seville power brake unit mounting

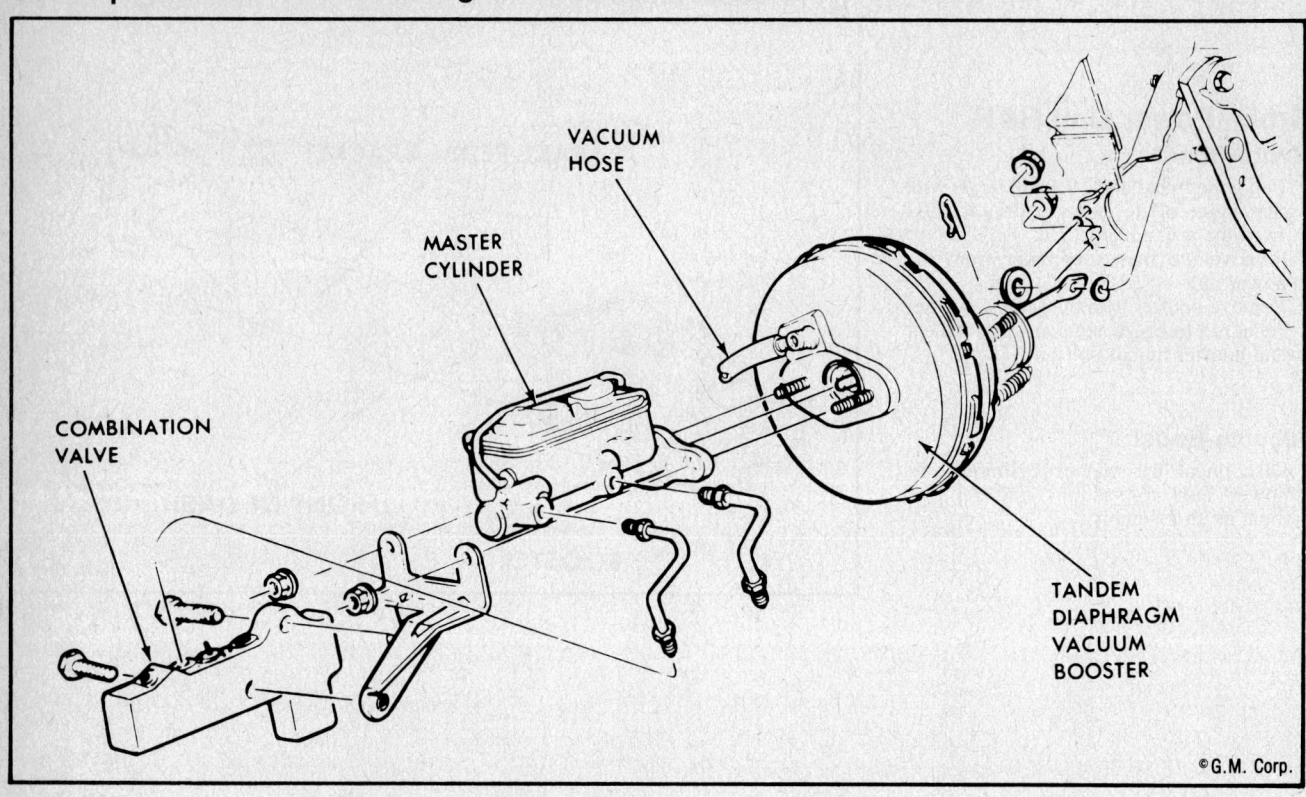

VACUUM HOSE

MASTER CYLINDER

COMBINATION VALVE

TANDEM DIAPHRAGM VACUUM BOOSTER

© G.M. Corp.

Parking brake cable except Eldorado and Seville

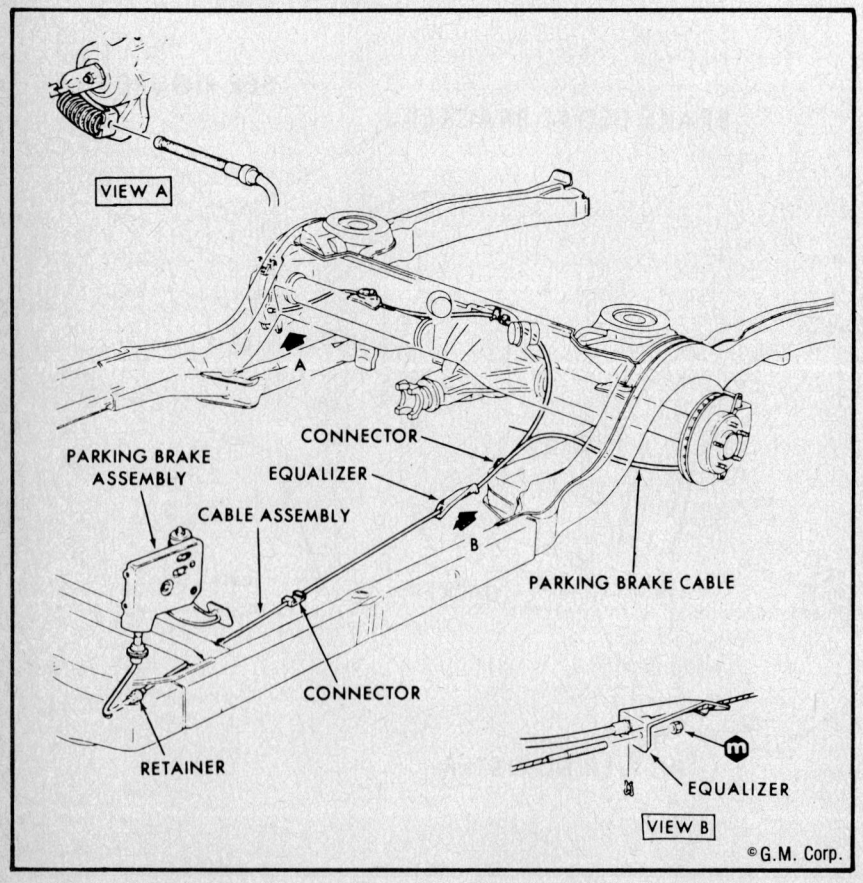

VIEW A

PARKING BRAKE ASSEMBLY

CABLE ASSEMBLY

CONNECTOR

EQUALIZER

CONNECTOR

PARKING BRAKE CABLE

RETAINER

EQUALIZER

VIEW B

© G.M. Corp.

Parking Brake Cable

- Disconnect cable from equalizer.
- For front cable replacement, disconnect the cable at the pedal assembly and route new cable through in place of the old.
- For rear cable replacement, disconnect the cable at the brake assembly, and route a new cable through in place of the old.

Parking brake cable-drum brake

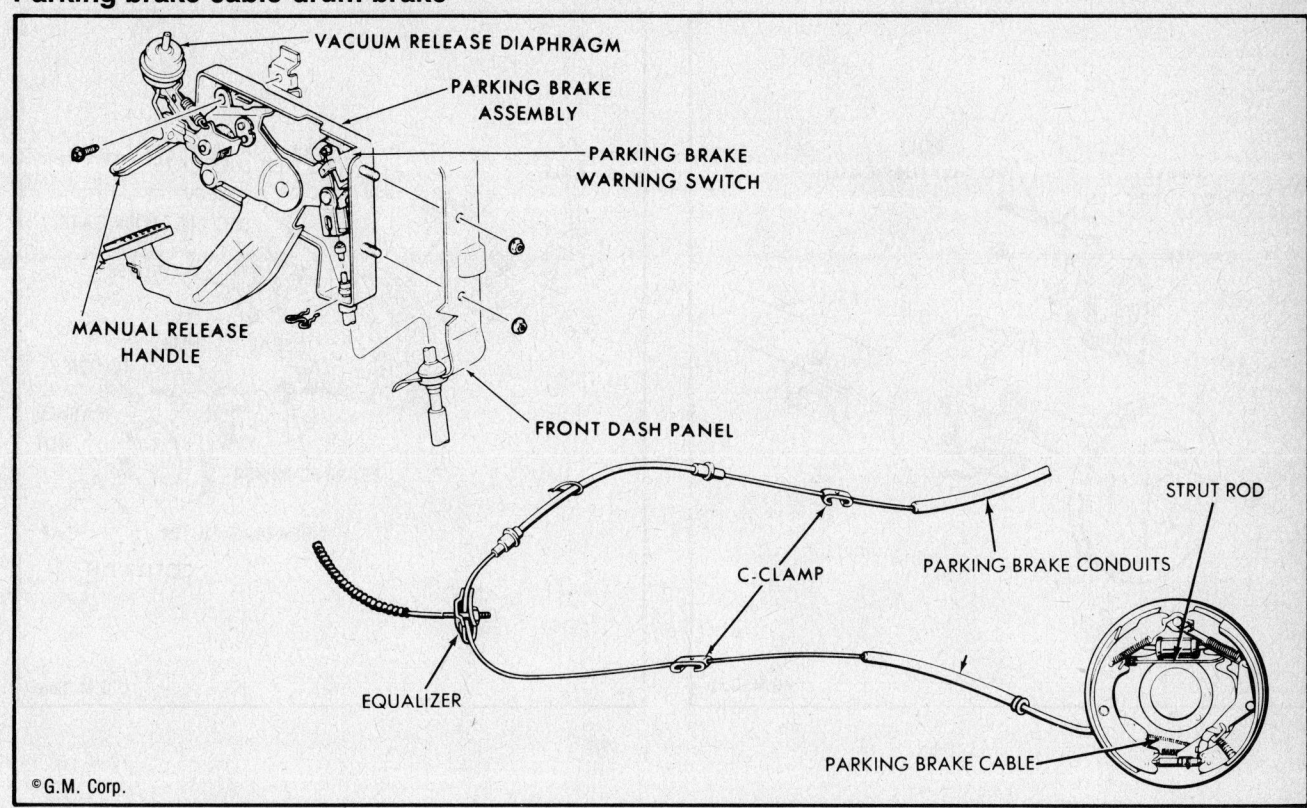

VACUUM RELEASE DIAPHRAGM
PARKING BRAKE ASSEMBLY
PARKING BRAKE WARNING SWITCH
MANUAL RELEASE HANDLE
FRONT DASH PANEL
STRUT ROD
PARKING BRAKE CONDUITS
C-CLAMP
EQUALIZER
PARKING BRAKE CABLE

© G.M. Corp.

Parking Brake Adjustment
Except Rear Disc Brakes

- Correctly adjust service brakes
- Apply parking brake two notches from fully released position.
- Tighten cable at equalizer until a slight drag is felt at the rear wheels.
- Release the parking brake lever, and check that the rear wheels turn without resistance.

Rear Disc Brakes

- Lubricate the cables at the equalizer hooks and underbody rub points, and check for free movement of all cables.
- With the parking brake pedal in the fully released position, hold the brake cable stud from turning and tighten the equalizer nut until all slack in the cable is removed.
- Make sure the caliper levers are against the stops on the caliper housing. If the levers are off the stops, loosen the cable until the levers return to the stops.
- Operate the parking brake pedal several times to check the adjustment.
- After adjustment, the parking brake pedal should travel 4–5 inches with about 125 lbs. force.

Rear disc brake except Eldorado and Seville

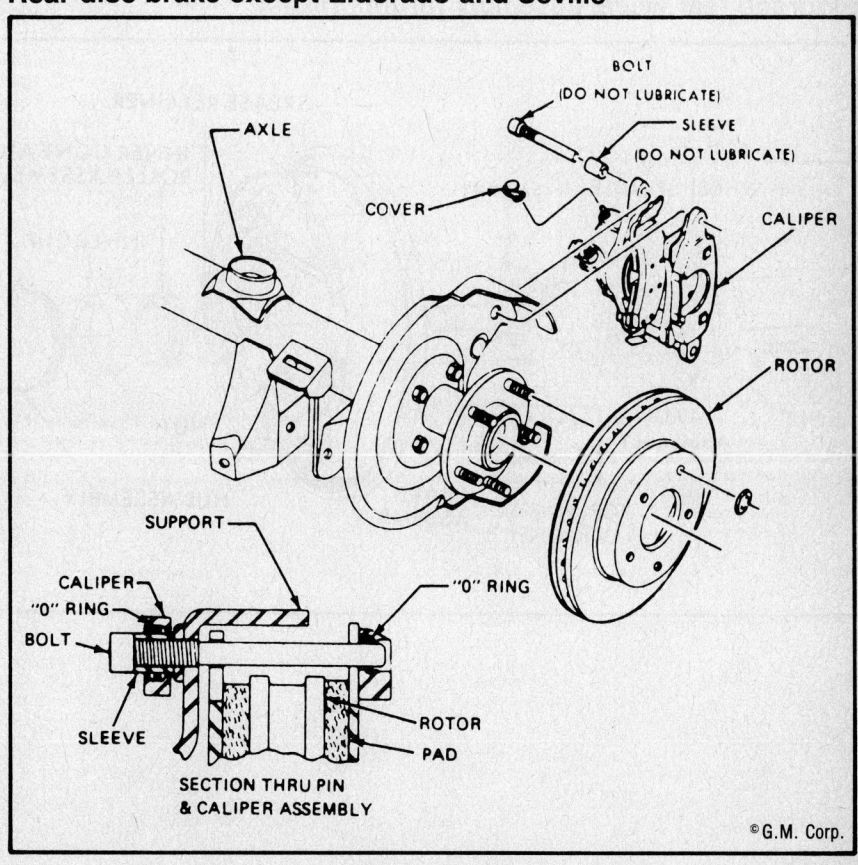

AXLE
BOLT (DO NOT LUBRICATE)
SLEEVE (DO NOT LUBRICATE)
COVER
CALIPER
ROTOR
SUPPORT
CALIPER
"0" RING
BOLT
"0" RING
SLEEVE
ROTOR
PAD

SECTION THRU PIN & CALIPER ASSEMBLY

© G.M. Corp.

A147

CADILLAC

EXCEPT CIMARRON

Seville rear disc brake (rear drive cars)

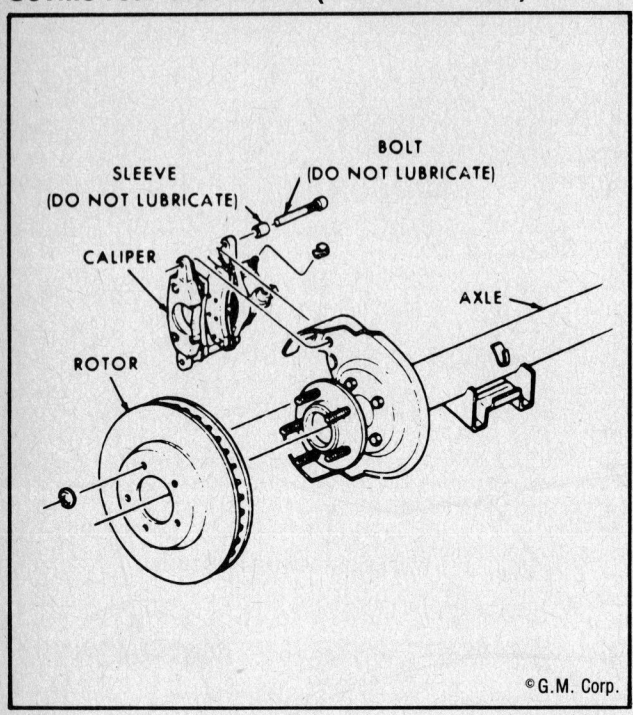

Eldorado rear disc brake

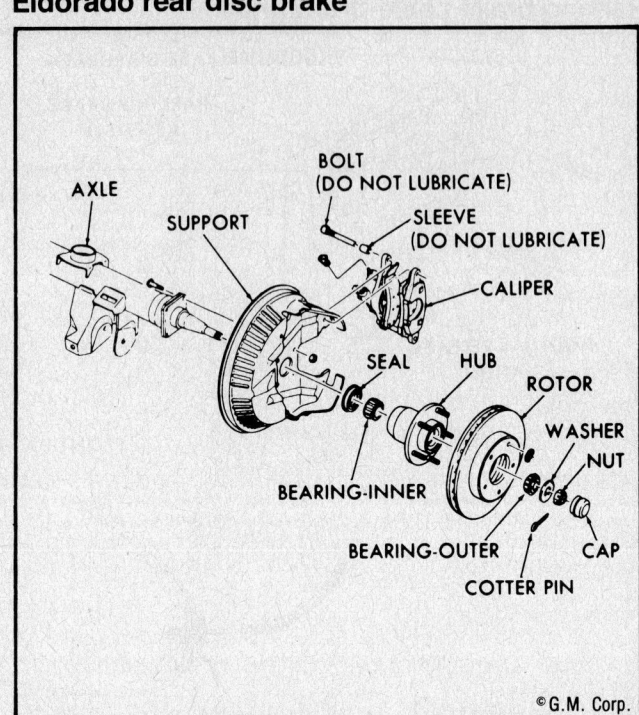

Eldorado rear wheel assembly (drum brakes)

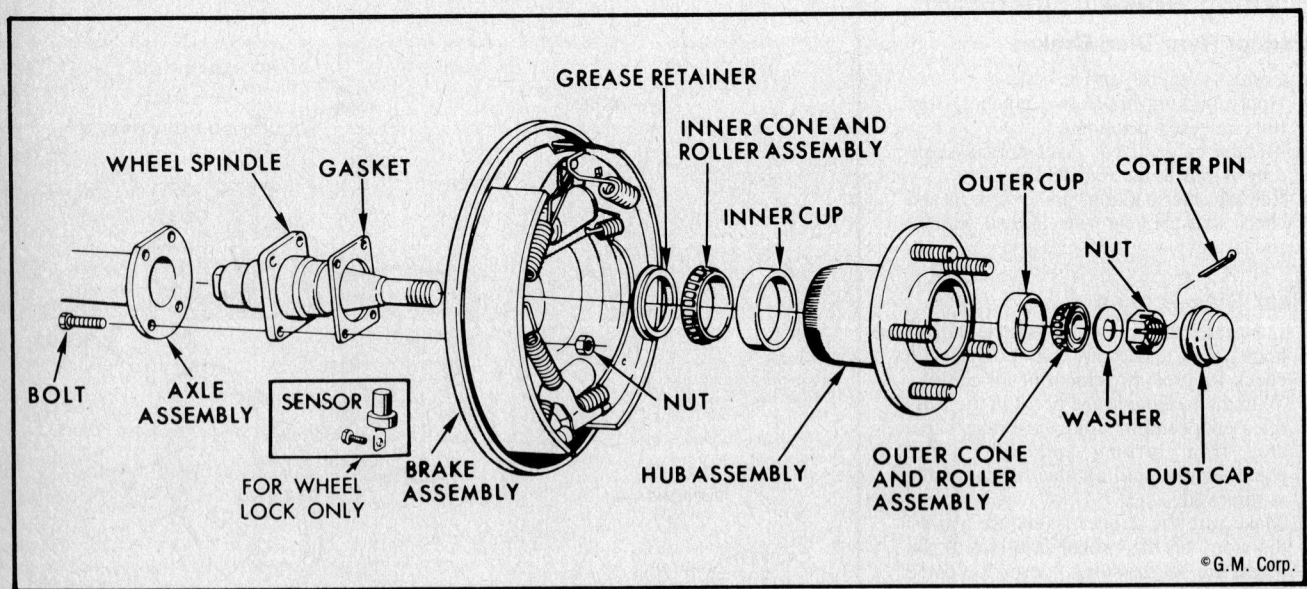

Automatic level control system component locations except Eldorado and Seville

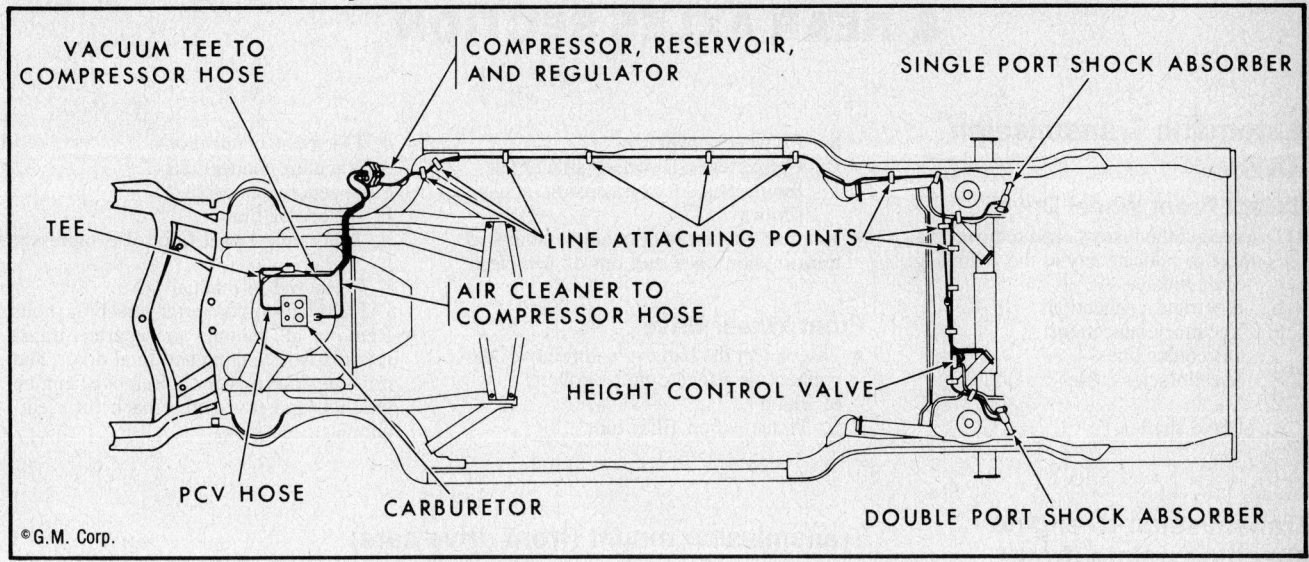

Automatic level control compressor mounting (front drive cars)

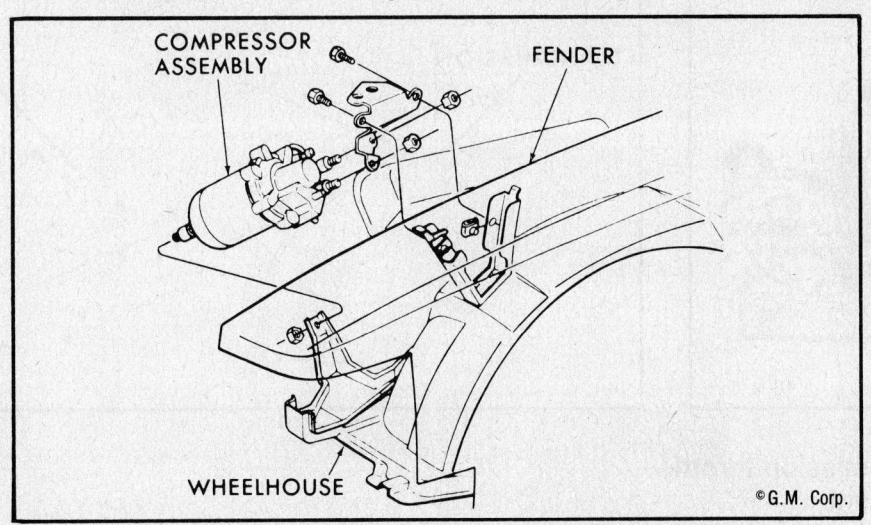

Automatic level control system component locations (front drive cars)

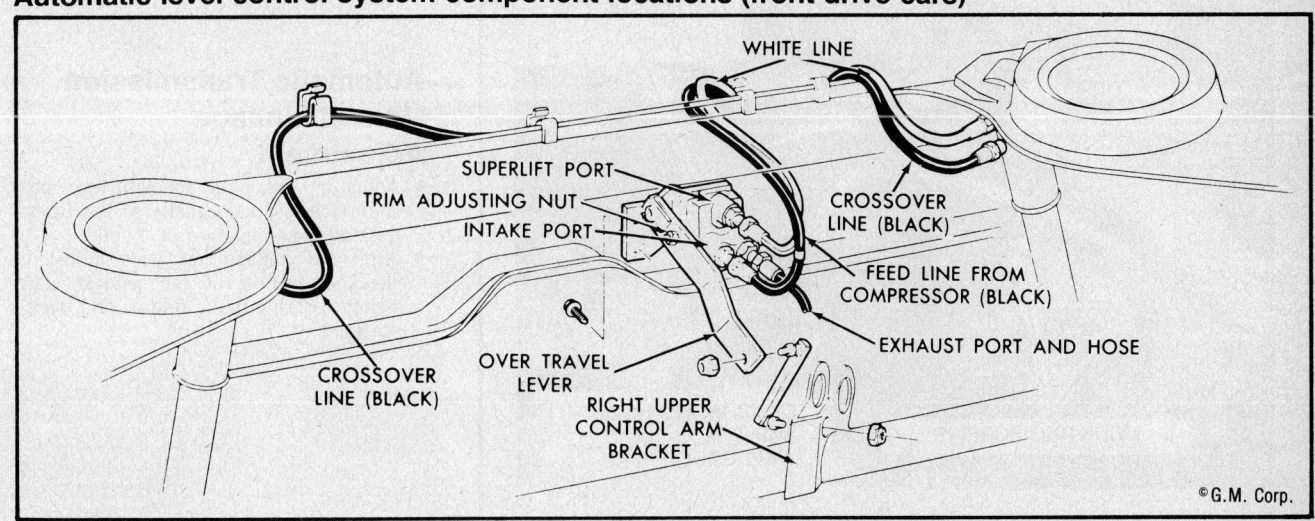

TRANSMISSION, PROPELLER SHAFT & REAR AXLES SECTION

Automatic Transmission R&R

Except Front Wheel Drive

- Disconnect the battery, and remove, disconnect or relocate any of the following:
  a. Shift linkage
  b. Electrical connections
  c. Vacuum connections
  d. Oil cooler lines
  e. Speedometer cable
  f. Starter
  g. Drive shaft

  h. Flywheel cover pan
  i. Converter-to-flywheel attachments
  j. Engine mount-to-extension housing screws
- Remove the mounting bolts, and slide transmission back and out of vehicle.

Front Wheel Drive

- Disconnect the battery, and remove, disconnect or relocate the following:
  a. Hood
  b. Transmission filler tube

  c. Electrical connections
  d. Vacuum connections
  e. Speedometer cable
  f. Oil cooler lines
  g. Automatic Level Control compressor
  h. Starter
  i. Relay rod-to-manual yoke
  j. Flexplate-to-converter attaching bolts
- Remove all mounts to separate transmission from engine and final drive, and remove transmission. Remove engine mounts, and pry engine back for clearance as necessary.

Transmission-to-engine attaching points (front drive cars)

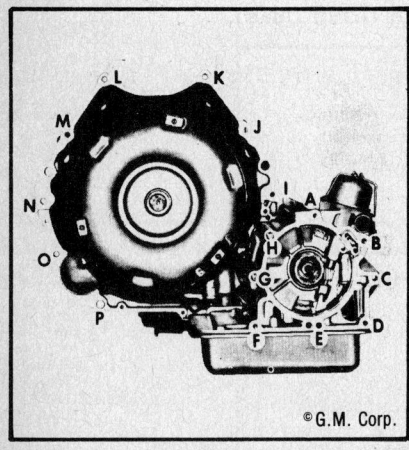

© G.M. Corp.

Transmission mount (front drive cars)

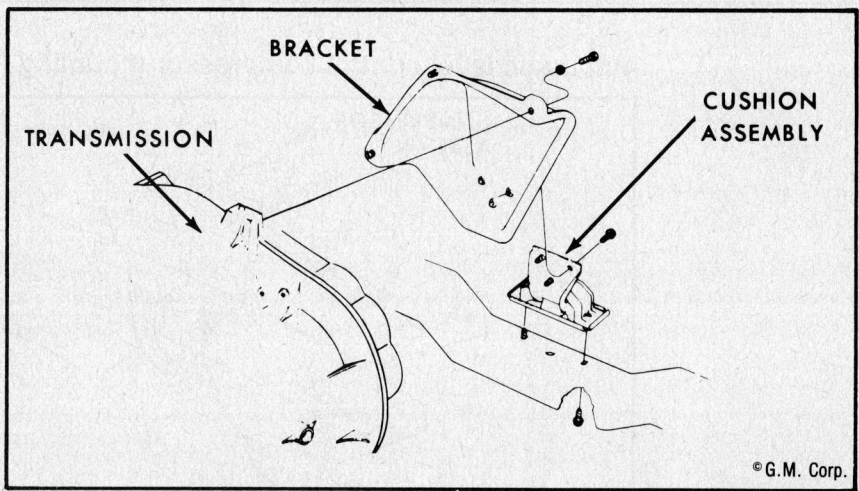

© G.M. Corp.

Automatic transmission throttle linkage adjustment

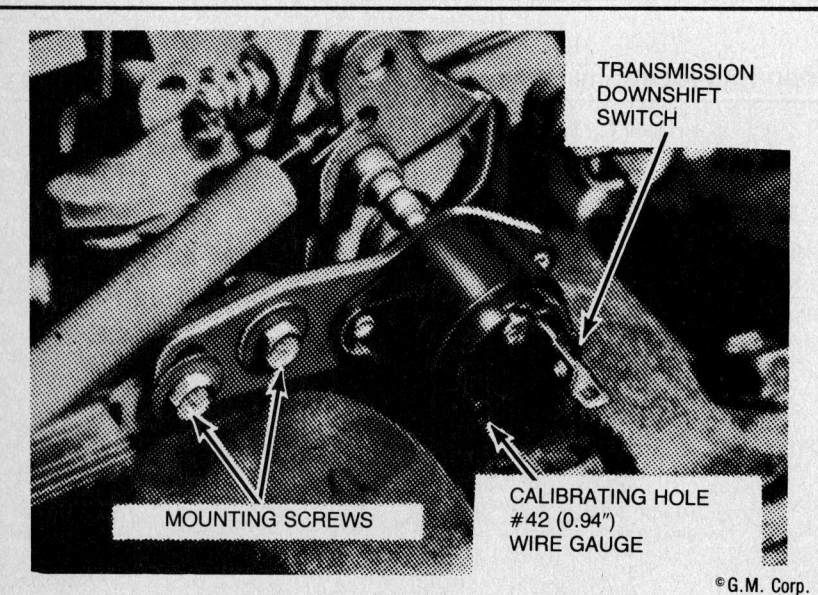

TRANSMISSION DOWNSHIFT SWITCH

MOUNTING SCREWS

CALIBRATING HOLE #42 (0.94") WIRE GAUGE

© G.M. Corp.

Automatic Transmission Manual Linkage Adjustment

- Adjust the linkage so the shift lever positions correspond exactly to the transmission positions.
- After the linkage has been adjusted, check operation of the neutral start switch, parking brake release and backup lights.

Automatic transmission shift linkage front drive cars

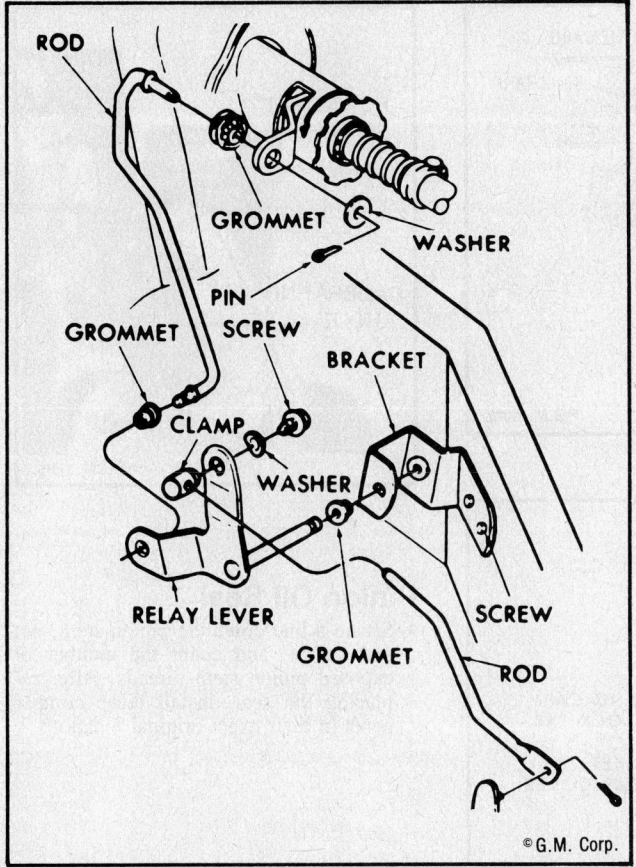

Automatic transmission shift linkage rear drive cars

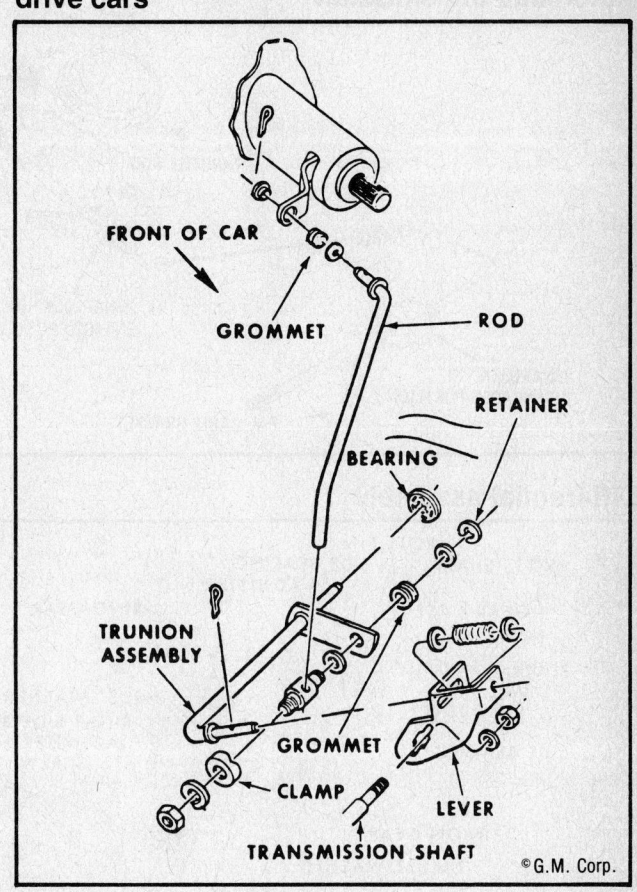

Shift linkage adjustment-200 series automatic transmission (diesel)

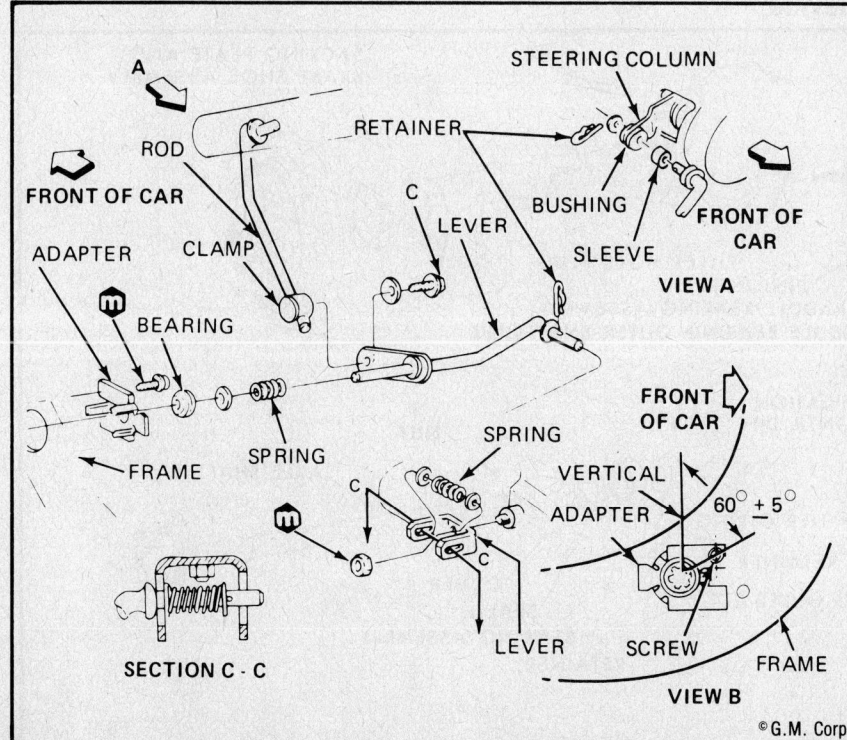

Automatic Transmission Throttle Linkage Adjustment

- With the idle speed correctly set and the carburetor operating on the low-speed circuit, loosen the switch mounting screws and place a 0.094 inch wire gauge into the hole in the lower wire terminal.
- Adjust the switch position so that the lever just touches the carburetor adaptor plate arm. The switch should make contact above 60° of throttle opening.
- Tighten the mounting screws and remove the wire gauge.

Adjustment Procedures

- Assemble all parts. Do not tighten screw marked C.
- With column lever in neutral position and transmission lever in neutral position, tighten screw marked C.
- Linkage is correctly adjusted if shift lever is raised and centered in the transmission's neutral detent, the shift lever can be lowered and will engage the steering column neutral notch. The adjustment is unacceptable if any rotation of the shift lever is required to engage the steering column neutral notch.

A151

CADILLAC
EXCEPT CIMARRON

Throttle valve adjustment with 200 series automatic transmission

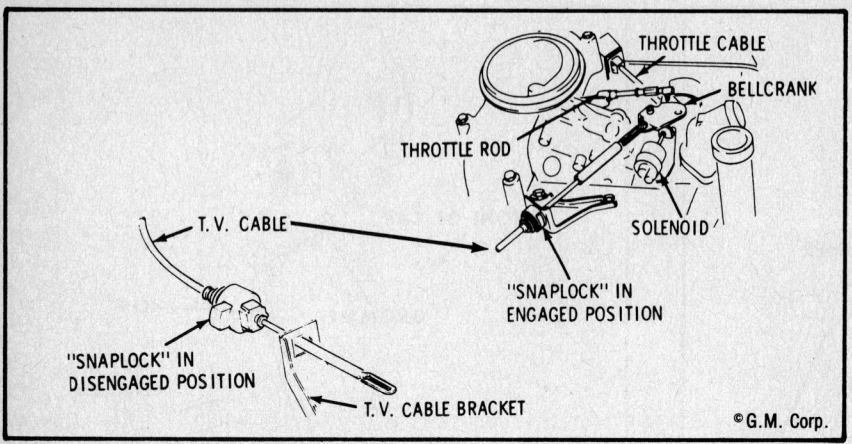

THROTTLE CABLE
BELLCRANK
THROTTLE ROD
T. V. CABLE
SOLENOID
"SNAPLOCK" IN ENGAGED POSITION
"SNAPLOCK" IN DISENGAGED POSITION
T. V. CABLE BRACKET
© G.M. Corp.

Typical transmission downshift switch

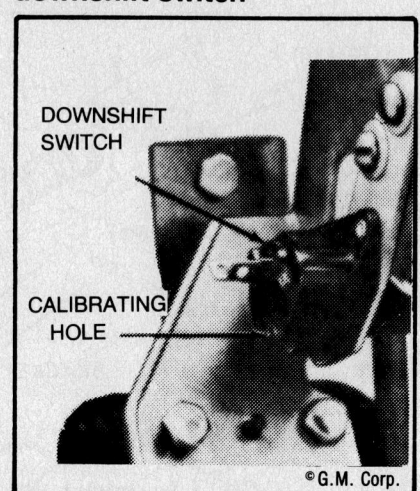

DOWNSHIFT SWITCH
CALIBRATING HOLE
© G.M. Corp.

Differential assembly

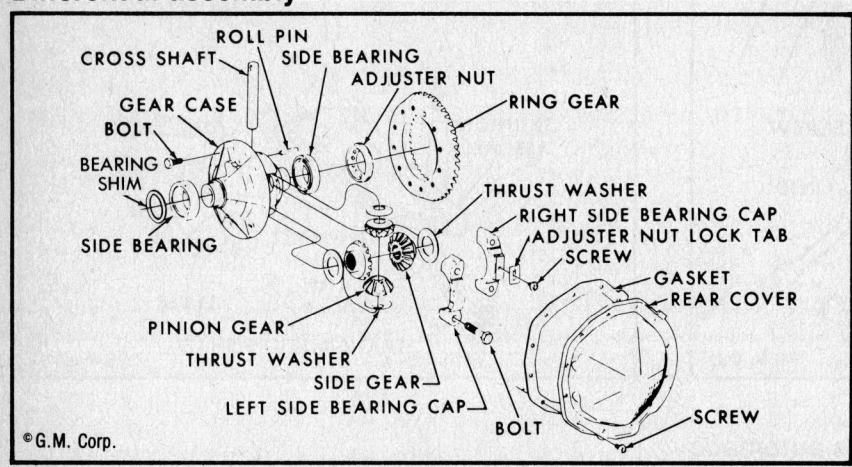

CROSS SHAFT
ROLL PIN
SIDE BEARING
ADJUSTER NUT
RING GEAR
GEAR CASE
BOLT
BEARING SHIM
THRUST WASHER
RIGHT SIDE BEARING CAP
ADJUSTER NUT LOCK TAB
SCREW
SIDE BEARING
GASKET
REAR COVER
PINION GEAR
THRUST WASHER
SIDE GEAR
LEFT SIDE BEARING CAP
BOLT
SCREW
© G.M. Corp.

Pinion Oil Seal

● Scribe a line down the pinion stem, nut and flange, and count the number of exposed pinion stem threads. After replacing the seal, install these components in their exact original locations.

Rear axle (rear drive cars) except Seville

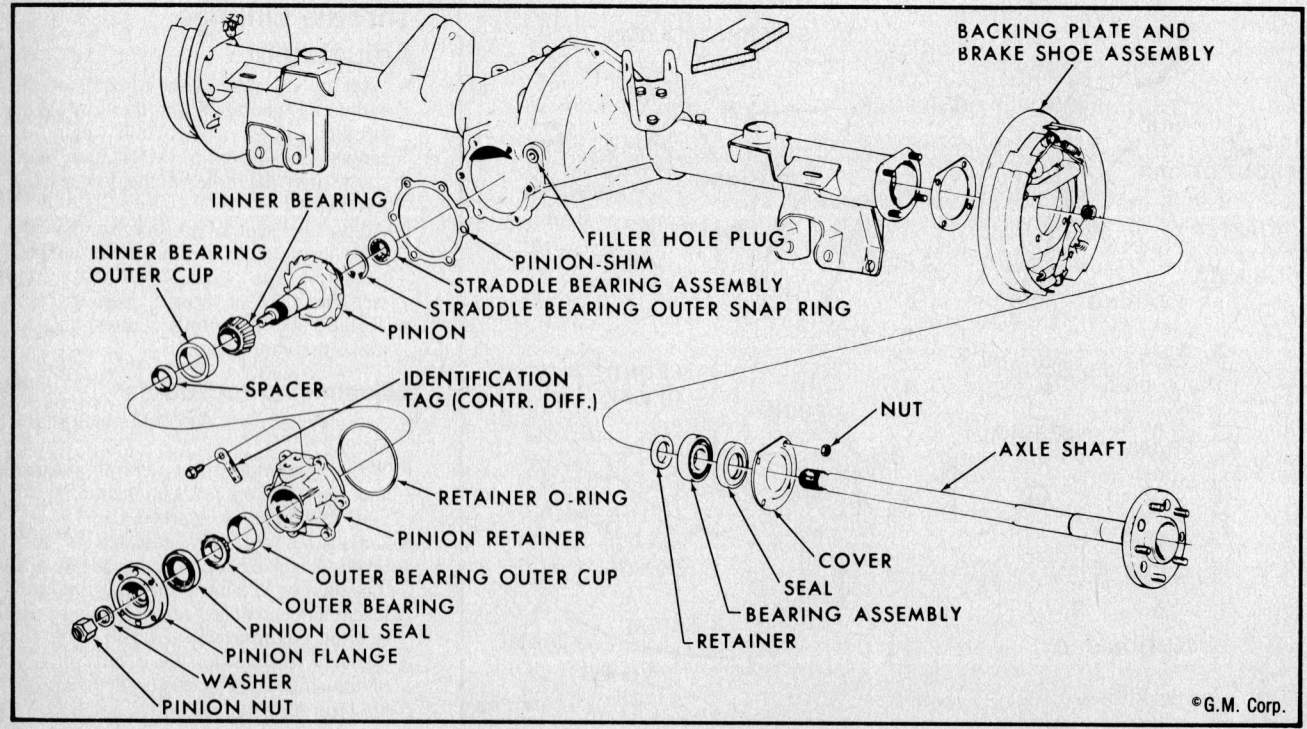

BACKING PLATE AND BRAKE SHOE ASSEMBLY
INNER BEARING
INNER BEARING OUTER CUP
FILLER HOLE PLUG
PINION-SHIM
STRADDLE BEARING ASSEMBLY
STRADDLE BEARING OUTER SNAP RING
PINION
SPACER
IDENTIFICATION TAG (CONTR. DIFF.)
NUT
AXLE SHAFT
RETAINER O-RING
PINION RETAINER
OUTER BEARING OUTER CUP
OUTER BEARING
PINION OIL SEAL
PINION FLANGE
WASHER
PINION NUT
COVER
SEAL
BEARING ASSEMBLY
RETAINER
© G.M. Corp.

Front wheel drive components

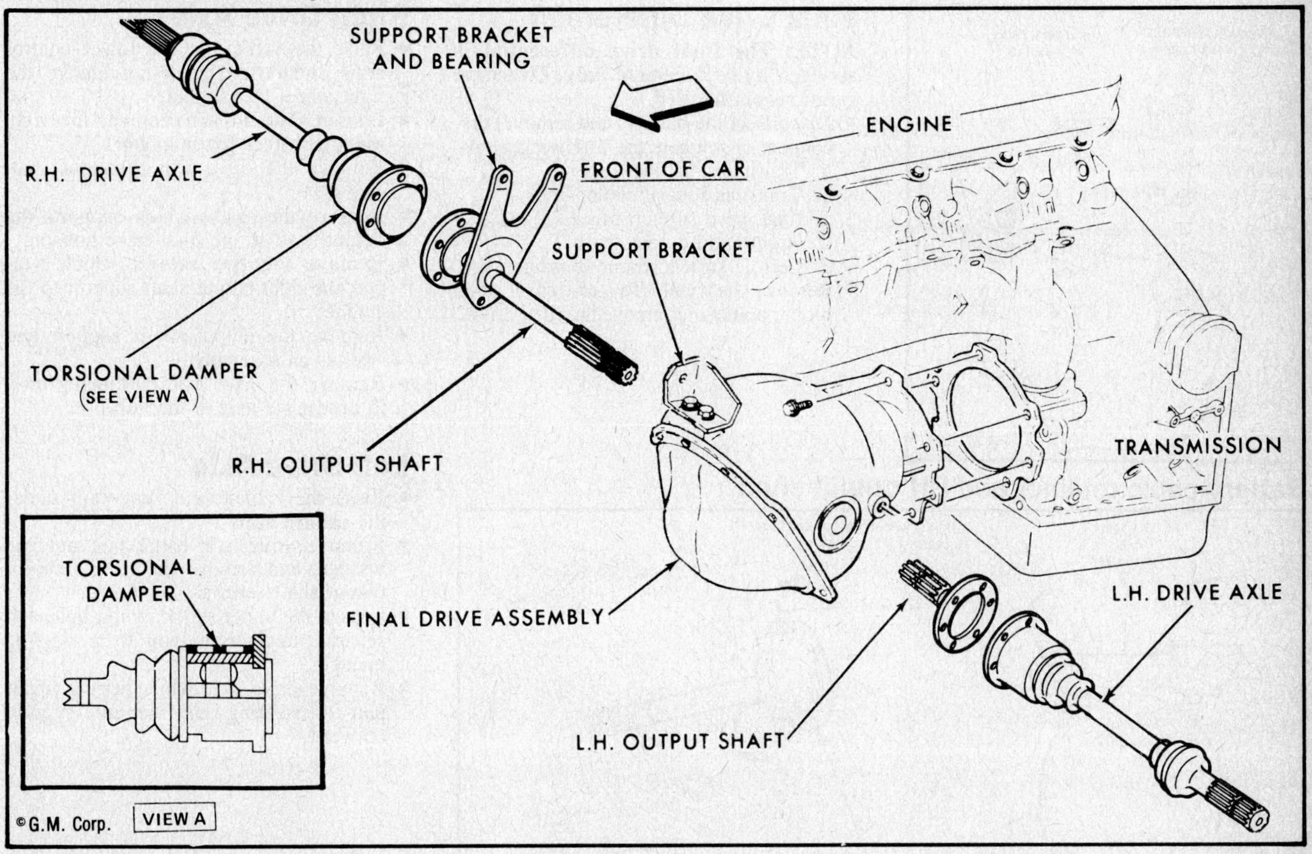

R.H. DRIVE AXLE

SUPPORT BRACKET AND BEARING

FRONT OF CAR

ENGINE

SUPPORT BRACKET

TORSIONAL DAMPER (SEE VIEW A)

R.H. OUTPUT SHAFT

TRANSMISSION

TORSIONAL DAMPER

FINAL DRIVE ASSEMBLY

L.H. DRIVE AXLE

L.H. OUTPUT SHAFT

© G.M. Corp. VIEW A

Final drive components

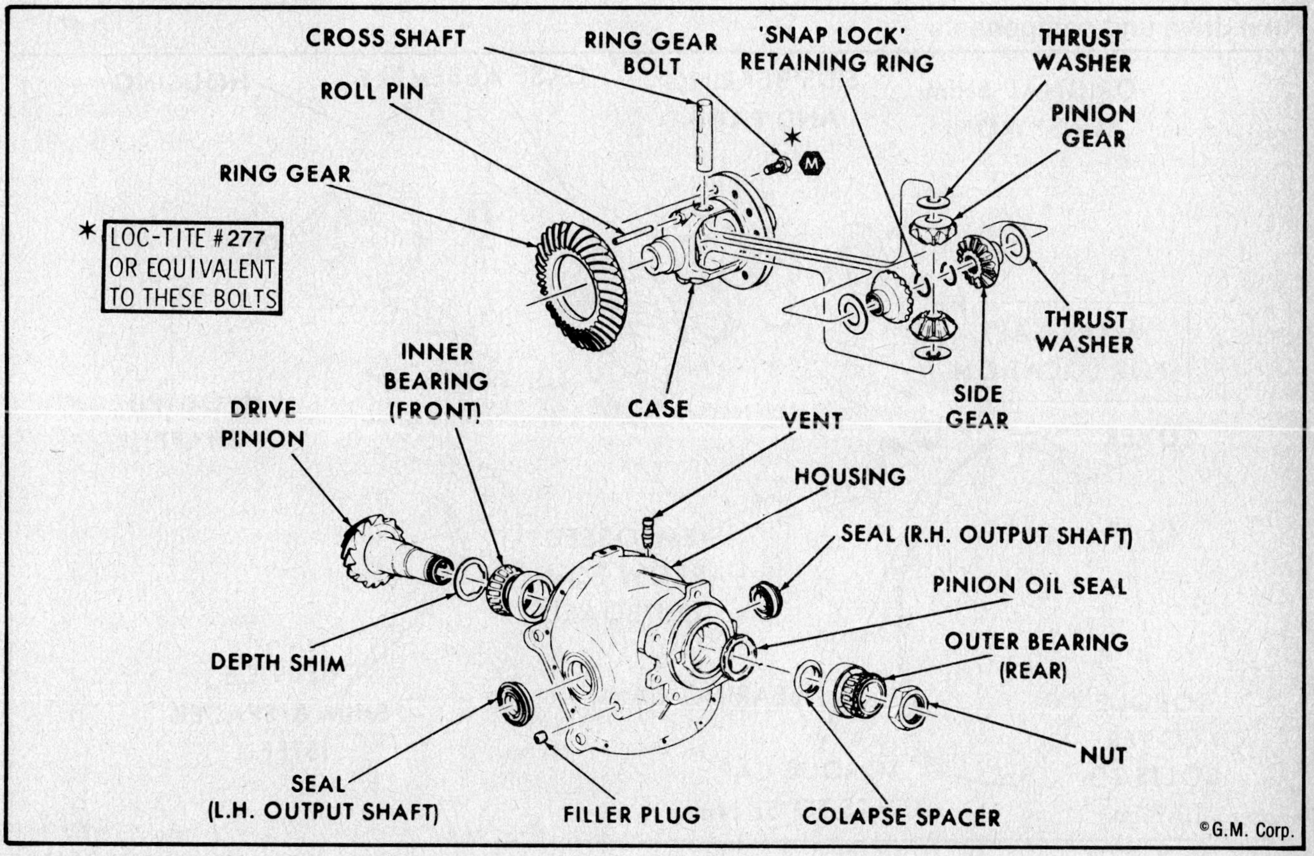

CROSS SHAFT

ROLL PIN

RING GEAR BOLT

'SNAP LOCK' RETAINING RING

THRUST WASHER

PINION GEAR

RING GEAR

* LOC-TITE #277 OR EQUIVALENT TO THESE BOLTS

THRUST WASHER

INNER BEARING (FRONT)

CASE

SIDE GEAR

DRIVE PINION

VENT

HOUSING

SEAL (R.H. OUTPUT SHAFT)

PINION OIL SEAL

DEPTH SHIM

OUTER BEARING (REAR)

SEAL (L.H. OUTPUT SHAFT)

FILLER PLUG

COLAPSE SPACER

NUT

© G.M. Corp.

Removing final drive shield

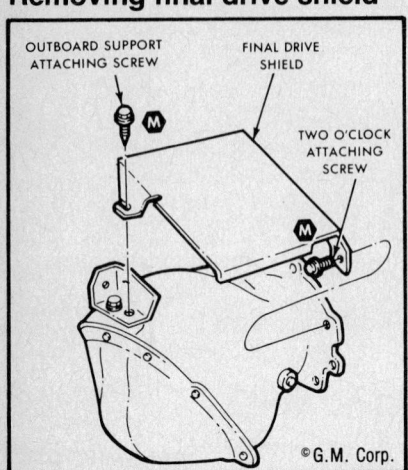

OUTBOARD SUPPORT
ATTACHING SCREW

FINAL DRIVE
SHIELD

TWO O'CLOCK
ATTACHING
SCREW

© G.M. Corp.

Final Drive Differential

NOTE: The final drive differential is serviced by replacement only. Overhaul is not recommended.

- Disconnect the battery, and remove, disconnect or relocate the following:
  a. Transmission filler tube
  b. Transmission oil cooler lines
  c. final drive support brace
  d. Right hand output shaft
  e. Left tie strut-to-frame crossmember
- Remove the final drive-to-transmission mount bolts, and remove the final drive.

Right Drive Axle

- Raise the vehicle at the lower control arms, and loosen, but do not remove, the right wheel spindle nut.
- Loosen, but do not remove, the right shock absorber lower mount.
- Remove the drive axle-to-output shaft screws.
- Remove the screw which supports the output shaft to the final drive housing.
- Remove the two screws which support the right output shaft support to the engine.
- Remove the output shaft, support and strut as an assembly.
- Remove the drive axle by tapping on it to unseat the axle at the hub.

Left Drive Axle

- Raise the vehicle and support it under the control arms.
- Remove drive axle cotter pin, nut and washer, and remove the drive axle-to-output shaft screws.
- Loosen the upper shock mount bolt, and separate upper ball joint from steering knuckle.
- Remove drive axle while tipping upper part of steering knuckle and support outward.

Battery cable retainer and RH output shaft

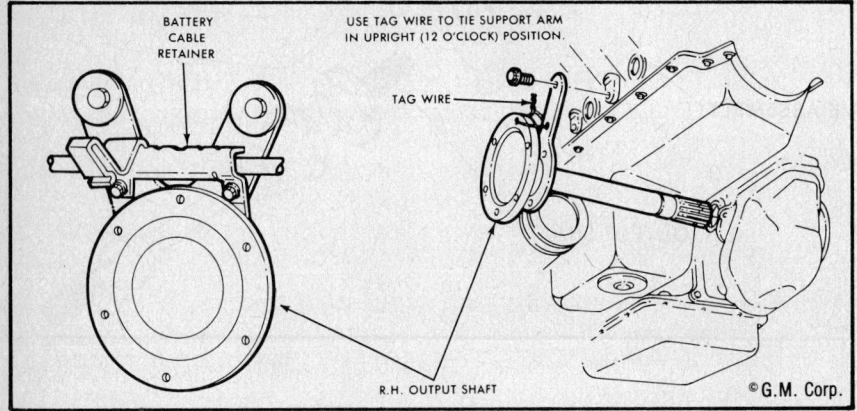

BATTERY
CABLE
RETAINER

USE TAG WIRE TO TIE SUPPORT ARM
IN UPRIGHT (12 O'CLOCK) POSITION.

TAG WIRE

R.H. OUTPUT SHAFT

© G.M. Corp.

Final drive unit components

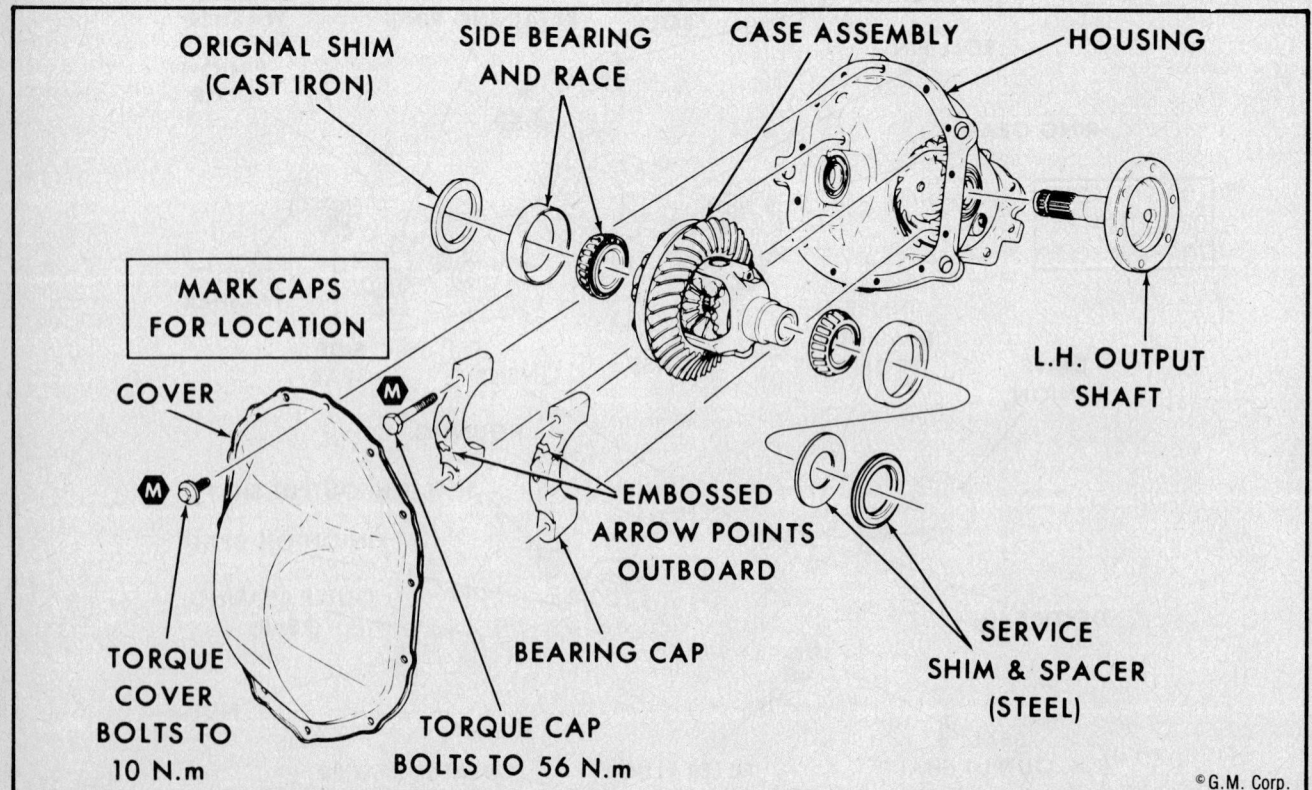

ORIGNAL SHIM
(CAST IRON)

SIDE BEARING
AND RACE

CASE ASSEMBLY

HOUSING

MARK CAPS
FOR LOCATION

COVER

L.H. OUTPUT
SHAFT

EMBOSSED
ARROW POINTS
OUTBOARD

BEARING CAP

SERVICE
SHIM & SPACER
(STEEL)

TORQUE
COVER
BOLTS TO
10 N.m

TORQUE CAP
BOLTS TO 56 N.m

© G.M. Corp.

INDEX

MODEL IDENTIFICATION

1976 CHEVROLET

W.B. **121.5″**, S/W **125″**. Length 223″, S/W 229″. Ship. Wgt. V8 4 Dr. 4222 Lbs.

1977 CHEVROLET

W.B. **116″**. S/W **215″**. Length 213″, Width 76″, S/W 80″. Ship. Wgt. V8 2 Dr. 3650

1978 CAPRICE

W.B. **116″** Length 212.1″ Ship. Wgt. 8 Cyl. 2 Dr. 3578 Lbs.

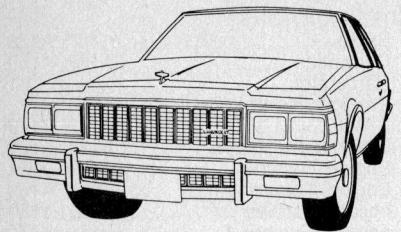

1979 CAPRICE

W.B. **116.0″** Length 212.1″ Ship. Wgt. 8 Cyl. 2 Dr. 3578 Lbs.

1980 CAPRICE

W.B. **116″**. Length 212.1″. Ship. Wgt. V6 2 Dr. 3643 Lbs.

1981-82 CAPRICE

W.B. **116.0″**. Length 212.1″. 6 Cyl. 2 Dr. Curb Wgt. 3451 Lbs.

1978 IMPALA

W.B. **116″** Length 212.1″ Ship. Wgt. 8 Cyl. 2 Dr. 3510 Lbs.

1979 IMPALA

W.B. **116.0″** Length 212.1″ Ship. Wgt. 8 Cyl. 2 Dr. 3510 Lbs.

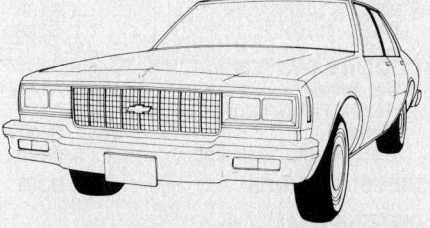

1980 IMPALA

W.B. **116″**. Length 212.1″. Ship. Wgt. V6 2 Dr. 3599 Lbs.

1981-82 IMPALA

W.B. **116.0″**. Length 212.1″. 6 Cyl. 2 Dr. Curb Wgt. 3451 Lbs.

1976 CAMARO

W.B. **108″**. Length 196″. Ship. Wgt. 6 Cyl. 2 Dr. 3421 Lbs. V8 2 Dr. 3511 Lbs.

1977 CAMARO

W.B. **108″**. Length 196″. Width 75″ Ship. Wgt. 6 Cyl. 2 Dr. 3369 Lbs. V8 2Dr. 3486 Lbs.

1978 CAMARO

W.B. **108″** Length 197.6″ Ship. Wgt. 8 Cyl. 2 Dr. 3399 Lbs.

1979 CAMARO

W.B. **108″** Length 197.6″ Ship. Wgt. 8 Cyl. 2 Dr. 3399 Lbs.

1980 CAMARO

W.B. **108″**. Length 197.6″. Ship. Wgt. Sport Coupe Approx. 3407 Lbs.

1981 CAMARO

W.B. 108.0". Length 197.0". 6 Cyl. Curb Wgt. 3374 Lbs.

1982 CAMARO

W.B. 108.0". Length 197.0". 6 Cyl. Curb Wgt. 3374 Lbs.

1976 CHEVELLE

W.B. 116", 2D 112". Length 210", 2D 206", S/W 216". Ship. Wgt. 6 Cyl. 2 Dr. 3650 Lbs. V8 2 Dr. 3755 Lbs.

1977 CHEVELLE

W.B. 116", 2D 112". Length 210", 2D 206", S/W 216". Width 77" Ship. Wgt. 6 Cyl. 2 Dr. 3551 Lbs. V8 2 Dr. 3650 Lbs.

1976 MONTE CARLO

W.B. 116". Length 214". Ship. Wgt. V8 2 Dr. 3907 Lbs.

1977 MONTE CARLO

W.B. 116". Length 214". Width 78". Ship. Wgt. V8 2 Dr. 3448 Lbs.

1978 MONTE CARLO

W.B. 108.1" Length 200.4" Ship. Wgt. 8 Cyl. 2 Dr. 3129 Lbs.

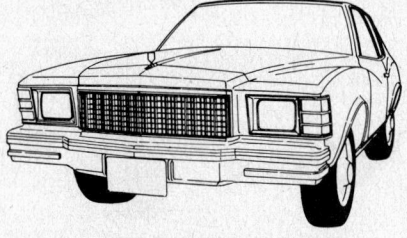

1979 MONTE CARLO

W.B. 108.1" Length 200.4" Ship. Wgt. 8 Cyl. 2 Dr. 3129 Lbs.

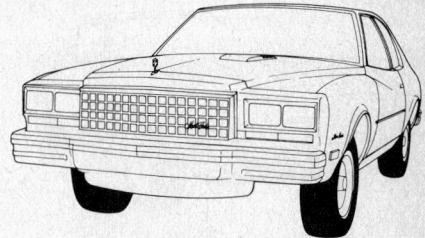

1980 MONTE CARLO

W.B. 108.1". Length 200.4". Ship. Wgt. Approx. 3132 Lbs.

1981 MONTE CARLO

W.B. 108.1". Length 200.4". 6 Cyl. 2 Dr. Curb Wgt. 3190 Lbs.

1982 MONTE CARLO

W.B. 108.1". Length 200.4". 6 Cyl. 2 Dr. Curb Wgt. 3190 Lbs.

1978 MALIBU

W.B. 108.1" Length 192.7" Ship. Wgt. 8 Cyl. 2 Dr. 3263 Lbs.

1979 MALIBU

W.B. 108.1" Length 192.7" Ship. Wgt. 8 Cyl. 2 Dr. 3263 Lbs.

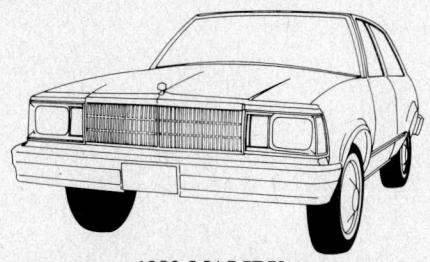

1980 MALIBU

W.B. 108.1". Length 192.7". Ship. Wgt. V6 2 Dr. Approx. 3076 Lbs.

1981 MALIBU

W.B. 108.1". Length 192.7". 6 Cyl. 2 Dr. Curb Wgt. 3104 Lbs.

CHEVROLET
EXCEPT CAVALIER, CELEBRITY, CHEVETTE, CITATION, MONZA & VEGA

1982 MALIBU

W.B. 108.1″. Length 192.7″. 6 Cyl. 2 Dr. Curb Wgt. 3104 Lbs.

1976 NOVA

W.B. 111″. Length 197″. Ship. Wgt. 6 Cyl. 2 Dr. 3188 Lbs. V8 2 Dr. 3272 Lbs.

1977 NOVA

W.B. 111″. Length 197″. Width 73″. Ship. Wgt. 6 Cyl. 2 Dr. 3139 Lbs. V8 2 Dr. 3265 Lbs.

1978 NOVA

W.B. 111″ Length 196.7″ Ship. Wgt. 8 Cyl. 2 Dr. 3133 Lbs.

1979 NOVA

W.B. 111″ Length 196.7″ Ship. Wgt. 8 Cyl. 2 Dr. 3133 Lbs.

1976 CORVETTE

W.B. 98″. Length 186″. Ship. Wgt. V8 2 Dr. 3445 Lbs.

1977 CORVETTE

W.B. 98″. Length 186″. Width 69″. Ship. Wgt. V8 2 Dr. 3445 Lbs.

1978 CORVETTE

W.B. 98″ Length 185.2″ Ship. Wgt. 8 Cyl. 2 Dr. 3401 Lbs.

1979 CORVETTE

W.B. 98″ Length 185.2″ Ship. Wgt. 2 Dr. 3401 Lbs.

1980 CORVETTE

W.B. 98″. Length 185.2″. Ship. Wgt. Approx. 3519 Lbs.

1981-82 CORVETTE

W.B. 98.0″. Length 185.3″. 8 Cyl. Curb Wgt. 3334 Lbs.

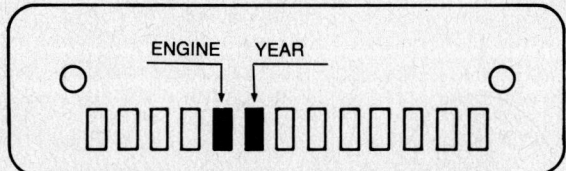

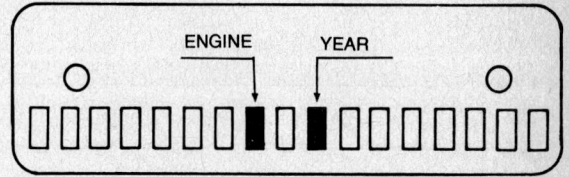

	ENGINE CODE				MODEL YEAR CODE	
Code	Eng. Disp. (cu in)	Eng. Config.	Carb	Eng. Mfgr.	Code	Year
D	250	L6	1V	Chev	6	1976
Q	305	V8	2V	Chev		
V	350	V8	2V	Chev		
L	350	V8	4V	Chev		
X	350	V8	4V	Chev		
U	400	V8	4V	Chev		
S	454	V8	4V	Chev		
T	350	V8	4V	Chev		
D	250	L6	1V	Chev	7	1977
U	305	V8	2V	Chev		
L	350	V8	4V	Chev		
X	350	V8	4V	Chev		
M	200	V6	2V	Chev	8	1978
A	231	V6	2V	Buick		
D	250	L6	1V	Chev		
U	305	V8	2V	Chev		
L	350	V8	4V	Chev		
4	350	V8	4V	Chev		
C	196	V6	2V	Buick	9	1979
M	200	V6	2V	Chev		
A	231	V6	2V	Buick		
2	231	V6	2V	Buick		
D	250	L6	1V	Chev		
J	267	V8	2V	Chev		
G	305	V8	2V	Chev		
H	305	V8	4V	Chev		
L	350	V8	4V	Chev		
4	350	V8	4V	Chev		
8	350	V8	4V	Chev		

	ENGINE CODE				MODEL YEAR CODE	
Code	Eng. Disp. cu in	Eng. Config.	Carb	Eng. Mfgr.	Code	Year
K	229	V6	2V	Chev	0	1980
A	231	V6	2V	Buick		
3	231	V6	4V	Buick		
S	265	V8	2V	Pont		
J	267	V8	2V	Chev		
W	301	V8	4V	Pont		
H	305	V8	4V	Chev		
N	350	V8	Diesel	Olds		
L	350	V8	4V	Chev		
6	350	V8	4V	Chev		
8	350	V8	4V	Chev		
K	229 3.8L	V6	2V	Chev	1	1981
A	231 3.8L	V6	2V	Buick		
3	231 3.8L	V6	4V	Buick		
J	267 4.4L	V8	2V	Chev		
T	301 4.9L	V8	4V	Pont		
H	305 5.0L	V8	4V	Chev		
L	350 5.7L	V8	4V	Chev		
6	350 5.7L	V8	4V	Chev		
N	350 5.7L	V8	Diesel	Olds		
K	229 3.8L	V6	2V	Chev	2	1982
A	231 3.8L	V6	2V	Buick		
3	231 3.8L	V6	4V	Buick		
J	267 4.4L	V8	2V	Chev		
T	301 4.9L	V8	4V	Pont		
H	305 5.0L	V8	4V	Chev		
N	350 5.7L	V8	Diesel	Olds		

① If a 17- or 19- digit VIN is used, the 7th digit is the engine code.

ENGINE FIRING ORDER

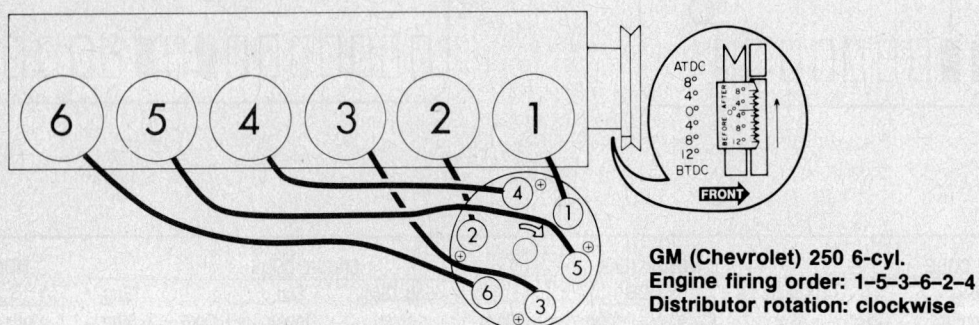

GM (Chevrolet) 250 6-cyl.
Engine firing order: 1–5–3–6–2–4
Distributor rotation: clockwise

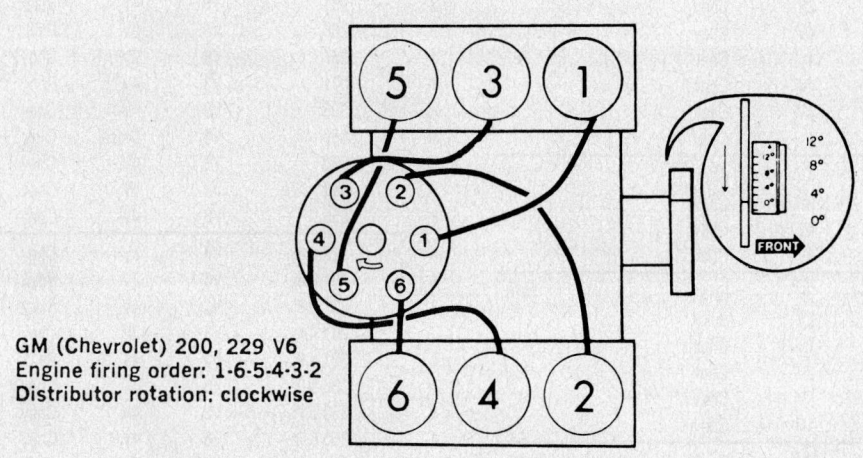

GM (Chevrolet) 200, 229 V6
Engine firing order: 1-6-5-4-3-2
Distributor rotation: clockwise

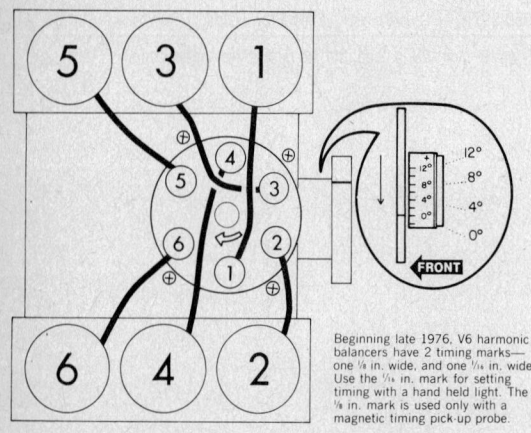

Beginning late 1976, V6 harmonic balancers have 2 timing marks—one ⅛ in. wide, and one ¹⁄₁₆ in. wide. Use the ¹⁄₁₆ in. mark for setting timing with a hand held light. The ⅛ in. mark is used only with a magnetic timing pick-up probe.

GM (Buick) 196, 231, 252 CID V6
Engine firing order: 1-6-5-4-3-2
Distributor rotation: clockwise

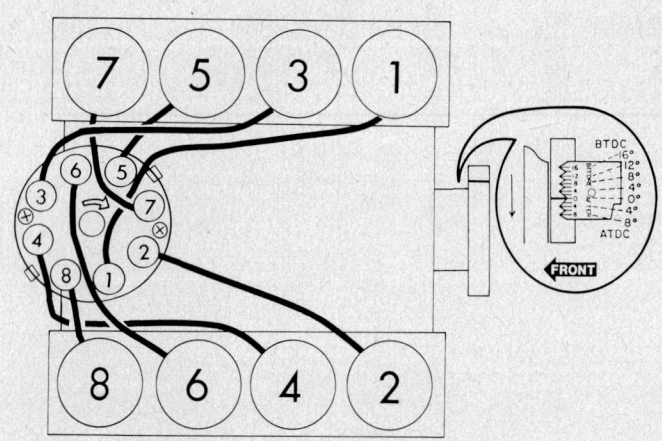

GM (Chevrolet) Corvette 350, 454 V8
Engine firing order: 1–8–4–3–6–5–7–2
Distributor rotation: clockwise

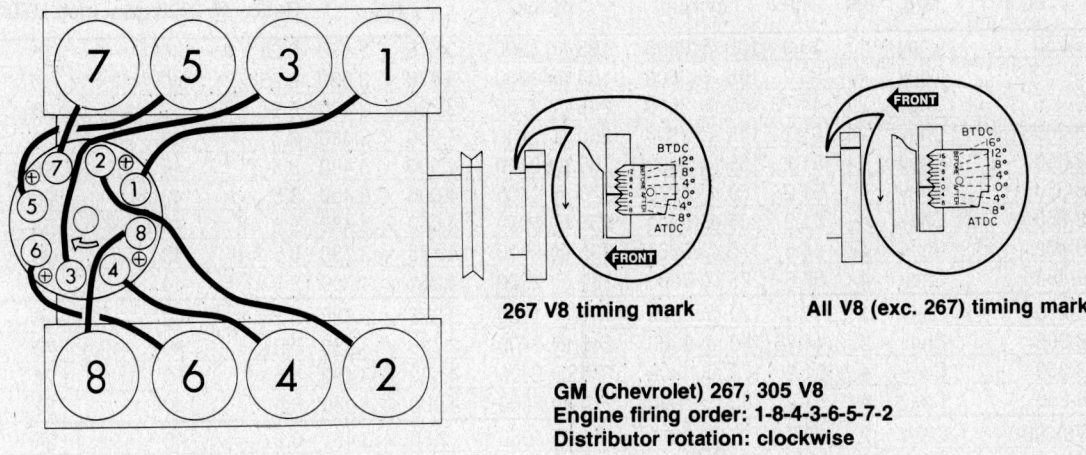

267 V8 timing mark   All V8 (exc. 267) timing mark

GM (Chevrolet) 267, 305 V8
Engine firing order: 1-8-4-3-6-5-7-2
Distributor rotation: clockwise

GM (Pontiac) 265, 301
Engine firing order: 1-8-4-3-6-5-7-2
Distributor rotation: counterclockwise

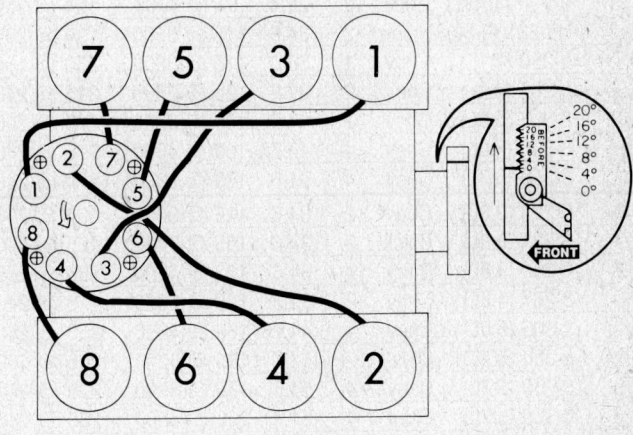

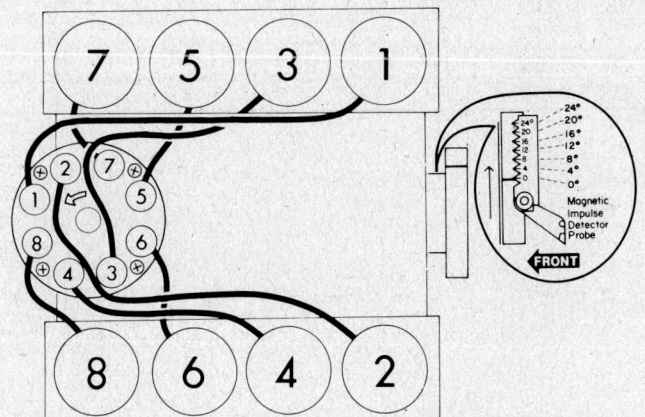

GM (Oldsmobile) 260, 307, 350 V8
Engine firing order: 1-8-4-3-6-5-7-2
Distributor rotation: counterclockwise

CHEVROLET
EXCEPT CAVALIER, CELEBRITY, CHEVETTE, CITATION, MONZA & VEGA

ENGINE SPECIFICATIONS
EXCEPT CORVETTE

Year	Eng. V.I.N. Code	Engine No. Cyl. Disp. cu in	Eng. Mfg.	Carb Bbl.	Tax H.P.	Horsepower @ rpm	Torque @ rpm (ft lbs)	Bore and Stroke (in)	Comp. Ratio	Oil Pressure @ 2000 rpm	Valves Intake Opens (deg BTDC)	Fuel Pump Pres.
76	D	6-250	Chev	1	36.0	105 @ 3800	185 @ 1200	3.875 × 3.530	8.25	40	16	3.5-4.5
	D	6-250①	Chev	1	36.0	105 @ 3800	185 @ 1200	3.875 × 3.530	8.25	40	16	3.5-4.5
	Q	8-305	Chev	2	44.76	140 @ 3800	245 @ 2000	3.736 × 3.480	8.5	40	28	7-8.5
	V	8-350	Chev	2	51.2	145 @ 3800	250 @ 2200	4.000 × 3.480	8.5	40	28	7-8.5
	L	8-350	Chev	4	51.2	165 @ 3800	260 @ 2400	4.000 × 3.480	8.5	40	28	7-8.5
	L	8-350	Chev	4	51.2	180 @ 4000	275 @ 2400	4.000 × 3.480	8.5	40	28	7-8.5
	X	8-350	Chev	4	51.2	205 @ 5200	255 @ 3600	4.000 × 3.480	9.0	40	52	7-8.5
	U	8-400	Chev	4	54.5	175 @ 3600	305 @ 2000	4.125 × 3.750	8.5	40	28	7-8.5
	S	8-454	Chev	4	57.8	225 @ 4000	360 @ 2800	4.251 × 4.000	8.5	40	55	7-8.5
77	D	6-250	Chev	1	36.0	110 @ 3800	195 @ 1600	3.875 × 3.530	8.25	40	16	3.5-4.5
	U	8-305	Chev	2	44.76	145 @ 3800	245 @ 2400	3.736 × 3.480	8.5	40	28	7-8.5
	L	8-350	Chev	4	51.2	170 @ 3800	270 @ 2400	4.000 × 3.480	8.5	40	28	7-8.5
	X	8-350	Chev	4	51.2	180 @ 4000	270 @ 2400	4.000 × 3.480	8.5	40	52	7-8.5
78	M	V6-200	Chev	2	29.4	95 @ 3800	160 @ 2000	3.50 × 3.48	8.2	40	34	4.5-6
	A	V6-231	Buick	2	34.6	105 @ 3400	185 @ 2000	3.8 × 3.40	8.0	40	17	4.5-5.5
	D	6-250	Chev	1	36.0	110 @ 3800①	190 @ 1600①	3.875 × 3.53	8.1	40	16	3.5-4.5
	U	8-305	Chev	2	44.76	145 @ 3800②	245 @ 2400②	3.736 × 3.48	8.4	40	28	7-8.5
	L	8-350	Chev	4	51.2	170 @ 3800③	270 @ 2400③	4.00 × 3.48	8.2	40	28	7-8.5
79	M	V6-200 (3.3L)	Chev	2	29.4	94 @ 4000	154 @ 2000	3.50 × 3.48	8.2	45	34	4.5-5.5
	A	V6-231 (3.8L)	Buick	2	34.6	115 @ 3800	190 @ 2000	3.8 × 3.40	8.0	34	17	4.5-5.5
	D	6-250 (4.1L)	Chev	1	36.0	115 @ 3800①	200 @ 1600①	3.875 × 3.53	8.0④	40	16	3.5-4.5
	J	8-267 (4.4L)	Chev	2	39.2	125 @ 3800	215 @ 2400	3.50 × 3.48	8.2	45	34	7.5-9
	G	8-305 (5.0L)	Chev	2	44.76	130 @ 3200②	245 @ 2000②	3.736 × 3.48	8.4	45	28	7.5-9
	H	8-305 (5.0L)	Chev	4	44.76	160 @ 4000	235 @ 2400	3.736 × 3.48	8.4	45	28	7.5-9
	L	8-350 (5.7L)	Chev	4	51.6	170 @ 3800③	270 @ 2400③	4.000 × 3.48	8.2	45	28	7.5-9
80	K	6-229 (3.8L)	Chev	2	34.6	115 @ 3800	190 @ 2000	3.74 × 3.48	8.5	45	34	4.5-5.5
	A	6-231 (3.8L)	Buick	2	34.6	105 @ 3400	185 @ 2000	3.800 × 3.400	8.0	37	17	3
	3	6-231 (3.8L)	Buick	4	34.6	165 @ 4000	265 @ 2800	3.800 × 3.400	8.0	37	17	5
	J	8-267 (4.4L)	Chev	2	39.2	125 @ 3800	215 @ 2400	3.500 × 3.480	8.5	45	34	7.5-9
	H	8-305 (5.0L)	Chev	4	44.76	160 @ 4000	235 @ 2400	3.736 × 3.480	8.5	45	28	7.5-9
	N	8-350 (5.7L)	Olds	③	52.7	105 @ 3200	205 @ 1600	4.057 × 3.385	22.5	37	16	5-6
	L	8-350 (5.7L)	Chev	4	51.6	170 @ 3800	270 @ 2400	4.000 × 3.480	8.5	45	28	7.5-9
	6	8-350 (5.7L)	Chev	4	51.6	190 @ 4000	280 @ 2400	4.000 × 3.480	8.2	45	28	7-8
	8	8-350 (5.7L)	Chev	4	51.6	230 @ 5000	275 @ 3500	4.000 × 3.480	9.0	45	—	7.5-8.5
81	K	6-229 (3.8L)	Chev	2	34.6	115 @ 3800	190 @ 2000	3.74 × 3.48	8.5	45	34	4.5-5.5
	A	6-231 (3.8L)	Buick	2	34.6	105 @ 3400	185 @ 2000	3.80 × 3.40	8.0	37	17	3
	3	6-231 (3.8L)	Buick	4	34.6	170 @ 4000	265 @ 2800	3.80 × 3.40	8.0	37	17	5
	J	8-267 (4.4L)	Chev	2	39.2	125 @ 3800	215 @ 2400	3.50 × 3.48	8.5	45	34	7.5-9
	H	8-305 (5.0L)	Chev	4	49.76	160 @ 4000	235 @ 2400	3.736 × 3.48	8.5	45	28	7.5-9
	L	8-350 (5.7L)	Chev	4	51.6	170 @ 3800	270 @ 2400	4.0 × 3.48	8.5	45	28	7.5-9
	6	8-350 (5.7L)	Chev	4	51.6	190 @ 4000	280 @ 1600	4.0 × 3.48	8.2	45	28	7.5-9
	N	8-350 (5.7L)	Olds	③	52.7	105 @ 3200	205 @ 1600	4.057 × 3.385	22.5	37	16	5-6

① Horsepower and torque figures for 1977 and later years are Chilton estimates
③ Fuel-injected diesel engine

TUNE-UP SPECIFICATIONS — EXCEPT CORVETTE

Year	V.I.N. Code	No. Cyl Disp. (cu in)	Spark Plugs Orig. Type	Spark Plugs Gap (in)	Distributor	Timing Man. Trans.	Timing Auto Trans.	Idle Man. Trans.	Idle Auto Fed.	Idle Auto Cal.	Idle Auto Hi. Alt.
76	D	6-250	R46TS	.035	E.I.	6	6	850	600	600	600
	D	6-250	R46TS	.035	E.I.	6	8	850	550	600	600
	Q	8-305	R45TS	.045	E.I.	6	8 (0)	800	600	600	600
	V	8-350	R45TS	.045	E.I.	—	6	—	600	—	—
	L	8-350	R45TS	.045	E.I.	8 (6)	8 (6)	800	600	600	600
	L	8-350	R45TS	.045	E.I.	8 (6)	8 (6)	800	600	600	600
	X	8-350	R45TS	.045	E.I.	12	12	1000	700	700	700
	U	8-400	R45TS	.045	E.I.	—	8	—	600	600	600
	S	8-454	R45TS	.045	E.I.	—	12	—	550	—	—
77	D	6-250	R46TS	.035	E.I.	6	8 (6)⑤	750⑥	575	575	600
	U	8-305	R45TS	.045	E.I.	8	8 (6)	600/700	500/650	500/650	—
	L	8-350	R45TS	.045	E.I.	8	8	700	500/650	500/650	600/650
	X	8-350	R45TS	.045	E.I.	12	12	800	700/800	—	—
78	M	V6-200	R45TS	.045	E.I.	8	8	700	600	600	600
	A	V6-231	R46TSX	.060	E.I.	15	15	800	600	600	600
	D	6-250	R46TS	.035	E.I.	6	10 (6)	800	550	600	—
	U	8-305	R45TS	.045	E.I.	4	4 (6)⑦	600	500	600	700
	L	8-350	R45TS	.045	E.I.	6	6 (8)	700	600	600	650
79	M	V6-200	R45TS	.045	E.I.	8	12	700/800	600/700	—	—
	A	V6-231	R45TSX	.060	E.I.	—	15	—	550/670	600	600
	D	6-250	R46TS	.035	E.I.	12	8 (6)	800	675	600	—
	J	8-267	R45TS	.045	E.I.	4	8	600/700	500/600	—	—
	G	8-305	R45TS	.045	E.I.	4	4	600/700	500/600	600/650	—
	H	8-305	R45TSX	.045	E.I.	4	4⑦	700	500/600	500/600	600/650
	L	8-350	R45TS	.045	E.I.	6	6 (8)⑦	700	500/600	500/600	600/650
80	K	6-229	R45TS	.045	E.I.	—	12D	—	600/700D	600/700D	600/700D
	A	6-231	R45TSX	.060	E.I.	—	15°	—	600D	600D	600D
	3	6-231	R45TS	.060	E.I.	—	15°	—	600D	600D	600D
	J	8-267	R45TS	.045	E.I.	—	4°		500/600D	500/600D	600D
	H	8-305	R45TS	.045	E.I.	6°	6°	700	500/600D	550/650D	—
	L	8-350	R45TS	.045	E.I.	6°	6°	700	500/600D	500/600D	500/600D
	6	8-350	R45TS	.045	E.I.	12°	12°	900	600/650D	—	600/650D
	N	8-350	DIESEL	—	—	—	—	—	600D	600D	
81	K	6-229	R45TS	.045	I.S.T.	6°	6°D	—	I.S.C.	I.S.C.	
	A	6-231	R45TSX	⑧	E.S.T.	—	15°	—	500D	500D	500D
	3	6-231	R45TS	.060⑧	E.S.T.	15°	15°	—	500D	500D	500D
	J	8-267	R45TS	.045	E.S.T.	—	6°	550	550D	550D	550D
	H	8-305	R45TS	.045	E.S.T.	6°	6°	700	500D	500D	500D
	L	8-350	R45TS	.045	E.S.T.	6°	6°	700	500/600D	600D	
	6	8-350	R45TS	.045	E.S.T.	—	6°	—	500D	500D	—
	N	8-350	DIESEL	—	INJECTOR	—	—	—	600D	600D	

CHEVROLET

EXCEPT CAVALIER, CELEBRITY, CHEVETTE, CITATION, MONZA & VEGA

ENGINE SPECIFICATIONS   EXCEPT CORVETTE

Year	Eng. V.I.N. Code	Engine No. Cyl. Disp. cu in	Eng. Mfg.	Carb Bbl.	Tax H.P.	Horsepower @ rpm	Torque @ rpm (ft lbs)	Bore and Stroke (in)	Comp. Ratio	Oil Pressure @ 2000 rpm	Valves Intake Opens (deg BTDC)	Fuel Pump Pres.
82	K	6-229 (3.8L)	Chev	2	34.6	115 @ 3800	190 @ 2000	3.74 × 3.48	8.5	45	34	4.5-5.5
	A	6-231 (3.8L)	Buick	2	34.6	105 @ 3400	185 @ 2000	3.80 × 3.40	8.0	37	17	3
	3	6-231 (3.8L)	Buick	4	34.6	170 @ 4000	265 @ 2800	3.80 × 3.40	8.0	37	17	5
	J	8-267 (4.4L)	Chev	2	39.2	125 @ 3800	215 @ 2400	3.50 × 3.48	8.5	45	34	7.5-9
	H	8-305 (5.0L)	Chev	4	49.76	160 @ 4000	235 @ 2400	3.736 × 3.48	8.5	45	28	7.5-9
	N	8-350 (5.7L)	Olds	③	52.7	105 @ 3200	205 @ 1600	4.057 × 3.385	22.5	37	16	5-6

① Horsepower and torque figures for 1977 and later years are Chilton estimates

③ Fuel-injected diesel engine

ENGINE SPECIFICATIONS   CORVETTE

Yr.	Eng. V.I.N. Code	Engine No. Cyl. Disp. (cu in)	Eng. Mfgr.	Carb Bbl	Tax H.P.	Horsepower① @ rpm	Torque @ rpm① (ft lbs)	Bore and Stroke (in)	Valves Intake Opens (deg. BTDC)	Fuel Pump Press. (psi)	Comp. Ratio	Oil Pressure @ 2000 rpm
76	L	8-350	Chev	4v	51.2	180 @ 4000	270 @ 2400	4.000 × 3.480	28	7.0-8.5	8.5	40
	T	8-350	Chev	4v	51.2	210 @ 5200	255 @ 3600	4.000 × 3.480	52	7.0-8.5	9.0	40
77	L	8-350	Chev	4v	51.2	180 @ 4000	270 @ 2400	4.000 × 3.480	28	7.0-8.5	8.5	32-40
	X	8-350	Chev	4v	51.2	210 @ 5200	255 @ 3600	4.000 × 3.480	52	7.0-8.5	9.0	32-40
78	L	8-350	Chev	4v	51.2	185 @ 4000	280 @ 2400	4.000 × 3.480	28	7.5-9.0	8.2	32-40
	4	8-350	Chev	4v	51.2	220 @ 5200	260 @ 3600	4.000 × 3.480	52	7.5-9.0	8.9	32-40
79	8	8-350	Chev	4v	51.2	185 @ 4000	280 @ 2400	4.000 × 3.480	28	7.5-9.0	8.5	32-40
	4	8-350	Chev	4v	51.2	220 @ 5200	260 @ 3600	4.000 × 3.480	52	7.5-9.0	9.0	32-40
80	6	8-350	Chev	4v	51.2	185 @ 4000	280 @ 2400	4.000 × 3.480	28	7-9	8.2	32-40
	8	8-350	Chev	4v	51.2	230 @ 5200	260 @ 3600	4.000 × 3.480	52	7-9	9.0	32-40
	H	8-305	Chev	4v	44.76	160 @ 4000	235 @ 2400	3.736 × 3.480	28	7-9	8.6	45
81-82	6	8-350	Chev	4v	51.2	185 @ 4000	280 @ 2400	4.0 × 3.480	28	7-9	8.2	34-40

① Horsepower and torque figures for 1977 and later years are Chilton estimates

TUNE-UP SPECIFICATIONS   EXCEPT CORVETTE

Year	V.I.N. Code	No. Cyl Disp. (cu in)	Spark Plugs Orig. Type	Gap (in)	Distributor	Timing① (deg BTDC @ rpm) Man. Trans.	Auto Trans.	Idle Speed② (rpm) Man. Trans.	Auto. Trans. Fed.	Cal.	Hi. Alt.
82	K	6-229	R45TS	.045	I.S.T.	—	6°	I.S.C.			
	A	6-231	R45TSX	.045	E.S.T.	—	15°	⑧			
	3	6-231	R45TS	.060	E.S.T.	—	15°	⑧			
	J	8-267	R45TS	.045	E.S.T.	⑧	⑧	⑧			
	T	8-301	R45TSX	.060	E.S.T.	—	⑧	⑧			
	H	8-305	R45TS	.045	E.S.T.	—	⑧	⑧			
	L	8-350	R45TS	.045	E.S.T.	⑧	⑧	⑧			
	N	8-350	DIESEL	—	INJECTOR	—	—	—	600D	600D	

NOTE: The underhood certification/specification decal is the authority for performance specifications affecting vehicle emissions. Use this manual's information only when that decal is not available.

—   Not applicable

E I   =Electronic Ignition

①   Time at curb idle speed unless otherwise indicated. Figures in parentheses are California applications

②   Set idle speed with automatic transmission in Drive; manual transmission in Neutral. Where two figures appear, the lower figure indicates idle speed with A/C solenoid deenergized

⑤   High altitude—10. Check underhood certification/specification decal as some California applications require a setting of 8

⑥   Air conditioned models—800

⑦   High altitude—8

⑧   See underhood certification/specification decal

     E.S.T.- Electric Spark Timing

     I.S.C.- Idle speed Control (not adjustable)

TUNE-UP SPECIFICATIONS   CORVETTE

Year	V.I.N. Code	No. Cyl Disp. (cu in)	Spark Plugs Orig. Type	Gap (in)	Distributor	Timing① (deg BTDC @ rpm) Man. Trans.	Auto Trans.	Idle Speed② (rpm) Man. Trans.	Auto. Trans. Fed.	Cal.	Hi. Alt.
76	L	8-350	R45TS	.045	E.I.	8	8	800	600	600	600
	T	8-350	R45TS	.045	E.I.	12	12	1000	700	700	700
77	L	8-350	R45TS	.045	E.I.	8	8	700	500	500	600
	X	8-350	R45TS	.045	E.I.	12	12	800	700	700	700
78	L	8-350	R45TS	.045	E.I.	6	6 (8)	700	500/600	500/600	500/650
	4	8-350	R45TS	.045	E.I.	12	12	900	700/800	—	—
79	8	8-350	R45TS	.045	E.I.	6	6④	700	500/600	500/600	600/650
	4	8-350	R45TS	.045	E.I.	12	12	900	700/800	—	—
80	H	8-305	R45TS	.045	E.I.	—	4	700N	500D	500/600D	500/600D
	6	8-350	R45TS	.045	E.I.	8	6	—	500D	500/600D	500/600D
	8	8-350	R45TS	.045	E.I.	12	12	700N	600D	600D	600D
81-82	6	8-350	R45TS	.045	E.S.T.	6	6	700N	600D	600D	600D

NOTE: The underhood certification/specification decal is the authority for performance specifications affecting vehicle emissions. Use this manual's information only when that decal is not available.

—   Not applicable

E I   =Electronic Ignition

①   Time at curb idle speed unless otherwise indicated. Figures in parentheses are California applications

②   Set idle speed with automatic transmission in Drive; manual transmission in Neutral. Where two figures appear, the lower figure indicates idle speed with A/C solenoid deenergized

④   High altitude application—8

⑤   See underhood certification/specification decal

     E.S.T.- Electronic Spark Timing

CHEVROLET
EXCEPT CAVALIER, CELEBRITY, CHEVETTE, CITATION, MONZA & VEGA

VALVE SPECIFICATIONS

EXCEPT CORVETTE

Year	Engine No. Cyl. Disp. (cu in)	Seat Angle (deg)	Face Angle (deg)	Valve Adjustment	Spring Test Pressure (lbs @ in)	Spring Installed Height (in)	Stem to Guide Clearance (in) Intake	Stem to Guide Clearance (in) Exhaust	Stem Diameter (in) Intake	Stem Diameter (in) Exhaust
76	6-250	46	45	⑤	170-180 @ 1.26	1²¹/₃₂	.0010-.0027	.0015-.0032	.3414	.3414
	8-262	46	45	⑤	194-206 @ 1.25	1²³/₃₂	.0010-.0027	.0010-.0027	.3414	.3414
	8-305	46	45	⑤	194-206 @ 1.25	1²³/₃₂	.0010-.0027	.0010-.0027	.3414	.3414
	8-350	46	45	⑤	194-206 @ 1.25	1²³/₃₂	.0010-.0027	.0010-.0027	.3414	.3414
	8-400	46	45	⑤	194-206 @ 1.25	1²³/₃₂	.0010-.0027	.0010-.0027	.3414	.3414
	8-454	46	45	⑤	288-312 @ 1.38	1⅞	.0010-.0027	.0010-.0027	.3719	.3719
77	6-250	46	45	⑤	170-180 @ 1.26	1²¹/₃₂	.0010-.0027	.0015-.0032	.3414	.3414
	8-305	46	45	⑤	194-206 @ 1.25①	1²³/₃₂②	.0010-.0027	.0010-.0027	.3414	.3414
	8-350	46	45	⑤	194-206 @ 1.25①	1²³/₃₂②	.0010-.0027	.0010-.0027	.3414	.3414
78	6-250	46	45	⑥	170-180 @ 1.26	1²¹/₃₂	.0010-.0027	.0015-.0032	.3414	.3414
	6-200	46	45	⑥	194-206 @ 1.25	1²³/₃₂	.0010-.0027	.0010-.0027	.3414	.3414
	6-231	45	45	⑥	162-174 @ 1.327	1²³/₃₂	.0015-.0032	.0015-.0032	.3407	.3407
	8-305	46	45	⑥	194-206 @ 1.25	1²³/₃₂	.0010-.0027	.0010-.0027	.3414	.3414
	8-350	46	45	⑥	194-206 @ 1.25	1²³/₃₂	.0010-.0027	.0010-.0027	.3414	.3414
79	6-250	46	45	⑥	170-180 @ 1.26	1²¹/₃₂	.0010-.0027	.0015-.0032	.3414	.3414
	6-200	46	45	⑥	194-206 @ 1.25	1²³/₃₂	.0010-.0027	.0010-.0027	.3414	.3414
	6-231	45	45	⑥	162-174 @ 1.327	1²³/₃₂	.0015-.0032	.0015-.0032	.3407	.3407
	8-305	46	45	⑥	194-206 @ 1.25	1²³/₃₂	.0010-.0027	.0010-.0027	.3414	.3414
	8-350	46	45	⑥	194-206 @ 1.25	1²³/₃₂	.0010-.0027	.0010-.0027	.3414	.3414
80	6-229 (3.8L)	46	45	⑥	194-206 @ 1.25	1²³/₃₂	.0010-.0027	.0010-.0027	.3414	.3414
	6-231 (3.8L)	45	45	⑥	162-174 @ 1.327	1.727	.0015-.0032	.0015-.0032	.3407	.3407
	8-267,305,350⑧	46	45	⑥	194-206 @ 1.25	1²³/₃₂	.0010-.0027	.0010-.0027	.3414	.3414
	8-350(VIN N) (5.7L)	③DIESEL	④	⑦	180-194 @ 1.270	1.670	.0010-.0027	.0015-.0032	.3429	.3424
81	6-229 (3.8L)	46	45	⑥	194-206 @ 1.25	1²³/₃₂	.0010-.0027	.0010-.0027	.3414	.3414
	6-231 (3.8L)	45	45	—	162-174 @ 1.327	1.727	.0015-.0032	.0015-.0032	.3407	.3407
	8-267,305⑧	46	45	⑥	194-206 @ 1.25	1²³/₃₂	.0010-.0027	.0010-.0027	.3414	.3414
	8-350(VIN N) (5.7L)	③DIESEL	④	⑦	180-194 @ 1.270	1.670	.0010-.0027	.0015-.0032	.3429	.3424
82	6-229 (3.8L)	46	45	⑥	194-206 @ 1.25	1²³/₃₂	.0010-.0027	.0010-.0027	.3414	.3414
	6-231 (3.8L)	45	45	—	162-174 @ 1.327	1.727	.0015-.0032	.0015-.0032	.3407	.3407
	8-267,305⑧	46	45	⑥	194-206 @ 1.25	1²³/₃₂	.0010-.0027	.0010-.0027	.3414	.3414
	8-350(VIN N) (5.7L)	③DIESEL	④	⑦	180-194 @ 1.270	1.670	.0010-.0027	.0015-.0032	.3429	.3424

① Intake shown; exhaust—194-206 @ 1.16
② Intake shown; exhaust—1 ¹⁹/₃₂
③ Intake—45; exhaust—31
④ Intake—44; exhaust—30
⑤ Turn rocker stud nut until all lash is eliminated. Then tighten the nut an additional ¾ turn.
⑥ Turn rocker stud nut until all lash is eliminated. Then tighten the nut an additional full turn.
⑦ Diesel engine, no valve adjustment possible.
⑧ 267 (4.4L) and 305 (5.0L) Chevrolet engines

A166

VALVE SPECIFICATIONS   CORVETTE

Year	Engine No. Cyl. Disp. (cu in)	Seat Angle (deg)	Face Angle (deg)	Spring Test Pressure (lbs @ in)	Spring Installed Height (in)	Stem to Guide Clearance (in)	Stem Diameter (in)
76	8-350	I-46	45	194-206 @ 1.25	1 23/32	.0010-.0027	.3414
		E-46	45	194-206 @ 1.25	1 23/32	.0012-.0029	.3414
77-80	8-350	I-46	45	194-206 @ 1.25 ③	1 23/32 INT	.0010-.0027	.3414
	8-305	E-46	45	194-206 @ 1.16 ③	1 19/32 EXH	.0010-.0027	.3414
81-82	8-350	I-46	45	194-206 @ 1.25 ③	1 23/32 INT	.0010-.0027	.3414
		E-46	45	194-206 @ 1.16 ③	1 19/32 EXH	.0010-.0027	.3414

I = Intake
E = Exhaust
① 250 horsepower engine exhaust valve spring pressure—194-206 @ 1.25
② 250 horsepower engine exhaust valve spring installed height—1 23/32
③ 305 spring test pressure—175 @ 1.25
  350 L48 spring test pressure—180 @ 1.25

DISC BRAKE SPECIFICATIONS   EXCEPT CORVETTE

Year	Caliper Type	Mounting Bolt Torque	Disc Pad Original Thickness	Mfg.'s Recommended Disc Pad Minimum Thickness	Rotor Runout	Rotor Allowable Minimum Machined Thickness	Rotor Thickness Variation Maximum
76	Sliding	35	—	1/32 ①	.005	.980	.0005
77	Sliding	35	—	.020 ①	.005	.980	.0005
78-80	Sliding	35	—	.020 ①	.004	.980	.0005
81	Sliding	35	—	.020 ①	.004	.980	.0005
82	Sliding	35	—	.020 ①	.004	.980	.0005

— Not applicable
① Above rivet head or thickness of remaining lining on bonded pads

DISC BRAKE SPECIFICATIONS   CORVETTE

Year	Caliper Type	Mounting Bolt Torque ft. lbs (N•m)	Housing Bolt Torque ft. lbs (N•m)	Mfr. Recommended Disc Pad Minimum Thickness	Rotor Runout	Rotor Allowable Minimum Machined Thickness	Rotor Thickness Variation Maximum
76-80	F Fixed	70(95)	130(175)	.020 ①	.005	1.230	.0005
	R Fixed	70(95)	60(80)	.020 ①	.005	1.230	.0005
81	F Fixed	70(95)	130(175)	.020 ①	.005	1.230	.0005
	R Fixed	70(95)	60(80)	.020 ①	1.005	1.230	.0005
82	F Fixed	70(95)	130(175)	.020 ①	.005	1.230	.0005
	R Fixed	70(95)	60(80)	.020 ①	1.005	1.230	.0005

① .020 over rivet thickness.
F = Front brakes
R = Rear brakes

FLUID CAPACITIES—Fuel & Lubricant   EXCEPT CORVETTE

Year	Model	Engine Crankcase[9]	TRANSMISSION (Pts to Refill After Draining) Manual 3-Speed	4-Speed	Automatic	Drive Axle (pts)	Gasoline Tank (gals)
76	Camaro	4	3	3	8	4.25	21
	Chevelle	4	3	—	8	4.25	22[4]
	Chevrolet	4	—	—	8[1]	4.25[2]	26[3]
	Monte Carlo	4	—		8	4.25	22
	Nova	4	3	3	8[5]	4.25	21
77	Camaro	4	3	3	8	4.25	21
	Chevelle	4	3	—	8	4.0	22[4]
	Impala, Caprice	4	—	—	8	4.0[6]	21[3]
	Monte Carlo	4	—	—	8	4.25	22
	Nova	4	3	3	8[5]	4.0[6]	21
78	Camaro	4	3	3	8[7]	4.25	21
	Impala, Caprice	4	—	—	8[7]	4.0[6]	21[3]
	Monte Carlo	4	3	3	4[7]	3.25	17.5
	Nova	4	3	3	8[7]	4.0[6]	21
79	Camaro	4	3	3	6[7]	4.25	21
	Impala, Caprice	4	—	—	6[7]	4.25[8]	21[3]
	Monte Carlo	4	3	3	6[7]	4.25[8]	17.5
	Nova	4	3	3	6[7]	4.25[8]	21
80	Camaro	4	3	3	6[7]	4.25[8]	21
	Impala, Caprice	4	—	—	6[7]	4.25[8]	[10]
	Monte Carlo	4	3	3	6[7]	4.25[8]	18.1
	Malibu	4	3	3	6[7]	4.25[8]	18.1
81	Camaro	4	3	3	6[7]	4.25[8]	21
	Impala, Caprice	4	—	—	6[7]	4.25[8]	[10]
	Monte Carlo	4	3	3	6[7]	4.25[8]	18.1
	Malibu	4	3	3	6[7]	4.25[8]	18.1
82	Camaro	4	3	3	6[7]	4.25[8]	21
	Impala, Caprice	4	—	—	6[7]	4.25[8]	[10]
	Monte Carlo	4	3	3	6[7]	4.25[8]	18.1
	Malibu	4	3	3	6[7]	4.25[8]	18.1

— Not Applicable

[1] With Z28 Camaro or 400 (LT-4) and 454 (L54) engine—9
[2] 8 ½ inch ring gear shown. 8 ⅞ inch ring gear—4.90
[3] Passenger car shown. Station wagon—22
[4] El Camino—26
[5] With 250 or 305 CID engine—7
[6] 8 ½ inch ring gear shown. 7 ½ inch ring gear—3.25
[7] THM 200—3
[8] 8 ½ inch and 8 ¾ inch gears shown. 7 ½ inch ring gear—3.50
[9] Most engines will require some additional oil when the filter is changed. Fill to correct level on dipstick
[10] Sdn. and coupes—25 gals; wagon—22 gals

FLUID CAPACITIES—Coolant, Fuel & Lubricant   CORVETTE

Year	Engine No. Cyl. Disp. (Cu In)	Engine Crankcase (Add 1 Qt For New Filter)	TRANSMISSION (Pts To Refill After Draining) Manual 3-Speed	4-Speed	Automatic ①	Drive Axle (pts)	Gasoline Tank (gals)	COOLING SYSTEM (qts) With Heater	With A/C	Rad. Cap Press.	Therm. Temp.
'76	8-350	4	—	3	②	4	17	20.7	21	15	195
'77	8-350	4	—	3	②	3.75	17	20.7	21	15	195
'78	8-350	4	—	3	8	3.75	24	21.6	21.6	15	195
'79	8-350	4	—	3	6	4	24	21	21	15	195
'80	8-305,8-350	4	—	3	6	4	24	21	21	15	195
'81-'82	8-350	4	—	3	6	4	24	21	21	15	195

— Not applicable.

① Specifications represent amount needed to refill after draining only the pan

② Standard engine — 8. 210 horsepower engine — 9

TORQUE SPECIFICATIONS   EXCEPT CORVETTE

All readings in ft/lbs

Year	Engine No. Cyl. Disp. (cu in)	Cylinder Head Bolts	Rod Bearing Bolts	Main Bearing Bolts	Crankshaft Pulley or Damper Bolt	Flywheel to Crankshaft Bolts	MANIFOLD Intake	Exhaust
76	6-250	90-100④	35	65	60	60	35	30①
	8-262,305,350,400	65	45	70③	60	60	30	20②
	8-454	80	50	110	85	65	30	20
77	6-250	90-100④	35	65	60	60	35	30①
	8-305,350	65	45	70③	60	60	30	20②
78	6-250	95④	35	65	60	60	—	30①
	6-200	65	45	70	60	60	30	20②
	6-231	80	40	100	175	60	45	25
	8-305,350	65	45	70	60	60	30	20②
79	6-250	95④	35	65	60	60	—	30①
	6-200	65	45	70	60	60	30	20②
	6-231	80	40	100	175	60	45	25
	8-267,305,350	65	45	70	60	60	30	20②
80	6-229	65	45	70	60	60	30	20②
	6-231	80	40	100	175	60	45	25
	8-267,305,350	65	45	70	60	60	30	20②
	8-350(Vin N)	130⑥	42	80⑦	255	60	40⑥	25
81-82	6-229	65	45	70	60	60	30	20②
	6-231	80	40	100	175	60	45	25
	8-267,305,350	65	45	70	60	60	30	20②
	8-350(Vin N)	130⑥	42	80⑦	255	60	40⑥	25

— Not applicable

① Exhaust-to-intake

② Center bolts—30

③ Outer bolts with four bolt main—65

④ Left front head bolt—85

⑤ Rear main—100

⑥ Clean and dip bolts in engine oil before tightening

⑦ Rear main—120

CHEVROLET

EXCEPT CAVALIER, CELEBRITY, CHEVETTE, CITATION, MONZA & VEGA

TORQUE SPECIFICATIONS   CORVETTE

All readings in ft/lbs

Year	Engine No. Cyl. Disp. (cu in)	Cylinder Head Bolts	Rod Bearing Bolts	Main Bearing Bolts	Crankshaft Bolt	Flywheel to Crankshaft Bolts	MANIFOLD	
							Intake	Exhaust
76-77	350	65	45	70 ①	60	60	30	③
78-80	350	65	45	80 ②	60	60	30	③
81-82	350	65	45	80 ②	60	60	30	③

① W/4 bolt main, outer 65 ft. lbs., inner 70 ft. lbs.
② W/4 bolt main, outer 70 ft. lbs., inner 80 ft. lbs.
③ Center bolts 30 ft. lbs., outer bolts 20 ft. lbs.

DISTRIBUTOR SPECIFICATIONS   EXCEPT CORVETTE

Year	Distributor Identification	CENTRIFUGAL ADVANCE		VACUUM ADVANCE	
		Start Crank. Deg. @ Eng. RPM	Finish Crank. Deg. @ Eng. RPM	Start @ In. Hg.	Finish Crank. Deg. @ In. Hg.
76	1110652	0 @ 1100	24 @ 4100	5	24 @ 15
	1110650	0 @ 1100	16 @ 4200	4	18 @ 12
	1110662	0 @ 1100	24 @ 4100	4	18 @ 12
	1103203	0 @ 1000	15 @ 2800	4	18 @ 7
	1112882	0 @ 1000	15 @ 2800	8	15 @ 15.5
	1112886	0 @ 1800	12 @ 4200	4	18 @ 7
	1110666	0 @ 1000	20 @ 4200	4	24 @ 15
	1112863	0 @ 1100	16 @ 4200	4	18 @ 12
	1112977	0 @ 1000	20 @ 3800	4	18 @ 12
	1112999	0 @ 1080	20 @ 3800	4	10 @ 8
	1112880	0 @ 1200	22 @ 4200	4	18 @ 12
	1112905	0 @ 1200	22 @ 4200	4	12 @ 15
	1112888	0 @ 1100	22 @ 4600	4	18 @ 12
	1112880	0 @ 1200	22 @ 4200	4	18 @ 12
	1112880	0 @ 1200	22 @ 4200	4	18 @ 12
	1112880	0 @ 1100	20 @ 4200	4	24 @ 15
	1112905	0 @ 1200	22 @ 4200	6	15 @ 12
	1112883	0 @ 1100	22 @ 4600	4	15 @ 10
	1112886	0 @ 1300	12 @ 4800	4	18 @ 7
77	1110678	0 @ 1000	20 @ 4100	4	24 @ 15
	1110681	0 @ 1000	20 @ 4200	4	15 @ 12
	1110725	0 @ 1000	20 @ 4200	5	24 @ 12
	1103239	0 @ 1000	20 @ 4200	4	15 @ 10
	1103244	0 @ 1000	20 @ 3800	4	20 @ 10
	1103246	0 @ 1200	22 @ 4200	4	18 @ 12
	1103248	0 @ 1200	22 @ 4200	4	10 @ 8
	1103256	0 @ 1200	16 @ 2000	4	10 @ 8

DISTRIBUTOR SPECIFICATIONS   EXCEPT CORVETTE

Year	Distributor Identification	CENTRIFUGAL ADVANCE		VACUUM ADVANCE	
		Start Crank. Deg. @ Eng. RPM	Finish Crank. Deg. @ Eng. RPM	Start @ In. Hg.	Finish Crank. Deg. @ In. Hg.
78	1103281	0 @ 1000	20 @ 3800	4	18 @ 12
	1103282	0 @ 1000	20 @ 3800	4	20 @ 10
	1103285	0 @ 1200	22 @ 4200	4	10 @ 8
	1103286	0 @ 1100	22 @ 4600	4	18 @ 12
	1103337	0 @ 1100	16 @ 2400	4	24 @ 10
	1103353	0 @ 1100	16 @ 2400	4	20 @ 10
	1110695	0-6 @ 1000	12-18 @ 3600	7-9	24 @ 10-13
	1110696	0 @ 1000	20 @ 3800	3	16 @ 6.5
	1110715	0 @ 1000	20 @ 4200	4	24 @ 15
	1110716	0 @ 1000	20 @ 4200	4	15 @ 12
	1110718	0 @ 1000	20 @ 4200	4	18 @ 12
	1110731	0-4 @ 1000	12-18 @ 3600	4-6	16 @ 7-9
79	1103281	0 @ 1000	20 @ 3800	4	18 @ 12
	1103282	0 @ 1000	20 @ 3800	4	20 @ 10
	1103285	0 @ 1200	22 @ 4200	4	10 @ 8
	1103337	0 @ 1100	22 @ 4600	4	24 @ 11
	1103353	0 @ 1100	22 @ 4600	4	20 @ 10
	1103368	0 @ 1000	20 @ 3800	4	10 @ 8
	1103370	0 @ 1300	16 @ 4200	3	24 @ 10
	1103371	0 @ 1000	22 @ 4400	3	24 @ 10
	1103379	0 @ 1000	20 @ 3800	3	20 @ 8.5
	1110695	0 @ 1680	15 @ 3600	3.9	24 @ 10.9
	1110696	0 @ 1000	20 @ 3800	2	16 @ 7.5
	1110716	0 @ 1000	20 @ 4200	4	15 @ 12
	1110731	0 @ 1680	15 @ 3600	4.9	16 @ 8.3
	1110737	0 @ 1000	20 @ 3800	3	30 @ 9.5
	1110748	0 @ 1000	20 @ 4200	4	20 @ 11
	1110756	0 @ 1400	14 @ 3800	2	24 @ 10
	1110766	0-4 @ 2000	14 @ 3600	4	24 @ 12
	1110767	0-4 @ 2000	14-18 @ 3600	3	20 @ 12
80	1110696	0 @ 1000	10 @ 1700	0 @ 2	16 @ 7.5
	1110756	0 @ 1400	14 @ 3800	0 @ 2	24 @ 10
	1110766	0-4 @ 2000	13-17 @ 3600	0-2 @ 4	24 @ 12
	1110767	0-4 @ 2000	13-17 @ 3600	0-2 @ 3	20 @ 12
	1110716	0 @ 1000	20 @ 4200	0 @ 4	15 @ 12
	1103371	0 @ 1000	22 @ 4400	0 @ 3	24 @10
	1103370	0 @ 1300	16 @ 4200	0 @ 3	24 @ 10
	1103282	0 @ 1000	20 @ 3800	0 @ 4	20 @ 11
	1103379	0 @ 1000	20 @ 3800	0 @ 3	20 @ 8.5
	1103368	0 @ 1000	20 @ 3800	0 @ 4	10 @ 8
	1103353	0 @ 1100	22 @ 4600	0 @ 4	20 @ 10
	103337	0 @ 1100	22 @ 4600	0 @ 4	24 @ 11

NOTE: 1981-82 ELECTRONIC CONTROLLED DISTRIBUTORS

CHEVROLET
EXCEPT CAVALIER, CELEBRITY, CHEVETTE, CITATION, MONZA & VEGA

DISTRIBUTOR SPECIFICATIONS

CORVETTE

Year	Distributor Identification	CENTRIFUGAL ADVANCE		VACUUM ADVANCE	
		Start Crank. Deg. @ Eng. RPM	Finish Crank. Deg. @ Eng. RPM	Start @ In. Hg.	Finish Crank. Deg. @ In. Hg.
76	1103200	0 @ 1200	16 @ 4000	4	10 @ 8
	1112905	0 @ 1200	22 @ 4200	6	15 @ 12
77	1103246	0 @ 1200	22 @ 4200	4	18 @ 12
	1103248	0 @ 1200	22 @ 4200	4	10 @ 8
	1103256	0 @ 1200	16 @ 4000	4	10 @ 8
78	1103285	0 @ 1200	22 @ 4800	4	10 @ 8
	1103291	0 @ 1200	16 @ 4000	4	10 @ 8
	1103337	0 @ 1100	16 @ 4800	4	24 @ 10
	1103353	0 @ 1100	16 @ 4800	4	20 @ 10
79	1103285	0 @ 1200	22 @ 4200	4	10 @ 8
	1103291	0 @ 1200	16 @ 2000	4	10 @ 8
	1103353	0 @ 1100	22 @ 4600	4	20 @ 10
80	1103287	0 @ 1200	22 @ 4200	0 @ 6	15 @ 12
	1103291	0 @ 1200	16 @ 2000	0 @ 3.5	10 @ 27
	1103353	0 @ 1100	22 @ 4600	0 @ 4	20 @ 10
	1103386	0 @ 1000	20 @ 3800	0 @ 4	16 @ 7.5

NOTE: 1981-82 ELECTRONIC CONTROLLED DISTRIBUTORS.

CRANKSHAFT & CONNECTING ROD SPECIFICATIONS

EXCEPT CORVETTE

Year	Engine No. Cyl. Disp. (cu in)	Main Brg. Journal Pos.	Main Brg. Journal Dia.	Crankshaft Main Brg. Oil Clearance	Shaft End-Play	Thrust on No.	CONNECTING ROD		
							Journal Diameter	Oil Clearance	Side Clearance
76	6-250		2.2983-2.2993	.0003-.0029	.002-.006	7	1.9928-2.000	.0007-.0027	.007-.016
	8-262,305	1	2.4484-2.4493	.0019-.0031	.002-.006	5			
		2-4	2.4481-2.4490	.0013-.0025					
		5	2.4479-2.4488	.0023-.0033					
	8-350 w/A.T.	1	2.4484-2.4493	.0019-.0031	.002-.006	5	2.099-2.100	.0013-.0035	.008-.014
		2-4	2.4481-2.4490	.0013-.0025					
		5	2.4479-2.4488	.0023-.0033					
	8-350 w/M.T.	1	2.4484-2.4493	.0013-.0025	.002-.006	5	2.009-2.100	.0013-.0035	.008-.014
		2-4	2.4481-2.4490	.0013-.0025					
		5	2.4479-2.4488	.0023-.0033					
	8-400	1	2.6484-2.6493	.0008-.0020	.002-.006	5	2.099-2.100	.0013-.0035	.008-.014
		2-4	2.6484-2.6493	.0011-.0023					
		5	2.6479-2.6488	.0017-.0033					
	8-454	1	2.7485-2.7494	.0013-.0025	.006-.010	5	2.199-2.200	.0009-.0025	.015-.021
		2-4	2.7481-2.7490	.0013-.0025					
		5	2.7478-2.7488	.0024-.0040					
77	6-250		2.2983-2.2993	.0003-.0029	.002-.006	7	1.9928-2.000	.0007-.0027	.007-.016
	8-305, 350	1	2.4484-2.4493	.0008-.0020	.002-.006	5	2.099-2.100	.0013-.0035	.008-.014
		2-4	2.4481-2.4490	.0011-.0023					
		5	2.4479-2.4488	.0017-.0032					

CRANKSHAFT & CONNECTING ROD SPECIFICATIONS · EXCEPT CORVETTE

Year	Engine No. Cyl. Disp. (cu in)	Main Brg. Journal Pos.	Main Brg. Journal Dia.	Crankshaft Main Brg. Oil Clearance	Shaft End-Play	Thrust on No.	CONNECTING ROD Journal Diameter	Oil Clearance	Side Clearance
78-79	6-250	1-6	2.2979-2.994	.0010-.0024	.002-.006	7	1.998-2.000	.0010-.0026	.006-.017
		7	2.2979-2.994	.0016-.0035					
	V6-200	1	2.4484-2.4493	.0008-.0020	.002-.006	4	2.0986-2.0998	.0013-.0035	.008-.014
		2-3	2.4481-2.4490	.0011-.0023					
		4	2.4479-2.4488	.0017-.0032					
	V6-231	1-4	2.4995	.0004-.0015	.004-.008	2	2.2487-2.2495	.0005-.0026	.006-.027
	8-305,350	1	2.4484-2.4493	.0008-.0020	.002-.006	5	2.0986-2.0998	.0013-.0035	.008-.014
		2-4	2.4481-2.4490	.0011-.0023					
		5	2.4479-2.4488	.0017-.0032					
80	6-229 (4.4L)	1	2.4484-2.4493	.0008-.0020	.002-.007	4	2.0986-2.0998	.0013-.0035	.008-.014
		2-3	2.4481-2.4490	.0011-.0023					
		4	2.4479-2.4488	.0017-.0032					
	6-231	1-4	2.4995	.0003-.0018	.003-.009	2	2.2487-2.2495	.0005-.0026	.006-.023
	8-267, 305, 350	1	2.4484-2.4493	.002 (max.)	.002-.007	5	2.099-2.100	.0035 (max.)	.006-.014
		2-4	2.4481-2.4490	.0023 (max.)					
		5	2.4479-2.4488	.0032 (max.)					
	8-350 (VIN N)	1-4	2.9993-3.0003	.0005-.0021	.0035-.0135	3	2.1238-2.1248	.0005-.0026	.006-.020
		5	2.9993-3.0003	.0015-.0031					
81-82	6-229	1	2.4484-2.4493	.008-.0020	.002-.007	4	2.0986-2.0998	.0013-.0035	.008-.014
		2-3	2.4481-2.4490	.0011-.0023					
		4	2.4479-2.4488	.0017-.0032					
	6-231	1-4	2.4995	.003-.0018	.003-.009	2	2.2487-2.2495	.0005-.0026	.006-.023
	8-267,305,350	1	2.4484-2.4493	.002 (max.)	.002-.007	5	2.009-2.100	.0035 (max.)	.006-.014
		2-4	2.4481-2.4490	.0023 (max.)					
		5	2.4479-2.4488	.0032 (max.)					
	8-350 (VIN N) DIESEL	1-4	2.9993-3.0003	.0005-.0021	.0035-.0135	3	2.1238-2.1248	.0005-.0026	.006-.020
		5	2.9993-3.0003	.0015-.0031					

COOLANT CAPACITIES

Year	Engine	Model	COOLING SYSTEM (qts) With Heater	With A/C	Radiator Cap Pressure	Therm. Temp.
76	L6-250	Camaro, Chevelle Nova	14.6	15.0	15	195
		Camaro	14.6	14.7	15	195
	V8-305	Camaro, Monte Carlo	17.2	18.0	15	195
		Chevelle, Nova	17.2	17.8	15	195
	V8-350,400	Camaro, Nova, Monte Carlo	17.3	18.0	15	195
		Chevrolet	18	18	15	195
		Chevelle	17.2	17.8	15	195
	V8-454	Chevrolet	23	23	15	195
	8-350	Corvette	21	21	15	195
77	L6-250	Chevrolet, Chevelle	14.24	14.4	15	195
		Camaro	14.6	14.7	15	195
		Nova	14.2	15.0	15	195
	V8-305	Nova, Camaro	17.2	17.9	15	195
	V8-350	Nova, Camaro	17.3	18.0	15	195
	V-8 305,350	Chevrolet, Chevelle	16.60	18.0	15	195
	8-350	Corvette	21	21	15	195

CHEVROLET
EXCEPT CAVALIER, CELEBRITY, CHEVETTE, CITATION, MONZA & VEGA

COOLANT CAPACITIES

Year	Engine	Model	COOLING SYSTEM (qts)		Radiator Cap Pressure	Therm. Temp.
			With Heater	With A/C		
78	L6-250	Nova	13.6	13.6	15	195
		Camaro	14.6	14.6	15	195
		Caprice, Impala	14.2	14.2	15	195
	V6-200	Malibu	15	16	15	195
		Monte Carlo	15	16	15	195
	V6-231	Malibu	14.79	14.79	15	195
		Monte Carlo	15.6	15.6	15	195
	V8-305,350	Caprice, Impala	16.6	16.6	15	195
		Nova	16.1	16.1	15	195
		Monte Carlo	19.2	19.2	15	195
		Camaro	17.3	17.3	15	195
		Malibu	18.13	18.13	15	195
	8-350	Corvette	21	21	15	195
79	L6-250	Nova	14	15	15	195
		Camaro	15	16	15	195
		Caprice, Impala	14	15	15	195
	V6-200	Malibu	15	16	15	195
		Monte Carlo	15	16	15	195
	V6-231	Malibu	15	16	15	195
		Monte Carlo	15	16	15	195
	V8-267,305,350	Caprice, Impala	16.5	18.5	15	195
		Nova	16	18	15	195
		Monte Carlo	18	20	15	195
		Camaro	17.5	18.5	15	195
		Malibu	18	20	15	195
	8-350	Corvette	21	21	15	195
80	V6-229	Camaro	17.5	18.5	15	195
		Malibu	15	16	15	195
		Monte Carlo	15	16	15	195
		Caprice	16.5	18.5	15	195
		Impala	16.5	18.5	15	195
	V6-231	Camaro	15	16	15	195
		Malibu	15	16	15	195
		Monte Carlo	15	16	15	195
		Caprice	17	18	15	195
		Impala	17	18	15	195
	V8-267,305,350	Camaro	17.5	18.5	15	195
		Malibu	18	20	15	195
		Monte Carlo	18	20	15	195
		Caprice	16.5	18.5	15	195
		Impala	16.5	18.5	15	195
	V8-350 Diesel	Caprice	18	18	15	195
		Impala	18	18	15	195
	8-350	Corvette	17½	18½	15	195
81-82	V6-229	Camaro	17.5	18.5	15	195
		Impala, Caprice	16.5	18.5	15	195
		Malibu	15	16	15	195
		Monte Carlo	15	16	15	195
	V6-231	Camaro	15	16	15	195
		Impala, Caprice	17	18	15	195
		Malibu	15	16	15	195
		Monte Carlo	15	16	15	195
	V8-267,305,350	Impala	16.5	18.5	15	195
		Malibu	18	20	15	195
		Monte Carlo	18	20	15	195
	V8-301	Camaro	21	21	15	195
	V8-350 (Diesel)	Impala, Caprice	18	18	15	195
	8-350	Corvette	21	21	15	195

CRANKSHAFT & CONNECTING ROD SPECIFICATIONS

All measurements given in inches

Year	Engine No. Cyl. Disp. (cu in)	Bearing Number	CRANKSHAFT Main Brg. Journal Dia	Main Brg. Oil Clearance	Shaft End-Play	Thrust on No.	CONNECTING ROD Journal Diameter	Oil Clearance	Side Clearance
76	8-350/A.T.	1	2.4484-2.4493	.0019-.0031	.002-.006	5	2.099-2.100	.0013-.0035	.008-.014
		2-4	2.4481-2.4490	.0013-.0025					
		5	2.4479-2.4480	.0023-.0033					
	8-350/M.T.	1	2.4484-2.4493	.0013-.0025	.002-.006	5	2.099-2.100	.0013-.0035	.008-.014
		2-4	2.4481-2.4490	.0013-.0025					
		5	2.4479-2.4480	.0023-.0033					
77-80	8-350	1	2.4484-2.4493	.0008-.0020	.002-.007	5	2.099-2.100	.0013-.0035	.008-.014
		2-4	2.4481-2.4490	.0011-.0023					
		5	2.4479-2.4488	.0017-.0032					
81-82	8-350	1	2.4484-2.4493	.0008-.0020	.002-.007	5	2.099-2.100	.0013-.0035	.008-.014
		2-4	2.4481-2.4490	.0011-.0023					
		5	2.4479-2.4488	.0017.0032					

BRAKE SPECIFICATIONS

Model	Year	MASTER CYLINDER BORE DIAMETER Manual	Power	CALIPER OR WHEEL CYLINDER Front	Rear	BRAKE DRUM/ROTOR DIAMETER Front	Rear
Camaro	76-77	1.0	1.125	2.9375	7/8	—	9.5
	78	1.0	1.125	2.9375	15/16	—	9.5
	79-80	1.0	1.125	2.9375	15/16	—	9.5
	81-82	1.0	1.125	2.9375	15/16	—	9.5
Chevelle	76-77	.9375	1.125	2.9375	15/16 ①	—	11.0
	78	.87	.94	2.500	3/4	—	9.5
	79-80	.87 ②	.94 ③	2.500	3/4	—	9.5
	81-82	.87 ②	.94 ③	2.500	3/4	—	9.5
Chevrolet, Caprice Impala exc. Station Wagon	76	1.125	1.125	2.9375	15/16	—	11.0
	77		1.125	2.9375	7/8	—	9.5
	78		1.125	2.9375	7/8	—	9.5
	79-80		1.125	2.9375	7/8	—	9.5
	81-82		1.125	2.9375	7/8	—	9.5
Chevrolet, Caprice Impala Station Wagon	76	1.125	1.125	2.9375	1.0	—	12.0
	77		1.125	2.9375	15/16	—	11.0
	78		1.125	2.9375	15/16	—	11.0
	79-80		1.125	2.9375	15/16	—	11.0
	81-82		1.125	2.9375	15/16	—	11.0
Monte Carlo	76-77		1.125	2.9375	15/16	—	11
	78	.87	.94	2.500	3/4	—	9.5
	79-80	.87 ②	.94 ③	2.500	3/4	—	9.5
	81-82	.87 ②	.94 ③	2.500	3/4	—	9.5
Nova	76-77	1.00	1.125	2.9375	15/16	—	9.5
	78	1.00	1.125	2.9375	15/16	—	9.5
	79-80	1.00	1.125	2.9375	15/16	—	9.5
Corvette	76-77	1.00	1.125	1.875	1.375	11.75	11.75
	78-80	1.125	1.125	1.875	1.375	11.75	11.75
	81-82	1.125	1.125	1.875	1.375	11.75	11.75

— Not applicable
① Manual brakes use 1 inch rear wheel cylinder
② V6 engine without air conditioning; manual or power brakes
③ V8 and V6 engines with air conditioning

Corvette fuse panel

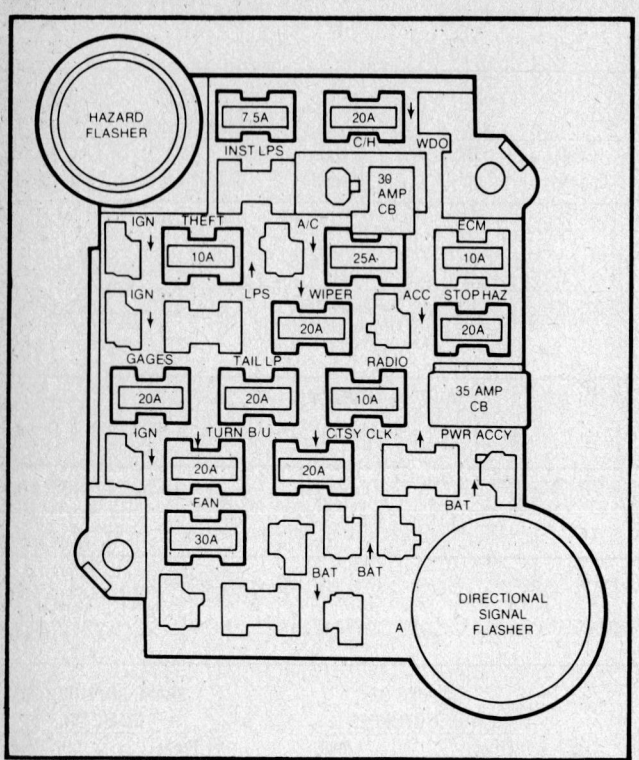

Chevrolet fuse panel

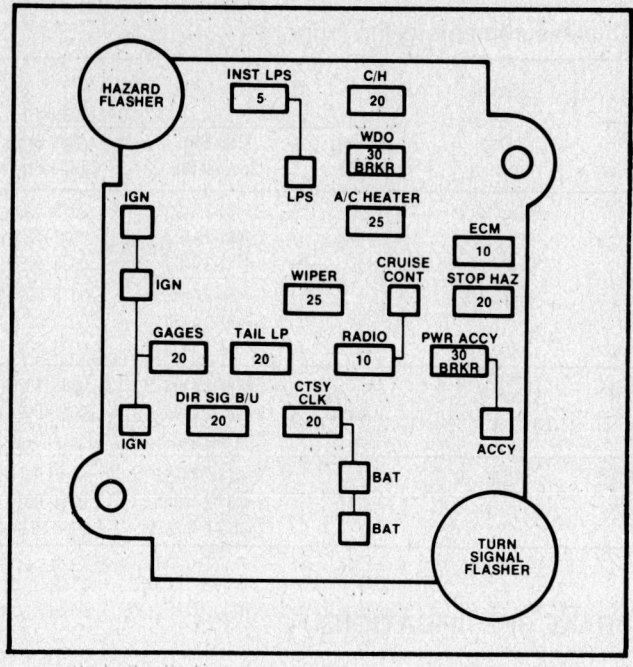

Corvette Fuse Panel

For easy identification, the amperage rating is clearly marked in large bold color coded letters on the end of each fuse. Test terminals are provided on the right and left side for use with a test light or volt-ohm-meter for checking the fuse while it is still installed in the fuse block.

The headlight circuits are protected by a circuit breaker in the light switch. An electrical overload on the breaker will cause the lamps to go on and off, or in some cases to remain off.

In addition to a fuse, the windshield wiper motor is also protected by a circuit breaker. If the motor overheats due to overloading caused by heavy snow, etc., the wipers will remain stopped until the motor cools. Be sure to correct the cause of overloading. Circuit breakers in the fuse panel protect the power window circuit and the rear defogger circuit.

FUSE AND CIRCUIT BREAKER DATA

Circuit	Ampere Rating
Headlamp circuit	Circuit breaker
Power window circuit	35 amp C.B.
Backup light and turn signals	AGC 20 amp FUSE
Heater/air conditioning	3AG 25 amp FUSE
Radio	AGC 10 amp FUSE
Rear defogger circuit	35 amp C.B.
Instrument lights	AGC 7.5 amp FUSE
Tail lights (side marker and parking lights), underhood lights	SFE 20 amp FUSE
Clock, lighter, courtesy, anti-theft alarm, glove box, dome, power antenna, horn relay, power door locks	SFE 20 amp FUSE
Stop hazard warning, key warning buzzer	SFE 20 amp FUSE
Gages/telltale lights, seat belt buzzer light, and relays (power window relay), cruise control	AGC 10 amp FUSE
Wipers/Washers	AGC 25 amp FUSE
Auxiliary Cooling Fan	AGC 30 amp FUSE
ECM	AGC 10 amp FUSE

Chevrolet accessory junction board

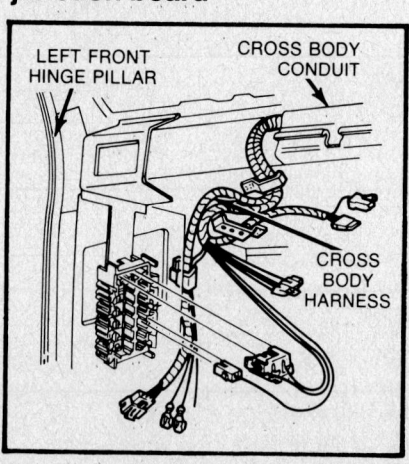

LEFT FRONT HINGE PILLAR

CROSS BODY CONDUIT

CROSS BODY HARNESS

Fuse test points

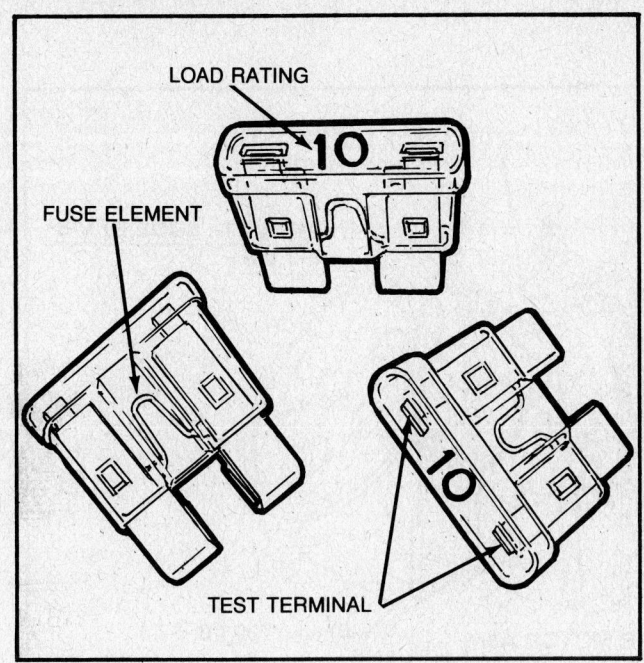

Fusible link

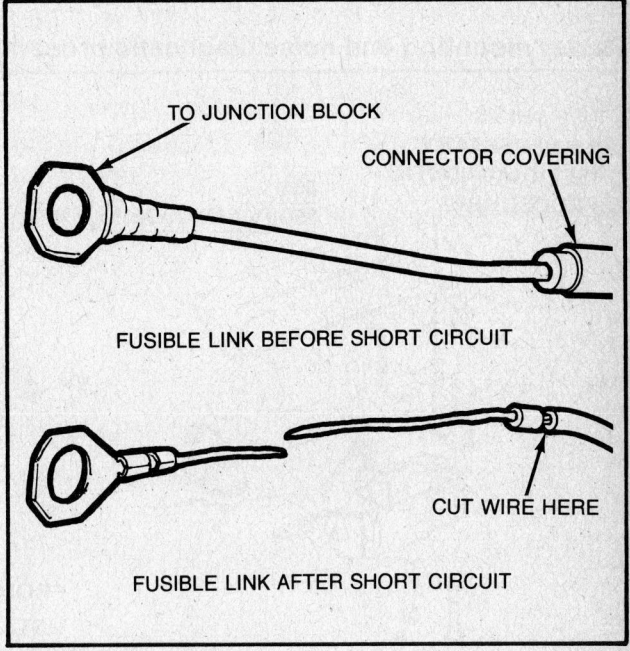

Located near starter

FUSE SIZE AND USAGE

Fuse Name	Amp Rating	Circuits Protected
INST LPS	5	Instrument panel illumination, light reminder buzzer
A/C HEATER	25	Four seasons air conditioner, heater
WIPER	25	Windshield wiper/washer, delayed pulse wiper/washer
STOP HAZ	20	Hazard/stop lights
PWR ACCY CIRCUIT BREAKER	30	Rear window defogger, power door locks, power seats
RADIO	10	Radio, power antenna, delayed pulse wiper/washer
DIR SIG B/U	20	Turn signal and backup lights
TAIL	20	Park, marker, license, and tail lights
CLK LTR CTSY	20	Power antenna, power door locks, light reminder buzzer, ignition key warning, courtesy lights, horns, courtesy light delay
GAGES	20	Cruise control, rear window defroster, trunk lock release, tailgate lock, seatbelt warning, courtesy light delay, light reminder buzzer, temperature, generator, brake warning lights and computer command control system
WDO CIRCUIT BREAKER	30	Power windows, sunroof
C/H	20	Choke heater
ECM	10	Electronic control module

ELECTRICAL SECTION

Starter mounting and noise diagnostic procedure

USE SHIMS AS NECESSARY (SEE DIAGNOSTIC PROCEDURE)

305 V-8
350 (V.I.N. CODE L) V-8

SHIMS—SEE DIAGNOSTIC PROCEDURE

350 (V.I.N. CODE R) V-8
403 V-8

FRONT

STARTER MOTOR ASM.

40 N•m (29 LB. FT.)

40 N•m (29 LB. FT.)

SHIMS—SEE DIAGNOSTIC PROCEDURE

STARTER MOTOR

231 V-6
350 (V.I.N. CODE X) V-8

FRONT OF ENGINE

40 N•m (29 LB. FT.)

© G.M. Corp.

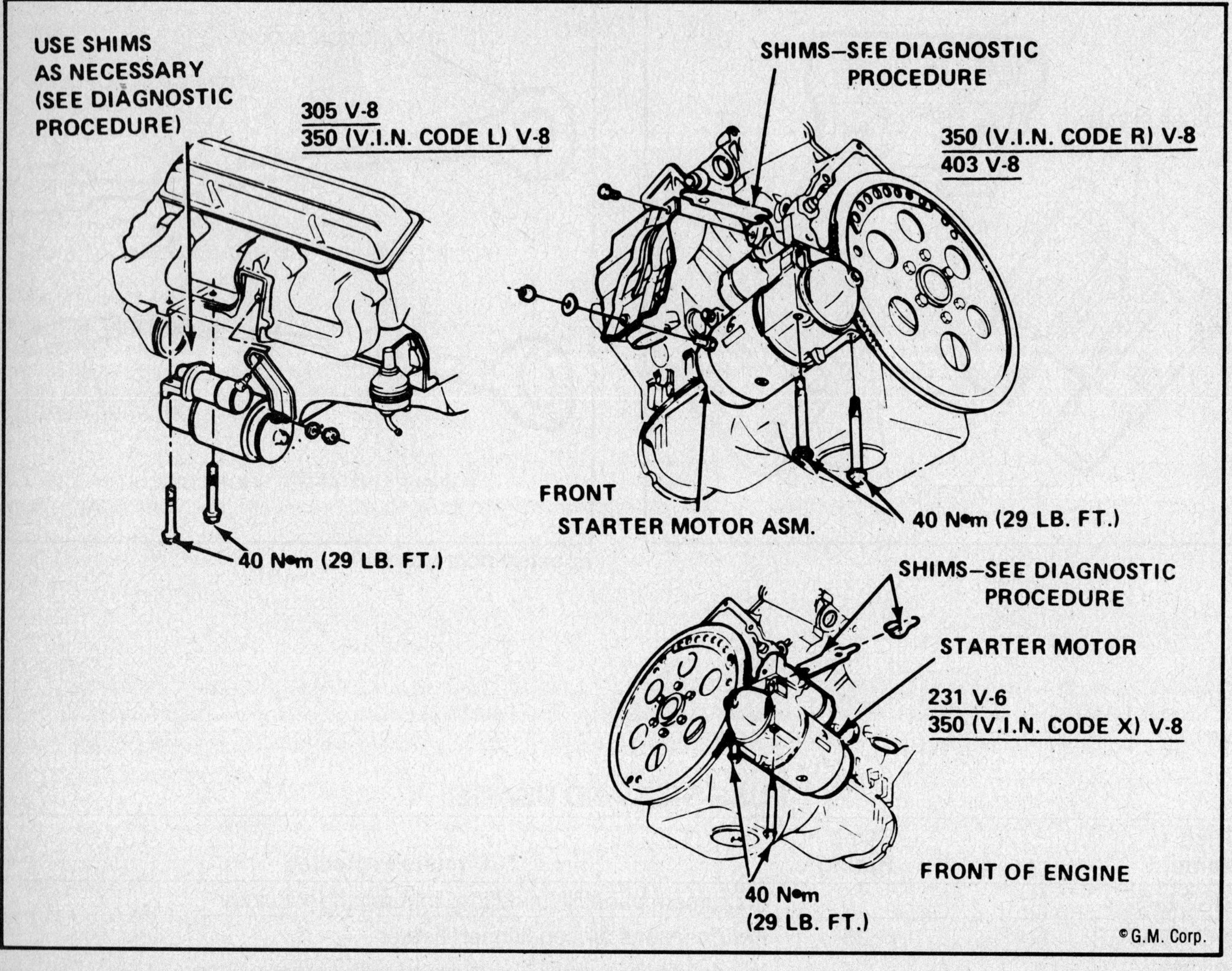

Flywheel to pinion clearance

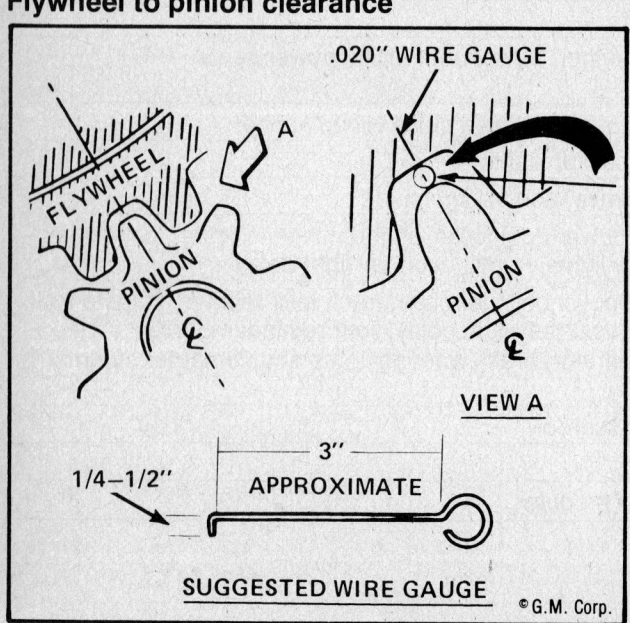

.020″ WIRE GAUGE

A

FLYWHEEL

PINION

PINION

VIEW A

1/4–1/2″

3″

APPROXIMATE

SUGGESTED WIRE GAUGE

© G.M. Corp.

Starter

- Disconnect electrical wiring, and remove, disconnect or relocate any of the following necessary for starter removal and clearance:
  a. Exhaust plumbing
  b. Flywheel housing cover
  c. Transmission oil cooler lines
  d. Crossmember

Meshing starter and flywheel teeth

SHIM

SCREW DRIVER

© G.M. Corp.

Diagnostic connector circuitry

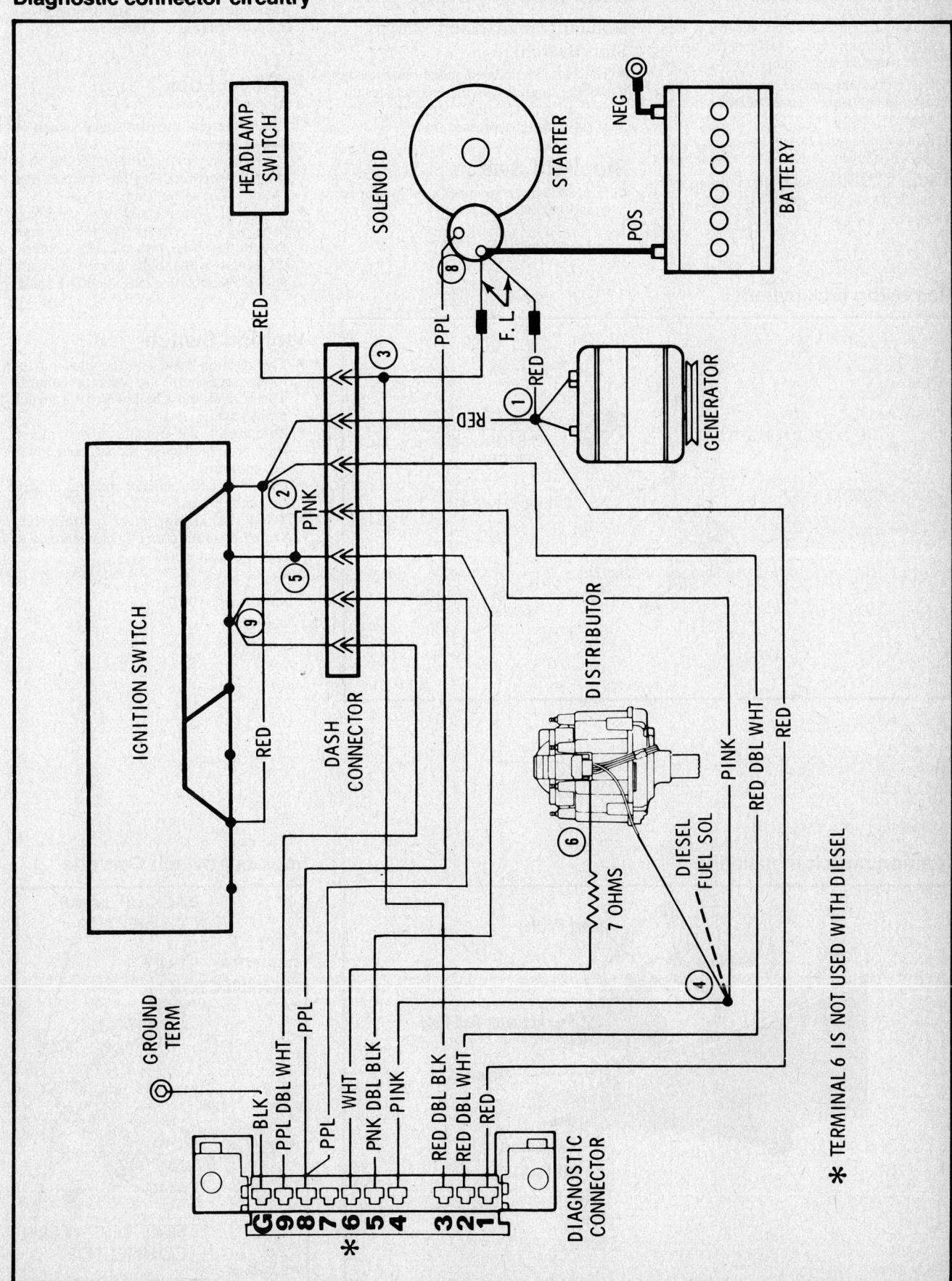

CHEVROLET
EXCEPT CAVALIER, CELEBRITY, CHEVETTE, CITATION, MONZA & VEGA

Ignition Distributor

- Remove distributor cap, electrical wiring, vacuum hose, tachometer drive, etc. from the distributor.
- Put alignment marks on rotor and distributor housing for installation reference.
- Remove the hold-down device, and pull the distributor up out of the engine.
- After installation, set ignition timing and check dwell, idle speed, etc.

Removing lock cylinder

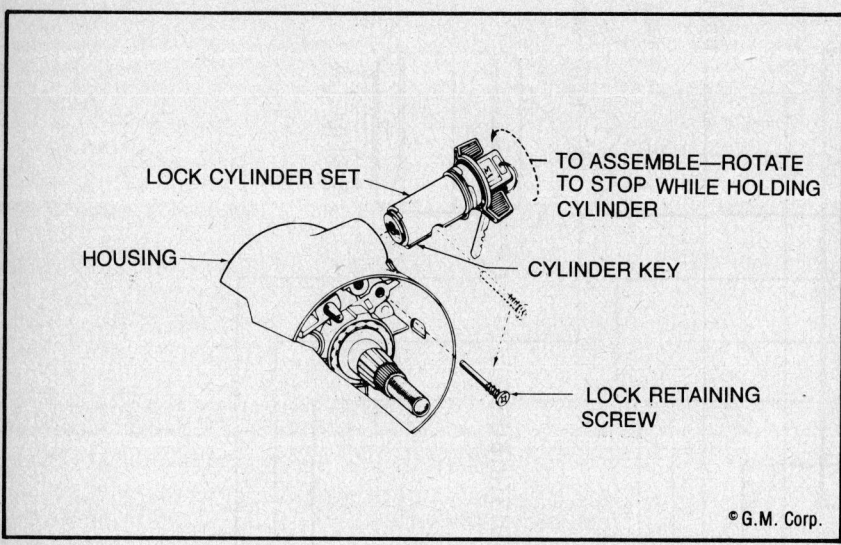

LOCK CYLINDER SET

HOUSING

TO ASSEMBLE—ROTATE TO STOP WHILE HOLDING CYLINDER

CYLINDER KEY

LOCK RETAINING SCREW

© G.M. Corp.

Neutral Safety Switch
Manual Transmission (Clutch Start Switch)

- The switch is located on the clutch pedal bracket, and allows the engine start circuit to activate only when the clutch pedal is fully depressed.

Stoplight Switch

- The switch is mounted on the brake pedal bracket.

- Adjust the switch so the stoplights illuminate at the first approximately ½ inch of brake pedal travel.

Ignition Lock

- Remove the steering wheel and lock plate, and pull the turn signal switch up out of the way.
- With the key cylinder in the RUN position, depress retaining tab and pull lock cylinder out of housing.
- To install, turn the key fully clockwise to stop. Insert cylinder into housing until it bottoms, then turn the key counterclockwise with slight inward pressure until drive section clicks into drive shaft.

Ignition Switch

- The ignition switch is mounted on the lower section of the steering column. The column must be lowered for switch replacement.
- Disconnect the column lower mount first, then the upper mount, and lower the column.
- Disconnect the actuator rod and electrical connections.
- When installing, make certain that switch position correctly corresponds to lock cylinder position.

Ignition switch installation

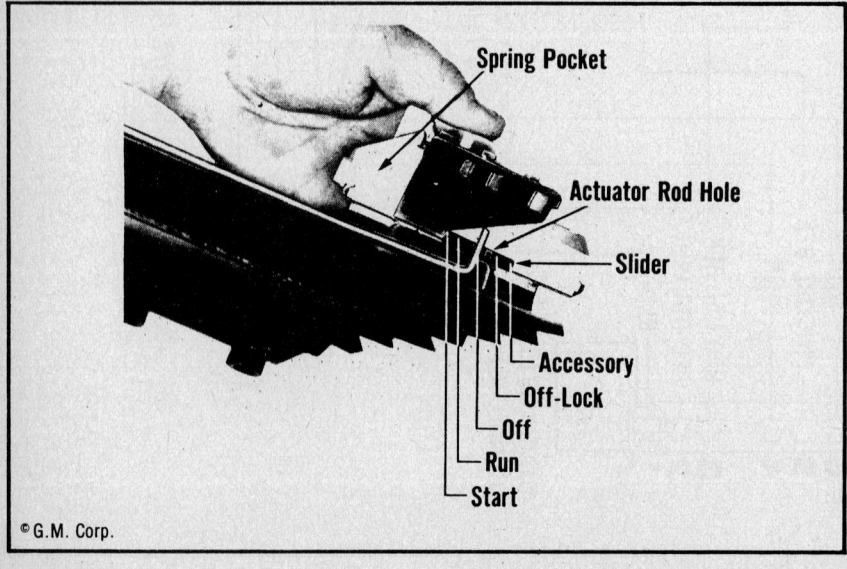

Spring Pocket

Actuator Rod Hole

Slider

Accessory
Off-Lock
Off
Run
Start

© G.M. Corp.

Lock-out switch Corvette

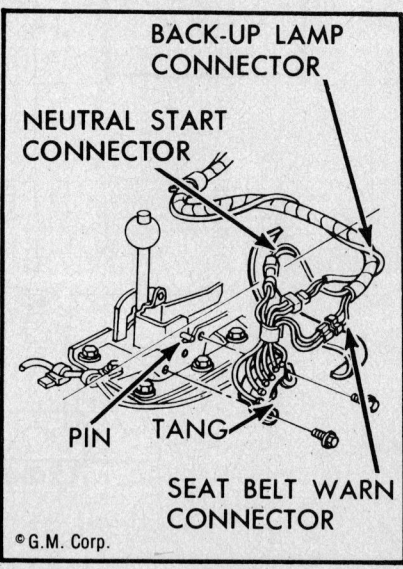

BACK-UP LAMP CONNECTOR

NEUTRAL START CONNECTOR

PIN   TANG

SEAT BELT WARN CONNECTOR

© G.M. Corp.

Steering Column Electrical Components

1. REMOVE AND INSTALL LOCK PLATE AND/OR CANCELLING CAM

REMOVE

1. Disconnect negative battery cable.
2. Remove parts as shown.

INSTALL

1. Install parts as shown.
2. Connect negative battery cable.

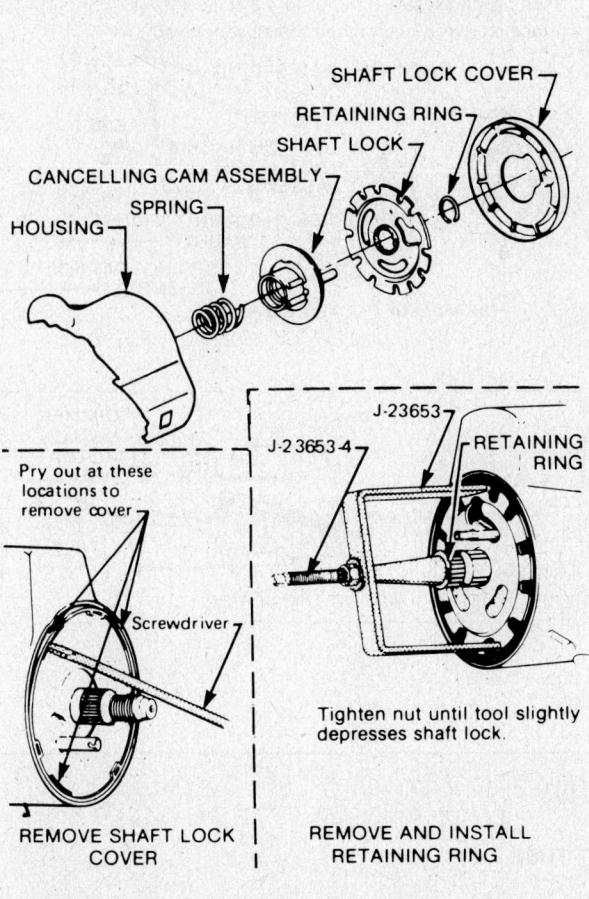

SHAFT LOCK COVER
RETAINING RING
SHAFT LOCK
CANCELLING CAM ASSEMBLY
HOUSING
SPRING

Pry out at these locations to remove cover

Screwdriver

REMOVE SHAFT LOCK COVER

J-23653-4
J-23653
RETAINING RING

Tighten nut until tool slightly depresses shaft lock.

REMOVE AND INSTALL RETAINING RING

2. REMOVE AND INSTALL TURN SIGNAL SWITCH

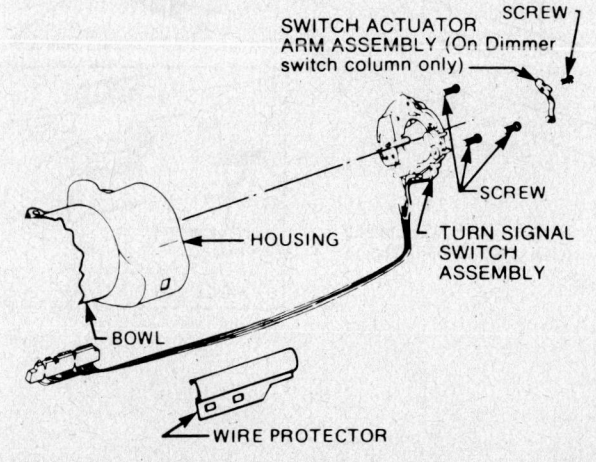

SCREW
SWITCH ACTUATOR ARM ASSEMBLY (On Dimmer switch column only)
SCREW
HOUSING
TURN SIGNAL SWITCH ASSEMBLY
BOWL
WIRE PROTECTOR

3. REMOVE AND INSTALL IGNITION LOCK AND KEY WARNING BUZZER

REMOVE

1. Turn lock to "RUN" position and remove key warning buzzer switch.
2. Remove parts as shown.

To assemble, rotate to stop while holding cylinder.

INSTALL

1. Install lock cylinder.
2. Turn lock to "RUN" position and install key warning buzzer switch.

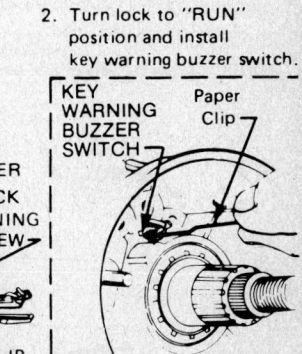

LOCK CYLINDER
LOCK RETAINING SCREW
CLIP
KEY WARNING BUZZER SWITCH
HOUSING

KEY WARNING BUZZER SWITCH
Paper Clip
REMOVE KEY WARNING BUZZER SWITCH

4. REMOVE AND INSTALL HOUSING AND WIPER SWITCH

REMOVE

1. Remove ignition and dimmer switch. Refer to step 5.
2. Remove parts as shown.
3. For KEY RELEASE - refer below

INSTALL

1. For KEY RELEASE refer below.
2. Assemble rack so that first rack tooth engages between first and second tooth of sector.
3. Install parts as shown.
4. Install ignition and dimmer switch. Refer to step 5.

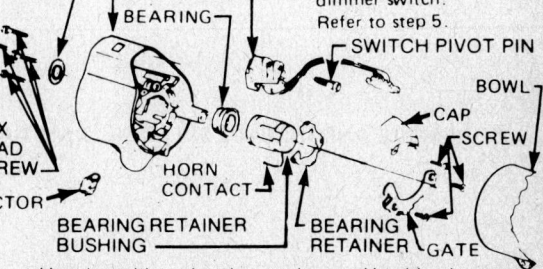

HOUSING
THRUST WASHER
PIVOT SWITCH ASSEMBLY (On wash/wipe column only)
BEARING
SWITCH PIVOT PIN
BOWL
CAP
SCREW
HEX HEAD SCREW
HORN CONTACT
SECTOR
BEARING RETAINER BUSHING
BEARING RETAINER
GATE

Housing without bearing retainer and bushing has spun-in bearing. If repair is necessary, complete housing assembly replacement is necessary.

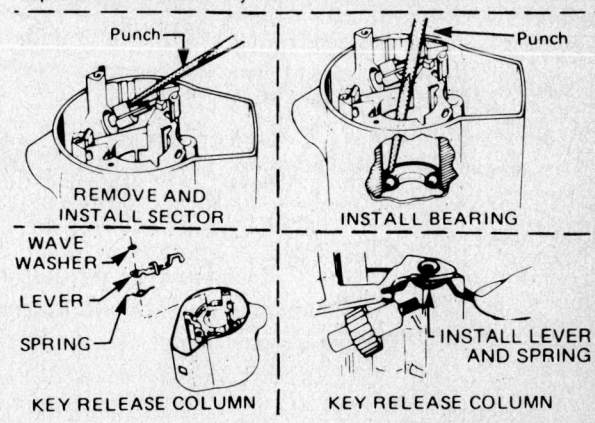

Punch
REMOVE AND INSTALL SECTOR

Punch
INSTALL BEARING

WAVE WASHER
LEVER
SPRING
KEY RELEASE COLUMN

INSTALL LEVER AND SPRING
KEY RELEASE COLUMN

5. REMOVE AND INSTALL IGNITION AND DIMMER SWITCH

REMOVE

1. Remove parts as shown.

INSTALL

1. Install parts as shown.
2. Position rod in slider hole and install ignition switch. Install lower stud and tighten to 4.0 N·m.
3. Install dimmer switch and depress switch slightly to insert 3/32" drill. Force switch up to remove lash, then tighten screw, and nut to 4.0 N·m.
4. Place shifter in neutral and install shift lever.

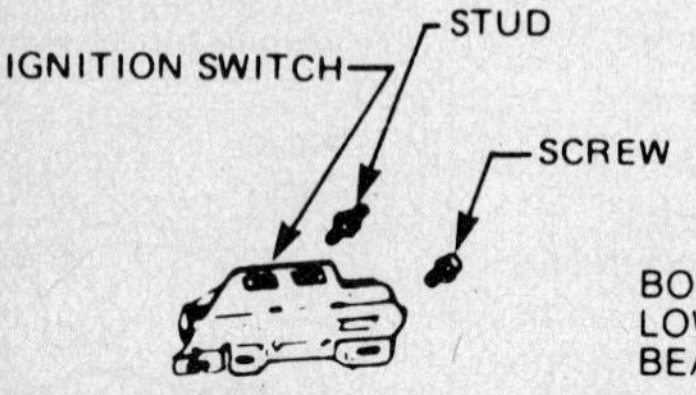

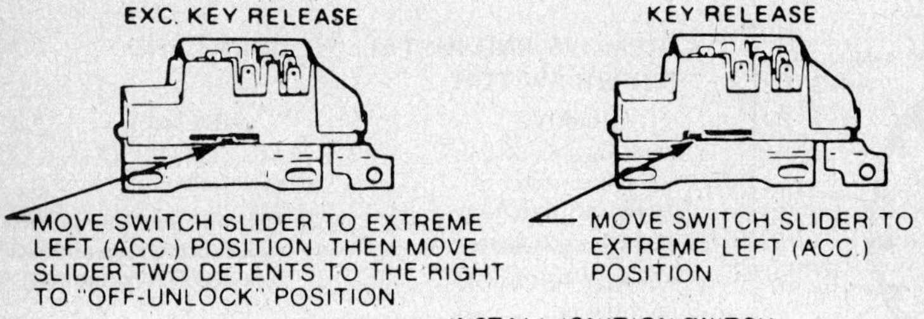

IGNITION SWITCH — STUD

SCREW

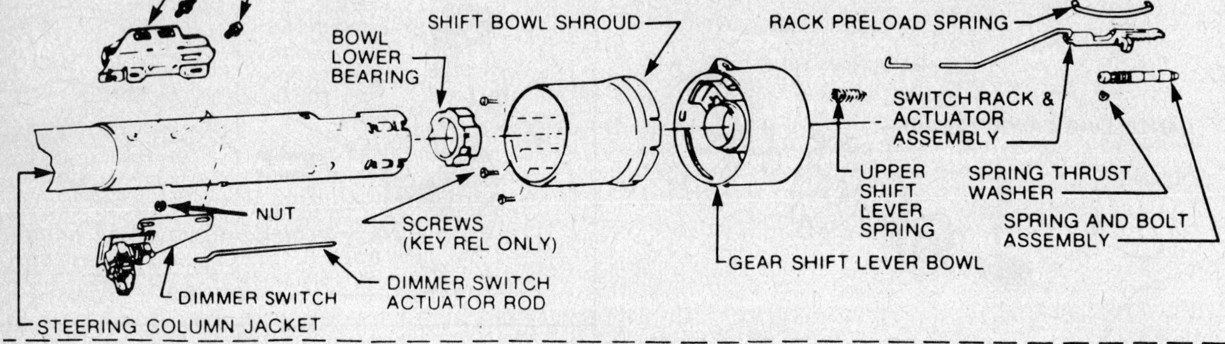

BOWL LOWER BEARING

SHIFT BOWL SHROUD

RACK PRELOAD SPRING

SWITCH RACK & ACTUATOR ASSEMBLY

UPPER SHIFT LEVER SPRING

SPRING THRUST WASHER

SPRING AND BOLT ASSEMBLY

GEAR SHIFT LEVER BOWL

NUT

SCREWS (KEY REL ONLY)

DIMMER SWITCH

DIMMER SWITCH ACTUATOR ROD

STEERING COLUMN JACKET

EXC. KEY RELEASE

MOVE SWITCH SLIDER TO EXTREME LEFT (ACC.) POSITION. THEN MOVE SLIDER TWO DETENTS TO THE RIGHT TO "OFF-UNLOCK" POSITION

KEY RELEASE

MOVE SWITCH SLIDER TO EXTREME LEFT (ACC.) POSITION

INSTALL IGNITION SWITCH

3/32" Drill

DIMMER SWITCH ACTUATOR ROD

DIMMER SWITCH

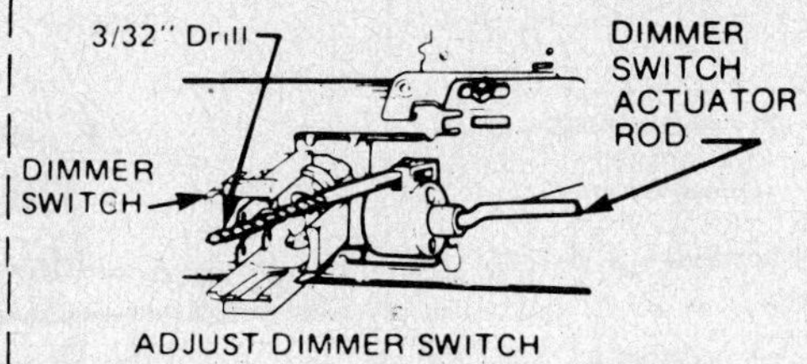

ADJUST DIMMER SWITCH

6. REMOVE AND INSTALL STEERING SHAFT AND SHIFT TUBE

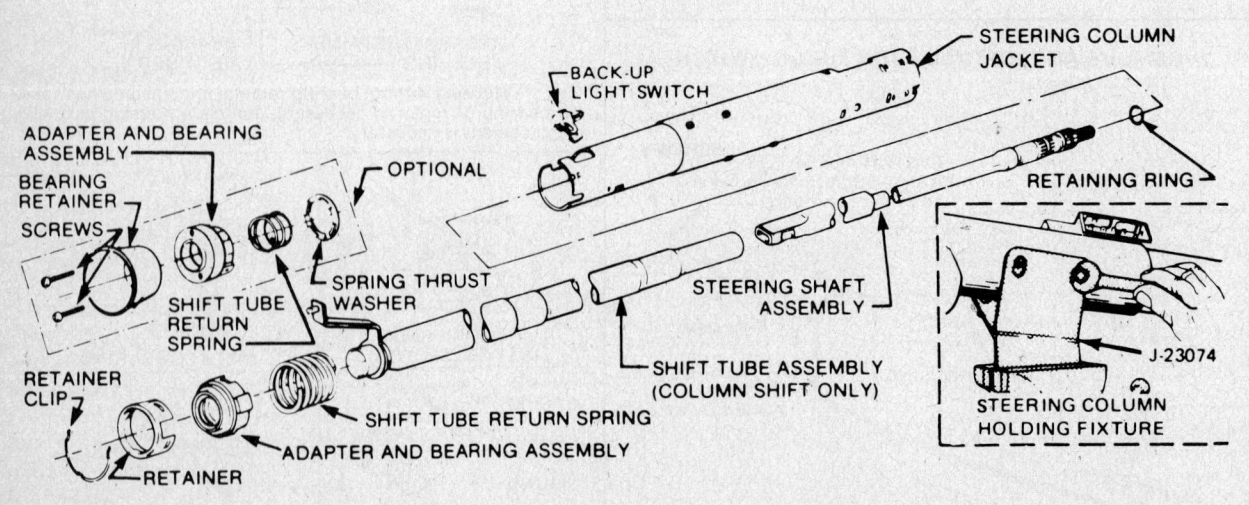

BACK-UP LIGHT SWITCH

STEERING COLUMN JACKET

ADAPTER AND BEARING ASSEMBLY

BEARING RETAINER

SCREWS

OPTIONAL

RETAINING RING

SPRING THRUST WASHER

SHIFT TUBE RETURN SPRING

STEERING SHAFT ASSEMBLY

SHIFT TUBE ASSEMBLY (COLUMN SHIFT ONLY)

J-23074

RETAINER CLIP

SHIFT TUBE RETURN SPRING

ADAPTER AND BEARING ASSEMBLY

RETAINER

STEERING COLUMN HOLDING FIXTURE

Stoplight switch installation

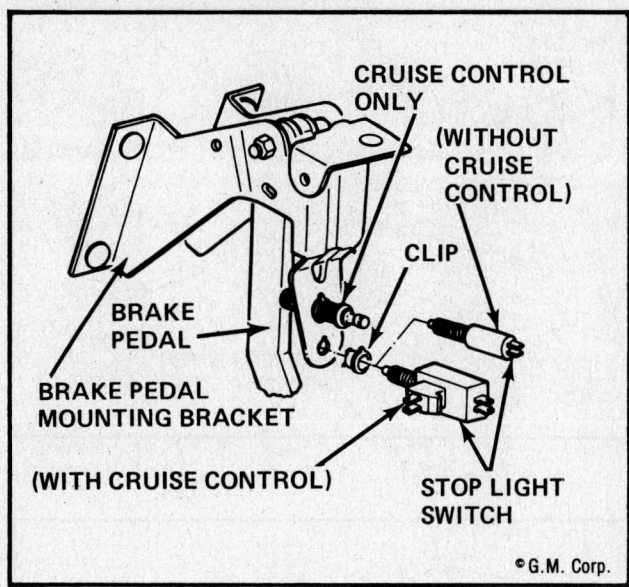

© G.M. Corp.

Corvette stoplight switch

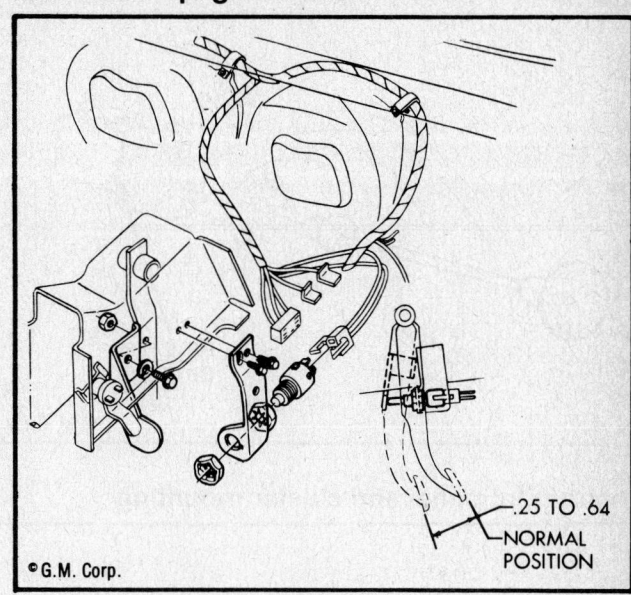

© G.M. Corp.

Light Switch
- Relocate anything preventing full access to the switch such as air conditioner ducting, trim panel, windshield wiper switch, radio speaker, etc.

- On Corvette the steering column must be lowered.
- Place switch in fully ON position. Pull on knob and press shaft release button to release shaft and knob assembly.
- Separate switch from instrument panel and electrical connections.

Horn switch and cushioned rim steering wheel

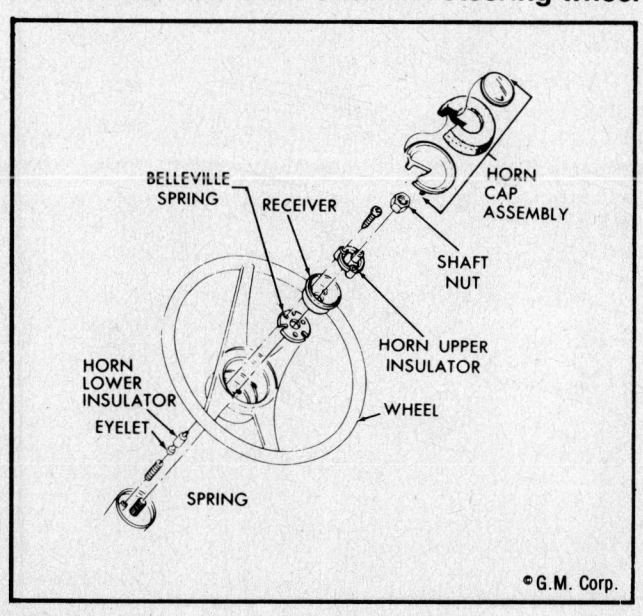

© G.M. Corp.

Standard steering wheel and horn switch

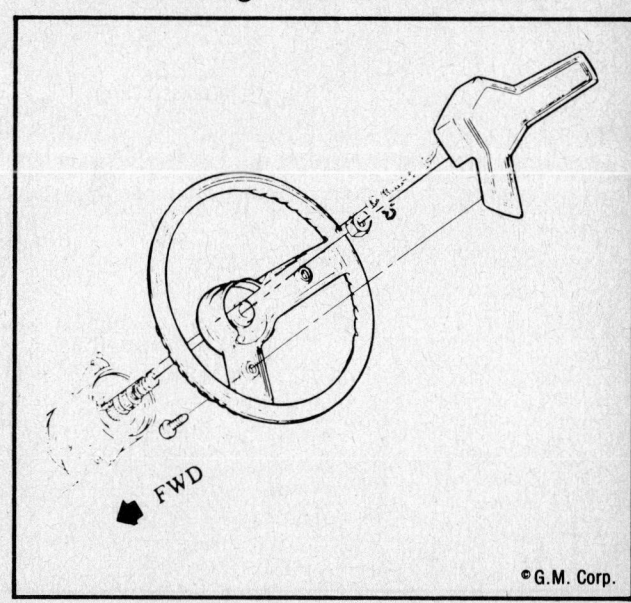

© G.M. Corp.

CHEVROLET
EXCEPT CAVALIER, CELEBRITY, CHEVETTE, CITATION, MONZA & VEGA

Light switch mounting

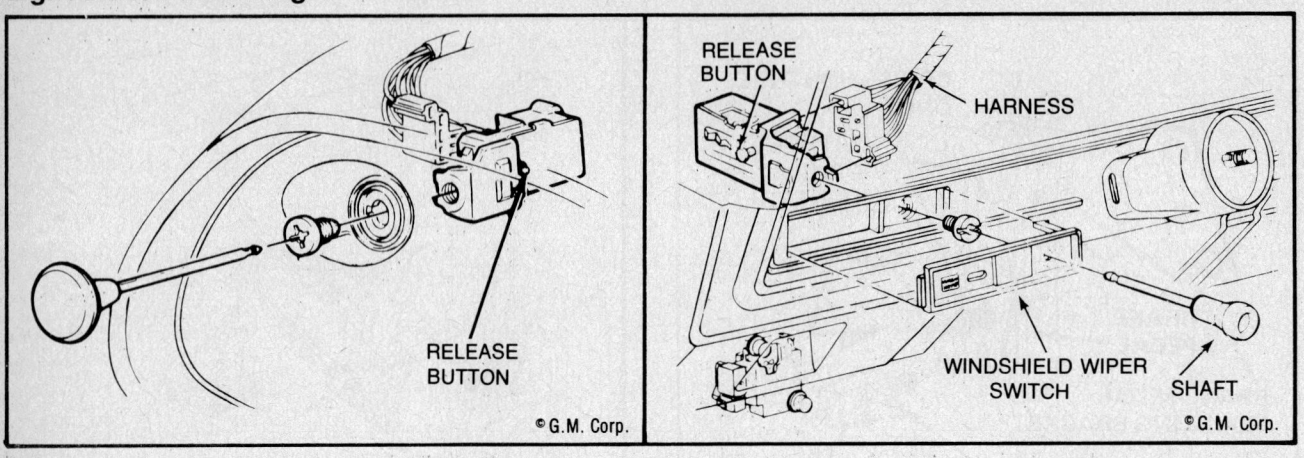

RELEASE BUTTON

RELEASE BUTTON

HARNESS

© G.M. Corp.

WINDSHIELD WIPER SWITCH

SHAFT

© G.M. Corp.

Instrument panel and cluster mounting

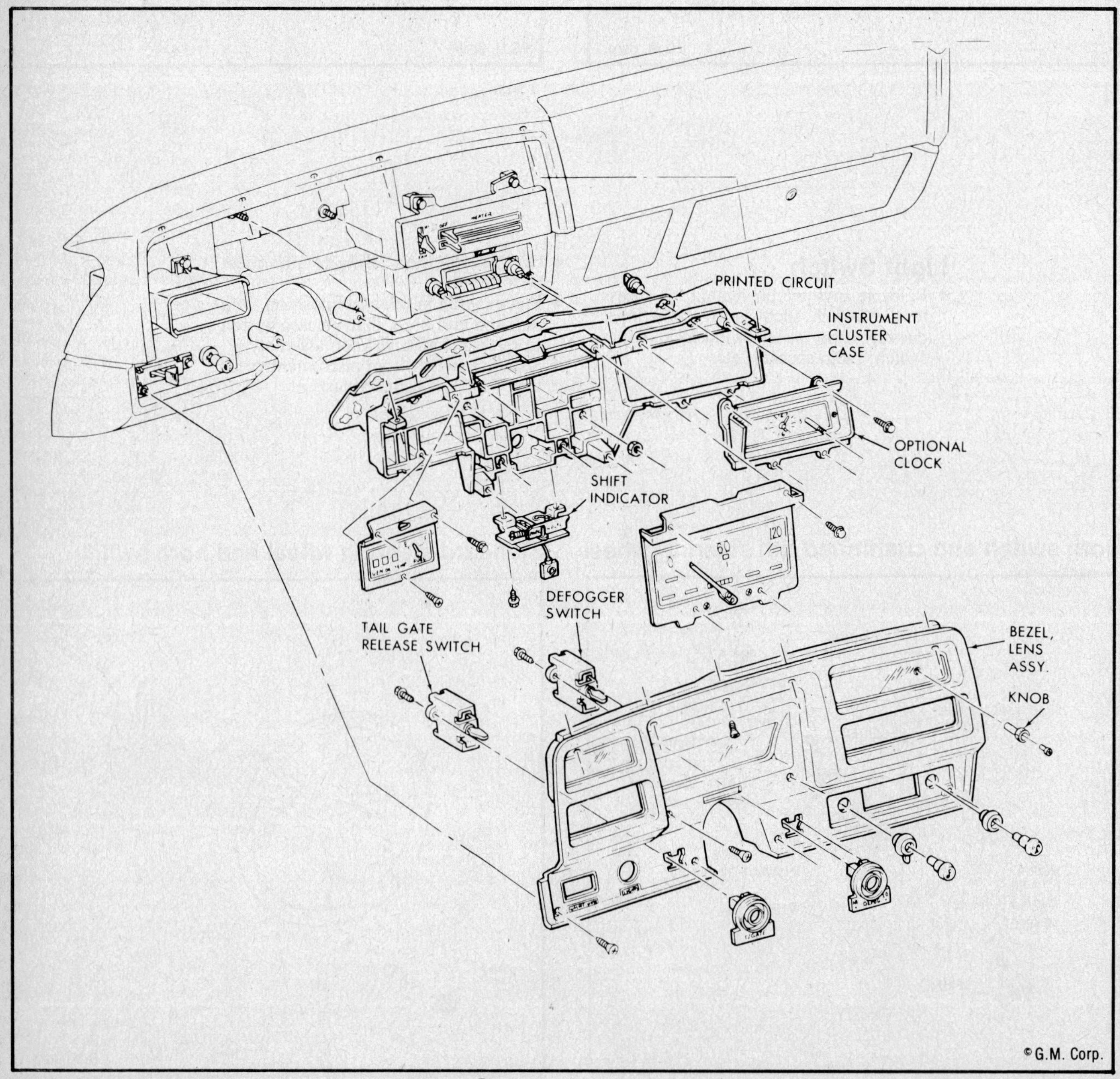

PRINTED CIRCUIT

INSTRUMENT CLUSTER CASE

OPTIONAL CLOCK

SHIFT INDICATOR

DEFOGGER SWITCH

TAIL GATE RELEASE SWITCH

BEZEL, LENS ASSY.

KNOB

© G.M. Corp.

Windshield wiper switch installation

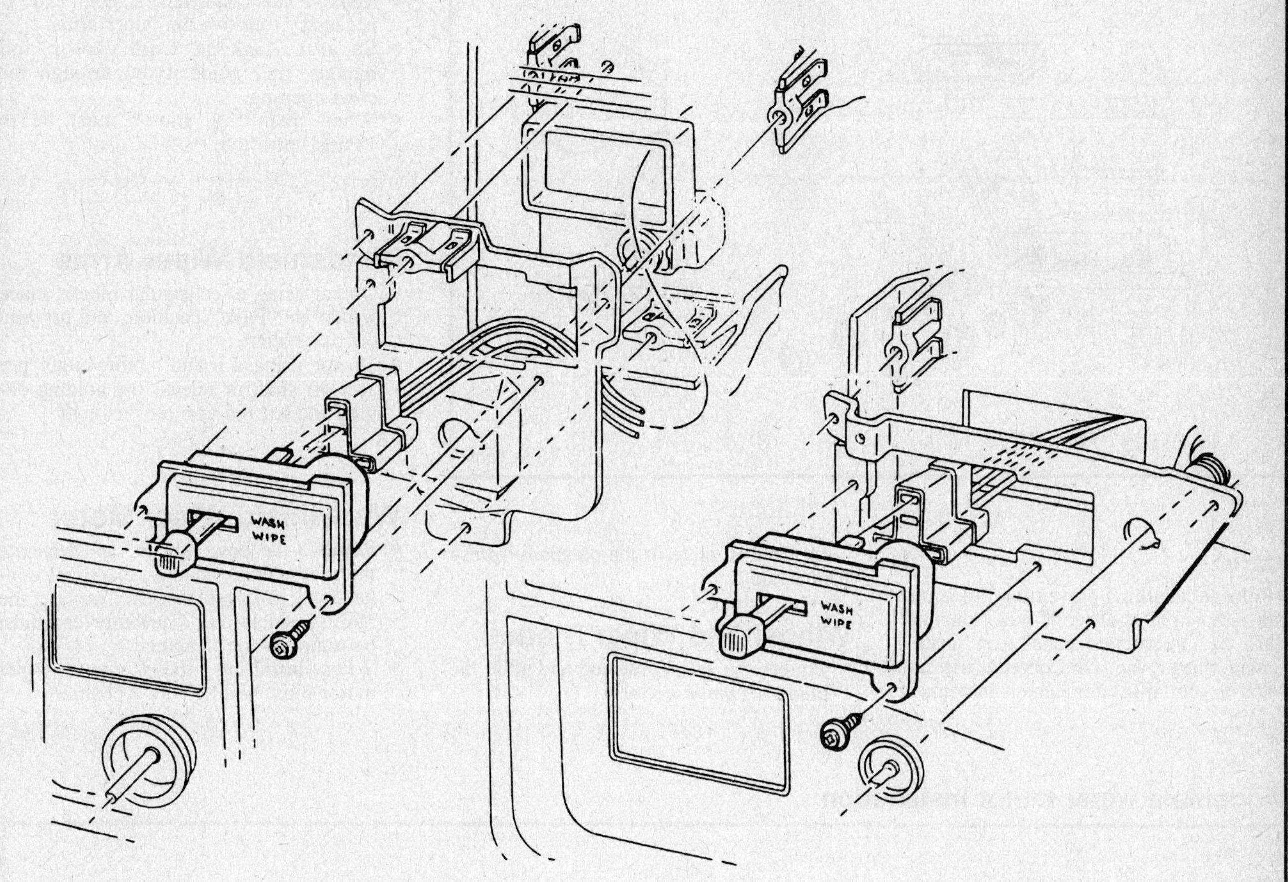

© G.M. Corp.

Windshield Wiper Switch

All Except 1978 And Later Corvette

- Relocate anything preventing access to the switch such as trim panel, instrument cluster, air conditioner ducting, light switch, etc.
- Separate switch from instrument panel and electrical wiring.

1978 And Later Corvette

- The steering column must be lowered for access to the switch which is located inside the steering column.
- Remove the steering wheel, ignition lock and turn signal switch.
- Remove the wiper switch and pull the wiring up through the column shroud.

Corvette windshield wiper switch

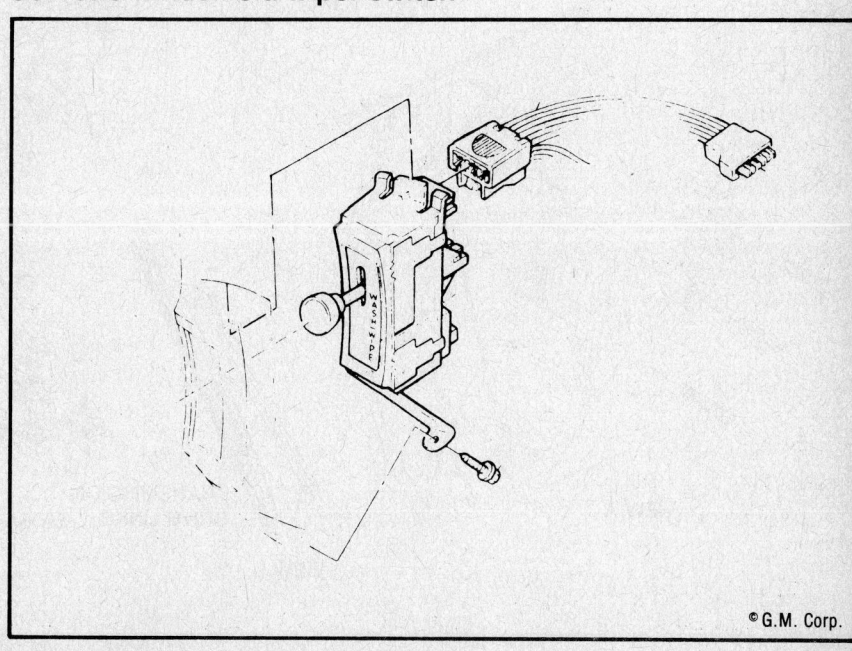

© G.M. Corp.

CHEVROLET
EXCEPT CAVALIER, CELEBRITY, CHEVETTE, CITATION, MONZA & VEGA

Radio installation

© G.M. Corp.

Radio
- Relocate anything preventing full access to radio such as air conditioner ducting, ash try, instrument panel trim, instrument cluster, etc. On Corvette, use care not to collapse the center instrument cluster trim plate or the plastic oil pressure line.

Windshield Wiper Blades
- Trigger the release device and slide the blade off the wiper arm.

Windshield Wiper Linkage
- Remove the cowl vent screen, and, if necessary, remove the wiper arms.
- Separate linkage from motor and mounts, and guide it out through the cowl opening.
- When installing, motor must be in "Park" position.

Windshield Wiper Arms
- On car using a rectangular motor, place wipers in "Park" position, and pry arm off drive shaft.
- On car using a round motor, either pry arm off shaft or release the holding device and lift the arm off the shaft.

Windshield Wiper Motor
- Remove the cowl screen, and separate the motor from mounts, electrical connections, linkages, etc. On Corvette, the ignition shield and distributor cap must be removed for clearance.
- When installing, the Corvette wiper motor must be in "Park" position.

Windshield wiper motor installation

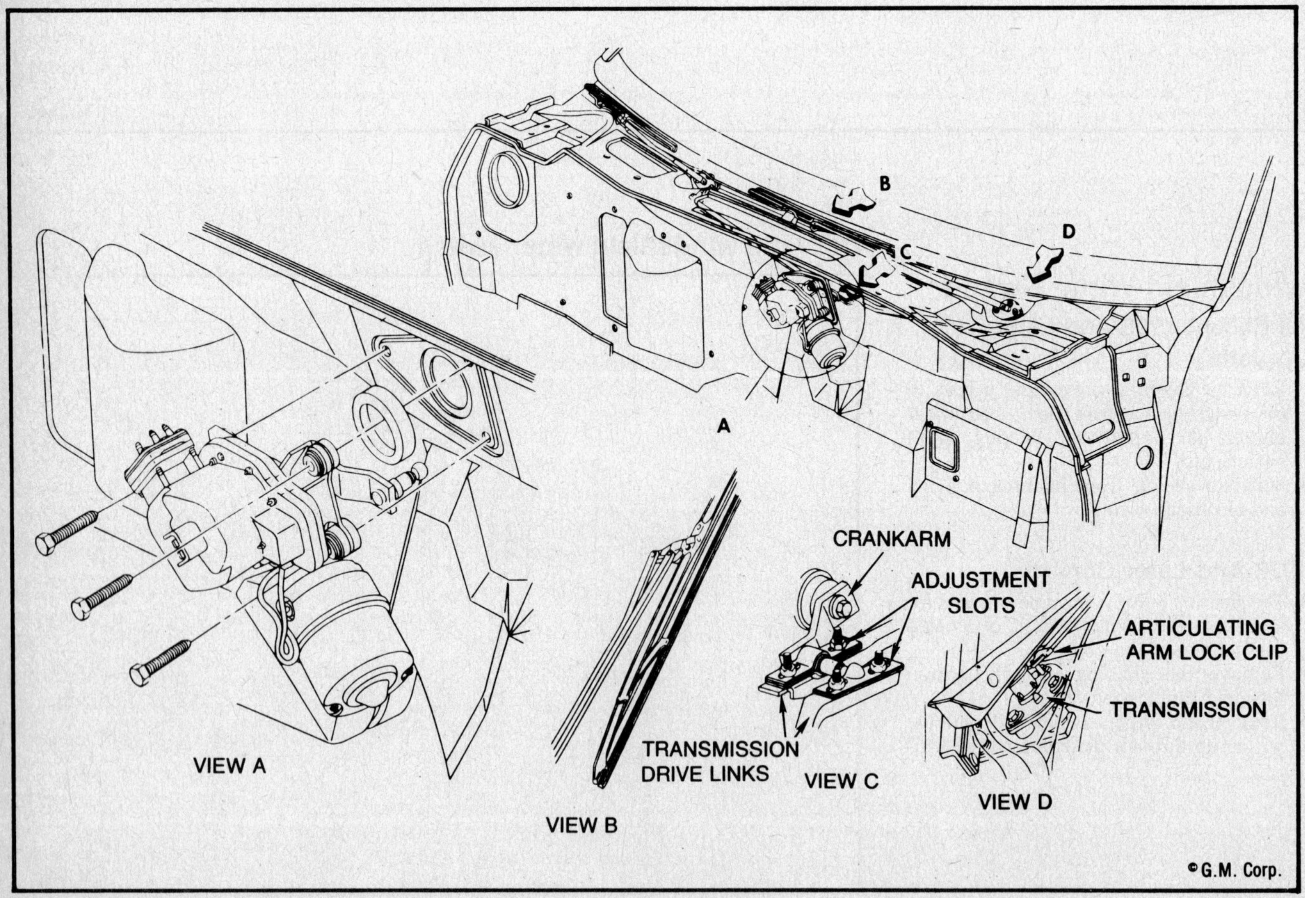

VIEW A

VIEW B

TRANSMISSION DRIVE LINKS

CRANKARM

ADJUSTMENT SLOTS

VIEW C

ARTICULATING ARM LOCK CLIP

TRANSMISSION

VIEW D

© G.M. Corp.

Typical radio trim plate

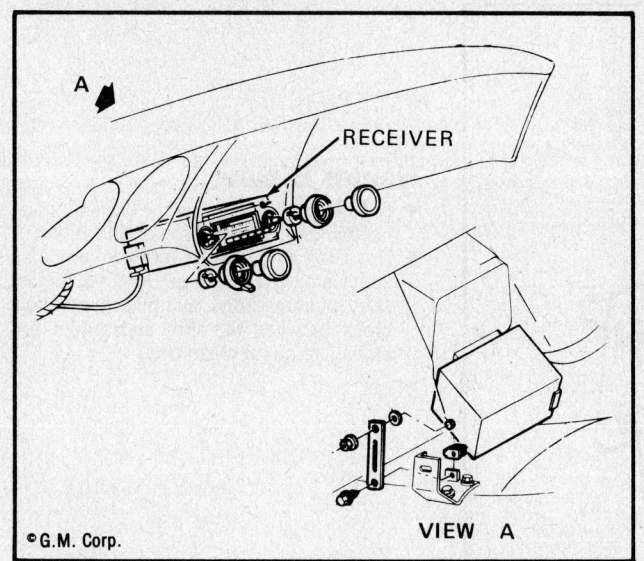

RECEIVER

A

VIEW A

© G.M. Corp.

Corvette radio mounting

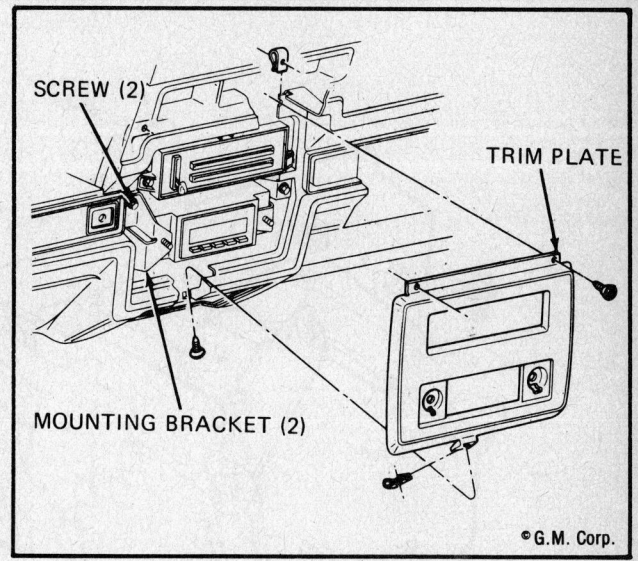

SCREW (2)

TRIM PLATE

MOUNTING BRACKET (2)

© G.M. Corp.

Temperature Control Unit/Blower Switch

- Relocate anything preventing full access to the control unit such as trim panel, radio, etc.
- Remove mounting screws, pull control unit out and separate it from control cables, vacuum lines and electrical connections.

Heater control unit typical in 1977 and later full size cars and 1978 and later mid-size cars

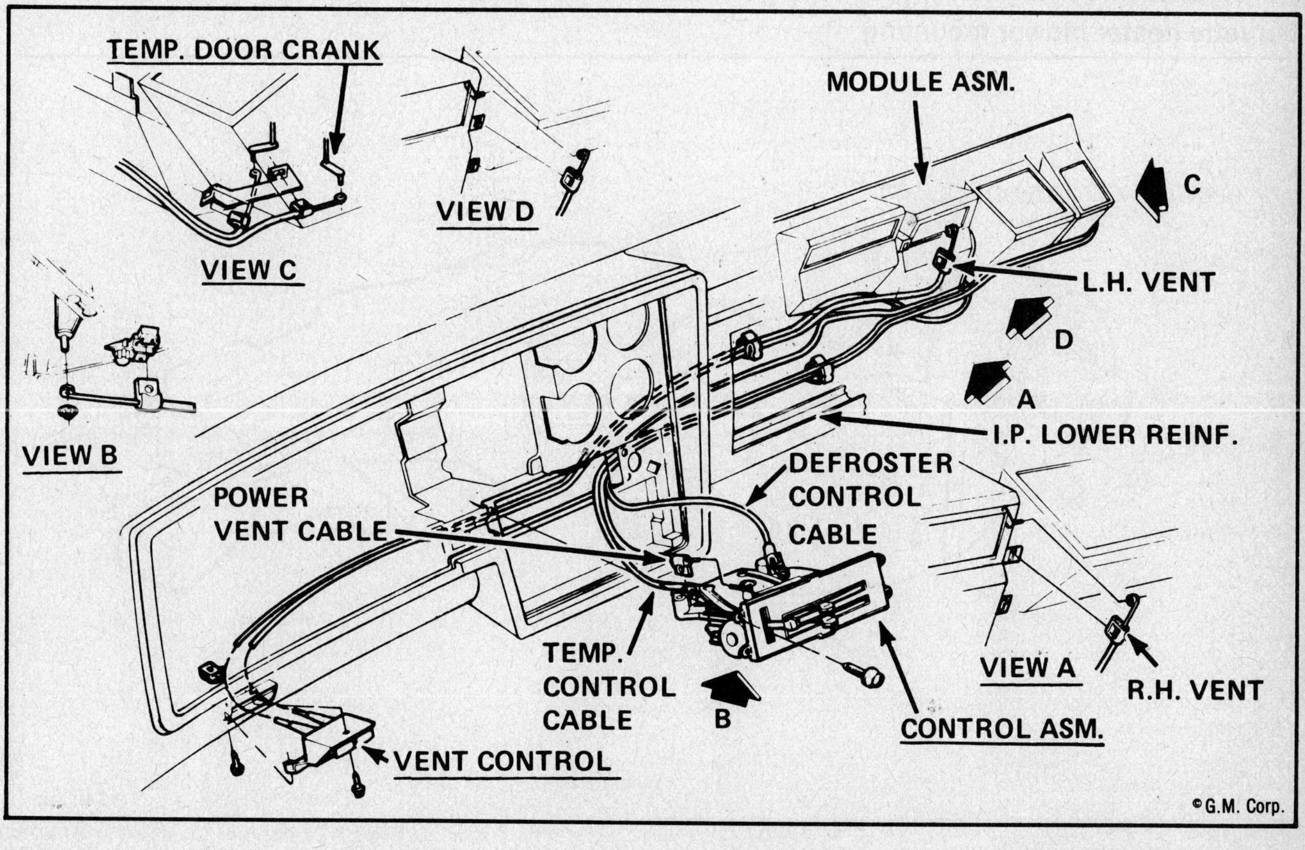

TEMP. DOOR CRANK

VIEW D

VIEW C

VIEW B

MODULE ASM.

C

L.H. VENT

D

A

I.P. LOWER REINF.

DEFROSTER CONTROL CABLE

POWER VENT CABLE

TEMP. CONTROL CABLE

B

VIEW A

R.H. VENT

CONTROL ASM.

VENT CONTROL

© G.M. Corp.

CHEVROLET
EXCEPT CAVALIER, CELEBRITY, CHEVETTE, CITATION, MONZA & VEGA

Heater control unit

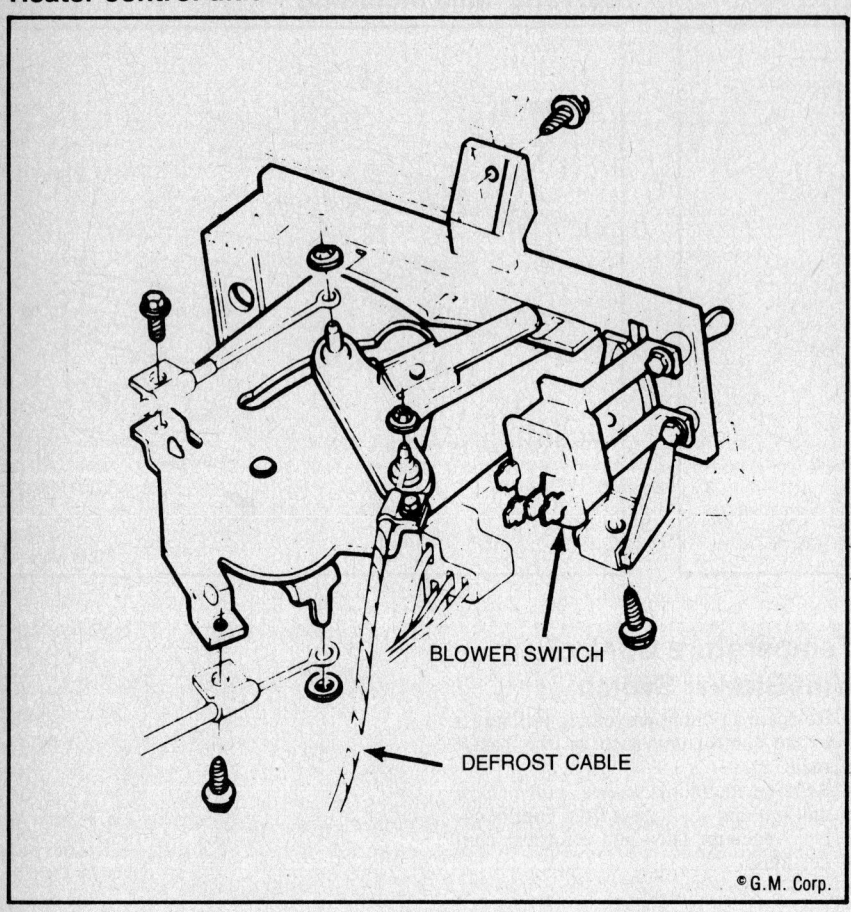

BLOWER SWITCH

DEFROST CABLE

© G.M. Corp.

Heater Blower
- Disconnect mounts and electrical connector, and remove blower and motor.
- On 1976 and earlier full-size models, and Camaro and Nova, remove fender skirt retaining bolts, and place a wooden block between the skirt and fender for blower removal clearance.

Corvette heater blower mounting

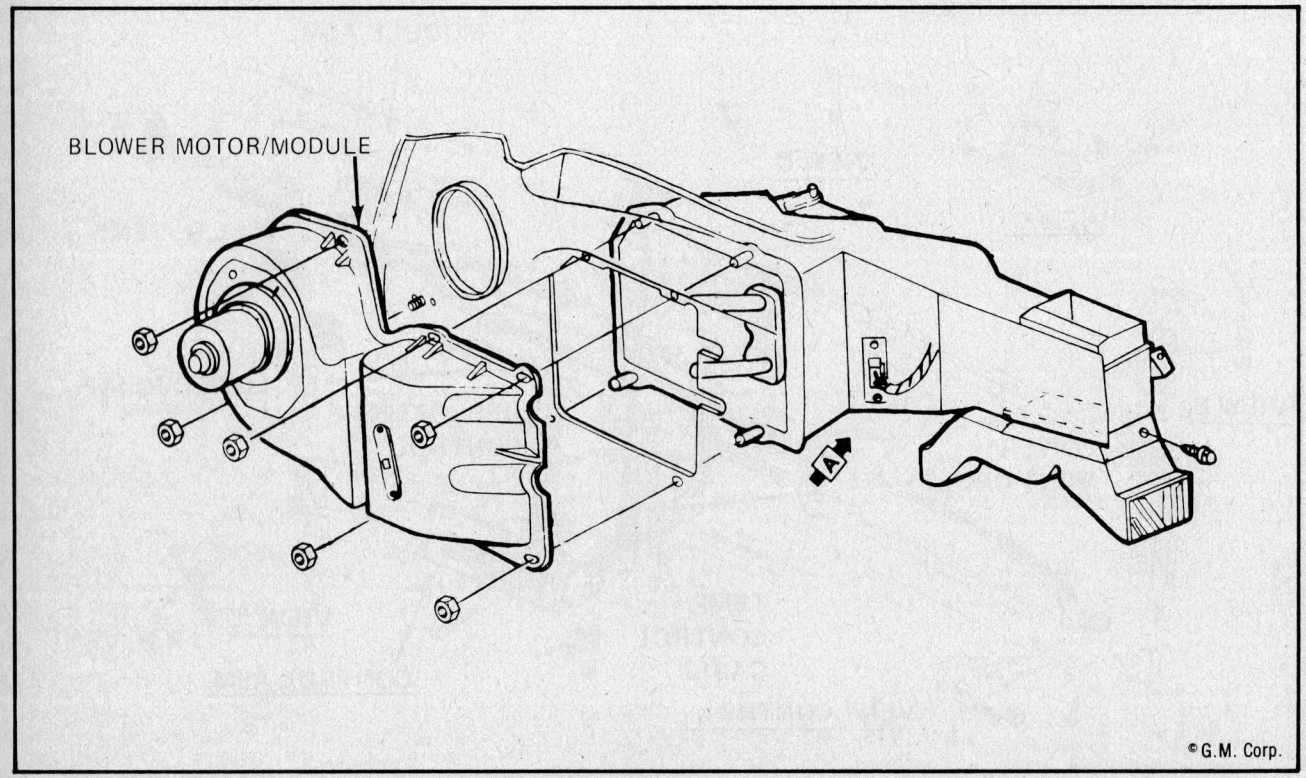

BLOWER MOTOR/MODULE

© G.M. Corp.

Chevrolet heater blower mounting

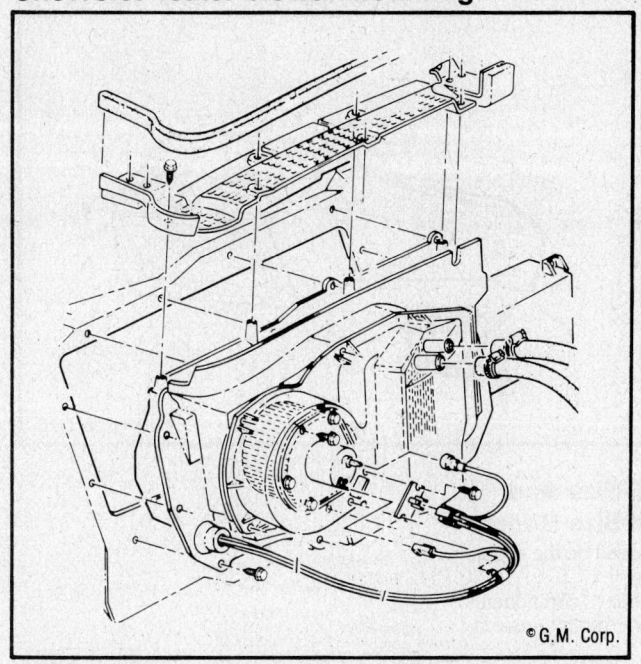

© G.M. Corp.

Heater blower motor, inlet assembly and core

Camaro heater blower mounting

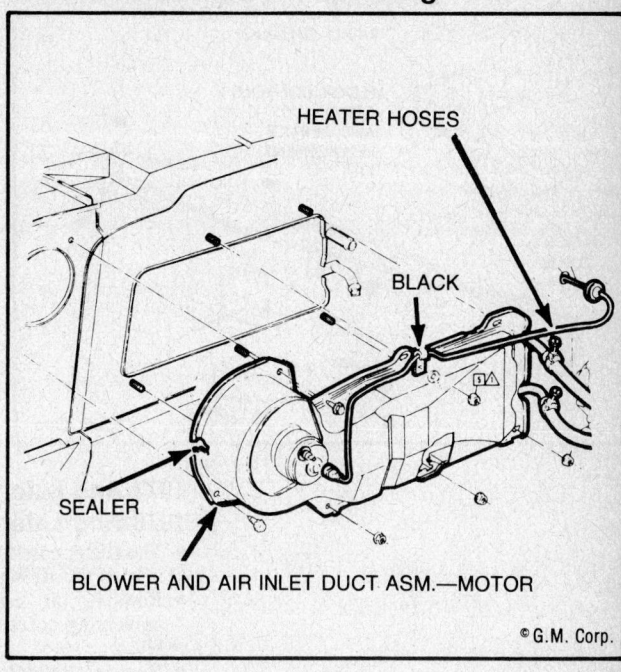

HEATER HOSES

BLACK

SEALER

BLOWER AND AIR INLET DUCT ASM.—MOTOR

© G.M. Corp.

Air conditioner module mounting

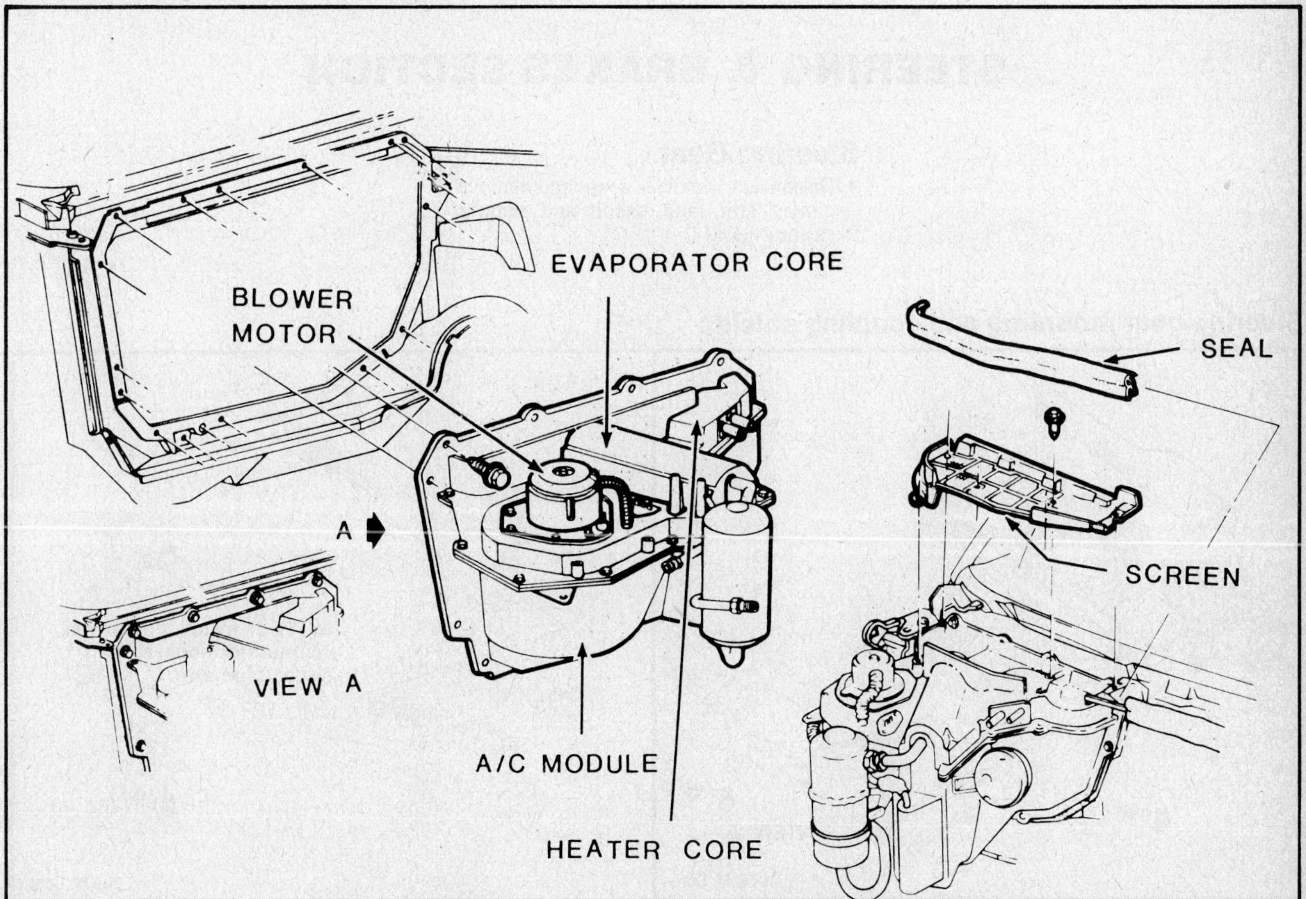

EVAPORATOR CORE

BLOWER MOTOR

SEAL

SCREEN

A

VIEW A

A/C MODULE

HEATER CORE

© G.M. Corp.

CHEVROLET
EXCEPT CAVALIER, CELEBRITY, CHEVETTE, CITATION, MONZA & VEGA

Camaro heater assembly

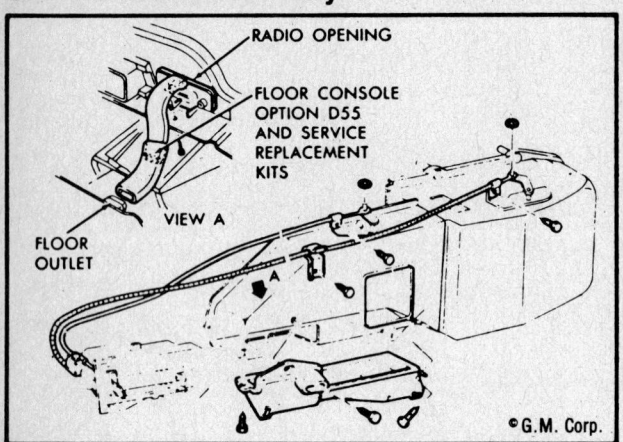

Chevelle heater assembly mounting

1977 And Later Full-Size And
1978 And Later Mid-Size Models
- The heater core is removed on the engine side of the firewall.
- Remove air conditioner components preventing access to the module assembly.
- Remove module cover and separate heater core from the module.

STEERING & BRAKES SECTION

Steering Gear
- Disconnect flexible coupling, remove pitman arm, and unbolt and remove steering gear.

Steering gear mounting and coupling shields

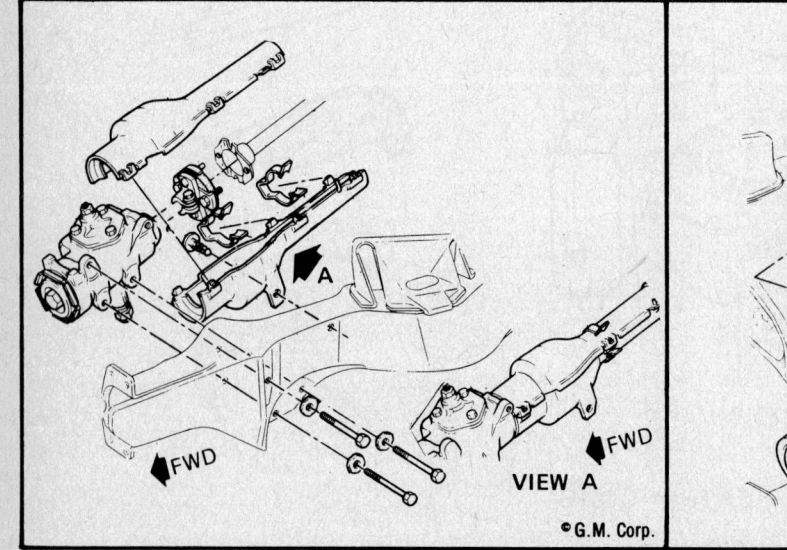

Malibu (manual steering)

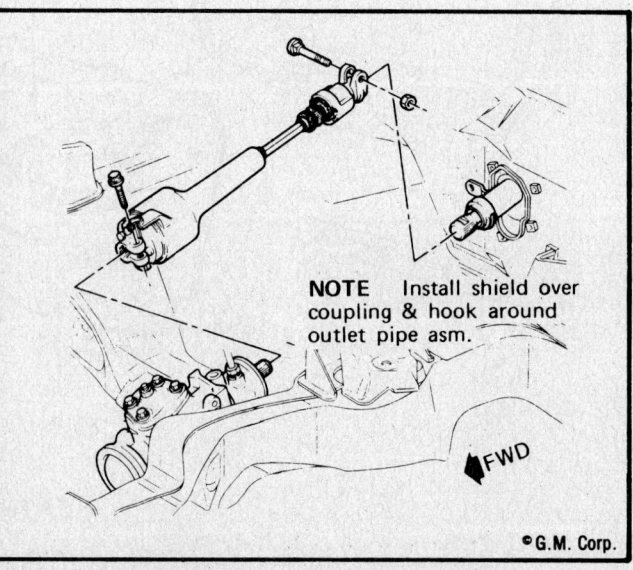

Chevrolet (all) Monte Carlo (all) Malibu (power steering)

Aligning steering shaft coupling slots

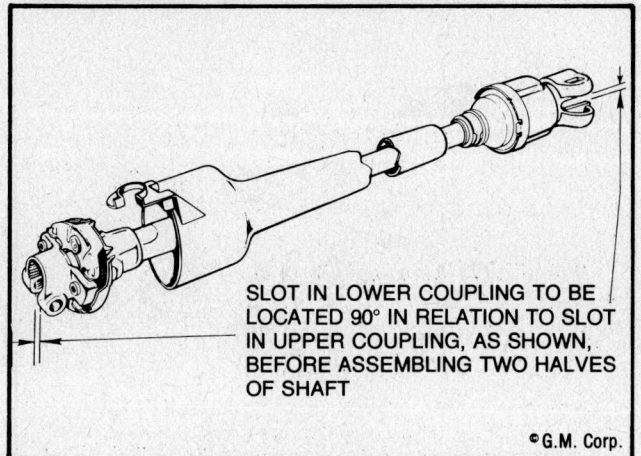

SLOT IN LOWER COUPLING TO BE LOCATED 90° IN RELATION TO SLOT IN UPPER COUPLING, AS SHOWN, BEFORE ASSEMBLING TWO HALVES OF SHAFT

© G.M. Corp.

Pot joint steering column coupling

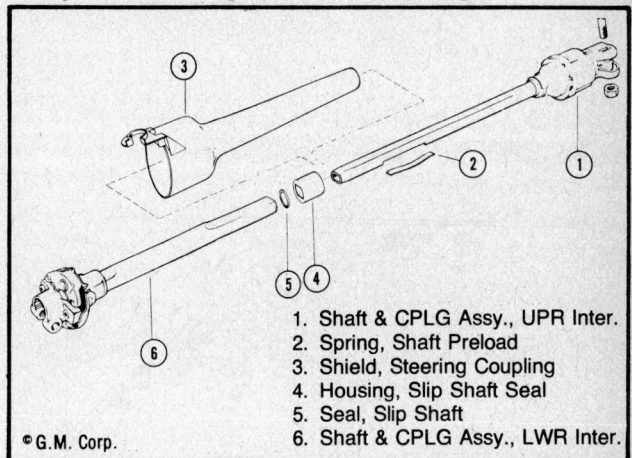

1. Shaft & CPLG Assy., UPR Inter.
2. Spring, Shaft Preload
3. Shield, Steering Coupling
4. Housing, Slip Shaft Seal
5. Seal, Slip Shaft
6. Shaft & CPLG Assy., LWR Inter.

© G.M. Corp.

Steering gear mounting and coupling shields

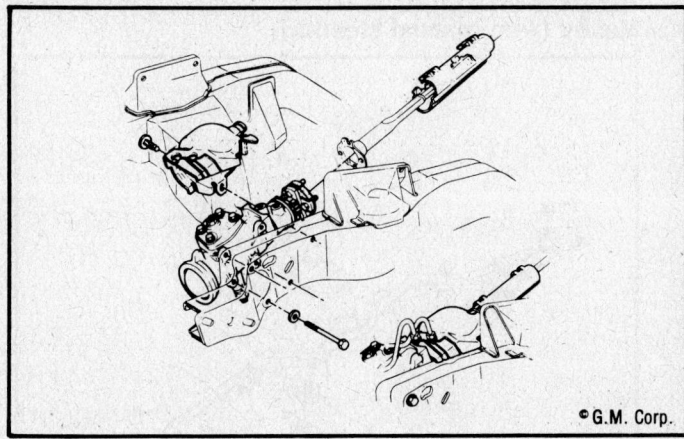

© G.M. Corp.

Camaro

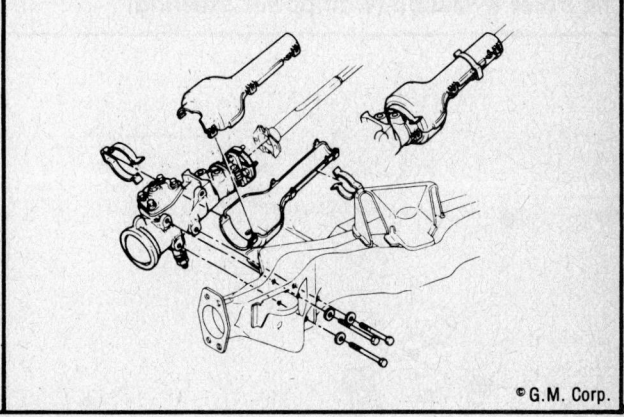

© G.M. Corp.

Nova

Steering Column

NOTE: Handle the steering column very carefully. Rapping on the end of it or leaning on it could shear off the inserts which allow the column to collapse in a crash.

- Disconnect the battery and flexible coupling.
- Disconnect shift linkages, wiring, etc.
- Remove lower column mounts, then upper column mounts, and pull column up and out of car.
- When installing, check that flexible coupling alignment is correct.

NOTE: When installing, use only the specified hardware. Over-length bolts could prevent the column from properly collapsing in a crash.

Steering column mounting typical in full size car models

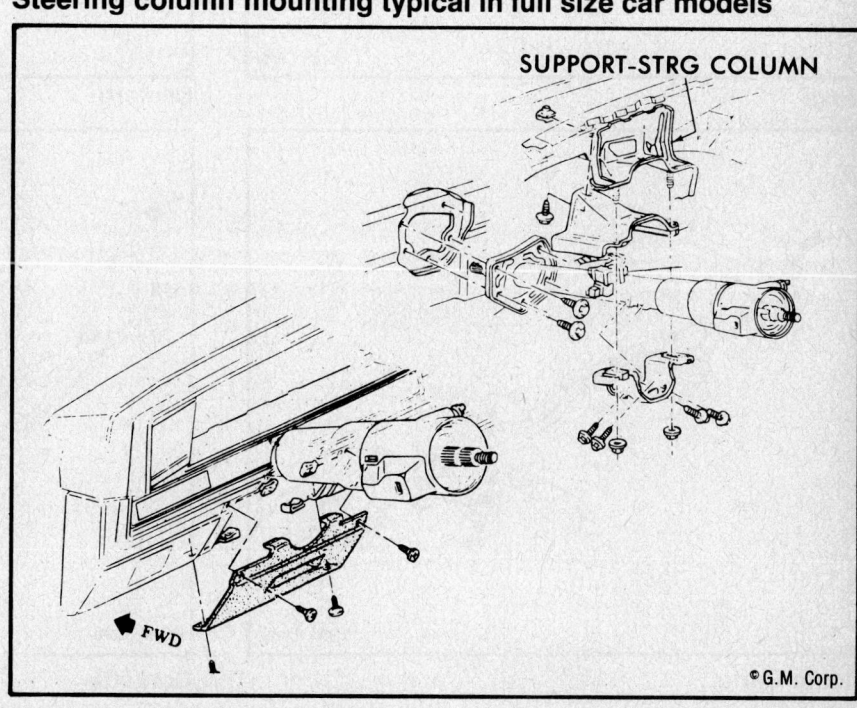

SUPPORT-STRG COLUMN

FWD

© G.M. Corp.

CHEVROLET
EXCEPT CAVALIER, CELEBRITY, CHEVETTE, CITATION, MONZA & VEGA

Steering linkage arrangements

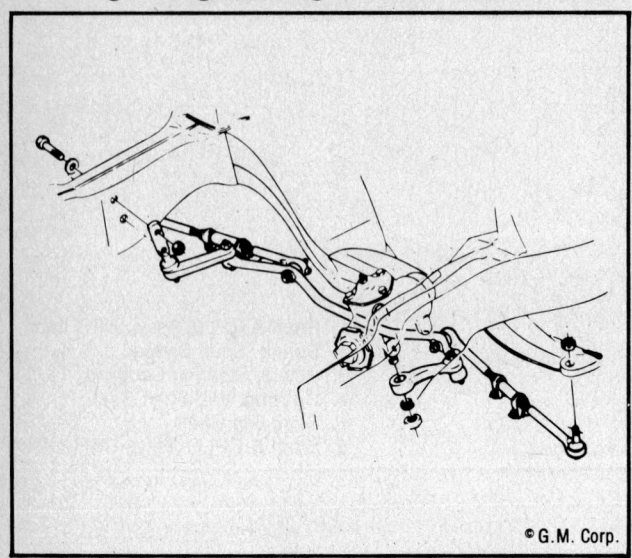

Chevrolet & Malibu (with power steering)

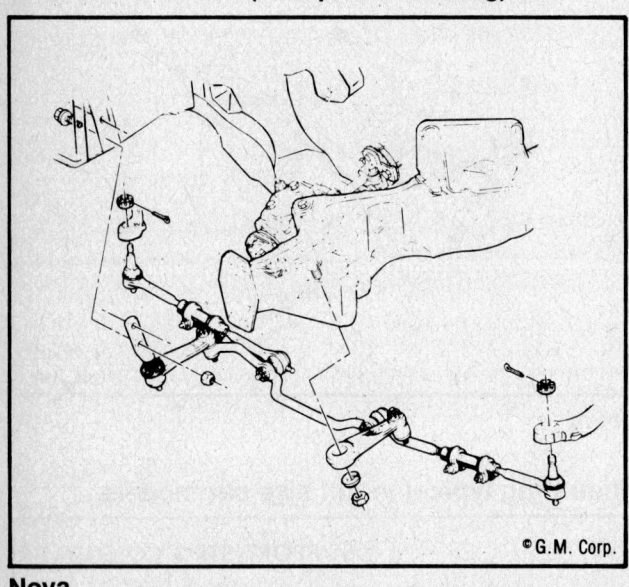

Nova

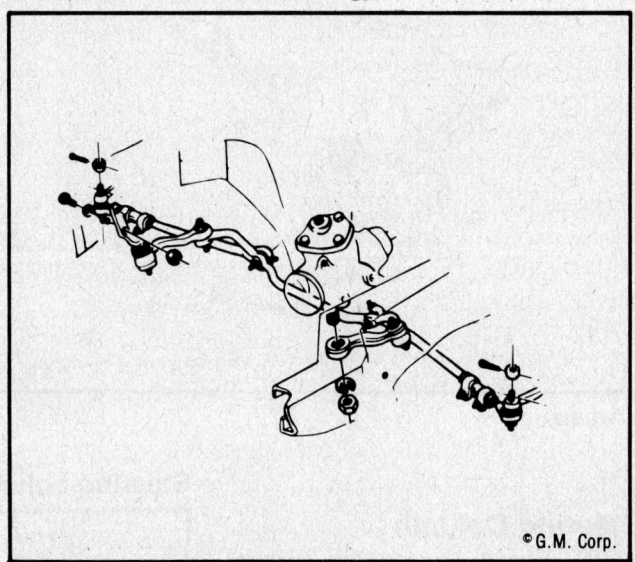

Malibu (with manual steering)

Camaro

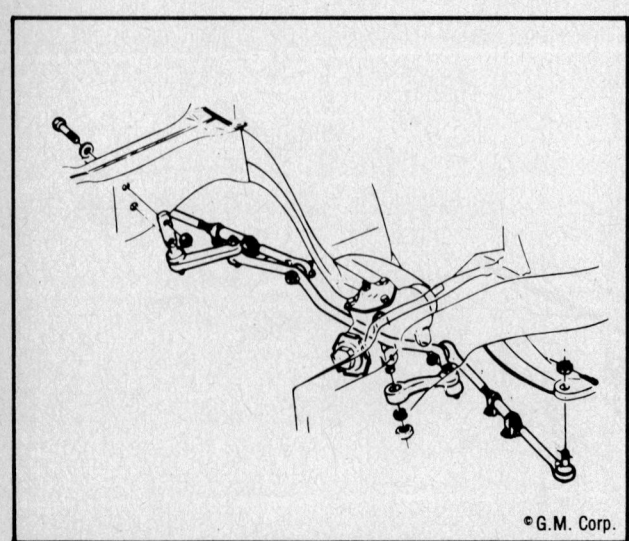

Monte Carlo

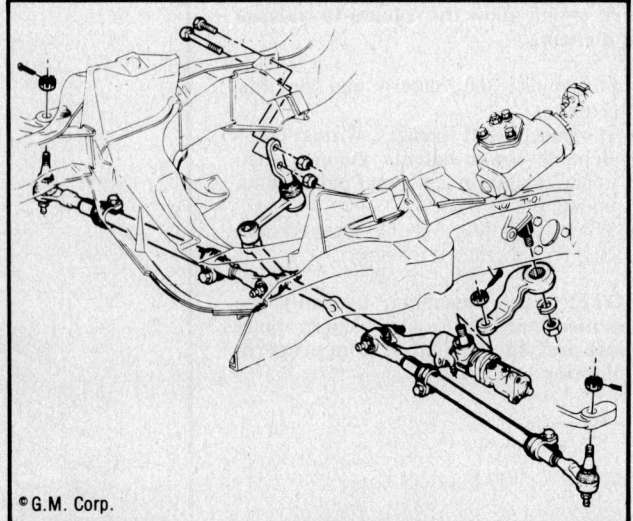

Corvette

Tilt steering column

© G.M. Corp.

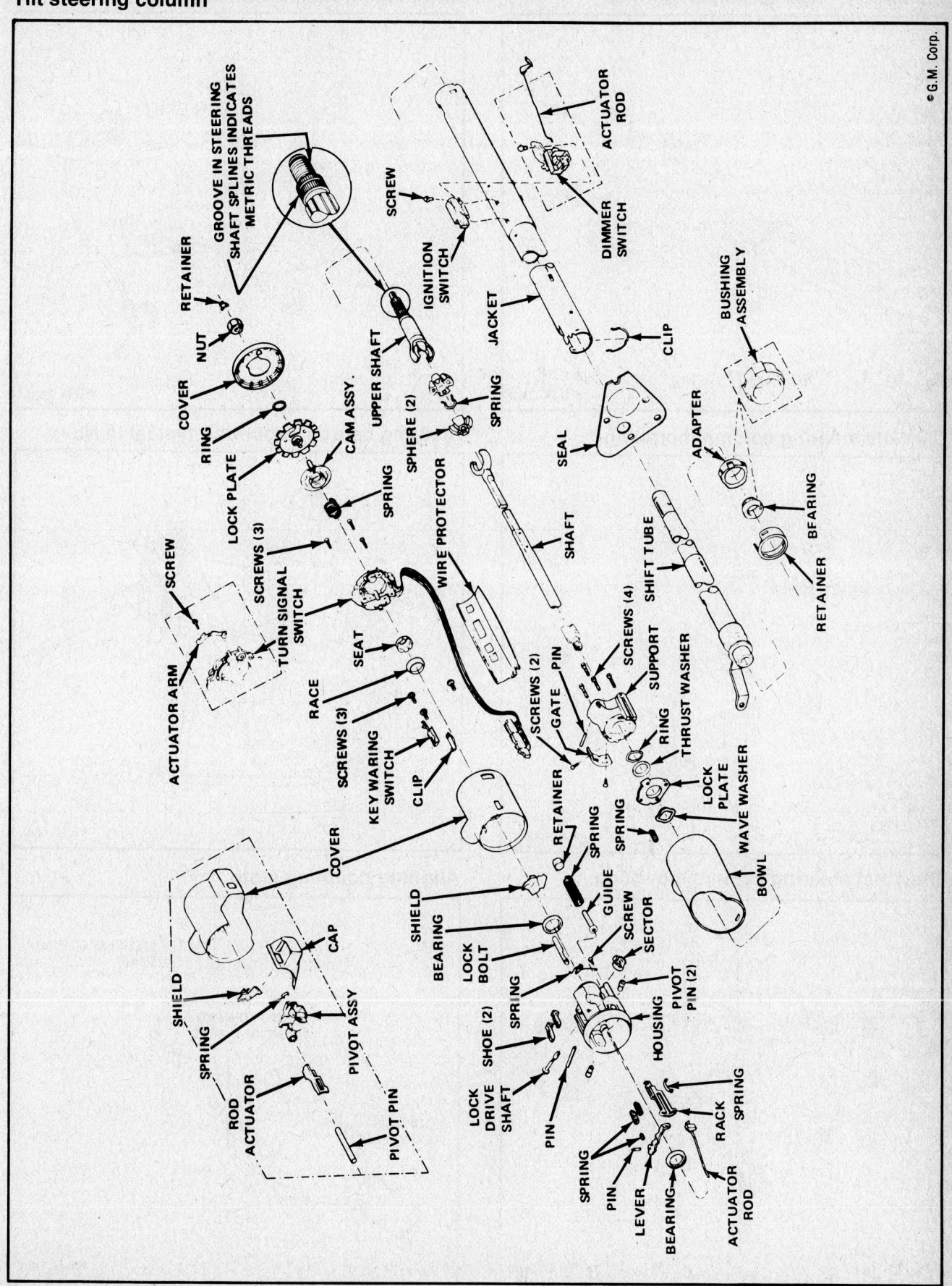

Camaro steering column mounting

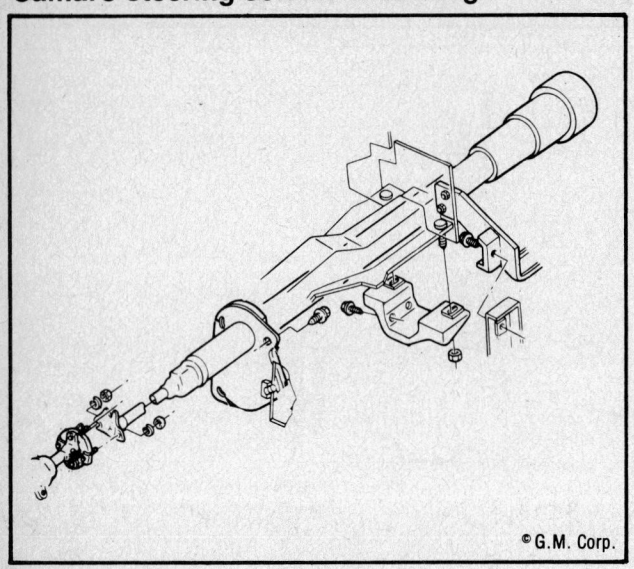

© G.M. Corp.

Automatic transmission indicator connection

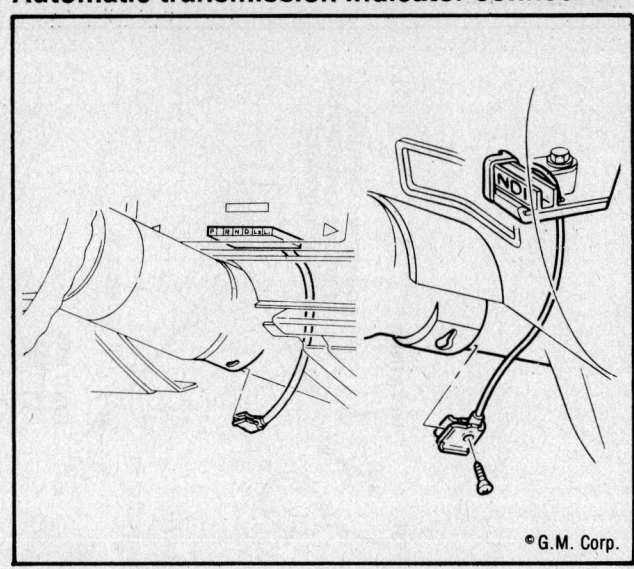

© G.M. Corp.

Corvette steering column mounting

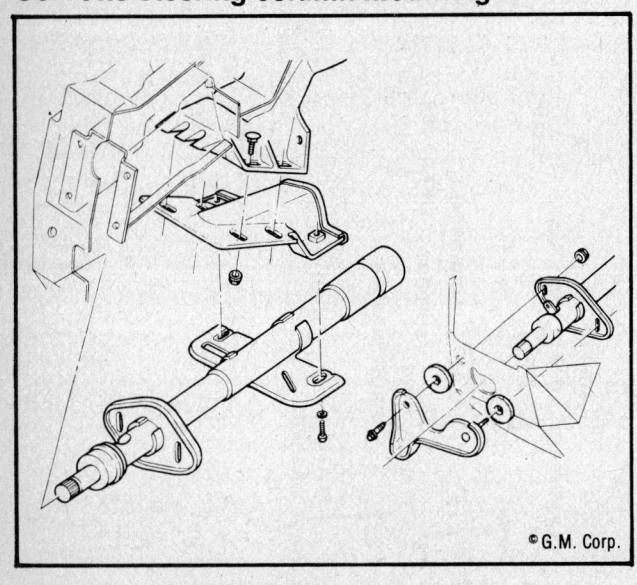

© G.M. Corp.

Steering column mounting typical in Nova

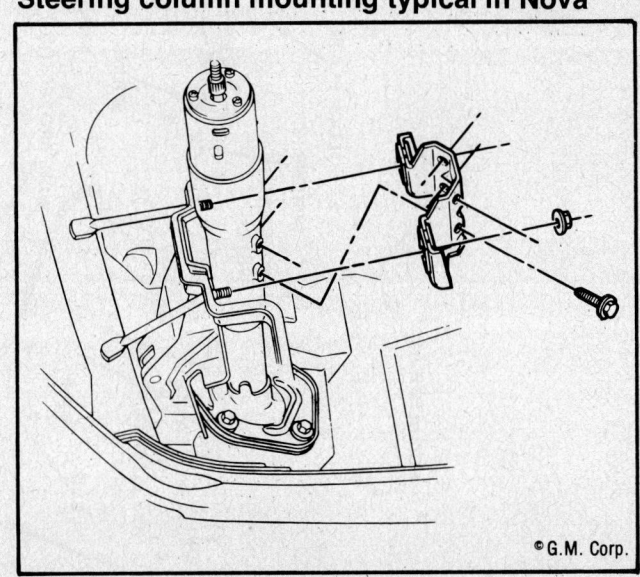

© G.M. Corp.

Chevrolet steering column mounting

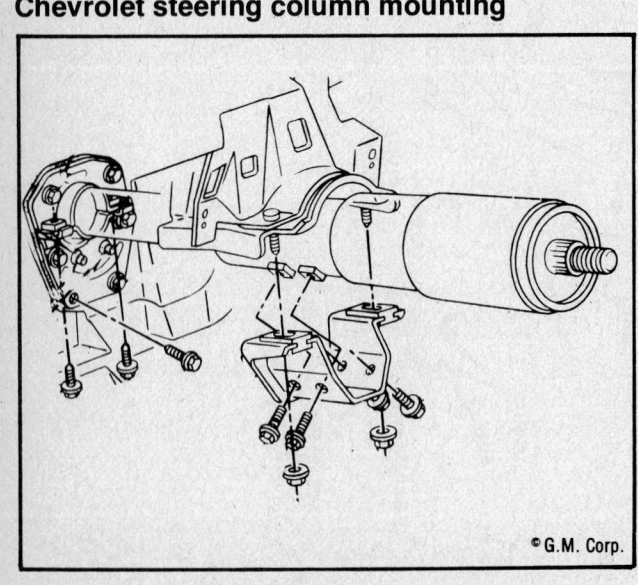

© G.M. Corp.

Aligning coupling slots

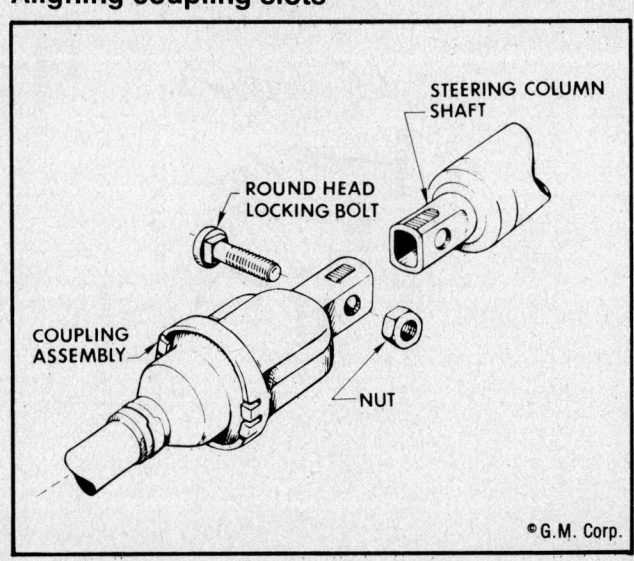

© G.M. Corp.

Brake power unit mounting typical in all except Corvette

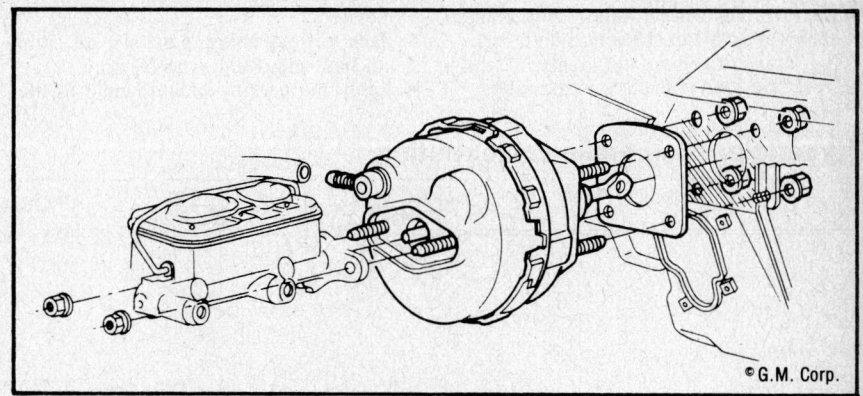

© G.M. Corp.

Brake Power Unit R&R

- Separate power unit and master cylinder, and unbolt power unit from firewall
- Disconnect the power brake push rod from the brake pedal.

Parking Brake Cable R&R

- Disconnect cables from equalizer
- For front cable replacement, disconnect the cable from the parking brake pedal or lever. On Corvette, the parking brake lever must be removed. Route new cable through in place of the old.
- For rear cable replacement, remove the brake drum, and separate the cable from brake shoes. On rear disc equipped Corvette, disconnect the cable at the rear wheel flange plate. Route new cable through in place of the old.

Parking Brake Adjustment

Except Corvette

- Correctly adjust service brakes.
- Apply parking brake two notches from fully released position.
- Tighten cable at equalizer until drag is felt at rear wheels.
- Release parking brake lever, and check that rear wheels turn without resistance.

Corvette power brake unit installation

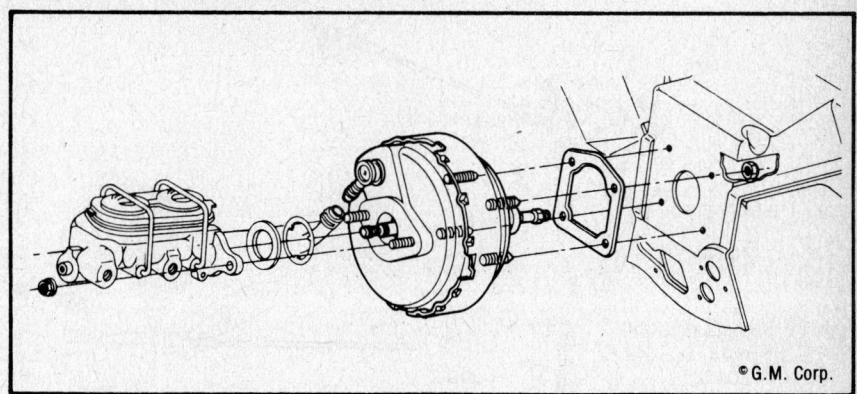

© G.M. Corp.

Parking brake cable routing except Corvette

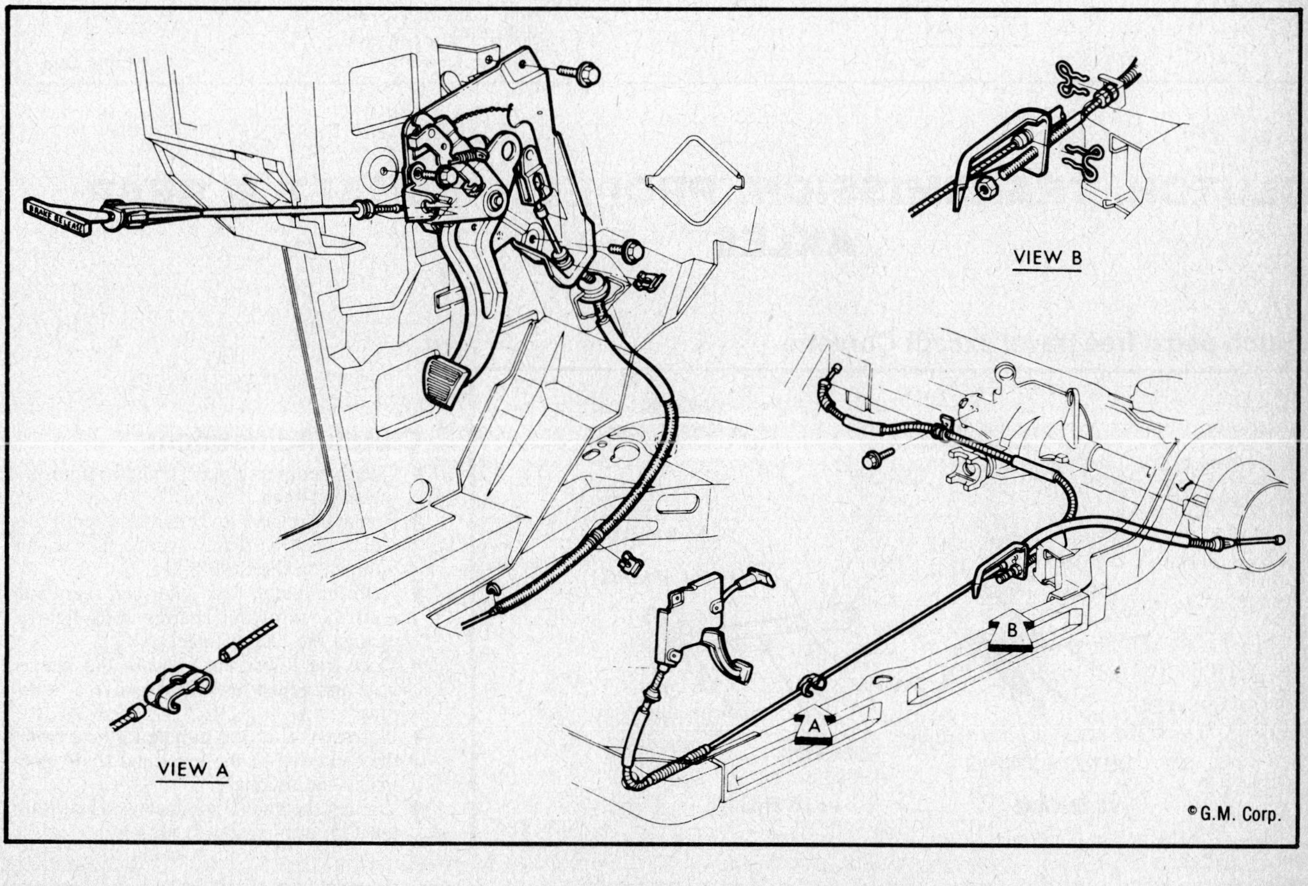

VIEW B

VIEW A

© G.M. Corp.

EXCEPT CAVALIER, CELEBRITY, CHEVETTE, CITATION, MONZA & VEGA

Corvette

- Remove rear wheels, and loosen brake cables at equalizer check nuts until parking brake levers move freely to the "off" position with slack in the cables.

- Line up the disc hole with the adjusting screw, and tighten until the disc will not move.
- Back off adjusting nuts six to eight notches, and install wheels.
- Apply the parking brake handle to the thirteenth notch, and tighten the check nuts until an 80 lb. pull is obtained while pulling into the fourteenth notch. Tighten the check nuts.
- Check that rear wheels turn in either direction without resistance.

Corvette parking brake cable routing

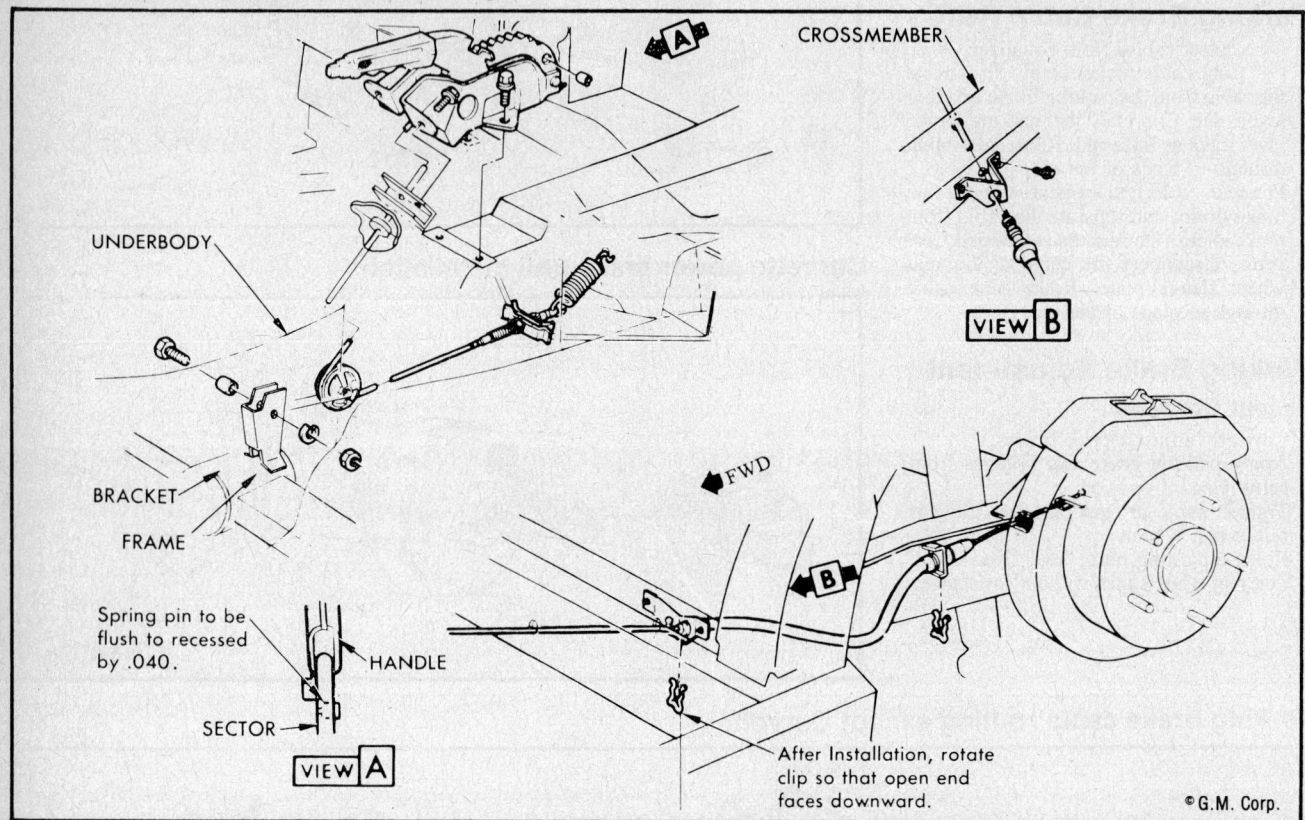

CLUTCH, TRANSMISSION, PROPELLER SHAFT & REAR AXLES

Clutch pedal free travel except Corvette

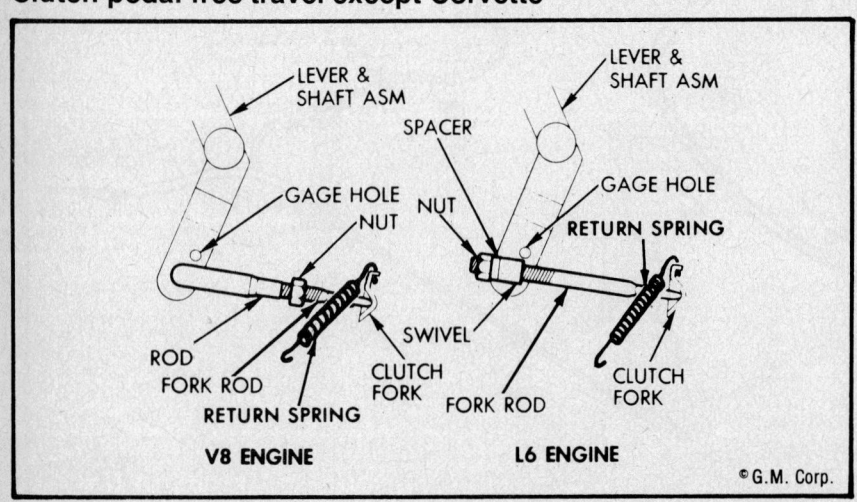

Clutch Adjustment

- Clutch pedal free play should be approximately 1 inch.
- Rotate the clutch lever and shaft until the clutch pedal is firmly against the rubber bumper on the dash brace.
- Push the clutch fork outer end rearward until the throwout bearing rests lightly against the clutch finger.
- Place the lower push rod in the gauge hole and adjust length to remove all free play.
- Place swivel or rod in hole farthest from the centering of the lever and shaft, and install the retainer.
- Tighten the swivel locknut, and reinstall the fork arm spring.

Clutch Adjustment Procedure

- Rotate Clutch Lever & Shaft Assembly until Clutch Pedal is firmly against Rubber Bumper on dash brace.
- Install Swivel (C) in hole in Clutch Lever & Shaft Assembly & install retainer.
- With Nuts (A) & (B) loose on Rod (D) apply 5 lbs. load in direction of Arrow (E) until bearing lightly contacts Belleville Spring Fingers.
- Tighten Lock Nut (B) toward Swivel (C) until dimension "X" is .400" ± .03".
- Tighten Nut (A) to lock Swivel (C) against Nut (B) using recommended torque.
- Above procedure to produce 1.25" ± .25" of Clutch Pedal "Free Travel" when measured at the center of the Pedal Pad.

Typical clutch linkage

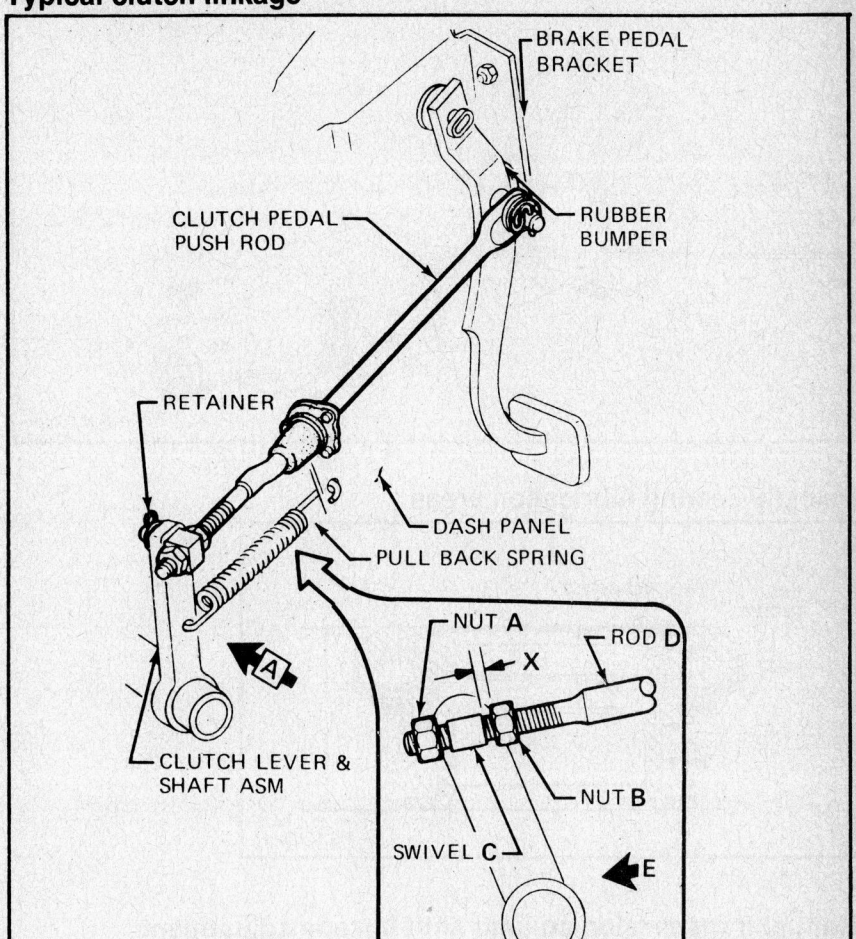

© G.M. Corp.

Corvette clutch adjustment procedure

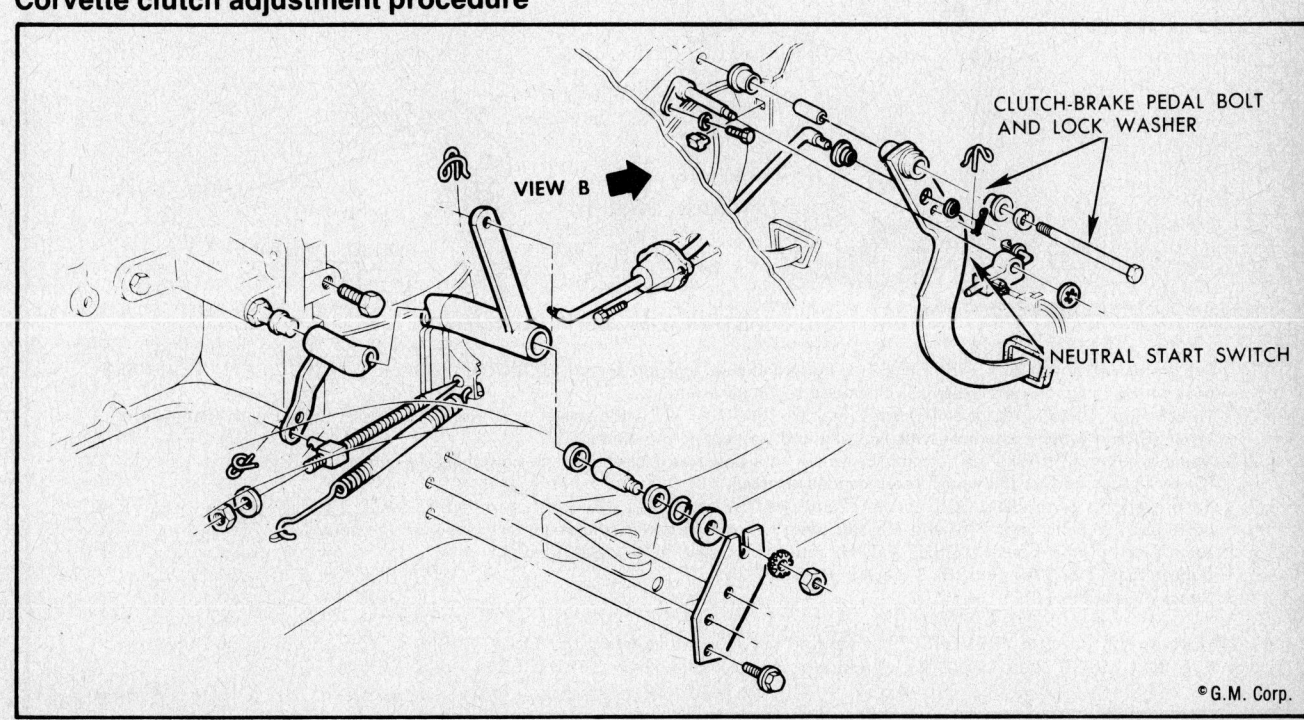

© G.M. Corp.

CHEVROLET
EXCEPT CAVALIER, CELEBRITY, CHEVETTE, CITATION, MONZA & VEGA

Typical manual transmission attachment

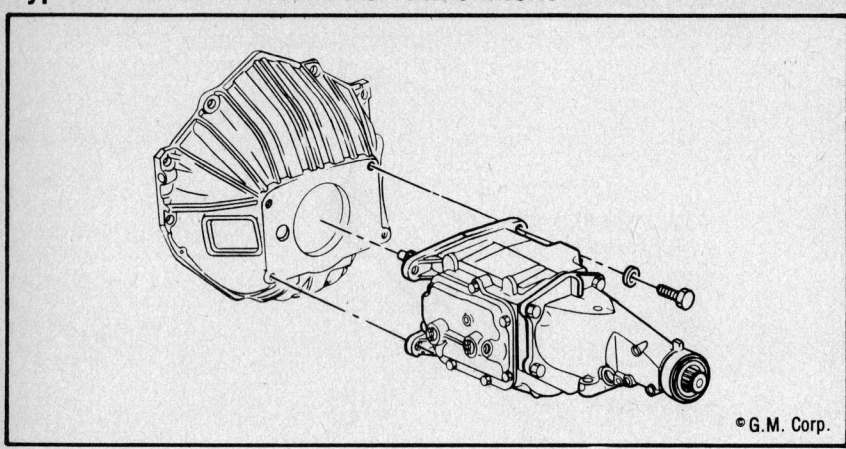

© G.M. Corp.

Release bearing lubrication areas

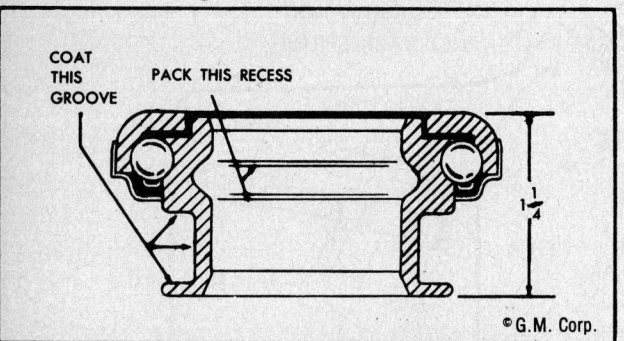

COAT THIS GROOVE
PACK THIS RECESS

© G.M. Corp.

Manual Transmission R&R
- Remove, relocate or disconnect the following:
  a. Shift lever knob, spring and T-handle.
  b. Speedometer cable
  c. Electrical connections
  d. Propeller shaft
  e. Shift rods
  f. Exhaust plumbing
  g. Crossmember
- On all except Corvette, remove the transmission-to-clutch housing upper retaining bolts, and insert guide pins. Remove the lower bolts, and slide the transmission back and out.
- On Corvette, remove the transmission-to-clutch mounting bolts and the lower left extension bolt. Rotate the transmission while moving it rearward and out of the vehicle.

Manual Transmission Linkage Adjustment
- Adjust the linkages so the shift lever positions correspond exactly to the transmission positions.
- Adjustment holes are provided in most shift assemblies through which drill rods can be placed for exact adjustment.

Manual transmission column shift linkage adjustment

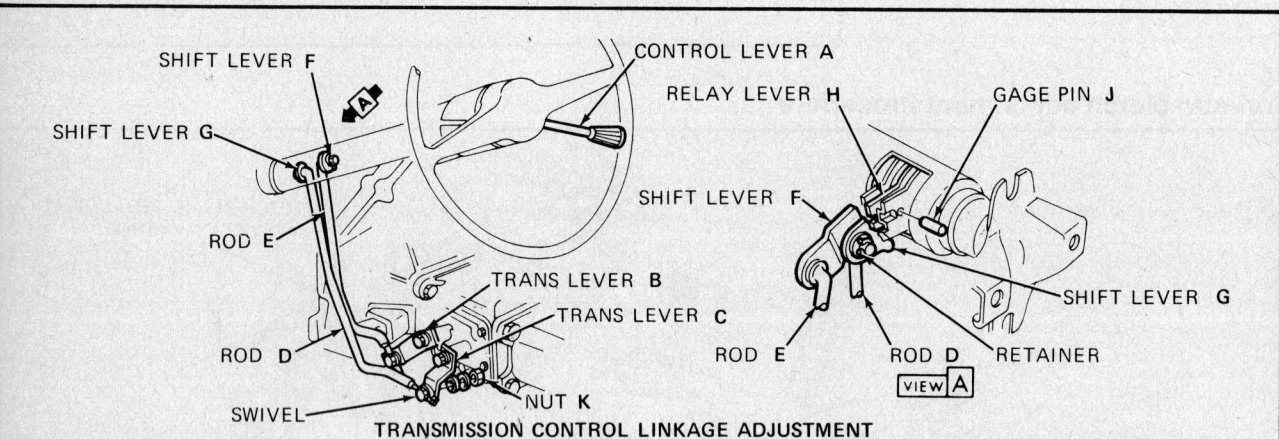

TRANSMISSION CONTROL LINKAGE ADJUSTMENT

1. Set Levers (A) and (C) in "REVERSE" position and turn ignition switch to "LOCK" position. **NOTE** Obtain "REVERSE" position by moving Trans Lever (C) clockwise to forward detent.
2. Attach Rod (D) to Shift Lever (G) with retainer. See View A. Slide swivel onto Rod (D). Insert Swivel with Clamp into Lever (C) and loosely assemble with Nut (K) and washers at this time.
3. Remove column "LASH" by rotating Lever (G) in a downward direction and complete attachment of Rod (D) to Lever (C) by tightening Nut (K) using recommended torque.
4. Turn ignition key to "UNLOCK" position and position Levers (A), (B) and (C) in "NEUTRAL". **NOTE** Obtain "NEUTRAL" position by moving Levers (B) and (C) clockwise to forward detent then counter-clockwise one detent.
5. Align gage holes in Levers (F), (G) and (H) and insert Gage Pin (J). See View A.
6. Repeat steps 2 & 3 for Rod (E) & Levers (B) & (F).
7. Remove Gage Pin (J).

NOTE With shift lever in "REVERSE" the ignition key must move freely to "LOCK" position. It must not be possibly to obtain ignition "LOCK" position in "NEUTRAL" or any gear other than "REVERSE".

© G.M. Corp.

Corvette manual transmission shift linkage adjustment

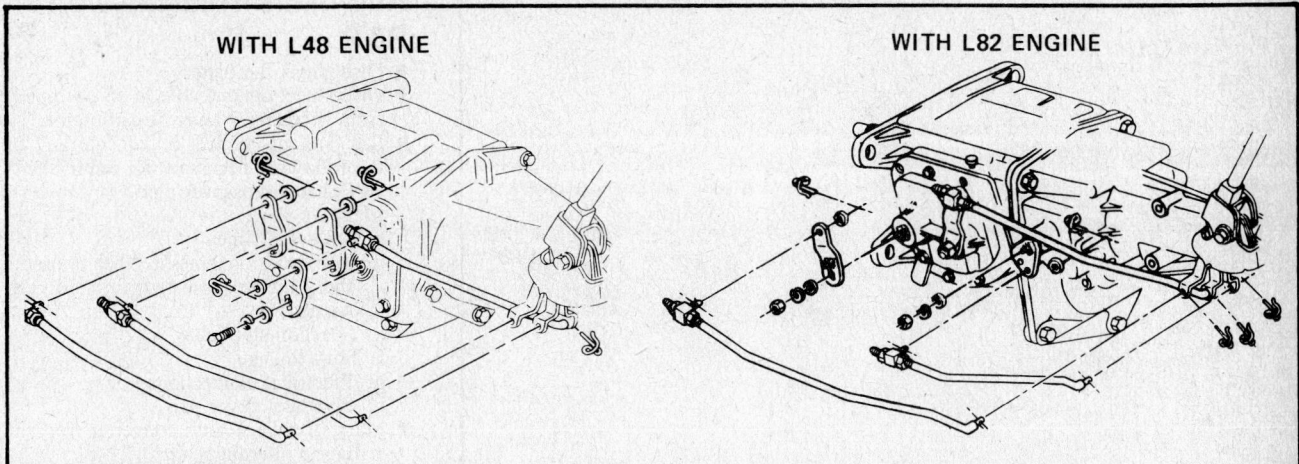

WITH L48 ENGINE   WITH L82 ENGINE

LINKAGE ADJUSTMENT

1. Set Levers (K), (M) & (P) in "NEUTRAL" position. **NOTE** Obtain "NEUTRAL" position by moving levers counter-clockwise to forward detent then clockwise one detent.
2. Move Lever (E) to "NEUTRAL" position. Align notches in Levers (C), (D) & (F) with notch in Lever & Brkt Asm & insert appropriate tool (H) to secure levers in "NEUTRAL" position.
3. Attach Rod (N) to Lever (C) with Retainer (G).
4. Loosely assemble Nuts (Q) & (S) & Swivel (R) on Rod (N).
5. Insert Swivel (R) into Lever (P), attach Washer (B) & secure with Retainer (A). Apply load on Lever (P) in direction of Arrow (Z). Tighten Nut (S) against Swivel then tighten Nut (Q) against Swivel using recommended torque.
6. Repeat steps 3, 4 & 5 for Rod (J) & Levers (F) & (K).
7. Repeat steps 3, 4 & 5 for Rod (L) & Levers (D) & (M).
8. Remove alignment tool from levers. **NOTE** After adjustments have been made, the centerlines of the shift levers must be aligned to each other to provide free crossover motion.
9. Be sure cables have adequate clearance around control rods.

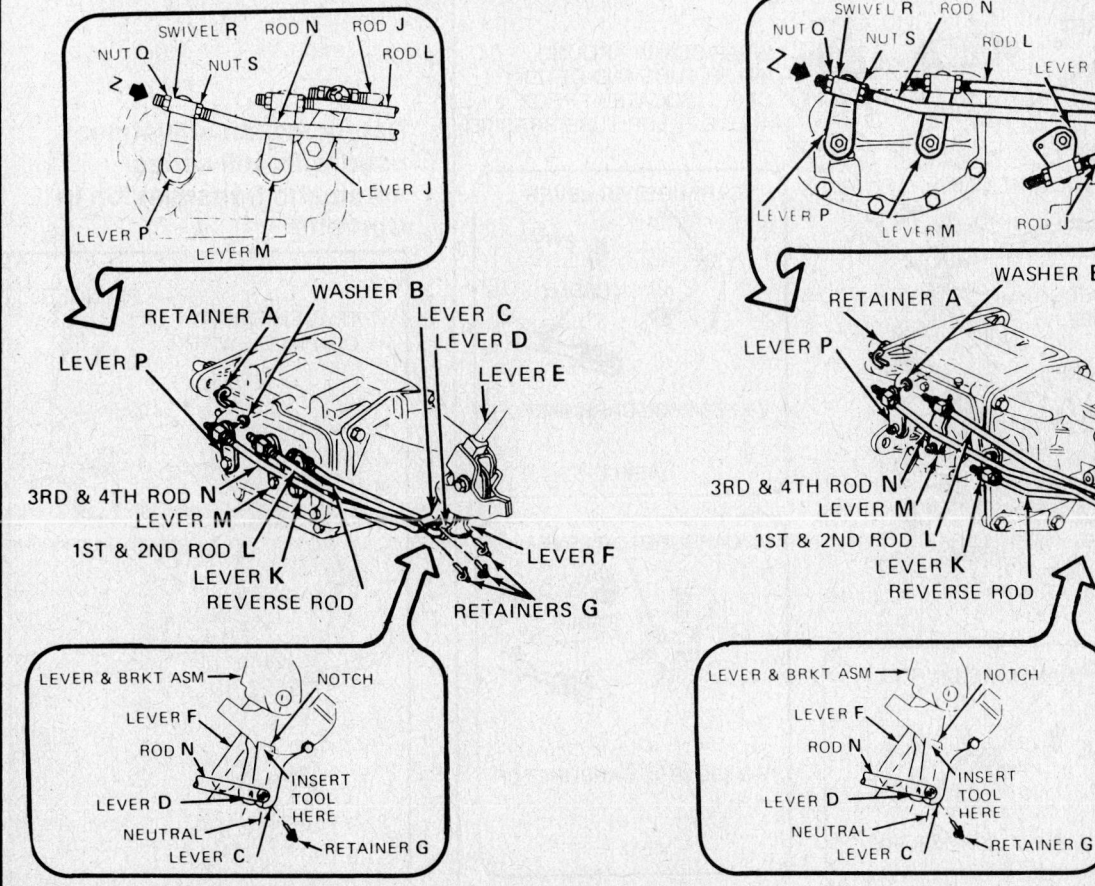

© G.M. Corp.

CHEVROLET

EXCEPT CAVALIER, CELEBRITY, CHEVETTE, CITATION, MONZA & VEGA

Automatic transmission typical attachment

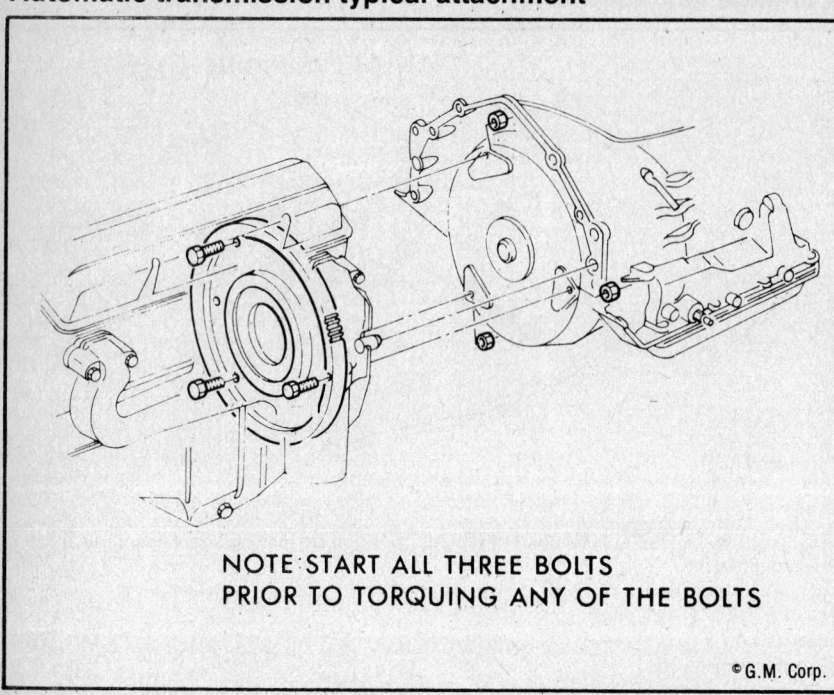

NOTE: START ALL THREE BOLTS
PRIOR TO TORQUING ANY OF THE BOLTS

© G.M. Corp.

Remove flexplate to converter bolts. Remove converter with transmission

Automatic Transmission R&R

- Disconnect the battery
- Disconnect detent cable (if so equipped) from accelerator lever or carburetor.
- Remove, disconnect or relocate any of the following necessary for removal:
  a. Exhaust crossover pipe
  b. Drive shaft
  c. Oil cooler lines
  d. Transmission crossmember (support the engine and transmission as needed)
  e. Speedometer cable
  f. Shift linkage
  g. Electrical connections
  h. Flywheel cover pan
- Mark flywheel and converter for installation reference.
- Remove mounting bolts, and slide transmission back and out of vehicle.

Automatic Transmission Cable Detent Adjustment

- Disengage the snap lock, and position the carburetor in the full open position.
- Push the snap lock on the cable down until the top is flush with the cable.

Automatic transmission detent cable adjustment

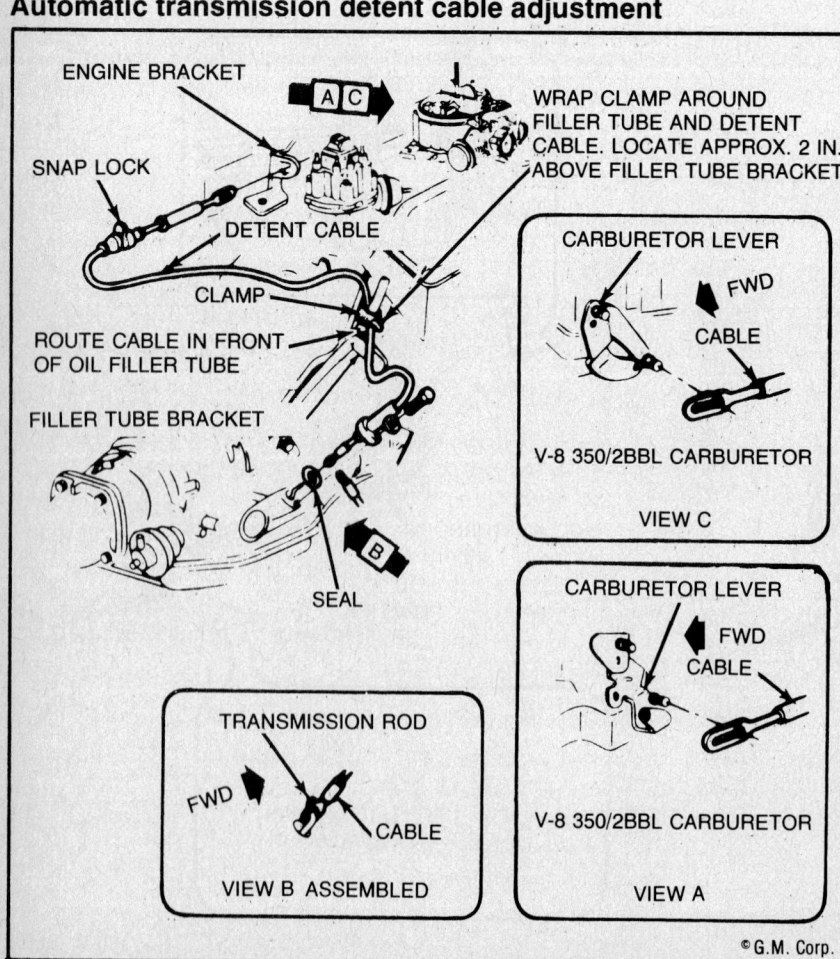

Detent switch adjustment used with 400 series automatic transmission in Corvette

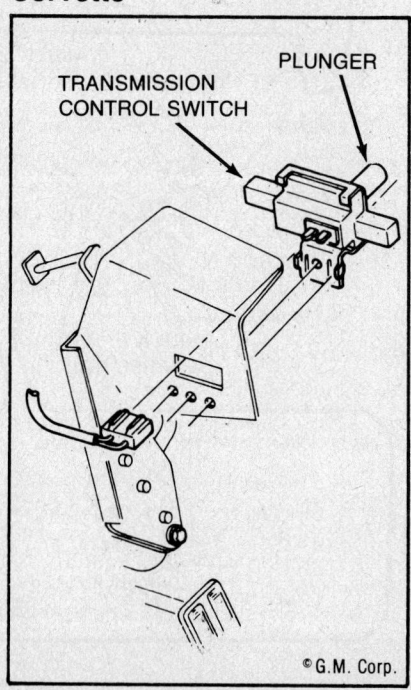

© G.M. Corp.

Automatic Transmission Manual Linkage Adjustment

- Adjust the linkage so the shift lever positions correspond exactly to the transmission positions.
- Some linkage arrangements have adjustment gage pin holes. In these a free pin fit will insure proper adjustment.
- After the linkage is adjusted, check operation of the neutral start switch and the backup lights.

Automatic transmission floorshift adjustment in Corvette

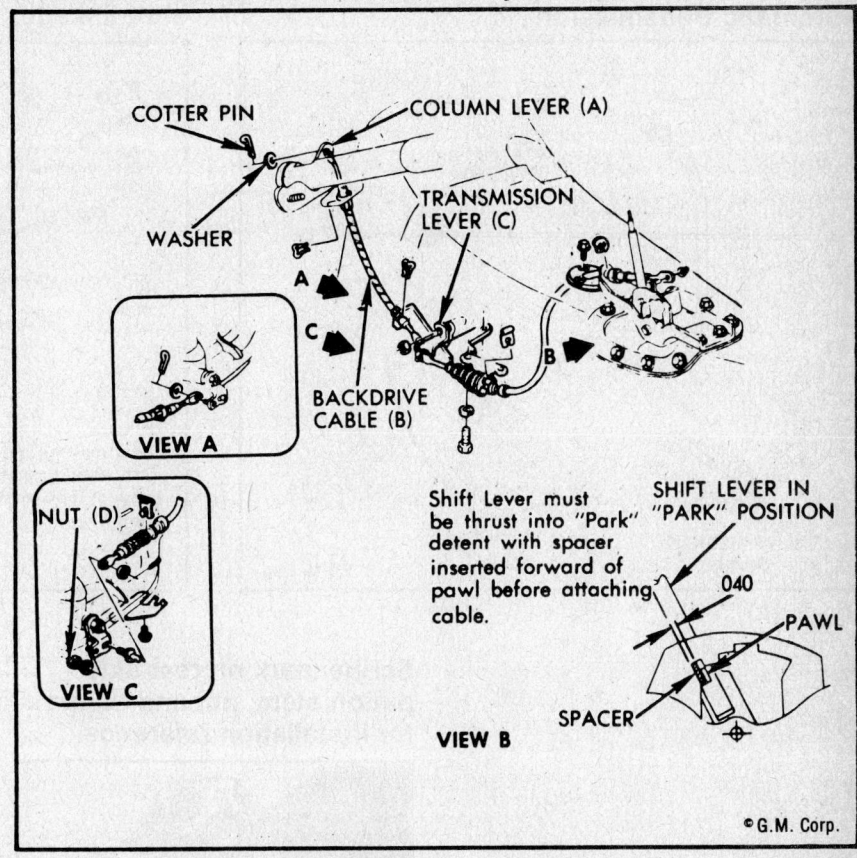

Shift Lever must be thrust into "Park" detent with spacer inserted forward of pawl before attaching cable.

© G.M. Corp.

Corvette automatic console shift linkage

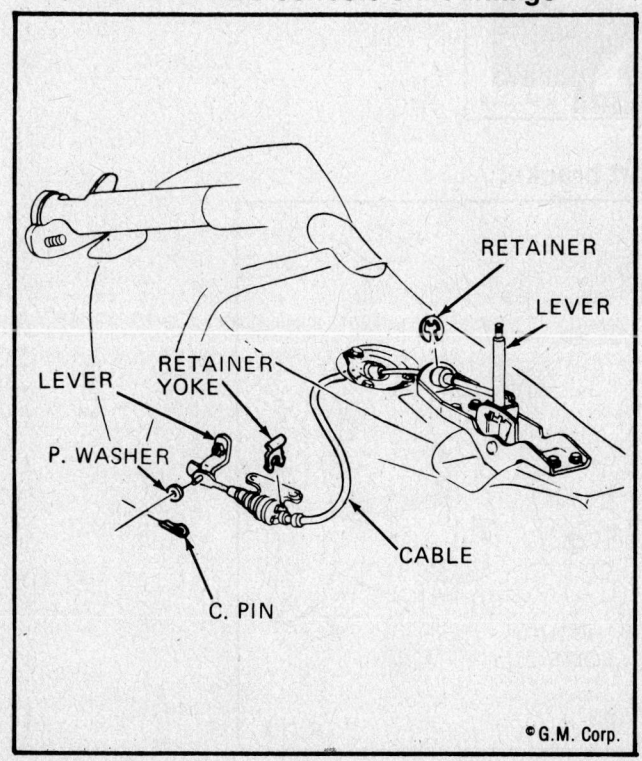

© G.M. Corp.

Automatic console shift linkage except Corvette

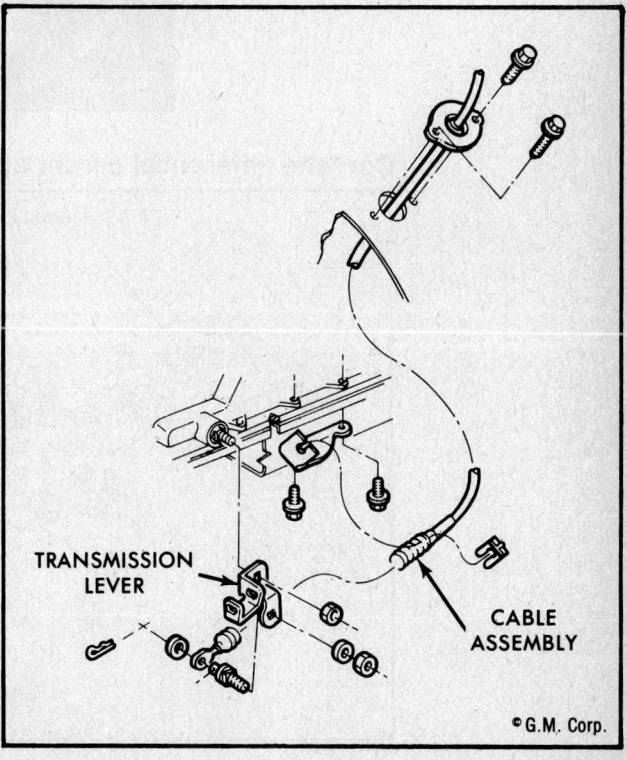

© G.M. Corp.

CHEVROLET

EXCEPT CAVALIER, CELEBRITY, CHEVETTE, CITATION, MONZA & VEGA

Column shift linkage with automatic transmission

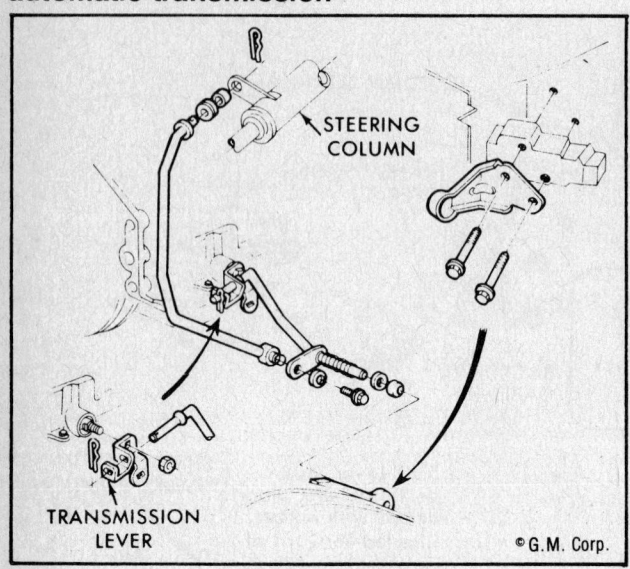

200 series automatic transmission shift linkage

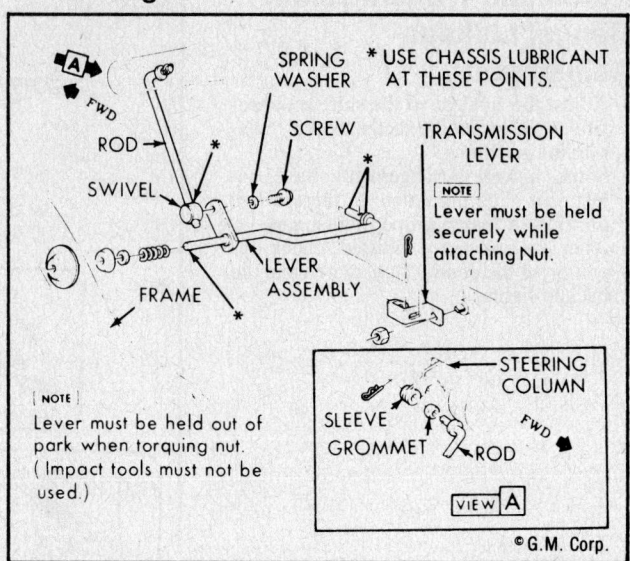

Scribe mark on rear axle pinion stem, nut and flange for installation reference

Pinion Oil Seal

- Scribe a line down the pinion stem, nut and flange, and count the number of exposed pinion stem threads. After replacing the seal, install these components in their exact original locations.

Corvette differential carrier support bracket

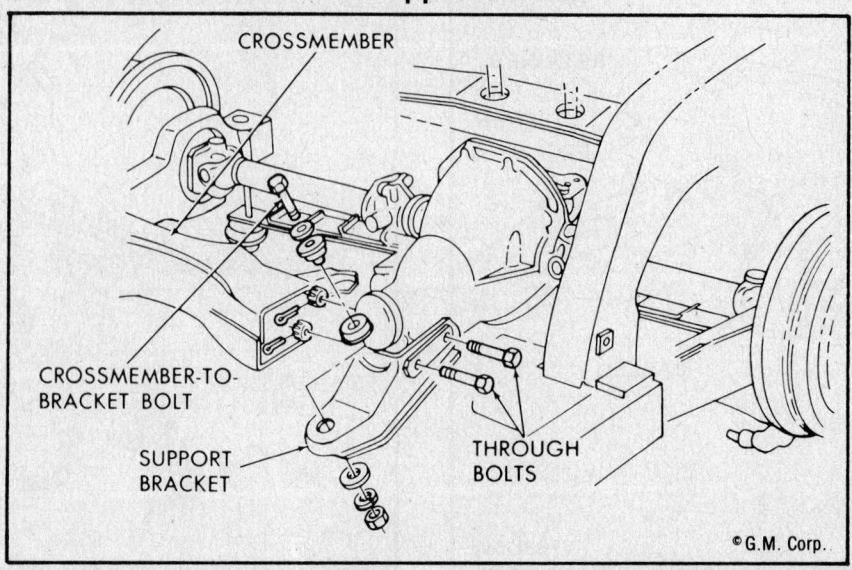

INDEX

CHRYSLER FRONT DRIVE CARS
ARIES, HORIZON, OMNI, RELIANT

MODEL IDENTIFICATION

1979 HORIZON
W.B. **96.7"** Length 172.7" 2+2, H/B, Ship. Wgt. 2247 Lbs.

1980 HORIZON
W.B. **99.2"**. Length 165". Ship. Wgt. Approx. 2191 Lbs.

1981 HORIZON
W.B. **99.7"**. Length 164.8". 4 Cyl. 4 Dr. Hatchback. Curb Wgt. 2170 Lbs.

1982 HORIZON
W.B. **99.7"**. Length 164.8". 4 Cyl. 4 Dr. Hatchback Curb Wgt. 2170 Lbs.

1980 HORIZON TC3
W.B. **96.7"**. Length 173". Ship. Wgt. Approx. 2133 Lbs.

1981 HORIZON TC3
W.B. **96.6"**. Length 173.5". 4 Cyl. 2 Dr. Hatchback. Curb Wgt. 2197 Lbs.

1982 HORIZON TC3
W.B. **96.6"**. Length 173.5". 4 Cyl. 2 Dr. Hatchback Curb Wgt. 2197 Lbs.

1979 OMNI
W.B. **96.7"** Length 173.3" 2+2, H/B, Ship. Wgt. 2247 Lbs.

1980 OMNI
W.B. **99.2"**. Length 165". Ship. Wgt. Approx. 2191 Lbs.

1980 OMNI 024
W.B. **96.7"**. Length 173". Ship. Wgt. Approx. 2133 Lbs.

1981 OMNI
W.B. **99.6"**. Length 164.8". 4 Cyl. 4 Dr. Curb Wgt. 2120 Lbs.

1982 OMNI
W.B. **99.6"**. Length 176.0". 4 Cyl. 2 Dr. Curb Wgt. 2328 Lbs.

1981-82 OMNI 024
W.B. **96.6**". Length 174.0". 4 Cyl. 2 Dr. Curb Wgt. 2197 Lbs.

1981-82 AIRIES
W.B. **99.6**". Length 176.0". 4 Cyl. 2 Dr. Curb Wgt. 2328 Lbs.

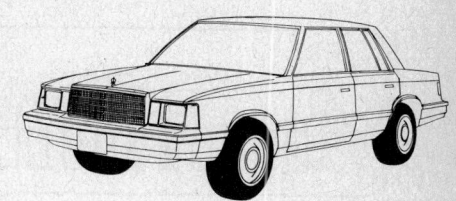

1981-82 RELIANT
W.B. **99.6**". Length 176.0". 4 Cyl. 2 Dr. Curb Wgt. 2328 Lbs.

1982 DODGE 400
W.B. **99.6**". Length 179.7". Curb Wgt. 2500 Lbs.

1982 LE BARON
W.B. **99.9**". Length 179.7". Curb Wgt. 2500 Lbs.

ENGINE FIRING ORDER

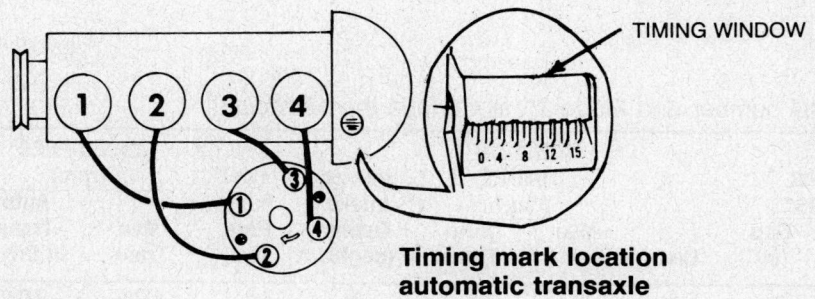

TIMING WINDOW

Timing mark location automatic transaxle

Four cylinder 104.7 CID (1700cc) engine
Engine firing order: 1-3-4-2
Distributor rotation: clockwise

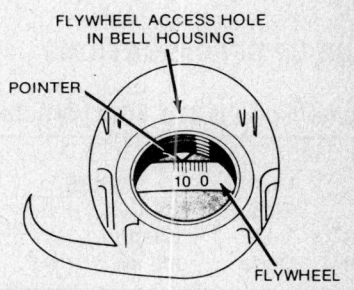

FLYWHEEL ACCESS HOLE IN BELL HOUSING

POINTER

FLYWHEEL

Timing mark location manual transaxle

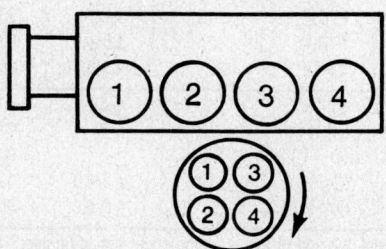

Four cylinder 135.9 CID (2200 cc) engine
Distributor rotation: clockwise (Chrysler)

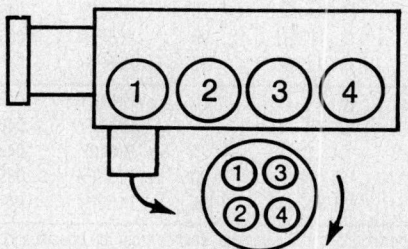

Four cylinder 155.9 CID (2600 cc) engine
Distributor rotation: clockwise (Mitsubishi)

CHRYSLER FRONT DRIVE CARS
ARIES, HORIZON, OMNI, RELIANT

VEHICLE IDENTIFICATION NUMBER (VIN)

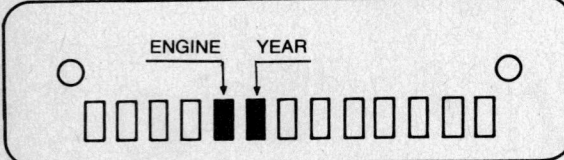 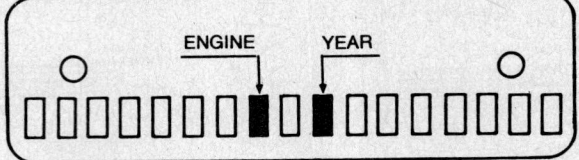

ENGINE SPECIFICATIONS

A 17-digit VIN is used, the 8th digit is the engine code and the 10th digit is the model year code

Year	Eng. V.I.N. Code	Engine No. Cyl. Disp. (cu in)	Carb Type	TAX H.P.	Horsepower @ rpm	Torque @ rpm (ft lbs)	Bore and Stroke	Comp. Ratio	Oil Pressure @2000 rpm
'78	A	104.7	2bbL	15.67	75@5600	90@3200	3.130×3.400	8.2:1	60–90①
'79	A	104.7	2bbL	15.67	75@5600†	90@3200†	3.130×3.400	8.2:1	60–90①
'80	A	104.7	2bbL	15.67	75@5600†	90@3200†	3.130×3.400	8.2:1	60–90
'81	A	104.7 (1.7L)	2bbL	15.67	75@5600	90@3200†	3.130×3.400	8.2:1	60–90
	B	135.0 (2.2L)	2bbL	18.92	90@4400	120@2200†	3.44×3.62	8.5:1	50
	D	155.9 (2.6L)	2bbL	21.53	105@5000	139@2500†	3.59×3.86	8.2:1	50–64
'82	A	104.7 (1.7L)	2bbL	15.67	75@5600	90@3200†	3.130×3.400	8.2:1	60–90
	B	135.0 (2.2L)	2bbL	18.92	90@4400	120@2200†	3.44×3.62	8.5:1	50
	D	155.9 (2.6L)	2bbL	21.53	105@5000	139@2500†	3.59×3.86	8.2:1	50–64

† Chilton estimate

TUNE-UP SPECIFICATIONS

Engine Code is the 8th character of the VIN number and Model Year Code is the 10th digit

Year	Eng. V.I.N. Code	ENGINE No. Cyl Disp. (cu in)	H.P.	SPARK PLUGS* Orig. Type	Gap (in)	Dist.	IGNITION TIMING (deg) Man Trans	Auto Trans	Valves Intake Opens (deg)B.	Fuel Pump Pres. (psi)	IDLE SPEED (rpm) Man Trans	Auto Trans in Drive
'78	A	104.7 (1.7L)	75	RN-12Y	.035	ELB	15B①	15B	14B	4–6	900②	900②
'79	A	104.7 (1.7L)	75	RN-12Y	.035	ELB	15B	15B	14B	4.4–5.9	900②	900②
'80	A	104.7 (1.7L)	75	RN-12Y	.035	ELB	10B	10B	14B	4–6	900②	900②
'81	A	104.7 (1.7L)	75	RN-12Y	.048⑥	ELB	10°B③	12°B③	14B	4–6	900②	900②
	A	104.7 (1.7L)	75	RN-12Y	.048⑥	ELB	10°B③	12°B③	14B	4–6	900②	900②
	A	104.7 (1.7L)	75	RN-12Y	.048⑥	④	10°B③	12°B③	14B	4–6	900②	900②
	B	135 (2.2L)	90	P65PR4	.035	④	10°B③	10°B③	12	4.5–6.0	900	900
	D	155.9 (2.6L)	105	P65PR4	.041⑦	④	7°B③	7°B③	25	4.6–6.0	800	800
'82	A	104.7 (1.7L)	75	RN-12Y	.048⑥	ELB	③	③	14B	4–6	900②	900②
	A	104.7 (1.7L)	75	RN-12Y	.048⑥	ELB	③	③	14B	4–6	900	900②
	A	104.7 (1.7L)	75	RN-12Y	.048⑥	④	③	③	14B	4–6	900	900②
	B	135 (2.2L)	90	P65PR4	.035	④	③	③	12	4.5–6.0	900	900
	D	155.9 (2.6L)	105	P65PR4	.041⑦	④	③	③	25	4.6–6.0	800	800

NOTE: Should the specifications in this manual deviate from the specifications on the engine compartment decal, the specifications on the decal should be used.
ELB—Electronic Lean Burn
① Canada—10B
② W/air conditioning—850 rpm; propane enriched idle speed For all models—1075 rpm
③ See engine decal. Check timing computer number
④ Chrysler Combustion Computer
⑤ Millimeter
⑥ Canada .035
⑦ Canada .030

FLUID CAPACITIES—COOLANT, FUEL & LUBRICANT

Year	VIN Code	Engine No. of Cyl. Displacement (cu in)	Engine Crankcase Add ½ Qt For New Filter	TRANSMISSION Pts. to Refill after Draining Manual 3-Speed	4-Speed	Automatic	Drive Axle (pts)	Gasoline Tank (gal)	COOLING SYSTEM Qts. With Heater	With A/C
'78	A	4-104.7 (1.7L)	4	—	2.8①	5③	2.37②	13	6.5④	6.5④
'79	A	4-104.7 (1.7L)	4	—	2.8①	6.2③	2.00②	13	6.5④	6.5④
'80	A	4-104.7 (1.7L)	4	—	2.8①	6.2③	2.00②	13	6.5④	6.5④
'81	A	4-104.7 (1.7L)	4	—	⑤	⑥	⑦	13	6.0	6.0
	B	4-135.0 (2.2L)	4	—	⑤	⑥	⑦	13	7.0	7.0
	D	4-155.9 (2.6L)	4.5	—	⑤	⑥	⑦	13	8.5	8.5
'82	A	4-104.7 (1.7L)	4	—	⑤	⑥	⑦	13	6.0	6.0
	B	4-135.0 (2.2L)	4	—	⑤	⑥	⑦	13	7.0	7.0
	D	4-155.9 (2.6L)	4.5	—	⑤	⑥	⑦	13	8.5	8.5

① Integral with front drive axle
② With automatic transmission only
③ 14.5 pts. if converter is drained
④ Includes .5 qt. for coolant reserve tank
⑤ A 412-1.5 qts.
   A 460-2.0 qts.
⑥ W/104.7 engine 7.3 qts.
   W/135.0 engine 7.5 qts.
   W/155.9 engine 8.5 qts.
⑦ Differential only auto. 1.2 qts.

BRAKE SPECIFICATIONS

Year	Model	Master Cylinder Bore Diameter	CALIPER OR WHEEL CYLINDER BORE DIAMETER Front	Rear	BRAKE DRUM/ROTOR DIAMETER Front	Rear	DISC SPECIFICATIONS Resurfacing Min. Thickness	Parallel Variation	Runout Maximum
'78-'80	ALL	.877"	1.89"	.628"	9.0"	7.87"	.461①	.005"	.004"
'81	Horizon/Omni "L"Body	.877"	1.89"	5/8"	9.0"	7.87"	.461	.005"	.004"
	Aries/Reliant "K"Body	.875"	2.130"	5/8"	9.4"	7.9"	.461	.005"	.004"
'82	Horizon/Omni "L"Body	.877"	1.89"	5/8"	9.0"	7.87"	.461	.005"	.004"
	Aries/Reliant "K"Body	.875"	2.130"	5/8"	9.4"	7.9"	.461	.005"	.004"

NOTE: Do not hone master cylinder bore
① Discard thickness is .431"

VALVE SPECIFICATIONS

Year	Engine No. Cyl. Displacement (cu in)	Eng. VIN No.	Intake Seat Angle (deg)	Exhaust Seat Angle (deg)	Intake Face Angle (deg)	Exh. Face Angle (deg)	Spring Test Pressure③ (lbs @ in)	Spring Installed Height (in)	STEM TO GUIDE CLEARANCE (in) Intake	Exhaust	STEM DIAMETER (in) Intake	Exhaust
'78-'80	104.7 (1.7L)	A	45	45	45⅓	43⅓①	100@.878②	1 9/32	.001–.002	.001–.002	.314	.314
'81	104.7 (1.7L)	A	45	45	43⅓	43⅓	100@.878	1 9/32	.001–.002	.001–.002	.314	.314
	135 (2.2L)	B	45	45	45	45	17501.22	1.65	.001–.003	.002–.004	.312	.311
	155.9 (2.6L)	D	45④	45④	45	45	55.@.8⅛	1.590"	.0012–.0024	.004–.006	.0012–.0024	.0020–.0035
'82	104.7 (1.7L)	A	45	45	43⅓	43⅓	100@.878	1 9/32	.001–.002	.001–.002	.314	.314
	135 (2.2L)	B	45	45	45	45	17501.22	1.65	.001–.003	.002–.004	.312	.311
	155.9 (2.6L)	D	45④	45④	45	45	55.@.8⅛	1.590"	.0012–.0024	.004–.006	.0012–.0024	.0020–.0035

① Exhaust valves are to be ground by hand only
② Inner spring 48.49 lbs.@.720"
③ Valve open
④ Jet valve 45°

CRANKSHAFT AND CONNECTING ROD SPECIFICATIONS

All measurements are given in inches

Year	Engine No. of Cyl. Displacement (cu in)	VIN	CRANKSHAFT Main Brg. Journal Dia	Main Brg. Oil Clearance	Shaft End Play	Thrust on No.	CONNECTING ROD Journal Diameter	Oil Clearance	Side Clearance
'78	104.7	A	2.13	.0008–.003	.003–.007	3	1.81	.0004–.0025	.002–.009
'79	104.7	A	2.13	.0008–.003	.004–.011	3	1.81	.0007–.0029	.0020–.0122
'80	104.7	A	2.13	.0008–.003	.004–.011	3	1.81	.007–.0029	.0020–.0122
'81	104.7 (1.7L)	A	2.1244/2.1236	.002	.007	3	1.8094–1.8087	0.028	0.014
	135 (2.2L)	B	2.362/2.363	.0004–.0026	.002–.007	3	1.968	.0004–.0026	.005–.013
	155.9 (2.6L)	D	2.3622	.0008–.0026	.002–.007	3	2.0866	.0008–.0028	.004–.010
'82	104.7 (1.7L)	A	2.1244/2.1236	.002	.007	3	1.8094–1.8087	0.028	0.014
	135 (2.2L)	B	2.362/2.363	.0004–.0026	.002–.007	3	1.968	.0004–.0026	.005–.013
	155.9 (2.6L)	D	2.3622	.0008–.0026	.002–.007	3	2.0866	.0008–.0028	.004–.010

VALVE ADJUSTMENT SPECIFICATIONS

Year	Eng. VIN No.	Engine (cu in)	INTAKE (in)	INTAKE (mm)	EXHAUST (in)	EXHAUST (mm)
'78–80(HOT)①	A	104.7 (1.7L)	.008–.012 Hot	.20–.30	.016–.020 Hot	.40–.50 Hot
'81	A	104.7 (1.7L)	.003–.012 Hot	.20–.30 Hot	.016–.020	.40–.50 Hot
	B	135 (2.2L)	③	③	③	③
	D	155.9 (2.6L)	.006 Hot②	.15 Hot②	.010 Hot	.25 Hot
'82	A	104.7 (1.7L)	.003–.012 Hot	.20–.30 Hot	.016–.020	.40–.50 Hot
	B	135 (2.2L)	③	③	③	③
	D	155.9 (2.6L)	.006②	.15②	.010	.25

① Engine off; do not rotate engine by turning camshaft pulley as this will stretch the drive belt
② Jet valve adjustment (hot)-.006in. (.15 mm). Adjust jet valve first
③ Hydraulic lash adjusters—not adjustable

TORQUE SPECIFICATIONS

Readings in ft/lbs. (N-M)

Year	VIN Code	Engine Displacement (cu in)	Cylinder Head Bolts	Rod Bearing Bolts (nuts)	Main Bearing Bolts	Crankshaft Pulley Bolts	Flywheel To C/Shaft	Flywheel To Pressure Plate	MANIFOLD Intake	MANIFOLD Exhaust
'78	A	4-104.7 (1.7L)	60(81)②	35(47)	47(64)	20(27)①	55(76)	15(20)	16.7(23)	12.25
'79	A	4-104.7 (1.7L)	60(81)②	35(47)	47(64)	20(27)①	55(76)	15(20)	16.7(23)	12.25
'80	A	4-104.7 (1.7L)	60(81)②	35(47)	47(64)	20(27)①	55(76)	15(20)	16.7(23)	12.25
'81	A	4-104.7 (1.7L)	60(81)	35(47)	47(64)	58(98)	55(76)	15(20)	16.7(23)	15.25
	B	4-135 (2.2L)	④	40(54)③	30(41)③	50(67)	55(76)	15(20)	15.8(23)	15.8
	B	4-155.9 (2.6L)	⑤	34(46)	58(79)	87(107)	60(80)	15(20)	15.8(23)	15.0

TORQUE SPECIFICATIONS

Readings in ft/lbs. (N-M)

Year	VIN Code	Engine Displacement (cu in)	Cylinder Head Bolts	Rod Bearing Bolts (nuts)	Main Bearing Bolts	Crankshaft Pulley Bolts	Flywheel To C/Shaft	Flywheel To Pressure Plate	MANIFOLD Intake	MANIFOLD Exhaust
'82	A	4-104.7 (1.7L)	60(81)	35(47)	47(64)	58(98)	55(76)	15(20)	16.7(23)	15.25
	B	4-135 (2.2L)	④	40(54)③	30(41)③	50(67)	55(76)	15(20)	15.8(23)	15.8
	B	4-155.9 (2.6L)	⑤	34(46)	58(79)	87(107)	60(80)	15(20)	15.8(23)	15.0

① Timing belt sprocket bolt (crankshaft center) 58 ft/lbs.

② After tightening all bolts in proper sequence, re-tighten all bolts ¼ turn in proper sequence.

③ +¼ turn

④ 4 torque sequence
1 = 30 ft lbs
2 = 45 ft lbs
3 = 45 ft lbs
4 = +¼ turn

⑤ Cold 69 lbs.-(94N-M)
Hot 76 lbs.

1979 ELECTRONIC SPARK CONTROL SYSTEM

CUSTOM I.C. SPARK CONTROL COMPUTER PART NUMBER	5206467	5206501	5206516	5206525	5606526	5206666
Spark Timer Advance Schedule	8°	8°	8°	8°	8°	8°
Delay Time in Seconds	60	60	60	60	60	60
Throttle Advance Schedule	0°	0°	4°–6°@100°F	4°–6°@100°F	0°	4°–6°@100°F
Test Transducer Core Out 1 Inch	0″	0″	4°–6°@140°F	4°–6°@140°F	0°	4°–6°@140°F
Vacuum Advance Schedule (A) Operating Vacuum Range	0″–14″	0″–14″	0″–14″	0″–14″	0″–14″	0″–14″
(B) Advance Off Idle (Carb Switch Isolated With Paper)	None	6°–10°	2°–6°	2°–6°	2°–6°	6°–10°
(C) Accumulation Time in Minutes	8	7	8	8	8	7
(D) Advance After Accumulation Time	18°–22°	18°–22°	18°–22°	18°–22°	18°–22°	18°–22°
Speed Advance (Ground Carb Switch and Disconnect Throttle Transducer Before Checking) @2000 RPM	6°–10°	6°–10°	6°–10°	5°–9°	6°–10°	5°–9°
@4000 RPM	18°–22°	18°–22°	18°–22°	13°–17°	18°–22°	13°–17°

NOTE: The above specifications are published from the latest information available at the time of publication. If anything differs from those on the Emission Control Information Label, use the specification on the label.

1979 ELECTRONIC SPARK CONTROL SYSTEM

CUSTOM I.C. SPARK CONTROL COMPUTER PART NUMBER	5206721	5206784	5206785	5206790	5206793
Vacuum Advance (Range)	0″–10″	0″–10″	0″–10″	0″–10″	0″–10″
Crank + Electrical = (Basic Timing)	10° + 5°	10° + 5°	10° + 5°	10° + 5°	10° + 0°
Speed Advance (Ground Carb Switch) @ 1100 RPM	0°–3°	0°–3°	0°–3°	0°–3°	0°–3°
@ 2000 RPM	8°–12°	8°–12°	8°–12°	8°–12°	8°–12°
Zero Time Offset	6°–10°	2°–6°	3°–7°	0°–3°	0°–3°
Accumulator Clock Up (in minutes)	8	8	8	8	8
Vacuum Advance—Full Accumulator @ 2000 RPM	18°–22°	18°–22°	18°–22°	18°–22°	18°–22°
@ 3000 RPM	23°–27°	23°–27°	28°–32°	28°–32°	23°–27°
Throttle Maximum Advance (Throttle Open 20°)	0°	0°	0°	0°	0°

CHRYSLER FRONT DRIVE CARS

ARIES, HORIZON, OMNI, RELIANT

1980 ELECTRONIC SPARK CONTROL SYSTEM

CUSTOM I.C. SPARK CONTROL COMPUTER PART NUMBER		5213008	5213012
Crank + Run = (Basic Timing)		10° + 0°	10° + 0°
Vacuum Advance (Range)		0″–10″	0″–10″
Zero Time Advance		18°–22°	23°–27°
Accumultor Clock Up (in minutes)		0	0
Vacuum Advance—Full Accumulator	@ 2000 RPM	5°–9°	5°–9°
	@ 3000 RPM	18°–22°	23°–27°
Speed Advance (Ground Carb Switch)	@ 1100 RPM	0°–3°	0°–3°
	@ 2000 RPM	8°–12°	13°–17°
	@ 4800 RPM	18°–22°	20°–24°
Warm Up Schedule (in seconds)		25	25
Throttle Maximum Advance (Throttle Open 20°)		0°	0°

NOTE: The above specifications are published from the latest information available at the time of publication. If anything differs from those on the Emission Control Information Label, use the specification on the label.

1981 ELECTRONIC SPARK CONTROL SYSTEM

Computer Part Number	5213101	5213111	5213116	5213123	5213268	5213337
Engine Application	1.7L Fed (M)	1.7L Fed (A)	1.7L Can (M)	1.7L Can (A)	1.7L Fed (M)	1.7L Can (A)
Basic Timing	12° BTDC	10° BTDC	5° BTDC	10° BTDC	12° BTDC	10° BTDC
Curb Idle Speed	900 RPM	900 RPM	900 RPM	900 RPM	900 RPM	900 RPM
Vacuum Range	0″–10″	0″–10″	0″–10″	0″–10″	0″–10″	0″–10″
Accumultor Clock Up (in minutes)	0	0	7	7	0	7
Spark Advance Test 2000 RPM 16″ Vacuum	38° ± 4°	35° ± 4°	45° ± 4°	35° ± 4°	43° ± 4°	35° ± 4°
Electronic EGR	No	No	No	No	No	No
Electronic Throttle Control	No	No	No	No	No	No
Detonation Suppression	No	No	No	No	No	No
O₂ Feedback Air Switching (Electronic)	No	No	No	No	No	No
Temperature Sensor	Switch 65°C(150°F)	Switch 65°C(150°F)	Switch 65°C(150°F)	Switch 65°C(150°F)	Switch 65°C(150°F)	Switch 65°C(150°F)

NOTE: The following specifications are published from the latest information available at the time of publication. If anything differs from those on the Emission Control Information Lable, use the specification on the label.

A—Automatic Transmission
M—Manual Transmission
BTDC—Before Top Dead Center
Can.—Canada
Fed.—Federal
Cal.—California

WHEEL LUG TORQUE DATA

Year	Model	Torque ft. lbs.
'78	ALL	80
'79	ALL	80
'80	ALL	80
'81	ALL	80
'82	ALL	80

1981 ELECTRONIC SPARK CONTROL SYSTEM

Computer Part Number	5213148	5213249	5213342	5213343	5213345
Engine Application	2.2L Can (M-A)	2.2L Fed (M)	2.2L Can (M-A)	2.2L Fed (A)	2.2L Cal (A)
Basic Timing	10° BTDC	10° BTDC	10° BTDC	10° BTDC	10° BTDC
Curb Idle Speed	900 RPM	900 RPM	900 RPM	900 RPM	900 RPM
Vacuum Range	0″–10″	0″–10″	0″–10″	0″–10″	0″–10″
Accumultor Clock Up (in minutes)	0	0	7	7	0
Spark Advance Test 2000 RPM 16″ Vacuum	33° ± 4°	33° ± 4°	33° ± 4°	25° ± 4°	25° ± 4°
Electronic EGR	No	No	No	No*	No*
Electronic Throttle Control	No	No	No	No	No
Detonation Suppression	No	No	No	No	No
O$_2$ Feedback Air Switching (Electronic)	No	No	No	No	No
Temperature Sensor	Switch 52°C(125°F)	Switch 52°C(125°F)	Switch 52°C(125°F)	Collant Sensor	Switch 52°C(125°F)

NOTE: The following specifications are published from the latest information available at the time of publication. If anything differs from those on the Emission Control Information Lable, use the specification on the label.
A—Automatic Transmission
M—Manual Transmission
BTDC—Before Top Dead Center
Can.—Canada
Fed.—Federal
Cal.—California

1981 ELECTRONIC SPARK CONTROL SYSTEM

Computer Part Number	5213347	5213128	5213133	5213138	5213143
Engine Application	1.7L Can (M)	2.2L Fed (M)	2.2L Fed (A)	2.2L Cal (M)	2.2L Cal (A)
Basic Timing	5° BTDC	10° BTDC	10° BTDC	10° BTDC	10° BTDC
Curb Idle Speed	900 RPM	900 RPM	900 RPM	900 RPM	900 RPM
Vacuum Range	0″–10″	0″–10″	0″–10″	0″–10″	0″–10″
Accumultor Clock Up (in minutes)	7	0	0	0	0
Spark Advance Test 2000 RPM 16″ Vacuum	45° ± 4°	28° ± 4°	25° ± 4°	23° ± 4°	25° ± 4°
Electronic EGR	No	No	No*	No	No
Electronic Throttle Control	No	No	No	No	No
Detonation Suppression	No	No	No	No	No
O$_2$ Feedback Air Switching (Electronic)	No	No	No	No	No
Temperature Sensor	Switch 65°C(150°F)	Switch 52°C(125°F)	Coolant Sensor	Switch 52°C(125°F)	Switch 52°C(125°F)

NOTE: The following specifications are published from the latest information available at the time of publication. If anything differs from those on the Emission Control Information Lable, use the specification on the label.
A—Automatic Transmission
M—Manual Transmission
BTDC—Before Top Dead Center
Can.—Canada
Fed.—Federal
Cal.—California

FUSE IDENTIFICATION

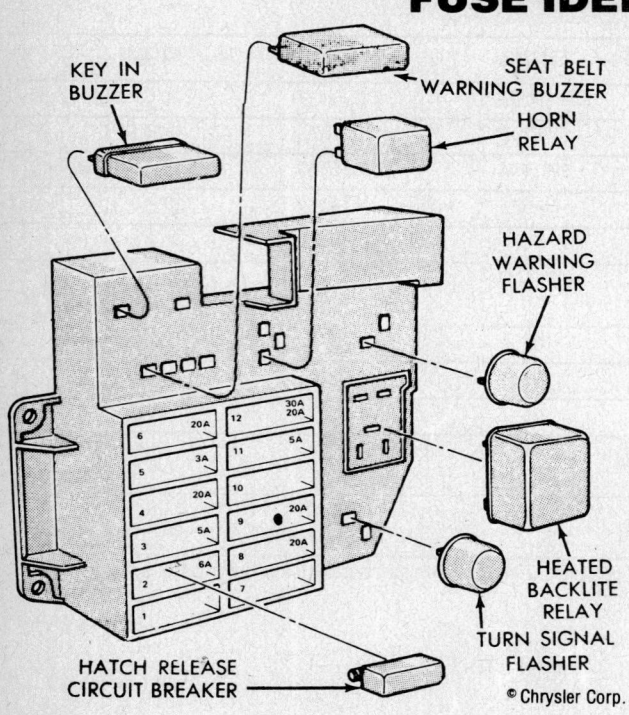

KEY IN BUZZER

SEAT BELT WARNING BUZZER

HORN RELAY

HAZARD WARNING FLASHER

HEATED BACKLITE RELAY

TURN SIGNAL FLASHER

HATCH RELEASE CIRCUIT BREAKER

© Chrysler Corp.

CAVITY	FUSE	ITEMS FUSED
1		
2	6 Amp C/Brkr	Rear Wash & Wipe (Mod 44) Hatch Release (Mod 24)
3	5 Amp	Radio
4	20 Amp	A/C Clutch, Turn Signal & Back-up Lamps & Tachometer
5	3 Amp	Cluster, Radio, A/C, Hrt, Ash Rec, Gear Sel, Heated RR Wdo, Rear Wash/Wipe & Hatch Release Lamps
6	20 Amp	Hazard Flasher
7		
8	20 Amp	Stop, Dome, Cargo, Glove Box, Map & Ign Lamps; Time Delay Relay, clock, cigar Lighter & Key-in Buzzer
9	20 Amp	Horn & Horn Relay; Park, Tail, Side Marker (RR), License & Cluster Lamps
10		
11	5 Amp	Seat Belt, Oil Pressure & Brake Warning Lamps; Seat Belt Buzzer, Voltage Limiter & Fuel & Temp Gauge
12	30 amp 20 amp	A/C & Heater Blower Motor Heater Blower Motor

ELECTRICAL SECTION

Starter Removal
- Disconnect the battery ground cable and starter electrical connections. Remove the starter mounting bolts.

Ignition Distributor
- Remove the distributor cap, electrical wiring and vacuum hose from the distributor.
- Put alignment marks on the rotor and distributor housing for installation reference.

- Remove the hold-down bolt. Carefully pull the distributor up and out of the engine block.
- Install the distributor in the correct position. Set the ignition timing within specifications.

Ignition Computer
CHILTON CAUTION· *Do not remove grease from the 10-wire harness connector or the connector cavity in the computer. The grease is used in order to prevent* *moisture from corroding the terminals. If there isn't at least 1/4 inch of grease on the bottom of the computer connector cavity, apply a liberal amount of Mopar multi-purpose grease over the entire end of connector plug before reinstalling.*

REMOVAL
When replacement of ignition computer is necessary proceed as follows.
- Remove the battery from vehicle.
- Disconnect the 10-wire harness and out-

1.7L engine A-412 manual transaxle starter

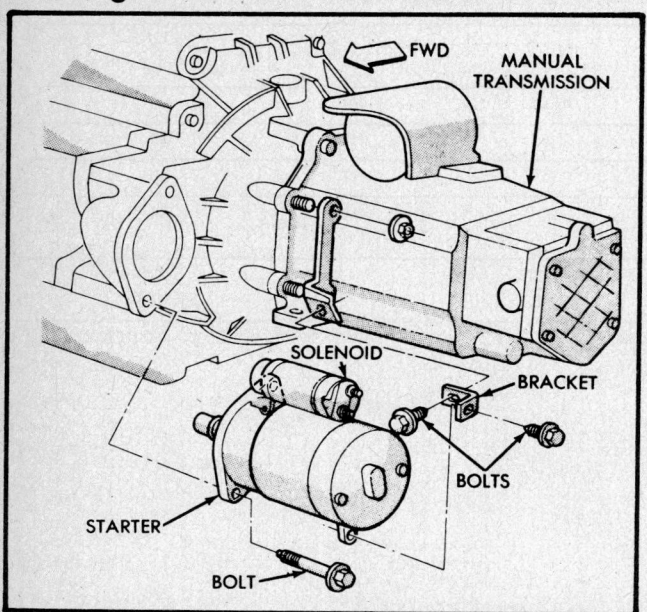

FWD

MANUAL TRANSMISSION

SOLENOID

BRACKET

BOLTS

STARTER

BOLT

1.7L engine A-404 automatic transaxle starter

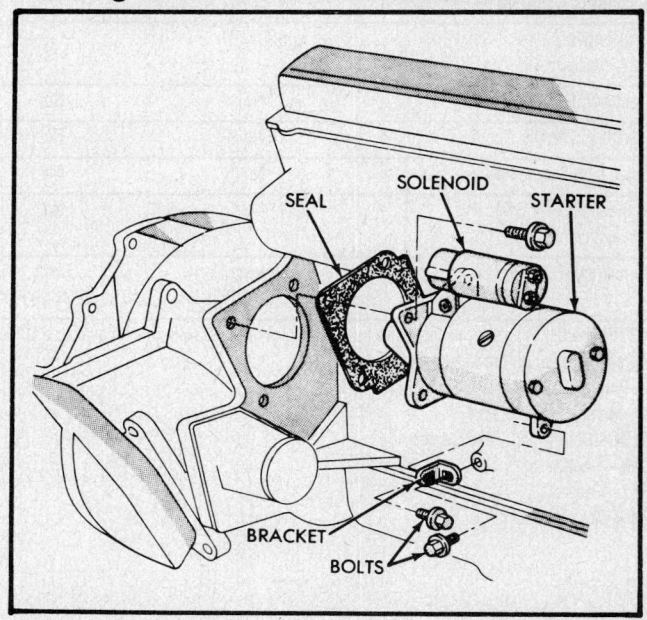

SEAL

SOLENOID

STARTER

BRACKET

BOLTS

1.7L engine A-460 manual and 2.2L engine manual and automatic transaxle starter

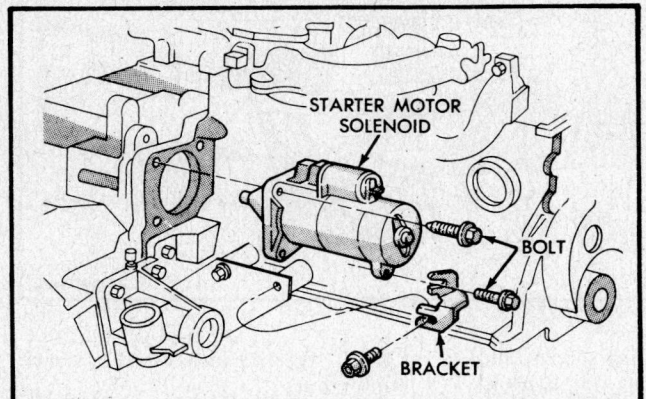

2.6L engine A-470 automatic transaxle starter

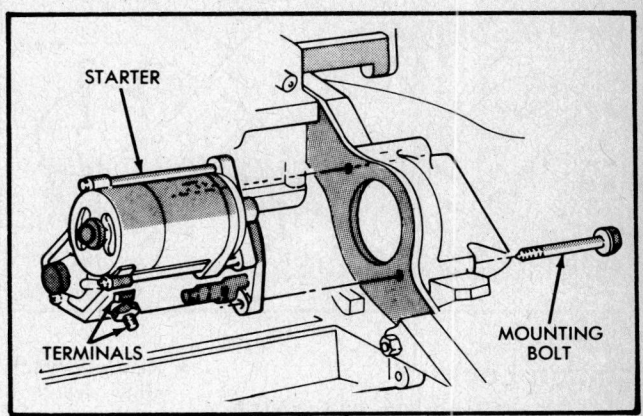

side air duct from the spark control computer and remove the vacuum line from vacuum transducer.

NOTE: To maintain proper sealing between the towers and nipples, cable and nipple assemblies should not be removed from the distributor or coil towers unless nipples are damaged or cable testing indicates high resistance or broken insulation. Plug wires do not pull from distributor cap, they must be released from inside.

CHILTON CAUTION: *Do not leave any one spark plug wire disconnected any longer than necessary during test or possible heat damage to catalytic converter will occur. Total test time must not exceed ten minutes.*

Ignition computer removal

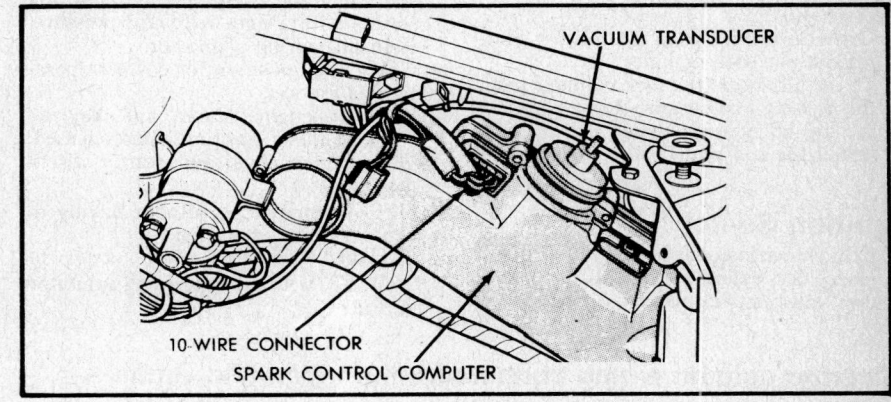

Coil and spark plug terminals

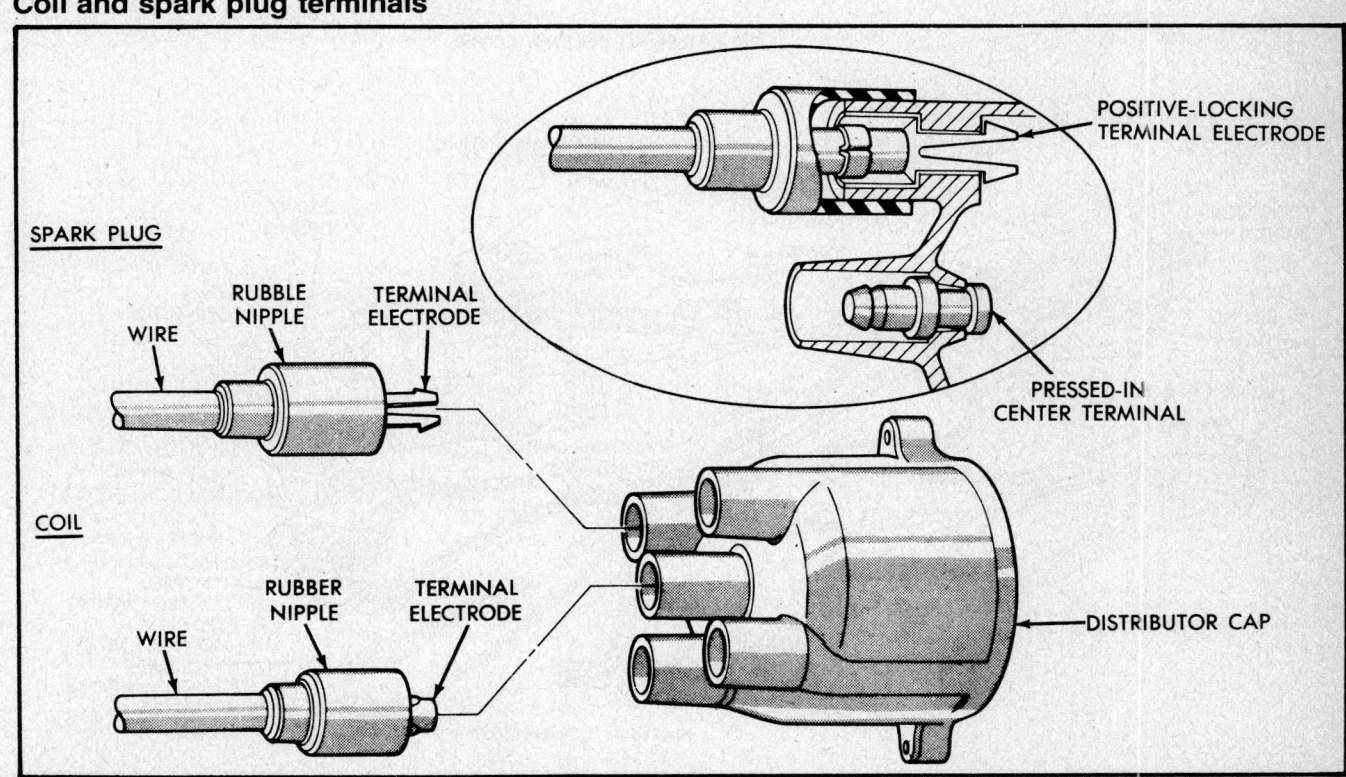

CHRYSLER FRONT DRIVE CARS

ARIES, HORIZON, OMNI, RELIANT

Ignition lock roll pin

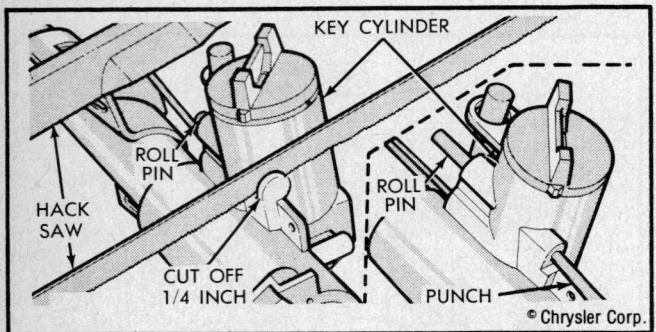

Ignition switch

Ignition Lock

- Remove steering wheel, both column covers, and the turn signal switch.
- Using a hacksaw blade, cut the upper ¼ inch from the key cylinder retainer pin boss.
- Drive the roll pin from the housing, and remove the lock cylinder.
- To install, insert the lock cylinder into the housing making sure that it engages the lug on ignition switch driver, and install the roll pin.

Ignition Switch

- Remove wiring connector from switch, place lock cylinder in "LOCK" position and remove the key.
- Remove switch mounting screws, and allow switch and push rod to drop below jacket. Separate switch from rod.
- To install, position switch in "LOCK" position (second detent from top), insert push rod, and tighten mounting screws with a light rearward pressure. Reinstall wiring connector.
- Check each position for correct operation as follows:
  START—engine starts, and key returns to "ON" position when released.
  ON—engine runs, and starter disengages.
  OFF—engine stops without having to depress inhibitor button.
  INHIBIT—Cannot turn key to "LOCK" without depressing inhibitor button.

LOCK—Steering locks, and key can be removed.
ACCESSORY—accessories operate with steering locked.

Neutral Start Switch

- The neutral start switch is located on the automatic transmission. Fluid will drain from the transmission when the switch is removed.
- Use a new seal when installing, and replenish lost fluid.

Stoplight Switch

- The stoplight switch is mounted to the brake pedal bracket. The switch is actuated by the brake pedal blade.

Steering column wiring connectors—Horizon and Omni

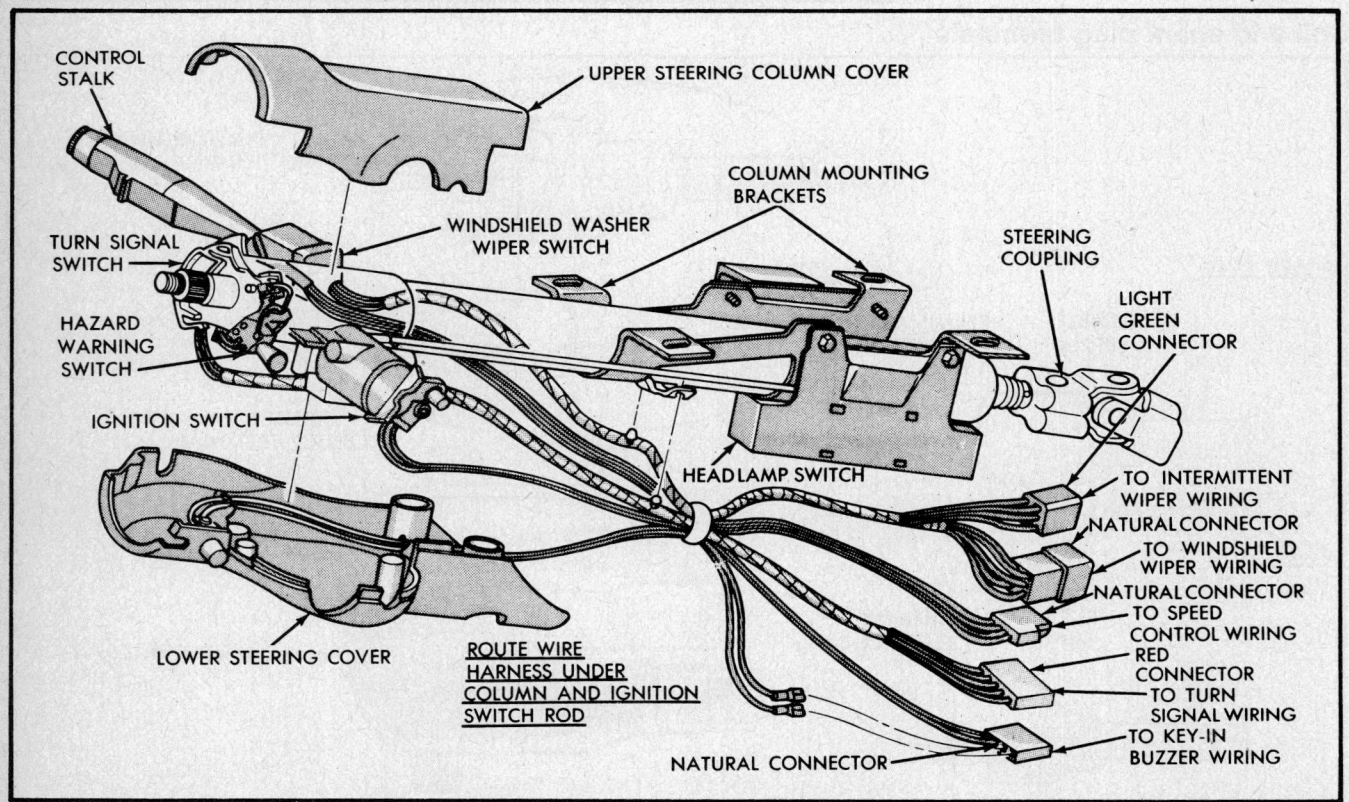

Removing steering wheel

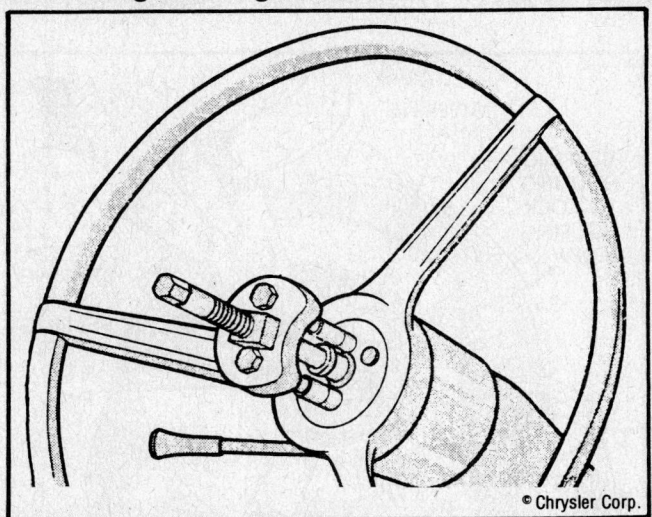

Turn signal switch

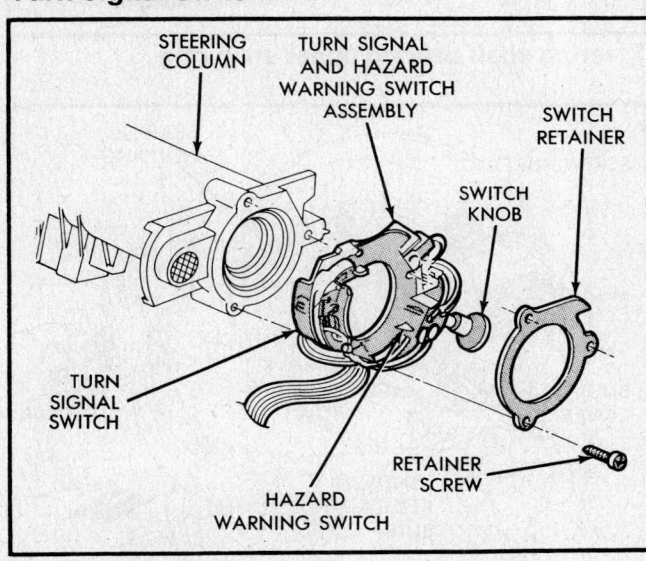

Windshield wiper switch

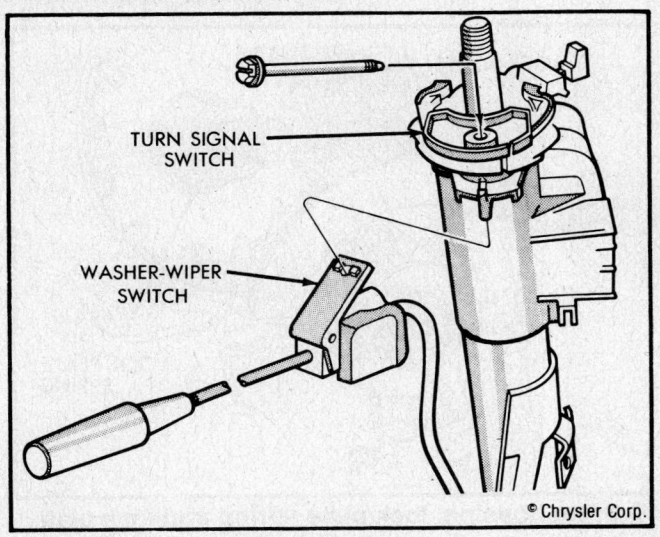

Turn signal lever access hole

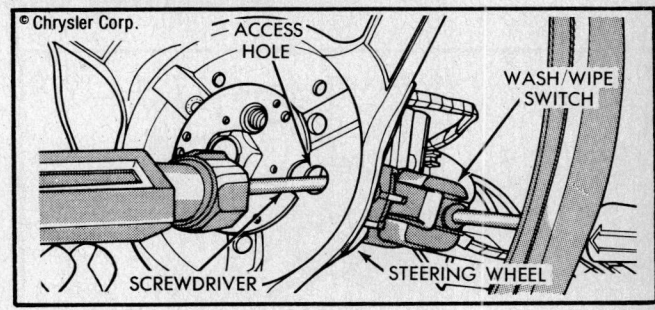

Horn switch

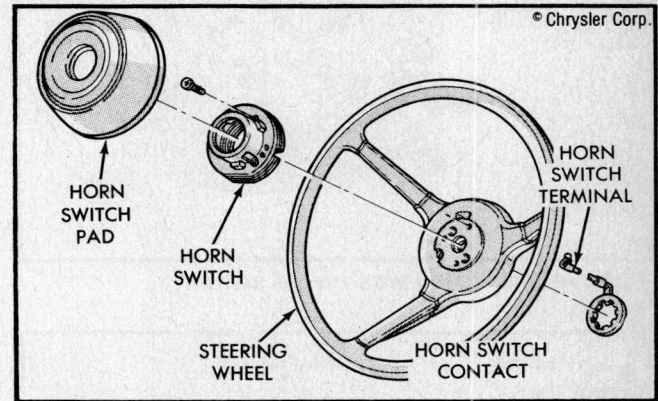

Horn Switch and Steering Wheel

- Disconnect turn signal switch electrical connector, remove horn button, and remove horn switch.
- Remove steering wheel nut, and use a puller to remove the steering wheel.

NOTE: When installing, do not torque against the column lock mechanism.

Turn Signal Switch

- Disconnect electrical connector; remove steering wheel, lower column cover and windshield wiper switch. Remove turn signal switch retaining screws.

Light Switch

- Place switch in full "ON" position. Pull on knob while pressing shaft release button on switch body to release shaft and knob assembly.
- Remove mounting device, and disconnect electrical wiring.

Light switch

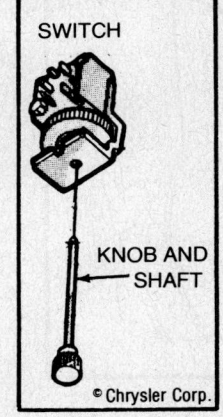

Windshield Wiper Switch

- Remove lower column cover and horn button.
- Place ignition lock in "OFF" position, and turn steering wheel to place access hole in hub area at 9 o'clock position.
- Loosen the turn signal lever screw through the access hole, and disengage dimmer push rod from wiper switch.
- Disconnect electrical wiring and remove switch.

Steering Column Switches

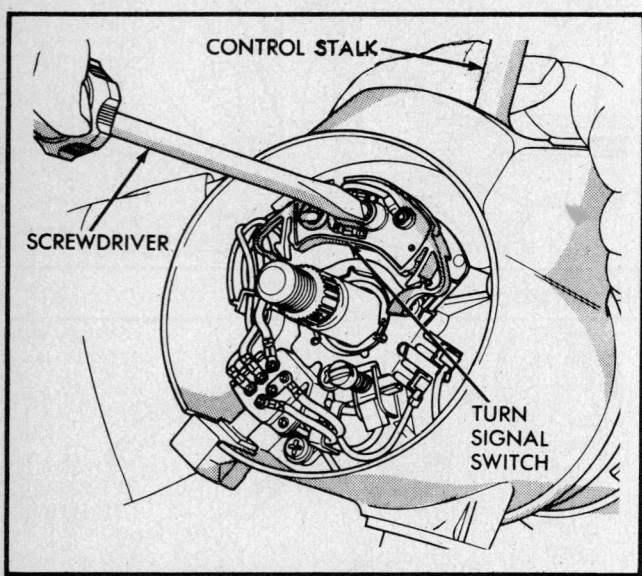

Remove and install wash/wipe switch

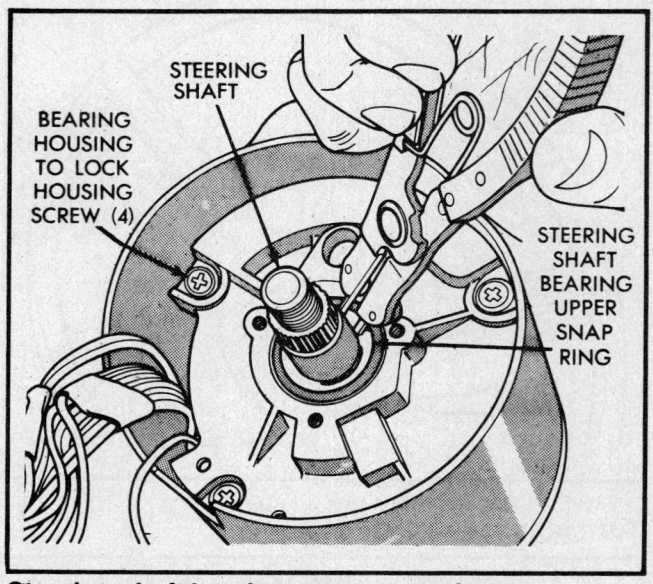

Steering shaft bearing upper snap ring

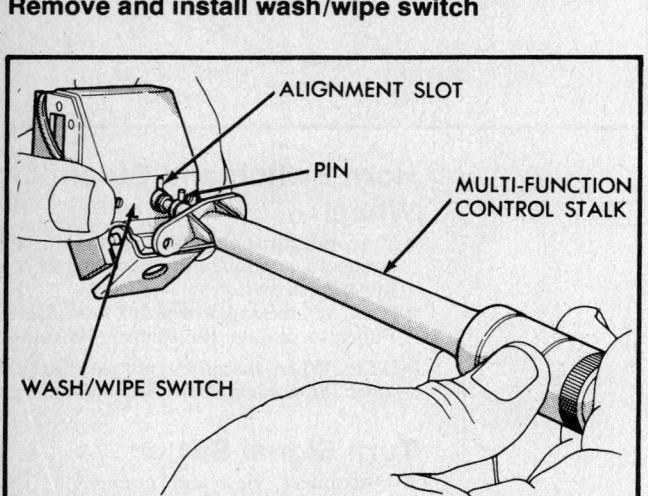

Remove or install control stalk

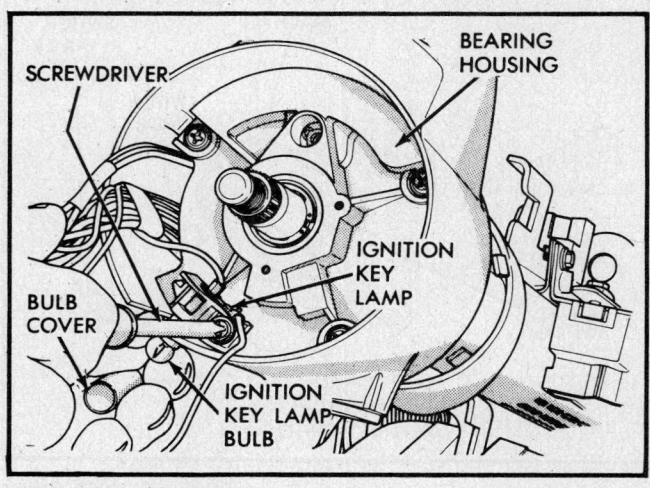

Ignition key lamp

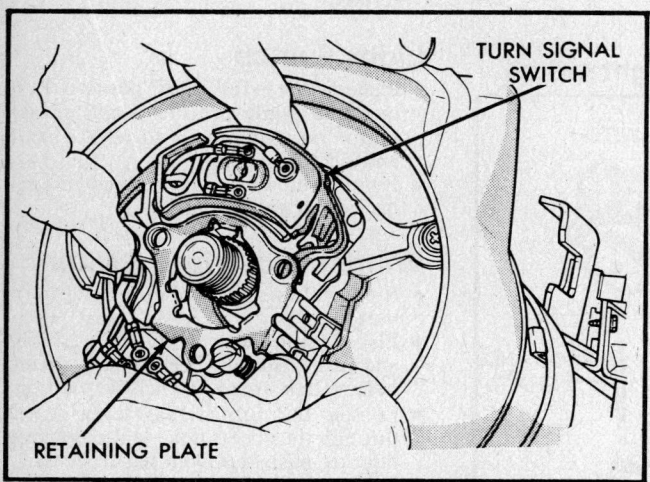

Retainer and turn signal switch

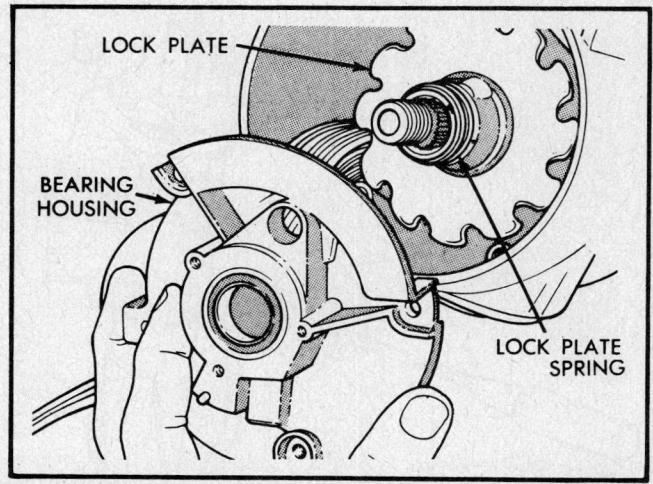

Bearing housing, lock plate spring and lock plate

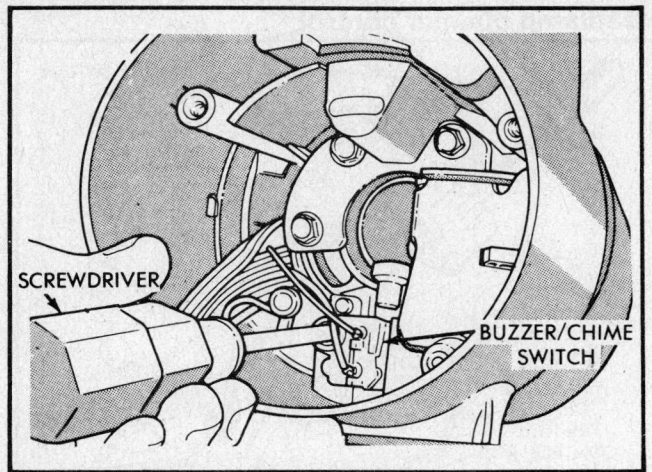

Ignition key buzzer/chime switch

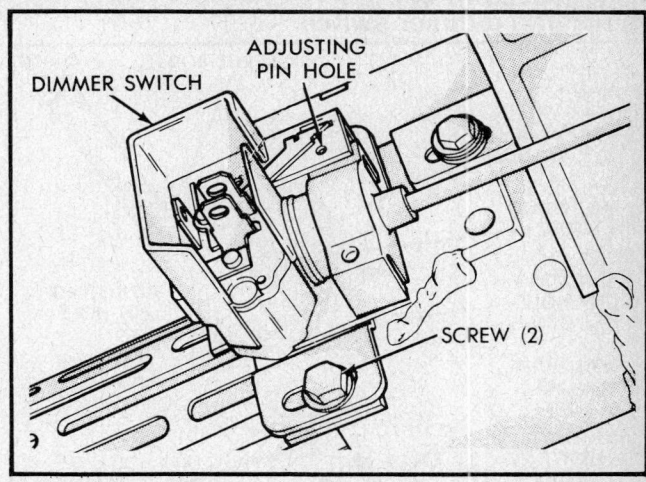

Dimmer switch

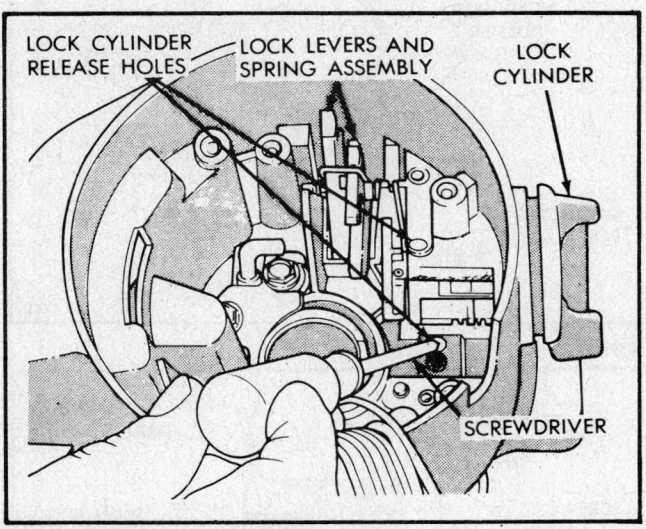

Lock cylinder and lock levers

Shift tube set screw

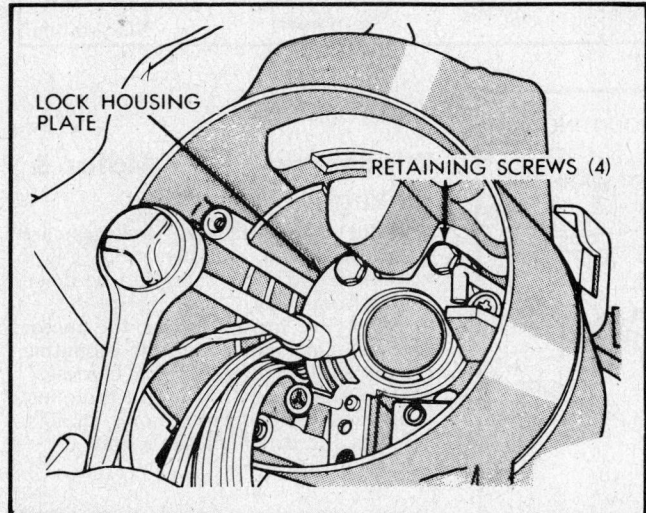

Lock housing to column jacket

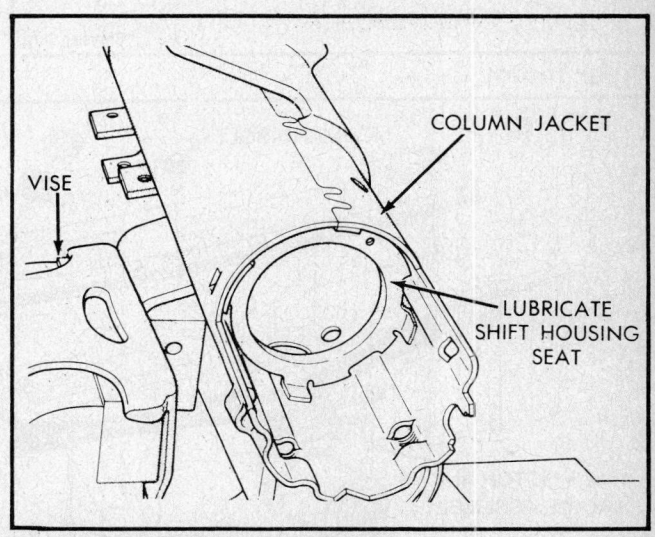

Lubricate shift housing seat

CHRYSLER FRONT DRIVE CARS

ARIES, HORIZON, OMNI, RELIANT

Headlamp dimmer switch

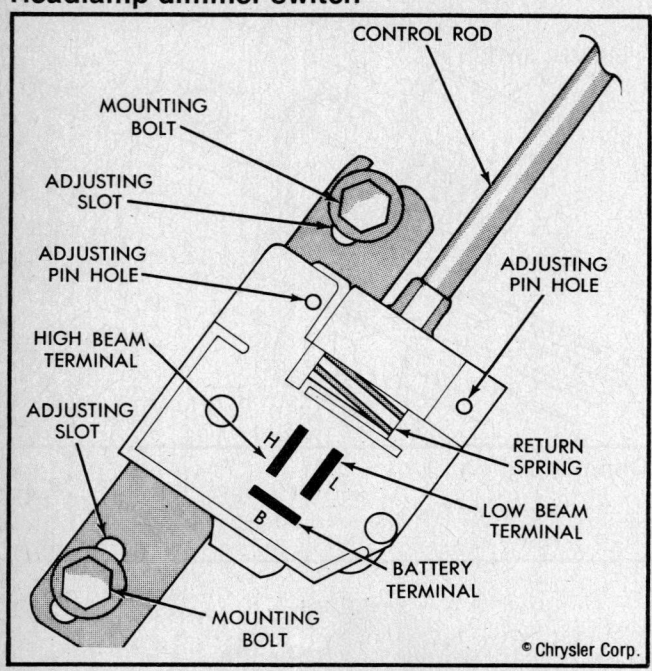

Dimmer switch adjustment. After installing drill shafts into both adjusting pin holes, tighten mounting bolts while pushing the switch body up the column. There should be no free play between the switch and the control rod

Headlamp dimmer control

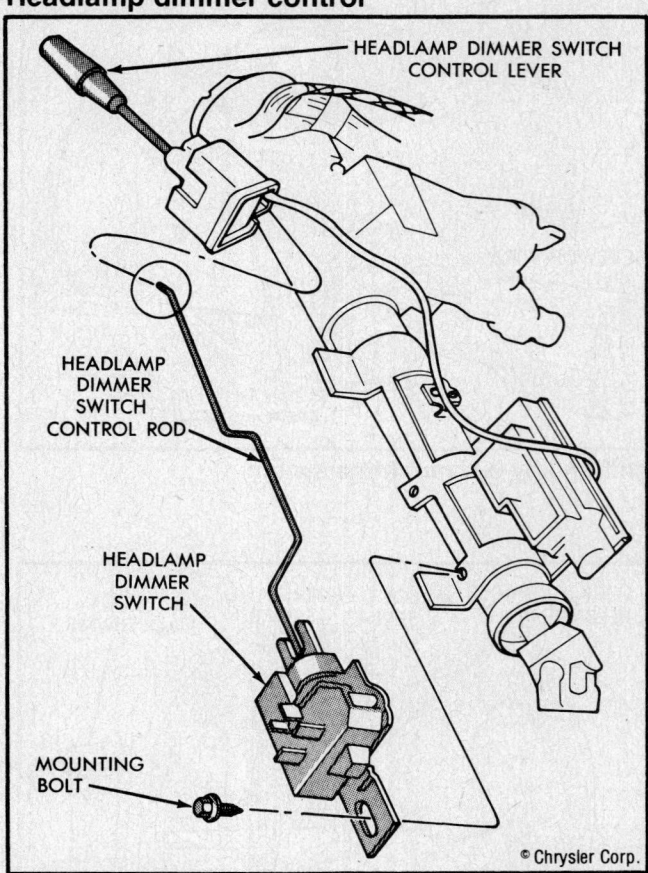

Dimmer switch installation alignment

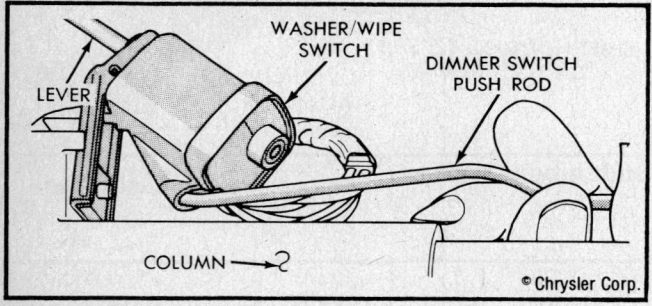

Dimmer switch push rod

Wiper motor

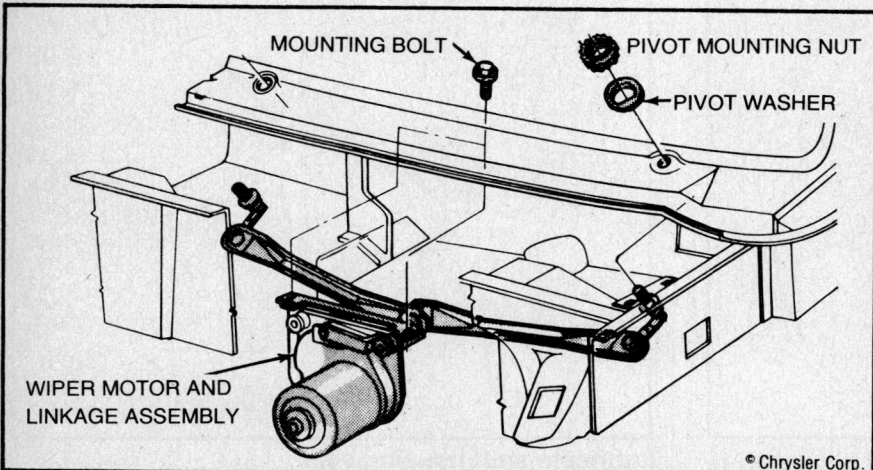

Windshield Wiper Motor & Linkage

- Motor and attaching linkages are removed as an assembly.
- Remove the wiper arms and tie down nuts from pivots.
- Under the hood, remove the motor cover, and remove motor mounting bolts and disconnect wiring harness.
- Disengage pivots from cowl top mounting, and remove wiper motor, cranks, pivots and drive links as a unit.

Windshield Wiper Arms

- Lift the arm to permit the latch to be pulled out to the holding position, and remove the arm from the pivot using a rocking motion.

NOTE: Removing a wiper arm with a prying tool may distort it in a manner that could allow it to come off the pivot shaft during operation.

Windshield Wiper Blades

- Depress release lever on center bridge, and remove blade from arm.

Radio

- Remove right bezel, remove radio mounting screws, and pull radio from instrument panel. Disconnect electrical and antenna leads.

Temperature Control Unit/Blower Switch

- Remove light switch and left bezel.
- Remove control unit mounting screws, and remove unit from instrument panel after disconnecting electrical leads, control cable and vacuum lines.

Wiper arms and blades

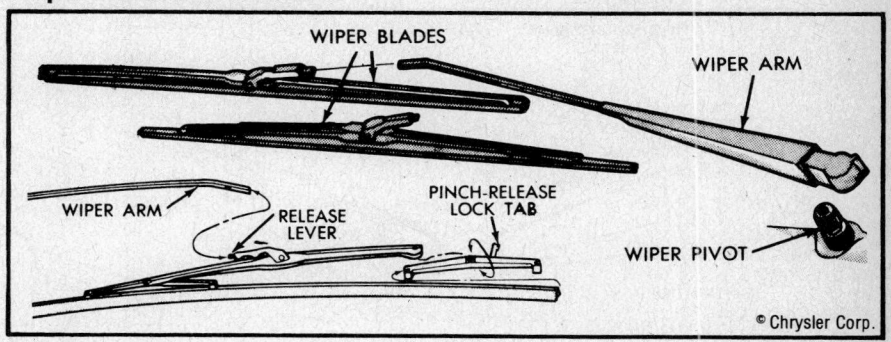

© Chrysler Corp.

Radio removal

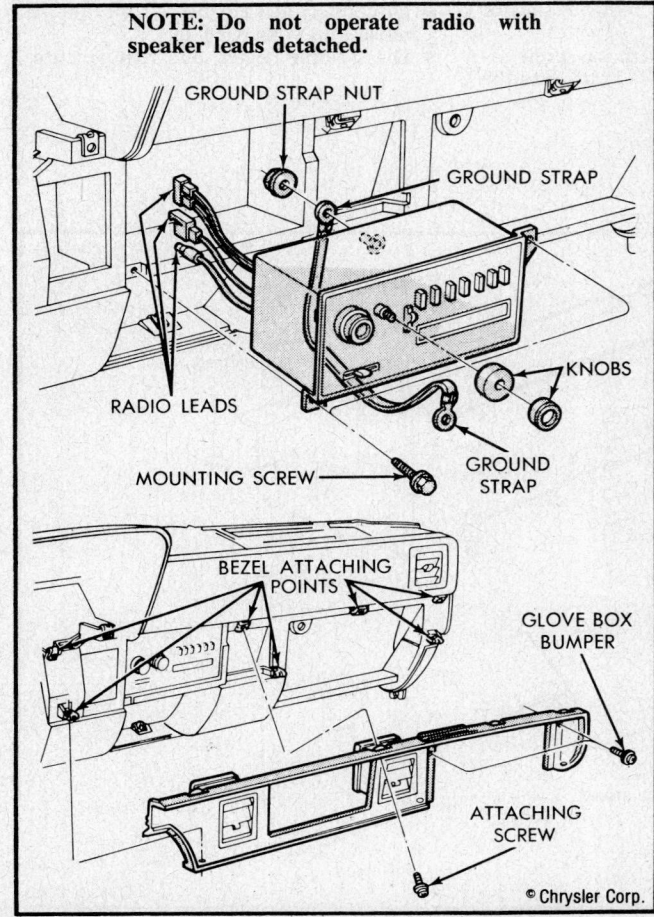

© Chrysler Corp.

Temperature control unit

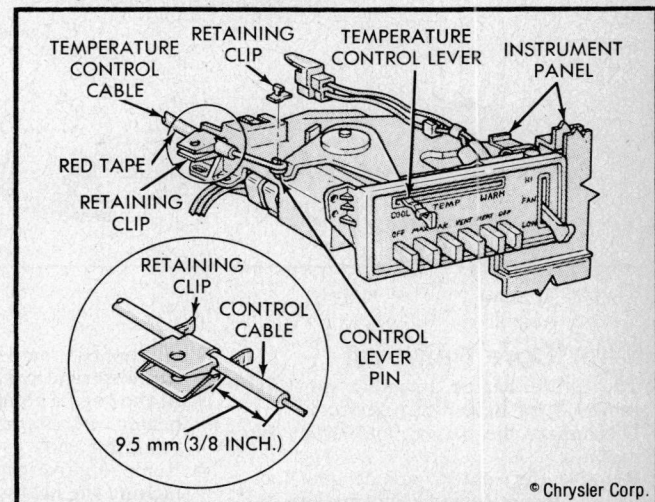

© Chrysler Corp.

Temperature controls

© Chrysler Corp.

Flag tab depressed for removal

Heater assembly

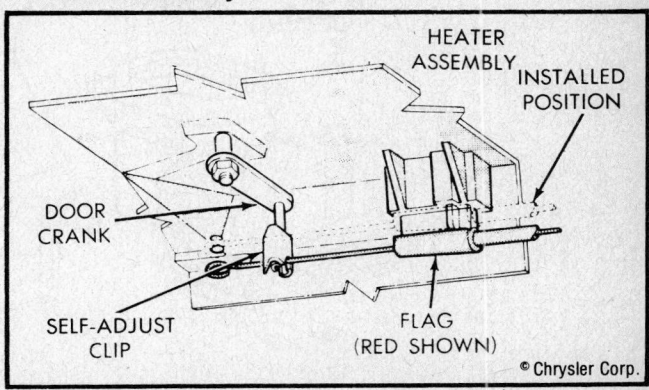

© Chrysler Corp.

A219

CHRYSLER FRONT DRIVE CARS
ARIES, HORIZON, OMNI, RELIANT

Heater control cable routing

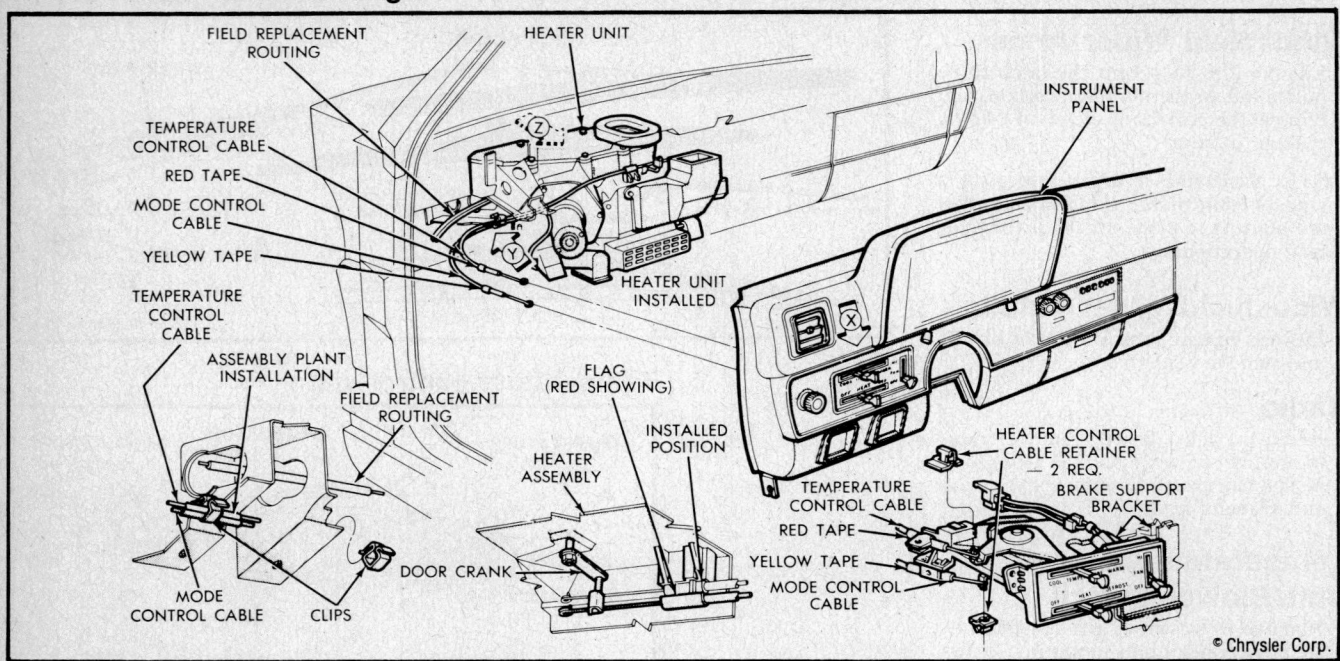

Heater Core Removal
- The entire heater assembly must be removed for heater core service.
- Disconnect the battery and drain the radiator.
- Remove the center, outside air, floor vent housing. Remove ash tray and defroster duct adapter.

- Disconnect temperature control cable and electrical wiring.
- In the engine compartment, disconnect heater hoses, and remove heater mounting nuts.
- Remove glove box. Remove screw attaching the heater brace bracket to the instrument panel.

- Remove unit support strap nut, disconnect strap from plenum stud, and lower heater from under instrument panel.
- Disconnect mode control cable, and remove unit from vehicle.
- Disassemble heater, and remove core.

Heater unit mounting

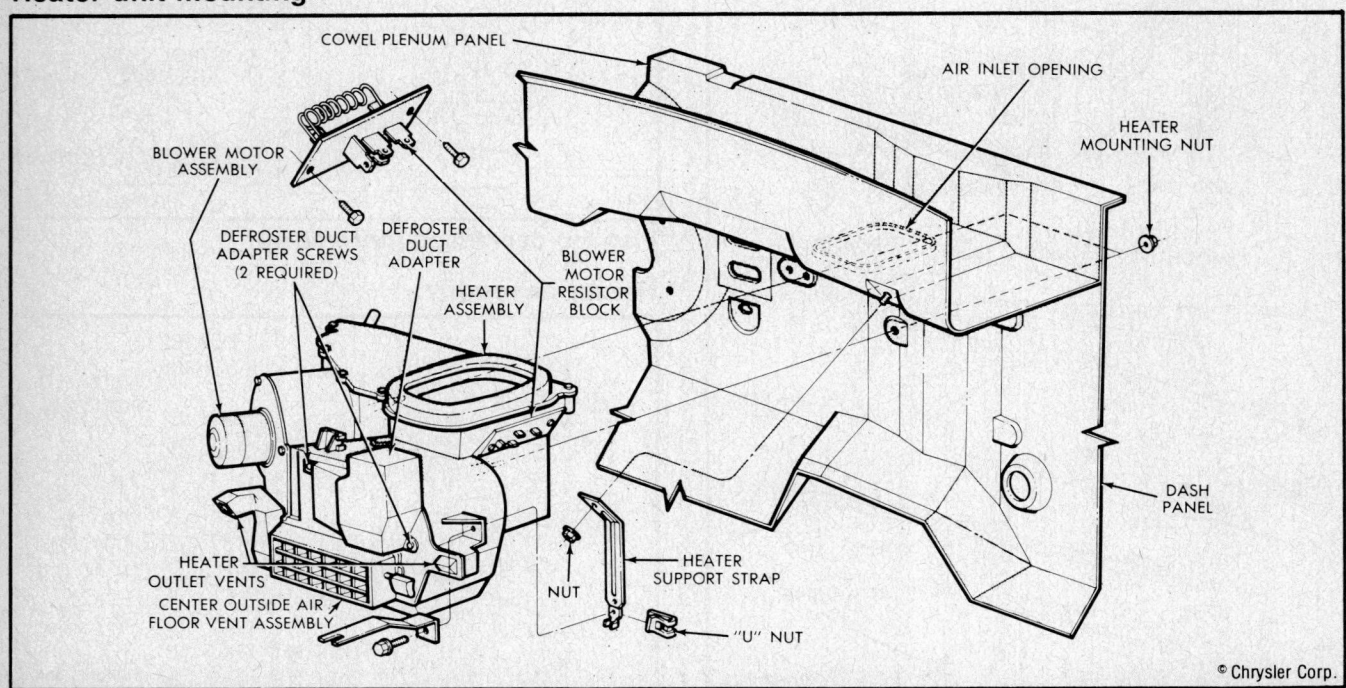

Heater blower assembly and left heater outlet duct location

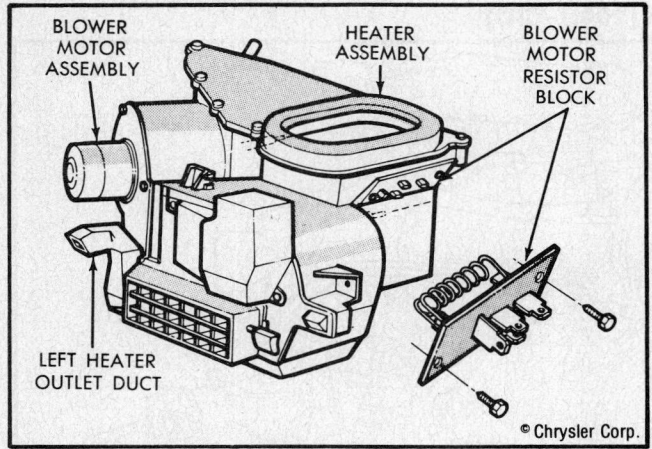

BLOWER MOTOR ASSEMBLY

HEATER ASSEMBLY

BLOWER MOTOR RESISTOR BLOCK

LEFT HEATER OUTLET DUCT

© Chrysler Corp.

Heater Blower
- Remove left heater outlet duct, remove blower mounting screws, and remove the blower motor.

Removing blower motor assembly

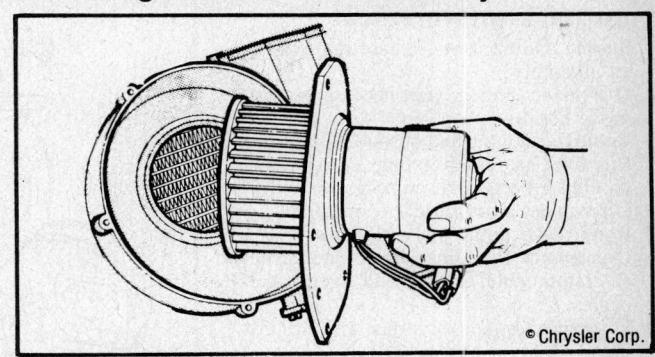

© Chrysler Corp.

Removing blower wheel

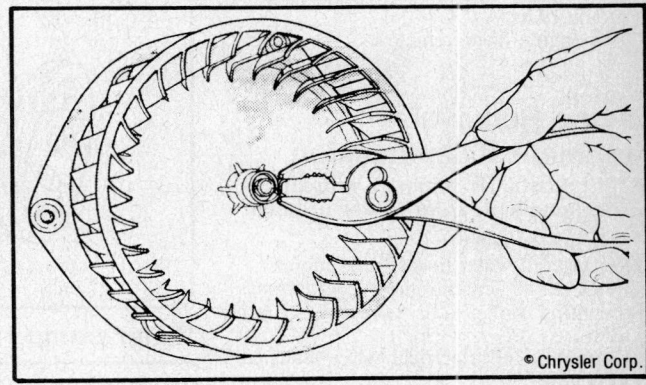

© Chrysler Corp.

Heater core removal

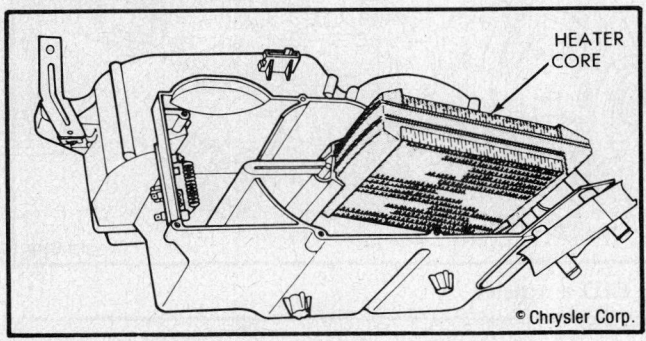

HEATER CORE

© Chrysler Corp.

Heater and defroster duct and upper air vents

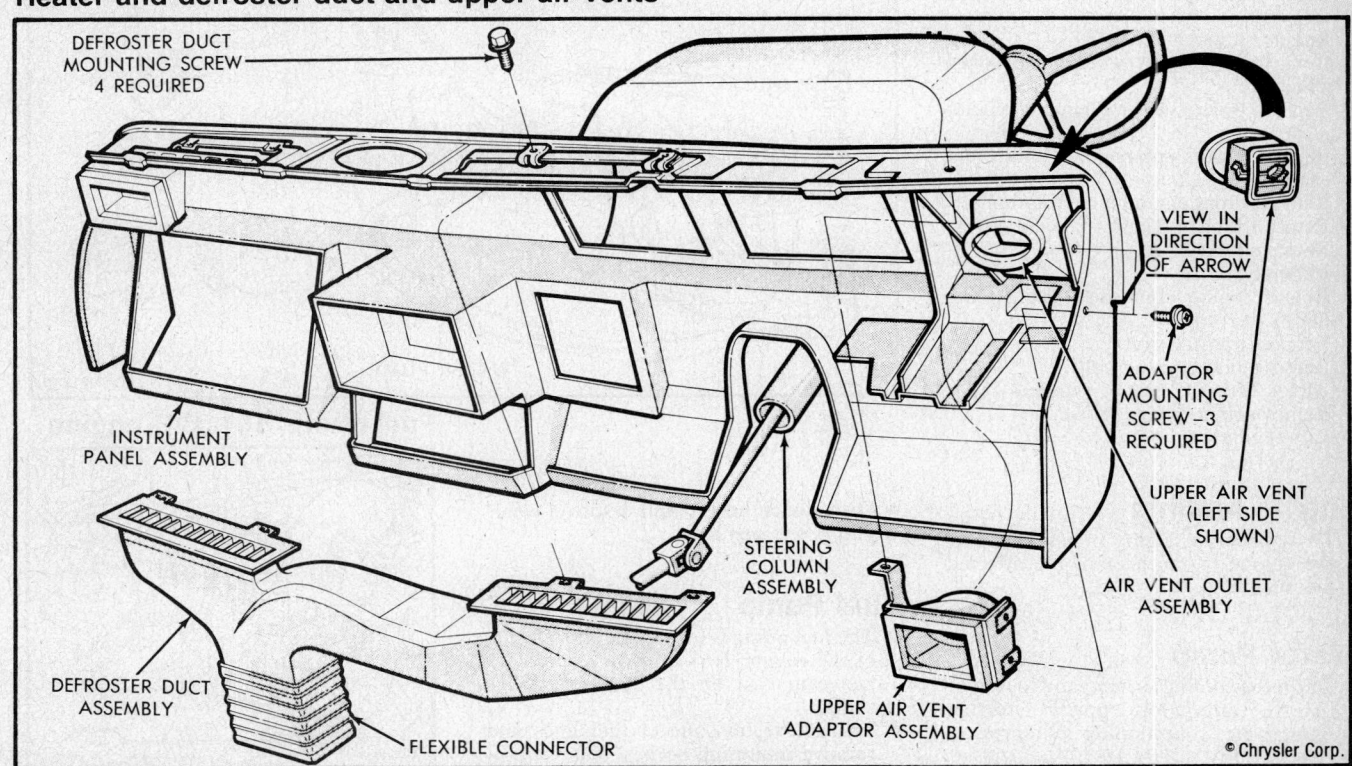

DEFROSTER DUCT MOUNTING SCREW 4 REQUIRED

VIEW IN DIRECTION OF ARROW

ADAPTOR MOUNTING SCREW–3 REQUIRED

UPPER AIR VENT (LEFT SIDE SHOWN)

AIR VENT OUTLET ASSEMBLY

INSTRUMENT PANEL ASSEMBLY

STEERING COLUMN ASSEMBLY

DEFROSTER DUCT ASSEMBLY

FLEXIBLE CONNECTOR

UPPER AIR VENT ADAPTOR ASSEMBLY

© Chrysler Corp.

ENGINE SECTION

Engine assembly (104.7 CID)

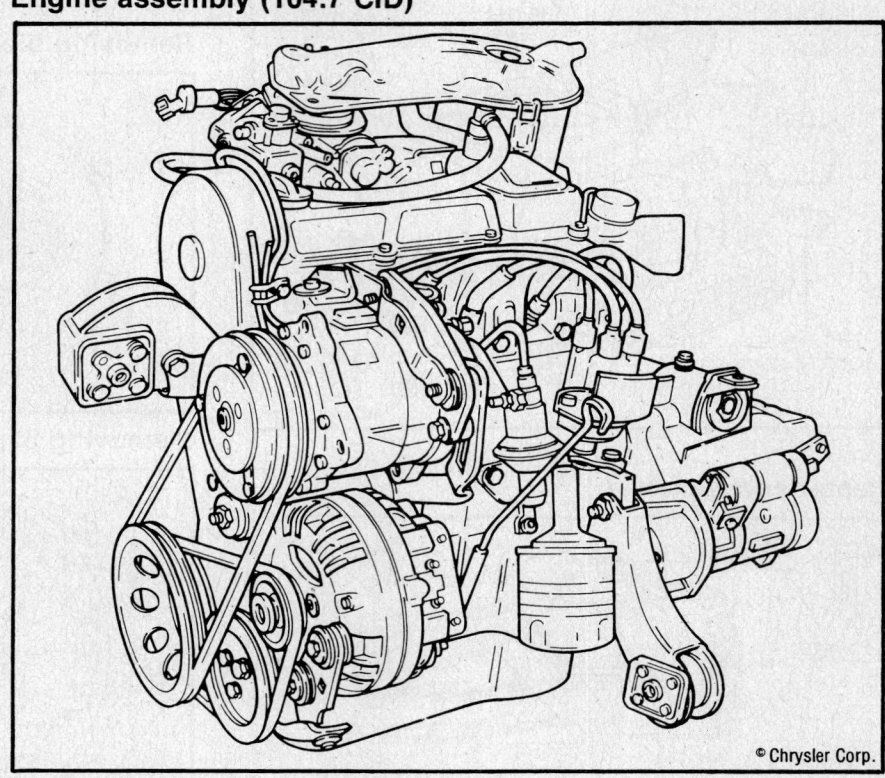

© Chrysler Corp.

Engine Removal
Manual Transmission

- Engine and transmission are removed as an assembly.
- Disconnect battery (not necessary to remove hood).
- Remove radiator and shroud assembly.
- Remove air conditioning compressor, mounting bolts, TIE compressor aside.
- Disconnect all electrical connections.
- Remove air pump and alternator.
- Disconnect fuel line, heater hose, accelerator cable, clutch and speedmeter cables.
- Disconnect universal joints, and exhaust pipe.
- Remove transmission linkage.
- Lift engine slightly and remove engine mount bolts.
- Lift engine from vehicle.

Engine Removal
Automatic Transmission

NOTE: Engine is removed without removing automatic transmission or hood.

- Disconnect battery.
- Remove all water hoses from engine.
- Remove air conditioning compressor, mounting bolts, TIE compressor, set aside.
- Disconnect all electrical wires attached to engine.
- Disconnect fuel line, and accelerator.
- Remove air diverter valve and lines from air pump.
- Remove alternator.
- Remove both front wheels and splash shields.
- Remove power steering pump, set pump aside.
- Remove water pump pulley and crank shaft pulley.
- Remove front engine mounting bolts.
- Remove transmission inspection cover.
- Remove flex plate bolts.
- Remove starter.
- Rotate engine crankshaft until timing marks line up.
- Support transmission.
- Remove bell housing bolts.
- Attach lifting fixture to engine.
- Remove right engine mount.
- Lift engine.

Engine Mounts

- To replace an engine mount, support the engine in the area of the affected mount only.

Water Pump

- Drain the cooling system, and loosen or remove alternator, power steering pump, air conditioning compressor, etc.

Water pump, 104. CID engine

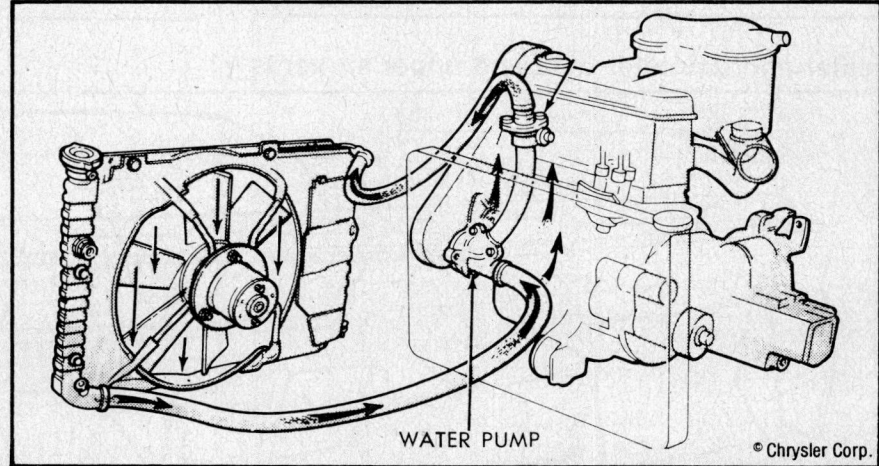

WATER PUMP

© Chrysler Corp.

- Disconnect hoses, and remove water pump retainer bolts.

Fuel Pump

- The fuel pump is located on the left side of the engine. It is driven by an eccentric cam cast on the accessory drive shaft.
- To remove, disconnect fuel lines and remove mounting bolts.

Fuel pump, 104. CID engine

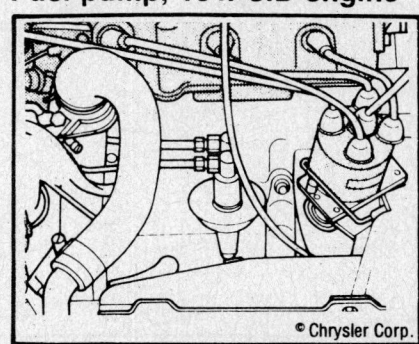

© Chrysler Corp.

Timing marks on crankshaft and intermediate sprockets

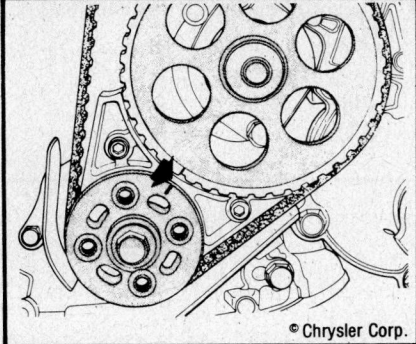

© Chrysler Corp.

Timing Belt
- Place engine in number one cylinder TDC position.
- Remove drive belts, pulleys and timing belt cover.
- Remove timing belt after loosening tensioner retaining screw.
- When installing, the belt is correctly tensioned when drive side of belt can be twisted ninety degrees with fingers.

Timing marks on camshaft sprocket, 104.7 CID engine

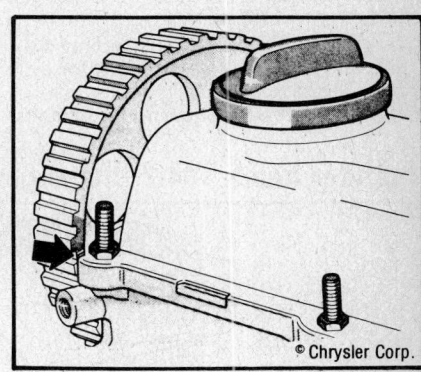

© Chrysler Corp.

Timing belt and components, 104.7 CID engine

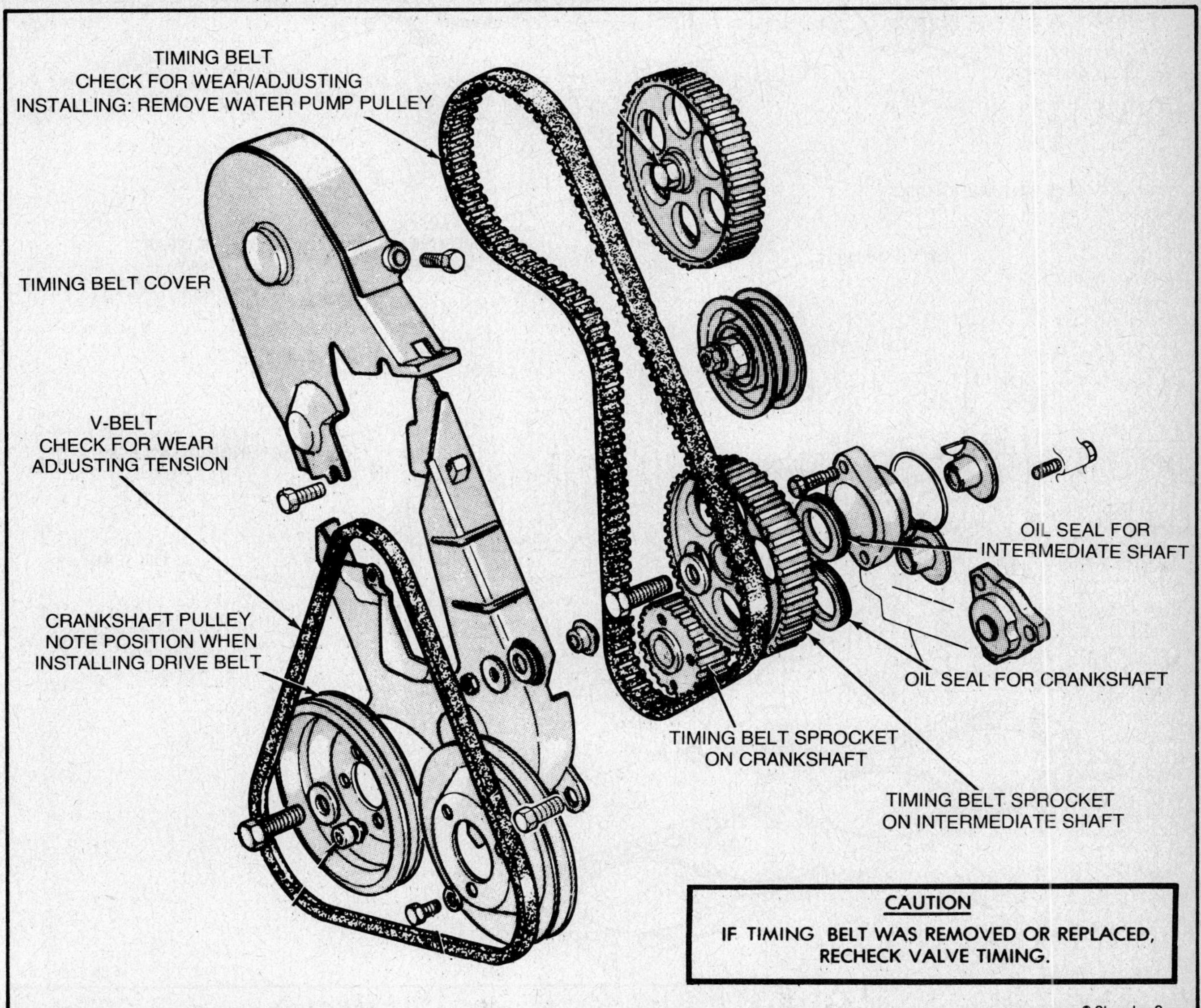

TIMING BELT
CHECK FOR WEAR/ADJUSTING
INSTALLING: REMOVE WATER PUMP PULLEY

TIMING BELT COVER

V-BELT
CHECK FOR WEAR
ADJUSTING TENSION

CRANKSHAFT PULLEY
NOTE POSITION WHEN
INSTALLING DRIVE BELT

OIL SEAL FOR
INTERMEDIATE SHAFT

OIL SEAL FOR CRANKSHAFT

TIMING BELT SPROCKET
ON CRANKSHAFT

TIMING BELT SPROCKET
ON INTERMEDIATE SHAFT

CAUTION
IF TIMING BELT WAS REMOVED OR REPLACED, RECHECK VALVE TIMING.

© Chrysler Corp.

CHRYSLER FRONT DRIVE CARS
ARIES, HORIZON, OMNI, RELIANT

Cylinder Head or Gasket

- The cylinder head can be removed with intake and exhaust manifolds either attached or removed.
- It is necessary to drain the cooling system and remove the timing belt for cylinder head removal.
- When installing, torque mounting bolts in prescribed sequence and to correct specifications.

Valve Adjustment

- Valve clearance is changed by installing different size adjustment discs.
- To remove an adjustment disc, press cam follower down with Tool L-4417, and remove disc with a magnet.

Camshaft

- Timing belt and camshaft sprocket must be removed before removing camshaft.
- When installing, use a new camshaft oil seal.

Cylinder head, 104.7 CID engine

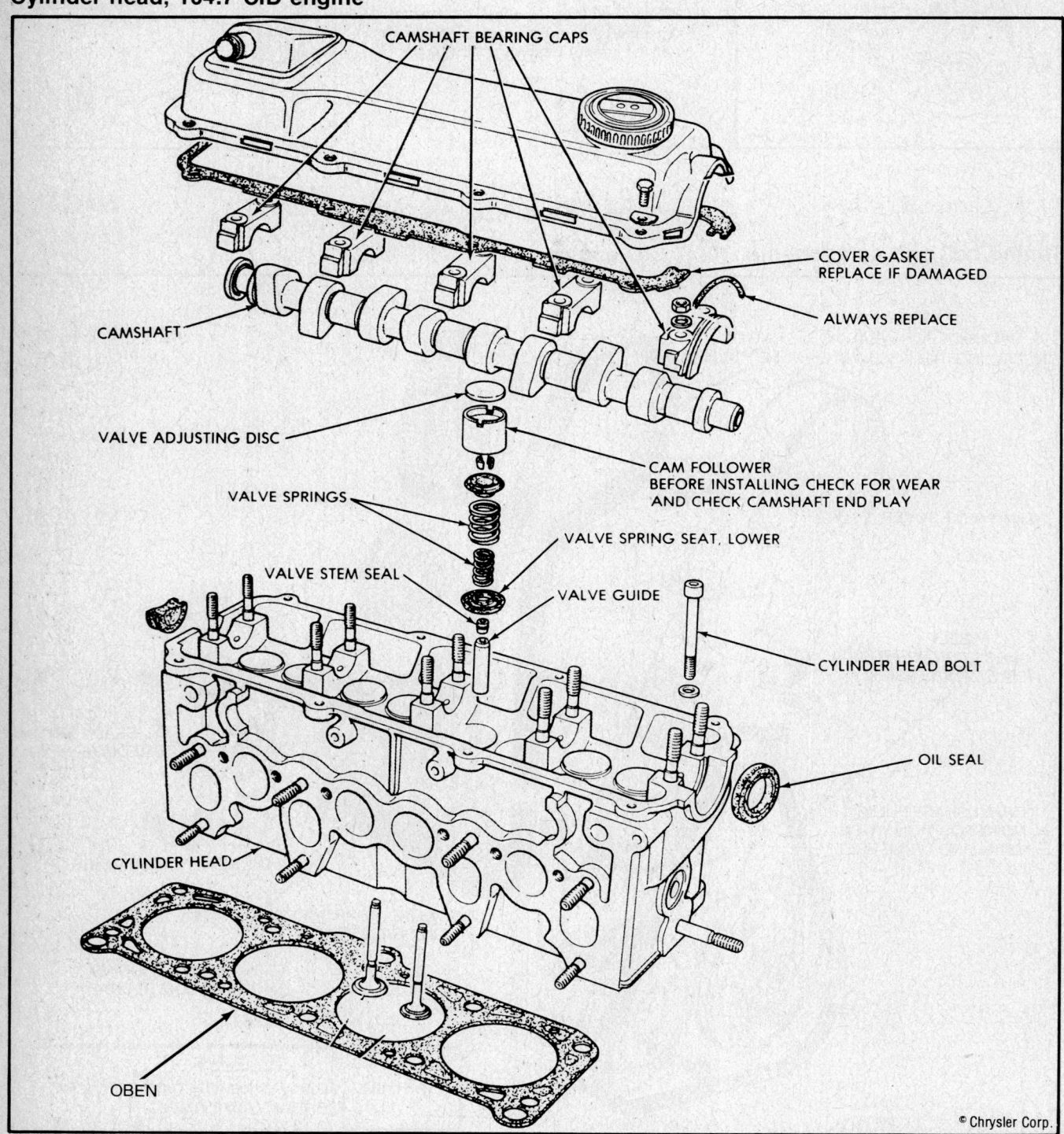

CAMSHAFT BEARING CAPS

COVER GASKET REPLACE IF DAMAGED

ALWAYS REPLACE

CAMSHAFT

VALVE ADJUSTING DISC

CAM FOLLOWER BEFORE INSTALLING CHECK FOR WEAR AND CHECK CAMSHAFT END PLAY

VALVE SPRINGS

VALVE SPRING SEAT, LOWER

VALVE STEM SEAL

VALVE GUIDE

CYLINDER HEAD BOLT

OIL SEAL

CYLINDER HEAD

OBEN

© Chrysler Corp.

The word "oben" towards cylinder head

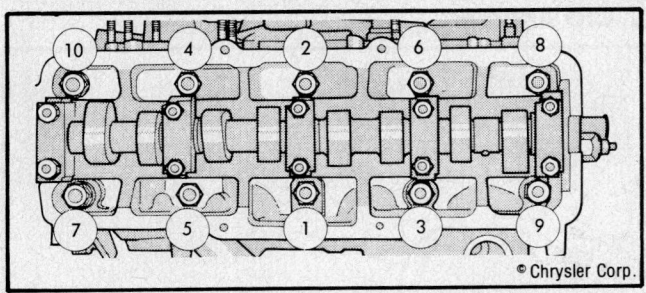

Cylinder head bolt tightening sequence. Install bolts 8 and 10 first to center head. After tightening to correct torque, tighten all bolts in proper sequence another ¼ turn.

Valve arrangement

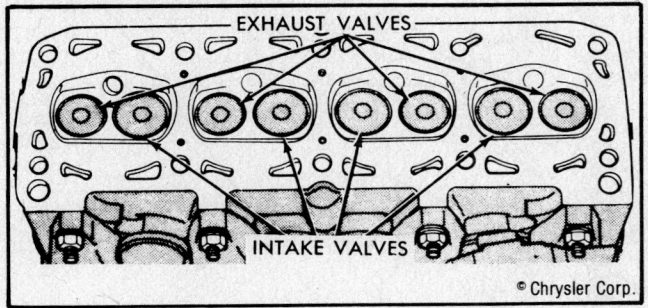

Measuring valve clearance

Valve adjustment

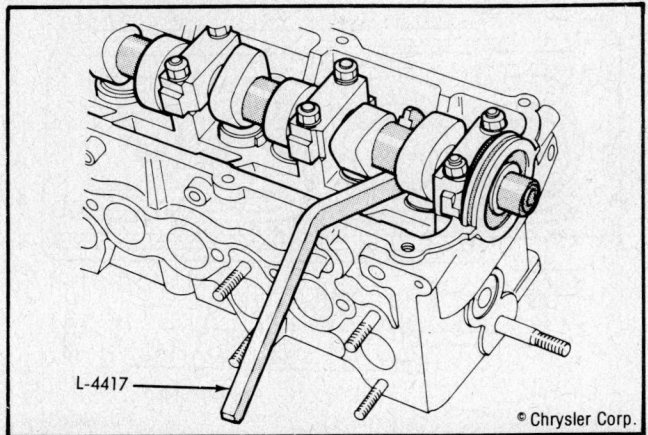

Changing valve adjustment disc. Press cam follower down with Tool L-4417, and remove disc with magnet

Valve Adjusting Discs

THICKNESS (mm)	
3.00	3.65
3.05	3.70
3.10	3.75
3.15	3.80
3.20	3.85
3.25	3.90
3.30	3.95
3.35	4.00
3.40	4.05
3.45	4.10
3.50	4.15
3.55	4.20
3.60	4.25

Valve adjusting disc

Camshaft caps, 104.7 CID engine

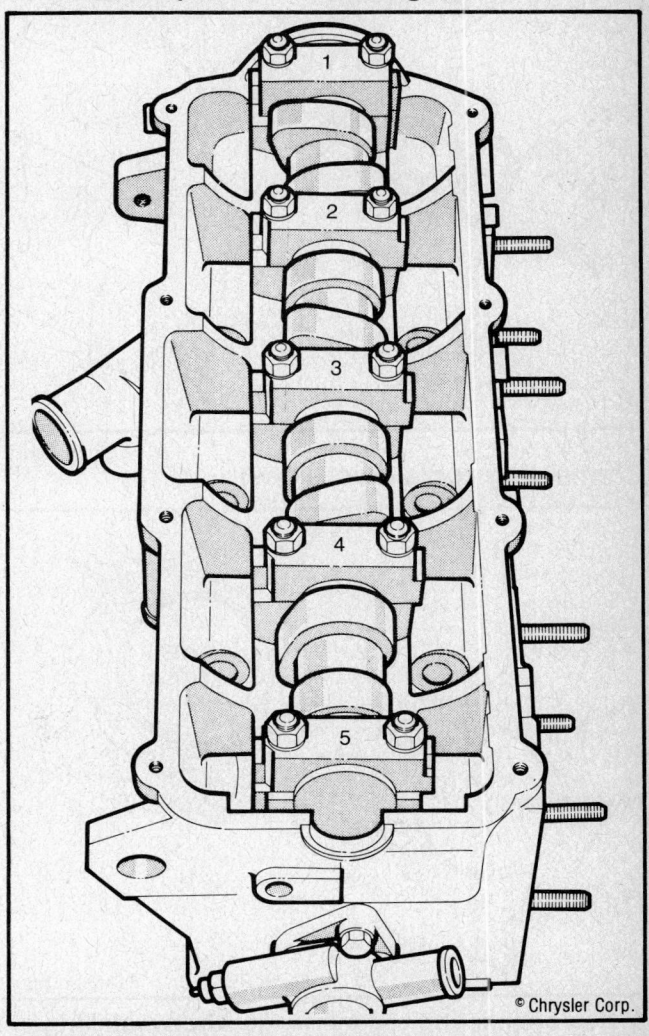

Camshaft bearing caps. Remove caps 5, 1 and 3 first, then diagonally loosen caps 2 and 4.

CHRYSLER FRONT DRIVE CARS

ARIES, HORIZON, OMNI, RELIANT

Crankshaft, bearings and intermediate shaft, 104.7 CID engine

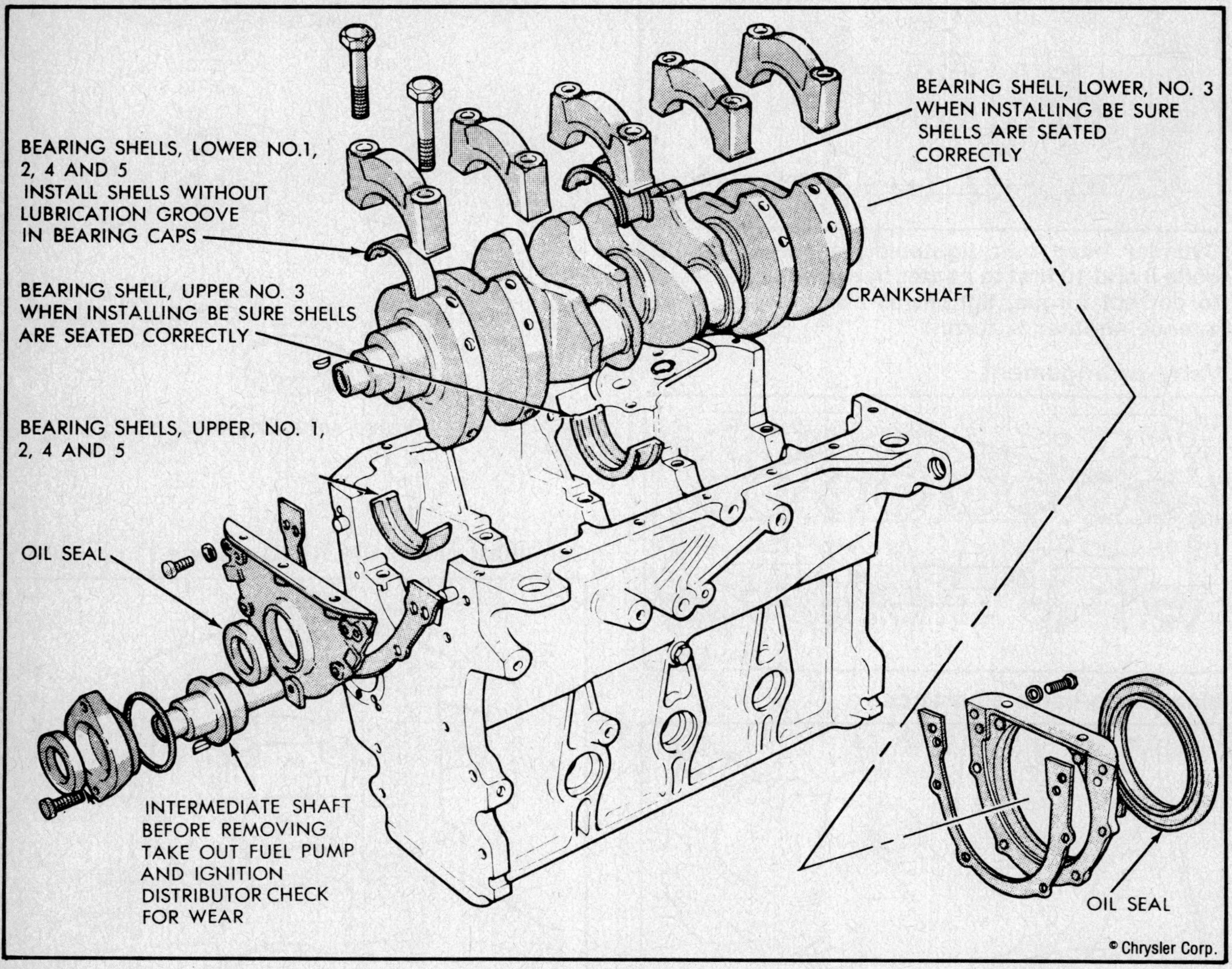

BEARING SHELL, LOWER, NO. 3
WHEN INSTALLING BE SURE
SHELLS ARE SEATED
CORRECTLY

BEARING SHELLS, LOWER NO.1,
2, 4 AND 5
INSTALL SHELLS WITHOUT
LUBRICATION GROOVE
IN BEARING CAPS

BEARING SHELL, UPPER NO. 3
WHEN INSTALLING BE SURE SHELLS
ARE SEATED CORRECTLY

BEARING SHELLS, UPPER, NO. 1,
2, 4 AND 5

CRANKSHAFT

OIL SEAL

INTERMEDIATE SHAFT
BEFORE REMOVING
TAKE OUT FUEL PUMP
AND IGNITION
DISTRIBUTOR CHECK
FOR WEAR

OIL SEAL

© Chrysler Corp.

Connecting rod's (two types)

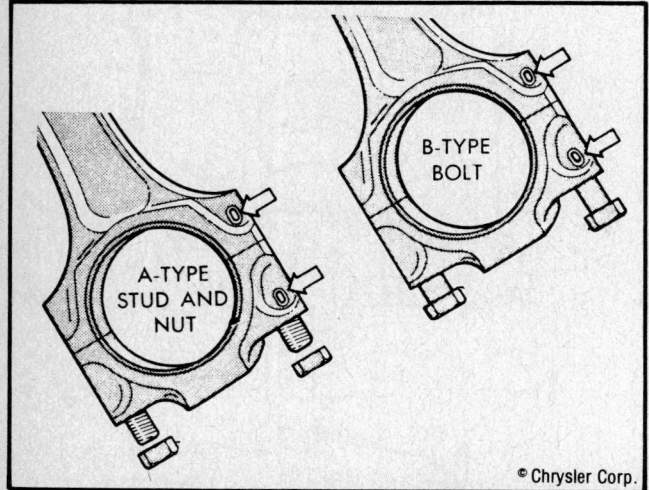

B-TYPE
BOLT

A-TYPE
STUD AND
NUT

© Chrysler Corp.

Match connecting rod markings when installing.
Marks must point toward intermediate shaft.

Piston markings

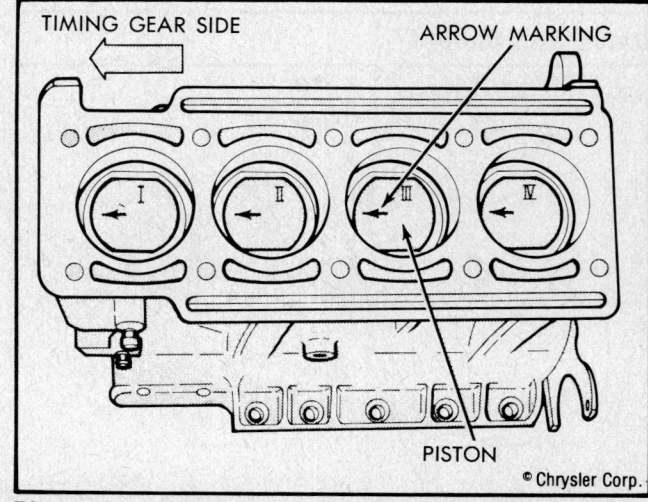

TIMING GEAR SIDE

ARROW MARKING

I   II   III   IV

PISTON

© Chrysler Corp.

Piston installation. Arrow markings on pistons
must point toward the timing gear side of the
engine.

Oil Pan
- The oil pan can be removed without disturbing any other components.

Oil Pump
- The oil pan must be removed for access to the oil pump.

Rear Oil Seal
- The rear oil seal is the one on the flywheel side.

Pistons, Rods & Bearings
- Pistons are removed through the top.
- Connecting rods are matched sets.

Connecting rod and piston, 104.7 CID engine

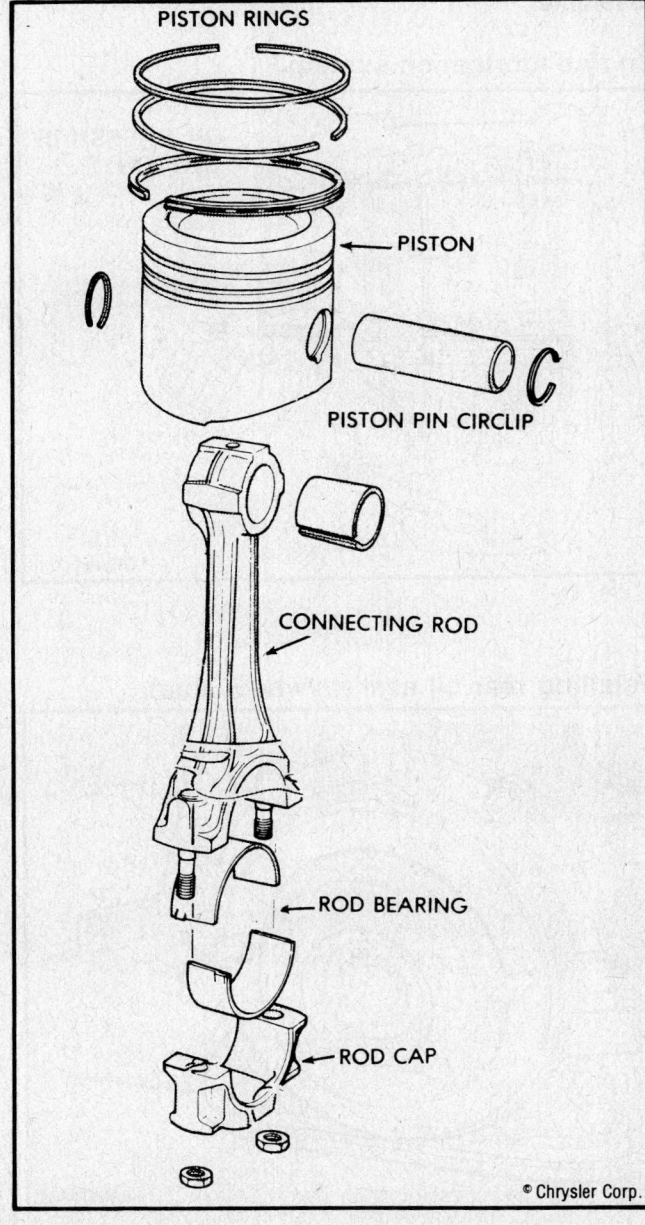

PISTON RINGS

PISTON

PISTON PIN CIRCLIP

CONNECTING ROD

ROD BEARING

ROD CAP

© Chrysler Corp.

Oil pump end play

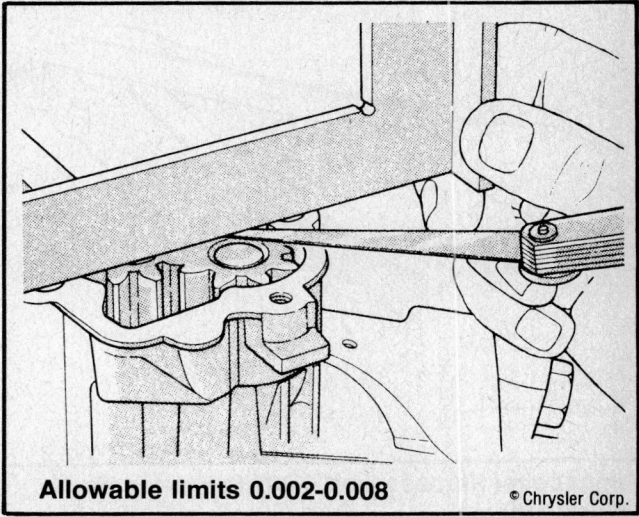

Allowable limits 0.002-0.008   © Chrysler Corp.

Oil pump gear backlash

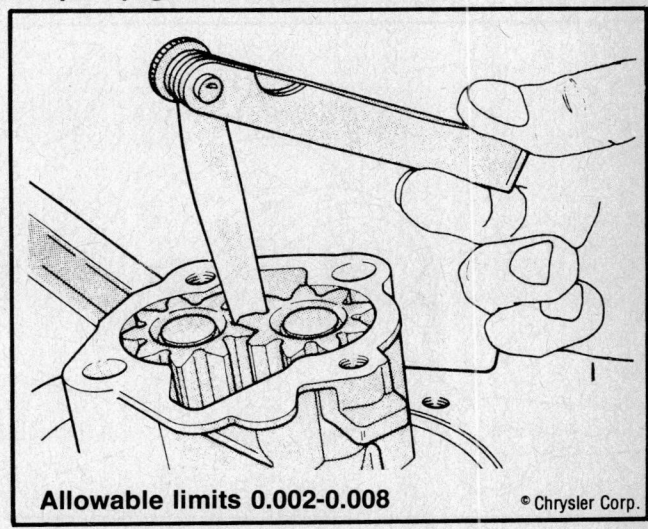

Allowable limits 0.002-0.008   © Chrysler Corp.

Engine oil pump, 104.7 CID engine

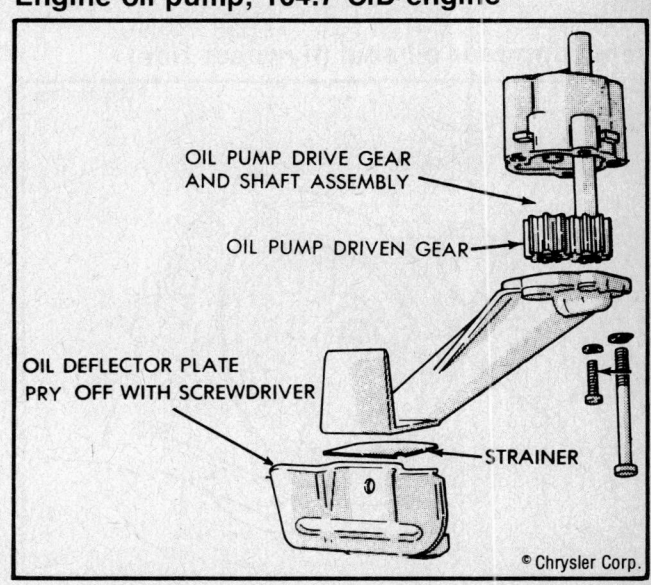

OIL PUMP DRIVE GEAR AND SHAFT ASSEMBLY

OIL PUMP DRIVEN GEAR

OIL DEFLECTOR PLATE PRY OFF WITH SCREWDRIVER

STRAINER

© Chrysler Corp.

CHRYSLER FRONT DRIVE CARS
ARIES, HORIZON, OMNI, RELIANT

Oil pump cover

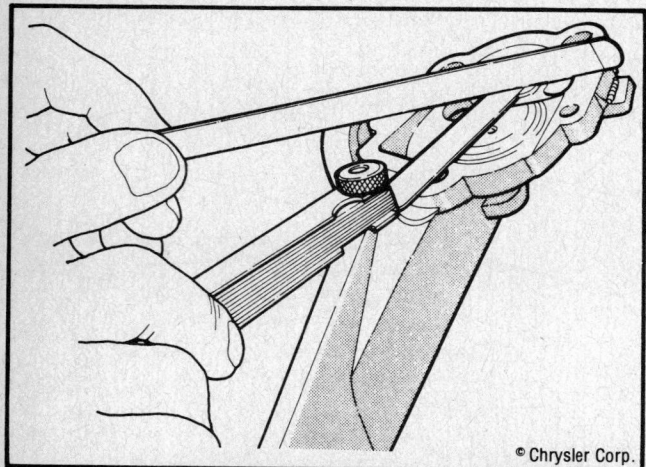

Pump cover flatness limit 0.002 in. (cover can be reserviced)

Checking relief valve

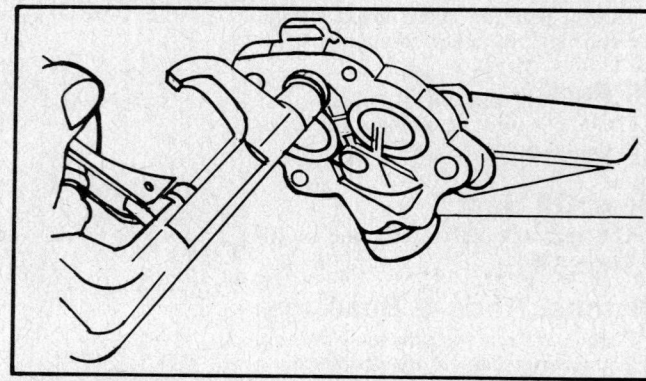

With a rubber tip seal, place nozzle of air hose at relief valve inlet port. Increase air pressure and observe plunger movement at the relief valve outlet port. If valve does not move replace cover assembly.

Removing timing gear

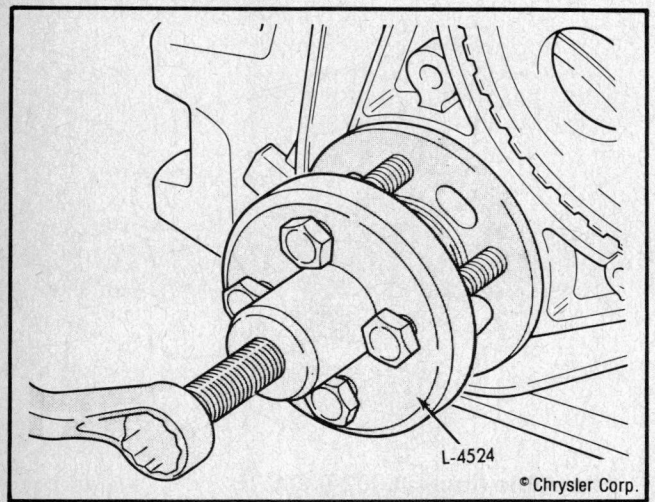

L-4524

© Chrysler Corp.

Remove engine. Special tool required to install oil seal

Engine lubrication system

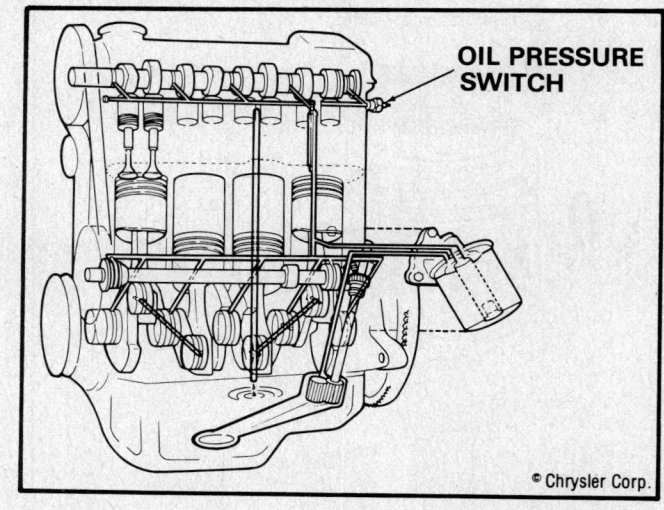

OIL PRESSURE SWITCH

© Chrysler Corp.

Removing rear oil seal (flywheel side)

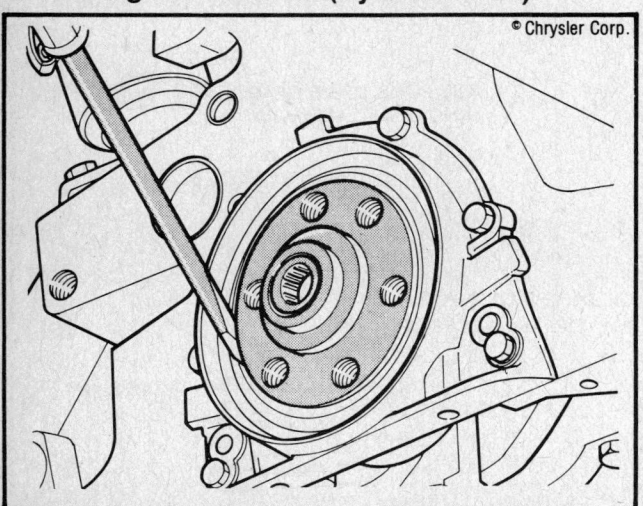

© Chrysler Corp.

Installing rear oil seal (flywheel side)

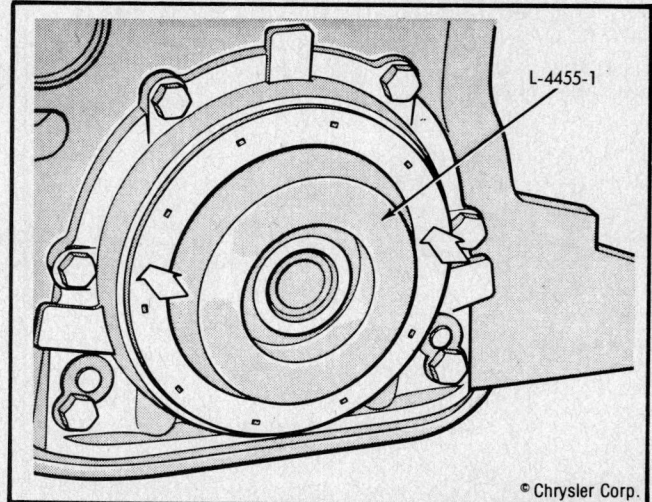

L-4455-1

© Chrysler Corp.

Cylinder head and valve assembly, 135 CID (2.2L) engine

10
6
2
3
7
9
5
1
4
8

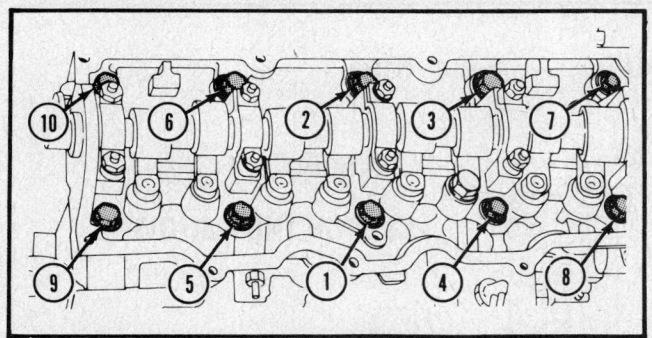

Cylinder head bolt tightening sequence—four step torque procedure in sequence shown
1. 41 N • m (30 Ft. Lbs.)
2. 61 N • m (45 Ft. Lbs.)
3. 61 N • m (45 Ft. Lbs.)
4. + ¼ Turn

1
2
3
4
5

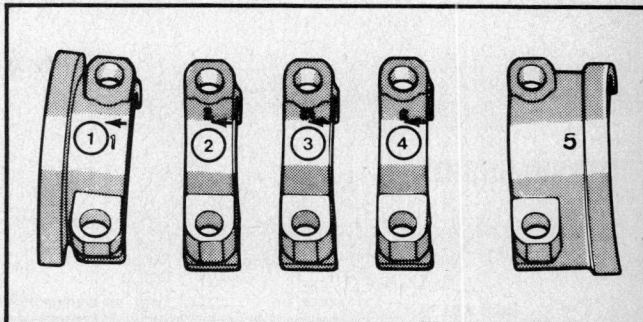

Camshaft bearing caps must be installed before camshaft seals are installed

Chrysler 135 CID engine with automatic transaxle

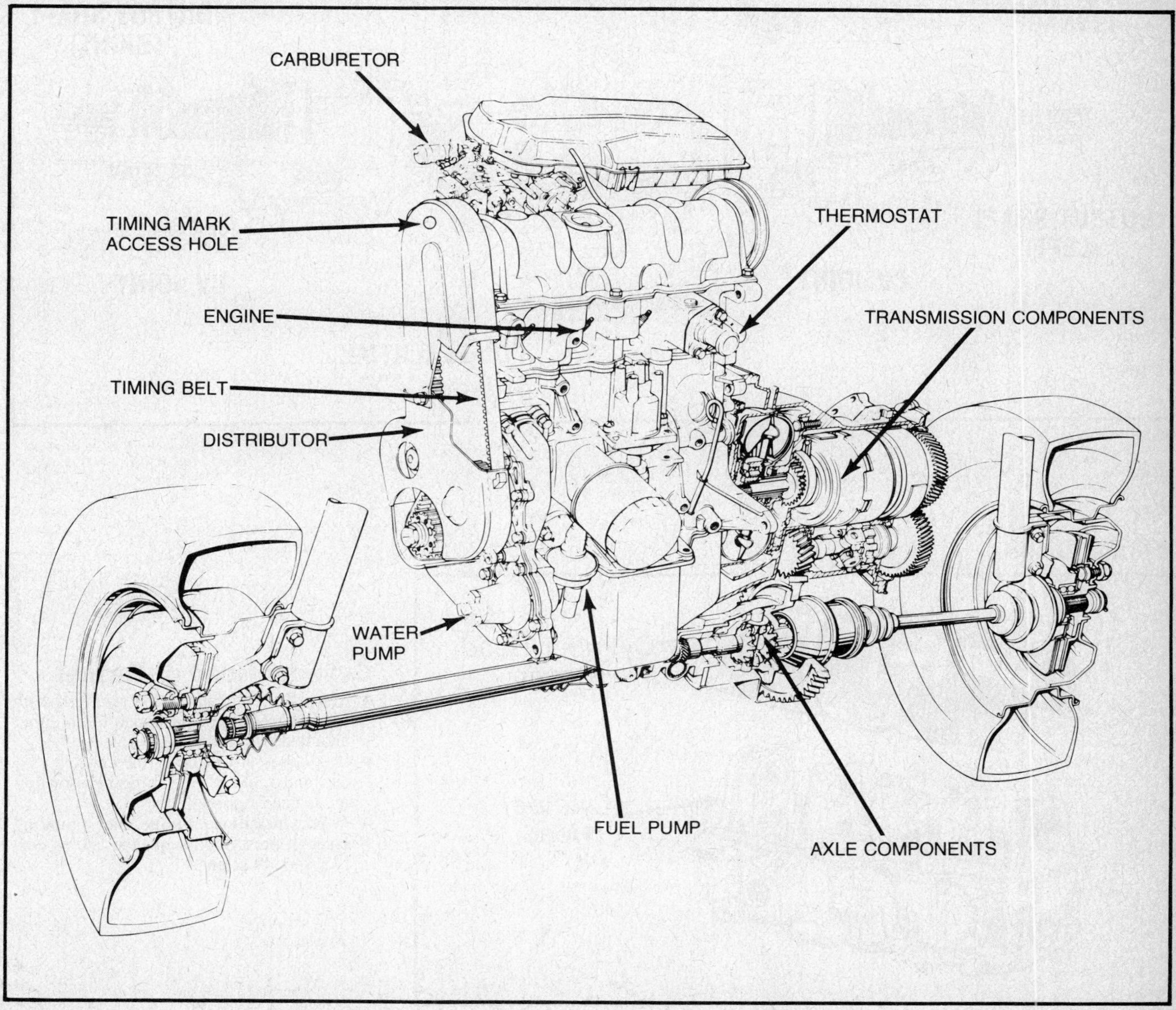

CARBURETOR
TIMING MARK ACCESS HOLE
THERMOSTAT
ENGINE
TRANSMISSION COMPONENTS
TIMING BELT
DISTRIBUTOR
WATER PUMP
FUEL PUMP
AXLE COMPONENTS

CHRYSLER FRONT DRIVE CARS
ARIES, HORIZON, OMNI, RELIANT

Four-speed manual transaxle

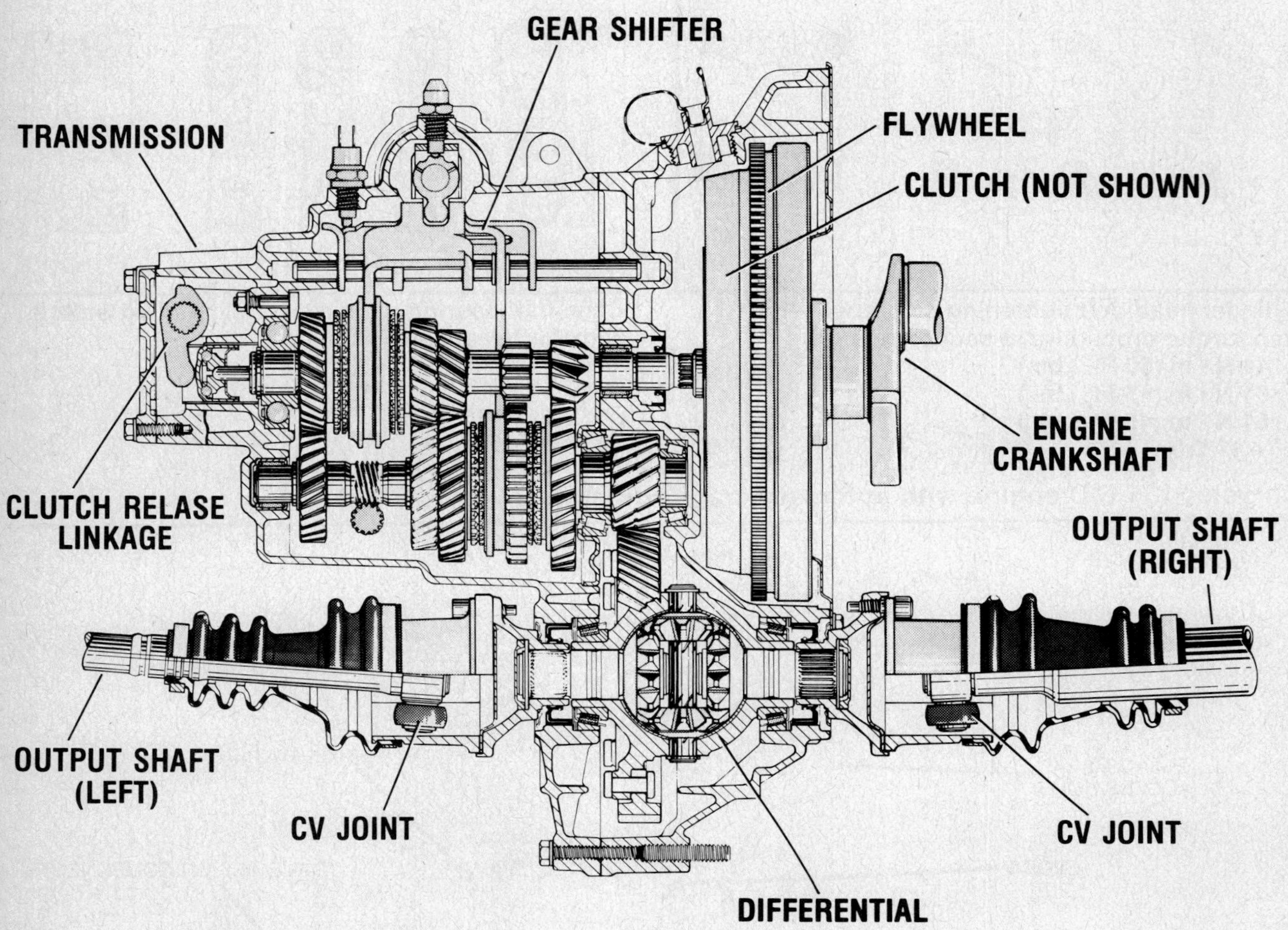

GEAR SHIFTER

TRANSMISSION

FLYWHEEL

CLUTCH (NOT SHOWN)

ENGINE CRANKSHAFT

CLUTCH RELASE LINKAGE

OUTPUT SHAFT (RIGHT)

OUTPUT SHAFT (LEFT)

CV JOINT

CV JOINT

DIFFERENTIAL

Cylinder head

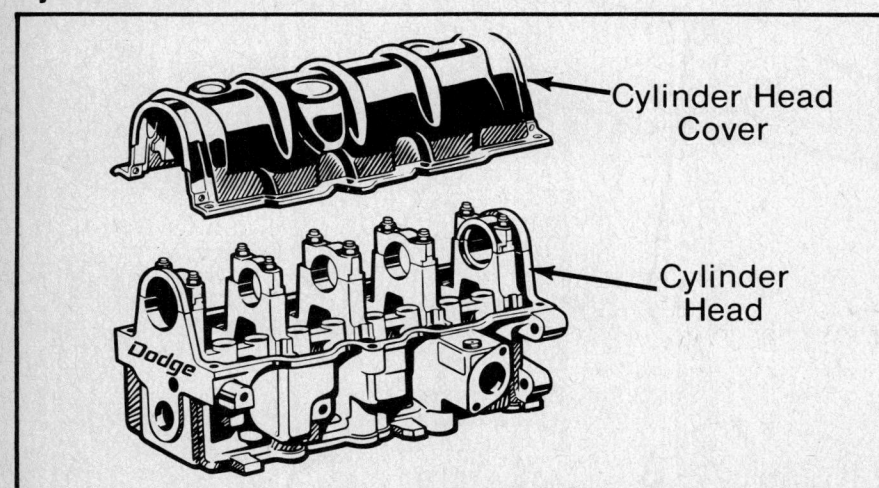

Cylinder Head Cover

Cylinder Head

Cylinder Head or Gasket
- The cylinder head can be removed with the intake and exhaust manifolds either attached or removed.
- It is necessary to drain the cooling system and remove the timing belt for cylinder head removal.
- When installing, torque the mounting bolts in prescribed sequence and to correct specifications.

Camshaft

- The timing belt and camshaft sprocket must be removed before removing the camshaft.
- When installing, use a new camshaft oil seal.

Camshaft, seal and retainer

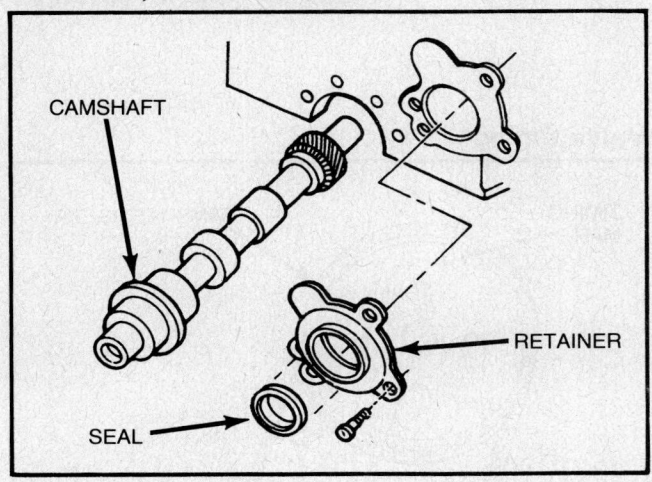

Chrysler-built 135 CID engine

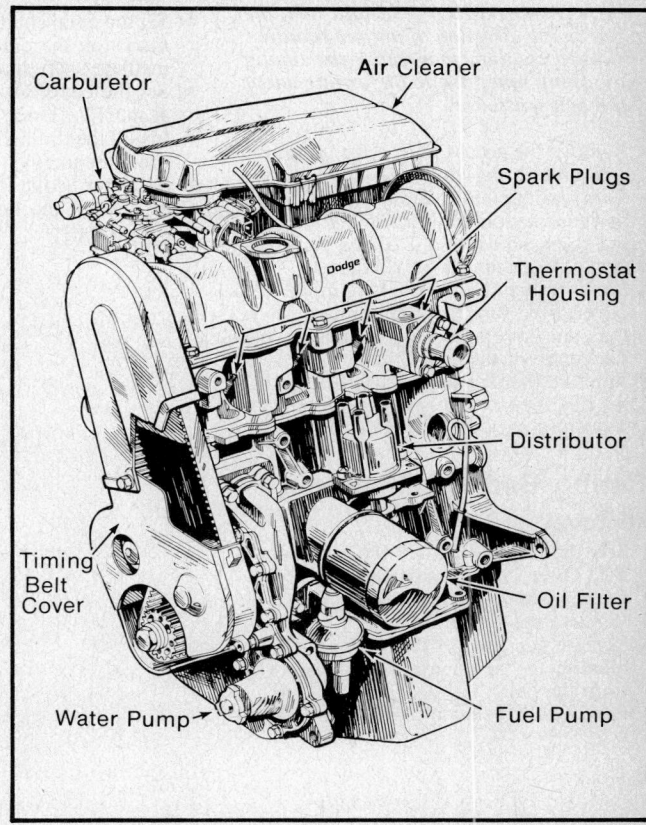

Valve system, 135 CID engine

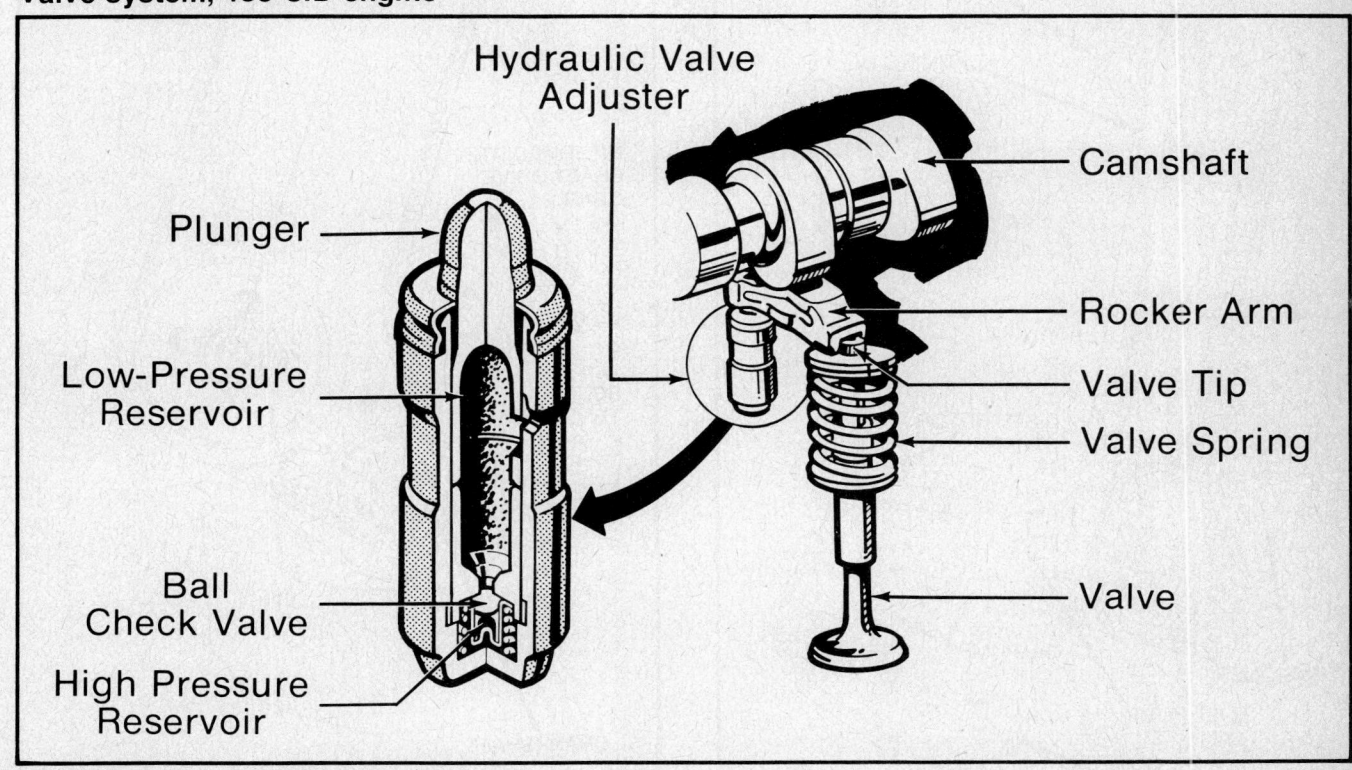

Note that valves are not adjustable

CHRYSLER FRONT DRIVE CARS
ARIES, HORIZON, OMNI, RELIANT

CAMSHAFT TIMING CHECK
CHILTON CAUTION: *Always turn the engine in the direction of normal rotation. Backward rotation may cause the timing belt to jump time, due to the arrangement of the belt tensioner.*

- Remove the access plug at the top of the cam belt timing cover.
- Turn the engine in the direction of the normal rotation until the timing mark on the crankshaft is at T.D.C. on compression stroke number 1 cylinder.
- Look through the access hole in the belt cover to be sure that the timing hole on the cam drive sprocket is lined up with the center of the access hole.
- Remove the distributor cap. Check that the distributor rotor is facing the number 1 position on the distributor cap.

Timing Belt Replacement
Removal
- Set the crankshaft at the number 1 T.D.C. on compression stroke.
- Remove the crankshaft pulley.
- Remove the upper timing belt cover.
- Release tension on the timing belt by moving the belt tensioner pulley away from the belt.
- Remove the belt.

Installation
- Set the crankshaft on T.D.C. Line up the marks on the crankshaft gear and intermediate shaft sprocket.
- Set the camshaft sprocket with the hole at the 12 o'clock position.
- Install the timing belt over the crankshaft sprocket and then counterclockwise over the intermediate and camshaft sprockets. Align the belt fore and aft on the sprockets.
- Move the belt tensioner against the belt.
- Rotate the crankshaft two complete turns in normal rotation to remove the slack from the belt. Torque the tensioner adjustment. Check the alignment of the timing marks.
- Install the upper and lower timing belt covers.
- Install the crankshaft pulley, belts, etc.

Valve timing

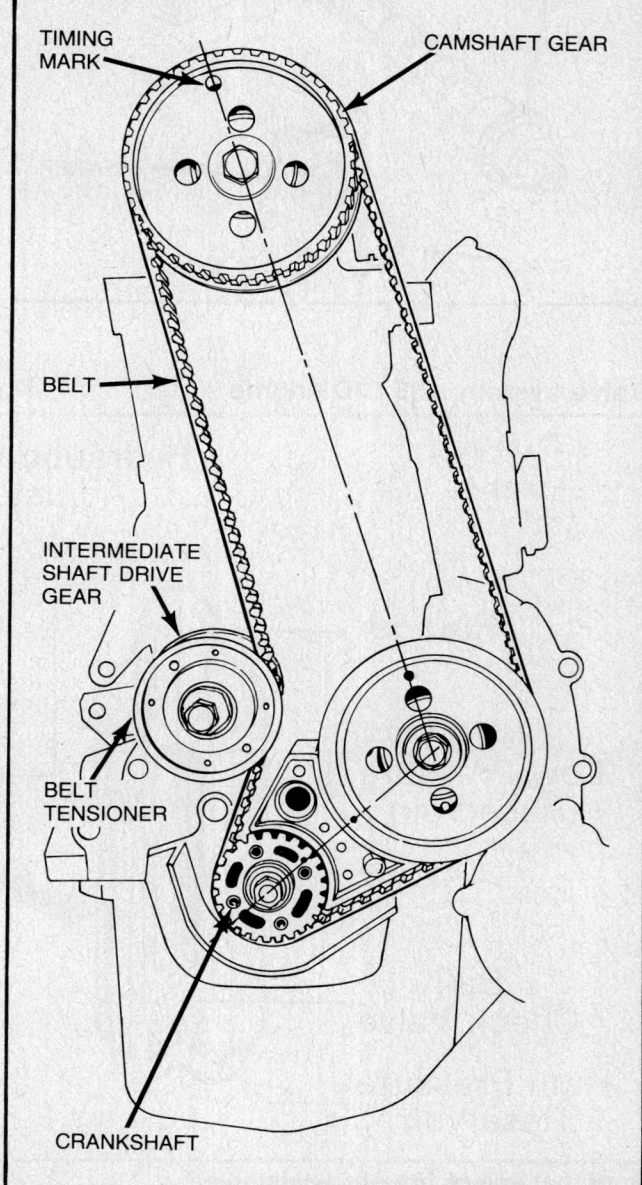

Distributor and oil pump drive

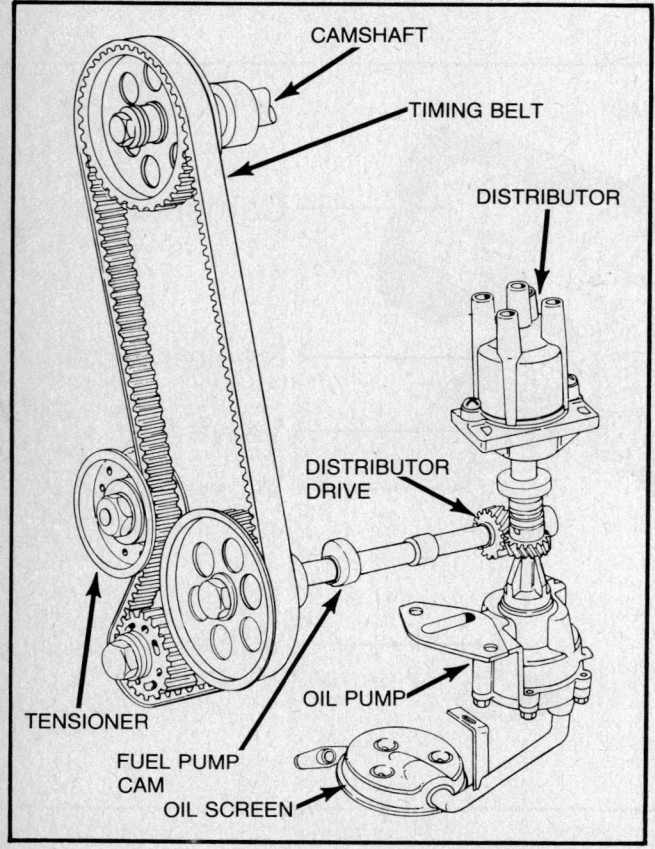

Piston and connecting rod assembly, 135 CID engine

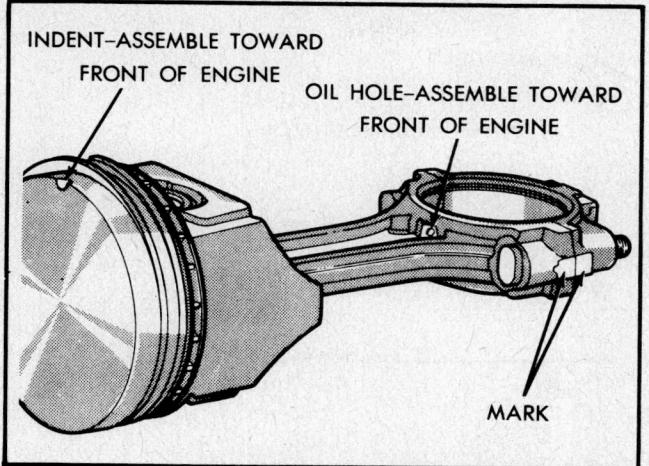

Mark connecting rod and cap before removing

Camshaft and intermediate shaft sprocket removal and installation, 135 CID engine

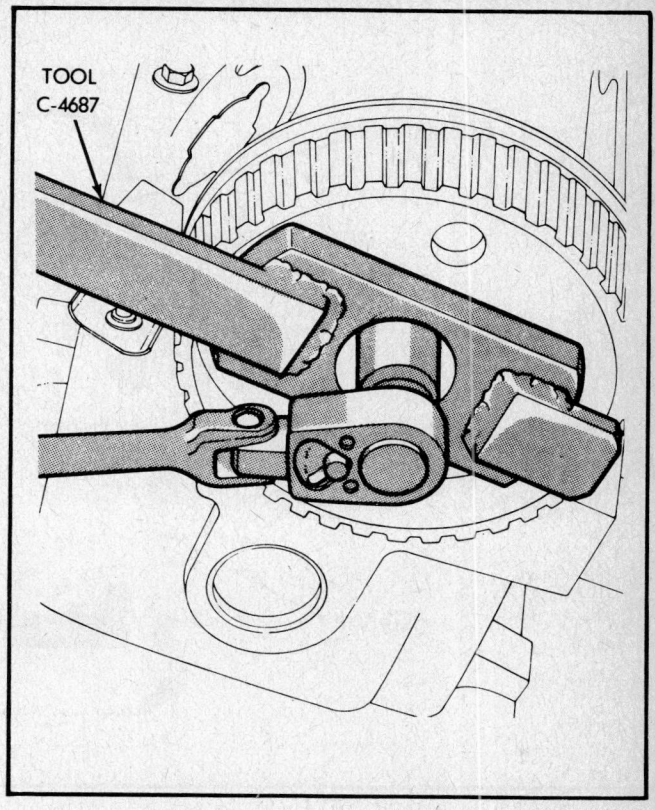

Piston marking, 135 CID engine

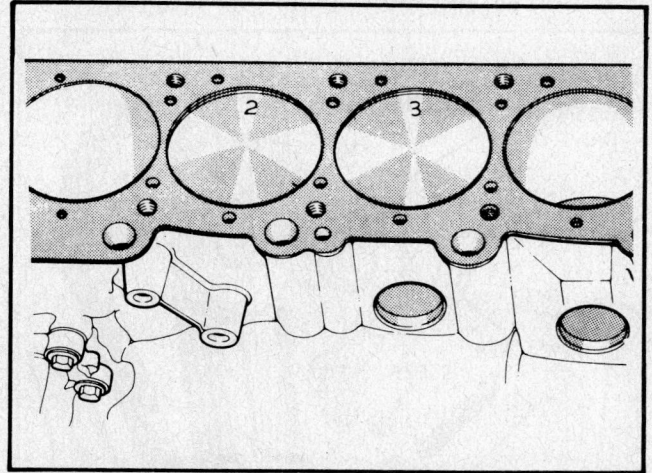

Indent on piston top must face timing belt side of engine

Drive belt tension adjustment, 135 CID engine

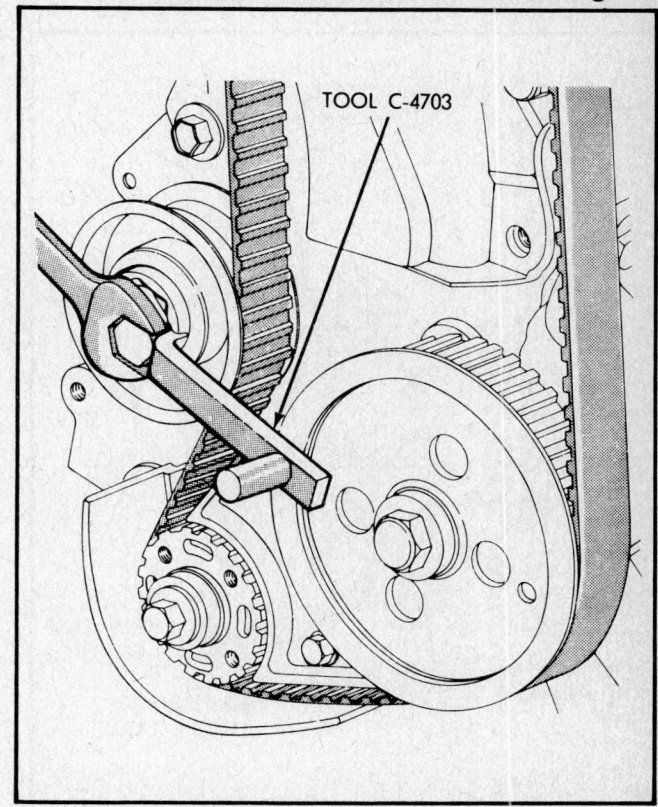

CHRYSLER FRONT DRIVE CARS
ARIES, HORIZON, OMNI, RELIANT

Mitsubishi silent shaft 155.9 CID engine

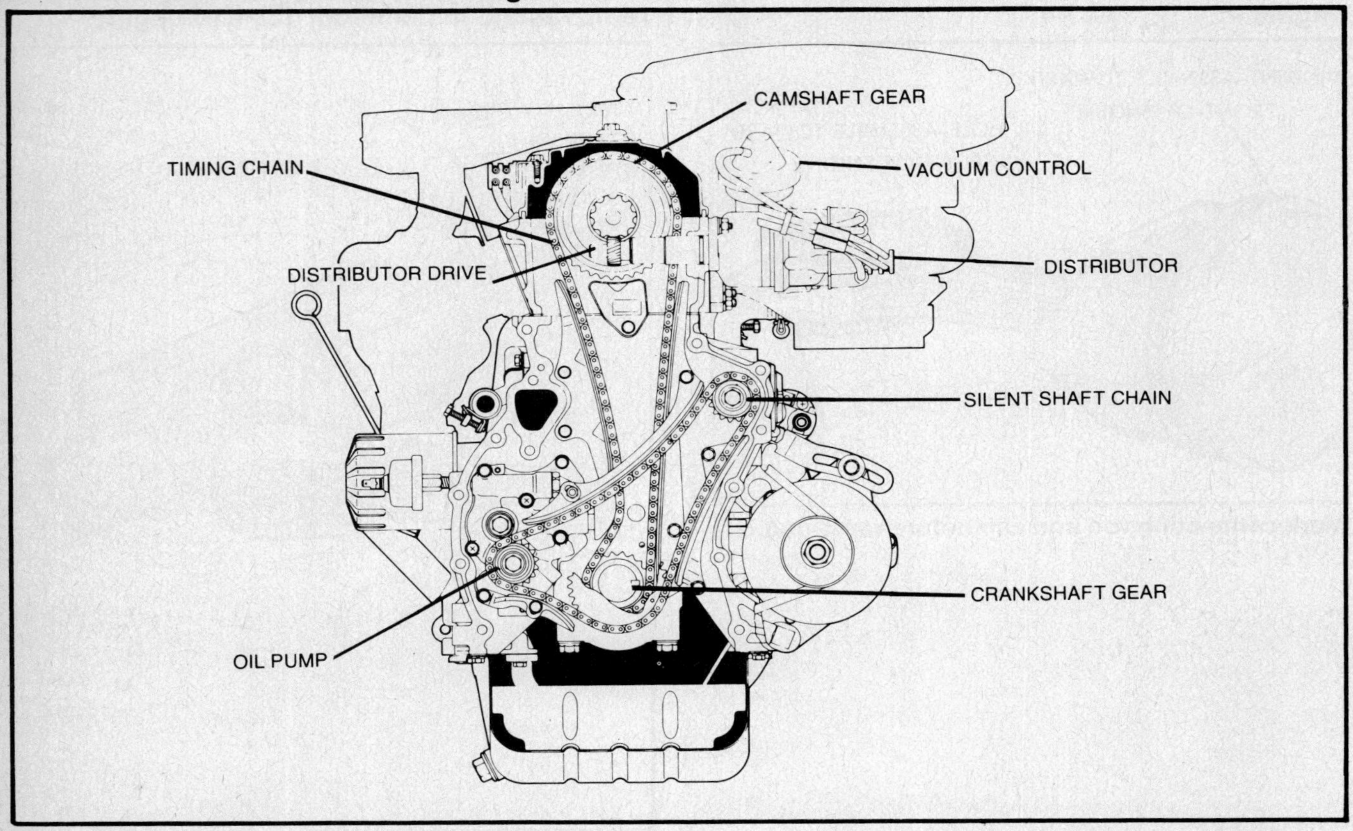

CAMSHAFT GEAR

VACUUM CONTROL

TIMING CHAIN

DISTRIBUTOR

DISTRIBUTOR DRIVE

SILENT SHAFT CHAIN

CRANKSHAFT GEAR

OIL PUMP

Chain case cover, 155.9 CID engine

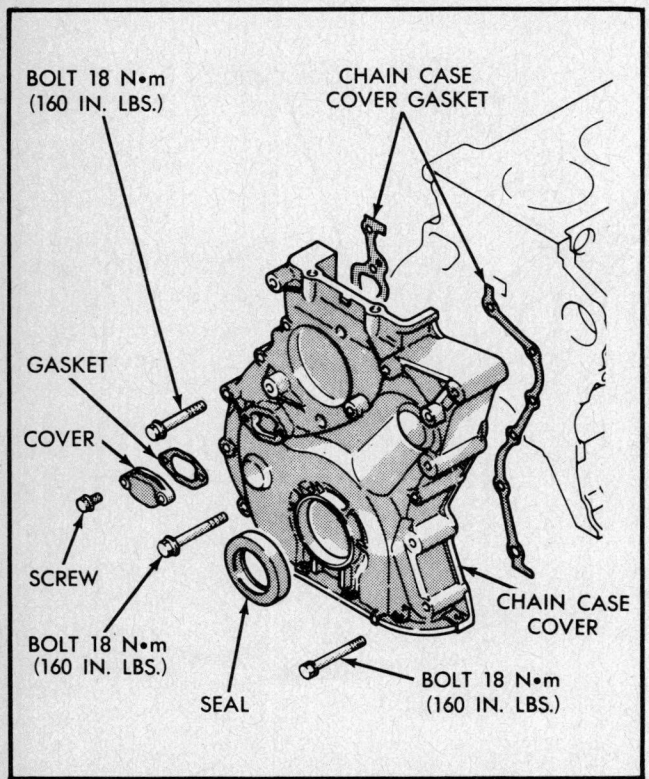

BOLT 18 N•m (160 IN. LBS.)

CHAIN CASE COVER GASKET

GASKET

COVER

SCREW

BOLT 18 N•m (160 IN. LBS.)

SEAL

BOLT 18 N•m (160 IN. LBS.)

CHAIN CASE COVER

Camshaft drive chain, 155.9 CID engine

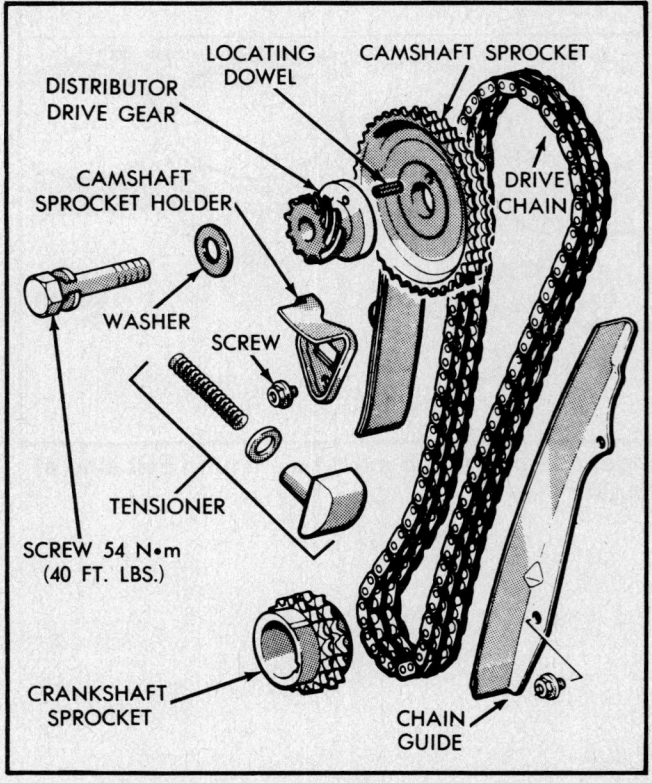

LOCATING DOWEL

CAMSHAFT SPROCKET

DISTRIBUTOR DRIVE GEAR

CAMSHAFT SPROCKET HOLDER

DRIVE CHAIN

WASHER

SCREW

TENSIONER

SCREW 54 N•m (40 FT. LBS.)

CRANKSHAFT SPROCKET

CHAIN GUIDE

Timing Chain

Removal

- Drain the coolant and remove the radiator. Disconnect the ground battery cable.
- Remove the alternator and accessory belts.
- Rotate the crankshaft to bring the number 1 piston to T.D.C. on the compression stroke.
- Mark and remove the distributor.
- Remove the crankshaft pulley.
- Remove the water pump assembly.
- Remove the cylinder head.
- Raise the front of the car and support it safely.
- Drain the engine oil. Remove the oil pan and screen.
- Remove the timing case cover.
- Remove the chain guides.
- Remove the locking bolts from the chain sprockets.
- Remove the crankshaft sprocket, counter balance shaft sprocket and the outer chain.
- Remove the crankshaft and camshaft sprockets and the inner chain.
- Remove the camshaft sprocket holder and the chain guides, both left and right. Remove the tensioner spring and sleeve from the oil pump.
- Remove the oil pump by first removing the bolt locking the oil pump driven gear and the right counter balance shaft. Then remove the oil pump mounting bolts. Remove the counter balance shaft from the engine block.

NOTE: If the bolt locking the oil pump driven gear and the counter balance shaft is hard to loosen, remove the oil pump and the shaft as a unit.

- Remove the left counter balance shaft thrust washer and withdraw the shaft from the engine block.

Installation

- Install the right counter balance shaft into the engine block.
- Install the oil pump assembly. Do not lose the Woodruff key from the end of the counter balance shaft. Torque the oil pump mounting bolts to 6 to 7 lbs.
- Tighten the counter balance shaft and the oil pump driven gear mounting bolt.

NOTE: The counter balance shaft and the oil pump can be installed as a unit.

- Install the left counter balance shaft into the engine block.
- Install a new O-ring on the thrust plate. Install the unit into the engine block using a pair of bolts without heads to act as alignment guides.

CHILTON CAUTION: If the thrust plate is turned to align the bolt holes, the O-ring may be damaged.

- Remove the guide bolts. Install the regular bolts into the thrust plate and tighten them securely.

- Rotate the crankshaft to bring the number 1 piston to T.D.C.
- Install the cylinder head.
- Install the sprocket holder and the right and left chain guides.
- Install the tensioner spring and sleeve on the oil pump body.
- Install the camshaft and crankshaft sprockets on the timing chain, aligning the sprocket punch marks to the chain plated links.
- While holding the sprocket and chain as a unit, install the crankshaft sprocket over the crankshaft. Align it with the keyway.
- Having the dowel pin hole on the camshaft in a vertical position, install camshaft sprocket and chain on the camshaft.

NOTE: The sprocket timing mark and the plated chain link should be at the 2 to 3 o'clock position when correctly installed.

Timing chain, 155.9 CID engine

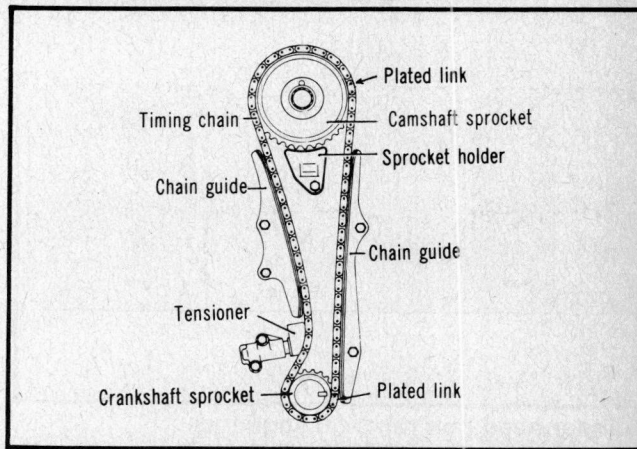

Line up the plated links with the marks on the camshaft and crankshaft sprockets

Drive system for balancer system

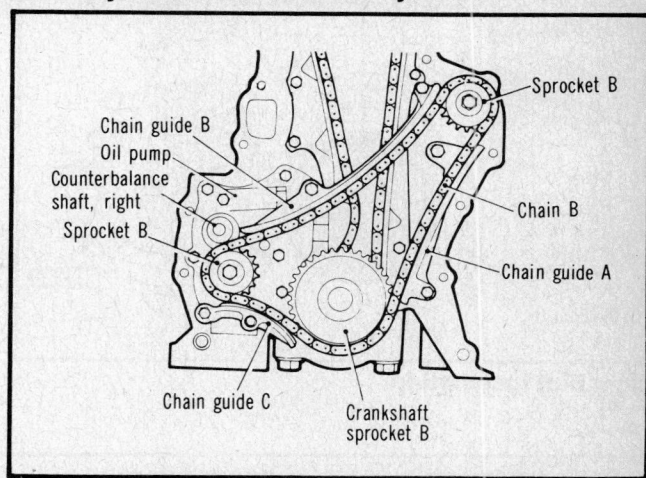

The countershaft rotates twice as fast as the crankshaft. Line up the plated links with the markings on the sprockets.

CHILTON CAUTION: *The chain must be aligned in the right and left chain guides with the tensioner pushing against the chain. The tension for the inner chain is predetermined by the spring tension.*

- Install the crankshaft sprocket for the outer or "B" chain.
- Install the two counter balance shaft sprockets. Align the punched mating marks with the plated links of the chain.
- Holding the two shaft sprockets and chain, install the outer chain in alignment with the mating mark of the crankshaft sprocket. Then install the shaft sprockets on the counter balance shaft and the oil pump driven gear. Install the lock bolts. Recheck the alignment of the punch marks and the plated links.

Cylinder head and valve assembly, 155.9 CID (2.6L) engine

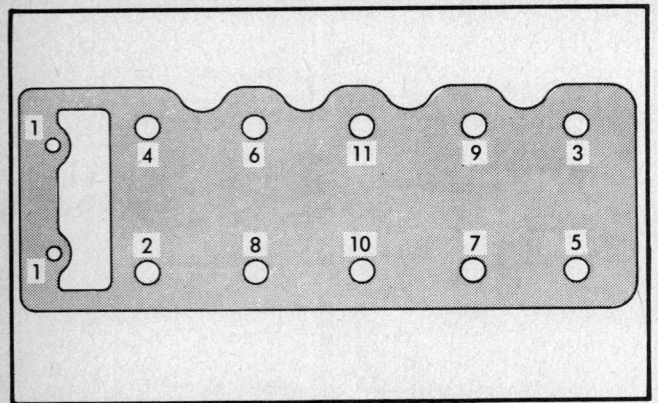

Cylinder head bolt removal sequence

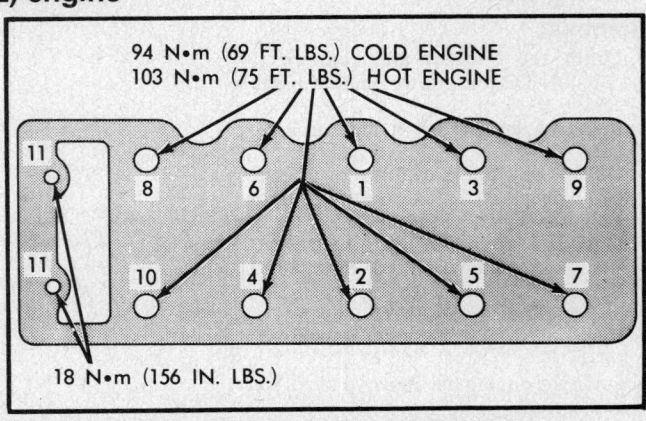

94 N•m (69 FT. LBS.) COLD ENGINE
103 N•m (75 FT. LBS.) HOT ENGINE

18 N•m (156 IN. LBS.)

Cylinder head bolt tightening sequence

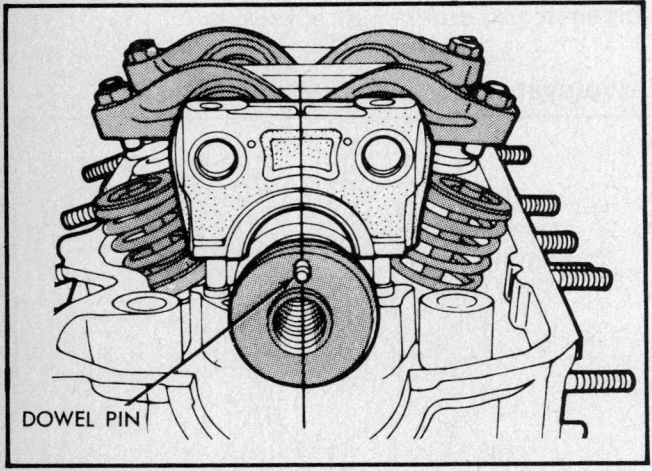

DOWEL PIN

Camshaft installation

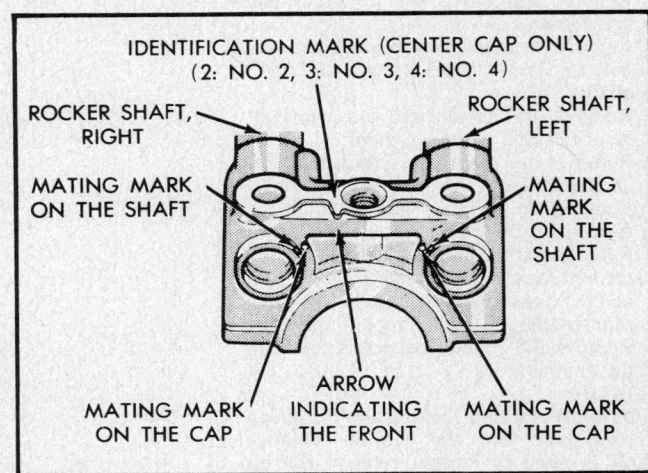

IDENTIFICATION MARK (CENTER CAP ONLY)
(2: NO. 2, 3: NO. 3, 4: NO. 4)

ROCKER SHAFT, RIGHT

ROCKER SHAFT, LEFT

MATING MARK ON THE SHAFT

MATING MARK ON THE SHAFT

MATING MARK ON THE CAP

ARROW INDICATING THE FRONT

MATING MARK ON THE CAP

Camshaft bearing cap

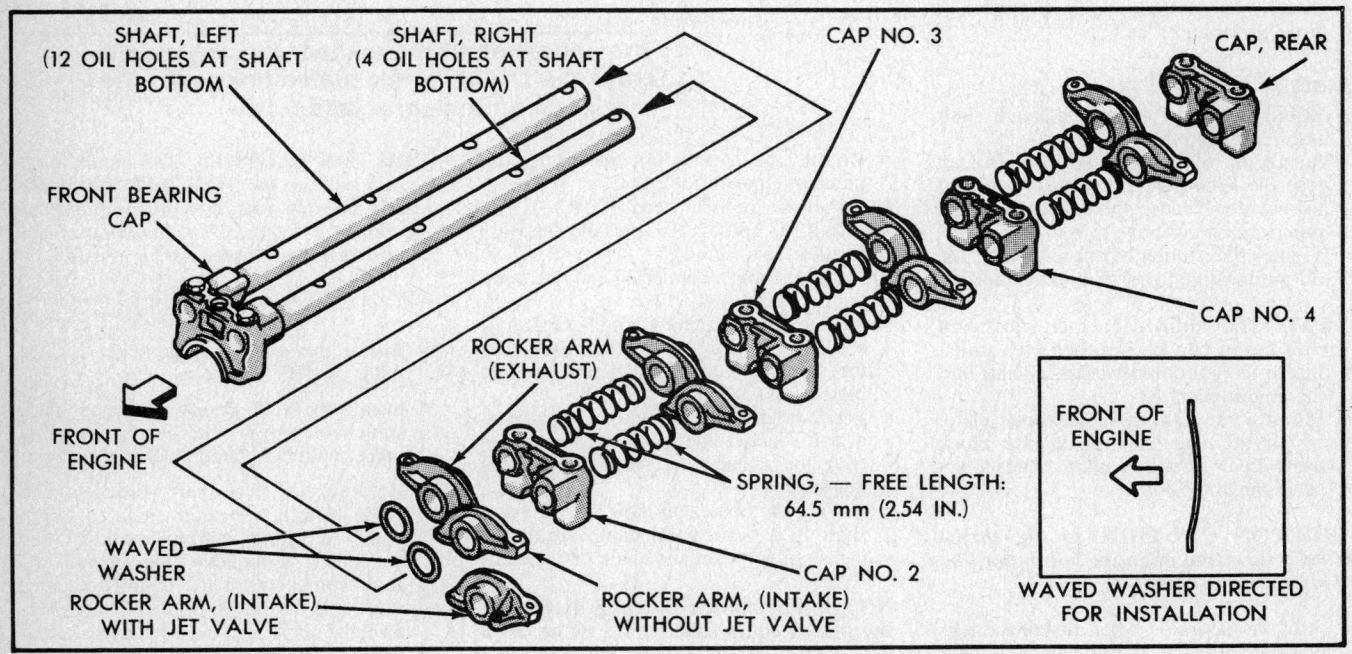

SHAFT, LEFT
(12 OIL HOLES AT SHAFT BOTTOM)

SHAFT, RIGHT
(4 OIL HOLES AT SHAFT BOTTOM)

CAP NO. 3

CAP, REAR

FRONT BEARING CAP

FRONT OF ENGINE

ROCKER ARM (EXHAUST)

CAP NO. 4

SPRING, — FREE LENGTH: 64.5 mm (2.54 IN.)

WAVED WASHER

ROCKER ARM, (INTAKE) WITH JET VALVE

CAP NO. 2

ROCKER ARM, (INTAKE) WITHOUT JET VALVE

FRONT OF ENGINE

WAVED WASHER DIRECTED FOR INSTALLATION

Assembling the rocker arm shaft

A236

Valve arrangement

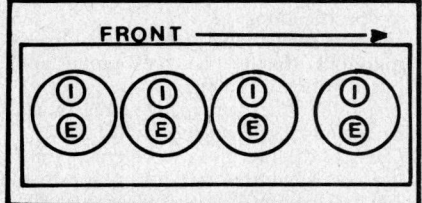

FRONT →

Valve Adjustments

This engine has three types of valves. There are four intake valves, four exhaust valves and four jet valves.

NOTE: The jet valve must be adjusted before the intake valve adjustment is made.

JET VALVE ADJUSTMENT

- With the engine at operating temperature, loosen all intake valve adjusting screws about two turns.
- One cylinder at a time, move the engine to T.D.C. on each cylinder, (both intake and exhaust valves completely close). Adjust the jet valve so that a .006″ feeler gauge fits between the valve stem and the adjusting screws.

INTAKE AND EXHAUST VALVES ADJUSTMENT

- With the engine at normal operating temperature, remove the rocker arm cover.
- Watch the valve operation on number 1 cylinder while rotating the crankshaft to close the exhaust valve and have the intake valve just begin to open. This places the number 4 cylinder on its firing stroke and permits the adjustment of the valves.
- Measure the clearance between the valve stem tip and the rocker arm face. The clearance is 0.006 inch for the intake valves and 0.010 inch for the exhaust valves when properly adjusted.

Adjusting engine valve clearance

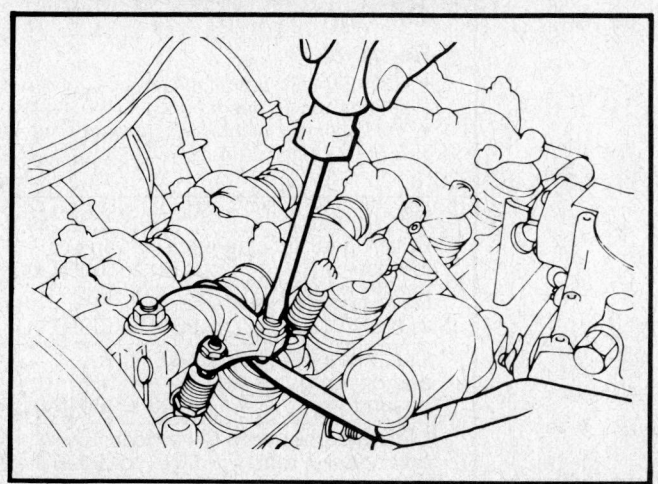

- Adjust as necessary. Then tighten the lock nuts and recheck the clearance.
- Repeat the valve adjustment for the remaining cylinders as per the Valve Adjusting Sequences chart.

Valve Adjusting Sequences

Exhaust Valve Closing	Adjust
No. 1 Cylinder	No. 4 Cylinder Valves
No. 2 Cylinder	No. 3 Cylinder Valves
No. 3 Cylinder	No. 2 Cylinder Valves
No. 4 Cylinder	No. 1 Cylinder Valves

Adjusting engine jet valve clearance

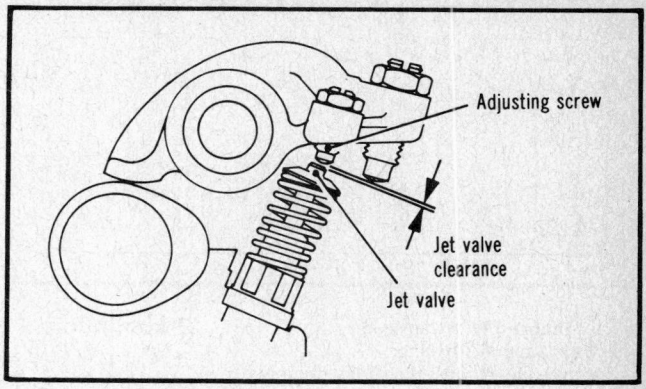

Adjusting screw

Jet valve clearance

Jet valve

Cylinder Head
Removal

CHILTON CAUTION: *Set the engine on number one T.D.C. before removing the timing chain. Keep the chain tight on the lower sprocket so that the valve timing will not be disturbed.*

- Disconnect the battery ground cable. Remove the air cleaner assembly and the attached hoses.
- Drain the coolant. Then remove the upper radiator hose and the heater hoses.
- Remove the fuel line. Then disconnect the accelerator linkage, distributor vacuum lines, purge valve and water temperature gauge wire.
- Remove the spark plug wires and the fuel pump. Then remove the distributor.

Cylinder head components

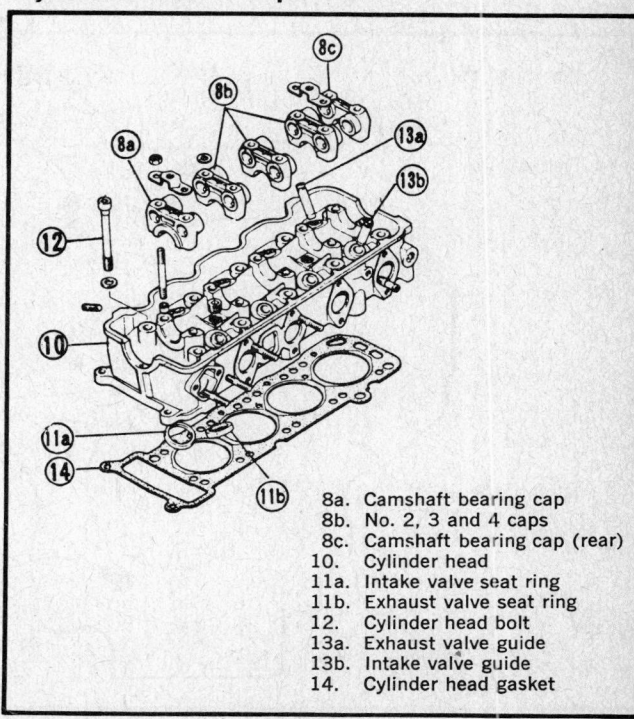

8a. Camshaft bearing cap
8b. No. 2, 3 and 4 caps
8c. Camshaft bearing cap (rear)
10. Cylinder head
11a. Intake valve seat ring
11b. Exhaust valve seat ring
12. Cylinder head bolt
13a. Exhaust valve guide
13b. Intake valve guide
14. Cylinder head gasket

Head bolt tightening sequences

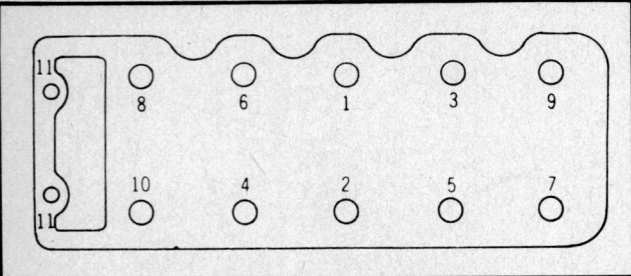

- Disconnect the exhaust pipe from the exhaust manifold flange.
- Remove the exhaust manifold assembly.
- Remove the intake manifold and carburetor as a unit.
- Turn the crankshaft to put number 1 piston at T.D.C. on the compression stroke.

NOTE: During the following procedures, do not turn the crankshaft after locating T.D.C.

- Remove the rocker arm cover.
- Position the camshaft sprocket dowel pin at the 12 o'clock position with the crankshaft pulley notch aligned with the timing mark "T" at the front of the timing chain case.
- Mate-match the timing chain with the mating mark on the camshaft sprocket.
- Remove the camshaft sprocket bolt, distributor gear and sprocket from the camshaft.
- Loosen and remove the cylinder head bolts in two or three stages to avoid cylinder head warpage.
- Remove the cylinder head from the engine block.

Installation

- Clean the cylinder head and block mating surfaces. Install a new cylinder head gasket.
- Position the cylinder head on the engine block. Engage the dowel pins front and rear. Install the cylinder head bolts in their respective holes.
- Tighten the head bolts in three stages. Then torque them to specifications.
- Install the timing belt upper under cover on the 1977–79 1600 cc engine.
- Locate the camshaft in the position as when removed. Pull the camshaft sprocket and bolt or chain upward and install on the camshaft.
- Install the camshaft sprocket bolt and distributor gear and tighten.
- Install the timing belt upper front cover and spark plug cable support, where applicable.
- Apply sealant to the intake manifold gasket on both sides. Position the gasket and install the intake manifold. Tighten nuts to specifications.

CHILTON CAUTION: *Be sure that no sealant enters the jet air passages.*

Engine oil pump

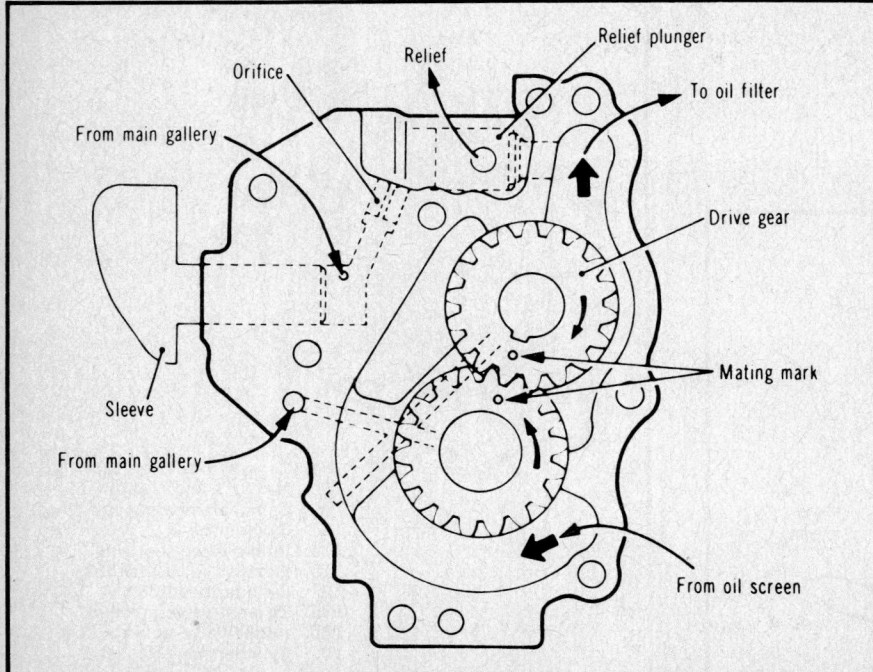

- Install the exhaust manifold gaskets and the manifold assembly. Tighten the nuts to specifications.
- Connect the exhaust pipe to the exhaust manifold. Install the fuel pump and purge valve.
- Install the water temperature gauge wire, heater hoses and upper radiator hose.
- Connect the fuel lines, accelerator linkage, vacuum hoses and spark plug wires.
- Fill the cooling system and connect the ground battery cable. Install the distributor to fire number 1 cylinder.
- Temporarily adjust the valve clearance to the cold engine specifications.

Cold Engine Specifications

Jet valve (if equipped)	.003 in. (.07 mm)
Intake valve	.003 in. (.07 mm)
Exhaust valve	.007 in. (.17 mm)

- Install the gasket on the rocker arm cover. Temporarily install the cover on the engine.
- Start the engine and bring it to normal operating temperature. Stop the engine and remove the rocker arm cover.
- Adjust the valves to hot engine specifications.

Hot Engine Specifications

Jet valve (if equipped)	.006 in. (.15 mm)
Intake valve	.006 in. (.15 mm)
Exhaust valve	.010 in. (.25 mm)

NOTE: Set the jet valves before setting the intake valves.

- Reinstall the rocker arm cover and tighten securely.

Oil Pan
Removal

- The oil pan can be removed without disturbing the engine mounts.
- For oil pump instructions, read the chapter on timing chain removal.

Gear end play	.0024 to .0059 in.
Driven gear tip clearance to body	.0041 to .0059 in.
Drive gear tip clearance to body	.0041 to .0059 in.
Clearance between drive and driven gears and bearing front	.0008 to .0018 in.
Clearance between drive gear and bearing rear	.0017 to .0026 in.

STEERING & BRAKES SECTION

Steering Gear
- Remove tie rod ends, and drive out lower roll pin attaching pinion shaft to lower universal joint. Remove tubes to pump on power gears.
- Remove bolts attaching gear to front suspension crossmember, and remove gear.

Steering Column
- Disconnect all electrical wiring connectors.
- Remove lower roll pin from upper universal joint.
- Dismount the column from the panel.

Ball Joint Inspection
- Ball joints are intended to operate with no free play.

Steering gears

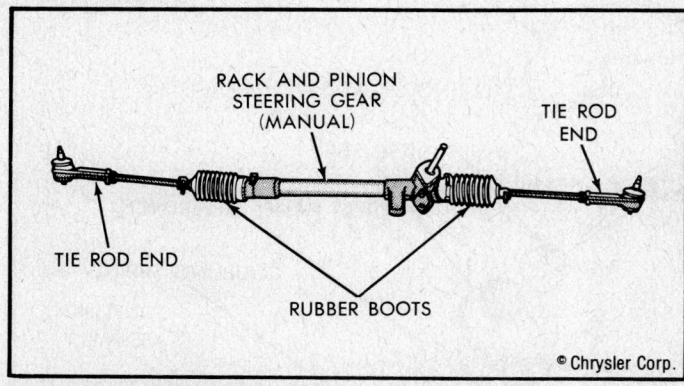

Manual steering gear

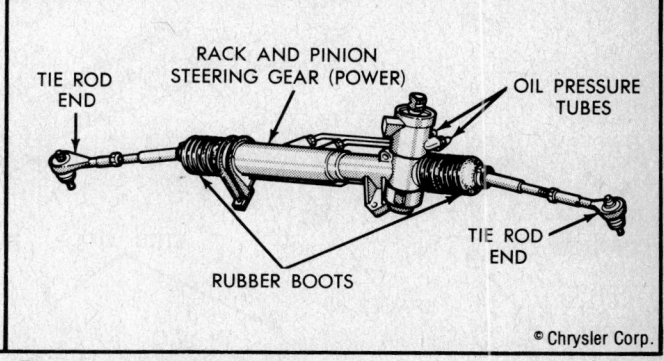

Power steering gear

Steering column assembly—L Car

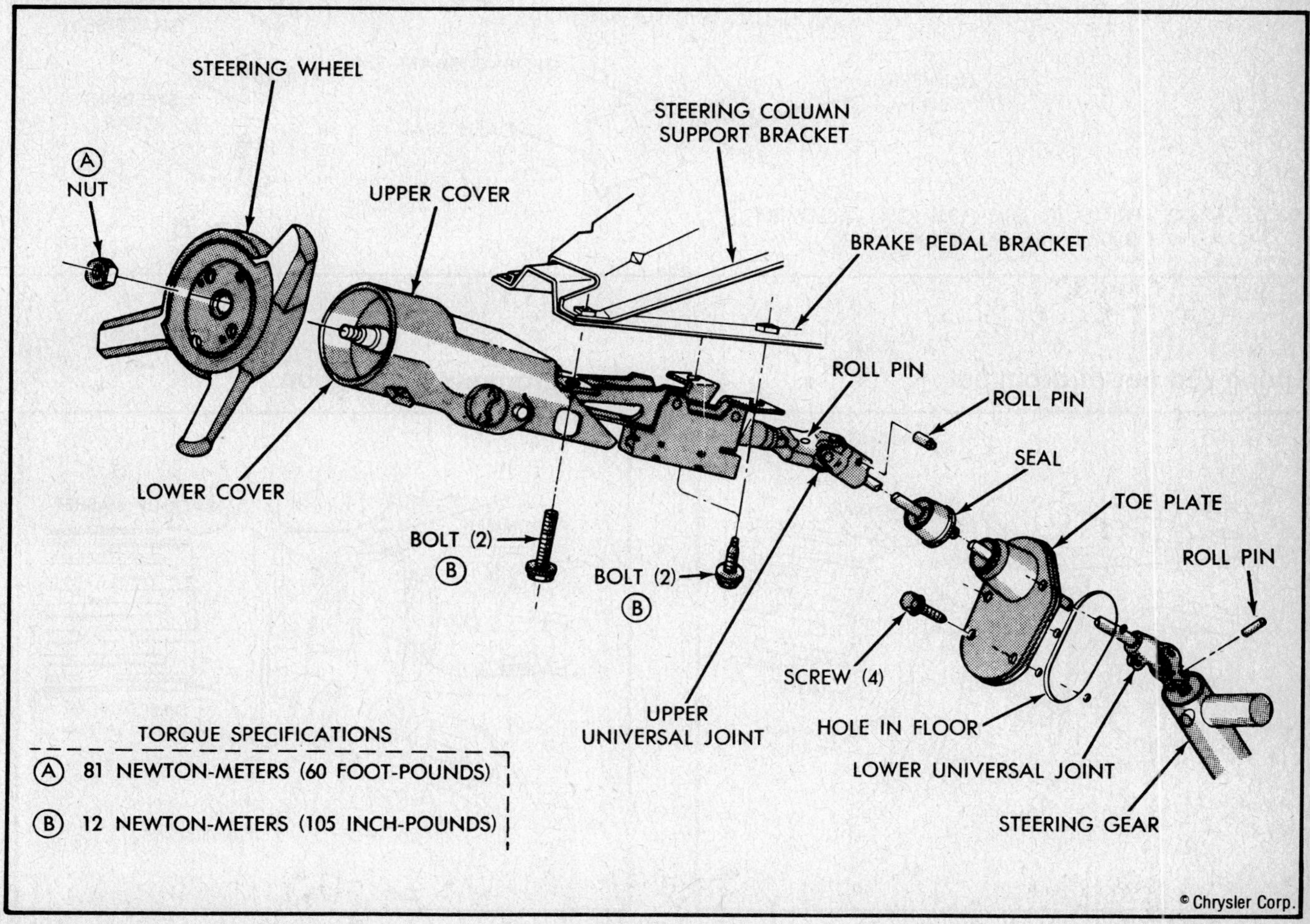

TORQUE SPECIFICATIONS

Ⓐ 81 NEWTON-METERS (60 FOOT-POUNDS)

Ⓑ 12 NEWTON-METERS (105 INCH-POUNDS)

© Chrysler Corp.

A239

Steering column assembly—K Car

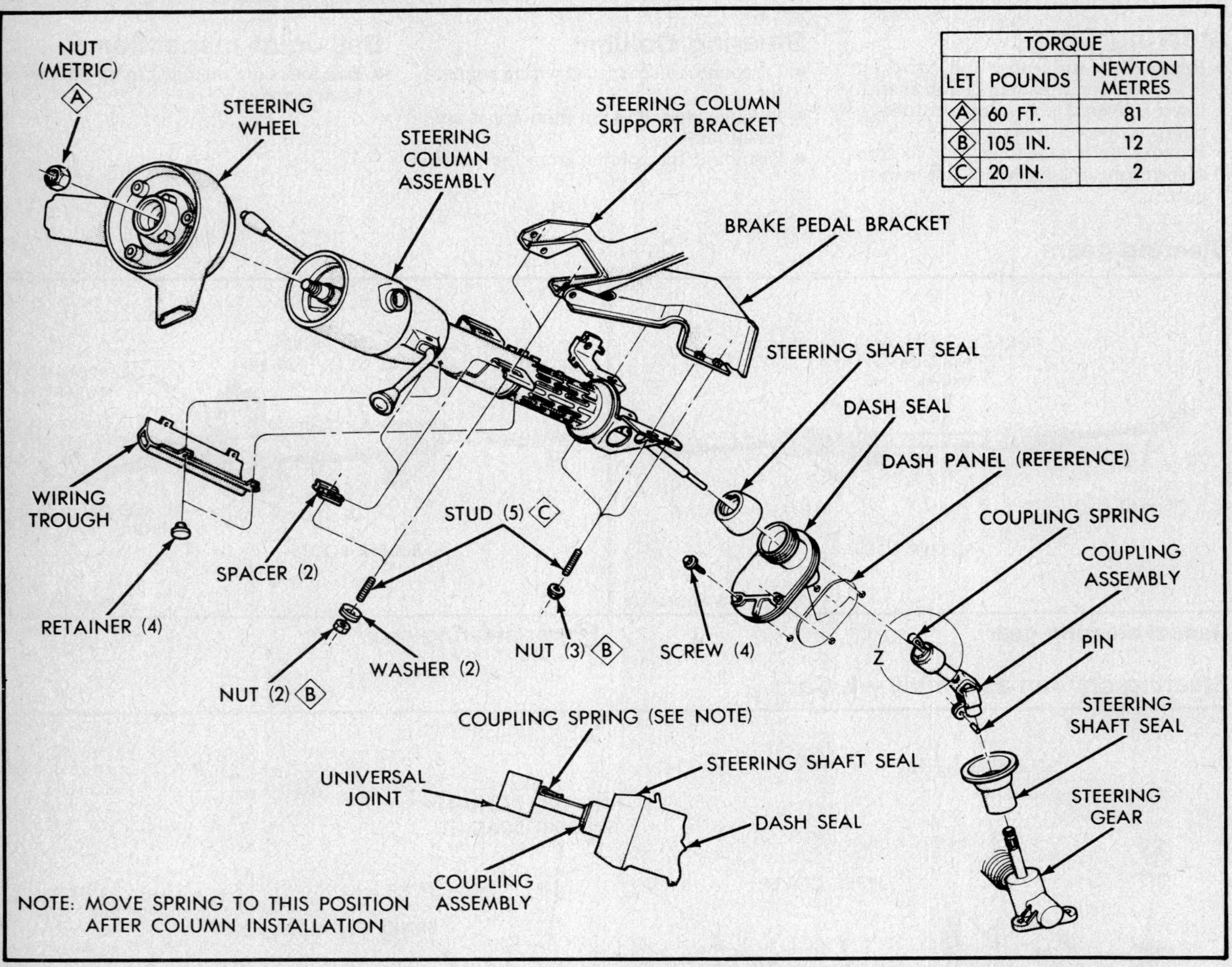

TORQUE		
LET	POUNDS	NEWTON METRES
A	60 FT.	81
B	105 IN.	12
C	20 IN.	2

NUT (METRIC) ◇A◇

STEERING WHEEL

STEERING COLUMN ASSEMBLY

STEERING COLUMN SUPPORT BRACKET

BRAKE PEDAL BRACKET

STEERING SHAFT SEAL

DASH SEAL

DASH PANEL (REFERENCE)

COUPLING SPRING

COUPLING ASSEMBLY

PIN

STEERING SHAFT SEAL

STEERING GEAR

WIRING TROUGH

RETAINER (4)

SPACER (2)

STUD (5) ◇C◇

NUT (3) ◇B◇

SCREW (4)

NUT (2) ◇B◇

WASHER (2)

COUPLING SPRING (SEE NOTE)

UNIVERSAL JOINT

STEERING SHAFT SEAL

DASH SEAL

COUPLING ASSEMBLY

NOTE: MOVE SPRING TO THIS POSITION AFTER COLUMN INSTALLATION

Prying rod out of grommet

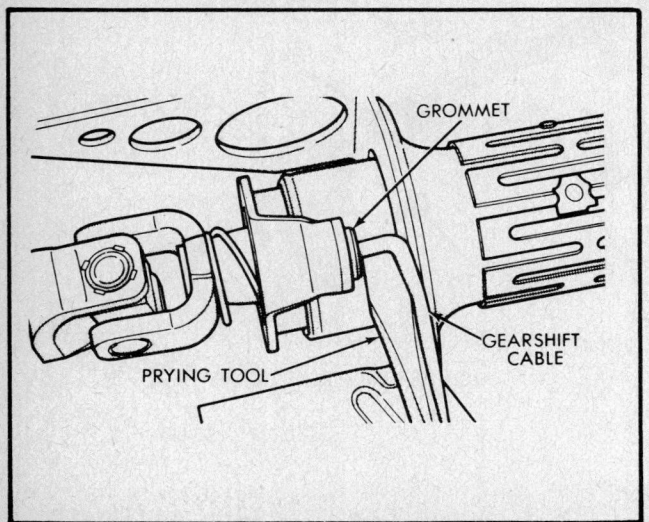

GROMMET

GEARSHIFT CABLE

PRYING TOOL

New grommet installation

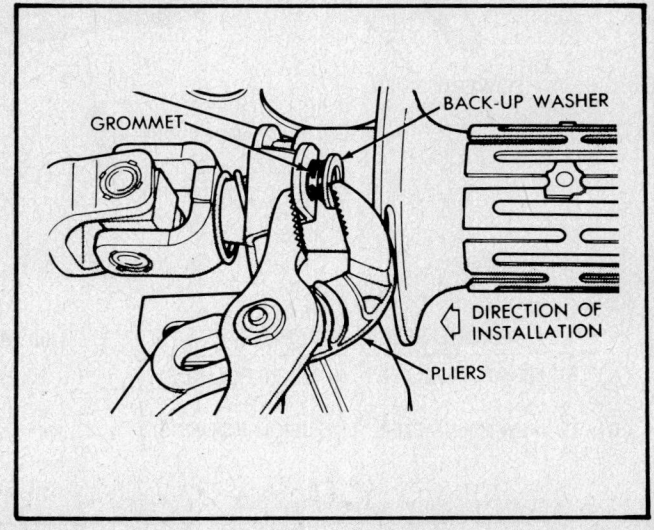

GROMMET

BACK-UP WASHER

DIRECTION OF INSTALLATION

PLIERS

Brake Power Unit

- Remove master cylinder from power unit. Do not disconnect or open any fluid lines.
- Disconnect linkage at brake pedal.
- Remove power unit attaching nuts.
- When installing, use a new retainer clip at the brake pedal.

Brake power unit

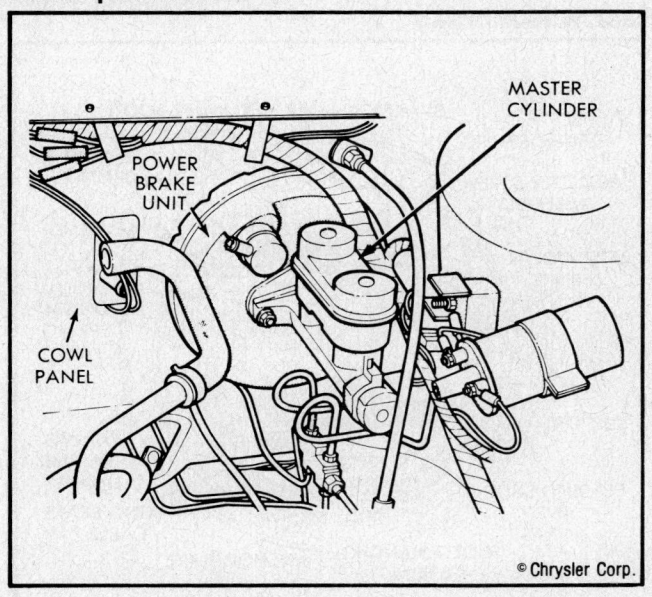

© Chrysler Corp.

Brake power unit attachment

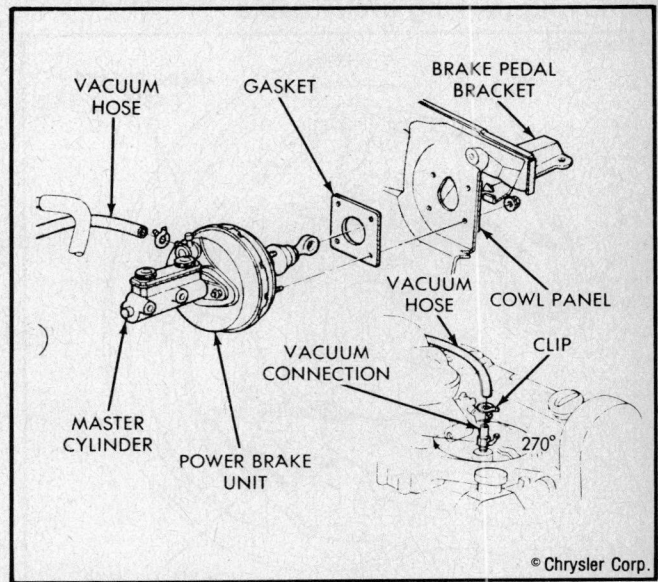

© Chrysler Corp.

Rear brake and drum assembly

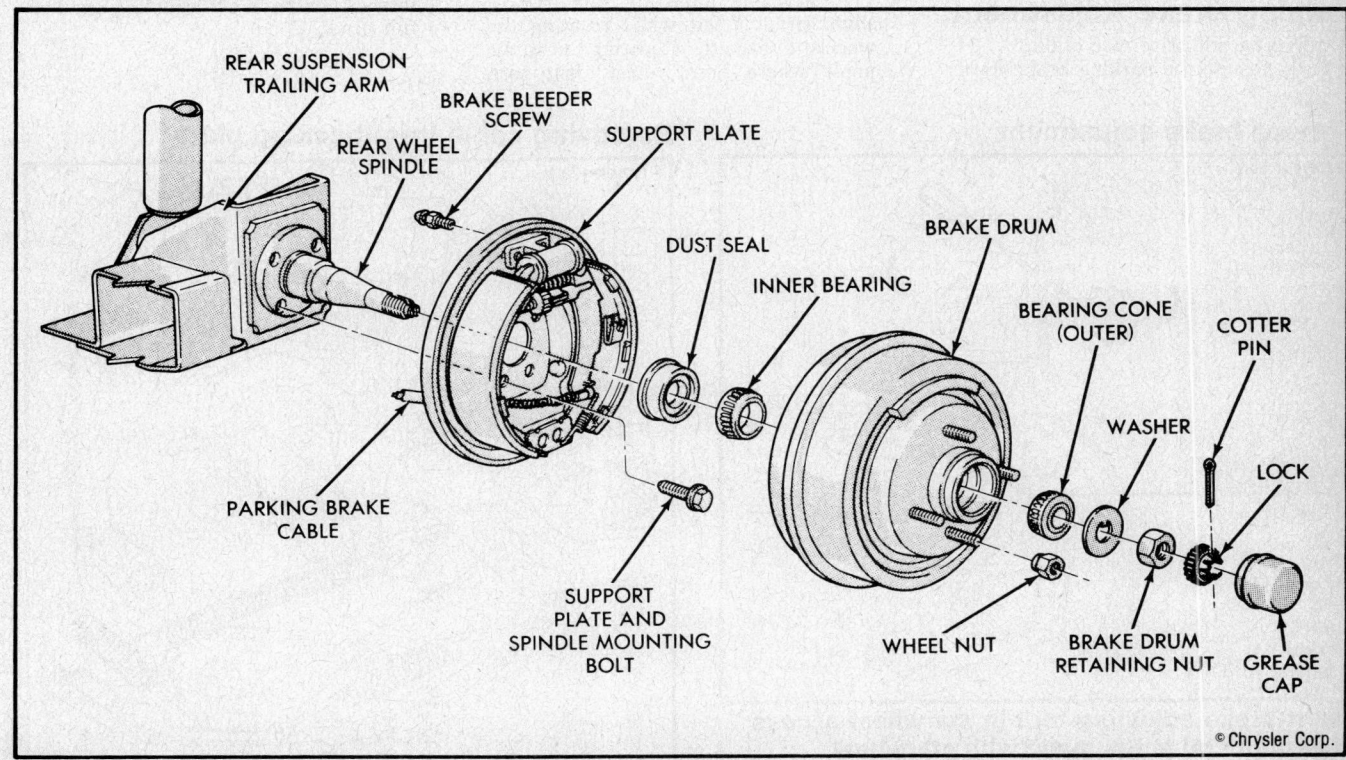

© Chrysler Corp.

CHRYSLER FRONT DRIVE CARS

ARIES, HORIZON, OMNI, RELIANT

Parking Brake Cable R&R

Rear Cable
- Raise vehicle.
- Disconnect brake cable from connector.
- Remove retaining clip from brake cable bracket.
- Remove brake drum from rear axle.
- Remove brake shoe return springs.
- Remove brake shoe retaining springs.
- Remove brake shoe strut and spring from brake support plate, and disconnect brake cable from operating arm.
- Compress retainers on end of brake cable housing, and remove cable from support plate.

Front Cable
- Disengage front cable from connector, and force cable housing and attaching clip forward out of body crossmember.
- Fold back left front edge of floor covering, and either remove rubber cable cover from floor pan or pry rubber grommet out of hole in dash panel.
- Remove cable-to-floor pan clip.
- Engage parking brake, and work cable up and out of clevis linkage.
- Remove cable from pedal assembly bracket, and work cable up through floor pan.

Removing parking brake cable

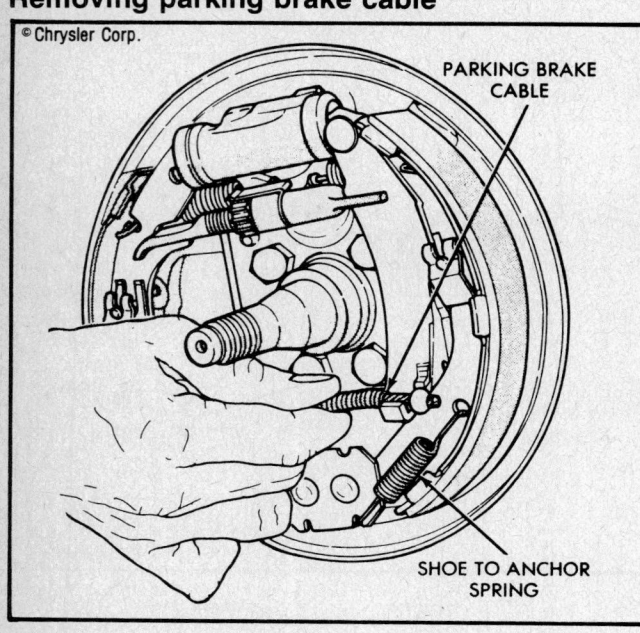

© Chrysler Corp.

PARKING BRAKE CABLE

SHOE TO ANCHOR SPRING

Rear wheel brake

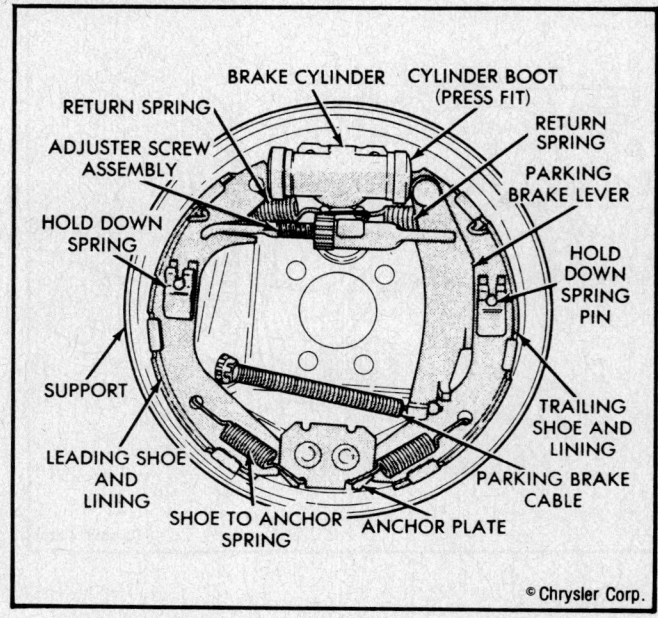

BRAKE CYLINDER   CYLINDER BOOT (PRESS FIT)

RETURN SPRING

ADJUSTER SCREW ASSEMBLY

HOLD DOWN SPRING

SUPPORT

LEADING SHOE AND LINING

SHOE TO ANCHOR SPRING

RETURN SPRING

PARKING BRAKE LEVER

HOLD DOWN SPRING PIN

TRAILING SHOE AND LINING

PARKING BRAKE CABLE

ANCHOR PLATE

© Chrysler Corp.

Parking Brake Adjustment
- Correctly adjust service brakes.
- Fully release the parking brake lever.

Tighten cable adjusting nut until a slight drag is felt while rotating the wheels. Loosen the adjusting nut to the point where both wheels just turn freely, then back off adjusting nut two full turns.

Service brake adjustment

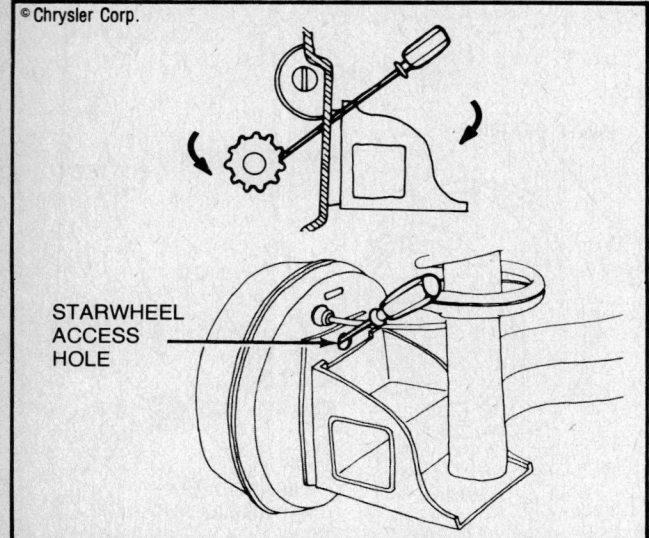

© Chrysler Corp.

STARWHEEL ACCESS HOLE

Insert brake adjusting tool in starwheel access hole until contact is made with starwheel.

Removing cable from backing plate

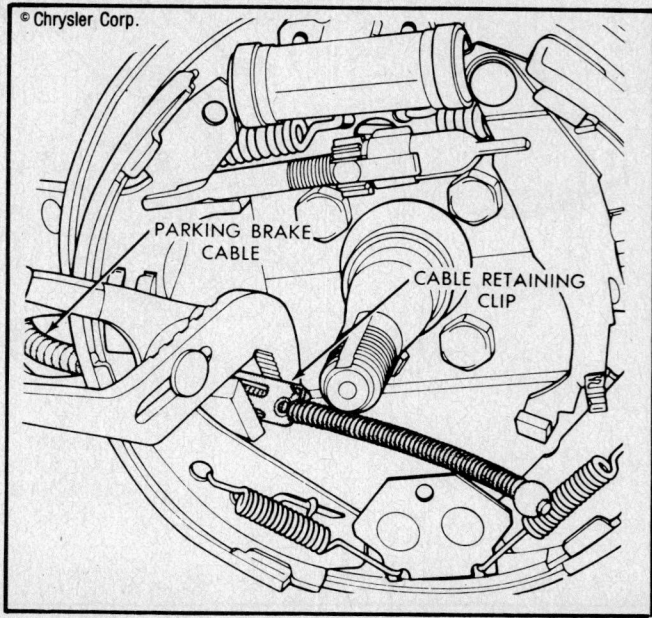

© Chrysler Corp.

PARKING BRAKE CABLE

CABLE RETAINING CLIP

POWER TRANSMISSION SECTION

Clutch adjustment

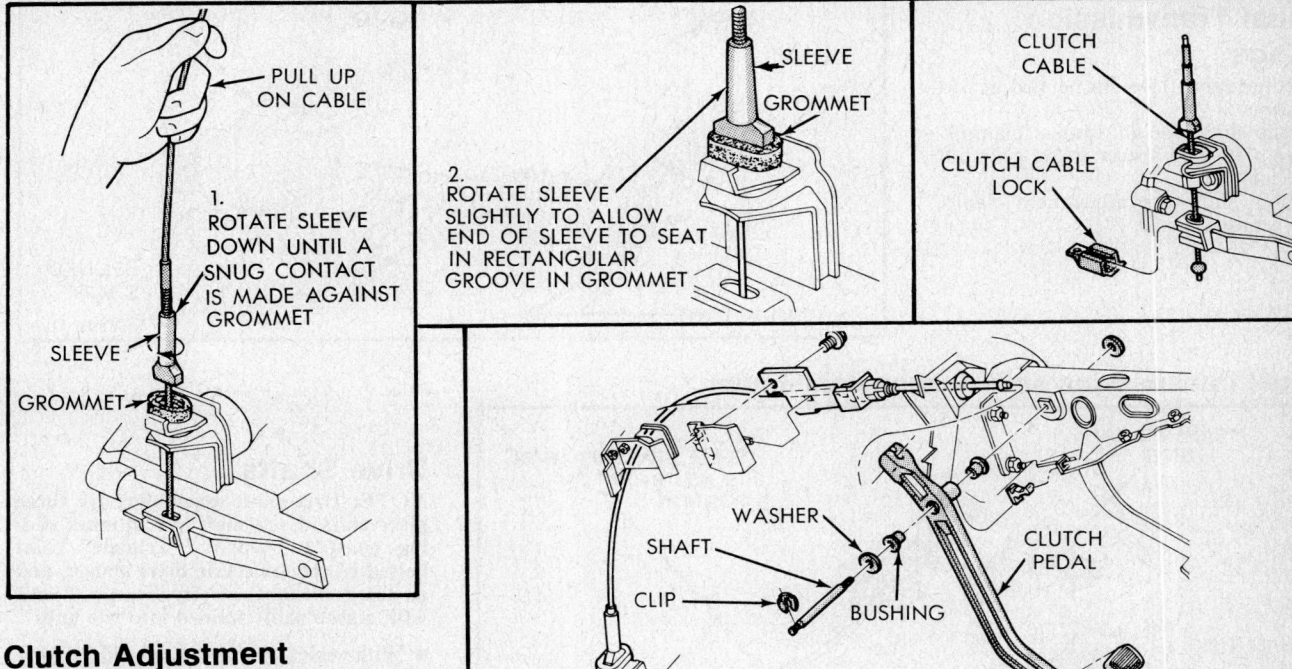

© Chrysler Corp.

Clutch Adjustment

- The clutch pedal linkage is provided with an adjustment to provide free play.

Manual Transaxle Removal

NOTE: The transaxle assembly consists of the clutch, transmission and differential.

- Remove engine timing access hole plug, and rotate engine to align drilled mark on flywheel with pointer on clutch housing.
- Disconnect all electrical connections, clutch cable and speedometer cable. Remove starter.
- Support engine, and raise vehicle.
- Disconnect right drive shaft, and remove left drive shaft.
- Remove left splash shield, and drain fluids from transaxle.
- Disconnect left engine mount, and remove bolts mounting transaxle to engine.
- Slide transaxle to left until mainshaft clears clutch, and lower the unit from the vehicle.

Manual transaxle

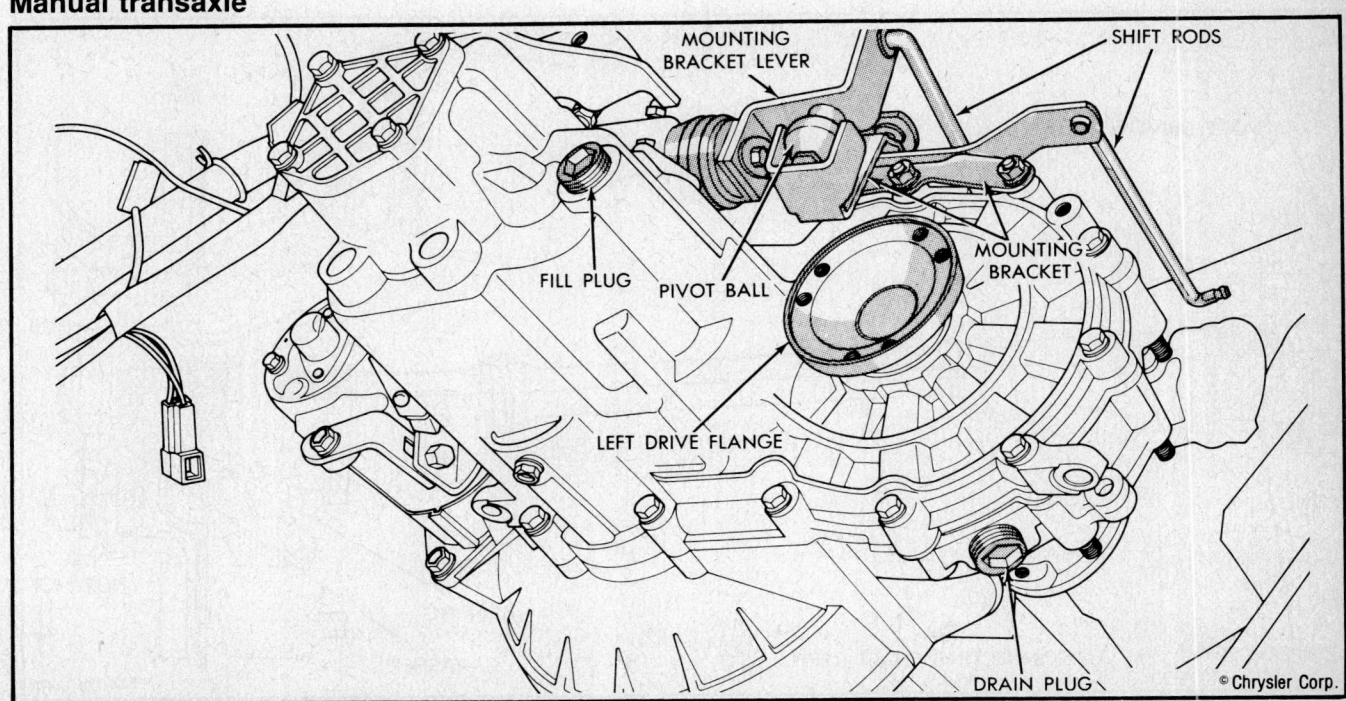

© Chrysler Corp.

CHRYSLER FRONT DRIVE CARS
ARIES, HORIZON, OMNI, RELIANT

Manual Transmission Linkage

- Place gearshift lever in neutral at 3–4 position.
- Loosen shift tube adjustment clamp.
- Place a ½ inch spacer to set gearshift unit lockout.
- Tighten shift tube adjustment clamp, and remove spacer.

Removing drive shaft

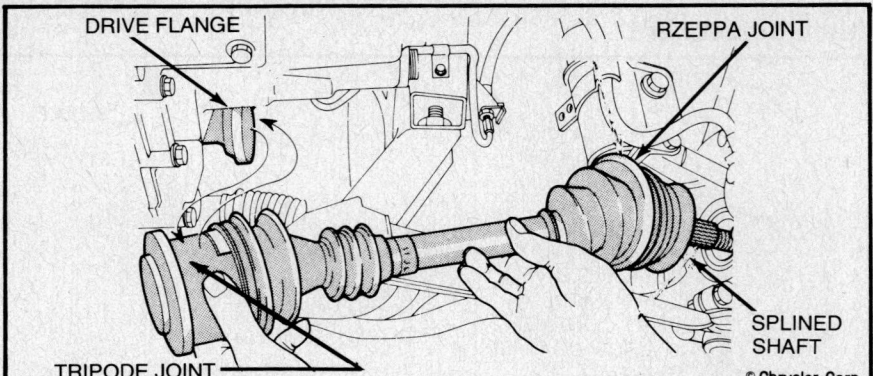

© Chrysler Corp.

Manual transmission shift linkage adjustment

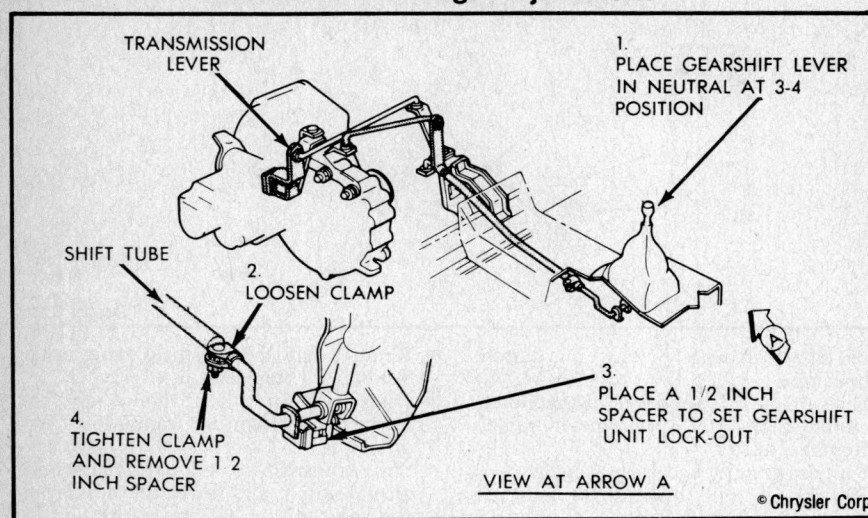

VIEW AT ARROW A

© Chrysler Corp.

Drive Shafts

NOTE: Driveshaft assemblies are three piece units. Each shaft has an inner sliding constant velocity "Tripode" joint bolted to the transaxle drive flange, and an outer constant velocity "Rzeppa" joint with a stub shaft splined into the hub.

- With vehicle on the floor and the brakes applied, loosen, but do not remove, the hub nut.
- Raise vehicle and remove hub nut.
- Remove allen screws attaching inboard constant velocity joint to transaxle drive flange.
- Remove splined shaft from splined hub.
- Stake hub nut after installing.

Drive shaft

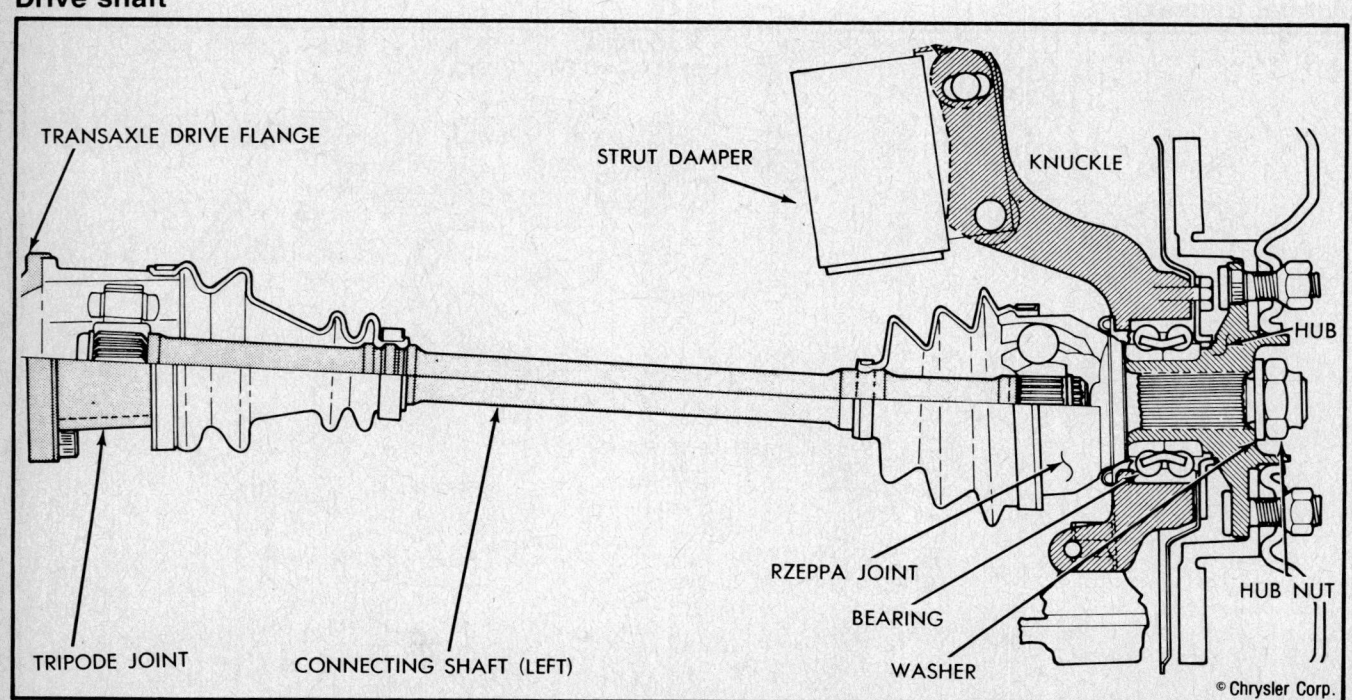

© Chrysler Corp.

Automatic Transaxle Removal

NOTE: The transaxle assembly consists of the clutch, transmission and differential.

- Disconnect the battery positive cable and the throttle and shift linkage from the transaxle.
- Disconnect the upper oil cooler tube.
- Support the engine, and remove the upper bell housing bolts.
- Remove both front wheel hub nuts and front wheels.
- Remove the left splash shield, drain the differential and remove the differential cover.
- Remove the speedometer adapter, cable and pinion as an assembly.
- Remove the sway bar, disconnect both lower ball joints from the steering knuckles and remove drive shafts from hubs.
- Rotate driveshafts to expose circlip ends in differential. Remove circlips and remove the drive shafts.
- Mark torque converter and drive plate for installation reference, and remove torque converter mounting bolts. (Remove access plug in right splash shield to rotate engine.)
- Disconnect the lower oil cooler tube and the neutral start switch.
- Remove the engine mount bracket from the front crossmember, and remove the front mount insulator through bolt and bezel housing bolts.
- Place a transmission jack under the transaxle, and remove the left engine mount.
- Remove the lower bell housing bolts, and lower the transaxle out of the vehicle. It may be necessary to pry on the engine for clearance.

Upper bell housing mount bolts

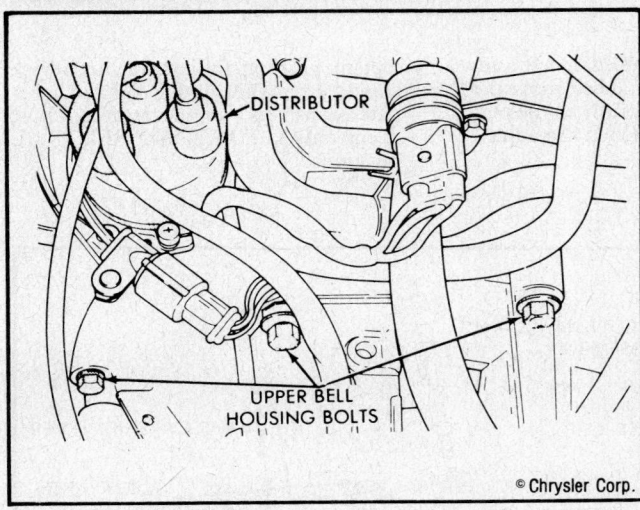

Removing drive shaft from hub

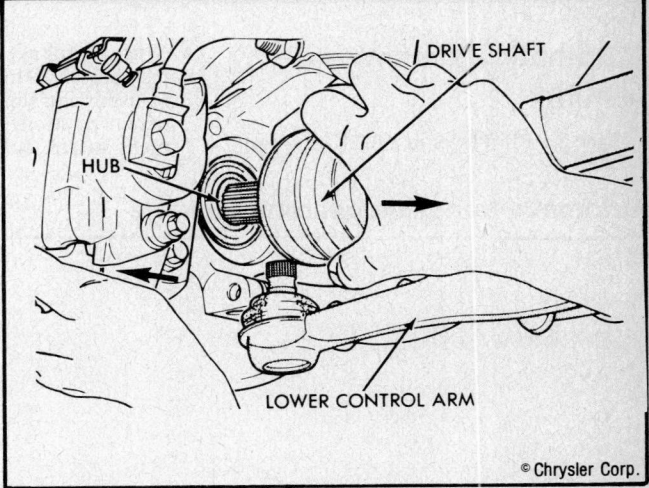

Removing circlips

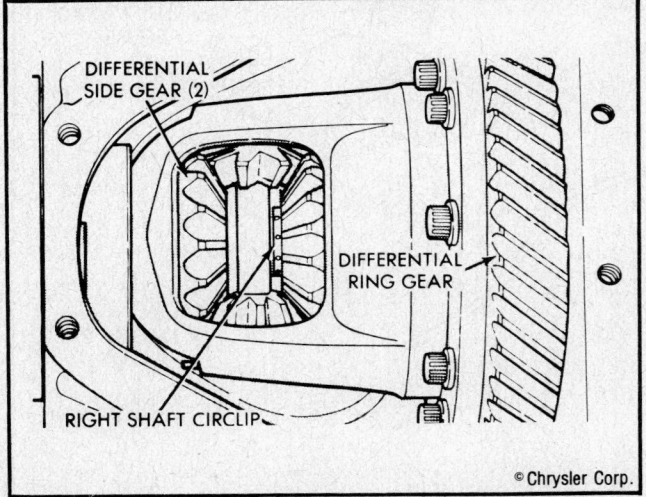

Remove circlips from differential gears prior to removing drive shafts.

Torque converter

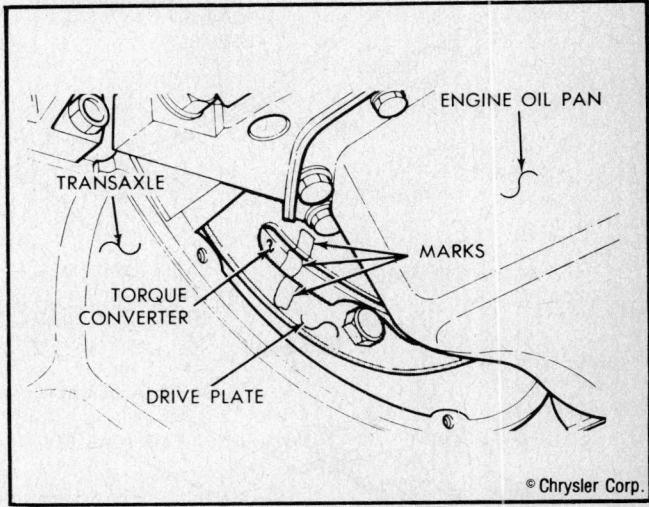

Mark torque converter and drive plate for installation reference before removing torque converter mounting bolts

CHRYSLER FRONT DRIVE CARS
ARIES, HORIZON, OMNI, RELIANT

Disconnect engine mounts for transaxle removal

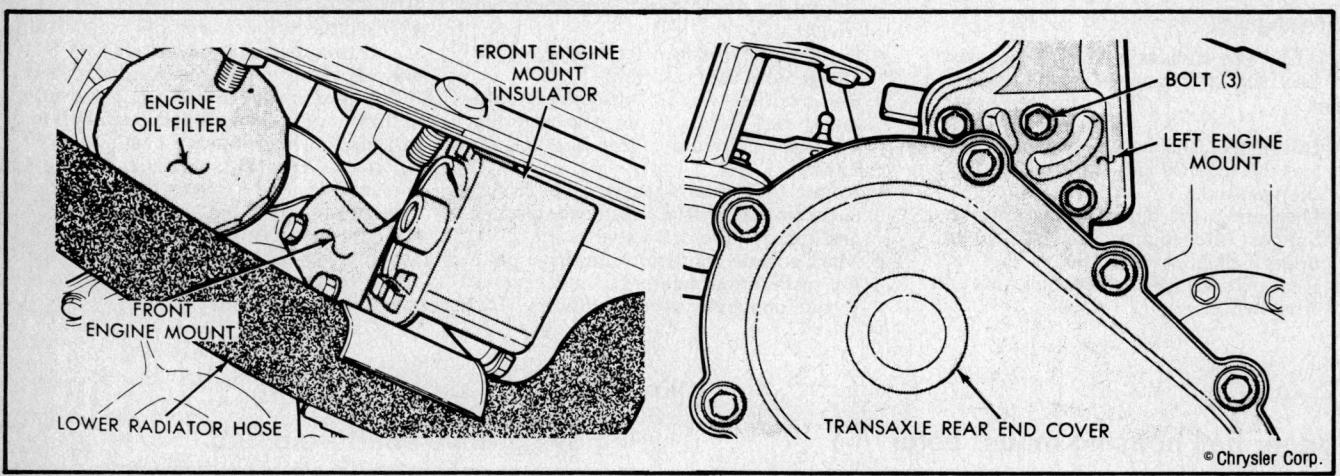

© Chrysler Corp.

Automatic Transmission Linkage

- Place gearshift lever in PARK position.

- With all linkage assembled and the adjustable swivel lock bolt loose, move the transmission shift lever fully to the rear detent position, and tighten the adjustment swivel lock bolt.

- Detent position for neutral and drive should be within limits of hand lever gate stops, and engine starting must occur only in PARK and NEUTRAL positions.

Automatic transaxle gearshift linkage

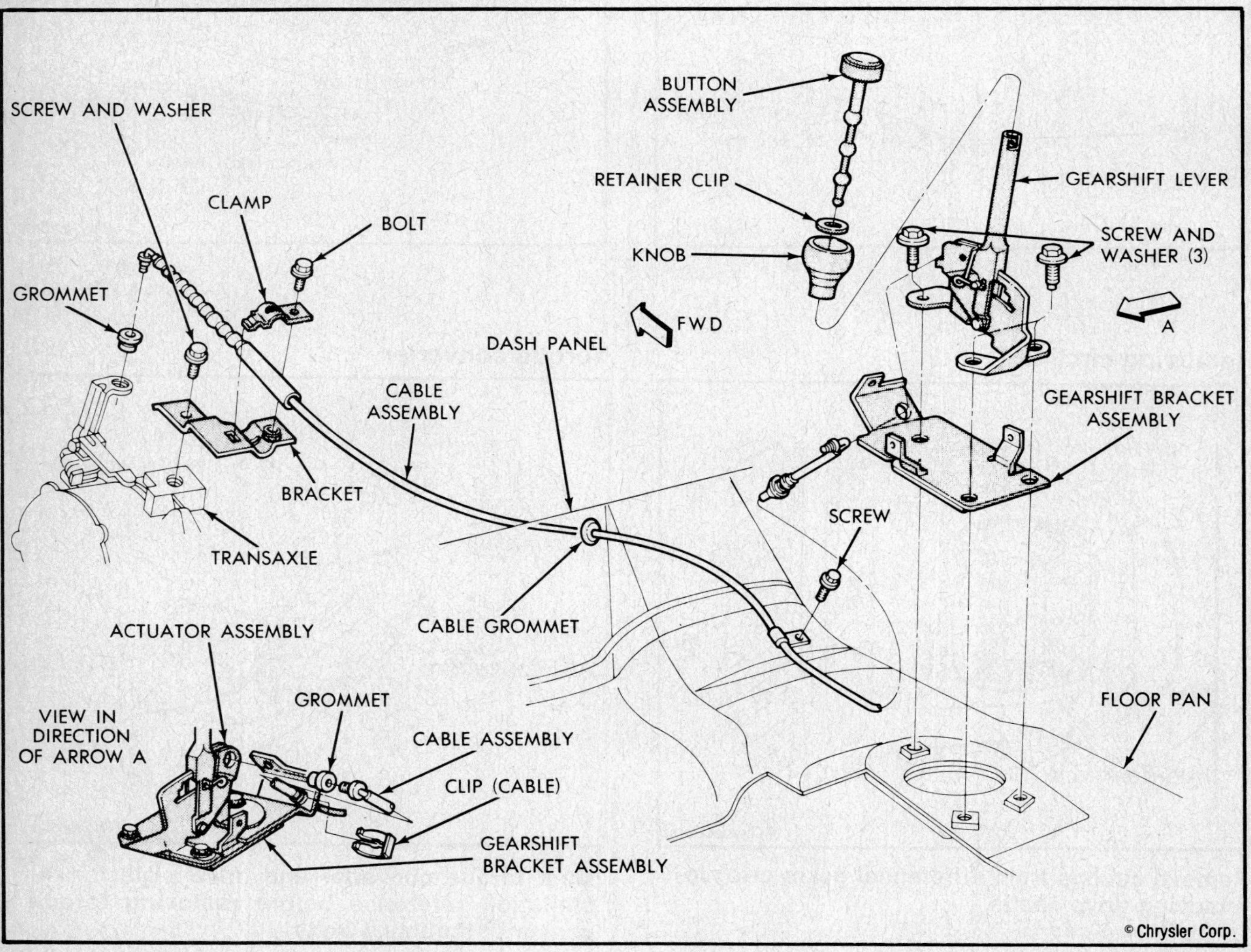

© Chrysler Corp.

A-460 MANUAL TRANSAXLE

Gearshift Linkage Adjustment

- Working over the left front fender, remove the lock pin from the transaxle selector shaft housing.
- Reverse the lock pin (so long end is down) and insert lock pin into same threaded hole while pushing the selector shaft into the selector housing. A hole in the selector shaft will align with the lock pin, allowing the lock pin to be screwed into the housing. This operation locks the selector shaft in the 1-2 neutral position.
- Raise vehicle on hoist.
- Loosen the clamp bolt that secures the gearshift tube to the gearshift connector.
- Check to see that gearshift connector slides and turns freely in gearshift tube.

- Position the shifter mechanism connector assembly so that the isolator is contacting the upstanding flange and the rib on the isolator is aligned fore and aft with the hole in the block-out bracket. Hold the connector isolator in this position while tightening the clamp bolt on the gearshift tube to 19 N•m (170 in-lbs). No significant force should be exerted on the linkage during this operation.
- Lower vehicle to floor.
- Remove lock pin from selector shaft housing and reinstall lock pin upside down in selector shaft housing. Tighten lock pin to 12 N•m (105 in-lbs).
- Check for shift into first and reverse. Check for blockout into reverse.
- Gearshift linkage is now properly adjusted.

Service in Vehicle

The selector shaft housing, both synchronizers, intermediate shaft speed gears, input shaft, reverse idler gear and shaft, shift forks and pads, and the shift fork rail can be serviced in the vehicle without removing the transaxle from the vehicle. Observe the following procedure:

CAUTION: _Safety goggles should be worn at all times when working on this unit._

- Disconnect negative (−) cable from battery.
- Loosen left engine mount.
- Remove selector shaft housing bolts (note the two pilot bolts) and remove selector shaft housing.

A-460 transaxle pinned in the 1-2 Neutral position to adjust gearshift linkage

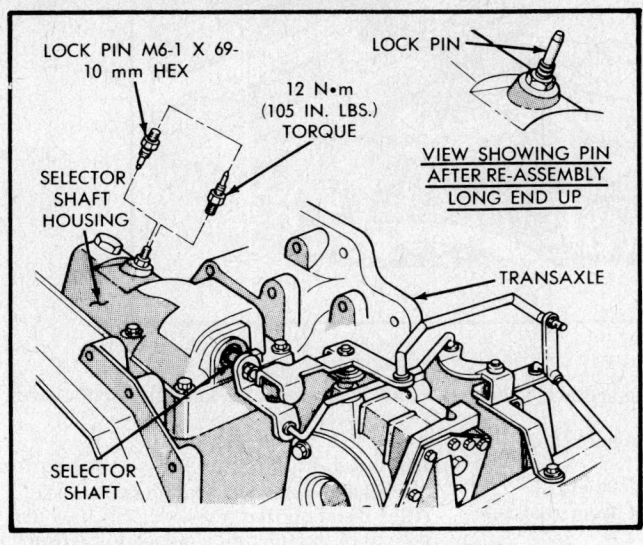

Gearshift linkage adjustment

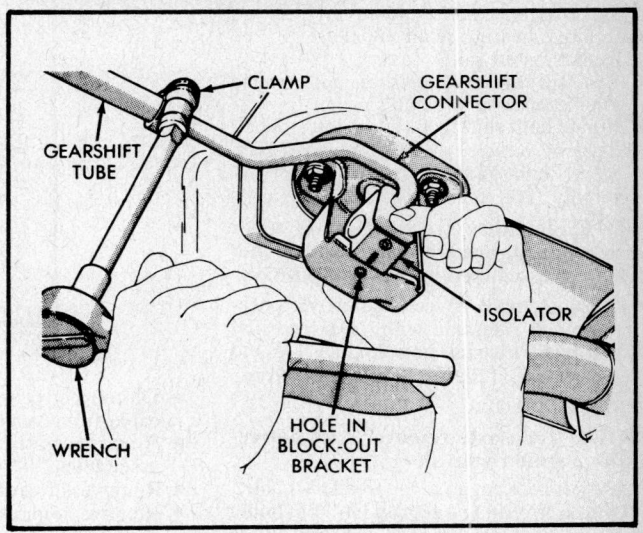

Impact bracket removal

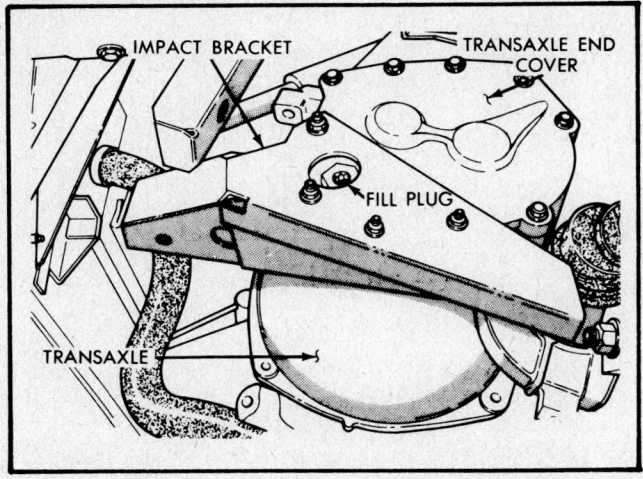

Anti-rotational link removal

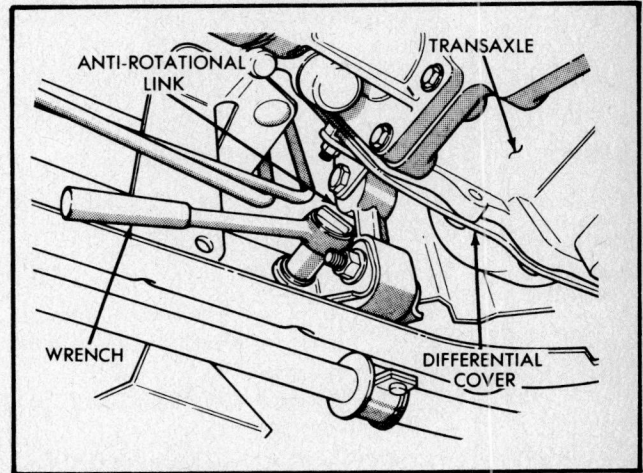

Clutch housing upper bolts removal

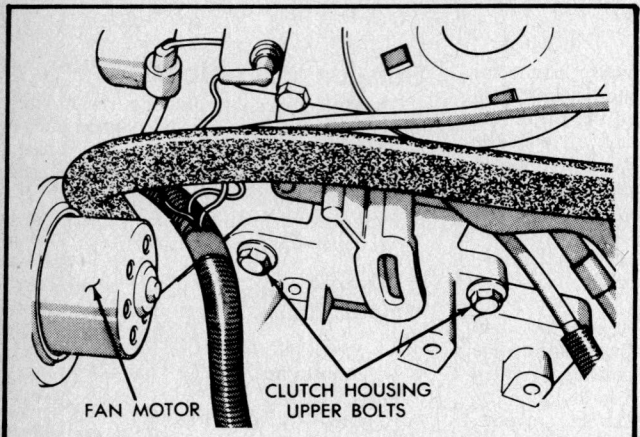

FAN MOTOR — CLUTCH HOUSING UPPER BOLTS

Position transmission jack under transaxle

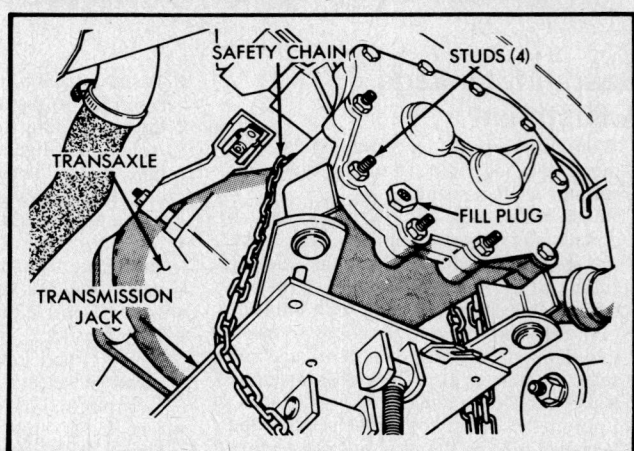

SAFETY CHAIN — STUDS (4) — FILL PLUG — TRANSAXLE — TRANSMISSION JACK

Engine support fixture

SUPPORT FIXTURE — ENGINE

- Raise vehicle on hoist and remove left wheel and tire assembly.
- Remove left splash shield.
- Remove impact bracket from transaxle end cover.
- Place drain pan under transaxle and remove transaxle rear end cover.
- Remove bearing retainer plate.
- Remove shift rail.
- Remove reverse idler shaft and reverse idler gear as an assembly.
- Rotate both shift forks to the left (toward front of vehicle) and firmly grasp both input shaft and intermediate shaft assembly. Pull gearset out of transaxle.

NOTE: If either synchronizer is to be disassembled, mark all parts so that they will be reassembled in the same position.

- To reassemble, reverse the above procedure. Fill transaxle with "Dexron® II" automatic transmission fluid (A.T.F.) to the bottom of the fill hole in end cover.

REMOVAL

NOTE: Transaxle removal does not require engine removal.

- Disconnect negative (−) battery cable.
- Install a "lifting eye" on No. 4 cylinder exhaust manifold bolt and install the engine support fixture.

- Disconnect gearshift linkage and clutch cable from transaxle.
- Remove both front wheel and tire assemblies.
- Remove left front splash shield.
- Remove impact bracket from transaxle end cover.
- Remove both driveshafts.

- Remove transaxle-to-engine bolts and remove transaxle.

INSTALLATION

Reverse the removal procedures to install. After installing the transaxle, fill it to the bottom of the filler plug hole with Dexron® II Automatic Transmission Fluid.

INDEX

CHRYSLER REAR DRIVE CARS

MODEL IDENTIFICATION

1976 NEWPORT
W.B. **124**". Length 228", Cust. 227". Ship. Wgt. V8 2 Dr. 4455 Lbs.

1977 NEWPORT
W.B. **124**". Length 227", S/W 228". Width 80". Ship. Wgt. V8 2 Dr. 4465 Lbs.

1978 NEWPORT
W.B. **123.9**" Length 227.1" Ship. Wgt. 8 Cyl. 2 Dr. 4465 Lbs.

1979 NEWPORT
W.B. **118.5**" Length 220.2" Ship. Wgt. 6 Cyl. 2 Dr. 3640 Lbs.

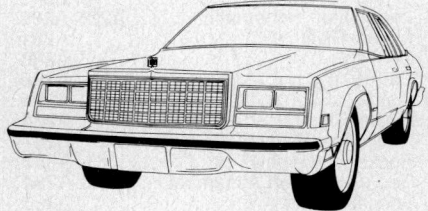

1980 NEWPORT
W.B. **118**". Length 221.5". Ship. Wgt. 6 Cyl. Approx. 3640 Lbs.

1981 NEWPORT
W.B. **118.5**". Length 220.2". 6 Cyl. 4 Dr. Curb Wgt. 3558 Lbs.

1979 NEW YORKER
W.B. **118.5**" Length 221.5" Ship. Wgt. 8 Cyl. 2 Dr. 3808 Lbs.

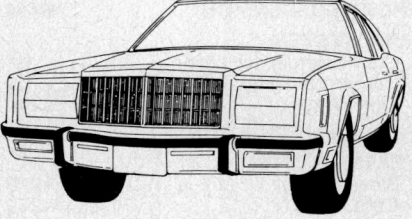

1980 NEW YORKER
W.B. **118.5**". Length 221.5". Ship. Wgt. 6 Cyl. 2 Dr. Approx. 3808 Lbs.

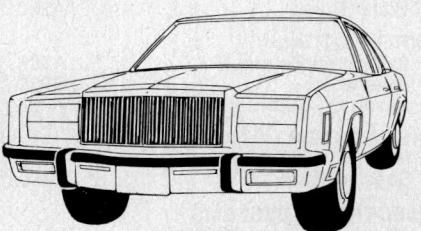

1981 NEW YORKER
W.B. **118.5**". Length 221.5". 6 Cyl. 4 Dr. Curb Wgt. 3559 Lbs.

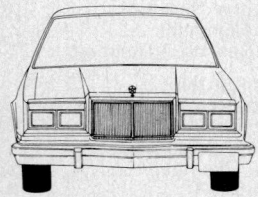

1982 NEW YORKER
W.B. **112.7**". Length 205.7". 6 Cyl. 4 Dr. Curb Wgt. 3507 Lbs.

1976 NEW YORKER BROUGHAM
W.B. **124**". Length 231". Ship. Wgt. V8 2 Dr. 4865 Lbs.

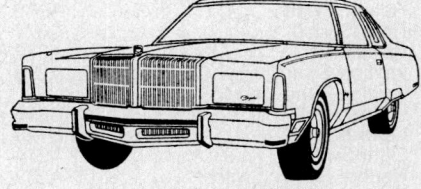

1977 NEW YORKER BROUGHAM
W.B. **124**". Length 231". Width 80". Ship. Wgt. V8 2 Dr. 4625 Lbs.

1978 NEW YORKER BROUGHAM
W.B. **123.9**" Length 231.0" Ship. Wgt. 8 Cyl. 2 Dr. 4625 Lbs.

1981-1982 IMPERIAL
W.B. **112.7**". Length 213.3". 8 Cyl. 2 Dr. Curb Wgt. 3968 Lbs.

1976 CORDOBA
W.B. **115**". Length 216". Ship. Wgt. V8 2 Dr. 4130 Lbs.

1977 CORDOBA

W.B. **115"**. Length 215". Width 78". Ship. Wgt. V8 2 Dr. 3880 Lbs.

1978 CORDOBA

W.B. **114.9"** Length 215.8" Ship. Wgt. 8 Cyl. 2 Dr. 3880 Lbs.

1979 CORDOBA

W.B. **114.9"** Length 215.8" Ship. Wgt. 8 Cyl. 2 Dr. 3839 Lbs.

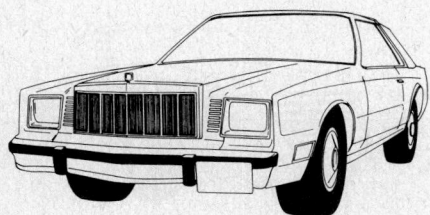

1980 CORDOBA

W.B. **112.7"**. Length 215". Ship. Wgt. 6 Cyl. Approx. 3439 Lbs.

1981-1982 CORDOBA

W.B. **112.7"**. Length 210.1". 6 Cyl. 2 Dr. Curb Wgt. 3397 Lbs.

1977 LEBARON

W.B. **112.7"**. Length 207", **2D 204"**. Width 73", **2D 74"**. Ship. Wgt.

1978 LE BARON

W.B. **112.7"** Length 204.1" Ship. Wgt. 8 Cyl. 2 Dr. 3510 Lbs.

1979 LEBARON

W.B. **112.7"** Length 204.1" Ship. Wgt. 8 Cyl. 2 Dr. 3380 Lbs.

1980 LEBARON

W.B. **108.7"**. Length 204". Ship. Wgt. Approx. 3180 Lbs.

1981 LEBARON

W.B. **112.7"**. Length 205.7". 6 Cyl. 4 Dr. Curb Wgt. 3389 Lbs.

1976 MONACO

W.B. **121.5"**, **S/W 124"**. Length 226", S/W 230". Ship. Wgt. V8 2 Dr. 4280 Lbs.

1977 MONACO

W.B. **117.4"**, **Htp 115"**. Length 219", Htp. 214", S/W 226". Width 78", S/W 79". Ship. Wgt. 6 Cyl 2 Dr. 3630 Lbs. V8 2 Dr. 4040 Lbs.

1978 MONACO

W.B. **114.9"** Length 213.2" Ship. Wgt. 8 Cyl. 2 Dr. 4040 Lbs.

1976 ROYAL MONACO BROUGHAM

W.B. **121.5"**, **S/W 124"**. Length 226", S/W 230". Ship. Wgt. V8 2 Dr. 4430 Lbs.

1977 ROYAL MONACO BROUGHAM

W.B. **121.4"**, **S/W 124"**. Length 226", S/W 230". Width 80". Ship. Wgt. V8 2 Dr. 4365 Lbs.

CHRYSLER REAR DRIVE CARS

1976 CHARGER

W.B. **115"**. Length 214", Specialty 216". Ship. Wgt. 6 Cyl. 2 Dr. 3595 Lbs. V8 2 Dr. 3830 Lbs.

1977 CHARGER

W.B. **115"**. Length 216". Width 78". Ship. Wgt. V8 2 Dr. 3895 Lbs.

1978 CHARGER SE

W.B. **114.9"** Length 215.3" Ship. Wgt. 8 Cyl. 2 Dr. 3895 Lbs.

1976 CORONET

W.B. **117.5"**, Htp. **115"**. Length 219", Hdt 214", S/W 226". Ship. Wgt. 6 Cyl. 4 Dr. 3625 Lbs. V8 4 Dr. 3860 Lbs.

1978 MAGNUM XE

W.B. **114.9"** Length 215.8" Ship. Wgt. 8 Cyl. 2 Dr. 3895 Lbs.

1979 MAGNUM XE

W.B. **114.9"** Length 215.8" Ship. Wgt. 8 Cyl. 2 Dr. 3895 Lbs.

1976 DART

W.B. **111"**, Model & LL29 **108"**. Length 204", Model LL29 201". Width 70", Model LL27 72". 6 Cyl. 2 Dr. 3035 Lbs. V8 2 Dr. 3160 Lbs.

1976 ASPEN

W.B. **112.5"**, Cpe. **108.5**. Length 202", Cpe. 198". 6 Cyl. 2 Dr. 3160 Lbs. V8 2 Dr. 3285 Lbs.

1977 ASPEN

W.B. **112.7"**, Cpe. **108.7"**. Length 202", Cpe. 198". Width 73". Ship. Wgt. 6 Cyl. 2 Dr. 3180 Lbs. V8 2 Dr. 3400 Lbs.

1978 ASPEN

W.B. **108.7"** Length 197.2" Ship. Wgt. 8 Cyl. 2 Dr. 3400 Lbs.

1979 ASPEN

W.B. **108.7"** Length 197.2" Ship. Wgt. 8 Cyl. 2 Dr. 3400 Lbs.

1980 ASPEN

W.B. **108"**. Length 200". Ship. Wgt. 6 Cyl. 2 Dr. Approx. 3145 Lbs.

1977 DIPLOMAT

W.B. **112"**. Length 207", 2D 204". Width 73", 2D 74". Ship. Wgt.

1978 DIPLOMAT

W.B. **112.7"** Length 204.1" Ship. Wgt. 8 Cyl. 2 Dr. 3510 Lbs.

1979 DIPLOMAT

W.B. **112.7"** Length 204.1" Ship. Wgt. 8 Cyl. 2 Dr. 3510 Lbs.

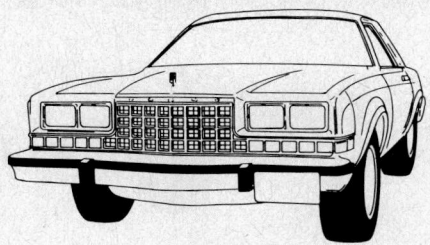

1980 DIPLOMAT
W.B. 108.7″. Length 201.2″. Ship. Wgt. 6 Cyl. 2 Dr. Approx. 3255 Lbs.

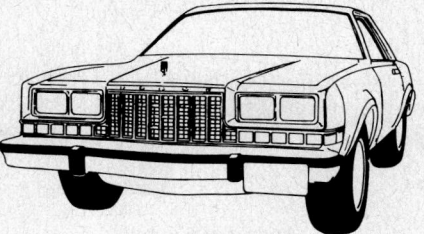

1981-82 DIPLOMAT
W.B. 108.7″. Length 201.7″. 6 Cyl. 2 Dr. Curb Wgt. 3282 Lbs.

1976 FURY
W.B. 117.5″, 2D 115″. Length 219″, 2D 214″, S/W 226″. Ship. Wgt. 6 Cyl. 2 Dr. 3590 Lbs. V8 2 Dr. 3830 Lbs.

1977 FURY
W.B. 17.4″, 2D 115″, S/W 117.5″. Length 219″, 2D 214″ S/W 226″. Width 78″. S/W 79″. Ship. Wgt. V8 2 Dr. 3855 Lbs.

1978 FURY
W.B. 114.9″ Length 213.2″ Ship. Wgt. 8 Cyl. 2 Dr. 3855 Lbs.

1976 GRAN FURY
W.B. 121.5, S/W 124″. Length 223″, S/W 227″. Ship. Wgt. V8 2 Dr. 4265 Lbs.

1977 GRAN FURY
W.B. 121.4″, S/W 124″. Length 223″, S/W 227″. Width 80″. Ship. Wgt. V8 2 Dr. 4070 Lbs.

1980 GRAN FURY
W.B. 118.5″. Length 221″. Ship. Wgt. 6 Cyl. 4 Dr. Approx. 3640 Lbs.

1981 GRAN FURY
W.B. 118.5″. Length 220.2″. 6 Cyl. 4 Dr. Curb Wgt. 3558 Lbs.

1982 GRAN FURY
W.B. 112.7″. Length 205.7″. 6 Cyl. 4 Dr. Curb Wgt. 3507 Lbs.

1979 ST. REGIS
W.B. 118.5″ Length 220.2″ Ship. Wgt. 6 Cyl. 2 Dr. 3671 Lbs.

1980 ST. REGIS
W.B. 118.5″. Length 220.2″. Ship. Wgt. 6 Cyl. 2 Dr. Approx. 3658 Lbs.

1981 ST. REGIS
W.B. 118.5″. Length 220.2″. 6 Cyl. 2 Dr. Curb Wgt. 3558 Lbs.

1976 VALIANT
W.B. 111″, Duster 108″. Length 200″, Duster 197″. Ship. Wgt. 6 Cyl. 2 Dr. 3020 Lbs.

1976 VOLARE
W.B. 112.5″, Spt. Cpe. 108.5″. Length 202″, Spt. Cpe. 198″. Ship. Wgt. 6 Cyl. 2 Dr. 3160 Lbs. V8 2 Dr. 3285 Lbs.

CHRYSLER REAR DRIVE CARS

1977 VOLARE

W.B. 112.7″, Spt. Cpe. 108.7″. Length 202″, Spt. Cpe. 198″. Width 73″. Ship. Wgt. 6 Cyl. 2 Dr. 3180 Lbs. V8 2 Dr. 3290 Lbs.

1978 VOLARE

W.B. 108.7″ Length 197.2″ Ship. Wgt. 8 Cyl. 2 Dr. 3290 Lbs.

1979 VOLARE

W.B. 108.7″ Length 197.2″ Ship. Wgt. 8 Cyl. 2 Dr. 3290 Lbs.

1980 VOLARE

W.B. 108.7″. Length 196″. Ship. Wgt. 6 Cyl. 2 Dr. Approx. 3290 Lbs.

1980 MIRADA

W.B. 112.7″. Length 209.5″. Ship. Wgt. 6 Cyl. 2 Dr. Approx. 3295 Lbs.

1981 MIRADA

W.B. 112.7″. Length 209.5″. 6 Cyl. 2 Dr. Curb Wgt. 3377 Lbs.

1982 MIRADA

W.B. 112.7″. Length 209.6″. 6 Cyl. 2 Dr. Curb Wgt. 3395 Lbs.

VEHICLE IDENTIFICATION NUMBER (VIN)

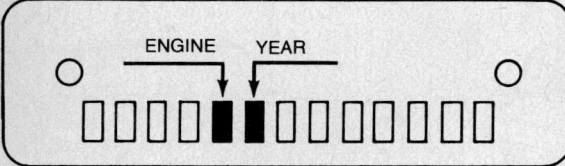

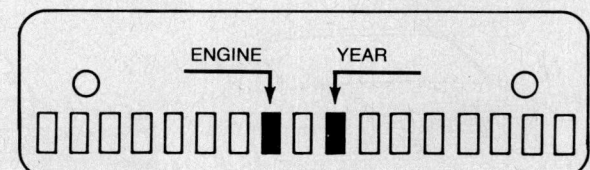

ENGINE FIRING ORDER

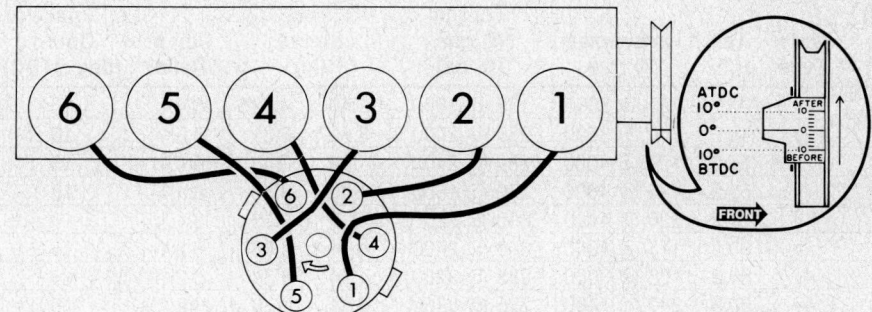

CHRYSLER CORP. 6-cyl. Engine firing order: 1–5–3–6–2–4 Distributor rotation: clockwise

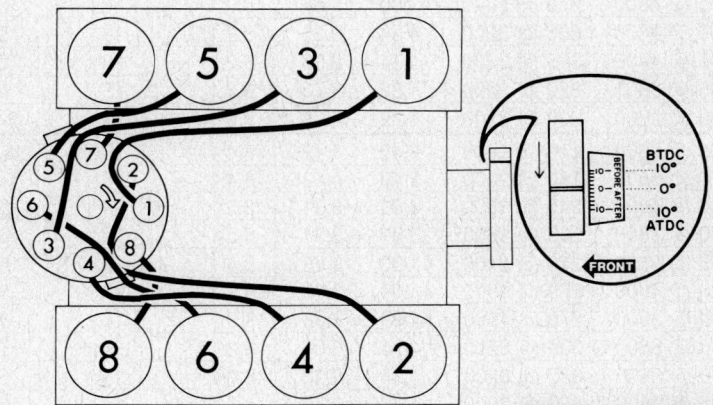

CHRYSLER CORP. 318, 340, 360 V8 Engine firing order: 1–8–4–3–6–5–7–2 Distributor rotation: clockwise

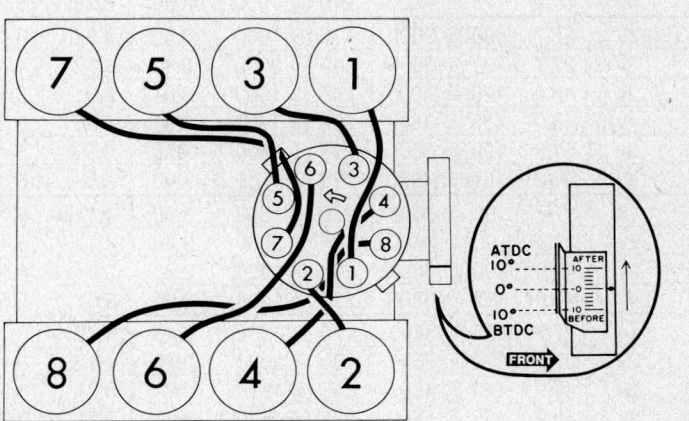

CHRYSLER CORP. 400, 440 V8 Engine firing order: 1–8–4–3–6–5–7–2 Distributor rotation: counterclockwise

CHRYSLER REAR DRIVE CARS

ENGINE SPECIFICATIONS

Year	Eng. V.I.N. Code	Engine No. Cyl. Disp. (cu in)	Carb Type	Tax H.P.	Horsepower @ rpm	Torque @ rpm (ft lbs)	Bore and Stroke (in)	Comp. Ratio	Valves Intake Opens (deg BTDC)	Fuel Pump Pres. (psi)	Oil Pressure @ 2000 rpm
'76	C	6-225	1v	27.7	90 @ 3600	165 @ 1600	3.40 × 4.125	8.4:1	16	3½-5	30-70
	G	8-318	2v	48.9	140 @ 3600	250 @ 2000	3.91 × 3.31	8.6:1	10	3½-5	30-80
	K	8-360	2v	51.2	170 @ 4000	280 @ 2400	4.000 × 3.58	8.4:1	18	5-7	30-80
	J	8-360	4v	51.2	175 @ 4000	270 @ 1600	4.000 × 3.58	8.4:1	18	5-7	30-80
	L	8-360	4v	51.2	220 @ 4400	280 @ 3200	4.000 × 3.58	8.4:1	18	5-7	30-80
	M	8-400	2v	60.3	175 @ 4000	300 @ 2400	4.34 × 3.38	8.2:1	18	5-7	30-80
	N	8-400	4v	60.3	185 @ 3600	285 @ 3200	4.34 × 3.38	8.2:1	18	5-7	30-80
	P	8-400	4v	60.3	240 @ 4400	325 @ 3200	4.34 × 3.38	8.2:1	18	5-7	30-80
	T	8-440	4v	59.7	200 @ 3600	310 @ 2400	4.32 × 3.75	8.2:1	18	5-7	30-80
	U	8-440	4v	59.7	250 @ 4000	350 @ 3200	4.32 × 3.75	8.2:1	21	6-7½	30-80
'77	C	6-225	1v	27.7	90 @ 3600	170 @ 1600	3.40 × 4.125	8.4:1	16	3½-5	30-70
	D	6-225	2v	27.7	110 @ 3600	170 @ 1600	3.40 × 4.125	8.4:1	16	3½-5	30-80
	G	8-318	2v	48.9	135 @ 3600	235 @ 1600	3.91 × 3.31	8.6:1	10	5-7	30-80
	K	8-360	2v	51.2	155 @ 3600	275 @ 2000	4.000 × 3.58	8.4:1	18	5-7	30-80
	J	8-360	4v	51.2	170 @ 4000	270 @ 1600	4.000 × 3.58	8.4:1	18	5-7	30-80
	L	8-360	4v	51.2	175 @ 4000	275 @ 2000	4.000 × 3.58	8.0:1	18	5-7	30-80
	N	8-400	4v	60.3	190 @ 3600	305 @ 3200	4.34 × 3.38	8.2:1	18	5-7	30-80
	P	8-400	4v	60.3	240 @ 4400	325 @ 3200	4.34 × 3.38	8.2:1	18	5-7	30-80
	T	8-440	4v	59.7	195 @ 3600	320 @ 2000	4.32 × 3.75	8.2:1	18	5-7	30-80
	U	8-440	4v	59.7	230 @ 4000	330 @ 3200	4.32 × 3.75	7.8:1	21	6-7½	30-80
'78	C	6-225	1v	27.7	100 @ 3600	170 @ 1600	3.40 × 4.125	8.4:1	16	4-5½	35-65
	D	6-225	2v	27.7	110 @ 3600	180 @ 2000	3.40 × 4.125	8.4:1	16	4-5½	35-65
	G	8-318	2v	48.9	140 @ 4000	245 @ 1600	3.91 × 3.31	8.5:1	10	5-7	30-80
	H	8-318	4v	48.9	150 @ 3800	235 @ 1600	3.91 × 3.31	8.5:1	10	5-7	30-80
	K	8-360	2v	51.2	155 @ 3600	270 @ 2400	4.000 × 3.58	8.4:1	18	5-7	30-80
	J	8-360	4v	51.2	170 @ 4000	270 @ 1600	4.000 × 3.58	8.4:1	18	5-7	30-80
	L	8-360	4v	51.2	160 @ 3800	270 @ 1600	4.000 × 3.58	8.0:1	18	5-7	30-80
	N	8-400	4v	60.3	190 @ 3600	305 @ 3200	4.34 × 3.38	8.2:1	18	5-7	30-80
	P	8-400	4v	60.3	190 @ 3600	305 @ 3200	4.34 × 3.38	8.0:1	18	5-7	30-80
	T	8-440	4v	59.7	195 @ 3600	320 @ 2000	4.32 × 3.75	8.2:1	18	5-7	30-80
	U	8-440	4v	59.7	255 @ 4400	360 @ 3200	4.32 × 3.75	7.8:1	21	5-7	30-80
'79	C	6-225	1v	27.7	90 @ 3600	170 @ 1600	3.40 × 4.125	8.4:1	16	4-5.5	35-65
	D	6-225	2v	27.7	110 @ 3600	180 @ 2000	3.40 × 4.125	8.4:1	16	4-5.5	35-65
	G	8-318	2v	48.9	135 @ 4000	245 @ 1600	3.91 × 3.31	8.5:1	10	5.8-7.3	35-65
	H	8-318	4v	48.9	155 @ 3800	235 @ 1600	3.91 × 3.31	8.5:1	10	5.8-7.3	35-65
	K	8-360	2v	51.2	150 @ 3600	270 @ 2400	4.000 × 3.58	8.4:1	18	5.8-7.3	35-65
	J	8-360	4v	51.2	170 @ 4000	270 @ 1600	4.000 × 3.58	8.0:1	18	5.8-7.3	35-65
	L	8-360	4v	51.2	175 @ 4000	270 @ 1600	4000 × 3.58	8.0:1	18	5-7	30-80
'80	C	6-225	1v	27.7	90 @ 3600	170 @ 1600	3.40 × 4.125	8.4:1	16	4.5-5	35-65
	D	6-225	2v	27.7	90 @ 3600	180 @ 2000	3.40 × 4.125	8.4:1	16	4.5-5	35-65
	G	8-318	2v	48.9	120 @ 4000	245 @ 1600	3.91 × 3.31	8.5:1	10	5-7	35-65
	H	8-318	4v	48.9	155 @ 3800	235 @ 1600	3.91 × 3.31	8.5:1	10	5-7	35-65
	K	8-360	2v	51.2	130 @ 3600	270 @ 2400	4.000 × 3.58	8.4:1	18	5-7	35-65
	L	8-360	4v	51.2	185 @ 4000	270 @ 1600	4.000 × 3.58	8.0:1	18	5-7	30-80
'81	C	6-225	1v	27.7	90 @ 3600	170 @ 1600	3.40 × 4.125	8.4:1	16	4.5-5	35-65
	D	6-225	2v	27.7	90 @ 3600	180 @ 2000	3.40 × 4.125	8.4:1	16	4.5-5	35-65
	G	8-318	2v	48.9	120 @ 4000	245 @ 1600	3.91 × 3.31	8.5:1	10	5-7	35-65
	H	8-318	4v	48.9	155 @ 3800	235 @ 1600	3.91 × 3.31	8.5:1	10	5-7	35-65
'82	C	6-225	1v	27.7	90 @ 3600	170 @ 1600	3.40 × 4.125	8.4:1	16	4.5-5	35-65
	D	6-225	2v	27.7	90 @ 3600	180 @ 2000	3.40 × 4.125	8.4:1	16	4.5-5	35-65
	G	8-318	2v	48.9	120 @ 4000	245 @ 1600	3.91 × 3.31	8.5:1	10	5-7	35-65
	H	8-318	4v	48.9	155 @ 3800	235 @ 1600	3.91 × 3.31	8.5:1	10	5-7	35-65

TUNE-UP SPECIFICATIONS

Engine Code, 5th character of the VIN number④

Year	Eng. V.I.N. Code	Engine No. Cyl. Disp. (cu in)	Spark Plugs Orig. Type	Gap (in)	Ignition Timing (deg B.T.D.C.) Federal Man	Auto	California Man	Auto	Carburetion Hot Idle Speed Federal Man	Auto	California Man	Auto
'76	C	6-225	RBL-15Y	.035	6	6	2	2	800	750	800	750
	G	8-318	N-12Y	.035	5①	5①	T.D.C.	T.D.C.	900	900	750	750
	K	8-360	N-12Y	.035	—	6	—	6	—	850	700	750
	J	8-360	N-12Y	.035	—	6	—	6	—	850	700	750
	L	8-360	N-12Y	.035	—	6	—	6	—	850	—	850
	M	8-400	J-13Y	.035	—	10	—	—	—	850	—	750
	N	8-400	J-13Y	.035	—	6	—	8	—	850	—	750
	P	8-400	RJ-87P	.035	—	6	—	8	—	850	—	750
	T	8-440	RJ-87P	.035	—	8	—	8	—	850	—	750
	U	8-440	J-11Y	.035	—	10	—	8	—	850	—	750
'77	C	6-225	RBL-15Y	.035	12	12	4	4	700	700	750	750●
	D	6-225	RBL-15Y	.035	12	12	4	4	700	700	750	750
	G	8-318	RN-12Y	.035	8	8	T.D.C.	T.D.C.	—	700	850	850●
	K	8-360	RN-12Y	.035	—	10	—	10	—	750	—	750
	L	8-360	RN-12Y	.035	—	20	—	—	—	750	—	750
	L	8-360	RN-12Y	.035	—	16	—	8	—	750	—	750
	N	8-400	RJ-13Y	.035	—	①	—	①	—	750	—	750●
	P	8-400	RJ-13Y	.035	—	①	—	①	—	750	—	750
	T	8-440	RJ-13Y	.035	—	16	—	8	—	750	—	750
	U	8-440	RJ-11Y	.035	—	16	—	8	—	750	—	750
'78	C	6-225	RBL-16Y	.035	12	12	8	8	700	700	750	750●
	D	6-225	RBL-16Y	.035	12	12	—	—	750	750	—	—
	G	8-318	RN-12Y	.035	16②③	16②③	16②③	16②③	700	750	750	750●
	H	8-318	RN-12Y	.035	10②③	10②③	—	10②③	—	—	—	750
	K	8-360	RN-12Y	.035	20②③	20②③	—	20	—	750	—	750
	J	8-360	RN-12Y	.035	—	16①②	—	16①②	—	750	—	750
	L	8-360	RN-12Y	.035	—	16①②	—	16①②	—	750	—	750●
	N	8-400	OJ-13Y	.035	—	20②	—	—	—	750	—	750
	P	8-400	OJ-11Y	.035	—	20②	—	—	—	750	—	750
	T	8-440	OJ-13Y	.035	—	①	—	8②	—	750	—	750●
	U	8-440	OJ-11Y	.035	—	①	—	8②	—	750	—	750●
'79	C	6-225	RBL-16Y	.035	12	12	—	8	675	675	—	750
	D	6-225	RN-12Y	.035	12	12	—	8	675	675	—	750
	G	8-318	12N-12Y	.035	16②	16②	16②	16②	725	725	—	—
	H	8-318	RN-12Y	.035	—	16②	16②	16②	750	750	—	750
	K	8-360	RN-12Y	.035	—	16②	—	16②	750	750	—	750
	L	8-360	RN-12Y	.035	16②	16②	—	—	750	750	—	—
'80	C	6-225	RBL-16Y	.035	12	12	—	8	675	675	—	750
	D	6-225	RN-12Y	.035	12	12	—	8	675	675	—	750
	G	8-318	12N-12Y	.035	16②	16	—	16②	725	725	—	750
	H	8-318	RN-12Y	.035	—	16	—	16②	750	750	—	750
	K	8-360	RN-12Y	.035	—	12	—	12②	750	750	—	750
	L	8-360	RN-12Y	.035	16②	16②	—	16②	750	750	—	750
'81	E	6-225	RBL-16Y	.048	①	①	—	8	675	675	—	750
	G	6-225	RN-12Y	.048	①	①	—	8	675	675	—	750
	K	8-318	12N-12Y	.035	①	①	—	16②	725	725	—	750
	M	8-318	RN-12Y	.048	①	①	—	16②	750	750	—	750

NOTE: Spark plugs shown are original equipment. For other manufacturers' equivalent plugs, see Popular Replacement Spark Plug Tables.

① See engine decal
② If equiped with lean burn, ground carburetor idle switch
③ Disconnect distributor vacuum, transmission in neutral
● = High altitude
Ⓝ = Neutral
④ If a 17-digit VIN is used, the 8th digit is the engine code and the 10th digit is the model year code

TUNE-UP SPECIFICATIONS

Engine Code, 5th character of the VIN number④

Year	Eng. V.I.N. Code	Engine No. Cyl. Disp. (cu in)	SPARK PLUGS		IGNITION TIMING (deg B.T.D.C.)				CARBURETION HOT IDLE SPEED			
			Orig. Type	Gap (in)	Federal③		California③		Federal		California	
					Man	Auto	Man	Auto	Man	Auto	Man	Auto
'82	E	6-225	RBL-16Y	.048	①	①	—	8	675	675	—	750
	G	6-225	RN-12Y	.048	①	①	—	8	675	675	—	750
	K	8-318	12N-12Y	.035	①	①	—	16②	725	725	—	750
	M	8-318	RN-12Y	.048	①	①	—	16②	750	750	—	750
	J	8-318	RN-12Y	.048	①	①	—	16②	750	750	—	750

NOTE: Spark plugs shown are original equipment. For other manufacturers' equivalent plugs, see Popular Replacement Spark Plug Tables.
① See engine decal
② If equiped with lean burn, ground carburetor idle switch
③ Disconnect distributor vacuum, transmission in neutral
● = High altitude
Ⓝ = Neutral
④ If a 17-digit VIN is used, the 8th digit is the engine code and the 10th digit is the model year code

Six cylinder switches and sensors

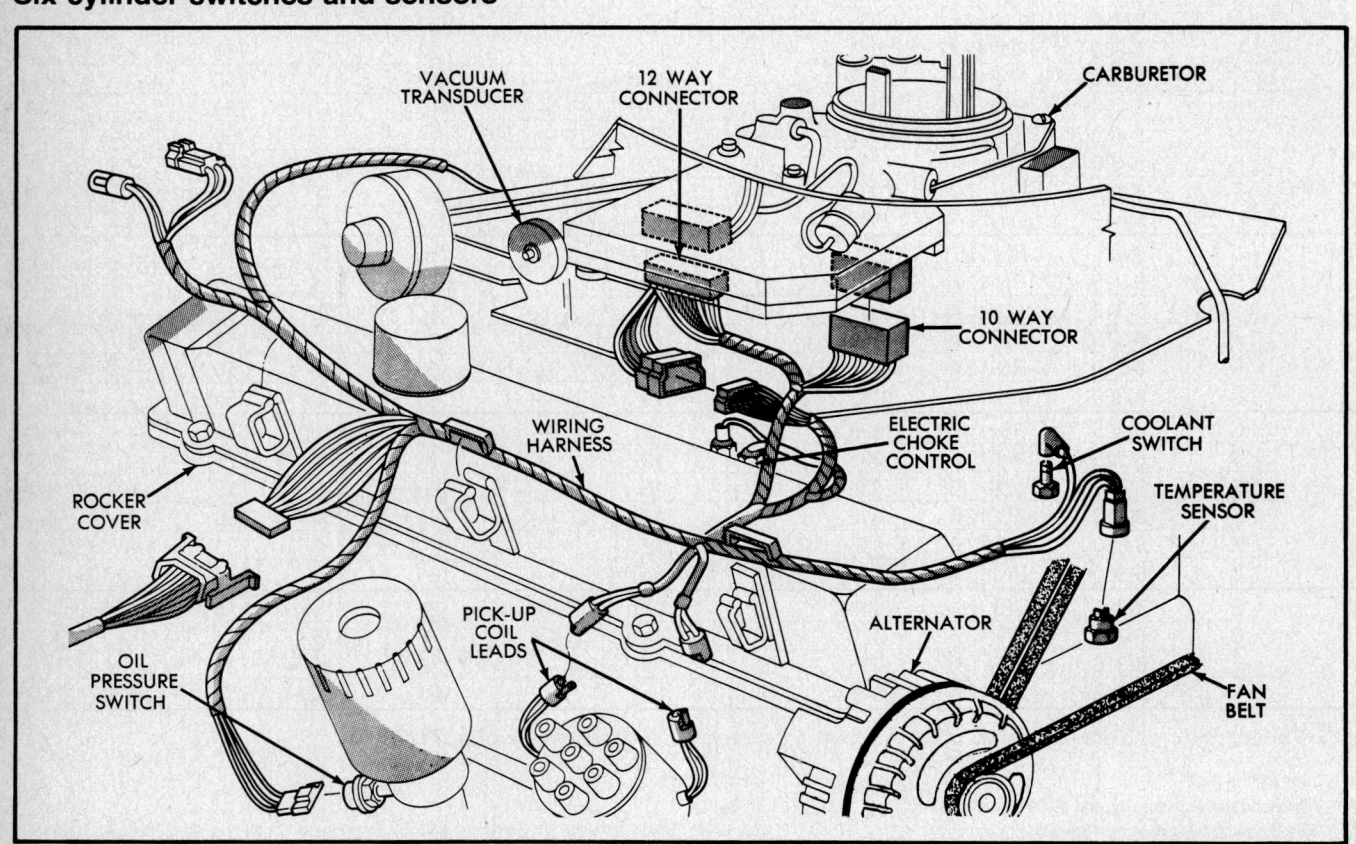

Eight cylinder switches and sensors

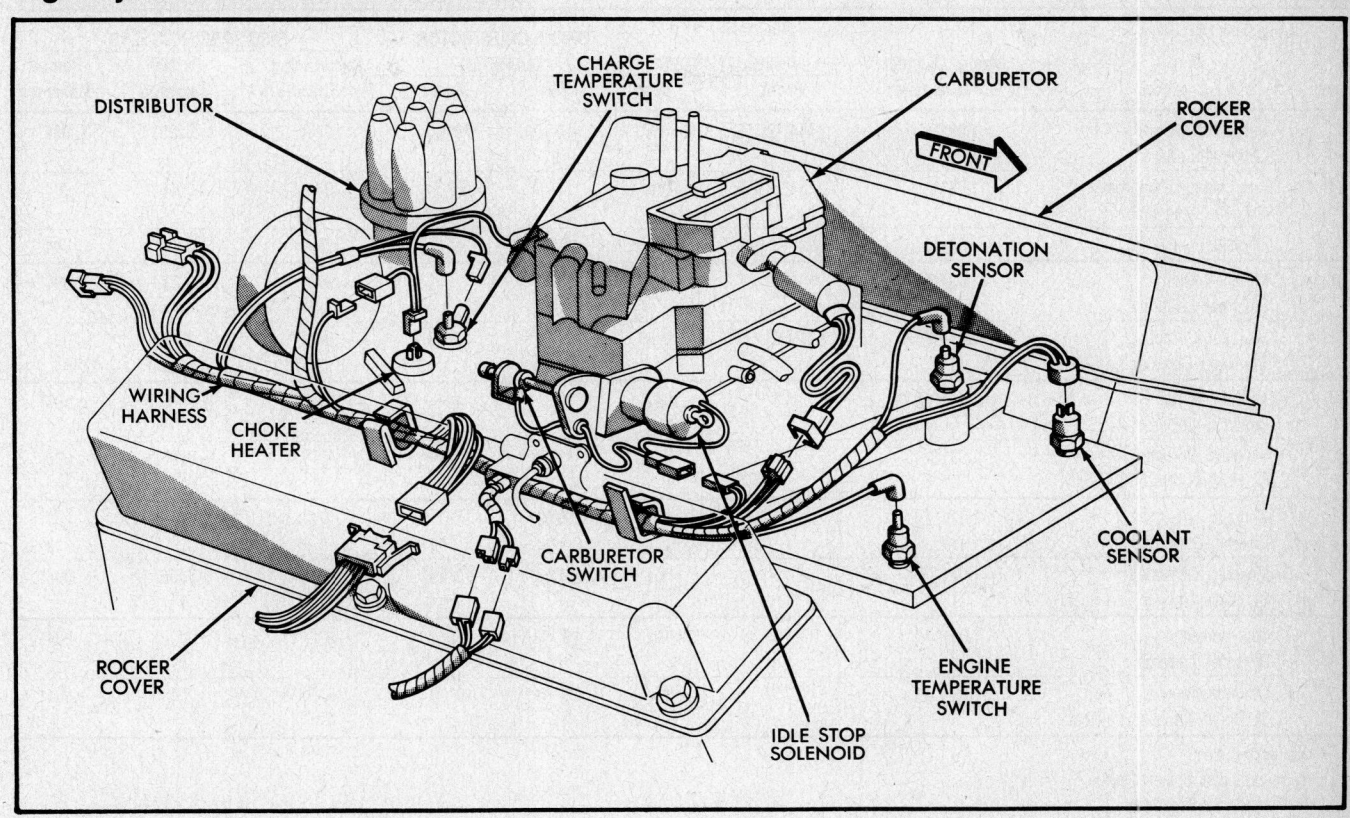

BRAKE SPECIFICATIONS

Year	Model	Master Cylinder Bore Diameter	WHEEL CYLINDER Front	WHEEL CYLINDER Rear	BRAKE DRUM/ROTOR DIAMETER Front	BRAKE DRUM/ROTOR DIAMETER Rear	DISC SPECIFICATIONS Resurfacing Min. Thickness	DISC SPECIFICATIONS Parallel Variation	DISC SPECIFICATIONS Runout Maximum
76	Dart & Valiant w/Drum Brks.	1.031″	$^{15}/_{16}$″	$^{15}/_{16}$″③	10″	10″⑤	—	—	—
	Dart, Valiant, Aspen, Volare w/Manual Disc Brks.	1.031″	2.754″-2.756″	$^{15}/_{16}$″	10.98″	10″⑧	.940″	.0005″	.004″
	Dart, Valiant, Aspen, Volare w/Power Disc Brks.	.937″⑥	2.754″-2.756″	$^{15}/_{16}$″	10.98″	10″⑧	.940″	.0005″	.004″
	Cordoba, Charger, Coronet, Fury up to 1-1-76	1.031″⑦	2.754″-2.756″	$^{15}/_{16}$″	10.98″	11″	.940″	.0005″	.004″
	Cordoba, Charger, Coronet, Fury after 1-1-76	1.031″	2.754″-2.756	$^{15}/_{16}$″	11.75″	11″	.940″	.0005″	.004″
	Gran Fury, Monaco and Chrysler	1.031″	3.102″-3.104″	$^{15}/_{16}$″	11.75″	11″	1.180″	.0005″	.004″
77	Aspen, Volare, Diplomat, LeBaron	1.031″	2.754″-2.756″	$^{15}/_{16}$″	10.98″	10″⑧	.970″	.0005″	.004″
	Fury, Monaco, Cordoba, Charger SE	1.031″	2.754″-2.756″	$^{15}/_{16}$″	11.75″	11″	.970″	.0005″	.004″
	Royal Monaco, Gran Fury, Chrysler	1.031″	3.102″-3.104″	$^{15}/_{16}$″	11.75″	11″	1.210″	.0005″	.004″

BRAKE SPECIFICATIONS

Year	Model	Master Cylinder Bore Diameter	WHEEL CYLINDER Front	Rear	BRAKE DRUM/ROTOR DIAMETER Front	Rear	DISC SPECIFICATIONS Resurfacing Min. Thickness	Parallel Variation	Runout Maximum
78	Aspen, Volare, Diplomat, LeBaron	1.031"	2.754"-2.755	15/16"	10.98"	10"⑨	.970"	.0005"	.004"
	Fury, Monaco, Charger, Cordoba, Magnum	1.031"	2.754"-2.755	15/16"	11.75"	10"⑨	.970"	.0005"	.004"
	Chrysler	1.031"	3.102"-3.104"	15/16"	11.75"	11"	1.210"	.0005"	.004"
79	Aspen, Volare, Diplomat, LeBaron	1.031"⑩	2.75"	15/16"	10.82"	10"	.970"	.0005"	.004"
	Maxnum, Cordoba, St. Regis, Chrysler, La-Scala	1.031"⑩	2.75"	15/16"	11.58"	10"⑩	.970"	.0005"	.004"
80	Aspen, Volare, Diplomat, LeBaron	1.031"⑩	2.75"	15/16"	10.82"	10"	.970"	.0005"	.004"
	Maxnum, Cordoba, St. Regis, Chrysler, La-Scala	1.031"⑩	2.75"	15/16"	11.58"	10"⑩	.970"	.0005"	.004"
81	Chrysler, Diplomat, LeBaron	1.031"⑩	2.75"	15/16"	10.82"	10"	.970"	.0005"	.004"
	Maxnum, Cordoba, St. Regis, Chrysler, La-Scala	1.031"⑩	2.75"	15/16"	11.58"	10"⑩	.970"	.0005"	.004"
82	New Yorker, Diplomat, LeBaron	1.031"⑩	2.75"	15/16"	10"-11"	10"	.970"	.0005"	.004"
	Cordoba, Imperial, St. Regis, Chrysler, La-Scala	1.031"⑩	2.75"	15/16"	10"-11"	10"⑩	.970"	.0005"	.004"

— Not applicable
① W/manual disc brakes 1 1/32"
② W/manual disc brakes 1"
③ 13/16" for 6 cyl. Dart and Valiant vehicles built before Jan. 1, 1976
④ Maximun after honing
⑤ 9" dia. rear drum on 6 cyl. Dart and Valiant before Jan. 1, 1976
⑥ Aspen and Volare 1.031"
⑦ W/manual disc brakes on Coronet and Fury 1.00"
⑧ Aspen and Volare wagons have 11" rear brakes
⑨ 11" drum on police and/or taxi Aspen, Volare, Monaco and Fury. Also on Cordoba, Magnum, Charger, Monaco and Fury equipped w/9 1/4" rear axle (12 bolt rear cover)
⑩ With power brakes 1.03"

CRANKSHAFT & CONNECTING ROD SPECIFICATIONS

All measurements given in inches

Engine No. Cyl. Displacement (cu in)	Year	CRANKSHAFT Main Brg. Journal Dia	Main Brg. Oil Clearance	Shaft End Play	Thrust on No.	CONNECTING ROD Journal diameter	Oil Clearance	Side Clearance
6-198, 225	ALL	2.7495-2.7505	.0005-.0020	.002-.007	3	2.1865-2.1875	.0005-.0020	.006-.012
6-225	ALL	2.7495-2.7505	.0005-.0020	.002-.009	3	2.1865-2.1875	.0005-.0025	.006-.025
8-318	ALL	2.4995-2.5005	.0005-.0020	.002-.007	3	2.124-2.125	.0005-.0025	.006-.014
8-360	ALL	2.8095-2.8105	.0005-.0020	.002-.007	3	2.124-2.125	.0005-.0020	.006-.014
8-400	ALL	2.6245-2.6255	.0005-.0020	.002-.007	3	2.375-2.376	.0002-.0022	.009-.017
8-440	ALL	2.7495-2.7505	.0005-.0020	.002-.007	3	2.375-2.376	.0004-.0029	.009-.017

DISTRIBUTOR SPECIFICATIONS

Year	Distributor Identification	CENTRIFUGAL ADVANCE Start Dist Deg @ Dist RPM	Finish Dist Deg @ Dist RPM	VACUUM ADVANCE Start @ In Hg	Finish Dist Deg @ In Hg
76	3874598	1.0–4.5 @ 600	9.5–11.5 @ 2,300	7	7.0–10.0 @ 11.5
	3874714	1.0–4.5 @ 450	7.0–9.0 @ 2,500	7	7.0–10.0 @ 11.5
	3874754	0–4.0 @ 500	11.5–13.5 @ 2,400	8	10.0–12.0 @ 13.5
	3874115	1.0–3.5 @ 600	10.0–12.0 @ 2,000	7	10.0–12.0 @ 12.5
	3874115	1.0–3.5 @ 600	10.0–12.0 @ 2,000	7	10.0–12.0 @ 12.5
	3874097	1–4.5 @ 650	13.5–16.5 @ 2,150	7	10.0–12.0 @ 12.5
	3874101	0.5–3.0 @ 600	10.0–12.0 @ 2,000	8	9.0–11.0 @ 14
	3874110	1.0–3.5 @ 600	10.0–12.0 @ 2,000	8	9.0–11.0 @ 14
	3874110	1.0–3.5 @ 600	10.0–12.0 @ 2,000	8	9.0–11.0 @ 14
	3874848	0.5–3.0 @ 550	5.5–9.0 @ 2,300	—	—
	3874596	0.5–4.0 @ 600	8.0–10.9 @ 2,000	8	9.0–11.0 @ 14
	3874173	1.0–3.5 @ 600	8.0–10.0 @ 2,000	8	9.0–11.0 @ 14
	3874795	1.5–3.5 @ 65	3.5–5.5 @ 2,300	7	9.0–12.0 @ 8.5
	3874119	1.0–3.5 @ 600	9.5–11.5 @ 2,400	7	10.0–12.0 @ 12.5
77	3874115	1.3–3.1 @ 600	10.0–12.0 @ 2000	7	10.0–12.0 @ 12.5
	3874173	1.3–3.1 @ 600	8.0–10.0 @ 2000	8	9.0–11.0 @ 14
	3874714	0.3–2.4 @ 500	6.9–8.9 @ 2500	7	7.3–9.8 @ 11.5
	3874858	1.4–3.4 @ 600	6.5–8.5 @ 2400	7	10.0–12.5 @ 12.5
	3874876	0.2–2.2 @ 600	3.7–5.7 @ 2500	7	7.3–9.8 @ 11.5
	3874909	0.2–2.2 @ 600	7.6–9.6 @ 2300	8	10.0–12.0 @ 13.5
	3874913	1.7–4.1 @ 600	11.6–13.6 @ 2350	8	10.0–12.0 @ 13.5
	3874917	0.6–2.0 @ 500	8.0–10.0 @ 2000	7	10.0–12.5 @ 12.5
	3874929	1.4–3.4 @ 600	9.7–11.7 @ 2300	7	7.3–9.8 @ 11.5
	4091039	0.2–2.2 @ 600	3.7–5.7 @ 2500	7	7.3–9.8 @ 11.5
	4091101	1.0–1.2 @ 600	5.8–7.8 @ 2060	9	7.5–9.5 @ 12.5
78	3874115	1.3–3.1 @ 600	10.0–12.0 @ 2000	7	10.0–12.0 @ 12.5
	3874173	1.3–3.1 @ 600	8.0–10.0 @ 2000	8	9.0–11.0 @ 14
	3874858	1.4–3.4 @ 600	6.5–8.5 @ 2400	7	10.0–12.5 @ 12.5
	3874876	0.2–2.2 @ 600	3.7–5.7 @ 2500	7	7.3–9.8 @ 11.5
	3874929	1.4–3.4 @ 600	9.7–11.7 @ 2300	7	7.3–9.8 @ 11.5
	4091101	1.0–1.2 @ 600	5.8–7.8 @ 2060	9	7.5–9.5 @ 12.5
79	3874876	.2–2.2 @ 600	3.7–5.7 @ 2500	7	7.3–9.8 @ 11.5
80	3874876	0.2–2.2 @ 600	3.7–5.7 @ 2500	7	7.3–9.8 @ 11.5
	4111501	0–1.5 @ 700	7.5–10 @ 2200	7	10–12 @ 15

Combustion computer

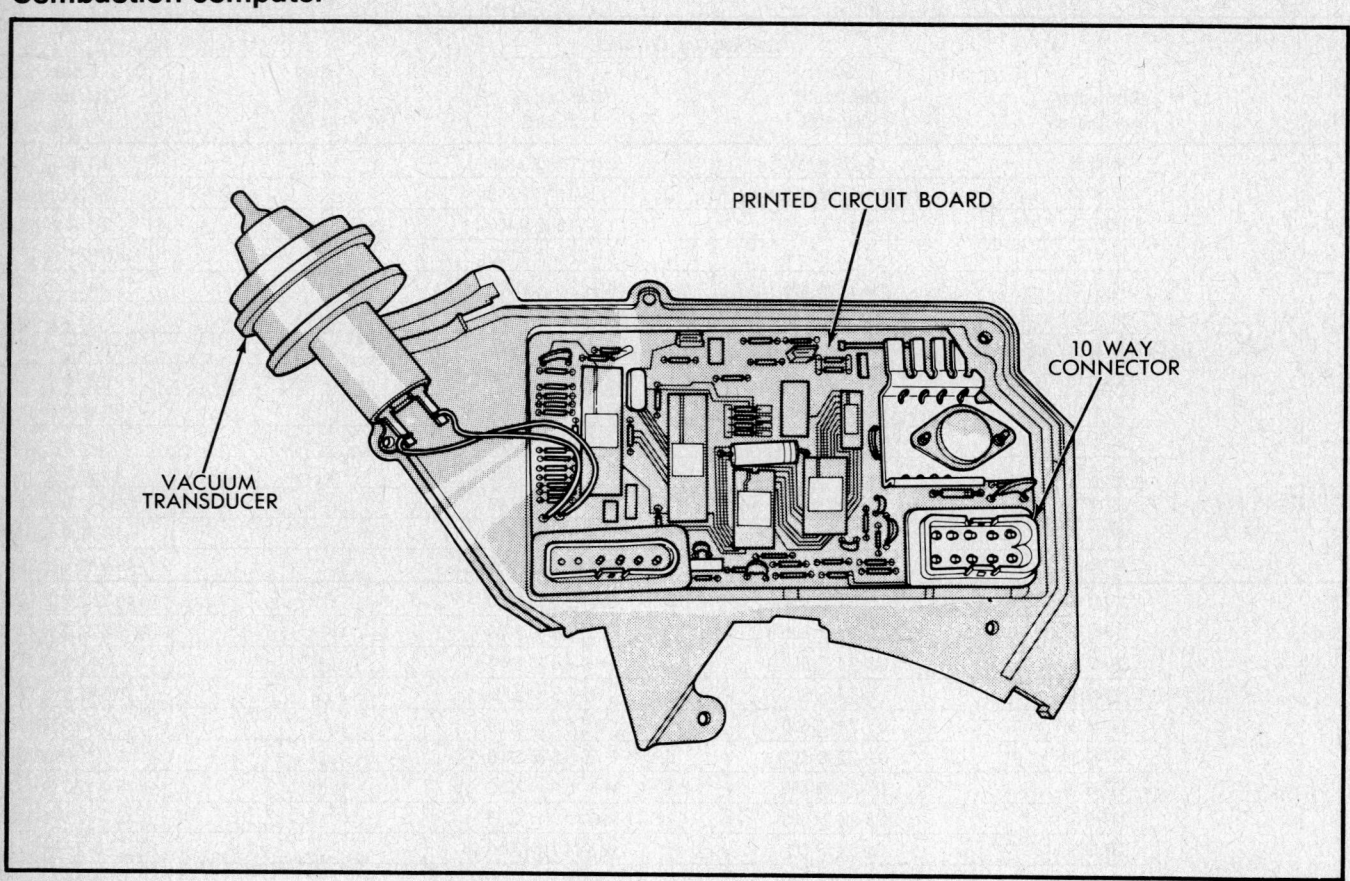

PRINTED CIRCUIT BOARD

10 WAY CONNECTOR

VACUUM TRANSDUCER

1978 ELECTRONIC SPARK CONTROL SYSTEM

Custom I.C. Spark Control Computer Part Number	4091730	4091731	4091732	4091786	4091787	4091788
Spark Timer Advance Schedule	8°	8°	8°	8°	8°	8°
Delay Time in Seconds	60	60	60	60	60	60
Throttle Advance Schedule	7°–9°@100°F	4°–6°@100°F	5°–7°@100°F	5°–7°@100°F	5°–7°@100°F	7°–9°@100°F
Test Transducer Core Out 1 Inch	3°–6°@140°F	2°–4°@140°F	2°–5°@140°F	2°–4°@140°F	2°–4°@140°F	4°–6°@140°F
Vacuum Advance Schedule (A) Operating Vacuum Range	0"–12"	0"–14"	0"–14"	0"–15.5"	0"–10"	0"–14'
(B) Advance Off Idle (Carb Switch Isolated With Paper	None	7°–11°	None	5°–9°	None	7°–11°
(C) Accumulation Time (In minutes)	8	8	8	7	8	8
(D) Advance After Accumulation Time	28°–32°	23°–27°	26°–30°	18°–22°	23°–27°	20°–24°
Speed Advance (Ground Carb Switch and @2000 Disconnect RPM Throttle Transducer @4000 Before Checking) RPM	4°–8° / 8°–12°	4°–8° / 10°–14°	0°–3° / 2°–6°	0°–1° / 0°–2°	2°–5° / 7°–11°	1°–5° / 4°–8°

1978 ELECTRONIC SPARK CONTROL SYSTEM

Custom I.C. Spark Control

Computer Part Number	4091791	4091923	4091924	4091954	4091955
Spark Timer Advance Schedule	8°	8°	8°	8°	8°
Delay Time in Seconds	60	60	60	60	60
Throttle Advance Schedule	4°–6°@100°F	5°–7°@100°F	9°–11°@100°F	5°–7°@100°F	7°–9°@100°F
Test Transducer Core Out 1 Inch	1°–4°@140°F	2°–5°@140°F	5°–8°@140°F	2°–5°@140°F	4°–6°@140°F
Vacuum Advance Schedule (A) Operating Vacuum Range	0″–12″	0″–14″	0″–14″	0″–15.5″	0″–14″
(B) Advance Off Idle (Carb Switch Isolated With Paper)	None	8°–12°	None	None	7°–11°
(C) Accumulation Time (In Minutes)	8	8	8	8	7
(D) Advance After Accumulation Time	20°–24°	24°–28°	21°–25°	18°–22°	20°–24°
Speed Advance (Ground Carb Switch and Disconnect @2000 RPM	7°–11°	1°–4°	10°–15°	0°–1°	1°–5°
Throttle Transducer Before Checking) @4000 RPM	8°–12°	6°–10°	16°–21°	0°–2°	4°–8°

Custom I.C. Spark Control

Computer Part Number	4111012	4111013	4111014	4111015	4111159
Spark Timer Advance Schedule	8°	8°	8°	8°	8°
Delay Time in Seconds	60	60	60	60	60
Throttle Advance Schedule	0°	9°–11°@100°F	5°–7°@100°F	5°–7°@100°F	5°–7°@100°F
Test Transducer Core Out 1 Inch	0°	5°–8°@140°F	2°–5°@140°F	2°–5°@140°F	2°–5°@140°F
Vacuum Advance Schedule (A) Operating Vacuum Range	0″–15.5″	0″–14″	0″–12″	0″–14″	0″–15.5″
(B) Advance Off Idle (Carb Switch Isolated With Paper)	None	None	2°–6°	2°–6°	None
(C) Accumulation Time (In Minutes)	8	8	8	8	8
(D) Advance After Accumulation Time	18°–22°	21°–25°	18°–22°	18°–22°	18°–22°
Speed Advance (Ground Carb Switch and Disconnect @2000 RPM	4°–8°	10°–14°	8°–12°	8°–12°	0°–1°
Throttle Transducer Before Checking) @4000 RPM	6°–10°	16°–21°	12°–16°	12°–16°	0°–2°

Custom I.C. Spark Control

Computer Part Number	4111169	4111170	4111172	4111217	4111218
Spark Timer Advance Schedule	None	None	None	8°	8°
Delay Time in Seconds	None	None	None	60	60
Throttle Advance Schedule	5°–7°@100°F	5°–7°@100°F	2°–5°@140°F	0°	0°
Test Transducer Core Out 1 Inch	5°–7°@100°F	2°–5°@140°F	2°–5°@140°F	0°	0°
Vacuum Advance Schedule (A) Operating Vacuum Range	0″–10″	0″–10″	0″–10″	4″–14″	4″–14″
(B) Advance Off Idle (Carb Switch Isolated With Paper)	5°–9°	5°–9°	5°–9°	6°–10°	2°–6°
(C) Accumulation Time (In Minutes)	8	8	8	7	7
(D) Advance After Accumulation Time	16°–20°	16°–20°	16°–20°	18°–22°	18°–22°
Speed Advance (Ground Carb Switch and Disconnect @2000 RPM	1°–5°	1°–5°	1°–5°	8°–12°	8°–12°
Throttle Transducer Before Checking) @4000 RPM	4°–8°	4°–8°	4°–8°	12°–16°	12°–16°

CHRYSLER REAR DRIVE CARS

1979 ELECTRONIC SPARK CONTROL SYSTEM

Custom I.C. Spark Control Computer Part Number		4111373	4111392	4111439	4111440
Engine Application		225 E-24-25	318-4 E46	360-4 E58	318-2 E44
Vacuum Advance (Range)		5″–11″	4″–13″	4″–12″	4″–12″
Crank + Electrical = (Basic Timing)		10° + 5°	10° + 6°	10° + 6°	10° + 6°
Speed Advance (Ground Carb Switch and Disconnect Throttle Transducer Before Checking	@1100 RPM	0°–2°	0°–1°	2°–6°	0°–1°
	@2000	1°–4°	1°–5°	6°–10°	1°–5°
Zero Time Offset		0°–3°	8°–12°	0°–3°	8°–12°
Accumulator Clock Up (in minutes)		8	8	8	8
Vacuum Advance—Full	@1100 RPM	11°–15°	16°–20°	8°–12°	12°–16°
Accumulator	@1500	18°–22°	23°–27°	18°–22°	18°–22°
Throttle Maximum Advance (Throttle Open 20°)		6°–10°	3°–7°	6°–10°	3°–7°

Custom I.C. Spark Control Computer Part Number		4111441	4111442	4111492	4111540
Engine Application		360-2 E57	360-4 E58	318-4 E47	318-2 E45
Vacuum Advance (Range)		4″–12″	4″–12″	4″–13″	4″–12″
Crank + Electrical = (Basic Timing)		12″ + 0°	10° + 6°	10° + 6°	10° + 6°
Speed Advance (Ground Carb Switch and Disconnect Throttle Transducer Before Checking	@1100 RPM	3°–7°	2°–6°	0°–1°	0°–1°
	@2000	8°–12°	6°–10°	1°–5°	1°–5°
Zero Time Offset		6°–10°	6°–10°	8°–12°	8°–12°
Accumulator Clock Up (in minutes)		8	8	8	8
Vacuum Advance—Full	@1100 RPM	11°–17°	8°–12°	16°–20°	12°–16°
Accumulator	@1500	18°–22°	18°–22°	23°–27°	18°–22°
Throttle Maximum Advance (Throttle Open 20°)		0°	6°–10°	3°–7°	3°–7°

Custom I.C. Spark Control Computer Part Number		4111574	4111575	4111650	4111652
Engine Application		318-4 E46	360-4 E56	318-2 E44	360-2 E57
Vacuum Advance (Range)		4″–13°	4″–10°	4″–12°	4″–14°
Crank + Electrical = (Basic Timing)		10° + 6°	10° + 6°	10° + 6°	12° + 0°
Speed Advance (Ground Carb Switch and Disconnect Throttle Transducer Before Checking	@100 RPM	0°–1°	2°–6°	0°–1°	0°–1°
	@2000	1°–5°	6°–10°	1°–5°	11°–15°
Zero Time Offset		0°–3°	2°–6°	18°–22°	0°–3°
Accumulator Clock Up (in minutes)		8	8	8	8
Vacuum Advance—Full	@1100 RPM	16°–20°	11°–15°	12°–16°	17°–21°
Accumulator	@1500	23°–27°	18°–22°	18°–22°	26°–30°
Throttle Maximum Advance (Throttle Open 20°)		3°–7°	6°–10°	3°–7°	3°–7°

1979 ELECTRONIC SPARK CONTROL SYSTEM

Custom I.C. Spark Control

Computer Part Number		4111656	4111657	4111674	4111750
Engine Application		360-2 E57	360-4 E58	318-4 E47	318-2 E45
Vacuum Advance (Range)		4°–14°	0°–12°	4°–13°	4°–12°
Crank + Electrical = (Basic Timing)		12° + 0°	10° + 0°	10° + 6°	10° + 6°
Speed Advance (Ground Carb Switch and Disconnect Throttle Transducer Before Checking	@1100 RPM	3°–7°	1°–5°	0°–1°	0°–1°
	@2000	8°–12°	11°–15°	1°–5°	1°–5°
Zero Time Offset		18°–22°	0°–3°	0°–3°	18°–22°
Accumulator Clock Up (in minutes)		0	8	8	0
Vacuum Advance—Full	@1100 RPM	13°–17°	17°–21°	16°–22°	12°–16°
Accumulator	@1500	18°–22°	26°–30°	23°–27°	18°–22°
Throttle Maximum Advance (Throttle Open 20°)		0°	3°–7°	3°–7°	3°–7°

1980 ELECTRONIC SPARK CONTROL SYSTEM

Custom I.C. Spark

Control Computer Number		414500	4145003	4145004	4105007	4145087
Engine Application		360-4 FED	318-4 CALIF	360-2 FED	225-1 CAL	360-4 FED
Vacuum Advance (Range)		4″-14″	4″-14″	4″-14″	0″-10″	4″-14″
Crank + Electrical = (Basic Timing)		8°+8°	8°+8°	12°+0°	12°+0°	8°+8°
Speed Advance (Ground Carb Switch and Disconnect Throttle Transducer Before Checking	@1100 RPM	1-4°	0°-2°	0°-4°	0°-2°	0°-2°
	@2000	4-8°	1°-5°	4°-8°	1°-5°	4°-8°
Zero Time Offset		23°-27°	28°-32°	23°-27°	0°-2°	21°-25°
Accumulator Clock Up (in minutes)		0	0	0	1 min.	0
Vacuum Advance—Full	@1100 R.P.M.	10°-14°	14°-18°	0°-2°	0°-2°	0°-2°
	@2500	23°-27°	28°-32°	23°-27°	20°-24°	21°-25°

1981 ELECTRONIC SPARK CONTROL SYSTEM

Computer Part Number	4145467	4145725	4145726
Engine Application	318-4 Cal.	318 EFI Cal.	318 EFI Fed. Can.
Basic Timing	16° BTDC①	12° BTDC	12° BTDC
Curb Idle Speed	600 RPM②	580 RPM	580 RPM
Vacuum Range	4″-14″	2″-12″	2″-12″
Accumultor Clock Up (in minutes)	0	0	0
Spark Advance Test 2000 RPM Vacuum	29° ± 4°	29° ± 4°	23° ± 4°
Electronic EGR	90 Sec	No	No
Electronic Throttle Control	No	AIS	AIS
Detonation Suppression	No	Yes	Yes
O₂ Feedback Air Switching (Electronic)	No	70 Sec	70 Sec
Temperature Sensor	No	Coolant Sensor	Coolant Sensor

CHRYSLER REAR DRIVE CARS

1981 ELECTRONIC SPARK CONTROL SYSTEM

Computer Part Number	4145788	4145817	4145850
Engine Application	318-4 Cal.	225-1 Cal.	318-4 Cal.
Basic Timing	16° BTDC	16° BTDC	16° BTDC
Curb Idle Speed	600 RPM	600 RPM	600 RPM
Vacuum Range	4"–14"	3"–10"	4"–14"
Accumultor Clock Up (in minutes)	0	0.5	0
Spark Advance Test 2000 RPM Vacuum	34° ± 4°	20° ± 4°	34° ± 4°
Electronic EGR	60 Sec	90 Sec	60 Sec
Electronic Throttle Control	60 Sec	90 Sec	60 Sec
Detonation Suppression	Yes	No	Yes
O_2 Feedback Air Switching (Electronic)	20 Sec	65 Sec	20 Sec
Temperature Sensor	Coolant Sensor	Coolant Sensor	Coolant Sensor

A—Automatic Transmission
M—Manual Transmission
BTDC—Before Top Dead Center
Can.—Canada
Fed.—Federal
Cal.—California
E48 318 CID Can.
① 12"
② 710 RPM

1981 ELECTRONIC SPARK CONTROL SYSTEM

Computer Part Number	4145431	4145452	4145457	4145466
Engine Application	225-1 Cal.	318-2 Can.	318-4 Fed.	318-2 Fed.
Basic Timing	16° BTDC	16° BTDC	16° BTDC	16° BTDC
Curb Idle Speed	600 RPM	600 RPM	600 RPM	600 RPM
Vacuum Range	3"–10"	4"–14"	4"–14"	4"–14"
Accumultor Clock Up (in minutes)	0.5	0	0	0
Spark Advance Test 2000 RPM Vacuum	20° ± 4°	29° ± 4°	34° ± 4°	34° ± 4°
Electronic EGR	60 Sec	35 Sec	60 Sec	20 Sec
Electronic Throttle Control	90 Sec	No	60 Sec	20 Sec
Detonation Suppression	No	No	Yes	No
O_2 Feedback Air Switching (Electronic)	65 Sec	No	30 Sec	90 Sec
Temperature Sensor	Coolant Sensor	No	Coolant Sensor	Coolant Sensor

NOTE: The following specifications are published from the latest information available at the time of publication. If anything differs from those on the Emission Control Information Label, use the specification on the label.

VALVE SPECIFICATIONS

Year	Engine No. Cyl. Displacement (cu in)	Seat Angle (deg)①	Face Angle (deg)①	Spring Test Pressure (lbs @ in)	Maximum Spring Installed Height (in)	STEM TO GUIDE CLEARANCE (in) Intake	Exhaust	MEDIAN STEM DIAMETER (in) Intake	Exhaust
'76	6-225 Ⓐ	45	②	137-150 @ 1.31	1¹¹⁄₁₆	.001-.003	.002-.004	.3725	.3715
	8-318	45	②	170-184 @ 1.31⑩	1¹¹⁄₁₆	.001-.003	.002-.004	.3725	.3715
	8-360	45	②	③	1¹¹⁄₁₆	.001-.003⑮	.002-.004⑮	.3725⑯	.3715⑯
	8-400, 440 std	45	45	192-208 @ 1.44	1⁵⁷⁄₆₄	.0011-.0028	⑧	.3727	⑥
	8-400, 440 HP	45	45	236-256 @ 1.36	1⁵⁷⁄₆₄	.0016-.0033	⑨	.3722	⑦
'77	6-225 Ⓐ	45	②	137-150 @ 1.31	1¹¹⁄₁₆	.001-.003	.002-.004	.3725	.3715
	8-318	45	②	170-184 @ 1.31⑩	1¹¹⁄₁₆	.001-.003	.002-.004	.3725	.3715
	8-360	45	②	186-200 @ 1.25	1¹¹⁄₁₆	.001-.003⑮	.002-.004⑮	.3725⑯	.3715⑯
	8-400, 440 std	45	45	192-208 @ 1.44	1⁵⁷⁄₆₄	.0011-.0028	⑧	.3727	⑥
	8-400, 440 HP	45	45	236-256 @ 1.36	1⁵⁷⁄₆₄	.0016-.0033	⑨	.3722	⑦
'78	6-225 Ⓐ	45	②	137-150 @ 1.31	1¹¹⁄₁₆	.001-.003	.002-.004	.3725	.3715
	8-318	45	②	170-184 @ 1.31⑩	1¹¹⁄₁₆	.001-.003	.002-.004	.3725	.3715
	8-360	45	②	186-200 @ 1.25	1¹¹⁄₁₆	.001-.003⑮	.002-.004⑮	.3725⑯	.3715⑯
	8-400, 440 std	45	45	192-208 @ 1.44	1⁵⁷⁄₆₄	.0011-.0028	⑧	.3727	⑥
	8-400, 440 HP	45	45	236-256 @ 1.36	1⁵⁷⁄₆₄	.0016-.0033	⑨	.3722	⑦
'79	6-225 Ⓐ	45	②	137-150 @ 1.31	1¹¹⁄₁₆	.001-.003	.002-.004	.3725	.3715
	8-318	45	②	185 @ 1.28	1¹¹⁄₁₆	.001-.003	.002-.004	.3725	.3715
	8-360	45	②	195 @ 1.24	1¹¹⁄₁₆	.001-.003	.002-.004	.3725	.3715
'80	6-225 Ⓐ	45	②	137-150 @ 1.31	1¹¹⁄₁₆	.001-.003	.002-.004	.3725	.3715
	8-318	45	②	185 @ 1.28	1¹¹⁄₁₆	.001-.003	.002-.004	.3725	.3715
	8-360	45	②	195 @ 1.24	1¹¹⁄₁₆	.001-.003	.002-.004	.3725	.3715
'81	6-225 Ⓑ	45	②	137-150 @ 1.31	1¹¹⁄₁₆	.001-.003	.002-.004	.3725	.3715
	8-318	45	②	185 @ 1.28	1¹¹⁄₁₆	.001-.003	.002-.004	.3725	.3715
	8-360	45	②	195 @ 1.24	1¹¹⁄₁₆	.001-.003	.002-.004	.3725	.3715
'82	6-225 Ⓑ	45	②	137-150 @ 1.31	1¹¹⁄₁₆	.001-.003	.002-.004	.3725	.3715
	8-318	45	②	185 @ 1.28	1¹¹⁄₁₆	.001-.003	.002-.004	.3725	.3715
	8-360	45	②	195 @ 1.24	1¹¹⁄₁₆	.001-.003	.002-.004	.3725	.3715

Ⓐ Adjustable valves
Ⓑ Non-adjustable valves hydraulic lifters
    Intake Hot—.010″
    Exhaust Hot—.020″
① Angle measured from the horizontal
② Intake 45°, Exhaust 43°
③ 360 × 2 bbl and 360 × 4 bbl std. engines (VIN codes "J" & "C")
    Spring test pressure 170-184 @ 1.31″
    360 × 4 bbl h.p. (VIN code "L") spring test pressure 231-245 @ 1.22″
④ Hot end—.0020-.0037. Cold end—.0010-.0027.
⑤ Hot end—.0025-.0042. Cold end—.0015-.0032.
⑥ Hot end—.3713-.3720. Cold end—.3723-.3730.
⑦ Hot end—.3708-.3715. Cold end—.3718-.3725.
⑧ Hot end—.0021-.0038. Cold end—.0011-.0028.
⑨ Hot end—.0026-.0043. Cold end—.0016-.0033.
⑩ W/surge damper removed
⑪ 360 × 4 bbl, 201-215 @ 1.31″, surge damper removed
⑫ V.I.N. codes M, N, T
⑬ All 360 × 2 bbl and 360 × 4 bbl in California, 170-184 @ 1.31″
    360 × 4 bbl h.p. (VIN code "L"), 231-245 @ 1.31″. surge damper removed for all tests
⑭ 360 × 4 bbl—.3710″
⑮ 360 × 4 bbl h.p. (code "L") valve stem to guide clearance—intake .0015″-.0035″
    exhaust .0025″-.0045″
⑯ 360 × 4 bbl h.p. (code "L") valve stem diameter—intake .3715″-.3725″
    exhaust .3705″-.3715″

CHRYSLER REAR DRIVE CARS

TORQUE SPECIFICATIONS

All readings in ft/lbs

Year	Engine Displacement (cu in)	Cylinder Head Bolts	Rod Bearing Bolts	Main Bearing Bolts	Crankshaft Pulley Bolt	Flywheel To Crankshaft Bolts	MANIFOLD Intake	MANIFOLD Exhaust
76	225	70	45	85	Press Fit	55	10①	10
	318-360	95	45	85	100	55	40	20②
	400-440	70	45	85	135	55	45	30
77	225	70	45	85	Press Fit	55	10③	10
	318-360	95	45	85	100	55	45	20②
	400-440	70	45	85	135	55	45	30
78	225	70	45	85	Press Fit	55	10③	10
	318-360	105	45	85	100	55	45	20②
	400-440	70	45	85	135	55	45	30
79	225	70	45	85	Press Fit	55	10③	10
	318-360	105	45	85	100	55	45	20②
80	225	70	45	85	Press Fit	55	10③	10
	318-360	105	45	85	100	55	45	20②
81	225(3.7L)	70	45	85	Press Fit	55	10③	10
	318(5.2L)	105	45	85	100	55	45	20②
82	225(3.7L)	70	45	85	Press Fit	55	10③	10
	318(5.2L)	105	45	85	100	55	45	20②

① Intake to exhaust manifold stud—30 ft/lbs
  Intake to exhaust manifold bolt—20 ft/lbs
② Mounting nut 15 ft/lbs
③ Intake to exhaust manifold stud—20 ft/lbs
  Intake to exhaust manifold bolt—17 ft/lbs

FLUID CAPACITIES—Coolant, Fuel & Lubricant   CHRYSLER

Year	Engine No. Cyl. Displacement (cu in)	Engine Crankcase (Add 1 Qt For New Filter)	Automatic Transmission (Pts To Refill After Draining includes converter)	Drive Axle (pts)	Gasoline Tank (gals)	Rad. Cap Pressure (lbs)	Thermo. Opening Temp.	COOLING SYSTEM (qts) With Heater	COOLING SYSTEM (qts) With A/C
'76	8-318	4	17③	4.5	26.5②	16	195	17.5	7.5
	8-360	4	19③	4.5	26.5②	16	195	16.0	16.0
	8-400	4	19③	4.5	26.5②	16	195	16.5	16.5
	8-400 HP	5	19③	4.5	26.5②	16	195	16.5	16.5
	8-440	4	19③	4.5	26.5②	16	195	16.0	16.0
	8-440 HP	5	19③	4.5	26.5②	16	195	16.0	16.0
'77	8-318	4	17	4.5	25.5②	16	195	16.5	18.0
	8-360	4	16.5④	4.5	26.5②	16	195	16.0	16.0
	8-400	4	16.5	4.5	26.5②	16	195	16.5	16.5
	8-440	4	16.5	4.5	26.5②	16	195	16.0	16.0
'78	8-360	4	16.5	4.5	26.5	16	195	16.0	16.0
	8-400	4	16.5	4.5	26.5	16	195	16.5	16.5
	8-440	4	16.5	4.5	26.5	16	195	16.0	16.0
'79	6-225	4	17	⑤	21.0	16	195	11.5	14.5
	8-318	4	①	⑤	21.0	16	195	15	17.5
	8-360	4	①	⑤	21.0	16	195	16	16
'80	6-225	4	①	⑤	21.0⑥	16	195	13	14
	8-318	4	①	⑤	21.0⑥	16	195	15	16
	8-360	4	①	⑤	21.0	16	195	15	16

FLUID CAPACITIES—Coolant, Fuel & Lubricant   CHRYSLER

Year	Engine No. Cyl. Displacement (cu in)	Engine Crankcase (Add 1 Qt For New Filter)	Automatic Transmission (Pts To Refill After Draining includes converter)	Drive Axle (pts)	Gasoline Tank (gals)	Rad. Cap Pressure (lbs)	Thermo. Opening Temp.	COOLING SYSTEM (qts) With Heater	With A/C
'81	6-225	4	①	⑤	21.0	16	195	13	14
	8-318	4	①	⑤	21.0	16	195	15	16
'82	6-225	4	①	⑤	18.0	16	195	13	14
	8-318	4	①	⑤	18.0	16	195	15	16

— Not applicable
① W/727 lock-up converter 16.7 pts
   W/904 lock-up converter 17.1 pts
② Wagons—24 gals.
③ 19 pts with A-727 transmission, 20.5 pts with trailer towing package
④ 17.0 W/A-998 auto trans.

⑤ Rear axle
   7½" ring gear—2.1 pts
   8¼" ring gear—4.4 pts
   9¼" ring gear—4.5 pts
⑥ LeBaron 18.0 gal.

FLUID CAPACITIES—Coolant, Fuel & Lubricant   VALIANT AND VOLARE

Year	Engine No. Cyl. Disp. (cu in)	Engine Crankcase (Add 1 Qt For New Filter)	TRANSMISSION Manual 3-Speed	4-Speed	Automatic (pts)	Drive Axle (pts)	Gasoline Tank (gals)	Rad. Cap Pressure (lbs)	Thermo. Opening Temp.	COOLING SYSTEM (qts) With Heater	With A/C
'76	6-225	4	4.75	—	17	4.4	20.5	16	195	12	14.5
	8-318	4	4.75	—	19⑥	4.4	25.5⑤	16	195	16.5	18
	8-360	4	—	—	19⑥	4.4	25.5⑤	16	195	16	16
	8-400	4	—	—	19	4.4	25.5④	16	195	16.5	16.5
	8-440	4	—	—	16.5	4.5	25.5④	16	195	16	16
'77	6-225	4	4.75	—	17	4.5	25.5③	16	195	13	14.5
	8-318	4	4.75	—	17	4.5	25.5⑤	16	195	16.5	18
	8-360	4	—	—	17	4.5	25.5⑤	16	195	16	16
	8-400	4	—	—	16.5	4.5	25.5⑤	16	195	16.5	16.5
'78	6-225	4	4.66	—	17	4.4	20.5	16	195	13	14.5
	8-318	4	—	—	17	4.4	25.5⑧	16	195	16	17.5
	8-360	4	—	—	17	4.4	25.5⑧	16	195	15.5	15.5
	8-400	4	—	—	16.5	4.4⑨	25.5⑧	16	195	16	16
	8-440	4	—	—	16.5	4.5	25.5⑧	16	195	15.5	15.5
'79	6-225	4	4.75	—	17	⑪	18⑩	16	195	13.0	14.5
	8-318	4	—	—	17.0	⑪	21.0	16	195	15.0	17.5
	8-360	4	—	—	17.0	⑪	21.0	16	195	16.0	16.0
'80	6-225	4	4.75	7	17	4.4	20.5	16	195	12.0	12.5
	8-318	4	4.75	7	17	4.5	19.5	16	195	15.0	15.5
	8-360	4	4.75	7	17	4.5	19.5	16	195	14.0	14.0
'81	6-225	4	4.75	7	17	4.4	20.5	16	195	12.0	12.5
	8-318	4	4.75	7	17	4.5	19.5	16	195	15.0	15.5
	8-360	4	4.75	7	17	4.5	19.5	16	195	14.0	14.0

— Not applicable
② Charger, Coronet, Satellite with 4 bbl—16.3 pts
③ Station wagons—21 gals
④ 400 4 bbl w/dual exhaust—20.5 gals
⑤ Wagon with catalyst-20
   Wagon without catalyst-20.5

⑥ 17 pts. w/ 904 trans.
⑦ Not available
⑧ Models w/dual exhausts 20.5 gal & station wagon—20.5 gal
⑨ 4.5 For wagons and vehicles w/ high alt. pkg.
⑩ Station wagon—19.5 gals.

⑪ Rear axle
   7½" ring gear—2.1 pts
   8¼" ring gear—4.4pts
   9¼" ring gear—4.5pts

FLUID CAPACITIES—Coolant, Fuel & Lubricant   **DODGE AND PLYMOUTH**

Year	Engine No. Cyl. Disp. (cu in)	Engine Crankcase (Add 1 Qt For New Filter)	Automatic Transmission (Pts To Refill After Draining)	Drive Axle (pts)	Gasoline Tank (gals)	Rad. Cap Pressure (lbs)	Thermo. Opening Temp.	COOLING SYSTEM (qts)	
								With Heater	With A/C
'76	8-318	4	17①	4.5	26.5	16	195	16.5	16.5
	8-360	4	19⑩	4.5	26.5②	16	195	16.0	16.0
	8-400	4	19⑩	4.5	26.5②	16	195	16.5	16.5
	8-400 HP	5	19⑩	4.5	26.5②	16	195	16.5	16.5
	8-440	4	19⑩	4.5	26.5②	16	195	16.0	16.0
	8-440 HP	5	19⑩	4.5	26.5②	16	195	16.0	16.0
'77	8-318	4	⑪	4.5	20.5	16	195	17.5	17.5
	8-360	4	⑪	4.5	26.5②	16	195	16.0	16.0
	8-400	4	⑪	4.5	26.5②	16	195	16.5	16.5
	8-400	4	⑪	4.5	26.5②	16	195	16.0	16.0
'78	8-318	4	⑪	4.5	20.5	16	195	17.5	17.5
	8-360	4	⑪	4.5	26.5②	16	195	16.0	16.0
	8-400	4	⑪	4.5	26.5②	16	195	16.5	16.5
	8-400	4	⑪	4.5	26.5②	16	195	16.0	16.0
'79	6-225	4	17	4.5	18.0⑫	16	195	11.5	12.5
	8-318	4	17	4.5	19.5	16	195	15.0	17.5
	8-360	4	17	4.5	19.5	16	195	15.0	15.0
'80	6-225	4	17	4.5	18.0⑫	16	195	11.5	14.5
	8-318	4	17	4.5	19.5	16	195	15.0	17.5
	8-360	4	17	4.5	19.5	16	195	16.0	16.0
'81	6-225	4	17	4.5	18.0⑫	16	195	11.5	14.5
	8-318	4	17	4.5	19.5	16	195	15.0	17.5
'82	6-225	4	17	4.5	18.0⑫	16	195	11.5	14.5
	8-318	4	17	4.5	19.5	16	195	15.0	17.5

— Not applicable
Figures in parentheses indicate California usage.
① Fury, Polara, Monaco—4.5 PTS
② Station wagons—24 gals
③ Fury, Polara, Monaco—23 gals
⑤ Charger, Coronet, Satellite with 4 bbl—16.3 pts
⑥ Fury, Polara, Monaco—19 pts
⑦ Station wagons—21 gals
⑧ Fury, Polara, Monaco—16 qts
⑨ Fury, Polara, Monaco—15.5 qts
⑩ 19 pts with A-727 transmission, 20.5 pts with trailer towing package
⑪ A-727-16.5; A-998-17.0
⑫ 6 cylinder wagon—19.5 gal

FUSES & CIRCUIT BREAKERS

CAVITY	FUSE	ITEMS FUSED
1	5 AMP	ACCESSORY SWITCH TITLE, A/C OR HEATER CONTROL, ASH TRAY, RADIO, CLUSTER, GEAR SELECTOR AND DIGITAL CLOCK LAMPS
2	20 AMP	HORN RELAY, HORN (DUAL)
3	20 AMP	TAIL, PARK, SIDE MARKER AND LICENSE LAMPS; CLOCK FEED (DIGITAL & CONVENTIONAL) AND KEY-IN BUZZER
4	20 AMP	STOP DOME, TRUNK, AFT DOME COURTESY (XS ONLY) MAP AND GLOVE BOX LAMPS; CIGAR LIGHTER AND IGNITION TIME DELAY RELAY
5	20 AMP	HAZARD FLASHER
6	20 AMP	BACK-UP AND TURN SIGNAL LAMPS
7	5 AMP	RADIO
8	5 AMP	OIL, BRAKE, EGR AND SEAT BELT LAMPS; SEAT BELT BUZZER AND TIME DELAY VOLTAGE LIMITER, OIL, TEMPERATURE AND FUEL GAUGES
9	30 AMP	A/C BLOWER MOTOR
10	20 AMP	HEATER BLOWER MOTOR, WINDOW LIFT SAFETY RELAY, POWER TAILGATE SOLENOID, DECK LID RELAY SOLENOID, HEATED REAR WINDOW AND TAILGATE AJAR

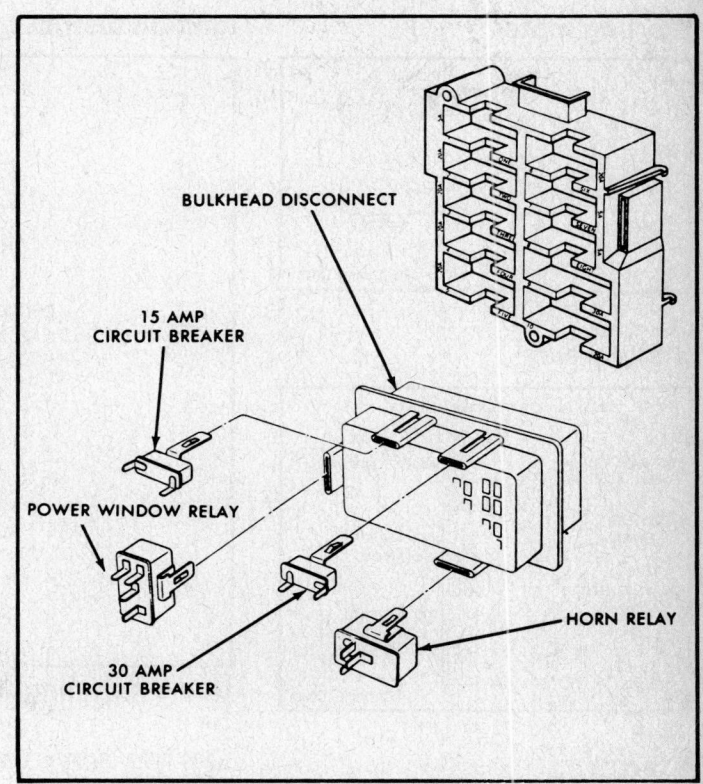

CAVITY	FUSE	ITEMS FUSED
1	30 AMP	A/C BLOWER MOTOR (HEATER BLOWER MOTOR 20 AMP)
2	20 AMP	PARK, TAIL, LICENSE, SIDE MARKER & INSTRUMENT PANEL LAMPS
3	20 AMP	STOP, DOME, MAP, GLOVE BOX, IGNITION UNDER HOOD, TRUNK LAMPS, KEY-IN BUZZER, IGNITION LAMP TIME DELAY RELAY, CLOCK (CONVENTIONAL), VANITY MIRROR LAMP, UNDER PANEL LAMP, & COURTESY LAMPS
4	20 AMP	HORN (DUAL), HORN RELAY & CIGAR LIGHTER
5	30 AMP C/BRKR	POWER WINDOW MOTORS, POWER DOOR LOCK RELAYS & POWER SEATS
6	20 AMP	POWER DOOR LOCK SWITCHES
7	5 AMP	ASH RECEIVER, GEAR SELECTOR, A/C & HEAT CONTROL, INSTRUMENT, CLOCK, RADIO (AM-FM-MPX), SWITCH TITLE
8	5 AMP	SEAT BELT, BRAKE WARNING & OIL PRESSURE LAMPS; VOLTAGE LIMITER, FUEL & TEMP GAUGE, SEAT BELT BUZZER, TIME DELAY RELAY, DOOR AJAR, CLOCK DISPLAY & LOW WASHER FLUID
9	20 AMP	SPEED CONTROL, REAR WINDOW DEFOGGER & ELECTRIC DECK LID RELEASE SOLENOID; WIDOW LIFT SAFTEY, HEATED BACKLITE RELAY & CORNERING LAMPS
10	20 AMP	A/C CLUTCH, T/SIG & BACK-UP LAMPS
11	5 AMP	RADIO
12	20 AMP	HAZARD FLASHER

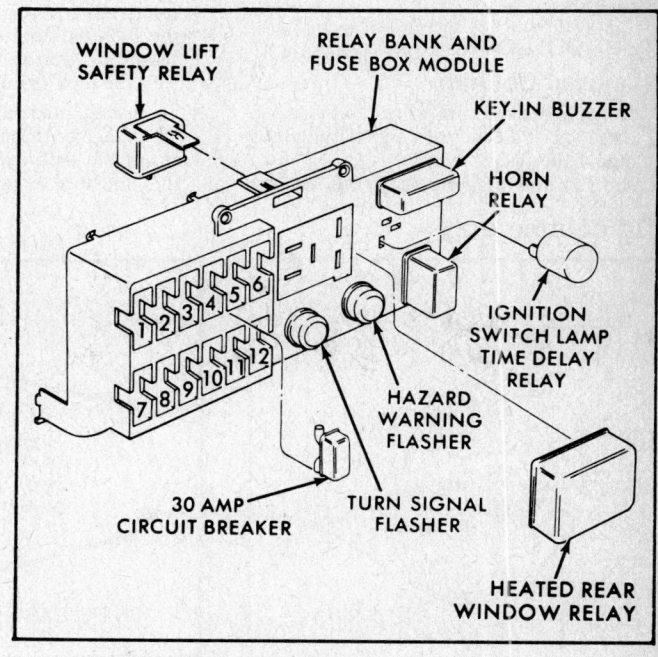

ELECTRICAL SECTION

Starting motor

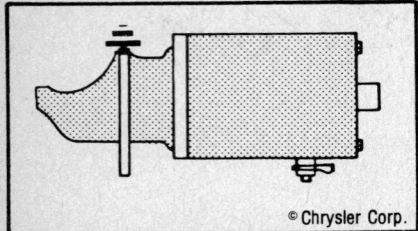

© Chrysler Corp.

Starter relay

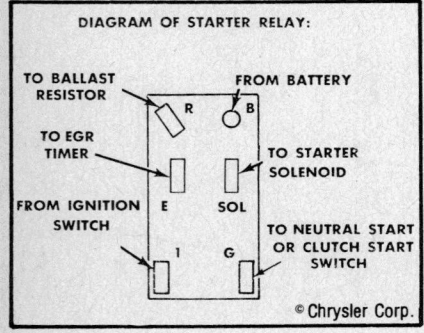

DIAGRAM OF STARTER RELAY:

TO BALLAST RESISTOR — R

FROM BATTERY — B

TO EGR TIMER — E

TO STARTER SOLENOID — SOL

FROM IGNITION SWITCH — 1

TO NEUTRAL START OR CLUTCH START SWITCH — G

© Chrysler Corp.

Ignition distributor

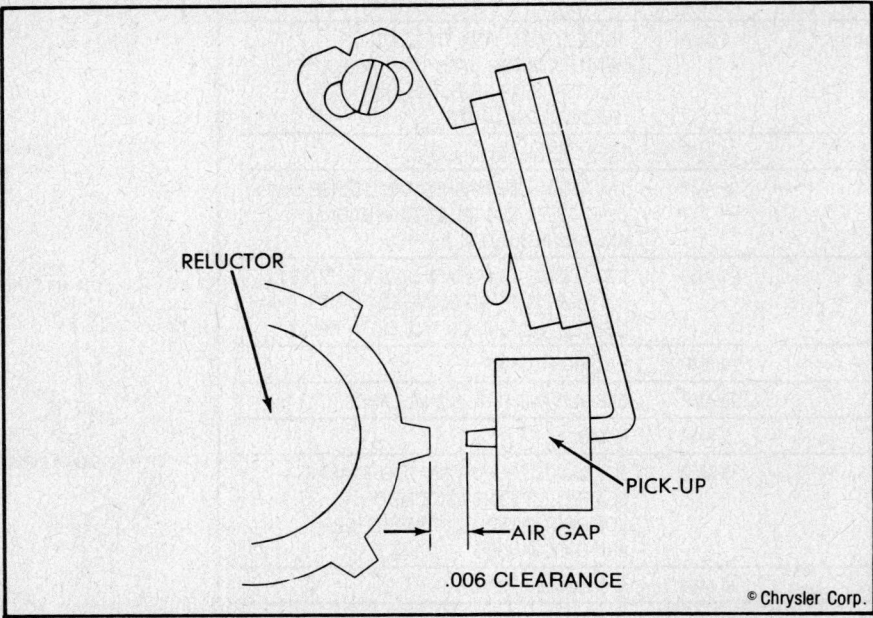

RELUCTOR

PICK-UP

AIR GAP

.006 CLEARANCE

© Chrysler Corp.

Use a non-magnetic feeler gauge

Starter

- Disconnect wiring and remove stud nut and bolt attaching starter to flywheel housing. Slide automatic transmission oil cooler tube bracket off the stud (if so equipped), and remove the starter.

NOTE: Do not damage flywheel housing seal.

Ignition Lock

Standard Column

- Remove the steering wheel and turn signal lever. Pull the turn signal switch up out of the way.
- Remove the retaining snap ring, and pry

the upper bearing housing off the steering shaft.
- Press out the pin that attaches the lock plate to the steering shaft, and remove the lockplate. Remove the lock lever guide plate.
- With the ignition lock cylinder in the "LOCK" position and the ignition key removed, insert a thin screwdriver into the lock cylinder release opening to release the spring-loaded lock retainer. Pull the lock cylinder out of its housing.
- To install, place the lock cylinder in the "LOCK" position, and remove the key. Insert the lock cylinder far enough into the housing to contact the switch ac-

tuator. Insert the key, and press and turn until the retainer snaps into place.

Ignition Distributor

- Remove distributor cap, electrical wiring and vacuum hose from distributor.
- Put alignment marks on rotor and distributor housing for installation reference.
- Remove the hold-down bolt, and carefully pull the distributor up out of the engine block.
- Install the distributor in the correct position, and set ignition timing within specifications.

Tilt column only

© Chrysler Corp.

Removing lock plate retaining

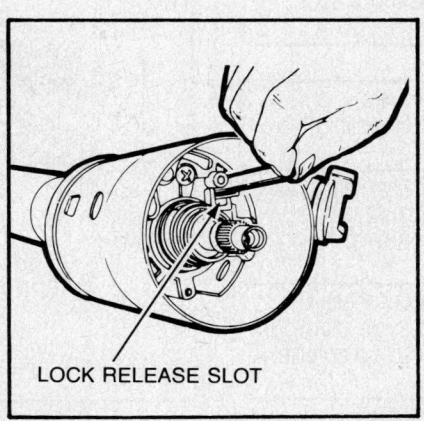

LOCK RELEASE SLOT

Slide in a thin piece of shim stock and depress the latch to remove the ignition lock column

Standard steering column

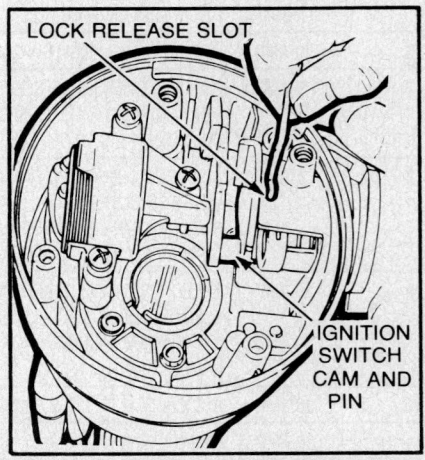

LOCK RELEASE SLOT

IGNITION SWITCH CAM AND PIN

Removing ignition lock column

Stoplight Switch

- The stoplight switch and its mounting bracket are attached to the brake pedal bracket. Adjustment is correct when stop lights illuminate after ½ inch brake pedal travel.

Neutral Start Switch

- The neutral start switch is located on the left side of the automatic transmission. Fluid will drain from the transmission when the switch is removed.
- Use a new seal when installing, and replenish lost fluid.

Tilt Column

- Remove the steering wheel, shaft lock cover, turn signal lever, tilt control lever and hazard warning knob.
- Remove the lockplate, cancelling cam and spring, and disconnect and pull the turn signal switch up out of the way.
- With the ignition lock cylinder in the "LOCK" position and the key removed, insert a thin screwdriver into the lock cylinder release opening to release the spring-loaded lock retainer. Pull the lock cylinder out of its housing.
- To install, place the lock cylinder in the "LOCK" position and remove the key. Insert the cylinder into the housing until it contacts the switch actuator. Move the switch actuator rod up and down to align the parts. When aligned, move the lock cylinder inward and snap into place.

Distributor alignment

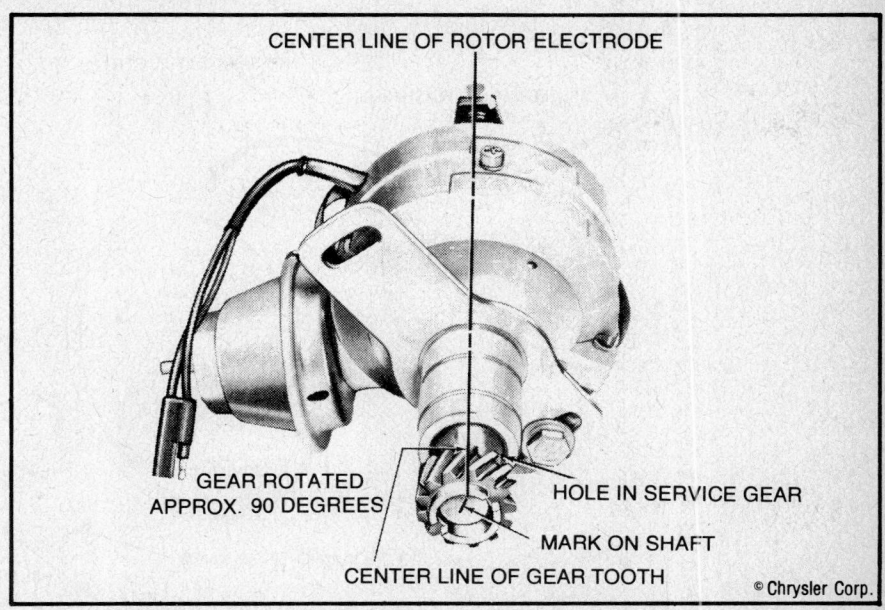

CENTER LINE OF ROTOR ELECTRODE

GEAR ROTATED APPROX. 90 DEGREES

HOLE IN SERVICE GEAR

MARK ON SHAFT

CENTER LINE OF GEAR TOOTH

© Chrysler Corp.

Aligning gear teeth with centerline of rotor electrode

Ignition Switch

- On a standard column, remove the ignition lock cylinder, then remove the ignition switch.
- On a tilt column, the ignition switch is mounted externally on the lower section of the steering column. To install, place both the switch and lock in "ACCESSORY" position.

Stoplight switch adjustment

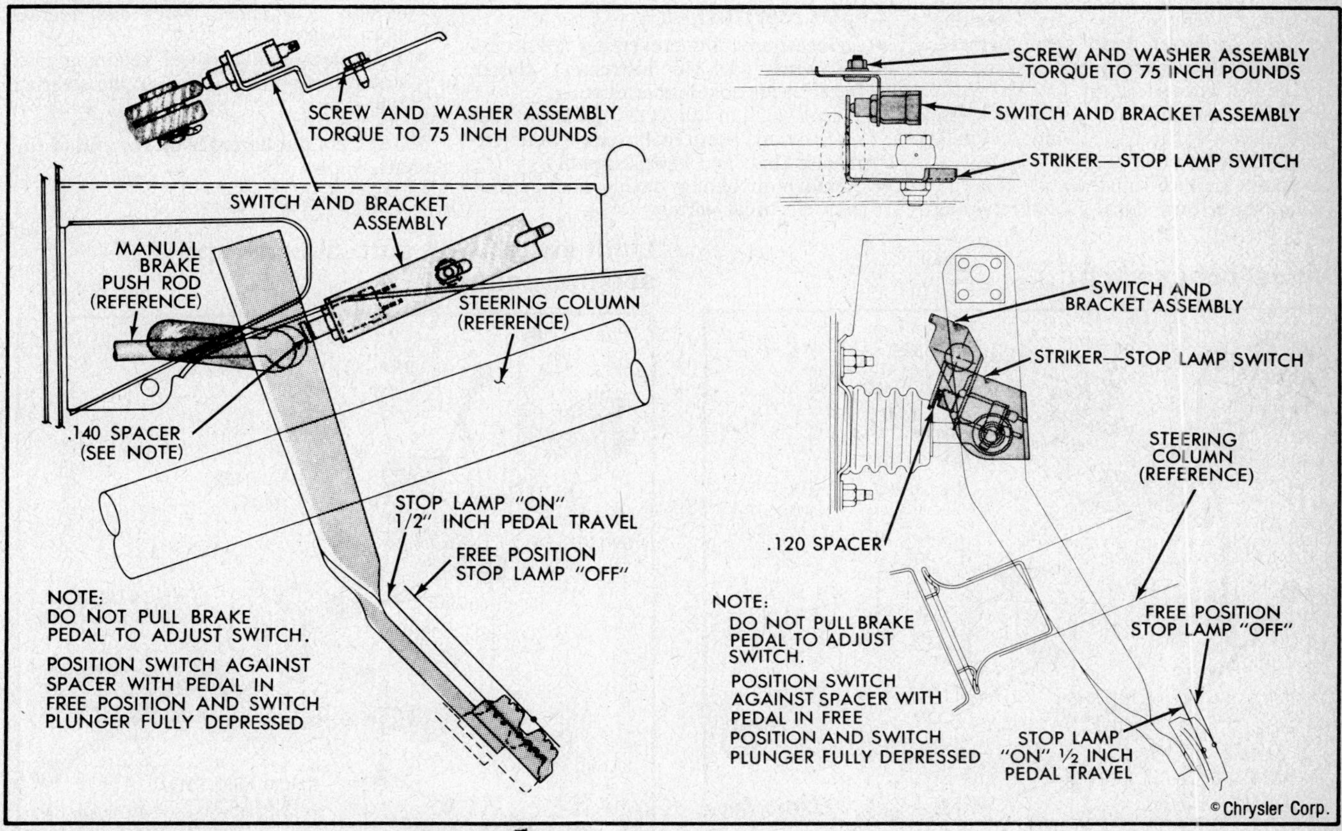

SCREW AND WASHER ASSEMBLY TORQUE TO 75 INCH POUNDS

SWITCH AND BRACKET ASSEMBLY

MANUAL BRAKE PUSH ROD (REFERENCE)

STEERING COLUMN (REFERENCE)

.140 SPACER (SEE NOTE)

STOP LAMP "ON" 1/2" INCH PEDAL TRAVEL

FREE POSITION STOP LAMP "OFF"

NOTE:
DO NOT PULL BRAKE PEDAL TO ADJUST SWITCH.

POSITION SWITCH AGAINST SPACER WITH PEDAL IN FREE POSITION AND SWITCH PLUNGER FULLY DEPRESSED

SCREW AND WASHER ASSEMBLY TORQUE TO 75 INCH POUNDS

SWITCH AND BRACKET ASSEMBLY

STRIKER—STOP LAMP SWITCH

SWITCH AND BRACKET ASSEMBLY

STRIKER—STOP LAMP SWITCH

STEERING COLUMN (REFERENCE)

.120 SPACER

FREE POSITION STOP LAMP "OFF"

NOTE:
DO NOT PULL BRAKE PEDAL TO ADJUST SWITCH.

POSITION SWITCH AGAINST SPACER WITH PEDAL IN FREE POSITION AND SWITCH PLUNGER FULLY DEPRESSED

STOP LAMP "ON" ½ INCH PEDAL TRAVEL

© Chrysler Corp.

CHRYSLER REAR DRIVE CARS

Horn switch and steering wheel

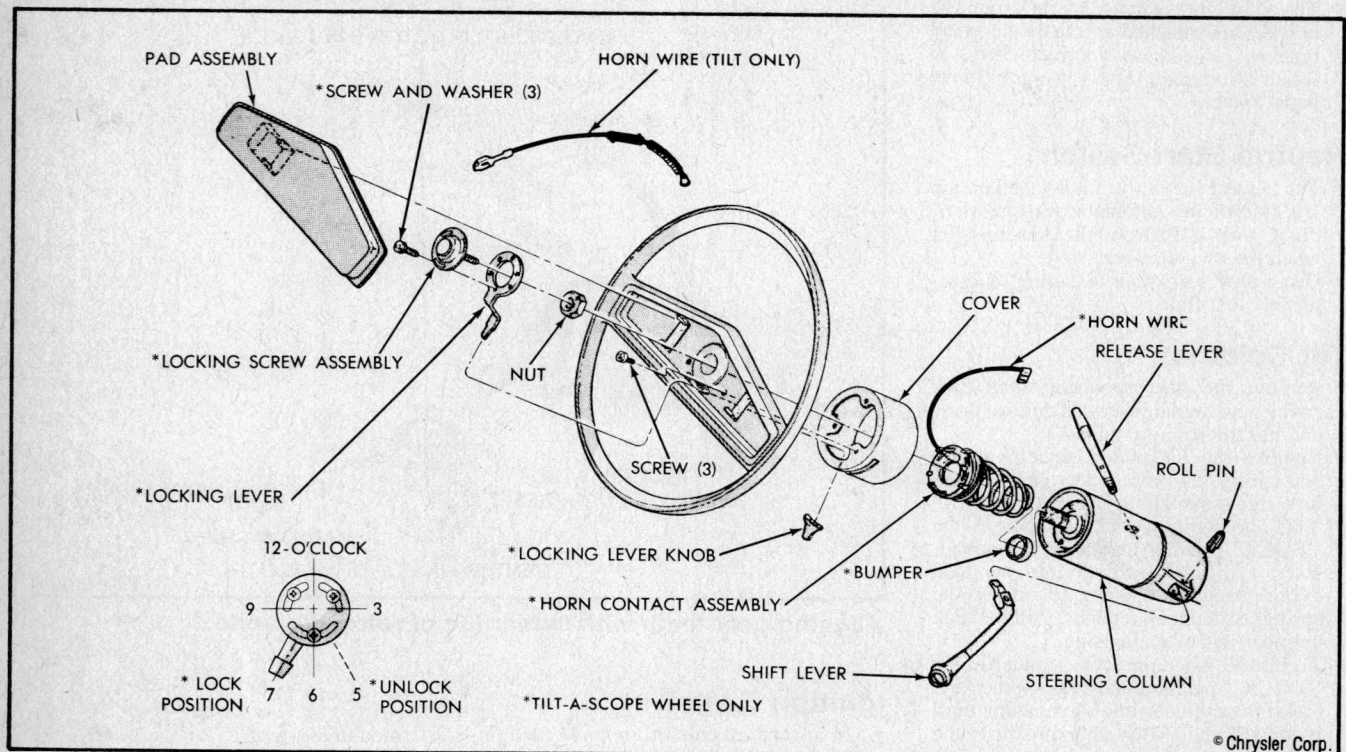

PAD ASSEMBLY
*SCREW AND WASHER (3)
HORN WIRE (TILT ONLY)
COVER
*HORN WIRE
RELEASE LEVER
ROLL PIN
*LOCKING SCREW ASSEMBLY
NUT
*LOCKING LEVER
SCREW (3)
*LOCKING LEVER KNOB
*HORN CONTACT ASSEMBLY
*BUMPER
SHIFT LEVER
STEERING COLUMN

12-O'CLOCK
9   3
*LOCK POSITION   *UNLOCK POSITION
7   6   5
*TILT-A-SCOPE WHEEL ONLY

© Chrysler Corp.

Turn Signal Switch

- Remove the steering wheel and the steering column cover.
- On a tilt column, remove the gearshift indicator, remove the nuts mounting column to lower panel reinforcement, remove the mounting bracket and remove the wiring trough.
- Position gearshift lever to full clockwise position on a standard column, and midpoint on a tilt column.
- Remove the turn signal lever.
- Remove the turn signal switch retaining screws and pull the switch and wiring up through the column.

Light Switch

- Relocate anything preventing full access to switch such as instrument cluster bezel or air conditioner ducting.
- Place switch in full "ON" position. Pull on knob and press shaft release button to release shaft and knob assembly.
- Remove mounting device and disconnect electrical wiring.

Horn Switch and Steering Wheel

- Remove steering wheel center pad assembly. Disconnect wires and remove horn switch.
- Remove steering wheel retaining nut, and use a puller to remove the steering wheel.

NOTE: Do not hammer on the end of the shaft.

Typical light switch

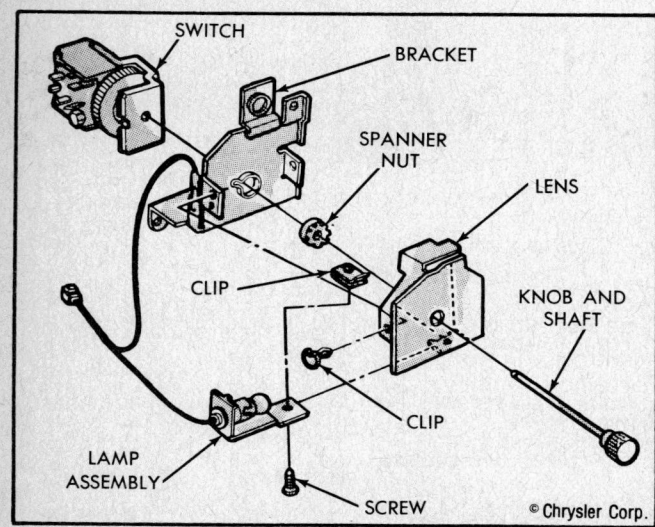

SWITCH
BRACKET
SPANNER NUT
LENS
CLIP
CLIP
KNOB AND SHAFT
LAMP ASSEMBLY
SCREW
CLIP

© Chrysler Corp.

Light switch with auto dimmer and sentinel control

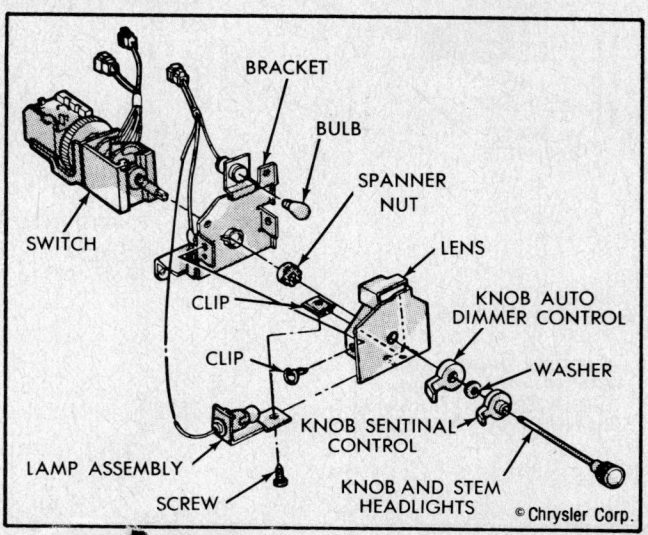

BRACKET
BULB
SPANNER NUT
SWITCH
LENS
CLIP
CLIP
KNOB AUTO DIMMER CONTROL
WASHER
LAMP ASSEMBLY
SCREW
KNOB SENTINAL CONTROL
KNOB AND STEM HEADLIGHTS

© Chrysler Corp.

Full-size Chrysler windshield wiper linkage

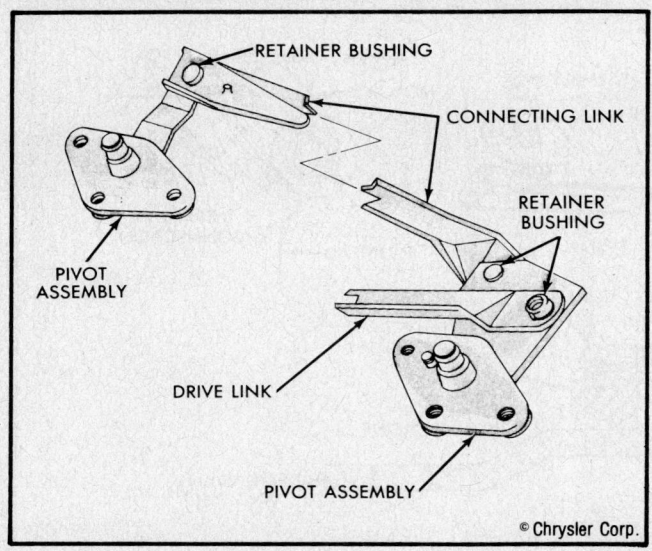

Typical windshield wiper linkage-mid-size models

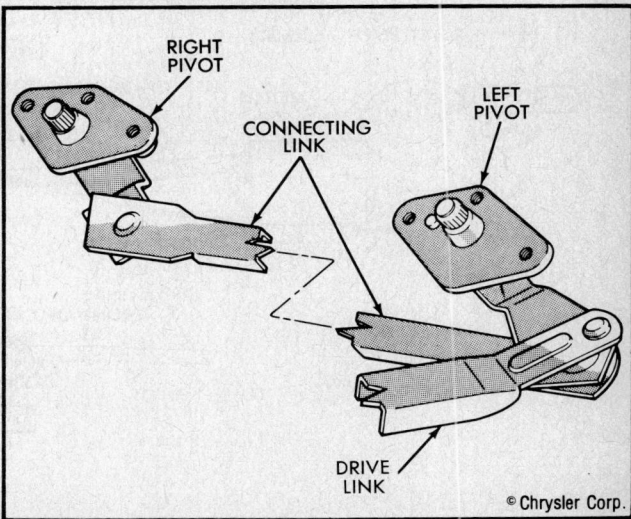

Windshield Wiper Switch
- Relocate anything preventing full access to switch such as instrument cluster, cluster bezel, air conditioner ducting or steering column cover.
- Separate the switch from the instrument panel and electrical wiring.

Windshield Wiper Motor
- On concealed wiper systems, remove wiper arms, blades and cowl screen. Remove crank arm from motor, and remove mounting nuts and electrical wiring.
- On non-concealed wiper systems, remove the mounting nuts and pull the motor far enough off the studs to remove crank arm. On cars without air conditioning this can be done from under the instrument panel.

Windshield Wiper Linkage
- Remove the drive crank from the wiper motor and the drive link.
- Remove the pivot assembly mounts, and remove the linkage assembly.

Windshield Wiper Arms
- Tool C-3982 is required to remove the wiper arm on 1973-74 non-concealed wiper. Install the tool, and lift wiper arm off pivot.

- On all other models, lift the arm far enough to allow the retaining latch to be pulled out to the holding position, and remove the arm from the pivot with a back and forth rocking motion.

Radio
- Remove or disconnect anything blocking access to the radio such as instrument cluster bezel, ash tray or air conditioner ducting.
- Loosen or remove mounting screws, knobs, etc., and remove radio from antenna, speaker and power connections.

NOTE: Do not operate the radio with speaker leads detached.

Turn signal switch

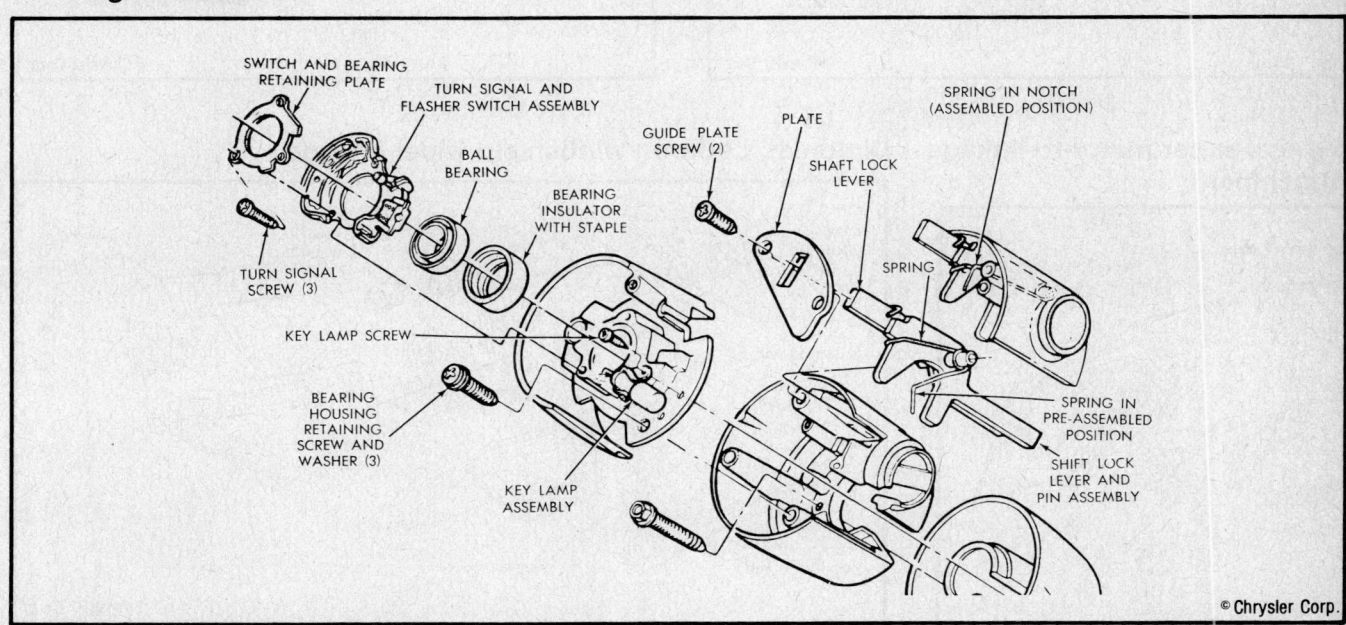

CHRYSLER REAR DRIVE CARS

Dart, Valiant windshield wiper system

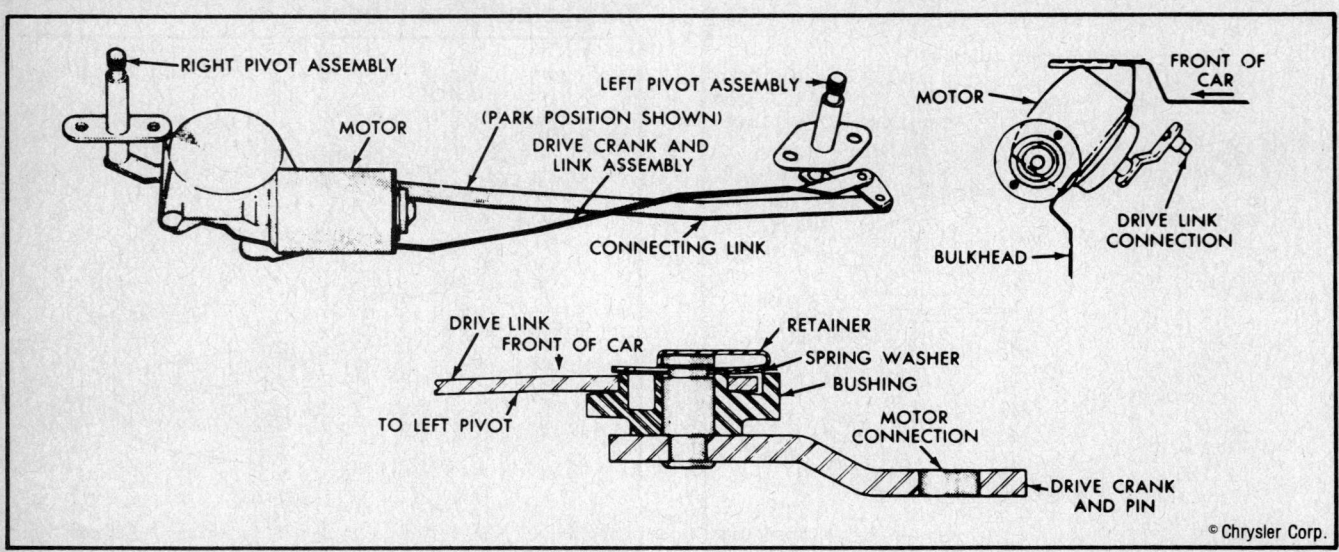

© Chrysler Corp.

Dart, Valiant windshield wiper linkage

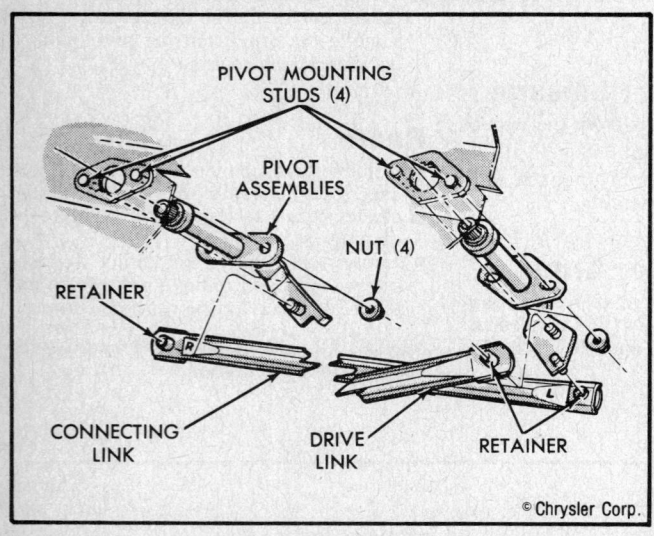

© Chrysler Corp.

Aspen, Volare windshield wiper linkage

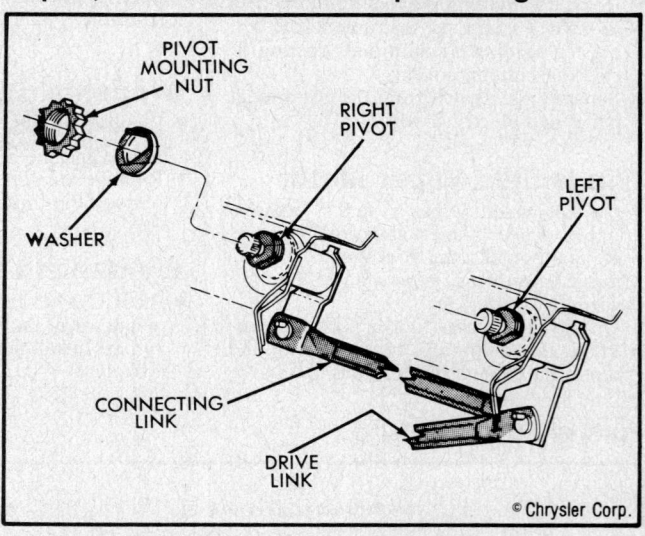

© Chrysler Corp.

Typical wiper motor-to-linkage attachment

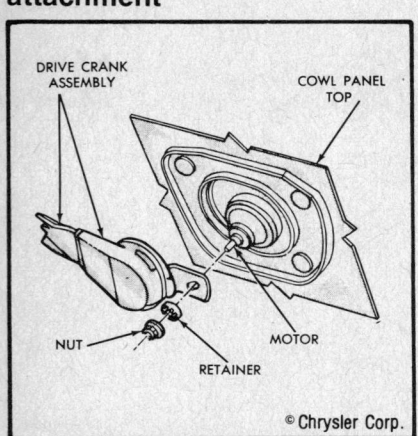

© Chrysler Corp.

Diplomat, LeBaron windshield wiper linkage

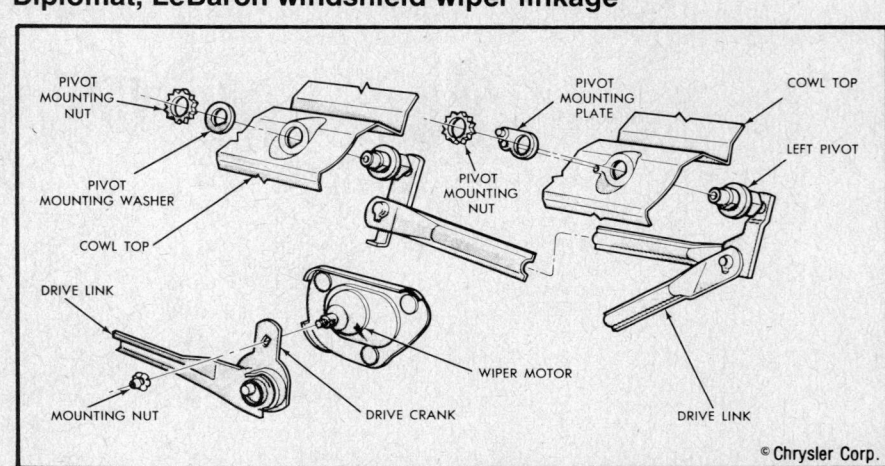

© Chrysler Corp.

Windshield wiper blade replacement

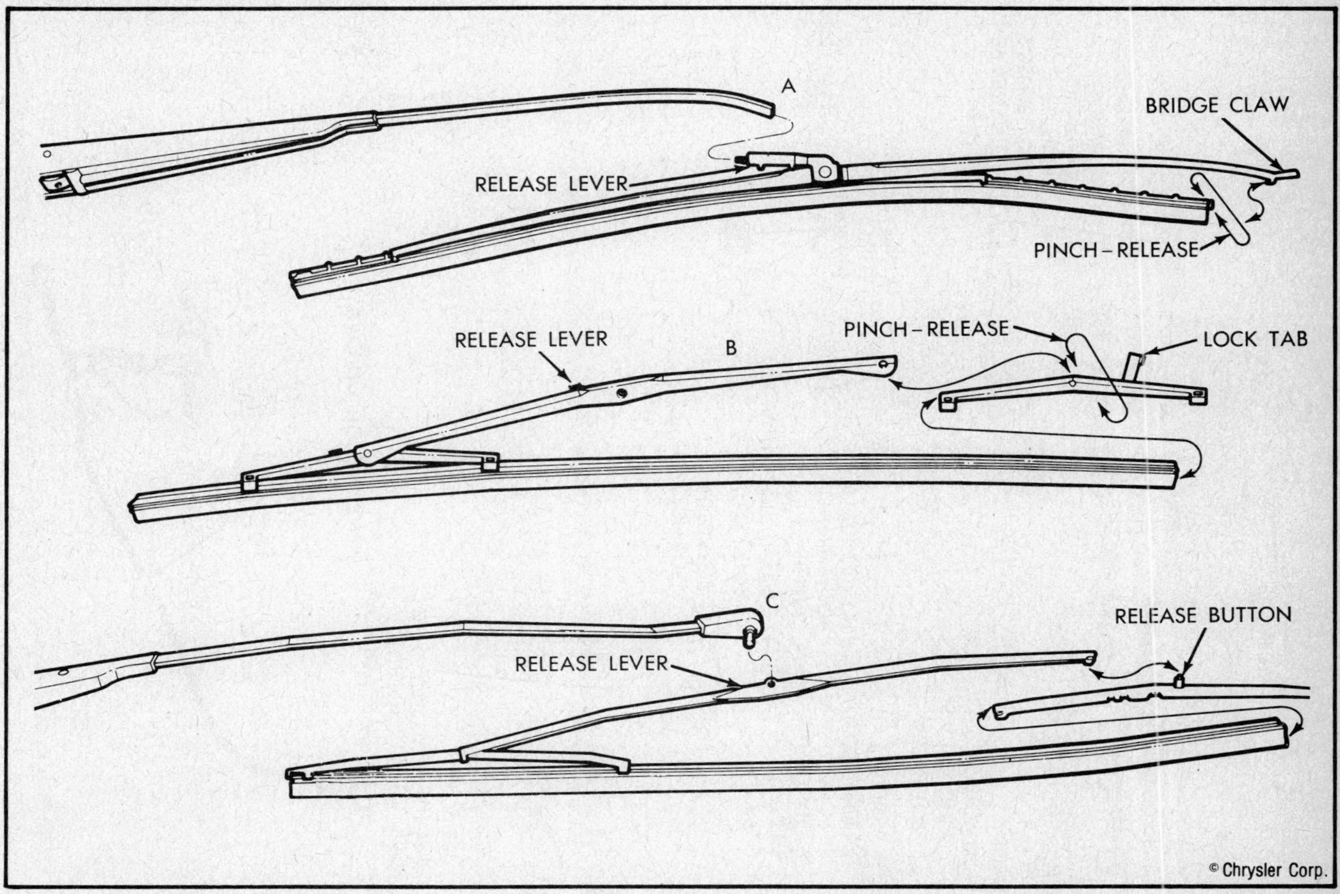

A

RELEASE LEVER

BRIDGE CLAW

PINCH–RELEASE

RELEASE LEVER

B

PINCH–RELEASE

LOCK TAB

C

RELEASE LEVER

RELEASE BUTTON

© Chrysler Corp.

Radio

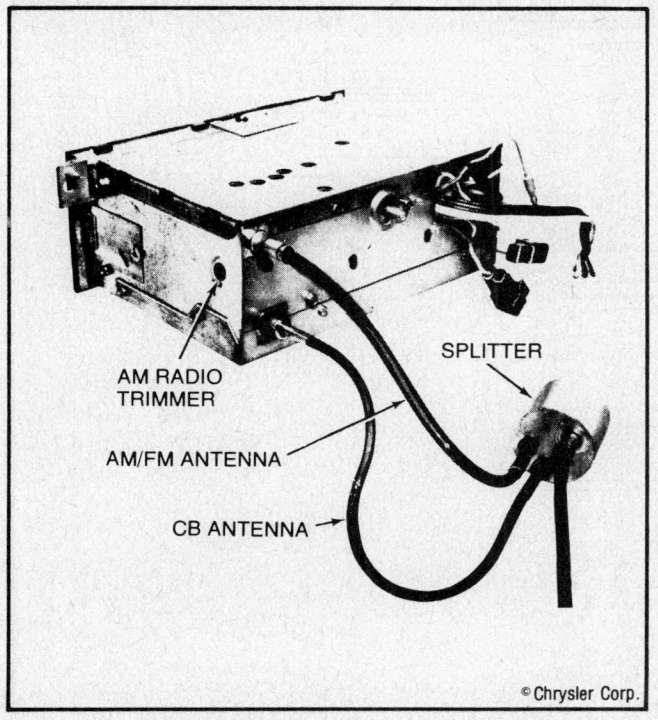

AM RADIO TRIMMER

SPLITTER

AM/FM ANTENNA

CB ANTENNA

© Chrysler Corp.

Power antenna

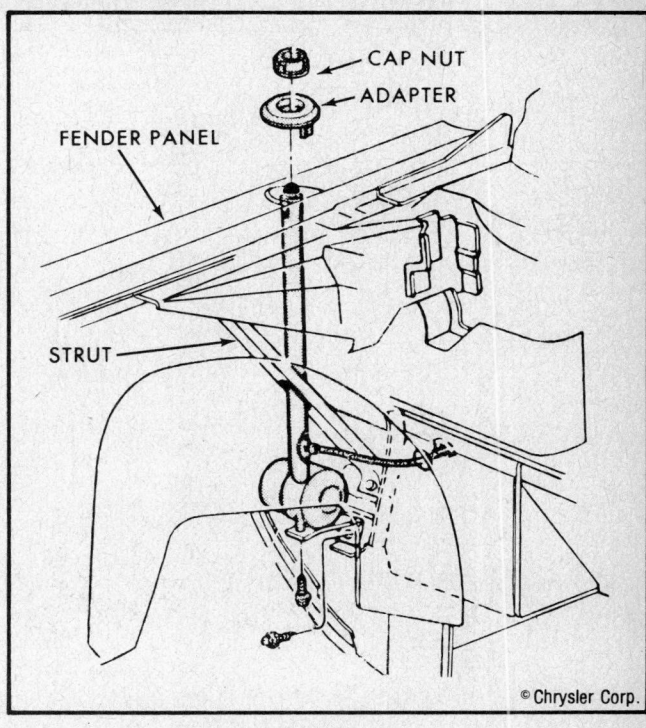

CAP NUT

ADAPTER

FENDER PANEL

STRUT

© Chrysler Corp.

Typical air/heater components

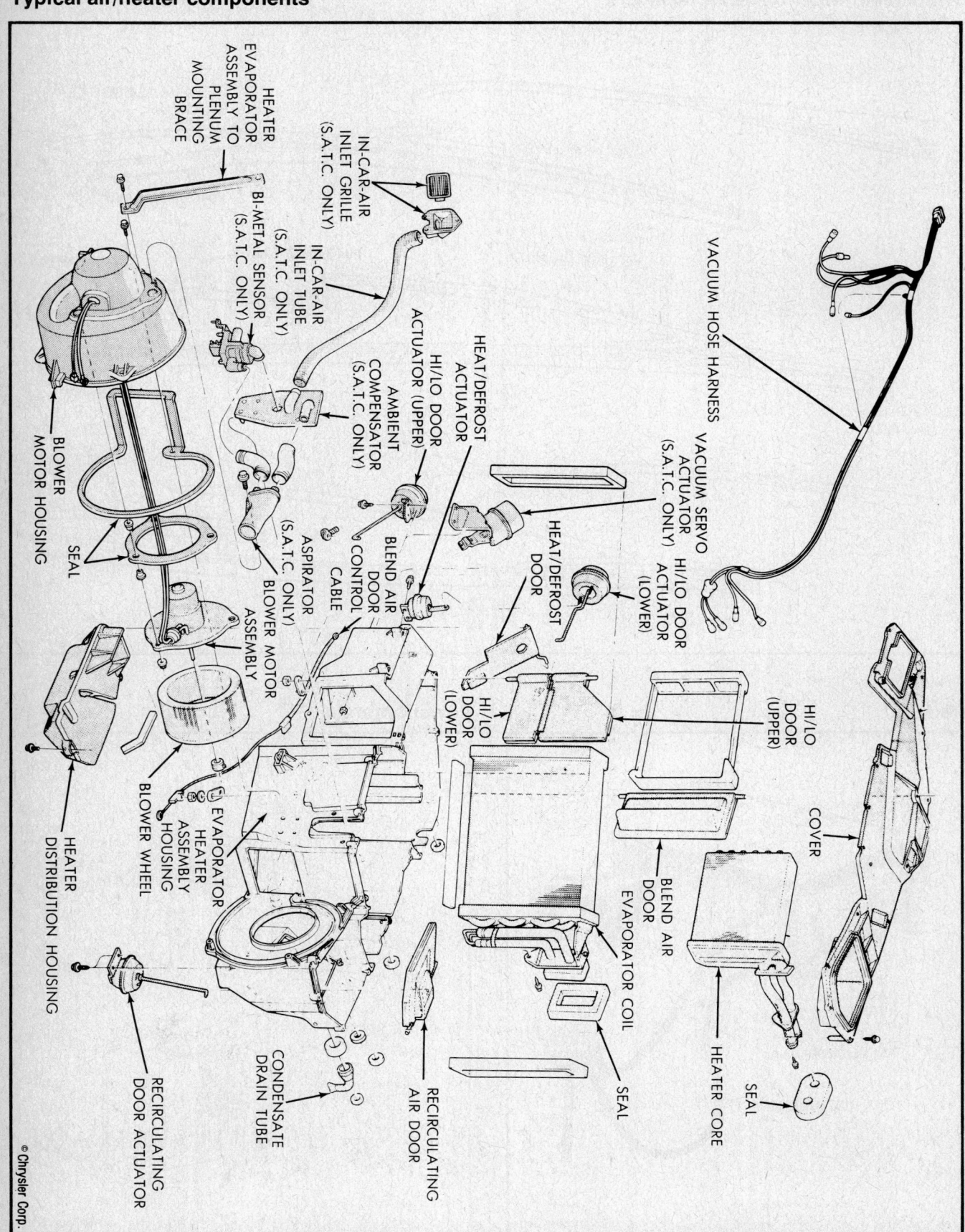

© Chrysler Corp.

Temperature control lever type

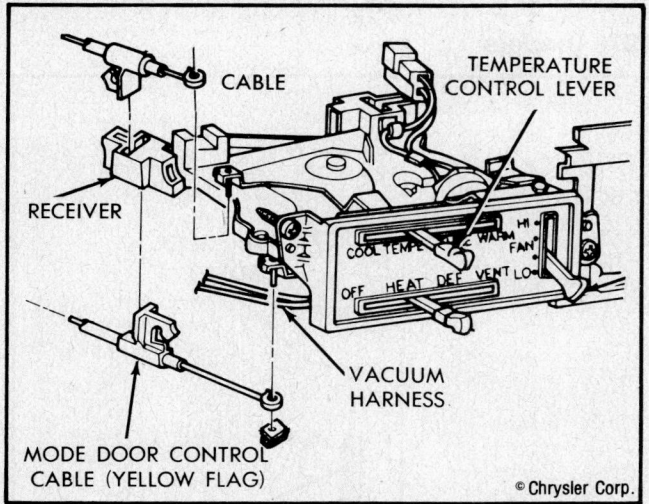

© Chrysler Corp.

Temperature control pushbutton type

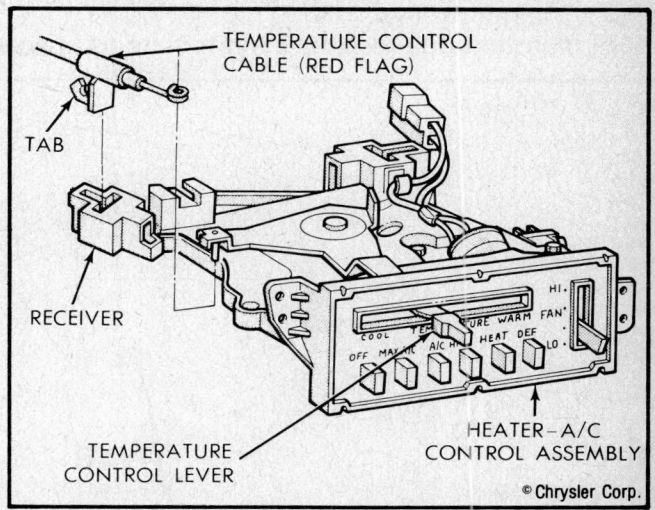

© Chrysler Corp.

Charger, Cordoba, Coronet, Fury, Magnum, Monaco— 1977 and later

- The entire heater assembly must be removed for core or blower motor service.
- Drain radiator, and disconnect heater hoses and blower motor vent tube.
- Remove mounting nuts from three studs around blower motor and one near center of dash panel. Remove lower instrument panel bezel, glove box and glove box door.
- Remove screw from housing to plenum support rod on right side of housing above outside air opening.
- Disconnect door cables and electrical wiring, and tip heater assembly down and out from under instrument panel.
- Remove screws that hold the front cover to the housing, and cut the sponge rubber plenum-to-housing air seal in two places where the front cover separates cover from housing.
- Remove one core tube retaining screw from behind housing between core tubes, and remove core from housing.
- Remove six sheet metal screws and clips holding blower motor mounting plate to the housing, and remove motor.
- Seal plenum air seal cuts with a good grade rubber cement when reassembling.

Heater Blower and Core
Dart, Valiant

- The entire heater assembly must be removed for core or blower motor service.
- Drain the radiator, and disconnect the heater hoses.
- Remove the heater dash panel seal and retainer plate.
- Disconnect electrical wiring and control cables, and remove mounting nuts and the heater housing support rod from the air duct.

- Remove the seal from around heater motor mounting studs.
- Remove backplate from distribution housing, and remove fan and motor.
- Remove air door seal from either inner or outer heater housing half only, and separate heater housing halves.
- Remove screws attaching heater core housing, and remove core.

Aspen, Diplomat, LeBaron, Volare

- The entire heater assembly must be removed for core or blower motor service.
- Drain radiator, disconnect heater hoses, and remove heater core tube dash panel seals and retainer.
- Remove cluster bezel assembly, instrument panel upper cover, steering column cover, right intermediate side cowl trim panel, lower instrument panel, and instrument panel center-to-lower reinforcement.

- Disconnect control cables, electrical wiring and mounts, and pull heater assembly from dash panel.
- Separate heater housing halves, and remove core and blower wheel and motor.

Heater/Air Conditioner Control Unit

- Remove, loosen or disconnect any of the following which prevent full access to the heater/air conditioner control unit:
    Radio
    Cluster Bezel
    Lamp Panel
    Air Ducts
    Steering Column Cover
- Separate the control unit from vacuum and electrical leads and control linkages, and remove it as a unit from its mounting in the instrument panel.

Heater blower

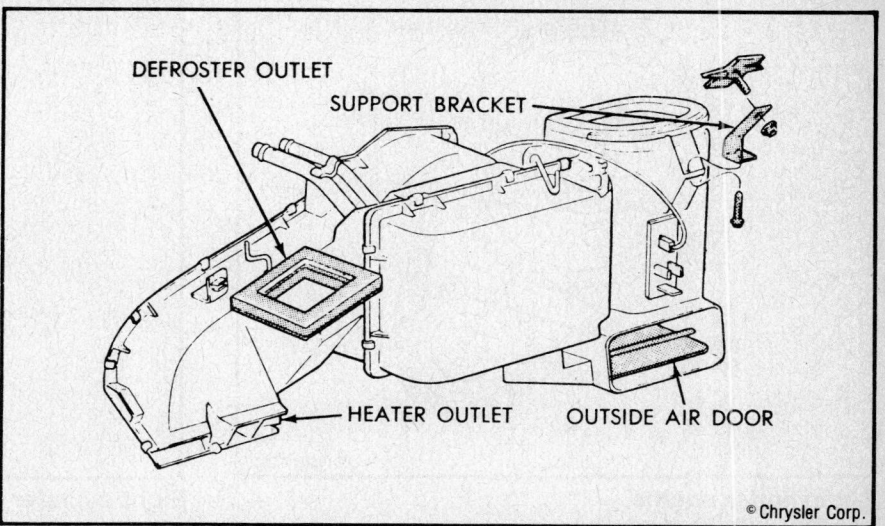

© Chrysler Corp.

ENGINE SECTION

EGR maintenance reminder system used in some 1976 models

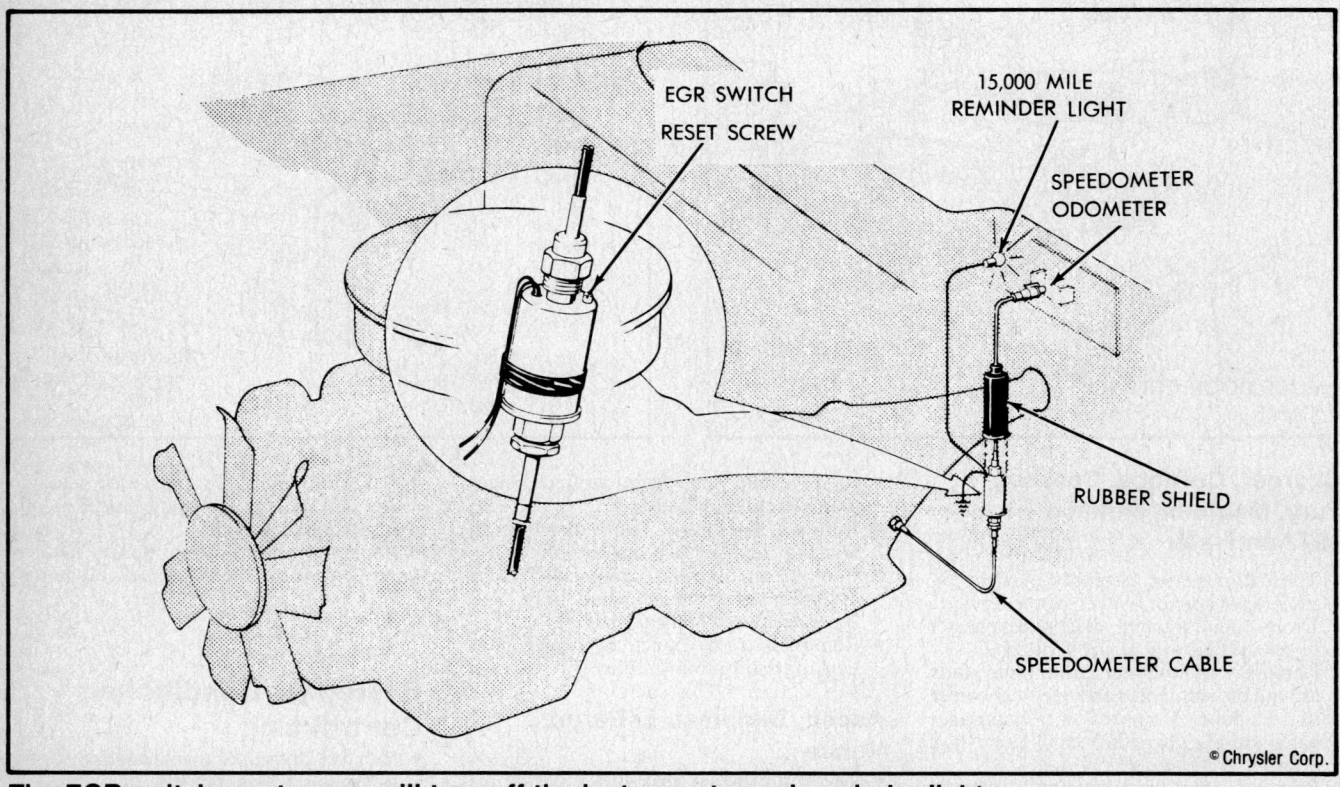

EGR SWITCH RESET SCREW

15,000 MILE REMINDER LIGHT

SPEEDOMETER ODOMETER

RUBBER SHIELD

SPEEDOMETER CABLE

© Chrysler Corp.

The EGR switch reset screw will turn off the instrument panel reminder light

Water Pump

NOTE: When replacing a water pump because of a bearing or shaft failure, also replace the engine fan to prevent possible blade separation.

- Drain cooling system.
- Remove or reposition fan shroud, drive belts, air pump, alternator, battery or any other components preventing full access to the water pump.
- After removing a silicone type fan clutch, do not place drive unit with shaft pointing down.
- The water pump on all models can be replaced without discharging the air conditioning system.

Timing mark alignment

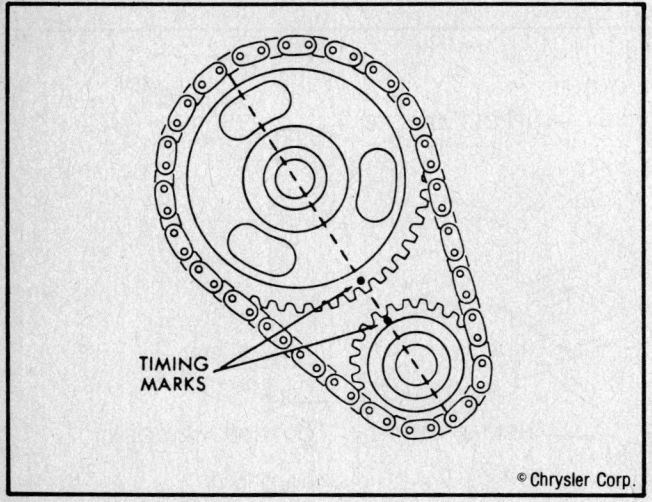

TIMING MARKS

© Chrysler Corp.

Six cylinder engine

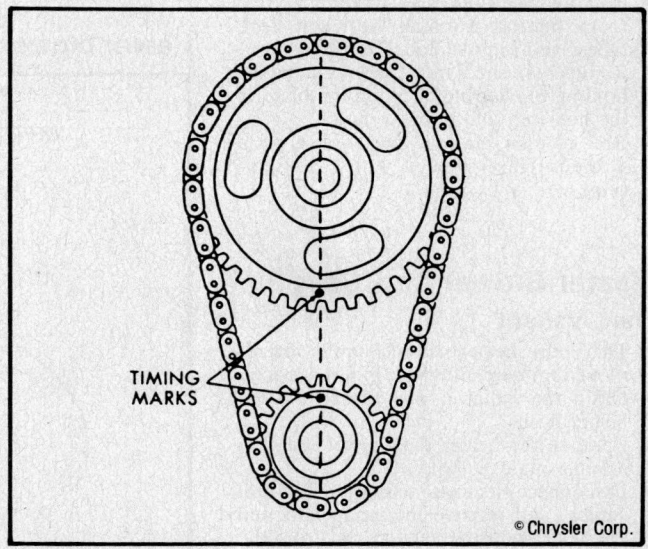

TIMING MARKS

© Chrysler Corp.

Eight cylinder engine

Fuel Pump
- Before installing a fuel pump, crank the engine until the camshaft eccentric lobe is out of the way of the fuel pump rocker arm.
- After installation, check for fuel leaks.

Timing Chain
NOTE: For front cover oil seal replacement only, some engines require front cover removal and some do not. Inspection is suggested before needlessly removing a front cover.

Six Cylinder Engine
- Remove radiator, fan and vibration damper assembly.
- Loosen oil pan bolts for clearance when removing front cover.
- Remove timing chain with camshaft sprocket.
- Install timing chain and sprocket with timing marks aligned.
- When installing cover, use sealant at the junction of rubber pan seal and cork oil pan gasket.

318-340-360 CID Engine
- Remove radiator, water pump, power steering pump, pulley and vibration damper, fuel pump and fuel lines.
- Loosen oil pan bolts, and remove the front bolt at each side. Use extreme care to avoid damaging oil pan gasket when removing front cover.
- It is normal to find particles of neoprene collected between the crankshaft seal retainer and oil slinger.
- Remove crankshaft sprocket attaching cup washer and fuel pump eccentric, and remove timing chain with crankshaft and camshaft sprockets.
- Install timing chain with timing marks aligned.

400-440 CID Engine
- Remove power steering pump, alternator, crankshaft pulley and vibration damper. Remove water pump and housing as an assembly.

- Remove front cover, and remove timing chain with crankshaft and camshaft sprockets.

- Install timing chain with timing marks aligned.

NOTE: **When installing timing chain, use Tool C-3509 to prevent camshaft from contacting the welch plug in the rear of the engine block. Remove distributor and oil pump/distributor drive gear. Locate tool against rear side of cam gear, and attach tool with distributor retainer plate bolt.**
- When installing front cover, use a sealer on the exposed portion of the oil pan gasket.

Engine Mounts
Front Mounts
- Position fan to clear radiator hose and radiator top tank when engine is raised, and disconnect throttle linkage at transmission and carburetor.
- Remove torque nuts from insulator studs, and raise engine enough to remove the mount.

Rear Mount
- Support transmission, and remove engine rear crossmember from frame and rear mount from transmission.

Six cylinder engine mounts

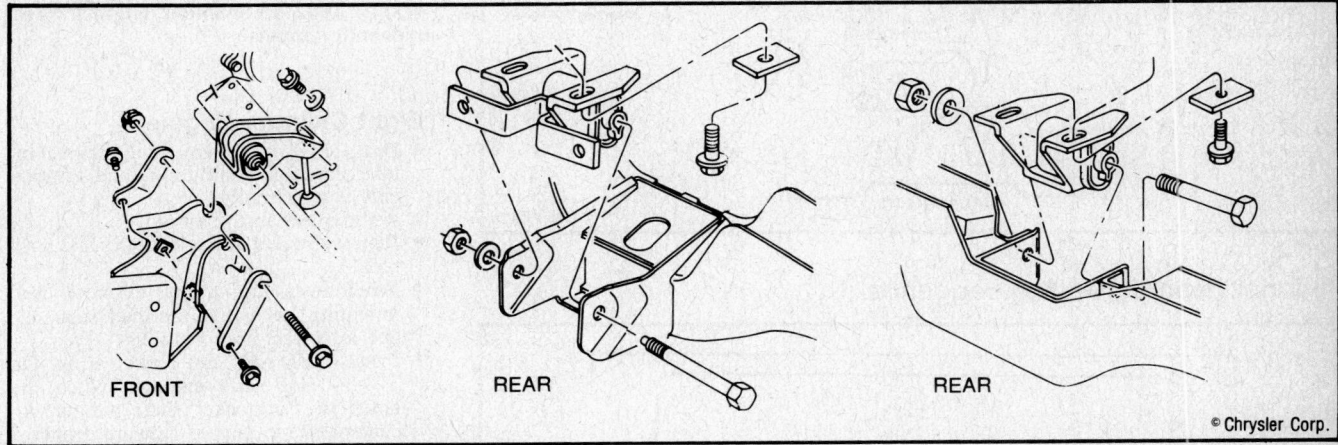

FRONT   REAR   REAR

© Chrysler Corp.

Eight cylinder engine mounts

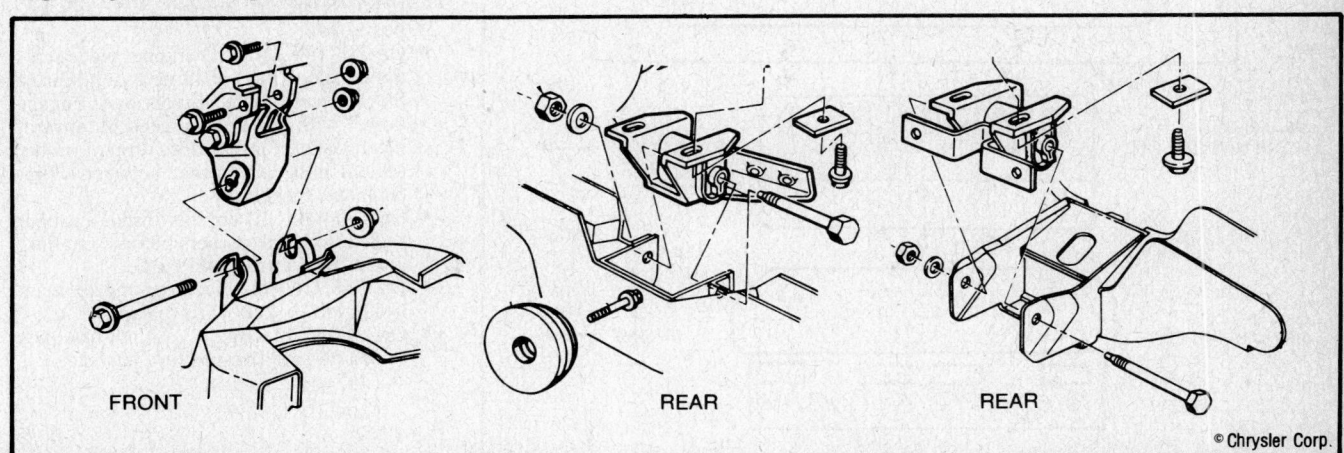

FRONT   REAR   REAR

© Chrysler Corp.

A281

Intake manifold tightening sequence

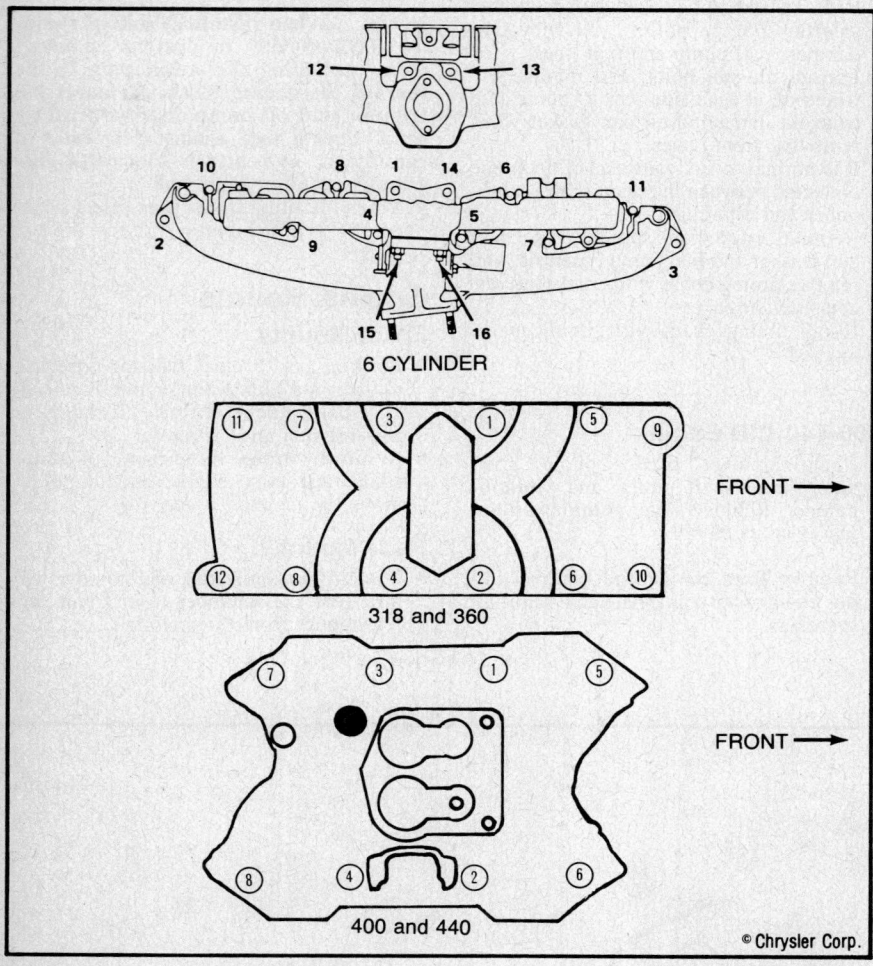

6 CYLINDER

318 and 360

400 and 440

© Chrysler Corp.

Cylinder head tightening sequence

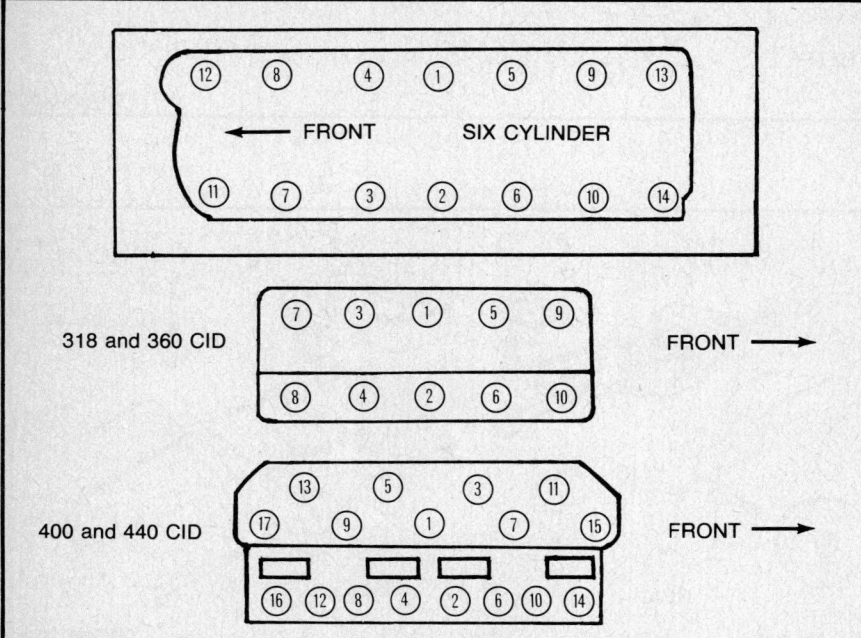

SIX CYLINDER

318 and 360 CID

400 and 440 CID

Cylinder Head
Six Cylinder Engine
- Drain the cooling system, and disconnect the exhaust pipe at the manifold.
- The intake and exhaust manifolds can be removed as a unit from the cylinder head either before or after the cylinder head is removed from the engine.
- Remove rocker arm assemblies and push rods.
- When installing cylinder head, torque mounting bolts in the prescribed sequence and to the correct specifications.
- When installing the intake and exhaust manifolds, loosen the three bolts connecting the two manifolds. This allows correct installation alignment. Tighten them beginning with the inner nut.
- After replacing rocker arms and push rods in their original locations, temporarily adjust tappets to:
  Intake—.012 inch
   Intake—.012 inch
   Exhaust—.028
  Idle the engine at normal operating temperature for five minutes, then adjust tappets to the correct setting:
   Intake—.010 inch
   Exhaust—.020 inch

NOTE: 1982 six cylinder engines have hydraulic tappets.

Eight Cylinder Engine
- Drain cooling system, and remove intake manifold, carburetor and ignition coil as an assembly.
- Remove exhaust manifold.
- Remove rocker arm assemblies and push rods.
- When installing, torque cylinder head mounting bolts in prescribed sequence and to correct specifications.
- Install push rods and rocker arms. On 318-340-360 CID engines, place the notch on the rocker shaft pointing to center-line of engine (toward front of engine on the left bank and to the rear on the right bank). On all eight cylinder engines install the long stamped steel retainers in the number two and four positions.
- On 318-340-360 CID engine, place sealant on block rails at front and at rear of block. Center hole in seals must engage dowel with end holes locked in tangs of head gasket. Place a large drop of rubber sealant into each corner between cylinder head gasket tabs.
- On 400-440 CID engine, install a rubber sealant to block corners before installing a new intake manifold gasket.
- On 318 CID engine, coat intake manifold side gaskets with sealant.
- On 360 CID engine, do not use any sealer on side composition gaskets.

Rocker Arms

Six Cylinder Engine

- Remove the cylinder head cover, and remove rocker arm shaft bolts and retainers.
- Rocker arms and shaft must be installed so that the oil hole, or flat on the end of the rocker shaft, is on top and points toward front of engine.
- After installing, temporarily adjust valve tappets to:
    Intake—.011 inch
    Exhaust—.028 inch
  Idle engine at normal operating temperature for five minutes, and reset tappet adjustment to correct specifications:
    Intake—.010 inch
    Exhaust—.020 inch

NOTE: Starting with 1981 engines, the valve clearance is controlled by hydraulic valve lifters which are non-adjustable.

Eight Cylinder Engine

- Remove the cylinder head cover, and remove rocker shaft bolts and retainers.
- On 318–340–360 CID engine; install rocker arm and shaft assembly with notched end of rocker shaft pointing to centerline of engine (toward front of engine on the left bank, and rear on right bank).
- On 400–440 CID engine, install rocker shaft so that the 3/16 inch diameter rocker arm lubrication holes point downward into the rocker arm. This will correctly place the 15 degree angle of these holes outward towards the valve end of the rocker arms. (The 15 degree angle of the rocker arm lubrication holes is determined from the centerline of the bolt holes which are used to attach the shaft assembly to the cylinder head.)
- Install long, stamped steel retainers in the number two and four positions.

Rocker arm and shaft assembly

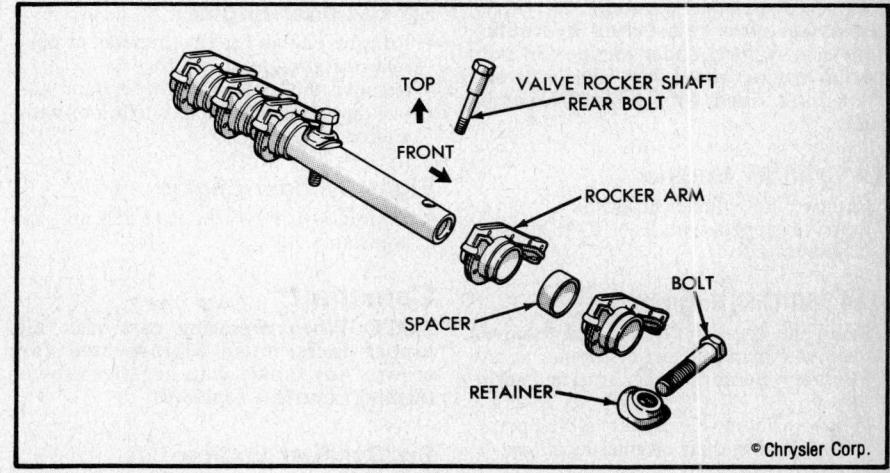

© Chrysler Corp.

Eight cylinder rocker arm and shaft

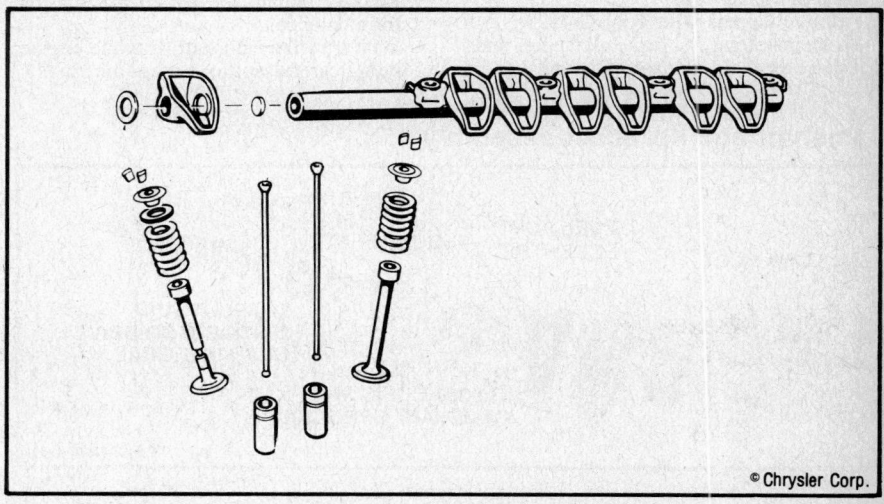

© Chrysler Corp.

Rocker arm lubricating holes—400, 440 CID engine

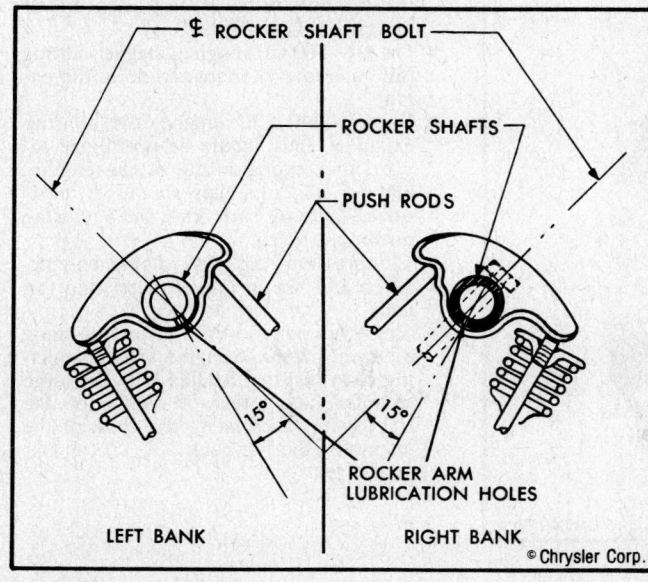

© Chrysler Corp.

Valve arrangement—six cylinder

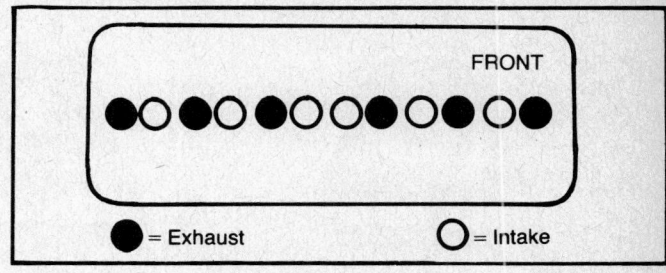

Valve arrangement—eight cylinder

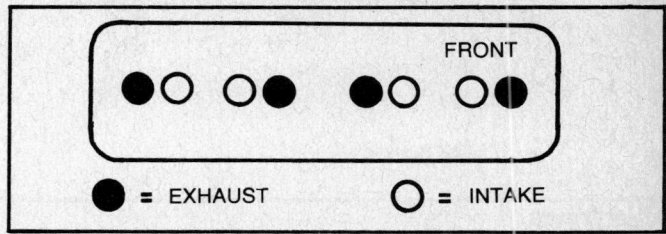

Valve Lifters

NOTE: To prevent damage to valve mechanism after reinstalling hydraulic tappets in eight cylinder engine, do not operate engine above fast idle until all lifters have filled with oil and become quiet.

Six Cylinder Engine

- Remove the cylinder head.
- Remove tappets with Tool C-4129 or a magnetic rod.

318–360 CID Engine

- Drain the cooling system, and remove the intake manifold and distributor as an assembly. Remove rocker arms and push rods.
- When installing, lubricate all tappets, and replace in their original locations.

400–440 CID Engine

- Remove the cylinder head cover, rocker arms and push rods.
- Remove tappets with Tool C-4129.
- When installing, lubricate all tappets and replace in their original locations.

Valve Adjustment

Six Cylinder Engine

- Run the engine for five minutes at normal operating temperature.
- Remove the rocker arm cover, and adjust tappets to correct specifications with engine running.

Eight Cylinder Engine

- Hydraulic Lifters are used and are not adjustable.

Camshaft

NOTE: When replacing camshaft, all tappet faces must be inspected for crown. Any tappet with negative crown (dishing) must be replaced.

Six Cylinder Engine

- Remove cylinder head, tappets, timing chain, distributor, oil pump and fuel pump.
- Remove radiator, grills, etc. as required for clearance.
- Withdraw the camshaft from the engine, being careful not to damage bearings.

Eight Cylinder Engine

- Remove the intake manifold, distributor, oil pump and distributor drive shaft, rocker arms, push rods and tappets.
- Remove timing chain and camshaft thrust plate.
- Remove radiator, grille, etc. as required for clearance.
- Withdraw the camshaft from the engine, being careful not to damage bearings.
- To install, insert camshaft to within two inches of its final position within the cylinder block, and install Tool C-3509 with the tongue behind the distributor drive gear. This tool will prevent the camshaft from being pushed in too far and knocking out the welch plug in the rear of the cylinder block. Remove the tool after the timing chain has been installed.

Pistons, Rods and Bearings

- Pistons are removed through the top on all engines.
- Piston pins are a press fit in the rods and a sliding fit in the pistons.

Six Cylinder Engine

- Compression ring gaps should be located on the engine left side and staggered 60 degrees apart. Neither gap should line up with an oil ring rail gap. Rotate oil ring expander so the ends are at engine right side, and rotate steel rails so that gaps are approximately opposite and positioned above piston pin holes.
- The notch on top of the piston must point toward the front of the engine, and the oil hole in the connecting rod must be toward the right side of the engine.

Eight Cylinder Engine

- On 318–360 CID engine, the keys on the oil ring spacer expander must be inserted into the hole in the oil ring groove over the piston pin front boss.
- On 318–360 CID engine, stagger oil ring rail gaps toward inboard side of the engine.
- On 400–440 CID engine, the oil ring expander ends should be positioned toward the outboard side of the engine, and oil ring rail gaps should be positioned opposite each other and above the piston pin holes.
- Compression ring gaps should be staggered and not in line with oil ring rail gaps.
- The notch or groove on piston top must be toward front of engine. The connecting rod must be installed with the large chamfer facing rear of engine on the right bank, and facing the front of the engine on the left bank.

Camshaft and sprocket assembly

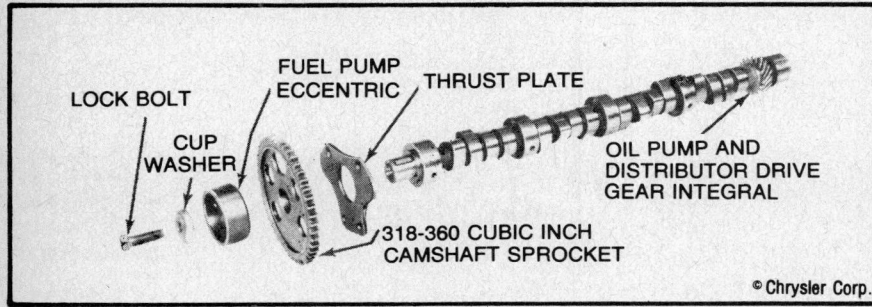

LOCK BOLT
CUP WASHER
FUEL PUMP ECCENTRIC
THRUST PLATE
318-360 CUBIC INCH CAMSHAFT SPROCKET
OIL PUMP AND DISTRIBUTOR DRIVE GEAR INTEGRAL

© Chrysler Corp.

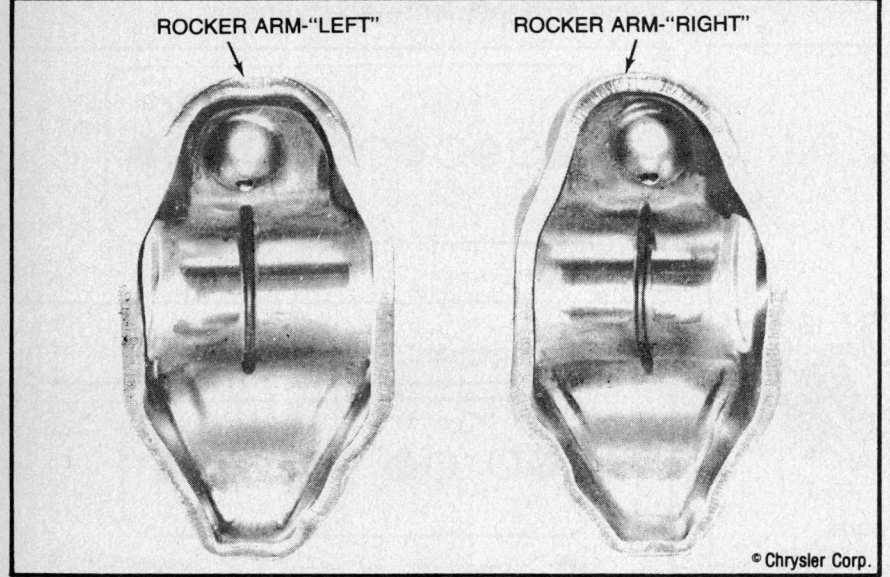

ROCKER ARM-"LEFT"   ROCKER ARM-"RIGHT"

© Chrysler Corp.

All engines

Ring gap location

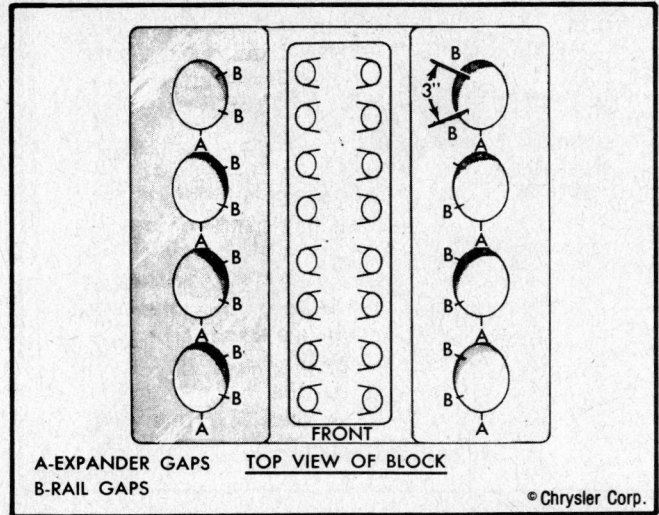

A-EXPANDER GAPS
B-RAIL GAPS

TOP VIEW OF BLOCK

FRONT

© Chrysler Corp.

Eight cylinder engine oil ring installation

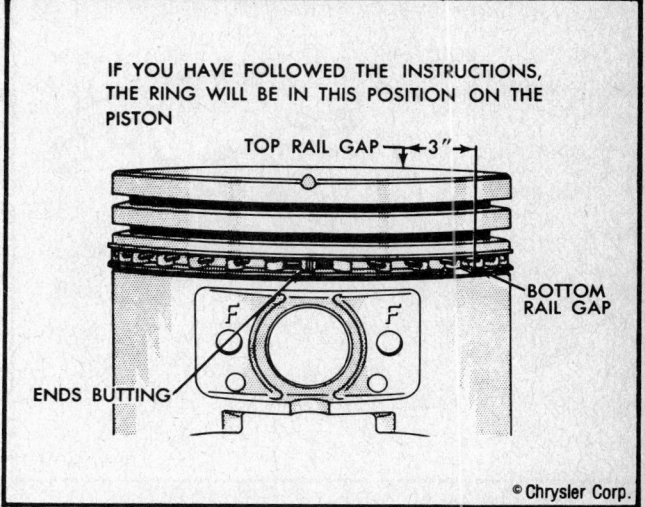

IF YOU HAVE FOLLOWED THE INSTRUCTIONS, THE RING WILL BE IN THIS POSITION ON THE PISTON

TOP RAIL GAP ──► ◄── 3"

BOTTOM RAIL GAP

ENDS BUTTING

© Chrysler Corp.

Oil Pump

- The six cylinder engine must be raised about two inches to remove the externally mounted oil pump. Do not support the engine at the crankshaft pulley or vibration damper.

- On 318–360 CID engine, remove the oil pan, and separate the oil pump from the rear main bearing cap. Prime the pump before installing.

- On 400–440 CID engine, the oil pump is mounted externally and can be unbolted after the oil filter has been removed. Prime the pump before installing.

Lubrication system six cylinder engine

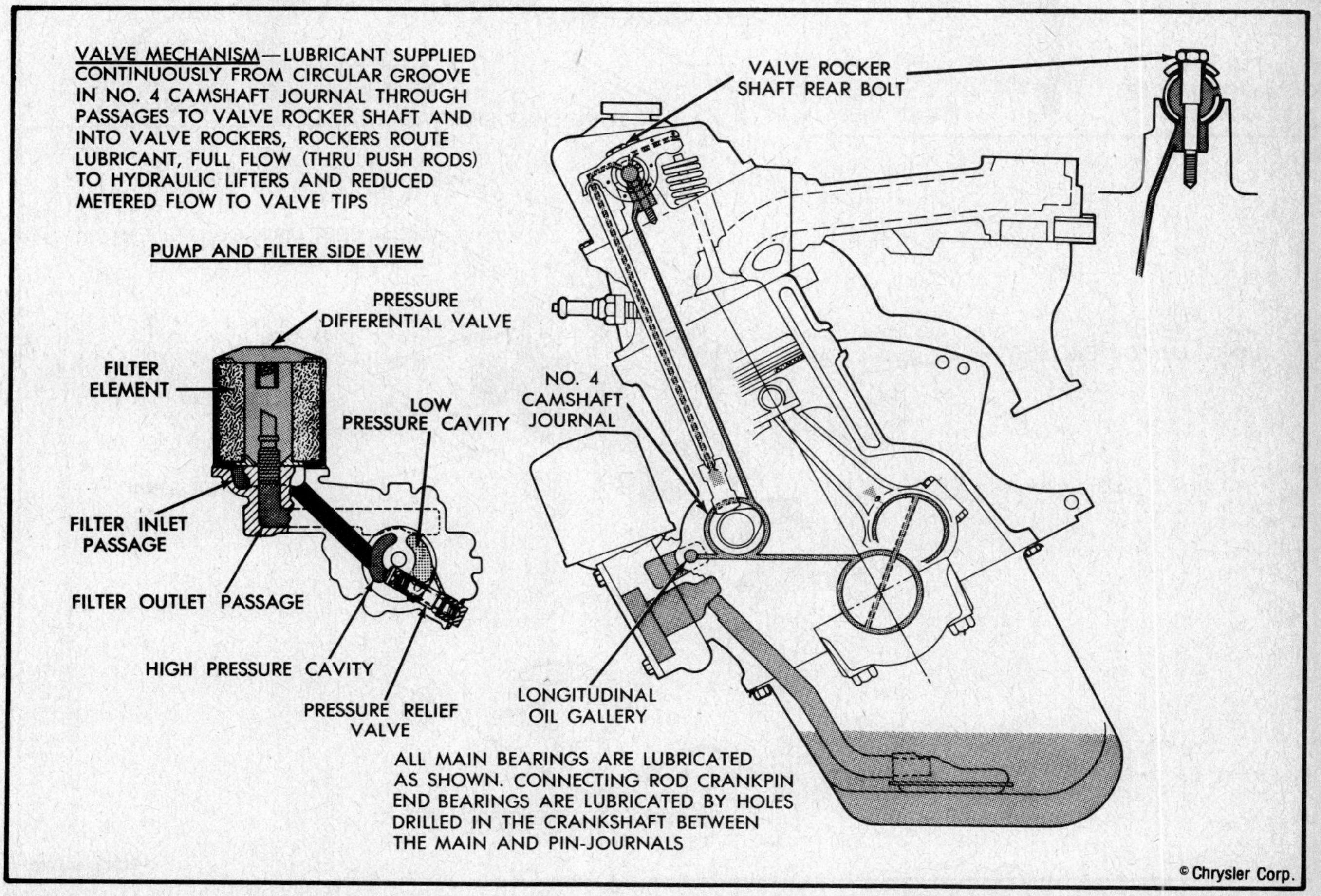

VALVE MECHANISM—LUBRICANT SUPPLIED CONTINUOUSLY FROM CIRCULAR GROOVE IN NO. 4 CAMSHAFT JOURNAL THROUGH PASSAGES TO VALVE ROCKER SHAFT AND INTO VALVE ROCKERS, ROCKERS ROUTE LUBRICANT, FULL FLOW (THRU PUSH RODS) TO HYDRAULIC LIFTERS AND REDUCED METERED FLOW TO VALVE TIPS

PUMP AND FILTER SIDE VIEW

VALVE ROCKER SHAFT REAR BOLT

PRESSURE DIFFERENTIAL VALVE

FILTER ELEMENT

LOW PRESSURE CAVITY

NO. 4 CAMSHAFT JOURNAL

FILTER INLET PASSAGE

FILTER OUTLET PASSAGE

HIGH PRESSURE CAVITY

PRESSURE RELIEF VALVE

LONGITUDINAL OIL GALLERY

ALL MAIN BEARINGS ARE LUBRICATED AS SHOWN. CONNECTING ROD CRANKPIN END BEARINGS ARE LUBRICATED BY HOLES DRILLED IN THE CRANKSHAFT BETWEEN THE MAIN AND PIN-JOURNALS

© Chrysler Corp.

Oil pump—318 and 360 CID engine

BODY
INNER ROTOR AND SHAFT
GASKET
DRIVE GEAR
OUTER ROTOR
SEAL RING
COVER
VALVE
SPRING
SCREW AND LOCKWASHER
PLUG
GASKET
SCREW AND LOCKWASHER
© Chrysler Corp.

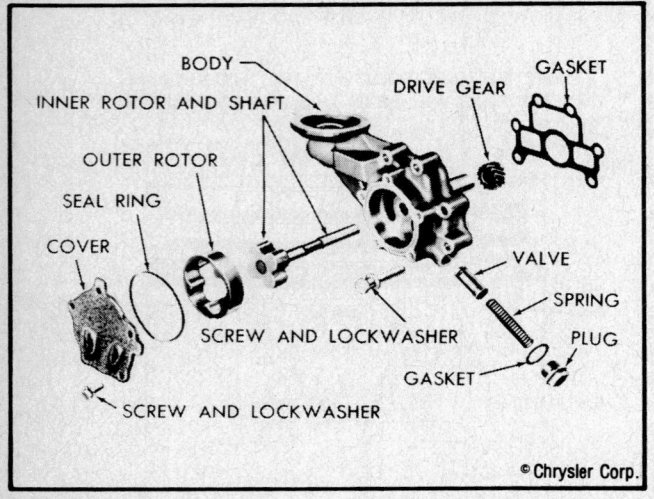

Oil pump—400, 440 CID engine

PLUG
GASKET
BOLTS AND WASHERS
COVER
OIL FILTER
SPRING
RELIEF VALVE PLUNGER
OUTER ROTOR
INNER ROTOR AND SHAFT
BODY
SEAL RING
DRIVE SHAFT AND GEAR
GASKET
"O" RING
PIN
© Chrysler Corp.

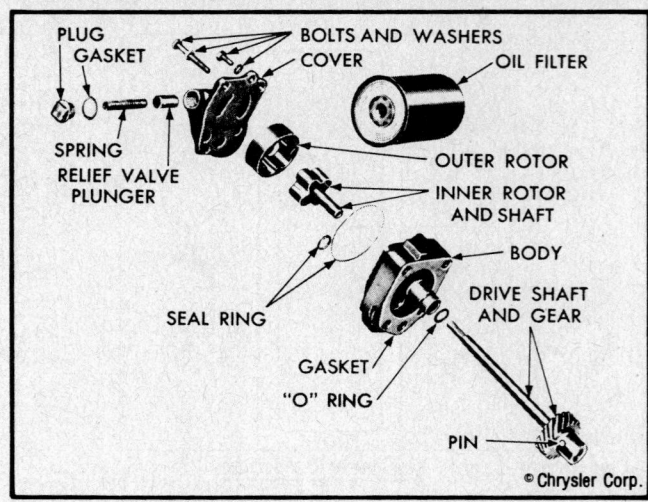

400, 440 CID engine oiling system

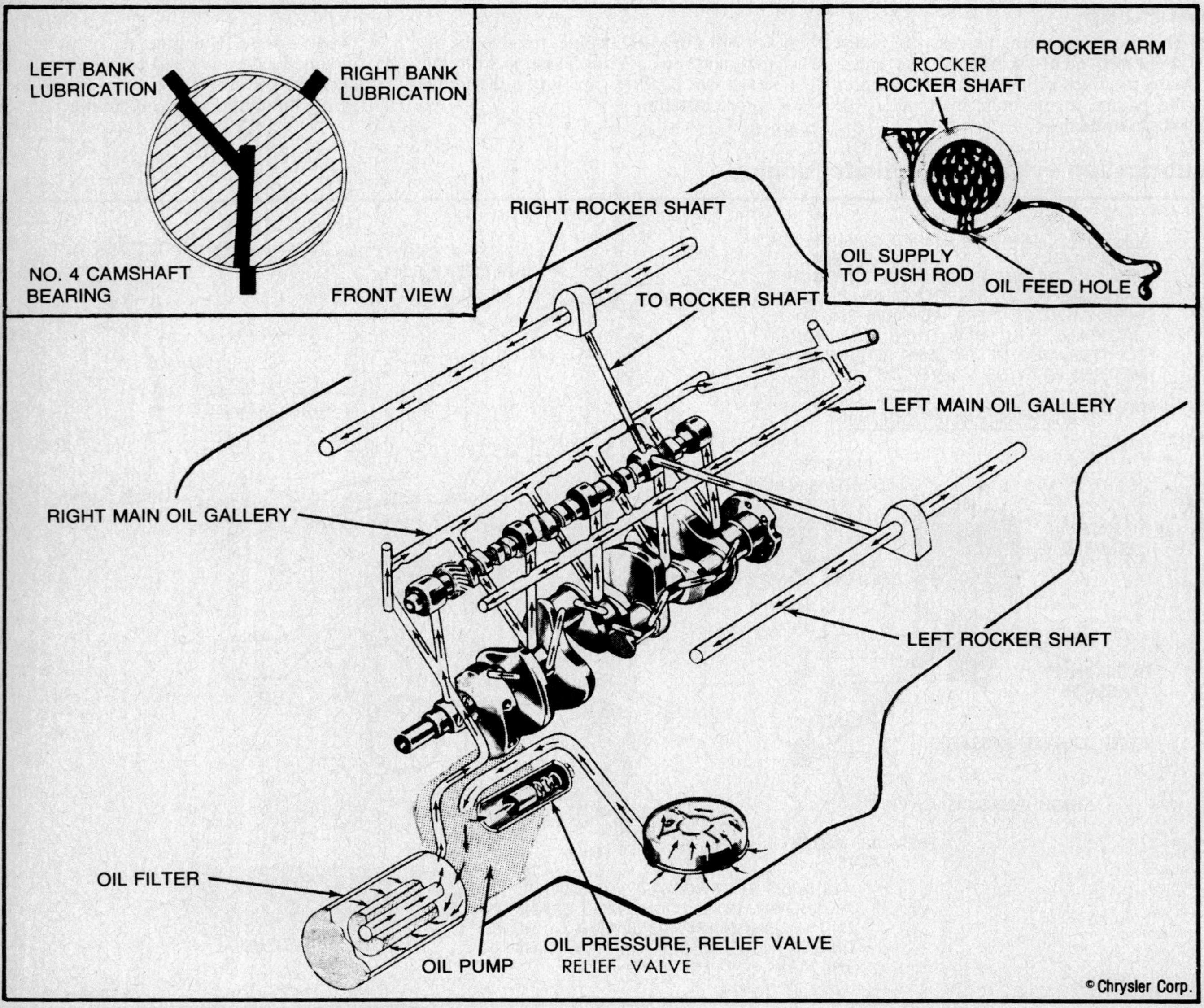

LEFT BANK LUBRICATION
RIGHT BANK LUBRICATION
NO. 4 CAMSHAFT BEARING
FRONT VIEW
ROCKER ARM
ROCKER
ROCKER SHAFT
OIL SUPPLY TO PUSH ROD
OIL FEED HOLE
RIGHT ROCKER SHAFT
TO ROCKER SHAFT
LEFT MAIN OIL GALLERY
RIGHT MAIN OIL GALLERY
LEFT ROCKER SHAFT
OIL FILTER
OIL PUMP
OIL PRESSURE, RELIEF VALVE
RELIEF VALVE
© Chrysler Corp.

318 and 360 engine oiling system

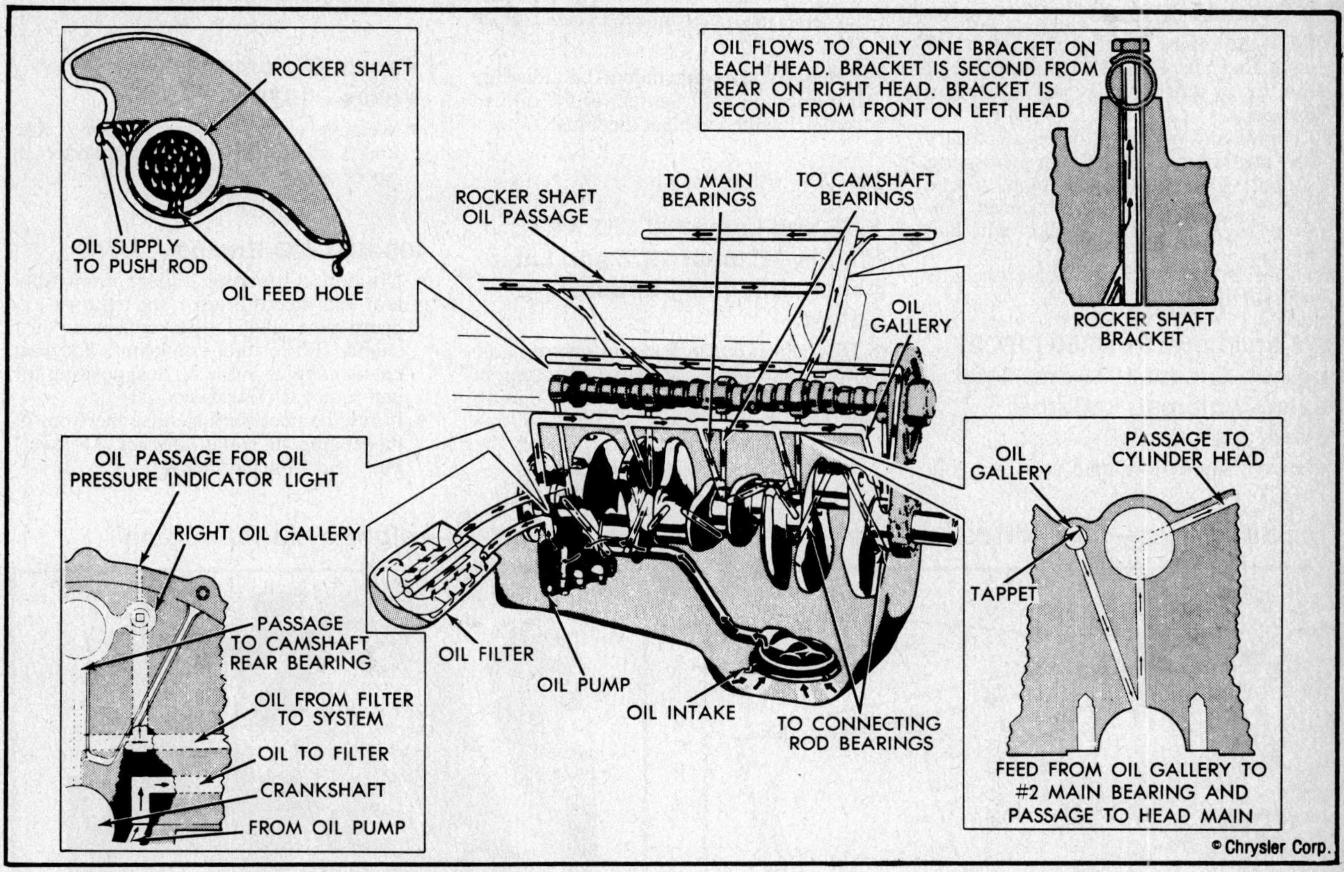

ROCKER SHAFT

OIL SUPPLY TO PUSH ROD

OIL FEED HOLE

OIL FLOWS TO ONLY ONE BRACKET ON EACH HEAD. BRACKET IS SECOND FROM REAR ON RIGHT HEAD. BRACKET IS SECOND FROM FRONT ON LEFT HEAD

ROCKER SHAFT OIL PASSAGE

TO MAIN BEARINGS

TO CAMSHAFT BEARINGS

OIL GALLERY

ROCKER SHAFT BRACKET

OIL PASSAGE FOR OIL PRESSURE INDICATOR LIGHT

RIGHT OIL GALLERY

PASSAGE TO CAMSHAFT REAR BEARING

OIL FILTER

OIL FROM FILTER TO SYSTEM

OIL PUMP

OIL INTAKE

OIL TO FILTER

CRANKSHAFT

FROM OIL PUMP

TO CONNECTING ROD BEARINGS

OIL GALLERY

PASSAGE TO CYLINDER HEAD

TAPPET

FEED FROM OIL GALLERY TO #2 MAIN BEARING AND PASSAGE TO HEAD MAIN

© Chrysler Corp.

Crankshaft Rear Oil Seal

- Using a split, rubber composition seal, the oil seal can be replaced without removing the crankshaft. Rope type and rubber composition seals may not be intermixed.
- Always place paint stripe to rear on rubber composition seals, and use no sealer or cement on seal ends or lip.
- Side seals on 400–440 CID engine *must* be pre-oiled with mineral spirits or diesel fuel, and installed rapidly before the seals swell.
- On 318 CID engine the cap seal with yellow paint goes on the right side with the bearing cap in engine position. Install seals with narrow sealing edge up. Cap seal edges must line up exactly with shoulder in bearing cap.
- On 360 CID engine, apply sealer adjacent to rubber seal—but not on the seal.

Crankshaft rear oil seal

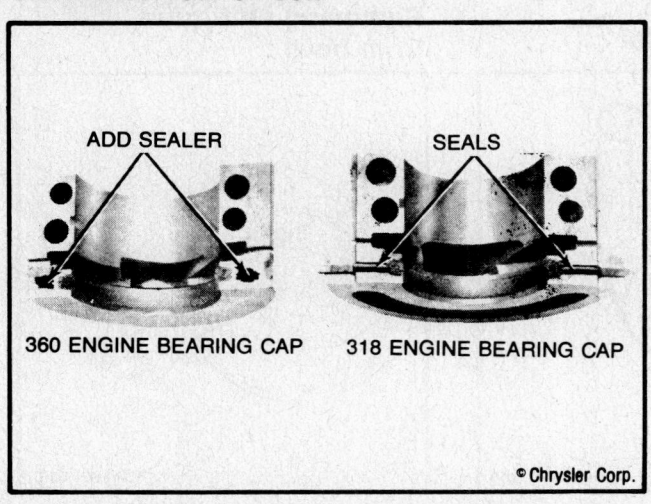

ADD SEALER

SEALS

360 ENGINE BEARING CAP

318 ENGINE BEARING CAP

© Chrysler Corp.

Crankshaft rear oil seal—six cylinder engine

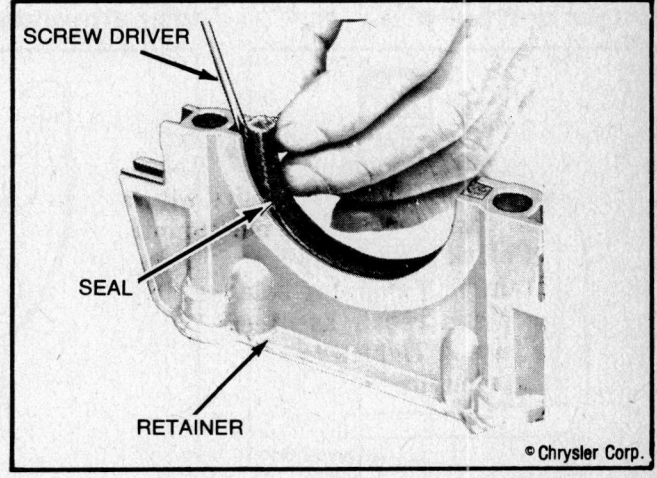

SCREW DRIVER

SEAL

RETAINER

© Chrysler Corp.

CHRYSLER REAR DRIVE CARS

Oil Pan
Six Cylinder Engine
- Raise the engine about two inches for oil pan clearance. Do not support engine at the crankshaft pulley or vibration damper.
- Remove any of the following necessary for clearance: Engine-to-transmission support bracket, exhaust pipe, torque converter inspection shield, center link from steering arm and idler arm ball joints.
- Turn crankshaft to clear counter-weights when removing oil pan.

1976 and Later 318–360 CID, 2V Engine—Except 1978 and Later Aspen, Diplomat, LeBaron, Volaré
- Remove engine-to-torque converter left housing strut, remove steering and idle arm ball joints from steering linkage center link, and disconnect exhaust pipes from manifolds.
- Remove rear engine mount, and raise the transmission until the rear of the oil pan can be lowered to clear the transmission.

1976 and Later 360 CID, 4V Engine—Except 1978 and Later Aspen, Diplomat, LeBaron, Volaré
- Disconnect fan shroud and steering linkage center link. Remove rear engine mount bolts, and raise the transmission until the rear of the oil pan can be lowered to clear the transmission. Return the transmission to its normal position.

- Raise the front of the engine far enough to remove the oil pan.

Aspen, Diplomat, LeBaron, Volaré—1978 and later
- Remove exhaust crossover pipe, center link, starter and torque converter inspection plate.

400–440 CID Engine
- Disconnect steering linkage from idler arm and steering arm, and remove exhaust pipe and torque converter dust shield. Place the crankshaft forward counterweight in the highest position for pan removal clearance.
- It may be necessary to raise the front of the engine in some Charger, Coronet, Fury and Monaco models.

Oil pan gasket—six cylinder engine

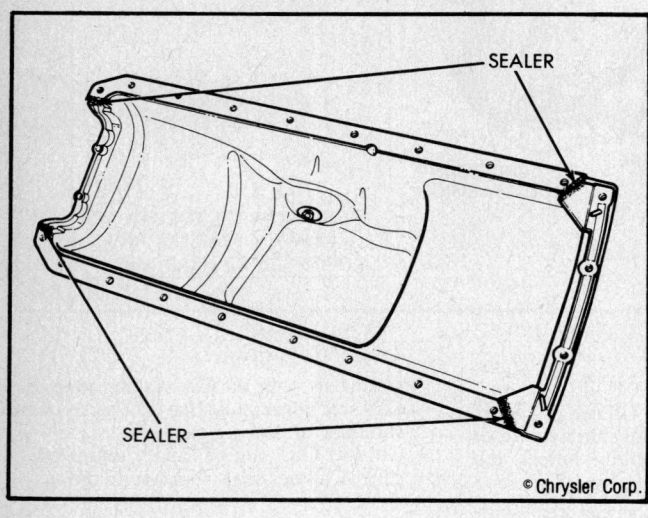

Oil pan gasket—eight cylinder engine

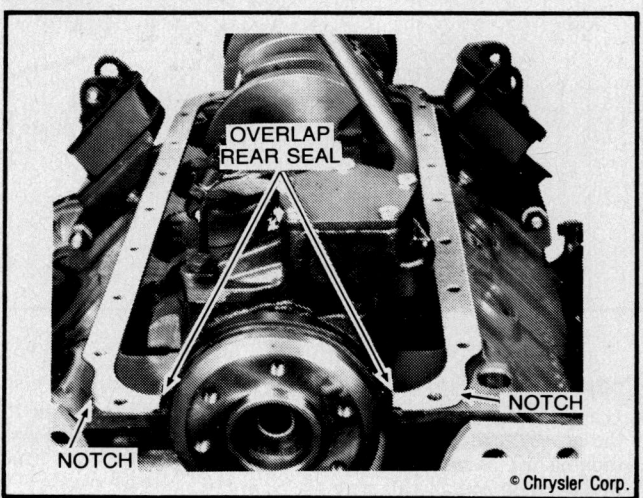

STEERING & BRAKES SECTION

Pitman arm puller

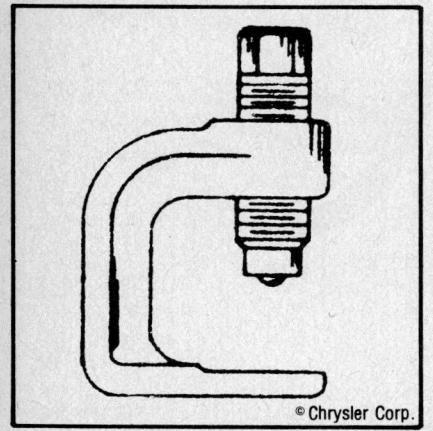

Idler arm end puller

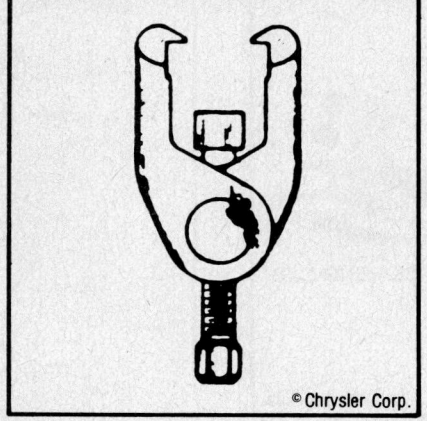

Removing shift tube from bowl

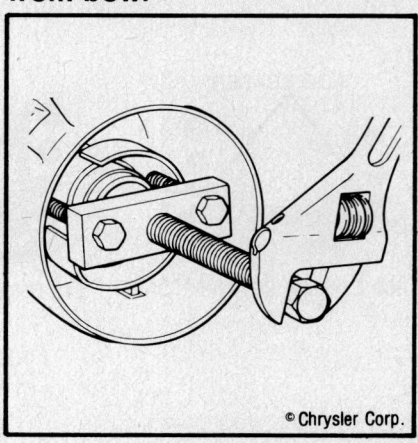

Steering linkage typical in full-size models

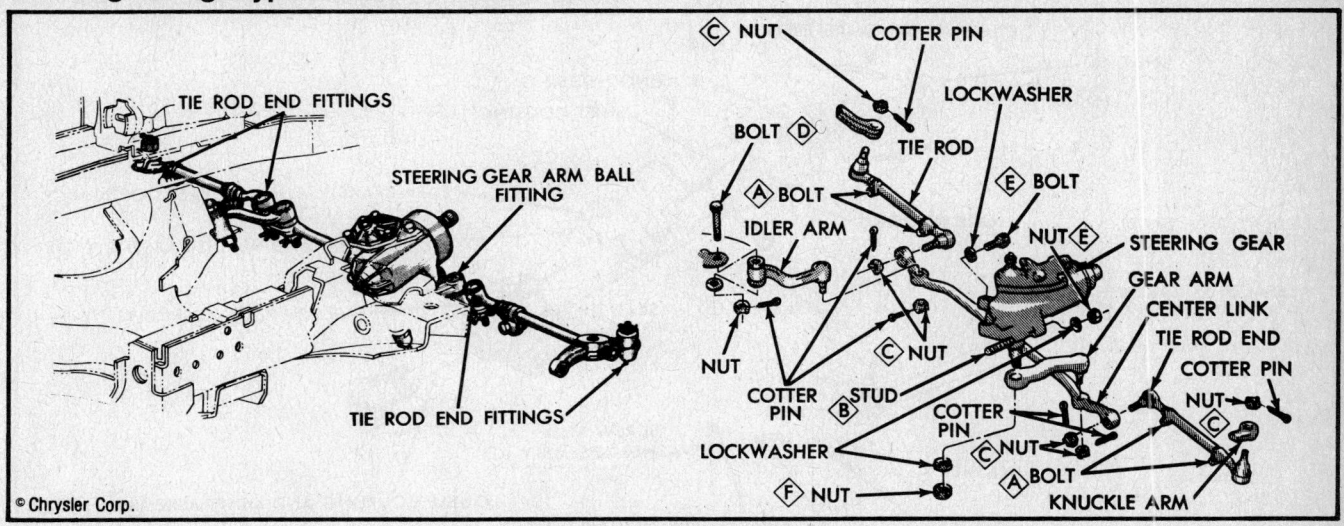

© Chrysler Corp.

Steering Gear

- Remove steering column, and use Tool C-4150 to remove steering arm.
- Eight cylinder engines in Dart and Valiant may have to be raised to remove power steering gear.

CHILTON CAUTION: Spring loaded components should be serviced with caution to prevent injury.

Steering Column

NOTE: Handle the steering column very carefully. Rapping on the end of it or leaning on it could damage the shear pins which allow the column to collapse in a crash.

- Disconnect linkages, electrical wiring, and vacuum connections.
- Remove steering shaft lower coupling-to-wormshaft roll pin.
- Remove steering wheel, turn signal lever, etc. for clearance and easier handling.
- Remove cluster bezel and instrument panels parts necessary for clearance and access to mounting bracket.
- Pry lower coupling from steering gear wormshaft, and remove column lower mounting, first, then remove upper mounting.
- New grommets must be used when shift lever rod is disconnected from lever.
- In models without a steering shaft lower bearing, Tool C-4134 or C-4157 must be used to hold the steering shaft in the center of the shift tube while installing and aligning the column.

Dart, Valiant steering column installation

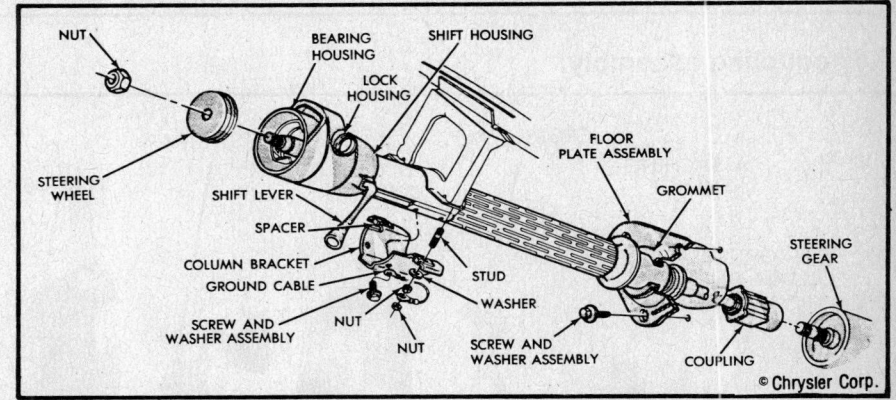

© Chrysler Corp.

Manual steering gear

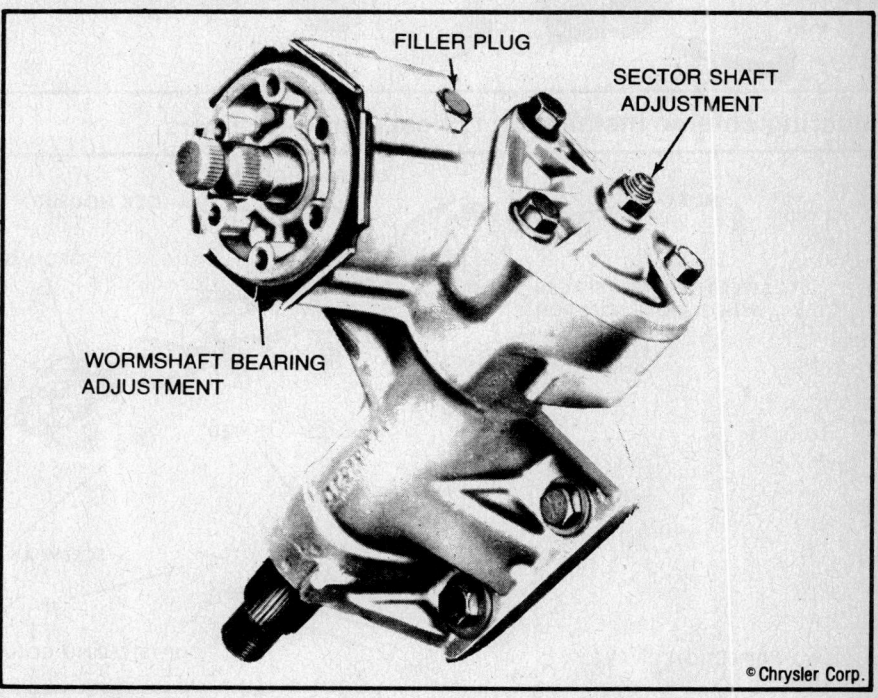

© Chrysler Corp.

CHRYSLER REAR DRIVE CARS

Steering column installation in full-size cars and Aspen, Diplomat, LeBaron, Volare

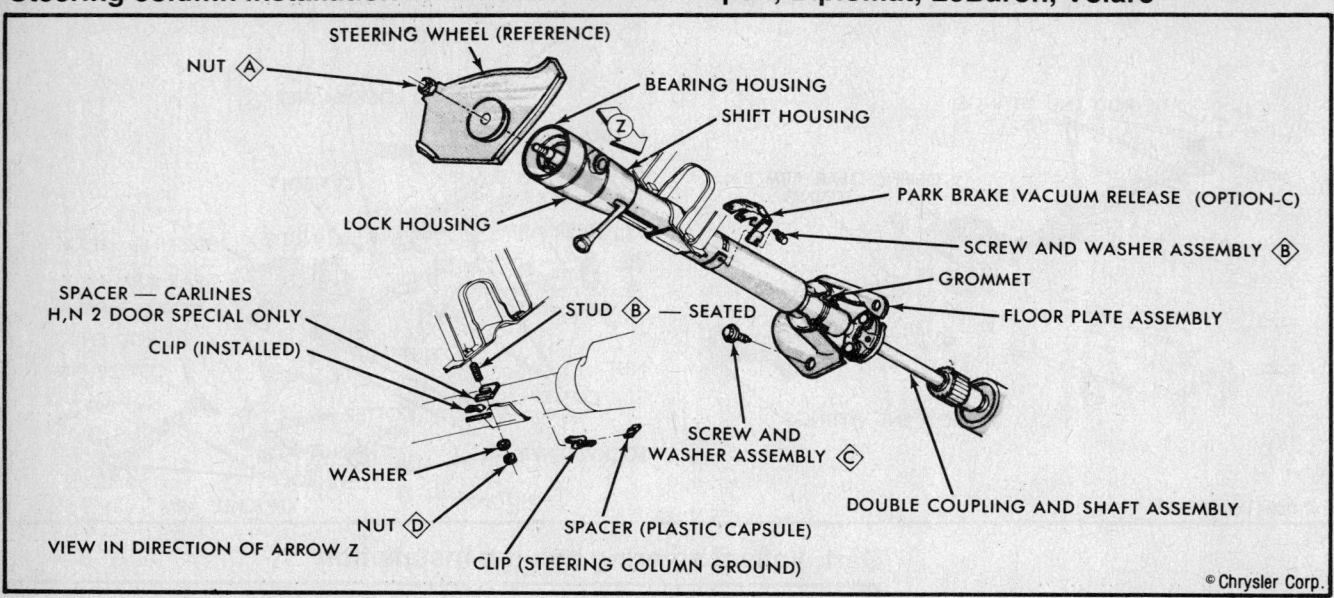

NUT Ⓐ

STEERING WHEEL (REFERENCE)

BEARING HOUSING

SHIFT HOUSING

PARK BRAKE VACUUM RELEASE (OPTION-C)

LOCK HOUSING

SCREW AND WASHER ASSEMBLY Ⓑ

GROMMET

SPACER — CARLINES
H, N 2 DOOR SPECIAL ONLY

FLOOR PLATE ASSEMBLY

CLIP (INSTALLED)

STUD Ⓑ — SEATED

SCREW AND
WASHER ASSEMBLY Ⓒ

WASHER

NUT Ⓓ

SPACER (PLASTIC CAPSULE)

DOUBLE COUPLING AND SHAFT ASSEMBLY

VIEW IN DIRECTION OF ARROW Z

CLIP (STEERING COLUMN GROUND)

© Chrysler Corp.

Flex coupling assembly

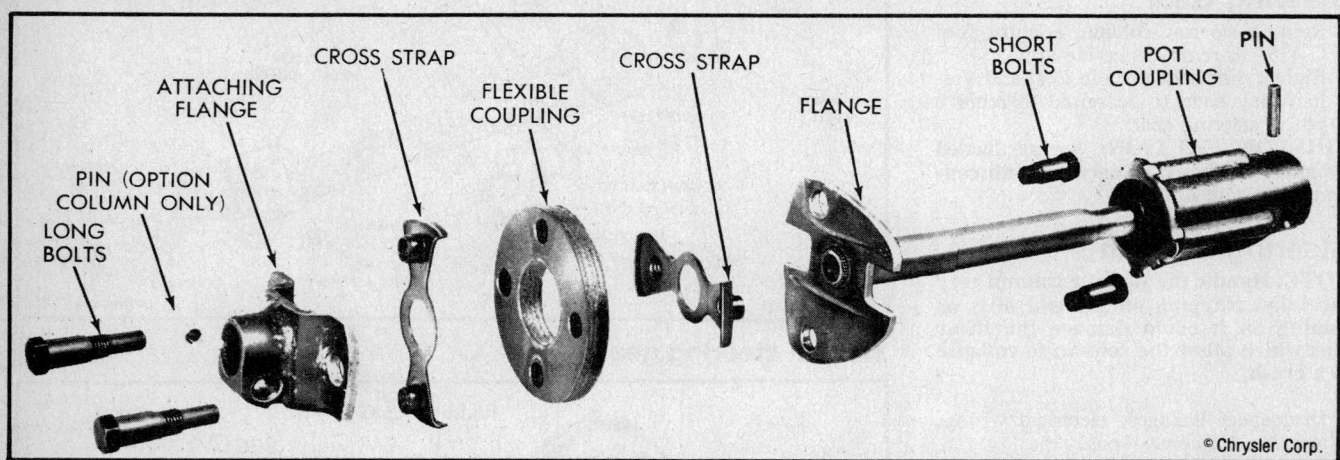

ATTACHING
FLANGE

CROSS STRAP

FLEXIBLE
COUPLING

CROSS STRAP

FLANGE

SHORT
BOLTS

POT
COUPLING

PIN

PIN (OPTION
COLUMN ONLY)

LONG
BOLTS

© Chrysler Corp.

Steering column installation typical in mid-size cars

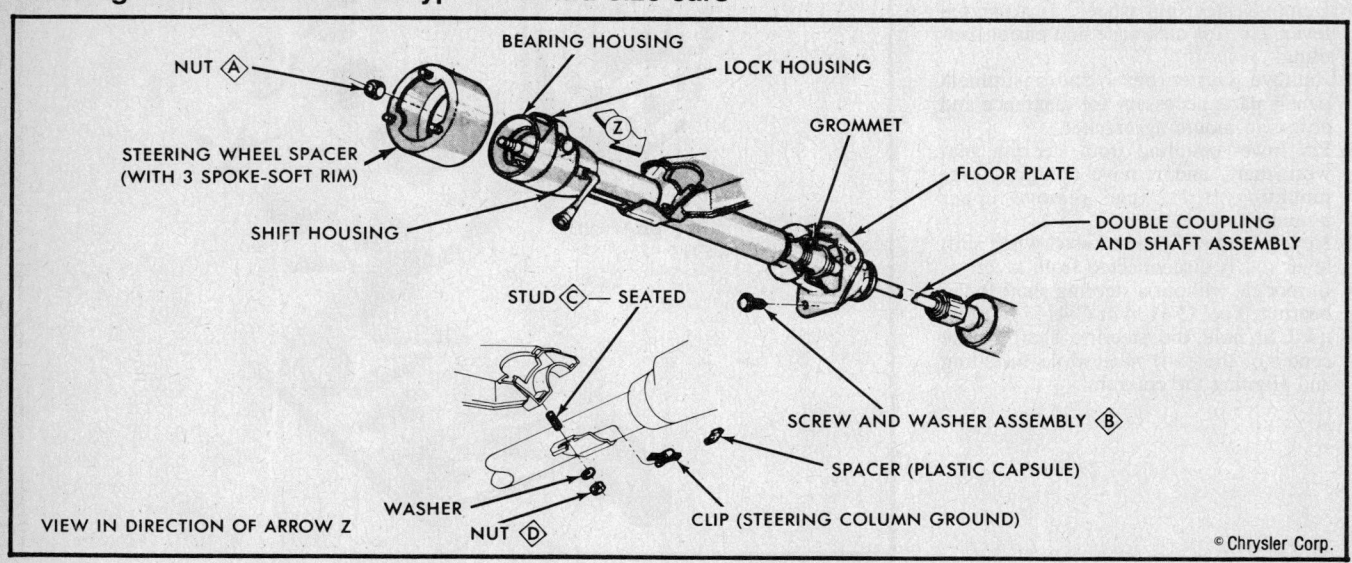

NUT Ⓐ

BEARING HOUSING

LOCK HOUSING

GROMMET

STEERING WHEEL SPACER
(WITH 3 SPOKE-SOFT RIM)

FLOOR PLATE

SHIFT HOUSING

DOUBLE COUPLING
AND SHAFT ASSEMBLY

STUD Ⓒ — SEATED

SCREW AND WASHER ASSEMBLY Ⓑ

SPACER (PLASTIC CAPSULE)

WASHER

CLIP (STEERING COLUMN GROUND)

NUT Ⓓ

VIEW IN DIRECTION OF ARROW Z

© Chrysler Corp.

A290

Tilt-a-scope steering

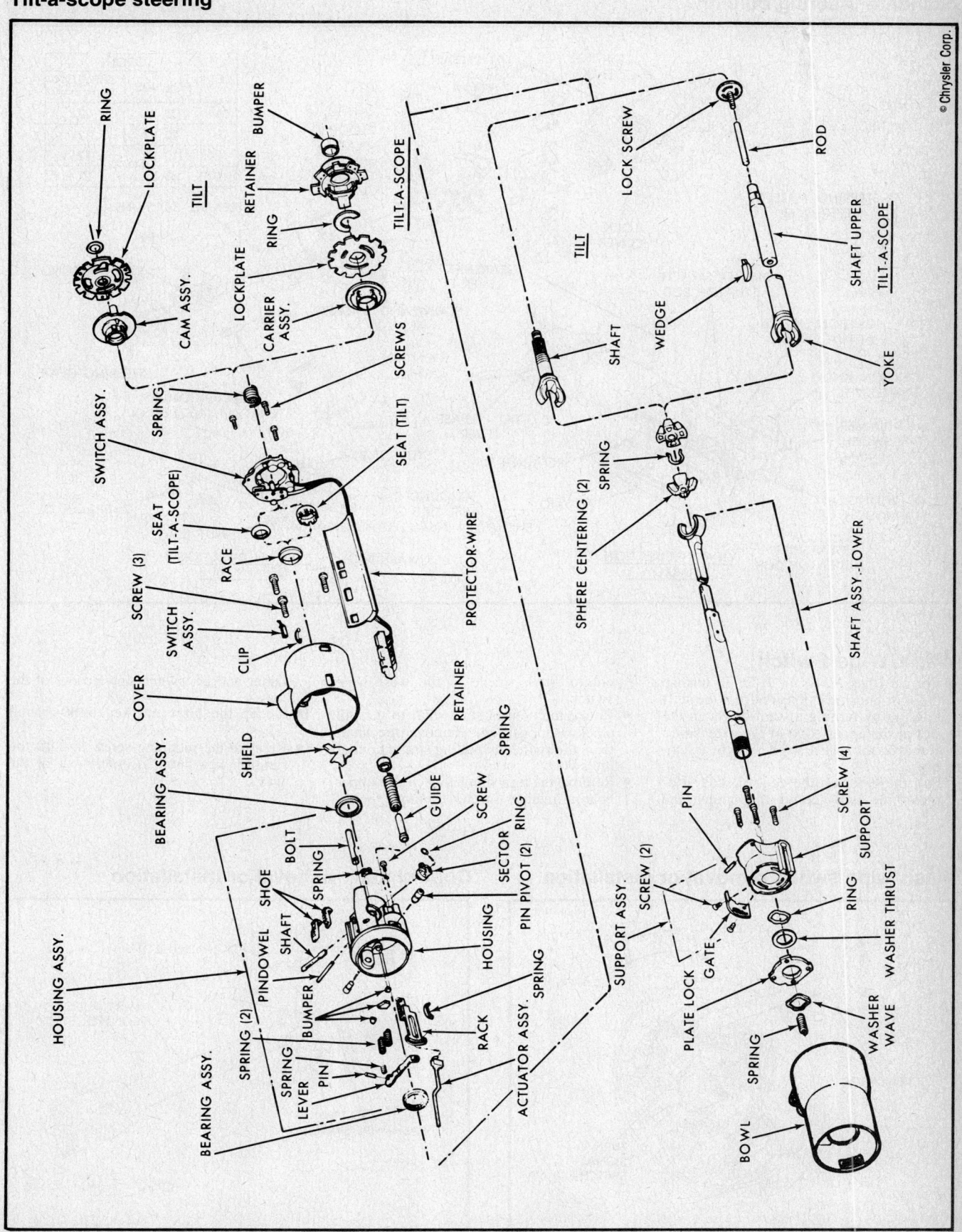

Standard steering column

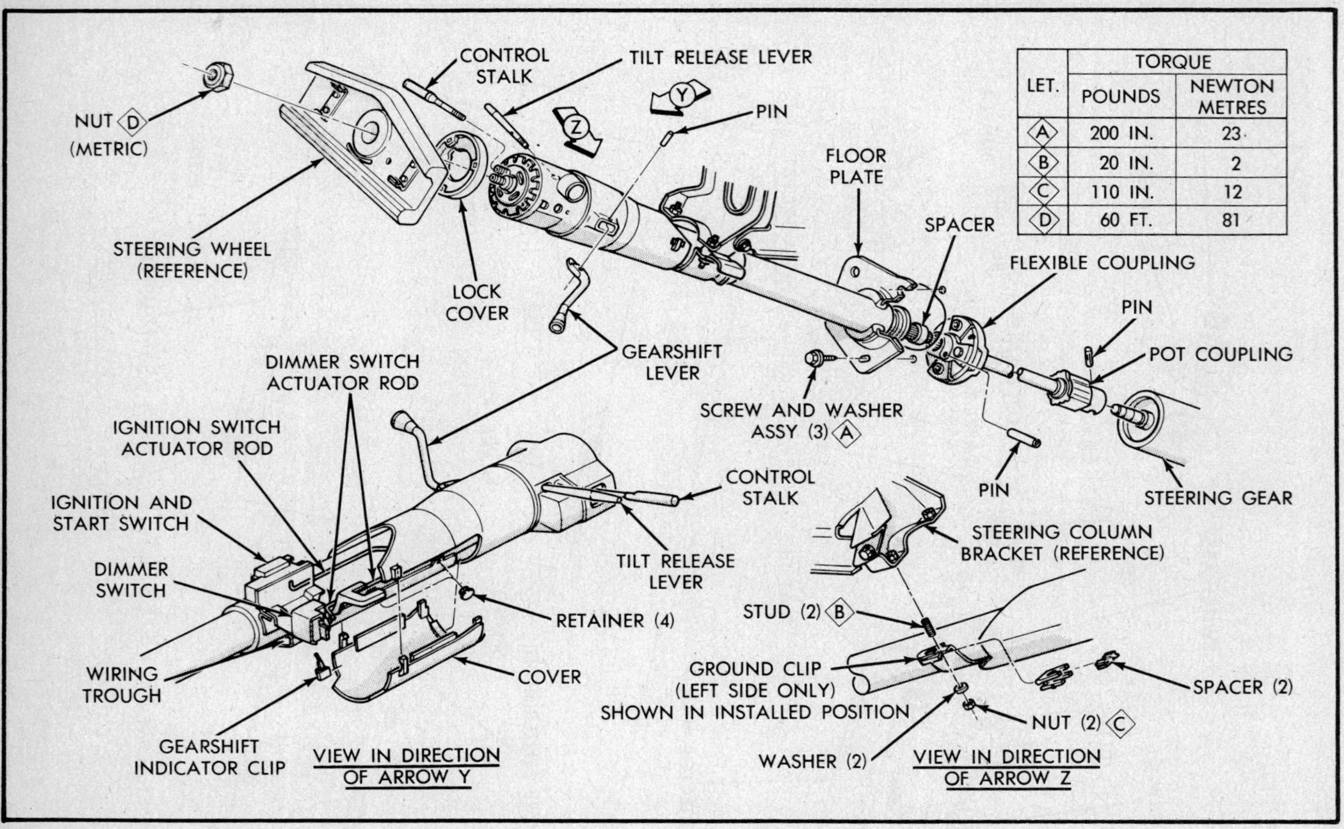

CONTROL STALK

TILT RELEASE LEVER

NUT ◇D◇ (METRIC)

PIN

FLOOR PLATE

LET.	TORQUE	
	POUNDS	NEWTON METRES
◁A◁	200 IN.	23
◁B◁	20 IN.	2
◁C◁	110 IN.	12
◁D◁	60 FT.	81

STEERING WHEEL (REFERENCE)

SPACER

FLEXIBLE COUPLING

LOCK COVER

PIN

POT COUPLING

DIMMER SWITCH ACTUATOR ROD

GEARSHIFT LEVER

IGNITION SWITCH ACTUATOR ROD

SCREW AND WASHER ASSY (3) ◁A◁

PIN

STEERING GEAR

IGNITION AND START SWITCH

CONTROL STALK

STEERING COLUMN BRACKET (REFERENCE)

DIMMER SWITCH

TILT RELEASE LEVER

STUD (2) ◁B◁

WIRING TROUGH

RETAINER (4)

GROUND CLIP (LEFT SIDE ONLY) SHOWN IN INSTALLED POSITION

SPACER (2)

GEARSHIFT INDICATOR CLIP

COVER

NUT (2) ◁C◁

VIEW IN DIRECTION OF ARROW Y

WASHER (2)

VIEW IN DIRECTION OF ARROW Z

Wash/Wipe Switch

- For car lines X, S, Y, J, E, T, unsnap the shift housing extension from the shift housing by turning a screwdriver in the slot at the upper edge of the extension.
- Remove the wash/wipe switch assembly.
- Pull the hider up the control stalk. Remove the two screws that attach the control stalk sleeve to the wash/wipe switch.
- Rotate the control stalk shaft to the full clockwise position. Remove the shaft from the switch by pulling straight out of the switch.
- Remove the turn signal switch and upper bearing retainer screws. Remove the retainer and lift switch upward out of the way.
- Unclip the horn and key light ground wires.
- Remove the retaining screw and lift the ignition key lamp assembly out of the way.

Wash/wipe switch removal or installation

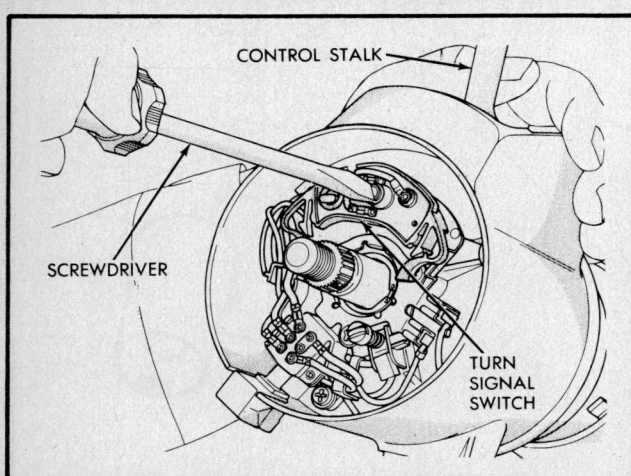

CONTROL STALK

SCREWDRIVER

TURN SIGNAL SWITCH

Control stalk removal or installation

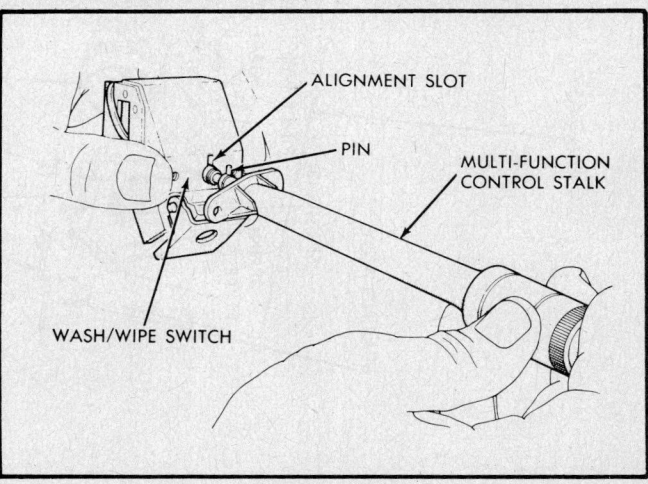

ALIGNMENT SLOT

PIN

MULTI-FUNCTION CONTROL STALK

WASH/WIPE SWITCH

Retainer and turn signal switch

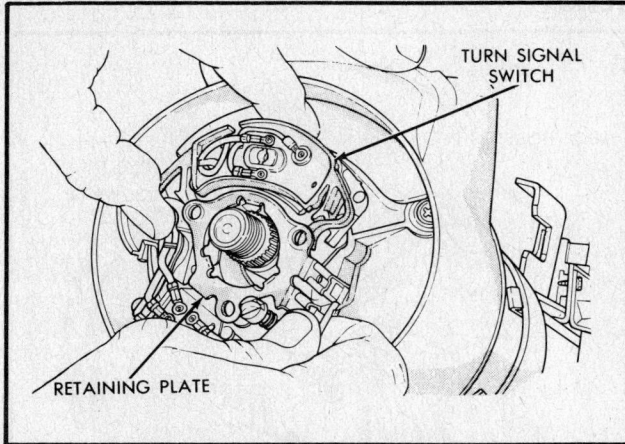

Ignition key lamp

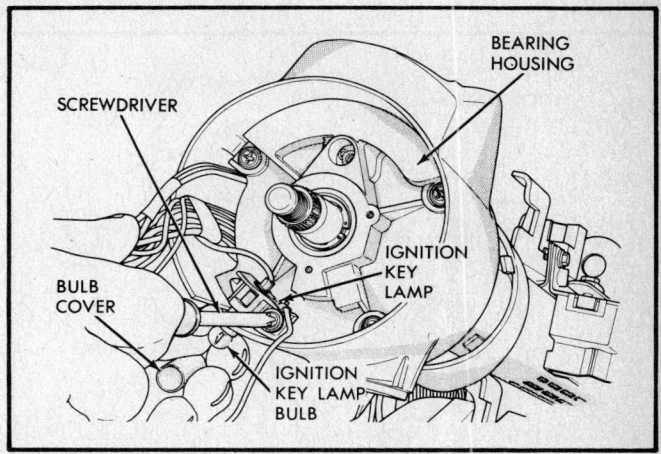

Lock Housing

- Remove the ignition key. Remove the screw and lift out buzzer/chime switch.
- Remove the two screws attaching the ignition switch.
- Remove the ignition switch by rotating the switch 90 degrees on the rod and sliding off the rod.
- Remove the two mounting screws from the dimmer switch. Disengage the switch from the actuator rod.
- Remove the two screws that mount the bellcrank. Slide the bellcrank up in the lock housing until it can be disconnected from the ignition switch actuator rod.
- Place the cylinder in the "lock" position and remove the key. Insert two small diameter screwdrivers or similar tools into both lock cylinder release holes and push in to release thespring-loaded lock retainers. At the same time pull the lock cylinder out of the housing bore.
- Grasp the lock lever and spring assembly and pull straight out of the housing.
- Remove the four lock housing to column jacket hex head retaining screws and remove the lock housing plate and housing from the jacket.

- When removing the lock housing, turn the lock housing 90 degrees to disengage it from the ignition switch actuator rod.

Steering shaft bearing upper snap ring

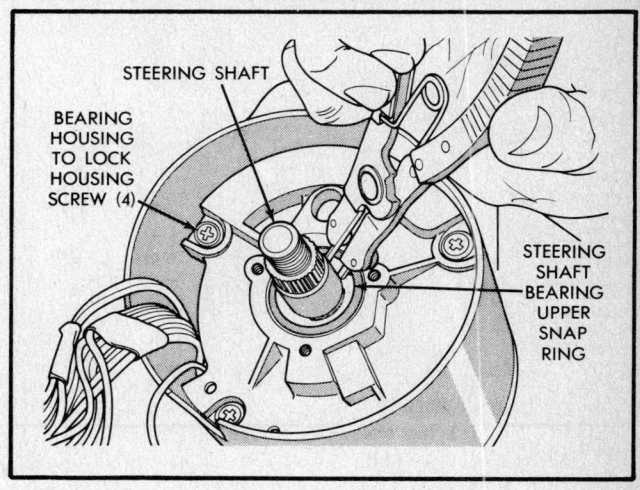

Ignition key buzzer/chime switch

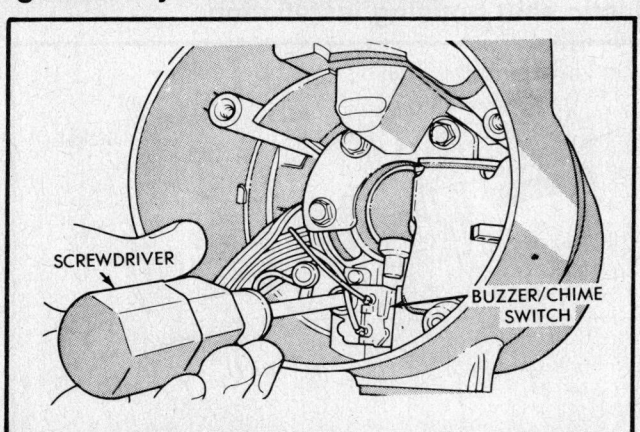

Lock cylinder and lock levers

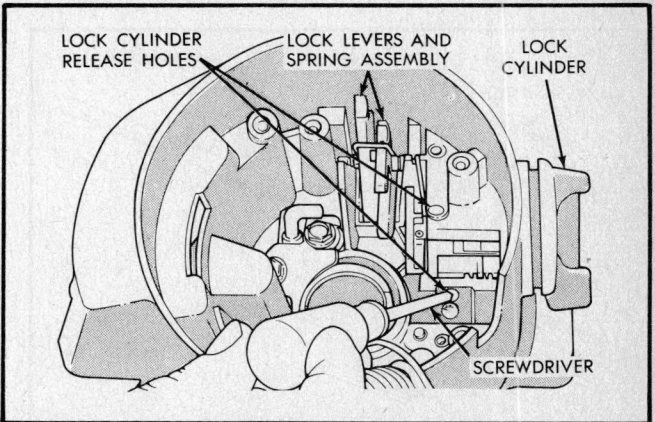

CHRYSLER REAR DRIVE CARS

Bearing housing, lock plate spring and lock plate

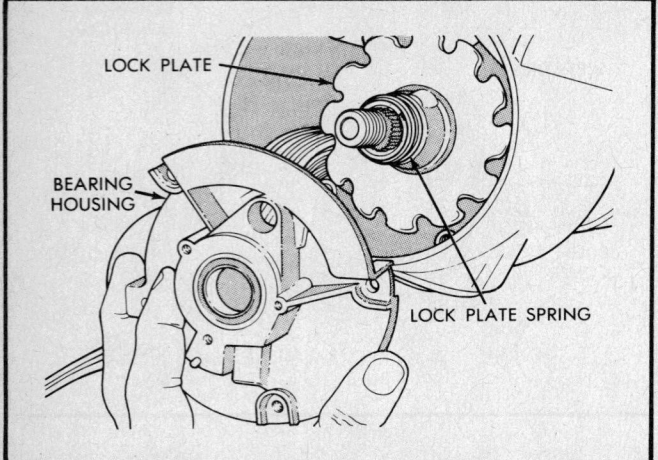

Lock housing to column jacket retaining screws

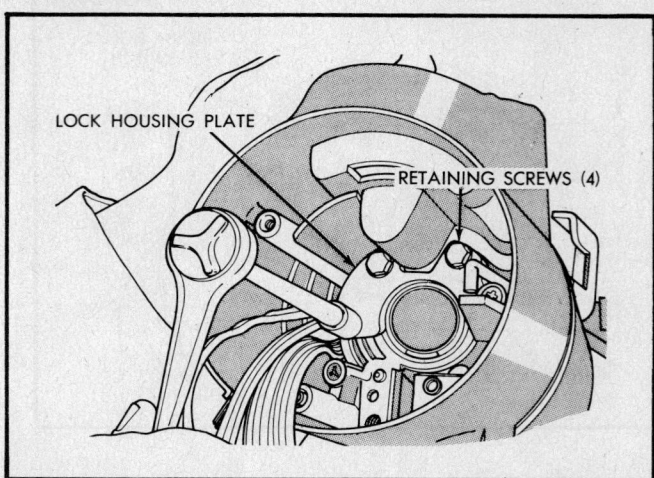

Plastic shift housing removal

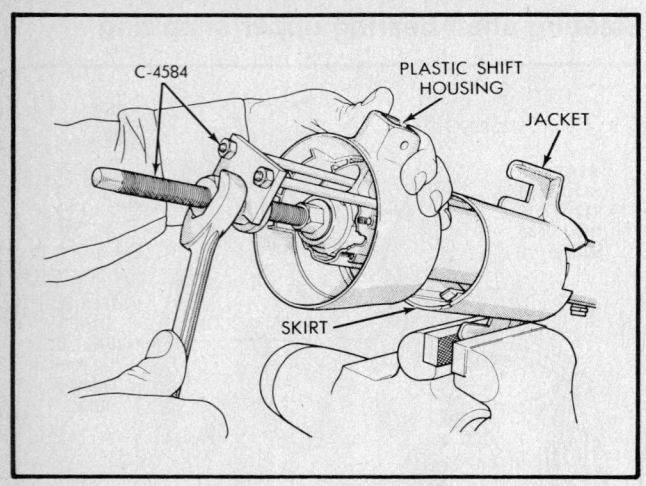

Shift Tube

- For car lines F and G remove the shift tube from column shift automatic models by loosening the shift tube set screw in the shift housing. Remove the shift tube through the lower end of the jacket.
- To install the shift tube, install the shift tube into the shift housing. Tighten the shift tube set screw.
- Remove the floor plate and grommet from the jacket.
- For car lines X, S, Y, J, E, T, remove the shift tube by using tool C-4584 to press the shift tube out of the lock housing.
- Remove the shift housing extension from the jacket.
- Reassembly is the reverse of this procedure.

Dimmer switch

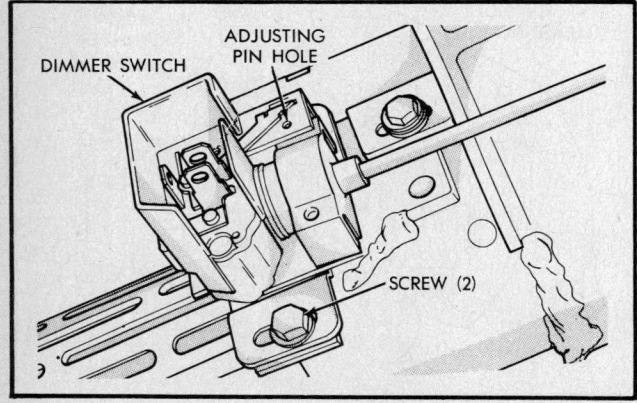

Plastic shift housing installation

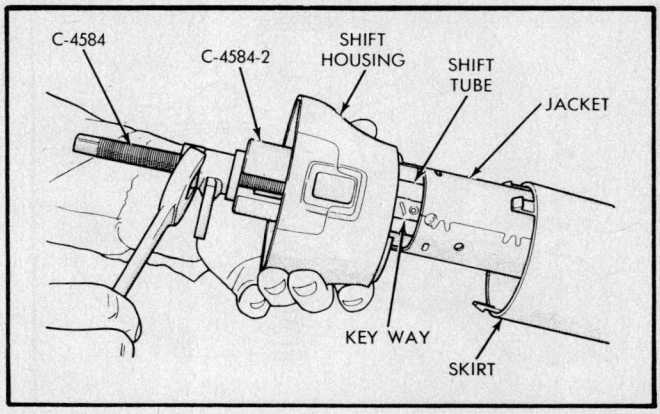

Steering column upper end—car lines F and G

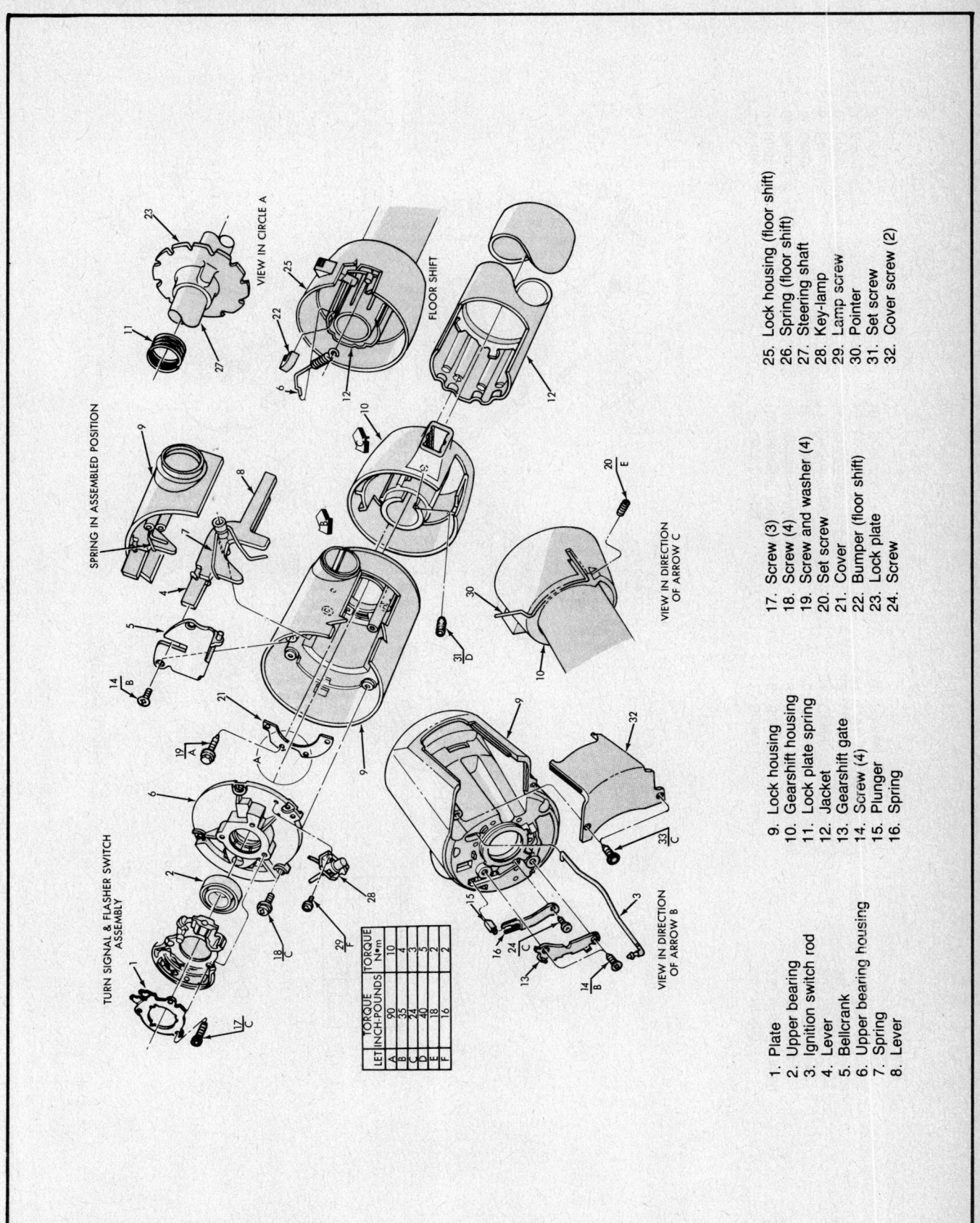

VIEW IN CIRCLE A

FLOOR SHIFT

SPRING IN ASSEMBLED POSITION

VIEW IN DIRECTION OF ARROW C

TURN SIGNAL & FLASHER SWITCH ASSEMBLY

VIEW IN DIRECTION OF ARROW B

LET	TORQUE INCH-POUNDS	TORQUE N·m
A	90	10
B	35	4
C	27	3
D	40	5
E	18	2
F	16	2

1. Plate
2. Upper bearing
3. Ignition switch rod
4. Lever
5. Bellcrank
6. Upper bearing housing
7. Spring
8. Lever
9. Lock housing
10. Gearshift housing
11. Lock plate spring
12. Jacket
13. Gearshift gate
14. Screw (4)
15. Plunger
16. Spring
17. Screw (3)
18. Screw (4)
19. Screw and washer (4)
20. Set screw
21. Cover
22. Bumper (floor shift)
23. Lock plate
24. Screw
25. Lock housing (floor shift)
26. Spring (floor shift)
27. Steering shaft
28. Key-lamp
29. Lamp screw
30. Pointer
31. Set screw
32. Cover screw (2)

Steering column upper end—car lines X, S, Y, J, E and T

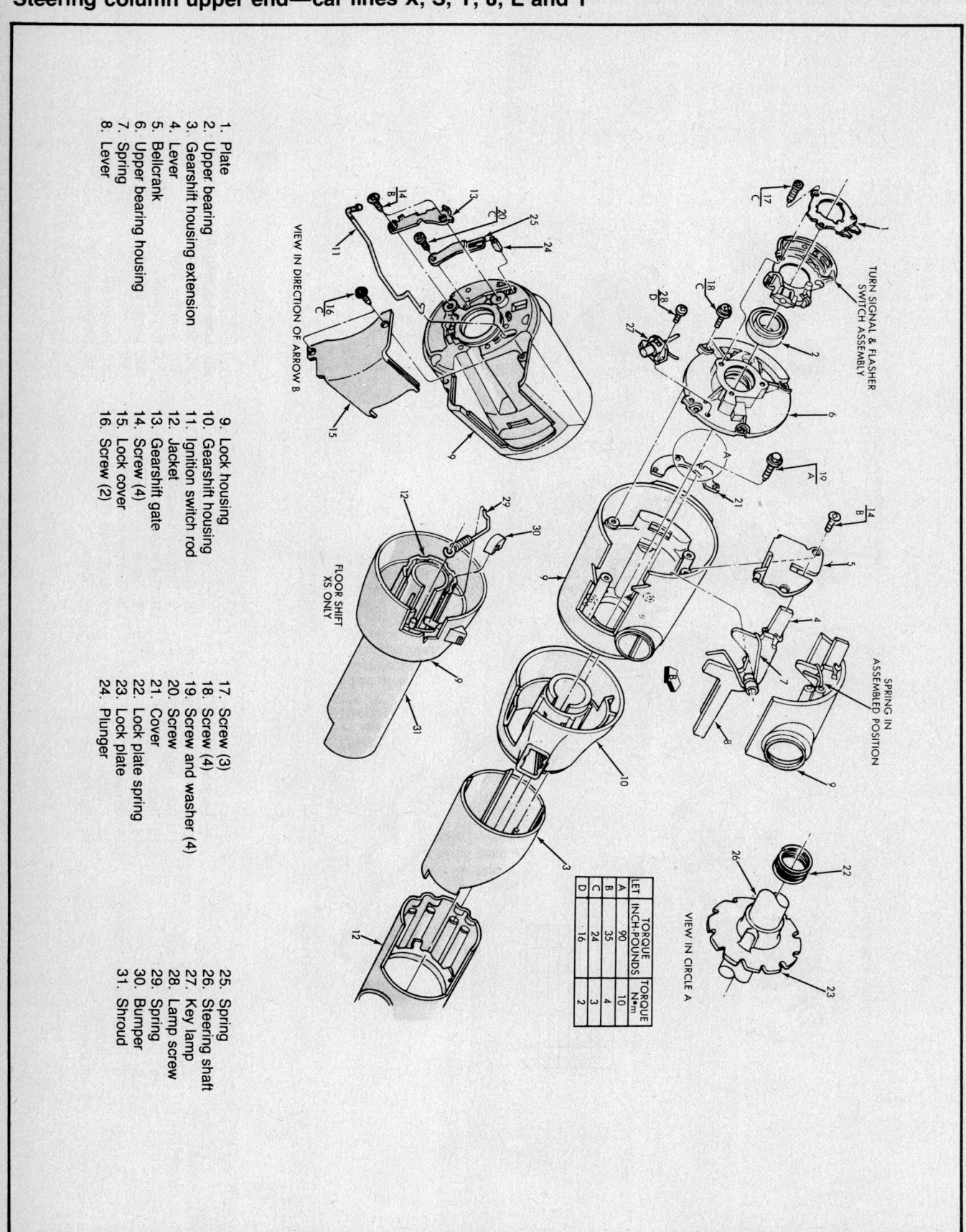

1. Plate
2. Upper bearing
3. Gearshift housing extension
4. Lever
5. Bellcrank
6. Upper bearing housing
7. Spring
8. Lever

9. Lock housing
10. Gearshift housing
11. Jacket
12. Ignition switch rod
13. Gearshift gate
14. Screw (4)
15. Lock cover
16. Screw (2)

17. Screw (3)
18. Screw (4)
19. Screw and washer (4)
20. Screw
21. Cover
22. Lock plate spring
23. Lock plate
24. Plunger

25. Spring
26. Steering shaft
27. Key lamp
28. Lamp screw
29. Spring
30. Bumper
31. Shroud

VIEW IN DIRECTION OF ARROW B

TURN SIGNAL & FLASHER SWITCH ASSEMBLY

FLOOR SHIFT XS ONLY

SPRING IN ASSEMBLED POSITION

VIEW IN CIRCLE A

LET	TORQUE INCH-POUNDS	TORQUE N·m
A	90	10
B	35	4
C	24	3
D	16	2

Lock housing and shift gate

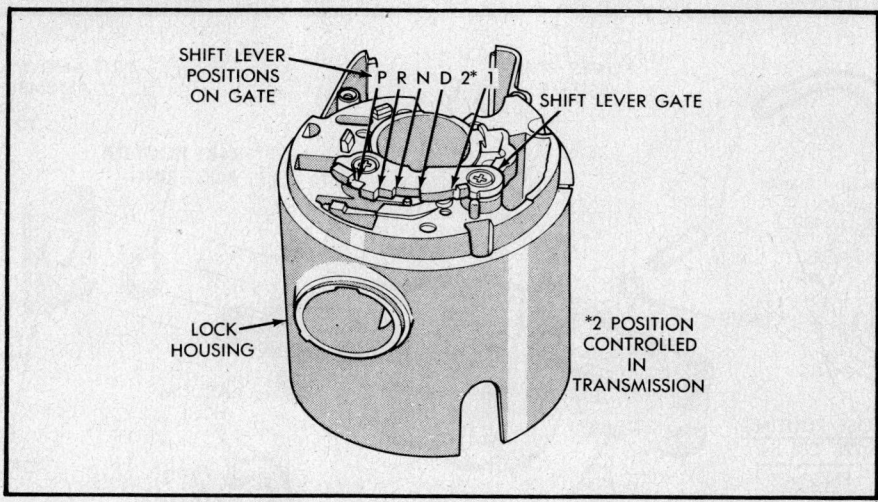

SHIFT LEVER POSITIONS ON GATE

P R N D 2* 1

SHIFT LEVER GATE

LOCK HOUSING

*2 POSITION CONTROLLED IN TRANSMISSION

Shift lever installation

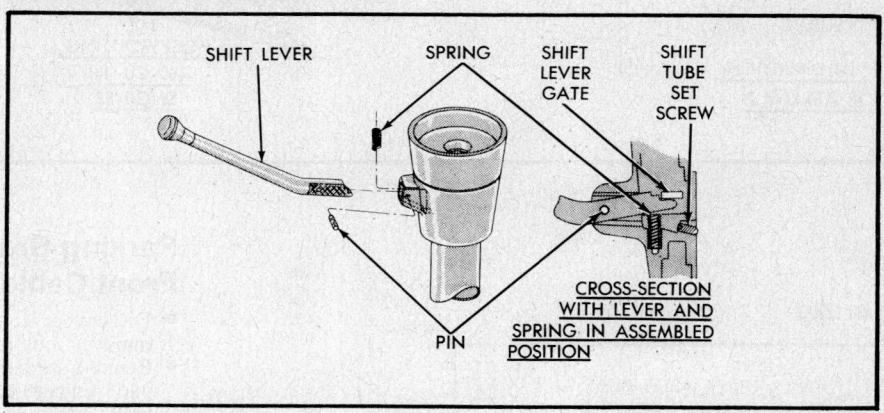

SHIFT LEVER

SPRING

SHIFT LEVER GATE

SHIFT TUBE SET SCREW

PIN

CROSS-SECTION WITH LEVER AND SPRING IN ASSEMBLED POSITION

Lock levers and spring assembly

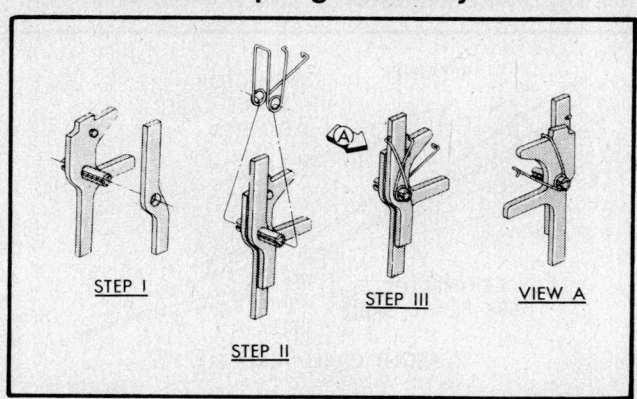

STEP I

STEP II

STEP III

VIEW A

Ground clip and plastic spacer illustration

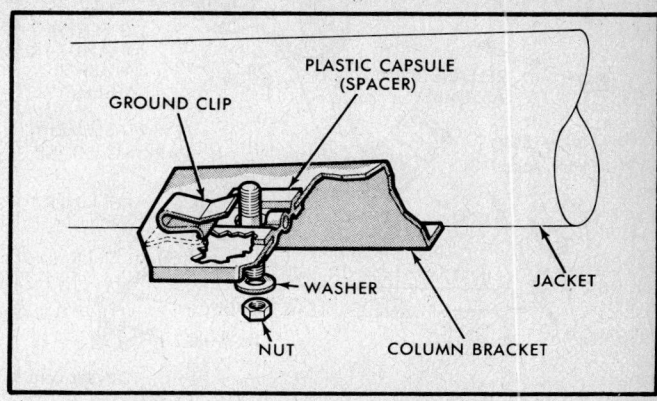

PLASTIC CAPSULE (SPACER)

GROUND CLIP

JACKET

WASHER

NUT

COLUMN BRACKET

CHRYSLER REAR DRIVE CARS

Typical power brake

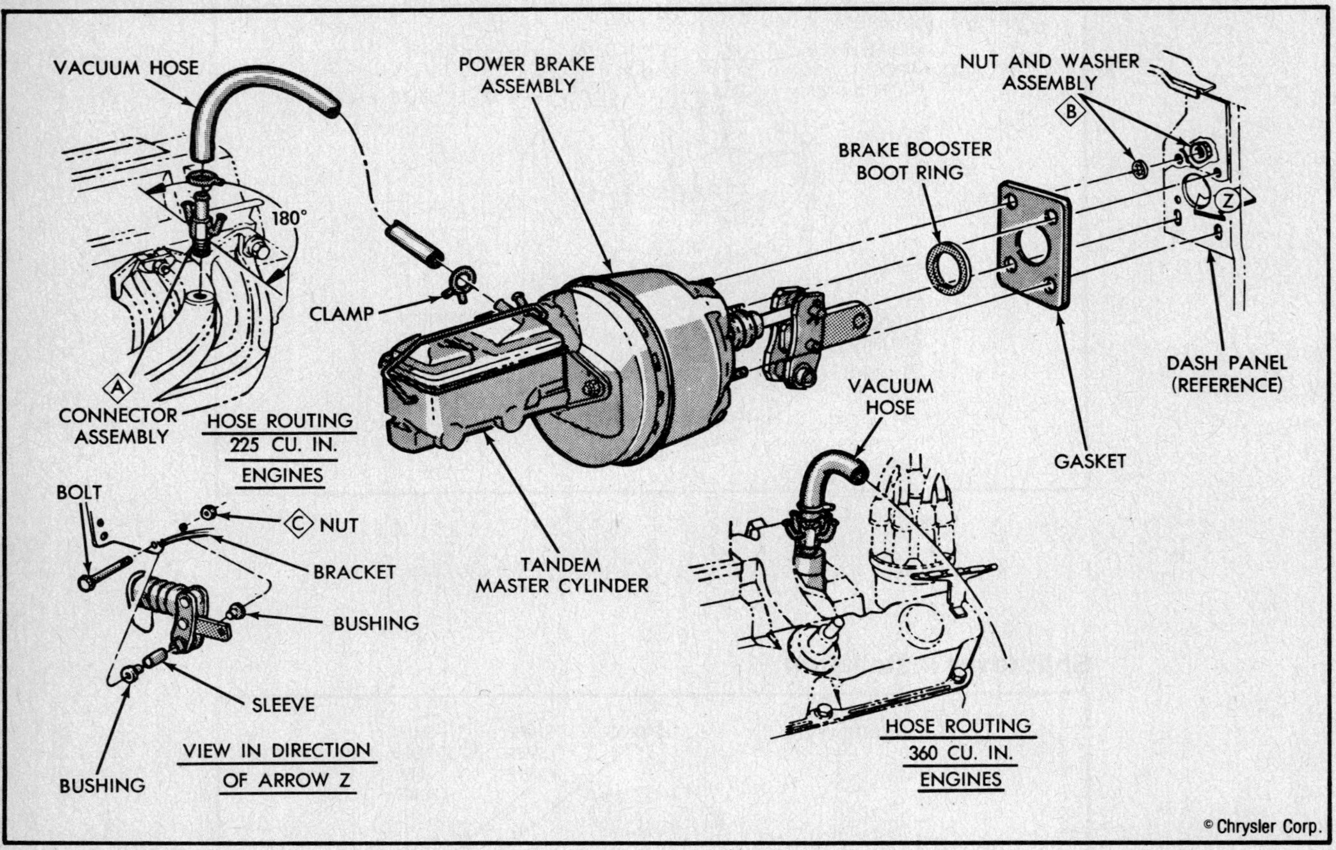

VACUUM HOSE

POWER BRAKE ASSEMBLY

NUT AND WASHER ASSEMBLY
B

BRAKE BOOSTER BOOT RING

180°

CLAMP

DASH PANEL (REFERENCE)

CONNECTOR ASSEMBLY
A

HOSE ROUTING 225 CU. IN. ENGINES

VACUUM HOSE

GASKET

BOLT

C NUT

BRACKET

BUSHING

TANDEM MASTER CYLINDER

SLEEVE

HOSE ROUTING 360 CU. IN. ENGINES

BUSHING

VIEW IN DIRECTION OF ARROW Z

© Chrysler Corp.

Typical parking brake

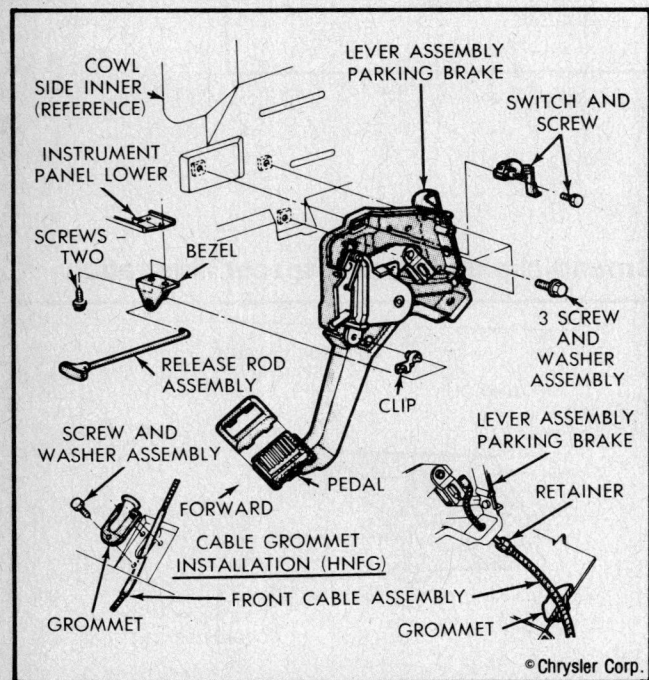

COWL SIDE INNER (REFERENCE)

LEVER ASSEMBLY PARKING BRAKE

SWITCH AND SCREW

INSTRUMENT PANEL LOWER

SCREWS - TWO

BEZEL

3 SCREW AND WASHER ASSEMBLY

CLIP

LEVER ASSEMBLY PARKING BRAKE

SCREW AND WASHER ASSEMBLY

RELEASE ROD ASSEMBLY

FORWARD

PEDAL

RETAINER

CABLE GROMMET INSTALLATION (HNFG)

GROMMET

FRONT CABLE ASSEMBLY

GROMMET

© Chrysler Corp.

Parking Brake Front Cable R&R

- Disconnect cable from equalizer, and remove from guide clips.
- Remove rubber cable cover from floor pan. Engage parking brake, and work brake cable up and out of brake, and work brake cable up and out of brake pedal linkage. Work cable up through floor pan.
- After installation, test operation of vacuum release.

Parking brake adjuster

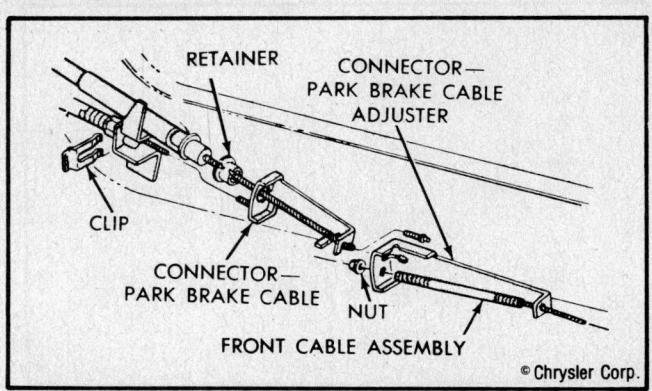

RETAINER

CONNECTOR— PARK BRAKE CABLE ADJUSTER

CLIP

CONNECTOR— PARK BRAKE CABLE

NUT

FRONT CABLE ASSEMBLY

© Chrysler Corp.

Parking Brake Adjustment
- Correctly adjust service brakes.
- Release the parking brake lever.

- Tighten cable adjusting nut until a slight drag is felt while rotating the wheels. Loosen adjusting nut to the point where

both wheels just turn freely, then back off adjusting nut two full turns.

Typical parking brake and cables

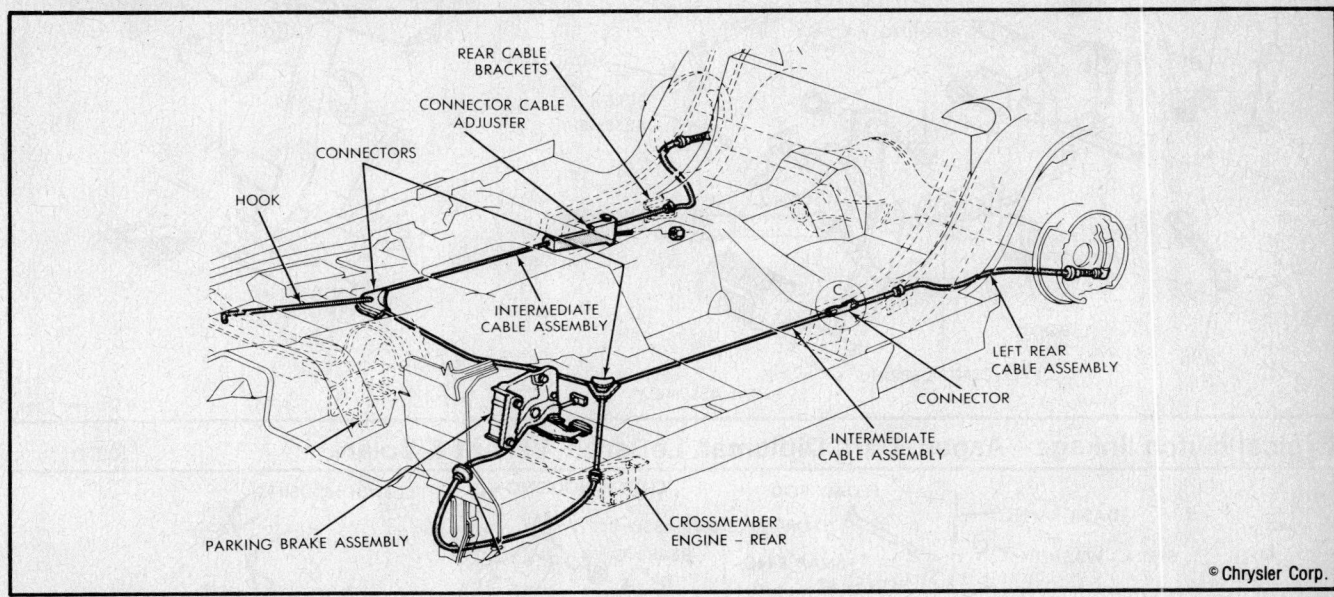

© Chrysler Corp.

CLUTCH, TRANSMISSION, PROPELLER SHAFT & REAR AXLES SECTION

Clutch Adjustment
- Clutch pedal free play is the only adjustment necessary.

- Turn self-locking adjusting nut to obtain $^5/_{32}$ inch free movement at end of fork.

This will provide the correct 1 inch free play at the pedal.

Release fork, bearing and sleeve

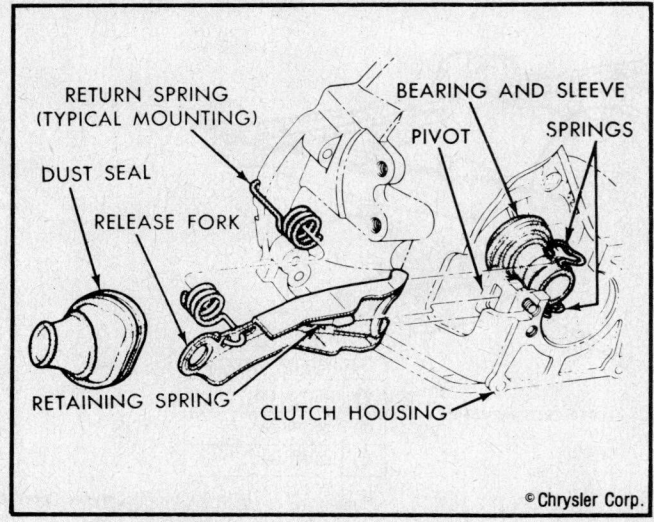

© Chrysler Corp.

Lubrication points

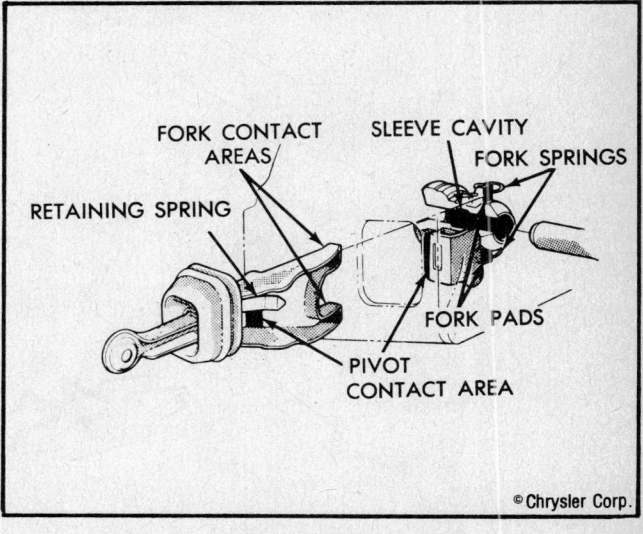

© Chrysler Corp.

CHRYSLER REAR DRIVE CARS

Clutch pedal and attaching linkage—Aspen, Diplomat, LeBaron & Volare

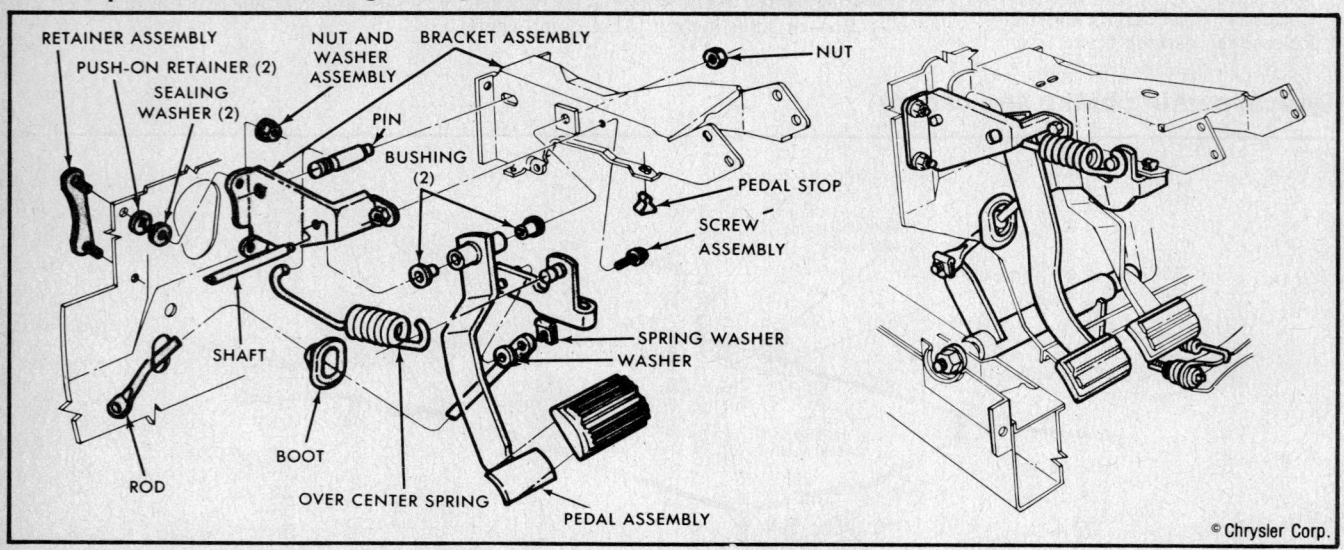

RETAINER ASSEMBLY
PUSH-ON RETAINER (2)
SEALING WASHER (2)
NUT AND WASHER ASSEMBLY
BRACKET ASSEMBLY
NUT
PIN
BUSHING (2)
PEDAL STOP
SCREW ASSEMBLY
SHAFT
SPRING WASHER
WASHER
ROD
BOOT
OVER CENTER SPRING
PEDAL ASSEMBLY

© Chrysler Corp.

Typical clutch linkage—Aspen, Dart, Diplomat, LeBaron, Valiant & Volare

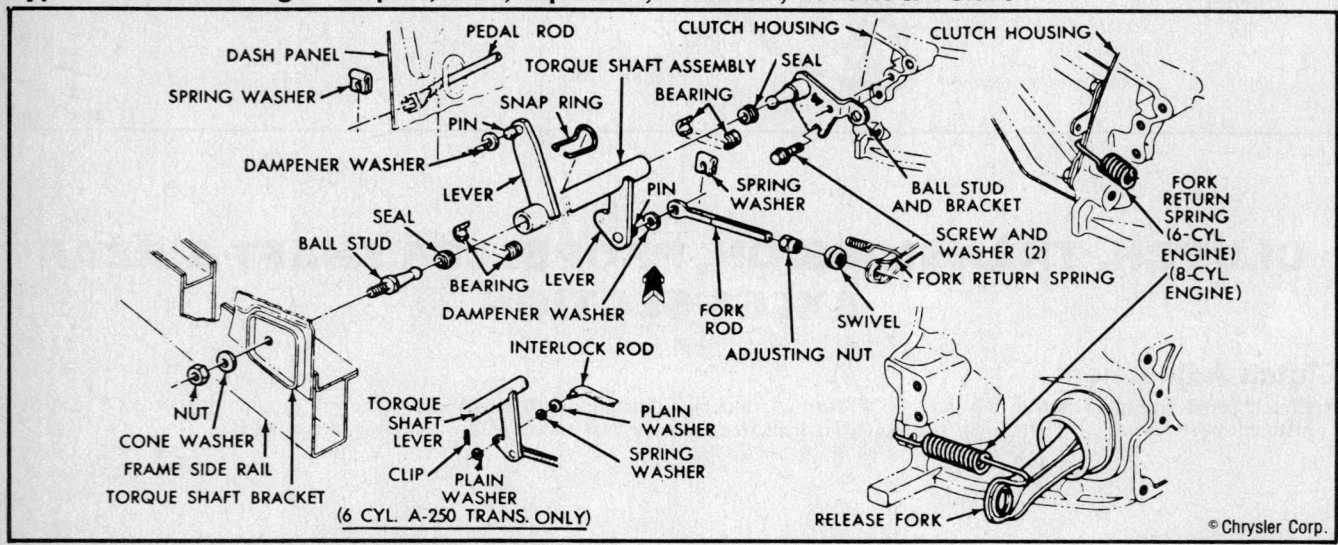

DASH PANEL
PEDAL ROD
CLUTCH HOUSING
CLUTCH HOUSING
SPRING WASHER
TORQUE SHAFT ASSEMBLY
SEAL
SNAP RING
BEARING
PIN
DAMPENER WASHER
LEVER
PIN
SPRING WASHER
SEAL
BALL STUD AND BRACKET
BALL STUD
BEARING
LEVER
SCREW AND WASHER (2)
FORK RETURN SPRING (6-CYL ENGINE) (8-CYL ENGINE)
DAMPENER WASHER
FORK ROD
SWIVEL
FORK RETURN SPRING
INTERLOCK ROD
ADJUSTING NUT
NUT
CONE WASHER
FRAME SIDE RAIL
TORQUE SHAFT BRACKET
TORQUE SHAFT LEVER
CLIP
PLAIN WASHER
PLAIN WASHER
SPRING WASHER
(6 CYL. A-250 TRANS. ONLY)
RELEASE FORK

© Chrysler Corp.

Crossmember and rear engine mount

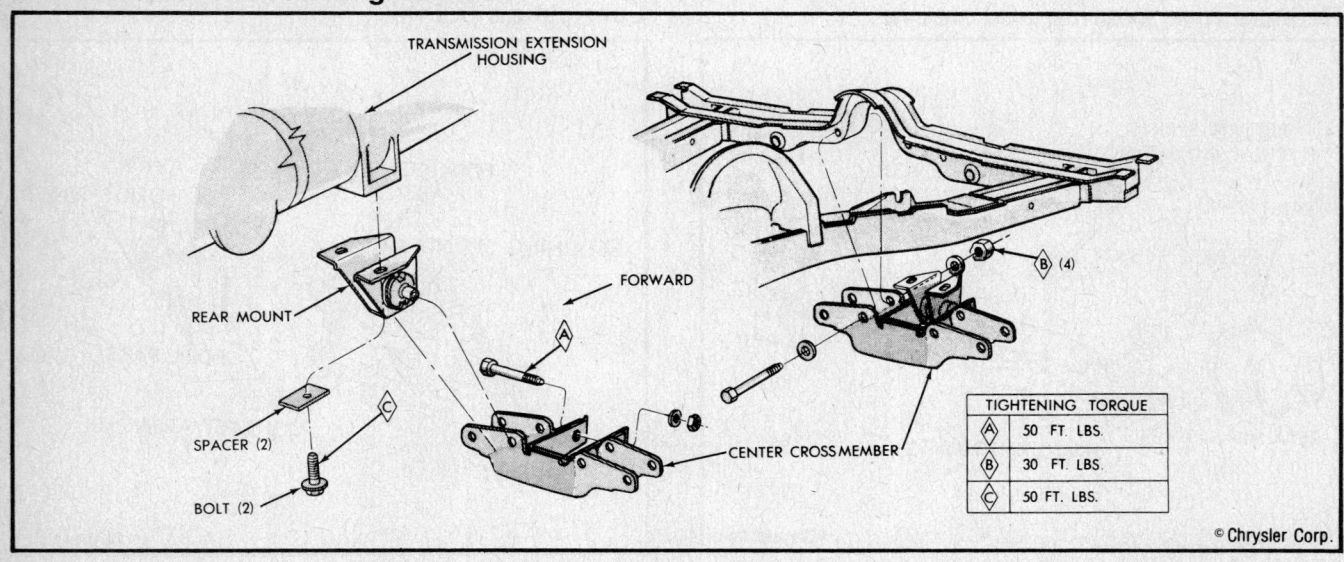

TRANSMISSION EXTENSION HOUSING
FORWARD
(B) (4)
REAR MOUNT
SPACER (2)
BOLT (2)
CENTER CROSSMEMBER

TIGHTENING TORQUE	
A	50 FT. LBS.
B	30 FT. LBS.
C	50 FT. LBS.

© Chrysler Corp.

Clutch torque shaft and linkage

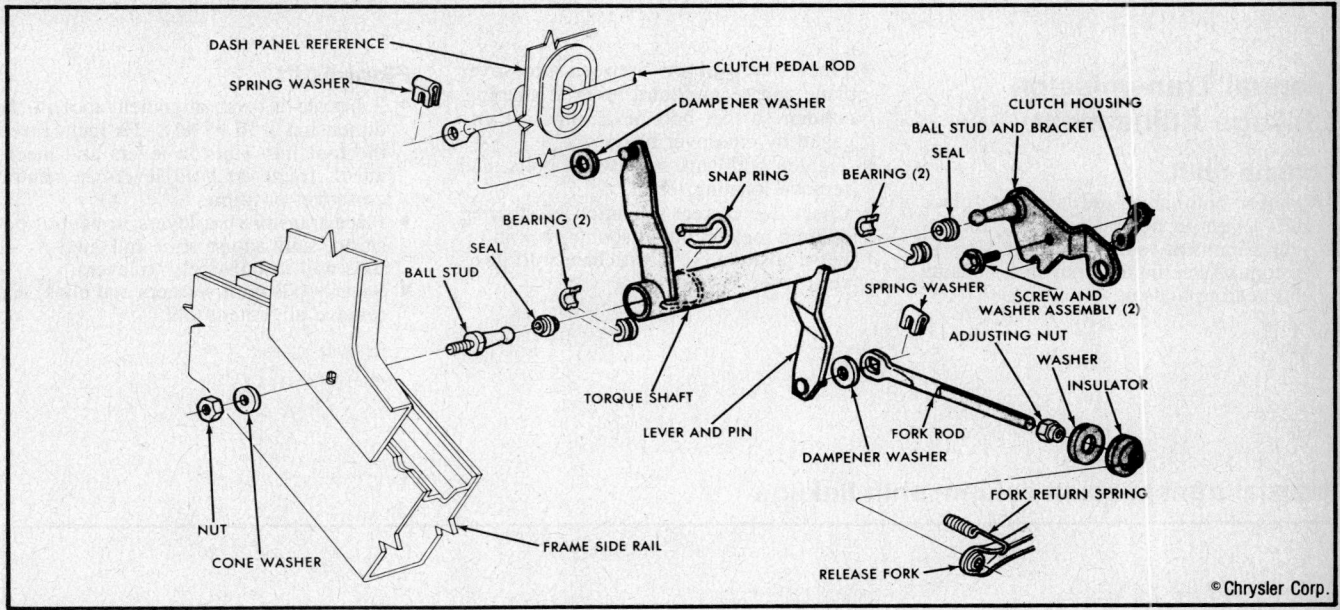

© Chrysler Corp.

Manual Transmission R&R

- Drain fluid, remove drive shaft, and disconnect electrical and mechanical connections and shift linkages. On four speed models, remove console and shifter.
- Remove or disconnect any part of exhaust system necessary for clearance.
- After raising the engine and supporting the transmission, remove the center crossmember.
- Remove the transmission-to-clutch housing bolts, and slide transmission toward rear until drive pinion shaft clears clutch disc.

Automatic Transmission R&R

- Transmission converter must be removed as an assembly. Do not permit transmission to rest on drive plate at any time.
- Disconnect battery, remove any exhaust system parts necessary for clearance, remove starter and engine-to-transmission struts, drain transmission and converter, and disconnect cooler lines at transmission.
- Mark converter and drive plate to aid in reassembly. Rotate engine clockwise with socket wrench on vibration damper bolt to position the bolts attaching torque converter to drive plate, and remove them.

- Remove drive shaft and disconnect all electrical and mechanical connections. Disconnect gearshift rod and torque shaft assembly, and throttle linkage from transmission.
- After raising engine and supporting transmission, remove crossmember.
- Remove bell housing bolts, and work transmission and converter assembly rearward off engine block dowels. Disengage converter hub from end of crankshaft.
- Some models have a torsion bar anchor crossmember, which remains in place, and requires a careful downward tilt of the front of the transmission as it is being removed. If these models have a vibration dampening device bolted to rear of extension housing, it must be removed for clearance.

Manual transmission & support

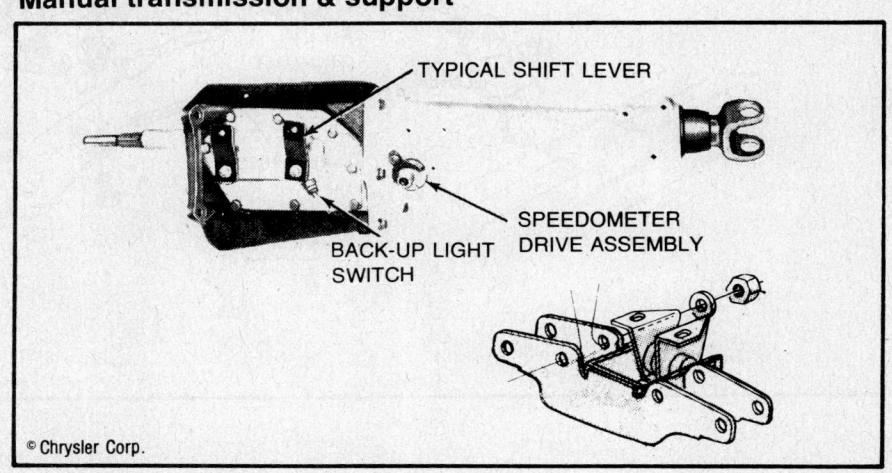

© Chrysler Corp.

Manual Transmission Linkage Adjustment

Column Shift

- Loosen both shift rod swivels, place shift levers in neutral position, and install alignment tool in locating slots in bottom of steering column shift housing and bearing housing.

- Place screwdriver between crossover blade and second/third lever at steering column so that both lever pins are engaged by crossover blade.
- Tighten both shift rod swivel bolts, and remove locating tools.
- Check for correct operation of steering column lock. Ignition should lock in reverse position only, with hands off gearshift lever.

Floor Shift

- Fabricate a lever alignment tool in the dimension 1/16 × ⅝ × 2⅜ inch. Insert the tool into slots in levers and mechanism frame to hold levers in neutral crossover position.
- Place transmission levers in neutral position, and adjust shift rod swivels so rods will install freely to levers.
- Secure rods with washers and clips, and remove alignment tool.

Manual transmission column shift linkage

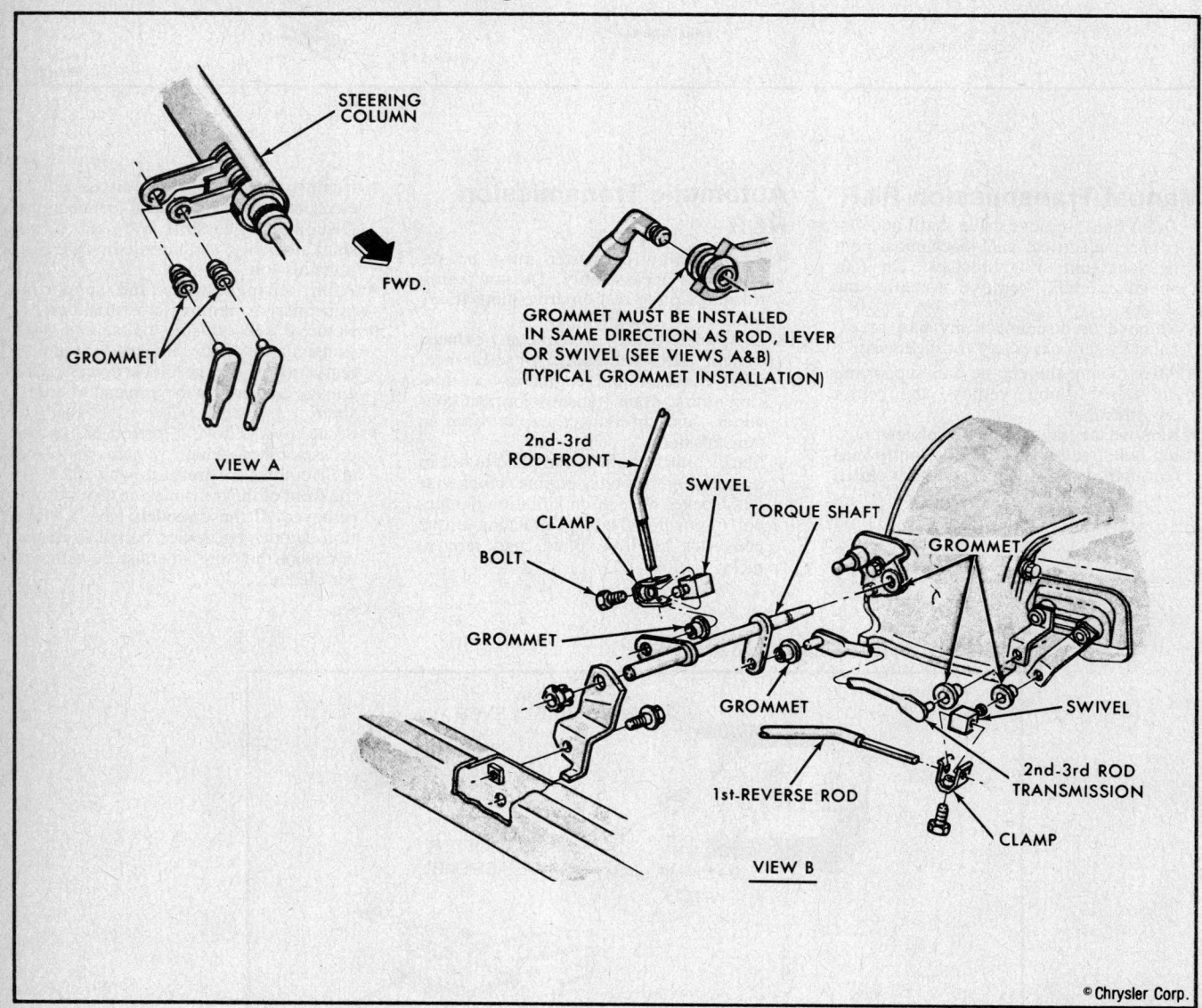

Three speed manual transmission floorshift linkage and adjustment tool

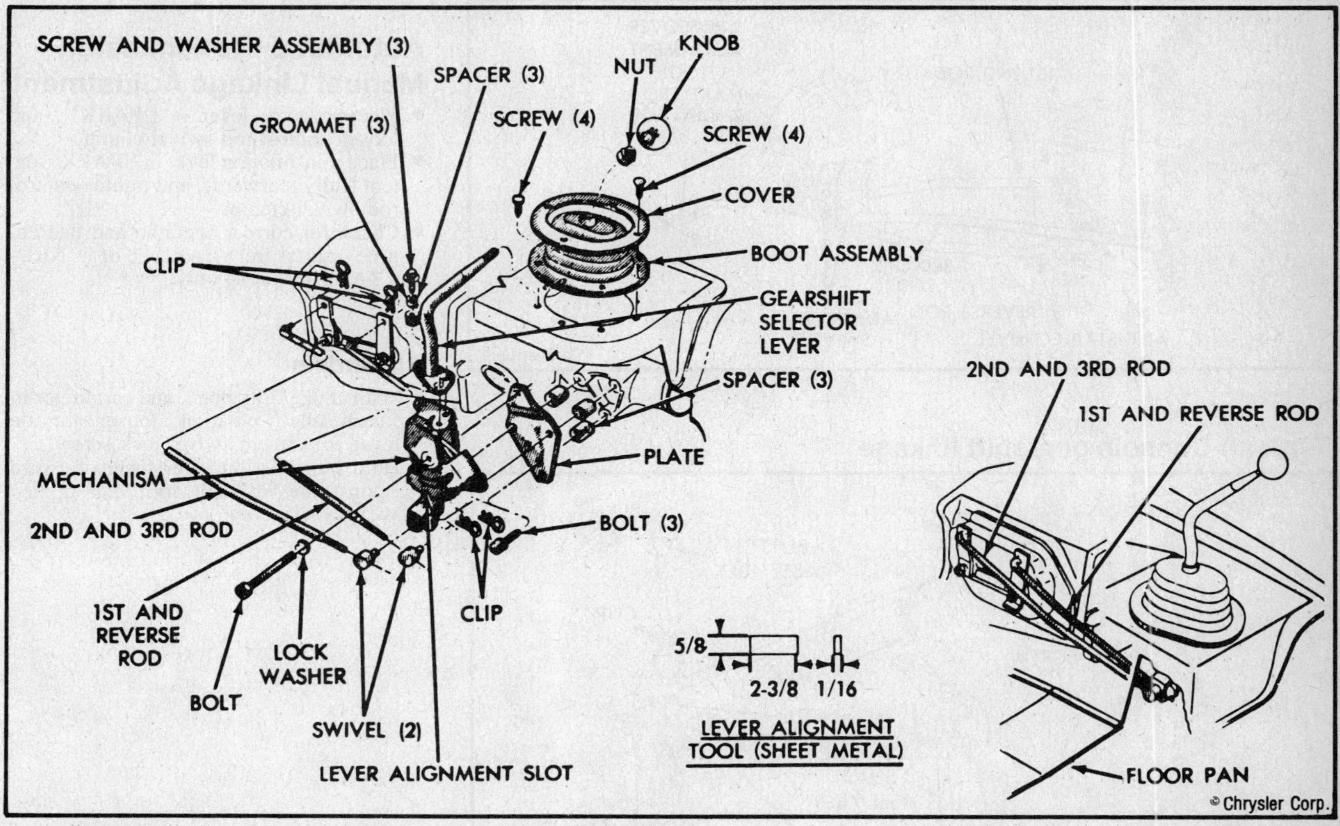

SCREW AND WASHER ASSEMBLY (3)

SPACER (3)

GROMMET (3)

SCREW (4)

NUT

KNOB

SCREW (4)

COVER

BOOT ASSEMBLY

CLIP

GEARSHIFT
SELECTOR
LEVER

SPACER (3)

2ND AND 3RD ROD

1ST AND REVERSE ROD

PLATE

MECHANISM

2ND AND 3RD ROD

BOLT (3)

1ST AND
REVERSE
ROD

LOCK
WASHER

CLIP

BOLT

SWIVEL (2)

LEVER ALIGNMENT SLOT

5/8

2-3/8   1/16

LEVER ALIGNMENT
TOOL (SHEET METAL)

FLOOR PAN

© Chrysler Corp.

Four speed manual transmission linkage

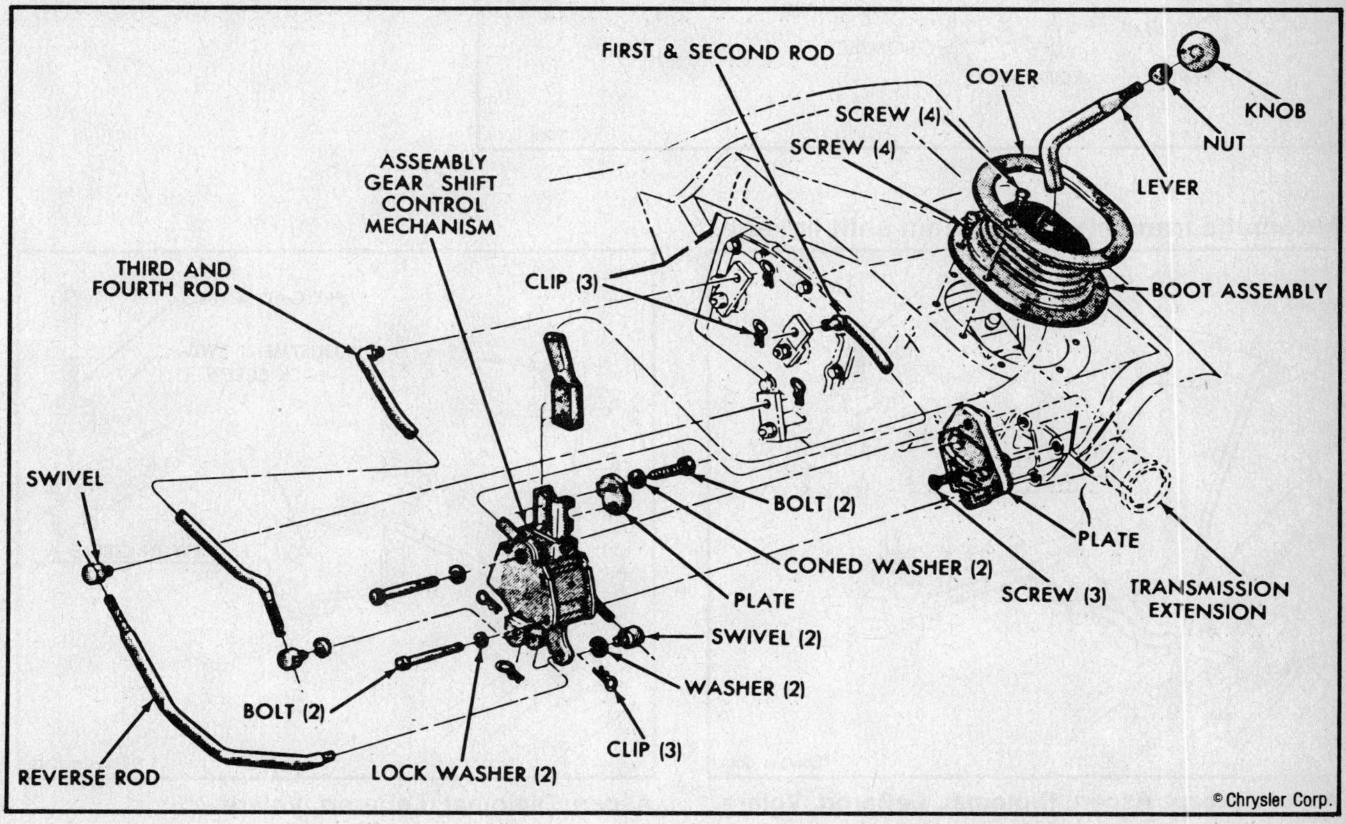

FIRST & SECOND ROD

COVER

ASSEMBLY
GEAR SHIFT
CONTROL
MECHANISM

SCREW (4)

SCREW (4)

KNOB

NUT

LEVER

THIRD AND
FOURTH ROD

CLIP (3)

BOOT ASSEMBLY

SWIVEL

BOLT (2)

CONED WASHER (2)

PLATE

PLATE

SWIVEL (2)

SCREW (3)

TRANSMISSION
EXTENSION

BOLT (2)

WASHER (2)

REVERSE ROD

LOCK WASHER (2)

CLIP (3)

© Chrysler Corp.

Floorshift linkage adjustment—four speed manual transmission

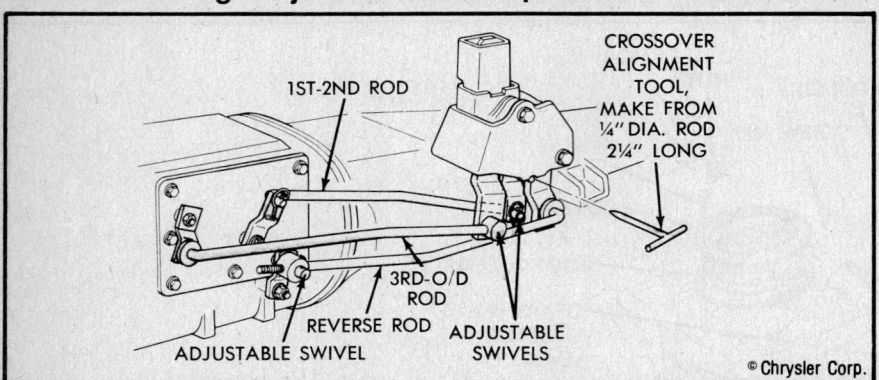

© Chrysler Corp.

Automatic Transmission Manual Linkage Adjustment

- Place selector lever in "PARK", and loosen control rod swivel clamp.
- Place transmission lever in "PARK" detent (fully rearward), and tighten control rod swivel clamp.
- Check for correct operaton and that engine starts in "PARK" or "NEUTRAL" positions only.

All Models

- With choke fully open, and carburetor in "curb idle" position, loosen throttle lever adjustment swivel lock screw.
- Hold transmission lever firmly forward against the internal stop, and tighten swivel lock screw.

(Typical) Console gearshift linkage

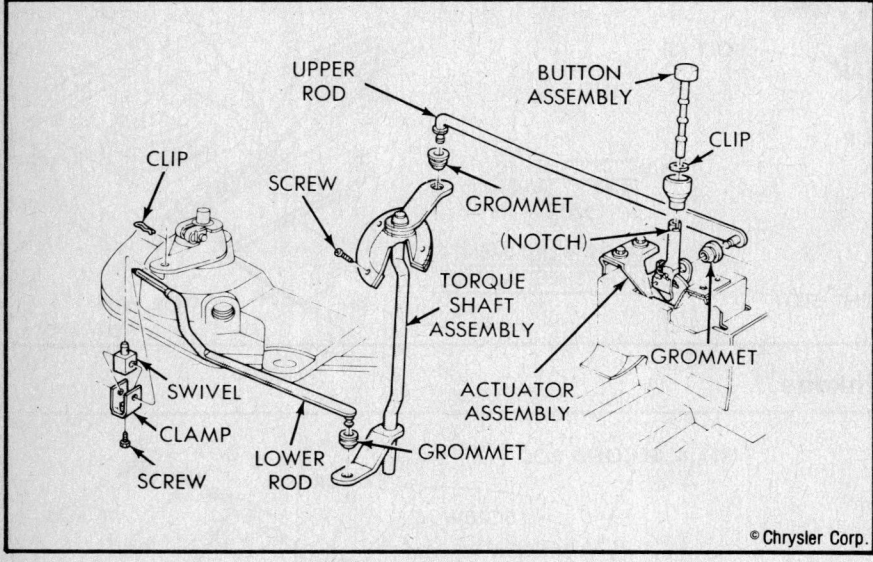

© Chrysler Corp.

Automatic transmission column shift linkage

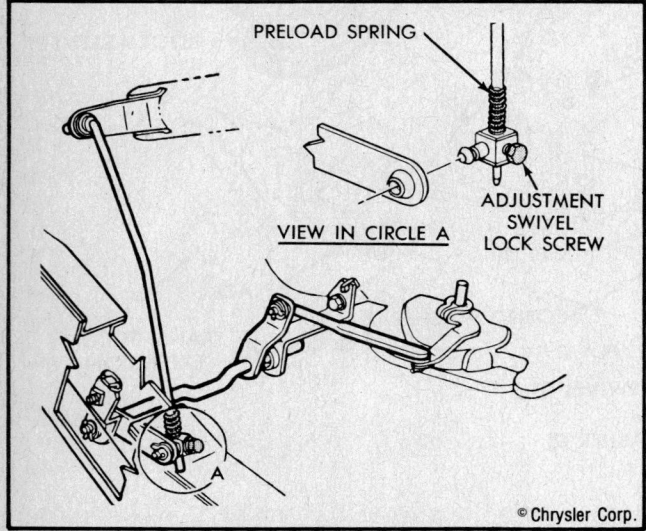

© Chrysler Corp.

Models except Aspen, Diplomat, LeBaron, Volare

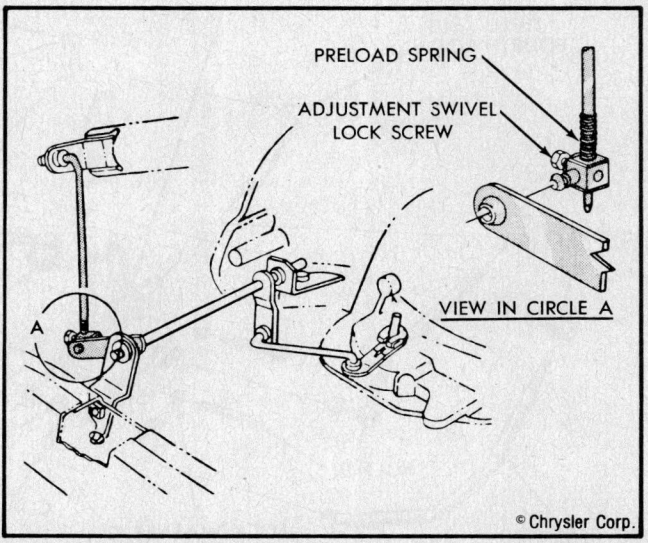

© Chrysler Corp.

Aspen, Diplomat, LeBaron, Volare

Throttle rod adjustment— eight cylinder engine

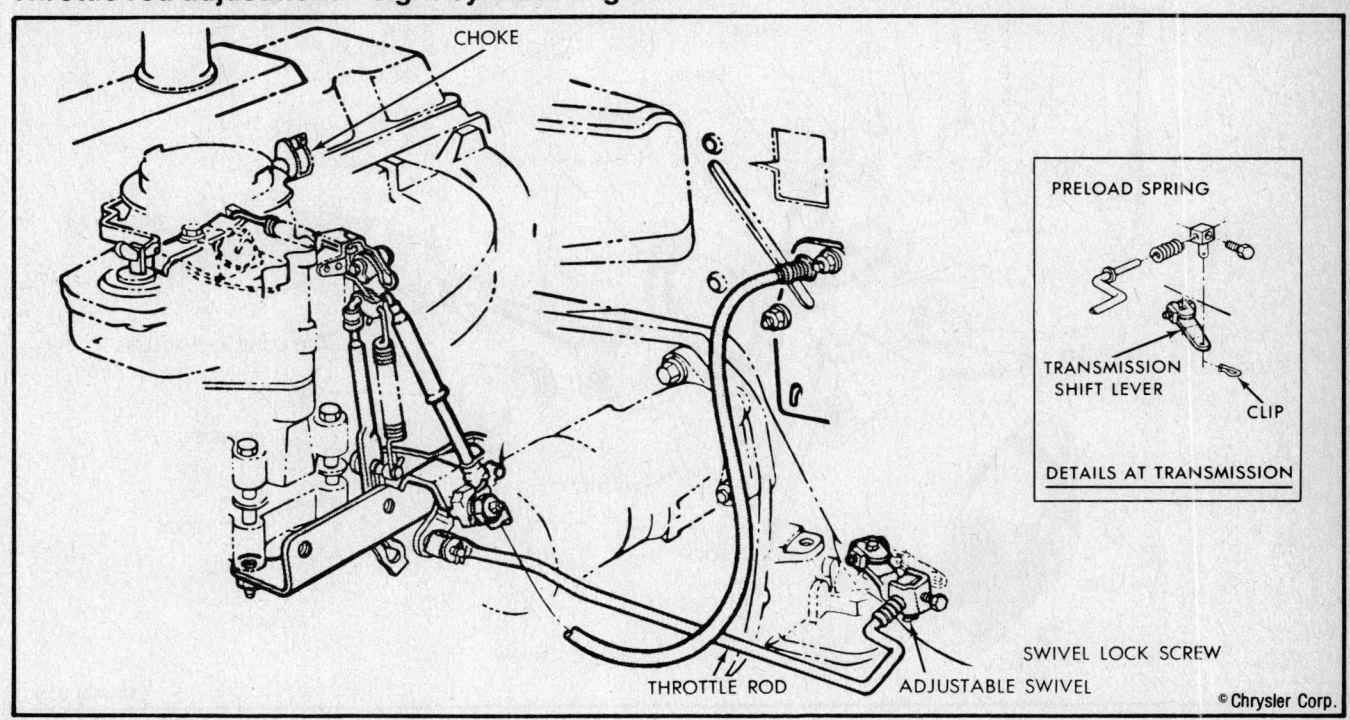

CHOKE

PRELOAD
SPRING

TRANSMISSION
SHIFT LEVER

CLIP

DETAILS AT TRANSMISSION

SWIVEL
LOCK SCREW

ADJUSTABLE SWIVEL

THROTTLE ROD

© Chrysler Corp.

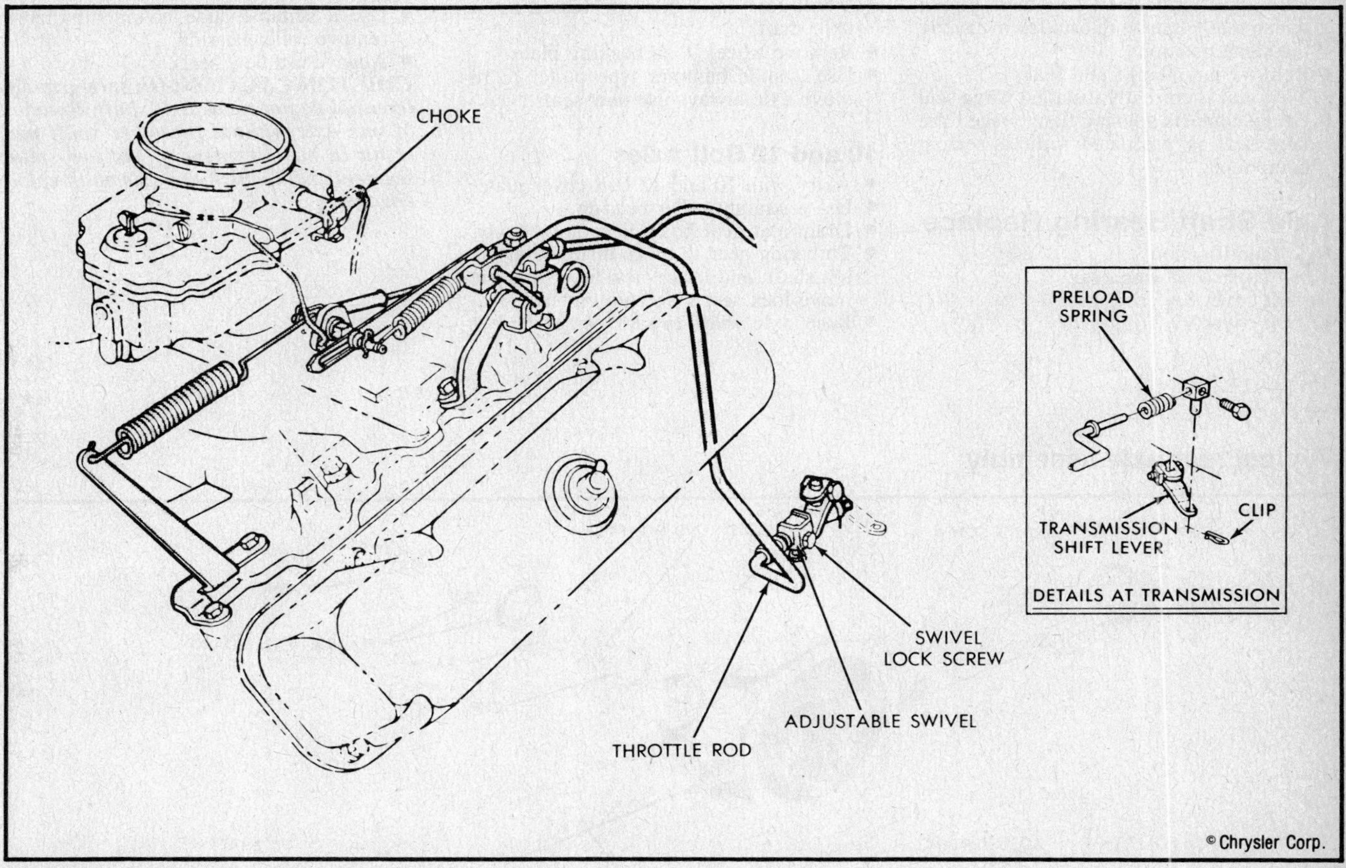

Rod type

Throttle rod adjustment—eight cylinder engine

CHOKE

PRELOAD SPRING

TRANSMISSION
SHIFT LEVER

CLIP

DETAILS AT TRANSMISSION

SWIVEL LOCK SCREW

THROTTLE ROD   ADJUSTABLE SWIVEL

© Chrysler Corp.

Cable type

CHRYSLER REAR DRIVE CARS

Pinion Oil Seal

- Disconnect drive shaft, and mark pinion nut so that it can be reinstalled in *exactly* the same position.
- Remove nut, flange and seal.
- New seal is correctly installed when seal flange contacts housing flange face. The new seal is precoated with a sealing compound.

Axle Shaft/Bearing Replace

Axle Identification
9 bolt cover 7¼″ ring gear
10 bolt cover 8¼″ ring gear
12 bolt cover 9¼″ ring gear

9 Bolt Axle

- 9 bolt uses a ball bearing pressed on the axle shaft.
- Remove wheel, then backing plate.
- Use a slide hammer type puller to remove axle always use new seals.

10 and 12 Bolt Axles

- Axles with 10 and 12 bolt cover plate.
- Use a straight roller bearing.
- Drain rear gear box and remove cover.
- Turn ring gear to make differential pinion shaft, and lock screw accessible, remove lock screw and pinion shaft.
- Push axle shaft toward center and re-

move the "C" washer from axle.
- Remove the axle.
- Use a suitable slide hammer puller to remove roller bearing.
- Always use new seals.

CHILTON CAUTION: *On sure grip differential do not rotate axle shaft. Rotation of one axle without the other shaft may result in misalignment of the tow spline segments with which the axle shaft spline engages.*

Typical rear axle assembly

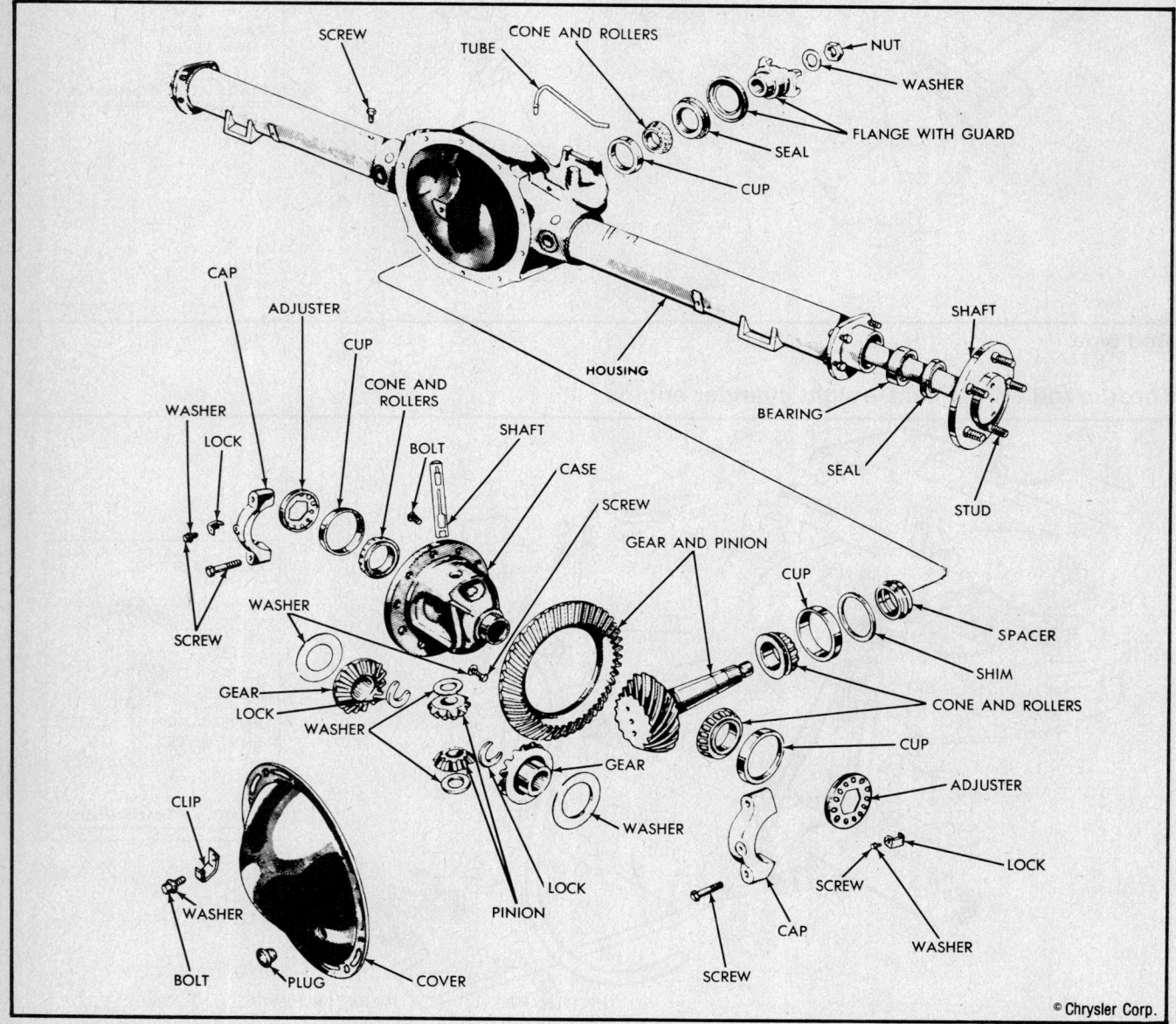

© Chrysler Corp.

Not used 9 bolt axle

INDEX

MODEL IDENTIFICATION

1981-82 LYNX
W.B. **94.2"**. Length 163.9". 4 Cyl. 3 Dr. Hatchback. Curb Wgt. 2005 Lbs.

1981-82 ESCORT
W.B. **94.2"**. Length 163.9". 4 Cyl. 3 Dr. Hatchback. Curb Wgt. 2005 Lbs.

1982 FORD EXP
W.B. **94.2"**. Length 163.9". 4 Cyl. Hatchback. Curb Wgt. 1955 Lbs.

1982 MERCURY LN7
W.B. **94.2"**. Length 163.9". 4 Cyl. Hatchback. Curb Wgt. 1955 Lbs.

ENGINE SPECIFICATIONS

Engine Code, 8th character of the VIN number

Year	Eng. V.I.N. Code	Engine No. Cyl. Disp.	Carb Type	Horsepower② @ rpm	Torque② @ rpm (ft lbs)	Bore and Stroke (in)	Valves Intake Opens (deg. BTDC)	Fuel Pump Pres. (psi)	Comp. Ratio	Oil Pressure @ 2000 rpm
'81	1	1.3L–79"	2V	58 @ 5700	63 @ 3600	3.15 × 2.4	24	5.5	8.8:1	40
'81	2	1.6L–98"	2V	69 @ 5000	86 @ 3200	3.15 × 3.13	22	5.5	8.8:1	40
'82	1	1.3L–79"	2V	58 @ 5700	63 @ 3600	3.15 × 2.4	24	5.5	8.8:1	40
'82	2	1.6L–98"	2V	69 @ 5000	86 @ 3200	3.15 × 3.13	22	5.5	8.8:1	40

TUNE-UP SPECIFICATIONS

Engine Code, 8th character of the VIN number

Year	Eng. V.I.N. Code	No. Cyl. Disp.	Spark Plugs Orig. Type	Gap (in)	Timing Man. Trans.	Timing Auto. Trans.	Idle Speed Manual	Idle Speed Auto Cal.	Idle Speed Auto Fed.
'81	1	1.3L–79"	AGSP32	.044	10°②	10°②	700	750①	750①
'81	2	1.6L–98"	AGSP32	.044	10°② (6°)	10°②	900	750①	750①
'82	1	1.3L–79"	AGSP32	.044	10°②	10°②	700	750①	750①
'82	2	1.6L–98"	AGSP32	.044	10°② (6°)	10°②	900	750①	750①

① With cooling fan on
② + or − 2°
( ) Calif. engines

VEHICLE IDENTIFICATION NUMBER (VIN)

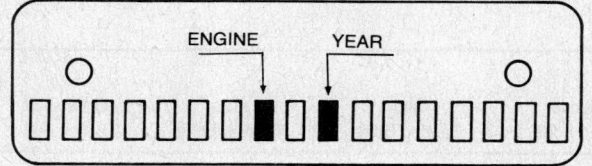

ENGINE FIRING ORDER

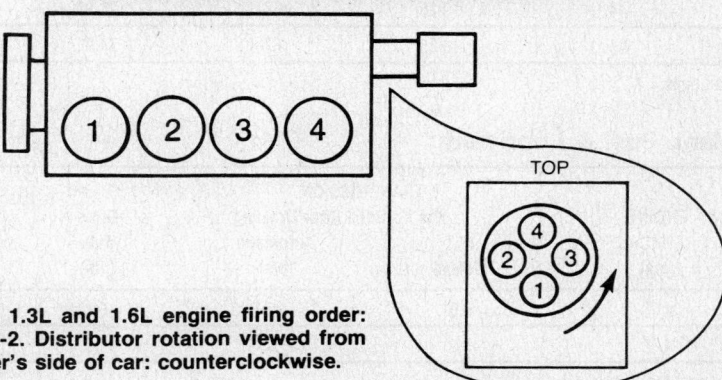

Ford 1.3L and 1.6L engine firing order: 1-3-4-2. Distributor rotation viewed from driver's side of car: counterclockwise.

VALVE SPECIFICATIONS

Year	Engine No. Cyl. Disp.	Eng. V.I.N Code	Seat Angle (deg)	Face Angle (deg)	Spring Test Pressure (lbs @ in)	Spring Installed Height	STEM TO GUIDE CLEARANCE (in) Intake	Exhaust	STEM DIAMETER (in) Intake	Exhaust
'81	4-1.3L–79″	1	45°	45°	180 @ 1.090″	1.417–1.504″	.0008-.0027	.0018-.0037	3160	3160
'81	4-1.6L–98″	2	45°	45°	180 @ 1.090″	1.417–1.504″	.0008-.0027	.0018-.0037	3160	3160
'82	4-1.3L–79″	1	45°	45°	180 @ 1.090″	1.417–1.504″	.0005-.0027	.0018-.0037	3160	3160
'82	4-1.6L–98″	2	45°	45°	180 @ 1.090″	1.417–1.504″	.0008-.0027	.0018-.0037	3160	3160

CRANKSHAFT & CONNECTING ROD SPECIFICATIONS

All measurements given in inches

Engine No. Cyl. Disp.	Year	Eng. V.I.N. Code	CRANKSHAFT Main Brg. Journal Dia.	Main Brg. Oil Clearance	Shaft End-Play	Thrust on No.	CONNECTING ROD Journal Diameter	Oil Clearance	Side Clearance
4-1.3L–79″	'81	1	2.286-2.2834	.057-.011	.004-.008	5	1.885-1.886	.064-.006	.004-.011
4-1.6L–98″	'81	2	2.286-2.2834	.057-.011	.004-.008	5	1.885-1.886	.064-.006	.004-.011
4-1.3L–79″	'82	1	2.2826-2.2834	.057-.011	.004-.008	5	1.885-1.886	.064-.006	.004-.011
4-1.6L–98″	'82	2	2.2826-2.2834	.057-.011	.004-.008	5	1.885-1.886	.064-.006	.004.011

BRAKE SPECIFICATIONS

Year	Model	Master Cylinder Bore Diameter	CALIPER/ WHEEL CYLINDER Front	Rear	BRAKE DRUM/ROTOR DIAMETER Front	Rear
'81	ESCORT & LYNX	.827②	2.125	.810	9.29″	7.1″①
'82	ESCORT & LYNX	.827②	2.125	.810	9.29″	7.1″①

① Liftgate model 8.0 in.
② With power brakes 1.35 in.

FORD—MERCURY FRONT DRIVE CARS

TORQUE SPECIFICATIONS

All readings in ft/lbs

Engine No. Cyl. Displacement	Year	Eng. V.I.N. Code	Cylinder Head Bolts	Rod Bearing Bolts	Main Bearing Bolts	Crankshaft Pulley Bolt	Flywheel To Crankshaft Bolts	MANIFOLD Intake	MANIFOLD Exhaust
1.3L-79"	'81	1	44①	19-25	67-80	74-90	59-69	12-15	15-20
1.6L-98"	'81	2	44①	19-25	67-80	74-90	59-69	12-15	15-20
1.3L-79"	'82	1	44①	19-25	67-80	74-90	59-69	12-15	15-20
1.6L-98"	'82	2	44①	19-25	67-80	74-90	59-69	12-15	15-20

① See special method for tightening head bolts.

FLUID CAPACITIES—Coolant, Fuel & Lubricant

Year	Engine No. Cyl. Disp.	ENGINE CRANKCASE (qts)	TRANSMISSION Pts To Refill After Draining Manual	Automatic (pts)	Drive Axle (pts)	Gasoline Tank (gals)	Cooling System (qts)
'81	1.3L-79"	4.②	5.0	20	①	10.0	8
'81	1.6L-98"	4.②	5.0	20	①	10.0	8
'82	1.3L-79"	4.②	5.0	20	①	10.0	8
'82	1.6L-98"	4.②	5.0	20	①	10.0	8

① Included in transmission capacity
② Includes filter

Dash panel-To-Engine Wiring Harness

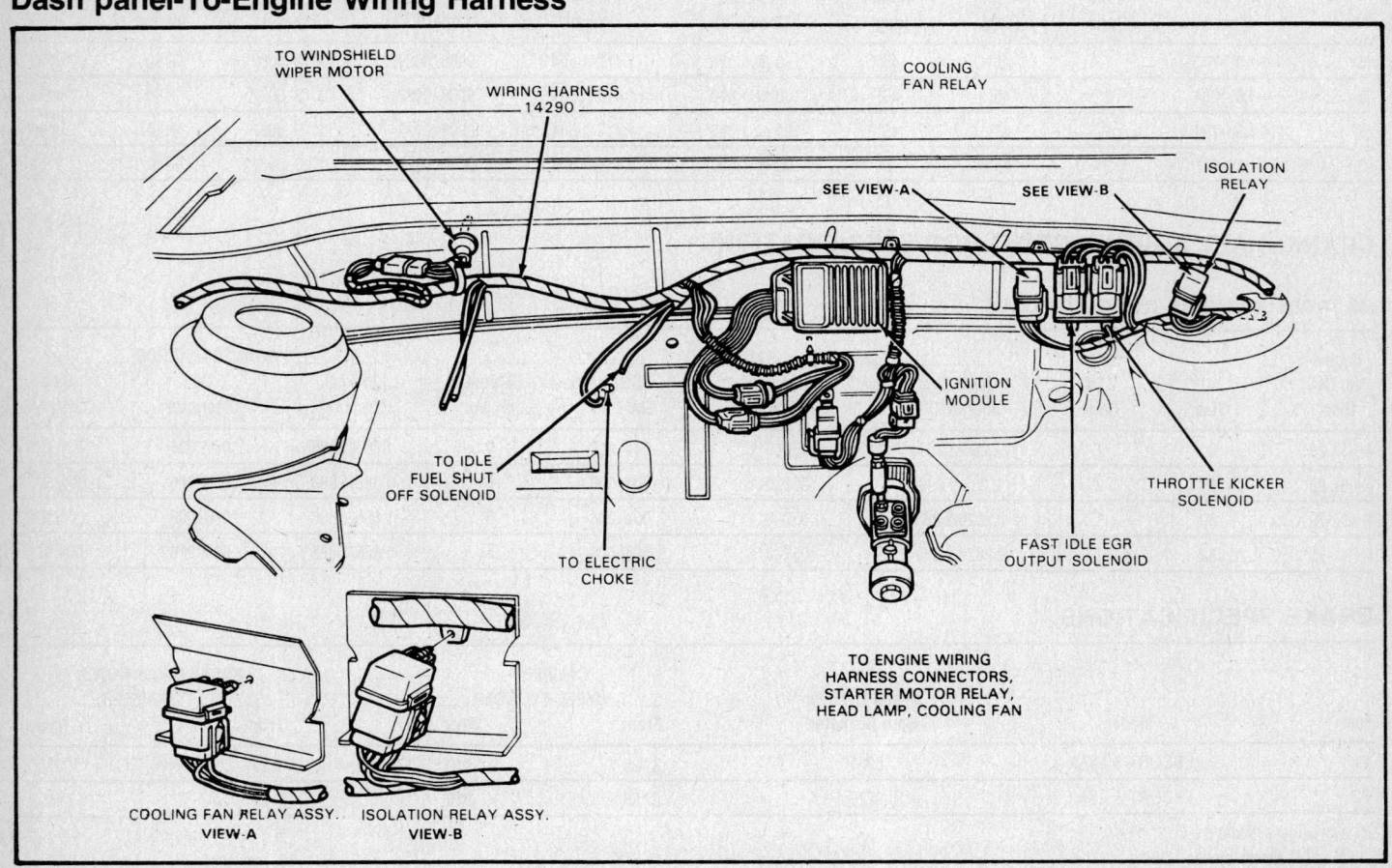

FORD—MERCURY FRONT DRIVE CARS

ELECTRICAL SECTION

Fuses and Circuit Breakers

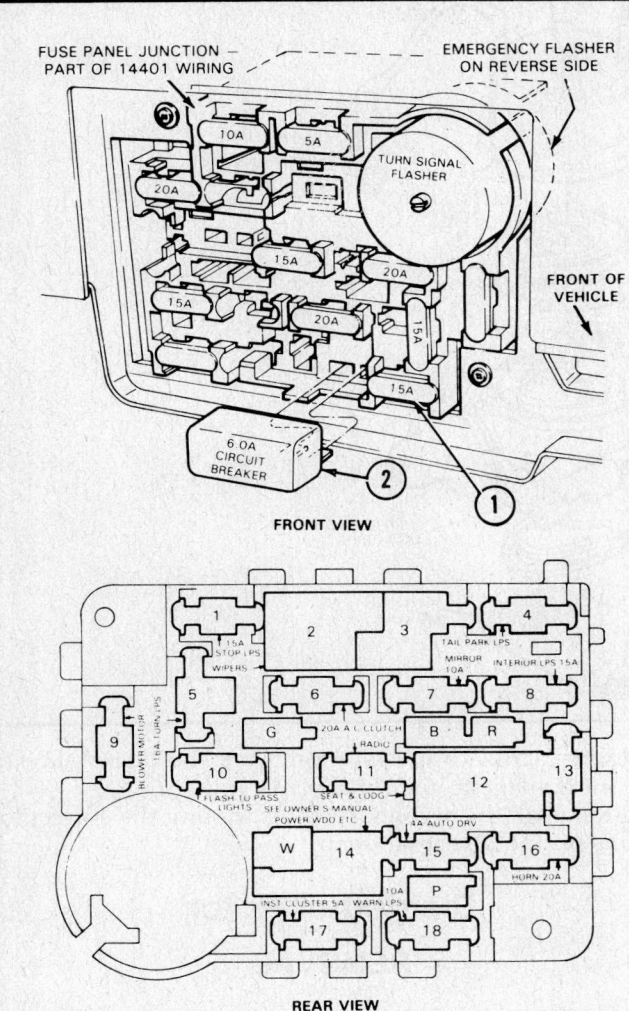

FUSE PANEL JUNCTION — PART OF 14401 WIRING

EMERGENCY FLASHER ON REVERSE SIDE

TURN SIGNAL FLASHER

FRONT OF VEHICLE

6.0A CIRCUIT BREAKER

FRONT VIEW

REAR VIEW

FUSE/CIRCUIT BREAKER USAGE

1. Stop Lamps, Hazard Warning Lamps 15 Amp Fuse
2. Windshield Wiper, Windshield Washer Pump, Interval Wiper 6 Amp Circuit Breaker
3. Not Used
4. Taillamps, Parking Lamps, Side Marker Lamps, Cluster Illumination Lamp, License Lamp. 15 Amp Fuse
5. Turn Signal Lamps, Back-up Lamps 15 Amp Fuse
6. Air Conditioner Clutch. Heated Backlite Relay, Liftgate Release, Speed Control Module, Rear Wiper/Washer, Electronic Digital Clock Display, Graphics Display Module, Air Conditioner Throttle Positioner. 20 Amp Fuse
7. Not used
8. Courtesy Lamps, Key Warning Buzzer 15 Amp Fuse

9. Air Conditioner Blower Motor 30 Amp Fuse

   Heater Blower Motor 15 Amp Fuse
10. Flash-to-pass 20 Amp Fuse
11. Radio, Tape Player, Premium Sound with one Amplifier. 15 Amp Fuse
12. Not Used
13. Not Used
14. Not Used
15. Not Used
16. Horn, Front Cigar Lighter 20 Amp Fuse
17. Instrument Cluster Illumination Lamps, Radio, Climate Control 5 Amp Fuse
18. Warning Indicator Lamps, Low Fuel Module, Auto Lamp System, Dual Timer Buzzer, Tachometer.

Starter

Torque studs or bolts to 41-51 N·M (30-40 lb-ft).

Starter

REMOVAL

1. Disconnect the negative battery cable.
2. Raise the vehicle on a hoist.
3. Disconnect the starter cable at the starter terminal. On vehicles equipped with manual transmissions, remove the three nuts that attach the roll restricter brace to the starter studs at the transmission and remove the brace.
4. Remove the two bolts attaching the starter rear support bracket. Remove the retaining nut from the rear of starter stud thru bolt and remove the bracket.
5. On vehicles equipped with manual transmission, remove the three starter mounting studs and remove the starter assembly. On vehicles equipped with automatic transmissions, remove three starter mounting bolts and remove the starter.

INSTALLATION

1. Position starter to transmission housing and install the three attaching studs or bolts.

Starting Circuit

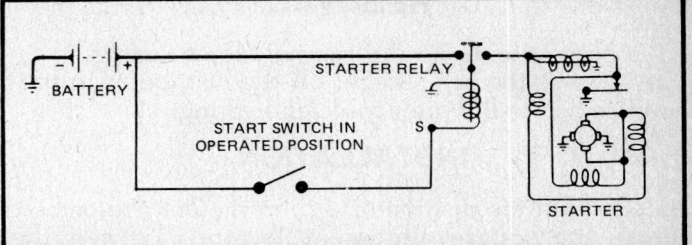

BATTERY

STARTER RELAY

START SWITCH IN OPERATED POSITION

STARTER

Ingition System

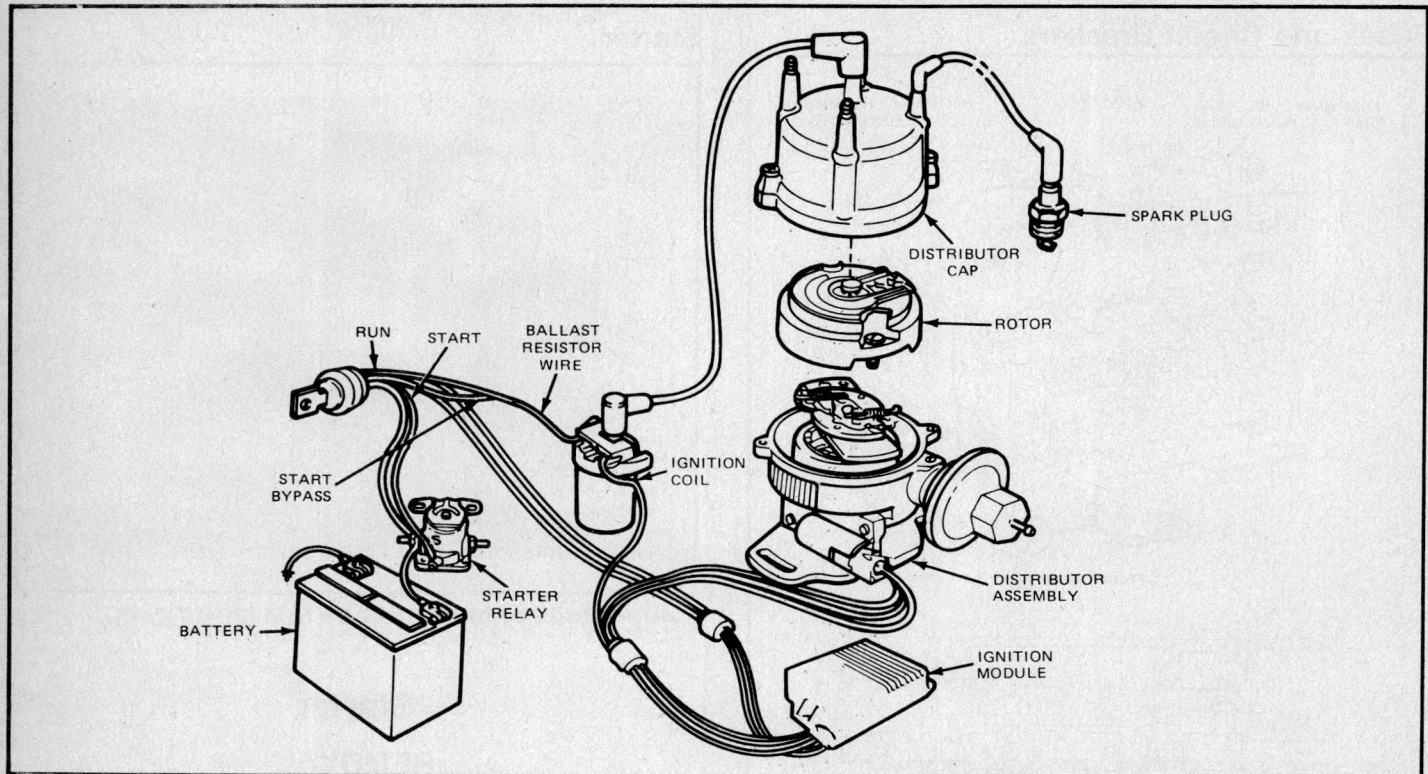

2. On manual transmissions, install the roll restricter brace on the starter mounting studs at the transmission housing and attach the three nuts.

3. Position the starter rear support bracket to the starter and attach the retaining nut and two attaching bolts.

4. Connect the starter cable at the starter terminal.

5. Connect the negative battery cable.

Distributor Cap and Rotor

When installing a new distributor rotor, coat the brass rotor electrode surface on all sides outboard of the plastic, including the outer edge, with a silicone dielectric compound of approximately $1/32$ inch thickness.

NOTE *Do not reapply or attempt to remove any silicone coating from the distributor cap electrodes. As this compound ages, it has the appearance of being a deposit on the cap and rotor electrodes. This condition is normal and causes no performance loss.*

REMOVAL

1. Loosen the distributor cap holddown screws.
2. Remove the cap straight off the distributor to prevent damage to the rotor blade and spring.

INSTALLATION

1. Position the distributor cap on the distributor base noting the square alignment locator. Tighten the

holddown screw to specification. Care should be taken to prevent damage to the rotor blade and spring.

2. Reinstall the secondary wires, noting the correct locations on the distributor cap.

Distributor Rotor

REMOVAL

1. Remove the secondary wire and cap from the distributor as outlined.
2. Loosen the rotor holddown screws and remove the rotor straight off the distributor weight plate to prevent damage to the advance mechanism.

INSTALLATION

1. Position the distributor rotor with the square and round locator pins matched to the distributor weight plate.

2. Tighten the holddown screws to specification. Care should be taken to prevent damage to the advance mechanism.

NOTE *When it is necessary to clean a distributor rotor for inspection or when a new rotor is being installed, silicone grease must be applied.*

NOTE *Silicone oxide deposit on the rotor blade is a normal condition and presents no performance loss. Do not attempt to remove silicone coating from the rotor blade. If the rotor is to be replaced, the new rotor must have silicone grease applied to the tip of the blade.*

Distributor

REMOVAL

1. Disconnect the primary wiring connector from the distributor.

2. Disconnect the vacuum advance hose at the distributor diaphragm assembly.

3. Using a suitable tool, remove the distributor cap and position it and the attached wires aside so as not to interfere with removing the distributor.

4. Remove the distributor rotor by unthreading the two holddown screws.

5. Remove the two distributor holddown bolts. The distributor can now be taken off the head.

INSTALLATION

1. Rotate the distributor by hand to make sure it turns freely.

2. Visually inspect for the presence of the base O-ring and the drive coupling spring.

3. Place the distributor in the cylinder head, seating the off-set tang of the drive coupling into the groove on the end of the camshaft.

4. Install the distributor holddown bolts and tighten so that the distributor can barely be rotated.

5. Install the distributor rotor and tighten the two screws.

Distributor

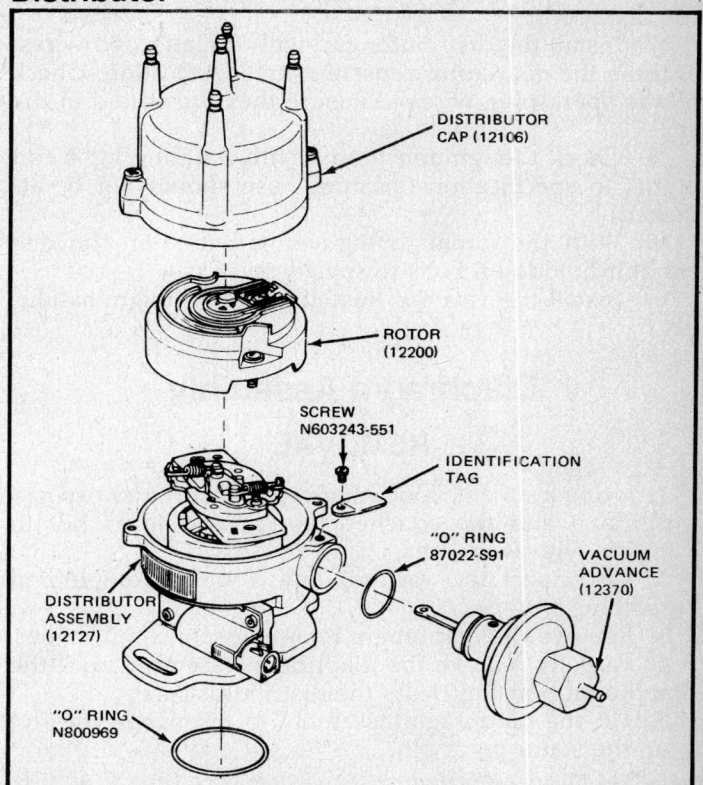

Distributor Removal

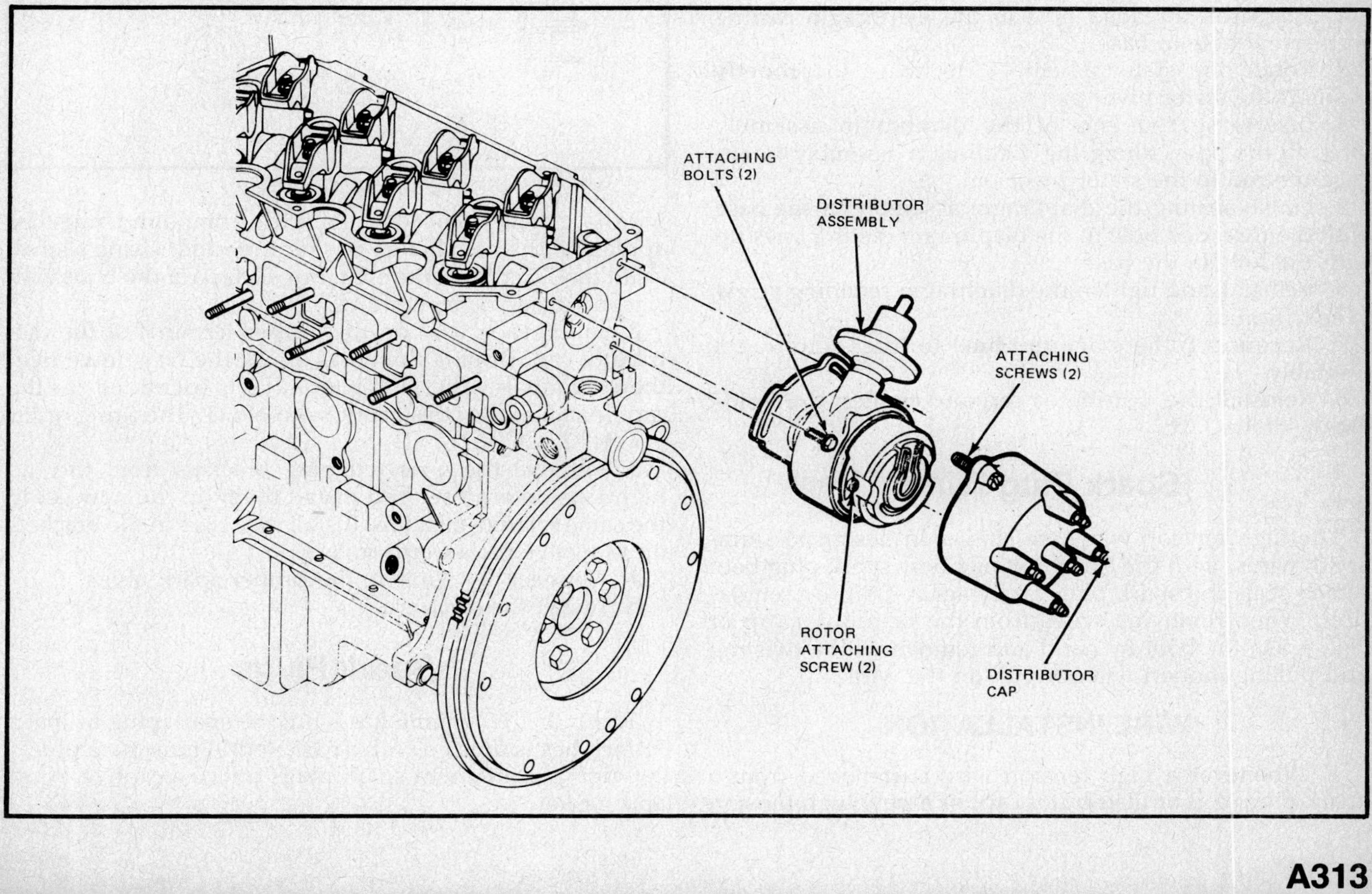

6. Reconnect the vehicle wiring harness connector to the distributor.

7. Install the distributor cap with the attached wires. Tighten the distributor capscrews to specification. Check all the spark plug wires to ensure they are seated in the cap.

8. Check the ignition timing with a timing light and adjust to specification (vacuum hose should not be attached).

9. With the initial timing verified, tighten the distributor holddown bolts to specification.

10. Install the vacuum hose to the diaphragm assembly.

Diaphragm Assembly

REMOVAL

1. Using a suitable tool, remove the distributor cap and position it and the attached wires aside so as not to interfere with work area.

2. Disconnect the vacuum line from the diaphragm assembly.

3. Remove the diaphragm retaining screws.

4. Partially remove the diaphragm assembly until the diaphragm housing clears the distributor base.

5. Tilt the diaphragm assembly to disengage the rod from the stator pivot pin.

INSTALLATION

1. Check the O-ring for tears or cracks.

2. Align the threaded hole in the diaphragm casting with screw hole in base.

3. Rotate the stator assembly clockwise to properly position the stator pivot pin.

4. Insert the rod end of the diaphragm assembly through the base, tilting the diaphragm assembly to engage the rod to the stator pivot pin.

5. Finish seating the diaphragm assembly in the base until the threaded hole in the diaphragm casting lines up with the hole in the base.

6. Reinstall and tighten the diaphragm retaining screw to specification.

7. Reconnect the vacuum line to the diaphragm assembly.

8. Reinstall the distributor cap and tighten the holddown screws.

Spark Plug Wires

The high tension wires are similar in design to Duraspark wires, with the exception of a new spark plug boot which seals the spark plug cavity against dirt accumulation. When removing wires from the distributor cap or coil, grasp the boot by hand and remove with a twisting and pulling motion. Do not pull on the wire.

WIRE INSTALLATION

1. Whenever a high tension wire is removed from a spark plug, coil or distributor cap, or a new high tension

Spark Plug Wire Removal

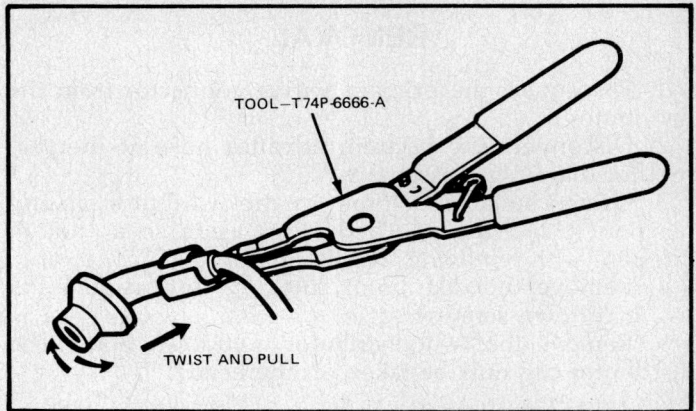

TOOL—T74P-6666-A

TWIST AND PULL

Stoplamp Switch W/O Power Brakes

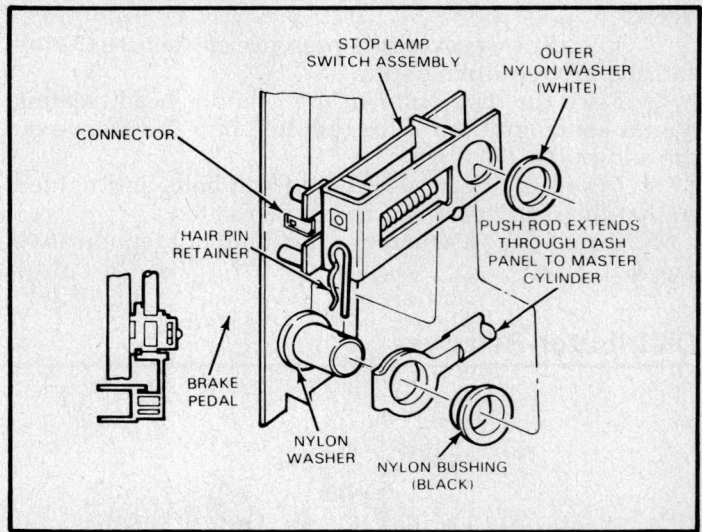

STOP LAMP SWITCH ASSEMBLY

OUTER NYLON WASHER (WHITE)

CONNECTOR

HAIR PIN RETAINER

PUSH ROD EXTENDS THROUGH DASH PANEL TO MASTER CYLINDER

BRAKE PEDAL

NYLON WASHER

NYLON BUSHING (BLACK)

wire is installed, silicone dielectric compound must be applied to the boot before it is reconnected. Using a small clean tool, coat the entire interior surface of the boot with silicone dielectric compound.

2. Insert each wire on the proper terminal of the distributor cap. Be sure the wires are all the way down over their terminals. The No. 1 terminal is identified on the cap. Install the wires starting with No. 1. The firing order is 1-3-4-2, CCW.

3. Remove the wire retaining brackets from the old high tension wire set and install them on the new set in the same relative position. Install the wires in the brackets on the valve rocker arm covers.

4. Connect the wires to the proper spark plugs.

5. Install the coil wire.

Spark Plugs

The 1.3L/1.6L engine has a unique spark plug in that a ⅝ inch hex is utilized with a gasketed 14 mm spark plug.

Original equipment spark plugs utilize a captive, reusable gasket.

Stoplamp Switch W/Power Brakes

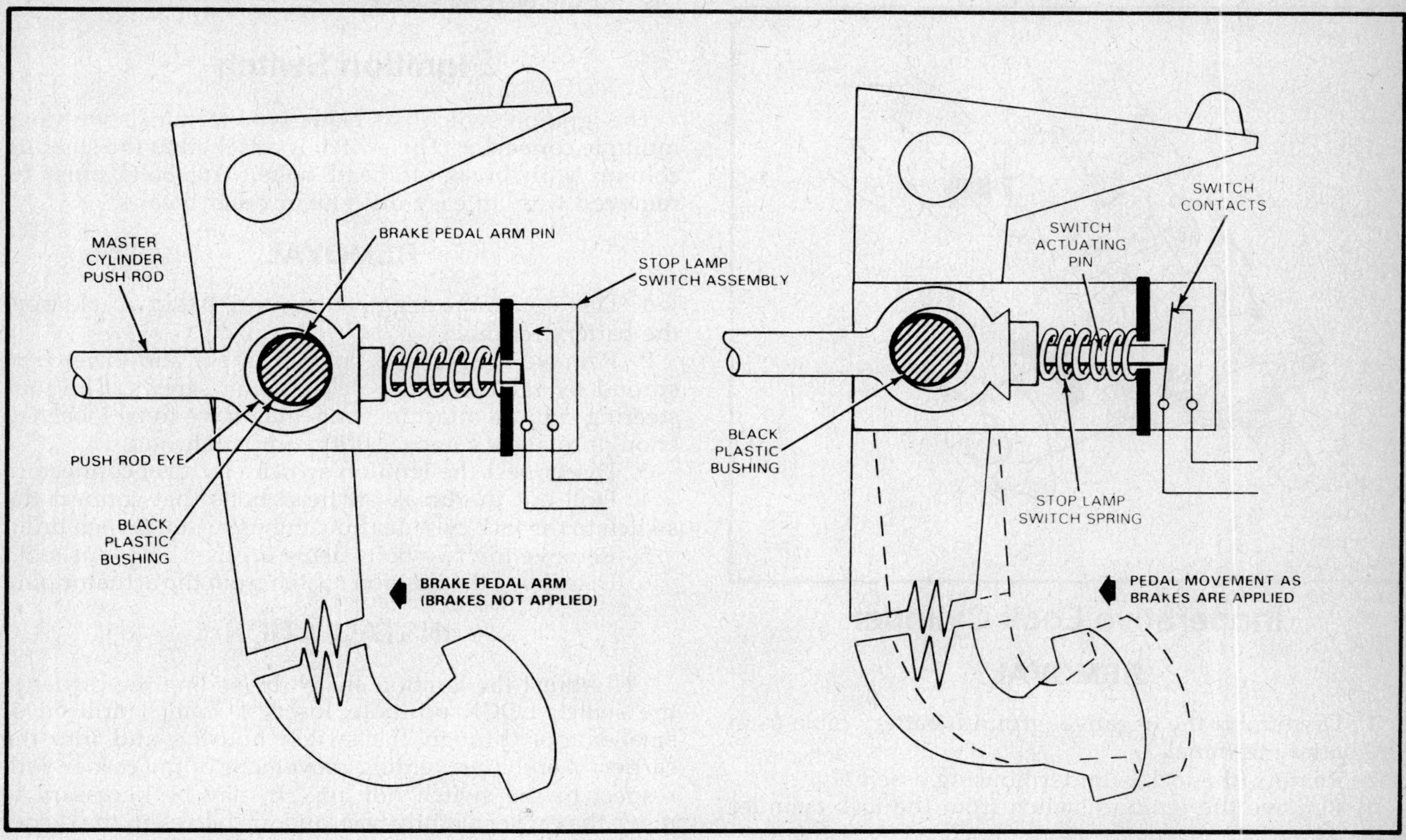

MASTER CYLINDER PUSH ROD

BRAKE PEDAL ARM PIN

STOP LAMP SWITCH ASSEMBLY

PUSH ROD EYE

BLACK PLASTIC BUSHING

BRAKE PEDAL ARM (BRAKES NOT APPLIED)

SWITCH ACTUATING PIN

SWITCH CONTACTS

BLACK PLASTIC BUSHING

STOP LAMP SWITCH SPRING

PEDAL MOVEMENT AS BRAKES ARE APPLIED

Service pacakged spark plugs utilize a screw-on type gasket that is supplied loose in the individual box with the spark plug. This gasket must be screwed onto the plug prior to plug installation.

Ignition Lock Cylinder Assembly

REMOVAL (WITH KEY)

1. Disconnect the negative (ground) batter cable from the battery terminal.
2. Remove the lower shroud.
3. Disconnect the warning buzzer electrical connector.
4. Turn the lock cylinder key to the RUN position.
5. Place an ⅛ inch (3.17 mm) diameter wire pin or small drift punch in the hole in the casting surrounding the lock cylinder. Depress the retaining pin while pulling out on lock cylinder to remove it from the column housing.

INSTALLATION

1. Install the lock cylinder by turning it to the RUN position and depressing the retaining pin. Insert the lock cylinder into the lock cylinder housing. Make sure that the cylinder is fully seated and aligned in the interlocking washer before turning the key to the OFF position. This action will permit the cylinder retaining pin to extend into the cylinder housing hole.

2. Rotate the lock cylinder, using the lock cylinder key, to ensure correct mechanical operation in all positions.
3. Install the electrical connector for the key warning buzzer.
4. Install the lower shroud.
5. Connect the negative (ground) battery cable to battery terminal.
6. Check for proper start in PARK or NEUTRAL. Also, make certain that the start circuit cannot be actuated in the DRIVE and REVERSE positions and that the column is locked in the LOCK position.

Remove Lock Cylinder

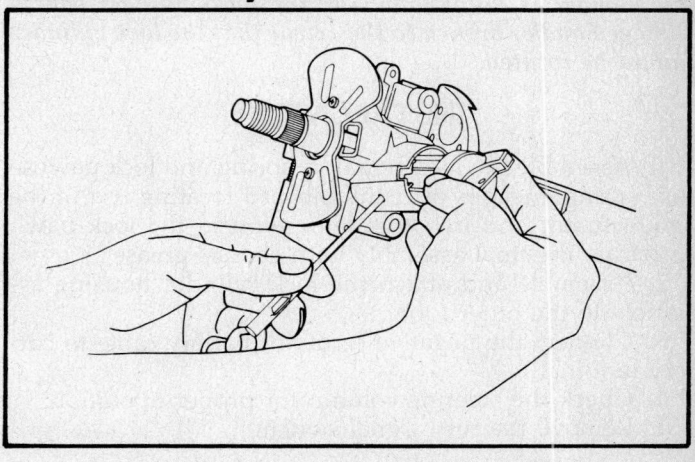

Lift Casting Off Steering Shaft

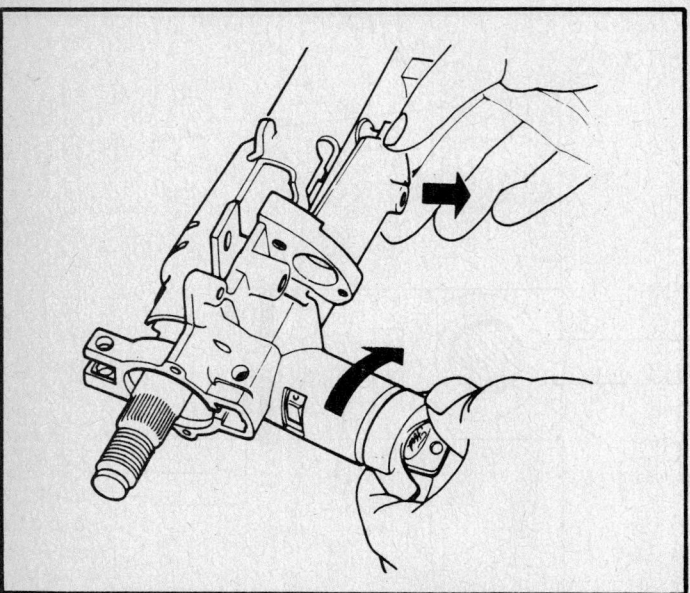

Inoperative Lock Cylinder

REMOVAL

1. Disconnect the negative (ground) battery cable from the battery terminal.
2. Remove the lock cylinder housing assembly.
3. Remove the ignition switch from the lock cylinder housing.
4. Replace the following components.
   a. Lock cylinder housing
   b. Gear, steering column lock
   c. Bearing, steering column lock housing
   d. Retainer, steering column lock gear
   e. Lock cylinder and key assembly
   f. Spring steering column lock
   g. Pawl, steering column lock
   h. Actuator assembly
   i. Bolt M6-1.0 x 10 break-off head

NOTE   These procedures apply to vehicles in which the ignition lock is inoperative and the lock cylinder cannot be rotated due to a lost or broken lock cylinder key; the key number is not known; or the lock cylinder cap is damaged and/or broken to the extent that the lock cylinder cannot be rotated.

INSTALLATION

1. Assemble the lock actuator, spring and lock pawl so that spring engages over the inboard locating rod of the lock actuator and into the depression in the lock pawl. Lubricate the final assembly with chassis grease.
2. Assemble and attach the lock cylinder housing assembly to the outer tube.
3. Connect the negative (ground) battery cable to battery terminal.
4. Check the steering column for proper operation.
5. Remove the turn signal switch.

6. Remove the upper steering shaft bearing sleeve. Discard the bearing sleeve.

Ignition Switch

The ignition switch has blade type terminals with one multiple connector. The switch is attached to the steering column with break-off head bolts. The bolts must be removed with an easy-out tool or other means.

REMOVAL

1. Disconnect the negative (ground) battery cable from the battery terminal.
2. Remove the steering column upper and lower trim shroud by removing five self-tapping screws. The four steering column attaching nuts may have to be loosened enough to allow removal of the upper shroud.
3. Disconnect the ignition switch electrical connector.
4. Drill out the break-off head bolts that connect the switch to the lock cylinder housing using an 1/8-inch drill.
5. Remove the two bolts using an Ex-3 easy-out tool.
6. Disengage the ignition switch from the actuator pin.

INSTALLATION

1. Adjust the ignition switch by sliding the carrier to the switch LOCK position. Insert a 1/6-inch drill bit or smaller tool through the switch housing and into the carrier, thereby preventing movement of the carrier with respect to the switch housing. It may be necessary to move the carrier slightly back and forth to align the carrier and housing adjustment holes.

NOTE   A new replacement switch assembly includes an adjusting pin already installed.

2. Rotate the lock cylinder to the LOCK position.
3. Install the ignition switch on the actuator pin.
4. Install the new break-off head bolts and hand tighten.

Blade Type Ignition Switch Connector

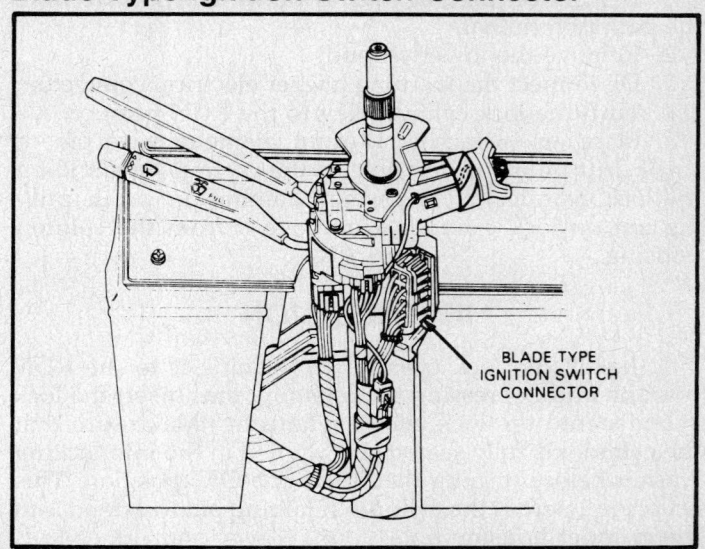

BLADE TYPE IGNITION SWITCH CONNECTOR

Ignition Switch Installation

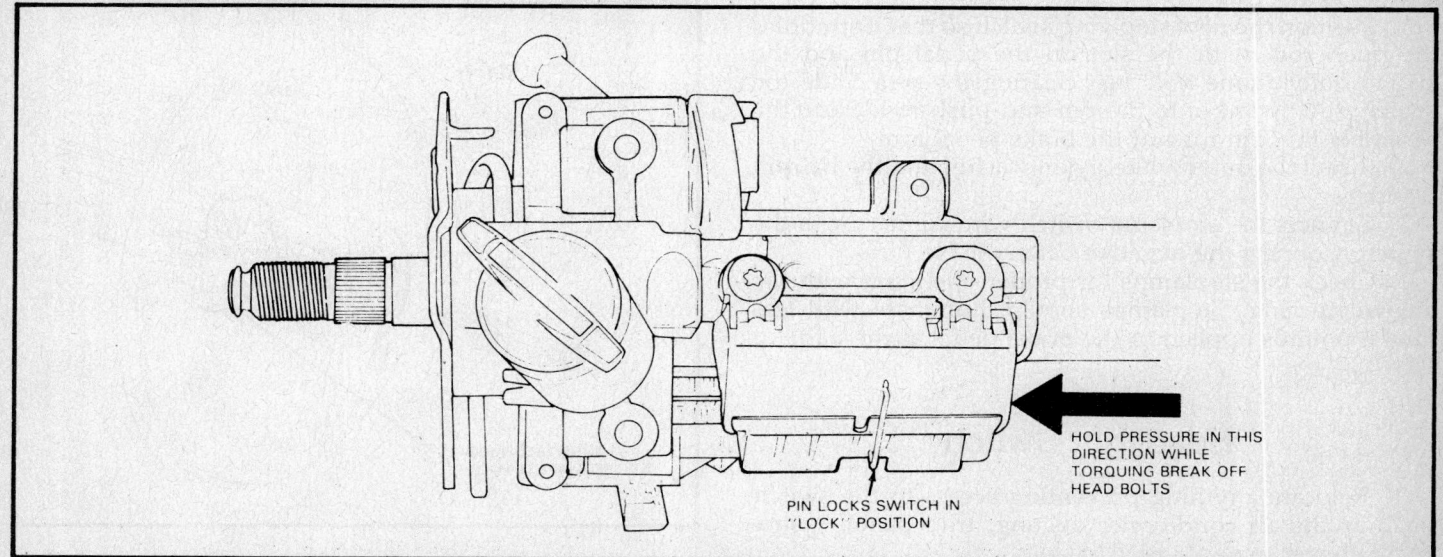

PIN LOCKS SWITCH IN "LOCK" POSITION

HOLD PRESSURE IN THIS DIRECTION WHILE TORQUING BREAK OFF HEAD BOLTS

5. Move the ignition switch up the steering column until all the travel in the screw slots is used. Hold the switch in this position and tighten the break-off head bolts until the heads break off.

6. Remove the adjustment drill bit or pin.

7. Connect the electrical connector to the ignition switch.

8. Position the upper shroud and tighten the steering column attaching nuts to 23-33 N•m (17-25 lb-ft) if they were loosened. Mate the lower shroud to the upper shroud and tighten the five attaching screws.

9. Connect the negative (ground) battery cable to the battery terminal.

10. Check the ignition switch for proper starting in PARK or NEUTRAL. Also make certain that the start circuit can not be actuated in the DRIVE or REVERSE position and that the column is locked in the LOCK position.

Stoplight Switch Without Power Brakes

REMOVAL

1. Disconnect the wire harness at the connector from the switch.

NOTE   The locking tab must be lifted before the connector can be removed.

2. Remove the hairpin retainer. Slide the stoplamp switch, the push rod and the white nylon washer and black bushing away from the pedal. Remove the switch by sliding the switch up/down.

NOTE   Since the switch side plate nearest the brake pedal is slotted, it is not necesary to remove the brake master cylinder push rod black bushing and one white spacer washer nearest the pedal arm from the brake pedal pin.

INSTALLATION

1. Position the switch so that the U-shaped side is nearest the pedal and directly over/under the pin. The black bushing must be in position in the push rod eyelet with the washer face on the side closest to the retaining pin.

2. Then slide the switch up/down, trapping the master cylinder push rod and black bushing between the switch side plates. Push the switch and push rod assembly firmly towards the brake pedal arm. Assemble outside the white plastic washer to pin and install the hairpin retainer to trap the whole assembly.

CHILTON CAUTION   Do not substitute other types of pin retainer. Replace only with production hairpin retainer.

3. Assemble the wire harness connector to the switch.

4. Check the stoplamp switch for proper operation. Stoplamps should illuminate with less than 6 pounds applied to the brake pedal at the pad.

NOTE   The stoplamp switch wire harness must have sufficient length to travel with the switch during full stroke at the pedal. If the wire length is insufficient, re-route the harness.

Stoplight Switch With Power Brakes

REMOVAL

1. Disconnect the negative battery cable.

2. Disconnect the stoplamp switch wire connector from the switch.

3. Remove the hairpin retainer and outer white nylon washer from the pedal pin. Slide the stoplamp switch off the brake pedal pin just far enough for the outer side plate of the switch to clear the pin. Then remove the switch.

INSTALLATION

1. Position the new stoplamp switch so that it straddles the push rod, with the slot on the pedal pin and the switch outer frame hole just clearing the pin. Slide the switch downward onto the pin and push rod. Slide the assembly inboard toward the brake pedal arm.

2. Install the outer white nylon washer and the hairpin retainer.

3. Connect the stoplamp switch wire connector to the switch. Connect the negative battery cable.

4. Check the stoplamps for proper operation with the engine running. Stoplamps should illuminate with less than 6 pounds applied to the brake pedal at the pad.

Headlight Switch

1. Relocate anything preventing access to the switch, such as the air conditioner ducting, trim panel, instrument cluster, etc.

2. Place the switch in full ON position. Pull on the knob while pressing the shaft release button to release the shaft and knob assembly.

3. Separate the switch from the mounting bracket and electrical connectors.

Head Light Switch

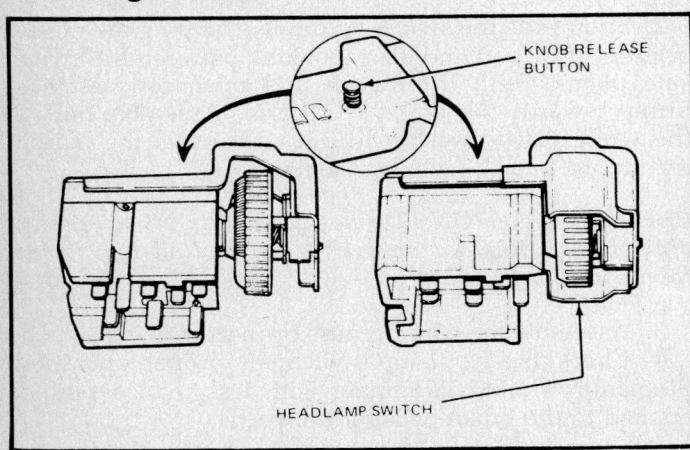

KNOB RELEASE BUTTON

HEADLAMP SWITCH

Steering Wheel

REMOVAL

1. Disconnect the negative (ground) battery cable from the battery terminal.

2. Remove the steering hub cover assembly.

3. Remove and discard the steering wheel attaching nut.

4. Remove the steering wheel from the upper shaft using tool T67L-3600-A. Do not use a knock-off type steering wheel puller or strike the end of steering column upper shaft with a hammer, or damage will occur to the bearing of the collapsible steering column.

Steering Wheel Removal

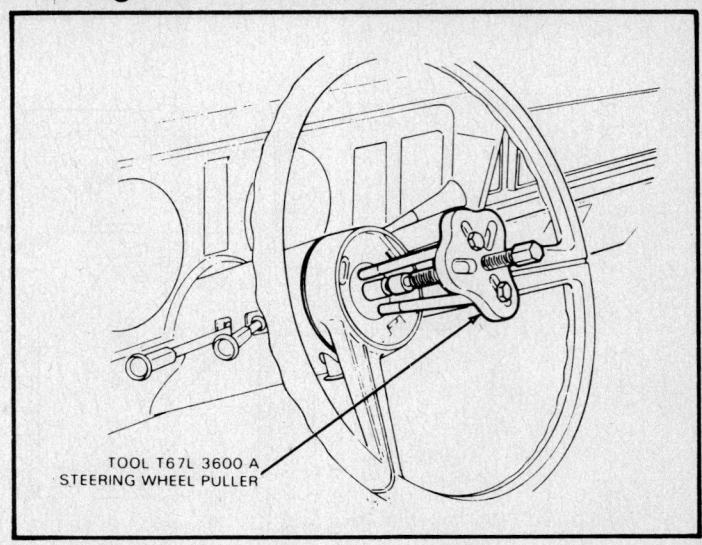

TOOL T67L 3600 A
STEERING WHEEL PULLER

INSTALLATION

1. Position the steering wheel on the end of the steering wheel shaft. Align the mark on the steering wheel with the mark on the shaft to assure that the straight-ahead steering wheel position corresponds to the straight-ahead position of the front wheels.

2. Install a new service wheel nut. Tighten the nut to a torque of 41-54 N•m (30-40 lb-ft).

3. Install the steering wheel cover assembly. Tighten to a torque of 15-23 N•m (13-20 lb-in).

4. Connect the negative (ground) battery cable to the battery terminal.

5. Check the steering column for proper operation.

Steering Column

REMOVAL

1. Disconnect the negative (ground) battery cable from the battery terminal.

2. Remove the steering column cover on the lower portion of the instrument panel (2 screws) to expose the instrument panel reinforcement section.

3. Remove the instrument panel reinforcement section (2 screws).

4. Remove the lower steering column shroud (five screws).

5. Loosen, but do not remove, the two nuts and two bolts retaining the steering column to the support bracket. Remove upper shroud.

6. Disconnect all steering column electrical connections (ignition, wash/wipe, turn signal, key warning buzzer and speed control).

7. Loosen the steering column to intermediate shaft clamp connection and remove the bolt or nut.

8. Remove the two nuts and two bolts retaining the steering column to the support bracket (40) and lower the steering column to the floor.

Electrical Circuits

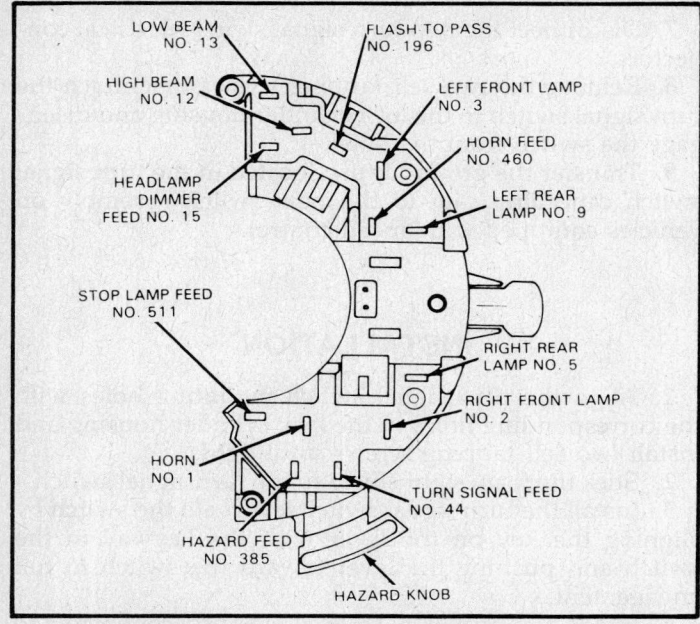

LOW BEAM NO. 13
FLASH TO PASS NO. 196
HIGH BEAM NO. 12
LEFT FRONT LAMP NO. 3
HEADLAMP DIMMER FEED NO. 15
HORN FEED NO. 460
LEFT REAR LAMP NO. 9
STOP LAMP FEED NO. 511
RIGHT REAR LAMP NO. 5
RIGHT FRONT LAMP NO. 2
HORN NO. 1
TURN SIGNAL FEED NO. 44
HAZARD FEED NO. 385
HAZARD KNOB

9. Pry open the steering column shaft clamp on each side of the bolt groove with the steering column locked. Open enough to disengage the shafts with a minimal effort. Do not use excessive force, as damage to components may result.

10. Inspect the two steering column bracket clips for damage. If clips have been bent or excessively distorted, they must be replaced.

INSTALLATION

1. Check the distance that the steering shaft protrudes past the outer tube assembly. This distance must be between 36.6 and 41.5 mm (1.44-1.63 in).

2. Engage the lower steering shaft to the intermediate shaft and hand start the clamp bolt and nut.

3. Place the steering column under the instrument panel, align the two bolts on the steering column support bracket asembly with the outer tube mounting holes, and hand start the two nuts. Check for the presence of the two clips on the outer bracket. The clips must be present to insure adequate performance of vital parts and systems. Hand start the two bolts through the outer tube upper bracket and clips and into the support bracket nuts.

4. Connect all quick connect electrical connectors (turn signal, wash/wipe, key warning buzzer, ignition, speed control).

5. Install the upper shroud.

6. Tighten the steering column mounting nut and bolts to a torque of 23-33 N•m (17-25 lb-ft).

7. Cycle the steering column one turn left and one turn right to align the intermediate shaft into the column shaft. (Power steering cars must have the engine running.) Torque the steering shaft clamp nut to 27-40 N•m (20-30 lb-ft).

8. Install the lower trim shroud with five screws.

9. Install the instrument panel reinforcement section with two screws.

10. Install the steering column cover on the instrument panel with two screws.

11. Connect the negative (ground) battery cable to the battery terminal.

12. Check the steering column for proper operation.

Steering Shaft Distance Past Outer Tube

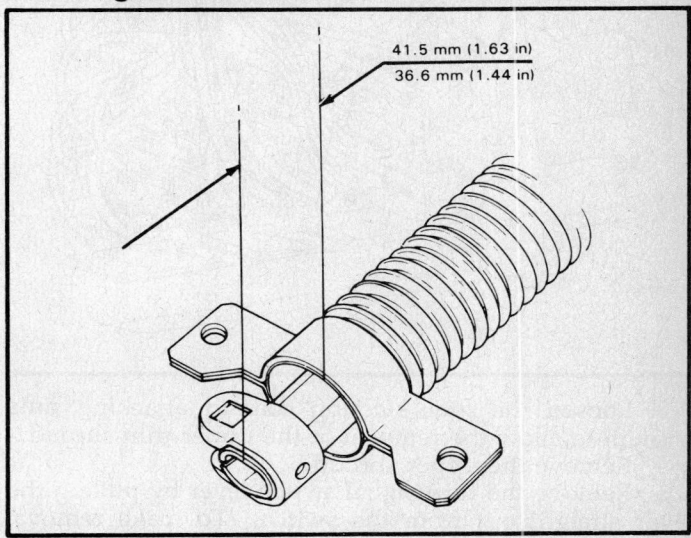

41.5 mm (1.63 in)
36.6 mm (1.44 in)

Turn Signal, Hazard, Horn, Dimmer, Flash-To-Pass Switch Assembly

REMOVAL

1. Disconnect the negative (ground) battery cable from the battery terminal.

2. Remove the five shroud screws and remove the lower shroud.

Stalk Mounted Horn Switch Lever and Wiring

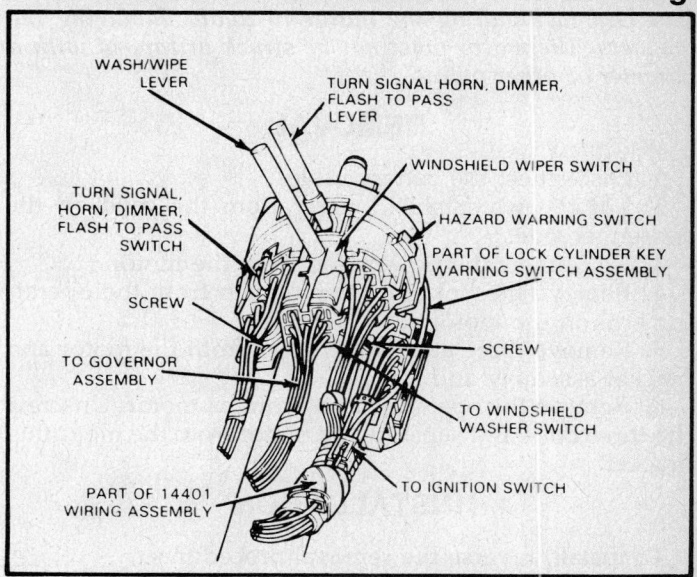

WASH/WIPE LEVER
TURN SIGNAL HORN, DIMMER, FLASH TO PASS LEVER
WINDSHIELD WIPER SWITCH
TURN SIGNAL, HORN, DIMMER, FLASH TO PASS SWITCH
HAZARD WARNING SWITCH
PART OF LOCK CYLINDER KEY WARNING SWITCH ASSEMBLY
SCREW
SCREW
TO GOVERNOR ASSEMBLY
TO WINDSHIELD WASHER SWITCH
PART OF 14401 WIRING ASSEMBLY
TO IGNITION SWITCH

Fuse Panel (Back)

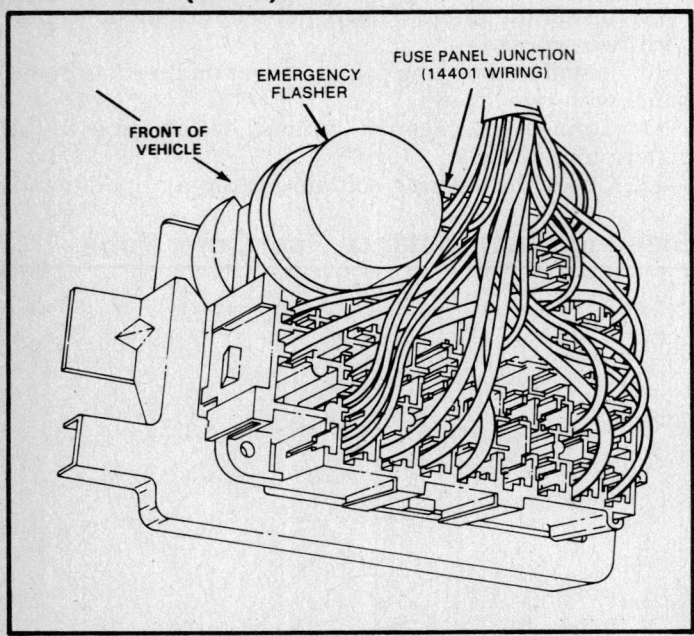

FRONT OF VEHICLE

EMERGENCY FLASHER

FUSE PANEL JUNCTION (14401 WIRING)

3. Loosen the four steering column attaching nuts enough to allow the removal of the upper trim shroud.

4. Remove the upper shroud.

5. Remove the turn signal switch lever by pulling the lever straight out from the switch. (To make removal easier, work the outer end of the lever around with a slight rotary movement before pulling it out.)

6. Peel back the foam sight shield from the turn signal switch.

7. Disconnect the two turn signal switch electrical connectors.

8. Remove the two self-tapping screws that attach the turn signal switch to the lock cylinder housing and disengage the switch from the housing.

9. Transfer the ground brush located in the turn signal switch cancelling cam to the new switch assembly on vehicles equipped with speed control.

INSTALLATION

1. Align the turn signal switch mounting holes with the corresponding holes in the lock cylinder housing and install two self-tapping screws until tight.

2. Stick the foam sight shield to the turn signal switch.

3. Install the turn signal switch lever into the switch by aligning the key on the lever with the keyway in the switch and pushing the lever toward the switch to full engagement.

4. Install two turn signal switch electrical connectors to full engagement.

5. Install the steering column trim shrouds.

6. Torque the steering column attaching nuts to 23-33 N•m (17-25 lb-ft).

7. Connect the negative (ground) battery cable to the battery terminal.

8. Check the steering column for proper operation.

WIPER SECTION

Windshield Wiper Motor

NOTE The internal permanent magnets used in the wiper motor are a ceramic (glass-like) material. Care must be exercised in handling the motor to avoid damaging the magnets. The motor must not be struck or tapped with a hammer or other object.

REMOVAL

1. Disconnect the battery cables.

2. Lift the water shield cover from the cowl on the passenger side.

3. Disconnect the power lead from the motor.

4. Remove the linkage retaining clip from the operating arm on the motor.

5. Remove three attaching screws from the motor and bracket assembly and remove.

6. Remove the operating arm from the motor. Unscrew the three bolts and separate the motor from the mounting bracket.

INSTALLATION

To install, reverse the removal procedures.

Windshield Wiper Motor

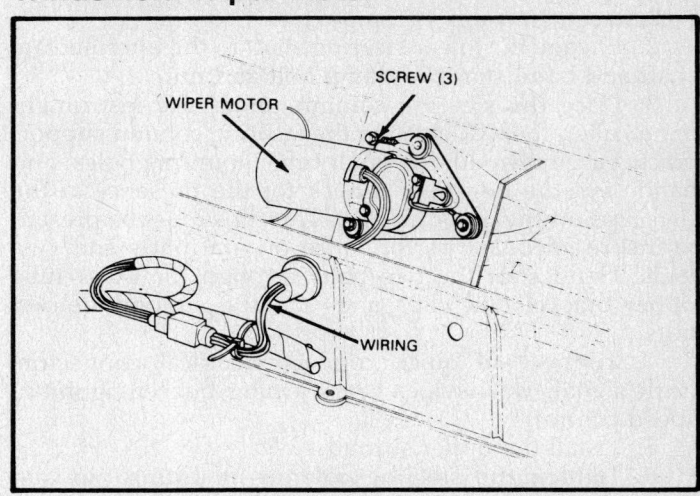

WIPER MOTOR

SCREW (3)

WIRING

Wiper Switch

NOTE The switch handle is an integral part of the switch and can not be removed separately.

Windshield Wiper Motor Mounting

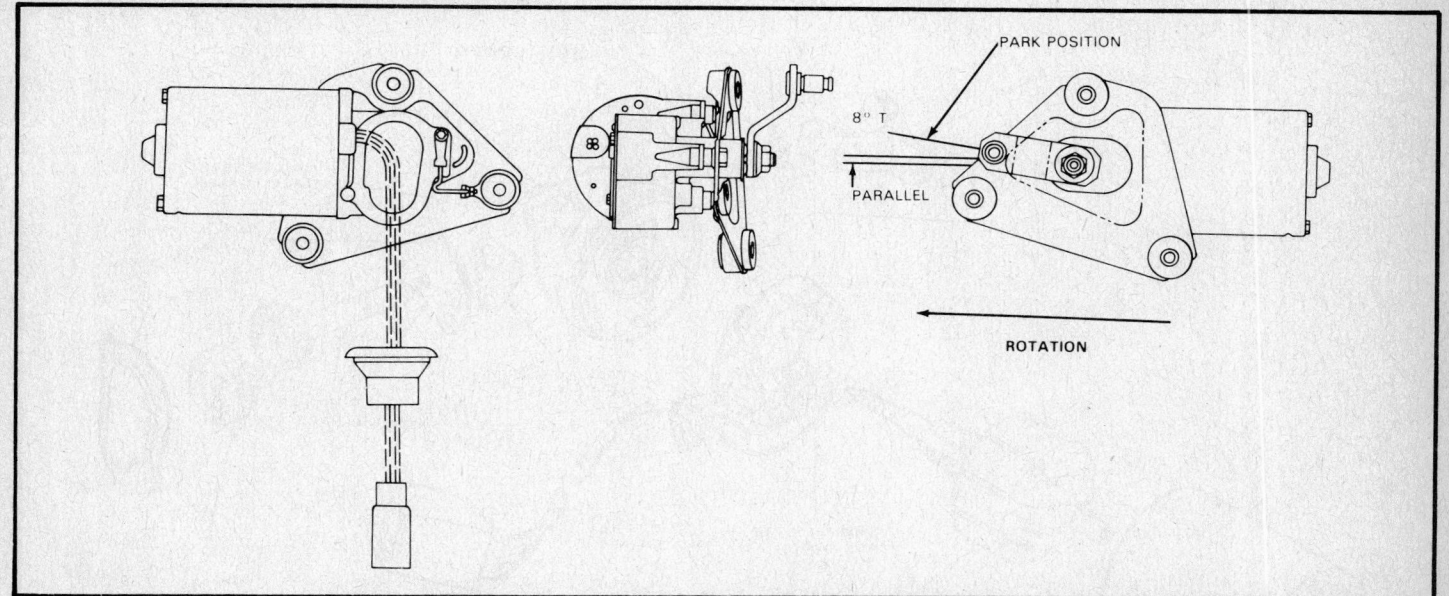

REMOVAL

1. Disconnect the negative (ground) battery cable from the battery terminal.
2. Loosen the steering column attaching nuts enough to remove the upper trim shroud.
3. Remove the trim shrouds.
4. Disconnect the quick connect electrical connector.
5. Peel back the foam sight shield. Remove the two hex-head screws holding the switch and remove the wash/wipe switch.

INSTALLATION

1. Position the switch on the column and install the two hex-head screws. Replace the foam sight shield over the switch.
2. Connect the quick connect electrical connector.
3. Install the upper and lower trim shrouds.
4. Tighten the steering column attaching nuts to 23-33 N•m (17-25 ft-lb).
5. Connect the negative (ground) battery cable to the battery terminal.
6. Check the steering column for proper operation.

Interval Governor

The interval governor is located on the left-hand side of the steering column support bracket.

REMOVAL

1. Remove the steering column screws.
2. Remove the two attaching screws (one has a ground pigtail under it).
3. Disconnect the connectors.

INSTALLATION

To install, reverse removal procedure.

Wiper Motor Wiring

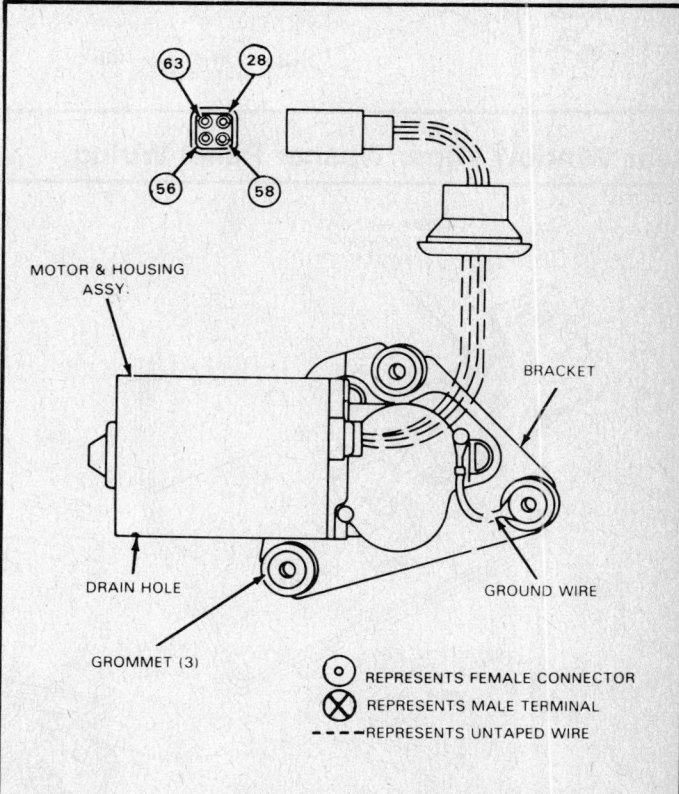

○ REPRESENTS FEMALE CONNECTOR
⊗ REPRESENTS MALE TERMINAL
--- REPRESENTS UNTAPED WIRE

CIRCUIT NO.	DESCRIPTION	COLOR
28	WIPER SWITCH TO WIPER MOTOR (PARK RETURN)	BLACK
58	WIPER SWITCH TO WIPER MOTOR (LOW)	WHITE
56	WIPER SWITCH TO WIPER MOTOR (HIGH)	BLUE
63	WIPER SWITCH TO WIPER MOTOR (PARK FEED)	RED

Disassembled Wiper Motor

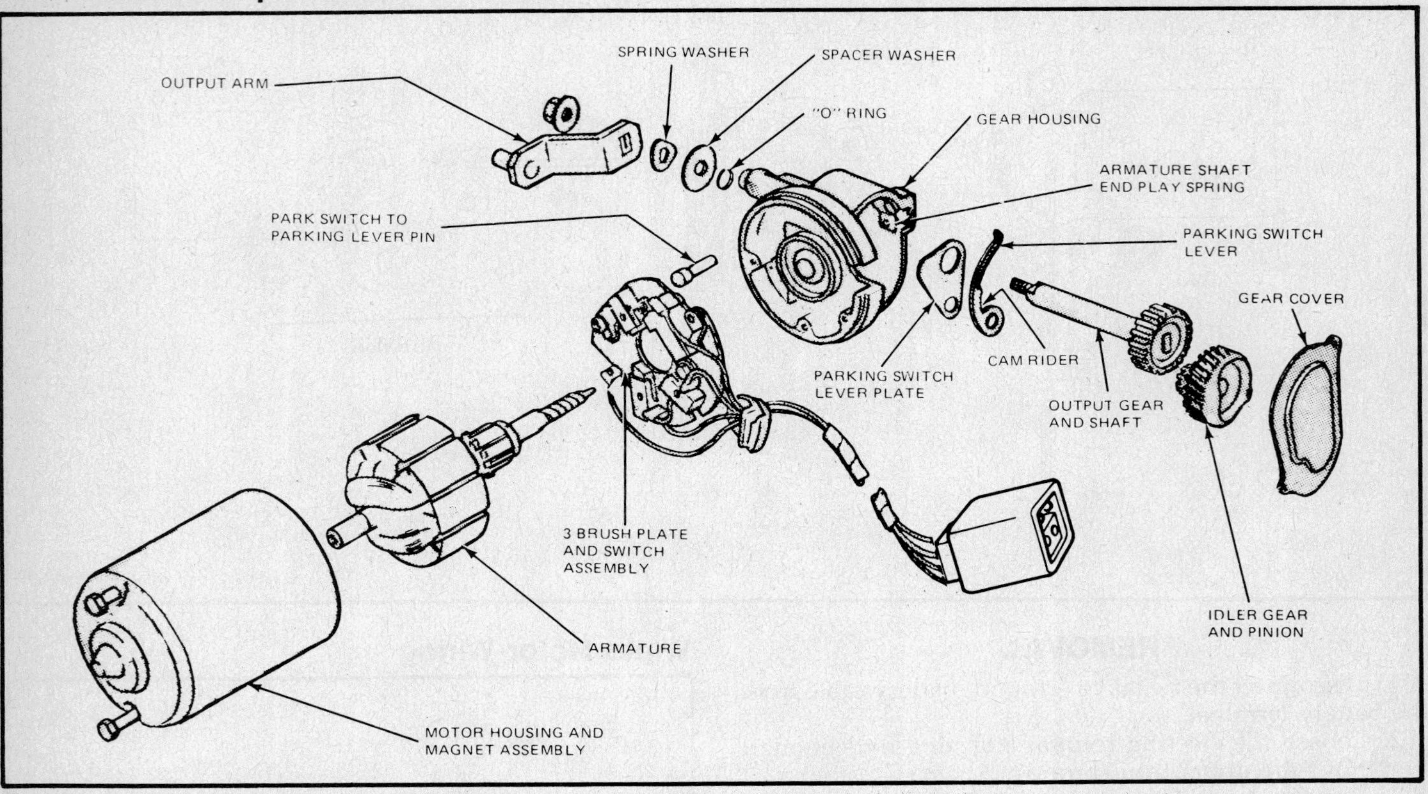

OUTPUT ARM

SPRING WASHER

SPACER WASHER

"O" RING

GEAR HOUSING

ARMATURE SHAFT END PLAY SPRING

PARK SWITCH TO PARKING LEVER PIN

PARKING SWITCH LEVER

GEAR COVER

PARKING SWITCH LEVER PLATE

CAM RIDER

OUTPUT GEAR AND SHAFT

3 BRUSH PLATE AND SWITCH ASSEMBLY

ARMATURE

IDLER GEAR AND PINION

MOTOR HOUSING AND MAGNET ASSEMBLY

Rear Window Wiper/Washer Panel Wiring

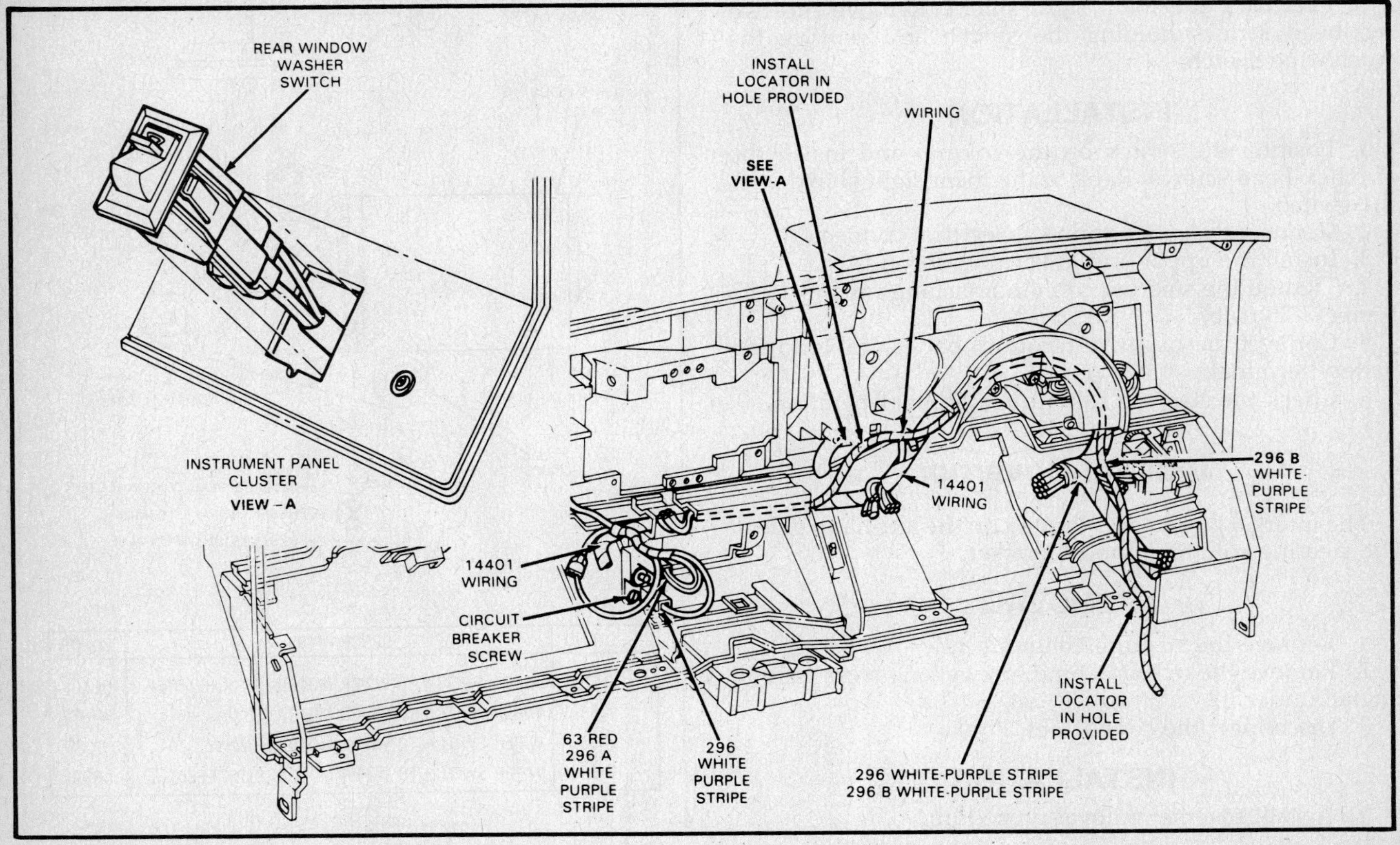

REAR WINDOW WASHER SWITCH

INSTALL LOCATOR IN HOLE PROVIDED

WIRING

SEE VIEW-A

14401 WIRING

296 B WHITE-PURPLE STRIPE

INSTRUMENT PANEL CLUSTER
VIEW - A

14401 WIRING

CIRCUIT BREAKER SCREW

63 RED 296 A WHITE PURPLE STRIPE

296 WHITE PURPLE STRIPE

INSTALL LOCATOR IN HOLE PROVIDED

296 WHITE-PURPLE STRIPE
296 B WHITE-PURPLE STRIPE

Wiper Linkage Removal and Installation

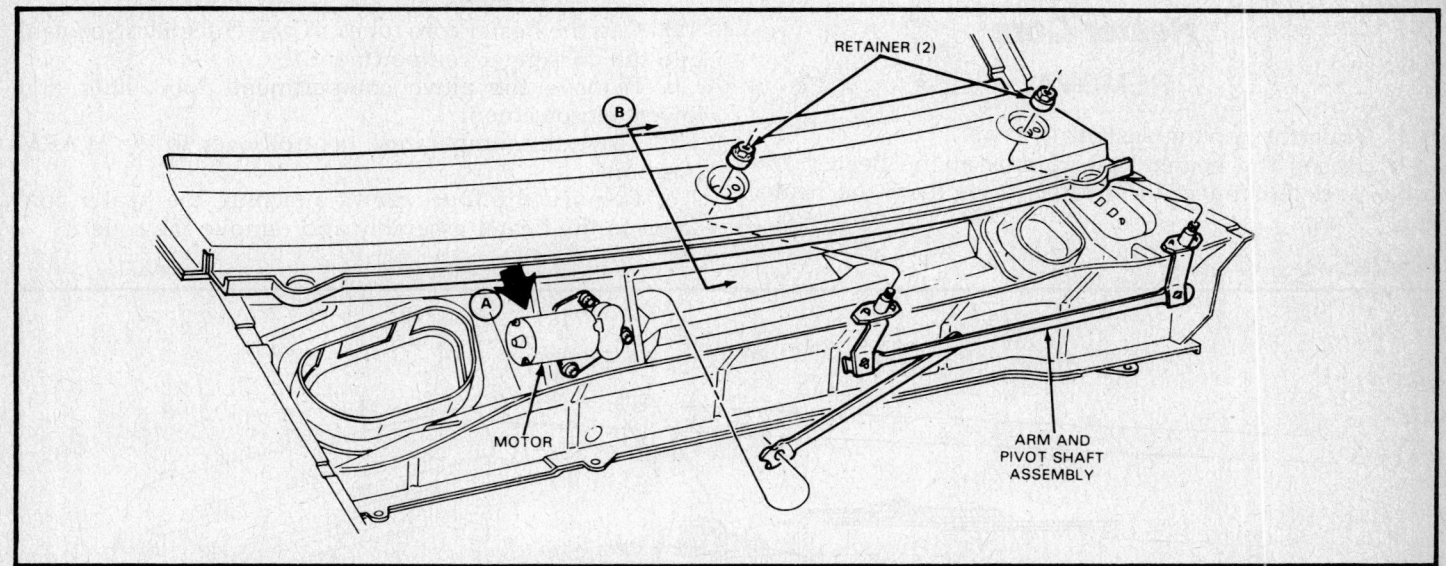

Rear Wiper Switch

REMOVAL—IGNITION OFF

1. Remove two cluster opening finish panel retaining screws and remove the finish panel by rocking the upper edge toward the driver.
2. Disconnect the wiring connector from the rear washer switch.

INSTALLATION

1. Install the cluster opening finish panel and two retaining screws.
2. Connect the wiring connector.
3. Push the rear washer switch into the cluster finish panel until it snaps into place.

Rear Wiper Motor (3-Door Model)

REMOVAL

1. Remove the wiper arm and blade.
2. Remove the pivot shaft attaching nut and spacers.
3. Remove the liftgate inner trim panel.
4. Disconnect the electrical connector to the wiper motor.
5. Remove the three screws retaining the bracket to the door inner skin. Remove the complete motor, bracket and linkage assembly.

INSTALLATION

To install, reverse the removal procedure.

Rear Wiper Motor (3-Door)

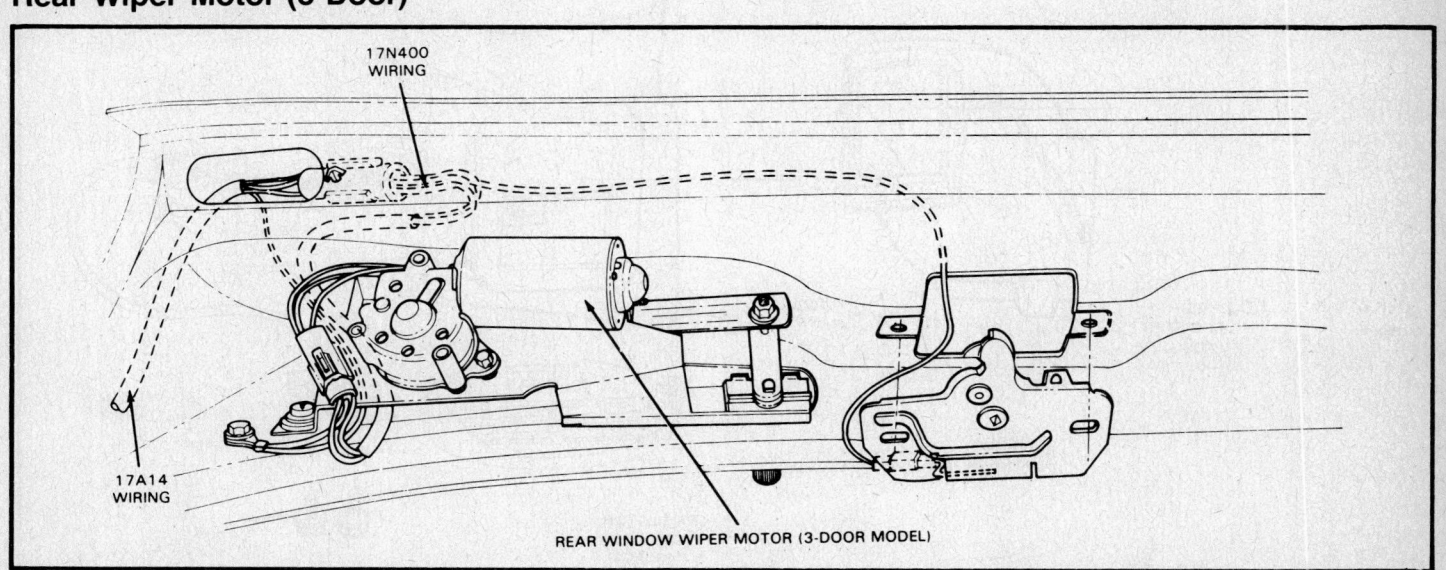

HEATER SECTION

Heater Core

REMOVAL

1. Drain the cooling system.
2. Loosen the heater hose clamps at the heater core tubes and disconnect the heater hoses from the heater core tubes.

3. Cap the heater core tubes to prevent spilling coolant into the passenger compartment.
4. Remove the glove compartment door, liner and lower reinforcement.
5. Move the temperature control lever to the WARM position.
6. Remove the four screws attaching the heater core cover to the heater assembly and remove the cover.

Heater

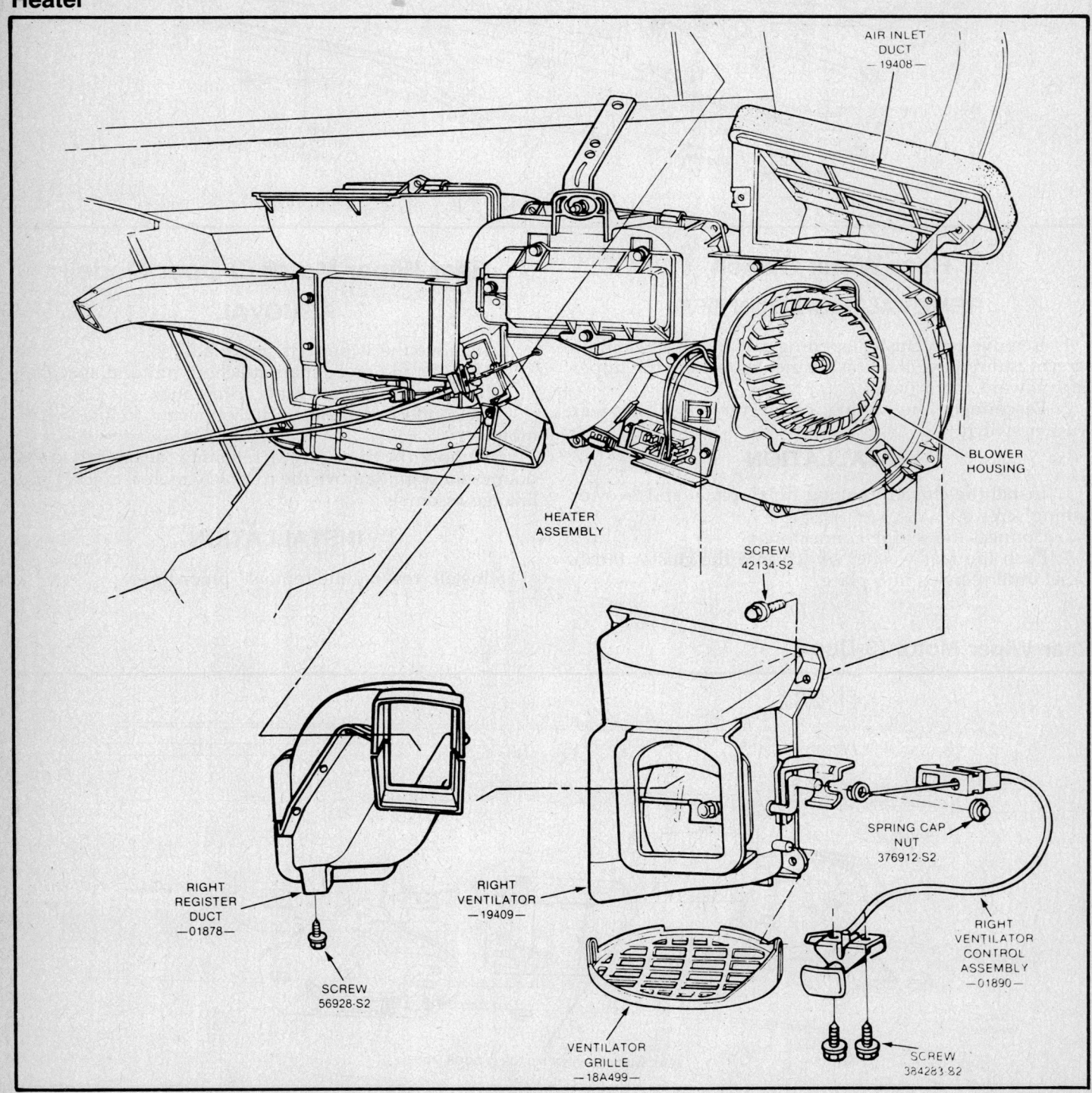

7. Working in the engine compartment, loosen the two nuts attaching the heater case assembly to the dash panel.

8. Push the heater core tubes toward the passenger compartment to loosen the heater core from the heater case assembly.

9. Pull the heater core from the heater case assembly and remove the heater core through the glove compartment opening.

INSTALLATION

To install, reverse the removal procedure.

Blower Motor Assembly

REMOVAL

1. Remove the right ventilator assembly.
2. Remove the hub clamp spring from the blower wheel hub.
3. Pull the blower wheel from the blower motor shaft.
4. Remove the three blower motor flange attaching screws located inside the blower housing.

Blower Motor Removal

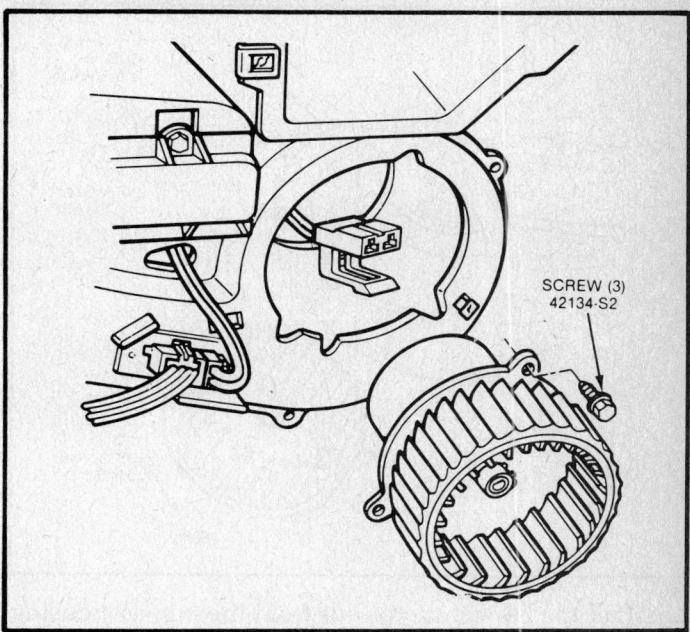

SCREW (3)
42134-S2

Heater Core Removal

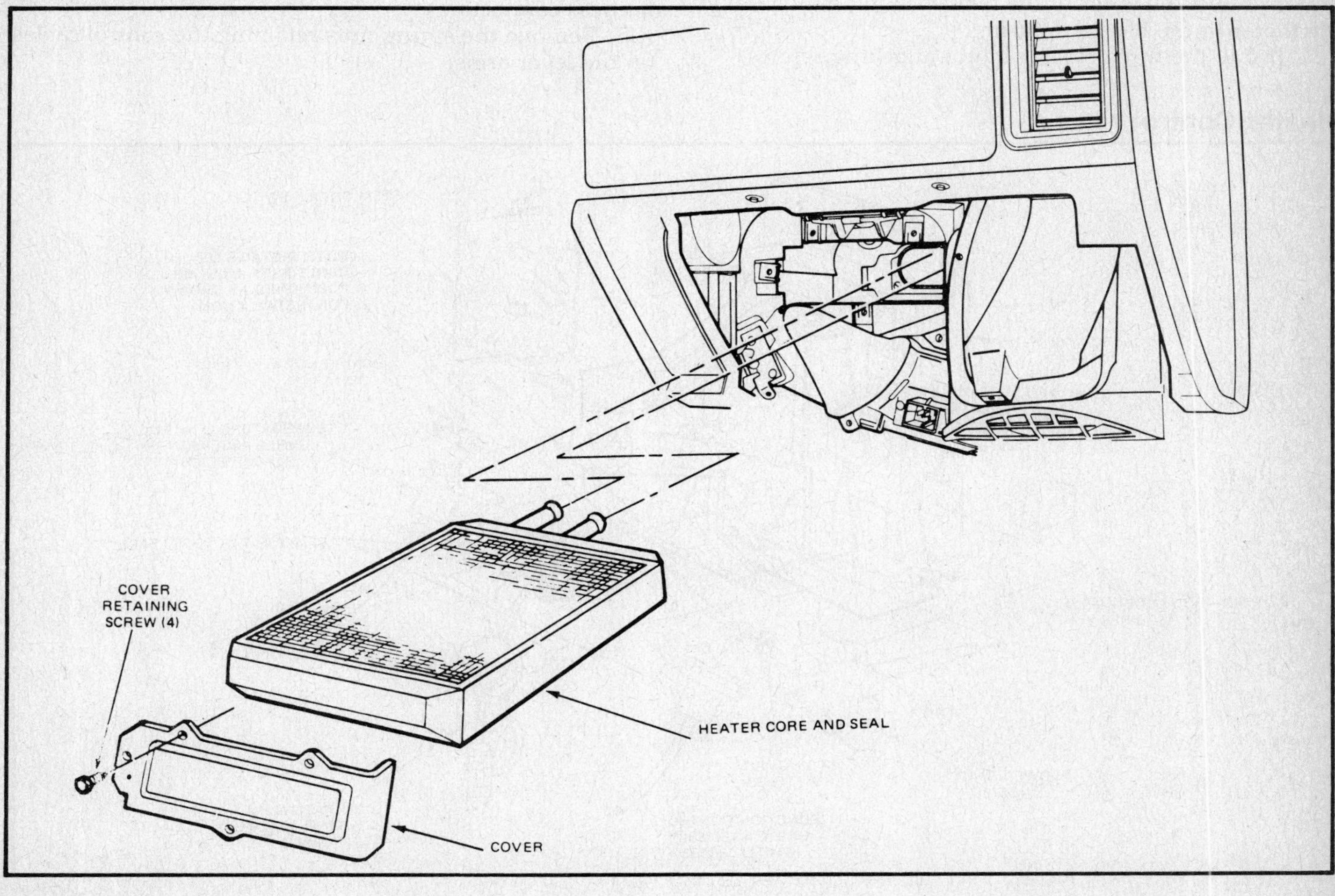

COVER
RETAINING
SCREW (4)

HEATER CORE AND SEAL

COVER

Blower Motor Wheel Removal

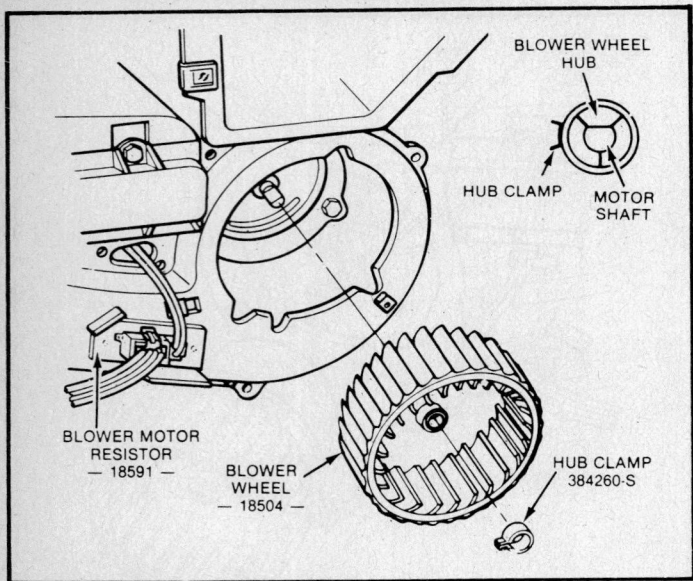

5. Pull the blower motor out from the blower housing (heater case) and disconnect the blower motor wires from the motor.

INSTALLATION

1. Connect the wires to the blower motor and position the motor in the blower housing.
2. Install the three blower motor attaching screws.

3. Position the blower wheel on the motor shaft and install the hub clamp spring.
4. Install the right ventilator assembly.
5. Check the system for proper operation.

Blower Wheel Removal

1. Remove the clamp spring from the blower wheel hub.
2. Pull the blower wheel from the blower motor shaft.

Heater Control Assembly

REMOVAL

1. Remove the two screws attaching the center finish panel to the instrument panel. Then, remove the center finish panel (unsnap).
2. Remove the four screws attaching the control assembly to the instrument panel.
3. Disconnect the function and temperature control cables from the heater case assembly.
4. Pull the control assembly out from the instrument panel and disconnect the wire connectors from the blower switch, the system ON-OFF switch, the heated back-lite switch (if so equipped) and the illumination wire harness connector.
5. Remove the spring nuts retaining the control cables on the lever arms.

Heater Control

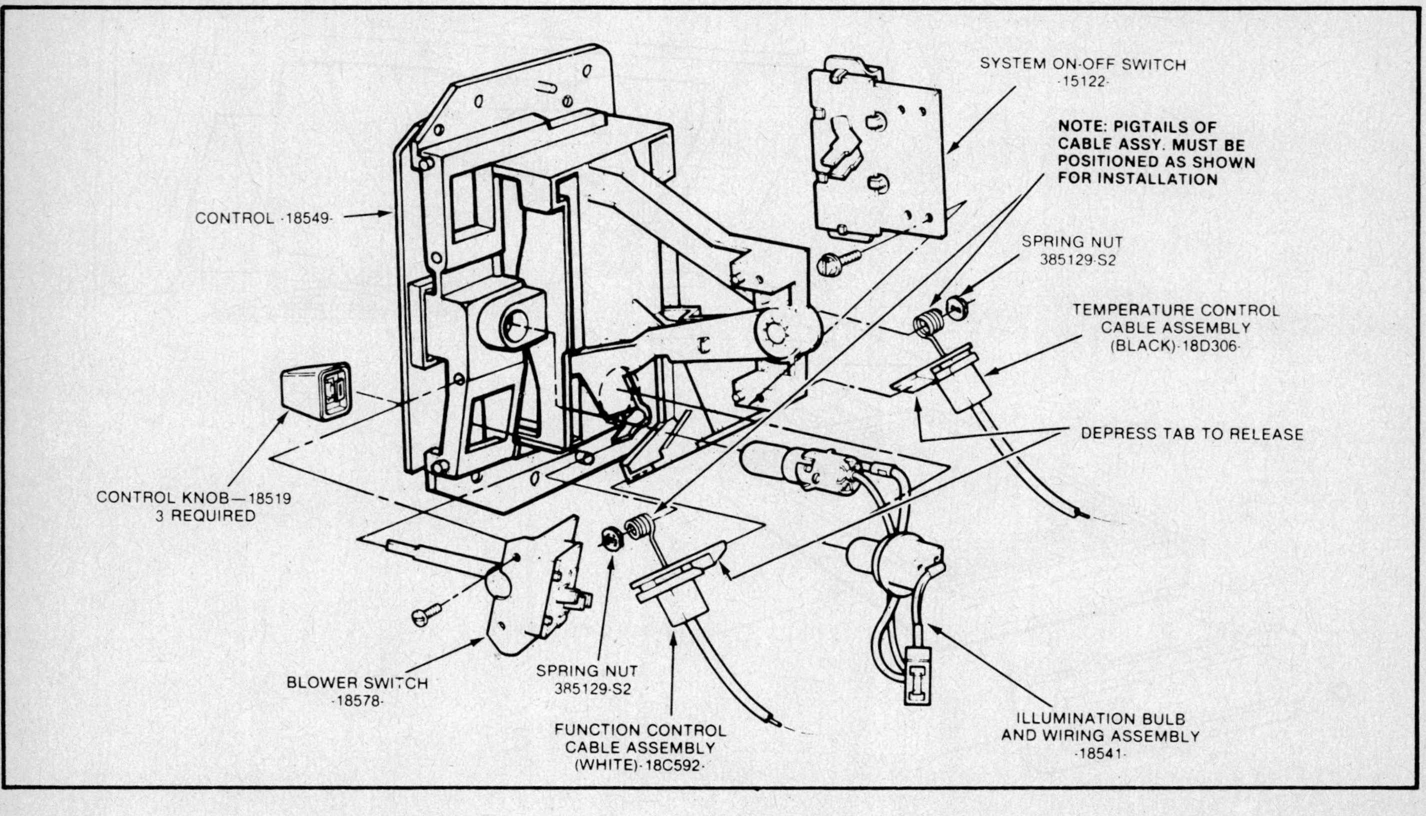

6. Disconnect the function and temperature control cable end retainers from the control assembly.

7. If the control assembly is to be replaced, transfer the necessary components to the new control assembly.

INSTALLATION

1. Connect the cable end retainers to the control assembly.

2. Place the end loop of the temperature control cable on the arm of the temperature selector lever and install a new spring nut to retain the cable end loop on the lever arm.

3. Connect the function control cable.

4. Connect the wire connectors to the blower switch, ON-OFF switch, heated back-lite switch and the illumination wire harness.

5. Position the control assembly to the instrument panel and install the four attaching screws.

6. Install the center finish panel on the instrument panel.

7. Pre-set the self-adjusting clips on the control cables.

8. Connect the control cables to the heater case assembly and adjust the cables.

9. Check the system for proper operation.

System On-Off Switch Assembly

REMOVAL

1. Remove the control assembly from the instrument panel following the procedure given for Control Assembly Removal.

2. Remove the two screws attaching the on-off switch to the control assembly and remove the switch.

INSTALLATION

1. Align the function selector lever tab with the slot of the system on-off switch. Position the switch assembly to the control assembly, taking care to align the locator pins with the holes in the switch.

2. Install the two on-off switch retaining screws and tighten them securely.

3. Install the control assembly following the procedure given for Control Assembly Installation.

Blower Switch Assembly

REMOVAL

1. Remove the control assembly from the instrument panel.

2. Remove the blower switch knob from the switch shaft by placing a suitable tool blade between the knob spring retainer and the control assembly. Then, pull on the tool, applying pressure on the spring retainer, and pull the knob off the switch shaft.

3. Remove one screw attaching the blower switch to the control assembly and remove the switch.

INSTALLATION

1. Position the blower switch to the control assembly, engaging the alignment pin with the hole in the switch mounting bracket.

2. Install the switch attaching screw and tighten the screw securely.

3. Install the control assembly following the procedure given for Control Assembly Installation.

4. Push the control knob on the blower switch shaft.

5. Check the system for proper operation.

INSTRUMENT PANEL SECTION

Radio And/Or Tape Player

REMOVAL

1. Disconnect the battery ground cable.

2. Remove the A/C floor duct, if so equipped.

3. Disconnect the power lead, speaker leads and antenna lead-in cable from the radio receiver.

4. Remove the control knobs, discs, control shaft nuts and washers.

5. Remove the ash receptacle and bracket.

6. Remove the radio.

7. Remove the radio rear support attaching nut.

INSTALLATION

1. Install the rear support to the radio and tighten the nut.

2. Position the radio on the instrument panel.

3. Install the washers and nuts on the control shafts and tighten.

4. Install the ash receptacle and bracket.

5. Install the heater or air conditioning floor ducts.

6. Connect the power leads, speaker leads and antenna-to-radio receiver.

7. Install the discs and knobs.

8. Connect the battery ground cable. Check the radio for proper operation and set the pushbuttons.

Instrument Cluster

REMOVAL

1. Disconnect the batter ground cable.

2. Remove the two lower steering column cover retaining screws and remove the steering column cover.

3. Remove the four cluster opening finish panel retaining screws and remove the finish panel.

4. Remove the two upper and lower screws which retain the cluster to the instrument panel.

5. Reach under the instrument panel and disconnect

Radio Receiver Installation

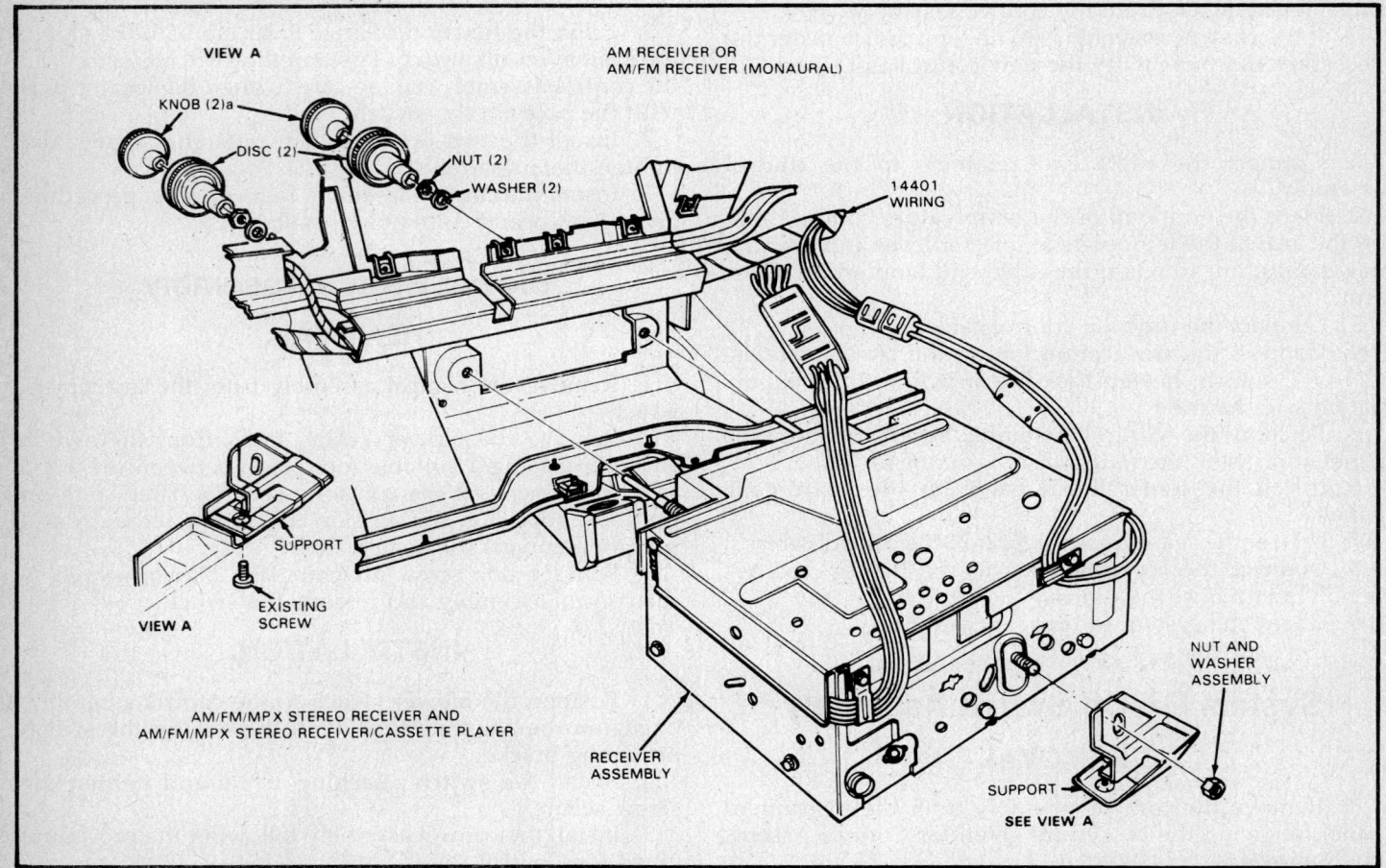

VIEW A

AM RECEIVER OR
AM/FM RECEIVER (MONAURAL)

KNOB (2)a

DISC (2)

NUT (2)

WASHER (2)

14401
WIRING

SUPPORT

EXISTING
SCREW

VIEW A

AM/FM/MPX STEREO RECEIVER AND
AM/FM/MPX STEREO RECEIVER/CASSETTE PLAYER

RECEIVER
ASSEMBLY

NUT AND
WASHER
ASSEMBLY

SUPPORT

SEE VIEW A

the speedometer cable by pressing on the flat surface of the plastic connector (quick connect).

6. Pull the cluster away from the instrument panel. Disconnect the cluster feed plug from its receptacle in the printed circuit.

INSTALLATION

To install, reverse the removal procedure.

Printed Circuit

REMOVAL

1. Disconnect the battery ground cable.
2. Remove the instrument cluster assembly.
3. Unsnap the printed circuit from the instrument voltage regulator (IVR). Remove the IVR attaching screw and remove the IVR.
4. Remove the illumination and indicator bulb and socket assemblies.
5. Remove the two screws retaining the cluster resistor and remove the resistor.
6. Remove the two fuel gauge attaching nuts. Remove the attaching nuts on the temperature gauge and tachometer, if so equipped.
7. Remove the printed circuit.

INSTALLATION

1. Position the printed circuit over the locating pins. If equipped with two printed circuits, position the smaller one first on the cluster backplate.
2. Reverse the removal procedure.

Instrument Voltage Regulator

The instrument voltage regulator (IVR) is calibrated at the manufacturing plant. Do not attempt to recalibrate the regulator. If the regulator does not function properly, it should be replaced.

To replace the IVR, remove the instrument cluster assembly. Remove the regulator to cluster retaining screw and snap off the printed circuit connector buttons.

Graphic Warning Display Module

REMOVAL

1. Remove the console finish trim panel by prying at the bottom to disengage the three retainers.
2. Remove the three module retaining screws.
3. Pull the module outward, disconnect the electrical connectors and remove the module.

Instrument Cluster

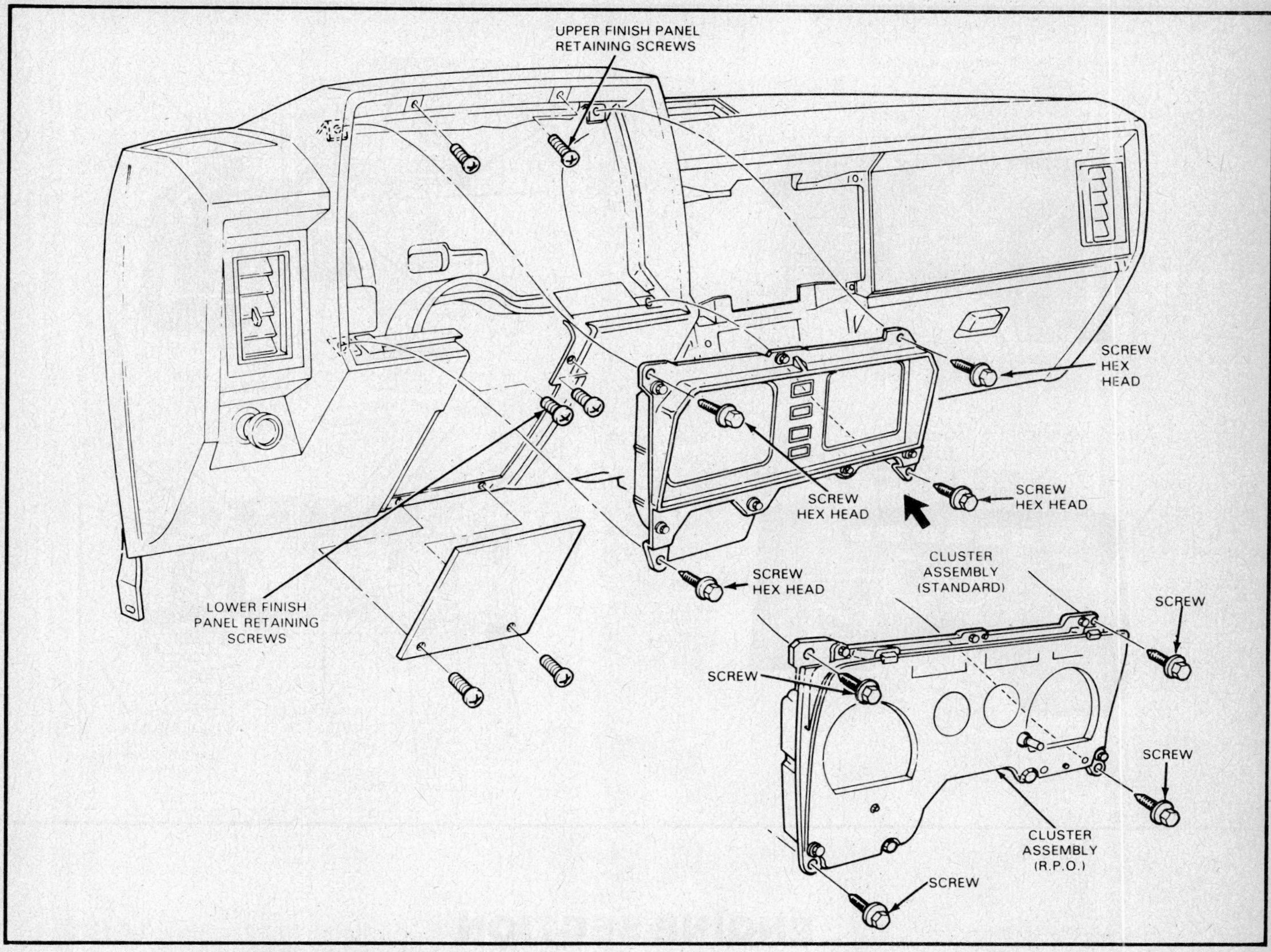

UPPER FINISH PANEL RETAINING SCREWS

SCREW HEX HEAD

SCREW HEX HEAD

SCREW HEX HEAD

SCREW HEX HEAD

CLUSTER ASSEMBLY (STANDARD)

SCREW

SCREW

SCREW

CLUSTER ASSEMBLY (R.P.O.)

SCREW

LOWER FINISH PANEL RETAINING SCREWS

INSTALLATION

Reverse the removal procedure. Make sure the locator pegs are properly seated in their respective holes before tightening the retaining screws.

CHILTON CAUTION   Do not hook up additional lights or attach external trailer lights to the vehicle. Improper hook-up may result in false warning or no warning. Substitution of headlamp bulbs other than original equipment (such as halogen for conventional) bulbs will result in a false warning or no warning.

NOTE   Do not replace resistance wire with regular wire. Replace only with complete wiring harness.

Graphic Warning Display Module

RETAINERS (3)

Printed Circuit

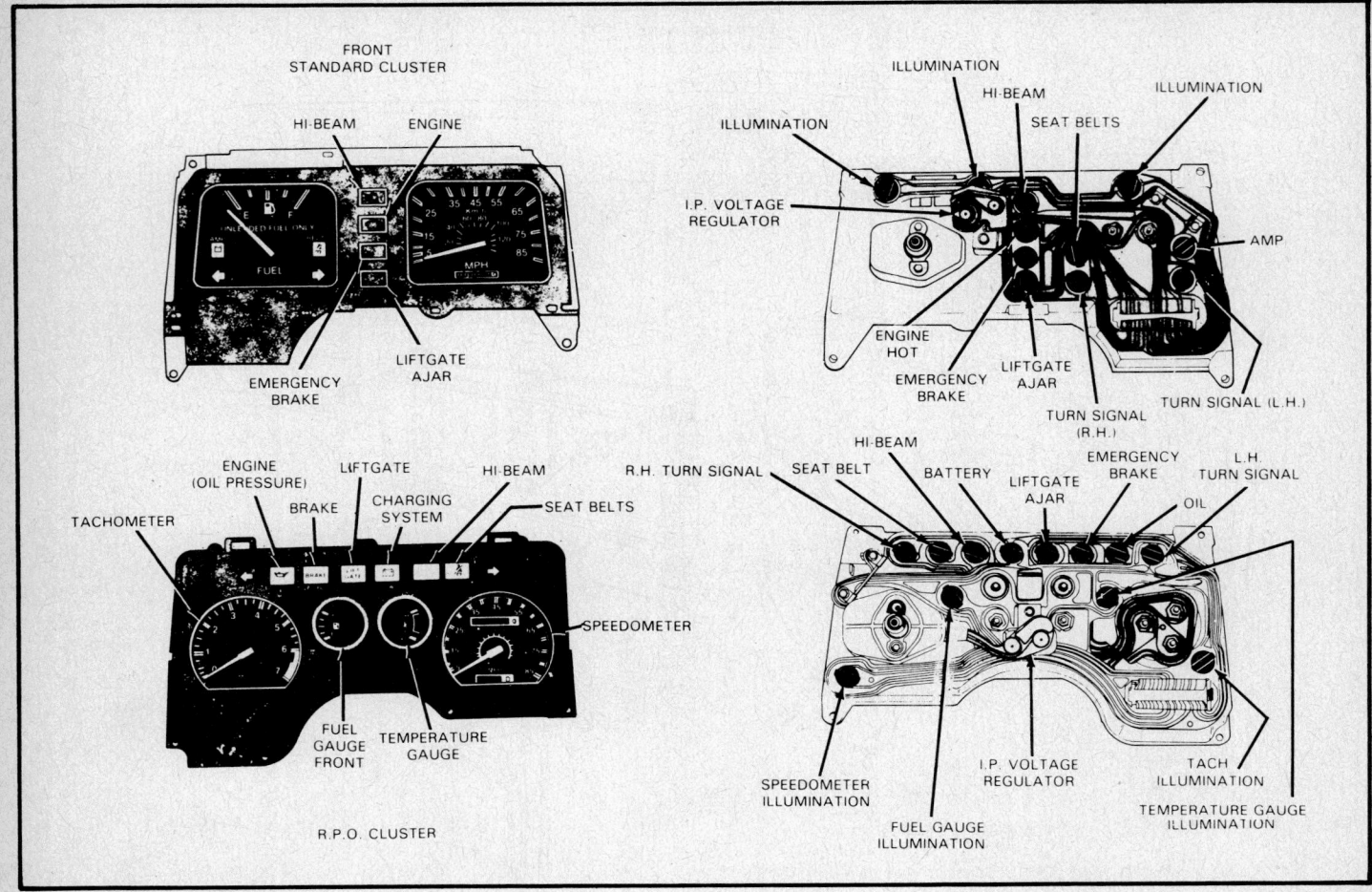

ENGINE SECTION

Engine

REMOVAL

1. Mark the location of the hinges and remove the hood.

2. Remove the air cleaner assembly, hot air tube and alternator fresh air intake tube.

3. Remove the battery and battery tray.

4. Drain the engine coolant from the radiator and the engine oil from the crankcase.

5. Remove the ignition coil and mounting bracket. Disconnect the secondary coil wire at the distributor.

6. Discharge the air conditioning system (if so equipped).

7. Disconnect the air conditioning suction hose at the hose coupler located above the air conditioning compressor. Observe all safety precautions.

8. Disconnect the radiator upper and lower hoses at the engine.

9. Disconnect the heater hoses.

10. If equipped with an automatic transaxle, disconnect the transaxle cooler lines at the rubber coupler.

11. Disconnect the electric cooling fan switch wire connector.

12. Remove the alternator fresh air intake tube.

13. Remove the fan motor and shroud assembly. Remove the radiator.

14. If equipped with power steering, remove the power steering pump filler tube.

15. Disconnect the following electrical connections.

a. Engine main wiring harness

b. Neutral safety switch (automatic transmission only)

c. Choke cap wire

d. Starter cable

e. Alternator wiring

16. Disconnect the fuel supply and fuel return lines at the rubber to metal connector on the engine.

17. Disconnect the three altitude compensator lines (if so equipped) from the carburetor. Identify each line as it is disconnected.

18. Disconnect the vacuum tree from the dash panel.

19. Disconnect the vacuum hoses from the power brake booster.

20. If equipped with speed control, remove the servo attaching screws and set the servo aside.

21. Disconnect the accelerator cable at the carburetor.

22. Disconnect the fuel EVAP hose from the metal tube at the left fender apron and lift the air conditioning liquid line over the metal EVAP tube.

23. If equipped with a manual transaxle, disconnect the clutch cable.

24. Remove the throttle cable and speed control bracket.

25. Remove the thermactor pump bracket bolt.

26. Install the engine support bar or chain.

27. Raise the vehicle on the hoist.

28. Remove the splash shields.

29. If equipped with a manual transaxle, remove the roll restrictor at the engine and body.

30. Remove the stabilizer bar.

31. Remove the lower control arm thru-bolts at the body brackets.

32. Disconnect the left tie rod from the steering knuckle.

33. Disconnect the secondary air tube (catalyst) at the check valve.

34. Disconnect the exhaust system at the exhaust pipe and at the tail pipe.

35. Remove the right half-shaft from the transaxle.

NOTE   Support the end of the shaft by suspending from an underbody component with a length of wire. Do not allow the shaft to hang unsupported, as damage to the outboard CV joint may result.

36. Remove the left side half-shaft from the transaxle, using driver T81P-4026-A or equivalent and a hammer.

37. Disconnect the speedometer cable. If equipped with an automatic transaxle, disconnect the shift selector cable.

NOTE   Mark the position of the shift control rod before disconnecting.

38. If equipped with a manual transaxle, disconnect the shift control rod.

39. If equipped with power steering, disconnect the pump return line at the pump and the pressure line at the intermediate fitting.

40. Remove the left front (No. 1) mount insulator attaching bracket, and the left front (No. 1) mount insulator with its thru-bolts.

41. Remove the left rear (No. 4) mount insulator stud nut.

42. Reach into the engine compartment and loosen the engine support bar J-bolt until the left rear (No. 4) mount insulator stud clears the mounting bracket.

43. Remove the left rear (No. 4) mount to transaxle case attaching bracket.

44. Attach the universal load positioning sling 140036 or equivalent.

45. Disconnect the 3-A engine mount.

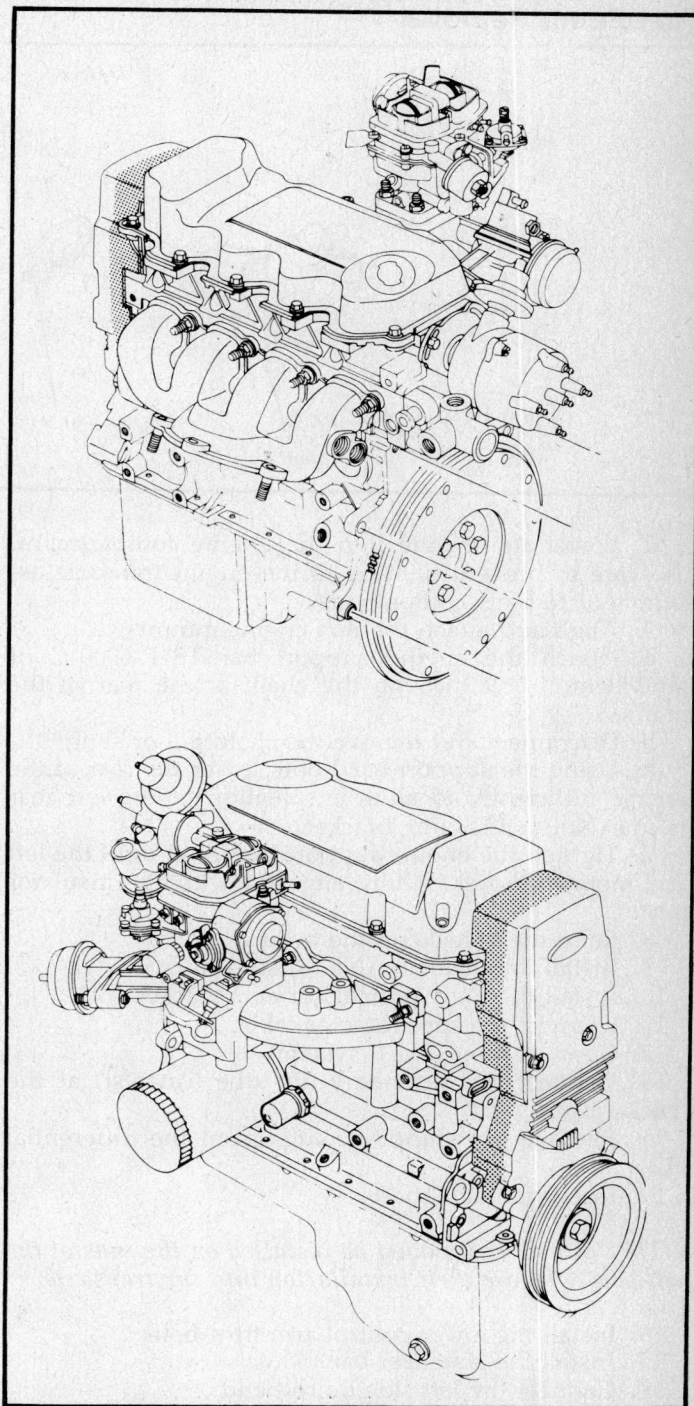

NOTE   To aid removal, maintain the engine in its relative installation position.

46. Lift the engine from the vehicle.

INSTALLATION

1. With the vehicle on a hoist and engine attached to the universal load positioning sling 140036 or equivalent or a chain fall, position the engine over the engine compartment.

Fuel Pump Removal

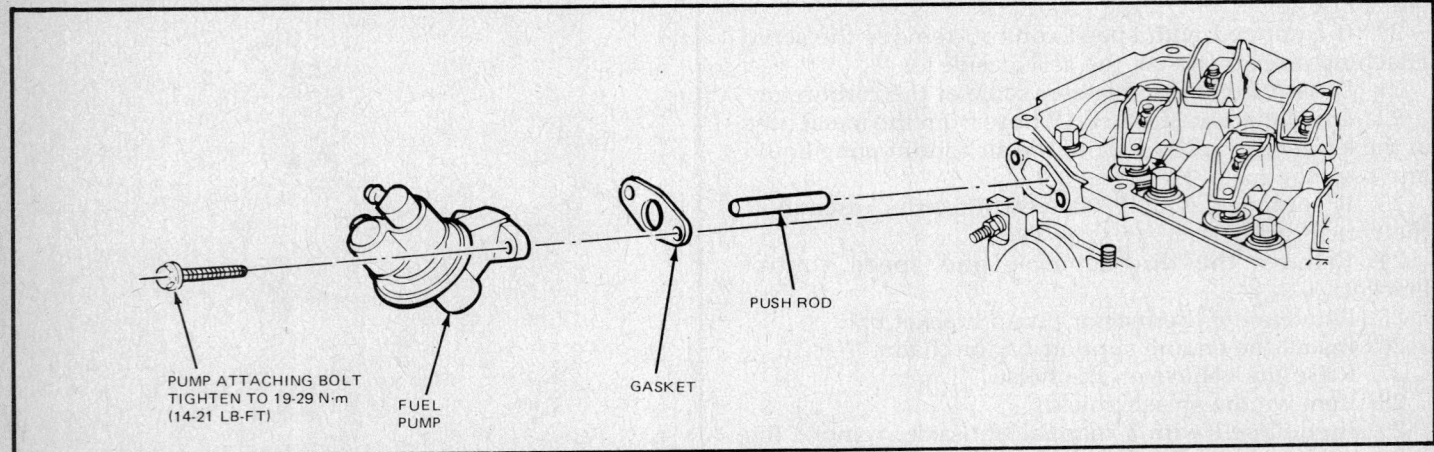

PUSH ROD

PUMP ATTACHING BOLT
TIGHTEN TO 19-29 N·m
(14-21 LB-FT)

FUEL PUMP

GASKET

2. Lower the engine into the engine compartment. Use care to prevent damage to the engine/transaxle assembly or to body components.

3. Align and attach the 3-A engine mounts.

4. Attach the engine support bar T81P-6000-C or equivalent, J-bolt through the chain at the rear of the engine.

5. Disconnect and remove the chain fall or sling.

6. Using the support bar J-bolt, lower the rear of the engine sufficiently to allow installation of the left rear mount (No. 4) attaching bracket.

7. Tighten the engine support bar J-bolt until the left rear mount bracket is fully engaged with the insulator stud.

8. Raise the vehicle on the hoist.

9. Install the insulator (No. 4) stud nut.

10. Install the (No. 1) insulator and bracket.

11. Connect the speedometer cable.

12. Connect the exhaust system.

13. Connect the secondary air tube (catalyst) at the check valve.

14. Remove the shipping plugs from the differential seals.

15. Install the half-shafts.

NOTE   A new cirlip must be installed on the ends of the half-shafts before their installation into the transaxle.

16. Install the lower control arm thru-bolts.

17. Install the stabilizer bar.

18. Connect the left side tie rod end.

19. If equipped with an automatic transaxle, connect the transaxle cooler lines.

20. Connect the starter cable at the starter.

21. If equipped with an automatic transaxle, connect the manual shift linkage attaching bracket and cable, using reference marks made during removal.

22. If equipped with an automatic transaxle, connect the ATX selector cable.

23. If equipped with power steering, connect the power steering return lines.

24. Connect the heater hoses.

25. Install the splash shields.

26. Lower the vehicle.

27. Remove the engine support bar.

28. If equipped with a manual transaxle, install the roll restrictor.

29. Install the thermactor pump bracket bolt.

30. Connect the throttle cable and, if equipped, the speed control bracket.

31. If equipped with a manual transaxle, connect the clutch cable.

32. Route the air conditioning liquid line under the metal EVAP tube and connect the fuel EVAP rubber hose to the metal EVAP tube at the fender apron.

33. Connect the vacuum tree to the dash panel and all vacuum lines to the tree.

34. Connect the altitude compensator lines to the carburetor, if so equipped. Refer to the removal procedure for proper line identification.

35. Connect the fuel line and fuel return line at the rubber connector.

36. Connect the necessary electrical connectors.

37. Install the radiator, fan motor and shroud assembly.

38. Connect the electric cooling fan connection.

39. Install the alternator fresh air intake tube.

40. Connect the radiator upper and lower hoses.

NOTE   Check all fluid levels and correct as necessary.

41. Start the engine and check for coolant, vacuum and oil leaks.

42. Raise the front wheels.

43. Cycle the transaxle through all operating ranges.

44. Charge the air conditioning system.

Motor Mounts

1. Place a jack and a wood block under the engine.

2. Raise the engine just enough to relieve the strain.

3. Remove the insulator bolts.

4. Replace the mount.

5. Lower the engine and remove the jack.

Engine Mounts

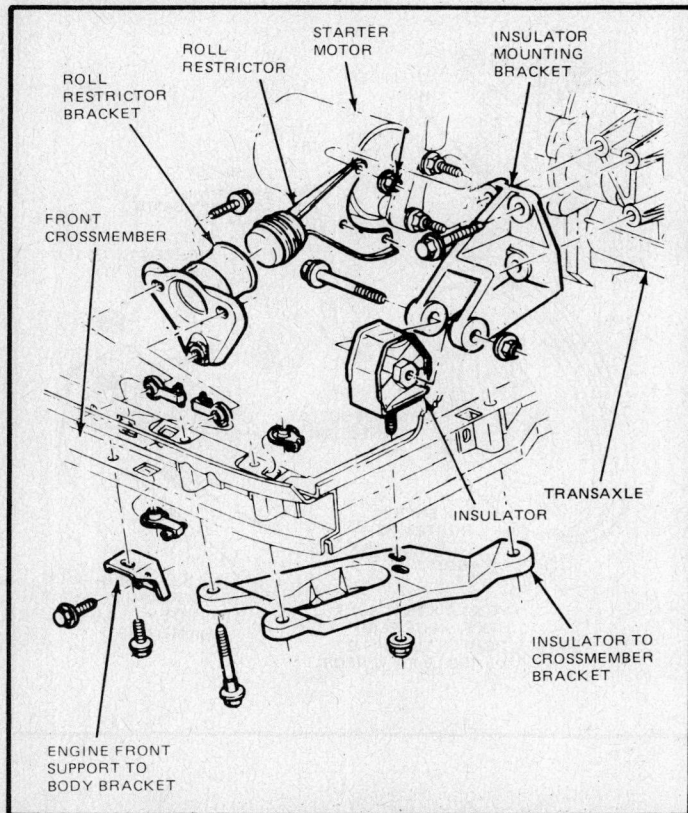

Left-hand front no. 1 insulator manual transaxle

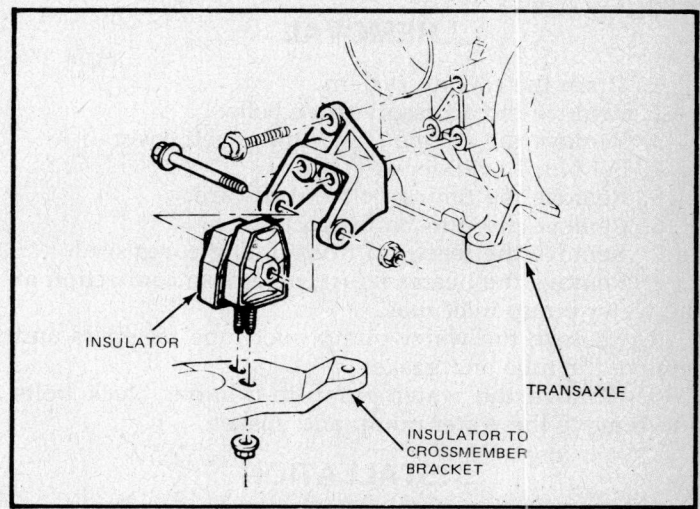

Left-hand front no. 1 insulator automatic transaxle

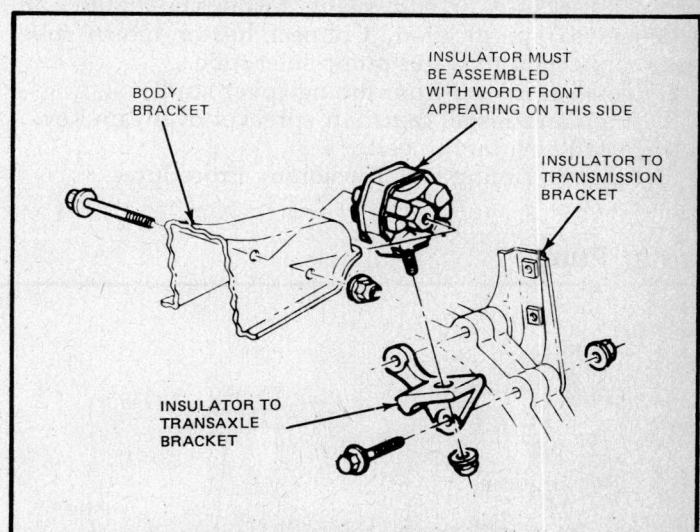

Left-hand rear no. 4 insulator automatic transaxle

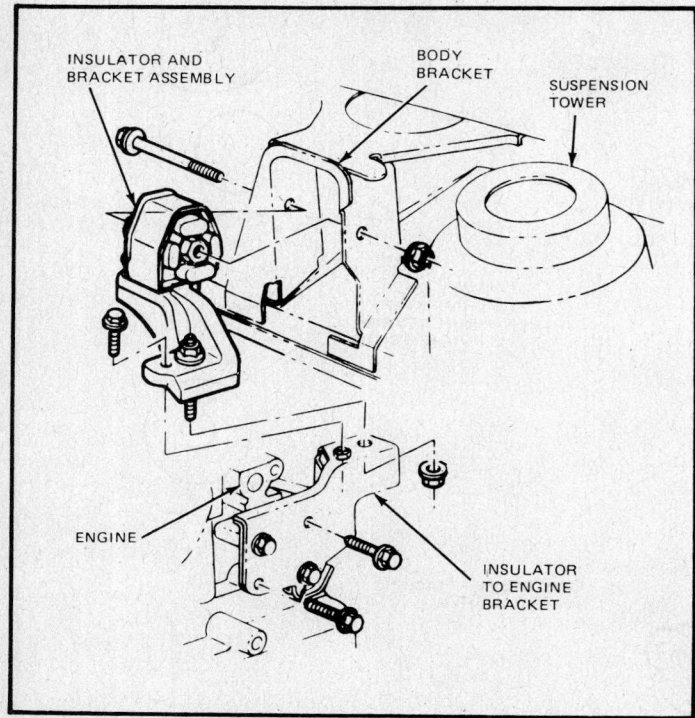

Right-hand no. 3A insulator

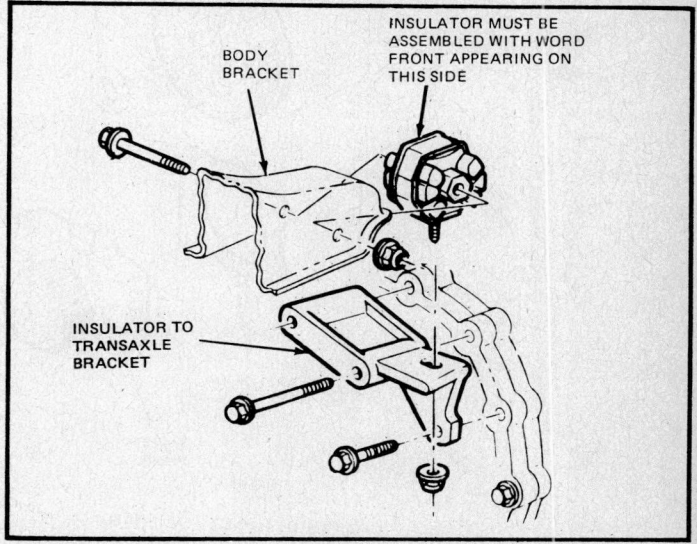

Left-hand rear no. 4 insulator manual transaxle

Water Pump

REMOVAL

1. Drain the cooling system.
2. Remove the accessory drive belts.
3. Remove the engine front timing belt cover.
4. Set No. 1 cylinder at TDC.
5. Remove the timing belt and discard.
6. Remove the camshaft sprocket.
7. Remove the rearward front timing cover stud.
8. Remove the heater return tube hose connection at the water pump inlet tube.
9. Remove the water pump inlet tube fasteners and remove the tube and gasket.
10. Remove the water pump-to-cylinder block bolts and remove the water pump and gasket.

INSTALLATION

1. Install water pump inlet tube and new gasket. Use Tool T81L-6254-A or equivalent. Install and tighten all fasteners to specification. Connect heater return tube hose connection to water pump inlet tube.
2. Install rearward front timing cover stud.
3. Align and install camshaft sprocket over cam key.
4. Install new timing belt.
5. Refer to Timing Belt Tensioning Procedures.

Thermostat Removal

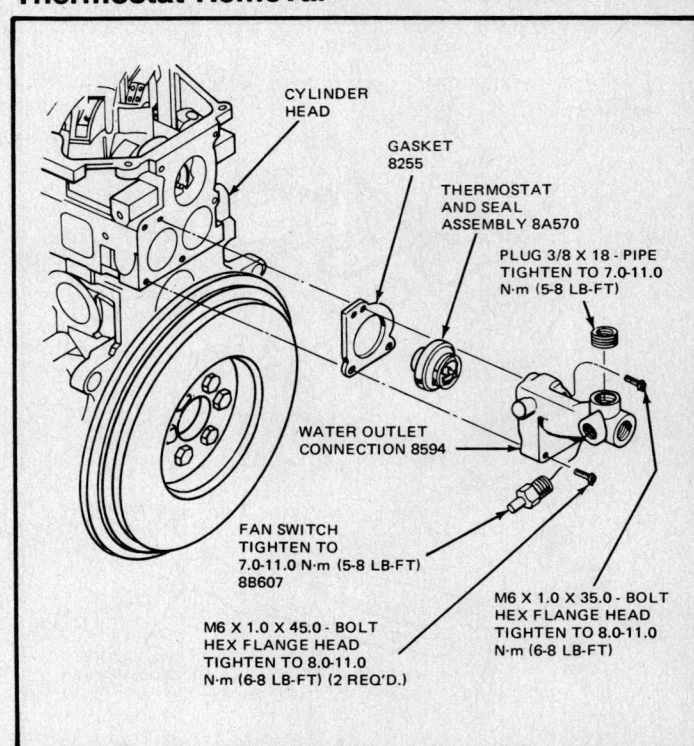

CYLINDER HEAD

GASKET 8255

THERMOSTAT AND SEAL ASSEMBLY 8A570

PLUG 3/8 X 18 - PIPE TIGHTEN TO 7.0-11.0 N·m (5-8 LB-FT)

WATER OUTLET CONNECTION 8594

FAN SWITCH TIGHTEN TO 7.0-11.0 N·m (5-8 LB-FT) 8B607

M6 X 1.0 X 45.0 - BOLT HEX FLANGE HEAD TIGHTEN TO 8.0-11.0 N·m (6-8 LB-FT) (2 REQ'D.)

M6 X 1.0 X 35.0 - BOLT HEX FLANGE HEAD TIGHTEN TO 8.0-11.0 N·m (6-8 LB-FT)

Water Pump

CAMSHAFT SPROCKET

WASHER

ATTACHING BOLT – DO NOT TIGHTEN

WATER PUMP GASKET

WATER PUMP

CRANKSHAFT GEAR

CAMSHAFT POINTER MUST BE ALIGNED WITH THE TIMING MARK.

TURN THE CRANKSHAFT UNTIL KEYWAY IS AT 12 O'CLOCK.

TIGHTEN THE ATTACHING BOLTS TO 7-10 N·m (5-7 LB-FT)

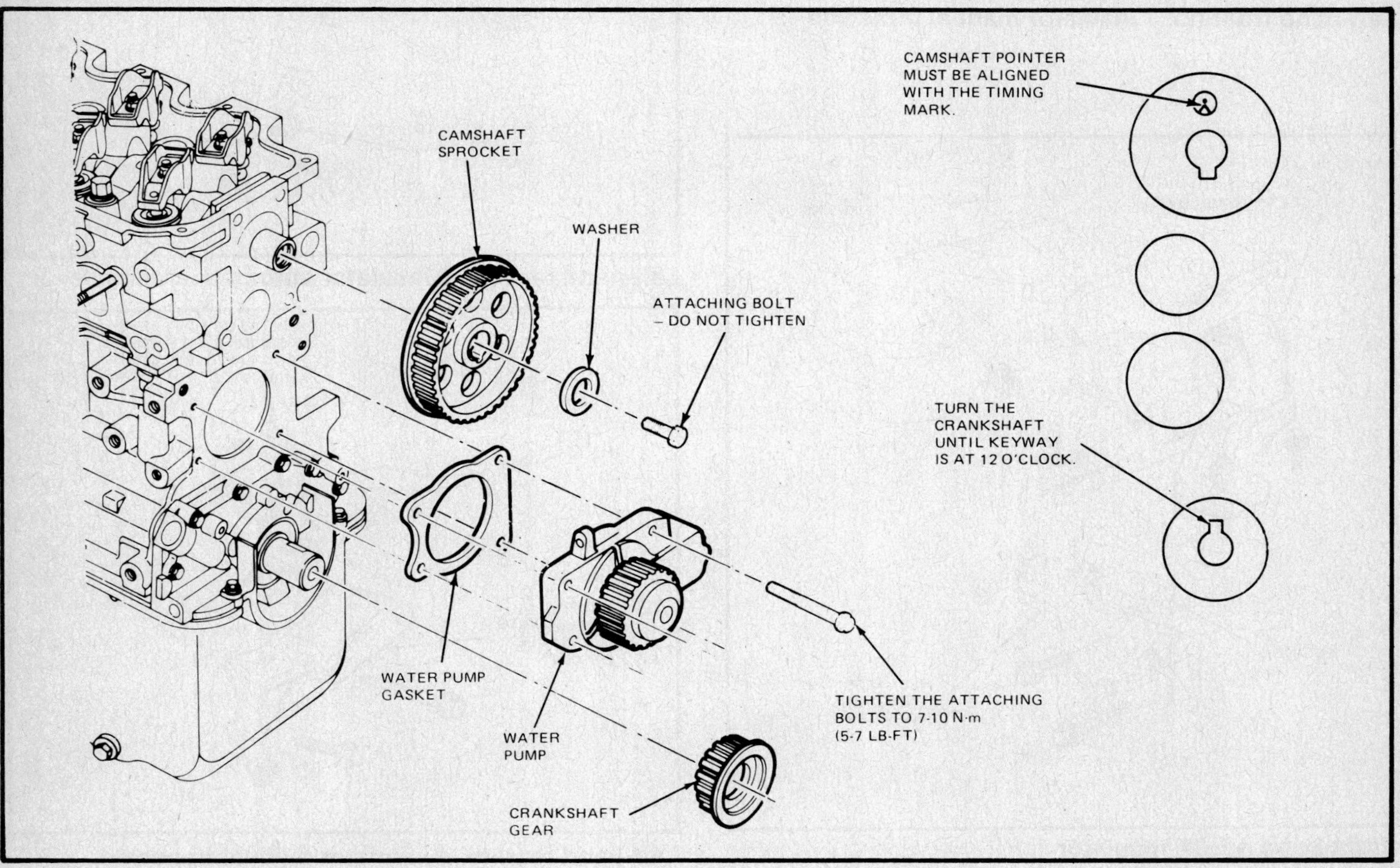

Oil Pan

REMOVAL

1. Disconnect the negative cable at the battery.
2. Raise the vehicle on a hoist.
3. Drain the crankcase.
4. Disconnect the cable at the starter.
5. Remove the knee brace.
6. Remove the starter attaching bolts and the starter.
7. Remove the knee braces at the transaxle.
8. Remove the oil pan retaining bolts and the oil pan.
9. Remove the oil pan front seal.
10. Remove the oil pan rear seal.
11. Remove the two oil pan side gaskets.

INSTALLATION

1. Clean the oil pan gasket surface and the mating surface on the cylinder block.
2. Remove and clean the oil pump pick-up tube and screen assembly. After cleaning, install the tube and screen assembly.
3. Apply sealer approximately 3.0 mm wide at the corner of the oil pan front and rear seals and at the seating point of the oil pump to the block retainer joint.
4. Install the front oil pan seal by pressing firmly into the oil pump slot cut into the bottom of the oil pump.
5. Install the oil pan rear seal by pressing firmly into the slot cut into the rear retainer assembly.
6. Apply adhesive evenly to the oil pan flange and to the pan side of the gaskets. Allow the adhesive to dry past the "wet" stage. Then install the gaskets on the oil pan.
7. Install the oil pan on the cylinder block.
8. Install the oil pan attaching bolts. Tighten the bolts in the proper sequence and to the specified torque.
9. Position the transaxle inspection plate and the rear section of the knee-brace on the transaxle and install the two attaching bolts. Tighten the bolts to specification.
10. Install the starter.
11. Install the knee-brace to the starter.
12. Connect the starter cable.
13. Lower the vehicle and fill the crankcase with oil.
14. Connect the negative cable at the battery.
15. Start the engine and check for oil leaks.

Cylinder Head

REMOVAL

1. Disconnect the negative cable at the battery.
2. Drain the cooling system and disconnect the heater hose at the fitting located under the intake manifold.
3. Disconnect the radiator upper hose at the cylinder head.
4. Disconnect the wiring terminal from the cooling fan switch.
5. Remove the air cleaner assembly.
6. Remove the PCV hose.
7. Disconnect the required vacuum hoses.

Oil Pan Removal

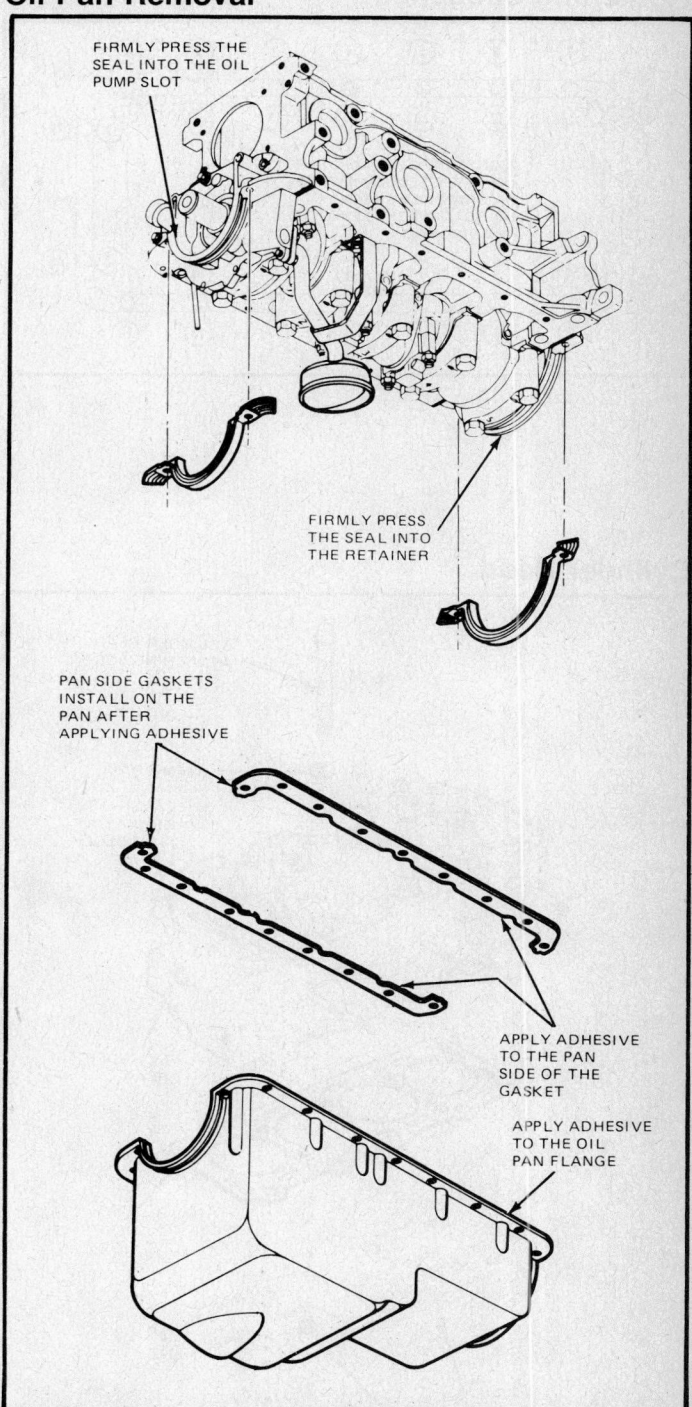

FIRMLY PRESS THE SEAL INTO THE OIL PUMP SLOT

FIRMLY PRESS THE SEAL INTO THE RETAINER

PAN SIDE GASKETS INSTALL ON THE PAN AFTER APPLYING ADHESIVE

APPLY ADHESIVE TO THE PAN SIDE OF THE GASKET

APPLY ADHESIVE TO THE OIL PAN FLANGE

8. Remove the rocker arm cover.
9. Disconnect all accessory drive belts.
10. Remove the crankshaft pulley.
11. Remove the timing belt cover.
12. Set the engine No. 1 cylinder to TDC prior to removing the timing belt.
13. Remove the distributor cap and spark plug wires as an assembly.
14. Loosen both belt tensioner attaching bolts using Tool T81P-6254-A or equivalent.

Tightening Sequence

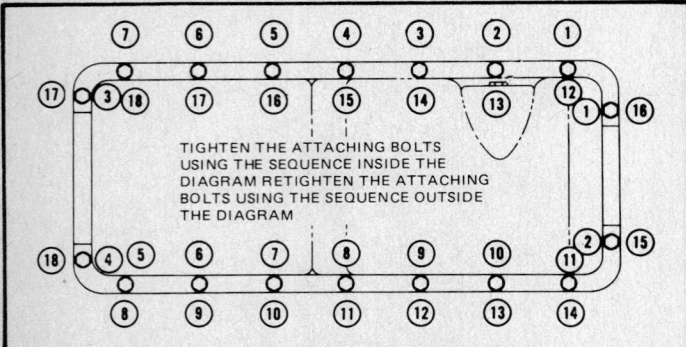

TIGHTEN THE ATTACHING BOLTS USING THE SEQUENCE INSIDE THE DIAGRAM RETIGHTEN THE ATTACHING BOLTS USING THE SEQUENCE OUTSIDE THE DIAGRAM

Cylinder Head

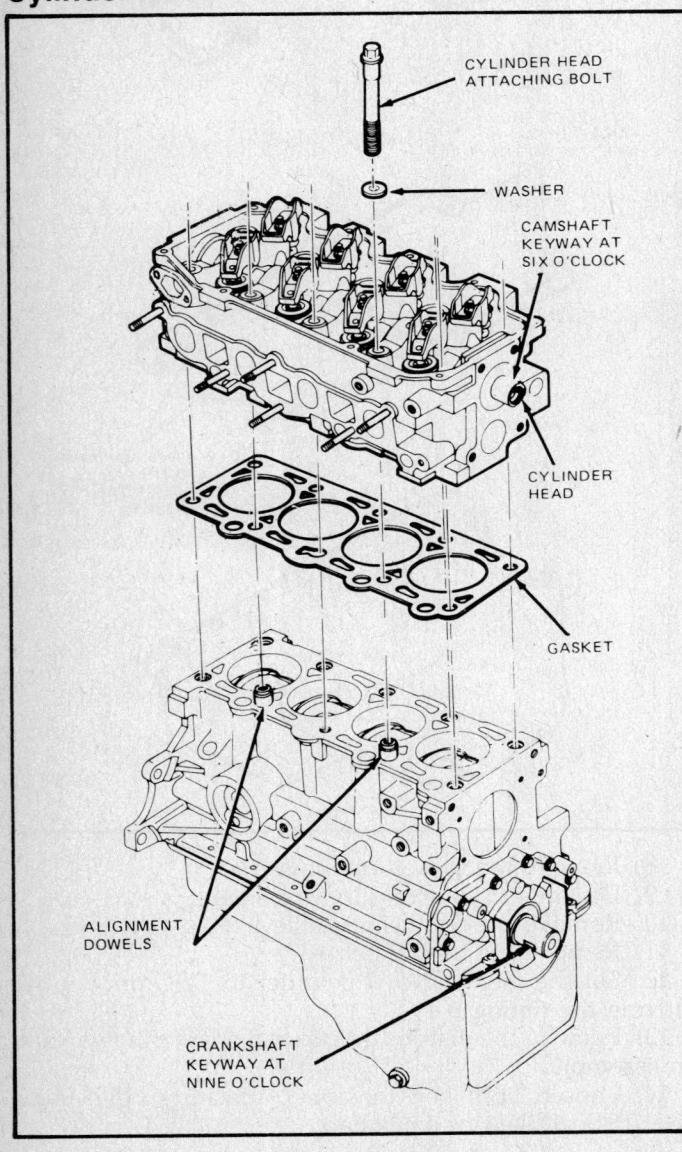

CYLINDER HEAD ATTACHING BOLT

WASHER

CAMSHAFT KEYWAY AT SIX O'CLOCK

CYLINDER HEAD

GASKET

ALIGNMENT DOWELS

CRANKSHAFT KEYWAY AT NINE O'CLOCK

15. Secure the belt tensioner as far left as possible.

16. Remove the timing belt and discard.

17. Disconnect the EGR tube at the EGR valve.

18. Disconnect the PVS hose connectors, using tool T81P-8564-A or equivalent. Label the connectors and set aside.

19. Disconnect the choke cap wire.

20. Disconnect the fuel supply and return lines at the metal connectors, located on the right side of the engine. Set the rubber lines aside.

21. Disconnect the accelerator cable and, if equipped, the speed control cable.

22. Disconnect the altitude compensator, if so equipped, from the dash panel and place on the heater/AC air intake.

23. Disconnect the alternator air intake tube and the alternator wiring harness.

24. Remove the alternator and its mounting bracket.

25. If equipped with power steering, remove the thermactor pump drive belt, the pump and the pump mounting bracket.

26. Disconnect the exhaust system at the exhaust pipe.

27. Remove the cylinder head bolts and washers. Discard the bolts, as they cannot be reused.

28. Remove the cylinder head with the exhaust and intake manifolds attached.

29. Remove the cylinder head gasket.

***CHILTON CAUTION** Do not lay the cylinder head flat. Damage to the spark plugs or gasket surfaces may result.*

INSTALLATION

NOTE Before installing the cylinder head, the crankshaft must be rotated so that the No. 1 piston is ninety degrees before top dead center (BTDC). To position the piston, turn the crankshaft until the pulley keyway is at nine o'clock. To time the valve train to this piston position, turn the camshaft until the keyway is at the six o'clock position. The camshaft and crankshaft MUST NOT BE TURNED until after the installation of the timing gears and belt.

1. Position the cylinder head gasket on the cylinder block.

2. Install the cylinder head and install new bolts and washers.

NOTE The cylinder head attaching bolts cannot be tightened to the specified torque more than once and must therefore be replaced when installing a cylinder head.

NOTE Apply Loctite® (or equivalent) to the attaching bolts.

3. Connect the exhaust system at the exhaust pipe.

4. Install the thermactor pump mounting bracket, pump and drive belt, if removed.

5. Install the alternator mounting bracket and the alternator.

6. Connect the alternator wiring harness and alternator air intake tube.

7. Connect the altitude compensator, if so equipped.

8. Connect the accelerator cable and, if equipped, the speed control cable.

9. Connect the fuel supply and return lines at the metal connector, located on the right side of the engine.

10. Connect the choke cap wire.

11. Connect the labeled PVS hose connectors using Tool T81L-8620-A or equivalent.

12. Connect the EGR tube to the EGR valve.

NOTE   Each time the timing belt tension is released or the belt is removed, a new belt must be installed. Refer to the Timing Belt Tensioning and Replacement procedures.

13. Install the timing belt cover.

14. Install the crankshaft pulley.

15. Install the distributor cap and spark plug wires.

16. Install the rocker cover gasket on the rocker cover. Use contact cement to hold the gasket in position.

17. Position the rocker arm cover on the cylinder head and install attaching bolts. Tighten the bolts to specification and in the proper sequence.

18. Connect the required vacuum hoses.

19. Connect the wiring terminal to the cooling fan switch.

20. Connect the radiator upper hose at the cylinder head.

21. Connect the heater hose to the fitting located below the intake manifold.

22. Fill the cooling system to the proper level.

23. Connect the negative ground cable.

24. Start the engine and check for vacuum, coolant and oil leaks.

25. After the engine has reached operating temperature, check and add coolant if necessary.

26. Adjust the ignition timing and connect the distributor vacuum line.

27. Install the PCV hose.

28. Install the air cleaner assembly.

Camshaft

REMOVAL

CHILTON CAUTION   Make sure the crankshaft is positioned at TDC and do not turn the crankshaft until the timing belt is installed.

1. Disconnect the cable from the battery negative terminal.

2. Remove the air cleaner assembly.

3. Remove the PCV hose.

4. Remove the accessory drive belts.

5. Remove the crankshaft pulley.

6. Remove the timing belt cover.

7. Remove the valve cover attaching bolts and studs. Remove the valve cover.

8. Set the engine No. 1 cylinder at TDC prior to removing the timing belt.

Tightening Sequence

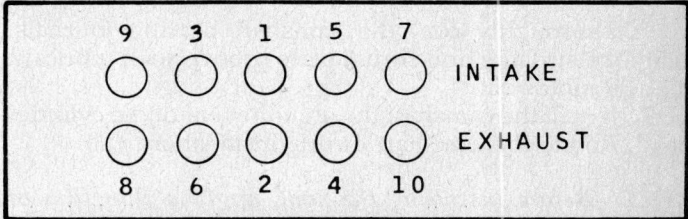

Tighten the attaching bolts to 60 N·m (44 lb-ft) in the sequence shown. After tightening, turn the bolts 90 degrees in the same sequence. Complete the bolt tightening by turning an additional 90 degrees in the same sequence.

9. Remove rocker arms and tappets as follows.

a. Remove the hex flange nuts.

b. Remove the fulcrums.

c. Remove the rocker arms.

d. Remove the fulcrum washer.

e. Remove the tappets.

10. Remove the distributor assembly.

11. Loosen both timing belt tensioner attaching bolts using Tool T81P-6254-A or equivalent.

12. Remove the crankshaft pulley.

13. Remove the timing belt and discard.

14. Remove the camshaft sprocket and key.

15. Remove the camshaft thrust plate.

16. Remove the fuel pump as follows.

a. Loosen the fuel supply line attaching nut at the fuel pump outlet.

b. Loosen the fuel pump mounting bolts two turns.

c. Manually rotate the engine to position the pump push rod on the low side of the cam.

d. Remove the rubber hose and clamp from the fuel pump inlet.

e. Disconnect the fuel line from the fuel pump inlet.

f. Disconnect the fuel line from the fuel pump outlet.

g. Remove the fuel pump mounting bolts, and fuel pump, gasket and push rod.

17. Remove the ignition coil and coil bracket.

18. Remove the camshaft through the back of the head towards the transaxle.

19. Inspect the camshaft seal. Replace the seal if it shows any signs of wear or damage.

Camshaft Gear

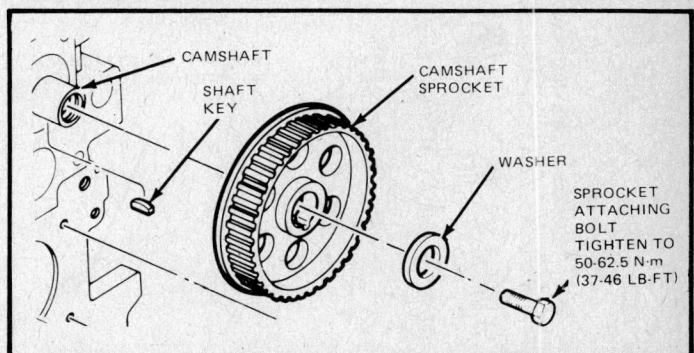

INSTALLATION

1. Thoroughly coat the camshaft bearing journals, cam lobe surfaces and thrust plate groove with lubricant SAE 30 motor oil.

2. Install the camshaft through the rear of the cylinder head. Rotate the camshaft during installation.

NOTE   Before installing the cam, apply a thin film of lubricant SAE 30 motor oil to the lip of the camshaft seal.

Camshaft Installation

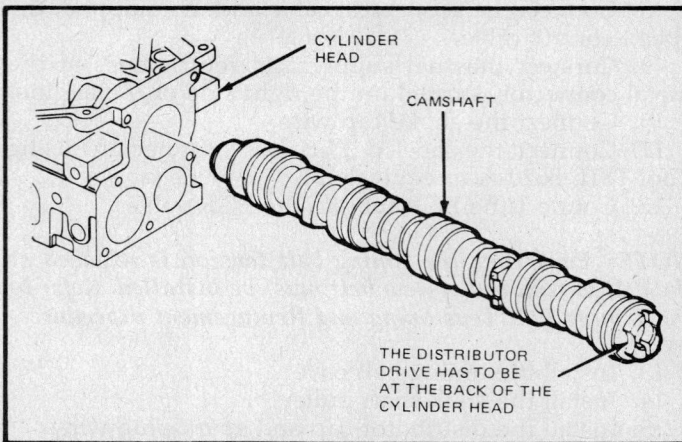

Cylinder Head

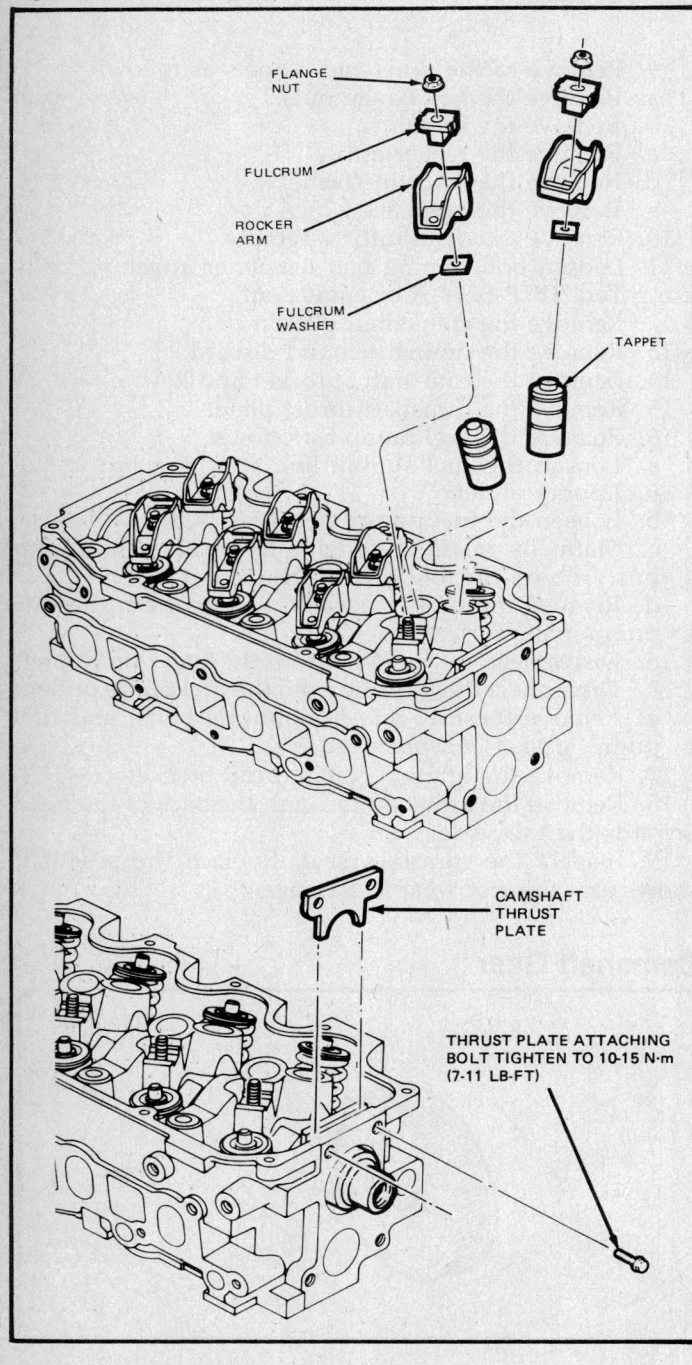

3. Install the camshaft thrust plate. Tighten the attaching bolts to specification.

4. Align and install the cam gear over the cam key. Install the attaching washer and bolt. While holding the camshaft. Tighten the bolt to specification.

NOTE   Each time the timing belt tension is released or the belt is removed, a new belt must be installed.

5. Install the timing belt cover.
6. Install the fuel pump and push rod.
a. Connect the fuel line to the outlet fitting.
b. Connect the rubber hose to the fuel pump inlet tube and install the hose clamp. Tighten the fitting to 20-24 N•m (15-18 lb-ft).
7. Install the rocker arm assembly as follows.

NOTE   Replace used hex flange nuts with new ones.

Camshaft End Play

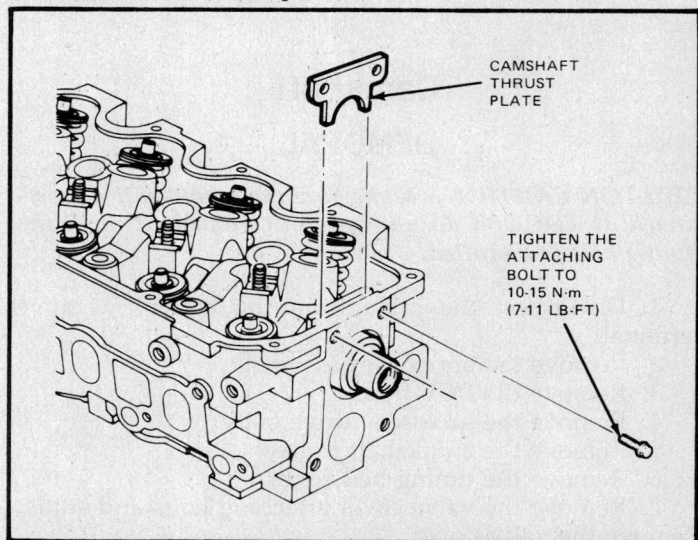

Camshaft end play should be 0.050-0.150mm (0.002-0.006 in.).

a. Install the tappets.

b. Install the fulcrum washers.

c. Install the rocker arms.

d. Install the fulcrums.

e. Install new rocker arm stud hex flange nuts. Tighten the nuts to the specified torque.

8. Install the distributor assembly.

9. Install the rocker arm cover attaching bolts and studs. Tighten the bolts and studs to the specified torque.

10. Install the PCV hose.

11. Install the air cleaner assembly.

Timing Belt Tensioning and Replacement Procedures

REMOVAL

NOTE Each time the timing belt tension is released or the belt is removed, a new belt must be installed.

CHILTON CAUTION With the timing belt removed and pistons at TDC, DO NOT rotate the camshaft. If the camshaft must be rotated, align the crankshaft pulley 90 degrees BTDC.

1. Disconnect the negative ground cable at the battery.

2. Remove the accessory drive belts.

3. Remove the timing belt cover.

NOTE Align timing mark on the camshaft sprocket with the timing mark on the cylinder head.

4. Install the timing belt cover and confirm that the timing mark on the crankshaft pulley aligns with the TDC on the front cover.

5. Remove the timing belt cover.

6. Loosen both timing belt tensioner attaching bolts using Tool T81P-6254-A or equivalent.

7. Pry the belt tensioner away from the belt as far as possible and tighten one of the tensioner attaching bolts.

8. Remove the crankshaft pulley.

9. Remove the timing belt and discard.

Installation

1. Install the timing belt over the gears in a counter-clockwise direction starting at the crankshaft. Keep the belt span from the crankshaft to the camshaft tight as the belt is installed over the remaining gears.

2. Loosen belt tensioner attaching bolts one-quarter to one-half turn maximum. Allow the tensioner to snap against the belt.

3. Tighten one of the tensioner attaching bolts using torque wrench adapter T81P-6254-A or equivalent.

4. Install the crankshaft pulley, the drive plate and the pulley attaching bolt.

5. Hold the crankshaft pulley stationary using crankshaft belt wrench YA-826 or equivalent. Tighten the pul-

Timing Belt

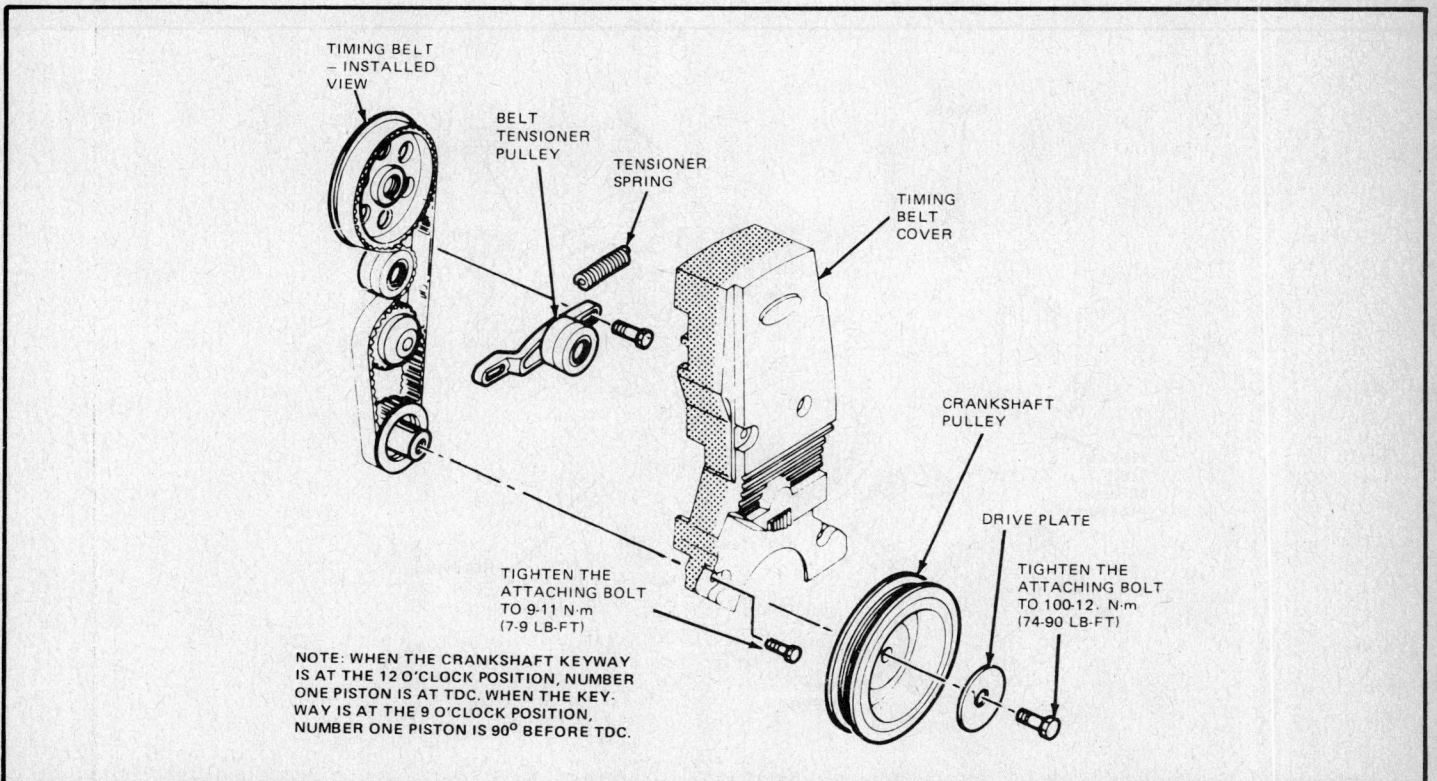

TIMING BELT – INSTALLED VIEW

BELT TENSIONER PULLEY

TENSIONER SPRING

TIMING BELT COVER

CRANKSHAFT PULLEY

DRIVE PLATE

TIGHTEN THE ATTACHING BOLT TO 9-11 N·m (7-9 LB-FT)

TIGHTEN THE ATTACHING BOLT TO 100-12. N·m (74-90 LB-FT)

NOTE: WHEN THE CRANKSHAFT KEYWAY IS AT THE 12 O'CLOCK POSITION, NUMBER ONE PISTON IS AT TDC. WHEN THE KEYWAY IS AT THE 9 O'CLOCK POSITION, NUMBER ONE PISTON IS 90° BEFORE TDC.

When the crankshaft keyway is at the 2 o'clock position, number one piston is at TDC. When the keyway is at the 9 o'clock position, number one piston is 90° before TDC.

ley attaching bolt 100-121 N•m (74-87 lb-ft) using crankshaft pulley wrench T81P-6312-A or equivalent.

6. Rotate the crankshaft two complete revolutions. Make sure the cam sprocket pointer is aligned with the TDC mark.

7. Loosen the belt tensioner attaching bolt one-quarter to one-half turn maximum.

8. To prevent rotation of the crankshaft, have a helper hold the crankshaft using wrench T81P-6312-A or equivalent. While the torque is applied, the crankshaft must not be allowed to turn.

9. With the crankshaft held, apply torque to the camshaft sprocket as follows.

1.3L: Turn the cam sprocket counterclockwise until the torque wrench reads 70-75 N•m (52-55 lb-ft). While holding the torque, tighten the tensioner attaching bolts.

1.6L: Turn the cam sprocket counterclockwise until the torque wrench reads 60-65 N•m (44-48 lb-ft). While holding the torque, tighten the tensioner attaching bolts.

NOTE Do not apply the torque to the camshaft sprocket attaching bolt. Apply it to the hex on the sprocket.

10. Install the timing belt cover.

11. Install the accessory drive belts and adjust to the specified tension.

12. Connect the negative cable at the battery. Start the engine and set the ignition timing to calibration specification.

Oil Pump
REMOVAL

1. Disconnect the negative cable at the battery.

2. Loosen the alternator bolt on the alternator adjusting arm. Lower the alternator to remove the accessory drivebelt from the crankshaft pulley.

3. Remove the timing belt cover.

4. Loosen both belt tensioner attaching bolts using Tool T81P-6254-A or equivalent on the left bolt.

NOTE Set No. 1 cylinder at TDC prior to removing the timing belt.

5. Disengage the timing belt from the camshaft pulley, water pump gear and the crankshaft pulley.

6. Raise the vehicle on a hoist.

7. Drain the crankcase.

8. Using crankshaft pulley wrench T81P-6312-A or equivalent, remove the crankshaft pulley attaching bolt.

9. Remove the timing belt and discard.

10. Remove the crankshaft drive plate assembly.

11. Remove the crankshaft pulley.

12. Remove the crankshaft gear.

13. Disconnect the starter cable at the starter.

14. Remove the knee-brace from the engine.

15. Remove the starter.

16. Remove the rear section of the knee-brace and inspection plate at the transmission.

Engine Oil Pump

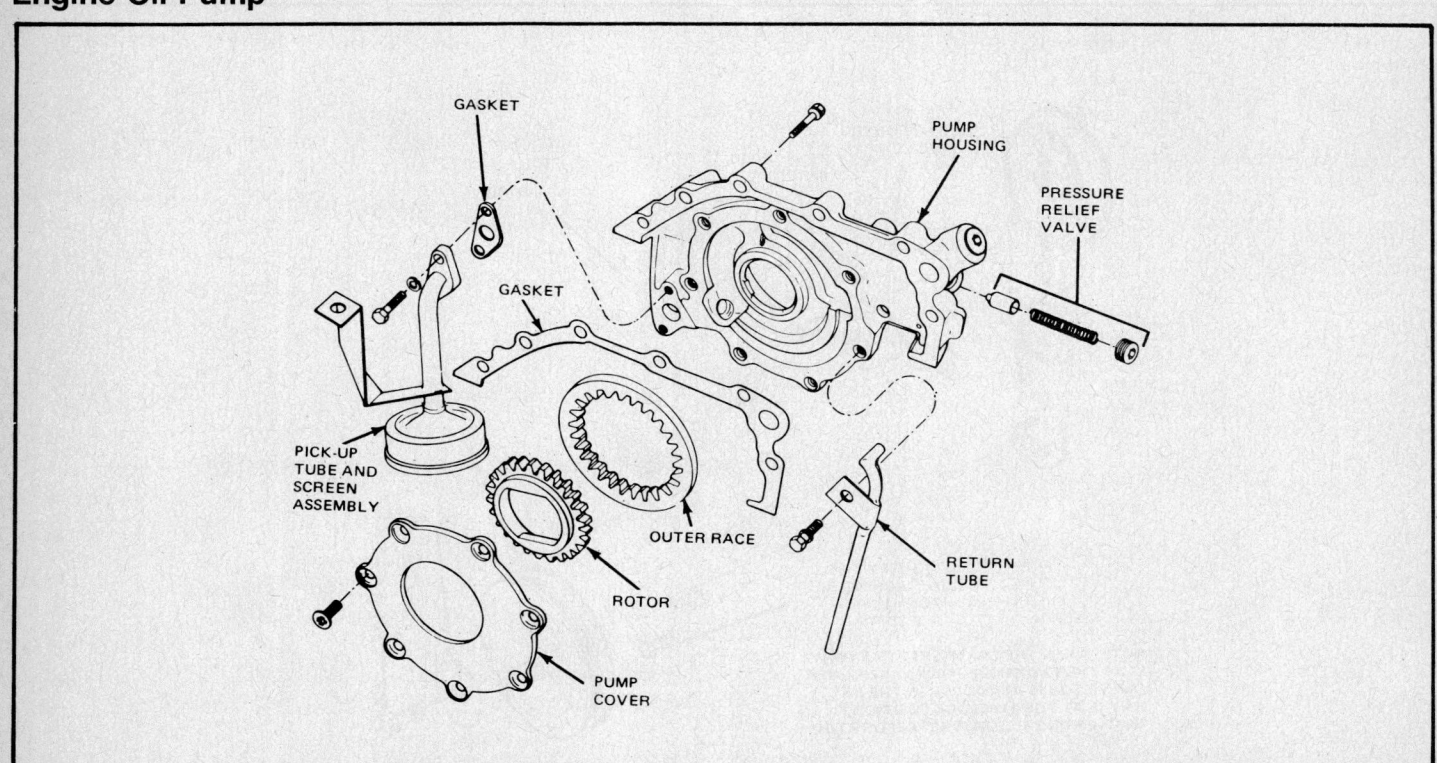

The outer race to housing clearance should not be more than 0.069-0.140mm (0.0016-0.0025 in.). The rotor end clearance should not be more than 0.040-0.066mm (0.001-0.0025 in.).

17. Remove the oil pan and gaskets.

18. Remove the bolt attaching the oil pick-up tube brace to the cylinder block.

19. Remove the oil pump attaching bolts, the oil pump and gasket.

20. Remove the oil pump seal.

INSTALLATION

1. Lubricate the outside diameter of the oil pump seal with engine oil.

2. Install the oil pump seal using seal installer T81P-6700-A or equivalent.

3. Install the pick-up tube and screen assembly on the oil pump.

4. Lubricate the oil pump seal lip with light engine oil.

5. Position the oil pump gasket over the locating dowels.

6. Position the oil pump and install the attaching bolts. Tighten the bolts to the specified torque.

7. Install the pick-up tube brace attaching bolt. Tighten the bolt to the specified torque.

8. Apply a bead of sealer, approximately 3.0 mm wide at the corner of the front and rear oil pan seals, and at the seating point of the oil pump to the block retainer joint.

9. Install the front oil pan seal by pressing firmly into the slot cut into the bottom of the pump.

10. Install the rear oil seal by pressing firmly into the slot cut into rear retainer assembly.

NOTE   Install the seal before the sealer has cured (within 10 minutes of application).

11. Apply the adhesive evenly to the oil pan flange and to the oil pan side of the gaskets. Allow the adhesive to dry past the "wet" stage and then install the gaskets on the oil pan.

12. Position the oil pan on the cylinder block.

13. Install the oil pan.

14. Position the transmission inspection plate and the rear section of the knee-brace on the transmission. Install the two attaching bolts and tighten to the specified torque.

15. Install the starter.

16. Install the knee-brace.

17. Connect the starter cable.

18. Install the crankshaft gear.

19. Install the crankshaft pulley.

20. Install the crankshaft drive plate assembly.

21. Install the timing belt over the crankshaft pulley.

NOTE   Each time the timing belt tension is released or the belt is removed, a new belt must be installed. Refer to the Timing Belt Tensioning and Replacement procedures.

22. Using the crankshaft pulley wrench T81P-6312-A or equivalent, install the crankshaft pulley attaching bolt. Tighten the bolt to the specified torque.

23. Install the engine front timing cover.

24. Position the accessory drive belts over the alternator and crankshaft pulleys. Tighten the drive belt to the specified tension.

25. Connect the negative cable at the battery.

26. Fill the crankcase to the proper level with the specified oil.

27. Start the engine and check for oil leaks. Make sure the oil pressure indicator light has gone out. If the light remains on, immediately shut off the engine, investigate the cause and correct the condition.

STEERING SECTION

Steering Wheel

REMOVAL

1. Disconnect the negative (ground) battery cable from the battery terminal.

2. Remove the steering hub cover assembly.

3. Remove and discard steering wheel attaching nut.

4. Remove steering wheel from upper shaft using Tool T67L-3600-A. Do not use a knock-off type steering wheel puller or strike the end of steering column upper shaft with a hammer, or damage will occur to the bearing of the collapsible steering column.

INSTALLATION

1. Position the steering wheel on the end of steering wheel shaft. Align the mark on the steering wheel with the mark on the shaft to assure that the straight-ahead steering wheel position corresponds to the straight-ahead position of the front wheels.

Steering Wheel Removal

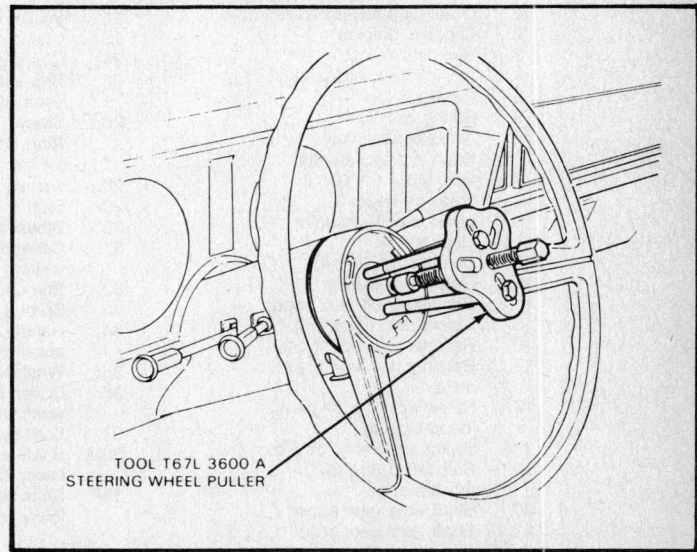

TOOL T67L 3600 A
STEERING WHEEL PULLER

Steering Column

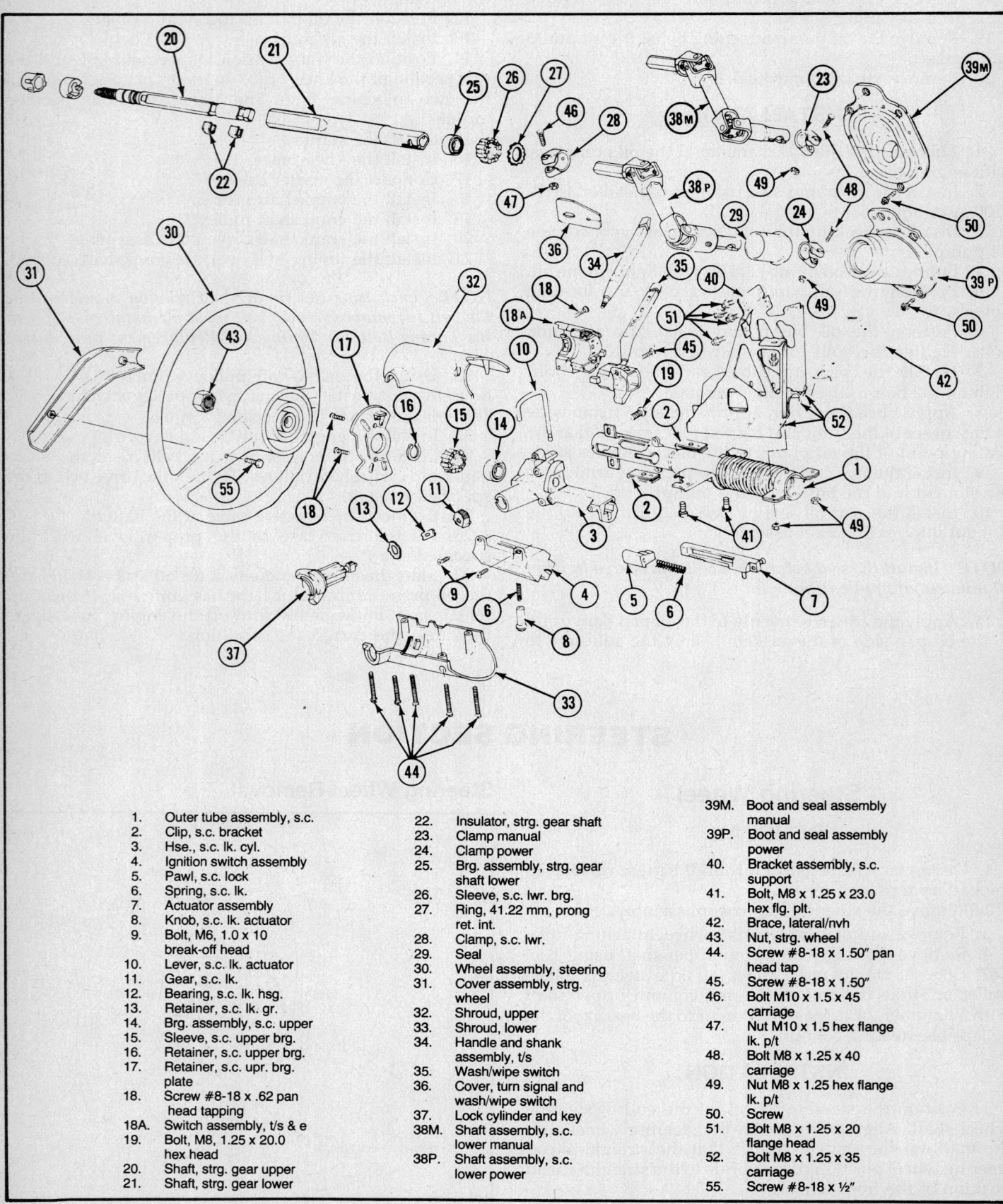

1.	Outer tube assembly, s.c.	22.	Insulator, strg. gear shaft	39M.	Boot and seal assembly manual	
2.	Clip, s.c. bracket	23.	Clamp manual	39P.	Boot and seal assembly power	
3.	Hse., s.c. lk. cyl.	24.	Clamp power	40.	Bracket assembly, s.c. support	
4.	Ignition switch assembly	25.	Brg. assembly, strg. gear shaft lower	41.	Bolt, M8 x 1.25 x 23.0 hex flg. plt.	
5.	Pawl, s.c. lock	26.	Sleeve, s.c. lwr. brg.	42.	Brace, lateral/nvh	
6.	Spring, s.c. lk.	27.	Ring, 41.22 mm, prong ret. int.	43.	Nut, strg. wheel	
7.	Actuator assembly	28.	Clamp, s.c. lwr.	44.	Screw #8-18 x 1.50" pan head tap	
8.	Knob, s.c. lk. actuator	29.	Seal	45.	Screw #8-18 x 1.50"	
9.	Bolt, M6, 1.0 x 10 break-off head	30.	Wheel assembly, steering	46.	Bolt M10 x 1.5 x 45 carriage	
10.	Lever, s.c. lk. actuator	31.	Cover assembly, strg. wheel	47.	Nut M10 x 1.5 hex flange lk. p/t	
11.	Gear, s.c. lk.	32.	Shroud, upper	48.	Bolt M8 x 1.25 x 40 carriage	
12.	Bearing, s.c. lk. hsg.	33.	Shroud, lower	49.	Nut M8 x 1.25 hex flange lk. p/t	
13.	Retainer, s.c. lk. gr.	34.	Handle and shank assembly, t/s	50.	Screw	
14.	Brg. assembly, s.c. upper	35.	Wash/wipe switch	51.	Bolt M8 x 1.25 x 20 flange head	
15.	Sleeve, s.c. upper brg.	36.	Cover, turn signal and wash/wipe switch	52.	Bolt M8 x 1.25 x 35 carriage	
16.	Retainer, s.c. upper brg.	37.	Lock cylinder and key	55.	Screw #8-18 x ½"	
17.	Retainer, s.c. upr. brg. plate	38M.	Shaft assembly, s.c. lower manual			
18.	Screw #8-18 x .62 pan head tapping	38P.	Shaft assembly, s.c. lower power			
18A.	Switch assembly, t/s & e					
19.	Bolt, M8, 1.25 x 20.0 hex head					
20.	Shaft, strg. gear upper					
21.	Shaft, strg. gear lower					

2. Install a new service wheel nut. Tighten the nut to torque of 41-54 N•m (30-40 lb-ft).

3. Install the steering wheel cover assembly. Tighten to a torque of 15-23 N•m (13-20 lb-in).

4. Connect the negative (ground) battery cable to the battery terminal.

5. Check the steering column for proper operation.

Steering Column

REMOVAL

1. Disconnect the negative (ground) battery cable from the battery terminal.

2. Remove the steering column cover on the lower portion of the instrument panel (2 screws) to expose the instrument panel reinforcement section.

3. Remove the instrument panel reinforcement section (2 screws).

4. Remove the lower steering column shroud (five screws).

5. Loosen, but do not remove the two nuts and two bolts retaining the steering column to the support bracket. Remove the upper shroud.

6. Disconnect all steering column electrical connections (ignition, wash/wipe, turn signal, key warning buzzer).

7. Loosen the steering column to intermediate shaft clamp connection and remove the bolt or nut.

8. Remove two nuts and two bolts retaining the steering column to the support bracket and lower the steering column to the floor.

9. Pry open the steering column shaft clamp on each side of the bolt groove with the steering column locked. Open enough to disengage shafts with a minimal effort. Do not use excessive force. Damage to components may result.

10. Inspect two steering column bracket clips for damage. If clips have been bent or excessively distorted they must be replaced.

INSTALLATION

1. Check the distance that the steering shaft protrudes past the outer tube assembly. This distance must be between 36.6 and 41.5 mm (1.44-1.63 in).

2. Engage the lower steering shaft to the intermediate shaft and hand start the clamp bolt and nut.

3. Place the steering column under the instrument panel. Align the two bolts on the steering column support bracket assembly with the outer tube mounting holes, and hand start the two nuts. Check for the presence of the two clips on the outer bracket. The clips must be present to insure adequate performance of vital parts and systems. Hand start the two bolts through the outer tube upper bracket and clips and into the support bracket nuts.

4. Connect all quick connect electrical connectors (turn signal, wash/wipe, key warning buzzer, ignition, speed control).

5. Install the upper shroud.

Steering Shaft Distance Past Outer Tube

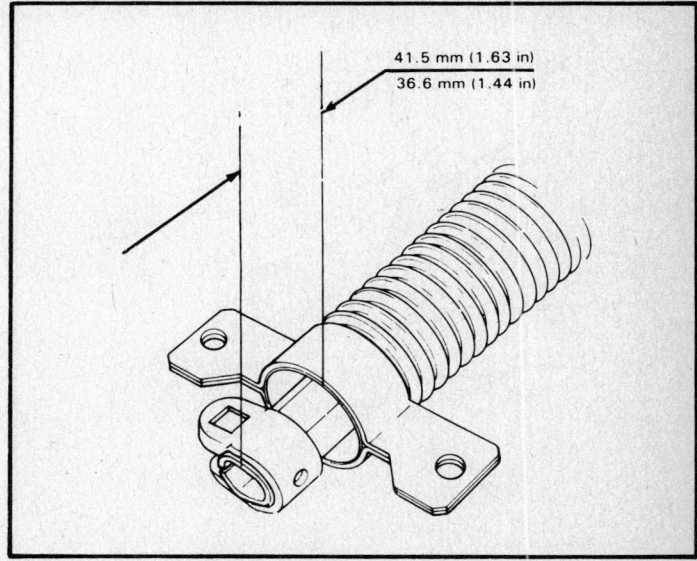

6. Tighten the steering column mounting nut and bolts to torque of 23-33 N•m (17-25 lb-ft).

7. Cycle the steering column one turn left and one turn right to align the intermediate shaft into the column shaft. (Power steering cars must have the engine running.) Torque the steering shaft clamp nut to 27-40 N•m (20-30 lb-ft).

8. Install the lower trim shroud with five screws.

9. Install the instrument panel reinforcement section with two screws.

10. Install the steering column cover on the instrument panel with two screws.

11. Connect the negative (ground) battery cable to the battery terminal.

12. Check the steering column for proper operation.

Upper Steering Shaft Bearing

REMOVAL

1. Remove the steering wheel using Tool T-67L-3600-A as described earlier.

2. Remove the upper and lower shroud.

3. Remove the upper bearing retainer plate.

4. Remove the upper bearing retainer snap ring and discard.

Installation of Upper Bearing

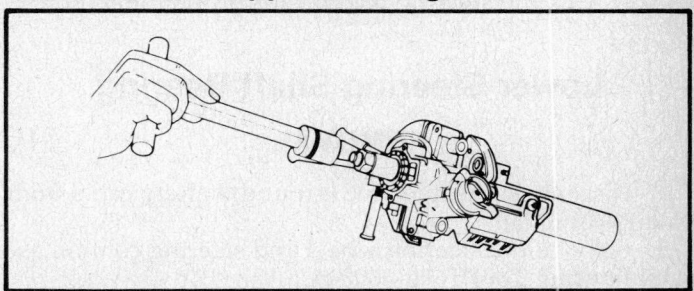

Pry Bearing From Shaft

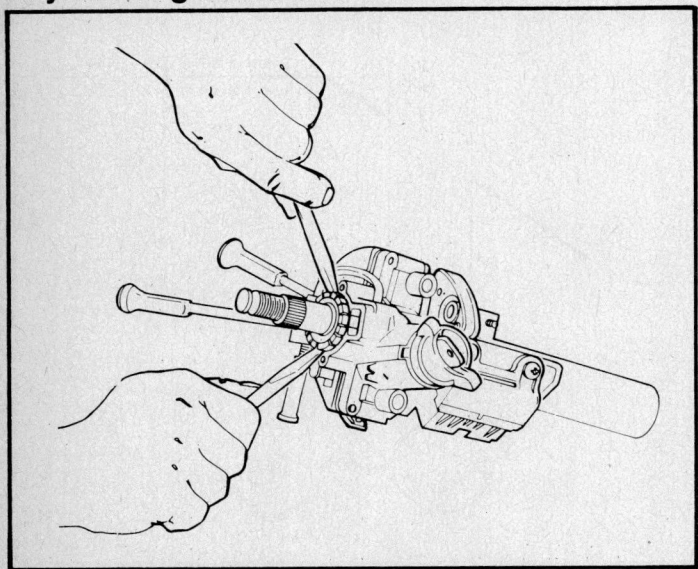

5. Insert two suitable tools under the bearing, using the two ramps provided in the casting. Gently pry the upper bearing and sleeve from the steering shaft. Discard the sleeve.

INSTALLATION

1. Prick punch the steering column upper shaft serration diameter sufficiently to ensure an interference fit between the bearing inner race and the steering column upper shaft.

2. Position the bearing and insulator on the steering column upper shaft. Work the bearing and insulator as far down the steering column upper shaft as possible. Then, place a piece of pipe .75 inch inside diameter x 1.5 inch over the end of the steering column upper shaft and install the steering wheel attaching nut.

3. Tighten the steering wheel attaching nut until the bearing is seated on the steering shaft.

4. Remove the steering wheel attaching nut and the piece of pipe from the steering column upper shaft.

5. Install a new snap ring in the groove at the top of the bearing column upper shaft above the bearing.

6. Install the upper bearing retainer plate.

7. Install the upper shroud.

8. Attach the lower shroud to the upper shroud with five screws.

9. Install the steering wheel.

10. Check the steering column for proper operation.

Lower Steering Shaft Bearing

REMOVAL

1. Disconnect the negative (ground) battery cable from battery terminal.

2. Remove the steering wheel and steering column assembly using Tool T67L-3600-A.

3. Remove the lower steering column clamp by prying open with two suitable tools placed through the bolt holes.

4. Remove the push-on retainer ring with a suitable tool. Discard the retainer.

5. Remove the lower bearing and sleeve.

INSTALLATION

1. Push the sleeve and bearing assembly onto the lower shaft and into the outer tube until they bottom on tabs in the outer tube. Make sure the sleeve is not deformed. The shaft to outer tube length should be 36.6-41.5 mm (1.44-1.63 in).

2. Push a new lower bearing retainer ring into the outer tube until it contacts the bearing. Make sure the retainer prongs are angled back, away from the direction of installation.

3. Install the steering column lower clamp.

4. Install the steering column and steering wheel.

5. Connect the negative (ground) battery cable to battery terminal.

6. check for proper operation of the steering column.

Intermediate Shaft—Seal and Clamp, Power Steering Clamp, Manual Steering

REMOVAL

1. Disconnect the negative (ground) battery cable from battery terminal.

2. Remove the steering column.

3. Remove the steering column boot and seal assembly on power steering equipped vehicles only (4 screws). Slide the boot up the intermediate shaft until the steering gear connection can be seen. On manual steering vehicles, removal of boot is unnecessary.

4. Remove and discard the intermediate-shaft-to-steering-gear clamp.

5. Remove the imperfect seal.

Intermediate Shaft

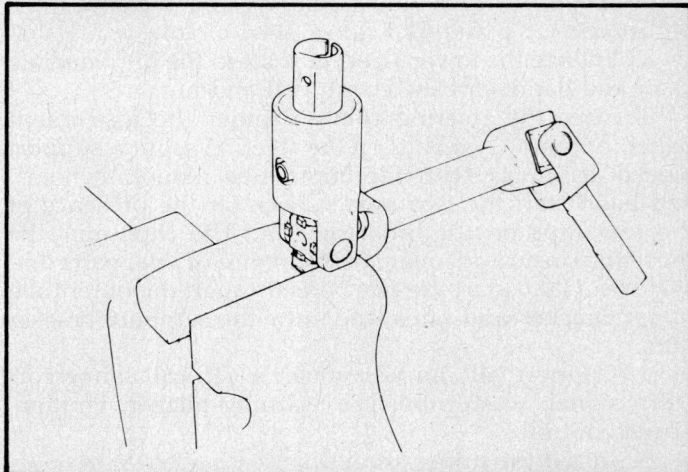

Drive In New Seal

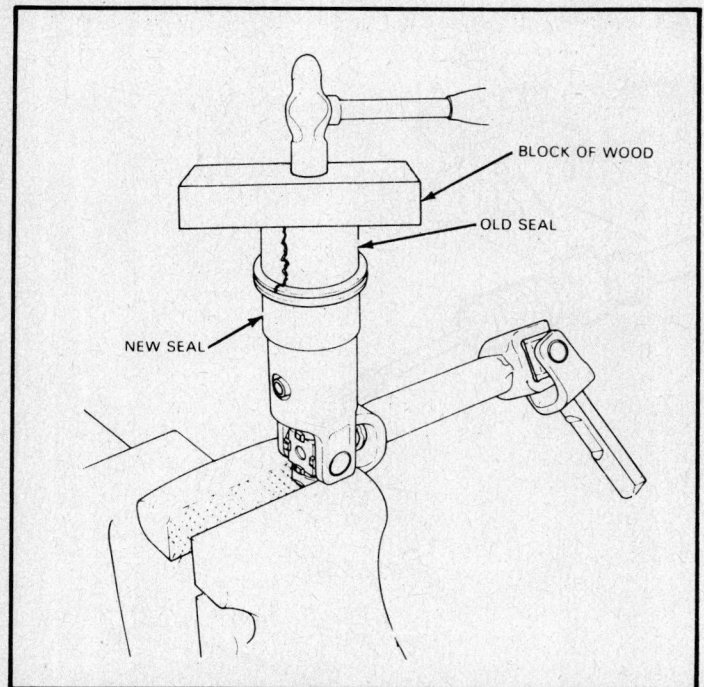

Inset ⅛ Inch Spacer

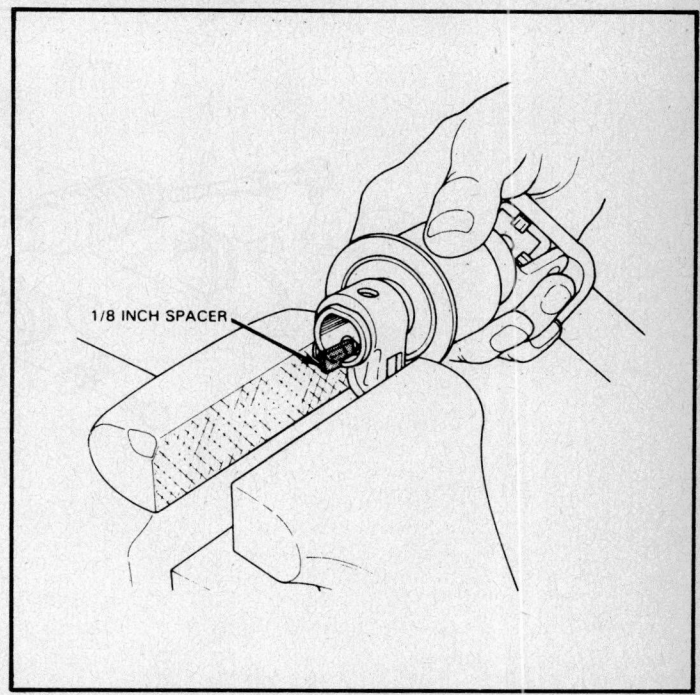

INSTALLATION

1. Clamp the intermediate shaft lightly in a vise.

CHILTON CAUTION Do not clamp tightly as damage could result to bearings. Do not clamp across the universal joint.

2. Drive a new seal on the isolator portion of the intermediate shaft until the end of the isolator is flush with end of the seal. Use the old seal (inverted) and a block of wood to do this. Check the new seal frequently to make sure it is going on straight.

3. Place the intermediate-shaft-to-steering-gear clamp on the intermediate shaft making sure dimple of the clamp aligns with the locator hole in the shaft.

4. Insert a ⅛ inch spacer into the total length of the slot in the intermediate shaft to prevent any collapse of the shaft.

5. Squeeze the clamp until a bolt can be inserted through the holes.

6. Remove the ⅛ inch spacer and hand start clamp bolt and nut.

7. Install the boot and seal assembly onto the intermediate shaft.

8. Install the steering column.

9. Connect the negative (ground) battery cable to battery terminal.

10. Check the steering column for proper operation.

Manual Rack and Pinion Steering

In a stationary vehicle, there should be no knock in the steering gear when the steering wheel is turned from stop to stop. If a knock is experienced, check adjustment of rack preload and pinion bearing preload. A faint knock produced by the steering gear while driving on an extremely rough road is acceptable, and in no way affects the proper functioning of the gear.

Adjustments

The rack and pinion gear provides two means of service adjustment. The gear must be removed from the vehicle to perform both adjustments.

1. Mount the gear in a vise, gripping it near the center of the steel tube. Do not overtighten the vise or damage to the tube could result.

2. Remove the yoke cover, gasket, shims and yoke spring.

Support Yoke Arrangement

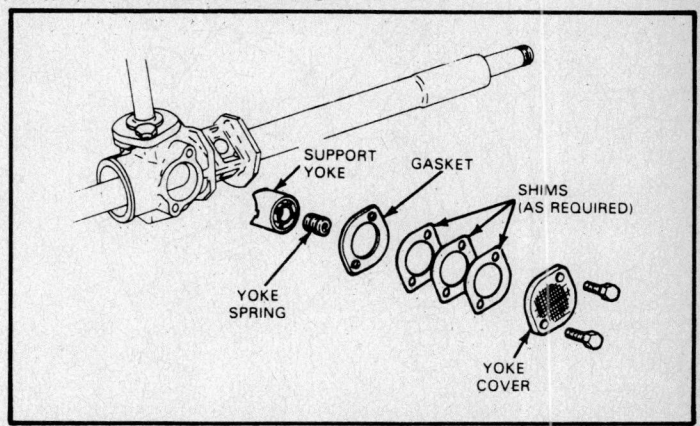

Manual Rack and Pinion Steering Gear

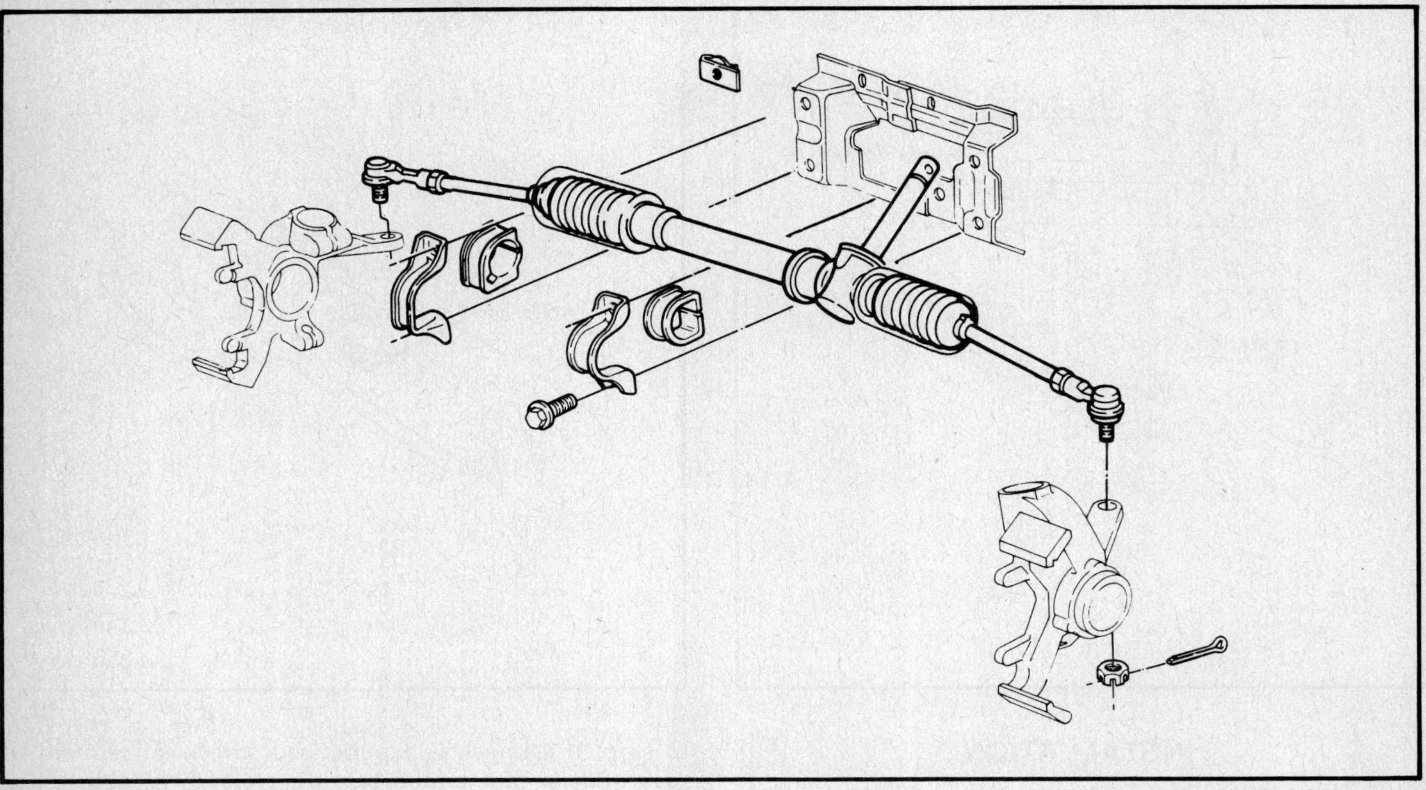

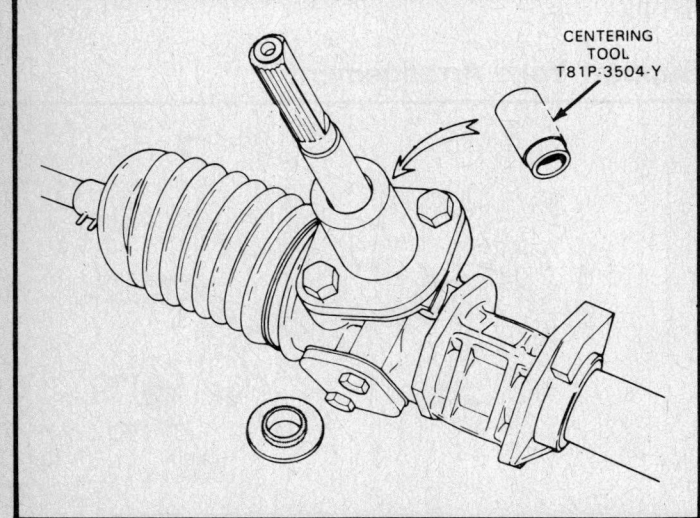

3. Install the yoke and cover, omitting the gasket, shims and spring.

4. Tighten the cover bolts lightly until the cover just touches the yoke.

5. Measure the gap between the cover and the housing flange. With the gasket, add selected shims to give a combined pack thickness 0.13-0.15 mm (.005-.006 inch) greater than the measured gap.

6. Remove the cover.

7. Assemble the gasket next to the housing flange, then the selected shims, spring and cover.

Pinion Cover Installation

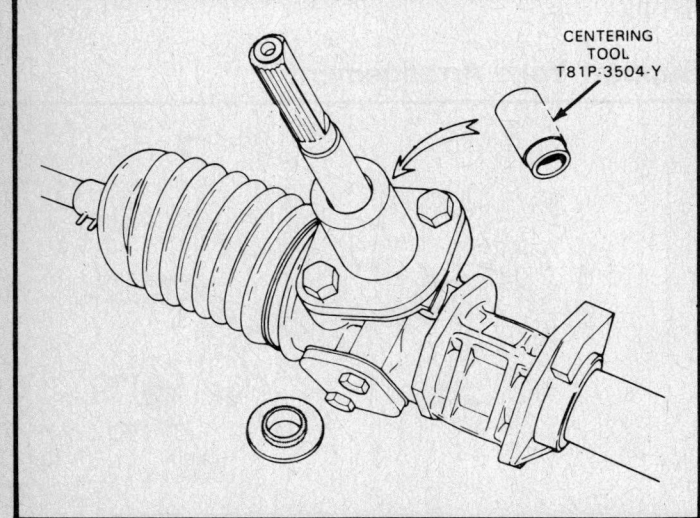

8. Install the cover bolts, sealing the threads with ESW-M46-132A or equivalent. Tighten to specifications.

9. Check to see that the gear operates smoothly without binding or slackness.

Pinion Bearing Preload

ASSEMBLY REMOVED

1. Loosen the bolts of the yoke cover to relieve spring pressure on the rack.

2. Remove the pinion cover and gasket. Clean the cover flange area thoroughly.

3. Remove the spacer and shims.

Pinion, Bearing Cover and Shim

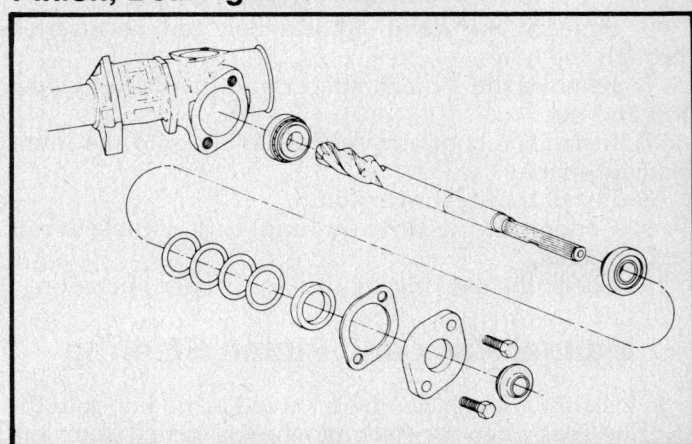

4. Install a new gasket and fit the shims between the upper bearing and spacer until the top of the spacer is flush with the gasket. Check with a straightedge, using light pressure.

5. Add one 0.13 mm (.005 inch) shim to the pack in order to preload the bearings. The spacer must be assembled next to the pinion cover.

6. Remove the oil seal from the cover. Install the cover, using a centering tool.

7. Tighten bolts to specification.

8. Install the pinion oil seal.

Tie Rod Articulation Effort

1. Loop a piece of wire through the hole in the rod end stud. Insert the hook of the pull scale, Tool T74P-3504-Y or equivalent, through the wire loop.

Total effort to move the tie rod should be 1-5 pounds. Do not damage the tie rod neck.

2. Replace ball joint/tie rod assembly if effort falls outside this range. Save tie rod end for use on new tie rod assembly.

Steering Gear Adjustment

The power rack and pinion steering gear provides for only one service adjustment. The gear must be removed from the vehicle to perform this adjustment.

1. Loosen and remove the yoke plug locknut.

Rod Articulation Check

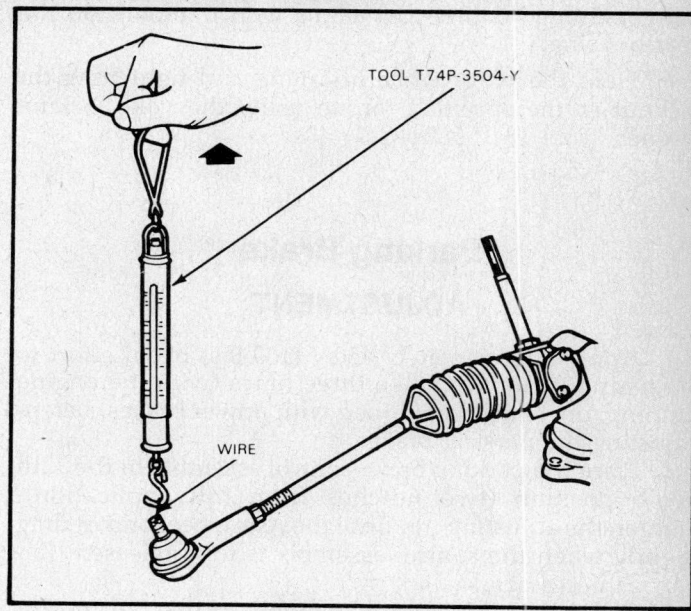

TOOL T74P-3504-Y

WIRE

2. Back off the yoke plug one turn.

3. Tighten the yoke plug to 5.8 N•m (45 in-lbs) using the yoke plug adapter Tool T81P-3504-U and an inch-pound torque wrench with a full scale reading to 100 inch-pounds maximum.

4. Mark the gear housing in line with the "O" mark on the yoke plug adapter tool.

Power Steering Gear

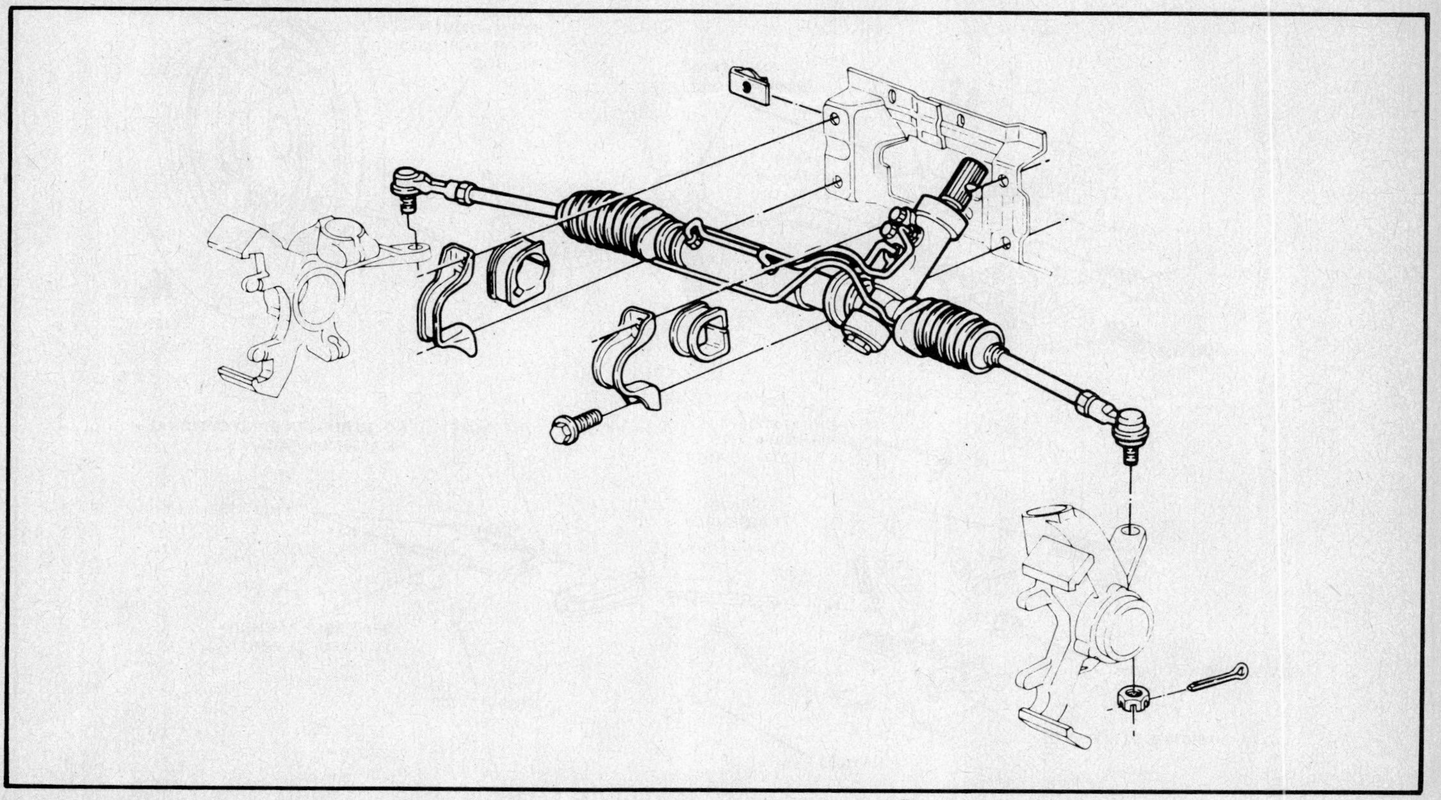

5. Back off the yoke plug so that the second mark on the yoke plug adapter tool aligns with the mark on the gear housing.

6. Hold the plug, while installing and tightening the locknut to the specified torque using the yoke locknut wrench, Tool T81P-3504-G.

Parking Brake
ADJUSTMENT

1. Apply approximately 450N (100 lbs) pedal effort to the hydraulic service brake three times (with the engine running, on vehicles equipped with power brakes) before adjusting the parking brake.
2. Place the parking brake control assembly in the 12th notch position (two notches from full application). Tighten the adjusting nut until the rear wheel brakes drag slightly when the control assembly is fully released. Repeat as necessary.
3. Reposition the control assembly in the 12th notch. Loosen the adjusting nut just enough to eliminate rear brake drag when the control assembly is fully released.

Yoke Adjustment

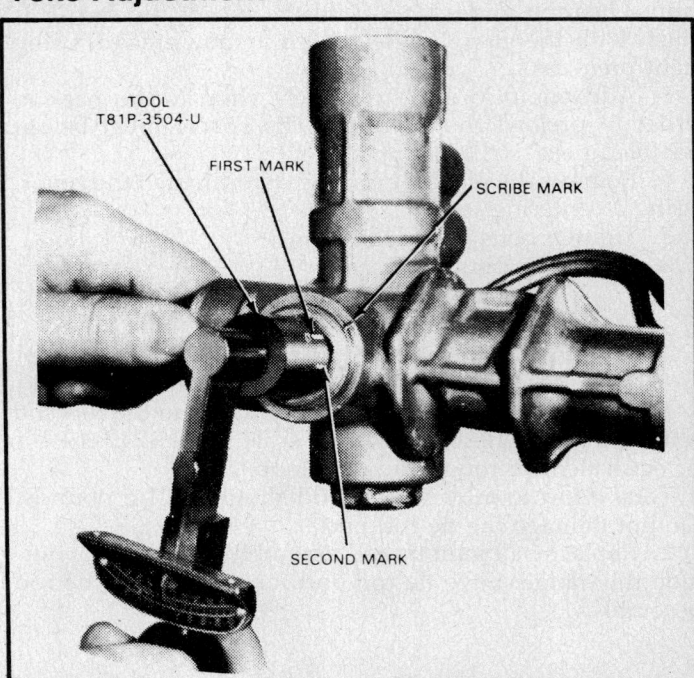

TOOL
T81P-3504-U

FIRST MARK

SCRIBE MARK

SECOND MARK

Parking Brake

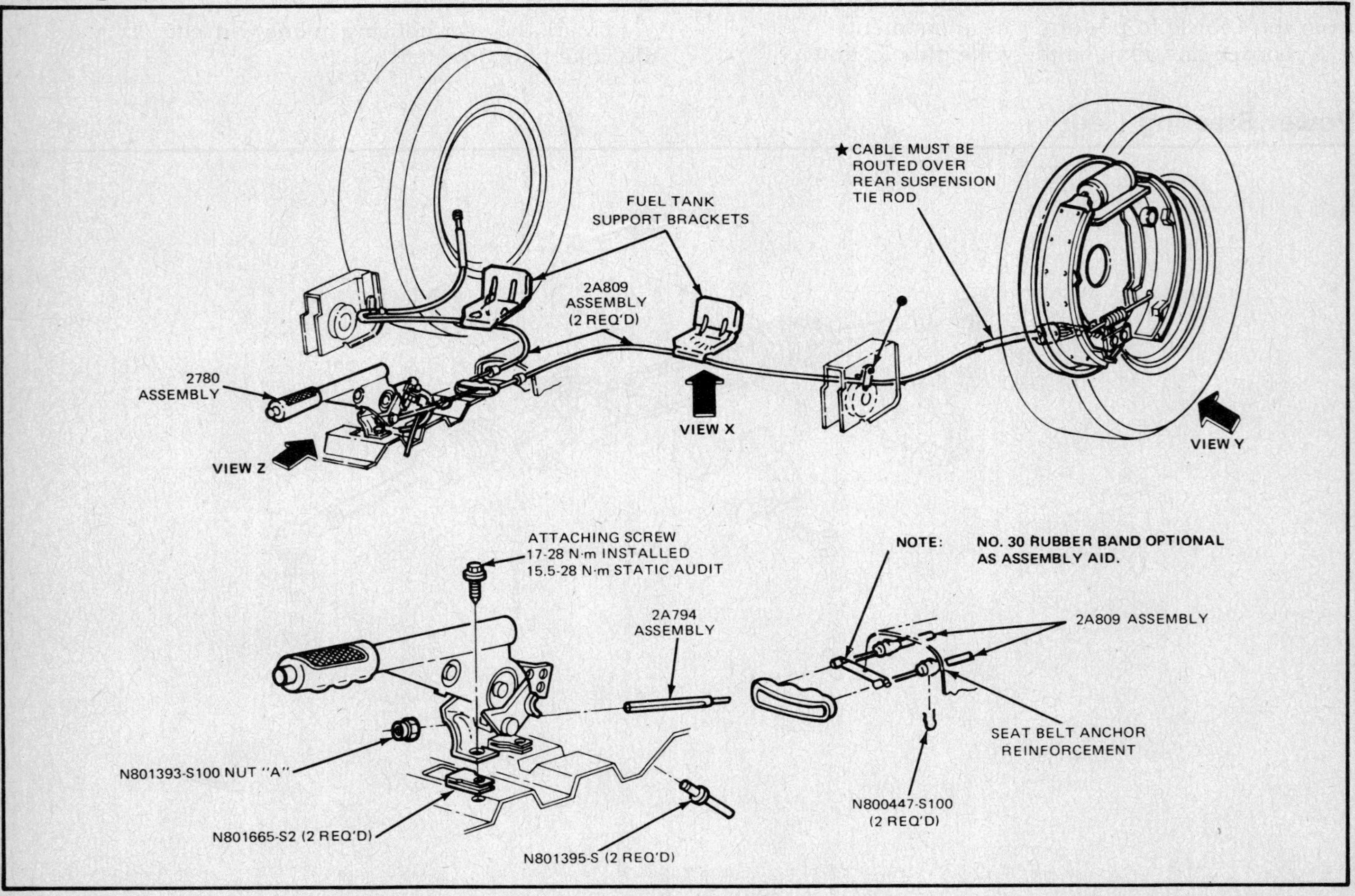

FUEL TANK
SUPPORT BRACKETS

★ CABLE MUST BE
ROUTED OVER
REAR SUSPENSION
TIE ROD

2A809
ASSEMBLY
(2 REQ'D)

2780
ASSEMBLY

VIEW X

VIEW Y

VIEW Z

ATTACHING SCREW
17-28 N·m INSTALLED
15.5-28 N·m STATIC AUDIT

2A794
ASSEMBLY

NOTE: NO. 30 RUBBER BAND OPTIONAL
AS ASSEMBLY AID.

2A809 ASSEMBLY

N801393-S100 NUT "A"

SEAT BELT ANCHOR
REINFORCEMENT

N801665-S2 (2 REQ'D)

N801395-S (2 REQ'D)

N800447-S100
(2 REQ'D)

DRIVESHAFT SECTION

Halfshaft

NOTE Due to the ATX case configuration, the right-hand halfshaft assembly must be removed first. Driver T81P-4026-A or equivalent is then inserted into the transaxle to drive the left-hand inboard CV joint assembly from the transaxle. If only the left-hand halfshaft assembly is to be removed for service, remove only the right-hand halfshaft assembly from the transaxle. After removal, support it with a length of wire. Then drive the left-hand halfshaft assembly from the transaxle.

Halfshafts and CV Joints

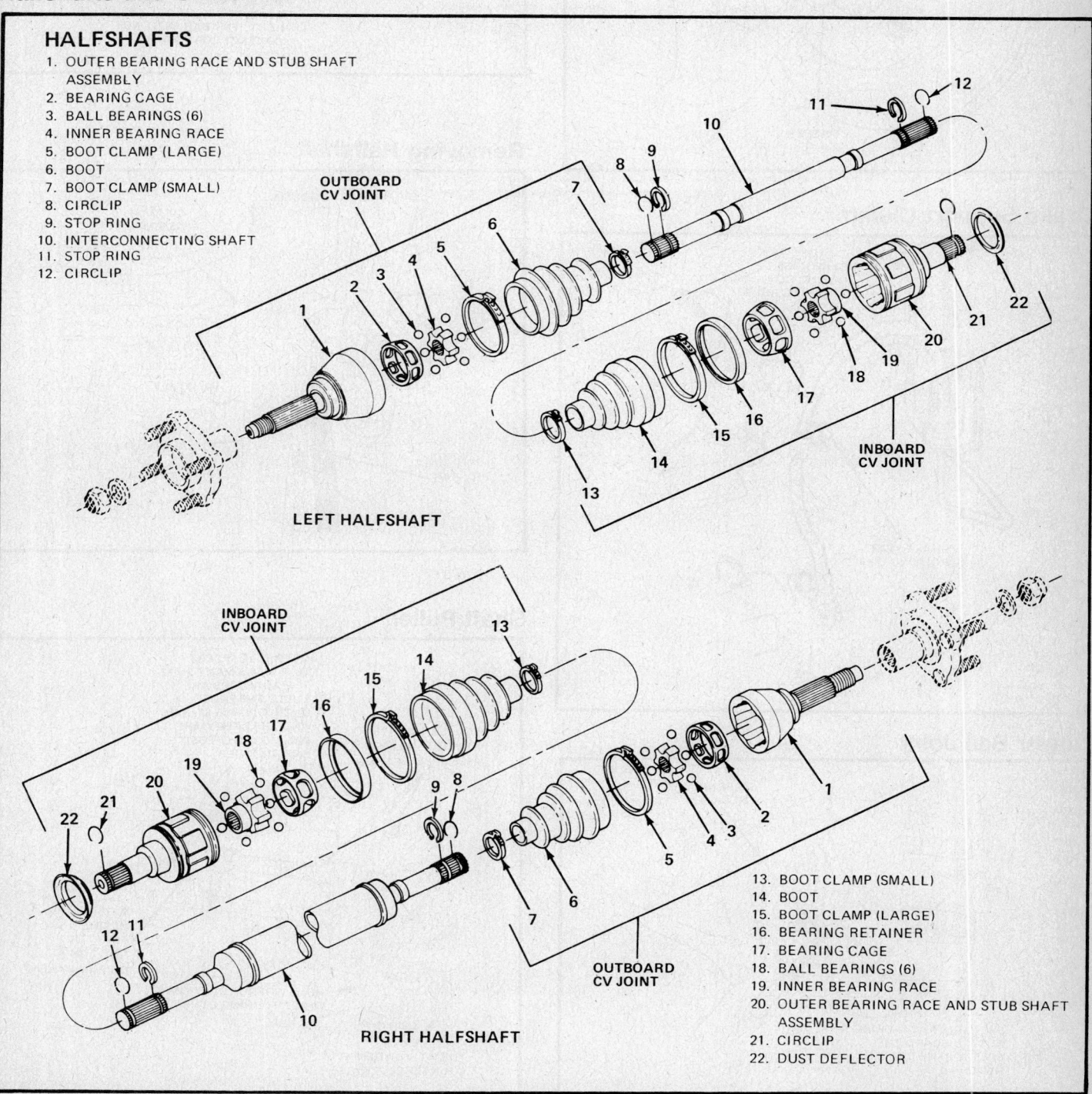

HALFSHAFTS
1. OUTER BEARING RACE AND STUB SHAFT ASSEMBLY
2. BEARING CAGE
3. BALL BEARINGS (6)
4. INNER BEARING RACE
5. BOOT CLAMP (LARGE)
6. BOOT
7. BOOT CLAMP (SMALL)
8. CIRCLIP
9. STOP RING
10. INTERCONNECTING SHAFT
11. STOP RING
12. CIRCLIP

OUTBOARD CV JOINT

INBOARD CV JOINT

LEFT HALFSHAFT

INBOARD CV JOINT

OUTBOARD CV JOINT

RIGHT HALFSHAFT

13. BOOT CLAMP (SMALL)
14. BOOT
15. BOOT CLAMP (LARGE)
16. BEARING RETAINER
17. BEARING CAGE
18. BALL BEARINGS (6)
19. INNER BEARING RACE
20. OUTER BEARING RACE AND STUB SHAFT ASSEMBLY
21. CIRCLIP
22. DUST DEFLECTOR

FORD—MERCURY FRONT DRIVE CARS

Hub Nut

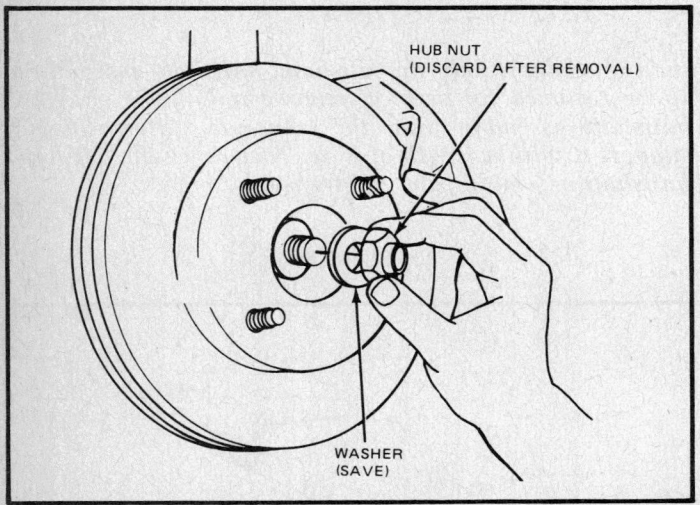

HUB NUT
(DISCARD AFTER REMOVAL)

WASHER
(SAVE)

Prying Lower Ball Joint

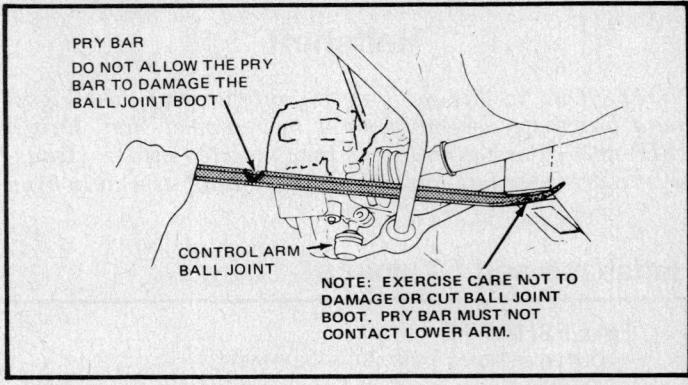

PRY BAR
DO NOT ALLOW THE PRY
BAR TO DAMAGE THE
BALL JOINT BOOT

CONTROL ARM
BALL JOINT

NOTE: EXERCISE CARE NOT TO
DAMAGE OR CUT BALL JOINT
BOOT. PRY BAR MUST NOT
CONTACT LOWER ARM.

Brake Support Clamp

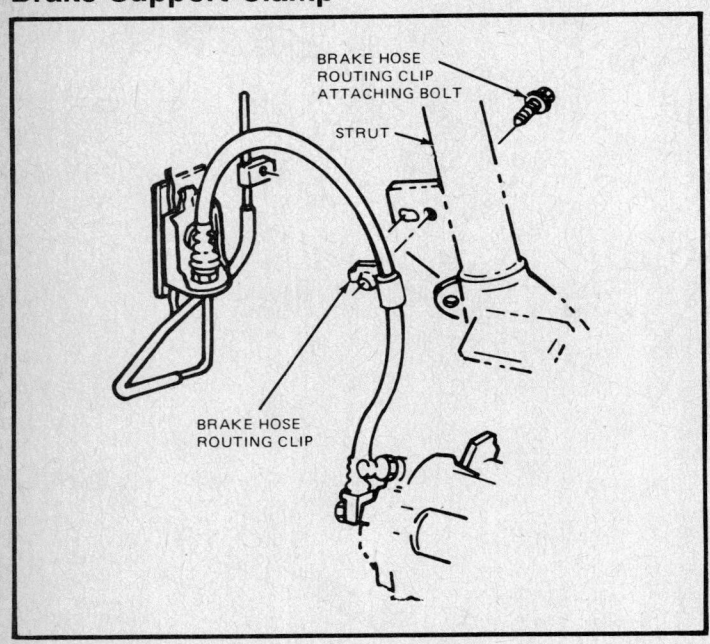

BRAKE HOSE
ROUTING CLIP
ATTACHING BOLT

STRUT

BRAKE HOSE
ROUTING CLIP

Removing Halfshaft

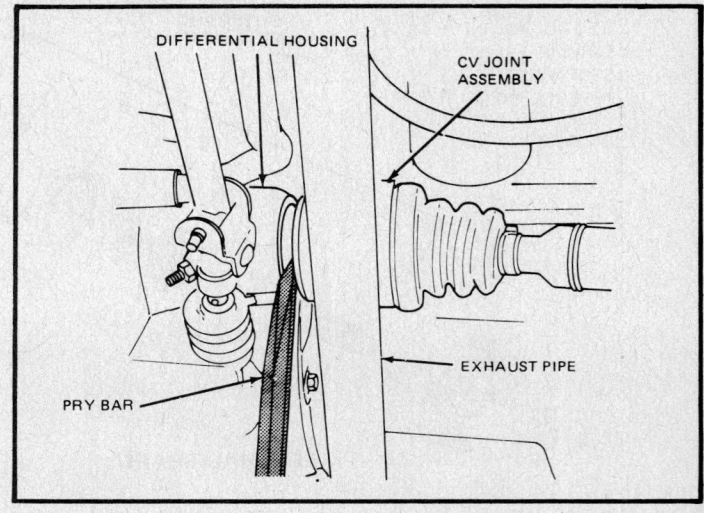

DIFFERENTIAL HOUSING

CV JOINT
ASSEMBLY

EXHAUST PIPE

PRY BAR

Lower Ball Joint

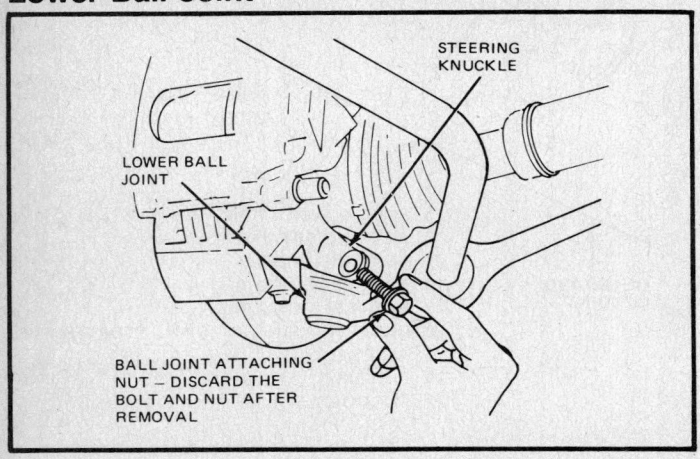

STEERING
KNUCKLE

LOWER BALL
JOINT

BALL JOINT ATTACHING
NUT – DISCARD THE
BOLT AND NUT AFTER
REMOVAL

Shaft Puller

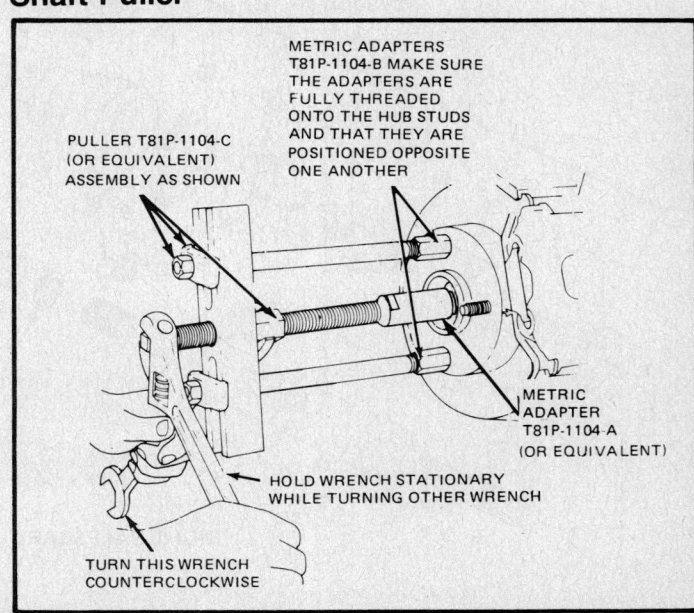

METRIC ADAPTERS
T81P-1104-B MAKE SURE
THE ADAPTERS ARE
FULLY THREADED
ONTO THE HUB STUDS
AND THAT THEY ARE
POSITIONED OPPOSITE
ONE ANOTHER

PULLER T81P-1104-C
(OR EQUIVALENT)
ASSEMBLY AS SHOWN

METRIC
ADAPTER
T81P-1104-A
(OR EQUIVALENT)

HOLD WRENCH STATIONARY
WHILE TURNING OTHER WRENCH

TURN THIS WRENCH
COUNTERCLOCKWISE

NOTE   The lower control arm ball joint fits into a pocket formed in the plastic disc brake rotor shield. This shield must be bent back away from the ball joint while prying the ball joint out of the steering knuckle.

6. Remove the halfshaft from the differential housing using a pry bar. Position the pry bar between the case and the shaft, but be careful not to damage the dust deflector location between the shaft and the case.

CHILTON CAUTION   Extreme care must be taken not to damage the differential oil seal, the CV joint boot or the CV joint dust deflector.

7. Support the end of the shaft by suspending it from a convenient underbody component with a length of wire.

NOTE   Do not allow the shaft to hang unsupported, as damage to the outboard CV joint may result.

8. Separate the outboard CV joint from the hub using puller T81P-1104-C or equivalent, and metric adapters T81P-1104-B and T81P-1104-A or equivalent.

CHILTON CAUTION   Never use a hammer to separate the outboard CV joint stub shaft from the hub. Damage to the CV joint internal components may result.

INSTALLATION

1. Install a new circlip on the inboard CV joint stub shaft. The outboard CV joint stub shaft does not have a circlip.

NOTE   To install the circlip properly, start one end in the groove and work the circlip over the stub shaft end and into the groove. This will avoid over expanding the circlip.

2. Carefully align the splines of the inboard CV joint stub shaft with the splines in the differential. Exerting some force, push the CV joint into the differential until the circlip is felt to seat in the differential side gear. Use care to prevent damage to the differential oil seal.

NOTE   A non-metallic mallet may be used to aid in seating the circlip into the differential side gear groove. If a mallet is necessary, tap only on the outboard CV joint stub shaft.

3. Carefully align the splines of the outboard CV joint stub shaft with the plines in the hub and push the shaft into the hub as far as possible. Use puller T81P-1104-C or equivalent and metric adapters T81P-1104-A and T81P-1104-B or equivalent to complete the installation.

REMOVAL

1. Remove the cap from the hub and loosen the hub nut. Set the parking brake to prevent the car from rolling while the nut is loosened. The nut must be loosened without unstaking. The use of a chisel or similar tool may damage the spindle thread.

Support Halfshaft

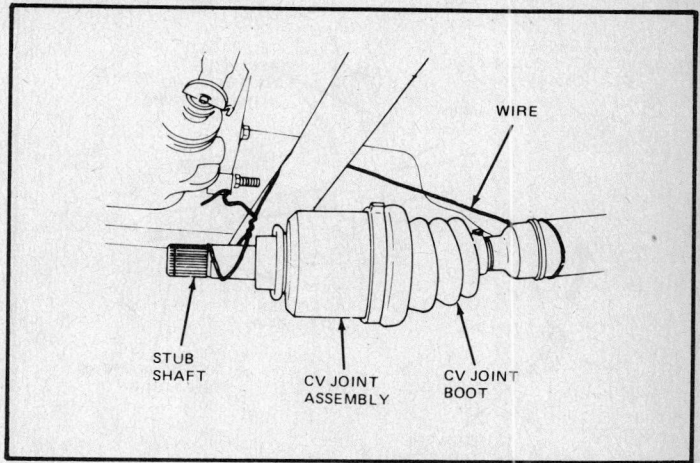

Stub Shaft Circlip

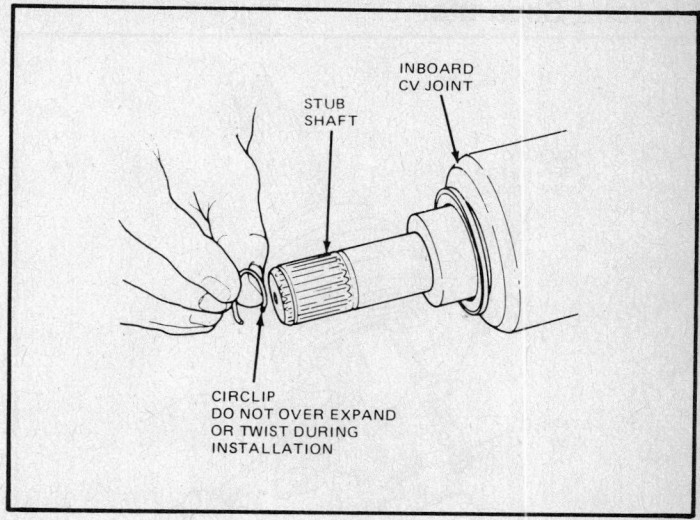

Seating Circlip

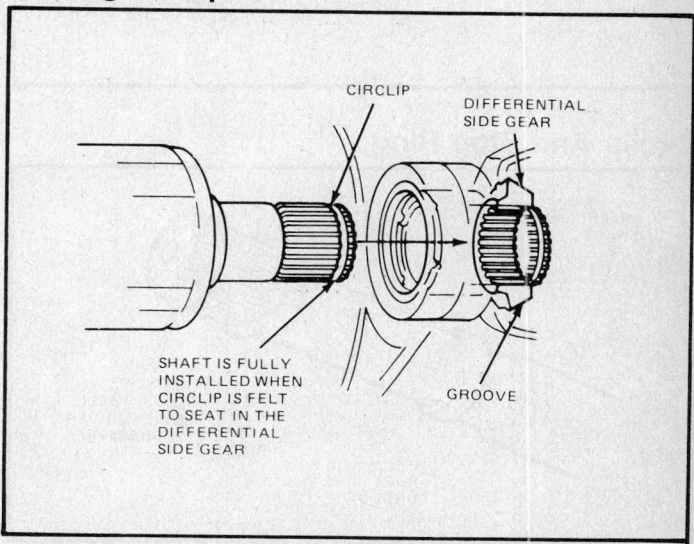

FORD—MERCURY FRONT DRIVE CARS

Pulling Stub Shaft

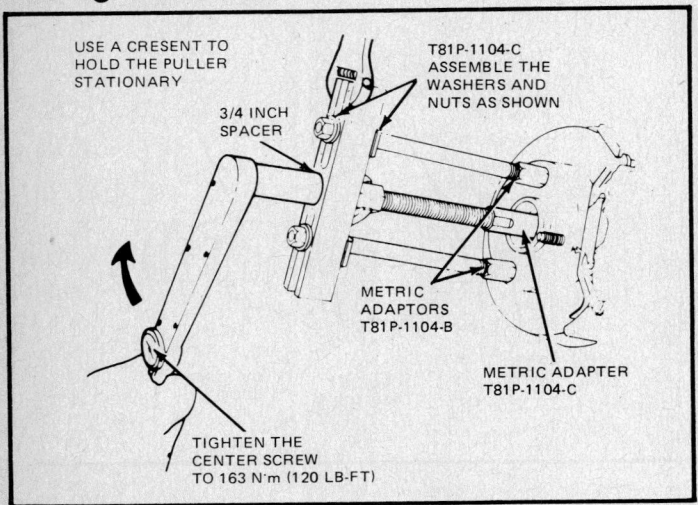

USE A CRESENT TO HOLD THE PULLER STATIONARY

3/4 INCH SPACER

T81P-1104-C ASSEMBLE THE WASHERS AND NUTS AS SHOWN

METRIC ADAPTORS T81P-1104-B

METRIC ADAPTER T81P-1104-C

TIGHTEN THE CENTER SCREW TO 163 N·m (120 LB-FT)

Removing Boot

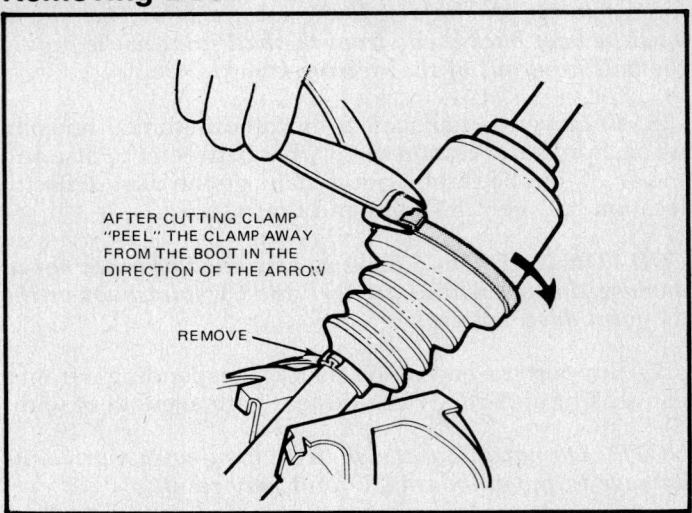

AFTER CUTTING CLAMP "PEEL" THE CLAMP AWAY FROM THE BOOT IN THE DIRECTION OF THE ARROW

REMOVE

CV Joint Separator

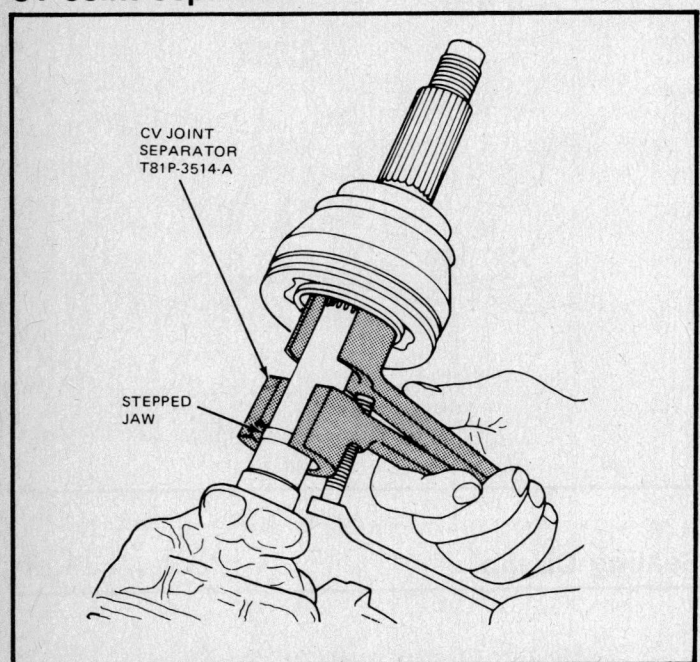

CV JOINT SEPARATOR T81P-3514-A

STEPPED JAW

Circlip And Stop Ring

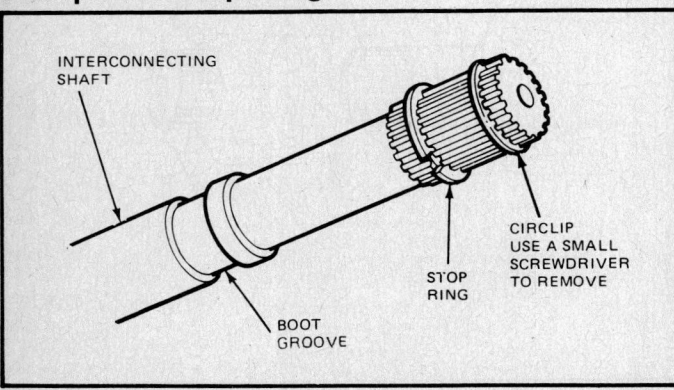

INTERCONNECTING SHAFT

BOOT GROOVE

STOP RING

CIRCLIP USE A SMALL SCREWDRIVER TO REMOVE

2. After raising the vehicle and removing the wheel and tire assembly, remove the hub nut and washer.

CHILTON CAUTION   Discard the nut, as it must not be reused.

3. Remove the bolt attaching the brake hose routing clip to the suspension strut.
4. Remove the nut from the ball joint to steering knuckle attaching bolt. Drive the bolt out of the steering knuckle using a punch and hammer.

CHILTON CAUTION   Discard the bolt and nut. They are of a torque prevailing design and cannot be reused.

5. Separate the ball joint from the steering knuckle using a pry bar. Position the end of the pry bar outside of the bushing pocket to avoid damage to the bushing. Use care to prevent damage to the ball joint boot.

CAUTION   The center thread of puller T81P-1104-C or equivalent must be oiled before installation and tightening. Failure to lubricate the threads could result in an inaccurate torque wrench reading.

4. Connect the control arm to the steering knuckle and install a new nut and bolt.

CHILTON CAUTION   A new bolt and nut must be installed.

5. Position the brake hose routing clip on the suspension strut and install the attaching bolts.
6. Install the hub nut washer and a new hub nut.

CHILTON CAUTION   A new nut must be installed.

7. Install the wheel and tire assembly and lower the vehicle.
8. Tighten the wheel nuts to specification.

Constant Velocity Joint

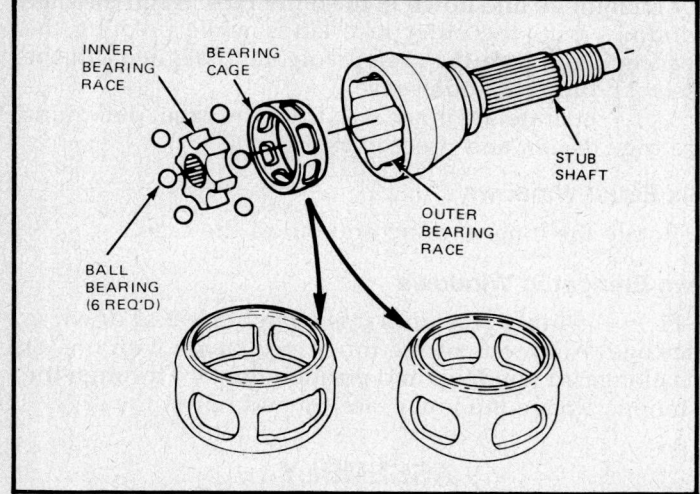

INNER BEARING RACE

BEARING CAGE

STUB SHAFT

OUTER BEARING RACE

BALL BEARING (6 REQ'D)

Removing Ball Bearings

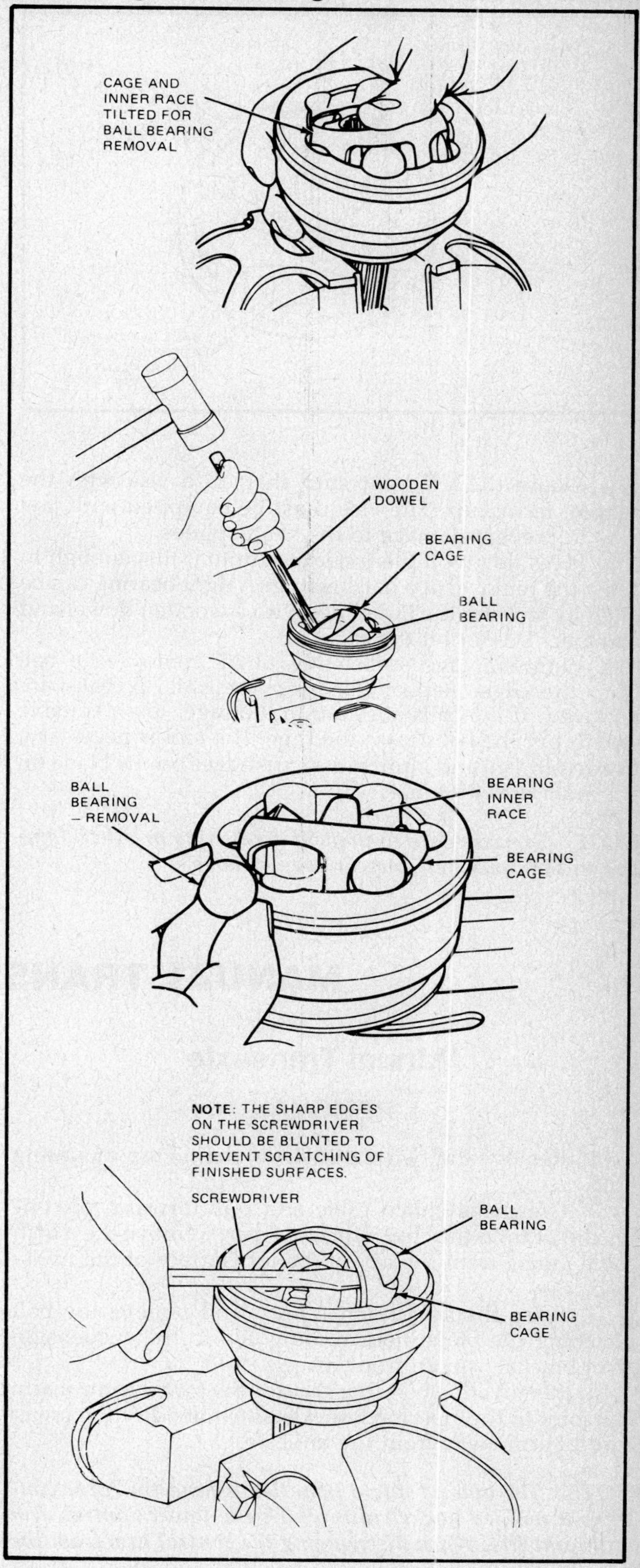

CAGE AND INNER RACE TILTED FOR BALL BEARING REMOVAL

WOODEN DOWEL

BEARING CAGE

BALL BEARING

BALL BEARING – REMOVAL

BEARING INNER RACE

BEARING CAGE

NOTE: THE SHARP EDGES ON THE SCREWDRIVER SHOULD BE BLUNTED TO PREVENT SCRATCHING OF FINISHED SURFACES.

SCREWDRIVER

BALL BEARING

BEARING CAGE

CV Joint Lubricant Check

When replacing damaged CV joint boots, the grease should be checked for contamination. If the CV joints were operating satisfactorily and the grease does not appear to be contaminated, add grease and replace the boot. If the lubricant appears contaminated, proceed with a complete CV joint disassembly and inspection.

1. Clamp the halfshaft in a vise. Do not allow the vice jaws to contact the boot or its clamp. The vice should be equipped with jaw caps to prevent damage to any machine surfaces.
2. Cut the large boot clamp using side cutters and peel away from the boot. After removing the clamp, roll the boot back over the shaft.
3. Separate the CV joint from the shaft using CV joint separator T81P-3514-A (or equivalent). The boot can now be removed from the shaft if necessary. Cut the remaining clamp and pull the boot from the shaft.
4. Remove the circlip located near the end of the shaft. Discard the circlip. A new clip is supplied with both the boot replacement kit and CV joint overhaul kit.
5. The stop ring, located just below the circlip, should be removed only if inspection determines it to be damaged, worn or otherwise unserviceable.

Constant Velocity Joint Service
DISASSEMBLY

NOTE Both inner and outer are serviced in the same manner.

NOTE The CV joint components are matched during manufacture and therefore cannot be interchanged with components from another CV joint. Extreme care should be taken not to mix or substitute like components between CV joints.

Installing Ball Bearings

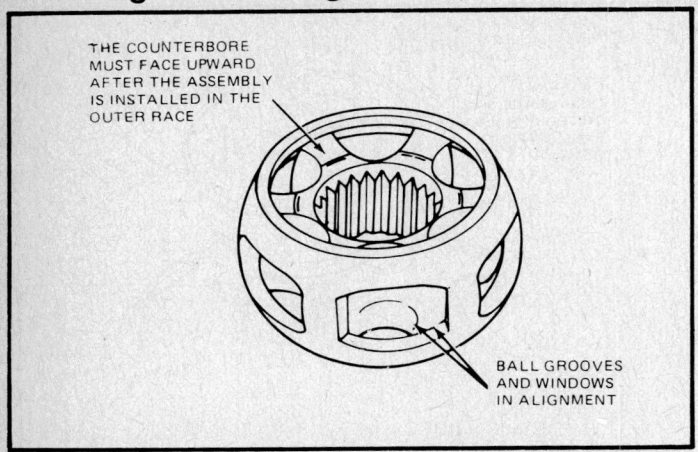

THE COUNTERBORE MUST FACE UPWARD AFTER THE ASSEMBLY IS INSTALLED IN THE OUTER RACE

BALL GROOVES AND WINDOWS IN ALIGNMENT

1. Clamp the CV joint stub shaft in a vise with the bearing facing up. The vise must be equipped with jaw caps to prevent damage to the shaft splines.
2. Press down on the inner race until it tilts enough to allow the removal of a ball bearing. A tight bearing can be tilted by tapping the inner race with a wooden dowel and hammer. Do not hit the cage.
3. With the cage sufficiently tilted, remove the ball from the cage. Repeat this step until all six balls are removed. If the balls are tight in the cage, use a suitable tool to pry the balls from the cage. If a tool is necessary, use an old tool and blunt any sharp edges on the blade on a grinder or with a file.

NOTE *Exercise care to prevent scratching or other damage to the inner ball race or cage spheres.*

4. Pivot the bearing cage and inner race assembly until it is straight up and down in the outer race. Align the cage windows with the outer race lands while pivoting the bearing cage. With the cage pivoted and aligned, lift the assembly from the outer race.
5. To separate the inner race from the cage, determine the cage design and proceed as follows.

Six Equal Windows

Rotate the inner race up and out of the cage.

Two Elongated Windows

Pivot the inner race until it is straight up and down in the cage. Align one of the inner race bands with one of the elongated windows and position the race through the window. Rotate the inner race up and out of the cage.

ASSEMBLY

1. Apply a light coating of grease on the inner and outer ball races. Install the inner race in the bearing cage.

CHILTON CAUTION *Use only the specified grease.*

2. Install the inner race and cage assembly in the outer race. Install the assembly vertically and pivot 90 degrees into position. When properly installed, the shallow counterbore cut into the inner race will be facing up.
3. Align the bearing cage and inner race with the outer race. Tilt the inner race and cage and install a ball bearing. Repeat this step until six balls are installed.
4. After installing the ball bearings, pack the CV joint with 1⅓ packets of the specified grease (supplied with the service kit). Pack the grease into the joint by forcing it through the splined hole in the inner race.

MANUAL TRANSMISSION SECTION

Manual Transaxle

REMOVAL

1. Remove the two transaxle to engine top mounting bolts.
2. Grasp the clutch cable and pull forward, disconnecting it from the clutch release lever. Remove the clutch cable casing from the rib on the top surface of the transaxle case.
3. Raise the vehicle on a hoist and remove the bolt attaching the brake hose routing clip to the suspension strut bracket at both front wheels.
4. Remove the bolt that secures the lower control arm ball joint to the steering knuckle assembly. Pry the lower control arm away from the knuckle.

NOTE *The plastic shield installed behind the rotor contains a molded pocket into which the lower control arm ball joint fits. When disengaging the control arm from the* knuckle, clearance for the ball joint can be provided by bending the shield back toward the rotor. Failure to provide clearance for the ball joint can result in damage to the shield.

CHILTON CAUTION *The nut and bolt must be discarded.*

NOTE *Exercise care not to damage or cut ball joint boot. The pry bar must not contact lower arm.*

5. Using a pry bar, pry the right inboard CV joint assembly from the transaxle.

NOTE *Lubricant will drain from the seal at this time. Install shipping plug T81P-1177-B2 or equivalent required.*

Remove the inner CV joint from the transaxle by grasping the right hand steering knuckle and swinging the knuckle and shaft outward from the transaxle.

Manual Transaxle

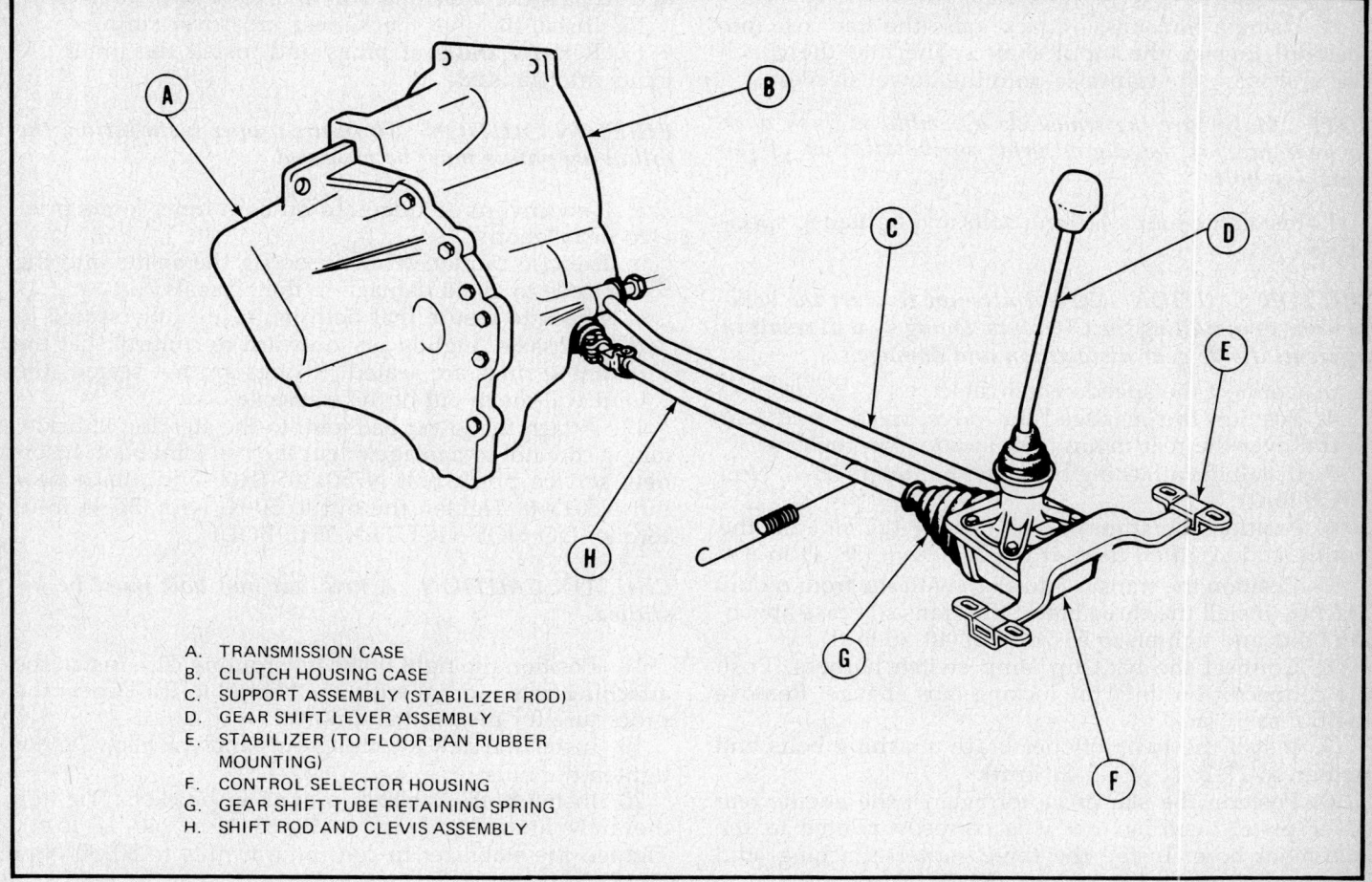

A. TRANSMISSION CASE
B. CLUTCH HOUSING CASE
C. SUPPORT ASSEMBLY (STABILIZER ROD)
D. GEAR SHIFT LEVER ASSEMBLY
E. STABILIZER (TO FLOOR PAN RUBBER MOUNTING)
F. CONTROL SELECTOR HOUSING
G. GEAR SHIFT TUBE RETAINING SPRING
H. SHIFT ROD AND CLEVIS ASSEMBLY

NOTE Use caution during the use of the pry bar and removal of the joint assembly to prevent damage to the oil seal.

6. Wire the joint assembly in a near level position to prevent over-extending the assembly during the remaining operations.

7. Repeat step 5 on the left inboard CV joint assembly. If it cannot be pried from the transaxle, insert service tool T81P-4026-A or equivalent through the right side and tap the joint out. Remove in the same manner as the right side. Wire the joint assembly as in step 6.

8. Disconnect the front stabilizer bar at both control arms. Discard the nuts.

9. Remove the two front stabilizer bar mounting brackets. Remove the stabilizer bar. Discard the bolts.

10. Disconnect the speedometer cable from the transaxle.

11. Disconnect the backup lamp switch connector from the transaxle switch.

12. Remove the three nuts from the starter mounting studs which hold the engine roll restrictor bracket.

13. Remove the engine roll restrictor. Remove the starter stud bolts.

14. Remove the two stiffener brace attaching bolts from the lower portion of the clutch housing.

15. Remove the shift mechanism crossover spring.

16. Remove the shift mechanism stabilizer bar to transaxle attaching bolt.

17. Remove the shift mechanism to shift shaft attaching bolt. Remove the shift mechanism from the shift shaft.

18. Position a transmission jack under the transaxle.

19. Loosen the nut on the rear mount stud.

20. Remove the attaching bolt from the bottom of the rear mount and loosen the two bolts at the top of the mount.

21. Remove the three bolts holding the front mount to the transaxle case.

22. Lower the MTX support jack until the transaxle clears the rear mount. Support the engine with a screw-type jack stand underneath the oil pan.

23. Remove the remaining four engine to transaxle attaching bolts.

24. Remove the transaxle from the rear face of the engine and lower from the vehicle.

NOTE The transaxle case casting may have sharp edges. Wear protective gloves when handling the transaxle assembly.

INSTALLATION

1. Using a transmission jack, raise the transaxle into position. Engage the input shaft spline into the clutch disc and work the transaxle onto the dowel sleeves.

NOTE *Make sure the transaxle assembly is flush with the rear face of the engine prior to installation of the attaching bolts.*

2. Install the four attaching bolts and tighten to specification.

CHILTON CAUTION *Do not attempt to start the vehicle prior to installing the CV joints. Doing so will result in differential side gear dislocation and damage.*

3. Connect the speedometer cable.
4. Position the managed air valve bracket and rear mount over the rear mount bolt locations in the case.
5. Install the attaching bolts and tighten to 55-70 N•m (40-50 lb-ft).
6. Position the transaxle to tighten the nut on the mount stud. Tighten the nut to 52-56 N•m (38-41 lb-ft).
7. Position the transaxle to align with the front mount bracket. Install the three bracket to transaxle case attaching bolts and tighten to 55-70 N•m (40-50 lb-ft).
8. Connect the back-up lamp switch harness. Push the connector on until the locking tabs engage. Remove the transaxle jack.
9. Install the two stiffener brace attaching bolts and tighten to 21-28 N•M (15-21 lb-ft).
10. Position the starter motor against the engine rear cover plate, insuring that it is correctly piloted in the alignment bore. Install the three starter attaching stud bolts and tighten to 41-54 N•m (30-40 lb-ft).
11. Install the engine roll restrictor.
12. Install the three roll restrictor attaching nuts and tighten to 34-40 N•m (25-30 lb-ft).
13. Install the shift mechanism stabilizer attaching bolt and tighten to 38-44 N•m (23-32 lb-ft).

14. Install the shift mechanism to the input shift rail and tighten the attaching bolt to 9-13 N•m (7-10 lb-ft).
15. Install the shift mechanism crossover spring.
16. Remove the seal plugs and install the inner CV joints into transaxle.

CHILTON CAUTION *To insure proper installation, the following points must be observed.*

a. New circlips are required on both inner joints prior to installation.
b. Exercise caution while inserting the shafts into the transaxle to avoid damage to the oil seals.
c. Check to insure that both joints are fully seated in the transaxle. Lightly pry outward to confirm that the retaining rings are seated. If rings are not seated, the joint will move out of the transaxle.

17. Attach the lower ball joint to the steering knuckle, taking care not to damage or cut the ball joint boot. Insert new service pinch bolt N7801305-S100 and attach new nut N801308. Tighten the nut to 50-60 N•m (37-44 lb-ft) torque. DO NOT TIGHTEN THE BOLT.

CHILTON CAUTION *A new nut and bolt must be installed.*

18. Position the right brake line routing clip. Install the attaching bolt and tighten to 11 N•m (8 lb-ft). Repeat the procedure for the left-hand wheel.
19. Install the new attaching nuts and washers. Do not tighten the nuts.
20. Install both stabilizer mounting brackets. Tighten the new attaching bolts to 54-60 N•m (40-44 lb-ft). Tighten the stabilizer to control arm nuts to 80-90 N•m (59-73 lb-ft).
21. Fill the transaxle with lubricant ESW-M2C33-F (automatic transmission fluid) or equivalent. Tighten the fill plug to 12-20 N•m (9-15 lb-ft).
22. Lower the vehicle.
23. Connect the clutch cable.

CLUTCH SECTION

Since the release bearing in this system is constant-running, transmission neutral rollover noise can be detected as such only by disengaging the release bearing from the clutch release fingers. This is best accomplished by disconnecting the cable from the release lever and moving the lever away from the cable. If neutral noise is evident under this condition, it is emanating from the transmission.

Noise associated with the release bearing/clutch system will be evident during all or some portion of pedal travel. During engagement and disengagement of the pawl and sector a "clicking" noise may be heard. This is normal and is in fact assurance that the adjusting mechanism is operating normally.

Release Bearing

REMOVAL

1. Remove the release fork to release the bearing retaining pin.
2. Slide the bearing from the transmission extension.

INSTALLATION

1. Apply a light film of C1AZ-19590-B or equivalent lubricant to the entire outer surface of the transmission extension and the tips of the release fork where they contact the bearing. Fill the bearing groove with the same.

Clutch

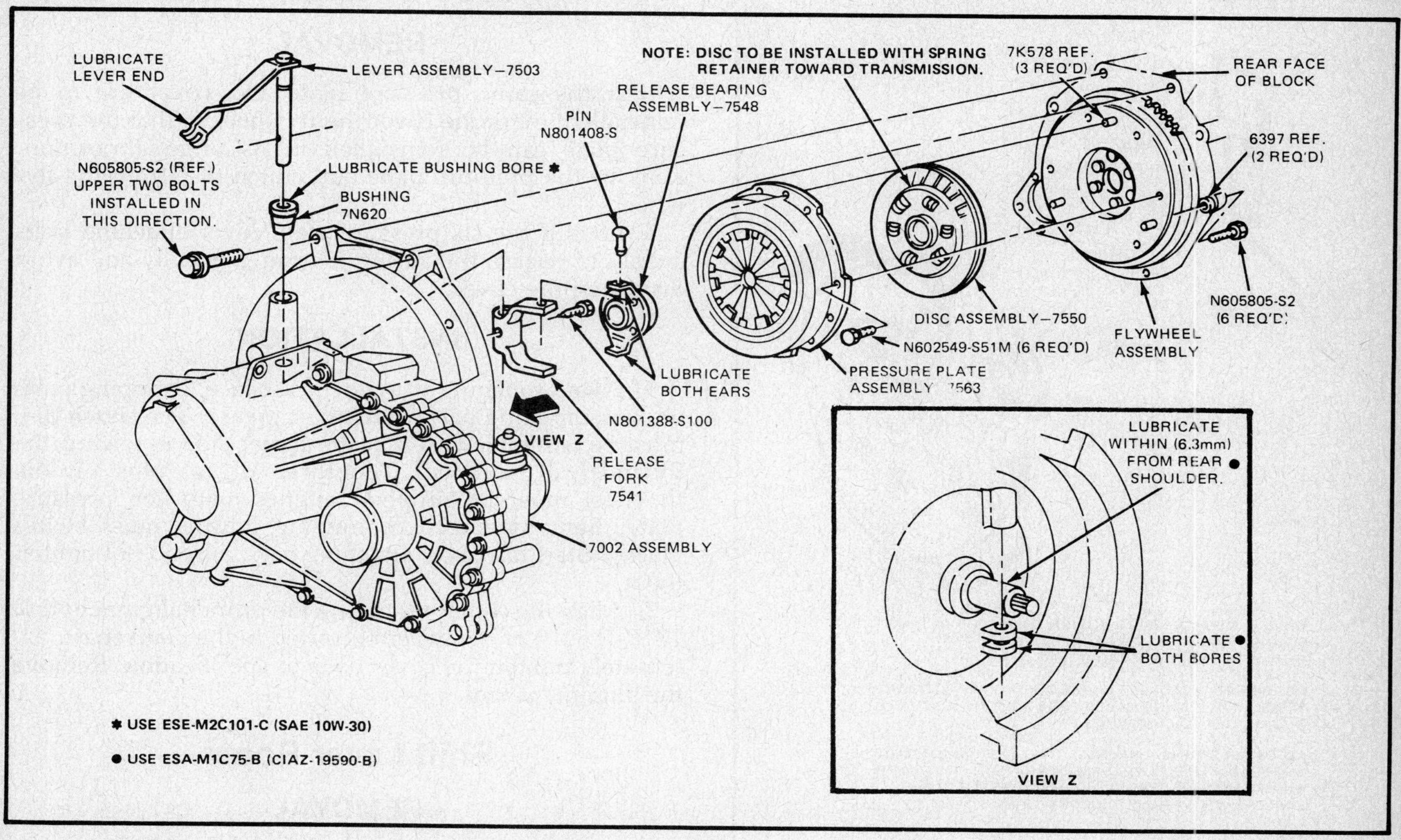

LUBRICATE LEVER END

LEVER ASSEMBLY—7503

PIN N801408-S

NOTE: DISC TO BE INSTALLED WITH SPRING RETAINER TOWARD TRANSMISSION.

RELEASE BEARING ASSEMBLY—7548

7K578 REF. (3 REQ'D)

REAR FACE OF BLOCK

N605805-S2 (REF.) UPPER TWO BOLTS INSTALLED IN THIS DIRECTION.

LUBRICATE BUSHING BORE ✱

BUSHING 7N620

6397 REF. (2 REQ'D)

DISC ASSEMBLY—7550

N605805-S2 (6 REQ'D)

FLYWHEEL ASSEMBLY

LUBRICATE BOTH EARS

N602549-S51M (6 REQ'D)

PRESSURE PLATE ASSEMBLY 7563

N801388-S100

RELEASE FORK 7541

7002 ASSEMBLY

VIEW Z

LUBRICATE WITHIN (6.3mm) FROM REAR SHOULDER.

LUBRICATE BOTH BORES

VIEW Z

✱ USE ESE-M2C101-C (SAE 10W-30)

● USE ESA-M1C75-B (CIAZ-19590-B)

Operation of Clutch Components

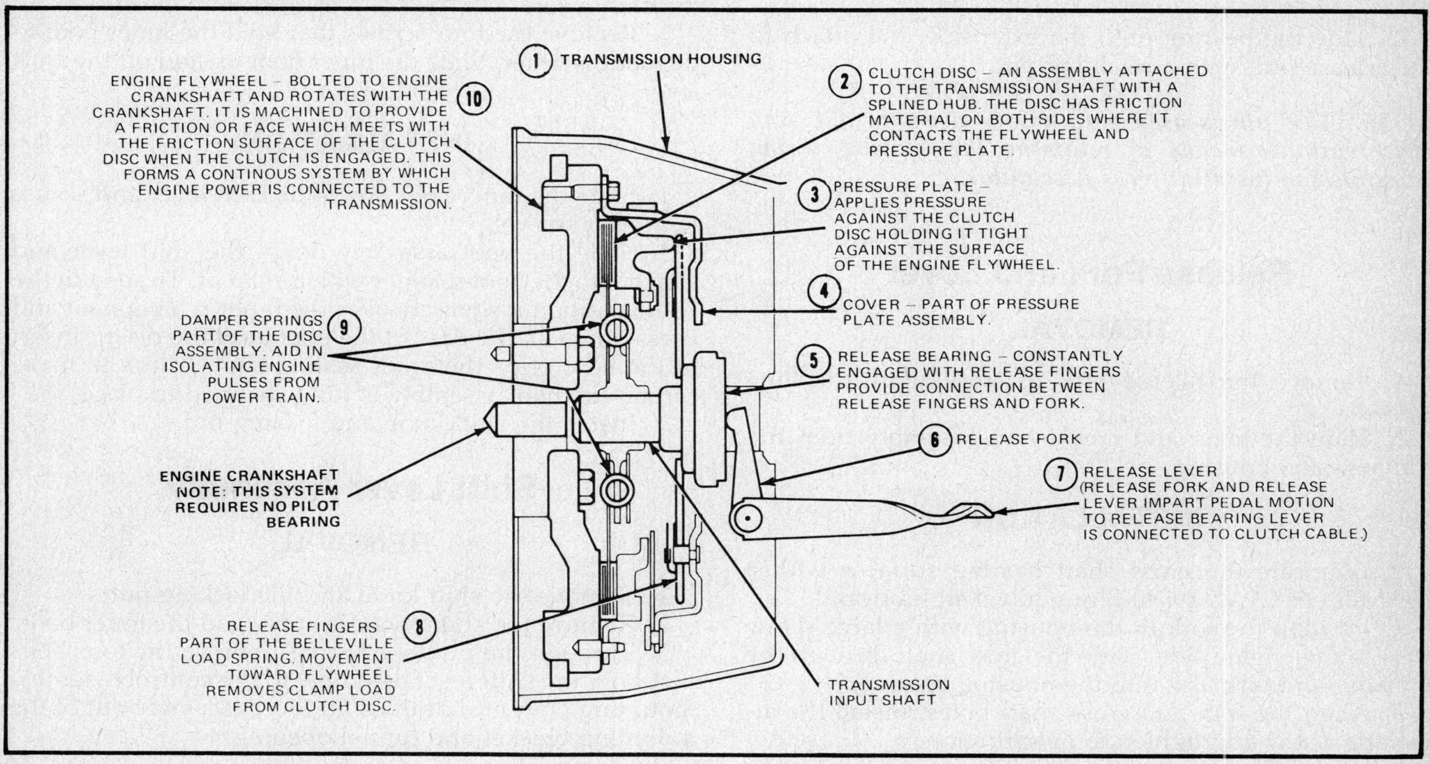

(10) ENGINE FLYWHEEL – BOLTED TO ENGINE CRANKSHAFT AND ROTATES WITH THE CRANKSHAFT. IT IS MACHINED TO PROVIDE A FRICTION OR FACE WHICH MEETS WITH THE FRICTION SURFACE OF THE CLUTCH DISC WHEN THE CLUTCH IS ENGAGED. THIS FORMS A CONTINOUS SYSTEM BY WHICH ENGINE POWER IS CONNECTED TO THE TRANSMISSION.

(1) TRANSMISSION HOUSING

(2) CLUTCH DISC – AN ASSEMBLY ATTACHED TO THE TRANSMISSION SHAFT WITH A SPLINED HUB. THE DISC HAS FRICTION MATERIAL ON BOTH SIDES WHERE IT CONTACTS THE FLYWHEEL AND PRESSURE PLATE.

(3) PRESSURE PLATE – APPLIES PRESSURE AGAINST THE CLUTCH DISC HOLDING IT TIGHT AGAINST THE SURFACE OF THE ENGINE FLYWHEEL.

(4) COVER – PART OF PRESSURE PLATE ASSEMBLY.

(5) RELEASE BEARING – CONSTANTLY ENGAGED WITH RELEASE FINGERS PROVIDE CONNECTION BETWEEN RELEASE FINGERS AND FORK.

(6) RELEASE FORK

(7) RELEASE LEVER (RELEASE FORK AND RELEASE LEVER IMPART PEDAL MOTION TO RELEASE BEARING LEVER IS CONNECTED TO CLUTCH CABLE.)

(9) DAMPER SPRINGS PART OF THE DISC ASSEMBLY. AID IN ISOLATING ENGINE PULSES FROM POWER TRAIN.

ENGINE CRANKSHAFT NOTE: THIS SYSTEM REQUIRES NO PILOT BEARING

(8) RELEASE FINGERS – PART OF THE BELLEVILLE LOAD SPRING. MOVEMENT TOWARD FLYWHEEL REMOVES CLAMP LOAD FROM CLUTCH DISC.

TRANSMISSION INPUT SHAFT

Clutch Control System

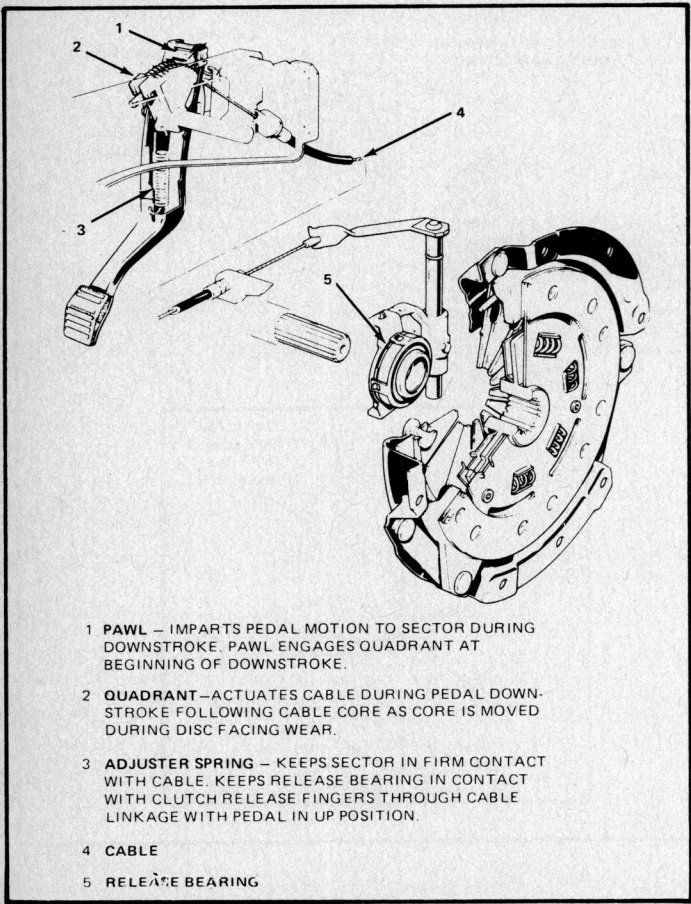

1 **PAWL** — IMPARTS PEDAL MOTION TO SECTOR DURING DOWNSTROKE. PAWL ENGAGES QUADRANT AT BEGINNING OF DOWNSTROKE.

2 **QUADRANT** — ACTUATES CABLE DURING PEDAL DOWN-STROKE FOLLOWING CABLE CORE AS CORE IS MOVED DURING DISC FACING WEAR.

3 **ADJUSTER SPRING** — KEEPS SECTOR IN FIRM CONTACT WITH CABLE. KEEPS RELEASE BEARING IN CONTACT WITH CLUTCH RELEASE FINGERS THROUGH CABLE LINKAGE WITH PEDAL IN UP POSITION.

4 **CABLE**

5 **RELEASE BEARING**

2. Slide the bearing onto the extension and attach to the release fork with a retaining pin.

NOTE This pin is used only as an assembly aid. Any other suitable means of retaining the bearing during transmission installation is acceptable.

Release Fork and Lever

REMOVAL

1. Remove the release fork to cross shaft attaching screw.
2. Slide the lever and cross shaft assembly from the transmission housing.

INSTALLATION

1. Lubricate the cross shaft bearing surfaces with a light film of C1AZ-19590-B or equivalent lubricant.
2. Position the fork in the housing with a large screw hole to the engine side. Slide the cross shaft through the bushing and fork and into the housing bearing.
3. Align the fork and cross shaft holes, install the attaching screw and tighten to specification.

Pressure Plate and Disc

REMOVAL

1. If the same pressure plate and cover are to be reinstalled, mark the cover the flywheel so that the pressure plate can be reinstalled in its original position. Remove the pressure plate and clutch disc from the flywheel.
2. Loosen the six pressure plate cover attaching bolts evenly to release the spring tension gradually and avoid distorting the cover.

INSTALLATION

1. Avoid touching the clutch disc face, dropping parts or contaminating parts with oil or grease. The clutch disc must be assembled so that the flatter side is toward the flywheel as stamped. The three dowel pins on the flywheel must be properly aligned with the pressure plate. Bent, damaged or missing dowels must be replaced. Start the cover attaching bolts, but do not tighten them.
2. Align the clutch disc using the proper alignment tool T81P-7550-A or equivalent inserted in the crankshaft. Alternately tighten the cover bolts to specification. Remove the alignment tool.

Shift Lever Boots

REMOVAL

1. Remove the shift knob and the locking nut.
2. Pull outward on each side of the shift boot assembly to release the snap-on feature. Slide the boot assembly off the shift lever.
3. Remove the four screws that hold the inner boot to the boot retainer. Slide the inner boot up and off the shift lever.

INSTALLATION

1. Slide the inner boot down the shift lever and secure with four screws.
2. Slide the boot assembly down the shift lever and attach it to the boot retainer with a snap fit. To snap fit the boot, position it squarely over the inner sealing boot and press down on the base of the boot until the plastic insert in the boot grips the inner sealing boot. Check to make certain the boot assembly is fully snapped in place.
3. Install the shift knob and locking nut.

Shift Lever Assembly

REMOVAL

1. Remove the shift knob and the locking nut.
2. Remove the shift boot assembly and the inner boot.
3. Through the tunnel opening, remove the four bolts that hold the shift lever assembly to the control assembly mounting bracket. Lift the shift lever assembly out of the mounting bracket and tunnel opening.

Manual Transaxle External Shift Linkage

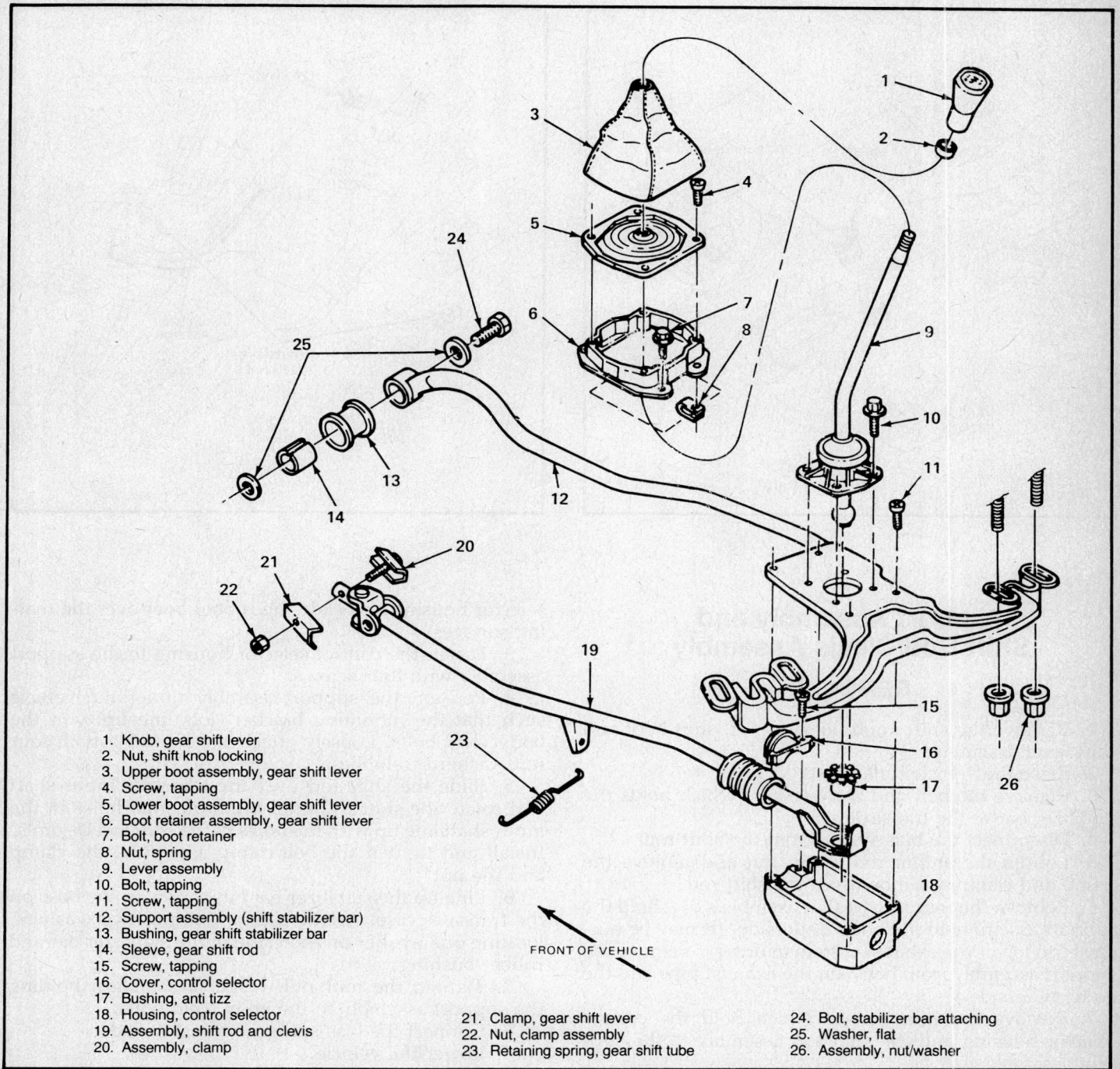

1. Knob, gear shift lever
2. Nut, shift knob locking
3. Upper boot assembly, gear shift lever
4. Screw, tapping
5. Lower boot assembly, gear shift lever
6. Boot retainer assembly, gear shift lever
7. Bolt, boot retainer
8. Nut, spring
9. Lever assembly
10. Bolt, tapping
11. Screw, tapping
12. Support assembly (shift stabilizer bar)
13. Bushing, gear shift stabilizer bar
14. Sleeve, gear shift rod
15. Screw, tapping
16. Cover, control selector
17. Bushing, anti tizz
18. Housing, control selector
19. Assembly, shift rod and clevis
20. Assembly, clamp

21. Clamp, gear shift lever
22. Nut, clamp assembly
23. Retaining spring, gear shift tube

24. Bolt, stabilizer bar attaching
25. Washer, flat
26. Assembly, nut/washer

FRONT OF VEHICLE

INSTALLATION

1. Insert the shift lever assembly through the tunnel opening into the control assembly, making sure the lower plastic pivot ball on the shift lever is inserted into the round socket on the end of the shift rod.

2. Fasten the shift lever to the control assembly with four self-tapping screws and tighten to 20-27 N•m (15-20 lb-ft).

3. Depress the clutch and actuate the shift lever as a check of function and tightness of all fasteners.

4. Install the inner boot and shift boot assembly.

5. Install the locking nut and shift knob.

Shifter Rod (Front)

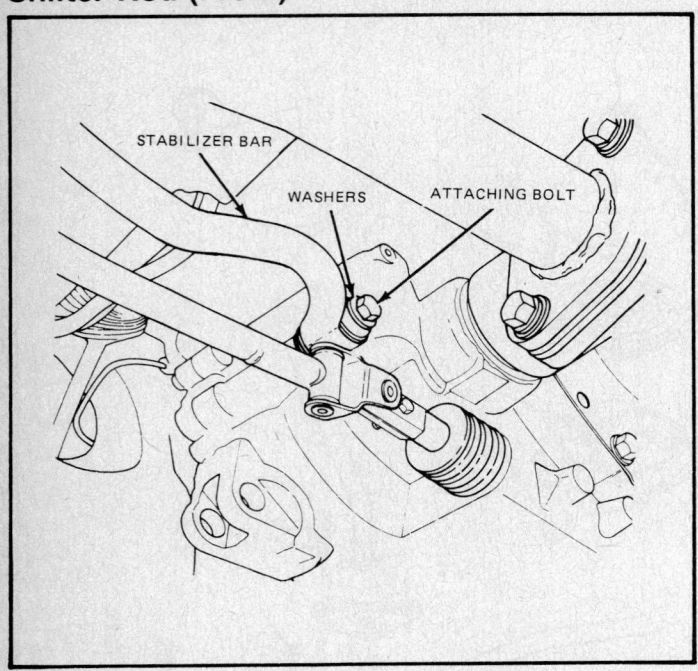

Shifter Rod (Rear)

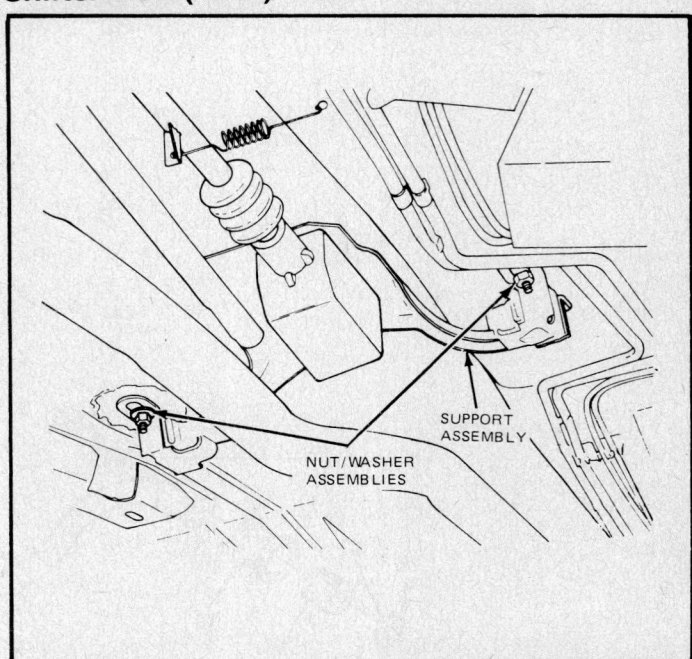

Support Assembly and Shift Rod/Clevis Assembly

REMOVAL

1. Remove the shift knob, locking nut, shift boot and shift lever assembly.
2. Raise the vehicle on a hoist.
3. Remove the bolt and two washers which holds the stabilizer bar to the transaxle.
4. Disconnect the bias spring from the shift rod.
5. Loosen the shifter rod clamp nut and remove the clamp and clamp assembly from the shift rod.
6. Remove the four nut/washer asemblies that hold the support assembly to the body underside. (It may be necessary to lower the exhaust system in order to remove the support assembly from between the exhaust pipe and the body underside.)
7. Remove the four screws which hold the control selector housing and the shift rod assembly to the support assembly.
8. Remove the two screws that hold the control selector cover to the control selector housing.
9. Remove the shift rod/clevis assembly from the control selector housing.

INSTALLATION

1. Install the shift rod/clevis assembly into the control selector housing.
2. Fasten the control selector cover onto the control selector housing and slide the rubber boot over the mating surfaces.
3. Fasten the control selector housing to the support assembly with four screws.
4. Position the support asembly under the vehicle such that the mounting bracket slots line up with the body weld bolts. Loosely attach the assembly with four nut/washer assemblies.
5. Slide the shift rod over the transaxle input shaft and rotate the shift rod until the horizontal holes in the input shaft line up with the holes in the shift rod U-joints. Install and tighten the bolt/clamp assembly, the clamp and the nut.
6. Line up the stabilizer bar bushing with the boss on the transaxle case. Attach with a bolt and two washers, locating one washer on each side of the stabilizer bar and rubber bushing.
7. Tighten the four nut/washer assemblies, holding the support assembly to the body weld bolts.
8. Connect the bias spring to the shift rod.
9. Lower the vehicle.
10. Insert the shift lever assembly through the tunnel opening into the support assembly, making sure the lower plastic pivot ball on the shift lever is inserted in the round socket on the end of the shift rod.
11. Fasten the shift lever assembly to the support assembly with four self-tapping screws and tighten to 20-27 N•m (15-20 lb-ft).
12. Depress the clutch and actuate the shift lever as a check of the function and tightness of all fasteners.
13. Install the lower boot assembly and the upper boot asembly.
14. Install the shift knob and locking nut.

AUTOMATIC TRANSAXLE SECTION

ATX Transaxle

REMOVAL

1. Disconnect the cable from the battery negative terminal.

NOTE Due to the ATX case configuration, the right-hand halfshaft assembly must be removed first. The differ- ential service tool T81P-4026-A or equivalent is then inserted into the transaxle to drive the left-hand inboard CV joint assembly from the transaxle.

2. Remove the bolts attaching the managed air valve to the ATX valve body cover.
3. Disconnect the wiring harness connector from the neutral safety switch.

Automatic Transaxle

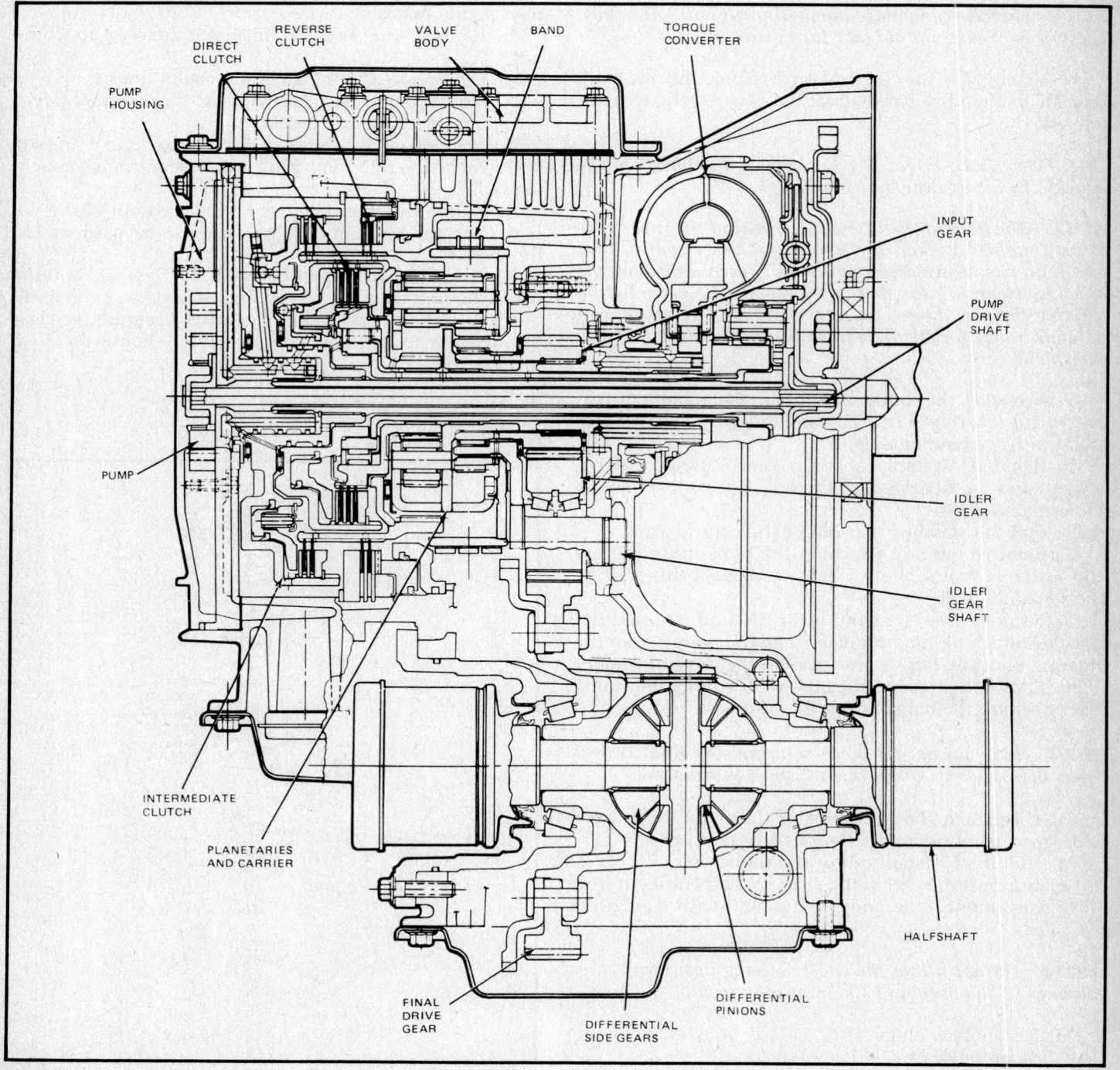

4. Disconnect the throttle valve linkage and the manual lever cable at their respective levers.

5. Remove the two transaxle to engine upper attaching bolts. The bolts are located below and on either side of the distributor.

6. Remove the nut from the control arm to steering knuckle attaching bolt (at the ball joint).

7. Drive the bolt out of the knuckle using a punch and hammer. Repeat this step on the remaining side.

CHILTON CAUTION The nut and bolt must be discarded.

NOTE Exercise care not to damage or cut ball joint boot. The pry bar must not contact lower arm.

8. Disengage the control arm from the steering knuckle using a pry bar. Repeat this step on the remaining side.

CHILTON CAUTION Do not use a hammer on the knuckle to remove the ball joints.

NOTE The plastic shield installed behind the rotor contains a molded pocket into which the lower control arm ball joint fits. When disengaging the control arm from the knuckle, clearance for the ball joint can be provided by bending the shield back toward the rotor. Failure to provide clearance for the ball joint can result in damage to the shield.

9. Remove the bolts attaching the stabilizer bar bracket to the frame rail. Discard the bolts. Repeat this step on the remaining side.

10. Remove the stabilizer bar to control the arm attaching nut and washer. Discard the nut. Repeat this step on the remaining side.

11. Pull the stabilizer bar out of the control arms.

12. Remove the bolt attaching the brake hose routing clip to the suspension strut bracket. Repeat this step on the remaining side.

13. Remove the steering gear tie rod to steering knuckle attaching nut and disengage the tie rod from the steering knuckle. Repeat this step on the remaining side.

14. Pry the halfshaft out of the right side of the transaxle. Position the halfshaft on the transaxle housing.

NOTE It is normal for some transmission fluid to leak from the transaxle when the halfshaft is removed.

15. Disengage the left halfshaft from the differential side gear using driver T81P-4026-A or equivalent.
 a. Pull the halfshaft out of the transaxle.
 b. Support the end of the shaft by suspending it from a convenient underbody component with a length of wire.

NOTE Do not allow the shaft to hang unsupported, as damage to the outboard CV joint may result.

16. Install seal plugs T81P-1177-B or equivalent into the differential seals.

17. Remove the starter support bracket and disconnect the starter cable.

18. Remove the starter attaching bolts and the starter.

19. Remove the transaxle support bracket.

20. Remove the dust cover from the torque converter housing.

21. Remove the torque converter to flywheel attaching nuts.

22. Turn the crankshaft pulley bolt to bring the attaching nuts into an accessible position.

23. Remove the nuts attaching the left front insulator to the body bracket.

24. Remove the bracket to body attaching bolts and remove the bracket.

25. Remove the left rear insulator bracket attaching nut.

26. Disconnect the transmission cooler lines.

27. Remove the bolts attaching the manual lever bracket to the transaxle case.

28. Position a transmission jack under the transaxle and remove the four remaining transaxle to engine attaching bolts.

29. Before the transaxle can be lowered out of the vehicle, the torque converter studs must be clear of the flywheel.

30. Insert a suitable tool between the flywheel and the converter and carefully move the transaxle and converter away from the engine. When the converter studs are clear of the flywheel, lower the transaxle slightly (2 to 3 inches).

Strut Assembly

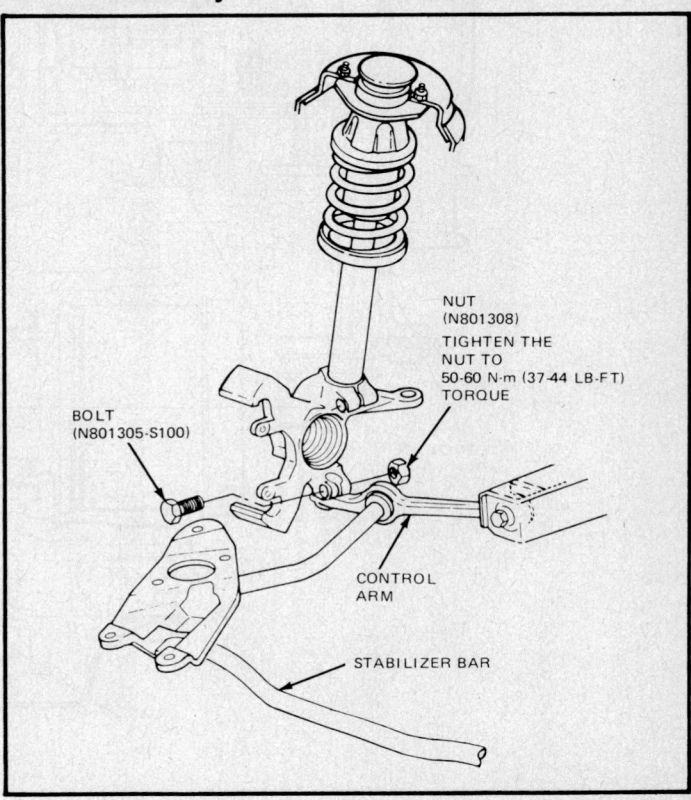

NUT
(N801308)
TIGHTEN THE NUT TO
50-60 N·m (37-44 LB-FT) TORQUE

BOLT
(N801305-S100)

CONTROL ARM

STABILIZER BAR

Circlip Installation

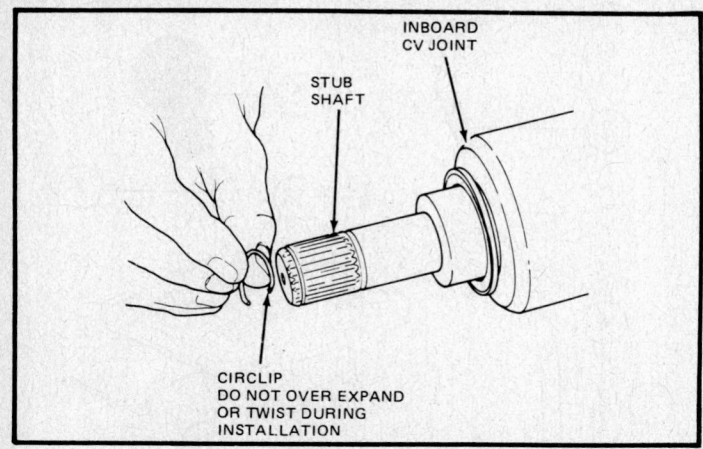

STUB SHAFT

INBOARD CV JOINT

CIRCLIP DO NOT OVER EXPAND OR TWIST DURING INSTALLATION

31. Disconnect the speedometer cable and finish lowering the transaxle.

NOTE When moving the transaxle away from the engine, watch the #1 insulator. If it contacts the body before the converter studs clear the flywheel, remove the insulator.

INSTALLATION

To install the ATX, reverse the removal procedure except for the following.
1. To install the halfshaft in the transaxle, carefully align the splines of the CV joint with the splines in the differential.
2. Exerting some force, push the CV joint into the differential until the circlip is felt to seat in the differential side gear.

NOTE Use care to prevent damage to the differential oil seal.

3. Attach the lower ball joint to the steering knuckle, taking care not to damage or cut the ball joint boot. Insert new service pinch bolt N7801305-S100 and attach new nut N801308.
4. Tighten the nut to 50-60 N•m (37-44 lb-ft) torque. DO NOT TIGHTEN THE BOLT.

CHILTON CAUTION A new nut and bolt must be installed.

Control Linkage

ADJUSTMENTS

The control linkage adjustment must be performed in the order in which they appear.
1. Position the selector lever in Drive position against the rearward stop. The shift lever must be held in the rearward position while the linkage is being adjusted.
2. Raise the vehicle and loosen the manual lever to control cable retaining nut.

Halfshaft Installation

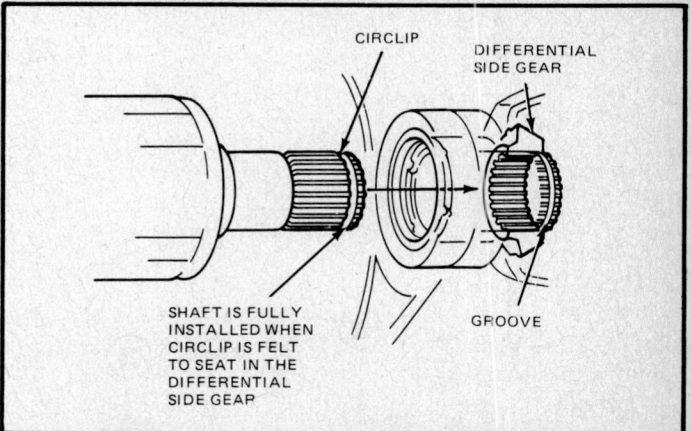

CIRCLIP

DIFFERENTIAL SIDE GEAR

SHAFT IS FULLY INSTALLED WHEN CIRCLIP IS FELT TO SEAT IN THE DIFFERENTIAL SIDE GEAR

GROOVE

3. Move the transmission manual lever to the Drive position, second detent from the most rearward position.
4. Tighten the attaching nut (20) to 14-20 N•m (10-15 lb-ft).
5. Lower the vehicle and check the operation of the transmission in each selector lever position. Be sure the park mechanism and Neutral start switch function properly.

Shift Knob
REMOVAL

1. Hold the shift knob securely and loosen the locknut by turning it counterclockwise.
2. Remove the shift knob by turning it counterclockwise.

INSTALLATION

1. Screw the locknut by hand until it bottoms out on the last thread of the selector lever.
2. Install the shift knob on the selector lever assembly until it bottoms out on the locknut.
3. Turn the shift knob counterclockwise until it is aligned. Then turn it one more complete turn counterclockwise.
4. Holding the shift knob, tighten the locknut against the shift knob.

Bezel Assembly
REMOVAL

1. Remove the shift knob and locknut.
2. Remove the console/consolette.
3. Remove the four screws from the bezel assembly.
4. Lift the bezel assembly slightly, disconnect the indicator bulb harness and remove the bezel assembly.

INSTALLATION

1. Install the bezel assembly over the shift lever. Con-

Automatic Transmission Control Linkage

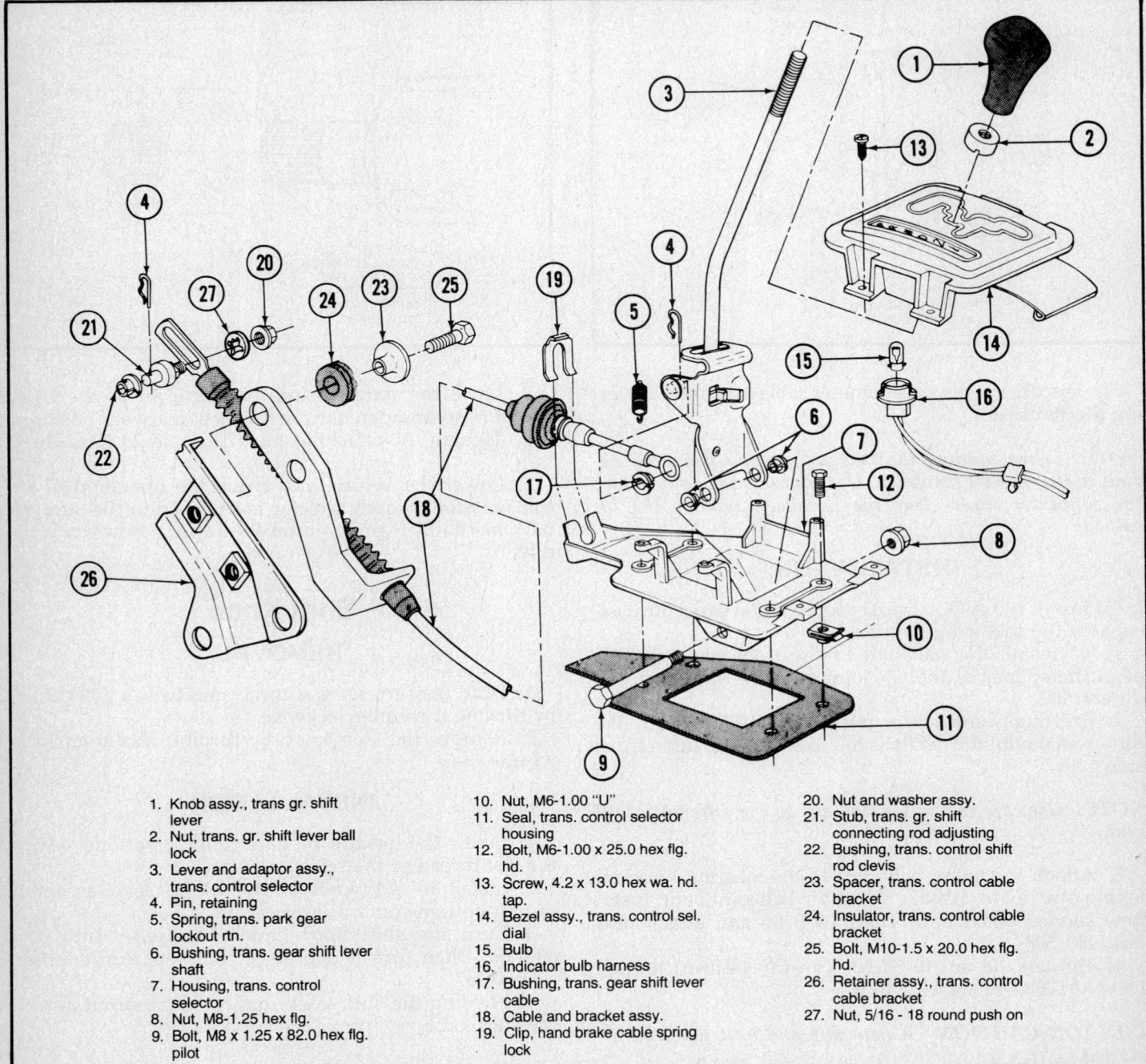

1. Knob assy., trans gr. shift lever
2. Nut, trans. gr. shift lever ball lock
3. Lever and adaptor assy., trans. control selector
4. Pin, retaining
5. Spring, trans. park gear lockout rtn.
6. Bushing, trans. gear shift lever shaft
7. Housing, trans. control selector
8. Nut, M8-1.25 hex flg.
9. Bolt, M8 x 1.25 x 82.0 hex flg. pilot
10. Nut, M6-1.00 "U"
11. Seal, trans. control selector housing
12. Bolt, M6-1.00 x 25.0 hex flg. hd.
13. Screw, 4.2 x 13.0 hex wa. hd. tap.
14. Bezel assy., trans. control sel. dial
15. Bulb
16. Indicator bulb harness
17. Bushing, trans. gear shift lever cable
18. Cable and bracket assy.
19. Clip, hand brake cable spring lock
20. Nut and washer assy.
21. Stub, trans. gr. shift connecting rod adjusting
22. Bushing, trans. control shift rod clevis
23. Spacer, trans. control cable bracket
24. Insulator, trans. control cable bracket
25. Bolt, M10-1.5 x 20.0 hex flg. hd.
26. Retainer assy., trans. control cable bracket
27. Nut, 5/16 - 18 round push on

nect the indicator bulb harness and secure the bezel assembly to the selector housing with four screws.

NOTE The bezel assembly indicator must be in the Park or Drive position when installed over the shift lever.

2. Install the console/consolette assembly.
3. Install the shift knob and locknut.
4. Adjust the control linkage.
5. Check the transmission operation for all selector lever detent positions.

Shift Lever and Housing Assembly
REMOVAL

1. Remove the shift knob, locknut and bezel assembly.
2. Remove the cable retaining clip from the lever and housing assembly.
3. Remove the retaining pin from the lever and housing assembly. Slide the control cable assembly and bushing from the boss.
4. Remove the four bolts which attach the lever and

housing assembly to the floor pan and remove the assembly.

INSTALLATION

1. Install the lever and housing assembly into the floor pan and secure with four bolts. Tighten to 4.1-9.5 N•m (3-7 lb-ft).
2. Slide the control cable assembly and bushing onto the attaching shaft.
3. Secure the cable assembly and bushing by installing the retainer pin.
4. Position the control cable assembly in the lever and housing assembly. Secure by installing the cable retaining clip.
5. Position the bezel assembly on the lever and housing assembly. Secure with four screws.
6. Position the console on the lever and housing assembly and attach with four screws.
7. Install the shift knob locknut and shift knob.
8. Adjust the control linkage.
9. Check the transmission operation for all selector lever detent positions.

Cable and Bracket Assembly

REMOVAL

1. Remove the shift knob, locknut, console, bezel assembly, control cable clip and cable retaining pin.
2. Disengage the rubber grommet from the floor pan by pushing it towards the engine compartment.
3. Raise the vehicle on a hoist.
4. Remove the retaining nut and control cable assembly from the transmission lever.

Installing Control Cable Assembly

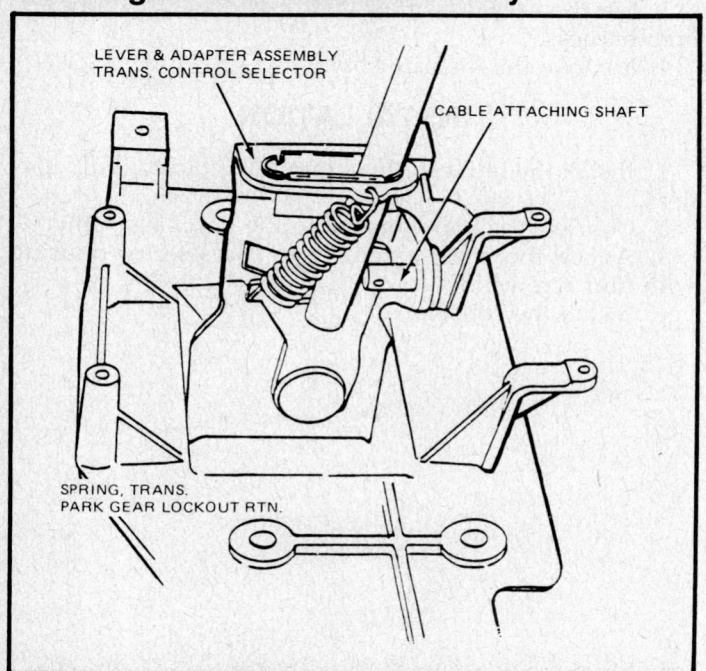

LEVER & ADAPTER ASSEMBLY
TRANS. CONTROL SELECTOR

CABLE ATTACHING SHAFT

SPRING, TRANS.
PARK GEAR LOCKOUT RTN.

Shift Control Cable—Installation At Floor Pan

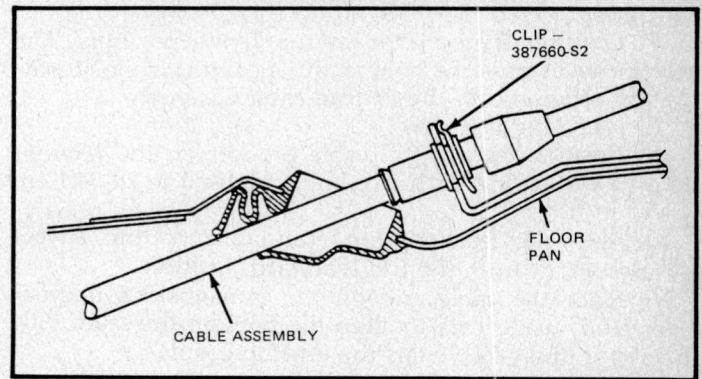

CLIP —
387660-S2

FLOOR
PAN

CABLE ASSEMBLY

5. Remove the control cable assembly bracket bolts.
6. Pull the cable through the floor pan.

INSTALLATION

1. Feed the round end of the control cable assembly through the floor pan.
2. Press the rubber boot on the control cable assembly into the body panel opening.
3. Lower the vehicle.
4. Position the control cable assembly in the selector lever housing assembly and install the spring clip.
5. Install the bushing and control cable assembly on the selector lever and housing assembly shaft and secure it with the retaining pin.

Shift Control Cable and Bracket Assembly

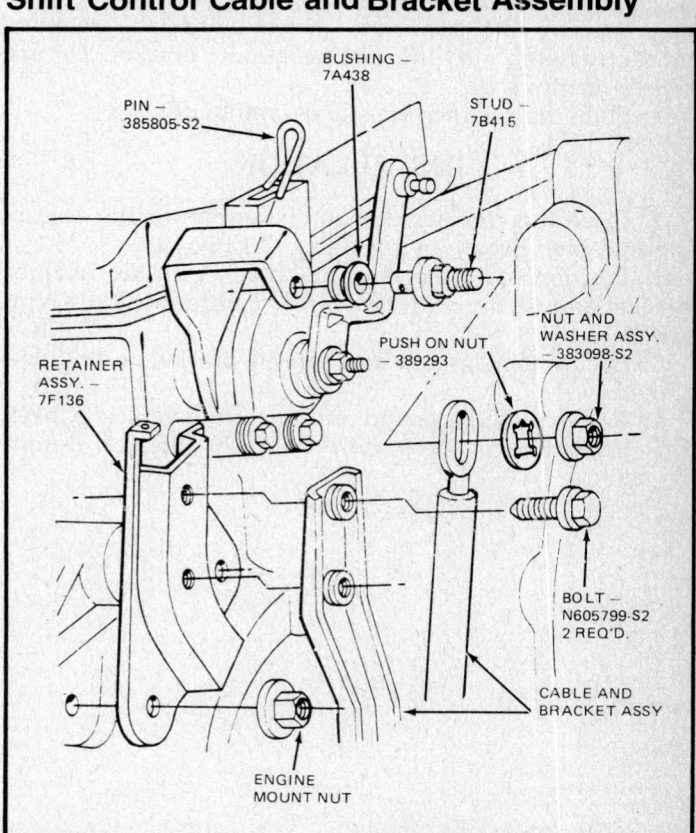

BUSHING —
7A438

PIN —
385805-S2

STUD —
7B415

NUT AND
WASHER ASSY.
— 383098-S2

PUSH ON NUT
— 389293

RETAINER
ASSY. —
7F136

BOLT —
N605799-S2
2 REQ'D.

CABLE AND
BRACKET ASSY.

ENGINE
MOUNT NUT

6. Install the bezel assembly, console, locknut and shift knob.

7. Position the selector in the Drive position. The selector lever must be held in this position while attaching the other end of the control cable assembly.

8. Raise the vehicle.

9. Position the control cable bracket on the retainer bracket and secure with two bolts. Tighten to 20-34 N•m (15-25 lb-ft).

10. Shift the transmission manual lever into Drive, second detent from the full rearward position.

11. Place the cable end on the transmission manual lever stud, using care to align the flats on the stud with the slot in the cable. Start the attaching nut.

12. Make sure the selector lever has not moved from the Drive detent. Then tighten the nut (20) to 14-19 N•m (10-14 lb-ft).

13. Lower the vehicle and check the transmission operation in each selector lever detent position. Insure Park mechanism and neutral start switch function properly.

Retainer Bracket Assembly

REMOVAL

1. Raise the vehicle.
2. Remove the bolts securing the cable bracket to the retainer bracket assembly.
3. Position a jackstand to support the engine.
4. Remove the screw which attaches a clip (securing the air pump hose and under body catalyst secondary hose) to the retainer bracket.
5. Remove the two nuts which attach the retainer bracket assembly to the engine mount bracket. *Do not remove the two bolts.*
6. Slide the retainer bracket assembly off.

INSTALLATION

1. Place the retainer bracket assembly on the engine mount bolts. Secure by installing the two nuts.
2. Position the cable assembly bracket on the retainer bracket and secure with two bolts. Tighten to 20-34 N•m (15-25 lb-ft).
3. Secure the clip and hoses in the bracket and tighten the screw.
4. Remove the jackstand and lower the vehicle. Check the transmission operation in each selector detent position.

Lever and Adapter Assembly

REMOVAL

1. Remove the shift knob, locknut, console and bezel assembly. Disconnect the control cable assembly from the selector lever and housing assemblies.
2. Remove the lever and adapter and housing assemblies.
3. Unscrew the lever and adapter assembly pivot nut. Remove the pivot bolt.
4. Pull the selector lever assembly out of the selector housing.
5. Remove the pivot bushings from the lever and adapter assembly.

INSTALLATION

1. Install the pivot bushings into the lever and adapter assembly.
2. Insert the lever and adapter assembly into the housing and align the bolt holes.
3. Install the pivot bolt and nut. Tighten the nut to 18-27 N•m (13-20 lb-ft).
4. Install the lever and housing assembly.
5. Install the control cable assembly, bezel assembly, console, locknut and shift knob.
6. Adjust the control linkage. Check the transmission operation for all selector lever detent positions.

Indicator Bulb

REMOVAL

1. Remove the console.
2. Remove the four screws which hold the bezel assembly.
3. Lift the bezel assembly and disconnect the indicator bulb harness.
4. Remove the indicator bulb.

INSTALLATION

1. Install the indicator bulb into the indicator bulb harness.
2. Connect the bulb harness to the bezel assembly.
3. Attach the bezel assembly to the selector housing with four screws.
4. Install the console.

INDEX

MODEL IDENTIFICATION

FORD

1976 FORD

W.B. **121″**. Length 224″, S/W 226″. Ship. Wgt. V8 2 Dr. 4257 Lbs.

1977 FORD

W.B. **121″**. Length 224″, Landau & S/W 226″. Width 80″. Ship. Wgt. V8 2 Dr. 4190 Lbs.

1978 LTD

W.B. **121.0″** Length 224.1 Ship. Wgt. 8 Cyl 2 Dr. 4349 Lbs.

1979 LTD

W.B. **114.0″** Length 209.0″ Ship. Wgt. 8 Cyl. 2 Dr. 3611 Lbs.

1980 LTD

W.B. **114.3″**. Length 209″. Ship. Wgt. 8 Cyl. 2 Dr. Approx. 3627 Lbs.

1981-82 FORD LTD

W.B. **114.3″**. Length 209.3″. 8 Cyl. 2 Dr. Curb Wgt. 3573 Lbs.

1977 LTD II

W.B. **118″, 2D 114″**. Length 216″, 4D 220″. S/W 224″. Width 78″, S/W 79″. Ship. Wgt. V8 2 Dr. 4785 Lbs.

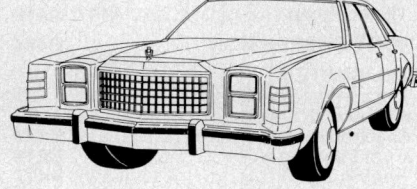

1978 LTD II

W.B. **114.0″** Length 215.5 Ship. Wgt. 8 Cyl. 2 Dr. 3971 Lbs.

1976 THUNDERBIRD

W.B. **120.4″**. Length 226″. Ship. Wgt. V8 2 Dr. 4808 Lbs.

1977 THUNDERBIRD

W.B. **114″**. Length 216″. Width 79″. Ship. Wgt. V8 2 Dr. 3907 Lbs.

1978 THUNDERBIRD

W.B. **114.0″** Length 215.5 Ship. Wgt. 8 Cyl. 2 Dr. 4061 Lbs.

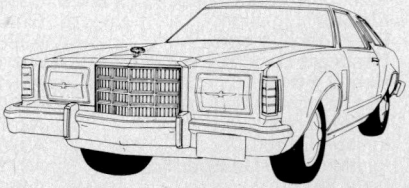

1979 THUNDERBIRD

W.B. **114.0″** Length 215.5″ Ship. Wgt. 8 Cyl. 2 Dr. 4028 Lbs.

1980 THUNDERBIRD

W.B. **108.4″**. Length 200.4″. Ship. Wgt. 8 Cyl. Approx. 3361 Lbs.

1981-82 THUNDERBIRD

W.B. **108.4″**. Length 200.4″. 6 Cyl. 2 Dr. Curb Wgt. 3169 Lbs.

1976 TORINO

W.B. **118″, 2D 114″**. Length 219″, 2D 215″, S/W 223″. Width 80″, S/W 79″. Ship. Wgt. 8 Cyl. 2 Dr. 3976 Lbs. 8 Cyl. 4 Dr. 4061 Lbs.

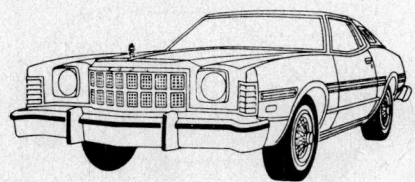

1976 ELITE
W.B. **114"**. Length 217". Ship. Wgt. V8 2 Dr. 4169 Lbs.

1976 MAVERICK
W.B. **109.9", 2D 103"**. Length 194", 2D 187". Ship. Wgt. 6 Cyl. 2 Dr. 2763 Lbs. 8 Cyl. 2 Dr. 2930 Lbs.

1977 MAVERICK
W.B. **109.9", 2D 103"**. Length 187", 2D 194". Width 71". Ship. Wgt. 6 Cyl. 2 Dr. 2782 Lbs. V8 2 Dr. 2947

1976 GRANADA
W.B. **109.9"**. Length 198". Ship. Wgt. 6 Cyl. 2 Dr. 3119 Lbs. 6 Cyl. 4 Dr. 3168 Lbs. V8 2 Dr. 3387 Lbs. V8 4 Dr. 3446 Lbs.

1977 GRANADA
W.B. **109.9"**. Length 198". Width 74". Ship. Wgt. 6 Cyl. 2 Dr. 3124 Lbs. V8 2 Dr. 3398 Lbs.

1978 GRANADA
W.B. **109.9"** Length 197.7" Ship. Wgt. 6 Cyl. 2 Dr. 3183 Lbs.

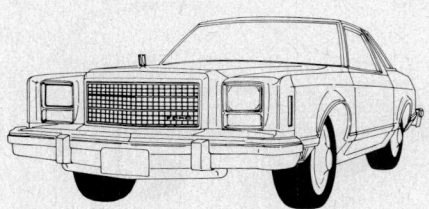

1979 GRANADA
W.B. **109.9"** Length 197.8" Ship. Wgt. 8 Cyl. 2 Dr. 3204 Lbs.

1980 GRANADA
W.B. **109.9"**. Length 197.8". Ship. Wgt. 8 Cyl. 2 Dr. Approx. 3222 Lbs.

1981-82 GRANADA
W.B. **105.5"**. Length 196.5". 4 Cyl. 2 Dr. Curb Wgt. 2834 Lbs.

1978 FAIRMONT
W.B. **105.5"** Length 193.8" Ship. Wgt. 8 Cyl. 2 Dr. 2720 Lbs.

1979 FAIRMONT
W.B. **105.5"** Length 193.8" Ship. Wgt. 8 Cyl. 2 Dr. 2615 Lbs.

1980 FAIRMONT
W.B. **105.5"**. Length 195". Ship. Wgt. 6 Cyl. 2 Dr. Approx. 2654 Lbs.

1981-82 FAIRMONT
W.B. **105.5"**. Length 195.5". 4 Cyl. 2 Dr. Curb Wgt. 2764 Lbs.

1980 FAIRMONT FUTURA
W.B. **105.5"**. Length 197.4". Ship. Wgt. Approx. 2592 Lbs.

1981-82 FAIRMONT FUTURA
W.B. **105.5"**. Length 195.5". 4 Cyl. 2 Dr. Curb Wgt. 2836 Lbs.

FORD—LINCOLN—MERCURY REAR DRIVE CARS

1976 PINTO
W.B. 94.5". Length 169", S/W 179". Ship. Wgt. 4 Cyl. 2 Dr. 2450 Lbs. V6 2 Dr. 2590 Lbs.

1977 PINTO
W.B. 94.5", S/W 94.8". Length 169", S/W 179". Width 70". Ship. Wgt. 4 Cyl. 2 Dr. 2315

1978 PINTO
W.B. 94.5" Length 169.3" Ship. Wgt. 6 Cyl. 2 Dr. 2421 Lbs.

1979 PINTO
W.B. 94.5" Length 168.8" Ship. Wgt. 2 Dr. 2472 Lbs.

1980 PINTO
W.B. 94.5". Length 169.3". Ship. Wgt. 6 Cyl. 2 Dr. Approx. 2425 Lbs.

1976 MUSTANG II
W.B. 96.2". Ship. Wgt. 4 Cyl. 2 Dr. 2678 Lbs. V6 2 Dr. 2756 Lbs.

1977 MUSTANG II
W.B. 96.2". Length 175". Width 71". Ship. Wgt. V6 2 Dr. 2627 Lbs. V8 2 Dr. 2911 Lbs.

1978 MUSTANG II
W.B. 96.2" Length 175.0" Ship. Wgt. 8 Cyl. 2 Dr. 2707 Lbs.

1979 MUSTANG
W.B. 100.4" Length 179.1" Ship. Wgt. 2 Dr. 2516 Lbs.

1980 MUSTANG
W.B. 100". Length 179.1". Ship. Wgt. 6 Cyl. Approx. 2606 Lbs.

1981 MUSTANG
W.B. 100.4". Length 179.1". 4 Cyl. 2 Dr. Curb Wgt. 2530 Lbs.

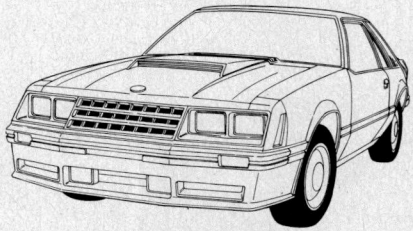

1982 MUSTANG
W.B. 100.4". Length 179.1". 4 Cyl. 2 Dr. Curb Wgt. 2583 Lbs.

1976 BOBCAT
W.B. 94.5", Villager 94.8". Length 169", S/W Ship. Wgt. 4 Cyl. S/W 2535 Lbs.

1977 BOBCAT
W.B. 94.5", S/W 94.8". Length 169". S/W 179". Width 70". Ship. Wgt. 4 Cyl. 3 Dr. 2369 Lbs. V6 3 Dr. 2508 Lbs.

1978 BOBCAT
W.B. 94.5" Length 169.3" Ship. Wgt. 6 Cyl. 3 Dr. 2487 Lbs.

1979 BOBCAT

W.B. 94.5″ Length 169.3″ Ship. Wgt. 6 Cyl. 2519 Lbs.

1980 BOBCAT

W.B. 94.5″. Length 169.3″. Ship. Wgt. 6 Cyl. 2 Dr. Approx. 2465 Lbs.

LINCOLN

1976 CONTINENTAL

W.B. 127.2″. Length 233″. Ship. Wgt. 8 Cyl. 4 Dr. 5083 Lbs.

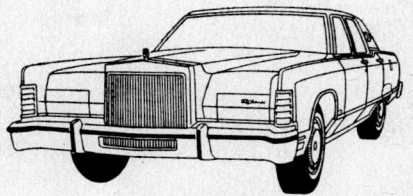

1977 CONTINENTAL

W.B. 127.2″. Length 233″. Width 80″. Ship. Wgt. V8 2 Dr. 4836 Lbs.

1978 LINCOLN CONTINENTAL

W.B.127.2″ Length 233.0 Ship. Wgt. 8 Cyl. 2 Dr. 4862 Lbs.

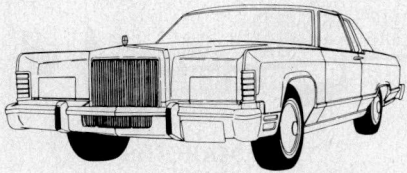

1979 LINCOLN CONTINENTAL

W.B. 127.2″ Length 233.0″ Ship. Wgt. 8 Cyl. 2 Dr. 4841 Lbs.

1980 CONTINENTAL

W.B. 117.4″. Length 219.2″. Ship. Wgt. 2 Dr. Approx. 3962 Lbs. 4 Dr. Approx. 4038 Lbs.

1981 LINCOLN TOWN CAR

W.B. 117.3″. Length 219.0″. 8 Cyl. 4 Dr. Curb Wgt. 4024 Lbs.

1982 LINCOLN CONTINENTAL

W.B. 108.5″. Length 201.2″. 6 Cyl. 4 Dr. Curb Wgt. 3563 Lbs.

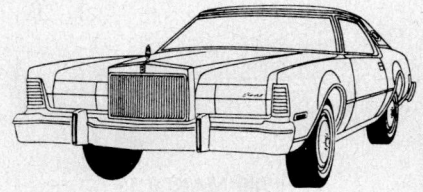

1976 MARK IV

W.B. 120.4″. Length 229″. Ship. Wgt. 8 Cyl. 2 Dr. 5051 Lbs.

1977 MARK V

W.B. 120.4″. Length 231″. Width 80″. Ship. Wgt. V8 2 Dr. 4652 Lbs.

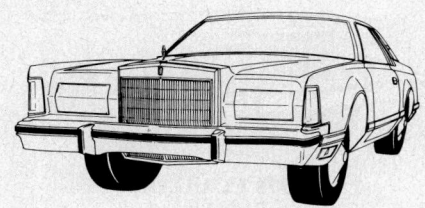

1978 MARK V

W.B. 120.4″ Length 230.3 Ship. Wgt. 8 Cyl. 2 Dr. 4770 Lbs.

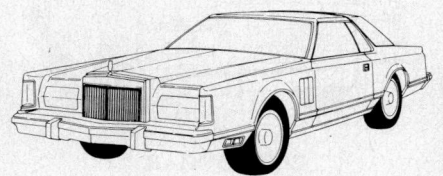

1979 MARK V

W.B. 120.4″ Length 230.3″ Ship. Wgt. 8 Cyl. 2 Dr. 4779 Lbs.

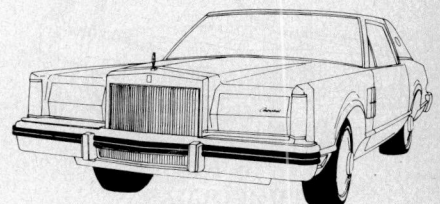

1980 MARK VI

W.B. 114″. Length 216″. Ship. Wgt. 8 Cyl. 2 Dr. Approx. 4004 Lbs.

FORD—LINCOLN—MERCURY REAR DRIVE CARS

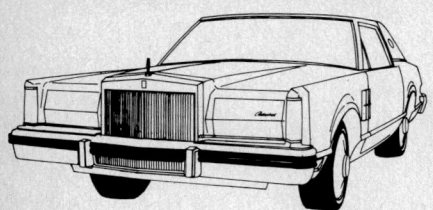

1981-82 CONTINENTAL MARK VI
W.B. 114.3″. Length 216.0″. 8 Cyl. 2 Dr. Curb Wgt. 4039 Lbs.

1977 1/2 VERSAILLES
W.B. 109.9″. Length 201″. Width ″ Ship. Wgt.

1978 VERSAILLES
W.B. 109.9″ Length 200.9″ Ship. Wgt. 8 Cyl. 2 Dr. 3891 Lbs.

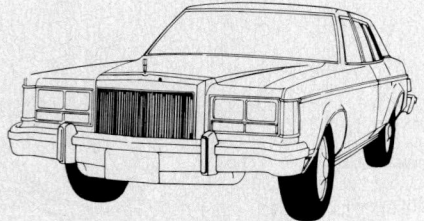

1979 VERSAILLES
W.B. 109.9″ Length 201.0″ Ship. Wgt. 8 Cyl. 4 Dr. 3848 Lbs.

1980 VERSAILLES
W.B. 109.9″. Length 200.7″. Ship. Wgt. 4 Dr. Approx. 3828 Lbs.

MERCURY

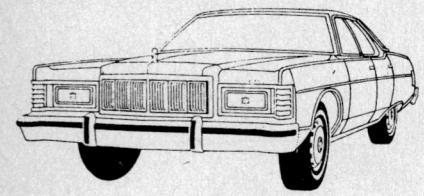

1976 MARQUIS
W.B. 124″, S/W **121**″. Length 229″. Ship. Wgt. V8 2 Dr. 4436 Lbs.

1977 MARQUIS
W.B. 124″, S/W **121**″. Length 229″. Width 80″. Ship. Wgt. V8 2 Dr. 4293 Lbs.

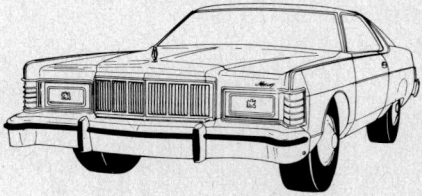

1978 MARQUIS
W.B. 124.0″ Length 229.0″ Ship. Wgt. 8 Cyl. 2 Dr. 4506 Lbs.

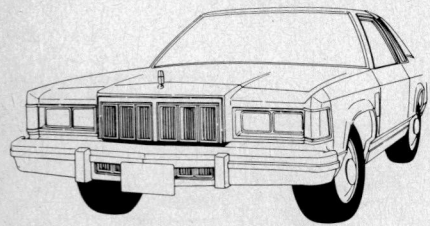

1979 MARQUIS
W.B. 114.4″ Length 212.0″ Ship. Wgt. 8 Cyl. 2 Dr. 3641 Lbs.

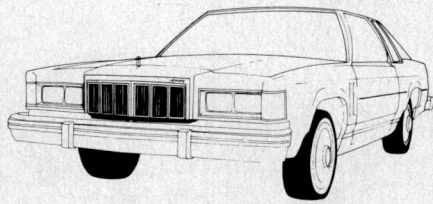

1980 MARQUIS
W.B. 114.3″. Length 212″. Ship. Wgt. 8 Cyl. 2 Dr. Approx. 3595 Lbs.

1981-82 MARQUIS
W.B. 114.3″. Length 212.3″. 8 Cyl. 2 Dr. Curb Wgt. 3728 Lbs.

1976 COUGAR
W.B. 114″. Length 216″. Ship. Wgt. V8 2 Dr. 4436 Lbs.

1977 COUGAR
W.B. 114″, 4D & S/W **118**″. Length 216″, 4D Htp 220″, S/W 224″. Width 78″. S/W 80″. Ship. Wgt. V8 2 Dr. 3811 Lbs.

1978 COUGAR
W.B. 114.0″ Length 215.5 Ship. Wgt. 8 Cyl. 2 Dr. 3914 Lbs.

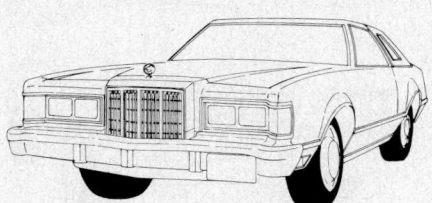

1979 COUGAR
W.B. **114.0"** Length 215.5" Ship. Wgt. 8 Cyl. 2 Dr. 3880 Lbs.

1980 COUGAR
W.B. **108.4"**. Length 200.4". Ship. Wgt. 8 Cyl. Approx. 3277 Lbs.

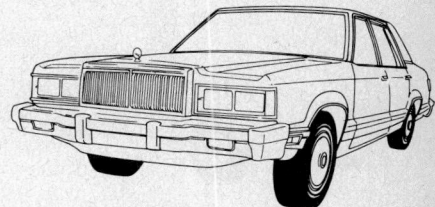

1981-82 COUGAR
W.B. **105.5"**. Length 196.5". 6 Cyl. 2 Dr. Curb Wgt. 2807 Lbs.

1981 COUGAR XR7
W.B. **108.4"**. Length 200.4". 6 Cyl. Curb Wgt. 3259 Lbs.

1982 COUGAR XR7
W.B. **108.4"**. Length 200.4". 6 Cyl. 2 Dr. Curb Wgt. 3152 Lbs.

1976 MONTEGO
W.B. **118"**, **2D 114"**. Length 220", 2D 216", S/W Ship. Wgt. V8 2 Dr. 4057 Lbs.

1976 COMET
W.B. **109.9"**, **2D 103"**. Length 197", 2D 190". Ship. Wgt. V8 2 Dr. 2952 Lbs.

1977 COMET
W.B. **109.9"**, **2D 103"**. Length 197", 2D 190". Width 71". Ship. Wgt. 6 Cyl. 2 Dr. 2799 Lbs. V8 2 Dr. 2964 Lbs.

1976 MONARCH
W.B. **109.9"**. Length 198". Ship. Wgt. 6 Cyl. 2 Dr. 3111 Lbs.

1977 MONARCH
W.B. **109.9"**. Length 198". Width 74". Ship. Wgt. 6 Cyl. 2 Dr. 3123 Lbs. V8 2 Dr. 3343 Lbs.

1978 MONARCH
W.B. **109.9"** Length 197.7" Ship. Wgt. 8 Cyl. 2 Dr. 3190 Lbs.

1979 MONARCH
W.B. **109.9"** Length 197.7" Ship. Wgt. 8 Cyl. 2 Dr. 3205 Lbs.

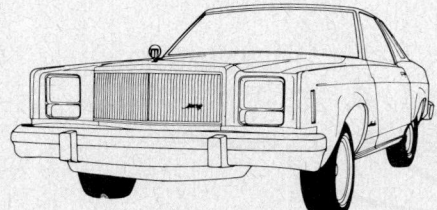

1980 MONARCH
W.B. **109.9"**. Length 197.8". Ship. Wgt. 6 Cyl. 2 Dr. Approx. 3211 Lbs.

1978 ZEPHYR
W.B. **105.5"** Length 193.8" Ship. Wgt. 8 Cyl. 2 Dr. 2720 Lbs.

1979 ZEPHYR
W.B. **105.5"** Length 193.8" Ship. Wgt. 8 Cyl. 2 Dr. 2647 Lbs.

FORD—LINCOLN—MERCURY REAR DRIVE CARS

1980 ZEPHYR
W.B. **104.5″**. Length 195.5″. Ship. Wgt. 6 Cyl. 2 Dr. Approx. 2643 Lbs.

1981 ZEPHYR
W.B. **105.5″**. Length 195.5″. 4 Cyl. 2 Dr. Curb Wgt. 2689 Lbs.

1979 CAPRI
W.B. **100.4″** Length 179.1″ Ship. Wgt. 6 Cyl. 2517 Lbs.

1980 CAPRI
W.B. **100.4″**. Length 179.1″. Ship. Wgt. 4 Cyl. Approx. 2640 Lbs.

1981-82 CAPRI
W.B. **100.4″**. Length 179.1″. 4 Cyl. Curb Wgt. 2688 Lbs.

ENGINE FIRING ORDER

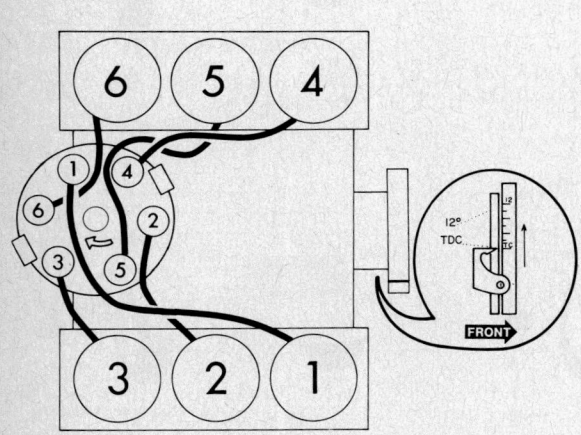

FORD MOTOR CO. 2800 cc V6
Engine firing order: 1–4–2–5–3–6
Distributor rotation: clockwise

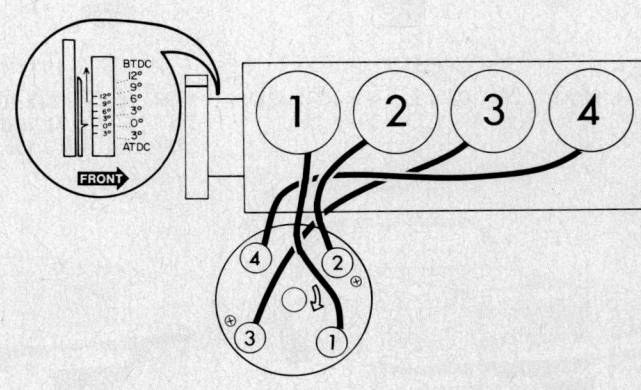

FORD MOTOR CO. 2300 cc 4-cyl.
Engine firing order: 1–3–4–2
Distributor rotation: clockwise

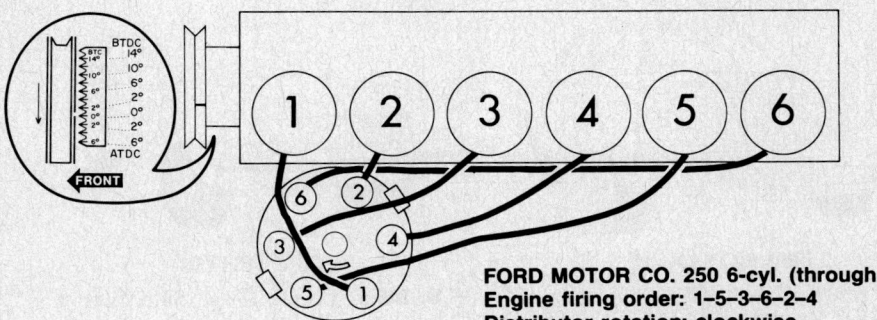

FORD MOTOR CO. 250 6-cyl. (through 1976)
Engine firing order: 1–5–3–6–2–4
Distributor rotation: clockwise

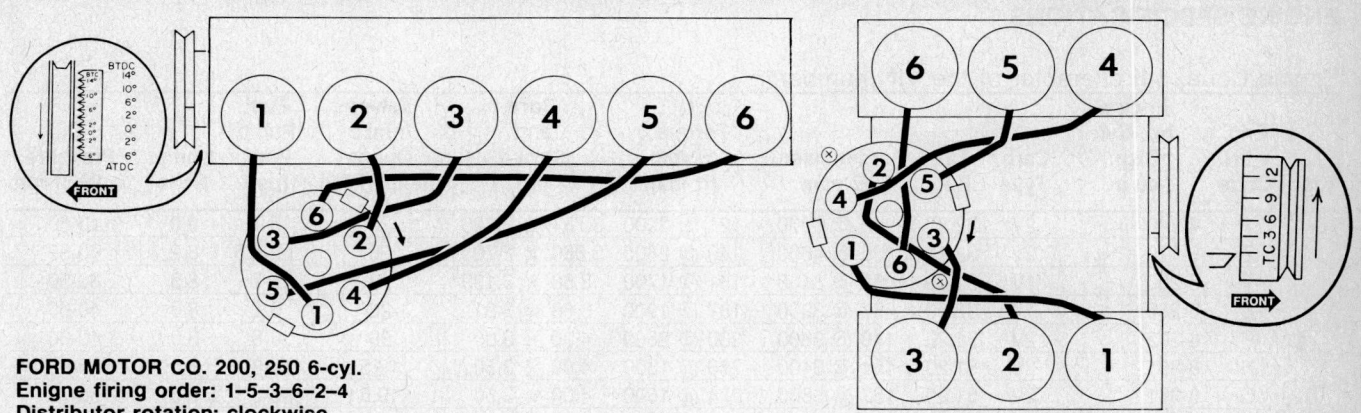

FORD MOTOR CO. 200, 250 6-cyl.
Enigne firing order: 1–5–3–6–2–4
Distributor rotation: clockwise

FORD MOTOR CO. 2800 cc V6
Engine firing order: 1–4–2–5–3–6
Distributor rotation: clockwise

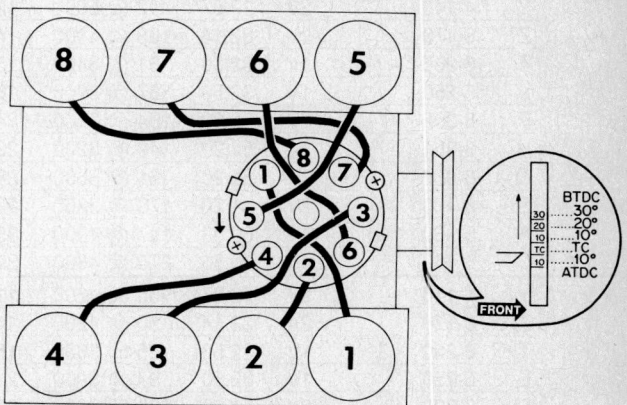

351M & 400 w/Frigidaire A/C only: timing pointer is viewed from left; all others viewed from right.

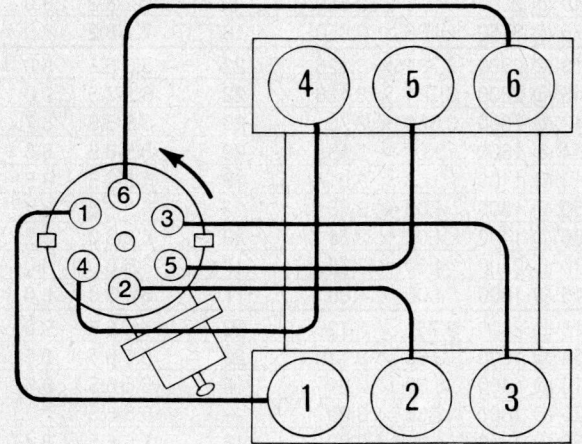

FORD MOTOR CO. 351, 400 V8
Engine firing order: 1–3–7–2–6–5–4–8
Distributor rotation: counterclockwise

FORD MOTOR CO. 255, 302, 460 V8
Engine firing order: 1–5–4–2–6–3–7–8
Distributor rotation: counterclockwise

FORD MOTOR COMPANY V6-232-3.8L
Engine firing order: 1–4–2–5–3–6
Distribution rotation: counterclockwise

VEHICLE IDENTIFICATION NUMBER (VIN)

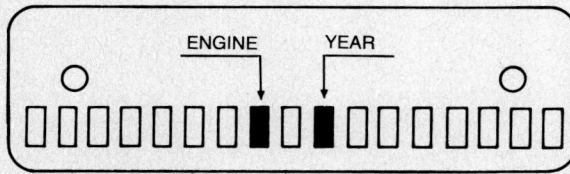

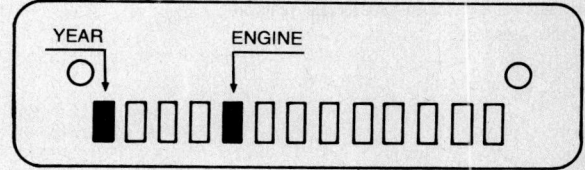

A375

FORD—LINCOLN—MERCURY REAR DRIVE CARS

ENGINE SPECIFICATIONS

Engine Code, 5th character of the VIN number①

Year	Eng. V.I.N. Code	Engine No. Cyl. Disp. cu in	Carb. Type	Tax H.P.	Horsepower② @ rpm	Torque② @ rpm (ft lbs)	Bore and Stroke (in)	Valves Intake Opens (deg. BTDC)	Fuel Pump Pres. (psi)	Comp. Ratio	Oil Pressure @ 2000 rpm
76	Y	4-140	2V	22.87	92 @ 5000	121 @ 3000	3.781 × 3.126	22	5-7	9.0	40-60
	Z	6-170	2V	32.14	105 @ 4600	140 @ 2600	3.660 × 2.70	20	3.5-5.5	8.2	40-55
	T	6-200	1V	32.50	81 @ 3400	151 @ 1700	3.68 × 3.130	28	5-7	8.3	30-50
	L	6-250	1V	32.50	87 @ 3000	187 @ 1900	3.68 × 3.91	26	5-7	8.0	40-60
	F	8-302	2V	51.20	140 @ 3800	230 @ 2600	4.00 × 3.00	20	6-8	8.0	40-60
	H	8-351	2V	51.20	154 @ 3400	286 @ 1800	4.00 × 3.50	19.5	6-8	8.0	40-60
	Q	8-351	2V	51.20	152 @ 3800	274 @ 1600	4.00 × 3.50	19.5	6-8	8.0	50-75
	S	8-400	2V	51.20	180 @ 3800	336 @ 1800	4.00 × 4.00	17	6-8	8.0	50-75
	A	8-460	4V	60.83	202 @ 3800	352 @ 1600	4.36 × 3.850	8	6-8	8.0	40-65
	C	8-460	4V	60.83	202 @ 3800	352 @ 1600	4.36 × 3.850	8	6-8	8.0	40-65
77	Y	4-140	2V	22.87	92 @ 5000	121 @ 3000	3.781 × 3.126	22	5-7	9.0	40-60
	Z	6-170	2V	32.14	103 @ 4400	149 @ 2800	3.660 × 2.70	20	3.5-5.5	8.7	40-60
	T	6-200	1V	32.50	81 @ 3400	151 @ 1700	3.68 × 3.130	20	5-7	8.3	30-50
	L	6-250	1V	32.50	87 @ 3000	187 @ 1200	3.68 × 3.91	18	5-7	8.0	40-60
	F	8-302	2V	51.20	134 @ 3600	245 @ 1600	4.00 × 3.00	16	6-8	8.0	40-65
	H	8-351	2V	51.20	149 @ 3200	291 @ 1600	4.00 × 3.50	23	6-8	8.0	40-65
	Q	8-351	2V	51.20	161 @ 3600	285 @ 1800	4.00 × 3.50	19.5	6-8	8.0	50-75
	S	8-400	2V	51.20	173 @ 3800	326 @ 1600	4.00 × 4.00	17	6-8	8.0	50-75
	A	8-460	4V	60.83	197 @ 4000	353 @ 2000	4.36 × 3.850	8	6-8	8.0	40-65
	C	8-460	4V	60.83	275 @ 4800	395 @ 2800	4.36 × 3.850	8	6-8	8.0	40-65
'78	Y	4-140	2V	22.87	88 @ 4800	118 @ 2800	3.781 × 3.126	22	5.5-6.5	9.0	40-60
	Z	6-170	2V	32.14	90 @ 4200	143 @ 2200	3.660 × 2.70	20	3.5-5.8	8.7	40-60
	T	6-200	1V	32.50	85 @ 3600	154 @ 1600	3.68 × 3.130	20	3.5-6.5	8.5	30-50
	L	6-250	1V	32.50	97 @ 3200	210 @ 1400	3.68 × 3.91	18	5.5-6.5	8.5	40-60
	F	8-302	2V	51.20	139 @ 3600	250 @ 1600	4.00 × 3.00	16	5.5-6.5	8.4	40-65
	H	8-351	2V	51.20	144 @ 3200	277 @ 1600	4.00 × 3.50	23	4-6	8.3	40-65
	Q	8-351	2V	51.20	152 @ 3600	278 @ 1800	4.00 × 3.50	19.5	6.5-7.5	8.0	50-75
	S	8-400	2V	51.20	166 @ 3800	319 @ 1800	4.00 × 4.00	17	6.5-7.5	8.0	50-75
	A	8-460	4V	60.83	202 @ 4000	348 @ 2000	4.36 × 3.850	8	7.2-8.2	8.0	40-65
	C	8-460	4V	60.83	255 @ 4800	375 @ 3750	4.36 × 3.850	18	7.2-8.2	8.0	40-65
'79	Y	4-140	2V	22.87	88 @ 4800	118 @ 2800	3.781 × 3.126	22	5.5-6.5	9.0	50
	W	4-140	2V	22.87	150 @ 4800	245 @ 2200	3.781 × 3.126	22	6.5-7.5	9.0	55
	Z	6-170	2V	32.14	109 @ 4800	142 @ 2800	3.660 × 2.70	28	3.5-5.8	8.7	40-60
	T	6-200	1V	32.50	85 @ 3600	154 @ 1600	3.68 × 3.130	20	5.5-6.5	8.5	30-50
	L	6-250	1V	32.50	97 @ 3200	210 @ 1400	3.68 × 3.91	18	5.5-6.5	8.6	40-60
	F	8-302	2V	51.20	140 @ 3600	250 @ 1800	4.00 × 3.00	16	5.5-6.5	8.4	40-60
	H	8-351	2V	51.20	135 @ 3200	286 @ 1400	4.00 × 3.50	23	6.5-8.0	8.3	50-75
	Q	8-351	2V	51.20	151 @ 3600	270 @ 2200	4.00 × 3.50	17	6.5-8.0	8.0	50-75
	S	8-400	2V	51.20	159 @ 3400	315 @ 1800	4.00 × 4.00	17	6.0-8.0	8.0	50-75
'80	A	4-140	2V	22.87	88 @ 4400	118 @ 2800	3.781 × 3.126	22	5.5-6.5	9.0	50
	B	6-200	1V	32.50	85 @ 3600	154 @ 1600	3.68 × 3.130	20	5.5-6.5	8.5	30-50
	C	6-250	1V	32.50	97 @ 3200	210 @ 1400	3.68 × 3.91	18	5.5-6.5	8.6	40-60
	D	8-255	2V	43.33	112 @ 3800	220 @ 1800	3.68 × 3.00	—	5.5-6.5		40-60
	F	8-302	2V	51.20	140 @ 3600	250 @ 1800	4.00 × 3.00	16	5.5-6.5	8.4	40-60
	G	8-351	2V	51.20	151 @ 3600	270 @ 2200	4.00 × 3.50	23	6.5-8.0	8.0	50-75
	W	4-140	2V	22.87	150 @ 4800	245 @ 2200	3.781 × 3.186	22	6.5-7.5	9.0	55

① This measurement in millimeters.
② Horsepower and torque figures for later years are Chilton estimates

TUNE-UP SPECIFICATIONS

Engine Code, 5th character of the VIN number②

Year	Eng. V.I.N. Code	Eng. No. Cyl. Disp. cu in	Spark Plugs Orig. Type	Gap (in)	Timing (deg. BTDC @ rpm) Man. Trans.	Auto. Trans.	Manual	Auto Cal.	Fed.
'76	Y	4-140	AGRF-52	.035	6 @ 550	20 @ 550	850N		750D/550N
	Z	6-170	AGR-42	.035	10 @ 700	6 @ 650	850N	800D/650N	700D/650N
	T	6-200	BRF-82	.044	6 @ 600	8 @ 650	800N	650D	
	L	6-250	BRF-82	.044	4 @ 650	6 @ 550	850N	600D	
	F	8-302	ARF-42	.044	12 @ 500	6 @ 500	750N	700D	650D
	H	8-351	ARF-42	.044	—	6 @ 650	—	650D	
	Q	8-351	ARF-42	.044	—	6 @ 650	—	650D	
	S	8-400	ARF-42	.044	—	10 @ 650	—	625D	650D
	A	8-460	ARF-52	.044	—	14 @ 650	—	650D/600N	
	C	8-460	ARF-52	.044	—	14 @ 650	—	650D/600N	
'77	Y	4-140	AWRF-42	.035	6 @ 550	20 @ 600	850N	750D/600N	800D/600N
	Z	6-170	AWSF-42	.035	12 @ 850	12 @ 700	850N	750D/600N	700D
	T	6-200	BRF-82	.050	6 @ 750	6 @ 750	800N	650D	
	L	6-250	BRF-82	.050	4 @ 750	6 @ 750	850N	600D	
	F	8-302	ARF-52	.050	6 @ 500	2 @ 500	800N	600D	
	H	8-351	ARF-52	.050	—	10 @ 800	—	650D	
	Q	8-351	ARF-52	.050	—	10 @ 800	—	650D	
	S	8-400	ARF-52	.050	—	6 @ 600	—	650D	600D
	A	8-460	ARF-52	.050	—	16 @ 525	—	650D/525N	
	C	8-460	ARF-52	.050	—	16 @ 525	—	650D/525N	
'78	Y	4-140	AWSF-42	.035	6 @ 550	20 @ 600	850N	750D/600N	800D/600N
	Z	6-170	AWSF-42	.035	10 @ 850	12 @ 650	850N	750D/600N	650D
	T	6-200	BSF-82	.050	10 @ 750	10 @ 750	800N	650D	
	L	6-250	BSF-82	.050	4 @ 750	14 @ 750	800N	600D	
	F	8-302	ARF-52	.050	10 @ 500	14 @ 500	900N	625D	
	H	8-351	ARF-52	.050	—	14 @ 800	—	600D	
	Q	8-351	ASF-52	.050	—	14 @ 800	—	600D	
	S	8-400	ASF-52	.050	—	13 @ 800	—	600D	575D
	A	8-460	ARF-52	.050	—	10 @ 580	—	580D	
	C	8-460	ARF-52	.050	—	10 @ 580	—	580D	
'79	Y	4-140	AWSF-42	.035	6 @ 550	20 @ 600	850N	750D/600N	800D/600N
	W	4-140	AWSF-42	.035	2 @ 650	—	900N	—	—
	Z	6-170	AWSF-42	.035	9 @ 650	9 @ 650	850N	750D/600N	650D
	T	6-200	BSF-82	.050	8 @ 750	10 @ 750	700N	650D	
	L	6-250	BSF-82	.050	4 @ 750	10 @ 750	800N	600D	
	F	8-302	ASF-52	.050	12 @ 500	8 @ 500	800N	600D	
	H	8-351	ASF-52	.050	—	15 @ 800	—	600D	
	Q	8-351	ASF-42	.050	—	12 @ 800	—	600D	
	S	8-400	ASF-52	.050	—	14 @ 800	—	650D	600D
'80	A	4-140	AWSF-42	.035	①			①	
	B	6-200	BSF-82	.050	①			①	
	C	6-250	BSF-82	.050	①			①	
	D	8-255	ASF-52	.050	①			①	
	F	8-302	ASF-52	.050	①			①	
	G	8-351	ASF-52	.050	①			①	
	W	4-140	AWSF-42	.035	①			①	

The underhood certification/specification decal is the authority for performance specifications affecting vehicle emissions. Use this manual's information only when that decal is not available.

① See underhood certification/specification decal

ENGINE SPECIFICATIONS

Engine Code, 5th character of the VIN number①

Year	Eng. V.I.N. Code	Engine No. Cyl. Disp. cu in	Carb. Type	Tax H.P.	Horsepower② @ rpm	Torque② @ rpm (ft lbs)	Bore and Stroke (in)	Valves Intake Opens (deg. BTDC)	Fuel Pump Pres. (psi)	Comp. Ratio	Oil Pressure @ 2000 rpm
'81	A	4-140	2V	22.87	88 @ 4400	118 @ 2800	3.781 × 3.126	22	5.5-6.5	9.0	40-60
	W	4-140	2V	22.87	150 @ 4800	245 @ 2200	3.781 × 3.126	22	6.5-7.5	9.0	55
	C	6-250	1V	32.50	97 @ 3200	210 @ 1400	3.68 × 3.91	18	5.5-6.5	8.6	40-60
	D	8-255	2V	43.33	112 @ 3800	220 @ 1800	3.68 × 3.00	—	5.5-6.5	8.4	40-60
	F	8-302	2V	51.20	140 @ 3600	250 @ 1800	4.00 × 3.00	16	5.5-6.5	8.4	40-60
	G	8-351	2V	51.20	151 @ 3600	270 @ 2200	400 × 3.50	23	5.5-6.5	8.0	50-75
'82	A	4-140	2V	22.87	88 @ 4400	118 @ 2800	3.781 × 3.126	22	5.5-6.5	9.0	40-60
	W	4-140	2V	22.87	150 @ 4800	245 @ 2200	3.781 × 3.126	22	6.5-7.5	9.0	55
	3	V6-232 (3.8L)	2V	34.6	112 @ 4000	175 @ 2600	96.8 × 86.0①	13	6.5-8.0	8.8	40-60
	D	8-255	2V	43.33	112 @ 3800	220 @ 1800	3.68 × 3.00	—	5.5-6.5	8.4	40-60
	F	8-302	2V	51.20	140 @ 3600	250 @ 1800	4.00 × 3.00	16	5.5-6.5	8.4	40-60
	G	8-351	2V	51.20	151 @ 3600	270 @ 2200	400 × 3.50	23	5.5-6.5	8.0	50-75

① This measurement in millimeters.
② Horsepower and torque figures for later years are Chilton estimates

TUNE-UP SPECIFICATIONS

Engine Code, 5th character of the VIN number②

Year	Eng. V.I.N. Code	Eng. No. Cyl. Disp. cu in	Spark Plugs Orig. Type	Gap (in)	Timing (deg. BTDC @ rpm) Man. Trans.	Timing (deg. BTDC @ rpm) Auto. Trans.	Manual	Idle Speed Auto Cal.	Idle Speed Auto Fed.
'81	A	4-140	AWSF-42	.035	①			①	
	W	4-140	AWSF-42	.035	①			①	
	B	6-200	BSF-82	.050	①			①	
	C	6-250	BSF-82	.050	①			①	
	D	8-255	ASF-52	.050	①			①	
	F	8-302	ASF-52	.050	①			①	
	G	8-351	ASF-52	.050	①			①	
'82	A	4-140	AWSF-42	.035	①			①	
	W	4-140	AWSF-42	.035	①			①	
	B	6-200	BSF-82	.050	①			①	
	3	V6-232 (3.8L)	AGSP-52	.044	①			①	
	D	8-255	ASF-52	.050	①			①	
	F	8-302	ASF-52	.050	①			①	
	G	8-351	ASF-52	.050	①			①	

The underhood certification/specification decal is the authority for performance specifications affecting vehicle emissions. Use this manual's information only when that decal is not available.

① See underhood certification/specification decal

FLUID CAPACITIES—Coolant, Fuel & Lubricant FORD SMALL CARS

Year	Engine No. Cyl. Disp. cu in	Engine Crankcase (Add 1 Qt For New Filter)	TRANSMISSION (Pts To Refill After Draining) Manual 3-Speed	4-Speed	Automatic (pts)	Drive Axle (pts)	Gasoline Tank (gals)	COOLING SYSTEM (qts) With Heater	With A/C
'76	4-140 (2300 cc)	4②	—	2.8⑨	⑦	2.2⑧	13⑤⑥	8.7	9.0
	6-170.8 (2800 cc)	4½②	—	2.8⑨	⑦	4.0	13⑤⑥	12.5	13.2
	8-302 (4950 cc)	4	—	3.5	⑦	4.0	13⑥	16.3	16.3
'77	4-140 (2300 cc)	4½②	—⑭	2.8⑨	⑦	⑭	13⑤⑥	8.7⑩	9.0⑪
	6-170 (2800 cc)	4½②	—⑭	2.8⑨	⑦	⑭	13⑤⑥	8.5⑫	9.2⑬
	8-302 (4950 cc)	4	—⑭	3.5	⑦	⑭	13⑤⑥	16.3	16.3
'78	4-140 (2.3L)	4②	—	3.5⑰	⑮	⑭	13.0⑤⑱	8.8⑲	9.1⑲
	6-170.8 (2.8L)	4.5②	—	3.5⑰	⑮	⑭	13.0⑤	8.8⑯⑳	9.0⑯⑳
	8-302	4	—	3.5	13.4	4.5	13.0⑤⑥	16.3	16.3
'79	4-140 (2.3L)	4②	—	3.5⑰	⑮	⑭	⑤㉑	8.8⑲	9.1⑲
	6-170.8 (2.8L)	4.5②	—	—	⑮	⑭	⑤㉑	8.8⑯⑳	9.0⑯⑳
	8-302	4	—	3.5	13.4	4.5	12.5	16.3	16.3
'80	4-140 (2.4L)	4②	—	3.5⑰	⑮	⑭	⑤㉑	8.8⑲	9.1⑲
	6-200	4	—	3.5	⑮	⑭	⑤㉑	8.8⑯⑳	9.0⑯⑳
	8-255	4	—	3.5	13.4	4.5	12.5	16.3	16.3
'81	4-140 (2.4L)	4②	—	3.5	⑮	⑭	①	10.2	10.2
	6-200	4	—	4.5	⑮	⑭	12.5	9.0	9.0
	8-255	4	—	—	⑮	⑭	17.5	14.2	14.3
'82	4-140 (2.3L)	4②	—	3.5	⑮	⑭	①	10.2	10.2
	6-200	4	—	4.5	⑮	⑭	12.5	9.0	9.0
	V6-232 (2.8L)	4	3.5	4.5	13.4	4.0	21	8.3	8.35
	8-255	4	—	—	⑮	⑭	17.5	14.2	14.3

— Not applicable
① Non-Turbo: 11.5 without air conditioning, 12.5 with air conditioning
Turbo: 11.5 with manual transmission, 12.5 with automatic
② Add 0.5 qt for filter
⑤ 14 gals on station wagon
⑥ 16.5 gals with auxiliary tank in Mustang II
⑦ C-3——16 pts
C-4——14.5 pts
⑧ 3.0 pts in Mustang II
⑨ 3.5 pts in Mustang II
⑩ 8.5 qts in Mustang II
⑪ 9.1 qts in Mustang II
⑫ 8.8 qts in Mustang II
⑬ 9.0 qts in Mustang II
⑭ 6.75 ring gear: 2.5 pts
7.5 ring gear: 3.5
8.0 ring gear: 4.5
⑮ W/c-3, 16.0 pts.
W/c-4, 13.4 pts.
⑯ 8.3 w/manual trans Mustang II
⑰ 2.8 pts. in Bobcat and Pinto
⑱ Bobcat in California—11.7 gal
⑲ Bobcat and Pinto w/o ac 8.6, w/ac 9.0
⑳ Bobcat and Pinto w/o ac 8.5, w/ac 9.2
㉑ Mustang and Capri 12.5 gal except w/2.3l non-turbo engine, w/2.3l non-turbo Mustang and Capri 11.5 gal
Pinto and Bobcat 13 gal except 3 door w/2.3l and manual trans. in California
Pinto and Bobcat 3 door w/2.3l and manual trans in California—11.7 gal

FORD—LINCOLN—MERCURY REAR DRIVE CARS

FLUID CAPACITIES—Coolant, Fuel & Lubricant LINCOLN CONTINENTAL

Year	Engine No. Cyl. Disp. cu in	Engine Crankcase (Add 1 Qt For New Filter)	TRANSMISSION (Pts To Refill After Draining) Manual 3-Speed	4-Speed	Automatic (pts)	Drive Axle (pts)	Gasoline Tank (gals)	COOLING SYSTEM (qts) With Heater	With A/C
'76	8-460 Linc.	4	—	—	25	5	24.2⑤	—	19.7
	8-460 MK IV	4	—	—	25	5	26.5	—	19.8
'77	8-400	4	—	—	25	5	⑥	17.2	17.2
	8-460	4	—	—	25	5	⑥	18.5	18.5
'78	8-400	4	—	—	24	5	⑦	—	16.9⑧
	8-460	4	—	—	24	5	⑦	—	18.6⑨
'79	8-400	4	—	—	24	5	⑦	—	16.9⑧
'80	8-302	4	—	—	24	15	18.0	—	16
	8-351	4	—	—	24	5	20.0	—	18
'81	8-302 (5.0L)	4	—	—	24	5	18.0	—	16
	8-351	4	—	—	24	5	20.0	—	18
'82	V6-232 (3.8L)	4	—	—	24	5	20⑩	8.3	7.9
	8-302 (5.0L)	4	—	—	24	5	20⑩	13.3	13.4

— Not applicable
③ Mark IV—20.5 qts; Lincoln—20.8 qts in 1975
④ 24.2 gals in 1975
⑤ 8 gal. tank opt.
⑥ Lincoln 24.2 gals 49 states, 22 gals California
Mark V 24 gals
⑦ Continental—24.2 gals.
Mark V—25.0 gals.
⑧ W/trailer tow, 17.3 qts. Continental; 17.4 Mark V
⑨ W/trailer tow, 19.0 qts Continental; 19.2, Mark V
⑩ 22.6 gal optional tank

FLUID CAPACITIES—Coolant, Fuel & Lubricant FORD COMPACT

Year	Engine No. Cyl. Disp. cu in	Eng. V.I.N. Code	Engine Crankcase (Add 1 Qt. For New Filter)	TRANSMISSION (Pts. to Refill After Draining) Manual 3-Speed	4-Speed	Automatic	Drive Axle (pts)	Gasoline Tank (gals)	COOLING SYSTEM (qts.) With Heater	With A/C
'76	Maverick, Comet									
	6-200	T	4	3.5	—	16	4.5	19.2	9.0	9.0
	6-250	L	4	3.5	—	18	4.5	19.2	9.7	9.7
	8-302	F	4	3.5	—	18	4.5	19.2	13.5	14.1
	Granada, Monarch									
	6-200	T	4	3.5	—	—	4③	19.2	9.9	9.9
	6-250	L	4	3.5	—	17	4③	19.2	10.5	10.7
	8-302	F	4	3.5	—	17	4	19.2	14.6	14.6
	8-351	H, Q	4	—	—	20	4	19.2	15.7	16.7
'77	Maverick, Comet									
	6-200	T	4	3.5	—	16	4.5	19.2	9.0	9.0
	6-250	L	4	3.5	—	18	4.5	19.2	9.7	9.7
	8-302	F	4	3.5	—	20	4.5	19.2	13.5	14.0
	Granada, Monarch, Versailles									
	6-200	T	4	—	4.0	—	③	19.2	9.7	—
	6-250	L	4	—	4.0	17	③	19.2	10.5	10.5
	8-302	F	4	—	4.0	20	③	19.2	14.6	14.6
	8-351	H, Q	4	—	4.0	20	4.0	19.2	15.7	15.7

A380

FLUID CAPACITIES—Coolant, Fuel & Lubricant **FORD COMPACT**

Year	Engine No. Cyl. Disp. cu in	Eng. V.I.N. Code	Engine Crankcase (Add 1 Qt. For New Filter)	TRANSMISSION (Pts. to Refill After Draining) Manual 3-Speed	4-Speed	Automatic	Drive Axle (pts)	Gasoline Tank (gals)	COOLING SYSTEM (qts.) With Heater	With A/C
'78	Fairmont, Zephyr									
	4-140	Y	4	3.5	3.0	16	3.5	16	8.6	10.2
	6-200	T	4	3.5	—	14	3.5	16	9.0	9.0
	8-302	F	4	3.5	—	20	3.5	16	13.9	14.0
	Granada, Monarch									
	6-250	L	4	3.5	4.5	20	④	18	10.5	10.6
	8-302	F	4	3.5	4.5	20	④	18	14.2	14.3
	Versailles									
	8-302	F	4	—	—	20	5.0	19.2	—	14.3
'79	Fairmont, Zephyr									
	4-140	Y	4	3.5	2.8	16	3.5	16	8.6	10.2
	6-200	T	4	3.5	4.5	14	3.5	16	9.0	9.0
	8-302	F	4	3.5	4.5	20	3.5	16	13.9	14.0
	Granada, Monarch									
	6-250	L	4	3.5	4.5	20	④	18	10.5	10.6
	8-302	F	4	3.5	4.5	20	④	18	14.2	14.3
	Versailles									
	8-302	F	4	—	—	20	5.0	19.2	—	14.3
'80	Fairmont, Zephyr									
	4-140	A	4	3.5	2.8	16	3.5	16	8.6	10.2
	6-200	B	4	3.5	4.5	14	3.5	16	9.0	9.0
	8-255	D	4	3.5	4.5	20	3.5	16	13.9	14.0
	Granada, Monarch									
	6-250	C	4	3.5	4.5	20	④	18	10.5	10.6
	8-255	D	4	3.5	4.5	20	④	18	14.2	14.3
	8-302	F	4	3.5	4.5	20	④	18	14.2	14.3
	Versailles									
	8-302	F	4	—	—	20	5.0	19.2	—	14.3
'81	Fairmont, Zephyr									
	4-140 (2.3L)	A	4	3.5	2.8	16	3.5	14	8.6	10.2
	6-200 (3.3L)	B	4	3.5	4.5	14	3.5	16	9.0	9.0
	8-255 (4.2L)	D	4	3.5	4.5	20	3.5	16	15	14.0
	Granada									
	6-200	B	4	3.5	4.5	20	④	14	8.5	10.6
	8-255 (4.2L)	D	4	3.5	4.5	20	④	16	14.2	14.3
	8-302 (5.0L)	F	4	3.5	4.5	20	④	16	15.0	15.0
	Versailles									
	8-302 (5.0L)	F	4	—	—	20	5.0	19.2	—	14.3
'82	Fairmont, Zephyr									
	4-140 (2.3L)	A	4	3.5	2.8	16	3.5	14	8.6	10.2
	6-200 (3.3L)	B	4	3.5	4.5	14	3.5	16	9.0	9.0
	V6-232 (3.8L)	3	4	3.5	4.5	20	3.5		8.3	8.35
	8-255 (4.2L)	D	4	3.5	4.5	20	3.5	16	15	14.0
	Granada									
	4-140 (2.3L)	A	4	3.5	4.5	16	3.5	14		
	6-200	B	4	3.5	4.5	20	④	14	8.5	10.6
	V6-232 (3.8L)	3	4	3.5	4.5	20	3.5		8.3	8.35
	8-255 (4.2L)	D	4	3.5	4.5	20	④	16	14.2	14.3
	8-302 (5.0L)	F	4	3.5	4.5	20	④	16	15.0	15.0

— Not applicable
③ 8 in. axle-4.5; 9 in. axle-5.0
④ 8 in. axle-4.5; 9 in. axle-5.0; 8.7 in. axle-4.0 pts.

FLUID CAPACITIES—Coolant, Fuel & Lubricant

FORD MID-SIZE

Year	Engine No. Cyl. Disp. cu in	Eng. V.I.N. Code	Engine Crankcase (Add 1 Qt. For New Filter)	TRANSMISSION (Pts. to Refill After Draining) Manual 3-Speed	4-Speed	Automatic	Drive Axle (pts)	Gasoline Tank (gals)	COOLING SYSTEM (qts.) With Heater	With A/C
'76	Cougar									
	8-351	H, Q	4	—	—	22⑩	5	26.5	17.1	17.5
	8-400	S	4	—	—	24.5⑪	5	26.5	17.1	17.5
	8-460	A, C	4	—	—	24.5	5	26.5	19.2	19.2
	Montego, Torino									
	8-351W	H, Q	4	—	—	⑤	5	26.5⑨	15.9	16.2
	8-351M	H, Q	4	—	—	⑤	5	26.5⑨	17.1	17.5
	8-400	S	4	—	—	25	5	26.5⑨	17.1	17.5
	8-460 4 bbl	A	4	—	—	25	5	26.5⑨	19.2	19.2
	8-460 P.I.	C	6⑮	—	—	25	5	26.5⑨	19.7	19.7
'77	Cougar									
	8-302	F	4	—	—	20	5	⑱	13.5	14.1
	8-351W	H, Q	4	—	—	22	5	⑱	15.9	16.3
	8-351M	H, Q	4	—	—	22	5	⑱	17.1	17.5
	8-400	S	4	—	—	25	5	⑱	17.1	17.5
	LTD II									
	8-302	F	4	—	—	20	5	⑱	13.5	14.1
	8-351W	H, Q	4	—	—	22	5	⑱	15.9	16.3
	8-351M	H, Q	4	—	—	22	5	⑱	15.9	16.3
	8-400	S	4	—	—	25	5	⑱	17.1	17.5
	Thunderbird									
	8-302	F	4	—	—	20	5	26	13.5	14.1
	8-351W	H, Q	4	—	—	22	5	26	15.9	17.2
	8-351M	H, Q	4	—	—	22	5	26	17.1	17.5
	8-400	S	4	—	—	25	5	26	17.1	17.5
'78	Cougar									
	8-302	F	4	—	—	20	5	21	14.3	14.6
	8-351W	H	4	—	—	22	5	21	15.4	15.7
	8-351M	Q	4	—	—	22	5	21	16.5	17.0
	8-400	S	4	—	—	24	5	21		
	LTD II									
	8-302	F	4	—	—	20	5	21	14.3	14.6
	8-351W	H	4	—	—	22	5	21	15.4	15.7
	8-351M	Q	4	—	—	22	5	21	16.5	17.0
	8-400	S	4	—	—	24	5	21	16.5	16.5
	Thunderbird									
	8-302	F	4	—	—	20	5	21	16.5	16.5
	8-351W	H	4	—	—	22	5	21	15.4	15.7
	8-351M	Q	4	—	—	22	5	21	15.4	15.4
	8-400	S	6	—	—	24	5	21	16.5	16.5
'79	Cougar									
	8-302	F	4	—	—	20	5	21	14.3	14.6
	8-351	H, Q	4	—	—	22	5	21	15.4	15.7
	LTD II									
	8-302	F	4	—	—	20	5	21	14.3	14.6
	8-351W	H	4	—	—	22	5	21	15.4	15.7
	8-351M	Q	4	—	—	22	5	21	16.5	17.0
	Thunderbird									
	8-302	F	4	—	—	20	5	21⑳	14.3	14.6
	8-351W	H	4	—	—	22	5	21⑳	16.5	16.5
	8-351M	Q	4	—	—	22	5	21⑳	15.4	15.7

FLUID CAPACITIES—Coolant, Fuel & Lubricant — FORD MID-SIZE

Year	Engine No. Cyl. Disp. cu in	Eng. V.I.N. Code	Engine Crankcase (Add 1 Qt. For New Filter)	TRANSMISSION (Pts. to Refill After Draining) Manual 3-Speed	4-Speed	Automatic	Drive Axle (pts)	Gasoline Tank (gals)	COOLING SYSTEM (qts.) With Heater	With A/C
'80	Cougar									
	8-255	D	4	—	—	20	5	17.5	—	14.0
	8-302	F	4	—	—	20	5	17.5		14.6
	LTD II									
	8-255	D	4	—	—	20	5	19.0㉑	—	14.0
	8-302	F	4	—	—	20	5	19.0㉑		14.6
	Thunderbird									
	8-255	D	4	—	—	20	5	17.5	—	14.0
	8-302	F	4	—	—	20	5	17.5	—	14.6
'81	Cougar									
	8-255 (4.2L)	D	4	—	—	20	5	17.5	14.1	14.9
	8-302	F	4	—	—	20	5	17.5		14.6
	LTD II									
	8-255	D	4	—	—	20	5	19.0㉑	—	14.0
	8-302	F	4	—	—	20	5	19.0㉑	--	14.6
	Thunderbird									
	8-255 (4.2L)	D	4	—	—	20	5	17.5	14.0	14.0
	8-302	F	4	—	—	20	5	17.5	14.6	14.6
'82	Cougar, Thunderbird									
	4-140 (2.3L)	A	4	3.5	4.5	20	5	21	8.4	8.4
	6-200 (3.3L)	B	4	3.5	4.5	20	5	21	8.4	8.4
	V6-232 (3.8L)	3	4	3.5	4.5	20	5	21	8.4	8,4
	8-255 (4.2L)	D	4	3.5	4.5	20	5	21	8.4	8.4

— Not applicable
⑧ Cougar—5 pts
⑨ Station Wagon—21.2 gallons
⑩ C4——21 pts.
⑪ FMX——22 pts.
⑫ C4—20 pts; C6—25 pts; FMX—22 pts
⑬ 17.1 qts with heater, 17.5 qts with AC on 351 C 2 bbl
⑭ C4—21 pts; C6—24.5 pts; FMX—22 pts
⑮ 7.5 with oil cooler
⑱ 26 gals sedan
    21.3 gals wagon
⑳ 27 gal optional
㉑ wagon 20 gals

FLUID CAPACITIES—Coolant, Fuel & Lubricant — FULL-SIZE FORD AND MERCURY

Year	Engine No. Cyl. Disp. cu in	Eng. V.I.N. Code	Engine Crankcase (Add 1 Qt. For New Filter)	TRANSMISSION (Pts. to Refill After Draining) Manual 3-Speed	4-Speed	Automatic	Drive Axle (pts)	Gasoline Tank (gals)■	COOLING SYSTEM (qts.) With Heater	With A/C
'76	8-351M	H, Q	4	—	—	22	4④	24.2③	17.1	17.6
	8-400	S	4	—	—	25	4④	24.2③	17.1	17.6
	8-460	A	4	—	—	25	4④	24.2③	18.5	18.5
	8-460 P	C	6②	—	—	25	4④	24.2③	20	20

FORD—LINCOLN—MERCURY REAR DRIVE CARS

FLUID CAPACITIES—Coolant, Fuel & Lubricant FULL-SIZE FORD AND MERCURY

Year	Engine No. Cyl. Disp. cu in	Eng. V.I.N. Code	Engine Crankcase (Add 1 Qt. For New Filter)	TRANSMISSION (Pts. to Refill After Draining) Manual 3-Speed	4-Speed	Automatic	Drive Axle (pts)	Gasoline Tank (gals)■	COOLING SYSTEM (qts.) With Heater	With A/C
'77	8-302	F	4	—	—	20	4④	24.2	15.9	16.3
	8-351W	H	4	—	—	22	4④	24.2	15.9	16.3
	8-351M	Q	4	—	—	22	4④	24.2	17.1	17.5
	8-400	S	4	—	—	22	4④	24.2⑦	17.1	17.5
	8-460	A	4	—	—	25	5	24.2	17.1	17.5
	8-460	C	6⑥	—	—	25	5	24.2	17.1	17.5
'78	8-302	F	4	—	—	20	4④	24.2	15.1⑩	15.1
	8-351W	H	4	—	—	22	4④	24.2	16.2⑨	16.2
	8-351M	Q	4	—	—	22	4④	24.2	16.9⑧⑬	16.9
	8-400	S	4	—	—	24	4④	24.2	16.9⑧⑬	16.9
	8-460	A	4	—	—	24	5	24.2	16.9⑧⑪	16.9
	8-460	C	6⑥	—	—	24	5	24.2	17.4⑫	17.4
'79	8-302	F	4	—	—	20	4④	19	15.1⑩	15.1
	8-351W	H	4	—	—	22	4④	19	16.2⑨	16.2
	8-351M	Q	4	—	—	22	4④	19	16.9⑧	16.9
'80	8-302	F	4	—	—	22	4	19	15⑩	15
	8-351	G	4	—	—	22	4	19	16.9⑧	16.9
'81	8-302	F	4	—	—	22	4	19	15⑩	15
	8-351	G	4	—	—	22	4	19	16.9⑧	16.9
'82	8-255 (4.2L)	D	4	3.5	4.5	22	4	19	13.0	13.4
	8-302 (5.0L)	F	4	3.5	4.5	22	4	19	13.3	13.8
	8-351 (5.8L)	G	4	3.5	4.5	22	4	19	16.9⑧	13.4

— Not applicable
② 7.5 w/oil cooler
③ With auxiliary fuel tank: sedan—32.3 gals; wagon—31.0 gals.
④ 5 with locking diff. and 3.00:1 axle ratio
⑤ Code C,—6 qts.
⑥ Add ¾ qt. w/ oil cooler
⑦ Mercury wagon w/ 400 CID engine, 19 gal.
⑧ Police and taxi—17.4 qts.

⑨ Police 16.7 qts.
⑩ Police 15.4 qts.
⑪ Mercury—18.6 with and without air conditioning; w/ trailer tow 19.0
⑫ Mercury 19.7
⑬ Mercury with trailer tow, 17.4 qts.
■ Station wagons: '75-78, 21 gal.: 1979—20 gal.
P Police

DISTRIBUTOR SPECIFICATIONS LINCOLN CONTINENTAL

Year	Distributor Identification	CENTRIFUGAL ADVANCE Start Dist. Deg. @ Dist. RPM	Finish Dist. Deg. @ Dist. RPM	VACUUM ADVANCE Start In. Hg.	Finish Dist. Deg. @ In. Hg.
'76	D6VE-12127BA	0-6 @ 1040	27.5-32.5 @ 4,000	3.8	21.5-26.5 @ 11
	D6VE-12127AA	0-4 @ 1000	25-30.5 @ 2,500	5.5	21.5-26.5 @ 13.5
'77	D6AE-12127AA	0-2 @ 500	11.5-14 @ 2,500	4.3	12.5-15.25 @ 11.5①
	D6VE-12127CA	0-1 @ 450	11.25-14 @ 2,500	3.5-5.5	10.75-13.25 @ 15
	D7AE-12127DA	0-1 @ 450	11.25-14 @ 2,500	3.2-5.5	12.75-15.25 @ 14.5
'78	D6VE-12127CA	0-1 @ 450	11.25-14 @ 2,500	4.5	10.75-13.25 @ 15.5
	D7AE-12127UA	0-1 @ 650	7.5-10.5 @ 2,500	4	10.75-13.5 @ 15
	D7VE-12127CA	0-1 @ 450	7.25-10 @ 2,500	4.5	10.75-13.25 @ 15.5
	D8AE-12127BA	0-1 @ 450	11.25-14 @ 2,500	3.5	15.75-17.25 @ 14.5
'79	D9AE-YA	0-2 @ 610	9.7-12.6 @ 2,500	2	14.7-17.7 @ 25
	D9AE-ACA	0-2 @ 725	7.5-10.2 @ 2,500	2.4	6.9-9.2 @ 25
	D8OE-AA	0-2.7 @ 500	13.6-16.3 @ 2,500	2	12.7-15.2 @ 25

NOTE: For 1980 models, the distributor does not control spark advance. All spark is controlled by EEC system.

FORD—LINCOLN—MERCURY REAR DRIVE CARS

FORD SMALL CARS

| Year | Distributor Identification | CENTRIFUGAL ADVANCE | | VACUUM ADVANCE | |
		Start Dist. Deg. @ Dist. RPM	Finish Dist. Deg. @ Dist. RPM	Start In. Hg.	Finish Dist. Deg. @ In. Hg.
'76	76TF-12100EA	.5 @ 550	10.5-12.5 @ 2,500	5	5 @ 8.5
	76TF-12100FA	0-2 @ 650	8-10 @ 2,000	5.5	4.5-7 @ 9.5
	76TF-12100GA	0-2 @ 650	8-10 @ 2,000	5.6	8-10 @ 12.5
	76TF-12100JA	0-2 @ 680	9.8-11.8 @ 2,000	4	2 @ 7.2
	D5DE-12127AFA	0-2.5 @ 550	10-12.4 @ 2,500	5.5	10.8-13.3 @ 15
	D6DE-12127JA	0-3.5 @ 500	16.3-18.8 @ 2,200	5	10.8 @ 13
	D6EE-12127AA	0-2.3 @ 650	13-15.5 @ 2,500	4	6.5-9.8 @ 7.2
	D6EE-12127BA	0-.5 @ 650	5-7.5 @ 2,500	5	10.8-13.3 @ 15.8
	D6EE-12127DA	0-2.5 @ 600	11.4-14 @ 2,500	4	10.8-12.3 @ 12.5
'77	77TF-12100AA	0-1 @ 625	8-10.5 @ 2,100	4	8-10 @ 12
	77TF-12100CA	0-1 @ 625	8-10.5 @ 2,100	4.5	5-7 @ 10
	77TF-12100DA	0-1 @ 510	11.5-14 @ 2,500	1.75	10.8-13.3 @ 12.4
	D0EA-12127GA	0-1 @ 425	13.5-16 @ 2,500	3	10.8-13 @ 16
	D7EE-12127CA	0-1 @ 800	5-7.5 @ 2,500	2.3	10.8-13.3 @ 15.75
	D7EE-12127DA	0-1 @ 525	11.5-14 @ 2,500	1.75	10.8-13.8 @ 12.4
	D7EE-12127EA	0-1 @ 525	11.5-14 @ 2,500	2	10.8-13.3 @ 15.75
	D7EE-12127GA	0-1 @ 525	11.5-14 @ 2,500	2.25	10.8-13.3 @ 15.75
	D7EE-12127HA	0-1 @ 775	5-7.5 @ 2,500	2	10.8-13.3 @ 15.75
	D7ZE-12127BA	0-1 @ 425	13.5-16 @ 2,500	3.5	10.8-13.3 @ 15.2
	D7ZE-12127CA	0-1 @ 575	9.3-12 @ 2,500	2.2	12.8-15.3 @ 16
'78	77TF-12100AA	0-1 @ 625	8-10.5 @ 2,100	4	8-10 @ 12
	77TF-12100CA	0-1 @ 625	8-10.5 @ 2,100	4.5	5-7 @ 10
	77TF-12100HA	0-1 @ 600	11-12 @ 2,100	4.5	5-7 @ 10
	D7DE-12127HA	0-1 @ 550	9.5-12.5 @ 2,500	3	12.8-15.3 @ 11
	D7DE-12127JA	0-1 @ 550	8.8-10.8 @ 2,500	3	10.8-13.3 @ 16
	D7EE-12127CA	0-1 @ 800	5-7.5 @ 2,500	2.3	10.8-13.3 @ 15.75
	D7EE-12127DA	0-1 @ 525	11.5-14 @ 2,500	1.75	10.8-13.8 @ 12.4
	D7EE-12127EA	0-1 @ 525	11.5-14 @ 2,500	2	10.8-13.3 @ 15.75
	D8ZE-12127BA	0-1 @ 425	13.5-16 @ 2,500	3.5	10.8-13.3 @ 14
	D8ZE-12127CA	0-1 @ 575	9.5-12.5 @ 2,500	2.5	9.8-12.3 @ 15.7
'79	D7EE-CA	0-2.1 @ 1235	5-7.5 @ 2,500	2.3	10.7-13.2 @ 16
	D7EE-DA	0-2.1 @ 530	11.5-14 @ 2,500	1.75	10.7-13.2 @ 12.4
	D7EE-EA	0-3 @ 500	11.2-14 @ 2,500	2	10.7-13.2 @ 16
	77TF-CA	0-1 @ 575	9.5-12.5 @ 2,500	3.5	5-7 @ 8.5
	79TF-FA	0-1 @ 600	10-12 @ 2,100	4.5	2-4 @ 10
	D9ZE-FA	0-2.5 @ 485	10-5-13 @ 2,500	1.8	8.7-11.2 @ 7.4
	D9ZE-EA	0-2.5 @ 485	10.5-13 @ 2,500	1.8	10.7-13.2 @ 16.2
'80	EE0E-BA	0-4.8 @ 1220	20.4-26.2 @ 5,000①	2-3.8	13.5-18.5 @ 25②
	EE0E-CA	0-5 @ 1160①	22.6-28 @ 5,000①	1.7-4.3	21.5-26.5 @ 25②
	EE0E-DA	0-6.4 @ 1200①	23.2-28 @ 5,000①	2.1-4.8	21.5-26.5 @ 25②
	EE0E-FA	0-5.2 @ 2280①	10.2-15.8 @ 5,000①	2.1-5	21.5-26.5 @ 25②
	E0ZA-BA	0-3.5 @ 1080①	17.2-22.6 @ 5,000①	1.7-4.3	17.5-22.5 @ 25②
	E0ZA-GA	0-6 @ 1000①	21.2-26.8 @ 5,000①	2.2-5	21.5-26.5 @ 25②
	E0ZA-HA	0-5.5 @ 1000①	13.2-18.6 @ 5,000①	2.2-4.6	13.5-18.5 @ 25②
	EE0E-EA	0-6.2 @ 1000①	22.2-27.5 @ 5,000①	2-5	13.5-18.5 @ 25②
	D9BE-DA	0-4 @ 1260①	11.8-19.5 @ 5,000①	1.8-4.3	17.5-22.5 @ 25②
	D8BE-EA	0-4 @ 1520①	13.4-19 @ 5,000①	2.4-5.4	17.5-22.5 @ 25②
	E0ZE-AA	0-6.6 @ 1000①	19.8-25.4 @ 5,000①	2.3-2.8	21.5-26.5 @ 25②
	E0SE-CA	0-4 @ 1270①	18.2-23.5 @ 5,000①	2.1-5	21.5-26.5 @ 25②

NOTE: Starting with 1981 models, distributor is electronic controlled.
① Engine r.p.m.
② Crankshaft degrees

FORD—LINCOLN—MERCURY REAR DRIVE CARS

DISTRIBUTOR SPECIFICATIONS   FORD COMPACT AND INTERMEDIATE CARS

Year	Distributor Identification	CENTRIFUGAL ADVANCE Start Dist. Deg. @ Dist. RPM	Finish Dist. Deg. @ Dist. RPM	VACUUM ADVANCE Start In. Hg.	Finish Dist. Deg. @ In. Hg.
'78	D7AE-12127UA	0-1 @ 650	7.5-10.5 @ 2,500	4	10.75-13.5 @ 15
	D7BE-12127GA	0-1 @ 500	6.25-8.75 @ 2,500	3	4.75-7.25 @ 7.0
	D7DE-12127AA	(−)1 to ½ @ 550	9.5-12.5 @ 2,500	3	13.25-15.25 @ 12
	D7DE-12127CA	(−)1 to ½ @ 450	12.5-15 @ 2,500	4	12.75-15.25 @ 11
	D7EE-12127CA	0-1 @ 800	5-7.5 @ 2,500	2.3	10.75-13.25 @ 15.75
	D7EE-12127DA	0-1 @ 510	11.5-14 @ 2,500	1.75	10.75-13.25 @ 12.4
	D7EE-12127EA	0-1 @ 525	11.5-14 @ 2,500	2	10.75-13.25 @ 15.75
	D8AE-12127BA	0-1 @ 450	11.25-14 @ 2,500	3.5	15.75-17.25 @ 14.5
	D8AE-12127CA	0-1 @ 1100	6.9-9.5 @ 2,500	3	14.5-17.5 @ 14
	D8AE-12127GA	0-1 @ 450	5.75-8.25 @ 2,500	5.5	13.25-15.25 @ 16.5
	D8AE-12127HA	0-1 @ 450	11.25-14 @ 2,500	3.25	14.75-17.25 @ 13.5
	D8AE-12127JA	0-1 @ 700	8-10.5 @ 2,400	3.25	12.75-15.25 @ 13
	D8AE-12127LA	0-1 @ 775	6.25-9.25 @ 2,500	3.75	14.75-17.25 @ 6.75
	D8BE-12127CA	0-1 @ 1000	2.25-4.75 @ 2,500	3	8.75-11.25 @ 11.5
	D8BE-12127EA	0-1 @ 550	7-9.5 @ 2,500	4.5	8.75-11.25 @ 12.5
	D8BE-12127FA	0-1 @ 500	7-9.5 @ 2,500	3.5	8.75-11.25 @ 13.5
	D8BE-12127JA	0-1 @ 550	7.5-10.5 @ 2,500	3.5	6.75-9.25 @ 13
	D8DE-12127CA	0-1 @ 475	6.5-9 @ 2,500	2	10.75-13.25 @ 10.8
	D8DE-12127EA	(−)1 to ½ @ 450	9.5-12.25 @ 2,500	3	10.75-13.25 @ 13
	D8EE-12127EA	0-1 @ 550	7-9.5 @ 2,500	4.5	8.75-11.25 @ 12.5
	D8ZE-12127CA	0-1 @ 575	9.5-11.5 @ 2,500	2.5	9.75-12.25 @ 15.7
'79	D9ZE-CA	0-3 @ 500	10-12.7 @ 2,500	2.8	14.7-17.2 @ 25
	D9SE-AA	0-2 @ 500	3.6-6.1 @ 2,500	2.8	14.7-17.2 @ 25
	D9AE-PA	0-3.6 @ 550	4.4-7.1 @ 2,500	2	14.7-17.2 @ 25
	D7AE-UA	0-2 @ 730	7.5-10.2 @ 2,500	2.3	11.2-13.2 @ 25
	D8OE-AA	0-2.7 @ 500	13.7-16.3 @ 2,500	2	12.7-15.2 @ 25
	D8BE-JA	0-1 @ 550	7.5-10.5	3.5	6.7-9.2 @ 13
	D9DE-CA	0-1 @ 1000	3.5-6.5 @ 2,500	3	8.7-11.2 @ 11.5
	D8DE-CA	0-1 @ 475	6.5-9 @ 2,500	2	10.7-13.2 @ 10.8
	D8DE-EA	0-1 @ 450	9.5-12.2 @ 2,500	3	10.7-13.2 @ 14
	D7DE-AA	0-1 @ 525	9.5-12.5 @ 2,500	3	12.7-15.2 @ 11
	D9BE-CA	0-1 @ 700	7.5 @ 2,500	4	12 @ 14
	D97E-CA	0-1 @ 450	10-13 @ 2,500	4	7.5-8.5 @ 13
	D7EE-DA	0-1 @ 510	11.5-14 @ 2,500	1.75	10.7-13.2 @ 12.4
	D7EE-EA	0-1 @ 525	11.5-14 @ 2,500	2	10.7-13.2 @ 7.9
	D7EE-CA	0-1 @ 800	5-7.5 @ 2,500	2.3	10.7-13.2 @ 7.9
	D7EE-HA	0-2.5 @ 1200	5-7.5 @ 2,500	2.3	10.7-13.2 @ 7.9
	D9TE-BA	0-1 @ 550	7-9.5 @ 2,500	4.5	8.7-11.2 @ 12.5
	D8BE-EA	0-1 @ 550	7-9.5 @ 2,500	4.5	8.7-11.2 @ 12.5
'80	EOEE-CA	0-5 @ 1160①	22.6-28 @ 5,000①	1.7	21.5-26.5② @ 25
	EOEE-DA	0-6.4 @ 1200①	23.2-28 @ 5,000①	2.1	21.5-26.5② @ 25
	EOEE-FA	0-5.2 @ 2280①	10.2-15.8 @ 5,000①	2.1	13.5-18.5② @ 25
	EOEE-BA	0-4.8 @ 1220①	20.4-26.2 @ 5,000①	2	13.5-18.5② @ 25
	EOZE-BA	0-3.5 @ 1080①	17.2-22.6 @ 5,000①	1.7	17.5-22.5② @ 25
	EOEE-EA	0-6.2 @ 1000①	22.2-27.5 @ 5,000①	2	13.5-18.5② @ 25
	D9BE-DA	0-4 @ 1260①	11.8-19.5 @ 5,000①	1.8	17.5-22.5② @ 25
	D8BE-EA	0-4 @ 1520①	13.4-19 @ 5,000①	2.4	17.5-22.5② @ 25
	EOZE-AA	0-4 @ 1270①	18.2-23.5 @ 5,000①	2.1	21.5-16.5② @ 25

NOTE: Starting with 1981 models, distributor is electronic controlled.

① Engine r.p.m.
② Crankshaft degrees

A386

FORD—LINCOLN—MERCURY REAR DRIVE CARS

DISTRIBUTOR SPECIFICATIONS   FORD COMPACT AND INTERMEDIATE CARS

Year	Distributor Identification	CENTRIFUGAL ADVANCE Start Dist. Deg. @ Dist. RPM	Finish Dist. Deg. @ Dist. RPM	VACUUM ADVANCE Start In. Hg.	Finish Dist. Deg. @ In. Hg.
'76	D60E-12127AA	0-2 @ 550	14-16.5 @ 2,500	4.5	21.5-26.5 @ 19
	D5OE-12127FA	0-3 @ 500	8.5-11.5 @ 2,500	5	21-26.5 @ 16
	D6AE-12127CA	0-3 @ 500	8.4-11.1 @ 2,500	4	14-25.5 @ 11.3
	D6AE-12127BA	0-3 @ 525	14-16.5 @ 2,500	5	21-26.5 @ 23
	D6AE-12127AA	0-2 @ 500	11.5-14 @ 2,500	4.3	25-30.5 @ 11.5
	D6VE-12127BA	0-3 @ 520	13.75-16.25 @ 2,000	3.8	21.5-26.5 @ 11.5
	D6VE-12127AA	0-2 @ 500	12.5-15.2 @ 2,500	5	21.5-26.5 @ 13.5
	D6DE-12127BA	0-2 @ 550	12.25-15.25 @ 2,500	4.5	17.5-22.5 @ 14
	D6DE-12127KA	0-1 @ 500	10.2-13 @ 2,500	3	13.6-14.5 @ 6.7
	D6DE-12127AA	0-2 @ 700	12-15 @ 2,500	3	17.5 @ 11.2
	D5DE-12127ACA	0-2 @ 600	11.6-14.2 @ 2,140	6	13.5-18.5 @ 12.5
	D6DE-12127GA	—	—	—	—
	D5DE-12127AGA	0-2 @ 680	10.8-13.5 @ 2,500	5	25.5 @ 13.75
	D6DE-12127JA	0-3.5 @ 500	16.3-18.8 @ 2,200	5	21.5 @ 13
	D5DE-12127AFA	0-2.5 @ 550	10-12.4 @ 2,500	5.6	21.5 @ 15.3
	D6DE-12127LA	0-3.75 @ 550	15.5-18.25 @ 2,500	4	25.5 @ 12
	D6DE-12127CA	0-3 @ 600	11.1-13.8 @ 2,500	5	21.5 @ 27.2
	D6BE-12127BA	—	—	—	—
	D5DE-12127YA	—	—	—	—
	D6DE-12127AA	0-2 @ 700	12-15 @ 2,500	3	8.75 @ 11.2
	D5DE-12127NA	0-2 @ 550	8.75-11.5 @ 2,500	.4	8.75-11.25 @ 14.5
'77	D5DE-12127AFA	0-2.5 @ 550	10-12.4 @ 2,500	5.6	13.25 @ 13.1
	D6AE-12127AA	0-2 @ 500	11.5-14 @ 2,500	4.3	12.5-15.25 @ 11.5
	D6DE-12127JA	0-3.5 @ 500	16.3-18.8 @ 2,200	5	13.25 @ 12.2
	D7AE-12127BA	0-1 @ 425	11-13.5 @ 2,250	3.5	12.75-15.25 @ 12
	D7AE-12127CA	0-1 @ 700	8.5-10.75 @ 2,500	3	12.75-15.25 @ 11
	D7AE-12127DA	0-1 @ 450	11.25-14 @ 2,500	3.2	12.25-15.25 @ 14.5
	D7BE-12127DA	0-1 @ 500	5.75-8.5 @ 2,500	3	8.75-11.25 @ 11
	D7BE-12127EA	0-1 @ 550	11.25-13.75 @ 2,450	3	8.75-11.25 @ 13.5
	D7BE-12127FA	0-1 @ 500	5.5-8.25 @ 2,500	3	4.75-7.25 @ 6.5
	D7DE-12127CA	0-1 @ 450	12.5-15.5 @ 2,500	3	12.75-15.25 @ 11
	D7DE-12127HA	(—)1 to ½ @ 550	3.5-6.5 @ 2,500	5	12.5-15 @ 14-15
	D7DE-12127FA	0-1 @ 425	11-13.75 @ 2,500	3	12.75-15.25 @ 13.5
	D7DE-12127GA	0-1 @ 525	4.5-7.25 @ 2,500	3	10.75-13.25 @ 8
	D7OE-12127CA	0-1 @ 450	13.5-16 @ 2,500	3.5	12.75-15.25 @ 14.5
	D7ZE-12127BA	0-1 @ 425	13.5-16 @ 2,500	3.5	10.75-13.25 @ 15.2

DISTRIBUTOR SPECIFICATIONS   FORD FULL-SIZE

Year	Distributor Identification	CENTRIFUGAL ADVANCE Start Dist. Deg. @ Dist. RPM	Finish Dist. Deg. @ Dist. RPM	VACUUM ADVANCE Start In. Hg.	Finish Dist. Deg. @ In. Hg.
'76	D5OE-12127FA	0-3 @ 500	8.5-11.5 @ 2,500	5	10.5-13.25 @ 16
	D6AE-12127CA	0-2 @ 500	11.5-14 @ 2,500	4.3	12.5-15.25 @ 11.5
	D6AE-12127BA	0-3 @ 525	14.25-16.5 @ 2,500	5	10.5-13.25 @ 13
	D6AE-12127AA	0-2 @ 500	11.5-14 @ 2,500	3	12.5-15.25 @ 11.5
	D6VE-12127BA	0-3 @ 520	13.75-16.25 @ 4,000	3.8	10.75-13.25 @ 11
	D6VE-12127AA	0-2 @ 500	12.5-15 @ 2,500	5.5	10.75-13.25 @ 13.5
'77	D6AE-12127AA	0-2 @ 500	11.5-14 @ 2,500	3.0-4.5	12.5-15.25 @ 11.5
	D6VE-12127CA	0-1 @ 450	11.25-14 @ 2,500	3.5-5.5	10.75-13.25 @ 15
	D7AE-12127BA	0-1 @ 425	11-13.5 @ 2,250	3.5-4.8	11.25-15.25 @ 12
	D7AE-12127CA	0-1 @ 700	8.25-11.75 @ 2,500	3-4.2	11.25-15.25 @ 11
	D7AE-12127DA	0-1 @ 450	11.25-14 @ 2,500	3.2-5.5	12.75-15.25 @ 14.5
	D7DE-12127CA	0-1 @ 450	12.5-15.5 @ 2,500	3-4	11.25-15.25 @ 11
	D7OE-12127CA	0-1 @ 450	13.5-16 @ 2,500	3.5-5.5	12.75-15.25 @ 14.5

FORD—LINCOLN—MERCURY REAR DRIVE CARS

DISTRIBUTOR SPECIFICATIONS

Year	Distributor Identification	CENTRIFUGAL ADVANCE Start Dist. Deg. @ Dist. RPM	Finish Dist. Deg. @ Dist. RPM	VACUUM ADVANCE Start In. Hg.	Finish Dist. Deg. @ In. Hg.
'78	D6VE-12127CA	0-1 @ 450	11.25-14 @ 2,500	3.5-5.5	10.75-13.25 @ 15
	D7AE-12127UA	0-1 @ 650	7.5-10.5 @ 2,500	4-5.2	10.75-13.5 @ 15
	D8AE-12127BA	0-1 @ 425	11.75-14.5 @ 2,500	3-4	14.75-17.25 @ 14.5
	D8AE-12127CA	0-1 @ 1100	6.9-9.5 @ 2,500	3-4	14.5-17.5 @ 14
	D8AE-12127GA	0-1 @ 450	5.75-8.25 @ 2,500	5.5-7.75	13.25-15.25 @ 16.5
	D8AE-12127HA	0-1 @ 450	11.25-14.25 @ 2,500	2.5-3.2	14.75-17.25 @ 14
	D8AE-12127JA	0-1 @ 700	8-10.5 @ 2,400	2.7-3.6	14.75-17.25 @ 14
	D8AE-12127LA	0-1 @ 775	6.75-9.25 @ 2,500	3-3.7	14.75-17.25 @ 13.7
	D8AE-12127NA	0-1 @ 490	9-12.75 @ 2,500	2.8-4	14.75-17.25 @ 15
'79	D9AE-AAA	0-2.7 @ 500	10.6-13.2 @ 2,500	2.3	12.7-15.2 @ 25
	D9AE-ZA	0-3 @ 500	12.2-14.7 @ 2,500	1.8	14.7-17.2 @ 25
	D9AE-ABA	0-2 @ 580	9.2-12.2 @ 2,500	2.8	6.7-9.2 @ 25①
	D9SE-AA	0-2 @ 500	3.6-6.1 @ 2,500	2.8	14.7-17.7 @ 25
'80	D94E-AA	All spark is controlled by EEC system			
	D9AE-DA	All spark is controlled by EEC system			
	D9AE-TA	0-6 @ 980②	20-26 @ 5,000②	2.2	25.5-30.5③ @ 25

① Retard maximum——2-4 @ 9.3
② Engine r.p.m.
③ Crankshaft degrees

CRANKSHAFT & CONNECTING ROD SPECIFICATIONS

FORD

All measurements given in inches

Engine No. Cyl. Disp. cu in	Year	Eng. V.I.N. Code	CRANKSHAFT Main Brg. Journal Dia.	Main Brg. Oil Clearance	Shaft End-Play	Thrust on No.	CONNECTING ROD Journal Diameter	Oil Clearance	Side Clearance
4-140 (2.3L)	75-80	Y,W,A	2.3982-2.3990	.0008-.0026	.004-.008	3	2.0465-2.0472	.0008-.0024	.0035-.0105
6-170 (2.7L)	75-79	Z	2.2433-2.2437	.0006-.0019	.004-.008	3	2.0464-2.1256	.0006-.0026	.004-.011
6-200 (3.3L)	75-80	T,B	2.2482-2.2490	.0008-.0015	.004-.008	5	2.1232-2.1240	.0008-.0015	.0035-.0105
6-250 (4.1L)	75-80	L,C	2.3982-2.3990	.0008-.0015	.004-.008	5	2.1232-2.1240	.0008-.0015	.0035-.0105
8-255 (4.2L)	80	D	2.2482-2.2486	.0005-.0024①	.004-.008	3	2.1228-2.1236	.0008-.0026	.010-.020
8-302 (5.0L)	75-80	F	2.2482-2.2490	.0005-.0015	.004-.008	3	2.1228-2.1236	.0008-.0015	.010-.020
8-351 W (5.8L)	75-80	H,Q	2.9994-3.0002	.0008-.0015	.004-.008	3	2.3103-2.3111	.0008-.0015	.0010-.0020
8-351 C,M (5.8L)	75-79	H,Q	2.9994-3.0002	.0008-.0015	.004-.008	3	2.3103-2.3111	.0008-.0015	.0010-.0020
8-400 (6.6L)	75-79	S	2.9994-3.0002	.0008-.0015	.004-.008	3	2.3103-2.3111	.0008-.0015	.0010-.0020
8-460 (7.5L)	75-78	A	2.9994-3.0002	.0012-.0015②	.004-.008	3	2.4992-2.5000	.0008-.0015	.010-.020
		C	2.9994-3.0002	.0009-.0015	.004-.008	3	2.4992-2.5000	.0008-.0015	.010-.020
4-140 (2.3L)	81-82	A,W	2.3982-2.3990	.0008-.0026	.004-.008	3	2.0465-2.0472	.0008-.0024	.0035-.0105
6-200 (3.3L)	81-82	B	2.2482-2.2490	.0008-.0015	.004-.008	5	2.1232-12.1240	.0008-.0015	.0035-.0105
V6-232 (3.8L)	82	3	2.2486	.0005-.0024	.004-.008	3	2.1232	.0007-.002	.0010-.0020
6-250 (4.1L)	81	C	2.3982-2.3990	.0008-.0015	.004-.008	5	2.1232-2.1240	.0008-.0015	.0035-.0105
8-255 (4.2L)	81-82	D	2.2482-2.2486	.0005-.0024①	.004-.008	3	2.1228-2.1236	.0008-.0026	.010-.020
8-302 (5.0L)	81-82	F	2.2482-2.2490	.0005-.0015	.004-.008	3	2.1228-2.1236	.0008-.0015	.010-.020
8-351 (5.8L)	81-82	G	2.9994-3.0002	.0008-.0015	.0004-.0008	3	2.3103-2.3111	.0008-.0015	.0010-.0020

TORQUE SPECIFICATIONS

FORD COMPACT & INTERMEDIATE

All readings in ft/lbs

Engine No. Cyl. Displacement cu in	Eng. VIN Code	Cylinder Head Bolts	Rod Bearing Bolts	Main Bearing Bolts	Crankshaft Pulley Bolt	Flywheel to Crankshaft Bolts	MANIFOLD	
							Intake	Exhaust
4-140 (2.3L)	Y,W,A	80-90	30-36	80-90	100-120①	54-64	14-21	16-23
6-170 (2.7L)	Z	65-80	21-25	65-75	92-103	47-51	15-18	14-18
6-200 (3.3L)	T,B	70-75	21-26	60-70	85-100①	75-85	--	18-24
V6-232 (3.8L)	3	③	④	⑤	85-100	75-85	⑥	⑦
6-250 (4.1L)	L,C	70-75	21-26	60-70	85-100①	75-85	18-24	18-24
8-255 (4.2L)	D	②	19-24	60-70	70-90①	75-85	12-18	18-24
8-302 (5.0L)	F	65-72	19-24	60-70	70-90①	75-85	23-25	18-24
8-351W (5.8L)	H,Q	105-112	40-45	95-105	70-90①	75-85	23-25	18-24
8-351C,M (5.8L)	H,Q	95-105	40-45	95-105(½) 35-45(⅜)	70-90①	75-85	21-25(5/16) 27-33(⅜) 6-9(¼)	12-24
8-400 (6.6L)S		95-105	40-45	95-105(½) 35-45(⅜)	70-90①	75-85	21-25(5/16)	12-24 27-33(⅜) 6-9(¼)
8-460 (7.5L)	A,C	130-140	40-45	95-105	70-90①	75-85	25-30	28-33

① Vibration damper-to-crankshaft shown.
　Pulley-to-vibration damper—35-50
② Torque in 2 steps; First step, 55-65 ft.lbs. (74-88 N•m).
　Second step, 65-72 ft.lbs. (88-96 N•m).
③ Special instructions (4 steps):
　1. Soak complete bolt in engine oil.
　2. Torque bolts in sequence to 65-81 ft.lbs. (92 to 110 N•m).
　3. Loosen all bolts two complete turns.
　4. Retorque all bolts in sequence to 61 to 81 ft.lbs. (92 to 110 N•m).
④ Special instructions (4 steps):
　1. Soak nuts in oil.
　2. Torque nuts to 30 to 36 ft.lbs. (41-49 N•m).
　3. Loosen nuts two complete turns.
　4. Retorque nuts to 30 to 36 ft.lbs. (41-49 N•m).
⑤ Special instructions (4 steps):
　1. Soak complete bolt in engine oil.
　2. Torque bolts to 62-81 ft.lbs. (88 to 110 N•m).
　3. Loosen bolts two complete turns.
　4. Retorque bolts to 62 to 81 ft.lbs. (88 to 110 N•m).
⑥ Special instructions (4 steps):
　1. Soak bolts in engine oil.
　2. First torque 5.2 ft.lbs. (7 N•m).
　3. Second torque 10 ft.lbs. (14 N•m).
　4. Third torque 18.4 ft.lbs. (25 N•m).
⑦ Torque bolt to 15-22 ft.lbs. (20-30 N•m).

FORD—LINCOLN—MERCURY REAR DRIVE CARS

VALVE SPECIFICATIONS

Year	Engine No. Cyl. Disp. (cu in)	Eng. VIN Code	Seat Angle (deg)	Face Angle (deg)	Spring Test Pressure (lbs @ in)	Spring Installed Height (in)	STEM TO GUIDE CLEARANCE (in) Intake	Exhaust	STEM DIAMETER (in) Intake	Exhaust
'76	4-140	Y	45	44	189 @ 1.16	1.563	.0010-.0027	.0015-.0032	.3419	.3415
	6-170	Z	45②	44②	144 @ 1.222	1.594	.0008-.0025	.0018-.0035	.3162	.3152
	6-200	T	45	44	I-150 @ 1.18 E-150 @ 1.22	1.578	.0008-.0025	.0010-.0027	.3104	.3102
	6-250	L	45	44	150 @ 1.18	1.578	.0008-.0025	.0010-.0027	.3104	.3102
	8-302	F	45	44	I-200 @ 1.31 E-200 @ 1.20	I-1.687 E-1.593	.0010-.0027	.0015-.0032	.3419	.3415
	8-351W	H,Q	45	44	200 @ 1.34	1.796	.0010-.0027	.0015-.0032	.3419	.3415
	8-351M	H,Q	45	44	226 @ 1.39	1.812	.0010-.0027	.0015-.0032	.3419	.3415
	8-400	S	45	44	226 @ 1.39	1.812	.0010-.0027	.0015-.0032	.3419	.3415
	8-460	A,C	45	44	229 @ 1.33	1.812	.0010-.0027	.0010-.0027	.3419	.3419
'77	4-140	Y	45	44	189 @ 1.16	1.560	.0010-.0027	.0015-.0032	.3419	.3415
	6-170	Z	45②	44②	144 @ 1.222	1.593	.0008-.0025	.0018-.0035	.3162	.3152
	6-200	T	45	44	I-156 @ 1.20 E-148 @ 1.23	1.578	.0008-.0025	.0010-.0027	.3104	.3102
	6-250	L	45	44	I-156 @ 1.20 E-154 @ 1.20	1.578	.0008-.0025	.0010-.0027	.3104	.3102
	8-302	F	45	44	I-200 @ 1.31 E-200 @ 1.20	I-1.687 E-1.593	.0010-.0027	.0015-.0032	.3419	.3415
	8-351W	H,Q	45	44	I-200 @ 1.34 E-200 @ 1.20	I-1.796 E-1.609	.0010-.0027	.0015-.0032	.3419	.3415
	8-351M	H,Q	45	44	226 @ 1.39	1.828	.0010-.0027	.0015-.0032	.3419	.3415
	8-400	S	45	44	226 @ 1.39	1.828	.0010-.0027	.0015-.0032	.3419	.3415
	8-460	A,C	45	44	229 @ 1.33	1.812	.0010-.0027	.0010-.0027	.3419	.3419
'78	4-140	Y	45	44	189 @ 1.16	1.560	.0010-.0027	.0015-.0032	.3419	.3415
	6-170	Z	45②	44②	144 @ 1.222	1.593	.0008-.0025	.0018-.0035	.3162	.3152
	6-200	T	45	44	150 @ 1.222	1.578	.0008-.0025	.0010-.0027	.3104	.3102
	6-250	L	45	44	150 @ 1.222	1.578	.0008-.0025	.0010-.0027	.3104	.3102
	8-302	F	45	44	I-200 @ 1.31 E-200 @ 1.20	I-1.796 E-1.609	.0010-.0027	.0015-.0032	.3419	.3415
	8-351W	H,Q	45	44	I-200 @ 1.34 E-200 @ 1.20	I-1.796 E-1.609	.0010-.0027	.0015-.0032	.3419	.3415
	8-351M	H,Q	45	44	226 @ 1.39	1.828	.0010-.0027	.0015-.0032	.3419	.3415
	8-400	S	45	44	226 @ 1.39	1.828	.0010-.0027	.0015-.0032	.3419	.3415
	8-460	A,C	45	44	229 @ 1.33	1.812	.0010-.0027	.0010-.0027	.3419	.3419
'79	4-140	Y,W	45	44	167 @ 1.16	1.56	.0010-.0027	.0015-.0032	.3419	.3415
	6-170	Z	45②	44②	144 @ 1.222	1.585	.0008-.0025	.0018-.0035	.3162	.3153
	6-200	T	45	44	I-156 @ 1.20 E-148 @ 1.23	1.58	.0008-.0025	.0010-.0027	.3105	.3105
	6-250	L	45	44	156 @ 1.20	1.58	.0008-.0025	.0010-.0027	.3103	.3102
	8-302	F	45	44	I-200 @ 1.3 E-200 @ 1.2	I-1.7 E-1.6	.0010-.0027	.0015-.0032	.34	.3414
	8-351W	H,Q	45	44	I-192 @ 1.37 E-200 @ 1.20	I-1.79 E-1.60	.0010-.0027	.0015-.0032	.34	.3414
	8-351M	H,Q	45	44	I-226 @ 1.39 E-226 @ 1.25	I-1.82 E-1.68	.0010-.0027	.0015-.0032	.34	.3414
	8-400	S	45	44	I-226 @ 1.39 E-226 @ 1.25	I-1.82 E-1.68	.0010-.0027	.0015-.0032	.3419	.3415

VALVE SPECIFICATIONS

Year	Engine No. Cyl. Disp. (cu in)	Eng. VIN Code	Seat Angle (deg)	Face Angle (deg)	Spring Test Pressure (lbs @ in)	Spring Installed Height (in)	STEM TO GUIDE CLEARANCE (in) Intake	Exhaust	STEM DIAMETER (in) Intake	Exhaust
'80	4-140	A,W	45	44	167 @ 1.16	1.56	.0010-.0027	.0015-.0032	.3419	.3415
	6-200	B	45	44	I-156 @ 1.20 E-148 @ 1.23	1.58	.0008-.0025	.0010-.0027	.3105	.3105
	6-250	C	45	44	156 @ 1.20	1.58	.0008-.0025	.0010-.0027	.3103	.3102
	8-255	D	45	44	①	①	①	①	①	①
	8-302	F	45	44	I-200 @ 1.3 E-200 @ 1.2	I-1.7 E-1.6	.0010-.0027	.0015-.0032	.34	.3414
	8-351	G	45	44	I-192 @ 1.37 E-200 @ 1.20	I-1.79 E-1.60	.0010-.0027	.0015-.0032	.34	.3414
'81	4-140	A,W	45	44	167 @ 1.16	1.56	.0010-.0027	.0015-.0032	.3419	.3415
	6-200	B	45	44	1-156 @ 1.20 E-148 @ 1.23	1.58	.0008-.0025	.0010-.0027	.3105	.3105
	6-250	C	45	44	156 @ 1.20	1.58	.0008-.0025	.0010-.0027	.3103	.3102
	8-255	D	45	44	190-212 @ 1.36	1.67	.0010	.0015	.3416	.3411
	8-302	F	45	44	I-200 @ 1.3 E-200 @ 1.2	I-1.79 E-1.60	.0010-.0027	.0015-.0032	.34	.3414
	8-351	G	45	44	I-192 @ 1.37 E-200 @ 1.2	I-1.79 E-1.60	.0010-.0027	.0015-.0032	.34	.3414
'82	4-140	A,W	45	44	167 @ 1.16	1.56	.0010-.0027	.0015-.0032	.3419	.3415
	6-200	B	45	44	1-156 @ 1.20 E-148 @ 1.23	1.58	.0008-.0025	.0010-.0027	.3105	.3105
	V6-232	3	45	44	190-210 @ 1.35	NA	.0026-.0068	.0038-.0081	8.705-8.677	8.682-8.664
	8-255	D	45	44	190-212 @ 1.36	1.67	.0010	.0015	.3416	.3411
	8-302	F	45	44	I-200 @ 1.3 E-200 @ 1.2	I-1.79 E-1.60	.0010-.0027	.0015-.0032	.34	.3414
	8-351	G	45	44	I-192 @ 1.37 E-200 @ 1.2	I-1.79 E-1.60	.0010-.0027	.0015-.0032	.34	.3414

① Information not available at publication time

I=Intake

E=Exhaust

C=Cold

② Mechanical lifters intake .014 C exhaust .016 C

BRAKE SPECIFICATIONS FORD SUB-COMPACT

Year	Model	Master Cylinder Bore Diameter	CALIPER/ WHEEL CYLINDER Front	Rear	BRAKE DRUM/ROTOR DIAMETER Front	Rear
76-78	All	.9375	2.6	.875	9.3	9.0
79-80	Pinto, Bobcat	.938	2.6	.875	9.3	9.0
	Mustang, Capri	.875	2.36	.813	9.3	9.0
	Mustang, Capri V-8	.875	2.36	.813	10.4	9.0
81	Mustang, Capri	.875	2.36	.813	9.3	9.0
82	Mustang, Capri	0.827	2.36	—	10.06	9.0

① Caliper bore: 2.127

② Rotor dia: 9.3

FORD—LINCOLN—MERCURY REAR DRIVE CARS

BRAKE SPECIFICATIONS   FORD FULL-SIZE

Year	Model	Master Cylinder Bore Diameter	CALIPER/ WHEEL CYLINDER		BRAKE DRUM/ROTOR DIAMETER	
			Front	Rear	Front	Rear
76-79	Ford and Mercury	1.0	3.1	1.0②	11.8	11.03①
80	Ford and Mercury	1.0	3.1	0.875②	11.08	10①
81-82	Ford and Mercury	1.0	3.1	0.875②	11.08	10①

① Rear rotor 11.50
② 2.6 with rear disc

BRAKE SPECIFICATIONS   FORD COMPACT & INTERMEDIATE CARS

Year	Model	Master Cylinder Bore Diameter	CALIPER/ WHEEL CYLINDER		BRAKE DRUM/ROTOR DIAMETER	
			Front	Rear	Front	Rear
'76-'78	Maverick, Comet, Granada, Monarch, Versailles①	.938⑥	2.6	15/16	11.03	10
	Cougar, Montego, Torino, LTD II, Elite, Thunderbird	1.0	3.1	15/16③	10.72⑤	11.03
78	Fairmont, Zephyr	.875	2.36	13/16	10.08	9④
'79	Fairmont, Zephyr	.875	2.36	13/16	10.08	9④
	Granada, Monarch, Versailles①	.938	2.6	15/16	11.03	10
	LTD II, Cougar, Thunderbird	1.0	3.1	15/16③	10.72⑤	11.03
'80	Fairmont, Zephyr	.875	2.36	13/16	10.08	9④
	Granada, Monarch, Versailles①	.938	2.6	15/16	11.03	10
	LTD II, Cougar, Thunderbird	1.0	2.6	15/16	11.03	11.03
'81	Fairmont, Zephyr	.875	2.36	13/16	10.08	9④
	Granada, Monarch, Versailles	.938	2.6	15/16	11.03	10
	LTD II, Cougar, Thunderbird	1.0	2.6	15/16	11.03	11.03
'82	Fairmont, Zephyr	0.827	2.36	0.813	10.06	9④
	Granada, Monarch	0.827	2.36	0.813	10.06	9④
	LTD II, Cougar, Thunderbird	0.827	2.36	0.8125	10.06-11.00	9"-10"

① Rear disc brake option available on Monarch, Granada and Versailles, rotor diameter 10.66", caliper bore 2.1"
② 11" on wagons with 351, 400, or 429V8 and all wagons 1975
③ Station wagon and/or police 1"
④ Station wagon—10
⑤ Police 11.80"
⑥ 1" w/rear disc option

FORD—LINCOLN—MERCURY REAR DRIVE CARS

FRONT DISC BRAKE SPECIFICATIONS   FORD SUB-COMPACT

Year	Model	Caliper Type	Mounting Bolt Torque (ft/lbs)	Disc Pad Original Thickness	Mfr.'s Recommended Disc Pad Minimum Thickness	Rotor Runout	Rotor Allowable Minimum Machined Thickness	Rotor Thickness Variation Maximum
76	Mustang II, Pinto, Bobcat	Ford Sliding	②	—	1/32①③	.003	.810	.0005
77-80	Mustang II, Pinto, Bobcat	Ford Sliding	②	.410⑤	1/8④	.003	.810	.0005
79-80	Mustang/Capri	Ford Sliding	35⑥	.410	1/8④	.003	.810	.0005
81-82	Mustang, Capri	Ford Sliding	35⑧	.410⑤	1/8④	.003	.810	.0005

① From rivets or shoe to lining surface
② Anchor plate mounting bolts:
   Upper—90-120
   Lower—55-75
   Caliper key retainer screw—14
③ 1976—1/8
④ From shoe surface
⑤ Outer pad shown, inner .403
⑥ Caliper locating pins

FRONT DISC BRAKE SPECIFICATIONS   FORD FULL-SIZE

Year	Model	Caliper Type	Mounting Bolt Torque	Mfr.'s Recommended Disc Pad Minimum Thickness	Rotor Runout	Rotor Allowable Minimum Machined Thickness	Rotor Thickness Variation Maximum
'76-'78	Ford & Mercury Full Size Cars	Ford Sliding	90-120	1/8①	.003	1.120	.0005
'76-'79	Lincoln Continental and Mark V	Ford Sliding	90-120	1/8①	.003	1.120	.0005
'79⑥	Ford and Mercury Full Size Cars	Ford Pin-slider	40-60	1/8①	.003	1.120	.0005
'80-'82	Lincoln Continental and Mark VI	Ford Sliding	90-120	1/8①	.003	1.120	.0005
'81-'82	Ford & Mercury	Ford Pin-Slider	40-60	1/8①	.003	1.120	.0005
	Continental & Mark VI	Ford Sliding	90-120	1/8①	.003	1.120	.0005

① From rivets or shoe to lining surface

A393

FORD—LINCOLN—MERCURY REAR DRIVE CARS

DISC BRAKE SPECIFICATIONS FORD COMPACT & INTERMEDIATE CARS

Year	Model	Caliper Type	Mounting Bolt Torque	Mfr.'s Recommended Disc Pad Minimum Thickness	Rotor Runout	Rotor Allowable Minimum Machined Thickness	Rotor Thickness Variation Maximum
'76–'78	Comet, Maverick, Granada, Monarch, Versailles	Ford Sliding	Upper: 90-120 Lower: 55-75	⅛①	.003	F.810 R.895	.0005
'76–'78	Cougar, LTD II, Montego, Thunderbird, Torino, Elite	Ford Sliding	90-120	⅛①	.003	1.120	.0005
'78	Fairmont, Zephyr	Ford Sliding	30-40③	⅛①	.003	.810	.0005
'79	Granada, Monarch, Versailles	Ford Sliding	Upper: 90-120 Lower: 55-75	⅛①	.003	F.810 R.895	.0005
	Cougar, LTD II, Thunderbird	Ford Sliding	90-120	⅛①	.003	.810	.0005
	Fairmont, Zephyr	Ford Sliding	30-40②	⅛①	.003	.810	.0005
'80	Granada, Monarch, Versailles	Ford Sliding	Upper: 90-120 Lower: 55-75	⅛①	.003	F.810 R.895	.0005
	Cougar, LTD II, Thunderbird	Ford Sliding	90-120	⅛①	.003	.810	.0005
	Fairmont, Zephyr	Ford Sliding	30-40②	⅛①	.003	.810	.0005
'81–'82	Granada, Monarch, Versailles	Ford Sliding	Upper: 90-120 Lower: 55-75	⅛①	.003	F.810 R.895	.0005
	Cougar, LTD II, Thunderbird	Ford Sliding	90-120	⅛①	.003	.810	.0005
	Fairmont, Zephyr	Ford Sliding	30-40②	⅛①	.003	.810	.0005

① From rivets or shoe to lining surface
② Caliper locating pin torque
F = front
R = rear

REAR DISC BRAKE SPECIFICATIONS FORD FULL-SIZE

Year	Model	Caliper Type	Mounting Bolt Torque	Mfr.'s Recommended Disc Pad Minimum Thickness	Rotor Runout	Rotor Allowable Minimum Machined Thickness	Rotor Thickness Variation Maximum
'76-77	Mercury Full-Size Cars	Ford Sliding	90-120	1/32①②	.004	.895	.0005
'76-77	Lincoln Continental, Mark IV, V & Ford Thunderbird	Ford Sliding	90-120	⅛①②	.004	.895	.0004
'78-80	Ford & Mercury Full Size Cars	Ford Sliding	75-95③	⅛	.004	.895	.0005
'78-80	Lincoln & Mark V	Ford Sliding	75-95③	⅛	.004	.895	.0004
'81-82	Ford & Mercury Lincoln, Mark VI	Ford Sliding —	75-95③ —	⅛ —	.004 —	.895 —	.0005 —

① From top of rivets
② 1975: 1/32
③ Caliper end retainer bolt torque

A394

FUSE IDENTIFICATION

Fuse panel—Fairmont/Zephyr, Mustang/Capri, Granada/Cougar

NOTE: EMERGENCY FLASHER LOCATED ON REVERSE SIDE OF FUSE PANEL BEHIND TURN SIGNAL FLASHER

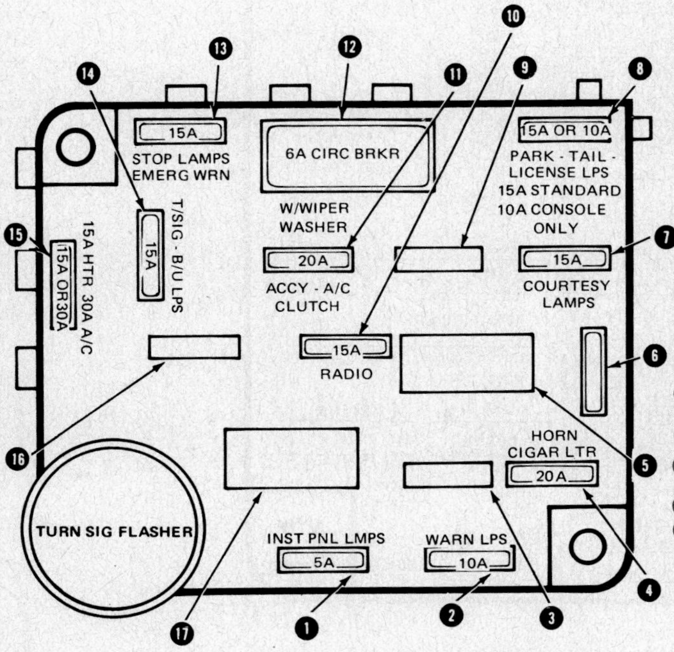

Diagram labels:
- 15A STOP LAMPS EMERG WRN
- 6A CIRC BRKR W/WIPER WASHER
- 15A OR 10A PARK - TAIL - LICENSE LPS 15A STANDARD 10A CONSOLE ONLY
- 15A HTR 30A A/C
- 15A OR 30A
- 15A T/SIG - B/U LPS
- 20A ACCY - A/C CLUTCH
- 15A RADIO
- 15A COURTESY LAMPS
- HORN CIGAR LTR 20A
- TURN SIG FLASHER
- INST PNL LMPS 5A
- WARN LPS 10A

1. 5 AMP. FUSE (D9ZB-14A094-BA) (TAN) INSTRUMENT PANEL, CLUSTER, AND INTERIOR ILLUMINATION
2. 10 AMP FUSE (D9ZB-14A094-CA) (RED) WARNING LAMPS
3. SPARE (NOT USED)
4. 20 AMP. FUSE (D9ZB-14A094-EA) (YELLOW) HORNS & CIGAR LIGHTER
5. SPARE (NOT USED)
6. SPARE (NOT USED)
7. 15 AMP FUSE (D9ZB-14A094-DA) (LIGHT BLUE) COURTESY LAMPS — AND IGNITION KEY WARNING BUZZER
   15 AMP FUSE--D9ZB-14A094-DA) (LIGHT BLUE COLOR) (FOR STANDARD CAR)
8. PARK, TAIL & LICENSE LAMPS 10 AMP FUSE – (D9ZB-14A094-CA) (RED COLOR) (FOR CONSOLE MODELS ONLY)
9. SPARE (NOT USED)
10. 15 AMP FUSE – (D9ZB-14A094-DA) (LIGHT BLUE) RADIO, STEREO TAPE PLAYER, PREMIUM SOUND & CB RADIO
11. 20 AMP FUSE – (D9ZB-14A094-EA) (YELLOW) ACCESSORY - A/C CLUTCH, HEATED BACKLITE RELAY COIL, REAR WIPER/WASHER, TRUNK LID RELEASE, POWER WINDOW SAFETY RELAY, & SPEED CONTROL
12. 6 AMP CIRCUIT BREAKER—(D9ZB-14526-AA) WINDSHIELD WIPER/WASHER
13. 15 AMP FUSE (D9ZB-14A094-DA) (LIGHT BLUE) STOP LAMPS & EMERGENCY WARNING LAMPS
14. 15 AMP FUSE (D9ZB-14A094-DA) (LIGHT BLUE) TURN SIGNAL LAMPS & BACK-UP LAMPS
15. 15 AMP FUSE (D9ZB-14A094-DA) (LIGHT BLUE) HEATER
    30 AMP FUSE (D9ZB-14A094-GA) (LIGHT GREEN) AIR CONDITIONER
16. SPARE (NOT USED)
17. 20 AMP CIRCUIT BREAKER FOR MUSTANG/CAPRI POWER WINDOWS ONLY (SPARE ON OTHER VEHICLES)

© Ford Motor Co.

Fuse panel—Thunderbird/XR7

NOTE: EMERGENCY FLASHER LOCATED ON THE REVERSE SIDE OF FUSE PANEL BEHIND TURN SIGNAL FLASHER

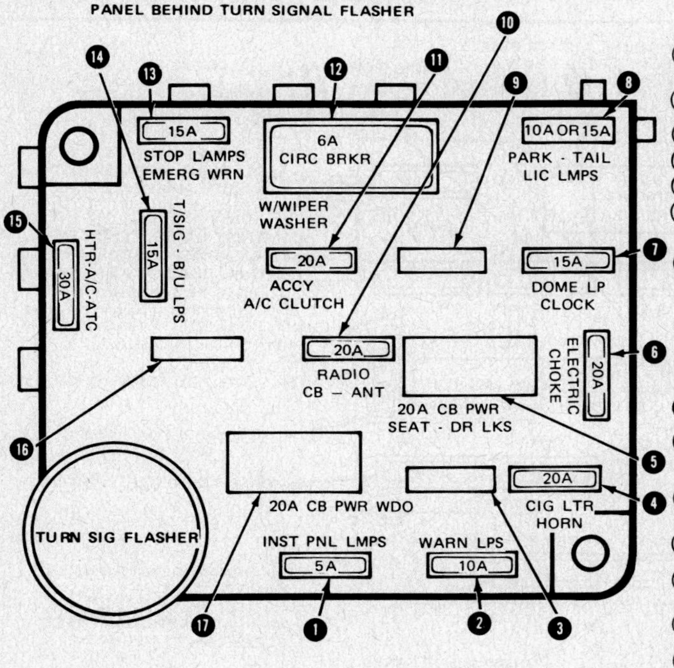

Diagram labels:
- 15A STOP LAMPS EMERG WRN
- 6A CIRC BRKR W/WIPER WASHER
- 10A OR 15A PARK - TAIL LIC LMPS
- HTR-A/C-ATC 30A
- 15A T/SIG - B/U LPS
- 20A ACCY A/C CLUTCH
- 15A DOME LP CLOCK
- ELECTRIC CHOKE 20A
- 20A RADIO CB – ANT
- 20A CB PWR SEAT - DR LKS
- 20A CB PWR WDO
- CIG LTR HORN 20A
- TURN SIG FLASHER
- INST PNL LMPS 5A
- WARN LPS 10A

1. 5 AMP FUSE (D9ZB-14A094-BA) (TAN) INSTRUMENT PANEL, CLUSTER AND INTERIOR ILLUMINATION
2. 10 AMP FUSE (D9ZB-14A094-CA) (RED) WARNING LAMPS — THROTTLE SOLENOID, SEAT BELT WARNING BUZZER OR CHIME
3. SPARE (NOT USED)
4. 20 AMP FUSE (D9ZB-14A094-EA) (YELLOW) CIGAR LIGHTER & HORNS
5. 20 AMP CIRCUIT BREAKER (D9AB-14526-BA) POWER SEAT & DOOR LOCKS
6. 20 AMP FUSE - (D9ZB-14A094-EA) (YELLOW) ELECTRIC CHOKE
7. 15 AMP FUSE (D9ZB-14A094-DA) (LIGHT BLUE) COURTESY LAMPS, CLOCK FEED, KEY WARNING BUZZER, HEADLIGHT "ON" WARNING BUZZER, SEAT BACK LATCH RELAY, ILLUMINATED ENTRY, * VISOR MIRROR LIGHT.
   * VISOR MIRROR LIGHT ALSO USED A LAMP FUSE LOCATED INSIDE THE VISOR ASSEMBLY
8. 15 AMP FUSE (D9ZB-14A094-DA) (LIGHT BLUE) (FOR STANDARD CAR) PARKS, TAIL & LICENSE LAMPS 10 AMP FUSE (D9ZB-14A094-CA) (RED) (FOR CONSOLE MODELS ONLY)
9. SPARE (NOT USED)
10. 20 AMP FUSE (D9ZB-14A094-EA) (YELLOW) RADIO, POWER ANTENNA, & CB RADIO
11. 20 AMP FUSE (D9ZB-14A094-EA) (YELLOW) ACCESSORY-A/C CLUTCH, HEATED BACKLITE RELAY COIL, TRUNK LID RELEASE SOLENOID, SPEED CONTROL, ILLUMINATED ENTRY
12. 6 AMP CIRCUIT BREAKER (D9ZB-14526-AA) WINDSHIELD WIPER/WASHER
13. 15 AMP FUSE (D9ZB-14A094-DA) (LIGHT BLUE) STOP LAMPS & EMERGENCY WARNING LAMPS
14. 15 AMP FUSE (D9ZB-14A094-DA) (LIGHT BLUE) TURN SIGNAL LAMPS & BACK-UP LAMPS
15. 30 AMP FUSE (D0ZB-14A094-GA) (LIGHT GREEN) HEATER-A/C-ATC
16. SPARE (NOT USED)
17. 20 AMP CIRCUIT BREAKER (D9AB-14526-BA) POWER WINDOWS

© Ford Motor Co.

FORD—LINCOLN—MERCURY REAR DRIVE CARS

Mini fuse panel—Ford/Mercury

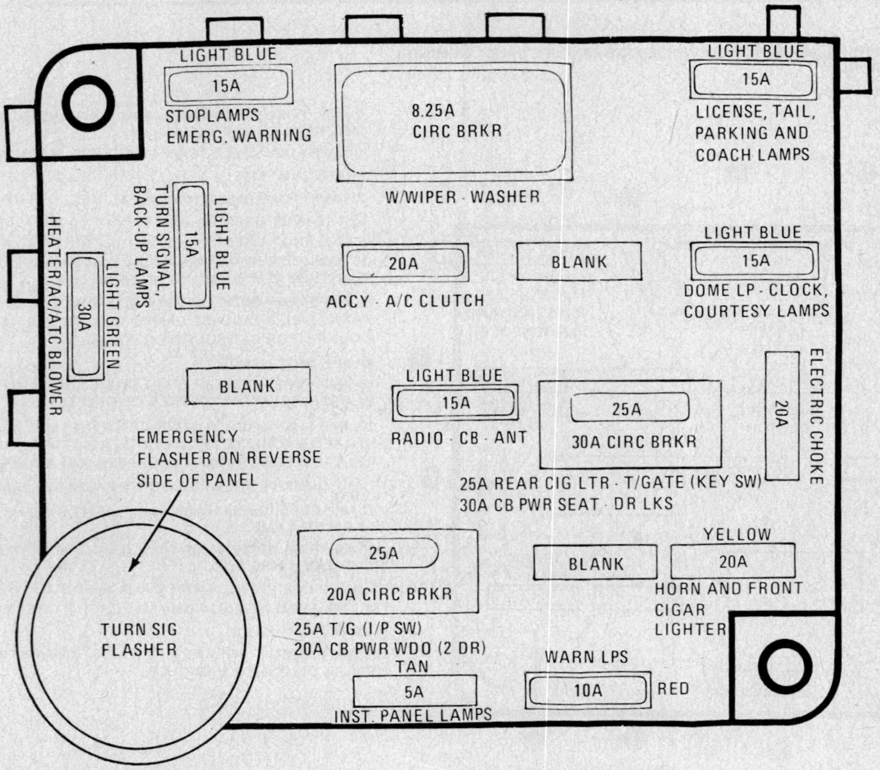

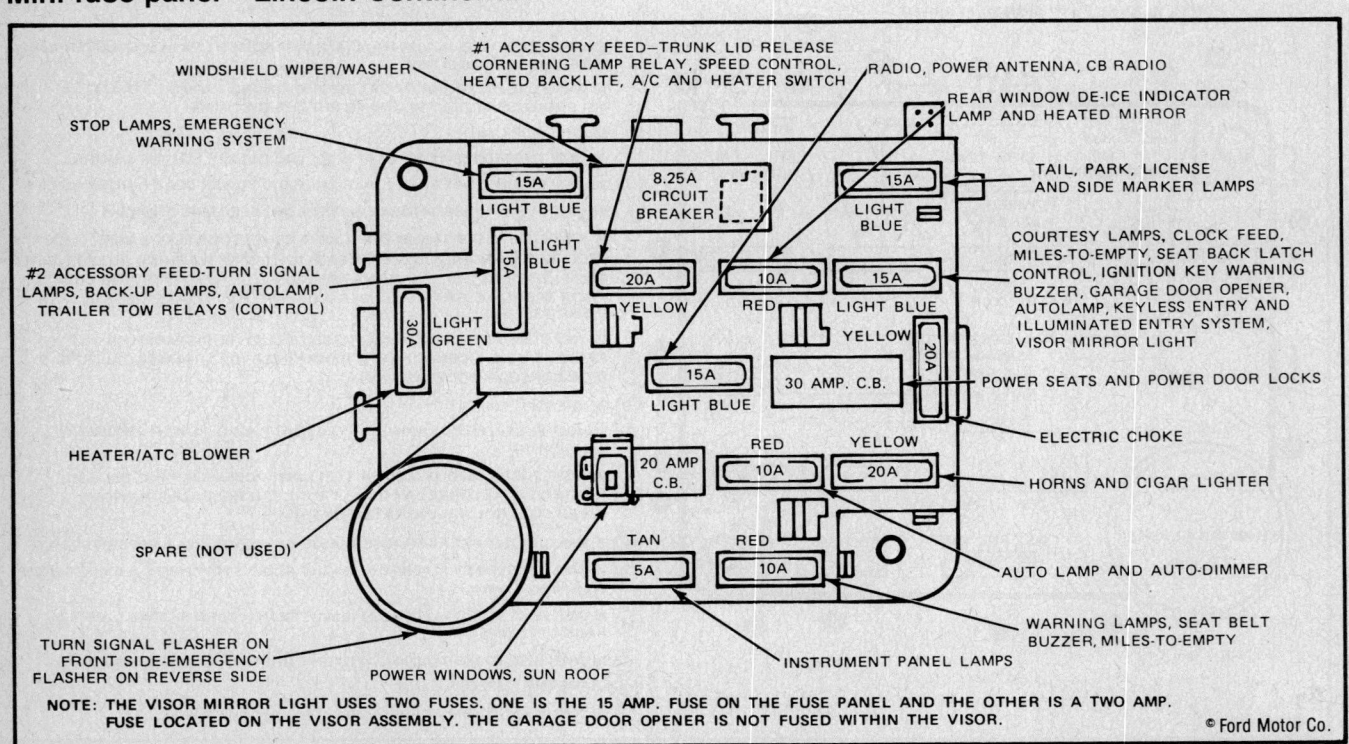

LIGHT BLUE
15A
STOPLAMPS
EMERG. WARNING

8.25A
CIRC BRKR
W/WIPER · WASHER

LIGHT BLUE
15A
LICENSE, TAIL,
PARKING AND
COACH LAMPS

TURN SIGNAL,
BACK-UP LAMPS
LIGHT BLUE
15A

HEATER/AC/ATC BLOWER
LIGHT GREEN
30A

20A
ACCY · A/C CLUTCH

BLANK

LIGHT BLUE
15A
DOME LP · CLOCK,
COURTESY LAMPS

BLANK

LIGHT BLUE
15A
RADIO · CB · ANT

25A
30A CIRC BRKR

ELECTRIC CHOKE
20A

EMERGENCY
FLASHER ON REVERSE
SIDE OF PANEL

25A REAR CIG LTR · T/GATE (KEY SW)
30A CB PWR SEAT · DR LKS

25A
20A CIRC BRKR
25A T/G (I/P SW)
20A CB PWR WDO (2 DR)
TAN
5A
INST. PANEL LAMPS

TURN SIG
FLASHER

BLANK

YELLOW
20A
HORN AND FRONT
CIGAR
LIGHTER

WARN LPS
10A RED

© Ford Motor Co.

Mini fuse panel—Lincoln Continental

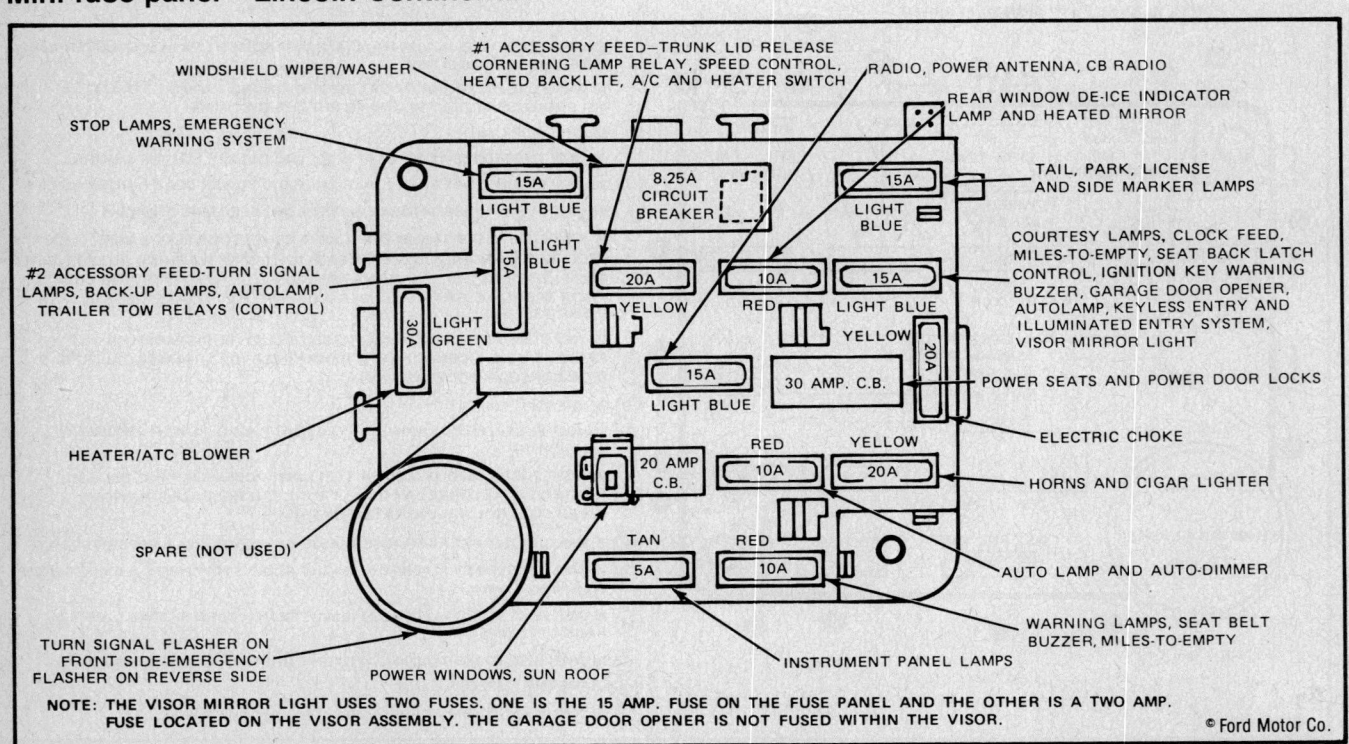

Windshield wiper/washer

#1 ACCESSORY FEED—TRUNK LID RELEASE
CORNERING LAMP RELAY, SPEED CONTROL,
HEATED BACKLITE, A/C AND HEATER SWITCH

RADIO, POWER ANTENNA, CB RADIO

REAR WINDOW DE-ICE INDICATOR
LAMP AND HEATED MIRROR

STOP LAMPS, EMERGENCY
WARNING SYSTEM

15A
LIGHT BLUE

8.25A
CIRCUIT
BREAKER

15A
LIGHT
BLUE

TAIL, PARK, LICENSE
AND SIDE MARKER LAMPS

#2 ACCESSORY FEED-TURN SIGNAL
LAMPS, BACK-UP LAMPS, AUTOLAMP,
TRAILER TOW RELAYS (CONTROL)

15A
LIGHT
BLUE

30A
LIGHT
GREEN

20A
YELLOW

10A
RED

15A
LIGHT BLUE

COURTESY LAMPS, CLOCK FEED,
MILES-TO-EMPTY, SEAT BACK LATCH
CONTROL, IGNITION KEY WARNING
BUZZER, GARAGE DOOR OPENER,
AUTOLAMP, KEYLESS ENTRY AND
ILLUMINATED ENTRY SYSTEM,
VISOR MIRROR LIGHT

15A
LIGHT BLUE

30 AMP. C.B.

YELLOW
20A

POWER SEATS AND POWER DOOR LOCKS

ELECTRIC CHOKE

HEATER/ATC BLOWER

20 AMP
C.B.

RED
10A

YELLOW
20A

HORNS AND CIGAR LIGHTER

SPARE (NOT USED)

TAN
5A

RED
10A

AUTO LAMP AND AUTO-DIMMER

TURN SIGNAL FLASHER ON
FRONT SIDE-EMERGENCY
FLASHER ON REVERSE SIDE

POWER WINDOWS, SUN ROOF

INSTRUMENT PANEL LAMPS

WARNING LAMPS, SEAT BELT
BUZZER, MILES-TO-EMPTY

NOTE: THE VISOR MIRROR LIGHT USES TWO FUSES. ONE IS THE 15 AMP. FUSE ON THE FUSE PANEL AND THE OTHER IS A TWO AMP.
FUSE LOCATED ON THE VISOR ASSEMBLY. THE GARAGE DOOR OPENER IS NOT FUSED WITHIN THE VISOR.

© Ford Motor Co.

ELECTRICAL SECTION

Starter

All except Bobcat, Mustang II and Pinto

- Disconnect electrical wiring, and remove mounting bolts, brackets, etc.
- When removing the starter it may be necessary to turn the steering wheel fully right or disconnect the idler arm for clearance.

BOBCAT, MUSTANG II AND PINTO

- In 1975 and later models the steering gear must be removed for starter removal clearance.

Ignition Distributor

- Remove distributor cap, electrical wiring, vacuum hose, etc. from the distributor.
- Put alignment marks on rotor and distributor housing for installation reference.

- Remove the hold-down device, and pull the distributor up out of the engine.

- After installation, set ignition timing and check dwell, idle speed, etc.

Distributor (breakerless ignition) used with eight cylinder engines

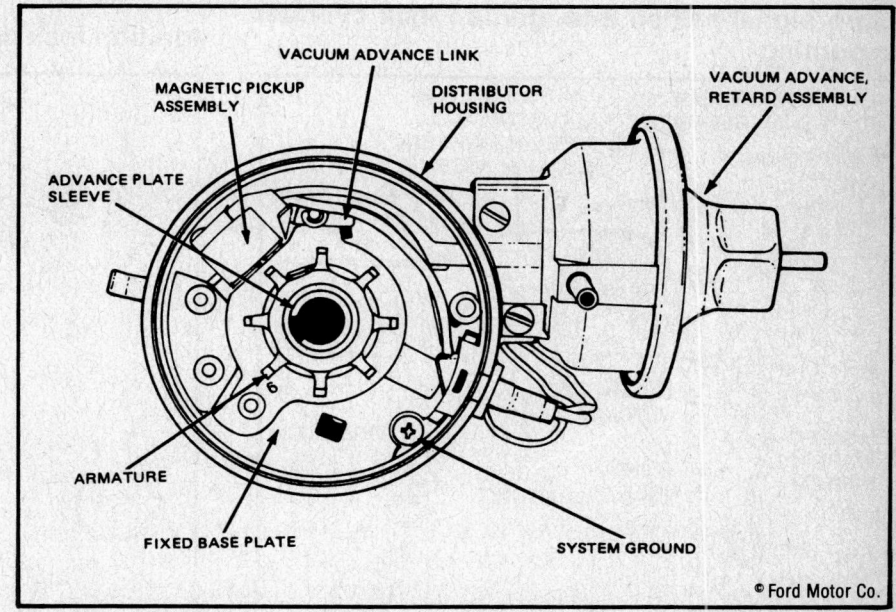

© Ford Motor Co.

Ignition distributor typical installation

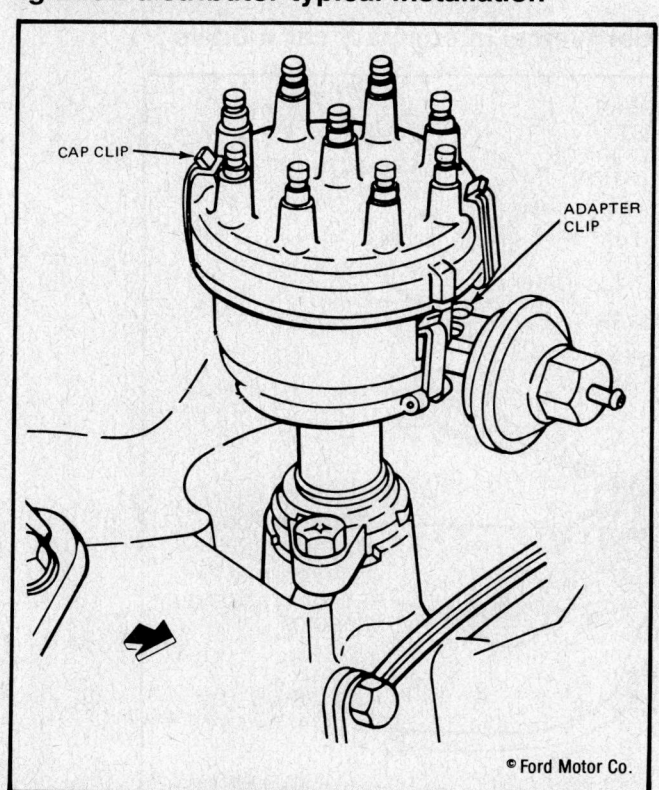

© Ford Motor Co.

Distributor rotor static timing position

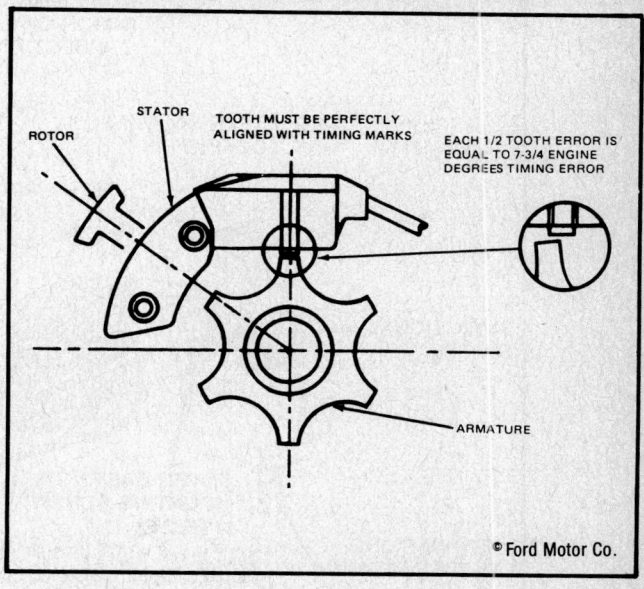

© Ford Motor Co.

FORD—LINCOLN—MERCURY REAR DRIVE CARS

Ignition Lock
- Disconnect the battery, remove the steering wheel and place the lock cylinder in the RUN position.
- Place the shift lever in PARK (automatic transmission) or REVERSE (manual transmission).
- Release the lock cylinder by inserting a wire pin in the lock cylinder hole located inside the column halfway down the lock cylinder housing on standard columns, and on the outside flange casting on tilt columns.

Ignition Switch
- The switch is located on the steering column lower section.
- For switch replacement, remove the steering column shroud, and lower the column from the brake support bracket. Remove the instrument cluster if necessary.
- When installing, adjust so that switch and lock cylinder positions exactly correspond.

Turn signal switch and ignition lock cylinder mounting

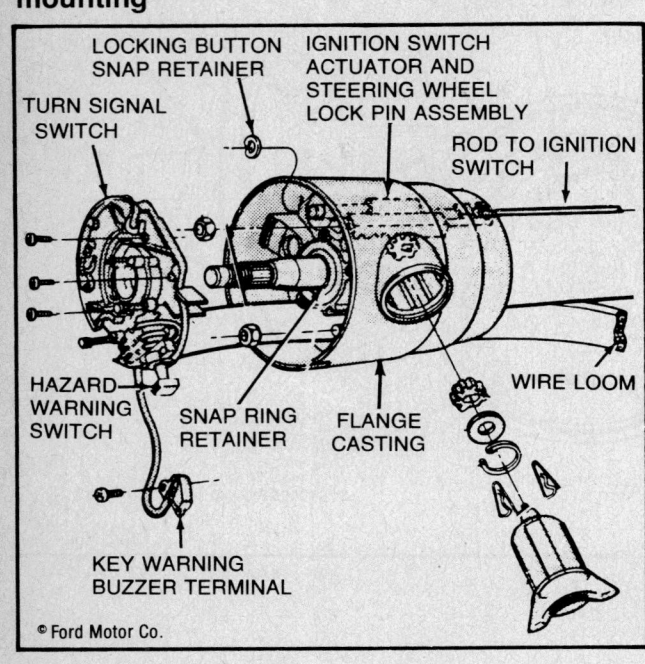

LOCKING BUTTON SNAP RETAINER
IGNITION SWITCH ACTUATOR AND STEERING WHEEL LOCK PIN ASSEMBLY
TURN SIGNAL SWITCH
ROD TO IGNITION SWITCH
HAZARD WARNING SWITCH
SNAP RING RETAINER
FLANGE CASTING
WIRE LOOM
KEY WARNING BUZZER TERMINAL
© Ford Motor Co.

Ignition lock drive gear

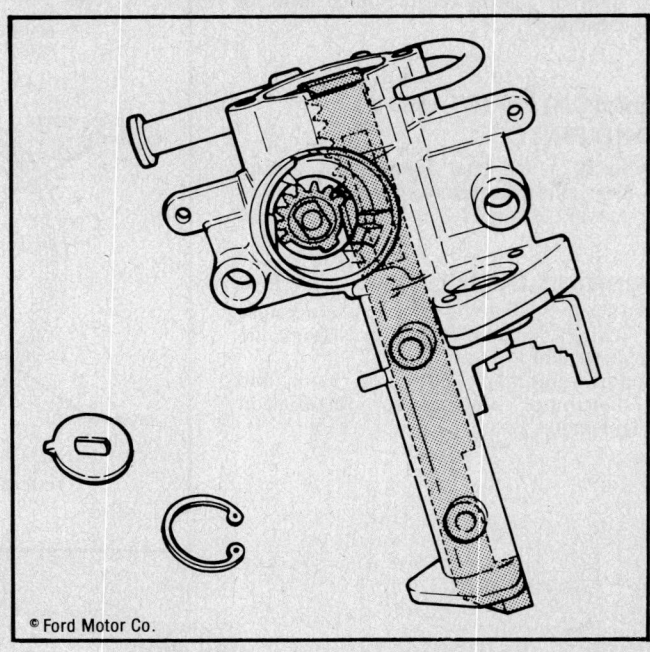

© Ford Motor Co.

Turn signal switch and ignition lock cylinder typical in compact car models

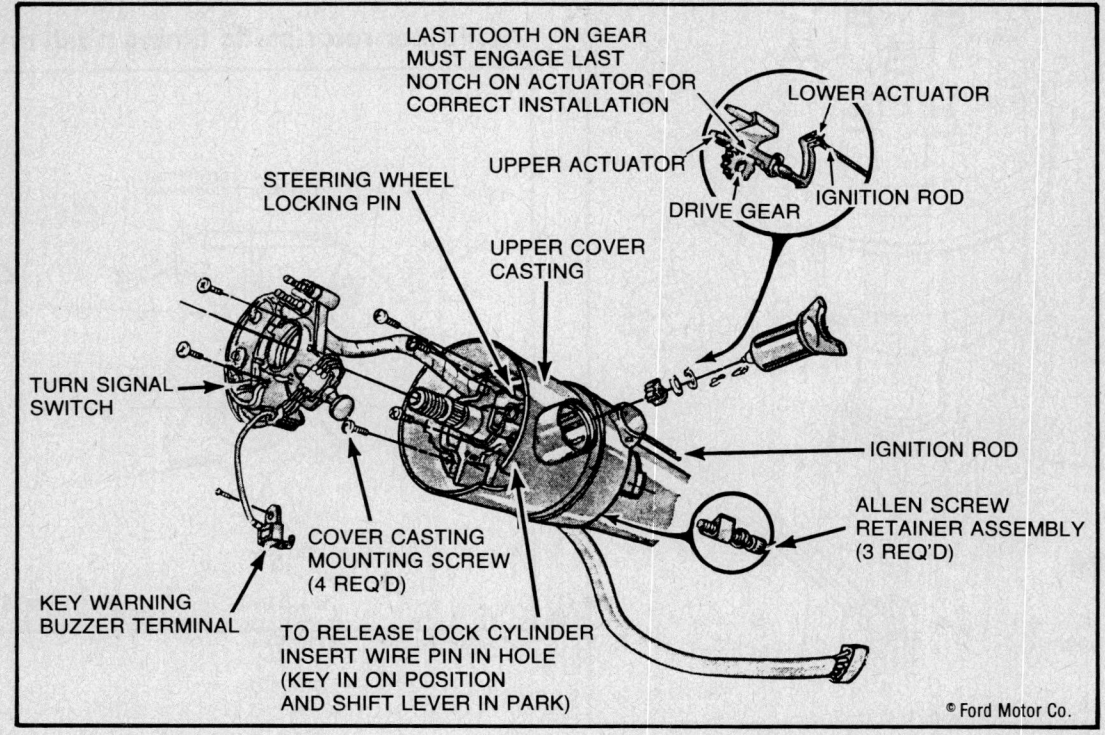

LAST TOOTH ON GEAR MUST ENGAGE LAST NOTCH ON ACTUATOR FOR CORRECT INSTALLATION
LOWER ACTUATOR
UPPER ACTUATOR
DRIVE GEAR
IGNITION ROD
STEERING WHEEL LOCKING PIN
UPPER COVER CASTING
TURN SIGNAL SWITCH
IGNITION ROD
ALLEN SCREW RETAINER ASSEMBLY (3 REQ'D)
COVER CASTING MOUNTING SCREW (4 REQ'D)
KEY WARNING BUZZER TERMINAL
TO RELEASE LOCK CYLINDER INSERT WIRE PIN IN HOLE (KEY IN ON POSITION AND SHIFT LEVER IN PARK)
© Ford Motor Co.

A398

Neutral safety switch adjustment typical in Bobcat, Mustang II and Pinto

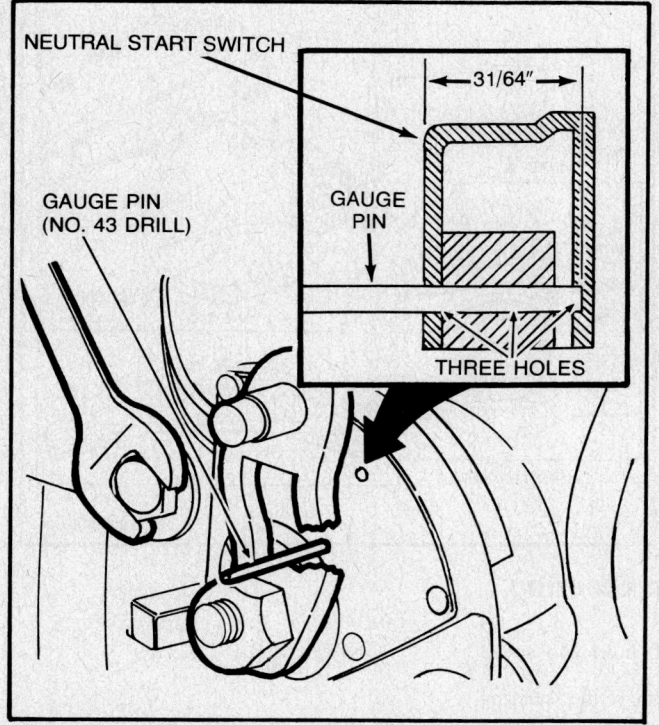

FMX transmission neutral start switch adjustment

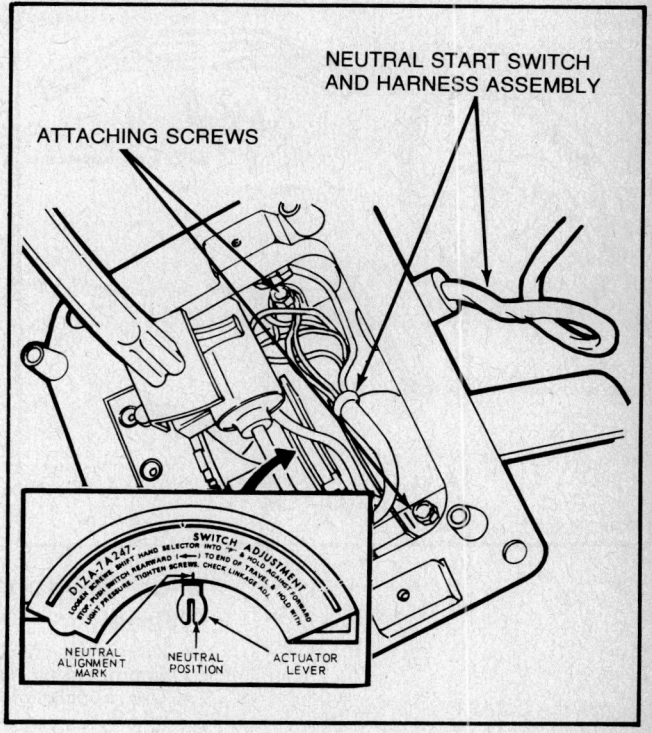

Stoplight Switch

- The switch assembly is installed on the pin of the brake pedal arm.
- Switch adjustment is not required.

Stoplight switch typical installation

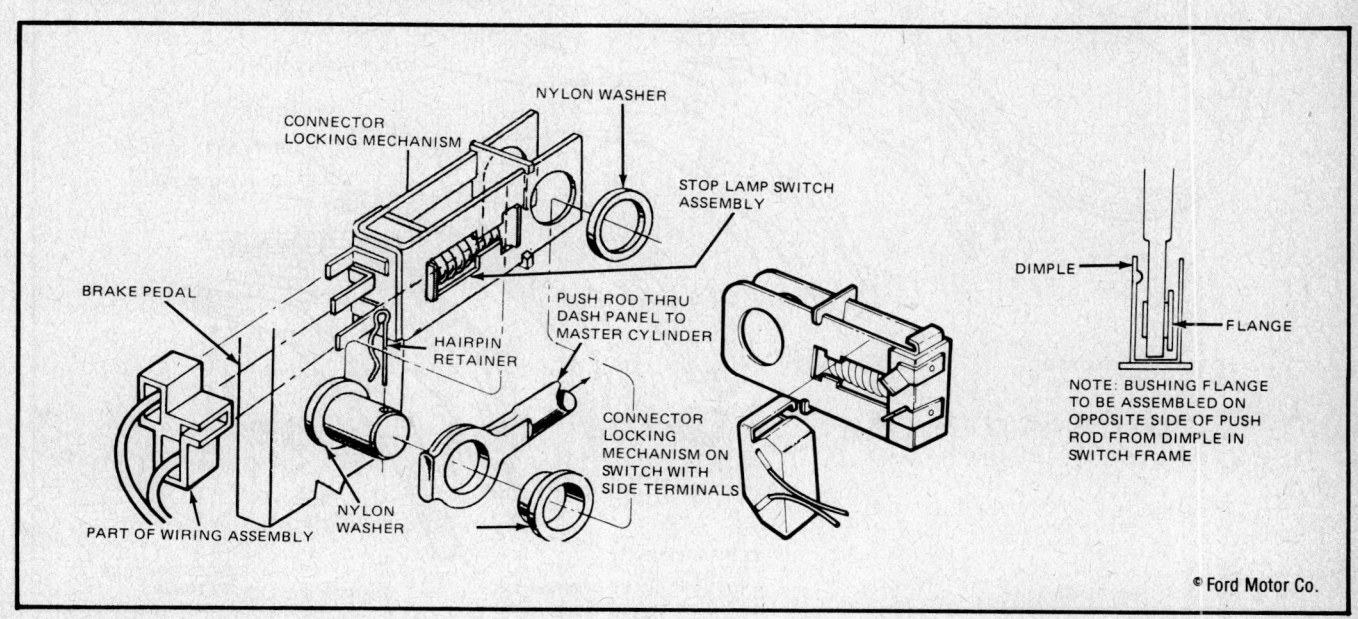

© Ford Motor Co.

Speed control switch removal and installation

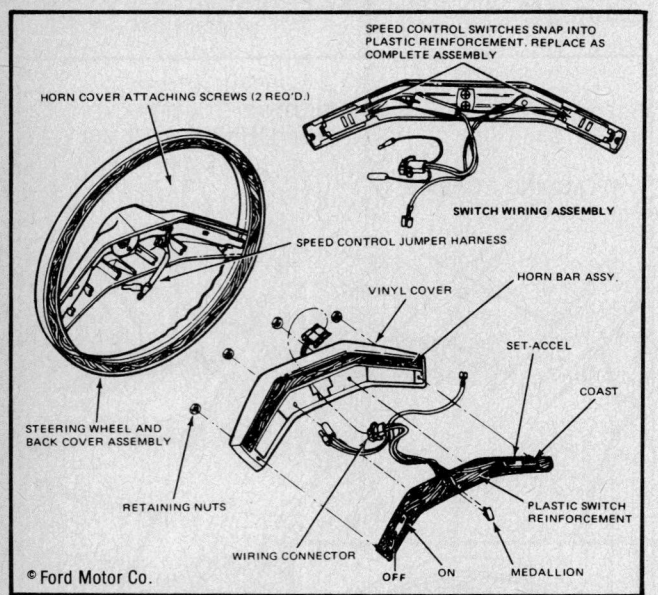

SPEED CONTROL SWITCHES SNAP INTO PLASTIC REINFORCEMENT. REPLACE AS COMPLETE ASSEMBLY

HORN COVER ATTACHING SCREWS (2 REQ'D.)

SWITCH WIRING ASSEMBLY

SPEED CONTROL JUMPER HARNESS

VINYL COVER

HORN BAR ASSY.

SET-ACCEL

COAST

STEERING WHEEL AND BACK COVER ASSEMBLY

RETAINING NUTS

PLASTIC SWITCH REINFORCEMENT

WIRING CONNECTOR

OFF   ON

MEDALLION

© Ford Motor Co.

Two spoke wheel and horn switch

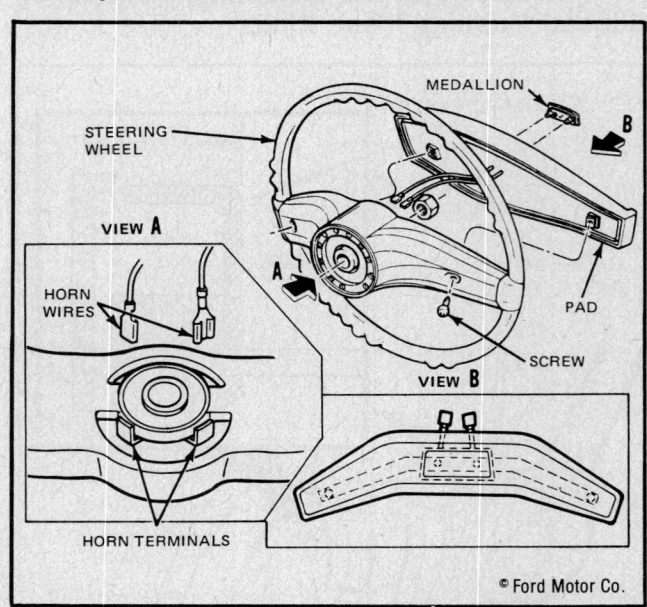

STEERING WHEEL

MEDALLION

B

VIEW A

HORN WIRES

A

PAD

SCREW

VIEW B

HORN TERMINALS

© Ford Motor Co.

Horn Switch and Steering Wheel

- Disconnect crash pad, horn and speed control wiring, etc.
- Use a puller to remove the steering wheel.

Luxury and speed control steering wheel and horn cover

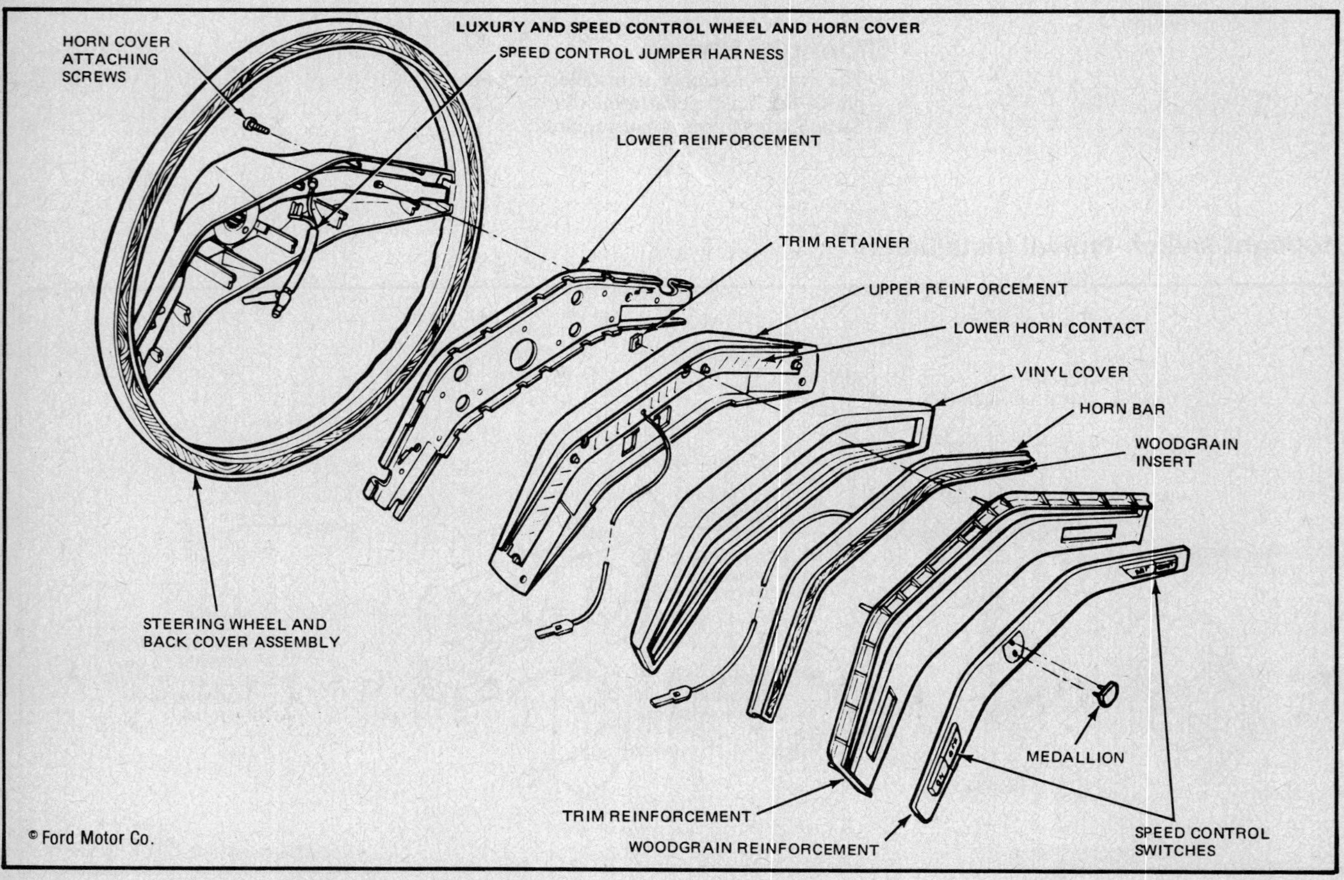

HORN COVER ATTACHING SCREWS

LUXURY AND SPEED CONTROL WHEEL AND HORN COVER

SPEED CONTROL JUMPER HARNESS

LOWER REINFORCEMENT

TRIM RETAINER

UPPER REINFORCEMENT

LOWER HORN CONTACT

VINYL COVER

HORN BAR

WOODGRAIN INSERT

STEERING WHEEL AND BACK COVER ASSEMBLY

MEDALLION

TRIM REINFORCEMENT

WOODGRAIN REINFORCEMENT

SPEED CONTROL SWITCHES

© Ford Motor Co.

Steering column wiring

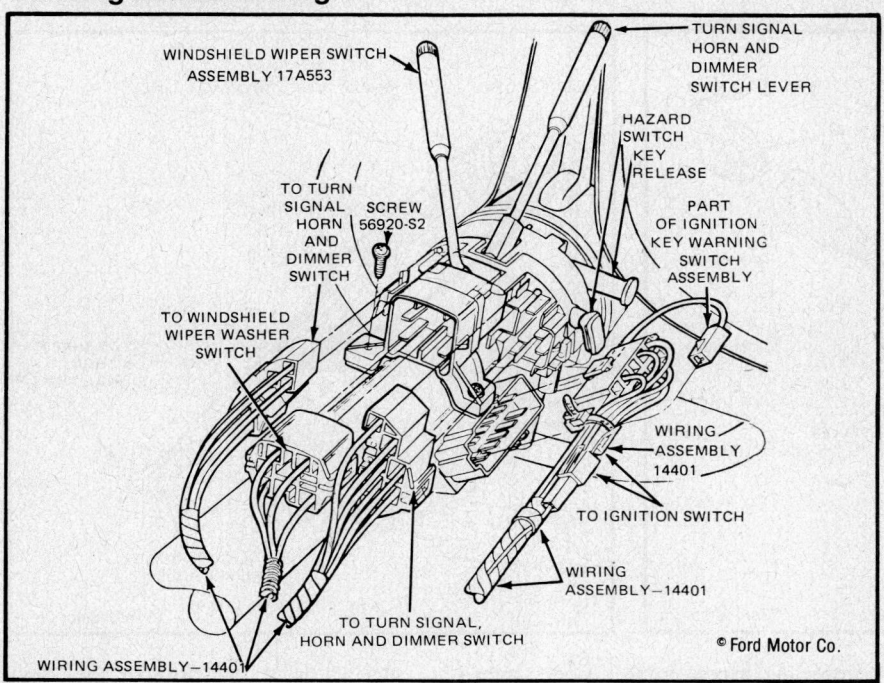

WINDSHIELD WIPER SWITCH
ASSEMBLY 17A553

TURN SIGNAL
HORN AND
DIMMER
SWITCH LEVER

HAZARD
SWITCH
KEY
RELEASE

TO TURN
SIGNAL
HORN AND
DIMMER
SWITCH

SCREW
56920-S2

PART
OF IGNITION
KEY WARNING
SWITCH
ASSEMBLY

TO WINDSHIELD
WIPER WASHER
SWITCH

WIRING
ASSEMBLY
14401

TO IGNITION SWITCH

WIRING
ASSEMBLY—14401

TO TURN SIGNAL,
HORN AND DIMMER SWITCH

WIRING ASSEMBLY—14401

© Ford Motor Co.

Turn Signal Switch

- Remove the steering wheel, turn signal lever, hazard warning knob, column shroud, etc.
- Disconnect the wiring connector, and pull the switch and wiring harness up out of the column. On tilt columns the connector will not fit up through the column so the wires must be separated from the connector.
- When installing, transfer the ground brush located in the cancelling cam to the new switch on speed control equipped vehicles.

Light Switch

- Relocate anything preventing access to the switch such as air conditioner ducting, trim panel, instrument cluster, etc.
- Place switch in full ON position. Pull on knob while pressing shaft release button to release shaft and knob assembly.
- Separate the switch from mounting bracket and electrical connectors.

Removing light switch knob

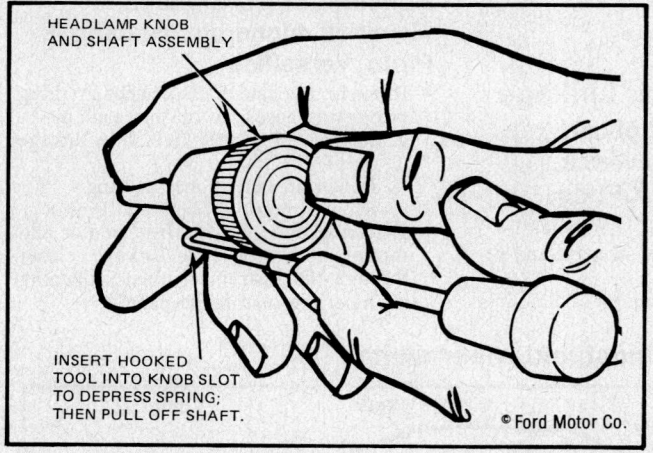

HEADLAMP KNOB
AND SHAFT ASSEMBLY

INSERT HOOKED
TOOL INTO KNOB SLOT
TO DEPRESS SPRING;
THEN PULL OFF SHAFT.

© Ford Motor Co.

Typical light switch

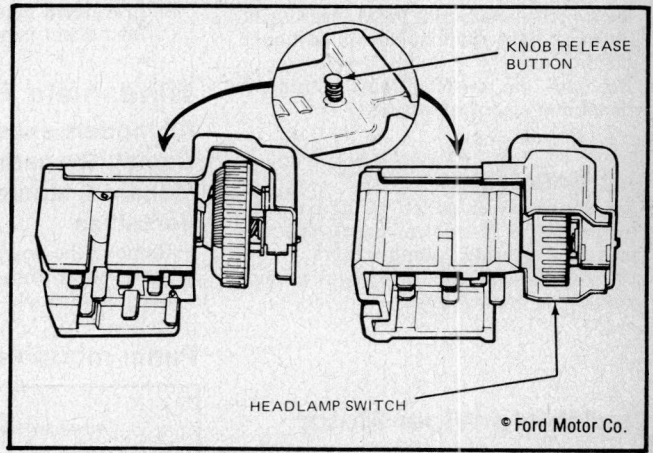

KNOB RELEASE
BUTTON

HEADLAMP SWITCH

© Ford Motor Co.

Light switch used with Autolamp system

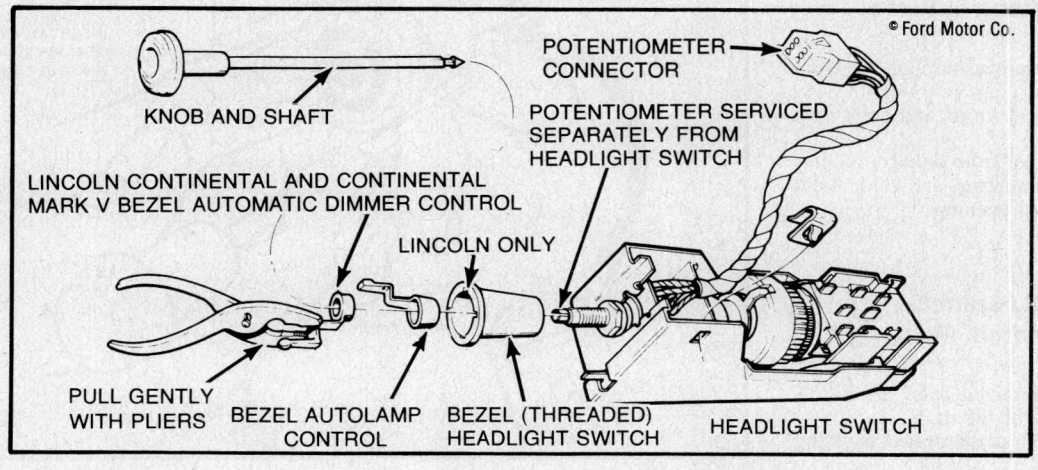

© Ford Motor Co.

KNOB AND SHAFT

POTENTIOMETER
CONNECTOR

POTENTIOMETER SERVICED
SEPARATELY FROM
HEADLIGHT SWITCH

LINCOLN CONTINENTAL AND CONTINENTAL
MARK V BEZEL AUTOMATIC DIMMER CONTROL

LINCOLN ONLY

PULL GENTLY
WITH PLIERS

BEZEL AUTOLAMP
CONTROL

BEZEL (THREADED)
HEADLIGHT SWITCH

HEADLIGHT SWITCH

Wiper switch removal

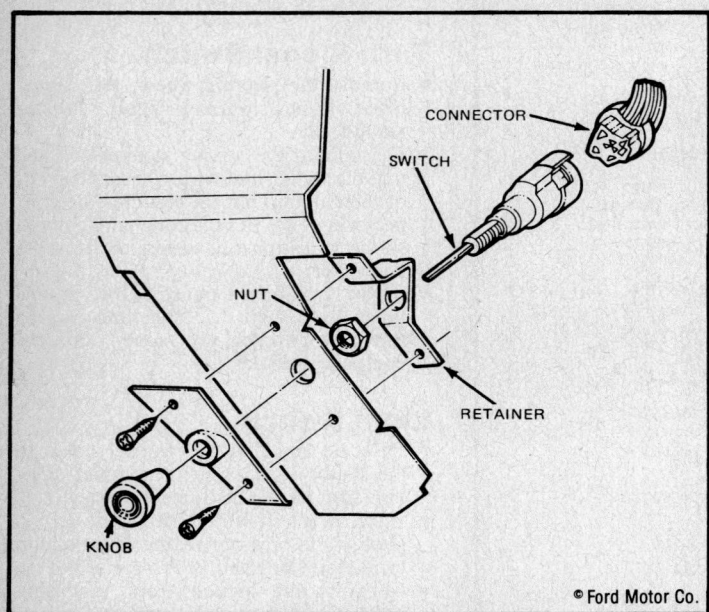

© Ford Motor Co.

Windshield wiper lever installation

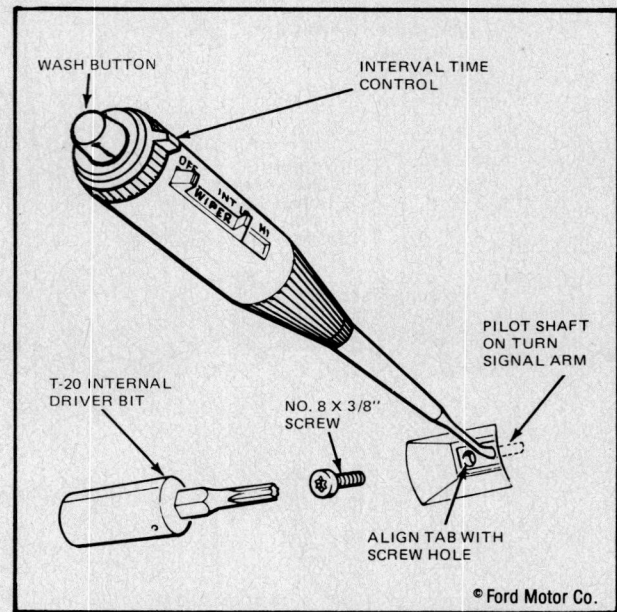

WASH BUTTON

INTERVAL TIME CONTROL

PILOT SHAFT ON TURN SIGNAL ARM

T-20 INTERNAL DRIVER BIT

NO. 8 X 3/8" SCREW

ALIGN TAB WITH SCREW HOLE

© Ford Motor Co.

Windshield Wiper Switch

Instrument Panel Mounted
- Relocate anything preventing access to the switch such as trim panel, instrument cluster, light switch, air conditioner ducting, etc.
- Separate the switch from instrument panel and electrical wiring.

Stalk Mounted
- Disconnect wiper switch wiring connector under the instrument panel, and remove the steering column covers.
- Remove the combined wiper/washer and turn signal control lever.

Windshield Wiper Motor

All models except Bobcat, Comet, Granada, Maverick, Monarch, Mustang II, Pinto, Versailles
- The motor is removed through the cowl vent opening
- Remove the wiper arms and cowl vent screens.
- Separate the motor from linkage, mounts and electrical connector, and guide it out through the cowl opening.

Bobcat, Comet, Granada, Maverick, Monarch, Mustang II, Pinto, Versailles
- The motor is removed from the instrument panel side of the dash.
- Remove, relocate or disconnect anything

preventing access to the wiper motor such as:
a. Evaporator case center distribution duct assembly.
b. Instrument cluster
c. Instrument panel braces

Windshield Wiper Linkage

All models except Bobcat, Comet, Granada, Maverick, Monarch, Mustang II, Pinto, Versailles
- Remove the cowl vent screens, and remove wiper arms.
- Separate linkage from motor and mounts

and guide it out through the cowl opening.

Bobcat, Comet, Granada, Maverick, Monarch, Mustang II, Pinto, Versailles
- Remove, relocate or disconnect anything preventing access to linkage such as:
a. Instrument cluster (left side linkage only)
b. Heater/air conditioner ducting
c. Blower motor (Bobcat and Pinto)
- Disconnect the linkage from motor and mounts. Remove the linkage either through the instrument cluster opening or under the instrument panel.

Panel mounted windshield wiper switch

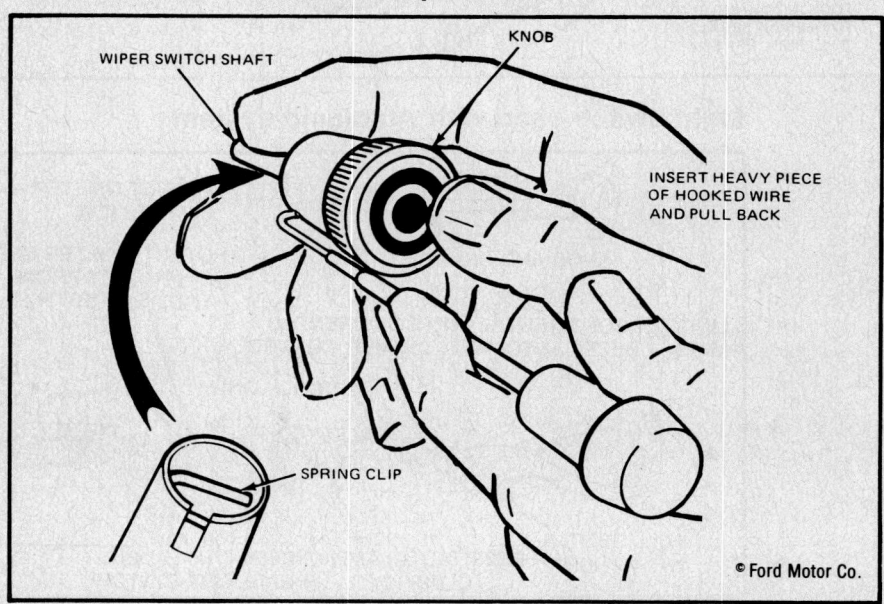

WIPER SWITCH SHAFT

KNOB

INSERT HEAVY PIECE OF HOOKED WIRE AND PULL BACK

SPRING CLIP

© Ford Motor Co.

Steering column mounted wiper switch

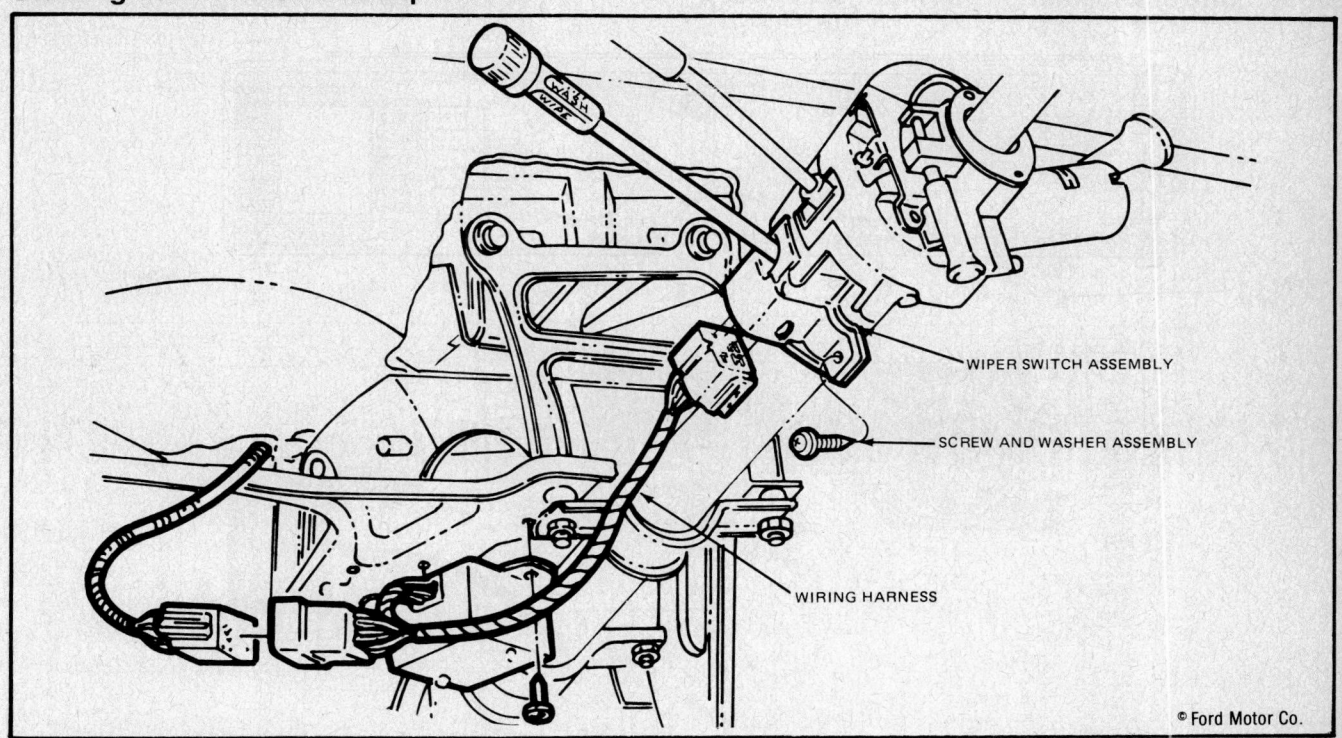

Radio typical installation

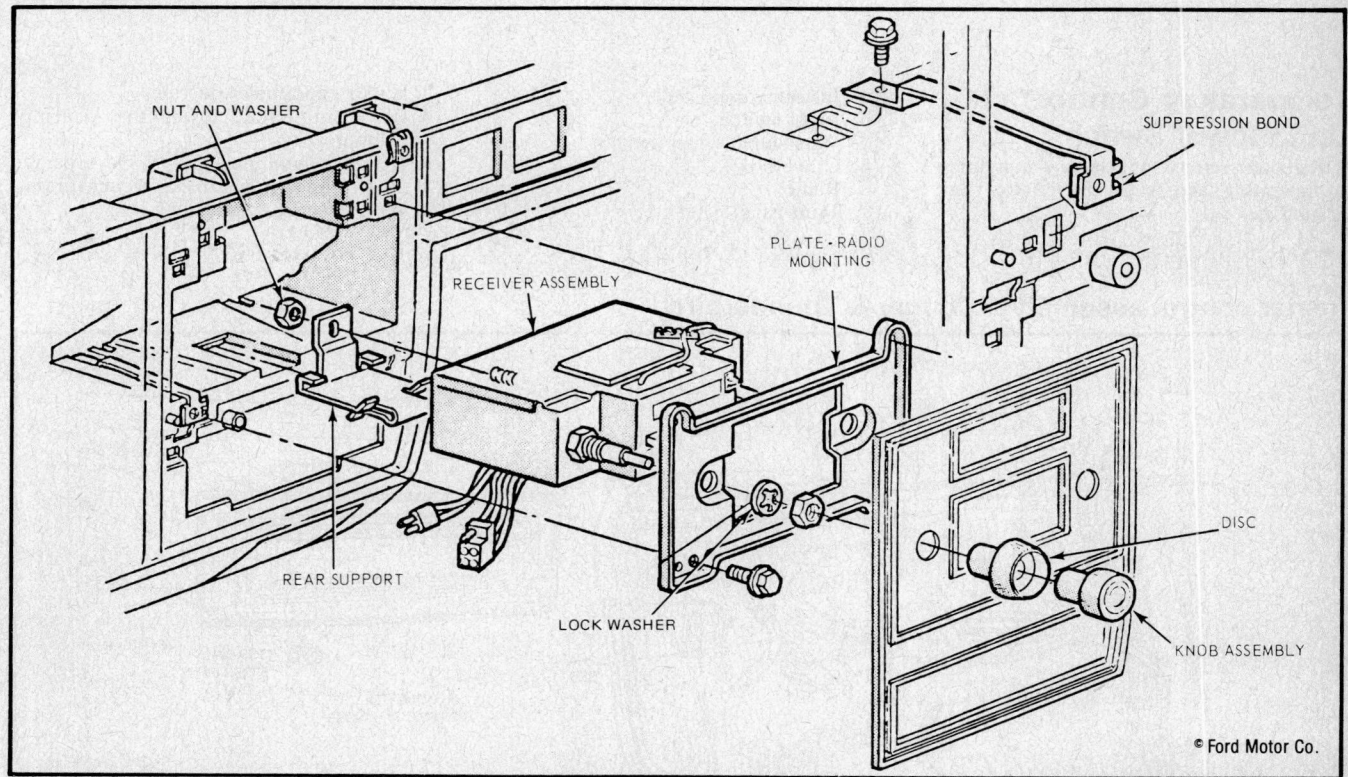

Radio

- Remove, relocate or disconnect anything preventing full access to the radio such as:
  a. Air conditioner ducting
  b. Headlight switch
  c. Twilight Sentinel amplifier
  d. Instrument cluster pad, instrument panel trim, etc.
  e. Heater/air conditioner control unit
  f. Steering column cover
  g. Air conditioner ducting
  h. Ash tray

- Remove mounting screws, knobs, etc., and remove radio from antenna, power and speaker connections.

Heater control assembly—Fairmont & Zephyr

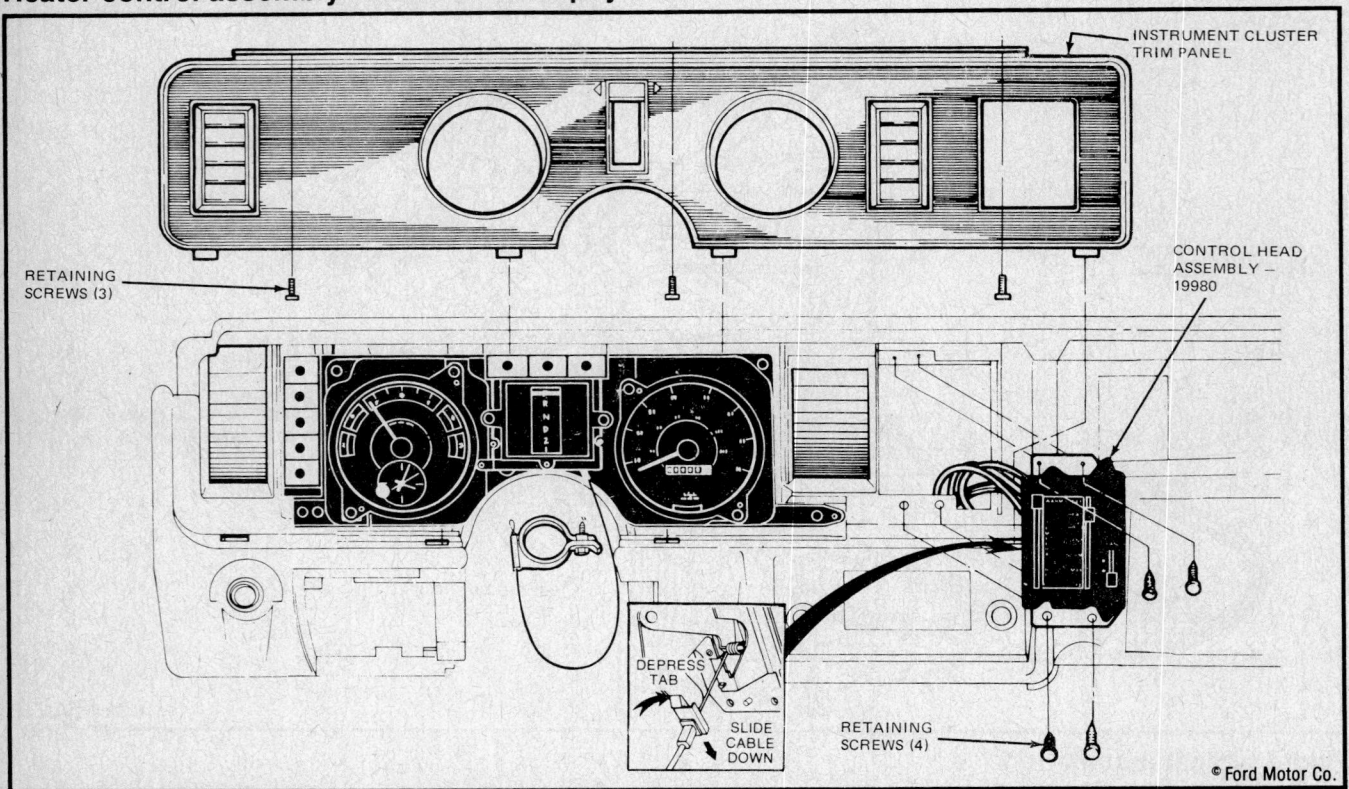

© Ford Motor Co.

Temperature Control Unit/Blower Switch

- Relocate, remove or disconnect anything preventing access to the control unit such as:

a. Instrument cluster
b. Light switch
c. Windshield wiper switch
d. Glove box
e. Radio
f. Trim panel

g. Air conditioner ducting
- On Continental, lower the steering column.
- Remove mounting screws and separate control unit from cables, vacuum lines, and electrical connections.

Heater control assembly—Cougar & Thunderbird

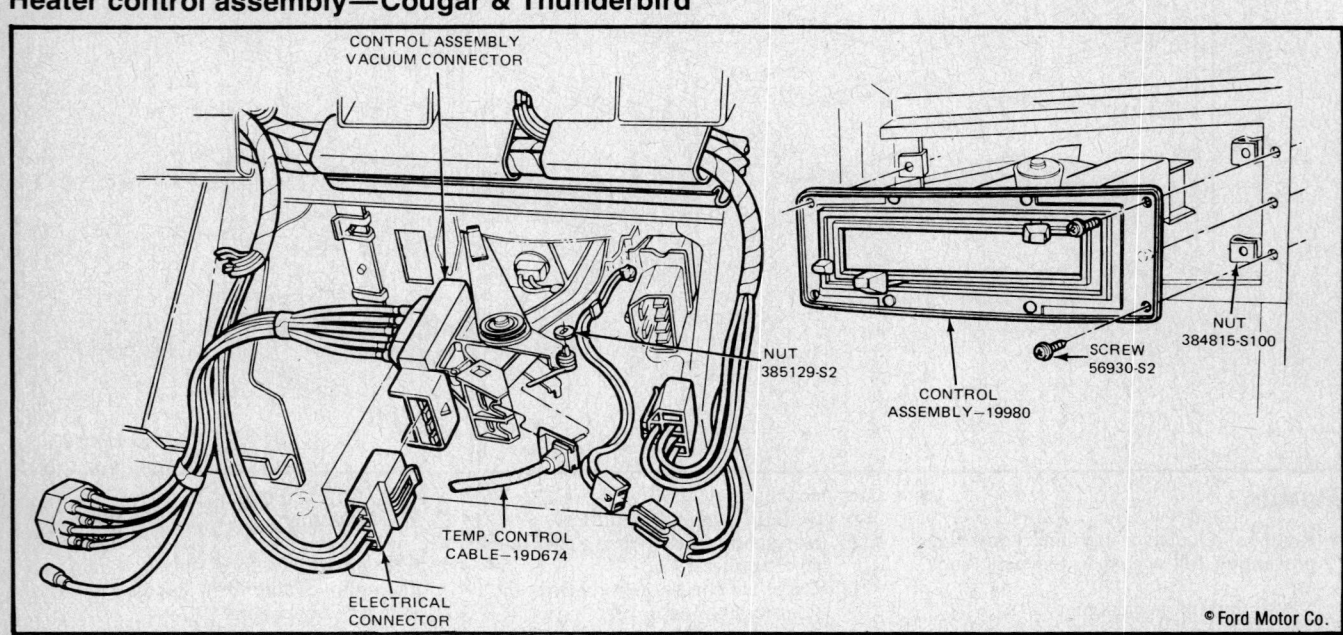

© Ford Motor Co.

Typical heater/air conditioner control unit

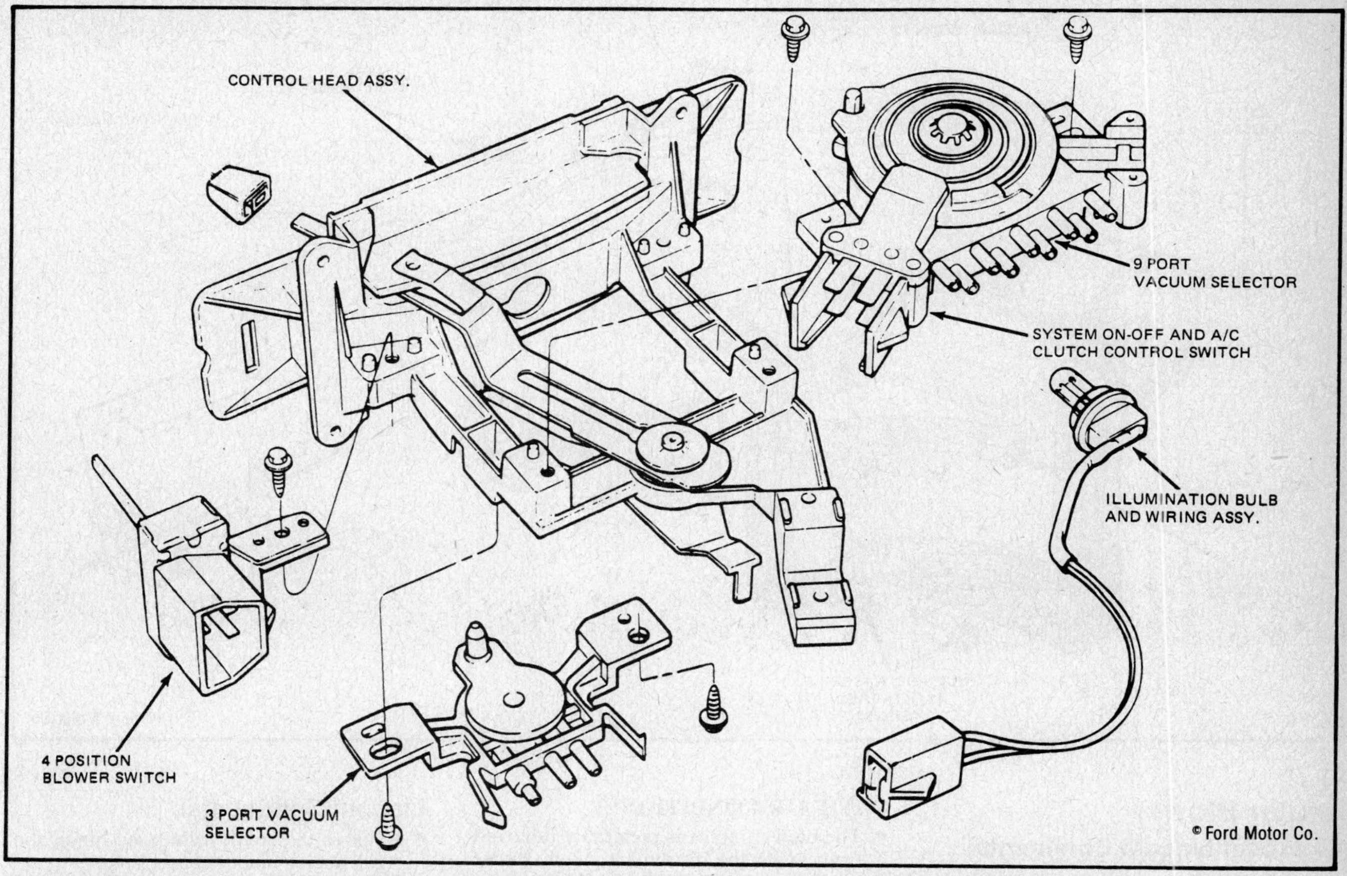

CONTROL HEAD ASSY.

9 PORT VACUUM SELECTOR

SYSTEM ON-OFF AND A/C CLUTCH CONTROL SWITCH

ILLUMINATION BULB AND WIRING ASSY.

4 POSITION BLOWER SWITCH

3 PORT VACUUM SELECTOR

© Ford Motor Co.

Heater/air conditioner control unit in automatic temperature control system

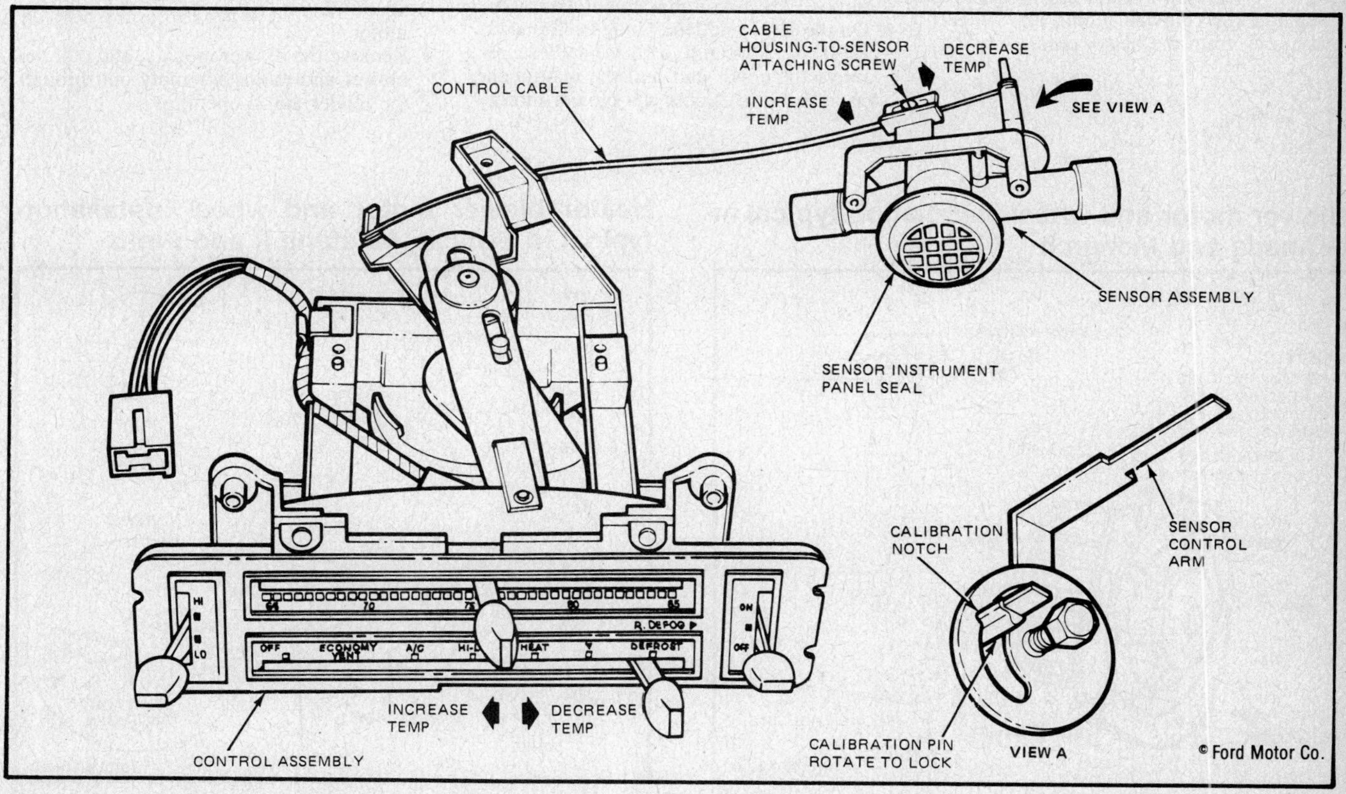

CABLE HOUSING-TO-SENSOR ATTACHING SCREW

DECREASE TEMP

CONTROL CABLE

INCREASE TEMP

SEE VIEW A

SENSOR ASSEMBLY

SENSOR INSTRUMENT PANEL SEAL

CALIBRATION NOTCH

SENSOR CONTROL ARM

INCREASE TEMP

DECREASE TEMP

CONTROL ASSEMBLY

CALIBRATION PIN ROTATE TO LOCK

VIEW A

© Ford Motor Co.

Heater core housing removal—Lincoln

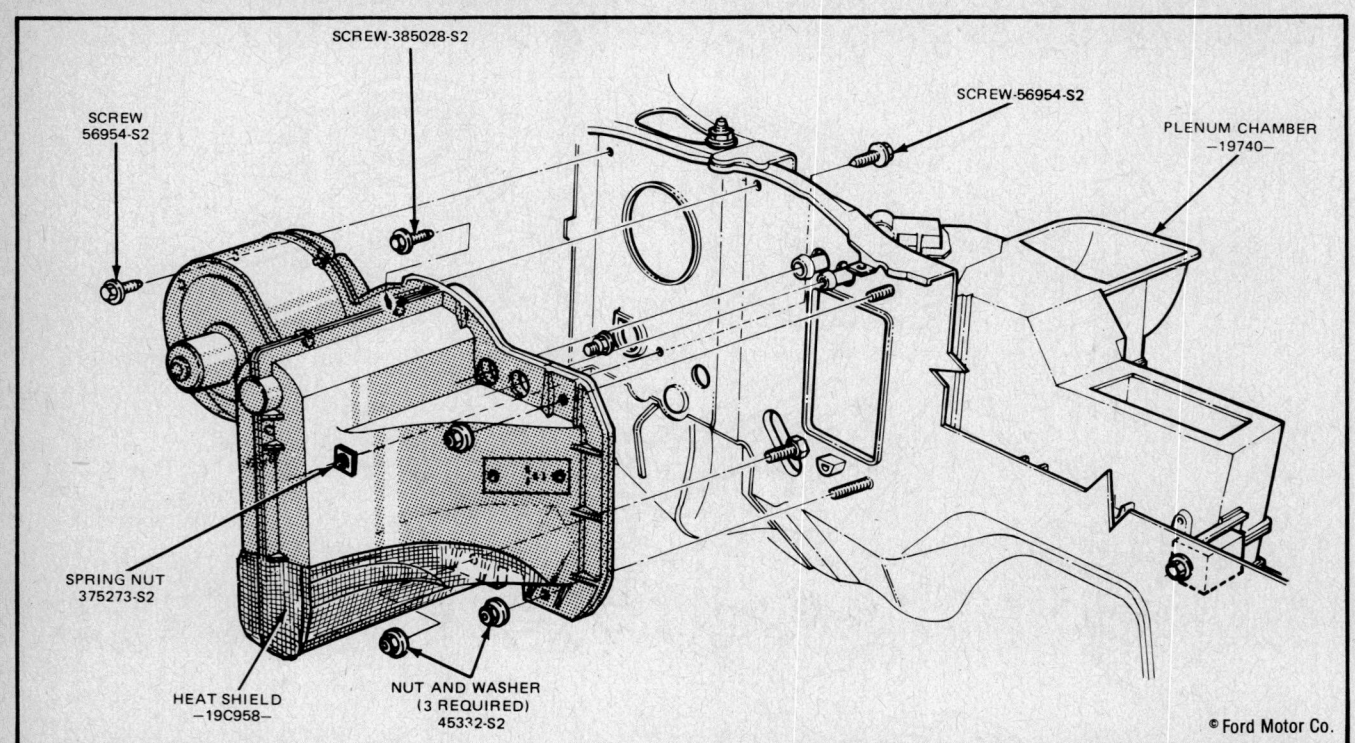

SCREW-385028-S2

SCREW 56954-S2

SCREW-56954-S2

PLENUM CHAMBER —19740—

SPRING NUT 375273-S2

HEAT SHIELD —19C958—

NUT AND WASHER (3 REQUIRED) 45332-S2

© Ford Motor Co.

Heater Blower
All except Lincoln Continental

WITHOUT AIR CONDITIONER
- Remove the entire heater assembly.
- Separate the blower motor and wheel assembly from the heater case.

WITH AIR CONDITIONER
- The blower motor is preferably removed from under the instrument panel. Either remove the entire blower housing or separate the blower housing halves, and remove the motor and blower assembly.
- On the 1977 and later Cougar, Granada, LTD II, Monarch and Versailles, remove the cowl, and pull the instrument panel back to expose the blower motor.

Lincoln Continental
- Remove the hood, right hood hinge and right fender inner support brace.
- Separate the fender apron from the fender wheel opening, and push the apron down away from the blower motor.
- Remove the blower mounts, and pull the blower and motor assembly out through the fender apron opening.

Blower motor and wheel installation typical in Granada and Monarch

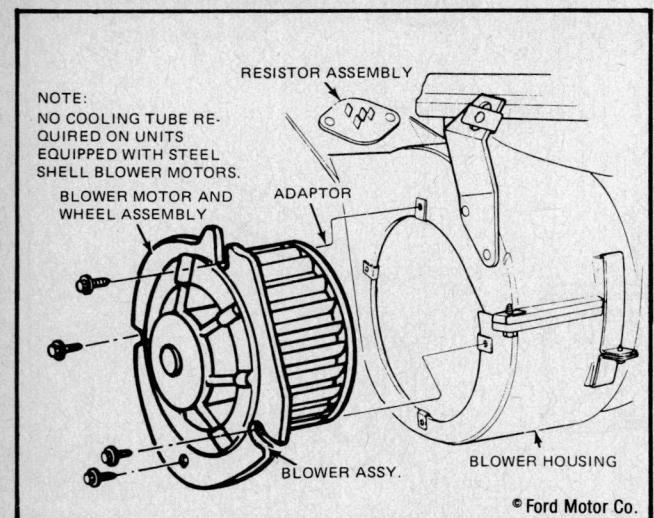

RESISTOR ASSEMBLY

NOTE:
NO COOLING TUBE REQUIRED ON UNITS EQUIPPED WITH STEEL SHELL BLOWER MOTORS.

BLOWER MOTOR AND WHEEL ASSEMBLY

ADAPTOR

BLOWER ASSY.

BLOWER HOUSING

© Ford Motor Co.

Heater blower motor and wheel installation typical in Bobcat, Mustang II and Pinto

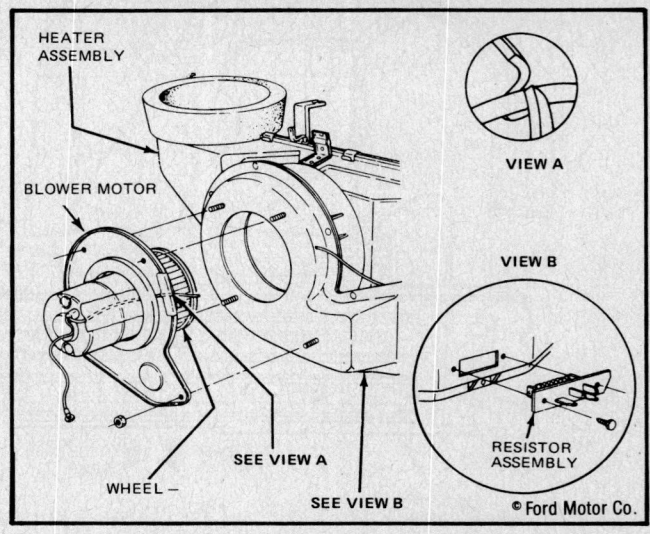

HEATER ASSEMBLY

BLOWER MOTOR

VIEW A

VIEW B

RESISTOR ASSEMBLY

SEE VIEW A

WHEEL —

SEE VIEW B

© Ford Motor Co.

Heater/air conditioner components typical in full-size car models

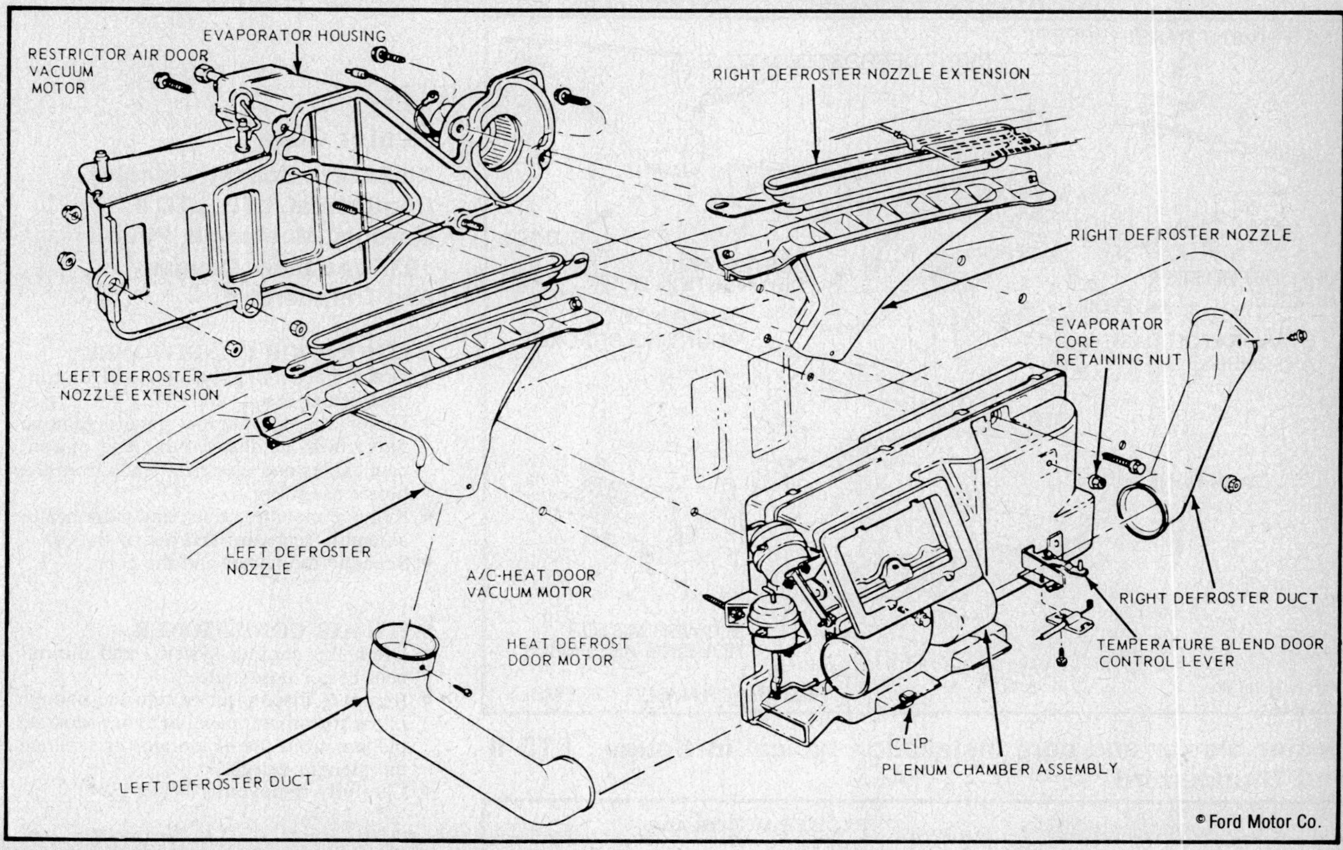

RESTRICTOR AIR DOOR
VACUUM MOTOR

EVAPORATOR HOUSING

RIGHT DEFROSTER NOZZLE EXTENSION

RIGHT DEFROSTER NOZZLE

EVAPORATOR CORE RETAINING NUT

LEFT DEFROSTER NOZZLE EXTENSION

LEFT DEFROSTER NOZZLE

A/C-HEAT DOOR VACUUM MOTOR

HEAT DEFROST DOOR MOTOR

LEFT DEFROSTER DUCT

RIGHT DEFROSTER DUCT

TEMPERATURE BLEND DOOR CONTROL LEVER

CLIP

PLENUM CHAMBER ASSEMBLY

© Ford Motor Co.

Bobcat, Mustang II and Pinto heater

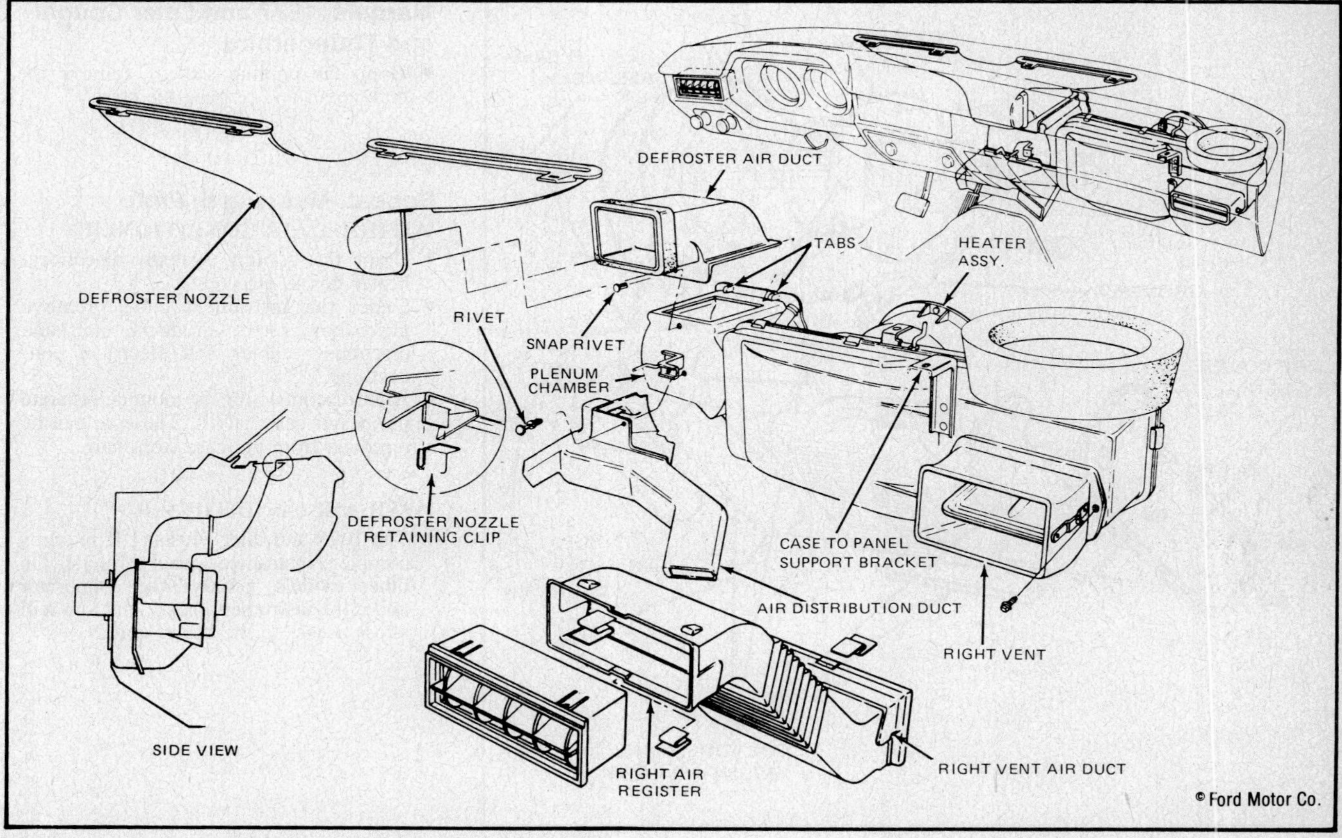

DEFROSTER AIR DUCT

DEFROSTER NOZZLE

TABS

HEATER ASSY.

RIVET

SNAP RIVET

PLENUM CHAMBER

DEFROSTER NOZZLE RETAINING CLIP

CASE TO PANEL SUPPORT BRACKET

AIR DISTRIBUTION DUCT

RIGHT VENT

SIDE VIEW

RIGHT AIR REGISTER

RIGHT VENT AIR DUCT

© Ford Motor Co.

FORD—LINCOLN—MERCURY REAR DRIVE CARS

Heater/air conditioner typical in Montego and Torino

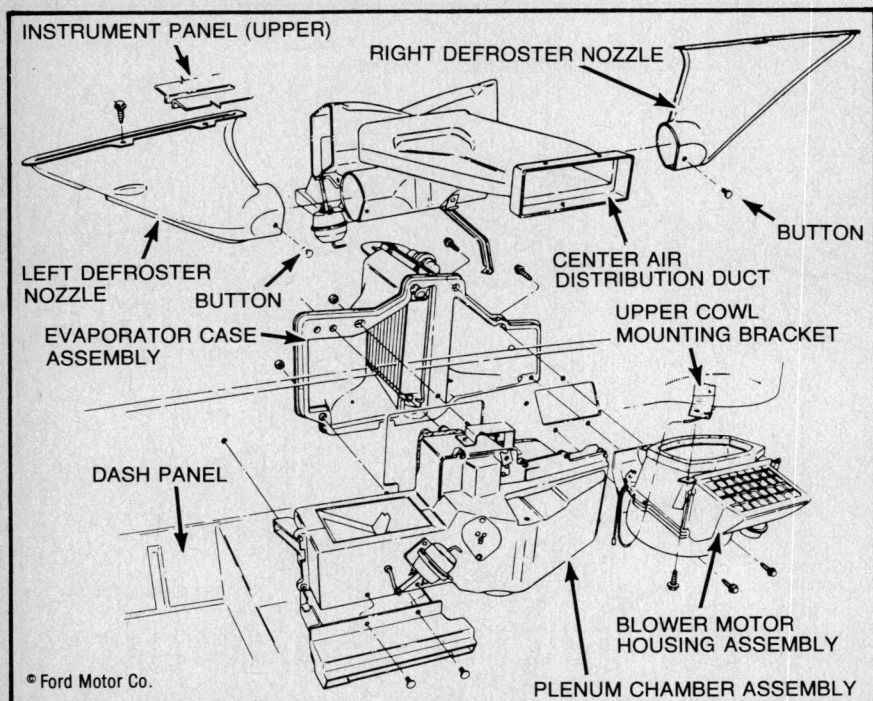

INSTRUMENT PANEL (UPPER)
RIGHT DEFROSTER NOZZLE
BUTTON
LEFT DEFROSTER NOZZLE
BUTTON
CENTER AIR DISTRIBUTION DUCT
EVAPORATOR CASE ASSEMBLY
UPPER COWL MOUNTING BRACKET
DASH PANEL
BLOWER MOTOR HOUSING ASSEMBLY
PLENUM CHAMBER ASSEMBLY
© Ford Motor Co.

Heater blower and core installation typical in Cougar, LTD II and Thunderbird

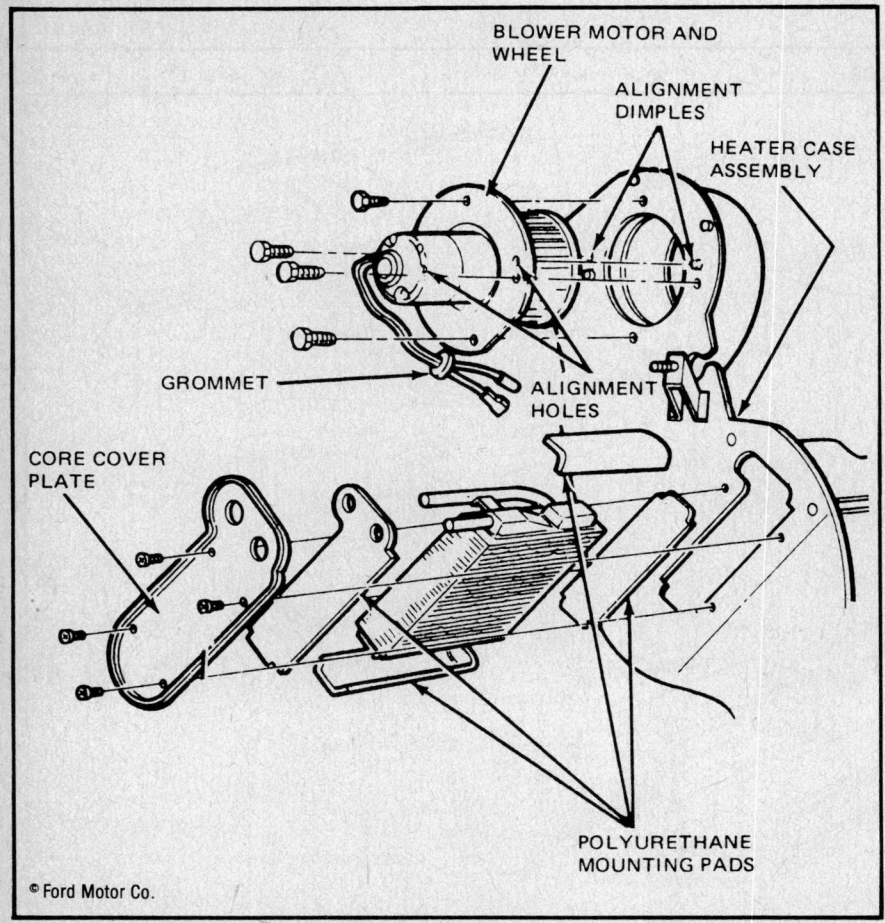

BLOWER MOTOR AND WHEEL
ALIGNMENT DIMPLES
HEATER CASE ASSEMBLY
GROMMET
ALIGNMENT HOLES
CORE COVER PLATE
POLYURETHANE MOUNTING PADS
© Ford Motor Co.

Heater Core
All Except Bobcat, Lincoln Continental, LTD, LTD II, Marquis, Mustang II, Pinto, 1977 and Later Cougar and Thunderbird

WITHOUT AIR CONDITIONER
- Drain the cooling system, and disconnect heater hoses, etc.
- Under the instrument panel, remove glove box, air ducts, etc., and disconnect cables and electrical leads from the heater assembly.
- Remove mounting nuts, and work heater assembly rearward and out of the car.
- Separate the heater and the core.

WITH AIR CONDITIONER
- Drain the cooling system, and disconnect heater hoses, etc.
- Remove, disconnect or relocate enough of the instrument panel to either separate plenum from the evaporator or separate the plenum halves.
- Carefully remove the heater core.

Lincoln Continental, LTD, LTD II, Marquis, 1977 and Later Cougar and Thunderbird
- Drain the cooling system, remove the core cover and remove the core.

Bobcat, Mustang II, Pinto
WITHOUT AIR CONDITIONER
- Drain the cooling system, disconnect heater hoses, etc.
- Under the instrument panel, remove glove box, radio, air ducts, etc., and disconnect cables and electrical connections.
- After disconnecting the mounts, separate the heater case halves. The core can be removed from the case front half.

WITH AIR CONDITIONER
- The 1975 and later Mustang II requires complete instrument panel removal. On other models, remove the evaporator under the instrument panel, and that will allow access to the heater core.

Heater/air conditioner in Comet and Maverick

Heater blower motor and wheel

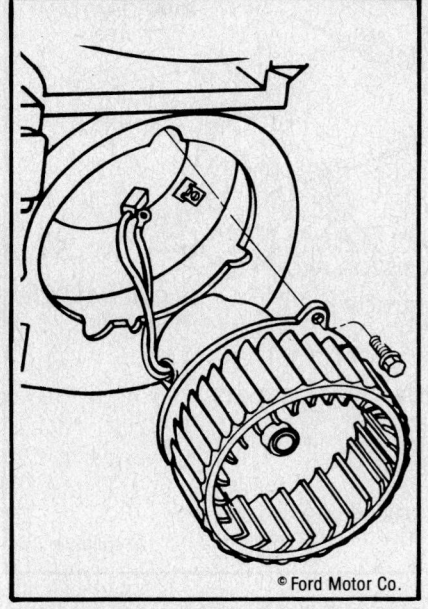

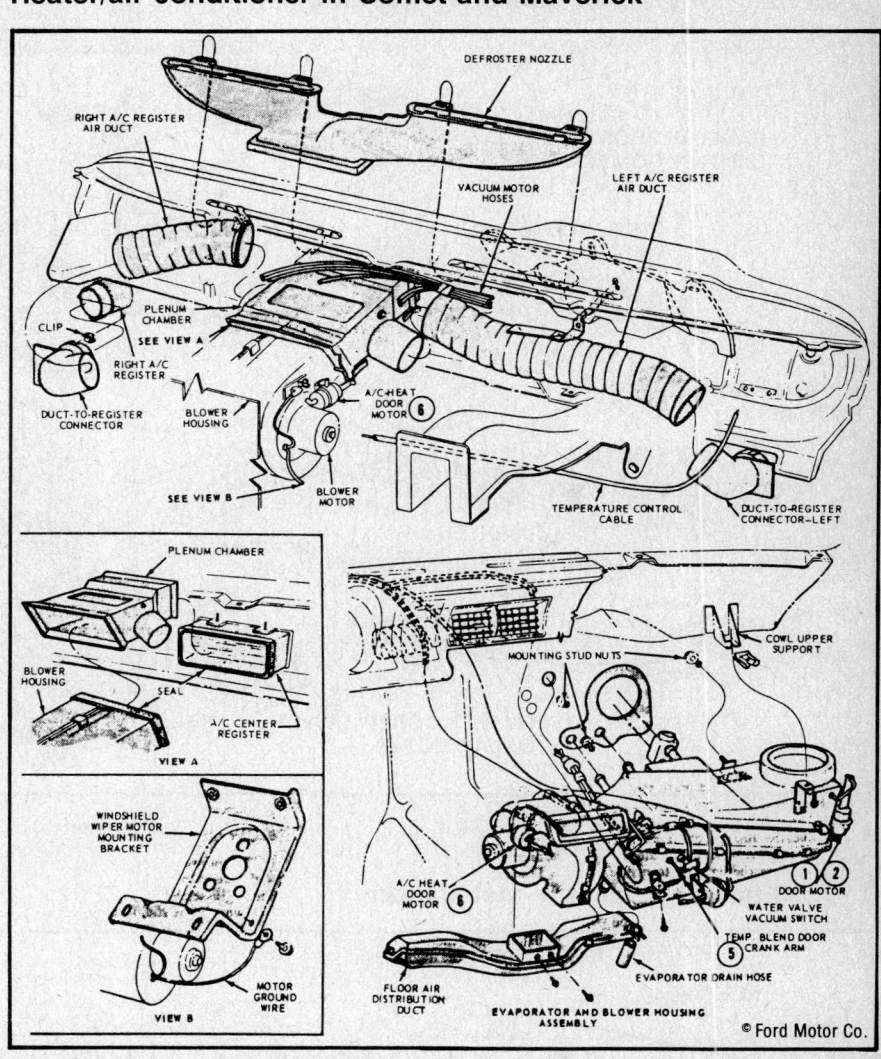

Installation typical in Fairmont, Zephyr and beginning 1979, Capri and Mustang

Cutting access hole in fender apron for heater blower removal

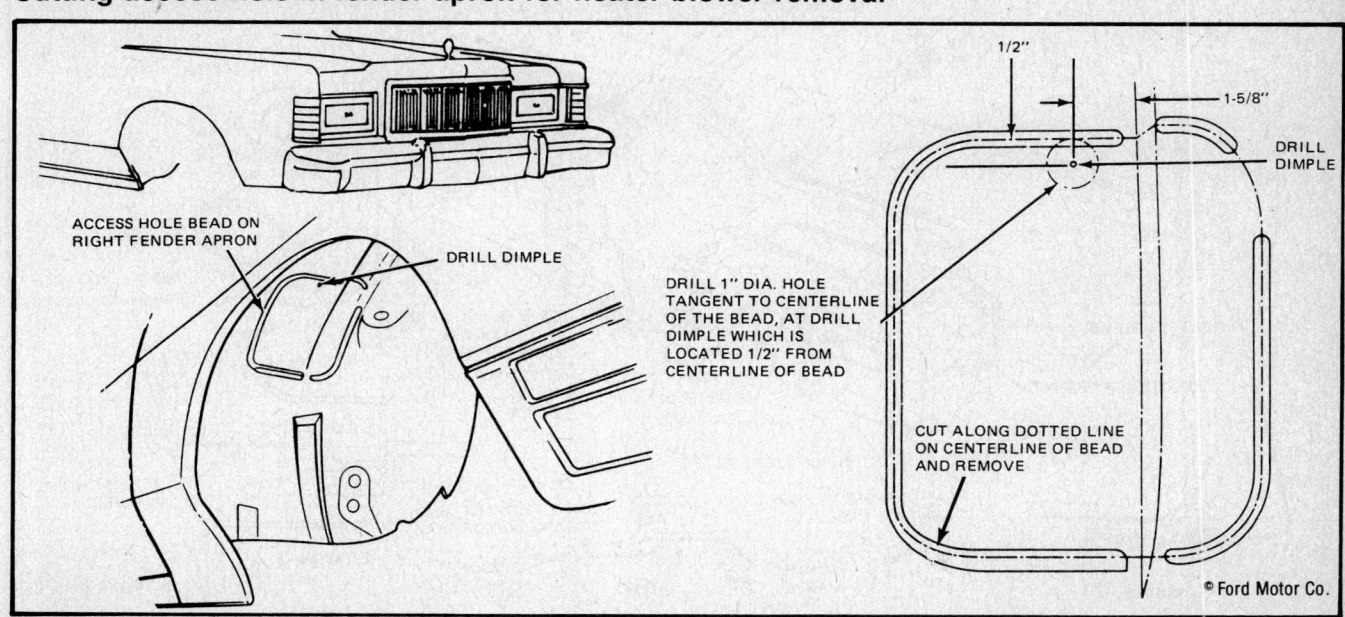

FORD—LINCOLN—MERCURY REAR DRIVE CARS

Heater/air conditioner typical in Mustang II

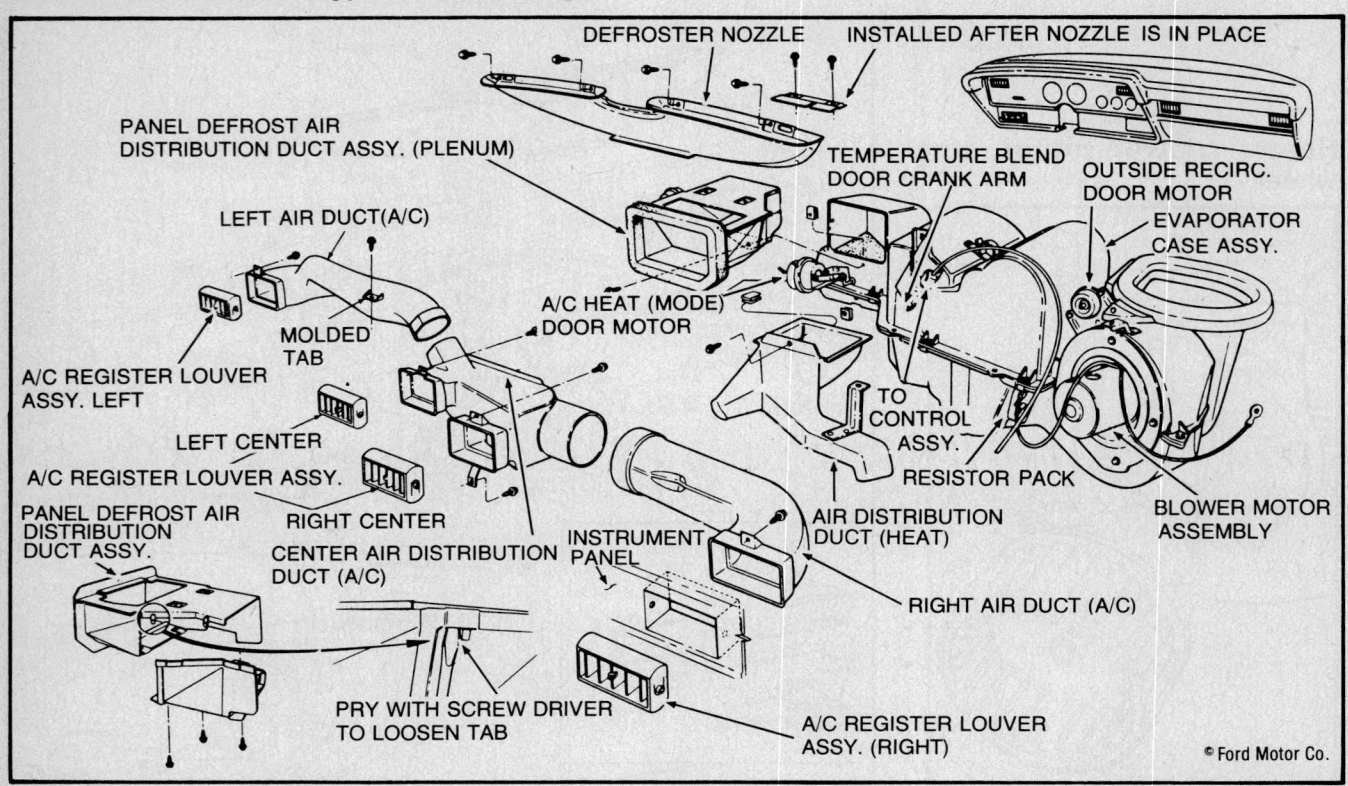

DEFROSTER NOZZLE   INSTALLED AFTER NOZZLE IS IN PLACE

PANEL DEFROST AIR DISTRIBUTION DUCT ASSY. (PLENUM)

LEFT AIR DUCT(A/C)

TEMPERATURE BLEND DOOR CRANK ARM

OUTSIDE RECIRC. DOOR MOTOR

EVAPORATOR CASE ASSY.

MOLDED TAB

A/C HEAT (MODE) DOOR MOTOR

A/C REGISTER LOUVER ASSY. LEFT

LEFT CENTER

A/C REGISTER LOUVER ASSY.

RIGHT CENTER

PANEL DEFROST AIR DISTRIBUTION DUCT ASSY.

CENTER AIR DISTRIBUTION DUCT (A/C)

INSTRUMENT PANEL

TO CONTROL ASSY.

RESISTOR PACK

BLOWER MOTOR ASSEMBLY

AIR DISTRIBUTION DUCT (HEAT)

RIGHT AIR DUCT (A/C)

PRY WITH SCREW DRIVER TO LOOSEN TAB

A/C REGISTER LOUVER ASSY. (RIGHT)

© Ford Motor Co.

Typical heater assembly installation

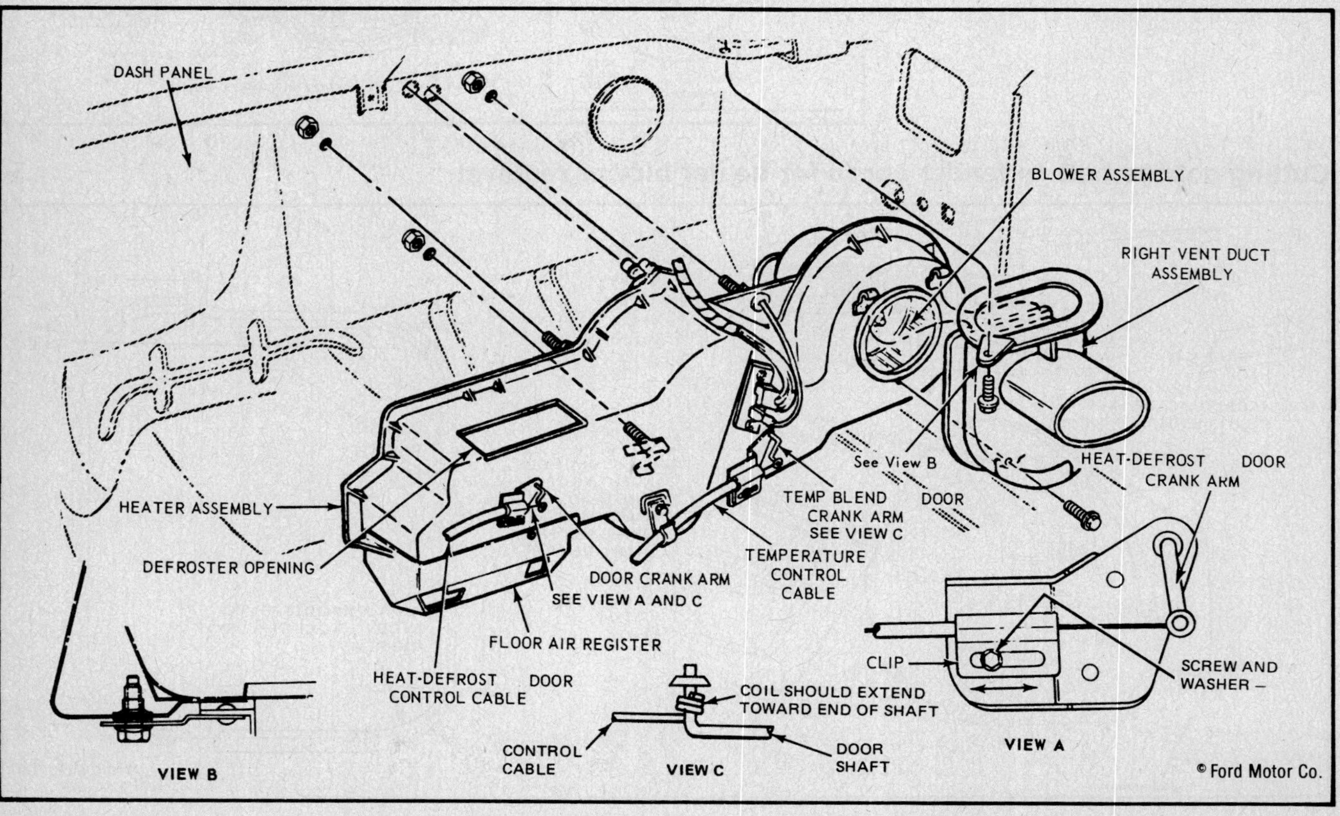

DASH PANEL

BLOWER ASSEMBLY

RIGHT VENT DUCT ASSEMBLY

See View B

HEAT-DEFROST DOOR CRANK ARM

HEATER ASSEMBLY

TEMP BLEND CRANK ARM SEE VIEW C

DOOR

DEFROSTER OPENING

TEMPERATURE CONTROL CABLE

DOOR CRANK ARM SEE VIEW A AND C

FLOOR AIR REGISTER

HEAT-DEFROST DOOR CONTROL CABLE

CLIP

SCREW AND WASHER —

COIL SHOULD EXTEND TOWARD END OF SHAFT

VIEW B

CONTROL CABLE

VIEW C

DOOR SHAFT

VIEW A

© Ford Motor Co.

ATC installation—Granada, Monarch & Versailles

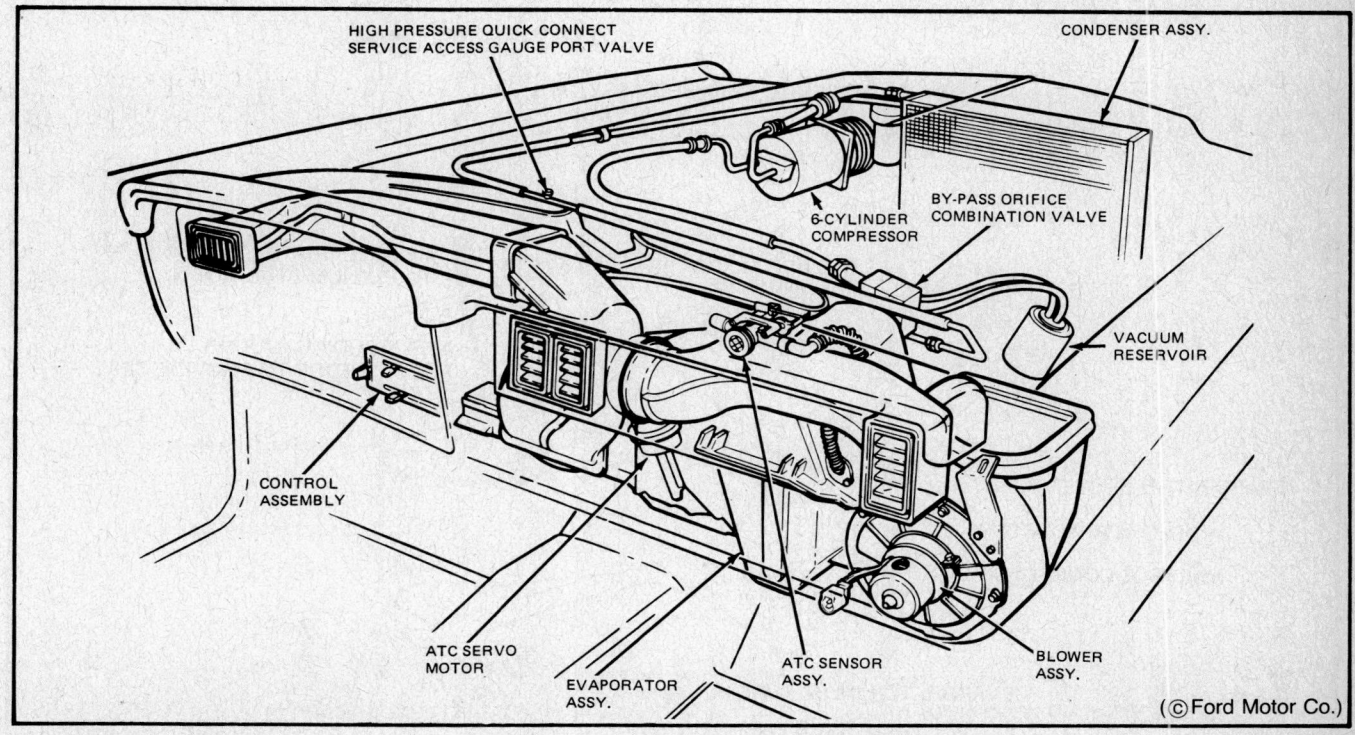

HIGH PRESSURE QUICK CONNECT SERVICE ACCESS GAUGE PORT VALVE

CONDENSER ASSY.

6-CYLINDER COMPRESSOR

BY-PASS ORIFICE COMBINATION VALVE

VACUUM RESERVOIR

CONTROL ASSEMBLY

ATC SERVO MOTOR

EVAPORATOR ASSY.

ATC SENSOR ASSY.

BLOWER ASSY.

(© Ford Motor Co.)

Heater core removal typical in Fairmont, Zephyr and beginning 1979, Capri and Mustang

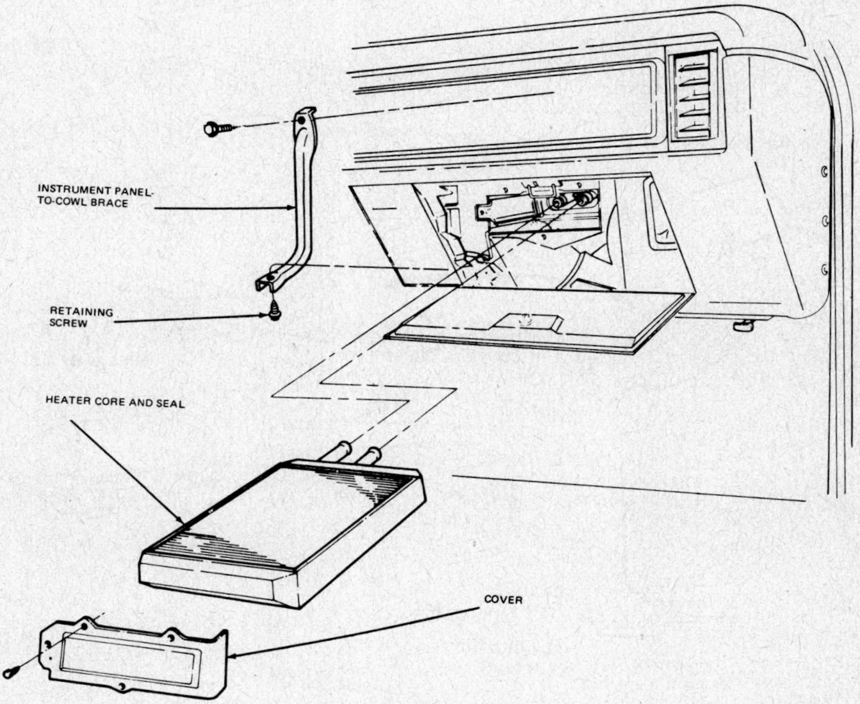

INSTRUMENT PANEL-TO-COWL BRACE

RETAINING SCREW

HEATER CORE AND SEAL

COVER

© Ford Motor Co.

Lincoln Continental evaporator case removal

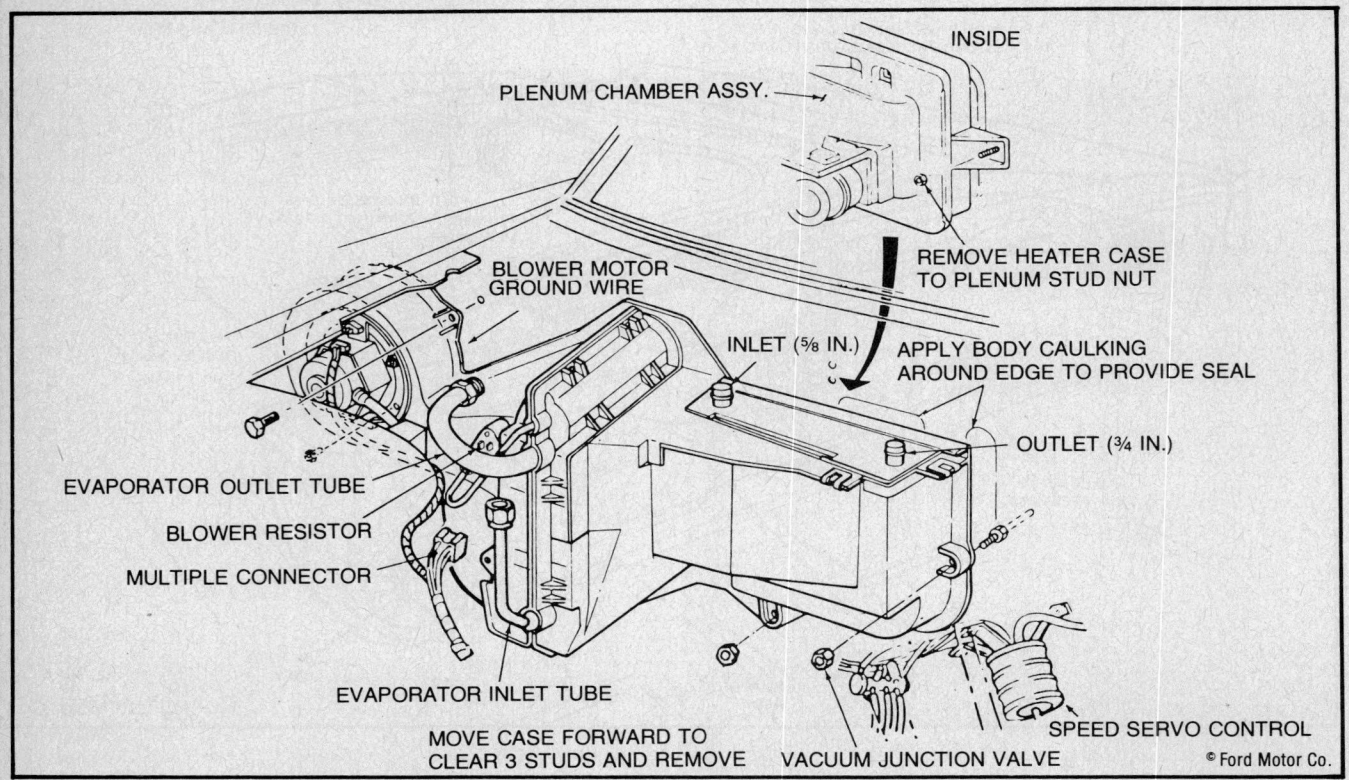

INSIDE

PLENUM CHAMBER ASSY.

REMOVE HEATER CASE TO PLENUM STUD NUT

BLOWER MOTOR GROUND WIRE

INLET (⅝ IN.)

APPLY BODY CAULKING AROUND EDGE TO PROVIDE SEAL

OUTLET (¾ IN.)

EVAPORATOR OUTLET TUBE

BLOWER RESISTOR

MULTIPLE CONNECTOR

EVAPORATOR INLET TUBE

MOVE CASE FORWARD TO CLEAR 3 STUDS AND REMOVE

VACUUM JUNCTION VALVE

SPEED SERVO CONTROL

© Ford Motor Co.

Granada and Monarch heater installation

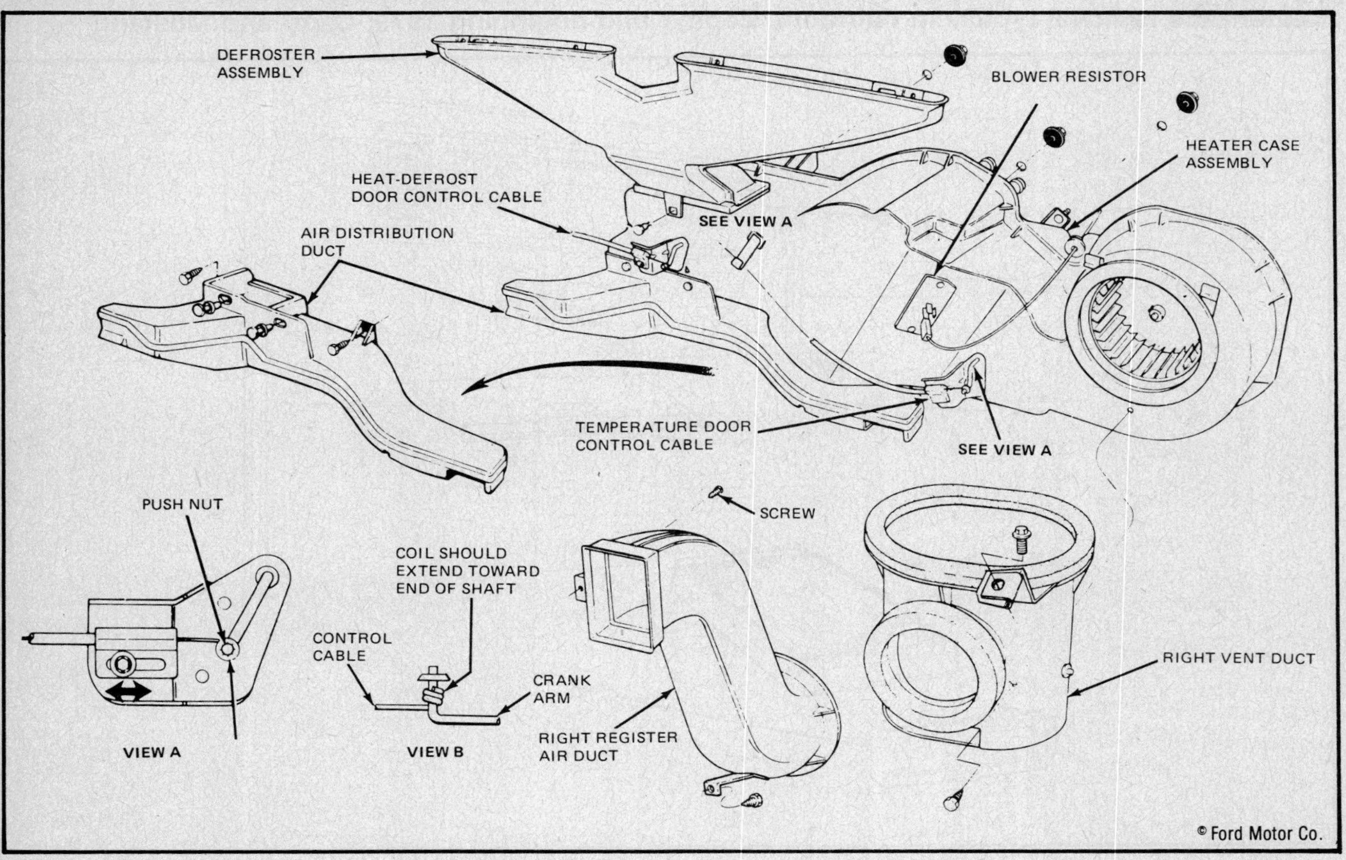

DEFROSTER ASSEMBLY

BLOWER RESISTOR

HEATER CASE ASSEMBLY

HEAT-DEFROST DOOR CONTROL CABLE

SEE VIEW A

AIR DISTRIBUTION DUCT

TEMPERATURE DOOR CONTROL CABLE

SEE VIEW A

PUSH NUT

SCREW

COIL SHOULD EXTEND TOWARD END OF SHAFT

CONTROL CABLE

CRANK ARM

RIGHT REGISTER AIR DUCT

RIGHT VENT DUCT

VIEW A

VIEW B

© Ford Motor Co.

Vacuum hose routing—Granada, Monarch & Versailles

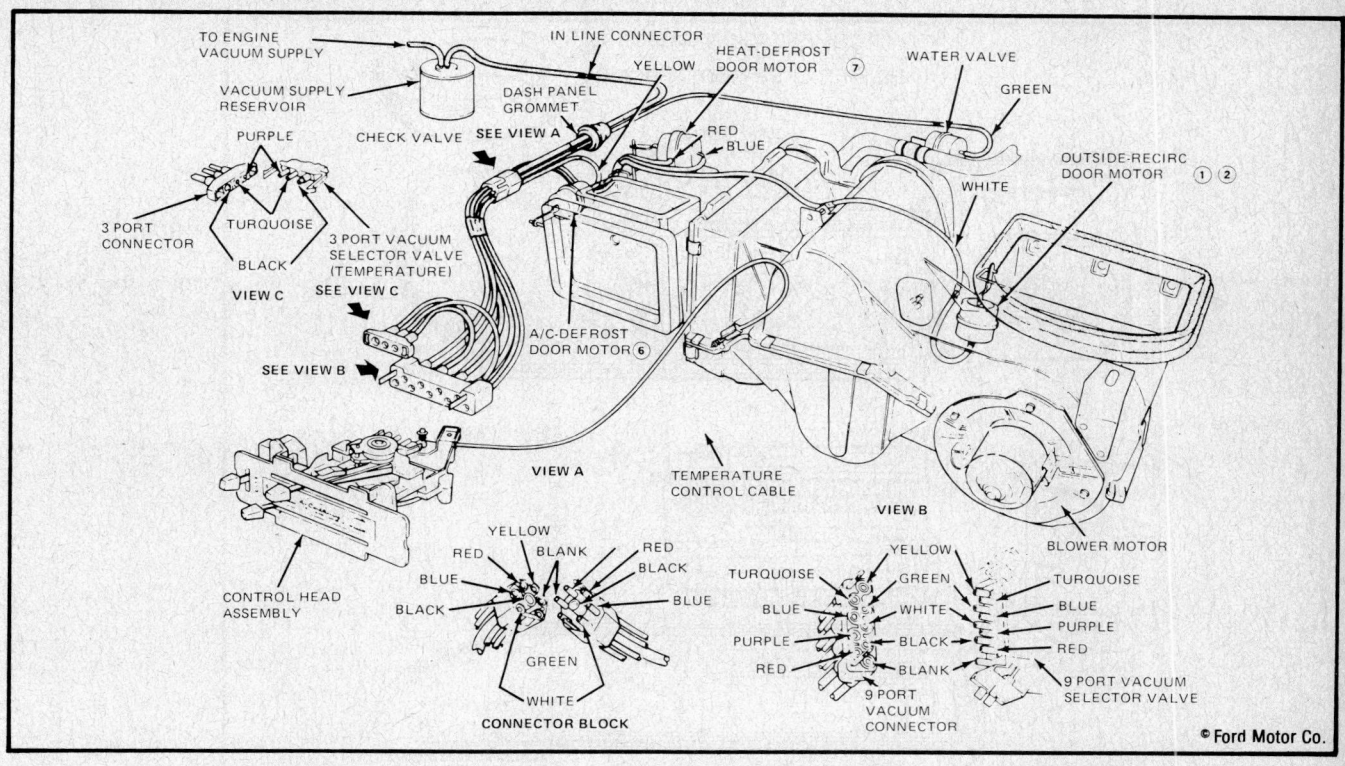

Manual air conditioner/heater temperature sensor

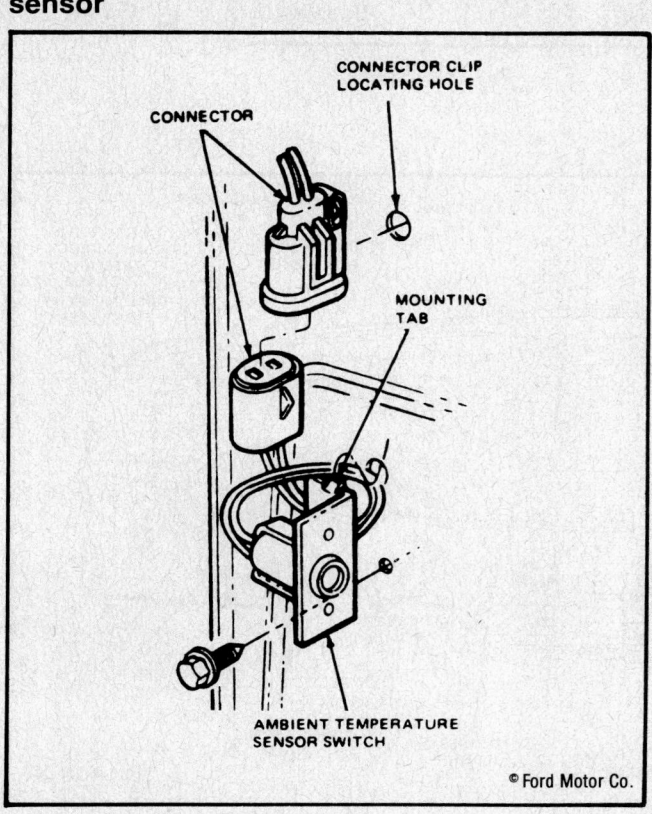

Lincoln Continental heater core removal

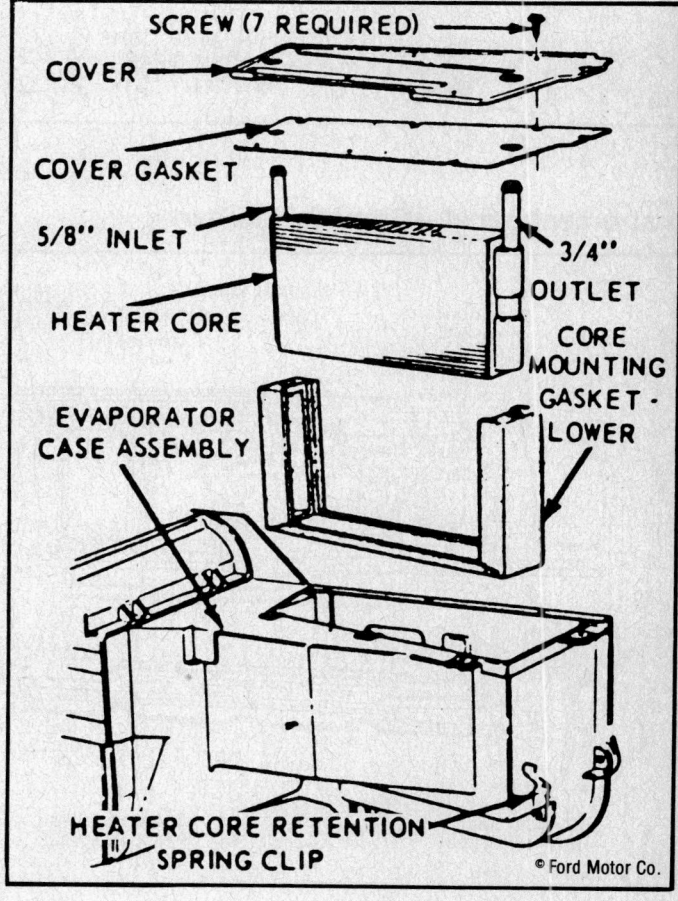

FORD—LINCOLN—MERCURY REAR DRIVE CARS

Heater core mounting typical in subcompact car models

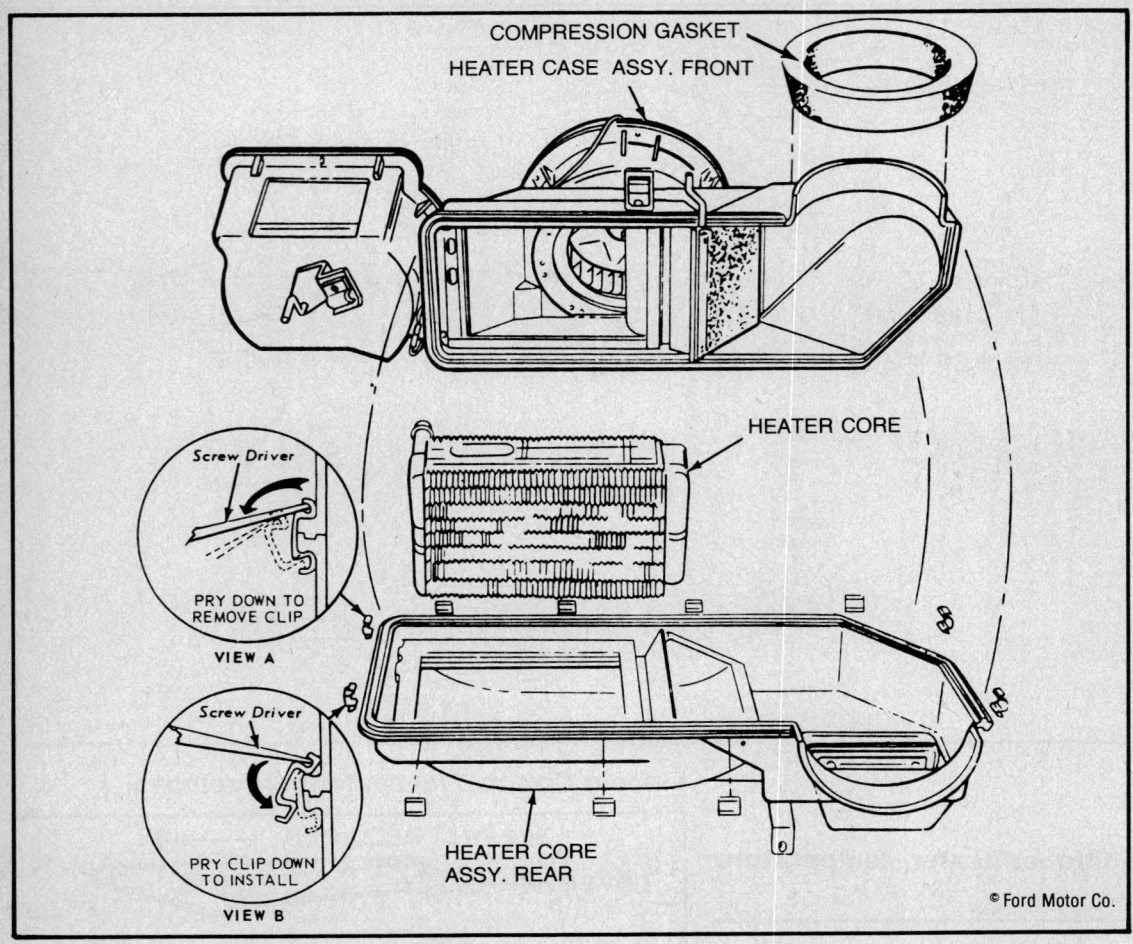

COMPRESSION GASKET
HEATER CASE ASSY. FRONT

HEATER CORE

Screw Driver

PRY DOWN TO
REMOVE CLIP

VIEW A

Screw Driver

PRY CLIP DOWN
TO INSTALL

VIEW B

HEATER CORE
ASSY. REAR

© Ford Motor Co.

Instrument panel—Granada/Cougar

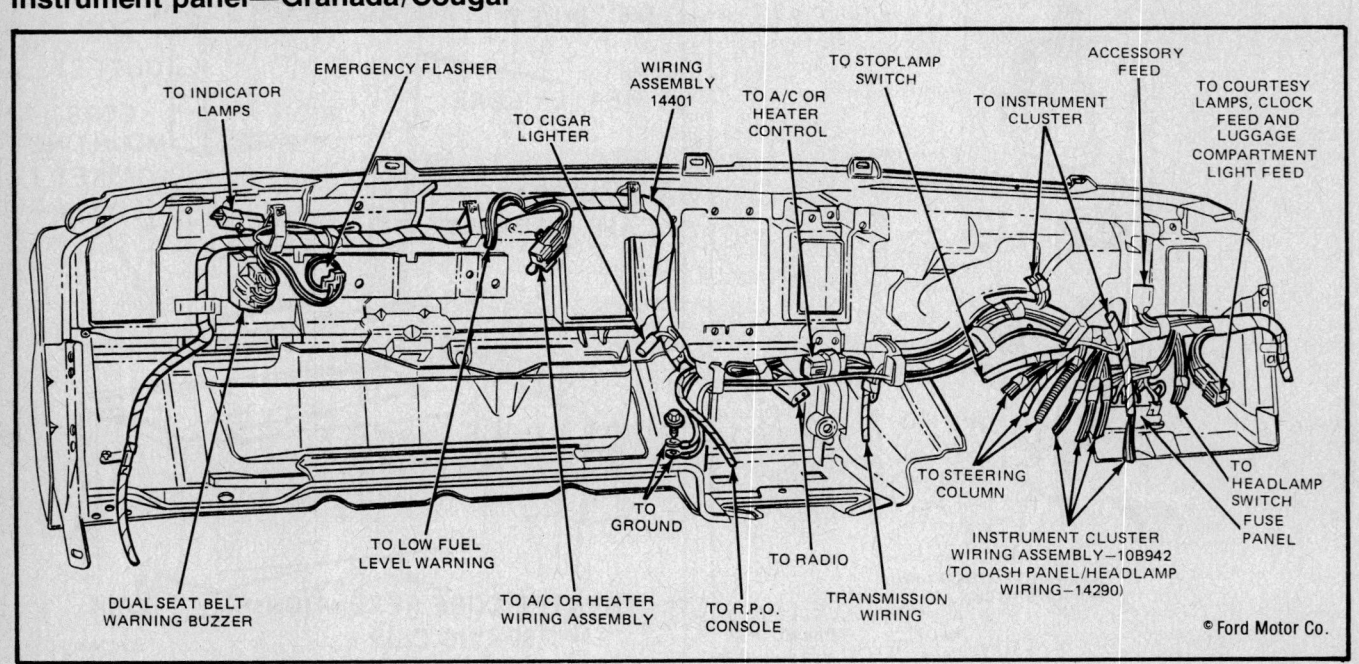

TO INDICATOR
LAMPS

EMERGENCY FLASHER

TO CIGAR
LIGHTER

WIRING
ASSEMBLY
14401

TO A/C OR
HEATER
CONTROL

TO STOPLAMP
SWITCH

ACCESSORY
FEED

TO INSTRUMENT
CLUSTER

TO COURTESY
LAMPS, CLOCK
FEED AND
LUGGAGE
COMPARTMENT
LIGHT FEED

TO STEERING
COLUMN

TO
HEADLAMP
SWITCH
FUSE
PANEL

DUAL SEAT BELT
WARNING BUZZER

TO LOW FUEL
LEVEL WARNING

TO A/C OR HEATER
WIRING ASSEMBLY

TO
GROUND

TO R.P.O.
CONSOLE

TO RADIO

TRANSMISSION
WIRING

INSTRUMENT CLUSTER
WIRING ASSEMBLY—10B942
(TO DASH PANEL/HEADLAMP
WIRING—14290)

© Ford Motor Co.

Instrument panel wire harness—Mustang/Capri

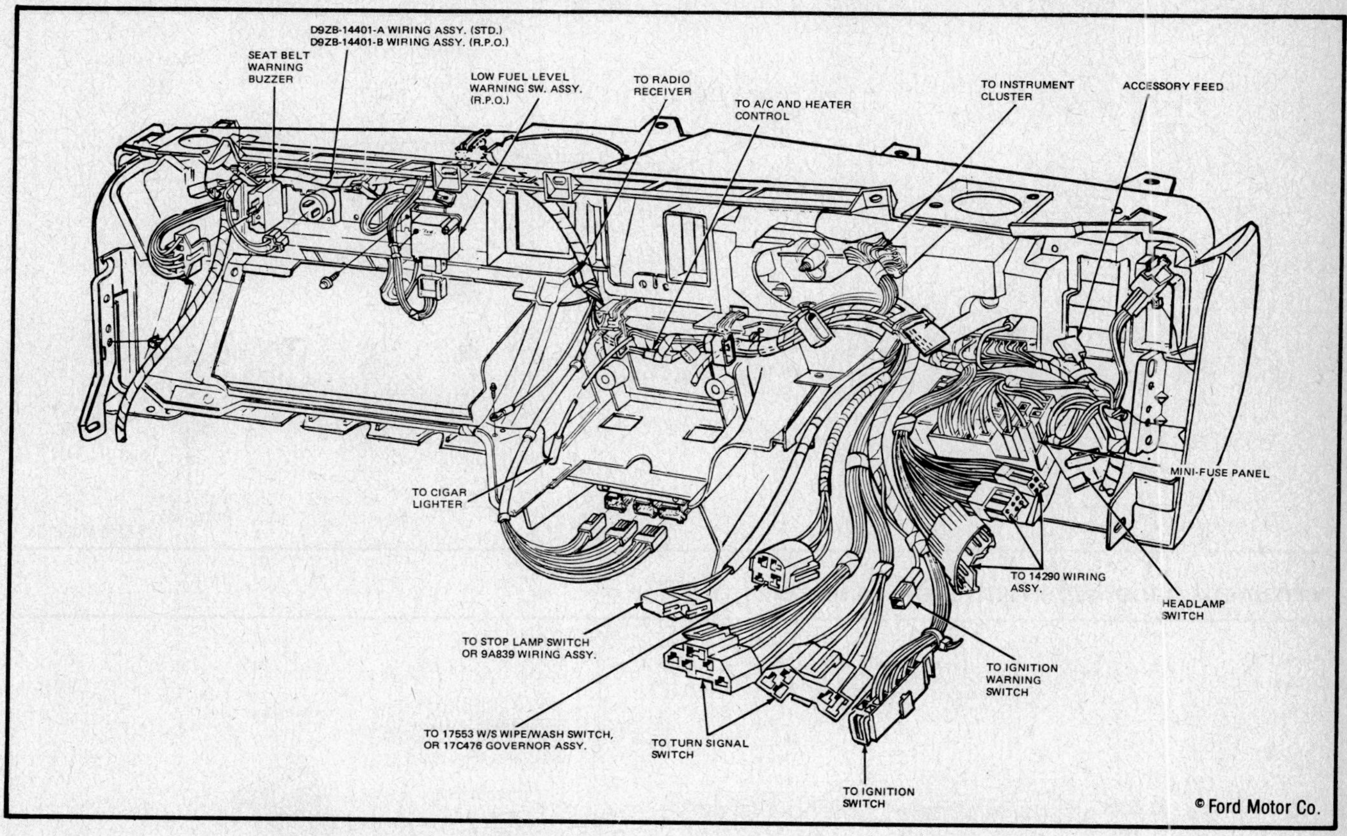

D9ZB-14401-A WIRING ASSY. (STD.)
D9ZB-14401-B WIRING ASSY. (R.P.O.)

SEAT BELT WARNING BUZZER

LOW FUEL LEVEL WARNING SW. ASSY. (R.P.O.)

TO RADIO RECEIVER

TO A/C AND HEATER CONTROL

TO INSTRUMENT CLUSTER

ACCESSORY FEED

MINI-FUSE PANEL

TO CIGAR LIGHTER

TO 14290 WIRING ASSY.

HEADLAMP SWITCH

TO STOP LAMP SWITCH OR 9A839 WIRING ASSY.

TO IGNITION WARNING SWITCH

TO 17553 W/S WIPE/WASH SWITCH, OR 17C476 GOVERNOR ASSY.

TO TURN SIGNAL SWITCH

TO IGNITION SWITCH

© Ford Motor Co.

Instrument panel wire harness—Fairmont/Zephyr

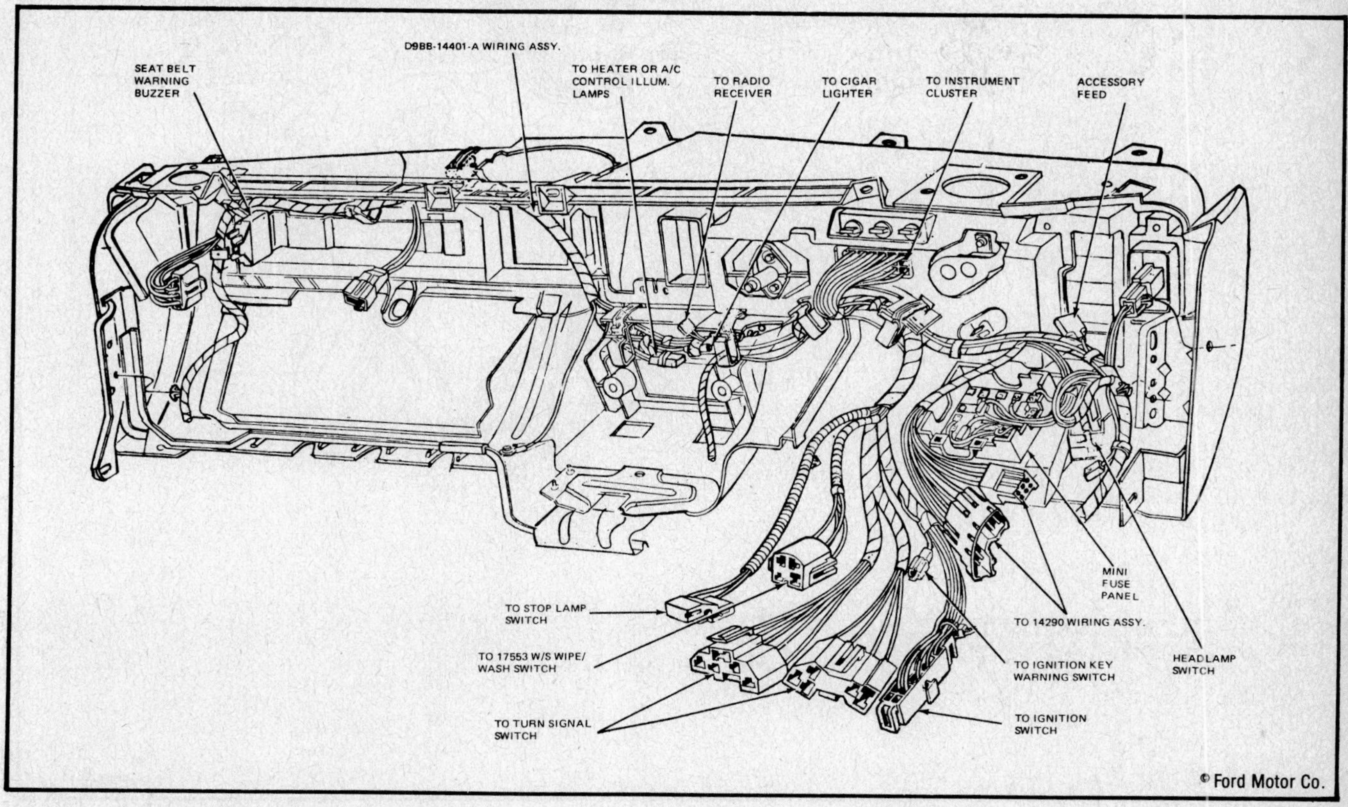

SEAT BELT WARNING BUZZER

D9BB-14401-A WIRING ASSY.

TO HEATER OR A/C CONTROL ILLUM. LAMPS

TO RADIO RECEIVER

TO CIGAR LIGHTER

TO INSTRUMENT CLUSTER

ACCESSORY FEED

MINI FUSE PANEL

TO 14290 WIRING ASSY.

HEADLAMP SWITCH

TO STOP LAMP SWITCH

TO 17553 W/S WIPE/WASH SWITCH

TO IGNITION KEY WARNING SWITCH

TO TURN SIGNAL SWITCH

TO IGNITION SWITCH

© Ford Motor Co.

Bobcat and Pinto typical instrument cluster

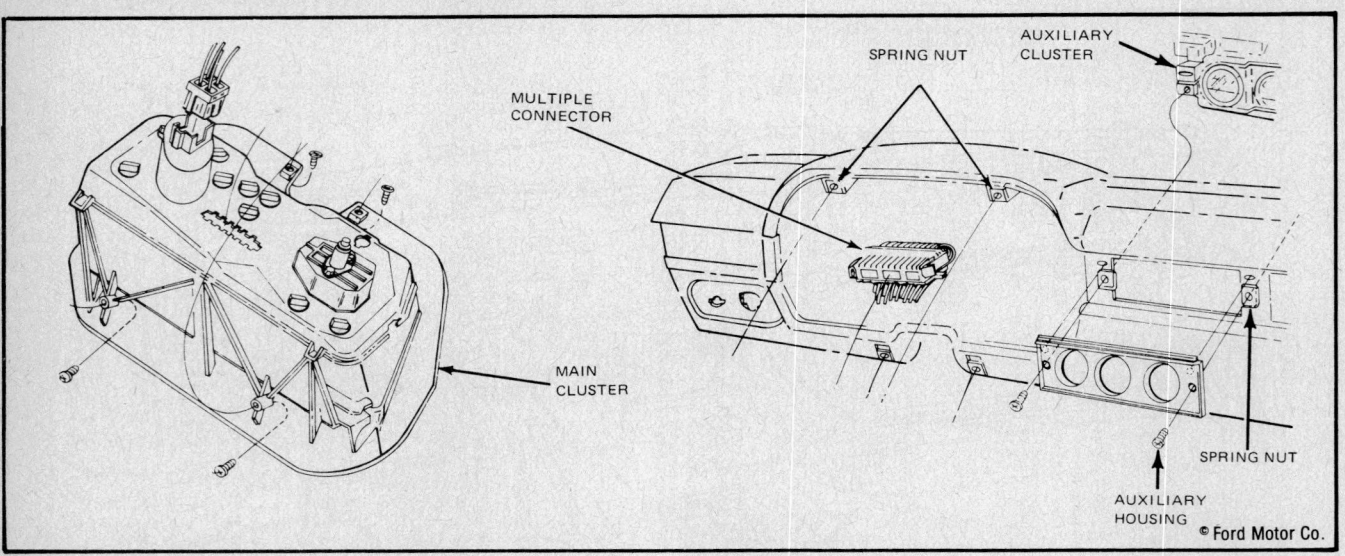

SPRING NUT

AUXILIARY CLUSTER

MULTIPLE CONNECTOR

MAIN CLUSTER

SPRING NUT

AUXILIARY HOUSING

© Ford Motor Co.

Instrument panel wire harness—Thunderbird/XR7

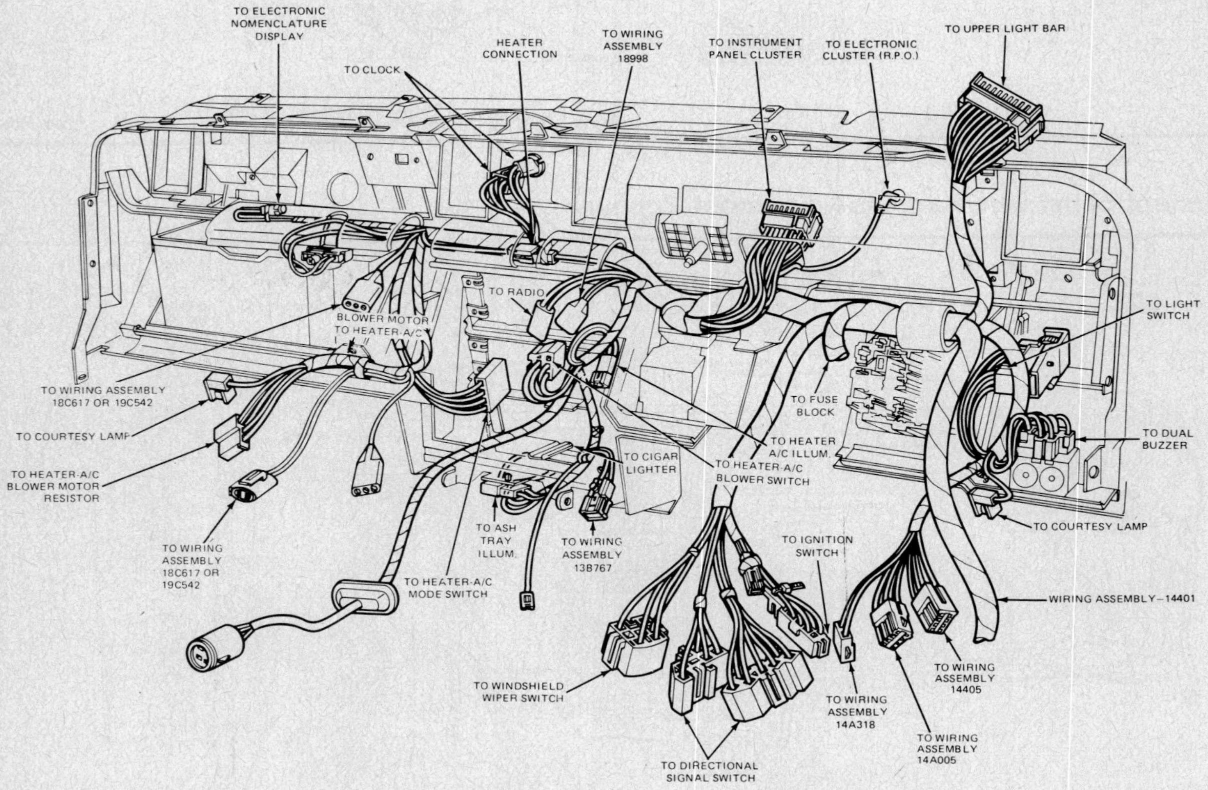

TO ELECTRONIC NOMENCLATURE DISPLAY

TO CLOCK

HEATER CONNECTION

TO WIRING ASSEMBLY 18998

TO INSTRUMENT PANEL CLUSTER

TO ELECTRONIC CLUSTER (R.P.O.)

TO UPPER LIGHT BAR

TO RADIO

BLOWER MOTOR TO HEATER-A/C

TO WIRING ASSEMBLY 18C617 OR 19C542

TO COURTESY LAMP

TO HEATER-A/C BLOWER MOTOR RESISTOR

TO WIRING ASSEMBLY 18C617 OR 19C542

TO FUSE BLOCK

TO HEATER A/C ILLUM.

TO LIGHT SWITCH

TO DUAL BUZZER

TO CIGAR LIGHTER

TO HEATER-A/C BLOWER SWITCH

TO COURTESY LAMP

TO ASH TRAY ILLUM.

TO WIRING ASSEMBLY 13B767

TO HEATER-A/C MODE SWITCH

TO IGNITION SWITCH

WIRING ASSEMBLY—14401

TO WIRING ASSEMBLY 14405

TO WINDSHIELD WIPER SWITCH

TO DIRECTIONAL SIGNAL SWITCH

TO WIRING ASSEMBLY 14A318

TO WIRING ASSEMBLY 14A005

NOTE: VEHICLE ELECTRICAL SYSTEM TESTING IS ACCOMPLISHED BY A.A.D. IN ACCORDANCE WITH SPECIFICATION ES-D9VB-14A228-AA (ELECTRICAL SYSTEM CERTIFICATION) USING THE V.E.T.S. (VEHICLE ELECTRICAL TEST SYSTEM) FOR CHICAGO PLANT ONLY.

© Ford Motor Co.

ENGINE SECTION

Water Pump

- Drain the cooling system.
- Remove fan shroud, drive belts, alternator, radiator, timing belt cover, etc. for access to water pump.

Fuel Pump

- When installing, crank the engine until the camshaft eccentric lobe is out of the way of the fuel pump rocker arm.
- When installing on a four cylinder engine, be sure the pushrod is correctly positioned against the pump actuating lever.

Fuel pump used with eight cylinder engines

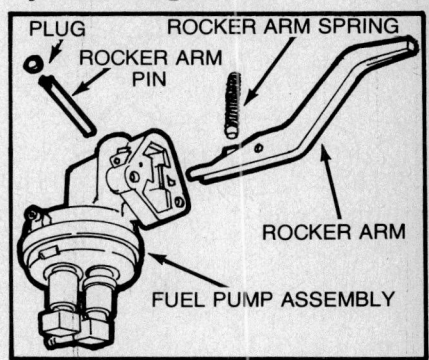

Water pump and thermostat installation on 2800 cc six cylinder engine

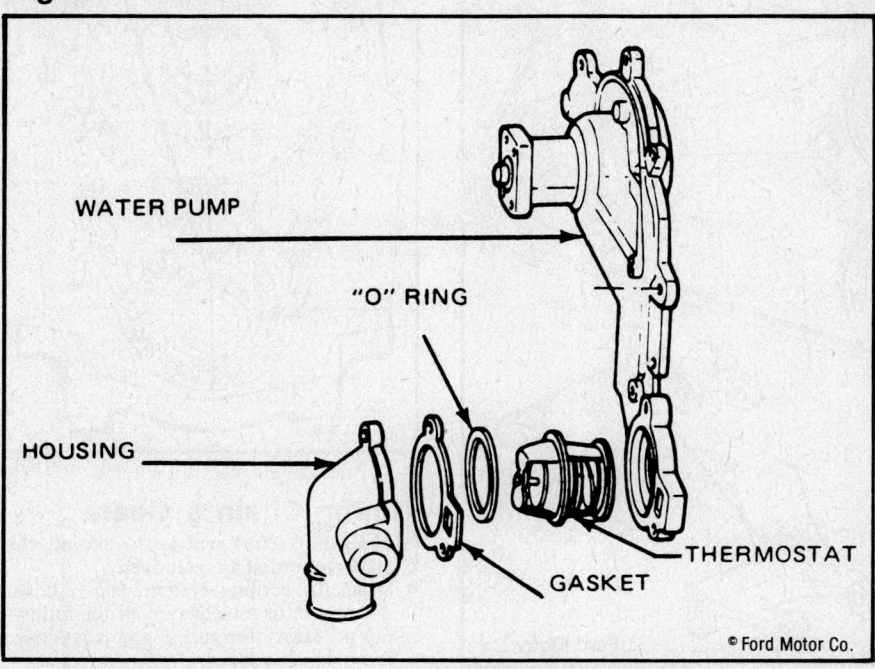

© Ford Motor Co.

Fuel pump mounting on 2300 cc engine

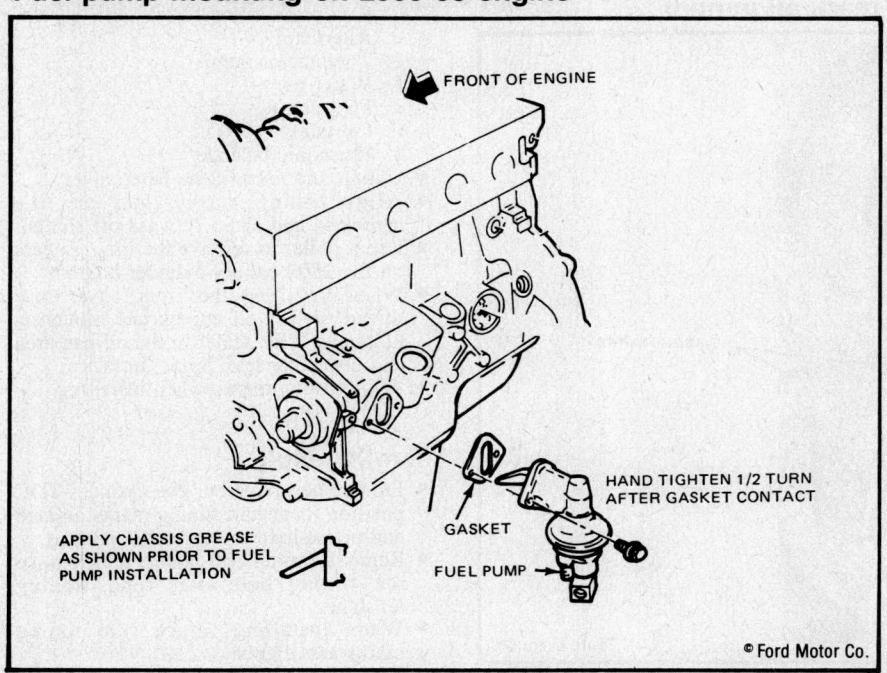

© Ford Motor Co.

Tank mounted electric fuel pump used in some car models

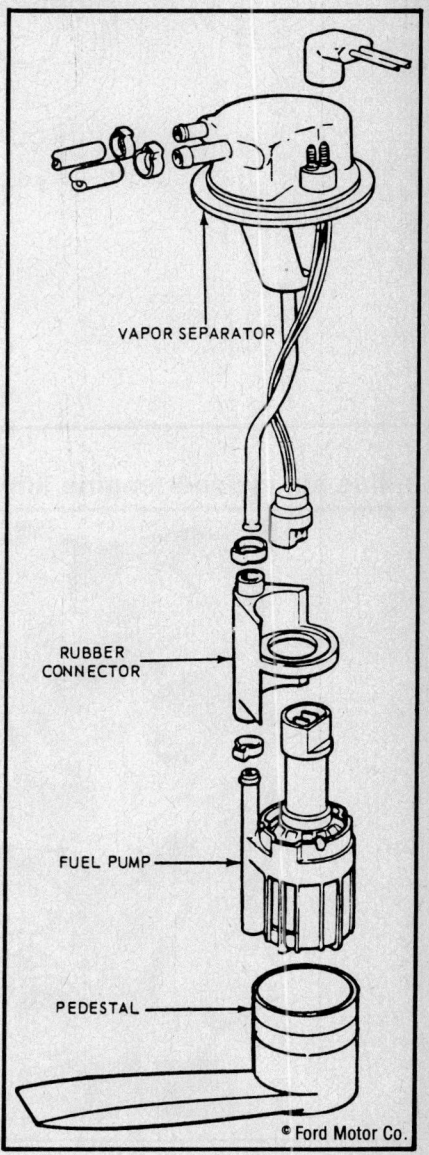

© Ford Motor Co.

Serpentine drive belt removal

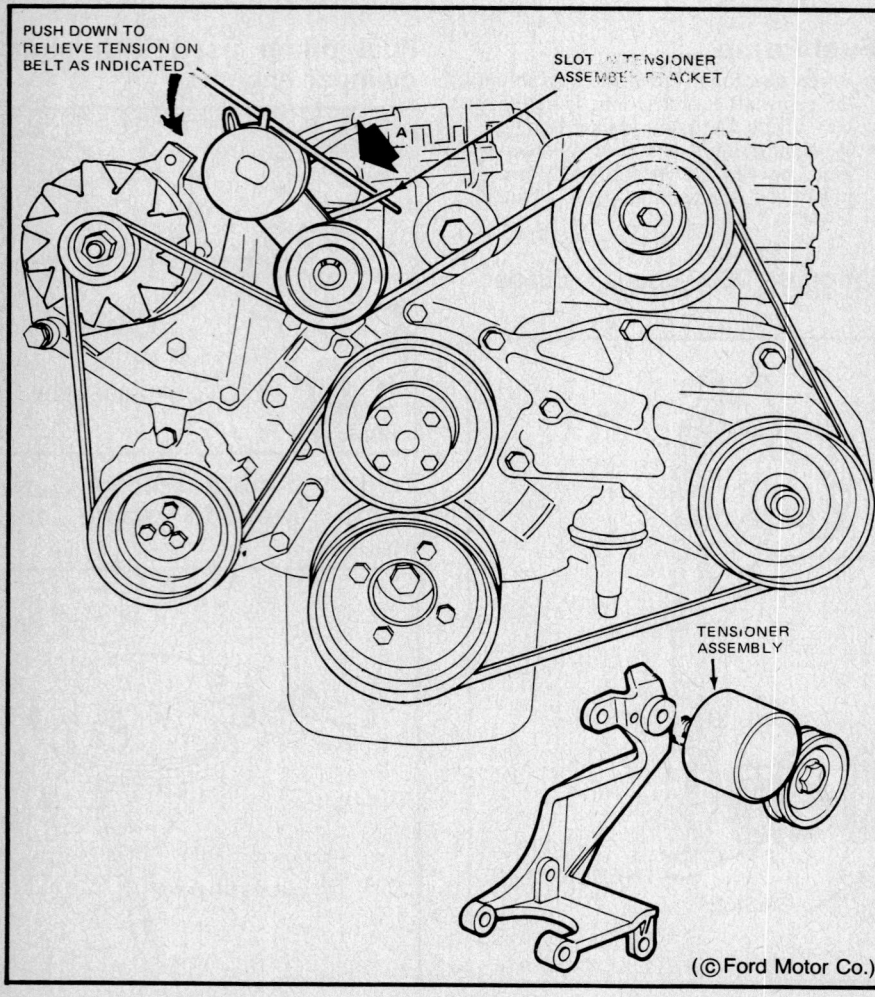

PUSH DOWN TO RELIEVE TENSION ON BELT AS INDICATED

SLOT IN TENSIONER ASSEMBLY BRACKET

TENSIONER ASSEMBLY

(© Ford Motor Co.)

In-line six cylinder engine timing mark alignment

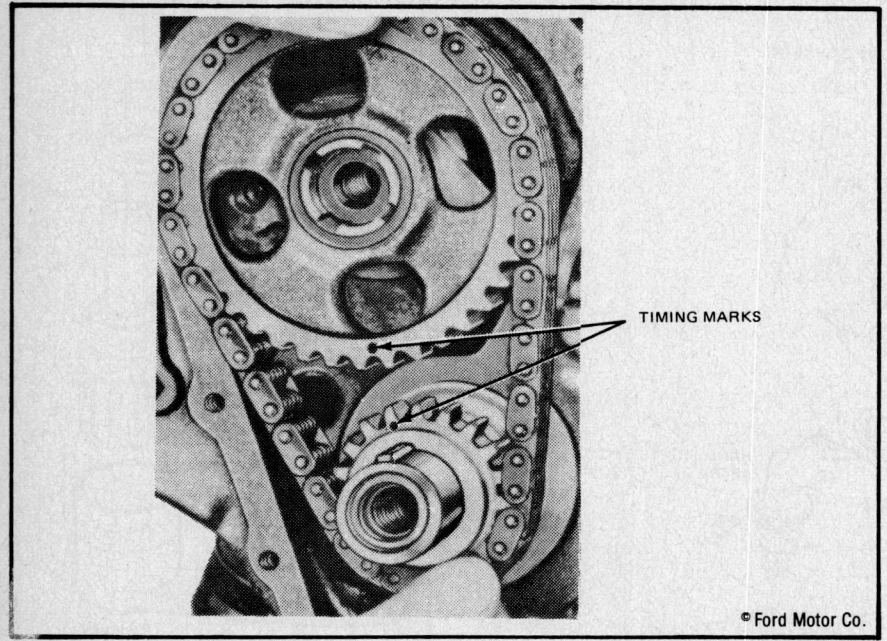

TIMING MARKS

© Ford Motor Co.

Eight cylinder engine timing mark alignment

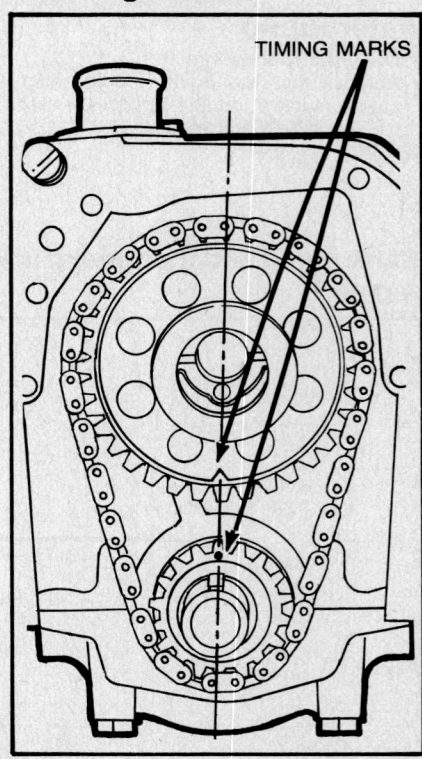

TIMING MARKS

Timing Chain & Gears

NOTE: For front seal replacement, the front cover must be removed.

- Drain the cooling system, and remove, disconnect or relocate any of the following necessary for access and front cover removal clearance:
  - a. Radiator
  - b. Heater and radiator hoses
  - c. Fan, pulleys and belts
  - d. Alternator
  - e. Thermactor pump
  - f. Water pump
  - g. Fuel pump
  - h. Oil pan
  - i. Harmonic balancer
- Unbolt and remove the front cover.
- Align timing marks, and pry the sprockets and chain forward off shafts.
- Use a puller to remove the timing gears on the 2800 cc, six cylinder engine.
- When installing the front cover, use thread sealant on appropriate mounting bolts and RTV sealer in the oil pan area and any other leak prone areas.
- Align timing marks when installing.

Timing Belt

- Put engine in number one cylinder TDC position (camshaft timing marks aligned and crankshaft timing mark on zero).
- Remove timing belt cover, and remove the timing belt after repositioning tensioner.
- When installing, make sure timing marks are aligned.

V6 engine timing marks alignment

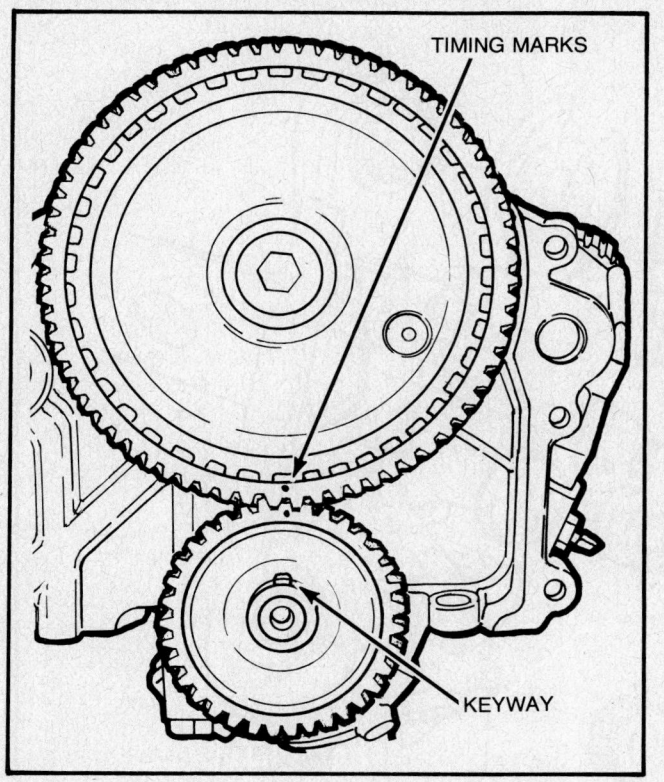

TIMING MARKS

KEYWAY

Water pump, thermostat and inner timing belt cover on 2300 cc engine

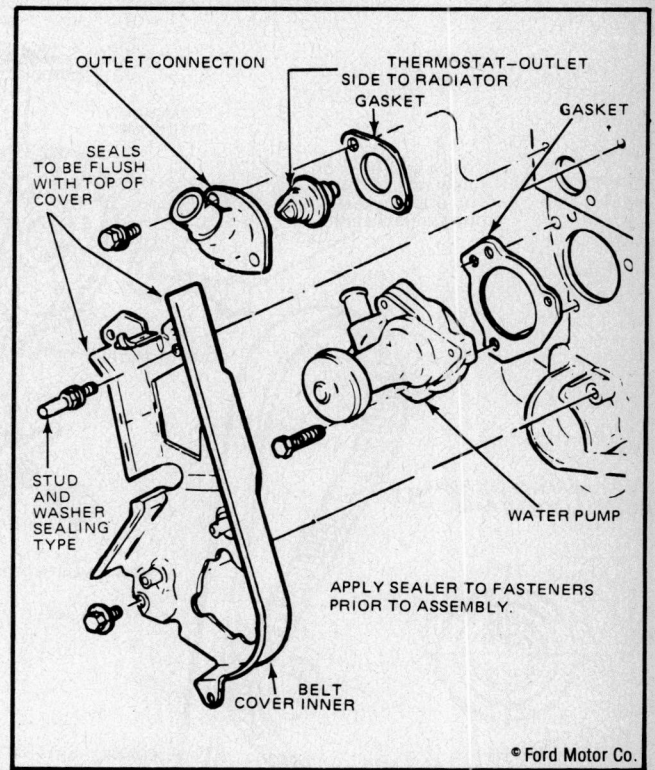

OUTLET CONNECTION

THERMOSTAT–OUTLET SIDE TO RADIATOR GASKET

GASKET

SEALS TO BE FLUSH WITH TOP OF COVER

STUD AND WASHER SEALING TYPE

WATER PUMP

APPLY SEALER TO FASTENERS PRIOR TO ASSEMBLY.

BELT COVER INNER

© Ford Motor Co.

2300 cc engine timing belt covers and attaching parts

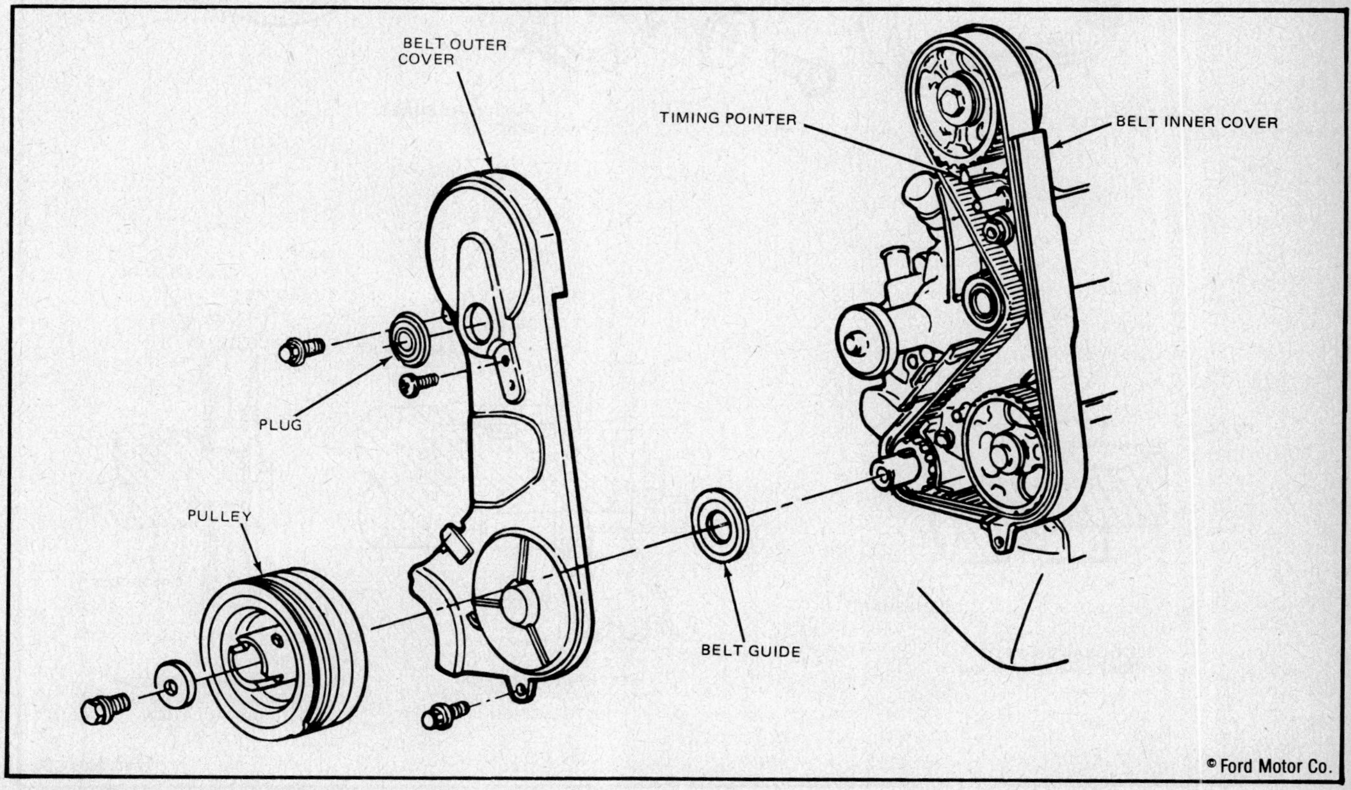

BELT OUTER COVER

TIMING POINTER

BELT INNER COVER

PLUG

PULLEY

BELT GUIDE

© Ford Motor Co.

Installing timing belt, sprockets and tensioner in 2300 cc engine

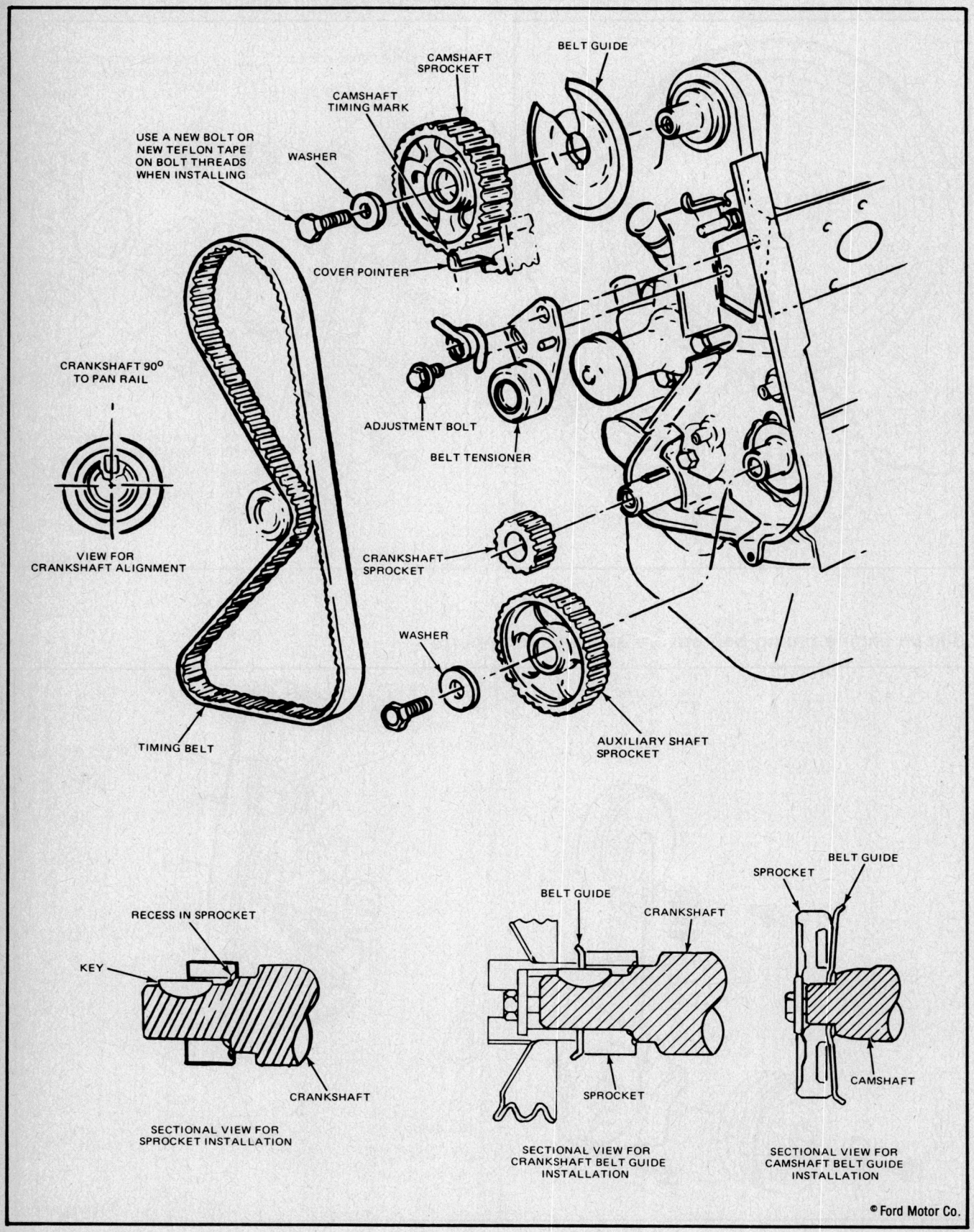

BELT GUIDE

CAMSHAFT
SPROCKET

CAMSHAFT
TIMING MARK

USE A NEW BOLT OR
NEW TEFLON TAPE
ON BOLT THREADS
WHEN INSTALLING

WASHER

COVER POINTER

CRANKSHAFT 90°
TO PAN RAIL

VIEW FOR
CRANKSHAFT ALIGNMENT

ADJUSTMENT BOLT

BELT TENSIONER

CRANKSHAFT
SPROCKET

WASHER

TIMING BELT

AUXILIARY SHAFT
SPROCKET

RECESS IN SPROCKET

KEY

CRANKSHAFT

SECTIONAL VIEW FOR
SPROCKET INSTALLATION

BELT GUIDE

CRANKSHAFT

SPROCKET

SECTIONAL VIEW FOR
CRANKSHAFT BELT GUIDE
INSTALLATION

BELT GUIDE

SPROCKET

CAMSHAFT

SECTIONAL VIEW FOR
CAMSHAFT BELT GUIDE
INSTALLATION

© Ford Motor Co.

Timing belt installation in 2300 cc engine

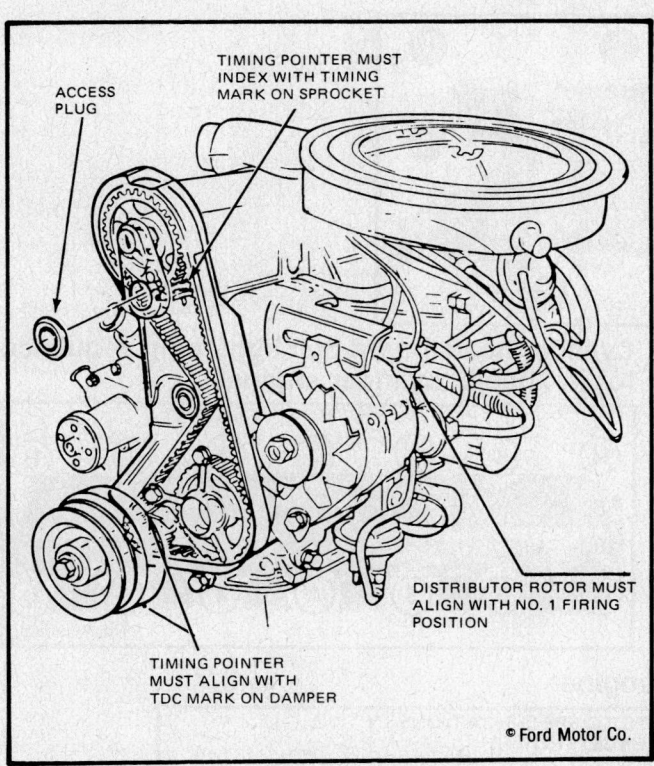

ACCESS PLUG

TIMING POINTER MUST INDEX WITH TIMING MARK ON SPROCKET

DISTRIBUTOR ROTOR MUST ALIGN WITH NO. 1 FIRING POSITION

TIMING POINTER MUST ALIGN WITH TDC MARK ON DAMPER

© Ford Motor Co.

Engine front mount typical with 250 CID, six cylinder engines

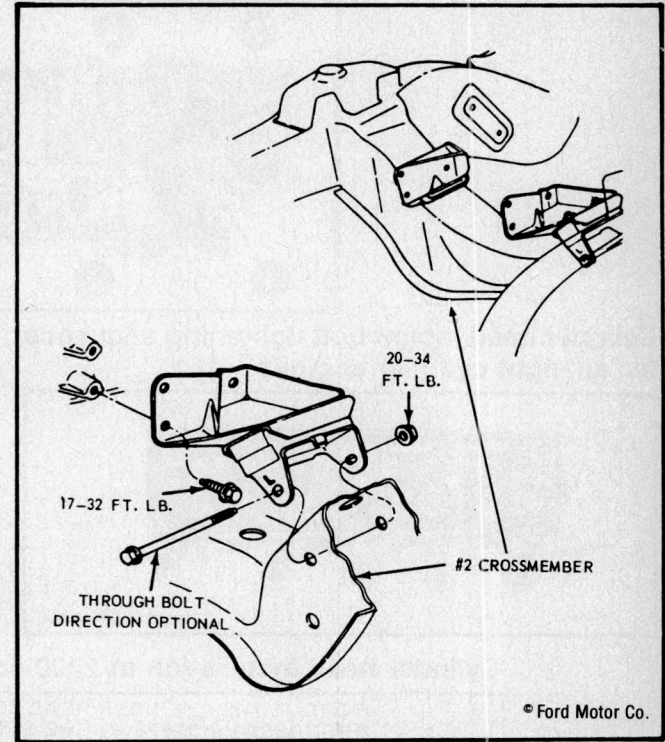

20—34 FT. LB.

17—32 FT. LB.

THROUGH BOLT DIRECTION OPTIONAL

#2 CROSSMEMBER

© Ford Motor Co.

Engine Mounts

- Support the engine either in the affected mount area or at the oil pan forward edge while changing an engine mount.

Cylinder Head

- Drain the cooling system, remove the intake manifold, and remove, relocate or disconnect any of the following applicable to a particular engine and necessary for access and clearance:
  a. Air conditioner compressor
  b. Power steering pump
  c. Alternator
  d. Exhaust manifold or pipe
  e. Timing belt cover
  f. Turbocharger and turbocharger plumbing
  g. Rocker arms and push rods
- On 429 and 460 CID engines, remove the cylinder head and exhaust manifold as an assembly.
- On 2300 cc engine, when installing, place camshaft locating pin at five o'clock position to minimize possible piston/valve contact.
- When installing, replace rocker arms and push rods in their original locations, and tighten cylinder head mount bolts in the prescribed sequence and to correct specifications.

2300 cc engine intake manifold mount bolt tightening sequence

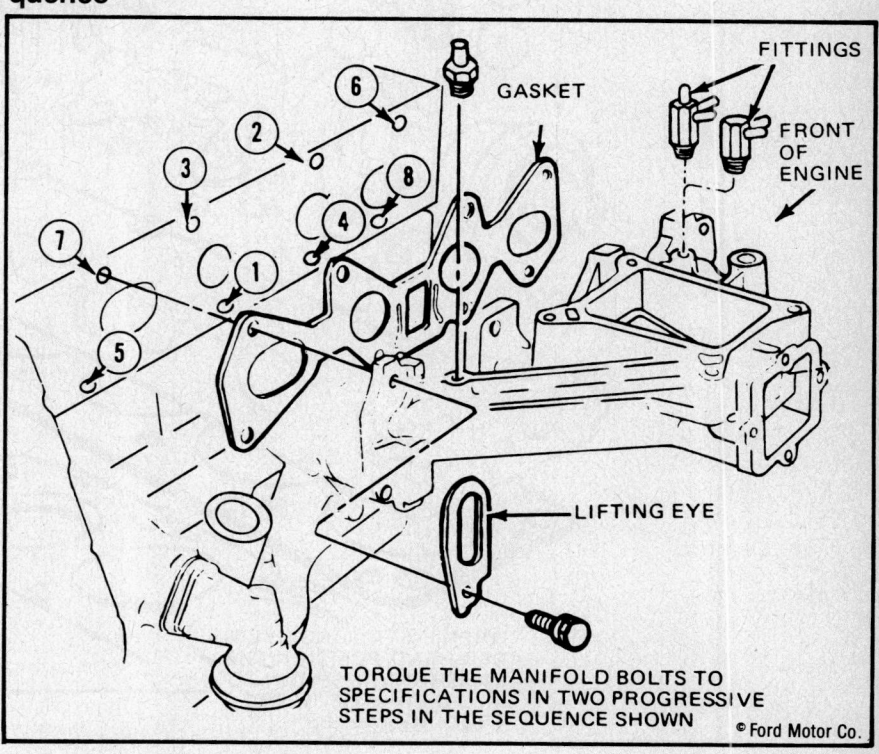

GASKET

FITTINGS

FRONT OF ENGINE

LIFTING EYE

TORQUE THE MANIFOLD BOLTS TO SPECIFICATIONS IN TWO PROGRESSIVE STEPS IN THE SEQUENCE SHOWN

© Ford Motor Co.

Intake manifold mount bolt tightening sequence in 2800 cc, six cylinder engines

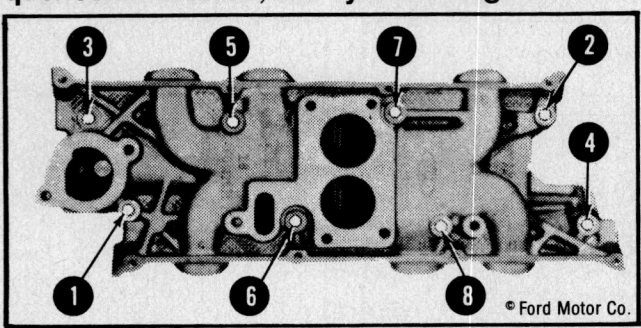

© Ford Motor Co.

Cylinder head mount bolt tightening sequence for all eight cylinder engines

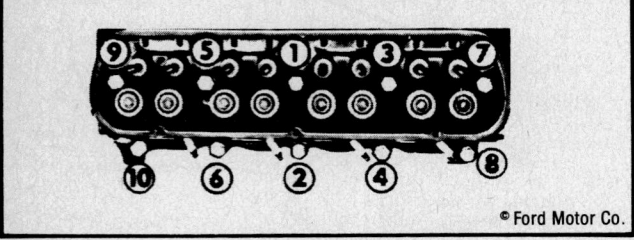

© Ford Motor Co.

Cylinder head mount bolt tightening sequence for in-line six cylinder engines

© Ford Motor Co.

Cylinder head installation in 2300 cc engine

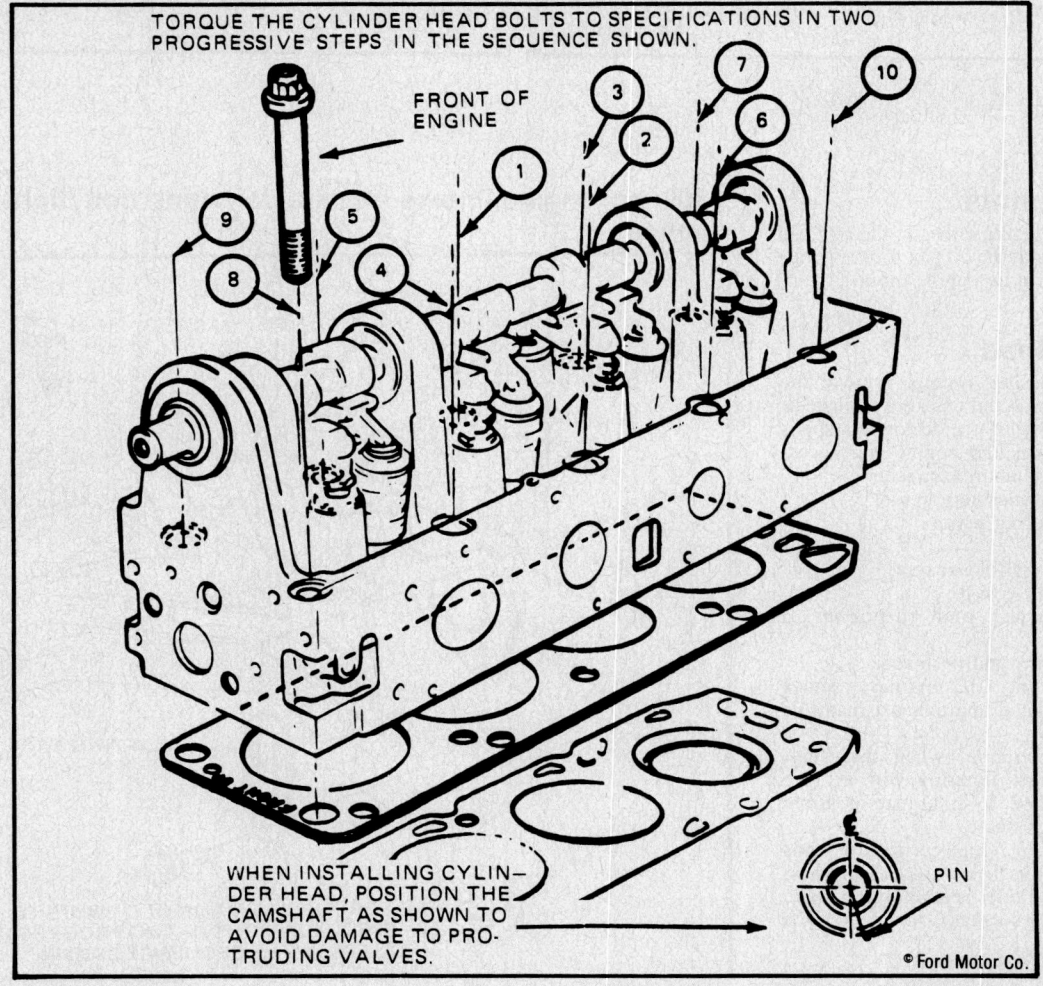

TORQUE THE CYLINDER HEAD BOLTS TO SPECIFICATIONS IN TWO PROGRESSIVE STEPS IN THE SEQUENCE SHOWN.

FRONT OF ENGINE

WHEN INSTALLING CYLINDER HEAD, POSITION THE CAMSHAFT AS SHOWN TO AVOID DAMAGE TO PROTRUDING VALVES.

PIN

© Ford Motor Co.

Intake manifold tightening sequence on all small block V-8 and 400 engines

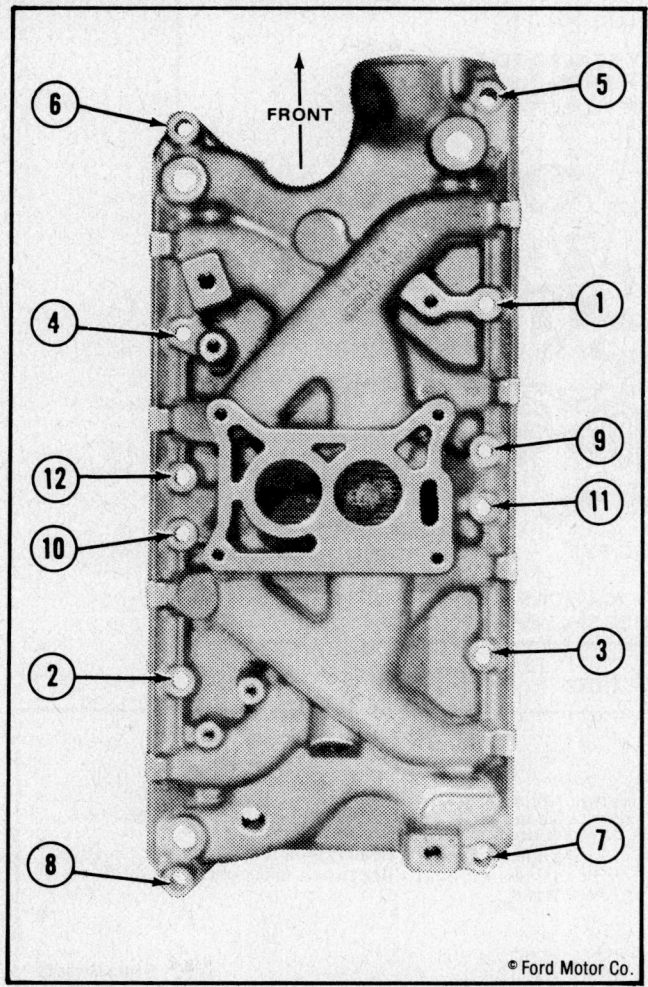

© Ford Motor Co.

Exhaust manifold mount bolt tightening sequence in 2800 cc, six cylinder engine

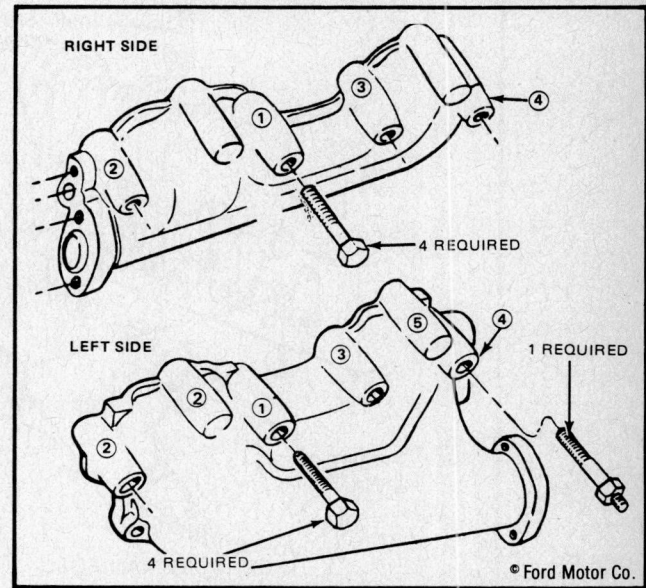

RIGHT SIDE
4 REQUIRED
LEFT SIDE
4 REQUIRED
1 REQUIRED
© Ford Motor Co.

Cylinder head mount bolt tightening sequence in 2800 cc, six cylinder engine

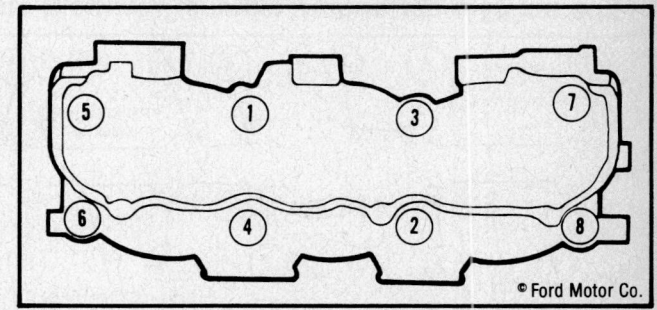

© Ford Motor Co.

429 and 460 CID engine intake manifold mount bolt tightening sequence

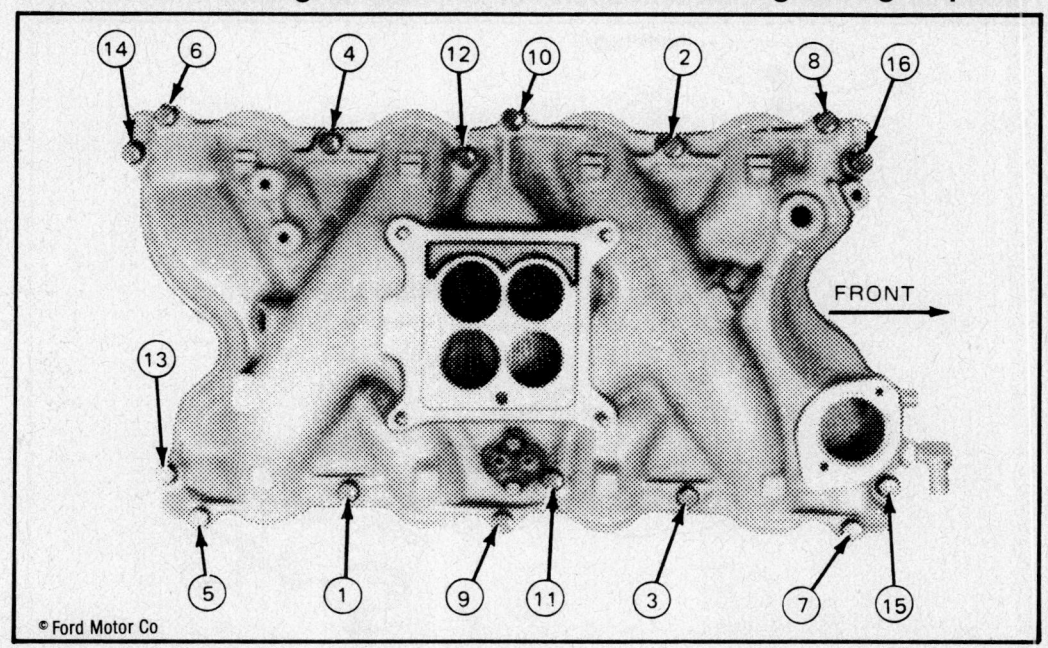

FRONT

© Ford Motor Co

FORD—LINCOLN—MERCURY REAR DRIVE CARS

2300 cc engine exhaust manifold mount bolt tightening sequence

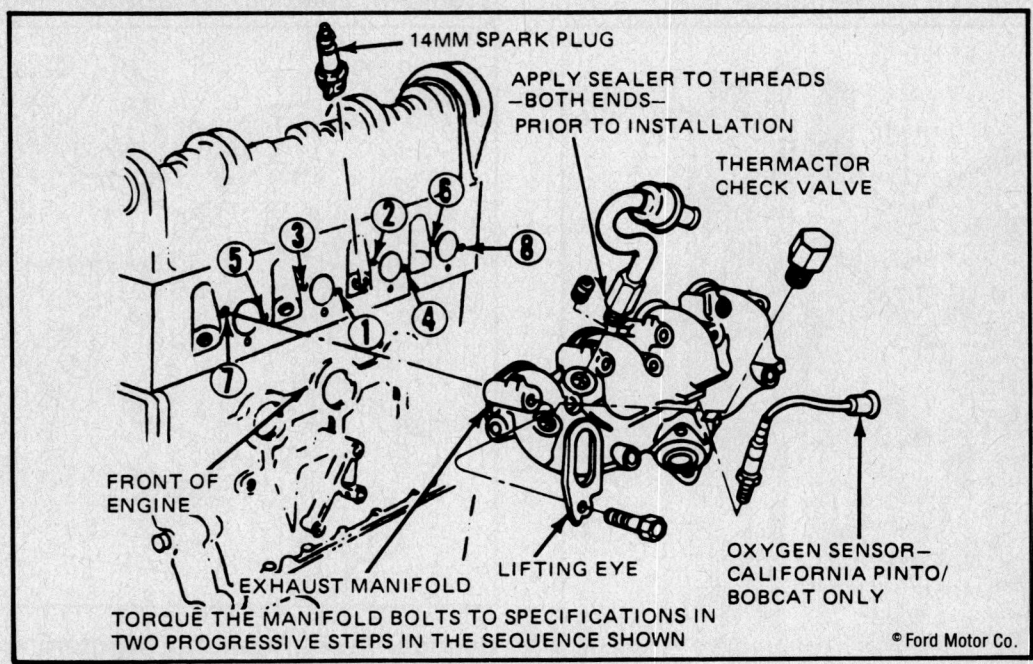

14MM SPARK PLUG

APPLY SEALER TO THREADS
—BOTH ENDS—
PRIOR TO INSTALLATION

THERMACTOR
CHECK VALVE

FRONT OF
ENGINE

EXHAUST MANIFOLD

LIFTING EYE

OXYGEN SENSOR—
CALIFORNIA PINTO/
BOBCAT ONLY

TORQUE THE MANIFOLD BOLTS TO SPECIFICATIONS IN
TWO PROGRESSIVE STEPS IN THE SEQUENCE SHOWN

© Ford Motor Co.

In-line six cylinder engine exhaust manifold installation

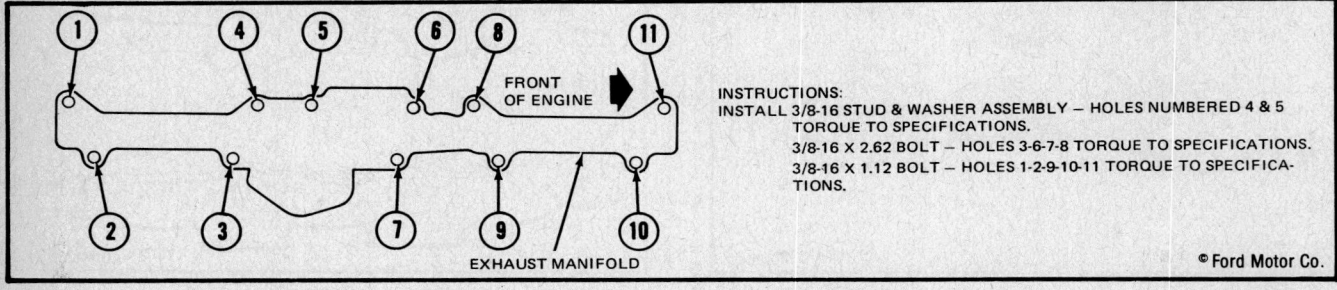

FRONT
OF ENGINE

EXHAUST MANIFOLD

INSTRUCTIONS:
INSTALL 3/8-16 STUD & WASHER ASSEMBLY — HOLES NUMBERED 4 & 5
TORQUE TO SPECIFICATIONS.
3/8-16 X 2.62 BOLT — HOLES 3-6-7-8 TORQUE TO SPECIFICATIONS.
3/8-16 X 1.12 BOLT — HOLES 1-2-9-10-11 TORQUE TO SPECIFICA-
TIONS.

© Ford Motor Co.

Turbocharger installation and operation on 2300 cc engine

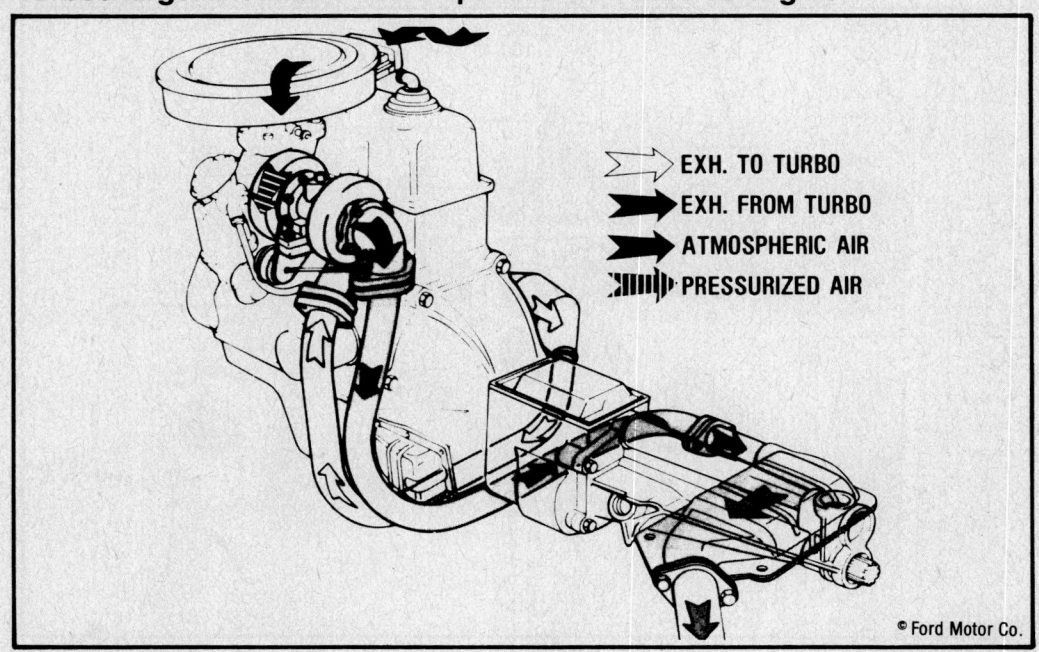

EXH. TO TURBO
EXH. FROM TURBO
ATMOSPHERIC AIR
PRESSURIZED AIR

© Ford Motor Co.

A424

Valve train installation—2300 cc engine

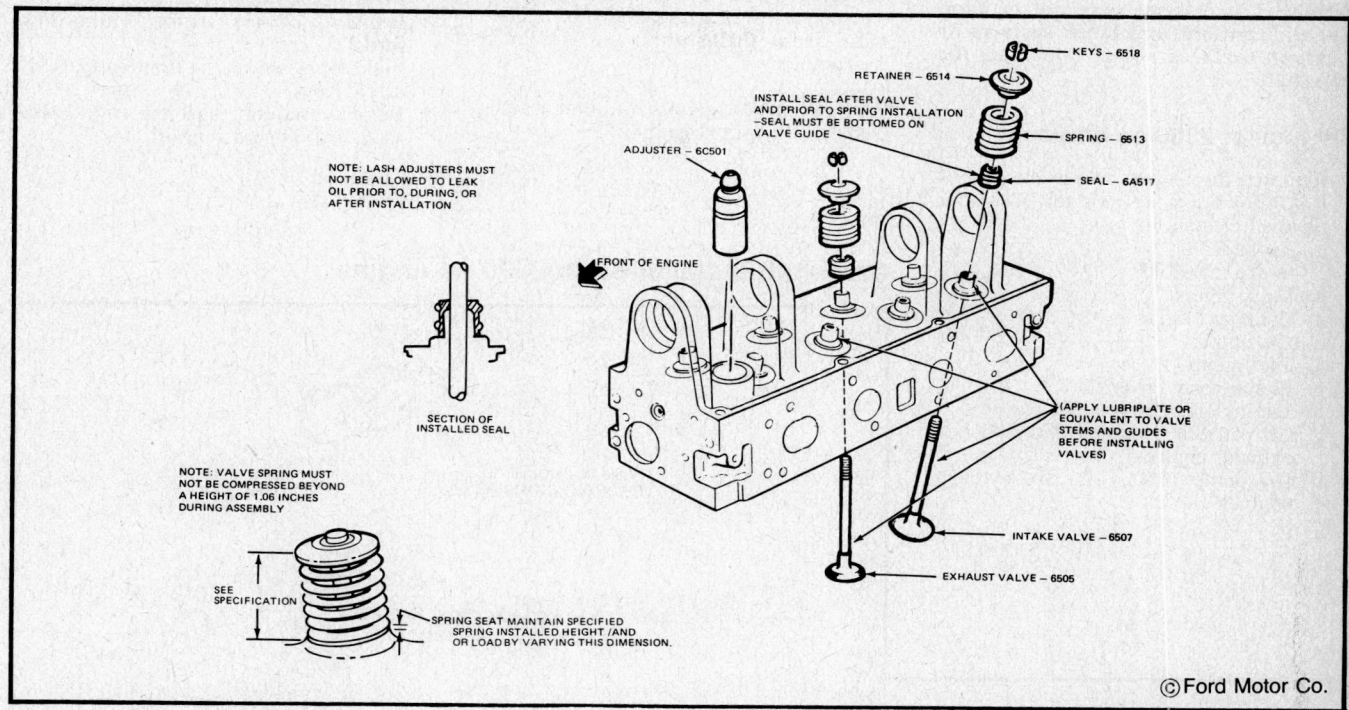

NOTE: LASH ADJUSTERS MUST NOT BE ALLOWED TO LEAK OIL PRIOR TO, DURING, OR AFTER INSTALLATION

FRONT OF ENGINE

ADJUSTER — 6C501

KEYS — 6518

RETAINER — 6514

INSTALL SEAL AFTER VALVE AND PRIOR TO SPRING INSTALLATION —SEAL MUST BE BOTTOMED ON VALVE GUIDE

SPRING — 6513

SEAL — 6A517

(APPLY LUBRIPLATE OR EQUIVALENT TO VALVE STEMS AND GUIDES BEFORE INSTALLING VALVES)

INTAKE VALVE — 6507

EXHAUST VALVE — 6505

SECTION OF INSTALLED SEAL

NOTE: VALVE SPRING MUST NOT BE COMPRESSED BEYOND A HEIGHT OF 1.06 INCHES DURING ASSEMBLY

SEE SPECIFICATION

SPRING SEAT MAINTAIN SPECIFIED SPRING INSTALLED HEIGHT AND OR LOAD BY VARYING THIS DIMENSION.

© Ford Motor Co.

Rocker Arms

NOTE: Always keep rocker arm components in order when removing. They must be reinstalled in exactly the same positions.

- On eight cylinder engines, remove the rocker arm nuts, fulcrum seats, etc., and remove the rocker arm.
- On six cylinder engines, remove the pin and spring washer from the rocker shaft ends and slide the rocker arms off the shaft.

Valve Adjustment
All Except 2800 cc Engines

- Hydraulic valve lifters are used, and no adjustment is necessary. Push rods are available in .060 overlength or underlength to compensate for valve train dimensional irregularities.

Valve Lifters

- On eight cylinder engines, remove the intake manifold, rocker arms and push rods, and use a magnet to raise valve lifters from their bores.

- On six cylinder engines, remove the cylinder head, and use a magnet to raise valve lifters from their bores.
- On the 1600 cc, four cylinder engine, the camshaft must first be removed and engine removal is required.

2800 cc Engine

- Adjust valves with engine cold to:
  Intake— .014 inch
  Exhaust— .016 inch
- Adjust the valves for each cylinder with that cylinder at TDC compression stroke.

Hydraulic tappets removal—six cylinder engines

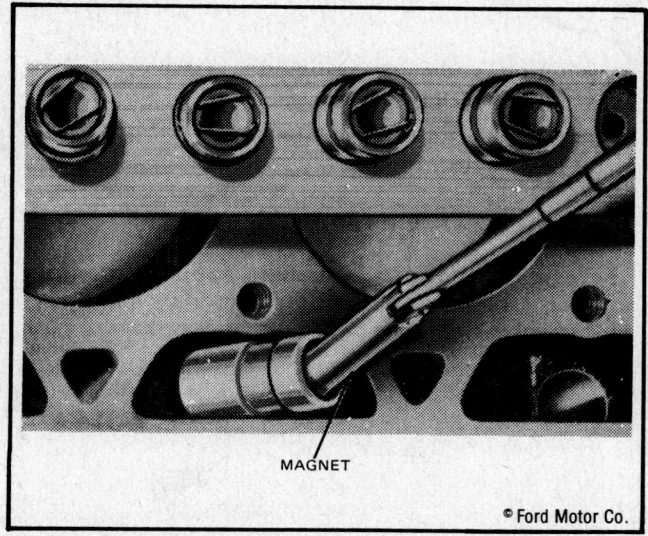

MAGNET

© Ford Motor Co.

Rocker arm assembly—255, 302 & 351 "W" engines

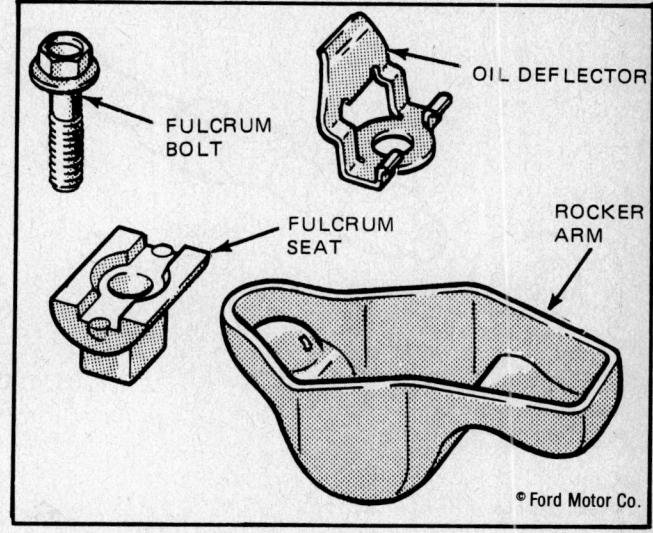

FULCRUM BOLT

OIL DEFLECTOR

FULCRUM SEAT

ROCKER ARM

© Ford Motor Co.

Camshaft

NOTE: Use extreme care not to damage the camshaft machined surfaces or bearing surfaces when removing the camshaft.

All Except 2300 cc Engines

- Remove, disconnect or relocate any of the following necessary for access or removal clearance:
  - a. Radiator
  - b. Intake manifold
  - c. Valve lifters
  - d. Cylinder heads
  - e. Distributor
  - f. Fuel pump
  - g. Engine front cover
  - h. Timing chain, sprockets, etc.
  - i. Oil pan (2800 cc and 250 CID, six cylinder engines)
  - j. Oil pump (250 CID, six cylinder engine)

- Slide the camshaft forward out of the bearing bores. It may be necessary in some cars to raise the engine or remove the front grille-work for sufficient clearance.

- Before installing, coat the entire camshaft with hypoid gear oil.

2300 cc Engines

- Remove the cylinder head.
- Remove rocker arms, timing belt sprocket, etc.
- Slide camshaft out the front on the 2300 cc engine.
- Before installing, coat the entire camshaft with hypoid gear oil.

Camshaft installation in 2300 cc engine

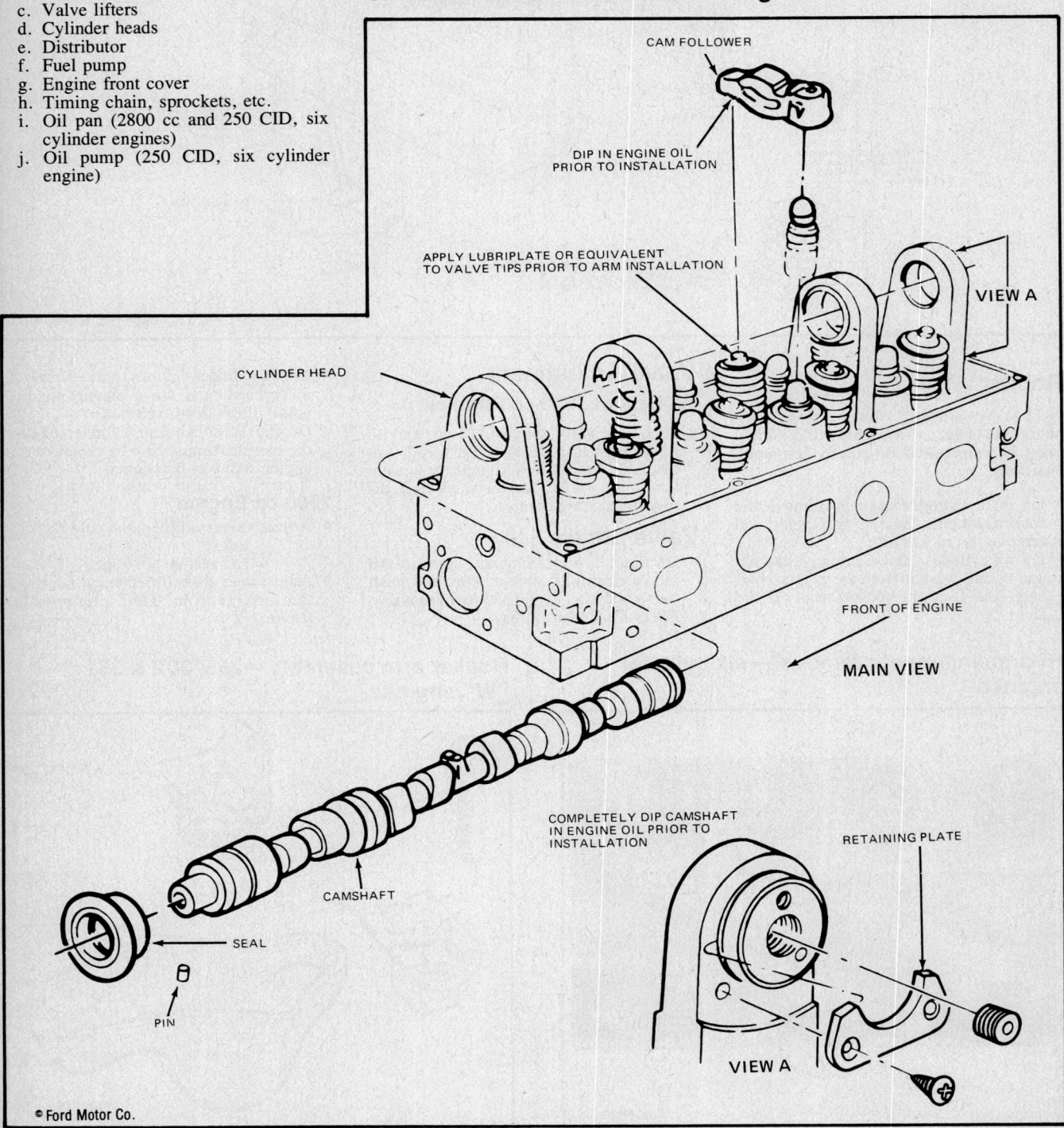

CAM FOLLOWER

DIP IN ENGINE OIL PRIOR TO INSTALLATION

APPLY LUBRIPLATE OR EQUIVALENT TO VALVE TIPS PRIOR TO ARM INSTALLATION

VIEW A

CYLINDER HEAD

FRONT OF ENGINE

MAIN VIEW

CAMSHAFT

SEAL

PIN

COMPLETELY DIP CAMSHAFT IN ENGINE OIL PRIOR TO INSTALLATION

RETAINING PLATE

VIEW A

© Ford Motor Co.

Piston and rod installation in 2800 cc six cylinder engine and all eight cylinder engines

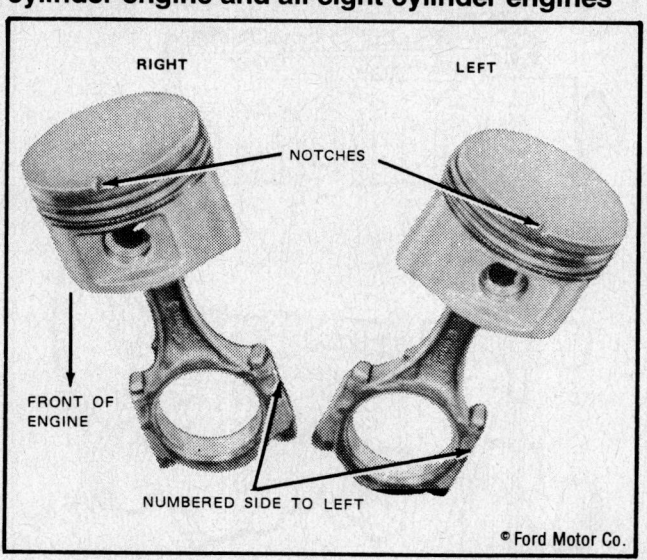

© Ford Motor Co.

Piston ring gap spacing

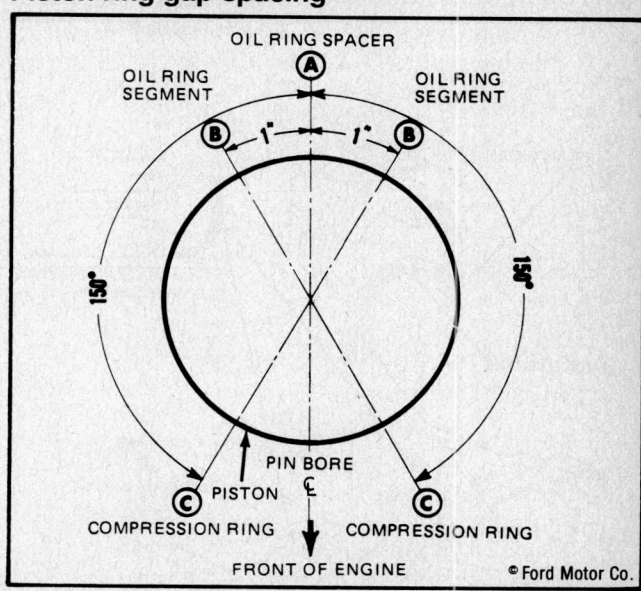

© Ford Motor Co.

Pistons, Rods & Bearings

- Pistons are removed through the top on all engines.
- Piston pins are a press fit in all engines, and the piston and pin must be replaced as an assembly.
- Assemble pistons and rods as illustrated.
- Piston ring gaps should be spaced as illustrated when installing pistons.

Oil Pump

- On all engines, remove the oil pan, and unbolt and remove the oil pump.

Oil pump typical in in-line six cylinder engine

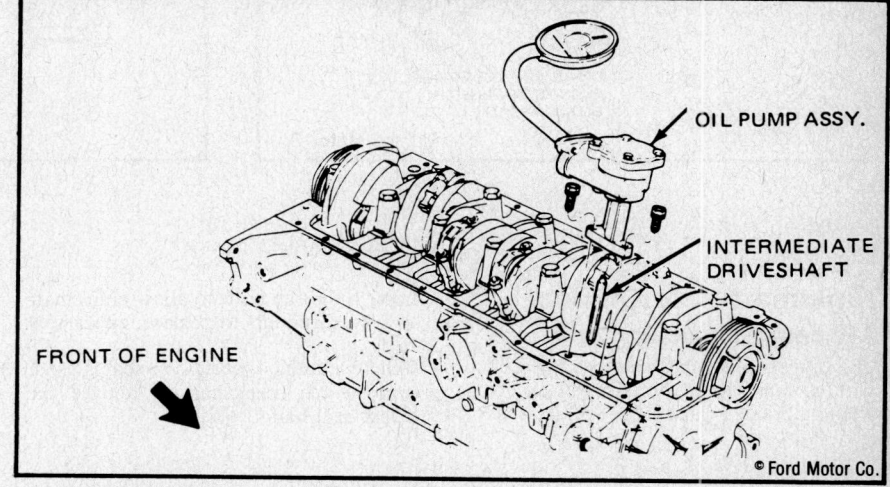

© Ford Motor Co.

Oil pump typical installation in 2300 cc engine

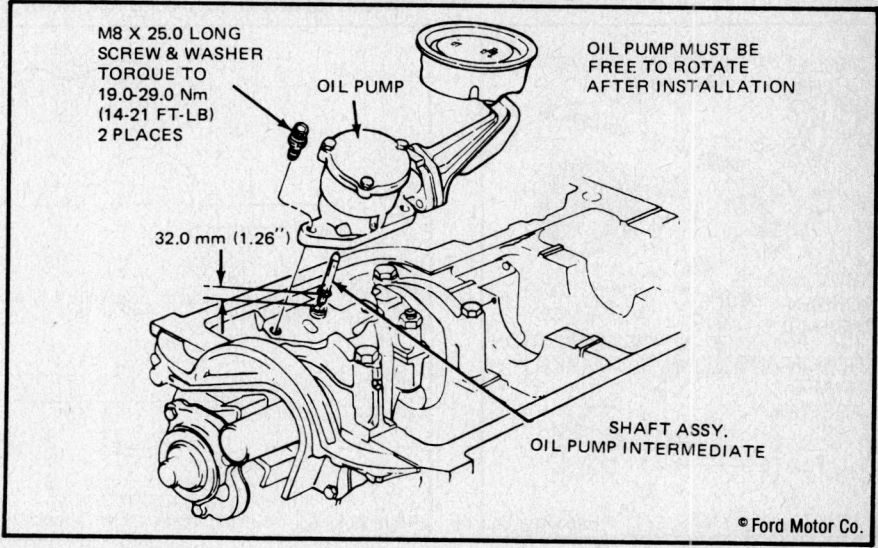

© Ford Motor Co.

A427

Rear oil seal installation—2.3 engine

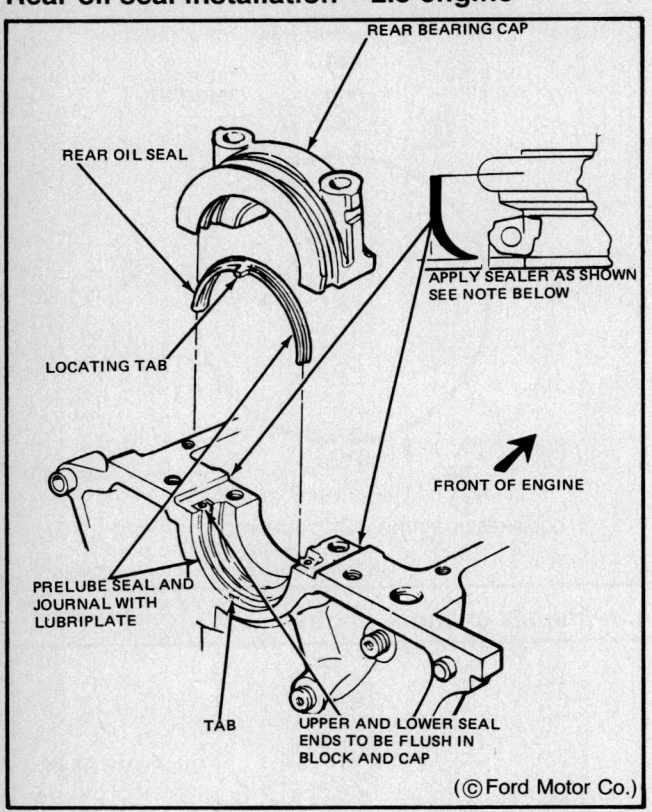

REAR BEARING CAP

REAR OIL SEAL

APPLY SEALER AS SHOWN
SEE NOTE BELOW

LOCATING TAB

FRONT OF ENGINE

PRELUBE SEAL AND
JOURNAL WITH
LUBRIPLATE

TAB

UPPER AND LOWER SEAL
ENDS TO BE FLUSH IN
BLOCK AND CAP

(© Ford Motor Co.)

2800 cc, V6 engine lubrication schematic

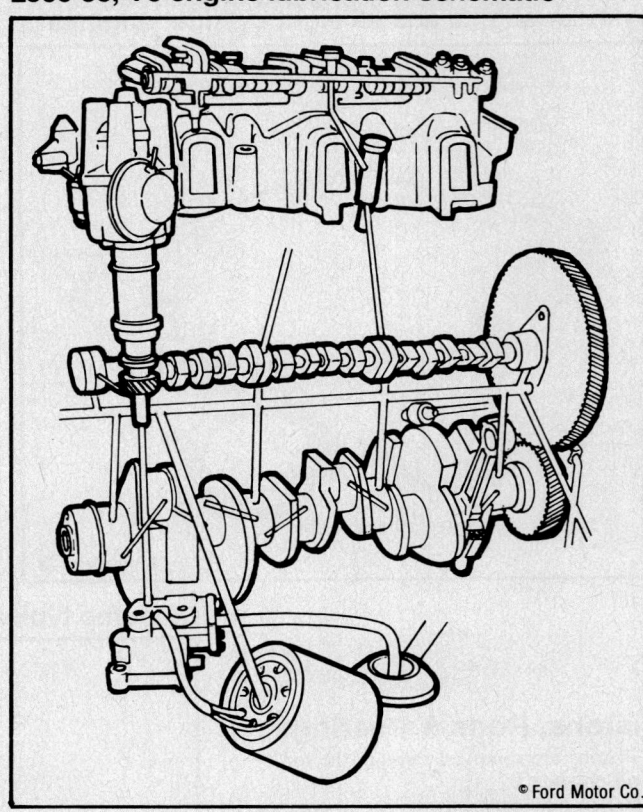

© Ford Motor Co.

Crankshaft Rear Oil Seal

All Except 2800 cc Engines

- The upper seal half can be replaced without removing the crankshaft except where a braided fabric type seal is used.

Loosen the cap bolts to allow crankshaft to lower enough to replace upper seal half.
- Where a braided fabric type seal is used, remove the crankshaft to replace the upper seal half.

2800 cc Engines

- An external seal is used.
- Remove transmission, flywheel, clutch, etc.
- Pry out the old seal, and press in the new seal.

Oil pump used in 351 CID (Cleveland) engine

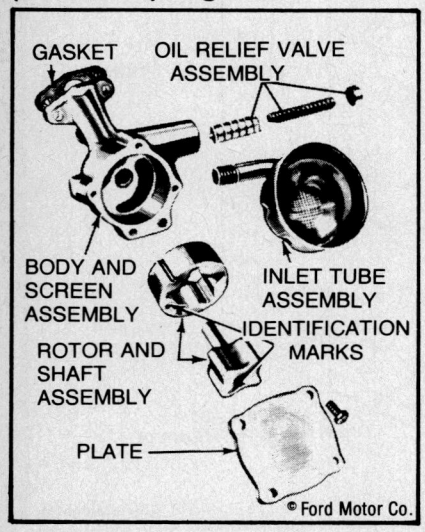

GASKET

OIL RELIEF VALVE ASSEMBLY

BODY AND
SCREEN
ASSEMBLY

INLET TUBE
ASSEMBLY

ROTOR AND
SHAFT
ASSEMBLY

IDENTIFICATION
MARKS

PLATE

© Ford Motor Co.

Typical crankshaft rear oil seal installation

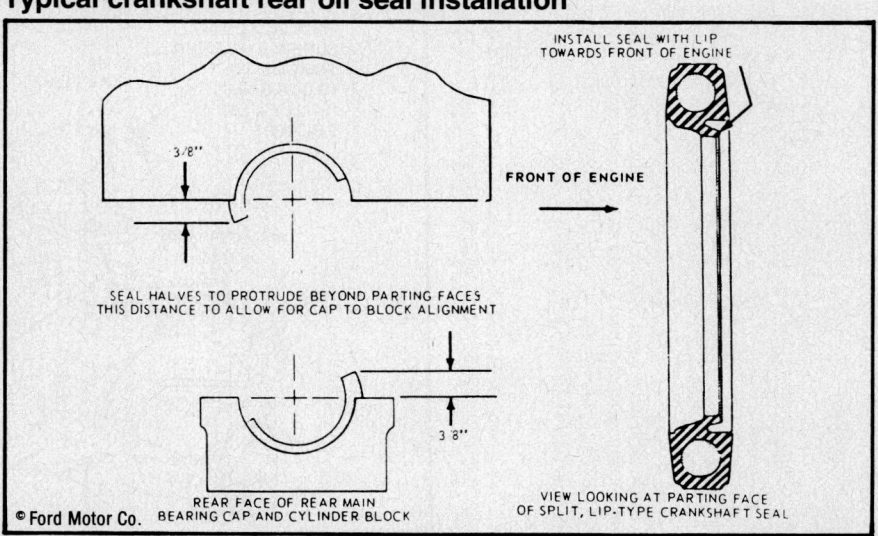

INSTALL SEAL WITH LIP
TOWARDS FRONT OF ENGINE

3/8"

FRONT OF ENGINE

SEAL HALVES TO PROTRUDE BEYOND PARTING FACES
THIS DISTANCE TO ALLOW FOR CAP TO BLOCK ALIGNMENT

3/8"

© Ford Motor Co.

REAR FACE OF REAR MAIN
BEARING CAP AND CYLINDER BLOCK

VIEW LOOKING AT PARTING FACE
OF SPLIT, LIP-TYPE CRANKSHAFT SEAL

Oil Pan

Four Cylinder Engines

- Engine raising is not necessary for oil pan removal.
- Remove, disconnect or relocate any of the following necessary for access and clearance:
  - a. Starter
  - b. Steering rack and pinion
  - c. Flywheel cover
  - d. Exhaust plumbing

Six Cylinder Engines

- In-line six cylinder engines do not have to be raised for oil pan removal except when used in Granada, Monarch and Mustang models.
- Remove, disconnect or relocate any of the following necessary for oil pan access or removal clearance:
  - a. Flywheel cover
  - b. Stabilizer bar
  - c. Radiator and fan shroud
  - d. Starter
  - e. Automatic transmission oil cooler lines
  - f. Steering gear (2800 cc engine)
- Tighten the mount bolts in the prescribed sequence when installing the oil pan.

Eight Cylinder Engines

- Remove, disconnect or relocate any of the following necessary to facilitate engine raising and oil pan removal:
  - a. Fan shroud
  - b. Starter
  - c. Stabilizer bar
  - d. Automatic transmission oil cooler lines
  - e. Oil filter
  - f. Exhaust plumbing
- Rotate crankshaft as needed for clearance while removing oil pan.

2300 cc Engine

- Apply gasket adhesive evenly to oil pan flange and to pan side gaskets. Allow adhesive to dry past wet stage, then install gaskets to oil pan.
- Apply sealer to joint of block and front cover. Install seals to front cover and rear bearing cap and press seal tabs firmly into block. Be sure to install the rear seal before the rear main bearing cap sealer has cured.
- Position two guide pins and install the oil pan. Secure the pan with the four M8 bolts.
- Remove the guide pins and install the torque the eighteen M6 bolts, beginning at hole "A" and working clockwise around the pan.

2300 cc engine oil pan installation

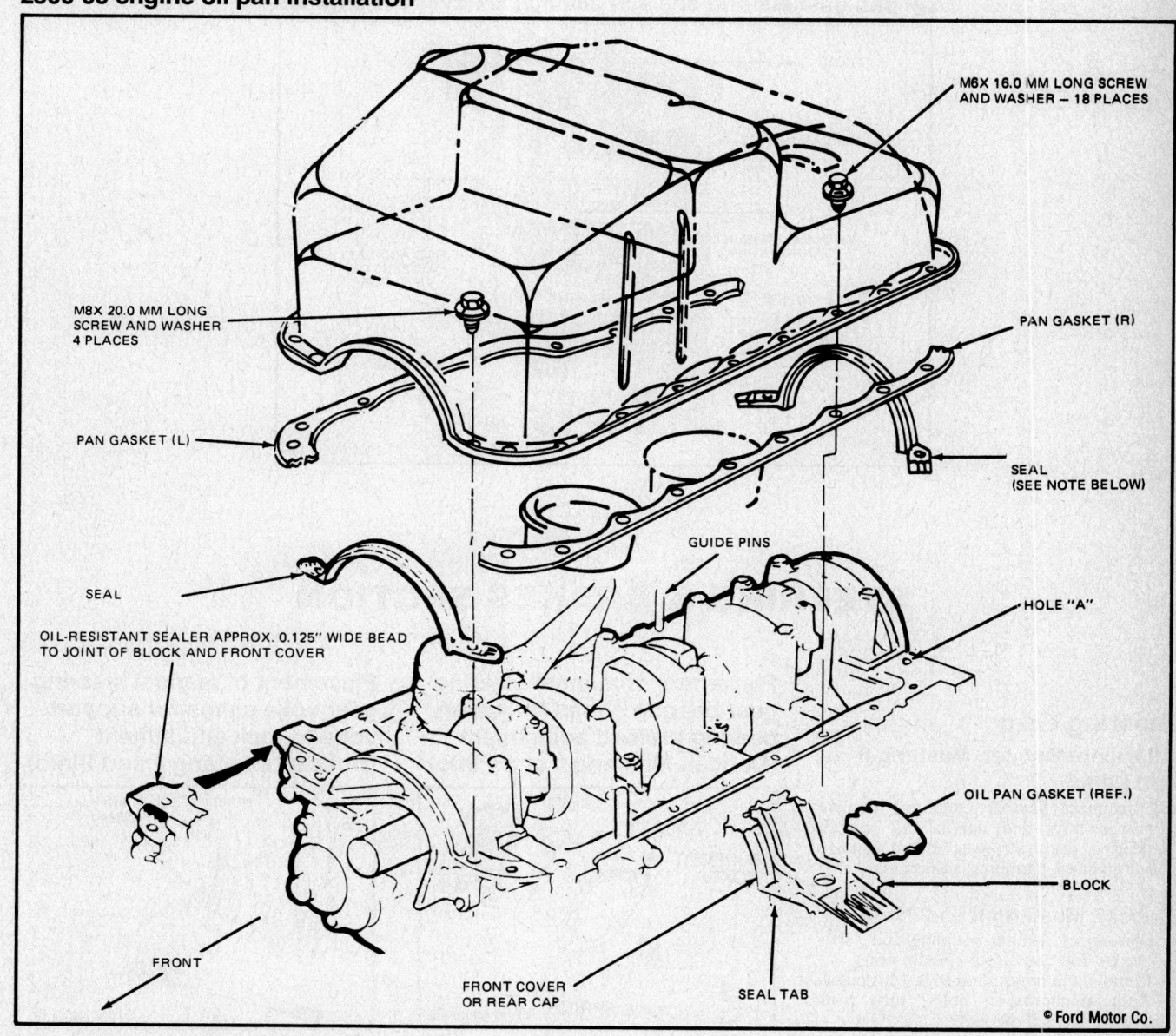

M6X 16.0 MM LONG SCREW AND WASHER – 18 PLACES

M8X 20.0 MM LONG SCREW AND WASHER 4 PLACES

PAN GASKET (R)

PAN GASKET (L)

SEAL (SEE NOTE BELOW)

SEAL

GUIDE PINS

HOLE "A"

OIL-RESISTANT SEALER APPROX. 0.125" WIDE BEAD TO JOINT OF BLOCK AND FRONT COVER

OIL PAN GASKET (REF.)

BLOCK

FRONT

FRONT COVER OR REAR CAP

SEAL TAB

© Ford Motor Co.

Oil pan mount bolt tightening sequence in 2800 cc six cylinder engine

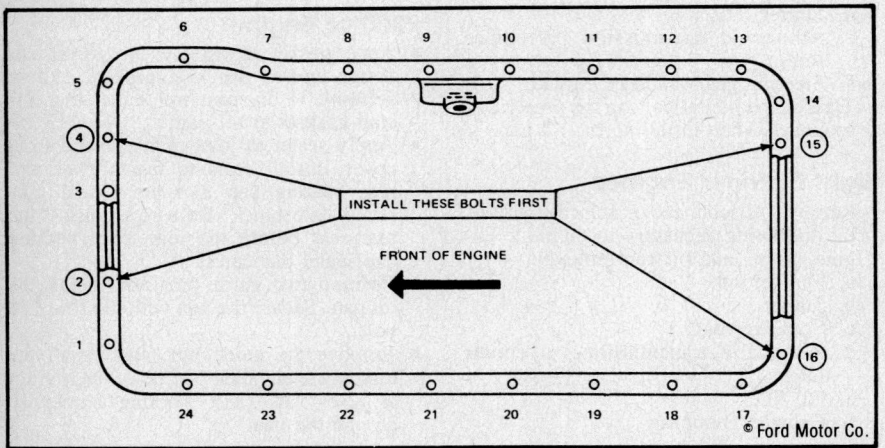

Oil pan mount bolt tightening sequence in 2000 cc engine

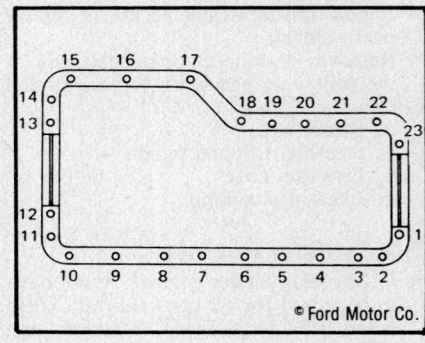

Oil pan gaskets and seals in 2800 cc six cylinder engines

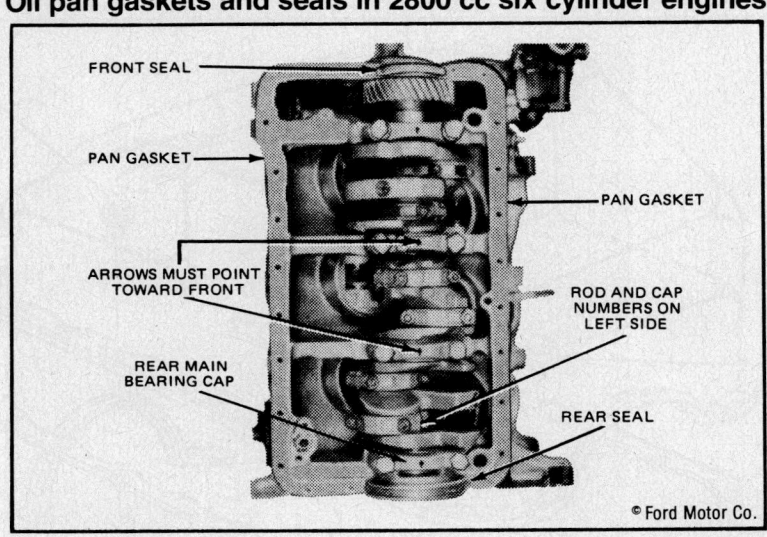

STEERING & BRAKES SECTION

Steering Gear

All except Bobcat, Mustang II and Pinto

- Disconnect flexible coupling, remove pitman arm, and unbolt and remove steering gear. Relocate clutch linkage and exhaust plumbing as necessary.

Bobcat, Mustang II and Pinto

- Disconnect flexible coupling and separate tie rod ends from spindle arms.
- Remove the crossmember in Mustang II
- Remove mounting bolts, turn front wheels and remove gear.

Placement of manual steering gear bearing shims for pinion bearing preload adjustment (Bobcat, Mustang II and Pinto)

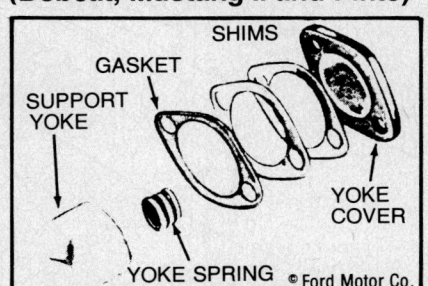

Placement of manual steering gear yoke shims for support yoke-to-rack adjustment (Bobcat, Mustang II and Pinto)

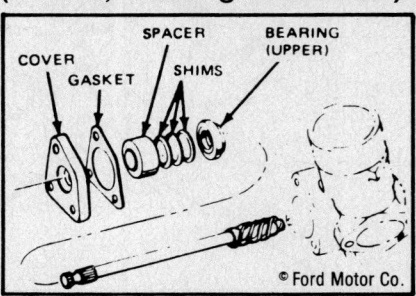

Steering linkage typical in all models except Bobcat, Fairmont, Mustang II, Pinto, Zephyr, and beginning 1979, Capri and Mustang

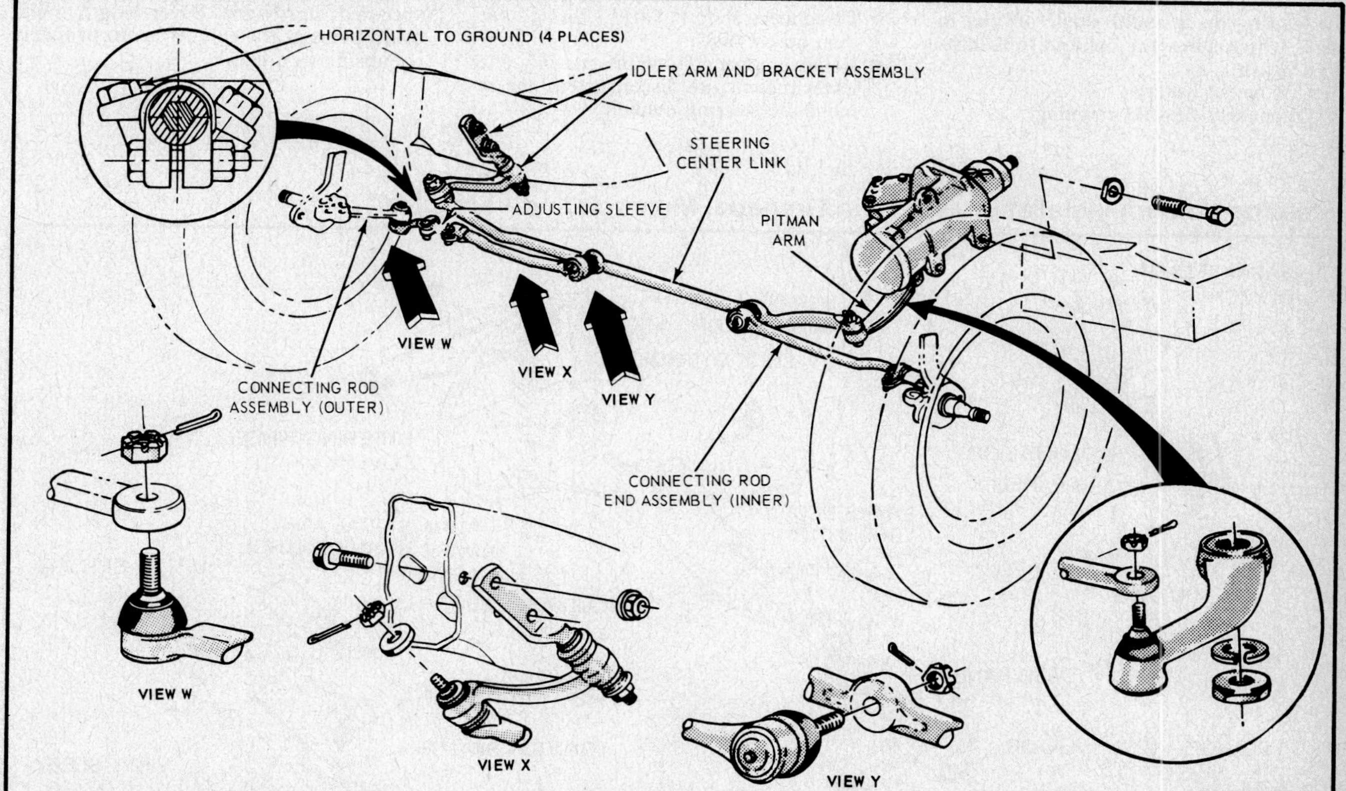

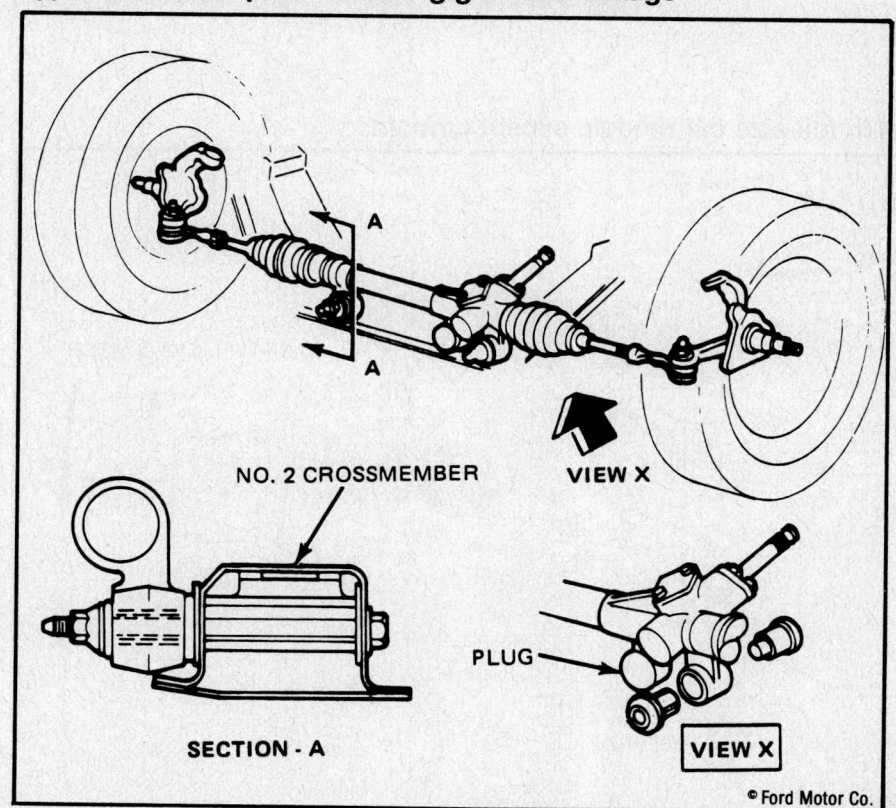

HORIZONTAL TO GROUND (4 PLACES)

IDLER ARM AND BRACKET ASSEMBLY

STEERING CENTER LINK

ADJUSTING SLEEVE

PITMAN ARM

VIEW W

VIEW X

VIEW Y

CONNECTING ROD ASSEMBLY (OUTER)

CONNECTING ROD END ASSEMBLY (INNER)

VIEW W

VIEW X

VIEW Y

© Ford Motor Co.

Typical rack and pinion steering gear and linkage

A

A

VIEW X

NO. 2 CROSSMEMBER

PLUG

SECTION - A

VIEW X

© Ford Motor Co.

Using puller to remove pitman arm

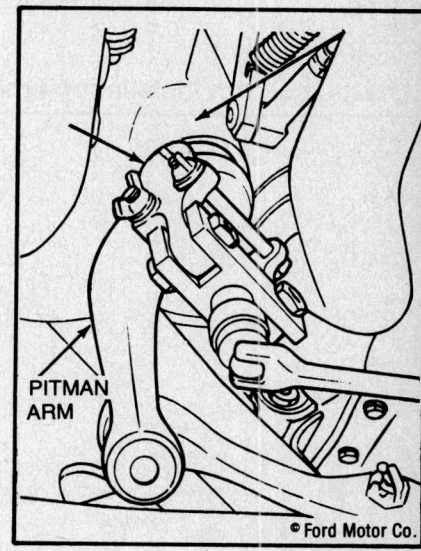

PITMAN ARM

© Ford Motor Co.

Steering Column

NOTE: Handle the steering column very carefully. Rapping on the end of it or leaning on it could shear off the inserts which allow the column to collapse in a crash.

- Disconnect battery.
- Disconnect flexible coupling.
- Remove cover and toe pan attachments.
- As necessary, remove instrument panel lower trim, instrument cluster, etc.
- Disconnect shift linkages, wiring, vacuum hoses, etc.
- Remove upper column mounts *only* after lower mounts are disconnected, and remove the steering column.
- When installing, check that flexible coupling alignment is correct.

NOTE: When installing, use only the specified hardware. Over-length bolts could prevent the column from properly collapsing in a crash.

Steering column installation typical in Granada, Monarch and Versailles

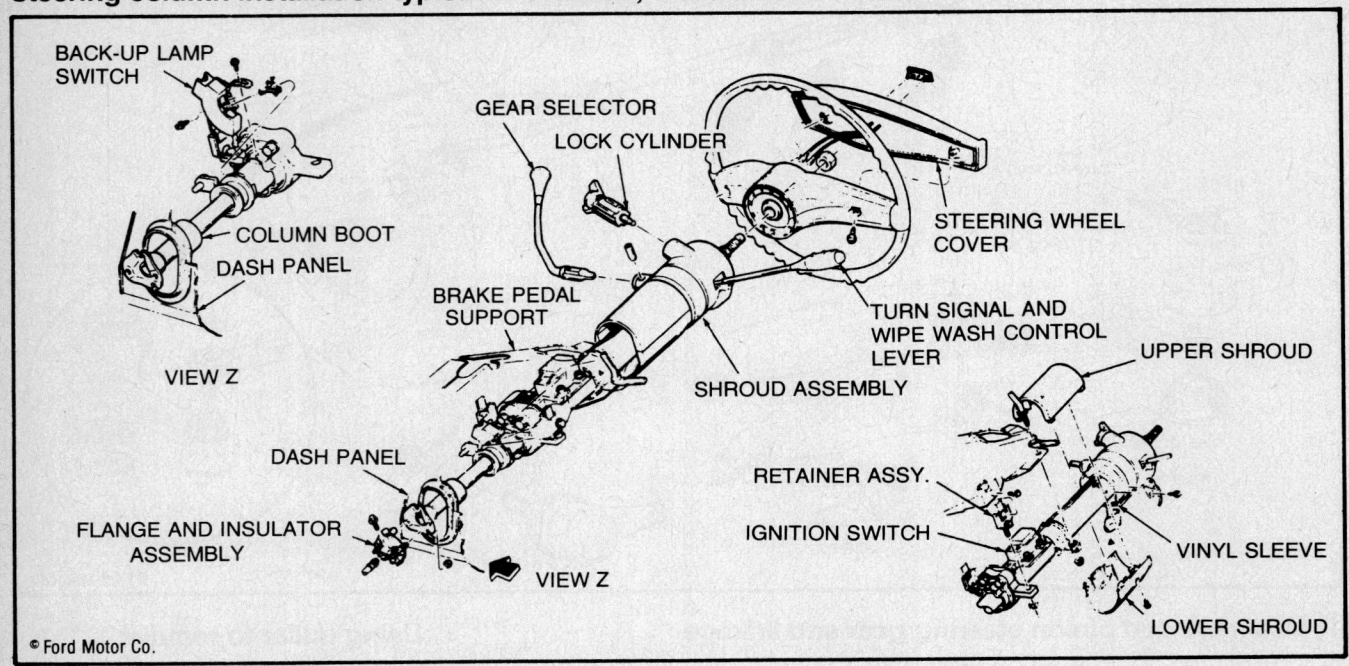

Steering column installation typical in full-size car models except Lincoln

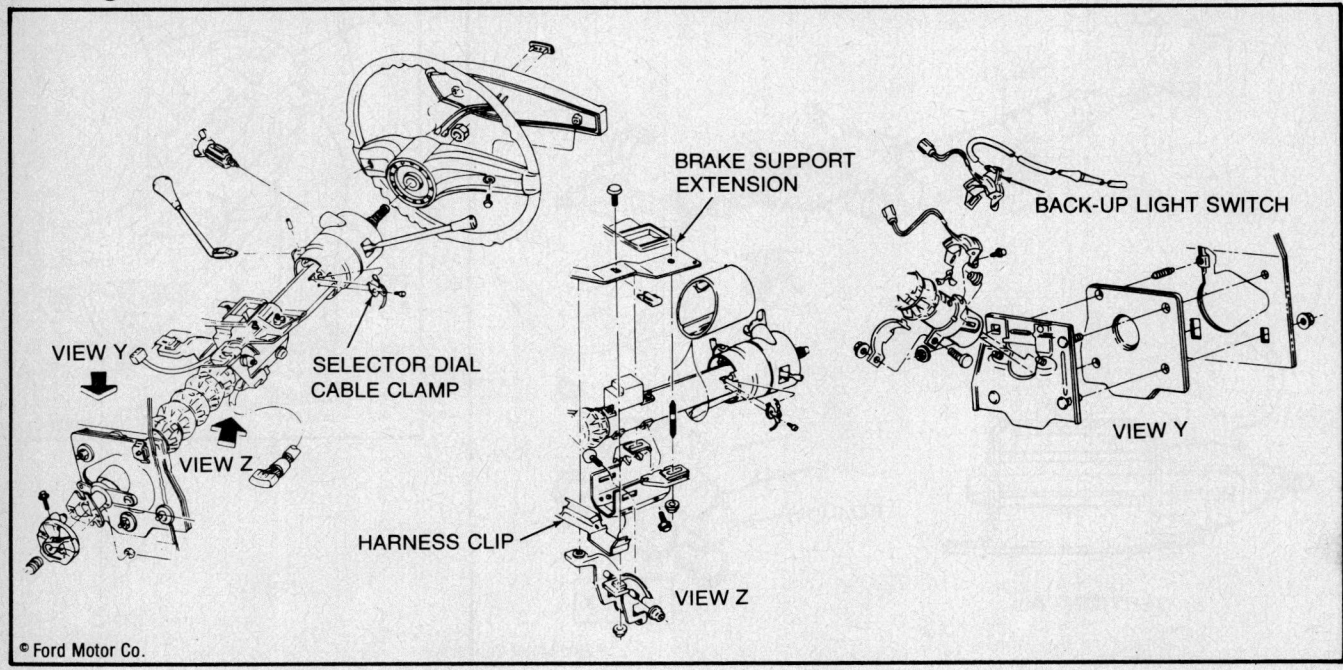

FORD—LINCOLN—MERCURY REAR DRIVE CARS

Steering column mounting typical in Bobcat, Mustang II and Pinto

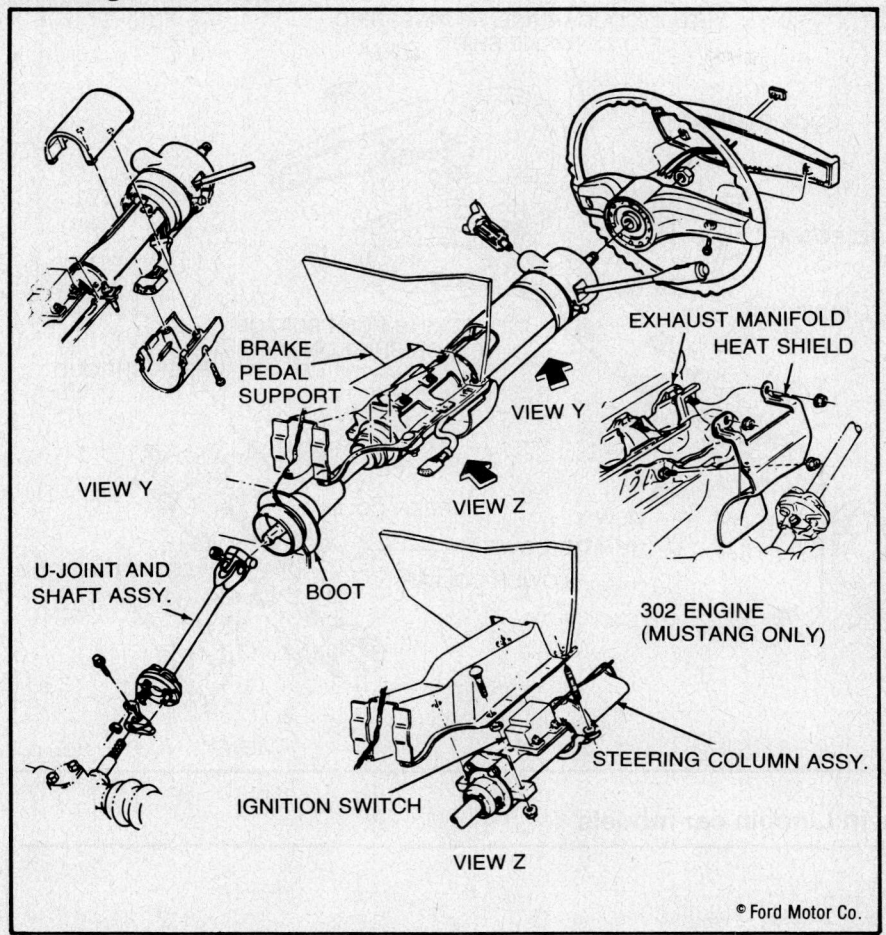

BRAKE PEDAL SUPPORT

EXHAUST MANIFOLD HEAT SHIELD

VIEW Y

VIEW Y

VIEW Z

U-JOINT AND SHAFT ASSY.

BOOT

302 ENGINE (MUSTANG ONLY)

STEERING COLUMN ASSY.

IGNITION SWITCH

VIEW Z

© Ford Motor Co.

Typical automatic transmission selector indicator

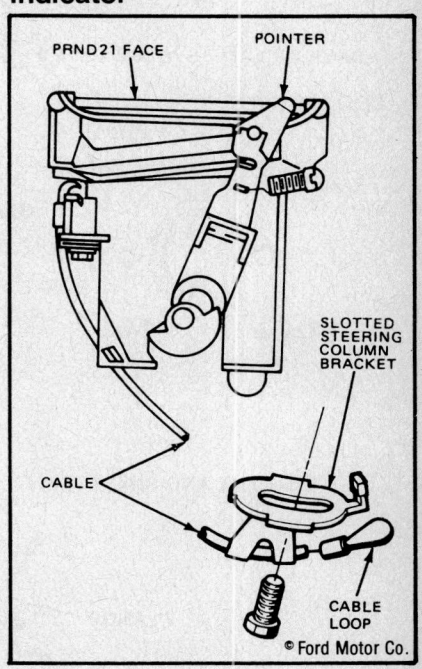

PRND21 FACE

POINTER

SLOTTED STEERING COLUMN BRACKET

CABLE

CABLE LOOP

© Ford Motor Co.

Steering column covers and wiring connectors

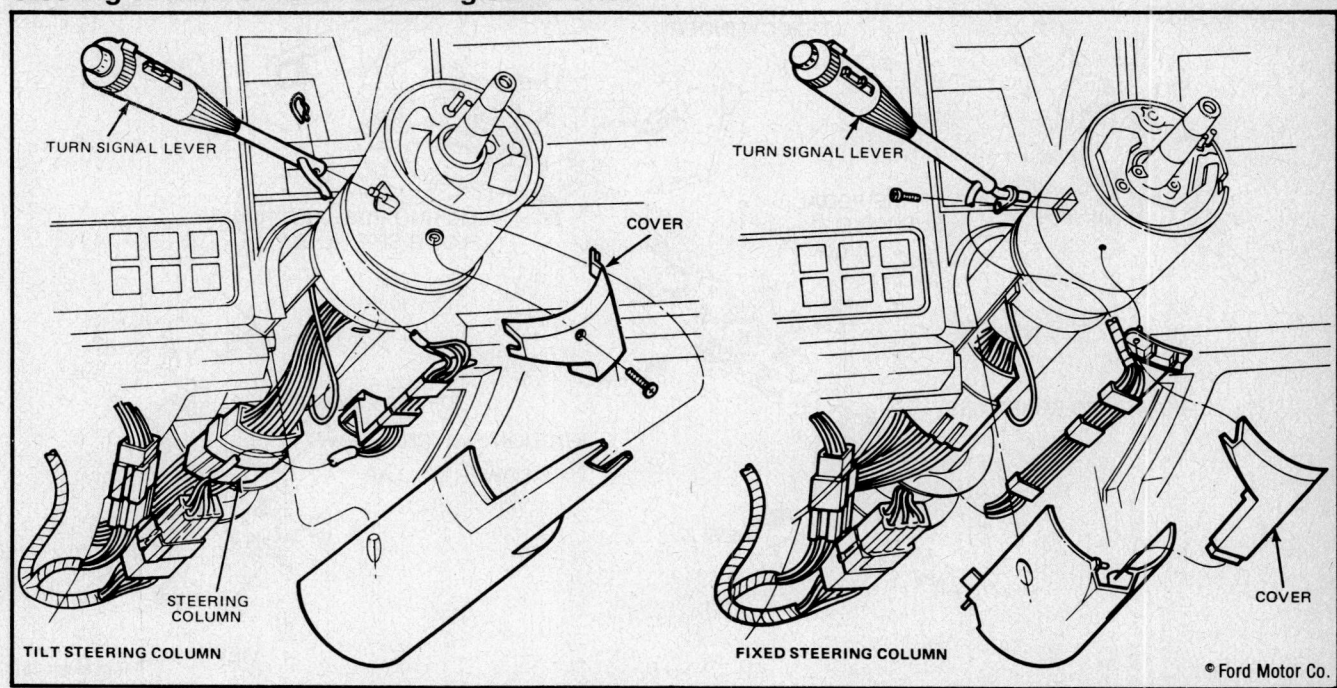

TURN SIGNAL LEVER

COVER

STEERING COLUMN

TILT STEERING COLUMN

TURN SIGNAL LEVER

COVER

FIXED STEERING COLUMN

© Ford Motor Co.

A433

FORD—LINCOLN—MERCURY REAR DRIVE CARS

Steering column mounting typical in Cougar, LTD II and Thunderbird

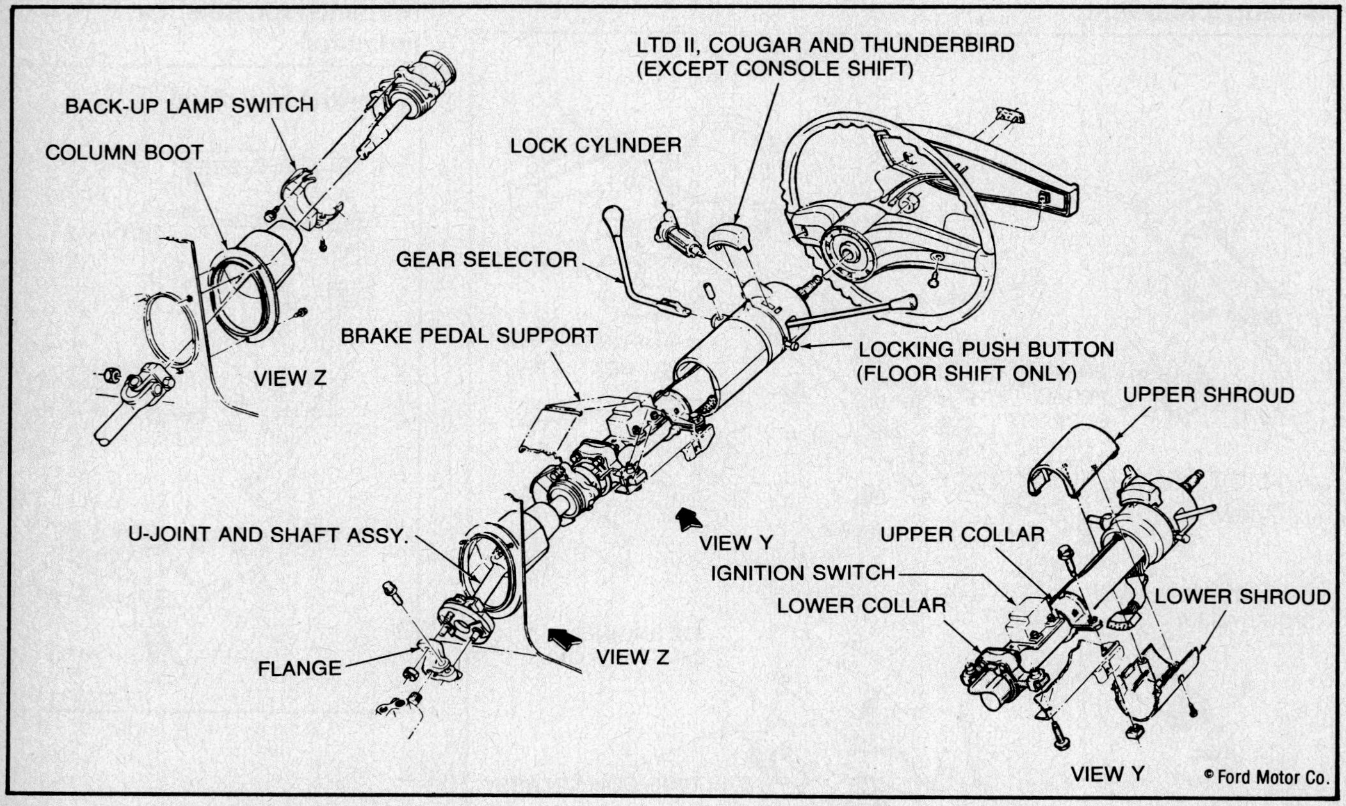

BACK-UP LAMP SWITCH

COLUMN BOOT

LTD II, COUGAR AND THUNDERBIRD
(EXCEPT CONSOLE SHIFT)

LOCK CYLINDER

GEAR SELECTOR

BRAKE PEDAL SUPPORT

VIEW Z

U-JOINT AND SHAFT ASSY.

FLANGE

VIEW Y

VIEW Z

LOCKING PUSH BUTTON
(FLOOR SHIFT ONLY)

UPPER SHROUD

UPPER COLLAR

IGNITION SWITCH

LOWER COLLAR

LOWER SHROUD

VIEW Y

© Ford Motor Co.

Steering column installation typical in Lincoln car models

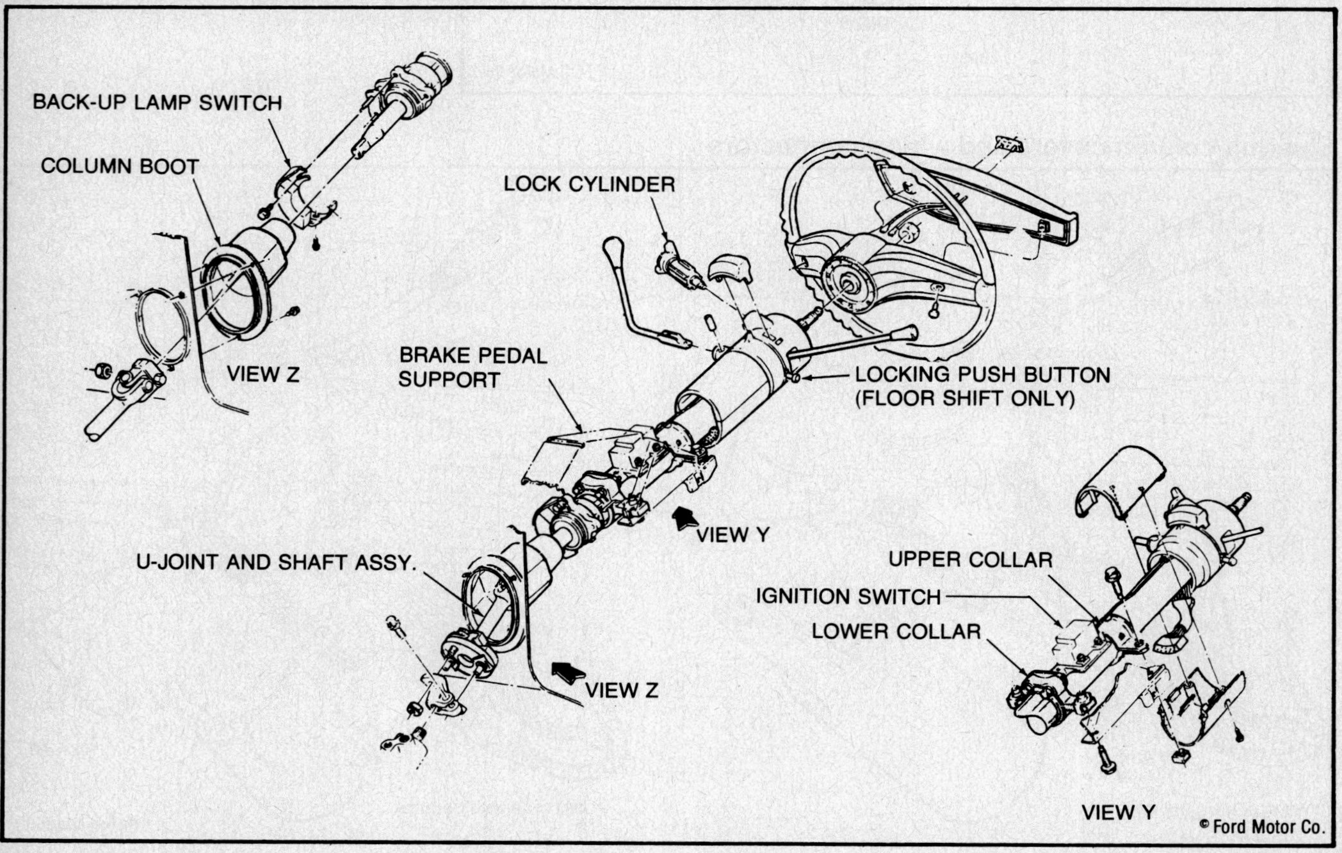

BACK-UP LAMP SWITCH

COLUMN BOOT

LOCK CYLINDER

BRAKE PEDAL
SUPPORT

VIEW Z

U-JOINT AND SHAFT ASSY.

VIEW Y

VIEW Z

LOCKING PUSH BUTTON
(FLOOR SHIFT ONLY)

UPPER COLLAR

IGNITION SWITCH

LOWER COLLAR

VIEW Y

© Ford Motor Co.

Steering column installation in Fairmont, Zephyr

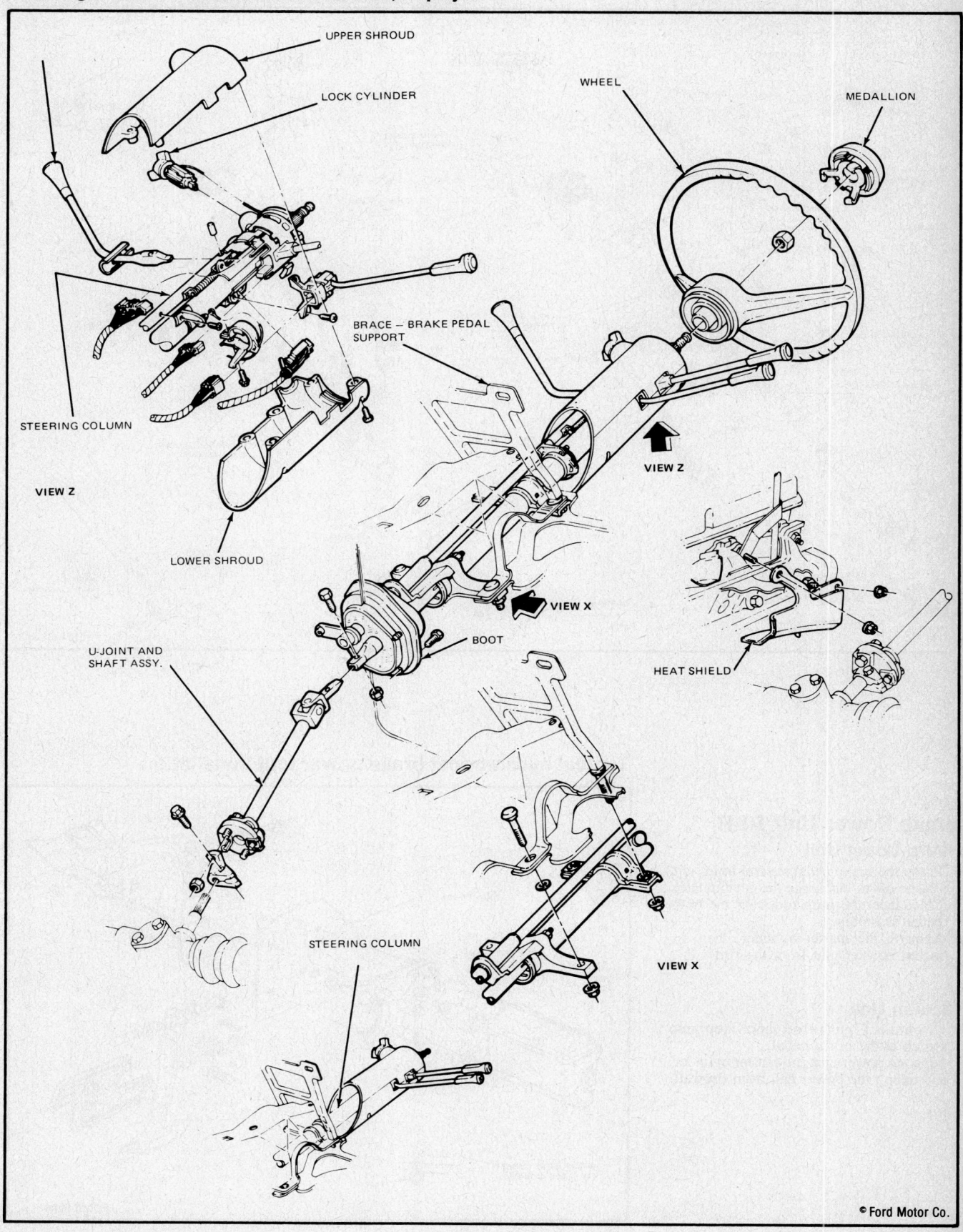

UPPER SHROUD

LOCK CYLINDER

WHEEL

MEDALLION

BRACE — BRAKE PEDAL SUPPORT

STEERING COLUMN

VIEW Z

VIEW Z

LOWER SHROUD

U-JOINT AND SHAFT ASSY.

BOOT

VIEW X

HEAT SHIELD

STEERING COLUMN

VIEW X

© Ford Motor Co.

Typical tilt steering column

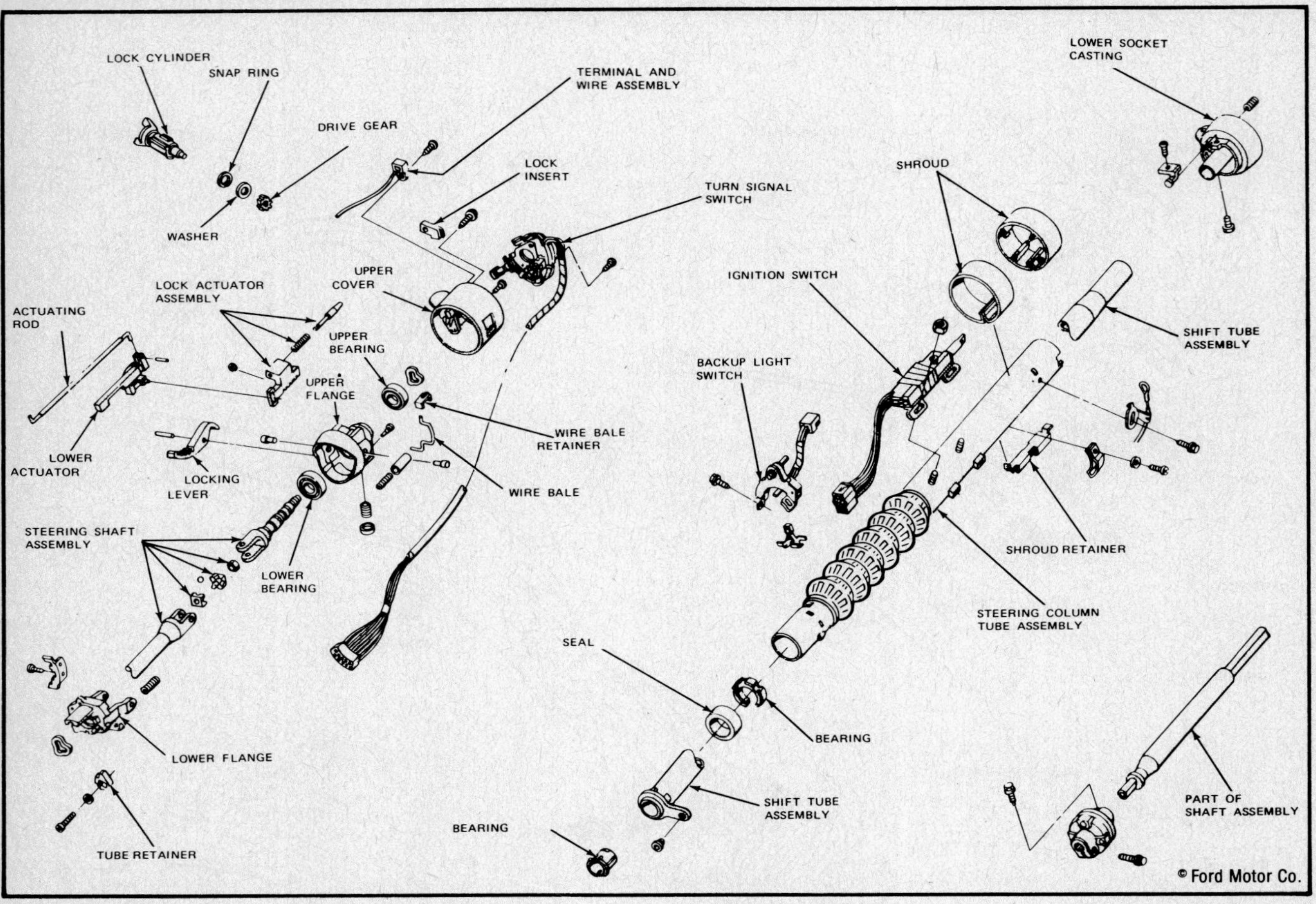

LOCK CYLINDER

SNAP RING

DRIVE GEAR

TERMINAL AND
WIRE ASSEMBLY

LOWER SOCKET
CASTING

WASHER

LOCK
INSERT

TURN SIGNAL
SWITCH

SHROUD

ACTUATING
ROD

LOCK ACTUATOR
ASSEMBLY

UPPER
COVER

IGNITION SWITCH

SHIFT TUBE
ASSEMBLY

UPPER
BEARING

BACKUP LIGHT
SWITCH

LOWER
ACTUATOR

UPPER
FLANGE

LOCKING
LEVER

WIRE BALE
RETAINER

STEERING SHAFT
ASSEMBLY

WIRE BALE

SHROUD RETAINER

LOWER
BEARING

STEERING COLUMN
TUBE ASSEMBLY

SEAL

LOWER FLANGE

BEARING

TUBE RETAINER

BEARING

SHIFT TUBE
ASSEMBLY

PART OF
SHAFT ASSEMBLY

© Ford Motor Co.

Brake Power Unit R&R

Hydro-Boost Unit

- Pump the brake pedal several times with engine off to discharge the accumulator.
- Disconnect the push rod from the brake pedal assembly.
- Remove the master cylinder, then dismount booster unit from the firewall.

Vacuum Unit

- Disconnect push rod and stoplamp switch at the brake pedal.
- Separate power unit and master cylinder, and unbolt the power unit from firewall.

Typical hydro-boost brake power unit installation

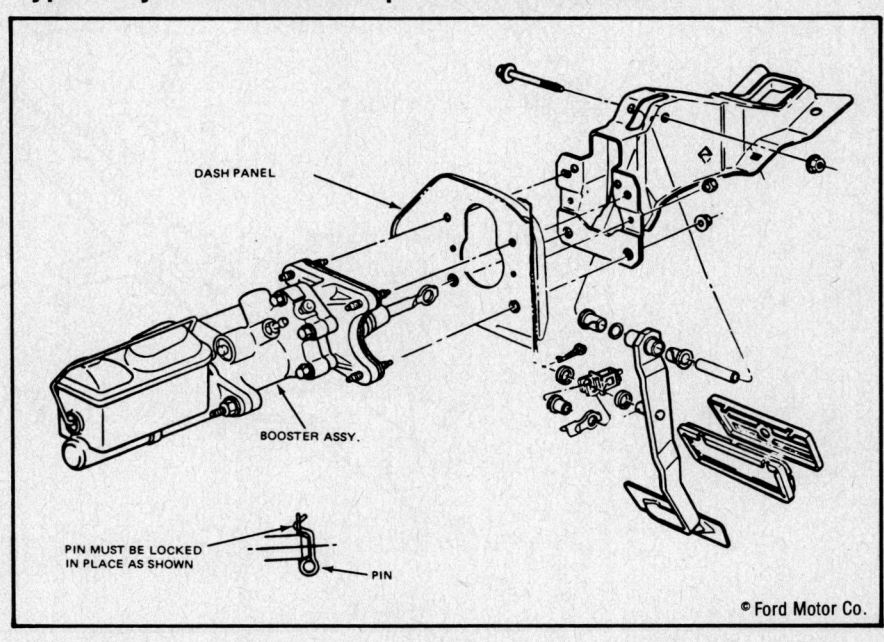

DASH PANEL

BOOSTER ASSY.

PIN MUST BE LOCKED
IN PLACE AS SHOWN

PIN

© Ford Motor Co.

Brake vacuum power unit typical in Fairmont and Zephyr

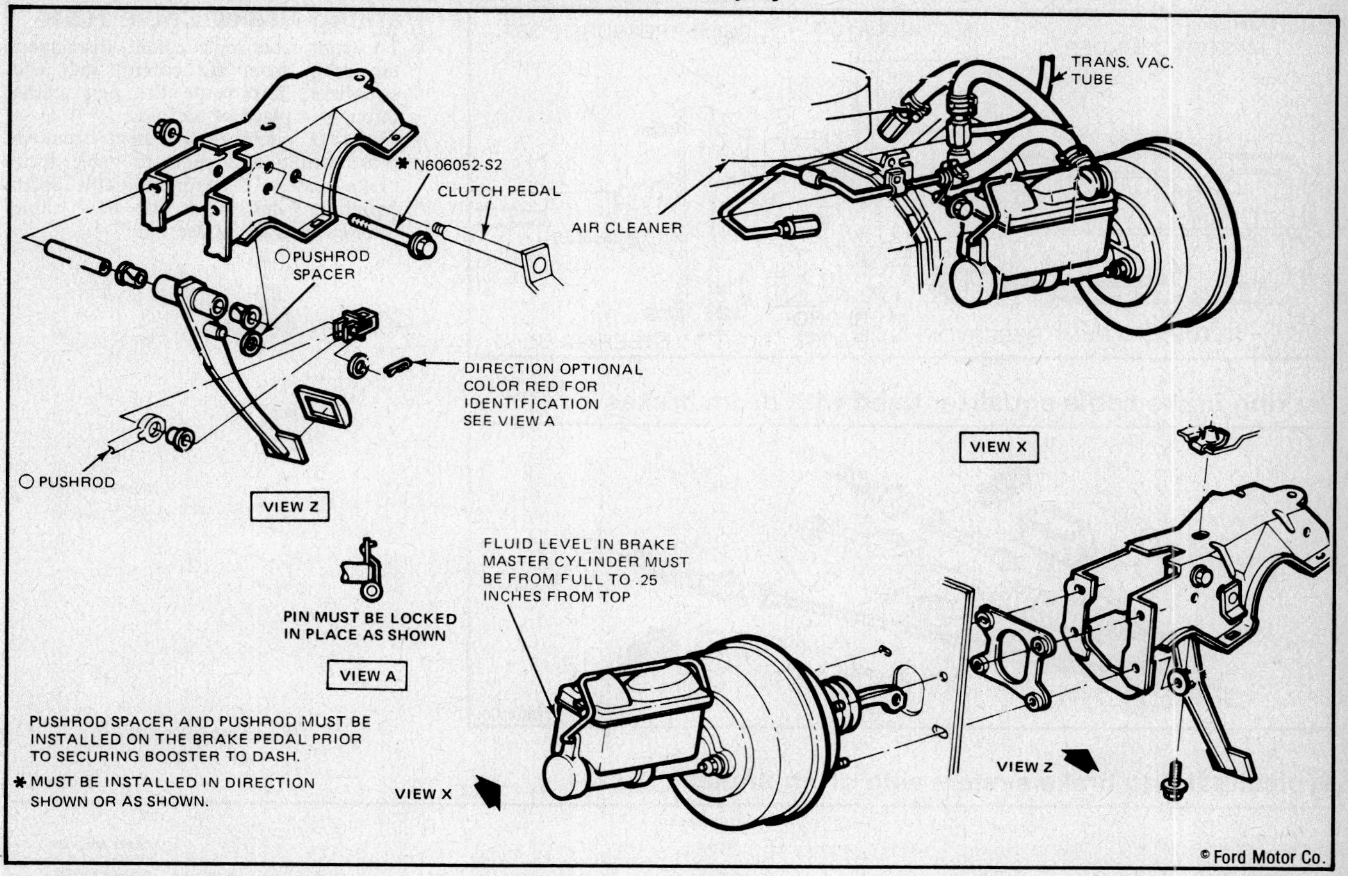

TRANS. VAC. TUBE

N606052-S2
CLUTCH PEDAL

AIR CLEANER

PUSHROD SPACER

DIRECTION OPTIONAL COLOR RED FOR IDENTIFICATION SEE VIEW A

PUSHROD

VIEW X

VIEW Z

FLUID LEVEL IN BRAKE MASTER CYLINDER MUST BE FROM FULL TO .25 INCHES FROM TOP

PIN MUST BE LOCKED IN PLACE AS SHOWN

VIEW A

PUSHROD SPACER AND PUSHROD MUST BE INSTALLED ON THE BRAKE PEDAL PRIOR TO SECURING BOOSTER TO DASH.

* MUST BE INSTALLED IN DIRECTION SHOWN OR AS SHOWN.

VIEW X

VIEW Z

© Ford Motor Co.

Typical hydro-boost brake system

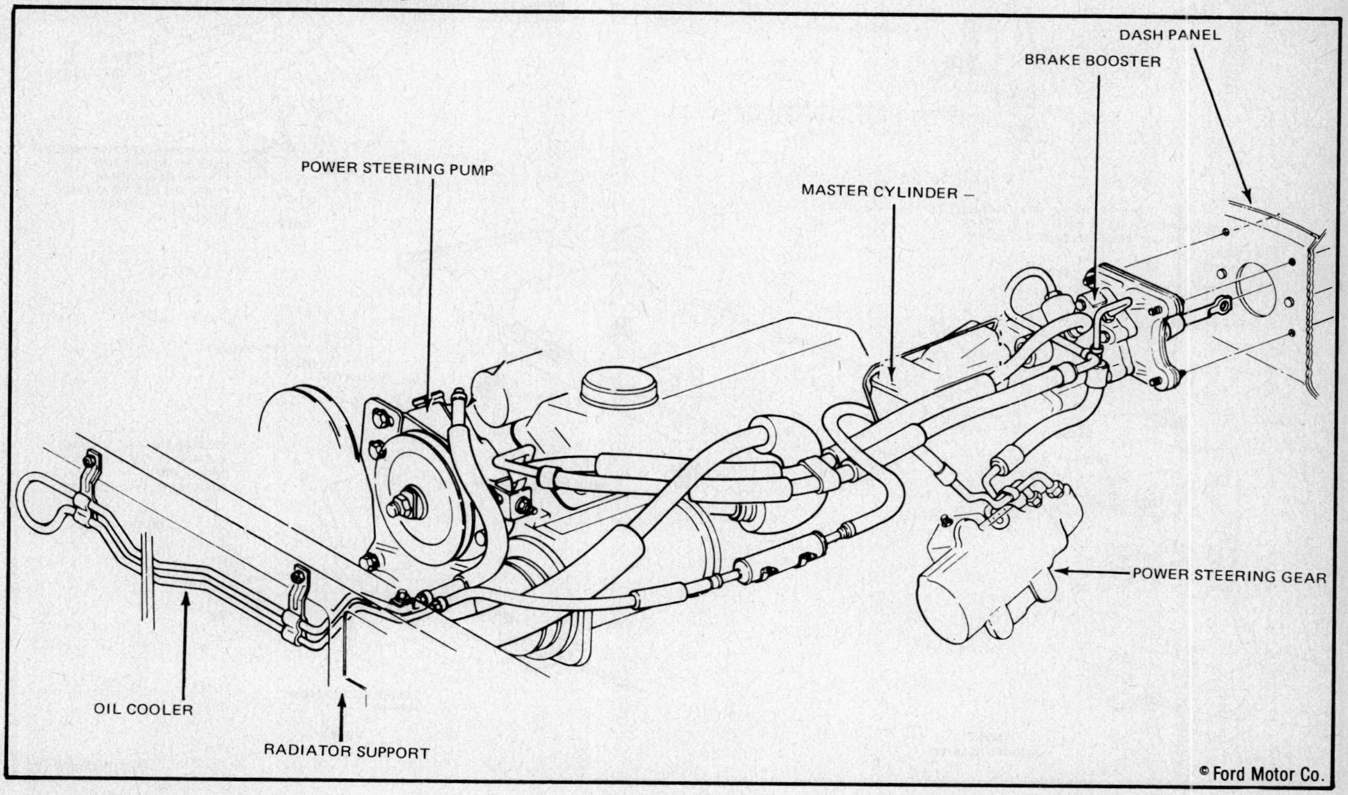

DASH PANEL

BRAKE BOOSTER

POWER STEERING PUMP

MASTER CYLINDER —

POWER STEERING GEAR

OIL COOLER

RADIATOR SUPPORT

© Ford Motor Co.

A437

Typical hydro-boost brake power unit

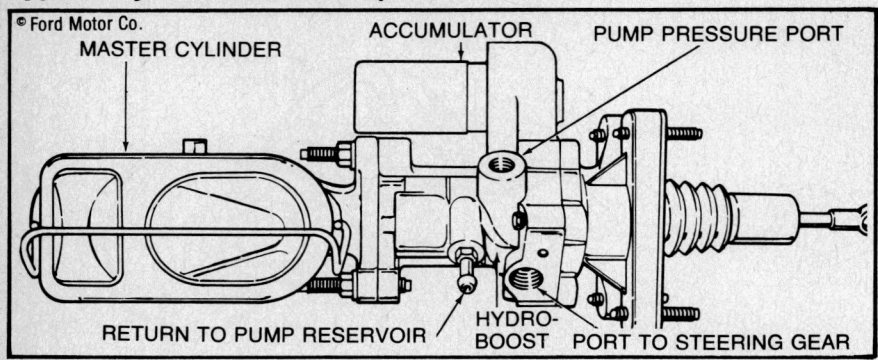

© Ford Motor Co.

MASTER CYLINDER — ACCUMULATOR — PUMP PRESSURE PORT

RETURN TO PUMP RESERVOIR — HYDRO-BOOST — PORT TO STEERING GEAR

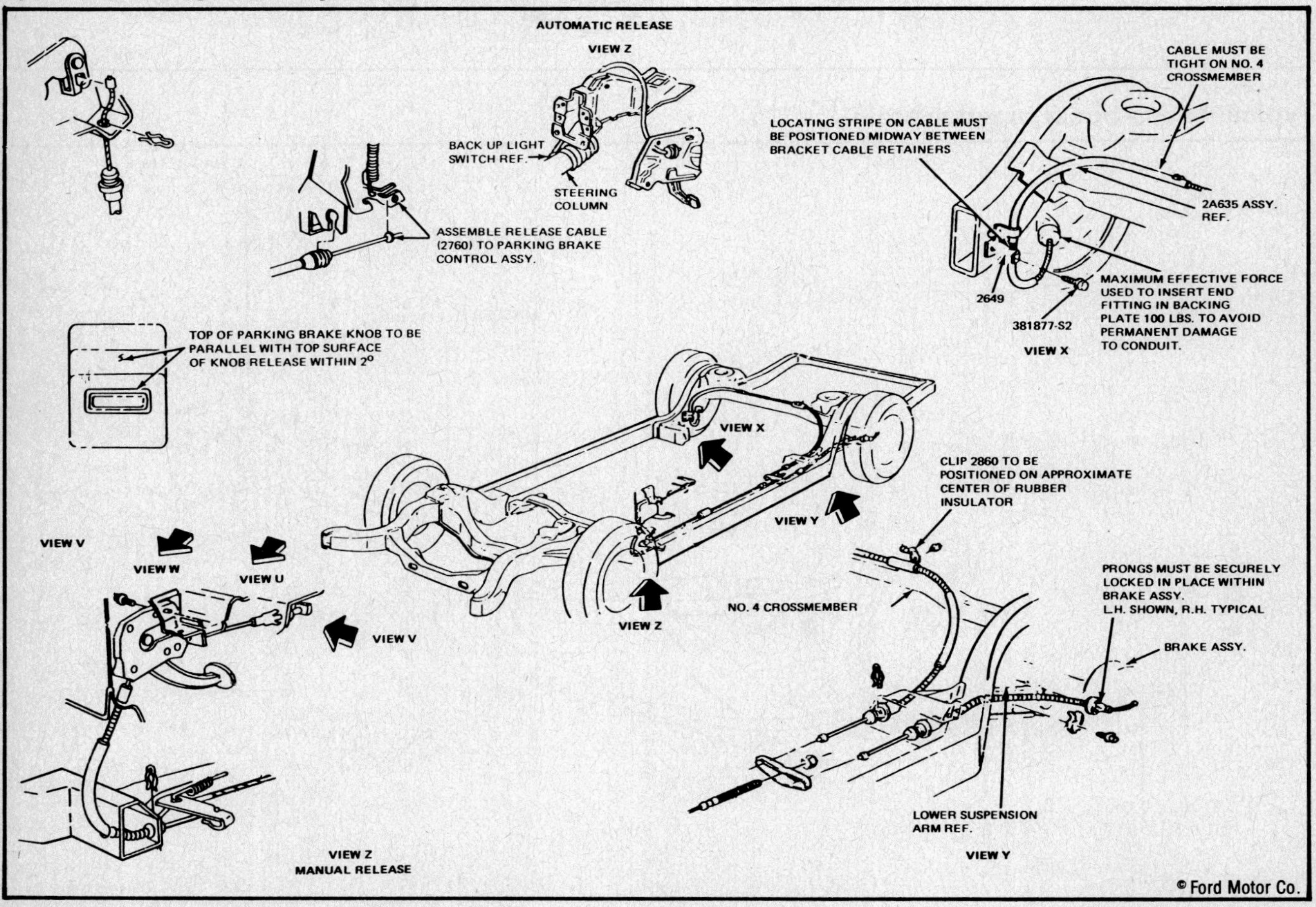

Parking Brake Cable R&R

- For front cable replacement, disconnect the cable from the control unit and equalizer, and route the new cable through in place of the old.
- For rear cable replacement, remove brake drum, and separate cable from brake shoes. Disconnect cable from equalizer, and route the new cable through in place of the old.

Parking brake cable equalizer used with drum brakes

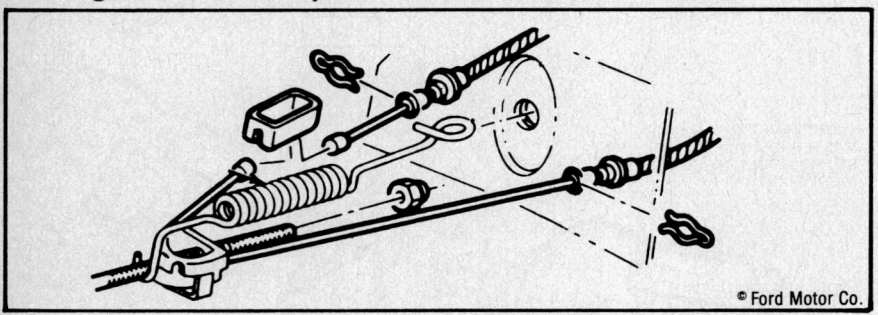

© Ford Motor Co.

Typical parking brake system with drum brakes

AUTOMATIC RELEASE
VIEW Z

BACK UP LIGHT SWITCH REF.

STEERING COLUMN

ASSEMBLE RELEASE CABLE (2760) TO PARKING BRAKE CONTROL ASSY.

TOP OF PARKING BRAKE KNOB TO BE PARALLEL WITH TOP SURFACE OF KNOB RELEASE WITHIN 2°

CABLE MUST BE TIGHT ON NO. 4 CROSSMEMBER

LOCATING STRIPE ON CABLE MUST BE POSITIONED MIDWAY BETWEEN BRACKET CABLE RETAINERS

2A635 ASSY. REF.

2649

381877-S2

VIEW X

MAXIMUM EFFECTIVE FORCE USED TO INSERT END FITTING IN BACKING PLATE 100 LBS. TO AVOID PERMANENT DAMAGE TO CONDUIT.

VIEW X

VIEW V

VIEW W   VIEW U

VIEW V

VIEW Y

VIEW Z

NO. 4 CROSSMEMBER

CLIP 2860 TO BE POSITIONED ON APPROXIMATE CENTER OF RUBBER INSULATOR

PRONGS MUST BE SECURELY LOCKED IN PLACE WITHIN BRAKE ASSY. L.H. SHOWN, R.H. TYPICAL

BRAKE ASSY.

LOWER SUSPENSION ARM REF.

VIEW Y

VIEW Z
MANUAL RELEASE

© Ford Motor Co.

Typical parking brake system with rear disc brakes

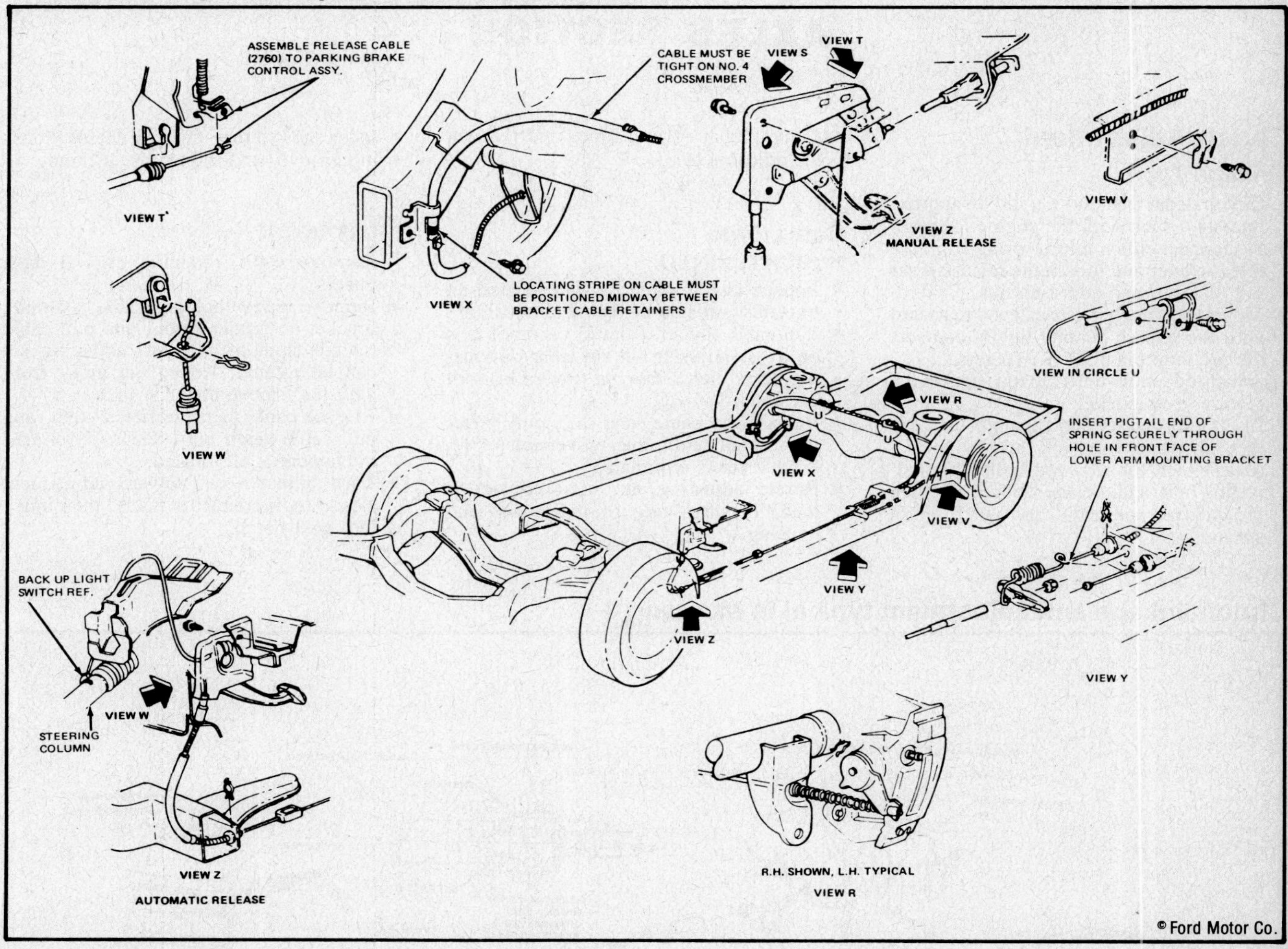

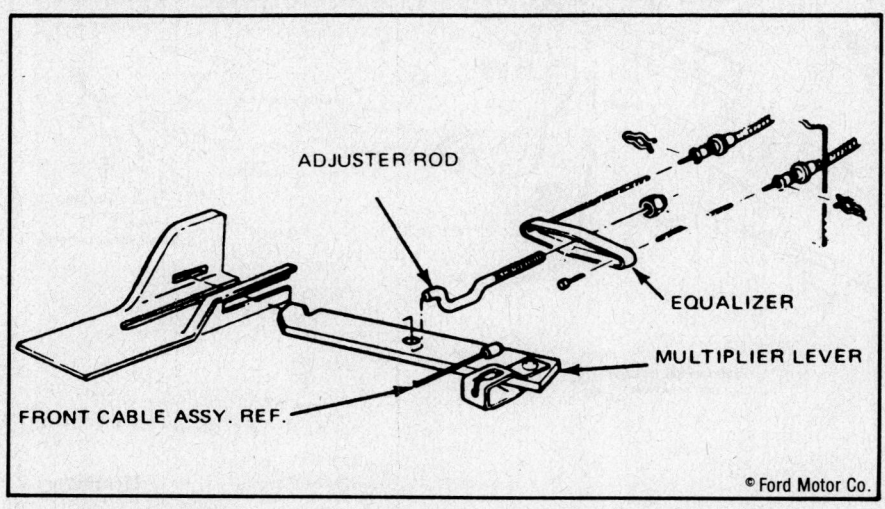

ASSEMBLE RELEASE CABLE (2760) TO PARKING BRAKE CONTROL ASSY.

VIEW T

CABLE MUST BE TIGHT ON NO. 4 CROSSMEMBER

VIEW S

VIEW T

VIEW V

VIEW Z MANUAL RELEASE

LOCATING STRIPE ON CABLE MUST BE POSITIONED MIDWAY BETWEEN BRACKET CABLE RETAINERS

VIEW X

VIEW W

VIEW IN CIRCLE U

INSERT PIGTAIL END OF SPRING SECURELY THROUGH HOLE IN FRONT FACE OF LOWER ARM MOUNTING BRACKET

VIEW R

VIEW X

VIEW V

VIEW Y

VIEW Z

VIEW Y

BACK UP LIGHT SWITCH REF.

VIEW W

STEERING COLUMN

VIEW Z

AUTOMATIC RELEASE

R.H. SHOWN, L.H. TYPICAL
VIEW R

© Ford Motor Co.

Parking brake cable equalizer used with disc

ADJUSTER ROD

EQUALIZER

MULTIPLIER LEVER

FRONT CABLE ASSY. REF.

© Ford Motor Co.

Parking Brake Adjustment
Except Rear Disc Brakes
- Correctly adjust service brakes.
- Fully release parking brake control.
- Tighten cable at equalizer until drag is felt at rear wheels.
- Release parking brake lever, and check that rear wheels turn without resistance.

Rear Disc Brakes
- Fully release parking brake.
- With vehicle raised, tighten the adjuster nut until caliper levers just begin to move. Loosen the nut just enough to obtain full return to the "off" position.
- Alternately apply service brakes and parking brake several times, and check that caliper parking brake levers fully return to "off" position.

A439

CLUTCH, TRANSMISSION, PROPELLER SHAFT & REAR AXLES SECTION

Clutch Adjustment
Linkage Type
- Clutch pedal free play should be approximately 1 inch with the engine idling.
- Disconnect clutch return spring from the release lever and loosen the release lever rod lock nut and adjusting nut.
- Move the clutch release lever rearward until the release bearing lightly contacts the pressure plate release fingers.
- Adust rod length until the rod seats in the release lever pocket.
- Insert the measurement gauge between the adjusting nut and swivel sleeve (0.136 inch for all), and tighten the adjusting nut against the gauge. Tighten the lock nut and install the clutch return spring.

- Cycle clutch several times and recheck the adjustment.

Cable Type
BOBCAT, PINTO
- Loosen clutch cable locknut located on transmission side of flywheel housing.
- Pull cable toward front of car until tabs on nylon adjuster nut are clear of housing boss, then rotate nut toward front of car about ¼ inch.
- Release the cable, and then pull it forward again until free movement of release lever is eliminated.
- Rotate adjusting nut until contact is made between face of index tabs and housing.

- Index tabs so they fall into nearest housing groove, and tighten the locknut.

MUSTANG II
- Remove cable retaining clip at dash panel.
- Remove screw holding cable attaching bracket on fender apron, and pull cable toward front of car until adjusting nut can be rotated. Rotate nut away from adjusting sleeve about ¼ inch.
- Release cable to neutralize system, and pull cable again until release lever free movement is eliminated.
- Turn adjuster nut toward adjustment sleeve until contact is made, then index into next notch.

Clutch linkage and adjustment typical in Mustang II

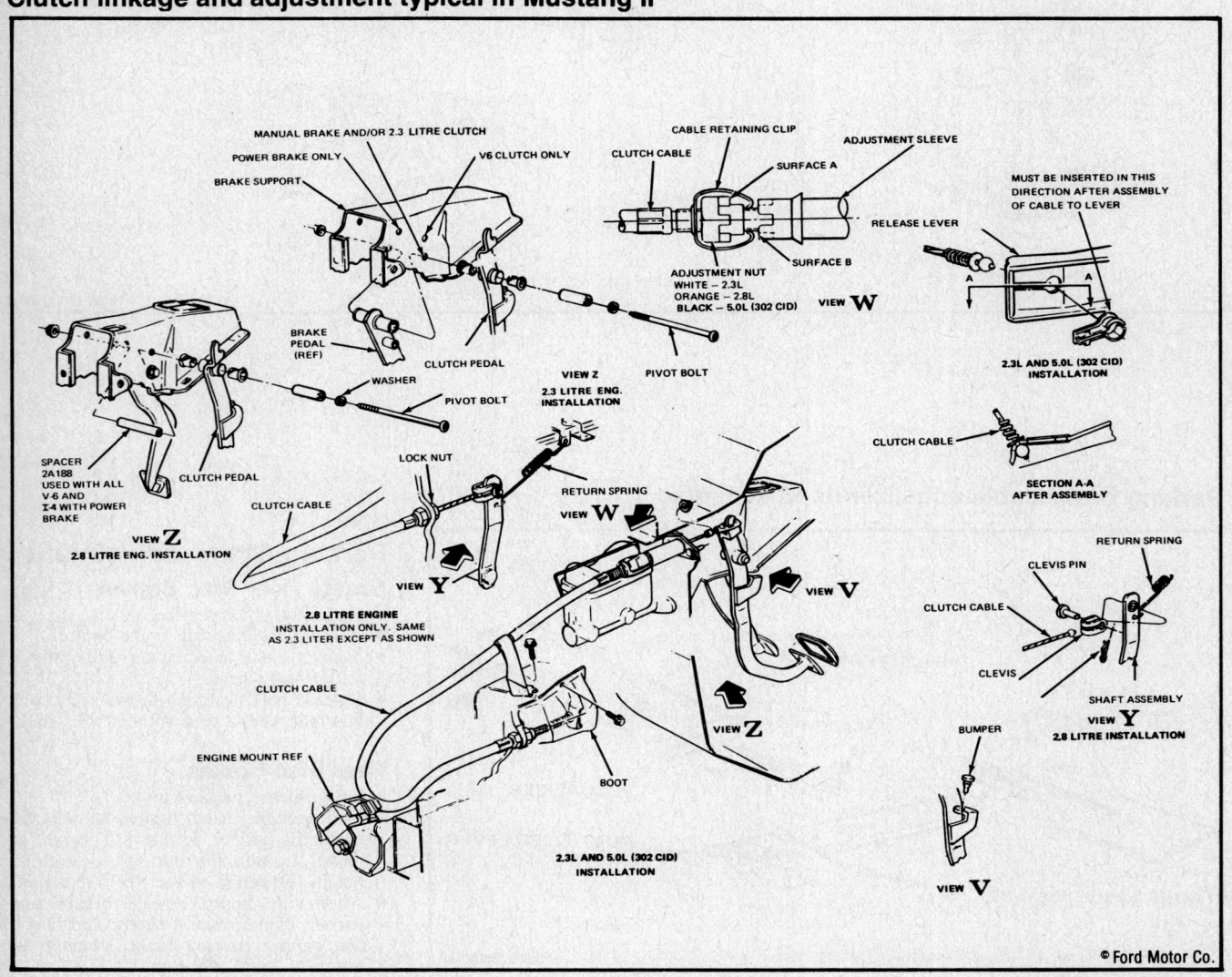

Clutch linkage typical in Fairmont and Zephyr

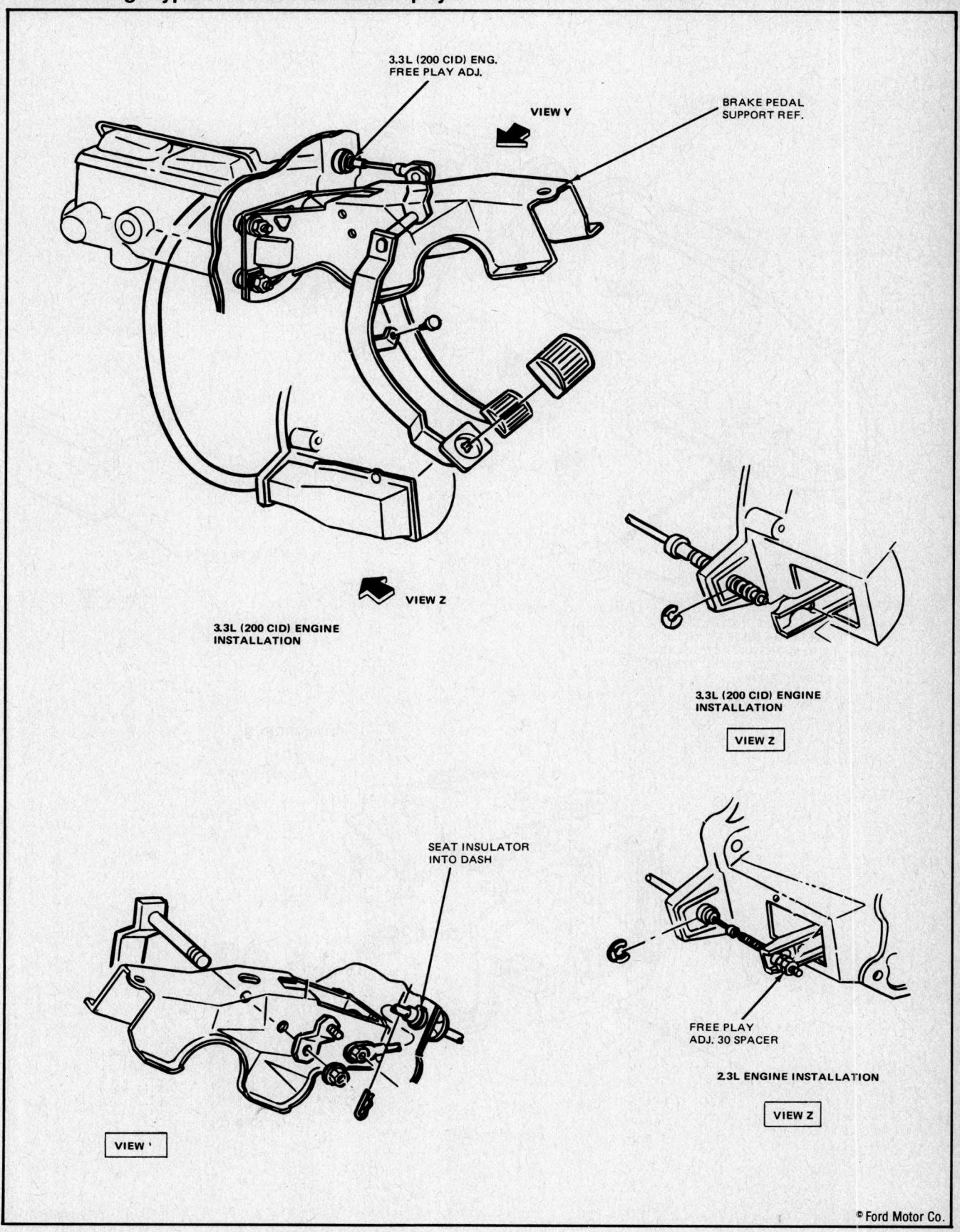

3.3L (200 CID) ENG. FREE PLAY ADJ.

VIEW Y

BRAKE PEDAL SUPPORT REF.

VIEW Z

3.3L (200 CID) ENGINE INSTALLATION

3.3L (200 CID) ENGINE INSTALLATION

VIEW Z

SEAT INSULATOR INTO DASH

FREE PLAY ADJ. 30 SPACER

2.3L ENGINE INSTALLATION

VIEW '

VIEW Z

© Ford Motor Co.

Clutch pedal and linkage typical in Bobcat and Pinto

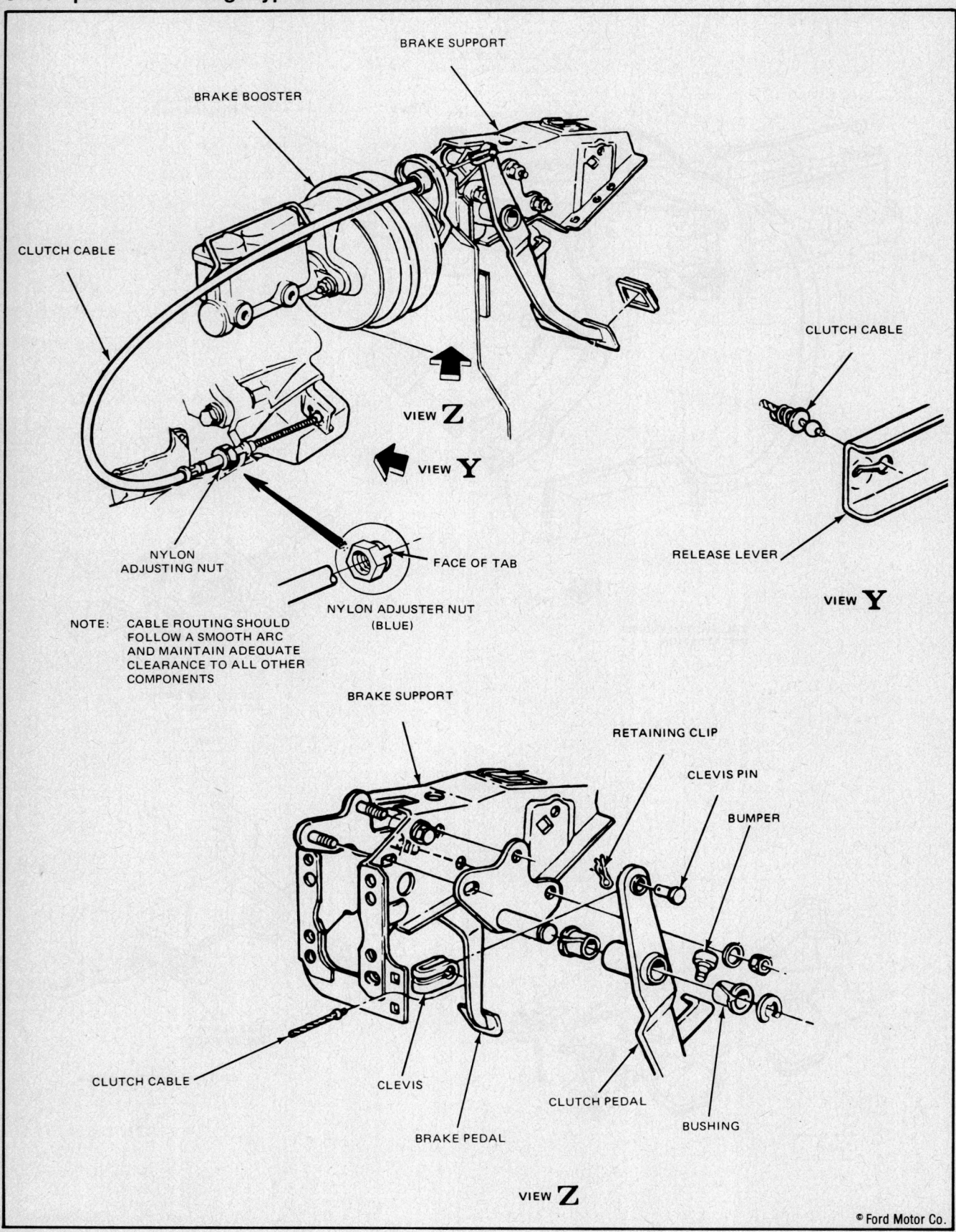

BRAKE SUPPORT

BRAKE BOOSTER

CLUTCH CABLE

VIEW Z

VIEW Y

CLUTCH CABLE

RELEASE LEVER

VIEW Y

NYLON ADJUSTING NUT

FACE OF TAB

NYLON ADJUSTER NUT (BLUE)

NOTE: CABLE ROUTING SHOULD FOLLOW A SMOOTH ARC AND MAINTAIN ADEQUATE CLEARANCE TO ALL OTHER COMPONENTS

BRAKE SUPPORT

RETAINING CLIP

CLEVIS PIN

BUMPER

CLUTCH CABLE

CLEVIS

BRAKE PEDAL

CLUTCH PEDAL

BUSHING

VIEW Z

© Ford Motor Co.

Clutch linkage adjustment typical in Cougar, Montego and Torino

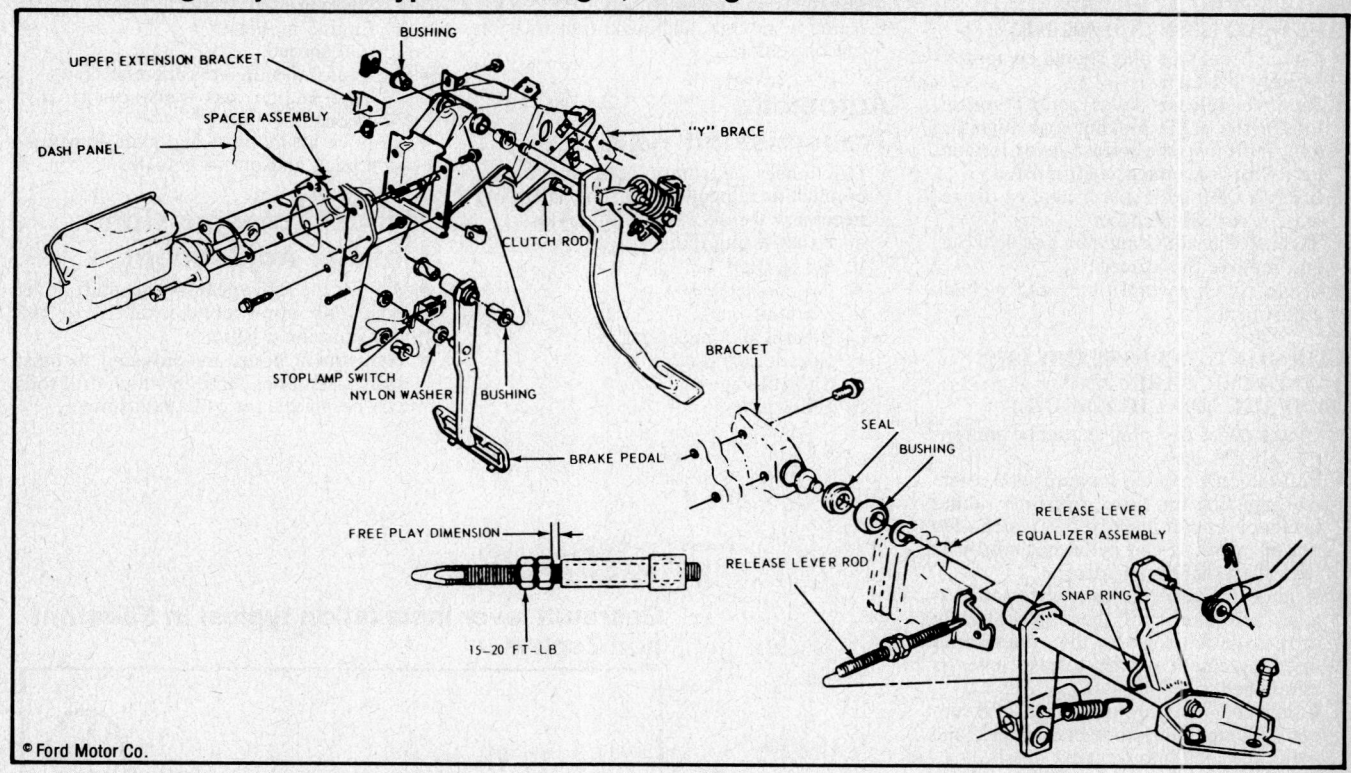

UPPER EXTENSION BRACKET
BUSHING
SPACER ASSEMBLY
DASH PANEL
"Y" BRACE
CLUTCH ROD
BRACKET
SEAL
BUSHING
STOPLAMP SWITCH
NYLON WASHER
BUSHING
BRAKE PEDAL
RELEASE LEVER
EQUALIZER ASSEMBLY
FREE PLAY DIMENSION
RELEASE LEVER ROD
SNAP RING
15–20 FT-LB

© Ford Motor Co.

Four-bar-link coil rear suspension in Fairmont, Zephyr, Mustang and Capri

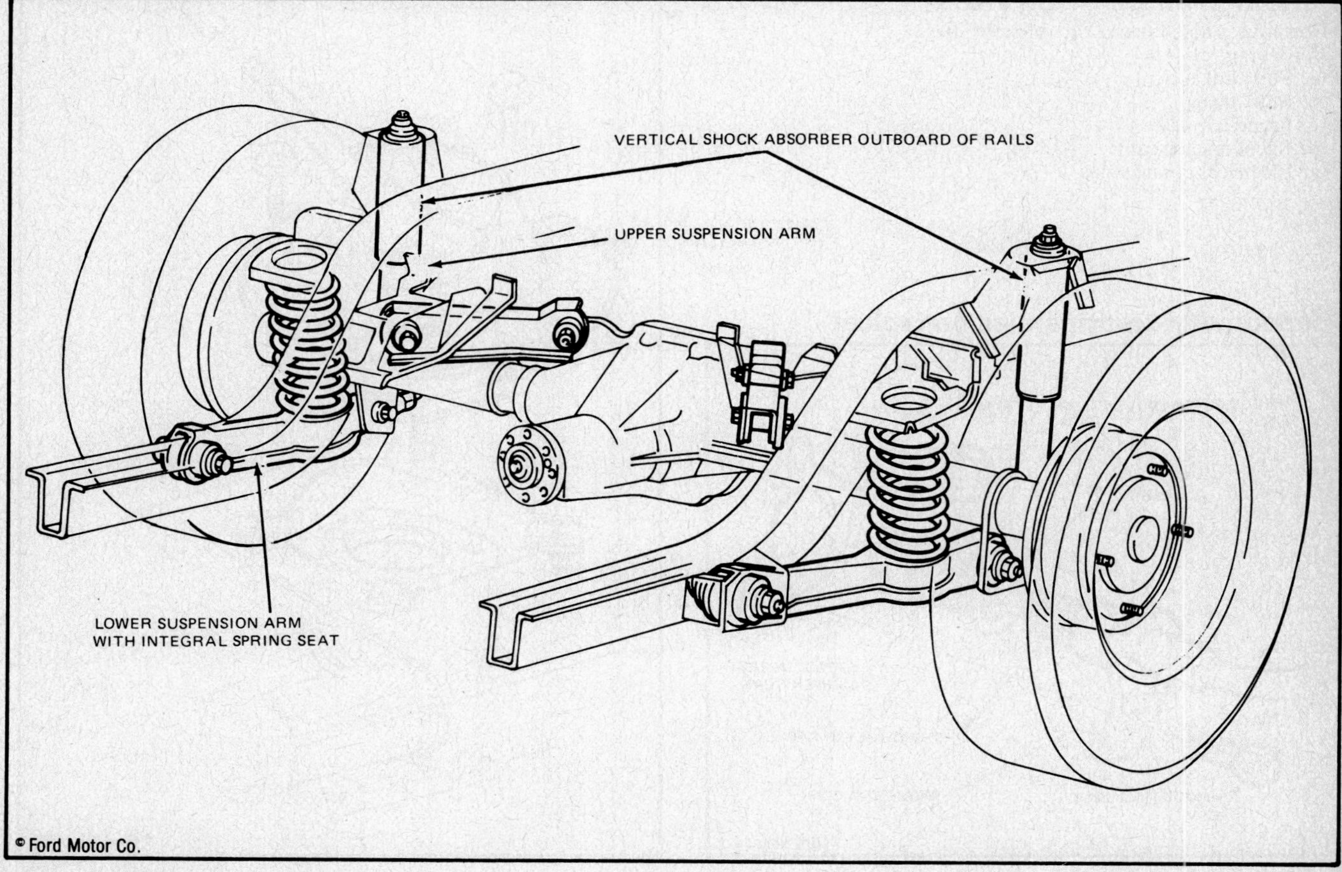

VERTICAL SHOCK ABSORBER OUTBOARD OF RAILS
UPPER SUSPENSION ARM
LOWER SUSPENSION ARM
WITH INTEGRAL SPRING SEAT

© Ford Motor Co.

FORD—LINCOLN—MERCURY REAR DRIVE CARS

FAIRMONT, ZEPHYR AND 1979 AND LATER CAPRI AND MUSTANG (2300 CC ENGINE)
- Clutch pedal free play should be approximately 1½ inch.
- Remove release lever return spring, loosen the cable locknut and adjusting nut, and move the release lever forward until free movement is eliminated.
- Insert a 0.30 inch spacer against the release lever cable spacer.
- Tighten the adjusting nut and locknut, and remove the spacer.
- Cycle clutch several times and recheck adjustment.

FAIRMONT, ZEPHYR AND 1979 AND LATER CAPRI AND MUSTANG (200 CID ENGINE)·
- Clutch pedal free play should be approximately 1½ inch.
- Pull the clutch cable forward, and rotate the adjusting nut away from the rubber insulator approximately 0.30 inch. Do not try to rotate the nylon nut until it is free of the rubber insulator.
- Release the cable to neutralize the system, and then pull the cable slightly to remove the slack in the system until free movement of the release lever is eliminated.
- Rotate the adjusting nut toward the rubber insulator until contact is made, and index the tabs into the next notch.
- Cycle clutch several times and recheck adjustment.

Manual Transmission R&R
- Remove, disconnect or relocate the following:
  a. Shift linkage
  b. Shift lever
  c. Propeller shaft
  d. Speedometer cable
  e. Electrical connections
- Support rear of engine, and remove transmission crossmember.
- Remove mounts, and lower transmission out of vehicle.

Automatic Transmission R&R
- Disconnect the battery, and remove, disconnect or relocate any of the following necessary for access and removal:
  a. Exhaust plumbing
  b. Drive shaft
  c. Oil cooler lines
  d. Vacuum lines
  e. Electrical connections
  f. Speedometer cable
  g. Shift linkages
  h. Filler tube
  i. Starter
  j. Steering idler arm
  k. Engine mounts
  l. Fan shroud
  m. Transmission crossmember (support engine and transmission as needed)
- Remove all mounts, and slide transmission back and out of vehicle.

Manual Transmission Linkage Adjustment
- Adjust the linkages so the shift lever positions correspond exactly to the transmission positions.
- Adjustment holes are provided in most shift assemblies through which drill rods can be placed for exact adjustment.

Gearshift lever installation typical in Fairmont and Zephyr

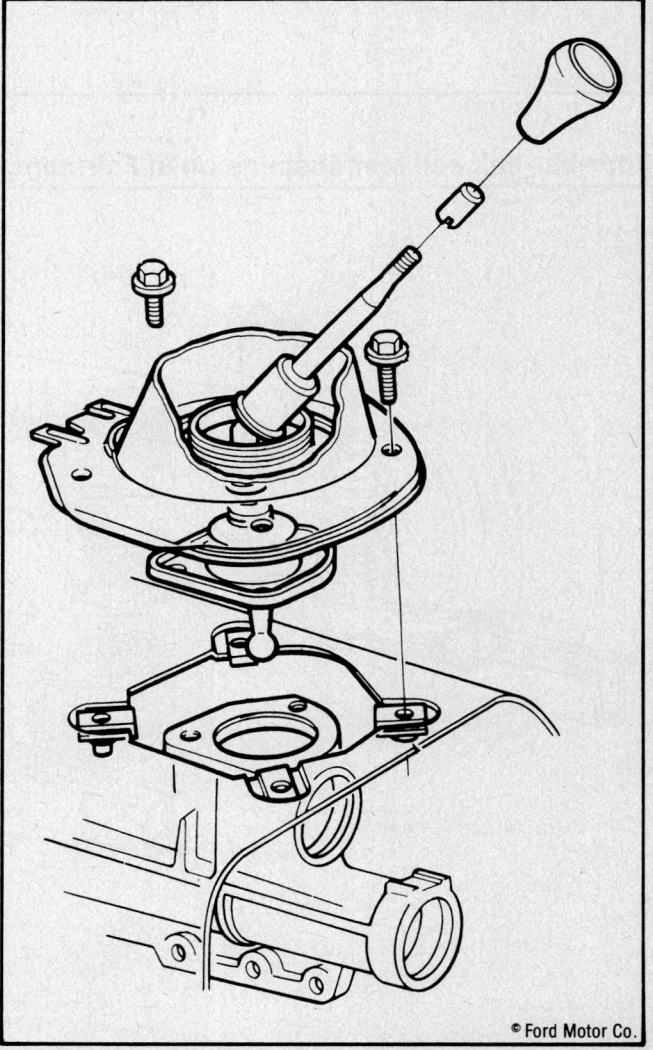

© Ford Motor Co.

Speedometer-to-transmission typical

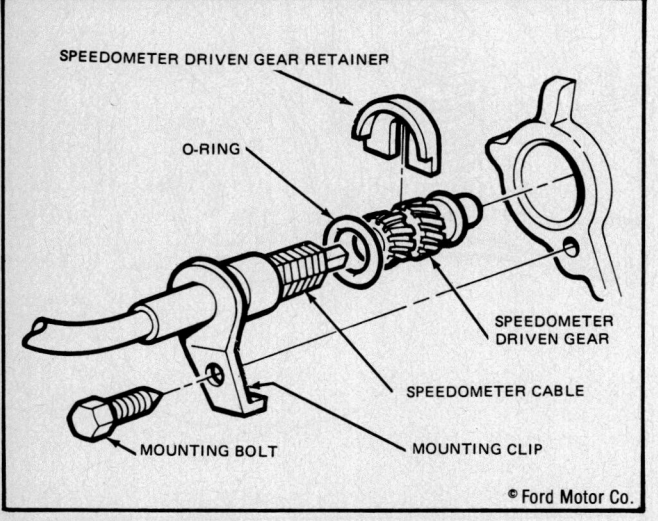

SPEEDOMETER DRIVEN GEAR RETAINER

O-RING

SPEEDOMETER DRIVEN GEAR

SPEEDOMETER CABLE

MOUNTING BOLT

MOUNTING CLIP

© Ford Motor Co.

Four speed overdrive transmission and linkage adjustment typical in Granada and Monarch

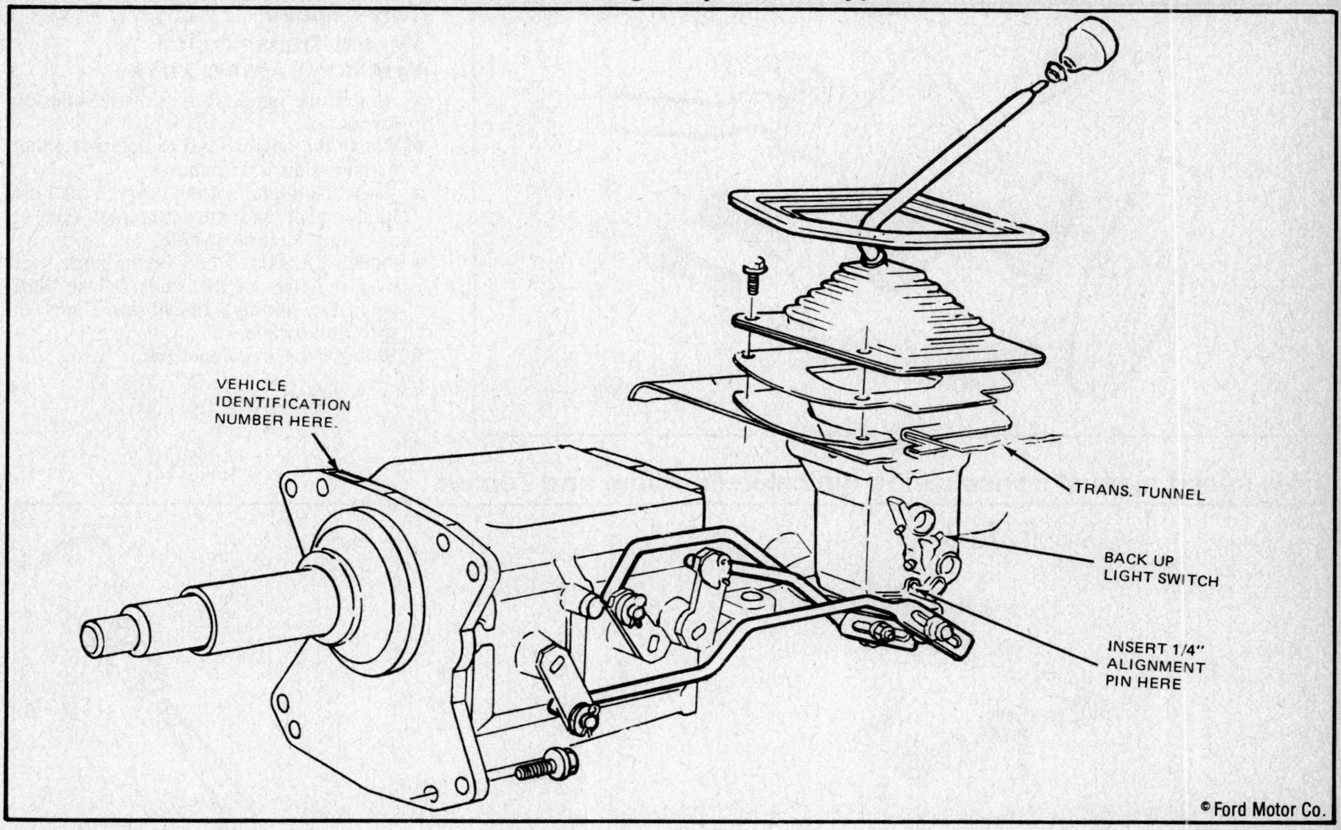

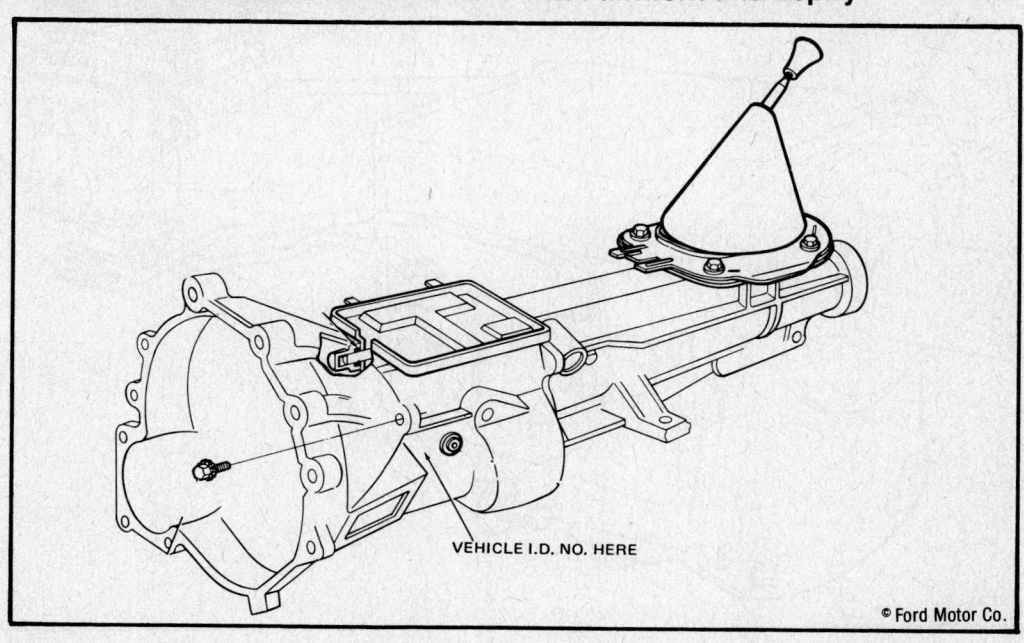

VEHICLE IDENTIFICATION NUMBER HERE.

TRANS. TUNNEL

BACK UP LIGHT SWITCH

INSERT 1/4" ALIGNMENT PIN HERE

© Ford Motor Co.

Four Speed Overdrive Transmission

GRANADA AND MONARCH

- Attach the shift rods to transmission levers.
- Shift the reverse (middle) lever clockwise to put the transmission in reverse.
- Insert the alignment pin through the hole in the boot and into the shift control assembly alignment hole.
- Attach the slotted ends of the 1-2 and 3-OD shift rods over the flats of the studs in the shift control assembly. Install lock nuts to 10-20 ft. lb. torque.
- Shift the transmission to neutral, attach reverse lever and torque to specifications.
- Remove the alignment pin. Lubricate linkage with chassis lube.

Model 78ET transmission installation in Fairmont and Zephyr

VEHICLE I.D. NO. HERE.

© Ford Motor Co.

A445

Shift tower

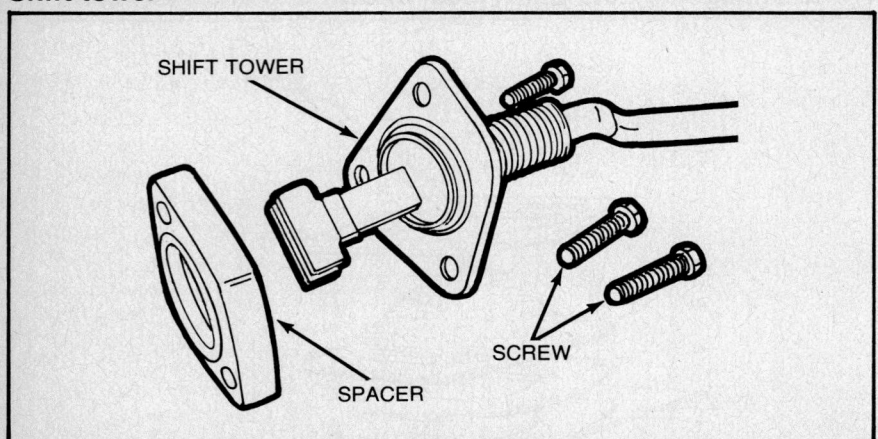

Three Speed Manual Transmission
FAIRMONT AND ZEPHYR
- Attach the shift rods to transmission levers.
- Rotate the output shaft to determine that transmission is in neutral.
- Insert the alignment pin through the hole in the boot and into the shaft control assembly alignment hole.
- Attach the slotted end of the shift rods over the flats of the studs on the shift control assembly. Install lock nuts to specified torque.
- Remove the alignment pin.

Three speed manual transmission typical in Fairmont and Zephyr

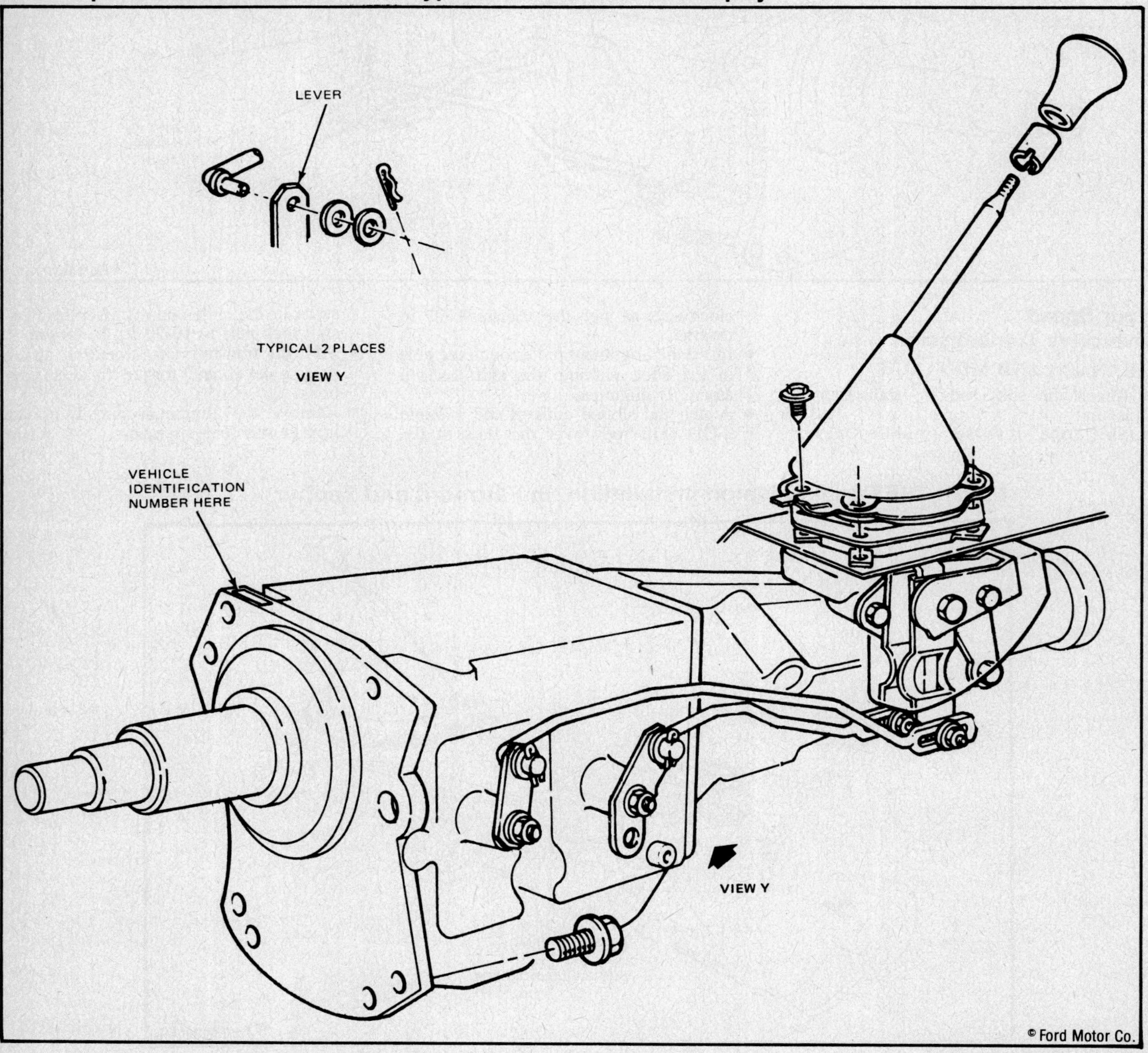

LEVER

TYPICAL 2 PLACES

VIEW Y

VEHICLE
IDENTIFICATION
NUMBER HERE

VIEW Y

© Ford Motor Co.

Three speed manual transmission floor shift linkage and adjustment

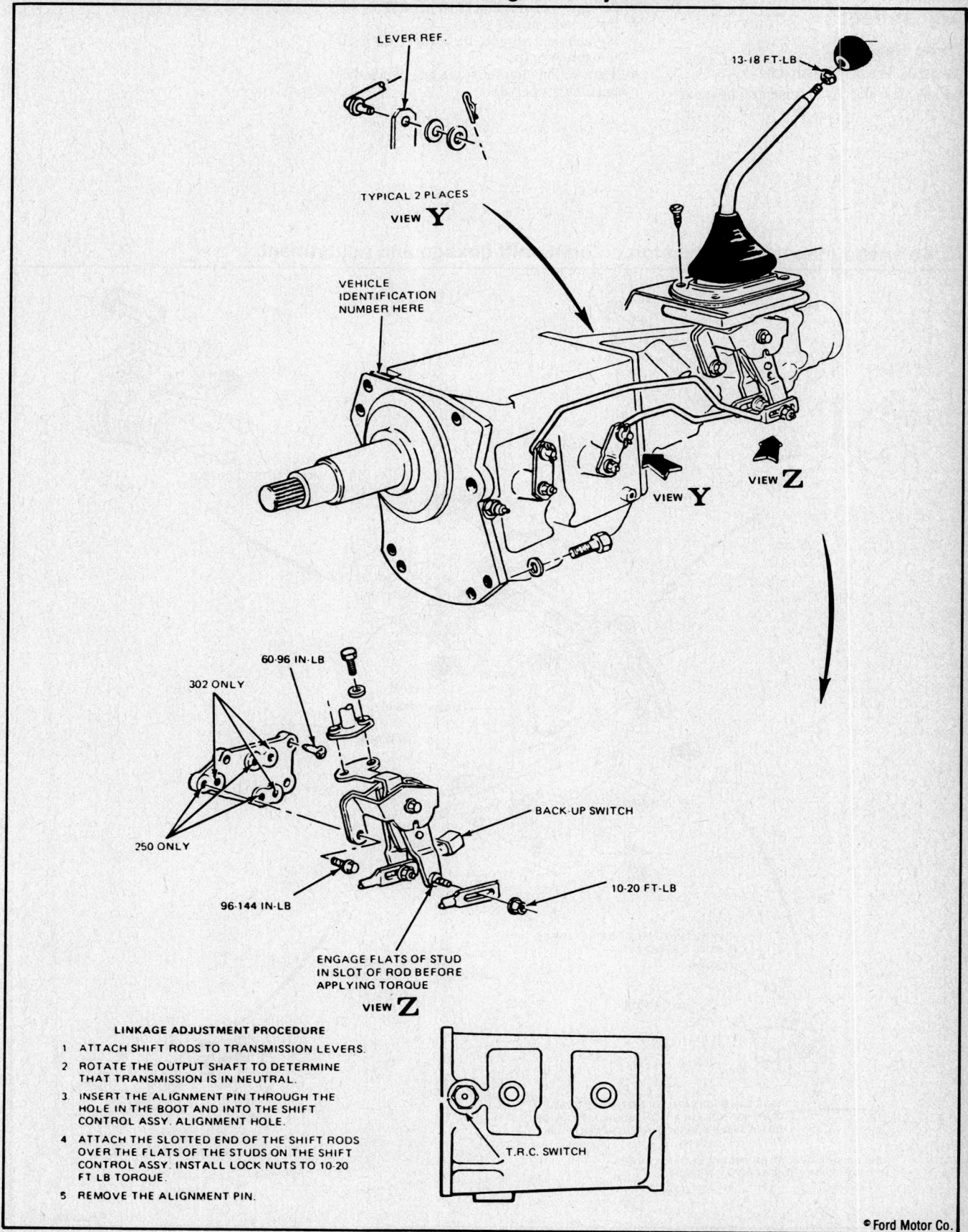

LEVER REF.

13-18 FT-LB

TYPICAL 2 PLACES
VIEW **Y**

VEHICLE
IDENTIFICATION
NUMBER HERE

VIEW **Y**

VIEW **Z**

60-96 IN-LB

302 ONLY

250 ONLY

BACK-UP SWITCH

96-144 IN-LB

10-20 FT-LB

ENGAGE FLATS OF STUD
IN SLOT OF ROD BEFORE
APPLYING TORQUE
VIEW **Z**

LINKAGE ADJUSTMENT PROCEDURE

1. ATTACH SHIFT RODS TO TRANSMISSION LEVERS.
2. ROTATE THE OUTPUT SHAFT TO DETERMINE THAT TRANSMISSION IS IN NEUTRAL.
3. INSERT THE ALIGNMENT PIN THROUGH THE HOLE IN THE BOOT AND INTO THE SHIFT CONTROL ASSY. ALIGNMENT HOLE.
4. ATTACH THE SLOTTED END OF THE SHIFT RODS OVER THE FLATS OF THE STUDS ON THE SHIFT CONTROL ASSY. INSTALL LOCK NUTS TO 10-20 FT LB TORQUE.
5. REMOVE THE ALIGNMENT PIN.

T.R.C. SWITCH

© Ford Motor Co.

Column Shift Linkage and Adjustment

Three Speed
Manual Transmission

- Place gear shift lever in neutral position.
- Loosen gear shift rod adjustment nuts.
- Be sure transmission is in neutral.
- Install adjustment pin.
- Tighten and torque the gear shift rod adjustment nuts.
- Remove the alignment pin and check the shift lever operation.

Three speed manual transmission column shift linkage and adjustment

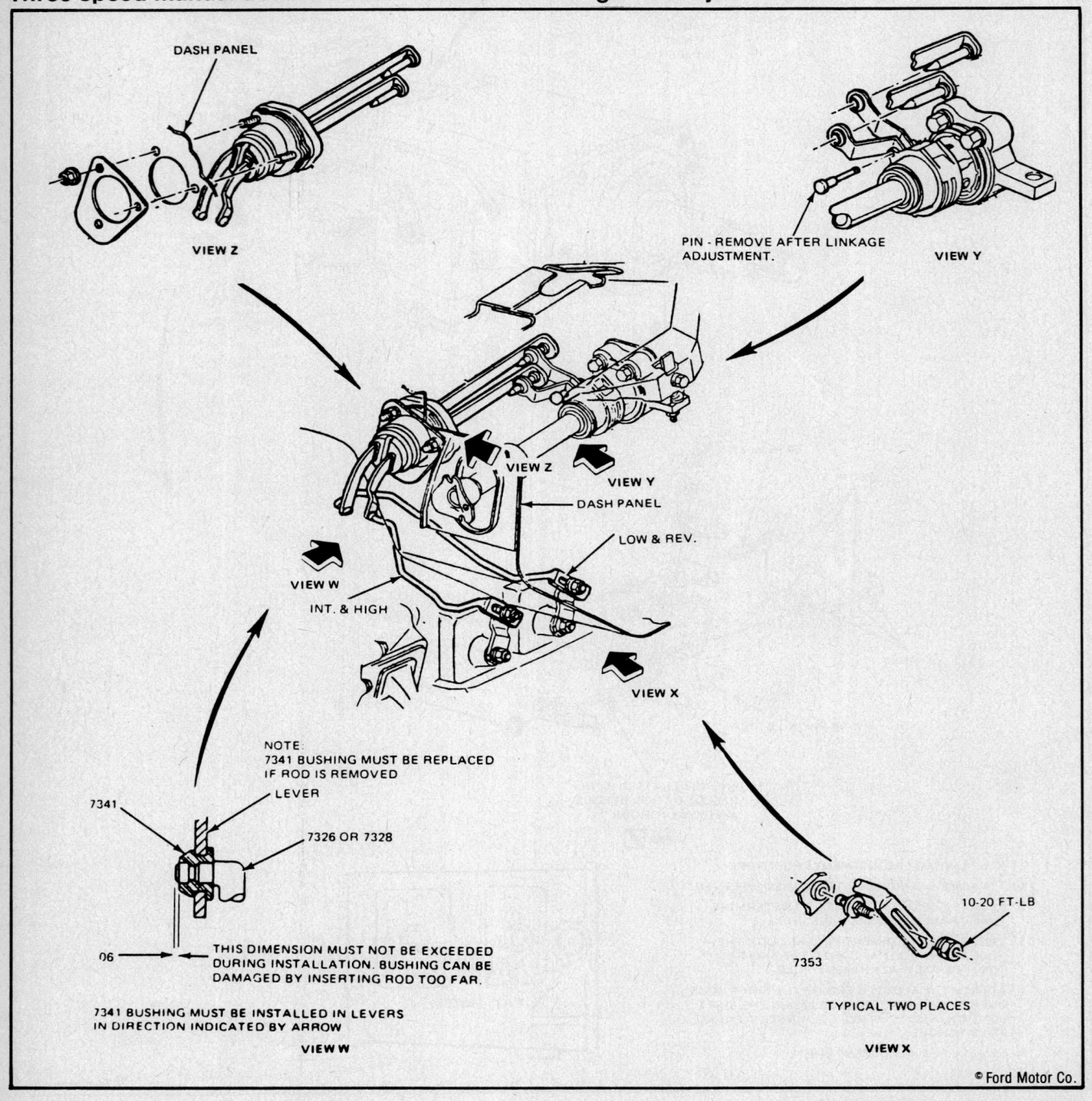

© Ford Motor Co.

Automatic Transmission Throttle Linkage Adjustment

- Check for wide open carburetor and linkage travel at full throttle. The carburetor full throttle stop must be contacted by the throttle linkage, and there must be a slight amount of movement left in the downshift linkage.

Automatic Transmission Manual Linkage Adjustment

- Adjust the linkage so the shift lever positions correspond exactly to the transmission position. Make this adjustment in the DRIVE position.
- After adjustment, check operation of the neutral start switch and the backup lights.

Transmission Kickdown Control Adjustment

- Assemble all components of kickdown controls.
- With carburetor held at W.O.T. position and the kickdown rod held downward with the specified 4.25 lb. weight against the through detent stop, adjust the kickdown adjusting screw to obtain .01-.08 clearance between screw and throttle ar.
- Return system to idle.

Automatic transmission shift linkage in subcompact car models

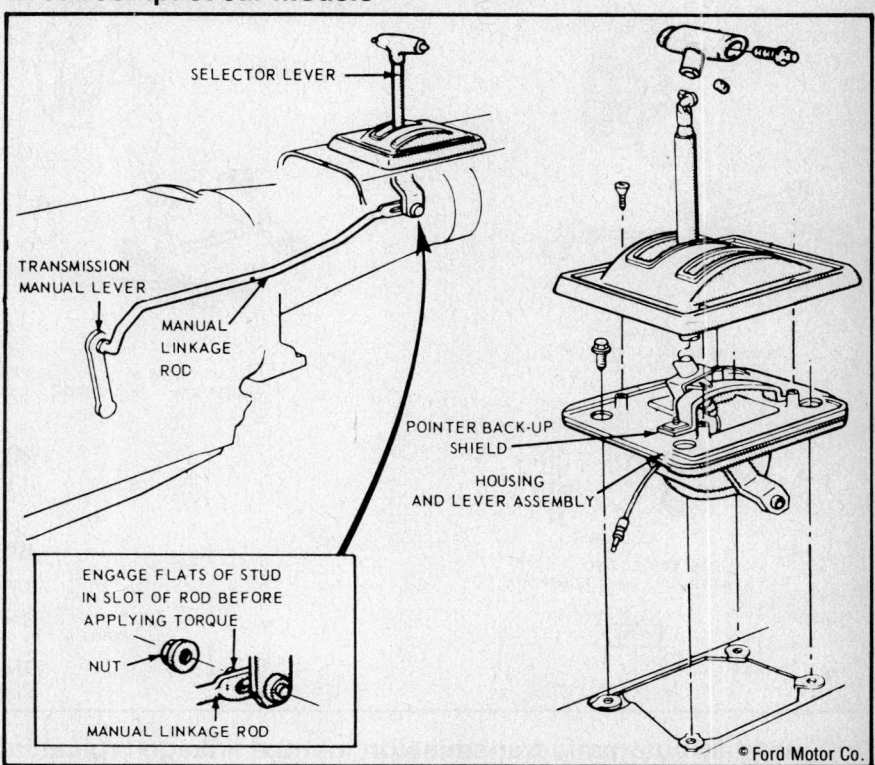

Automatic transmission typical throttle linkage and downshift adjustment

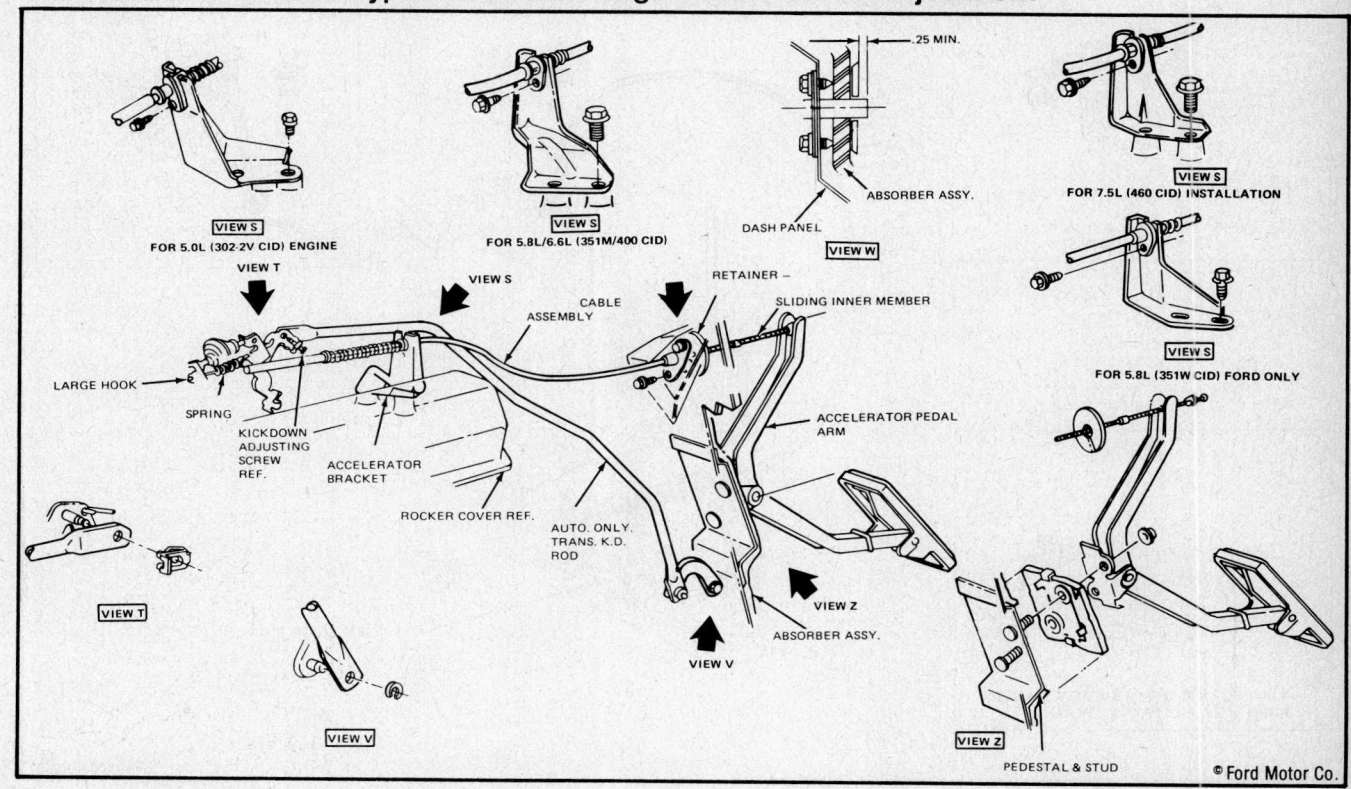

FORD—LINCOLN—MERCURY REAR DRIVE CARS

Column shift automatic transmission manual linkage typical in Fairmont and Zephyr

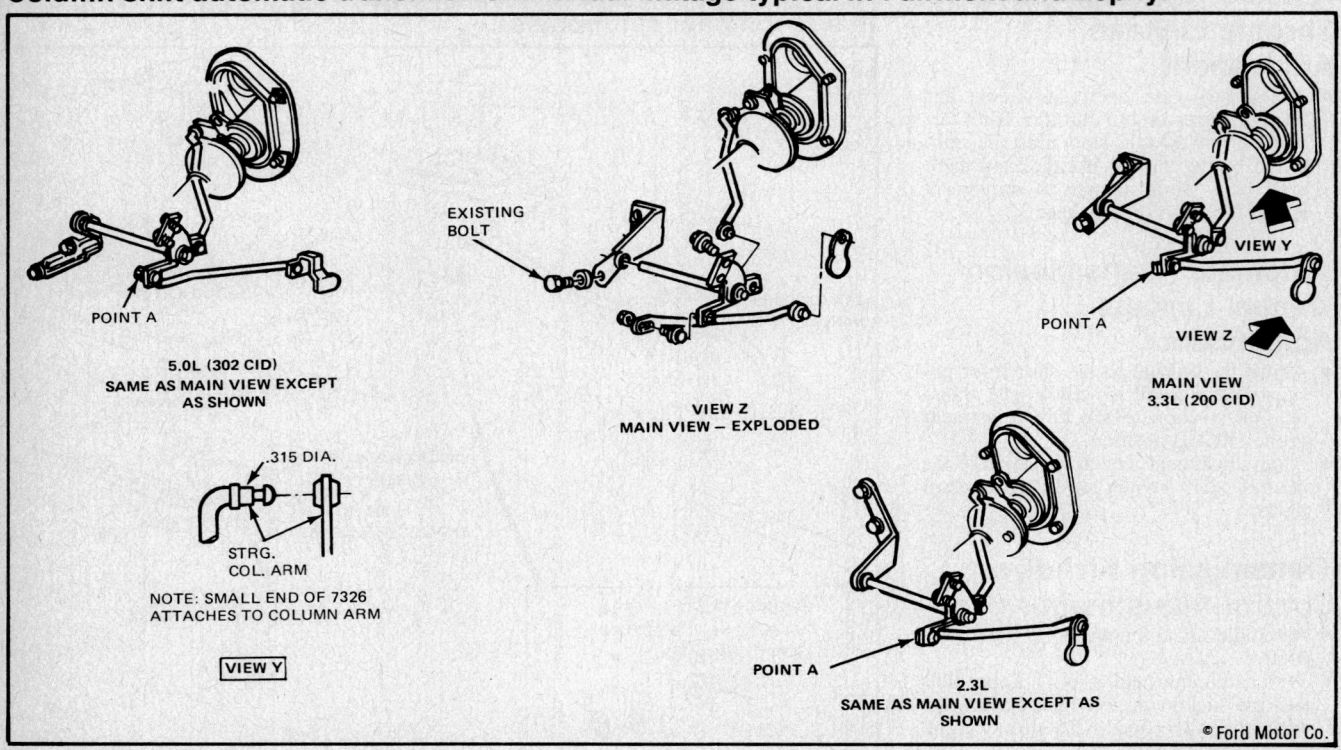

EXISTING BOLT

POINT A

5.0L (302 CID)
SAME AS MAIN VIEW EXCEPT
AS SHOWN

.315 DIA.

STRG.
COL. ARM

NOTE: SMALL END OF 7326
ATTACHES TO COLUMN ARM

VIEW Y

VIEW Z
MAIN VIEW — EXPLODED

VIEW Y

POINT A

VIEW Z

MAIN VIEW
3.3L (200 CID)

POINT A

2.3L
SAME AS MAIN VIEW EXCEPT AS
SHOWN

© Ford Motor Co.

Column shift automatic transmission manual linkage typical in Cougar, Continental Mark V, Granada, LTD II, Monarch, Thunderbird, and Versailles

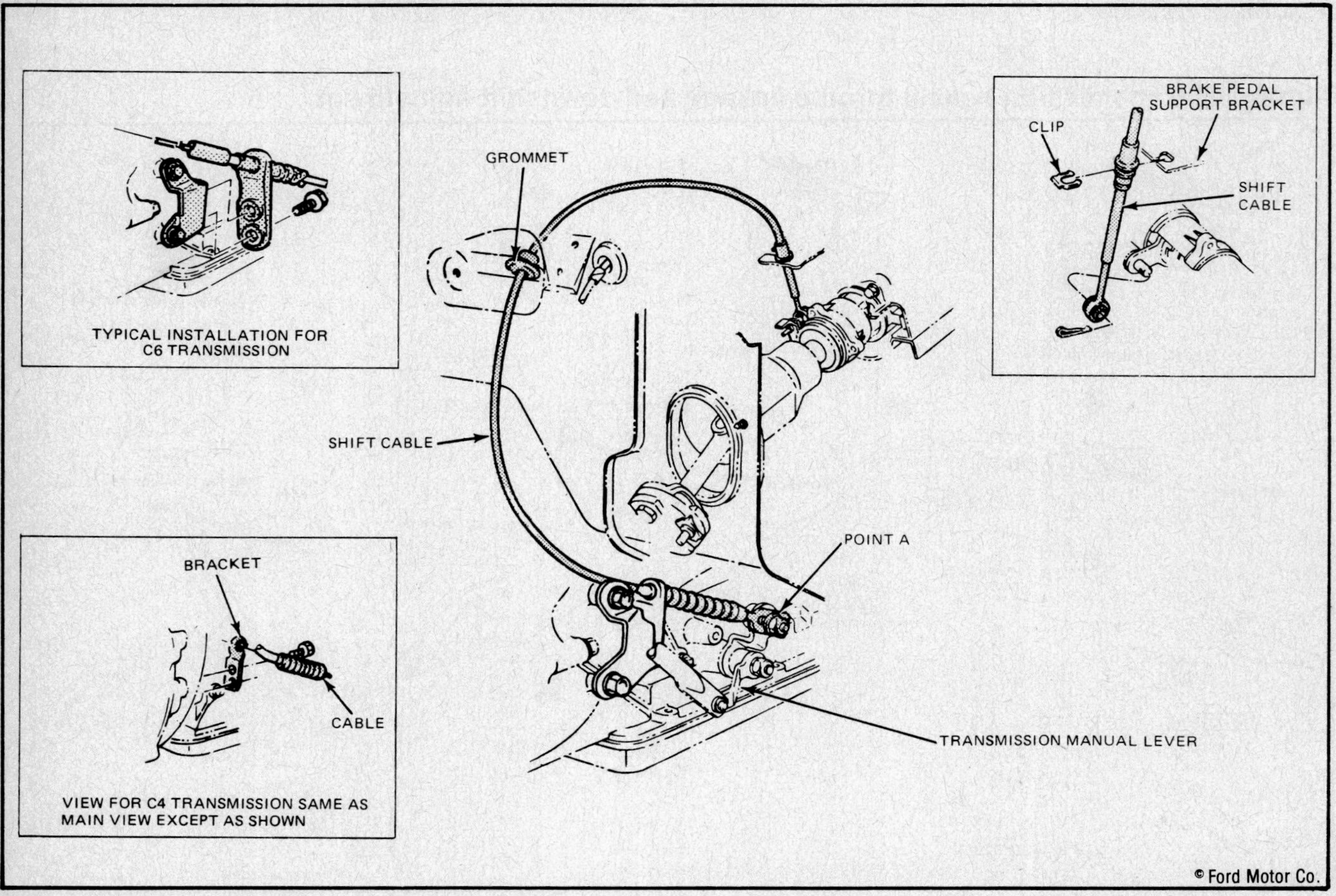

TYPICAL INSTALLATION FOR
C6 TRANSMISSION

GROMMET

BRAKE PEDAL
SUPPORT BRACKET

CLIP

SHIFT
CABLE

SHIFT CABLE

POINT A

BRACKET

CABLE

VIEW FOR C4 TRANSMISSION SAME AS
MAIN VIEW EXCEPT AS SHOWN

TRANSMISSION MANUAL LEVER

© Ford Motor Co.

GENERAL MOTORS "A" & "X" BODY

"A": Celebrity, Ciera, AF6000, Century; "X": Citation, Omega, Phoenix, Skylark

INDEX

Page Numbers Preceded by "B" Refer to Unit Repair Section

GENERAL MOTORS "A" AND "X" BODY CARS
"A": CELEBRITY, CENTURY, A6000, CIERA; "X": CITATION, OMEGA, PHOENIX, SKYLARK

MODEL IDENTIFICATION

1980 CITATION
W.B. **104.9"** Length 181.1" Ship. Wgt.
Coupe 2441, Sedan 2480

1981 CITATION
W.B. **104.9"**. Length 181.1". Ship. Wgt.
2495 Lbs.

1982 CITATION
W.B. **104.9"**. Length 181.1". Ship. Wgt.
Coupe 2441, Sedan 2480

1980 OMEGA
W.B. **104.9"** Length 181.1" Ship. Wgt.
Coupe 2441, Sedan 2480

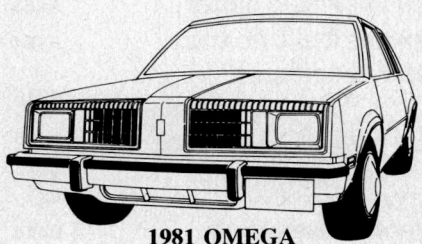

1981 OMEGA
W.B. **104.9"**. Length 181.1". Ship. Wgt.
2495 Lbs.

1982 OMEGA
W.B. **104.9"**. Length 181.1". Ship. Wgt.
2495 Lbs.

1980 PHOENIX
W.B. **104.9"** Length 182.1" Ship. Wgt.
Coupe 2496, Sedan 2539

1981 PHOENIX
W.B. **104.9"**. Length 181.1". Ship. Wgt.
2495 Lbs.

1982 PHOENIX
W.B. **104.9"**. Length 182.1". Ship. Wgt.
Coupe 2496, Sedan 2539

1980 SKYLARK
W.B. **104.9"** Length 181.1" Ship. Wgt.
Coupe 2441, Sedan 2480

1981 SKYLARK
W.B. **104.9"**. Length 181.1". Ship. Wgt.
2495 Lbs.

1982 SKYLARK
W.B. **104.9"**. Length 181.1". Ship. Wgt.
2495 Lbs.

1982 CHEVROLET CELEBRITY
W.B. **104.9"**. Length 190". Ship. Wgt.
2650 Lbs.

1982 PONTIAC A-6000
W.B. **104.9"**. Length 188.2". Ship. Wgt.
2641 Lbs.

A452

GENERAL MOTORS "A" AND "X" BODY CARS

"A": CELEBRITY, CENTURY, A6000, CIERA; "X": CITATION, OMEGA, PHOENIX, SKYLARK

1982 OLD'S CIERA
W.B. **104.9"**. Length 188.2". Ship. Wgt. 2640 Lbs.

1982 BUICK CENTURY
W.B. **104.9"**. Length 188.2". Ship. Wgt. 2630 Lbs.

ENGINE FIRING ORDER

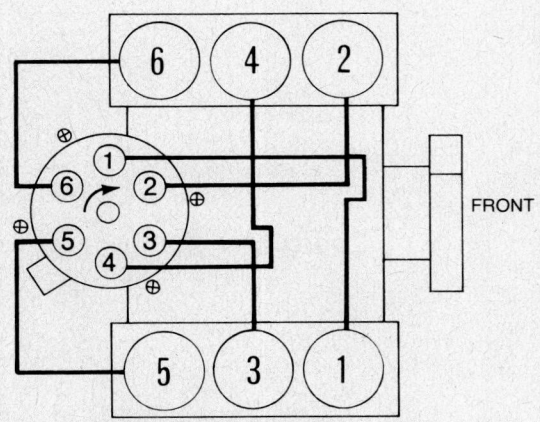

FRONT

GM (Chevrolet) 173 V6
Engine firing order: 1-2-3-4-5-6
Distributor rotation: clockwise

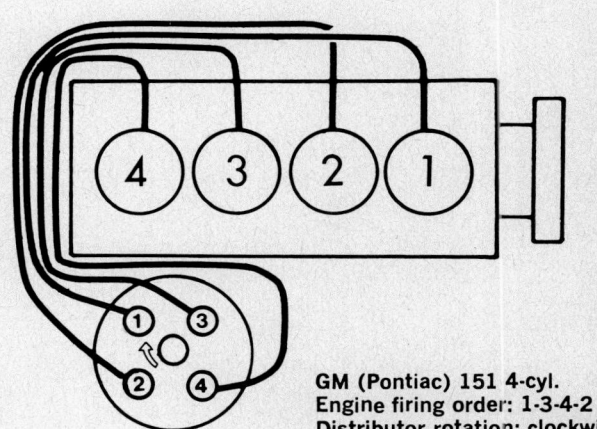

GM (Pontiac) 151 4-cyl.
Engine firing order: 1-3-4-2
Distributor rotation: clockwise

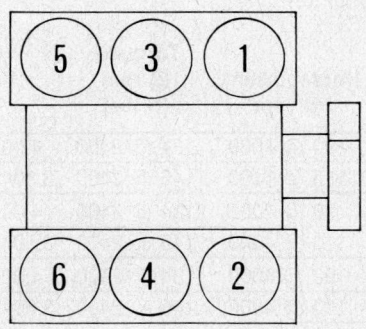

GM (Olds.) Diesel V6 260 CID 4.3L
Firing order: 1-6-5-4-3-2

A453

VEHICLE IDENTIFICATION NUMBER (VIN)

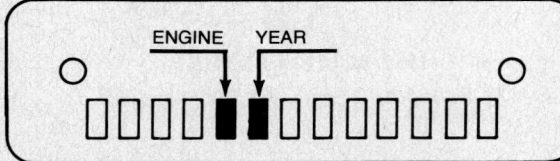 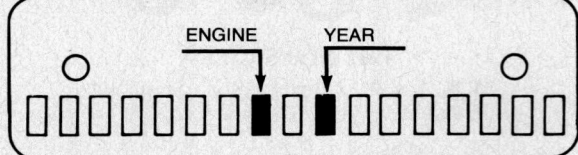

VIN Code	ENGINE CODE				MODEL YEAR CODE	
	Eng. Disp. (cu in)	Eng. Config.	Carb.	Eng. Mfgr.	Code	Year
5	151	L4	2V	Pont.	A	1980
7	173	V6	2V	Chev		
5	151	L4	2V	Pont	B	1981
X	173	V6	2V	Chev		
Z	173	V6	2V	Chev		
5	151	L4	2V	Pont.	C	1982
X	173	V6	2V	Chev.		
7	173	V6	2V	Chev.		
E	181	V6	2V	Buick		
T	260	V6	DIESEL	Olds.		

① If a 17- or 19-digit VIN is used, the 8th digit is the engine code

ENGINE SPECIFICATIONS

Yr.	Eng. V.I.N. Code	Engine No. Cyl. Disp. (cu in)	Eng. Mfr.	Carb Bbl	Tax H.P.	Horsepower② @ rpm	Torque② @ rpm (ft lbs)	Bore and Stroke (in)	Valves Intake Opens (deg BTDC)	Fuel Pump Pres. (psi)	Comp. Ratio	Oil Pressure @ 2000 rpm
80	5	4-151	Pont	2	25.6	90 @ 4000	134 @ 2400	4.00 × 3.00	33	6.5-8	8.3	36-41
	7	6-173	Chev	2	29.5	115 @ 5100	145 @ 2400	3.504 × 2.992	—	6-7.5	8.6	—
81	5	4-151-2.5L	Pont	2	25.6	90 @ 4000	134 @ 2400	4.00 × 3.00	33		8.2:1	36-40
	X-Z	6-173-2.8L	Chev	2	29.5	110 @ 4800	145 @ 2400	3.504 × 3.00	—		8.2:1	35-40
82	5	4-151-2.5L	Pont	2	29.5	90 @ 4000	134 @ 2400	4.00 × 3.00	33		8.2:1	36-40
	X-Z	6-163-2.8L	Chev	2	29.5	110 @ 4800	145 @ 2400	3.504 × 3.00	—		8.2:1	36-40
	E	6-181-3.0L	Buick	—	—	—	—	3.8 × 2.66	—		8.45:1	—
	Diesel T	6-263-4.3L	Olds		39.2	90 @ 2400	170 @ 1800	4.057 × 3.385	—		22.5:1	30-45

② Figures are Chilton estimates

TUNE-UP SPECIFICATIONS

Yr.	Eng. V.I.N. Code	Engine No. Cyl. Disp. (cu in)	Applic. & Trans.	SPARK PLUGS Orig. Type	Gap (in)	Timing deg BTDC @ rpm	IDLE SPEEDS Solenoid Screw A/C	Non A/C	Base	Curb	Fast
80	5	4-151	Lo.Alt./Man.	R43TSX	.060	10 @ 1000	1300N	1000N	500N	1000N	2400N
			Lo.Alt./Auto.	R43TSX	.060	10 @ 650	900D	650D	500D	650D	2600N
			Calif./Man.	R43TSX	.060	10 @ 1000	1200N	1000N	500N	1000N	2200N
			Calif./Auto.	R43TSX	.060	10 @ 650	900D	650D	500D	650D	2600N
	7	6-173	Lo.Alt./Man.	R44TS	.045	2 @ 750	1200N	1200N	750N	—	1900N
			Lo.Alt./Auto.	R44TS	.045	6 @ 700	850D	—	—	700D	2000P
			Calif./Man.	R44TS	.045	6 @ 750	—	—	750N	—	2000N
			Calif./Auto.	R44TS	.045	10 @ 700	800D	—	—	700D	2000P
81	5	4-151-2.5L	Man.	R44TX	.060	4 @ 1000-N	—	—	800N	1000N	2600N
	5	4-151-2.5L	Auto.	R44TX	.060	4 @ 675-D	—	—	550D	675D	2600P
	X-Z	6-173-2.8L	Man.	R43TX	.045	6 @ 1100	—	—	—	850N	2600N
	X-Z	6-173-2.8L	Auto.	R43TX	.045	10 @ 650-D	—	—	—	600D	2600P
82	5	4-151-2.5L	Man.	R44TX	.060	4 @ 1000-N	—	—	800N	1000N	2600N
	5	4-151-2.5L	Auto.	R44TX	.060	4 @ 675-D	—	—	550D	675D	2600P
	X-Z	6-173-2.8L	Man.	R43TX	.045	6 @ 1100	—	—	—	850N	2600N
	X-Z	6-173-2.8L	Auto.	R43TX	.045	10 @ 650-D	—	—	—	600D	2600P
	E	6-181-3.0L	Auto.	①	①	①	—	—	—	①	①
	T	6-263-3.4	Auto.	Diesel	—	—	—	—	—	①	—

NOTE: The underhood certification/specification decal is the authority for performance specifications affecting vehicle emissions. Use this manual's information only when that decal is not available.

— Not applicable
N = Neutral
D = Drive
P = Park
① See engine decal

DISTRIBUTOR SPECIFICATIONS①

Year	Distributor Identification	CENTRIFUGAL ADVANCE Start Crankshaft Deg. @ Eng. RPM	Finish Crankshaft Deg. @ Eng. RPM	VACUUM ADVANCE Start @ In. Hg.	Finish Crankshaft Deg. @ In. Hg.
80	1103361	0-4.5 @ 1100	20-24 @ 4800	3.5	8.5-11.5 @ 20
	1103362	0-4.5 @ 1100	24-28 @ 4800	3.5	8.5-11.5 @ 20
	1110782	0-4 @ 1050	19-23 @ 4000	3.5	16.5-22 @ 8
	1110783	0-3 @ 1400	19-23 @ 4000	4	19-20 @ 10
	1110786	0-3 @ 1050	19-23 @ 4000	3.5	22 @ 9
	1110787	0 @ 1050	22 @ 4000	3.5	20 @ 9

① 81-82 distributor is computer controlled, electric timing.

TORQUE SPECIFICATIONS

All readings in ft/lbs

Year	Engine No. Cyl. Disp. (cu in)	Eng. V.I.N. Code	Cylinder Head Bolts	Rod Bearing Bolts	Main Bearing Bolts	Crankshaft Pulley Bolt	Flywheel To Crankshaft Bolts	MANIFOLD Intake	MANIFOLD Exhaust
80	4-151-2.5L	5	75	32	70	200	44	29	44
	6-173-2.8L	7	65-75	34-40	63-74	66-84	45-55	20-25	22-28
81	4-151-2.5L	5	75	32	70	200	44	29	44
	6-173-2.8L	X	65-75	34-40	63-74	66-84	45-55	20-25	22-28
	6-173-2.8L	Z	65-75	34-40	63-74	66-84	45-55	20-25	22-28
82	4-151-2.5L	5	75	32	70	200	44	29	44
	6-173-2.5L	X-Z	65-75	34-40	63-74	66-84	45-55	20-25	22-28
	6-181-3.0L	E	80	40	100	225	60	45	25
	6-263-4.3L	T-Diesel	—	40	107	29	29	15	29

VALVE SPECIFICATIONS

Year	Engine No. Cyl. Disp. (cu in)	Eng. V.I.N. Code	Seat Angle (deg)	Face Angle (deg)	Spring Test Pressure (lbs @ in)	Spring Installed Height (in)	STEM TO GUIDE CLEARANCE (in) Intake	STEM TO GUIDE CLEARANCE (in) Exhaust	STEM DIAMETER (in) Intake	STEM DIAMETER (in) Exhaust
80	4-151-2.5L	5	46	45	122-180 @ 1.254	1.69	.0010-.0027	.0010-.0027	.3425-.3418	.3425-.3418
	6-173	7	46	45	194 @ 1.18	1.574	.0010-.0026	.0010-.0026	—	—
81	4-151-2.5L	5	46	45	122-180 @ 1.254	1.69	.0010-.0027	.0010-.0027	.3425-.3418	.3425-.3418
	6-173-2.8L	X	46	45	194 @ 1.18	1.574	.0010-.0026	.0010-.0026	.3410-.3418	.3425-.3418
82	4-151-2.5L	5	46	45	122-180 @ 1.254	1.69	.0010-.0027	.0010-.0027	.3425-.3418	.3425-.3418
	6-173-2.8L	X-Z	46	45	151 @ 1.15	1.60	.0010-.0026	.0010-.0026	.3410-.3418	.3410-.3418
	6-181-3.0L	E	45	45	164 @ 1.340②	1.727	.0015-.0035	.0015-.0032	.3412-.3401	.3412-.3405
	6-263-4.3L	T	①	①	①	①	①	①	①	①

① See diesel engine section
② Intake shown, exhaust 182 ± 8 @ 1.34°

CRANKSHAFT & CONNECTING ROD SPECIFICATIONS

All measurements given in inches

Year	Engine No. Cyl. Disp. (cu in)	Eng. V.I.N. Code	CRANKSHAFT Main Brg. Journal Dia	CRANKSHAFT Main Brg. Oil Clearance	CRANKSHAFT Shaft End-Play	CRANKSHAFT Thrust on No.	CONNECTING ROD Journal Diameter	CONNECTING ROD Oil Clearance	CONNECTING ROD Side Clearance
80	4-151	5	2.300	.0005-.0022	.0035-.0085	5	2.000	.0005-.0026	.006-.022
	6-173	7	2.490	.0017-.0029	.0019-.0078	3	1.999	.0014-.0035	.006-.017
81	4-151	5	2.300	.0005-.0022	.0035-.0085	5	2.000	.0005-.0026	.006-.022
	6-173	X	2.490	.0017-.0029	.0019-.0078	3	2.000	.0014-.0035	.006-.017
	6-173	Z	2.490	.0017-.0029	.0019-.0018	3	2.000	.0014-.0035	.006-.017
82	4-151	5	2.300	.0005-.0022	.0035-.0085	5	2.000	.0005-.00026	.006-.022
	6-173	X-Z	2.490	.0005-.0015	.0020-.0080	3	2.000	.0005-.00026	.006-.017
	6-181	E	2.4995	.0003-.0018	.003-.009	2	2.2487	.0005-.0026	.006-.023
Diesel	6-263-4.3L	T	2.9993-3.0003	.0005-.0021	.0035-.0135	3	2.1238-2.148	.0005-.0026	.006-.020

FLUID CAPACITIES—Coolant, Fuel & Lubricant

Year	Engine No. Cyl. Disp. (cu in)	Eng. V.I.N. Code	Engine① Crankcase	TRANSAXLE (Pts. to Refill After Draining) Manual	Automatic	Gasoline Tank (gals)	COOLING SYSTEM (qts) With Heater	with A/C	Rad. Cap. Press.	Therm. Temp.
80	4-151-2.5L	5	3	3	10	14	9.50	9.75	15	195
	6-173-2.8L	7	4	3	10	14	11.50	11.75	15	195
81	4-151-2.5L	5	3	3	10	14	9.50	9.75	15	195
	6-173-2.8L	X-Z	4	3	10	14	11.50	11.75	15	195
82	6-181-3.0L	E	②	3	6	15	11.5	11.75	15	195
Diesel	6-263-4.3L	T①	②	3	6	15	11.5	11.75	15	195

① See diesel section
② See owner's manual

BRAKE SPECIFICATIONS

Readings in inches (mm)

Year	Model	Master Cylinder Bore Diameter	CALIPER OR WHEEL CYLINDER Front	Rear	BRAKE DRUM/ROTOR DIAMETER Front	Rear
80	All	.874(22)	.689(17.5)	.689	11.0	7.8
81	All	.874(22)	.689(17.5)	.689	11.0	7.8
82	A Body	.874(22)	.689(17.5)	.689	10.00	9.0
	X Body	.874(22)	.689(17.5)	.689	9.72	7.8

① Additional oil may be needed when filter is changed. Fill to correct level on dipstick.

DISC BRAKE SPECIFICATIONS

Year	Model	Caliper Type	Mounting Bolt Torque ft/lbs(N•m)	Mfr.'s Recommended Disc Pad Minimum Thickness	Rotor Runout	Rotor Allowance Minimum Machined Thickness	Rotor Thickness Variation Maximum
80	All	Sliding	28(17)	①	.005	.965	.0005
81	All	Sliding	28(17)	①	.005	.965	.0005
82	A Body	Sliding	28(17)	①	.005	—	.005
	X Body	Sliding	28(17)	①	.005	.965	.005

① Replace when lining is worn to within .030" of any rivet

A457

Fuse and Circuit Breaker Data

Name	Color/Size (Amps)	Circuits Protected	Fuse Block Connector Protected
A/C	WHT (25)	Air Conditioner Blower and Compressor (L4 and V6); Heater; Trunk Release.	(GRY)
C/H	YEL (20)	Choke Heater (Gages and No Gages); Cooling Fan	
CIG-CLK-DM	YEL (20)	Air Conditioner (L4); Cigar Lighter; Clock; Computer Command Control (L4-A/C) Courtesy Lights; Ignition Key Warning; Lights-On Reminder; Power Antenna; Power Door Locks (2 DR and 4 DR); Radio Capacitor; Trunk Light; Vanity Mirror Lights	BAT (BLK)
GAGES	YEL (20)	Air Conditioner (L4); Charge; Computer Command Control; Defogger. Seatbelt Warning.	IGN 1 (WHT)
INST LPS	TAN (5)	Console Light; Instrument Panel Lights; Lights-On Reminder.	LPS (BRN)
PWR ACCY (CIRCUIT BREAKER)	(30)	Defogger; Power Door Locks; Power Seats.	BAT (RED)
RADIO	RED (10)	Cruise Control; Power Antenna Radio.	RADIO (ORN)
STOP-HAZ	YEL (20)	Hazard Lights; Stop Lights.	
TAIL LP	YEL (20)	Lights: Front Park/Front Marker; Lights: Rear Park/Rear Marker/License.	
TURN-B/U	YEL (20)	Backup Lights; Idle Stop Solenoid; Lights: Turn.	
WDO (CIRCUIT BREAKER)	(30)	Power Windows.	WDO (BLK)
WIPER	WHT (25)	Wiper/Washer; Wiper/Washer (Delay).	

Fuse Block

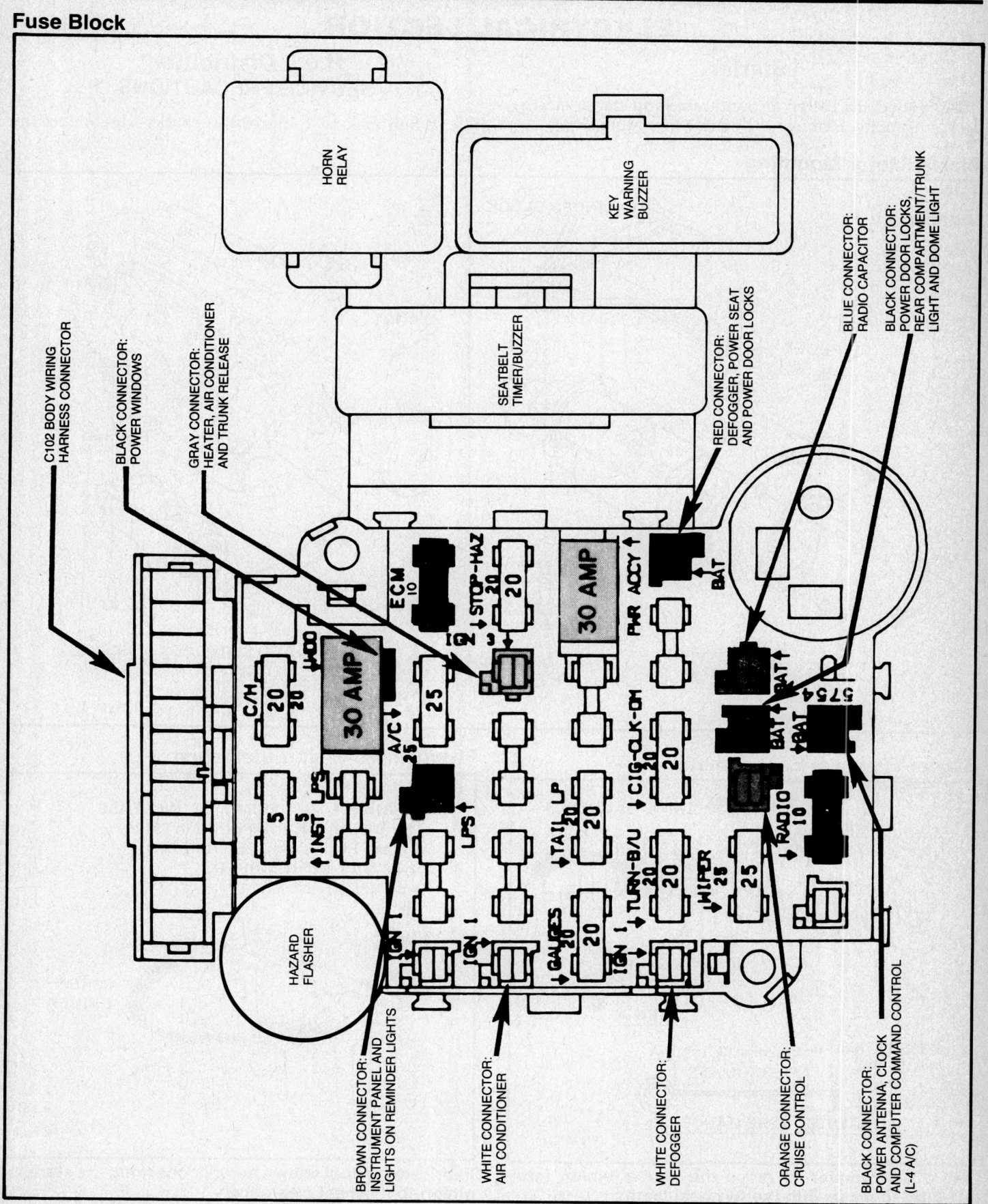

A459

ELECTRICAL SECTION

Starter

Disconnect the battery ground cable and starter electrical connections. Remove the starter mounting bolts.

H.E.I. Distributor
SERVICE PRECAUTIONS

1. When making compression checks, disconnect the

Starter Motor Mounting

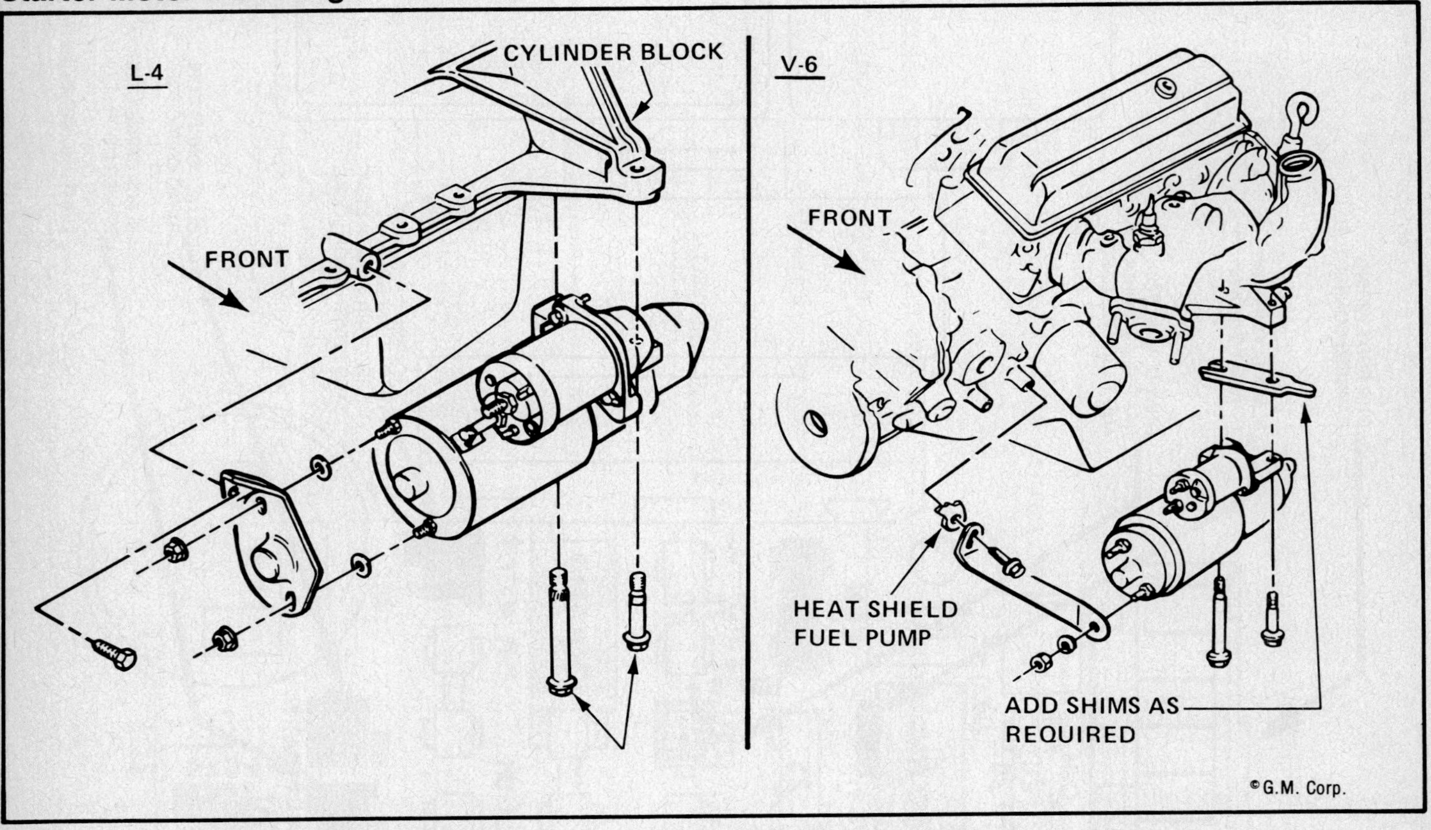

L-4　　　　　CYLINDER BLOCK　　V-6

FRONT

FRONT

HEAT SHIELD
FUEL PUMP

ADD SHIMS AS
REQUIRED

© G.M. Corp.

Starter-Flywheel Engagement

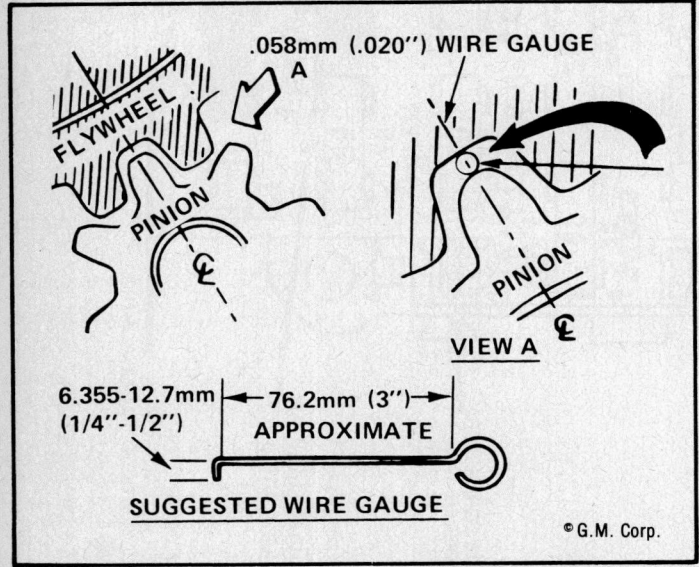

.058mm (.020") WIRE GAUGE

FLYWHEEL

PINION

A

PINION

VIEW A

6.355-12.7mm
(1/4"-1/2")

76.2mm (3")
APPROXIMATE

SUGGESTED WIRE GAUGE

© G.M. Corp.

Use a screwdriver to move the starter pinion into position to mesh with the flywheel teeth

Flywheel-To-Pinion Clearance

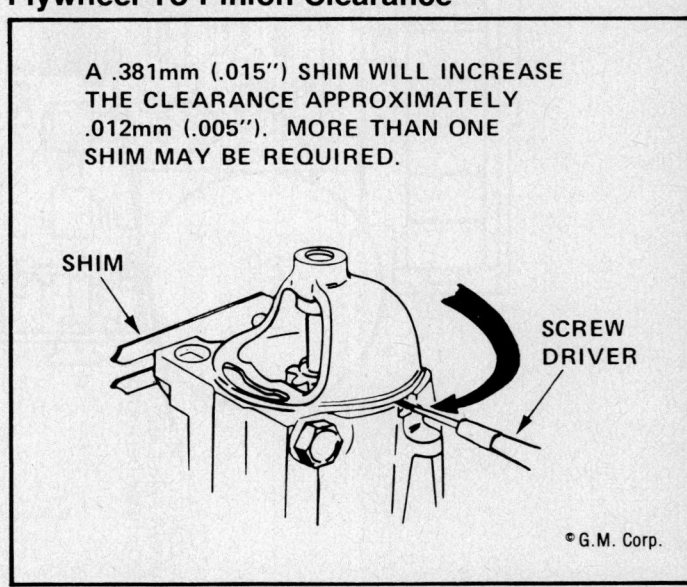

A .381mm (.015") SHIM WILL INCREASE
THE CLEARANCE APPROXIMATELY
.012mm (.005"). MORE THAN ONE
SHIM MAY BE REQUIRED.

SHIM

SCREW
DRIVER

© G.M. Corp.

Fabricate the tool shown here for checking the starter pinion-to-flywheel clearance

ignition switch feed wire. (Pink wire at the distributor on V6 engines, pink wire at the coil on L4 engines.)

2. No periodic lubrication is required. Engine oil lubricates the lower bushing and an oil-filled reservoir provides lubrication for the upper bushing.

3. The tachometer (TACH) terminal is next to the ignition switch (BAT) connector on the distributor cap on V6 engines and is at the brown wire connection at the coil on L4 engines.

NOTE The tachometer terminal must never be connected to ground, as damage to the module and/or ignition coil can result.

NOTE Some tachometers currently in use may not be compatible with the High Energy Ignition System. Consult the manufacturer of the tachometer if questions arise.

4. Dwell adjustment is controlled by the module and cannot be adjusted.

5. The material used to construct the spark plug cables is very soft. This cabe will withstand more heat and carry a higher voltage, but scuffing and cutting become easier. The spark plug cables must be routed correctly to prevent chaffing or cuttting.

6. When removing a spark plug wire from a spark plug, twist the boot on the spark plug and pull on the boot to remove the wire, or use a special tool designed to remove spark-plug boots.

R AND R

1. Remove the distributor cap, electrical wiring and vacuum hose from the distributor.
2. Put alignment marks on the rotor, distributor housing and engine for installation reference.
3. Remove the distributor clamp screw and hold-down clamp. Pull the distributor up out of the engine block.
4. Install the distributor in the correct position and set the ignition timing within specifications.

IGNITION TIMING

Timing specifications for each engine are listed on the tune-up label in the engine compartment. When using a timing light, connect an adapter between the no. 1 spark plug and the no. 1 spark plug wire, or use an inductive type pick-up. Do not pierce the plug lead. Once the insulation of the spark plug cable has been broken, volt-

Spark Plug Coding

```
      1  2  3    4    5
     ⌒  ⌒ ⌒  ⌒⌒  ⌒
      R  4  5    T S   X
```

1 — R--INDICATES RESISTOR-TYPE PLUG.
2 — "4" INDICATES 14 mm THREADS.
3 — HEAT RANGE
4 — TS--TAPERED SEAT.
     S--EXTENDED TIP
5 — SPECIAL GAP

Electronic Spark Timing 4 Cylinder Distributor

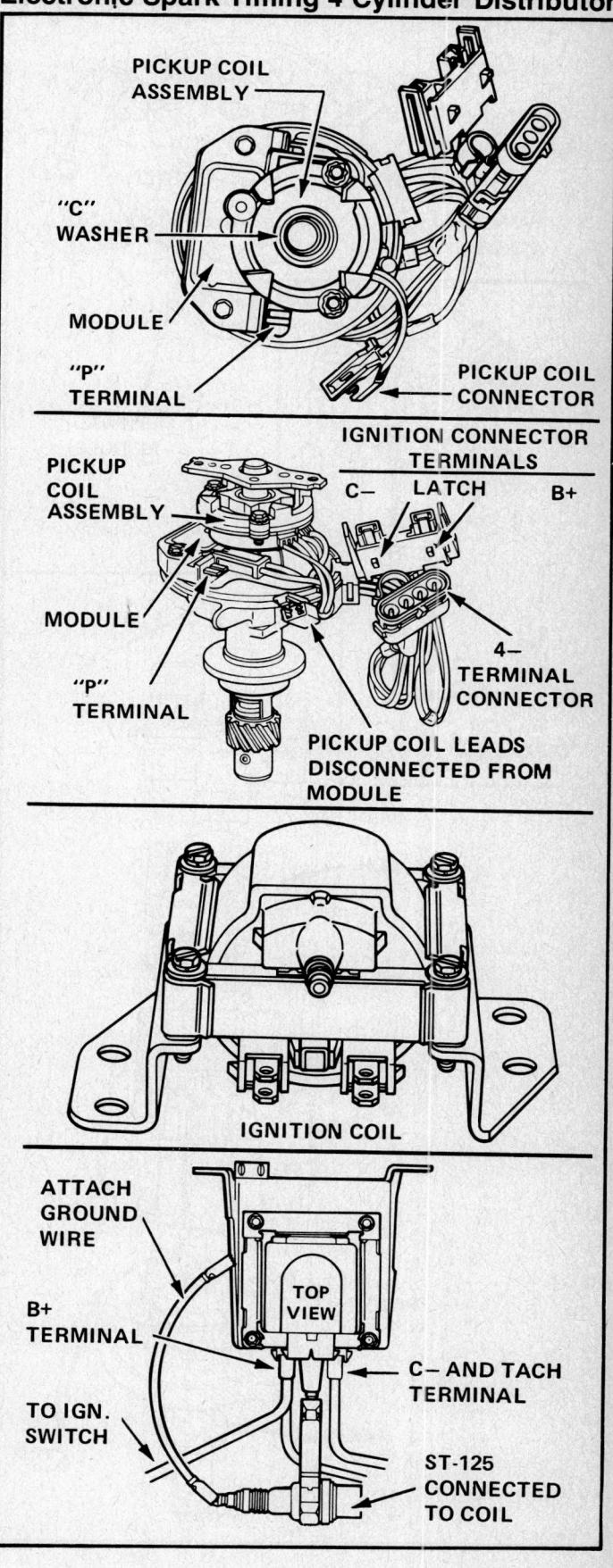

PICKUP COIL ASSEMBLY
"C" WASHER
MODULE
"P" TERMINAL
PICKUP COIL CONNECTOR

PICKUP COIL ASSEMBLY
MODULE
"P" TERMINAL
IGNITION CONNECTOR TERMINALS
C−   LATCH   B+
4− TERMINAL CONNECTOR
PICKUP COIL LEADS DISCONNECTED FROM MODULE

IGNITION COIL

ATTACH GROUND WIRE
B+ TERMINAL
TO IGN. SWITCH
TOP VIEW
C− AND TACH TERMINAL
ST-125 CONNECTED TO COIL

Electronic Spark Timing 6 Cylinder Distributor

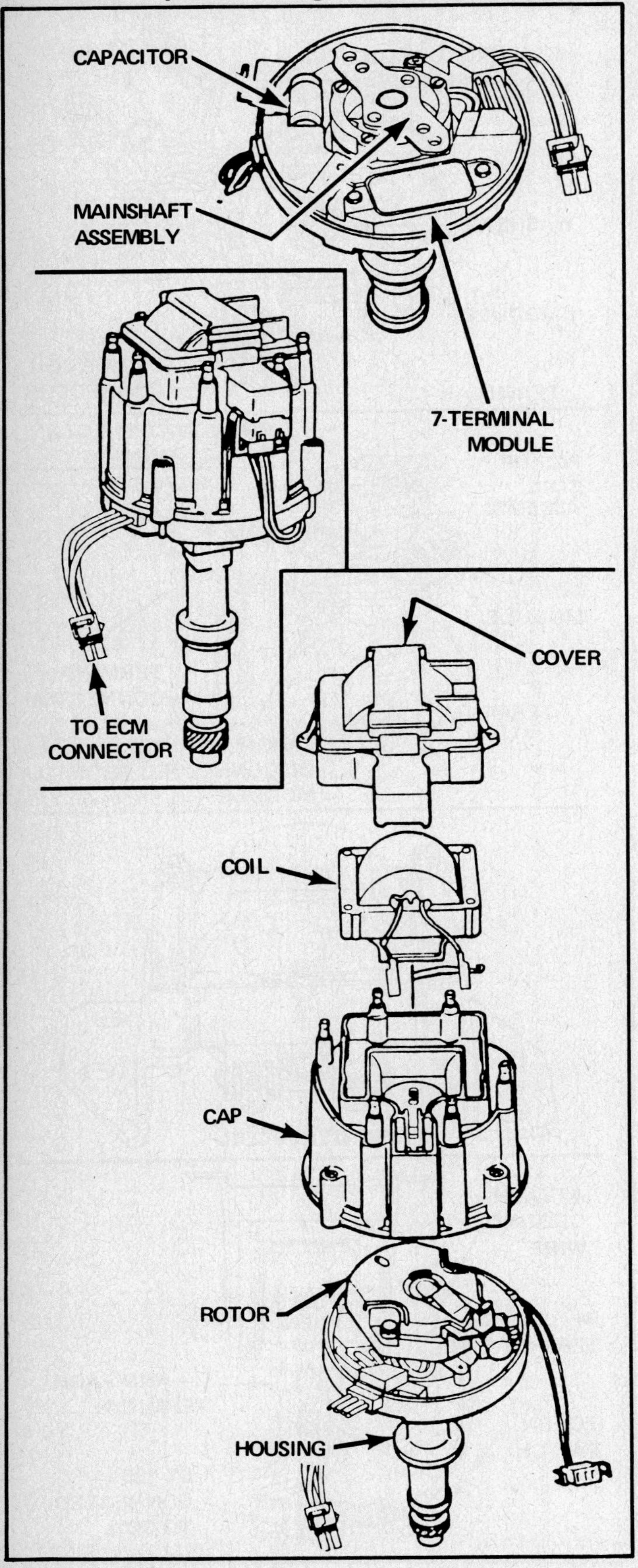

CAPACITOR

MAINSHAFT ASSEMBLY

7-TERMINAL MODULE

TO ECM CONNECTOR

COVER

COIL

CAP

ROTOR

HOUSING

age will jump to the nearest ground and the spark plug will not fire properly. Always follow tune-up label procedures when adjusting the timing. A magnetic timing probe hole is built in for use with special electronic timing equipment.

Magnetic Timing Probe Hole And Timing Marks

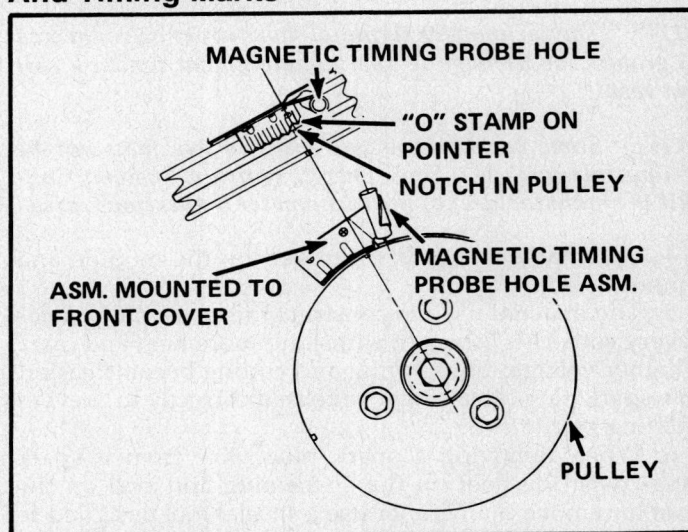

MAGNETIC TIMING PROBE HOLE

"O" STAMP ON POINTER

NOTCH IN PULLEY

MAGNETIC TIMING PROBE HOLE ASM.

ASM. MOUNTED TO FRONT COVER

PULLEY

Spark Plug

WIRING

The spark plug wiring used with the HEI system is a carbon impregnated cord conductor encased in an 8 mm (5/16") diameter silicone rubber jacket. The silicone jacket will withstand very high temperatures and also provides an excellent insulator for the higher voltage of the HEI system. The silicone spark plug boots form a tight seal on the plug and the boot should be twisted 1/2 turn before removing.

Care should also be exercised when connecting a timing light or other pick-up equipment. Do not force anything between the boot and wiring, or through the silicone jacket. Connections should be made in parallel using an adapter. Do not pull on the wire to remove it. Pull on the boot or use a tool designed for this purpose.

FLASH-OVER DETECTION

Do not mistake corona discharge for flash-over or a shorted insulator. Corona is a steady blue light appearing around the insulator, just above the shell crimp. It is the visible evidence of a high-tension field and has no effect on ignition performance. Usually it can be detected only in darkness. This discharge may repel dust particles, leaving a clear ring on the insulator just above the shell. This ring is sometimes mistakenly regarded as evidence that combustion gases have blown out between the shell and insulator.

Ignition and Headlight Dimmer Switches

Removal and Installation

1. Remove parts as shown in illustration.
2. Install parts as shown in illustration.
3. Position the rod in the slider hole and install the ignition switch. Install the lower stud and tighten to 3.9 N•m (35 in. lbs.)
4. Install the dimmer switch and depress the switch slightly to insert a 3/32" drill. Force the switch up to remove the lash. Then tighten the screw and nut to 3.9 N•m (35 in. lbs.)
5. Place the shifter in Neutral and install the shift lever.

Neutral Start Switch

Cars with automatic transmissions use a mechanical block on the gear selector which prevents starting in any position except Neutral or Park.

Cars with manual transmissions use a clutch start switch which is attached to the clutch pedal mechanism under the dash.

Steering Wheel and Horn Switch

Removal

1. Disconnect the negative battery cable.
2. Remove parts as shown in illustration.

Ignition And Headlight Dimmer Switches

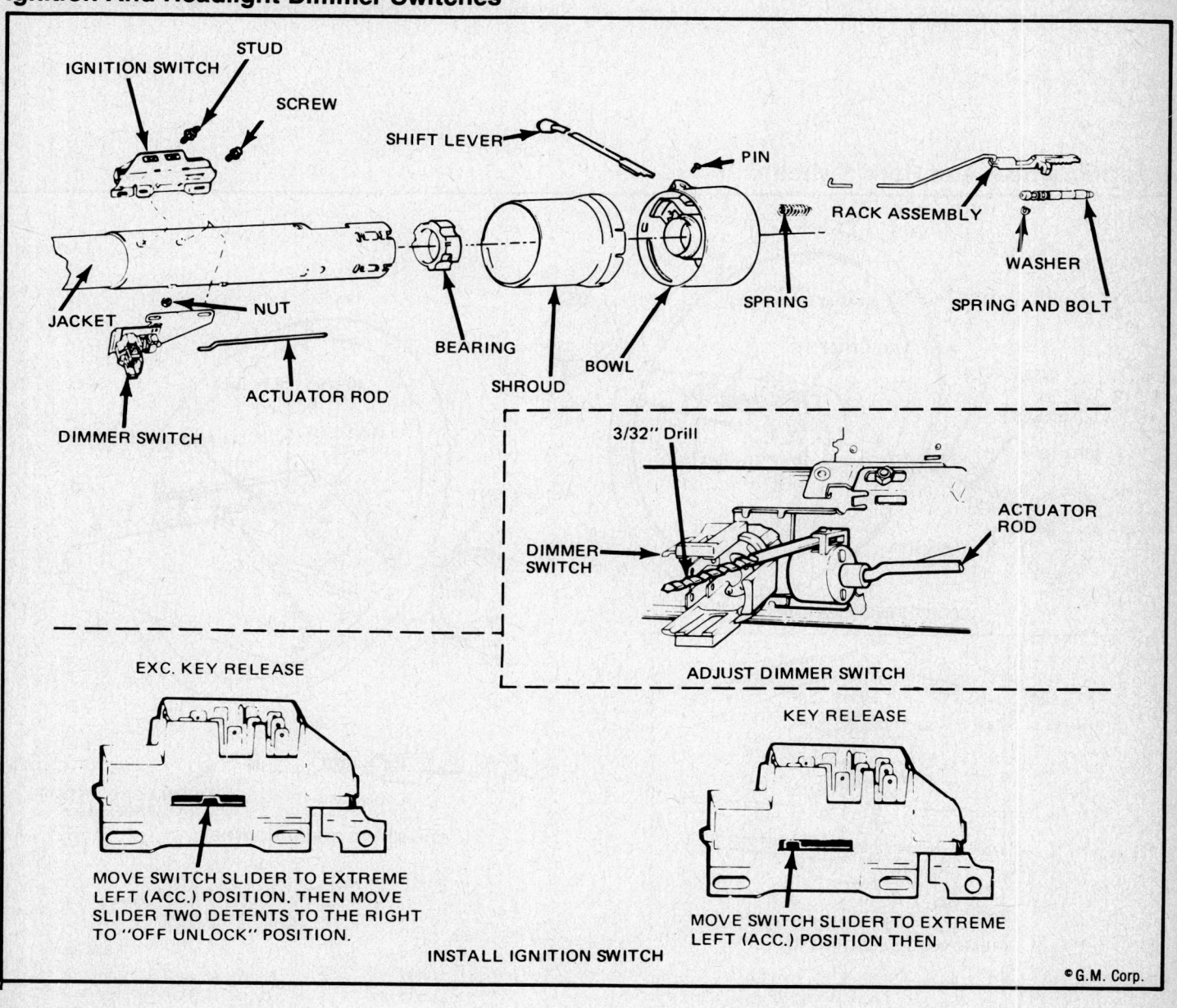

STUD
IGNITION SWITCH
SCREW
SHIFT LEVER
PIN
RACK ASSEMBLY
WASHER
SPRING AND BOLT
SPRING
BOWL
SHROUD
BEARING
JACKET
NUT
ACTUATOR ROD
DIMMER SWITCH

3/32" Drill
DIMMER SWITCH
ACTUATOR ROD
ADJUST DIMMER SWITCH

EXC. KEY RELEASE

MOVE SWITCH SLIDER TO EXTREME LEFT (ACC.) POSITION. THEN MOVE SLIDER TWO DETENTS TO THE RIGHT TO "OFF UNLOCK" POSITION.

KEY RELEASE

MOVE SWITCH SLIDER TO EXTREME LEFT (ACC.) POSITION THEN

INSTALL IGNITION SWITCH

© G.M. Corp.

Neutral Start Switch

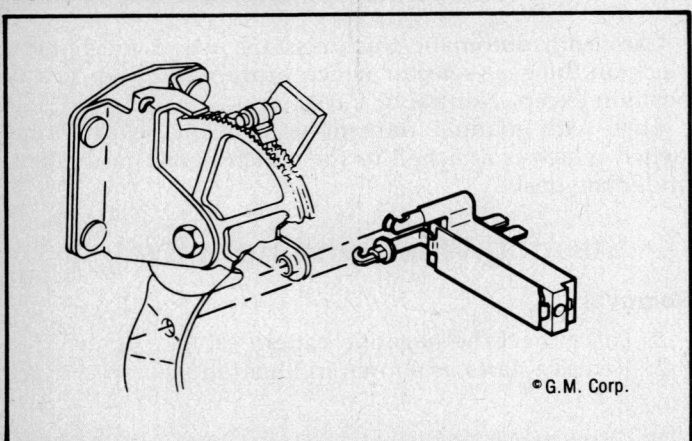

© G.M. Corp.

Clutch start switch is mounted on the clutch pedal mechanism. Automatic transmission vehicles have no neutral start switch.

Installation

1. Align the marks on the steering wheel with the marks on the shaft.
2. Install parts as shown in illustration.
3. Connect the negative battery cable.

Stoplight Switch

1. The switch is mounted in the brake pedal bracket.
2. To adjust, insert the switch into the tubular clip until it seats. Pull the brake pedal against the pedal stop which will automatically adjust the switch.

Light Switch

Remove the trim cover and the screws which attach the switch to the adapter assembly.

Steering Wheel And Horn Switch

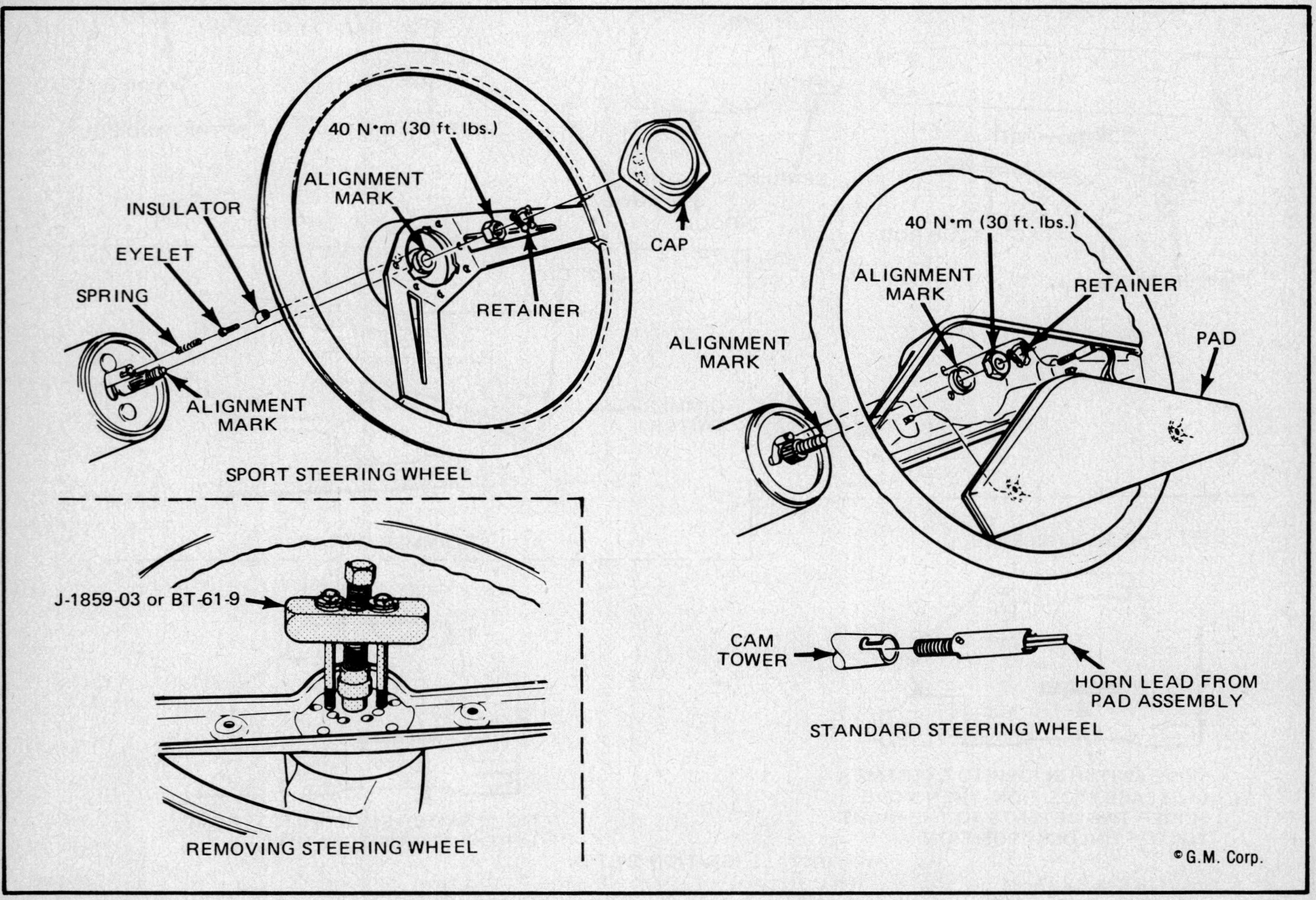

40 N·m (30 ft. lbs.)

ALIGNMENT MARK

INSULATOR

EYELET

SPRING

ALIGNMENT MARK

CAP

RETAINER

SPORT STEERING WHEEL

J-1859-03 or BT-61-9

REMOVING STEERING WHEEL

40 N·m (30 ft. lbs.)

ALIGNMENT MARK

RETAINER

PAD

ALIGNMENT MARK

CAM TOWER

HORN LEAD FROM PAD ASSEMBLY

STANDARD STEERING WHEEL

© G.M. Corp.

Ignition Lock

Removal and Installation

1. Turn lock to the Run position and remove the key warning buzzer.

2. Remove parts as shown in illustration.
3. Install the lock cylinder.
4. Turn lock to the Run position and install the key warning buzzer switch.

Turn Signal Switch

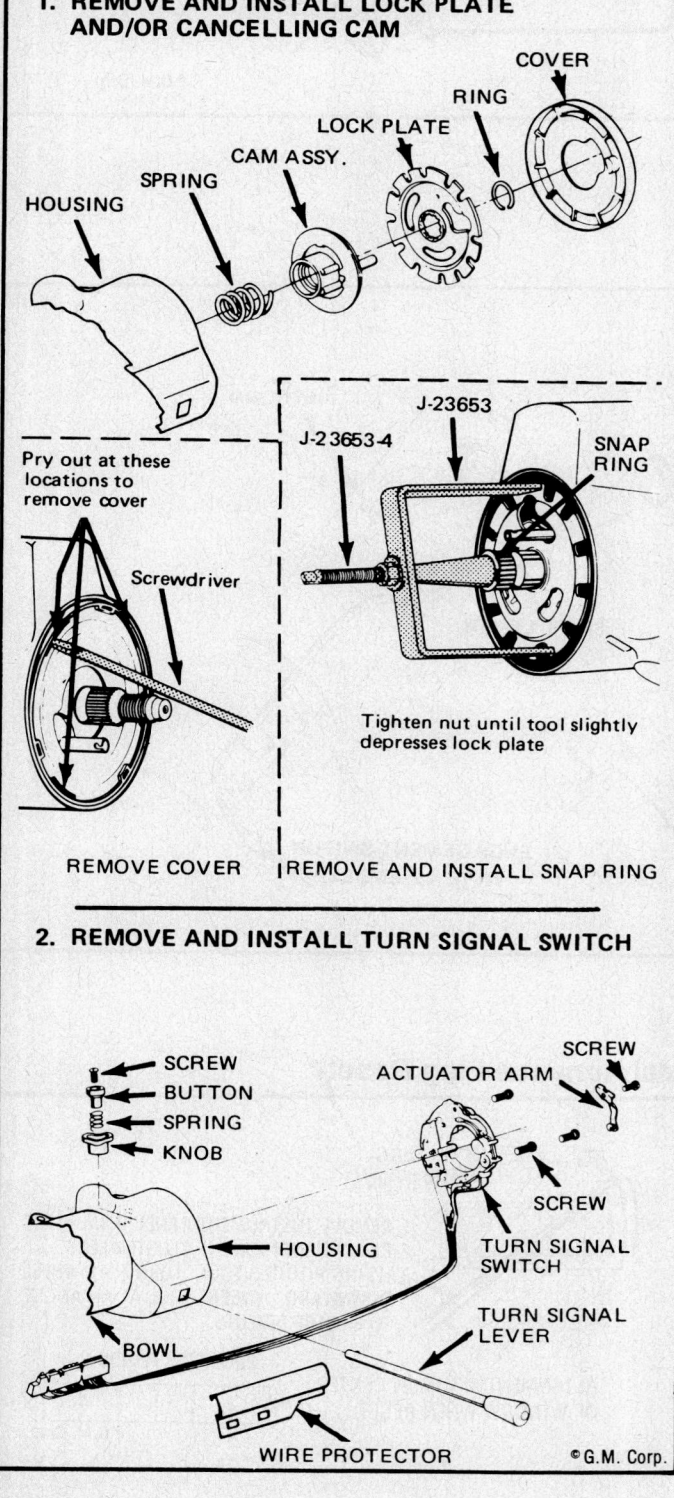

1. REMOVE AND INSTALL LOCK PLATE AND/OR CANCELLING CAM

COVER
RING
LOCK PLATE
CAM ASSY.
SPRING
HOUSING

Pry out at these locations to remove cover

Screwdriver

J-23653-4
J-23653
SNAP RING

Tighten nut until tool slightly depresses lock plate

REMOVE COVER | REMOVE AND INSTALL SNAP RING

2. REMOVE AND INSTALL TURN SIGNAL SWITCH

SCREW
BUTTON
SPRING
KNOB
ACTUATOR ARM
SCREW
SCREW
TURN SIGNAL SWITCH
HOUSING
TURN SIGNAL LEVER
BOWL
WIRE PROTECTOR
© G.M. Corp.

Stoplight Switch And Speed Control Valve

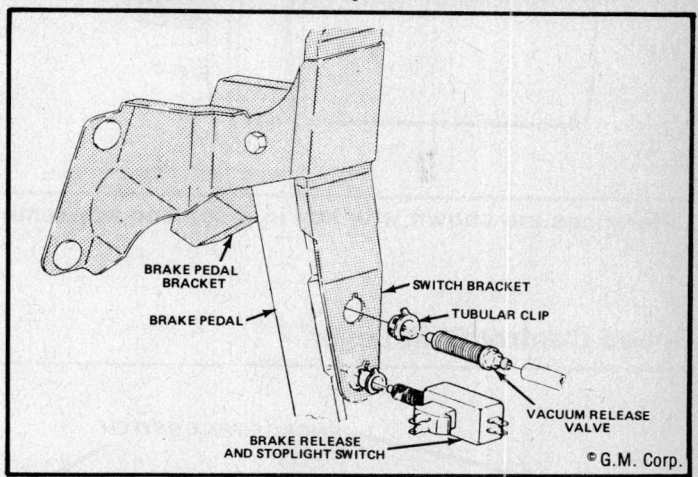

BRAKE PEDAL BRACKET
BRAKE PEDAL
SWITCH BRACKET
TUBULAR CLIP
VACUUM RELEASE VALVE
BRAKE RELEASE AND STOPLIGHT SWITCH
© G.M. Corp.

Ignition Lock

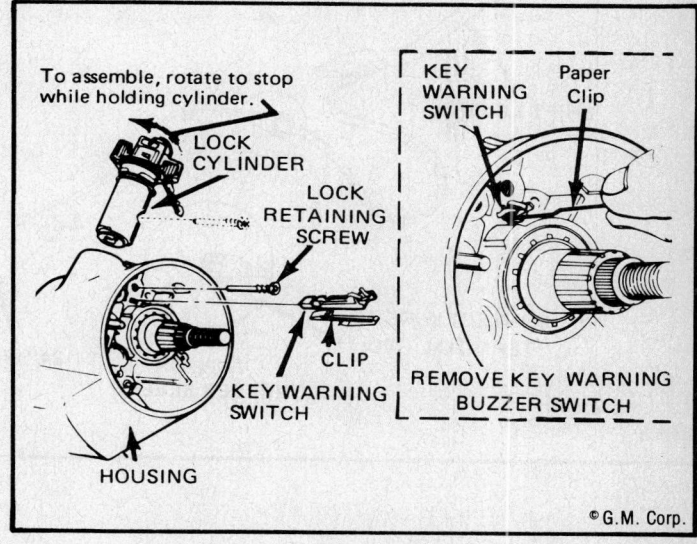

To assemble, rotate to stop while holding cylinder.
LOCK CYLINDER
LOCK RETAINING SCREW
CLIP
KEY WARNING SWITCH
HOUSING

KEY WARNING SWITCH
Paper Clip
REMOVE KEY WARNING BUZZER SWITCH
© G.M. Corp.

Rear Window Defrost Switch

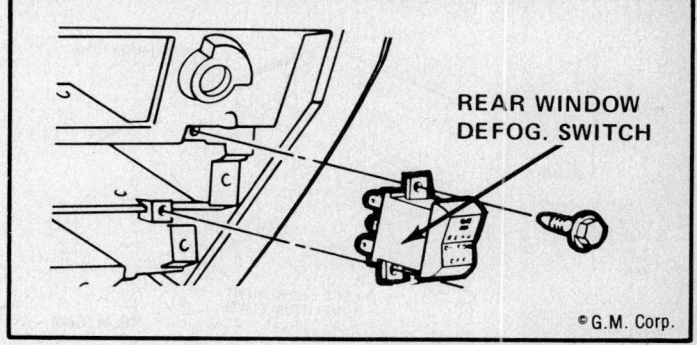

REAR WINDOW DEFOG. SWITCH
© G.M. Corp.

GENERAL MOTORS "A" AND "X" BODY CARS
"A": CELEBRITY, CENTURY, A6000, CIERA; "X": CITATION, OMEGA, PHOENIX, SKYLARK

Ignition Lock Cylinder

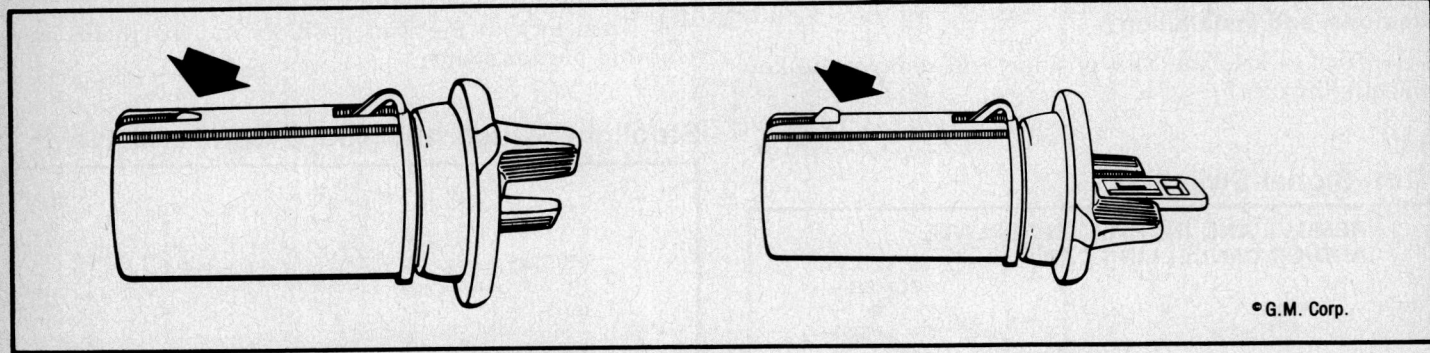

© G.M. Corp.

Differences are shown with key in place and key removed

Speed Control Shift Lever

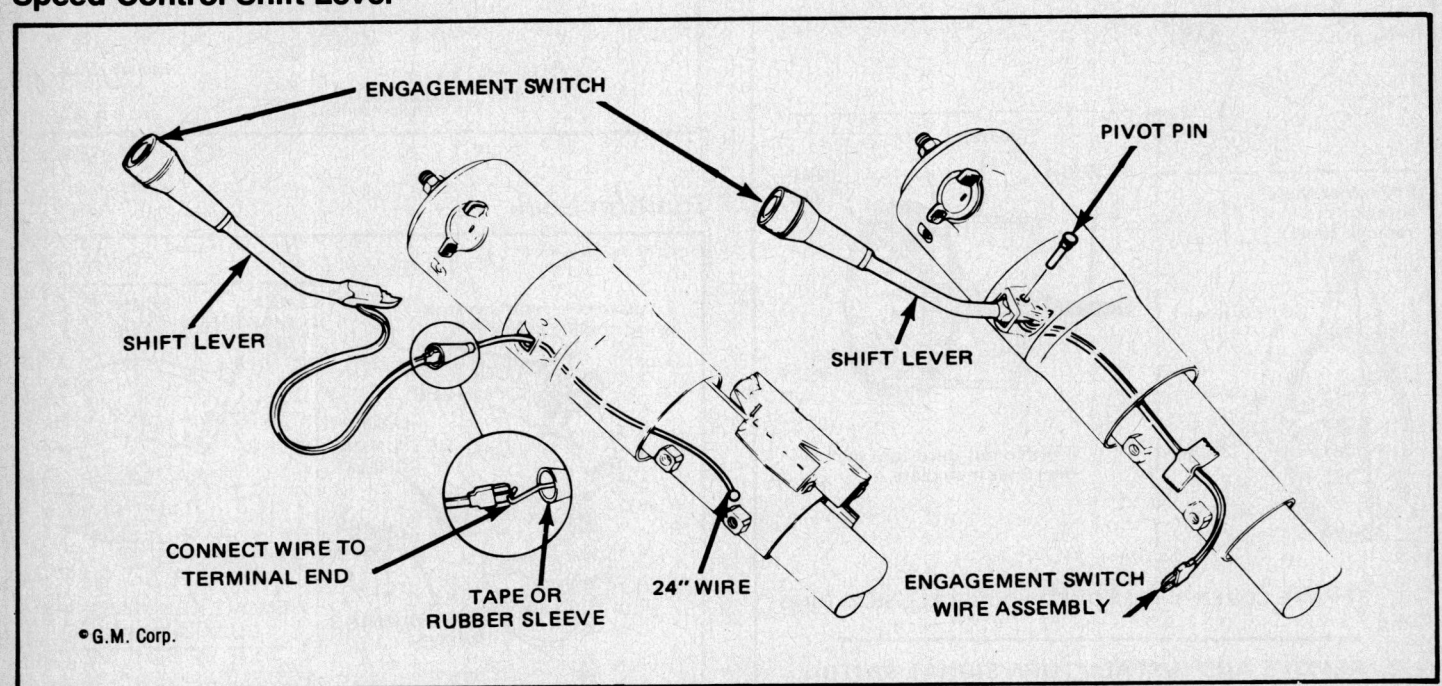

ENGAGEMENT SWITCH

PIVOT PIN

SHIFT LEVER

SHIFT LEVER

CONNECT WIRE TO TERMINAL END

TAPE OR RUBBER SLEEVE

24" WIRE

ENGAGEMENT SWITCH WIRE ASSEMBLY

© G.M. Corp.

Radio

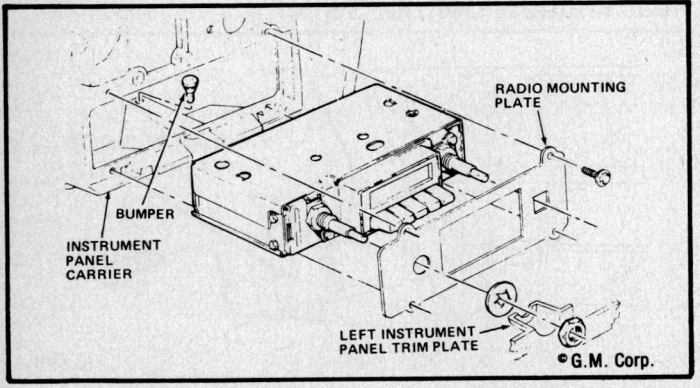

RADIO MOUNTING PLATE

BUMPER

INSTRUMENT PANEL CARRIER

LEFT INSTRUMENT PANEL TRIM PLATE

© G.M. Corp.

Maintenance Flag Reset

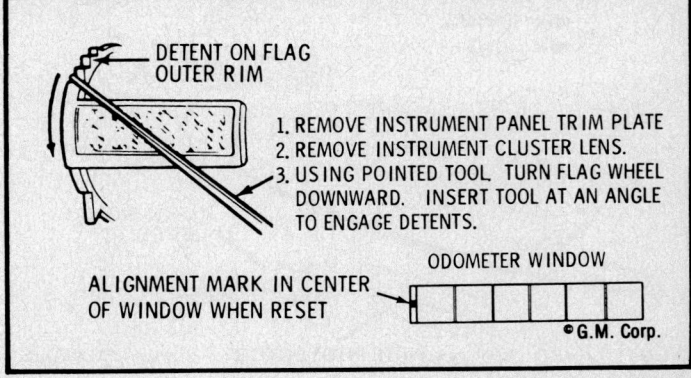

DETENT ON FLAG OUTER RIM

1. REMOVE INSTRUMENT PANEL TRIM PLATE
2. REMOVE INSTRUMENT CLUSTER LENS.
3. USING POINTED TOOL TURN FLAG WHEEL DOWNWARD. INSERT TOOL AT AN ANGLE TO ENGAGE DETENTS.

ALIGNMENT MARK IN CENTER OF WINDOW WHEN RESET

ODOMETER WINDOW

© G.M. Corp.

Temperature Control Unit

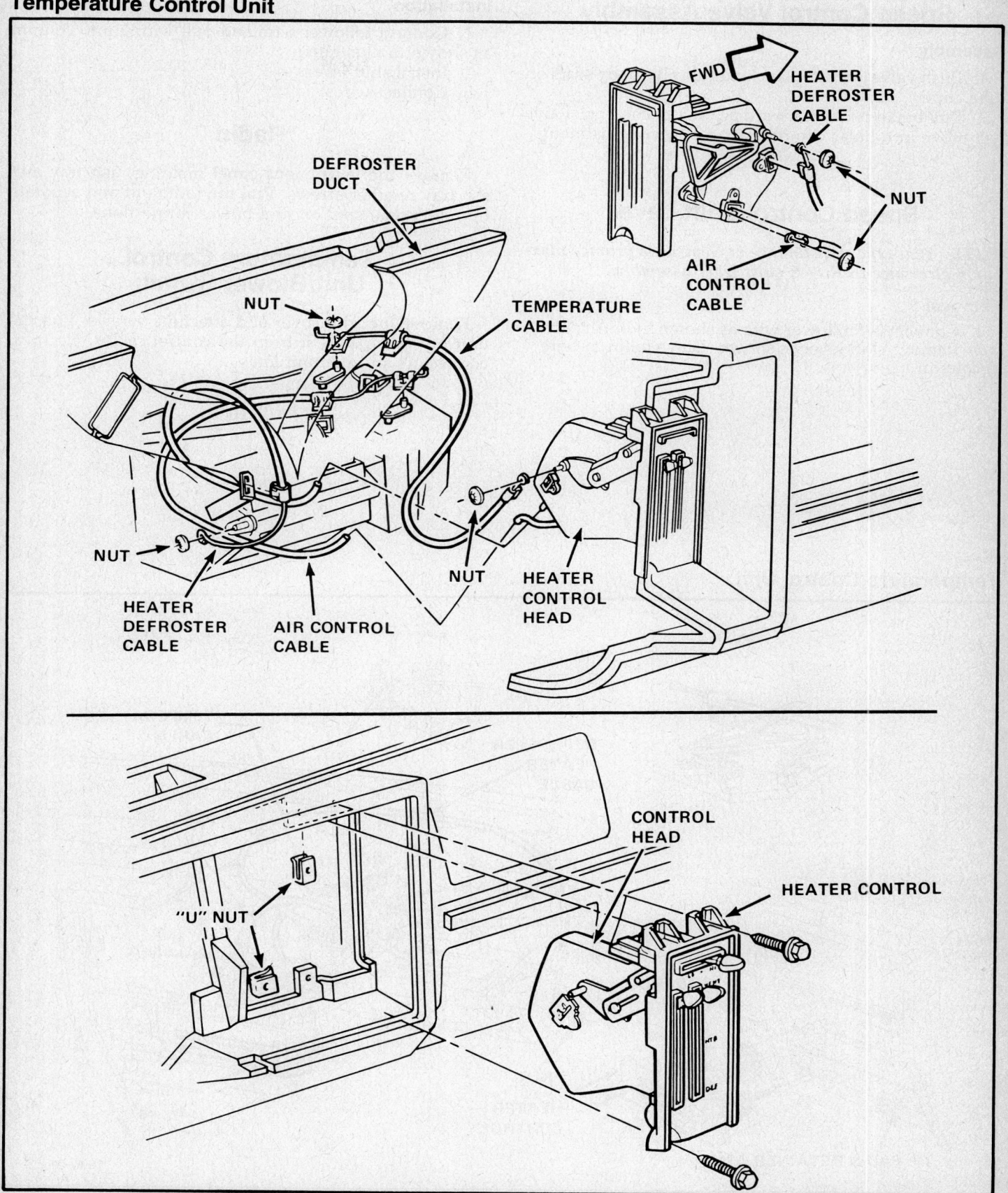

Vertical control panel mounting and control cable routing

GENERAL MOTORS "A" AND "X" BODY CARS

"A": CELEBRITY, CENTURY, A6000, CIERA; "X": CITATION, OMEGA, PHOENIX, SKYLARK

Speed Control Valve Assembly

Assembly

1. Push valve into tubular clip until valve body seats on tube clip.
2. Pull brake pedal rearward against pedal stop. Valve will move in tubular clip providing proper adjustment.

Speed Control Shift Lever

NOTE   Place the shift linkage in Neutral to provide maximum clearance to R & R shift lever assembly.

Removal

1. Connect 24" follower wire as shown in illustration.
2. Remove shift lever as shown. Leave follower wire in column.

Installation

1. Connect follower wire and pull wiring into column as shown in illustration.
2. Install shift lever.
3. Connect wires.

Radio

Remove the instrument panel molding, ash tray and ash tray retainer screws. Pull the radio out and separate from antenna, speaker and power connections.

Temperature Control Unit/Blower Switch

Remove the trim cover and attaching screws. Pull the unit out to separate it from the control cables, electrical connectors and vacuum lines.

Temperature Control Unit

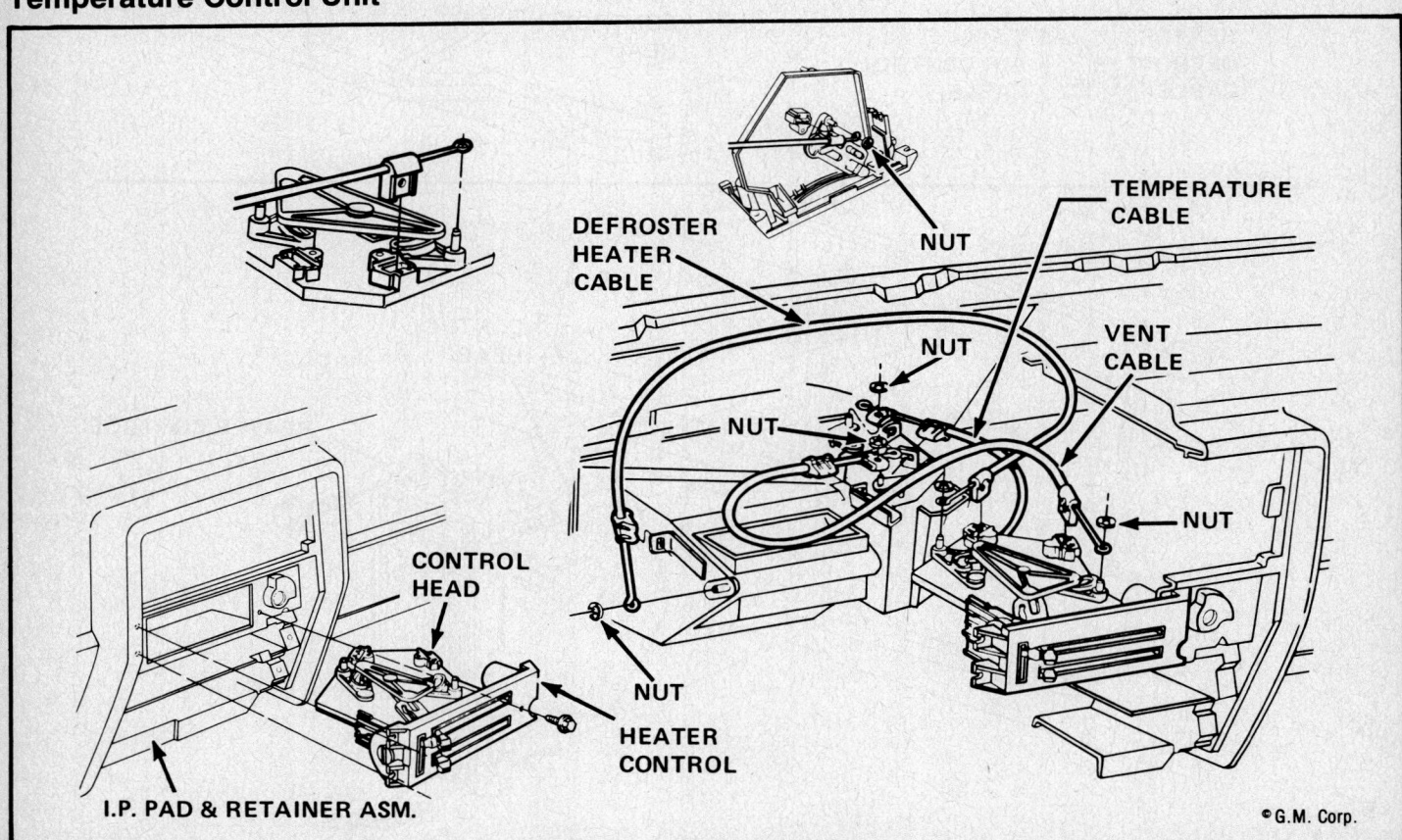

Horizontal control panel mounting and control cable routing

A468

WIPER SECTION

Windshield Wiper Switch

Removal

1. Remove ignition and dimmer switch.
2. Remove parts as shown in illustration.

Installation

1. Assemble rack so that the first rack tooth engages between the first and second tooth of the sector.
2. Install parts as shown in illustration.
3. Install ignition and dimmer switch.

Windshield Wiper Pulse Switch

Remove the trim cover and the screws which attach the switch to the adapter assembly.

Windshield Wiper Motor

1. After removing the wiper arms, lower the windshield reveal molding and front cowl panel. Loosen, but do not remove, the transmission drive link-to-motor crank arm retaining nuts.

Windshield Wiper Switch

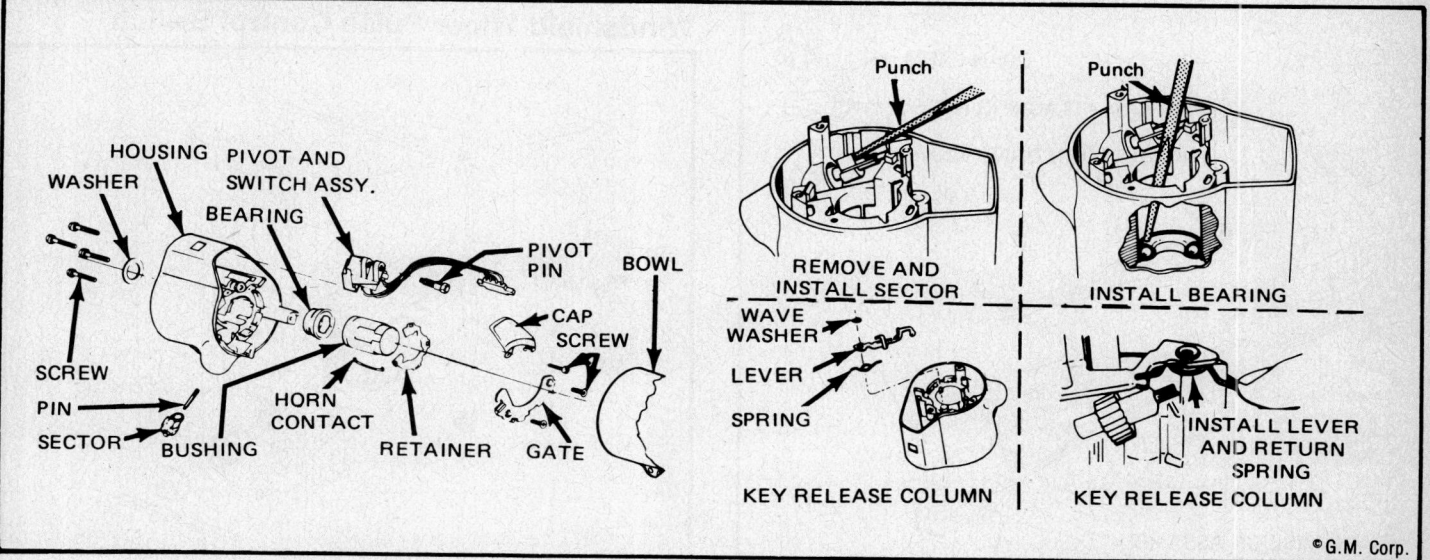

© G.M. Corp.

Windshield Wiper Motor

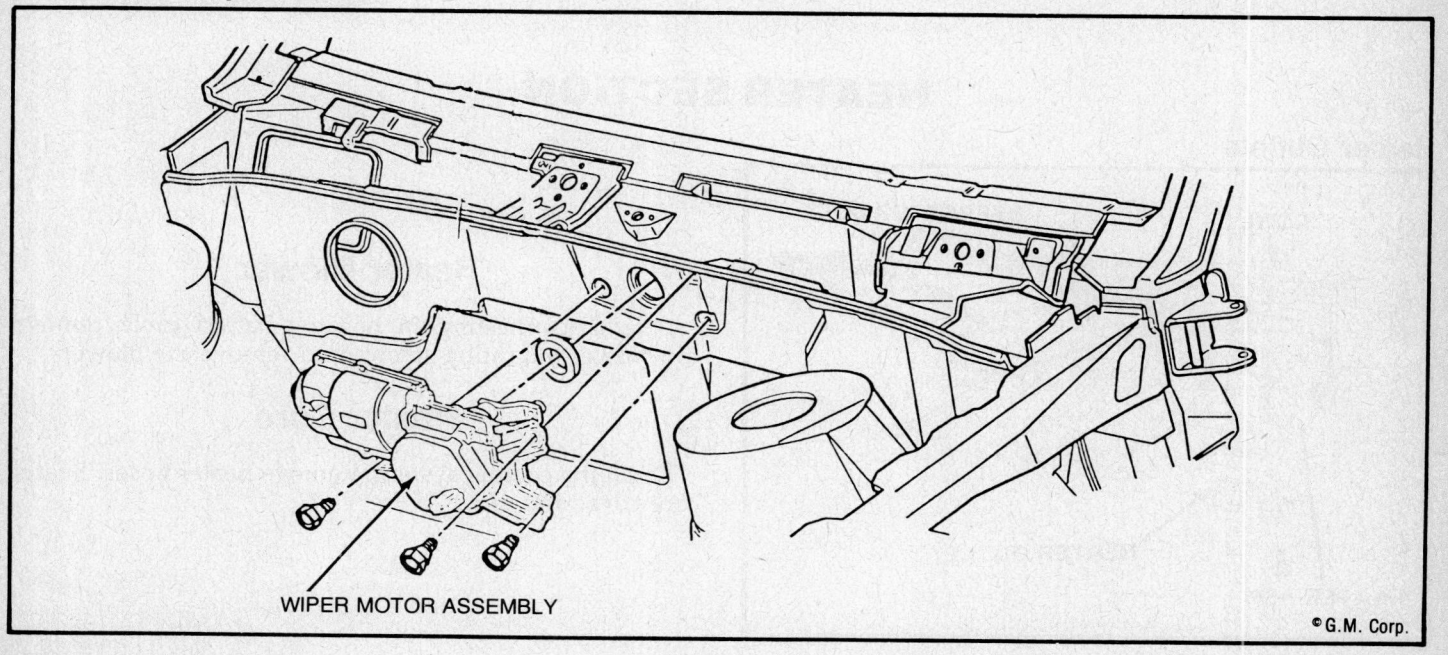

WIPER MOTOR ASSEMBLY

© G.M. Corp.

A469

GENERAL MOTORS "A" AND "X" BODY CARS

"A": CELEBRITY, CENTURY, A6000, CIERA; "X": CITATION, OMEGA, PHOENIX, SKYLARK

NOTE   On styles equipped with air conditioning remove the motor attaching bolts prior to removing the crank arm attaching nut. The crank arm must be removed before motor can be lifted past the A/C evaporator unit.

Windshield Wiper Linkage

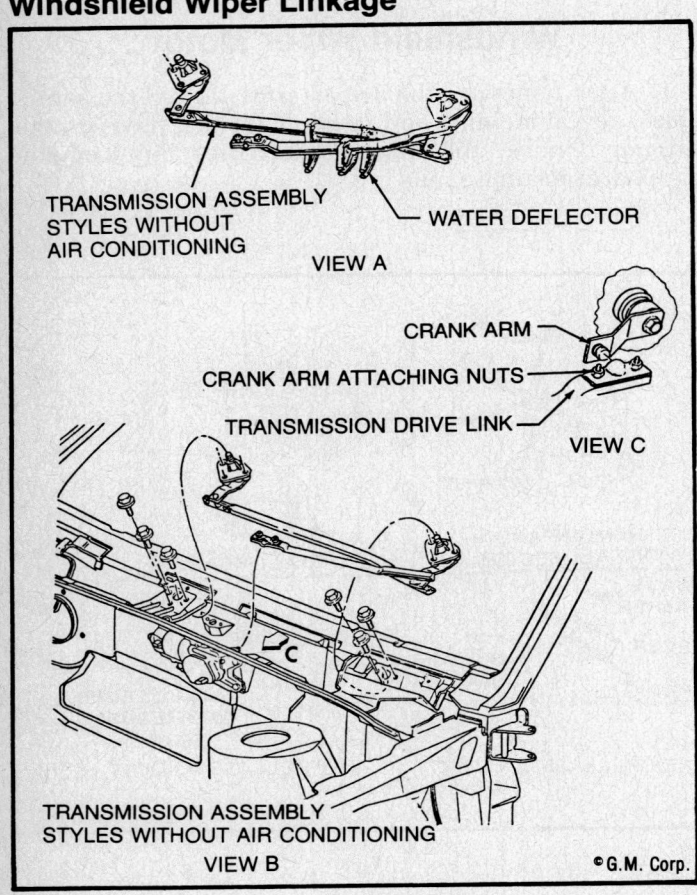

TRANSMISSION ASSEMBLY STYLES WITHOUT AIR CONDITIONING

WATER DEFLECTOR

VIEW A

CRANK ARM

CRANK ARM ATTACHING NUTS

TRANSMISSION DRIVE LINK

VIEW C

TRANSMISSION ASSEMBLY STYLES WITHOUT AIR CONDITIONING

VIEW B

© G.M. Corp.

2. After completely removing the motor attaching bolts, remove the crank arm retaining nut, disconnect electrical leads and rotate motor up and out.

Windshield Wiper Arms

The arms must be pried off the transmission shafts. Tool J-8966 can be used to accomplish this.

Windshield Wiper Blades

1. On wipers using a press-type release, press the release tab and the blade will separate from the arm.

2. On wipers using a coil spring retainer, insert a suitable tool on top of the spring and push down to separate the arm and blade.

Windshield Wiper Pulse Control Switch

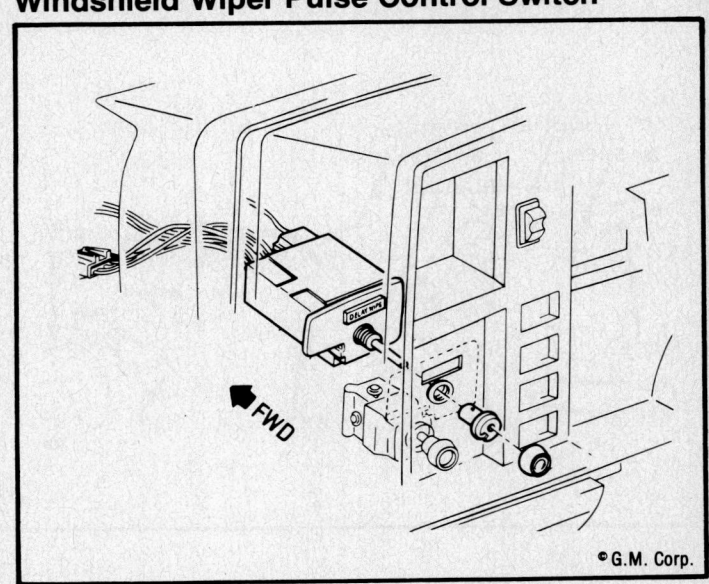

FWD

© G.M. Corp.

HEATER SECTION

Heater Outlets

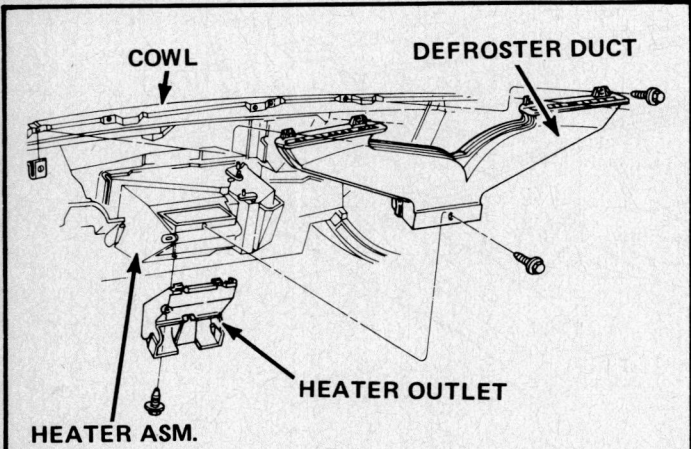

COWL

DEFROSTER DUCT

HEATER OUTLET

HEATER ASM.

Heater Blower

After disconnecting the negative battery cable, remove the blower mounting screws and remove the blower.

Heater Core

Drain the cooling system. Remove heater hoses, heater core cover and core.

Heater Assembly Components

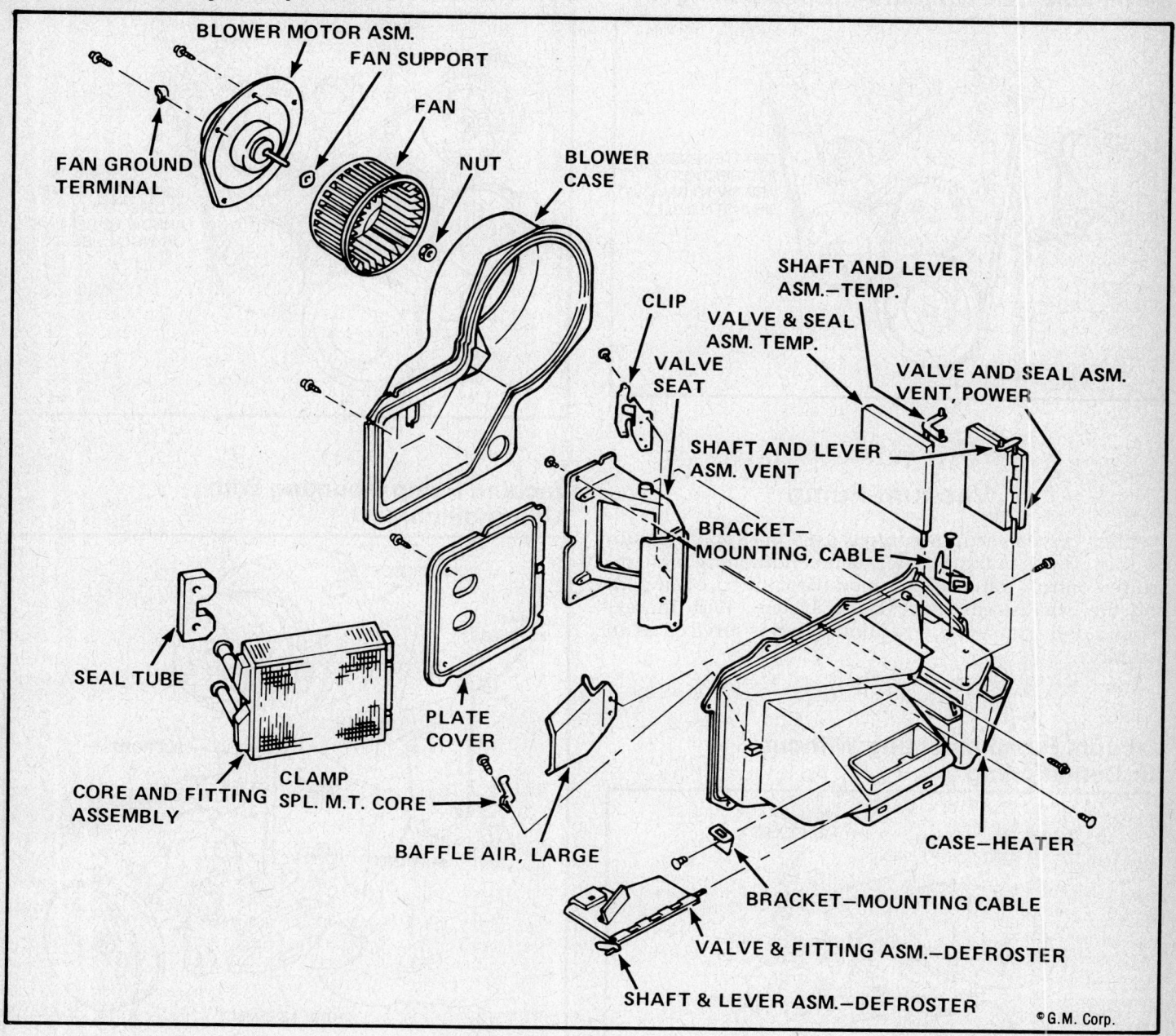

BLOWER MOTOR ASM.
FAN SUPPORT
FAN
NUT
BLOWER CASE
FAN GROUND TERMINAL
CLIP
VALVE SEAT
SHAFT AND LEVER ASM.—TEMP.
VALVE & SEAL ASM. TEMP.
VALVE AND SEAL ASM. VENT, POWER
SHAFT AND LEVER ASM. VENT
BRACKET—MOUNTING, CABLE
SEAL TUBE
PLATE COVER
CORE AND FITTING ASSEMBLY
CLAMP SPL. M.T. CORE
BAFFLE AIR, LARGE
CASE—HEATER
BRACKET—MOUNTING CABLE
VALVE & FITTING ASM.—DEFROSTER
SHAFT & LEVER ASM.—DEFROSTER
© G.M. Corp.

ON CAR SERVICE—DIESEL

Belt

A single serpentine wide belt is used to drive all engine accessories formerly driven by multiple drive belts. All belt-driven accessories are ridgedly mounted with belt tension maintained by a spring load tensioner. To remove and install the belt, lift (rotate) the tensioner idler pulley. Check the tensioner, using belt tension gauge BT-7825 or J-23600. Belt tension should be 360-540 N•m (80-120 lbs.).

GENERAL MOTORS "A" AND "X" BODY CARS
"A": CELEBRITY, CENTURY, A6000, CIERA; "X": CITATION, OMEGA, PHOENIX, SKYLARK

Serpentine Belt Without Air Conditioning

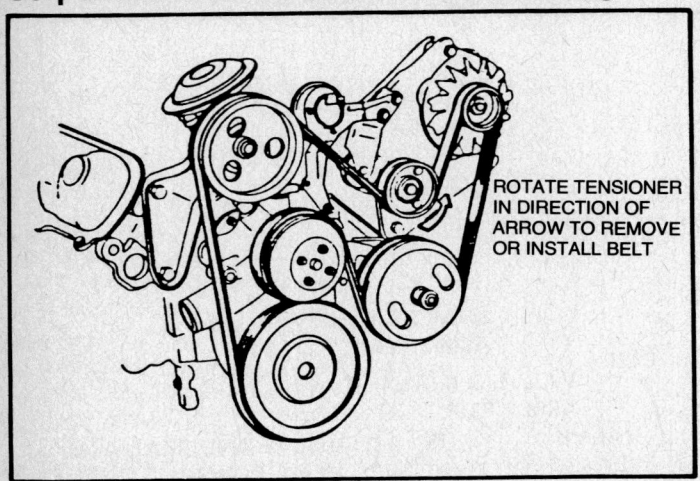

ROTATE TENSIONER IN DIRECTION OF ARROW TO REMOVE OR INSTALL BELT

Serpentine Belt With Air Conditioning

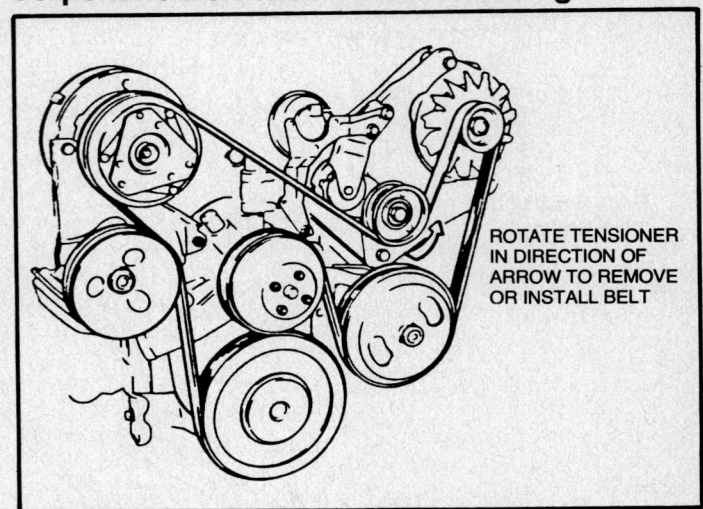

ROTATE TENSIONER IN DIRECTION OF ARROW TO REMOVE OR INSTALL BELT

Vacuum Pump

A belt-driven vacuum pump is used to supply vacuum to the power brake booster, air conditioning system, cruise control, transmission modulator (if so equipped) and the exhaust gas recirculation system. With the exception of the pulley, the vacuum pump is serviced as an assembly.

Vacuum Pump Mounting With Air Conditioning

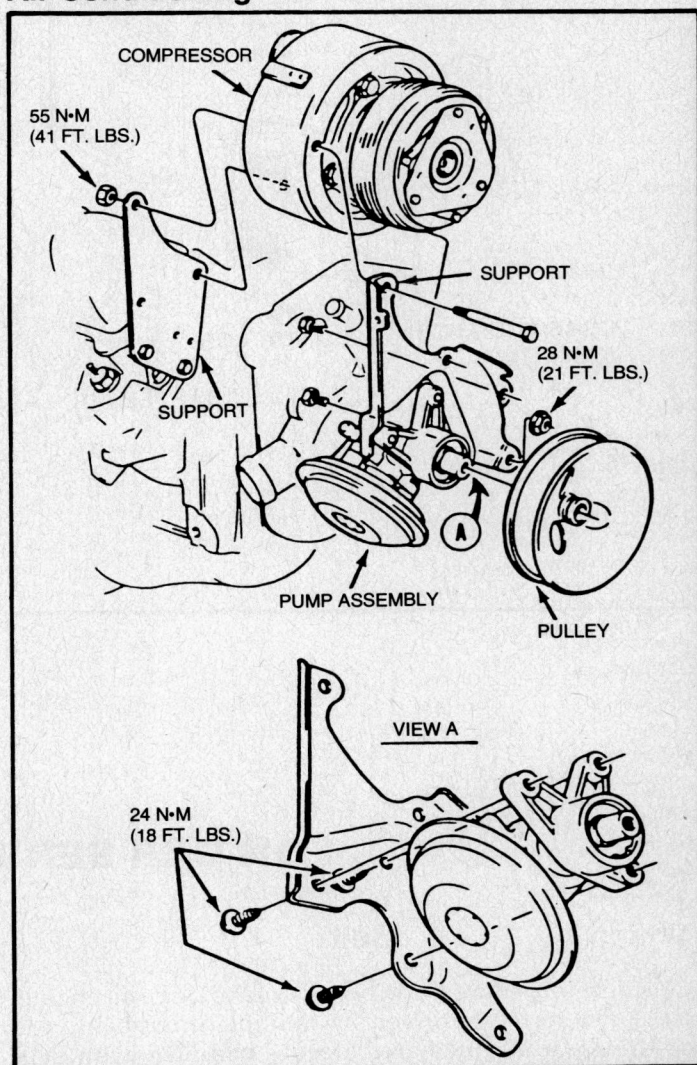

COMPRESSOR

55 N·M (41 FT. LBS.)

SUPPORT

SUPPORT

28 N·M (21 FT. LBS.)

PUMP ASSEMBLY

PULLEY

VIEW A

24 N·M (18 FT. LBS.)

Vacuum Pump Mounting Without Air Conditioning

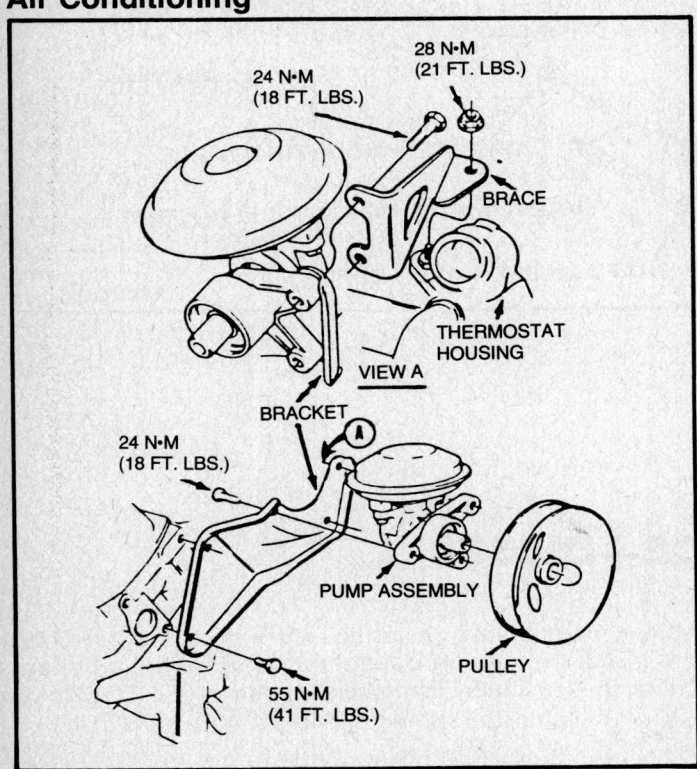

24 N·M (18 FT. LBS.)

28 N·M (21 FT. LBS.)

BRACE

THERMOSTAT HOUSING

VIEW A

BRACKET

24 N·M (18 FT. LBS.)

PUMP ASSEMBLY

PULLEY

55 N·M (41 FT. LBS.)

Oil Filter Base

Removal

1. Remove the oil cooler lines.
2. Bend the exhaust manifold lock tabs away from the bolts.
3. Disconnect the exhaust system from the exhaust manifold.
4. Remove the exhaust manifold.
5. Remove the oil filter.

Installation

1. If a new oil filter element is installed, add one quart of oil.
2. Clean sealing surfaces and re-bend manifold bolt lock tables.
3. Start engine, inspect for leaks and proper oil level.
4. Torque oil filter base attaching bolts to 40 N•m (29 ft. lbs.) and the exhaust manifold bolts to 39 N•m (29 ft. lbs.).

Vacuum Pump Pulley Removal And Installation

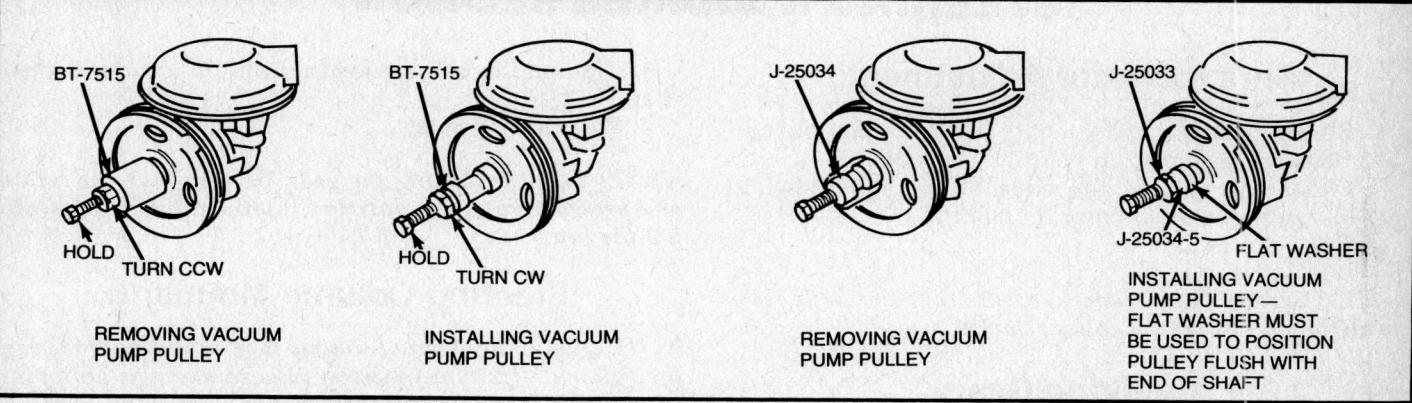

Diesel Engine Oil Cooler Lines

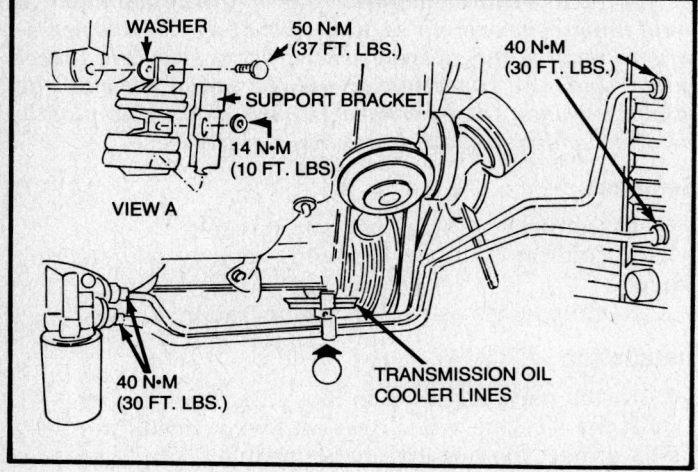

Diesel Engine Oil Filter Base

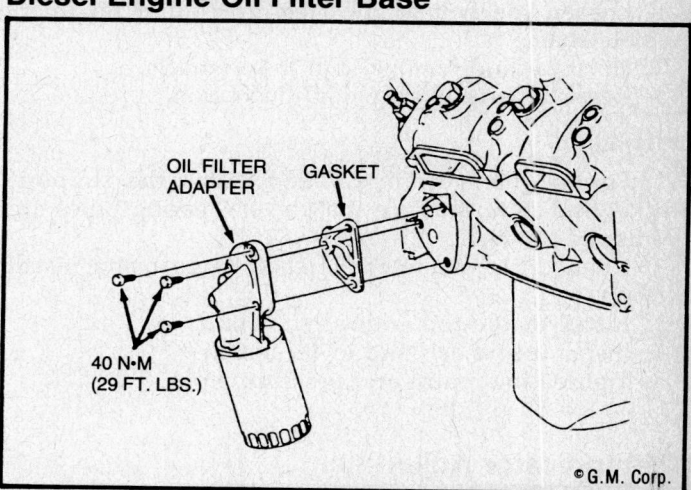

© G.M. Corp.

ENGINE SECTION

See General Motors Engine Section for information pertinent to engines used in these vehicles.

Removal

1. The engine is removed from the top after separating it from its mounts and the transaxle. The two upper engine-to-transaxle mount bolts will have to remain in place until the engine transaxle assembly can be raised far enough so that the engine front mount studs clear the cradle.

2. With six-cylinder engines using a manual transaxle, both drive shafts must be disconnected from the transaxle.

3. Engine removal requires disconnection, removal or displacement of some or all of the following:
a. Battery cables
b. Air cleaner
c. Vacuum hoses
d. Mechanical linkages
e. Electrical wiring
f. Cooling system and heater hoses
g. Speedometer cable
h. Crossmember
i. Exhaust plumbing
j. Fuel lines

STEERING & BRAKES SECTION

Shift Indicator Adjustment

1. Steering column attachments should be completed.
2. Position shift lever in Neutral gate notch.
3. Guide the clip on the edge of the shift bowl to centrally position the pointer on Neutral.
4. Push clip onto bowl.

NOTE Care must be taken to assure that the cable rests on the bowl, not on the column jacket.

Steering Gear

Removal

1. Loosen the bolt at the steering column to intermediate shaft.
2. Hoist car and remove both front wheels.
3. Remove parts as shown in illustration.

Installation

1. Position the gear in car and install the support, bracket and nuts. Be sure the power steering pipes are positioned properly.
2. Connect the intermediate shaft to gear and install the bolt.
3. Install the tie-rod ends as shown.
4. Install the wheels and lower hoist.
5. Tighten the return and pressure pipes.

Shift Indicator Adjustment

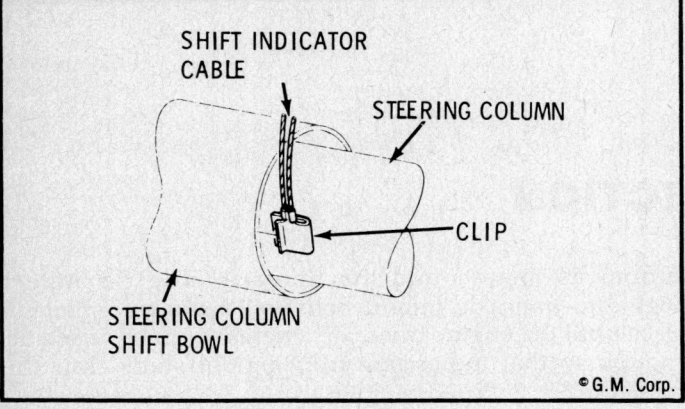

SHIFT INDICATOR CABLE
STEERING COLUMN
CLIP
STEERING COLUMN SHIFT BOWL

© G.M. Corp.

6. Tighten the bolt at steering column to intermediate shaft.
7. Bleed the system.

NOTE: When installing the gear, be sure that the return and pressure pipes are positioned properly before installing the brackets.

Steering Column Mounting

NOTE   Once the steering column is removed from the car, the column is extremely susceptible to damage. Dropping the column assembly on its end could collapse the steering shaft or loosen the plastic injections which maintain column rigidity. Leaning on the column assembly could cause the jacket to bend or deform. Any of the above damage could impair the column's collapsible design. If it is necessary to remove the steering wheel, use a standard wheel puller. Under no condition should the end of the shaft be hammered upon, as hammering could loosen the plastic injection which maintains column rigidity.

Removal

1. Disconnect the negative battery cable.
2. If column is to be repaired, remove the steering wheel.
3. Remove parts as shown in illustration.

Installation

1. Install parts a shown in illustration.
2. If the steering wheel was removed, install it.
3. Connect the negative battery cable.

Brake Booster

Removal

1. Disconnect the master cylinder from the booster. Disconnect the booster pushrod.
2. Remove the attaching nuts and remove the booster.

Installation

1. Install the booster to cowl. Torque the attaching nuts to 30-45 N•m (22-33 ft. lb.).
2. Connect the booster pushrod.
3. Install the master cylinder on the booster. Torque the attaching nuts to 30-45 N•m (22-33 ft. lb.).

Steering Gear

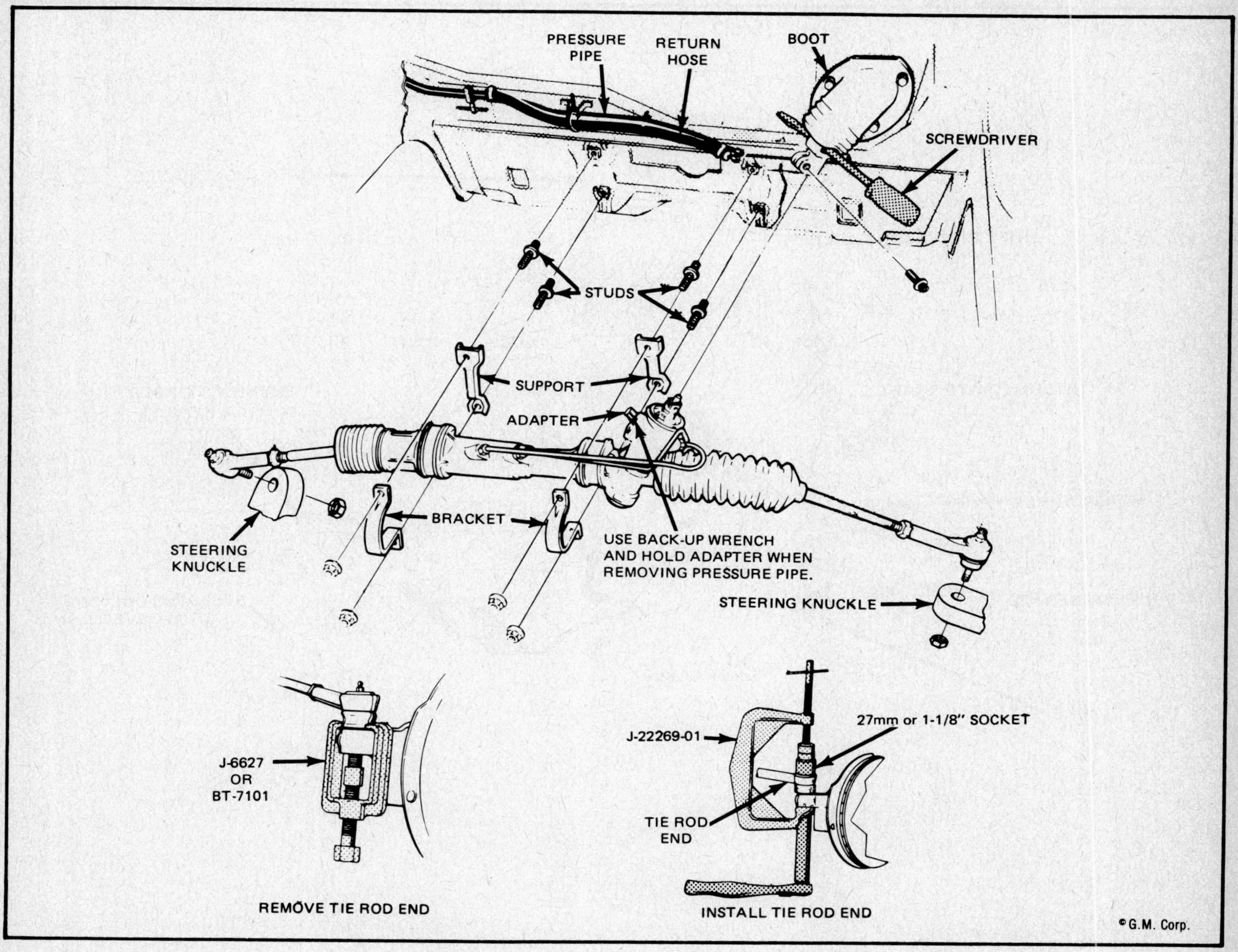

PRESSURE PIPE

RETURN HOSE

BOOT

SCREWDRIVER

STUDS

SUPPORT

ADAPTER

STEERING KNUCKLE

BRACKET

USE BACK-UP WRENCH AND HOLD ADAPTER WHEN REMOVING PRESSURE PIPE.

STEERING KNUCKLE

J-6627 OR BT-7101

REMOVE TIE ROD END

J-22269-01

27mm or 1-1/8" SOCKET

TIE ROD END

INSTALL TIE ROD END

© G.M. Corp.

Stoplight Switch

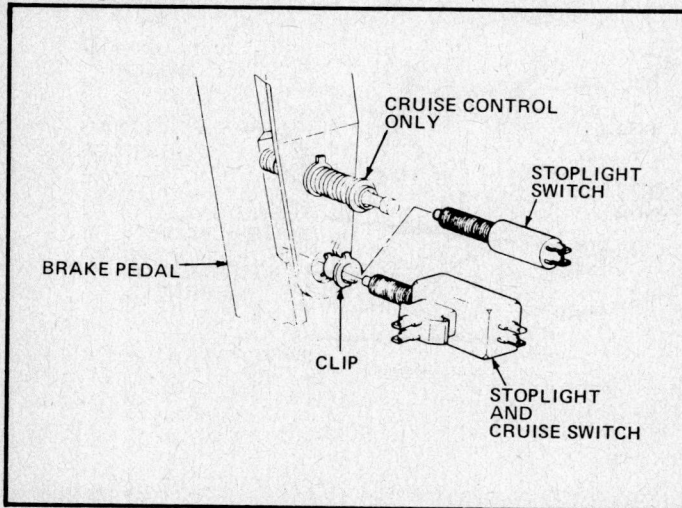

CRUISE CONTROL ONLY

STOPLIGHT SWITCH

BRAKE PEDAL

CLIP

STOPLIGHT AND CRUISE SWITCH

Brake Booster Replacement

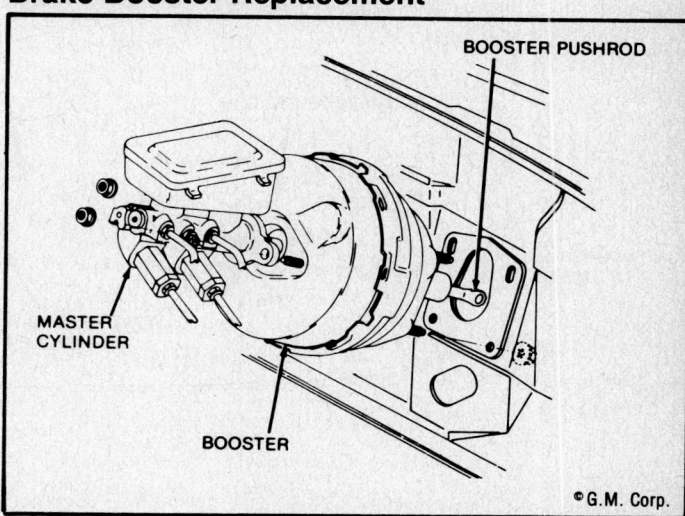

BOOSTER PUSHROD

MASTER CYLINDER

BOOSTER

© G.M. Corp.

A475

GENERAL MOTORS "A" AND "X" BODY CARS

"A": CELEBRITY, CENTURY, A6000, CIERA; "X": CITATION, OMEGA, PHOENIX, SKYLARK

Steering Column Mounting

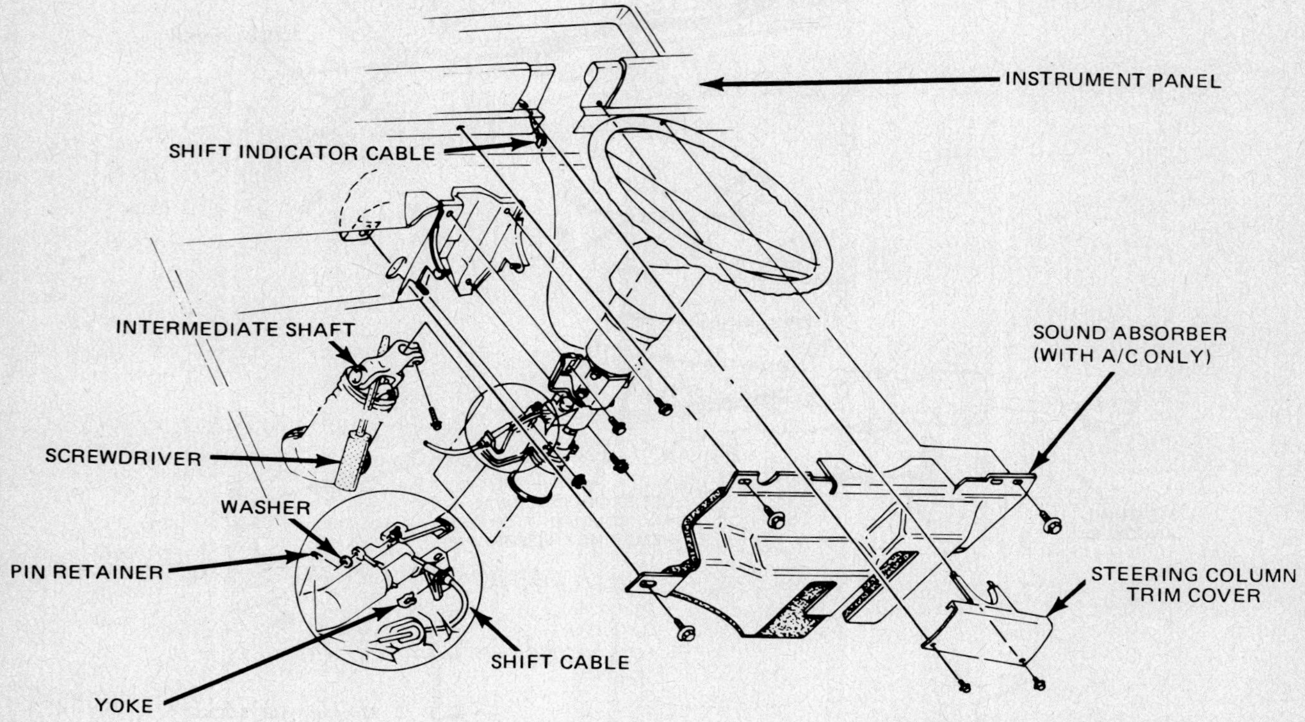

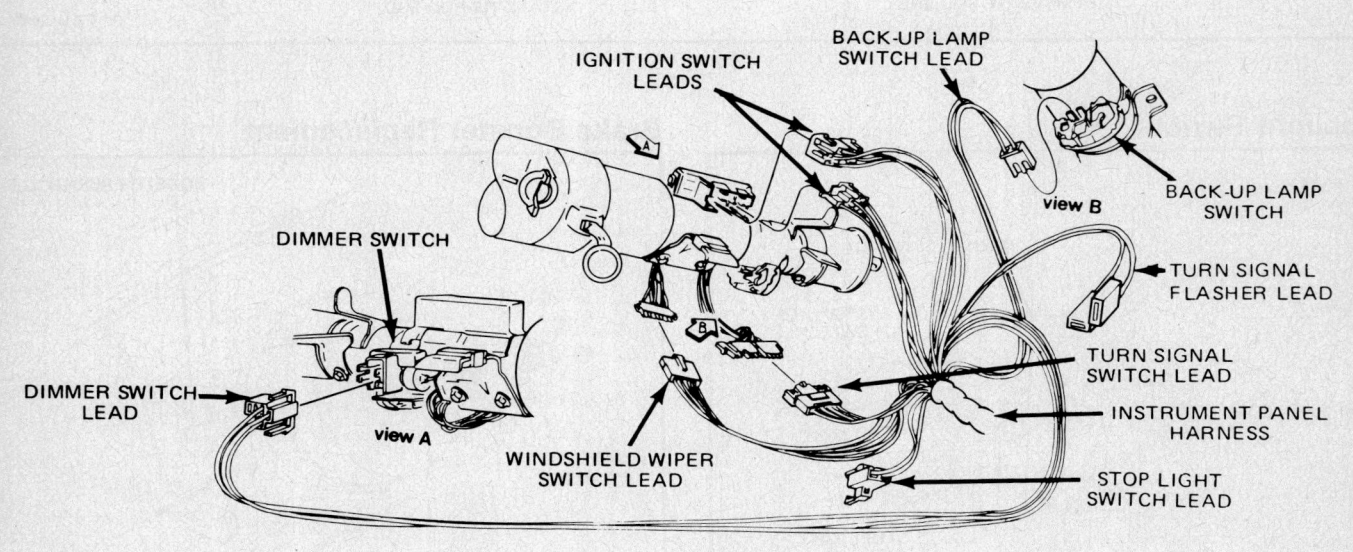

INSTRUMENT PANEL

SHIFT INDICATOR CABLE

SOUND ABSORBER
(WITH A/C ONLY)

INTERMEDIATE SHAFT

SCREWDRIVER

WASHER

PIN RETAINER

STEERING COLUMN
TRIM COVER

YOKE

SHIFT CABLE

IGNITION SWITCH
LEADS

BACK-UP LAMP
SWITCH LEAD

view B

BACK-UP LAMP
SWITCH

DIMMER SWITCH

TURN SIGNAL
FLASHER LEAD

DIMMER SWITCH
LEAD

view A

TURN SIGNAL
SWITCH LEAD

INSTRUMENT PANEL
HARNESS

WINDSHIELD WIPER
SWITCH LEAD

STOP LIGHT
SWITCH LEAD

© G.M. Corp.

A476

Tilt Steering Column

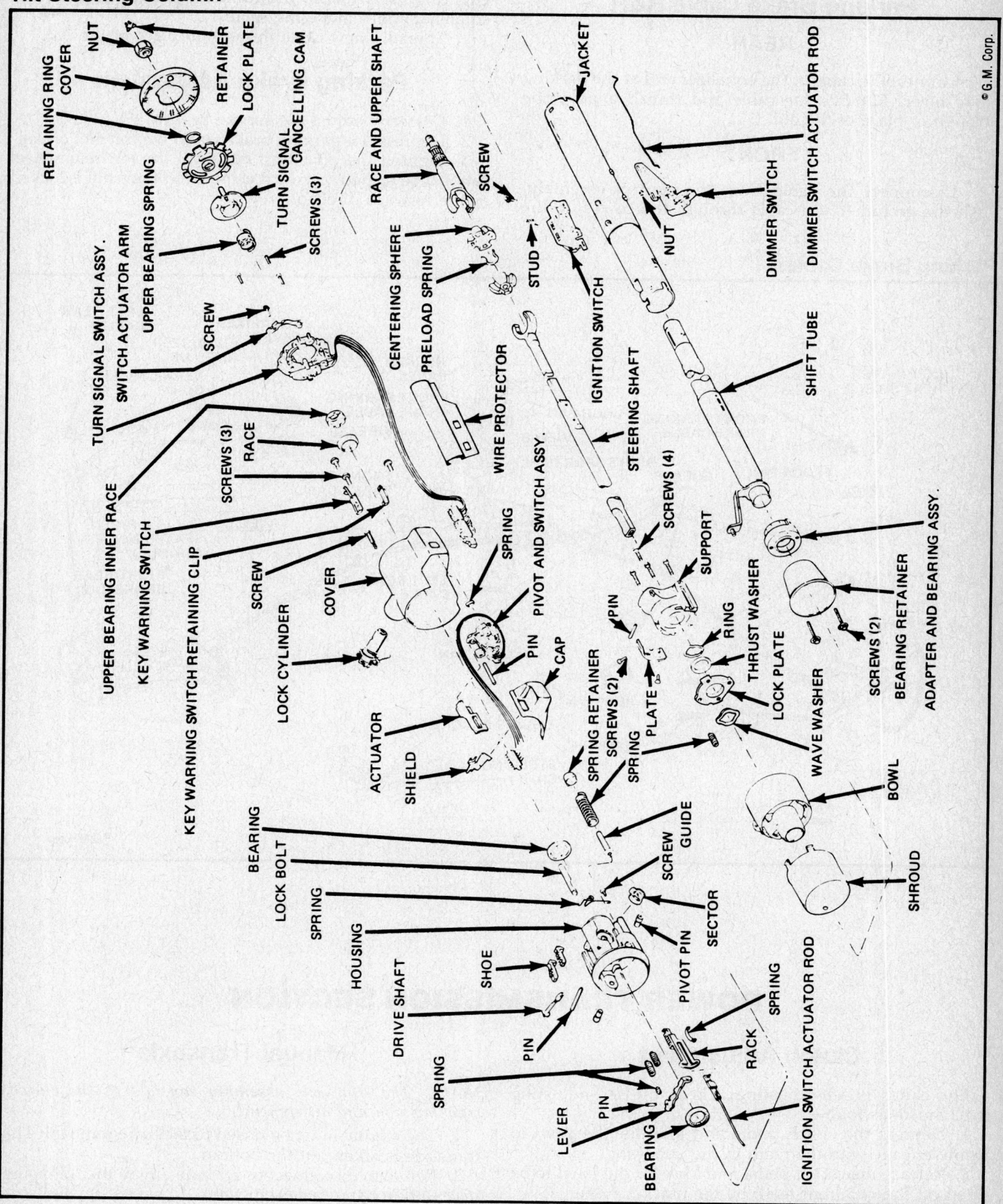

© G. M. Corp.

A477

Parking Brake Cable R&R

REAR

Disconnect the cable at the equalizer and at the parking brake lever. Remove the cable and thread a new one through in place of the old.

FRONT

1. Disconnect the cable from the control assembly. Push the grommet and cable through the cowl into the engine compartment. Disconnect the cable from the equalizer and remove the cable.
2. Thread a new cable through in place of the old.

Parking Brake Adjustment

1. Correctly adjust the service brakes.
2. Depress the parking brake pedal two ratchet clicks.
3. Tighten the adjusting nut until the left rear wheel can just be turned rearward using two hands but is locked in the forward direction.

Parking Brake Cables

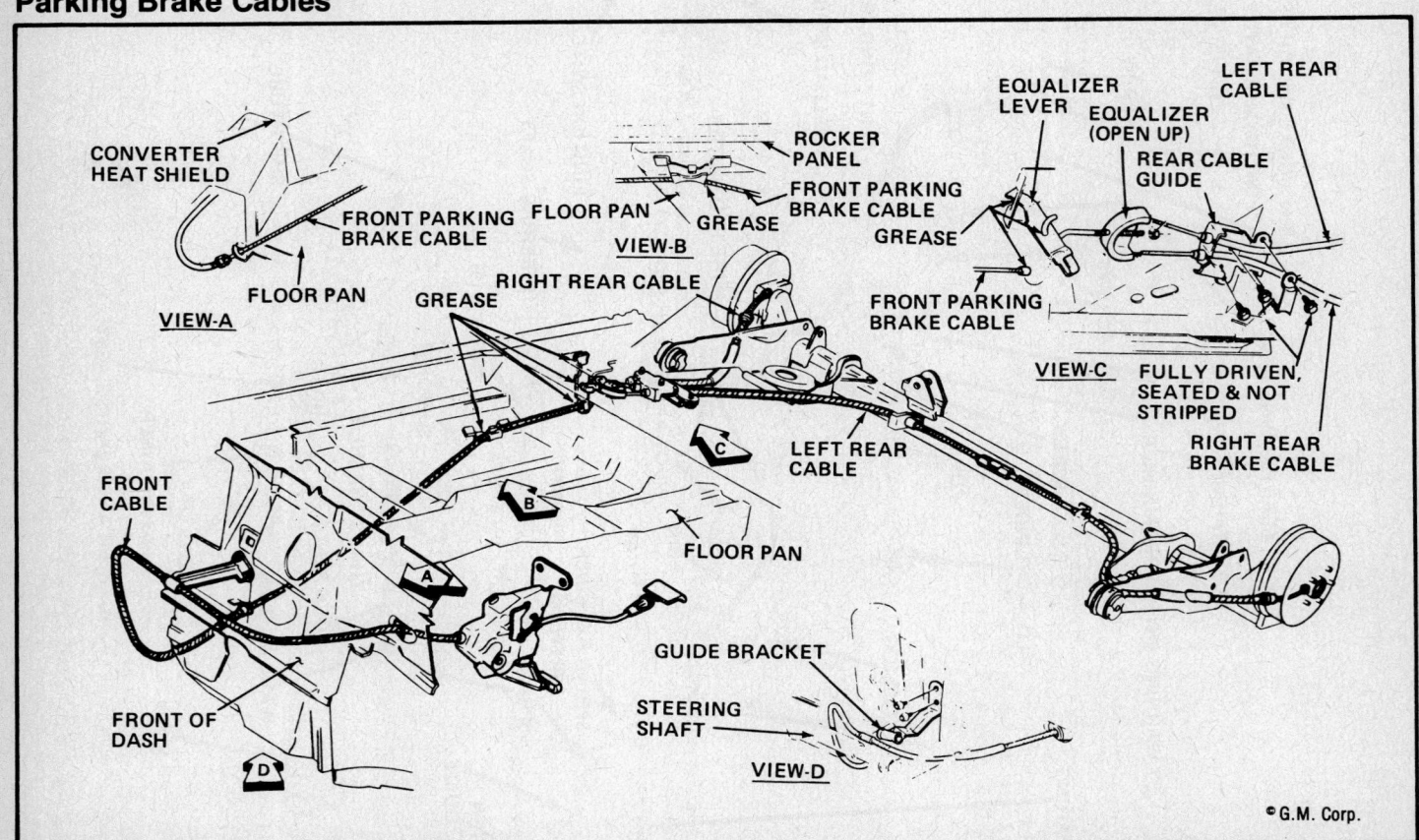

POWER TRANSMISSION SECTION

Clutch Adjustment

The clutch is self-adjusting. Check the self-adjusting mechanism as follows:
1. Depress the clutch pedal and look for the pawl to firmly engage with the teeth in the quadrant.
2. Release the clutch pedal and look for the pawl to be lifted off the quadrant teeth by the bracket stop.

Manual Transaxle

NOTE The transaxle assembly consists of the clutch, transmission and differential.

1. The engine must be raised to facilitate removal. The transaxle is taken out the bottom.
2. Remove, disconnect or relocate any of the following necessary for transaxle removal:

Transaxle Front Mounts With V6 Engine

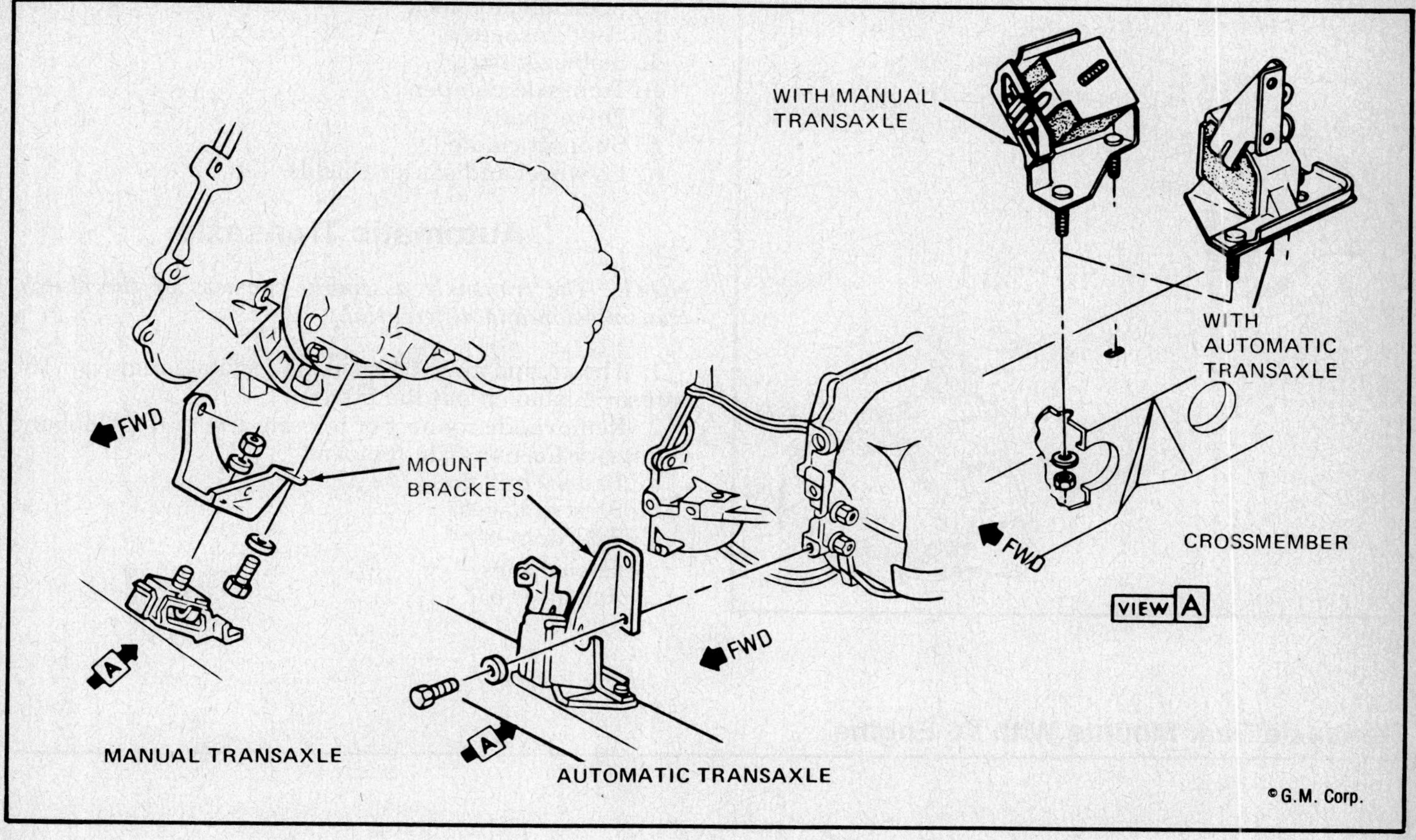

WITH MANUAL TRANSAXLE

WITH AUTOMATIC TRANSAXLE

FWD

CROSSMEMBER

VIEW A

FWD

MOUNT BRACKETS

FWD

A

MANUAL TRANSAXLE

A

AUTOMATIC TRANSAXLE

© G.M. Corp.

Stabilizer-To-Cradle Attachment

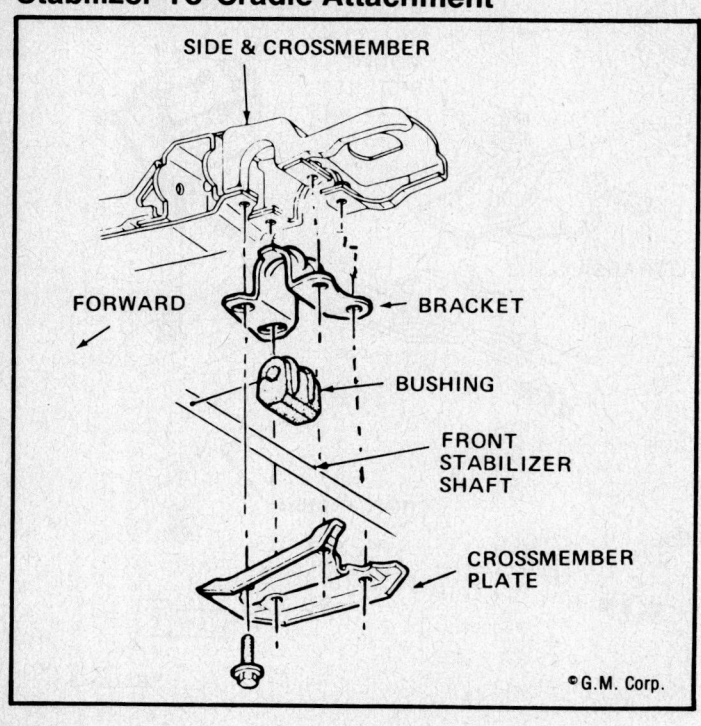

SIDE & CROSSMEMBER

FORWARD

BRACKET

BUSHING

FRONT STABILIZER SHAFT

CROSSMEMBER PLATE

© G.M. Corp.

Stabilizer-To-Control Arm Attachments

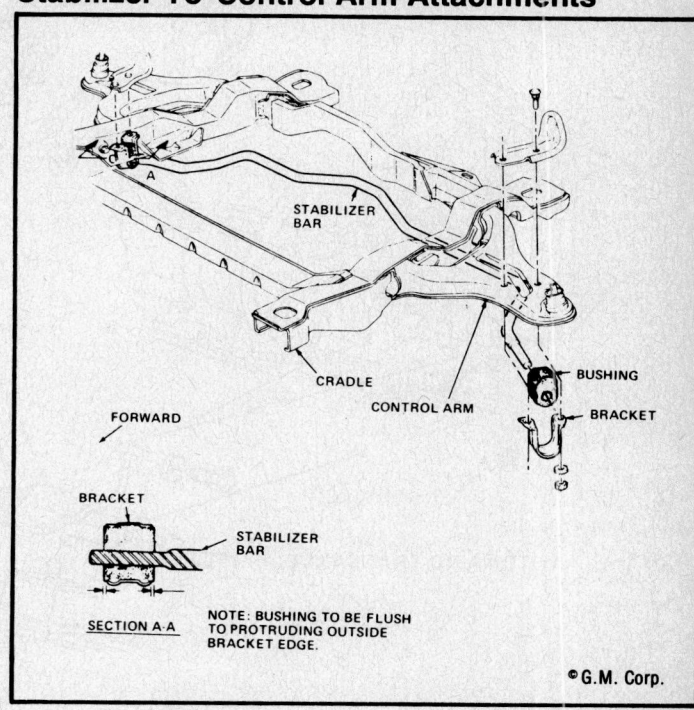

A

STABILIZER BAR

CRADLE

CONTROL ARM

BUSHING

BRACKET

FORWARD

BRACKET

STABILIZER BAR

SECTION A-A

NOTE: BUSHING TO BE FLUSH TO PROTRUDING OUTSIDE BRACKET EDGE.

© G.M. Corp.

GENERAL MOTORS "A" AND "X" BODY CARS

"A": CELEBRITY, CENTURY, A6000, CIERA; "X": CITATION, OMEGA, PHOENIX, SKYLARK

Manual Transaxle-To-Engine Attachments

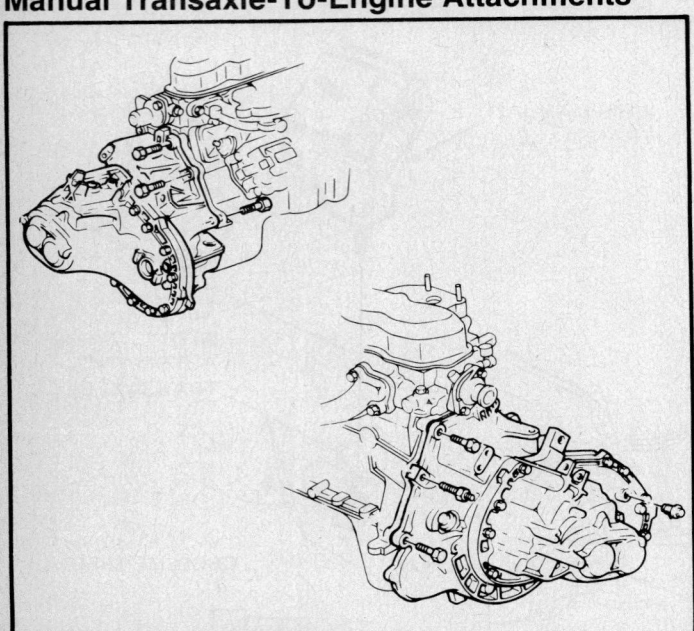

a. Battery cables
b. Speedometer cable
c. Shift linkages
d. Stabilizer bar
e. Transaxle damper
f. Drive shafts
g. Support cradle
h. Flywheel and starter shields

Automatic Transaxle

NOTE   The transaxle assembly consists of the clutch, transmission and differential.

1. The engine must be raised to facilitate removal. The transaxle is taken out the bottom.
2. Remove, disconnect or relocate any of the following necessary for transaxle removal:
a. Battery cables
b. Shift linkages
c. Speedometer
d. Cooler lines
e. Stabilizer bar

Transaxle Rear Mounts With V6 Engine

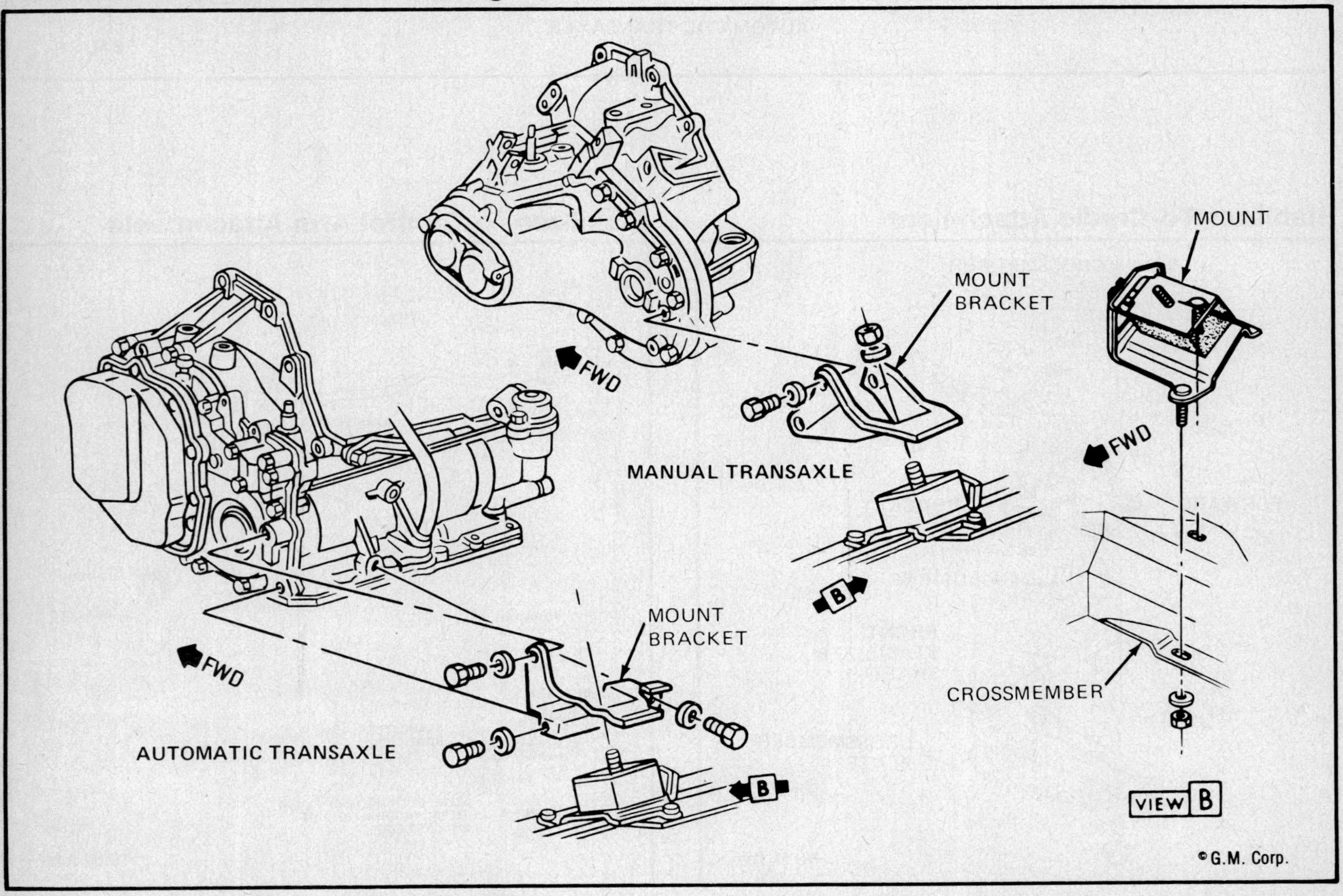

FWD

MOUNT

MOUNT BRACKET

MANUAL TRANSAXLE

FWD

B

MOUNT BRACKET

FWD

CROSSMEMBER

FWD

AUTOMATIC TRANSAXLE

B

VIEW B

© G.M. Corp.

Engine Cradle Transaxle Mount Holes

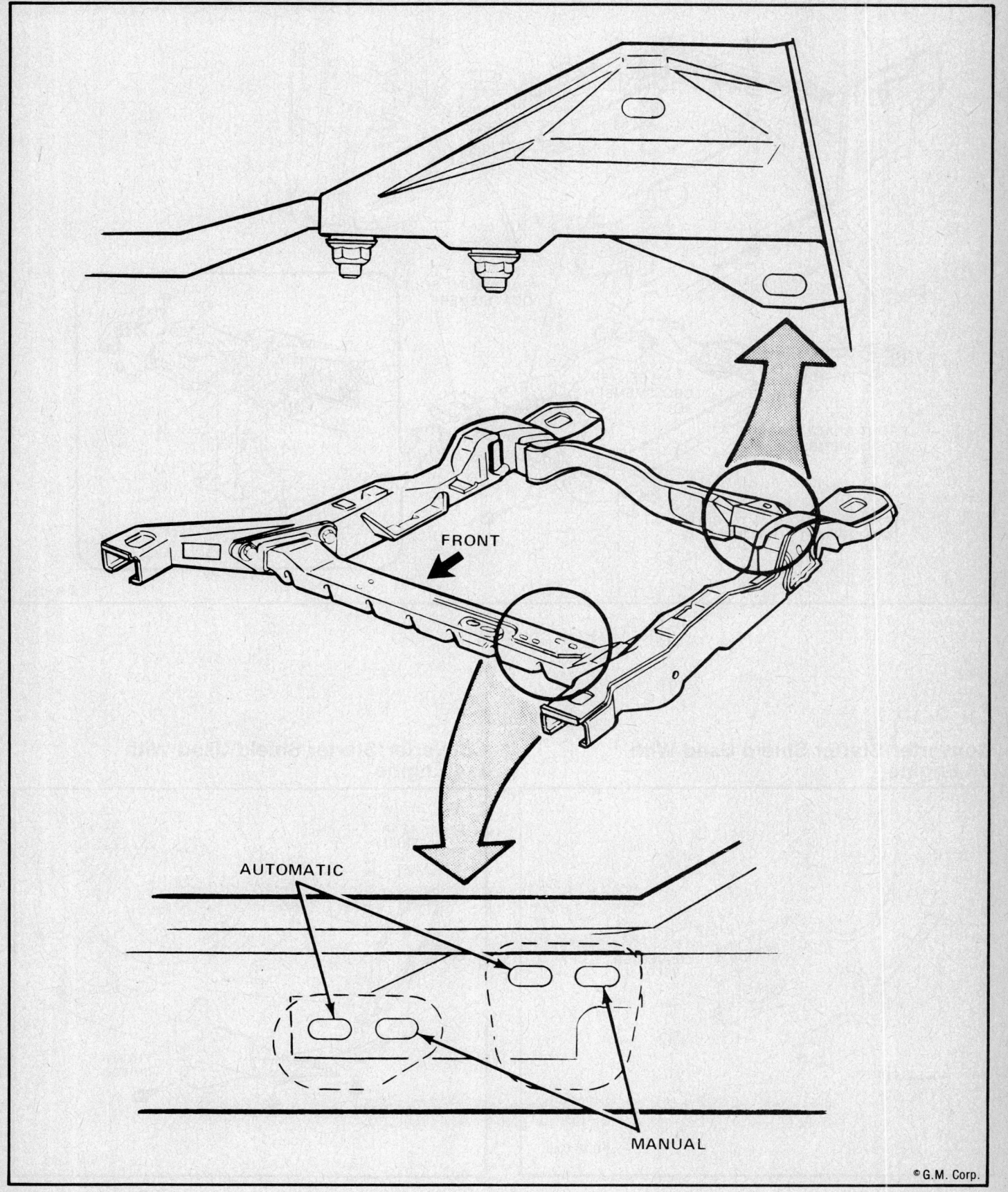

FRONT

AUTOMATIC

MANUAL

© G.M. Corp.

GENERAL MOTORS "A" AND "X" BODY CARS

"A": CELEBRITY, CENTURY, A6000, CIERA; "X": CITATION, OMEGA, PHOENIX, SKYLARK

Cradle Mounting Attachments

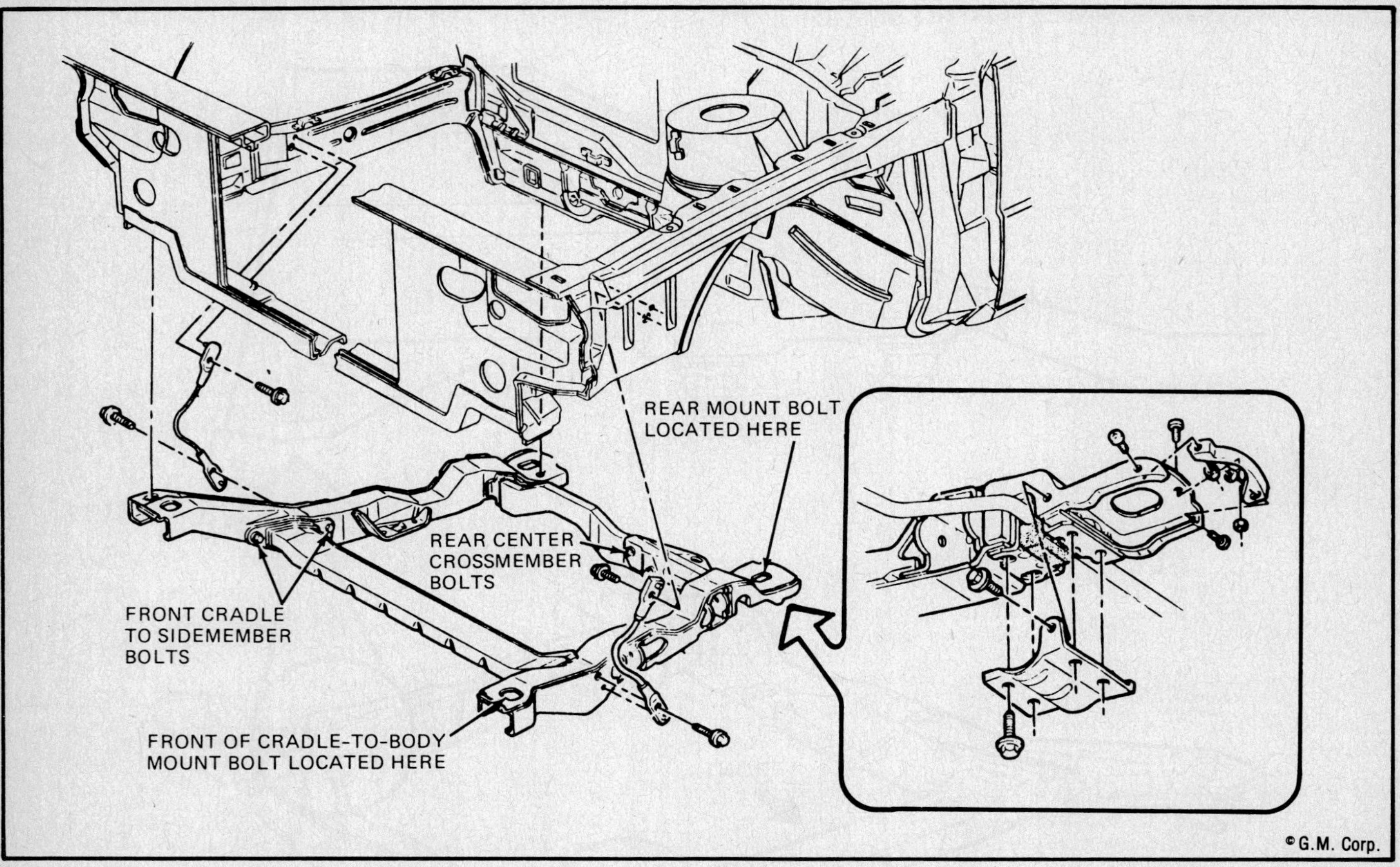

REAR MOUNT BOLT LOCATED HERE

REAR CENTER CROSSMEMBER BOLTS

FRONT CRADLE TO SIDEMEMBER BOLTS

FRONT OF CRADLE-TO-BODY MOUNT BOLT LOCATED HERE

© G.M. Corp.

Converter/Starter Shield Used With V6 Engine

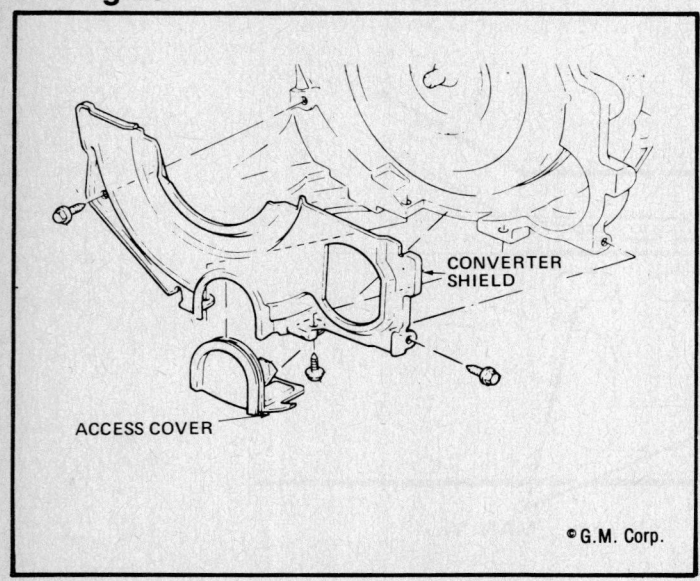

CONVERTER SHIELD

ACCESS COVER

© G.M. Corp.

Converter/Starter Shield Used With L-4 Engine

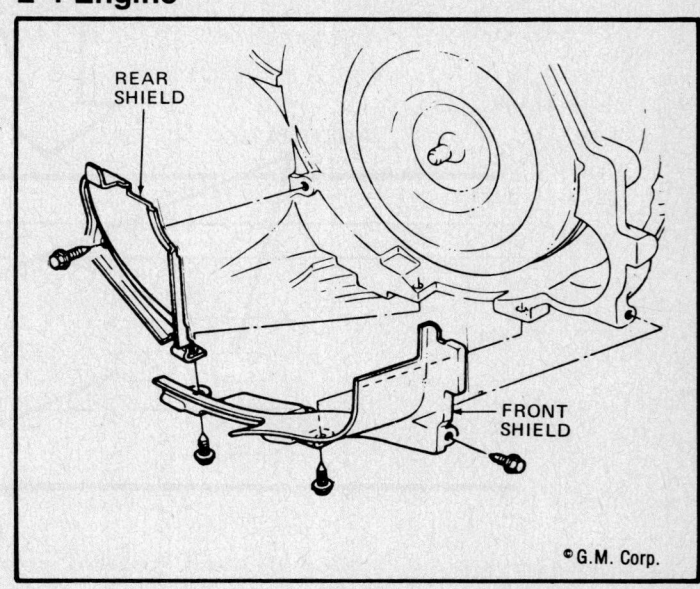

REAR SHIELD

FRONT SHIELD

© G.M. Corp.

A482

Manual Transaxle Shift Cable Adjustment

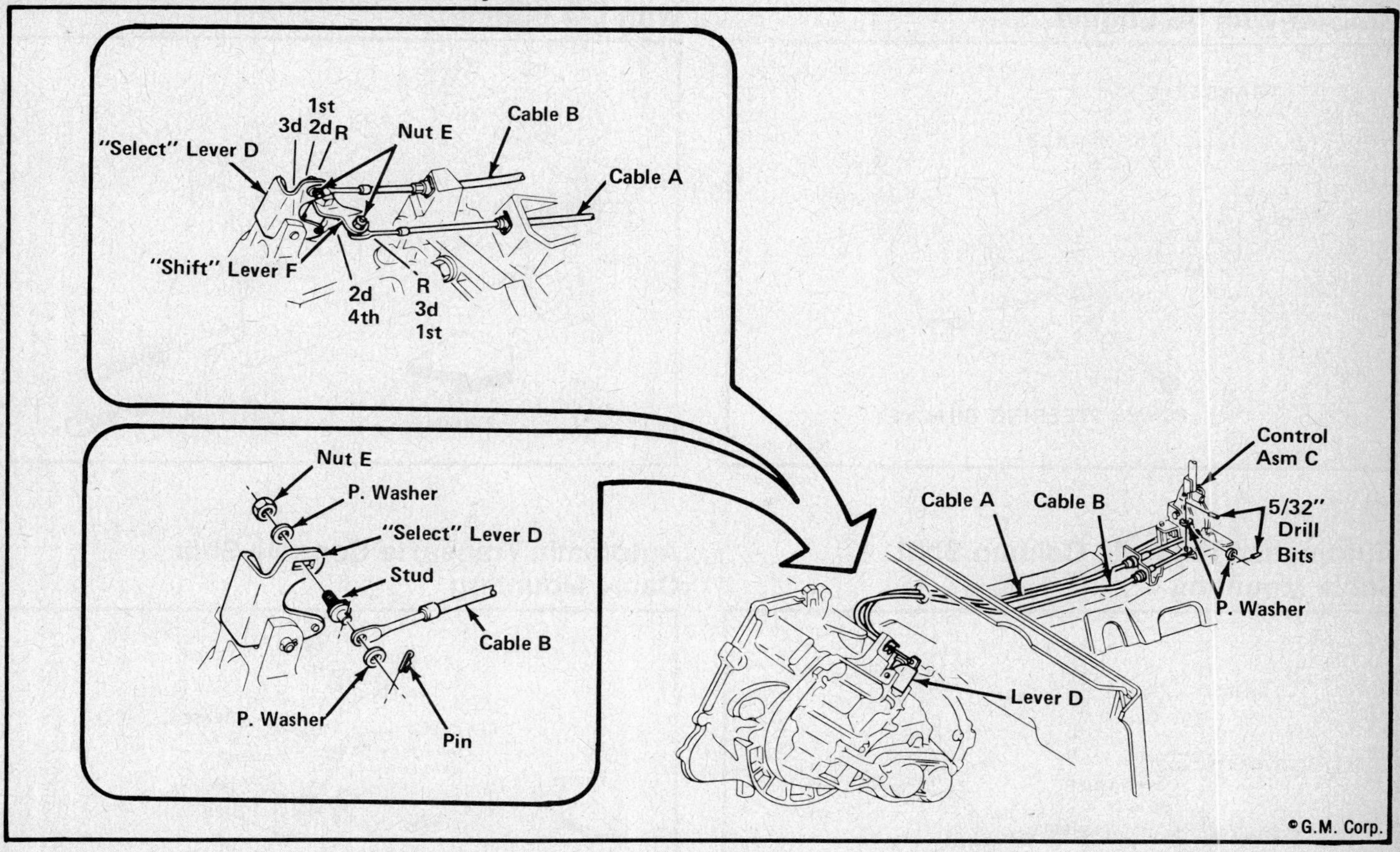

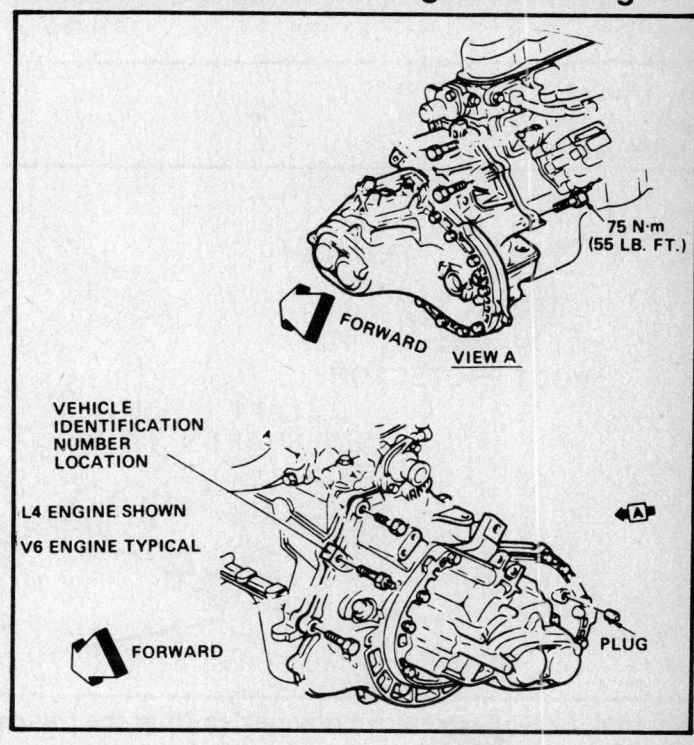

1st
3d 2d R — Nut E — Cable B

Cable A

"Select" Lever D

"Shift" Lever F

2d
4th — R
3d
1st

Nut E
P. Washer
"Select" Lever D
Stud
Cable B
P. Washer — Pin

Cable A — Cable B — Control Asm C — 5/32" Drill Bits — P. Washer

Lever D

© G.M. Corp.

f. Support cradle
g. Transaxle damper
h. Axle shafts
i. Converter and starter shields
j. Converter-to-flywheel bolts
k. Exhaust plumbing
l. Electrical connections
3. When installing, the right axle shaft must be inserted into the case *as the transaxle is being installed.*

Shift Linkage Adjustment

Adjust the linkage so the shift lever positions corresponds exactly to the transmission positions.

Drive Shafts

1. Remove the hub nut and wheel.
2. Remove the brake and support calipers.
3. Remove the cam bolt and upper attaching bolt after marking the cam for installation reference.
4. Pull the steering knuckle assembly out of the strut bracket.
5. Pull the axle shaft from the transaxle. Tool J-28468 can be used for this.
6. Remove the drive shaft from the hub and bearing assembly using Tool J-28733.

Automatic Transaxle-To-Engine Mounting

75 N·m
(55 LB. FT.)

FORWARD

VIEW A

VEHICLE IDENTIFICATION NUMBER LOCATION

L4 ENGINE SHOWN
V6 ENGINE TYPICAL

FORWARD

PLUG

GENERAL MOTORS "A" AND "X" BODY CARS

"A": CELEBRITY, CENTURY, A6000, CIERA; "X": CITATION, OMEGA, PHOENIX, SKYLARK

Automatic Transaxle Extension-To-Engine Bracket With V6 Engine

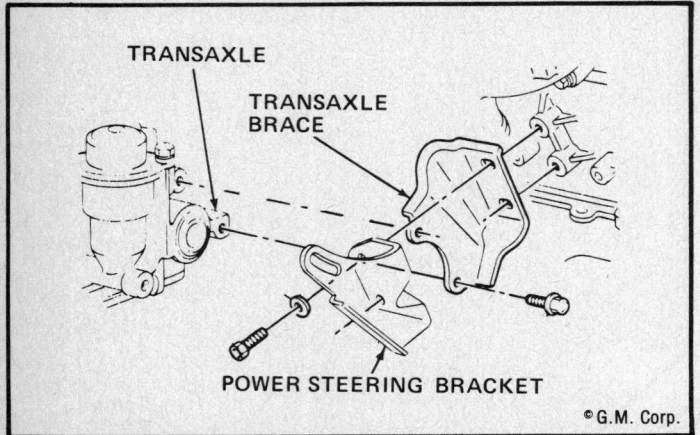

© G.M. Corp.

Automatic Transaxle Extension-To-Engine With L-4 Engine

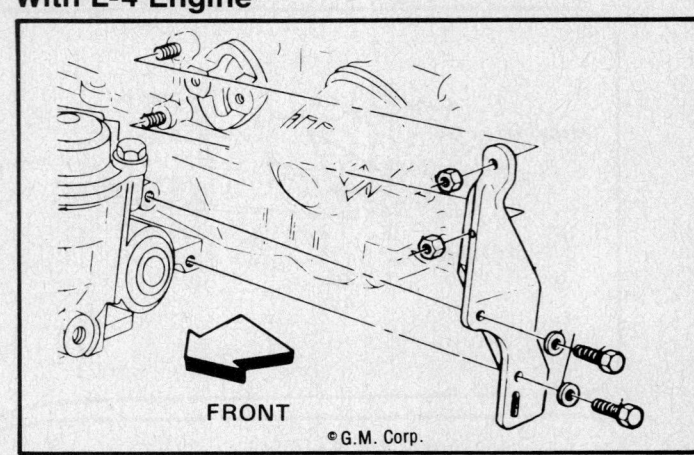

© G.M. Corp.

Automatic Transaxle Column Shift Cable Mounting

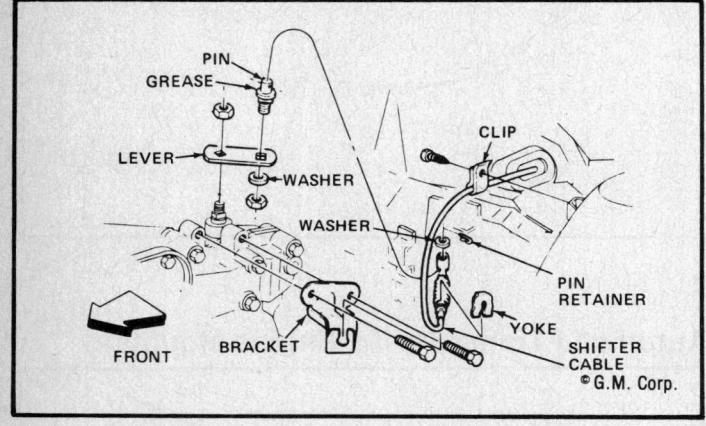

© G.M. Corp.

Automatic Transaxle Console Shift Cable Mounting

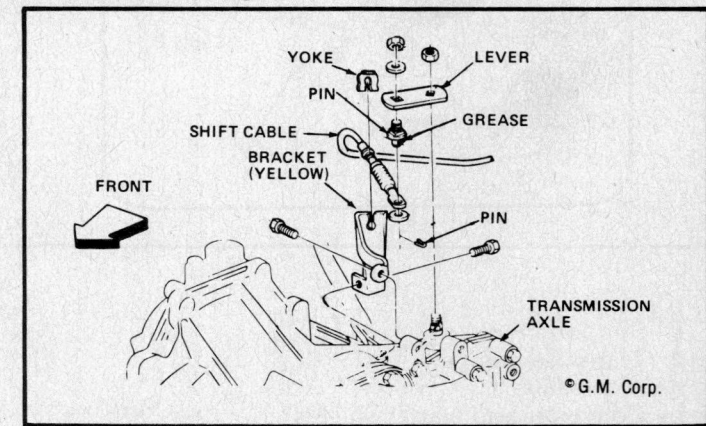

© G.M. Corp.

Drive Axles

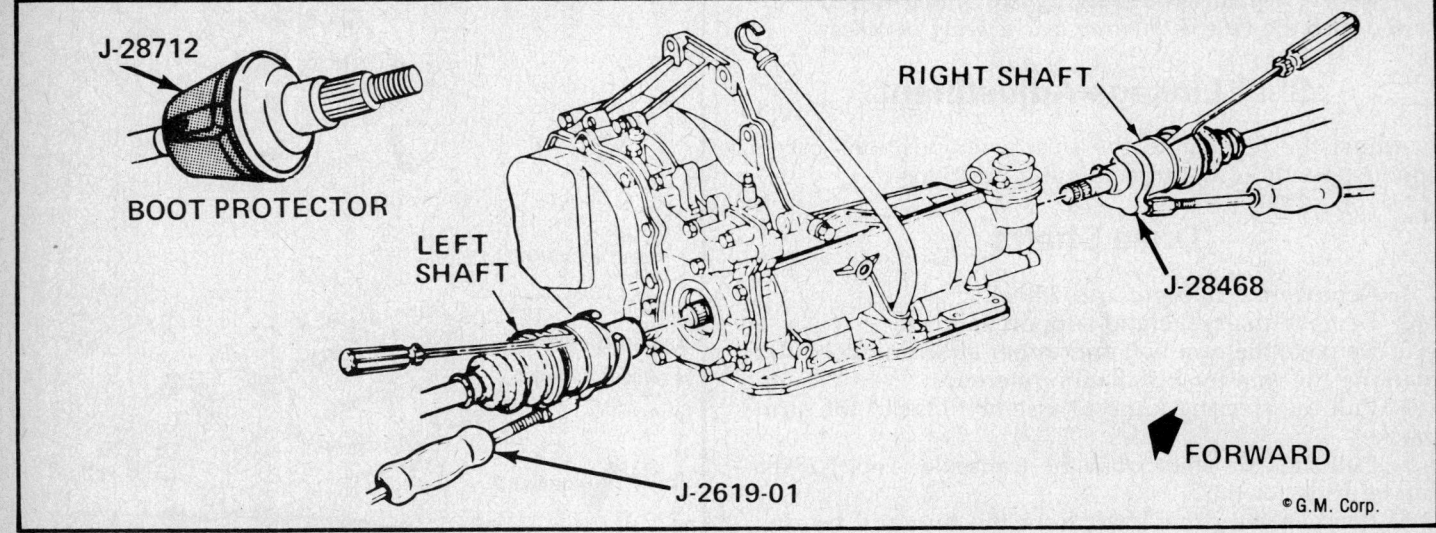

© G.M. Corp.

Use tool J-28468 to remove drive axles from the transaxle

A484

GENERAL MOTORS "H" BODY

Astre, Monza, Skyhawk, Starfire, Sunbird & Vega

INDEX

Page Numbers Preceded by "B" Refer to Unit Repair Section

GENERAL MOTORS "H" BODY CARS
ASTRE, MONZA, SKYHAWK, STARFIRE, SUNBIRD, VEGA

MODEL IDENTIFICATION

BUICK

1976 SKYHAWK
W.B. 97". Length 180". Ship. Wgt. V6 2 Dr. H/B 2889 Lbs.

1977 SKYHAWK
W.B. 97". Length 180". Width 66". Ship. Wgt. V6 2Dr. H/B 2805 Lbs.

1978 SKYHAWK
W.B. 97.0" Length 179.3" Ship. Wgt. 6 Cyl. 2 Dr. 2830 Lbs.

1979 SKYHAWK
W.B. 97.0" Length 179.3" Ship. Wgt. H.B. 2821 Lbs.

1980 SKYHAWK
W.B. 97". Length 179.5". Ship. Wgt. Hatchback Approx. 2821 Lbs.

CHEVROLET

1976 VEGA
W.B. 97", Length 176". Ship. Wgt. 4 Cyl. 2 Dr. 2443 Lbs.

1977 VEGA
W.B. 97". Length 176". Width 66". Ship. Wgt. 4 Cyl. 2 Dr. 2453 Lbs.

1976 MONZA
W.B. 97". Length Hatchback 180", Towne 179". Ship. Wgt. 4 Cyl. 2 Dr. 2625 Lbs.

1977 MONZA
W.B. 97". Length Hatchback 180", Towne 179". Ship. Wgt. 4 Cyl. 2 Dr. 2665 Lbs.

1978 MONZA
W.B. 97" Length 177.4" Ship. Wgt. 4 Cyl. 2 Dr. 2619 Lbs.

1979 MONZA

W.B. 97″ Length 177.4″ Ship. Wgt. 4 Cyl. 2 Dr. 2619 Lbs.

1980 MONZA

W.B. 97″. Length 177.5″. Ship. Wgt. Approx. 2680 Lbs.

OLDSMOBILE

1976 STARFIRE

W.B. 97″. Length 180″. Ship. Wgt. V6 2 Dr. 2857 Lbs.

1977 STARFIRE

W.B. 97″. Length 180″. Width 66″. V6 2 Dr. 2698 Lbs.

1978 STARFIRE

W.B. 97.0″ Length 179.3″ Ship. Wgt. 4 Cyl. 2 Dr. 2712 Lbs.

1979 STARFIRE

W.B. 97.0″ Length 179.6″ Ship. Wgt. 4 Cyl. 2 Dr. 2687 Lbs.

1980 STARFIRE

W.B. 97″. Length 179.6″. Ship. Wgt. Approx. 2680 Lbs.

PONTIAC

1976 ASTRE

W.B. 97″. Length 178″. Ship. Wgt. 4 Cyl. 2 Dr. 2439 Lbs.

1977 ASTRE

W.B. 97″. Length 178″. Width 66″. Ship. Wgt. 4 Cyl. 2 Dr. 3305 Lbs.

1976 SUNBIRD

W.B. 97″. Length 178″. Ship. Wgt. 4 Cyl. 2 Dr. 2653 Lbs.

GENERAL MOTORS "H" BODY CARS
ASTRE, MONZA, SKYHAWK, STARFIRE, SUNBIRD, VEGA

1977 SUNBIRD

W.B. 97". Length 178". Width 66". Ship. Wgt. 4 Cyl. 2 Dr. 2653 Lbs.

1978 SUNBIRD

W.B. 97.0" Length 177.8" Ship. Wgt. 6 Cyl. 2 Dr. 2662 Lbs.

1979 SUNBIRD

W.B. 97.0" Length 177.8" Ship. Wgt. 6 Cyl. 2 Dr. 2662 Lbs.

1980 SUNBIRD

W.B. 97". Length 179.2". Ship. Wgt. 6 Cyl. Approx. 2660 Lbs.

ENGINE FIRING ORDER

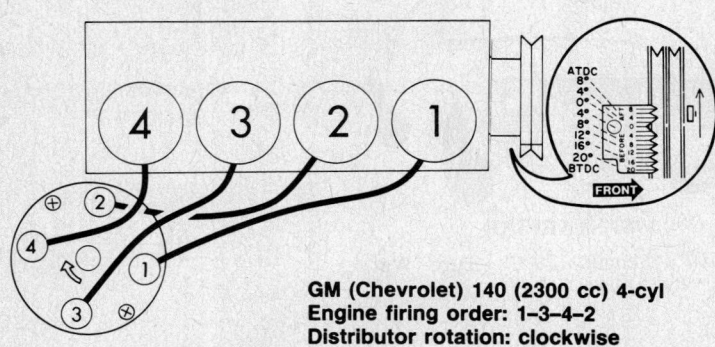

GM (Chevrolet) 140 (2300 cc) 4-cyl
Engine firing order: 1–3–4–2
Distributor rotation: clockwise

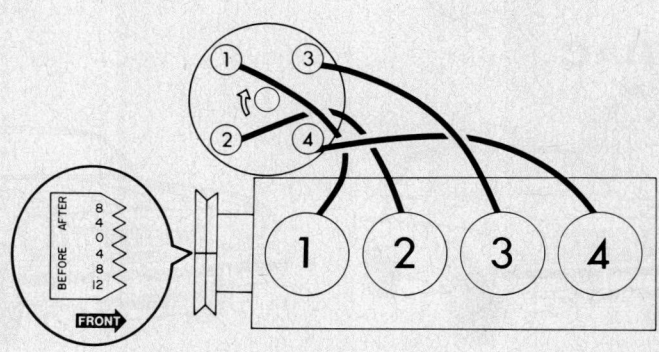

GM (Chevrolet) Cosworth Vega 122 4-cyl.
Engine firing order: 1–3–4–2
Distributor rotation: clockwise

GENERAL MOTORS "H" BODY CARS
ASTRE, MONZA, SKYHAWK, STARFIRE, SUNBIRD, VEGA

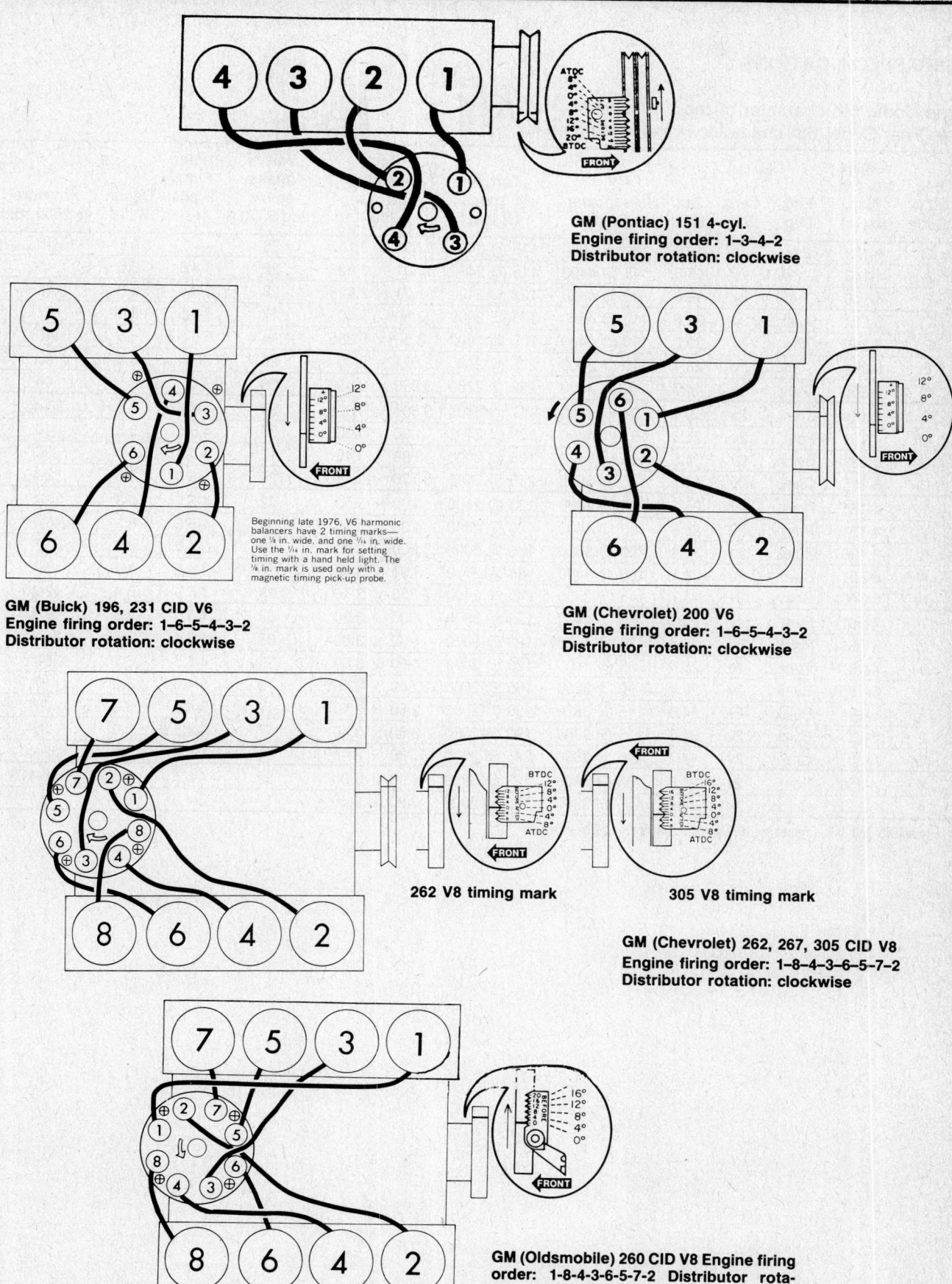

GM (Pontiac) 151 4-cyl.
Engine firing order: 1–3–4–2
Distributor rotation: clockwise

GM (Buick) 196, 231 CID V6
Engine firing order: 1–6–5–4–3–2
Distributor rotation: clockwise

Beginning late 1976, V6 harmonic balancers have 2 timing marks—one ⅛ in. wide, and one 1/16 in. wide. Use the 1/16 in. mark for setting timing with a hand held light. The ⅛ in. mark is used only with a magnetic timing pick-up probe.

GM (Chevrolet) 200 V6
Engine firing order: 1–6–5–4–3–2
Distributor rotation: clockwise

262 V8 timing mark

305 V8 timing mark

GM (Chevrolet) 262, 267, 305 CID V8
Engine firing order: 1–8–4–3–6–5–7–2
Distributor rotation: clockwise

GM (Oldsmobile) 260 CID V8 Engine firing order: 1-8-4-3-6-5-7-2 Distributor rotation: counterclockwise

A489

GENERAL MOTORS "H" BODY CARS

ASTRE, MONZA, SKYHAWK, STARFIRE, SUNBIRD, VEGA

ENGINE SPECIFICATIONS

Engine Code, 5th character of the VIN number
Model Year Code, 6th character of the VIN number

Yr.	Eng. V.I.N. Code	Engine No. Cyl. Disp. (cu in)	Eng. Mfg.	Carb. Bbl.	Tax H.P.	Horsepower[2] @ rpm	Torque @ rpm[1] (ft lbs)	Bore and Stroke (in)	Valves Intake opens (deg BTDC)	Fuel Pump Press. (psi)	Comp. Ratio	Oil Pressure @ 2000 rpm
76	O	4-122	Chev	FI	19.6	120 @ 5600	115 @ 3400	3.501 × 3.160	38	—	8.5	45
	A	4-140	Chev	1v	19.6	75 @ 4400	115 @ 2400	3.501 × 3.625	22	3-4.5	8.0	45
	B	4-140	Chev	2v	19.6	85 @ 4400	122 @ 2400	3.501 × 3.625	28	3-4.5	8.0	45
	C	6-231	Buick	2v	34.6	110 @ 4000	175 @ 2000	3.80 × 3.40	17	3-4.5	8.0	37
	F	8-260	Olds	2v	39.2	110 @ 3400	205 @ 1600	3.50 × 3.385	14	5.5-6.5	8.5	40
	G	8-262	Chev	2v	43.1	110 @ 3600	205 @ 2400	3.671 × 3.10	26	7-8	8.5	40
	Q	8-305	Chev	2v	44.7	140 @ 3800	250 @ 2200	3.736 × 3.480	26	7-8.5	8.5	40
77	B	4-140	Chev	2v	19.6	84 @ 4400	117 @ 2400	3.501 × 3.625	34	3-4.5	8.0	36-45
	V	4-151	Pont.	2v	25.6	87 @ 4400	128 @ 2400	4.00 × 3.00	33	4.5-5	8.3	40
	C	6-231	Buick	2v	34.6	105 @ 3400	185 @ 2000	3.80 × 3.40	17	3-4.5	8.0	37
	U	8-305	Chev	2v	44.7	145 @ 3800	245 @ 2400	3.736 × 3.480	28	7-8.5	8.5	32-40
78	1	4-151	Pont	2v	25.6	85 @ 4400	123 @ 2800	4.00 × 3.00	33	4-5.5	8.3	36-41
	V	4-151	Pont	2v	25.6	85 @ 4400	123 @ 2800	4.00 × 3.00	33	4-5.5	8.3	36-41
	C	6-196	Buick	2v	29.4	90 @ 3600	165 @ 2000	3.500 × 3.400	18	3-4.5	8.0	37
	A	6-231	Buick	2v	34.6	105 @ 3400	185 @ 2000	3.80 × 3.40	17	3-4.5	8.0	37
	U	8-305	Chevy	2v	44.7	145 @ 3800	245 @ 2400	3.736 × 3.480	28	7.5-9	8.4	32-40
79	1	4-151	Pont	2v	25.6	85 @ 4400	123 @ 3800	4.00 × 3.00	33	4-5.5	8.3	36-41
	V	4-151	Pont	2v	25.6	85 @ 4400	123 @ 3800	4.00 × 3.00	33	4-5.5	8.3	36-41
	9	4-151	Pont	2v	25.6	85 @ 4400	123 @ 2800	4.00 × 3.00	33	4-5.5	8.3	36-41
	C	6-196	Buick	2v	29.4	90 @ 3600	165 @ 2000	3.500 × 3.400	18	3-4.5	8.0	37
	A	6-231	Buick	2v	34.6	115 @ 3800	190 @ 2000	3.80 × 3.40	17	3-4.5	8.0	37
	2	6-231	Buick	2v	34.6	115 @ 3800	190 @ 2000	3.80 × 3.40	17	3-4.5	8.0	37
	G	8-305	Chevy	2v	44.7	145 @ 3800	245 @ 2400	3.736 × 3.480	28	7.5-9	8.4	32-40
80	V	4-151	Pont.	2v	25.6	85 @ 4400	123 @ 3800	4.00 × 3.00	33	4-5.5	8.3	36-41
	A	6-231	Buick	2v	34.6	115 @ 3800	190 @ 2000	3.80 × 3.40	17	3-4.5	8.0	37

[1] Horsepower and torque figures for 1977 and later years are Chilton estimates

TUNE-UP SPECIFICATIONS

Engine Code, 5th character of the VIN number
Model Year Code, 6th character of the VIN number⑦

Year	V.I.N. Code	No. Cyl Disp. (cu in)	Orig. Type	Gap (in)	Distributor	Timing① (deg BTDC @ rpm) Man. Trans.	Auto Trans.	Idle Speed② (rpm) Man. Trans.	Auto. Trans. Fed.	Cal.	Hi. Alt.
76	O	4-122	R43T8X	.035	E.I.	12	—	1600	—	—	—
	A	4-140	R43TS	.035	E.I.	10	12 (8)	750/1200	550/750	—	—
	B	4-140	R43TS	.035	E.I.	10	12 (8)	700④	600/750	600/750	600/750
	C	6-231	R44SX	.060	E.I.	12	12	800	600	600	600
	F	8-260	R46SX	.060	E.I.	16 @ 1100	14 @ 1100	750	550	550	550
	G	8-262	R45TS	.045	E.I.	8	8 (0)	800	600/650	—	—
	Q	8-305	R45TS	.045	E.I.	—	8 (0)	—	600/650	600/650	600/650
77	B	4-140	R43TS	.035	E.I.	0 (−2)	2 (0)	700/1250⑤	650/850	650/850	700/850
	V	4-151	R44TSX	.060	E.I.	14 @ 1000	14 (12)	500/1000	500/650	500/650	500/650
	C	6-231	R46TSX	.040	E.I.	12	12	600/800	600/670	600/670	600/670
	U	8-305	R45TS	.045	E.I.	8	8 (6)	600	500/700	500/700	600/700
78	1	4-151	R43TSX	.060	E.I.	14	14	—	500/650	—	—
	V	4-151	R43TSX	.060	E.I.	14	14	500/1000	500/650	—	—
	C	6-196	R46TSX	.060	E.I.	15	15	800	550/670	550/670	550/670
	A	6-231	R46TSX	.060	E.I.	15	15	800	600	600	600
	U	8-305	R45TS	.045	E.I.	4	6	600	500	500	600
79	1	4-151	R43TSX	.060	E.I.	14	14	1000/1200	—	650/850	650/850
	V	4-151	R43TSX	.060	E.I.	12	12	900/1250	650/850	—	650/850
	9	4-151	R43TSX	.060	E.I.	12	12	900/1250	650/850	650/850	650/850
	C	6-196	R46TSX	.060	E.I.	15	15	800	550/670	—	—
	A	6-231	R46TSX	.060	E.I.	15	15	800	—	600	600
	2	6-231	R46TSX	.060	E.I.	—	15	—	—	580/670	—
	G	8-305	R45TS	.045	E.I.	4	4②	600/700	500/600	600/650	—
80	V	4-151	R43TSX	.060	E.I.	12° @ 1000	12° @ 650	1000	—⑥	650/800	650/800
	A	6-231	R46TSX	.060	E.I.	15° @ 650	15° @ 550	800	⑥	600	—

NOTE: The underhood certification/specification decal is the authority for performance specifications affecting vehicle emissions. Use this manual's information only when that decal is not available

— Not applicable

① Time at curb idle speed unless otherwise indicated. Figure in parentheses is California application.

② Set idle speed with automatic transmission in Drive; manual transmission in Neutral. Where two figures appear, the lower figure indicates idle speed with solenoid deactivated.

④ 700/1000 for California applications

⑤ 800/1250 for California and High Altitude applications

⑥ See underhood certification/specification decal

⑦ If a 17-digit VIN is used, the 8th digit is the engine code and the 10th digit is the model year code

VEHICLE IDENTIFICATION NUMBER (VIN)

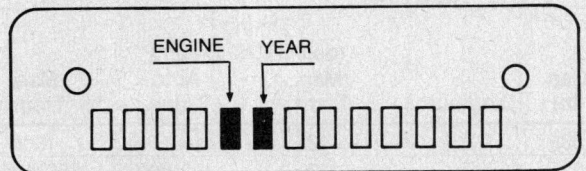

Code	Eng. Disp. (cu in)	Eng. Config.	Carb	Eng. Mfgr.	Code	Year
O	122	L4	FI	Chev	6	76
A	140	L4	1V	Chev		
B	140	L4	2V	Chev		
C	231	V6	2V	Buick		
F	260	V8	2V	Olds		
G	262	V8	2V	Chev		
Q	305	V8	2V	Chev		
B	140	L4	2V	Chev	7	77
V	151	L4	2V	Pont		
C	231	V6	2V	Buick		
U	305	V8	2V	Chev		
V	151	L4	2V	Pont.	8	78
C	196	V6	2V	Buick		
A	231	V6	2V	Buick		
U	305	V8	2V	Chev		
V	151	L4	2V	Pont	9	79
1	151	L4	2V	Pont		
9	151	L4	2V	Pont		
C	196	V6	2V	Buick		
M	200	V6	2V	Chev		
A	231	V6	2V	Buick		
2	231	V6	2V	Buick		
F	260	V8	2V	Olds		
U	267	V8	2V	Chev		
G	305	V8	2V	Chev		
H	305	V8	4V	Chev		
V	151	L4	2v	Pont	A	80
A	231	V6	2v	Buick		

Header for table: ENGINE CODE | MODEL YEAR CODE

BRAKE SPECIFICATIONS

All readings in inches

Year	Model	Master Cylinder Bore Diameter	CALIPER OR WHEEL CYLINDER		BRAKE DRUM/ROTOR DIAMETER	
			Front	Rear	Front	Rear
76	Sunbird, Monza, Starfire	.875	2.50	11/16	9.8	9.5
	Skyhawk	.875	1.875	13/16	9.8	9.5
	Astre	.750	1.875	11/16	9.8	9.0
	Vega	.750	1.875	11/16	9.8	9.5
77	Vega, Astre	.750	1.875	11/16	9.8	9.5
	Sunbird, Starfire, Monza, Skyhawk	.875	2.50	11/16	9.8	9.5
78	Sunbird, Starfire, Monza, Skyhawk	.875	2.50	11/16	9.8	9.5
79	Sunbird, Starfire, Monza, Skyhawk	.875	2.50	11/16	9.8	9.5
80	Sunbird, Starfire, Monza, Skyhawk	.875	2.50	11/16	9.8	9.5

DISC BRAKE SPECIFICATIONS

All readings in inches

Year	Model	Caliper Type	Mounting Bolt Torque	Disc Pad Original Thickness	Mfr.'s Recommended Disc Pad Minimum Thickness	Rotor Runout	Rotor Allowable Minimum Machined Thickness	Rotor Thickness Variation Maximum
76	Vega, Astre	Sliding	①	.370	②	.005	.455	.0005
	Monza, Sunbird, Starfire, Skyhawk	Sliding	①	.430	②	.005	.830	.0005
77	Vega, Astre	Sliding	①	.370	③	.004	.455	.0005
	Monza, Sunbird, Starfire, Skyhawk	Sliding	①	.430	③	.004	.830	.0005
78	Monza, Sunbird, Starfire, Skyhawk	Sliding	①	.430	③	.004	.830	.0005
79	Monza, Sunbird, Starfire, Skyhawk	Sliding	①	.430	③	.004	.830	.0005
80	Monza, Sunbird, Starfire, Skyhawk	Sliding	①	.430	③	.004	.830	.0005

① Pin type mounting
② 1/32" over the rivet head or shoe
③ .030 over the rivet head or shoe

GENERAL MOTORS "H" BODY CARS
ASTRE, MONZA, SKYHAWK, STARFIRE, SUNBIRD, VEGA

DISTRIBUTOR SPECIFICATIONS

Yr.	Dist. Ident.	Centrifugal Advance Start Crank. Deg. @ Eng. rpm	Centrifugal Advance Finish Crank. Deg. @ Eng. rpm	Vacuum Advance Start @ In Hg	Vacuum Advance Finish Crank. Deg. @ In Hg
76	1112862	0 @ 1600	22 @ 4800	5	24 @ 12
	1112983	0 @ 1200	22 @ 4000	4	15 @ 10
	1112862	0 @ 900	22 @ 4800	5	20 @ 14
	1110668	0 @ 1275	16 @ 3200	6	24 @ 12
	1110661	0 @ 1050	16 @ 4100	6	18 @ 10
	1112863	0 @ 1100	16 @ 4200	3-5	24 @ 14.5
	1112863	0 @ 1100	16 @ 4200	4	18 @ 12
	1110666	0 @ 1000	20 @ 4200	4	24 @ 15
	1110668	0 @ 1275	16 @ 3175	6	24 @ 11.5
	1110661	0 @ 1075	16 @ 4100	6	18 @ 10
	1112994	0 @ 650	28 @ 4400	4.5	24 @ 10.5
	1112995	0 @ 900	26 @ 4475	4	30 @ 11
	1112996	0 @ 1100	28 @ 4400	—	—
77	1110538	0 @ 900	17 @ 2000	5	24 @ 10
	1110539	0 @ 900	17 @ 2000	5	24 @ 10
	1103239	0 @ 1200	20 @ 4200	14	15 @ 10
	1103244	0 @ 1000	20 @ 3800	4	20 @ 10
	1103252	0 @ 1000	20 @ 3800	4	18 @ 12
	1103229	0 @ 1200	20 @ 4400	3.5	20 @ 12
	1103263	0 @ 1200	20 @ 4400	3.5	20 @ 9
	1103231	0 @ 1200	20 @ 4400	3.5	20 @ 12
	1103230	0 @ 1200	20 @ 4400	3.5	20 @ 9
	1103303	0 @ 1200	20 @ 4400	9	20 @ 16
	1110677	0 @ 1400	20 @ 3600	4	24 @ 11
	1110686	0 @ 1400	20 @ 3600	7	8 @ 9
78	1103281	0 @ 1000	20 @ 3800	4	18 @ 12
	1103282	0 @ 1000	20 @ 3800	4	20 @ 10
	1103326	0 @ 1700	20 @ 4650	3.4	20 @ 10.7
	1103328	0 @ 1200	20 @ 4400	3.5	20 @ 9
	1103329	0 @ 1200	20 @ 4400	3.5	20 @ 12
	1103365	0 @ 1700	20 @ 4650	5.5	14 @ 9.5
	1110695	0-4 @ 2000	12-18 @ 3600	6	16 @ 9
	1110731	0-4 @ 2000	12-18 @ 3600	6	16 @ 9
	1110732	0-4 @ 2000	12-18 @ 3600	9	14 @ 13
79	1103281	0 @ 1000	20 @ 3800	4	12 @ 12
	1103285	0 @ 1200	22 @ 4200	4	10 @ 8
	1103365	0 @ 1200	20 @ 4400	5	22 @ 11
	1103379	0 @ 1000	20 @ 3800	3	20 @ 7.5
	1110726	0 @ 1200	18 @ 4000	3.5	22 @ 11
	1110757	0 @ 1200	18 @ 4000	3.5	22 @ 11
	1110766	0 @ 1700	15 @ 3600	4	20 @ 11
	1110767	0-4 @ 2000	12-16 @ 3600	3	20 @ 12
	1110768	2 @ 1250	15 @ 3600	3.5	22 @ 12.5
	1110770	0 @ 1600	15 @ 3600	3	20 @ 9
80	1110558	0 @ 1000	14 @ 4000	3	15 @ 5
	1110559	0 @ 1200	14 @ 4000	3	15 @ 5
	1110560	0 @ 1000	14 @ 4400	4	20 @ 10

FLUID CAPACITIES—Coolant, Fuel & Lubricant

Year	Engine No. Cyl. Disp. (Cu In)	Eng. V.I.N. Code	Engine[6] Crankcase	Transmission Pts. to Refill After Draining — Manual 3-Speed	Manual 4-Speed	Automatic[7]	Drive Axle (pts.)	Gasoline Tank (gals)	Rad. Cap Press.	Therm. Temp.	Cooling System (qts.) With Heater	With A/C
76	4-122	O	3.5	—	3	—	2.8	16	15	195	6.8	6.8
	4-140	A, B	3.5	3	3	8	28	16	15	195	8	8
	6-231	C	4	—	3.12①	6	2.8	18.5	15	195	13.4	14.2
	8-262	G	4	—	3.12①	8	2.8	18.5	15	195	18	18
	8-305	Q	4	—	3.12①	8	2.8	18.5	15	195	18	18
77	4-140	B	3.5	—	3②	8	2.8	18.5	15	195	8③	8
	4-151	V	3	—	3②	6	3.5④	16	15	195	10.7	—
	V6-231	C, A	4	—	3①	6	2.8	18.5	15	195	12	11.5
	8-305	U	4	—	3②	8	2.8	18.5	15	195	18	18

FLUID CAPACITIES—Coolant, Fuel & Lubricant

Year	Engine No. Cyl. Disp. (Cu In)	Eng. V.I.N. Code	Engine⑥ Crankcase	TRANSMISSION PTS. TO REFILL AFTER DRAINING Manual 3-Speed		TRANSMISSION Manual 4-Speed	Automatic⑦	Drive Axle (pts.)	Gasoline Tank (gals)	Rad. Cap Press.	Therm. Temp.	COOLING SYSTEM (qts.) With Heater	With A/C
78	4-151	V	3	—		3①②	6.0⑤	3.5	18.5	15	195	11.0	11.5
	6-196	C	4	—		3①②	6.0	3.5	18.5	15	195	11.8	12.16
	6-231	A	4	—		3①②	6.0	3.5	18.5	15	195	11.8	12.16
	8-305	U	4	—		3②	6.0	3.5	18.5	15	195	16.2	16.2
79	4-151	V,1,9	3	—		3①②	4.5⑤	3.5	18.5	15	195	11.0	11.5
	6-191	C	4	—		3①②	6.0	3.5	18.5	15	195	11.8	12.16
	6-231	A, 2	4	3		3①②	6.0	3.5	18.5	15	195	11.8	12.16
	8-305		4	3		3②	6.0	3.5	18.5	15	195	16.2	16.2
80	4-151	V	3	3		3①②	3⑤	3.5	18.5	15	195	11.0	11.5
	6-231	A	4	3		3①②	3	3.5	18.5	15	195	11.8	12.16

— Not applicable
① Five speed Chevrolet and Buick — 3.5
② Five speed Oldsmobile and Pontiac — 3
③ Astre and Sunbird — 7
④ With 6.5 inch ring gear — 2.8
⑤ Chevrolet with 151 CID engine — 5.0.
  All others — 7.0
⑥ Most engines will require some additional oil when the filter is changed. Fill to correct level on dipstick.
⑦ Amount to drain and refill pan only

VALVE SPECIFICATIONS

Year	Engine No. Cyl. Disp. (cu in.)	Eng. V.I.N. Code	Seat Angle (deg)	Face Angle (deg)	Spring Test Pressure (lbs @ in)	Spring Installed height (in)	STEM TO GUIDE CLEARANCE (in.) Intake	Exhaust	STEM DIAMETER (in.) Intake	Exhaust
76-77	4-122	O	46	45	②	③	.0010-.0027	.0010-.0027	.2788-.2975	.2788-.2795
	4-140	A,B	46	45	190 @ 1.310	1.746	.0010-.0027	.0010-.0027	.3410-.3417	.3410-.3417
	6-231	C	45	45	164 @ 1.34④	1.727	.0015-.0035	.0015-.0032	.3402-.3412	.3405-.3412
	8-260	F	⑤	⑥	187 @ 1.27	1.67	.0010-.0027	.0015-.0032	.3432-.3425	.3427-.3420
	8-262	G	46	45	⑦	⑧	.0010-.0027	.0010-.0027	.3410-.3417	.3410-.3417
	8-305	Q,U	46	45	⑦	⑧	.0010-.0027	.0010-.0027	.3410-.3417	.3410-.3417
78	4-151	V	46	45	78-86 @ 1.66	1.69	.0010-.0027	.0010-.0027	.34	.34
	6-196	C	45	45	168 ± 6 @ 1.327	1.727	.0015-.0032	.0015-.0032	.3405-.3412	.3405-.3412
	6-231	A	45	45	168 ± 6 @ 1.327	1.727	.0015-.0032	.0015-.0032	.3405-.3412	.3405-.3412
	8-305	U	46	45	194-206 @ 1.25⑩	1²³⁄₃₂⑩	.0010-.0027	.0010-.0027	.3410-.3417	.3410-.3407
79	4-151	V,1,9	46	45	78-86 @ 1.66	1.69	.0010-.0027	.0010-.0027	.34	.34
	6-196	C	45	45	168 ± 6 @ 1.327	1.727	.0015-.0032	.0015-.0032	.3405-.3412	.3405-.3412
	6-231	A,2	45	45	168 ± 6 @ 1.327	1.727	.0015-.0032	.0015-.0032	.3405-.3412	.3405-.3412
	8-305	G	46	45	194-206 @ 1.25⑩	1²³⁄₃₂⑩	.0010-.0027	.0010-.0027	.3410-.3417	.3410-.3417
80	4-151	V	46	45	78-86 @ 1.66	1.69	.0010-.0027	.0010-.0027	.34	.34
	6-231	A	45	45	168 ± 6 @ 1.327	1.727	.0015-.0032	.0015-.0032	.3405-.3412	.3405-.3412

② Outer — 104-116 @ .92
  Inner — 78.5-80.5 @ .875
③ Outer — 1.30
  Inner — 1.25
④ 182 @ 1.34
⑤ Intake — 46
  Exhaust— 31
⑥ Intake — 45
  Exhaust — 30
⑦ Intake — 200 @ 1.25
  Exhaust — 200 @ 1.16
⑧ Intake — 1.70
  Exhaust — 1.61
⑩ Intake — 194-206 @ 1.16
  Installed height — 1⁹⁄₃₂

GENERAL MOTORS "H" BODY CARS

ASTRE, MONZA, SKYHAWK, STARFIRE, SUNBIRD, VEGA

CRANKSHAFT & CONNECTING ROD SPECIFICATIONS

All measurements given in inches

Year	Engine No. Cyl. Disp. (cu in)	Eng. V.I.N. Code	CRANKSHAFT Main Brg. Journal	Main Brg. Journal Dia.	Main Brg. Oil Clearance	Shaft End-Play	Thrust on No.	CONNECTING ROD Journal Diameter	Oil Clearance	Side Clearance
76-77	4-122	O	ALL	2.3011⑦	.0008-.0034⑧	.002-.008	4	1.999-2.000	.0007-.0027	.0009-.0013
	4-140	A, B	ALL	2.3004	.0003-.0029	.002-.008	4	1.999-2.000	.0007-.0027	.0009-.0013
	6-231	C, A	ALL	2.4995	.0004-.0015	.004-.008	2	1.9991-2.0000	.0002-.0023	.006-.014
	8-260	F	ALL	2.5000	.0005-.0021⑨	.004-.008	3	2.1240	.0007-.0027	.007-.016
	8-262	G	ALL	2.4502	③	.002-.007	5	2.099-2.100	.0013-.0035	.008-.014
	8-305	Q, U	ALL	2.4502	③	.002-.007	5	2.099-2.100	.0013-.0025	.006-.016
78	4-151	V	ALL	2.3000	.0002-.0022	.0035-.0085	5	2.000⑩	.0005-.0026	.006-.022
	6-196	C	ALL	2.4995	.0003-.0017	.004-.008	2	2.2487-2.2495	.0005-.0026	.006-.027
	6-231	A	ALL	2.4995	.0003-.0017	.004-.008	2	2.2487-2.2495	.0005-.0026	.006-.027
	8-305	U	1	2.4484-2.4493	.0008-.0020	.002-.006	5	2.0988-2.0998	.0013-.0035	.008-.014
			2-4	2.4481-2.4490	.0011-.0023					
			5	2.4479-2.4488	.0017-.0032					
79	4-151	V,1,9	ALL	2.2983-2.2993	.0005-.0022	.0035-.0085	5	2.000⑩	.0005-.0026	.006-.022
	6-196	C	ALL	2.4995	.0003-.0017	.004-.008	2	2.2487-2.2495	.0005-.0026	.006-.020
	6-231	A,2	ALL	2.4995	.0003-.0017	.004-.008	2	2.2487-2.2495	.0005-.0026	.006-.020
	8-305	G	1	2.4484-2.4493	.0008-.0020	.002-.006	5	2.0988-2.0998	.0013-.0035	.008-.014
			2-4	2.4481-2.4490	.0011-.0023					
			5	2.4479-2.4488	.0017-.0032					
80	4-151	V	ALL	2.2983-2.2993	.0005-.0022	.0035-.0085	5	2.000⑩	.0005-.0026	.006-.022
	6-231	A	ALL	2.4995	.0003-.0017	.004-.008	2	2.2487-2.2495	.0005-.0026	.006-.027

③ No. 1 — .0008-.0020
No. 2, 3, 4 — .0011-.0023
No. 5 — .0017-.0033
⑦ No. 4 — 2.3006
⑧ No. 4 — .0002-.0029
⑨ No. 5 — .0005-.0031
⑩ May also be 1.990

TORQUE SPECIFICATIONS

All readings in ft/lbs

Engine No. Cyl. Disp. (cu in)	Eng. V.I.N. Code	Year	Cylinder Head Bolts	Rod Bearing Bolts	Main Bearing Bolts	Crankshaft Pulley Bolt	Flywheel To Crankshaft Bolts	MANIFOLD	
								Intake	Exhaust
4-140	A,B	All	60	35	65	80	60	30	30
6-231	C	All	85	42	①	200-310	60	40	25
6-196, 6-231	C,A,2	All	80	40	100	225	60	45	25
4-151	V,1,9	All	95	30	65	160	55	40	40
8-260	F	All	85	42	120	160	40	25	25
8-262	G	All	60-70	45	75②	60	60	30	③
8-305	Q,U,G	All	65	45	80	60	60	30	20

① 1, 2, 3, 4—80; 5—120
② 4 bolt main outer bolts—65
③ Center bolts—25-30; end bolts—15-20

FUSE IDENTIFICATION

Fuse block H series

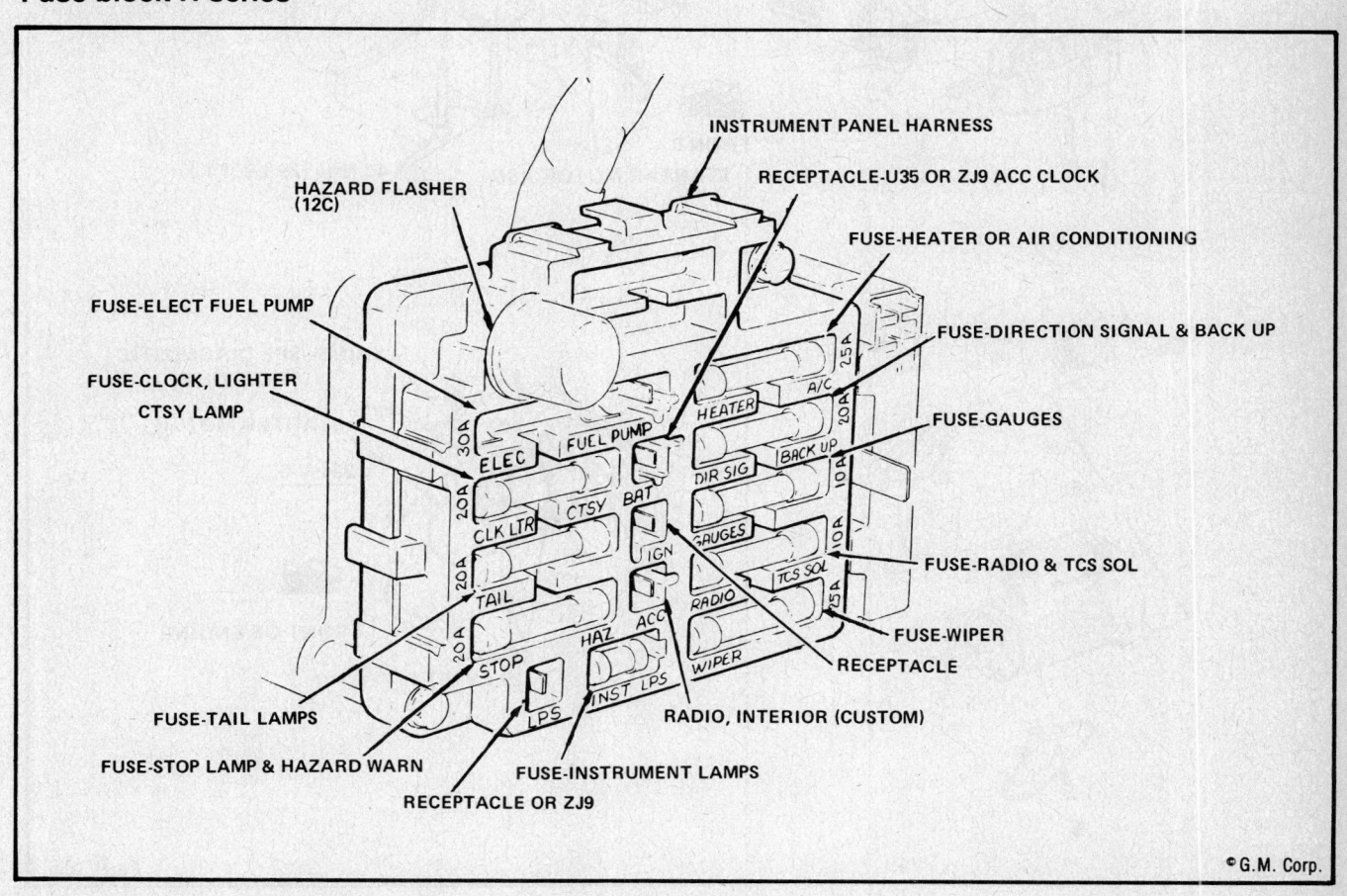

ELECTRICAL SECTION

Starter

- Disconnect electrical wiring, and remove or loosen anything preventing full access to starter such as shield, flywheel cover, exhaust pipe or engine crossmember.
- Electrical terminal nuts are not interchangeable. They must be installed in the same locations from which they were removed.

Ignition Distributor R&R

- Remove distributor cap, electrical wiring and vacuum hose from distributor.
- Put alignment marks on rotor and distributor housing so distributor can be installed in the correct position.
- Remove hold-down, and pull distributor up out of engine block.
- Install the distributor in the correct position and time engine to specifications.

Starter Noise Diagnostic Procedure

- If there is starter noise during cranking remove 1-.015″ double shim or add single .015″ shim to outer bolt only.
- If there is a high pitched whine after engine fires, add .015″ double shims until noise disappears.

Starter mounting

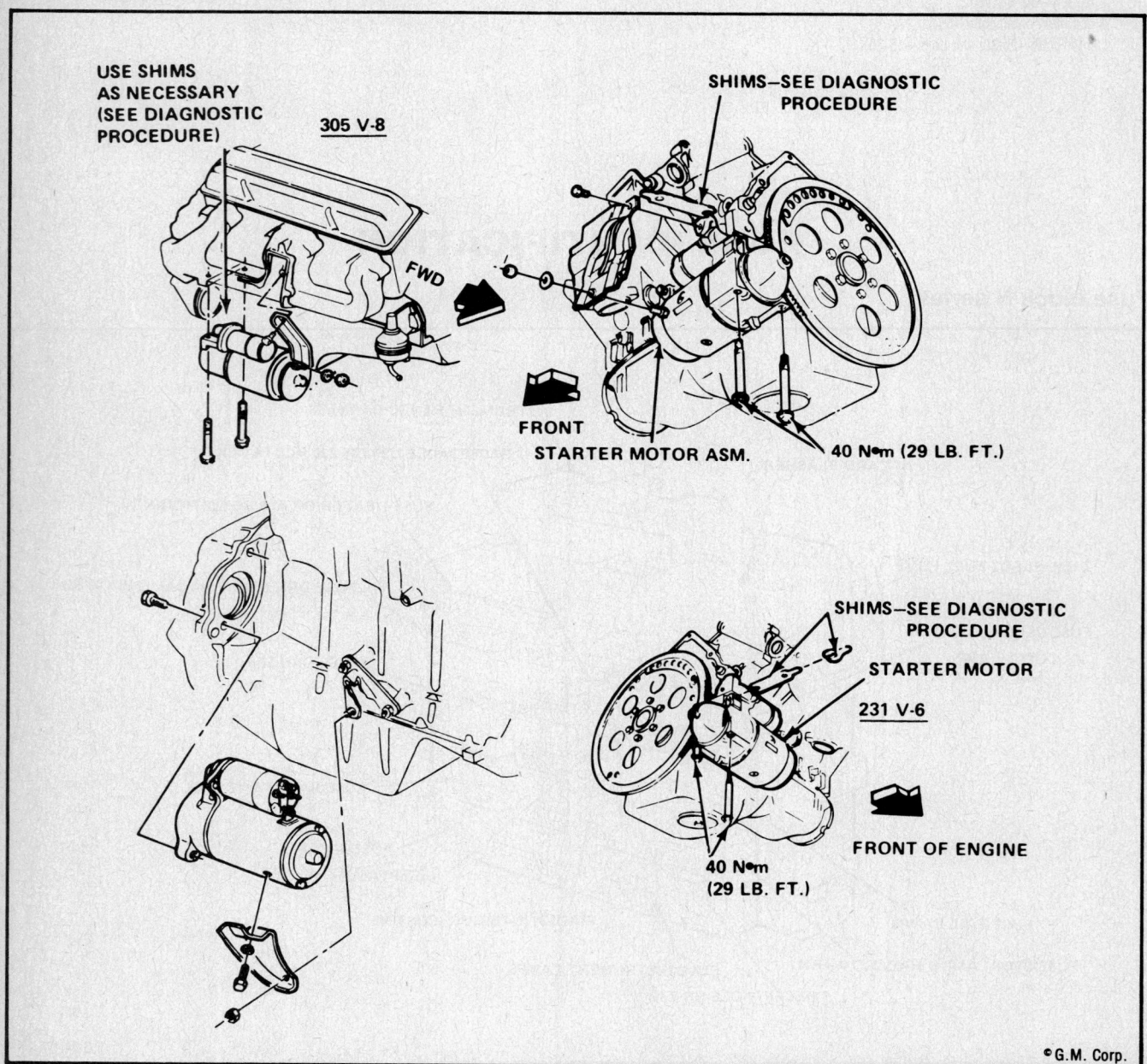

Regular key release column and electrical components

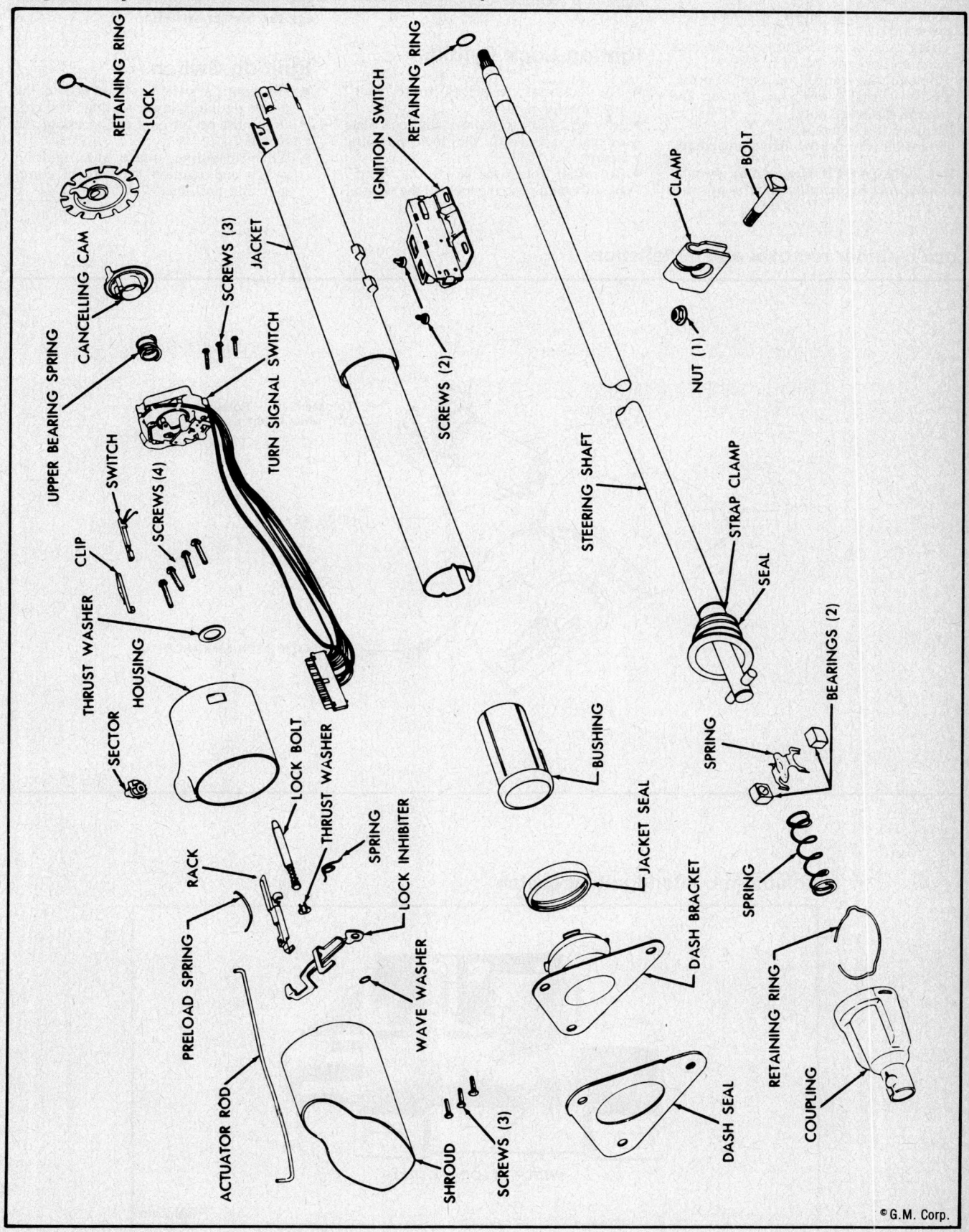

RETAINING RING
LOCK
CANCELING CAM
UPPER BEARING SPRING
SCREWS (3)
JACKET
RETAINING RING
IGNITION SWITCH
CLAMP
BOLT
NUT (1)
SWITCH
CLIP
THRUST WASHER
SCREWS (4)
TURN SIGNAL SWITCH
SCREWS (2)
STEERING SHAFT
STRAP CLAMP
SECTOR
HOUSING
SEAL
SPRING
BEARINGS (2)
PRELOAD SPRING
RACK
LOCK BOLT
THRUST WASHER
SPRING
LOCK INHIBITER
BUSHING
JACKET SEAL
SPRING
ACTUATOR ROD
WAVE WASHER
DASH BRACKET
RETAINING RING
SHROUD
SCREWS (3)
DASH SEAL
COUPLING

© G.M. Corp.

Turn Signal Switch

- Remove steering wheel and lock plate cover.
- Using special tool, compress the lock plate and pry off the snap ring.
- Remove the cancelling cam, spring, thrust washer, turn signal lever and hazard warning knob.
- Remove the switch.
- To install, reverse the above procedure.

CHILTON CAUTION: *Use only the correct hardware on installation. Use of over-length screws could prevent column collapse in a collision.*

Ignition Lock Cylinder

- The lock must be placed in the "run" position for removal.
- It is necessary to remove the lock plate to gain access to the lock retaining screw.
- To install, rotate the key to the "start" position and push the lock all the way in.

NOTE: Removing the lock cylinder in any position except "RUN" may damage the buzzer switch.

Ignition Switch

- The ignition switch is mounted to the steering column lower section. The column must be lowered for access to the switch.
- When installing, make sure ignition switch and ignition lock are in corresponding positions.

Lock cylinder removal and installation

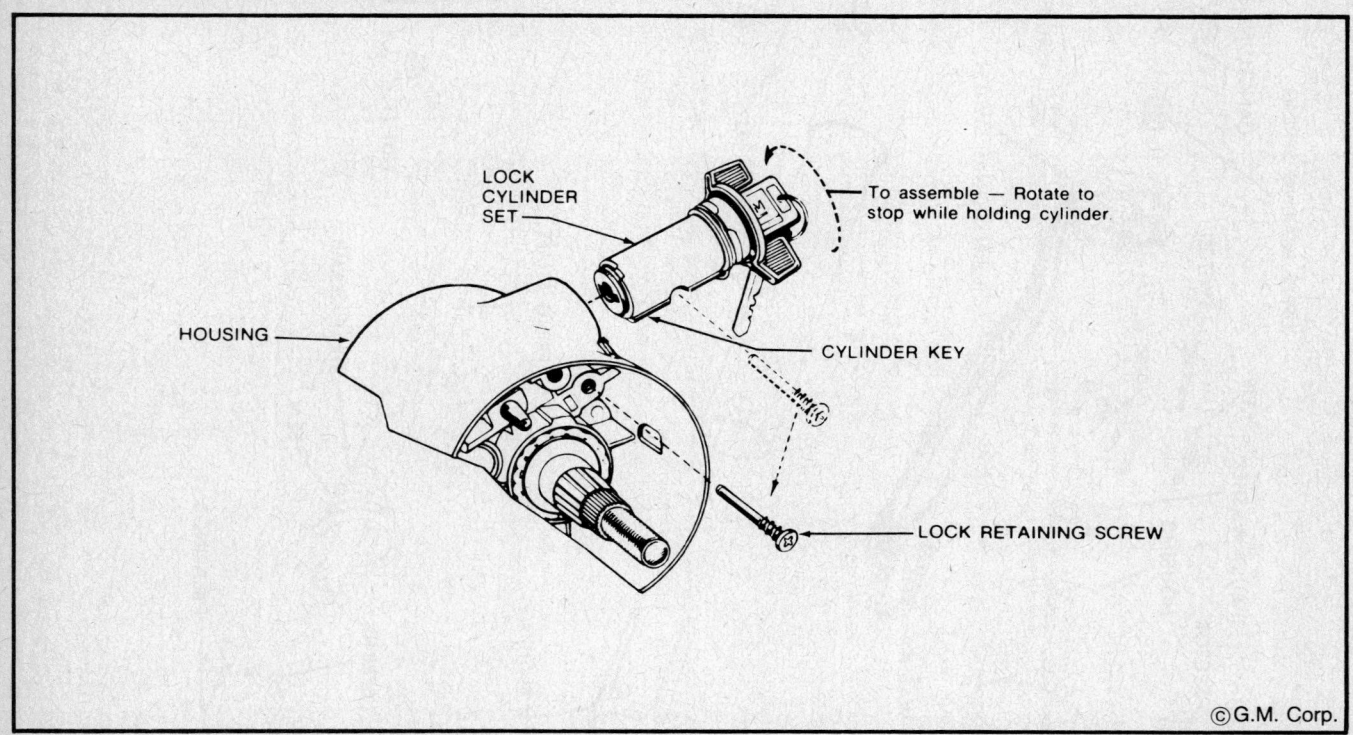

© G.M. Corp.

Column-mounted ignition switch

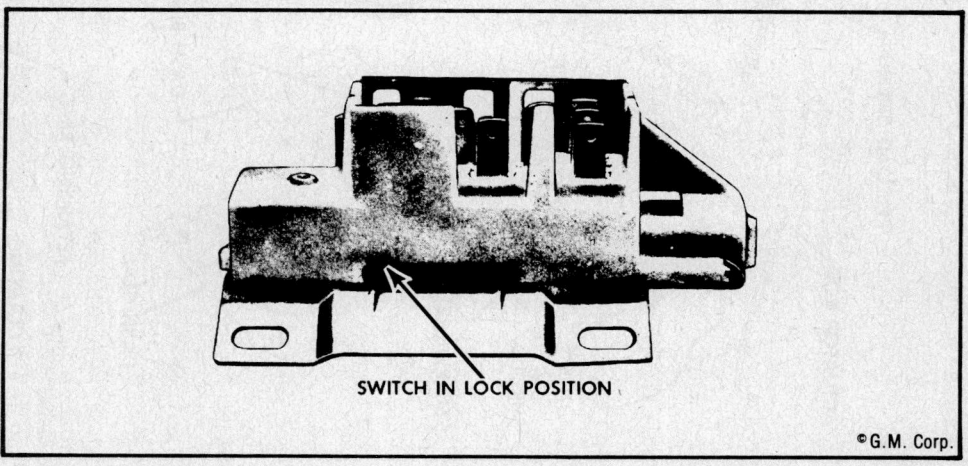

© G.M. Corp.

Automatic transmission neutral start switch

Neutral Start Switch

- The neutral start switch is located in the floor shifter mechanism.
- Remove the shifter console, place shift lever in neutral, disconnect electrical wiring and remove switch. The switch mounting screws may be concealed under the lever core.
- After installation, check that engine starts only in "Park" and "Neutral" positions.

Clutch Start Switch

- The switch assembly mounts with two tangs to the clutch pedal brace switch pivot bracket and the clutch pedal arm.
- To remove:
  - a. Remove the electrical plug from the switch
  - b. Compress switch assembly actuating shaft barb retainer, and push out of clutch pedal
  - c. Compress switch assembly pivot bracket barb and lift off switch assembly
- The switch assembly is self-aligning. No adjustment is required.

Stoplight Switch

- The switch is mounted at the brake pedal. It can be removed by disconnecting the electrical lead and pulling the switch out of its mounting bracket.
- Brake lights should illuminate within the first ⅜ to ⅝ inch of pedal travel.

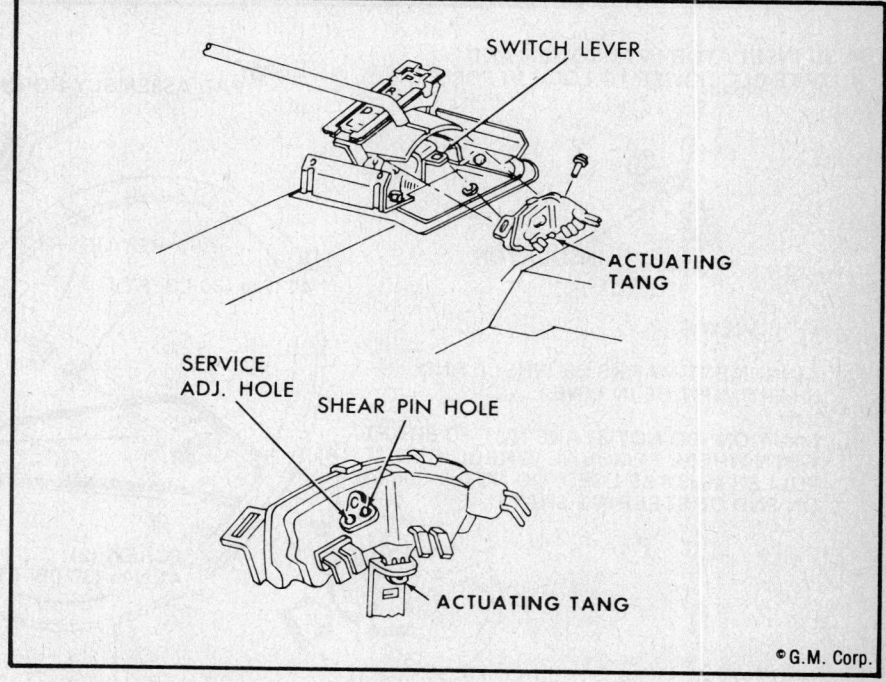

© G.M. Corp.

Horn Switch and Steering Wheel

- Disconnect battery.
- Remove wheel cover, nuts, snap ring, etc., and use a steering wheel puller to remove the wheel.

CHILTON CAUTION: *Do not hammer on the end of the shaft.*

Compressing lock plate with special tool

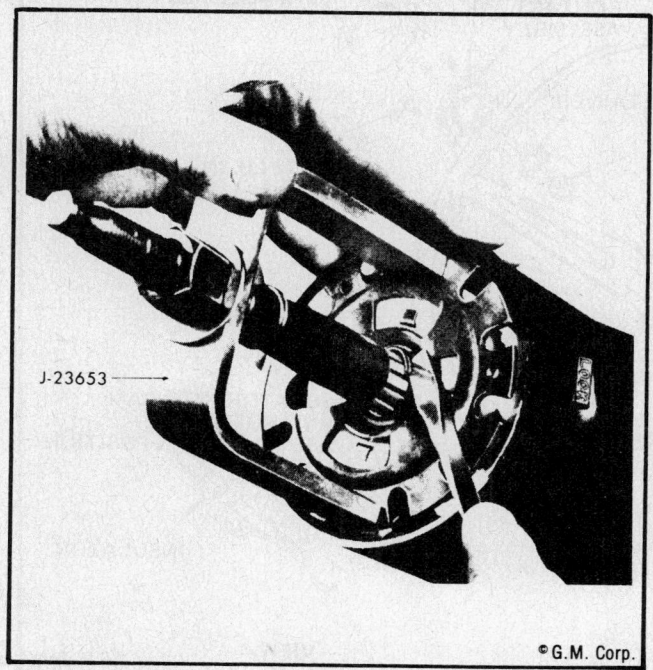

J-23653

© G.M. Corp.

Clutch operated start switch

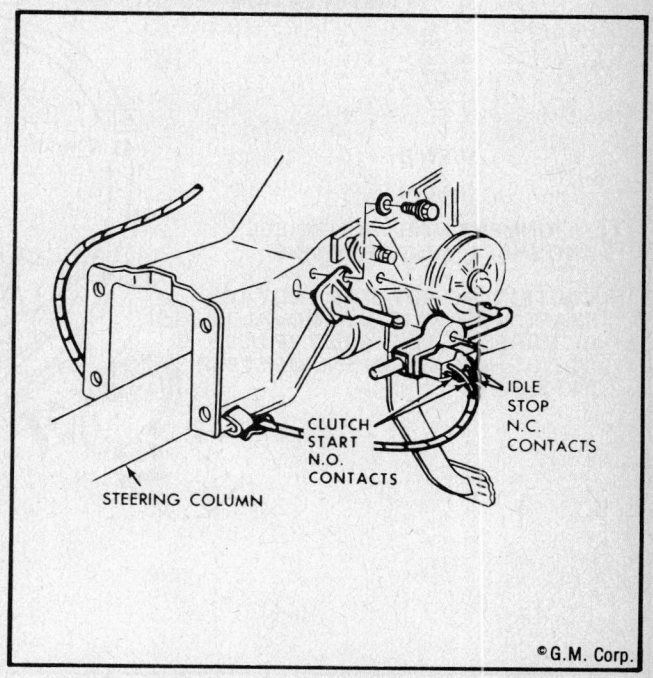

© G.M. Corp.

Standard steering wheel

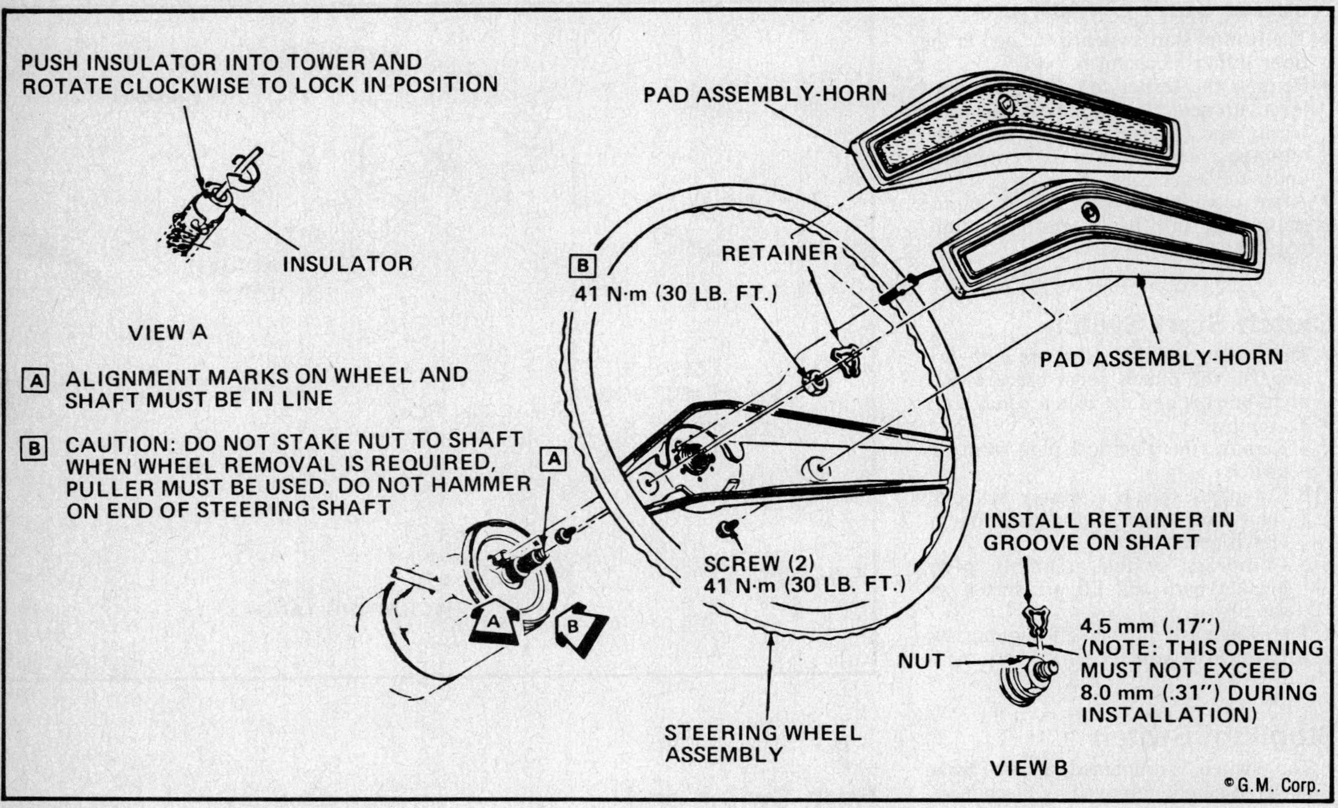

PUSH INSULATOR INTO TOWER AND
ROTATE CLOCKWISE TO LOCK IN POSITION

INSULATOR

VIEW A

PAD ASSEMBLY-HORN

[B] 41 N·m (30 LB. FT.)

RETAINER

PAD ASSEMBLY-HORN

[A] ALIGNMENT MARKS ON WHEEL AND
SHAFT MUST BE IN LINE

[B] CAUTION: DO NOT STAKE NUT TO SHAFT
WHEN WHEEL REMOVAL IS REQUIRED,
PULLER MUST BE USED. DO NOT HAMMER
ON END OF STEERING SHAFT

SCREW (2)
41 N·m (30 LB. FT.)

INSTALL RETAINER IN
GROOVE ON SHAFT

NUT

4.5 mm (.17")
(NOTE: THIS OPENING
MUST NOT EXCEED
8.0 mm (.31") DURING
INSTALLATION)

STEERING WHEEL
ASSEMBLY

VIEW B

© G.M. Corp.

Sport wheel

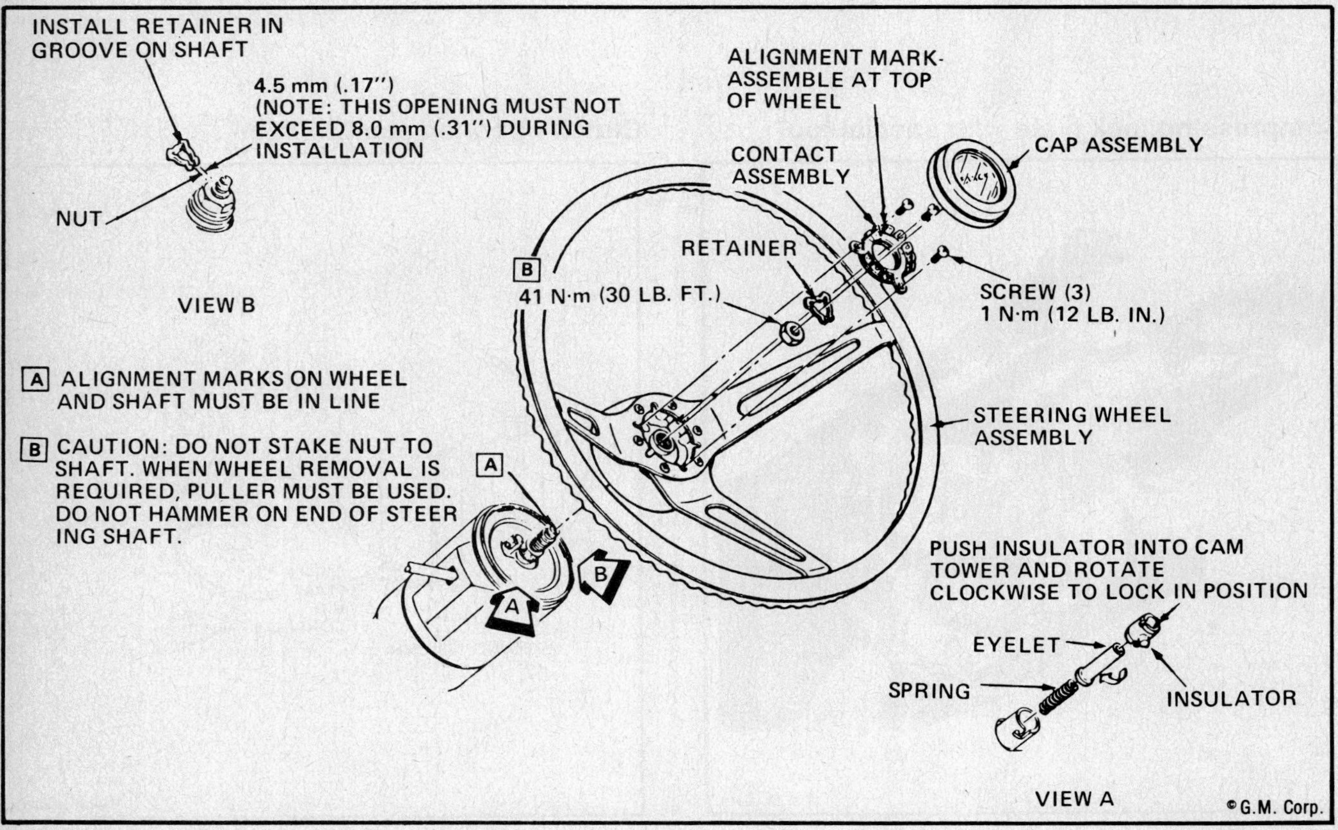

INSTALL RETAINER IN
GROOVE ON SHAFT

4.5 mm (.17")
(NOTE: THIS OPENING MUST NOT
EXCEED 8.0 mm (.31") DURING
INSTALLATION

NUT

VIEW B

ALIGNMENT MARK-
ASSEMBLE AT TOP
OF WHEEL

CONTACT
ASSEMBLY

CAP ASSEMBLY

RETAINER

[B] 41 N·m (30 LB. FT.)

SCREW (3)
1 N·m (12 LB. IN.)

[A] ALIGNMENT MARKS ON WHEEL
AND SHAFT MUST BE IN LINE

[B] CAUTION: DO NOT STAKE NUT TO
SHAFT. WHEN WHEEL REMOVAL IS
REQUIRED, PULLER MUST BE USED.
DO NOT HAMMER ON END OF STEER
ING SHAFT.

STEERING WHEEL
ASSEMBLY

PUSH INSULATOR INTO CAM
TOWER AND ROTATE
CLOCKWISE TO LOCK IN POSITION

EYELET

SPRING

INSULATOR

VIEW A

© G.M. Corp.

Turn signal switch

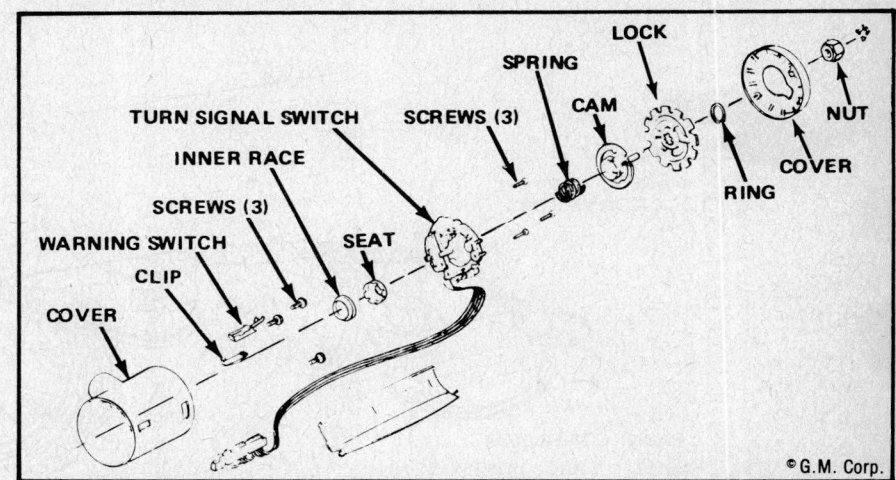

© G.M. Corp.

Turn Signal Switch

- Remove steering wheel, lock plate, cancelling cam, preload spring, thrust washer, etc.
- Remove the turn signal lever and the hazard warning knob.
- Remove the switch mounting screws, and pull the switch and wiring harness up out of the column.

Typical light switch installation

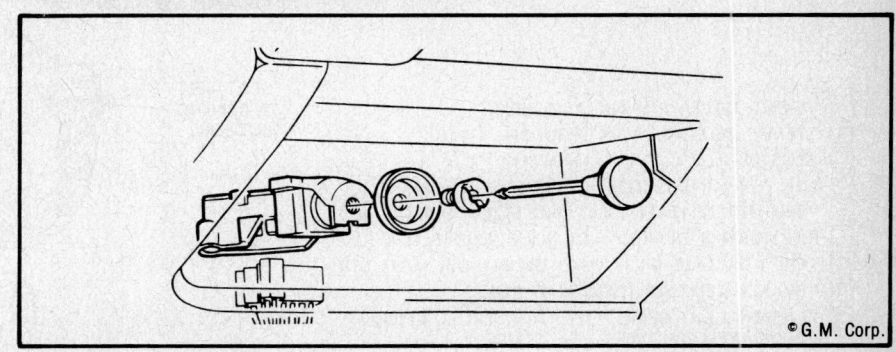

© G.M. Corp.

Light Switch

- Disconnect battery.
- Place switch in full "On" position. Pull on knob and press shaft release button (on switch body) to release shaft and knob assembly.
- Separate switch from instrument panel and electrical connector.

Instrument panel pads and bezel

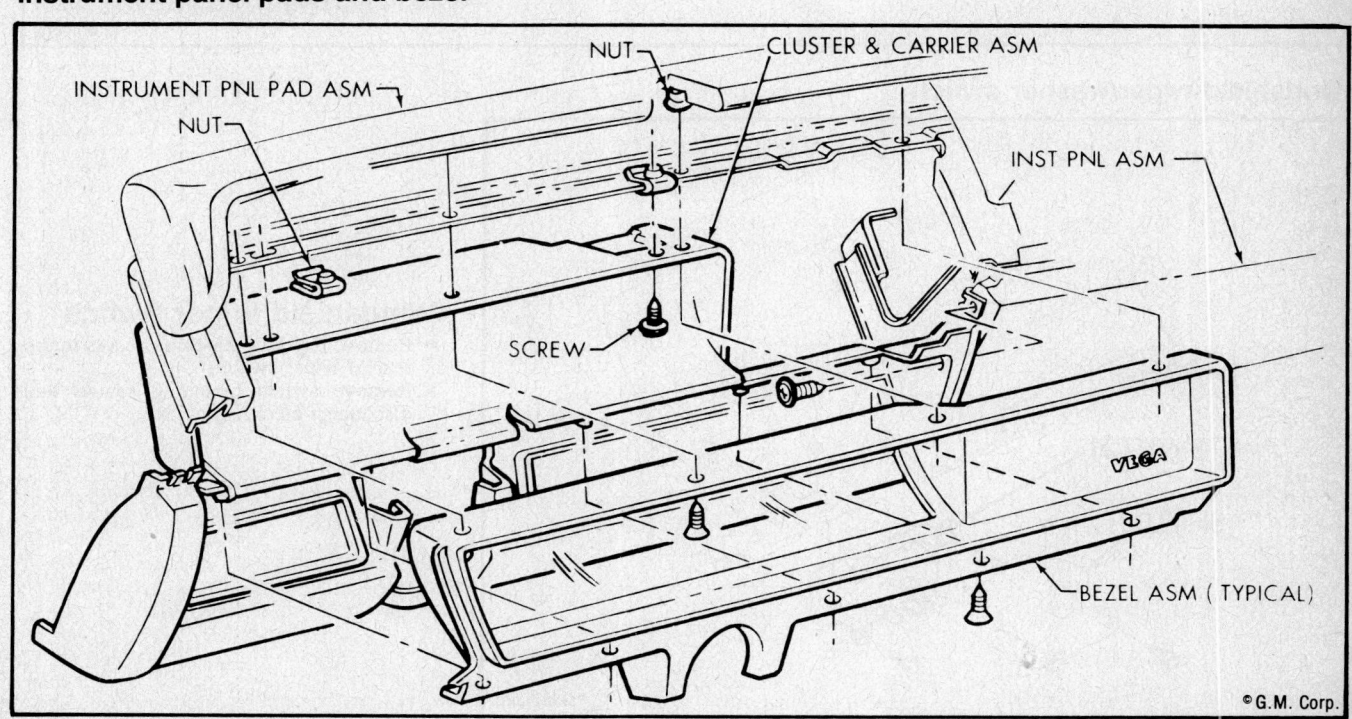

© G.M. Corp.

GENERAL MOTORS "H" BODY CARS
ASTRE, MONZA, SKYHAWK, STARFIRE, SUNBIRD, VEGA

Standard instrument cluster

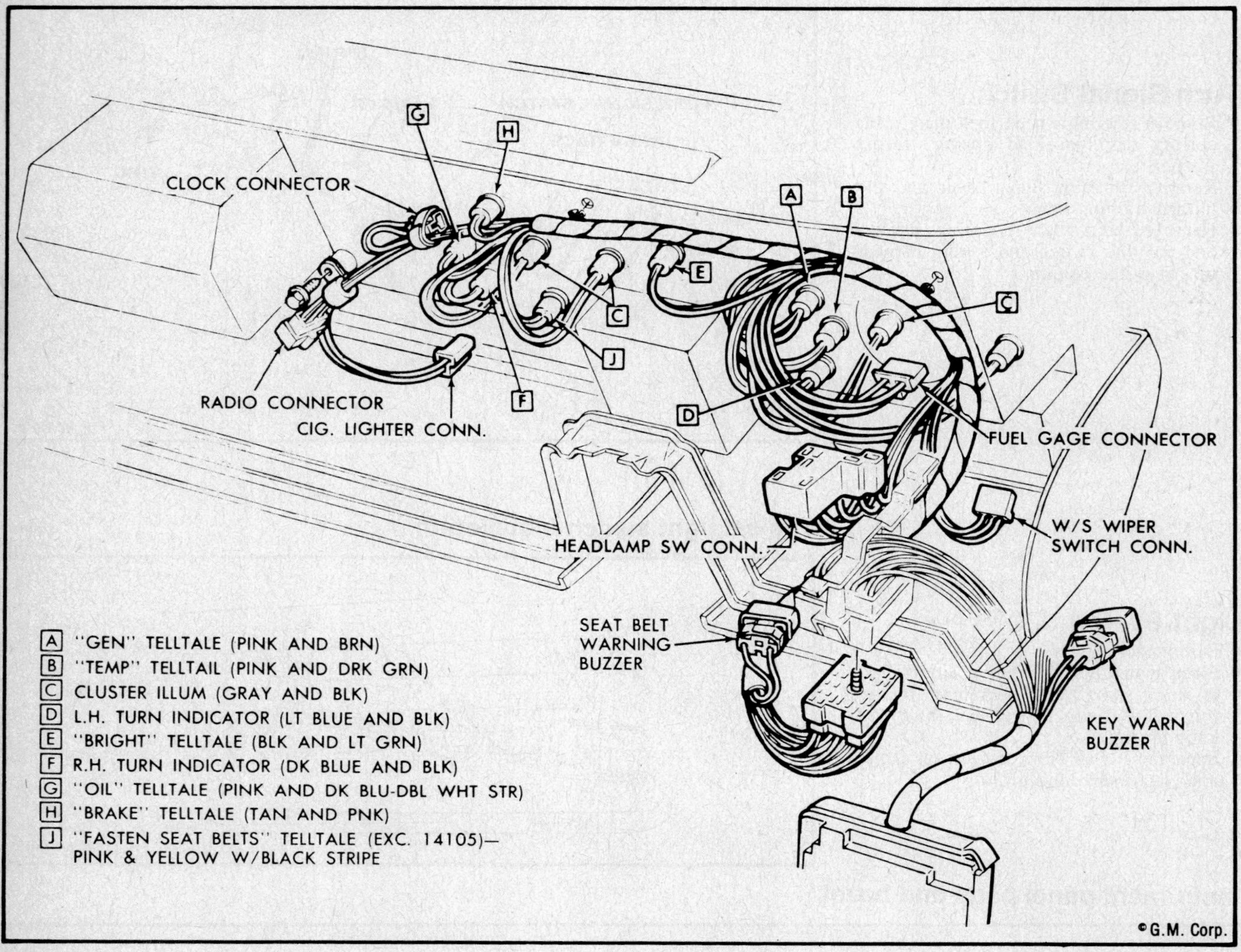

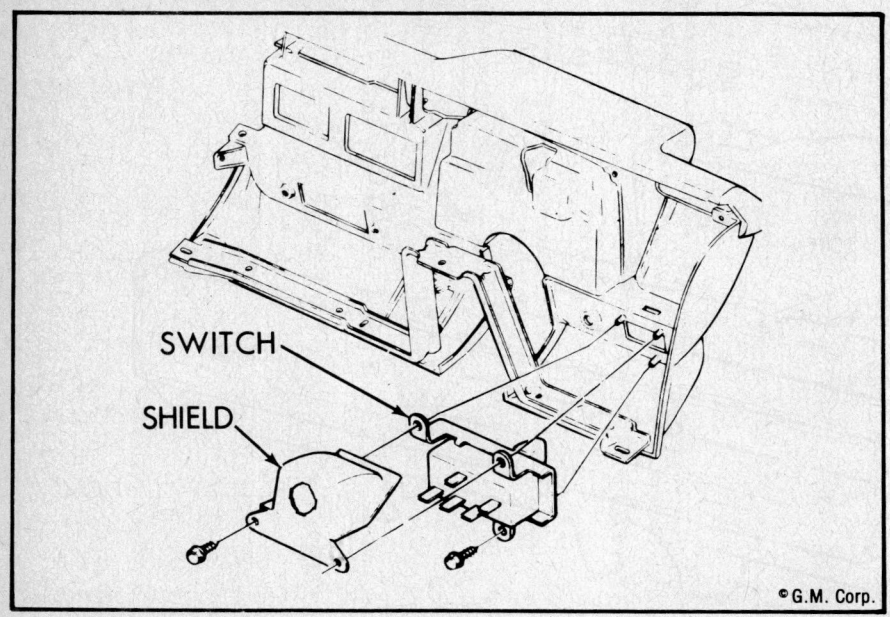

CLOCK CONNECTOR

RADIO CONNECTOR

CIG. LIGHTER CONN.

FUEL GAGE CONNECTOR

W/S WIPER SWITCH CONN.

HEADLAMP SW CONN.

SEAT BELT WARNING BUZZER

KEY WARN BUZZER

A ''GEN'' TELLTALE (PINK AND BRN)
B ''TEMP'' TELLTAIL (PINK AND DRK GRN)
C CLUSTER ILLUM (GRAY AND BLK)
D L.H. TURN INDICATOR (LT BLUE AND BLK)
E ''BRIGHT'' TELLTALE (BLK AND LT GRN)
F R.H. TURN INDICATOR (DK BLUE AND BLK)
G ''OIL'' TELLTALE (PINK AND DK BLU-DBL WHT STR)
H ''BRAKE'' TELLTALE (TAN AND PNK)
J ''FASTEN SEAT BELTS'' TELLTALE (EXC. 14105)—
PINK & YELLOW W/BLACK STRIPE

© G.M. Corp.

Windshield wiper/washer switch

SWITCH

SHIELD

Windshield Wiper Switch
- Remove anything blocking access to the rear of wiper switch.
- Remove switch mounting screws and disconnect electrical wiring.

© G.M. Corp.

Radio mounting

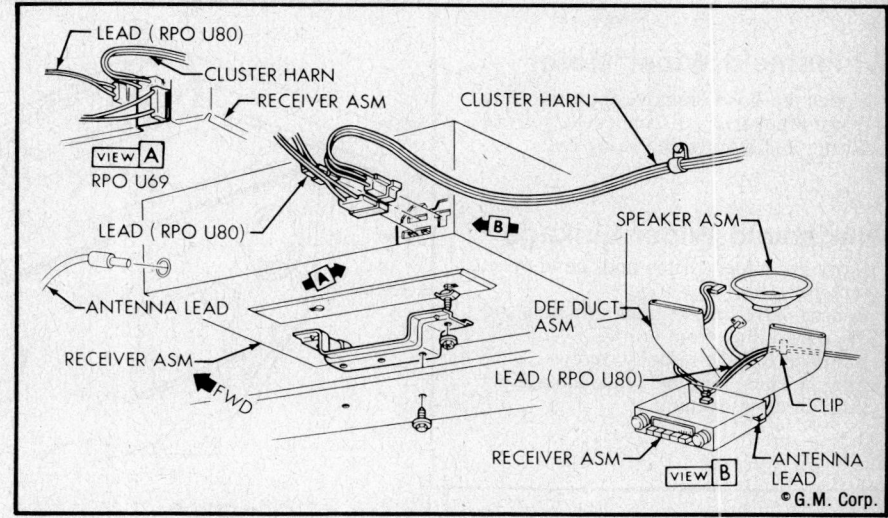

Radio

- Disconnect battery.
- Remove control knobs, bezels, nuts, washers, etc.

Temperature Control Unit/Blower Switch

- Disconnect, loosen, or remove anything preventing access to the control unit such as air conditioner ducting, radio, instrument panel bezel.
- Separate the control unit from the instrument panel, control cables and electrical leads.

Blower motor and housing

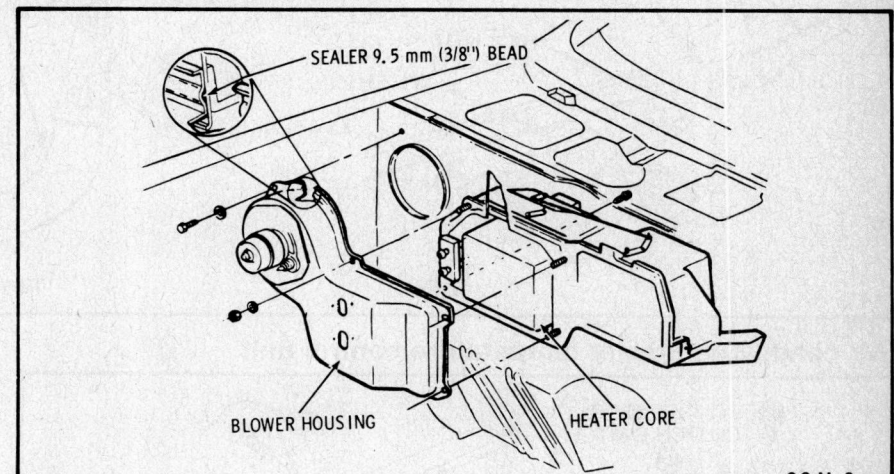

Heater temperature control panel

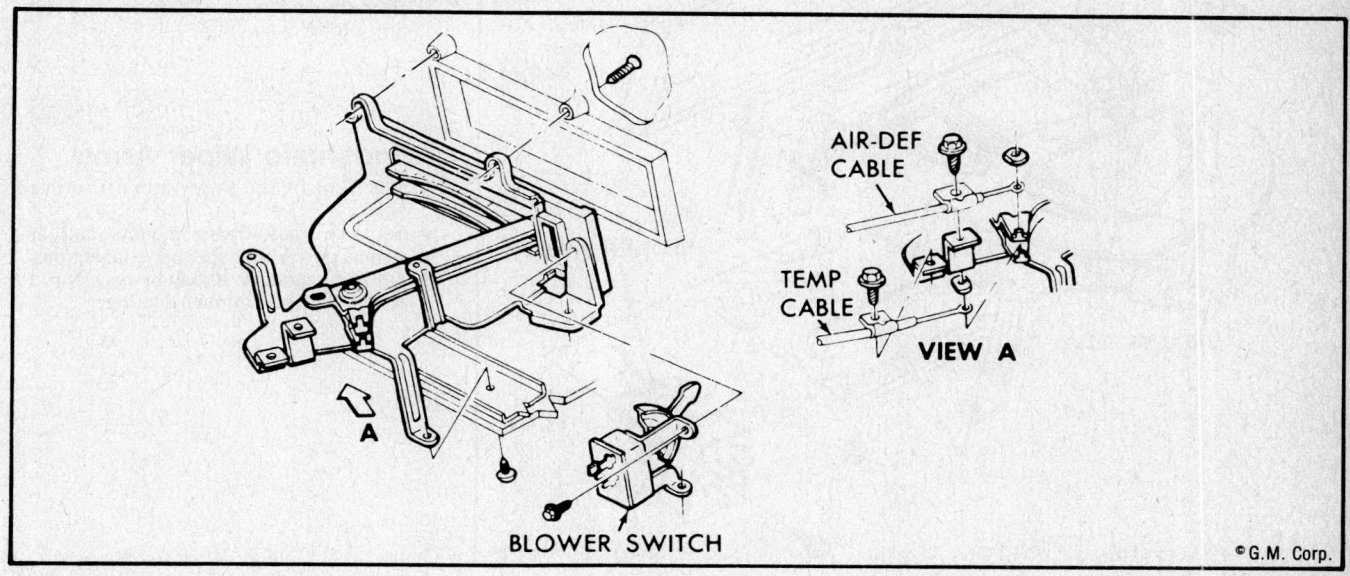

A505

GENERAL MOTORS "H" BODY CARS
ASTRE, MONZA, SKYHAWK, STARFIRE, SUNBIRD, VEGA

Wiper installation

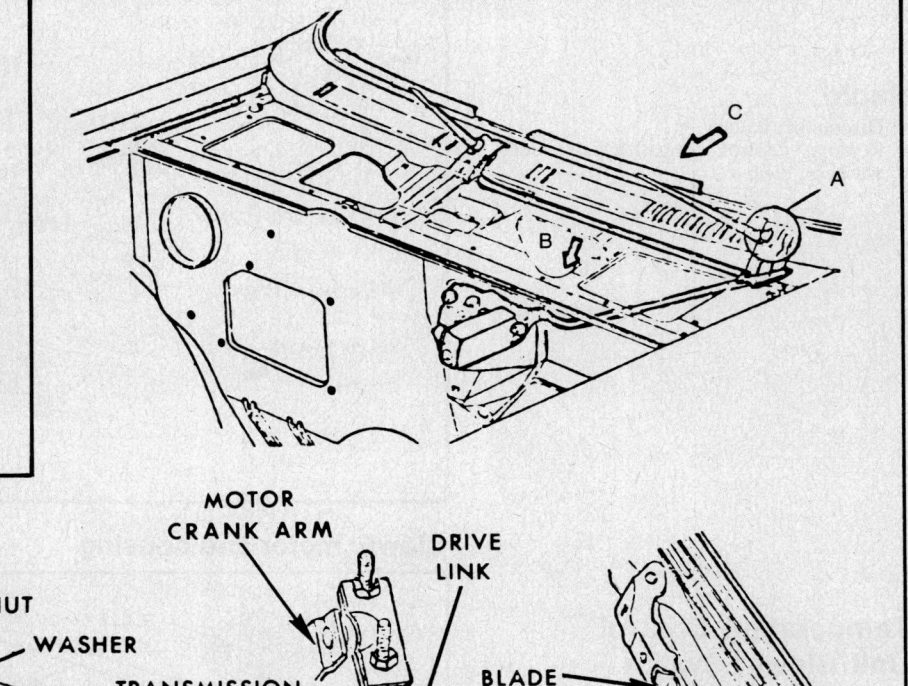

Windshield Wiper Motor
- Under the hood, remove the drive link from crankarm, disconnect electrical wiring and remove mounting bolts.

Windshield Wiper Linkage
- Remove wiper arms and cowl vent screen.
- Loosen drive link-to-crank arm nuts and disconnect link from arm.
- Remove linkage-to-body screws, snap ring, hex nut, etc., and guide linkage out through cowl opening.

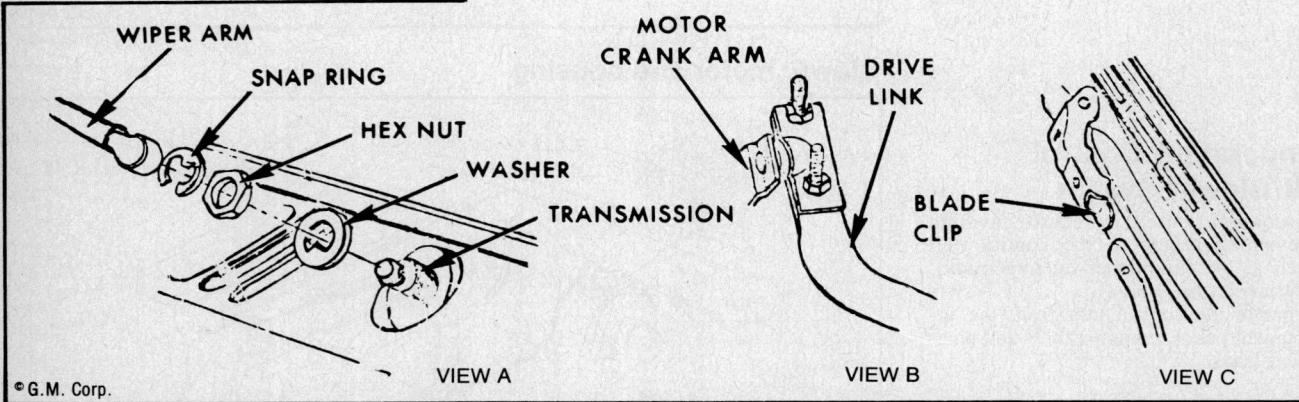

© G.M. Corp.

Air conditioner/heater temperature control unit

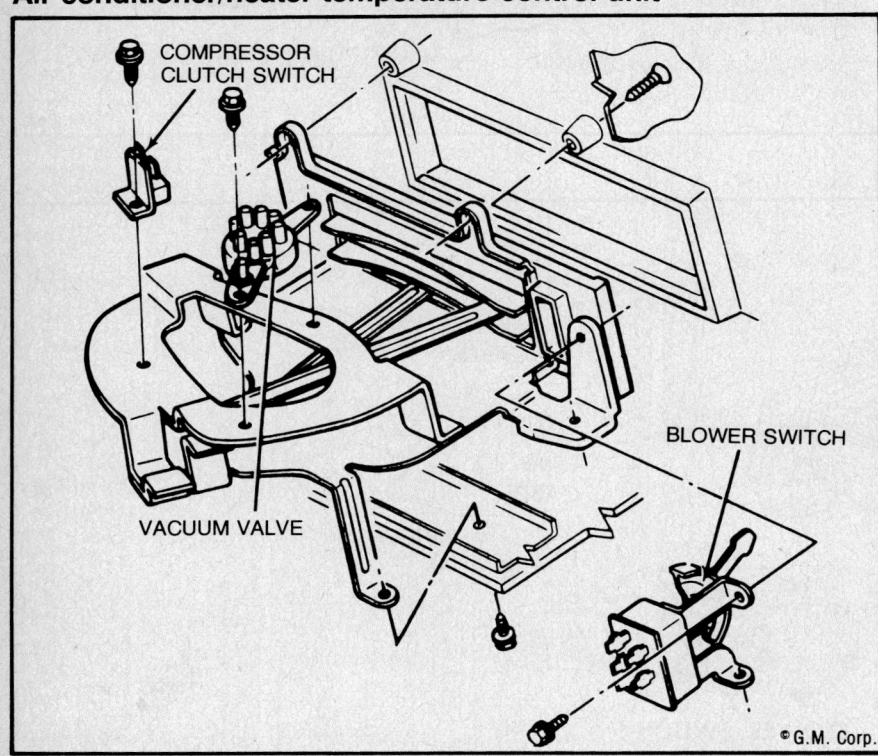

© G.M. Corp.

Windshield Wiper Blades
- Depress the spring type blade clip away from the underside of the arm, and slide arm out of blade clip.

Windshield Wiper Arms
- Use Tool J-8966 to pry arm off serrated shaft.
- Separate radio from mounts and antenna, power and speaker connections.
- On some models, it may be necessary to remove air conditioner ducting.

Heater motor, blower inlet and core

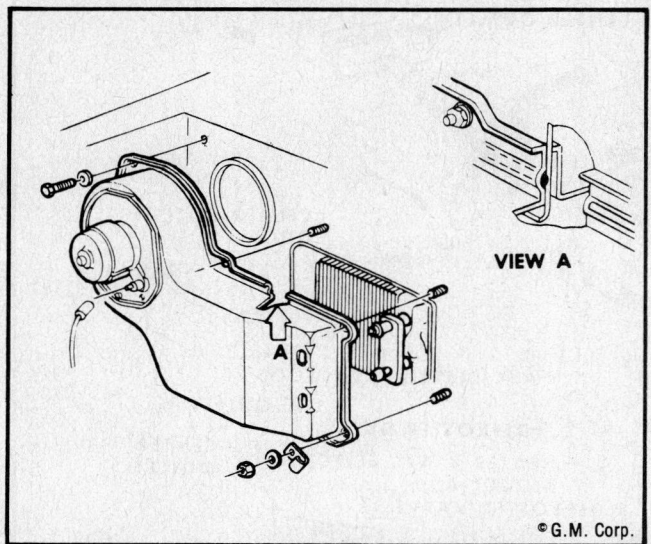

VIEW A

© G.M. Corp.

Heater distributor assembly

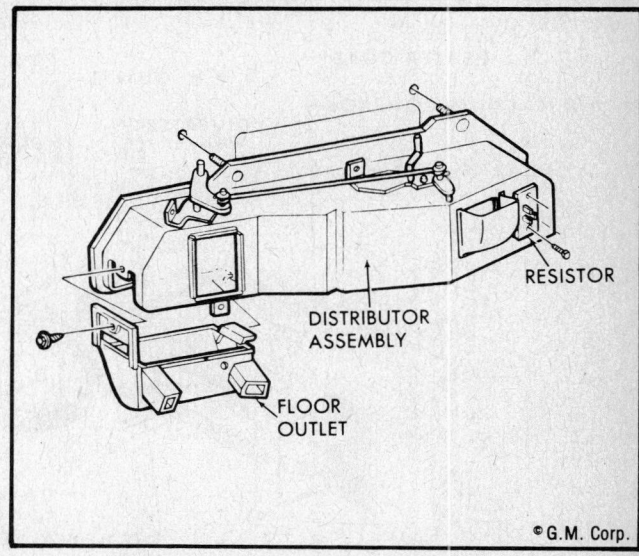

RESISTOR

DISTRIBUTOR ASSEMBLY

FLOOR OUTLET

© G.M. Corp.

Heater Blower

- Scribe alignment marks for blower motor flange-to-case position for installation reference. Remove the blower-to-case attaching screws, and remove te blower motor and wheel as an assembly.

Heater Core

Without Air Conditioner

- Disconnect the heater hoses. Remove the blower inlet-to-dash panel mounts, and remove the blower inlet, motor and wheel as an assembly.

- Remove the core restraining strap screws to remove the core.

With Air Conditioner

- The heater core is removed from inside the vehicle after extensive instrument panel dismantling. It is not necessary to purge the air conditioning system.
- Remove the floor outlet duct, glove box, left and right dash outlets and the instrument panel pad.
- Disconnect the vacuum hoses at the valves on left end of heater-evaporator unit.
- Remove insulation tray (below instru-

ment cluster), and loosen the console and slide it rearward.
- Lower the steering column, and then lower the instrument panel to rest on the column.
- Remove the right instrument panel and lap cooler as an assembly.
- Remove the modular duct-to-heater-evaporator mount, and remove the modular duct. Disconnect the control cables and electrical wiring. Disconnect heater hoses from core tubes.
- Remove heater case stud nuts and heater core case-to-evaporator core case attaching screws. Drive on studs to break loose from dash panel, and remove the heater core case assembly.
- Separate core from case.

Air conditioner condenser mounting

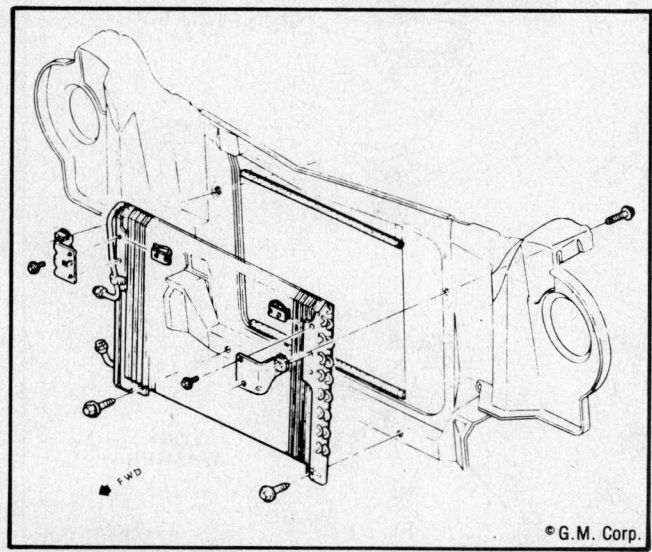

FWD

© G.M. Corp.

Air conditioner accumulator mounting

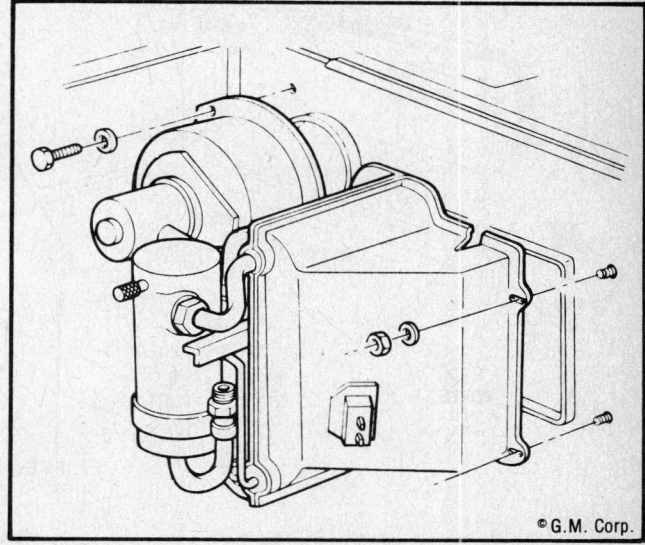

© G.M. Corp.

A507

GENERAL MOTORS "H" BODY CARS

ASTRE, MONZA, SKYHAWK, STARFIRE, SUNBIRD, VEGA

Heater/air conditioner components and ducting

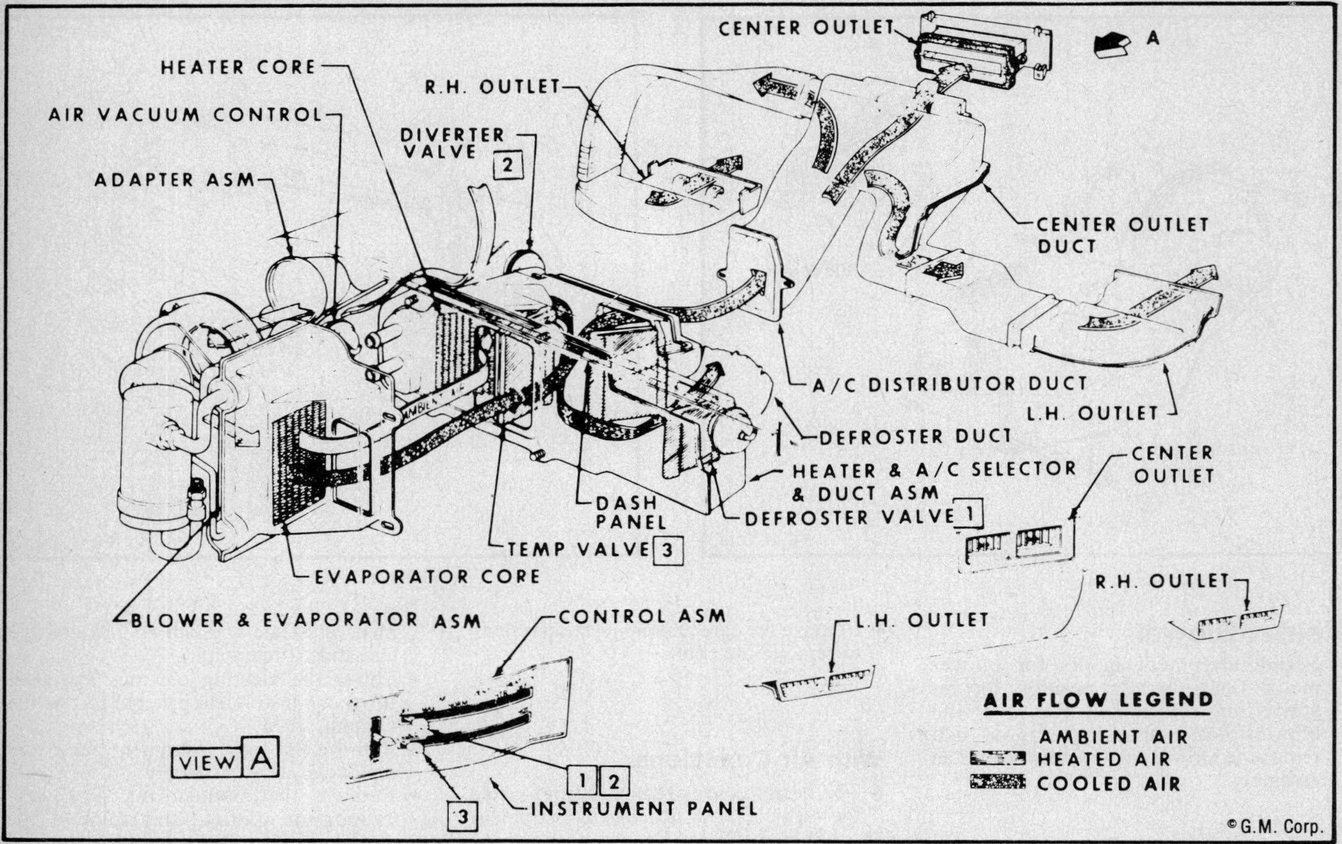

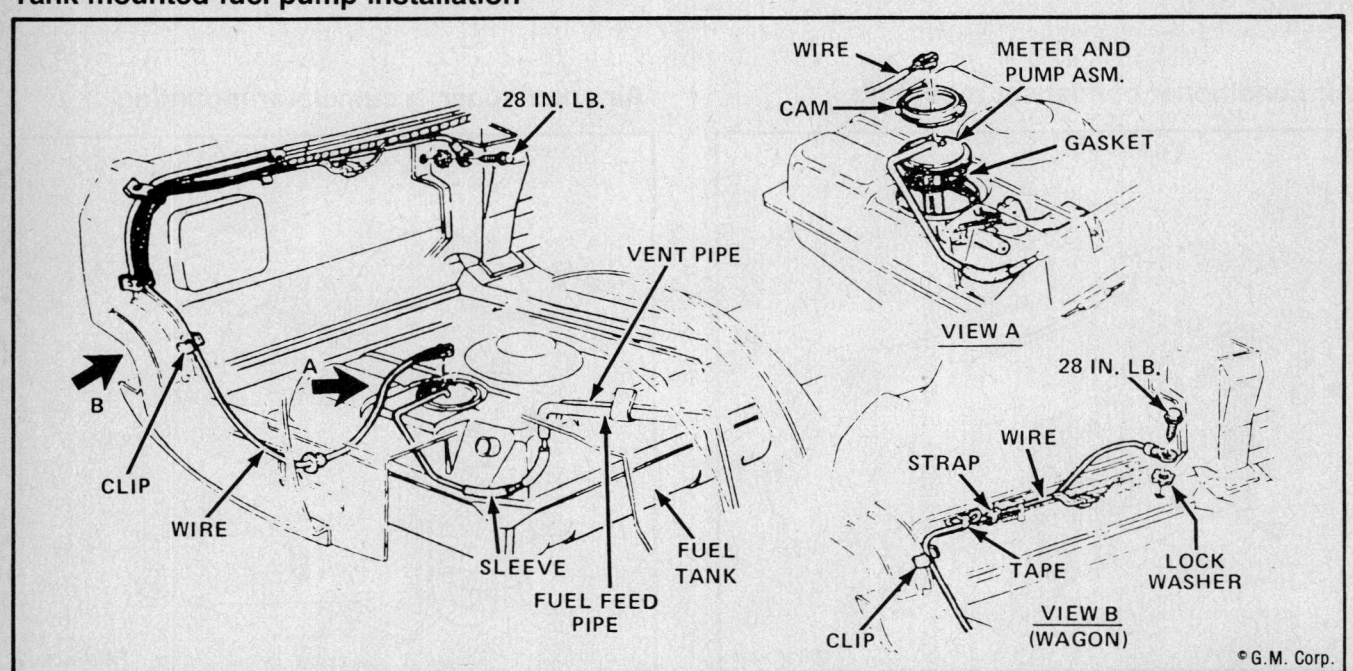

HEATER CORE

AIR VACUUM CONTROL

ADAPTER ASM

R.H. OUTLET

DIVERTER VALVE 2

CENTER OUTLET

A

CENTER OUTLET DUCT

A/C DISTRIBUTOR DUCT

L.H. OUTLET

DEFROSTER DUCT

HEATER & A/C SELECTOR & DUCT ASM

CENTER OUTLET

DEFROSTER VALVE 1

DASH PANEL

TEMP VALVE 3

EVAPORATOR CORE

BLOWER & EVAPORATOR ASM

CONTROL ASM

R.H. OUTLET

L.H. OUTLET

VIEW A

1 2

3

INSTRUMENT PANEL

AIR FLOW LEGEND
AMBIENT AIR
HEATED AIR
COOLED AIR

© G.M. Corp.

Fuel Pump

- The fuel pump is mounted in the fuel tank and is electrically operated. The tank must be removed for fuel pump replacement.

Tank mounted fuel pump installation

28 IN. LB.

WIRE

CAM

METER AND PUMP ASM.

GASKET

VENT PIPE

VIEW A

B

CLIP

WIRE

SLEEVE

FUEL FEED PIPE

FUEL TANK

28 IN. LB.

WIRE

STRAP

TAPE

LOCK WASHER

CLIP

VIEW B (WAGON)

© G.M. Corp.

A508

Steering Column

NOTE: Handle the steering column very carefully. Rapping on the end of it or leaning on it could shear off the plastic inserts which allow the column to collapse in a crash.

Standard Column

- Disconnect the battery.

- Remove the steering wheel.
- Disconnect the pot joint or flexible coupling.
- Remove the floor pan bracket screws and instrument panel nuts.
- Disconnect electrical wiring and remove the column.

Tilt Column

- Remove the steering wheel.

- Remove the turn signal lever and hazard warning knob.
- Depress the shaft lock plate and pry the retaining snap ring out of the groove.
- Slide the turn signal cancelling cam and upper bearing preload spring off the end of the shaft.
- Remove the mounting bolts and lower the column.

Regular key release column

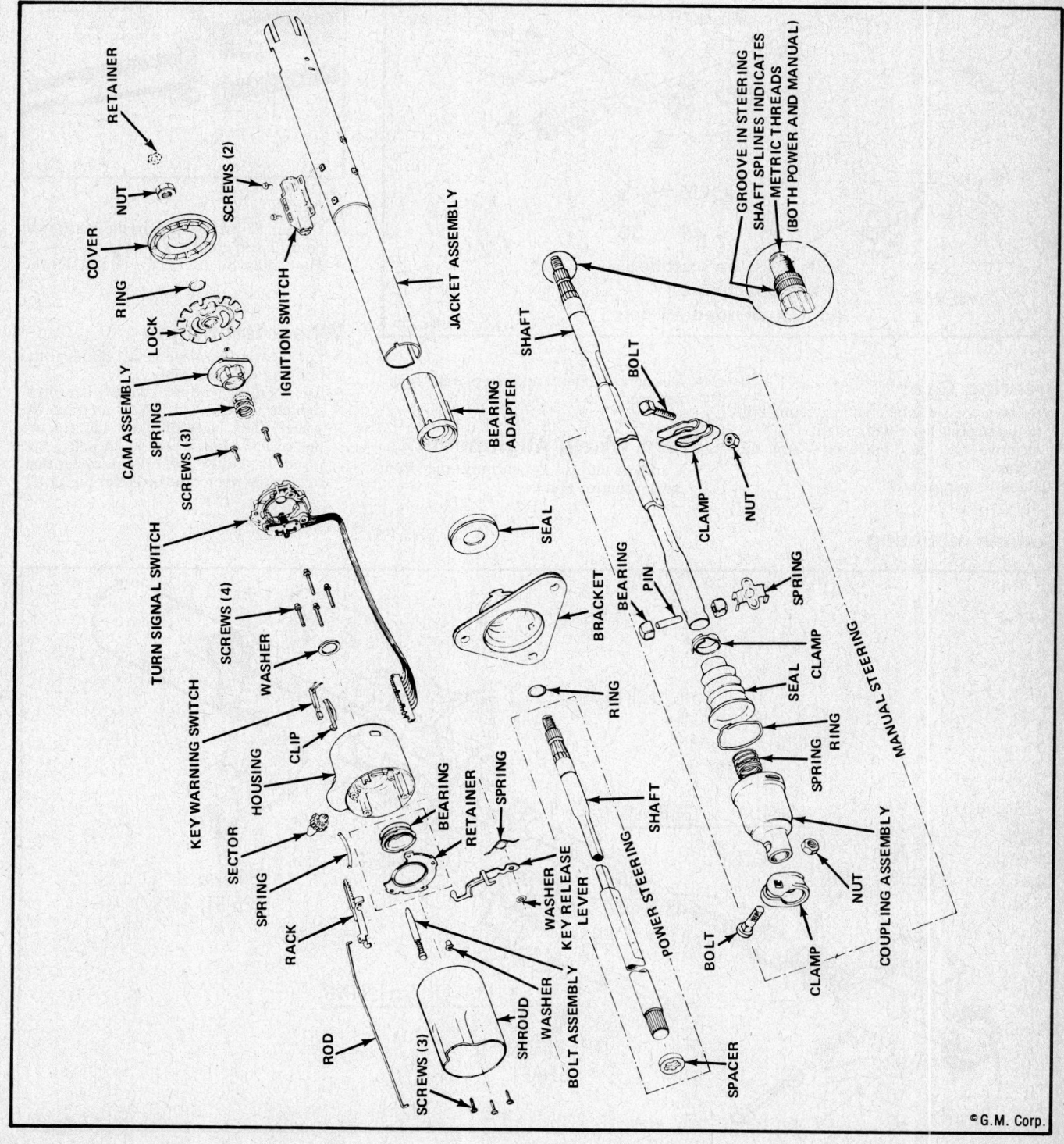

STEERING SECTION

Steering linkage arrangement

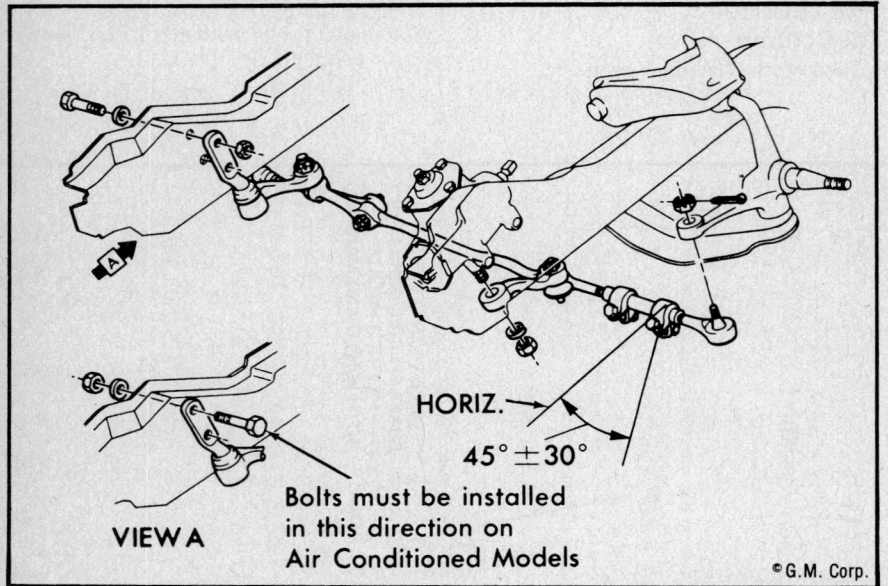

VIEW A

HORIZ.

45° ± 30°

Bolts must be installed in this direction on Air Conditioned Models

© G.M. Corp.

Column alignment spacer removal

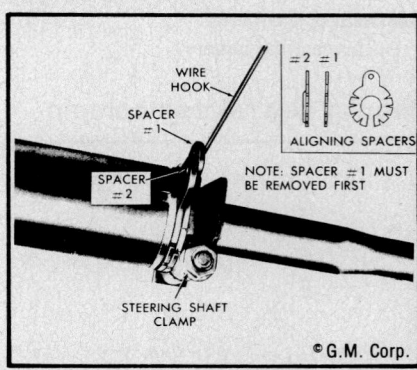

WIRE HOOK

SPACER #1

SPACER #2

≠2 ≠1

ALIGNING SPACERS

NOTE: SPACER ≠1 MUST BE REMOVED FIRST

STEERING SHAFT CLAMP

© G.M. Corp.

- Caster: adjust by turning the rear lower control arm cam.
- Toe: adjust by turning the tie rod sleeve.

Wheel Bearings

- For bearing replacement, remove the hub and disc assembly.
- To correctly adjust wheel bearings, tighten spindle nut while rotating the wheel, then back off until nut reaches the exact point where it loosens, and install the cotter pin. Loosen rather than tighten the nut to line up cotter pin slots.

Steering Gear

- Remove the pot joint coupling clamp bolt at the steering gear wormshaft.
- Remove the "K" brace on Astre and Vega.
- Remove pitman arm.
- Disconnect mounts and remove the steering gear.

Front Wheel Alignment

- Camber: adjust by turning the front lower control arm cam.

Column mounting

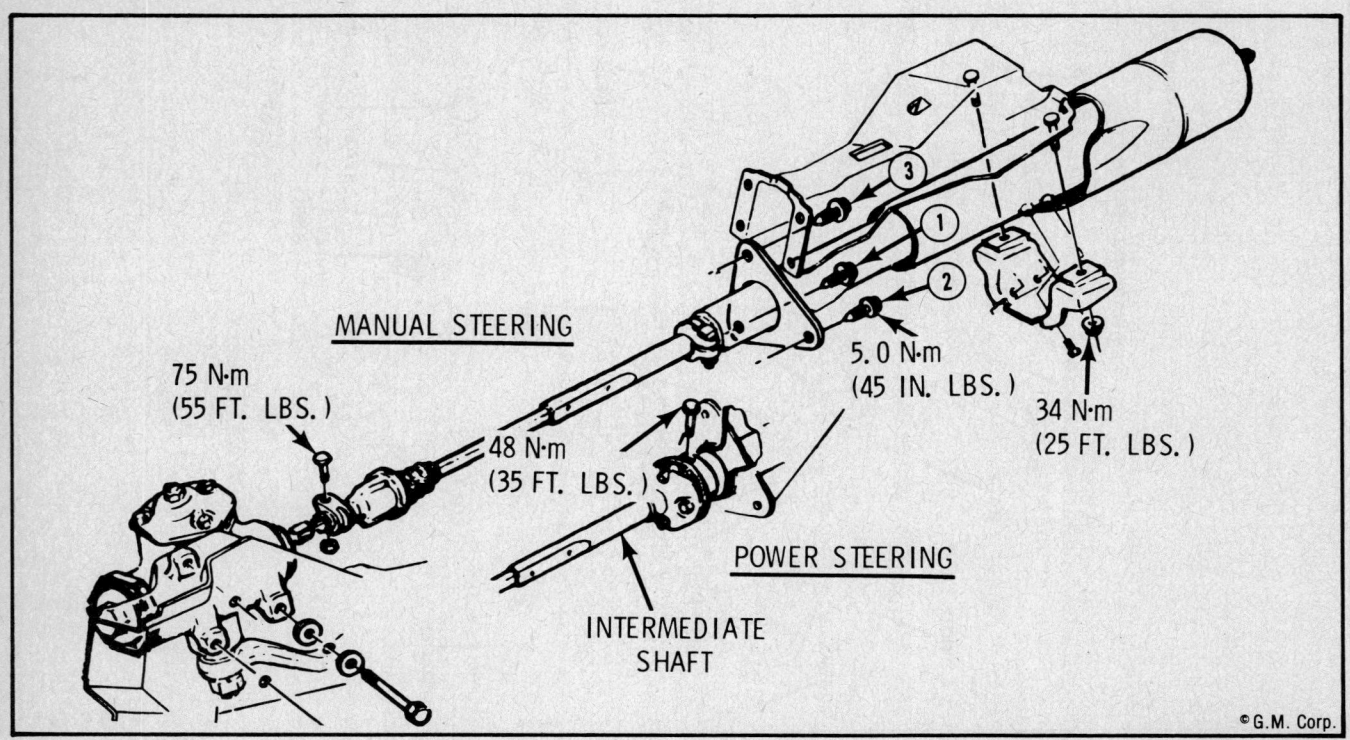

MANUAL STEERING

75 N·m (55 FT. LBS.)

48 N·m (35 FT. LBS.)

5.0 N·m (45 IN. LBS.)

34 N·m (25 FT. LBS.)

POWER STEERING

INTERMEDIATE SHAFT

© G.M. Corp.

Tie rod clamp and sleeve placement

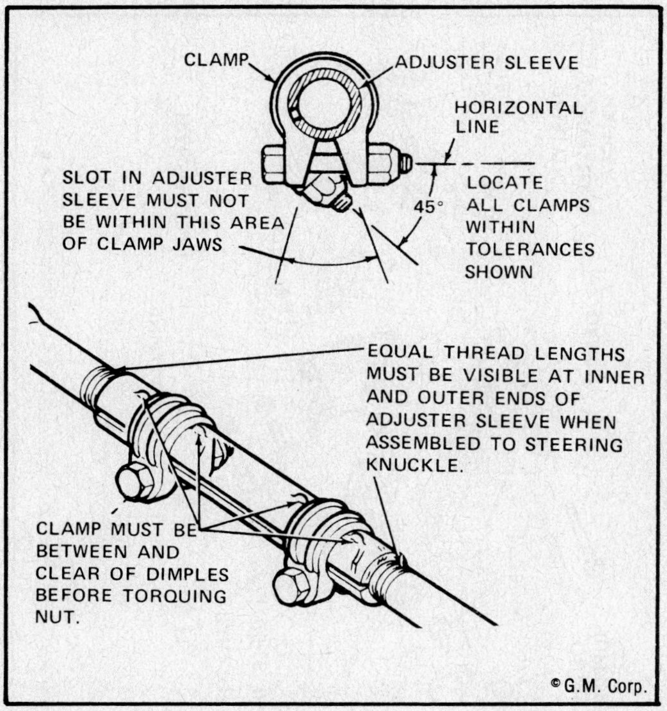

CLAMP

ADJUSTER SLEEVE

HORIZONTAL LINE

45°

SLOT IN ADJUSTER SLEEVE MUST NOT BE WITHIN THIS AREA OF CLAMP JAWS

LOCATE ALL CLAMPS WITHIN TOLERANCES SHOWN

EQUAL THREAD LENGTHS MUST BE VISIBLE AT INNER AND OUTER ENDS OF ADJUSTER SLEEVE WHEN ASSEMBLED TO STEERING KNUCKLE.

CLAMP MUST BE BETWEEN AND CLEAR OF DIMPLES BEFORE TORQUING NUT.

© G.M. Corp.

Built-in wear indicator for lower ball joint

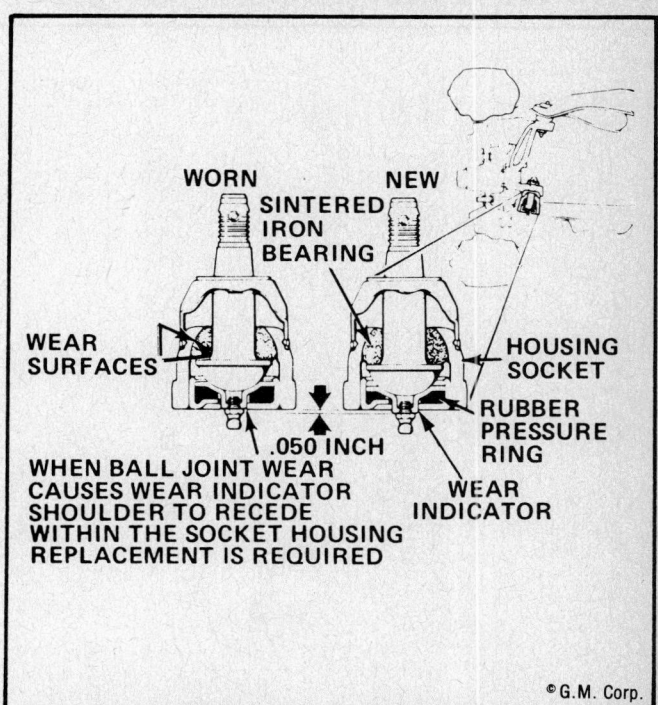

WORN

NEW

SINTERED IRON BEARING

WEAR SURFACES

HOUSING SOCKET

RUBBER PRESSURE RING

WEAR INDICATOR

.050 INCH

WHEN BALL JOINT WEAR CAUSES WEAR INDICATOR SHOULDER TO RECEDE WITHIN THE SOCKET HOUSING REPLACEMENT IS REQUIRED

© G.M. Corp.

Track rod and control arms

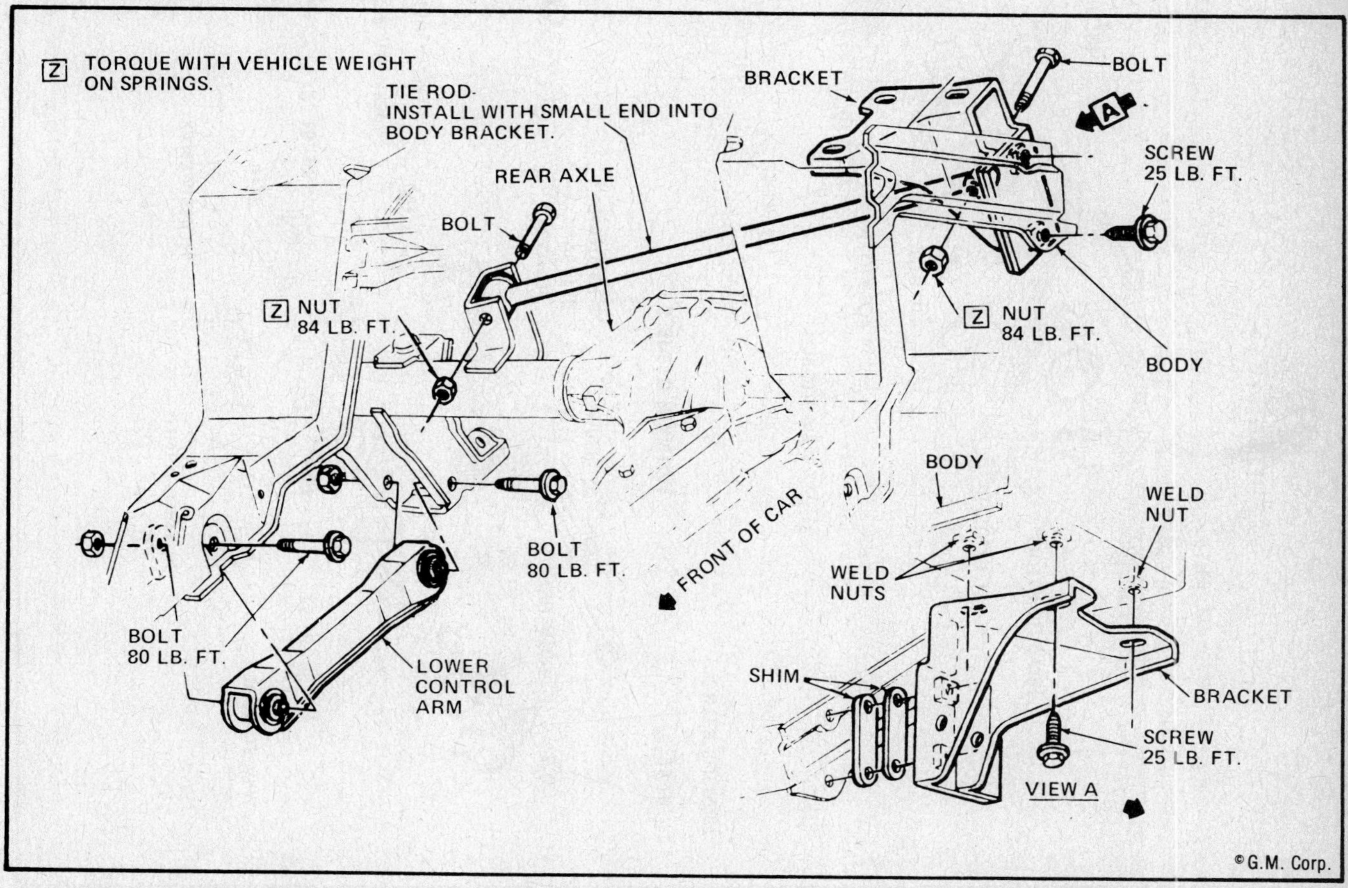

Z TORQUE WITH VEHICLE WEIGHT ON SPRINGS.

TIE ROD-INSTALL WITH SMALL END INTO BODY BRACKET.

BRACKET

BOLT

REAR AXLE

A

SCREW 25 LB. FT.

BOLT

Z NUT 84 LB. FT.

Z NUT 84 LB. FT.

BODY

FRONT OF CAR

BODY

WELD NUT

BOLT 80 LB. FT.

WELD NUTS

BOLT 80 LB. FT.

LOWER CONTROL ARM

SHIM

BRACKET

SCREW 25 LB. FT.

VIEW A

© G.M. Corp.

A511

GENERAL MOTORS "H" BODY CARS

ASTRE, MONZA, SKYHAWK, STARFIRE, SUNBIRD, VEGA

Torque arm-to-support attachment

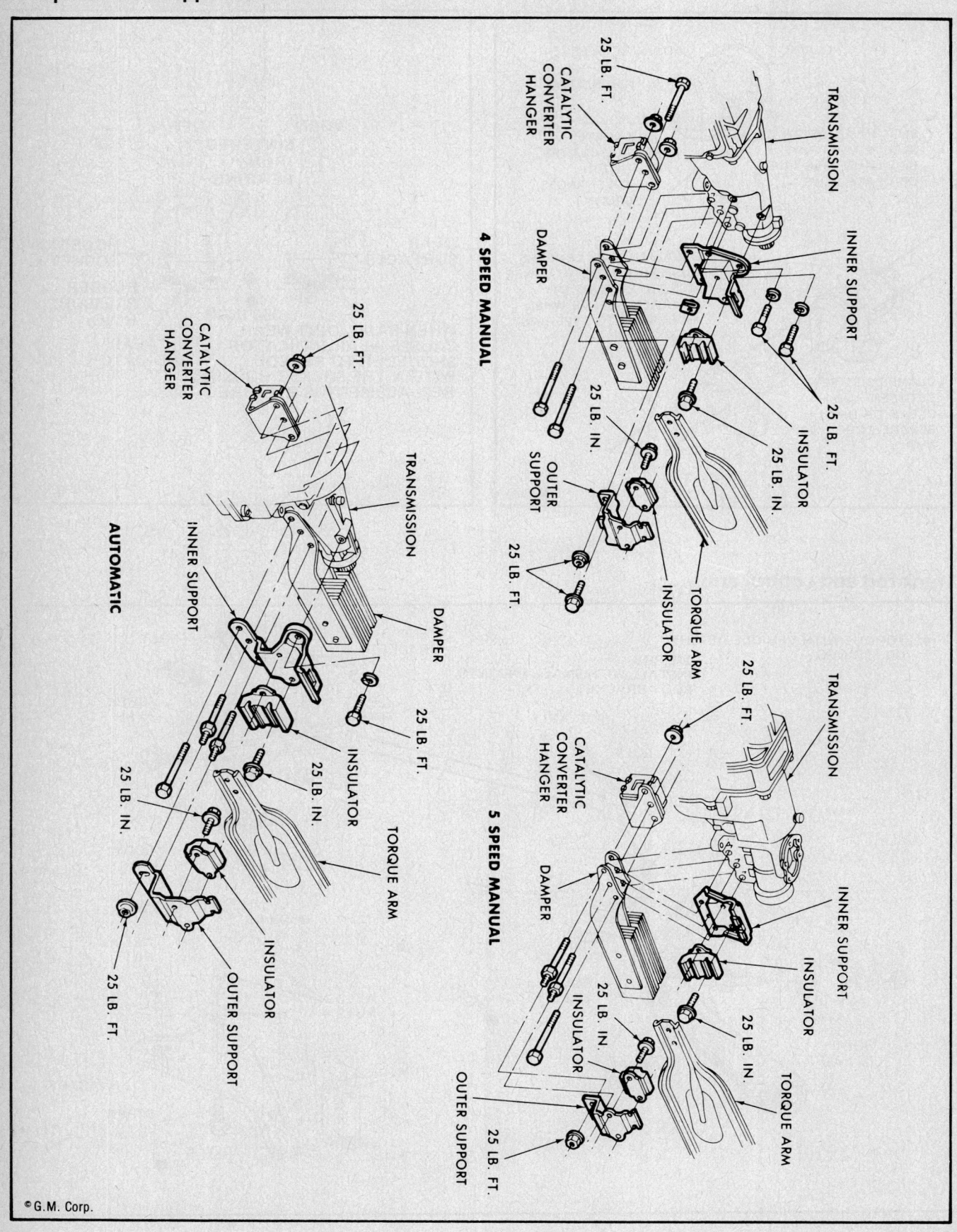

Brake Power Unit R&R

- Disconnect the power brake push rod from the brake pedal.
- Separate power unit and master cylinder, and unbolt power unit from firewall.

NOTE: See Unit Repair section of this manual for bleeding instructions.

Parking Brake Cable R&R

- Disconnect cables from equalizer.
- Remove brake drum, and disengage and remove cable.
- Adjust parking brake after installation.

Parking Brake Adjustment

- Correctly adjust service brakes.
- Apply parking brake one notch from fully released position.
- Tighten cable at equalizer until drag is felt at the rear wheels.
- Release parking brake lever, and check that rear wheels turn without resistance.

Master cylinder and brake pedal mounting

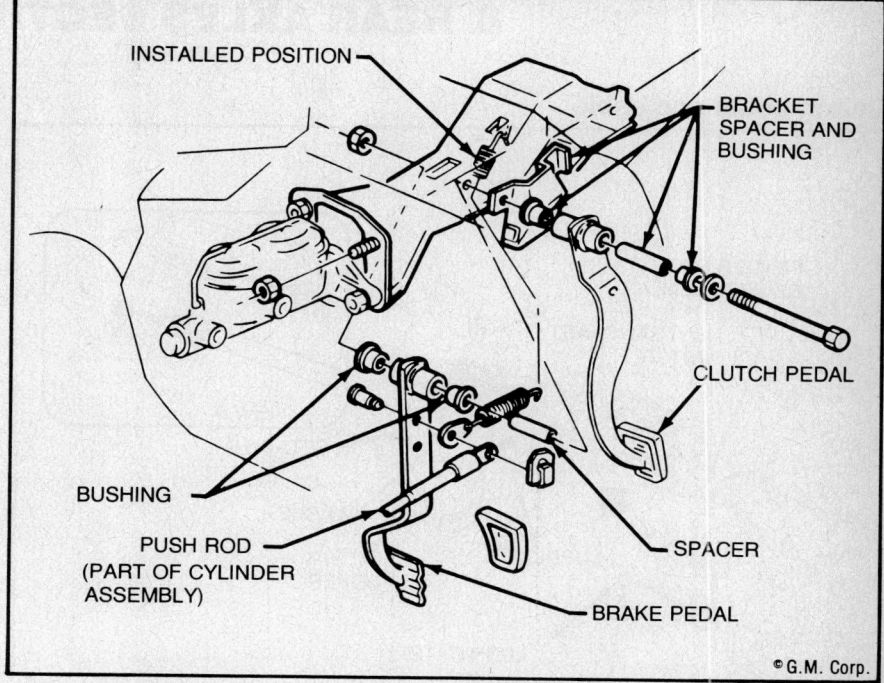

© G.M. Corp.

Parking brake

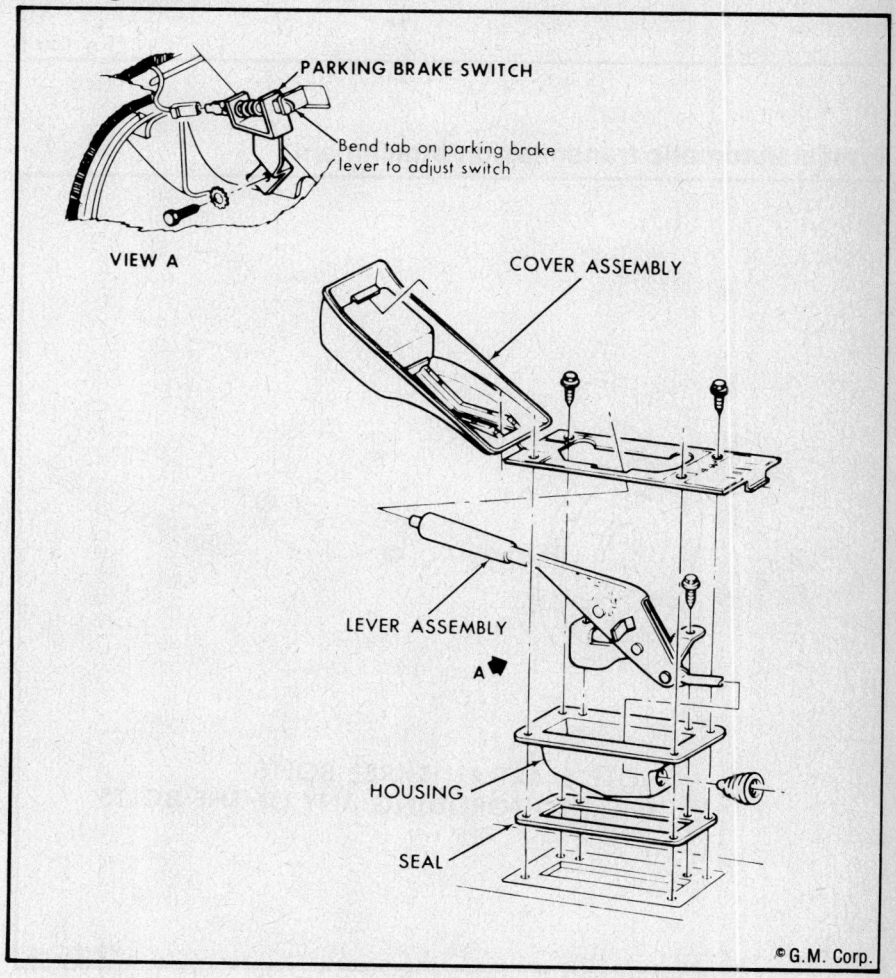

© G.M. Corp.

A513

CLUTCH, TRANSMISSION, PROPELLER SHAFT & REAR AXLES SECTION

Clutch pedal and cable

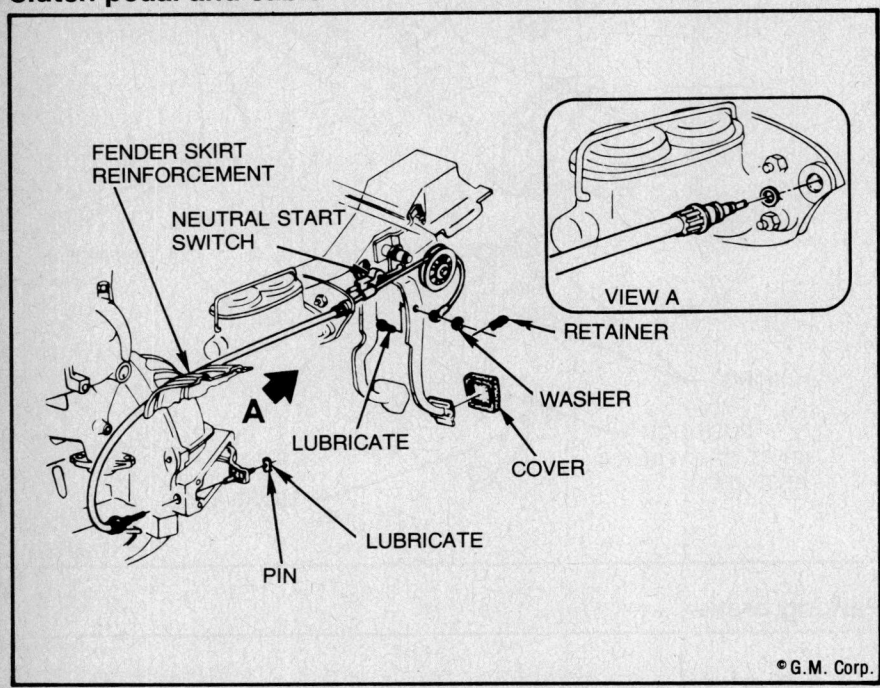

Clutch Adjustment

- Adjust for normal clutch wear by turning the clutch fork ball stud counterclockwise to give .90 inch free play at the pedal.

Manual Transmission R&R

- On five speed transmission, remove the shift lever.
- Remove drive shaft and disconnect the speedometer cable and electrical leads.
- On three and four speed transmissions, disconnect control rod and lever assemblies from the shifter shafts.
- Remove the damper assembly, converter bracket and torque arm bracket from the five speed transmission.
- Support the transmission, remove the crossmember on the three and four speed transmissions, and remove the mount bolts.

Automatic Transmission R&R

- Before raising the vehicle, disconnect, remove or relocate the following:
  a. Battery
  b. Detent cable at the carburetor and bracket.
  c. Dip stick
  d. Heater core cover (on air conditioned cars only)
- Raise the vehicle, and disconnect, remove or relocate the following:
  a. Driveshaft
  b. Speedometer cable
  c. Electrical leads
  d. Oil cooler lines
  e. Shift control linkages
  f. Exhaust plumbing
  g. Crossmember
- Support the transmission, and remove the rear mount bolts.
- Remove the torque converter underpan, and remove the converter-to-flexplate bolts.
- Mark drive plate and torque converter for installation reference.
- Lower transmission until the jack is barely supporting it, and remove the transmission-to-engine mounts.
- Raise transmission to its normal position and slide rearward.
- After installation, check fluid level and adjust linkages.

Typical automatic transmission attachment

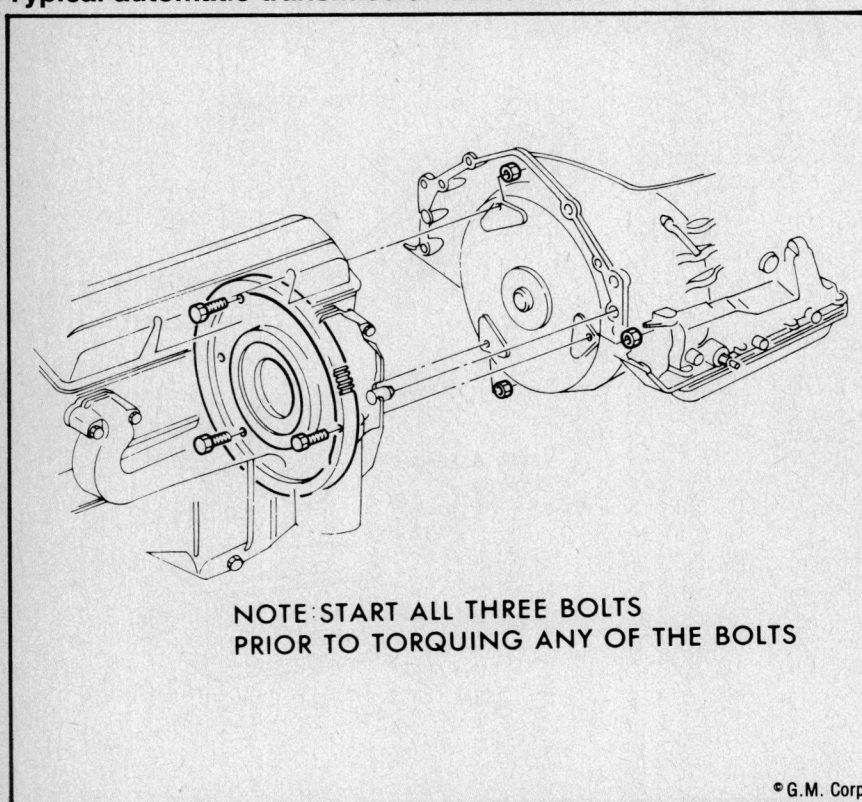

NOTE: START ALL THREE BOLTS PRIOR TO TORQUING ANY OF THE BOLTS

© G.M. Corp.

Four speed manual transmission shift control linkage

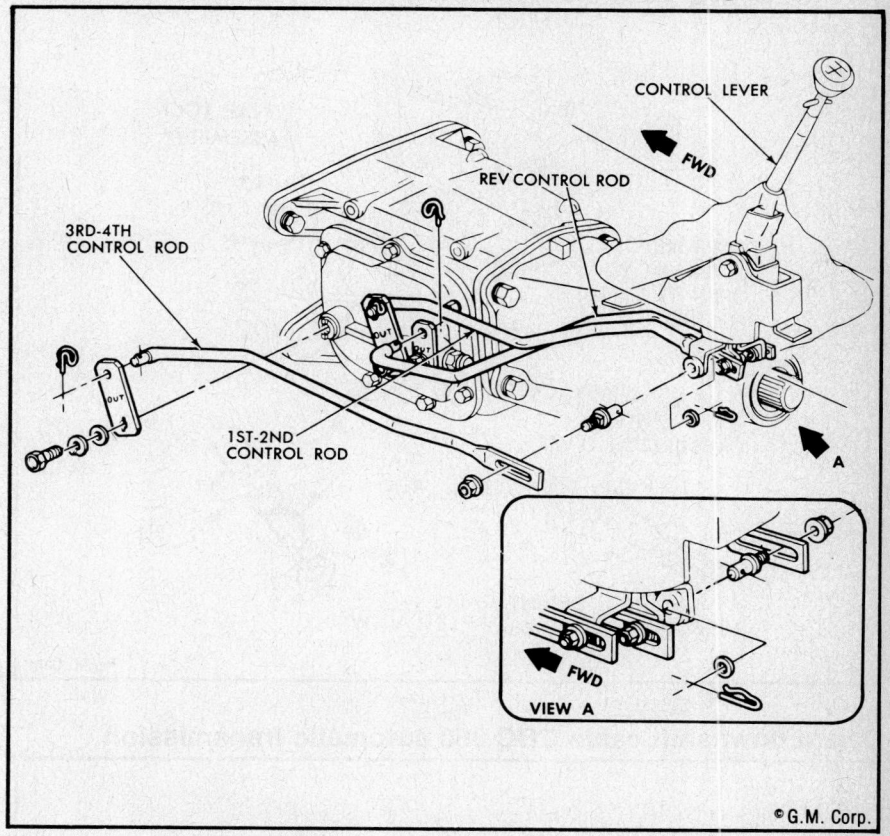

Manual Transmission Linkage Adjustment

- Loosen lock nuts at swivels on the shaft rods.
- Set transmission shift levers in neutral, and set shift control lever in neutral. Align control levers and install gage pin into levers and bracket.
- Tighten the shift rod nuts against their swivels.

Three speed manual transmission shift control linkage

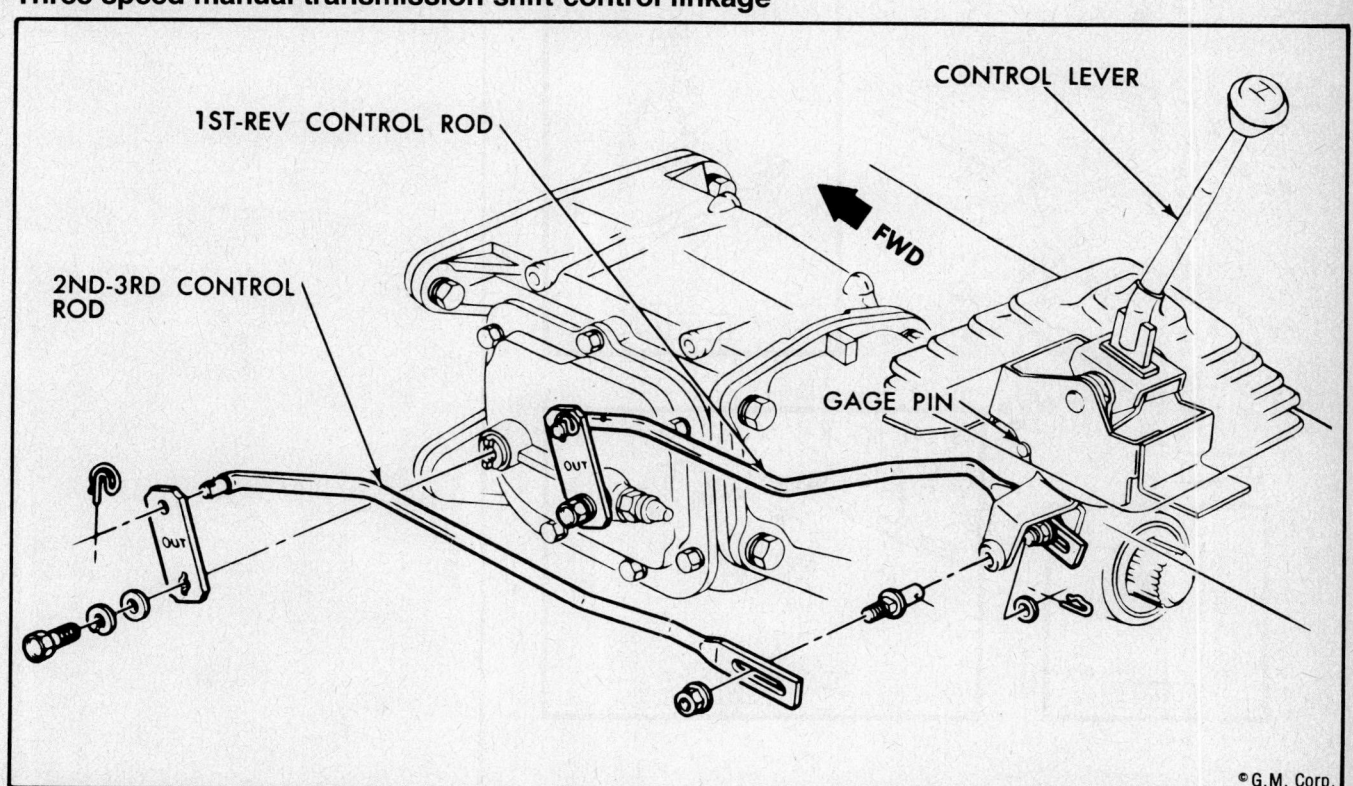

Use gauge pin for adjustment

GENERAL MOTORS "H" BODY CARS
ASTRE, MONZA, SKYHAWK, STARFIRE, SUNBIRD, VEGA

Detent downshift cable automatic transmission

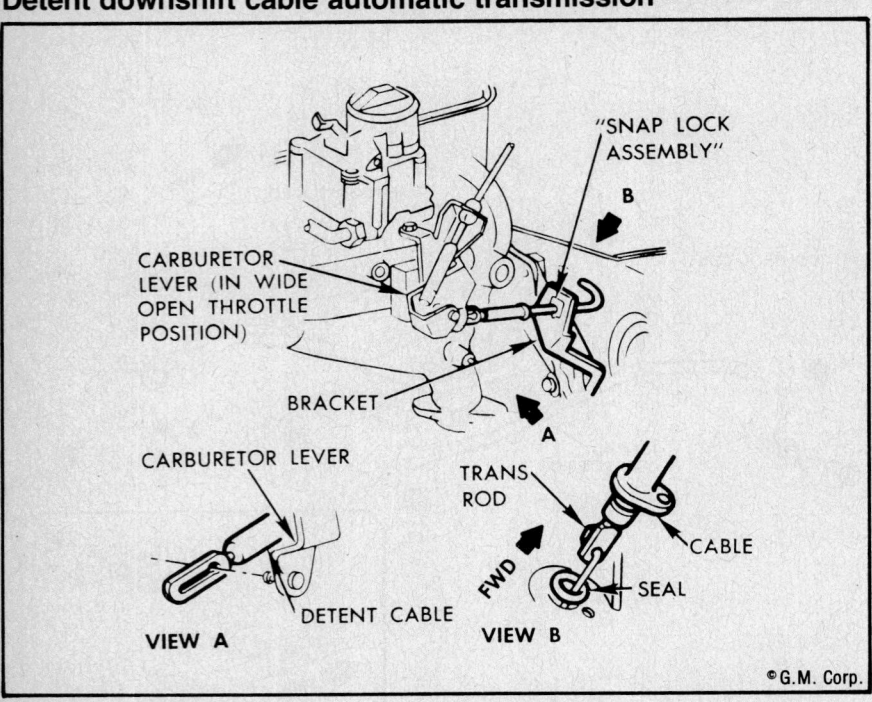

Automatic Transmission Cable Detent Adjustment
- Disengage the snap lock, and position the carburetor in the full open position.
- Push the snap lock on the cable down until the top is flush with the cable.

Automatic Transmission Manual Linkage Adjustment
- Loosen the nut and swivel at the transmission lever.
- Place both transmission shifter and transmission lever in neutral.
- Tighten the locknut, and if necessary, adjust the neutral start switch.

Detent downshift cable CBC 350 automatic transmission

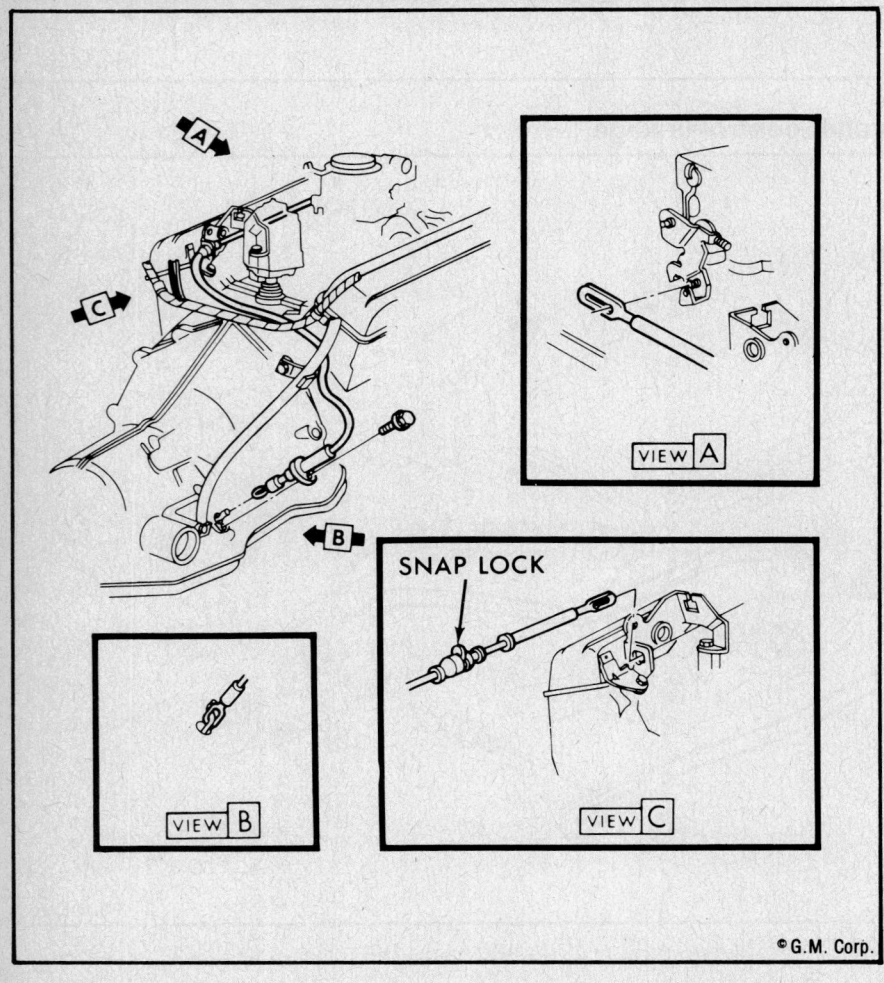

Shift linkage used with Turbo Hydra-matic 250 automatic transmission

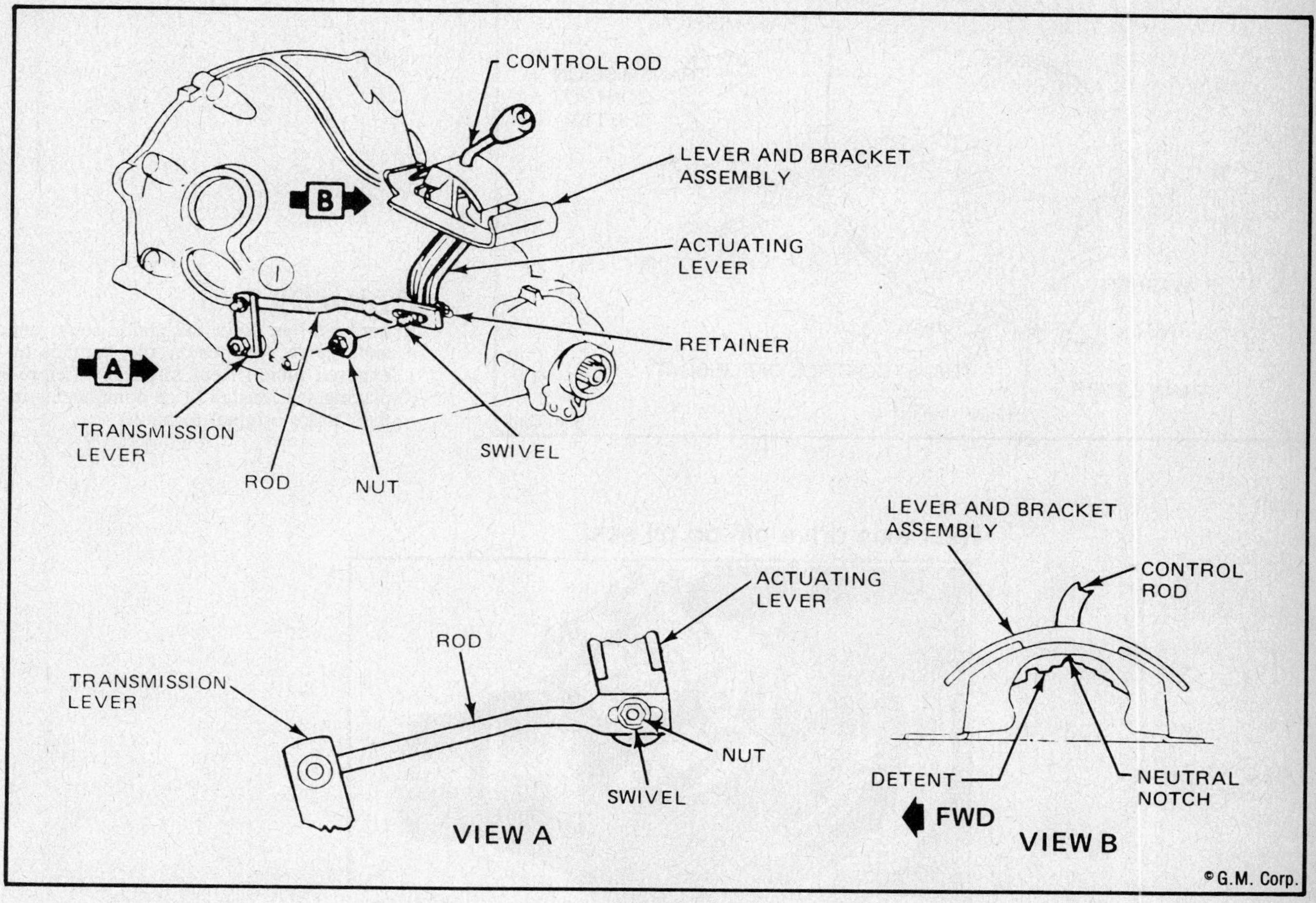

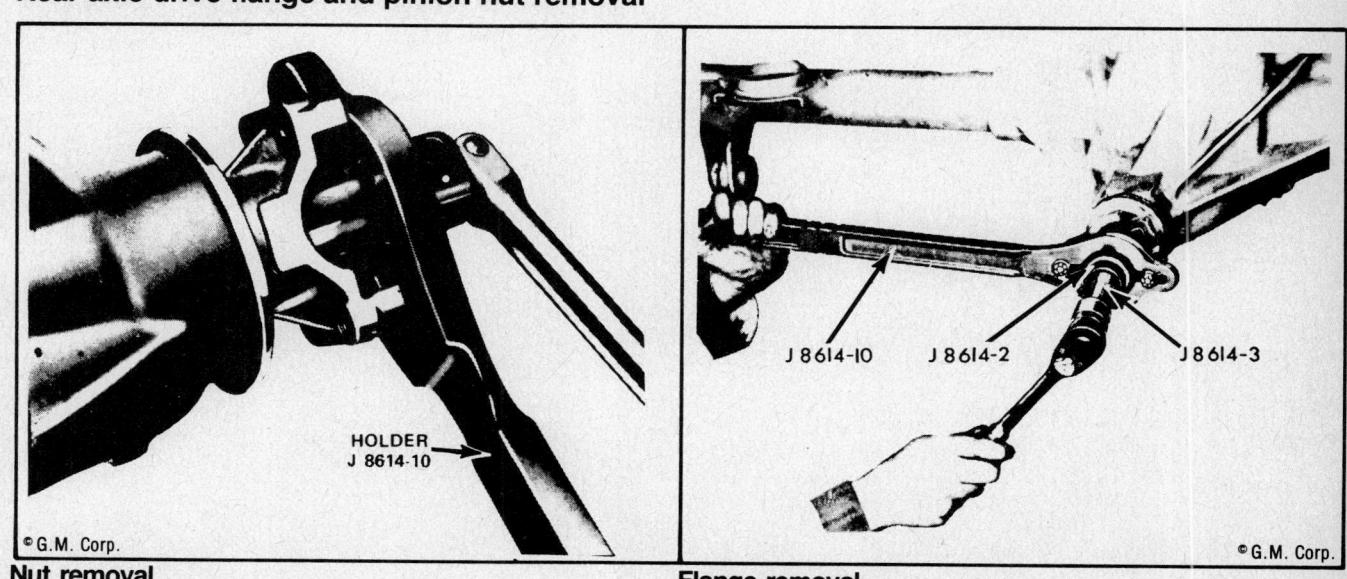

CONTROL ROD

LEVER AND BRACKET ASSEMBLY

ACTUATING LEVER

RETAINER

SWIVEL

TRANSMISSION LEVER

ROD

NUT

B

A

VIEW A

TRANSMISSION LEVER

ROD

ACTUATING LEVER

NUT

SWIVEL

VIEW B

LEVER AND BRACKET ASSEMBLY

CONTROL ROD

DETENT

NEUTRAL NOTCH

FWD

© G.M. Corp.

Rear axle drive flange and pinion nut removal

HOLDER J 8614-10

© G.M. Corp.

Nut removal

J 8614-10

J 8614-2

J 8614-3

© G.M. Corp.

Flange removal

A517

GENERAL MOTORS "H" BODY CARS
ASTRE, MONZA, SKYHAWK, STARFIRE, SUNBIRD, VEGA

Cable type automatic transmission shift linkage

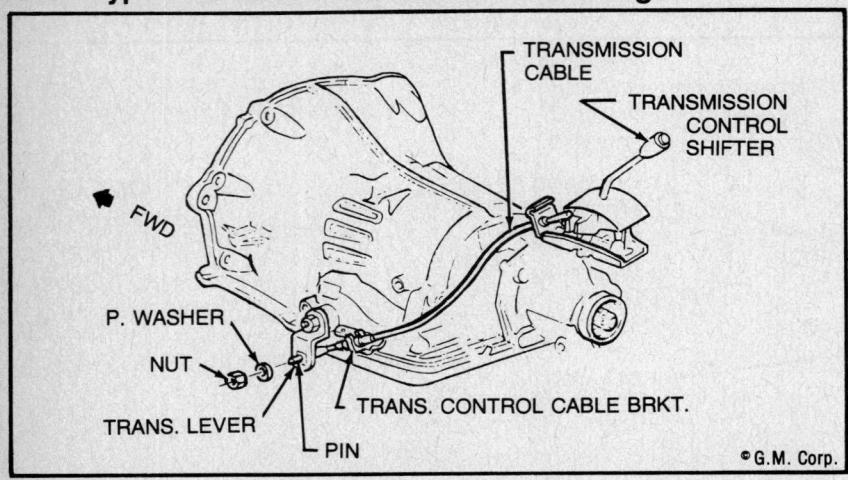

Pinion Oil Seal

- Scribe a line down the pinion stem, nut and flange, and count the number of exposed pinion stem threads. After replacing seal, install these components in their exact original locations.

Rear axle drive pinion oil seal

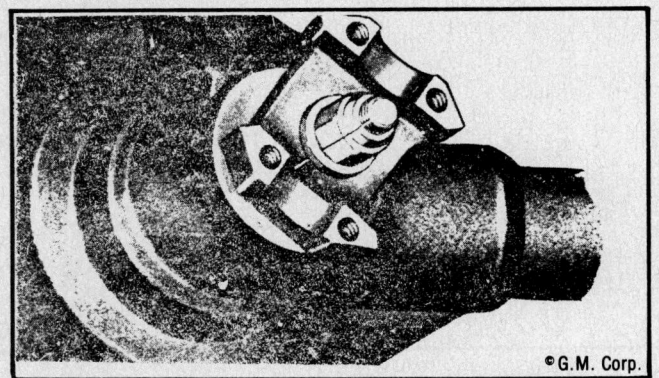

Scribe mark on pinion stem, nut and flange and count exposed threads on pinion stem for installation reference

INDEX

GENERAL MOTORS "J" BODY CARS

CAVALIER, J2000, CIMARRON

1982 Cimarron
W.B. 101.2″. Length 173.0″. 4 Dr. Curb Wgt. 2594 Lbs.

1982 Cavalier
W.B. 101.2″. Length 173.0″. 4 Dr. Curb Wgt. 2594 Lbs.

1982 J2000
W.B. 101.2″. Length 173.0″. 4 Dr. Curb Wgt. 2594 Lbs.

ENGINE SPECIFICATIONS

Year	Eng. V.I.N. Code	Engine No. Cyl. Disp.	Carb. BBL	Horsepower @ rpm	Torque @ rpm (ft. lbs.)	Bore and Stroke (in.)	Comp. Ratio	Fuel Pump Press. (p.s.i.)	Oil Pressure @ 2000 rpm
1982	G	4-112 (1.8L)	2	85 @ 5100	100 @ 2800	3.5 × 2.9	9.1:1	4.5-6.0	36

TUNE UP SPECIFICATIONS

Year	Eng. V.I.N. Code	Eng. No. Cyl Disp.	Spark Plugs Orig. Type	Gap (in.)	Distributor	IGNITION Timing① (deg. B.T.D.C.) Man. Trans.	Auto Trans.	Valves Intake Opens (deg. B.T.D.C.)	CARBURETION IDLE SPEED (r.p.m.) Manual Fed.	Cal.	Auto (in drive) Fed.	Cal.
1982	G	4-112 (1.8L)	R42TS	.045①	③	12°N	12°P	32	②	②	②	②

① Calif. A.T. (.035)
② Not adjustable, controlled by computer.
③ High energy ignition distributor, with electronic spark timing control.

ELECTRICAL SECTION

Idle Speed Control (ISC)

The idle speed control (ISC) is controlled by the electronic control module (ECM), which has the desired idle speed programmed in its memory. The ECM compares the actual idle speed from the engine rpm sensor (distributor TACH or EST reference signal) to the desired rpm reference in memory. When the two do not match, the ISC plunger is moved in or out. This automatically adjusts the throttle to hold an idle rpm independent of the engine loads.

An integral part of the ISC is the throttle contact switch. The position of the switch determines whether or not the ISC should control idle speed. When the throttle lever is resting against the ISC plunger, the switch contacts are closed, at which time the ECM moves the ISC to the programmed idle speed. When the throttle lever is not contacting the ISC plunger, the switch contacts are open; the ECM stops sending idle speed commands and the driver controls engine speed.

Fast Idle Adjustment

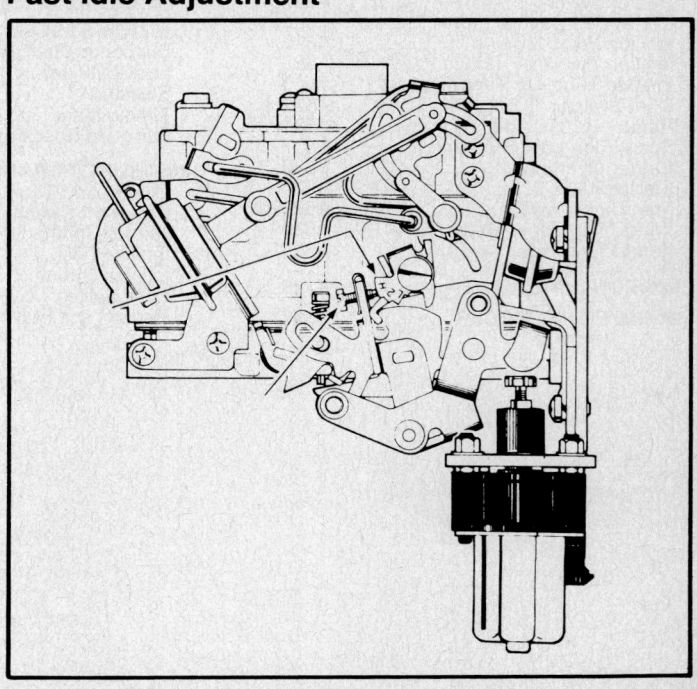

Replacement

1. With ignition off, disconnect wiring from ISC motor and remove two screws that attach the ISC bracket to the carburetor. Remove ISC and bracket assembly.

2. Install new ISC assembly to carburetor and re-attach throttle return spring and any other related parts removed during disassembly. Perform the "On-Car Speed Adjustments."

On-Car Speed Adjustments

NOTE   Before starting engine, place transmission selector lever in park or neutral, set parking brake, and block drive wheels.

When a new ISC assembly is installed, a base (minimum authority) and high (maximum authority) rpm speed check must be performed and adjustments made as required. These adjustments limit the low and high rpm speeds to the ECM. When making a low and high speed adjustment, the low speed adjustment is always made first. DO NOT use the ISC plunger to adjust curb idle speed as the idle speed is controlled by the ECM.

NOTE   Do not disconnect or connect ISC connector with ignition on as damage to the ECM may occur.

1. Connect tachometer (distributor side of tach filter, if used).
2. Connect dwell meter to mixture control (M/C) solenoid dwell lead. Remember to set dwell meter on the six cylinder scale, regardless of the engine being tested.
3. Turn A/C off.
4. Start engine and run until stabilized by entering "closed loop" (dwell meter needle starts to vary).
5. Turn ignition off.
6. Unplug connector from ISC motor.
7. Fully retract ISC plunger by applying 12 volts DC (battery voltage) to terminal "C" of the ISC motor connection and ground lead to terminal "D" of the ISC motor connection. It may be necessary to install jumper leads from the ISC motor in order to make proper connections.

NOTE   Do not apply battery voltage to motor longer than necessary to retract ISC plunger. Prolonged contact will damage motor. Also, never connect voltage source across terminals "A" and "B" as damage to the internal throttle contact switch will result.

8. Start engine and wait until dwell meter needle starts to vary, indicating "closed loop" operation.
9. With parking brake applied and drive wheels blocked, place transmission in Drive (Neutral, manual transmission models).
10. With ISC plunger fully retracted, adjust carburetor base (slow) idle stop screw to the specified rpm (see specifications). ISC plunger should not be left in full retracted position.
11. Place transmission in Park or Neutral and fully extend ISC plunger by applying 12 volts DC to terminal "D" of the ISC motor connection and ground lead to terminal "C" of the ISC motor connection.

Idle Motor

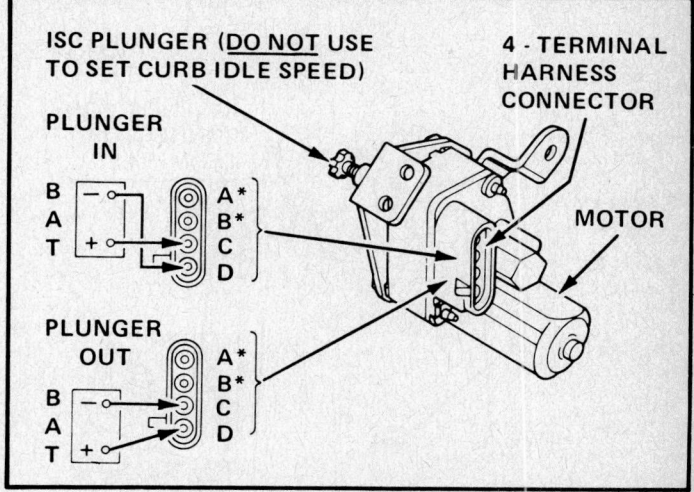

NOTE   Never connect voltage source across terminals "A" and "B" as damage to the internal throttle contact switch will result.

12. With ISC plunger fully extended, using Tool J-29831 or equivalent, turn ISC plunger to obtain ISC adjustment rpm (see specifications). Verify ISC adjustment rpm with voltage applied to motor; motor will ratchet in and out.
Auto trans. only: place transmission in Drive and readjust ISC plunger to ISC adjustment rpm.
13. Place transmission in Park or Neutral and turn ignition off. Disconnect 12 volt DC power source, jumper leads, ground lead, tachometer, and dwell meter.
14. Reconnect four terminal harness connector to ISC motor.
15. "Tricking" the ISC motor as described will cause the "Check Engine" light to come on and an ISC motor trouble code to be set. By restoring the system to normal operation, the light will go out, but the trouble code will continue to be stored as an intermittent problem. In this case, it will be necessary to clear the diagnostic trouble code.

Fast Idle Adjustment

1. Prepare the car for adjustments as specified on the underhood emission label. Place the transmission in Park or Neutral.
2. Place the fast idle screw on the highest step of the fast idle cam.
3. Turn the fast idle screw in or out to obtain the specified fast idle speed.

Ignition Timing

Ignition timing for this engine should be accomplished using the "averaging" method in which the timing of each cylinder can be brought into closer agreement with the base timing specification.

The averaging method involves the use of a double

A521

Ignition Distributor

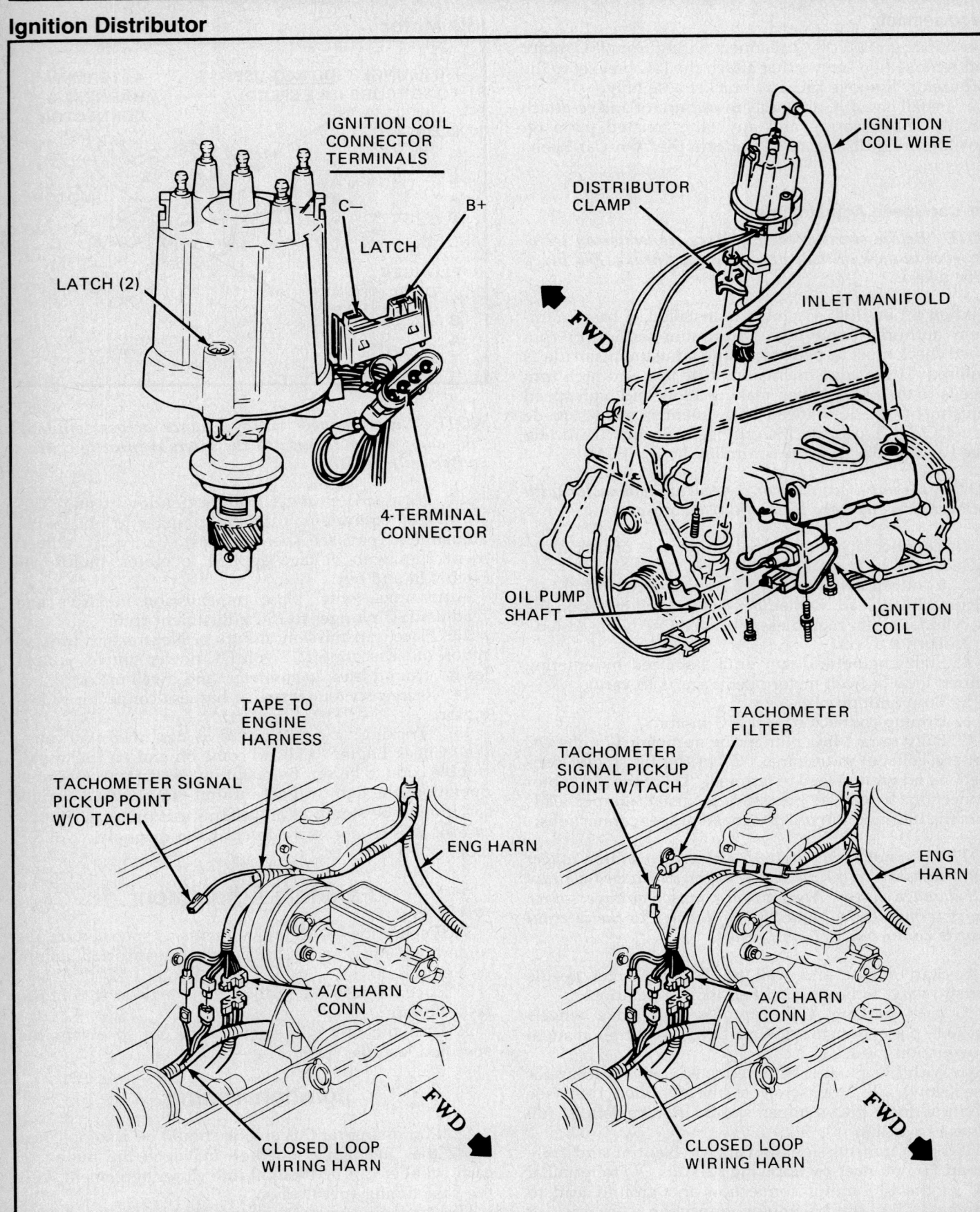

IGNITION COIL CONNECTOR TERMINALS

C—

B+

LATCH

LATCH (2)

4-TERMINAL CONNECTOR

IGNITION COIL WIRE

DISTRIBUTOR CLAMP

FWD

INLET MANIFOLD

OIL PUMP SHAFT

IGNITION COIL

TACHOMETER SIGNAL PICKUP POINT W/O TACH

TAPE TO ENGINE HARNESS

ENG HARN

A/C HARN CONN

CLOSED LOOP WIRING HARN

FWD

TACHOMETER FILTER

TACHOMETER SIGNAL PICKUP POINT W/TACH

ENG HARN

A/C HARN CONN

CLOSED LOOP WIRING HARN

FWD

Ignition Timing Using Averaging Method

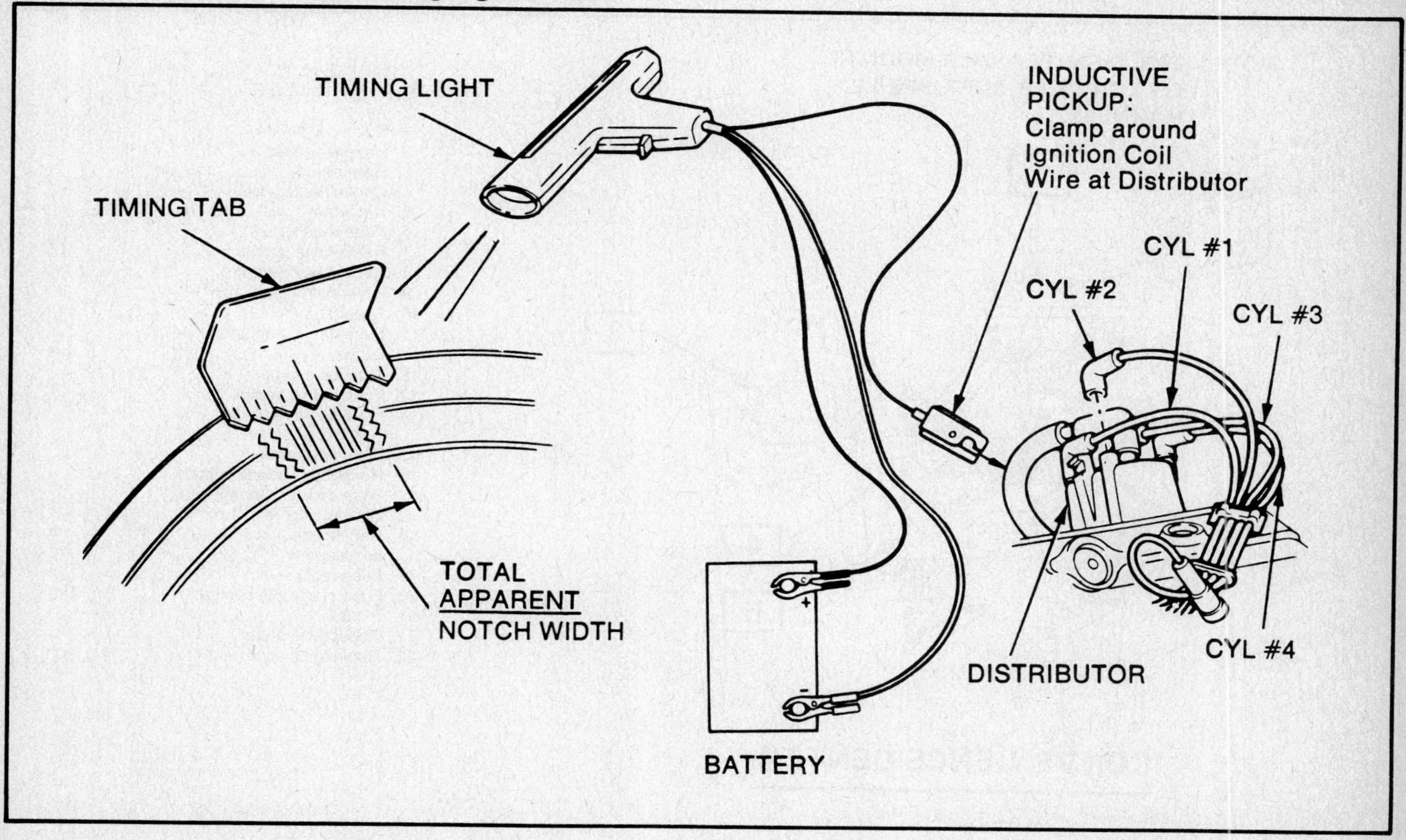

TIMING LIGHT

TIMING TAB

INDUCTIVE PICKUP: Clamp around Ignition Coil Wire at Distributor

CYL #1

CYL #2

CYL #3

CYL #4

DISTRIBUTOR

TOTAL APPARENT NOTCH WIDTH

BATTERY

notched crankshaft pulley. When timing the engine, the coil wire, instead of the No. 1 plug wire, should be used to trigger the timing light. The notch for the No. 1 cylinder is scribed across all three edges of the double sheave pulley. Another notch located 180 degrees away from the No. 1 cylinder notch is scribed only across the center section of the pulley to make it distinguishable from the No. 1 cylinder notch.

Since the trigger signal for the timing light is picked up at the coil wire, each spark firing results in a flash from the timing light. A slight jiggling of the timing notch may be apparent since each cylinder firing is being displayed. Optimum timing of all cylinders is accomplished by centering the total apparent notch width about the correct timing specification.

The following procedure should be used to correctly time this engine. A magnetic timing pickup will not work and cannot be used with this procedure.

1. On vehicles with electronic spark timing, it will be necessary to disconnect the four terminal EST connector at the distributor to cause the engine to operate the bypass timing mode.

2. Follow manufacturer's instructions for connecting the timing light to the appropriate power source.

3. Clamp timing light inductive pickup around the high tension coil wire. It will be necessary to peel back the protective plastic cover on the wire in order to install the timing light inductive pickup.

Double Sheave Pulley Timing Notches

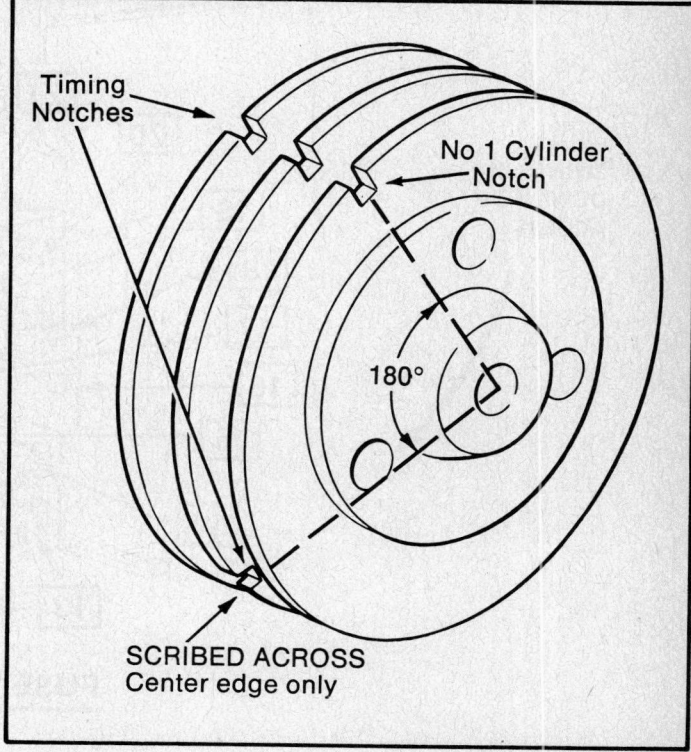

Timing Notches

No 1 Cylinder Notch

180°

SCRIBED ACROSS Center edge only

GENERAL MOTORS "J" BODY CARS

CAVALIER, J2000, CIMARRON

Fuse Block

NOTE: DIR. SIGN. FLASHER MOUNTS
ON LOWER I.P. SUPT. SEE I.P.
HARNESS.

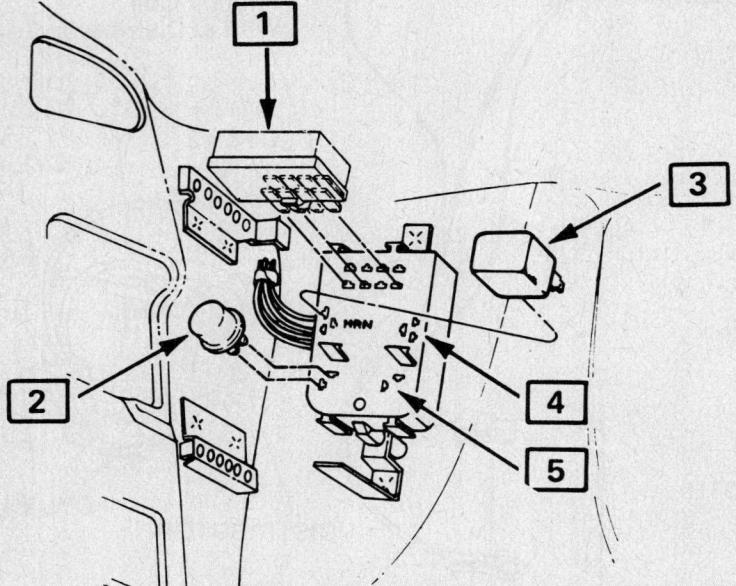

CONVENIENCE CENTER

1. Buzzer assembly
2. Hazard flasher
3. Horn relay
4. Choke heater relay
5. Not used
6. Fuse wipers
7. Receptacle lamps
8. Receptacle ignition
9. Fuse instrument lights
10. Fuse gauges
11. Fuse turn signal and back-up lamps
12. Fuse stop lamp
13. Fuse choke heater
14. Fuse heater and air conditioner
15. Fuse tail lamps
16. Receptacle power window
17. Fuse courtesy lamps and cigarette lighter
18. Receptacle power accessories
19. Fuse radio
20. Fuse electronic control module
21. Receptacle battery
22. Receptacle accessory

SWING
DOWN FOR
ACCESS

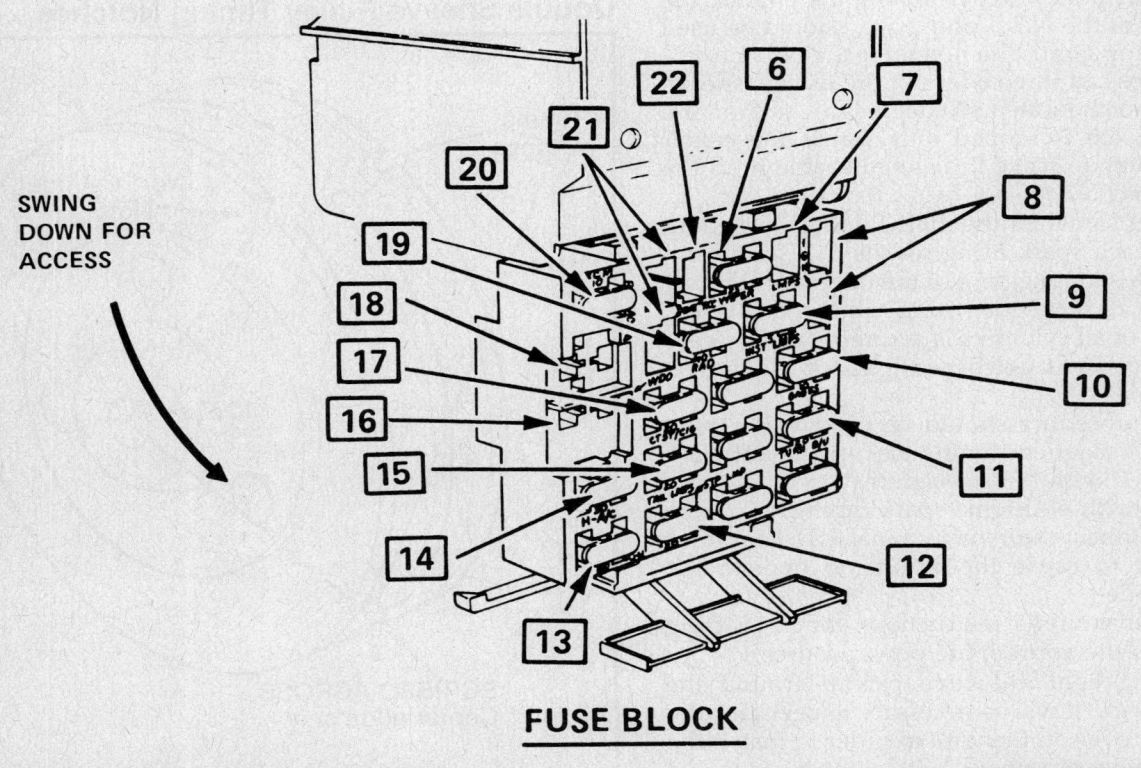

FUSE BLOCK

A524

4. Loosen the distributor clamp nut slightly so that the distributor may be rotated as necessary to adjust timing.

5. Start the engine and aim the timing light at the timing tab. A slight jiggling of the pulley notch may appear due to the fact that each cylinder firing is being displayed. The apparent notch width cannot be reduced by timing adjustment.

6. Adjust the position of the distributor by rotating in the direction of advance or retard as necessary to center the total apparent notch width about the correct timing specification. This insures that the average cylinder timing is as close to the specification as possible.

7. When the adjustment is complete, shut off the engine and tighten down the distributor clamp nut, taking care not to disturb the position of the distributor as adjusted. The timing should be rechecked after tightening. Reinstall the distributor four terminal EST connector and the protective plastic cover on the coil wire.

Distributor

Removal and Installation

1. Disconnect negative battery cable.
2. Remove air cleaner.
3. Remove distributor cap by rotating two latches counterclockwise.
4. Disconnect AIR pipe to exhaust manifold hose at AIR Management valve.
5. Remove rear engine lift bracket bolt and nut from the stud and move assembly aside for access.
6. Mark position of distributor in block and remove distributor hold down nut and clamp.
7. Rotate distributor to disengage from gear drive and remove the distributor.
8. Installation is the reverse.

Starter

Removal

1. Disconnect negative battery lead at battery.
2. From beneath the car, remove the solenoid wires and battery cable.
3. Remove rear motor support bracket.
4. Remove A/C compressor support rod (where equipped).
5. Remove two starter motor-to-engine bolts, and remove starter.

Installation

To replace, reverse the above procedure. Replace any shims that were removed.

Headlight Switch

Removal

1. Disconnect negative battery cable.

Starter Motor Mounting

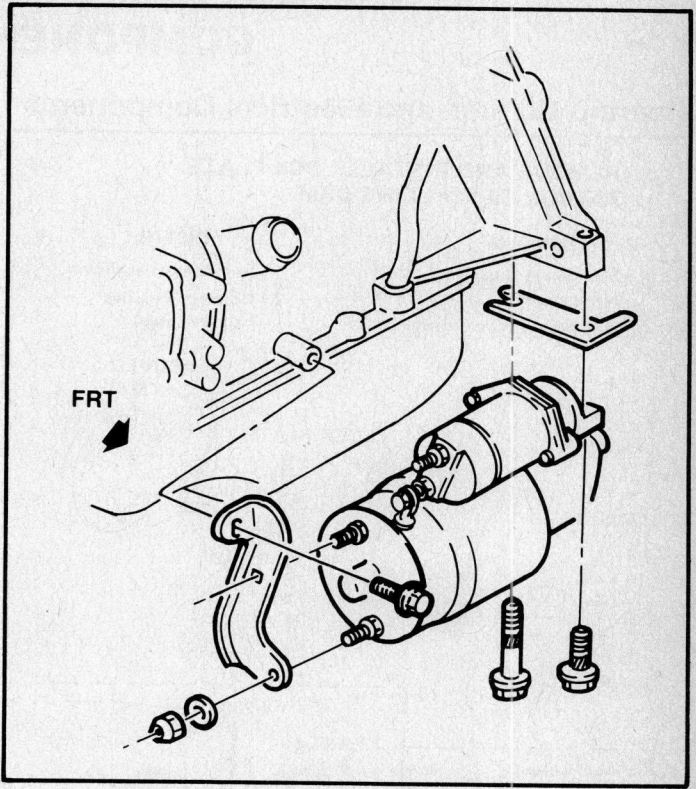

FRT

2. Pull knob out fully. Remove knob from rod by depressing retaining clip with paper clip from underside of knob.
3. Remove trimplate.
4. Remove switch by removing nut, rotating switch 180 degrees, then tilting forward and pulling out. Disconnect wire harness.

Installation

Reverse removal procedures.

Headlight Switch

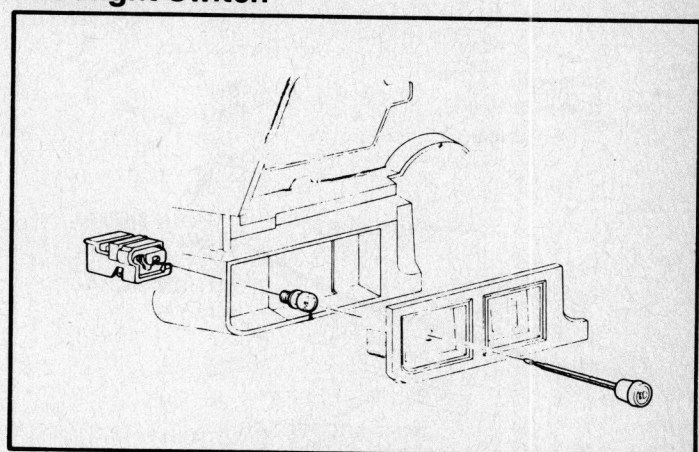

STEERING COLUMN AND ELECTRICAL COMPONENTS SECTION

Steering Column and Electrical Components

1. REMOVE AND INSTALL LOCK PLATE AND/OR CANCELLING CAM

REMOVE

1. Disconnect negative battery cable.
2. Remove parts as shown.

INSTALL

1. Install parts as shown.
2. Connect negative battery cable.

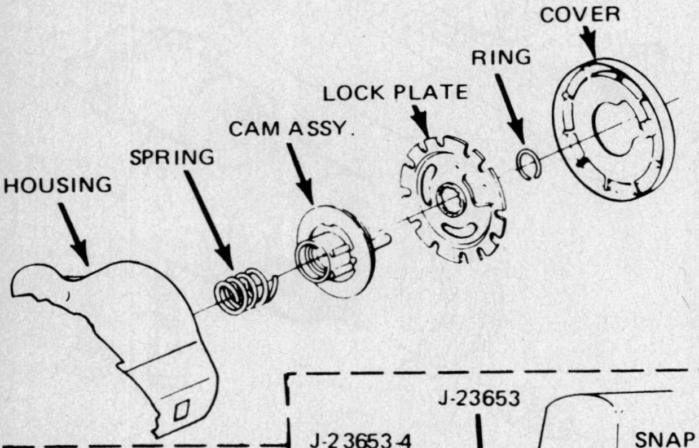

COVER · RING · LOCK PLATE · CAM ASSY. · SPRING · HOUSING

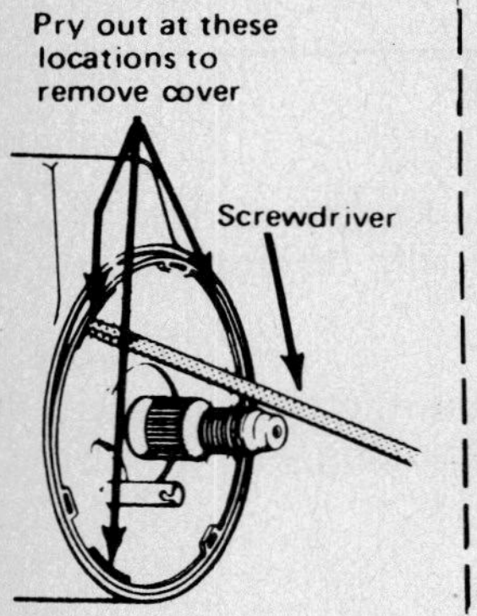

Pry out at these locations to remove cover

Screwdriver

REMOVE COVER

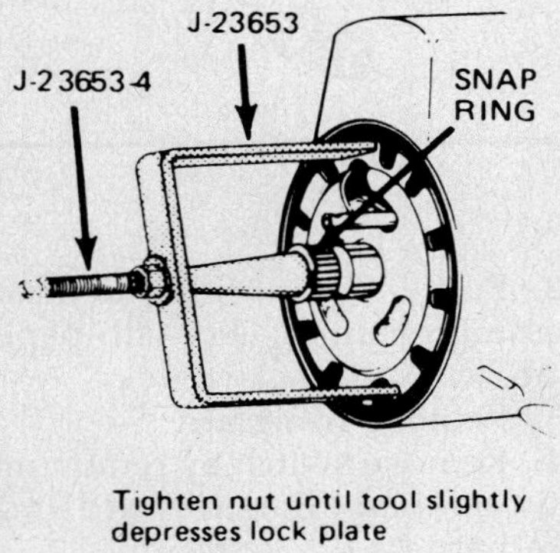

J-23653-4 · J-23653 · SNAP RING

Tighten nut until tool slightly depresses lock plate

REMOVE AND INSTALL SNAP RING

2. REMOVE AND INSTALL TURN SIGNAL SWITCH

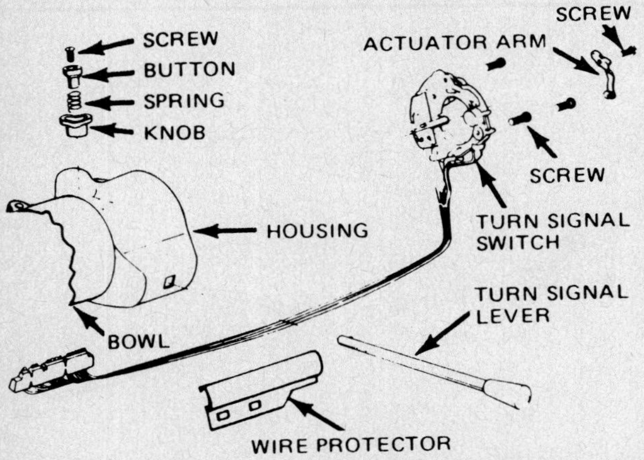

SCREW · BUTTON · SPRING · KNOB · ACTUATOR ARM · SCREW · SCREW · TURN SIGNAL SWITCH · HOUSING · TURN SIGNAL LEVER · BOWL · WIRE PROTECTOR

3. REMOVE AND INSTALL IGNITION LOCK AND KEY WARNING BUZZER

REMOVE

1. Turn lock to "RUN" position and remove key warning buzzer.
2. Remove parts as shown.

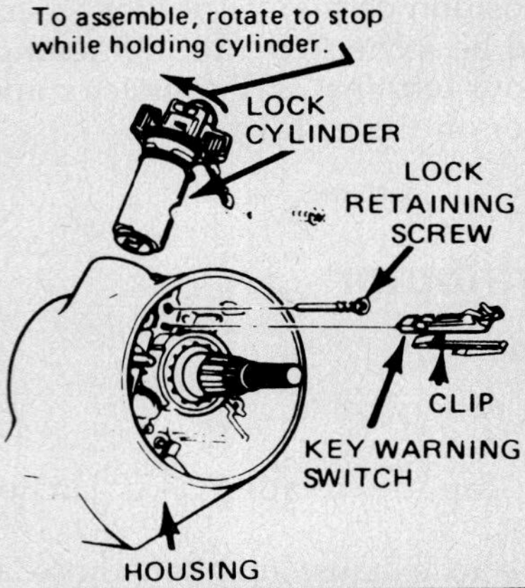

To assemble, rotate to stop while holding cylinder.

INSTALL

1. Install lock cylinder.
2. Turn lock to "RUN" position and install key warning buzzer switch.

LOCK CYLINDER · LOCK RETAINING SCREW · CLIP · KEY WARNING SWITCH · HOUSING

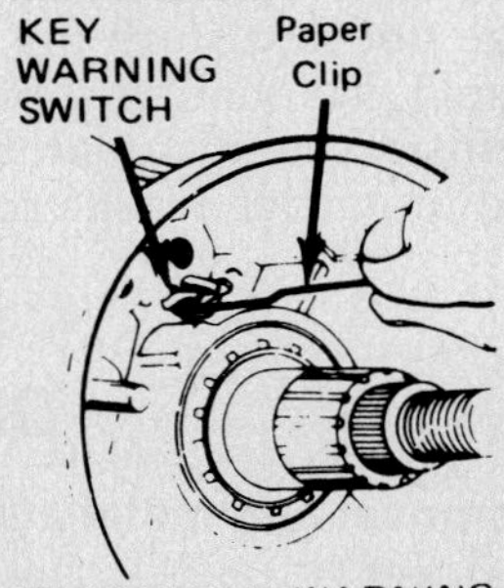

KEY WARNING SWITCH · Paper Clip · REMOVE KEY WARNING BUZZER SWITCH

4. REMOVE AND INSTALL COVER AND WIPER SWITCH

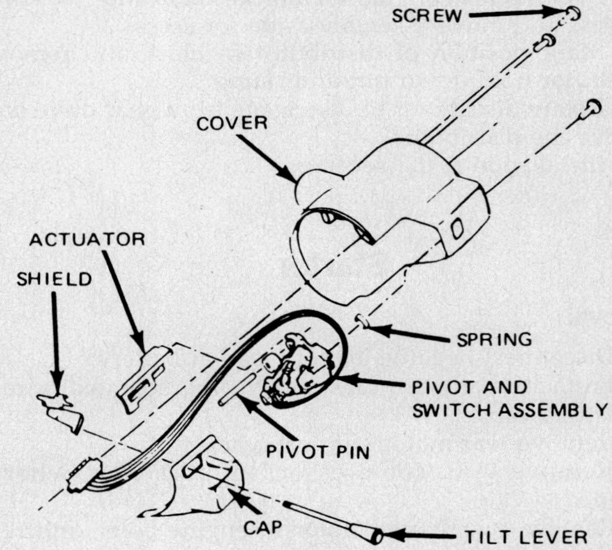

SCREW · COVER · ACTUATOR · SHIELD · SPRING · PIVOT AND SWITCH ASSEMBLY · PIVOT PIN · CAP · TILT LEVER

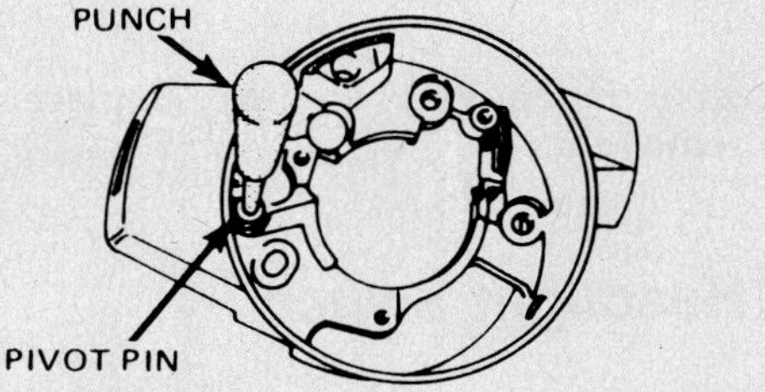

PUNCH · PIVOT PIN · REMOVE AND INSTALL PIVOT ASSEMBLY

Key Release Tilt Wheel Steering Column

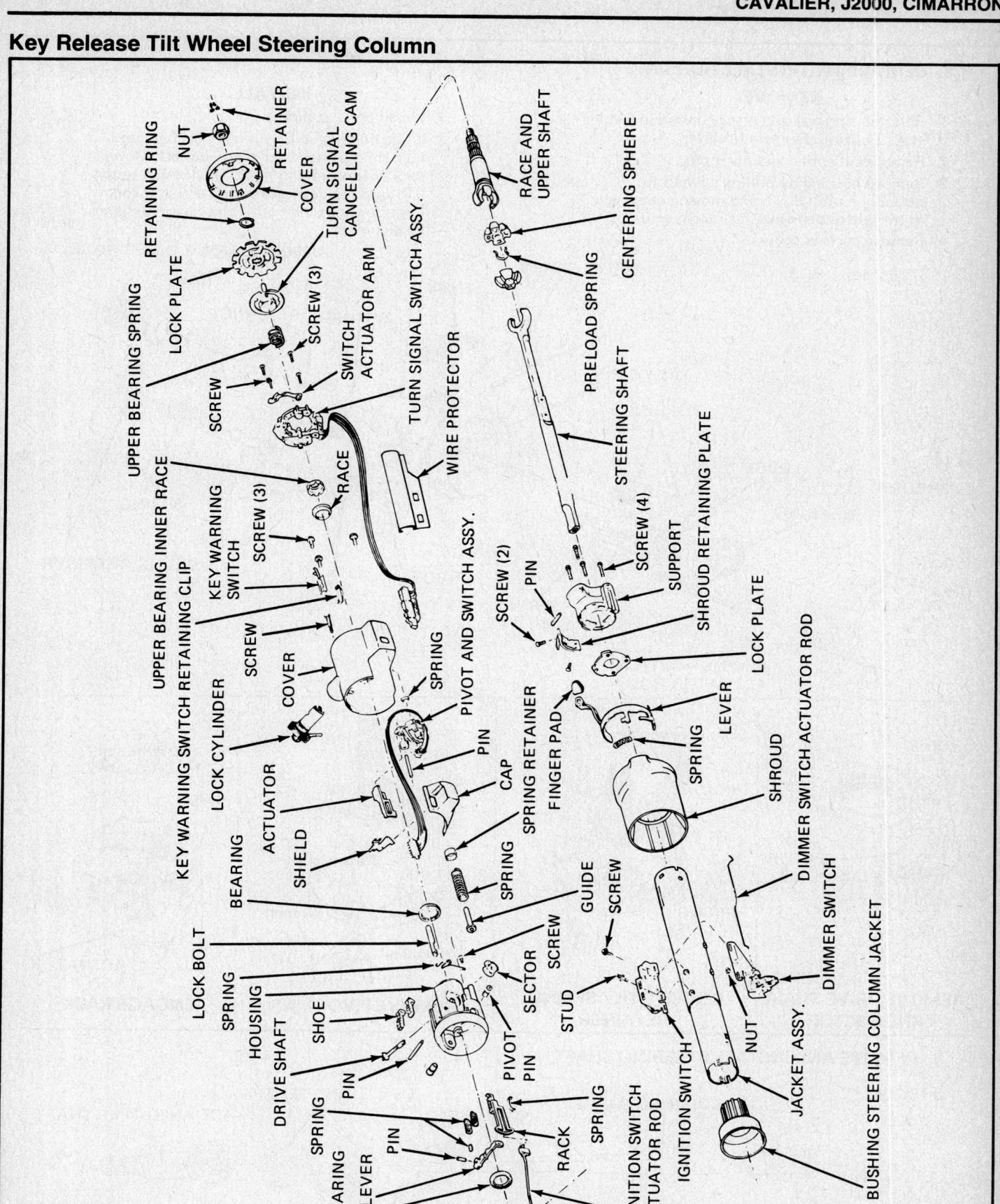

5. REMOVE AND INSTALL HOUSING

REMOVE

1. Reinstall tilt lever and place column in full "UP" position. Remove tilt lever.
2. Remove tilt spring and pivot pins.
3. Remove housing by pulling upward to extend rack full down and moving housing to the left to disengage rack from actuator.
4. Remove parts as shown.

INSTALL

1. Install parts as shown.
2. While holding up on tilt lever to disengage lock shoes install over steering shaft. Move rack downward and hold. Tip housing to the left until rack engages pin on actuator rod. Push housing down until pivot pin holes are in alignment.

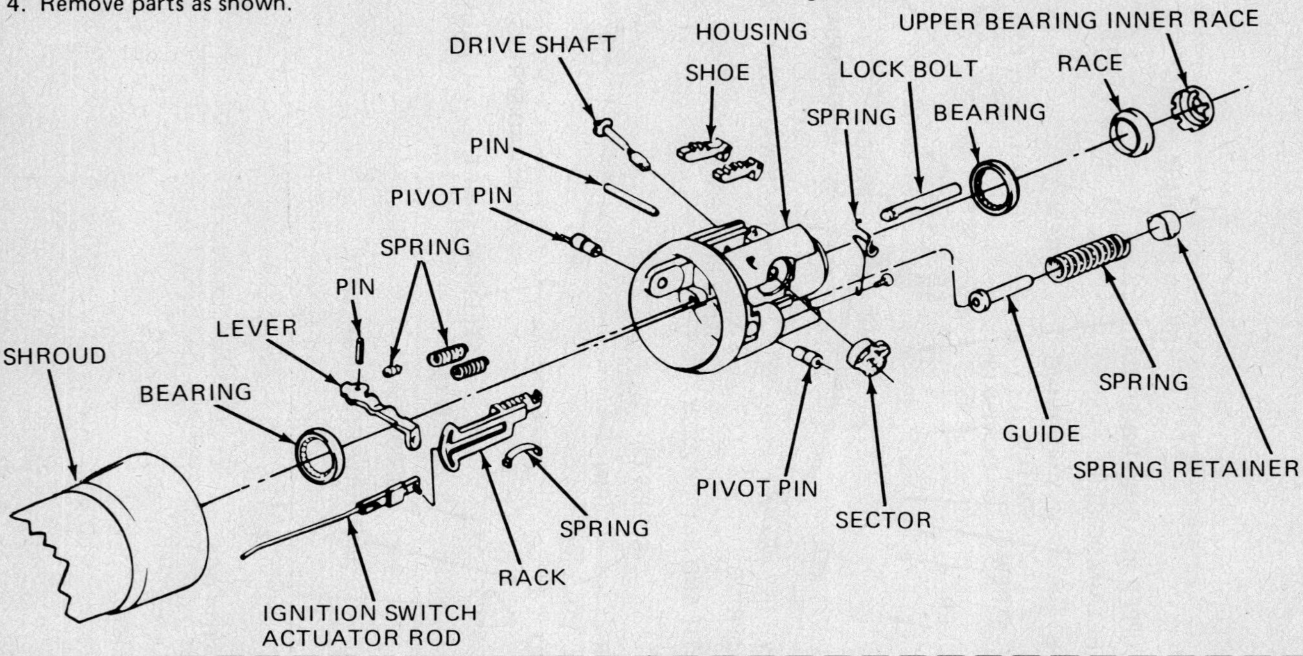

DRIVE SHAFT • HOUSING • UPPER BEARING INNER RACE

SHOE • LOCK BOLT • RACE

PIN • SPRING • BEARING

PIVOT PIN

SPRING

PIN

LEVER

SHROUD

BEARING

SPRING

RACK

IGNITION SWITCH ACTUATOR ROD

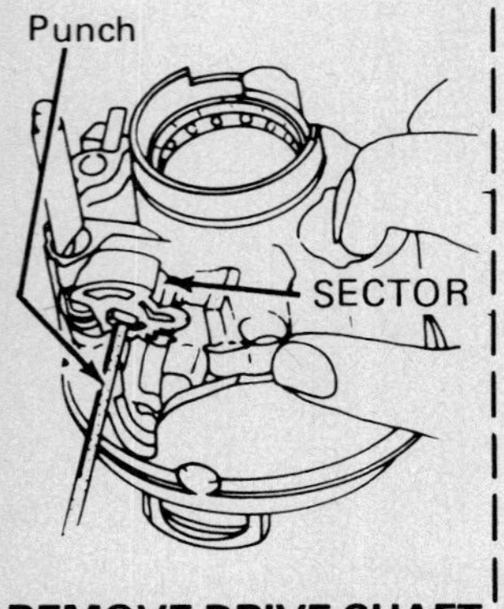

PIVOT PIN • SECTOR • GUIDE • SPRING • SPRING RETAINER

REMOVE DRIVE SHAFT AND SECTOR — Punch — SECTOR

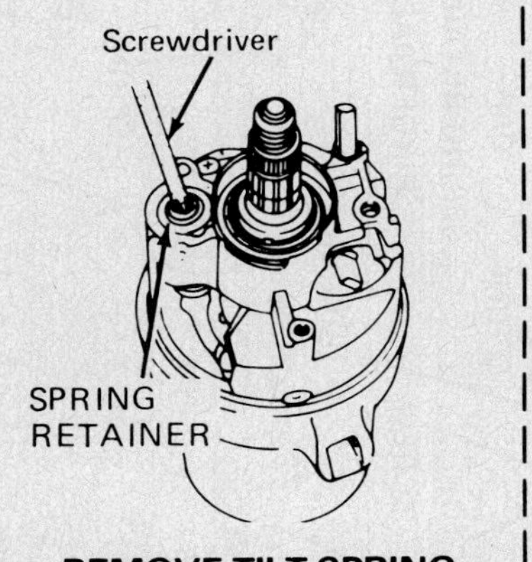

REMOVE TILT SPRING RETAINER — Screwdriver — SPRING RETAINER

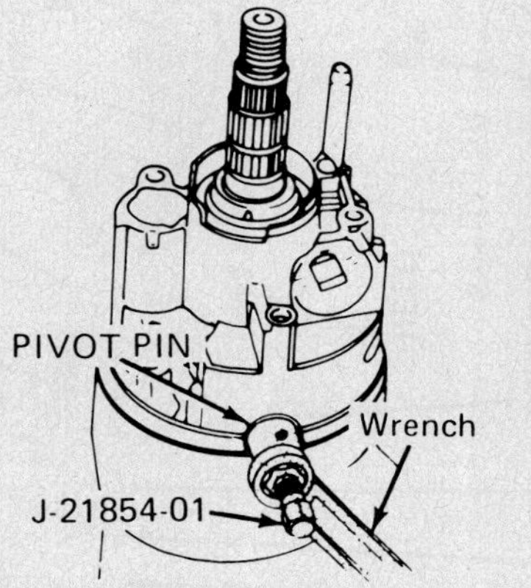

REMOVE PIVOT PINS — PIVOT PIN — Wrench — J-21854-01

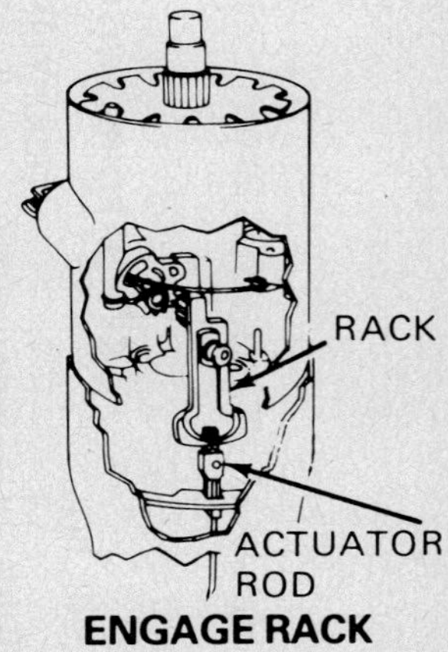

ENGAGE RACK — RACK — ACTUATOR ROD

6. REMOVE AND INSTALL STEERING SHAFT

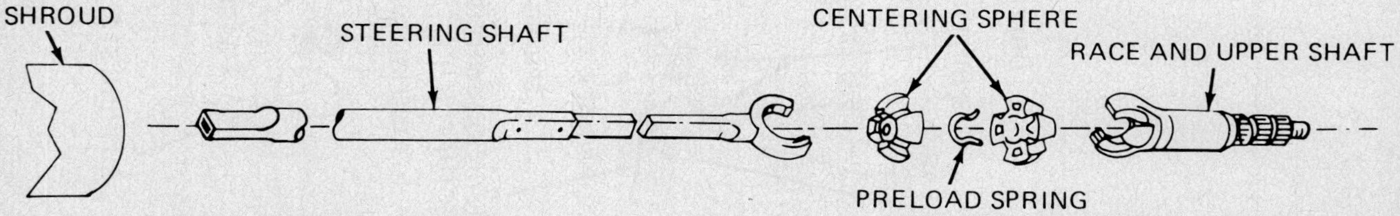

SHROUD

STEERING SHAFT

CENTERING SPHERE

RACE AND UPPER SHAFT

PRELOAD SPRING

7. REMOVE AND INSTALL IGNITION AND DIMMER SWITCH

REMOVE

1. Remove parts as shown.

INSTALL

1. Install parts as shown.
2. Position rod in slider hole and install ignition switch. Install lower stud and tighten to 3.9 N·m (35 in. lbs.)
3. Install dimmer switch and depress switch slightly to insert 3/32" drill. Force switch up to remove lash, then tighten screw, and nut to 3.9 N·m (35 in. lbs.).
4. Place shifter in neutral and install shift lever.

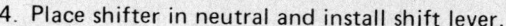
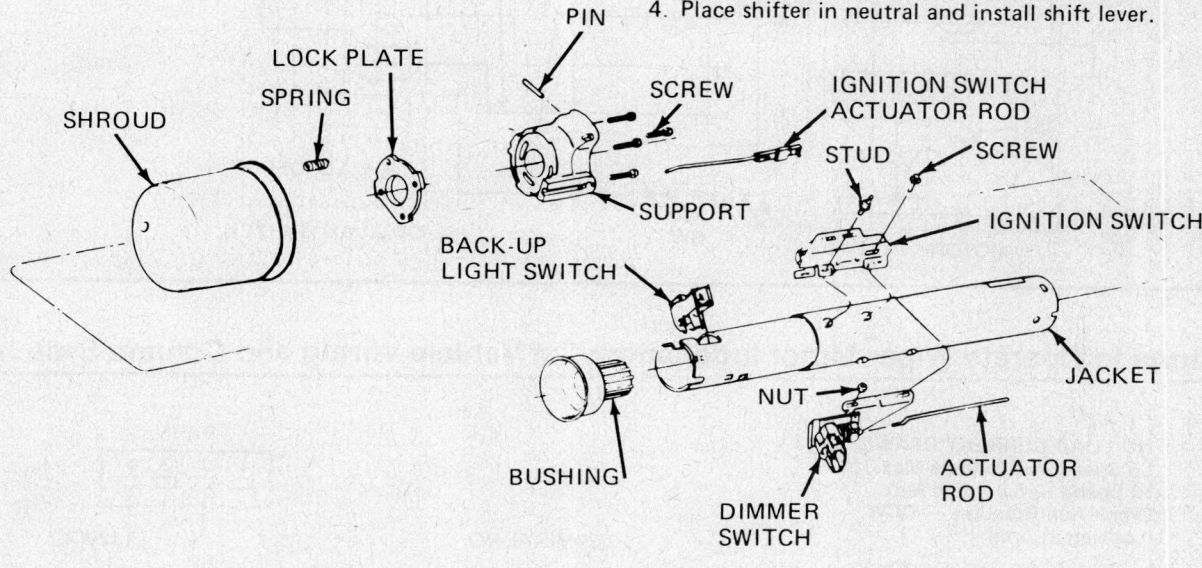

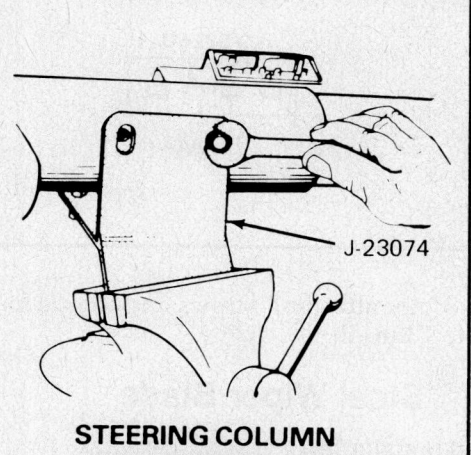

STEERING COLUMN HOLDING FIXTURE

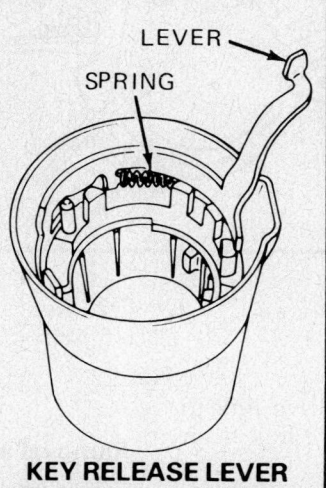

KEY RELEASE LEVER

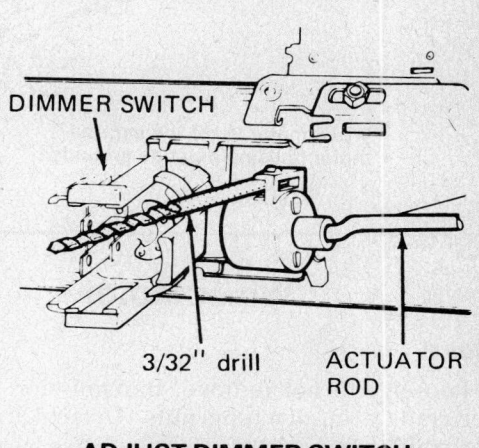

ADJUST DIMMER SWITCH

WIPER AND HEATER SECTION

Windshield Wiper Motor and Switch Circuits Diagram

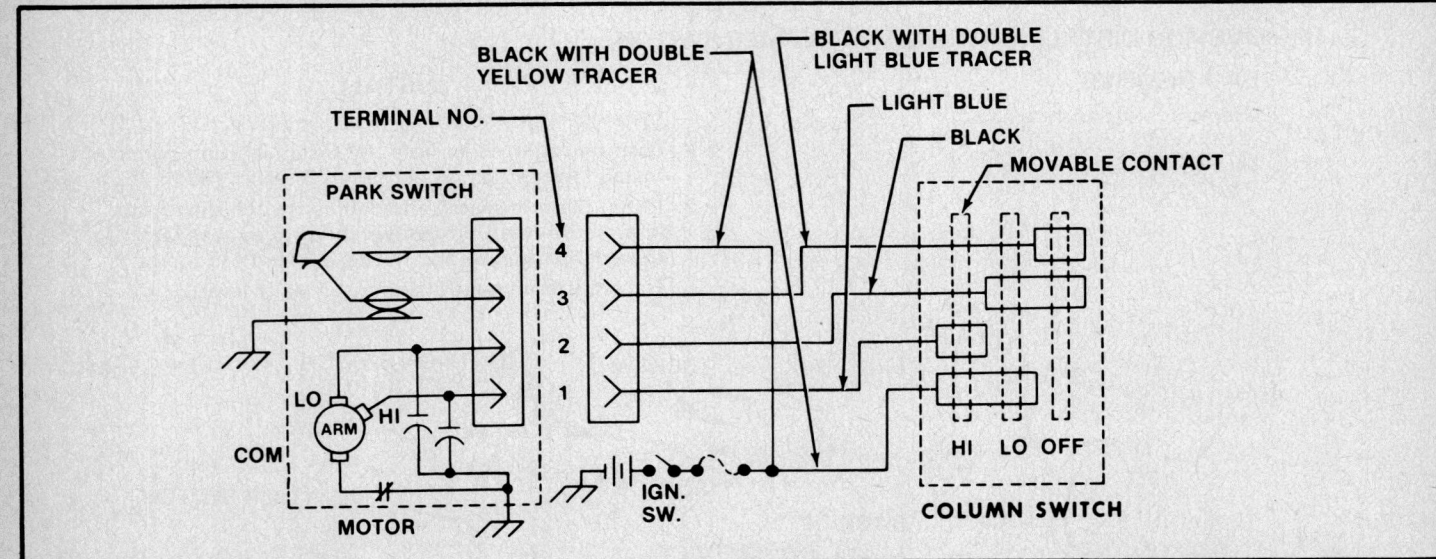

Connections to Operate Wiper Motor Independent of Vehicle Wiring and Column Switch

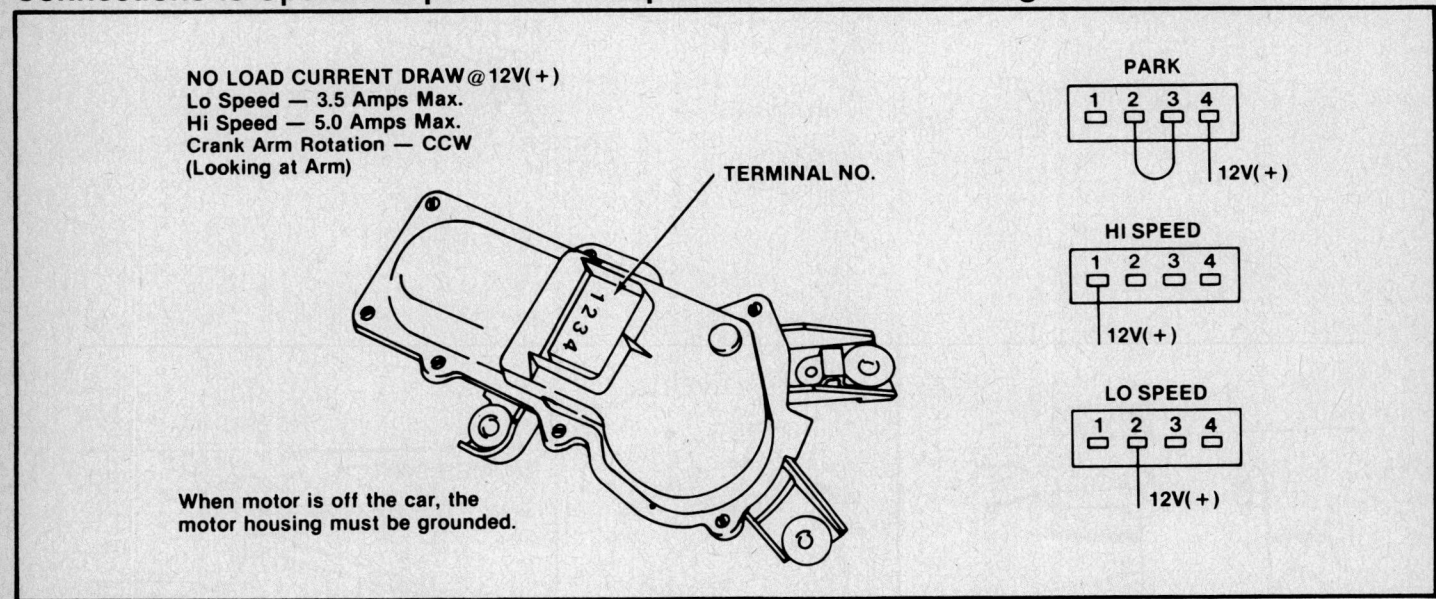

NO LOAD CURRENT DRAW @ 12V(+)
Lo Speed — 3.5 Amps Max.
Hi Speed — 5.0 Amps Max.
Crank Arm Rotation — CCW
(Looking at Arm)

When motor is off the car, the motor housing must be grounded.

Wiper Motor

Removal

1. Loosen, do not remove, transmission drive link to motor crank arm attaching nuts. Detach drive link from motor crank arm.
2. Disconnect electrical leads.
3. Rotate motor up and outward to remove.

Installation

1. Install motor by placing crank arm through opening in body.

2. Replace motor attaching screws and torque to 4.5 to 6.5 N•m (51 to 73 in.-lb.).

Steel Wiper Blade

Removal and Installation

Two methods are used to retain the steel wiper blades to the wiper arms. One method uses a press-type release tab. When the release tab is depressed, the blade assembly can be separated from the arm. The other method uses a coil spring retainer. A screwdriver must be inserted on top of the spring and the spring pushed down-

Plastic Wiper Blade Assembly

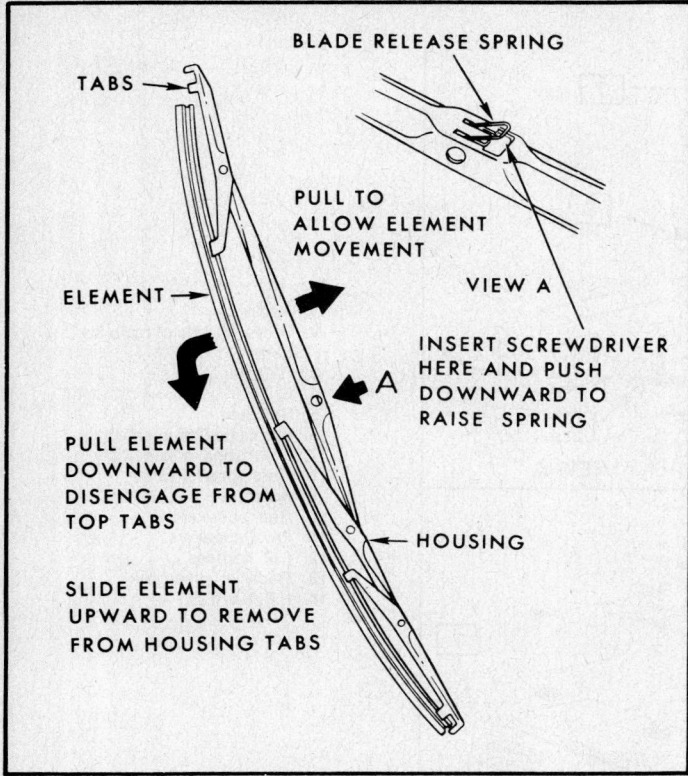

Plastic Wiper Blade

Removal and Installation

To remove the plastic wiper blade, insert a screwdriver under the retaining spring and then push downward on screwdriver handle to raise spring. the blade assembly can then be separated from the arm.

To install the blade assembly to the arm, insert blade over pin at top of arm and press until spring retainer engages groove in pin. The blade element is retained by tabs on the blade housing.

To remove the blade element from the housing, the housing must be pulled backwards to disengage tab; the element can then be slid out of the blade assembly.

Radio

Removal

1. Disconnect the negative battery cable.
2. Remove instrument panel trimplate.
3. Check right side of radio to determine whether a nut or stud is used for side retention. If a nut is used, remove the hush panel, and loosen nut from below on cars without A/C. On A/C cars, remove the hush panel, A/C duct, and A/C control head for access to nut. Loosen nut enough to pull radio out. Do not remove nut.

If a rubber stud is used, go to Step 4

4. Remove two radio bracket-to-instrument panel attaching screws, then pull radio forward far enough to disconnect wiring and antenna. Remove radio.

ward. The blade assembly can then be separated from the arm.

To install the blade assembly to the arm, insert blade over pin at tip of arm and press until spring retainer or clip engages groove in pin.

Two methods are used to retain the rubber element in the steel blade assembly. One method uses a press-type button. When the button is depressed, the blade element can be slid off the blade assembly. The other method uses a spring-type retainer clip in the end of the steel blade. When the retainer clip is squeezed together, the blade element can be slid out of the blade assembly.

Steel Wiper Blade Assemblies

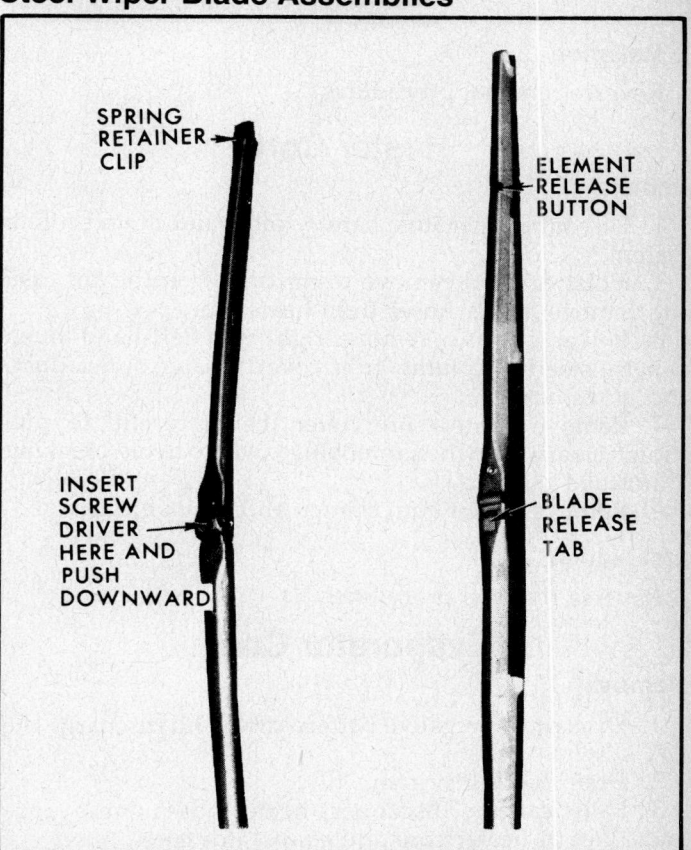

Wiper Motor Installation

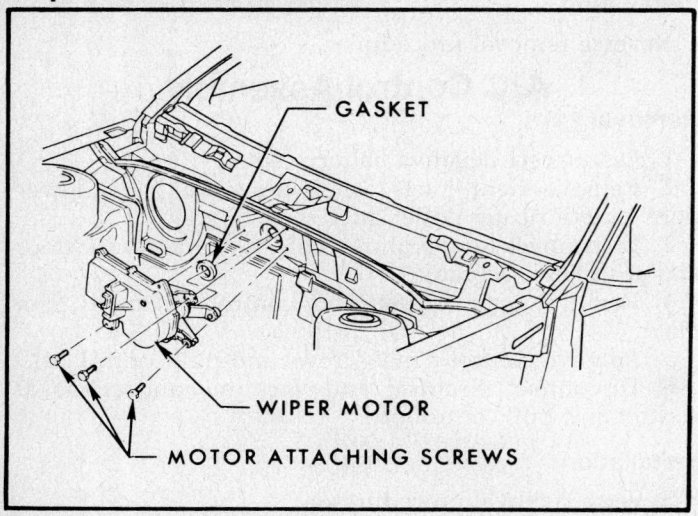

Radio and Front Speakers

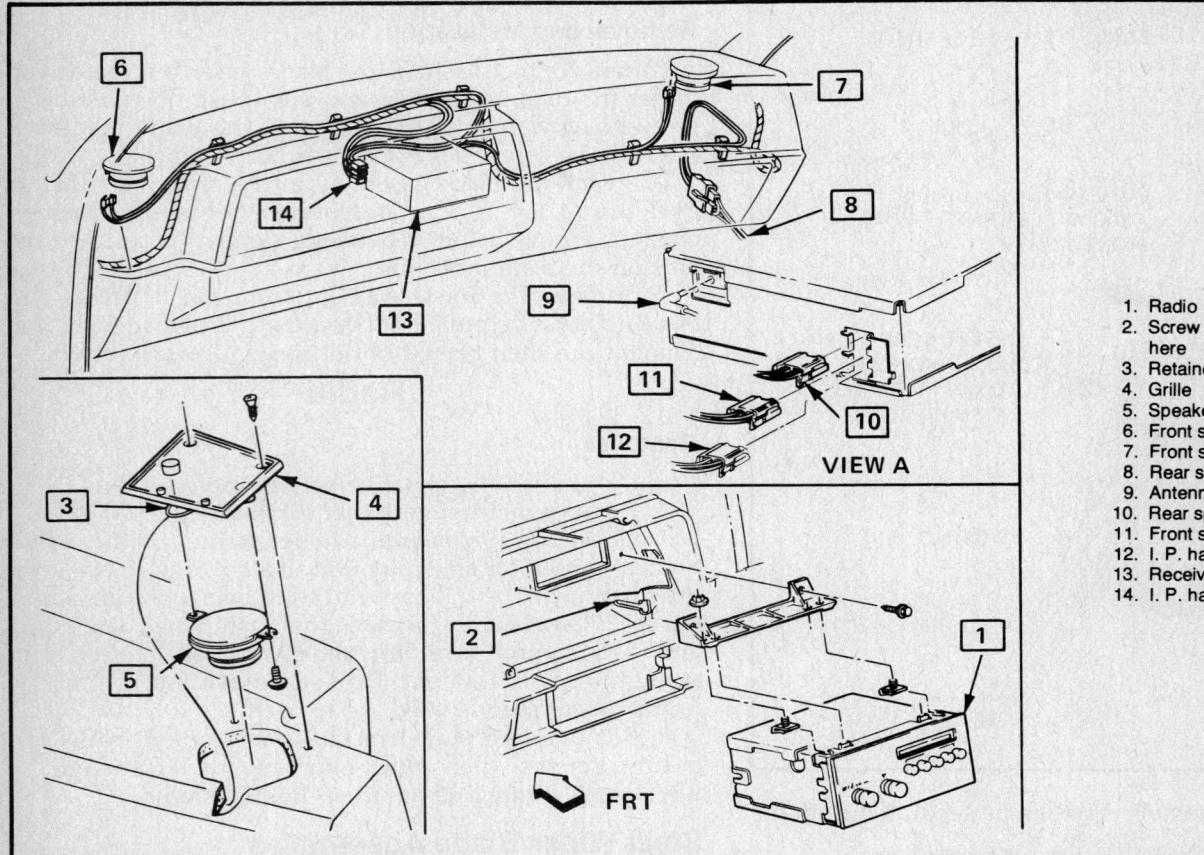

1. Radio
2. Screw on side of radio fits here
3. Retainer
4. Grille
5. Speaker
6. Front speaker assembly
7. Front speaker assembly
8. Rear speaker wire
9. Antenna
10. Rear speakers
11. Front speakers
12. I. P. harness
13. Receiver assembly
14. I. P. harness

VIEW A

FRT

Installation

Reverse removal procedures.

Heater Core

Removal

1. Disconnect negative battery cable and drain cooling system.
2. Hoist car and remove drain tube from heater case and remove heater hoses from heater core.
3. Lower car and remove right and left-hand hush panels, steering column trim cover, heater outlet duct, and glove box.
4. Remove heater core cover, being careful to pull straight rearward when removing cover to avoid breaking drain tube.
5. Remove heater core clamps and remove core.

Installation

Reverse removal procedures.

Evaporator Core

Removal

1. Disconnect negative battery cable and discharge the A/C system.
2. Drain cooling system.
3. Hoist car and disconnect heater hoses and evaporator lines at heater core and evaporator core.

4. Remove drain tube.
5. Remove right and left-hand hush panels, steering column trim cover, heater outlet, and glove box.
6. Remove heater core cover, pulling straight rearward on cover to avoid breaking drain tube.
7. Remove heater core clamps and remove heater core.
8. Remove screws holding defroster vacuum actuator to module case.
9. Remove evaporator cover and remove evaporator core.

Installation

Reverse removal procedures.

A/C Control Assembly

Removal

1. Disconnect negative battery cable.
2. Remove right hush panel, glove box, and lower right side of heater outlet duct.
3. Disconnect temperature cable at temperature door and at vacuum actuator.
4. Remove cigar lighter and control assembly trim plate.
5. Remove control panel screws and pull control out.
6. Disconnect electrical and vacuum connections at control and pull control out.

Installation

Reverse removal procedures.

Heater Evaporator Assembly, Blower Assembly and Air Inlet Assembly Installation

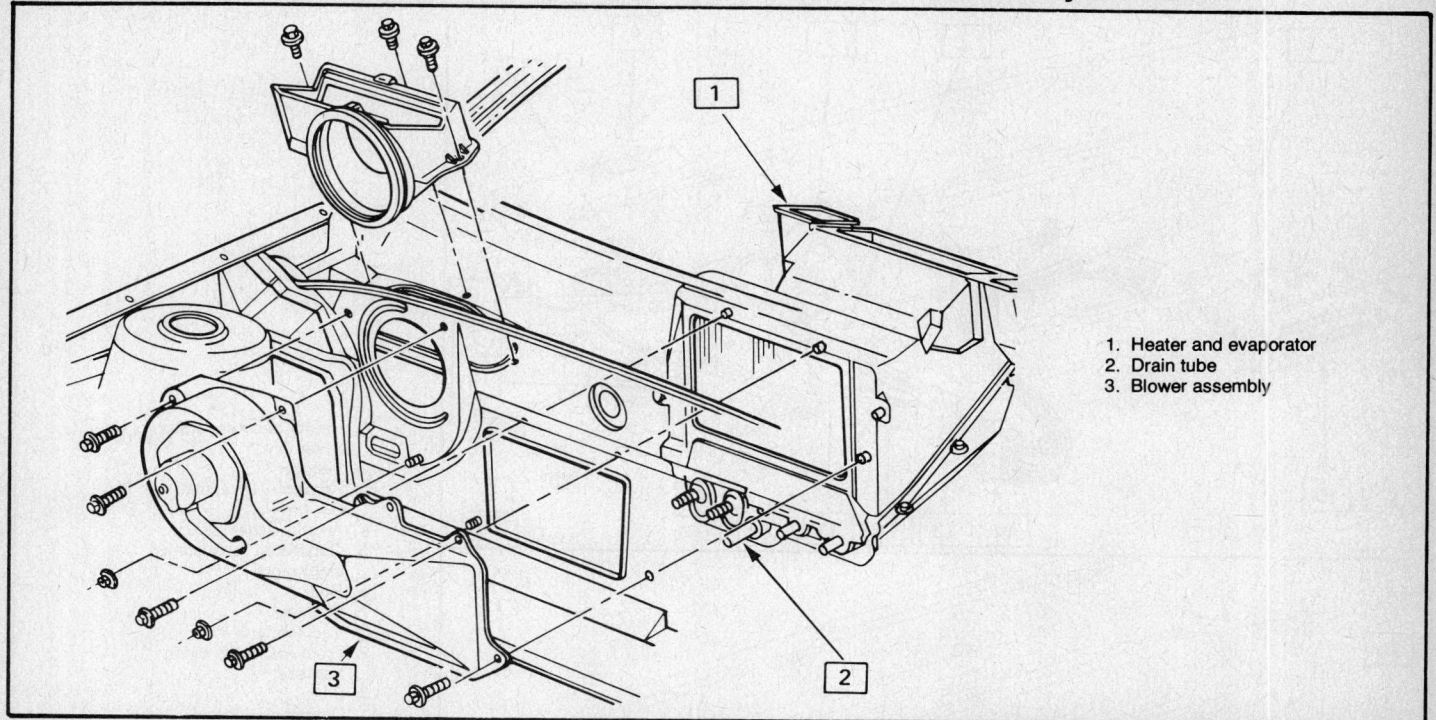

1. Heater and evaporator
2. Drain tube
3. Blower assembly

When removing the heater and evaporator assembly, pull the assembly straight toward the interior of the car until the plastic drain tube clears the cowl. If the assembly is tilted in any direction before the tube clears the cowl, the tube may break.

Instrument Panel and Trimplates

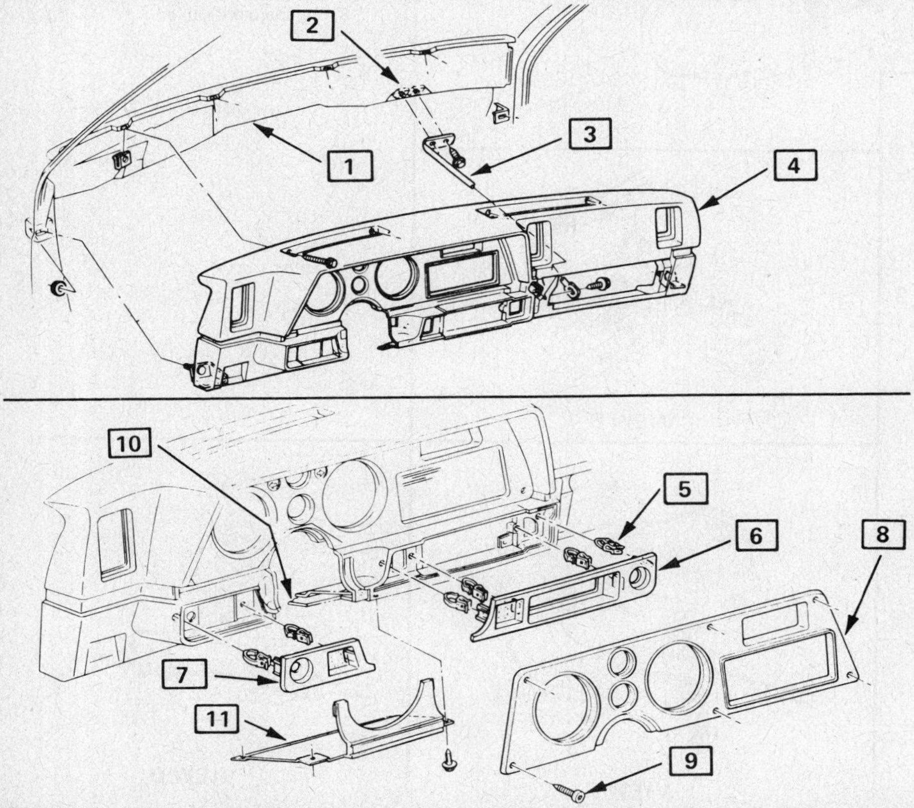

1. Dash panel
2. Weld nuts
3. Center reinforcement
4. Pad assembly
5. Snap-in clips
6. Right-hand lower I.P. trim plate
7. Left-hand lower I.P. trim plate
8. I.P. trim plate
9. Torx screw
10. Hush panel
11. Steering column trim cover

GENERAL MOTORS "J" BODY CARS

CAVALIER, J2000, CIMARRON

Interior Vacuum Harness and Temperature Control Cable Routing

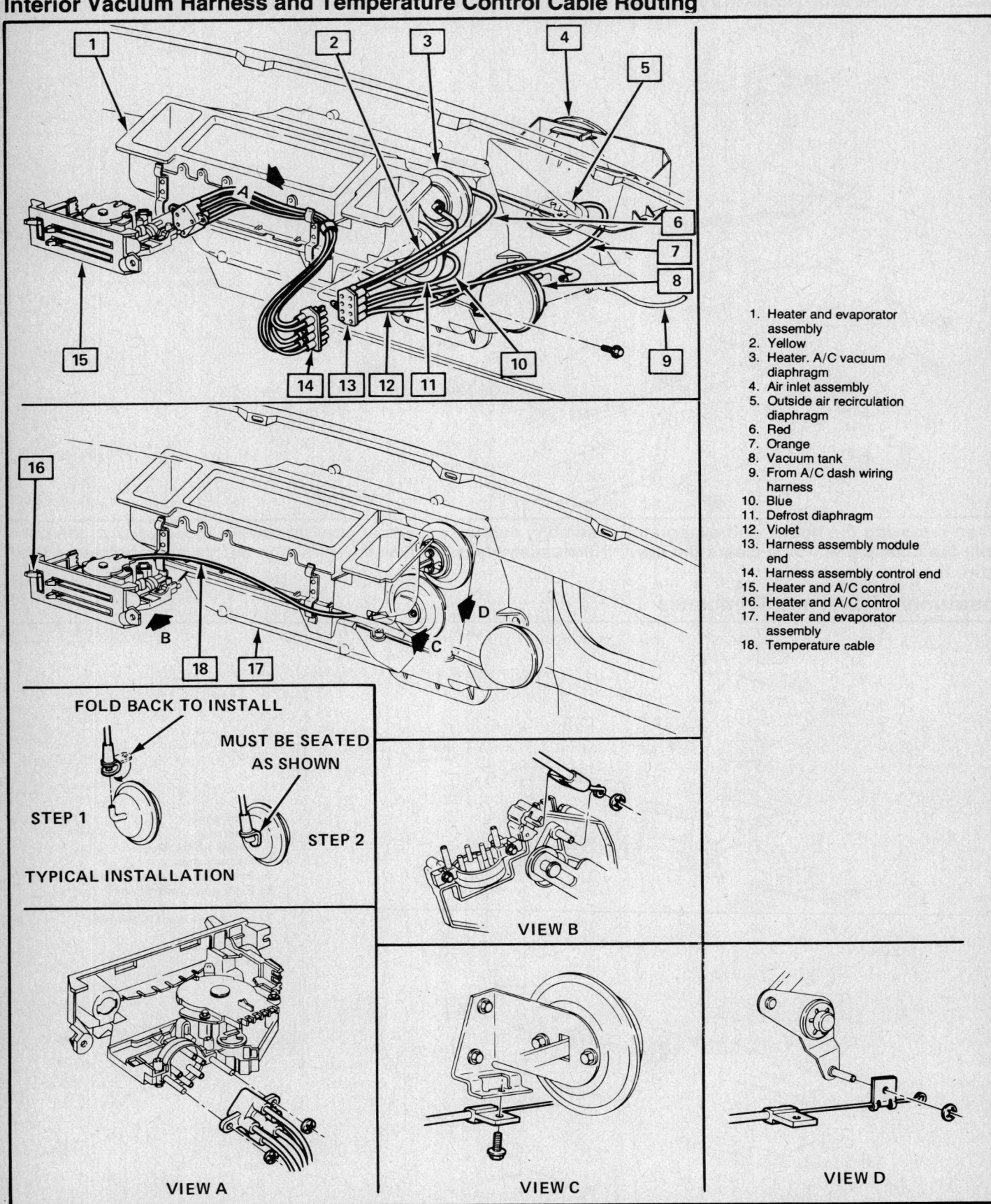

1. Heater and evaporator assembly
2. Yellow
3. Heater. A/C vacuum diaphragm
4. Air inlet assembly
5. Outside air recirculation diaphragm
6. Red
7. Orange
8. Vacuum tank
9. From A/C dash wiring harness
10. Blue
11. Defrost diaphragm
12. Violet
13. Harness assembly module end
14. Harness assembly control end
15. Heater and A/C control
16. Heater and A/C control
17. Heater and evaporator assembly
18. Temperature cable

FOLD BACK TO INSTALL

MUST BE SEATED AS SHOWN

STEP 1

STEP 2

TYPICAL INSTALLATION

VIEW A

VIEW B

VIEW C

VIEW D

ENGINE SECTION

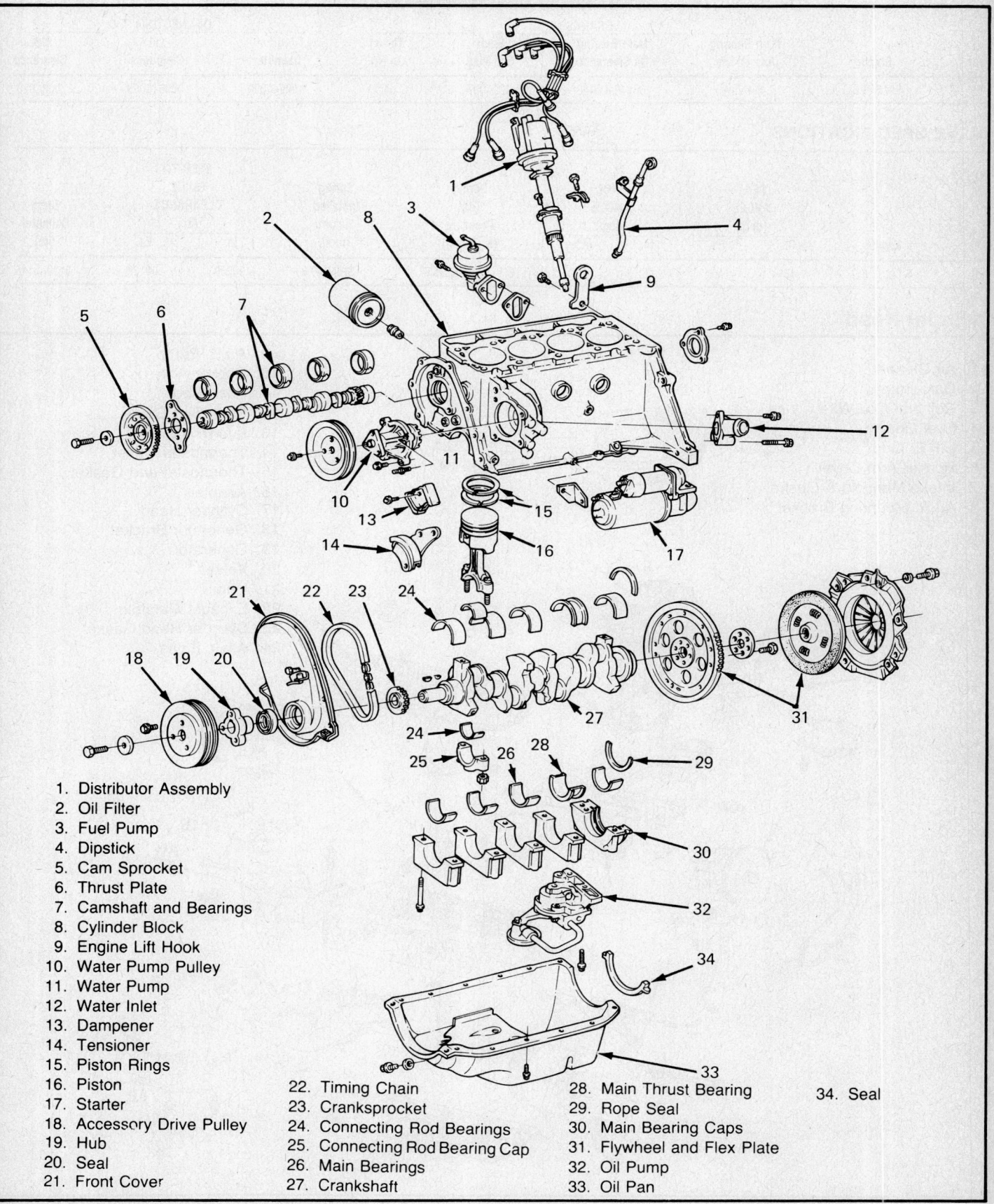

1. Distributor Assembly
2. Oil Filter
3. Fuel Pump
4. Dipstick
5. Cam Sprocket
6. Thrust Plate
7. Camshaft and Bearings
8. Cylinder Block
9. Engine Lift Hook
10. Water Pump Pulley
11. Water Pump
12. Water Inlet
13. Dampener
14. Tensioner
15. Piston Rings
16. Piston
17. Starter
18. Accessory Drive Pulley
19. Hub
20. Seal
21. Front Cover
22. Timing Chain
23. Cranksprocket
24. Connecting Rod Bearings
25. Connecting Rod Bearing Cap
26. Main Bearings
27. Crankshaft
28. Main Thrust Bearing
29. Rope Seal
30. Main Bearing Caps
31. Flywheel and Flex Plate
32. Oil Pump
33. Oil Pan
34. Seal

CRANKSHAFT & CONNECTING ROD SPECIFICATIONS

Year	Engine	CRANKSHAFT				CONNECTING ROD		
		Main Bearing Journal Dia.	Main Bearing Oil Clearance	Shaft End Play	Thrust On No.	Journal Diameter	Oil Clearance	Side Clearance
1982	4-112 (1.8L)	2.494-2.495	.00142-.00268	.002-.007	4	1.999-2.000	.0005-.0028	.008-.020

VALVE SPECIFICATIONS

Year	Engine	SEAT ANGLE (deg.)		FACE ANGLE (deg.)		Spring Test Pressure (N @ mm)	Spring Installed Height (mm)	STEM-TO GUIDE CLEARANCE (in.)		Stem Diameter (in.)
		In.	Ex.	In.	Ex.			In.	Ex.	
1982	4-112 (1.8L)	46°	46°	45°	45°	810 ± 27 @ 33.9	+ SHIM 40.6	.00059	.00138	.3139-.3146

Cylinder Head

1. Air Cleaner
2. Carburetor
3. Coil and Coil Wire
4. Fuel Line
5. E.F.E. Grid
6. Rocker Arm Cover
7. Intake Manifold & Gasket
8. A.I.R. Mounting Bracket
9. A.I.R. Pump
10. Rocker Arm
11. Push Rod
12. Push Rod Guide
13. E.G.R. Valve
14. Thermostat Outlet
15. Thermostat and Gasket
16. Adapter
17. Cylinder Head
18. Generator Bracket
19. Generator
20. Valves
21. Lifter
22. Exhaust Manifold
23. Cylinder Head Gasket
24. A.I.R. Pipes

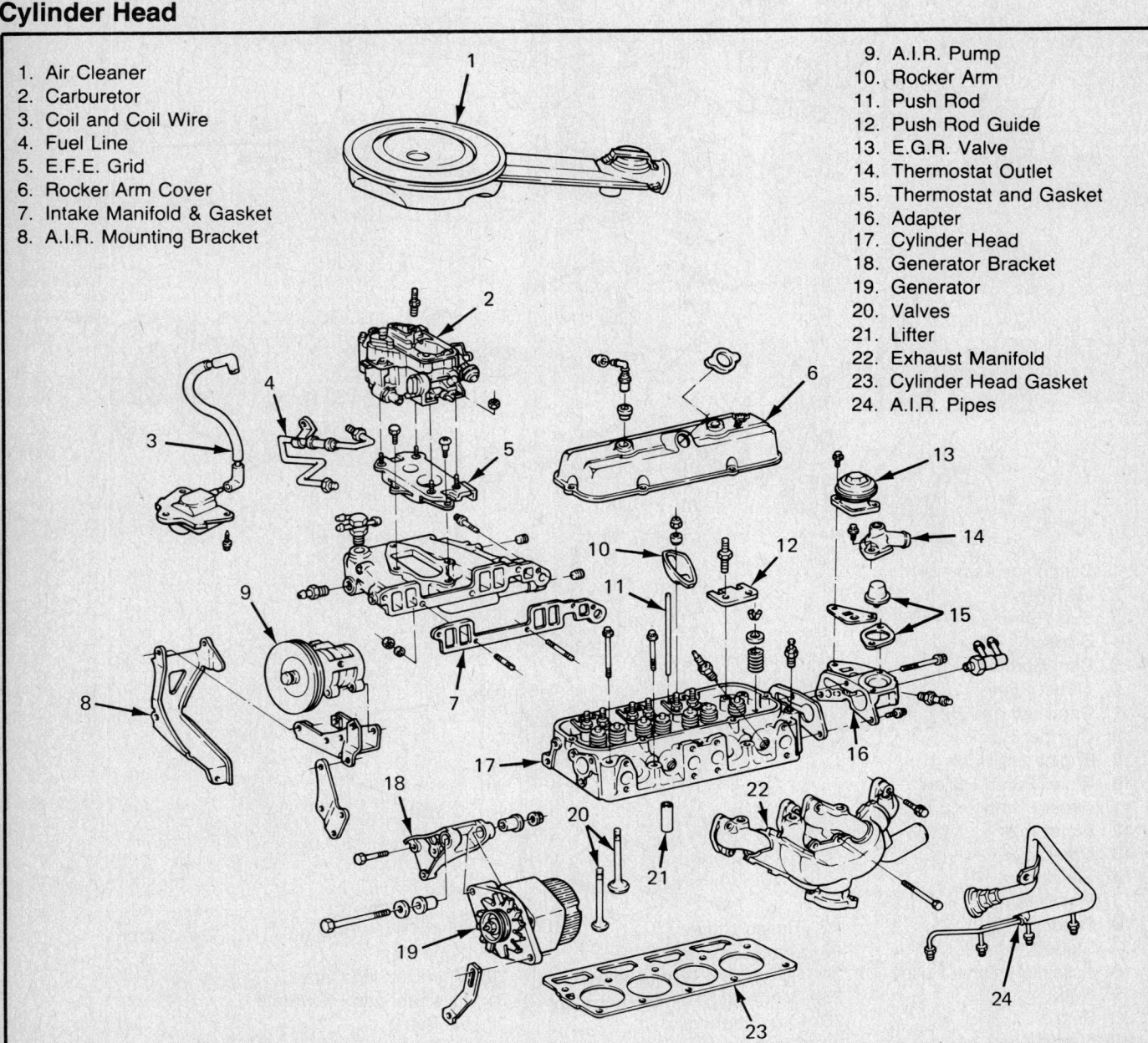

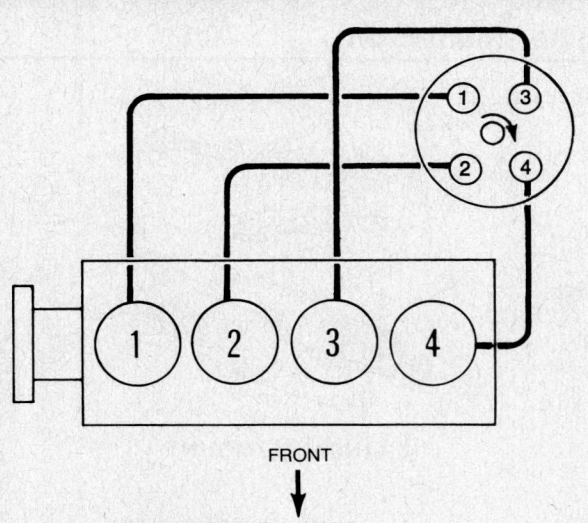

FRONT

GM (Chevrolet) 112
Engine firing order: 1-3-4-2
Distributor rotation: clockwise

Oil Pan

Removal

1. Disconnect negative battery cable.
2. Raise vehicle.
3. Drain crankcase.

Oil Pan

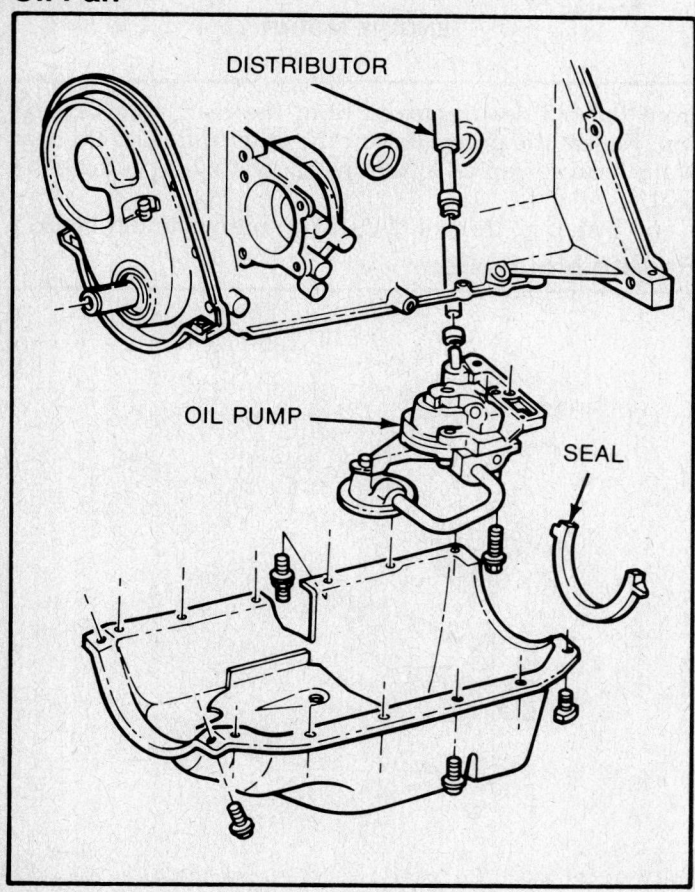

4. Remove A/C brace (if applicable).
5. Remove exhaust pipe and shield at exhaust manifold.
6. Remove starter.
7. Remove flywheel cover.
8. Remove oil pan.

Installation

1. With clean sealing surface, place a 2 mm diameter of RTV sealant on the engine block sealing surfaces.
2. Apply RTV sealant to oil pan surface which fits to engine front cover.
3. Using a new oil pan rear seal, install pan against cylinder case and attach retaining bolts.
4. Install flywheel cover.
5. Install starter.
6. Connect exhaust pipe to exhaust manifold.
7. Install A/C (if applicable).
8. On automatic transaxle, install oil filter and extension.
9. Lower vehicle.
10. Refill crankcase.
11. Connect negative battery cable.

Oil Pump

Removal

1. Remove oil pan as previously outlined.
2. Remove pump-to-rear main bearing cap bolt.
3. Remove pump and extension shaft.

Installation

Reverse removal procedures.

Front Cover Oil Seal

Removal With Cover Installed

1. Remove crankshaft pulley and hub.

Rear Main Oil Seal

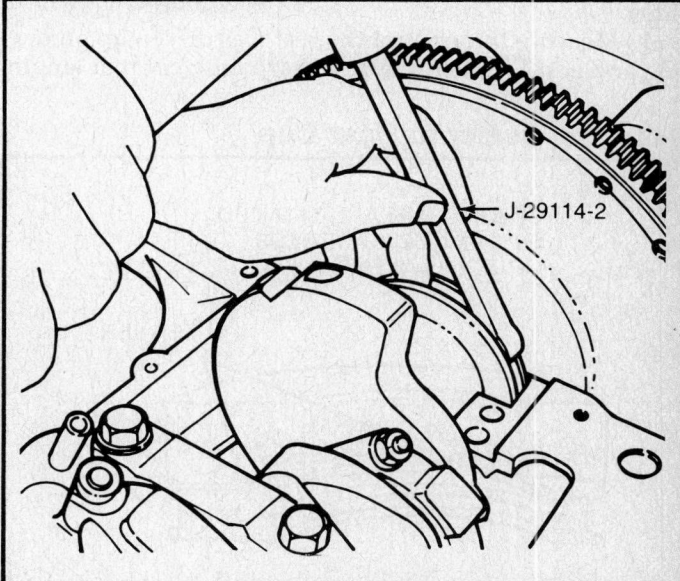

J-29114-2

GENERAL MOTORS "J" BODY CARS

CAVALIER, J2000, CIMARRON

Rear Main Oil Seal

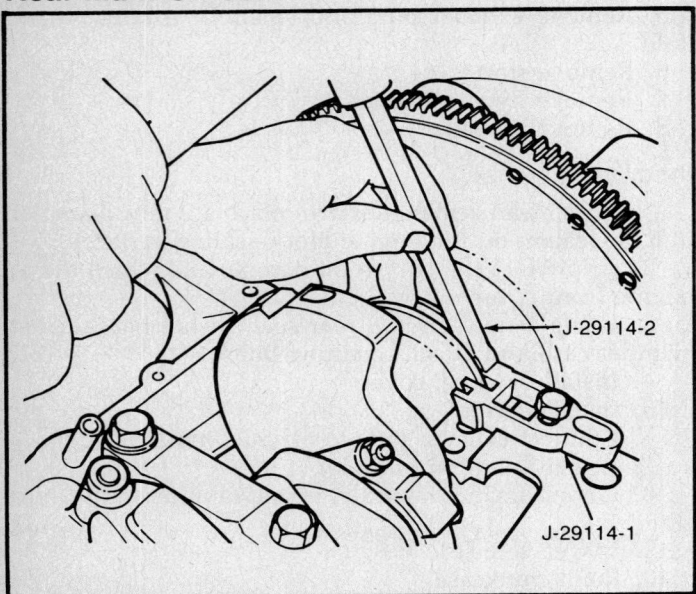

J-29114-2

J-29114-1

2. With hub removed, pry seal out of cover from the front with a small pry bar, being careful not to damage the surface on the crankshaft.

Installation

Install new seal so that open end of seal is toward the inside of cover. Drive it into position with tool J-23042.

Rear Main Oil Seal

Repair

1. Remove oil pan and oil pump as previously outlined.
2. Remove rear main bearing cap.
3. Use packing tool J-29114-2 and gently drive upper seal into groove approximately ¼ inch. Do this on both sides.
4. Measure the amount the seal was driven up on one side and add ¹/₁₆ inch. Using a sharp tool, cut that length

Applying Sealer to Rear Cup

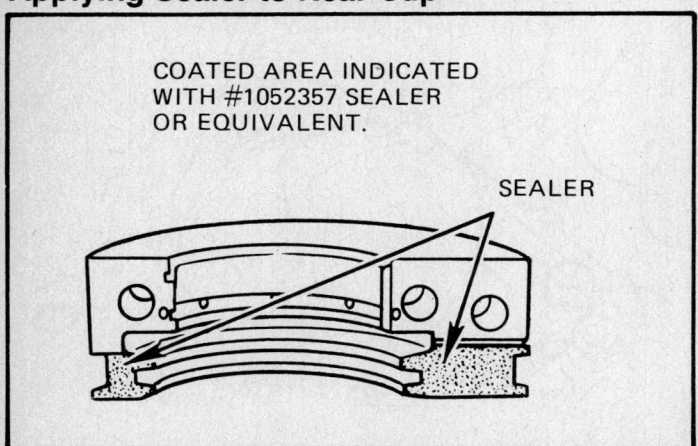

COATED AREA INDICATED WITH #1052357 SEALER OR EQUIVALENT.

SEALER

Engine Mount Front

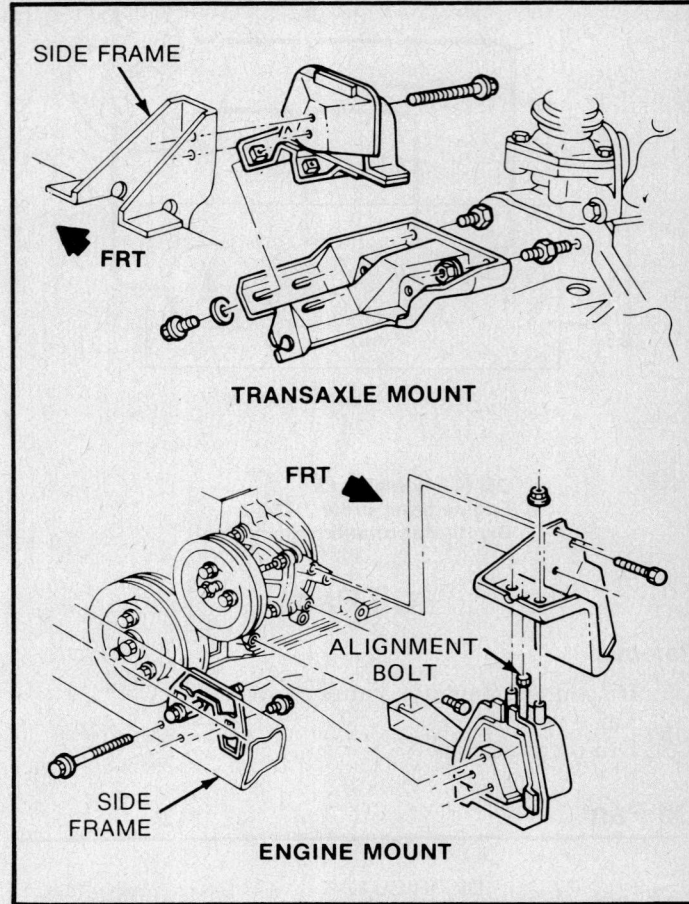

SIDE FRAME

FRT

TRANSAXLE MOUNT

FRT

ALIGNMENT BOLT

SIDE FRAME

ENGINE MOUNT

from the old seal removed from the rear main bearing cap. Repeat the procedure for the other side. Use the rear main bearing cap as a holding fixture when cutting the seal.

5. Install guide tool (J-29114-1) onto cylinder block.

Engine Mount Rear

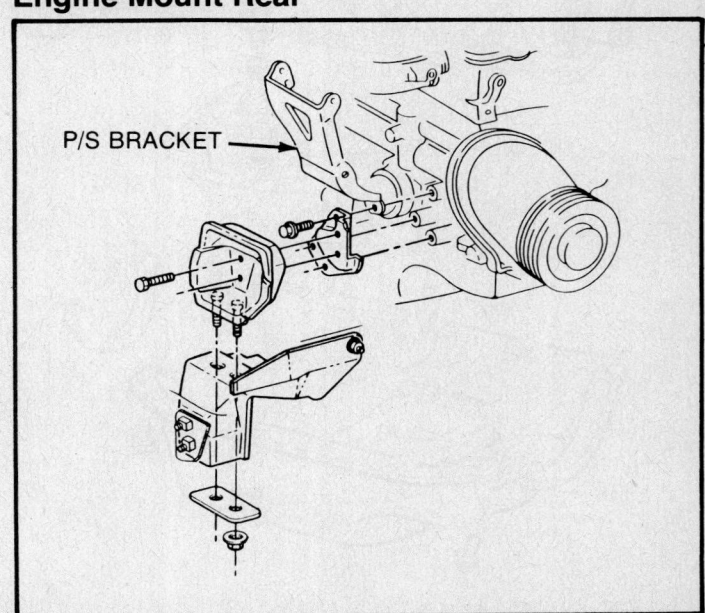

P/S BRACKET

Rocker Arm and Cover

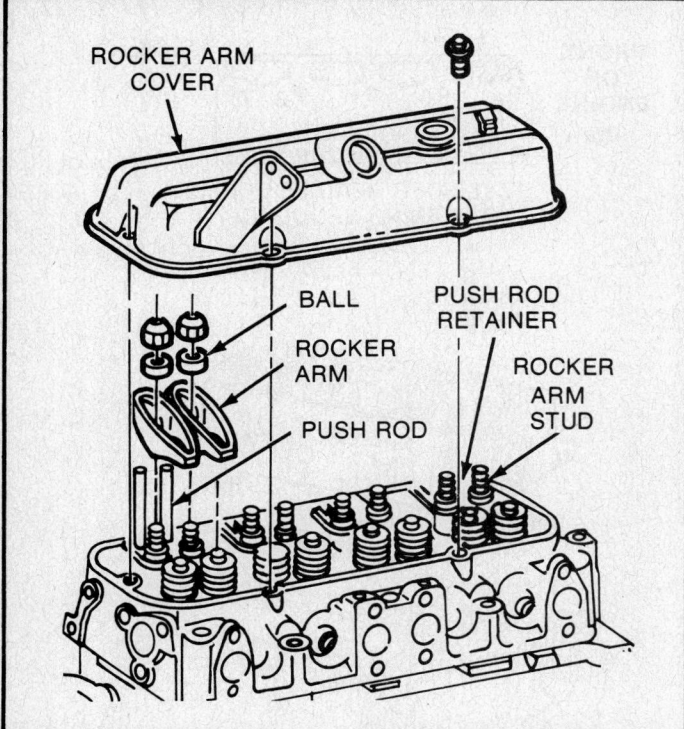

ROCKER ARM COVER

BALL

ROCKER ARM

PUSH ROD

PUSH ROD RETAINER

ROCKER ARM STUD

At the time of installation, the flanges must be free of oil. A 2.0-3.0 bead of sealant must be applied to the flanges. The sealant must be wet to the touch when the bolts are torqued.

6. Using packing tool, work the short pieces cut in Step 4 onto the guide tool and then pack into cylinder block. The guide tool and packing tool have been machined to provide a built-in stop. Use the procedure for both sides.

7. It may help to use oil on the short pieces of the rope seal when packing into the cylinder block.

8. Install a new rope seal in the rear main bearing cap.

9. Using tool J-29590, cut the ends of seal flush with cup.

10. Install the rear main bearing cap and torque to 95 N•m (70 ft.-lbs.).

Rocker Arm Cover

Removal

1. Disconnect negative battery cable.
2. Remove air cleaner.
3. Remove distributor cap with spark plug wires. Remove spark plug wire clip from rocker arm cover and lay wires and cap aside.
4. Disconnect vacuum hoses and pipes at generator bracket, front of valve cover, deceleration valve, and P.C.V. valve.
5. Disconnect the oxygen sensor and carburetor choke wires, and the ground wire at bracket.
6. Loosen accelerator linkage bracket.
7. Remove bolts and rocker arm cover. If cover adheres

to cylinder head, shear off by bumping end of rocker arm cover with a rubber mallet. If cover still will not come loose, carefully pry until loose. Do not distort sealing flange.

Installation

1. Clean sealing surface on cylinder head and intake manifold with degreaser.
2. Place a 3 mm diameter (⅛ inch) bead of RTV sealant all around the rocker arm sealing surface. (When going around the attaching bolt holes, always flow the RTV on the inboard side of the holes.)
3. Install cover and torque bolts to 10 N•m (8 ft.-lbs.) while RTV is still wet.

NOTE When applying RTV, keep sealant out of bolt holes as this could cause a hydraulic condition which would damage the head casting.

Valve Adjustment

NOTE Adjust valves when lifter is on base circle of camshaft lobe.

1. Crank engine until mark on crank pulley lines up with "O" mark on the timing tab. The engine should also be in the No. 1 firing position. This may be determined by placing fingers on the No. 1 rocker arms as the mark on the crank pulley comes near the "O" mark. If the valves are not moving, the engine is in the No. 1 firing position. If the valves move as the mark comes up to the timing tab, the engine is in No. 4 firing position and should be rotated one revolution to reach the No. 1 position.

2. With the engine in the No. 1 firing position, the following valves may be adjusted:
   Exhaust—1, 3
   Intake—3, 4
   Back out adjusting nut until lash is felt at the pushrod, then turn in adjusting nut until all lash is removed. This can be determined by rotating pushrod while turning

Valve Lash Adjustment

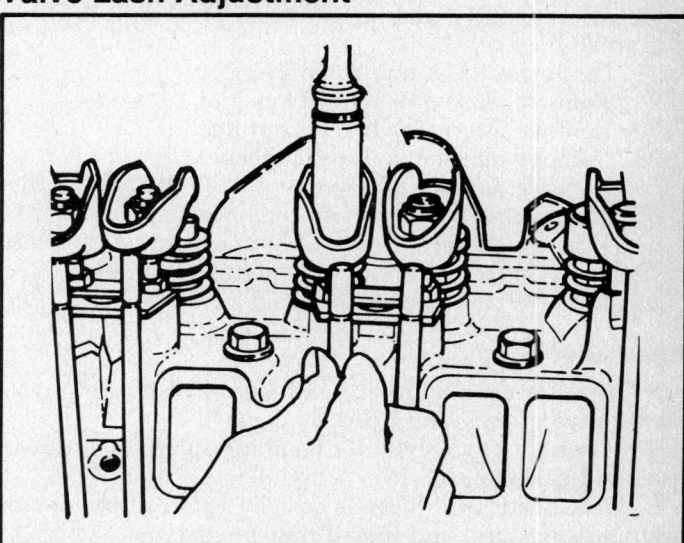

adjusting nut. When lash has been removed, turn adjusting nut in 1½ additional turns (to center lifter plunger).

3. Crank the engine one revolution until the timing tab "O" mark and crank pulley mark are again in alignment. This is the No. 4 firing position. With the engine in this position, the following valves may be adjusted:

Exhaust—2, 4
Intake—1, 2

Cylinder Head

Removal

1. Disconnect negative battery cable.
2. Drain coolant.
3. Remove air cleaner.
4. Raise vehicle.
5. Remove exhaust shield.
6. Remove exhaust pipe.
7. Remove heater hose from intake.
8. Lower vehicle.
9. Remove engine lift bracket.
10. Remove distributor.
11. Disconnect vacuum manifold at alternator bracket.
12. Disconnect remaining vacuum lines at intake manifold and thermostat housing.
13. Remove air management pipe at exhaust check valve.
14. Disconnect accelerator linkage at carburetor and remove accelerator linkage bracket.
15. Disconnect necessary wires.
16. Remove upper radiator hose at thermostat.
17. Remove bolt attaching dipstick tube and hot water bracket.
18. Remove idler pulley.
19. Remove AIR/power steering belt.
20. If equipped with power steering, remove power steering pump and lay aside.
21. Remove AIR bracket-to-intake bolt.
22. If equipped with power steering, remove AIR pump pulley.
23. If equipped with power steering, remove the AIR through bolt and power steering adjusting bracket.
24. Loosen AIR mounting bracket lower bolt (bracket will rotate).
25. Disconnect fuel line at carburetor.
26. Remove alternator with wires and lay aside.
27. Remove alternator brace from head.
28. Remove alternator upper bracket.
29. Remove rocker arm cover.
30. Remove rocker arms and pushrods.
31. Remove cylinder head. Cylinder head will include carburetor, intake manifold and exhaust manifold.
32. Remove cylinder head bolts.

Installation

1. Install a new cylinder head gasket in position over dowel pins on cylinder head.
2. Carefully guide cylinder head into place over dowel pins and gaskets.
3. Coat heads and threads of cylinder head bolts with sealing compound and install finger-tight.

Cylinder Head

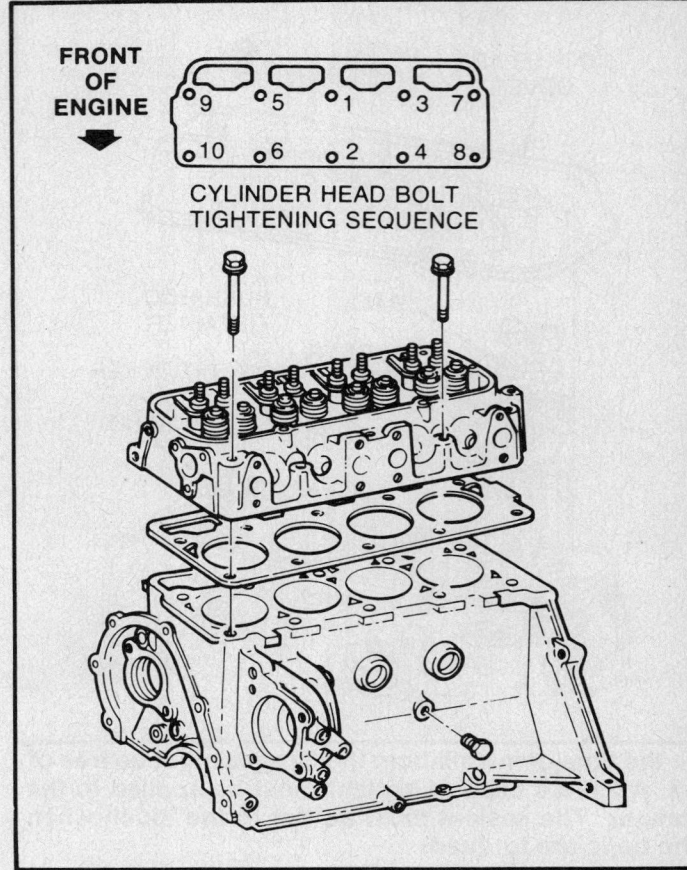

CYLINDER HEAD BOLT
TIGHTENING SEQUENCE

4. Tighten the cylinder head gradually with a torque wrench. Tighten bolts following sequence illustrated. The final torque is 88-107 N•m (65-75 ft.-lbs.).
5. Reverse removal procedure for remainder of installation.

Timing Chain

Removal

1. Disconnect negative battery cable.
2. Remove accessory drive belts.
3. Raise vehicle.
4. Remove tire and wheel.
5. Remove inner fender splash shield.
6. If equipped with A/C, remove A/C belt.
7. Remove accessory drive pulley retaining bolts.
8. Install Tool J-24420 on hub; turn puller screw and remove hub.
9. Remove front cover bolts.
10. Remove front cover. If difficult to remove, use a rubber mallet to loosen cover.
11. Align marks on crankshaft sprocket and cam sprocket.
12. Loosen timing chain tensioner nut as far as possible, but do not remove.
13. Remove camshaft sprocket and timing chain.
14. Crankshaft sprocket can be removed using a puller.

Crankshaft Pulley and Head

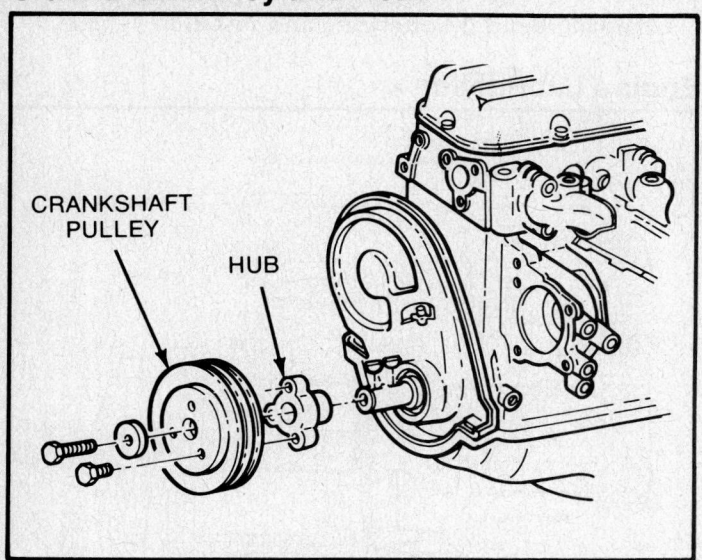

CRANKSHAFT PULLEY

HUB

Installation

1. If crankshaft sprocket was removed, install crankshaft sprocket using Tool J-5590.
2. Install timing chain on camshaft sprocket and crank sprocket. Lube thrust surface with Molykote or its equivalent. Align marks on camshaft sprocket and crankshaft sprocket.
3. Align dowel in camshaft with dowel hole in camshaft sprocket, then install sprocket on camshaft.
4. Draw the camshaft sprocket onto camshaft using the mounting bolts.
5. Lubricate timing chain with engine oil.
6. Install timing chain tensioner.

NOTE Use a wire looped around the nut to position nut on stud.

7. Install crankcase front cover.
8. Coat front cover seal contact area with engine oil.
9. Place hub in position over key on crankshaft.

Timing Chain and Sprockets

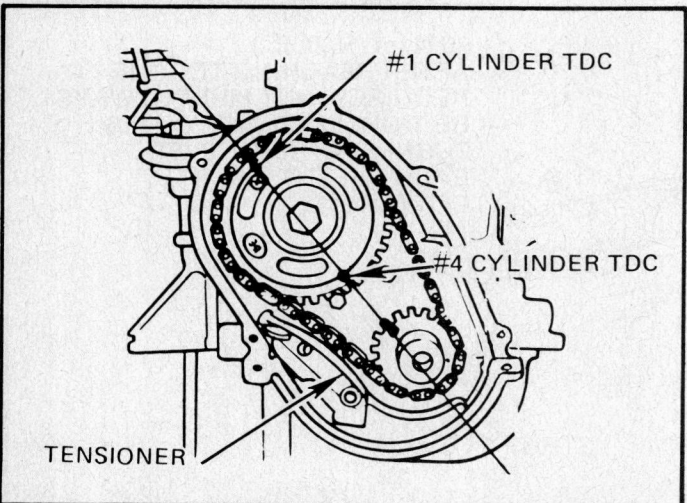

#1 CYLINDER TDC

#4 CYLINDER TDC

TENSIONER

ENGINE TORQUE SPECIFICATIONS

	N•m	Ft. Lbs.
A/C Bracket to Block	25–38	20–28
A/C Cmpr. to Eng. Mt	65–85	48–63
Camshaft Sprocket	90–15	66–85
Camshaft Cover (Rear)	50–65	4–5
Cylinder Head	88–107	65–75
Connecting Rod Cap	46–54	34–40
Crankshaft Pulley	27–41	20–30
Crankshaft Pulley Hub	90–115	66–84
EGR Valve	18–24	13–18
Engine Mounting Front—Nuts	34–48	25–35
Engine Mounting Lower—Nuts	20–28	15–20
Engine Mount (to Frame)	48–56	35–45
Exhaust Manifold	30–38	22–28
Flywheel	61–75	45–55
Front Cover	8–12	6–9
Fuel Pump	20–30	15–22
Generator Bracket (to Head)	27–40	20–30
Generator Brace (to Head)	27–41	20–30
Generator Pivot Bolt	27–41	20–30
Generator Adjust Bolt	20–34	20–25
Intake Manifold	27–34	20–25
Main Bearing Caps	85–100	63–74
Cam Thrust Plate	8–12	6–9
Oil Level Gage Tube	8–12	6–9
Oil Filter	16–23	12–17
Oil Pan	8–12	6–9
	18–24	13–18
Oil Pump	35–47	26–35
Oil Pump Cover	8–12	6–9
Oil Drain Plug	20–27	15–20
P/S Brace (to Head)	25–38	20–28
Rocker Arm Cover	8–12	6–9
Rocker Arm Stud	58–66	43–49
Spark Plug	10–20	7–15
Starter Motor Block	36–50	26–37
Thermostat Adapter	16–28	22–36
Thermostat Outlet	18–30	13–22
Transmission to Engine Block	65–85	48–63
Water Outlet	18–30	13–22
Water Pump	18–24	13–18
Water Pump Pulley	18–24	13–18
Rocker Nut	6–14	45–10
Oil Filter Adapter Auto	20–30	15–22
Water Outlet Adapter	16–28	12–20

10. Pull hub onto crankshaft as follows:
a. Install Tool J-29113 or equivalent into crankshaft so that at least 6mm of thread engagement is obtained.
b. Pull hub into position and remove tool from hub.
11. Install accessory drive pulley.
12. Hang drive belts on proper pulleys.
13. If equipped with A/C, install and adjust A/C belt.
14. Install inner fender splash shield.

15. Install tire and wheel.
16. Lower vehicle.
17. Adjust accessory drive belts to proper tension.
18. Connect battery negative cable.

Camshaft

Removal

1. Remove engine from vehicle.
2. Remove valve lifters.
3. Remove crankcase front cover.
4. Mark position of rotor and remove distributor.
5. Remove fuel pump and pushrod.
6. Remove timing chain and sprocket.
7. Remove camshaft.

Piston Marking

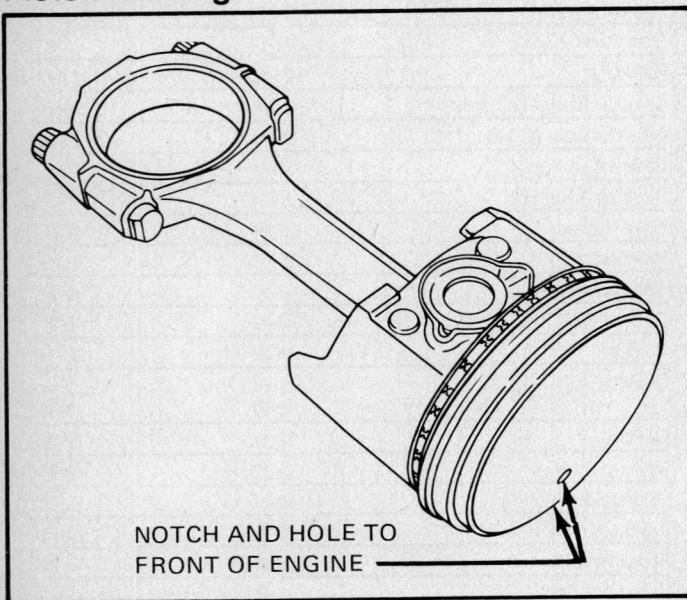

NOTCH AND HOLE TO FRONT OF ENGINE

Installation

Complete build up of engine and install in vehicle.

Engine Lubrication

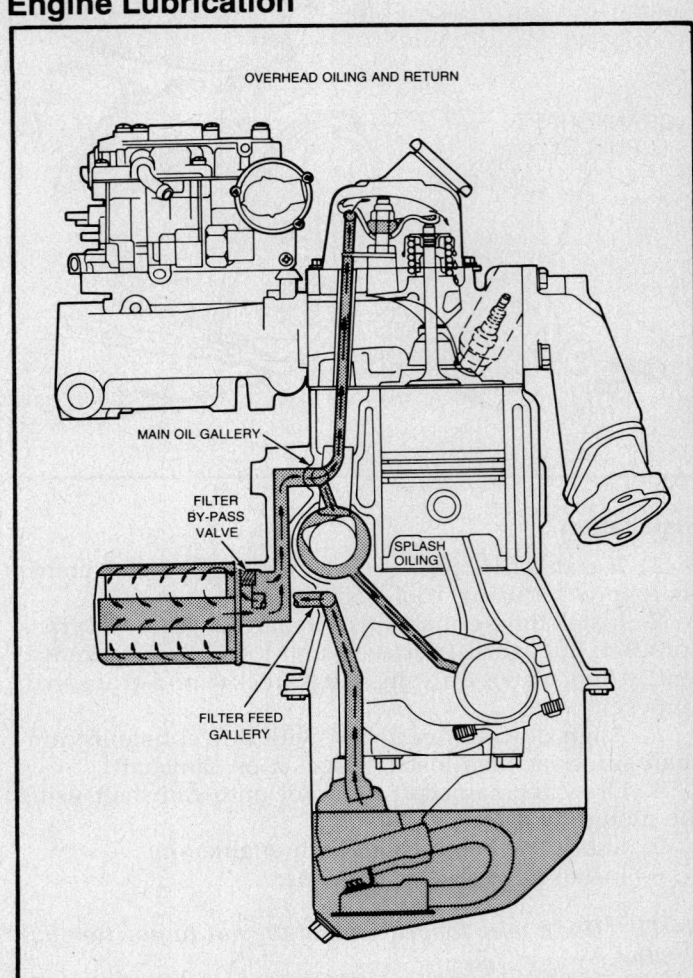

OVERHEAD OILING AND RETURN

MAIN OIL GALLERY

FILTER BY-PASS VALVE

SPLASH OILING

FILTER FEED GALLERY

STEERING AND BRAKE SECTION

Power Rack and Pinion Assembly Removal and Installation

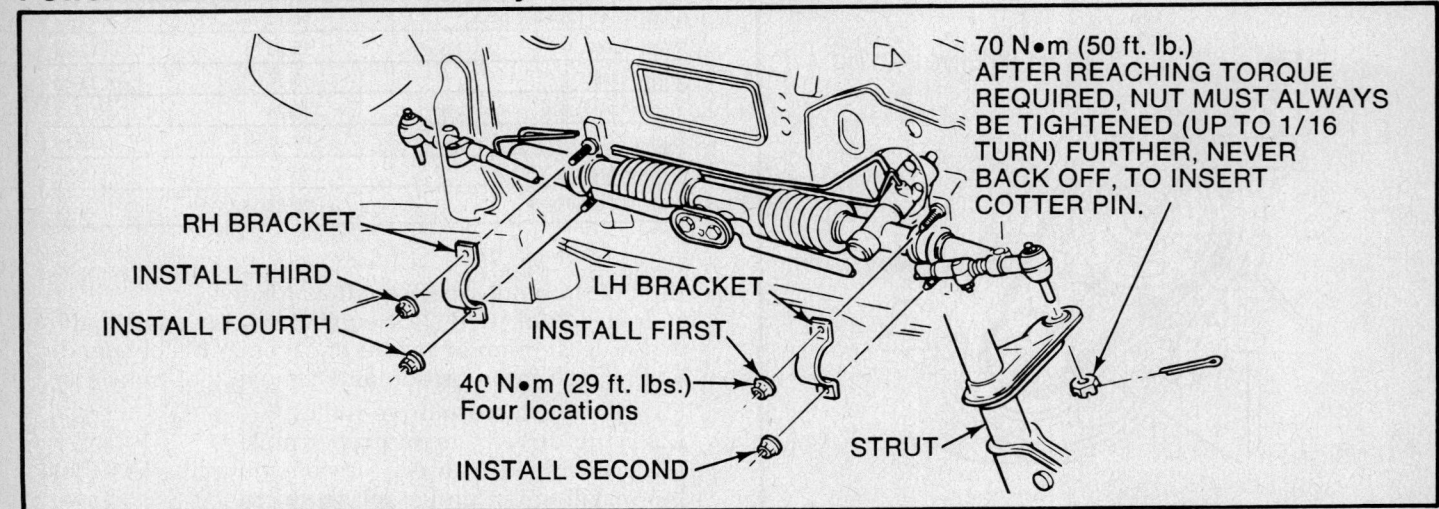

70 N•m (50 ft. lb.) AFTER REACHING TORQUE REQUIRED, NUT MUST ALWAYS BE TIGHTENED (UP TO 1/16 TURN) FURTHER, NEVER BACK OFF, TO INSERT COTTER PIN.

RH BRACKET

INSTALL THIRD

INSTALL FOURTH

LH BRACKET

INSTALL FIRST

40 N•m (29 ft. lbs.) Four locations

INSTALL SECOND

STRUT

Disconnect Tie Rod

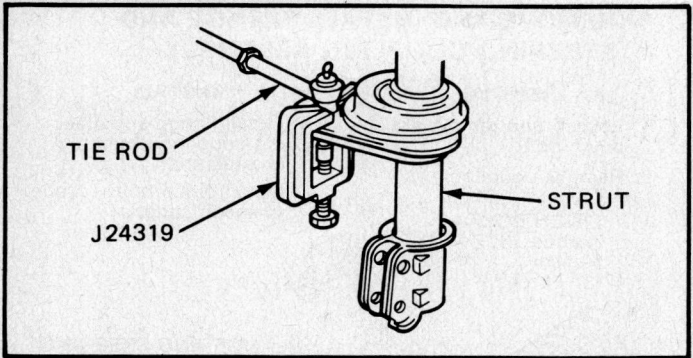

TIE ROD

J24319

STRUT

Power Rack and Pinion

Removal

1. Remove driver's side hush panel.
2. Pull down the plastic boot and remove the upper pinch bolt from the flexible coupling.
3. Remove air cleaner and washer jar.
4. Disconnect pressure line from rack assembly and from switch block. Remove the pressure line to gain access to return line fitting.
5. Disconnect return line from rack assembly.
6. Remove right-hand (passenger side) bracket attaching gear to cowl.
7. Remove left-hand (driver side) bracket.
8. Move rack assembly away from the cowl, and remove the lower pinch bolt from the flexible coupling. Separate the coupling from the rack assembly.
9. Disconnect both tie rods from the struts, using Tool J-24319, or the equivalent.
10. Remove splash shield from left inner fender.
11. Remove rack assembly through the access hole in the left inner fender.

Flexible Coupling

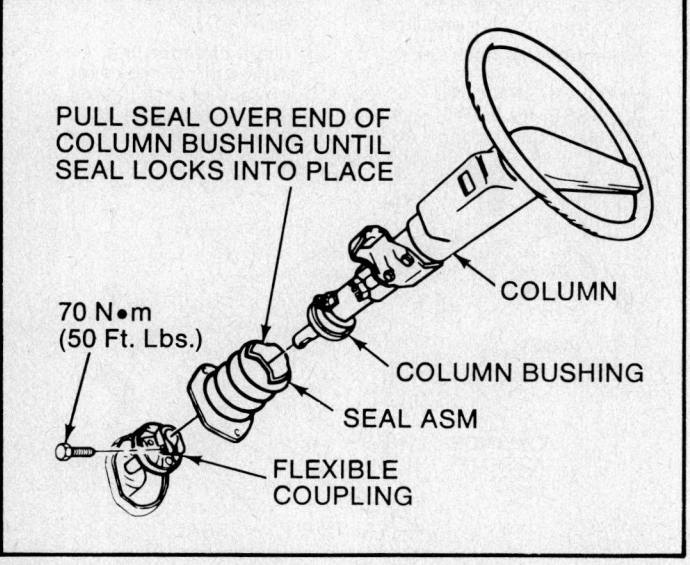

PULL SEAL OVER END OF COLUMN BUSHING UNTIL SEAL LOCKS INTO PLACE

70 N•m (50 Ft. Lbs.)

COLUMN

COLUMN BUSHING

SEAL ASM

FLEXIBLE COUPLING

Installation

1. Install the rack assembly through the access hole in the left inner fender.
2. Use a screwdriver to slightly spread the clamp areas of the flexible coupling.
3. Place the rack assembly into position. Have a helper inside the car to guide the flexible coupling onto the stub shaft and onto the steering column. Install both clamp bolts and tighten the coupling-to-stub shaft to 50 N•m (35 ft.-lbs.), and the coupling-to-column to 70 N•m (50 ft.-lbs.).
4. Install return line, and then install pressure line.
5. Install the left-hand attaching bracket to the cowl. Do not tighten.
6. Install the right-hand attaching bracket.
7. Tighten both brackets to specifications in order.
8. Install air cleaner and washer jar.
9. Install splash shield.
10. Install hush panel.
11. Check toe setting. Adjust as required.

Vacuum Pump

The vacuum pump is designed to aid the engine in maintaining a proper vacuum level for the power brake system. The vacuum pump will maintain a vacuum of 47 ± 6 kPa (13.0 ± 1.8 in. Hg) in the system. When the vacuum decreases to 47 ± 6 kPa, the vacuum pump is activated for 5–10 seconds to bring the vacuum back to proper level.

Parking Brake Release Lever

Removal

1. Place gear selector in Neutral and apply parking brake.
2. Remove front ash tray and remove two Torx screws.
3. Gently pry out emblem in the center of shift knob and remove snap ring securing knob. Lift trimplate out by pulling front end up first.
4. Remove three screws under trimplate and remove rear ashtray. Remove screw under ashtray and lift off console.
5. Remove parking brake switch.
6. Disconnect parking brake cable from lever assembly.
7. Remove three screws securing lever to floor panel and remove lever.

Installation

1. Reverse procedure for lever installation.

Parking Brake Cable

FRONT SECTION

Removal

1. Place gear selector in Neutral and apply parking brake.
2. Remove console.
3. Disconnect parking brake cable from lever.

GENERAL MOTORS "J" BODY CARS

CAVALIER, J2000, CIMARRON

Steering Tie Rods

1. REMOVE AND INSTALL OUTER TIE ROD

REMOVE

1. Loosen outer tie rod pinch bolt.
2. Remove tie rod using

   Tool J-24319-01 or BT-7101.

INSTALL

1. Install parts as shown.
2. Loosen inner tie rod pinch bolt.
3. Make toe-in adjustment by turning the tie rod adjuster.
4. Torque pinch bolts to 28 N·m (20 Ft. Lbs.)

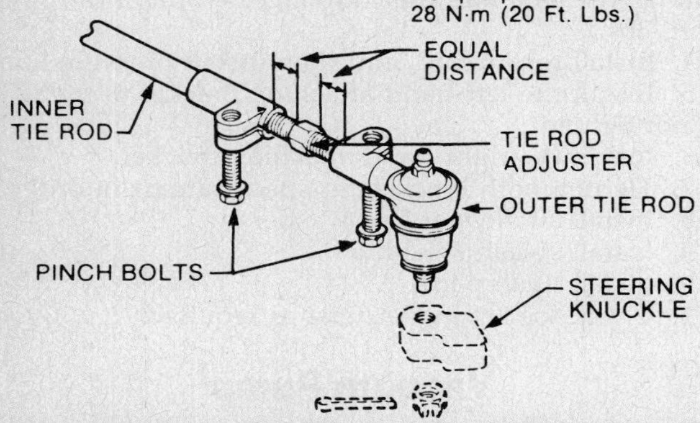

- INNER TIE ROD
- PINCH BOLTS
- EQUAL DISTANCE
- TIE ROD ADJUSTER
- OUTER TIE ROD
- STEERING KNUCKLE

2. REMOVE AND INSTALL INNER TIE ROD AND INNER PIVOT BUSHING

REMOVE

1. Bend back lock plate tabs.
2. Remove inner tie rod bolt.
3. Inner tie rod can now be removed by sliding out between bolt support plate and rack and pinion boot.

   If both inner tie rods are to be removed, after removing the first tie rod reinstall bolt to keep rack and pinion boot and other parts properly aligned.

INSTALL

1. Be sure center housing cover washers are fitted into rack and pinion boot.
2. Install parts as shown.
3. Bend lock plate tabs against flats of inner tie rod bolts after torquing.

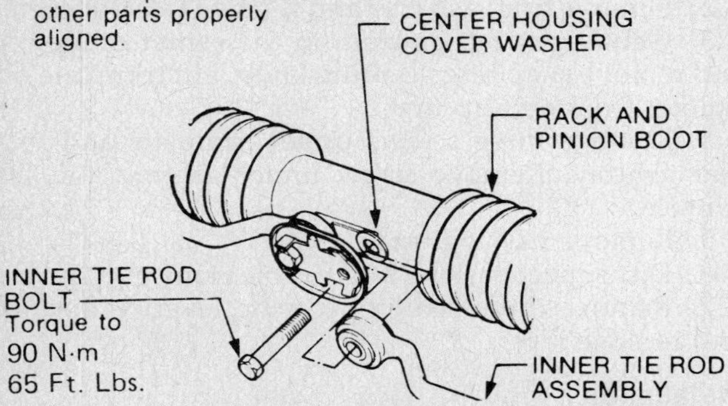

- CENTER HOUSING COVER WASHER
- RACK AND PINION BOOT
- INNER TIE ROD BOLT Torque to 90 N·m 65 Ft. Lbs.
- INNER TIE ROD ASSEMBLY

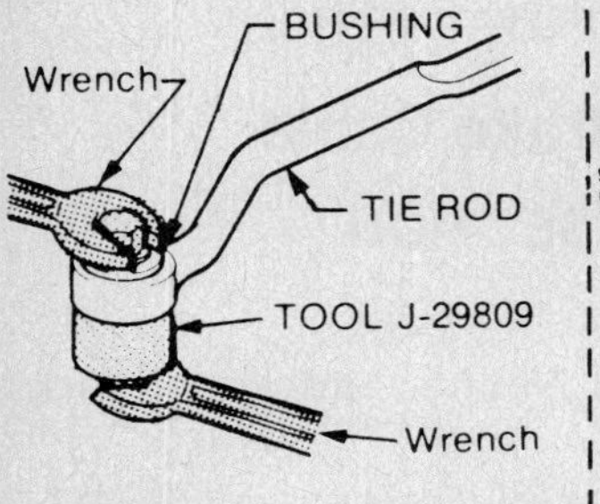

- Wrench
- BUSHING
- TIE ROD
- TOOL J-29809
- Wrench

Remove inner tie rod bushing.

For ease of installation, coat bushing lightly with grease.

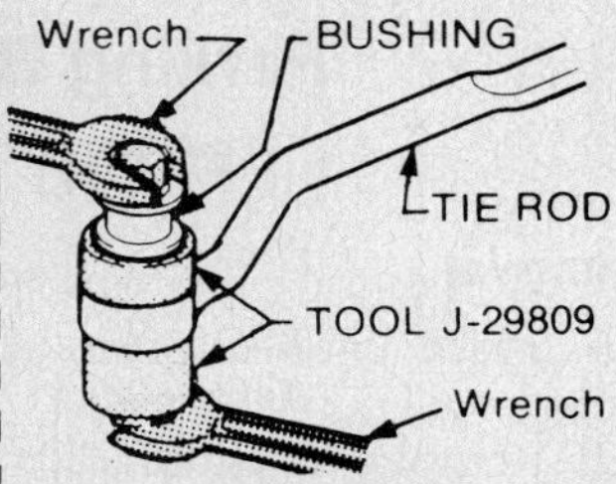

- Wrench
- BUSHING
- TIE ROD
- TOOL J-29809
- Wrench

Install inner tie rod bushing.

3. REMOVE AND INSTALL FLANGE AND STEERING COUPLING ASSEMBLY

REMOVE

1. Loosen and remove pinch bolt.
2. Remove coupling.

INSTALL

1. Install flange and steering coupling assembly on stub shaft.
2. Install pinch bolt. Torque to specifications.

- PINCH BOLT Torque to 50 N·m (37 Ft. Lbs.)
- FLANGE AND STEERING COUPLING ASSEMBLY
- STUB SHAFT

4. REMOVE AND INSTALL DASH SEAL

REMOVE

1. Remove dash seal.

INSTALL

1. Line up notch in dash seal and notch on housing.
2. Be sure top of seal is flush or below top of housing.

- DASH SEAL
- Notch

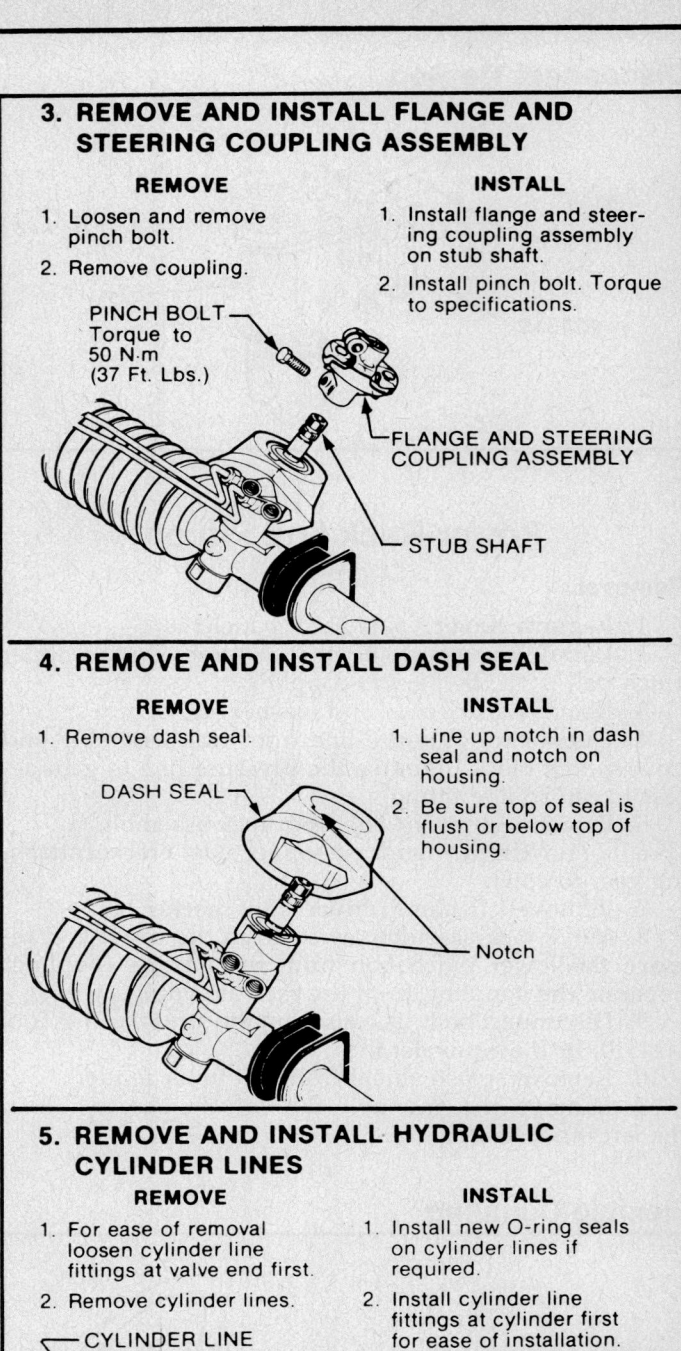

5. REMOVE AND INSTALL HYDRAULIC CYLINDER LINES

REMOVE

1. For ease of removal loosen cylinder line fittings at valve end first.
2. Remove cylinder lines.

INSTALL

1. Install new O-ring seals on cylinder lines if required.
2. Install cylinder line fittings at cylinder first for ease of installation. Torque fittings to 18 N·m (13 Ft. Lbs.).

- CYLINDER LINE ASSEMBLY (RT) Has Long Fitting
- CYLINDER END
- O-RING SEALS
- CYLINDER LINE ASSEMBLY (LT)
- VALVE END
- O-RING SEALS (2)
- O-RING SEALS (2)

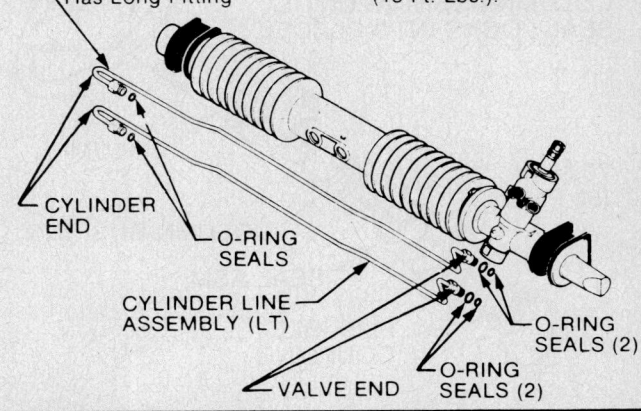

Brake Vacuum Pump

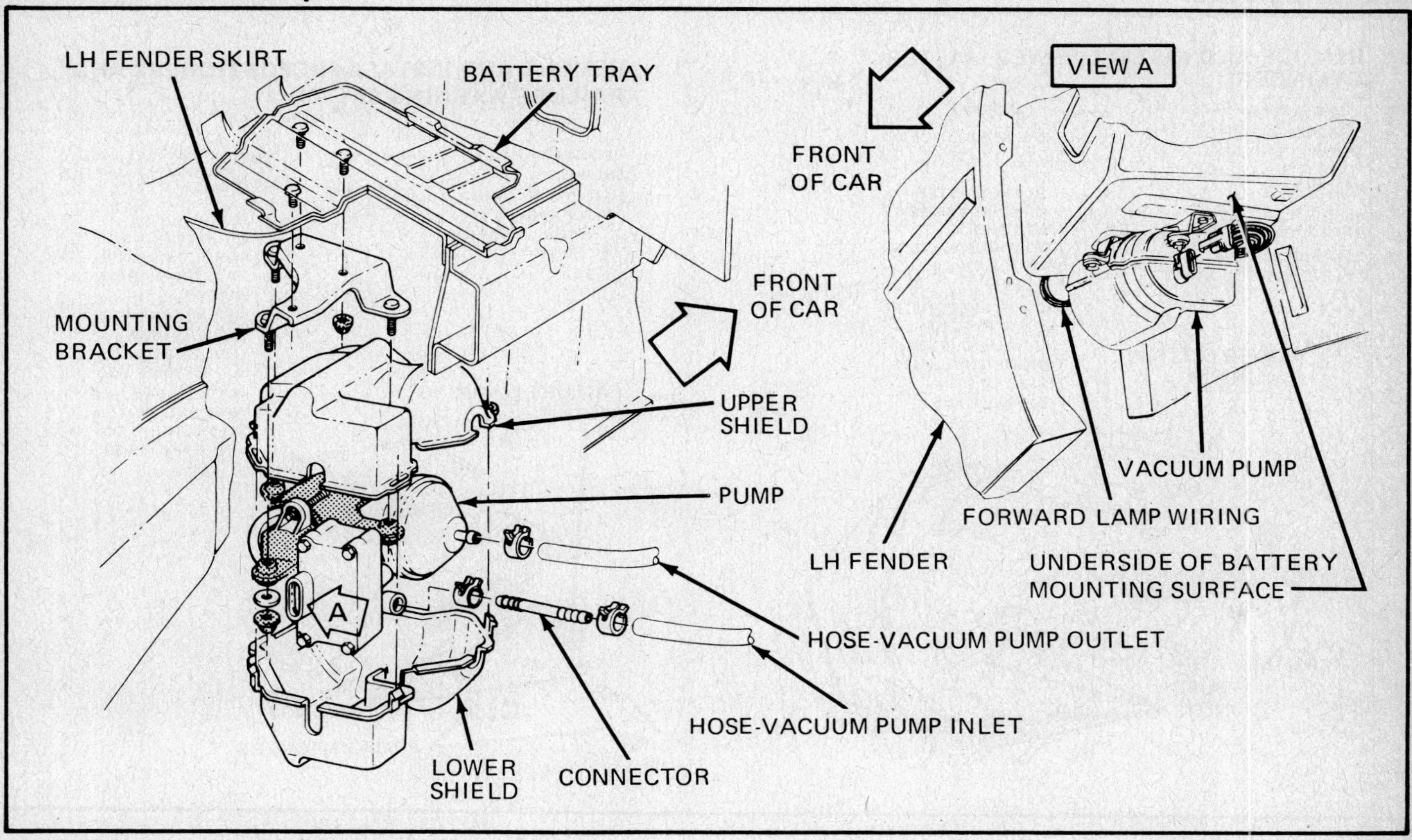

LH FENDER SKIRT

BATTERY TRAY

VIEW A

FRONT OF CAR

FRONT OF CAR

MOUNTING BRACKET

UPPER SHIELD

PUMP

VACUUM PUMP

FORWARD LAMP WIRING

LH FENDER

UNDERSIDE OF BATTERY MOUNTING SURFACE

HOSE-VACUUM PUMP OUTLET

HOSE-VACUUM PUMP INLET

A

LOWER SHIELD

CONNECTOR

Brake Vacuum Pump Wiring Connector

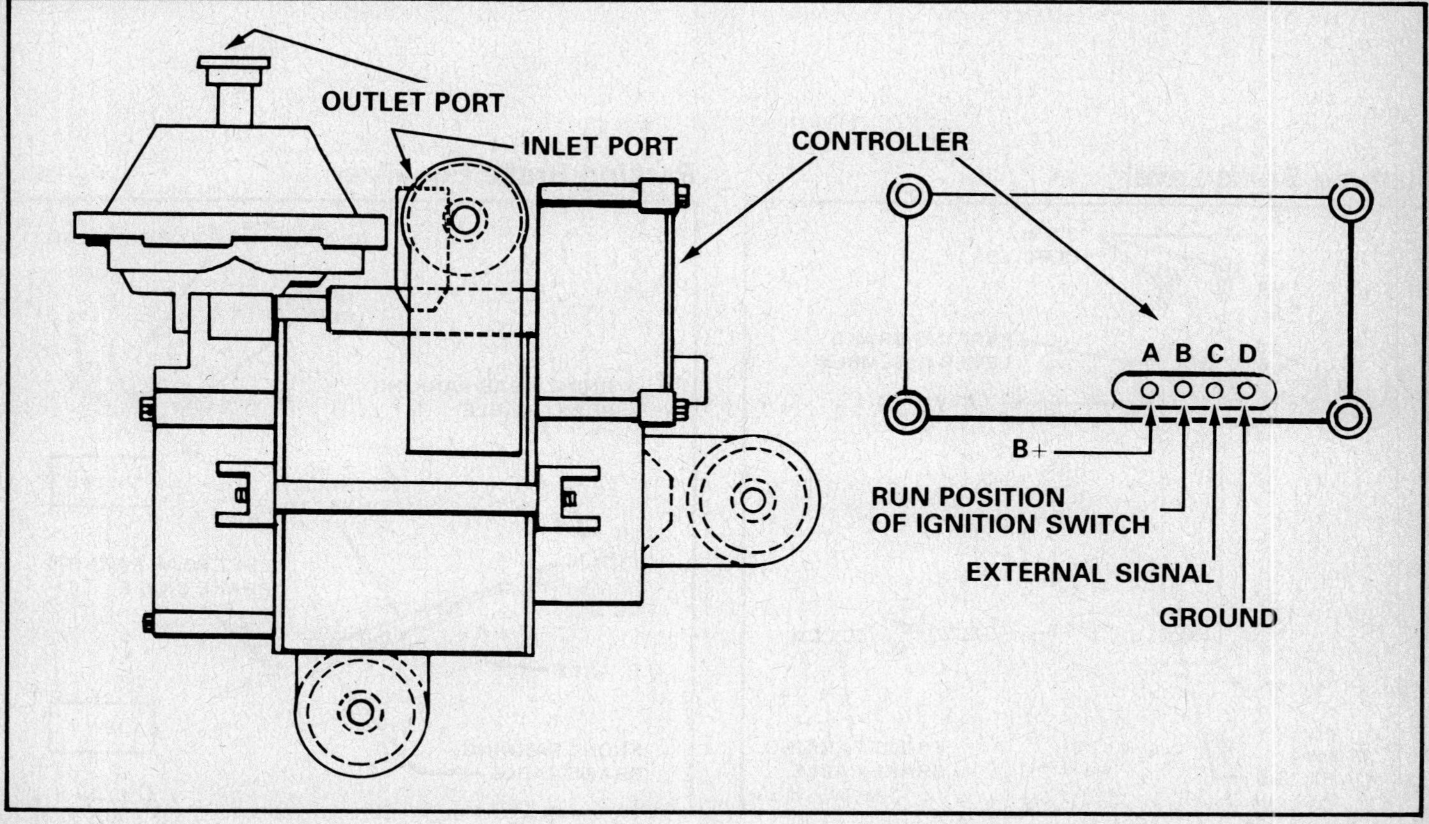

OUTLET PORT

INLET PORT

CONTROLLER

A B C D

B+

RUN POSITION OF IGNITION SWITCH

EXTERNAL SIGNAL

GROUND

GENERAL MOTORS "J" BODY CARS
CAVALIER, J2000, CIMARRON

Master Cylinder

REMOVE AND INSTALL POWER MASTER CYLINDER.

REMOVE

1. DISCONNECT ELECTRICAL LEAD AND FOUR HYDRAULIC LINES.
2. REMOVE TWO ATTACHING NUTS.
3. REMOVE MASTER CYLINDER AS SHOWN.

INSTALL

NOTICE: SEE NOTICE AT THE BEGINNING OF THIS SECTION.

1. INSTALL MASTER CYLINDER AS SHOWN AND TORQUE ATTACHING NUTS TO 30-40 N·m (22-30 FT. LBS.).
2. ATTACH ELECTRICAL LEAD AND FOUR HYDRAULIC LINES. TORQUE TUBE NUTS TO 13.6-20.3 N·m (120-180 IN. LBS.).

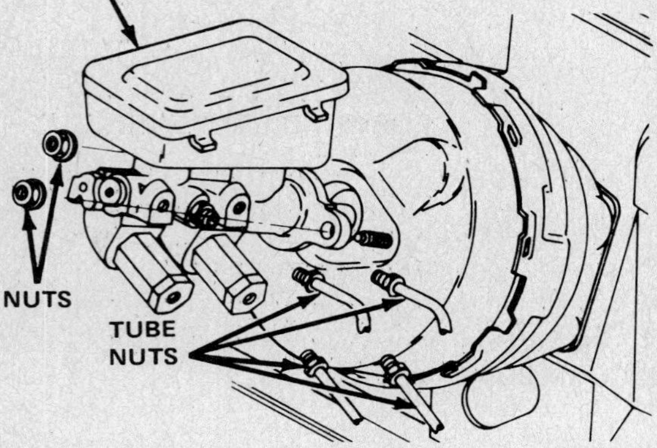

POWER MASTER CYLINDER

NUTS

TUBE NUTS

REMOVE AND INSTALL PROPORTIONERS AND FAILURE WARNING SWITCH.

REMOVE

1. REMOVE PARTS AS SHOWN.
2. FAILURE WARNING SWITCH O-RING IS OPTIONAL ON ORIGINAL EQUIPMENT.

INSTALL

NOTICE: SEE NOTICE AT THE BEGINNING OF THIS SECTION.

1. INSTALL NEW O-RINGS ON PROPORTIONERS AND FAILURE WARNING SWITCH.
2. INSTALL PROPORTIONERS AND TORQUE TO 24.1-41.0 N·m (18-30 IN. LBS.).
3. INSTALL FAILURE WARNING SWITCH AND TORQUE TO 1.7-5.6 N·m (15-50 IN. LBS.).

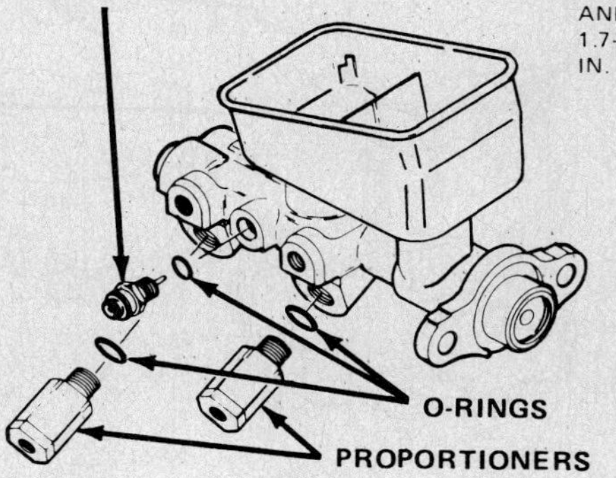

FAILURE WARNING SWITCH

O-RINGS

PROPORTIONERS

Parking Brake Lever

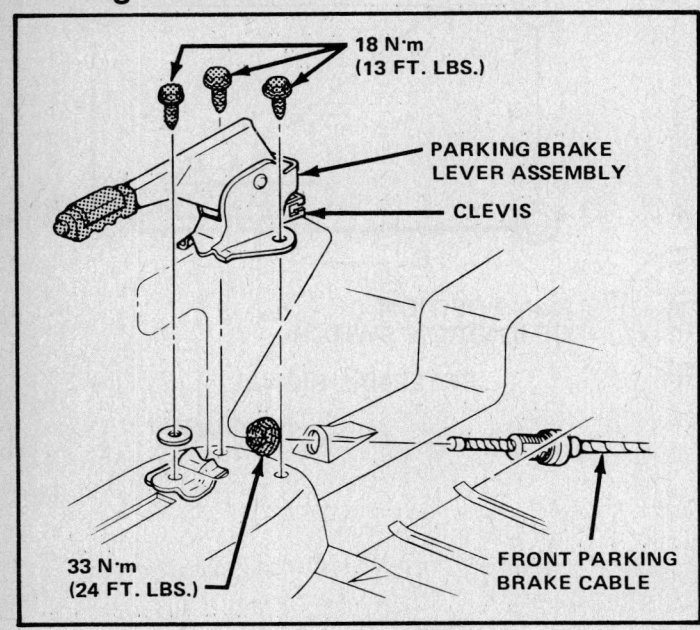

18 N·m (13 FT. LBS.)

PARKING BRAKE LEVER ASSEMBLY

CLEVIS

33 N·m (24 FT. LBS.)

FRONT PARKING BRAKE CABLE

Parking Brake Equalizer

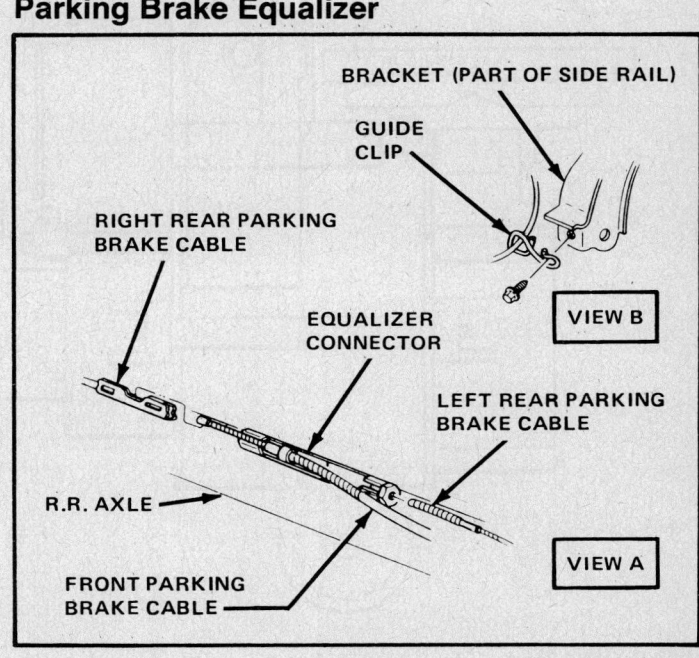

BRACKET (PART OF SIDE RAIL)

GUIDE CLIP

RIGHT REAR PARKING BRAKE CABLE

EQUALIZER CONNECTOR

LEFT REAR PARKING BRAKE CABLE

VIEW B

R.R. AXLE

FRONT PARKING BRAKE CABLE

VIEW A

A546

Front and Rear Brake Cables

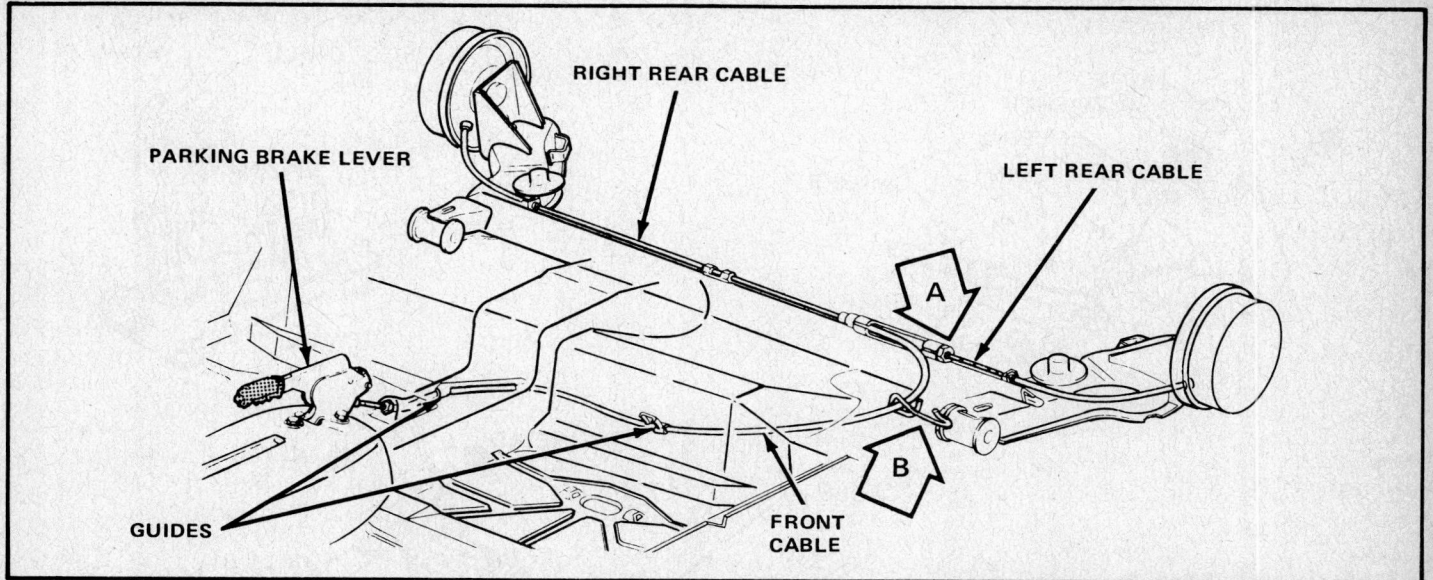

4. Remove cable retaining nut and bracket securing front cable to floor panel.

5. Raise car and loosen equalizer nut.

6. Loosen catalytic converter shield and remove parking brake cable from body.

7. Disconnect cable from equalizer and remove cable from guide and underbody clips.

Installation

To install, reverse the removal procedures. Adjust the cable tension after installation.

Parking Brake Cable

RIGHT-AND LEFT-HAND SECTIONS

Removal

1. Raise and suitably support car.

2. Back off equalizer nut until cable tension is eliminated.

3. Remove tire and wheel.

4. Remove brake drum.

5. Insert screwdriver between brake shoe and top part of brake adjuster bracket. Push bracket to the front and release the top adjuster bracket rod.

6. Remove rear hold down spring and remove actuator lever and lever return spring.

7. Remove adjuster screw spring.

8. Remove top rear brake shoe return spring.

9. Unhook parking brake cable from parking brake lever.

10. Depress conduit fitting retaining tangs and remove conduit fitting from backing plate.

11. Remove cable end button from connector.

12. Depress conduit fitting retaining tangs and remove conduit fitting from axle bracket.

Installation

Reverse removal procedure; adjust cable when installed.

MANUAL TRANSAXLE SECTION

Shift Cable Adjustment Procedure

1. Disconnect negative cable at battery.

2. Place transaxle into First gear.

3. Loosen shift cable attaching pins at transaxle lever "D" and "F".

4. Remove shifter boot and retainer.

5. Install a $5/32$-inch or No. 22 drill bit into alignment hole at side of shifter assembly, as shown in view C. Next install a yoke clip between tower and carrier as shown in view D.

6. Remove lash from transaxle by rotating lever "D" in direction of arrow while tightening nut "E".

7. Remove drill bit and yoke at shifter assembly.

8. Install shifter boot and retainer.

9. Connect negative cable at battery.

10. Road test vehicle to check for a good Neutral gate feel during shifting. It may be necessary to fine tune the adjustment after road testing.

GENERAL MOTORS "J" BODY CARS

CAVALIER, J2000, CIMARRON

Manual Transaxle On Car Adjustments

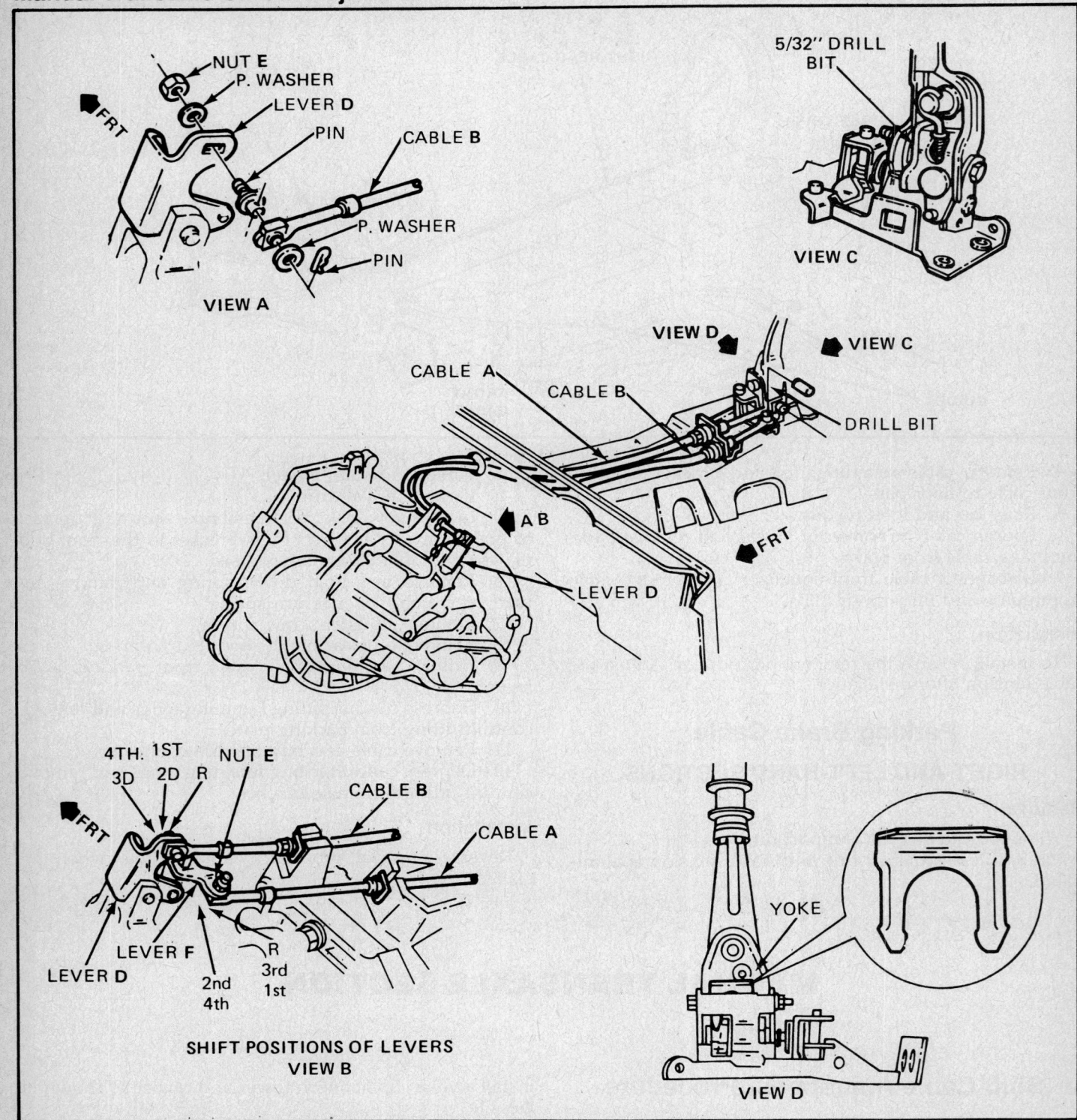

NUT **E**
P. WASHER
LEVER **D**
PIN
CABLE **B**
P. WASHER
PIN
FRT
VIEW A

5/32" DRILL BIT
VIEW C

VIEW D
VIEW C
CABLE **A**
CABLE **B**
DRILL BIT
A B
LEVER **D**
FRT

4TH. 1ST
3D 2D R
NUT **E**
CABLE **B**
CABLE **A**
FRT
R
3rd
1st
LEVER **F**
2nd
4th
LEVER **D**

SHIFT POSITIONS OF LEVERS
VIEW B

YOKE
VIEW D

Clutch Bracket and Cable Assembly

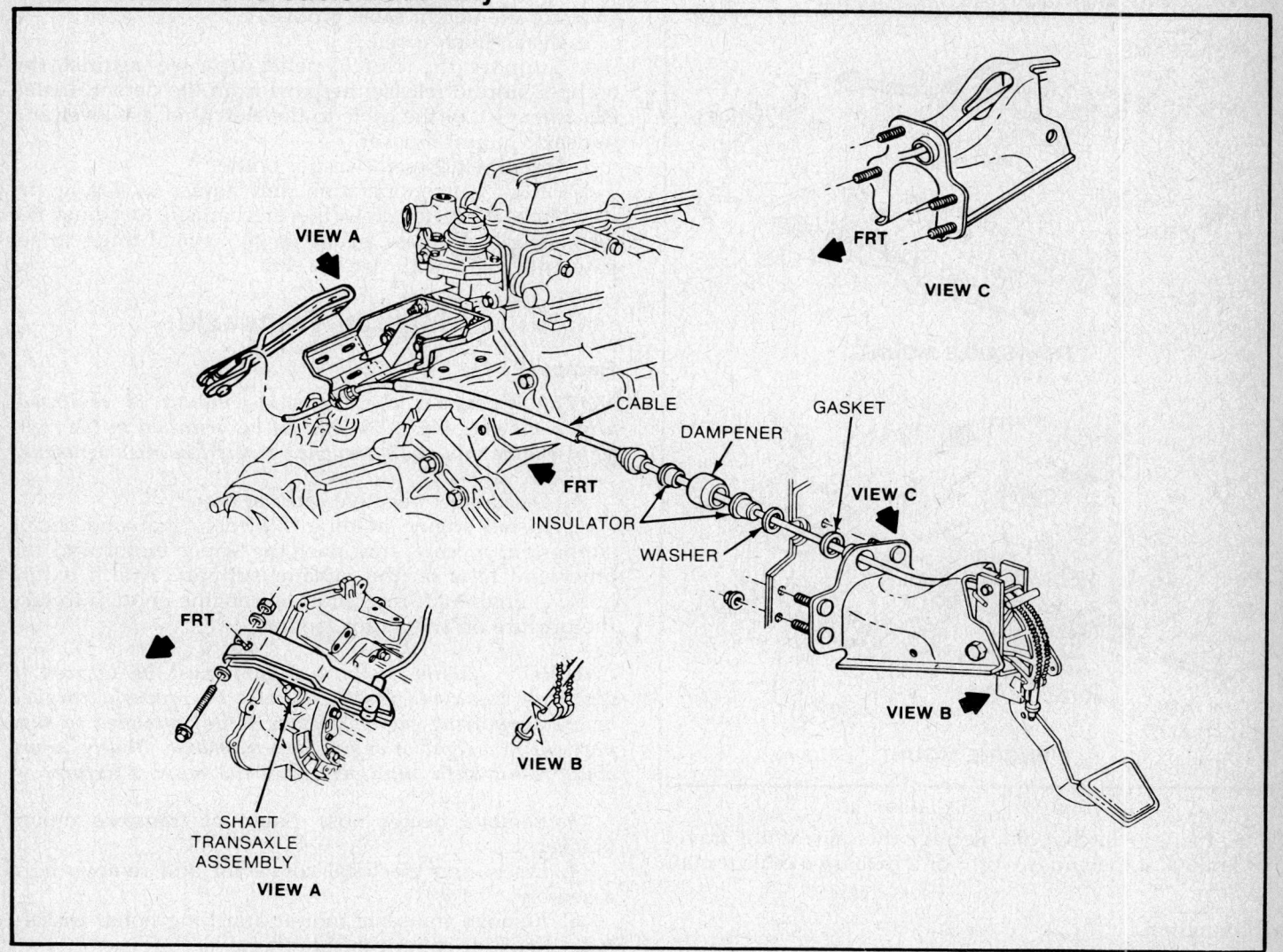

VIEW A

FRT

VIEW C

CABLE

DAMPENER

GASKET

VIEW C

FRT

INSULATOR

WASHER

VIEW B

FRT

VIEW B

SHAFT
TRANSAXLE
ASSEMBLY

VIEW A

Clutch Cable

The adjusting mechanism is mounted to the clutch pedal and bracket assembly. The cable is a fixed length and cannot be lengthened or shortened. However, the position of the cable can be changed by adjusting the position of the detent in relation to clutch pedal. The mechanism makes adjustments in the detent position (which changes the effective cable length). This is done by lifting the clutch pedal to disengage the pawl from the detent.

NOTE As the clutch friction material wears, the cable must be lengthened. This is accomplished by simply pulling the clutch pedal up to its rubber bumper. This action forces the pawl against its stop and rotates it out of mesh with the detent teeth, allowing the cable to play out until the detent spring load is balanced against the load applied by the release bearing. This adjustment procedure is required every 5,000 miles or less.

Removal

1. Support clutch pedal upward against the bumper stop to release the pawl from the detent. Disconnect the clutch cable from the clutch release lever at the transaxle assembly. Be careful and prevent the cable from snapping rapidly toward rear of car. The detent in the adjusting mechanism can be damaged by allowing the cable to snap back.
2. Remove hush panel from inside the car.
3. Disconnect the clutch cable from the detent end tangs. Lift the locking pawl away from the detent, then slide the cable forward between the detent and locking pawl.
4. Remove windshield washer bottle.
5. From the engine side of the cowl, pull the clutch cable out, disengaging it from the clutch pedal mounting bracket. The insulators, dampener and washers may separate from the cable when removing. Disconnect the cable from the transaxle mounting bracket and remove the cable.

Powertrain Mounts

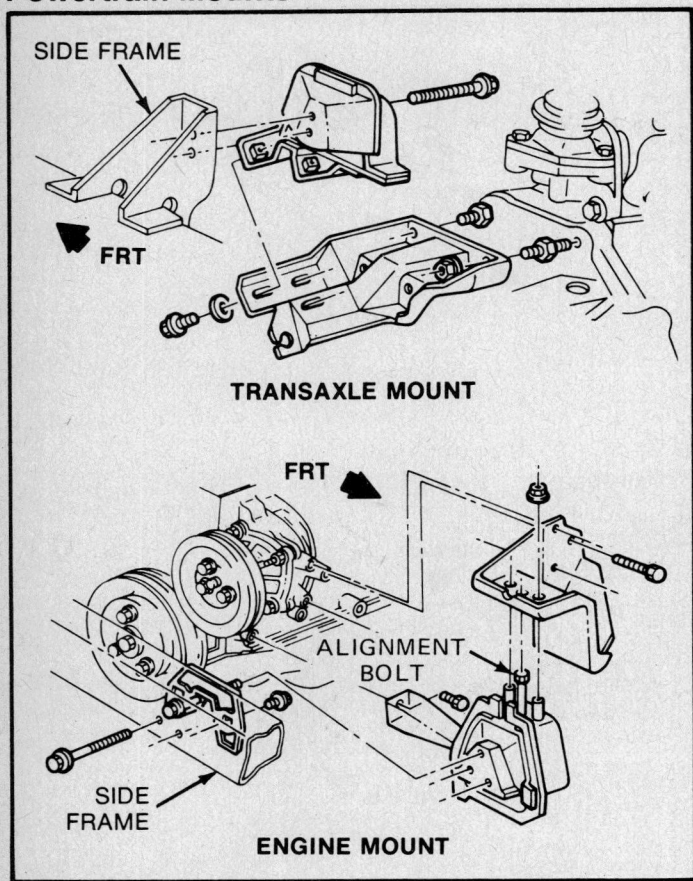

TRANSAXLE MOUNT

FRT

SIDE FRAME

ALIGNMENT BOLT

SIDE FRAME

ENGINE MOUNT

6. Inspect clutch cable. Replace the cable if it is frayed or kinked, if the end is worn, or if excessive cable friction exists.

Installation

1. Install cable into both insulators, damper and washer. Lubricate rear insulator with tire mounting lube or equivalent to ease assembly into pedal mounting bracket.
2. From inside car, attach the end of the cable to the

Manual Transaxle

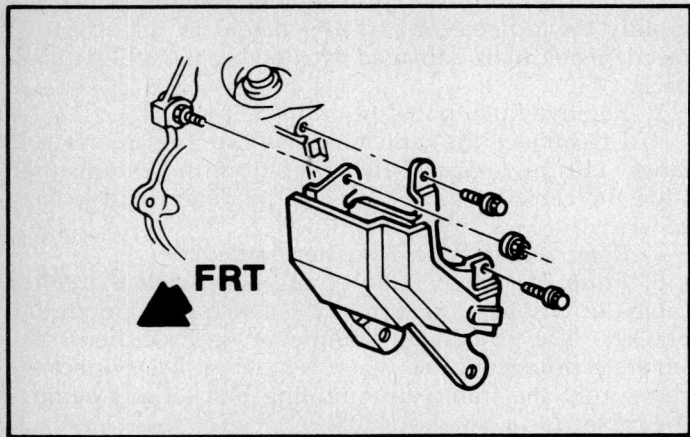

FRT

detent, being sure to route the cable underneath the pawl and into the detent cable groove.

3. Install hush panel.
4. Support the clutch pedal upward against the bumper stop to release the pawl from the detent. Install the other end of the cable to the clutch release lever and transaxle mount bracket.
5. Install windshield washer bottle.
6. Check clutch operation and adjust by lifting the clutch pedal up to allow the mechanism to adjust the cable length. Depress pedal slowly several times to set pawl into mesh with detent teeth.

Manual Transaxle

Removal

NOTE Whenever the transaxle mount is removed, alignment bolt M6X1X65.0 must be installed in the right front engine mount to prevent powertrain misalignment.

1. Disconnect negative cable at battery.
2. Install engine holding fixture so that one end is supported on cowl tray over the wiper motor and the other end rests on the radiator support. Attach fixture hook to engine lift ring and raise engine enough to take the presure off the motor mounts.

CAUTION Engine support fixture must be located in center of cowl and fasteners must be properly torqued before supporting engine. Fixture is not intended to support entire weight of engine and transaxle. Bodily injury could result with improper use of the support fixture.

3. Remove heater hose clamp at transaxle mount bracket.
4. Disconnect electrical connector and remove horn assembly.
5. Remove transaxle mount attaching bolts. Discard bolts attaching mount to side frame.

NOTE New bolts must be used at installation.

6. Disconnect the clutch cable from the clutch release lever.
7. Remove transaxle mount bracket attaching bolts and nuts.
8. Disconnect shift cables and retaining clips at the transaxle.
9. Disconnect ground cables at transaxle mounting stud.
10. Remove four upper transaxle-to-engine mounting bolts.
11. Raise vehicle.
12. Remove left front wheel and tire.
13. Remove left front inner splash shield.
14. Remove transaxle strut.
15. Remove transaxle strut bracket.
16. Remove clutch housing cover bolts.
17. Disconnect speedometer cable at transaxle.
18. Disconnect stabilizer bar at the left suspension support and control arm.

Transaxle-to-Engine Attachment

Engine Support Tools Installed

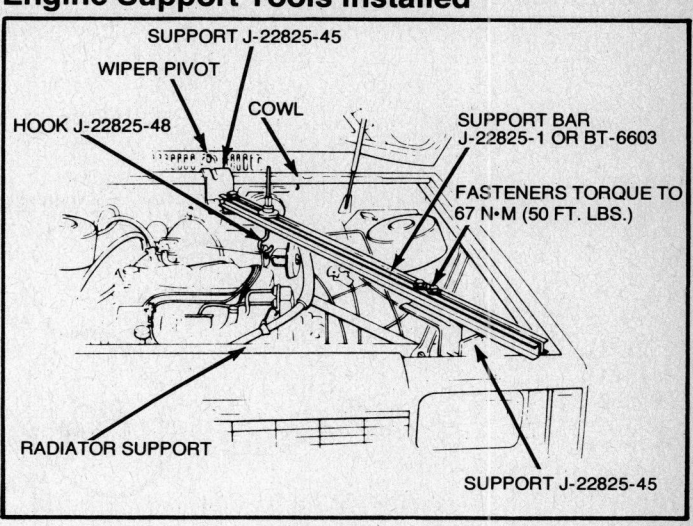

19. Disconnect the ball joint from the steering knuckle.

20. Remove left suspension support attaching bolts and remove the support and control as an assembly.

21. Install boot protectors and disengage drive axles at transaxle. Remove left shaft from transaxle.

22. Securely attach transaxle case to jack for removal.

23. Remove the lower two transaxle-to-engine mounting bolts.

24. Remove transaxle by sliding towards the driver's side, away from engine. Carefully lower the jack, guiding the right shaft out of the transaxle and move the transaxle to the bench.

Installation

1. When installing transaxle, guide the right drive axle shaft into its bore as the transaxle is being raised. The right-hand shaft *cannot* be readily installed after the transaxle is connected to engine.

2. Install the lower two transaxle-to-engine mounting bolts. Torque bolts to 75 N•m (55 ft.-lbs.).

3. Install left drive axle shaft into its bore at the transaxle. Seat right- and left-hand drive axle at transaxle.

4. Position suspension support to body and install attaching bolts. Torque bolts to 100 N•m (75 ft.-lbs.).

5. Install ball joint to steering knuckle.

6. Connect stabilizer bar to suspension support and control arm.

7. Connect speedometer cable to transaxle.

8. Install clutch housing cover bolts and torque to 15 N•m (10 ft.-lbs.).

9. Install strut bracket to transaxle assembly. Torque nut at mounting stud to 40 N•m (30 ft.-lbs) and bolts to 50 N•m (35 ft.-lbs.).

10. Install strut and torque bolts to 40 N•m (30 ft.-lbs.).

11. Install inner splash shield.

12. Install wheel and tire and torque wheel bolts.

13. Lower vehicle.

14. Install four upper transaxle-to-engine mounting bolts and torque to 75 N•m (55 ft.-lbs.).

15. Connect ground cables at transaxle mounting stud. Torque nut to 40 N•m (30 ft.-lbs.).

16. Connect shift cables and install retaining clips at transaxle.

17. Install transaxle mount bracket. Torque nuts to 40 N•m (30 ft.-lbs.) and bolts to 50 N•m (35 ft.-lbs.).

18. Connect clutch cable to release lever and mount bracket.

19. Position transaxle mount to side frame and attach with new bolts. Torque bolts to 50 N•m (40 ft.-lbs.).

20. Install bolts attaching mount to transaxle bracket. Before tightening bolts, check alignment bolt at the engine mount. If excessive effort is required to remove alignment bolt, re-align powertrain components. Tighten bolts to 50 N•m (40 ft.-lbs.) and then remove alignment bolt.

21. Install horn and connect wire.

22. Install hose clamp at mount bracket.

23. Remove engine support fixture and attaching hook from vehicle.

24. Connect negative cable at battery and adjust transaxle fluid level.

Pressure Plate/Clutch Disc

Removal

1. Remove transaxle assembly as outlined.

2. Mark the relationship of the pressure plate assembly to the flywheel, for reassembly in the same position.

3. Loosen the attaching bolts one turn at a time, until spring pressure is relieved.

4. Support the pressure plate, then remove the bolts. Remove the pressure plate and driven disc. Do not disassemble the pressure plate assembly. If defective, replace assembly.

5. Inspect the clutch disc, pressure plate, flywheel, clutch fork and pivot shaft assembly and release bearing. Replace parts as required. Also inspect the bearing retainer outer surface of the transaxle.

6. Clean the pressure plate and flywheel mating surfaces and the bearing retainer outer surface, of all oil, grease, metal deposits, and other foreign material.

Clutch and Flywheel

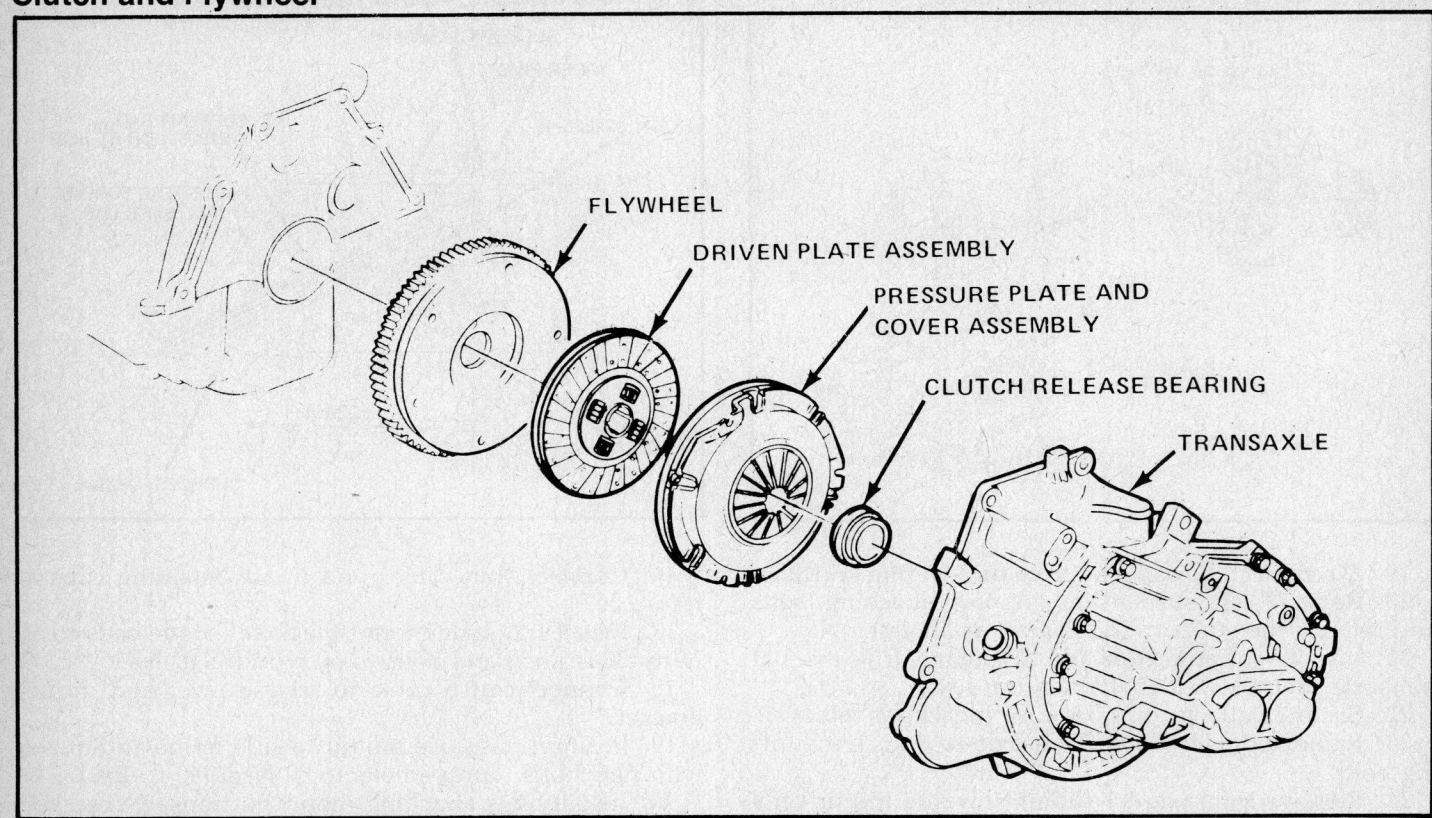

FLYWHEEL

DRIVEN PLATE ASSEMBLY

PRESSURE PLATE AND COVER ASSEMBLY

CLUTCH RELEASE BEARING

TRANSAXLE

Installation

1. Position the clutch disc and pressure plate in relative installed position, and support with alignment Tool no. J-29074 or the equivalent. The driven disc is installed with the damper springs offset toward the transaxle. Stamped letters on the driven disc identify "Flywheel Side."

2. Install the pressure plate assembly-to-flywheel bolts evenly and gradually. Remove the alignment tool. Torque bolts to 20 N•m (15 ft.-lbs.).

3. Lightly lubricate the outside diameter groove and completely pack full the inside diameter recess of the release bearing.

4. Install transaxle as outlined in this book.

5. Check clutch operation and adjust by lifting the clutch pedal up to allow the mechanism to adjust the cable length. Depress pedal slowly several times to set pawl into mesh with detent teeth.

AUTOMATIC TRANSAXLE SECTION

Adjustments

MANUAL LINKAGE

The transaxle manual linkage must be adjusted so that the indicator quadrant and stops correspond with the transaxle detents. If the linkage is not adjusted properly, an internal leak could occur which could cause a clutch or band to slip.

CAUTION   If a manual linkage adjustment is made with the selector lever in the Park position, the parking pawl should freely engage the reaction internal gear to prevent the car from rolling. Transmission, vehicle or personel injury may occur if not properly adjusted.

CHECKING T.V. CABLE IN VEHICLE

To check T.V. cable for freeness, pull ut on the upper end of the cable. The cable should travel a short distance with light spring resistance. This light resistance is due to the small coiled return spring on the T.V. lever and bracket that returns the lever to the zero T.V. or closed throttle position. Pulling the cable farther out moves the lever to contact the T.V. plunger, compressing the T.V. spring, which has more resistance. By releasing the upper-end of the T.V. cable, it should return to the zero T.V. position. This checks the cable in the housing, the T.V. lever and bracket, and the T.V. plunger in its bushing for freeness.

T.V. CONTROL CABLE ADJUSTMENT

This adjustment must be performed whenever the cable has been disconnected from the transaxle.
1. Install the cable into the transaxle.
2. Install the cable fitting into the engine bracket.

NOTE The slider must not ratchet through the fitting before or during assembly into the engine bracket. If ratcheting occurs, use the readjustment procedure to correct.

3. Install the cable terminal into the carburetor lever.
4. Open the carburetor lever to the full throttle position. This will automatically adjust the slider on the cable to the correct setting.

NOTE The lock tab must not be depressed during this operation.

5. Release the carburetor lever.

T.V. CONTROL CABLE READJUSTMENT

Readjustment may be necessary due to repairs to the throttle linkage or carburetor, or because of inadvertent adjustment before or during assembly of cable linkage to transaxle.
1. Depress and hold the metal lock tab.
2. Move the slider back through the fitting (away from the carburetor lever) until the slider stops against the fitting.
3. Release the metal lock tab.
4. Perform Steps 3, 4, and 5 of the "Adjustment" procedure.

Throttle Lever and Bracket Assembly

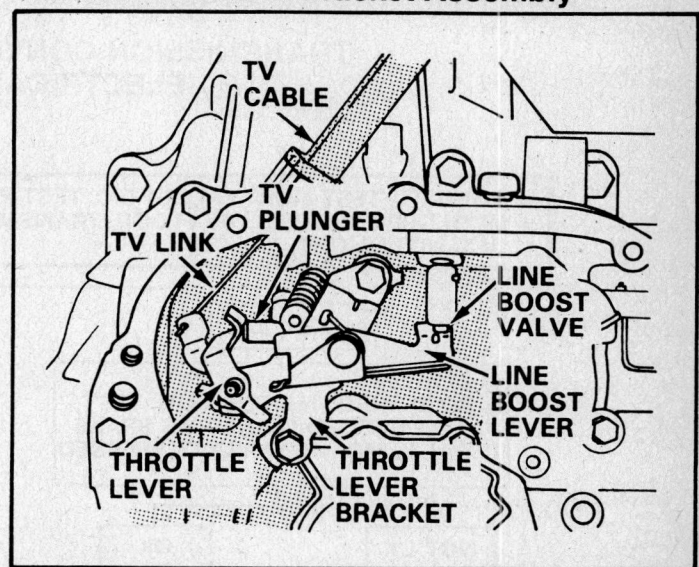

CHECKING T.V. CABLE ADJUSTMENT

1. Install line pressure gauge.
2. Check line pressure with selector lever in Park and engine at 1000 rpm.
3. check line pressure with selector lever in Neutral at 1000 rpm. Pressure should be the same to no more than 34 kPa (10 psi) higher than in Park.
4. Increase engine rpm to 1400; line pressure should increase.

T.V. Cable Adjustment

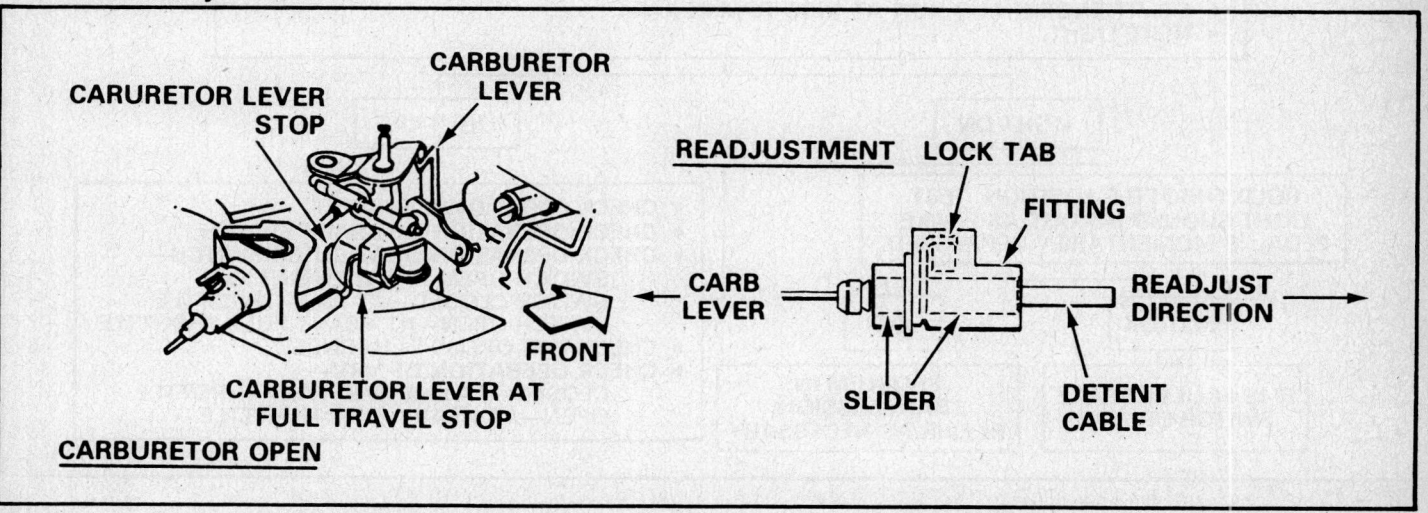

TRANSMISSION CONVERTER CLUTCH (T.C.C.) ELECTRICAL DIAGNOSIS

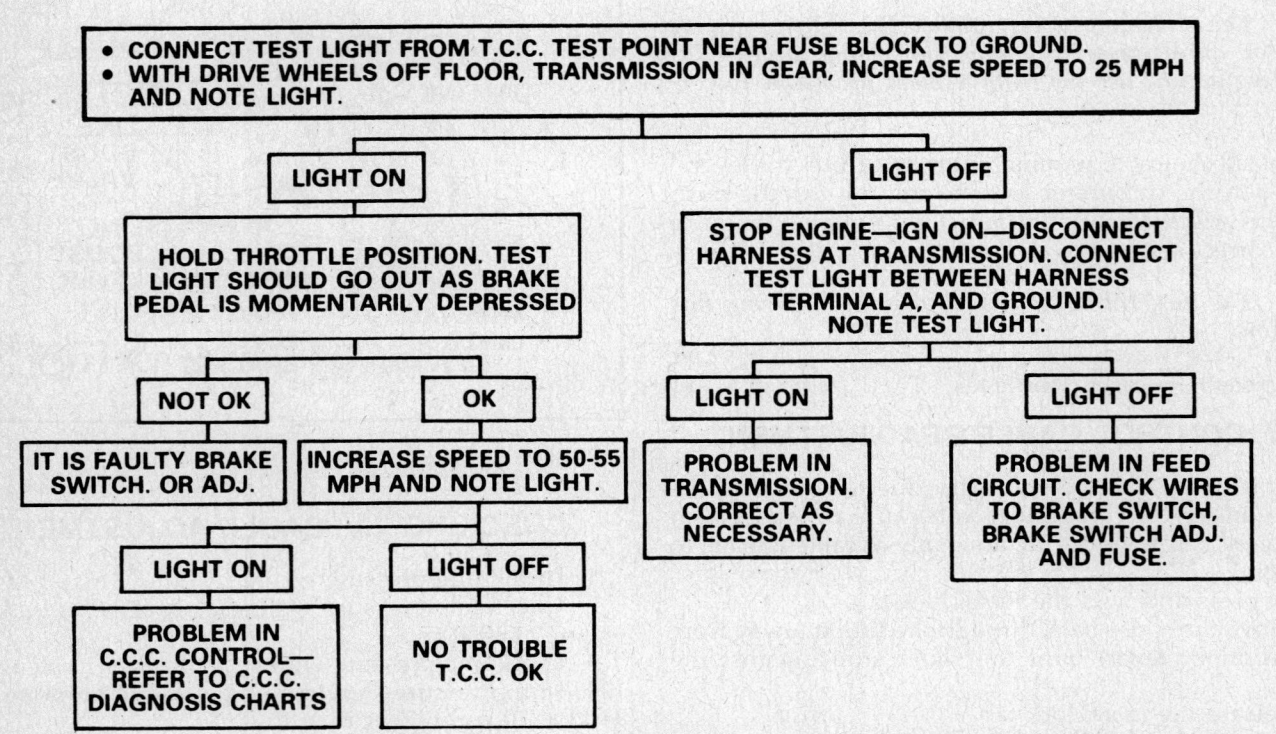

- CONNECT TEST LIGHT FROM T.C.C. TEST POINT NEAR FUSE BLOCK TO GROUND.
- WITH DRIVE WHEELS OFF FLOOR, TRANSMISSION IN GEAR, INCREASE SPEED TO 25 MPH AND NOTE LIGHT.

LIGHT ON

HOLD THROTTLE POSITION. TEST LIGHT SHOULD GO OUT AS BRAKE PEDAL IS MOMENTARILY DEPRESSED

NOT OK — IT IS FAULTY BRAKE SWITCH. OR ADJ.

OK — INCREASE SPEED TO 50-55 MPH AND NOTE LIGHT.

LIGHT ON — PROBLEM IN C.C.C. CONTROL—REFER TO C.C.C. DIAGNOSIS CHARTS

LIGHT OFF — NO TROUBLE T.C.C. OK

LIGHT OFF

STOP ENGINE—IGN ON—DISCONNECT HARNESS AT TRANSMISSION. CONNECT TEST LIGHT BETWEEN HARNESS TERMINAL A, AND GROUND. NOTE TEST LIGHT.

LIGHT ON — PROBLEM IN TRANSMISSION. CORRECT AS NECESSARY.

LIGHT OFF — PROBLEM IN FEED CIRCUIT. CHECK WIRES TO BRAKE SWITCH, BRAKE SWITCH ADJ. AND FUSE.

Cars Not Equipped With Computer Command Control (C.C.C.)

Mechanical checks such as linkage, oil level, etc. should be performed prior to using this table.

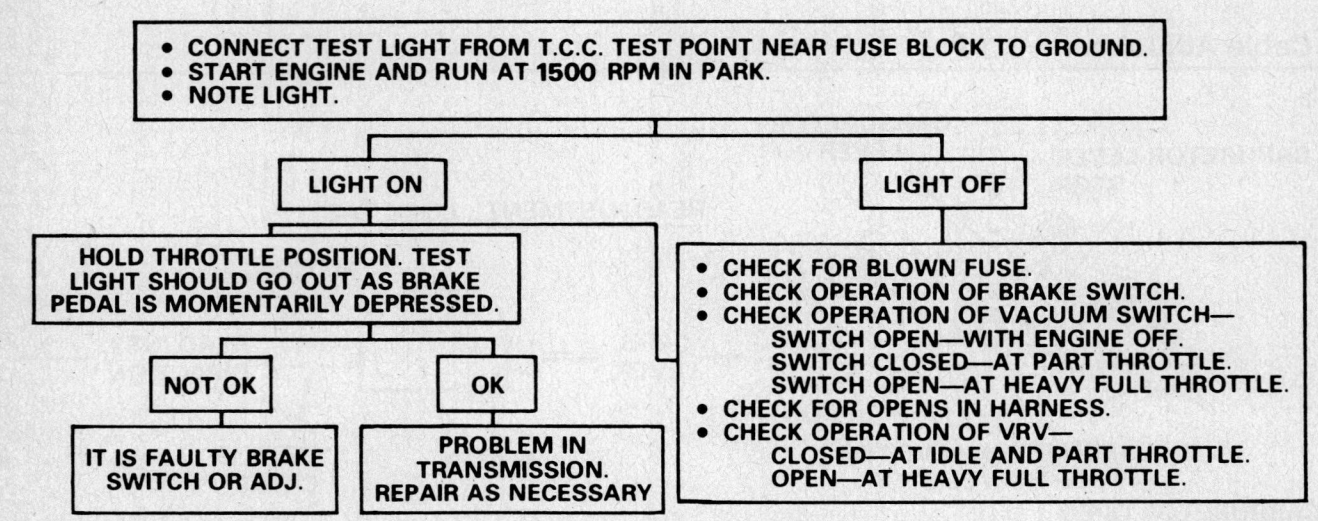

- CONNECT TEST LIGHT FROM T.C.C. TEST POINT NEAR FUSE BLOCK TO GROUND.
- START ENGINE AND RUN AT 1500 RPM IN PARK.
- NOTE LIGHT.

LIGHT ON

HOLD THROTTLE POSITION. TEST LIGHT SHOULD GO OUT AS BRAKE PEDAL IS MOMENTARILY DEPRESSED.

NOT OK — IT IS FAULTY BRAKE SWITCH OR ADJ.

OK — PROBLEM IN TRANSMISSION. REPAIR AS NECESSARY

LIGHT OFF

- CHECK FOR BLOWN FUSE.
- CHECK OPERATION OF BRAKE SWITCH.
- CHECK OPERATION OF VACUUM SWITCH—
  SWITCH OPEN—WITH ENGINE OFF.
  SWITCH CLOSED—AT PART THROTTLE.
  SWITCH OPEN—AT HEAVY FULL THROTTLE.
- CHECK FOR OPENS IN HARNESS.
- CHECK OPERATION OF VRV—
  CLOSED—AT IDLE AND PART THROTTLE.
  OPEN—AT HEAVY FULL THROTTLE.

Automatic Transaxle

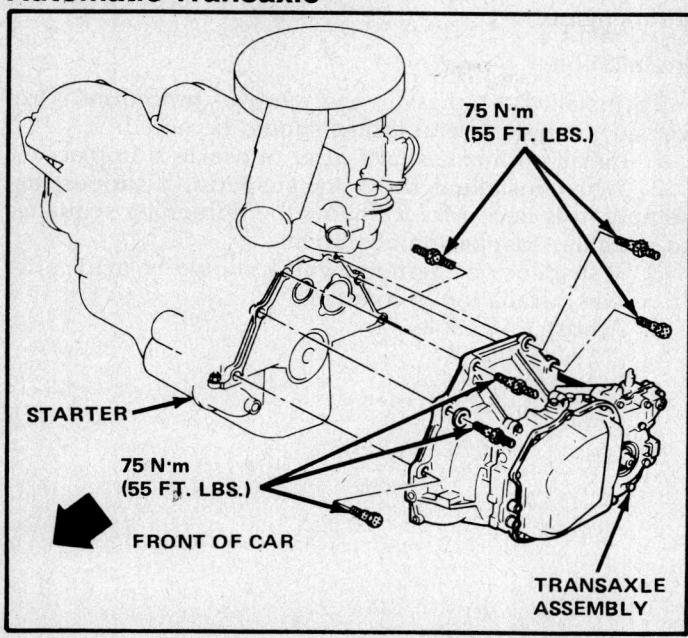

75 N·m (55 FT. LBS.)

STARTER

75 N·m (55 FT. LBS.)

FRONT OF CAR

TRANSAXLE ASSEMBLY

Transaxle Assembly

Removal

1. Disconnect negative battery cable from transaxle.
2. Using a ¼ x 2-inch long bolt, insert bolt in hole at front right-hand motor mount to prevent mount mislocation during transaxle removal.
3. Remove carburetor air cleaner and disconnect T.V. cable at carburetor.
4. Remove bolt securing T.V. cable to transaxle. Pull up on cable cover at transaxle until cable is seen. Disconnect cable from transaxle rod.
5. Remove bolt securing engine wire harness at top front of transaxle.
6. Remove hose from air management valve, allowing the engine wire harness to be pulled up and out of way.
7. Install engine support fixture and raise engine enough to take pressure from motor mounts.

CAUTION Engine support must be located in center of cowl and fasteners must be torqued before supporting engine. Fixture is not intended to support entire weight of engine and transaxle. Bodily injury could result with improper use of support fixture.

Engine Support Fixture

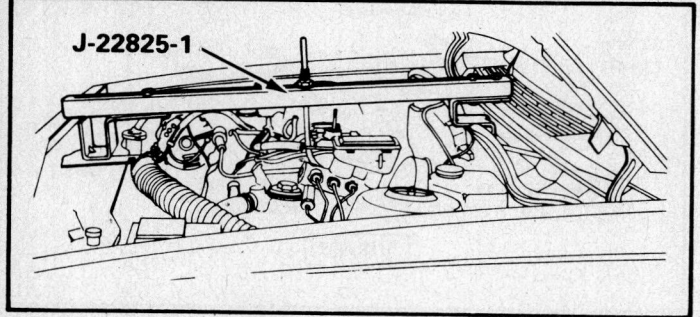

J-22825-1

Front Engine Mount

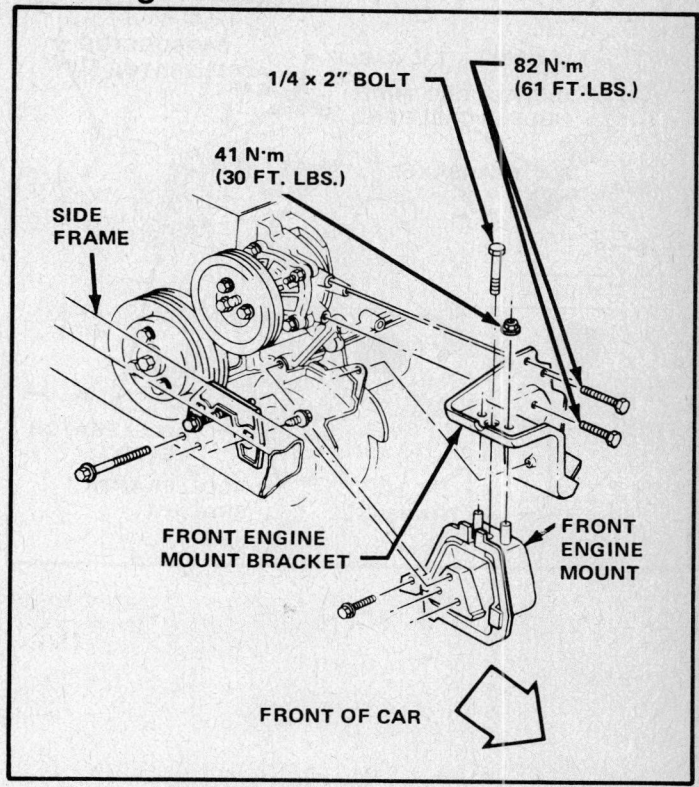

1/4 x 2" BOLT

82 N·m (61 FT.LBS.)

41 N·m (30 FT. LBS.)

SIDE FRAME

FRONT ENGINE MOUNT BRACKET

FRONT ENGINE MOUNT

FRONT OF CAR

8. Remove top transaxle mount and bracket assembly.
9. Disconnect shift control linkage from transaxle.
10. Remove top transaxle-to-engine mounting bolts. Loosen transaxle-to-engine bolt near starter but do not remove.

Flex Plate Installation

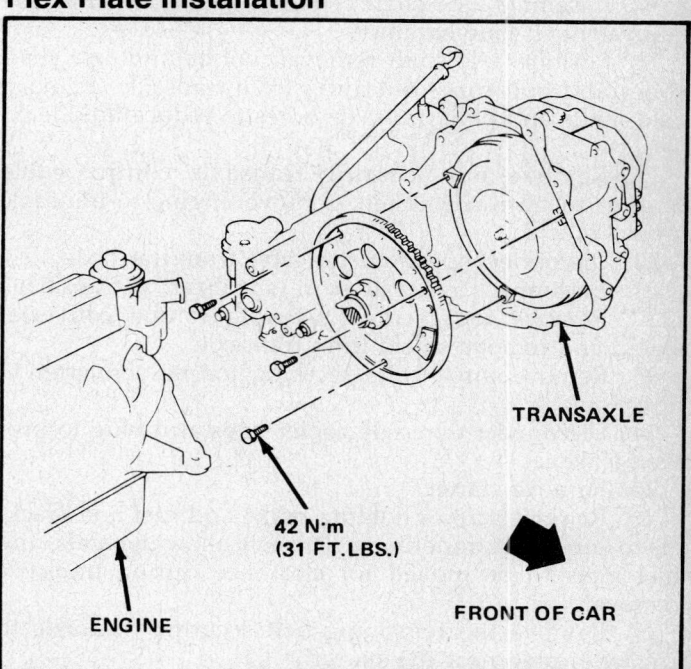

TRANSAXLE

42 N·m (31 FT.LBS.)

ENGINE

FRONT OF CAR

T.V. Control Cable

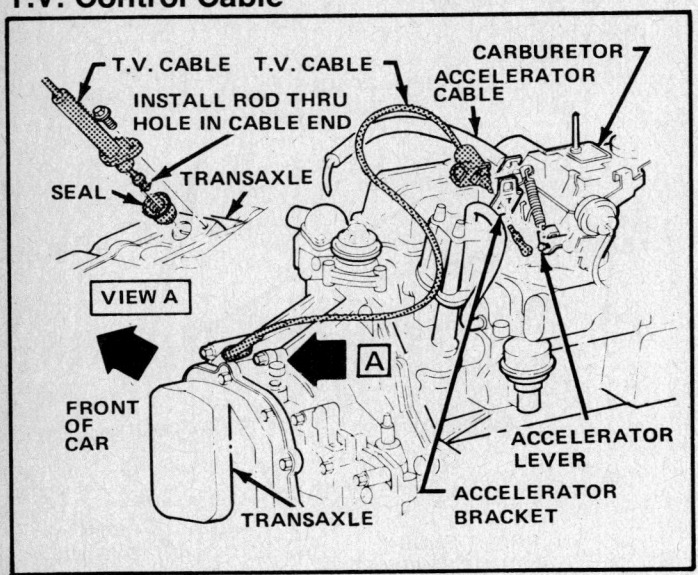

Installation

To install the transaxle, the removal procedure is reversed, though several things should be noted:

1. Install both axle shafts **after** transaxle is in place.
2. When installing the front suspension support assembly, it is necessary to follow the tightening sequence to maintain suspension alignment.
3. A suspension alignment check should be made after transaxle installation is complete.
4. Adjust T.V. cable.

28. Remove transaxle by sliding to left side and away from engine.

11. Unlock steering column and raise car.
12. Remove both front wheel/tire assemblies.
13. Remove cotter pin and loosen the castelled ball joint nut until ball joint separates from control arm.
14. Repeat on other side.
15. Remove bolt securing stabilizer bar to left-hand lower control arm.
16. Remove six bolts securing left front suspension support assembly.
17. Assemble axle shaft removal Tool J-28468 or the equivalent to slide hammer.
18. Position axle shaft removal tool behind axle shaft cones and pull cones out away from transaxle. Remove axle shafts and plug transaxle bores to reduce fluid leakage.
19. Remove nut securing transaxle control cable bracket to transaxle. Then, remove engine-to-transaxle stud.
20. Disconnect speedometer cable from transaxle.
21. Disconnect transaxle strut (stabilizer) at transaxle.
22. Remove four screws securing torque converter shield and remove shield from transaxle.
23. Remove three bolts securing torque converter to flex plate.
24. Disconnect transaxle cooler lines and plug to prevent leakage.
25. Remove starter.
26. Remove screws holding brake and fuel line brackets to left side of underbody. This will allow the brake and fuel lines to be moved for clearance during transaxle removal.
27. Remove the remaining bolt securing transaxle to engine located near the starter.

Transaxle Mounts

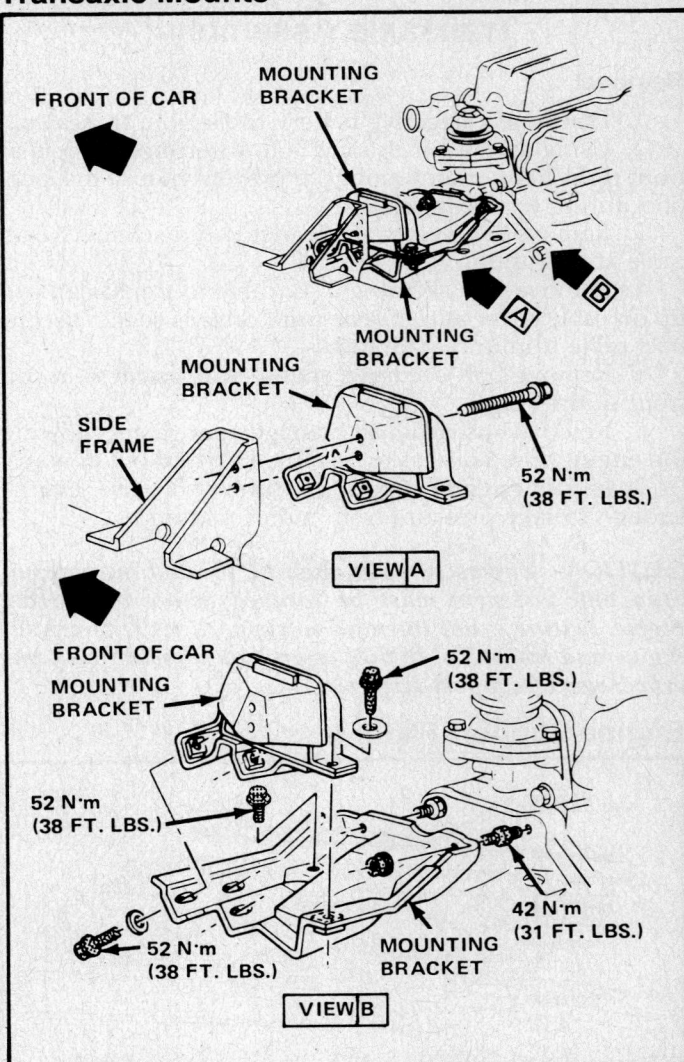

DRIVE AXLE SECTION

1. REMOVE AND INSTALL OUTER JOINT SEAL.

REMOVE

1. Remove parts as shown.

INSTALL

1. Flush grease from joint and repack joint with approx. half of grease provided.
2. Put remainder of grease in seal.
3. Install parts as shown. Use tool J-22610 to secure seal retaining clamp.

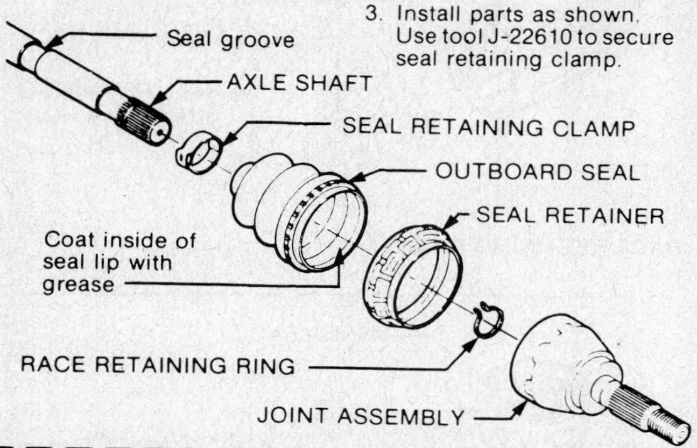

- Seal groove
- AXLE SHAFT
- SEAL RETAINING CLAMP
- OUTBOARD SEAL
- SEAL RETAINER
- Coat inside of seal lip with grease
- RACE RETAINING RING
- JOINT ASSEMBLY

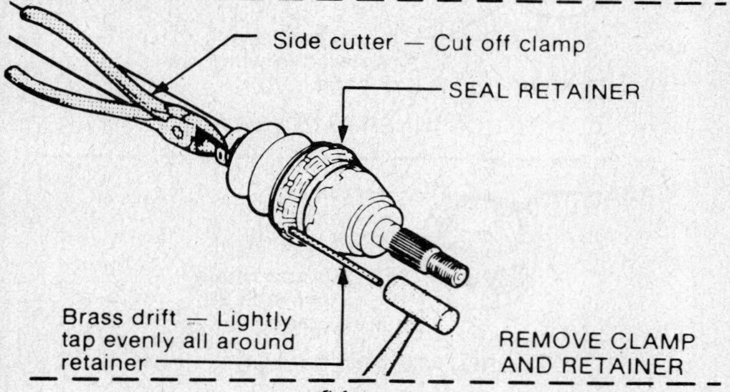

- Side cutter — Cut off clamp
- SEAL RETAINER
- Brass drift — Lightly tap evenly all around retainer
- REMOVE CLAMP AND RETAINER

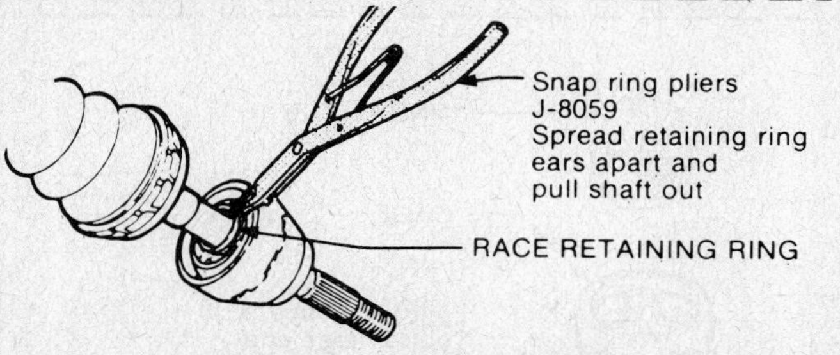

- Snap ring pliers J-8059 Spread retaining ring ears apart and pull shaft out
- RACE RETAINING RING

REMOVE JOINT ASSEMBLY

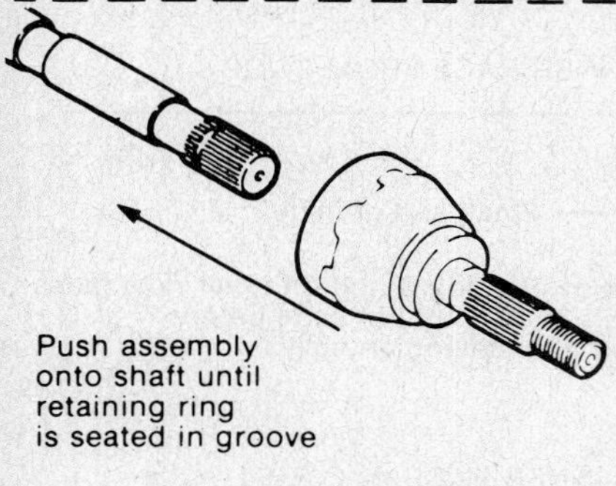

- Push assembly onto shaft until retaining ring is seated in groove

INSTALL JOINT ASSEMBLY

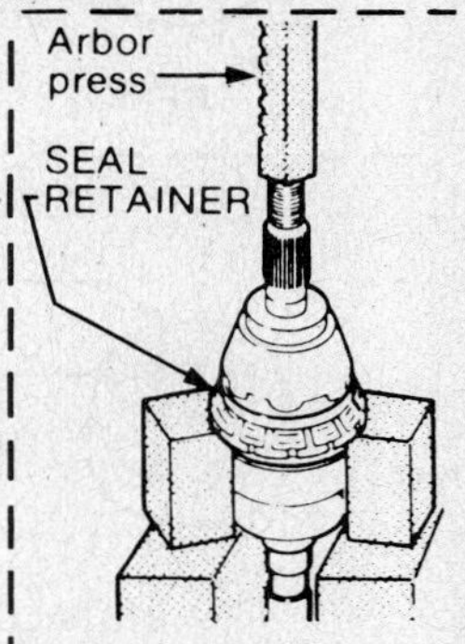

- Arbor press
- SEAL RETAINER

INSTALL SEAL RETAINER

2. DISASSEMBLE AND ASSEMBLE OUTER JOINT ASSEMBLY.

REMOVE

1. Remove parts as shown.

INSTALL

1. Put a light coat of recommended grease on ball grooves of inner and outer races.
2. Install parts as shown. Be sure retaining ring side of inner race faces axle shaft.
3. Pack joint with recommended grease.

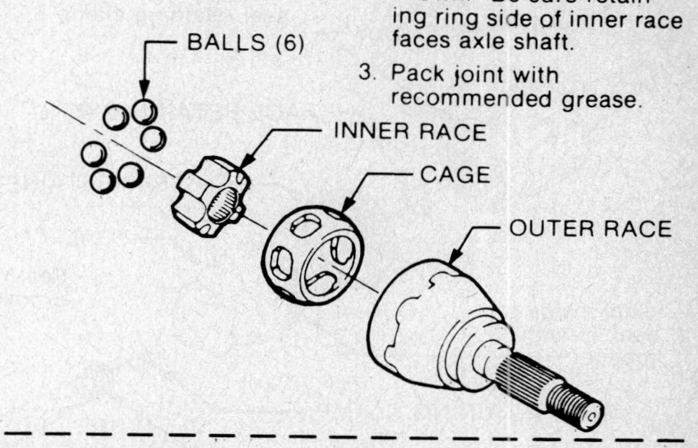

- BALLS (6)
- INNER RACE
- CAGE
- OUTER RACE

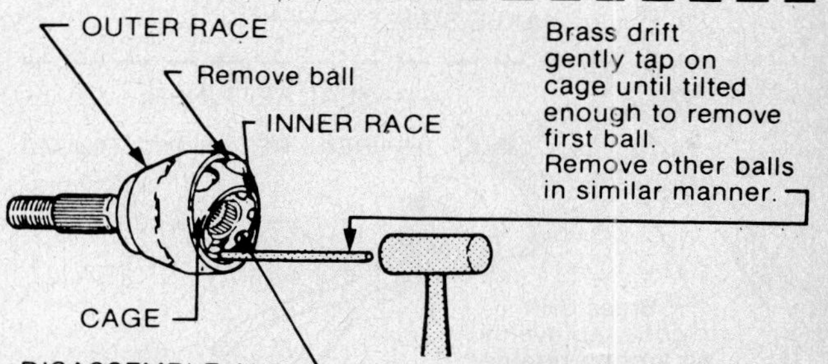

- OUTER RACE
- Remove ball
- INNER RACE
- CAGE
- Brass drift gently tap on cage until tilted enough to remove first ball. Remove other balls in similar manner.
- Retaining ring side of inner race.

DISASSEMBLE AND ASSEMBLE BALLS

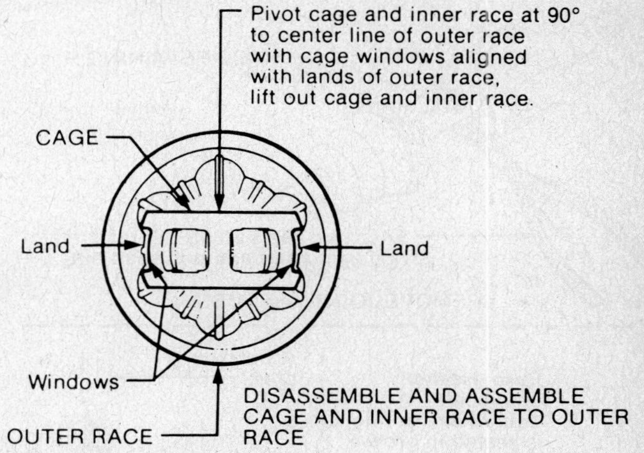

- Pivot cage and inner race at 90° to center line of outer race with cage windows aligned with lands of outer race, lift out cage and inner race.
- CAGE
- Land
- Land
- Windows
- OUTER RACE

DISASSEMBLE AND ASSEMBLE CAGE AND INNER RACE TO OUTER RACE

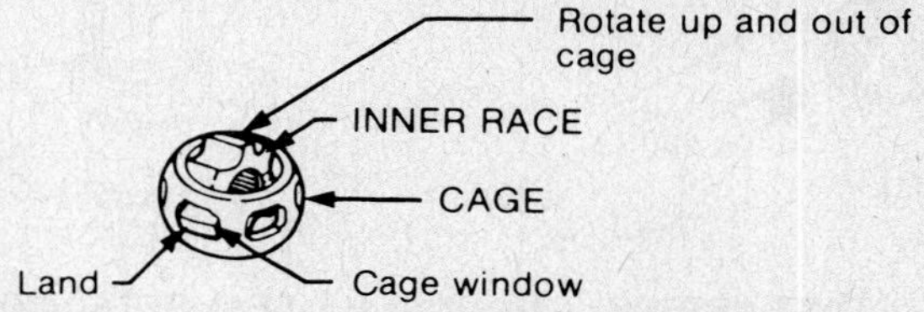

- Rotate up and out of cage
- INNER RACE
- CAGE
- Land
- Cage window

DISASSEMBLE AND ASSEMBLE INNER RACE AND CAGE

A557

GENERAL MOTORS "J" BODY CARS

CAVALIER, J2000, CIMARRON

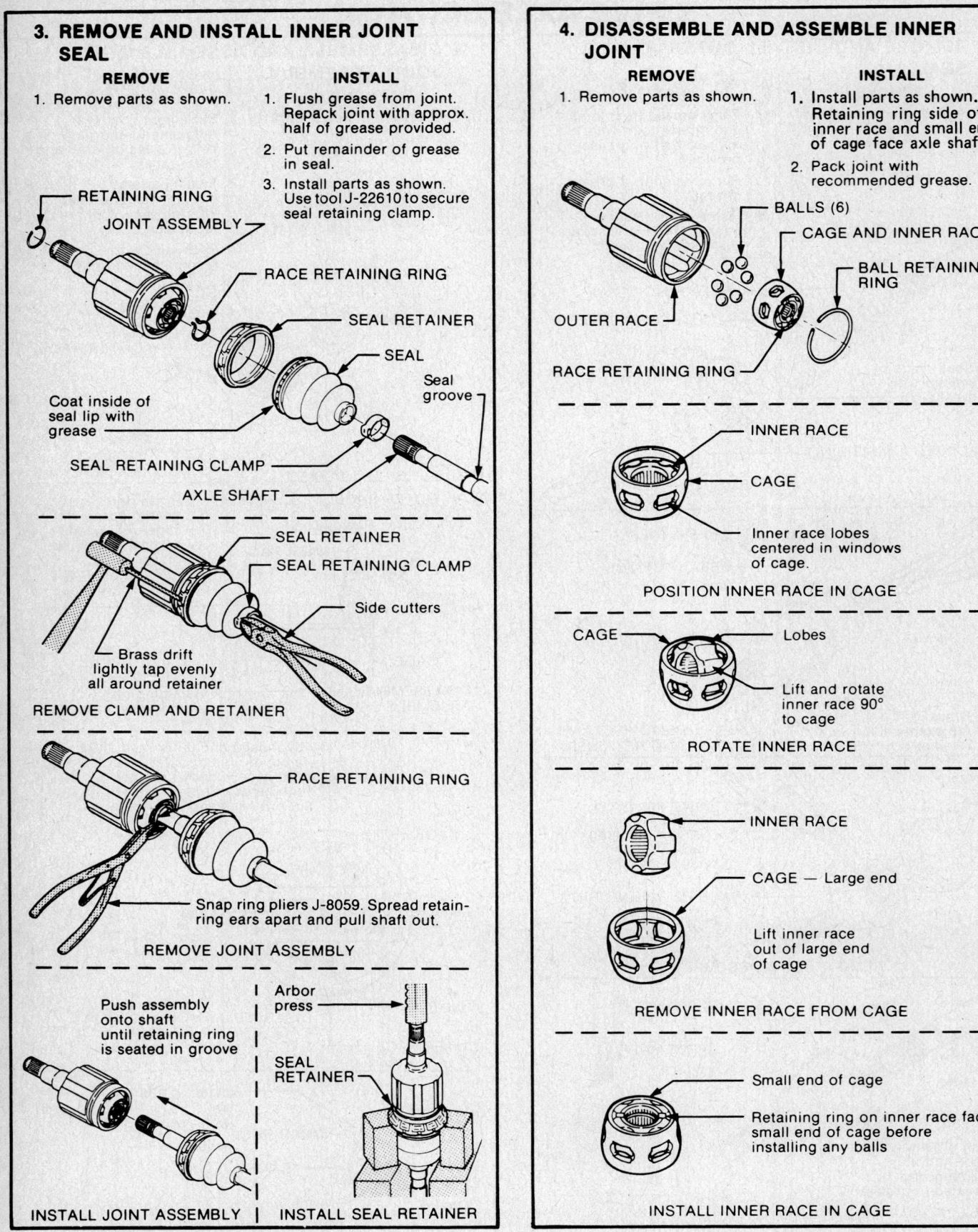

3. REMOVE AND INSTALL INNER JOINT SEAL

REMOVE

1. Remove parts as shown.

INSTALL

1. Flush grease from joint. Repack joint with approx. half of grease provided.
2. Put remainder of grease in seal.
3. Install parts as shown. Use tool J-22610 to secure seal retaining clamp.

RETAINING RING
JOINT ASSEMBLY
RACE RETAINING RING
SEAL RETAINER
SEAL
Seal groove
Coat inside of seal lip with grease
SEAL RETAINING CLAMP
AXLE SHAFT

SEAL RETAINER
SEAL RETAINING CLAMP
Side cutters
Brass drift lightly tap evenly all around retainer

REMOVE CLAMP AND RETAINER

RACE RETAINING RING
Snap ring pliers J-8059. Spread retaining-ring ears apart and pull shaft out.

REMOVE JOINT ASSEMBLY

Push assembly onto shaft until retaining ring is seated in groove

Arbor press
SEAL RETAINER

INSTALL JOINT ASSEMBLY | INSTALL SEAL RETAINER

4. DISASSEMBLE AND ASSEMBLE INNER JOINT

REMOVE

1. Remove parts as shown.

INSTALL

1. Install parts as shown. Retaining ring side of inner race and small end of cage face axle shaft.
2. Pack joint with recommended grease.

BALLS (6)
CAGE AND INNER RACE
BALL RETAINING RING
OUTER RACE
RACE RETAINING RING

INNER RACE
CAGE
Inner race lobes centered in windows of cage.

POSITION INNER RACE IN CAGE

CAGE
Lobes
Lift and rotate inner race 90° to cage

ROTATE INNER RACE

INNER RACE
CAGE — Large end
Lift inner race out of large end of cage

REMOVE INNER RACE FROM CAGE

Small end of cage
Retaining ring on inner race faces small end of cage before installing any balls

INSTALL INNER RACE IN CAGE

A558

INDEX

MODEL IDENTIFICATION

1976 CHEVETTE
W.B. **94.3"**. Length 159". Ship. Wgt. 4 Cyl. 2 Dr. 1920 Lbs.

1977 CHEVETTE
W.B. **94.3"**. Length 159". Width 62". Ship. Wgt. 4 Cyl. 2 Dr. 1958 Lbs.

1978 CHEVETTE
W.B. **94.3"** Length 158.8" Ship. Wgt. 4 Cyl. 2 Dr. 1964.9 Lbs.

1979 CHEVETTE
W.B. **97.3"** Length 162.6" Ship. Wgt. 4 Cyl. 2 Dr. 1964 Lbs.

1980 CHEVETTE
W.B. **97.3"**. Length 162.6". Ship. Wgt. 4 Cyl. 2 Dr. 1964 Lbs.

1981-82 CHEVETTE
W.B. **97.3"**. Length 162.6". 4 Cyl. 2 Dr. Ship. Wgt. 1964 Lbs.

1982 PONTIAC T1000
W.B. **97.3"**. Length 164.9". 4 Cyl. 2 Dr. Curb Wgt. 2119 Lbs.

Isuzu Diesel

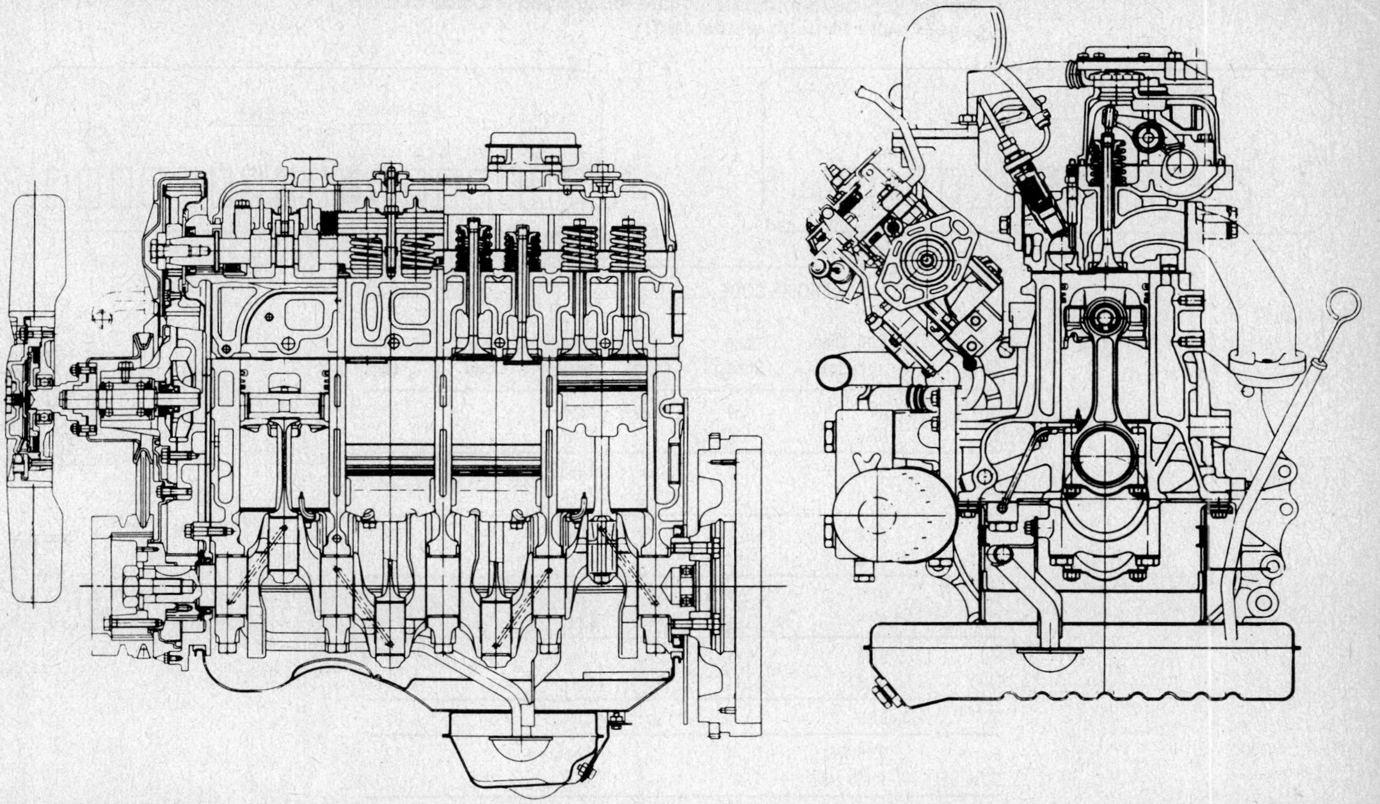

Fuse Panel

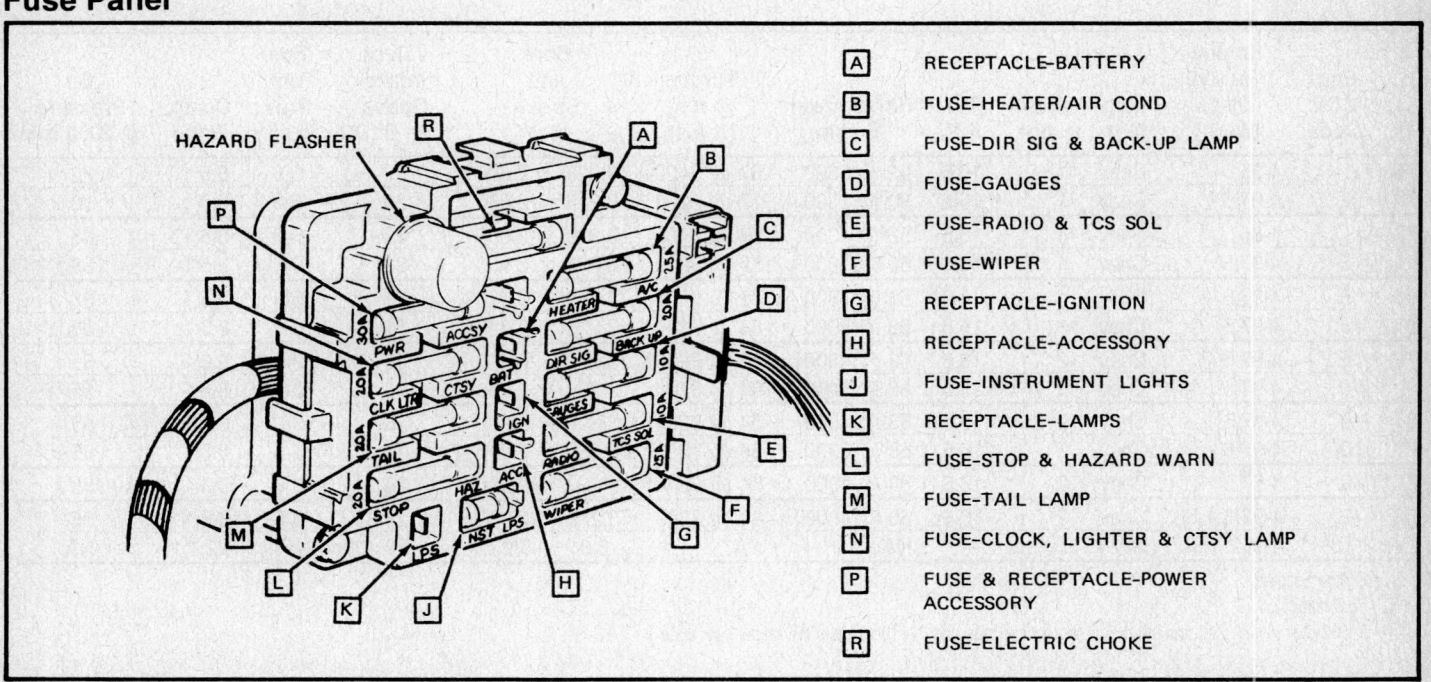

A	RECEPTACLE-BATTERY
B	FUSE-HEATER/AIR COND
C	FUSE-DIR SIG & BACK-UP LAMP
D	FUSE-GAUGES
E	FUSE-RADIO & TCS SOL
F	FUSE-WIPER
G	RECEPTACLE-IGNITION
H	RECEPTACLE-ACCESSORY
J	FUSE-INSTRUMENT LIGHTS
K	RECEPTACLE-LAMPS
L	FUSE-STOP & HAZARD WARN
M	FUSE-TAIL LAMP
N	FUSE-CLOCK, LIGHTER & CTSY LAMP
P	FUSE & RECEPTACLE-POWER ACCESSORY
R	FUSE-ELECTRIC CHOKE

GENERAL MOTORS "T" BODY CARS

CHEVETTE, T1000

VEHICLE IDENTIFICATION NUMBER (VIN)①

Typical Vehicle Identification Plate located top left side of dash panel visible through windshiled.

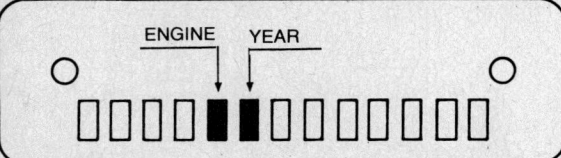
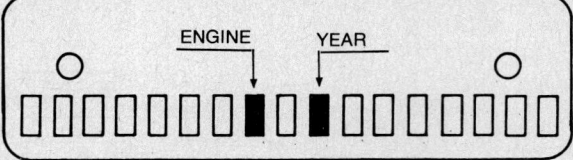

ENGINE CODE					MODEL YEAR CODE	
Code	Eng. Disp. (cu in)	Eng. Config.	Carb	Eng. Mfgr.	Code	Year
I	85	L-4	1v	Chev	6	76
E	97.6	L-4	1v	Chev		
I	85	L-4	1v	Chev	7	77
E	97.6	L-4	1v	Chev		
E	97.6	L-4	1v	Chev	8	78
J	97.6	L-4	1v	Chev		
E	97.6	L-4	2v	Chev	9	79
O	97.6	L-4	2v	Chev		
9	97.6	L-4	2v	Chev	A	80
O②	97.6	L-4	2v	Chev		
9	97.6	L-4	2v	Chev	B	81
9	97.6 1.6L	L-4	2v	Chev	2	82
D-DIESEL	112.0 1.8L	L-4	—	Isuzu	2	

① If a 17-digit VIN is used, the 8th digit is the engine code and the 10th digit is the model year code
② Dual takedown

ENGINE SPECIFICATIONS

Yr.	Eng. V.I.N. Code	Engine No. Cyl. Disp. (cu in)	Eng. Mfgr.	Carb Bbl	Tax H.P.	Horsepower @ rpm	Torque @ rpm (ft lbs)	Bore and Stroke (in)	Valves Intake Opens (deg BTDC)	Fuel Pump Pres. (p.s.i.)	Comp. Ratio	Oil Pressure @ 2000 rpm
76	I	4-85	Chev	1	16.6	52 @ 5300	67 @ 3400	3.228 × 2.606	32	5-6	8.5:1	38
	E	4-97.6	Chev	1	16.6	60 @ 5300	77 @ 3200	3.228 × 2.980	32	5-6	8.5:1	38
77	I	4-85	Chev	1	16.6	52 @ 5300	67 @ 3400	3.228 × 2.606	32	5-6	8.5:1	38
	E	4-97.6	Chev	1	16.6	60 @ 5300	77 @ 3200	3.228 × 2.980	32	5-6	8.5:1	38
78	E	4-97.6	Chev	1	16.6	63 @ 4800	82 @ 3200	3.228 × 2.980	28	5-6	8.5:1	38
	J	4-97.6	Chev	1	16.6	68 @ 5000	84 @ 3200	3.228 × 2.980	31	5-6	8.5:1	38
79	E	4-97.6	Chev	2	16.6	63 @ 4800†	82 @ 3200†	3.228 × 2.980	28	3-6	8.6:1	55
	O	4-97.6	Chev	2	16.6	68 @ 5000†	84 @ 3200†	3.228 × 2.980	31	3-6	8.6:1	55
80	9	4-97.6	Chev	2	16.6	63 @ 4800	84 @ 3200†	3.228 × 2.980	28	3-6	8.6:1	55
	O①	4-97.6	Chev	2	16.6	68 @ 5000	84 @ 3200†	3.228 × 2.980	31	3-6	8.6:1	55
81	9	4-97.6	Chev	2	16.6	63 @ 4800	84 @ 3200†	3.228 × 2.980	28	3-6	8.6:1	55
82	9	4-97.6 1.6L	Chev	2	16.6	63 @ 4800	84 @ 3200	3.228 × 2.980	28	3-6	8.5:1	55
	D	4-112 1.8L	Isuzu	Diesel	—	NA	NA	3.31 × 3.23	32	—	22.1:1	NA

† Chilton Estimate
① Dual takedown
② If a 17-digit VIN is used, the 8th digit is the engine code and the 10th digit is the model year code

Gas Engine Electrical Diagnostic Connector

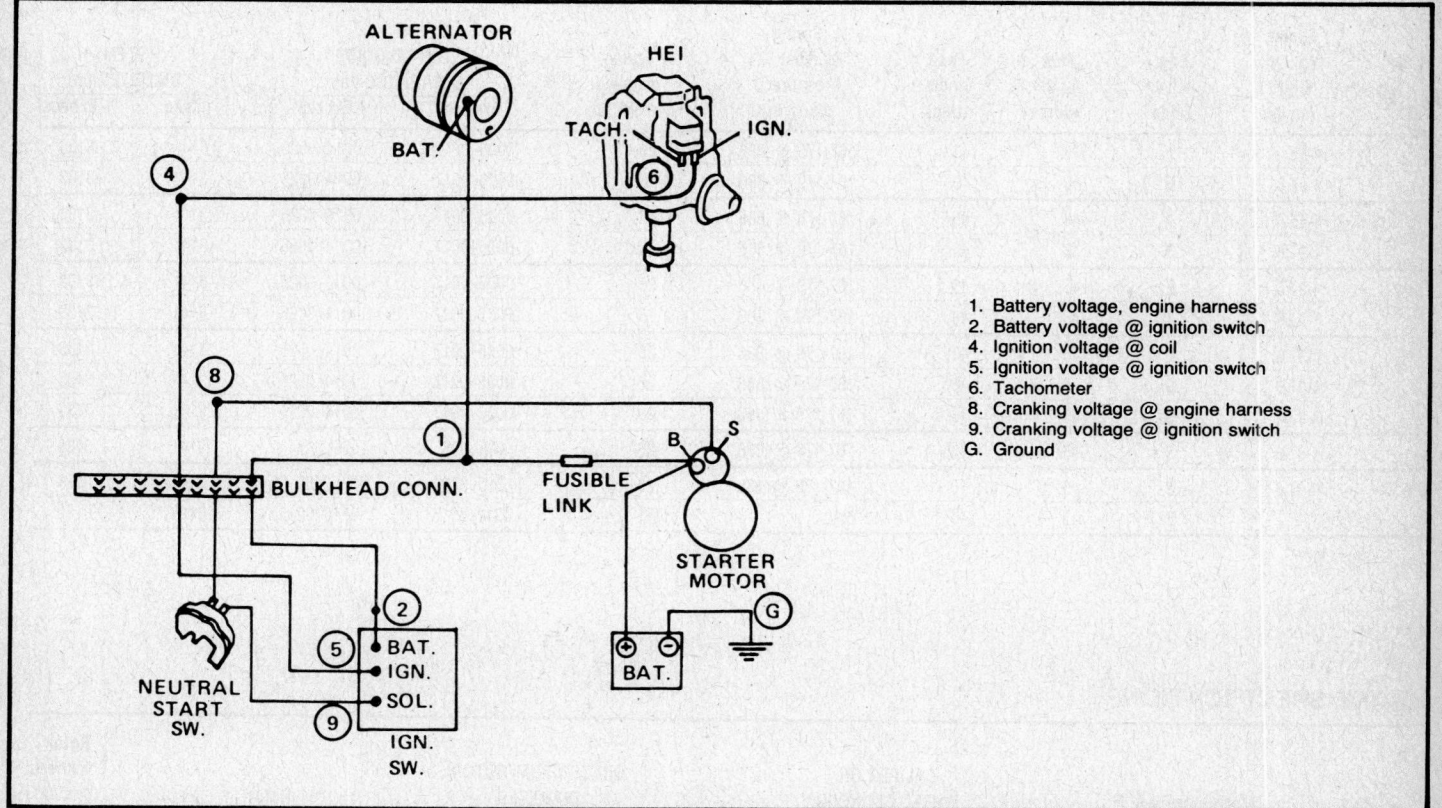

1. Battery voltage, engine harness
2. Battery voltage @ ignition switch
4. Ignition voltage @ coil
5. Ignition voltage @ ignition switch
6. Tachometer
8. Cranking voltage @ engine harness
9. Cranking voltage @ ignition switch
G. Ground

TUNE-UP SPECIFICATIONS

Year	Eng. V.I.N. Code	Eng. No. Cyl. Disp. (cu in)	Carb Bbl	SPARK PLUGS Orig. Type	Gap (in)	IGNITION TIMING DEG B.T.D.C. Man	Auto	CARBURETION IDLE SPEED③ Manual Trans.-In Fed.	Cal.	Auto Trans. (In Drive) Fed.	Cal.
76	I	4-85	1	R43TS	.035	10	10	800	800	750	750
	E	4-97.6	1	R43TS	.035	8	10	800	800	750	750
77	I	4-85	1	R43TS	.035	12	12	800	800	750	750
	E	4-97.6	1	R43TS	.035	8	8	800	800	750	750
78	E	4-97.6	1	R43TS	.035	8	8	800	800	750	750
	J	4-97.6	1	R43TS	.035	8	8	800	800	750	750
79	E	4-97.6	2	R43TS	.035	②	②	800	800	750	750
	0	4-97.6	2	R43TS	.035	②	②	800	800	750	750
80	9	4-97.6	2	R42TS	.035	12	18	800	800	750	750
	0	4-97.6	2	R42TS	.035	12	18	800	800	750	750
81	9	4-97.6	2	R42TS	.035	12	18	700	700	700	700
82	9	4-97.6 1.6L	2	R42TS	.035	18	18	700	700	700	700
	D	4-112 1.8L	Diesel	—	—	—	—	625	625	725-N	725-N

NOTE: Should the information in this manual deviate from the specifications on the underhood tune-up decal the decal specifications should be used as they may reflect production changes.

② Distributor no. 1110741-1110742-1110743 1110744-1110759 12 B.T.C.

③ Distributor no. 1110778-18 B.T.C. Distributor no. 1110760-16 B.T.C.

③ Air cond. cars, carb. solenoid energized- 1150 RPM. Fast idle all engines- 2250 RPM.

GENERAL MOTORS "T" BODY CARS

CHEVETTE, T1000

VALVE SPECIFICATIONS

Year	Engine No. Cyl. Disp. (cu in)	Eng. V.I.N. Code	Seat Angle (deg)	Face Angle (deg)	Spring Test Pressure① lbs @ in)	Spring Installed Height (in)	STEM TO GUIDE CLEARANCE (in) Intake	STEM TO GUIDE CLEARANCE (in) Exhaust	STEM DIAMETER (in) Intake	STEM DIAMETER (in) Exhaust
76	4-85	I	46	45	167-179 @ .886	1.25	.0006-.0017	.0014-.0025	.3141	.3133
	4-97.6	E	46	45	167-179 @ .886	1.25	.0006-.0017	.0014-.0025	.3141	.3133
77	4-85	I	46	45	167-179 @ .886	1.25	.0006-.0017	.0014-.0025	.3141	.3133
	4-97.6	E	46	45	167-179 @ .886	1.25	.0006-.0017	.0014-.0025	.3141	.3133
78	4-97.6	E	45	46	167-179 @ .886	1.25	.0006-.0017	.0014-.0025	.3141	.3133
	4-97.6	J	45	46	167-179 @ .886	1.25	.0006-.0017	.0014-.0025	.3141	.3133
79-80	4-97.6	E	45	46	167-179 @ .886	1.26	.0006-.0017	.0014-.0025	.3141	.3133
	4-97.6	0	45	46	167-179 @ .886	1.26	.0006-.0017	.0014-.0025	.3141	.3133
	4-97.6	9	45	46	167-179 @ .886	1.26	.0006-.0017	.0014-.0025	.3141	.3133
81	4-97.6	9	45	46	167-179 @ .886	1.26	.015-.045	.035-.065	.3141	.3133
82	4-97.6	9	45	46	167-179 @ .886	0.794mm	.015-.045	.035-.065	.3141	.3133
	112	D	45	45	NA	NA	.0010-.0015	.0010-.0015	.3128	.3132

① Valve Open

BRAKE SPECIFICATIONS

Year	Master Cylinder Bore Diameter	CALIPER OR WHEEL CYLINDER Front	CALIPER OR WHEEL CYLINDER Rear	BRAKE DRUM/ROTOR DIAMETER Front	BRAKE DRUM/ROTOR DIAMETER Rear	Rotor Runout	Rotor Thickness Variation Maximum
76	.750	1.875	.750	9.68	7.88	.005	.0005
77	.750	1.875	.750	9.68	7.88	.005	.0005
78	.750	1.875	.750	9.68	7.88	.005	.0005
79	.750	1.875	.750	9.68	7.88	.005	.0005
80	.750	1.875	.750	9.68	7.88	.005	.0005
81	.750	1.875	.750	9.68	7.88	.005	.0005
82	.750	1.875	.750	9.86	7.88	.005	.0005

TIMING BELT SPECIFICATIONS

Year	Belt Width	Acceptable Operating Tension Range	Adjustment Specification
76	15mm	40-60 lbs.	50-60 lbs.
77	19mm	50-80 lbs.	63-77 lbs.
78	19mm	50-80 lbs.	63-77 lbs.
79	19mm	50-80 lbs.	63-77 lbs.
80	19mm	50-80 lbs.	63-77 lbs.
81	19mm	50-80 lbs.	63-77 lbs.
82 Gas	19mm	50-80 lbs.	63-77 lbs.
82 Disel	19mm	45 lbs.	45-63 lbs.

WHEEL LUG TORQUE DATA

Year	Model	Torque ft/lbs
1976	ALL	65
1977	ALL	65
1978	ALL	65-70
1979	ALL	65-70
1980	ALL	65-70
1981	ALL	65-70
1982	ALL	70

A564

DISTRIBUTOR SPECIFICATIONS

Year	Distributor Identification	CENTRIFUGAL ADVANCE Start Crank. Deg. @ Eng. RPM	Finish Crank. Deg. @ Eng. RPM	VACUUM ADVANCE Start @ In. Hg.	Finish Crank. Deg. @ In. Hg.
'76	1110654	0 @ 1200	20 @ 4800	4	14 @ 8
	1110655	0 @ 1200	20 @ 4800	5	12 @ 12
	1110657	0 @ 1200	20 @ 4800	5	24 @ 12
	1110658	0 @ 1200	20 @ 4800	5	26 @ 14.5
	1110659	0 @ 1500	16 @ 4800	4	26 @ 12
'77	1110687	0 @ 1200	20 @ 4800	4	27 @ 12
	1110693	0 @ 1200	20 @ 4800	4	14 @ 8
	1110702	0 @ 1200	20 @ 4800	4	30 @ 12
	1110703	0 @ 1200	24 @ 5700	4	30 @ 12
'78	1110705	0 @ 1200	20 @ 4800	4	30 @ 12
	1110707	0 @ 1200	20 @ 4800	4	14 @ 8
	1110712	0 @ 1200	20 @ 4800	4	26 @ 12
	1110713	0 @ 1200	22 @ 5250	4	30 @ 12
'79	1110741	0 @ 1510	16 @ 5250	4	14 @ 8
	1110742	0 @ 1200	20 @ 4800	5	16 @ 11.5
	1110743	0 @ 1200	24 @ 5700	4	30 @ 10.0
	1110744	0 @ 1200	20 @ 4800	4	30 @ 10.0
	1110759	0 @ 1200	24 @ 5700	—	—
	1110760	0 @ 1510	16 @ 5250	5	16 @ 11.5
	1110778②	0 @ 1200	24 @ 5700	5	24 @ 12.0
	1110778③	0 @ 1200	20 @ 4800	5	24 @ 12.0
80	110788	0 @ 1520	16 @ 5250	5	24 @ 12
	110789	0 @ 1200	24 @ 5700	3	20 @ 7.5
	110792	0 @ 1520	16 @ 5250	3	25 @ 10
	110794	0 @ 1520	16 @ 5250	3	16 @ 6.5
	110795	0 @ 1200	24 @ 5700	3	25 @ 10

NOTE: 81-82 electronic spark timing
② W/vac. no. 604
③ W/vac. no. 608

CRANKSHAFT & CONNECTING ROD SPECIFICATIONS

All measurements given in inches

Year	Engine No. Cyl. Disp. (cu in)	Eng. V.I.N. Code	CRANKSHAFT Main Brg. Journal Dia	Main Brg. Oil Clearance	Shaft End-Play	Thrust on No.	CONNECTING ROD Journal Diameter	Oil Clearance	Side Clearance
76	4-85	I	2.0075-2.0085	.0009-.0025	.004-.008	4	1.809-1.810	.0014-.0030	.004-.012
	4-97.6	E	2.0075-2.0085	.0009-.0025	.004-.008	4	1.809-1.810	.0014-.0030	.004-.012
77	4-85	I	2.0075-2.0085	.0009-.0025	.004-.008	4	1.809-1.810	.0014-.0030	.004-.012
	4-97.6	E	2.0075-2.0085	.0009-.0025	.004-.008	4	1.809-1.810	.0014-.0030	.004-.012
78	4-97.6	E-J	2.0078-2.0088	.0009-.0026	.004-.008	4	1.809-1.810	.0014-.0031	.004-.012
79	4-97.6	E-0	2.0078-2.0088	.0009-.0026	.004-.008	4	1.809-1.810	.0014-.0031	.004-.012
80	4-97.6	9-0	2.0078-2.0088	.0009-.0026	.004-.008	4	1.809-1.810	.0014-.0031	.004-.010
81	4-97.6	9	2.0078-2.0088	.0009-.0026	.004-.008	4	1.809-1.810	.0014-.0031	.004-.010
82	4-97.6	9	2.0078-2.0088	.0009-.0026	.004-.008	4	1.809-1.810	.0014-.0031	.004-.101
	4-112	D-DIESEL	2.201-2.202	.0015-.0027	.0017	3	1.925-1.926	.0016-.0032	.005-.010

GENERAL MOTORS "T" BODY CARS

CHEVETTE, T1000

TORQUE SPECIFICATIONS

All readings in ft/lbs

Year	Eng. V.I.N. Code	Cam Cover	Cylinder Head Bolts	Rod Bearing Bolts	Main Bearing Bolts	Front Crankshaft Bolt	Flywheel To Crankshaft Bolts	Manifold Intake	Manifold Exhaust
76	I-E	14	70-80	34-40	40-52	65-85	40-52	13-18	①
77	I-E	14	70-80	34-40	40-52	65-85	40-52	13-18	①
78	E-J	14	75	40	50	75	50	15	②
79	E-0	14	75	40	50	75	50	15	②
80	0-9	14	75	40	50	75	50	15	②
81	9	14	75	40	50	75	50	15	②
82	9	14	75	40	50	75	50	15	②
	D④	5	③	65	75	110	40	30	②

① Center bolts—13-18; end bolts—19-25
② Center bolts—15; end bolts—22
③ First pull 21-36 lbs
   Second pull new bolt 83-98 lbs
   Second pull reused bolt 90-105 lbs
④ Diesel

FLUID CAPACITIES—Coolant, Fuel & Lubricant

Year	Engine No. Cyl. Disp. (cu in)	Engine Crankcase Add ½ Qt For New Filter	TRANSMISSION Pts to Refill After Draining Manual 3-Speed	4-Speed	Automatic	Drive Axle (pts)	Gasoline Tank (gals)	COOLING SYSTEM With Heater (qts)	With A/C (qts)	Thermo. Stat.	Cap Pressure
76	4-85	4	—	3	7	2.8	12	8.5	8.5	190	15
	4-97.6	4	—	3	7	2.8	12	9.0	9.0	190	15
77	4-85	4	—	3	7	2.8	12	8.5	8.5	190	15
	4-97.6	4	—	3	7	2.8	12	9.0	9.0	190	15
78	4-97.6	4	—	3.4	5.7	1.75	13	8.5	9.0	190	15
79	4-97.6	4	—	3.4	5.7	1.75	13	8.5	9.0	190	15
80	4-97.6	4	—	3.4	5.7	1.75	12.5	8.5	9.0	190	15
81	4-97.6	4	—	3.4	6.0	1.75	12.5	9.3	9.3	190	15
82	4-97.6	4	—	3.4	6.0	1.75	12.5	9.3	9.3	190	15
	4-112②	6	—	3.25①	6.0	1.75	12.5	9.3	9.3	195	17

① 5-Speed
② Diesel

ENGINE FIRING ORDER

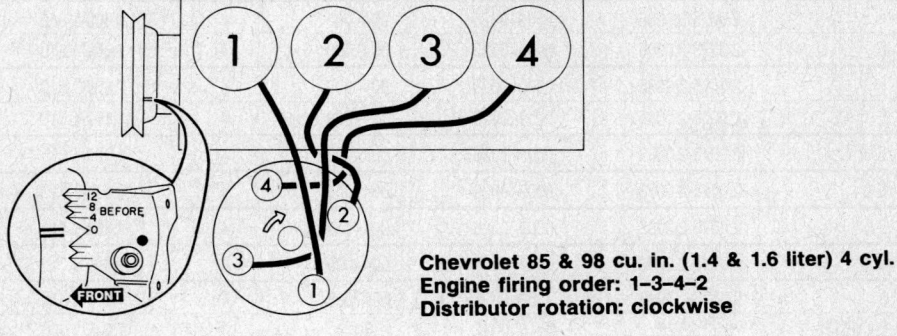

Chevrolet 85 & 98 cu. in. (1.4 & 1.6 liter) 4 cyl.
Engine firing order: 1–3–4–2
Distributor rotation: clockwise

ELECTRICAL SECTION

Starter—Gas Engine

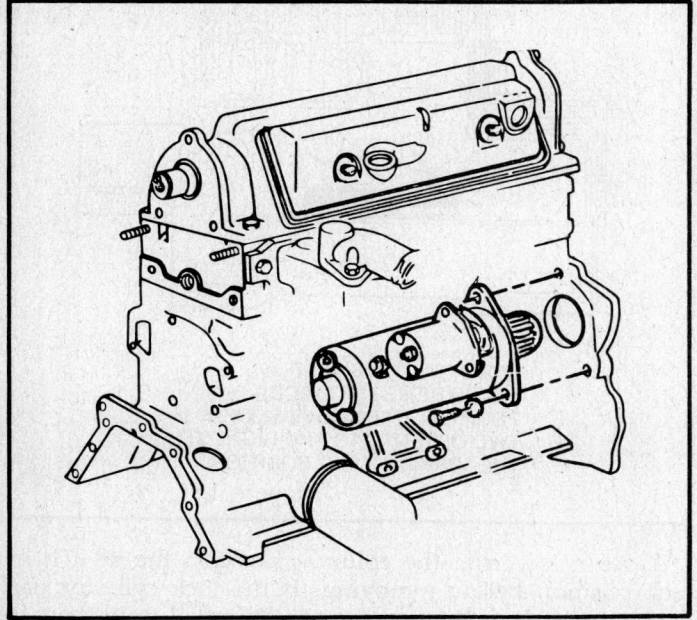

Starter—Diesel Engine

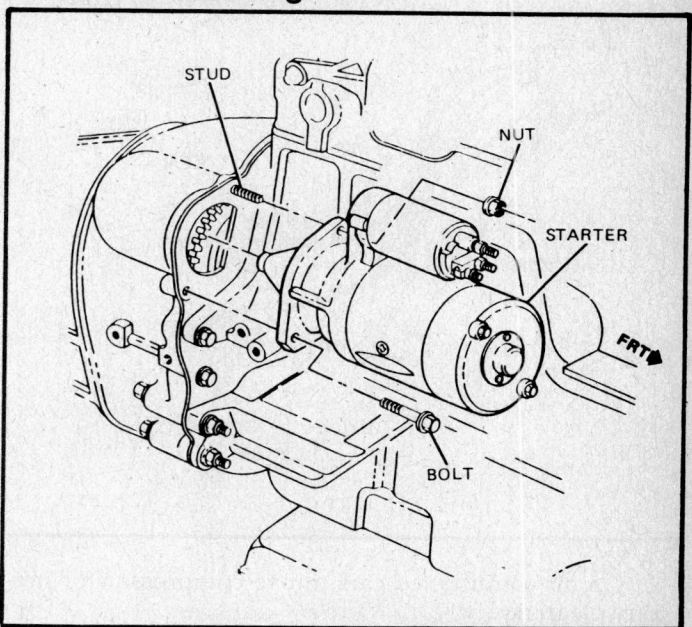

Starter

Replacement (Without Power Brakes)

1. Disconnect battery ground cable.
2. Remove air cleaner.
3. Disconnect gas line at carburetor and move aside.
4. Disconnect vacuum hoses at carburetor.
5. Remove splash shield from distributor coil and move aside.
6. Remove upper starter bolt.
7. Remove lower starter bolt.
8. Move starter for access and disconnect starter wiring.
9. Remove master cylinder mounting nuts to gain access for removing starter. It will be necessary to move the master cylinder aside to remove the starter.
10. Remove starter.
11. Reverse above steps to install.

Replacement (With Power Brakes)

1. Disconnect battery ground cable.
2. Remove air cleaner.
3. Disconnect gas line at carburetor and move aside for access.
4. Remove splash shield from distributor coil and move aside.
5. Remove upper starter bolt.
6. Remove steering column cover screws and remove cover.
7. Remove steering column upper nuts and toe pan screw.
8. Raise vehicle on hoist.
9. Remove steering shaft from steering coupling.

Lower vehicle and move steering column from inside car for access to starter.
10. Disconnect starter wiring.
11. Remove starter lower bolt and remove starter.
12. Reverse above procedure to install.

Ignition Distributor

1. Remove cap, electrical wiring and vacuum hose from distributor.

Starter Wiring

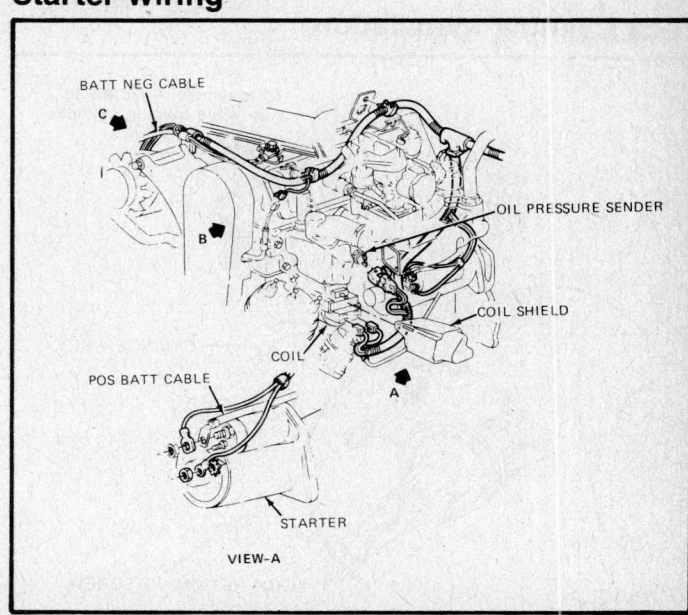

Ignition Distributor

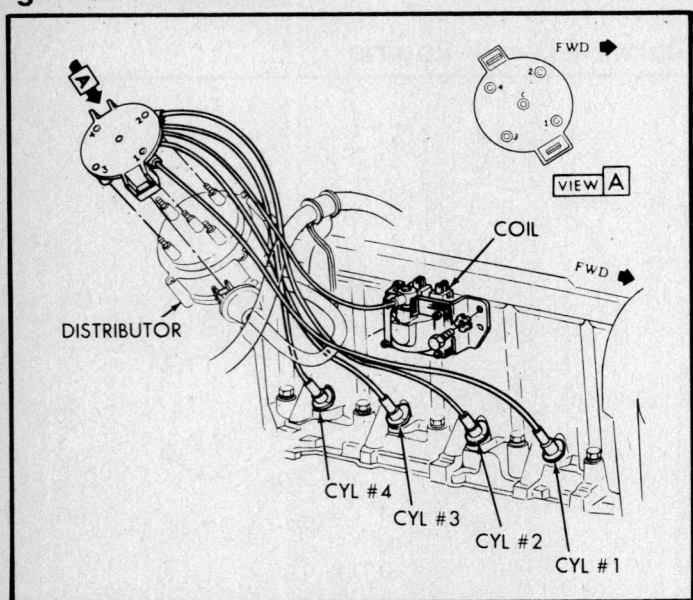

Ignition Switch

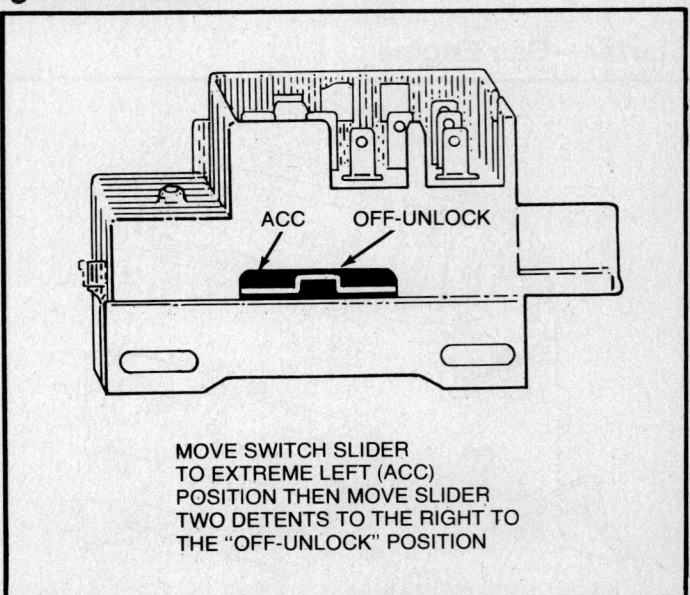

MOVE SWITCH SLIDER
TO EXTREME LEFT (ACC)
POSITION THEN MOVE SLIDER
TWO DETENTS TO THE RIGHT TO
THE "OFF-UNLOCK" POSITION

2. On air conditioned cars, move compressor for necessary clearance.

3. If necessary, remove fuel pump.

4. Put alignment marks on rotor and distributor housing so distributor can be installed in the correct position.

5. Remve the hold-down bolt, and pull distributor up out of engine.

6. After installing, check ignition timing, idle speed, etc.

Ignition Switch

1. The steering column must be lowered to replace the ignition switch. It is located inside the channel section of the brake pedal support and is mounted on top of the mast jacket.

Lock Cylinder Installation

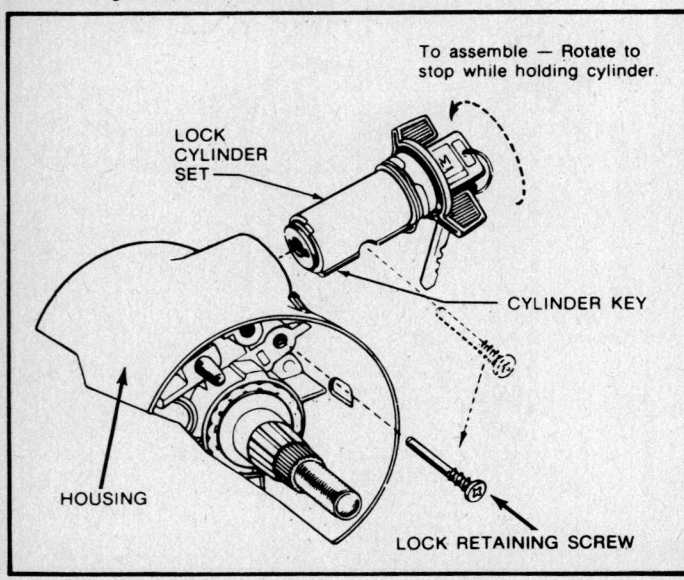

2. After lowering the column, position the switch in lock position before removing. If the lock cylinder has been removed, pull up on the actuating rod until there is a stop, then move down one detent into the lock position.

Ignition Lock

1. Remove steering wheel and lock plate, and pull turn signal switch up out of the way.

2. With key cylinder in RUN position, depress retainer, and pull the cylinder out of its housing.

3. Before installing, turn cylinder to full clockwise position.

Lock Cylinder

Disassembly

1. Place lock in Run position.

2. Remove lock plate, turn signal and buzzer switch.

3. Remove screw and lock cylinder.

CAUTION If screw is dropped during removal, it could fall into the column, requiring complete disassembly to retrieve the screw.

Assembly

1. Rotate and align cylinder key with the keyway housing.

2. Push lock all the way in.

3. Install screw and tighten to 4.5 N•m for regular columns (2.5 N•m for adjustable columns.)

Charging System—Diesel

The charging system used on this engine is a solid state integral regulator generator. A vacuum pump is attached to the rear cover of the generator and is driven off the generator shaft.

Generator/Vacuum Pump

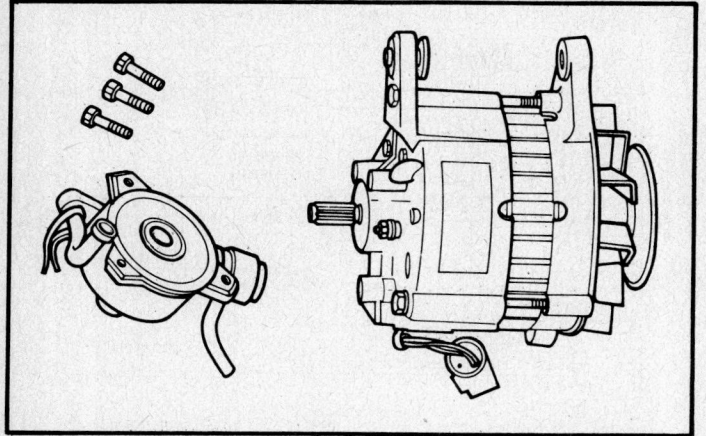

12 volt—50 amp

Stator and Diode Assembly

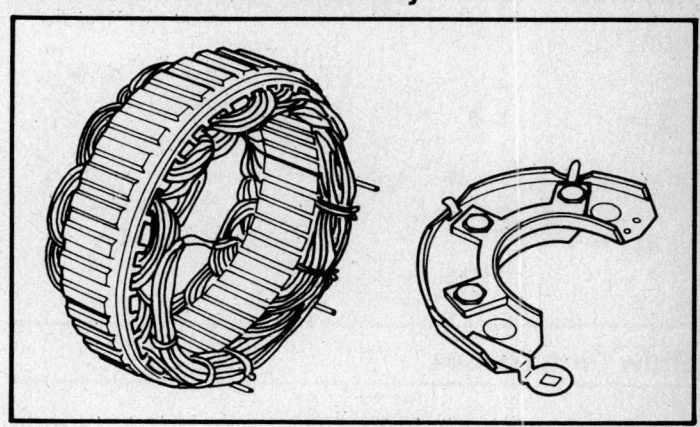

Rear Cover Assembly

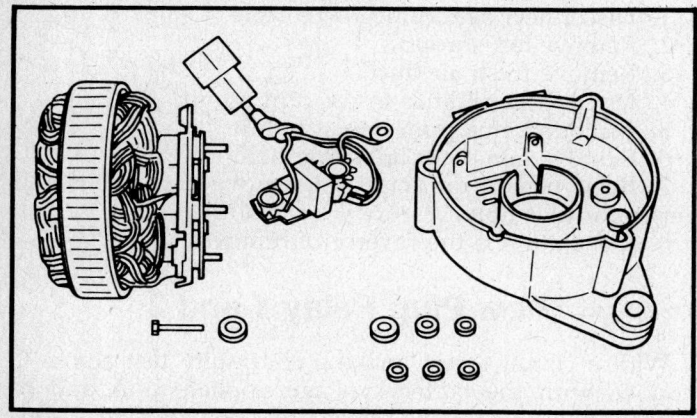

Vacuum Pump Disassembly

Controller

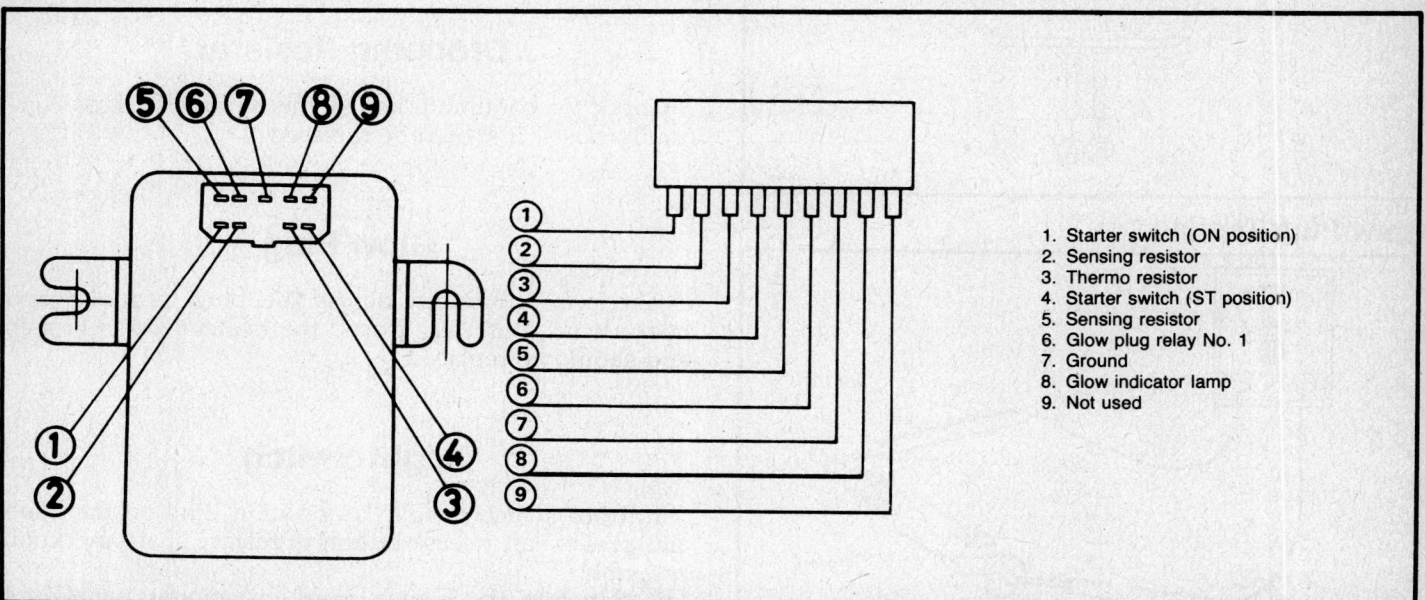

1. Starter switch (ON position)
2. Sensing resistor
3. Thermo resistor
4. Starter switch (ST position)
5. Sensing resistor
6. Glow plug relay No. 1
7. Ground
8. Glow indicator lamp
9. Not used

Position to which connector terminal is connected

GENERAL MOTORS "T" BODY CARS

CHEVETTE, T1000

Regulator Assembly

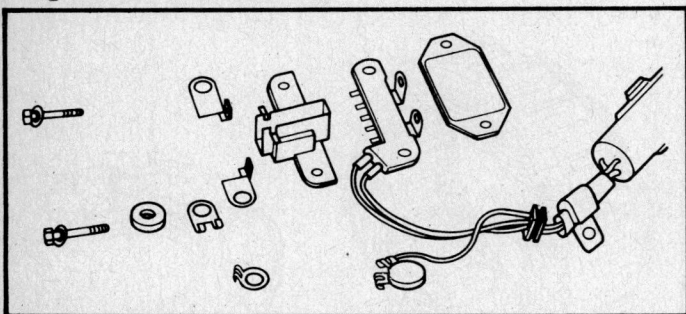

Glow Plug Relays

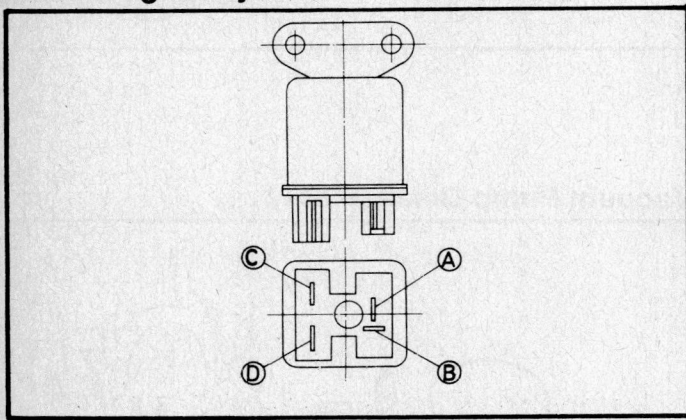

Dropping Resistor

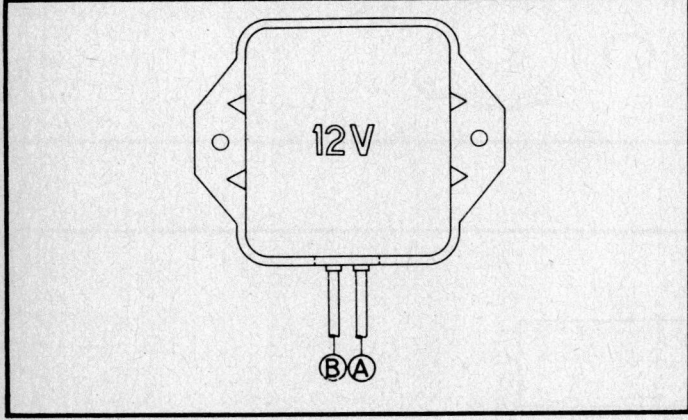

Glow Plug Testing

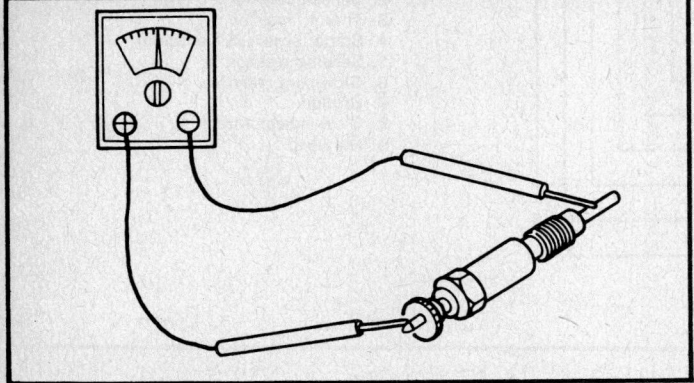

Electrical Circuit Diagram

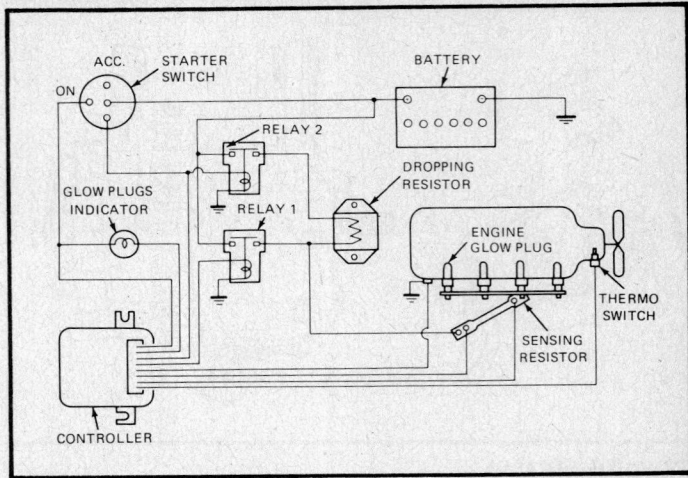

GENERATOR REMOVAL

1. Disconnect battery negative cable.
2. Remove fan shroud.
3. Remove fresh air duct.
4. Disconnect oil lines to vacuum pump.
5. Disconnect vacuum line at pump.
6. Remove generator adjusting bolt.
7. Raise vehicle on hoist and remove lower bolts and generator assembly.
8. Installation is the reverse of removal.

Glow Plug Relay 1 and 2

With a circuit tester, make a continuity test across C and D, with the battery voltage applied to A and B. Replace the parts if the tester does not indicate a continuity.

Dropping Resistor

Check for continuity across the terminals. If no continuity exists, it should be replaced.

Glow Plug

Check for continuity across the plug terminals and body. If no continuity exists, the heater wire is broken and should be replaced.

Light Switch

1. Place switch in full ON position. Pull on the knob and press shaft release button to release shaft and knob assembly.
2. Separate the switch from instrument panel and electrical connections.

Automatic Transmission Neutral Start Switch

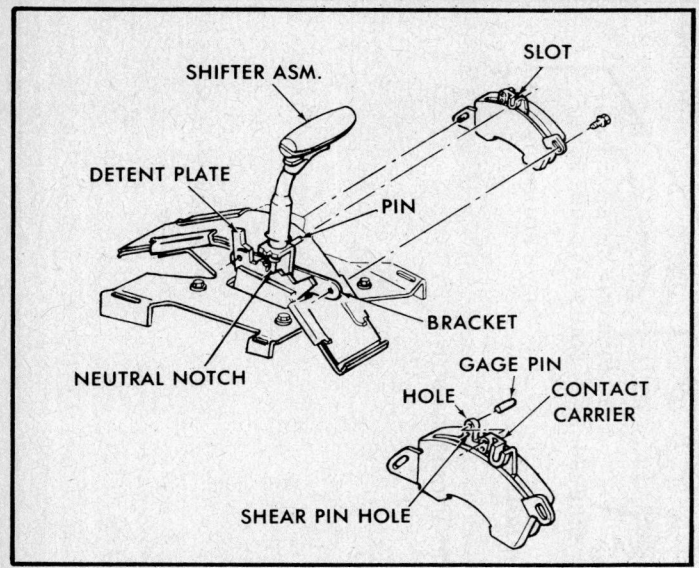

Clutch Start Switch Mounting

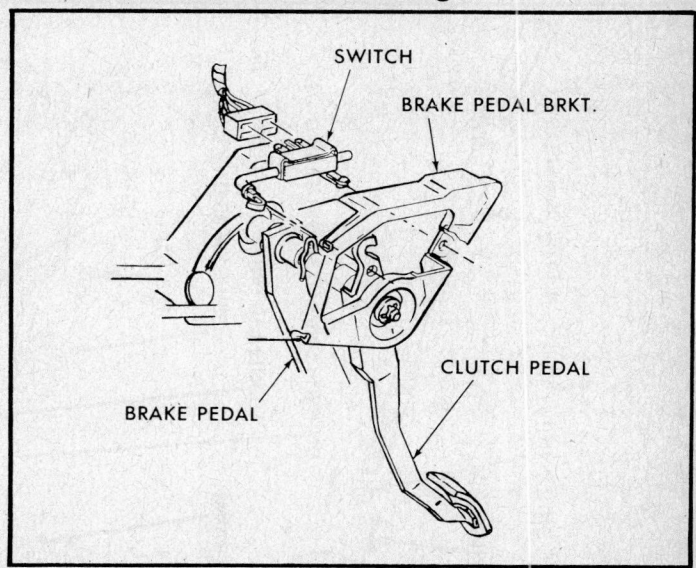

Turn Signal Switch

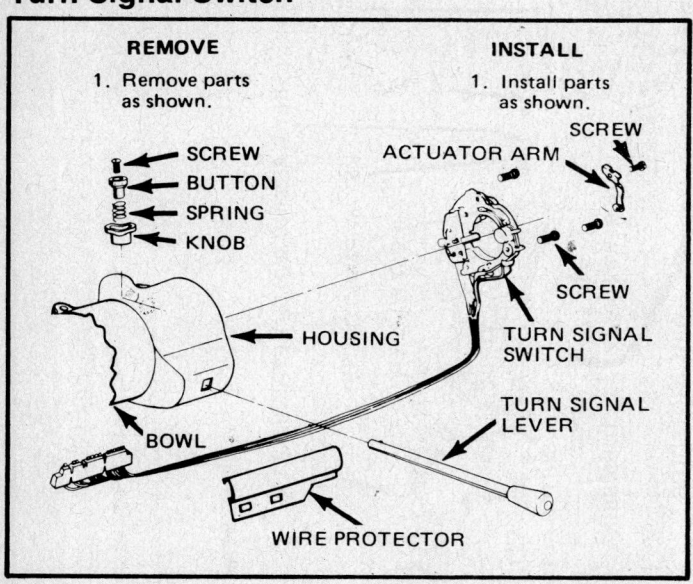

Light Switch and Attachments

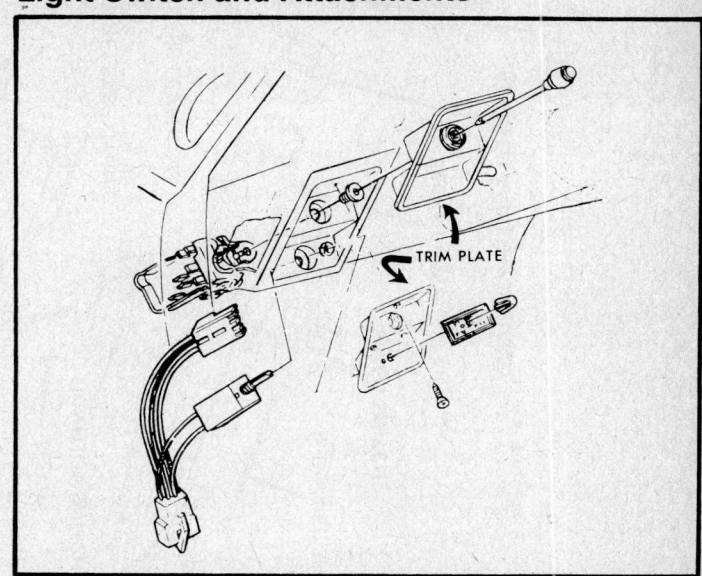

Stoplight Switch and Adjustment

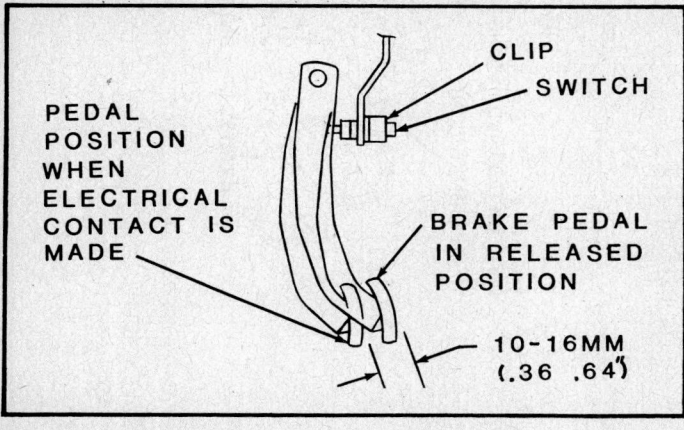

Steering Wheel Mounting

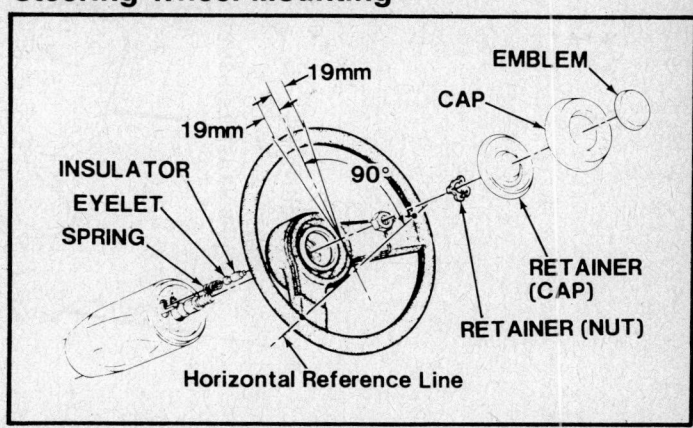

Key Release Steering Column

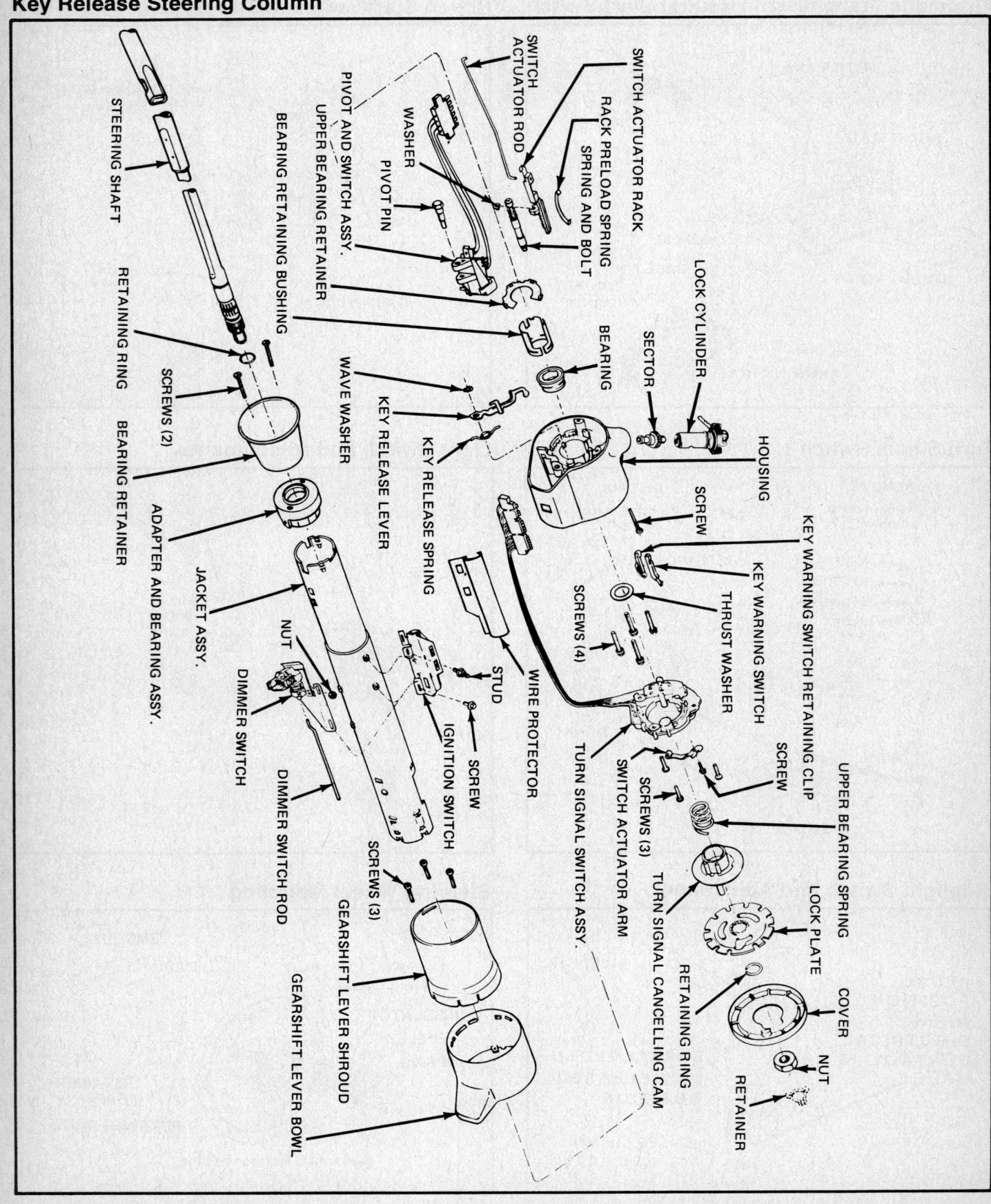

Standard Steering Column

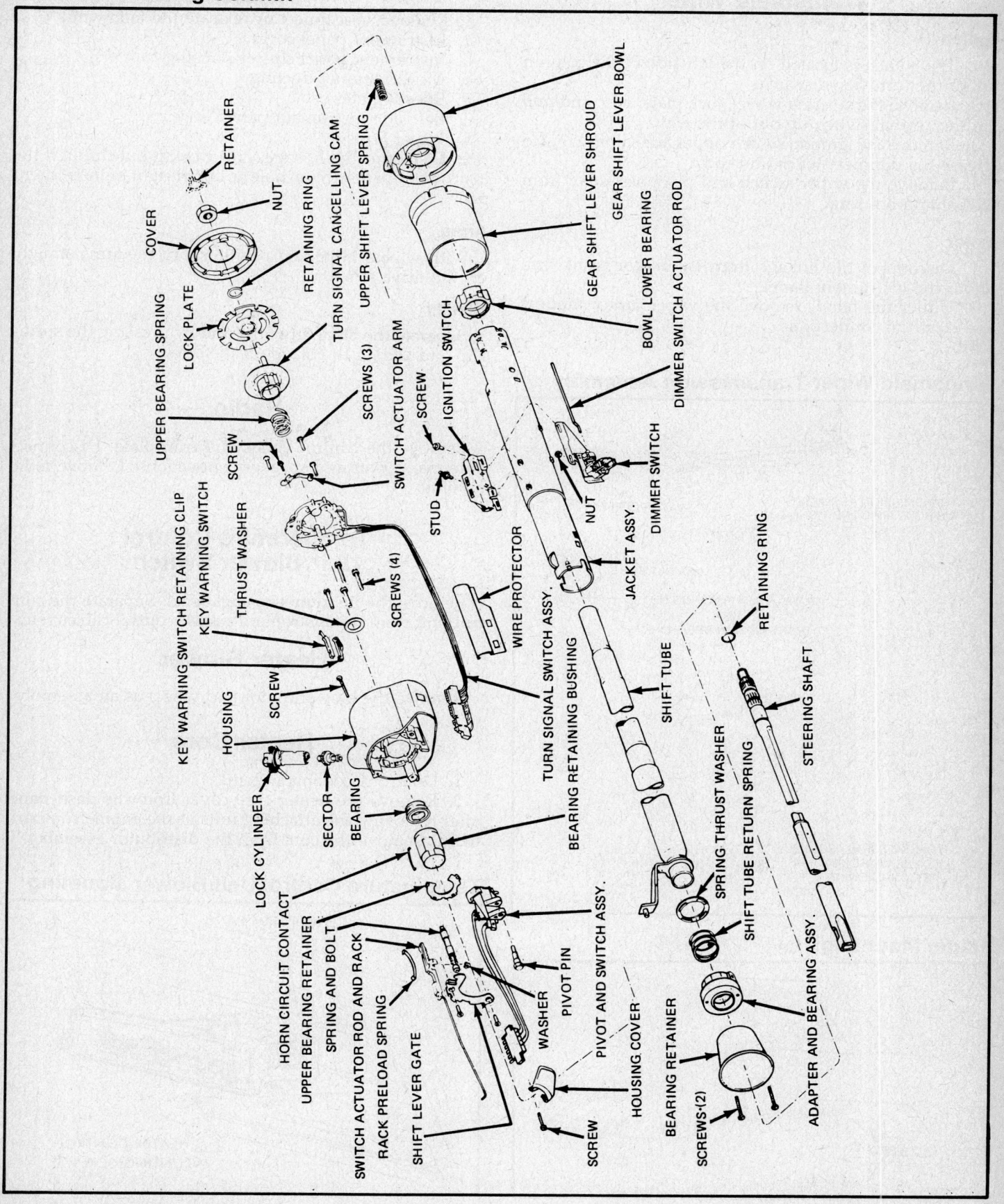

Windshield Wiper

Switch

1. The switch is located on the left side of the column under the turn signal switch.
2. Remove the steering wheel, lock plate, etc., and pull the turn signal switch up out of the way.
3. Remove the ignition switch upper attaching screw to release the dimmer switch and rod.
4. Remove the wiper switch and pivot assembly from the column housing.

Motor

1. Disconnect the linkage from the motor crank arm under the instrument panel.
2. Under the hood, remove the wiper motor mounts and electrical connections.

Windshield Wiper Transmission Assembly

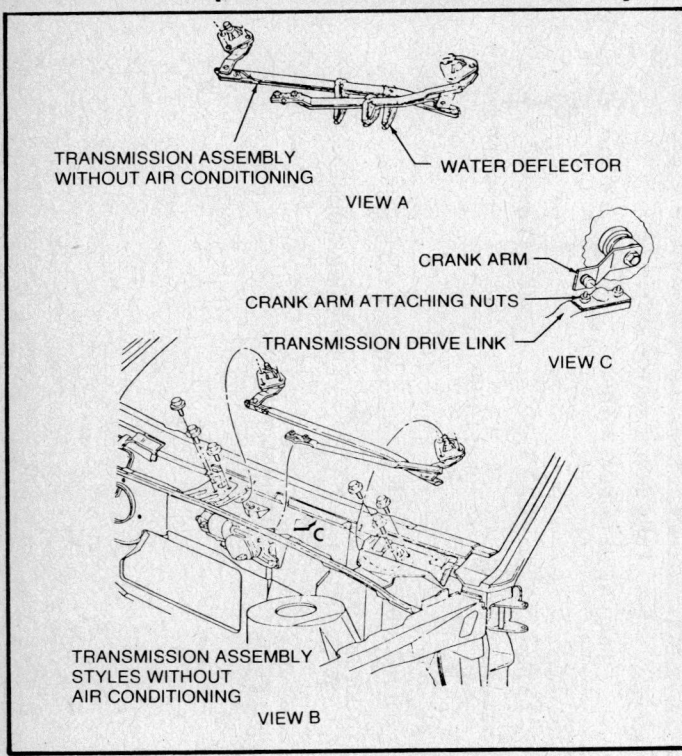

Radio Mounting

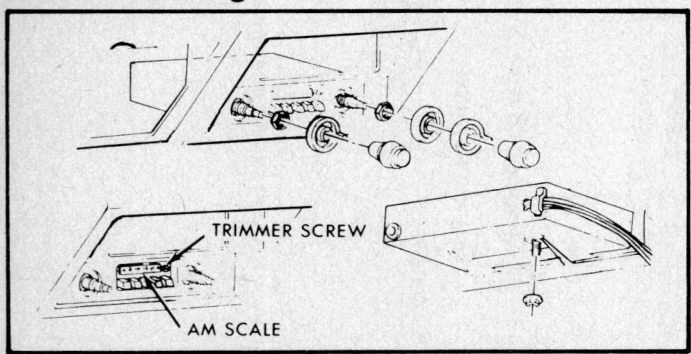

Linkage

1. Remove, disconnect or relocate the following:
a. Instrument panel cover
b. Instrument panel cluster housing
c. Air conditioner ducting
d. Speedometer cable
e. Left side instrument panel brace
f. Wiper arms
2. Dismount the linkage, and work it out through the instrument panel access hole at upper right of instrument panel.

Arms

With wipers in parked position, pry the arms straight off the drive arms.

Blades

Separate the blade from the arm by pressing the spring clip and sliding the blade off the arm.

Radio

Remove the control knobs and trim plate. Disconnect antenna, power and speaker connections. Remove radio mounts.

Temperature Control Unit/Blower Switch

Remove the instrument panel bezel. Separate the control unit from the instrument panel, control cables, etc.

Heater Blower

Remove the blower motor and wheel as an assembly.

Heater Core

1. Drain the cooling system.
2. Remove the heater core cover from the dash panel after removing the attaching nuts in the engine compartment. Remove the core from the distributor assembly.

Temperature Control Unit/Blower Mounting

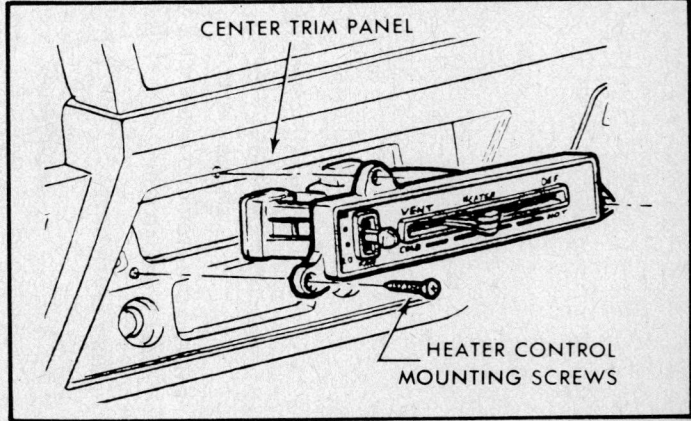

Cable Attachments Temperature Control Unit

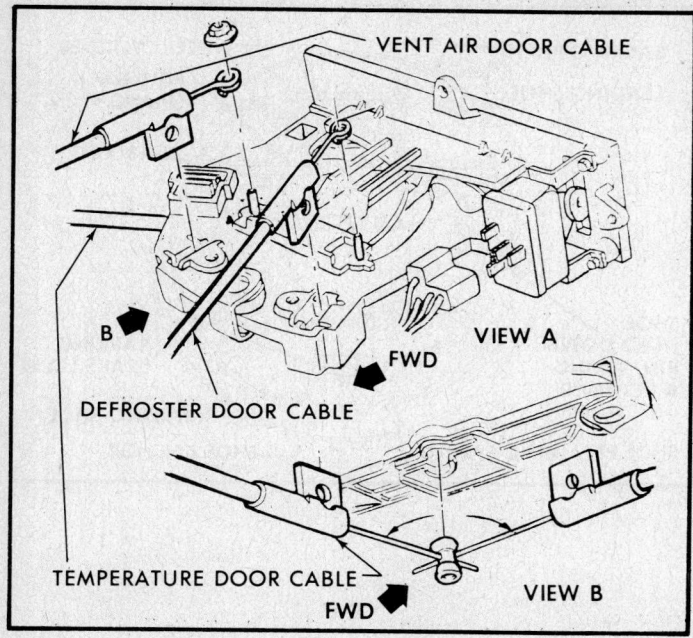

VENT AIR DOOR CABLE

B

VIEW A

FWD

DEFROSTER DOOR CABLE

TEMPERATURE DOOR CABLE

FWD

VIEW B

Air Conditioner Compressor Cutout Switch

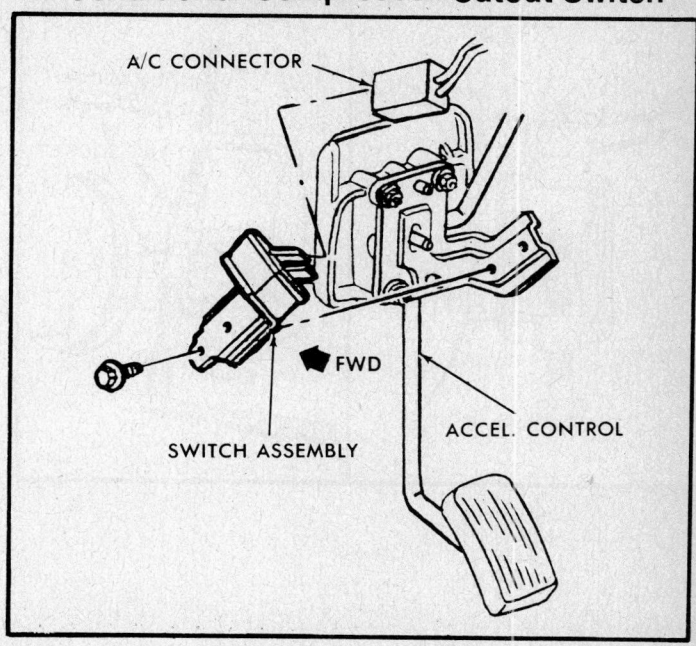

A/C CONNECTOR

FWD

SWITCH ASSEMBLY

ACCEL. CONTROL

Instrument Panel Trim Plates

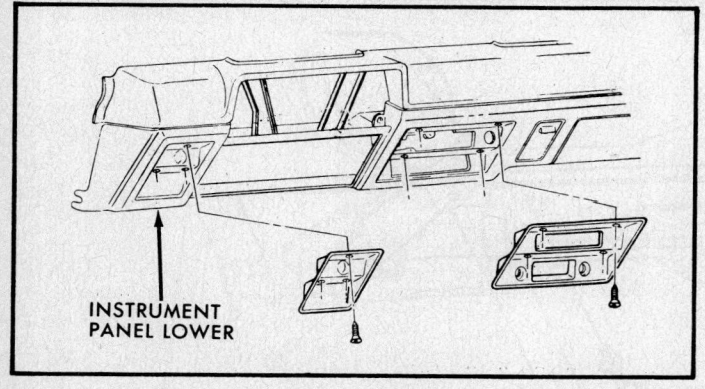

INSTRUMENT PANEL LOWER

Instrument Panel Pad

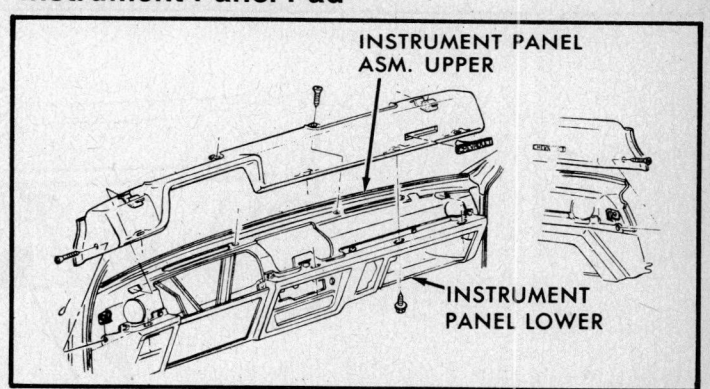

INSTRUMENT PANEL ASM. UPPER

INSTRUMENT PANEL LOWER

STEERING AND BRAKES SECTION

Steering Gear (Rack and Pinion Assembly)

1. Remove the shield. Disconnect the tie rods from the steering knuckles and remove the flexible coupling pinch bolt.
2. Remove the four clamp bolts and remove the rack and pinion assembly.

Steering Column

NOTE   Once the steering column is removed from the car, the column is extremely susceptible to damage. Dropping the column assembly on its end could collapse the steering shaft or loosen the plastic injections which maintain column rigidity. Leaning on the column assembly could cause the jacket to bend or deform. Any of the above damage could impair the column's collapsible design. If it is necessary to remove the steering wheel, use standard wheel puller. Under no condition should the end of the shaft be hammered upon, as hammering could loosen the plastic injections.

Removal and Installation

1. Disconnect negative battery cable.
2. If column is to be repaired remove steering wheel.
3. Remove parts as shown.
4. Install parts as shown.

GENERAL MOTORS "T" BODY CARS

CHEVETTE, T1000

Remove Tie Rod End   Install Tie Rod End

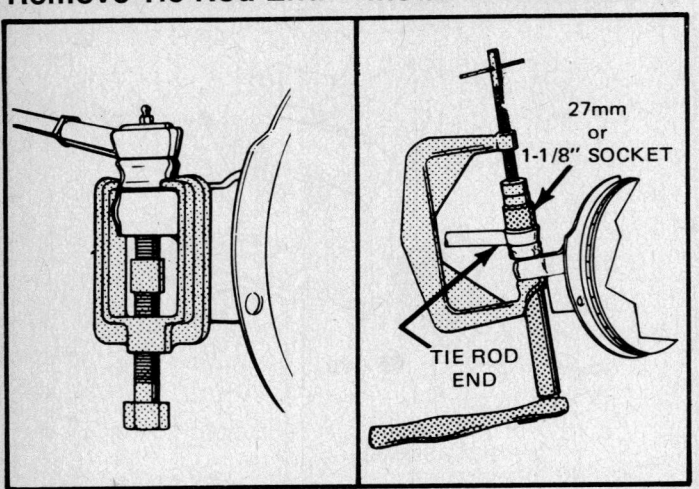

Rear Brake

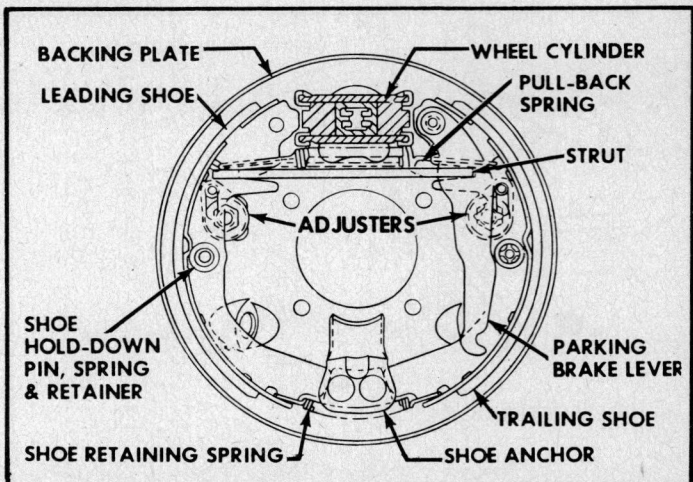

Remove and Install Manual Rack and Pinion

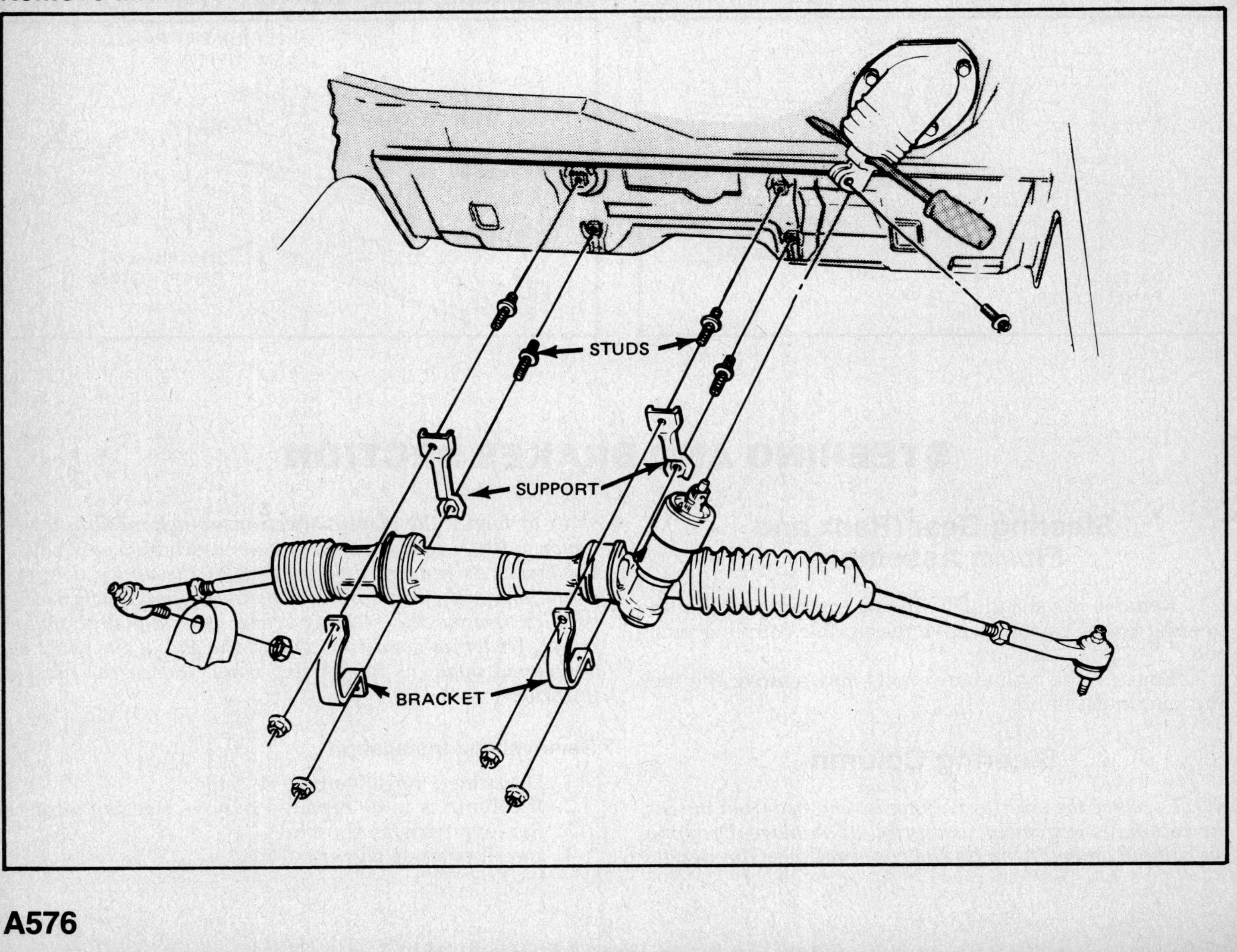

Steering Column

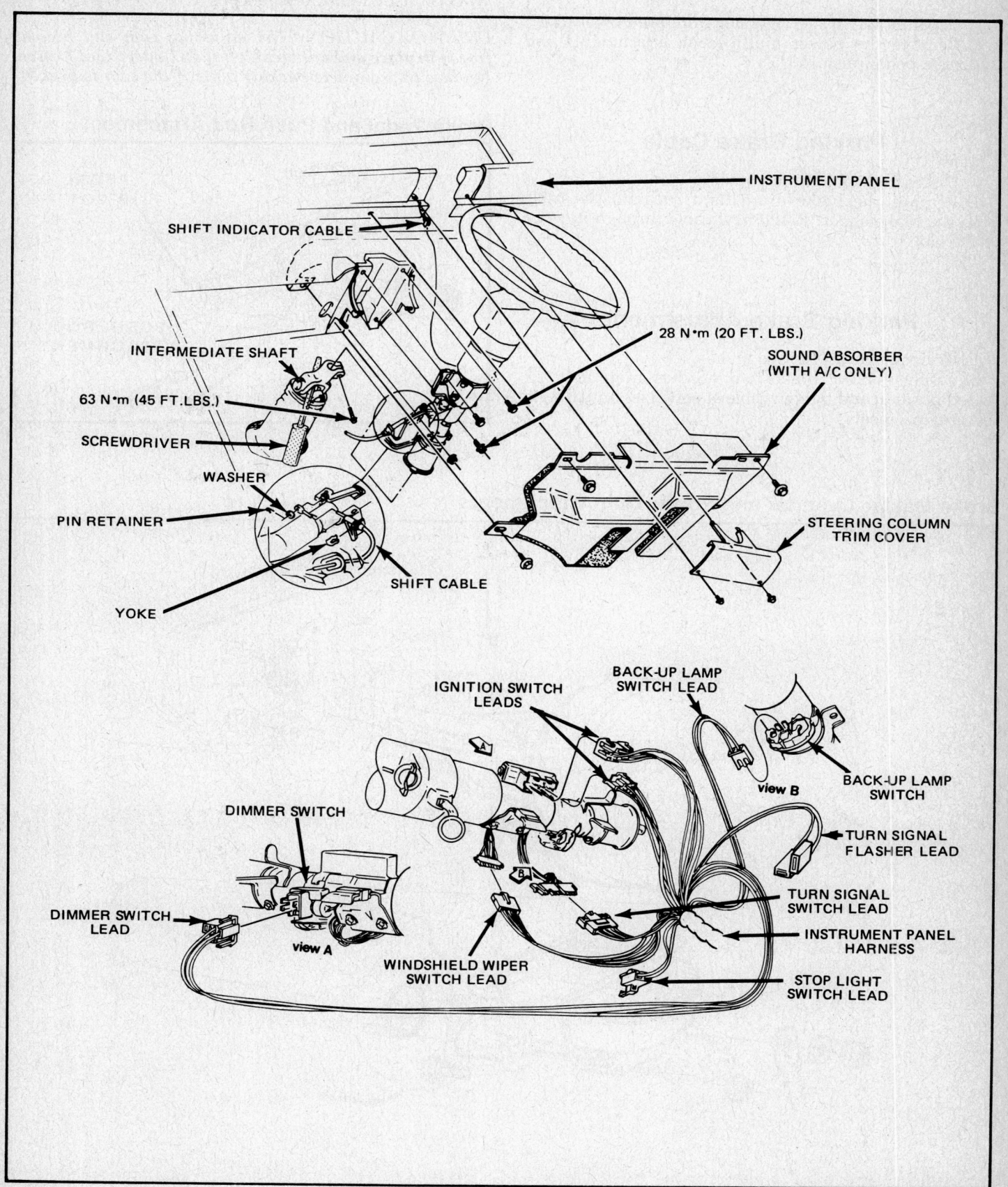

INSTRUMENT PANEL

SHIFT INDICATOR CABLE

28 N·m (20 FT. LBS.)

SOUND ABSORBER (WITH A/C ONLY)

INTERMEDIATE SHAFT

63 N·m (45 FT.LBS.)

SCREWDRIVER

WASHER

PIN RETAINER

YOKE

SHIFT CABLE

STEERING COLUMN TRIM COVER

IGNITION SWITCH LEADS

BACK-UP LAMP SWITCH LEAD

view B

BACK-UP LAMP SWITCH

DIMMER SWITCH

TURN SIGNAL FLASHER LEAD

DIMMER SWITCH LEAD

view A

WINDSHIELD WIPER SWITCH LEAD

TURN SIGNAL SWITCH LEAD

INSTRUMENT PANEL HARNESS

STOP LIGHT SWITCH LEAD

Brake Power Unit R&R

1. Separate the master cylinder from the power unit.
2. Remove the power unit-to-dash attachments and the brake pedal push rod.

Parking Brake Cable

1. Disconnect cable from equalizer.
2. Remove the brake drum, and separate the cable from the brake shoes. Route new cable through in place of the old.

Parking Brake Adjustment

1. Correctly adjust service brakes.
2. Apply parking brake two notches from fully released position and tighten cable at equalizer until drag is felt at rear wheels.

3. Release the parking brake lever, and check that rear wheels turn without resistance.

CHILTON CAUTION *The adjusting cam can become frozen in place and wil break off if an impact tool is used. Replace the complete backing plate if the cam is broken.*

Brake Pedal and Push Rod Attachment

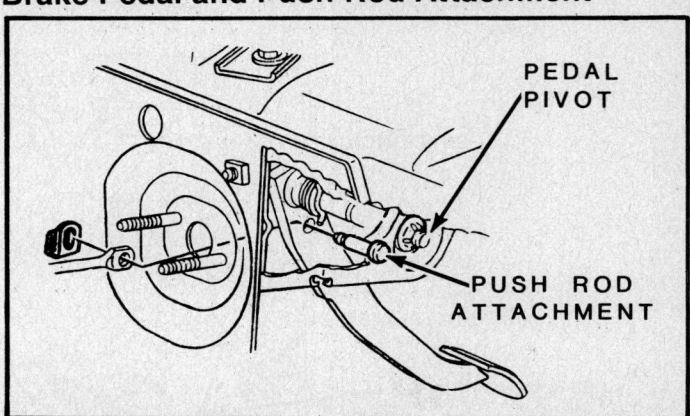

PEDAL PIVOT

PUSH ROD ATTACHMENT

Brake Master Cylinder and Power Unit Attachments

CLUTCH, TRANSMISSION, PROPELLER SHAFT AND REAR AXLES SECTION

Initial Ball Stud Adjustment

1. Install throw-out bearing assembly, clutch fork and ball stud to transmission.
2. Mount and secure transmission to engine.
3. Cycle clutch one time.
4. Place gauge J-28449 so flat end is against front face of clutch housing and the hooked end is aligned with the bottom depression in the clutch fork.
5. Turn ball stud clockwise by hand until clutch release bearing makes contact with clutch spring and fork is snug on gauge.
6. Install lock nut and tighten to 33.0 N•m (25 ft-lbs), being careful not to change ball stud adjustment.
7. Remove gauge by pulling outward at housing end.

Clutch Cable Attachment and Adjustment

NOTE   The following adjustments are to be made with the cable and loose parts assembled to the front of dash and with the cable attached to the clutch pedal.

1. Place cable (A) through hole in clutch fork and seat.
2. Install return spring (E).
3. From the engine compartment, pull the cable, with approx. 155 N (35 lbs) force away from the dash until the clutch pedal is firmly against the pedal bumper and hold in position.
4. Install ring (F) in the first fully visible groove in the cable from the sleeve. Release the cable.
5. Depress clutch pedal to the floor 4 times minimum to insure all parts of the clutch control system are properly seated.
6. The above procedure should produce 21.0 ± 6 mm (83 ± .25 in.) of lash at the clutch pedal.

NOTE   If the clutch pedal lash does not fall within 21 ± 6 mm range the following procedure will be necessary.

Minor Clutch Pedal Free Travel Adjustment

1. If there is insufficient clutch pedal lash, remove ring (F) from the cable and allow the cable to move into the dash by one cable notch and reinstall the ring (F).
2. If there is excessive clutch pedal lash, remove ring (F) from the cable and pull the cable out of the dash by one cable notch and reinstall the ring (F). It may be necessary during the clutch pedal lash adjustment to use either procedure to obtain the 21 ± 6 mm clutch pedal lash.

Clutch Adjustment

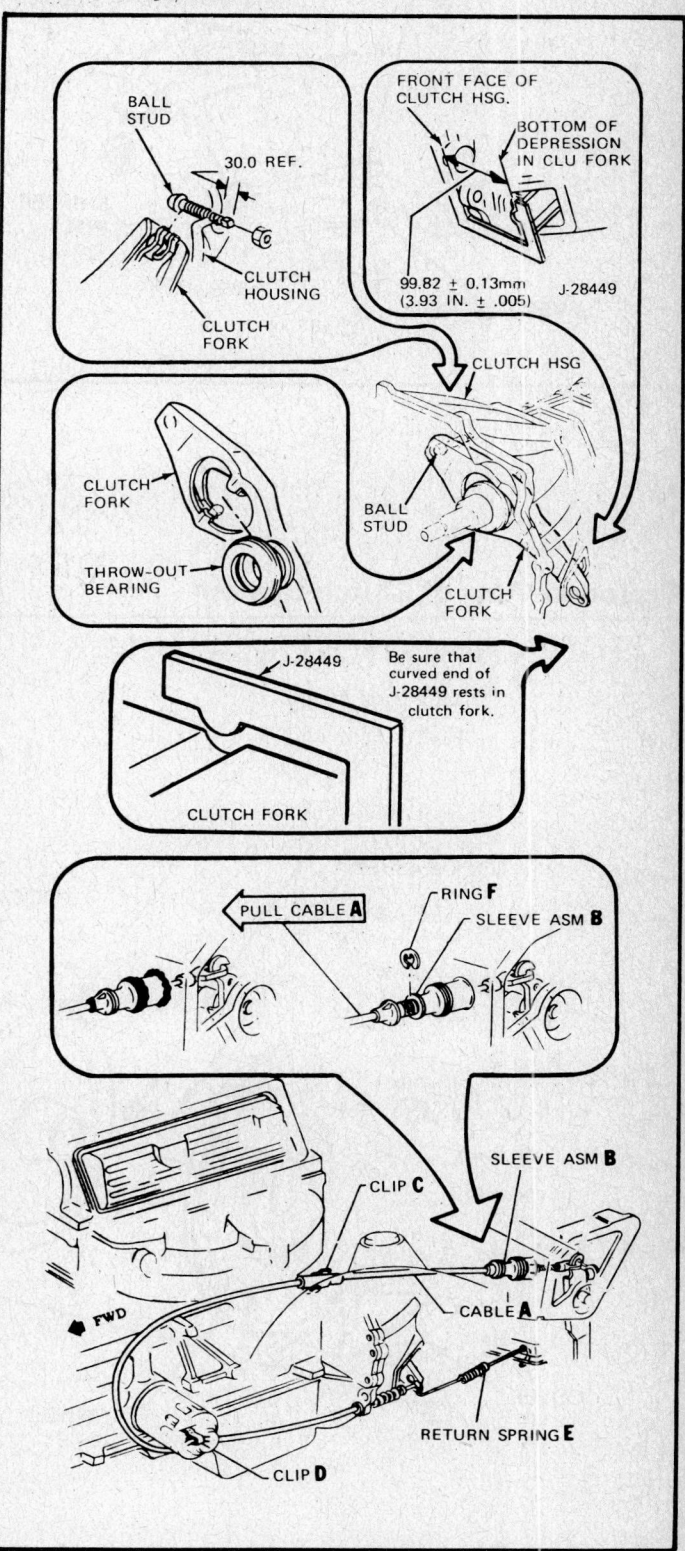

GENERAL MOTORS "T" BODY CARS

CHEVETTE, T1000

Automatic Transmission Shift Linkage

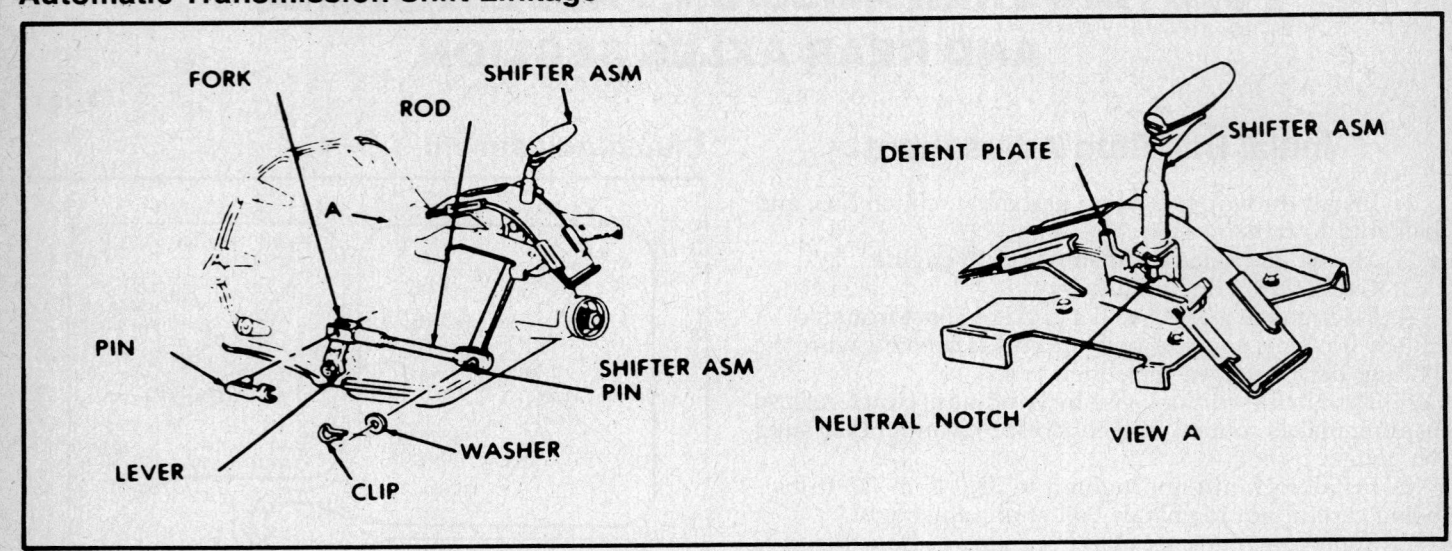

FORK

SHIFTER ASM

ROD

DETENT PLATE

SHIFTER ASM

A

PIN

SHIFTER ASM
PIN

LEVER

WASHER

CLIP

NEUTRAL NOTCH

VIEW A

Exploded View of Clutch System

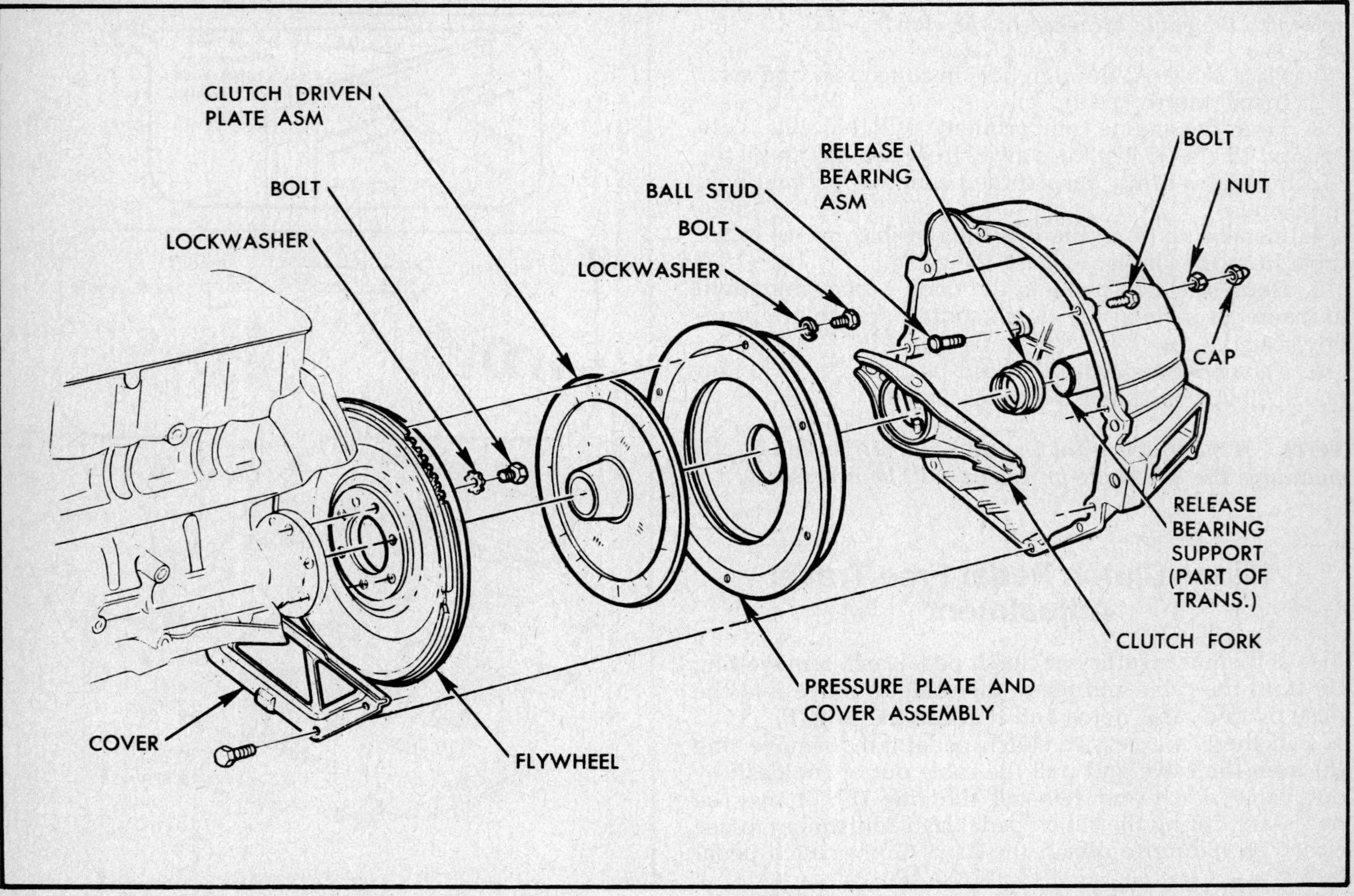

CLUTCH DRIVEN
PLATE ASM

BOLT

LOCKWASHER

BALL STUD

BOLT

LOCKWASHER

RELEASE
BEARING
ASM

BOLT

NUT

CAP

RELEASE
BEARING
SUPPORT
(PART OF
TRANS.)

CLUTCH FORK

COVER

FLYWHEEL

PRESSURE PLATE AND
COVER ASSEMBLY

CHILTON CAUTION After adjustment, stroke clutch pedal by hand and slowly release. If the clutch pedal does not return tight against the clutch pedal bumper, (test by raising the clutch pedal until contact is made with the clutch pedal bumper), and if motion results, a major clutch adjustment is now necessary. Follow the steps listed above under "Initial Ball Stud Adjustment."

Manual Transmission R&R

1. Remove, disconnect or relocate the following:
a. Shift lever
b. Driveshaft
c. Speedometer cable
d. Electrical connections
e. Clutch cable at release fork
f. Exhaust converter
g. Crossmember
2. Remove the clutch housing-to-engine retaining bolts, slide the transmission and clutch housing to the rear, and remove.

Manual Transmission Linkage Adjustment

There is no external linkage on the transmission. No adjustment is possible.

Driveshaft Installation

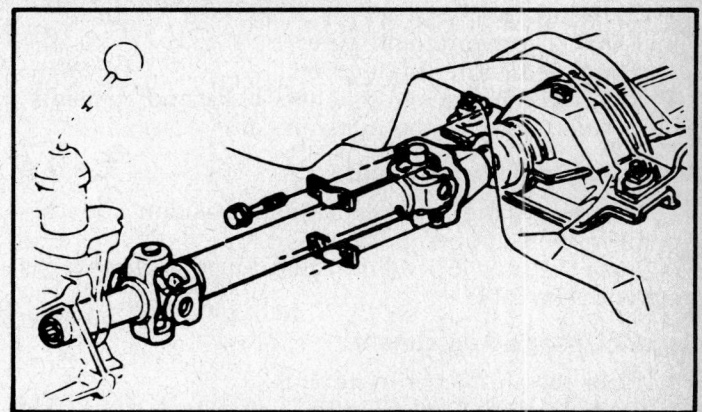

Automatic Transmission

R&R

1. Remove, disconnect or relocate the following:
a. Carburetor detent cable
b. Heater core on air conditioned cars
c. Driveshaft
d. Speedometer cable
e. Electrical leads

Automatic Transmission Downshift Cable Adjustment

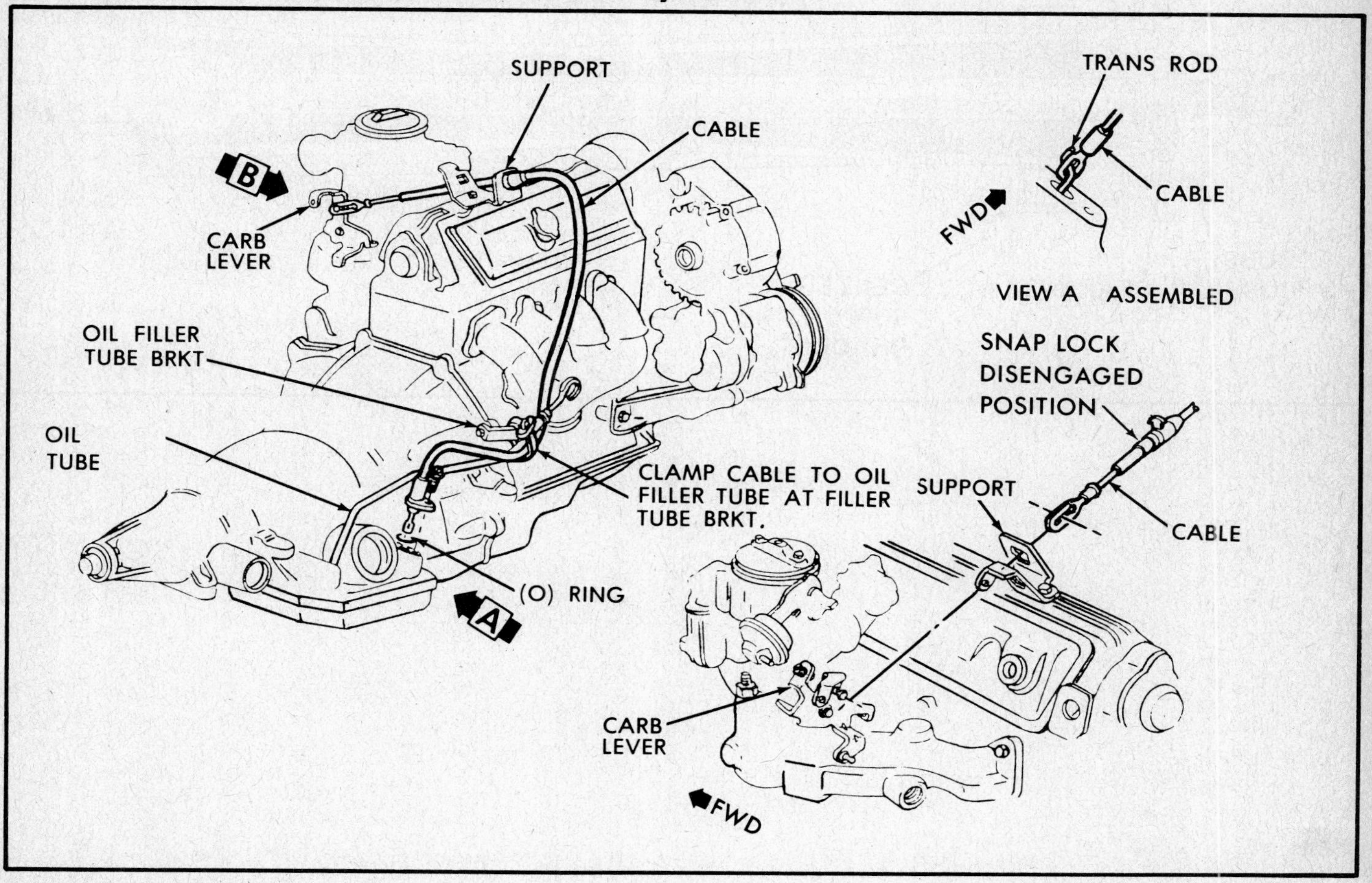

SUPPORT

CABLE

TRANS ROD

B

CARB LEVER

FWD

CABLE

OIL FILLER TUBE BRKT.

VIEW A   ASSEMBLED

OIL TUBE

SNAP LOCK DISENGAGED POSITION

CLAMP CABLE TO OIL FILLER TUBE AT FILLER TUBE BRKT.

SUPPORT

CABLE

(O) RING

A

CARB LEVER

FWD

f. Oil cooler lines
g. Shift linkage
h. Exhaust converter and pipe
i. Torque converter underpan
2. Remove converter-to-flywheel bolts and transmission mounts. Remove the transmission.

Downshift Cable Adjustment

1. Disengage the snap lock, and position the carburetor in the full open position.
2. Push the snap lock on the cable down until the top is flush with the cable.

Manual Linkage Adjustment

1. Place the shift lever in neutral.
2. Disconnect the rod from the lower end of the shift lever, and place the transmission lever in neutral.
3. Adjust the rod until the hole aligns with the pin on the shift lever. Install the rod and secure.

Drive Pinion Nut Tool

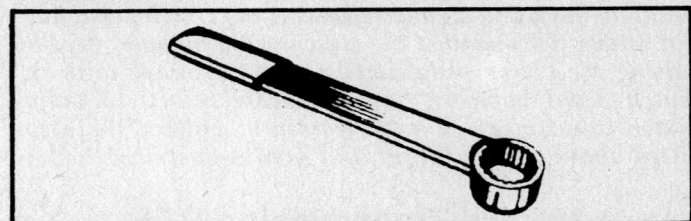

Pinion Oil Seal

1. Scribe a line down the pinion stem, nut and flange, and count the exposed pinion stem threads.
2. After replacing the seal, install the components in their exact locations.

Drive Shaft Extension Housing

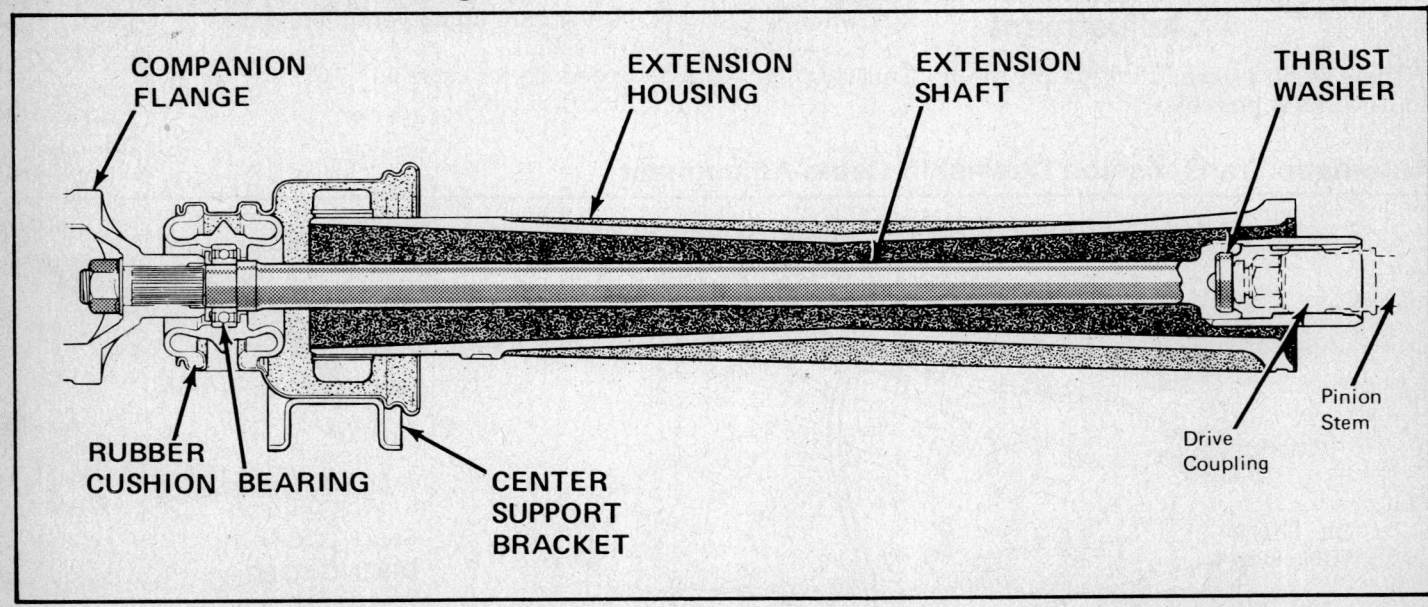

OLDSMOBILE
Except Ciera, Starfire & '80–'82 Omega

INDEX

OLDSMOBILE
EXCEPT CIERA, STARFIRE & '80-'82 OMEGA

MODEL IDENTIFICATION

1976 DELTA 88

W.B. **124″**, **C/Cruiser 127″**. Length 227″, C/Cruiser 231″. Ship. Wgt. V8 4 Dr. 4336 Lbs.

1977 DELTA 88

W.B. **116″**. Length 218″. Width 77″, C/Cruiser 80″. Ship. Wgt. V6 2 Dr. 3431 Lbs. V8 2 Dr. 3561 Lbs.

1978 DELTA 88

W.B. **116.0″** Length 217.5″ Ship. Wgt. 6 Cyl. 4 Dr. 3449 Lbs.

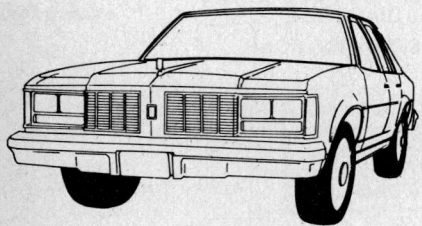

1979 DELTA 88

W.B. **116.0″** Length 217.5″ Ship. Wgt. 6 Cyl. 4 Dr. 3490 Lbs.

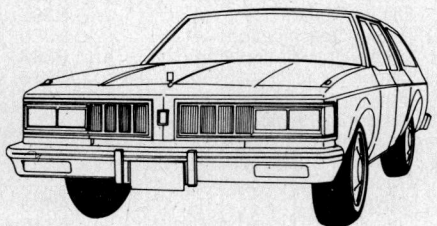

1980 88

W.B. **116″**. Length 217.5″. Ship. Wgt. Approx. 3420 Lbs.

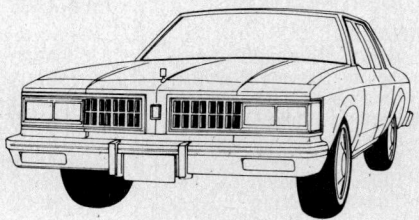

1981 DELTA 88

W.B. **116.0″**. Length 217.5″. 6 Cyl. 2 Dr. Ship. Wgt. 3541 Lbs.

1982 DELTA 88

W.B. **116.0″**. Length 217.5″. 6 Cyl. 2 Dr. Ship. Wgt. 3541 Lbs.

1976 "98"

W.B. **127″**. Length 233″. Ship. Wgt. V8 4 Dr. 4673 Lbs.

1977 "98"

W.B. **119″**. Length 221″. Width 77″. Ship. Wgt. V8 2 Dr. 3753 Lbs.

1978 "98"

W.B. **119.00″** Length 220.5″ Ship. Wgt. 8 Cyl. 2 Dr. 3837 Lbs.

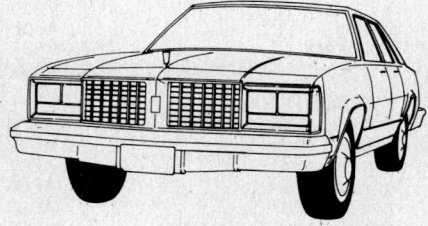

1979 "98"

W.B. **119.9″** Length 220.4″ Ship. Wgt. 8 Cyl. 2 Dr. 3852 Lbs.

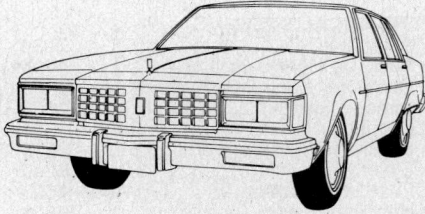

1980 98

W.B. **119.9″**. Length 220.4″. Ship. Wgt. 8 Cyl. 2 Dr. Approx. 3750 Lbs.

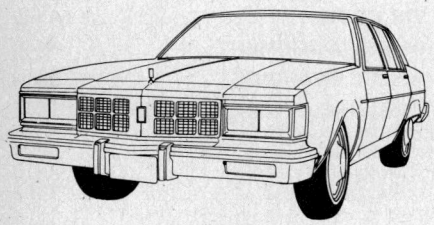

1981-82 "98"

W.B. **119.9″**. Length 221″. 6 Cyl. 4 Dr. Ship. Wgt. 3888 Lbs.

1976 TORONADO

W.B. **122″**. Length 228″. Ship. Wgt. V8 2 Dr. 4694 Lbs.

1977 TORONADO

W.B. **122″**, Length 228″. Width 80″. Ship. Wgt. V8 2 Dr. 4636 Lbs.

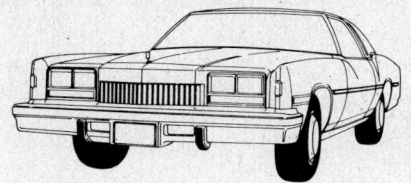

1978 TORONADO
W.B. **122.0″** Length 227.5″ Ship. Wgt. 8 Cyl. 2 Dr. 4628 Lbs.

1979 TORONADO
W.B. **114″** Length 205.6″ Ship. Wgt. 3711 Lbs.

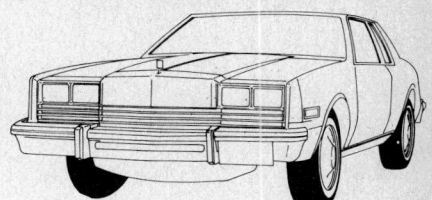

1980 TORONADO
W.B. **114″**. Length 205.6″. Ship. Wgt. Approx. 3720 Lbs.

1981-82 TORONADO
W.B. **114.0″**. Length 206.0″. 6 Cyl. 2 Dr. Ship. Wgt. 3695 Lbs.

1976 CUTLASS
W.B. **116″, 2D 112″**. Length 216″, 2D 210″/212″, S/W 220″. Ship. Wgt. 6 Cyl. 2 Dr. 3608 Lbs. V8 2 Dr. 3771 Lbs.

1977 CUTLASS
W.B. **116″, 2D 112″**. Length 216″, 2D 210″, S/W 220″. Width 77″, S/W 78″. Ship. Wgt. V6 2 Dr. 3535 Lbs. V8 2 Dr. 3680 Lbs.

1978 CUTLASS
W.B. **108.01″** Length 200.1″ Ship. Wgt. 6 Cyl. 2 Dr. 3109 Lbs.

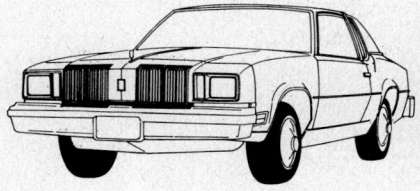

1979 CUTLASS
W.B. **108.1″** Length 197.7″ Ship. Wgt. 6 Cyl. 2 Dr. 3084 Lbs.

1980 CUTLASS
W.B. **108.1″**. Length 197.7″. Ship. Wgt. 8 Cyl. 2 Dr. Approx. 3133 Lbs.

1981 CUTLASS SUPREME
W.B. **108.1″**. Length 197.7″. 6 Cyl. 2 Dr. Ship. Wgt. 3285 Lbs.

1981 CUTLASS SUPREME BROUGHAM
W.B. **108.1″**. Length 197.7″. 6 Cyl. 2 Dr. Ship. Wgt. 3337 Lbs.

1982 CUTLASS SUPREME BROUGHAM
W.B. **108.1″**. Length 197.7″. 6 Cyl. 2 Dr. Ship. Wgt. 3337 Lbs.

1976 OMEGA
W.B. **111″**. Length 200″. Ship. Wgt. 6 Cyl. 2 Dr. 3174 Lbs. V8 2 Dr. 3323 Lbs.

1977 OMEGA
W.B. **111″**. Length 200″. Width 73″. Ship. Wgt. 6 Cyl. 2 Dr. 3171 Lbs. V8 2 Dr. 3312 Lbs.

1978 OMEGA
W.B. **111.00″** Length 199.6″ Ship. Wgt. 6 Cyl. 2 Dr. 3142 Lbs.

1979 OMEGA
W.B. **111.0″** Length 199.6″ Ship. Wgt. 6
Cyl. 2 Dr. 3118 Lbs.

ENGINE FIRING ORDER

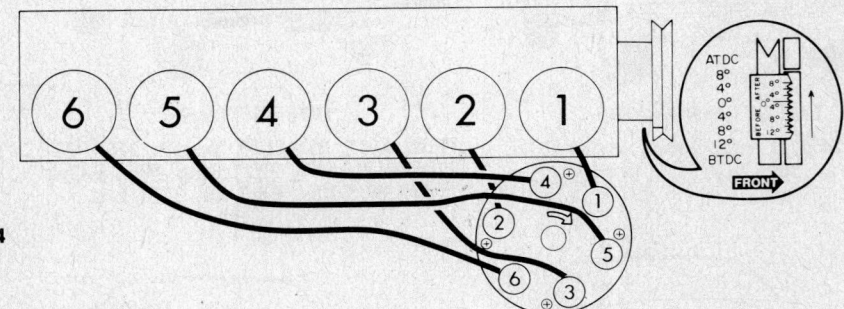

GM (Chevrolet) 250 6-cyl.
Engine firing order: 1–5–3–6–2–4
Distributor rotation: clockwise

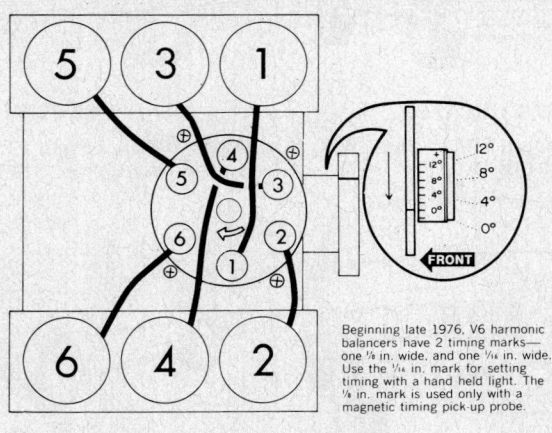

GM (Buick) 231, 252, V6
Engine firing order: 1-6-5-4-3-2
Distributor rotation: clockwise

Beginning late 1976, V6 harmonic
balancers have 2 timing marks—
one ⅛ in. wide, and one ¹⁄₁₆ in. wide.
Use the ¹⁄₁₆ in. mark for setting
timing with a hand held light. The
⅛ in. mark is used only with a
magnetic timing pick-up probe.

GM (Oldsmobile) 260, 307, 350, 403, 355, V8
Engine firing order: 1-8-4-3-6-5-7-2
Distributor rotation: counterclockwise

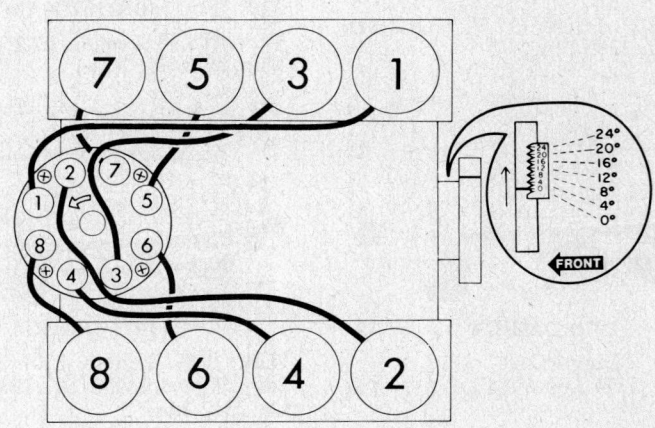

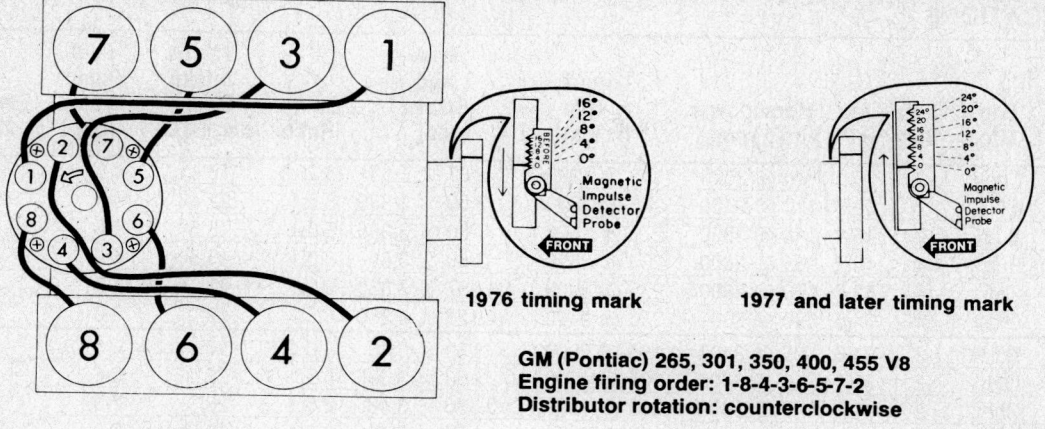

1976 timing mark   **1977 and later timing mark**

GM (Pontiac) 265, 301, 350, 400, 455 V8
Engine firing order: 1-8-4-3-6-5-7-2
Distributor rotation: counterclockwise

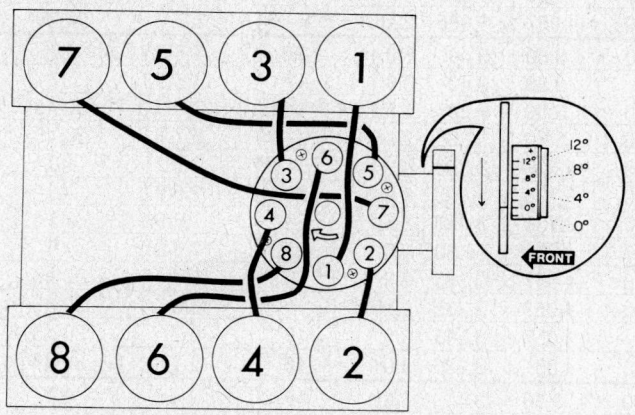

GM (Buick) 350 V8
Engine firing order: 1–8–4–3–6–5–7–2
Distributor rotation: clockwise

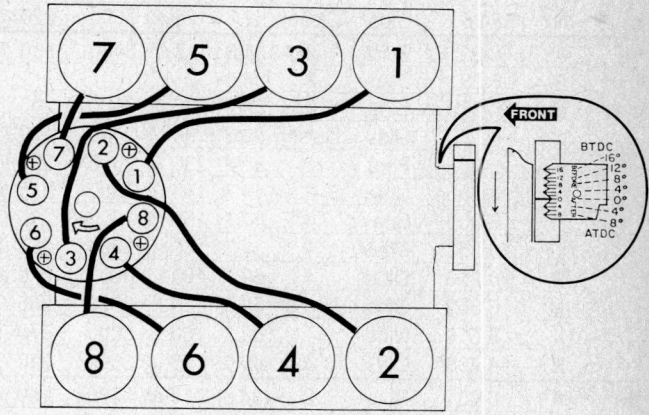

GM (Chevrolet) V8
Engine firing order: 1–8–4–3–6–5–7–2
Distributor rotation: clockwise

ENGINE SPECIFICATIONS

Year	Eng. V.I.N. Code	Engine No. Cyl. Disp. (cu in)	Eng. Mfg.	Carb Bbl	Tax H.P.	Horsepower @ rpm	Torque @ rpm (ft lbs)	Bore and Stroke (in)	Comp. Ratio	Valves Intake Opens (deg BTDC)	Fuel Pump Press. (psi)	Oil Pressure @ 2000 rpm
76	D	6-250	Chev	1	36.0	110 @ 3800	185 @ 1200	3.87 × 3.53	8.25:1	16	4-5	38
	F	8-260	Olds	2	39.2	110 @ 3400	205 @ 1600	3.50 × 3.385	8.5:1	22	5-6	38
	H	8-350	Buick	2	46.2	145 @ 3800	275 @ 1600	3.80 × 3.385	8.0:1	13.5	4-5	37
	J	8-350	Buick	4	46.2	165 @ 3800	260 @ 2400	3.80 × 3.85	8.0:1	13.5	4-5	37
	R	8-350	Olds	4	52.7	170 @ 3800	275 @ 2000	4.057 × 3.385	8.0:1	22	5-6	40
	T	8-455	Olds	4	54.5	190 @ 3600	350 @ 2400	4.126 × 4.250	8.5:1	22	5-6	40
77	C-A	V6-231	Buick	2	34.6	105 @ 3400	185 @ 2000	3.80 × 3.40	8.0:1	17	4-5	35
	F	8-260	Olds	2	39.2	110 @ 3400	205 @ 1600	3.50 × 3.385	8.5:1	22	5-6	38
	U	8-305	Chev	2	44.7	145 @ 3800	280 @ 1800	3.736 × 3.48	8.5:1	28	7-9	36
	L	8-350	Chev.	4	51.2	170 @ 3800	270 @ 2400	4.00 × 3.48	8.0:1	28	7-9	38
	R	8-350	Olds	4	52.7	170 @ 3800	275 @ 2000	4.057 × 3.385	8.0:1	13.5	5-6	40
	K	8-403	Olds	4	60.6	185 @ 3600	320 @ 2000	4.351 × 3.385	8.0:1	20	5-6	40
78	A	6-231	Buick	2	34.6	105 @ 3400	185 @ 2000	3.80 × 3.40	8.0:1	17	4-5	37
	F	8-260	Olds	2	39.2	110 @ 3400	205 @ 1800	3.50 × 3.385	7.5:1	14	5.5-6.5	30-45
	U	8-305	Chev	2	44.7	145 @ 3800	245 @ 2400	3.736 × 3.480	8.5:1	28	7.5-9.0	32-40
	H	8-305	Chev	4	44.7	160 @ 4000	235 @ 2400	3.736 × 3.480	8.5:1	28	7.5-9.0	32-40
	L	8-350	Chev	4	51.2	160 @ 3800	260 @ 2400	4.00 × 3.480	8.5:1	28	7.5-9.0	32-40
	R	8-350	Olds	4	52.7	170 @ 3800	275 @ 2000	4.057 × 3.385	8.0:1	16	5.5-5.6	30-45
	K	8-403	Olds	4	60.6	185 @ 3600②	320 @ 2000②	4.351 × 3.385	8.0:1	16	5.5-6.5	30-45
	N	8-350	Olds	Diesel	52.7	120 @ 3600	220 @ 1600	4.057 × 3.385	22.5:1	—	5-7	30-45
79	A	6-231	Buick	2	34.6	115 @ 3480	190 @ 2000	3.80 × 3.40	8.0:1	17	4.5-5.7	37
	2	6-231	Buick	2	34.6	①	①	3.80 × 3.40	8.0:1	17	4.5-5.7	37
	F	8-260	Olds	2	39.2	105 @ 3600	205 @ 1800	3.50 × 3.385	7.5:1	14	7.5-9.0	30-45
	P	8-260	Olds	Diesel	39.2	90 @ 2400	170 @ 1800	3.50 × 3.385	22.5:1	—	5.7-7.0	30-45
	Y	8-301	Pont	2	51.2	230 @ 2000	230 @ 2000	4.000 × 3.000	8.2:1	31/27	7-8	40
	G	8-305	Chev	2	44.7	145 @ 3800	245 @ 2400	3.736 × 3.480	8.5:1	28	7.5-9.0	45
	H	8-305	Chev	4	44.7	160 @ 4000	235 @ 2400	3.736 × 3.480	8.5:1	28	7.5-9.0	45
	L	8-350	Chev	4	51.2	160 @ 3800	260 @ 2400	4.00 × 3.480	8.5:1	29	7.5-9.0	45
	R	8-350	Olds	4	52.7	160 @ 3600	270 @ 2000	4.057 × 3.385	8.0:1	16	5-7	30-45
	N	8-350	Olds	Diesel	52.7	125 @ 3600	225 @ 1600	4.057 × 3.385	22.5:1	—	6-8	30-45
	X	8-350	Olds		52.7	160 @ 3600	270 @ 200	4.057 × 3.385	8.0:1	16	5-7	30-45
	K	8-403	Olds	4	60.6	175 @ 3600	310 @ 2000	4.351 × 3.385	8.0:1	16	5-7	30-45
80	A	6-231	Buick	2	34.6	115 @ 3480	190 @ 2000	3.80 × 3.40	8.0:1	17	3-4.5	37
	F	8-260	Olds	2	39.2	105 @ 3600	205 @ 1800	3.50 × 3.385	8.0:1	17	5.5-6.5	30-45
	P	8-260	Olds	Diesel	39.2	90 @ 2400	170 @ 1800	3.50 × 3.385	22.5:1	—	5.5-6.5	30-45
	H	8-305	Chev	4	44.6	145 @ 3800	245 @ 2400	3.736 × 3.480	8.5:1	28	7.5-9.0	30-45
	Y	8-307	Olds	4	46.2	148 @ 3800	250 @ 2400	3.800 × 3.385	8.5:1	—	5.5-6.5	30-45
	R	8-350	Olds	4	52.7	160 @ 3600	270 @ 2000	4.057 × 3.385	8.5:1	16	5-7	30-45
	N	8-350	Olds	Diesel	52.7	120 @ 3600	220 @ 1600	4.057 × 3.385	22.5:1	—	5-6	30-45
'81	A	6-231	Buick	2	34.6	115 @ 3480	190 @ 2000	3.80 × 3.40	8.0:1	17	3-4.5	37
	4	6-252	Buick	4	36.0	110 @ 3400	195 @ 2000	3.965 × 3.40	8.0:1	17	5.0	37
	F	8-260	Olds	2	39.2	105 @ 3600	205 @ 1800	3.50 × 3.385	8.0:1	17	5.5-6.5	30-45
	H	8-305	Chev	4	44.6	145 @ 3800	245 @ 2400	3.736 × 3.480	8.5:1	28	7.5-9.0	30-45
	Y	8-307	Olds	4	46.2	148 @ 3800	250 @ 2400	3.80 × 3.385	8.5:1	—	5.5-6.5	30-45
	N	8-350	Olds	Diesel	52.7	170 @ 3600	220 @ 1600	4.057 × 3.385	22.5:1	—	5-6	30-45

① Not available

② All except Toronado, Toronado 190 H.P. @ 3600, 325 ft/lbs @ 2000

③ If a 17-digit VIN is used, the 8th digit is the engine code and the 10th digit is the model year code

TUNE-UP SPECIFICATIONS

Year	Eng. V.I.N. Code	Engine No. Cyl. Disp. (cu in)	SPARK PLUGS Orig. Type	Gap (in)	IGNITION TIMING (deg B.T.D.C. @ rpm) Federal Manual	Federal Auto.	Calif. Hi. Alt. Manual	Calif. Hi. Alt. Auto.	CARBURETION HOT IDLE SPEED Federal Manual	Federal Auto.(D)	Calif. Hi. Alt Manual	Calif. Hi. Alt Auto.(D)
76	D	6-250	R46TS	.035	6 @ 450	10 @ 450	—	—	850	550	850	550
	F	8-260	R46SX	.080	16 @ 1100	18 @ 1100	14 @ 1100	16 @ 1100	—	650	—	650
	H	8-350	R45TSX	.060	—	12 @ 600	—	—	—	650	—	650
	J	8-350	R45TSX	.060	—	12 @ 600	—	12 @ 600	—	650	—	650
	R	8-350	R46SX	.080	—	20 @ 1100	—	20 @ 1100	—	650	—	650
	T	8-455	R46SX	.080	—	16 @ 1100[2]	—	16 @ 1100[7]	—	650	—	650
77	C-A	6-231	R46TS	.040	12 @ 600	12 @ 800	12 @ 600	12 @ 600	—	600	—	600
	F	8-260	R46SZ	.060	16 @ 1100	18 @ 1100	16 @ 1100	16 @ 1100	750	650	750	650
	U	8-305	R45TS	.045	8 idle	8 @ 600	—	6 @ idle	700	650	700	650
	L	8-350	R45TS	.045	—	8 @ 600	—	6 @ 1100	—	650	—	650
	R	8-350	R46SZ	.060	—	20 @ 1100	—	—	—	650	—	650
	K	8-403	R46SZ	.060	—	20 @ 1100[4]	—	20 @ 1100[4]	—	675	—	675
78	A	6-231	R46TSX	.060	—	15 @ 800	—	18 @ 1100	800	800	800	800
	F	8-260	R46SZ	.060	18 @ 1100	20 @ 1100	—	—	800	500	800	500
	U	8-305	R45TS	.045	4 @ 600	4 @ 500	—	8 @ 575	700	600	—	650
	H	8-305	R45TS	.045	4 @ 600	8 @ 600	—	—	—	—	—	700●
	L	8-350	R45TS	.045	—	—	—	8 @ 500[5]	—	600	—	650
	R	8-350	R46SZ	.060	—	20 @ 1100	—	20 @ 1100	—	650	—	675●
	K	8-403	R46SZ	.060	—	18 @ 1100	—	20 @ 1100	—	650	—	675●
	N	8-350	—	DIESEL	—	—	—	—	—	[1]	—	[1]
79	A	6-231	R46TSX	.060	15 @ 600	15 @ 800	15 @ 600	15 @ 600	800	800	800	800
	2	6-231	[1]	[1]	[1]	[1]	[1]	[1]	—	—	—	—
	F	8-260	R46SZ	.060	18 @ 1100	20 @ 1100	—	18 @ 1100	800	625	—	625●
	P	8-260	DIESEL		—	[1]	—	[1]	—	[1]	—	[1]
	Y	8-301	R46TSX	.060	—	12 @ 650	—	20 @ 1100	650	650	—	650
	G	8-305	R45TS	.045	4 @ 600	4 @ 500	—	4 @ 500	—	600	—	650●
	H	8-305	R45TS	.045	4 @ 500	4 @ 500	—	4 @ 500[6]	—	—	—	—
	L	8-350	R43TS	.045	—	—	—	8 @ 500	—	650	—	600[6]
	R	8-350	R46SZ	.060	—	20 @ 1100	—	20 @ 1100	—	650	—	600[6]
	N	8-350	DIESEL		—	[1]	—	[1]	—	[1]	—	[1]
	X	8-350	R46TSX	.060	—	15 @ 550	—	—	—	650	—	—
	K	8-403	R46SZ	.060	—	20 @ 1100	—	20 @ 1100	—	650	—	600[6]
80	A	6-231	R45TS[10]	.040	15 @ 800	15 @ 550	15 @ 550	15 @ 550	600	670	—	620
	F	8-260	R46SX	.080	20 @ 1100[11]	20 @ 1100[11]	20 @ 1100[11]	20 @ 1100[11]	625	625	625	625
	P	8-260	DIESEL	—	—	[8]	—	—	—	650	—	650
	S	8-265	R45TSX	.060	10 @ 600	10 @ 600	—	10 @ 600	700	625	[1]	[1]
	H	8-305	R45TS	.045	4 @ 500	4 @ 500	4 @ 550	4 @ 550	600	600	650	650
	Y	8-307	R46SX	.080	20 @ 1100	20 @ 1100	—	20 @ 1100	—	600	[1]	650
	R	8-350	R46SX	.080	18 @ 1100	18 @ 1100	16 @ 1100	16 @ 1100[12]	—	600	—	650
	N	8-350	DIESEL	—	—	[8]	—	—	—	650	—	650
81	A	6-231	R45TS[10]	.040	15 @ 800	15 @ 550	15 @ 800	15 @ 550	800	600	800	600
	4	6-252	R45TS8	.080	—	15 @ IDLE	15 @ IDLE	15 @ IDLE	—	690	—	690
	F	8-260	R46SX	.080	18 @ 1100	18 @ 1100	18 @ 1100	18 @ 1100	[14]	[14]	[14]	[14]
	Y	8-307	R46SX	.080	15 @ 1100	15 @ 1100	15 @ 1100	15 @ 1100	[14]	[14]	[14]	[14]
	N	8-350	DIESEL	—	[1]	[1]	[1]	[1]	[1]	[1]

NOTE: Should the information provided in this manual deviate from the specifications on the underhood tune-up label, the label specifications should be used, as they may reflect production changes.

—   Not applicable
D = Auto. transmission in drive
N = Transmission in neutral
[1] See engine decal
[2] Toronado 14 @ 1100 rpm
[3] Toronado 10 @ 1100 rpm
[4] Not adjustable with electronic spark timing
[5] Hi.Alt.—idle 700 rpm
[6] Hi.Alt.—idle 600 rpm
[7] Calif., Tornado—12 B.T.C. @ 1100 rpm
[8] Int. timing 16 BTC-38 A.T.D.C.
   Ext. timing 64 BTC-17 A.T.D.C.
[10] Calif.-R45TSX
[11] Cutlass Wgn.-18 @ 1100
[12] Toronado only. All others 18 @ 1100
[14] Idle speed controlled by computer.

OLDSMOBILE
EXCEPT CIERA, STARFIRE & '80-'82 OMEGA

VEHICLE IDENTIFICATION NUMBER (VIN)①

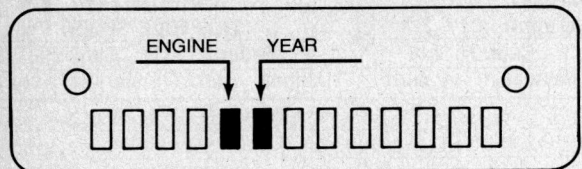

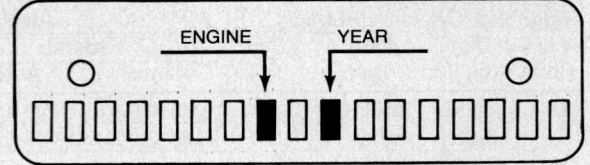

| Code | ENGINE CODE | | | | MODEL YEAR CODE | |
	Eng. Disp. cu in	Eng. Config.	Carb	Eng. Mfgr.	Code	Year
D	250	L-6	1v	Chev.	6	1976
F	260	V-8	2v	Olds.		
H	350	V-8	2v	Buick		
J	350	V-8	4v	Buick		
R	350	V-8	4v	Olds.		
Q	400	V-8	4v	Pont.		
T	455	V-8	4v	Olds.		
C-A	231	V-6	2v	Buick	7	1977
D	250	L-6	1v	Chev.		
F	260	V-8	2v	Olds.		
Y	301	V-8	2v	Pont.		
U	305	V-8	2v	Chev.		
L	350	V-8	4v	Chev.		
R	350	V-8	4v	Olds.		
K	403	V-8	4v	Olds.		
A	231	V-6	2v	Buick	8	1978
D	250	L-6	1v	Chev.		
F	260	V-8	2v	Olds.		
U	305	V-8	2v	Chev.		
H	305	V-8	4v	Chev.		
L	350	V-8	4v	Chev.		
R	350	V-8	4v	Olds.		
K	403	V-8	4v	Olds.		
N	350 Diesel	V-8	—	Olds.		

① If a 17- or 19- digit VIN is used, the 7th digit is the engine code

| Code | ENGINE CODE | | | | MODEL YEAR CODE | |
	Eng. Disp. cu in	Eng. Config.	Carb	Eng. Mfgr.	Code	Year
A	231	V6	2v	Buick	9	1979
2	231	V6	2v	Buick		
F	260	V8	2v	Olds.		
P	260	V8	Diesel	Olds.		
Y	301	V8	2v	Pont.		
G	305	V8	2v	Chev.		
H	305	V8	4v	Chev.		
L	350	V8	4v	Chev.		
N	350	V8	Diesel	Olds.		
R	350	V8	4v	Olds.		
X	350	V8	4v	Buick		
8	350	V8	4v	Chev.		
K	403	V8	4v	Olds.		
A	231 (3.8L)	V6	2v	Buick	A	1980
F	260 (4.3L)	V8	2v	Olds.		
P	260 (4.3L)	V8	Diesel	Olds.		
S	265 (4.3L)	V8	2v	Pont.		
H	305 (5.0L)	V8	4v	Chev.		
Y	307 (5.0L)	V8	4v	Olds.		
R	350 (5.7L)	V8	4v	Olds.		
N	350 (5.7L)	V8	Diesel	Olds.		
A	231 (3.8L)	V6	2v	Buick	B	1981
4	252 (4.3L)	V6	4v	Buick		
F	260 (4.3L)	V8	2v	Olds.		
Y	307 (5.0L)	V8	4v	Olds.		
N	350 (5.7L)	V8	Diesel	Olds.		
A	231 (3.8L)	V6	2v	Buick	2	1982
4	252 (4.3L)	V6	4v	Buick		
F	260 (4.3L)	V8	2v	Olds.		
Y	307 (5.0L)	V8	4v	Olds.		
V	263 (4.3L)	V6	Diesel	Olds.		
N	350 (5.7L)	V8	Diesel	Olds.		

① If a 17- or 19- digit VIN is used, the 7th digit is the engine code

TORQUE SPECIFICATIONS

All readings in ft/lbs

Year	Engine No. Cyl. Disp. (cu in)	Cylinder Head Bolts	Rod Bearing Bolts	Main Bearing Bolts	Crankshaft Pulley Or Damper Bolt	Flywheel To Crankshaft Bolts	MANIFOLD	
							Intake	Exhaust
'76	6-250	95	35	65	Press fit	60	①	④
	8-350	80	40	115	175	60	45	25
	8-260, 350, 455	85	42	120②	200-310	③	40	25
'77	6-231	80	40	115	175	60	45	25
	8-260	85	42	②	200-310	③	40	25
	8-305, 350	65	45	70	60	60	30	20
	8-350, 403	130	42	②	200-310	③	40	25
'78	6-231	80	40	115	175	60	45	25
	8-260	85	42	②	200-310	③	40	25
	8-305, 350(VIN-L)	65	45	70	60	60	30	20
	8-350(VIN-R), 403	130	42	②	200-310	③	40	25
	8-350 Diesel	130	42	120	200-310	60	40	25
'79	6-231	80	40	115	175	60	45	25
	8-260	85	42	②	200-310	③	40	25
	8-260 Diesel	130	42	120	175	60	40	25
	8-301 (VIN-Y)	90	35	⑤	60	95	45	25
	8-305, 350 (VIN-L)	65	45	70	60	60	30	20
	8-350 (VIN-R), 403	130	42	②	200-310	③	40	25
	8-350 Diesel	130	42	120	200-310	60	40	25
	8-350 (VIN-X)	80	40	100	225	⑦	45	25
'80	6-231	80	40	100	225	60	45	25
	8-260	85⑧	42	②	200-310	③	40	25
	8-260 Diesel	130	42	120	175	60	40	25
	8-305 H	65	45	70	60	95	45	25
	8-307 Y	130	43	⑥	200-310	⑦	40	25
	8-350 R	130	42	⑥	200-310	⑦	40	25
	8-350 N V8 Diesel	130	42	120	200-310	60	40	25
'81	6-231-252	80 (108 N•m)	40 (54 N•m)	100 (136 N•m)	225 (306 N•m)	60 (81 N•m)	45 (61 N•m)	25 (34 N•m)
	8-260	85⑧ (115 N•m)	42 (57 N•m)	②	200-310 (217-310 N•m)	③	40 (54 N•m)	25 (34 N•m)
	8-307 Y	130 (176 N•m)	42 (57 N•m)	⑥	200-310 (217-310 N•m)	⑦	40 (54 N•m)	25 (34 N•m)
	8-350 N V8 Diesel	130 (180 N•m)	42 (57 N•m)	120 (163 N•m)	200-310 (217-310 N•m)	60 (81 N•m)	40 (54 N•m)	25 (34 N•m)
'82	6-231-252	80 (108 N•m)	40 (54 N•m)	100 (136 N•m)	225 (306 N•m)	60 (81 N•m)	45 (61 N•m)	25 (34 N•m)
	8-260	85⑧ (115 N•m)	42 (57 N•m)	②	200-310 (217-310 N•m)	③	40 (54 N•m)	25 (34 N•m)
	8-307 Y	130 (176 N•m)	42 (57 N•m)	⑥	200-310 (217-310 N•m)	⑦	40 (54 N•m)	25 (34 N•m)
	6-263 Diesel	See Diesel Section of This Manual						
	8-350 N V8 Diesel	130 (180 N•m)	42 (57 N•m)	120 (163 N•m)	200-310 (217-310 N•m)	60 (81 N•m)	40 (54 N•m)	25 (34 N•m)

① Intake manifold integral with cylinder head
② 8-260, 350, 403—80 on no. 1-4, 120 on no. 5
③ A.T. 60 ft lbs.; M.T. 90 ft lbs.
④ Inner bolts—30 ft lbs.; outer bolts—20 ft lbs.
⑤ Rear main—100 ft lbs, all others—60 ft lbs.
⑥ #1, 2, 3, 4—80 ft lbs.
   #5—120 ft lbs.
⑦ Auto trans—60 ft lbs.—(81 N•m)
   Manual trans—90 ft lbs.
⑧ Dip bolts in motor oil

OLDSMOBILE
EXCEPT CIERA, STARFIRE & '80-'82 OMEGA

ENGINE SPECIFICATIONS — OLDSMOBILE (EXCEPT STARFIRE & '80-'81 OMEGA)

Year	Eng. V.I.N. Code	Engine No. Cyl. Disp. (cu in)	Eng. Mfg.	Carb Bbl	Tax H.P.	Horsepower @ rpm	Torque @ rpm (ft lbs)	Bore and Stroke (in)	Comp. Ratio	Valves Intake Opens (deg BTDC)	Fuel Pump Press. (psi)	Oil Pressure @ 2000 rpm
'82	A	6-231	Buick	2	34.6	115 @ 3480	190 @ 2000	3.80 × 3.40	8.0:1	17	3-4.5	37
	3	6-231	Buick	4	34.6	170 @ 4000	265 @ 2800	3.80 × 3.40	8.0:1	17	5	37
	F	8-260	Olds	2	39.2	105 @ 3600	205 @ 1800	3.50 × 3.385	7.5:1	17	5.5-6.5	30-45
	Y	8-307	Olds	4	46.2	148 @ 3800	250 @ 2400	3.80 × 3.385	8.5:1	—	5.5-6.5	30-45
	V	6-263	Olds	Diesel	39.2	—	—	4.070 × 3.385	21.6:1	—	—	30-45
	N	8-350	Olds	Diesel	52.7	170 @ 3600	220 @ 1600	4.057 × 3.385	22.5:1	—	5-6	30-45

① Not available
② All except Toronado, Toronado 190 H.P. @ 3600, 325 ft/lbs @ 2000
③ If a 17-digit VIN is used, the 8th digit is the engine code and the 10th digit is the model year code

TUNE-UP SPECIFICATIONS — OLDSMOBILE (EXCEPT STARFIRE & '80-'82 OMEGA)

Year	Eng. V.I.N. Code	Engine No. Cyl. Disp. (cu in)	SPARK PLUGS Orig. Type	SPARK PLUGS Gap (in)	IGNITION TIMING (deg B.T.D.C. @ rpm) Federal Manual	Federal Auto.	Calif. Hi. Alt. Manual	Calif. Hi. Alt. Auto.	CARBURETION HOT IDLE SPEED Federal Manual	Federal Auto.(D)	Calif. Hi. Alt Manual	Calif. Hi. Alt Auto.(D)
82	A	6-231	R45TS⑩	.040	①	①	①		①	①	①	①
	4	6-252	R45TS8	.080	①	①	①		①	①	①	①
	F	8-260	R46SX	.080	①	①	①		⑭	⑭	⑭	⑭
	Y	8-307	R46SX	.080	①	①	①		⑭	⑭	⑭	⑭
	V	V6-263	DIESEL		See Diesel Section of This Manual							
	N	8-350	DIESEL	—	①	①	①		①		①	

NOTE: Should the information provided in this manual deviate from the specifications on the underhood tune-up label, the label specifications should be used, as they may reflect production changes.

— Not applicable
D = Auto. transmission in drive
N = Transmission in neutral
① See engine decal
② Toronado 14 @ 1100 rpm
③ Toronado 10 @ 1100 rpm
④ Not adjustable with electronic spark timing
⑤ Hi.Alt.—idle 700 rpm
⑥ Hi.Alt.—idle 600 rpm
⑦ Calif., Tornado—12 B.T.C. @ 1100 rpm
⑧ Int. timing 16 BTC-38 A.T.D.C.
Ext. timing 64 BTC-17 A.T.D.C.
⑩ Calif.-R45TSX
⑪ Cutlass Wgn.-18 @ 1100
⑫ Toronado only. All others 18 @ 1100
⑭ Idle speed controlled by computer.

FLUID CAPACITIES—Coolant, Fuel & Lubricant

OLDSMOBILE COMPACT

Year	Engine No. Cyl. Disp. (Cu In)	Eng. VIN Code	Engine Crankcase (Add 1 Qt For New Filter)	TRANSMISSION (Pts To Refill After Draining) Manual 3-Speed	4-Speed	Automatic	Drive Axle (pts)	Gasoline Tank (gals)	Rad. Cap Press.	Thermo. Temp.	COOLING SYSTEM (qts) With Heater	With A/C
'76	6-231	C	4	3.12	3.12③	6	4.25	21	15	195	17.09	18.0
	6-250	D	4	3.0	—	8	4.25	21	15	195	14.6④	15⑤
	8-260	F	4	3.0	3.5⑥	7.5	4.25	20.5	15	195	19.6	20.1
	8-305	Q	4	3.0-	3.0	8	4.25	21	15	195	17.2	17.9
	8-350	All	4	3.0	3.0	7.5⑦	4.25	20.5⑧	15	195	17.8	18
'77	6-231	C,A	4	3	—	6	4.25	21	15	195	12.8	12.7
	8-260	F	4	—	—	6	4.25	21	15	195	16.9	17
	8-305	U	4	3	—	6	4.25	21	15	195	14.6	15.3
	8-350	L, R	4	—	—	6	4.25	21	15	195	16	16.7
'78	6-231	A	4	3	—	6	4.25	21	15	195	12.8	12.7
	8-305	U	4	3	—	6	4.25	21	15	195	15.8	16.1
	8-350	L	4	3	—	6	4.25	21	15	195	16	16.7
'79	6-231	A	4	3	—	6	4.25	21	15	195	12.8	12.7
	8-305	G	4	3	—	6	4.25	21	15	195	15.8	16.1
	8-350	L	4	3	—	6	4.25	21	15	195	16	16.7
'80	See GM X-body car—front drive, "Omega" section											

FLUID CAPACITIES—Coolant, Fuel & Lubricant

OLDSMOBILE MID-SIZE

Year	Engine No. Cyl. Disp. cu in	Engine Crankcase (Add 1 Qt For New Filter)	TRANSMISSION (Pts To Refill After Draining) Manual 3-Speed	4-Speed	Automatic ①	Drive Axle (pts)	Gasoline Tank (gals)	Rad. Cap Pressure	Thermo. Opening Temp.	COOLING SYSTEM (qts) With Heater	With A/C
'76	6-250	4	3.5	—	6	4.25	22	15	195	17	17
	8-260	4	3.5	—	6	4.25	22	15	195	17	17
	8-350	4	—	—	6	4.25③	22	15	195	20	20
	8-455	4	—	—	6	5.5	22	15	195	21⑥	21.5
'77	6-231	4	3.5	—	6	4.3	22	15	195	12.7	12.7
	8-260	4	3.0	⑦	6	4.3	22	15	195	17	17
	8-350	4	3.0	—	6	4.3	22	15	195	15	15.5
	8-403	4	—	—	6	4.3	22	15	195	16.2	16.5
'78	6-231	4	3.0	2.4⑦	3	3.5③	17.4	15	195	11.93	11.83
	8-260	4	3.0	2.4⑦	3	3.5③	17.4	15	195	16.2	17.0
	8-305	4	3.0	2.4	3	3.5③	17.4	15	195	15.6	15.5
	8-350	4	—	—	3	3.5③	17.4	15	195	15.6	17.2
'79	6-231	4	3	3	3	3.5③	④	15	195	13.3	13.3
	8-260	4	3.0	3	3	3.5③	④	15	195	16.2	17.0
	8-260 DIESEL	6	—	—	③	3.5③	④	15	195	20.0	20.0
	8-305	4	—	—	3	3.5③	④	15	195	15.5	15.5
	8-350	4	—	—	3	3.5③	④	15	195	15.0	15.0
	8-350 DIESEL	6	—	—	3	3.5③	④	15	195	18.0	17.9

OLDSMOBILE
EXCEPT CIERA, STARFIRE & '80-'82 OMEGA

FLUID CAPACITIES—Coolant, Fuel & Lubricant　　　　　**OLDSMOBILE MID-SIZE**

Year	Engine No. Cyl. Disp. cu in	Engine Crankcase (Add 1 Qt For New Filter)	TRANSMISSION (Pts To Refill After Draining) Manual 3-Speed	4-Speed	Automatic ①	Drive Axle (pts)	Gasoline Tank (gals)	Rad. Cap Pressure	Thermo. Opening Temp.	COOLING SYSTEM (qts) With Heater	With A/C
'80	6-231 (3.8L)	4	3	3	3	③	④	15	195	13.3	13.3
	8-301 (5.0L)	4	3	3	3	③	④	15	195	20.0	20.0
	8-260 (4.2L)	4	3	3	3	③	④	15	195	20.0	20.0
	8-260 (4.2L) DIESEL	6	—	—	3	③	19.25	15	195	20.0	20.0
	8-305 (5.0L)	4	3	3	3	③	④	15	195	15.5	15.5
	8-350 (5.7L)	4	3	3	3	③	④	15	195	15.0	15.0
	8-350 (5.7L) DIESEL	6	—	—	3	③	④	15	195	18.0	18.0
'81	6-231 (3.8L)	4	3	3	3	③	④	15	195	13.3	13.3
	6-252 (4.1L)	4	3	3	3	③	④	15	195	13.6	13.6
	8-260 (4.2L)	4	3	3	3	③	④	15	195	20.0	20.0
	8-307 (5.0L)	4	3	3	3	③	④	15	195	15.5	15.5
	8-350 DIESEL (5.7L)	6	—	—	3	③	④	15	195	18.0	18.0
'82	6-231 (3.8L)	4	3	3	3	③	④	15	195	13.3	13.3
	6-252 (4.1L)	4	3	3	3	③	④	15	195	13.6	13.6
	8-260 (4.3L)	4	3	3	3	③	④	15	195	20.0	20.0
	8-307 (5.0L)	4	3	3	3	③	④	15	195	15.5	15.5
	V6-263 (4.3L)		See Diesel Section of This Section								
	8-350 (5.7L) DIESEL	6	—	—	3	③	④	15	195	18.0	18.0

① Does not include converter
② Add approx. 1 qt. H.D. cooling
③ 7½" Ring Gear　　3.5 pts.
　 8½" Ring Gear　　4.25 pts.
④ Cutlass　　　　　　18.0 gals.
　 Cutlass Cruiser　　18.25 gals.

FLUID CAPACITIES—Coolant, Fuel & Lubricant　　　　　**OLDSMOBILE FULL-SIZE**

Year		Engine No. Cyl. Disp. cu in	Engine Crankcase (Add 1 Qt. For New Filter)	Transmission (Pts to Refill After Draining) Automatic ⑤	Drive Axle (pts)	Full Gasoline Tank (gals)	Rad. Cap Press.	Thermo. Temp.	COOLING SYSTEM (qts) With Heater	With A/C
76	88 & 98	8-350	4	6	5.40	26①	15	195	20.0	22.5
		8-455	4	6	5.40	26①	15	195	20.0	22.5
	Toronado	8-455	5	8	4.0	26	15	195	21.0	21.5
77	88 & 98	6-231	4	6	③	21②	15	195	12.2	12.1
		8-260	4	6	③	21②	15	195	16.4	16.2
		8-350	4	6	③	21②	15	195	14.6	15.3
		8-403	4	6	③	24.5	15	195	15.7	16.4
	Toronado	8-403	4	8	4.0	26	15	195	—	17.2
78	88 & 98	6-231	4	6	③	21②	15	195	12.2	12.1
		8-260	4	6	③	21②	15	195	16.4	16.2
		8-350	4	6	③	21②	15	195	14.6	15.3
		8-350 Diesel	6	6	③	21②	15	195	18.0	17.9
		8-403	4	6	③	24.5	15	195	16.4	16.4
	Toronado	8-403	4	8	4.0	26	15	195	—	17.2

FLUID CAPACITIES—Coolant, Fuel & Lubricant

OLDSMOBILE FULL-SIZE

Year		Engine No. Cyl. Disp. cu in	Engine Crankcase (Add 1 Qt. For New Filter)	Transmission (Pts to Refill After Draining) Automatic⑤	Drive Axle (pts)	Full Gasoline Tank (gals)	Rad. Cap Press.	Thermo. Temp.	COOLING SYSTEM (qts) With Heater	With A/C
79	88 & 98	6-231	4	6	③	④	15	195	13.3	13.3
		8-260	4	6	③	④	15	195	16.4	16.2
		8-305	4	6	③	④	15	195	14.6	15.3
		8-350	4	6	③	④	15	195	14.6	15.3
		8-350 Diesel	6	6	③	④	15	195	18.0	17.9
		8-403	4	6	③	④	15	195	15.7	16.4
	Toronado	8-350	4	10	③	④	15	195	14.9	15.6
		8-350 Diesel	6	6	③	④	15	195	18.4	18.4
80		6-231 (3.8L)	4	6	③	⑥	15	195	16.35	17.25
		8-301 (5.0L)	4	6	③	④⑥	15	195	—	16.25
		8-305 (5.0L)	4	6	③	④⑥	15	195	15.5	16.25
		8-307 (5.0L)	4	6	③	④⑥	15	195	17.5	17.5
		8-350 (5.7L)	4	6	③	④⑥	15	195	18.0	18.0
		8-350 (5.7L) Diesel	6	6	③	④⑥	15	195	18.0	18.0
		Toronado	—	10	3.25	④⑥	15	195	14.9	15.6
81		6-231 (3.8L)	4	6	③	⑥	15	195	16.35	17.25
		6-252 (4.1L)	4	6	4.25	25⑨	15	195	13.7	13.7
		8-260 (4.2L)	4	6	③	④⑥	15	195	16	16.5
		8-307 (5.0L)	4	6	③	④⑥	15	195	17.5	17.5
		8-350 (5.7L) Diesel	6	6	③	④⑥	15	195	18.0	18.0
		Toronado	6	10	3.75	④⑥	15	195	14.9	15.6
82		6-231 (3.8L)	4	6	4.25	25⑨	15	195	13.7	13.7
		6-252 (4.1L)	4	6	4.25	25⑨	15	195	⑩	⑩
		8-307 (5.0L)	4	6	4.25	25⑨	15	195	17.5	17.5
		V6-263 (4.3L)		See Diesel Section in This Manual						
		8-350 (N)(5.7L)	7.5	6	4.25	25⑨	15	195	18.0	
		Toronado	6	10	3.75	④⑥	15	195	14.9	15.6

① Sta. wagon 22 gal.
② California models 24 gal.
③ With 7½" ring gear 3.5 pts
   With 8½-8¾ ring gear 4.25 pts
④ Gas engine models:
   88 Sedan & Calif. Coupe   21.0 gals.
   Other 88 & 98 Models   25.3 gals.
   Toronado   20.0 gals.
   Diesel Engine Models
   88 & 98   27.25 gals.
   Toronado   22.75 gals.
⑤ Does not include converter

⑥ Cutlass Coupe and Sedan (Exc. Diesel)   18
   Cutlass Coupe and Sedan (Diesel)   19-3/4
   Cutlass Cruiser (Incl. Diesel)   18-1/4
   88 Coupe and Sedan (all) with VIN A and 88
   Royale and Royal Brougham Coupe and
   Sedan with VIN Y   20-3/4
   88 Coupe and Sedan (all) with VIN S, 88
   Coupe and Sedan with VIN Y, 98 (all)
   with VIN Y, 88 Coupe and Sedan (all)
   with VIN R, and 98 (all) with VIN R   25
   88 Coupe & Sedan (all) and 98 (all) with VIN
   N (Diesel)   27
   Custom Cruiser with VIN Y, R and N
   (Diesel)   22
   Toronado with VIN Y and R   21
   Toronado with VIN N (Diesel)   23

OLDSMOBILE
EXCEPT CIERA, STARFIRE & '80-'82 OMEGA

CRANKSHAFT & CONNECTING ROD SPECIFICATIONS

All measurements given in inches

Year	Engine No. Cyl. Disp. (cu in)	Eng. V.I.N. Code		CRANKSHAFT Main Brg. Journal Dia.	Main Brg. Oil Clearance	Shaft End-Play	Thrust on No.	CONNECTING ROD Journal Diameter	Oil Clearance	Side Clearance
76	6-250		1	2.2983-2.2993	.002 max.	.002-.006	7	1.999-2.000	.0035	.009-.014
			2-7	2.2983-2.2993	.0035 max.					
	8-260	F	1	2.4988-2.4998	.0005-.0021	.004-.008	3	2.1238-2.1248	.0004-.0033	.006-.020
			2-4	2.4985-2.4995	.0005-.0021					
			5	2.4985-2.4995	.0015-.0031					
	8-350	R	1	2.4988-2.4998	.0005-.0021	.004-.008	3	2.1238-2.1248	.0004-.0033	.006-.020
			2-4	2.4985-2.4995	.0005-.0021					
			5	2.4985-2.4995	.0015-.0031					
	8-350	H, J		3.000	.0004-.0015	.003-.009	3	1.991-2.000	.0005-.0026	.006-.027
	8-455		1-4	2.9993-3.003	.0005-.0021	.004-.008	3	2.4988-2.4998	.0004-.0033	.006-.020
			5	2.9993-3.0003	.0020-.0034					
77	6-231	C, A	All	2.4995	.0004-.0015	.004-.008	2	2.0000	.0005-.0026	.006-.027
	8-260	F	1	2.4988-2.4998	.0005-.0021	.0035-.0135	3	2.1238-2.1248	.0004-.0033	.006-.020
			2-4	2.4985-2.4995	.0005-.0021					
			5	2.4985-2.4995	.0015-.0035					
	8-305	U	1	2.4485-2.4493	.002 max.	.002-.006	5	2.199-2.200	.0035 max.	.008-.014
			2-4	2.4481-2.4490	.0035 max.					
			5	2.4479-2.4488	.0035 max.					
	8-350	L	1	2.4484-2.4493	.002 max.	.002-.006	5	2.199-2.200	.0035 max.	.008-.014
			2-4	2.4481-2.4490	.0035 max.					
			5	2.4479-2.4488	.0035 max.					
	8-350	R	1	2.4988-2.4998	.0005-.0021	.0035-.0135	3	2.1238-2.1248	.0004-.0033	.006-.020
		R	2-4	2.4985-2.4995	.0005-.0021					
			5	2.4985-2.4995	.0015-.0035					
	8-403	K	1	2.4988-2.4998	.0005-.0021	.0035-.0135	3	2.1238-2.1248	.0004-.0033	.006-.020
			2-4	2.4985-2.4995	.0005-.0021					
			5	2.4985-2.4995	.0015-.0035					
78	6-231	A		2.4995	.0004-.0015	.004-.008	2	2.0000	.0005-.0026	.006-.027
	8-260	F	1	2.4988-2.4998	.0005-.0021	.0035-.0135	3	2.1238-2.1248	.0004-.0033	.006-.020
			2-4	2.4985-2.4995	.0005-.0021					
			5	2.4985-2.4995	.0015-.0035					
	8-305	U	1	2.4484-2.4493	.002 max.	.002-.006	5	2.199-2.200	.0035 max.	.008-.014
			2-4	2.4481-2.4490	.0035 max.					
			5	2.4479-2.4488	.0035 max.					
	8-350	L	1	2.4484-2.4493	.002 max.	.002-.006	5	2.199-2.200	.0035 max.	.008-.014
			2-4	2.4481-2.4490	.0035 max.					
			5	2.4479-2.4488	.0035 max.					
	8-350	R	1	2.4988-2.4998	.0005-.0021	.0035-.0135	3	2.1238-2.1248	.0004-.0033	.006-.020
			2-4	2.4985-2.4995	.0005-.0021					
			5	2.4985-2.4995	.0015-.0035					
	8-350 (Diesel-N)		1-4	2.9993-3.0003	.0005-.0021	.0035-.0135	3	2.1238-2.1248	.0005-.0026	.006-.020
			5	2.9993-3.0003	.0015-.0031					
	8-403	K	1	2.4988-2.4998	.0005-.0021	.0035-.0135	3	2.1238-2.1248	.0004-.0033	.006-.020
			2-4	2.4985-2.4995	.0005-.0021					
			5	2.4985-2.4995	.0015-.0035					

A596

CRANKSHAFT & CONNECTING ROD SPECIFICATIONS

All measurements given in inches

Year	Engine No. Cyl. Disp. (cu in)	Eng. V.I.N. Code		CRANKSHAFT				CONNECTING ROD		
				Main Brg. Journal Dia.	Main Brg. Oil Clearance	Shaft End-Play	Thrust on No.	Journal Diameter	Oil Clearance	Side Clearance
79	6-231	A		2.4995	.0004-.0015	.004-.008	2	2.000	.0005-.0026	.006-.027
	8-260	F	1	2.4988-2.4998	.0005-.0021	.0035-.0135	3	2.1238-2.1248	.0004-.0033	.006-.020
			2-4	2.4985-2.4995	.0005-.0021					
			5	2.4985-2.4995	.0015-.0035					
	8-260 Diesel	P	1-4	2.9993-3.0003	.0005-.0021	.0035-.0138	3	2.1238-2.1248	.0004-.0032	.006-.027
			5	2.9993-3.0003	.0015-.0031					
	8-301	Y		3.00	.0002-.0020	.003-.009	4	2.240-2.250	.0005-.0025	.006-.022
	8-305	G	1	2.4484-2.4493	.002 max.	.002-.006	5	2.199-2.200	.0035 max.	.008-.014
			2-4	2.4481-2.4490	.0035 max.					
			5	2.4479-2.4488	.0035 max.					
	8-350	L	1	2.4484-2.4493	.002 max.	.002-.006	5	2.199-2.200	.0035 max.	.008-.014
			2-4	2.4481-2.4490	.0035 max.					
			5	2.4479-2.4488						
	8-350	R	1	2.4988-2.4998	.0005-.0021	.0035-.0135	3	2.1238-2.11248	.0004-.0033	.006-.020
			2-4	2.4985-2.4995	.0005-.0021					
			5	2.4985-2.4995	.0015-.0035					
	8-350	X		2.9995	.004-.0015	.002-.006	3	1.991-2.000	.0005-.0026	.006-.020
	8-350 Diesel	N	1-4	2.9993-3.0003	.0005-.0021	.0035-.0135	3	2.1238-2.1248	.0004-.0033	.006-.020
			5	2.9993-3.0003	.0015-.0031					
	8-403	K	1	2.4988-2.4998	.0005-.0021	.0035-.0135	3	2.1238-2.1248	.0004-.0033	.006-.020
			2-4	2.4985-2.4995	.0005-.0021					
			5	2.4985-2.4995	.0015-.0035					
80	6-231	A		2.4995	.0004-.0018	.004-.008	2	2.000	.0005-.0026	.006-.027
	8-260	F	1	2.4988-2.4998	.0005-.0021	.0035-.0135	3	2.1238-2.1248	.0004-.0033	.006-.020
			2-4	2.4985-2.4995	.0005-.0021					
			5	2.4985-2.4995	.0015-.0035					
	8-260 Diesel		1-4	2.9993-3.0003	.0005-.0021	.0035-.0138	3	2.1238-2.1248	.0004-.0032	.006-.027
			5	2.9993-3.0003	.0015-.0031					
	8-265	S		3.00	.0002-.0020	.003-.009	4	2.240-2.250	.0005-.0025	.006-.022
	8-305		1	2.4484-2.4493	.002 max.	.002-.006	5	2.199-2.200	.0035 max.	.008-.014
			2-4	2.4481-2.4490	.0035 max.					
			5	2.4479-2.4488	.0035 max.					
	8-307	Y	1	2.4988-2.4998	.0005-.0021	.0035-.0135	3	2.1238-2.1248	.0004-.0033	.006-.020
			2-4	2.4985-2.4995	.0005-.0021					
			5	2.4985-2.4995	.0015-.0035					
	8-350	R	1	2.498-2.4998	.0005-.0021	.0035-.0135	3	2.1238-2.1248	.0004-.0033	.006-.020
			2-4	2.4985-2.4995	.0005-.0021					
			5	2.4985-2.4995	.0015-.0035					
	8-350 Diesel	N	1-4	2.9993-3.0003	.0005-.0021	.0035-.0135	3	2.1238-2.1248	.0005-.0026	.006-.020
			5	2.9993-3.0003	.0015-.0031					
81	6-231	A,3		2.4995	.0004-.0018	.004-.008	2	2.000	.0005-.0026	.006-.027
	6-252	4		2.2495-2.2487	.0004-.0018	.003-.008	2	2.000	.0005-.0026	.006-.027
	8-260	F	1	2.4988-2.4998	.0005-.0021	.0035-.0135	3	2.1238-2.1248	.0004-.0033	.006-.020
			2-4	2.4985-2.4995	.0005-.0021					
			5	2.4985-2.4995	.0015-.0035					
	8-307	Y	1	2.4988-2.4998	.0005-.0021	.0035-.0135	3	2.1238-2.1248	.0004-.0033	.006-.020
			2-4	2.4985-2.4995	.0005-.0021					
			5	2.4985-2.4995	.0015-.0035					
	8-350	N	1-4	2.9993-3.0003	.0005-.0021	.0035-.0135	3	2.1238-2.1248	.0005-.0026	.006-.020
			5	2.9993-3.0003	.0015-.0035					

CRANKSHAFT & CONNECTING ROD SPECIFICATIONS   OLDSMOBILE

All measurements given in inches

Year	Engine No. Cyl. Disp. (cu in)	Eng. V.I.N. Code		CRANKSHAFT Main Brg. Journal Dia.	CRANKSHAFT Main Brg. Oil Clearance	CRANKSHAFT Shaft End-Play	CRANKSHAFT Thrust on No.	CONNECTING ROD Journal Diameter	CONNECTING ROD Oil Clearance	CONNECTING ROD Side Clearance
82	6-231	A,3		2.4995	.0004-.0018	.004-.008	2	2.000	.0005-.0026	.006-.027
	6-252	4		2.2495-2.2487	.0004-.0018	.003-.008	2	2.000	.0005-.0026	.006-.027
	8-260	F	1	2.4988-2.4998	.0005-.0021	.0035-.0135	3	2.1238-2.1248	.0004-.0033	.006-.020
			2-4	2.4985-2.4995	.0005-.0021					
			5	2.4985-2.4995	.0015-.0035					
	8-307	Y	1	2.4988-2.4998	.0005-.0021	.0035-.0135	3	2.1238-2.1248	.0004-.0033	.006-.020
			2-4	2.4985-2.4995	.0005-.0021					
			5	2.4985-2.4995	.0015-.0035					
	V6-263	V		See Diesel Section of This Manual						
	8-350	N	1-4	2.9993-3.0003	.0005-.0021	.0035-.0135	3	2.1238-2.1248	.0005-.0026	.006-.020
			5	2.9993-3.0003	.0015-.0035					

BRAKE SPECIFICATIONS

Year	Model		Master Cylinder Bore Diameter	CALIPER OR WHEEL CYLINDER Front	CALIPER OR WHEEL CYLINDER Rear	BRAKE DRUM/ROTOR Diameter Front	BRAKE DRUM/ROTOR Diameter Rear	Rotor Runout	Rotor Minimum Machined Thickness	Rotor Thickness Variation Maximum
76	Omega		1.125	2.9375	7/8	—	9.5	.004	.980	.0005
	Cutlass	Man	.9375	2.9375	15/16	—	11.0	.004	.980	.0005
		Pwr.	1.125	2.9375	1	—	11.0	.004	.980	.0005
	Vista Cruiser		1.125	2.9375	1	—	11.0	.004	.980	.0005
	88 & 98 Pass.		1.125	2.9375	15/16	—	11.0	.005	1.230	.0005
	88 & 98 Station Wagon		1.125	2.9375	1	—	12.0	.005	1.230	.0005
	Toronado		1.125	2.9375	15/16	—	11.0	.002	1.185	.0005
77	Omega		1.125	2.9375	7/8	—	9.5	.004	.980	.0005
	Cutlass,	Man.	.9375	2.9375	15/16	—	11.0	.005	.980	.0005
	Vista Cruiser	Pwr.	1.125	2.9375	1	—	11.0	.005	.980	.0005
	88 & 98, Custom Cruiser		1.125	2.9375	15/16	—	11.0	.005	.980	.0005
	Toronado		1.125	2.9375	15/16	—	11.0	.002	1.185	.0005
78	Omega		1.125	2.9375	7/8	—	9.5	.004	.980	.0005
	Cutlass, Cutlas Wagon	Man.	.87	2.50	3/4	—	9.5	.004	.980	.0005
		Pwr.	.94	2.50	3/4	—	9.5	.004	.980	.0005
	88		1.125	2.9375	15/16	—	9.5	.004	.980	.0005
	98 Station Wagon		1.125	2.9375	15/16	—	11.0	.004	.980	.0005
	Toronado		1.125	2.9375	15/16	—	11.0	.002	1.185	.0005
79	Omega		1.125	2.9375	7/8	—	9.5	.004	.980	.0005
	Cutlass, Cutlass Wagon	Man.	.87	2.43	3/4	—	9.5	.004	.980	.0005
		Pwr.	.94	2.43	3/4	—	9.5	.004	.980	.0005
	88		1.125	2.9375	15/16	—	9.5	.004	.980	.0005
	98 & Station Wagon		1.125	2.9375	15/16	—	11.0	.004	.980	.0005
	Toronado		.945	2.50	3/4	—	9.5	.002	1.185	.0005
80	Cutlass, Cutlass Wagon	Man.	.87	2.43	3/4	—	9.5	.004	.980	.0005
		Pwr.	.94	2.43	3/4	—	9.5	.004	.980	.0005
	88		1.125	2.9375	15/16	—	9.5	.004	.980	.0005
	98 & Station Wagon		1.125	2.9375	15/16	—	11.0	.004	.980	.0005
	Toronado		.945	2.50	3/4	—	9.5	.002	1.185	.0005

BRAKE SPECIFICATIONS

OLDSMOBILE (EXCEPT STARFIRE & '80-'82 OMEGA)

Year	Model		Master Cylinder Bore Diameter	CALIPER OR WHEEL CYLINDER		BRAKE DRUM/ROTOR Diameter		Rotor Runout	Rotor Minimum Machined Thickness	Rotor Thickness Variation Maximum
				Front	Rear	Front	Rear			
81	Cutlass, Cutlass Wagon	Man.	.87	2½"	¾	—	9.5	.004	.980	.0005
		Pwr.	⅞"	2½"	¾	—	9.5	.004	.980	.0005
	88		1⅛"	2⁵/₁₆"	¹⁵/₁₆	—	9.5	.004	.980	.0005
	98 & Station Wagon		1⅛"	2⁵/₁₆"	¹⁵/₁₆	—	11.0	.004	.980	.0005
	Toronado		1"	2⁵/₁₆"	¹⁵/₁₆"	—	9.5	.002	1.185	.0005
82	Cutlass, Cutlass Wagon	Man.	.87	2½"	¾	—	9.5	.004	.980	.0005
		Pwr.	⅞"	2½"	¾	—	9.5	.004	.980	.0005
	88		1⅛"	2⁵/₁₆"	¹⁵/₁₆	—	9.5	.004	.980	.0005
	98 & Station Wagon		1⅛"	2⁵/₁₆"	¹⁵/₁₆	—	11.0	.004	.980	.0005
	Toronado		1"	2⁵/₁₆"	¹⁵/₁₆"	—	9.5	.002	1.185	.0005

VALVE SPECIFICATIONS

Year	Engine No. Cyl. Displacement (cu in)	V.I.N. Code	Seat Angle (deg)	Face Angle (deg)	Spring Test Pressure (lbs @ in)	Spring Installed Height (in)	STEM TO GUIDE CLEARANCE (in)		STEM DIAMETER (in)	
							Intake	Exhaust	Intake	Exhaust
'76	6-250		46	45	175 @ 1.26	1²¹/₃₂	.0010-.0027	.0015-.0032	.3413	.3413
	8-260		⑥	⑦	187 @ 1.27	1⁴⁶/₆₄	.0010-.0027	.0015-.0032	.3428	.3423
	8-350		45	45	180 @ 1.34⑫	1⁴⁶/₆₄	.0015-.0035	.0015-.0032	.3725	.3726
	8-350		⑥	⑦	187 @ 1.27	1²¹/₃₂	.0010-.0027	.0015-.0032	.3429	.3424
	8-455		⑥	⑦	187 @ 1.27	1²¹/₃₂	.0010-.0027	.0015-.0032	.3429	.3424
'77	6-231		45	45	168 @ 1.327	1⁴⁶/₆₄	.0015-.0032	.0015-.0032	.3409	.3409
	8-260		⑥	⑦	187 @ 1.270	1⁴³/₆₄	.0010-.0027	.0015-.0032	.3429	.3427
	8-305		46	45	200 @ 1.250	1⁴⁵/₆₄	.0010-.0037	.0010-.0037	.3414	.3414
	8-350		46	45	200 @ 1.250	1⁴⁵/₆₄	.0010-.0037	.0010-.0037	.3414	.3414
	8-350		⑥	⑦	187 @ 1.270	1⁴³/₆₄	.0010-.0027	.0015-.0032	.3429	.3427
	8-403		⑥	⑦	187 @ 1.270	1⁴³/₆₄	.0010-.0027	.0015-.0032	.3429	.3427
'78	6-231		45	45	168 + 6 @ 1.327	1.727	.0015-.0032	.0015-.0032	.3405-.3412	.3405-.3412
	8-260		⑥	⑦	180-194 @ 1.270	1.670	.0010-.0027	.0015-.0032	.3425-.3432	.3420-.3427
	8-305, 350(VIN-L)		46	45	194-206 @ 1.25⑬	1.70⑬	.0010-.0037	.0010-.0037	.3414	.3414
	8-350(VIN-R) 403		⑥	⑦	180-194 @ 1.270	1.670	.0010-.0027	.0015-.0032	.3425-.3432	.3420-.3427
	8-350 Diesel		⑥	⑦	144-158 @ 1.300	1.670	.0010-.0027	.0015-.0032	.3425-.3432	.3420-.3427
'79	6-231		45	45	168 + 6 @ 1.327	1.727	.0015-.0032	.0015-.0032	.3405-.3412	.3405-.3412
	8-260		⑥	⑦	180-194 @ 1.270	1.670	.0010-.0027	.0015-.0032	.3425-.3432	.3420-.3427
	8-260 Diesel	P	⑥	⑦	144-158 @ 1.300	1.670	.0010-.0027	.0015-.0032	.3425-.3432	.3420-.3427
	8-301	Y	46	45	162-170 @ 1.296	1.66	.0010-.0027	.0010-.0027	.3425-.3418	.3425-.3428
	8-305, 350	L	46	45	194-206 @ 1.25⑬	1.70⑬	.0010-.0037	.0010-.0037	.3414	.3414
	8-350 403	R	⑥	⑦	180-194 @ 1.270	1.670	.0010-.0027	.0015-.0032	.3425-.3432	.3420-.3427
	8-350 Diesel		⑥	⑦	144-158 @ 1.300	1.670	.0010-.0027	.0015-.0032	.3425-.3432	.3420-.3427
	8-350	X	45	45	175 @ 1.34	1.727	.0015-.0032	.0015-.0032	.3405-.3412	.3405-.3412

VALVE SPECIFICATIONS   OLDSMOBILE (EXCEPT STARFIRE & '80-'82 OMEGA)

Year	Engine No. Cyl. Displacement (cu in)	V.I.N. Code	Seat Angle (deg)	Face Angle (deg)	Spring Test Pressure (lbs @ in)	Spring Installed Height (in)	STEM TO GUIDE CLEARANCE (in) Intake	Exhaust	STEM DIAMETER (in) Intake	Exhaust
'80	6-231	A	45	45	168 ± 6 @ 1.327	1.727	.0015-.0032	.0015-.0032	.3405-.3412	.3405-.3412
	8-260	F	⑥	⑦	180-194 @ 1.270	1.670	.0010-.0027	.0015-.0032	.3425-.3432	.3420-.3427
	8-260 Diesel	P	⑥	⑦	144-158 @ 1.300	1.670	.0010-.0027	.0015-.0032	.3425-.3432	.3420-.3427
	8-265	S	46	45	165 @ 1.29	1.660	.0010-.0027	.0010-.0027	.3425	.3425
	8-305	H	46	45	I-174-186 @ 1.25 E-184-196 @ 1.16	I-1.70 E-1.61	.0010-.0027	.0010-.0027	.3410-.3417	.3410-.3417
	8-307	Y	⑥	⑦	180-194 @ 1.270	1.670	.0010-.0027	.0015-.0032	.3425-.3432	.3420-.3427
	8-350	R	⑥	⑦	180-194 @ 1.270	1.670	.0010-.0027	.0015-.0032	.3425-.3432	.3420-.3427
	8-350 Diesel	N	⑥	⑦	144-158 @ 1.300	1.670	.0010-.0027	.0015-.0032	.3425-.3432	.3420-.3427
81	6-231	A,3	45	45	162-174 @ 1.327	1.727	.0015-.0032	.0015-.0032	.3405-.3412	.3405-.3412
	8-260	F	⑥	⑦	180-194 @ 1.270	1.670	.0010-.0027	.0015-.0032	.3425-.3432	.3420-.3427
	8-252	4	45	45	164 ± 5 @ 1.340⑩	1.727	.0015-.0035	.0015-.0032	.3412-.3401	.3412-.3405
	8-307	Y	⑥	⑦	180-194 @ 1.270	1.670	.0010-.0027	.0015-.0032	.3425-.3432	.3420-.3427
	8-350 Diesel	N	⑥	⑦	144-158 @ 1.300	1.670	.0010-.0027	.0015-.0032	.3425-.3432	.3425-.3427
82	6-231	A,3	45	45	162-174 @ 1.327	1.727	.0015-.0032	.0015-.0032	.3405-.3412	.3405-.3412
	8-260	F	⑥	⑦	180-194 @ 1.270	1.670	.0010-.0027	.0015-.0032	.3425-.3432	.3420-.3427
	8-252	4	45	45	164 ± 5 @ 1.340⑩	1.727	.0015-.0035	.0015-.0032	.3412-.3401	.3412-.3405
	8-307	Y	⑥	⑦	180-194 @ 1.270	1.670	.0010-.0027	.0015-.0032	.3425-.3432	.3420-.3427
	6-263 Diesel	V	⑥	⑦	144-158 @ 1.300	1.670	.0010-.0027	.0015-.0032	.3425-.3432	.3420-.3427
	8-350 Diesel	N	⑥	⑦	144-158 @ 1.300	1.670	.0010-.0027	.0015-.0032	.3425-.3432	.3425-.3427

① Intake—45 Exhaust—30
② Intake—46 Exhaust—30
③ California Usage
④ Intake—30 Exhaust—45
⑤ Intake—30 Exhaust—46
⑥ Intake—45 Exhaust—31
⑦ Intake—44 Exhaust—30
⑧ Intake—31 Exhaust—45
⑨ Intake—30 Exhaust—44
⑩ Engines using small valves: Intake—45 Exhaust—45 Engines using large valves: Intake—30 Exhaust—45
⑪ Engines using small valves:
  Intake—44 Exhaust—44 Engines using large valves: Intake—29 Exhaust—44
⑫ Exhaust 177 @ 1.45.
⑬ Intake: exhaust—194-206 LB. @ 1.16", installed HT. 1.61"
⑭ Information not available at publication time

DISTRIBUTOR SPECIFICATIONS

Year	Distributor Identification	Vacuum Model Identification	CENTRIFUGAL ADVANCE Start Crank. Deg. @ Eng. RPM	Finish Crank. Deg. @ Eng. RPM	VACUUM ADVANCE Start @ In Hg	Finish Crank. Deg. @ In Hg
'76	1103204		0 @ 650	28 @ 4400	6	20 @ 14.8
	1103208		0 @ 650	28 @ 4400	6	18 @ 10.2
	1103210		0 @ 1000	16 @ 4000	6	24 @ 13.7
	1103211		0 @ 650	28 @ 4400	6	14 @ 9.2
	1103212		0 @ 1000	13 @ 3600	8	28 @ 15
	1110666		0 @ 1000	20 @ 4200	3-5	24 @ 14-15
	1112863		0 @ 1100	16 @ 4200	6-8	24 @ 14-16
	1112936		0 @ 1000	16 @ 4000	6.5	24 @ 15.8
	1112937		0 @ 1000	13 @ 3600	8	18 @ 13
	1112952		0 @ 1100	14 @ 3600	8	18 @ 13
	1112953		0 @ 1000	16 @ 4000	8	18 @ 8
	1112956		0 @ 650	28 @ 4400	—	—
	1112988		0 @ 1000	13 @ 3600	8	18 @ 13
	1112991		0-4 @ 1750	17-22 @ 5000	6.9	18.5-21.5 @ 14.3
	1112994		0 @ 650	28 @ 4400	4.5	24 @ 10.5
	1112995		0 @ 900	26 @ 4465	4	30 @ 11

DISTRIBUTOR SPECIFICATIONS

OLDSMOBILE (EXCEPT STARFIRE & '80-'82 OMEGA)

Year	Distributor Identification	Vacuum Model Identification	CENTRIFUGAL ADVANCE		VACUUM ADVANCE	
			Start Crank. Deg. @ Eng. RPM	Finish Crank. Deg. @ Eng. RPM	Start @ In Hg	Finish Crank. Deg. @ In Hg
'77	1103239		0 @ 1200	20 @ 4200	14	15 @ 10
	1103246		0 @ 1200	22 @ 4200	4	18 @ 12
	1103248		0 @ 1200	20-24 @ 4200	3-5	8-12 @ 7.9
	1103259		0 @ 1000	19 @ 4000	6	24 @ 13
	1103260		0 @ 1000	13 @ 3600	6	24 @ 13
	1103262		0 @ 900	26 @ 4450	4	30 @ 11
	1103264		0 @ 1000	13 @ 3600	5	16 @ 11
	1103266		0 @ 1000	19 @ 4000	5	16 @ 11
'78	1103281		0 @ 1000	20 @ 3800	4	18 @ 12
	1103282		0 @ 1000	20 @ 3900	4	20 @ 10
	1103285		0 @ 1200	22 @ 4200	4	24 @ 8
	1103320		0 @ 900	26 @ 4450	4	30 @ 11
	1103322		0 @ 600	29 @ 4000	6	24 @ 13
	1103323		0 @ 1000	19 @ 4000	5	16 @ 11
	1103324		0 @ 600	23 @ 3600	6	24 @ 13
	1103325		0 @ 1000	13 @ 3600	5	16 @ 11
	1103346		0 @ 1000	19 @ 4000	6	24 @ 13
	1103347		0 @ 1000	13 @ 3600	6	24 @ 13
	1103353		0-3 @ 1250	11-12 @ 4500	3-6	20 @ 9-12
'79	1103281	1973621	0 @ 1000	20 @ 3800	4	18 @ 12
	1103282	1973624	0 @ 1000	20 @ 3800	4	20 @ 10
	1103285	1973626	0 @ 1200	2 @ 4200	4	24 @ 8
	1103314	1973635	0 @ 825	21.5 @ 3400	4	25 @ 12
	1103320	1973610	0 @ 910	26 @ 4465	4	30 @ 11
	1103322	1973597	0 @ 600	29 @ 4000	6	24 @ 13
	1103323	1973603	0 @ 1000	19 @ 4000	5	16 @ 11
	1103324	1973597	0 @ 600	23 @ 3600	6	24 @ 13
	1103325	1973603	0 @ 1000	13 @ 3600	5	16 @ 11
	1103346	1973597	0 @ 1000	19 @ 4000	6	24 @ 13
	1103347	1973597	0 @ 1000	13 @ 3600	6	24 @ 13
	1103353	1973624	0 @ 1250	11-12 @ 4500	3-6	20 @ 9-12
	1103355	1973662	0 @ 910	26 @ 4465	4	30 @ 9
	1103368	1973626	0 @ 1000	20 @ 3800	4	10 @ 8
	1103379	1973691	0 @ 1000	20 @ 3800	3	20 @ 7.5
	1103396	1973686	0 @ 910	26 @ 4465	5	30 @ 12
	1110766	1973688	0 @ 1680	15 @ 3600	4	24 @ 11
	110767	1973687	0 @ 1680	15 @ 3600	3	20 @ 12
	110768	1973687	0 @ 1000	15 @ 3600	3	20 @ 12
	110769	1973688	0 @ 1000	15 @ 3600	4	24 @ 11
'80	1110555	1973688	0 @ 1000	15 @ 3600	4	24 @ 11
	1110554	1973718	0 @ 1680	15 @ 3600	3	24 @ 12
	1110552	1973709	0 @ 925	14 @ 3400	3	24 @ 8
	1103419	1973610	0 @ 600	23 @ 3600	4	30 @ 11
	1103384	1973620	0 @ 800	20 @ 4000	4	15 @ 12
	1103386	1973693	0 @ 1000	20 @ 3800	4	16 @ 7.5
	1103412	197314	0 @ 600	29 @ 4000	4	30 @ 12.5
	1103398	1973715	0 @ 600	23 @ 3600	5	30 @ 13.7
	1103413 (1)	1973708	0 @ 1000	13 @ 3600	6	30 @ 13
	1103414 (2)	1973597 (2)	0 @ 600	23 @ 3600	6	24 @ 13

NOTE: Starting with 1981 engines, the distributor is controlled electronically.

OLDSMOBILE
EXCEPT CIERA, STARFIRE & '80-'82 OMEGA

FUSE IDENTIFICATION

Fuse panel (Cutlass)

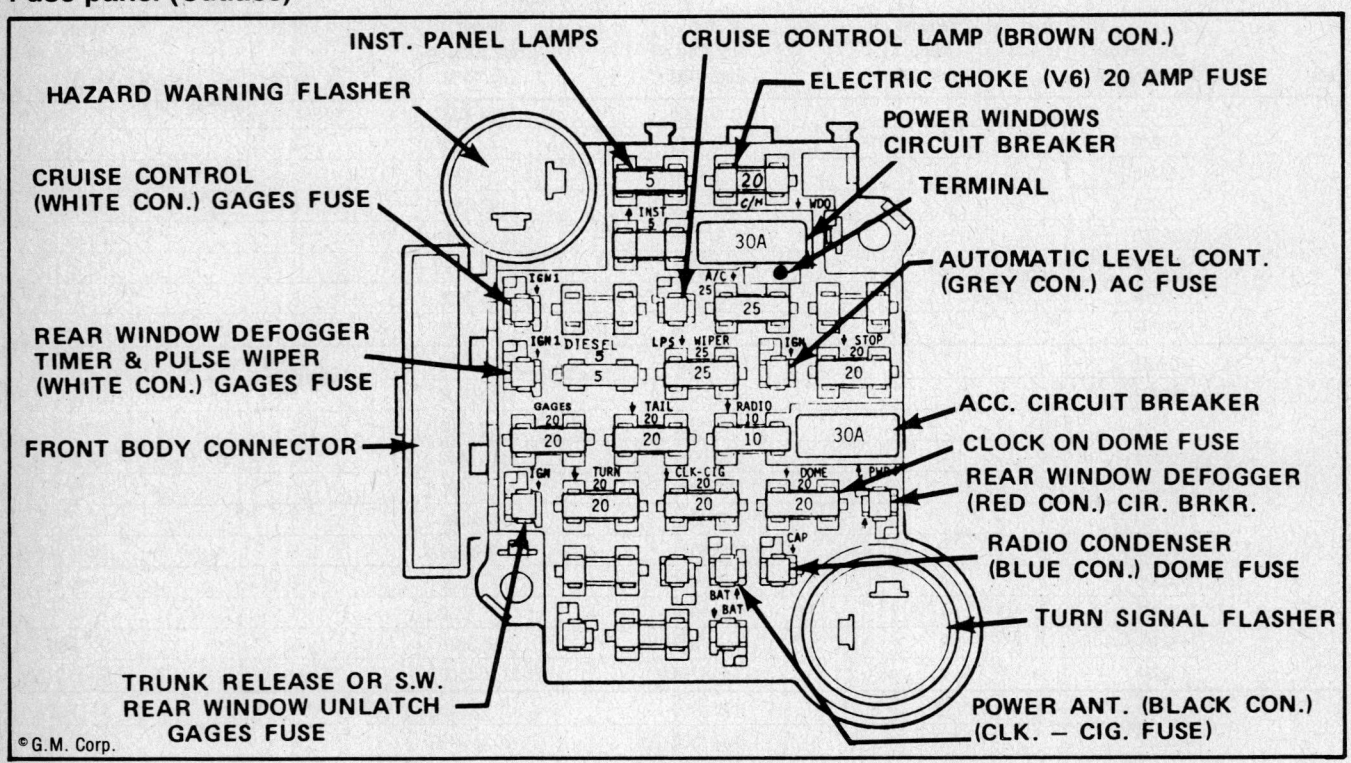

INST. PANEL LAMPS

CRUISE CONTROL LAMP (BROWN CON.)

HAZARD WARNING FLASHER

ELECTRIC CHOKE (V6) 20 AMP FUSE

POWER WINDOWS CIRCUIT BREAKER

CRUISE CONTROL (WHITE CON.) GAGES FUSE

TERMINAL

AUTOMATIC LEVEL CONT. (GREY CON.) AC FUSE

REAR WINDOW DEFOGGER TIMER & PULSE WIPER (WHITE CON.) GAGES FUSE

FRONT BODY CONNECTOR

ACC. CIRCUIT BREAKER

CLOCK ON DOME FUSE

REAR WINDOW DEFOGGER (RED CON.) CIR. BRKR.

RADIO CONDENSER (BLUE CON.) DOME FUSE

TURN SIGNAL FLASHER

TRUNK RELEASE OR S.W. REAR WINDOW UNLATCH GAGES FUSE

POWER ANT. (BLACK CON.) (CLK. – CIG. FUSE)

© G.M. Corp.

Fuse panel (Omega)

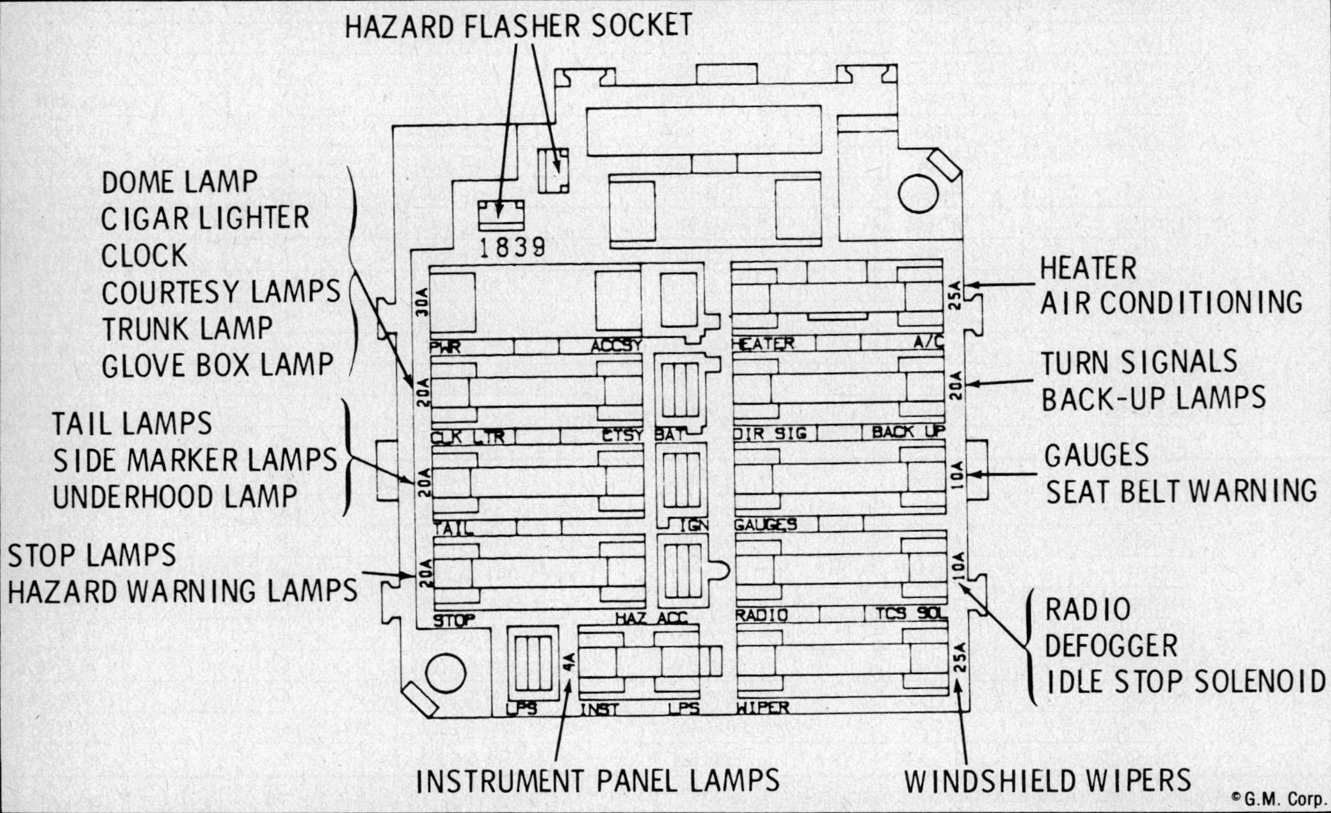

HAZARD FLASHER SOCKET

DOME LAMP
CIGAR LIGHTER
CLOCK
COURTESY LAMPS
TRUNK LAMP
GLOVE BOX LAMP

HEATER
AIR CONDITIONING

TURN SIGNALS
BACK-UP LAMPS

TAIL LAMPS
SIDE MARKER LAMPS
UNDERHOOD LAMP

GAUGES
SEAT BELT WARNING

STOP LAMPS
HAZARD WARNING LAMPS

RADIO
DEFOGGER
IDLE STOP SOLENOID

INSTRUMENT PANEL LAMPS

WINDSHIELD WIPERS

© G.M. Corp.

Fuse panel (88-98)

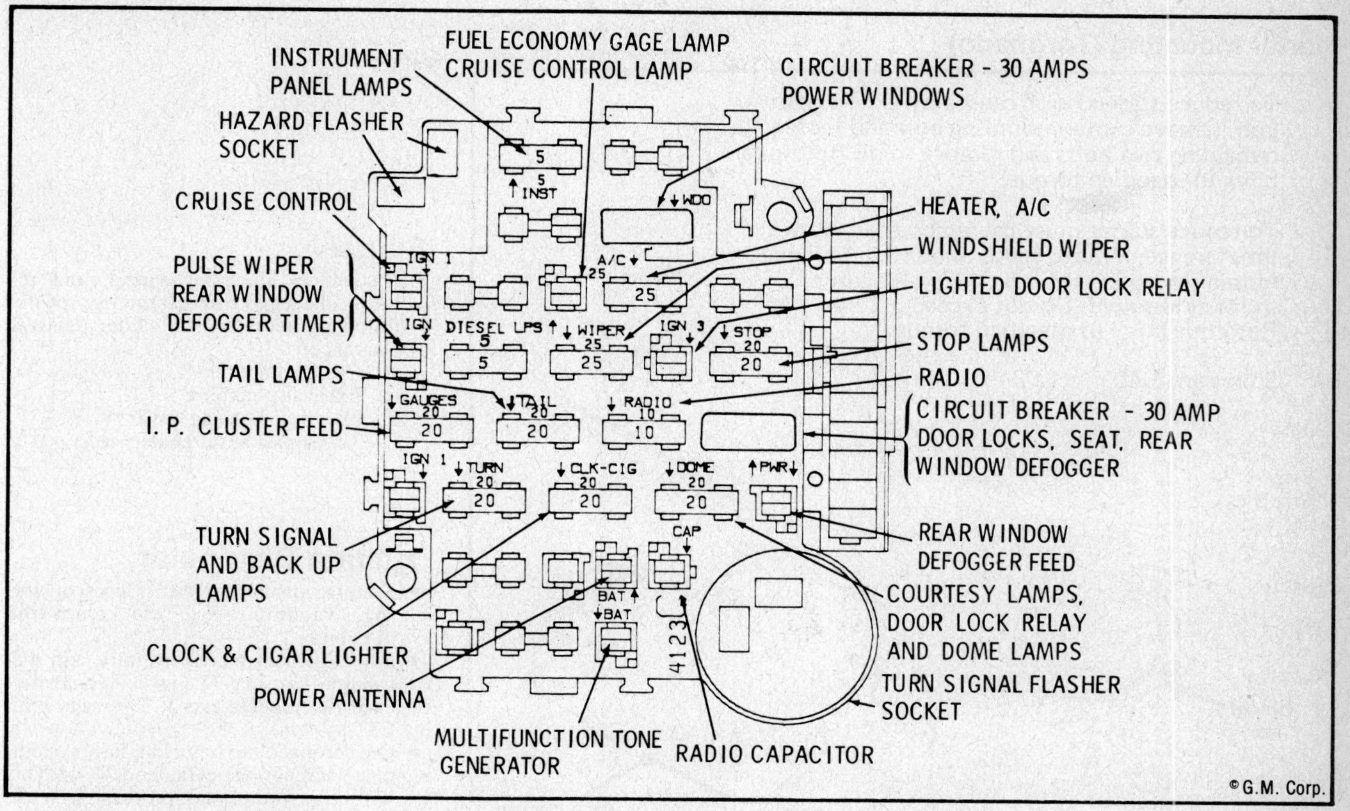

INSTRUMENT PANEL LAMPS

HAZARD FLASHER SOCKET

CRUISE CONTROL

PULSE WIPER REAR WINDOW DEFOGGER TIMER

TAIL LAMPS

I. P. CLUSTER FEED

TURN SIGNAL AND BACK UP LAMPS

CLOCK & CIGAR LIGHTER

POWER ANTENNA

MULTIFUNCTION TONE GENERATOR

RADIO CAPACITOR

FUEL ECONOMY GAGE LAMP
CRUISE CONTROL LAMP

CIRCUIT BREAKER - 30 AMPS POWER WINDOWS

HEATER, A/C

WINDSHIELD WIPER

LIGHTED DOOR LOCK RELAY

STOP LAMPS

RADIO

CIRCUIT BREAKER - 30 AMP DOOR LOCKS, SEAT, REAR WINDOW DEFOGGER

REAR WINDOW DEFOGGER FEED

COURTESY LAMPS, DOOR LOCK RELAY AND DOME LAMPS

TURN SIGNAL FLASHER SOCKET

5
5
↑ INST
↓ WDO
IGN 1
A/C ↓ 25
25
IGN 3
DIESEL LPS ↑ ↓ WIPER 25
5
5
25
↓ STOP 20
20
↓ GAUGES 20
20
↓ TAIL 20
20
↓ RADIO 10
10
IGN 1
↓ TURN 20
20
↓ CLK-CIG 20
20
↓ DOME 20
20
↑ PWR ↓
CAP
↓ BAT
↓ BAT
4123

© G.M. Corp.

Fuse panel (Toronado)

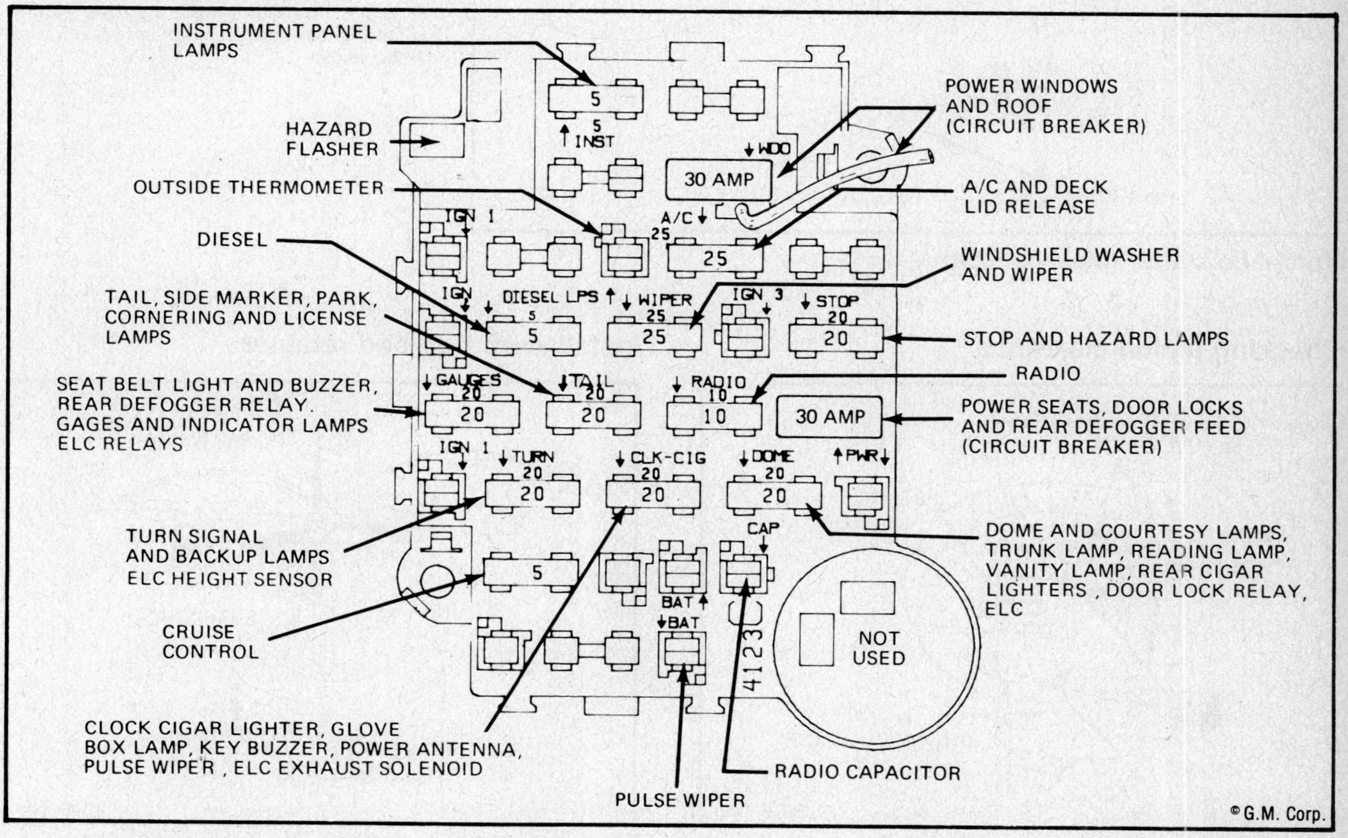

INSTRUMENT PANEL LAMPS

HAZARD FLASHER

OUTSIDE THERMOMETER

DIESEL

TAIL, SIDE MARKER, PARK, CORNERING AND LICENSE LAMPS

SEAT BELT LIGHT AND BUZZER, REAR DEFOGGER RELAY. GAGES AND INDICATOR LAMPS ELC RELAYS

TURN SIGNAL AND BACKUP LAMPS ELC HEIGHT SENSOR

CRUISE CONTROL

CLOCK CIGAR LIGHTER, GLOVE BOX LAMP, KEY BUZZER, POWER ANTENNA, PULSE WIPER , ELC EXHAUST SOLENOID

PULSE WIPER

RADIO CAPACITOR

POWER WINDOWS AND ROOF (CIRCUIT BREAKER)

A/C AND DECK LID RELEASE

WINDSHIELD WASHER AND WIPER

STOP AND HAZARD LAMPS

RADIO

POWER SEATS, DOOR LOCKS AND REAR DEFOGGER FEED (CIRCUIT BREAKER)

DOME AND COURTESY LAMPS, TRUNK LAMP, READING LAMP, VANITY LAMP, REAR CIGAR LIGHTERS , DOOR LOCK RELAY, ELC

5
5
↑ INST
↓ WDO
30 AMP
IGN 1
A/C ↓ 25
25
IGN
DIESEL LPS ↑ ↓ WIPER 25
5
5
25
IGN 3
↓ STOP 20
20
↓ GAUGES 20
20
↓ TAIL 20
20
↓ RADIO 10
10
30 AMP
IGN 1
↓ TURN 20
20
↓ CLK-CIG 20
20
↓ DOME 20
20
↑ PWR ↓
5
CAP
↓ BAT
↓ BAT
4123
NOT USED

© G.M. Corp.

A603

ELECTRICAL SECTION

Starter mounting (Toronado)

To reduce starter noise caused by excess gear lash, remove center mounting bolt and loosen remaining two bolts and remove shim. Retorque bolts to specified torque.

To reduce starter noise caused by gear tooth interference, remove center mounting bolt and loosen remaining two bolts. Install additional shims as required. Do not exceed 1.2 mm (.047"). Retorque bolts to specified torque.

Shims are .040 mm (.0015") thick.

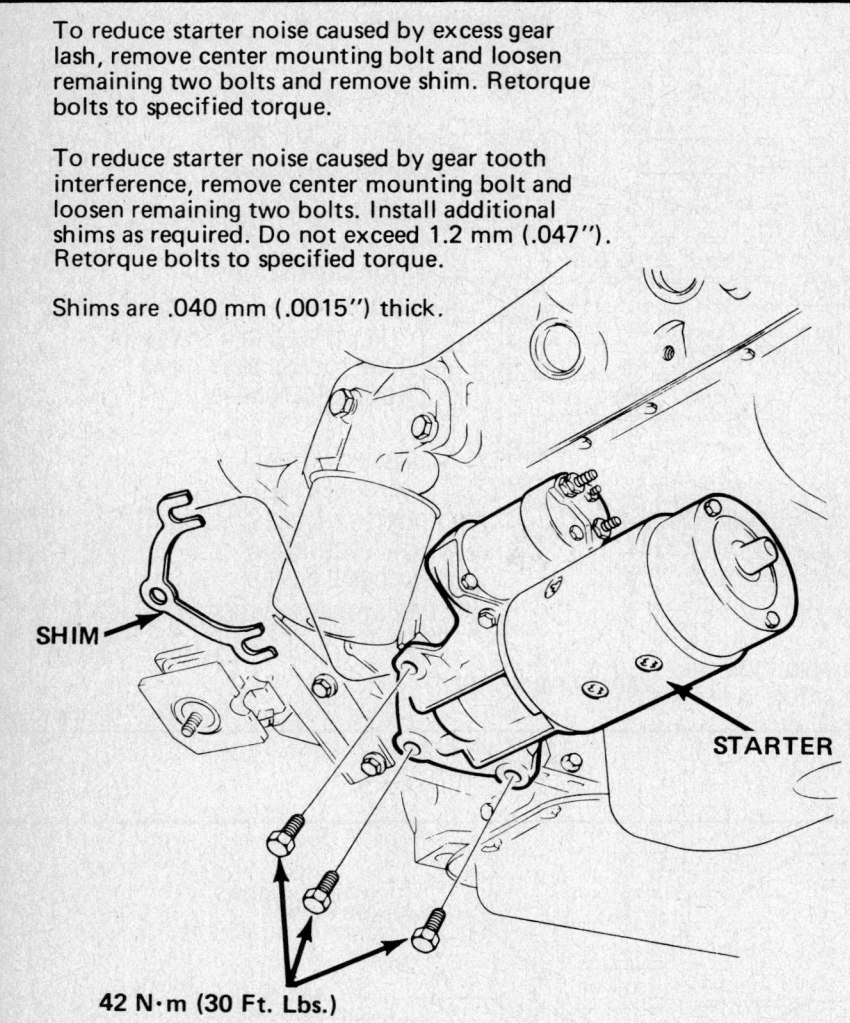

SHIM

STARTER

42 N·m (30 Ft. Lbs.)

Toronado starter (diesel shown)

Starter
- Disconnect electrical wiring, and remove, disconnect or relocate any of the following necessary for starter removal clearance:
  a. Crossmember
  b. Exhaust plumbing
  c. Flywheel housing cover
  d. Transmission oil cooler lines

Ignition Distributor
- Remove distributor cap, electrical wiring, vacuum hose, etc. from the distributor.
- Put alignment marks on rotor and distributor housing for installation reference (all models except Toronado with EST system).
- On Toronado models using EST system, place number one cylinder at TDC. This will align white mark on rotor with the white pointer in the distributor.
- Remove the hold-down device, and pull the distributor up out of the engine.
- After installation, set ignition timing and check dwell, idle speed, etc. as necessary.

Checking pinion clearance

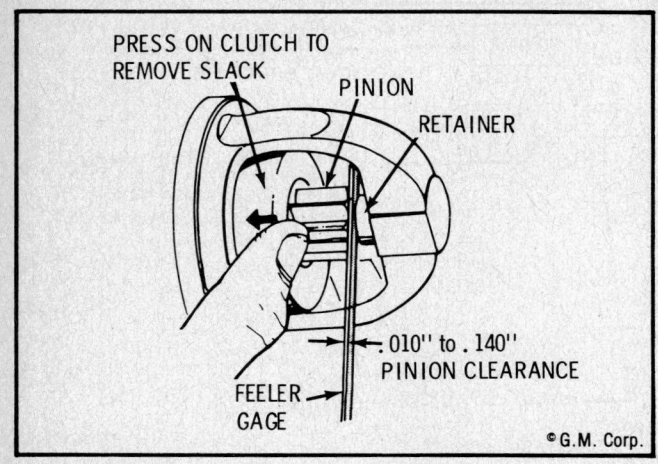

PRESS ON CLUTCH TO REMOVE SLACK

PINION

RETAINER

.010" to .140" PINION CLEARANCE

FEELER GAGE

© G.M. Corp.

Install snap ring and retainer

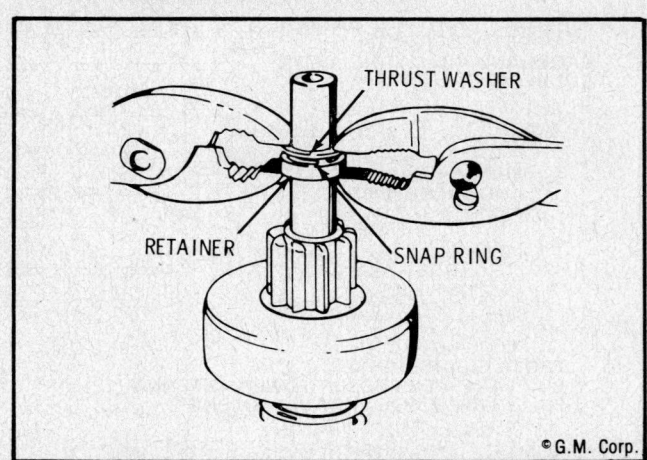

THRUST WASHER

RETAINER

SNAP RING

© G.M. Corp.

Engine starter mounting and diagnostic procedure

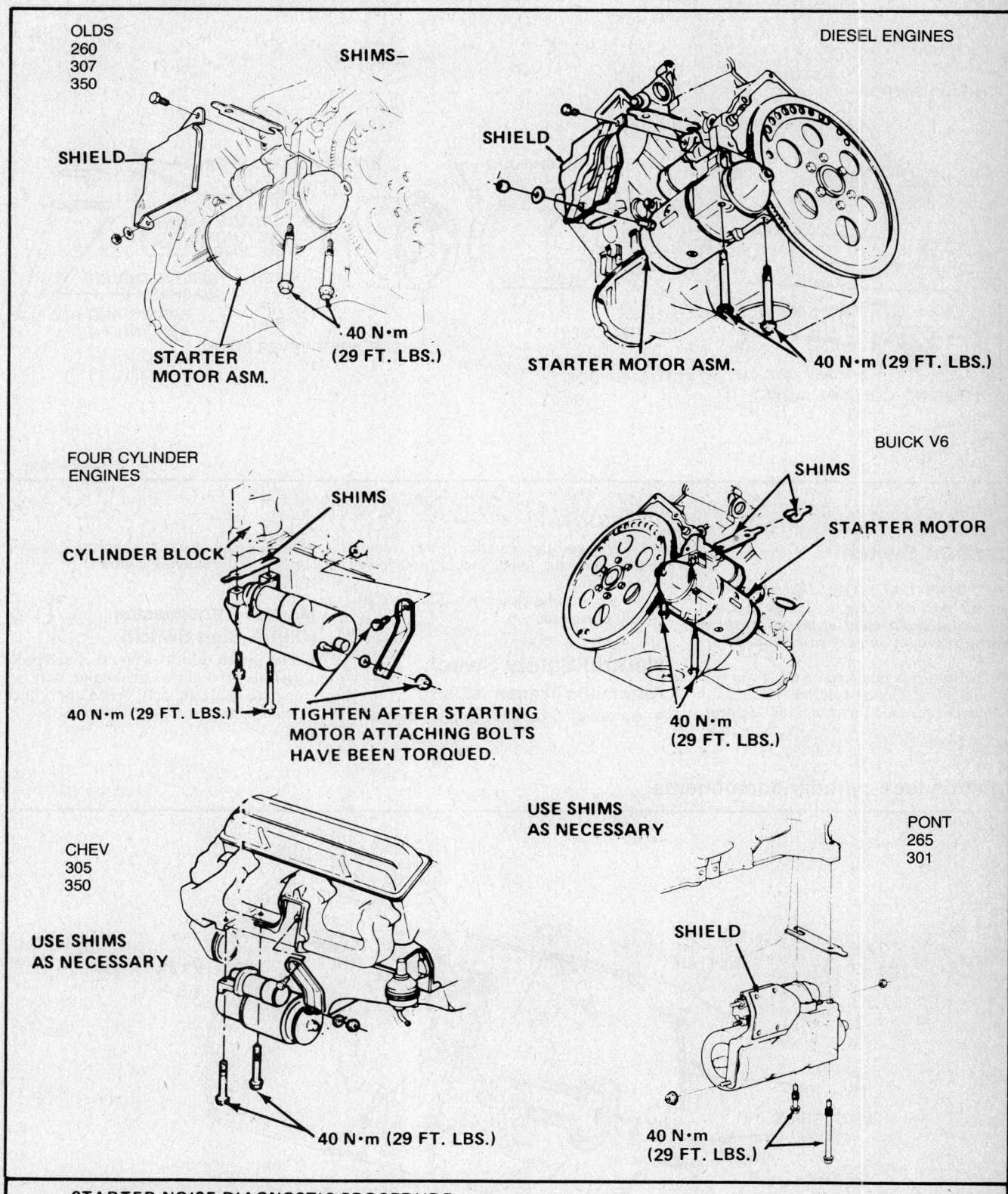

OLDS
260
307
350

SHIMS—

DIESEL ENGINES

SHIELD

SHIELD

40 N·m
(29 FT. LBS.)

STARTER
MOTOR ASM.

STARTER MOTOR ASM.

40 N·m (29 FT. LBS.)

FOUR CYLINDER
ENGINES

BUICK V6

SHIMS

SHIMS

STARTER MOTOR

CYLINDER BLOCK

40 N·m (29 FT. LBS.)

TIGHTEN AFTER STARTING
MOTOR ATTACHING BOLTS
HAVE BEEN TORQUED.

40 N·m
(29 FT. LBS.)

USE SHIMS
AS NECESSARY

PONT
265
301

CHEV
305
350

USE SHIMS
AS NECESSARY

SHIELD

40 N·m (29 FT. LBS.)

40 N·m
(29 FT. LBS.)

STARTER NOISE DIAGNOSTIC PROCEDURE

1. STARTER NOISE DURING CRANKING: REMOVE 1 — .015" DOUBLE SHIM OR ADD SINGLE .015" SHIM TO OUTER BOLT ONLY.

2. HIGH PITCHED WHINE AFTER ENGINE FIRES: ADD .015" DOUBLE SHIMS UNTIL NOISE DISAPPEARS.

© G.M. Corp.

OLDSMOBILE
EXCEPT CIERA, STARFIRE & '80-'82 OMEGA

Ignition and dimmer switch installation—exploded view

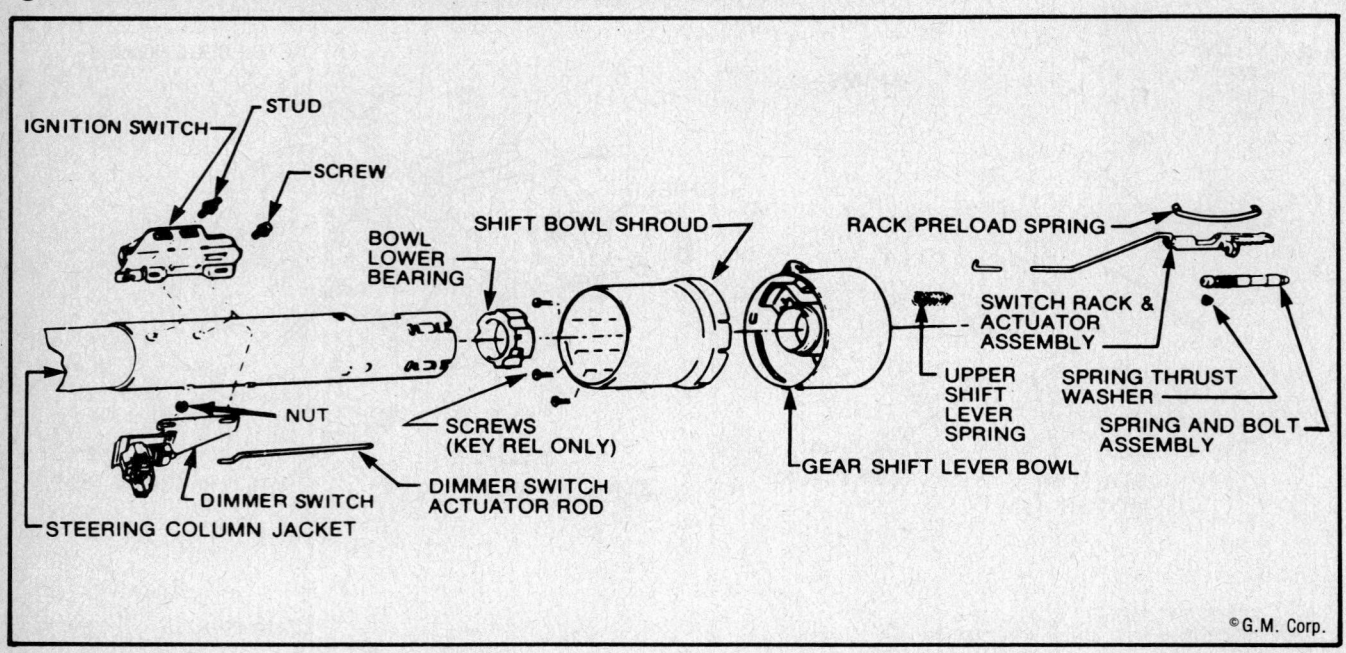

© G.M. Corp.

Ignition Switch

CHILTON CAUTION: *Disconnect the battery positive cable to insure against accidental deployment of the air cushion restraint system on cars so equipped.*

- The switch is mounted on the lower section of the steering column. The column must be lowered for switch replacement.

- Disconnect the column lower mount first, then the upper mount, and lower the column.
- Disconnect the actuator rod and electrical connection.

Neutral Safety Switch
Automatic Transmission

- Automatic vehicles with automatic

transmission use a mechanical lock cylinder in the steering column.

Manual Transmission (Clutch Start Switch)

- The switch is located on the clutch pedal bracket, and allows the engine start circuit to activate only when the clutch pedal is depressed.

Ignition lock cylinder components

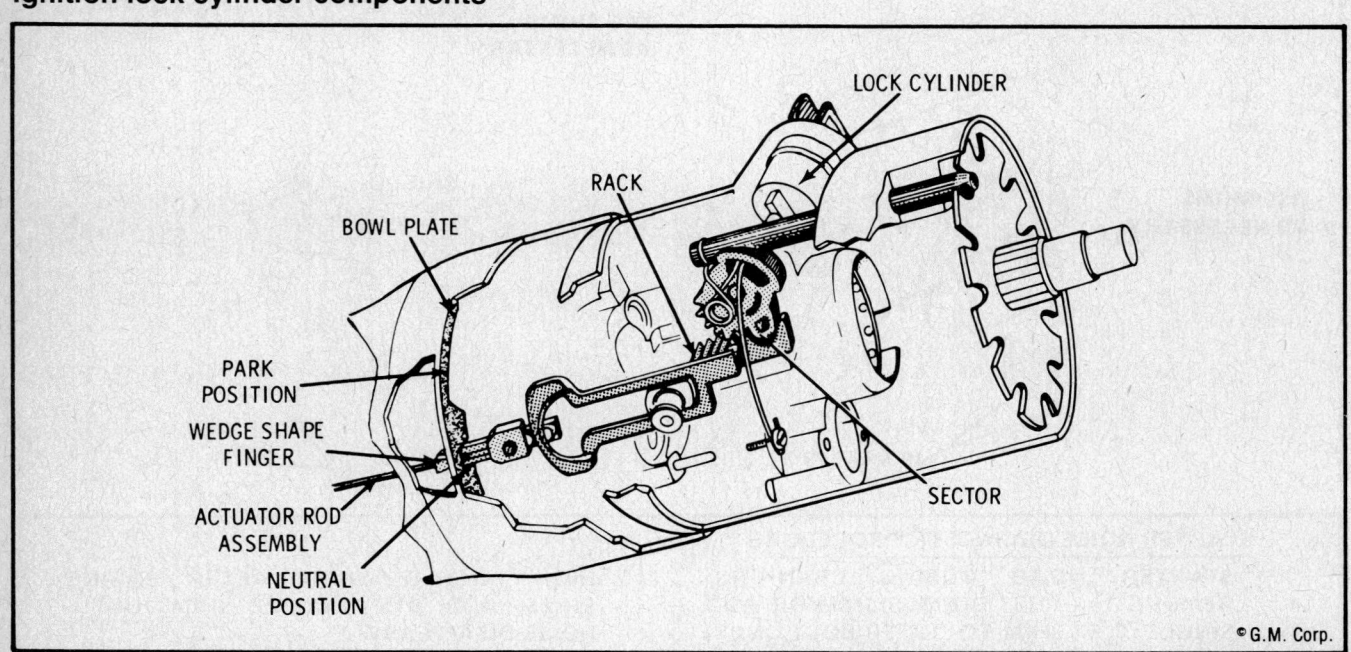

© G.M. Corp.

Omega stoplight switch

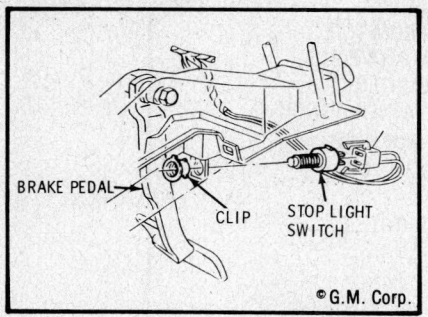

© G.M. Corp.

Stoplight switch in 88 and 98 models

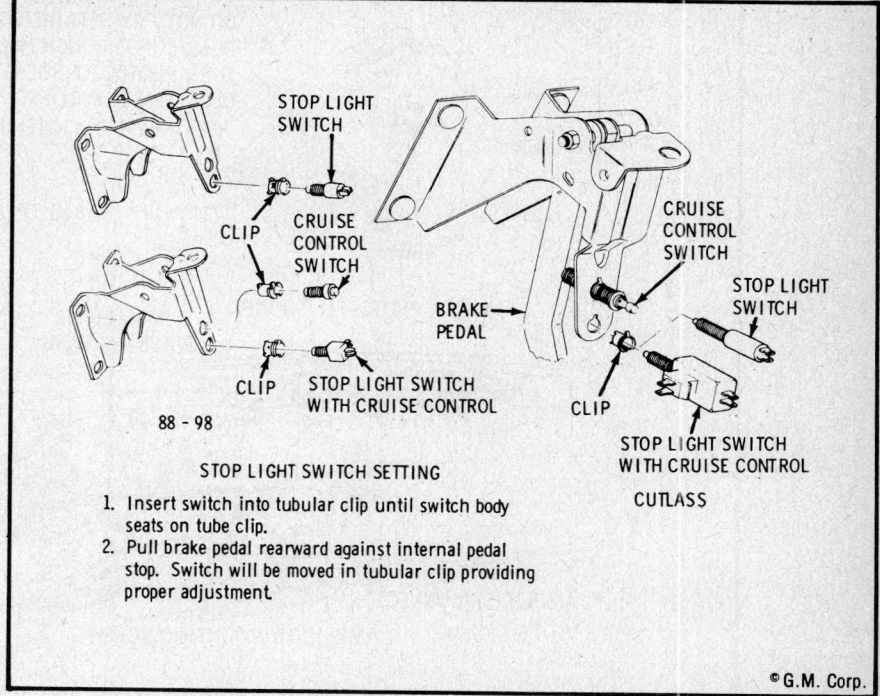

88 - 98

STOP LIGHT SWITCH SETTING

1. Insert switch into tubular clip until switch body seats on tube clip.
2. Pull brake pedal rearward against internal pedal stop. Switch will be moved in tubular clip providing proper adjustment.

© G.M. Corp.

Stoplight Switch

- The switch is mounted on the brake pedal bracket.
- To adjust, depress the pedal and push the switch through the circular retaining clip until it contacts the brake pedal, then pull the pedal up against the internal pedal stop. This places the switch in the correct position within the clip.

Horn Switch and Steering Wheel

CHILTON CAUTION: *Disconnect the battery positive cable to insure against accidental deployment of the air cushion restraint system on cars so equipped.*

- Remove the horn pad, contact assembly, etc.
- On tilt and telescope column, remove the lock lever and plate.
- Remove the steering wheel with a puller.

Tilt and telescope steering column horn contacts

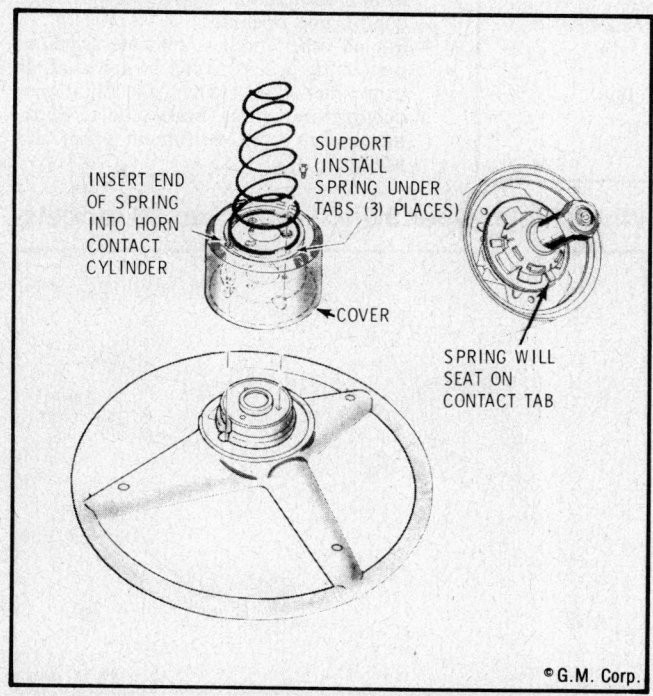

© G.M. Corp.

Omega horn switch steering wheel and pad

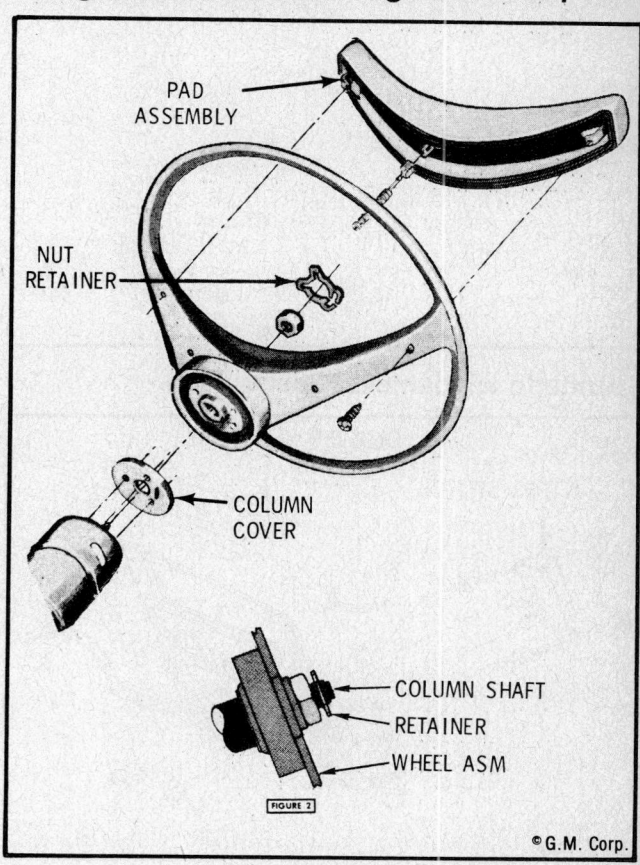

© G.M. Corp.

OLDSMOBILE
EXCEPT CIERA, STARFIRE & '80-'82 OMEGA

Twilight Sentinel mounting in Toronado

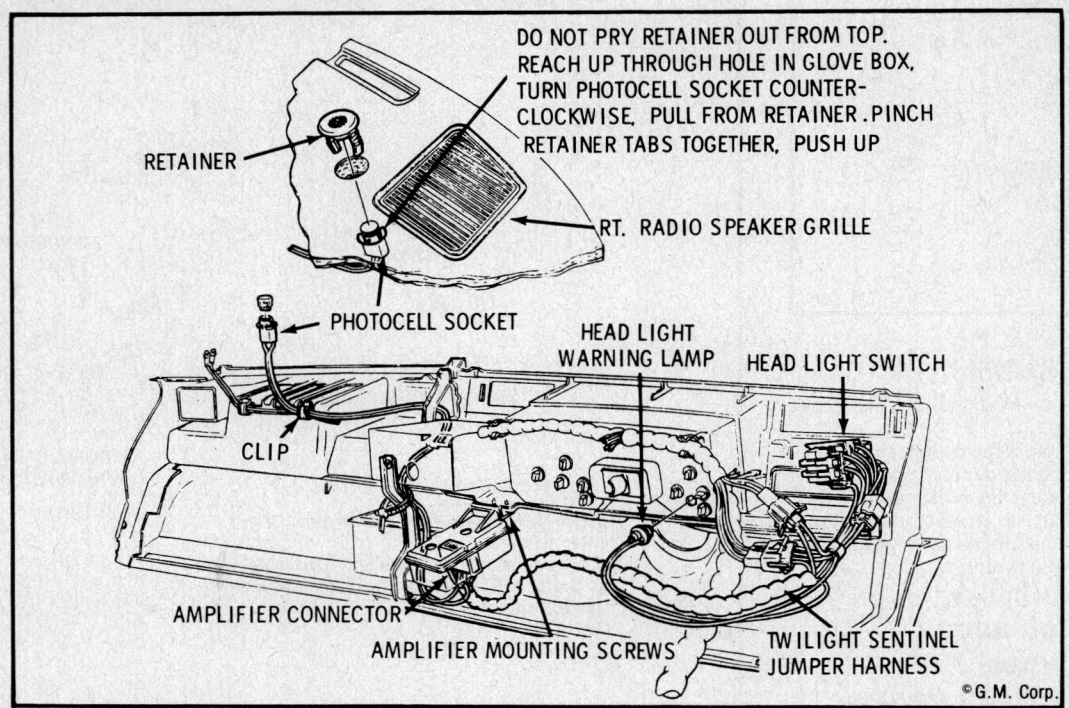

DO NOT PRY RETAINER OUT FROM TOP.
REACH UP THROUGH HOLE IN GLOVE BOX,
TURN PHOTOCELL SOCKET COUNTER-
CLOCKWISE. PULL FROM RETAINER. PINCH
RETAINER TABS TOGETHER, PUSH UP

RT. RADIO SPEAKER GRILLE

RETAINER

PHOTOCELL SOCKET

HEAD LIGHT WARNING LAMP

HEAD LIGHT SWITCH

CLIP

AMPLIFIER CONNECTOR

AMPLIFIER MOUNTING SCREWS

TWILIGHT SENTINEL JUMPER HARNESS

© G.M. Corp.

Light switch in 88 and 98 models

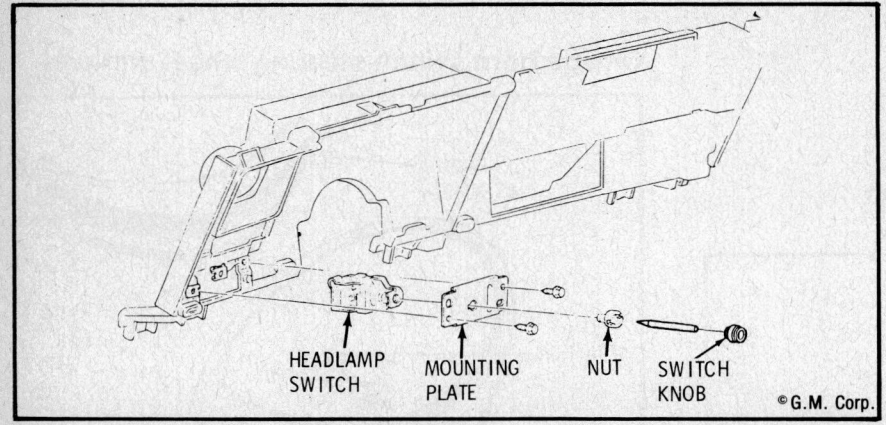

HEADLAMP SWITCH

MOUNTING PLATE

NUT

SWITCH KNOB

© G.M. Corp.

Windshield Wiper Switch

- On 1978 and later Cutlass, remove the cluster pad assembly and separate switch from instrument panel.
- On 1977 and later 88 and 98 models, remove the left trim cover, remove the switch mounting plate screws, and separate the switch from the mount plate.
- For Toronado and 1976 and earlier full-size models, remove the light switch, and then remove the wiper switch through the heater/air conditioner control unit opening.
- For all other models, relocate anything preventing access to the switch such as trim panel, light switch, air conditioner ducting or parking brake cable. Separate switch from instrument panel and wiring.

Toronado windshield wiper switch

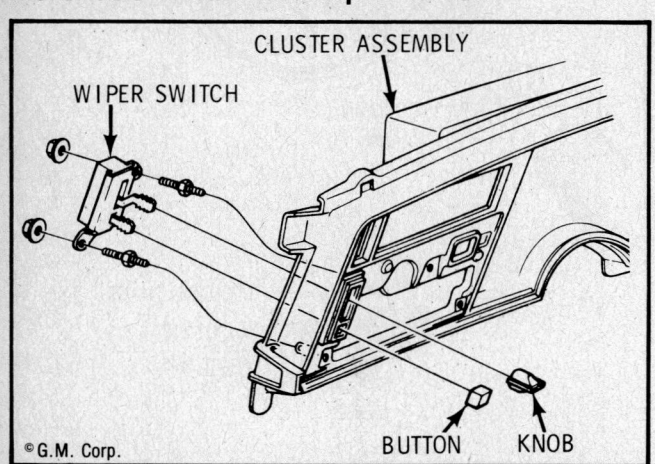

CLUSTER ASSEMBLY

WIPER SWITCH

BUTTON   KNOB

© G.M. Corp.

Windshield wiper switch in 88 and 98 models

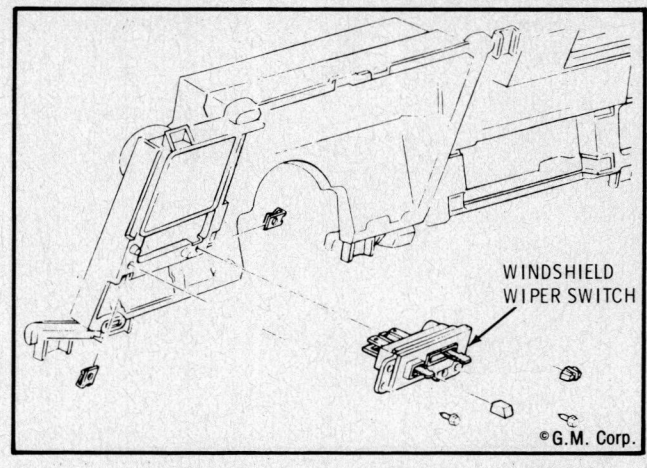

WINDSHIELD WIPER SWITCH

© G.M. Corp.

A608

1978 and later Cutlass windshield wiper switch

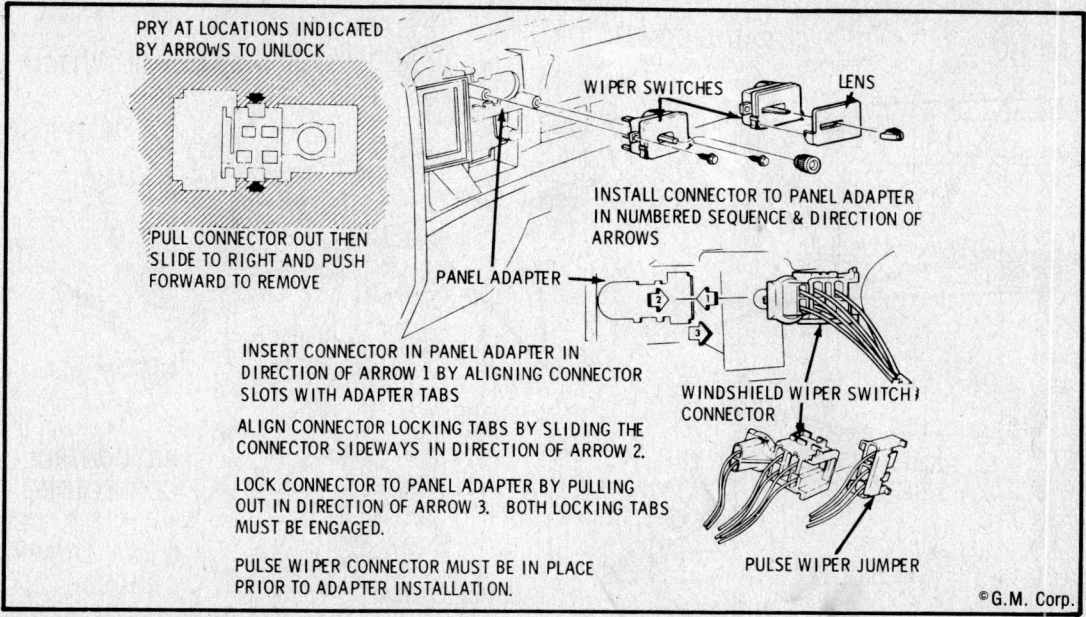

PRY AT LOCATIONS INDICATED BY ARROWS TO UNLOCK

PULL CONNECTOR OUT THEN SLIDE TO RIGHT AND PUSH FORWARD TO REMOVE

WIPER SWITCHES

LENS

INSTALL CONNECTOR TO PANEL ADAPTER IN NUMBERED SEQUENCE & DIRECTION OF ARROWS

PANEL ADAPTER

INSERT CONNECTOR IN PANEL ADAPTER IN DIRECTION OF ARROW 1 BY ALIGNING CONNECTOR SLOTS WITH ADAPTER TABS

ALIGN CONNECTOR LOCKING TABS BY SLIDING THE CONNECTOR SIDEWAYS IN DIRECTION OF ARROW 2.

LOCK CONNECTOR TO PANEL ADAPTER BY PULLING OUT IN DIRECTION OF ARROW 3. BOTH LOCKING TABS MUST BE ENGAGED.

PULSE WIPER CONNECTOR MUST BE IN PLACE PRIOR TO ADAPTER INSTALLATION.

WINDSHIELD WIPER SWITCH CONNECTOR

PULSE WIPER JUMPER

© G.M. Corp.

Omega wiper switch mounting

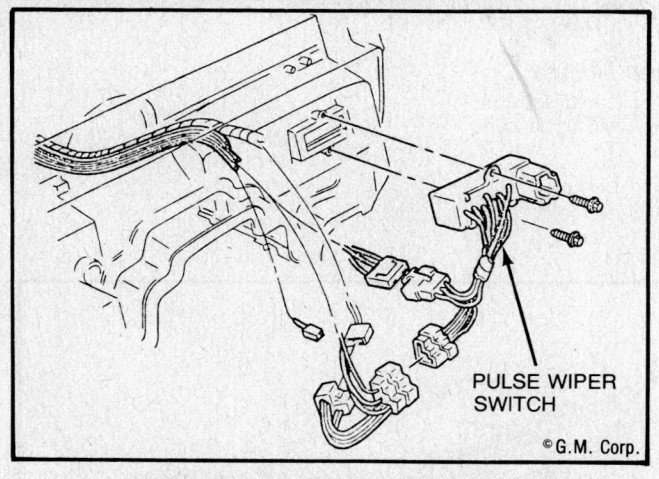

PULSE WIPER SWITCH

© G.M. Corp.

Pulse wiper switch

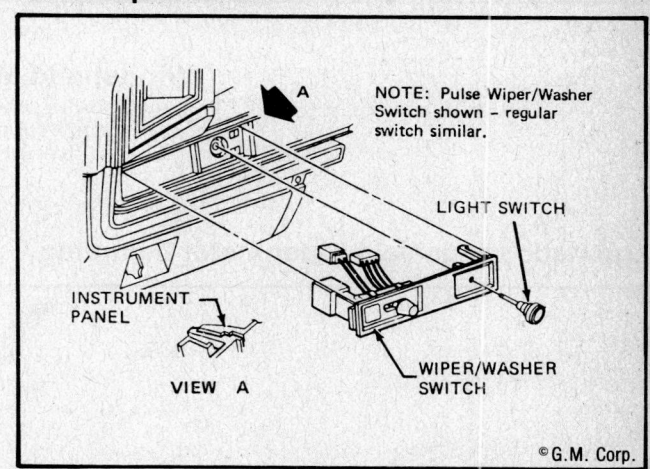

NOTE: Pulse Wiper/Washer Switch shown - regular switch similar.

LIGHT SWITCH

INSTRUMENT PANEL

VIEW A

WIPER/WASHER SWITCH

© G.M. Corp.

Instrument panel wiring typical

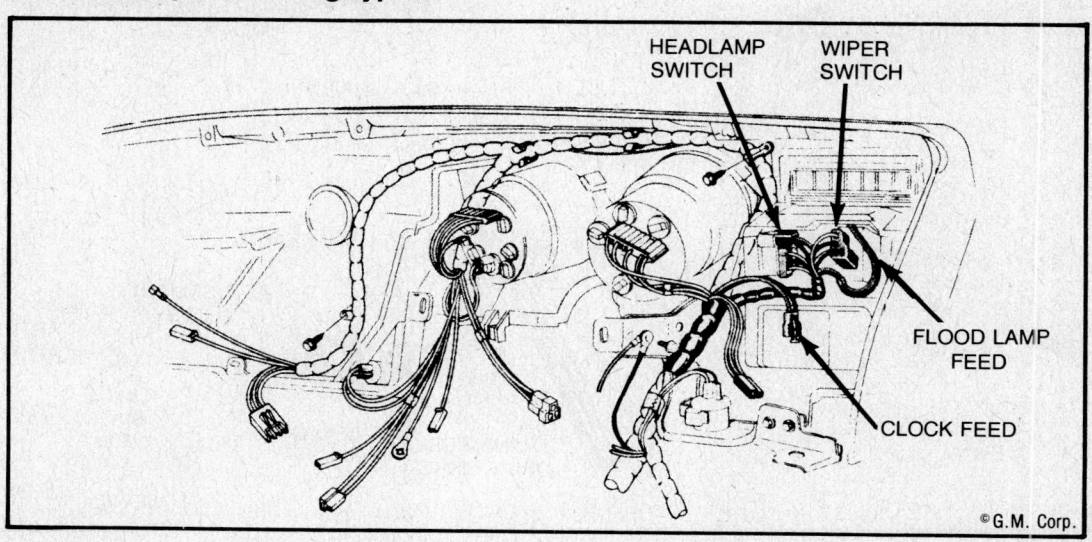

HEADLAMP SWITCH

WIPER SWITCH

FLOOD LAMP FEED

CLOCK FEED

© G.M. Corp.

Toronado instrument panel wiring

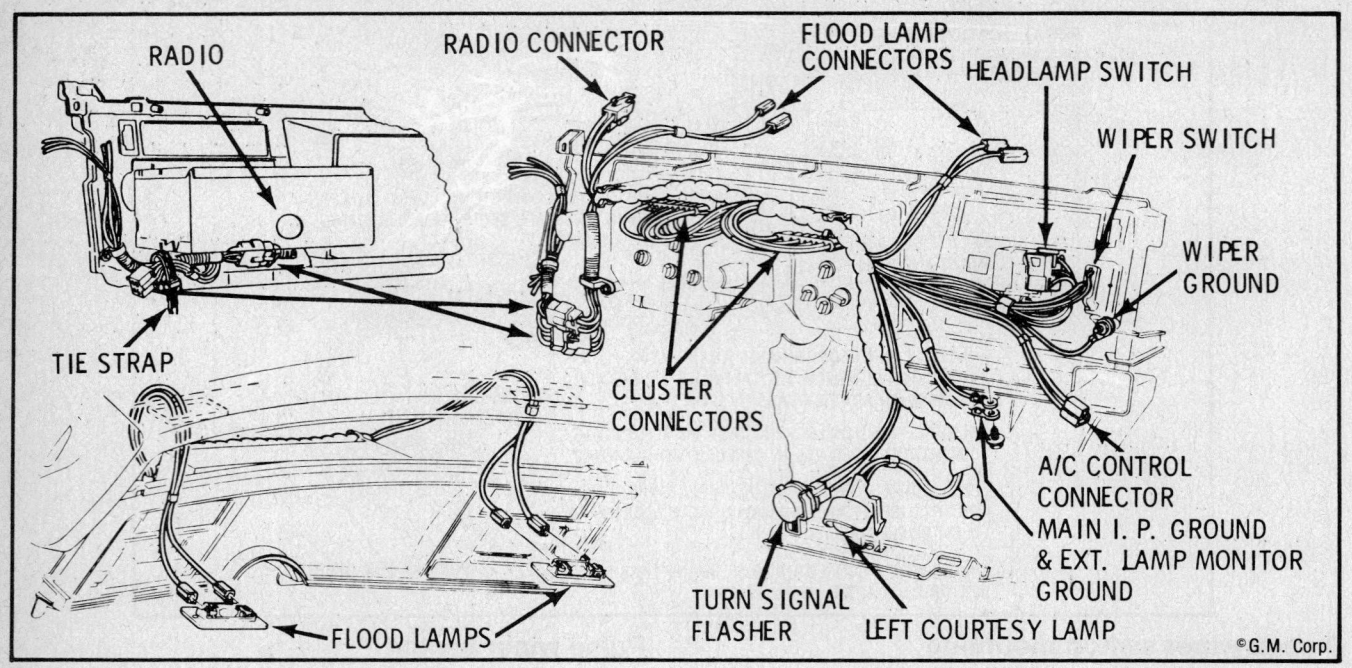

RADIO

RADIO CONNECTOR

FLOOD LAMP CONNECTORS

HEADLAMP SWITCH

WIPER SWITCH

WIPER GROUND

TIE STRAP

CLUSTER CONNECTORS

A/C CONTROL CONNECTOR
MAIN I. P. GROUND & EXT. LAMP MONITOR GROUND

TURN SIGNAL FLASHER

LEFT COURTESY LAMP

FLOOD LAMPS

© G.M. Corp.

Windshield Wiper Motor

- Remove the cowl screen, and separate the motor from mounts, electrical connections, linkages, etc.

Toronado windshield wiper motor mounting

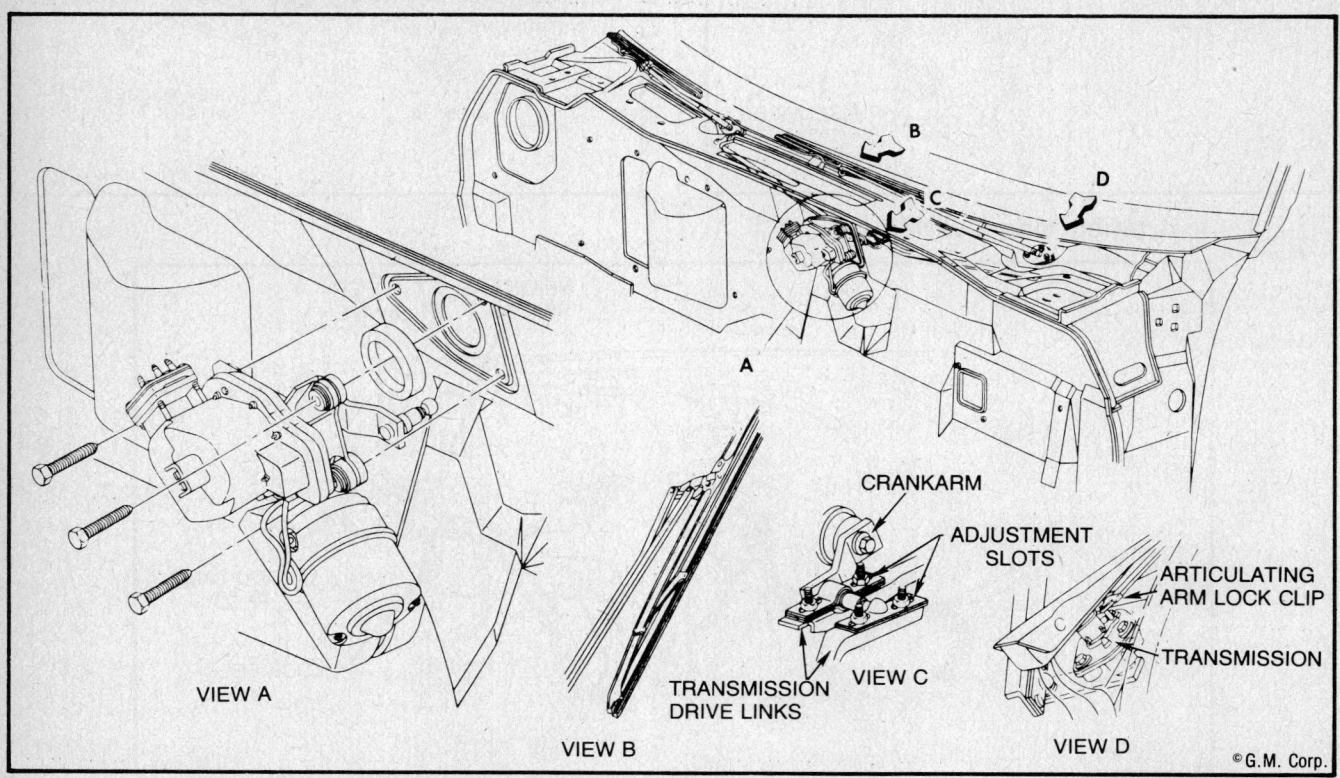

B

C

D

A

CRANKARM

ADJUSTMENT SLOTS

ARTICULATING ARM LOCK CLIP

TRANSMISSION

VIEW A

TRANSMISSION DRIVE LINKS

VIEW C

VIEW D

VIEW B

© G.M. Corp.

Windshield wiper motor installation typical in 88 and 98 models

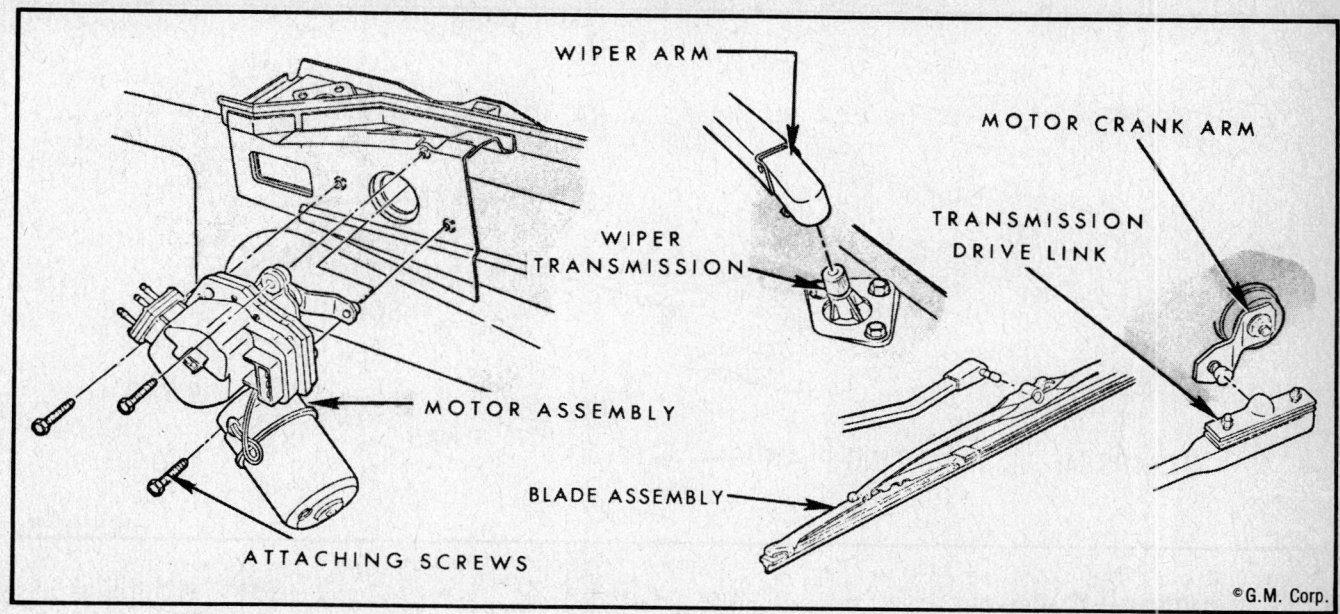

© G.M. Corp.

Windshield wiper linkage installation typical in 88 and 98 models

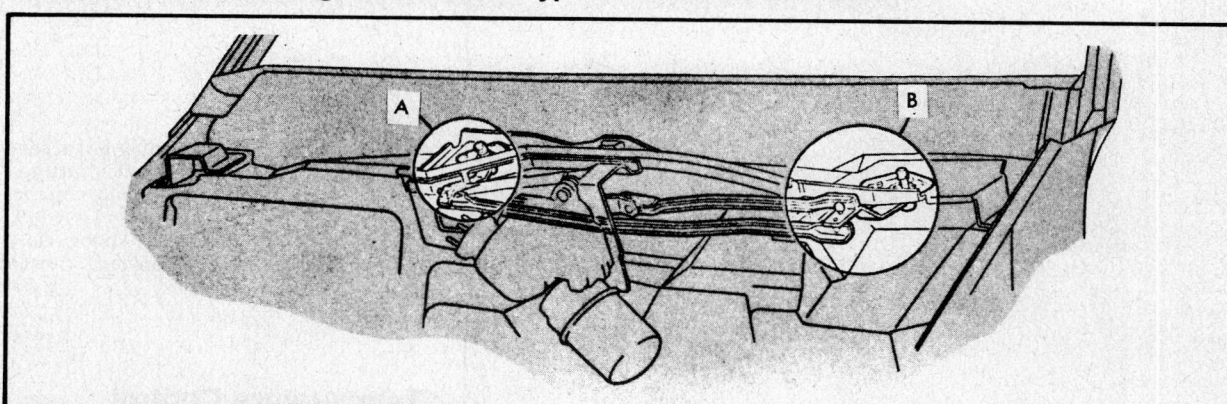

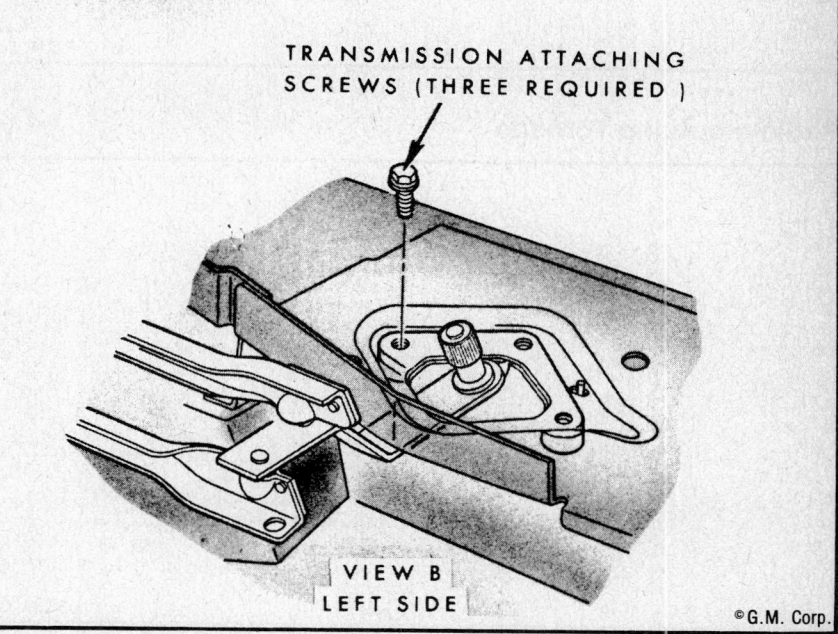

Windshield Wiper Linkage

- Remove the cowl vent screen, and, if necessary, remove the wiper arms.
- Separate linkage from motor and mounts and guide it out through the cowl opening.

Windshield Wiper Arms

- Wipers must be in "Park" position.
- On car using a rectangular motor, pry the arm off the drive shaft.
- On car using a round motor, release whatever holding device is employed, and lift the arm off the drive shaft.

Windshield Wiper Blades

- Trigger the release device, and slide the blade off the wiper arm.

© G.M. Corp.

OLDSMOBILE
EXCEPT CIERA, STARFIRE & '80-'82 OMEGA

Radio mounting 88 and 98 models

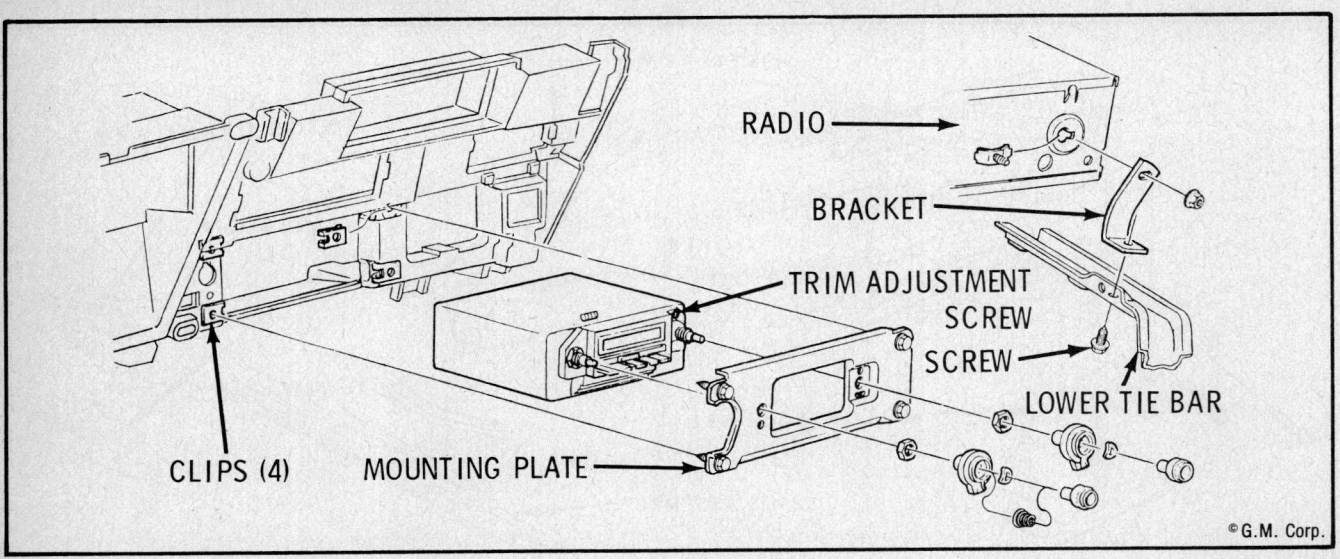

RADIO

BRACKET

TRIM ADJUSTMENT SCREW

SCREW

LOWER TIE BAR

CLIPS (4)

MOUNTING PLATE

© G.M. Corp.

Radio mounting—Cutlass

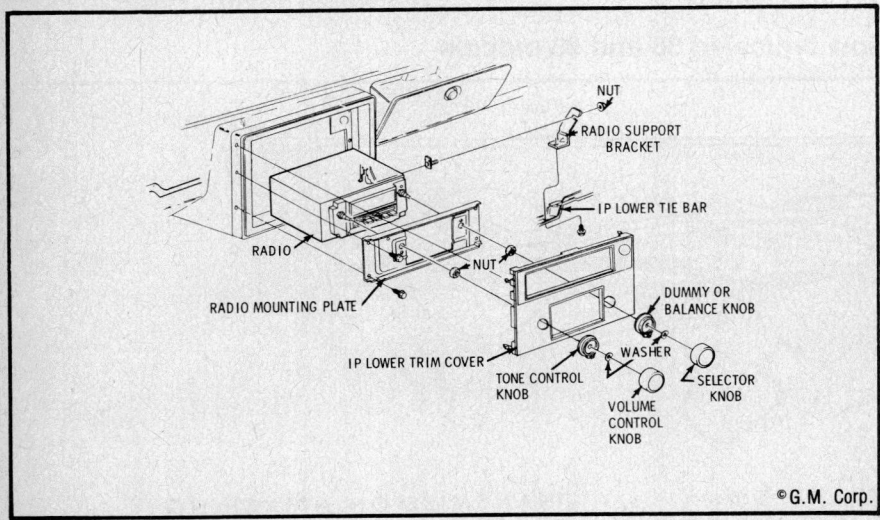

NUT

RADIO SUPPORT BRACKET

IP LOWER TIE BAR

RADIO

NUT

DUMMY OR BALANCE KNOB

RADIO MOUNTING PLATE

IP LOWER TRIM COVER

TONE CONTROL KNOB

WASHER

SELECTOR KNOB

VOLUME CONTROL KNOB

© G.M. Corp.

Radio mounting Tornado

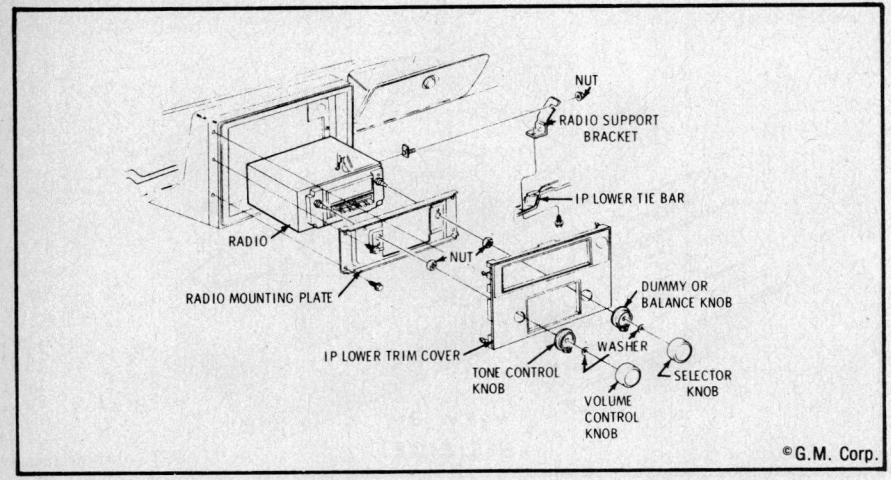

NUT

RADIO SUPPORT BRACKET

IP LOWER TIE BAR

RADIO

NUT

DUMMY OR BALANCE KNOB

RADIO MOUNTING PLATE

IP LOWER TRIM COVER

TONE CONTROL KNOB

WASHER

SELECTOR KNOB

VOLUME CONTROL KNOB

© G.M. Corp.

Radio
- Relocate anything preventing full access to radio such as air conditioner ducting, ash tray, instrument panel trim, throttle cable, etc.
- Remove mounting screws, knobs, etc., and remove radio from antenna, power and speaker connections.

Temperature Control Unit/Blower Switch
- Relocate anything preventing full access to radio such as:
  a. Instrument panel trim covers
  b. Headlight switch and instrument panel applique
  c. Radio
- Remove mounting screws, pull control unit out and separate it from control cables, vacuum lines and electrical connections.

Temperature Cable Adjustment

- Move temperature lever to cold or left end of slot.
- Rotate the temperature door crank clockwise to full cold.
- Reach through glove box opening and adjust the cable until loop aligns with the pin on crank. Install push-on nut on pin.
- Move the temperature control lever to the right (hot) end of control panel slot. Door should be heard hitting its seat. If not, readjust cable.

NOTE: The defrost and vent cables are not adjustable.

ATC Temperature Cable Adjustment

- Remove the glove compartment.
- Align the holes in the programmer lever and the programmer chassis.
- Check the temperature lever to make sure it is at 75. If it is not, turn the adjusting buckle until lever reads 75.

Temperature cable adjustment—all models with ATC

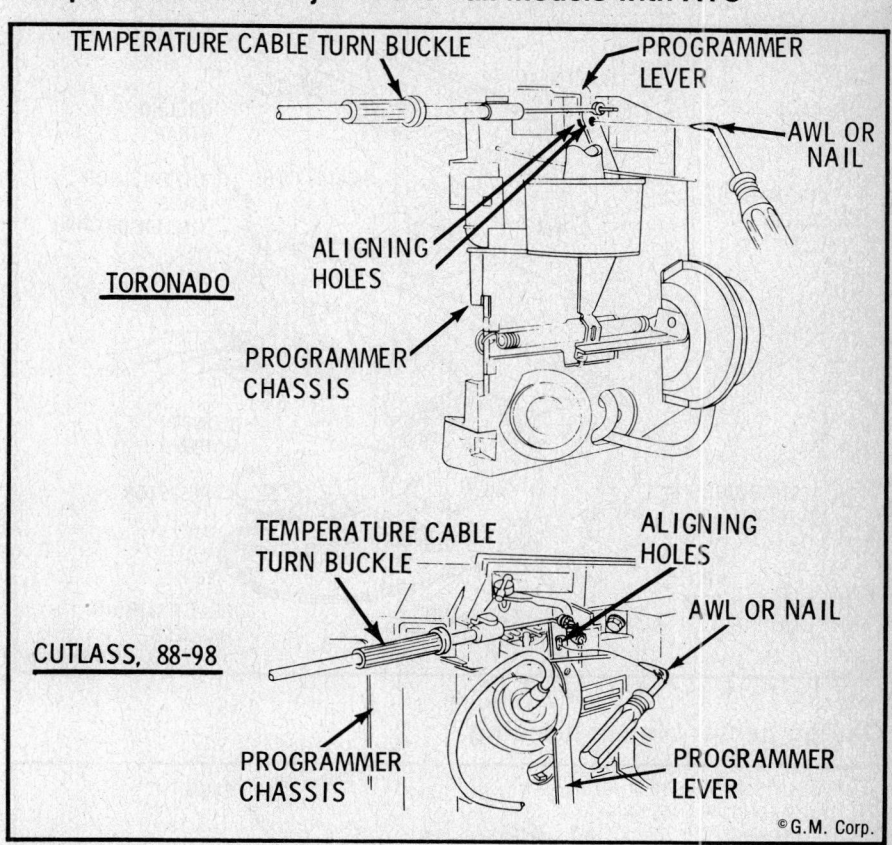

© G.M. Corp.

Heater—A/C control and vacuum hoses

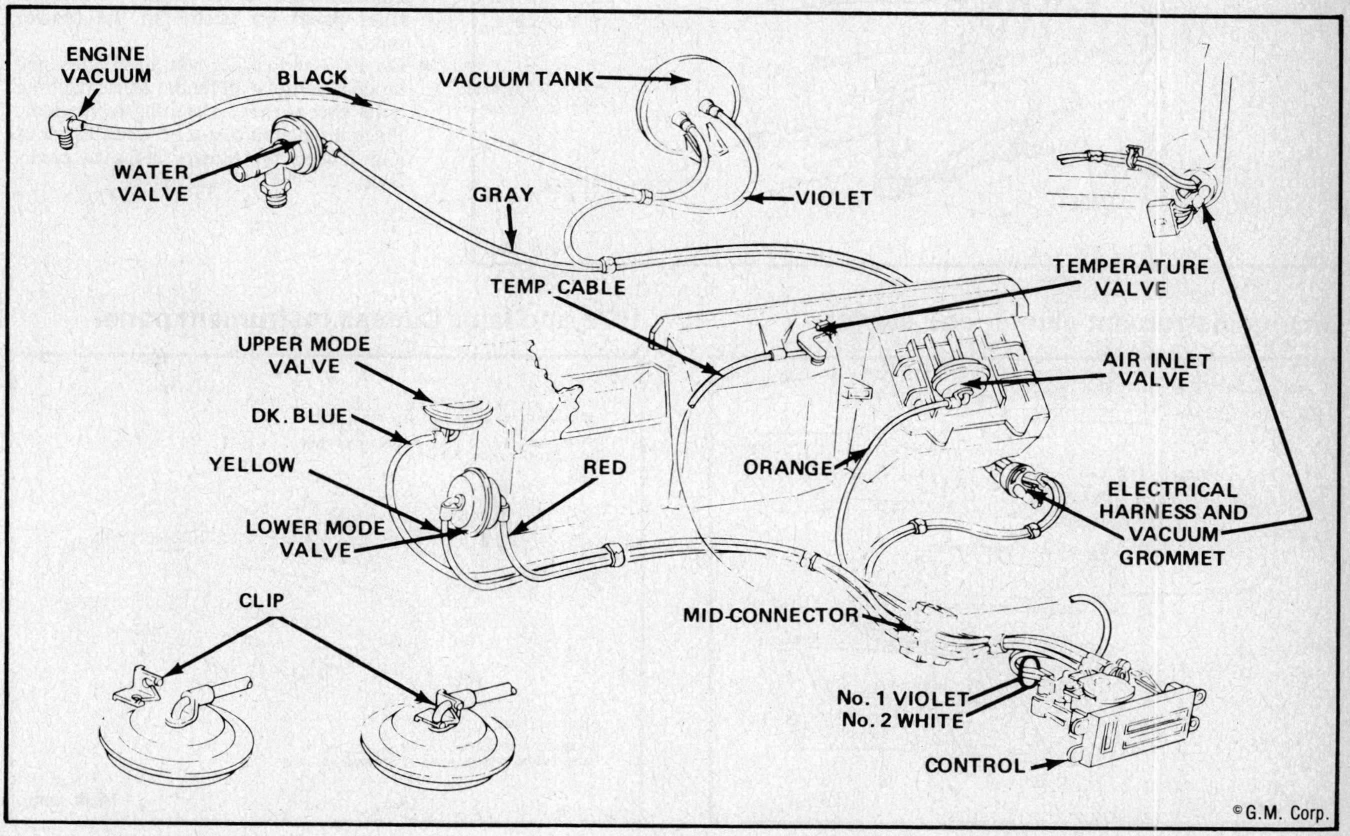

© G.M. Corp.

OLDSMOBILE
EXCEPT CIERA, STARFIRE & '80-'82 OMEGA

Heater module mounting in 1977 and later 88 and 98 models

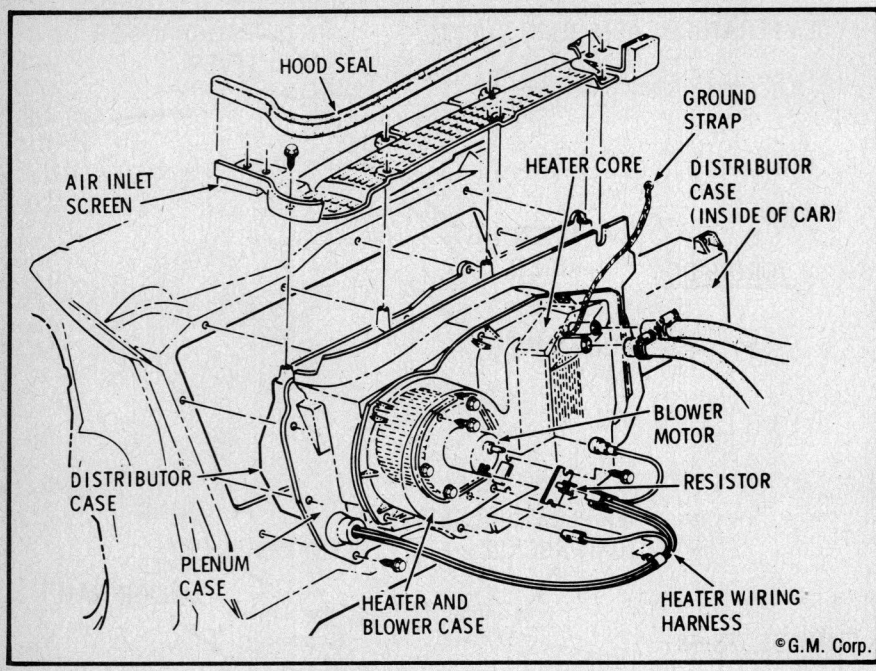

HOOD SEAL
GROUND STRAP
HEATER CORE
DISTRIBUTOR CASE (INSIDE OF CAR)
AIR INLET SCREEN
BLOWER MOTOR
RESISTOR
DISTRIBUTOR CASE
PLENUM CASE
HEATER AND BLOWER CASE
HEATER WIRING HARNESS
© G.M. Corp.

Omega heater blower housing

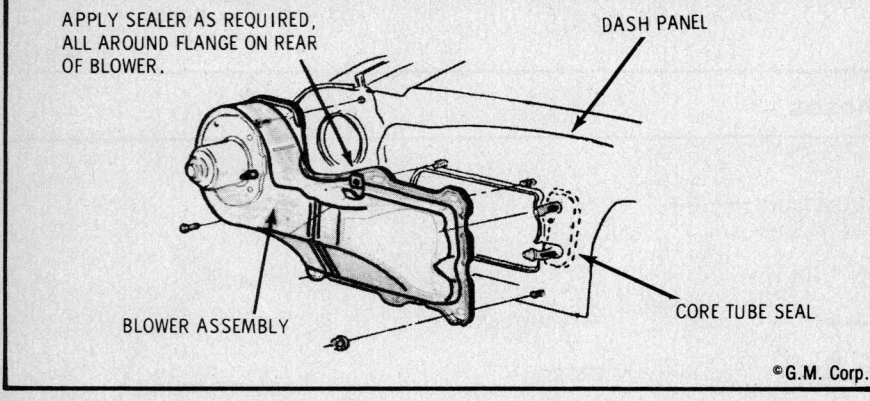

APPLY SEALER AS REQUIRED, ALL AROUND FLANGE ON REAR OF BLOWER.
DASH PANEL
BLOWER ASSEMBLY
CORE TUBE SEAL
© G.M. Corp.

Heater Blower

1977 And Later 88 And 98
- Disconnect mounts and electrical connections, and remove blower and motor.

'78 And Earlier Toronado And '76 88 And 98
- Cut through the wheel well filler panel to expose heater blower motor.
- Disconnect mounts and electrical connections, and remove motor through opening.
- After installation, seal the hole.

Cutlass
- On 1978 and later models, disconnect mounts and electrical connections, and remove blower and motor after disconnecting air conditioner cooling tube.
- On 1977 and earlier air-conditioned models, disconnect mounts and electrical connections, and remove blower and motor.
- On 1977 and earlier non-air-conditioned models, remove the right wheel well filler panel for access to the blower motor.

Omega
- On 1977 and earlier air-conditioned models, remove the right wheel well filler panel for access to the blower motor.
- On 1977 and earlier non-air-conditioned models, remove all fender skirt attaching bolts except those attaching to radiator. Place a wooden block between the skirt and fender for blower removal clearance.

Omega instrument cluster and carrier

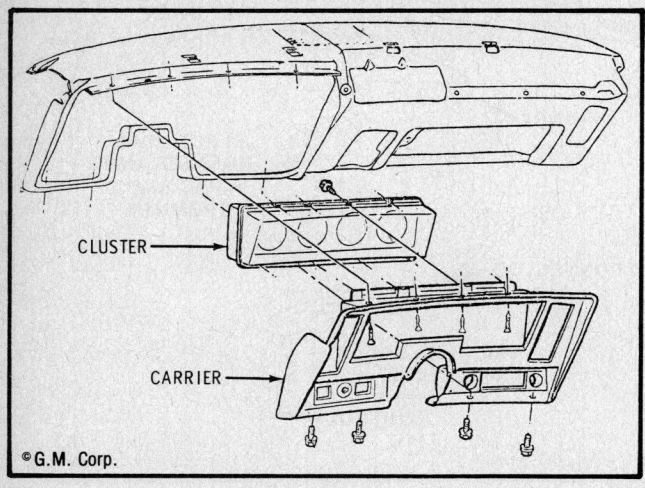

CLUSTER
CARRIER
© G.M. Corp.

1978 and later Cutlass instrument panel

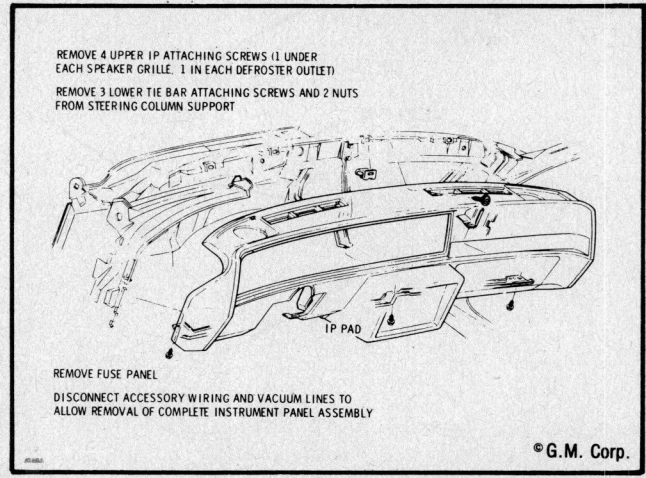

REMOVE 4 UPPER IP ATTACHING SCREWS (1 UNDER EACH SPEAKER GRILLE, 1 IN EACH DEFROSTER OUTLET)

REMOVE 3 LOWER TIE BAR ATTACHING SCREWS AND 2 NUTS FROM STEERING COLUMN SUPPORT

IP PAD

REMOVE FUSE PANEL

DISCONNECT ACCESSORY WIRING AND VACUUM LINES TO ALLOW REMOVAL OF COMPLETE INSTRUMENT PANEL ASSEMBLY

© G.M. Corp.

Heater Core

- On 1977 and later 88 and 98, and 1978 and later Cutlass, remove the module on the Cutlass and remove the module top on the 88 and 98. The core can now be removed from the module.
- On all other models, follow this procedure:
  a. Drain the cooling system and disconnect heater hoses, etc.
  b. Under the instrument panel, remove air conditioner ducting, and disconnect cables, vacuum lines and electrical leads from the heater assembly.
  c. Remove mounting nuts, and work heater assembly rearward and out of the car.
  d. Separate the core from the heater case.
  e. When installing, seal along mating surfaces between dash and heater.

Heater module used in 1977 and later 88 and 98 models

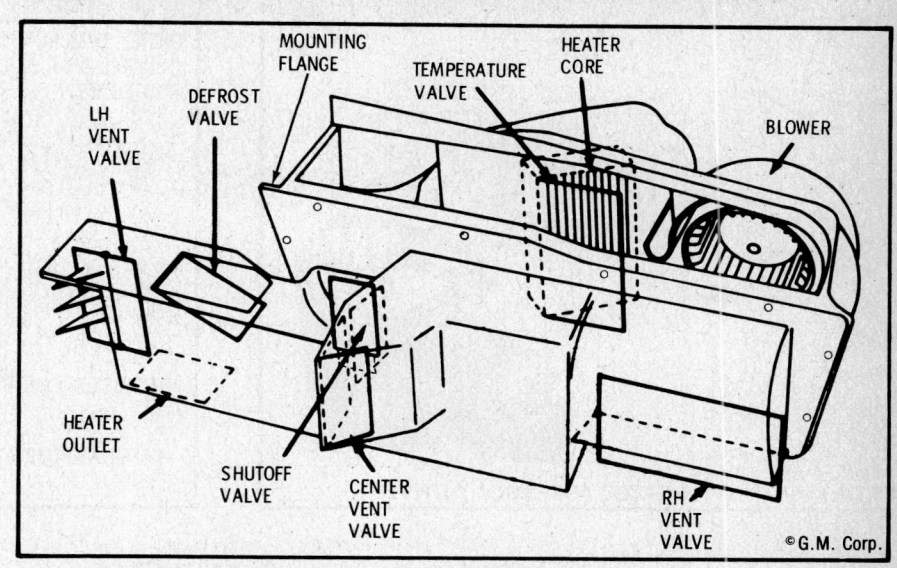

© G.M. Corp.

Heater/air conditioner air distribution manifold in Toronado

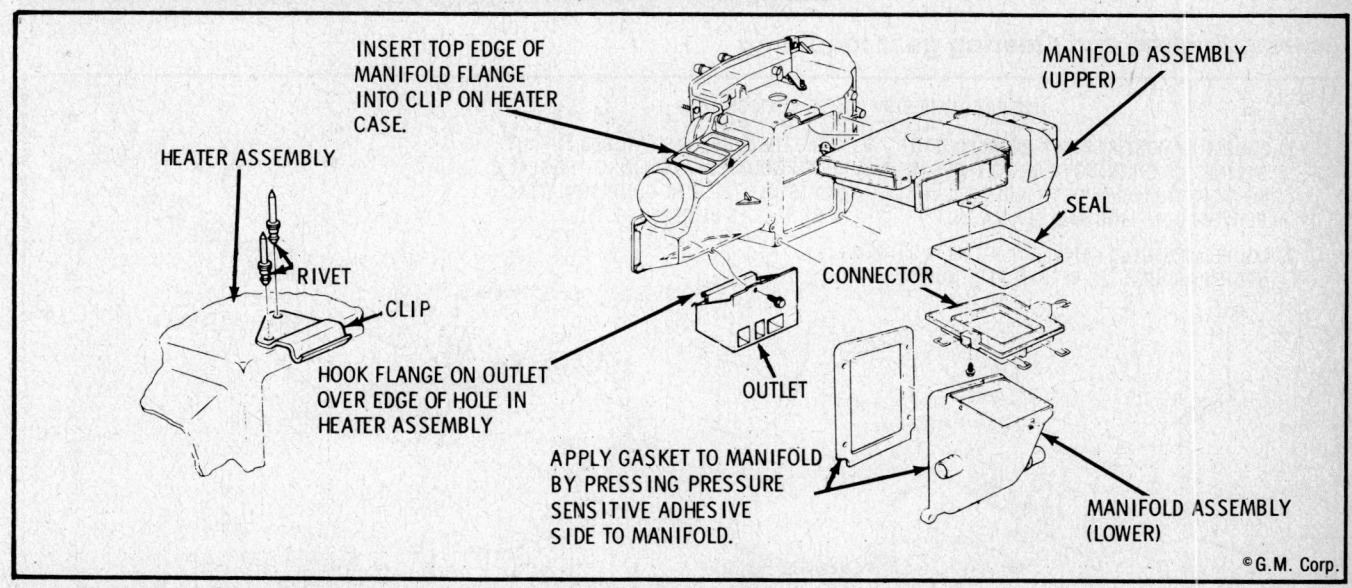

© G.M. Corp.

Heater core removal in 1977 and later 88 and 98 models

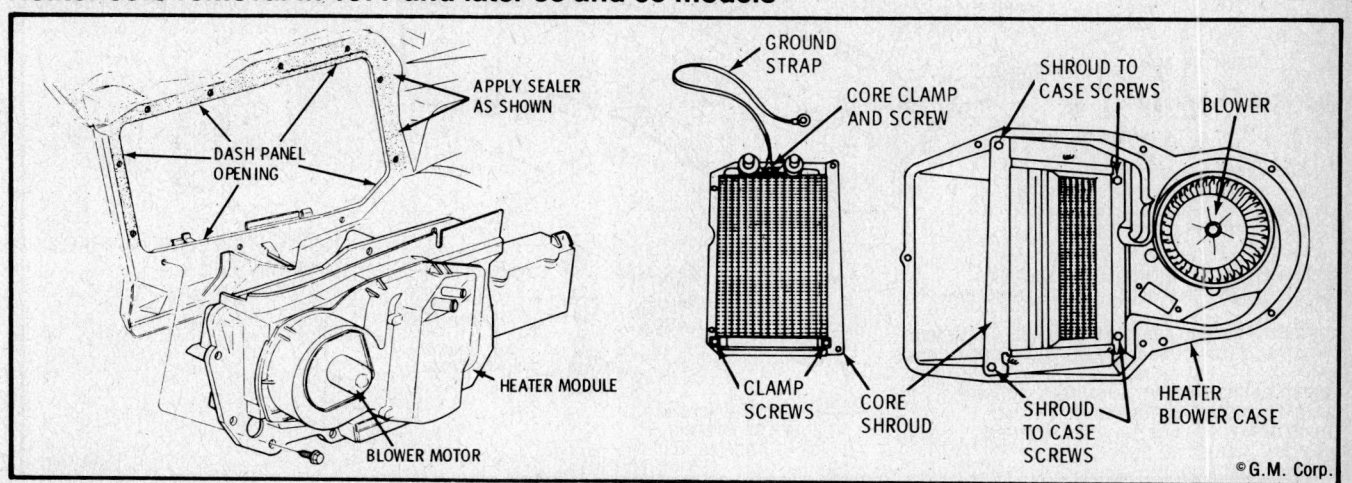

© G.M. Corp.

A615

OLDSMOBILE
EXCEPT CIERA, STARFIRE & '80-'82 OMEGA

Toronado heater case mounting inside car

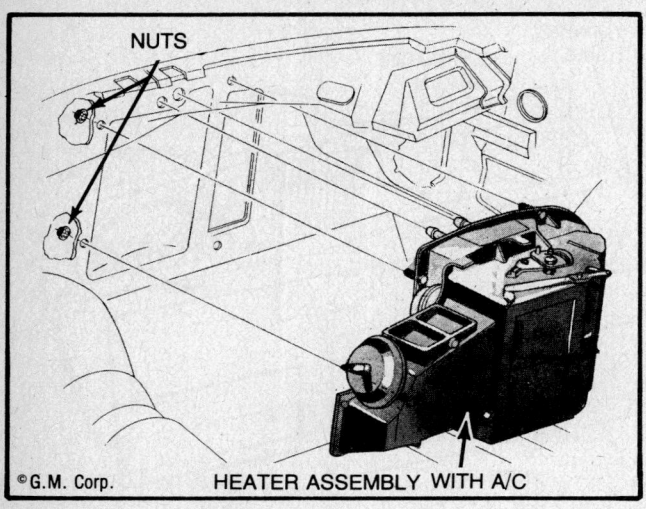

NUTS

© G.M. Corp.

HEATER ASSEMBLY WITH A/C

Typical heater assembly installation

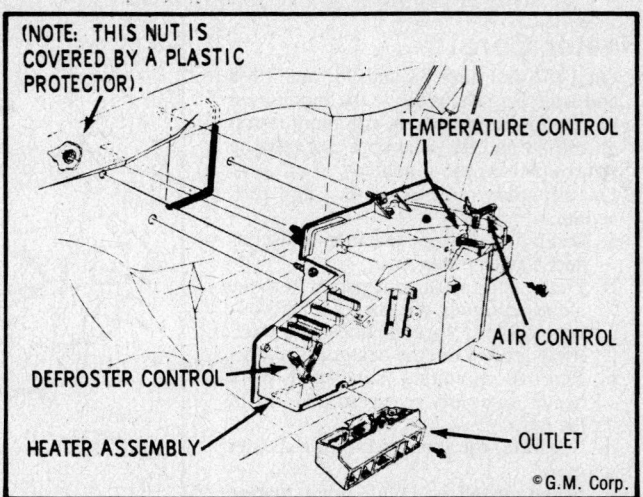

(NOTE: THIS NUT IS COVERED BY A PLASTIC PROTECTOR).

TEMPERATURE CONTROL

AIR CONTROL

DEFROSTER CONTROL

HEATER ASSEMBLY

OUTLET

© G.M. Corp.

STEERING & BRAKES SECTION

Steering linkage and steering gear mounting

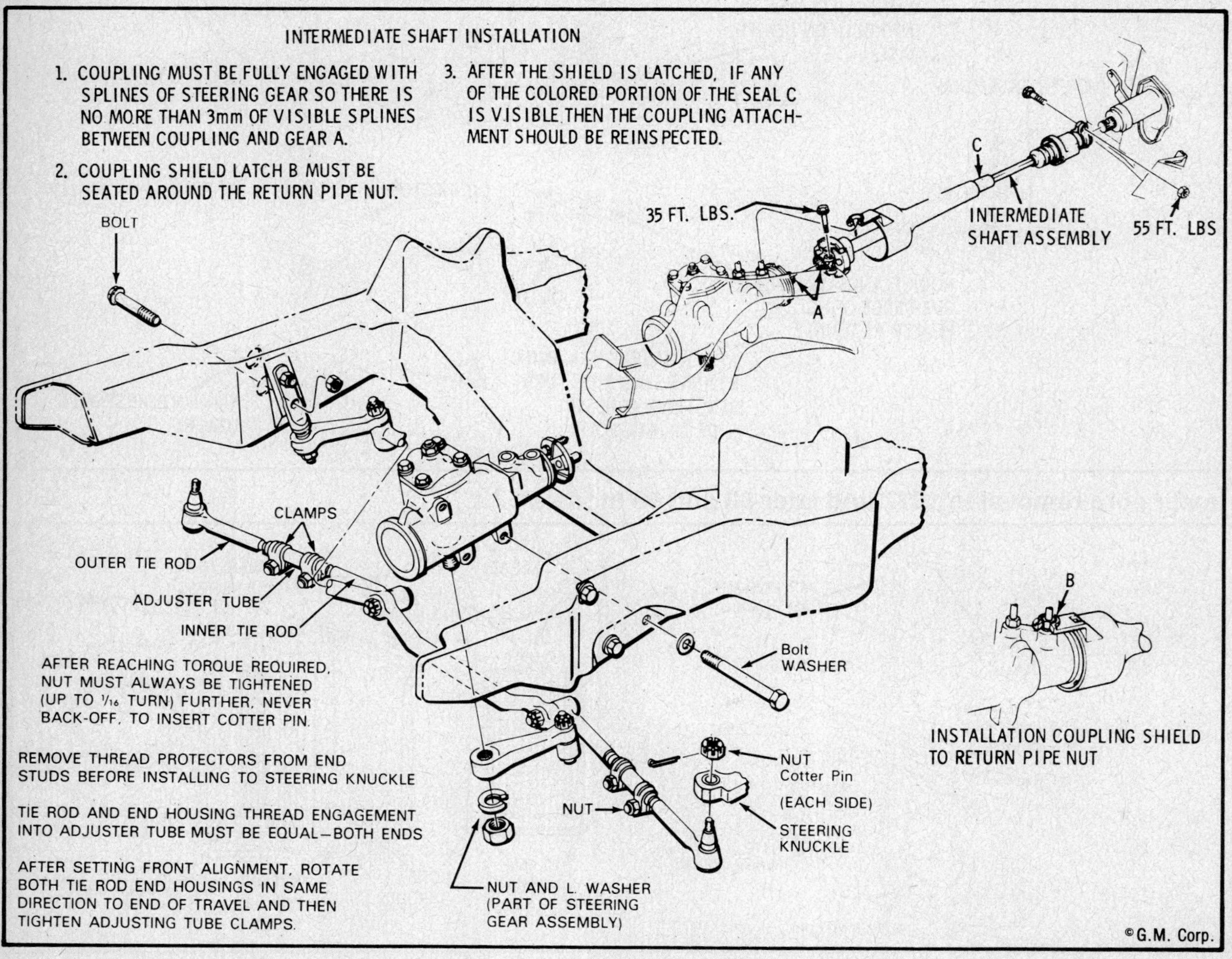

INTERMEDIATE SHAFT INSTALLATION

1. COUPLING MUST BE FULLY ENGAGED WITH SPLINES OF STEERING GEAR SO THERE IS NO MORE THAN 3mm OF VISIBLE SPLINES BETWEEN COUPLING AND GEAR A.

2. COUPLING SHIELD LATCH B MUST BE SEATED AROUND THE RETURN PIPE NUT.

3. AFTER THE SHIELD IS LATCHED, IF ANY OF THE COLORED PORTION OF THE SEAL C IS VISIBLE THEN THE COUPLING ATTACHMENT SHOULD BE REINSPECTED.

35 FT. LBS.

C

INTERMEDIATE SHAFT ASSEMBLY

55 FT. LBS

A

BOLT

CLAMPS

OUTER TIE ROD

ADJUSTER TUBE

INNER TIE ROD

AFTER REACHING TORQUE REQUIRED, NUT MUST ALWAYS BE TIGHTENED (UP TO 1/16 TURN) FURTHER, NEVER BACK-OFF, TO INSERT COTTER PIN.

REMOVE THREAD PROTECTORS FROM END STUDS BEFORE INSTALLING TO STEERING KNUCKLE

TIE ROD AND END HOUSING THREAD ENGAGEMENT INTO ADJUSTER TUBE MUST BE EQUAL—BOTH ENDS

AFTER SETTING FRONT ALIGNMENT, ROTATE BOTH TIE ROD END HOUSINGS IN SAME DIRECTION TO END OF TRAVEL AND THEN TIGHTEN ADJUSTING TUBE CLAMPS.

Bolt WASHER

NUT

NUT Cotter Pin (EACH SIDE)

STEERING KNUCKLE

NUT AND L. WASHER (PART OF STEERING GEAR ASSEMBLY)

B

INSTALLATION COUPLING SHIELD TO RETURN PIPE NUT

© G.M. Corp.

Steering column mounting typical in Cutlass, 88 and 98 models

Steering Column

CHILTON CAUTION: *Disconnect the battery positive cable to insure against accidental deployment of the air cushion restraint system on vehicles so equipped.*

NOTE: Handle the steering column very carefully. Rapping on the end of it or leaning on it could shear off the inserts which allow the column to collapse in a crash.

- Disconnect battery
- Disconnect flexible coupling.
- Remove cover and toe-pan attaching screws.
- If necessary, remove instrument panel lower trim.
- Disconnect shift linkages, wiring, etc.
- Remove lower column mounts, then upper column mounts, and pull column up and out of car.
- When installing, check that flexible coupling alignment is correct.

NOTE: When installing, use only the specified hardware. Over-length bolts could prevent the column from properly collapsing in a crash.

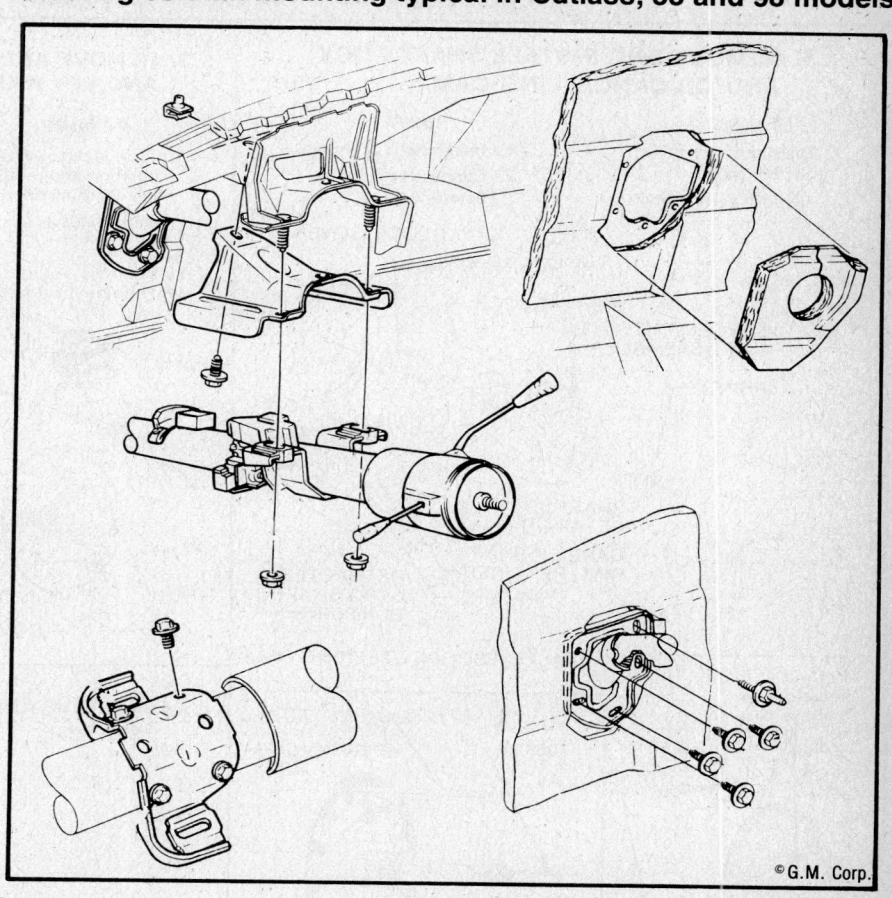

© G.M. Corp.

Toronado steering column mounting

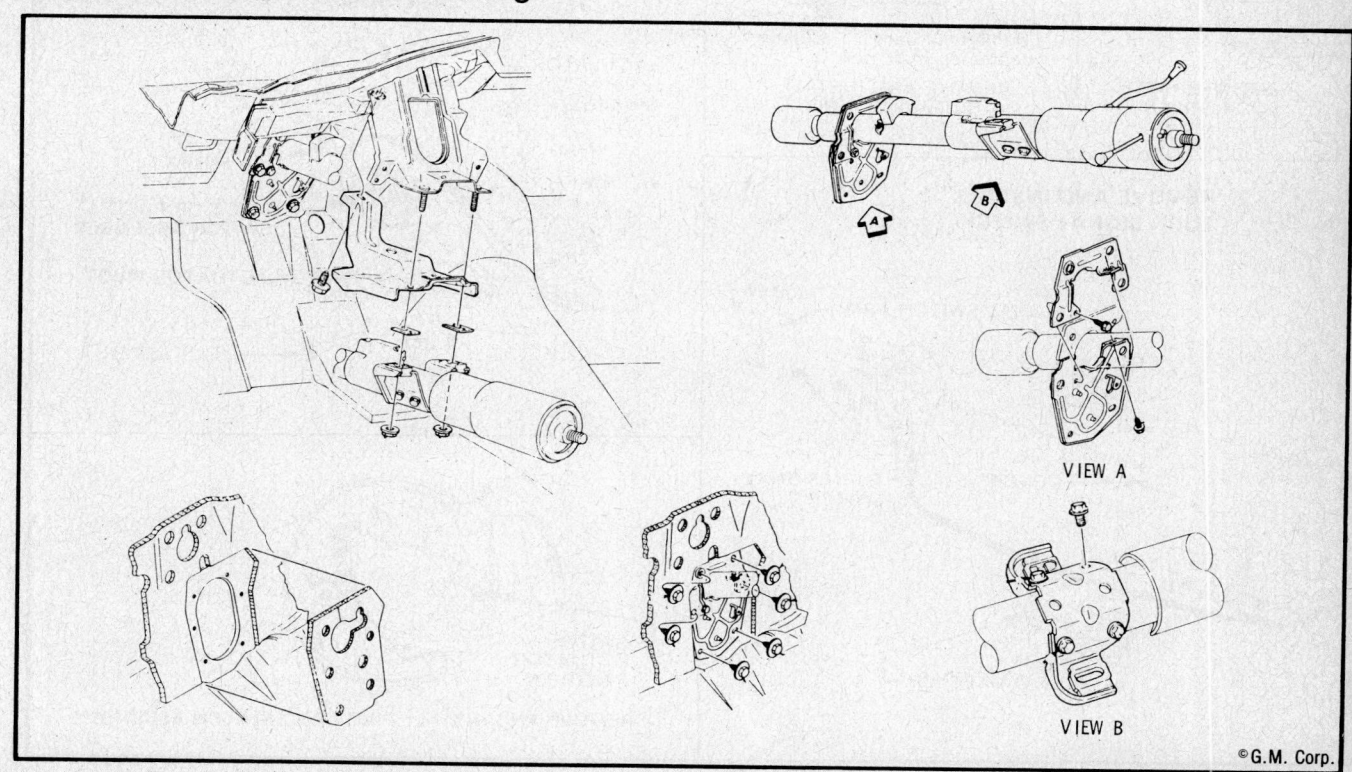

VIEW A

VIEW B

© G.M. Corp.

Steering column and electrical components

1. REMOVE AND INSTALL SHAFT LOCK AND/OR CANCELLING CAM

REMOVE

1. Disconnect negative battery cable.
2. Remove parts as shown.

INSTALL

1. Install parts as shown.
2. Connect negative battery cable.

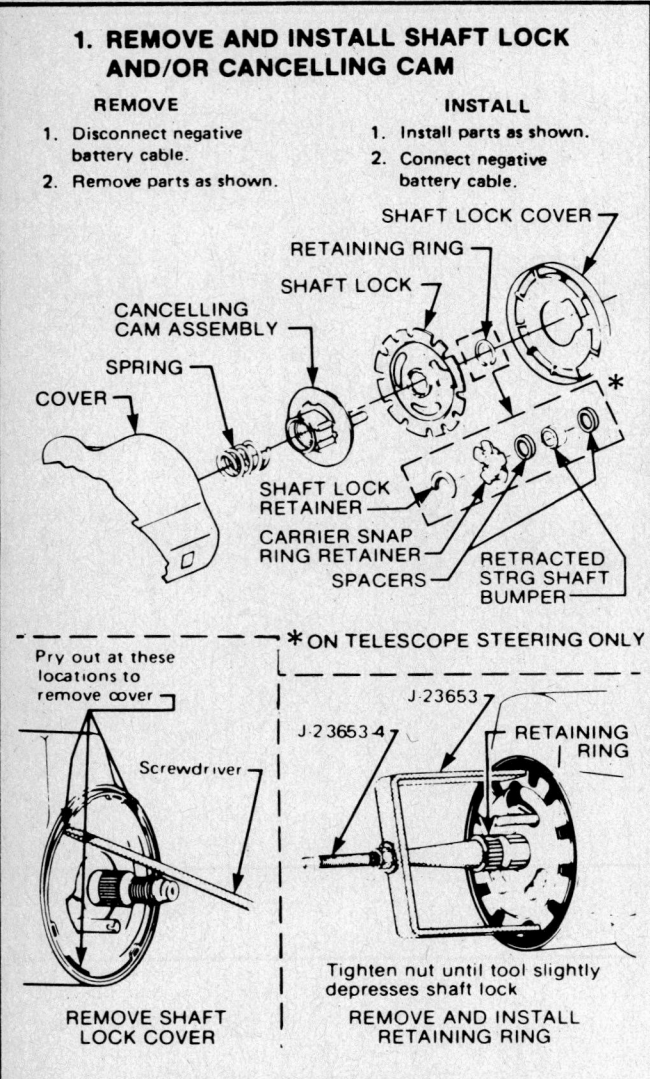

SHAFT LOCK COVER
RETAINING RING
SHAFT LOCK
CANCELLING CAM ASSEMBLY
SPRING
COVER
*
SHAFT LOCK RETAINER
CARRIER SNAP RING RETAINER
SPACERS
RETRACTED STRG SHAFT BUMPER

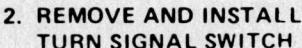

*ON TELESCOPE STEERING ONLY

Pry out at these locations to remove cover
Screwdriver

J-23653-4
J-23653
RETAINING RING

Tighten nut until tool slightly depresses shaft lock

REMOVE SHAFT LOCK COVER

REMOVE AND INSTALL RETAINING RING

2. REMOVE AND INSTALL TURN SIGNAL SWITCH

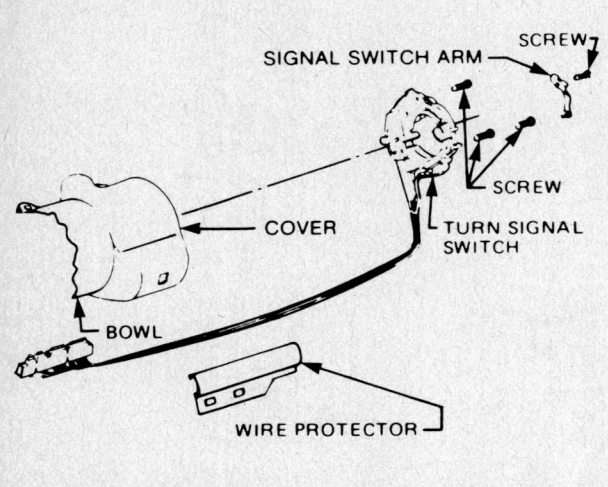

SIGNAL SWITCH ARM
SCREW
SCREW
COVER
TURN SIGNAL SWITCH
BOWL
WIRE PROTECTOR

3. REMOVE AND INSTALL IGNITION LOCK AND KEY WARNING BUZZER

REMOVE

1. Turn lock to "RUN" position and remove key warning buzzer.
2. Remove parts as shown.

To assemble, rotate to stop while holding cylinder

INSTALL

1. Install lock cylinder.
2. Turn lock to "RUN" position and install key warning buzzer switch.

LOCK CYLINDER
LOCK RETAINING SCREW
CLIP
COVER
KEY WARNING BUZZER SWITCH

KEY WARNING BUZZER SWITCH
Paper Clip
REMOVE KEY WARNING BUZZER SWITCH

4. REMOVE AND INSTALL COVER AND WIPER SWITCH

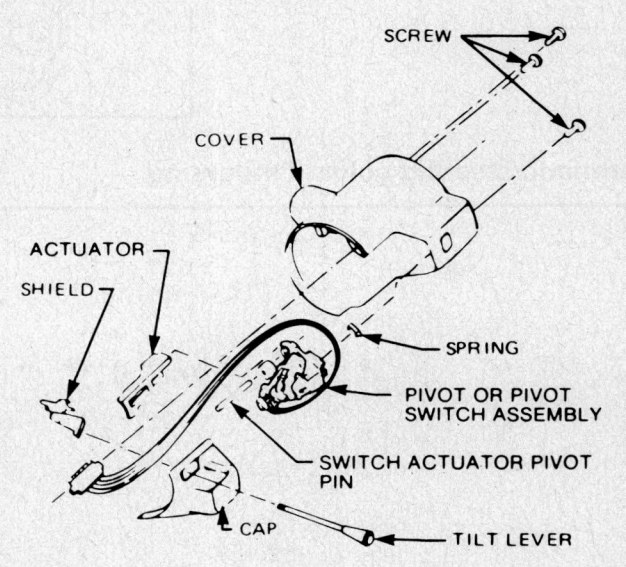

SCREW
COVER
ACTUATOR
SHIELD
SPRING
PIVOT OR PIVOT SWITCH ASSEMBLY
SWITCH ACTUATOR PIVOT PIN
CAP
TILT LEVER

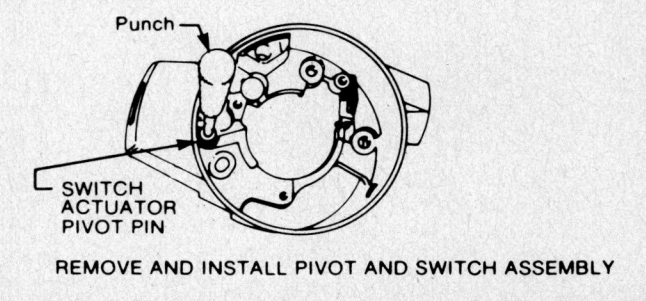

Punch
SWITCH ACTUATOR PIVOT PIN

REMOVE AND INSTALL PIVOT AND SWITCH ASSEMBLY

5. REMOVE AND INSTALL HOUSING

REMOVE

1. Reinstall tilt lever and place column in full "UP" position.
2. Remove tilt spring and pivot pins.
3. Remove housing by pulling upward on tilt lever and pull housing upward until it stops. Move housing to the right to disengage rack from actuator.
4. Remove tilt lever.
5. Remove parts as shown.

INSTALL

1. Install parts as shown.
2. While holding up on tilt lever to disengage lock shoes install over steering shaft. Move rack downward and hold. Tip housing to the left until rack engages pin on actuator rod. Push housing down until pivot pin holes are in alignment.

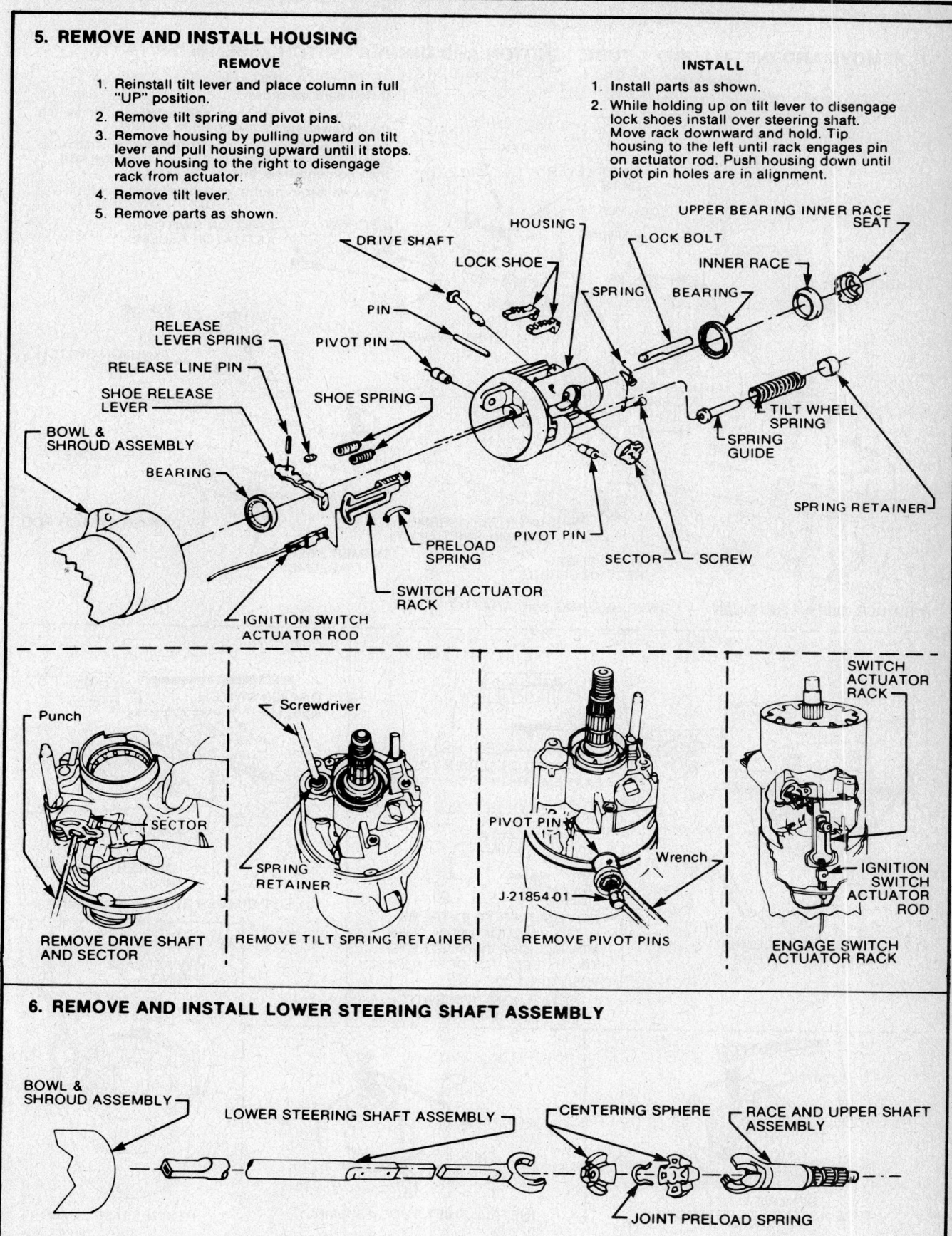

6. REMOVE AND INSTALL LOWER STEERING SHAFT ASSEMBLY

7. REMOVE AND INSTALL SHIFT TUBE, IGNITION AND DIMMER SWITCH ASSEMBLIES

REMOVE

1. Remove parts as shown.

INSTALL

1. Install parts as shown.
2. Position rod in slider hole and install ignition switch. Install lower stud and tighten to 4.0 N·m.
3. Install dimmer switch and depress switch slightly to insert 3/32" drill. Force switch up to remove lash, then tighten screw, and nut to 4.0 N·m.
4. Place shifter in neutral and install shift lever.

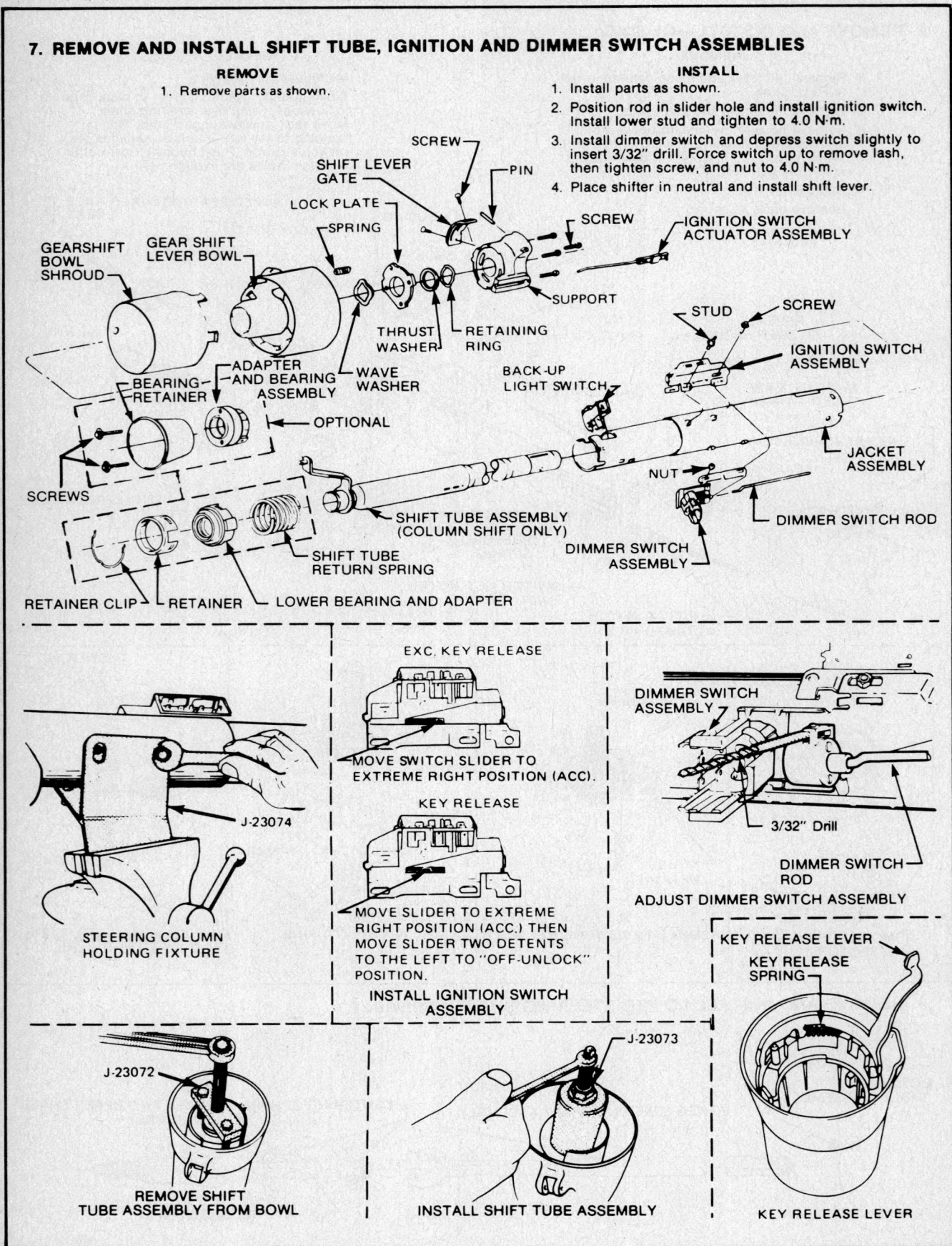

Tilt-away steering column

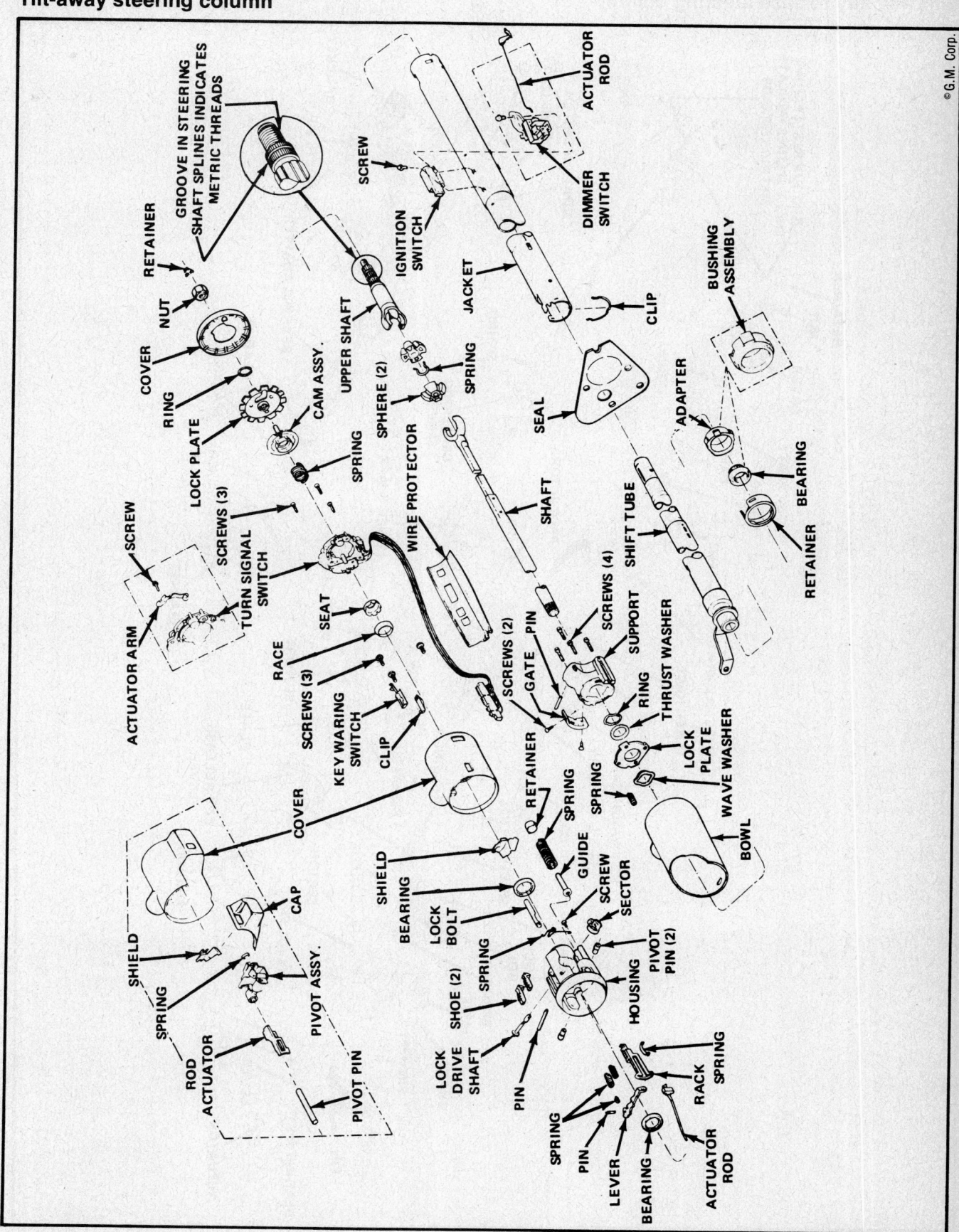

© G. M. Corp.

Tilt-away key release steering column

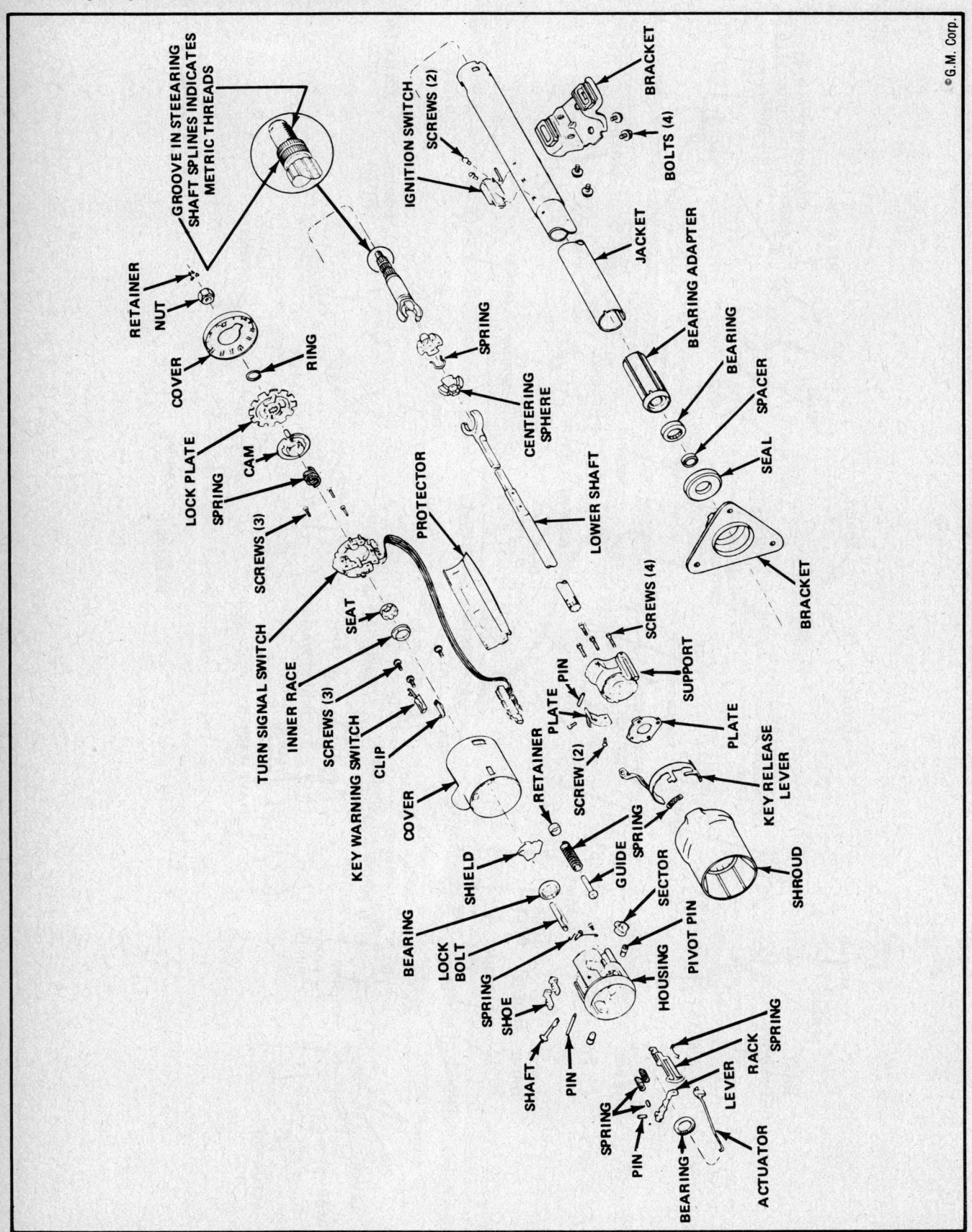

© G.M. Corp.

Brake Power Unit R&R
Vacuum Booster
- Remove the power unit and master cylinder as an assembly after disconnecting vacuum and hydraulic lines and brake pedal push rod.

Hydro-Boost
- With engine off, pump brake pedal four or five times to deplete accumulator of pressurized fluid.
- Separate the power unit from master cylinder, hydraulic lines, firewall and brake pedal rod.

Parking Brake Cable R&R
- Disconnect cables from equalizer.
- For front cable replacement, remove the wheelhouse panel and disconnect cable from parking brake pedal assembly. Route new cable through in place of the old.
- For rear cable replacement, remove brake drum, and separate cable from brake shoes. Route new cable through in place of the old.

Parking Brake Adjustment
Except Rear Disc Brakes
- Correctly adjust service brakes.
- Apply parking brake two notches from fully released position.
- Tighten cable at equalizer until drag is felt at rear wheels.
- Release parking brake lever, and check that rear wheels turn without resistance.

Rear Disc Brakes
- Lubricate the cables at the equalizer hooks and underbody rub points, and check for free movement of all the cables.
- With the parking brake pedal in the fully released position, hold the brake cable stud from turning and tighten the equalizer nut until all slack in the cable is removed.
- Make sure the caliper levers are against the stops on the caliper housing. If the levers are off the stops, loosen the cable until the levers return to the stops.
- Operate the parking brake pedal several times to check the adjustment.
- After adjustment, the parking brake pedal should travel 4-5 inches with about 125 lbs. force.

Vacuum operated brake power unit typical mounting

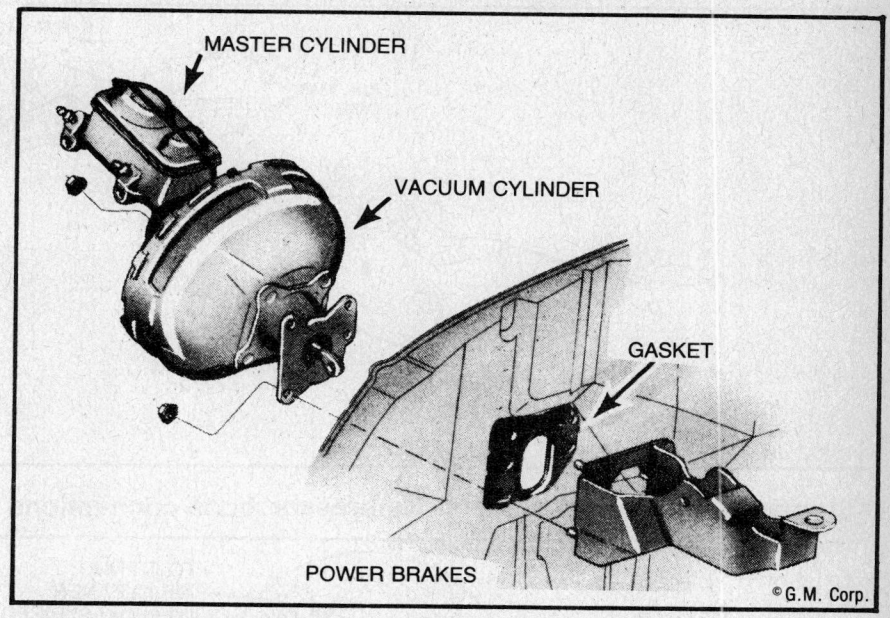

Hydro-Boost brake power unit mounting

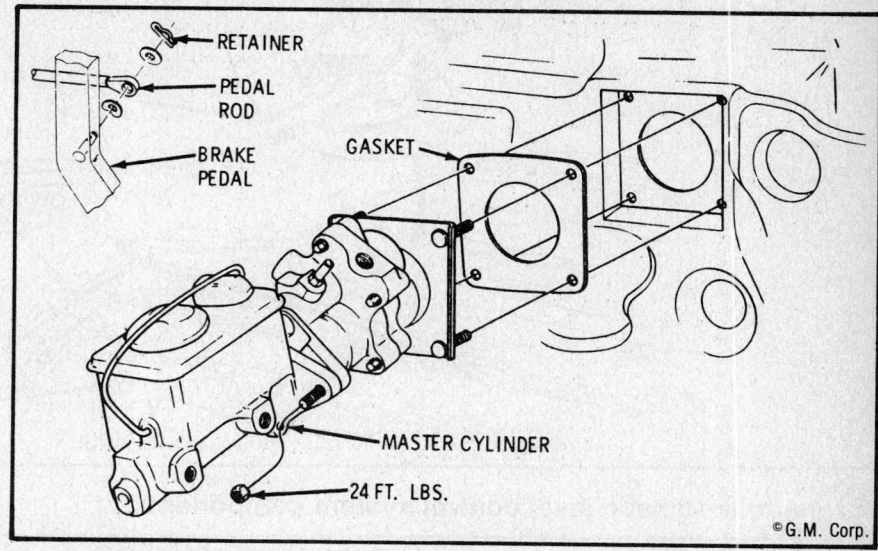

Parking brake cable

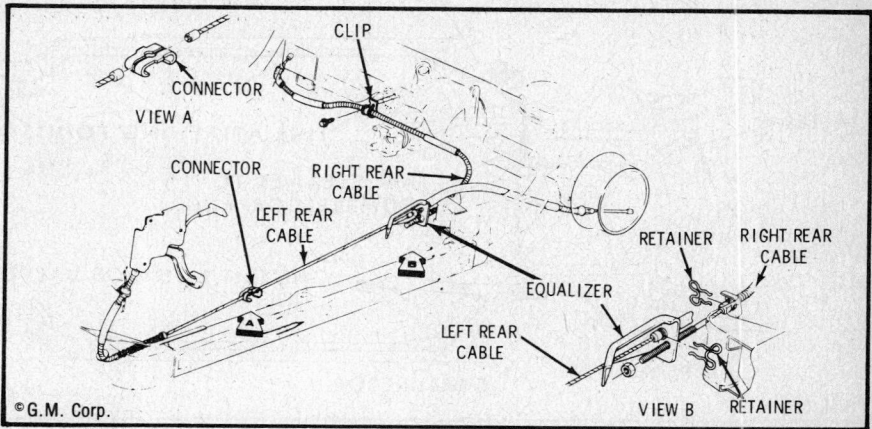

OLDSMOBILE
EXCEPT CIERA, STARFIRE & '80-'82 OMEGA

Toronado parking brake cable routing

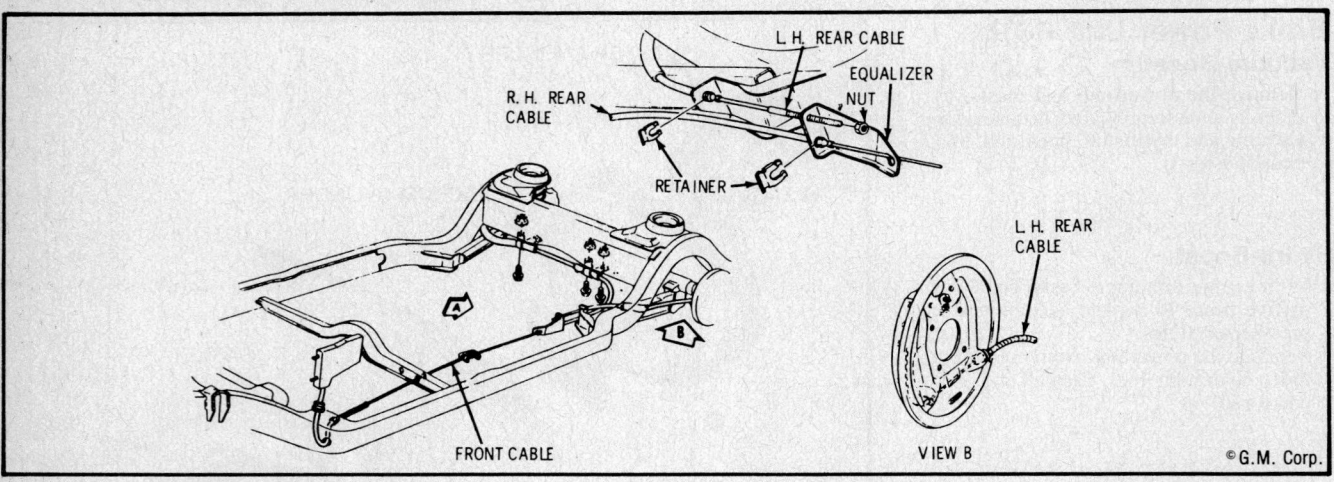

Automatic level control system compressor hose connections

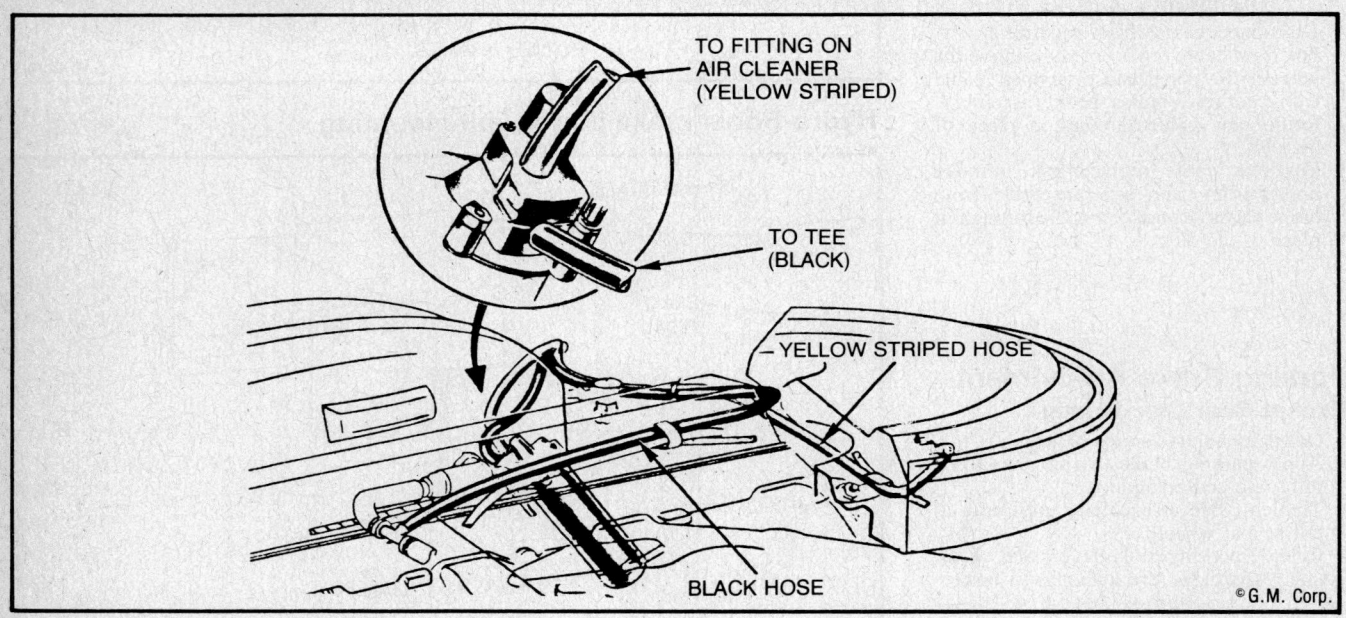

Toronado automatic level control system components

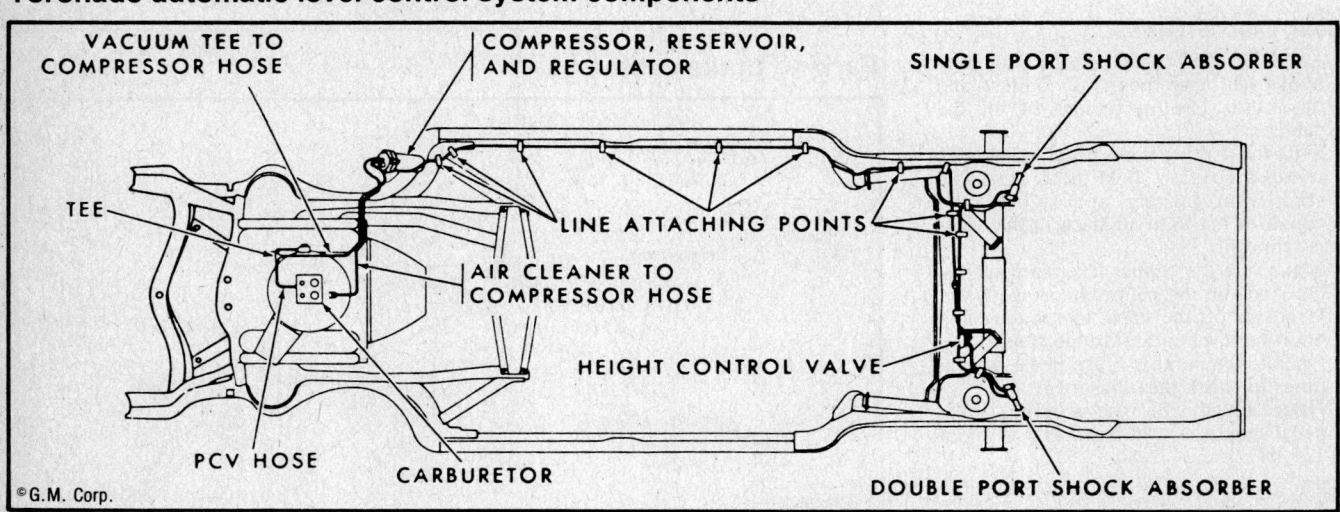

CLUTCH, TRANSMISSION, PROPELLER SHAFT & REAR AXLES SECTION

Clutch Adjustment

- Clutch pedal free play should be approximately 1 inch.

Manual Transmission R&R

- Remove, disconnect, or relocate the following:
  a. Throttle and shift linkages
  b. Propeller shaft
  c. Speedometer cable
  d. Electrical connections
  e. Exhaust plumbing
  f. Crossmember
- Remove mount bolts and slide transmission back and out of the car.

Cutlass clutch lower linkage

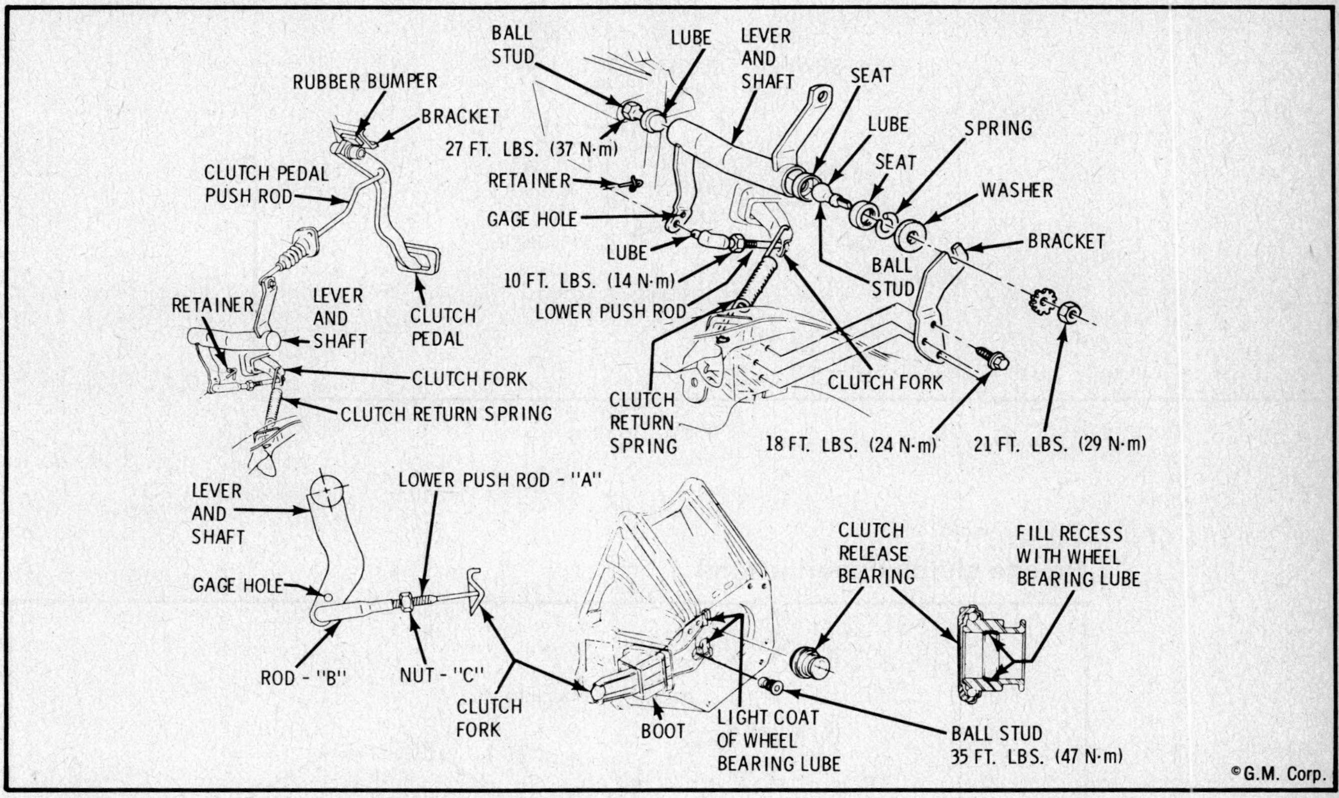

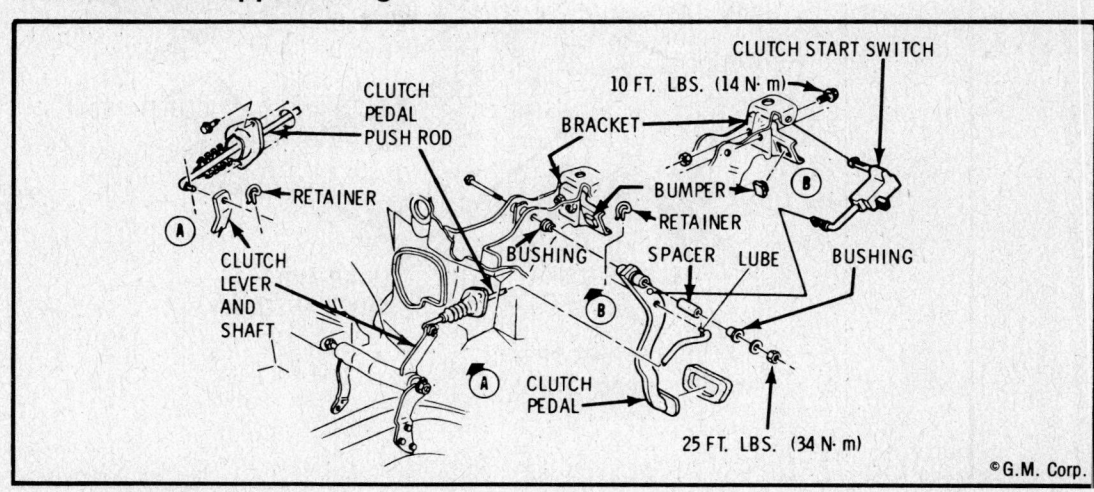

© G.M. Corp.

Cutlass clutch upper linkage

© G.M. Corp.

A625

Omega clutch lower linkage

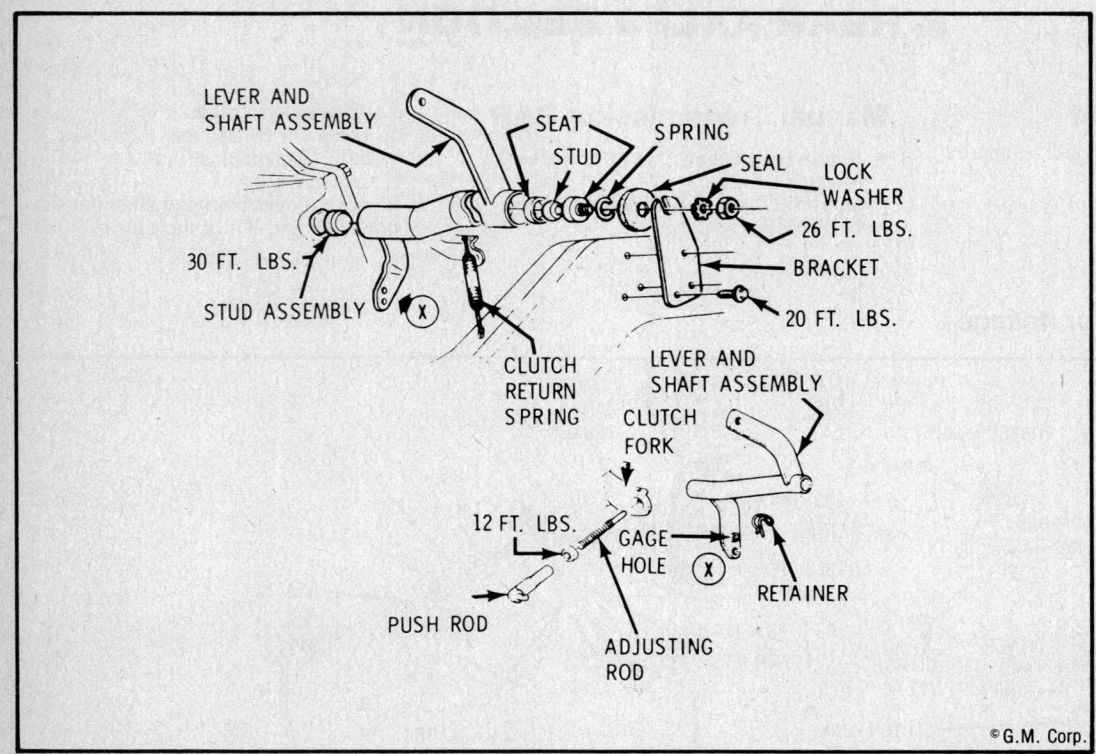

Omega clutch upper linkage

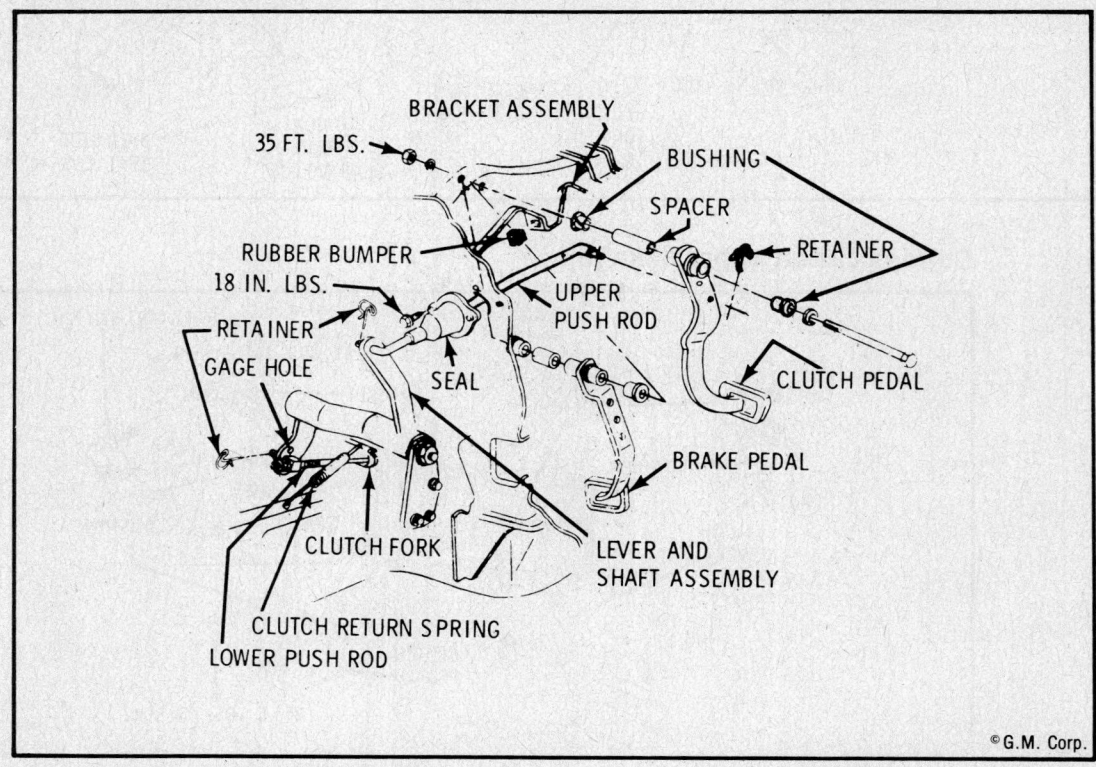

Manual Transmission Linkage Adjustment

- Adjust the linkages so the shift lever positions correspond exactly to the transmission positions.
- Adjustment holes are provided in most shift assemblies through which drill rods can be placed for exact adjustment.

Cutlass manual transmission shift linkage

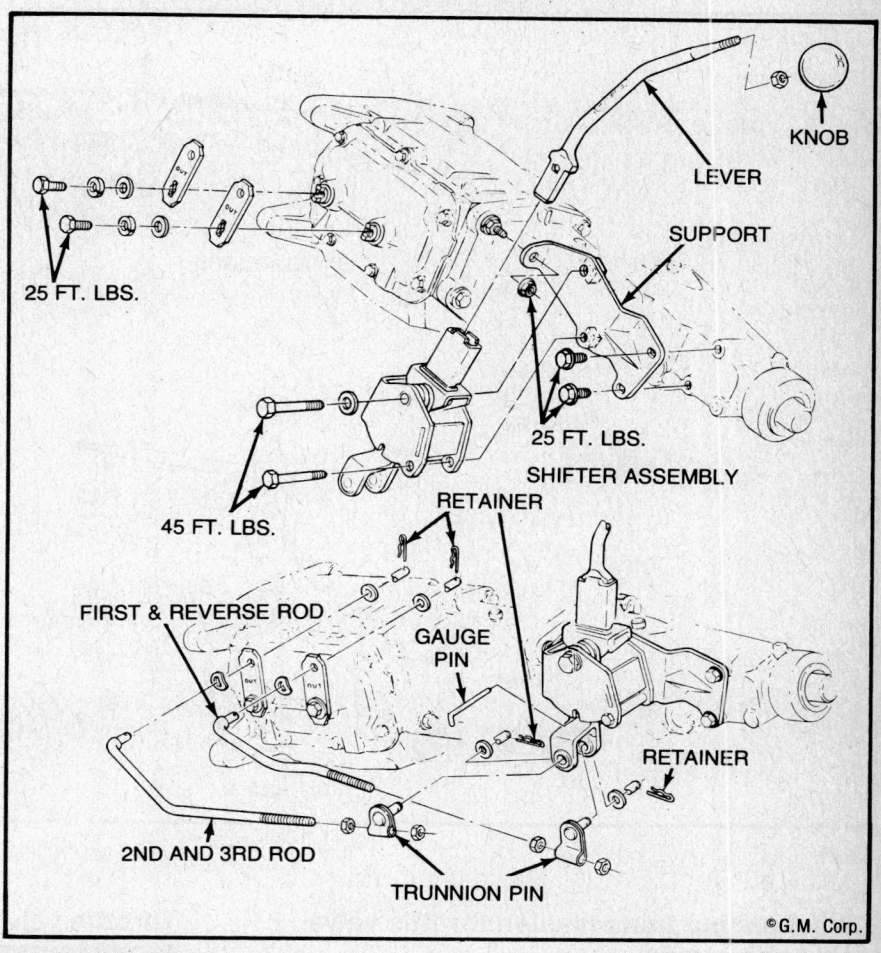

Omega manual transmission column shift linkage

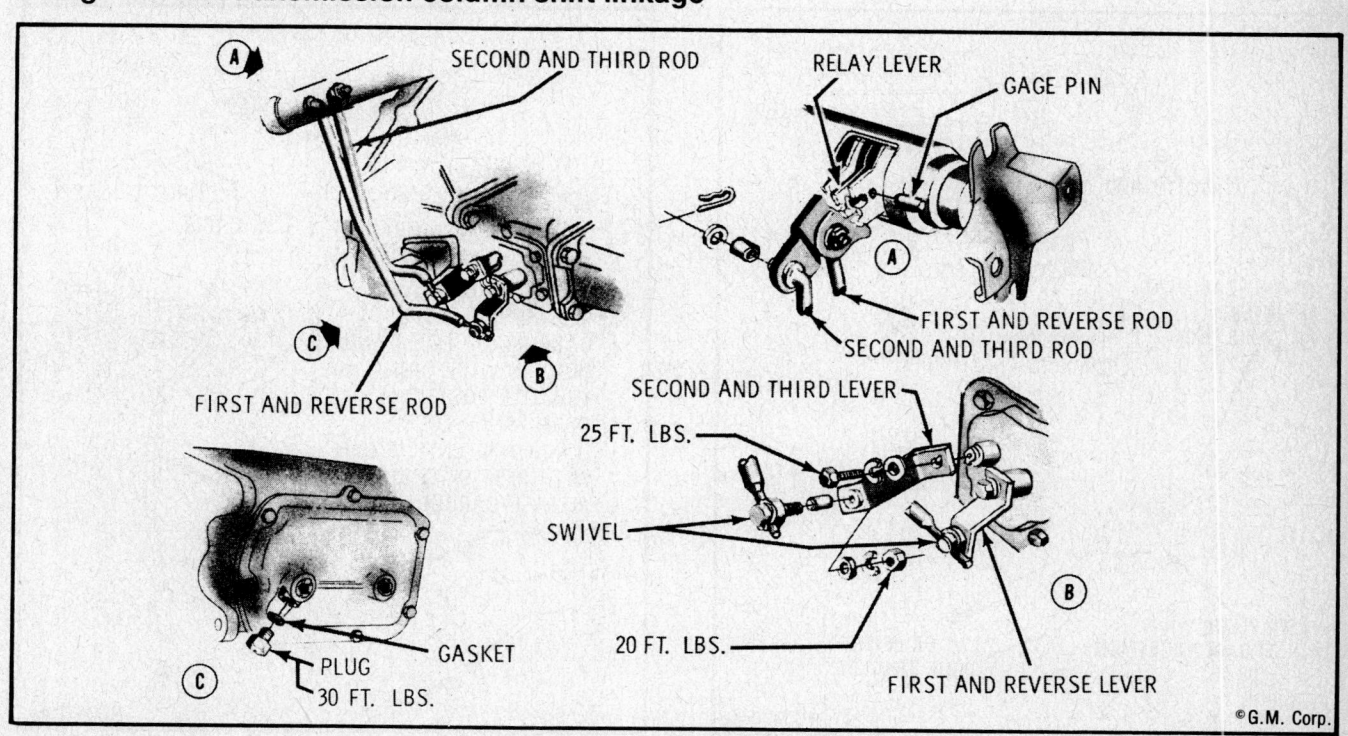

OLDSMOBILE
EXCEPT CIERA, STARFIRE & '80-'82 OMEGA

Cutlass four speed manual transmission shift linkage

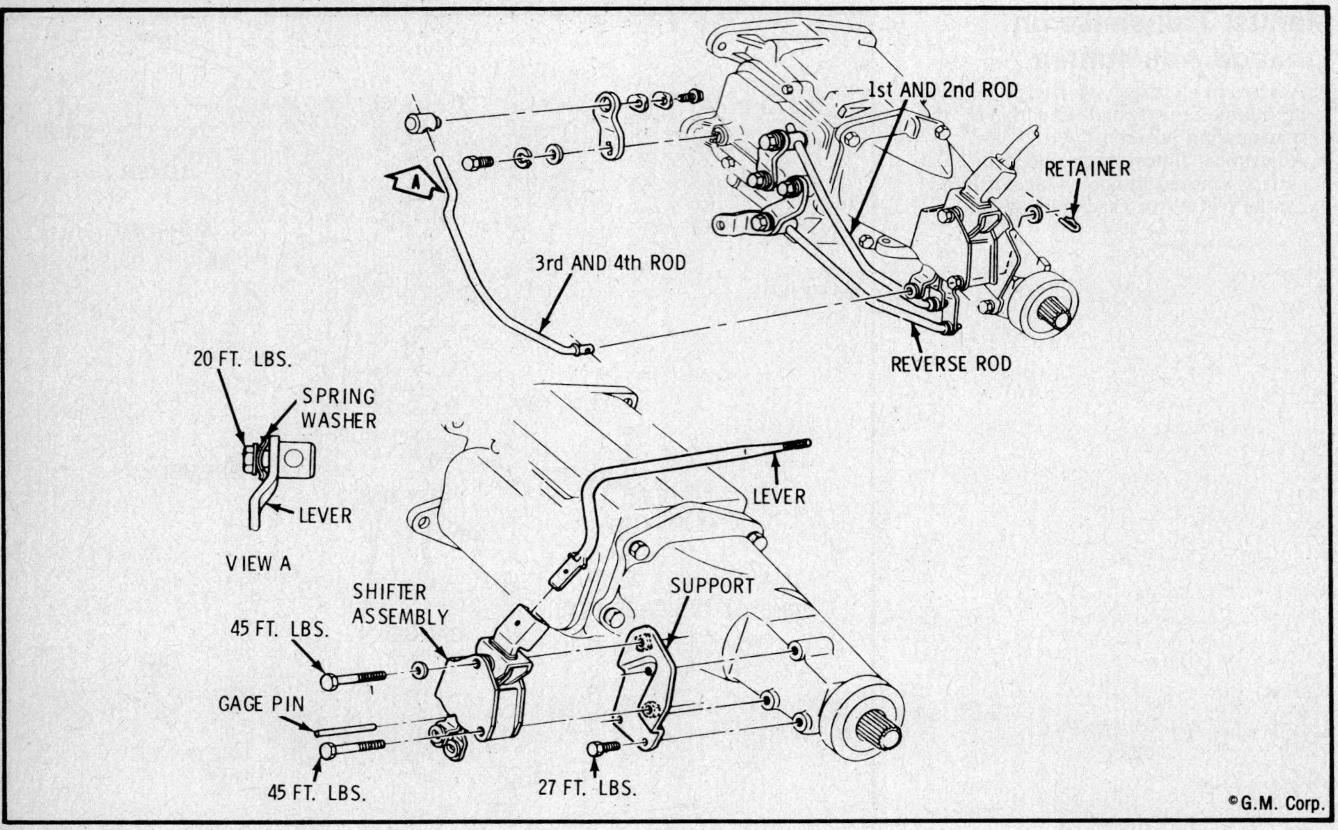

1st AND 2nd ROD

RETAINER

3rd AND 4th ROD

REVERSE ROD

20 FT. LBS.

SPRING WASHER

LEVER

LEVER

VIEW A

SHIFTER ASSEMBLY

SUPPORT

45 FT. LBS.

GAGE PIN

45 FT. LBS.

27 FT. LBS.

© G.M. Corp.

Diesel engine transmission throttle valve cable adjustment

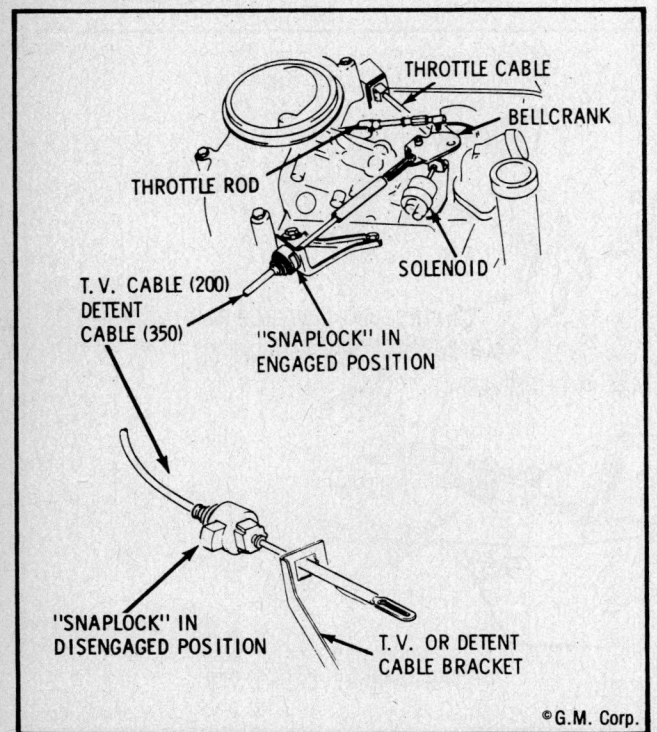

THROTTLE CABLE

BELLCRANK

THROTTLE ROD

SOLENOID

T. V. CABLE (200)
DETENT CABLE (350)

"SNAPLOCK" IN ENGAGED POSITION

"SNAPLOCK" IN DISENGAGED POSITION

T. V. OR DETENT CABLE BRACKET

© G.M. Corp.

Throttle valve cable adjustment with 200 series transmission

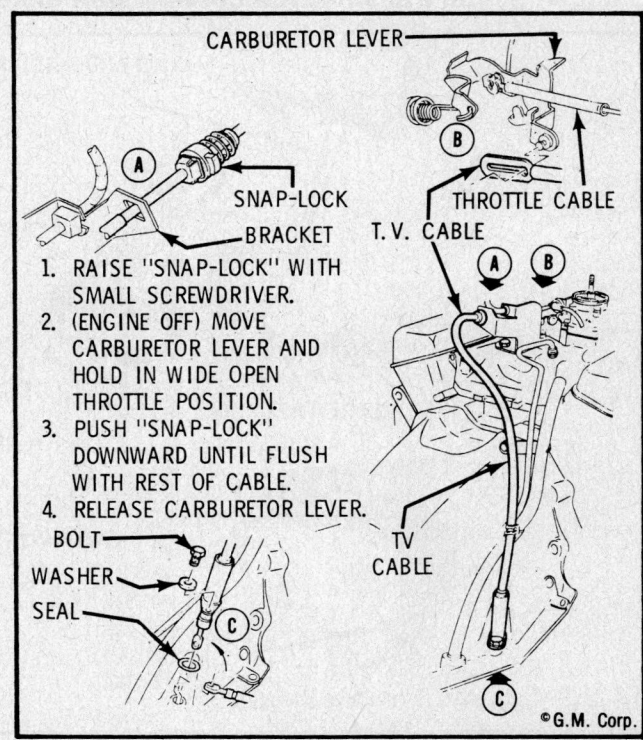

CARBURETOR LEVER

Ⓐ

Ⓑ

SNAP-LOCK

THROTTLE CABLE

BRACKET

T. V. CABLE

Ⓐ Ⓑ

1. RAISE "SNAP-LOCK" WITH SMALL SCREWDRIVER.
2. (ENGINE OFF) MOVE CARBURETOR LEVER AND HOLD IN WIDE OPEN THROTTLE POSITION.
3. PUSH "SNAP-LOCK" DOWNWARD UNTIL FLUSH WITH REST OF CABLE.
4. RELEASE CARBURETOR LEVER.

BOLT

WASHER

SEAL

Ⓒ

TV CABLE

Ⓒ

© G.M. Corp.

Automatic Transmission Cable Detent Adjustment

- Disengage the snap lock, and position the carburetor in the full open position.
- Push the snap lock on the cable down until the top is flush with the cable.

Automatic Transmission R&R
Except Front Wheel Drive

- Disconnect the battery.
- Disconnect detent cable (if so equipped) from accelerator lever or carburetor.
- Remove, disconnect or relocate any of the following necessary for removal:
  - a. Exhaust crossover pipe
  - b. Drive Shaft
  - c. Oil cooler lines
  - d. Transmission crossmember (support engine and transmission as needed)
  - e. Speedometer cable
  - f. Shift linkage
  - g. Electrical connections
  - h. Flywheel cover pan
- Mark flywheel and converter for installation reference.
- Remove mounting bolts, and slide transmission back and out of vehicle.

NOTE: Transmission and torque converter are removed as an assembly.

Front Wheel Drive

- Disconnect the battery, and remove, disconnect or relocate the following:
  - a. Filler tube
  - b. Speedometer cable
  - c. Electrical and vacuum leads
  - d. Oil cooler tubes
  - e. Starter
  - f. Converter cover plate
  - g. Shift linkage
- Remove mount bolts to separate transmission from the engine and final drive unit, and remove the transmission. As required, disconnect engine mounts and pry engine back for clearance.

Automatic transmission (400 series) mounting

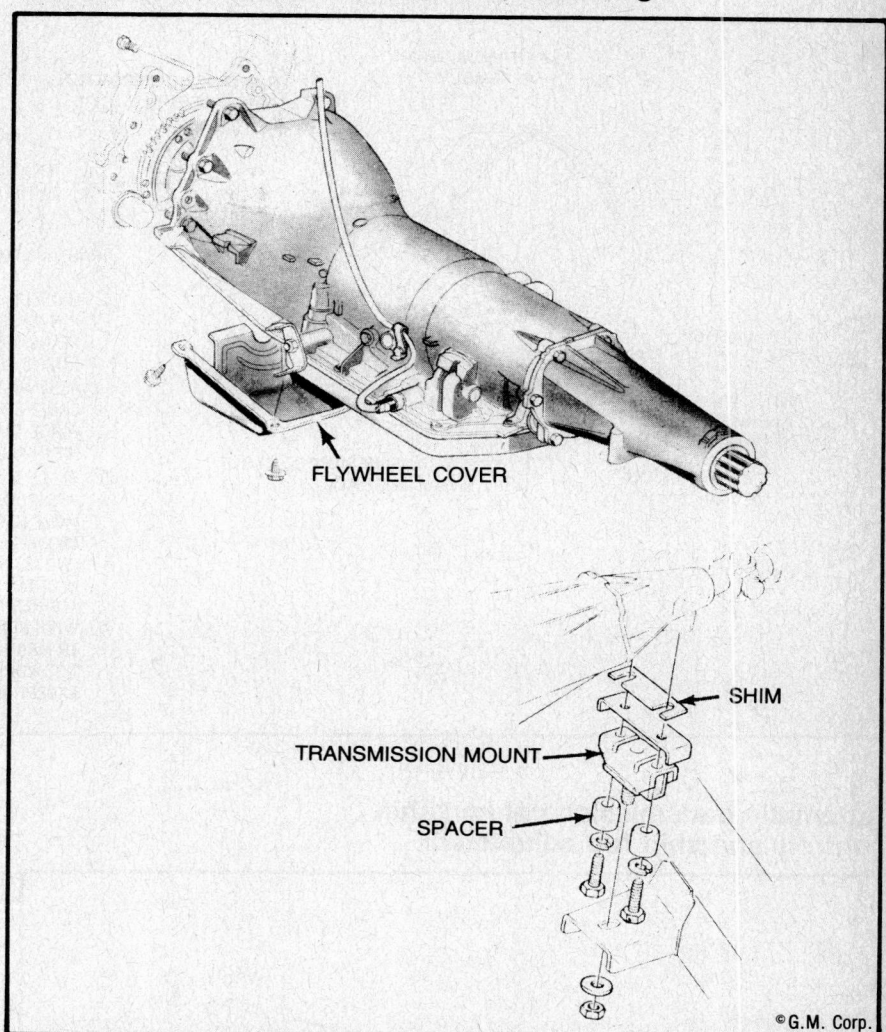

FLYWHEEL COVER

SHIM

TRANSMISSION MOUNT

SPACER

© G.M. Corp.

Toronado transmission-to-engine mounting

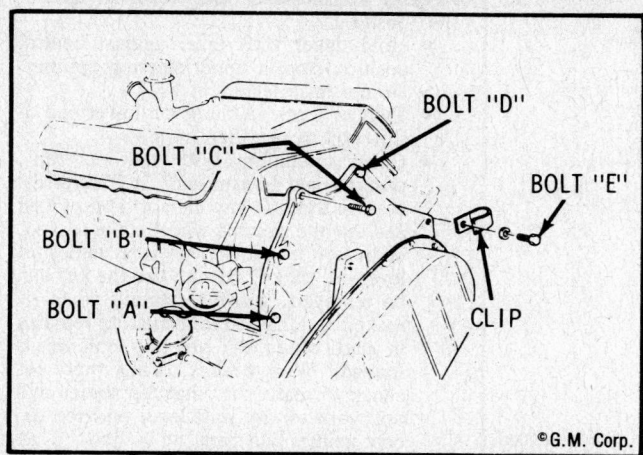

BOLT "D"

BOLT "C"

BOLT "E"

BOLT "B"

BOLT "A"

CLIP

© G.M. Corp.

Toronado transmission mount

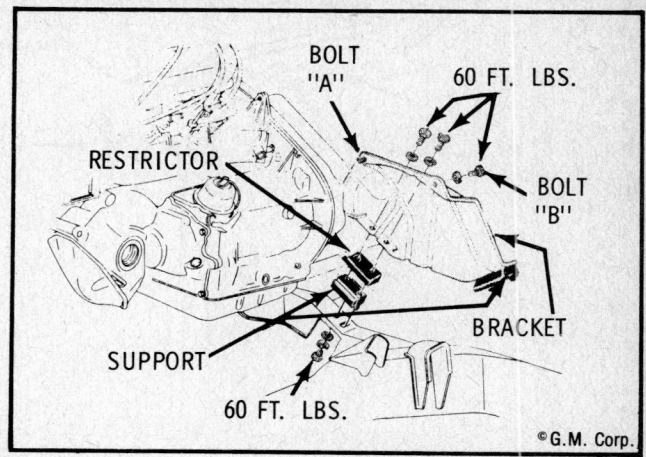

BOLT "A"

60 FT. LBS.

RESTRICTOR

BOLT "B"

BRACKET

SUPPORT

60 FT. LBS.

© G.M. Corp.

A629

Automatic transmission console shift linkage and control cable adjustment

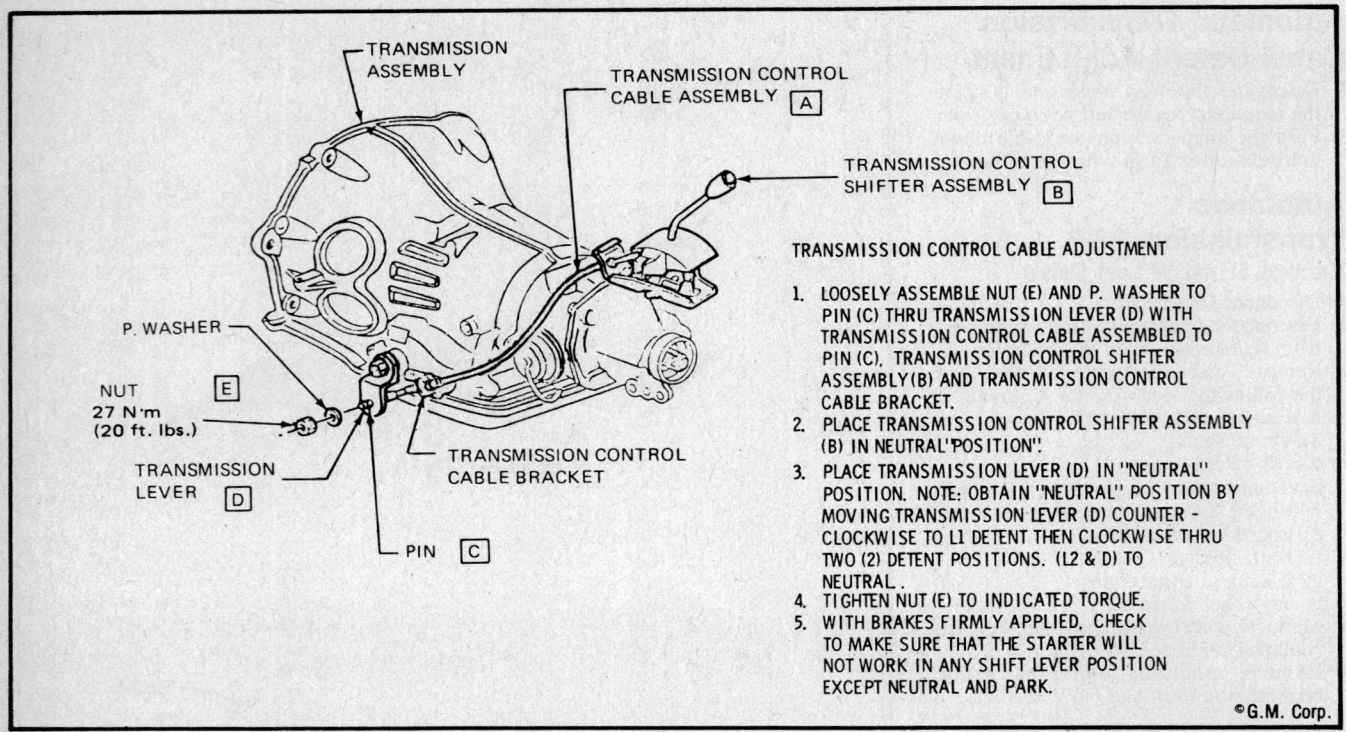

TRANSMISSION CONTROL CABLE ADJUSTMENT

1. LOOSELY ASSEMBLE NUT (E) AND P. WASHER TO PIN (C) THRU TRANSMISSION LEVER (D) WITH TRANSMISSION CONTROL CABLE ASSEMBLED TO PIN (C), TRANSMISSION CONTROL SHIFTER ASSEMBLY (B) AND TRANSMISSION CONTROL CABLE BRACKET.
2. PLACE TRANSMISSION CONTROL SHIFTER ASSEMBLY (B) IN NEUTRAL "POSITION".
3. PLACE TRANSMISSION LEVER (D) IN "NEUTRAL" POSITION. NOTE: OBTAIN "NEUTRAL" POSITION BY MOVING TRANSMISSION LEVER (D) COUNTER - CLOCKWISE TO L1 DETENT THEN CLOCKWISE THRU TWO (2) DETENT POSITIONS. (L2 & D) TO NEUTRAL.
4. TIGHTEN NUT (E) TO INDICATED TORQUE.
5. WITH BRAKES FIRMLY APPLIED, CHECK TO MAKE SURE THAT THE STARTER WILL NOT WORK IN ANY SHIFT LEVER POSITION EXCEPT NEUTRAL AND PARK.

©G.M. Corp.

Automatic transmission column shift controls and shift rod adjustment

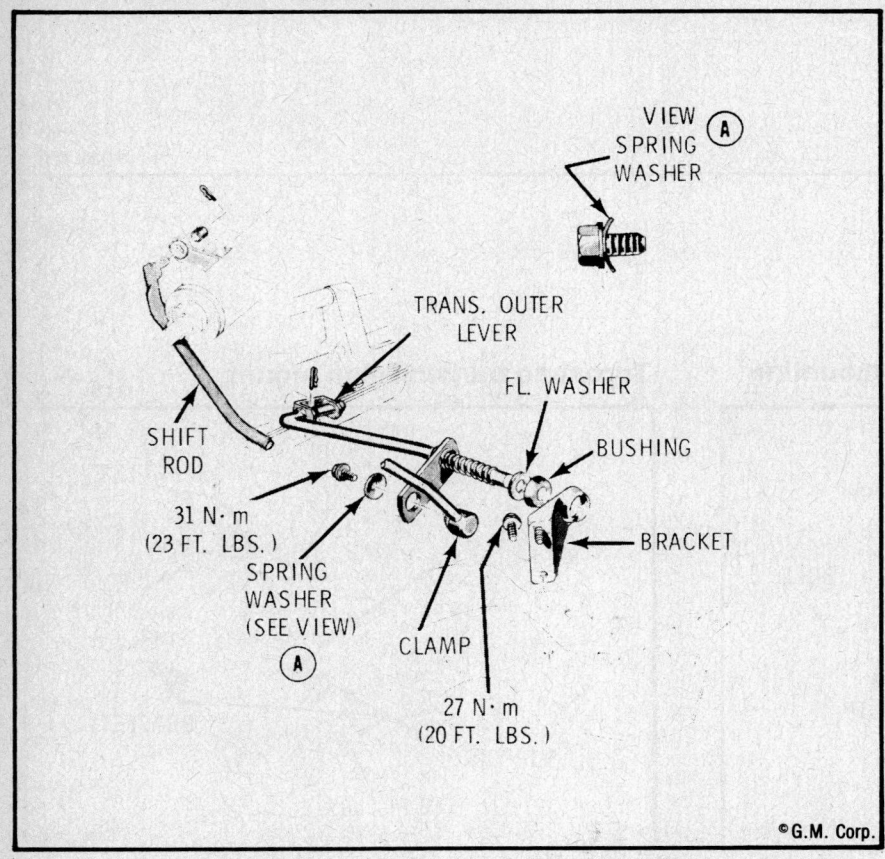

©G.M. Corp.

Automatic Transmission Manual Linkage Adjustment
- Adjust the linkage so the shift lever positions correspond exactly to the transmission positions.
- Some linkage arrangements have adjustment gage pin holes. In these a free pin fit will insure proper adjustment.
- After linkage adjustment, check operation of the neutral start switch, backup lights and automatic parking brake release.

Shift Rod Adjustment
- With shift rod clamp screw loosened, set transmission outer lever in neutral position.
- Hold upper shift lever against neutral position stop in upper steering column. Do not raise lever.
- Tighten screw in clamp on lower end of shift rod to specified torque.
- Check operation: With key in "run" position and transmission in "reverse" be sure that the key cannot be removed and that the steering wheel is not locked. With key in "lock" position and shift lever in "park", be sure that the key can be removed, that the steering wheel is locked and that the transmission remains in park when the steering column is locked. With brakes firmly applied, check to make sure that the starter will not work in any shift lever position except neutral and park.

Automatic transmission console shift cable and adjustment

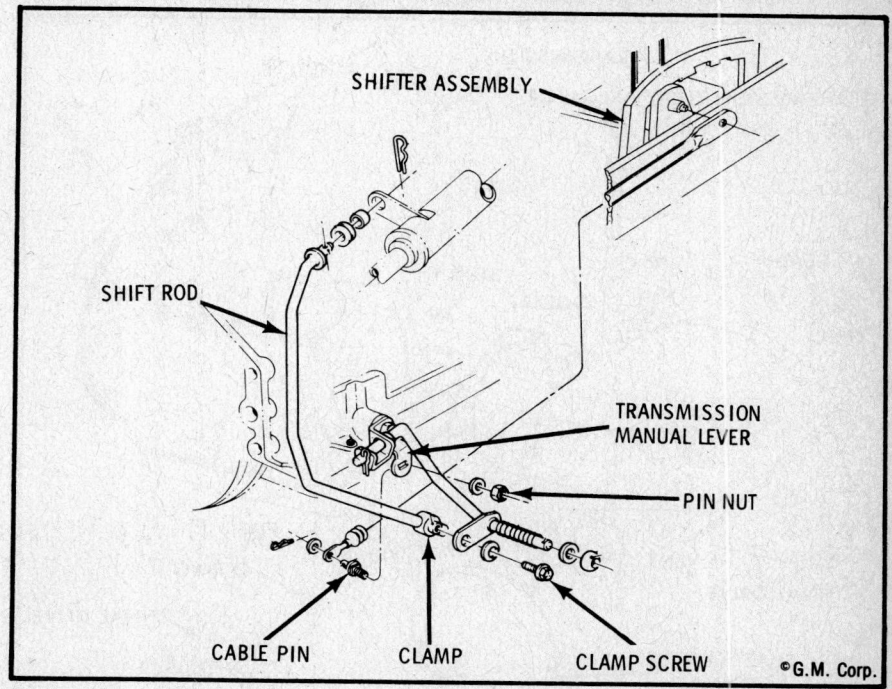

© G.M. Corp.

Shift Cable Adjustment

- Loosen shift rod clamp screw, loosen pin in transmission manual lever.
- Place shift lever in "park" position. Place transmission manual lever in "park" position and ignition key in lock position.
- Tighten cable pin nut to 20 ft. lbs.
- Rotate the transmission manual lever fully against the "park" stop, then release the lever.
- Pull shift rod down against lock stop to eliminate lash and tighten clamp screw to 20 ft. lbs.
- Check operation: Move shift handle into each gear position and see that transmission manual lever is also in detent position. With key in "run" position and transmission in "reverse" be sure that the key cannot be removed and that steering wheel is not locked. With key in "lock" position and transmission in "park", be sure that key can be removed and that steering wheel is locked. Engine must start in park and neutral. With brakes firmly applied, check to make sure that the starter will not work in any shift lever position except neutral and park.

Toronado shift linkage and adjustment

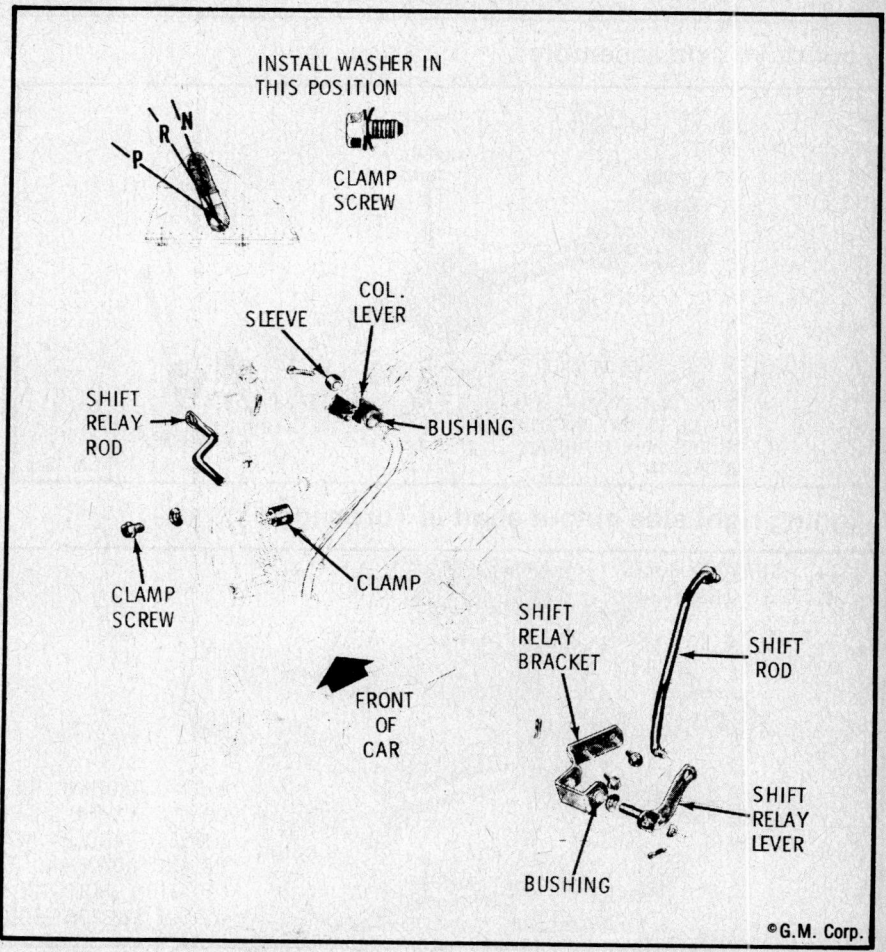

© G.M. Corp.

Shift Linkage and Adjustment
Toronado

- Loosen clamp screw and be sure rod is free to slide in clamp.
- Place upper shift lever against neutral stop in steering column. A detent will hold it there.
- Set transmission outer lever in neutral position.
- Tighten clamp screw to 20 ft. lbs.
- Check operation: With key in "run" position and transmission in "reverse" be sure that the key cannot be removed and that the steering wheel is not locked. With key in "lock" position and shift lever in "park" be sure that key can be removed, that steering wheel is locked, and that the upper shift lever cannot be removed from "park". With brakes firmly applied, check to make sure that the starter will not work in any shift lever position except neutral and park.

OLDSMOBILE
EXCEPT CIERA, STARFIRE & '80-'82 OMEGA

Final drive differential mounting

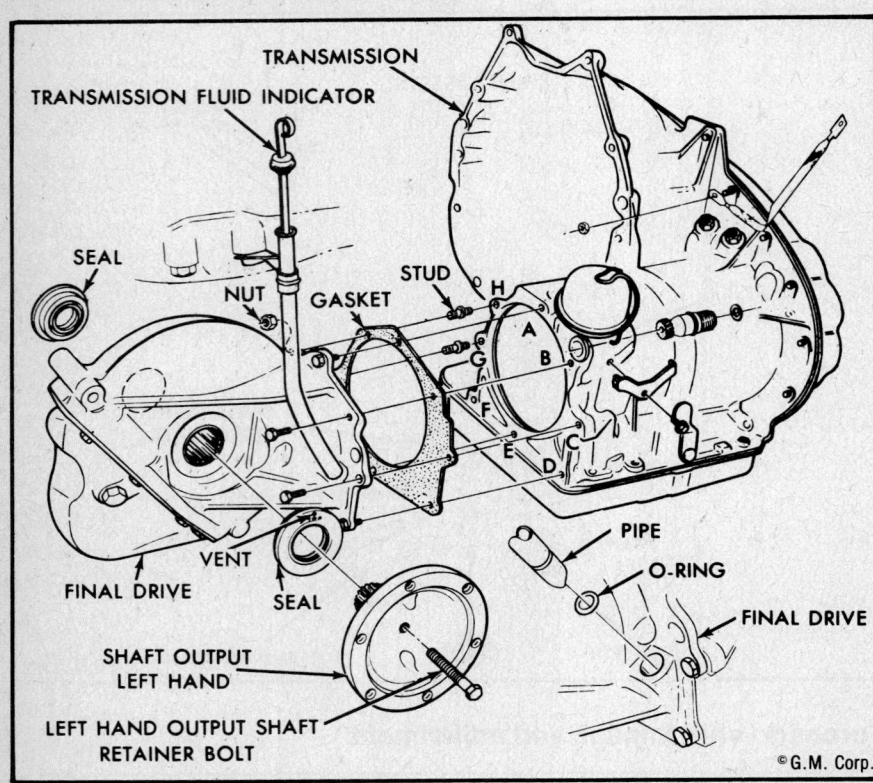

TRANSMISSION
TRANSMISSION FLUID INDICATOR
SEAL
NUT
GASKET
STUD
H
G
A
B
F
E
D
C
SEAL
VENT
FINAL DRIVE
PIPE
O-RING
FINAL DRIVE
SHAFT OUTPUT LEFT HAND
LEFT HAND OUTPUT SHAFT RETAINER BOLT
© G.M. Corp.

Front drive axle assembly

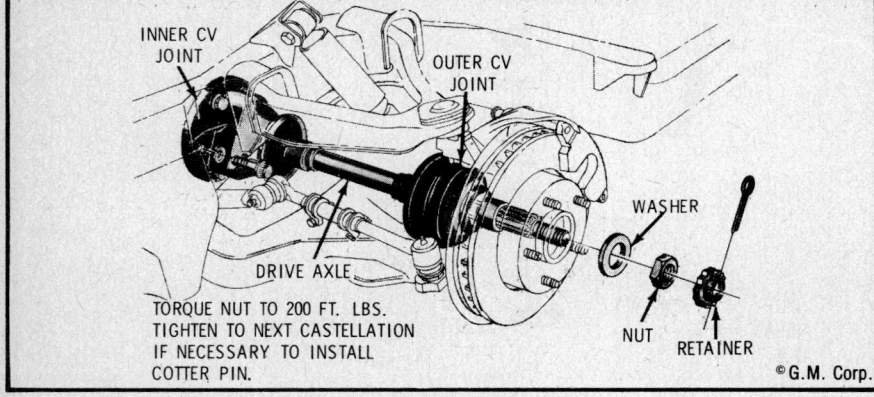

INNER CV JOINT
OUTER CV JOINT
WASHER
DRIVE AXLE
NUT
RETAINER
TORQUE NUT TO 200 FT. LBS. TIGHTEN TO NEXT CASTELLATION IF NECESSARY TO INSTALL COTTER PIN.
© G.M. Corp.

Aligning right side output shaft in Toronado

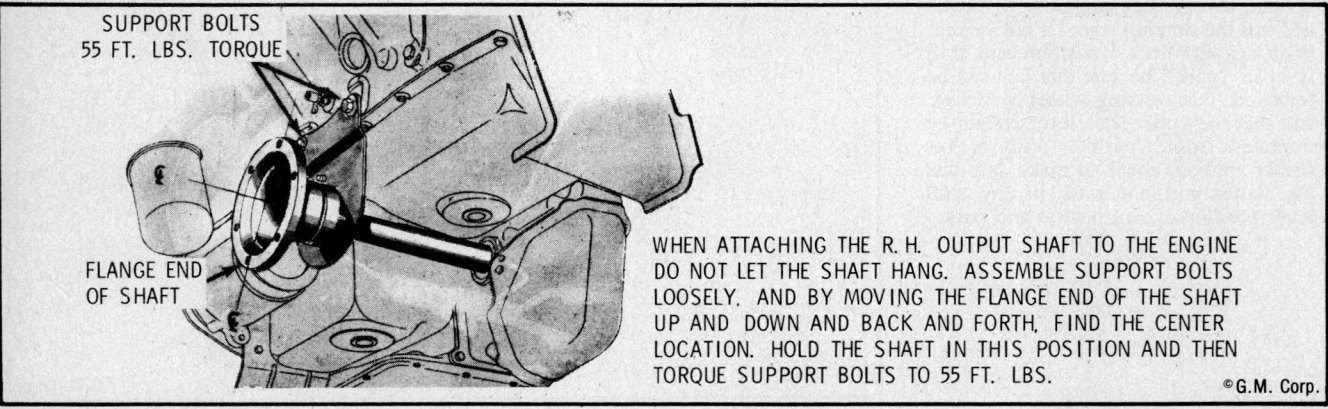

SUPPORT BOLTS 55 FT. LBS. TORQUE
FLANGE END OF SHAFT
WHEN ATTACHING THE R. H. OUTPUT SHAFT TO THE ENGINE DO NOT LET THE SHAFT HANG. ASSEMBLE SUPPORT BOLTS LOOSELY, AND BY MOVING THE FLANGE END OF THE SHAFT UP AND DOWN AND BACK AND FORTH, FIND THE CENTER LOCATION. HOLD THE SHAFT IN THIS POSITION AND THEN TORQUE SUPPORT BOLTS TO 55 FT. LBS.
© G.M. Corp.

Pinion Oil Seal
- Scribe a line down the pinion stem, nut and flange, and count the number of exposed pinion stem threads. After replacing the seal, install these components in their exact original locations.

Final Drive Differential
NOTE: The final drive differential is serviced by replacement only. Overhaul is never recommended.

- Disconnect the battery, and remove, disconnect or relocate the following:
  a. Transmission filler tube
  b. Transmission oil cooler lines
  c. Final drive support brace
  d. Right hand output shaft
  e. Steering or suspension linkage
- Remove the final drive-to-transmission mount bolts, and remove the final drive.

Drive Axles

Right Drive Axle
- Raise and support the car at the control arms, and remove the drive axle nut.
- Remove the oil filter.
- Remove the inner constant velocity joint attaching bolts, and push the joint outward enough to disengage from final drive output shaft.
- Remove output shaft and drive axle assembly.

Left Drive Axle
- Raise and support the car at the control arms, and remove the drive axle nut.
- Disconnect tie rod end from spindle.
- Remove drive axle assembly-to-output shaft bolts.
- Separate upper ball joint from the steering knuckle, and remove the steering knuckle.
- Remove the shock absorber.
- Remove the drive axle assembly.

INDEX

PONTIAC
EXCEPT ASTRE, A6000, '80-'82 PHOENIX & T1000

MODEL IDENTIFICATION

1976 CATALINA
W.B. 123.4″, S/W & Gr. Safari 127″.
Length 226″, S/W & Gr. Safari 232″.
Ship. Wgt. V8 2 Dr. 4256 Lbs.

1977 CATALINA
W.B. 115.9″. Length 215″. Width 76″.
Ship. Wgt. V8 2 Dr. 4266 Lbs.

1978 CATALINA
W.B. 115.9″ Length 214.3″ Ship. Wgt. 8
Cyl. 2 Dr. 3430.68 Lbs.

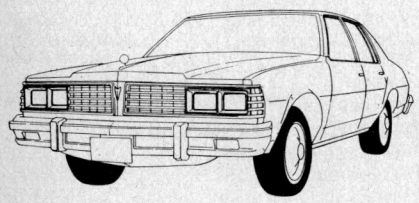

1979 CATALINA
W.B. 115.9″ Length 214.3″ Ship. Wgt. 8
Cyl. 2 Dr. 3430 Lbs.

1980 CATALINA
W.B. 115.9″. Length 214.3″. Ship. Wgt. 8
Cyl. 2 Dr. Approx. 3328 Lbs.

1981 CATALINA
W.B. 116.0″. Length 214.0″. 6 Cyl. 2 Dr.
Curb Wgt. 2968 Lbs.

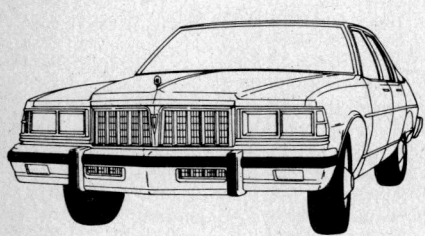

1978 BONNEVILLE
W.B. 115.9″ Length 214.3 Ship. Wgt. 8
Cyl. 2 Dr. 3573 Lbs.

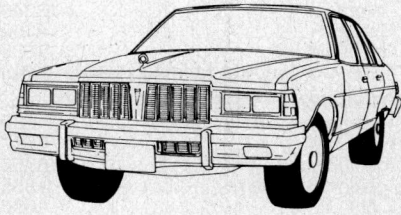

1979 BONNEVILLE
W.B. 115.9″ Length 214.3″ Ship. Wgt. 8
Cyl. 2 Dr. 3573 Lbs.

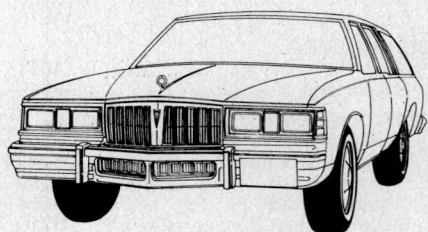

1980 BONNEVILLE
W.B. 115.9″. Length 214″. Ship. Wgt. 2
Dr. Approx. 3470 Lbs.

1981 BONNEVILLE
W.B. 116.0″. Length 216.7″. 6 Cyl. 2 Dr.
Curb Wgt. 3003.5 Lbs.

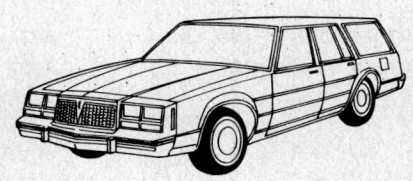

1982 BONNEVILLE
W.B. 108.1″. Length 198.6″. V6 Cyl. 4
Dr. Curb Wgt. 3003 Lbs.

1976 FIREBIRD
W.B. 108.1″. Length 196″. Ship. Wgt. 6
Cyl. 2 Dr. 3383 Lbs. V8 2 Dr. 3563 Lbs.

A634

1977 FIREBIRD
W.B. 108.1". Length 197". Width 73". Ship. Wgt. 6 Cyl. 2 Dr. 3274 Lbs. V8 2 Dr. 4977 Lbs.

1978 FIREBIRD
W.B. 108.1" Length 196.8" Ship. Wgt. 8 Cyl. 2 Dr. 3254 Lbs.

1979 FIREBIRD
W.B. 108.1" Length 196.8" Ship. Wgt. 8 Cyl. 2 Dr. 3254 Lbs.

1980 FIREBIRD
W.B. 108.1". Length 196.8". Ship. Wgt. Approx. 3250 Lbs.

1981 FIREBIRD
W.B. 108.2". Length 198.1". 6 Cyl. 2 Dr. Curb Wgt. 3385 Lbs.

1982 FIREBIRD
W.B. 101.0". Length 189.9". V6 Cyl. 2 Dr. Curb Wgt. 3169 Lbs.

1976 GRAND PRIX
W.B. 116". Length 213". Ship. Wgt. V8 2 Dr. 4048 Lbs.

1977 GRAND PRIX
W.B. 116". Length 219". Width 78". Ship. Wgt. V8 2 Dr. 3829 Lbs.

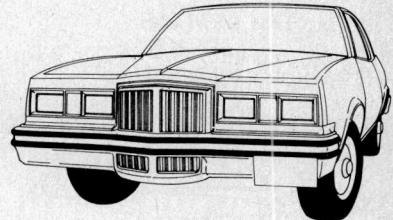

1978 GRAND PRIX
W.B. 108.1" Length 201.2" Ship. Wgt. 8 Cyl. 2 Dr. 3118.28 Lbs.

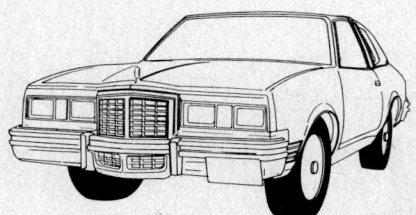

1979 GRAND PRIX
W.B. 108.1" Length 201.2" Ship. Wgt. 8 Cyl. 2 Dr. 3118 Lbs.

1980 GRAND PRIX
W.B. 108.7". Length 201.2". Ship. Wgt. 8 Cyl. Approx. 3115 Lbs.

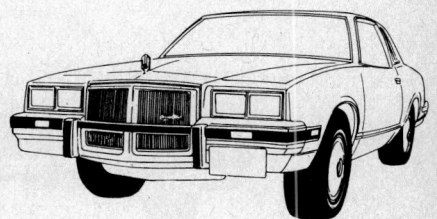

1981 GRAND PRIX
W.B. 108.1". Length 201.8". 6 Cyl. 2 Dr. Curb Wgt. 3258.8 Lbs.

PONTIAC
EXCEPT ASTRE, A6000, '80-'82 PHOENIX & T1000

1982 GRAND PRIX
W.B. 108.1″. Length 201.9″. V6 Cyl. 2 Dr. Curb Wgt. 3258 Lbs.

1976 LE MANS
W.B. 116″. 2D 112″. Length 212″, 2D 208″, S/W 216″. Ship. Wgt. 6 Cyl. 2 Dr. 3651 Lbs. V8 2 Dr. 3826 Lbs.

1977 LE MANS
W.B. 116″, 2D 112″. Length 212″, 4D 208″, S/W 216″. Width 78″. Ship. Wgt. 6 Cyl. 2 Dr. 3564 Lbs. V8 2 Dr. 3696 Lbs.

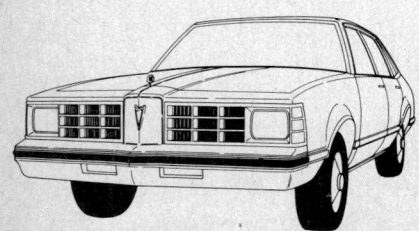

1978 LEMANS
W.B. 111.1″ Length 203.4″ Ship. Wgt. 8 Cyl. 2 Dr. 3011 Lbs.

1979 LEMANS
W.B. 111.1″ Length 203.4″ Ship. Wgt. 8 Cyl. 2 Dr. 3011 Lbs.

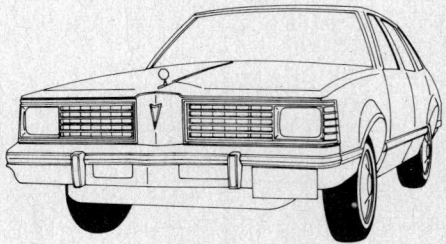

1980 LE MANS
W.B. 111.1″. Length 203.4″. Ship. Wgt. 8 Cyl. 2 Dr. Approx. 3000 Lbs.

1981 LEMANS
W.B. 108.1″. Length 198.5″. 6 Cyl. 2 Dr. Curb Wgt. 3083.8 Lbs.

1979 GRAND AM
W.B. 111.1″ Length 203.4″ Ship. Wt. 8 Cyl. 2 Dr. 3011 Lbs.

1980 GRAND AM
W.B. 111.1″. Length 203.4″. Ship. Wgt. 8 Cyl. 2 Dr. Approx. 3000 Lbs.

1976 VENTURA
W.B. 111.1″. Length 200″. Ship. Wgt. 6 Cyl. 4 Dr. 3271 Lbs.

1977 VENTURA
W.B. 111.1″. Length 200″. Width 73″. Ship. Wgt. 6 Cyl. 4 Dr. 3145 Lbs. V8 4 Dr. 3145 Lbs.

1977 PHOENIX
W.B. 111.1″. Length 203.4″ Ship. Wgt. 8 Cyl. 2 Dr. 3202 Lbs.

1978 PHOENIX
W.B. 111.1″ Length 203.4″ Ship. Wgt. 8 Cyl. 2 Dr. 3202 Lbs.

1979 PHOENIX
W.B. 111.1″ Length 203.4″ Ship. Wgt. 8 Cyl. 2 Dr. 3202 Lbs.

VEHICLE IDENTIFICATION NUMBER (VIN)①

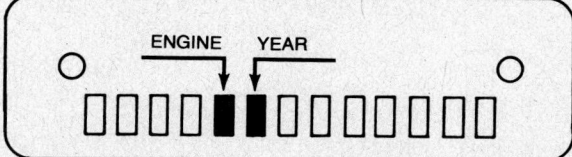

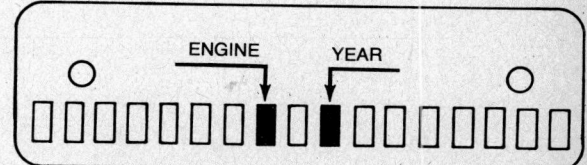

Code	Eng. Disp. cu in	Eng. Config.	Carb	Eng. Mfgr.	Code	Year
C	231	V-6	2v	Buick	6	1976
D	250	L-6	1v	Chev.		
F	260	V-8	2v	Olds.		
M	350	V-8	2v	Pont.		
E	350	V-8	4v	Pont.		
H	350	V-8	2v	Buick		
J	350	V-8	4v	Buick		
R	400	V-8	2v	Pont.		
,S	400	V-8	4v	Pont.		
W	455	V-8	4v	Pont.		
D	250	L-6	1v	Chev.	7	1977
A-C	231	V-6	2v	Buick		
Y	301	V-8	2v	Pont.		
U	305	V-8	2v	Chev.		
L	350	V-8	4v	Chev.		
P	350	V-8	4v	Pont.		
R	350	V-8	4v	Olds.		
Z	400	V-8	4v	Pont.		
K	403	V-8	4v	Olds.		
V	151	L-4	2v	Pont.	8	1978
A	231	V-6	2v	Buick		
Y	301	V-8	2v	Pont.		
W	301	V-8	4v	Pont.		
U	305	V-8	2v	Chev.		
R	350	V-8	4v	Olds.		
L	350	V-8	4v	Chev.		
Z	400	V-8	4v	Pont.		
K	403	V-8	4v	Olds.		

Code	Eng. Disp. cu in	Eng. Config.	Carb	Eng. Mfgr.	Code	Year
A	231	V-6	2v	Buick	9	1979
2	231	V-6	2v	Buick		
F	260	V-8	2v	Olds.		
Y	301	V-8	2v	Pont.		
W	301	V-8	4v	Pont.		
G	305	V-8	2v	Chev.		
H	305	V-8	4v	Chev.		
L	350	V-8	4v	Chev.		
R	350	V-8	4v	Olds.		
X	350	V-8	4v	Buick		
Z	400	V-8	4v	Pont.		
K	403	V-8	4v	Olds.		
K	229	V-6	2v	Chev.	A	1980
A	231	V-6	2v	Buick		
S	265	V-8	2v	Pont.		
J	267	V-8	2v	Chev.		
W	301	V-8	2v	Pont.		
T	301 Turbo	V-8	4v	Pont.		
H	305	V-8	2v	Chev.		
X	350	V-8	4v	Buick		
N	350	V-8	4v	Olds		
R	350	V-8	Diesel	Olds		
A	231 (3.8L)	V-6	2v	Buick	B	1981
S	265 (4.3L)	V-8	2v	Pont.		
W	301 (4.9L)	V-8	4v	Pont.		
T	301 (4.9L)	V-8	4v	Pont.		
H	305 (5.0L)	V-8	4v	Chev.		
Y	307	V-8	4v	Olds.		
N	350 (5.7L)	V-8	Diesel	Olds.		
A	231 (3.8L)	V-6	2v	Buick	2	1982
S	252 (4.3L)	V-6	4v	Buick		
H	305 (5.0L)	V-8	4v	Chev.		

① If a 17- or 19- digit VIN is used, the 7th digit is the engine code

ENGINE FIRING ORDER

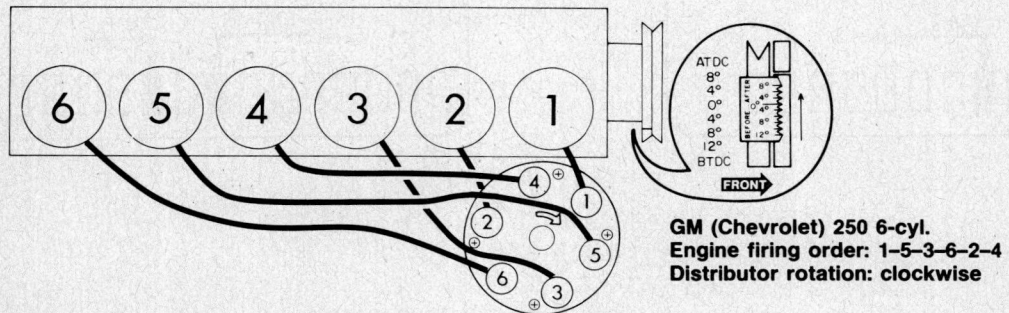

GM (Chevrolet) 250 6-cyl.
Engine firing order: 1-5-3-6-2-4
Distributor rotation: clockwise

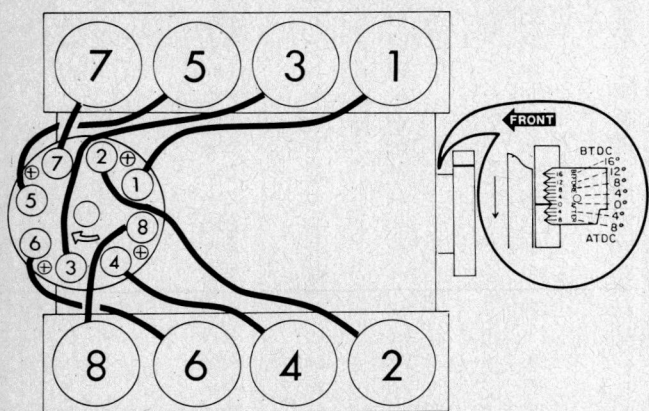

GM (Chevrolet) 267, 305, 350 V8
Engine firing order: 1-8-4-3-6-5-7-2
Distributor rotation: clockwise

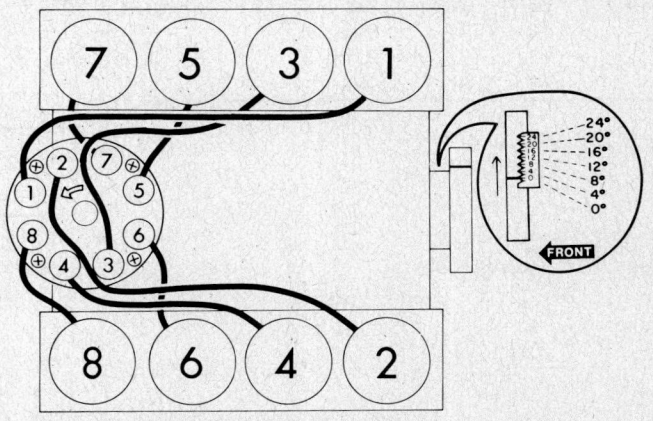

GM (Oldsmobile) 260, 307, 350, 403, V8
Engine firing order: 1-8-4-3-6-5-7-2
Distributor rotation: counterclockwise

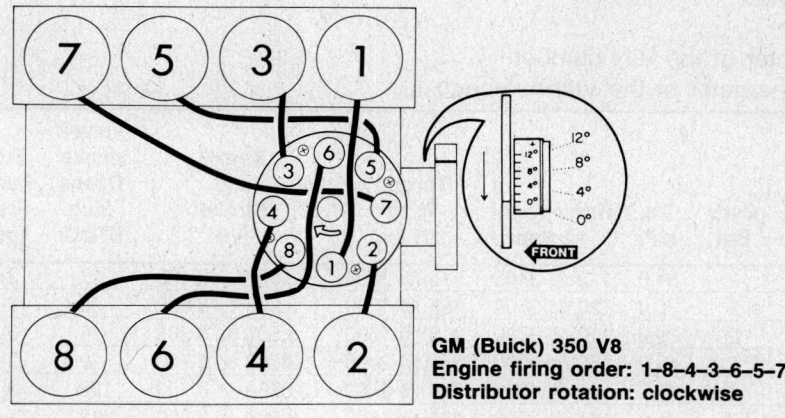

GM (Buick) 350 V8
Engine firing order: 1-8-4-3-6-5-7
Distributor rotation: clockwise

GM (Buick) 231 V6
Engine firing order: 1-6-5-4-3-2
Distributor rotation: clockwise

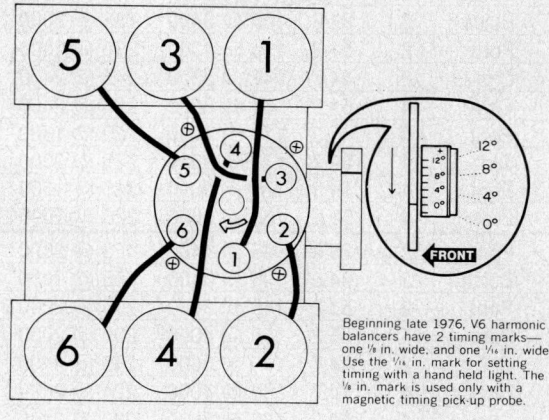

Beginning late 1976, V6 harmonic balancers have 2 timing marks— one 1/8 in. wide, and one 1/16 in. wide. Use the 1/16 in. mark for setting timing with a hand held light. The 1/8 in. mark is used only with a magnetic timing pick-up probe.

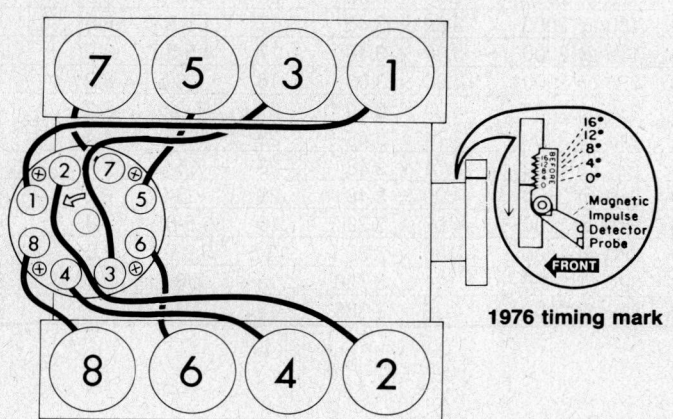

1976 timing mark

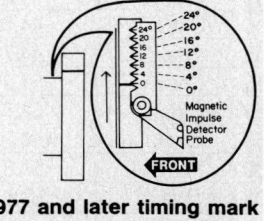

1977 and later timing mark

GM (Pontiac) 265, 301, 350, 400, 455 V8
Engine firing order: 1-8-4-3-6-5-7-2
Distributor rotation: counterclockwise

PONTIAC
EXCEPT ASTRE, A6000, '80-'82 PHOENIX & T1000

ENGINE SPECIFICATIONS

Engine Code, 5th character of the VIN number
Model Year Code, 6th character of the VIN number③

Yr.	Eng. V.I.N. Code	Engine No. Cyl. Disp. (cu in)	Eng. Mfg.	Carb Bbl	Tax H.P.	Horsepower @ rpm	Torque② @ rpm (ft lbs)	Bore② and Stroke (in)	Valves Intake Opens (deg BTDC)	Fuel Pump Pres. (psi)	Comp. Ratio	Oil Pressure @ 2000 rpm
76	C	6-231	Buick	2	34.6	110 @ 3400	175 @ 2000	3.800 × 3.400	17	3-6	8.0	40
	D	6-250	Chev	1	36.0	110 @ 3600	185 @ 1200	3.875 × 3.530	25	3-5	8.3	40
	F	8-260	Olds	2	39.2	110 @ 3400	205 @ 1600	3.500 × 3.385	14	3-6	7.5	40
	M	8-350	Pont	2	48.0	160 @ 4000	280 @ 2000	3.8762 × 3.750	22	3-6	7.6	40
	E	8-350	Pont	4	48.0	165 @ 4000	260 @ 2400	3.8762 × 3.750	26	3-6	7.6	40
	H	8-350	Buick	2	46.2	140 @ 3200	280 @ 1600	3.800 × 3.850	13	3-6	8.0	40
	J	8-350	Buick	4	46.2	155 @ 3400	280 @ 1800	3.800 × 3.850	13	3-6	8.0	40
	R	8-400	Pont	2	54.3	170 @ 4000	310 @ 1600	4.1212 × 3.750	26	3-6	7.6	40
	S	8-400	Pont	4	54.3	185 @ 3600	310 @ 1600	4.1212 × 3.750	23/30	3-6	7.6	40
	W	8-455	Pont	4	55.2	200 @ 3500	330 @ 2000	4.1522 × 4.210	23	3-6	7.6	40
77	V	4-151	Pont	2	25.6	88 @ 4400	128 @ 2400	4.00 × 3.00	27	4-5.5	8.3	40
	A	6-231	Buick	2	34.6	105 @ 3400	185 @ 2000	3.800 × 3.400	17	4-6	8.0	40
	C	6-231	Buick	2	34.6	105 @ 3400	185 @ 2000	3.800 × 3.400	17	4-6	8.0	40
	Y	8-301	Pont	2	51.2	135 @ 4000	230 @ 2000	4.000 × 3.000	31/27	7-8	8.2	40
	U	8-305	Chev	2	44.7	140 @ 3800	245 @ 2400	3.736 × 3.480	28	7-9	8.5	40
	L	8-350	Chev	4	51.2	165 @ 3800	270 @ 2400	4.000 × 3.480	28	7-9	8.5	40
	P	8-350	Pont	4	48.0	170 @ 4000	280 @ 1800	3.8762 × 3.750	29	7-8	7.6	40
	R	8-350	Olds	4	52.7	170 @ 3800	275 @ 2000	4.057 × 3.385	29	5-6	8.0	40
	Z	8-400	Pont	4	54.3	180 @ 3600	325 @ 1600	4.1212 × 3.750	29	7-8	7.6	60
	K	8-403	Olds	4	60.6	185 @ 3600	320 @ 2000	4.351 × 3.385	16	5-6	8.0	40
78	V	4-151	Pont	2	25.6	85 @ 4400	123 @ 2800	4.00 × 3.00	28	5-6.5	8.3	40
	A	6-231	Buick	2	34.6	105 @ 3400	185 @ 2000	3.80 × 3.40	17	4.5-5.7	8.0	40
	Y	8-301	Pont	2	51.2	140 @ 3600	235 @ 2000	4.00 × 3.00	27	7-8.5	8.2	40
	W	8-301	Pont	4	51.2	150 @ 4000	239 @ 2000	4.00 × 3.00	14	7-8.5	8.2	40
	U	8-305	Chev	2	44.7	145 @ 3800	245 @ 2400	3.74 × 3.48	28	7.5-9	8.4	40
	H	8-305	Chev	4	44.7	150 @ 4000	224 @ 2400	3.74 × 3.48	28	7.5-9	8.4	40
	L	8-350	Chev	4	51.2	160 @ 3800	260 @ 2400	4.00 × 3.48	28	7.5-9	8.2	40
	X	8-350	Buick	4	46.2	155 @ 3400	280 @ 1800	3.80 × 3.85	13.5	5.9-7.4	8.0	40
	R	8-350	Olds	4	52.7	170 @ 3800	275 @ 2000	4.07 × 3.39	16	5.5-6.5	7.9	40
	Z	8-400	Pont	4	54.3	180 @ 3600	325 @ 1600	4.121 × 3.750	21	7-8.5	7.7	40
	Z①	8-400	Pont	4	54.3	220 @ 4000	320 @ 2800	4.121 × 3.750	16	7-8.5	8.1	60
	K	8-403	Olds	4	60.6	185 @ 3600	320 @ 2000	4.36 × 3.385	16	5.5-6.5	7.9	40
79	V	4-151	Pont	2	25.6	90 @ 4400	123 @ 2800	4.00 × 3.00	33	5-6.5	8.3	40
	2	6-231	Buick	2	34.6	115 @ 3400	180 @ 2000	3.80 × 3.40	17	4.5-5.7	8.0	40
	A	6-231	Buick	2	34.6	115 @ 3400	185 @ 2000	3.80 × 3.40	17	4.5-5.7	8.0	40
	Y	8-301	Pont	2	51.2	140 @ 3600	235 @ 2000	4.00 × 3.00	16	7-8.5	8.2	40
	W	8-301	Pont	4	51.2	150 @ 4000	239 @ 2000	4.00 × 3.00	27	7-8.5	8.2	40
	G	8-305	Chev	2	44.7	130 @ 3800	245 @ 2400	3.74 × 3.48	28	7.5-9	8.4	40
	H	8-305	Chev	4	44.7	155 @ 4000	224 @ 2400	3.74 × 3.48	28	7.5-9	8.4	40
	L	8-350	Chev	4	51.2	170 @ 3800	260 @ 2400	4.00 × 3.48	28	7.5-9	8.2	40
	R	8-350	Olds	4	52.7	170 @ 3800	275 @ 2000	4.07 × 3.39	16	5.5-6.5	7.9	40
	X	8-350	Buick	4	46.2	155 @ 3400	280 @ 1800	3.80 × 3.85	13.5	5.9-7.4	8.0	40
	Z①	8-400	Pont	4	54.3	220 @ 4000	320 @ 2800	4.121 × 3.750	16	7-8.5	8.1	60
	K	8-403	Olds	4	60.6	185 @ 3600	320 @ 2000	4.36 × 3.385	16	7-8.5	7.9	40

* Chilton Estimate
① Firebird W-72 dual exhaust engine.
② Horsepower and torque figures for 1977 and later
years are Chilton estimates.

A640

TUNE-UP SPECIFICATIONS

Year	Eng. V.I.N Code	Engine No. Cyl Disp. (cu in)	SPARK Plugs Orig. Type	SPARK Plugs Gap (in)	Dist.	IGNITION TIMING (deg BTDC) Man Trans.	IGNITION TIMING (deg BTDC) Auto Trans.	Lo-Alt Man. Trans In(N)	Lo-Alt Auto Trans In (Drive)	Calif Man Trans N	Calif Auto Trans In Drive	Hi-Alt Man Trans N	Hi-Alt Auto Trans In Drive
76	C	V6-231	R44SX	.060	E.I.	12	12	600/800	500/650	500/1000	500/650	——	——
	D	6-250	R46TX	.060	E.I.	6	10	850	550	850	600	——	——
	F	8-260	R46SX	.080	E.I.	16@1100	16@1100	750	650	750	650	——	——
	M	8-350	R46TSX	.060	E.I.	—	12	——	600	——	——	——	——
	E	8-350	R46TSX	.060	E.I.	—	12	——	600	——	——	——	——
	H	8-350	R45TSX	.060	E.I.	—	12	——	600	——	——	——	——
	J	8-350	R45TSX	.060	E.I.	16	16	——	550	——	——	——	——
	R	8-400	R46TSX	.060	E.I.	16	16	——	550	——	550	——	——
	S	8-400	R45TSX	.060	E.I.	12	16	750	575	750	575	——	——
	W	8-455	R45TSX	.060	E.I.	—	16③	——	——	——	600	——	550
77	V	4-151	R44TSX	.060	E.I.	14	14	500/1000	500/650	——	——	——	——
	A	V6-231	R46TSX	.060	E.I.	12	12	600/800	600/675	600/800	500/675	——	——
	C	V6-231	R46TSX	.060	E.I.	15	15	500/1000	500/650	500/1000	500/650	——	——
	Y	8-301	R46TSX	.060	E.I.	16@850	12@550	800	750/875	800	750/875	——	——
	U	8-305	R45TS	.045	E.I.	8	8	700	550/650	700	550/650	——	——
	L	8-350	R45TS	.045	E.I.	14	14	700	500/650	——	——	——	——
	P	8-350	R45TSX	.060	E.I.	—	16	——	575/650	——	——	——	——
	R	8-350	R46SZ	.060	E.I.	20@1100	—	——	550/650	——	550/650	——	——
	Z	8-400	R45TSX	.060	E.I.	—	16	——	575/675	——	——	——	——
	K	8-403	R46SZ	.060	E.I.	—	22	——	550/650	——	——	——	——
78	V	4-151	R43TSX	.060	E.I.	—	14	——	650/850	——	——	——	——
	A	6-231	R46TSX	.060	E.I.	15	15	800	600/675	800	600/675	——	——
	Y	8-301	R46TSX	.060	E.I.	—	12	——	550/650	——	——	——	——
	W	8-301	R45TSX	.060	E.I.	—	12	——	550/650	——	——	——	——
	U	8-305	R45TS	.045	E.I.	4	4	600/700	500/600	——	——	——	——
	H	8-305	R46SZ	.080	E.I.	—	6	——	——	——	500/650	——	——
	L	8-350	R45TS	.045	E.I.	6	8	700	500/600	700	500/600	700	600/650
	X	8-350	R46TSX	.060	E.I.	—	15	——	550	——	——	——	——
	R	8-350	R46SZ	.060	E.I.	—	20@1100	——	550/650	——	550/650	——	——
	Z	8-400	R45TSX	.060	E.I.	18	16	775	575/650	——	——	——	——
	Z	8-400	R45TSX	.060	E.I.	18	18	775	600/700	——	——	——	——
	K	8-403	R46SZ	.060	E.I.	—	20	——	——	——	550/650	——	700
79	V	4-151	R43TSX	.060	E.I.	13 C 14	12 C 14	900	600/675	1000	850	——	——
	2	6-231	R46TSX	.060	E.I.	15	15	800	600	800	600	800	600
	A	6-231	R46TSX	.060	E.I.	15	15	800	600	800	600	800	600
	Y	8-301	R46TSX	.060	E.I.	12	14	800	650	800	650	——	——
	W	8-301	R45TSX	.060	E.I.	—	12	——	650	——	——	——	——
	G	8-305	R45TS	.045	E.I.	4	4	700	600/675	——	600/700	——	——
	H	8-305	R46SZ	.080	E.I.	4	4	——	——	——	600	——	500
	L	8-350	R46SZ	.080	E.I.	—	15②	——	600	——	600	——	600
	R	8-350	R45TSX	.060	E.I.	—	20@1100	——	600/675	——	——	——	——
	X	8-350	R46TSX	.080	E.I.	—	15	——	600/675	——	——	——	——
	Z	8-400	R45TSX	.060	E.I.	18	18	775	650	——	——	——	——
	K	8-403	R46SZ	.080	E.I.	—	18 C 20	——	650	——	600	——	——

NOTE: Should the information provided in this manual deviate from the specifications on the underhood tune-up label, the label specifications should be used, as they may reflect production changes.

NOTE: Where two idle speeds are listed, the higher speed is with the air conditioner on.

① Cal. and high alt. R45TSX
② Cal. 20°—high alt. 8°
③ Calif.—12
C = California
⑤ See engine decal

PONTIAC
EXCEPT ASTRE, A6000, '80-'82 PHOENIX & T1000

ENGINE SPECIFICATIONS

Engine Code, 5th character of the VIN number
Model Year Code, 6th character of the VIN number③

Yr.	Eng. V.I.N. Code	Engine No. Cyl. Disp. (cu in)	Eng. Mfg.	Carb Bbl	Tax H.P.	Horsepower @ rpm	Torque② @ rpm (ft lbs)	Bore② and Stroke (in)	Valves Intake Opens (deg BTDC)	Fuel Pump Pres. (psi)	Comp. Ratio	Oil Pressure @ 2000 rpm
80	K	6-229	Chev	2	34.6	100 @ 3400	180 @ 2000	3.73 × 3.48	42	4.5-6.0	8.5	40
	A	6-231	Buick	2	34.6	105 @ 3400	185 @ 2000	3.80 × 3.40	17	4-5	8.0	40
	S	8-265	Pont	2	44.7	110 @ 3400	207 @ 1800	3.740 × 3.00	27	7-8.5	8.2	40
	J	8-267	Chev	2	39.2	112 @ 3400	209 @ 2000	3.500 × 3.480	27	7-8.5	8.5	40
	W	8-301	Pont	4	51.2	140 @ 3600	235 @ 2000	4.00 × 3.00	16	7-8.5	8.2	40
	T	8-301	Pont	4	51.2	170 @ 4400	240 @ 2000	4.00 × 3.00	17	7-8.5	7.5	40
	H	8-305	Chev	2	44.7	145 @ 3800	245 @ 2400	3.74 × 3.48	27	7-8.5	8.5	40
	X	8-350	Buick	4	46.2	155 @ 3400	280 @ 2800	3.80 × 3.85	13.5	6-7.5	8.0	40
	R	8-350	Olds	4	52.7	170 @ 3800	275 @ 2000	4.07 × 3.39	16	5-6.5	8.1	40
	N	8-350	Olds	Diesel	52.7	125 @ 3800	215 @ 2000	4.057 × 3.385	16	5-6	22.5	40
81	A	6-231	Buick	2	34.6	105 @ 3400	185 @ 2000	3.80 × 3.40	17	4-5	8.0	40
	S	8-265	Pont	2	44.7	110 @ 3400	207 @ 1800	3.74 × 3.00	27	7-8.5	8.2	40
	W	8-301	Pont	4	51.2	140 @ 3600	235 @ 2000	4.00 × 3.00	16	7-8.5	8.2	40
	T	8-301	Pont	4	51.2	170 @ 4400	240 @ 2000	4.00 × 3.00	17	7-8.5	7.5	40
	H	8-305	Chev	4	44.7	145 @ 3800	245 @ 2400	3.74 × 3.48	27	7-8.5	8.5	40
	Y	8-307	Olds	4	46.2	148 @ 3800	250 @ 2400	3.80 × 3.385	—	5.5-6.5	8.5	30-45
	N	8-350	Olds	Diesel	52.7	125 @ 3800	215 @ 2000	4.057 × 3.385	16	5-6	22.5	40
82	A	6-231	Buick	2	34.6	105 @ 3400	185 @ 2000	3.80 × 3.40	17	4-5	8.0	40
	4	8-252	Buick	4	36.0	110 @ 3400	195 @ 2000	3.965 × 3.400	17	5	8.0	37
	H	8-305	Chev	4	44.7	145 @ 3800	245 @ 2400	3.74 × 3.48	27	7-8.5	8.5	40
	N	8-350	Olds	Diesel	52.7	125 @ 3800	215 @ 2000	4.057 × 3.385	16	5-6	22.5	40

* Chilton Estimate
① Firebird W-72 dual exhaust engine.
② Horsepower and torque figures for 1977 and later years are Chilton estimates.

BRAKE SPECIFICATIONS

Year	Model	Master Cylinder Bore Diameter	CALIPER OR WHEEL CYLINDER		BRAKE DRUM/ROTOR DIAMETER	
			Front	Rear	Front	Rear
76-77	Ventura, Phoenix	1.125④	2.9375	.875②	11.0	9.5
78-79	Phoenix	1.125④	2.9375	.938	11.0	9.5
76-77	LeMans, Firebird, Grand Prix	1.125⑩	2.9375	.937⑭	11.0	11.0①
78	Firebird	1.125④	2.9375	.938	11.0	9.5
	Lemans	.945⑫	2.50	.75	10.5	11.0
	Grand Prix	.945⑫	2.50	.75	10.5	11.0
79-80	Firebird	1.125④	2.9375	.938	11.0	9.5
	Lemans	.945⑫	2.50	.75	10.5	9.5
	Grand Prix	.945⑫	2.50	.75	10.5	9.5
76	Full Size Pontiac	1.125	2.9375	.9375⑬	11.86	11.0
	Full Size Wagon	1.125	2.9375	1.00	11.86	12.0
77	Full Size Pontiac	1.125	2.9375	.875	11.0	11.0
	Full Size Wagon	1.125	2.9375	.9375	11.0	11.0
78	Full Size Pontiac	1.125	2.9375	.9375⑬	11.86	11.0
	Full Size Wagon	1.125	2.9375	.9375	11.0	11.0

TUNE-UP SPECIFICATIONS

Year	Eng. V.I.N Code	Engine No. Cyl Disp. (cu in)	SPARK Plugs Orig. Type	Gap (in)	Dist.	IGNITION TIMING (deg BTDC) Man. Trans.	Auto Trans.	CARBURETION HOT IDLE SPEED Lo-Alt Man. Trans In(N)	Auto Trans In (Drive)	Calif Man Trans N	Auto Trans In Drive	Hi-Alt Man Trans N	Auto Trans In Drive
80	K	6-229	R45TS	.045	E.I.	⑤	⑤	800	600	800	600	800	600
	A	6-231	R45TS	.060	E.I.	⑤	⑤	800	600	800	600	800	600
	S	8-265	R45TSX	.60	E.I.	⑤	⑤	700	600	700	600	——	——
	J	8-267	R45TSX	.045	E.I.	4	8	700	600	700	600	——	——
	W	8-301	R45TSX	.060	E.I.	—	12	——	600/675	——	600/700	——	——
	T	8-301	R45TSX	.60	E.I.	——	8		600/675	——	600/700	——	——
	H	8-305	R45TS	.045	E.I.	⑤	4	700	600/675	——	600/700	——	500
	X	8-350	R46TSX	.080	E.I.	—	15	——	600/675	——	——	——	——
	R	8-350	R45TSX	.060	E.I.	—	20@1100	——	600/675	——	600/700	——	——
	N	8-350	DIESEL	—	E.I.	—	—	——	575	——	——	——	——
81	A	6-231	R45TS8	.080	E.S.T.	15° @ 800N	15° @ 500P	800N	500D	800N	500D		
	S	8-265	R45TSX	.060	E.S.T.	——	12° @ 600P		450D		450D		
	W	8-301	R45TSX	.060	E.S.T.	——	12° @ 600P		450D		450D		
	T	8-301	R45TSX	.060	E.S.T.	——	6° @ 700P		450D		450D		
	Y	8-307	R46SX	.080	E.S.T.	——	15° @ 1100P		500D		500D		
	H	8-305	R45TS	.045	E.S.T.	6° @ 800N	——	800N	——	800N	——		
	N	8-350	DIESEL						600		600		
82	A	6-231	R45TS8	.080	E.S.T.	15° @ 800N	15° @ 500P	800N	500D	800N	500D		
	4	6-252	R45TS8	.080	E.S.T.	——	15° @ 500P		500D		500D		
	H	8-305	R45TS	.045	E.S.T.	6° @ 800N	——	800N	——	800N	——		
	N	8-350	DIESEL	——	——	——	——	600		600			

NOTE: Should the information provided in this manual deviate from the specifications on the underhood tune-up label, the label specifications should be used, as they may reflect production changes.

NOTE: Where two idle speeds are listed, the higher speed is with the air conditioner on.

① Cal. and high alt. R45TSX   C = California
② Cal. 20°—high alt. 8°   ⑤ See engine decal
③ Calif.—12

BRAKE SPECIFICATIONS

Year	Model	Master Cylinder Bore Diameter	CALIPER OR WHEEL CYLINDER Front	Rear	BRAKE DRUM/ROTOR DIAMETER Front	Rear
79-80	Full Size Pontiac	1.125	2.9375	.875⑮	11.0	9.5⑮
	Full Size Wagon	1.125	2.9375	.975⑯	11.0	11.0⑯
81-82	Firebird	1.125④	2.9375	.938	11.0	9.5
	LeMans	.945⑫	2.50	.75	10.5	9.5
	Grand Prix	.945⑫	2.50	.75	10.5	9.5
	Pontiac	1.125	2.9375	.875⑮	11.0	9.5⑮
	Pontiac Wagon	1.125	2.9375	.875⑯	11.0	11.0⑯

② 1976-77 w/disc brakes .938   ⑬ 1976—1"
③ 11" rotor   ⑭ Firebird—.938
④ 1" w/o power brakes   ⑮ With 4.75" wheel bolt circle
— "   ⑯ With 5.0" wheel bolt circle

⑧ 75 Grand Prix—.9375"
⑨ 75 Grand Prix—11.0"
⑩ Lemans w/o pwr. brakes—.9375"
    Firebird w/o pwr. brakes—1"
⑪ Firebird—11"
⑫ Lemans w/o power brks—.866"

TORQUE SPECIFICATIONS

All readings in ft/lbs

Year	Engine No. Cyl. Disp. (cu in)	Eng. V.I.N. Code	Cylinder Head Bolts	Rod Bearing Bolts	Main Bearing Bolts	Crankshaft Bolt	Flywheel to Crankshaft Bolts	MANIFOLD	
								Intake	Exhaust
76	V6 231	C	75	40	100	150	55	45	25
	6 250	D	95	35	65	PRESS FIT	60	②	②
	V8 260	F	85③	42	80④	310	60⑦	40③	40③
	V8 350	H, J	80	40	115	140	60	45	28
	V8 350, 400, 455	M,E, R,S,W	95	43	120	160	95	40	30
77	4-151	V	95	30	65	160	55	40⑥	40⑤
	6-231	C-A	75	40	100	150	55	45	25
	8-350, 8-403	R K	130③	42	80④	200-310	60⑦	40③	25
	8-301,	Y	85	30	70⑧	160	95	35	40
	8-350, 400	P,Z	100	40	100④	160	95	35	40
	8-305, 350	U,L	65	45	70	60	60	30	20
78	4-151	V	95	30	65	160	55	40⑥	40⑤
	6-231	A	80	40	100	225	60	45	25
	8-350	X	80	40	100	225	60	45	25
	8-305, 8-350	U,H L	65	45	70	60	60	30	20
	8-301	Y,W	95	30	70⑧	160	95	35	40
	8-400	Z	95	40	100④	160	95	35	40
	8-350 8-403	R K	130	42	80④	220	60⑦	40③	25
79	4-151	V	95	30	65	160	55	40⑥	40⑤
	6-231	A,2	80	40	100	225	60	45	25
	8-350	X	80	40	100	225	60	45	25
	8-305 8-350	G,H L	65	45	70	60	60	30	20
	8-301	Y,W	95	30	70⑧	160	95	35	40
	8-400	Z	95	40	100④	160	95	35	40
	8-350	R	130	42	80	220	60	40	25
	8-403	K	130	42	80	260			
80	6-229	K	80	40	100	175	60	45	25
	6-231	A	80	40	100	225	60	45	25
	8-265	S	95	30	70⑧	160	95	35	40
	8-267	J	65	45	70	60	60	30	20
	8-301	W	95	30	70	160	60	35	40
	8-301	T	95	30	70	160	60	35	40
	8-305	H	65	45	70	60	60	30	20
	8-350	X	80	40	100	225	60	45	25
	8-350	N	130⑨	42	120	—	60	40⑨	25
	8-350	R	130	42	80	220	60	40	25
81	6-231	A	80	40	100	225	60	45	25
	8-265	S	95	30	70⑧	160	95	35	40
	8-301	W	95	30	70	160	60	35	40
	8-301	T	95	30	70	160	60	35	40
	8-305	H	65	45	70	60	60	30	20
	8-307	Y	130⑨	42	70⑩	160	60	40	25
	8-350	N	130⑨	42	120	—	60	40⑨	25

TORQUE SPECIFICATIONS

All readings in ft/lbs

Year	Engine No. Cyl. Disp. (cu in)	Eng. V.I.N. Code	Cylinder Head Bolts	Rod Bearing Bolts	Main Bearing Bolts	Crankshaft Bolt	Flywheel to Crankshaft Bolts	MANIFOLD	
								Intake	Exhaust
82	6-231	A	80	40	100	225	60	45	25
	8-252	4	80	40	100	225	60	45	25
	8-305	H	65	42	70	200-310	60	40	25
	8-350	N	130⑤	42	120	200-310	60	30	25

① 455 engine 43 ft./lb.
② Integral with head
③ Lubricate bolt
④ Crank shaft bolt #5 main brg. 120 ft./lbs.
⑤ Nut 30 ft/lbs
⑥ Intake to exhaust manifold
⑦ With manual transmission 90 ft./lbs.
⑧ Rear main-100 ft./lbs.
⑨ Dip complete bolt in engine oil, to get correct torque reading.
⑩ Rear main 120 ft./lbs.

CRANKSHAFT & CONNECTING ROD SPECIFICATIONS

All measurements given in inches

Year	Engine No. Cyl. Disp. (cu in)	CRANKSHAFT				CONNECTING ROD		
		Main Brg. Journal Dia	Main Brg. Oil Clearance	Shaft End-Play	Thrust on No.	Journal Diameter	Oil Clearance	Side Clearance
76	6-231	2.4995	.0004-.0015	.004-.008	2	1.991-2.000	.0005	.006-.027
	6-250	2.2983-2.2993	.0003-.0029	.002-.006	7	1.999-2.000	.0007-.0027	.009-.014
	8-260	#1,2.4998-2.4988 #2-5,2.4995-2.4985	#1-4,.0005-.0021 #5,.0015-.0031	.0035-.0135	3	2.1248-2.1238	.0005-.0026	.006-.020
	8-350(M-E)	3.00	.0002-.0017	.003-.009	4	2.25	.0005-.0025	.012-.017
	8-350(H-J)	3.00	.0004-.0015	.003-.009	3	1.9910-2.000	.0005-.0026	.006-.020
	8-400	3.00	.0002-.0017	.003-.009	4	2.25	.0005-.0025	.012-.017
	8-455	3.25	.0005-.0021	.003-.009	4	2.25	.0005-.0025	.012-.017
77	4-151	2.2983-2.2993	.0002-.0022	.0015-.0085	5	2.00	.0005-.0026	.006-.022
	6-231	2.4995	.0004-.0015	.004-.008	2	1.991-2.00	.0005	.006-.027
	8-301	3.000	.0004-.0020	.003-.009	4	2.00	.0005-.0025	.006-.022
	8-305	#1,2.4484-2.4493 #2-4,2.4481-2.4490 #5,2.4479-2.4488	#1,.0010-.0015 #2-4,.0011-.0035 #5,.0017-.0035	.002-.006	5	2.199-2.20	.013-.035	.008-.014
	8-350(P)	3.000	.0004-.0020	.003-.009	4	2.25	.0005-.0025	.012-.017
	8-350(R)	#1,2.4998-2.4988 #2-5,2.4995-2.4985	#1-4,.0005-.0021 #5,.0015-.0031	.0035-.0135	3	2.1248-2.1238	.0004-.0033	.006-.020
	8-350(L)	#1,2.4484-2.4493 #2-4,2.4481-2.4490 #5,2.4479-2.4488	#1,.0008-.0020 #2-4,.0011-.0035 #5,.0017-.0035	.002-.006	5	2.199-2.20	.013-.035	.008-.014
	8-400	3.000	.0004-.0020	.003-.009	4	2.25	.0005-.0025	.012-.017
	8-403	#1,2.4998-2.4988 #5,2.4995-2.4985	#1-4,.0005-.0021 #5,.0015-.0031	.0035-.0135	3	2.1248-2.1238	.0004-.0033	.006-.020

CRANKSHAFT & CONNECTING ROD SPECIFICATIONS

All measurements given in inches

Year	Engine No. Cyl. Disp. (cu in)	CRANKSHAFT				CONNECTING ROD		
		Main Brg. Journal Dia	Main Brg. Oil Clearance	Shaft End-Play	Thrust on No.	Journal Diameter	Oil Clearance	Side Clearance
78	4-151	2.300	.0002-.0022	.0035-.0085	5	1.990-2.000	.0005-.0026	.006-.022
	6-231	2.4995	.0004-.0015	.003-.009	2	1.991-2.000	.0005-.0026	.006-.027
	8-350(X)	3.000	.0003-.0017	.003-.009	3	2.2487-2.2495	.0005-.0026	.006-.027
	8-305(U,H) 8-350(L)	#1-4, 2.4502 #5 2.4508	#1,.0008-.0020 #2-4,.0011-.0023 #5 .0017-.0033	.002-.007	5	2.099-2.100	.0013-.0035	.006-.016
	8-301(Y,W)	3.00	.0002-.0020	.003-.009	4	2.240-2.250	.0005-.0025	.006-.022
	8-400(Z)	3.00	.0002-.0020	.003-.009	4	2.240-2.250	.0005-.0025	.006-.022
	8-350(R), 8-403(K)	#1-, 2.4998-2.4988 #2-5-, 2.4995-2.4985	#1-4-, .0005-.0021 #5,.0015-.003	.0035-.0135	3	2.1248-2.1238	.0005-.0026	.006-.020
79	4-151	2.30	.0002-.0022	.0035-.0085	5	2.000	.0005-.0026	.006-.022
	6-231	2.4995	.0004-.0015	.003-.009	2	2.2487-2.2495	.0005-.0026	.006-.023
	8-350(X)	2.9995	.0004-.0015	.002-.006	3	1.991-2.000	.0005-.0026	.006-.020
	8-305(G,H) 8-350(L)	#1-4 2.4502 #5 2.4508	#1-.0008-.0020 #2-4- .0011-.0023 #5- .0017-.0033	.002-.007	5	2.009-2.1000	0.013-.035	.006-.016
	8-301(Y,W)	3.00	.0002-.0020	.003-.009	4	2.240-2.250	.0005-.0025	.006-.022
	8-400(Z)	3.00	.0002-.0020	.003-.009	4	2.240-2.250	.0005-.0025	.006-.022
	8-350(R) 8-403(K)	#1- 2.4998-2.4988 #2-5 2.4995-2.4985	#1-4- .0005-.0021 #5 .0015-.003	.0035-.0135	5	2.1248-2.1238	.0005-.0026	.006-.020
80	6-229(K)	2.2495-2.2487	.0004-.0015	.004-.008	4	2.2495-2.2487	.0013-.0035	.008-.014
	6-231(A)	2.495	.0003-.0017	.004-.008	2	2.2491	.0005-.0025	.006-.0027
	8-265(S)	3.00	.0003-.0017	.004-.008	4	2.2491	.0005-.0025	.006-.022
	8-301(W)	3.00	.0004-.0020	.006-.022	4	2.25	.0005-.0025	.006-.022
	8-301(T)	3.00	.0004-.0020	.006-.022	4	2.25	.0005-.0025	.006-.022
	8-305 8-267	#1-2.4484-2.4493 #2-4-2.4481-2.4490 #5-2.4479-2.4488	#1-.0010-.0015 #2-4-.0011-.0035 #5-.0017-.0035	.002-006	5	2.199-2.20	.013-.035	.008-.014
	8-350(X)	3.00	.004-.0015	.003-.009	3	1.996	.0004-.0015	.006-.0027
	8.350(N)	2.9993-3.0003	.0005-.0021	.0035-.0135	3	2.1238-2.1248	.0005-.0026	.006-.020
	8-350(R)	2.4990	.0005-.0021	.004-.008	3	2.1243	.0004-.0033	.006-.020
81	6-231(A)	2.495	.0003-.0017	.004-.008	2	2.2491	.0005-.0025	.006-.027
	8-265(S)	3.00	.0003-.0017	.004-.008	4	2.2491	.0005-.0025	.006-.022
	8-301(W)	3.00	.0004-.0020	.006-.022	4	2.25	.0005-.0025	.006-.022
	8-301(T)	3.00	.0004-.0020	.006-.022	4	2.25	.0005-.0025	.006-.022
	8-305	#1-2.4484-2.4493 #2-4-2.4481-2.4490 #5-2.4479-2.4488	.0010-.0015 .0011-.0035 .0017-.0035	.002-.006	5	2.199-2.20	.013-.035	.008-.014
	8-307	#1-2.4988-2.4998 #2-4-2.4985-2.4995 #5-2.4985-2.4995	.0005-.0021 .0005-.0021 .0015-.0031	.0035-.0135	3	2.1238-2.1248	.0004-.0033	.006-.020
	8-350(N)	2.9993-3.0003	.0005-.0021	.0035-.0135	3	2.1238-2.1248	.0005-.0026	.006-.020

CRANKSHAFT & CONNECTING ROD SPECIFICATIONS

All measurements given in inches

Year	Engine No. Cyl. Disp. (cu in)	CRANKSHAFT				CONNECTING ROD		
		Main Brg. Journal Dia	Main Brg. Oil Clearance	Shaft End-Play	Thrust on No.	Journal Diameter	Oil Clearance	Side Clearance
82	6-231, 252 A-4	2.495	.0003-.0018	.003-.009	2	2.2487-2.2495	.0005-.0026	.006-.023
	8-305	#1-2.4484-2.4493 #2-4-2.4481-2.4490 #5-2.4479-2.4488	.0010-.0015 .0011-.0035 .0017-.0035	.002-.006	5	2.199-2.20	.013-.035	.008-.014
	8-350(N)	2.9993-3.0003	.0005-.0021	.0035-.0135	3	2.1238-2.1248	.0005-.0026	.006-.020

VALVE SPECIFICATIONS

Year	Engine No. Cyl. Disp. (cu in)	Seat Angle (deg) ⑯	Face Angle (deg) ⑰	Spring Test Pressure (lbs @ in)	Spring Installed Height (in)	STEM TO GUIDE CLEARANCE (in)		STEM DIAMETER (in)	
						Intake	Exhaust	Intake	Exhaust
'76	4-140	46③	45③	75 @ 1.75	1¾	.0010-.0027	.0017-.0027	.3414	.3414
	6-231	45③	45③	64 @ 1.72	1⁴⁷/₆₄	.0015-.0032	.0015-.0032	.3409	.3409
	6-250	46③	45③	57 @ 1.66	1²¹/₃₂	.0010-.0027	.0010-.0027	.3414	.3414
	8-260	46⑨	45⑩	80 @ 1.67	1³¹/₃₂	.0010-.0027	.0015-.0032	.3429	.3424
	8-350	30	29	66 @ 1.56	1¹⁹/₃₂	.0016-.0033	.0021-.0038	.3416	.3411
	8-400	30	29	70 @ 1.54	1⁹/₁₆	.0016-.0033	.0021-.0038	.3416	.3411
	8-455	30	29	65 @ 1.27	1⁹/₁₆	.0016-.0033	.0021-.0038	.3416	.3411
'77	4-140	46③	45③	75 @ 1.75	1¾	.0010-.0027	.0010-.0027	.3414	.3414
	4-151	46③	45③	82 @ 1.66	1²¹/₃₂	.0010-.0027	.0010-.0027②	.3422	.3422
	6-231	45	45	64 @ 1.72	1⁴⁷/₆₄	.0015-.0035	.0015-.0032	.3407	.3409
	8-301	46	45	82 @ 1.66	1²¹/₃₂	.0010-.0027	.0010-.0027	.3422	.3422
	8-305	46③	45③	80 @ 1.70	1²³/₃₂⑪	.0010-.0027	.0010-.0027	.3414	.3414
	8-350 Chev.	46③	45③	80 @ 1.70	1²³/₃₂⑪	.0010-.0027	.0010-.0027	.3414	.3414
	8-350 Olds.	⑫	⑫	80 @ 1.67	1²¹/₃₂	.0010-.0027	.0015-.0032	.3429	.3424
	8-350 Pont.	30	29	68 @ 1.54	1¹⁹/₃₂	.0016-.0033	.0021-.0038	.3416	.3412
	8-400	30	29	68 @ 1.55	1¹⁹/₃₂	.0016-.0033	.0021-.0038	.3416	.3412
	8-403 Olds.	⑫	⑫	80 @ 1.67	1²¹/₃₂	.0010-.0027	.0015-.0032	.3429	.3424
'78	4-151	46③	45③	78-86 @ 1.66⑭	1.69	.0010-.0027	⑬	.3400	.3400
	6-231	45	44	174-190 @ 1.340⑭	1.727	.0015-.0032	.0015-.0032	.3402-.3412	.3412-.3405
	8-301	46③	45③	165 @ 1.29	1.66	.0010-.0027	⑬	.3425	.3425
	8-305	46③	45③	184-196 @ 1.16	I-1.72 E-1.59	.0010-.0027	.0010-.0027	.3410-.3417	.3410-.3417
	8-350	46③	45③	184-196 @ 1.16	I-1.72 E-1.59	.0010-.0027	.0010-.0027	.3410-.3417	.3410-.3417
	I8-350	45	44	I-173-187 @ 1.34 E-168-182 @ 1.34	1.727	.0015-.0035	.0015-.0032	.3720-.3730	.3723-.3730
	8-350	45⑮	46⑮	180-194 @ 1.27	1.67	.0010-.0027	.0015-.0032	.3425-.3432	.3420-.3427
	8-400	I-30 E-45	I-29 E-44	OUT-135 @ 1.18 IN-97 @ 1.14	1.54	.0010-.0027	⑬	.3425	.3425
	8-403	45⑮	46⑮	180-194 @ 1.27	1.67	.0010-.0027	.0015-.0032	.3425-.3432	.3420-.3427

PONTIAC
EXCEPT ASTRE, A6000, '80-'82 PHOENIX & T1000

VALVE SPECIFICATIONS

Year	Engine No. Cyl. Disp. (cu in)	Seat Angle (deg) ⑯	Face Angle (deg) ⑰	Spring Test Pressure (lbs @ in)	Spring Installed Height (in)	STEM TO GUIDE CLEARANCE (in) Intake	STEM TO GUIDE CLEARANCE (in) Exhaust	STEM DIAMETER (in) Intake	STEM DIAMETER (in) Exhaust
'79	4-151	46③	45③	172-180 @ 1.254	1.66	.0010-.0027	⑬	.3418-.3425	.3418-.3425
	6-231	45	44	159-169 @ 1.34	1.727	.0015-.0035	.0015-.0032	.3402-.3412	.3405-.3412
	8-301	46③	45③	162-170 @ 1.296	1.66	.0010-.0027	.0010-.0027	.3425-.3418	.3425-.3418
	8-305	46③	45③	I-174-186 @ 1.25 E-184-196 @ 1.16	I-1.70 E-1.61	.0010-.0027	.0010-.0027	.3410-.3417	.3410-.3417
	8-305	46③	45③	I-174-186 @ 1.25 E-184-196 @ 1.16	I-1.70 E-1.61	.0010-.0027	.0010-.0027	.3410-.3417	.3410-.3417
	8-350	46③	45③	I-174-186 @ 1.25 E-184-196 @ 1.16	I-1.70 E-1.61	.0010-.0027	.0010-.0027	.3410-.3417	.3410-.3417
	8-350	45⑮	46⑮	180-194 @ 1.270	1.67	.0010-.0027	.0015-.0032	.3425-.3432	.3420-.3427
	8-350	45	44	I-173-187 @ 1.34 E-168-182 @ 1.34	1.727	.0015-.0035	.0015-.0032	.3720-.3730	.3723-.3730
	8-400	I-30 E-45	I-29 E-44	OUT-126-136 @ 1.185 IN-92-102 @ 1.145	1.549	.0016-.0033	.0021-.0038	.3412-.3419	.3407-.3414
	8-403	45⑮	46⑮	180-194 @ 1.270	1.67	.0010-.0027	.0015-.0032	.3425-.3432	.3420-.3427
'80	6-229-K	46	45	200 @ 1.25	1	.0010-.0027	.0010-.0027	.3410-.3417	.3410-.3417
	6-231-A	45	44	159-169 @ 1.34	1.727	.0015-.0035	.0015-.0032	.3402-.3412	.3405-.3412
	8-265-S	46	45	159-169 @ 1.34		.0015-.0035	.0015-.0032	.3402-.3412	.3405-.3412
	8-267-J	46	45	1-174-186 @ 1.25	1 23/32	.0015-.0035	.0015-.0032	.3410-.3417	.3410-.3417
	8-301-W	46③	45③	162-170 @ 1.296	1.66	.0010-.0027	.0010-.0027	.3425-.3418	.3425-.3418
	8-301-T	4③	45③	162-170 @ 1.296	1.66	.0010-.0027	.0010-.0027	.3425-.3418	.3425-.3418
	8-305	46③	45③	I-174-186 @ 1.25 E-184-196 @ 1.16	I-1.70 E-1.61	.0010-.0027	.0010-.0027	.3410-.3417	.3410-.3417
	8-350-X	45	45	180+7 @ 1.340⑱	1.727	.0015-.0035	.0015-.0032	.3730-.3720	.3730-.3720
	DIE 8-350-N	⑮	⑮	144-158 @ 1.300	1.670	.0010-.0015	.0010-.0032	.3425-.3432	.3420-.3427
	8-350-R	45	44	180-194 @ 1.270	1.670	.0010-.0027	.0015-.0032	.3432-.3425	.3427-.3420
'81	6-231-A	45	44	159-169 @ 1.34	1.727	.0015-.0035	.0015-.0032	.3402-.3412	.3405-.3412
	8-265-S	46	45	159-169 @ 1.34	—	.0015-.0035	.0015-.0032	.3402-.3412	.3405-.3412
	8-301-W	46③	45③	162-170 @ 1.296	1.66	.0010-.0027	.0010-.0027	.3425-.3418	.3425-.3418
	8-301-T	46③	45③	162-170 @ 1.296	1.66	.0010-.0027	.0010-.0027	.3425-.3418	.3425-.3418
	8-307-Y	⑲	⑳	180-194 @ 1.270	1.670	.0010-.0027	.0015-.0032	.3425-.3432	.3420-.3427
	8-305-H	46③	45③	I-174-186 @ 1.25 E-184-196 @ 1.16	1.70 1.161	.0010-.0027	.0010-.0027	.3410-.3417	.0010-.3417
	8-350-N	⑮	⑮	144-158 @ 1.300	1.670	.0010-.0015	.0010-.0032	.3425-.3432	.3420-.3427
'82	6-231-252 A-4	45	45	168 + 6 @ 1.327	1.727	.0015-.0032	.0015-.0032	.3405-.3412	.3405-.3412
	8-305-H	46	45	I-174-186 @ 1.25 E-184-196 @ 1.16	I-1.70 E-1.161	.0010-.0027	.0010-.0027	.3410-.3417	.3410-.3417
	8-350-N	⑮	⑮	144-158 @ 1.300	1.670	.0010-.0027	.0015-.0032	.3425-.3432	.3425-.3427

① Manual transmission with 400 cu in. engine
② Figure given is at top of guide; .0020-.0037 at bottom
③ Exhaust valve seat and face angles are the same as intake valve seat and face angles
④ Ventura II only
⑤ Firebird only
⑥ 59 @ 1.50 with manual trans
⑦ .3416 in. for 455 s.d. engine
⑧ 60 @ 1.60 with manual trans
⑨ Exhaust—31
⑩ Exhaust—30
⑪ Exhaust: 1 19/32
⑫ Intake seat 45°, intake face 44°; Exhaust seat 31°, exhaust face 30°
— Not Specified
I -Intake

⑬ Top of exhaust valve -.0010/.0027 bottom of exhaust valve -.0020/.0037
⑭ With damper removed
⑮ Intake—45 Exhaust—31
⑯ Intake valve seat angles are shown. All exhaust valve seat angles are 45° unless otherwise indicated.
⑰ Intake valve face angles are shown. All exhaust valve face angles are 44° unless otherwise indicated.
⑱ Exhaust—177 + 7 @ 1.450
⑲ Intake—45 Exhaust—31
⑳ Intake—44 Exhaust—30

A648

DISTRIBUTOR SPECIFICATIONS

Year	Dist. Ident.	CENTRIFUGAL ADVANCE Start Crank. Deg. @ Eng. RPM	Finish Crank. Deg. @ Eng. RPM	VACUUM ADVANCE Start @ in hg	Finish Crank. Deg. @ in hg
'76	1103201	0 @ 1200	20 @ 3800	6	24 @ 13
	1103205	0 @ 1200	16 @ 4400	7	20 @ 11
	1103206	0 @ 1200	17 @ 3600	7	20 @ 11
	1103207	0 @ 1000	14 @ 4400	8	20 @ 15
	1110650	0 @ 1200	14 @ 4200		16 @ 15
	1110661	0 @ 1050	16 @ 4100	6	18 @ 10
	1110666	0 @ 1000	20 @ 4200	4	24 @ 15
	1110668	0 @ 1270	16 @ 3200	6	24 @ 12
	1112495	0 @ 1100	8 @ 4400	7	25 @ 12
	1112497	0 @ 1200	20 @ 3800	5	25 @ 11
	1112500	0 @ 1200	20 @ 4400	7	25 @ 12
	1112862	0 @ 900	22 @ 4800	5	20 @ 14
	1112863	0 @ 770	16 @ 4400	4	18 @ 12
	1112896	0 @ 1100	12 @ 4425	6.5	14 @ 12
	1112923	0 @ 1000	14 @ 4400	7	25 @ 12
	1112928	0 @ 1200	16 @ 4400	7	25 @ 12
	1112930	0 @ 1400	10 @ 4400	7	25 @ 12
	1112950	0 @ 1200	20 @ 3800	7	20 @ 11
	1112956	0 @ 650	28 @ 4400	①	①
	1112958	0 @ 1200	16 @ 4400	5	25 @ 11
	1112960	0 @ 1000	14 @ 4400	9	20 @ 16
	1112991	0 @ 1425	20 @ 4430	7	20 @ 13
	1112992	0 @ 900	20 @ 4400	8	14 @ 11
	1112994	0 @ 650	28 @ 4400	5	24 @ 11
	1112995	0 @ 900	26 @ 4450	4	30 @ 11
'77	1103231	0 @ 1200	20 @ 4400	3.5	20 @ 12
	1103239	0 @ 1200	20 @ 4200	4.5	20 @ 10
	1103244	0 @ 1000	20 @ 3800	4.5	20 @ 10
	1103246	0 @ 1200	22 @ 4200	3.5	18 @ 11
	1103248	0 @ 1200	20 @ 4200	3.5	10 @ 7
	1103257	0 @ 1200	17 @ 3600	5	20 @ 10
	1103259	0 @ 1000	19 @ 4000	6	24 @ 13
	1103260	0 @ 1000	13 @ 3600	6	24 @ 13
	1103263	0 @ 1000	20 @ 4400	3.5	20 @ 9
	1103264	0 @ 1000	25 @ 3600	5	16 @ 11
	1103266	0 @ 1000	19 @ 4000	5	16 @ 11
	1103269	0 @ 1000	17 @ 4600	5	20 @ 10
	1103271	0 @ 1000	20 @ 4400	5	25 @ 11
	1103272	0 @ 830	22.5 @ 3425	4	25 @ 12
	1103273	0 @ 1000	19 @ 3600	4	25 @ 12
	1103276	0 @ 800	4 @ 1000	5	20 @ 10
	1103278	0 @ 1200	16 @ 4400	5	20 @ 10
	1110677	0 @ 1400	20 @ 3600	4	24 @ 11
	1110686	0 @ 1400	20 @ 3600	7	8 @ 9
'78	1103264	0 @ 1000	13 @ 3600	5	16 @ 11
	1103266		19 @ 4000	5	16 @ 11
	1103281	0 @ 1000	20 @ 3800	4	18 @ 12
	1103282	0 @ 1000	20 @ 3800	4	20 @ 10
	1103285	0 @ 1200	22 @ 4200	4	10 @ 8
	1103310	0 @ 1000	14 @ 4400	4	25 @ 12

DISTRIBUTOR SPECIFICATIONS

Year	Dist. Ident.	CENTRIFUGAL ADVANCE Start Crank. Deg. @ Eng. RPM	Finish Crank. Deg. @ Eng. RPM	VACUUM ADVANCE Start @ in hg	Finish Crank. Deg. @ in hg
	1103314	0 @ 825	21.5 @ 3400	4	25 @ 12
	1103315	0 @ 1000	20 @ 4400	5	25 @ 11
	1103316	0 @ 1000	17 @ 4600	4	25 @ 12
	1103323	0 @ 1000	19 @ 4000	5	16 @ 11
	1103325	0 @ 1000	13 @ 3600	5	16 @ 11
	1103329	0 @ 1200	20 @ 4400	3.5	20 @ 9
	1103337	0 @ 1100	16 @ 4400	4	24 @ 10
	1103342	0-8 @ 2000	19 @ 4400	7	24 @ 13
	1103343	0 @ 800	16.5 @ 3650	4	25 @ 11
	1103346	0 @ 1000	19 @ 4000	6	24 @ 13
	1103347	0 @ 1000	13 @ 3600	6	24 @ 13
	1103359	0 @ 1000	17 @ 4600	5	20 @ 10
	1110695	0-6 @ 2000	12-18 @ 3600	6	20 @ 13
	1110731	0-4 @ 2000	12-18 @ 3600	6	16 @ 9
'79	1103281	0 @ 1000	20 @ 3800	4	18 @ 12
	1103282	0 @ 1000	20 @ 3800	4	20 @ 10
	1103285	0 @ 1200	22 @ 4200	4	20 @ 8
	1103310	0 @ 1000	14 @ 4400	4	25 @ 12
	1103314	0 @ 825	21.5 @ 3400	4	25 @ 12
	1103315	0 @ 1000	20 @ 4400	5	25 @ 11
	1103323	0 @ 1000	19 @ 4000	5	16 @ 11
	1103325	0 @ 1000	13 @ 3600	5	16 @ 11
	1103337	0 @ 1100	16 @ 2400	4	24 @ 10
	1103346	0 @ 1000	19 @ 4000	6	24 @ 13
	1103347	0 @ 1000	13 @ 3600	6	24 @ 13
	1103353	0 @ 1100	22 @ 4600	4	20 @ 10
	1103731	0 @ 1675	15 @ 3600	6	16 @ 9
	1110695	0-6 @ 1675	15 @ 3600	6	24 @ 13
	1110713	0-4 @ 2000	12-18 @ 3600	6	16 @ 9
	1110766	0 @ 1675	15 @ 3600	3.9	24 @ 10.9
'80	1103283	2.5 @ 1200	20 @ 3800	5	20 @ 11
	1103407	2 @ 1200	23 @ 4400	4.5	20 @ 10.5
	1103417	2 @ 2200	17 @ 4400	6	20 @ 13.5
	1103413	2 @ 1400	12 @ 5000	6.5	30 @ 15.8
	1103425	2 @ 1250	18 @ 4600	4.5	20 @ 10.5
	1103444	1 @ 1200	14 @ 4400	7.5	19 @ 13.5
	1103447	2 @ 2200	17 @ 4400	7	24 @ 14.6
	1103450	2 @ 1050	18 @ 5000	4.5	20 @ 10.5
	110552	2 @ 1200	14 @ 3400	3.5	24 @ 8.5
	110554	2 @ 1950	15 @ 5000	3.5	24 @ 13.5
	110555	2 @ 1200	15 @ 3600	4.5	24 @ 9.5
	110558	2 @ 1350	14 @ 4000	3.5	16 @ 6
	1110559	0.5 @ 1200	14 @ 4000	3.5	16 @ 7
	1110560	2 @ 1450	14 @ 4400	5	21 @ 10.5
	1110752	2 @ 1550	14 @ 4100	4	16 @ 7.5
	1110769	2 @ 1200	15 @ 3600	4.5	24 @ 9.5

NOTE: Beginning with 1981, all engines are equipped with electronic spark timing (E.S.T.).

① Not equipped with vacuum control

FLUID CAPACITIES—Coolant, Fuel & Lubricant PONTIAC MID-SIZE

Year	Engine No. Cyl. Disp. (Cu. In.)	V.I.N.	Engine Crankcase (Add 1 Qt For New Filter)	TRANSMISSION (Pts To Refill After Draining) Manual 3-Speed	4-Speed	Automatic ㉓	Drive Axle (pts)	Gasoline Tank (gals)	Rad. Cap Press.	Thermo. Stat. Temp.	COOLING SYSTEM (qts) With Heater	With A/C
'76	6-250		4	3.5	3.5⑨	7.5	4.25⑧	21.8⑦	15	195	15	15
	8-260	F	5	3.5	3.5⑨	7.5	4.25⑧	21.8⑦	15	195	19.6	20.1
	8-350	M-E-H	5	—	—	7.5	4.25⑧	21.8⑥⑦	15	195	21.3	23.2
	8-400	R-S	5	—	—	7.5	4.25⑧	22⑥⑦	15	195	21.3	23.2
	8-455	W	5	—	—	7.5	4.25⑧	22⑥⑦	15	195	22.3	23.6
'77	6-231	A-C	4	3.5	—	7.5	4.25	21.8④⑦	15	195	13.9	NA
	8-301	Y	5	—	—	7.5	4.25	21.8④⑥⑦	15	195	21.9	NA
	8-350		5⑫	—	—	7.5	4.25	21.8④⑥⑦	15	195	21.0⑪	NA
	8-400		5	—	—	7.5	4.25	21.8④⑥⑦	15	195	19.4	NA
	8-403		5	—	—	7.5	4.25	21.8④⑥⑦	15	195	17.2	NA
'78	6-231	A	4	3.5	2.5	6.0	3.5⑰	17.0⑬	15	195	13.1⑮	13.1⑮
	8-301	Y	4	—	—	6.0	3.5	15.0⑬	15	195	18.4	19.3
	8-301	W	4	—	—	6.0	3.5	15.0⑬	15	195	18.4	19.3
	8-305	U	4	3.5	2.5	6.0	3.5⑰	15.0⑬	15	195	14.0	14.9
	8-305	R	4	—	—	6.0	3.5	15.0⑬	15	195	14.0	14.9
	8-350	L	4	—	2.5	6.0	3.5⑰	15.0⑬	15	195	17.5⑯	17.7⑯
	8-400	Z	5	—	2.5	6.0	4.25	18	15	195	19.7	20.3⑱
	8-403	K	4	—	2.5	6.0	4.25	18	15	195	16.8⑭	17.5⑭
'79	6-231	A-2	4	3.5	—	6.0	3.4⑰	18	15	195	13.6⑲	13.6
	8-301	Y-W	4	—	3.5	6.0	3.4⑰	18	15	195	21.8⑳	21.8
	8-305	G-H	4	—	—	6.0	3.4⑰	18	15	195	16.1㉑	16.1
	8-350	L-R-X	4	—	—	6.0	3.4⑰	18	15	195	16.1㉑	16.1
	8-400	Z	5	—	3.5	6.0	4.25	18	15	195	18.4	18.4
	8-403	K	4	—	—	6.0	4.25	18	15	195	20.4	20.4
'80	6-229	K	4	3.5	—	6.0	3.4⑰	㉔	15	195	13.6⑲	13.6⑲
	6-231	A	4	3.5	—	6.0	3.4⑰	㉔	15	195	13.6	13.6
	8-265	S	4	3.5	—	6.0	3.4⑰	㉔	15	195	12.8	12.8
	8-267	J	4	3.5	3.5	6.0	3.4⑰	㉔	15	195	16.1㉑	16.1㉑
	8-301	W	5	—	3.5	6.0	3.4⑰	㉔	15	195	21.8	21.8
	8-301	T	—	5	3.5	—	—	㉔	15	195	—	—
	8-305	H	4	—	—	6.0	3.4⑰	㉔	15	195	16.1㉑	16.1㉑
	8-350	X	4	—	—	6.0	3.4⑰	㉔	15	195	16.1㉑	16.1㉑
'81	6-231	A	4	3.5	—	6.0	3.4⑰	㉔	15	195	13.6	13.6
	8-265	S	4	3.5	—	6.0	3.4⑰	㉔	15	195	12.8	12.8
	8-301	W	5	—	3.5	6.0	3.4⑰	㉔	15	195	21.8	21.8
	8-301	T	—	5	3.5	—	—	㉔	15	195	23	23
	8-307	Y	4	3.5	3.5	6.0	3.4	㉔	15	195	15.3	16.0
	8-305	H	—	—	—	6.0	3.4⑰	㉔	15	195	16.1㉑	16.1㉑
'82	6-231		4	3.5	3.5	6.0	4.25	25⑨	15	195	13.7	13.7
	8-252		4	3.5	3.5	6.0	4.25	25⑨	15	195	13.7	13.7
	8-305		4	3.5	3.5	6.0	4.25	25⑨	15	195	15.7	15.6
	8-350	N	7.5	—	—	6.0	4.25	25⑨	15	195	18.0	17.9

— Not Applicable
N.A. Not Available
② 5.5 pts. with 8.875 in. ring gear (station wagon)
④ station wagon—22 gal.
⑤ Grand AM—25 gal.
⑥ Grand Prix—25 gal.
⑦ Firebird—20.2 gal.
⑧ 5.31 with 8.88 in. ring gear
⑨ 5 speed

⑩ Lower figure is 2 bbl engine/higher 4 bbl engine
⑪ In California 16.1 qts.
⑫ California engine 4 qts.
⑬ Firebird 21 gal., Grand Prix 15.0 gal., wagons—18 gal.
⑭ Heavy duty—19.4 qts.
⑮ Lemans—12.7 qts., Grand Prix—12.9 qts.
⑯ Lemans—14.0 qts. w/o air conditioning
14.9 qts. w/air conditioning
⑰ Firebird—4.25 pts.

⑱ w/auto trans—22.1
⑲ Firebird—15.8 qts.
㉑ Firebird—17.5 qts.
㉓ Specifications do not include torque converter
㉔ Lemans cp & sdn—18.1 gals.
Leman wagon—18.2 gals
Grand Prix—18.1 gals.
Firebird—20.8 gals.

A650

FLUID CAPACITIES—Coolant, Fuel & Lubricant

Year	Engine No. Cyl. Disp. (Cu. In.)	Engine Crankcase (Add 1 Qt For New Filter)	Transmission (Pts To Refill After Draining) Automatic ●	Drive Axle (pts)	Gasoline Tank (gals) ▲	Rad. Cap Press.	Thermo-Stat Temp.	COOLING SYSTEM (qts)	
								With Heater	With A/C
'76	8-400	5	7.5	5.31	25.8	15	195	21.6	22.4
	8-455	5	7.5	5.31	25.8	15	195	19.8	22.3
'77	6-231	5	7.5	4.25	20	15	195	12.1	13.1
	8-301	5	6.0	4.25	20	15	195	19.8	20.8
	8-350	5	6.0	4.25	20	15	195	14.3	15.3
	8-403	5	7.5	3.5	24.5	15	195	15.4	16.4
'78	6-231(A)	4	6.0	3.5	21.0	15	195	14.2	14.1
	8-301(Y-W)	5	6.0	3.5④	21.0	15	195	20.2	20.1
	8-350(R)	4	6.0	3.5④	21.0	15	195	16.5	16.4
	8-350(X)	4	6.0	3.5④	21.0	15	195	16.6③	18.5③
	8-400(Z)	5	6.0	3.5④	21.0	15	195	26.3	20.3
	8-403(K)	4	6.0	3.5④	21.0	15	195	17.7	23.0
'79	6-231	4	6.0	3.5	21.0	15	195	12.8	12.8
	8-301	5	6.0	3.5④	21.0	15	195	20.9	20.9
	8-350(X)	4	6.0	3.5④	21.0	15	195	16.6③	18.5③
	8-350(R)	4	6.0	3.5④	21.0	15	195	16.5	16.4
	8-403(K)	4	6.0	3.5④	21.0	15	195	16.3	16.3
'80	6-229(K)	4	6.0	3.5	⑤	15	195	12.8	12.8
	6-231(A)	4	6.0	3.5	⑤	15	195	12.8	12.8
	8-265(S)	4	6.0	3.5	⑤	15	195	12.8	12.8
	8-267(J)	4	6.0	3.5	⑤	15	195	20.9	20.9
	8-301(W)	5	6.0	3.5④	⑤	15	195	20.9	20.9
	8-350(X)	4	6.0	3.5④	⑤	15	195	16.5③	18.5③
	8-350(N)	6	6.0	3.5	⑤	15	195	18.0	18.0
	8-350(R)	4	6.0	3.5④	⑤	15	195	16.5③	18.5③
'81	6-231(A)	4	6.0	3.5	⑤	15	195	12.8	12.8
	8-265(S)	4	6.0	3.5	⑤	15	195	12.8	12.8
	8-301(W)	5	6.0	3.5④	⑤	15	195	20.9	20.9
	8-305	4	6.0	3.5	⑤	15	195	17.2	17.2
	8-307(Y)	4	6.0	3.5	⑤	15	195	15.3	16.0
	8-350(N)	6	6.0	3.5	⑤	15	195	18.0	18.0
'82	6-231	4	6.0	3.5	⑤	15	195	13.1	13.3
	8-252	4	6.0	3.5	⑤	15	195	13.1	13.3
	V8-305	4	6.0	3.5	⑤	15	195	17.2	17.2
	8-350(N)	6	6.0	3.5	⑤	15	195	17.0	17.0

● Specifications do not include torque converter

— Not Applicable

② 4.25 pts with 8.50 in. ring gear

▲ Station wagon fuel tank (gals)

  '75-'78   22 gals

③ Station wagon

  18.6 w/heater

  19.1 w/air cond.

④ Station wagons - 4.25 pts

⑤ Pontiac Cp & Sdn - 20.7 gals

  Pontiac Wagon - 22.0 gals

  Lemans Cp & Sdn - 18.1 gals

  Leman Wagon - 18.2 gals

  Grand Prix - 18.1 gals

  Firebird - 20.8 gals

Typical electric circuit panels

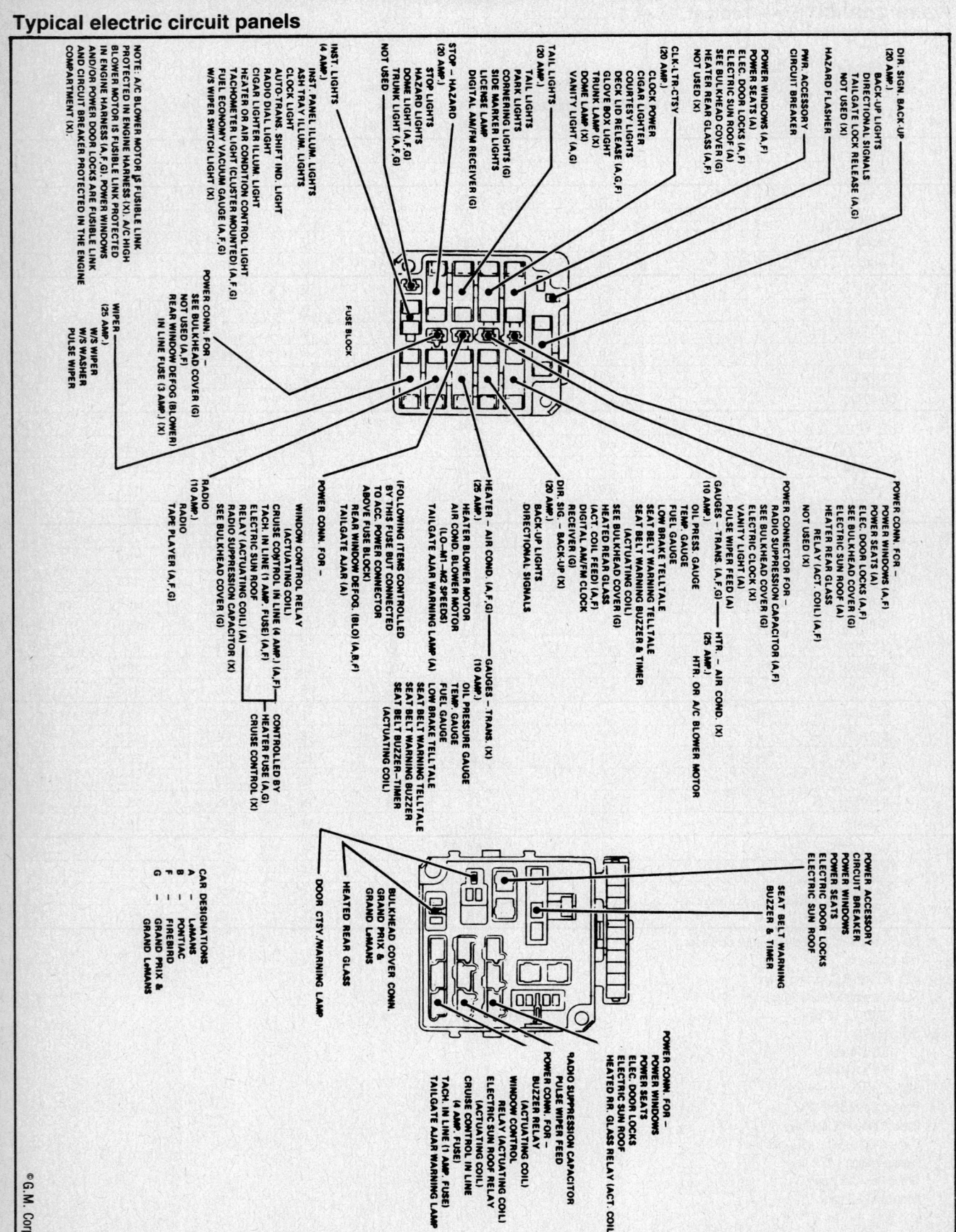

© G.M. Corp.

Typical fuse panel

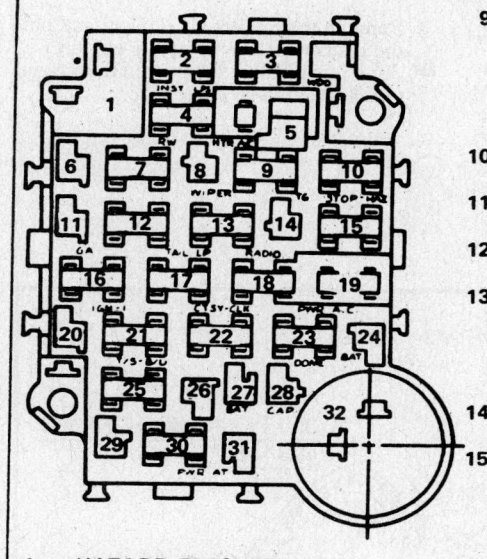

1 - HAZARD FLASHER

2 - INST. LIGHTS
(5 AMP.)
INST. PANEL ILLUM. LIGHTS
ASH TRAY ILLUM. LIGHT
CLOCK LIGHT
AUTO. TRANS. SHIFT
IND. LIGHT
RADIO DIAL LIGHT
CIGAR LIGHTER ILLUM.
HEATER OR AIR COND.
CONTROL LIGHT
FUEL ECONOMY VACUUM
GAUGE LIGHT (B)
W/S WIPER & HEADLAMP SW.
LIGHT

3 - ELECTRIC CHOKE
(20 AMP)
ELECTRIC CHOKE FEED—
V-6 (A & G)
THROTTLE SOL. (M.T.)—
V-6 (A & G)
NOT USED (B)

4 - NOT USED

5 - PWR. ACSRY.-CIRCUIT BREAKER
(30 AMP.)
POWER WINDOWS
POWER RR WINDOW (STA.
WAGON (B))
ELECTRIC SLIDING SUNROOF

6 - 11 - 20 -
IGN. NO. 1 POWER CONN. FOR —
(GAUGE FUSE)
HEATED RR GLASS RELAY
(ACTUATING COIL)
RADIO SUPPRESSION CAP.
(B-V-6)
PULSE WIPER (A & G)
BLOWER DEFOG (A)

7 - NOT USED

8 - HTD. RR GLASS TIMER

9 - HEATER - AIR COND.
(25 AMP.)
HEATER BLOWER MOTOR
AIR COND. BLOWER MOTOR
IDLE STOP SOLENOID

10 - NOT USED

11 - SEE ITEM NO. 6

12 - NOT USED

13 - WIPER
(25 AMP.)
W/S WIPER
W/S WASHER

14 - CRUISE CONTROL

15 - STOP - HAZARD
(20 AMP.)
STOP LIGHTS
HAZARD LIGHTS
KEY WARNING BUZZER

16 - GAUGES
(20 AMP.)
OIL PRES. GAUGE
TEMP. GAUGE
FUEL GAUGE
LOW BRAKE TELLTALE
SEAT BELT WARNING TELLTALE
SEAT BELT WARNING BUZZER
(ACTUATING COIL FEED)
SEAT BELT BUZZER TIMER
(ACTUATING COIL)
DECK LID RELEASE
TAILGATE UNLOCK (A)

17 - TAIL LIGHTS
(20 AMP.)
TAIL LIGHTS
PARK LIGHTS
CORNERING LIGHTS
SIDE MARKER LIGHTS
LICENSE LAMP

18 - RADIO
(10 AMP.)
RADIO
TAPE PLAYER
TAILGATE AJAR LIGHT (B)

19 - CIRCUIT BREAKER
(30 AMP.)
POWER CONNECTION FOR
ITEM NO. 8 AND 24

20 - SEE ITEM NO. 6

21 - DIR. - SIGN. - BACK-UP
(20 AMP.)
BACK-UP LIGHTS
DIRECTIONAL SIGNALS

22 - CLOCK - LTR. - CTSY.
(20 AMP.)
CLOCK POWER
CIGAR LIGHTER
CTSY. LIGHTS
GLOVE BOX LAMP
PULSE WIPER FEED
POWER ANTENNA
TO HORNS
DIGITAL AM/FM CLOCK
RECEIVER

23 - DOME LAMP
(20 AMP.)
VANITY LIGHT
DOME LAMP
RADIO SUPPRESSION
CAPACITOR
TRUNK LIGHT
DOOR COURTESY & WARNING
LAMP (B & G)

24 - POWER CONN. FOR —

ELECTRIC DOOR LOCKS
POWER SEATS

25 - NOT USED

26 - NOT USED

27 - 31 -
POWER CONN. FOR
(CLK-LTR-CTSY FUSE)
PULSE WIPER (B)
POWER ANTENNA
RADIO SUPPRESSION CAP
(A & G)

28 - POWER CONN. FOR —
(DOME LAMP FUSE)
RADIO SUPPRESSION
CAPACITOR
(B—V-8 ONLY)

29 - POWER CONN. FOR—
(RADIO FUSE)
TAILGATE AJAR LAMP (B)

30 - NOT USED

31 - SEE ITEM NO. 27

32 - DIRECTIONAL SIGNAL
FLASHER

CAR DESIGNATIONS

A — LeMANS, GRAND LeMANS,
GRAND AM
G — GRAND PRIX
B — CATALINA
BONNEVILLE

ELECTRICAL SECTION

Starter

- Disconnect electrical wiring, starter braces and shields that may be in the way, and the engine crossmember with the Buick built V6 engine.
- When reinstalling the same starter, replace all mounting pad shims in their original locations.

Ignition Distributor

- Remove distributor cap, electrical wiring, vacuum hose, etc. from the distributor.
- Put alignment marks on rotor and distributor housing for installation reference.

- Remove the hold-down device, and pull the distributor up out of the engine.
- After installation, set ignition timing and check dwell, idle speed, etc.

Starter mounting and noise diagnostic procedure

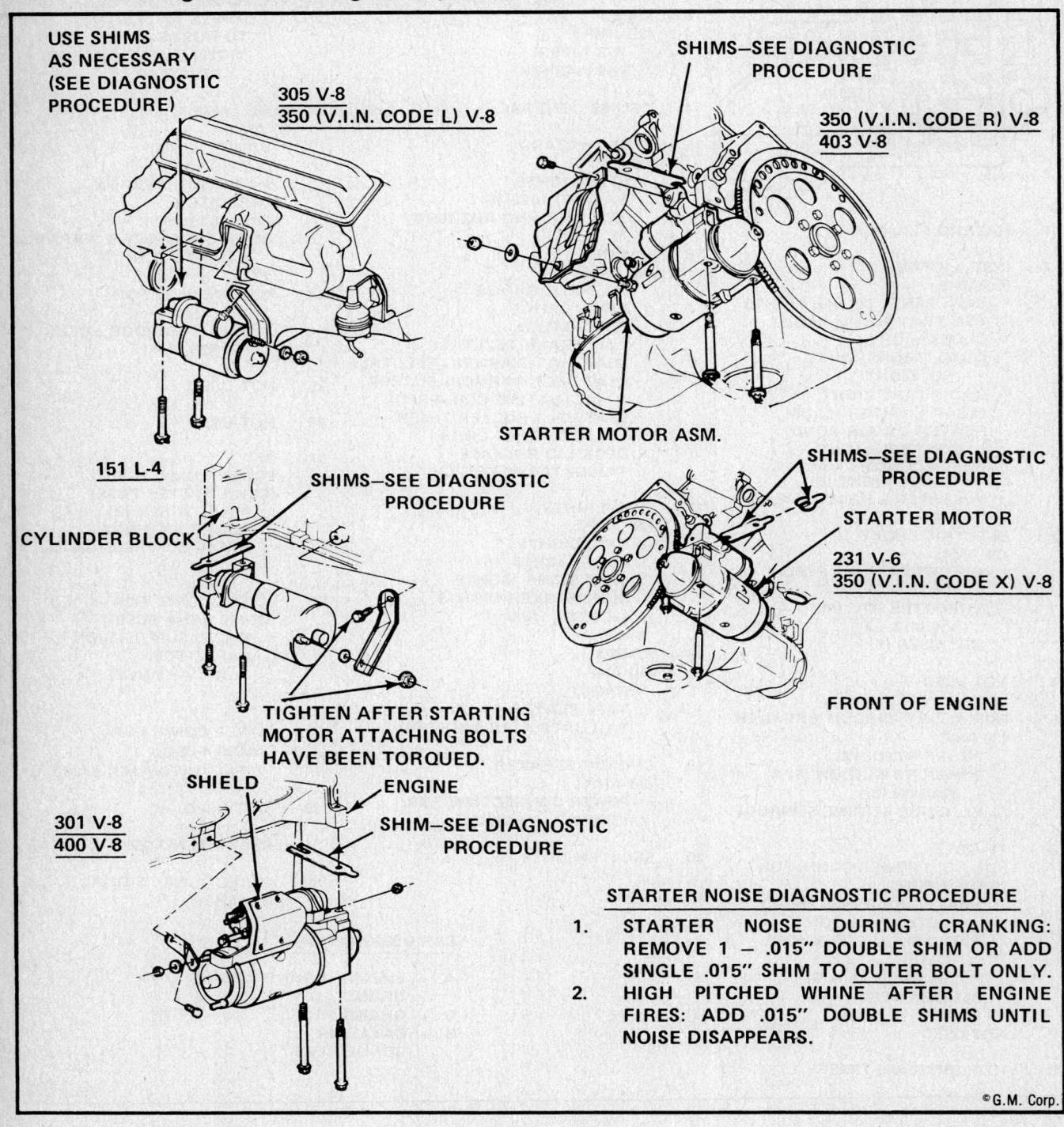

USE SHIMS AS NECESSARY (SEE DIAGNOSTIC PROCEDURE)

305 V-8
350 (V.I.N. CODE L) V-8

SHIMS—SEE DIAGNOSTIC PROCEDURE

350 (V.I.N. CODE R) V-8
403 V-8

STARTER MOTOR ASM.

151 L-4

SHIMS—SEE DIAGNOSTIC PROCEDURE

CYLINDER BLOCK

TIGHTEN AFTER STARTING MOTOR ATTACHING BOLTS HAVE BEEN TORQUED.

SHIELD

ENGINE

SHIM—SEE DIAGNOSTIC PROCEDURE

301 V-8
400 V-8

SHIMS—SEE DIAGNOSTIC PROCEDURE

STARTER MOTOR

231 V-6
350 (V.I.N. CODE X) V-8

FRONT OF ENGINE

STARTER NOISE DIAGNOSTIC PROCEDURE

1. STARTER NOISE DURING CRANKING: REMOVE 1 — .015″ DOUBLE SHIM OR ADD SINGLE .015″ SHIM TO OUTER BOLT ONLY.
2. HIGH PITCHED WHINE AFTER ENGINE FIRES: ADD .015″ DOUBLE SHIMS UNTIL NOISE DISAPPEARS.

© G.M. Corp.

Ignition Switch

- The ignition switch is mounted on the lower section of the steering column. The column must be lowered for switch replacement.
- Disconnect the shift indicator linkage and lower the steering column.
- Disconnect actuator rod and electrical connection.

Ignition Lock

- Remove the steering wheel and lock plate, and pull the turn signal switch up out of the way.
- With key cylinder in RUN position, depress retaining tab and pull lock cylinder out of housing.
- To install, turn the key fully clockwise to stop. Insert cylinder into housing until it bottoms, then turn key counterclockwise with slight inward pressure until drive section clicks into drive shaft.

Positioning ignition switch

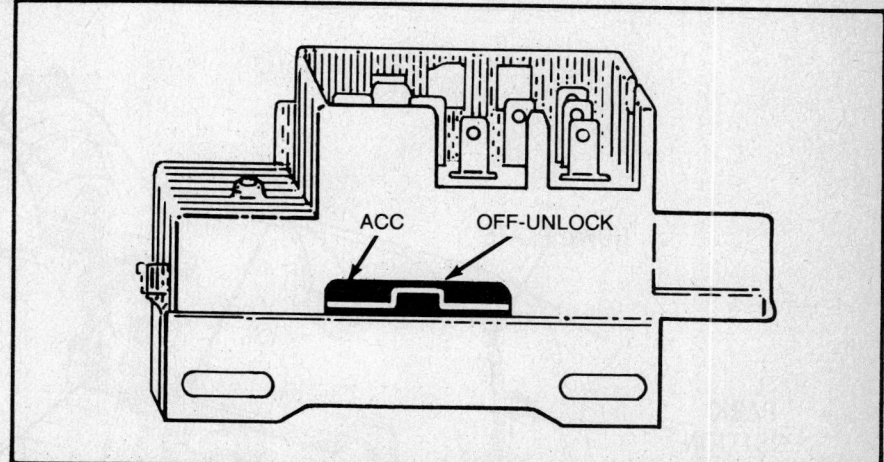

Move switch slider to extreme left (acc) position, then move slider two detents to the right of "off-unlock" position

Ignition lock

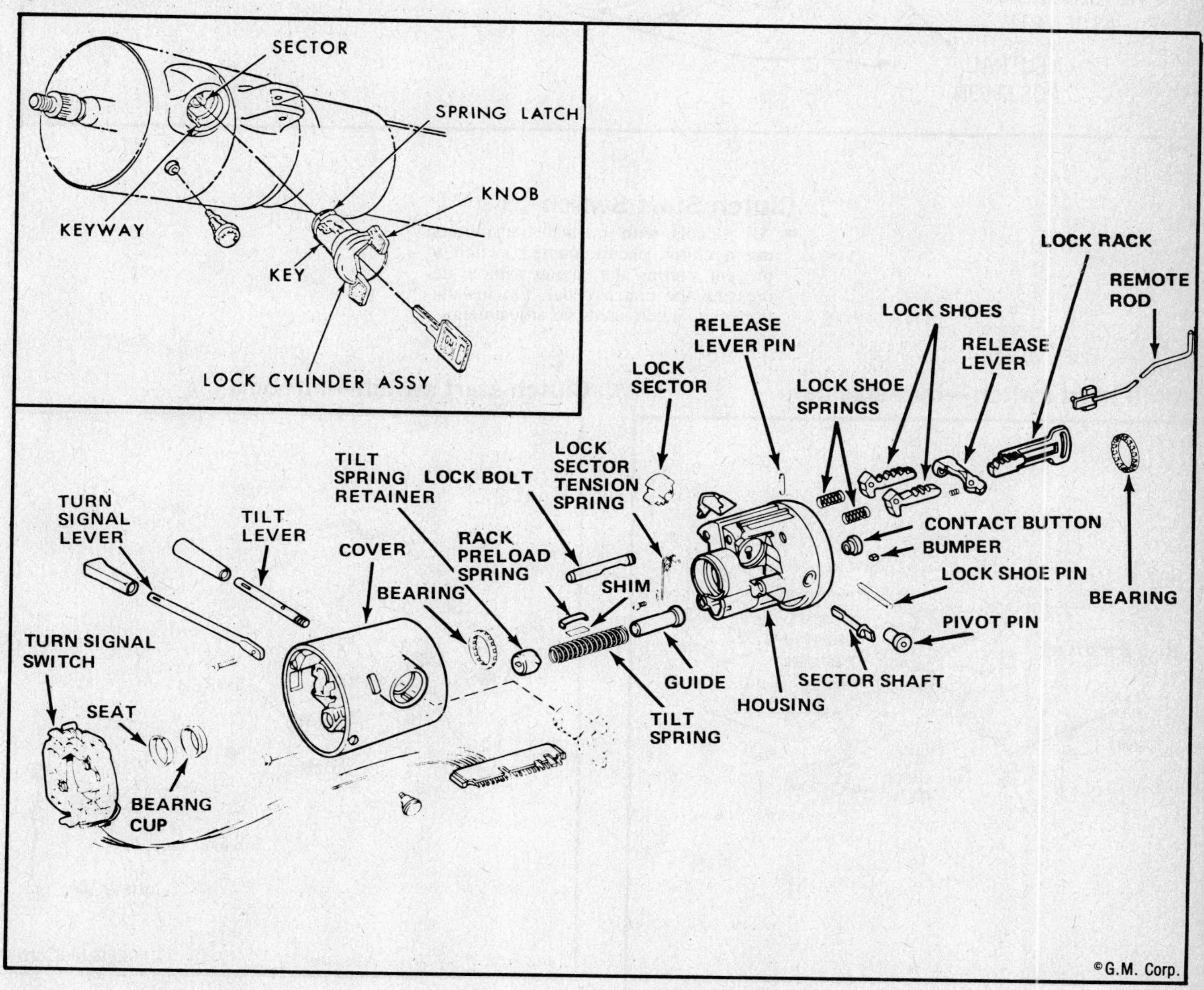

SECTOR

SPRING LATCH

KNOB

KEYWAY

KEY

LOCK CYLINDER ASSY

TURN SIGNAL LEVER

TILT LEVER

TILT SPRING RETAINER

LOCK BOLT

RACK PRELOAD SPRING

LOCK SECTOR TENSION SPRING

COVER

BEARING

LOCK SECTOR

RELEASE LEVER PIN

LOCK SHOE SPRINGS

LOCK SHOES

RELEASE LEVER

LOCK RACK

REMOTE ROD

CONTACT BUTTON

BUMPER

LOCK SHOE PIN

BEARING

PIVOT PIN

SHIM

TURN SIGNAL SWITCH

SEAT

BEARNG CUP

GUIDE

TILT SPRING

HOUSING

SECTOR SHAFT

©G.M. Corp.

PONTIAC
EXCEPT ASTRE, A6000, '80-'82 PHOENIX & T1000

Mechanical neutral start system

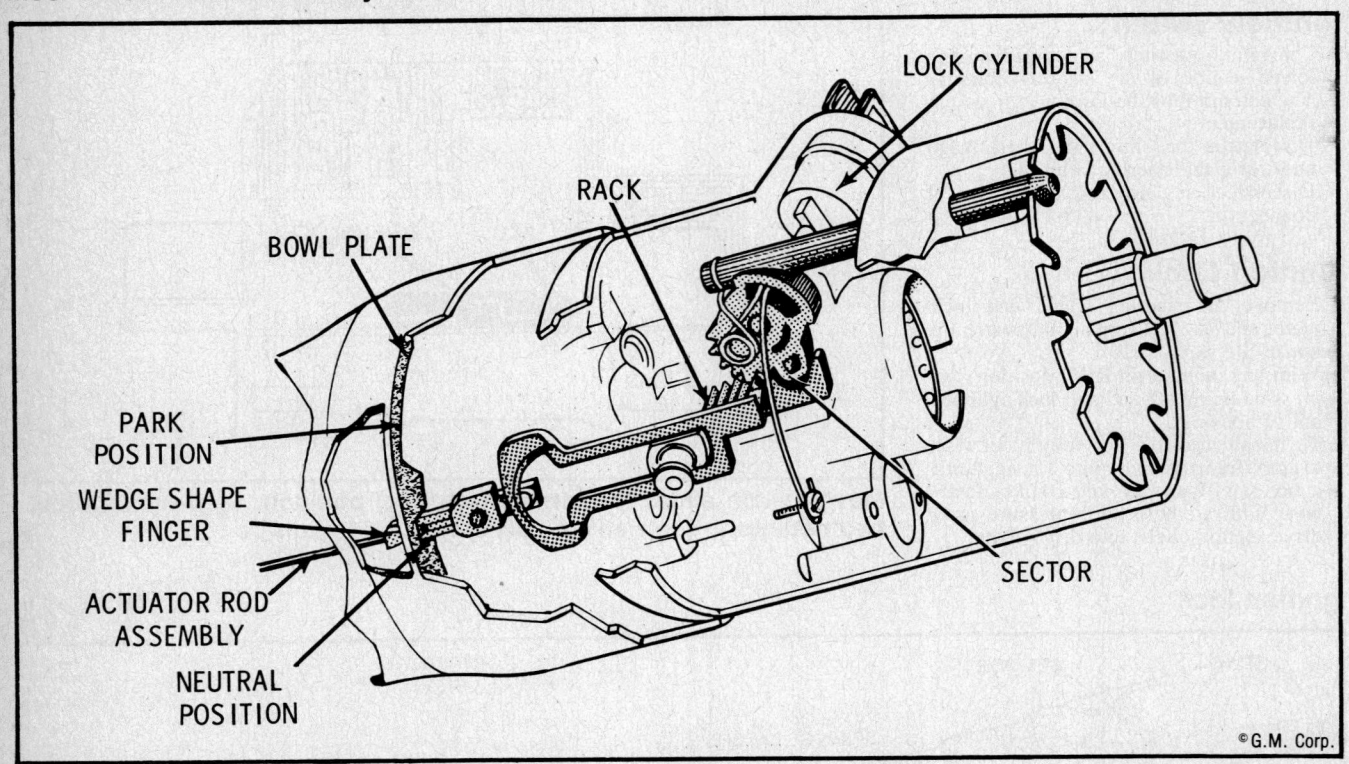

Clutch Start Switch
- All models with manual transmission use a clutch pedal-mounted switch to prevent starting the engine without depressing the clutch pedal. On installation, the switch needs no adjustment.

Clutch start switch—mid-size cars

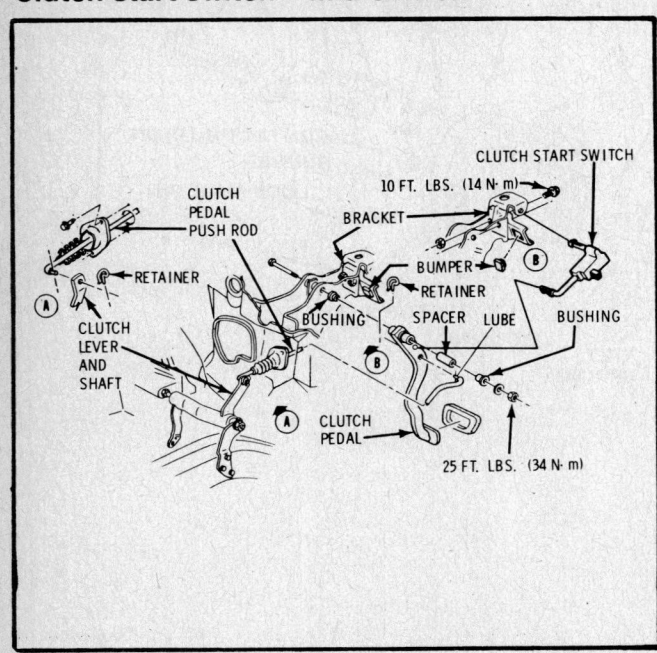

Clutch start switch—Firebird

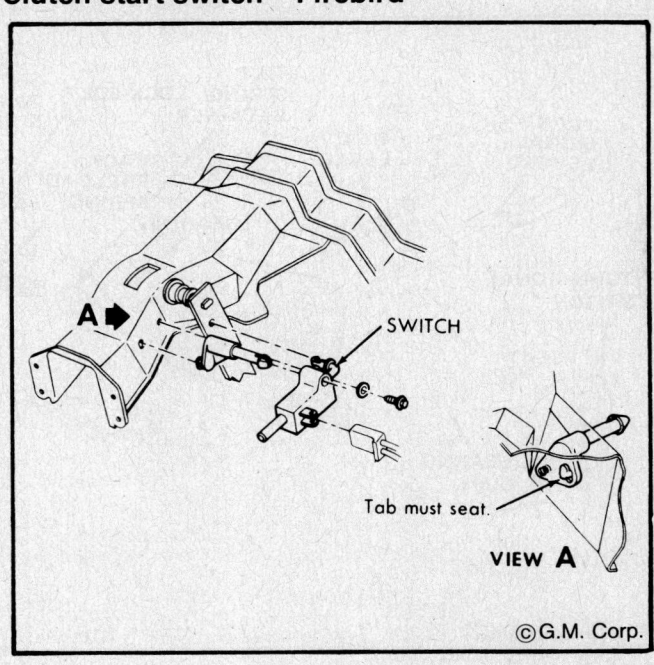

Stoplight Switch

- The switch is mounted on the brake pedal bracket.
- To adjust, depress the pedal and push the switch through the circular retaining clip until it contacts the brake pedal, then pull the pedal up against the internal pedal stop. This places the switch in the correct position within the clip.

Horn Switch And Steering Wheel

- Use a puller to remove the steering wheel.
- Disconnect horn electrical leads.

Steering wheel puller

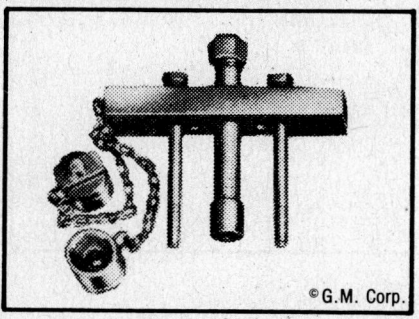

© G.M. Corp.

Stoplight switch mounting and adjustment

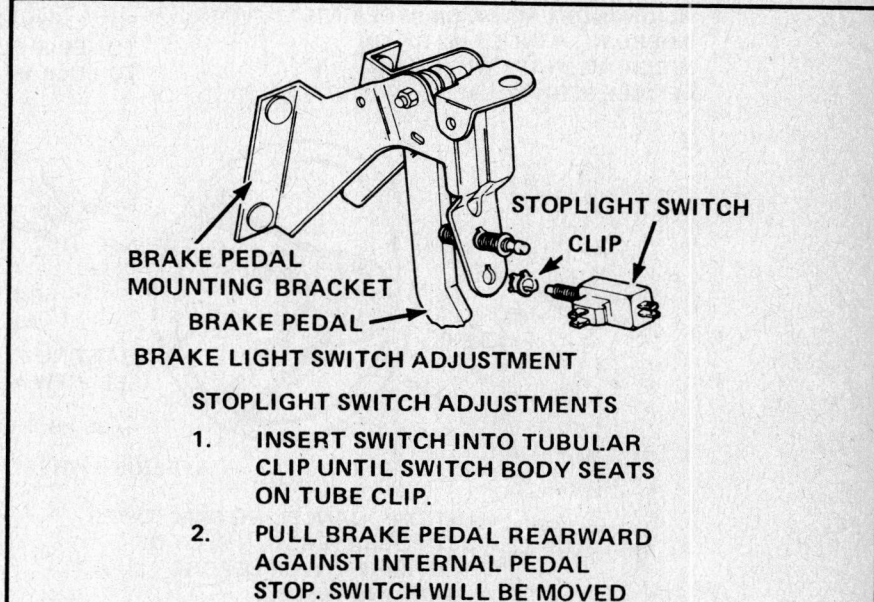

BRAKE PEDAL MOUNTING BRACKET
BRAKE PEDAL
STOPLIGHT SWITCH CLIP

BRAKE LIGHT SWITCH ADJUSTMENT

STOPLIGHT SWITCH ADJUSTMENTS

1. INSERT SWITCH INTO TUBULAR CLIP UNTIL SWITCH BODY SEATS ON TUBE CLIP.
2. PULL BRAKE PEDAL REARWARD AGAINST INTERNAL PEDAL STOP. SWITCH WILL BE MOVED IN TUBULAR CLIP PROVIDING PROPER ADJUSTMENT.

© G.M. Corp.

Horn switch and steering wheel mounting

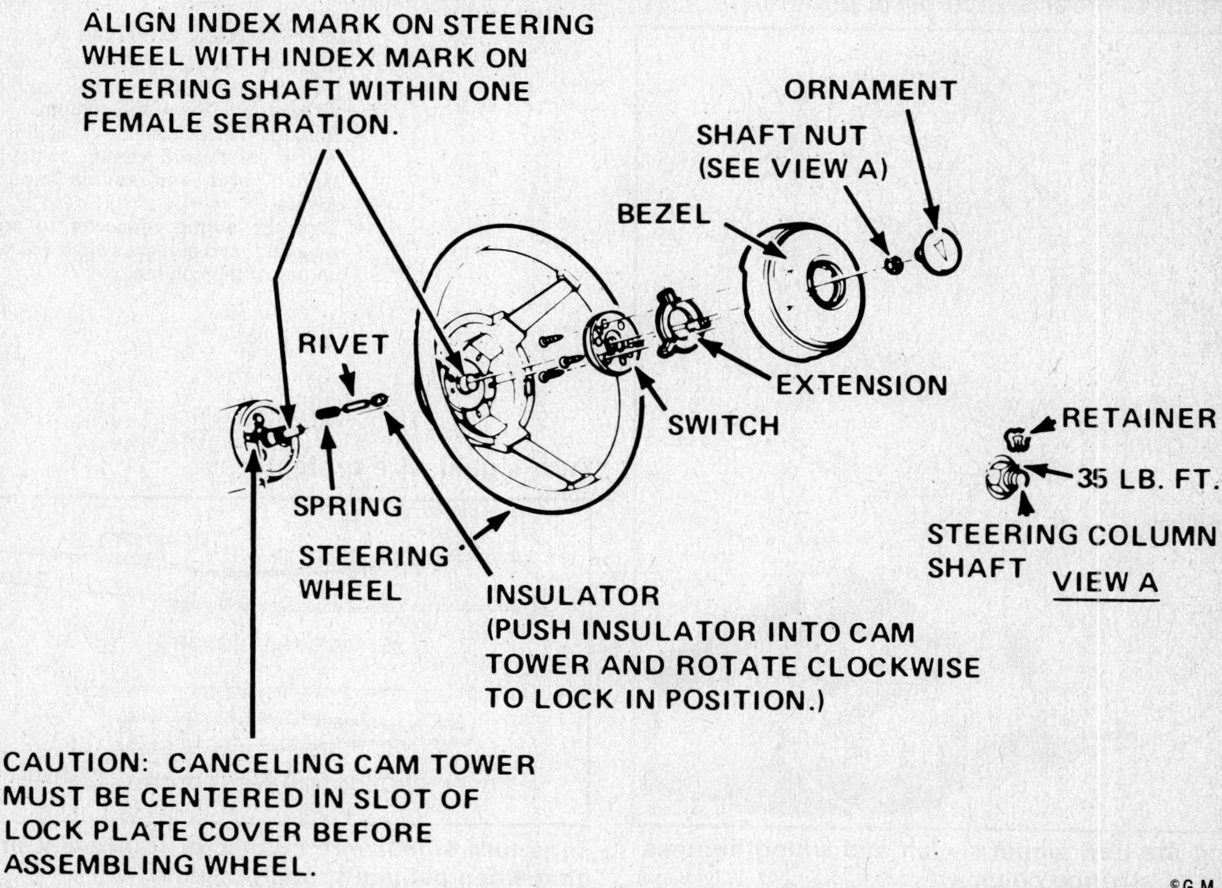

ALIGN INDEX MARK ON STEERING WHEEL WITH INDEX MARK ON STEERING SHAFT WITHIN ONE FEMALE SERRATION.

ORNAMENT
SHAFT NUT (SEE VIEW A)
BEZEL
RIVET
EXTENSION
SWITCH
SPRING
STEERING WHEEL
INSULATOR (PUSH INSULATOR INTO CAM TOWER AND ROTATE CLOCKWISE TO LOCK IN POSITION.)

RETAINER
35 LB. FT.
STEERING COLUMN SHAFT VIEW A

CAUTION: CANCELING CAM TOWER MUST BE CENTERED IN SLOT OF LOCK PLATE COVER BEFORE ASSEMBLING WHEEL.

© G.M. Corp.

A657

Typical horn switch and steering wheel mounting (cushion wheel)

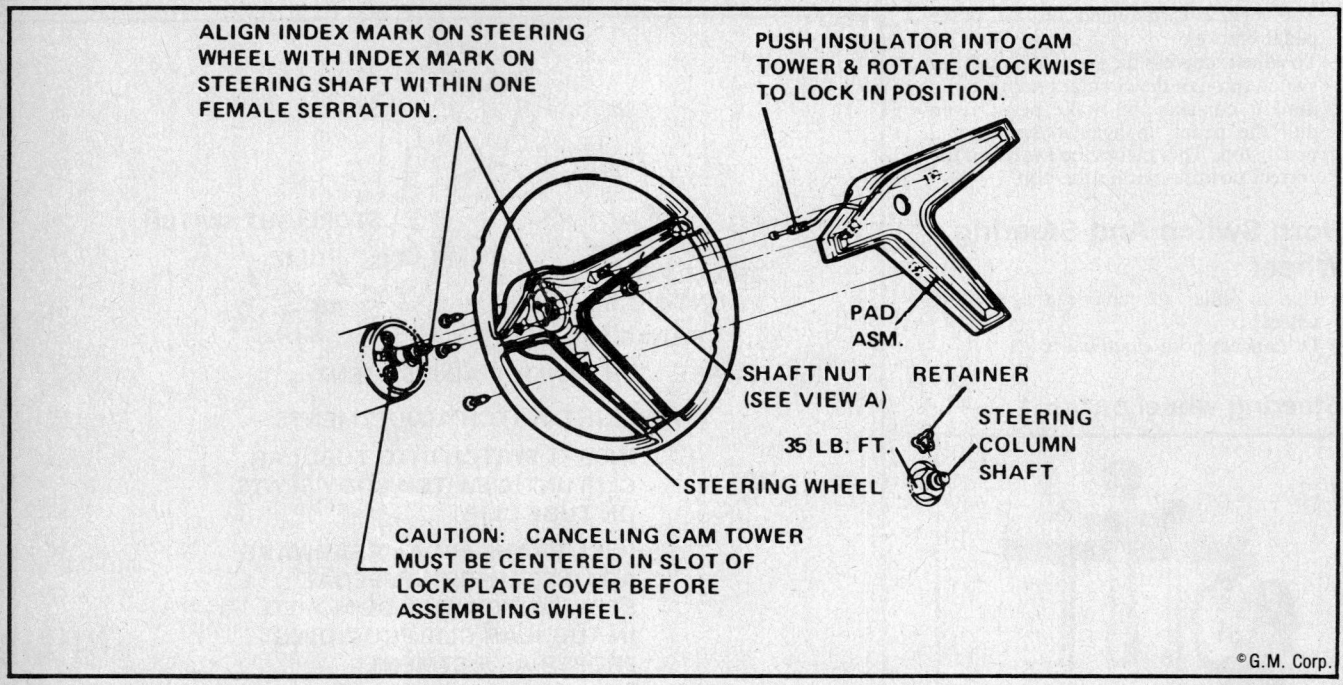

ALIGN INDEX MARK ON STEERING WHEEL WITH INDEX MARK ON STEERING SHAFT WITHIN ONE FEMALE SERRATION.

PUSH INSULATOR INTO CAM TOWER & ROTATE CLOCKWISE TO LOCK IN POSITION.

PAD ASM.

SHAFT NUT (SEE VIEW A)

RETAINER

STEERING COLUMN SHAFT

35 LB. FT.

STEERING WHEEL

CAUTION: CANCELING CAM TOWER MUST BE CENTERED IN SLOT OF LOCK PLATE COVER BEFORE ASSEMBLING WHEEL.

© G.M. Corp.

Headlight dimmer switch pivot pin

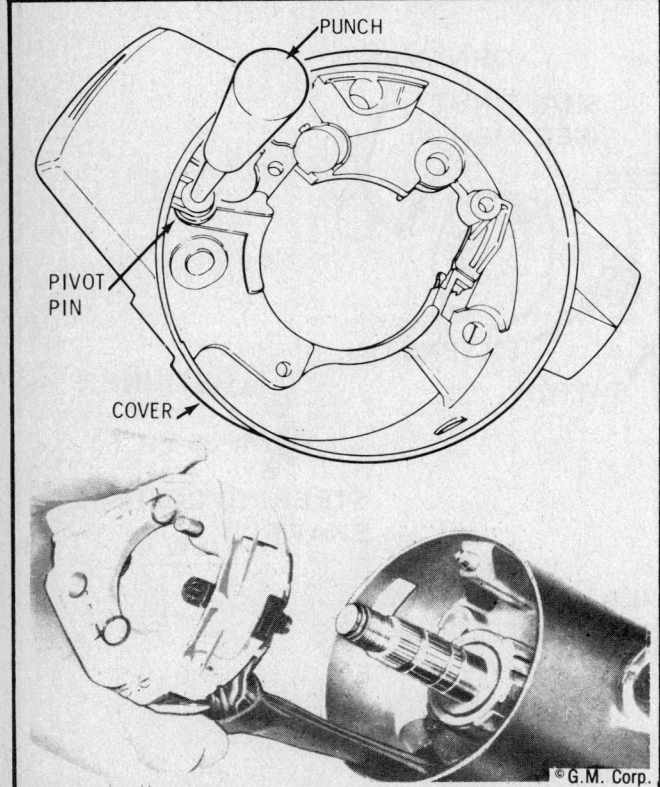

PUNCH

PIVOT PIN

COVER

© G.M. Corp.

Pulling the turn signal switch and wiring harness up out of steering column

Turn Signal Switch

- Remove the steering wheel and lock plate cover. On tilt columns, remove the tilt lever and lower the column.
- Remove the lock plate, cancelling cam and spring, hazard warning switch, turn signal lever and switch mounting screws.
- Tape the wiring connector to prevent snagging, and pull the switch and wiring up out of the column.

Turn signal wire protectors

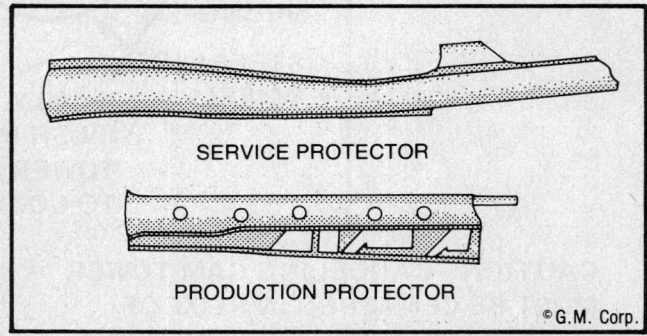

SERVICE PROTECTOR

PRODUCTION PROTECTOR

© G.M. Corp.

Tape turn signal wire connector to prevent snagging when pulling through column

Speed control cable and lever installation

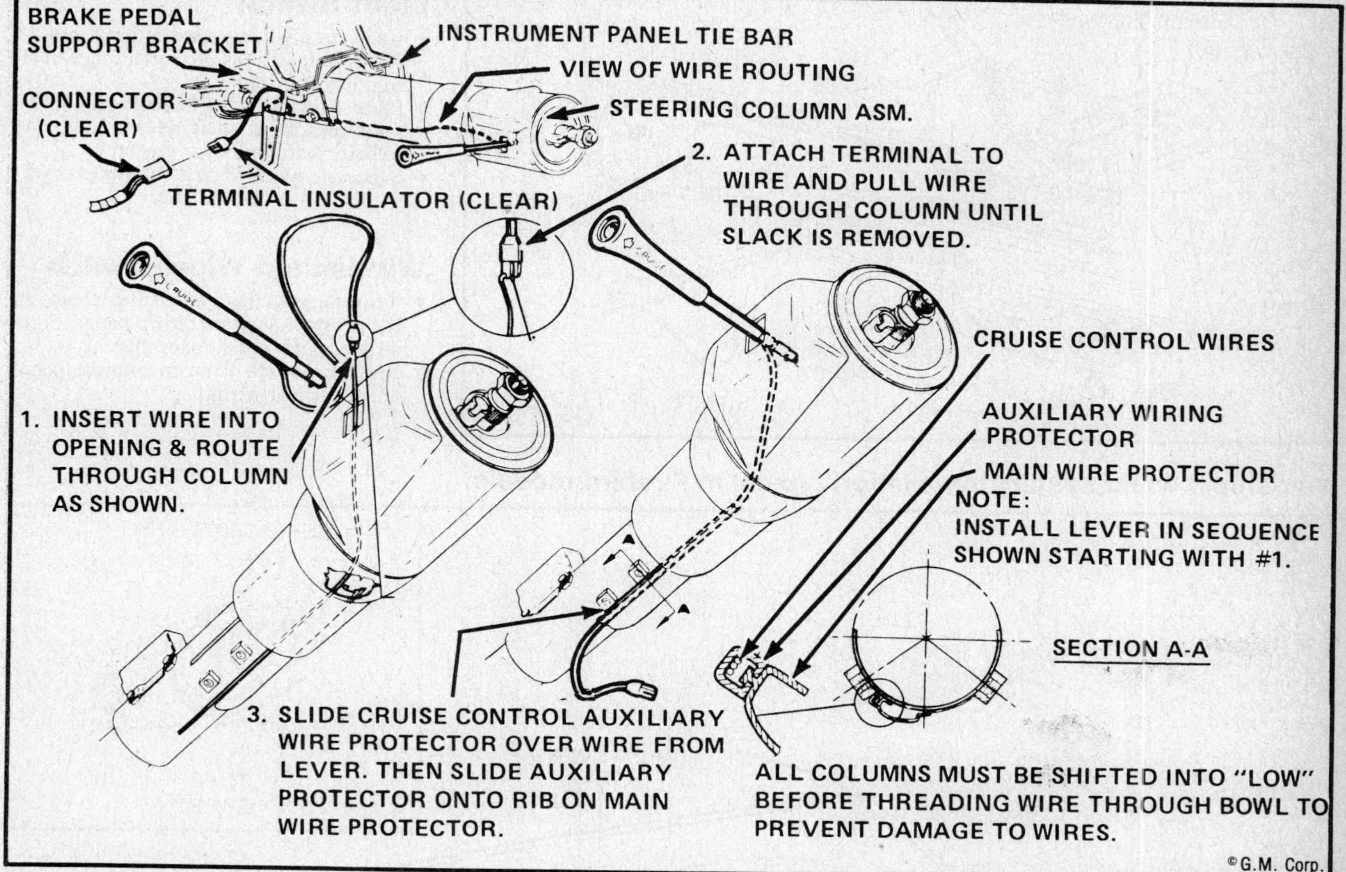

BRAKE PEDAL SUPPORT BRACKET

INSTRUMENT PANEL TIE BAR

VIEW OF WIRE ROUTING

STEERING COLUMN ASM.

CONNECTOR (CLEAR)

TERMINAL INSULATOR (CLEAR)

2. ATTACH TERMINAL TO WIRE AND PULL WIRE THROUGH COLUMN UNTIL SLACK IS REMOVED.

1. INSERT WIRE INTO OPENING & ROUTE THROUGH COLUMN AS SHOWN.

CRUISE CONTROL WIRES

AUXILIARY WIRING PROTECTOR

MAIN WIRE PROTECTOR

NOTE:
INSTALL LEVER IN SEQUENCE SHOWN STARTING WITH #1.

SECTION A-A

3. SLIDE CRUISE CONTROL AUXILIARY WIRE PROTECTOR OVER WIRE FROM LEVER. THEN SLIDE AUXILIARY PROTECTOR ONTO RIB ON MAIN WIRE PROTECTOR.

ALL COLUMNS MUST BE SHIFTED INTO "LOW" BEFORE THREADING WIRE THROUGH BOWL TO PREVENT DAMAGE TO WIRES.

© G.M. Corp.

Steering column-mounted headlight dimmer switch mounting

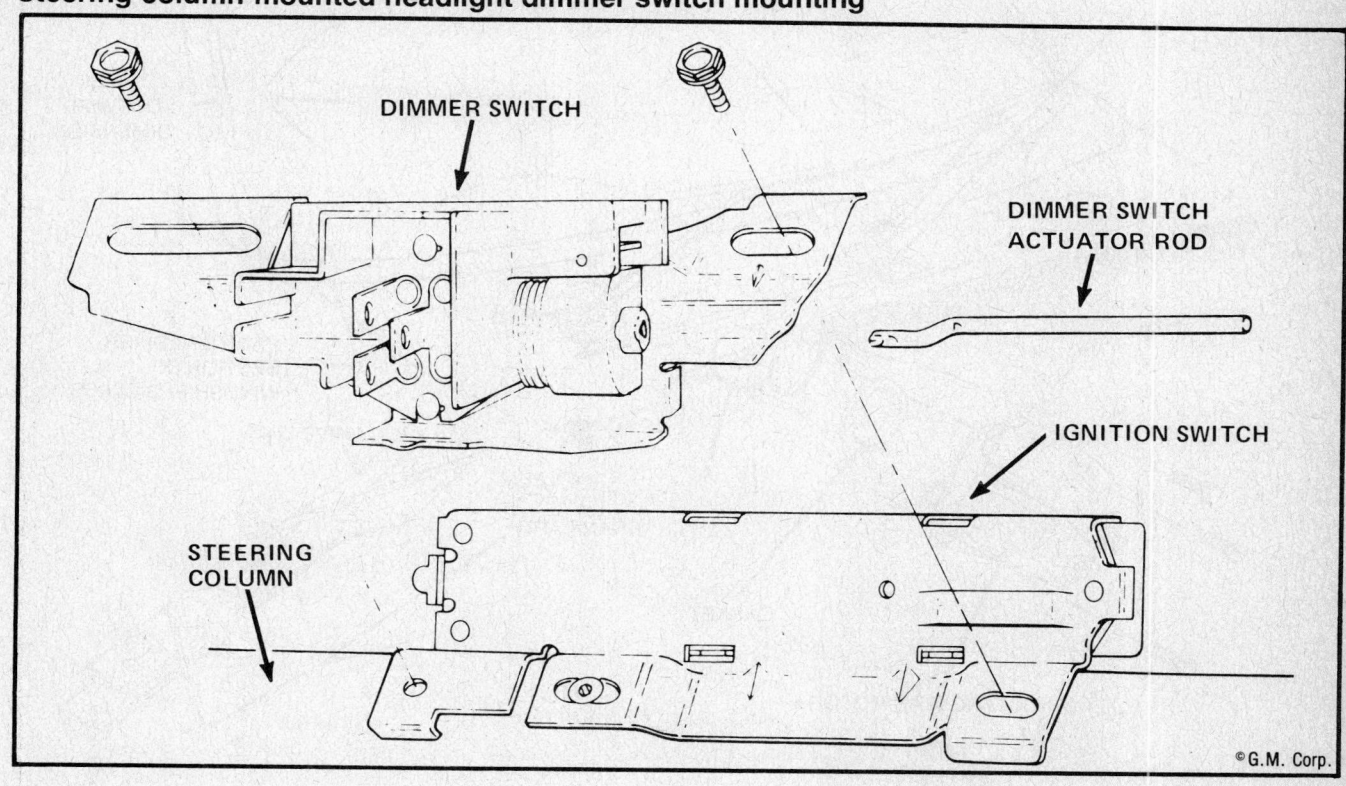

DIMMER SWITCH

DIMMER SWITCH ACTUATOR ROD

IGNITION SWITCH

STEERING COLUMN

© G.M. Corp.

PONTIAC
EXCEPT ASTRE, A6000, '80-'82 PHOENIX & T1000

Headlight switch mounting—mid-size cars

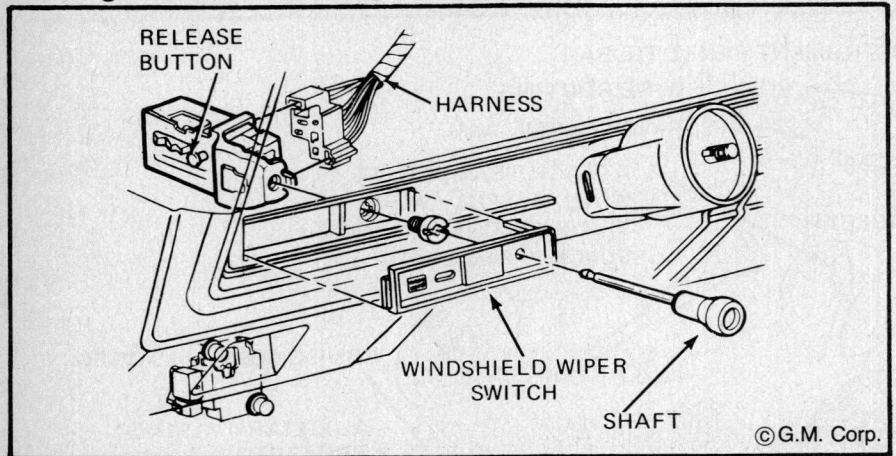

RELEASE BUTTON

HARNESS

WINDSHIELD WIPER SWITCH

SHAFT

©G.M. Corp.

Light Switch
- Relocate anything preventing access to the switch such as air conditioner ducting or trim panel.
- Place switch in full ON Position. Pull on knob and press shaft release button to release shaft and knob assembly.
- Separate switch from mounting bracket.

Windshield Wiper Switch
- Relocate anything preventing access to the switch such as trim panel, light switch or air conditioner ducting.
- Separate switch from instrument panel and electrical wiring.

Windshield wiper system installation typical in Firebird models

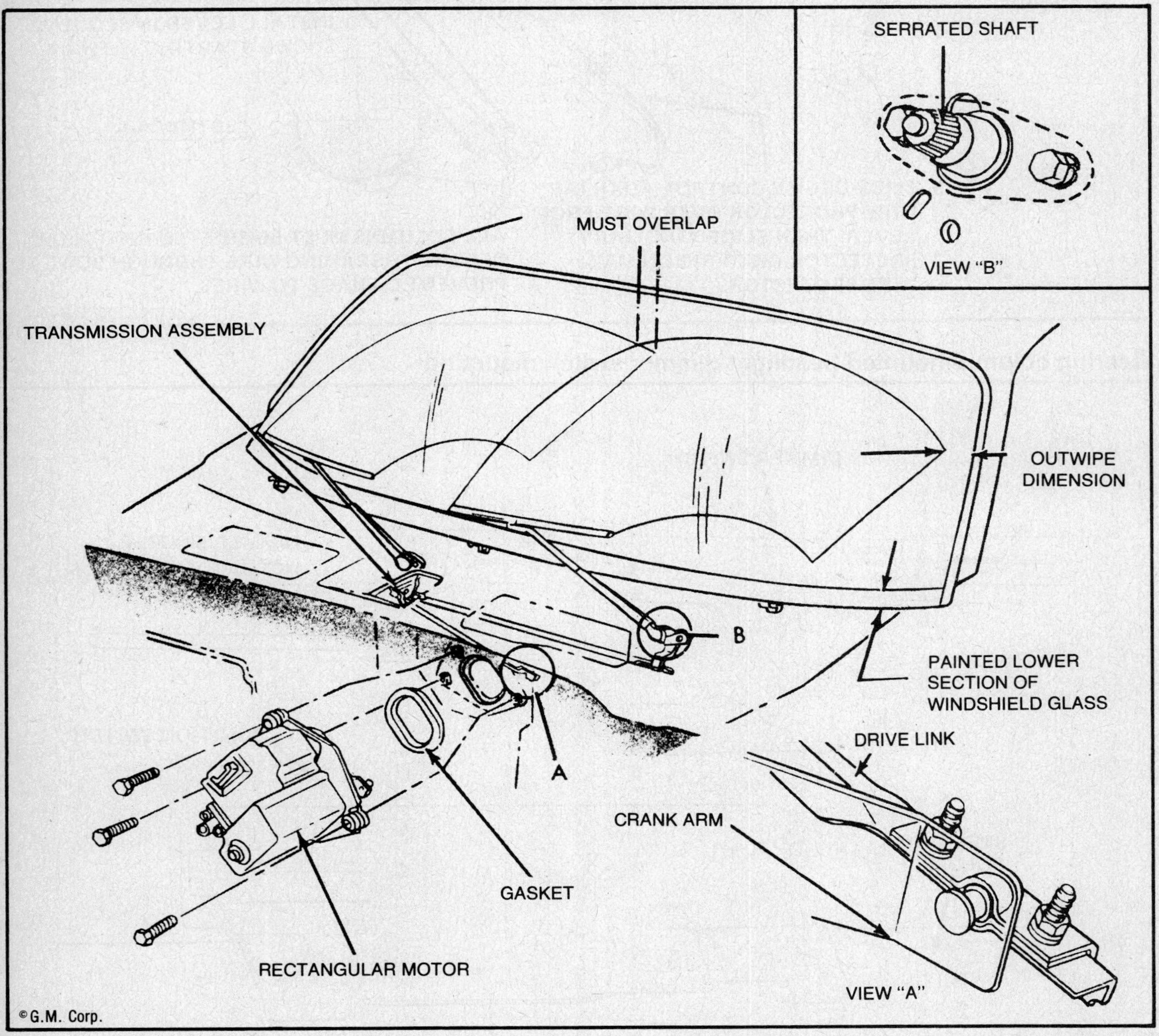

SERRATED SHAFT

VIEW "B"

MUST OVERLAP

TRANSMISSION ASSEMBLY

OUTWIPE DIMENSION

B

PAINTED LOWER SECTION OF WINDSHIELD GLASS

A

DRIVE LINK

CRANK ARM

GASKET

RECTANGULAR MOTOR

VIEW "A"

©G.M. Corp.

Windshield wiper system mounting typical in mid-size car models

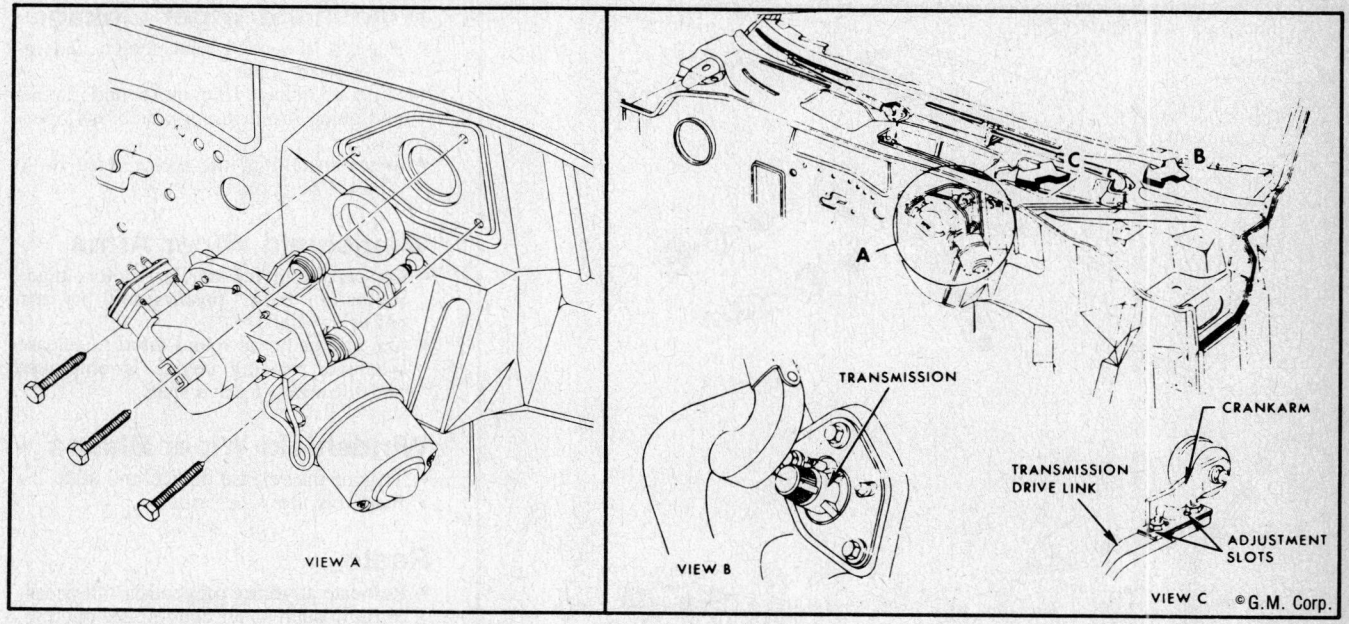

VIEW A

VIEW B

CRANKARM

TRANSMISSION DRIVE LINK

ADJUSTMENT SLOTS

TRANSMISSION

VIEW C   © G.M. Corp.

Windshield Wiper Motor

- Remove the cowl screen, and separate the motor from mounts, electrical connections, linkage, etc.
- Motor must be in "Park" position when assembling crank arm to drive link in vehicles using a round motor.

Windshield wiper linkage installation typical in full-size car models

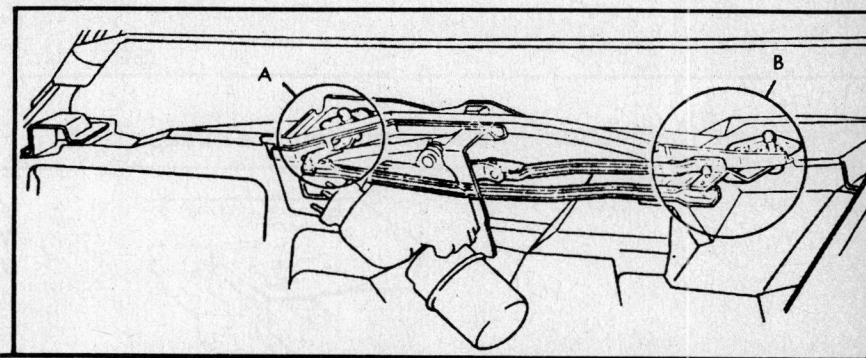

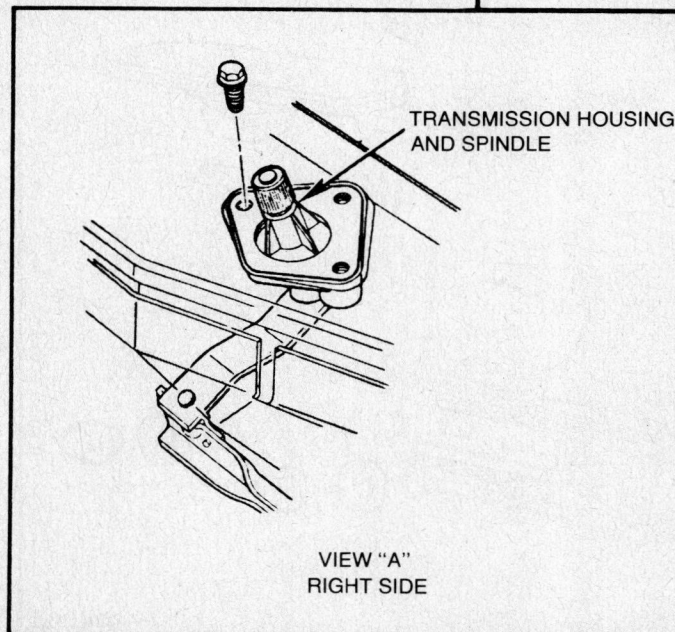

TRANSMISSION HOUSING AND SPINDLE

VIEW "A"
RIGHT SIDE

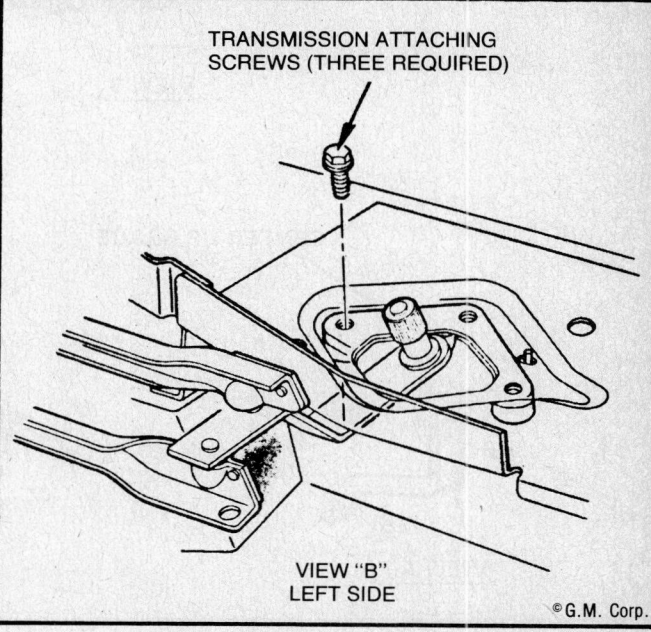

TRANSMISSION ATTACHING SCREWS (THREE REQUIRED)

VIEW "B"
LEFT SIDE

© G.M. Corp.

A661

Radio mounting—Firebird

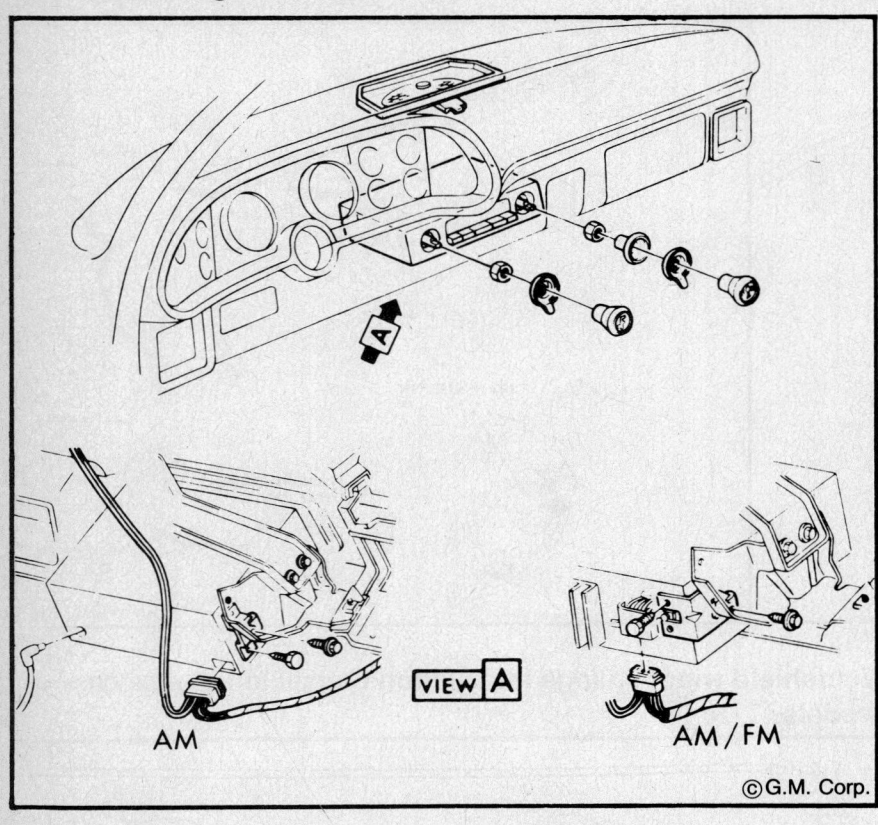

AM

VIEW A

AM/FM

©G.M. Corp.

Windshield Wiper Linkage
- Remove the cowl vent screen and remove wiper arms.
- Separate linkage from motor and mounts and guide it out through the cowl opening.
- When installing, the motor must be in "Park" position.

Windshield Wiper Arms
- On car using rectangular motor, place motor in "Park" position and pry arm off drive shaft.
- On car using a round motor, release whatever holding device is employed and lift arm off drive shaft.

Windshield Wiper Blades
- Trigger the release device and slide the blade off the wiper arm.

Radio
- Relocate anything preventing full access to radio such as air conditioner ducting, ash tray, instrument panel trim, glove box, etc.
- Remove mounting screws, knobs, etc., and remove radio from antenna, power and speaker connections.

Typical radio installation, Phoenix and Ventura except 1980

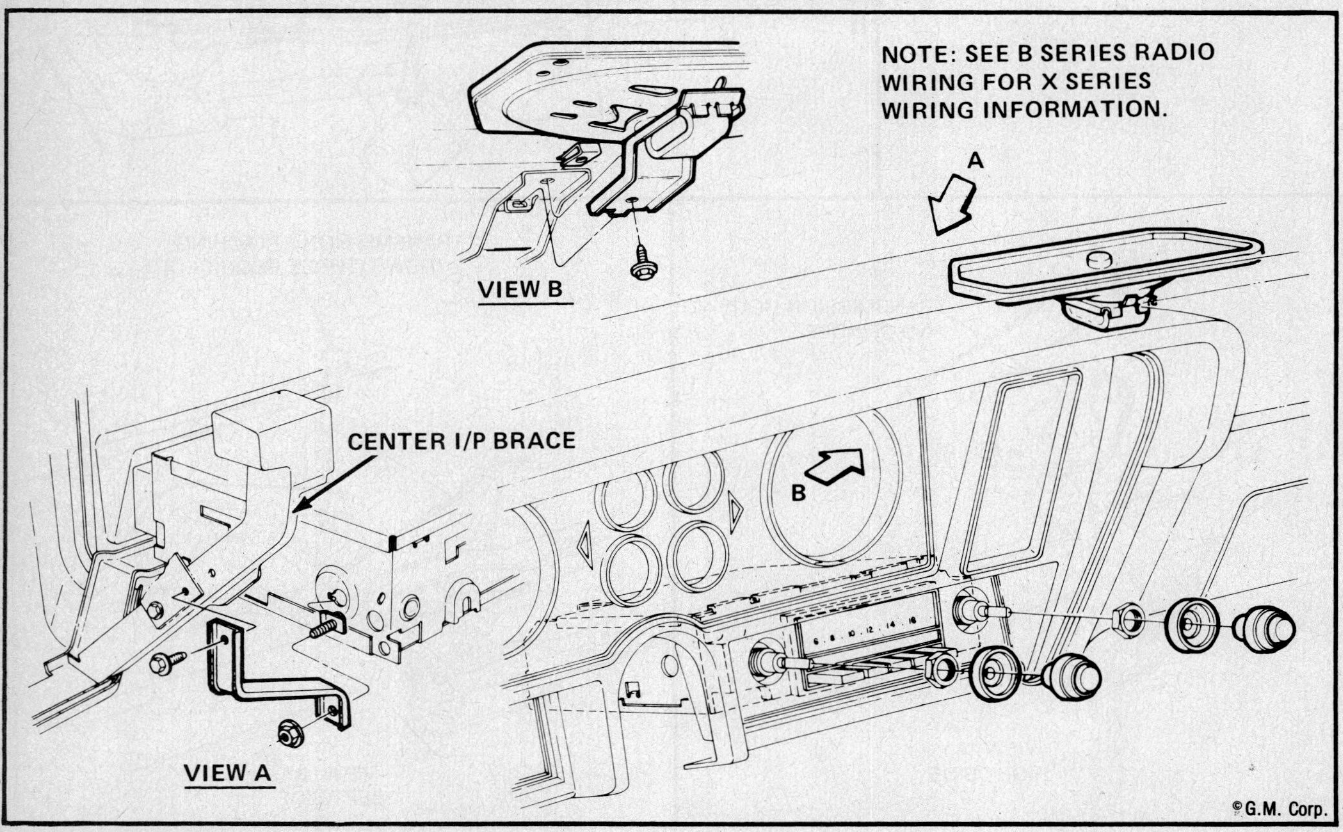

NOTE: SEE B SERIES RADIO WIRING FOR X SERIES WIRING INFORMATION.

VIEW B

A

CENTER I/P BRACE

B

VIEW A

©G.M. Corp.

Radio installation, mid-size cars

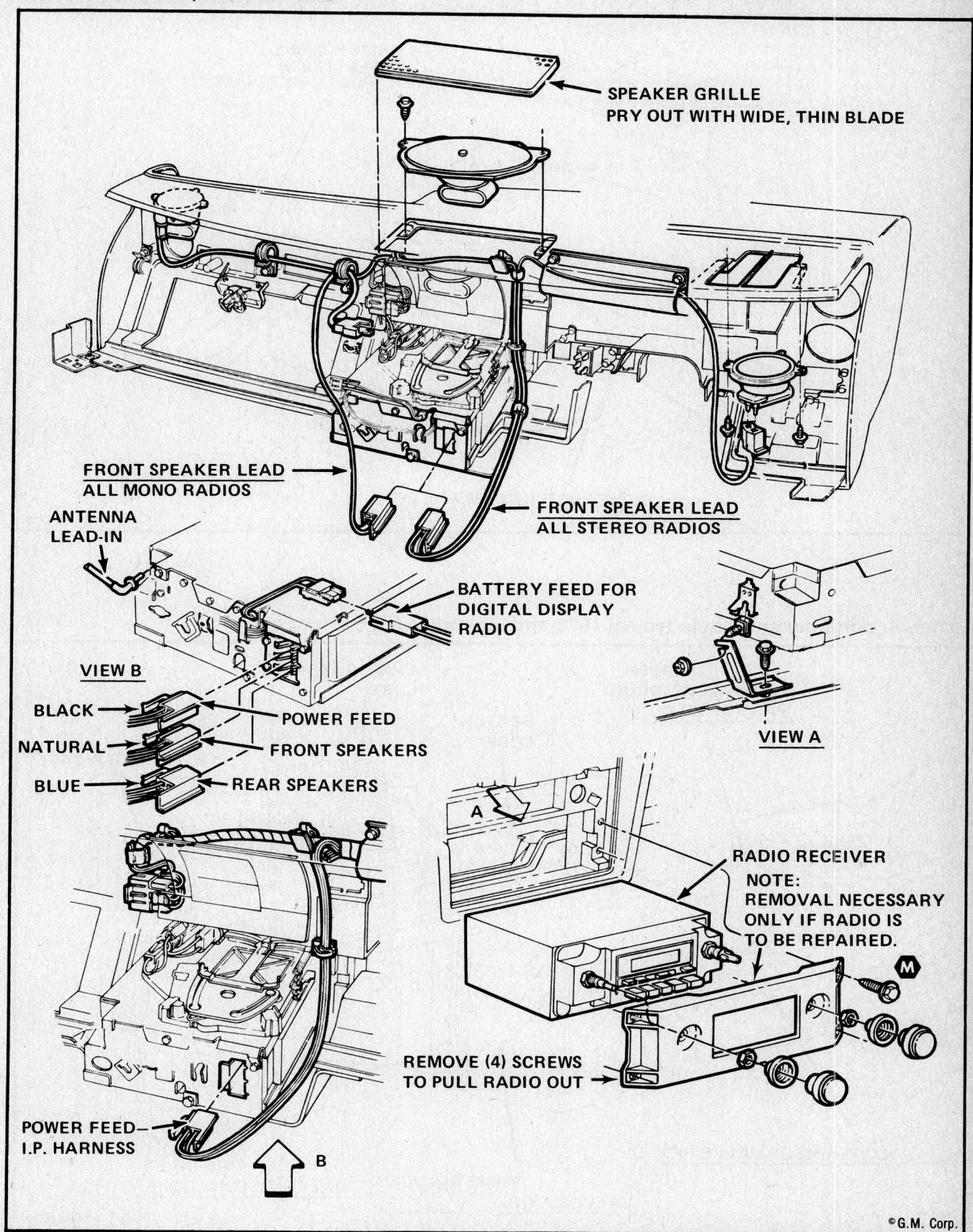

SPEAKER GRILLE
PRY OUT WITH WIDE, THIN BLADE

FRONT SPEAKER LEAD
ALL MONO RADIOS

ANTENNA
LEAD-IN

FRONT SPEAKER LEAD
ALL STEREO RADIOS

BATTERY FEED FOR
DIGITAL DISPLAY
RADIO

VIEW B

BLACK → POWER FEED

NATURAL → FRONT SPEAKERS

BLUE → REAR SPEAKERS

VIEW A

RADIO RECEIVER
NOTE:
REMOVAL NECESSARY
ONLY IF RADIO IS
TO BE REPAIRED.

REMOVE (4) SCREWS
TO PULL RADIO OUT

POWER FEED—
I.P. HARNESS

© G.M. Corp.

Heater exterior assembly attachments typical in Firebird

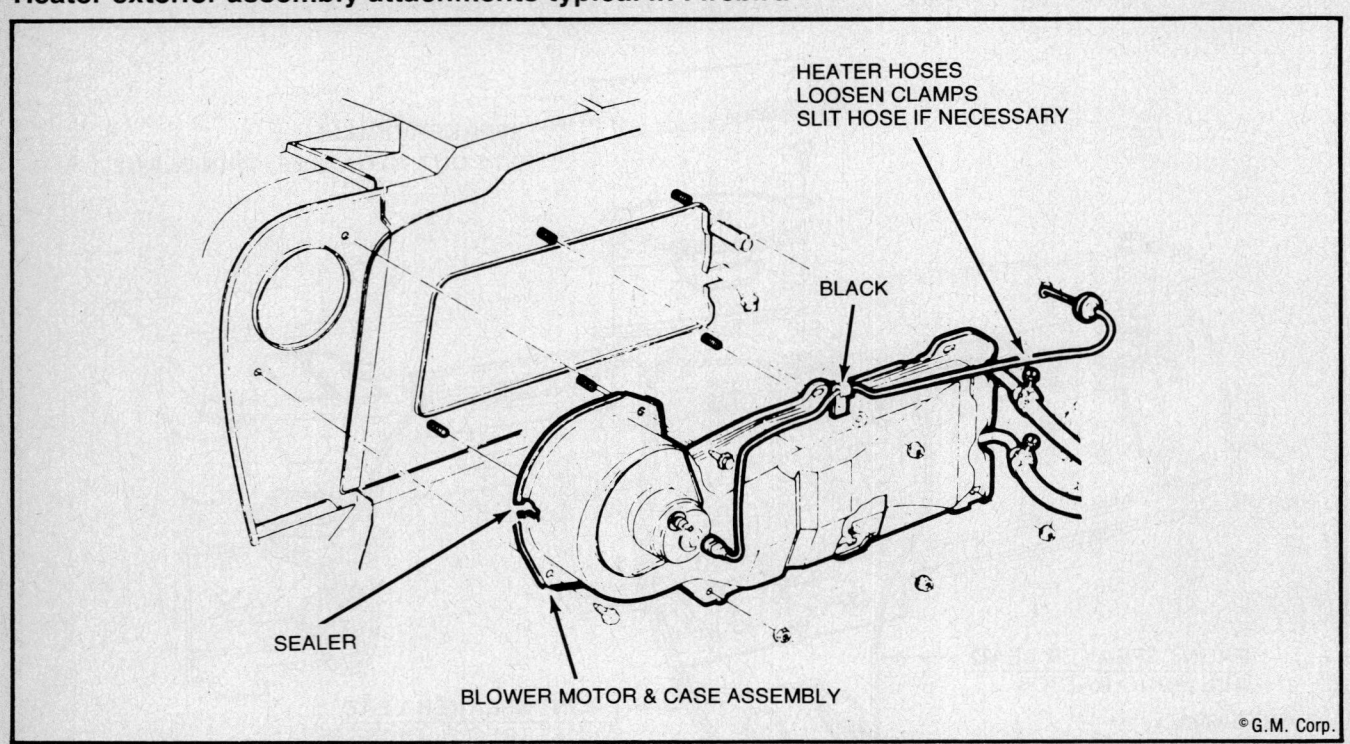

HEATER HOSES
LOOSEN CLAMPS
SLIT HOSE IF NECESSARY

BLACK

SEALER

BLOWER MOTOR & CASE ASSEMBLY

© G.M. Corp.

Heater/air conditioner module typical 1978 and later mid-size car models

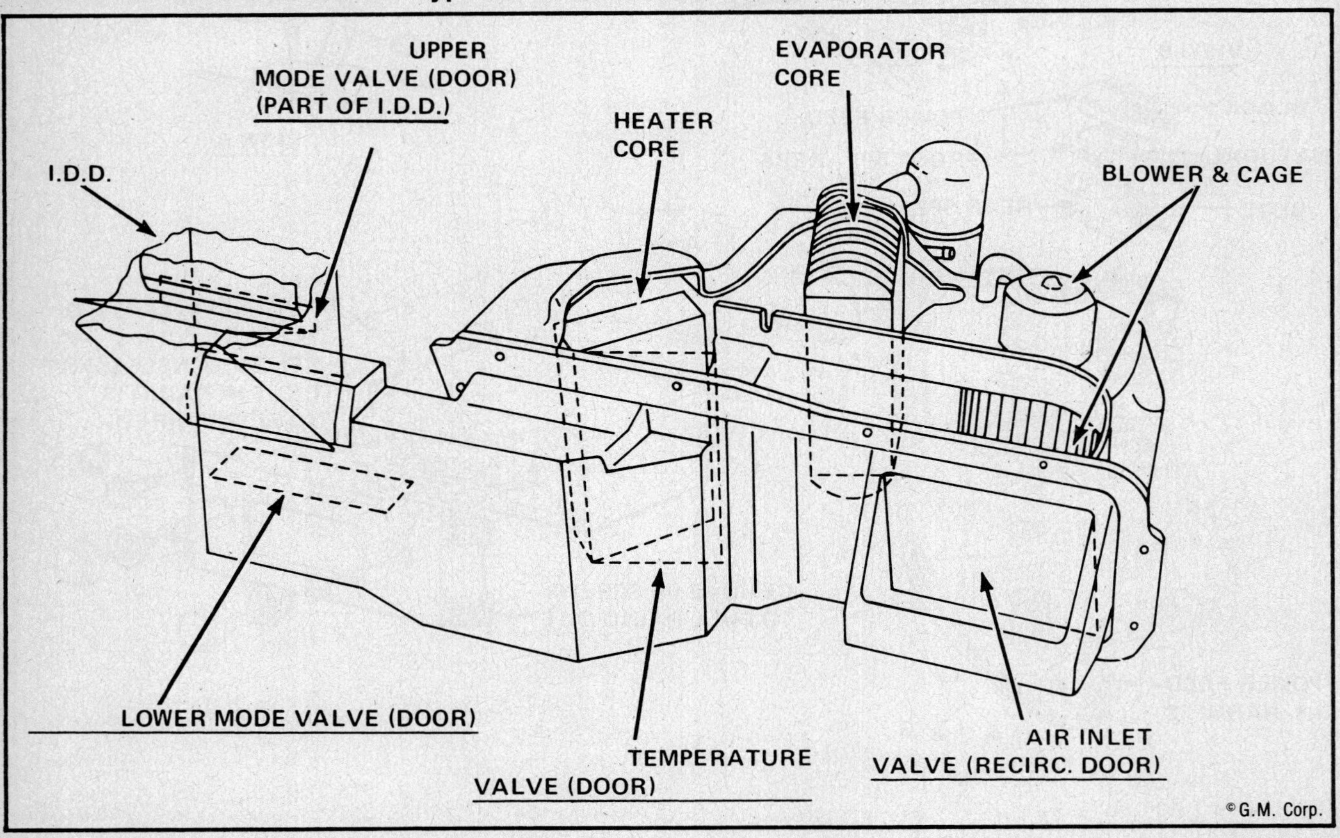

UPPER
MODE VALVE (DOOR)
(PART OF I.D.D.)

EVAPORATOR
CORE

HEATER
CORE

I.D.D.

BLOWER & CAGE

LOWER MODE VALVE (DOOR)

TEMPERATURE
VALVE (DOOR)

AIR INLET
VALVE (RECIRC. DOOR)

© G.M. Corp.

Heater exterior assembly attachments typical 1977 and later mid-size car models

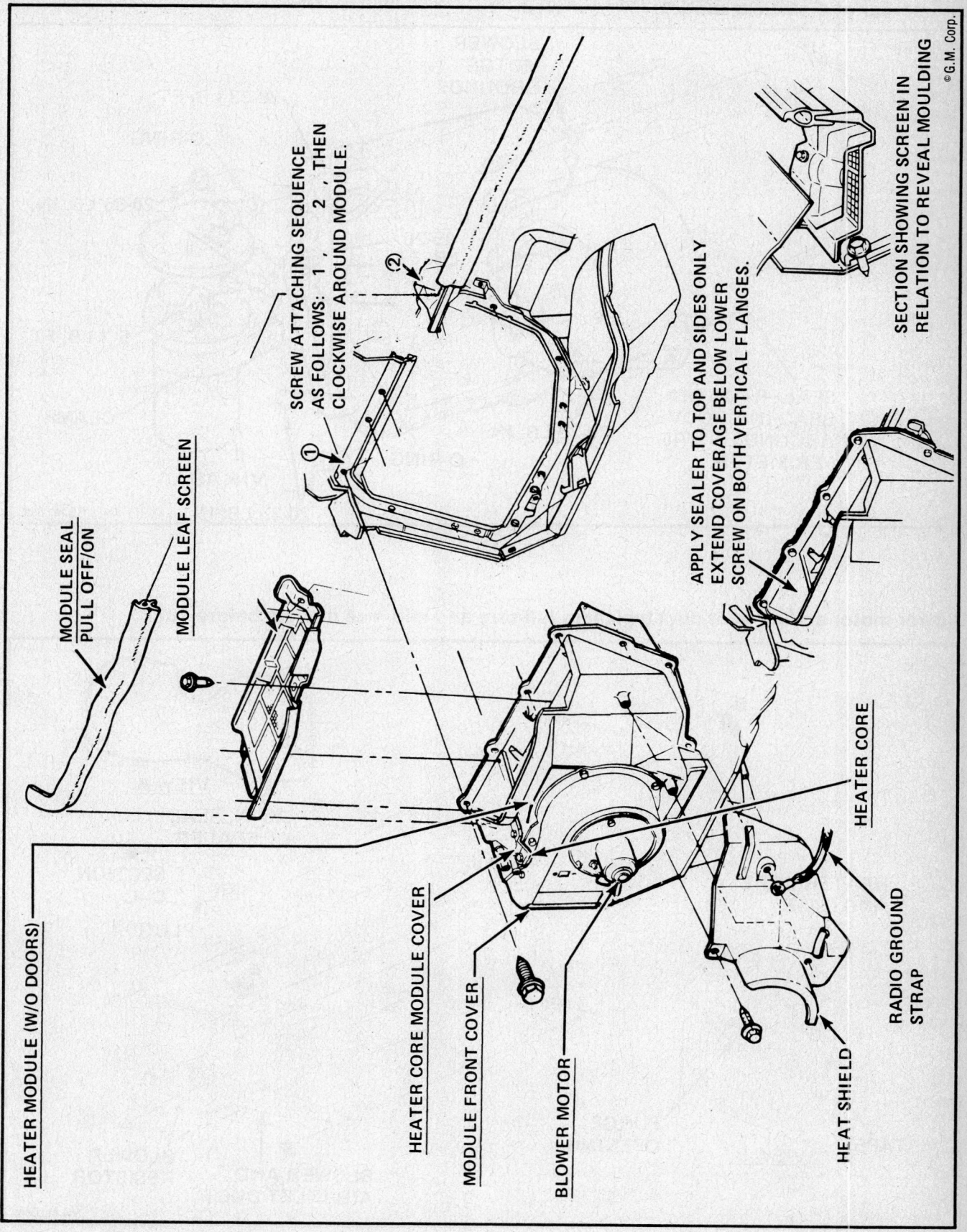

© G.M. Corp.

SCREW ATTACHING SEQUENCE AS FOLLOWS: 1 , 2 , THEN CLOCKWISE AROUND MODULE.

SECTION SHOWING SCREEN IN RELATION TO REVEAL MOULDING

APPLY SEALER TO TOP AND SIDES ONLY. EXTEND COVERAGE BELOW LOWER SCREW ON BOTH VERTICAL FLANGES.

MODULE SEAL PULL OFF/ON

MODULE LEAF SCREEN

HEATER CORE

HEATER MODULE (W/O DOORS)

HEATER CORE MODULE COVER

MODULE FRONT COVER

BLOWER MOTOR

HEAT SHIELD

RADIO GROUND STRAP

PONTIAC

Heater/air conditioner evaporator and blower assembly installation in 1977 and earlier mid-size car models

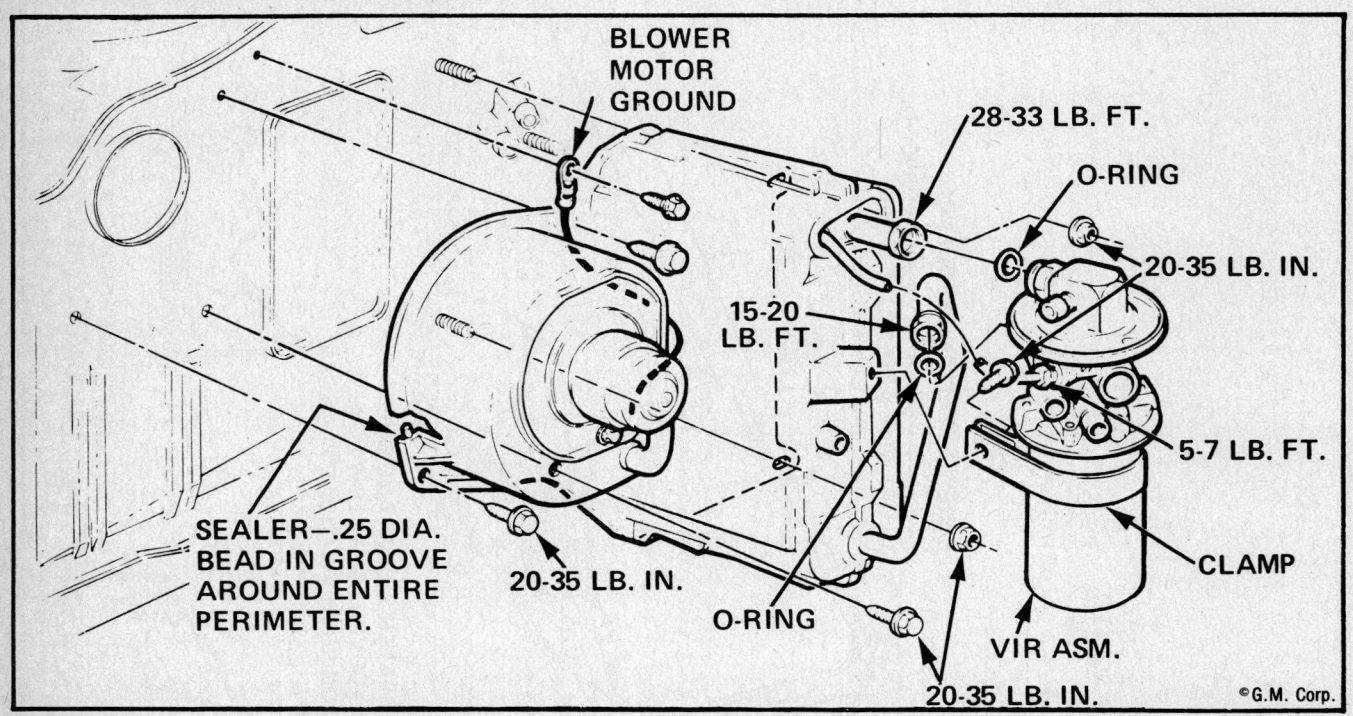

BLOWER MOTOR GROUND

28-33 LB. FT.

O-RING

20-35 LB. IN.

15-20 LB. FT.

5-7 LB. FT.

CLAMP

SEALER—.25 DIA. BEAD IN GROOVE AROUND ENTIRE PERIMETER.

20-35 LB. IN.

O-RING

VIR ASM.

20-35 LB. IN.

© G.M. Corp.

Blower motor and air inlet duct typical in full-size and mid-size models before 1977

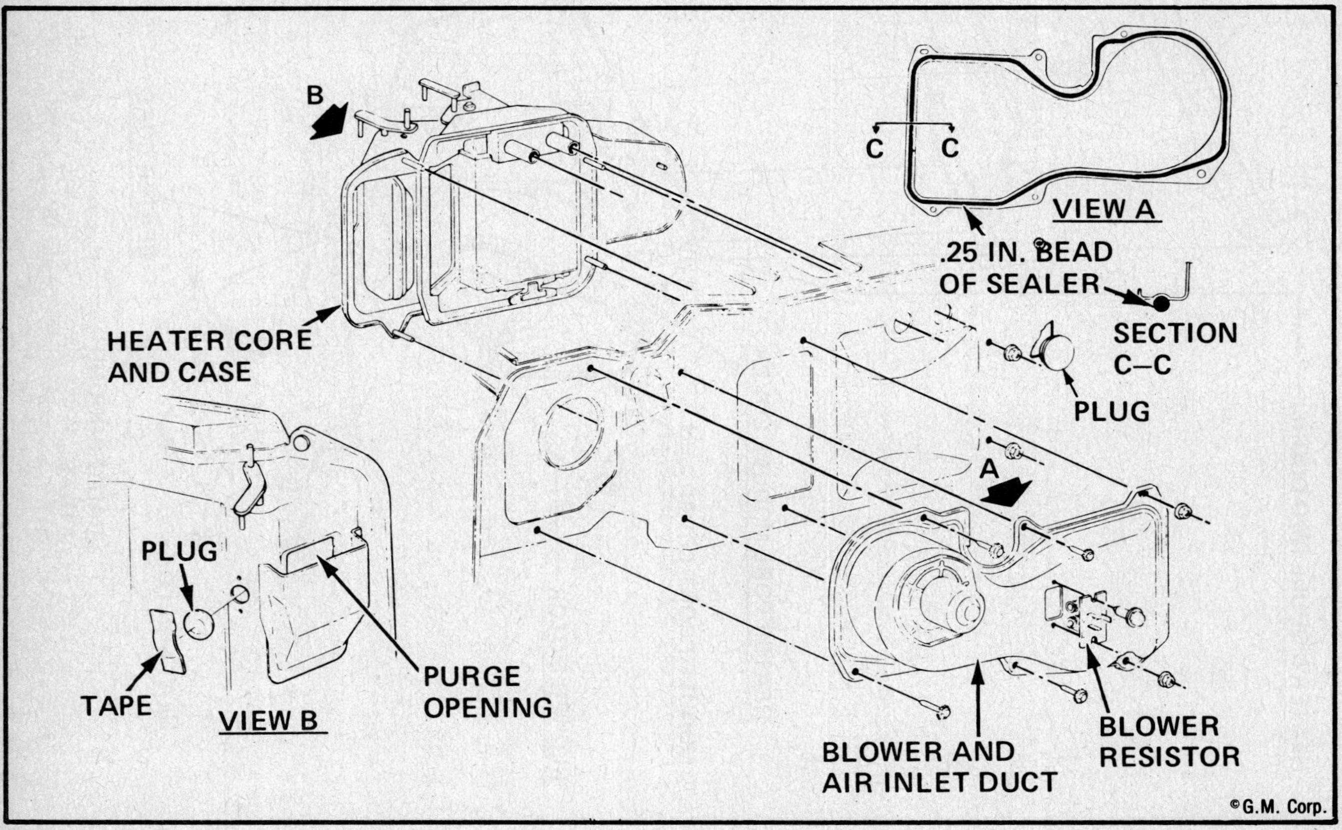

B

HEATER CORE AND CASE

C   C

VIEW A

.25 IN. BEAD OF SEALER

SECTION C–C

PLUG

A

PLUG

TAPE   VIEW B

PURGE OPENING

BLOWER AND AIR INLET DUCT

BLOWER RESISTOR

© G.M. Corp.

Heater Core

All except 1977 and later Full-Size and 1978 and later Mid-Size

- Drain the cooling system, disconnect heater hoses etc.
- Under the instrument panel, remove air conditioner ducting, and disconnect cables, vacuum lines and electrical leads from the heater assembly.
- Remove mounting nuts, and work heater assembly rearward and out of the car.
- Separate the heater and core.
- When installing, seal along mating surfaces between dash and heater.

1977 and later Full-Size and 1978 and later Mid-Size

- Relocate attaching air conditioner components, etc., and remove the module cover.
- Remove the heater core.

Heater core and case installation in 1977 and earlier full-size models

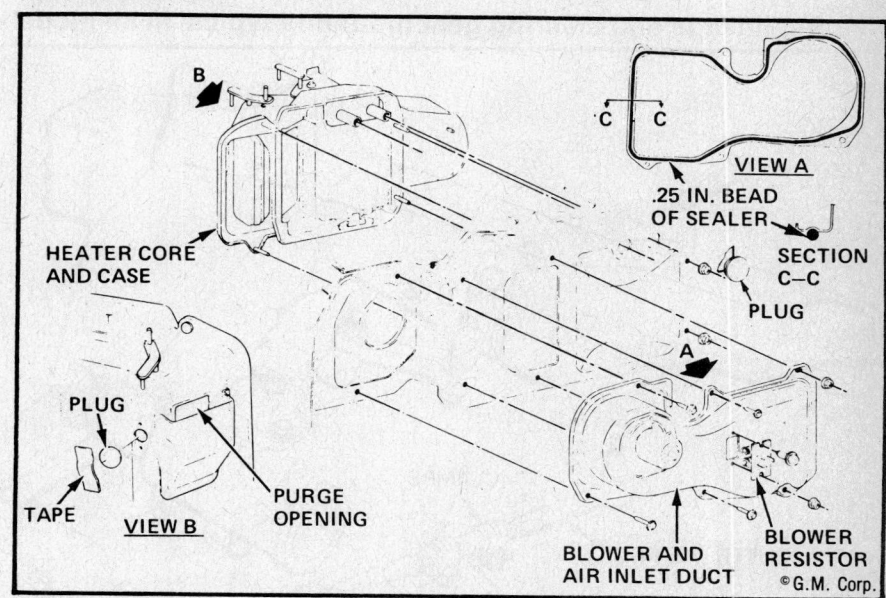

VIEW A

.25 IN. BEAD OF SEALER

SECTION C–C

PLUG

HEATER CORE AND CASE

PLUG

TAPE

VIEW B

PURGE OPENING

BLOWER AND AIR INLET DUCT

BLOWER RESISTOR

©G.M. Corp.

Heater exterior assembly attachments in 1977 and later full-size models

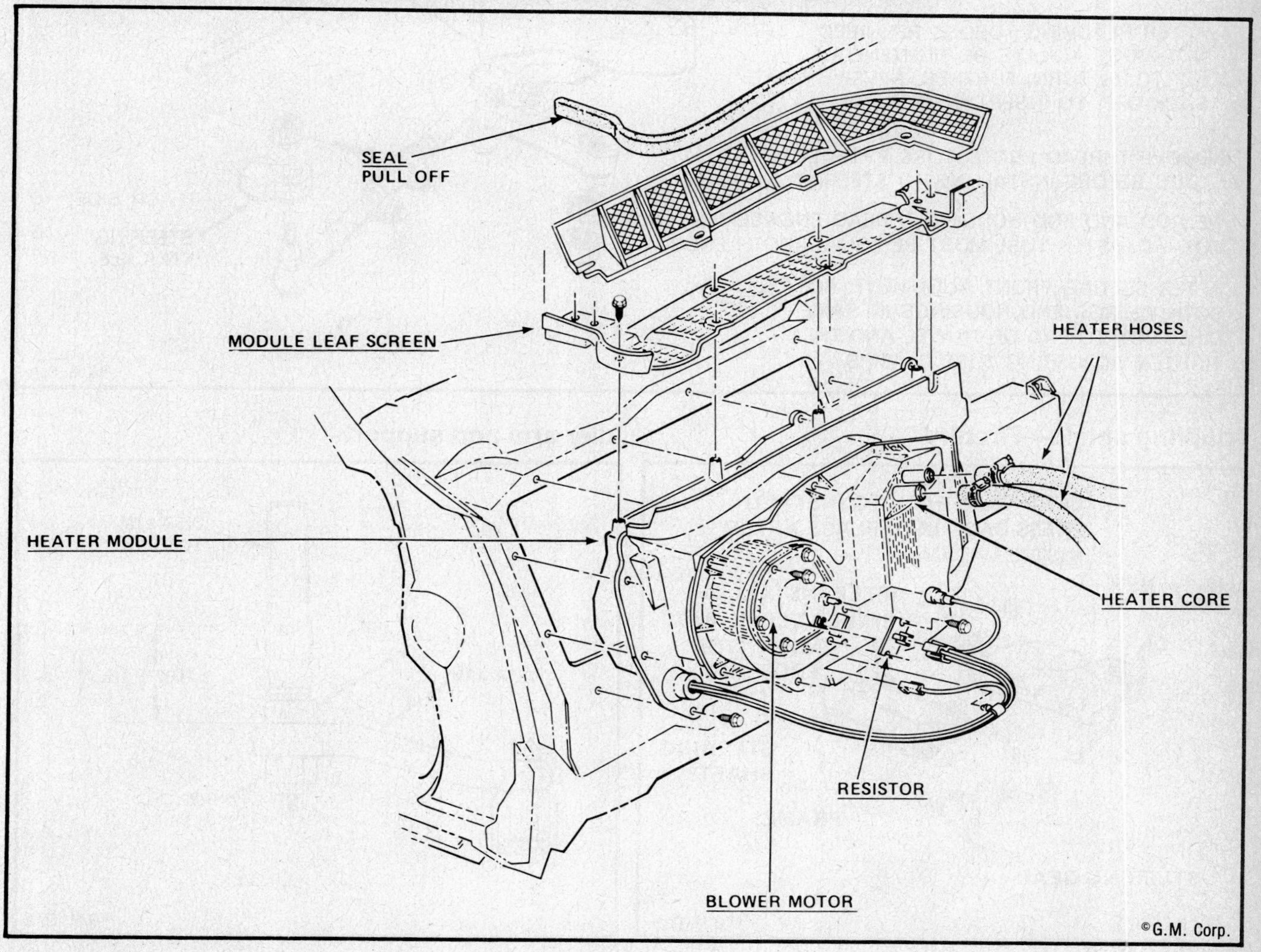

SEAL PULL OFF

MODULE LEAF SCREEN

HEATER HOSES

HEATER MODULE

HEATER CORE

RESISTOR

BLOWER MOTOR

©G.M. Corp.

A667

STEERING & BRAKES SECTION

Steering linkage and steering gear mounting typical in all models

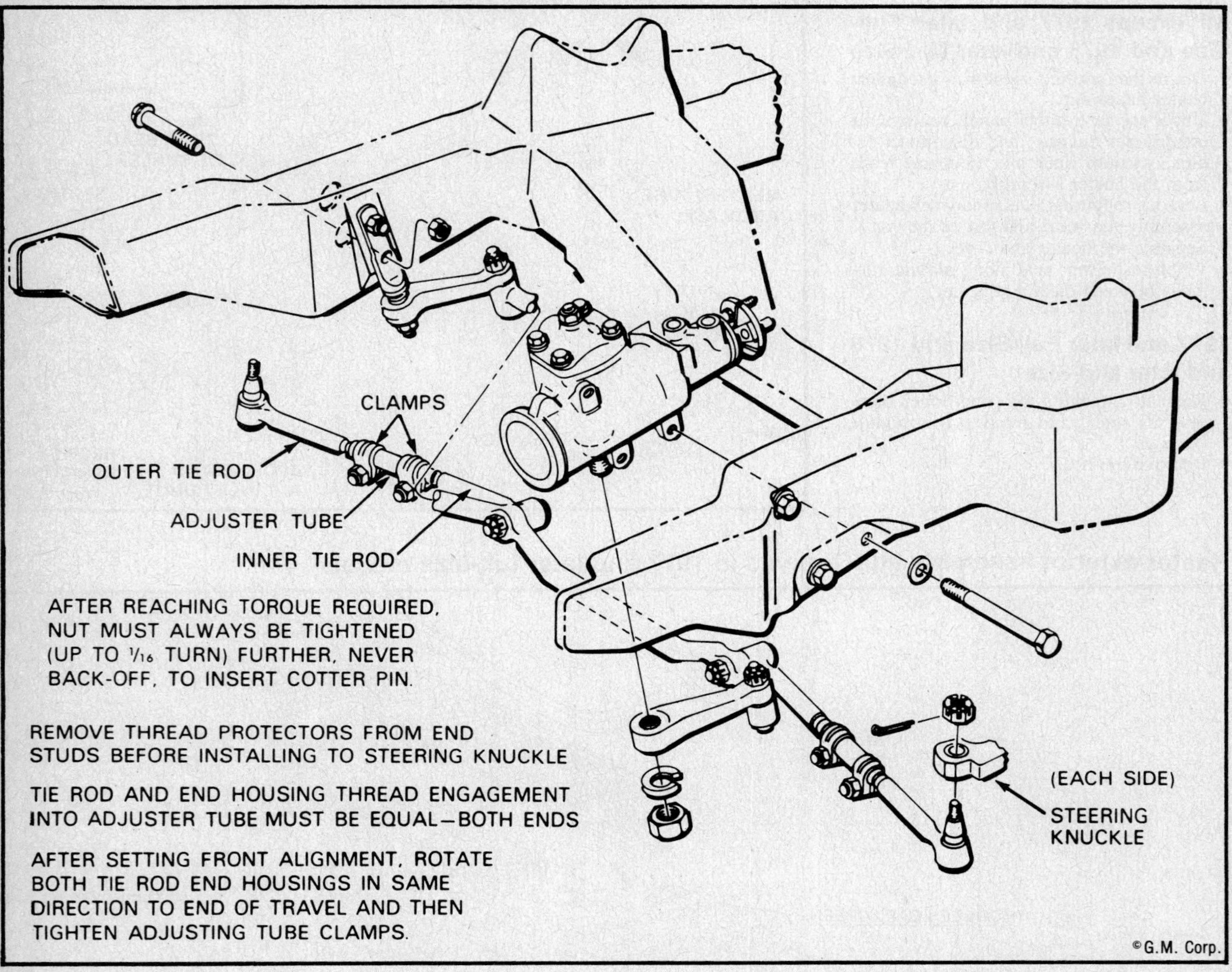

CLAMPS

OUTER TIE ROD

ADJUSTER TUBE

INNER TIE ROD

AFTER REACHING TORQUE REQUIRED, NUT MUST ALWAYS BE TIGHTENED (UP TO 1/16 TURN) FURTHER, NEVER BACK-OFF, TO INSERT COTTER PIN.

REMOVE THREAD PROTECTORS FROM END STUDS BEFORE INSTALLING TO STEERING KNUCKLE

TIE ROD AND END HOUSING THREAD ENGAGEMENT INTO ADJUSTER TUBE MUST BE EQUAL—BOTH ENDS

AFTER SETTING FRONT ALIGNMENT, ROTATE BOTH TIE ROD END HOUSINGS IN SAME DIRECTION TO END OF TRAVEL AND THEN TIGHTEN ADJUSTING TUBE CLAMPS.

(EACH SIDE)

STEERING KNUCKLE

© G.M. Corp.

Coupling shield—Firebird

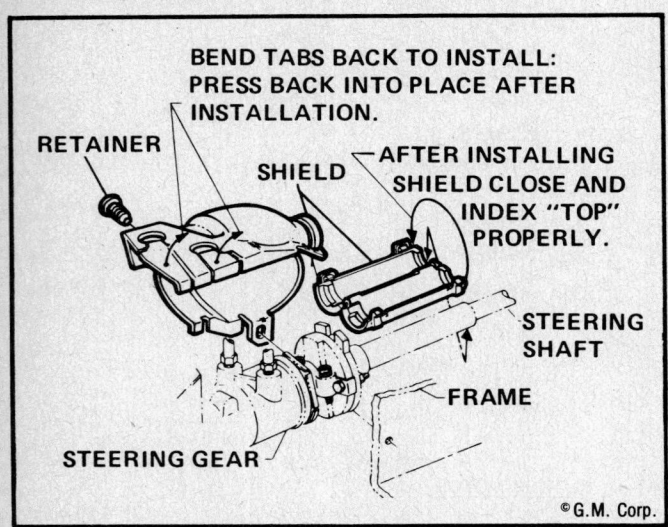

BEND TABS BACK TO INSTALL: PRESS BACK INTO PLACE AFTER INSTALLATION.

RETAINER

SHIELD

AFTER INSTALLING SHIELD CLOSE AND INDEX "TOP" PROPERLY.

STEERING SHAFT

FRAME

STEERING GEAR

© G.M. Corp.

Idler arm and support

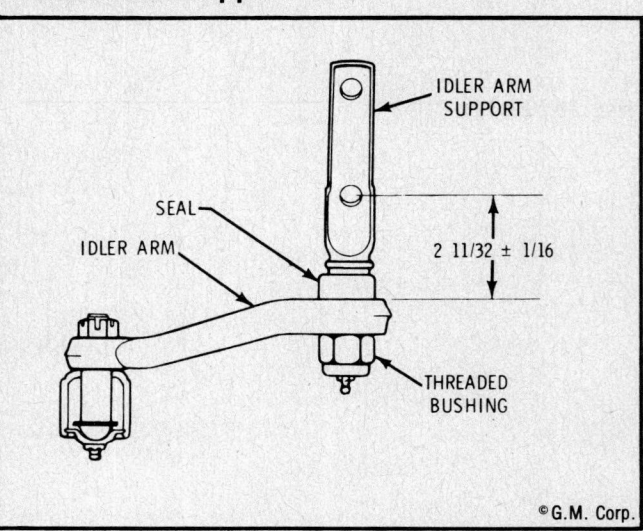

IDLER ARM SUPPORT

SEAL

IDLER ARM

2 11/32 ± 1/16

THREADED BUSHING

© G.M. Corp.

Standard steering column

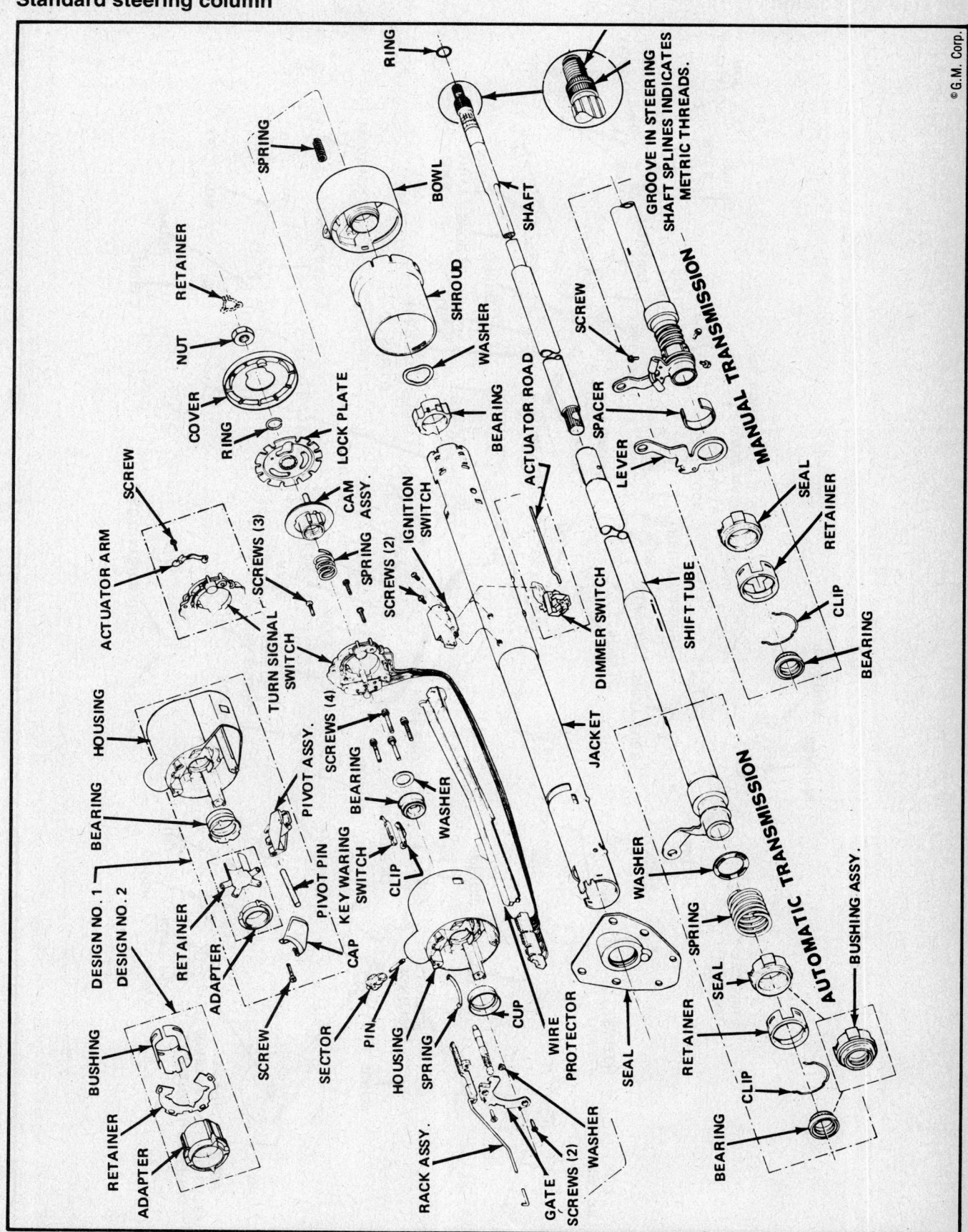

RING

SPRING

RETAINER

NUT

RETAINER

COVER

RING

SPRING

BOWL

SHROUD

WASHER

LOCK PLATE

CAM ASSY.

SPRING

BEARING

ACTUATOR ROAD

SHAFT

GROOVE IN STEERING SHAFT SPLINES INDICATES METRIC THREADS.

SCREW

SPACER

MANUAL TRANSMISSION

LEVER

SEAL

RETAINER

CLIP

BEARING

SCREW

ACTUATOR ARM

SCREWS (3)

TURN SIGNAL SWITCH

SCREWS (2)

IGNITION SWITCH

SCREWS (4)

PIVOT ASSY.

HOUSING

BEARING

DESIGN NO. 1

BEARING

DESIGN NO. 2

RETAINER

ADAPTER

PIVOT PIN

KEY WARING SWITCH

CAP

CLIP

DIMMER SWITCH

JACKET

SHIFT TUBE

WASHER

BUSHING

ADAPTER

RETAINER

ADAPTER

SCREW

SECTOR

PIN

HOUSING

SPRING

CUP

WIRE PROTECTOR

SEAL

WASHER

SPRING

RETAINER

SEAL

CLIP

BEARING

AUTOMATIC TRANSMISSION

BUSHING ASSY.

RACK ASSY.

GATE SCREWS (2)

WASHER

© G.M. Corp.

Tilt steering column

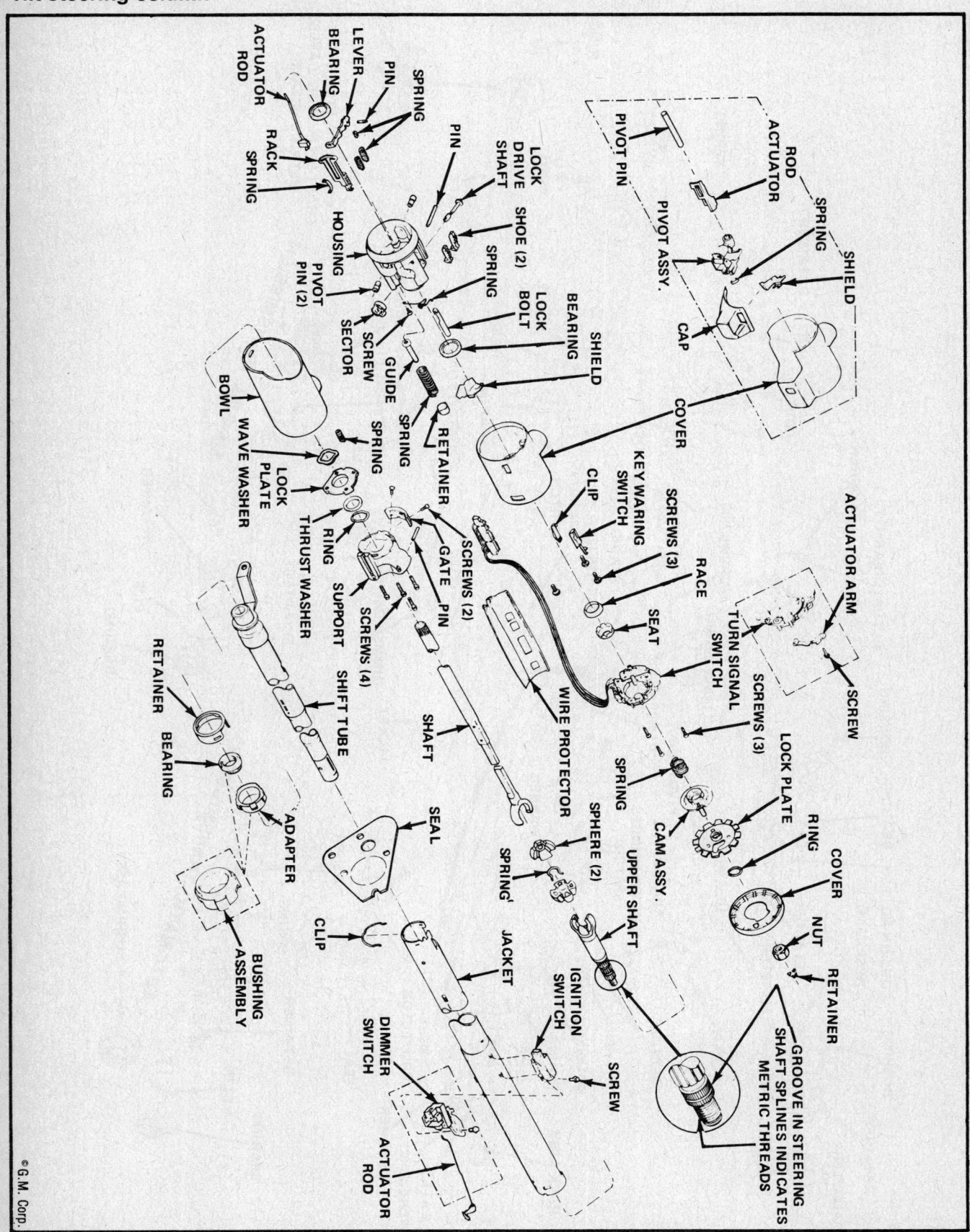

© G.M. Corp.

Steering column, upper and lower mounts

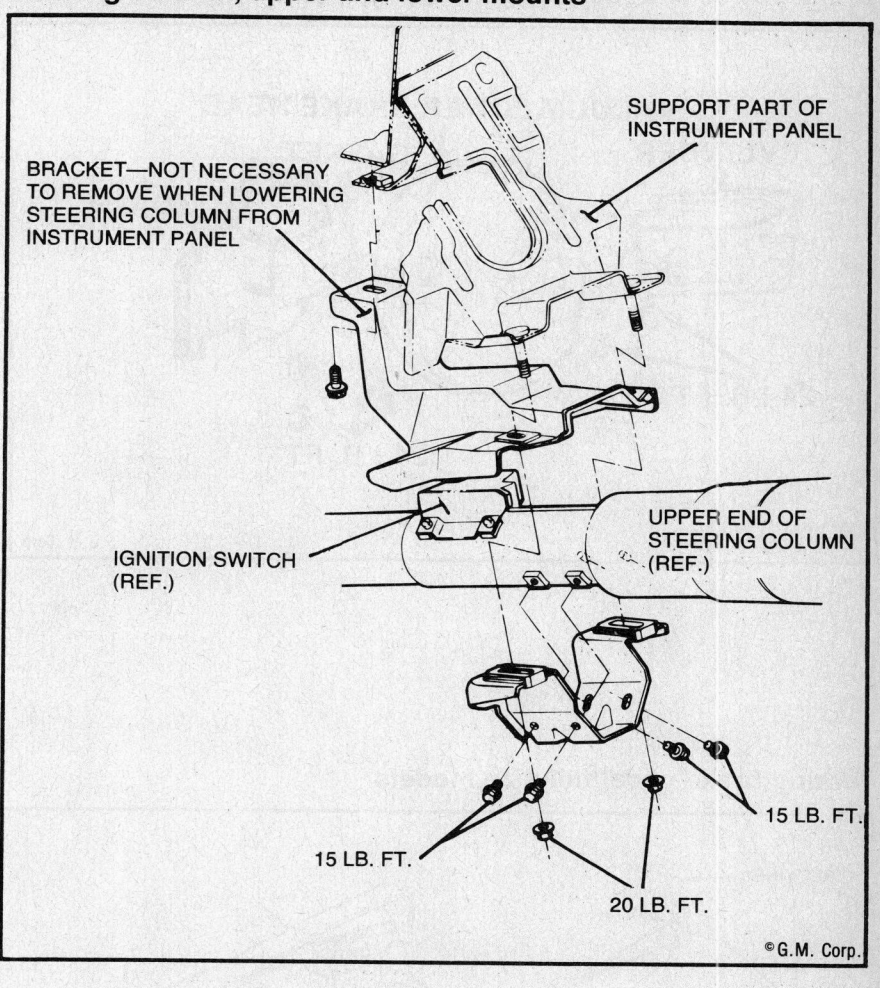

BRACKET—NOT NECESSARY TO REMOVE WHEN LOWERING STEERING COLUMN FROM INSTRUMENT PANEL

SUPPORT PART OF INSTRUMENT PANEL

UPPER END OF STEERING COLUMN (REF.)

IGNITION SWITCH (REF.)

15 LB. FT.

15 LB. FT.

20 LB. FT.

© G.M. Corp.

Steering Column

NOTE: Handle the steering column very carefully. Rapping on the end of it or leaning on it could shear off the inserts which allow the column to collapse in a crash.

- Disconnect battery.
- Remove clamp bolt from coupling at lower end of column shaft, and remove flex-coupling shield.
- Remove cover and toe-pan attaching screws.
- Disconnect shift linkages, electrical wiring, etc.
- Remove column upper mounts, and remove the column from the vehicle.
- When installing, check that flexible coupling alignment is correct.

NOTE: When installing use only the specified hardware. Over-length bolts could prevent the column from properly collapsing in a crash.

CHILTON CAUTION: *Do not exceed maximum of 25 lb. ft. of torque to prevent crushing of capsules.*

Steering column, upper and lower mounts

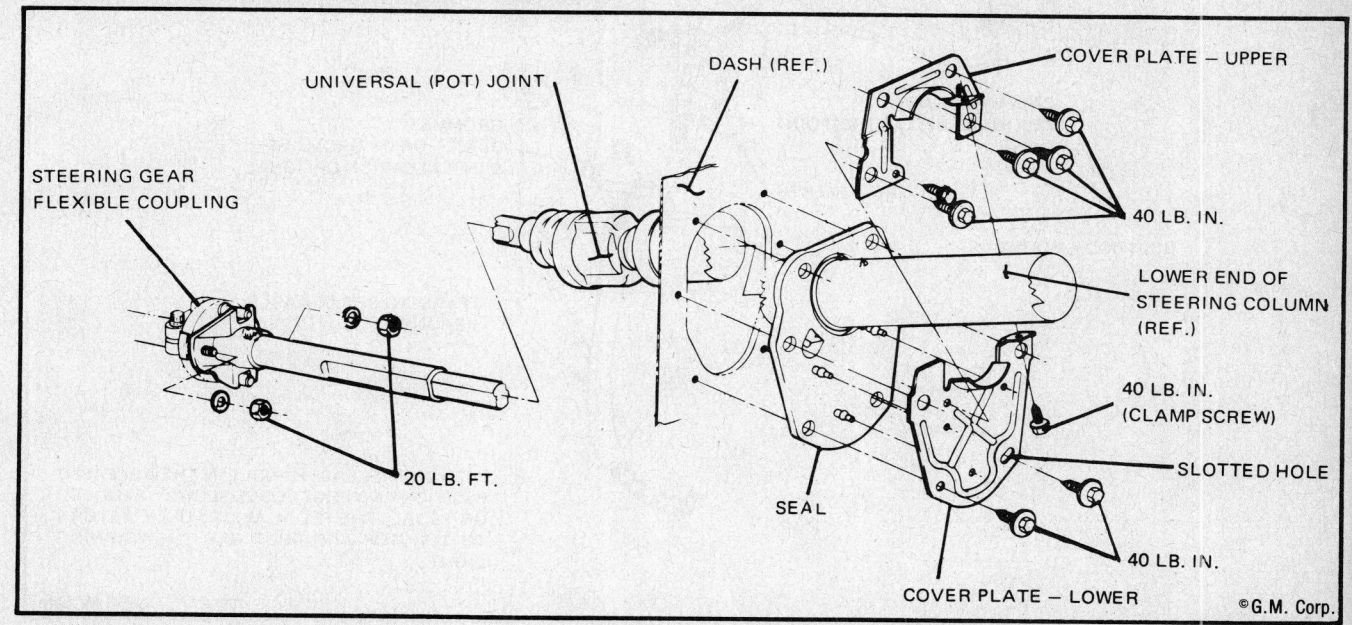

UNIVERSAL (POT) JOINT

DASH (REF.)

COVER PLATE — UPPER

STEERING GEAR FLEXIBLE COUPLING

40 LB. IN.

LOWER END OF STEERING COLUMN (REF.)

40 LB. IN. (CLAMP SCREW)

SLOTTED HOLE

20 LB. FT.

SEAL

40 LB. IN.

COVER PLATE — LOWER

© G.M. Corp.

A671

Brake power unit mounting

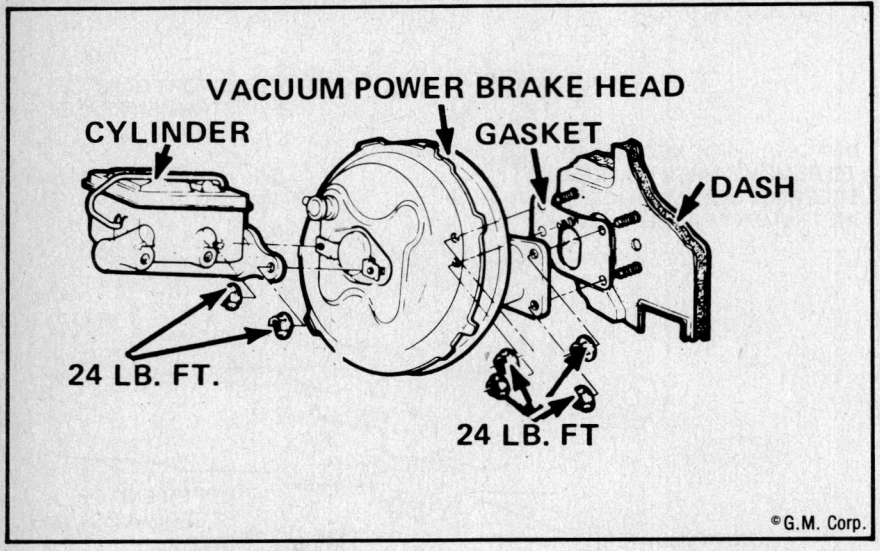

VACUUM POWER BRAKE HEAD

CYLINDER   GASKET

DASH

24 LB. FT.

24 LB. FT

© G.M. Corp.

Brake Power Unit R&R
- Separate power unit and master cylinder, and unbolt power unit from fire-wall.
- Disconnect the power brake push rod from the brake pedal.

Parking Brake Cable R&R
- Disconnect cables from equalizers.
- For front cable removal, remove the wheelhouse panel and disconnect cable from parking brake pedal assembly. Route new cable through in place of the old.
- For rear cable removal, remove brake drum, and separate cable from brake shoes. Route new cable through in place of the old.

Parking Brake Adjustment
- Correctly adjust service brakes.
- Apply parking brake two notches from fully released position.
- Tighten cable at equalizer until drag is felt at rear wheels.
- Release parking brake lever, and check that rear wheels turn without resistance.

Parking brake pedal full-size models

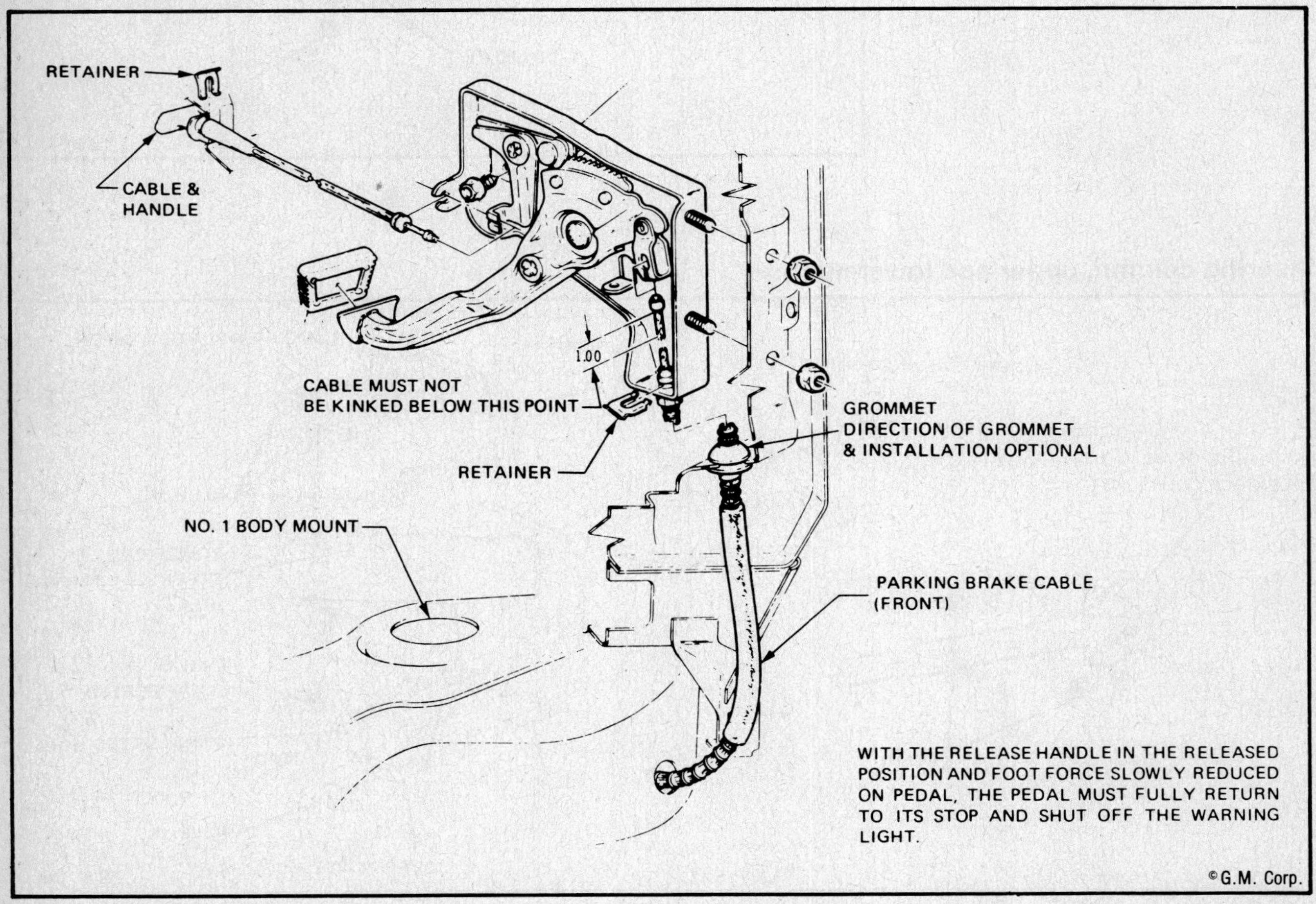

RETAINER

CABLE & HANDLE

CABLE MUST NOT BE KINKED BELOW THIS POINT

RETAINER

NO. 1 BODY MOUNT

1.00

GROMMET
DIRECTION OF GROMMET & INSTALLATION OPTIONAL

PARKING BRAKE CABLE (FRONT)

WITH THE RELEASE HANDLE IN THE RELEASED POSITION AND FOOT FORCE SLOWLY REDUCED ON PEDAL, THE PEDAL MUST FULLY RETURN TO ITS STOP AND SHUT OFF THE WARNING LIGHT.

© G.M. Corp.

Front parking brake cable in Ventura

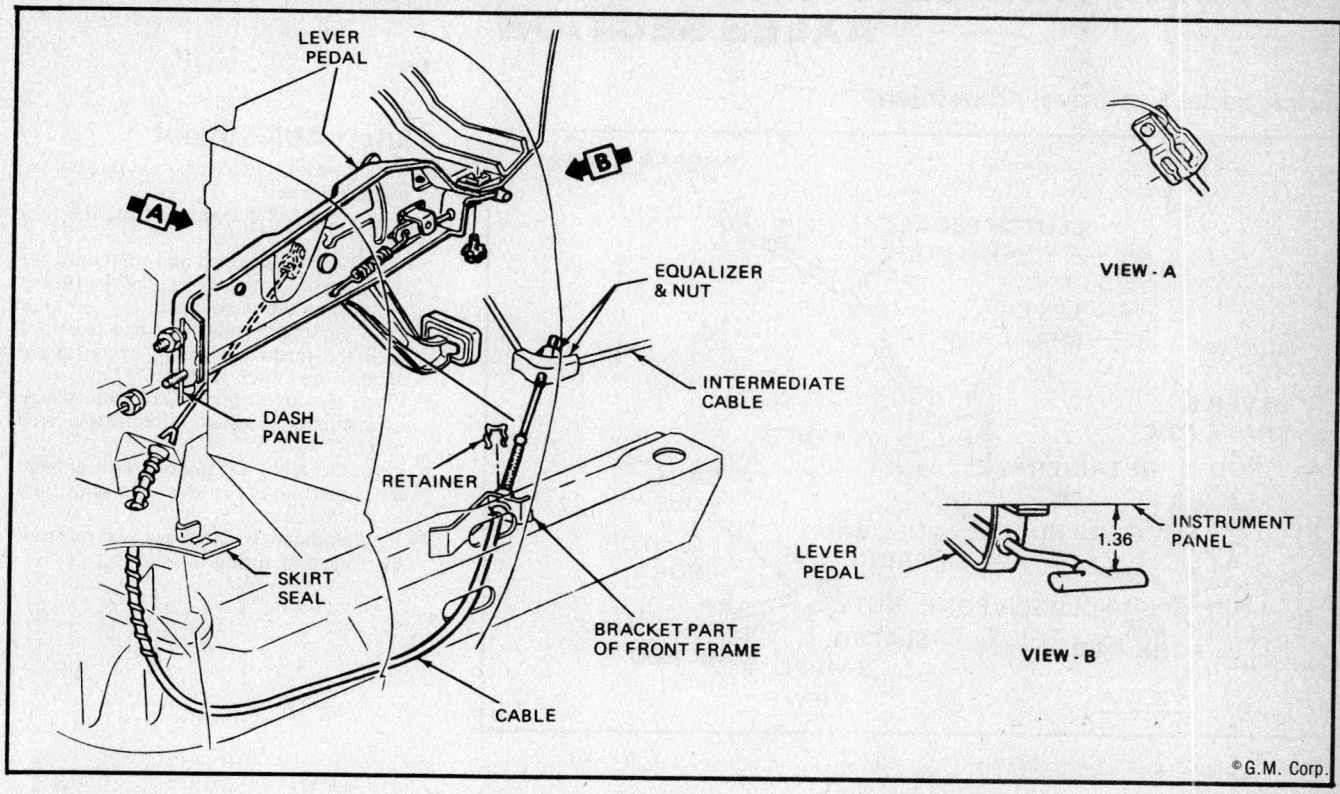

LEVER PEDAL

A

B

EQUALIZER & NUT

INTERMEDIATE CABLE

DASH PANEL

RETAINER

SKIRT SEAL

BRACKET PART OF FRONT FRAME

CABLE

VIEW - A

LEVER PEDAL

1.36

INSTRUMENT PANEL

VIEW - B

© G.M. Corp.

Parking brake cable routing in mid-size models

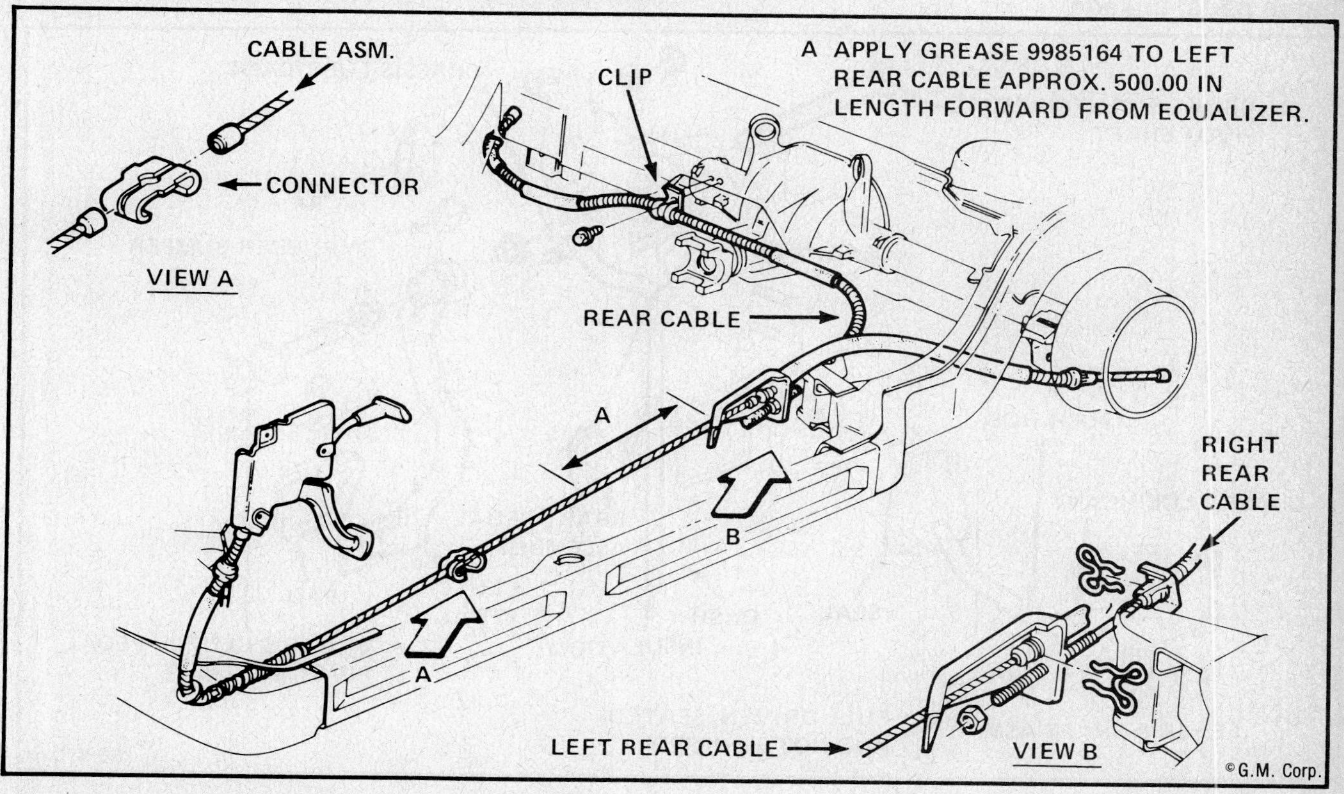

CABLE ASM.

CONNECTOR

VIEW A

CLIP

A APPLY GREASE 9985164 TO LEFT REAR CABLE APPROX. 500.00 IN LENGTH FORWARD FROM EQUALIZER.

REAR CABLE

A

B

A

RIGHT REAR CABLE

LEFT REAR CABLE

VIEW B

© G.M. Corp.

CLUTCH, TRANSMISSION, PROPELLER SHAFT & REAR AXLES SECTION

Clutch pedal free travel adjustment

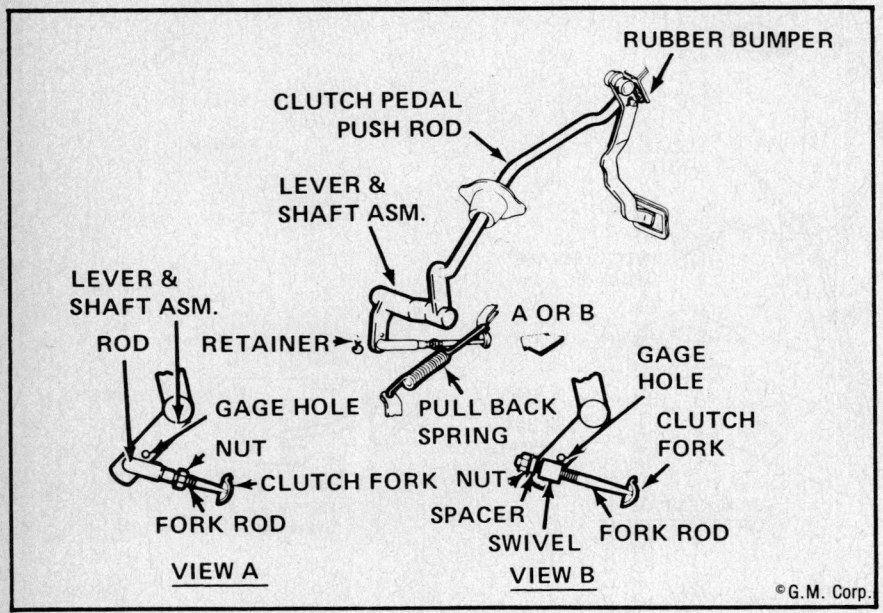

RUBBER BUMPER

CLUTCH PEDAL PUSH ROD

LEVER & SHAFT ASM.

LEVER & SHAFT ASM.

ROD   RETAINER   A OR B

GAGE HOLE

GAGE HOLE   PULL BACK SPRING   CLUTCH FORK

NUT

CLUTCH FORK   NUT

FORK ROD   SPACER   FORK ROD

SWIVEL

VIEW A   VIEW B

© G.M. Corp.

Clutch Adjustment

- Clutch pedal free play should be approximately 1 inch.
- Remove the clutch spring from the fork arm.
- Rotate the clutch lever and shaft until the clutch pedal is firmly against the rubber bumper on the dash brace.
- Push the clutch fork outer end rearward until the throwout bearing rests lightly against the clutch fingers.
- Place the lower push rod in the gauge hole and adjust length to remove all free play.
- Place swivel or rod in hole farthest from the centerline of the lever and shaft, and install the retainer.
- Tighten the swivel locknut, and reinstall the fork arm spring.

Clutch pedal linkage

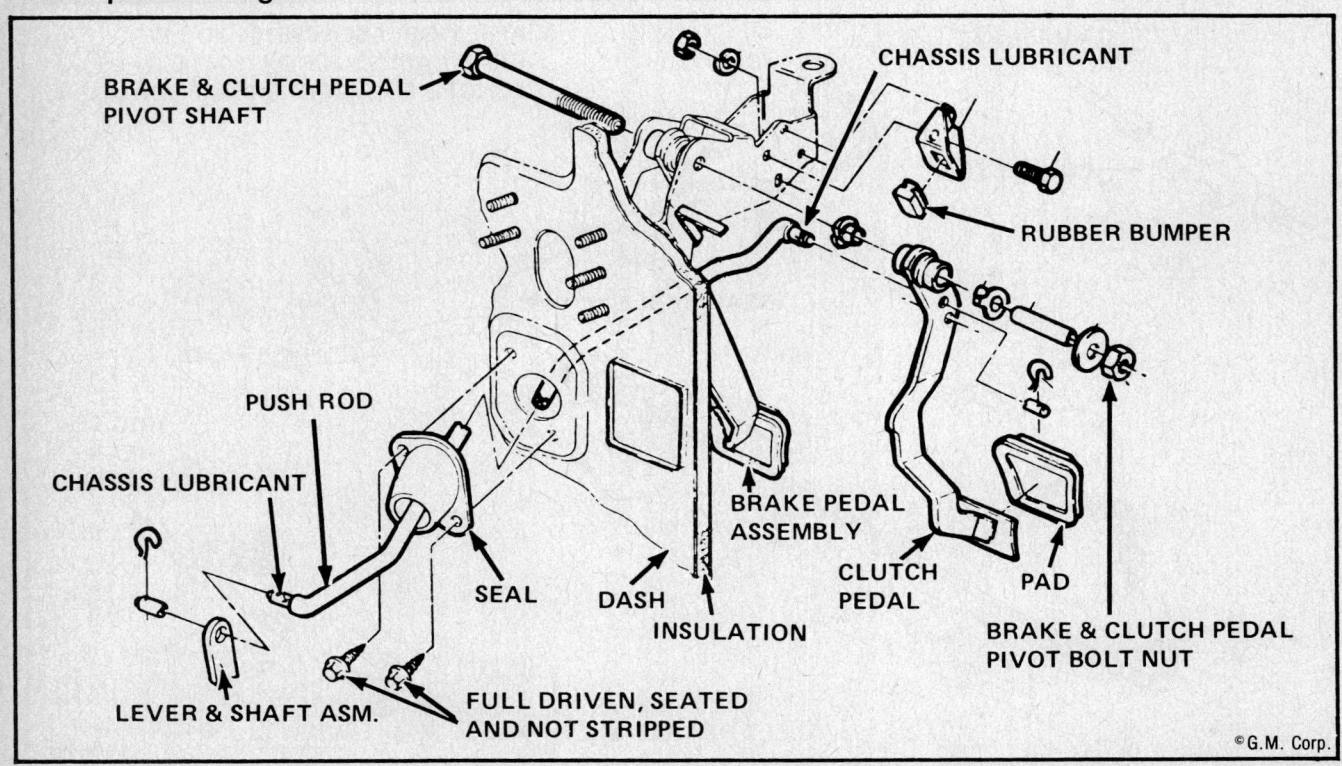

BRAKE & CLUTCH PEDAL PIVOT SHAFT

CHASSIS LUBRICANT

RUBBER BUMPER

PUSH ROD

CHASSIS LUBRICANT

BRAKE PEDAL ASSEMBLY

CLUTCH PEDAL

PAD

SEAL   DASH   INSULATION

BRAKE & CLUTCH PEDAL PIVOT BOLT NUT

LEVER & SHAFT ASM.   FULL DRIVEN, SEATED AND NOT STRIPPED

© G.M. Corp.

Manual Transmission R&R

- Remove, disconnect, or relocate the following:
  - a. Speedometer gear
  - b. Shift rods
  - c. Propeller shaft
- Support rear of engine and remove the transmission crossmember.
- Remove the two upper mount bolts, and insert guide pins. Remove the lower bolts, and slide the transmission back and out.

Manual Transmission Linkage Adjustment

- Adjust the linkages so the shift lever positions correspond exactly to the transmission positions.
- Adjustment holes are provided in most shift assemblies through which drill rods can be placed for exact adjustment.

Manual transmission column shift linkage

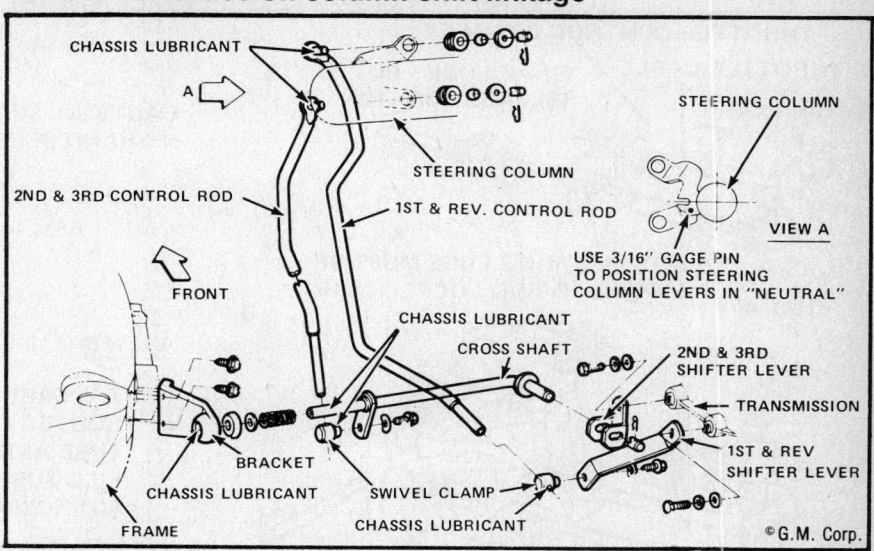

CHASSIS LUBRICANT

A

2ND & 3RD CONTROL ROD

FRONT

STEERING COLUMN

1ST & REV. CONTROL ROD

STEERING COLUMN

VIEW A

USE 3/16" GAGE PIN TO POSITION STEERING COLUMN LEVERS IN "NEUTRAL"

CHASSIS LUBRICANT

CROSS SHAFT

2ND & 3RD SHIFTER LEVER

TRANSMISSION

1ST & REV SHIFTER LEVER

BRACKET

SWIVEL CLAMP

CHASSIS LUBRICANT

CHASSIS LUBRICANT

FRAME

© G.M. Corp.

Manual transmission floor shift mechanism and adjustment

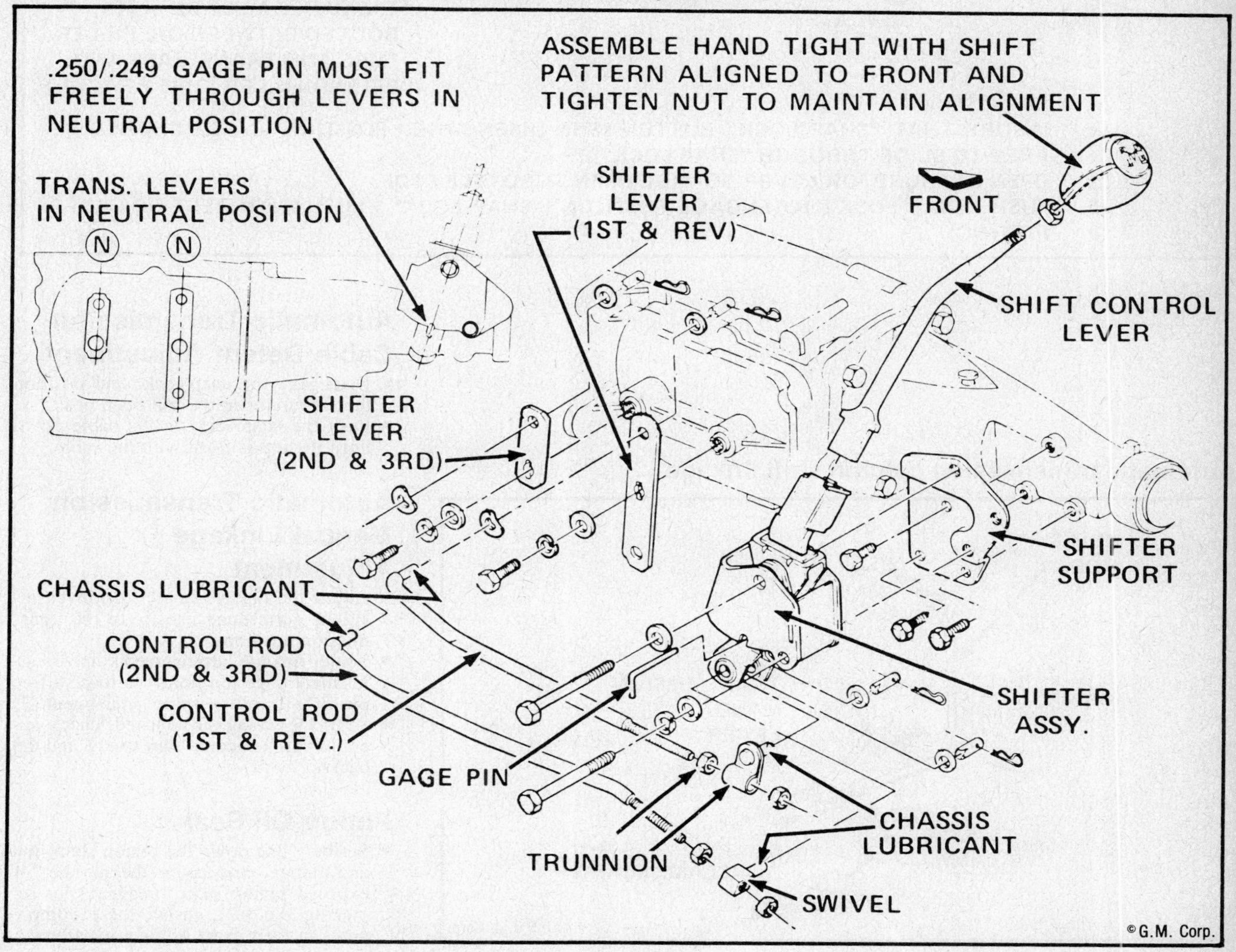

.250/.249 GAGE PIN MUST FIT FREELY THROUGH LEVERS IN NEUTRAL POSITION

ASSEMBLE HAND TIGHT WITH SHIFT PATTERN ALIGNED TO FRONT AND TIGHTEN NUT TO MAINTAIN ALIGNMENT

TRANS. LEVERS IN NEUTRAL POSITION

N   N

SHIFTER LEVER (1ST & REV)

FRONT

SHIFT CONTROL LEVER

SHIFTER LEVER (2ND & 3RD)

CHASSIS LUBRICANT

CONTROL ROD (2ND & 3RD)

CONTROL ROD (1ST & REV.)

GAGE PIN

TRUNNION

SHIFTER SUPPORT

SHIFTER ASSY.

CHASSIS LUBRICANT

SWIVEL

© G.M. Corp.

A675

Transmission throttle valve cable adjustment

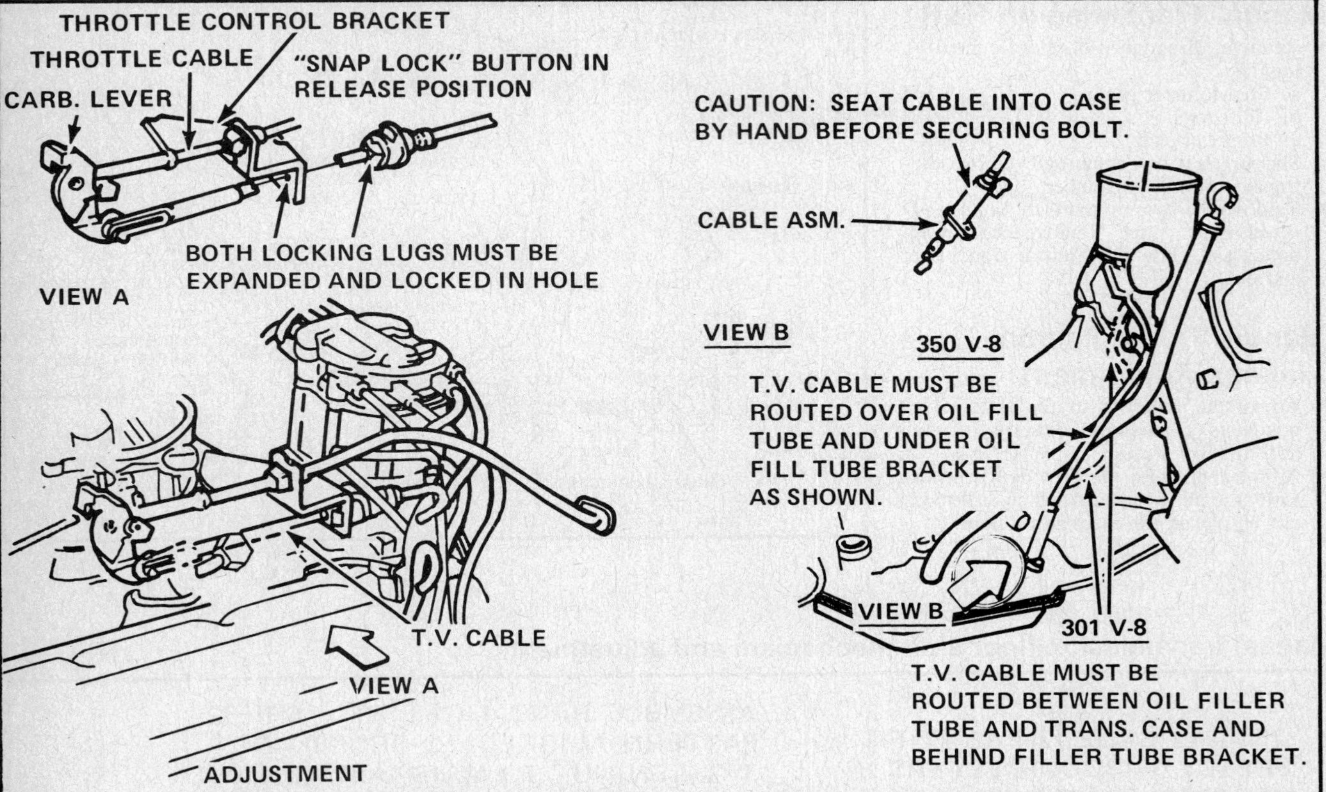

THROTTLE CONTROL BRACKET

THROTTLE CABLE

CARB. LEVER

"SNAP LOCK" BUTTON IN RELEASE POSITION

BOTH LOCKING LUGS MUST BE EXPANDED AND LOCKED IN HOLE

VIEW A

CAUTION: SEAT CABLE INTO CASE BY HAND BEFORE SECURING BOLT.

CABLE ASM.

VIEW B

350 V-8

T.V. CABLE MUST BE ROUTED OVER OIL FILL TUBE AND UNDER OIL FILL TUBE BRACKET AS SHOWN.

T.V. CABLE

VIEW A

VIEW B

301 V-8

T.V. CABLE MUST BE ROUTED BETWEEN OIL FILLER TUBE AND TRANS. CASE AND BEHIND FILLER TUBE BRACKET.

ADJUSTMENT

1. INSURE THAT "SNAP LOCK" BUTTON IS IN DISENGAGED POSITION (CABLE SHOULD BE FREE TO SLIDE THROUGH "SNAP LOCK").
2. OPEN CARBURETOR LEVER TO WIDE OPEN THROTTLE STOP.
3. PUSH "SNAP LOCK" TO ENGAGE POSITION ("SNAP LOCK" FLUSH WITH REST OF CABLE FITTING).

©G.M. Corp.

Automatic Transmission Cable Detent Adjustment

- Disengage the snap lock, and position the carburetor in the full open position.
- Push the snap lock on the cable down until the top is flush with the cable.

Automatic Transmission Manual Linkage Adjustment

- Adjust the linkage so the shift lever positions correspond exactly to the transmission positions.
- Some linkage arrangements have adjustment gage pin holes. In these a free pin fit will insure proper adjustment.
- After the linkage is adjusted, check operation of the neutral start switch and the backup lights.

Pinion Oil Seal

- Scribe a line down the pinion stem, nut and flange, and count the number of exposed pinion stem threads. After replacing the seal, install these components in their exact original locations.

Automatic transmission column shift linkage

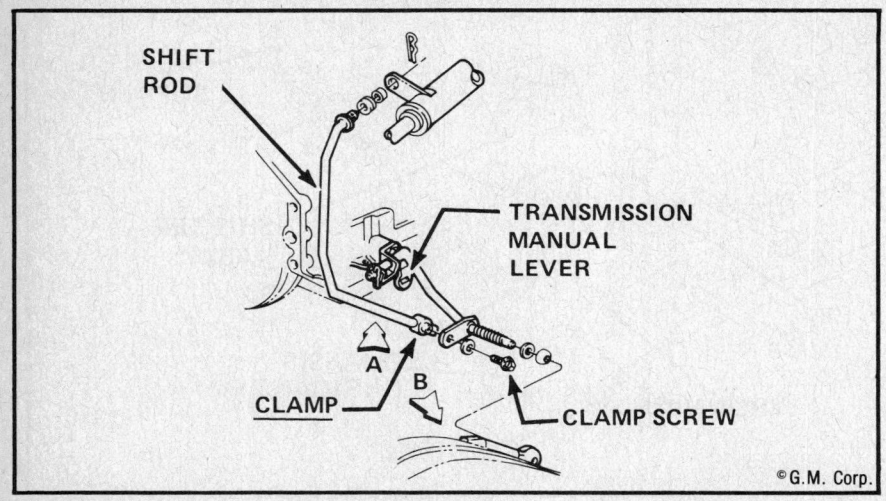

SHIFT ROD

TRANSMISSION MANUAL LEVER

A

B

CLAMP

CLAMP SCREW

©G.M. Corp.

Automatic
Transmission R&R

- Disconnect the battery.
- Disconnect detent cable (if so equipped) from accelerator lever or carburetor.
- Remove, disconnect or relocate any of the following necessary for removal:
  a. Exhaust crossover pipe

  b. Drive shaft
  c. Oil cooler lines
  d. Transmission crossmember (support engine and transmission as needed)
  e. Speedometer cable
  f. Shift linkage

  g. Electrical connections
  h. Flywheel cover pan
- Remove mounting bolts, and slide transmission back and out of vehicle.
- Mark flywheel and converter for installation reference.

Automatic transmission console shift mechanism

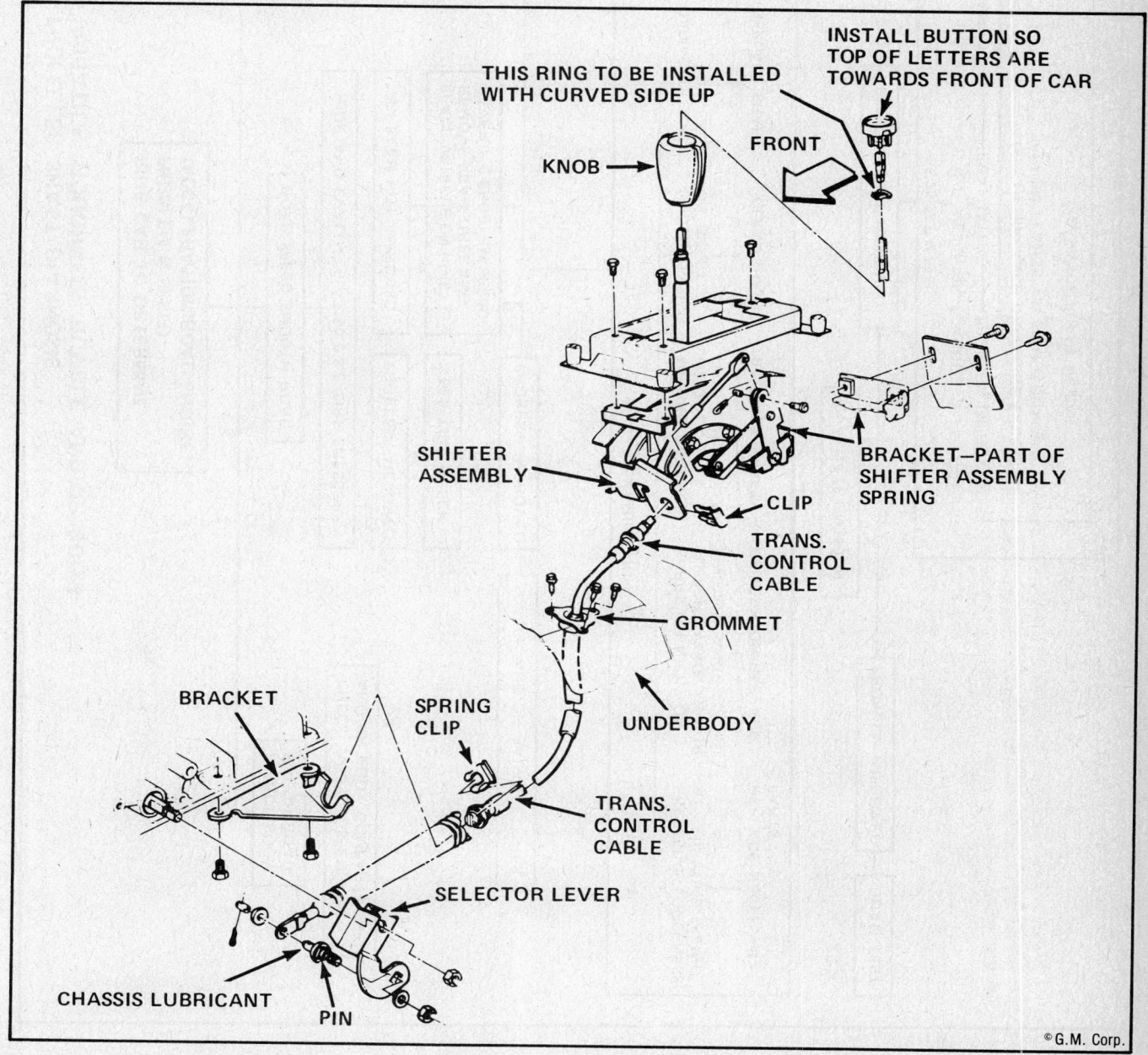

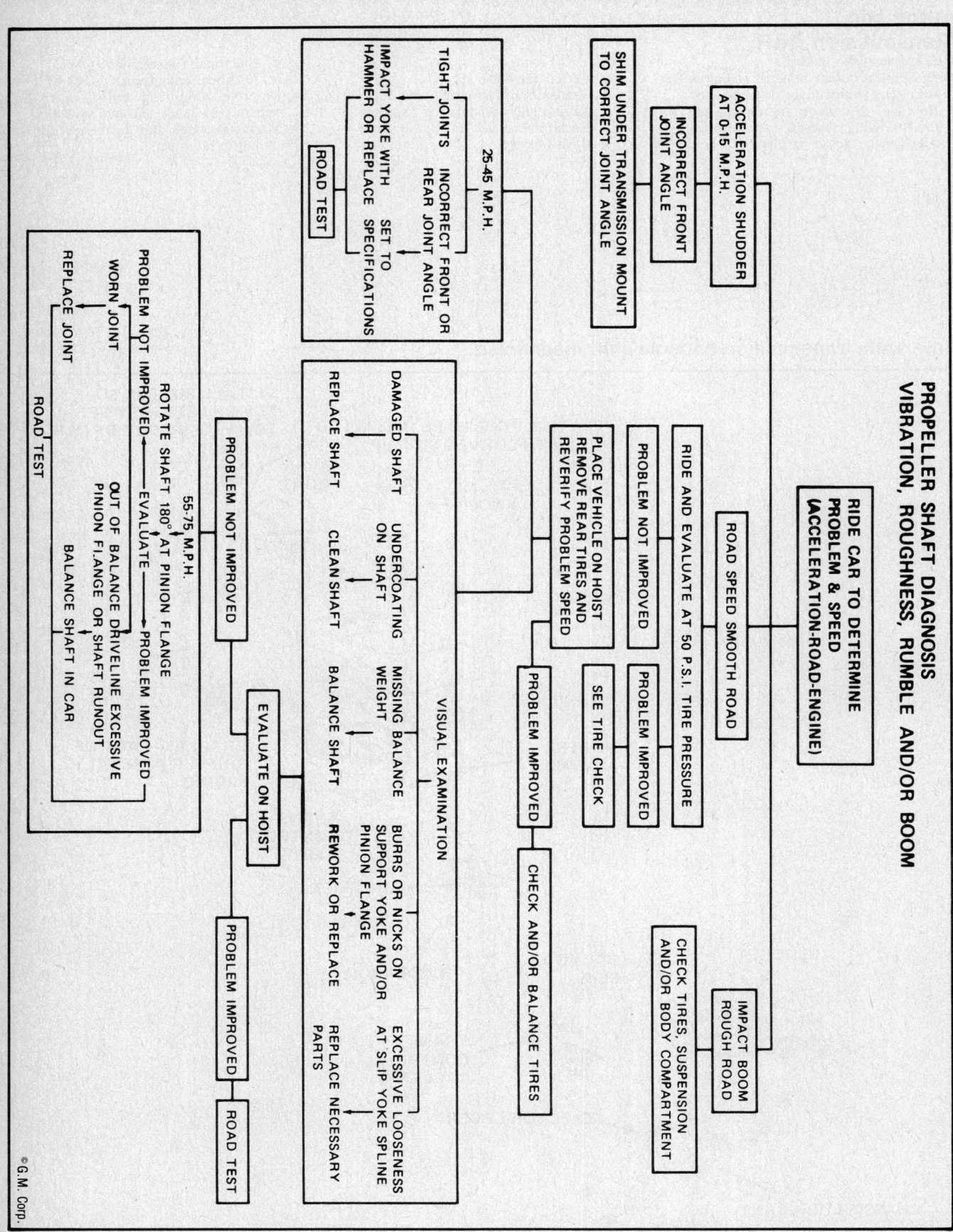

PROPELLER SHAFT DIAGNOSIS
VIBRATION, ROUGHNESS, RUMBLE AND/OR BOOM

© G.M. Corp.

UNIT REPAIR SECTION

INDEX

CARBURETORS

INDEX

CARTER CARBURETORS

MODEL BBD

The BBD carburetor is a two barrel unit. It is equipped with a dashpot on some applications.

Vacuum Step-Up Piston Adjustment

1. Remove the dust cover.
2. Be sure not to disturb the adjusting screw on top of the piston. If it is disturbed, reset the gap at the top of the piston to 0.035–0.040 in.
3. Back off the curb idle adjustment until the throttle valves are completely closed. Count the number of turns so that the screw can later be returned to the original position. Then turn the idle screw in one full turn on AMC products only.
4. Fully depress the step-up piston while holding moderate pressure on the rod lifter tab and loosen and tighten the rod lifter lockscrew.
5. Release the piston and rod lifter; return the curb idle screw to its original position.
6. Replace the dust cover, unless the accelerator pump is to be adjusted.

Accelerator Pump Adjustment

1. Back off the idle adjusting screw. Open the choke valve so that the fast idle cam allows the throttle valves to close. Be sure that the accelerator pump "S" link is in the outer hole of the pump arm if there are two holes.

2. Turn the idle adjusting screw in two complete turns after it contacts the stop.
3. Remove the dust cover. With the throttle valves closed tightly, measure the distance between the top of the air horn and the top of the pump plunger shaft. If the dimension is not as specified, loosen the pump arm adjusting lockscrew (near the plunger shaft) and rotate the sleve to obtain the correct dimension.

Fast Idle Cam Position Adjustment

1. With the fast idle speed adjusting screw contacting the second highest speed step on the fast idle cam, move the choke valve toward the closed position with light pressure on the choke shaft lever. On AMC, loosen the choke cover and turn ¼ turn rich.
2. Insert the specified drill (refer to Specifications), between the top of the choke valve and the wall of the air horn. An adjustment will be necessary if a slight drag is not obtained as the drill is being removed.
3. If an adjustment is required, bend the fast idle connector rod at the angle.
4. Reset the choke cover to specification.

Accelerator Pump & Bowl Vent
1978 AND LATER CHRYSLER

1. The accelerator pump stroke adjustment and the curb idle speed must be adjusted first.

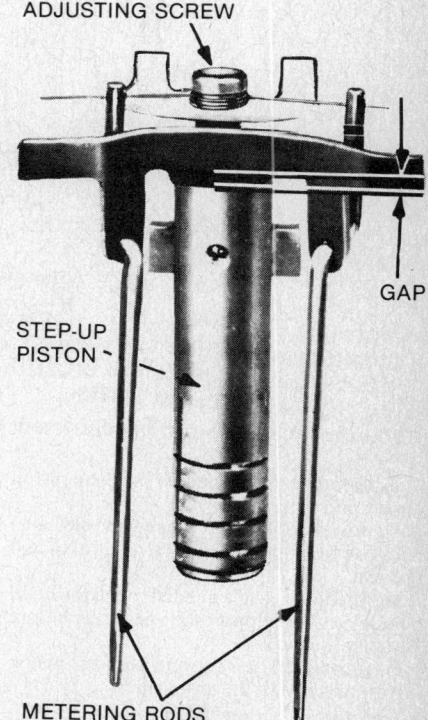

BBD vacuum step-up piston and metering rod assembly (© AMC)

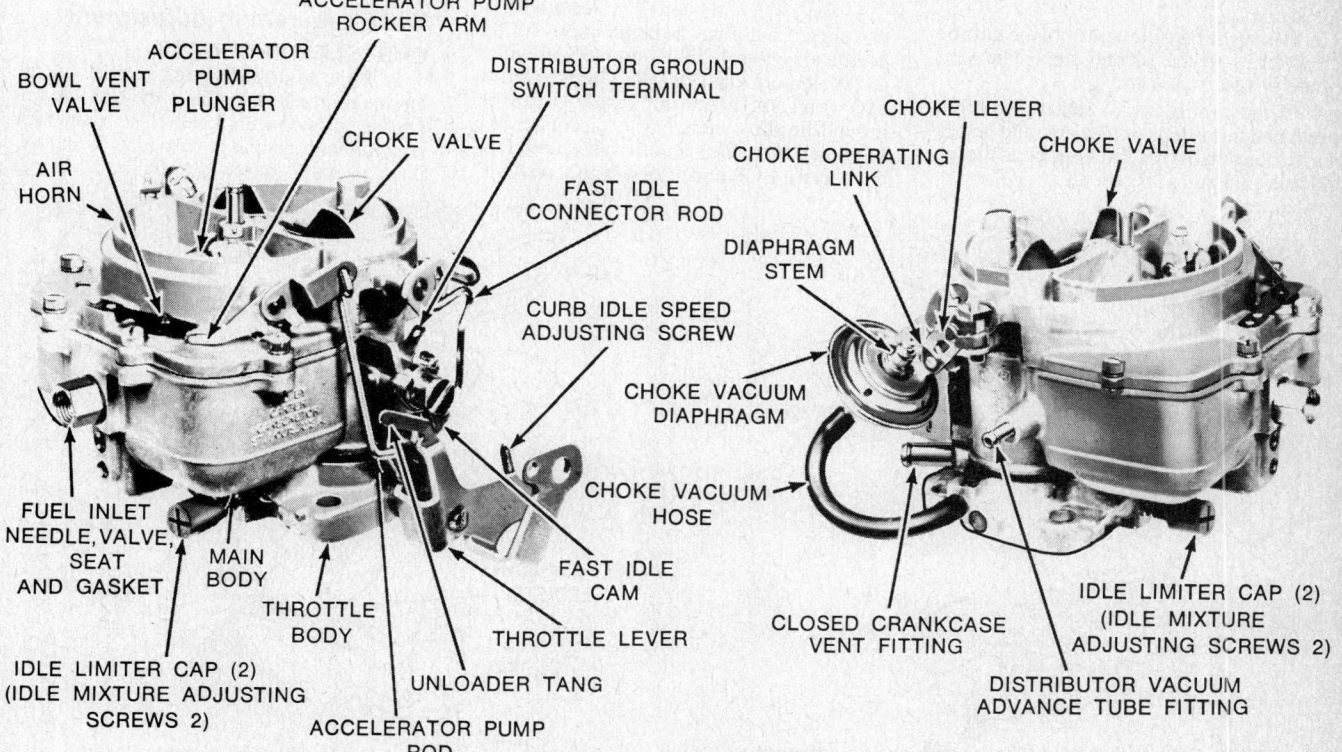

BBD carburetor assembly

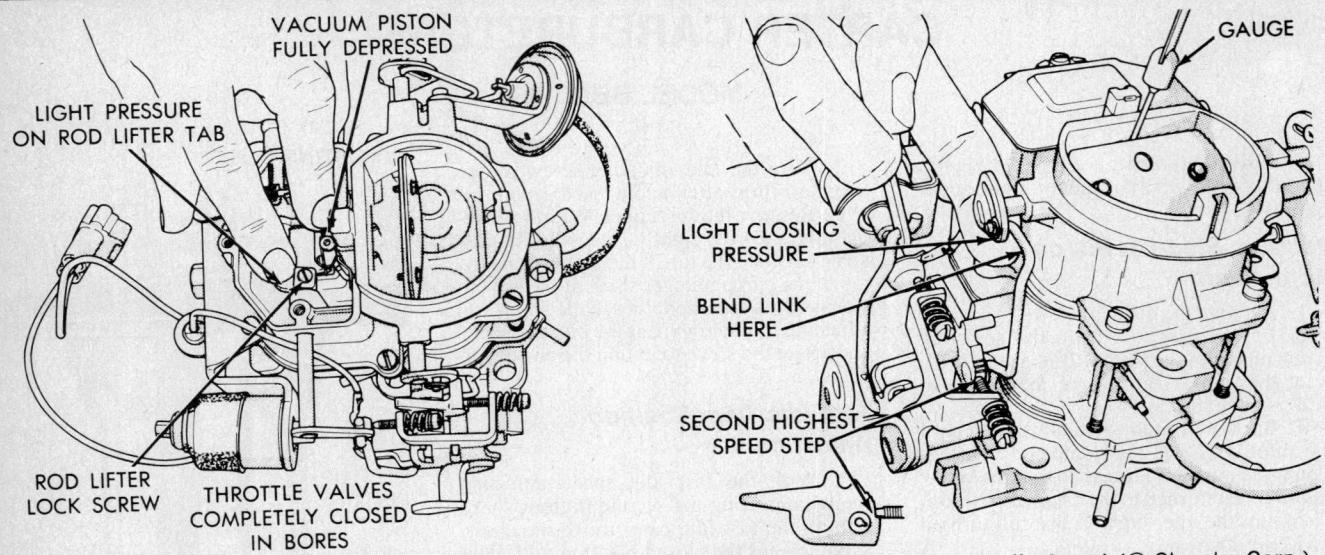

BBD vacuum step-up piston adjustment (© Chrysler Corp.)

BBD fast idle cam position adjustment (© Chrysler Corp.)

2. Remove the air cleaner, step-up piston cover, and the gasket.

3. Insert the specified gauge (0.080 in.) between the top of the bowl vent valve and the seat.

4. If adjustment is needed, bend the bowl vent lever tab. Support the vent lever before bending the tab.

5. Install the gasket and step-up piston cover, and install the air cleaner.

1975 AND LATER AMC

1. Remove the rollover check valve from the air horn for access to the metering rod.

2. Place the throttle on the high step of the fast idle cam. The bowl vent should be closed.

3. Move the fast idle cam until the throttle screw drops to the second step. The vent should just start to open.

4. If the vent is not closed on the high, fourth and third steps of the cam, and beginning to open on the second step, bend the tab until the adjustment is correct.

Choke Unloader (Wide Open Kick)

1. Hold the throttle valves in the wide open position. Insert the specified drill (see Specifications) between the upper edge of the choke valve and the inner wall of the air horn.

2. With a finger lightly pressing against the control lever, a slight drag should be felt as the drill is being withdrawn. If an adjustment is necessary, bend the unloader tang on the throttle lever until the correct opening has been obtained.

Fast Idle Speed (On Vehicle)

1. On 1975 and later Chrysler products, disconnect and plug the connections for the heated air control, EGR, and OSAC valve or distributor. On 1980–81 Chrysler products with ESA (Electronic Spark Advance), ground the idle switch. Do not disconnect the vacuum hose to the vacuum transducer. Disconnect the EGR and TCS solenoid on AMC

cars through 1980. On 1981 AMC disconnect the EGR. With the engine off and the transmission in Park or Neutral position, open the throttle slightly.

2. Close the choke valve until the fast idle screw can be positioned on the second highest speed step of the fast idle cam.

3. Start the engine and let the idle stabilize. Turn the fast idle speed screw in or out to obtain the specified speed.

4. Stopping the engine between adjustments is not necessary. However, reposition the fast idle speed screw on the cam after each speed adjustment to provide the correct throttle closing torque.

Vacuum Kick (Initial Choke Valve Clearance) Adjustment
CHRYSLER PRODUCTS

1. If the adjustment is to be made with the engine running, disconnect the fast idle linkage to allow the choke to close to the kick position with engine at curb idle. If an auxiliary vacuum source is to be used, as rec-

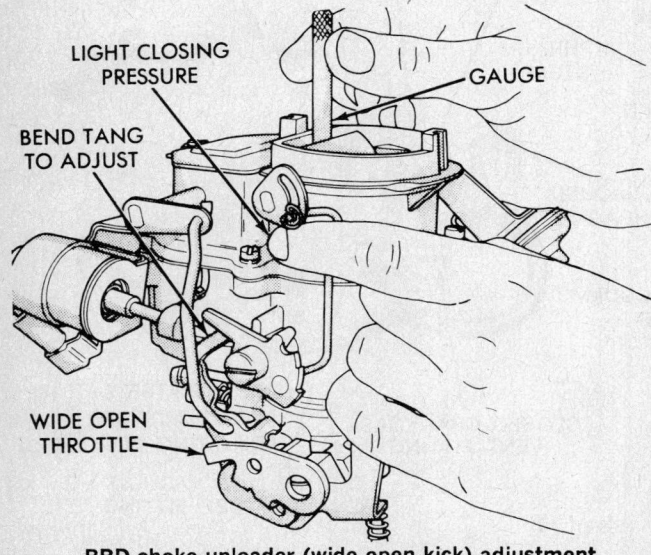

BBD choke unloader (wide open kick) adjustment (© Chrysler Corp.)

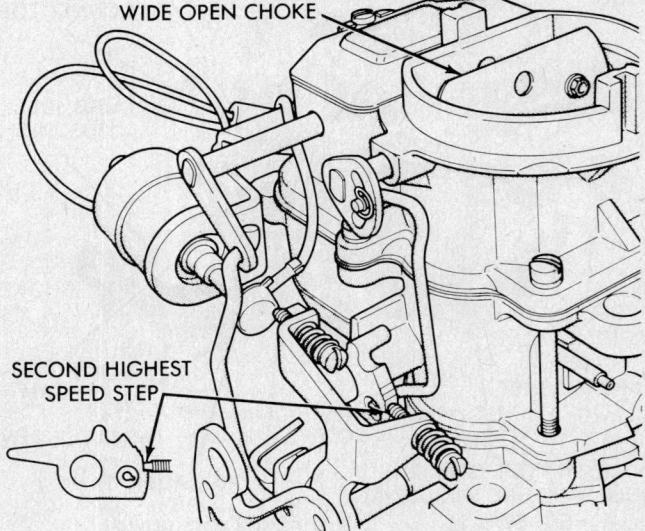

BBD on-car fast idle adjustment (© Chrysler Corp.)

ommended for 1977 and later, open the throttle valves (engine not running) and move the choke to the closed position. Release the throttle first, then release the choke.

2. When using an auxiliary vacuum source, disconnect the vacuum hose from the carburetor and connect it to the hose from the vacuum supply with a small length of tube to act as a fitting. Removel of the hose from the diaphragm may require sufficient force to damage the system. Apply a vacuum of 15 or more in. of mercury.

3. Insert the specified drill (refer to Specifications) between the top of the choke valve and the wall of the air horn. Apply sufficient closing pressure on the lever to which the choke rod attachs to provide a minimum choke valve opening without distortion of the diaphragm link. Note that the cylindrical stem of the diaphragm will extend as the internal spring is compressed. This spring must be fully compressed for proper measurement of the vacuum kick adjustment.

4. An adjustment will be necessary if a slight drag is not obtained as the drill is being removed. Shorten or lengthen the diaphragm link to obtain the correct choke opening. Length changes should be made carefully by bending (opening or closing) the U-bend provided in the diaphragm link.

CAUTION
Do not apply twisting or bending force to the diaphragm.

5. Reinstall the vacuum hose on the correct carburetor fitting. Return the fast idle linkage to its original condition if it was disturbed, as suggested in Step 1.

6. Make the following check: With no vacuum applied to the diaphragm, the choke valve should move freely between the open and closed positions. If its movement is not free, examine the linkage for misalignment or interference caused by the bending operation. Repeat the adjustment if necessary to provide proper link operations.

AMC PRODUCTS
This adjustment is called Initial Choke Valve Clearance Adjustment on AMC products.

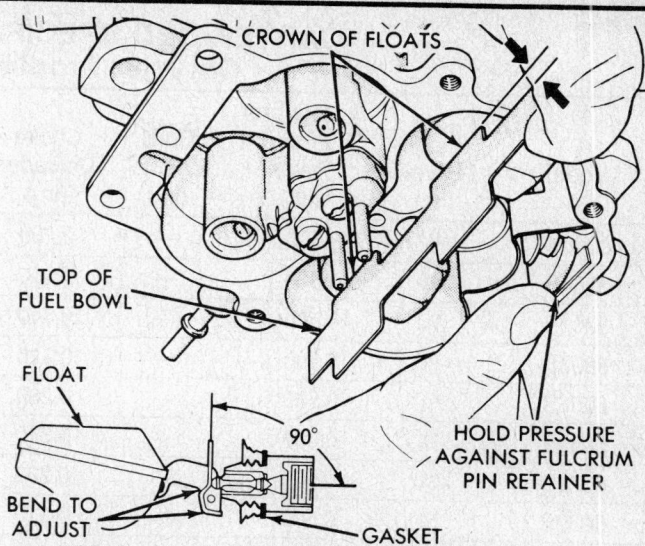

BBD float level adjustment (© Chrysler Corp.)

1. Remove the choke cover. On 1978 and later models, loosen the choke cover, turn ¼ turn rich, and tighten one cover screw.

2. Apply a vacuum of at least 19 inches of mercury to pull the diaphragm in against the stop.

3. Open the throttle valve slightly to place the fast idle screw on the high step of the cam.

4. Hold the choke coil tang in the closed position, on models through 1977. Measure the clearance between the choke plate upper edge and the air horn wall.

5. Adjust the clearance by bending the diaphragm connector link at the angle. Reset the choke or replace the cover.

Float Level
CHRYSLER PRODUCTS
1. Invert the carburetor so that the weight of the floats is the only force on the needle and seat.

2. Use a T-scale to check the float level. Measure from the surface of the fuel bowl to the crown of each float at center.

3. To adjust, hold the floats on the bottom of the bowl and bend the float lip to give the specified dimension.

AMERICAN MOTORS PRODUCTS
1. Remove the air horn.

2. Hold the float lip gently against the needle to raise the float.

3. Place a straightedge across the float bowl to measure the float level at the top of the float.

4. To adjust, bend the float lip, being careful not to exert pressure on the synthetic needle tip.

Dashpot Adjustment
1976 AMERICAN MOTORS PRODUCTS
1. Make sure that the idle speed adjustment is correct.

2. Hold the dashpot plunger in against the stop.

3. Measure the clearance between the plunger and the throttle lever with the throttle in idle position. It should be .104 in.

4. Adjust by turning the dashpot.

CHRYSLER PRODUCTS
The dashpot is used on manual transmission models only.

1. Make sure that the curb idle speed is correctly adjusted.

2. Start the engine. Position the throttle lever so that the actuating tab is just contacting the dashpot plunger stem. Let the engine speed stabilize for 30 seconds.

3. The speed should be 2500 rpm.

4. Adjust the setting by loosening the locknut and moving the dashpot.

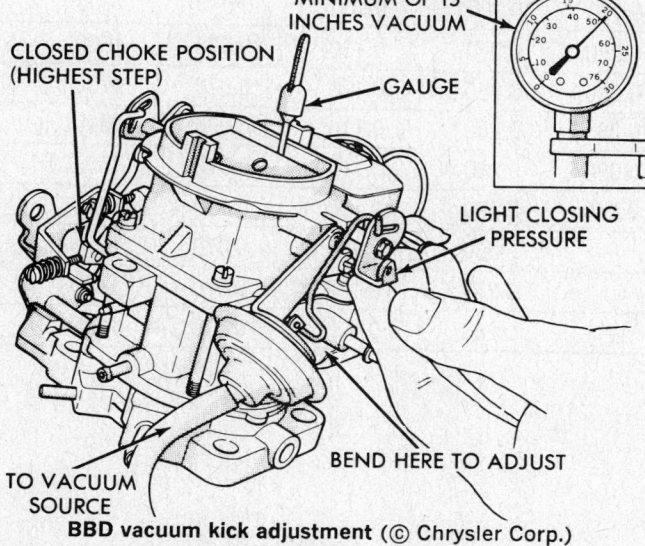

BBD vacuum kick adjustment (© Chrysler Corp.)

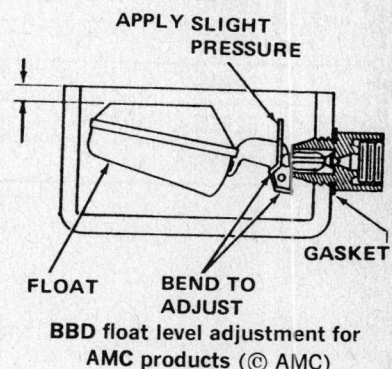

BBD float level adjustment for AMC products (© AMC)

CARTER CARBURETORS

CARTER BBD SPECIFICATIONS
Chrysler Products

Year	Model ④	Float Level (in.)	Accelerator Pump Travel (in.)	Bowl Vent (in.)	Choke Unloader (in.)	Choke Vacuum Kick	Fast Idle Cam Position	Fast Idle Speed (rpm)	Automatic Choke Adjustment
1975	8000S	¼	0.500①	—	0.280	0.130	0.070	1500	Fixed
	8064S	¼	0.500①	—	0.310	0.070	0.070	1500	Fixed
	8001S	¼	0.500①	—	0.310	0.110	0.070	1500	Fixed
	8003S	¼	0.500①	—	0.310	0.110	0.070	1500	Fixed
	8066S	¼	0.500①	—	0.280	0.130	0.070	1500	Fixed
	8062S	¼	0.500①	—	0.310	0.110	0.070	1500	Fixed
1976	8071S	¼	0.500①	—	0.280	0.130	0.070	1500	Fixed
	8069S	¼	0.500①	—	0.310	0.070	0.070	1200	Fixed
	8070S	¼	0.500①	—	0.310	0.110	0.070	1500	Fixed
	8077S, 8099S	¼	0.500①	—	0.280	0.110	0.070	1250	Fixed
	8072S	¼	0.500①	—	0.310	0.070	0.070	1500	Fixed
1977	8087S	¼	0.469①	—	0.280	0.100	0.070	1600	Fixed
	8089S	¼	0.469①	—	0.280	0.130	0.070	1600	Fixed
	8090S	¼	0.469①	—	0.280	0.130	0.070	1700	Fixed
	8127S	¼	0.469①	—	0.280	0.110	0.070	1500	Fixed
	8093S	¼	0.469①	—	0.310	0.130	0.070	1400	Fixed
	8094S	¼	0.469①	—	0.310	0.070	0.070	1400	Fixed
	8096S	¼	0.469①	—	0.310	0.110	0.070	1500	Fixed
	8126S	¼	0.469①	—	0.310	0.110	0.070	1500	Fixed
1978	8136S	¼	0.500①	0.080	0.280	0.110	0.070	1500	Fixed
	8137S	¼	0.500①	0.080	0.280	0.100	0.070	1600	Fixed
	8177S	¼	0.500①	0.080	0.280	0.100	0.070	1600	Fixed
	8175S	¼	0.500①	0.080	0.280	0.160	0.070	1400	Fixed
	8143S	¼	0.500①	0.080	0.280	0.150	0.070	1500	Fixed
1979	8198S	¼	0.500①	0.080	0.280	0.100	0.070	1600	Fixed
	8199S	¼	0.500①	0.080	0.280	0.100	0.070	1600	Fixed
1980	8233S	¼	0.500①	0.080	0.280	0.130	0.070	1500	Fixed
	8235S	¼	0.500①	0.080	0.280	0.130	0.070	1700	Fixed
	8237S	¼	0.500①	0.080	0.280	0.110	0.070	1500	Fixed
	8239S	¼	0.500①	0.080	0.280	0.110	0.070	1500	Fixed
	8286S	¼	0.500①	0.080	0.280	0.100	0.070	1400	Fixed
1981	8290S	¼	0.500①	—	0.280	0.100	0.070	1600	Fixed
	8291S	¼	0.500①	—	0.280	0.130	0.070	1400	Fixed
	8292S	¼	0.500①	—	0.280	0.130	0.070	1600	Fixed

CARTER BBD SPECIFICATIONS
American Motors

Year	Model ②	Float Level (in.)	Accelerator Pump Travel (in.)	Choke Unloader (in.)	Choke Vacuum Kick	Fast Idle Cam Position	Fast Idle Speed (rpm)	Automatic Choke Adjustment
1976	8067	¼	0.500	0.250	0.128	0.095	1700	2 Rich
	8073	¼	0.500	0.250	0.128	0.095	1700	1 Rich
1977	8103	¼	0.496	0.280	0.150	0.120	1600	1 Rich
	8104	¼	0.520	0.280	0.128	0.095	1500	1 Rich
	8117	¼	0.480	0.280	0.152	0.112	1600	1 Rich
1978	8128	¼	0.496	0.280	0.150	0.110	1600	Index
	8129	¼	0.520	0.280	0.128	0.095	1500	1 Rich
1979	8185	¼	0.470	0.280	0.140	0.110	1600	1 Rich
	8186	¼	0.520	0.280	0.150	0.110	1500	1 Rich
	8187	¼	0.470	0.280	0.140	0.110	1600	1 Rich
	8221	¼	0.530	0.280	0.150	0.110	1600	1 Rich
1980	8216	¼	0.520	0.280	0.140	0.090	1850	2 Rich
	8246	¼	0.520	0.280	0.140	0.095	1850	2 Rich
	8247	¼	0.520	0.280	0.150	0.095	1700	1 Rich
	8248	¼	0.520	0.280	0.150	0.095	1700	1 Rich
	8253	¼	0.470	0.280	0.128	0.095	1850	2 Rich
	8256	¼	0.470	0.280	0.128	0.093	1850	2 Rich
	8278	¼	0.542	0.280	0.140	0.093	1850	Index
1981	8310	¼	0.525	0.280	0.140	0.095	1850	Index
	8302	¼	0.500	0.280	0.128	0.095	1850	1 Rich
	8303	¼	0.500	0.280	0.128	0.090	1700	1 Rich
	8306	¼	0.500	0.280	0.128	0.090	1700	1 Rich
	8307	¼	0.500	0.280	0.128	0.095	1850	1 Rich
	8308	¼	0.500	0.280	0.128	0.095	1850	2 Rich
	8309	¼	0.520	0.280	0.128	0.093	1700	2 Rich

② Model numbers located on the tag or casting

MODEL YF, YFA

The YF carburetor is a single barrel downdraft carburetor with a diaphragm type accelerator pump and diaphragm operated metering rods.

Float Adjustment

1. Invert the air horn assembly and check the clearance from the top of the float to the surface of the air horn with a T-scale. The air horn should be held at eye level when gauging and the float arm should be resting on the needle pin.
2. Do not exert pressure on the needle valve when measuring or adjusting the float. Bend the float arm as necessary to adjust the float level.

— CAUTION —

Do not bend the tab at the end of the float arm as it prevents the float from striking the bottom of the fuel bowl when empty and keeps the needle in place.

Metering Rod Adjustment

1. Remove the air horn. Back out the idle speed adjusting screw until the throttle plate is seated fully in its bore.
2. Press down on the upper end of the diaphragm shaft until the diaphragm bottoms in the vacuum chamber.
3. The metering rod should contact the bottom of the metering rod well. The lifter link at the outer end nearest the springs and at the supporting link should be bottomed.

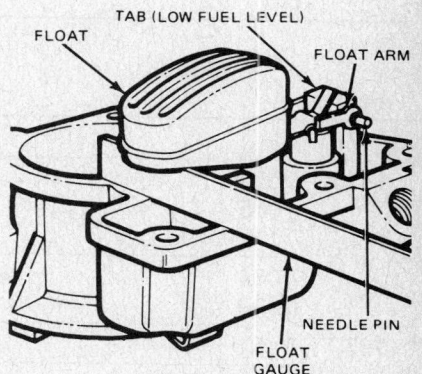

YFA float level adjustment

CARTER CARBURETORS

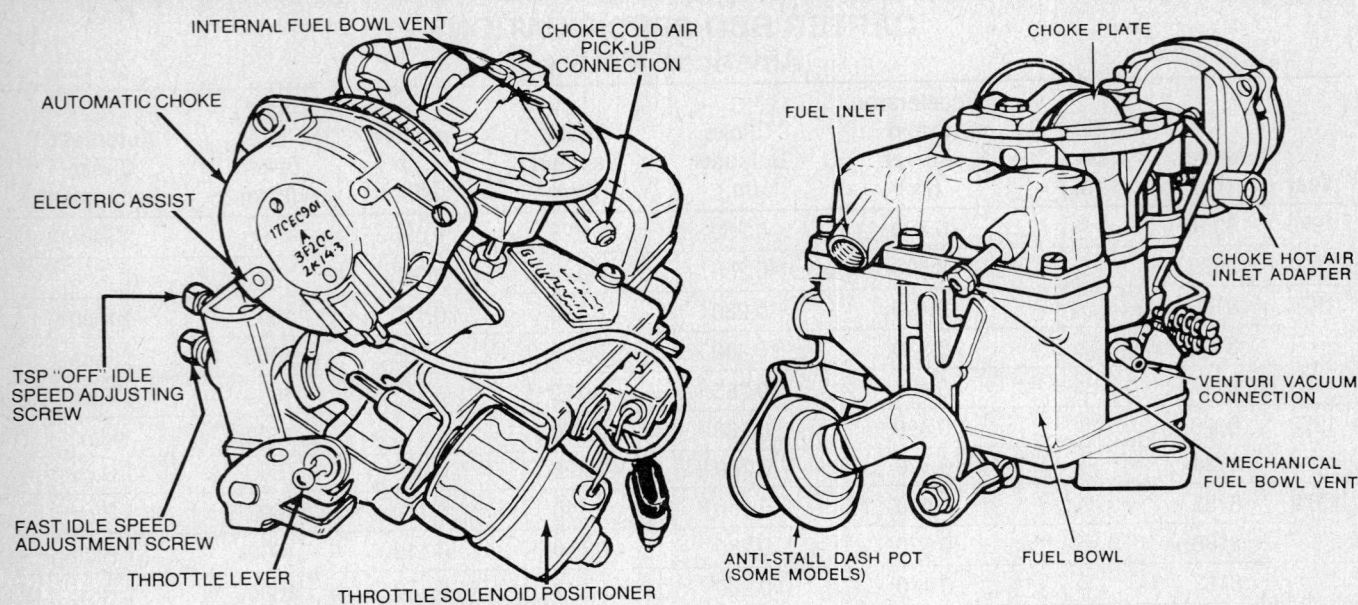

Carter YFA carburetor

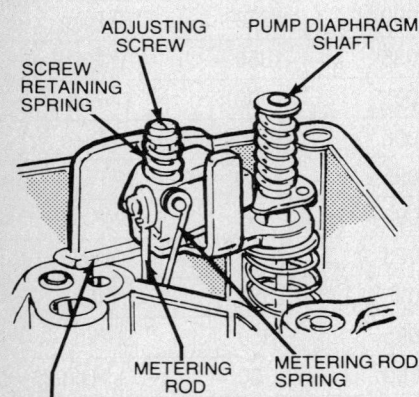

ROD ACTION CAUSED BY SCREW
ACTING AS PIVOT POINT FOR LEVER
YFA metering rod adjustment

4. On models not equipped with an adjusting screw, adjust by bending the lip of the metering rod is attached.

5. On models with an adjusting screw, turn the screw until the metering rod just bottoms in the body casting. For final adjustment, turn the screw one additional turn clockwise.

Fast Idle Cam Adjustment

1. Put the fast idle screw on the second highest step of the fast idle cam against the shoulder of the high step.

2. Adjust by bending the choke plate connecting rod to obtain the specified clearance between the lower edge of the choke plate and the air horn wall.

Choke Unloader Adjustment

1. With the throttle valve held wide open and the choke valve held in the closed position, bend the unloader tang on the throttle lever to obtain the specified clearance between the lower edge of the choke valve and the air horn wall.

Automatic Choke Adjustment

1. Loosen the choke cover retaining screws.

2. Turn the choke cover so that the index mark on the cover lines up with the specified mark on the choke housing.

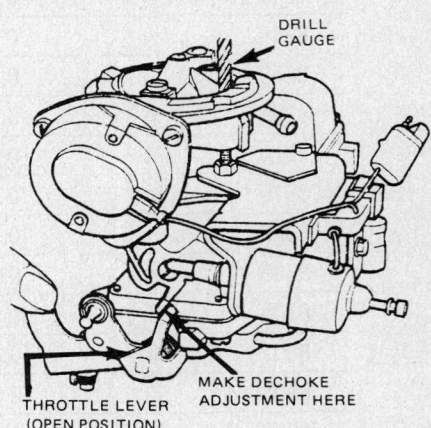

YFA choke unloader adjustment

CARTER YF, YFA SPECIFICATIONS
American Motors

Year	Model ①	Float Level (in.)	Fast Idle Cam (in.)	Unloader (in.)	Choke
1975	All	0.476	0.190	0.275	1 Rich
1976	7083, 7085, 7112	0.476	0.185	0.275	1 Rich
	7084, 7086	0.476	0.185	0.275	2 Rich
1977	7151	0.476	0.195	0.275	1 Rich
	7152	0.476	0.195	0.275	1 Rich

CARTER YF, YFA SPECIFICATIONS
American Motors

Year	Model ①	Float Level (in.)	Fast Idle Cam (in.)	Unloader (in.)	Choke
1977	7153	0.476	0.195	0.275	Index
	7195	0.476	0.195	0.275	1 Rich
	7223	0.476	0.195	0.275	Index
	7111	0.476	0.201	0.275	2 Rich
	7189	0.476	0.201	0.275	1 Rich
1978-79	7201	0.476	0.195	0.275	Index
	7228	0.476	0.195	0.275	1 Rich
	7229	0.476	0.195	0.275	1 Rich
	7235	0.476	0.195	0.275	Index
	7267	0.476	0.195	0.275	1 Rich
	7232	0.476	0.201	0.275	2 Rich
	7233	0.476	0.201	0.275	1 Rich

CARTER YF, YFA SPECIFICATIONS
Ford Motor Co.

Year	Model ①	Float Level (in.)	Fast Idle Cam (in.)	Unloader (in.)	Choke
1975	D5DE-EA	3/8	0.140	0.250	2 Rich
	D5DE-MA	3/8	0.140	0.250	2 Rich
	D5DE-ZA	3/8	0.140	0.250	2 Rich
	D5DE-DA	3/8	0.140	0.250	2 Rich
	D5DE-GA	3/8	0.140	0.250	2 Rich
1976	D6BE-AA	25/32	0.140	0.250	1 Rich
	D6BE-BB	25/32	0.140	0.250	2 Rich
	D5DE-DB	25/32	0.140	0.250	2 Rich
	D5DE-MB	25/32	0.140	0.250	2 Rich
	D6DE-AB	25/32	0.140	0.250	Index
	D6DE-BB	25/32	0.140	0.250	Index
1977-78	D7BE-AA,AB,BA	25/32	0.140	0.250	Index
	D7BE-FA,HB, GB,GC	25/32	0.140	0.250	2 Rich
	D7BE-NA,DA	25/32	0.140	0.250	1 Rich
1979	D9BE-RA D9DE-CB,DB, AA,BA,CA,EA	25/32	0.140	0.250	1 Rich
1980	DEDE-GA, HA, EODE-JA, NA, LA, MA	25/32	0.140	0.250	2 Rich

① Model number located on the tag or casting

MODEL TQ

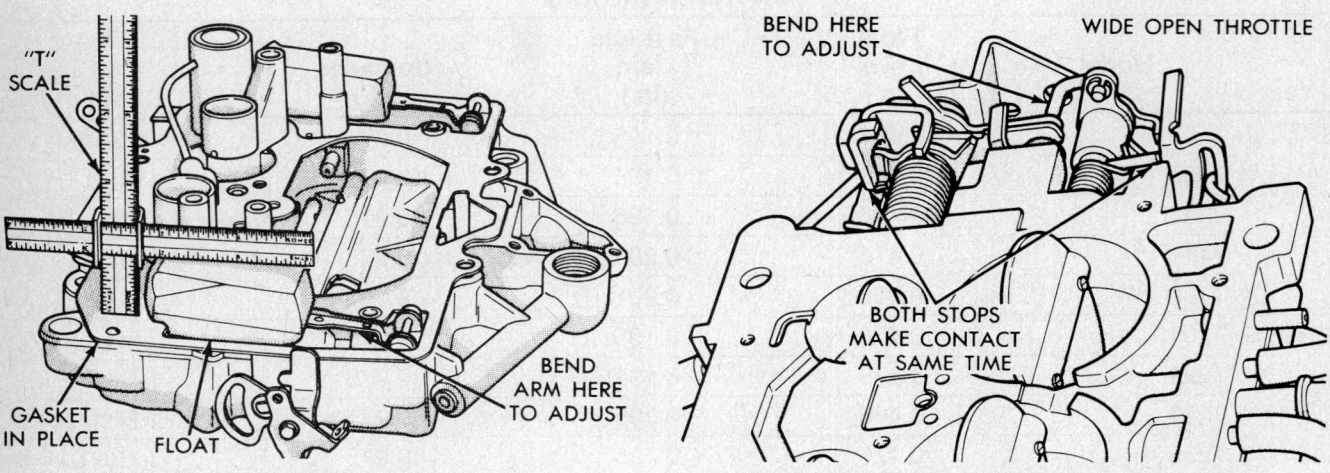

TQ float adjustment (© Chrysler Corp.)

TQ secondary throttle adjustment (© Chrysler Corp.)

The TQ (Thermo-Quad) has a fuel bowl made of phenolic resin. This acts as a heat insulator. Fuel is kept 20 degrees cooler than in metal carburetors. It also has a suspended design metering system which aids in cooling. All the calibration points are in the upper aluminum casting or air horn and are in effect suspended in the cavities in the main body.

Float Adjustment

1. With the bowl cover inverted, the gasket installed, and the floats resting on the seated needle, the dimension of each float from the bottom side of the float to the cover gasket should be as shown in the specifications chart.

2. To adjust, bend the float lever. Do not allow the float lever lip to be pressed against the needle during adjustment.

Secondary Throttle Linkage

1. Block the choke valve in the wide open position and invert the carburetor.

2. Slowly open the primary throttle valves until the secondary valves start to open. Measure between the lower edge of the primary valve and its bore. On 1978 and later models, open the throttle to the wide open position. The primary and secondary levers should contact the stops at the same time.

3. If it is necessary to adjust, bend the secondary throttle operating rod at the lower angle until the correct dimension is obtained.

Secondary Air Valve Opening

1. With the air valve in the closed position, the opening along the air valve at its long side must be at its maximum and parallel with the air horn gasket surface.

2. With the air valve wide open, the opening of the air valve at the short side and the air horn must match the dimensions in the Specifications Charts. The corner of the air valve is notched for adjustment. Bend the corner with a pair of pliers to give proper opening.

Accelerator Pump Adjustment

1975

1. Move the choke valve wide open to release the fast idle cam.

2. Back off the idle speed adjusting screw until the throttle valves are seated in the bores.

3. Be sure that the throttle connector rod is in the center (three holes) or the inner (two holes) hole of the pump arm.

4. Close the throttle valve tightly and

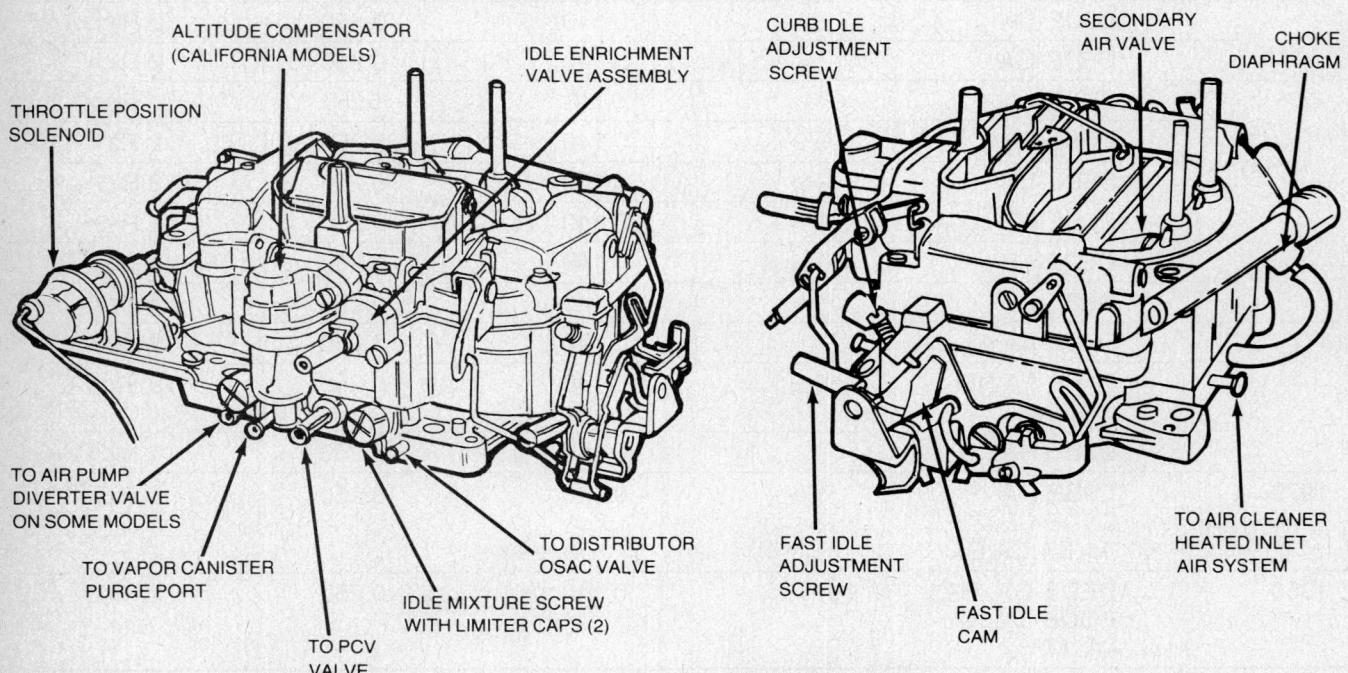

TQ carburetor assembly

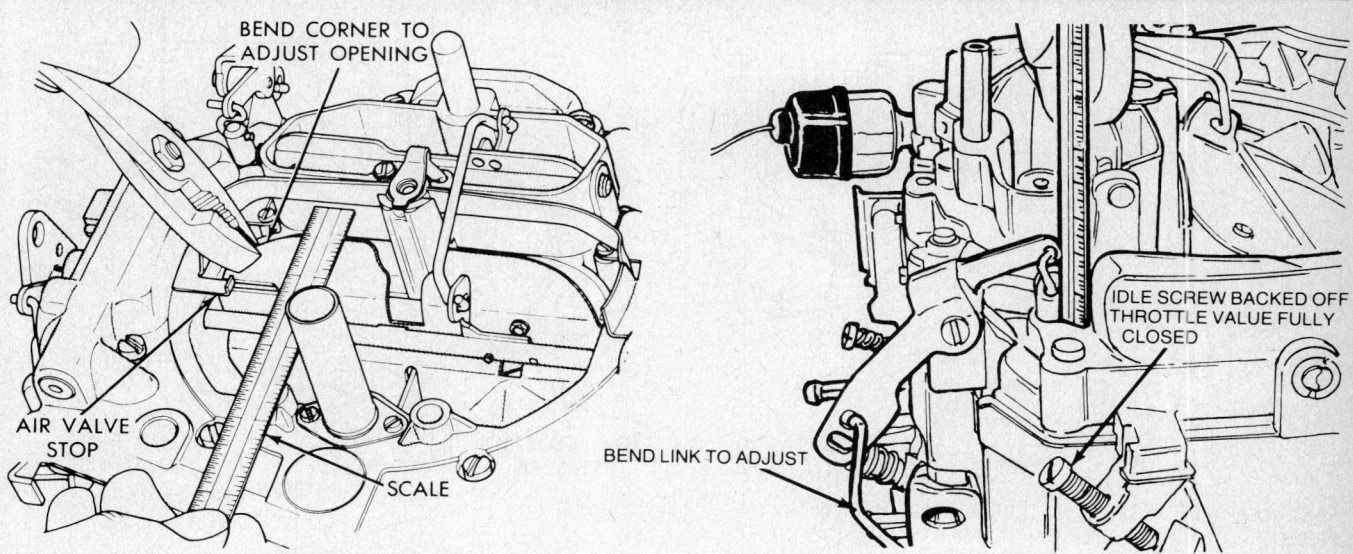

TQ secondary air valve adjustment (© Chrysler Corp.)

TQ accelerator pump adjustment

measure the distance between the top of the bowl cover and the end of the plunger shaft. The dimension should be as shown in the Specifications Chart.

5. Bend the throttle connector rod at the lower angle to adjust.

1976 AND LATER

1. Make sure the throttle connector rod is in the correct hole of the pump arm.
2. Measure the height of the accelerator pump plunger at curb idle. The ignition switch must be on if there is an idle stop solenoid.
3. Adjust plunger height by bending the throttle connector rod.

Choke Control Lever

1. Disconnect the diaphragm rod.
2. Close the choke by pushing on the choke lever with the throttle partly open.
3. Measure the vertical distance from the top of the rod hole in the control lever down

to the carburetor base. The dimension should be as shown in the Specifications Chart.

4. To adjust, bend the link which connects the two choke shafts. If an adjustment is needed, the vacuum kick, fast idle cam, and choke unloader must be readjusted.

Choke Vacuum Kick Adjustment

NOTE: The test can be made on or off the vehicle.

1. If the adjustment is to be made with the engine running, back off the fast idle speed screw until the choke can be closed to the kick position with the engine at curb ide. (Note the number of screw turns required so that the fast idle can be returned to the original adjustment.)

2. If an auxiliary vacuum source is to be used, as recommended for 1977 and later open the throttle valve (engine not running) and move the choke to the closed position.

Release the throttle first, then release the choke.

When using an auxiliary vacuum source, disconnect the vacuum hose from the carburetor and connect it to the hose from the vacuum supply with a small length of tube to act as a fitting. Removel of the hose from the diaphragm may require sufficient force to bend the bracket. Apply a vacuum of 15 or more in. of mercury.

3. Insert the specified drill between the long side, lower edge, of the choke valve and the air horn wall.

4. Apply sufficient pressure on the choke control lever to provide a minimum choke valve opening. The spring connecting the control lever to the adjustment lever must be fully extended for proper adjustment.

5. Bend the tang to change contact with the end of the diaphragm rod. Do not adjust the diaphragm rod. A slight drag should be felt as the drill is being removed.

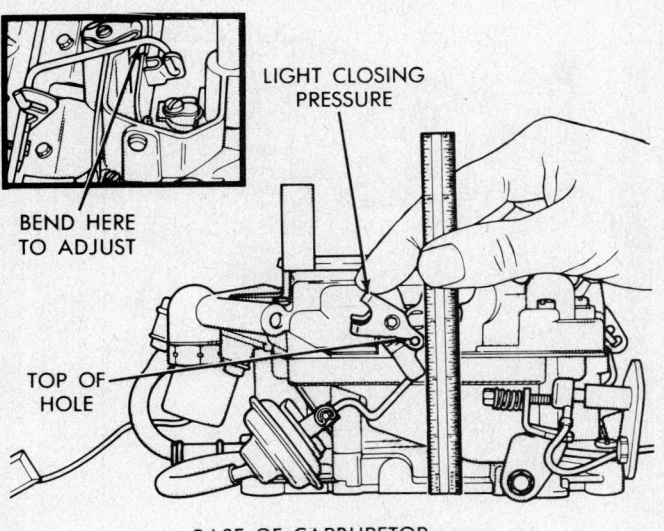

TQ choke control lever (© Chrysler Corp.)

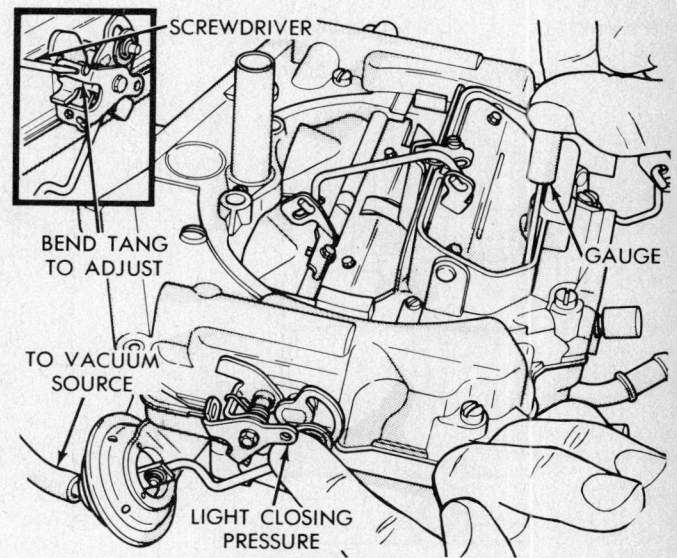

TQ vacuum kick adjustment (© Chrysler Corp.)

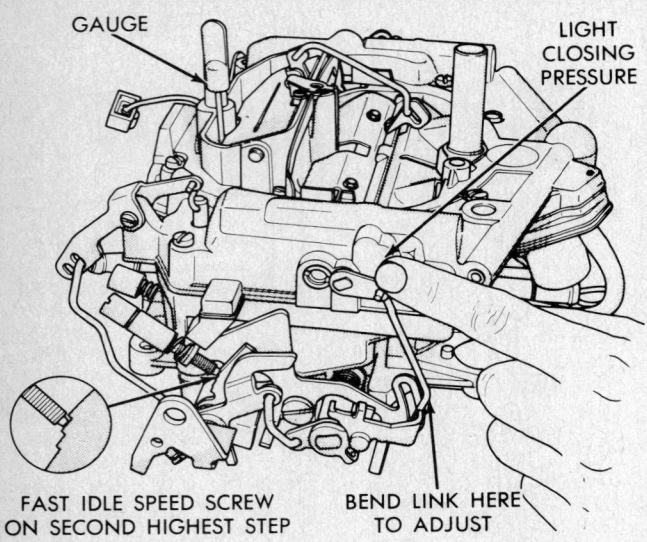

TQ fast idle cam linkage adjustment (© Chrysler Corp.)

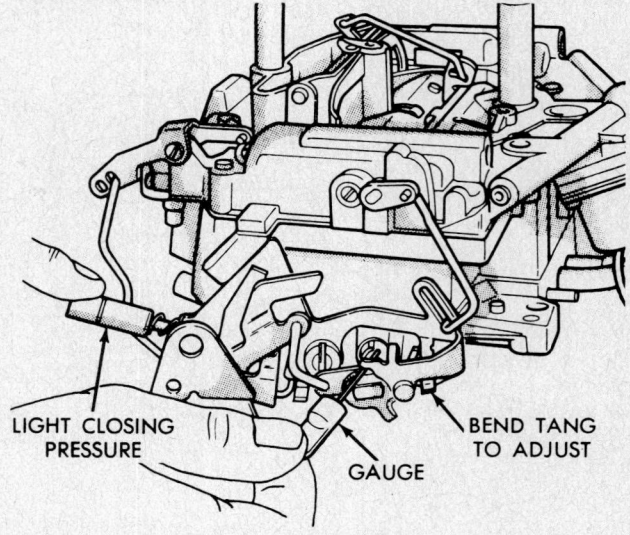

TQ secondary throttle lockout adjustment (© Chrysler Corp.)

Fast Idle Cam Linkage

1. With the fast screw on the second fastest step of the cam against the shoulder of the first step, there should be 0.100 in. between the air horn wall and edge of the choke valve.
2. To adjust, bend the fast idle connector rod at the lower angle.

Secondary Throttle Lockout

1. Move the choke control lever to the open choke position.
2. Measure the clearance between the lockout lever and the stop.
3. Bend the tang on the fast idle control lever to provide the proper clearance. Clearance should be 0.060–0.090 in. through 1977, or 0.075 in. thereafter.

Bowl Vent Valve Adjustment

THROUGH 1978

1. Remove the bowl vent valve checking hole plug in the bowl cover.
2. With the throttle valve in the idle position insert a narrow ruler down through the hole.
3. Allow the ruler to rest lightly on the top of the valve. Measure from the top of the valve to the top of the bowl cover at the opening. The correct dimension should be $1\frac{3}{16}$ in.
4. Bend the bowl vent operating lever at the notch to adjust.
5. Install a new plug.

TQ fast idle cam adjustment

1979 AND LATER

1. Remove the air cleaner. Disconnect the hose to the solenoid bowl vent diaphragm.

2. Connect an auxiliary vacuum source. With 15 in. Hg. applied, the valve should move down. This can be observed down through the air horn vent tube.
3. Turn the ignition switch on and disconnect the auxiliary vacuum source. The valve should remain down. With the ignition off, the valve should move back up.
4. If the valve does not move down when vacuum is applied, the diaphragm is leaking and must be replaced. If the valve does not stay down with the ignition on and the vacuum removed, the solenoid or the wiring is defective.

Fast Idle Speed Cam

1. Disconnect and plug the heated air, EGR, OSAC valve, or distributor connections. With lean burn, do not disconnect the spark control computer hose. Use a jumper wire to ground the carburetor idle stop switch. With the engine off and the transmission in Park or Neutral, open the throttle slightly.

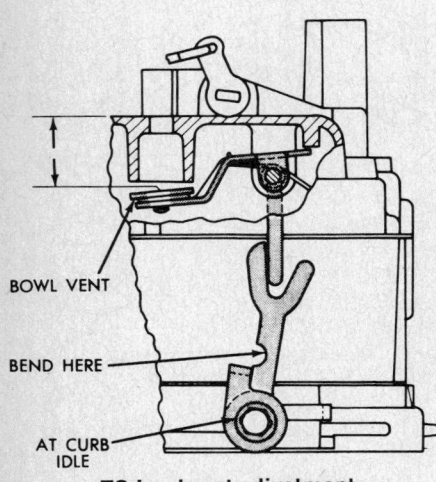

TQ bowl vent adjustment

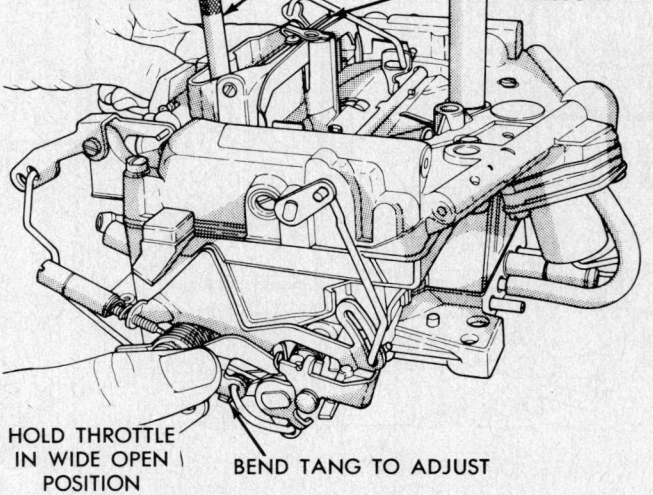

TQ choke unloader adjustment (© Chrysler Corp.)

2. Close the choke valve until the fast idle screw can be positioned on the second step of the cam against the shoulder of the first step.

3. Start the engine and adjust the screw to obtain the specified fast idle speed.

Choke Unloader Adjustment

1. Hold the throttle valves in the wide open position and insert the specified drill between the bottom of the choke valve and inner wall of the air horn.

2. With a finger pressing lightly against the choke control lever, a slight drag should be felt as the drill is being withdrawn.

3. To adjust, bend the tang on the fast idle lever.

--- **CAUTION** ---

Hold the adjustment plug with a screwdriver when loosening the lock plug. If you don't, the spring may snap out of position and require carburetor disassembly to retrieve it.

Secondary Air Valve Spring Tension

1. Loosen the air valve lock plug and allow the air valve to position itself in the wide open position.

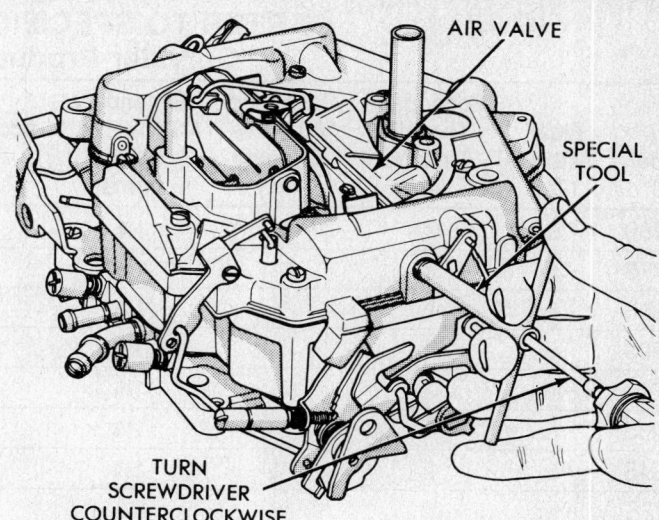

TQ air valve spring tension adjustment (© Chrysler Corp.)

2. With a long screwdriver that will enter the center of tool C-4152 positioned on the air valve adjustment plug, turn the plug counterclockwise until the air valve contacts the stop lightly, then tighten the specified amount.

3. Hold the adjustment plug with the screwdriver and tighten the lock plug with the tool. Make sure the adjustment does not move and that the air valve moves freely.

CARTER TQ SPECIFICATIONS
Chrysler Products

Year	Model ①	Float Setting (in.)	Secondary Throttle Linkage (in.)	Secondary Air Valve Opening (in.)	Secondary Air Valve Spring (turns)	Accelerator Pump (in.)	Choke Control Lever (in.)	Choke Unloader (in.)	Vacuum Kick (in.)	Fast Idle Speed (rpm)
1975	9004S	$^{29}/_{32}$	②	½	1¼	$^{35}/_{64}$	3⅜	0.310	0.100	1600
	9002S	$^{29}/_{32}$	②	½	1¼	$^{35}/_{64}$	3⅜	0.310	0.100	1600
	9046S	$^{29}/_{32}$	②	½	1¼	$^{35}/_{64}$	3⅜	0.310	0.100	1800
	9008S	$^{29}/_{32}$	②	½	1¼	$^{35}/_{64}$	3⅜	0.310	0.100	1800
	9053S	$^{29}/_{32}$	②	½	1¼	$^{35}/_{64}$	3⅜	0.310	0.100	1800
	9009S	$^{29}/_{32}$	②	½	1¼	$^{35}/_{64}$	3⅜	0.310	0.100	1600
	9010S	$^{29}/_{32}$	②	½	1¼	$^{35}/_{64}$	3⅜	0.310	0.100	1600
	9011S	$^{29}/_{32}$	②	½	1¼	$^{35}/_{64}$	3⅜	0.310	0.100	1600
	9012S	$^{29}/_{32}$	②	½	1¼	$^{35}/_{64}$	3⅜	0.310	0.100	1800
1976	9002S	$^{29}/_{32}$	②	$^{33}/_{64}$	1¼	$^{33}/_{64}$	3⅜	0.310	0.100	1700
	9055S	$^{29}/_{32}$	②	$^{33}/_{64}$	1¼	$^{33}/_{64}$	3⅜	0.310	0.100	1700
	9074S	$^{29}/_{32}$	②	$^{33}/_{64}$	1¼	$^{33}/_{64}$	3⅜	0.310	0.100	1600
	9057S	$^{29}/_{32}$	②	$^{33}/_{64}$	1¼	$^{33}/_{64}$	3⅜	0.310	0.100	1600
	9054S	$^{29}/_{32}$	②	$^{33}/_{64}$	1¼	$^{33}/_{64}$	3⅜	0.310	0.100	1800
	9058S	$^{29}/_{32}$	②	$^{33}/_{64}$	1¼	$^{31}/_{64}$	3⅜	0.310	0.100	1600
	9059S	$^{29}/_{32}$	②	$^{33}/_{64}$	1¼	$^{31}/_{64}$	3⅜	0.310	0.100	1600
	9066S	$^{29}/_{32}$	②	$^{33}/_{64}$	1¼	$^{33}/_{64}$	3⅜	0.310	0.100	1600
	9062S	$^{29}/_{32}$	②	$^{33}/_{64}$	1¼	$^{33}/_{64}$	3⅜	0.310	0.100	1600
	9052S	$^{29}/_{32}$	②	$^{33}/_{64}$	1¼	$^{33}/_{64}$	3⅜	0.310	0.100	1600

CARTER CARBURETORS

CARTER TQ SPECIFICATIONS
Chrysler Products

Year	Model ①	Float Setting (in.)	Secondary Throttle Linkage (in.)	Secondary Air Valve Opening (in.)	Secondary Air Valve Spring (turns)	Accelerator Pump (in.)	Choke Control Lever (in.)	Choke Unloader (in.)	Vacuum Kick (in.)	Fast Idle Speed (rpm)
1977	9076S	$27/32$	②	$1/2$	$1\frac{1}{2}$	$33/64$	$3\frac{3}{8}$	0.310	0.150	1700
	9077S	$27/32$	②	$31/64$	$1\frac{1}{2}$	$33/64$	$3\frac{3}{8}$	0.310	0.100	1400
	9078S	$27/32$	②	$1/2$	$1\frac{1}{4}$	$33/64$	$3\frac{3}{8}$	0.310	0.100	1400
	9080S	$27/32$	②	$1/2$	$1\frac{1}{4}$	$33/64$	$3\frac{3}{8}$	0.310	0.100	1200
	9081S	$27/32$	②	$1/2$	$1\frac{1}{4}$	$33/64$	$3\frac{3}{8}$	0.310	0.100	1600
	9093S	$27/32$	②	$17/32$	$1\frac{1}{4}$	$33/64$	$3\frac{3}{8}$	0.310	0.150	1500
	9101S	$27/32$	②	$1/2$	$1\frac{1}{4}$	$33/64$	$3\frac{3}{8}$	0.310	0.100	1600
1978	9147S	$29/32$	②	$1/2$	$1\frac{1}{2}$	$31/64$	$3\frac{3}{8}$	0.310	0.100	1600
	9137S	$29/32$	②	$1/2$	$1\frac{1}{2}$	$31/64$	$3\frac{3}{8}$	0.310	0.100	1600
	9134S	$29/32$	②	$1/2$	$1\frac{1}{2}$	$31/64$	$3\frac{3}{8}$	0.310	0.100	1500
	9104S	$29/32$	②	$1/2$	$1\frac{1}{2}$	$31/64$	$3\frac{3}{8}$	0.310	0.150	1500
	9140S	$29/32$	②	$1/2$	$1\frac{1}{2}$	$33/64$	$3\frac{3}{8}$	0.310	0.150	1500
	9108S	$27/32$	②	$1/2$	$1\frac{1}{2}$	$33/64$	$3\frac{3}{8}$	0.310	0.100	1400
	9109S	$27/32$	②	$1/2$	$1\frac{1}{2}$	$33/64$	$3\frac{3}{8}$	0.310	0.100	1400
	9110S	$27/32$	②	$1/2$	$1\frac{1}{2}$	$33/64$	$3\frac{3}{8}$	0.310	0.100	1600
	9111S	$27/32$	②	$1/2$	$1\frac{1}{2}$	$33/64$	$3\frac{3}{8}$	0.310	0.100	1400
	9112S	$29/32$	②	$1/2$	$1\frac{1}{2}$	$33/64$	$3\frac{3}{8}$	0.310	0.100	1200
	9148S	$29/32$	②	$1/2$	$1\frac{1}{2}$	$33/64$	$3\frac{3}{8}$	0.310	0.100	1600
1979	9195S	$29/32$	②	$3/8$	2	$33/64$	$3\frac{3}{8}$	0.310	0.100	1600
	9197S	$29/32$	②	$1/2$	$1\frac{1}{2}$	$33/64$	$3\frac{3}{8}$	0.310	0.100	1600
	9196S, 9198S, 9202S	$29/32$	②	$1/2$	2	$33/64$	$3\frac{3}{8}$	0.310	0.100	1600
1980	9236S	$29/32$	②	$1/2$	3	$11/32$ ③	$3\frac{3}{8}$	0.310	0.100	1600
	9243S	$29/32$	②	$1/2$	$2\frac{5}{8}$	$11/32$ ④	$3\frac{3}{8}$	0.310	0.100	1600
	9244S	$29/32$	②	$1/2$	$2\frac{1}{2}$	$11/32$ ④	$3\frac{3}{8}$	0.310	0.100	1200
1981	92835	$29/32$	②	$1/2$	$1\frac{3}{4}$	$33/64$ ④	$3\frac{3}{8}$	0.312	0.130	1400
	9293S	$29/32$	②	$1/2$	$1\frac{3}{4}$	$33/64$ ④	$3\frac{3}{8}$	0.312	0.130	1400
	9284S	$29/32$	②	$1/2$	$1\frac{7}{8}$	$33/64$ ③	$3\frac{3}{8}$	0.312	0.100	1500

NOTE: All choke settings are fixed.
① Model numbers located on the tag or on the casting
② Adjust link so primary and secondary stops both contact at same time
③ Slot #1
④ Slot #2

FORD, AUTOLITE, MOTORCRAFT CARBURETORS

MODEL 740

The model 740 has five basic systems: choke system, idle system, main metering system, acceleration system and power enrichment system. The choke system is used for cold starting and features a bi-metallic spring and an electric heater for faster cold starts and improved warm-up. The idle system is a separate and adjustable system for the correct air/fuel mixture for both idle and low speed performance.

The main metering system provides the correct air/fuel mixture for normal cruising speeds. A main metering system is provided for both primary and secondary stage operation.

The accelerating system is mechanically operated from the primary throttle linkage and provides fuel to the primary stage during acceleration. Fuel is provided by a diaphragm-type pump. The power enrichment system consists of a vacuum operated power valve and an airflow-regulated pullover system in the secondary. This system is used along with the main metering system to provide satisfactory performance during moderate to heavy acceleration.

Distributor and EGR vacuum ports are located in the primary venturi area of the carburetor.

Fast Idle Cam

1. Set the fast idle screw on the kickdown step of the cam against the shoulder of the top step.
2. Manually close the primary choke plate, and measure the distance between the downstream side of the choke plate and the air horn wall.
3. Adjust the right fork of the choke bi-metal shaft, which engages the fast idle cam, by bending the fork up and down to obtain the specified clearance.

Fast Idle

1. Place the transmission in neutral or park.
2. Bring the engine to normal operating temperature.
3. Disconnect and plug the vacuum hose at the EGR and purge valves.
4. Identify the vacuum source to the air by-pass section of the air supply control valve. If a vacuum hose is connected to the carburetor, disconnect the hose and plug the hose at the air supply control valve.
5. Place the fast idle adjustment on the second step of the fast idle cam. Run the engine until the cooling fan comes on.

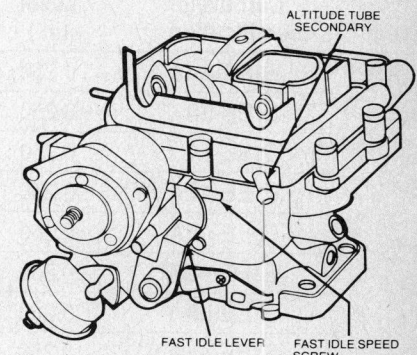

Model 740 carburetor—¾ front view

6. While the cooling fan is on, check the fast idle rpm. If adjustment is necessary, loosen the locknut and adjust to specification on underhood decal.
7. Remove all plugs and reconnect hoses to their original position.

Dashpot

With the throttle set at the curb idle position, fully depress the dashpot stem and measure the distance between the stem and the throttle lever. Adjust by loosening the locknut and turning the dashpot.

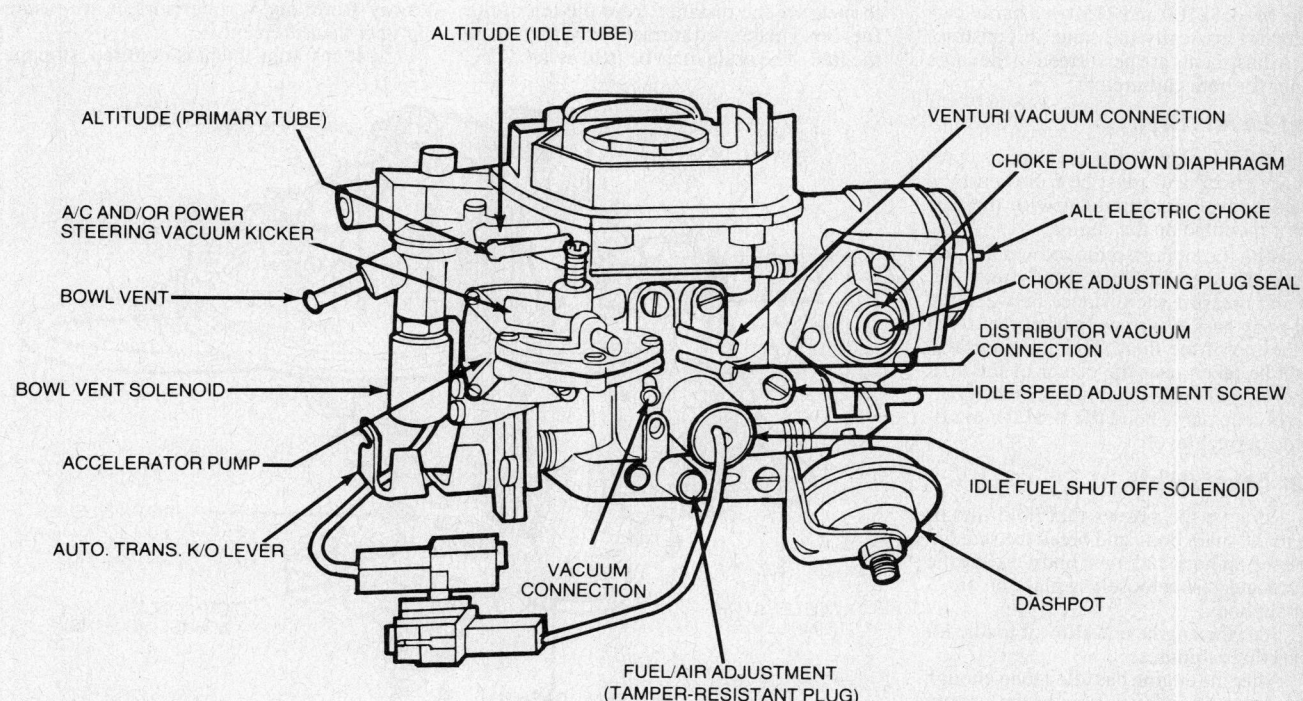

Model 740 carburetor—full rear

MOTORCRAFT MODEL 740 SPECIFICATIONS
Escort, Lynx

Year	(9510)* Carburetor Identification ①	Dry Float Level (in.)	Choke Plate Pulldown (in.)	Fast Idle Cam Linkage (in.)	Fast Idle (rpm)	Dechoke (in.)	Choke Setting	Dashpot (in.)
1981	E1EE-AAA	0.250	0.120	0.80	①	0.140	Index	0.140
	E1EE-SA	0.250	0.120	0.80	①	0.140	Index	0.140
	E1EE-TA	0.250	0.120	0.80	①	0.140	Index	0.140
	E1EE-AEA	0.250	0.120	0.80	①	0.140	Index	0.140
	E1EE-AFA	0.250	0.120	0.80	①	0.140	Index	0.140
	E1EE-ADA	0.250	0.120	0.80	①	0.140	Index	0.140
	E1EE-LA	0.250	0.120	0.80	①	0.140	Index	0.140
	E1EE-AHA	0.250	0.100	0.80	①	0.140	Index	0.160
	E1EE-ZA	0.250	0.160	0.80	①	0.140	1 Lean	0.160
	E1EE-MA	0.250	0.160	0.80	①	0.140	1 Lean	0.160
	E1EE-NA	0.250	0.160	0.80	①	0.140	1 Lean	0.160
	E1EE-PA	0.250	0.160	0.80	①	0.140	1 Lean	0.160
	E1EE-ACA	0.250	0.160	0.80	①	0.140	1 Lean	0.160
	E1EE-RA	0.250	0.160	0.80	①	0.140	1 Lean	0.160

① See underhood decal.

MODELS 2100, 2150

The Model 2100 and 2150 two barrel carburetor are basically the same in construction. Adjustments are performed in the same manner for both carburetors.

Float Level (Dry)

The dry float level measurement is a preliminary check and must be followed by a wet float level measurement with the carburetor mounted on the engine.

1. With the air horn removed and the fuel inlet needle seated lightly, gently raise the float and measure the distance between the main body gasket surface (gasket removed) and the top of the float. This measurement should be taken near the center of the float at a point ⅛ in. from the free end of the float.

2. If necessary, bend the float tab to obtain the correct level.

Float Level (Wet)

1. Remove the screws that hold the air horn to the main body and break the seal between the air horn and main body. Leave the air horn and gasket loosely in place on top of the main body.

2. Start the engine and allow it to idle for at least three minutes.

3. After the engine has idled long enough to stabilize the fuel level, remove the air horn assembly.

4. With the engine idling, use a T-scale to measure the distance from the top of the fuel bowl machined surface to the surface of the fuel. The scale must be held at last ¼ in. away from any vertical surface to ensure proper measurement.

5. If any adjustment is required, stop the

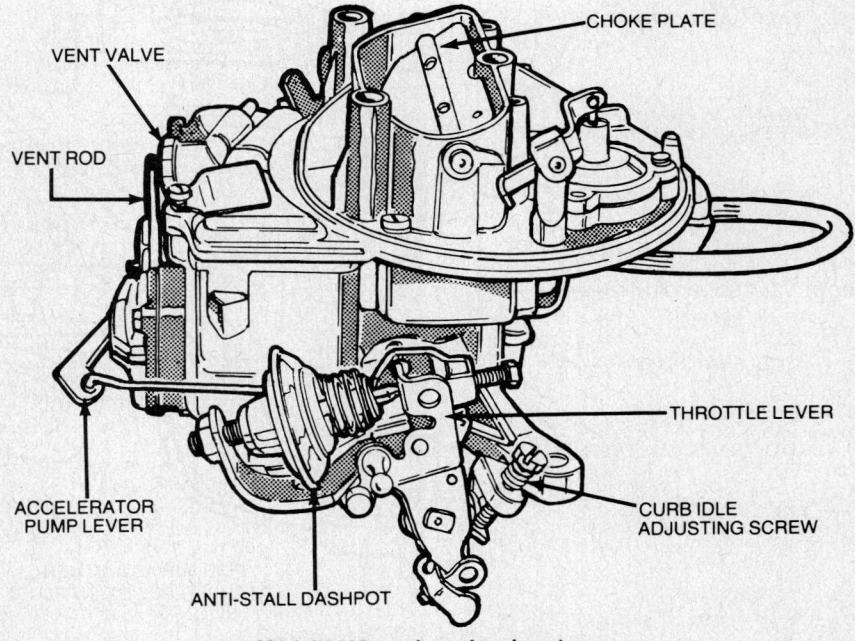

Model 2100 two barrel carburetor

VENT VALVE

VENT ROD

CHOKE PLATE

THROTTLE LEVER

CURB IDLE ADJUSTING SCREW

ACCELERATOR PUMP LEVER

ANTI-STALL DASHPOT

engine to avoid a fire from fuel spraying on the engine.

6. Bend the float tab upward to raise the level and downward to lower the level.

CAUTION

Be sure to hold the fuel inlet needle off its seat when bending the float tab so as not to damage the Viton® tip.

---

7. Each time the float level is changed, the air horn must be temporarily positioned and the engine started to stabilize the fuel level before again checking it.

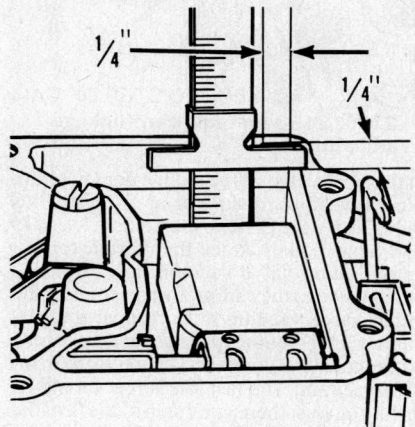

Fuel level measurement (wet)
(© Ford Motor Co)

Choke Plate Pulldown
FORD MODEL 2100

1. Loosen the screws on the choke cover and rotate the cover ¼ turn counterclockwise (rich), then tighten the screws.

2. Operate the throttle to allow full closing the choke plate.

3. Press down on the choke modulator arm until the choke modulator diaphragm is bottomed and then measure the distance from the lower edge of the choke plate to the inside air horn wall.

4. Adjustment is achieved by turning the diaphragm stop screw on the underside of the air horn.

5. Turn the screw clockwise to decrease clearance and counter-clockwise to increase clearance.

NOTE: Do not reset the choke cover until the fast idle cam adjustment is made.

AMC MODEL 2100

1. Loosen the choke cover screws and rotate the cover ¼ turn counter-clockwise (rich).

2. Disconnect the choke heat inlet tube. Set the fast idle speed screw on the second step of the fast idle cam.

3. Start the engine without moving the throttle linkage. Turn the fast idle cam lever adjusting screw out three turns.

4. Check the clearance between the lower edge of the choke valve and the air horn wall.

5. Adjust by twisting the modulator arm. Be very careful not to damage the nylon modulator piston rod.

6. Stop the engine and connect the heat tube.

7. Make the fast idle cam adjustment before resetting the choke cover.

MODEL 2150

1. Remove the air cleaner assembly.

2. Set the throttle on the top step of the fast idle cam.

3. Noting the position of the choke housing cap, loosen the retaining screws and rotate the cap 90 degrees in the rich (closing) direction.

4. Activate the pull-down motor by manually forcing the pull-down control diaphragm link in the direction of applied vacuum or by applying vacuum to the external vacuum tube.

5. Using a drill gauge of the specified diameter, measure the clearance between the choke plate and the center of the air horn wall nearest the fuel bowl.

6. To adjust, reset the diaphragm stop on the end of the choke pull-down diaphragm.

NOTE: Loctite® was applied to the adjusting screw during manufacture and this will have to be loosened before the adjustment can be made. Heat the area around the screw with an electric soldering gun until the Loctite® softens enough to permit the screw to turn freely.

7. After adjusting, check and adjust the fast idle cam. Check and reset fast idle speed, if necessary. Install the air cleaner.

Fast Idle Cam
THROUGH 1976

1. Push down on the fast idle cam lever until the fast idle screw is in contact with the second step of the fast idle cam and against the shoulder of the high step.

2. The specified clearance should be present between the lower edge of the choke plate and the air horn wall.

3. The adjustment is made by turning the fast idle cam lever screw.

4. The choke cover may now be replaced and adjusted according to specification.

1977 AND LATER

1. The choke setting should still be 90° rich, as in step 1 of the pulldown procedure. Press and release the throttle to set the fast idle cam.

2. Activate the choke pulldown mechanism as in step 4 of the pulldown procedure.

3. Press and release the throttle to set the fast idle cam. It should drop to the kickdown step, and the fast idle speed screw should be opposite the V notch in the cam.

4. To adjust, turn the hex head screw on the plastic fast idle cam lever. After adjustment, allow the choke plate to close and check that it closes tightly. Reset the choke cover and connect the vacuum hose if removed.

Choke Unloader (Dechoke)

1. With the throttle held completely open, move the choke plate to the closed position.

2. Measure the distance between the lower edge of the choke plate and the air horn wall.

3. Adjust by bending the tang on the fast idle speed lever which is located on the throttle shaft.

NOTE: Final unloader adjustment must be performed on the car and the throttle should be opened by using the accelerator pedal of the car. This is to be sure that full throttle operation is achieved.

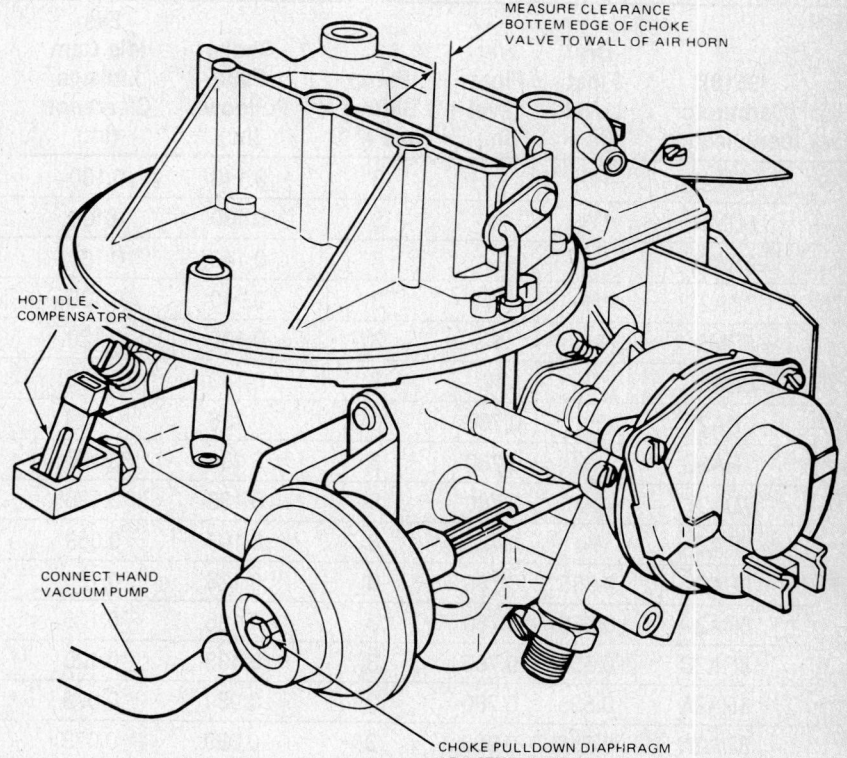

Adjusting choke plate pulldown (© Ford Motor Co.)

FORD, AUTOLITE, MOTORCRAFT CARBURETORS

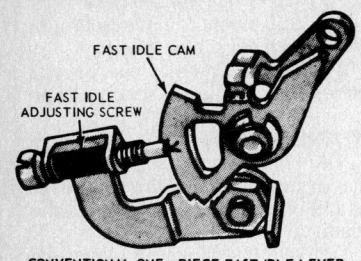

FAST IDLE CAM
FAST IDLE ADJUSTING SCREW

CONVENTIONAL ONE - PIECE FAST IDLE LEVER

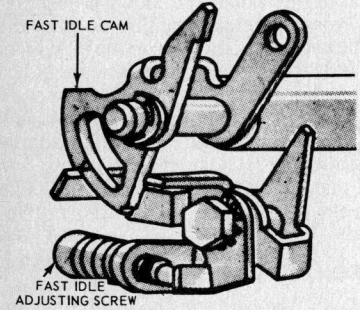

FAST IDLE CAM
FAST IDLE ADJUSTING SCREW

TWO - PIECE FAST IDLE LEVER FOR 351-C ENGINE

Fast idle adjustment
(© Ford Motor Co)

Accelerator Pump

The accelerator pump operating rod must be positioned in the proper holes of the accelerator pump lever and the throttle over-travel lever to assure correct pump travel. If adjusting is required, additional holes are provided in the throttle over-travel lever.

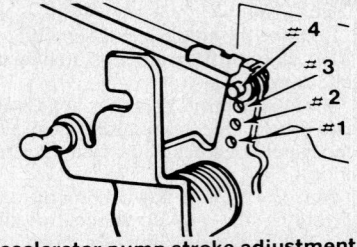

Accelerator pump stroke adjustment
(© Ford Motor Co)

Dashpot Adjustment

With the throttle set at the curb idle position, fully depress the dashpot stem and measure the distance between the stem and the throttle lever. Adjust by loosening the locknut and turning the dashpot.

Fast Idle

Adjust the fast idle with the engine at normal operating temperature. On AMC cars, plug the spark port on the carburetor, and remove the EGR vacuum line at the valve and plug it. On Ford cars, if the engine is equipped with a spark delay valve, remove it and reroute the partial throttle vacuum signal line directly to the advance side of the distributor. If the distributor is a dual diaphragm type, leave the manifold vacuum line connected to the retard side of the distributor, and remove and plug the line to the advance side. If an EGR/PVS valve or cold weather modulator is located in the vacuum hose routing, disconnect and plug the hose

FAST IDLE CAM LEVER SCREW

SECOND STEP OF CAM

2100, 2150 fast idle cam linkage adjustment

at the EGR valve. If the engine does not have a cold weather modulator or an EGR/PVS valve, leave the EGR hose attached. On 1979 and later models, trace the thermactor (air pump) dump valve vacuum hose from the dump valve to the carburetor; disconnect the dump valve vacuum hose nearest the carburetor, and plus the original vacuum source and connect the dump valve directly to manifold vacuum. The fast idle screw should be resting against the second step of the fast idle cam on all models except 1975 and later Fords with the 302 engine, which have the screw set on the high step of the cam. Adjust the fast idle speed by turning the fast idle screw.

FORD, AUTOLITE, MOTORCRAFT MODELS 2100, 2150 SPECIFICATIONS
American Motors

Year	(9510)* Carburetor Identification	Dry Float Level (in.)	Wet Float Level (in.)	Pump Setting Hole #①	Choke Plate Pulldown (in.)	Fast Idle Cam Linkage Clearance (in.)	Fast Idle (rpm)	Dechoke (in.)	Choke Setting	Dashpot (in.)
1975	5DA2	13/32	3/4	3	0.140	0.130	1600	0.250	1 Rich	—
	5DMS	13/32	3/4	3	0.130	0.130	1600	0.250	2 Rich	3/32
	5RAS	13/32	3/4	3	0.140	0.130	1600	0.250	1 Rich	—
1976	6DA2	13/32	3/4	3	0.140	0.130	1600	0.250	1 Rich	—
	6DM2	35/64	15/16	3	0.130	0.120	1600	0.250	2 Rich	—
	6RA2	13/32	3/4	3	0.140	0.130	1600	0.250	1 Rich	—
1977	7RA2	5/16	0.780	3	0.136	0.126	1600	0.250	1 Rich	—
	7RA2C	5/16	0.780	3	0.130	0.120	1800⑥	0.250	1 Rich	—
	7DA2	5/16	0.780	3	0.136	0.126	1600	0.250	Index	—
	7RA2A	5/16	0.780	3	0.104	0.089	1800	0.250	1 Rich	—
1978	8DA2	0.555	0.780	3	0.136	0.126	1600	0.250	Index	—
	8RA2	0.555	0.780	3	0.136	0.126	1600	0.250	1 Rich	—
	8RA2C	0.555	0.780	3	0.136	0.120	1800	0.250	1 Rich	—
	8RA2A	0.555	0.780	3	0.089	0.078	1800	0.170	2 Rich	—
	8DA2A	0.555	0.930	3	0.089	0.078	1600	0.170	2 Rich	—
1979	9DA2	0.313	0.780	3	0.125	0.113	1600⑦	0.300	1 Rich	—

FORD, AUTOLITE, MOTORCRAFT MODELS 2100, 2150 SPECIFICATIONS
Ford Products

Year	(9510)* Carburetor Identification	Dry Float Level (in.)	Wet Float Level (in.)	Pump Setting Hole #①	Choke Plate Pulldown (in.)	Fast Idle Cam Linkage Clearance (in.)	Fast Idle (rpm)	Dechoke (in)	Choke Setting
1975	D5ZE-AC	3/8	3/4	2	0.145	②	1500	②	2 Rich
	D5ZE-BC	3/8	3/4	2	0.145	②	1500	②	2 Rich
	D5ZE-CC	3/8	3/4	3	0.145	②	1500	②	2 Rich
	D5ZE-DC	3/8	3/4	2	0.145	②	1500	②	2 Rich
	D5DE-AA	7/16	13/16	2	0.140	②	1500	②	3 Rich
	D5DE-BA	7/16	13/16	2	0.140	②	1500	②	3 Rich
	D5DE-JA	7/16	13/16	2	0.140	②	1500	②	3 Rich
	D5ZE-JA	7/16	13/16	2	0.140	②	1500	②	3 Rich
	D50E-AA	7/16	13/16	2	0.140	②	1500	②	3 Rich
	D50E-DA	7/16	13/16	2	0.140	②	1500	②	3 Rich
	D5DE-HA	7/16	13/16	3	0.140	②	1500	②	3 Rich
	D5DE-UA	7/16	13/16	2	0.140	②	1500	②	3 Rich
	D50E-BA	7/16	13/16	3	0.125	②	1500	②	3 Rich
	D50E-CA	7/16	13/16	3	0.125	②	1500	②	3 Rich
	D50E-GA	7/16	13/16	2	0.125	②	1500	②	3 Rich
	D5AE-AA	7/16	13/16	3	0.125	②	1500	②	3 Rich
	D5AE-EA	7/16	13/16	3	0.125	②	1500	②	3 Rich
	D5ME-BA	7/16	13/16	2	0.125	②	1500	②	3 Rich
	D5ME-FA	7/16	13/16	2	0.125	②	1500	②	3 Rich
1976	D5ZE-BE	3/8	3/4	2	0.105	②	1600③	②	3 Rich
	D6ZE-AA	3/8	3/4	2	0.100	②	1600③	②	3 Rich
	D6ZE-BA	3/8	3/4	2	0.100	②	1600③	②	3 Rich
	D6ZE-CA	13/32	3/4	2	0.110	②	1600③	②	3 Rich
	D6ZE-DA	3/8	3/4	3	0.110	②	1600③	②	3 Rich
	D5DE-AEA	7/16	13/16	2	0.160	②	2000④	②	3 Rich
	D5DE-AFA	7/16	13/16	2	0.160	②	2000④	②	3 Rich
	D5WE-FA	7/16	13/16	2	0.160	②	2000④	②	3 Rich
	D6ZE-JA	7/16	13/16	2	0.160	②	2000④	②	3 Rich
	D60E-AA	7/16	13/16	3	0.160	②	2000④	②	3 Rich
	D60E-BA	7/16	13/16	3	0.160	②	2000④	②	3 Rich
	D60E-CA	7/16	13/16	3	0.160	②	2000④	②	3 Rich
	D6WE-AA	7/16	13/16	2	0.160	②	1350⑤	②	3 Rich
	D6WE-BA	7/16	13/16	2	0.160	②	1350⑤	②	3 Rich
	D6AE-HA	7/16	13/16	2	0.160	②	1350⑤	②	3 Rich
	D6ME-AA	7/16	13/16	2	0.160	②	1350⑤	②	3 Rich

FORD, AUTOLITE, MOTORCRAFT CARBURETORS

FORD, AUTOLITE, MOTORCRAFT MODELS 2100, 2150 SPECIFICATIONS
Ford Products

Year	(9510)* Carburetor Identification	Dry Float Level (in.)	Wet Float Level (in.)	Pump Setting Hole # ①	Choke Plate Pulldown (in.)	Fast Idle Cam Linkage Clearance (in.)	Fast Idle (rpm)	Dechoke (in)	Choke Setting
1977	D7YE-AA	0.375	0.750	3	0.122	0.142	1600	—	2 Rich
	D7YE-BA	0.375	0.750	3	0.122	0.142	1700	—	Index
	D7YE-EA	0.375	0.750	3	0.122	0.142	1600	—	2 Rich
	D7BE-JA	0.438	0.813	2	0.147	0.167	2100	—	1 Rich
	D7BE-LA	0.438	0.813	2	0.147	0.167	2100	—	1 Rich
	D7BE-MA	0.438	0.813	2	0.147	0.167	2000	—	1 Rich
	D7BE-PA	0.438	0.813	2	0.147	0.167	2100	—	1 Rich
	D7BE-YA	0.438	0.813	2	0.147	0.167	2100	—	1 Rich
	D7DE-KA	0.438	0.813	2	0.147	0.167	2100	—	1 Rich
	D7DE-LA	0.438	0.813	2	0.147	0.167	2000	—	1 Rich
	D7WE-EA	0.438	0.813	2	0.147	0.167	2100	—	1 Rich
	D7WE-EB	0.438	0.813	2	0.147	0.167	2100	—	1 Rich
	D7AE-ADA	0.438	0.813	3	0.179	0.189	1400	—	2 Rich
	D7AE-AHA	0.438	0.813	3	0.179	0.189	1400	—	Index
	D7AE-CA	0.438	0.813	3	0.179	0.189	1400	—	Index
	D7AE-DA	0.438	0.813	3	0.179	0.189	1350	—	Index
	D7DE-RA	0.438	0.813	3	0.179	0.189	1400	—	3 Rich
	D7DE-RB	0.438	0.813	3	0.179	0.189	1400	—	3 Rich
	D7OE-CA	0.750	0.750	3	0.167	0.187	1350	—	2 Rich
	D7OE-LA	0.750	0.750	3	0.167	0.187	2000	—	2 Rich
	D7OE-NA	0.750	0.750	3	0.167	0.187	1350	—	2 Rich
	D7OE-RA	0.750	0.750	3	0.167	0.187	1350	—	2 Rich
	D7AE-ACA	0.438	0.813	2	0.156	0.170	1350	—	Index
	D7AE-AKA	0.438	0.813	3	0.179	0.189	1400	—	Index
	D7AE-GA	0.438	0.813	3	0.179	0.189	1350	—	Index
	D7OE-HA	0.438	0.813	3	0.185	0.205	1350	—	2 Rich
	D7OE-HB	0.438	0.813	3	0.185	0.205	1350	—	Index
	D7OE-MA	0.438	0.813	3	0.185	0.205	1400	—	Index
	D7OE-TA	0.438	0.813	3	0.185	0.205	1350	—	2 Rich
1978-79	D84E-EA	7/16	13/16	2	0.110	⑧	⑨	—	3 Rich
	D8AE-JA	3/8	3/4	3	0.167	⑧	⑨	—	3 Rich
	D8BE-ACA	7/16	3/4	4	0.155	⑧	⑨	—	2 Rich
	D8BE-ADA	7/16	13/16	2	0.110	⑧	⑨	—	3 Rich
	D8BE-AEA	7/16	13/16	2	0.110	⑧	⑨	—	4 Rich
	D8BE-AFA	7/16	13/16	2	0.110	⑧	⑨	—	4 Rich
	D8BE-MB	3/8	13/16	3	0.122	⑧	⑨	—	Index
	D8DE-HA	19/32	13/16	3	0.157	⑧	⑨	—	Index

FORD, AUTOLITE, MOTORCRAFT CARBURETORS

FORD, AUTOLITE, MOTORCRAFT MODELS 2100, 2150 SPECIFICATIONS
Ford Products

Year	(9510)* Carburetor Identification	Dry Float Level (in.)	Wet Float Level (in.)	Pump Setting Hole # ①	Choke Plate Pulldown (in.)	Fast Idle Cam Linkage Clearance (in.)	Fast Idle (rpm)	Dechoke (in)	Choke Setting
1978-79	D8KE-EA	19/32	13/16	2	0.135	⑧	⑨	—	3 Rich
	D8OE-BA	3/8	3/4	3	0.167	⑧	⑨	—	3 Rich
	D8OE-EA	19/32	13/16	2	0.136	⑧	⑨	—	Index
	D8OE-HA	7/16	13/16	3	0.180	⑧	⑨	—	2 Rich
	D8SE-CA	19/32	13/16	3	0.150	⑧	⑨	—	2 Rich
	D8ZE-TA	3/8	3/4	4	0.135	⑧	⑨	—	Index
	D8ZE-UA	3/8	3/4	4	0.135	⑧	⑨	—	Index
	D8WE-DA	7/16	13/16	4	0.143	⑧	⑨	—	1 Rich
	D8YE-AB	3/8	13/16	3	0.122	⑧	⑨	—	Index
	D8SE-DA, EA	7/16	13/16	3	0.147	⑧	⑨	—	3 Rich
	D8SE-FA, GA	3/8	13/16	3	0.147	⑧	⑨	—	3 Rich
1980	EO4E-PA, RA	—	13/16	2	0.104	⑧	⑨	1/4	⑨
	EOBE-AUA	—	13/16	3	0.116	⑧	⑨	1/4	⑨
	EODE-SA, TA	—	13/16	2	0.104	⑧	⑨	1/4	⑨
	EOKE-CA, DA	—	13/16	3	0.116	⑧	⑨	1/4	⑨
	EOKE-GA, HA	—	13/16	3	0.116	⑧	⑨	1/4	⑨
	EOKE-JA, KA	—	13/16	3	0.116	⑧	⑨	1/4	⑨
	D84E-TA, UA	—	13/16	2	0.125	⑧	⑨	1/4	⑨
	EO4E-ADA, AEA	—	13/16	2	0.104	⑧	⑨	1/4	⑨
	EO4E-CA	—	13/16	2	0.104	⑧	⑨	1/4	⑨
	EO4E-EA, FA	—	13/16	2	0.104	⑧	⑨	1/4	⑨
	EO4E-JA, KA	—	13/16	2	0.137	⑧	⑨	1/4	⑨
	EO4E-SA, TA	—	13/16	2	0.104	⑧	⑨	1/4	⑨
	EO4E-VA, YA	—	13/16	2	0.104	⑧	⑨	1/4	⑨
	EODE-TA, VA	—	13/16	2	0.104	⑧	⑨	1/4	⑨
	EOSE-GA, HA	—	13/16	2	0.104	⑧	⑨	1/4	⑨
	EOSE-LA, MA	—	13/16	2	0.104	⑧	⑨	1/4	⑨
	EOSE-NA	—	13/16	2	0.104	⑧	⑨	1/4	⑨
	EOSE-PA	—	13/16	2	0.137	⑧	⑨	1/4	⑨
	EOVE-FA	—	13/16	2	0.104	⑧	⑨	1/4	⑨
	EOWE-BA, CA	—	13/16	2	0.137	⑧	⑨	1/4	⑨
	D9AE-ANA, APA	—	13/16	3	0.129	⑧	⑨	1/4	⑨
	D9AE-AVA, AYA	—	13/16	3	0.129	⑧	⑨	1/4	⑨
	EOAE-AGA	—	13/16	3	0.159	⑧	⑨	1/4	⑨
1981	EIKE-CA	7/16	0.810	3	0.124	⑧	⑨	0.250	⑨
	EIKE-EA	7/16	0.810	3	0.124	⑧	⑨	0.250	⑨
	EIKE-DA	7/16	0.810	3	0.124	⑧	⑨	0.250	⑨

FORD, AUTOLITE, MOTORCRAFT CARBURETORS

FORD, AUTOLITE, MOTORCRAFT MODELS 2100, 2150 SPECIFICATIONS
Ford Products

Year	(9510)* Carburetor Identification	Dry Float Level (in.)	Wet Float Level (in.)	Pump Setting Hole # ①	Choke Plate Pulldown (in.)	Fast Idle Cam Linkage Clearance (in.)	Fast Idle (rpm)	Dechoke (in)	Choke Setting
1981	EIKE-FA	7/16	0.810	3	0.124	⑧	⑨	0.250	⑨
	EIWE-FA	7/16	0.810	2	0.120	⑧	⑨	0.250	⑨
	EIWE-EA	7/16	0.810	2	0.120	⑧	⑨	0.250	⑨
	EIWE-CA	7/16	0.810	2	0.120	⑧	⑨	0.250	⑨
	EIWE-DA	7/16	0.810	2	0.120	⑧	⑨	0.250	⑨
	EIAE-YA	7/16	0.810	3	0.124	⑧	⑨	0.250	⑨
	EIAE-ZA	7/16	0.810	3	0.124	⑧	⑨	0.250	⑨
	EIAE-ADA	7/16	0.810	3	0.124	⑧	⑨	0.250	⑨
	EIAE-AEA	7/16	0.810	3	0.124	⑧	⑨	0.250	⑨
	EIAE-TA	—	0.810	2	0.104	⑧	⑨	0.250	⑨
	EIAE-UA	—	0.810	2	0.104	⑧	⑨	0.250	⑨

* Basic carburetor number for Ford products
① With link in inboard hole of pump lever
② Electric choke; see pulldown procedure in text
③ Figure given is for manual transmission; for automatics add 100 RPM.
④ Figure given is for 49 states Granada and Monarch; for Calif. Granada and Monarch and all Torino, Montego and Cougar models, figure is 1400 RPM.
⑤ Figure given is for 49 states model; Calif. specification is 1150 RPM.
⑥ 1600 with 360V8
⑦ 1500 with manual transmission.
⑧ Opposite "V" notch; see text
⑨ See underhood decal

MODEL 2700 VV

Since the design of the 2700 VV (variable venturi) carburetor differs considerably from the other carburetors in the Ford lineup, an explanation in the theory and operation is presented here.

In exterior appearance, the variable venturi carburetor is similar to conventional carburetors and, like a conventional carburetor, it uses a normal float and fuel bowl system. However, the similarity ends there. In place of a normal choke plate and fixed area venturis, the 2700VV carburetor has a pair of small oblong castings in the top of the upper carburetor body where you would normally expect to see the choke plate. These castings slide back and forth across the top of the carburetor in response to fuel-air demands. Their movement is controlled by a spring-loaded diaphragm valve regulated by a vacuum signal taken below the venturis in the throttle bores. As the throttle is opened, the strength of the vacuum signal increases, opening the venturis and allowing more air to enter the carburetor.

Fuel is admitted into the venturi area by means of tapered metering rods that fit into the main jets. These rods are attached to the venturis, and, as the venturis open or close in response to air demand, the fuel needed to maintain the proper mixture increases or decreases as the metering rods slide in the jets. In comparison to a conventional carburetor with fixed venturis and a variable air supply, this system provides much more precise control of the fuel-air supply during all modes of operation. Because of the variable venturi principle, there are fewer fuel metering systems and fuel passages. The only auxiliary fuel metering systems required are an idle trim, accelerator pump (similar to a conventional carburetor), starting enrichment, and cold running enrichment.

NOTE: Adjustment, assembly and disassembly of this carburetor require special tools for some of the operations. These tools are available (see the Tools and Equipment Section). Do not attempt any operations on this carburetor without first checking to see if you need the special tools for that particular operation. The adjustment and repair procedures given here mention when and if you will need the special tools.

Float Level Adjustment

1. Remove and invert the upper part of the carburetor, with the gasket in place.
2. Measure the vertical distance between the carburetor body, outside the gasket, and the bottom of the float.
3. To adjust, bend the float operating lever that contacts the needle valve. Make sure that the float remains parallel to the gasket surface.

Float Drop Adjustment

1. Remove and hold upright the upper part of the carburetor.
2. Measure the vertical distance between the carburetor body, outside the gasket, and the bottom of the float.
3. Adjust by bending the stop tab on the float lever that contacts the hinge pin.

Fast Idle Speed Adjustment

1. With the engine warmed up and idling, place the fast idle lever on the step of the fast idle cam specified on the engine compartment sticker or in the specifications chart. Disconnect and plug the EGR vacuum line.

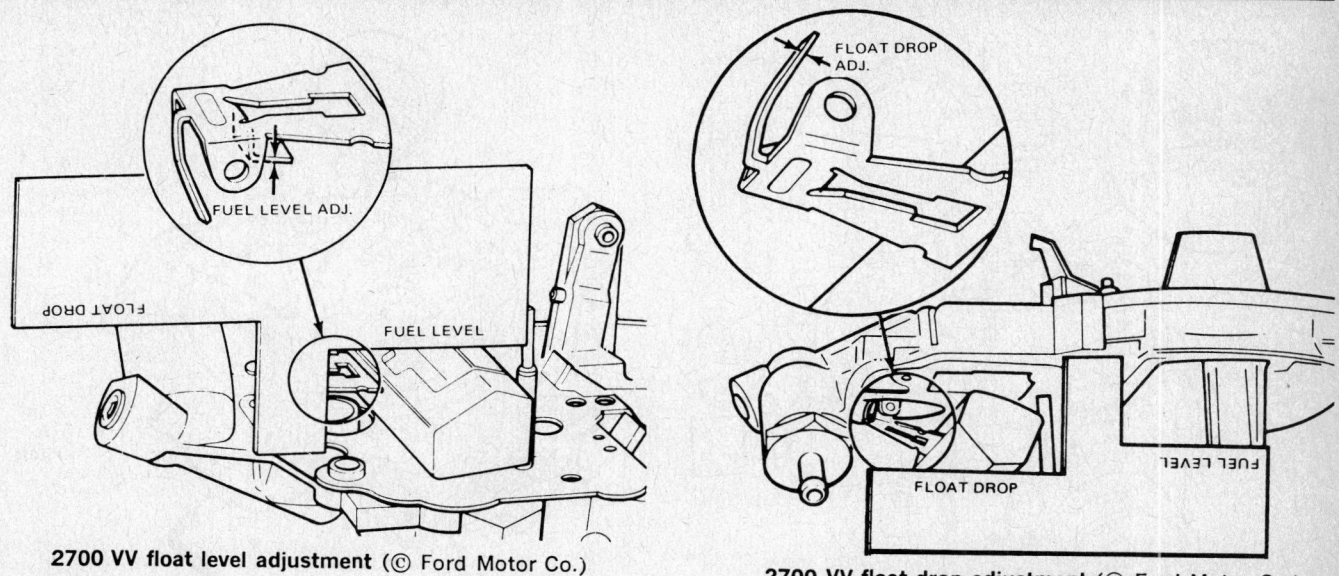

2700 VV float level adjustment (© Ford Motor Co.)

2700 VV float drop adjustment (© Ford Motor Co.)

2. Make sure the high speed cam positioner lever is disengaged.

3. Turn the fast idle speed screw to adjust to the specified speed.

Fast Idle Cam Adjustment

You will need a special tool for this job; Ford calls it a stator cap (#T77L-9848-A). It fits over the choke thermostatic lever when the choke cap is removed.

1. Remove the choke coil cap. On 1980 and later California models, the choke cap is riveted in place. The top rivets will have to be drilled out; the bottom rivet will have to be driven out from the rear. New rivets must be used upon installation.

2. Place the fast idle lever in the corner of the specified step of the fast idle cam (the highest step is first) with the high speed cam positioner retracted.

3. If the adjustment is being made with the carburetor removed, hold the throttle lightly closed with a rubber band.

4. Turn the stator cap clockwise until the lever contacts the fast idle cam adjusting screw.

5. Turn the fast idle cam adjusting screw until the index mark on the cap lines up with the specified mark on the casting.

6. Remove the stator cap. Install the choke coil cap and set to the specified housing mark.

Cold Enrichment Metering Rod Adjustment

A dial indicator and the stator cap are required for this adjustment.

1. Remove the choke coil cap. See Step 1 of the ''Fast Idle Cam Adjustment.''

2. Attach a weight to the choke coil mechanism to seat the cold enrichment rod.

3. Install and zero a dial indicator with the tip on top of the enrichment rod. Raise and release the weight to verify zero on the dial indicator.

4. With the stator cap at the index position, the dial indicator should read the specified dimension. Turn the adjusting nut to correct.

5. Install the choke cap at the correct setting.

Control Vacuum Adjustment
1977 ONLY

1. Make sure the idle speed is correct.

2. Using a 5/32 in. Allen wrench, turn the venturi valve diaphragm adjusting screw clockwise until the valve is firmly closed.

3. Connect a vacuum gauge to the vacuum tap on the venturi valve cover.

4. Idle the engine and use a 1/8 in. Allen wrench to turn the venturi by-pass adjusting screw to the specified vacuum setting. You may have to correct the idle speed.

5. Turn the venturi valve diaphragm adjusting screw counter-clockwise until the vacuum drops to the specified setting. You

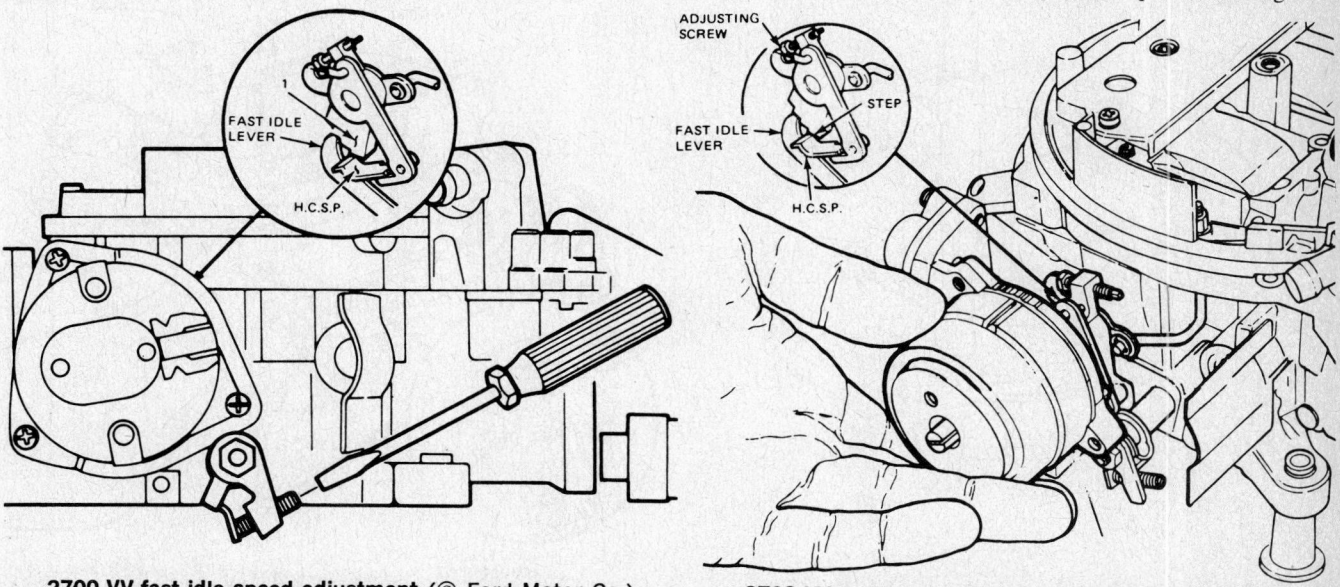

2700 VV fast idle speed adjustment (© Ford Motor Co.)

2700 VV fast idle cam adjustment (© Ford Motor Co.)

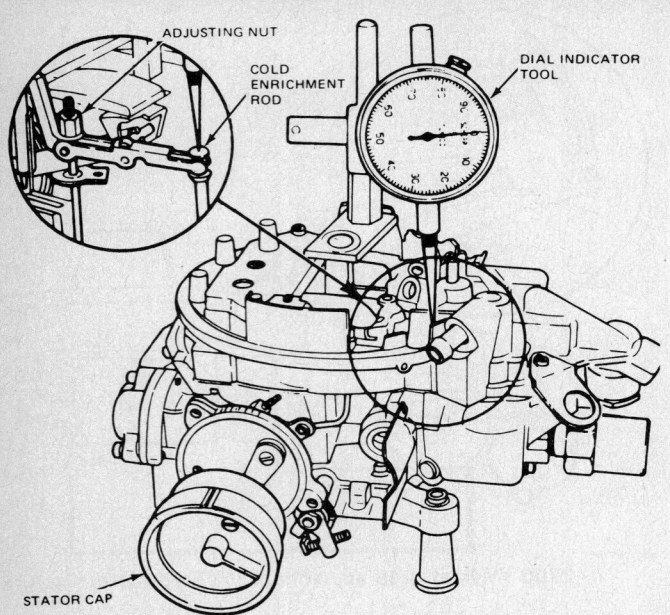

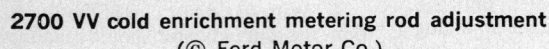

2700 VV cold enrichment metering rod adjustment
(© Ford Motor Co.)

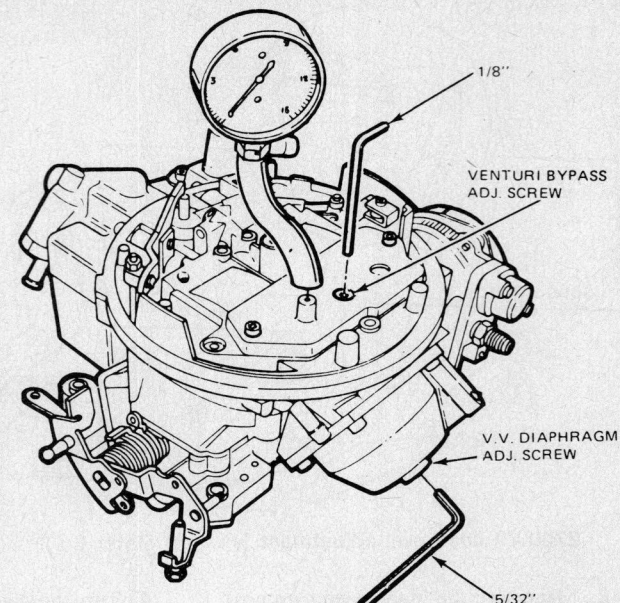

2700 VV control vacuum adjustment (© Ford Motor Co.)

will have to work the throttle to get the vacuum to drop.

6. Reset the idle speed.

1980–81 ONLY

This adjustment is necessary only on non-feedback systems.

1. Remove the carburetor. Remove the venturi valve diaphragm plug with a center-punch.

2. If the carburetor has a venturi valve bypass plug, remove it by removing the two cover retaining screws; invert and remove the by-pass screw plug from the cover with a drift. Install the cover.

3. Install the carburetor. Start the engine and allow it to reach normal operating temperature. Connect a vacuum gauge to the

venturi valve cover. Set the idle speed to 500 rpm with the transmission in Drive.

4. Push and hold the venturi valve closed. Adjust the bypass screw to obtain a reading of 8 in. H_2O on the vacuum gauge. Make sure the idle speed remains constant. Open and close the throttle and check the idle speed.

5. With the engine idling, adjust the venturi valve diaphragm screw to obtain a reading of 6 in. H_2O. Set the curb idle to specification. Install new venturi valve bypass and diaphragm plugs.

Internal Vent Adjustment
THROUGH 1978 ONLY

This adjustment is required whenever the idle speed adjustment is changed.

1. Make sure the idle speed is correct.

2. Place a 0.010 in. feeler gauge between the accelerator pump stem and the operating link.

3. Turn the nylon adjusting nut until there is a slight drag on the gauge.

Venturi Valve Limiter Adjustment

1. Remove the carburetor. Take off the venturi valve cover and the two rollers.

2. Use a center punch to loosen the expansion plug at the rear of the carburetor main body on the throttle side. Remove it.

3. Use an Allen wrench to remove the venturi valve wide open stop screw.

4. Hold the throttle wide open.

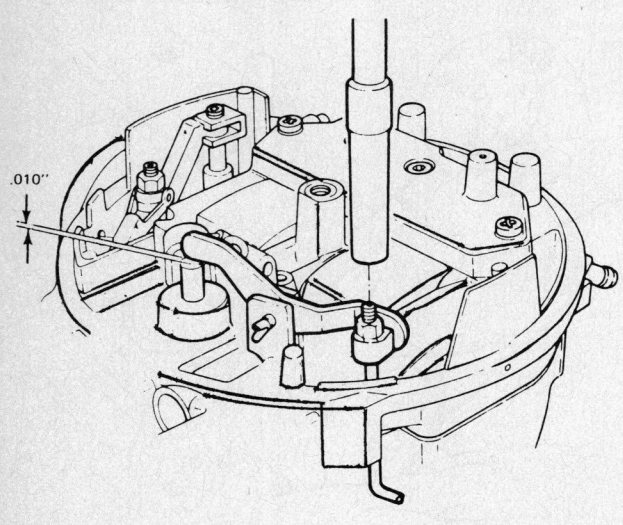

2700 VV internal vent adjustment (© Ford Motor Co.)

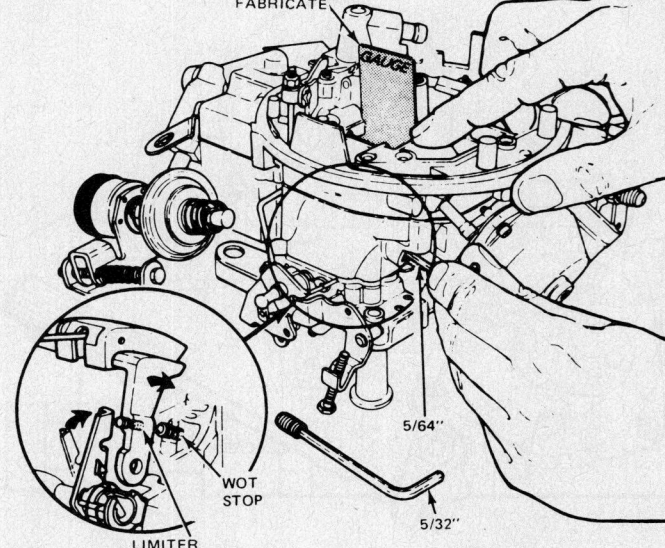

2700 VV venturi valve limiter adjustment (© Ford Motor Co.)

5. Apply a light closing pressure on the venturi valve and check the gap between the valve and the air horn wall. To adjust, move the venturi valve to the wide open position and insert an Allen wrench into the stop screw hole. Turn clockwise to increase the gap. Remove the wrench and check the gap again.

6. Replace the wide open stop screw and turn it clockwise until it contacts the valve.

7. Push the venturi valve wide open and check the gap. Turn the stop screw to bring the gap to specifications.

8. Reassemble the carburetor with a new expansion plug.

Control Vacuum Regulator Adjustment

There are two systems used. The earlier system's C.V.R. rod threads directly through the arm. The revised system, introduced in late 1977, has a ⅜ in. nylon hex adjusting nut on the C.V.R. rod and a flange on the rod.

EARLY SYSTEM

1. Make sure that the cold enrichment metering rod adjustment is correct.

2. Rotate the choke coil cap half a turn clockwise from the index mark. Work the throttle to set the fast idle cam.

3. Press down lightly on the regulator rod. If there is no down travel, turn the adjusting screw counter-clockwise until some travel is felt.

4. Turn the regulator rod clockwise with an Allen wrench until the adjusting nut just begins to rise.

5. Press lightly on the regulator rod. If there is any down travel, turn the adjusting screw clockwise in ¼ turn increments until it is eliminated.

6. Return the choke coil cap to the specified setting.

REVISED SYSTEM

The cold enrichment metering rod adjustment must be checked and set before making this adjustment.

1. After adjusting the cold enrichment metering rod, leave the dial indicator in place but remove the stator cap. Do not re-zero the dial indicator.

2. Press down on the C.V.R. rod until it bottoms on its seat. Measure this amount of travel with the dial indicator.

3. If the adjustment is incorrect, hold the ⅜ in. C.V.R. adjusting nut with a box wrench to prevent it from turning. Use a 3/32 in. Allen wrench to turn the C.V.R. rod; turning counter-clockwise will increase the travel, and vice versa.

High Speed Cam Positioner Adjustment

THROUGH 1979 ONLY

1. Place the high speed cam positioner in the corner of the specified cam step, counting the highest step as the first.

2. Place the fast idle lever in the corner of the positioner.

3. Hold the throttle firmly closed.

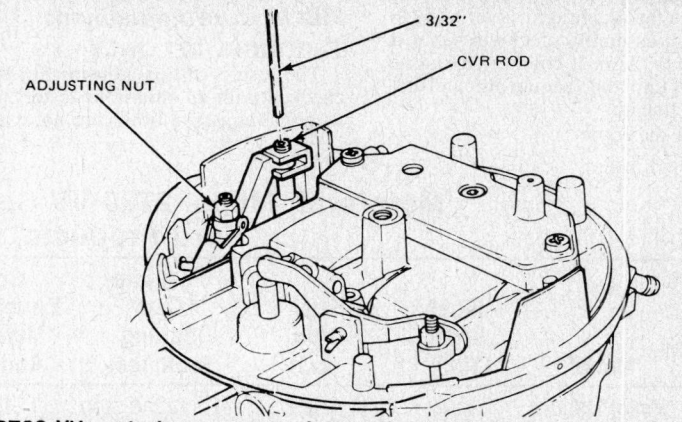

2700 VV control vacuum regulator adjustment (© Ford Motor Co.)

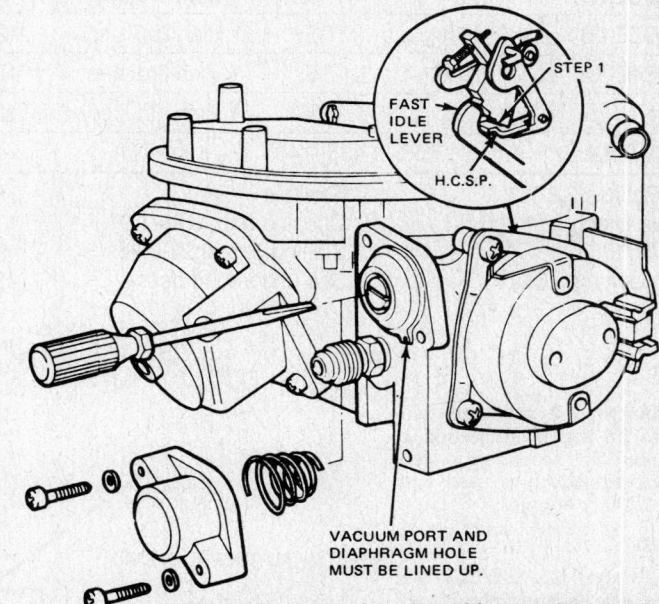

2700 VV high speed cam positioner adjustment
(© Ford Motor Co.)

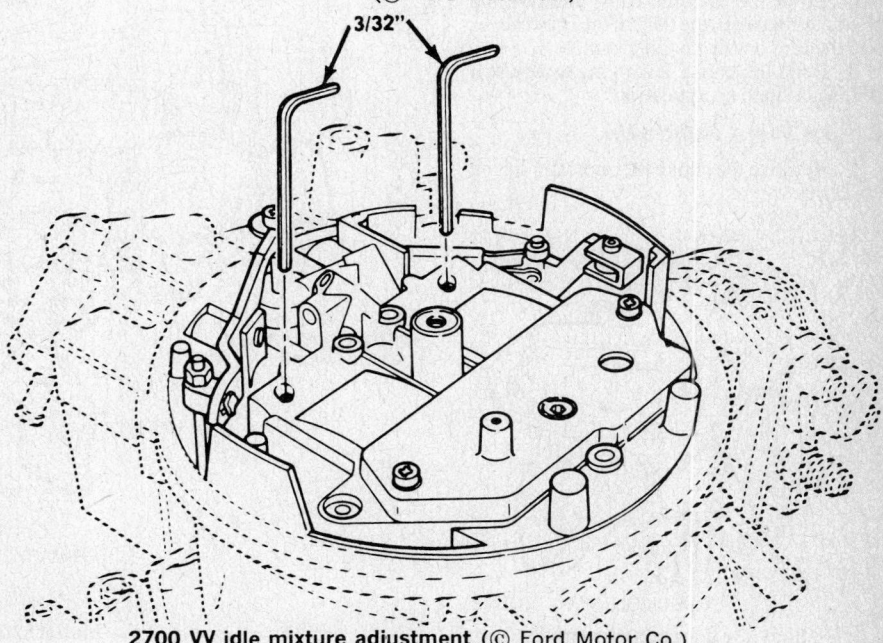

2700 VV idle mixture adjustment (© Ford Motor Co.)

FORD, AUTOLITE, MOTORCRAFT CARBURETORS

4. Remove the diaphragm cover. Adjust the diaphragm assembly clockwise until it lightly bottoms. Turn it counter-clockwise ½ to 1½ turns until the vacuum port and diaphragm hole line up.

5. Replace the cover.

Idle Mixture Adjustment
THROUGH 1977 ONLY

The results of this adjustment should be checked with an emissions tester, to make sure that emission limits are not exceeded.

Idle mixture (idle trim) is not adjustable on 1978 and later models.

1. Remove the air cleaner cover only.

2. Use a ³⁄₃₂ in. Allen wrench to adjust the mixture for each barrel by turning the air adjusting screw. Turn clockwise to richen.

Motorcraft Model 2700 VV Specifications
Ford Products

Year	Model	Float Level (in.)	Float Drop (in.)	Fast Idle Cam Setting (notches)	Cold Enrichment Metering Rod (in.)	Control Vacuum (in. H₂O)	Venturi Valve Limiter (in.)	Choke Cap Setting (notches)	Control Vacuum Regulator Setting (in.)
1977-78	Pinto, Bobcat	1³⁄₆₄	1¹⁵⁄₃₂	4 Rich/2nd step	.125	5.0	13/32	Index	—
	All other	1³⁄₆₄	1¹⁵⁄₃₂	1 Rich/3rd step	.125	5.0	61/64	Index	—
1979	D9ZE-LB	1³⁄₆₄	1¹⁵⁄₃₂	1 Rich/2nd step	.125	①	②	Index	.230
	D84E-KA	1³⁄₆₄	1¹⁵⁄₃₂	1 Rich/3rd step	.125	5.5	61/64	Index	—
1980	All	1³⁄₆₄	1¹⁵⁄₃₂	1 Rich/4th step	.125	③	④	⑤	.075
1981	EIAE-AAA	1.015-1.065	1.435-1.485	—	—	③	④	⑤	—

① Venturi Air Bypass 6.8-7.3
　Venturi Valve Diaphragm 4.6-5.1
② Limiter Setting .38-.42
　Limiter Stop Setting .73-.77
③ See text
④ Opening gap: 0.99-1.01
　Closing gap: 0.94-0.98
⑤ See underhood decal

MODEL 5200

The 5200 carburetor is a two-stage, two-venturi carburetor in which the secondary venturi is the larger. The secondary system is mechanically operated. It is used with 2000, 2300 and 2800 cc engines.

Fast Idle Cam

1. Insert a ⁵⁄₃₂ in. drill between the lower edge of the choke plate and the air horn wall.

2. With the fast idle screw held on the second step of the fast idle cam, measure the clearance between the tang of the choke lever and the arm on the fast idle cam.

3. Bend the choke lever tang to adjust it if it is not up to specification.

Choke Plate Pulldown

1. Remove the choke thermostatic spring cover.

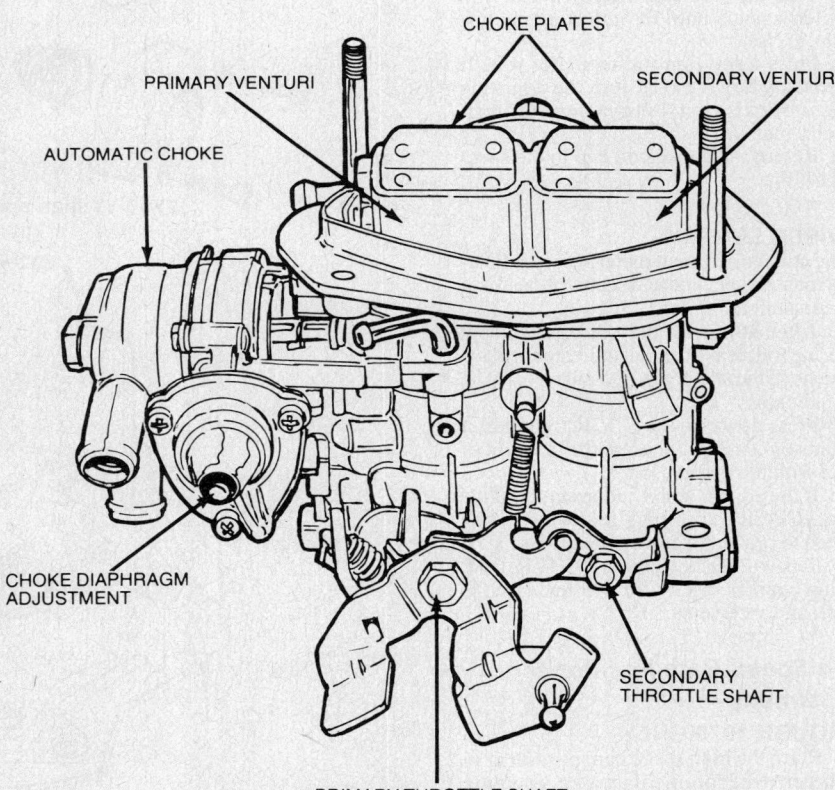

Model 5200 carburetor

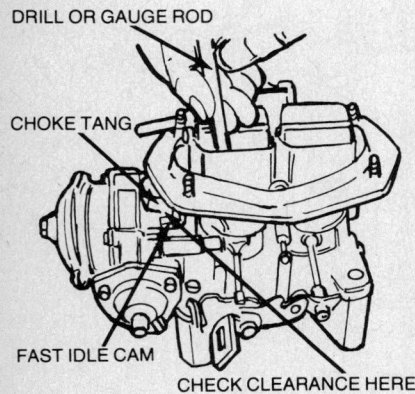

Fast idle cam adjustment

2. Pull the water cover and the thermostatic spring cover assembly or the electric choke assist assembly out of the way.

3. Set the fast idle cam on the high step through 1977, or second step 1978 and later.

4. Push the diaphragm stem against its stop and insert the specified gauge between the lower edge of the choke valve and the air horn wall.

5. Appoy Apply sufficient pressure to the upper edge of the choke valve to take up any slack in the choke linkage.

6. Turn the adjusting screw in or out to adjust the choke plate-to-air horn clearance.

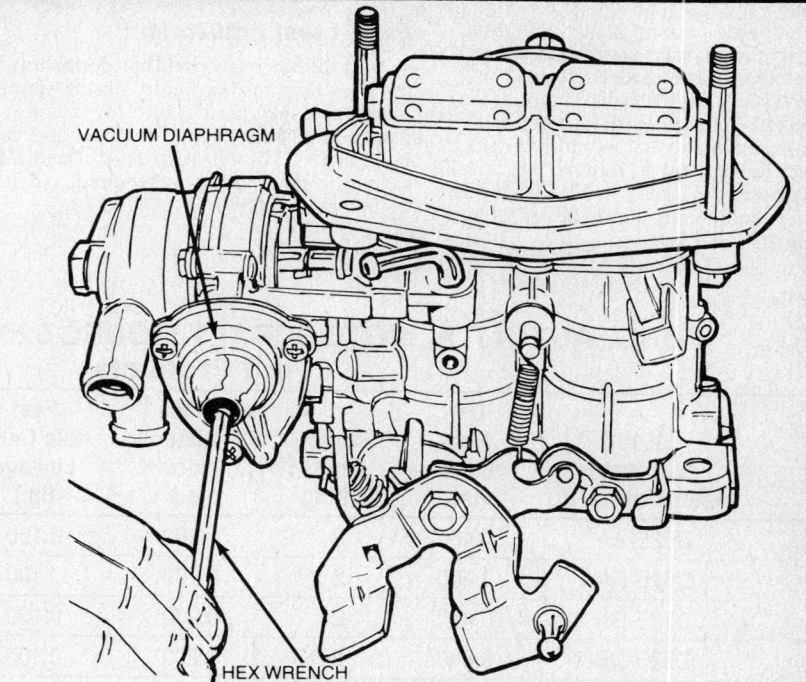

Choke plate pulldown adjustment

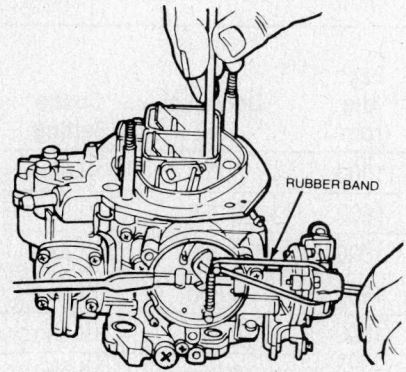

Choke plate pulldown adjustment

Dechoke (Unloader) Adjustment

Dechoke clearance adjustment is controlled by the fast idle cam adjustment. The figures in the specification chart refer to choke plate clearance between the plate and the air horn wall. Clearance can be measured as follows:

1. Hold the throttle wide open. Remove any slack from the choke linkage by applying pressure to the upper edge of the choke valve.

2. Measure the distance between the lower edge of the choke plate and the air horn wall.

3. Adjust by bending the tab on the fast idle lever where it touches the cam.

Fast Idle Speed

Set the fast idle speed with the fast idle screw positioned on the second step of the fast idle cam and with the engine at operating temperature.

On 1975 and later models, you must also remove the EGR line at the valve and plug it. If the car is equipped with a spark delay valve, remove the valve and route the dis-

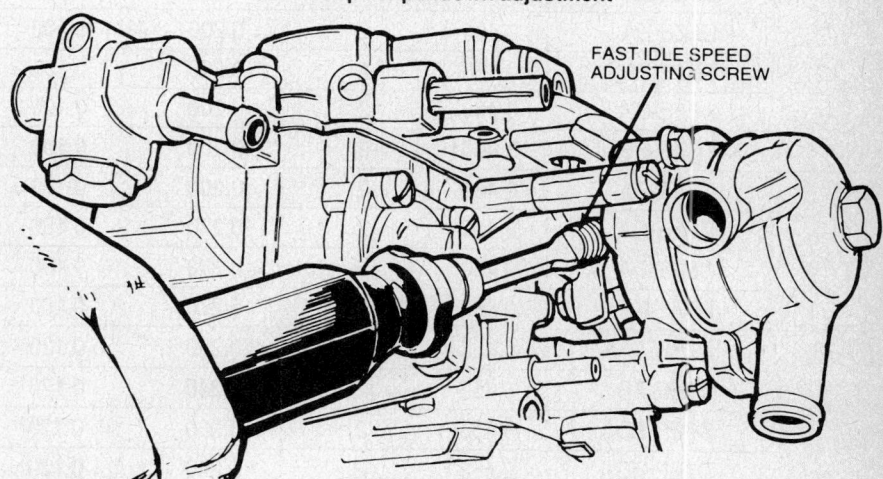

Fast idle adjustment

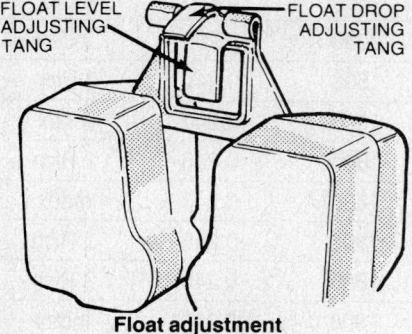

Float adjustment

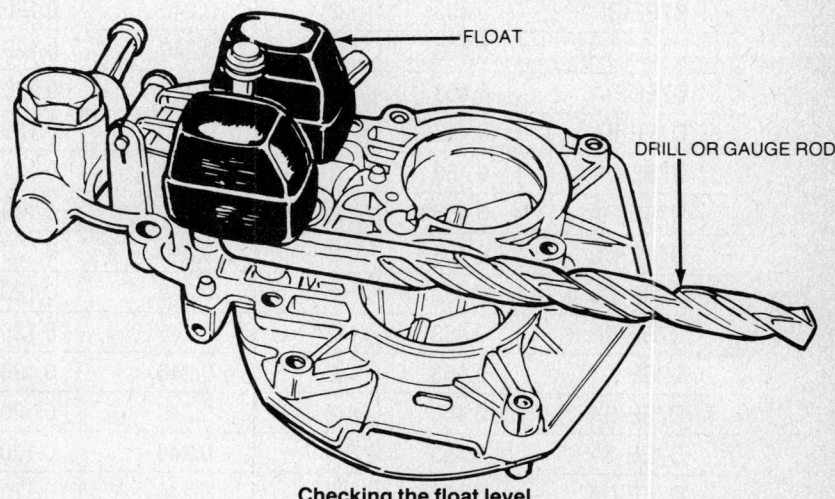

Checking the float level

FORD, AUTOLITE, MOTORCRAFT CARBURETORS

tributor advance vacuum signal directly to the distributor advance diaphragm. On all manual transmission models, remove and plug the vacuum line to the distributor. If the distributor also has a retard diaphragm, leave the hose connected to it alone. If the engine has a deceleration valve, remove this hose at the carburetor and plug it. Finally, if the car has air conditioning it must be off before adjusting the fast idle.

Float Level Adjustment

With the bowl cover held upside down and the float tang resting lightly on the spring loaded fuel inlet needle, measure the clearance between the edge of the float and the bowl cover. To adjust the level, bend the float tang up or down as required. Adjust both floats equally.

Secondary Throttle Stop Screw

1. Turn the secondary throttle stop screw counterclockwise until the secondary throttle plate seats in its bore.
2. Turn the screw clockwise until it touches the tab on the secondary throttle lever.
3. Add ¼ turn clockwise for four-cylinder engines and ¾ turn for V6 engines through 1976.

FORD, AUTOLITE, MOTORCRAFT MODEL 5200 SPECIFICATIONS
Ford Products

Year	(9510)* Carburetor Identification①	Dry Float Level (in.)	Pump Hole Setting	Choke Plate Pulldown (in.)	Fast Idle Cam Linkage (in.)	Fast Idle (rpm)	Dechoke (in.)	Choke Setting
1975	D52E-AA	0.460	2	0.200	0.100	1800	0.260	1 Lean
	D52E-BA	0.460	2	0.200	0.100	1800	0.260	1 Lean
	D52E-CA	0.460	2	0.200	0.100	1800	0.260	1 Lean
	D52E-DB	0.460	2	0.200	0.100	1800	0.260	1 Lean
	D5ZE-EA	0.460	2	0.200	0.100	1800	0.260	1 Lean
	D5ZE-EA	0.460	2	0.200	0.100	1800	0.260	1 Lean
	D5ZE-FA	0.460	2	0.200	0.100	1800	0.260	1 Lean
	D5ZE-GA	0.460	2	0.200	0.100	1800	0.260	1 Lean
	D5ZE-HB	0.460	2	0.200	0.100	1800	0.260	1 Lean
1976	D6EE-BA	0.460	2	0.200	0.100	1500①	0.260	1 Lean
	D6EE-CA	0.460	2	0.270	0.160	1500①	0.260	1 Lean
	D6EE-DA	0.460	2	0.200	0.100	1500①	0.260	1 Lean
	D6ZE-EA	0.460	2	0.270	0.160	1500①	0.260	1 Lean
1977-78	D7EE-AAA	0.453	2	0.200	0.120	2000	0.180	Index
	D7EE-AB	0.453	2	0.240	0.120	1800	0.240	2 Rich
	D7EE-BDA	0.453	2	0.280	0.120	1500	0.240	2 Rich
	D7EE-BGA	0.453	2	0.240	0.120	1500	0.240	Index
	D7EE-BHA	0.453	2	0.240	0.120	1500	0.240	Index
	D7EE-BLA	0.453	2	0.240	0.120	2000	0.240	Index
	D7EE-BMA	0.453	2	0.240	0.120	2000	0.240	Index
	D7EE-DA	0.453	2	0.240	0.120	1500	0.240	2 Rich
	D7EE-EA	0.453	2	0.240	0.120	2000	0.240	Index
	D7EE-FA	0.453	2	0.240	0.120	1800	0.240	Index
	D7EE-GA	0.453	2	0.200	0.120	2000	0.200	Index
	D7EE-HA	0.453	2	0.240	0.120	1500	0.240	2 Rich
	D7EE-JA	0.453	2	0.240	0.120	1800	0.240	Index
	D7EE-KB	0.453	2	0.240	0.120	1800	0.240	2 Rich
	D7EE-LA	0.453	2	0.240	0.120	1800	0.240	Index
	D7EE-SA	0.453	2	0.240	0.120	1800	0.240	2 Rich
	D7EE-TA	0.453	2	0.240	0.120	1800	0.240	2 Rich
	D7EE-UA	0.453	2	0.240	0.120	1800	0.240	Index

FORD, AUTOLITE, MOTORCRAFT MODEL 5200 SPECIFICATIONS
Ford Products

Year	(9510)* Carburetor Identification ①	Dry Float Level (in.)	Pump Hole Setting	Choke Plate Pulldown (in.)	Fast Idle Cam Linkage (in.)	Fast Idle (rpm)	Dechoke (in.)	Choke Setting	Dashpot (in.)
1977-78	D7EE-VA	0.453	2	0.240	0.120	1800	0.240	Index	
1979	D9ZE-ND	0.460	3	0.236	0.118	1800	0.236	2 Rich	—
	D9BE-AAA, D9BE-ABA, D9EE-AMA	0.460	2	0.236	0.118	1800	0.236	2 Rich	—
	D9EE-ANA, D9EE-ASA, D9EE-AYA	0.460	2	0.236	0.118	1800	0.236	1 Rich	—
1980	D9EE-APA, ANA	0.460	2	0.236	0.118	②	0.236	1 Rich	—
	EOEE-GA, RA	0.460	2	0.196	0.078	②	0.196	②	—
	EOEE-JA, TA	0.460	2	0.196	0.078	②	0.196	②	—
	EOEE-JC, TC	0.460	—	0.196	0.078	②	0.196	②	—
	EOEE-JD, TD	0.460	2	0.177	0.078	②	0.196	②	—
	EOEE-AEA, AFA	0.460	2	0.196	0.078	②	0.196	②	—
	EOZE-ACB	0.460	—	0.275	0.157	②	0.236	②	—
	EOZE-AZA	0.460	2	0.275	0.157	②	0.393	②	—
	EOZE-AAA	0.460	3	0.275	0.157	②	0.236	②	—
	EOZE-ACA	0.460	2	0.275	0.157	②	0.236	②	—
	EOZE-ATA	0.460	2	0.275	0.118	②	0.236	②	—
1981	EIZE-YA	.41-.51	2	0.200	.080	②	0.200	②	
	EOEE-RB	.41-.51	2	0.200	.080	②	0.200	②	
	EIZE-VA	.41-.51	2	0.200	.080	②	0.200	②	
	D9EE-ANA	.41-.51	2	0.240	0.720	②	0.200	②	
	D9EE-APA	.41-.51	2	0.240	0.120	②	0.200	②	

* Basic carburetor number
① Figure given is for all manual transmissions; for automatic trans. the figures are: (49 states) 2000 RPM; (Calif.) 1800 RPM.
② See underhood decal

MODEL 4300, 4350

The model 4300 and 4350 4 barrel carburetor is composed of three main assemblies: the air horn, the main body, and the throttle body. The air horn assembly serves as the fuel bowl cover as well as the housing for the choke valve and shaft. It contains the accelerator pump linkage, fuel inlet seat, float and lever, booster venturi, and internal fuel bowl vents.

The main body houses the fuel metering passages, accelerator pump mechanism, and the power valve.

The throttle body contains the primary and secondary throttle valves and shafts, the curb idle adjusting screw, the fast idle adjusting screw, the idle mixture adjusting screws, and the automatic choke assembly.

This carburetor is last used in 1978.

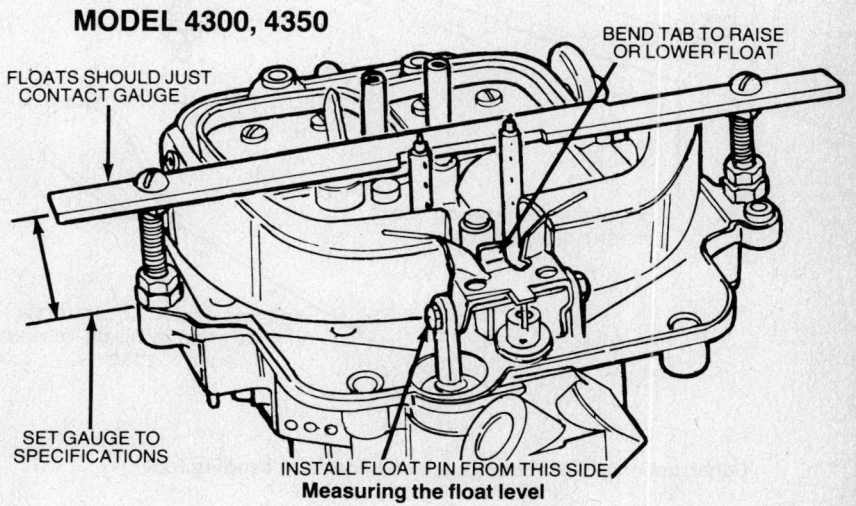

FLOATS SHOULD JUST CONTACT GAUGE

BEND TAB TO RAISE OR LOWER FLOAT

SET GAUGE TO SPECIFICATIONS

INSTALL FLOAT PIN FROM THIS SIDE
Measuring the float level

Float Adjustment

1. Adjustments to the fuel lever are best made with the carburetor removed from the engine and the carburetor cleaned upon disassembly.

2. Invert the air horn assembly and remove the gasket from the surface.

3. Use a T-scale to measure the distance from the floats to the air horn casting. Position the scale horizontally over the flat surface of both floats at the free ends and parallel to the air horn casting. Hold the lower end of the vertical scale in full contact with the smooth surface of the air horn.

CAUTION

The end of the vertical scale must not come into contact with any gasket sealing ridges while measuring the float level.

4. The free end of each float should just touch the horizontal scale; if one float is lower than the other, twist the float and lever assembly slightly to correct.

5. Adjust the float level by bending the tab which contacts the needle and seat assembly.

NOTE: The illustrations in this section show an alternate method of adjusting the floats on the model 4300 carburetor.

The procedure includes the fabrication of a gauge and a bending device. After fabricating the gauge, it is possible to adjust it to the specified dimensions and insert it into the air horn outboard holes. Both pontoons should just touch the gauge.

A float tab bending tool is also shown and may be used in the following manner.

To raise the float: insert the open end of the bending tool to the RIGHT side of the float lever tab and between the needle and float hinge. Raise the float lever off of the needle and bend the tab downward.

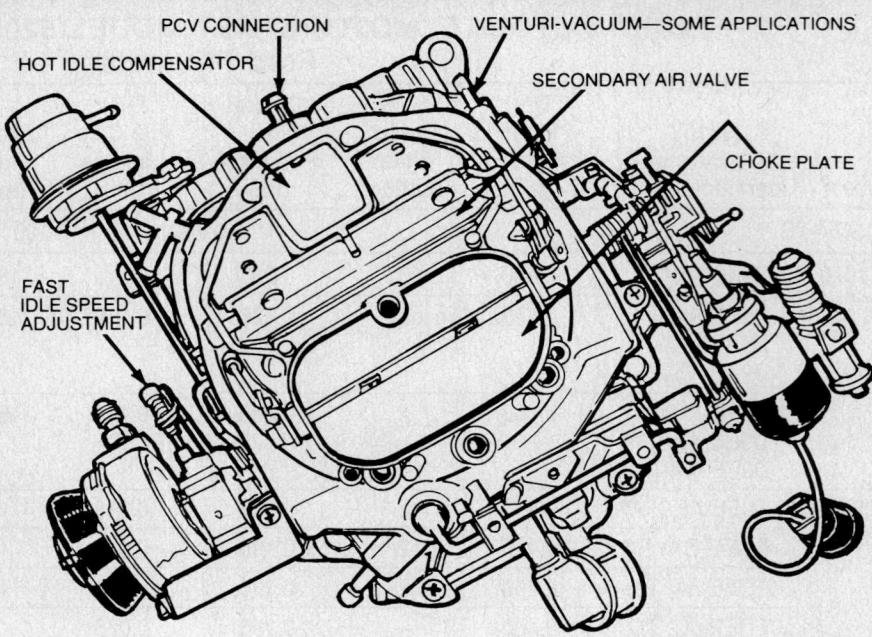

Top view—Model 4300 carburetor

To lower the float: insert the bending tool to the LEFT side of the float lever tab between the needle and float hinge, support the float lever, and bend the tab upward.

Choke Plate Pulldown

1. Remove the air cleaner and choke thermostatic spring housing.

2. Bend a wire gauge (0.036 in. diameter) at a 90 degree angle about ⅛ in. from one end.

3. Block the throttle open so that the fast idle screw does not contact the fast idle cam.

4. Insert the bent end of the wire gauge between the lower edge of the piston slot and the upper edge of the right hand slot in the choke housing.

5. Pull the choke piston lever counterclockwise until the gauge is snug in the piston slot. Hold the wire in place by exerting light pressure in a rearward direction on the choke piston lever. Check the distance from the lower edge of the choke valve to the air horn wall.

6. Adjustment is done by loosening the hex head screw (left-hand thread) on the choke valve shaft and prying the link away from the shaft. Use a drill gauge 0.010 in. under the specified clearance between the lower edge of the choke valve and the air horn wall. Hold the choke valve against the gauge and maintain a light rearward pressure on the choke lever.

7. With the choke piston snug against the 0.036 in. wire and the choke valve against the drill, tighten the hex screw on the choke valve shaft. The use of a gauge 0.010 in. undersize compensates for tolerance in the linkage.

8. Use the correct size gauge for final measurement.

9. Replace the housing on the thermostatic spring.

Delayed Choke Pulldown

The 4350 is also equipped with a vacuum-diaphragm operated delayed choke pulldown that opens the choke to a wider setting after about 6–18 seconds of engine operation.

1. With the throttle set on the fast idle cam, note the position of the index marks on the cap. Loosen the retaining screws and rotate the cap ninety degrees (¼ turn), in the closing (rich) direction.

2. Disconnect the vacuum supply hose from the port on the delayed choke pulldown diaphragm assembly. After removing the fil-

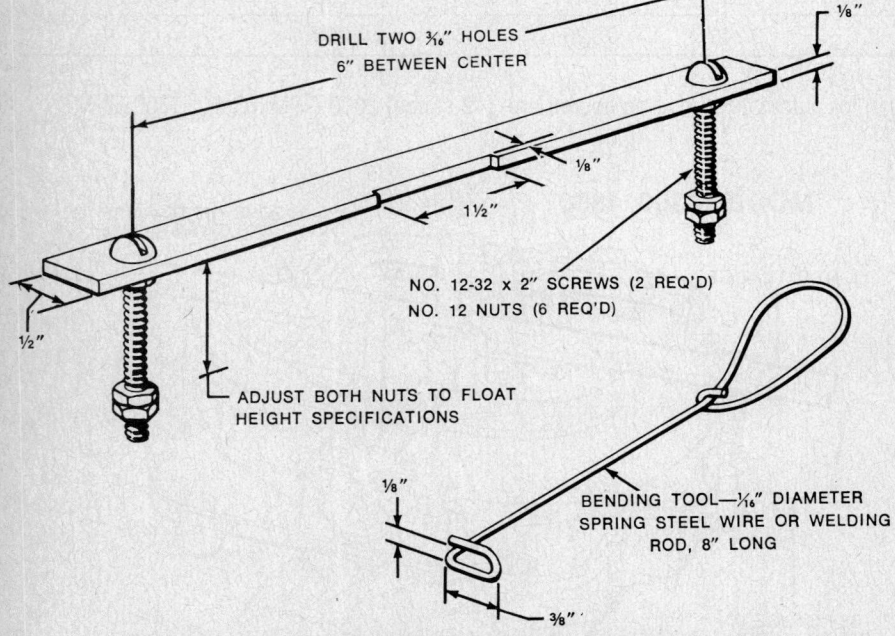

Construction of float level gauge and float arm bending tool
(© Ford Motor Co)

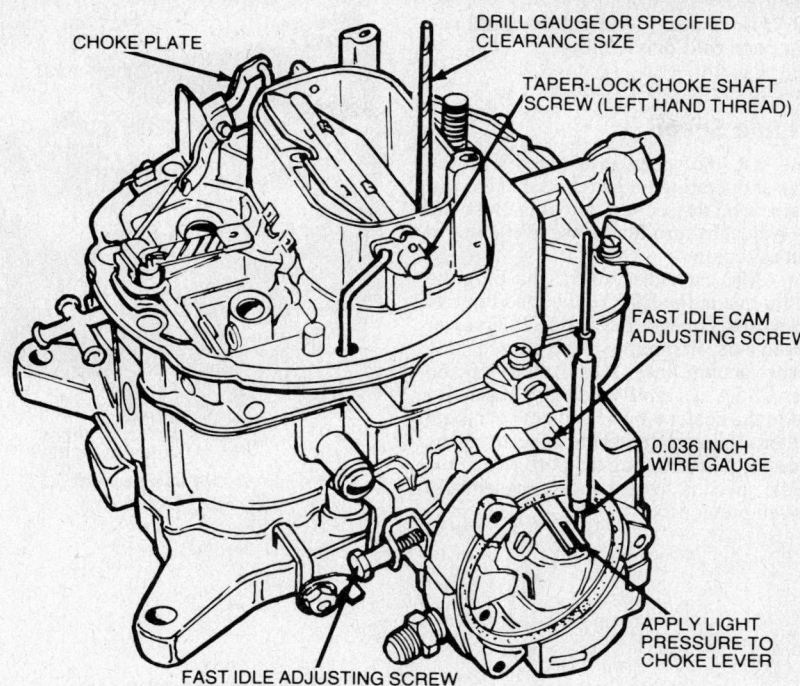

Choke plate pulldown and fast idle cam adjustment

ter cap, place a piece of tape over the purge hole, and apply vacuum to the port.

3. Measure the dimension at the lower edge of the choke plate at the center of the air horn. To adjust this figure, turn the stop screw on the delayed choke pulldown diaphragm.

Fast Idle Cam Adjustment

1. Loosen the screws on the choke thermostatic spring cover and rotate the housing ¼ turn counter-clockwise. Tighten the screws.

2. Open the throttle and allow the choke valve to close completely.

3. Push down on the fast idle cam counterweight until the fast idle screw is in contact with the second step of the cam and against the high step.

4. Measure the clearance between the lower edge of the choke plate and the air horn wall.

5. Adjust by turning the fast idle cam adjusting screw (inward to increase clearance, outward to decrease clearance).

6. Return the housing on the thermostatic spring to its original position.

Choke Unloader (Dechoke) Adjustment

1. Open the throttle fully and hold it in this position.

2. Rotate the choke plate toward the closed position until the pawl on the fast idle speed lever contacts the fast idle cam.

3. Check the clearance between the lower edge of the choke plate and the air horn wall.

4. Adjust by bending the pawl on the fast idle speed lever forward to increase the clearance and backward to decrease the clearance.

Accelerator Pump Stroke Adjustment

The accelerator pump adjustment is preset at the factory for reduced exhaust emissions. Adjustment is provided only for different engine installations. The adjustment is internal, with three piston-to-shaft pin positions in the pump piston.

To check that the shaft pin is located in the specified piston hole, remove the carburetor air horn and invert it. Disconnect the accelerator pump from the operating arm by pressing downward on the spring and sliding the arm out of the pump shaft slot. Disassemble the spring and nylon keeper retaining the adjustment pin. If the pin is not in its specified hole, remove it, reposition the shaft to the correct hole in the piston assembly and reinstall the pin. Then, slide the nylon retainer over the pin and position the spring on the shaft. Finally, compress the spring on the shaft and install the pump on the pump arm.

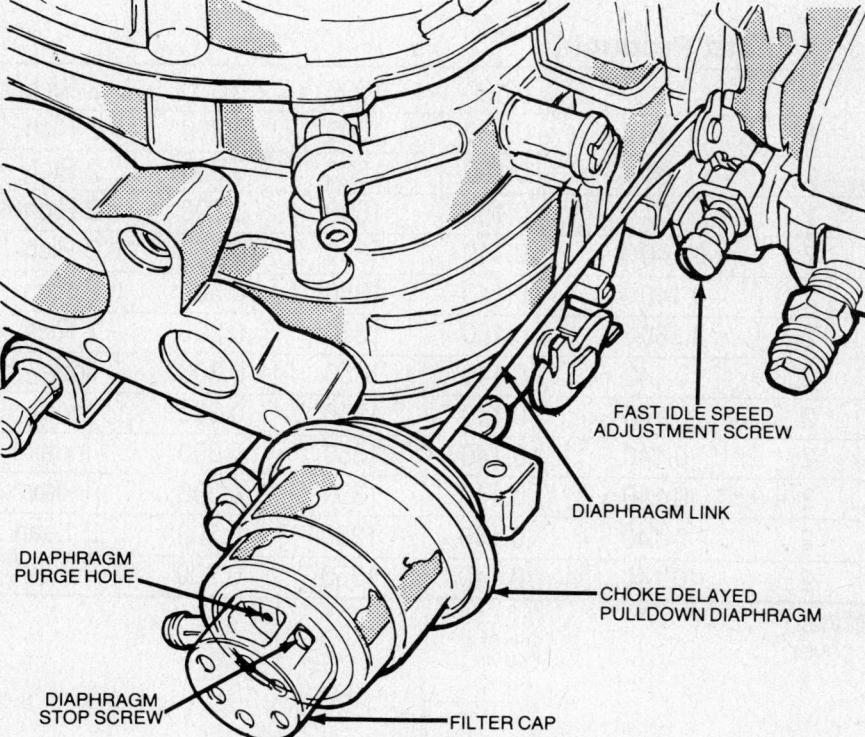

Motorcraft 4350 delayed choke assembly

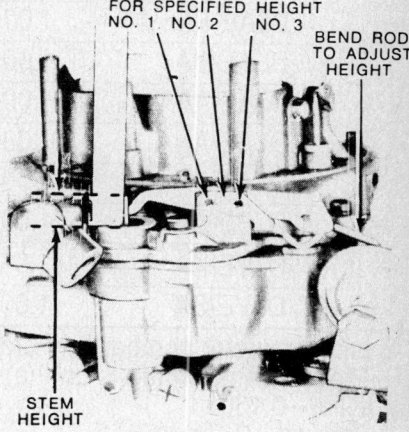

Accelerator pump adjustment
(© Ford Motor Co)

B31

FORD, AUTOLITE, MOTORCRAFT CARBURETORS

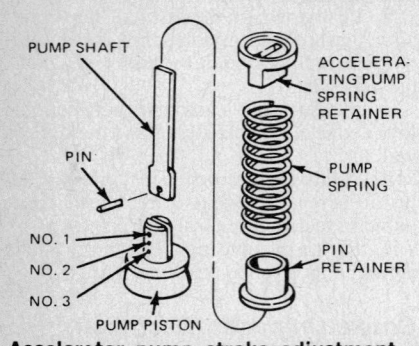

PUMP SHAFT
PIN
NO. 1
NO. 2
NO. 3
PUMP PISTON
ACCELERATING PUMP SPRING RETAINER
PUMP SPRING
PIN RETAINER

Accelerator pump stroke adjustment—Motorcraft 4350

NOTE: Under no circumstances should you adjust the stroke of the accelerator pump by turning the vacuum limiter lever adjusting nut. This adjustment is preset

at the factory and modification could result in poor cold driveability.

Fast Idle Speed

The fast idle speed is adjusted with the engine at operating temperature and the fast idle screw on the second step of the fast idle cam. Adjust by turning the fast idle screw in or out as required.

On AMC cars, disconnect and plug the vacuum line at the EGR valve, and remove the electrical connector from the TCS valve. On Ford cars, first remove and plug the distributor vacuum lines. Remove the top and center CSSA system PVS switch hoses (located in the heater elbow) and connect them together. Remove the EGR hose from the carburetor port and plug the port. When the fast idle speed is set, reconnect those hoses removed previously.

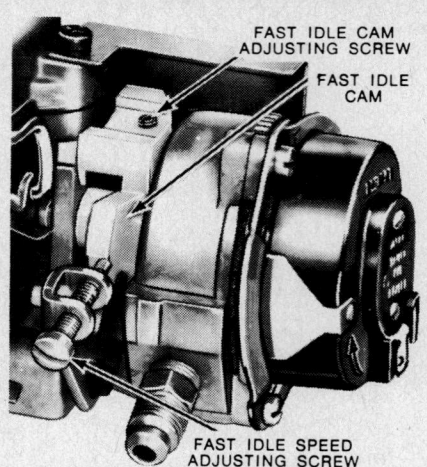

FAST IDLE CAM ADJUSTING SCREW
FAST IDLE CAM
FAST IDLE SPEED ADJUSTING SCREW

Fast idle adjustment
(© Ford Motor Co)

FORD, AUTOLITE, MOTORCRAFT MODELS 4300, 4350 SPECIFICATIONS
American Motors

Year	(9510)* Carburetor Identification ①	Dry Float Level (in.)	Pump Hole Setting	Choke Plate Pulldown (in.)	Fast Idle Cam Linkage	Fast Idle (rpm)	Dechoke (in.)	Choke Setting
1975	5TA4	0.90	Lower	0.140	0.160	1600	0.325	2 Rich
1976	6TA4	0.090	Lower	0.130	0.135	1600	0.325	2 Rich

Ford Products

Year	(9510)* Carburetor Identification ①	Dry Float Level (in.)	Pump Hole Setting	Choke Plate Pulldown (in.)	Fast Idle Cam Linkage	Fast Idle (rpm)	Dechoke (in.)	Choke Setting
1975	D5VE-AD	15/16	1	②	0.160	1600	0.300	2 Rich
	D5VE-BA	15/16	1	②	0.160	1600	0.300	2 Rich
	D5AE-CA	31/32	1	②	0.160	1600	0.300	2 Rich
	D5AE-DA	31/32	1	②	0.160	1600	0.300	2 Rich
1976	D6AE-CA	1.00	2	0.140③	0.140	1350	0.300	2 Rich
	D6AE-FA	1.00	2	0.140③	0.140	1350	0.300	2 Rich
	D6AE-DA	1.00	2	0.160④	0.160	1350	0.300	2 Rich
1977-78	D7AE-AAA	1.00	2	0.140	0.140	1350	0.300	Index
	D7AE-ANA	1.00	2	0.140	0.140	1350	0.300	Index
	D7AE-ZA	1.00	2	0.140	0.140	1350	0.300	Index
	D7PE-AA	1.00	2	0.140	0.140	1350	0.300	Index
	D7VE-KA	1.00	2	0.140	0.140	1350	0.300	2 Lean
	D7VE-SA	1.00	2	0.140	0.140	1350	0.300	Index

* Basic carburetor number for Ford products.
① The identification tag is on the bowl cover.
② Initial—0.160 in.
   Delayed—0.190 in.
③ Initial Figure given: delayed—0.190
④ Initial Figure given: delayed—0.210

MODEL 7200

The Motorcraft model 7200 variable venturi (VV) carburetor shares most of its design features with the model 2700 VV. The major difference between the two is that the 7200 is designed to work with Ford's EEC (electronic engine control) feedback system. The feedback system precisely controls the air/fuel ratio by varying signals to the feedback control monitor located on the carburetor, which opens or closes the metering valve in response. This expands or reduces the amount of control vacuum above the fuel bowl, leaning or richening the mixture accordingly.

Float Level, Float Drop, Fast Idle Speed Adjustments

These adjustments are performed in the same manner as for the 2700 VV. See that section for procedures.

Fast Idle Cam Adjustment

This procedure is the same as for the 2700 VV. Use the procedure in that section. The 7200 VV used on California models has a choke cover held on with rivets. The carburetor must be removed to remove the rivets. With the carburetor removed, the top two rivets can be drilled out with a ⅛ in. drill bit. Drill only through the rivet head. The bottom rivet is located in a blind hole and must be removed by lightly tapping the backside of the retainer ring with a punch. The cover must be installed with replacement rivets, Ford part no. 388575, or the equivalent.

Cold Enrichment Metering Rod Adjustment

This adjustment is made in the same manner as for the 2700 VV. See the paragraph under the Fast Idle Cam Adjustment above concerning the riveted choke cover used on California models.

Internal Vent, Venturi Valve Limiter Adjustments

These adjustments are the same as for the 2700 VV. See that section for details.

Control Vacuum Regulator Adjustment

Use the Revised System procedure in the 2700 VV section. Note that the control vacuum is not adjustable on any 7200 carburetor; only the regulator is adjustable.

High Speed Cam Positioner, Idle Mixture Adjustments

Procedures are the same as for the 2700 VV. See that section for details. Like the 2700 VV, the 7200 idle trim is preset at the factory and non-adjustable.

MOTORCRAFT MODEL 7200 VV SPECIFICATIONS

Year	Model	Float Level (in.)	Float Drop (in.)	Fast Idle Cam Setting (notches)	Cold Enrichment Metering Rod (in.)	Control Vacuum (in. H$_2$O)	Venturi Valve Limiter (in.)	Choke Cap Setting (notches)
1979	D9AE-ACA	1³⁄₆₄	1¹⁵⁄₃₂	1 Rich/3rd step	.125	7.5	.73-.77 ①	Index
	D9ME-AA	1³⁄₆₄	1¹⁵⁄₃₂	1 Rich/3rd step	.125	7.5	.73-.77 ①	Index
1980	All	1³⁄₆₄	1¹⁵⁄₃₂	1 Rich/3rd step	.125	②	③	④
1981	D9AE-AZA	1.015-1.065	1.435-1.485	1 Rich/3rd step	.125	②	⑤	Index
	EIAE-LA	1.015-1.065	1.435-1.485	0.360/2nd step	⑦	②	⑥	INR
	EIAE-SA	1.015-1.065	1.435-1.485	0.360/2nd step	⑦	②	⑥	INR
	EIVE-AA	1.015-1.065	1.435-1.485	0.360/2nd step	⑦	②	③	Index

① Limiter Stop Setting: .99-1.01
② See text
③ Opening gap: 0.99-1.01
   Closing gap: 0.39-0.41
④ See underhood decal
⑤ Maximum opening: .99/1.01
   Wide open on throttle: .94/.98

⑥ Maximum opening: .99/1.01
   Wide open on throttle: .74/.76
⑦ 0°F—0.490 @ starting position
   75°F—0.475 @ starting position

ROCHESTER CARBURETORS

MODEL IDENTIFICATION

General Motors Rochester carburetors are identified by their model number. The first number indicates the number of barrels, while one of the last letters indicates the type of choke used. These are V for the manifold mounted choke coil, C for the choke coil mounted on the carburetor, and E for electric choke, also mounted on the carburetor. Model numbers ending in A indicate an altitude-compensating carburetor.

MODEL 1ME

This is a Rochester Monojet carburetor, designed for use on the Chevette. It is also used on Chevrolet inline sixes, starting 1977. It is a single bore downdraft unit. Some models have a hot idle compensator. The 1ME has an integral automatic choke system with an electrically heated choke coil. The carburetor is last used in 1979.

Float Level Adjustment

1. Remove the top of the carburetor.
2. Hold the float retaining pin in place and push down on the float arm at the outer end against the top of the float needle valve.
3. Measure the distance from the bump on the top of the float at the end to the bowl gasket surface, without the gasket.

ROCHESTER CARBURETORS

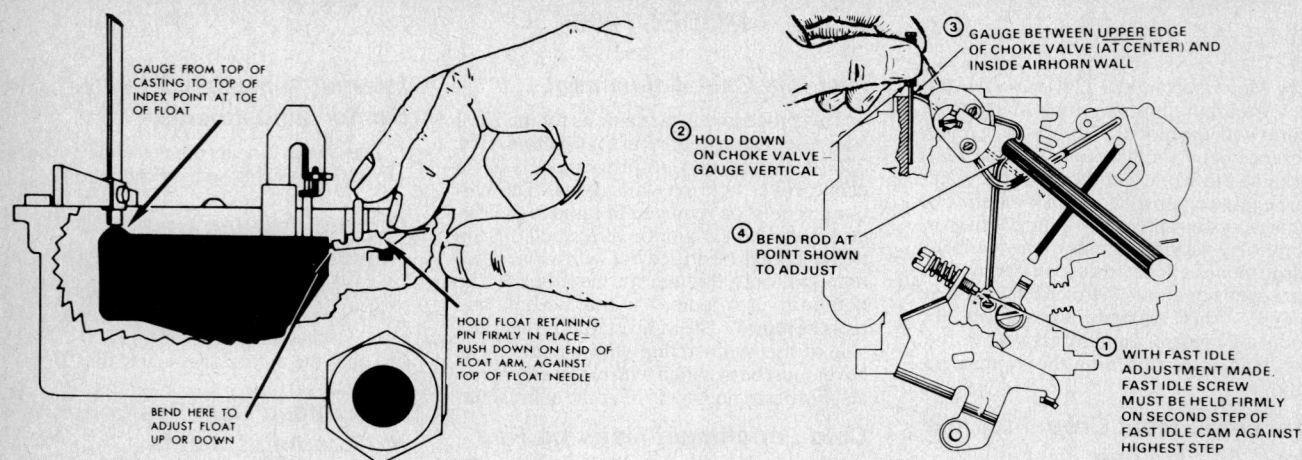

1ME Float level adjustment (© Chevrolet Div., G.M. Corp.)

1ME Fast idle cam adjustment (© Chevrolet Div., G.M. Corp.)

4. To adjust, bend the float arm at the point where it joins the float.

Metering Rod Adjustment

CHEVETTE

1. Remove the top of the carburetor.
2. Back out the idle stop solenoid and rotate the fast idle cam so that the fast idle screw does not contact the cam.
3. With the throttle valve completely closed, make sure the power piston is all the way up.
4. Insert the specified size gauge between the bowl gasket surface with no gasket and the lower surface of the metering rod holder, next to the metering rod.
5. To adjust, carefully bend the metering rod holder.

INLINE SIXES

1. Remove the top of the carburetor and the gasket.
2. Remove the metering rod. Hold the throttle valve wide open. Push down on the metering rod against spring tension, then slide the rod out of the slot in the holder and remove it from the main metering jet.

3. Back out the idle stop solenoid and hold the throttle valve completely closed.
4. Hold the power piston down and swing the metering rod holder over the flat surface of the bowl casting next to the carburetor bore. The gauge should be a slide fit between the rod holder and the flat surface.
5. Adjust by carefully bending the metering rod holder.

Fast Idle Speed Adjustment

NOTE: This adjustment is not possible on some California and high altitude carburetors. It should not be done on carburetors with an idle dashpot.

1. The engine should be at normal temperature with the air cleaner in place. Disconnect and plug EGR valve vacuum line.
2. Make sure that the curb idle speed is as specified.
3. Place the fast idle screw or cam follower on the highest cam step with the engine running.
4. Adjust the fast idle speed screw to the correct fast idle speed. If there is no screw, adjust by bending the tang.

Fast Idle Cam Adjustment

1. Hold the fast idle speed screw on the second cam step against the shoulder of the high step.
2. Hold the choke valve closed with a finger.
3. Insert the specified gauge between the center upper (lower starting 1978) edge of the choke valve and the air horn wall.
4. Bend the linkage rod at the upper angle to adjust.

Vacuum Break Adjustment

1976

1. Place the fast idle speed screw on the highest cam step.
2. Tape over the bleed hole in the diaphragm unit. Apply suction by mouth to seat the diaphragm.

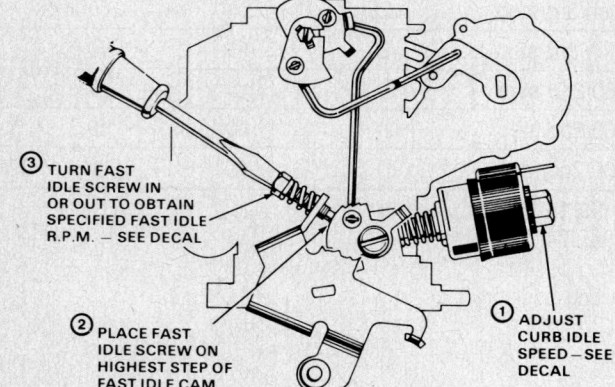

1ME Fast idle speed adjustment (© Chevrolet Div., G.M. Corp.)

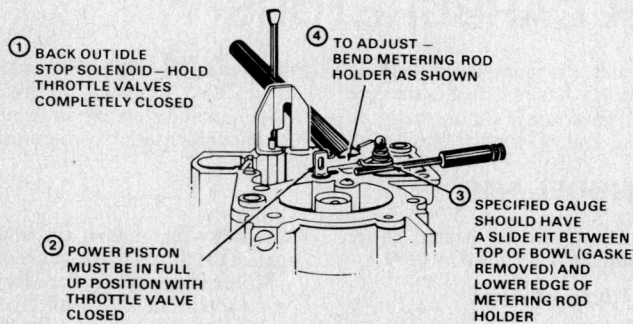

1ME Metering rod adjustment (© Chevrolet Div., G.M. Corp.)

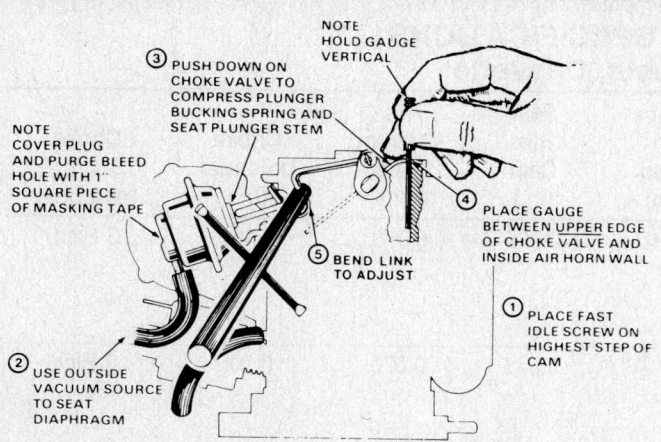

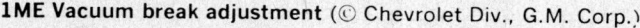

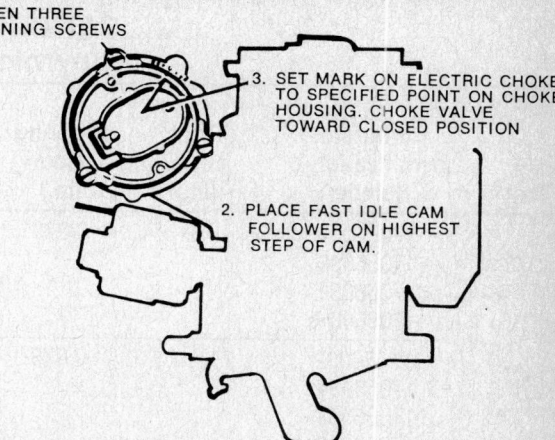

1ME Vacuum break adjustment (© Chevrolet Div., G.M. Corp.)

1ME Electric choke adjustment (© Chevrolet Div., G.M. Corp.)

3. Push down on the choke valve with a finger.

4. Insert the gauge between the upper edge of the choke valve and the airhorn wall.

5. Bend the link to adjust.

1977

1. Place the fast idle screw on the high step of the cam.

2. Apply vacuum to the vacuum break diaphragm until the plunger is fully seated. The diaphragm plunger should be out and seated with the bucking spring compressed.

3. Push up on the choke coil lever so the rod is in the end of the slot.

4. Insert the specified drill bit between the upper center edge of the choke valve and the air horn wall.

5. Bend the rod to adjust.

6. Check the fast idle cam (choke rod) adjustment.

1978–1979

1. Place the fast idle screw or cam follower on the high step of the cam.

2. Apply vacuum to the vacuum break diaphragm to seat the diaphragm. If the diaphragm has a bleed hole, it must be temporarily taped over.

3. Push down on the choke valve. Compress the plunger bucking spring and seat the plunger stem on models so equipped.

4. Measure between the lower edge of the choke valve and the inside air horn wall.

5. Bend the U-shaped link to adjust.

Choke Unloader Adjustment

1. Hold the throttle valve wide open.

2. Hold down the choke valve with a finger and insert the specified gauge between the upper (lower starting 1978) edge of the choke valve and the air horn wall.

3. Bend the linkage tang to adjust.

Choke Coil Lever Adjustment

1. Place the fast idle speed screw or cam follower on the highest cam step.

2. Hold the choke valve closed.

3. Insert a 0.120 in. gauge through the hole in the arm on the choke housing and into the hole in the casting.

4. Bend the link to adjust.

Electric Choke Adjustment

1. Place the fast idle cam follower on the high step.

2. Loosen the three retaining screws and rotate the cover counter-clockwise until the choke valve just closes.

3. Align the index mark on the cover with the specified housing mark.

4. Tighten the three screws.

NOTE: Failure of the electric choke heater circuit will cause the oil pressure light to go on.

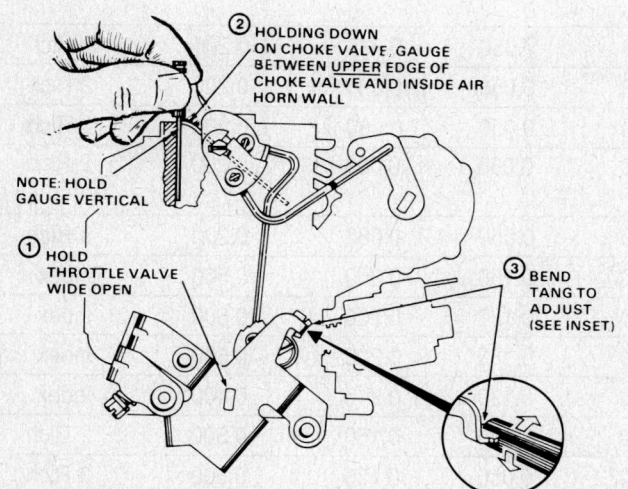

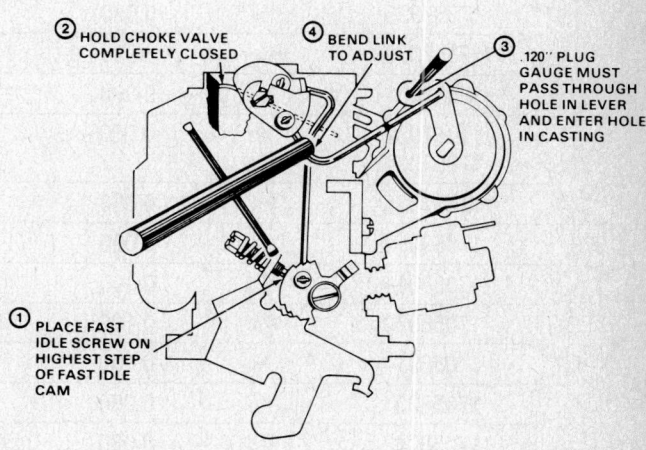

1ME Choke unloader adjustment (© Chevrolet Div., G.M. Corp.)

1ME Choke coil lever adjustment (© Chevrolet Div., G.M. Corp.)

ROCHESTER CARBURETORS

1ME CARBURETOR SPECIFICATIONS
Chevrolet Products, Chevette

Year	Carburetor Identification ① Number	Float Level (in.)	Metering Rod (in.)	Fast Idle Speed (rpm)	Fast Idle Cam (in.)	Vacuum Break (in.)	Choke Unloader (in.)	Choke Setting (notches)
1976	17056036 17056030 17056031 17056037	5/32	0.072	2000②	0.065	0.070	0.165	3 Rich
	17056032 17056034, 17056033, 17056035	5/32	0.073	2000③	0.045	0.070	0.200	3 Rich
	17056330 17056331	5/32	0.072	2000	0.065	0.070	0.165	3 Rich
	17056332 17056333, 17056334	5/32	0.073	2000	0.045	0.070	0.200	3 Rich
	17056335	5/32	0.073	2000	0.045	0.120	0.200	3 Rich
1977	17057016	3/8	0.070	2000	0.095	0.125	0.325	1 Lean
	17057013	3/8	0.070	2000	0.100	0.120	0.270	3 Rich
	17057015	3/8	0.070	2000	0.100	0.125	0.325	1 Rich
	17057018	3/8	0.070	2000	0.085	0.120	0.325	1 Rich
	17057014	3/8	0.070	2000	0.100	0.125	0.325	2 Rich
	17057020	3/8	0.070	2000	0.085	0.120	0.120	2 Rich
	17057310	3/8	0.070	2000	0.085	0.125	0.200	Index
	17057312	3/8	0.070	1800	0.100	0.100	0.110	Index
	17057314	3/8	0.070	1800	0.100	0.110	0.225	Index
	17057318	3/8	0.070	1800	0.100	0.110	0.110	Index
	17057042 17057044	5/32	0.080	2400	0.050	0.075	0.200	1 Rich
	17047045	5/32	0.080	2000	0.050	0.075	0.200	1 Rich
	17057332 17057334	5/32	0.080	2400	0.050	0.075	0.200	2 Rich
	17057335	5/32	0.080	2300	0.050	0.080	0.200	2 Rich
	17057030	5/32	0.080	2400	0.050	0.080	0.200	2 Rich
	17057031	5/32	0.080	2300	0.050	0.080	0.200	2 Rich
	17057032 17057034	5/32	0.080	2400	0.050	0.080	0.200	2 Rich
	17057035	5/32	0.080	2300	0.050	0.080	0.200	3 Rich
1978	17058013	3/8	0.080	2000	0.180	0.200	0.500	Index
	17058014	5/16	0.100	2100	0.180	0.200	0.500	Index
	17058020	5/16	0.100	2100	0.180	0.200	0.500	Index
	17058314	3/8	0.100	2000	0.190	0.245	0.400	Index
	17058031	5/32	0.080	2400	0.105	0.150	0.500	2 Rich
	17058032	5/32	0.080	2400	0.080	0.130	0.500	3 Rich

1ME CARBURETOR SPECIFICATIONS
Chevrolet Products, Chevette

Year	Carburetor Identification ① Number	Float Level (in.)	Metering Rod (in.)	Fast Idle Speed (rpm)	Fast Idle Cam (in.)	Vacuum Break (in.)	Choke Unloader (in.)	Choke Setting (notches)
	17058033	5/32	0.080	2400	0.080	0.130	0.500	2 Rich
	17058034	5/32	0.080	2400	0.080	0.130	0.500	3 Rich
	17058035	5/32	0.080	2300	0.080	0.130	0.500	3 Rich
	17058036	5/32	0.080	2400	0.080	0.130	0.500	3 Rich
	17058037	5/32	0.080	2400	0.080	0.130	0.500	2 Rich
	17058038	5/32	0.080	2400	0.080	0.130	0.500	3 Rich
	17058042	5/32	0.080	2400	0.080	0.160	0.500	2 Rich
	17058044	5/32	0.080	2400	0.080	0.160	0.500	2 Rich
	17058045	5/32	0.080	2300	0.080	0.160	0.500	2 Rich
	17058332	5/32	0.080	2400	0.080	0.160	0.500	2 Rich
	17058334	5/32	0.080	2400	0.080	0.160	0.500	2 Rich
	17058335	5/32	0.080	2300	0.080	0.160	0.500	2 Rich
1979	17059014	3/8	0.095	2000	0.180	0.200	0.400	Index
	17059020	3/8	0.095	2000	0.180	0.200	0.400	Index
	17059013	3/8	0.095	1800	0.180	0.200	0.400	Index
	17059314	3/8	0.100	2000	0.190	0.245	0.400	Index

① Stamped on float bowl, next to fuel inlet nut
② 2200 rpm for the first two numbers
③ 2200 rpm for the last two numbers

MODEL MV, 1 MV

The model MV carburetor is a single bore, down-draft carburetor with an aluminum throttle body, automatic choke, internally balanced venting, and a hot idle compensating system for cars equipped with automatic transmissions. Newer models are also equipped with Combination Emission Control valves (C.E.C.) and an Exhaust Gas Recirculation (EGR) system. An electrically operated idle stop solenoid replaces the idle stop screw of older models.

The MV carburetor is used on General Motors inline four and six cylinder cars through 1976.

Fast Idle Speed Adjustment
NOTE: The fast idle adjustment must be made with the transmission in Neutral.

1. Disconnect and plug the distributor vacuum line on 1976 models. Position the fast idle lever on the high step of the fast idle cam.
2. Be sure that the choke is properly adjusted and in the wide open position with the engine warm.
3. Bend the fast idle lever until the specified speed is obtained.

Choke Rod (Fast Idle Cam) Adjustment
NOTE: Adjust the fast idle before making choke rod adjustments.

1. Place the fast idle cam follower on the second step of the fast idle cam and hold it firmly against the rise to the high step.

2. Rotate the choke valve in the direction of a closed choke by applying force to the choke coil lever.
3. Bend the choke rod to give the specified opening between the lower edge (upper edge for 1976) of the choke valve and the inside air horn wall.

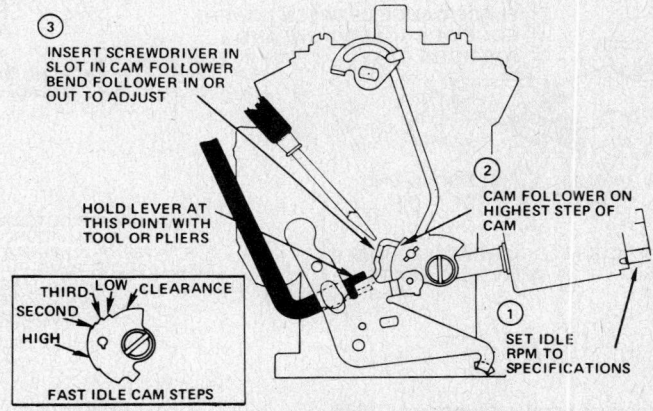

Fast Idle Adjustment (© Chevrolet Div., G.M. Corp)

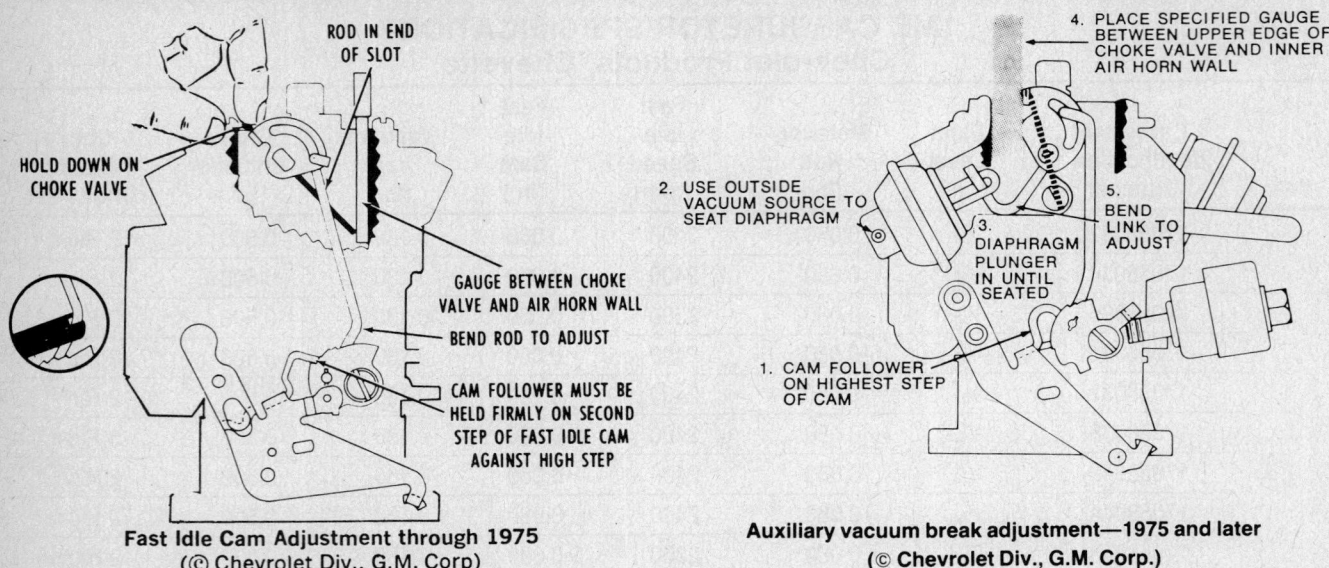

Fast Idle Cam Adjustment through 1975
(© Chevrolet Div., G.M. Corp)

Auxiliary vacuum break adjustment—1975 and later
(© Chevrolet Div., G.M. Corp.)

NOTE: Measurement must be made at the center of the choke valve.

Choke Vacuum Break Adjustment

The adjustment of the vacuum break diaphragm unit insures correct choke valve opening after engine starting.

1. Remove the air cleaner on vehicles with Therm AC air cleaner; plug the sensor's vacuum take off port.
2. Using an external vacuum source, apply vacuum to the vacuum break diaphragm until the plunger is fully seated.
3. When the plunger is seated, push the choke valve toward the closed position.
4. Holding the choke valve in this position, place the specified gauge between the lower edge (upper edge for 1976) of the choke valve and the air horn wall.
5. If the measurement is not correct, bend the vacuum break rod.

Choke Auxiliary Vacuum Break Adjustment

This adjustment is required in addition to the preceding vacuum break adjustment.

1. Using an external source of vacuum, apply vacuum to the auxiliary vacuum break diaphragm until the plunger is seated fully.
2. Place the cam follower on the highest step of the fast idle cam.
3. With the diaphragm seated, insert the specified gauge between the upper edge of the choke valve and the inner air horn wall.
4. To adjust the clearance, bend the link between the vacuum break and the choke lever.

NOTE: The auxiliary vacuum break diaphragm is on the same side of the carburetor as the throttle stop solenoid.

Choke Unloader Adjustment

1. Apply pressure to the choke valve and hold it in the closed position.
2. Open the throttle valve to the wide open position.
3. Check the dimension between the lower edge (upper edge for 1976) of the choke plate and the air horn wall; if adjustment is needed, bend the unloader tang on the throttle lever.

Choke Coil Rod Adjustment

1. Disconnect the thermostatic coil rod from the upper choke lever and hold the choke valve closed.
2. Push down on the coil rod to the end of its travel.
3. The top of the rod should be even with the bottom hole in the choke lever.

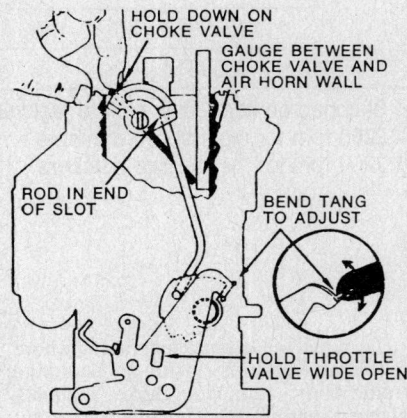

Adjusting Choke Unloader
(© Chevrolet Div., G.M. Corp)

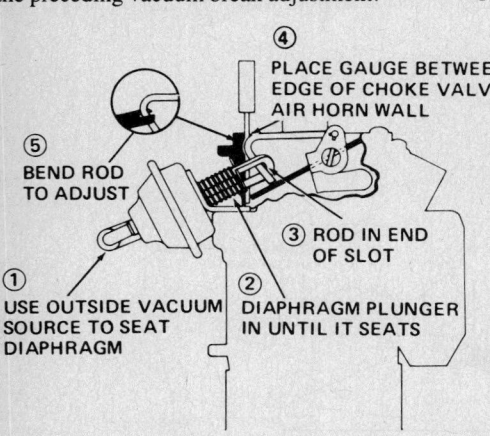

Vacuum break adjustment—1975
(© Chevrolet Div., G.M. Corp.)

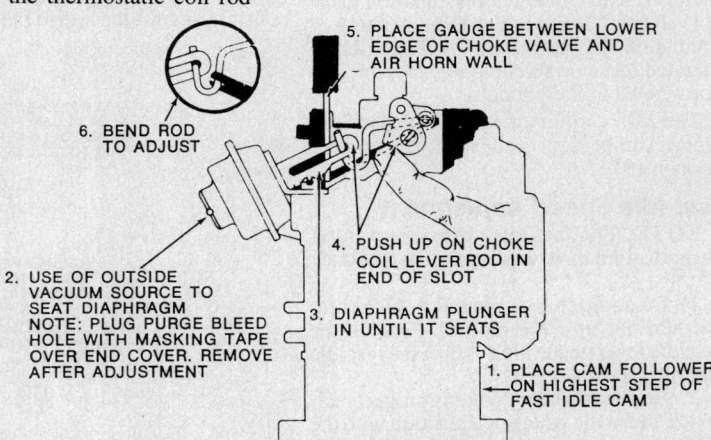

Primary vacuum break adjustment—1976 and later (© Chevrolet Div., G.M. Corp.)

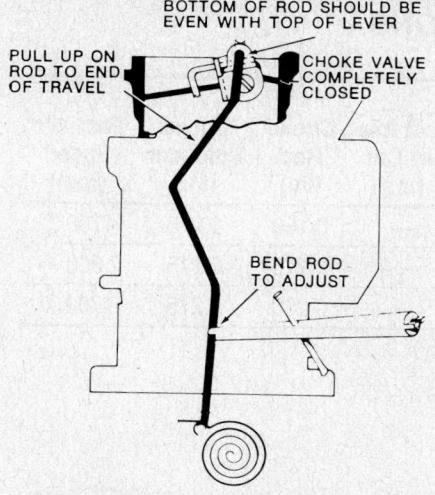

Choke coil rod adjustment
(© Chevrolet Div., G.M. Corp.)

4. To make adjustments, bend the rod.

Float Adjustment

1. Hold the float retainer in place and the float arm against the top of the float needle by pushing down on the float arm at the outer end toward the float bowl casting.

2. Using an adjustable T scale, measure the distance from the toe of the float to the float bowl gasket surface.

NOTE: The float bowl gasket should be removed and the gauge held on the index point on the float for accurate measurement.

3. Adjust the float level by bending the float arm up or down at the float arm junction.

Metering Rod Adjustment

1. Hold the throttle valve wide open and push down on the metering rod against spring tension, then remove the rod from the main metering jet.

2. In order to check adjustment, the slow idle screw must be backed out and the fast idle cam rotated so that the fast idle cam follower does not contact the steps on the cam.

3. With the throttle valve closed, push down on the power piston until it contacts its stop.

4. With the power piston depressed, swing the metering rod holder over the flat surface of the bowl casting next to the carburetor bore.

5. Insert a specified size drill between the bowl casting sealing bead and the lower surface of the metering rod holder. The drill should slide smoothly between both surfaces.

6. If adjustment is needed, carefully bend the metering rod holder up or down. After adjustment, reinstall the metering rod.

Idle Vent Adjustment

1. The engine idle must be set at the specified RPM and the choke valve held wide open so that the fast idle cam follower is not contacting the cam.

NOTE: If the carburetor is off the car, a preliminary idle setting can be made by turning the idle speed screw in 1½ turns from the closed throttle valve position.

2. With the throttle stop screw held against the idle stop screw, the idle vent valve should be open to specification. To check, a drill of specified size may be inserted between the top of the air horn casting and the bottom surface of the valve.

3. If adjustment is necessary, turn the slotted vent valve head with a screwdriver. Turning the head clockwise increases the clearance.

NOTE: On models equipped with an idle stop solenoid, the solenoid must be activated when checking and adjusting the valve.

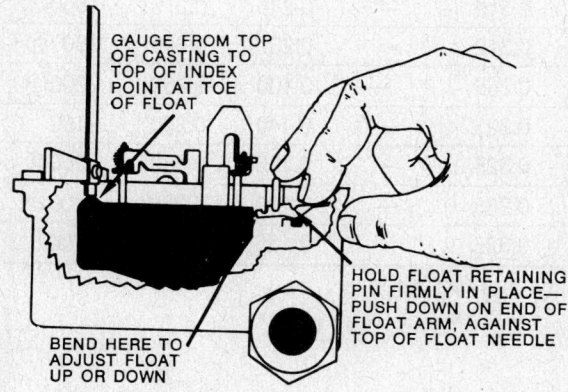

Float Level
(© Pontiac Div., G.M. Corp)

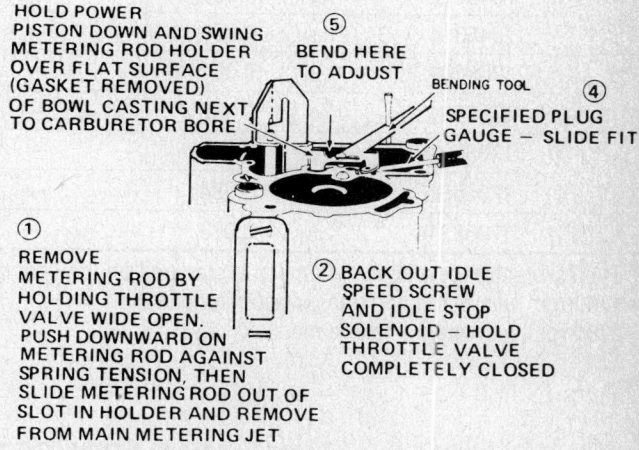

Metering Rod Adjustment (© Chevrolet Div., G.M. Corp)

MV, 1MV CARBURETOR SPECIFICATIONS
Chevrolet Vega, Monza

Year	Carburetor Identification ①	Float Level (in.)	Metering Rod (in.)	Pump Rod	Idle Vent (in.)	Vacuum Break (in.)	Fast Idle Off Car (in.)	Choke Rod (in.)	Choke Unloader (in.)	Fast Idle Speed (rpm)
1975	Manual	⅛	—	—	0.100	0.450	—	0.080	0.375	2000
	Automatic	⅛	—	—	0.100	0.450	—	0.080	0.375	2000
1976	Manual	⅛	—	—	0.060	0.450	—	0.045	0.215	1200
	Automatic	⅛	—	—	0.060	0.450	—	0.045	0.215	750

① The carburetor identification number is stamped on the float bowl, next to the fuel inlet nut.

ROCHESTER CARBURETORS

MV, 1MV CARBURETOR SPECIFICATIONS
Buick

Year	Carburetor Identification①	Float Level (in.)	Metering Rod (in.)	Pump Rod	Idle Vent (in.)	Vacuum Break (in.)	Auxiliary Vacuum Break (in.)	Fast Idle Off Car (in.)	Choke Rod (in.)	Choke Unloader (in.)	Fast Idle Speed (rpm)
1975	7045012	11/32	0.080	—	—	0.200	0.215	—	0.160	0.275	1700②
	7045013	11/32	0.080	—	—	0.350	0.312	—	0.275	0.275	1800②
	7045314	11/32	0.080	—	—	0.275	0.312	—	0.230	0.275	1700②

① The Carburetor Identification number is stamped on the float bowl, next to the fuel inlet nut.
② In Neutral or Park

MV, 1MV CARBURETOR SPECIFICATIONS
Chevrolet

Year	Carburetor Identification①	Float Level (in.)	Metering Rod (in.)	Pump Rod	Idle Vent (in.)	Vacuum Break (in.)	Auxiliary Vacuum Break (in.)	Fast Idle Off Car (in.)	Choke Rod (in.)	Choke Unloader (in.)	Fast Idle Speed (rpm)
1975	7045013	11/32	0.080	—	—	0.200	0.215	—	0.160	0.215	1800②
	7045012	11/32	0.080	—	—	0.350	0.312	—	0.275	0.275	1800②
	7045314	11/32	0.080	—	—	0.275	0.312	—	0.230	0.275	1800②
1976	17056012	11/32	0.084	—	—	0.140	0.265	—	0.100	0.260	2200③
	17066013	11/32	0.082	—	—	0.140	0.325	—	0.140	0.260	2100
	17056016	11/32	0.080	—	—	0.140	0.325	—	0.115	0.260	2200③
	17056018	11/32	0.084	—	—	0.140	0.265	—	0.100	0.260	2200③
	17056314	11/32	0.083	—	—	0.150	0.325	—	0.135	0.260	1700

① The carburetor identification number is stamped on the float bowl, next to the fuel inlet nut.
② 1700 rpm with automatic transmission in neutral.
③ 2100 rpm with integral intake manifold.

MV, 1MV CARBURETOR SPECIFICATIONS
Oldsmobile

Year	Carburetor Identification①	Float Level (in.)	Metering Rod (in.)	Pump Rod	Idle Vent (in.)	Vacuum Break (in.)	Auxiliary Vacuum Break (in.)	Fast Idle Off Car (in.)	Choke Rod (in.)	Choke Unloader (in.)	Fast Idle Speed (rpm)
1975	Manual	11/32	0.080	—	—	0.350	0.312	—	0.275	0.275	1800②
	Automatic	11/32	0.080	—	—	0.200	0.215	—	0.160	0.275	1800②
1976	4-140 Man.	1/8	—	—	—	0.055	0.450	—	0.045	0.215	—
	4-140 Auto.	1/8	—	—	—	0.060	0.450	—	0.045	0.215	—
	6-250 Man.	11/32	—	—	—	0.165	0.320	—	0.140	0.265	—
	6-250 Auto.	11/32	—	—	—	0.140	0.265	—	0.100	0.265	—
	6-250 Calif.	11/32	—	—	—	0.150	0.260	—	0.135	0.265	—

① The carburetor identification number is stamped on the float bowl, next to the fuel inlet nut.
① Preset

MV, 1MV CARBURETOR SPECIFICATIONS
Pontiac

Year	Carburetor Identification ①	Float Level (in.)	Metering Rod (in.)	Pump Rod	Idle Vent (in.)	Vacuum Break (in.)	Auxiliary Vacuum Break (in.)	Fast Idle Off Car (in.)	Choke Rod (in.)	Choke Unloader (in.)	Fast Idle Speed (rpm)
1975	7045012	11/32	0.080	—	—	0.200	0.215	—	0.160	0.275	1800 ②
	7045013	11/32	0.080	—	—	0.350	0.312	—	0.275	0.275	1800 ②
	7045014	11/32	0.080	—	—	0.257	0.312	—	0.230	0.275	1800 ②
	Astre Man.	1/8	—	—	—	0.130	—	—	0.080	0.375	2000 ③
	Astre Auto.	1/8	—	—	—	0.130	—	—	0.080	0.375	2000 ③
1976	4-140 Man.	1/8	—	—	—	0.055	0.450	—	0.045	0.215	—
	4-140 Auto.	1/8	—	—	—	0.060	0.450	—	0.045	0.215	—
	6-250 Man.	11/32	—	—	—	0.165	0.320	—	0.140	0.265	—
	6-250 Auto	11/32	—	—	—	0.140	0.265	—	0.100	0.265	—
	6-250 Calif.	11/32	—	—	—	0.150	0.260	—	0.135	0.265	—

① The carburetor identification number is stamped on the float bowl, next to the fuel inlet nut.
② High step of cam.
③ No vacuum to the distributor

MODEL 2GC, 2GV, 2GE

This two barrel carburetor is used on General Motors cars through 1978. The newer carburetors use a plastic float and a longer needle and seat to provide better fuel control. See the beginning of the Rochester section for an explanation of the type designations.

Fast Idle Speed Adjustment

1. Except on some Oldsmobile cars, the fast idle is set automatically when the curb idle and mixture is set.
2. Some Oldsmobile 2GC carburetors have a screw to adjust the fast idle.

Choke Rod (Fast Idle Cam)

1. Turn in the idle cam stop screw, if any, until it just contacts the bottom step of the fast idle cam. Then turn the screw one full turn.
2. Place the idle screw on the second step of the fast idle cam against the shoulder of the high step.
3. Hold the choke valve closed and check the clearance between the upper edge of the choke valve and the air horn wall.
4. Adjust the clearance by bending the tang on the choke lever.

2GC, 2GE Intermediate Choke Rod (Choke Coil Lever) Adjustment

1. Remove the thermostatic cover coil, gasket, and inside baffle plate assembly.
2. Place the idle speed screw on the highest step of the fast idle cam.
3. Close the choke valve by pushing up on the intermediate choke lever.
4. The edge of the coil lever inside the choke housing must line up with the edge of a 0.120 in. drill bit inserted into the hole inside the choke housing.
5. Adjust by bending the intermediate choke rod at the first bend from the bottom of the rod.

Vacuum Break Adjustment

1. Remove the air cleaner. Vehicles with a Therm AC air cleaner should have the sensor's vacuum take-off port plugged.
2. Using an external vacuum source, apply vacuum to the vacuum break diaphragm until the plunger is fully seated. If the diaphragm has a bleed hole, tape it over.
3. When the plunger is seated, push the choke valve toward the closed position. For 1975–76 models, place the idle speed screw on the high step of the fast idle cam.
4. Holding the choke valve in the closed position, place the specified size gauge be-

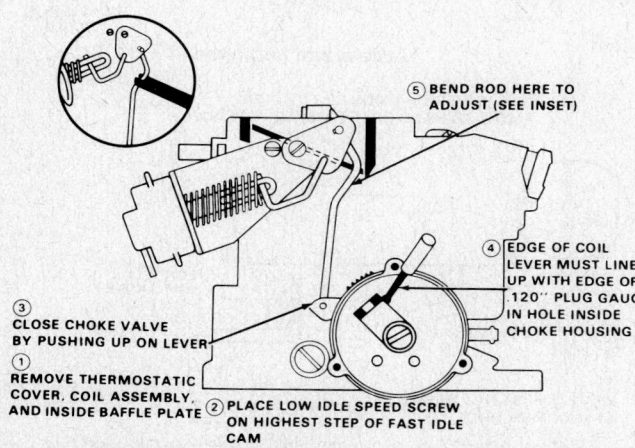

Intermediate choke rod adjustment (© Chevrolet Div., G.M. Corp.)

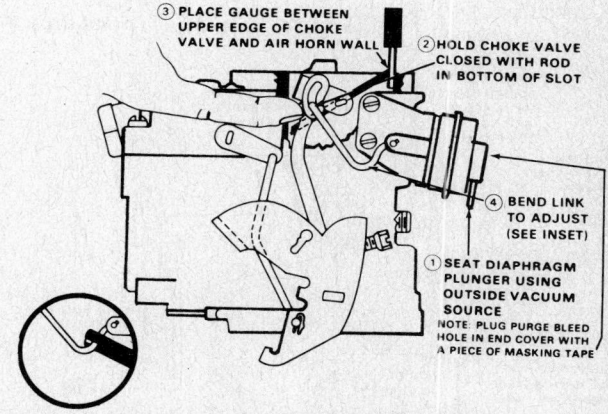

Primary vacuum break adjustment (© Buick Div., G.M. Corp.)

ROCHESTER CARBURETORS

tween the upper edge of the choke valve and the air horn wall.

5. If the measurement is not correct, bend the vacuum break rod.

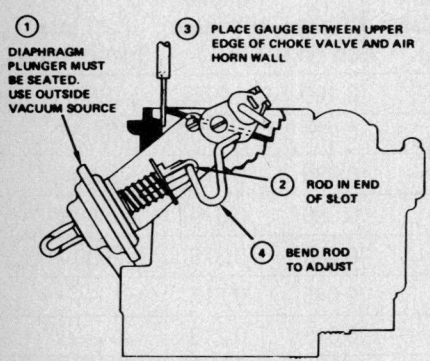

Vacuum Break Adjustment
(© Chevrolet Div., G.M. Corp)

Auxiliary Vacuum Break

1. Seat the auxiliary vacuum diaphragm by applying an outside source of vacuum. Tape over the vacuum bleed hole so the vacuum will not bleed down.
2. Place the idle speed screw on the high step of the fast idle cam.
3. Hold the choke toward the closed choke position.
4. Measure the distance between the upper edge of the choke valve and the air horn wall.
5. Adjust by bending the auxiliary vacuum break rod at the bottom of the U-shaped bend. Remove the piece of tape from the auxiliary vacuum diaphragm.

Choke Unloader Adjustment

1. Hold the throttle valves wide open.
2. Close the choke valve.
3. Bend the unloader tang to obtain the proper clearance between the upper edge of the choke valve and air horn wall.

2GV Choke Coil Rod Adjustment

1. Hold the choke valve completely open.
2. Disconnect the coil rod from the upper lever and push down on the rod to the end of its travel.
3. When the rod is all the way down, the top of the rod should line up with the bottom of the slotted hole on the choke valve linkage.

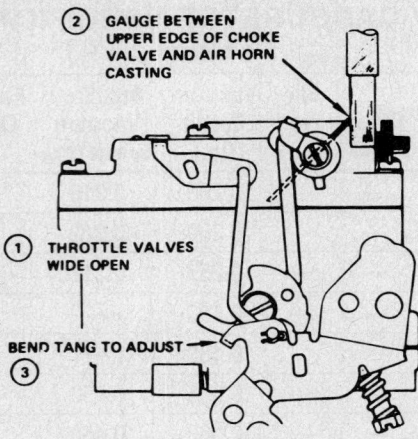

Choke Unloader Adjustment
(© Chevrolet Div., G.M. Corp.)

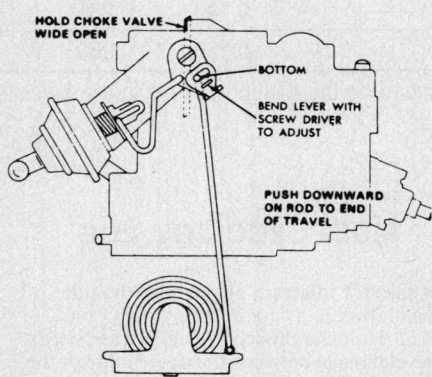

Choke Coil Rod Adjustment
(© Chevrolet Div., G.M. Corp)

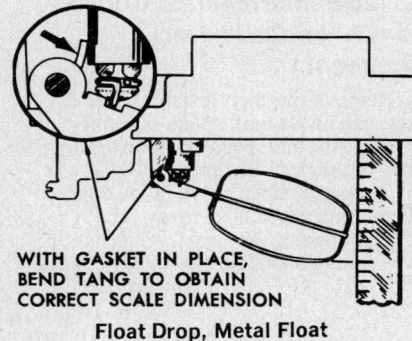

WITH GASKET IN PLACE, BEND TANG TO OBTAIN CORRECT SCALE DIMENSION

Float Drop, Metal Float

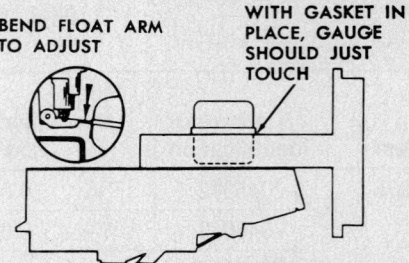

Float Level Measurement, Metal Float

4. Adjust by bending the lever.

Float Level

With the air horn assembly upside down, measure the distance from the air horn gasket to the lip at the toe of the float. Bend the float arm to adjust to specifications.

Float Drop

Holding the air horn assembly upright, measure the distance from the gasket to the lip or notch at the toe of the float. If correction is necessary, bend the float tang at the rear, next to the needle and seat.

Accelerator Pump Rod

1. Back out the idle speed screw and completely close the throttle valves.
2. Place the pump gauge across the air horn ring.
3. With the T-scale set to the specified height, the lower leg of the gauge should just touch the top of the accelerator pump rod.

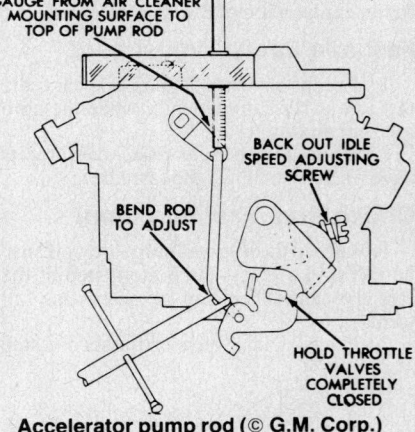

Accelerator pump rod (© G.M. Corp.)

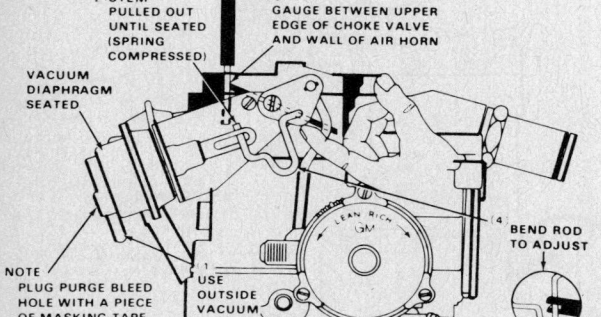

Auxiliary vacuum break adjustment (© Buick Div., G.M. Corp.)

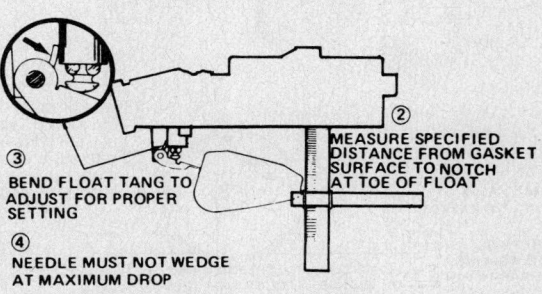

Float Drop, Plastic Float

B42

4. Bend the pump rod to adjust.

Bowl Vent Valve Adjustment

NOTE: Check and adjust, if necessary, the pump rod clearance and curb idle speed before adjusting the bowl vent valve.

1. Remove the two bowl vent valve cover attaching screws in the top of the air horn and remove the cover and gasket. Remove the bowl vent valve spring.

2. Place the idle speed screw on the second step of the fast idle cam next to the highest step. In this position, the bowl vent valve should just be closed.

3. If the vent valve is just closed with the idle the fast idle cam, rotate the fast idle cam so that the idle speed screw is on the next lower step. In this position, the vent valve should just begin to open.

4. If it is necessary to adjust the bowl vent valve, turn the adjustment screw in the top f of the valve, to obtain the conditions mentioned in Steps 2 and 3.

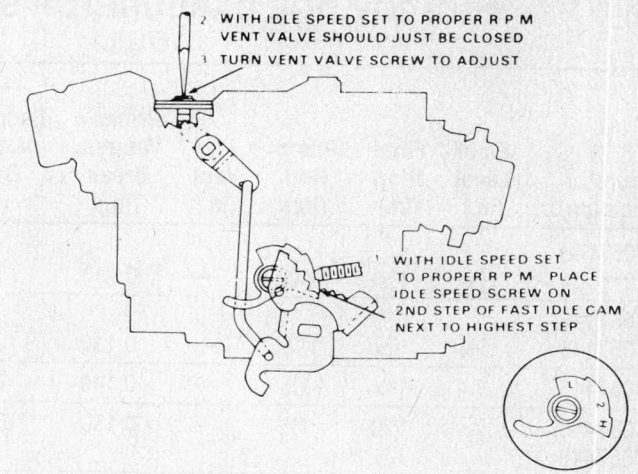

Bowl vent valve adjustment (© Buick Div., G.M. Corp.)

2GC, 2GV, 2GE CARBURETOR SPECIFICATIONS
Buick

Year	Carburetor Identification ①	Float Level (in.)	Float Drop (in.)	Pump Rod (in.)	Idle Vent (in.)	Primary Vacuum Break (in.)	Secondary Vacuum Break (in.)	Automatic Choke (notches)	Choke Rod (in.)	Choke Unloader (in.)	Fast Idle Speed (rpm)
1975	7045145	¹⁵/₃₂	1⁹/₃₂	1¹⁵/₃₂	—	0.120	0.120	Index	0.080	0.120	—
	7045146	¹⁵/₃₂	1⁹/₃₂	1¹⁵/₃₂	—	0.120	0.120	—	0.080	0.120	—
	7045147	¹⁵/₃₂	1⁹/₃₂	1¹⁵/₃₂	—	0.120	0.120	1 Lean	0.080	0.120	—
	7045148	¹⁵/₃₂	1⁹/₃₂	1¹⁵/₃₂	—	0.120	0.120	1 Rich	0.080	0.120	—
	7045149	¹⁵/₃₂	1⁹/₃₂	1¹⁵/₃₂	—	0.120	0.120	1 Rich	0.080	0.120	—
	7045446	¹⁵/₃₂	1⁹/₃₂	1¹⁵/₃₂	—	0.120	0.120	—	0.080	0.120	—
	7045448	¹⁵/₃₂	1⁹/₃₂	1¹⁵/₃₂	—	0.120	0.120	Index	0.080	0.120	—
	7045449	¹⁵/₃₂	1⁹/₃₂	1¹⁵/₃₂	—	0.120	0.120	1 Lean	0.080	0.120	—
	7045143	¹⁵/₃₂	1⁹/₃₂	1¹⁵/₃₂	—	0.140	0.120	1 Rich	0.080	0.140	—
	7045140	¹⁵/₃₂	1⁹/₃₂	1¹⁵/₃₂	—	0.140	0.120	1 Rich	0.080	0.140	—
1976	17056447	⁷/₁₆	1⁹/₃₂	1¹⁹/₃₂	—	0.130	0.100	1 Rich	0.080	0.140	—
	17056145	¹³/₃₂	1⁹/₃₂	1¹⁹/₃₂ ②	—	0.110	0.100	1 Rich	0.080	0.140	—
	17056148	⁷/₁₆	1⁹/₃₂	1¹⁹/₃₂	—	0.120	0.100	1 Rich	0.080	0.140	—
	17056149	⁷/₁₆	1⁹/₃₂	1¹⁹/₃₂	—	0.120	0.100	1 Rich	0.800	0.140	—
	17056448	⁷/₁₆	1⁹/₃₂	1¹⁹/₃₂	—	0.130	0.110	1 Rich	0.080	0.140	—
	17056449	⁷/₁₆	1⁹/₃₂	1¹⁹/₃₂	—	0.130	0.110	1 Rich	0.080	0.140	—
	17056143	¹⁵/₃₂	1⁹/₃₂	1¹⁹/₃₂	—	0.140	0.100	1 Rich	0.080	0.180	—
	17056140	¹⁵/₃₂	1⁹/₃₂	1¹⁹/₃₂	—	0.140	0.100	1 Rich	0.080	0.180	—
1977	17057140	¹⁵/₃₂	1⁵/₃₂	1⁹/₁₆	—	0.140	0.100	1 Rich	0.080	0.180	—
	17057141, 17057145, 17057147	⁷/₁₆	1⁵/₃₂	1½	—	0.110	0.040	1 Rich	0.080	0.140	—

ROCHESTER CARBURETORS

2GC, 2GV, 2GE CARBURETOR SPECIFICATIONS
Buick

Year	Carburetor Identification ①	Float Level (in.)	Float Drop (in.)	Pump Rod (in.)	Idle Vent (in.)	Primary Vacuum Break (in.)	Secondary Vacuum Break (in.)	Automatic Choke (notches)	Choke Rod (in.)	Choke Unloader (in.)	Fast Idle Speed (rpm)
1977	17057143, 17075144	7/16	1 5/32	1 17/32	—	0.130	0.100	1 Rich	0.080	0.140	—
	17057146, 17057148	7/16	1 5/32	1 17/32	—	0.110	0.040	1 Rich	0.080	0.140	—
	17057445	7/16	1 5/32	1 1/2	—	0.140	0.100	1 Rich	0.080	0.140	—
	17057446, 17057448	7/16	1 5/32	1 1/2	—	0.130	0.110	1 Rich	0.080	0.140	—
	17057447	7/16	1 5/32	1 1/2	—	0.130	0.100	1 Rich	0.080	0.140	—
1978	17058104	15/32	1 9/32	1 21/32	—	0.160	—	Index	0.260	0.325	—
	17058105	15/32	1 9/32	1 21/32	—	0.160	—	Index	0.260	0.325	—
	17058108	19/32	1 9/32	1 21/32	—	0.160	—	Index	0.260	0.325	—
	17058110	19/32	1 9/32	1 21/32	—	0.160	—	Index	0.260	0.325	—
	17058112	19/32	1 9/32	1 21/32	—	0.160	—	Index	0.260	0.325	—
	17058114	19/32	1 9/32	1 21/32	—	0.160	—	Index	0.260	0.325	—
	17058126	19/32	1 9/32	1 17/32	—	0.150	—	Index	0.260	0.325	—
	17058128	19/32	1 9/32	1 17/32	—	0.150	—	Index	0.260	0.325	—
	17058404	1/2	1 9/32	1 21/32	—	0.160	—	1/2 Lean	0.260	0.325	—
	17058405	1/2	1 9/32	1 21/32	—	0.160	—	1/2 Lean	0.260	0.325	—
	17058408	21/32	1 9/32	1 21/32	—	0.160	—	1/2 Lean	0.260	0.325	—
	17058410	21/32	1 9/32	1 21/32	—	0.160	—	1/2 Lean	0.260	0.325	—
	17058412	21/32	1 9/32	1 21/32	—	0.160	—	1/2 Lean	0.260	0.325	—
	17058414	21/32	1 9/32	1 21/32	—	0.160	—	1/2 Lean	0.260	0.325	—
	17058140	7/16	1 5/32	1 19/32	—	0.070	0.110	1 Rich	0.080	0.140	—
	17058143	7/16	1 5/32	1 9/16	—	0.080	0.110	1 Rich	0.080	0.140	—
	17058144	7/16	1 5/32	1 5/8	—	0.060	0.110	1 Rich	0.080	0.140	—
	17058145	7/16	1 5/32	1 19/32	—	0.060	0.110	1 Rich	0.080	0.160	—
	17058148	7/16	1 5/32	1 19/32	—	0.080	0.110	1 Rich	0.080	0.150	—
	17058149	7/16	1 5/32	1 19/32	—	0.080	0.110	1 Rich	0.080	0.150	—
	17058141	7/16	1 5/32	1 19/32	—	0.100	0.140	1 Rich	0.080	0.140	—
	17058147	7/16	1 5/32	1 19/32	—	0.100	0.140	1 Rich	0.080	0.140	—
	17058182	7/16	1 5/32	1 19/32	—	0.080	0.110	1 Rich	0.080	0.140	—
	17058183	7/16	1 5/32	1 19/32	—	0.080	0.110	1 Rich	0.080	0.140	—
	17058444	7/16	1 5/32	1 19/32	—	0.100	0.140	1 Rich	0.080	0.140	—
	17058446	7/16	1 5/32	1 19/32	—	0.110	0.130	1 Rich	0.080	0.140	—
	17058447	7/16	1 5/32	1 19/32	—	0.110	0.150	1 Rich	0.080	0.140	—
	17058448	7/16	1 5/32	1 9/16	—	0.100	0.140	1 Rich	0.080	0.140	—
	17058185	7/16	1 5/32	1 19/32	—	0.050	0.110	1 Rich	0.080	0.140	—
	17058187	7/16	1 5/32	1 19/32	—	0.050	0.110	1 Rich	0.080	0.140	—

2GC, 2GV, 2GE CARBURETOR SPECIFICATIONS
Buick

Year	Carburetor Identification ①	Float Level (in.)	Float Drop (in.)	Pump Rod (in.)	Idle Vent (in.)	Primary Vacuum Break (in.)	Secondary Vacuum Break (in.)	Automatic Choke (notches)	Choke Rod (in.)	Choke Unloader (in.)	Fast Idle Speed (rpm)
1978	17058189	7/16	1 5/32	1 19/32	—	0.080	0.110	1 Rich	0.080	0.140	—
	17058188	7/16	1 5/32	1 5/8	—	0.050	0.120	1 Rich	0.080	0.140	—

① The carburetor identification number is stamped on the float bowl, next to the fuel inlet nut.
② 1¾ in. on Skyhawk.

2GC, 2GV, 2GE CARBURETOR SPECIFICATIONS
Chevrolet

Year	Carburetor Identification ①	Float Level (in.)	Float Drop (in.)	Pump Rod (in.)	Idle Vent (in.)	Primary Vacuum Break (in.)	Secondary Vacuum Break (in.)	Automatic Choke (notches)	Choke Rod (in.)	Choke Unloader (in.)	Fast Idle Speed (rpm)
1975	7045105	19/32	1 7/32	1 19/32	—	0.130	—	—	0.375	0.350	—
	7045106	19/32	1 7/32	1 19/32	—	0.130	—	—	0.380	0.350	—
	7045111	21/32	31/32	1 5/8	—	0.130	—	—	0.400	0.350	—
	7045112	21/32	31/32	1 5/8	—	0.130	—	—	0.400	0.350	—
	7045114	21/32	31/32	1 5/8	—	0.130	—	—	0.400	0.350	—
	7045115	21/32	31/32	1 5/8	—	0.130	—	—	0.400	0.350	—
	7045123	21/32	31/32	1 5/8	—	0.130	—	—	0.400	0.350	—
	7045124	21/32	31/32	1 5/8	—	0.130	—	—	0.400	0.350	—
	7045405	21/32	1 7/32	1 19/32	—	0.130	—	—	0.380	0.350	—
	7045406	21/32	1 7/32	1 19/32	—	0.130	—	—	0.380	0.350	—
1976	17056108	9/16	1 19/32	1 21/32	—	0.140	—	Index	0.260	0.325	—
	17056110	9/16	1 9/32	1 21/32	—	0.140	—	Index	0.260	0.325	—
	17056111	9/16	1 9/32	1 21/32	—	0.140	—	Index	0.260	0.325	—
	17056112	9/16	1 9/32	1 21/32	—	0.140	—	Index	0.260	0.325	—
	17056113	9/16	1 9/32	1 21/32	—	0.140	—	Index	0.260	0.325	—
	17056114	21/32	31/32	1 11/16	—	0.130	—	1 Rich	0.260	0.325	—
	17056430	9/16	1 9/32	1 21/32	—	0.140	—	Index	0.260	0.325	—
	17056432	9/16	1 9/32	1 21/32	—	0.140	—	Index	0.260	0.325	—
1977	17057108, 17057110, 17057111, 17057112, 17057113	9/16	1 9/32	1 21/32	—	0.140	—	Index	0.260	0.325	—
	17057114	21/32	31/32	1 11/16	—	0.130	—	1 Rich	0.260	0.325	—
	17057123	19/32	1 9/32	1 21/32	—	0.160	—	Index	0.260	0.325	—

ROCHESTER CARBURETORS

2GC, 2GV, 2GE CARBURETOR SPECIFICATIONS
Chevrolet

Year	Carburetor Identification ①	Float Level (in.)	Float Drop (in.)	Pump Rod (in.)	Idle Vent (in.)	Primary Vacuum Break (in.)	Secondary Vacuum Break (in.)	Automatic Choke (notches)	Choke Rod (in.)	Choke Unloader (in.)	Fast Idle Speed (rpm)
1977	17057408, 17057410, 17057412, 17057414	$^{21}/_{32}$	$1^9/_{32}$	$1^{21}/_{32}$	—	0.160	—	½ Lean	0.260	0.325	—
1978	17058102	$^{15}/_{32}$	$1^9/_{32}$	$1^{17}/_{32}$	—	0.150	—	Index	0.260	0.325	—
	17058103	$^{15}/_{32}$	$1^9/_{32}$	$1^{17}/_{32}$	—	0.150	—	Index	0.260	0.325	—
	17058104	$^{15}/_{32}$	$1^9/_{32}$	$1^{21}/_{32}$	—	0.160	—	Index	0.260	0.325	—
	17058107	$^{15}/_{32}$	$1^9/_{32}$	$1^{17}/_{32}$	—	0.160	—	Index	0.260	0.325	—
	17058109	$^{15}/_{32}$	$1^9/_{32}$	$1^{17}/_{32}$	—	0.160	—	Index	0.260	0.325	—
	17058404	½	$1^9/_{32}$	$1^{21}/_{32}$	—	0.160	—	½ Lean	0.260	0.325	—
	17058405	½	$1^9/_{32}$	$1^{21}/_{32}$	—	0.160	—	Index	0.260	0.325	—
	17058447	$^7/_{16}$	$1^5/_{32}$	$1^5/_8$	—	0.110	0.150	1 Rich	0.080	0.140	—
	17058143	$^7/_{16}$	$1^5/_{32}$	$1^5/_8$	—	0.040	0.110	1 Rich	0.080	0.140	—
	17058147	$^7/_{16}$	$1^5/_{32}$	$1^5/_8$	—	0.100	0.140	1 Rich	0.080	0.140	—
	17058144	$^7/_{16}$	$1^5/_{32}$	$1^5/_8$	—	0.060	0.110	1 Rich	0.080	0.140	—

① The carburetor identification number is stamped on the float bowl, next to the fuel inlet nut.

2GC, 2GV, 2GE, CARBURETOR SPECIFICATIONS
Chevrolet Vega, Monza

Year	Carburetor Identification ①	Float Level (in.)	Float Drop (in.)	Pump Rod (in.)	Idle Vent (in.)	Primary Vacuum Break (in.)	Secondary Vacuum Break (in.)	Automatic Choke (notches)	Choke Rod (in.)	Choke Unloader (in.)	Fast Idle Speed (rpm)
1975	7045105	$^{19}/_{32}$	$1^7/_{32}$	$1^{19}/_{32}$	—	0.130	—	Index	0.375	0.350	—
	7045405	$^{21}/_{32}$	$1^7/_{32}$	$1^{19}/_{32}$	—	0.130	—	Index	0.380	0.350	—
	7045106	$^{19}/_{32}$	$1^7/_{32}$	$1^{19}/_{32}$	—	0.130	—	Index	0.375	0.350	—
	7045406	$^{21}/_{32}$	$1^7/_{32}$	$1^{19}/_{32}$	—	0.130	—	Index	0.380	0.350	—
1976	17056101	$^{17}/_{32}$	$1^9/_{32}$	$1^5/_8$	—	0.130	—	Index	0.260	0.325	—
	17056102	$^{17}/_{32}$	$1^9/_{32}$	$1^5/_8$	—	0.130	—	Index	0.260	0.325	—
	17056104	$^{17}/_{32}$	$1^5/_{32}$	$1^5/_8$	—	0.140	—	Index	0.260	0.325	—
	17056404	$^9/_{16}$	$1^3/_{16}$	$1^{21}/_{32}$	—	0.140	—	Index	0.260	0.325	—
1977	17057104	$^7/_{16}$	$1^9/_{32}$	$1^{21}/_{32}$	—	0.130	—	Index	0.260	0.325	—
	17057105	½	$1^9/_{32}$	$1^{21}/_{32}$	—	0.150	—	Index	0.260	0.325	—
	17057107	$^7/_{16}$	$1^9/_{32}$	$1^5/_8$	—	0.130	—	Index	0.260	0.325	—
	17057109	½	$1^9/_{32}$	$1^{21}/_{32}$	—	0.160	—	Index	0.260	0.325	—
	17057404	½	$1^9/_{32}$	$1^{21}/_{32}$	—	0.160	—	1 Lean	0.260	0.325	—
	17057405	½	$1^9/_{32}$	$1^{21}/_{32}$	—	0.160	—	½ Lean	0.260	0.325	—
1978	17058102	$^{15}/_{32}$	$1^9/_{32}$	$1^{17}/_{32}$	—	0.150	—	Index	0.260	0.325	—
	17058103	$^{15}/_{32}$	$1^9/_{32}$	$1^{17}/_{32}$	—	0.150	—	Index	0.260	0.325	—

2GC, 2GV, 2GE, CARBURETOR SPECIFICATIONS
Chevrolet Vega, Monza

Year	Carburetor Identification ①	Float Level (in.)	Float Drop (in.)	Pump Rod (in.)	Idle Vent (in.)	Primary Vacuum Break (in.)	Secondary Vacuum Break (in.)	Automatic Choke (notches)	Choke Rod (in.)	Choke Unloader (in.)	Fast Idle Speed (rpm)
1978	17058104	15/32	1 9/32	1 21/32	—	0.160	—	Index	0.260	0.325	—
	17058107	15/32	1 9/32	1 17/32	—	0.160	—	Index	0.260	0.325	—
	17058109	15/32	1 9/32	1 17/32	—	0.160	—	Index	0.260	0.325	—
	17058404	1/2	1 9/32	1 21/32	—	0.160	—	½ Lean	0.260	0.325	—
	17058405	1/2	1 9/32	1 21/32	—	0.160	—	Index	0.260	0.325	—
	17058447	7/16	1 5/32	1 5/8	—	0.110	0.150	1 Rich	0.080	0.140	—
	17058143	7/16	1 5/32	1 5/8	—	0.040	0.110	1 Rich	0.080	0.140	—
	17058147	7/16	1 5/32	1 5/8	—	0.100	0.140	1 Rich	0.080	0.140	—
	17058144	7/16	1 5/32	1 5/8	—	0.060	0.110	1 Rich	0.080	0.140	—

① The carburetor identification number is stamped on the float bowl, next to the fuel inlet nut.

2GC, 2GV, 2GE CARBURETOR SPECIFICATIONS
Oldsmobile

Year	Carburetor Identification ①	Float Level (in.)	Float Drop (in.)	Pump Rod (in.)	Idle Vent (in.)	Primary Vacuum Break (in.)	Secondary Vacuum Break (in.)	Automatic Choke (notches)	Choke Rod (in.)	Choke Unloader (in.)	Fast Idle Speed (rpm)
1975	7045143	15/32	1 9/32	1 19/32	—	0.140	0.120	1 Rich	0.080	0.080	Preset
	7045147	7/16	1 9/32	1 19/32	—	0.120	0.120	1 Lean	0.080	0.140	1800 ②
	7045149	7/16	1 9/32	1 19/32	—	0.120	0.120	1 Rich	0.080	0.140	1800 ②
	7045160	9/16	1 7/32	1 11/32	—	0.145	0.265	1 Rich	0.085	0.180	Preset
	7045161	9/16	1 7/32	1 11/32	—	0.145	0.265	1 Rich	0.085	0.180	Preset
	7045449	7/16	1 9/32	1 19/32	—	0.120	0.120	1 Lean	0.080	0.140	Preset
1976	17056143	15/32	1 5/32	1 11/32	—	0.140	0.100	1 Rich	0.080	0.180	—
	17056145	7/16	1 5/32	1 19/32	—	0.110	0.100	1 Rich	0.080	0.140	—
	17056149	7/16	1 5/32	1 19/32	—	0.120	0.100	1 Rich	0.080	0.140	—
	17056447	7/16	1 5/32	1 19/32	—	0.130	0.110	1 Rich	0.080	0.140	—
	17056449	7/16	1 5/32	1 19/32	—	0.130	0.110	1 Rich	0.080	0.140	—
1977	17057146	7/16	1 5/32	1 9/16	—	0.110	0.110	1 Rich	0.080	0.140	—
	17057148	7/16	1 5/32	1 19/32	—	0.110	0.090	1 Rich	0.080	0.140	—
	17057143	7/16	1 5/32	1 19/32	—	0.130	—	1 Rich	0.080	0.140	—
	17057144	7/16	1 5/32	1 19/32	—	0.130	0.120	1 Rich	0.080	0.140	—
	17057447	7/16	1 5/32	1 19/32	—	0.130	0.100	1 Rich	0.080	0.140	—
	17057445	7/16	1 5/32	1 19/32	—	0.140	0.110	1 Lean	0.080	0.140	—
	17057446	7/16	1 5/32	1 19/32	—	0.130	0.130	1 Rich	0.080	0.140	—
	17057448	7/16	1 5/32	1 19/32	—	0.130	0.110	1 Rich	0.080	0.140	—
	17057104	7/16	1 9/32	1 21/32	—	0.130	—	Index	0.260	0.325	—
	17057105	7/16	1 9/32	1 21/32	—	—	0.130	Index	0.260	0.325	—
	17057107	7/16	1 9/32	1 5/8	—	0.130	—	Index	0.260	0.325	—

ROCHESTER CARBURETORS

2GC, 2GV, 2GE CARBURETOR SPECIFICATIONS
Oldsmobile

Year	Carburetor Identification①	Float Level (in.)	Float Drop (in.)	Pump Rod (in.)	Idle Vent (in.)	Primary Vacuum Break (in.)	Secondary Vacuum Break (in.)	Automatic Choke (notches)	Choke Rod (in.)	Choke Unloader (in.)	Fast Idle Speed (rpm)
1977	17057109	7/16	1 9/32	1 5/8	—	—	0.130	Index	0.260	0.325	—
	17057112	19/32	1 9/32	1 21/32	—	0.130	0.100	Index	0.260	0.325	—
	17057114	19/32	1 9/32	1 21/32	—	—	0.130	Index	0.260	0.325	—
	17057113, 17057123	19/32	1 9/32	1 5/8	—	—	0.130	Index	0.260	0.325	—
	17057404	1/2	1 9/32	1 21/32	—	—	0.140	1 Lean	0.260	0.325	—
	17057405	1/2	1 9/32	1 5/8	—	—	0.140	1 Lean	0.260	0.325	—
1978	17058102	15/32	1 9/32	1 17/32	—	0.130	—	Index	0.260	0.325	—
	17058103	15/32	1 9/32	1 17/32	—	0.130	—	Index	0.260	0.325	—
	17058104	15/32	1 9/32	1 21/32	—	0.130	—	Index	0.260	0.325	—
	17058105	15/32	1 9/32	1 21/32	—	0.130	—	Index	0.260	0.325	—
	17058107	15/32	1 9/32	1 17/32	—	0.130	—	Index	0.260	0.325	—
	17058108	19/32	1 9/32	1 21/32	—	0.130	—	Index	0.260	0.325	—
	17058109	15/32	1 9/32	1 17/32	—	0.130	—	Index	0.260	0.325	—
	17058110	19/32	1 9/32	1 21/32	—	0.130	—	Index	0.260	0.325	—
	17058111	19/32	1 9/32	1 17/32	—	0.130	—	Index	0.260	0.325	—
	17058113	19/32	1 9/32	1 17/32	—	0.130	—	Index	0.260	0.325	—
	17058121	19/32	1 9/32	1 17/32	—	0.130	—	Index	0.260	0.325	—
	17058123	19/32	1 9/32	1 17/32	—	0.130	—	Index	0.260	0.325	—
	17058126	19/32	1 9/32	1 17/32	—	0.130	—	Index	0.260	0.325	—
	17058128	19/32	1 9/32	1 17/32	—	0.130	—	Index	0.260	0.325	—
	17058140	7/16	1 5/32	1 19/32	—	0.070	0.110	1 Rich	0.080	0.140	—
	17058145	7/16	1 5/32	1 19/32	—	0.060	0.110	1 Rich	0.080	0.160	—
	17058147	7/16	1 5/32	1 19/32	—	0.100	0.140	1 Rich	0.080	0.140	—
	17058182	7/16	1 5/32	1 19/32	—	0.080	0.110	1 Rich	0.080	0.140	—
	17058183	7/16	1 5/32	1 19/32	—	0.080	0.110	1 Rich	0.080	0.140	—
	17058185	7/16	1 5/32	1 19/32	—	0.050	0.110	1 Rich	0.080	0.140	—
	17058187	7/16	1 5/32	1 19/32	—	0.080	0.110	1 Rich	0.080	0.140	—
	17058189	7/16	1 5/32	1 19/32	—	0.080	0.110	1 Rich	0.080	0.140	—
	17058404	1/2	1 9/32	1 21/32	—	0.140	—	1/2 Lean	0.260	0.325	—
	17058405	1/2	1 9/32	1 21/32	—	0.140	—	1/2 Lean	0.260	0.325	—
	17058408	21/32	1 9/32	1 21/32	—	0.140	—	1/2 Lean	0.260	0.325	—
	17058410	21/32	1 9/32	1 21/32	—	0.140	—	1/2 Lean	0.260	0.325	—
	17058444	7/16	1 5/32	1 19/32	—	0.100	0.140	1 Rich	0.080	0.140	—
	17058446	7/16	1 5/32	1 19/32	—	0.110	0.130	1 Rich	0.080	0.140	—
	17058447	7/16	1 5/32	1 19/32	—	0.110	0.150	1 Rich	0.080	0.140	—
	17058448	7/16	1 5/32	1 9/16	—	0.100	0.140	1 Rich	0.080	0.140	—

① The carburetor identification is stamped on the float bowl, next to the fuel inlet nut.
② In Park

2GC, 2GV, 2GE CARBURETOR SPECIFICATIONS (Cont'd)

Pontiac

Year	Carburetor Identification ①	Float Level (in.)	Float Drop (in.)	Pump Rod (in.)	Idle Vent (in.)	Primary Vacuum Break (in.)	Secondary Vacuum Break (in.)	Automatic Choke (notches)	Choke Rod (in.)	Choke Unloader (in.)	Fast Idle Speed (rpm)
1975	7045160	9/16	1 7/32	1 3/4	0.025	0.145	0.265	1 Rich	0.085	0.180	—
	7045162	9/16	1 7/32	1 13/16	0.025	0.145	0.260	1 Rich	0.085	0.180	—
	7045171	9/16	1 7/32	1 13/16	0.025	0.145	0.260	1 Rich	0.085	0.180	—
	7045143	15/32	1 7/32	1 13/16	0.025	0.140	0.120	1 Rich	0.080	0.180	—
1976	6-231 Man.	7/16	1 9/32	1 19/32	—	0.110	0.100	1 Rich	0.080	0.140	—
	6-231 Auto.	7/16	1 9/32	1 19/32	—	0.120	0.100	1 Rich	0.080	0.140	—
	6-231 Calif.	7/16	1 9/32	1 19/32	—	0.130	0.110	1 Rich	0.080	0.140	—
	8-350 Ventura	15/32	1 9/32	1 11/32	—	0.140	0.100	1 Rich	0.080	0.180	—
	8-350, 400 Auto.	9/16	1 9/32	1 11/32	—	0.165	0.285	1 Rich	0.085	0.180	—
1977	17057141	7/16	1 5/32	1 5/8	—	0.110	—	1 Rich	0.080	0.140	—
	17057147	7/16	1 5/32	1 5/8	—	0.110	0.090	1 Rich	0.080	0.140	—
	17057143	15/32	1 9/32	1 11/32	—	0.140	—	Index	0.080	0.180	—
	17057144	7/16	1 5/32	1 19/32	—	0.130	0.100	1 Rich	0.080	0.140	—
	17057145	7/16	1 5/32	1 19/32	—	0.110	0.090	1 Rich	0.080	0.140	—
	17057446	7/16	1 3/32	1 19/32	—	0.130	—	1 Rich	0.080	0.140	—
	17057448	7/16	1 5/32	1 19/32	—	0.130	0.110	1 Rich	0.080	0.140	—
	17057447	7/16	1 5/32	1 19/32	—	0.130	0.100	1 Rich	0.080	0.140	—
	17057148	7/16	1 5/32	1 9/16	—	0.110	0.090	1 Rich	0.080	0.140	—
	17057149	7/16	1 5/32	1 9/16	—	0.110	0.040	1 Lean	0.080	0.140	—
	17057445	7/16	1 5/32	1 9/16	—	0.140	0.110	1 Lean	0.080	0.140	—
1978	17058102	19/32	1 9/32	1 17/32	—	0.130	—	Index	0.260	0.325	—
	17058103	19/32	1 9/32	1 17/32	0.130	—	Index	0.260	0.325	—	
	17058108	19/32	1 9/32	1 21/32	—	0.130	—	Index	0.260	0.325	—
	17058110	19/32	1 9/32	1 21/32	—	0.130	—	Index	0.260	0.325	—
	17058111	19/32	1 9/32	1 5/8	—	0.130	—	Index	0.260	0.325	—
	17058112	19/32	1 9/32	1 21/32	—	0.130	—	Index	0.260	0.325	—
	17058113	19/32	1 9/32	1 5/8	—	0.130	—	Index	0.260	0.325	—
	17058114	19/32	1 9/32	1 21/32	—	0.130	—	Index	0.260	0.325	—
	17058121	19/32	1 9/32	1 5/8	—	0.130	—	Index	0.260	0.325	—
	17058123	19/32	1 9/32	1 5/8	—	0.130	—	Index	0.260	0.325	—
	17058126	19/32	1 9/32	1 17/32	—	0.130	—	Index	0.260	0.325	—
	17058128	19/32	1 9/32	1 17/32	—	0.130	—	Index	0.260	0.325	—
	17058145	7/16	1 5/32	1 5/8	—	0.110	0.110	1 Lean	0.080	0.160	—
	17058147	7/16	1 5/32	1 5/8	—	0.140	0.140	1 Rich	0.080	0.140	—
	17058182	7/16	1 5/32	1 5/8	—	0.110	0.110	1 Rich	0.080	0.140	—
	17058183	7/16	1 5/32	1 5/8	—	0.110	0.110	1 Rich	0.080	0.140	—
	17058185	7/16	1 5/32	1 19/32	—	0.110	0.110	1 Rich	0.080	0.140	—

2GC, 2GV, 2GE CARBURETOR SPECIFICATIONS (Cont'd)

Pontiac

Year	Carburetor Identification ①	Float Level (in.)	Float Drop (in.)	Pump Rod (in.)	Idle Vent (in.)	Primary Vacuum Break (in.)	Secondary Vacuum Break (in.)	Automatic Choke (notches)	Choke Rod (in.)	Choke Unloader (in.)	Fast Idle Speed (rpm)
1978	17058187	$7/16$	$1^5/32$	$1^{19}/32$	—	0.110	0.110	1 Rich	0.080	0.140	—
	17058189	$7/16$	$1^5/32$	$1^{19}/32$	—	0.110	0.110	1 Rich	0.080	0.140	—
	17058408	$2^1/32$	$1^9/32$	$1^{21}/32$	—	0.140	0.140	½ Lean	0.260	0.325	—
	17058410	$2^1/32$	$1^9/32$	$1^{21}/32$	—	0.140	0.140	½ Lean	0.260	0.325	—
	17058412	$2^1/32$	$1^9/32$	$1^{21}/32$	—	0.140	0.140	½ Lean	0.260	0.325	—
	17058414	$2^1/32$	$1^9/32$	$1^{21}/32$	—	0.140	0.140	½ Lean	0.260	0.325	—
	17058444	$7/16$	$1^5/32$	$1^5/8$	—	0.140	0.140	1 Rich	0.080	0.140	—
	17058446	$7/16$	$1^5/32$	$1^5/8$	—	0.140	0.140	1 Rich	0.080	0.140	—
	17058447	$7/16$	$1^5/32$	$1^5/8$	—	0.150	0.150	1 Rich	0.080	0.140	—
	17058448	$7/16$	$1^5/32$	$1^5/8$	—	0.140	0.140	1 Rich	0.080	0.140	—

① The carburetor identification number is stamped on the float bowl, next to the fuel inlet nut.

MODEL 2SE, E2SE

The Rochester 2SE and E2SE Varajet II carburetors are two barrel, two stage downdraft units. Most carburetor components are aluminum, although a zinc choke housing is used on four cylinder engines installed in 1980 models. The E2SE is used both in conventional installations and in the Computer Controlled Catalytic Converter System. In that installation the E2SE is equipped with an electrically operated mixture control solenoid, controlled by the Electronic Control Module. The 2SE and E2SE are also used on the AMC four cylinder in 1980–81.

Float Adjustment

1. Remove the air horn from the throttle body.
2. Use your fingers to hold the retainer in place, and to push the float down into light contact with the needle.
3. Measure the distance from the toe of the float (furthest from the hinge) to the top of the carburetor (gasket removed).
4. To adjust, remove the float and gently bend the arm to specification. After adjustment, check the float alignment in the chamber.

Pump Adjustment

1. With the throttle closed and the fast idle screw off the steps of the fast idle cam, measure the distance from the air horn casting to the top of the pump stem.
2. To adjust, remove the retaining screw and washer and remove the pump lever. Bend the end of the lever to correct the stem height. Do not twist the lever or bend it sideways.
3. Install the lever, washer and screw and check the adjustment. When correct, open

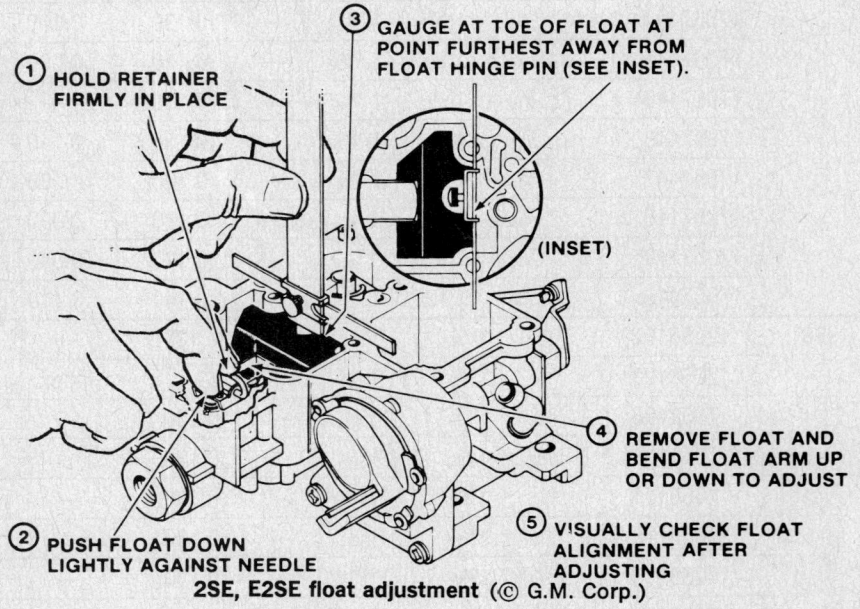

① HOLD RETAINER FIRMLY IN PLACE
② PUSH FLOAT DOWN LIGHTLY AGAINST NEEDLE
③ GAUGE AT TOE OF FLOAT AT POINT FURTHEST AWAY FROM FLOAT HINGE PIN (SEE INSET).
(INSET)
④ REMOVE FLOAT AND BEND FLOAT ARM UP OR DOWN TO ADJUST
⑤ VISUALLY CHECK FLOAT ALIGNMENT AFTER ADJUSTING

2SE, E2SE float adjustment (© G.M. Corp.)

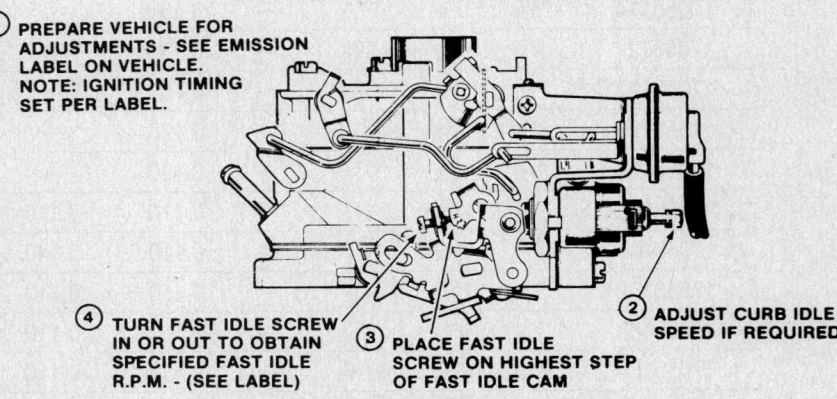

① PREPARE VEHICLE FOR ADJUSTMENTS - SEE EMISSION LABEL ON VEHICLE. NOTE: IGNITION TIMING SET PER LABEL.
② ADJUST CURB IDLE SPEED IF REQUIRED
③ PLACE FAST IDLE SCREW ON HIGHEST STEP OF FAST IDLE CAM
④ TURN FAST IDLE SCREW IN OR OUT TO OBTAIN SPECIFIED FAST IDLE R.P.M. - (SEE LABEL)

2SE, E2SE fast idle adjustment (© G.M. Corp.)

NOTE: ON MODELS USING A CLIP TO RETAIN PUMP ROD IN PUMP LEVER, NO PUMP ADJUSTMENT IS REQUIRED. ON MODELS USING THE "CLIPLESS" PUMP ROD, THE PUMP ADJUSTMENT SHOULD NOT BE CHANGED FROM ORIGINAL FACTORY SETTING UNLESS GAUGING SHOWS OUT OF SPECIFICATION. THE PUMP LEVER IS MADE FROM HEAVY DUTY, HARDENED STEEL MAKING BENDING DIFFICULT. DO NOT REMOVE PUMP LEVER FOR BENDING UNLESS ABSOLUTELY NECESSARY.

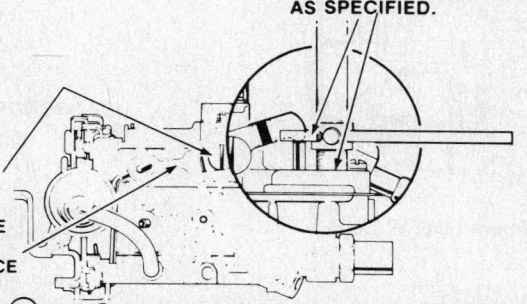

② GAUGE FROM AIR HORN CASTING SURFACE TO TOP OF PUMP STEM. DIMENSION SHOULD BE AS SPECIFIED.

① THROTTLE VALVES COMPLETELY CLOSED. MAKE SURE FAST IDLE SCREW IS OFF STEPS OF FAST IDLE CAM.

③ IF NECESSARY TO ADJUST, REMOVE PUMP LEVER RETAINING SCREW AND WASHER AND REMOVE PUMP LEVER BY ROTATING LEVER TO REMOVE FROM PUMP ROD. PLACE LEVER IN A VISE, PROTECTING LEVER FROM DAMAGE, AND BEND END OF LEVER (NEAREST NECKED DOWN SECTION).

NOTE: DO NOT BEND LEVER IN A SIDEWAYS OR TWISTING MOTION.

⑤ OPEN AND CLOSE THROTTLE VALVES CHECKING LINKAGE FOR FREEDOM OF MOVEMENT AND OBSERVING PUMP LEVER ALIGNMENT.

④ REINSTALL PUMP LEVER, WASHER AND RETAINING SCREW. RECHECK PUMP ADJUSTMENT ① AND ②. TIGHTEN RETAINING SCREW SECURELY AFTER THE PUMP ADJUSTMENT IS CORRECT.

2SE, E2SE pump adjustment (© G.M. Corp.)

and close the throttle a few times to check the linkage movement and alignment.

Fast Idle Adjustment

1. Set the ignition timing and curb idle speed, and disconnect and plug hoses as directed on the emission control decal.
2. Place the fast idle screw on the highest step of the cam.
3. Start the engine and adjust the engine speed to specification with the fast idle screw.

Choke Coil Lever Adjustment

1. Remove the three retaining screws and remove the choke cover and coil. On models with a riveted choke cover, drill out the three rivets and remove the cover and choke coil.

NOTE: A choke stat cover retainer kit is required for reassembly.

2. Place the fast idle screw on the high step of the cam.
3. Close the choke by pushing in on the intermediate choke lever. On front wheel drive V6 models, the intermediate choke lever is behind the choke vacuum diaphragm.
4. Insert a drill or gauge of the specified size into the hole in the choke housing. The choke lever in the housing should be up against the side of the gauge.
5. If the lever does not just touch the

gauge, bend the intermediate choke rod to adjust.

Fast Idle Cam (Choke Rod) Adjustment

NOTE: A special angle gauge should be used.

1. Adjust the choke coil lever and fast idle first.
2. Rotate the degree scale until it is zeroed.
3. Close the choke and install the degree scale onto the choke plate. Center the leveling bubble.
4. Rotate the scale so that the specified degree is opposite the scale pointer.
5. Place the fast idle screw on the second step of the cam (against the high step). Close the choke by pushing in the intermediate lever.
6. Push on the vacuum break lever in the direction of opening choke until the lever is against the rear tang on the choke lever.
7. Bend the fast idle cam rod at the U to adjust angle to specifications.

Air Valve Rod Adjustment

1. Seat the vacuum diaphragm with an outside vacuum source. Tape over the purge bleed hole if present.
2. Close the air valve.
3. Insert the specified gauge between the rod and the end of the slot in the plunger on fours, or between the rod and the end of the slot in the air valve on V6s.
4. Bend the rod to adjust the clearance.

Primary Side Vacuum Break Adjustment

1. Follow Steps 1–4 of the Fast Idle Cam Adjustment.
2. Seat the choke vacuum diaphragm with an outside vacuum source.
3. Push in on the intermediate choke lever to close the choke valve, and hold closed during adjustment.
4. Adjust by bending the vacuum break rod until the bubble is centered.

Electric Choke Setting

This procedure is only for those carburetors with choke covers retained by screws. Riveted choke covers are preset and nonadjustable.

1. Loosen the three retaining screws.
2. Place the fast idle screw on the high step of the cam.
3. Rotate the choke cover to align the cover mark with the specified housing mark.

Secondary Vacuum Break Adjustment

This procedure is for V6 installations in front wheel drive models only.

1. Follow Steps 1–4 of the Fast Idle Cam Adjustment.
2. Seat the choke vacuum diaphragm with an outside vacuum source.
3. Push in on the intermediate choke lever to close the choke valve, and hold closed during adjustment. Make sure the plunger spring is compressed and seated, if present.

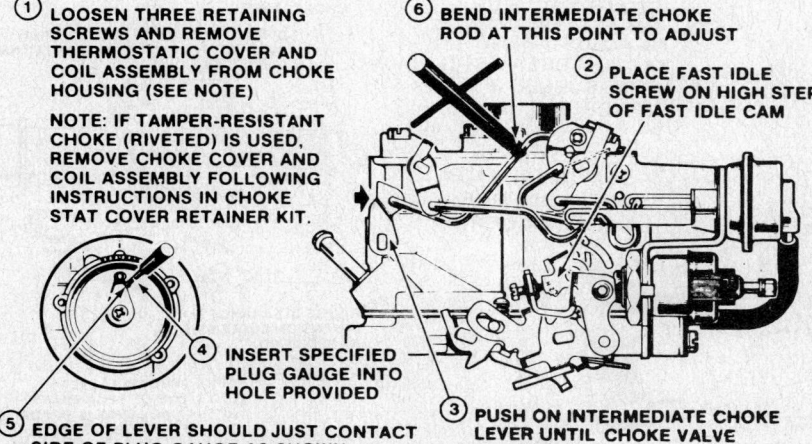

① LOOSEN THREE RETAINING SCREWS AND REMOVE THERMOSTATIC COVER AND COIL ASSEMBLY FROM CHOKE HOUSING (SEE NOTE)

NOTE: IF TAMPER-RESISTANT CHOKE (RIVETED) IS USED, REMOVE CHOKE COVER AND COIL ASSEMBLY FOLLOWING INSTRUCTIONS IN CHOKE STAT COVER RETAINER KIT.

⑥ BEND INTERMEDIATE CHOKE ROD AT THIS POINT TO ADJUST

② PLACE FAST IDLE SCREW ON HIGH STEP OF FAST IDLE CAM

④ INSERT SPECIFIED PLUG GAUGE INTO HOLE PROVIDED

⑤ EDGE OF LEVER SHOULD JUST CONTACT SIDE OF PLUG GAUGE AS SHOWN

③ PUSH ON INTERMEDIATE CHOKE LEVER UNTIL CHOKE VALVE IS CLOSED

2SE, E2SE choke coil lever adjustment (© G.M. Corp.)

ROCHESTER CARBURETORS

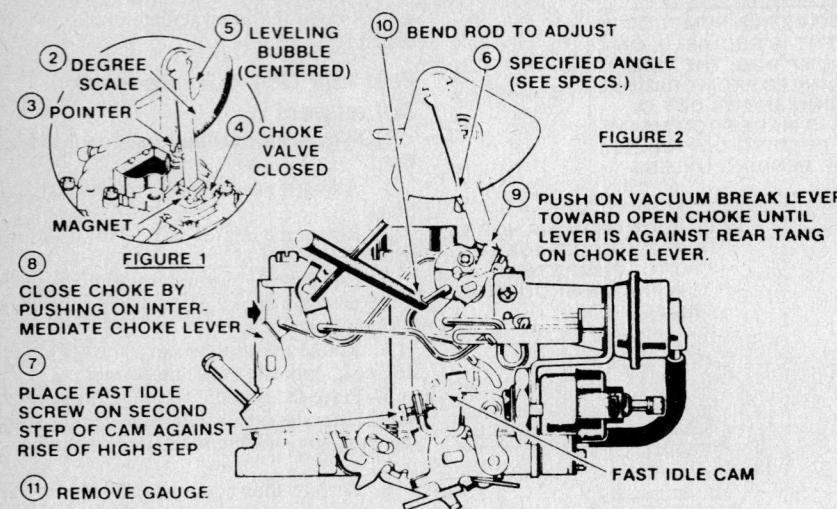

2SE, E2SE fast idle cam adjustment (©G.M. Corp.)

4. Bend the vacuum break rod at the U next to the diaphragm until the bubble is centered.

Choke Unloader Adjustment

1. Follow Steps 1–4 of the Fast Idle Cam Adjustment.
2. Install the choke cover and coil, if removed, aligning the marks on the housing and cover as specified.
3. Hold the primary throttle wide open.
4. If the engine is warm, close the choke valve by pushing in on the intermediate choke lever.
5. Bend the unloader tang until the bubble is centered.

Secondary Lockout Adjustment

1. Pull the choke wide open by pushing out on the intermediate choke lever.
2. Open the throttle until the end of the secondary actuating lever is opposite the toe of the lockout lever.
3. Gauge clearance between the lockout lever and secondary lever should be as specified.
4. To adjust, bend the lockout lever where it contacts the fast idle cam.

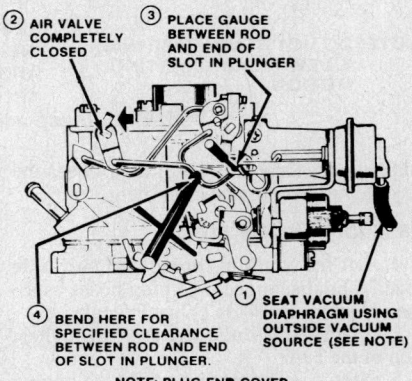

2SE, E2SE air valve rod adjustment
(© G.M. Corp.)

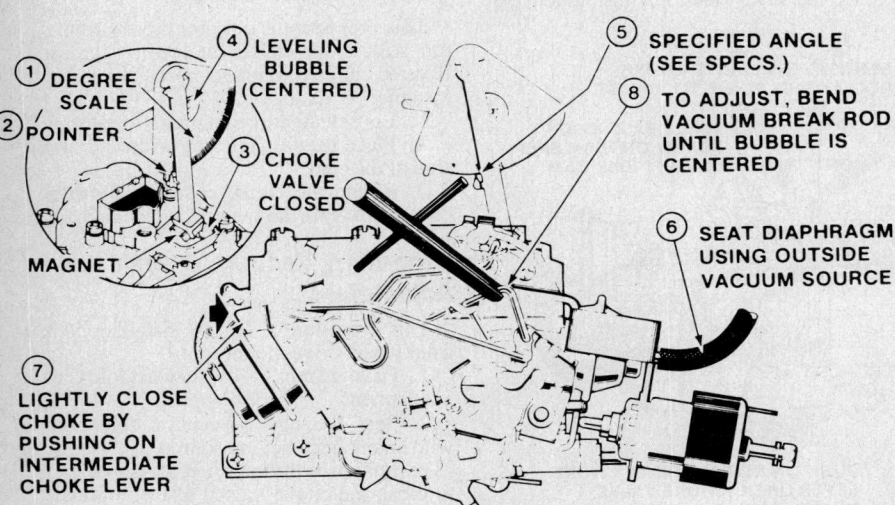

Four cylinder 2SE and E2SE primary vacuum break adustment (© G.M. Corp.)

V6 2SE and E2SE primary vacuum break adjustment (© G.M. Corp.)

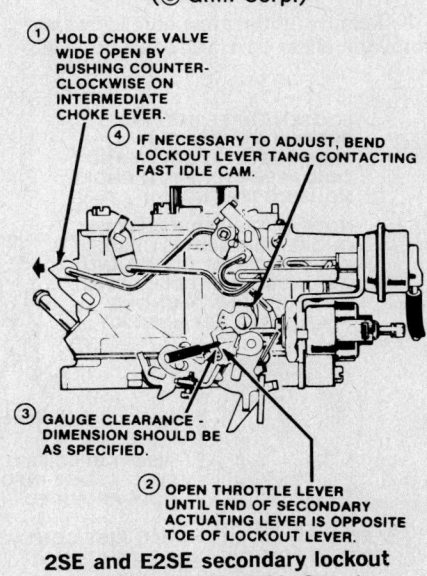

2SE and E2SE secondary lockout adjustment (© G.M. Corp.)

2SE, E2SE CARBURETOR ADJUSTMENTS
American Motors

Year	Carburetor Identification	Float Level (in.)	Pump Rod (in.)	Fast Idle (rpm)	Choke Coil Lever (in.)	Fast Idle Cam (deg./in.)	Air Valve Rod (in.)	Primary Vacuum Break (deg./in.)	Choke Setting (notches)	Choke Unloader (deg./in.)	Secondary Lockout (in.)
1980	17080681	3/16	17/32	2400	.142	18/0.096	.018	20/.110	Fixed	32/.195	N.A.
	17080683	3/16	1/2	2400	.142	18/0.096	.018	20/.110	Fixed	32/.195	N.A.
	17080686	3/16	1/2	2600	.142	18/0.096	.018	20/.110	Fixed	32/.195	N.A.
	17080688	3/16	1/2	2600	.142	18/0.096	0.18	20/.110	Fixed	32/.195	N.A.
1981	17081790	0.256	0.128	2600	0.085	25/0.142	.011	19/.103	Fixed	32/.195	0.065
	17081791	0.256	0.128	2400	0.085	25/0.142	.011	19/.103	Fixed	32/.195	0.065
	17081792	0.256	0.128	2400	0.085	25/0.142	.011	19/.103	Fixed	32/1.95	0.065
	17081794	0.256	0.128	2600	0.085	25/0.142	.011	19/.103	Fixed	32/.195	0.065
	17081795	0.256	0.128	2600	0.085	25/0.142	.011	19/.103	Fixed	32/.195	0.065
	17081796	0.208	0.128	2400	0.065	25/0.142	.011	19/.103	Fixed	32/.1950	.065
	17081797	0.208	0.128	2600	0.085	25/0.142	.011	19/.103	Fixed	32/.195	0.085
	17081793	0.256	0.128	2400	0.085	25/0.142	.011	19/.103	Fixed	32/.195	0.065

N.A.: Not Available

2SE, E2SE CARBURETOR ADJUSTMENTS
Chevrolet Monza

Year	Carburetor Identification	Float Level (in.)	Pump Rod (in.)	Fast Idle (rpm)	Choke Coil Lever (in.)	Fast Idle Cam (deg./in.)	Air Valve Rod (in.)	Primary Vacuum Break (deg./in.)	Choke Setting (notches)	Secondary Vacuum Break (deg./in.)	Choke Unloader (deg./in.)	Secondary Lockout (in.)
1979	17059674	13/64	1/2	2400	.120	18/0.096	.025	19/.103	2 Rich	—	32/.195	.030
	17059675	13/64	17/32	2200	.120	18/0.096	.025	21/.117	1 Rich	—	32/.195	.030
	17059676	13/64	1/2	2400	.120	18/0.096	.025	19/.103	2 Rich	—	32/.195	.030
	17059677	13/64	17/32	2200	.120	18/0.096	.025	21/.117	1 Rich	—	32/.195	.030
1980	All	3/16	1/2	①	.085	18/0.096	0.18	—	Fixed	—	32/.195	.120

① See Underhood Decal

2SE, E2SE CARBURETOR ADJUSTMENTS
Oldsmobile (except Omega)

Year	Carburetor Identification	Float Level (in.)	Pump Rod (in.)	Fast Idle (rpm)	Choke Coil Lever (in.)	Fast Idle Cam (deg./in.)	Air Valve Rod (in.)	Primary Vacuum Break (deg./in.)	Choke Setting (notches)	Secondary Vacuum Break (deg./in.)	Choke Unloader (deg./in.)	Secondary Lockout (in.)
1979	17059674	13/64	1/2	2400	.085	18/0.096	.025	22/.123	2 Rich	—	32/.195	.030
	17059675	13/64	17/32	2200	.085	18/0.096	.025	22/.123	1 Rich	—	32/.195	.030
	17059676	13/64	1/2	2400	.085	18/0.096	.025	22/.123	2 Rich	—	32/.195	.030
	17059677	13/64	17/32	2200	.085	18/0.096	.025	22/.123	1 Rich	—	32/.195	.030
1980	17080674	3/16	1/2	2600	.085	18/0.096	.018	19/.103	Fixed	—	32/.195	.025
	17080675	3/16	1/2	2600	.085	18/0.096	.018	21/.117	Fixed	—	32/.195	.025
	17080676	3/16	1/2	2600	.085	18/0.096	.018	19/.103	Fixed	—	32/.195	.025

ROCHESTER CARBURETORS

2SE, E2SE CARBURETOR ADJUSTMENTS
Oldsmobile (except Omega)

Year	Carburetor Identification	Float Level (in.)	Pump Rod (in.)	Fast Idle (rpm)	Choke Coil Lever (in.)	Fast Idle Cam (deg./in.)	Air Valve Rod (in.)	Primary Vacuum Break (deg./in.)	Choke Setting (notches)	Secondary Vacuum Break (deg./in.)	Choke Unloader (deg./in.)	Secondary Lockout (in.)
1980	17080677	3/16	1/2	2600	.085	18/0.096	.018	21/.117	Fixed	—	32/.195	.025
	17059774	5/32	1/2	①	.085	18/0.096	.018	19/.103	Fixed	—	32/.195	.025
	17059775	5/32	17/32	①	.085	18/0.096	.018	21/.117	Fixed	—	32/.195	.025
	17059776	5/32	1/2	①	.085	18/0.096	.018	19/.103	Fixed	—	32/.195	.025
	17059777	5/32	17/32	①	.085	18/0.096	.018	21/.117	Fixed	—	32/.195	.025

① See Underhood Decal

Pontiac (except Phoenix)

Year	Carburetor Identification	Float Level (in.)	Pump Rod (in.)	Fast Idle (rpm)	Choke boil Lever (in.)	Fast Idle Cam (deg./in.)	Air Valve Rod (in.)	Primary Vacuum Break (deg./in.)	Choke Setting (notches)	Secondary Vacuum Break (deg./in.)	Choke Unloader (deg./in.)	Secondary Lockout (in.)
1979	17059674	3/16	1/2	2400	.120	18/0.096	.025	19/.103	2 Rich	—	32/.195	.01-.04
	17059675	3/16	17/32	2200	.120	18/0.096	.025	21/.117	1 Rich	—	32/.195	.01-.04
	17059676	3/16	1/2	2400	.120	18/0.096	.025	19/.103	2 Rich	—	32/.195	.01-.04
	17059677	3/16	17/32	2200	.120	18/0.096	.025	21/.117	1 Rich	—	32/.195	.01-.04
1980	17080674	3/16	1/2	①	.085	18/0.096	.018	19/.103	Fixed	—	32/.195	.012
	17080675	3/16	1/2	①	.085	18/0.096	.018	21/.117	Fixed	—	32/.195	.012
	17080676	3/16	1/2	①	.085	18/0.096	.018	19/.103	Fixed	—	32/.195	.012
	17080677	3/16	1/2	①	.085	18/0.096	.018	21/.117	Fixed	—	32/.195	.012
	17059774	5/32	1/2	①	.085	18/0.096	.018	19/.103	Fixed	—	32/.195	.012
	17059775	5/32	17/32	①	.085	18/0.096	.018	21/.117	Fixed	—	32/.195	.012
	17059776	5/32	1/2	①	.085	18/0.096	.018	19/.103	Fixed	—	32/.195	.012
	17059777	5/32	17/32	①	.085	18/0.096	.018	21/.117	Fixed	—	32/.195	.012

① See Underhood Decal

Citation, Omega, Phoenix, Skylark

Year	Carburetor Identification	Float Level (in.)	Pump Rod (in.)	Fast Idle (rpm)	Choke Coil Lever (in.)	Fast Idle Cam (deg./in.)	Air Valve Rod (in.)	Primary Vacuum Break (deg./in.)	Choke Setting (notches)	Secondary Vacuum Break (deg./in.)	Choke Unloader (deg./in.)	Secondary Lockout (in.)
1980	17059614	3/16	1/2	2600	.085	18/.096	.025	17/.090	Fixed	—	36/.227	.120
	17059615	3/16	5/32	2600	.085	18/.096	.025	19/.103	Fixed	—	36/.227	.120
	17059616	3/16	1/2	2600	.085	18/.096	.025	17/.090	Fixed	—	36/.227	.120
	17059617	3/16	5/32	2600	.085	18/.096	.025	19/.103	Fixed	—	36/.227	.120
	17059650	3/16	3/32	2000	.085	27/.157	.025	30/.179	Fixed	38/.243	30/.179	.120
	17059651	3/16	3/32	1900	.085	27/.157	.025	22/.123	Fixed	23/.120	30/.179	.120
	17059652	3/16	3/32	2000	.085	27/.157	.025	30/.179	Fixed	38/.243	30/.179	.120
	17059653	3/16	3/32	1900	.085	27/.157	.025	22/.123	Fixed	23/.120	30/.179	.120
	17059714	11/16	5/32	2600	.085	18/.096	.025	23/.129	Fixed	—	32/.195	.120
	17059715	11/16	3/32	2200	.085	18/.096	.025	25/.142	Fixed	—	32/.195	.120

2SE, E2SE CARBURETOR ADJUSTMENTS
Citation, Omega, Phoenix, Skylark

Year	Carburetor Identification	Float Level (in.)	Pump Rod (in.)	Fast Idle (rpm)	Choke Coil Lever (in.)	Fast Idle Cam (deg./in.)	Air Valve Rod (in.)	Primary Vacuum Break (deg./in.)	Choke Setting (notches)	Secondary Vacuum Break (deg./in.)	Choke Unloader (deg./in.)	Secondary Lockout (in.)
1980	17059716	11/16	5/32	2600	.085	18/.096	.025	23/.129	Fixed	—	32/.195	.120
	17059717	11/16	3/32	2200	.085	18/.096	.025	25/.142	Fixed	—	32/.195	.120
	17059760	1/8	5/64	2000	.085	17.5/.093	.025	20/.110	Fixed	33/.203	35/.220	.120
	17059762	1/8	5/64	2000	.085	17.5/.093	.025	20/.110	Fixed	33/.203	35/.220	.120
	17059763	1/8	5/64	2000	.085	17.5/.093	.025	20/.110	Fixed	33/.203	35/.220	.120
	17059618	3/16	1/2	2600	.085	18/.096	.025	17/.090	Fixed	—	36/.227	.120
	17059619	3/16	5/32	2600	.085	18/.096	.025	19/.103	Fixed	—	36/.227	.120
	17059620	3/16	1/2	2600	.085	18/.096	.025	17/.090	Fixed	—	36/.227	.120
	17059621	3/16	5/32	2600	.085	18/.096	.025	19/.103	Fixed	—	36/227	.120
1981	17081650	1/4	Fixed	2600	.085	17/.090	1①	25/.142	Fixed	34/.211	35/.220	.012
	17081651	1/4	Fixed	2400	.085	17/.090	1①	29/.171	Fixed	35/.220	35/.220	.012
	17081652	1/4	Fixed	2600	.085	17/.090	1①	25/.142	Fixed	34/.211	35/.220	.012
	17081653	1/4	Fixed	2600	.085	17/.090	1/z1	29/.171	Fixed	35/.220	35/.220	.012
	17081670	5/32	Fixed	2600	.085	18/.096	1①	19/.103	Fixed	—	32/.195	.012
	17081671	5/32	Fixed	2600	.085	33.5/.207	1①	21/.117	Fixed	—	32/.195	.012
	17081672	5/32	Fixed	2600	.085	18/.096	1①	19/.103	Fixed	—	32/.195	.012
	17081673	5/32	Fixed	2600	.085	33.5/.207	1①	21/.117	Fixed	—	32/.195	.012
	17081740	1/4	Fixed	2400	.085	17/.090	1①	25/.142	Fixed	35/.220	35/.220	.012
	17081742	1/4	Fixed	2400	.085	17/.090	1①	25/.142	Fixed	35/.220	35/.220	.012

① Measurement in degrees

MODEL 2MC, M2MC, M2ME, E2ME

The Rochester model 2MC carburetor is a two-barrel single stage carburetor which incorporates the design features of the primary side of the Rochester Quadrajet four-barrel carburetor. It is used on small displacement V8s. The M2MC version with front and rear vacuum break diaphragms, was introduced in 1977 on the 301 V8.

The Dualjet E2ME Model 210 is a variation of the M2ME, modified for use with the Electronic Fuel Control System (also called the Computer Controlled Catalytic Converter, or C-4, System). An electrically operated mixture control solenoid is mounted in the float bowl. Mixture is thus controlled by the Electronic Control Module, in response to signals from the oxygen sensor mounted in the exhaust system upstream of the catalytic converter.

Float Level Adjustment

See the illustration for float level adjustment for all carburetors. The E2ME procedure is the same except for adjustment (step 4 in the figure). For the E2ME only, if the float level is too high, hold the retainer firmly in place and push down on the center of the float to adjust.

If the float level is too low on the E2ME, lift out the metering rods. Remove the solenoid connector screws. Turn the lean mixture solenoid screw in clockwise, counting the exact number of turns until the screw is lightly bottomed in the bowl. Then turn the screw out counterclockwise and remove it. Lift out the solenoid and connector. Remove the float and bend the arm up to adjust. Install

the parts, installing the mixture solenoid screw in until it is lightly bottomed, then turning it out the exact number of turns counted earlier.

Fast Idle Speed

1. Place the fast idle lever on the high step of the fast idle cam.

2MC, M2MC float level adjustment (© G.M. Corp.)

ROCHESTER CARBURETORS

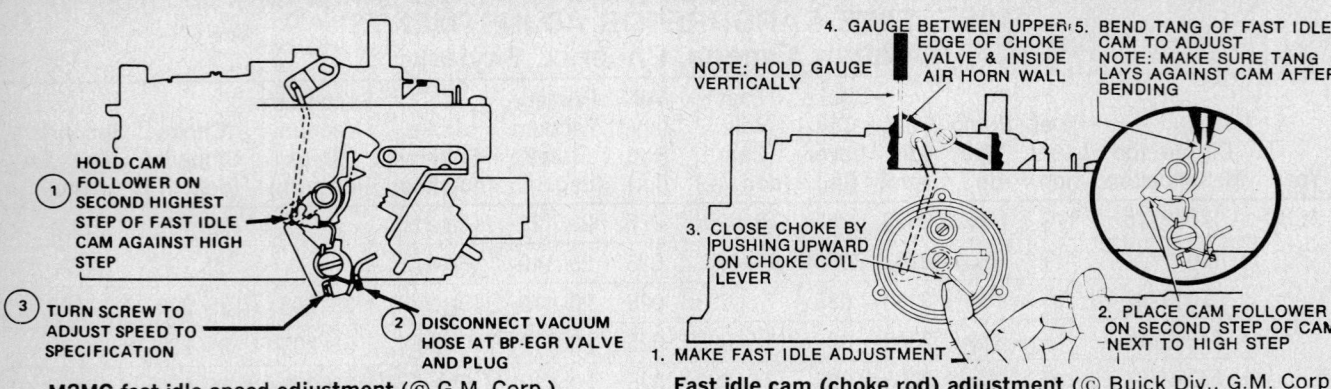

Fast idle cam (choke rod) adjustment (© Buick Div., G.M. Corp.)

M2MC fast idle speed adjustment (© G.M. Corp.)

2. Turn the fast idle screw out until the throttle valves are closed.

3. Turn the screw in to contact the lever, then turn it in three more turns through 1978, or two more turns 1979 and later. Check this preliminary setting against the sticker figure.

Fast Idle Cam (Choke Rod) Adjustment

1. Adjust the fast idle speed.
2. Place the cam follower lever on the second step of the fast idle cam, holding it firmly against the rise of the high step.
3. Close the choke valve by pushing upward on the choke coil lever inside the choke housing, or by pushing up on the vacuum break lever tang.
4. Gauge between the upper edge of the choke valve and the inside of the air horn wall.

5. Bend the tang on the fast idle cam to adjust.

Pump Adjustment

This adjustment is not required on E2ME carburetors used in conjunction with the C-4 system.

1. With the fast idle cam follower off the steps of the fast idle cam, back out the idle speed screw until the throttle valves are completely closed.
2. Place the pump rod in the proper hole of the lever.
3. Measure from the top of the choke valve wall, next to the vent stack, to the top of the pump stem.
4. Bend the pump lever to adjust.

Choke Coil Lever Adjustment

1. Remove the choke cover and thermo-static coil from the choke housing. On models with a fixed choke cover, drill out the rivets and remove the cover. A stat cover kit will be required for assembly.

2. Push up on the coil tang (counterclockwise) until the choke valve is closed. The top of the choke rod should be at the bottom of the slot in the choke valve lever. Place the fast idle cam follower on the high step of the cam.
3. Insert a 0.120 in. plug gauge in the hole in the choke housing.
4. The lower edge of the choke coil lever should just contact the side of the plug gauge.
5. Bend the choke rod to adjust.

2MC Lean/Rich Vacuum Break Adjustment

1. Place the cam follower on the highest step of the fast idle cam.

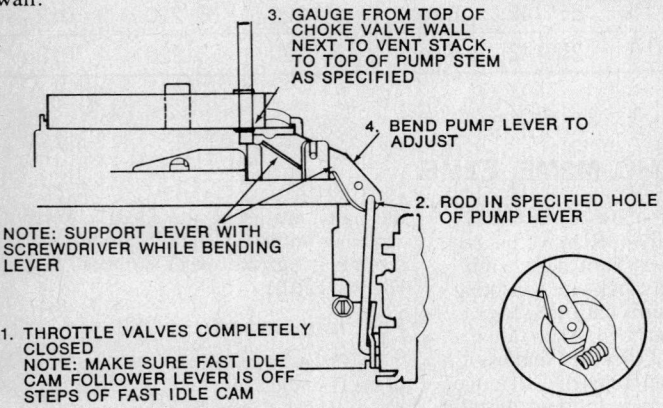

Pump adjustment (© Buick Div., G.M. Corp.)

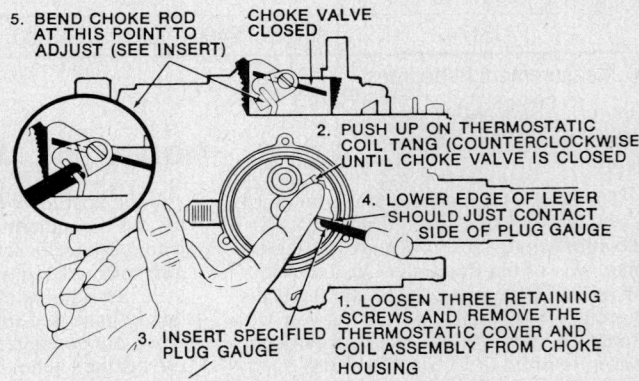

Choke coil lever adjustment (© Buick Div., G.M. Corp.)

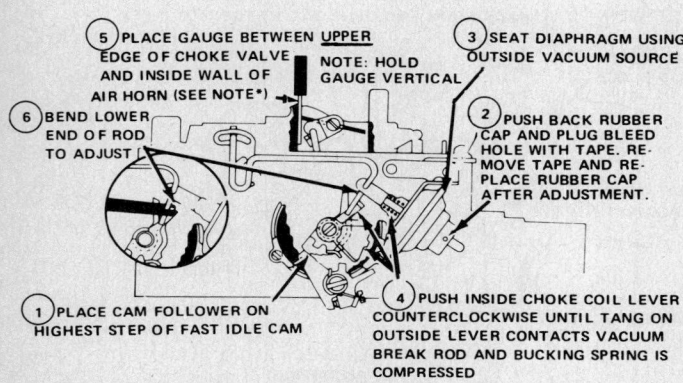

2MC rich vacuum break setting (© Oldsmobile Div., G.M. Corp.)

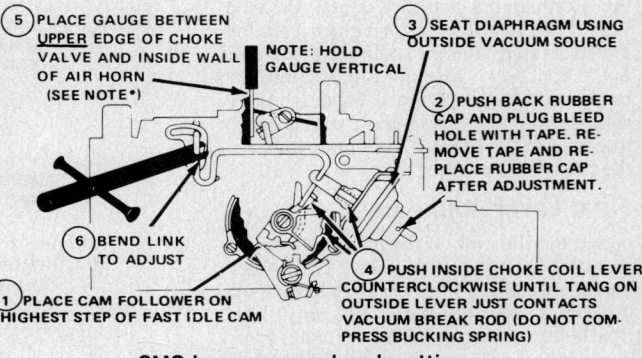

2MC lean vacuum break setting (© Oldsmobile Div., G.M. Corp.)

2. Seat the vacuum break diaphragm by using an outside vacuum source. Tape over the bleed hole, if any, under the rubber cover on the diaphragm.

3. Remove the choke cover and thermostatic coil and push up on the coil lever inside the choke housing until the tang on the vacuum break lever contacts the tang on the vacuum break plunger stem. Do not compress the bucking spring for lean adjustment. Compress the bucking spring for rich adjustment.

4. With the choke rod in the bottom of the slot in the choke lever, gauge between the upper edge of the choke valve and the inside wall of the air horn.

5. Bend the link rod at the vacuum break plunger stem to adjust the rich setting. Bend the link rod at the opposite end from the diaphragm to adjust the lean setting.

M2MC, M2ME, E2ME

Front/Rear Vacuum Break Adjustment

1. Seat the front diaphragm, using an outside vacuum source. If there is an air bleed hole on the diaphragm, tape it over.

2. Remove the choke cover and coil. Rotate the inside coil lever counter-clockwise. On models with a fixed choke cover, push up on the vacuum break lever tang and hold it in position with a rubber band.

3. Check that the specified gap is present between the top of the choke valve and the air horn wall.

4. Turn the front vacuum break adjusting screw to adjust.

5. To adjust the rear vacuum break diaphragm, perform Steps 1–3 on the rear diaphragm, but make sure that the plunger bucking spring is compressed and seated in Step 2. Adjust by bending the link at the bend nearest the diaphragm.

Unloader Adjustment

1. With the choke valve completely

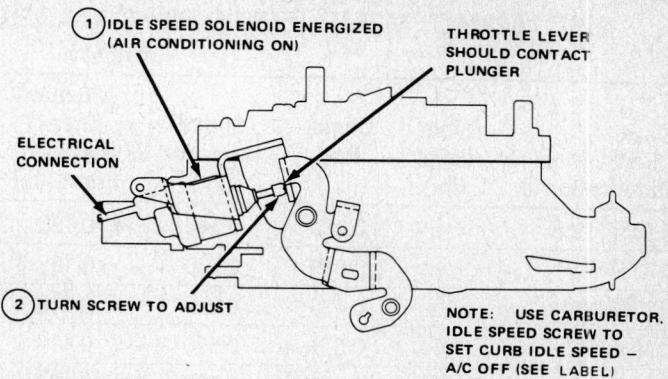

2MC, M2MC air conditioning idle speed-up solenoid adjustment
(© Oldsmobile Div., G.M. Corp.)

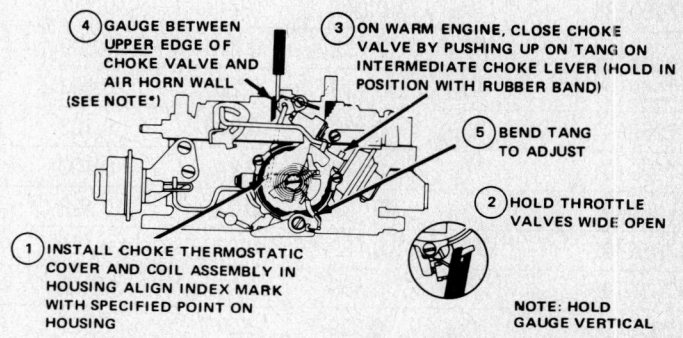

2MC, M2MC unloader adjustment (© G.M. Corp.)

closed, hold the throttle valves wide open.

2. Measure between the upper edge of the choke valve and air horn wall.

3. Bend the tang on the fast idle lever to obtain the proper measurement.

Air Conditioning Idle Speed-Up Solenoid Adjustment

1. With the engine at normal operating temperature and the air conditioning turned on but the compressor clutch lead disconnected, the solenoid should be electrically energized (plunger stem extended). Open the throttle slightly to allow the solenoid plunger to fully extend.

2. Adjust the plunger screw to obtain the specified idle speed.

3. Turn off the air conditioner. The solenoid plunger should move away from the tang on the throttle lever.

4. Adjust the curb idle speed with the idle speed screw, if necessary.

2MC, M2MC, M2ME, E2ME E2MC CARBURETOR SPECIFICATIONS
Buick

Year	Carburetor Identification ①	Float Level (in.)	Choke Rod (in.)	Choke Unloader (in.)	Vacuum Break Lean or Front (in.)	Vacuum Break Rich or Rear (in.)	Pump Rod (in.)	Choke Coil Lever (in.)	Automatic Choke (notches)
1975	7045156	5/32	0.130	0.285	0.235	0.150	9/32 ②	0.120	1 Rich
	7045248	5/32	0.130	0.285	0.235	0.150	9/32 ②	0.120	1 Rich
	7045358	3/16	0.130	0.285	0.300	0.150	5/16 ③	0.120	1 Rich
	7045354	3/16	0.130	0.285	0.300	0.150	5/16 ③	0.120	1 Rich
1976	17056156	1/8	0.105	0.210	0.175	0.110	9/32 ②	0.120	1 Rich
	17056158	1/8	0.105	0.210	0.175	0.110	9/32 ②	0.120	1 Rich
	17056458	1/8	0.105	0.210	0.175	0.110	3/16 ③	0.120	1 Rich
	17056454	1/8	0.105	0.210	0.175	0.110	3/16 ③	0.120	1 Rich

ROCHESTER CARBURETORS

2MC, M2MC, M2ME, E2ME E2MC CARBURETOR SPECIFICATIONS
Buick

Year	Carburetor Identification [1]	Float Level (in.)	Choke Rod (in.)	Choke Unloader (in.)	Vacuum Break Lean or Front (in.)	Vacuum Break Rich or Rear (in.)	Pump Rod (in.)	Choke Coil Lever (in.)	Automatic Choke (notches)
1977	17057172	11/32	0.075	0.240	0.135	0.240	3/8 [3]	0.120	2 Rich
	17057173	11/32	0.075	0.240	0.165	0.240	3/8 [3]	0.120	2 Rich
1978	17058160	11/32	0.133	0.220	0.149	0.227	1/4 [3]	0.120	2 Lean
	17058192	1/4	0.074	0.350	0.117	0.103	9/32 [2]	0.120	1 Rich
	17058496	1/4	0.077	0.243	0.136	0.211	3/8 [3]	0.120	1 Rich
1979	17059134	15/32	0.243	0.243	0.157	—	1/4	0.120	1 Lean
	17059136	15/32	0.243	0.243	0.157	—	1/4	0.120	1 Lean
	17059193	13/32	0.139	0.220	0.103	0.090	1/4 [2]	0.120	2 Rich
	17059194	11/32	0.139	0.220	0.103	0.090	1/4 [2]	0.120	2 Rich
	17059190	11/32	0.139	0.243	0.103	0.090	1/4 [2]	0.120	2 Rich
	17059191	11/32	0.139	0.243	0.103	0.090	9/32 [2]	0.120	2 Rich
	17059491	11/32	0.139	0.277	0.129	0.117	9/32 [2]	0.120	1 Rich
	17059492	11/32	0.139	0.277	0.129	0.117	9/32 [2]	0.120	1 Rich
	17059196	11/32	0.139	0.277	0.129	0.117	1/4 [2]	0.120	1 Rich
	17059498	11/32	0.139	0.277	0.129	0.117	9/32 [2]	0.120	2 Rich
	17059180	11/32	0.139	0.243	0.103	0.090	1/4 [2]	0.120	2 Rich
	17059184	11/32	0.139	0.220	0.103	0.090	1/4 [2]	0.120	2 Rich
	17059496	5/16	0.139	0.243	0.117	0.179	3/8 [2]	0.120	2 Rich
1980	17080496	5/16	0.139	0.243	0.117	0.203	3/8	0.120	Fixed
	17080498	5/16	0.139	0.243	0.117	0.203	3/8	0.120	Fixed
	17080490	5/16	0.139	0.243	0.117	0.203	3/8	0.120	Fixed
	17080492	5/16	0.139	0.243	0.117	0.203	3/8	0.120	Fixed
	17080491	5/16	0.139	0.243	0.117	0.220	3/8	0.120	Fixed
	17080190	9/32	0.139	0.243	0.123	0.110	1/4 [2]	0.120	Fixed
	17080191	11/32	0.139	0.243	0.096	0.096	1/4 [2]	0.120	Fixed
	17080195	9/32	0.139	0.243	0.103	0.071	1/4 [2]	0.120	Fixed
	17080197	9/32	0.139	0.243	0.103	0.071	1/4 [2]	0.120	Fixed
	17080192	9/32	0.139	0.243	0.123	0.110	1/4 [2]	0.120	Fixed
	17080160	5/16	0.074	0.239	0.168	0.207	1/4 [2]	0.120	Fixed
1981	17080491	5/16	0.139	0.243	0.117	0.220	Fixed	0.120	Fixed
	17080496	5/16	0.139	0.243	0.117	0.203	Fixed	0.120	Fixed
	17080498	5/16	0.139	0.243	0.117	0.203	Fixed	0.120	Fixed
	17081130	11/32	0.110	0.243	0.142	—	Fixed	0.120	Fixed
	17081131	11/32	0.110	0.243	0.142	—	Fixed	0.120	Fixed
	17081132	11/32	0.110	0.243	0.142	—	Fixed	0.120	Fixed
	17081133	11/32	0.110	0.243	0.142	—	Fixed	0.120	Fixed
	17081138	11/32	0.110	0.260	0.142	—	Fixed	0.120	Fixed
	17081140	11/32	0.110	0.260	0.142	—	Fixed	0.120	Fixed

ROCHESTER CARBURETORS

2MC, M2MC, M2ME, E2ME E2MC CARBURETOR SPECIFICATIONS
Buick

Year	Carburetor Identification ①	Float Level (in.)	Choke Rod (in.)	Choke Unloader (in.)	Vacuum Break Lean or Front (in.)	Vacuum Break Rich or Rear (in.)	Pump Rod (in.)	Choke Coil Lever (in.)	Automatic Choke (notches)
1981	17081160	11/32	0.074	0.220	0.136	0.234	Fixed	0.120	Fixed
	17081190	5/16	0.139	0.243	0.117	0.187	Fixed	0.120	Fixed
	17081191	5/16	0.139	0.243	0.164	0.136	Fixed	0.120	Fixed
	17081192	3/8	0.139	0.243	0.164	0.136	Fixed	0.120	Fixed
	17081193	5/16	0.139	0.243	0.117	0.187	Fixed	0.120	Fixed
	17081194	5/16	0.139	0.243	0.117	0.179	Fixed	0.120	Fixed
	17081196	5/16	0.139	0.243	0.164	0.136	Fixed	0.120	Fixed
	17081197	3/8	0.096	0.243	0.164	0.136	Fixed	0.120	Fixed
	17081198	3/8	0.139	0.243	0.164	0.136	Fixed	0.120	Fixed
	17081150	13/32	0.071	0.220	0.136	0.227	Fixed	0.120	Fixed
	17081152	13/32	0.071	0.220	0.136	0.227	Fixed	0.120	Fixed

2MC, M2MC, M2ME, E2ME CARBURETOR SPECIFICATIONS
Chevrolet (except Monza)

Year	Carburetor Identification ①	Float Level (in.)	Choke Rod (in.)	Choke Unloader (in.)	Vacuum Break Lean or Front (in.)	Vacuum Break Rich or Rear (in.)	Pump Rod (in.)	Choke Coil Lever (in.)	Automatic Choke (notches)
1978	All	1/4	0.314	0.314	0.136	—	9/32 ②	0.120	Index
1979	17059180	11/32	0.139	0.243	0.103	0.090	1/4 ②	0.120	1 Lean
	17059190	11/32	0.139	0.243	0.103	0.090	1/4 ②	0.120	1 Lean
	17059196	11/32	0.139	0.277	0.129	0.117	1/4 ②	0.120	1 Lean
	17059134	13/32	0.243	0.243	0.157	—	1/4 ②	0.120	1 Lean
	17059135	13/32	0.243	0.243	0.157	—	1/4 ②	0.120	1 Lean
	17059136	13/32	0.243	0.243	0.157	—	1/4 ②	0.120	1 Lean
	17059137	13/32	0.243	0.243	0.157	—	1/4 ②	0.120	1 Lean
	17059434	13/32	0.243	0.243	0.171	—	1/4 ②	0.120	1 Lean
	17059436	13/32	0.243	0.243	0.171	—	1/4 ②	0.120	1 Lean
	17059130	9/32	0.243	0.243	0.157	—	1/4 ②	0.120	Index
	17059131	9/32	0.243	0.243	0.157	—	1/4 ②	0.120	Index
	17059132	9/32	0.243	0.243	0.157	—	1/4 ②	0.120	1 Lean
	17059133	9/32	0.243	0.243	0.157	—	1/4 ②	0.120	1 Lean
	17059138	9/32	0.243	0.243	0.164	—	1/4 ②	0.120	1 Lean
	17059139	9/32	0.243	0.243	0.164	—	1/4 ②	0.120	1 Lean
	17059140	9/32	0.243	0.243	0.164	—	1/4 ②	0.120	1 Lean
	17059141	9/32	0.243	0.243	0.164	—	1/4 ②	0.120	1 Lean
	17059430	9/32	0.243	0.243	0.157	—	1/4 ②	0.120	1 Lean
	17059432	9/32	0.243	0.243	0.157	—	1/4 ②	0.120	1 Lean
	17059496	5/16	0.139	0.243	0.117	0.179	3/8 ②	0.120	2 Rich

ROCHESTER CARBURETORS

2MC, M2MC, M2ME, E2ME CARBURETOR SPECIFICATIONS
Chevrolet (except Monza)

Year	Carburetor Identification ①	Float Level (in.)	Choke Rod (in.)	Choke Unloader (in.)	Vacuum Break Lean or Front (in.)	Vacuum Break Rich or Rear (in.)	Pump Rod (in.)	Choke Coil Lever (in.)	Automatic Choke (notches)
1980	17080108	3/8	0.243	0.243	0.142	—	5/16 ②	0.120	Fixed
	17080110	3/8	0.243	0.243	0.142	—	5/16 ②	0.120	Fixed
	17080130	5/16	0.243	0.243	0.142	—	5/16 ②	0.120	Fixed
	17080131	5/16	0.243	0.243	0.142	—	5/16 ②	0.120	Fixed
	17080132	5/16	0.243	0.243	0.142	—	5/16 ②	0.120	Fixed
	17080133	5/16	0.243	0.243	0.142	—	5/16 ②	0.120	Fixed
	17080138	3/8	0.243	0.243	0.142	—	5/16 ②	0.120	Fixed
	17080140	3/8	0.243	0.243	0.142	—	5/16 ②	0.120	Fixed
	17080493	5/16	0.139	0.243	0.117	0.179	Fixed	0.120	Fixed
	17080495	5/16	0.139	0.243	0.117	0.179	Fixed	0.120	Fixed
	17080496	5/16	0.139	0.243	0.117	0.203	Fixed	0.120	Fixed
	17080498	5/16	0.139	0.243	0.117	0.203	Fixed	0.120	Fixed
1981	17080185	9/32	0.139	0.243	0.103	0.071	1/4	0.120	Fixed
	17080187	9/32	0.139	0.243	0.103	0.071	1/4	0.120	Fixed
	17080191	9/32	0.139	0.243	0.096	0.096	1/4	0.120	Fixed
	17080496	5/16	0.139	0.243	0.117	0.203	Fixed	0.120	Fixed
	17080498	5/16	0.139	0.243	0.117	0.203	Fixed	0.120	Fixed
	17081130	3/8	0.110	0.243	0.142	—	Fixed	0.120	Fixed
	17081131	3/8	0.110	0.243	0.142	—	Fixed	0.120	Fixed
	17081132	3/8	0.110	0.243	0.142	—	Fixed	0.120	Fixed
	17081133	3/8	0.110	0.243	0.142	—	Fixed	0.120	Fixed
	17081138	3/8	0.110	0.260	0.142	—	Fixed	0.120	Fixed
	17081140	3/8	0.110	0.260	0.142	—	Fixed	0.120	Fixed
	17081191	5/16	0.139	0.243	0.139	0.136	Fixed	0.120	Fixed
	17081192	5/16	0.139	0.243	0.139	0.136	Fixed	0.120	Fixed
	17081194	5/16	0.139	0.243	0.139	0.136	Fixed	0.120	Fixed
	17081196	5/16	0.139	0.243	0.139	0.136	Fixed	0.120	Fixed
	17081197	5/16	0.096	0.243	0.096	0.136	Fixed	0.120	Fixed
	17081198	3/8	0.139	0.243	0.139	0.136	Fixed	0.120	Fixed
	17081199	3/8	0.096	0.243	0.096	0.136	Fixed	0.120	Fixed
	17080491	5/16	0.139	0.243	0.117	0.220	Fixed	0.120	Fixed

Chevrolet Monza

Year	Carburetor Identification ①	Float Level (in.)	Choke Rod (in.)	Choke Unloader (in.)	Vacuum Break Lean or Front (in.)	Vacuum Break Rich or Rear (in.)	Pump Rod (in.)	Choke Coil Lever (in.)	Automatic Choke (notches)
1980	17080191	11/32	0.139	0.243	0.096	0.096	1/4 ②	0.120	Fixed
	17080195	9/32	0.139	0.243	0.103	0.090	1/4 ②	0.120	Fixed
	17080197	9/32	0.139	0.243	0.103	0.090	1/4 ②	0.120	Fixed
	17080491	5/16	0.139	0.243	0.117	—	3/8	0.120	Fixed
	17080496	5/16	0.139	0.243	0.117	0.203	3/8	0.120	Fixed
	17080498	5/16	0.139	0.243	0.117	0.203	3/8	0.120	Fixed

2MC, M2MC, M2ME, E2ME CARBURETOR SPECIFICATIONS
Oldsmobile

Year	Carburetor Identification ①	Float Level (in.)	Choke Rod (in.)	Choke Unloader (in.)	Vacuum Break Lean or Front (in.)	Vacuum Break Rich or Rear (in)	Pump Rod (in.)	Choke Coil Lever (in.)	Automatic Choke (notches)
1975	7045297	3/16	0.130	0.300	0.300	0.150	9/32 ②	0.120	1 Rich
	7045354	3/16	0.130	0.300	0.300	0.150	5/16 ③	0.120	1 Rich
	7045358	3/16	0.130	0.300	0.300	0.150	5/16 ③	0.120	1 Rich
	7045156	5/32	0.130	0.300	0.300	0.150	9/32 ②	0.120	1 Rich
	7045598	5/32	0.130	0.300	0.300	0.150	3/16 ②	0.120	Index
	7045298	5/32	0.130	0.300	0.300	0.150	3/16 ②	0.120	1 Rich
	7045356	5/32	0.130	0.300	0.300	0.150	3/16 ②	0.120	Index
1976	17056156	1/8	0.105	0.210	0.175	0.110	9/32 ②	0.120	1 Rich
	17056157	1/8	0.105	0.210	0.175	0.110	3/16 ③	0.120	1 Rich
	17056158	1/8	0.105	0.210	0.175	0.110	9/32 ②	0.120	1 Rich
	17056454	1/8	0.105	0.210	0.210	0.110	3/16 ③	0.120	1 Rich
	17056455	1/8	0.120	0.210	0.210	0.130	9/32 ②	0.120	1 Rich
	17056456	1/8	0.105	0.210	0.210	0.110	3/16 ③	0.120	Index
	17056457	1/8	0.105	0.210	0.245	0.110	3/16 ③	0.120	Index
	17056458	1/8	0.105	0.210	0.210	0.110	3/16 ③	0.120	1 Rich
	17056459	1/8	0.105	0.210	0.210	0.110	3/16 ③	0.120	Index
1977	17057150, 17057151	1/8	0.085	0.190	0.160	0.090	11/32 ③	0.120	2 Rich
	17057157	1/8	0.090	0.190	0.190	0.100	3/8 ③	0.120	1 Rich
	17057156, 17057158	1/8	0.085	0.190	0.160	0.090	11/32 ③	0.120	1 Rich
1978	17058150	3/8	0.065	0.203	0.203	0.133	1/4 ②	0.120	2 Rich
	17058151	3/8	0.065	0.203	0.229	0.133	11/32 ③	0.120	2 Rich
	17058152	3/8	0.065	0.203	0.203	0.133	1/4 ②	0.120	2 Rich
	17058154	3/8	0.065	0.203	0.146	0.245	11/32 ③	0.120	2 Rich
	17058155	3/8	0.065	0.203	0.146	0.245	11/32 ③	0.120	2 Rich
	17058156	3/8	0.065	0.203	0.229	0.133	11/32 ③	0.120	2 Rich
	17058158	3/8	0.065	0.203	0.229	0.133	11/32 ③	0.120	2 Rich
	17058450	3/8	0.065	0.203	0.146	0.289	11/32 ③	0.120	2 Rich
1979	17059134	15/32	0.243	0.243	0.157	—	1/4 ②	0.120	1 Lean
	17059135	15/32	0.243	0.243	0.157	—	1/4 ②	0.120	1 Lean
	17059136	15/32	0.243	0.243	0.157	—	1/4 ②	0.120	1 Lean
	17059137	15/32	0.243	0.243	0.157	—	1/4 ②	0.120	1 Lean
	17059150	3/8	0.071	0.220	0.195	0.129	1/4 ②	0.120	2 Rich
	17059151	3/8	0.071	0.220	0.243	0.142	11/32 ③	0.120	2 Rich
	17059152	3/8	0.071	0.220	0.195	0.129	1/4 ②	0.120	2 Rich
	17059154	3/8	0.071	0.220	0.157	0.260	11/32 ③	0.120	2 Rich
	17059160	11/32	0.110	0.195	0.129	0.187	1/4 ②	0.120	2 Rich
	17059430	9/32	0.243	0.243	0.157	—	9/32	0.120	1 Lean

ROCHESTER CARBURETORS

2MC, M2MC, M2ME, E2ME CARBURETOR SPECIFICATIONS
Oldsmobile

Year	Carburetor Identification ①	Float Level (in.)	Choke Rod (in.)	Choke Unloader (in.)	Vacuum Break Lean or Front (in.)	Vacuum Break Rich or Rear (in)	Pump Rod (in.)	Choke Coil Lever (in.)	Automatic Choke (notches)
1979	17059432	9/32	0.243	0.243	0.157	—	9/32	0.120	1 Lean
	17059450	3/8	0.071	0.220	0.157	—	11/32 ③	0.120	2 Rich
	17059180	11/32	0.039	0.243	0.103	0.090	1/4 ②	0.120	2 Rich
	17059190	11/32	0.039	0.243	0.103	0.090	1/4 ②	0.120	2 Rich
	17059191	11/32	0.039	0.243	0.103	0.090	9/32 ②	0.120	2 Rich
	17059196	11/32	0.039	0.277	0.129	0.117	1/4 ②	0.120	1 Rich
	17059491	11/32	0.039	0.277	0.129	0.117	9/32 ②	0.120	1 Rich
	17059492	11/32	0.039	0.277	0.129	0.117	9/32 ②	0.120	1 Rich
	17059498	11/32	0.039	0.277	0.129	0.117	9/32 ②	0.120	2 Rich
1980	17080150	3/8	0.071	0.220	0.243	0.157	11/32 ③	0.120	Fixed
	17080152	3/8	0.071	0.220	0.243	0.157	11/32 ③	0.120	Fixed
	17080153	3/8	0.071	0.220	0.243	0.157	11/32 ③	0.120	Fixed
	17080190	9/32	0.139	0.243	0.123	0.110	1/4 ②	0.120	Fixed
	17080191	11/32	0.139	0.243	0.096	0.096	1/4 ②	0.120	Fixed
	17080192	9/32	0.139	0.243	0.123	0.110	1/4 ②	0.120	Fixed
	17080195	9/32	0.139	0.243	0.103	0.071	1/4 ②	0.120	Fixed
	17080197	9/32	0.139	0.243	0.103	0.071	1/4 ②	0.120	Fixed
	17080491	5/16	0.139	0.243	0.117	0.220	Fixed	0.120	Fixed
	17080493	5/16	0.139	0.243	0.117	0.179	Fixed	0.120	Fixed
	17080495	5/16	0.139	0.243	0.117	0.179	Fixed	0.120	Fixed
	17080496	5/16	0.139	0.243	0.117	0.203	Fixed	0.120	Fixed
	17080498	5/16	0.139	0.243	0.117	0.203	Fixed	0.120	Fixed
1981	17081191	5/16	0.139	0.243	0.164	0.136	⑤	0.120	Fixed
	17081192	5/16	0.139	0.243	0.117	0.179	⑤	0.120	Fixed
	17081194	5/16	0.139	0.243	0.117	0.179	⑤	0.120	Fixed
	17081196	5/16	0.139	0.243	0.117	0.220	⑤	0.120	Fixed
	17081197	5/16	0.139	0.243	0.117	0.179	⑤	0.120	Fixed
	17081198	3/8	0.139	0.243	0.164	0.136	⑤	0.120	Fixed
	17081150	13/32	0.071	0.220	0.136	0.227	⑤	0.120	Fixed
	17081152	13/32	0.071	0.220	0.136	0.227	⑤	0.120	Fixed

2MC, M2MC, M2ME, E2ME, E2MC CARBURETOR SPECIFICATIONS
Pontiac

Year	Carburetor Identification	Float Level (in.)	Choke Rod (in.)	Choke Unloader (in.)	Vacuum Break Lean or Front (in.)	Vacuum Break Rich or Rear (in)	Pump Rod (in.)	Choke Coil Lever (in.)	Automatic Choke (notches)
1975	7045156	5/32	0.130	0.275	0.230	0.150	9/32 ②	0.120	1 Rich
	7045297	3/16	0.130	0.275	0.275	0.180	9/32 ②	0.120	1 Rich
	7045298	5/32	0.130	0.275	0.275	0.150	9/32 ②	0.120	1 Rich
	7045598	5/32	0.160	0.275	0.230	0.150	9/32 ②	0.120	1 Rich
	7045356	5/32	0.160	0.275	0.275	0.180	9/32 ②	0.120	1 Rich

2MC, M2MC, M2ME, E2ME, E2MC CARBURETOR SPECIFICATIONS
Pontiac

Year	Carburetor Identification①	Float Level (in.)	Choke Rod (in.)	Choke Unloader (in.)	Vacuum Break Lean or Front (in.)	Vacuum Break Rich or Rear (in)	Pump Rod (in.)	Choke Coil Lever (in.)	Automatic Choke (notches)
1976	8-260 Man.	1/8	0.105	0.210	0.175	0.110	3/16③	0.120	1 Rich
	8-260 Auto.	1/8	0.105	0.210	0.175	0.110	9/32②	0.120	1 Rich
	8-260 Calif.	1/8	0.105	0.210	0.210	0.110	3/16③	0.120	1 Rich④
1977	17057172	11/32	0.075	0.240	0.135	0.240	3/8③	0.120	2 Rich
	17057173	11/32	0.075	0.240	0.165	0.240	3/8③	0.120	2 Rich
1978	17058160	11/32	0.126	0.203	0.142	0.195	1/4②	0.120	2 Rich
1979	17059134, 135, 136, 137	13/32	0.243	0.243	0.157	—	9/32②	0.120	1 Lean
	17059180, 190, 191	11/32	0.139	0.243	0.103	0.090	1/4②	0.120	2 Rich
	17059160	11/32	0.110	0.195	0.129	0.203	9/32②	0.120	2 Rich
	17059196	11/32	0.139	0.277	0.129	0.117	1/4②	0.120	1 Rich
	17059434, 436	13/32	0.243	0.243	0.164	—	9/32②	0.120	2 Lean
	17059492, 498	11/32	0.139	0.277	0.129	0.117	9/32②	0.120	2 Rich
	17059430, 432	9/32	0.243	0.243	0.171	—	9/32②	0.120	1 Lean
	17059491	11/32	0.139	0.277	0.129	0.117	9/32②	0.120	1 Rich
1980	17080130, 131, 132, 133 146, 147 148, 149	11/32	0.110	0.243	0.142	—	1/4②	0.120	Fixed
	17080160	5/16	0.110	0.243	0.168	0.207	1/4②	0.120	Fixed
	17080190	9/32	0.074	0.243	0.123	0.110	1/4②	0.120	Fixed
	17080191	11/32	0.139	0.243	0.096	0.096	1/4②	0.120	Fixed
	17080192	9/32	0.139	0.243	0.096	0.110	1/4②	0.120	Fixed
	17080195	9/32	0.139	0.243	0.103	0.071	1/4②	0.120	Fixed
	17080197	9/32	0.139	0.243	0.103	0.071	1/4②	0.120	Fixed
	17080490	5/16	0.139	0.243	0.117	0.203	1/4②	0.120	Fixed
	17080491	5/16	0.139	0.243	0.117	0.220	1/4②	0.120	Fixed
	17080492	5/16	0.139	0.243	0.117	0.203	1/4②	0.120	Fixed
	17080493	5/16	0.139	0.243	0.117	0.179	3/8	0.120	Fixed
	17080494	5/16	0.139	0.243	0.117	0.179	1/4②	0.120	Fixed
	17080495	5/16	0.139	0.243	0.117	0.179	3/8	0.120	Fixed
	17080496	5/16	0.139	0.243	0.117	0.203	3/8	0.120	Fixed
	17080498	5/16	0.139	0.243	0.117	0.203	3/8	0.120	Fixed
1981	17080185, 187	9/32	0.139	0.243	0.103	0.071	1/4②	0.120	Fixed
	17080191	11/32	0.139	0.243	0.096	0.096	1/4②	0.120	Fixed
	17080491	5/16	0.139	0.243	0.117	0.220	⑤	0.120	Fixed
	17080496, 498	5/16	0.139	0.243	0.117	0.203	⑤	0.120	Fixed
	17081131, 133	13/32	0.110	0.243	0.142	—	⑤	0.120	Fixed

2MC, M2MC, M2ME, E2ME CARBURETOR SPECIFICATIONS
Oldsmobile

Year	Carburetor Identification ①	Float Level (in.)	Choke Rod (in.)	Choke Unloader (in.)	Vacuum Break Lean or Front (in.)	Vacuum Break Rich or Rear (in)	Pump Rod (in.)	Choke Coil Lever (in.)	Automatic Choke (notches)
1981	17081138, 140	13/32	0.110	0.260	0.142	—	⑤	0.120	Fixed
	17081150, 152	13/32	0.071	0.220	0.136	0.227	⑤	0.120	Fixed
	17081160	11/32	0.074	0.220	0.136	0.234	⑤	0.120	Fixed
	17081191, 194	5/16	0.139	0.243	0.164	0.136	⑤	0.120	Fixed
	17081196	5/16	0.139	0.243	0.164	0.136	⑤	0.120	Fixed
	17081192, 197	3/8	0.139	0.243	0.164	0.136	⑤	0.120	Fixed
	17081198	3/8	0.139	0.243	0.164	0.136	⑤	0.120	Fixed
	17081199	3/8	0.096	0.243	0.164	0.136	⑤	0.120	Fixed
	1708130, 132	13/32	0.110	0.243	0.142	—	⑤	0.120	Fixed

① The carburetor identification number is stamped on the float bowl, next to the fuel inlet nut.
② Inner hole
③ Outer hole
④ Index on LeMans
⑤ Not Adjustable

The Rochester Quadrajet carburetor is a two stage, four-barrel downdraft carburetor. It has been built in many variations designated as 4MC, 4MV, M4MC, M4MCA, M4ME, M4MEA, E4MC, and E4ME. See the beginning of the Rochester section for an explanation of these designations.

The primary side of the carburetor is equipped with two primary bores and a triple venturi with plain tube nozzles. During off idle and part throttle operation, the fuel is metered through tapered metering rods operating in specially designed jets positioned by a manifold vacuum responsive piston.

The secondary side of the carburetor contains two secondary bores. An air valve is used on the secondary side for metering control and supplements the primary bore.

The secondary air valve operates tapered metering rods which regulate the fuel in constant proportion to the air being supplied.

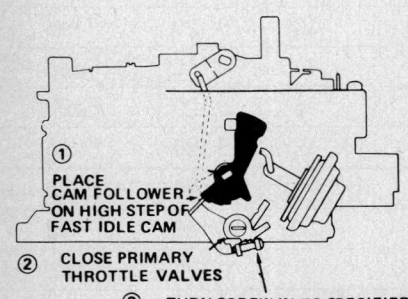

① PLACE CAM FOLLOWER ON HIGH STEP OF FAST IDLE CAM
② CLOSE PRIMARY THROTTLE VALVES
③ TURN SCREW IN TO SPECIFIED FAST IDLE RPM TO ADJUST

Fast Idle Adjustment
(© Chevrolet Div., G.M. Corp)

QUADRAJET

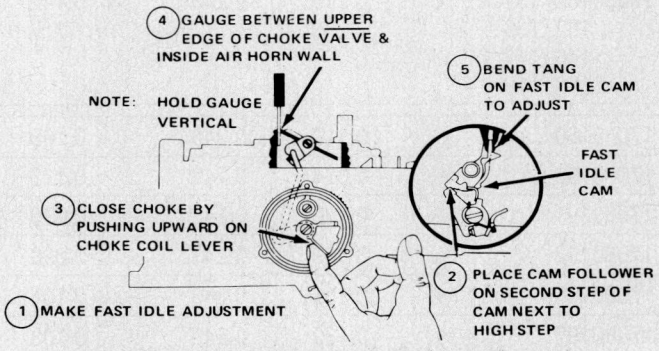

④ GAUGE BETWEEN UPPER EDGE OF CHOKE VALVE & INSIDE AIR HORN WALL

NOTE: HOLD GAUGE VERTICAL

⑤ BEND TANG ON FAST IDLE CAM TO ADJUST

FAST IDLE CAM

③ CLOSE CHOKE BY PUSHING UPWARD ON CHOKE COIL LEVER

② PLACE CAM FOLLOWER ON SECOND STEP OF CAM NEXT TO HIGH STEP

① MAKE FAST IDLE ADJUSTMENT

Quadrajet choke rod (fast idle cam) adjustment
(© G.M. Corp.)

Fast Idle Speed

1. Position the fast idle lever on the high step of the fast idle cam.
2. Be sure that the choke is wide open and the engine warm. Plug the EGR vacuum hose. Disconnect the vacuum hose to the front vacuum break unit, if there are two.
3. Make a preliminary adjustment by turning the fast idle screw out until the throttle valves are closed, then screwing it in the specified number of turns after it contacts the lever (see the carburetor specifications).
4. Use the fast idle screw to adjust the fast idle to the speed, and under the conditions, specified on the engine compartment sticker or in the specifications chart.

Choke Rod (Fast Idle Cam)

1. Adjust the fast idle and place the cam follower on the second step of the fast idle

cam against the shoulder of the high step.
2. Close the choke valve by exerting counter-clockwise pressure on the external choke lever. Remove the coil assembly from the choke housing and push upon the choke coil lever. On models with a fixed (riveted) choke cover, push up on the vacuum break lever tang and hold in position with a rubber band.
3. Insert a gauge of the proper size between the lower (upper beginning 1975) edge of the choke valve and the inside air horn wall.
4. To adjust, bend the tang on the fast idle cam. Be sure that the tang rests against the cam after bending.

Primary (Front) Vacuum Break Adjustment

1. Loosen the three retaining screws and

remove the thermostatic cover and coil assembly from the choke housing through 1979.

2. Place the cam follower lever on the highest step of the fast idle cam through 1977.

3. Seat the front vacuum diaphragm using an outside vacuum source. If there is a diaphragm unit bleed hole, tape it over.

4. Push up on the inside choke coil lever until the tang on the vacuum break lever contacts the tang on the vacuum break plunger. On models with a fixed choke coil cover, push up on the vacuum break lever tang.

5. Place the proper size gauge between the upper edge of the choke valve and the irside of the air horn wall.

6. To adjust, turn the adjustment screw on the vacuum break plunger lever.

7. Install the vacuum hose to the vacuum break unit.

Secondary (Rear) Vacuum Break Adjustment

1. Remove the thermostatic cover and coil assembly from the choke housing through 1979.

2. Place the cam follower on the highest step of the fast idle cam through 1977.

3. Tape over the bleed hole in the rear vacuum break diaphragm and seat the diaphragm using an outside vacuum source. Make sure the diaphragm plunger bucking spring, if any, is compressed.

4. Close the choke by pushing up on the choke coil lever inside the choke housing. On models with a fixed choke coil cover, push up on the vacuum break lever tang.

5. With the choke rod in the bottom of the slot in the choke lever, measure between the upper edge of the choke valve and the air horn wall with a wire type gauge.

NOTE: On 1975 454 cu. in. engines only, the choke valve should be held wide open.

6. To adjust, bend the vacuum break rod at the first bend near the diaphragm except on 1980 models with a screw at the rear of the diaphragm; on those models, turn the screw to adjust.

7. Remove the tape covering the bleed hole of the diaphragm and connect the vacuum hose.

Choke Unloader

1. Push up on the vacuum break lever to

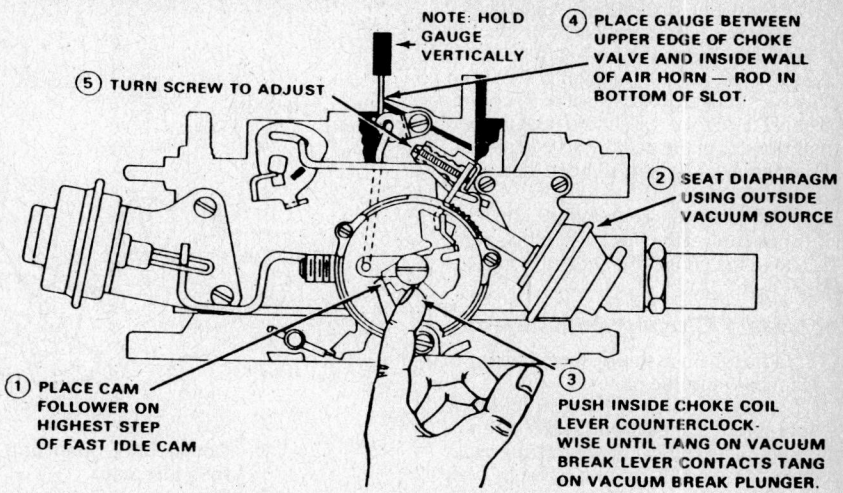

Front vacuum break adjustment (© Buick Div., G.M. Corp.)

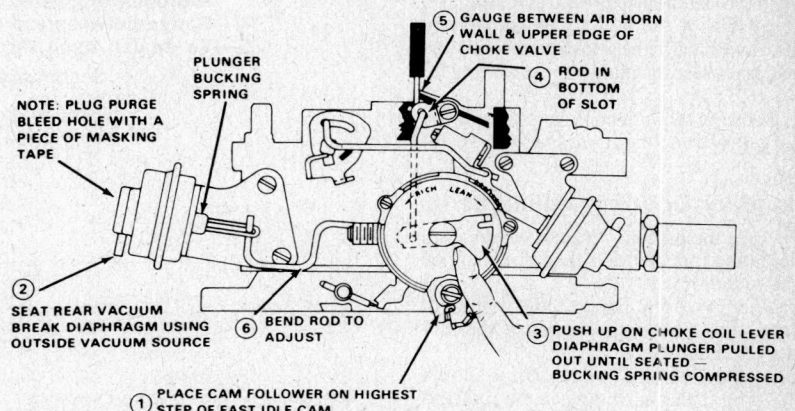

Rear vacuum break adjustment—exc. 454 cu. in. eng. (© Buick Div., G.M. Corp.)

close the choke valve, and fully open the throttle valves.

2. Measure the distance from the lower (upper beginning 1975) edge of the choke valve to the air horn wall.

3. To adjust, bend the tang on the fast idle lever.

4MV Choke Coil Rod

1. Close the choke valve by rotating the choke coil lever counter-clockwise.

2. Disconnect the thermostatic coil rod from the upper lever.

3. Pus down on the rod until it contacts the bracket of the coil.

4. The rod must fit in the notch of the upper lever.

5. If it does not, it must be bent on the curved portion just below the upper lever.

MC, ME Choke Coil Lever Adjustment

1. Remove the choke cover and thermostatic coil from the choke housing. On models with a fixed (riveted) choke cover,

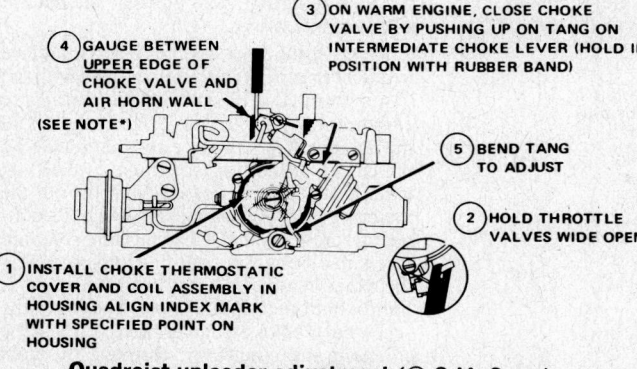

Quadrajet unloader adjustment (© G.M. Corp.)

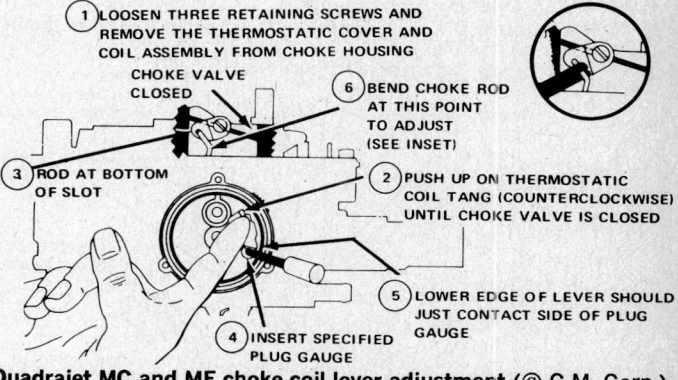

Quadrajet MC and ME choke coil lever adjustment (© G.M. Corp.)

the rivets must be drilled out. A choke stat kit is necessary for assembly. Place the fast idle cam follower on the high step.

2. Push up on the coil tang (counter-clockwise) until the choke valve is closed. The top of the choke rod should be at the bottom of the slot in the choke valve lever.

3. Insert a 0.120 in. drill bit in the hole in the choke housing.

4. The lower edge of the choke coil lever should just contact the side of the plug gauge.

5. Bend the choke rod at the top angle to adjust.

Secondary Closing Adjustment

This adjustment assures proper closing of the secondary throttle plates.

1. Set the slow idle as per instructions in the appropriate car section. Make sure that the fast idle cam follower is not resting on the fast idle cam and the choke valve is wide open.

2. There should be 0.020 in. clearance between the secondary throttle actuating rod and the front of the slot on the secondary throttle lever with the closing tang on the throttle lever resting against the actuating lever.

3. Bend the secondary closing tang on the primary throttle actuating rod or lever to adjust.

Secondary Opening Adjustment

1. Open the primary throttle valves until the actuating link contacts the upper tang on the secondary lever.

2. With two point linkage, the bottom of the link should be in the center of the secondary lever slot.

3. With three point linkage, there should be 0.070 in. clearance between the link and the middle tang.

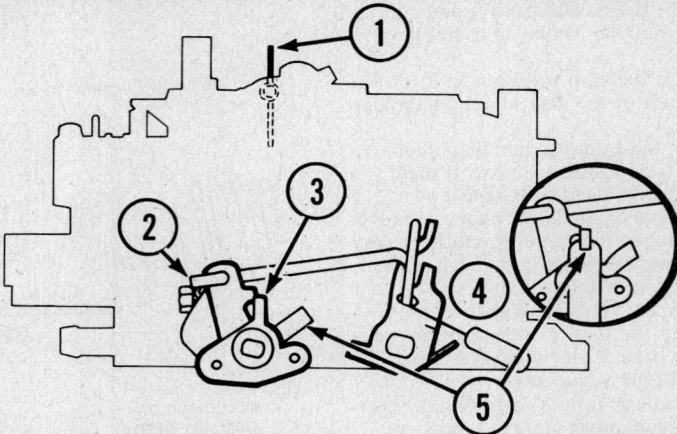

1—Choke fully open and fast idle cam follower off steps of fast idle cam.
2—Slow idle set properly.
3—Make sure throttle lever tang is against secondary throttle rod operating lever as shown in 3.
4—Gauge between rod and end of slot as shown in 4.
5—To adjust, open throttle slightly and bend tang.

Secondary Closing Adjustments

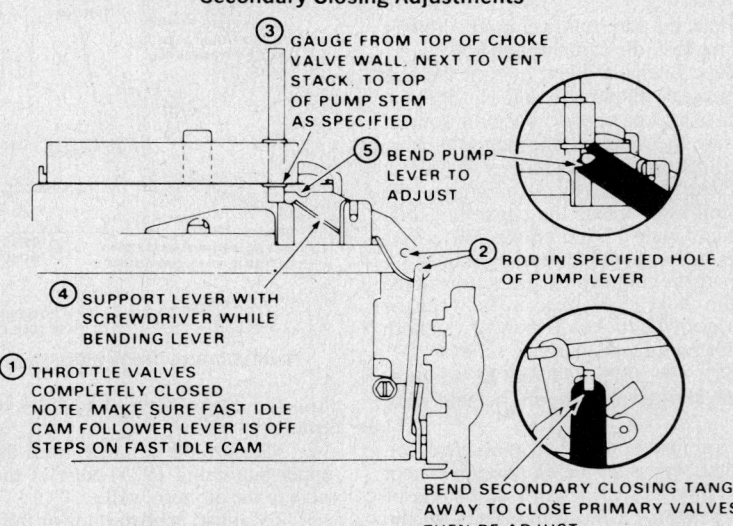

③ GAUGE FROM TOP OF CHOKE VALVE WALL, NEXT TO VENT STACK, TO TOP OF PUMP STEM AS SPECIFIED

⑤ BEND PUMP LEVER TO ADJUST

② ROD IN SPECIFIED HOLE OF PUMP LEVER

④ SUPPORT LEVER WITH SCREWDRIVER WHILE BENDING LEVER

① THROTTLE VALVES COMPLETELY CLOSED NOTE MAKE SURE FAST IDLE CAM FOLLOWER LEVER IS OFF STEPS ON FAST IDLE CAM

BEND SECONDARY CLOSING TANG AWAY TO CLOSE PRIMARY VALVES. THEN RE-ADJUST

Accelerator Pump Rod Adjustment (© Pontiac Div., G.M. Corp.)

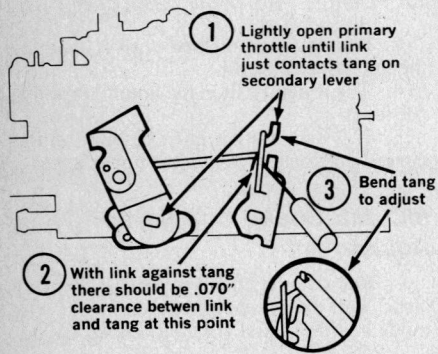

1 Lightly open primary throttle until link just contacts tang on secondary lever

3 Bend tang to adjust

2 With link against tang there should be .070" clearance between link and tang at this point

Secondary Opening Adjustments
(© Oldsmobile Div., G.M. Corp)

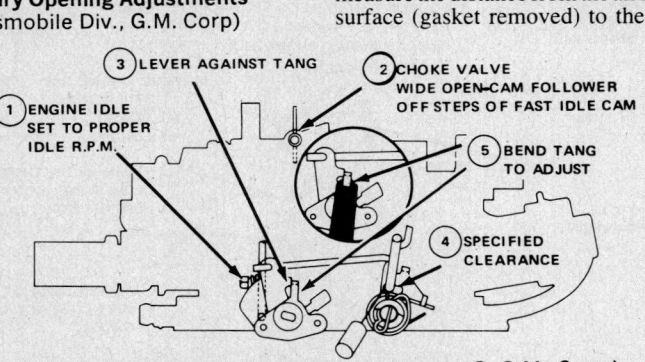

3 LEVER AGAINST TANG

2 CHOKE VALVE WIDE OPEN-CAM FOLLOWER OFF STEPS OF FAST IDLE CAM

1 ENGINE IDLE SET TO PROPER IDLE R.P.M.

5 BEND TANG TO ADJUST

4 SPECIFIED CLEARANCE

Quadrajet Secondary Closing Adjustment (© G.M. Corp.)

4. Bend the upper tang on the secondary lever to adjust as necessary.

Float Level

With the air horn assembly removed, measure the distance from the air horn gasket surface (gasket removed) to the top of the float at the toe ($\frac{1}{16}$ in. back from the toe on 1975 models; $\frac{3}{16}$ in. back on 1976 and later models).

NOTE: Make sure the retaining pin is firmly held in place and that the tang of the float is lightly held against the needle and seat assembly.

Remove the float and bend the float arm to adjust except on carburetors used with the C-4 system (E4MC and E4ME). For those carburetors, if the float level is too high, hold the retainer firmly in place and push down on the center of the float to adjust. If the float level is too low on C-4 models, lift out the metering rods. Remove the solenoid connector screw. Turn the lean mixture solenoid screw in clockwise, counting and recording the exact number of turns until the screw is lightly bottomed in the bowl. Then turn the screw out clockwise and remove. Lift out the solenoid and connector. Remove the float and bend the arm up to adjust. Install the

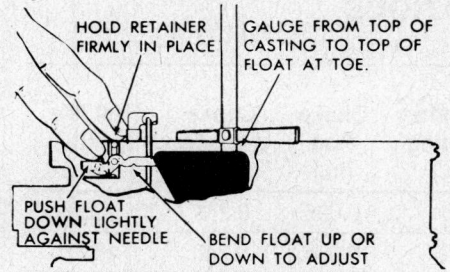

HOLD RETAINER FIRMLY IN PLACE — GAUGE FROM TOP OF CASTING TO TOP OF FLOAT AT TOE.

PUSH FLOAT DOWN LIGHTLY AGAINST NEEDLE — BEND FLOAT UP OR DOWN TO ADJUST

Adjusting Float Level
(ⓒ Pontiac Div., G.M. Corp)

parts, turning the mixture solenoid screw in until it is lightly bottomed, then unscrewing it the exact number of turns counted earlier.

Accelerator Pump

The accelerator pump is not adjustable on C-4 carburetors (E4MC and E4ME).

1. Close the primary throttle valves by backing out the slow idle screw and making sure that the fast idle cam follower is off the steps of the fast idle cam.

2. Bend the secondary throttle closing tang away from the primary throttle lever, if necessary, to insure that the primary throttle valves are fully closed.

3. With the pump in the appropriate hole in the pump lever, measure from the top of the choke valve wall to the top of the pump stem.

4. To adjust, bend the pump lever.

5. After adjusting, readjust the secondary throttle tang and the slow idle screw.

Air Valve Spring Adjustment

To adjust the air valve spring windup, loosen the Allen head lock screw and turn the adjusting screw counter-clockwise to remove all spring tension. With the air valve closed, turn the adjusting screw clockwise the specified number of turns after the torsion spring contacts the pin on the shaft. Hold the adjusting screw in this position and tighten the lockscrew.

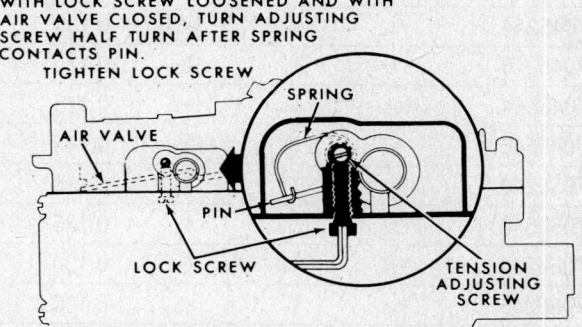

WITH LOCK SCREW LOOSENED AND WITH AIR VALVE CLOSED, TURN ADJUSTING SCREW HALF TURN AFTER SPRING CONTACTS PIN. TIGHTEN LOCK SCREW.

AIR VALVE — SPRING — PIN — LOCK SCREW — TENSION ADJUSTING SCREW

Air Valve Spring Setting (ⓒ Pontiac Div., G.M. Corp.)

QUADRAJET CARBURETOR SPECIFICATIONS
Cadillac

Year	Carburetor Identification ①	Float Level (in.)	Air Valve Spring (turn)	Pump Rod (in.)	Primary Vacuum Break (in.)	Secondary Vacuum Break (in.)	Secondary Opening (in.)	Choke Rod (in.)	Choke Unloader (in.)	Fast Idle Speed (rpm)
1975	7045230	15/32	7/16	3/8	0.160	0.130	③	0.080	0.215	1200-1250
	7045530	15/32	1/2	3/8	0.230	0.230	③	0.080	0.215	1200-1250
1976	7056232	13/32	3/8	3/8	0.160	0.160	③	0.080	0.230	1400
	7056230	13/32	3/8	3/8	0.160	0.160	③	0.080	0.230	1400
	7056530	7/16	3/8	9/32	0.160	0.160	③	0.080	0.230	1400
1977	17057232, 17057233	13/32	1/2	3/8	0.140	0.140	③	0.080	0.230	1400
	17057230	13/32	1/2	7/16	0.140	0.140	③	0.080	0.230	1400
	17057231	17/32	1/2	3/8	0.140	0.140	③	0.080	0.230	1400
	17057530	13/32	1/2	7/16	0.150	0.150	③	0.080	0.230	1500
1978	17058230	13/32	1/2	3/8	0.150	0.165	③	0.080	0.230	1500
	All others	13/32	1/2	3/8	0.140	0.250	③	0.080	0.230	1400
1979	17059230	13/32	1/2	9/32②	0.142	0.234	0.015	0.083	0.142	1000
	17059232	13/32	1/2	9/32②	0.142	0.234	0.015	0.083	0.142	1500
	17059530	13/32	1/2	9/32②	0.149	0.164	0.015	0.083	0.142	1500
	17059532	13/32	1/2	9/32②	0.149	0.164	0.015	0.083	0.142	1500
1980	17080230	7/16	1/2	9/32②	0.149	0.136	③	0.083	0.220	1450
	17080530	17/32	1/2	Fixed	0.142	0.400	③	0.083	0.260	1350
1981	17081248	3/8	5/8	Fixed	0.164	0.136	③	0.139	0.243	
	17081289	13/32	5/8	Fixed	0.164	0.136	③	0.139	0.243	

① The carburetor identification number is stamped on the float bowl, near the secondary throttle lever.   ④ See underhood decal.
② Inner hole
③ No measurement necessary on two point linkage; see text.

QUADRAJET CARBURETOR SPECIFICATIONS
Buick

Year	Carburetor Identification ①	Float Level (in.)	Air Valve Spring (turn)	Pump Rod (in.)	Primary Vacuum Break (in.)	Secondary Vacuum Break (in.)	Secondary Opening (in.)	Choke Rod (in.)	Choke Unloader (in.)	Fast Idle Speed ④ (rpm)
1975	7045240	$7/16$	$7/16$	$9/32$	0.135	0.120	②	0.095	0.240	1800
	7045548	$7/16$	$7/16$	$9/32$	0.135	0.120	②	0.095	0.240	1800
	7045244	$5/16$	$3/4$	$15/32$	0.130	0.115	②	0.095	0.240	1800
	7045246	$5/16$	$3/4$	$15/32$	0.130	0.115	②	0.095	0.240	1800
	7045544	$5/16$	$3/4$	$15/32$	0.145	0.130	②	0.095	0.240	1800
	7045546	$5/16$	$3/4$	$15/32$	0.145	0.130	②	0.095	0.240	1800
1976	17056240	$15/32$	$7/16$	$3/8$	0.135	0.120	②	0.095	0.250	1800
	17056540	$15/32$	$7/16$	$3/8$	0.135	0.120	②	0.095	0.250	1800
	17056244	$5/16$	$3/4$	$3/8$	0.130	0.120	②	0.095	0.250	1800
	17056246	$5/16$	$3/4$	$3/8$	0.130	0.120	②	0.095	0.250	1800
	17056544	$5/16$	$3/4$	$3/8$	0.130	0.130	②	0.095	0.250	1800
	17056546	$5/16$	$3/4$	$3/8$	0.130	0.130	②	0.095	0.250	1800
1977	17057241	$5/16$	$3/4$	$3/8$	0.120	0.105	②	0.095	0.240	⑤
	17057250, 17057253, 17057255, 17057256	$13/32$	$1/2$	$9/32$	0.120	0.170	②	0.095	0.205	⑤
	17057258	$13/32$	$1/2$	$9/32$	0.125	0.215	②	0.095	0.205	⑤
	17057550, 17057553	$13/32$	$1/2$	$9/32$	0.125	0.215	②	0.095	0.200	⑤
1978	17058240	$1/32$	$3/4$	$9/32$	0.117	0.117	②	0.074	0.243	⑤
	17058241	$5/16$	$3/4$	$3/8$	0.120	0.103	②	0.096	0.243	⑤
	17058250	$13/32$	$1/2$	$9/32$	0.129	0.183	②	0.096	0.220	⑤
	17058253	$13/32$	$1/2$	$9/32$	0.129	0.183	②	0.096	0.220	⑤
	17058254	$15/32$	$1/2$	$9/32$	0.136	—	②	0.103	0.220	⑤
	17058257	$13/32$	$1/2$	$9/32$	0.136	0.231	②	0.103	0.220	⑤
	17058258	$13/32$	$1/2$	$9/32$	0.136	0.231	②	0.103	0.220	⑤
	17058259	$13/32$	$1/2$	$9/32$	0.136	0.231	②	0.103	0.220	⑤
	17058582	$15/32$	$7/8$	$9/32$	0.179	—	②	0.314	0.277	⑤
	17058584	$15/32$	$7/8$	$9/32$	0.179	—	②	0.314	0.277	⑤
	17058282	$15/32$	$7/8$	$9/32$	0.157	—	②	0.314	0.277	⑤
	17058284	$15/32$	$7/8$	$9/32$	0.157	—	②	0.314	0.277	⑤
	17058228	$15/32$	1	$9/32$	0.179	—	②	0.314	0.277	⑤
	17058502	$15/32$	$7/8$	$9/32$	0.164	—	②	0.314	0.277	⑤
	17058504	$15/32$	$7/8$	$9/32$	0.164	—	②	0.314	0.277	⑤
	17058202	$15/32$	$7/8$	$9/32$	0.157	—	②	0.314	0.277	⑤
	17058204	$15/32$	$7/8$	$9/32$	0.157	—	②	0.314	0.277	⑤
	17058540	$7/32$	$3/4$	$9/32$	0.117	0.117	②	0.074	0.243	⑤
	17058550	$13/32$	$1/2$	$9/32$	0.136	0.231	②	0.103	0.220	⑤

QUADRAJET CARBURETOR SPECIFICATIONS
Buick

Year	Carburetor Identification ①	Float Level (in.)	Air Valve Spring (turn)	Pump Rod (in.)	Primary Vacuum Break (in.)	Secondary Vacuum Break (in.)	Secondary Opening (in.)	Choke Rod (in.)	Choke Unloader (in.)	Fast Idle Speed ④ (rpm)
1978	17058553	15/32	1/2	9/32	0.129	0.231	②	0.096	0.220	⑤
	17058559	15/32	1/2	9/32	0.136	—	②	0.096	0.231	⑤
1979	17059240	7/32	3/4	9/32	0.117	0.117	②	0.074	0.179	⑥
	17059243	7/32	3/4	9/32	0.117	0.117	②	0.074	0.179	⑥
	17059540	7/32	3/4	9/32	0.117	0.129	②	0.074	0.243	⑥
	17059543	7/32	3/4	9/32	0.117	0.129	②	0.074	0.243	⑥
	17059242	7/32	3/4	9/32	0.066	0.066	②	0.074	0.179	⑥
	17059553	13/32	1/2	9/32	0.136	0.230	②	0.103	0.220	⑥
	17059555	13/32	1/2	9/32	0.149	0.230	②	0.103	0.220	⑥
	17059250	13/32	1/2	9/32	0.129	0.182	②	0.096	0.220	⑥
	17059253	13/32	1/2	9/32	0.129	0.182	②	0.096	0.220	⑥
	17059208	15/32	7/8	9/32	—	0.129	②	0.314	0.277	⑥
	17059209	15/32	7/8	9/32	—	0.129	②	0.314	0.277	⑥
	17059210	15/32	1	9/32	0.157	—	②	0.243	0.243	⑥
	17059211	15/32	1	9/32	0.157	—	②	0.243	0.243	⑥
	17059228	15/32	1	9/32	0.157	—	②	0.243	0.243	⑥
	17059241	5/16	3/4	3/8	0.120	0.113	②	0.096	0.243	⑥
	17059247	5/16	3/4	3/8	0.110	0.103	②	0.096	0.243	⑥
	17059272	15/32	5/8	3/8	0.136	0.195	②	0.074	0.220	⑥
1980	17080240	3/16	9/16	9/32 ③	0.083	0.083	②	0.074	0.179	⑥
	17080241	7/16	3/4	9/32 ③	0.129	0.114	②	0.096	0.243	⑥
	17080242	13/32	9/16	9/32 ③	0.077	0.096	②	0.074	0.220	⑥
	17080243	3/16	9/16	9/32 ③	0.083	0.083	②	0.074	0.179	⑥
	17080244	5/16	5/8	9/32 ③	0.096	0.071	②	0.139	0.243	⑥
	17080249	7/16	3/4	9/32 ③	0.129	0.114	②	0.096	0.243	⑥
	17080253	13/32	1/2	9/32 ③	0.149	0.211	②	0.090	0.220	⑥
	17080259	13/32	1/2	9/32 ③	0.149	0.211	②	0.090	0.220	⑥
	17080270	15/32	5/8	3/8 ⑦	0.149	0.211	②	0.074	0.220	⑥
	17080271	15/32	5/8	3/8 ⑦	0.142	0.211	②	0.110	0.203	⑥
	17080272	15/32	5/8	3/8 ⑦	0.129	0.175	②	0.074	0.203	⑥
	17080502	1/2	7/8	Fixed	0.136	0.179	②	0.110	0.243	⑥
	17080504	1/2	7/8	Fixed	0.136	0.179	②	0.110	0.243	⑥
	17080540	3/8	9/16	Fixed	0.103	0.129	②	0.074	0.243	⑥
	17080542	3/8	9/16	Fixed	0.103	0.066	②	0.074	0.243	⑥
	17080543	3/8	9/16	Fixed	0.103	0.129	②	0.074	0.243	⑥
	17080553	15/32	1/2	Fixed	0.142	0.220	②	0.090	0.220	⑥
	17080554	15/32	1/2	Fixed	0.142	0.211	②	0.090	0.220	⑥
1981	17081202 204	11/32	7/8	Fixed	0.157 ⑧	—	②	0.110	0.243	⑩

ROCHESTER CARBURETORS

QUADRAJET CARBURETOR SPECIFICATIONS
Buick

Year	Carburetor Identification ①	Float Level (in.)	Air Valve Spring (turn)	Pump Rod (in.)	Primary Vacuum Break (in.)	Secondary Vacuum Break (in.)	Secondary Opening (in.)	Choke Rod (in.)	Choke Unloader (in.)	Fast Idle Speed ④ (rpm)
1981	17081203 207	11/32	7/8	Fixed	0.157⑧	—	②	0.110	0.243	⑩
	17081216 218	11/32	7/8	Fixed	0.157⑧	—	②	0.110	0.243	⑩
	17081242	3/8	9/16	Fixed	0.090⑧	0.077⑨	②	0.139	0.243	⑩
	17081243	5/16	9/16	Fixed	0.103⑧	0.090⑨	②	0.139	0.243	⑩
	17081245	3/8	5/8	Fixed	0.164⑧	0.136⑨	②	0.139	0.243	⑩
	17081247	3/8	5/8	Fixed	0.164⑧	0.136⑨	②	0.139	0.243	⑩
	17081248 249	3/8	5/8	Fixed	0.164⑧	0.136⑨	②	0.139	0.243	⑩
	17081253 254	15/32	1/2	Fixed	0.142⑧	0.227⑨	②	0.071	0.220	⑩
	17081270	7/16	5/8	Fixed	0.136⑧	0.211⑨	②	0.074	0.220	⑩
	17081272	5/8	5/8	Fixed	0.136⑧	0.260⑨	②	0.074	0.220	⑩
	17081274	5/8	5/8	Fixed	0.136⑧	0.220⑨	②	0.083	0.220	⑩
	17081289	5/8	5/8	Fixed	0.164⑧	0.136⑨	②	0.139	0.243	⑩

① The carburetor identification number is stamped on the float bowl, near the secondary throttle lever.
② No measurement necessary on two point linkage; see text
③ Inner hole
④ On high step of cam, automatic in Park
⑤ 3 turns after contacting lever for preliminary setting
⑥ 2 turns after contacting lever for preliminary setting
⑦ Outer hole
⑧ Front
⑨ Rear
⑩ 4½ turns after contacting lever for preliminary setting

QUADRAJET CARBURETOR SPECIFICATIONS
Chevrolet

Year	Carburetor Identification ①	Float Level (in.)	Air Valve Spring (turn)	Pump Rod (in.)	Primary Vacuum Break (in.)	Secondary Vacuum Break (in.)	Secondary Opening (in.)	Choke Rod (in.)	Choke Unloader (in.)	Fast Idle Speed ④ (rpm)
1975	7045200	17/32	9/16	0.275	0.200	0.550	⑤	0.300	0.325	1000
	7045202	15/32	7/8	0.275	0.180	0.170	⑤	0.300	0.325	1600
	7045203	15/32	7/8	0.275	0.180	0.170	⑤	0.300	0.325	1600
	7045206	15/32	7/8	0.275	0.180	0.170	⑤	0.300	0.325	1600
	7045207	15/32	7/8	0.275	0.180	0.170	⑤	0.300	0.325	1600
	7045208	15/32	7/8	0.275	0.180	0.170	⑤	0.300	0.325	1600
	7045209	15/32	7/8	0.275	0.180	0.170	⑤	0.300	0.325	1600
	7045210	15/32	7/8	0.275	0.180	0.170	⑤	0.300	0.325	1600
	7045211	15/32	7/8	0.275	0.180	0.170	⑤	0.300	0.325	1600
	7045222	15/32	7/8	0.275	0.180	0.170	⑤	0.300	0.325	1600
	7045223	15/32	7/8	0.275	0.180	0.170	⑤	0.300	0.325	1600
	7045224	15/32	3/4	0.275	0.180	0.170	⑤	0.325	0.325	1600
	7045228	15/32	3/4	0.275	0.180	0.170	⑤	0.325	0.325	1600
	7045502	15/32	7/8	0.275	0.180	0.170	⑤	0.300	0.325	1600

QUADRAJET CARBURETOR SPECIFICATIONS
Chevrolet

Year	Carburetor Identification ①	Float Level (in.)	Air Valve Spring (turn)	Pump Rod (in.)	Primary Vacuum Break (in.)	Secondary Vacuum Break (in.)	Secondary Opening (in.)	Choke Rod (in.)	Choke Unloader (in.)	Fast Idle Speed ④ (rpm)
1975	7045503	15/32	7/8	0.275	0.180	0.170	⑤	0.300	0.325	1600
	7045504	15/32	7/8	0.275	0.180	0.170	⑤	0.300	0.325	1600
	7045506	15/32	7/8	0.275	0.180	0.170	⑤	0.300	0.325	1600
	7044507	15/32	7/8	0.275	0.180	0.170	⑤	0.300	0.325	1600
1976	17056202	13/32	7/8	9/32	0.185	—	⑤	0.325	0.325	1600
	17056203	13/32	7/8	9/32	0.170	—	⑤	0.325	0.325	1600
	17056206	13/32	7/8	9/32	0.185	—	⑤	0.325	0.325	1600
	17056207	13/32	7/8	9/32	0.170	—	⑤	0.325	0.325	1600
	17056210	13/32	1.0	9/32	0.185	—	⑤	0.325	0.325	1600
	17056211	13/32	3/4	9/32	0.185	—	⑤	0.325	0.325	1600
	17056228	13/32	7/8	9/32	0.185	—	⑤	0.325	0.325	1600
	17056502	13/32	7/8	9/32	0.185	—	⑤	0.325	0.325	1600
	17056506	13/32	3/4	9/32	0.185	—	⑤	0.325	0.325	1600
	17056528	13/32	7/8	9/32	0.185	—	⑤	0.325	0.325	1600
	17056200	13/32	7/8	9/32	0.240	0.160	⑤	0.190	0.270	1600
1977	17057202	15/32	7/8	15/32	0.180	—	⑤	0.325	0.280	1600
	17057204	15/32	3/4	9/32	0.160	—	⑤	0.325	0.280	1600
	17057203	15/32	7/8	15/32	0.180	—	⑤	0.325	0.280	1300
	17057502	15/32	7/8	15/32	0.165	—	⑤	0.325	0.280	1600
	17057504	15/32	7/8	9/32	0.165	—	⑤	0.325	0.280	1600
	17057210	15/32	1	15/32	0.180	—	⑤	0.325	0.280	1600
	17057510, 17057528	15/32	1	9/32	0.180	—	⑤	0.325	0.280	1600
	17057211	15/32	1	15/32	0.180	—	⑤	0.325	0.280	1300
	17057228	13/32	1	15/32	0.180	—	⑤	0.325	0.280	1600
	17057582	15/32	7/8	13/32	0.180	—	⑤	0.325	0.280	1600
	17057584	15/32	1	9/32	0.180	—	⑤	0.325	0.280	1600
1978	17058202	15/32	7/8	9/32	0.179	—	⑤	0.314	0.277	⑥
	17058203	15/32	7/8	9/32	0.179	—	⑤	0.314	0.277	⑥
	17058204	15/32	7/8	9/32	0.179	—	⑤	0.314	0.277	⑥
	17058210	15/32	1/2	9/32	0.203	—	⑤	0.314	0.277	⑥
	17058211	15/32	1/2	9/32	0.203	—	⑤	0.314	0.277	⑥
	17058228	15/32	7/8	9/32	0.203	—	⑤	0.314	0.277	⑥
	17058502	15/32	7/8	9/32	0.187	—	⑤	0.314	0.277	⑥
	17058504	15/32	7/8	9/32	0.187	—	⑤	0.314	0.277	⑥
	17058582	15/32	7/8	9/32	0.203	—	⑤	0.314	0.277	⑥
	17058584	15/32	7/8	9/32	0.203	—	⑤	0.314	0.277	⑥
1979	17059203	15/32	7/8	1/4	0.157	—	⑤	0.243	0.243	⑦
	17059207	15/32	7/8	1/4	0.157	—	⑤	0.243	0.243	⑦

ROCHESTER CARBURETORS

QUADRAJET CARBURETOR SPECIFICATIONS
Chevrolet

Year	Carburetor Identification ①	Float Level (in.)	Air Valve Spring (turn)	Pump Rod (in.)	Primary Vacuum Break (in.)	Secondary Vacuum Break (in.)	Secondary Opening (in.)	Choke Rod (in.)	Choke Unloader (in.)	Fast Idle Speed ④ (rpm)
1979	17059216	15/32	7/8	1/4	0.157	—	⑤	0.243	0.243	⑦
	17059217	15/32	7/8	1/4	0.157	—	⑤	0.243	0.243	⑦
	17059218	15/32	7/8	1/4	0.164	—	⑤	0.243	0.243	⑦
	17059222	15/32	7/8	1/4	0.164	—	⑤	0.243	0.243	⑦
	17059502	15/32	7/8	1/4	0.164	—	⑤	0.243	0.243	⑦
	17059504	15/32	7/8	1/4	0.164	—	⑤	0.243	0.243	⑦
	17059582	15/32	7/8	11/32	0.203	—	⑤	0.243	0.314	⑦
	17059584	15/32	7/8	11/32	0.203	—	⑤	0.243	0.314	⑦
	17059210	15/32	1	9/32	0.157	—	⑤	0.243	0.243	⑦
	17059211	15/32	1	9/32	0.157	—	⑤	0.243	0.243	⑦
	17029228	15/32	1	9/32	0.157	—	⑤	0.243	0.243	⑦
1980	17080202	7/16	7/8	1/4 ⑧	0.157	—	⑤	0.110	0.243	⑩
	17080204	7/16	7/8	1/4 ⑧	0.157	—	⑤	0.110	0.243	⑩
	17080207	7/16	7/8	1/4 ⑧	0.157	—	⑤	0.110	0.243	⑩
	17080228	7/16	7/8	9/32 ⑧	0.179	—	⑤	0.110	0.243	⑩
	17080243	3/16	9/16	9/32 ⑧	0.016	0.083	⑤	0.074	0.179	⑩
	17080274	15/32	5/8	5/16 ⑨	0.110	0.164	⑤	0.083	0.203	⑩
	17080282	7/16	7/8	11/32 ⑨	0.142	—	⑤	0.110	0.243	⑩
	17080284	7/16	7/8	11/32 ⑨	0.142	—	⑤	0.110	0.243	⑩
	17080502	1/2	7/8	Fixed	0.136	0.179	⑤	0.110	0.243	⑩
	17080504	1/2	7/8	Fixed	0.136	0.179	⑤	0.110	0.243	⑩
	17080542	3/8	9/16	Fixed	0.103	0.066	⑤	0.074	0.243	⑩
	17080543	3/8	9/16	Fixed	0.103	0.129	⑤	0.074	0.243	⑩
1981	17081202	11/32	7/8	Fixed	0.149	—	⑤	0.110	0.243	⑪
	17081203	11/32	7/8	Fixed	0.149	—	⑤	0.110	0.243	⑪
	17081204	11/32	7/8	Fixed	0.149	—	⑤	0.110	0.243	⑪
	17081207	11/32	7/8	Fixed	0.149	—	⑤	0.110	0.243	⑪
	17081216	11/32	7/8	Fixed	0.149	—	⑤	0.110	0.243	⑪
	17081217	11/32	7/8	Fixed	0.149	—	⑤	0.110	0.243	⑪
	17081218	11/32	7/8	Fixed	0.149	—	⑤	0.110	0.243	⑪
	17081242	5/16	9/16	Fixed	0.090	0.077	⑤	0.139	0.243	⑪
	17081243	1/4	9/16	Fixed	0.103	0.090	⑤	0.139	0.243	⑪

① The carburetor identification number is stamped on the float bowl, near the secondary throttle lever.
② Without vacuum advance.
③ With automatic transmission; vacuum advance connected and EGR disconnected and the throttle positioned on the high step of cam.
④ With manual transmission; without vacuum advance and the throttle positioned on the high step of cam.
⑤ No measurement necessary on two point linkage; see text.
⑥ 3 turns after contacting lever for preliminary setting.
⑦ 2 turns after contacting lever for preliminary setting.
⑧ Inner hole

⑨ Outer hole
⑩ 4 turns after contacting lever for preliminary setting.
⑪ 4½ turns after contacting lever for preliminary setting

QUADRAJET CARBURETOR SPECIFICATIONS
Oldsmobile

Year	Carburetor Identification[1]	Float Level (in.)	Air Valve Spring (turn)	Pump Rod (in.)	Primary Vacuum Break (in.)	Secondary Vacuum Break (in.)	Secondary Opening (in.)	Choke Rod (in.)	Choke Unloader (in.)	Fast Idle Speed [4] (rpm)
1975	7045183	3/8	1/2	9/32	0.190	0.140	[4]	0.135	0.235	[3]
	7045250	3/8	1/2	9/32	0.250	0.180	[4]	0.170	0.300	[3]
	7045483	3/8	1/2	9/32	0.275	0.180	[4]	0.135	0.235	[3]
	7045550	3/8	1/2	9/32	0.275	0.180	[4]	0.135	0.235	[3]
	7045264	17/32	1/2	9/32	0.150	0.260	[4]	0.130	0.235	[3]
	7045184	3/8	3/4	9/32	0.190	0.140	[4]	0.135	0.235	[3]
	7045185	3/8	3/4	9/32	0.275	0.140	[4]	0.135	0.235	[3]
	7045251	3/8	3/4	9/32	0.190	0.140	[4]	0.135	0.235	[3]
	7045484	3/8	3/4	9/32	0.190	0.140	[4]	0.135	0.235	[3]
	7045485	3/8	3/4	9/32	0.190	0.180	[4]	0.160	0.235	[3]
	7045551	3/8	3/4	9/32	0.190	0.140	[4]	0.135	0.235	[5]
	7045546	5/16	3/4	3/8	0.145	0.130	[4]	0.095	0.240	[5]
1976	17056246	5/16	3/4	3/8	0.130	0.120	[4]	0.095	0.250	[5]
	17056250	13/32	1/2	9/32	0.190	0.140	[4]	0.130	0.230	[5]
	17056251	13/32	3/4	9/32	0.190	0.140	[4]	0.130	0.230	[5]
	17056252	13/32	3/4	9/32	0.190	0.140	[4]	0.130	0.230	[5]
	17056253	13/32	1/2	9/32	0.190	0.140	[4]	0.130	0.230	[5]
	17056255	13/32	3/4	9/32	0.190	0.140	[4]	0.130	0.230	[5]
	17056256	13/32	3/4	9/32	0.190	0.140	[4]	0.130	0.230	[5]
	17056257	13/32	3/4	9/32	0.190	0.140	[4]	0.130	0.230	[5]
	17056258	13/32	1/2	9/32	0.190	0.140	[4]	0.130	0.230	[5]
	17056259	13/32	1/2	9/32	0.190	0.140	[4]	0.130	0.230	[5]
	17056546	5/16	3/4	3/8	0.130	0.130	[4]	0.095	0.250	[5]
	17056550	13/32	1/2	9/32	0.190	0.140	[4]	0.130	0.230	[5]
	17056551	13/32	3/4	9/32	0.190	0.140	[4]	0.130	0.230	[5]
	17056552	13/32	3/4	9/32	0.200	0.140	[4]	0.130	0.230	[5]
	17056553	13/32	1/2	9/32	0.190	0.140	[4]	0.130	0.230	[5]
	17056556	13/32	3/4	9/32	0.190	0.140	[4]	0.130	0.230	[5]
1977	17057250	13/32	3/4	9/32	0.125	0.170	[4]	0.095	0.205	[5]
	17057252	13/32	3/4	9/32	0.135	0.180	[4]	0.100	0.220	[5]
	17057253	13/32	3/4	9/32	0.135	0.180	[4]	0.095	0.205	[5]
	17057255	13/32	3/4	9/32	0.125	0.170	[4]	0.095	0.205	[5]
	17057256	13/32	3/4	9/32	0.135	0.180	[4]	0.100	0.205	[5]
	17057257	13/32	3/4	9/32	0.135	0.225	[4]	0.100	0.220	[5]
	17057258	13/32	3/4	9/32	0.135	0.225	[4]	0.100	0.205	[5]
	17057550	13/32	3/4	9/32	0.135	0.225	[4]	0.100	0.200	[5]
	17057552, 17057553	13/32	1/2	9/32	0.135	0.225	[4]	0.100	0.200	[5]
	17057202	15/32	3/4	9/32	0.160	—	[4]	0.325	0.280	[5]

ROCHESTER CARBURETORS

QUADRAJET CARBURETOR SPECIFICATIONS
Oldsmobile

Year	Carburetor Identification [1]	Float Level (in.)	Air Valve Spring (turn)	Pump Rod (in.)	Primary Vacuum Break (in.)	Secondary Vacuum Break (in.)	Secondary Opening (in.)	Choke Rod (in.)	Choke Unloader (in.)	Fast Idle Speed [4] (rpm)
1977	17057204	$15/32$	$7/8$	$9/32$	0.160	—	[4]	0.325	0.280	[5]
	17057502	$15/32$	$3/4$	$9/32$	0.175	—	[4]	0.325	0.285	[5]
	17057504	$15/32$	$1/2$	$9/32$	0.175	—	[4]	0.325	0.285	[5]
	17057582	$15/32$	$3/4$	$9/32$	0.180	—	[4]	0.325	0.285	[5]
	17057584	$15/32$	$7/8$	$9/32$	0.175	—	[4]	0.325	0.280	[5]
1978	17058202	$15/32$	$7/8$	$9/32$	0.157	—	[4]	0.314	0.277	[5]
	17058204	$15/32$	$7/8$	$9/32$	0.157	—	[4]	0.314	0.277	[5]
	17058250	$13/32$	$1/2$	$9/32$	0.129	0.183	[4]	0.096	0.220	[5]
	17058253	$13/32$	$1/2$	$9/32$	0.129	0.183	[4]	0.096	0.220	[5]
	17058257	$13/32$	$1/2$	$9/32$	0.136	0.230	[4]	0.103	0.220	[5]
	17058258	$13/32$	$1/2$	$9/32$	0.136	0.230	[4]	0.103	0.220	[5]
	17058259	$13/32$	$1/2$	$9/32$	0.136	0.183	[4]	0.103	0.220	[5]
	17058502	$15/32$	$7/8$	$9/32$	0.164	—	[4]	0.314	0.277	[5]
	17058504	$15/32$	$7/8$	$9/32$	0.164	—	[4]	0.314	0.277	[5]
	17058553	$13/32$	$1/2$	$9/32$	0.136	0.230	[4]	0.103	0.220	[5]
	17058555	$13/32$	$1/2$	$9/32$	0.136	0.230	[4]	0.103	0.220	[5]
	17058582	$15/32$	$7/8$	$9/32$	0.179	—	[4]	0.314	0.277	[5]
	17058584	$15/32$	$7/8$	$9/32$	0.179	—	[4]	0.314	0.277	[5]
1979	17059202	$1/2$	$7/8$	$1/4$	0.164	—	[4]	0.314	0.243	[6]
	17059207	$15/32$	$7/8$	$1/4$	0.157	—	[4]	0.243	0.243	[6]
	17059216	$15/32$	$7/8$	$1/4$	0.157	—	[4]	0.243	0.243	[6]
	17059217	$15/32$	$7/8$	$1/4$	0.157	—	[4]	0.243	0.243	[6]
	17059218	$15/32$	$7/8$	$9/32$	0.164	—	[4]	0.243	0.243	[6]
	17059222	$15/32$	$7/8$	$9/32$	0.164	—	[4]	0.243	0.243	[6]
	17059250	$13/32$	$1/2$	$9/32$	0.129	0.183	[4]	0.096	0.220	[6]
	17059251	$13/32$	$1/2$	$9/32$	0.129	0.183	[4]	0.096	0.220	[6]
	17059253	$13/32$	$1/2$	$9/32$	0.129	0.183	[4]	0.096	0.220	[6]
	17059256	$13/32$	$1/2$	$9/32$	0.136	0.195	[4]	0.103	0.220	[6]
	17059258	$13/32$	$1/2$	$9/32$	0.136	0.195	[4]	0.103	0.220	[6]
	17059502	$15/32$	$7/8$	$1/4$	0.164	—	[4]	0.243	0.243	[6]
	17059504	$15/32$	$7/8$	$1/4$	0.164	—	[4]	0.243	0.243	[6]
	17059553	$13/32$	$1/2$	$9/32$	0.136	0.230	[4]	0.103	0.220	[6]
	17059554	$13/32$	$1/2$	$9/32$	0.136	0.230	[4]	0.103	0.220	[6]
	17059582	$15/32$	$7/8$	$11/32$	0.203	—	[4]	0.243	0.314	[6]
	17059584	$15/32$	$7/8$	$11/32$	0.203	—	[4]	0.243	0.314	[6]
1980	17080202	$7/16$	$7/8$	$1/4$ [7]	0.157	—	[4]	0.110	0.243	[5]
	17080204	$7/16$	$7/8$	$1/4$ [7]	0.157	—	[4]	0.110	0.243	[5]
	17080250	$13/32$	$1/2$	$9/32$ [7]	0.149	0.211	[4]	0.090	0.220	[5]
	17080251	$13/32$	$1/2$	$9/32$ [7]	0.149	0.211	[4]	0.090	0.220	[5]

QUADRAJET CARBURETOR SPECIFICATIONS
Oldsmobile

Year	Carburetor Identification ①	Float Level (in.)	Air Valve Spring (turn)	Pump Rod (in.)	Primary Vacuum Break (in.)	Secondary Vacuum Break (in.)	Secondary Opening (in.)	Choke Rod (in.)	Choke Unloader (in.)	Fast Idle Speed ④ (rpm)
1980	17080252	13/32	1/2	9/32 ⑦	0.149	0.211	④	0.090	0.220	⑤
	17080253	13/32	1/2	9/32 ⑦	0.149	0.211	④	0.090	0.220	⑤
	17080259	13/32	1/2	9/32 ⑦	0.149	0.211	④	0.090	0.220	⑤
	17080260	13/32	1/2	9/32 ⑦	0.149	0.211	④	0.090	0.220	⑤
	17080504	1/2	7/8	⑧	0.136	0.179	④	0.110	0.243	⑤
	17080553	15/32	1/2	⑧	0.142	0.220	④	0.090	0.220	⑤
	17080554	15/32	1/2	⑧	0.142	0.211	④	0.090	0.220	⑤
1981	17081250	13/32	1/2	9/32 ⑦	0.149 ⑨	0.211 ⑩	④	0.090	0.220	⑤
	17081253	15/32	1/2	⑧	0.142 ⑨	0.227 ⑩	④	0.071	0.220	⑤
	17081254	15/32	1/2	⑧	0.142 ⑨	0.227 ⑩	④	0.071	0.220	⑤
	17081248	3/8	—	⑧	0.164 ⑨	0.136 ⑩	④	0.139	0.243	⑤
	17081289	13/32	—	⑧	0.164 ⑨	0.136 ⑩	④	0.139	0.243	⑤

① The carburetor identification number is stamped on the float bowl, next to the secondary throttle lever.
③ 1800 rpm on Omega and 400 cu. in. engines with the cam follower on the highest step of the fast idle cam; 900 rpm on all others with the fast idle cam follower on the lowest step of the fast idle cam.
④ No measurement necessary on two point linkage; see text.
⑤ 3 turns after contacting lever for preliminary setting.
⑥ 2 turns after contacting lever for preliminary setting.
⑦ Inner hole
⑧ Not Adjustable
⑨ Front
⑩ Rear

QUADRAJET CARBURETOR SPECIFICATIONS
Pontiac

Year	Carburetor Identification ①	Float Level (in.)	Air Valve Spring (turn)	Pump Rod (in.)	Primary Vacuum Break (in.)	Secondary Vacuum Break (in.)	Secondary Opening (in.)	Choke Rod (in.)	Choke Unloader (in.)	Fast Idle Speed ② (rpm)
1975	7045246	5/16	1/2	15/32	0.130	0.115	④	0.095	0.240	1800
	7045546	5/16	1/2	15/32	0.145	0.130	④	0.095	0.240	1800
	7045263	1/2	1/2	9/32	0.150	0.260	④	0.130	0.230	1800
	7045264	1/2	1/2	9/32	0.150	0.260	④	0.130	0.230	1800
	7045268	1/2	3/8	9/32	0.150	0.260	④	0.130	0.230	1800
	7045269	1/2	3/8	9/32	0.160	0.265	④	0.130	0.230	1800
	7045274	1/2	1/2	9/32	0.150	0.260	④	0.130	0.230	1800
	7045260	1/2	1/2	9/32	0.150	0.260	④	0.130	0.230	1800
	7045262	1/2	1/2	9/32	0.150	0.260	④	0.130	0.230	1800
	7045266	1/2	1/2	9/32	0.150	0.260	④	0.130	0.230	1800
	7045562	1/2	1/2	9/32	0.150	0.260	④	0.130	0.230	1800
	7045564	1/2	1/2	9/32	0.150	0.260	④	0.130	0.230	1800
	7045568	1/2	1/2	9/32	0.150	0.260	④	0.130	0.230	1800
	7045566	1/2	1/2	9/32	0.150	0.260	④	0.130	0.230	1800

ROCHESTER CARBURETORS

QUADRAJET CARBURETOR SPECIFICATIONS
Pontiac

Year	Carburetor Identification ①	Float Level (in.)	Air Valve Spring (turn)	Pump Rod (in.)	Primary Vacuum Break (in.)	Secondary Vacuum Break (in.)	Secondary Opening (in.)	Choke Rod (in.)	Choke Unloader (in.)	Fast Idle Speed ② (rpm)
1976	7045246	5/16	3/4	3/8	0.130	0.120	④	0.095	0.250	1800
	7045546	5/16	3/4	3/8	0.130	0.130	④	0.095	0.250	1800
	7045268	17/32	1/2	3/8	0.160	0.250	④	0.125	0.230	1800
	7045264, 7045274, 7045266	17/32	1/2	3/8	0.160	0.250	④	0.125	0.230	1800
	7045263	17/32	5/8	3/8	0.170	0.250	④	0.125	0.230	1800
	7045564	17/32	1/2	3/8	0.150	0.260	④	0.130	0.230	1800
	7045260	1/2	1/2	9/32	0.150	0.230	④	0.130	0.230	1800
	7045262	17/32	1/2	3/8	0.160	0.250	④	0.125	0.230	1800
	7045562	17/32	1/2	9/32	0.150	0.260	④	0.130	0.230	1800
	7045566	17/32	1/2	3/8	0.170	0.250	④	0.120	0.230	1800
1977	17057250, 17057253, 17057255, 17057256	13/32	1/2	9/32	0.125	0.170	④	0.095	0.205	900
	17057258	13/32	1/2	9/32	0.125	0.215	④	0.095	0.205	1000
	17057550, 17057553	13/32	1/2	9/32	0.125	0.215	④	0.095	0.200	1000
	17057262	17/32	1/2	3/8	0.150	0.240	④	0.130	0.220	1800
	17057263	17/32	5/8	3/8	0.165	0.240	④	0.130	0.220	1800
	17057266	17/32	—	3/8	0.149	0.260	④	0.129	0.220	1800
	17057274	17/32	1/2	3/8	0.150	0.240	④	0.130	0.220	1800
1978	17058202	15/32	—	9/32	0.157	—	④	0.314	0.277	③
	17058204	15/32	—	9/32	0.157	—	④	0.314	0.277	③
	17058241	5/16	3/4	3/8	0.117	0.103	④	0.096	0.243	③
	17058250	13/32	1/2	9/32	0.119	0.167	④	0.088	0.203	③
	17058253	13/32	1/2	9/32	0.119	0.167	④	0.088	0.203	③
	17058258	13/32	1/2	9/32	0.126	0.212	④	0.092	0.203	③
	17058263	17/32	5/8	3/8	0.164	0.260	④	0.129	0.220	③
	17058264	17/32	1/2	3/8	0.149	0.260	④	0.129	0.220	③
	17058266	17/32	1/2	3/8	0.149	0.260	④	0.129	0.220	③
	17058272	15/32	5/8	3/8	0.126	0.195	④	0.071	0.222	③
	17058274	17/32	1/2	3/8	0.149	0.260	④	0.129	0.220	③
	17058276	17/32	1/2	3/8	0.149	0.260	④	0.129	0.220	③
	17058278	17/32	1/2	3/8	0.149	0.260	④	0.129	0.220	③
	17058502	15/32	—	9/32	0.164	—	④	0.314	0.277	③
	17058504	15/32	—	9/32	0.164	—	④	0.314	0.277	③
	17058553	13/32	1/2	9/32	0.126	0.212	④	0.092	0.203	③
	17058582	15/32	7/8	9/32	0.179	—	④	0.314	0.277	③
	17058584	15/32	7/8	9/32	0.179	—	④	0.314	0.277	③

QUADRAJET CARBURETOR SPECIFICATIONS
Pontiac

Year	Carburetor Identification①	Float Level (in.)	Air Valve Spring (turn)	Pump Rod (in.)	Primary Vacuum Break (in.)	Secondary Vacuum Break (in.)	Secondary Opening (in.)	Choke Rod (in.)	Choke Unloader (in.)	Fast Idle Speed② (rpm)
1979	17058263	$17/32$	$5/8$	$3/8$	0.164	0.243	④	0.129	0.220	⑤
	17059250,253	$13/32$	$1/2$	$9/32$	0.129	0.183	④	0.096	0.220	⑤
	17059241	$5/16$	$3/4$	$3/8$	0.120	0.113	④	0.096	0.243	⑤
	17059271	$9/16$	$5/8$	$3/8$	0.142	0.227	④	0.010	0.203	⑤
	17059272	$15/32$	$5/8$	$3/8$	0.136	0.195	④	0.074	0.220	⑤
	17059502,504	$15/32$	$7/8$	$1/4$	0.164	—	④	0.243	0.243	⑤
	17059553	$13/32$	$1/2$	$9/32$	0.136	0.230	④	0.103	0.220	⑤
	17059582,584	$15/32$	$7/8$	$11/32$	0.203	—	④	0.243	0.314	⑤
1980	17080249	$7/16$	$3/4$	$9/32$⑥	0.129	0.114	④	0.096	0.243	③
	17080270	$15/32$	$5/8$	$3/8$⑦	0.149	0.211	④	0.074	0.220	③
	17080272	$15/32$	$5/8$	$3/8$⑦	0.129	0.175	④	0.074	0.203	③
	17080274	$15/32$	$5/8$	$5/16$⑥	0.110	0.164	④	0.083	0.203	③
	17080502	$1/2$	$7/8$	⑧	0.136	0.179	④	0.110	0.243	③
	17080504	$1/2$	$7/8$	⑧	0.136	0.179	④	0.110	0.243	③
	17080553	$15/32$	$1/2$	⑧	0.142	0.220	④	0.090	0.220	③
1981	17081202,204	$11/32$	$7/8$	⑧	0.157⑩	—	④	0.110	0.243	⑨
	17081203,207	$11/32$	$7/8$	⑧	0.157⑩	—	④	0.110	0.243	⑨
	17081216, 217,218	$11/32$	$7/8$	⑧	0.157⑩	—	④	0.110	0.243	⑨
	17081242	$3/8$	$9/16$	⑧	0.090⑩	0.077⑪	④	0.139	0.243	⑨
	17081243	$5/16$	$9/16$	⑧	0.103⑩	0.090⑪	④	0.139	0.243	⑨
	17081245	$3/8$	$5/8$	⑧	0.164⑩	0.136⑪	④	0.139	0.243	⑨
	17081247	$3/8$	$5/8$	⑧	0.164⑩	0.136⑪	④	0.139	0.243	⑨
	17081248,249	$3/8$	$5/8$	⑧	0.164⑩	0.136⑪	④	0.139	0.243	⑨
	17081253,254	$15/32$	$1/2$	⑧	0.142⑩	0.227⑪	④	0.071	0.220	⑨
	17081270	$7/16$	$5/8$	⑧	0.136⑩	0.211⑪	④	0.074	0.220	⑨
	17081272	$7/16$	$5/8$	⑧	0.136⑩	0.260⑪	④	0.074	0.220	⑨
	17081274	$7/16$	$5/8$	⑧	0.136⑩	0.220⑪	④	0.083	0.220	⑨
	17081289	$13/36$	$5/8$	⑧	0.164⑩	0.136⑪	④	0.139	0.243	⑨

① The carburetor identification number is stamped on the float bowl, near the secondary throttle lever.
② On highest step.
③ 1½ turns after contacting lever for preliminary setting
④ No measurement necessary on two point linkage; see text.
⑤ 2 turns after contacting lever for preliminary setting.
⑥ Inner hole
⑦ Outer hole
⑧ Not adjustable
⑨ 4½ turns after contacting lever for preliminary setting
⑩ Front
⑪ Rear

HOLLEY CARBURETORS

MODEL 1945

The model 1945 carburetor is a concentric downdraft single barrel carburetor with an internal float bowl which completely surrounds the venturi. The unit uses dual nitrophyl floats which permit operation at extreme angles. It is used on 1975 and later Chrysler Corporation six-cylinder engines.

Float Adjustment

1. Remove the float bowl cover and invert the bowl. Hold the retaining spring in place.
2. Place a straightedge across the surface of the bowl. On 1976 and later models, the gasket should be in place. The straightedge should just clear the toes of the floats by the specified measurement.
3. If the adjustment is necessary, bend the float tang to obtain the correct adjustment.

Fast Idle Adjustment

1. Remove the air cleaner and disconnect the vacuum lines to the heated air control and the OSAC (Orifice Spark Advance Control) valve. If there is no OSAC valve, disconnect the hose to the distributor and the EGR hose. Cap all carburetor vacuum fittings.
2. With the engine off, transmission in Neutral and the parking brake set, open the throttle and close the choke.
3. Close the throttle. This will place the fast idle speed screw on the highest step.
4. Move the fast idle cam until the screw drops to the second highest speed step.
5. Start the engine and stabilize the engine speed. Rotate the fast idle speed screw to obtain the specified setting. See Specifications Chart.

Choke Unloader Adjustment

1. Hold the throttle valves wide-open and insert the specified gauge between the upper

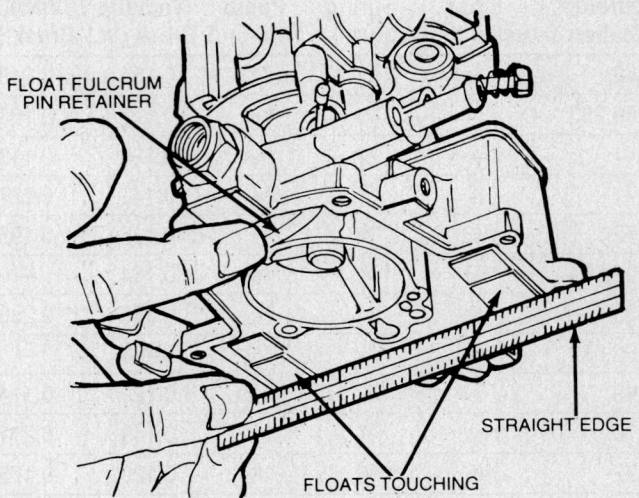

Checking the float adjustment—Holley 1945

edge of the choke valve and the inner wall of the air horn.
2. Place slight pressure against the control lever and attempt to remove the gauge. There should be a slight drag as the gauge is being withdrawn. If adjustment is necessary, bend the unloader tang on the throttle lever until the correct opening has been obtained.

Choke Vacuum Kick Adjustment

1. With the engine running, back off the fast idle screw to allow the choke to close to the kick position with the engine at curb idle. Note the number of turns. If the adjustment is made with the engine stopped as recommended for 1977 and later, open the throttle and move the choke to the closed position. Release the throttle first and then the choke.

2. If an auxiliary vacuum source is used, disconnect the vacuum hose from the carburetor and connect it to the hose from the vacuum supply with an extra length of tube. Apply a vacuum of 15 or more in. of mercury.
3. Insert the correct gauge (see Specifications Chart) between the choke valve upper edge and the wall of the air horn. Close and hold the choke rod lever with light pressure. The cylindrical stem of the diaphragm will extend as the internal spring is compressed. This spring must be fully compressed for proper measurement of the vacuum kick.
4. If adjustment is necessary, shorten or lengthen the diaphragm link to obtain the correct opening.

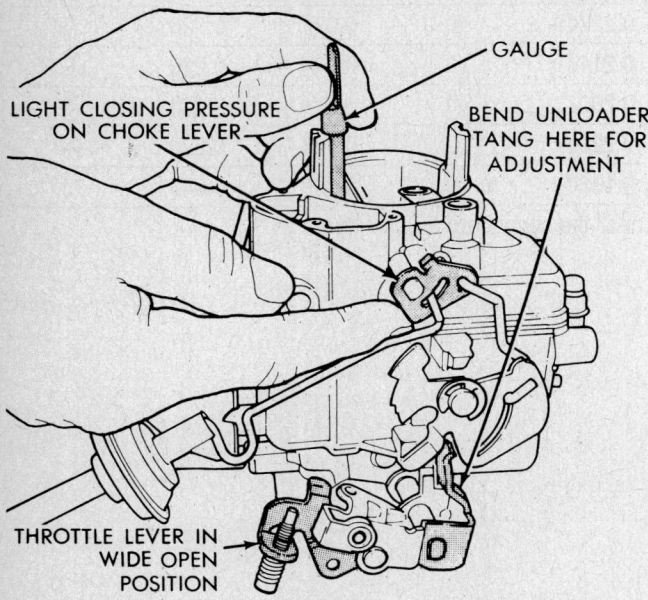

Choke unloader adjustment—Holley 1945

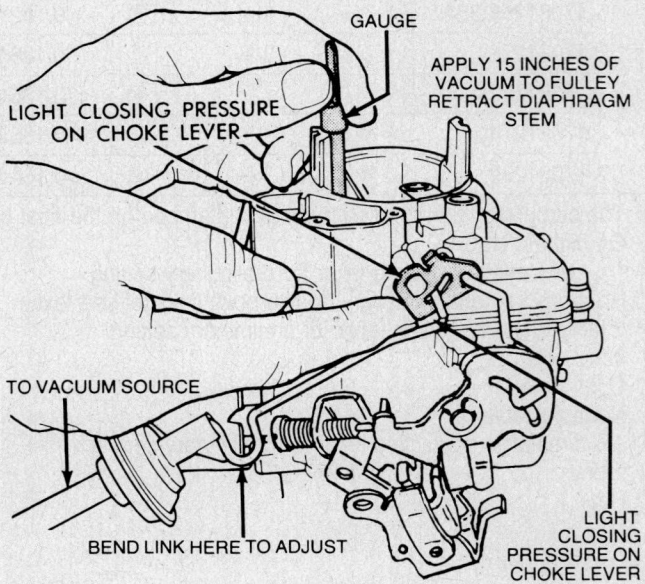

Choke vacuum kick adjustment-Holley 1945

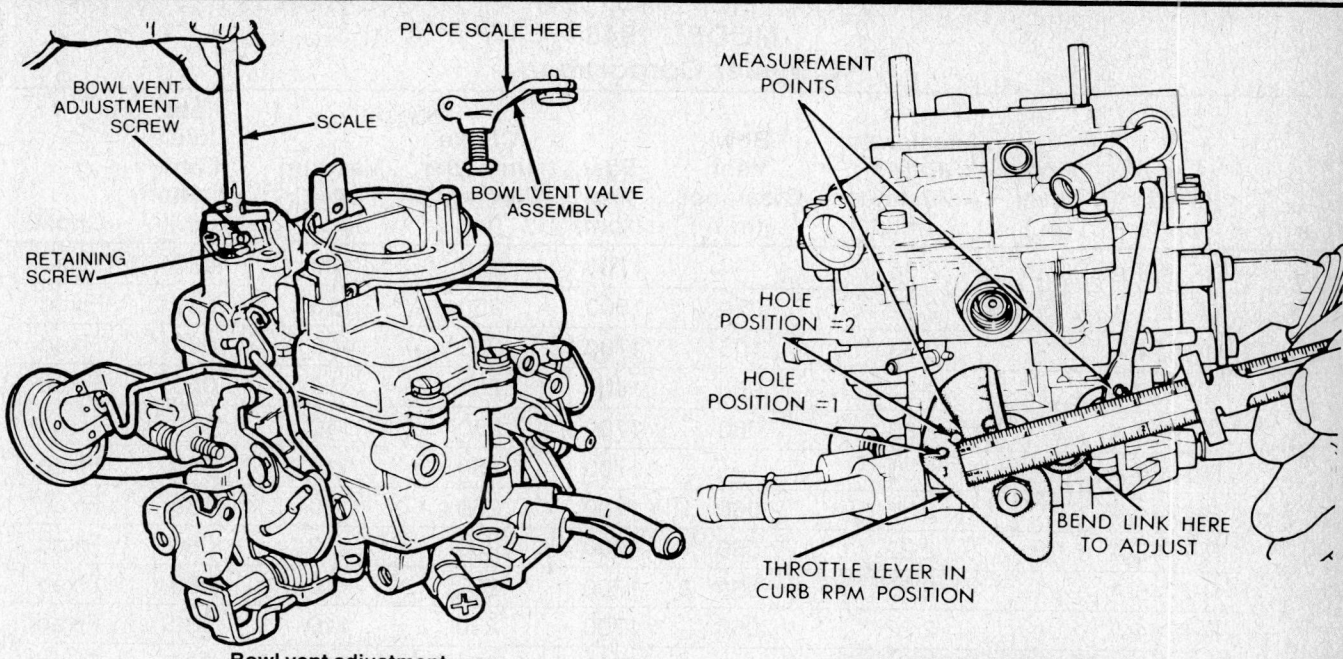

Bowl vent adjustment

Accelerator pump adjustment

CAUTION

Do not twist or bend the diaphragm.

5. Install the vacuum hose on the correct carburetor fitting and connect the fast idle linkage.

6. Check the operation in the following manner. With vacuum applied to the diaphragm, the choke valve should move freely between the open and closed positions. If there is binding, examine the linkage for misalignment or interference caused by bending.

Accelerator Pump Adjustment

1. With the throttle in the curb idle position, measure the distance between the pump link pivot and the link connection to the throttle lever. Models through 1976 have only one slot for the link at the throttle lever. 1977–78 models have three slots for the link at the throttle lever. 1979 models have three holes in the throttle lever; 1980 and later models have two holes. Make sure the link is in the correct hole or slot.

2. If the measurement is incorrect, the link may be bent at the "U" to adjust.

NOTE: If the pump link is adjusted, the Bowl Vent Adjustment must be checked and, if necessary, reset.

Bowl Vent Adjustment
1976 AND LATER ONLY

1. With the throttle set at curb idle speed, measure the distance from the cover support surface down to the flat on the bowl vent lever.

2. If adjustment is necessary, turn the bowl vent lever adjusting screw with a screwdriver.

3. Install the bowl vent spring and cover plate.

MODEL 1945
Chrysler Corporation

Year	Carb. Part No. ②	Float Level (in.)	Accelerator Pump Adjustment (in.)	Bowl Vent Clearance (in.)	Fast Idle (rpm)	Choke Unloader Clearance (in.)	Vacuum Kick (in.)	Fast Idle Cam Position (in.)	Choke
1975	R-7329-A	.046	2.22	—	1700	.250	.130	.080	Fixed
	R-7017-A	.046	2.22	—	1600	.250	.130	.080	Fixed
	R-7018-A	.046	2.33	—	1700	.250	.090	.080	Fixed
	R-7019-A	.046	2.22	—	1600	.250	.130	.080	Fixed
	R-7020-A	.046	2.33	—	1700	.250	.090	.080	Fixed
	R-7029-A	.046	2.22	—	1600	.250	.130	.080	Fixed
	R-7210-A	.046	2.33	—	1700	.250	.090	.080	Fixed
1976	R-7356-A	①	2.22	.060	1600	.250	.110	.080	Fixed
	R-7357-A	①	2.65	.060	1700	.250	.100	.080	Fixed
	R-7360-A	①	2.22	—	1600	.250	.110	.080	Fixed
	R-7361-A	.046	2.65	—	1700	.250	.100	.080	Fixed

HOLLEY CARBURETORS

MODEL 1945
Chrysler Corporation

Year	Carb. Part No. ②	Float Level (in.)	Accelerator Pump Adjustment (in.)	Bowl Vent Clearance (in.)	Fast Idle (rpm)	Choke Unloader Clearance (in.)	Vacuum Kick (in.)	Fast Idle Cam Position (in.)	Choke
1976	R-7363-A	.046	2.65	—	1700	.250	.100	.080	Fixed
	R-7823-A	①	2.22	.070	1600	.250	.110	.080	Fixed
	R-7824-A	①	2.33	.105	1700	.250	.100	.080	Fixed
1977	R-7632-A	①	2.22	.060	1400	.250	.110	.080	Fixed
	R-7633-A	①	2.33	.060	1700	.250	.110	.080	Fixed
	R-7635-A	①	2.33	—	1700	.250	.110	.080	Fixed
	R-7744-A	①	2.33	.060	1700	.250	.130	.080	Fixed
	R-7745-A	①	2.22	.060	1600	.250	.150	.080	Fixed
	R-7746-A	①	2.33	.060	1700	.250	.110	.080	Fixed
	R-7764-A	①	2.22	.060	1700	.250	.110	.080	Fixed
	R-7765-A	①	2.33	.060	1700	.250	.110	.080	Fixed
1978	R-7988-A	①	2.22	.062	1400	.250	.110	.080	Fixed
	R-7989-A	①	2.33	.062	1600	.250	.110	.080	Fixed
	R-8008-A	①	2.33	.062	1700	.250	.110	.080	Fixed
	R-8010-A	①	2.33	.062	1500	.250	.130	.080	Fixed
	R-8394-A	①	2.33	.062	1700	.250	.110	.080	Fixed
1979	R-8523-A	①	1.70③	1/16	1400	.250	.110	.080	Fixed
	R-8452-A	①	1.615④	1/16	1600	.250	.110	.080	Fixed
	R-8555-A	①	1.70③	1/16	1400	.250	.110	.080	Fixed
	R-8727-A	①	1.615④	1/16	1600	.250	.110	.080	Fixed
	R-8680-A	①	1.615④	1/16	1500	.250	.130	.080	Fixed
1980	R-8718-A	①	1.70③	1/16	1400	.250	.150	.090	Fixed
	R-8831-A	①	1.615④	1/16	1600	.250	.140	.090	Fixed
	R-8832-A	①	1.70③	1/16	1400	.250	.110	.090	Fixed
	R-8833-A	①	1.615④	1/16	1600	.250	.110	.090	Fixed
1981	R-9253-A	⑤	1.615④	—	1600	1250	.150	.090	Fixed

① Flush with the top of the bowl cover gasket, plus or minus 1/32
② Located on a tag attached to the carburetor.
③ Position #1
④ Position #2
⑤ Flush with the top of the main body casting to 0.050" above

MODEL 1946

This unit is a one barrel, altitude compensating model used on 1978 and later Fairmont, Zephyr, Mustang, and Capri cars with the 200 cid, 6-cylinder engine and the 1981 Thunderbird, XR-7, Granada and Cougar cars with the 200 cid 6-cylinder engine and automatic transmission.

Fast Idle Cam Position Adjustment

1. Position the fast idle adjusting screw on the second highest step of the fast idle cam.
2. Lightly move the choke plate toward the closed position.
3. Check the fast idle cam setting by placing the correct gauge (see specifications) between the upper edge of the choke plate and the air horn wall.
4. If the setting is not as specified, bend the fast idle cam link.

Fast Idle Adjustment

1. Remove the spark delay valve, if so equipped, and route the distributor vacuum hose directly to the advance side of the distributor.
2. Trace the EGR signal vacuum hose from the EGR valve to the carburetor. If an EGR/PVS valve or cold weather modulator is located in the hose, disconnect the EGR hose at the EGR valve and plug the hose. If not equipped with EGR/PVS or a cold weather modulator, do not detach the hose except on 1980 models; disconnect and plug the EGR hose on all 1980 models. On all 1981 models disconnect and plug the vacuum hoses at the EGR and purge valves.
3. Run the engine to normal operating temperature. With the choke plate fully open and the transmission in Park, place the fast idle screw on the next to the highest step of the fast idle cam. Allow the engine speed to stabilize and adjust the speed to the fast idle speed specification found on the underhood sticker.
4. Run the engine at 2500 rpm for about 15 seconds and recheck the fast idle speed.
5. When the speed is properly adjusted, turn off the engine and re-route the vacuum lines.

Accelerator Pump Stroke

The accelerator pump stroke is present at the factory and should not be adjusted to improve driveability.

Dechoke Adjustment

1. With the engine off, hold the throttle in the wide open position.
2. Insert the specified gauge between the upper edge of the choke plate and the wall of the air horn.

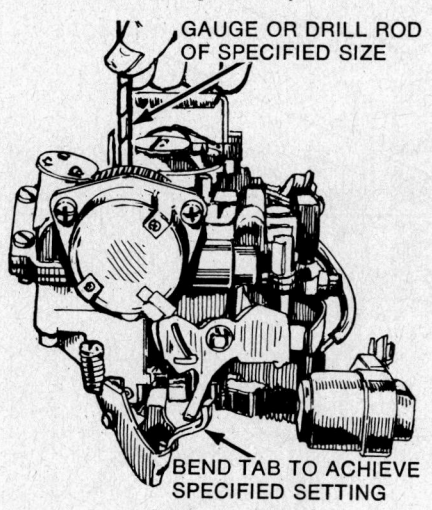

GAUGE OR DRILL ROD OF SPECIFIED SIZE

BEND TAB TO ACHIEVE SPECIFIED SETTING

Dechoke adjustment

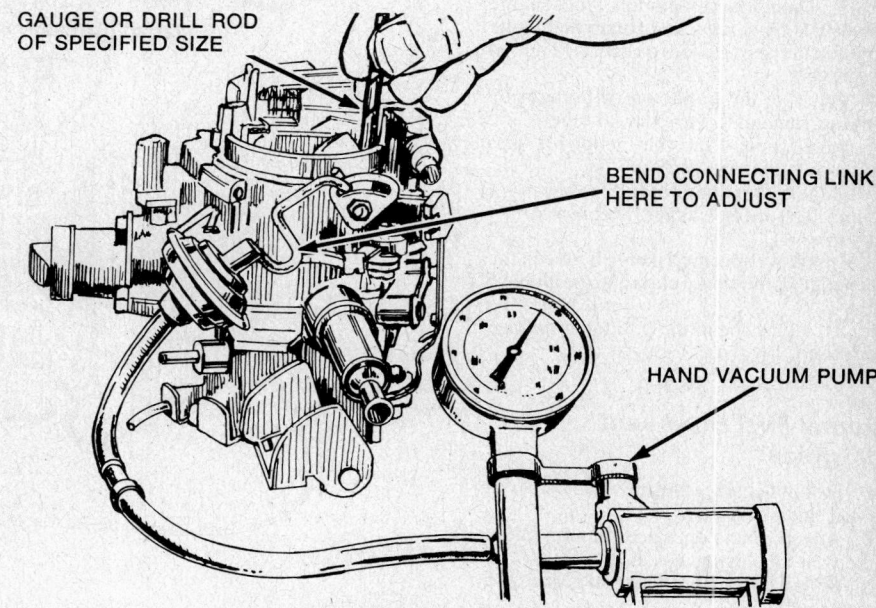

GAUGE OR DRILL ROD OF SPECIFIED SIZE

BEND CONNECTING LINK HERE TO ADJUST

HAND VACUUM PUMP

Choke pulldown adjustment

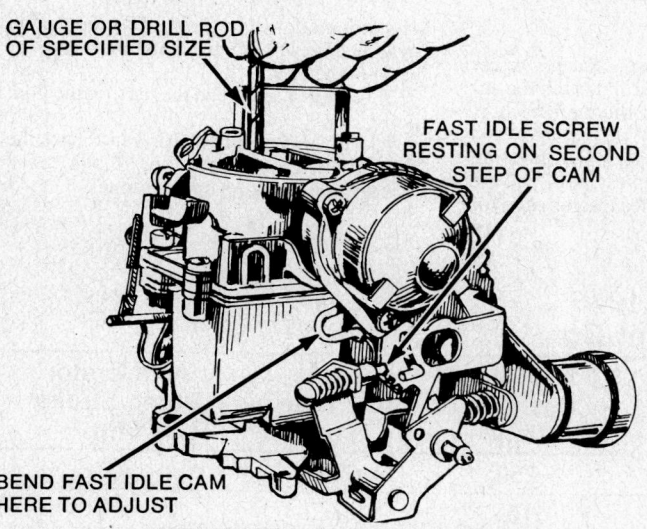

GAUGE OR DRILL ROD OF SPECIFIED SIZE

FAST IDLE SCREW RESTING ON SECOND STEP OF CAM

BEND FAST IDLE CAM HERE TO ADJUST

Fast idle cam position adjustment

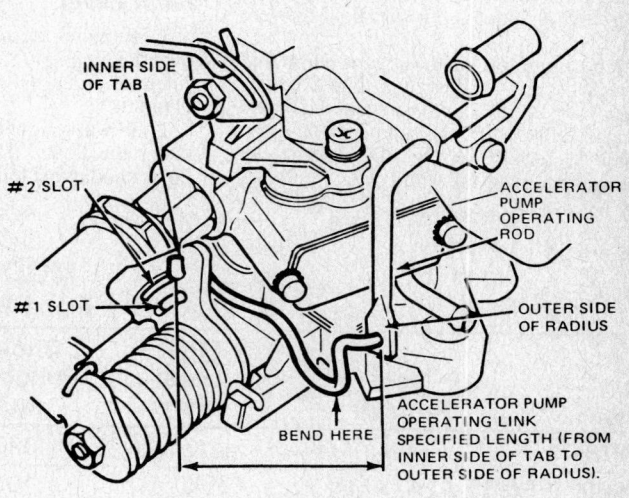

INNER SIDE OF TAB

#2 SLOT

#1 SLOT

ACCELERATOR PUMP OPERATING ROD

OUTER SIDE OF RADIUS

BEND HERE

ACCELERATOR PUMP OPERATING LINK SPECIFIED LENGTH (FROM INNER SIDE OF TAB TO OUTER SIDE OF RADIUS).

Accelerator pump adjustment (© Ford Motor Co.)

HOLLEY CARBURETORS

3. With a slight pressure against the choke shaft a slight drag should be felt when the gauge is withdrawn.

4. To adjust, bend the unloader tab on the throttle lever until the correct opening is obtained.

Choke Pulldown 1975-80

NOTE: On 1981 and later models this adjustment is preset at the factory and protected by a tamper resistant plug.

1. Set the fast idle screw on the highest step of the fast idle cam.

2. Cool the choke housing until the plate is fully closed.

3. Mark the choke setting for later resetting.

4. On 1980 California models, remove the choke thermostat housing, retaining ring and screws. Temporarily remove the index spacer. Reinstall the housing, retainer, and screws. Then, on all models, loosen the choke housing screws and rotate the choke cap 90° in the rich (closed) direction. Tighten the screws.

5. Activate the pulldown diaphragm by applying vacuum to the external tube.

6. Make sure that the pulldown diaphragm is fully retracted.

7. If the motor does not fully retract with vacuum, test it for leakage. Replace it if it leaks.

8. Insert the specified gauge between the upper edge of the choke plate and the air horn wall.

9. To adjust, bend the pulldown linkage as required.

External Fuel Bowl Vent Adjustment

1. Disconnect the canister vent hose from the fuel bowl vent.

2. Attach a hand operated vacuum pump to the vent tube using a ⅜ in adapter.

3. Remove the vent cover and gasket and vent spring.

4. The adjusting screw is located on the nylon arm. Turn it clockwise until no more than ⅛ in. of threads is visible above the vent arm.

5. Operate the hand vacuum pump and turn the screw ⅛ turn at a time counterclockwise, until vacuum is registered on the gauge. Release the vacuum and turn the screw ½ turn clockwise. Disconnect the pump and replace the vent cover.

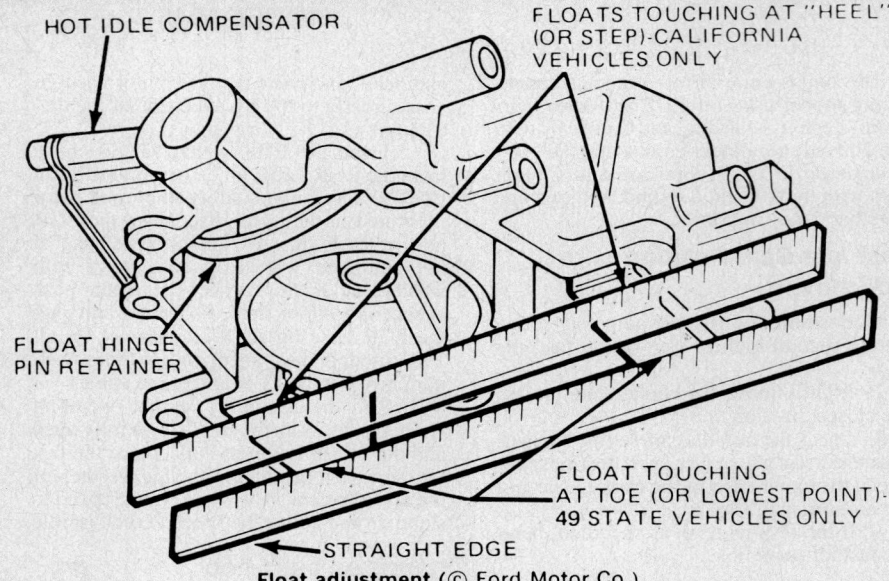

Float adjustment (© Ford Motor Co.)

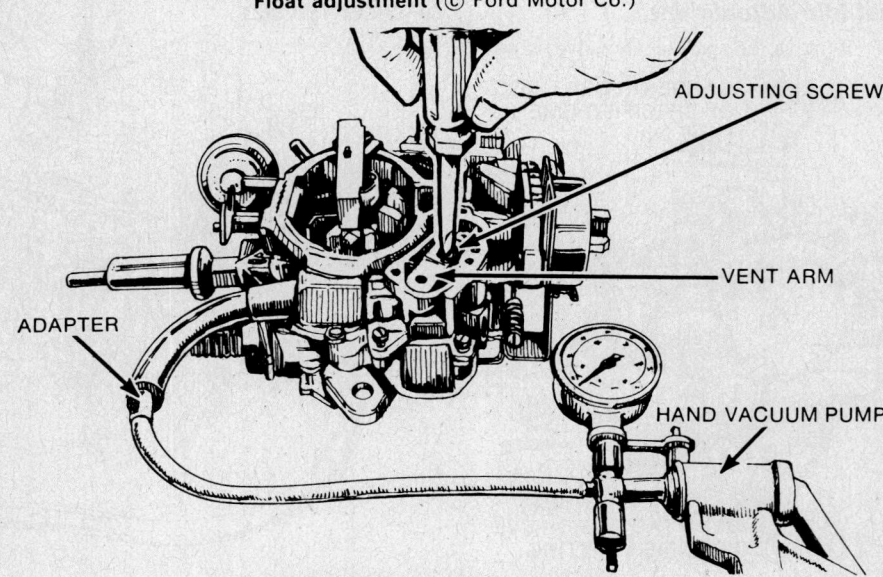

External fuel bowl vent adjustment

Float Level

1. Remove the air horn, place a finger over the hinge pin retainer and catch the accelerator pump ball when the main body is inverted.

2. Lay a straight edge across the housing under the floats. The lowest point of the floats should just touch the straight edge for 49 states models. For California models, the straight edge should just contact the step (or heel) of the float.

3. If necessary, bend the tang on the float arm.

4. Turn the main body back and check the float alignment. No binding should exist through the float movement range.

MODEL 1946
Ford Motor Co.

Year	Part Number	Float Level (in.)	Choke Pulldown (in.)	Dechoke (in.)	Fast Idle Cam (in.)	Accelerator Pump Stroke Slot
1978-79	All	①	.026	.250	.080	#2
1980	EOBE-ALA, AMA	①	.100	.150	.070	#2
	EOEE-ANA, APA	①	.100	.150	.070	#2

MODEL 1946
Ford Motor Co.

Year	Part Number	Float Level (in.)	Choke Pulldown (in.)	Dechoke (in.)	Fast Idle Cam (in.)	Accelerator Pump Stroke Slot
1980	EOZE-BBA, BAA	①	.120	.150	.086	#2
	EOZE-DA, EA	①	.110	.150	.070	#2
	EOZE-FA, GA	①	.110	.150	.070	#2
	EOBE-AA, CA	①	.100	.150	.070	#2
	EOBE-ZA, AAA	①	.115	.150	.090	#1
1981	EIBE-AFA	.69	.113	.150	.082	#2
	EIBE-AKA	.69	.113	.150	.082	#2
	EOBE-CA	.69	.100	.150	.070	#2
	EOBE-AA	.69	.100	.150	.070	#2

① See text

MODEL 2245

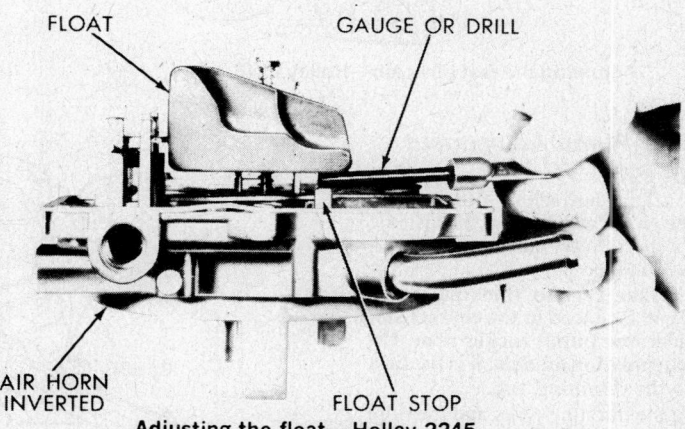

Adjusting the float—Holley 2245

The model 2245 carburetor is a two barrel unit used on 1975–79 Chrysler products with 360 or 400 cubic inch engines.

Float Adjustment

1. Invert the air horn so that the weight of the float is forcing the metering needle against its seat.
2. Measure the distance between the top of the float and the float stop. The clearance should be the same as given in the Specifications Chart. Make certain that the gauge is level when making the measurement.
3. If adjustment is necessary, bend the float adjusting tab toward or away from the needle until the correct clearance is obtained. A narrow-bladed screwdriver may be used to bend the tab.
4. Check the float drop by holding the air horn upright. The bottom edge of the float should be parallel to the underside of the air horn. If an adjustment is necessary, bend the tang on the float arm.

Fast Idle Cam Position Adjustment

1. Position the fast idle speed adjusting screw on the second highest notch on the fast idle cam. Move the choke valve toward the closed position by applying light pressure on the choke shaft lever.
2. Insert the correct gauge (see Specifications Chart) between the top of the choke valve and the wall of the air horn. An adjustment will be necessary if there is not a slight drag when the gauge is removed.
3. If an adjustment is necessary, bend the fast idle connector rod at the angle.

Vacuum Kick Adjustment

1. The adjustment must be made with some type of vacuum source. If the adjustment is made with the engine running, disconnect the fast idle linkage to allow the choke to close to the kick position with the engine at curb idle. If an auxiliary vacuum source is to be used as recommended for 1977 and later, open the throttle valves and move the choke to the closed position. Release the throttle first and then the choke.
2. If an auxiliary vacuum source is used, disconnect the vacuum hose from the carburetor and connect it to the hose from the vacuum supply with a small length of extra hose. Apply a vacuum of 15 or more in. of mercury.
3. Insert the correct gauge (see Specifications Chart) between the top of the choke valve and the wall of the air horn. Apply pressure to the lever to which the choke rod attaches without distorting the diaphragm link. The cylindrical stem of the diaphragm will extend as the internal spring is compressed. This spring must be fully compressed for proper measurement of the vacuum kick adjustment.
4. If a slight drag is not felt when the gauge is removed, adjustment is necessary. Adjust the diaphragm link to obtain the correct choke valve opening. Adjustments can be made by carefully opening or closing the U-bend in the link.

— CAUTION —
Do not twist or bend the diaphragm.

5. Connect the vacuum hose to the correct carburetor fitting. Replace the linkage.
6. Make the following check. With vacuum applied to the diaphragm, the choke valve should move freely between open and closed positions. If the movement is not free, examine the linkage for misalignment or interference caused by the bending operation.

Choke Unloader (Wide Open Kick) Adjustment

1. Place the throttle valves in the wide-open position and insert the proper gauge (see Specifications Chart) between the upper edge of the choke valve and the inner wall of the air horn.
2. While holding pressure on the choke lever, a slight drag should be felt as the gauge is removed.
3. If an adjustment is necessary, bend the unloader tang on the throttle lever until the correct opening has been obtained.

HOLLEY CARBURETORS

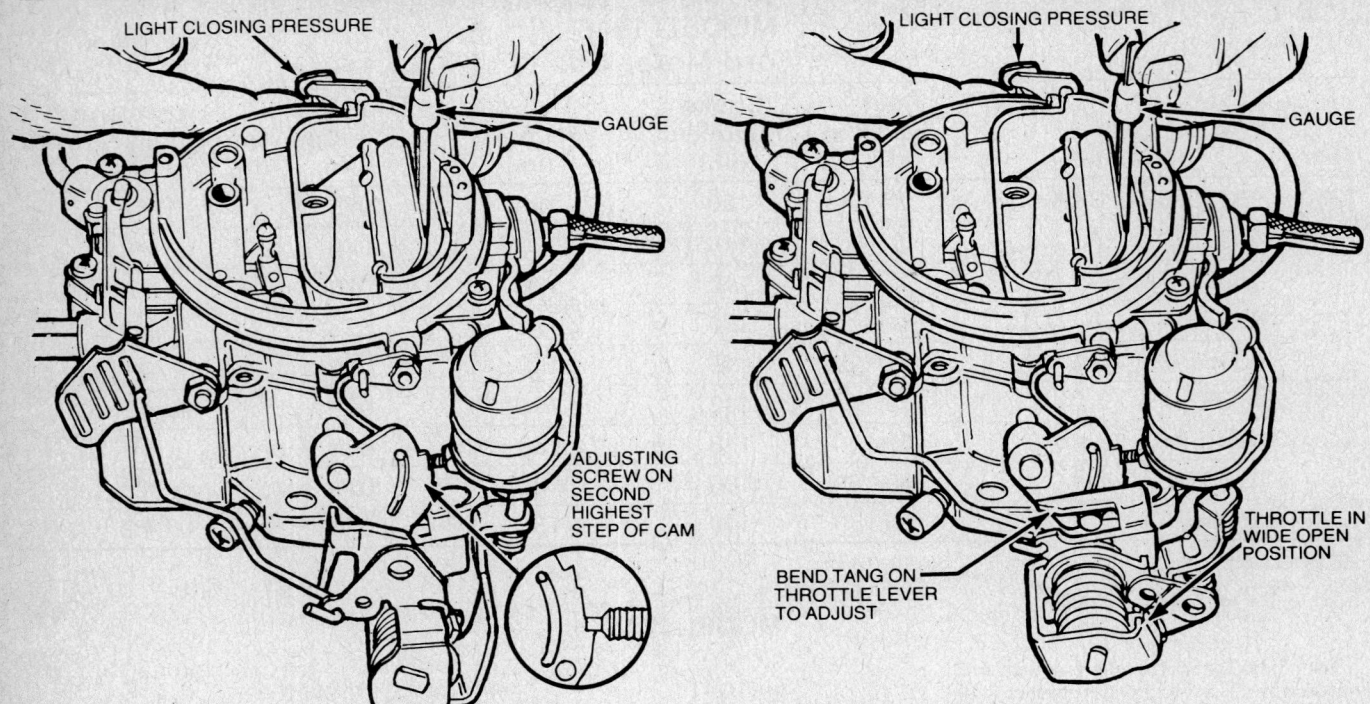

Adjusting the fast idle cam—Holley 2245

Adjusting the choke unloader—Holley 2245

Accelerator Pump Adjustment

THROUGH 1975

1. Back off the curb idle adjusting screw and open the choke valve so that the fast idle cam allows the throttle valves to be completely seated in their bores.

NOTE: Make certain that the pump connector rod is placed in the correct slot of the accelerator pump rocker arm. On manual transmission models, it is the first slot next to the retaining nut.

2. Close the throttle valves and measure the distance from the top of the air horn to the end of the plunger shaft. See Specifications Chart.

3. If adjustment is needed, bend the pump operating rod at its loop until the correct setting has been obtained.

1976 AND LATER

1. Make sure that the pump connector rod is in the first slot next to the retaining nut of the pump arm on 360 engines, and in the second slot for the 400.

2. Measure the drop of the pump plunger between curb idle and wide open throttle.

3. Adjust the travel by bending the operating rod.

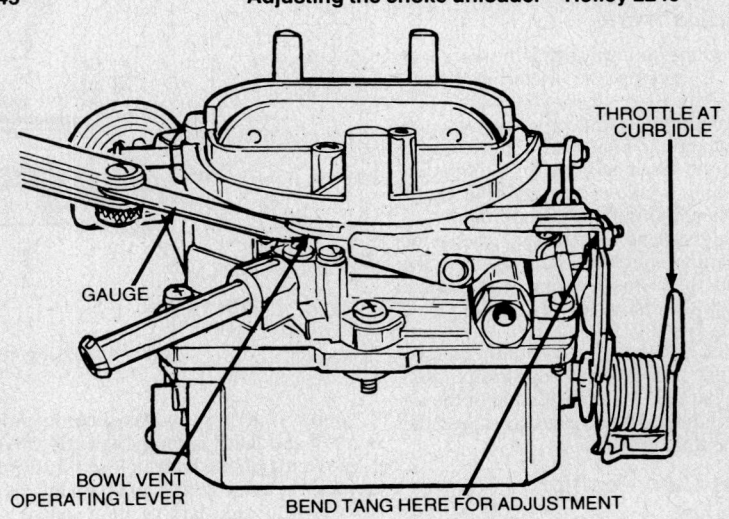

Adjusting the bowl vent clearance—Holley 2245

Bowl Vent Valve Clearance

1. With the throttle valves set at curb idle, insert the specified gauge between the bowl vent valve plunger stem and the operating rod.

2. If the gauge does not fit, bend the tang on the pump lever until the correct clearance has been obtained.

MODEL 2245
Chrysler Corporation

Year	Carb.★ Part No.	Float Level (in.)	Accelerator Pump Adjustment (in.)	Bowl Vent Clearance (in.)	Fast Idle (rpm)	Choke Unloader Clearance (in.)	Vacuum Kick (in.)	Fast Idle Cam Position (in.)	Choke
1975	R-7226-A	.190	.250	.015	1600	.170	.150	.110	Fixed
	R-7211-A	.190	.250	.015	1600	.170	.150	.110	Fixed
	R-7027-A	.190	.250	.015	1600	.170	.150	.110	Fixed
1976	R-7364-A	.190	.265	.025	1600	.170	.150	.110	Fixed
	R-7366-A	.190	.265	.025	1600	.170	.150	.110	Fixed
1977	R-7671-A	.190	.265	.025	1700	.170	.110	.110	Fixed
1978	R-7991-A	.188	.265	.025	1600	.170	.110	.110	Fixed
	R-8326-A	.188	.265	.025	1600	.170	.110	.110	Fixed
1979	R-8450-A	.188	.266	.025	1600	.170	.110	.110	Fixed
	R-8774-A	.188	.266	.025	1600	.170	.110	.110	Fixed

★ Located on a tag attached to the carburetor.

MODEL 2280

The model 2280 is a two barrel unit used on 1978–79 Chrysler 318 cid engines with automatic transmission in all states except California.

Float Adjustment

1. Remove the carburetor air horn.
2. Invert the carburetor body, taking care to catch the pump intake check ball, so that the weight of the floats only is forcing the needle against the seat. Hold a finger against the hinge pin retainer to fully seat the float in the float pin cradle.

3. Lay a straight edge across the float bowl. The toe of each float should be 5/16 in. from the straight edge. If necessary, bend the float tang to adjust.

Accelerator Pump Stroke Measurement

1. Remove the bowl vent cover plate and vent valve lever spring. Take care to avoid loosening the vent valve retainer.
2. Make sure that the accelerator pump connector rod is in the inner hole of the pump operating lever and the throttle is at curb idle.

3. Place a straight edge on the bowl vent cover surface of the air horn, over the accelerator pump lever.
4. The lever surface should be flush with the air horn. If not, adjust it by bending the pump connector rod at the 90 degree bend.
NOTE: If this adjustment is changed, both the bowl vent and the mechanical power valve adjustments must be reset.

Choke Unloader Adjustment

1. Hold the throttle valves in the wide open position.

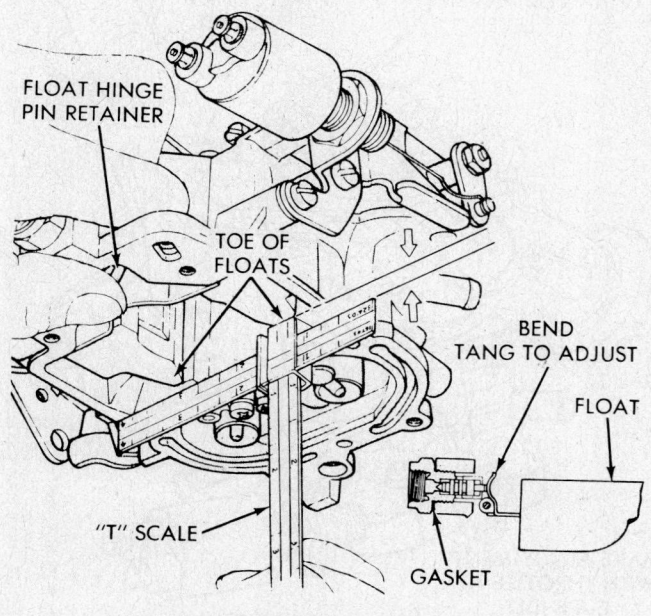

Float adjustment (© Chrysler Corp.)

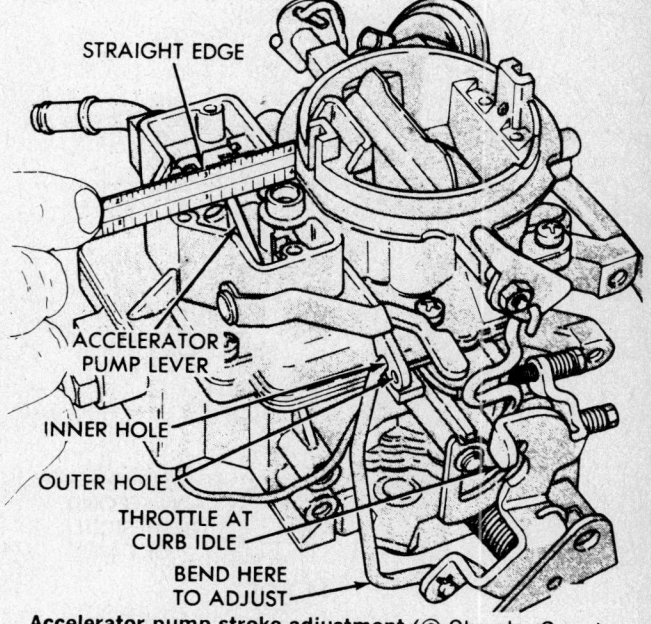

Accelerator pump stroke adjustment (© Chrysler Corp.)

HOLLEY CARBURETORS

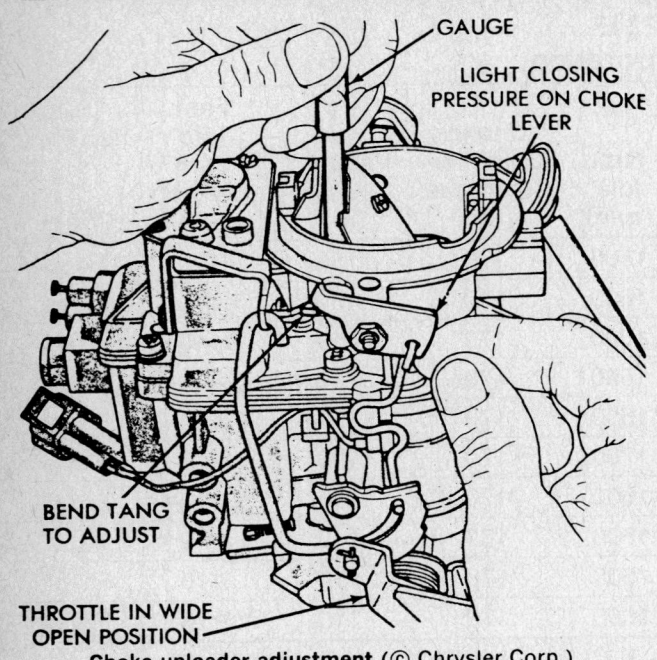

Choke unloader adjustment (© Chrysler Corp.)

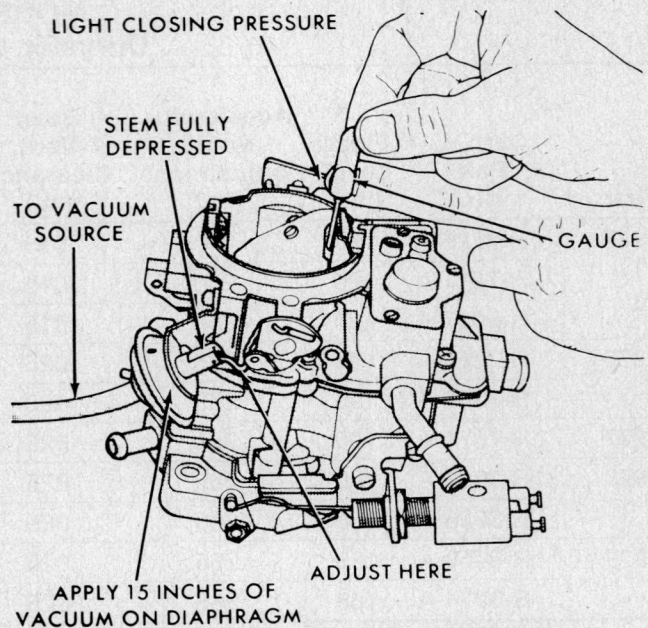

Choke vacuum kick adjustment (© Chrysler Corp.)

2. Lightly press a finger against the control lever to move the choke valve toward the closed position.

3. Insert a .310 inch gauge between the top of the choke valve and the air horn wall.

4. Adjust, if necessary, by bending the tang on the accelerator pump lever.

Choke Vacuum Kick Adjustment

1. Open the throttle, close the choke, then close the throttle to trap the fast idle cam at the closed choke position.

2. Disconnect the vacuum hose from the carburetor and connect it to an auxiliary vacuum source with a length of hose. Apply at least 15 in. Hg.

3. Completely compress the choke lever spring in the diaphragm stem without distorting the linkage.

4. Insert a .150 inch gauge between the top of the choke valve and the air horn wall.

5. Adjust by bending the diaphragm link. Check for free movement. Replace the vacuum hose.

Fast Idle Cam Position Adjustment

1. Position the adjusting screw on the second highest step of the fast idle cam.

2. Move the choke towards the closed position with light finger pressure.

3. Insert a .070 inch gauge between the choke valve and the air horn wall.

4. Adjust by opening or closing the U-bend in the fast idle connector link.

Bowl Vent Valve Adjustment

1. Remove the bowl vent cover and vent valve lever spring. Take care to avoid disturbing the lever retainer.

2. With the throttle at curb idle, press firmly down on the vent valve lever where the spring seats.

3. Insert a .030 inch gauge between the vent valve tang and the lever.

4. Adjust by bending the end of the vent valve lever up or down.

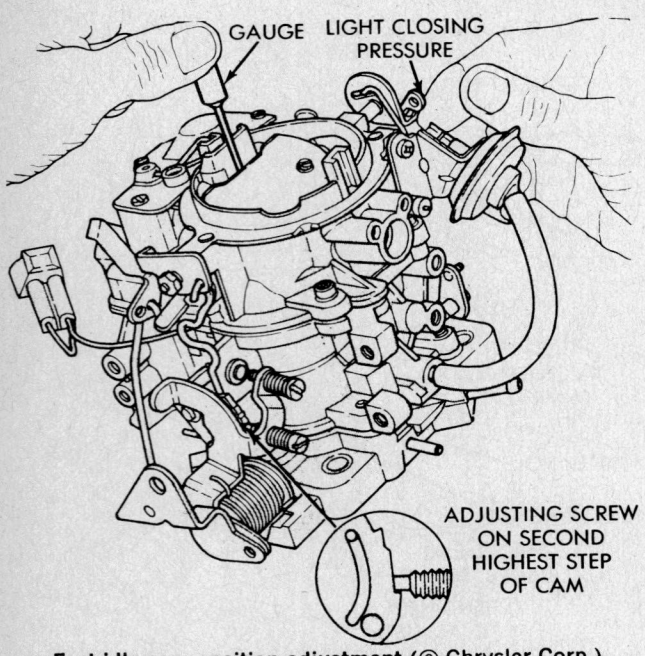

Fast idle cam position adjustment (© Chrysler Corp.)

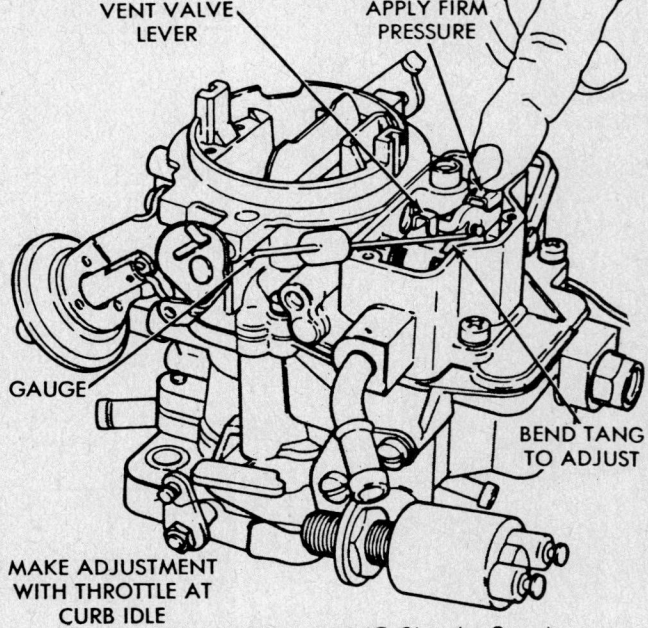

Bowl vent valve adjustment (© Chrysler Corp.)

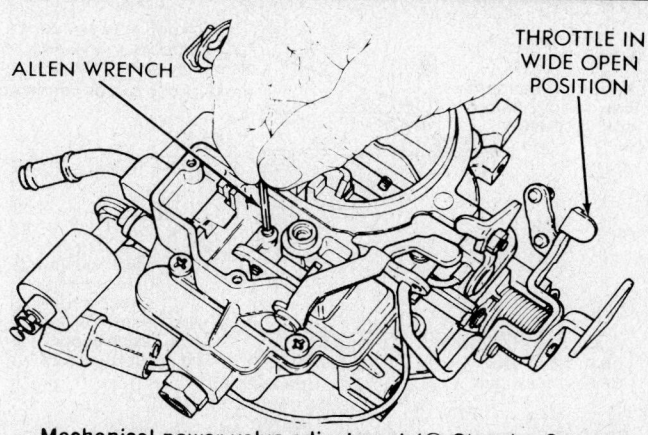

Mechanical power valve adjustment (© Chrysler Corp.)

Mechanical Power Valve Adjustment

1. Remove the bowl vent cover plate, vent valve lever, spring and retainer. Remove the lever pivot pin.

2. Hold the throttle in the wide open position.

3. Using a ⁵⁄₆₄ in. Allen wrench, press the mechanical power valve adjustment screw down, and release it to determine if clearance exists. Turn the screw clockwise until clear is zero.

4. Adjust by turning the screw one turn counter-clockwise.

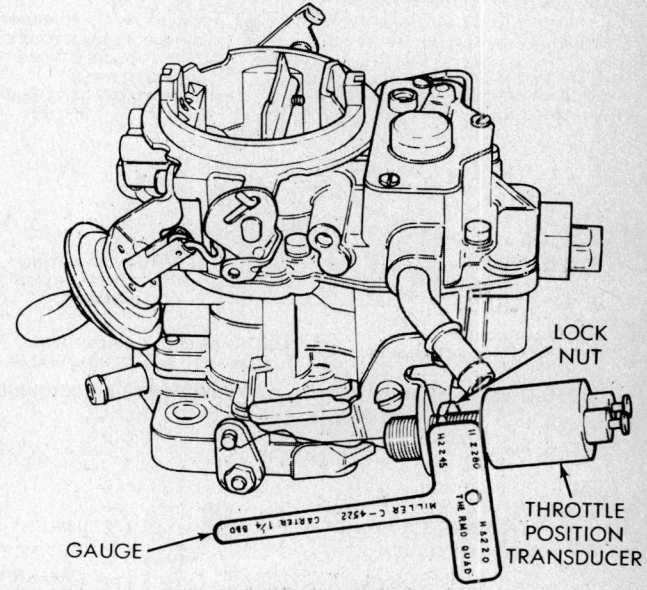

Throttle position transducer adjustment (© Chrysler Corp.)

5. Install all parts.

Throttle Position Transducer Adjustment

1. Disconnect the wire from the unit.
2. Loosen the locknut.

3. Insert an ¹¹⁄₁₆ inch gauge between the outer portion of the transducer and the transducer mounting bracket.
4. Adjust the transducer by turning it.
5. Tighten the locknut.

MODEL 2280
Chrysler Corporation

Year	Carb. Part No.	Float Level (in.)	Accelerator Pump Adjustment (in.)	Bowl Vent Clearance (in.)	Fast Idle (rpm)	Choke Unloader Clearance (in.)	Vacuum Kick (in.)	Fast Idle Cam Position (in.)	Choke
1978	R-7990-A	.313	Flush	.030	1600	.310	.150	.070	Fixed
1979	R-8448-A	.313	Flush	.030	1600	.310	.150	.070	Fixed

MODEL 5210-C

The Holley 5210-C is a progressive two barrel carburetor with an automatic choke system which is activated by a water heated thermostatic coil. An electrically heated choke is used on most later models. It also has an exhaust gas recirculation system with the valve located in the intake manifold. It is used on General Motors four cylinder engines through 1978, 1979–80 Chevettes, and 1977–79 AMC four cylinder engines.

Float Level

1. With the carburetor air horn inverted, and the float tang resting lightly on the inlet needle, insert the specified gauge between the air horn and the float.

2. Bend the float tang if an adjustment is needed.

Float Drop
GM THROUGH 1978 ONLY

1. With the air horn right side up, measure between the air horn and the top of the float.

2. Bend the float tang if an adjustment is needed.

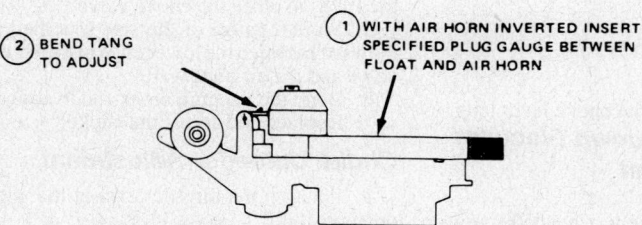

5210-C Float level adjustment (© G.M. Corp.)

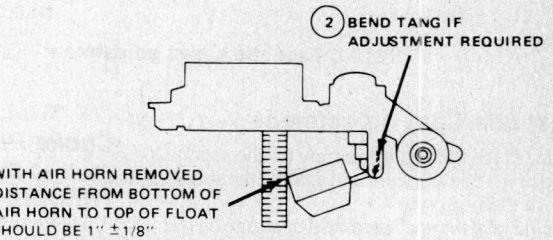

5210-C Float drop adjustment (© G.M. Corp.)

HOLLEY CARBURETORS

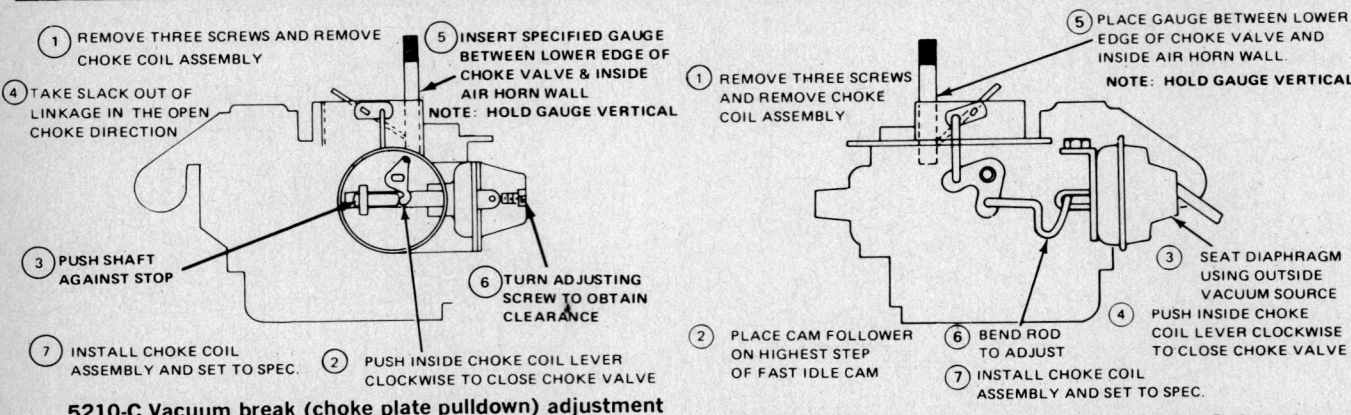

1 REMOVE THREE SCREWS AND REMOVE CHOKE COIL ASSEMBLY

4 TAKE SLACK OUT OF LINKAGE IN THE OPEN CHOKE DIRECTION

5 INSERT SPECIFIED GAUGE BETWEEN LOWER EDGE OF CHOKE VALVE & INSIDE AIR HORN WALL
NOTE: HOLD GAUGE VERTICAL

3 PUSH SHAFT AGAINST STOP

6 TURN ADJUSTING SCREW TO OBTAIN CLEARANCE

7 INSTALL CHOKE COIL ASSEMBLY AND SET TO SPEC.

2 PUSH INSIDE CHOKE COIL LEVER CLOCKWISE TO CLOSE CHOKE VALVE

5210-C Vacuum break (choke plate pulldown) adjustment
(© G.M. Corp.)

5 PLACE GAUGE BETWEEN LOWER EDGE OF CHOKE VALVE AND INSIDE AIR HORN WALL.
NOTE: HOLD GAUGE VERTICAL

1 REMOVE THREE SCREWS AND REMOVE CHOKE COIL ASSEMBLY

3 SEAT DIAPHRAGM USING OUTSIDE VACUUM SOURCE

4 PUSH INSIDE CHOKE COIL LEVER CLOCKWISE TO CLOSE CHOKE VALVE

2 PLACE CAM FOLLOWER ON HIGHEST STEP OF FAST IDLE CAM

6 BEND ROD TO ADJUST

7 INSTALL CHOKE COIL ASSEMBLY AND SET TO SPEC.

5210-C Secondary vacuum break adjustment (© G.M. Corp.)

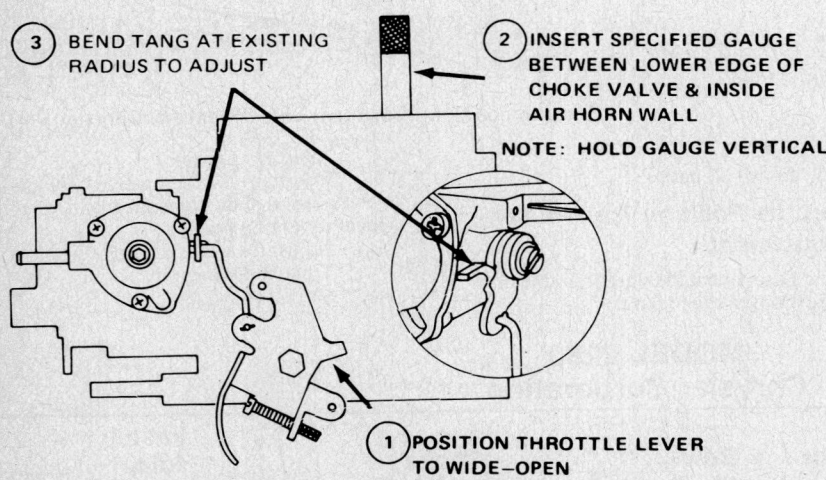

3 BEND TANG AT EXISTING RADIUS TO ADJUST

2 INSERT SPECIFIED GAUGE BETWEEN LOWER EDGE OF CHOKE VALVE & INSIDE AIR HORN WALL
NOTE: HOLD GAUGE VERTICAL

1 POSITION THROTTLE LEVER TO WIDE-OPEN

5210-C Choke unloader adjustment (© G.M. Corp.)

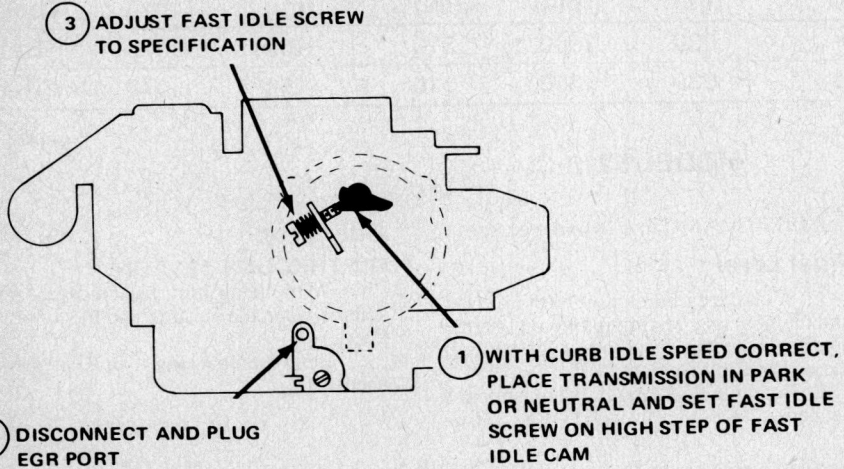

3 ADJUST FAST IDLE SCREW TO SPECIFICATION

2 DISCONNECT AND PLUG EGR PORT

1 WITH CURB IDLE SPEED CORRECT, PLACE TRANSMISSION IN PARK OR NEUTRAL AND SET FAST IDLE SCREW ON HIGH STEP OF FAST IDLE CAM

5210-C Fast idle speed adjustment (© G.M. Corp.)

Fast Idle Cam Adjustment

1. Place the fast idle screw on the second step of the fast idle cam and against the shoulder of the high step.
2. Place the specified drill or gauge on the down side of the choke plate.
3. To adjust, bend the choke lever tang.

Choke Plate Pulldown (Vacuum Break) Adjustment
THROUGH 1979

1. Remove the three hex headed screws and ring which retain the choke cover.

— CAUTION —
Do not remove the choke water housing screw if adjusting on the car. Pull the choke water housing and bimetal cover assembly back out of the way.

2. Push the diaphragm shaft against the stop. Push the coil lever clockwise.
3. Insert the specified size gauge on the down side of the primary choke plate.
4. Take the slack out of the linkage and turn the adjusting screw with a 5/22 in. Allen wrench.

1980

1. Attach a hand vacuum pump to the vacuum break diaphragm; apply vacuum and seat the diaphragm.
2. Push the fast idle cam lever down to close the choke plate.
3. Take any slack out of the linkage in the open choke position.
4. Insert the specified gauge between the lower edge of the choke plate and the air horn wall.
5. If the clearance is incorrect, turn the vacuum break adjusting screw, located in the break housing, to adjust.

Secondary Vacuum Break Adjustment
GM THROUGH 1978 ONLY

1. Remove the three screws and the choke coil assembly.
2. Place the cam follower on the highest step of the fast idle cam.
3. Seat the diaphragm by applying an outside source of vacuum.
4. Push the inside choke coil lever counter-clockwise through 1977; clockwise for 1978, to close the choke valve.
5. Place a gauge of the size specified in the chart between the lower edge of the choke valve and the air horn wall.
6. Bend the vacuum break rod to adjust.
7. Replace and adjust the choke.

Choke Unloader Adjustment

1. Position the throttle lever at the wide open position.
2. Insert a gauge of the size specified in

the chart between the lower edge of the choke valve and the air horn wall.

3. Bend the unloader tang for adjustment.

Secondary Throttle Stop Screw Adjustment

1. Back off the screw until it doesn't touch the throttle lever.

2. Turn the screw in until it touches the secondary throttle lever. Turn it in ¼ turn more.

Fast Idle Speed Adjustment

THROUGH 1975

1. Engine temperature must be normal with the air cleaner off. Disconnect and plug the vacuum advance line to the distributor.

2. Position the fast idle screw on the top step (second step for 1975) of the fast idle cam.

3. Adjust the fast idle speed to specifications.

4. Adjustments are made by turning the fast idle screw in or out.

1976 AND LATER

1. The engine must be at normal operating temperature with the air cleaner off.

2. With the engine running, position the fast idle screw on the high step of the cam for GM cars, or on the second step against the shoulder of the high step for AMC cars. Plug the EGR Port on the carburetor.

3. Adjust the speed by turning the fast idle screw.

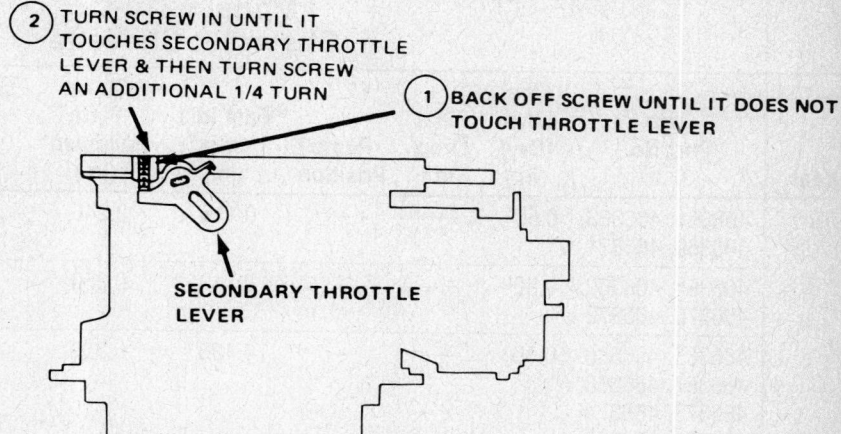

5210-C Secondary throttle stop screw adjustment (© G.M. Corp.)

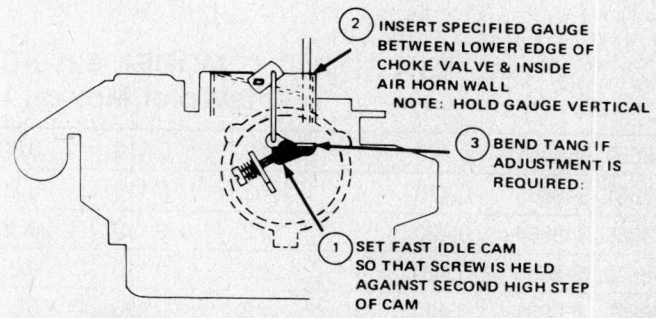

5210-C Fast idle cam adjustment (© G.M. Corp.)

MODEL 5210-C
AMC OHC 4 Cylinder

Year	Carb. Part No. ① ②	Float Level (Dry) (in.)	Float Drop (in.)	Pump Position	Fast Idle Cam (in.)	Choke Plate Pulldown* (in.)	Secondary Vacuum Break (in.)	Fast Idle Setting (rpm)	Choke Unloader (in.)	Choke Setting
1977	7711	0.420	—	—	0.140	0.246	—	1600	0.300	1 Rich
	7712	0.420	—	—	0.140	0.246	—	1600	0.300	1 Rich
	7799	0.420	—	—	0.135	0.215	—	1600	0.300	Index
	7846	0.420	—	—	0.101	0.204	—	1600	0.300	1 Rich
1978	8163	0.420	—	—	0.193	0.191	—	1800	0.300	1 NR
	8164	0.420	—	—	0.204	0.202	—	1800	0.300	1 NR
	8165	0.420	—	—	0.177	0.180	—	1800	0.300	Index
1979	8548	0.420	—	—	0.204	0.191	—	1800	0.300	1 Rich
	8549	0.420	—	—	0.191	0.266	—	1800	0.300	1 Rich
	7846	0.420	—	—	0.193	0.191	—	1800	0.300	1 Rich
	8675	0.420	—	—	0.173	0.177	—	1800	0.300	Index

HOLLEY CARBURETORS

Model 5210-C
Chevrolet Chevette

Year	Carb. Part No. ① ②	Float Level (Dry) (in.)	Float Drop (in.)	Pump Position	Fast Idle Cam (in.)	Choke Plate Pulldown* (in.)	Secondary Vacuum Break (in.)	Fast Idle Setting (rpm)	Choke Unloader (in.)	Choke Setting
1979	466361, 466363, 466369, 466371	0.50	—	—	0.110	0.245	—	2500	0.350	2 Rich
	466364, 466362, 466370, 466372	0.50	—	—	0.110	0.250	—	2500	0.350	2 Rich
	466365, 466366, 466367, 466368, 466373, 466374, 466375, 466376	0.50	—	—	0.130	0.300	—	2500	0.350	1 Rich
1980	All	0.50	—	—	0.110	0.120	—	⑤	0.350	Fixed

MODEL 5210-C
Chevrolet Monza, Vega

Year	Carb. Part No.	Float Level (Dry) (in.)	Float Drop (in.)	Pump Position	Fast Idle Cam (in.)	Choke Plate Pulldown* (in.)	Secondary Vacuum Break (in.)	Fast Idle Setting (rpm)	Choke Unloader (in.)	Choke Setting
1975	348659, 348663	0.420	1	#2	0.110	0.325	—	1600⑥	—	3 Rich
	348661, 348665	0.420	1	#2	0.110	0.275	—	1600⑥	—	3 Rich
	348660, 348664	0.420	1	#2	0.110	0.300	—	1600⑥	—	4 Rich
	348662, 348666	0.420	1	#2	0.110	0.275	—	1600⑥	—	4 Rich
1976	366829, 366831	0.420	1	#3	0.320	0.313	—	2200	0.375	2 Rich
	366833, 366841	0.420	1	#3	0.320	0.268	—	2200	0.375	2 Rich
	366830, 366832	0.420	1	#2	0.320	0.288	—	2200	0.375	3 Rich
	366834, 366840	0.420	1	#2	0.320	0.268	—	2200	0.375	3 Rich
1977	458103, 458105	0.420	1	#2	0.120	0.250	—	2500	0.350	3 Rich
	458107, 458109	0.420	1	#2	0.120	0.275	—	2500	0.400	3 Rich
	458102, 458104	0.420	1	#1	0.085	0.250	—	2500	0.350	3 Rich
	458106, 458108	0.420	1	#1	0.120	0.275	—	2500	0.400	3 Rich
	458110, 458112	0.420	1	#1	0.120	0.300	—	2500	0.400	3 Rich
1978	See notes	0.520	1	—	0.150	⑦	0.400	2500	0.350	⑧

Model 5210-C
Oldsmobile Starfire

Year	Carb. Part No.	Float Level (Dry) (in.)	Float Drop (in.)	Pump Position	Fast Idle Cam (in.)	Choke Plate Pulldown* (in.)	Secondary Vacuum Break (in.)	Fast Idle Setting (rpm)	Choke Unloader (in.)	Choke Setting
1976	Manual	0.420	1	#3	0.320	0.313③	—	2200	0.375	2 Rich
	Automatic	0.420	1	#2	0.320	0.288③	—	2200	0.375	3 Rich
1977	458102, 458104	0.420	1	④	0.085	0.250	0.400	2500	0.350	3 Rich
	458103, 458105	0.420	1	④	0.120	0.250	0.400	2500	0.350	3 Rich
	458106, 458107, 458108, 458109	0.420	1	④	0.120	0.275	0.400	2500	0.400	3 Rich
	458110, 458112	0.420	1	④	0.120	0.300	0.400	2500	0.400	3 Rich
1978	see notes	0.520	1	—	0.150	⑨	—	⑩	0.350	⑪

Model 5210-C
Pontiac Astre, Sunbird, Ventura

Year	Carb. Part No. ① ②	Float Level (Dry) (in.)	Float Drop (in.)	Pump Position	Fast Idle Cam (in.)	Choke Plate Pulldown* (in.)	Secondary Vacuum Break (in.)	Fast Idle Setting (rpm)	Choke Unloader (in.)	Choke Setting
1975	Manual	0.420	1	#3	0.140	0.300	—	2000 ⑥	—	2½ Rich
	Automatic	0.420	1	#2	0.140	0.400	—	2200 ⑥	—	3½ Rich
1976	Manual	0.410	1	#3	0.420	0.313 ③	—	2200 ⑥	0.375	2 Rich
	Automatic	0.410	1	#2	0.320	0.288 ③	—	2200 ⑥	0.375	3 Rich
1977	458102, 458103, 458104, 458105	0.420	1	④	0.085	0.250	—	2500	0.350	3 Rich
	458107, 458109	0.420	1	④	0.125	0.275	0.400	2500	0.350	3 Rich
	458110, 458112	0.420	1	④	0.120	0.300	0.400	2500	0.350	3 Rich
1978	see notes	0.520	1	—	0.150	⑫	—	⑬	0.350	⑭

① Located on tag attached to the carburetor, or on the casting or choke plate
② Beginning 1974, GM identification numbers are used in place of the Holley numbers
③ 0.268 in California
④ #1 manual, #2 automatic
⑤ See underhood decal
⑥ With no vacuum to the distributor
* Vacuum break initial choke valve clearance on AMC
⑦ Part #10001048, 10001050: .300
　　#10001047, 10001049, 10001052, 10001054: .325
⑧ Part #10001047, 10001049: 1 Rich
　　#10001048, 10001050, 10001052, 10001054: 2 Rich

⑨ Part #10001047, 10001049: .325
　　#10004048. 10004049: .300
⑩ Part #10001047, 10001049:2200
　　#10004048, 10004049: 2400
⑪ Part #10001047, 10001049: 1 Rich
　　#10004048, 10004049: 2 Rich
⑫ Part #10001047, 10001049: .325
　　#10004048, 10004049: .300
⑬ Part #10001047, 10001049: 2200
　　#10004048, 10004049: 2400
⑭ Part #10001047, 10001049: 1 Rich
　　#10004048, 10004049: 2 Rich

MODEL 5220

This is a staged two barrel unit used on Omni/Horizon cars.

Float Setting and Float Drop Adjustment

1. Remove and invert the air horn.
2. Insert a .480 inch gauge between the air horn and float.

3. If necessary, bend the tang on the float arm to adjust.
4. Turn the air horn right side up and allow the float to hang freely. Measure the float drop from the bottom of the air horn to the bottom of the float. It should be exactly 1⅞ inches. Correct by bending the float tang.

Vacuum Kick Adjustment

1. Open the throttle, close the choke, then close the throttle to trap the fast idle system at the closed choke position.
2. Disconnect the vacuum hose to the carburetor and connect it to an auxiliary vacuum source.

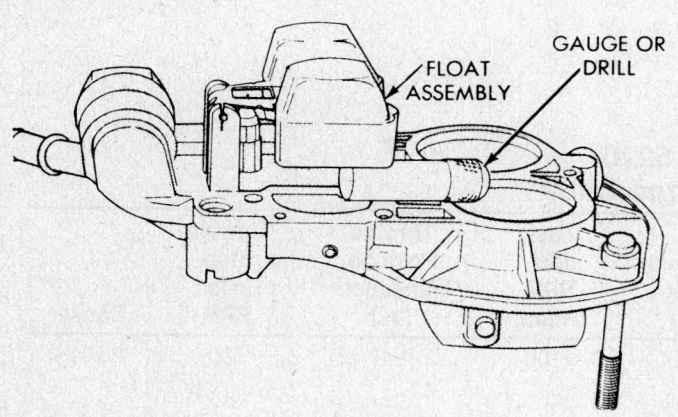

Float setting adjustment

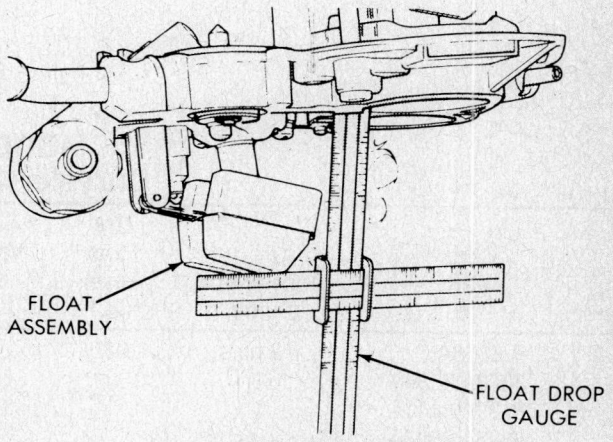

Float drop measurement

3. Apply at least 15 inches Hg. vacuum to the unit.

4. Apply sufficient force to close the choke valve without distorting the linkage.

5. Insert a gauge (see Specification Chart) between the top of the choke plate and the air horn wall.

6. Adjust by rotating the Allen screw in the center diaphragm housing.

7. Replace the vacuum hose.

Throttle Position Transducer Adjustment

1978 ONLY

1. Disconnect the wire from the transducer.

2. Loosen the locknut.

3. Place an $^{11}/_{16}$ inch gauge between the outer portion of the transducer and the mounting bracket.

4. To adjust the gap, turn the transducer.

5. Tighten the locknut.

Fast Idle Speed Adjustment

1. Remove the air cleaner, disconnect and plug the EGR line, but do not disconnect the spark control computer vacuum line. Use a jumper wire to ground the idle stop switch (through 1979). Turn the air conditioning off.

2. Disconnect the radiator fan electrical connector and use a jumper wire to complete the circuit at the fan. Do not short to ground, as this will damage the system.

3. With the parking brake set and the transmission in Neutral (engine still off), open the throttle and place the fast idle screw on the slowest step of the cam.

4. Start the engine and check the idle speed. If it continues to rise slowly, the idle stop switch is not grounded properly.

5. Adjust the fast idle with the screw, moving the screw off the cam each time to adjust. Allow the screw to fall back against the cam and the speed to stabilize between each adjustment.

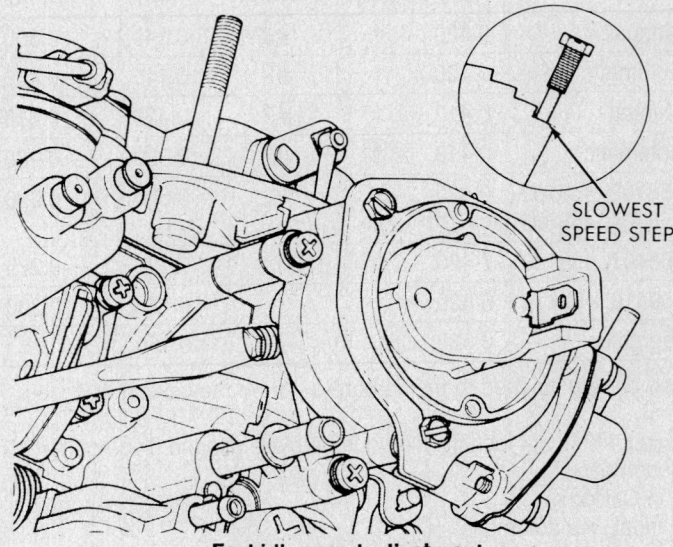

SLOWEST SPEED STEP

Fast idle speed adjustment

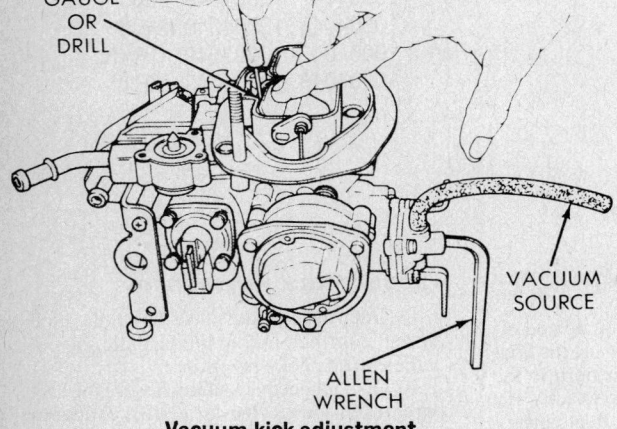

GAUGE OR DRILL

VACUUM SOURCE

ALLEN WRENCH

Vacuum kick adjustment

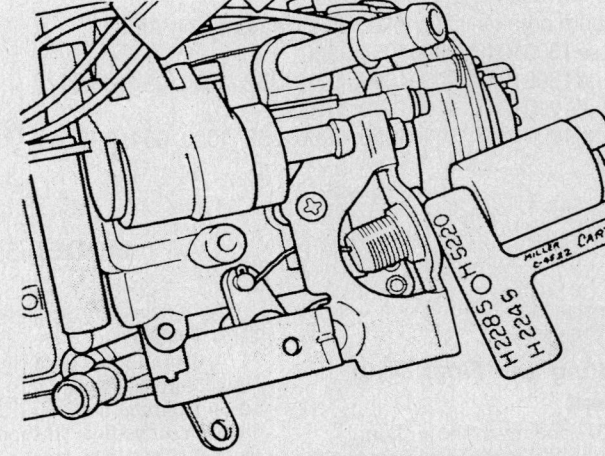

Throttle position transducer adjustment

MODEL 5220
Chrysler Corporation

Year	Carb. Part No.	Accelerator Pump	Dry Float Level (in.)	Vacuum Kick (in.)	Fast Idle RPM (w/fan)	Throttle Position Transducer (in.)	Throttle Stop Speed RPM	Choke
1978	R-8376A, 8378A,8384A, 8439A,8441A, 8505A,8507A	#2 hole	.480	.070	1100	.547	700	2 Rich

MODEL 5220
Chrysler Corporation

Year	Carb. Part No.	Accelerator Pump	Dry Float Level (in.)	Vacuum Kick (in.)	Fast Idle RPM (w/fan)	Throttle Position Transducer (in.)	Throttle Stop Speed RPM	Choke
1979	R-8524A, 8526A,8532A, 8534A,8528A, 8530A	#2 hole	.480	.040	1700	—	700	2 Rich
	R-8525A, 8541A,8531A, 8533A,8527A, 8529A	#2 hole	.480	.070	1400	—	700	2 Rich
1980	R8838A, 8839A, 9110A, 9111A, 9325A, 9327A	#2 hole	.480	.040	1700	—	700	Fixed
	R8726A, 8727A, 8837A, 9108A, 9321A, 9323A	#2 hole	.480	.070	1400	—	700	Fixed
	R9109A	#2 hole	.480	.100	1400	—	700	Fixed
1981	R-9056A	#2 hole	.480	.070	1400	—	700	Fixed
	R-9057A	#2 hole	.480	.070	1400	—	—	Fixed
	R-9058A	#2 hole	.480	.040	1400	—	700	Fixed
	R-9059A	#2 hole	.480	.040	1400	—	—	Fixed
	R-9064A	#2 hole	.480	.070	1300	—	—	Fixed
	R-9065A	#2 hole	.480	.070	1300	—	—	Fixed
	R-9066A	#2 hole	.480	.060	1300	—	700	Fixed
	R-9067A	#2 hole	.480	.060	1300	—	—	Fixed

MODEL 6500, 6510-C

Model 6500

This is a Holley-Weber Unit used on 1978 and later Pinto and Bobcat California models with the 2.3L engine. It is also used on all 1981 models with the 2.3L engine equipped with the Feedback Electronic Engine Control System. With the exception of an externally variable fuel metering system in place of the fuel enrichment valve, it is identical to the 1977 model Motorcraft 5200. For all adjustments, refer to this listing in the Motorcraft section of Carburetor Unit Repair.

MODEL 6510-C

The 6510-C is used on subcompact GM cars with the 4-151 engine through 1979. In 1980 and later, it is used only on the Chevette and T-1000.

This is a staged, two barrel unit which incorporates a feedback air/fuel metering system. The system uses five new and additional components.

Vacuum Break Adjustment
THROUGH 1979
   a. Oxygen sensor
   b. Electrical control unit
   c. Vacuum modulator
   d. Feedback diaphragm and idle needle
   e. Main feedback idle system

   1. Remove the choke coil assembly.
   2. Push the choke coil lever clockwise to close the choke valve.
   3. Push the choke shaft against its stop.
   4. Take the slack out of the linkage, in the open direction.
   5. Insert the specified gauge between the lower edge of the choke plate and the air horn wall. Turn the adjusting screw on the diaphragm housing to adjust.

1980-81
   1. Attach a hand vacuum pump to the vacuum break diaphragm. Apply vacuum until the diaphragm is seated.
   2. Push the fast idle cam lever down to close the choke plate.
   3. Take the slack out of the linkage in the open choke position.
   4. Insert the specified gauge between the lower edge of the choke plate and the air horn wall.
   5. If the clearance is incorrect, turn the screw in the end of the diagphragm to adjust.

Fast Idle Cam Adjustment

   1. Set the fast idle cam so that the screw is on the second highest step of the fast idle cam.
   2. Insert the specified gauge between the lower edge of the choke valve and the air horn wall.
   3. Bend the tang on the arm to adjust.

Unloader Adjustment

   1. Place the throttle in the wide open position.
   2. Insert a .350 inch gauge between the

HOLLEY CARBURETORS

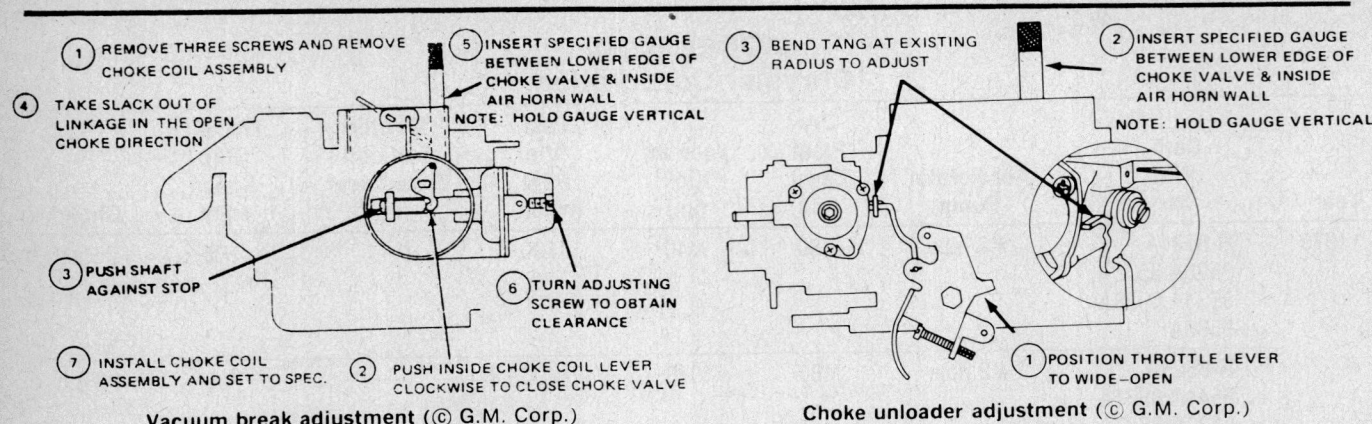

① REMOVE THREE SCREWS AND REMOVE CHOKE COIL ASSEMBLY

④ TAKE SLACK OUT OF LINKAGE IN THE OPEN CHOKE DIRECTION

③ PUSH SHAFT AGAINST STOP

⑦ INSTALL CHOKE COIL ASSEMBLY AND SET TO SPEC.

⑤ INSERT SPECIFIED GAUGE BETWEEN LOWER EDGE OF CHOKE VALVE & INSIDE AIR HORN WALL NOTE: HOLD GAUGE VERTICAL

⑥ TURN ADJUSTING SCREW TO OBTAIN CLEARANCE

② PUSH INSIDE CHOKE COIL LEVER CLOCKWISE TO CLOSE CHOKE VALVE

Vacuum break adjustment (© G.M. Corp.)

③ BEND TANG AT EXISTING RADIUS TO ADJUST

② INSERT SPECIFIED GAUGE BETWEEN LOWER EDGE OF CHOKE VALVE & INSIDE AIR HORN WALL NOTE: HOLD GAUGE VERTICAL

① POSITION THROTTLE LEVER TO WIDE-OPEN

Choke unloader adjustment (© G.M. Corp.)

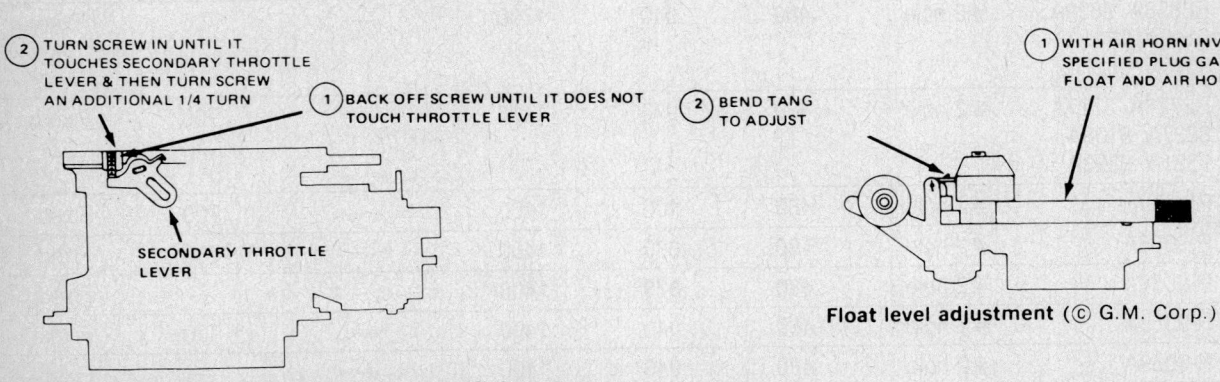

② TURN SCREW IN UNTIL IT TOUCHES SECONDARY THROTTLE LEVER & THEN TURN SCREW AN ADDITIONAL 1/4 TURN

① BACK OFF SCREW UNTIL IT DOES NOT TOUCH THROTTLE LEVER

SECONDARY THROTTLE LEVER

Secondary throttle stop screw adjustment (© G.M. Corp.)

① WITH AIR HORN INVERTED INSERT SPECIFIED PLUG GAUGE BETWEEN FLOAT AND AIR HORN

② BEND TANG TO ADJUST

Float level adjustment (© G.M. Corp.)

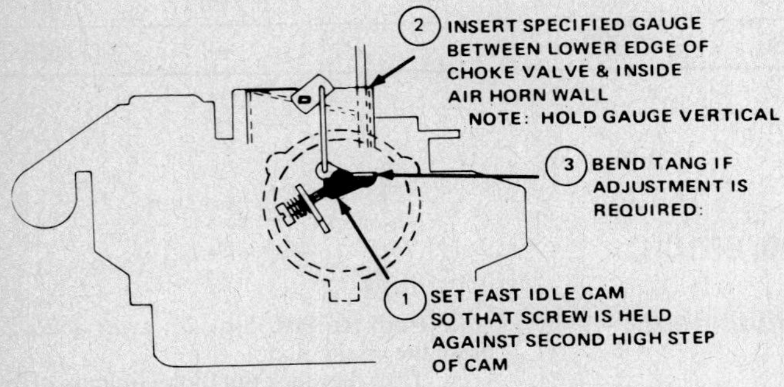

② INSERT SPECIFIED GAUGE BETWEEN LOWER EDGE OF CHOKE VALVE & INSIDE AIR HORN WALL NOTE: HOLD GAUGE VERTICAL

③ BEND TANG IF ADJUSTMENT IS REQUIRED:

① SET FAST IDLE CAM SO THAT SCREW IS HELD AGAINST SECOND HIGH STEP OF CAM

Fast idle cam adjustment (© G.M. Corp.)

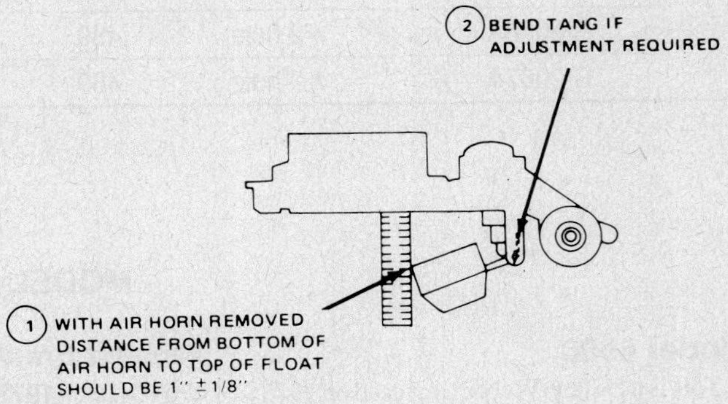

② BEND TANG IF ADJUSTMENT REQUIRED

① WITH AIR HORN REMOVED DISTANCE FROM BOTTOM OF AIR HORN TO TOP OF FLOAT SHOULD BE 1" ±1/8"

Float drop adjustment (© G.M. Corp.)

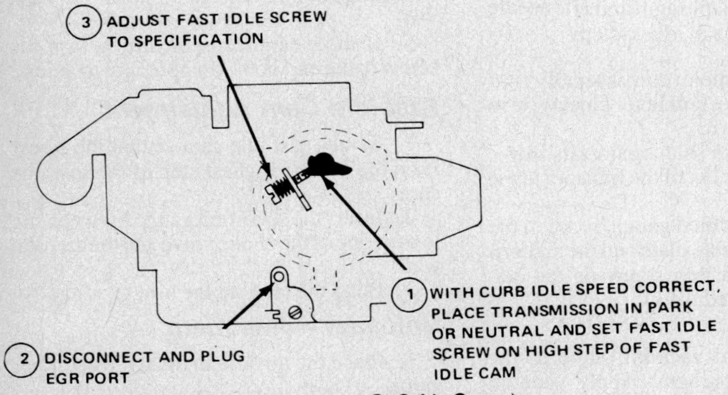

③ ADJUST FAST IDLE SCREW TO SPECIFICATION

① WITH CURB IDLE SPEED CORRECT, PLACE TRANSMISSION IN PARK OR NEUTRAL AND SET FAST IDLE SCREW ON HIGH STEP OF FAST IDLE CAM

② DISCONNECT AND PLUG EGR PORT

Fast idle speed adjustment (© G.M. Corp.)

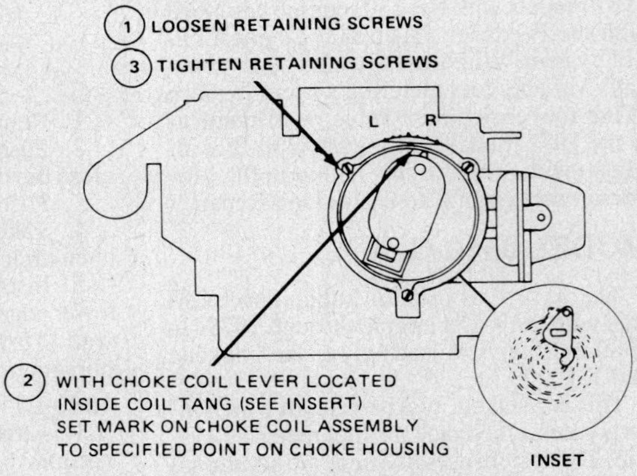

① LOOSEN RETAINING SCREWS

③ TIGHTEN RETAINING SCREWS

L R

② WITH CHOKE COIL LEVER LOCATED INSIDE COIL TANG (SEE INSERT) SET MARK ON CHOKE COIL ASSEMBLY TO SPECIFIED POINT ON CHOKE HOUSING

INSET

Choke cap setting (© G.M. Corp.)

B94

lower edge of the choke valve and the air horn wall.

3. Bend the tang on the choke arm to adjust.

Choke Cap Setting

1. Loosen the retaining screws.
2. Make sure that the choke coil lever is located inside the coil tang.
3. Turn the cap to the specified setting.
4. Tighten the retaining screws.

Fast Idle Adjustment

1. With the curb idle speed correct, place the fast idle screw on the highest cam step and adjust to the specified rpm.

NOTE: The EGR line must be disconnected and plugged.

Float Level Adjustment

1. Remove and invert the air horn.
2. Place the specified gauge between the air horn and the float.
3. If necessary, bend the float arm tang to adjust.

Float Drop Setting

THROUGH 1979 ONLY
1. Hold the air horn right side up. The distance between the bottom of the air horn and the top of the float should be 1 inch.

2. If necessary, bend the tang on the side of the float arm support, to adjust.

Secondary Throttle Stop Screw Adjustment

1. Back off the screw until it does not touch the lever.
2. Turn the screw in until it touches the lever, then turn it an additional ¼ turn.

MODEL 6500
Ford Bobcat and Pinto

Year	Carb. Iden.	Dry Float Level (in.)	Pump Hole Setting	Choke Plate Pulldown (in.)	Fast Idle Cam Linkage (in.)	Dechoke (in.)	Choke Setting
1978-79	D9EE-AFC	0.455	2	0.236	0.118	0.236	2 Rich
	D9EE-AJC, D9EE-AKC	0.460	2	0.236	0.118	0.236	1 Rich
	D9EE-AGC	0.460	2	0.236	0.118	0.236	2 Rich
1980	EOEE-NA, VA	0.460	2	0.236	0.118	0.393	①
	EOEE-NC, NV	0.460	2	0.236	0.118	0.157	①
	EOEE-ND, VD	0.460	2	0.236	0.118	0.393	①
	EOZE-AFA, SA	0.460	2	0.236	0.118	0.393	①
	EOZE-AFC, SC	0.460	—	0.236	0.118	0.393	①
1981	EIZE-RA	0.460	3	0.240	0.120	0.400	—
	EIZE-SA	0.460	3	0.240	0.120	0.400	—
	EIDE-DA	0.460	3	0.240	0.120	0.400	—
	EIDE-EA	0.460	3	0.240	0.120	0.400	—

① See underhood decal

MODEL 6510-C
General Motors Corp.

Year	Part Number	Vacuum Break Adjustment (in.)	Fast Idle Cam Adjustment (in.)	Unloader Adjustment (in.)	Fast Idle Adjustment (rpm)	Float Level Adjustment (in.)	Choke Setting
1978	10001056, 10001058	.325	.150	.350	2400	.520	1 Rich
1979	10008489, 10008490	.250	.150	.350	2400	.520	1 Rich
	10008491, 10008492	.250	.150	.350	2200	.520	2 Rich
	10009973, 10009974	.275	.150	.350	2400	.520	2 Rich
1980	All w/manual	.275	.130	.350	2600	.500	Fixed
	All w/automatic	.300	.130	.350	2500	.500	Fixed

HOLLEY CARBURETORS

MODEL 6510-C
General Motors Corp.

Year	Part Number	Vacuum Break Adjustment (in.)	Fast Idle Cam Adjustment (in.)	Unloader Adjustment (in.)	Fast Idle Adjustment (rpm)	Float Level Adjustment (in.)	Choke Setting
1981	14004768	.300	.130	.350	①	.500	Fixed
	14004769	.300	.130	.350	①	.500	Fixed
	14004770	.300	.130	.350	①	.500	Fixed
	14004771	.300	.130	.350	①	.500	Fixed
	14004777	.300	.130	.350	①	.500	Fixed

① See underhood decal

MODEL 6145
Chrysler Corporation

Year	Carb. Part No. ①	Float Level (in.)	Accelerator Pump Adjustment (in.)	Bowl Vent Clearance (in.)	Fast Idle (rpm)	Choke Unloader Clearance (in.)	Vacuum Kick (in.)	Fast Idle Cam Position (in.)	Choke
1981	R-9129A	②	1.615③	—	2000	.250	.150	.090	Fixed

① Located on a tag attached to the carburetor
② Flush with the top of the main body casting to .050″ above
③ Position #2

MODEL 6520
Chrysler Corporation

Year	Carb. Part No. ①	Accelerator Pump	Dry Float Level (in.)	Float Drop (in.)	Vacuum Kick (in.)	Fast Idle RPM
1981	R-9052A	#2 hole	.480	1.875	.070	1400②
	R-9053A	#2 hole	.480	1.875	.070	1400②
	R-9054A	#2 hole	.480	1.875	.040	1400②
	R-9055A	#2 hole	.480	1.875	.040	1400②
	R-9060A	#2 hole	.480	1.875	.030	1100②
	R-9061A	#2 hole	.480	1.875	.030	1100②
	R-9602A	#2 hole	.480	1.875	.035	1500②
	R-9603A	#2 hole	.480	1.875	.035	1500②
	R-9125A	#2 hole	.480	1.875	.030	1200②
	R-9126A	#2 hole	.480	1.875	.030	1200②
	R-9604A	#2 hole	.480	1.875	.035	1600②
	R-9605A	#2 hole	.480	1.875	.035	1600②

① Located on tag attached to the carburetor
② With radiator fan running

FORD TURBOCHARGERS

Description

The turbocharger is used on some 2300 cc engines which have increased cooling system capacity, modified lubrication system and strengthened valves, pistons and bearings. A boost pressure activated spark retard system prevents the detonation which could be caused by increased intake pressure. The turbocharger raises engine horsepower by about 35% and torque by about 25%.

Operation

The turbocharger is used to increase power on a demand basis and has little effect at low engine speeds. As load on the engine is increased and the throttle is opened, more air-fuel mixture flows into the conbustion chambers. As this increased flow is burned, a larger volume of higher energy exhaust gas enters the engine exhaust system and is directed through the turbocharger turbine housing. Some of this energy is used to increase the turbine wheel speed.

The turbine wheel is connected by a shaft to the compressor wheel. The increased compressor wheel speed compresses the air-fuel mixture it receives from the carburetor and delivers it to the intake manifold. The resulting higher pressure in the intake manifold allows a denser charge to enter the combustion chambers. This denser charge develops more power during the combustion cycle.

Turbocharger Individual Component Operation

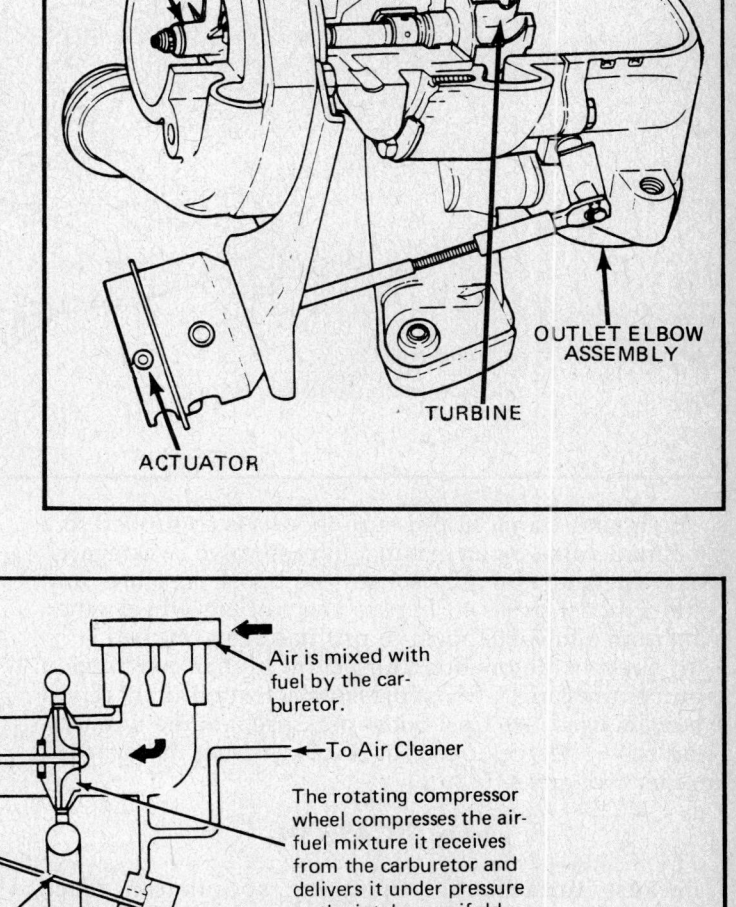

COMPRESSOR   CENTER HOUSING

OUTLET ELBOW ASSEMBLY

TURBINE

ACTUATOR

Turbocharger Operating Schematic

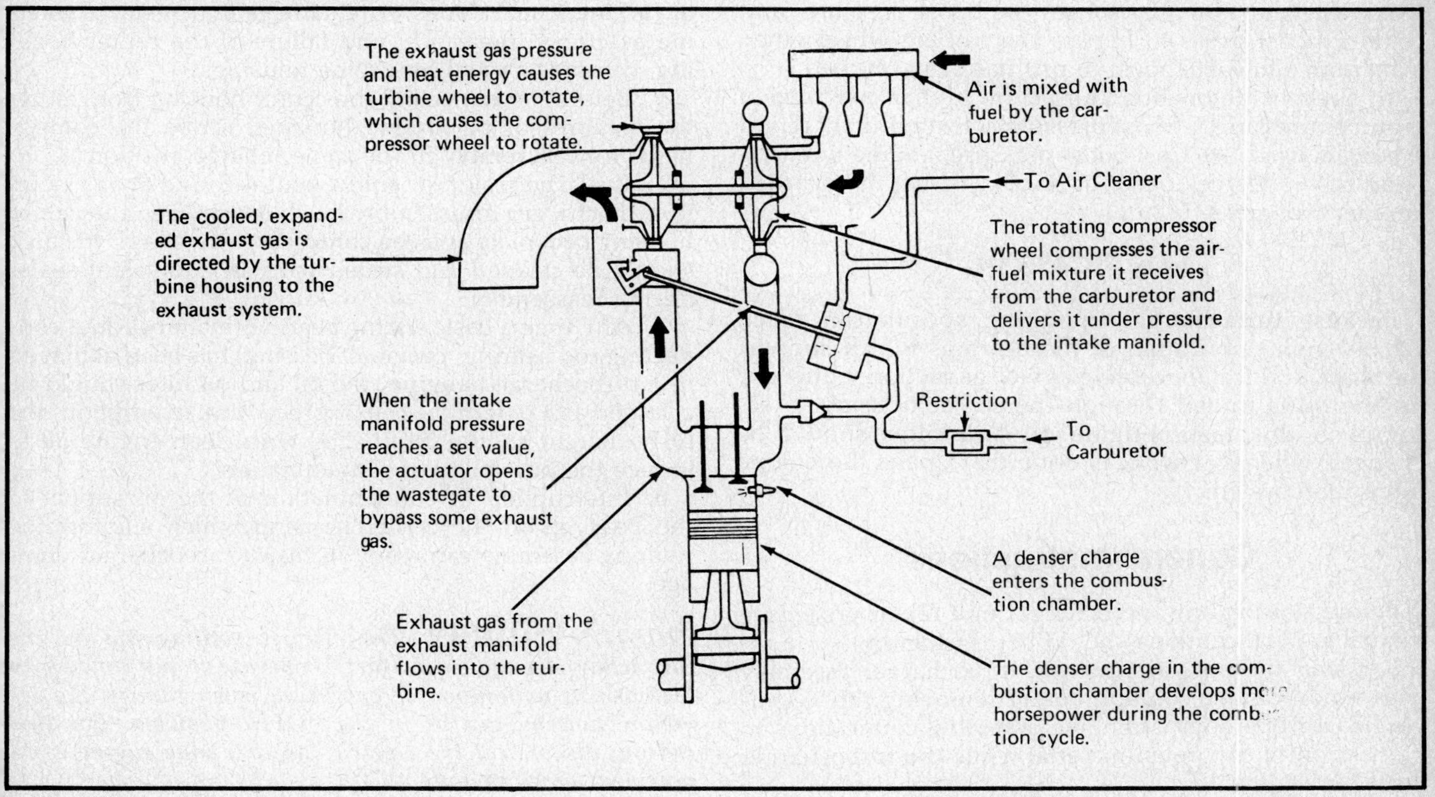

The exhaust gas pressure and heat energy causes the turbine wheel to rotate, which causes the compressor wheel to rotate.

Air is mixed with fuel by the carburetor.

To Air Cleaner

The cooled, expanded exhaust gas is directed by the turbine housing to the exhaust system.

The rotating compressor wheel compresses the air-fuel mixture it receives from the carburetor and delivers it under pressure to the intake manifold.

Restriction

To Carburetor

When the intake manifold pressure reaches a set value, the actuator opens the wastegate to bypass some exhaust gas.

Exhaust gas from the exhaust manifold flows into the turbine.

A denser charge enters the combustion chamber.

The denser charge in the combustion chamber develops more horsepower during the combustion cycle.

Turbocharger Lubrication System Connections

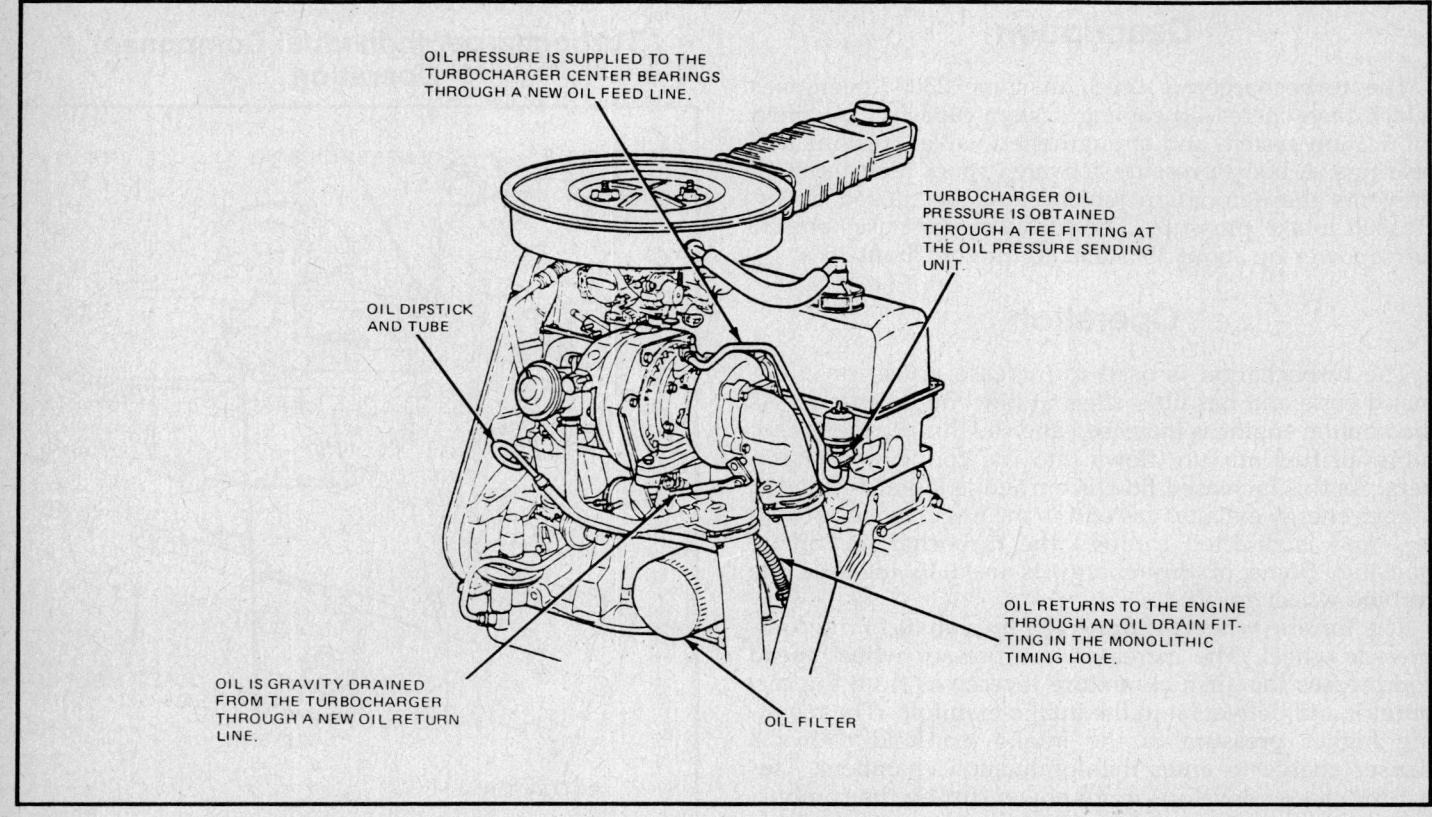

OIL PRESSURE IS SUPPLIED TO THE
TURBOCHARGER CENTER BEARINGS
THROUGH A NEW OIL FEED LINE.

TURBOCHARGER OIL
PRESSURE IS OBTAINED
THROUGH A TEE FITTING AT
THE OIL PRESSURE SENDING
UNIT.

OIL DIPSTICK
AND TUBE

OIL RETURNS TO THE ENGINE
THROUGH AN OIL DRAIN FIT-
TING IN THE MONOLITHIC
TIMING HOLE.

OIL IS GRAVITY DRAINED
FROM THE TURBOCHARGER
THROUGH A NEW OIL RETURN
LINE.

OIL FILTER

The intake manifold pressure (boost) is controlled to a maximum value by an exhaust bypass valve (wastegate). The wastegate assembly senses the boost pressure, and vents exhaust gases to bypass the turbine wheel when maximum allowable boost (6 psi) has been reached.

To prevent detonation caused by higher combustion chamber pressure, a boost pressure activated spark retard system is used. At 1 psi boost pressure, engine timing is retarded 6 degrees, and at 4 psi, timing is retarded another 6 degrees.

LUBRICATION

Because turbocharger operating speeds can reach 120,000 rpm, lubrication of the bearings which support the shaft is critical for cooling as well as friction reduction. Engine oil is routed through the center housing to accomplish this task. Engine oil and filter should be changed whenever work is done that opens the engine lubrication system.

General Instructions

Before starting any turbocharger unit repair procedure several general cautions should be considered.

1. Clean the area around the turbocharger assembly with a non-caustic solution before removing the assembly. Cover openings of engine assembly connections to prevent entry of foreign material while the turbocharger is off the engine.

2. When removing turbocharger assembly, take special care not to bend, nick or in any way damage compressor or turbine wheel blades. Any damage may result in rotating assembly imbalance, and failure of the center housing, compressor and/or turbine housings.

3. Before disconnecting the center housing from either the compressor or turbine housing, scribe the components for reassembly in the same relative position.

4. If silastic sealer, or equivalent, is found at any point in turbocharger disassembly (such as between the center housing backplate and the compressor housing), the area should be cleaned and sealed with an equivalent sealer during reassembly.

5. Any time a basic engine bearing (main bearing, connecting rod bearing, camshaft bearing) has been damaged in a turbocharged engine, the oil and oil filter should be changed as a part of the repair procedure. In addition, the turbocharger should be flushed with clean engine oil to reduce the possibility of contamination.

6. Interruption or contamination of the oil supply to the bearings in the center housing which support the rotating assembly can result in major turbocharger damage.

CHILTON CAUTION The electric cooling fan on the turbocharged engine can start to operate at any time by an increase in underhood temperature, even though the ignition switch may be in the "OFF" position. For this reason, disconnect the electric fan any time engine compartment work is done.

Troubleshooting and System Analysis
BOOST CONTROL SYSTEM

Vacuum/Pressure System Integrity Check

1. Remove the pressure hose from the intake manifold fitting. Apply 40 kPa (7.0 psi) pressure to this line. Observe the movement of the wastegate activating rod.

Wastegate Activating Rod Travel

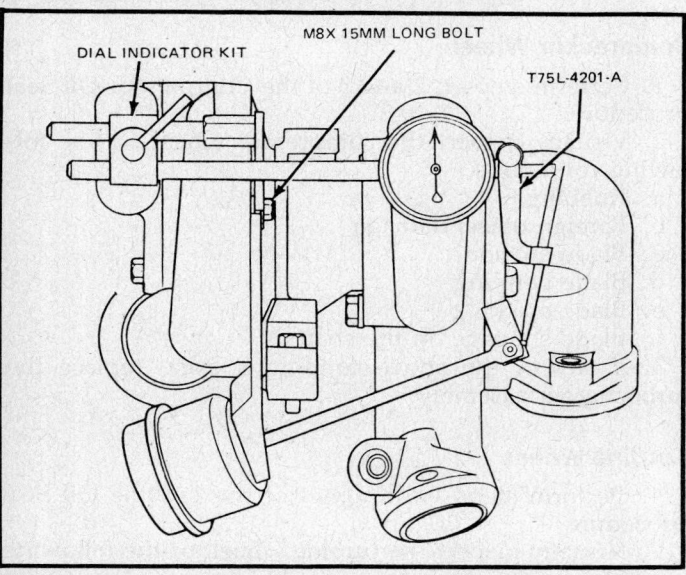

DIAL INDICATOR KIT
M8X 15MM LONG BOLT
T75L-4201-A

Ignition Module and Timing Switch Assembly

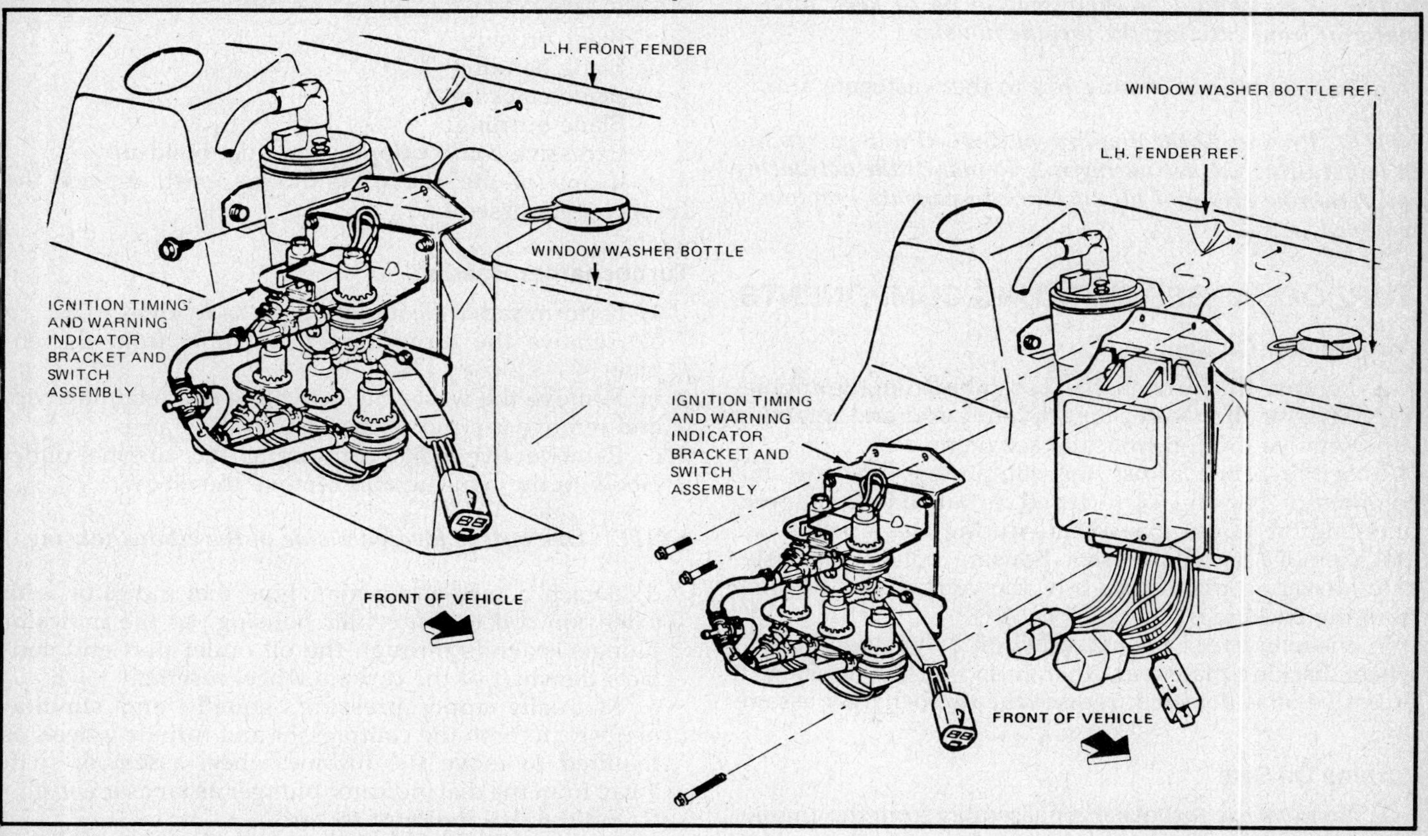

If the wastegate activating rod moves, perform steps 2, 3 and 4 of the Wastegate Activating Diaphragm procedure. Reinstall the pressure hose and fitting removed in step 1.

If the wastegate activating rod does not move, use the following procedures.

a. Check the hoses and fittings for obstructions or leakage. Service and/or replace as required.

b. Check for leakage at the distributor diaphragm. Service and/or replace as required.

c. Check boost retard switch assembly for leakage. Service and/or replace as required.

d. Check boost light switch assembly for leakage. Service and/or replace as required.

e. Perform steps 2, 3 and 4 of the Wastegate Activating Diaphragm procedure.

f. Perform steps 1 and 2 of the Outlet Elbow and Wastegate Assembly procedure.

Wastegate Activating Diaphragm

1. Verify that the wastegate activating rod is attached to the wastegate arm, with the retaining clip in place. If not, correct as required.

2. Remove the lines from the diaphragm. Install an external vacuum source to the vacuum side of the diaphragm. Apply 84 kPa (25 In-Hg) vacuum and trap. If the vacuum drops below 61 kPa (18 In-Hg) after 60 seconds, replace the wastegate activating diaphragm. If the vacuum drop is within specification, release the vacuum and remove the line.

3. Install an external pressure source to the pressure

L.H. FRONT FENDER
WINDOW WASHER BOTTLE REF.
L.H. FENDER REF.
WINDOW WASHER BOTTLE
IGNITION TIMING AND WARNING INDICATOR BRACKET AND SWITCH ASSEMBLY
IGNITION TIMING AND WARNING INDICATOR BRACKET AND SWITCH ASSEMBLY
FRONT OF VEHICLE
FRONT OF VEHICLE

side of the diaphragm. Apply 34 kPa (5 psi) of pressure and trap. If the pressure drops below 14 kPa (2.0 psi) after 60 seconds, replace the wastegate activating diaphragm. If the pressure drop is within specification, release the pressure.

4. Install a dial indicator to measure the travel of the wastegate activating rod. Very slowly apply pressure until the dial indicator shows .015 inch of linear displacement. Read the pressure gauge. The pressure should be 46.89 ± 3.45 kPa (6.8 ± 0.5 psi). If the pressure is not as specified, or if the wastegate activating arm stays closed and does not move freely, replace the wastegate activating diaphragm.

5. Release the pressure and remove all test equipment. Reinstall all system components previously removed.

Outlet Elbow and Wastegate Assembly

1. Verify that the wastegate activating rod is attached to the wastegate arm with a retaining clip in place. If not, correct as required.

2. Remove the diaphragm activating rod clip and remove the activating rod from the wastegate arm. Check the wastegate arm for freedom of rotation. It should move freely through a minimum of 40 degrees rotation. If not, replace the outlet elbow and wastegate assembly.

3. Remove the turbocharger outlet pipe assembly. Check to see that the wastegate sealing poppet is free to move on the pintle and is seating on the turbine housing bypass hole. If not, replace the outlet elbow and wastegate assembly and/or clean the bypass hole and sealing surface.

NOTE Care should be exercised, so as to keep foreign material from entering the turbine housing.

4. Reinstall the activating rod to the wastegate arm.

NOTE Pressurize the diaphragm to 41 kPa (6 psi) to aid in reinstalling the activating rod. Reinstall the activating rod retaining clip and all system components previously removed.

TURBOCHARGER ROTATING COMPONENTS

Compressor Oil Seal

1. Remove the turbocharger assembly from the engine.
2. Remove the wastegate activating rod and retaining clip. Remove the rod from the activating arm.
3. Scribe a line across the compressor housing and compressor backing plate (used as an aid in properly orienting the housing and plate during reassembly).
4. Remove six compressor housing bolts, the wastegate activating diaphragm and the compressor housing from the backing plate.
5. Visually check for excessive oil on the compressor wheel, backing plate and inner surface of the housing. If excessive oil is detected, replace the turbocharger assembly.

Turbine Oil Seal

1. Remove the turbocharger assembly from the engine.

2. Remove the wastegate activating rod and retaining clip. Remove the rod from the activating arm.
3. Scribe a line across the turbine housing and center housing (used as an aid in properly orienting the turbine and center housings during reassembly).
4. Remove six turbine housing bolts. Then remove the turbine housing from the center housing.
5. Visually check for excessive oil on the turbine wheel, turbine housing and turbine heat shield. If excessive oil is detected, replace the turbocharger assembly.

Compressor Wheel

1. Perform steps 1, 2 and 3 of the Compressor Oil Seal procedure.
2. Visually inspect the compressor wheel for the following conditions.
   a. Rubbing
   b. Foreign object damage
   c. Blade erosion
   d. Blade bending
   e. Blade cracking
   f. Blade slippage on the shaft
3. If any of the above conditions exist, replace the turbocharger assembly.

Turbine Wheel

1. Perform steps 1 through 4 of the Turbine Oil Seal procedure.
2. Visually inspect the turbine wheel for the following conditions.
   a. Rubbing
   b. Foreign object damage
   c. Blade erosion
   d. Blade bending
   e. Blade cracking
   f. Blade burning
   g. Excessive combustion by-product build-up
3. If any of the above conditions exist, replace the turbocharger assembly.

Turbocharger Bearing

1. Perform radial clearance check as follows.
   a. Remove the turbocharger assembly from the engine.
   b. Remove the wastegate activating rod retaining clip, and remove the rod from the activating arm.
   c. Remove five bolts connecting the turbine outlet elbow to the housing and remove the elbow.

NOTE One bolt is located inside of the elbow housing.

   d. Attach a rack-and-pinion type dial indicator with extension rod to the center housing, so the indicator plunger extends through the oil outlet port and contacts the shaft of the turbine wheel assembly.
   e. Manually apply pressure, equally and simultaneously, to both the compressor and turbine wheels as required to move the turbine wheel assembly shaft away from the dial indicator plunger as far as it will go.
   f. Set the dial indicator to zero.

Radial Clearance Check

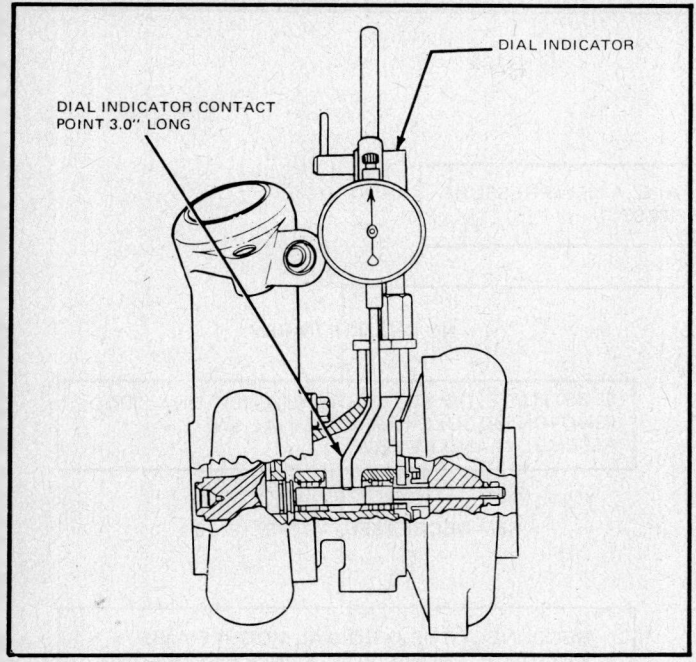

Axial Clearance Check

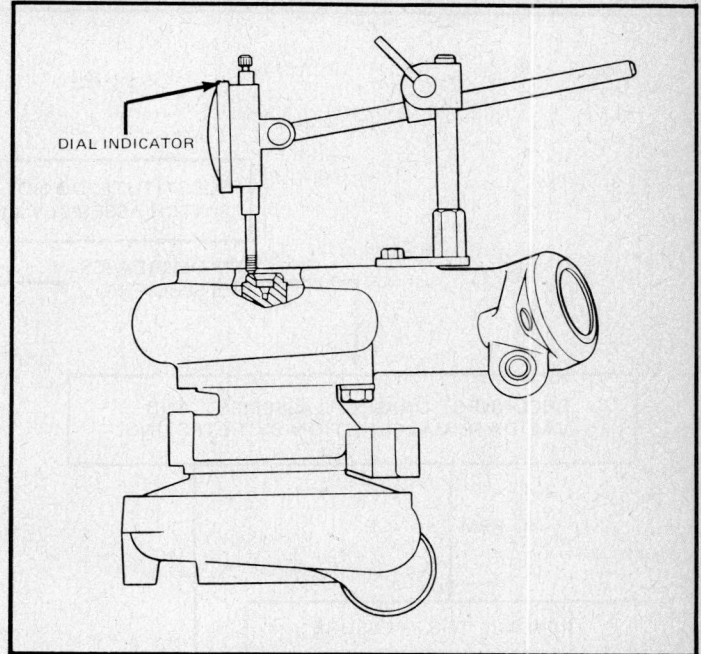

g. Manually apply pressure, equally and simultaneously, to both the compressor and turbine wheels as required to move the turbine wheel assembly shaft toward the dial indicator plunger as far as it will go. Note the maximum shaft excursion shown on the indicator dial.

h. Manually apply pressure, equally and simultaneously, to the compressor and turbine wheels as required to move the turbine wheel assembly shaft away from the dial indicator plunger as far as it will go. Note that the indicator pointer returns exactly to zero.

i. Repeat steps e. through h., as required to make sure that the maximum clearance between the center housing bores and the shaft bearing diameters, as indicated by the maximum shaft excursion, has been obtained.

j. If the maximum wheel radial clearance is less than 0.08 mm (.003 inch) or greater than 0.15 mm (.006 inch) replace the turbocharger assembly.

2. Perform axial clearance check as follows.

a. Remove the turbocharger assembly from the engine.

b. Remove the wastegate activating rod retaining clip, and remove the rod from the activating arm.

c. Remove five bolts connecting the turbine outlet elbow to the housing and remove the elbow.

NOTE   One bolt is located inside of the elbow housing.

d. Attach a rack-and-pinion type dial indicator at the turbine end of the turbocharger so that the dial indicator tip rests on the end of the turbine wheel assembly.

e. Manually move the compressor wheel and turbine wheel assembly alternately away from and toward the turbine end of the turbocharger. Note the travel of the turbine wheel assembly in each direction shown on the indicator dial.

f. Repeat step e, as required to make sure that the maximum clearance between the thrust bearing components, as indicated by the maximum turbine wheel assembly travel, has been obtained.

g. If the maximum thrust bearing axial clearance is less than 0.03 mm (.001 inch) or greater than 0.08 mm (.003 inch), replace the turbocharger assembly. Otherwise reassemble the turbocharger and reinstall on the engine.

h. Remove all the test equipment. Reinstall all the system components previously removed.

BOOST PRESSURE ACTIVATED SPARK RETARD SYSTEM

NOTE   If the vehicle is equipped with a spark knock sensing module, disconnect the module from the pressure switch before performing this diagnosis.

1. Check the basic engine timing.

2. Remove the pressure supply line to the ignition timing pressure switch assembly (three switches on one bracket). Cap the line and install an external pressure source to the ignition timing pressure switch assembly.

3. Remove and plug the vacuum advance line to the distributor. Connect a tachometer to the engine. Start the engine and let it warm up.

4. Increase the engine speed to between 1300 and 1400 rpm.

5. Apply pressure slowly (as shown in the table) and observe rpm changes. Distributor calibrations may affect readings.

If the rpm decreases as specified above, the retard system is functioning satisfactorily. Remove all test equipment and reconnect all vacuum and pressure lines.

Spark Retard System Troubleshooting

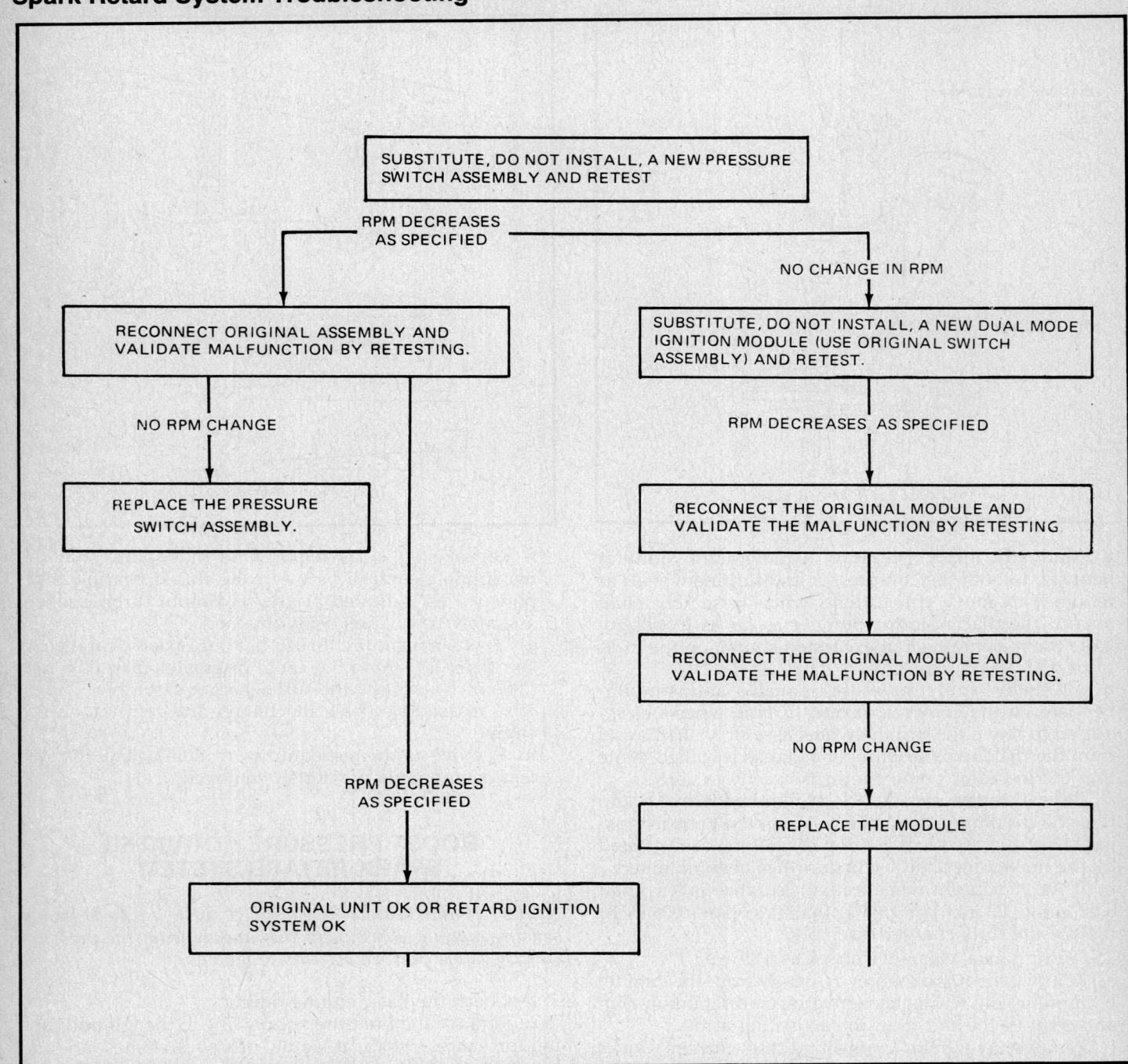

SUBSTITUTE, DO NOT INSTALL, A NEW PRESSURE SWITCH ASSEMBLY AND RETEST

RPM DECREASES AS SPECIFIED

NO CHANGE IN RPM

RECONNECT ORIGINAL ASSEMBLY AND VALIDATE MALFUNCTION BY RETESTING.

SUBSTITUTE, DO NOT INSTALL, A NEW DUAL MODE IGNITION MODULE (USE ORIGINAL SWITCH ASSEMBLY) AND RETEST.

NO RPM CHANGE

RPM DECREASES AS SPECIFIED

REPLACE THE PRESSURE SWITCH ASSEMBLY.

RECONNECT THE ORIGINAL MODULE AND VALIDATE THE MALFUNCTION BY RETESTING

RECONNECT THE ORIGINAL MODULE AND VALIDATE THE MALFUNCTION BY RETESTING.

NO RPM CHANGE

RPM DECREASES AS SPECIFIED

REPLACE THE MODULE

ORIGINAL UNIT OK OR RETARD IGNITION SYSTEM OK

If the rpm does not decrease as specified above, follow the spark retard system troubleshooting chart.

Pressure (psi)	Rpm Decrease
0 to 0.49	0
0.5 to 1.0	Greater than 75 rpm
1.0 to 3.74	No additional change
3.75 to 4.25	At least 100 rpm more
Release pressure to 0	Engine rpm should return to 1300–1400

Component Servicing
TURBOCHARGER R & R

UNDER THE VEHICLE

1. Remove four exhaust outlet nuts and crossover pipes to turbocharger.
2. Remove crossover pipe retaining nuts to the engine manifold (right side). Loosen and lower crossover. Remove retaining exhaust outlet pipe to catalyst inlet and outlet pipe.

Turbocharger Component Identification

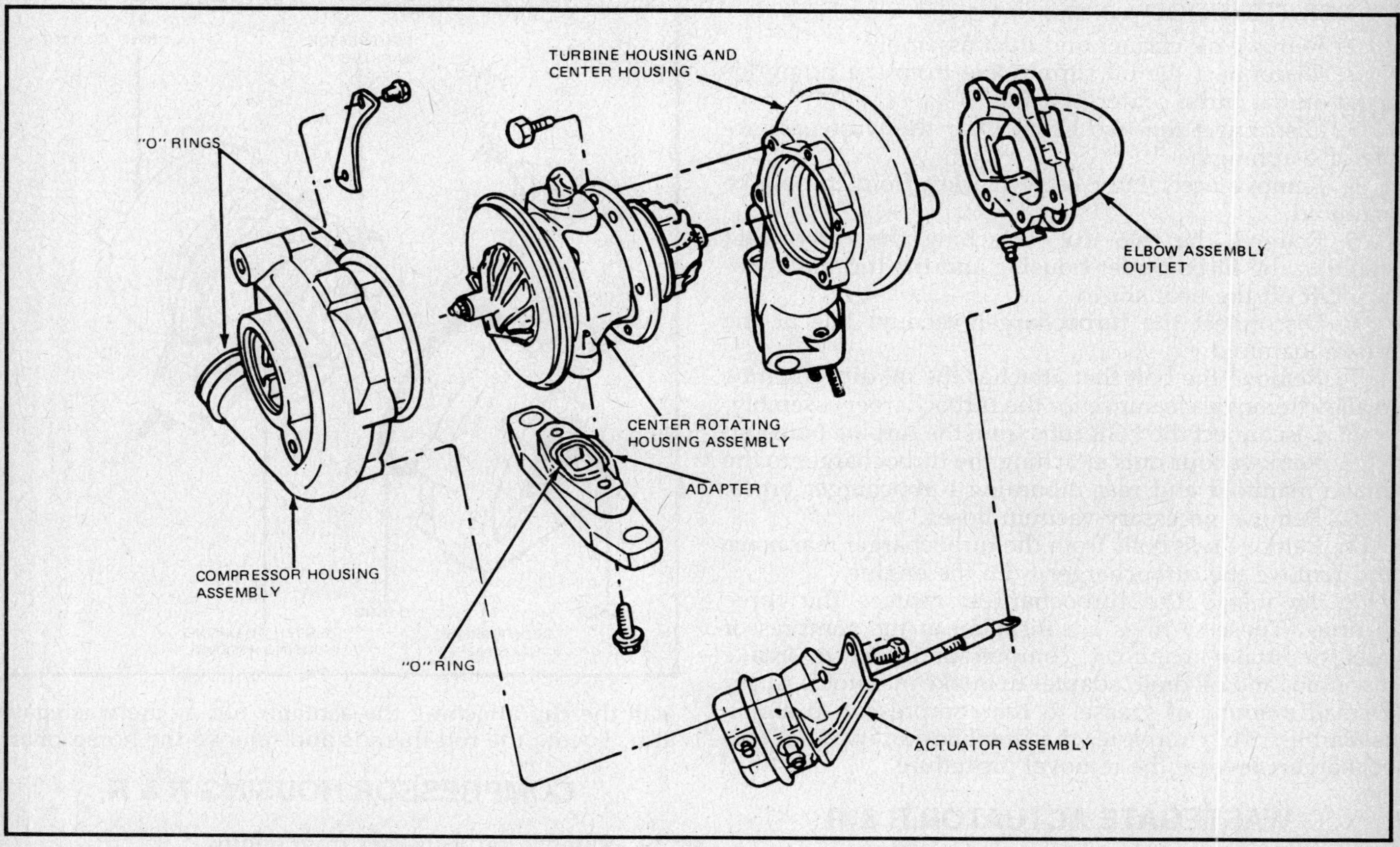

"O" RINGS

TURBINE HOUSING AND CENTER HOUSING

ELBOW ASSEMBLY OUTLET

CENTER ROTATING HOUSING ASSEMBLY

ADAPTER

COMPRESSOR HOUSING ASSEMBLY

"O" RING

ACTUATOR ASSEMBLY

Turbine Housing Removal

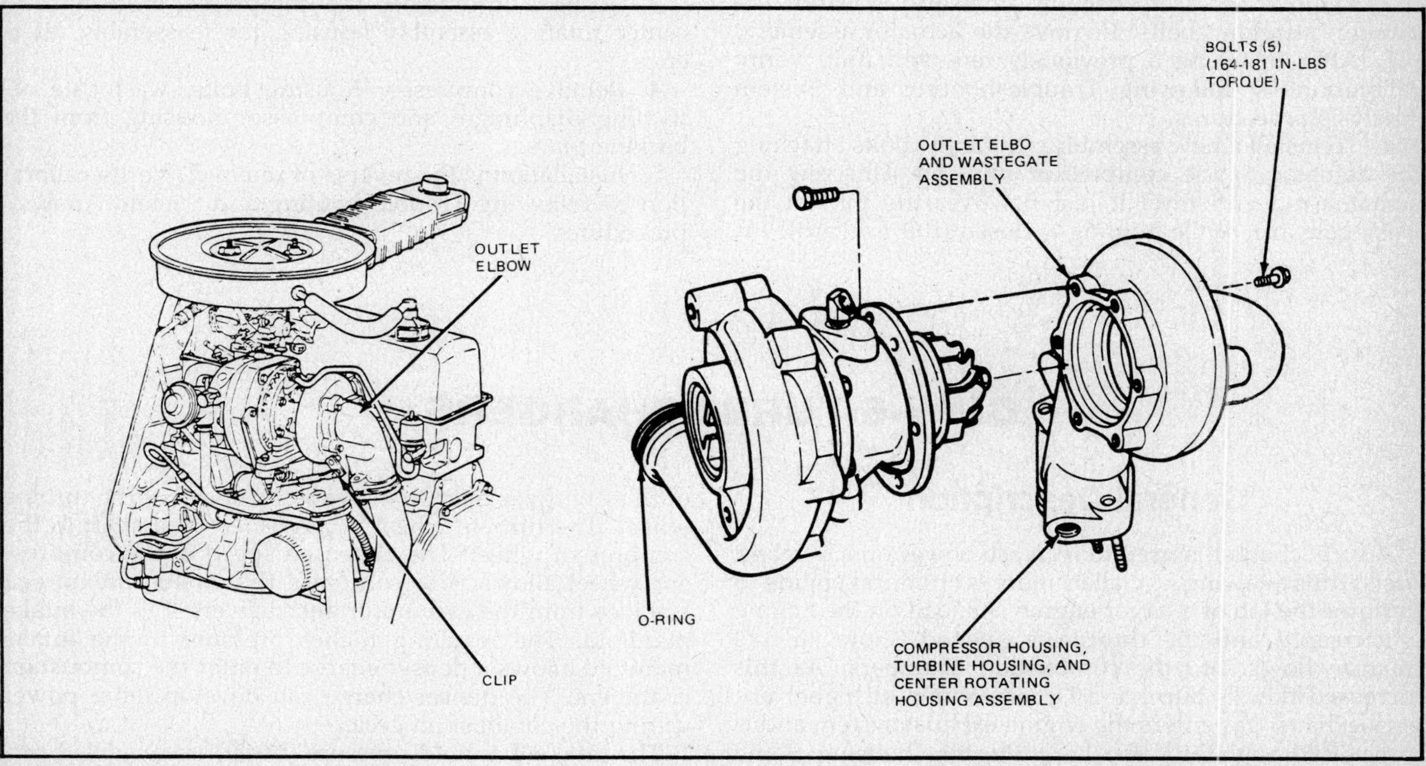

OUTLET ELBOW

CLIP

O-RING

OUTLET ELBO AND WASTEGATE ASSEMBLY

BOLTS (5) (164-181 IN-LBS TORQUE)

COMPRESSOR HOUSING, TURBINE HOUSING, AND CENTER ROTATING HOUSING ASSEMBLY

3. Remove the turbocharger rear mounting brace bolts.

UNDER THE HOOD

1. Remove air cleaner and duct assembly.
2. Disconnect the oil supply line from the fitting located on the turbo center housing.
3. Disconnect the two hoses from the wastegate actuator diaphragm.
4. Remove accelerator cable bracket from the intake manifold.
5. Remove the two nuts attaching the turbo heat shield to the turbo center housing and the turbine housing. Lift off the heat shield.
6. Disconnect the turbocharger vacuum line at the intake manifold.
7. Remove the bolt that attaches the oil dipstick tube to allow removal clearance for the turbocharger assembly.
8. Disconnect the EGR tube from the turbine housing.
9. Remove four nuts attaching the turbocharger to the intake manifold and rear mounting turbocharger brace.
10. Remove necessary vacuum hoses.
11. Remove two bolts from the turbocharger rear brace and remove the turbocharger from the engine.
12. To install the turbocharger, replace the three O-rings. These O-rings are installed at the compressor inlet to intake manifold, compressor outlet to intake manifold, and oil drain adapter to intake manifold. Apply a small amount of grease to the compressor to aid in assembly. To complete the installation of the turbocharger, reverse the removal procedure.

WASTEGATE ACTUATOR R & R

1. Remove heat shield and clip attaching actuator rod to wastegate arm.
2. Remove necessary vacuum lines and actuator diaphragm attaching bolts. Remove the actuator assembly.
3. After installing a previously removed unit, verify calibration by following Troubleshooting and System Analysis procedures.
4. To install a new assembly, install the bolts attaching the actuator to the compressor housing. Unscrew the actuator rod end until it just fits over the pin on the wastegate arm while holding it closed (full forward). In-

Compressor Housing Removal

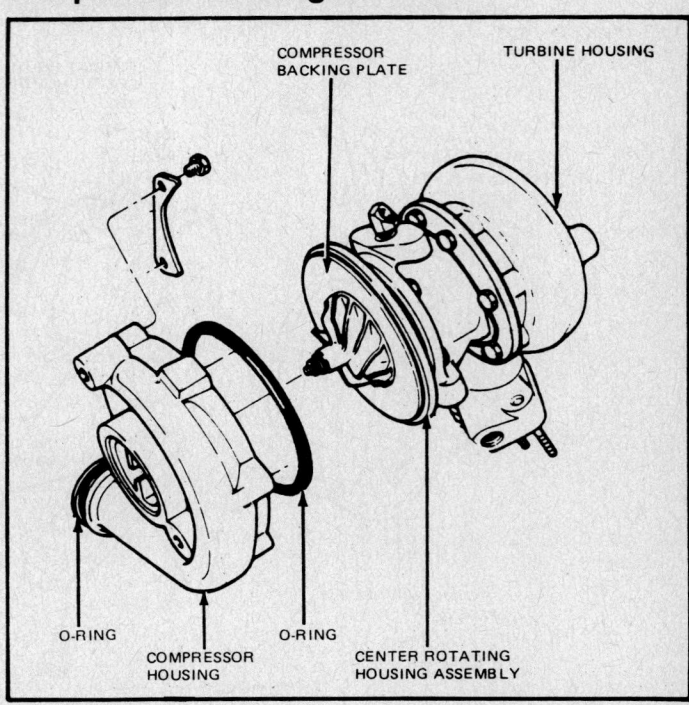

stall the clip attaching the actuator rod to the wastegate arm. Loctite the rod threads and remove the horsecollar.

COMPRESSOR HOUSING R & R

1. Remove turbocharger from engine.
2. Remove wastegate actuator rod retaining clip and remove rod from wastegate arm.
3. Scribe a line across the compressor housing and center rotating assembly housing for reassembly reference.
4. Remove compressor housing bolts, wastegate activating diaphragm and compressor housing from the backing plate.
5. Installation is the reverse of removal. Verify calibration by following Troubleshooting and System Analysis procedures.

GM V-6 TURBOCHARGERS

General Description

A turbocharger is used to increase power on a demand basis, thus allowing a smaller, more economical engine to perform the job of a larger engine. As load on the engine is increased and the throttle is opened, more air-fuel mixture flows into the combustion chambers. As this increased flow is burned, a larger volume of higher energy exhaust gas enters the engine exhaust system and is directed through the turbocharger turbine housing. Some

of this energy is used to increase the speed of the turbine wheel. The turbine wheel is connected by a shaft to the compressor wheel. The increased speed of the compressor wheel allows it to compress the air-fuel mixture it receives from the carburetor and delivers it to the intake manifold. The resulting higher pressure in the intake manifold allows a denser charge to enter the combustion chambers. The denser charge can develop more power during the combustion cycle.

The intake manifold pressure (boost) is controlled to a

correct maximum value by an exhaust bypass valve (wastegate). The valve allows a portion of the exhaust gas to bypass the turbine wheel, thus not increasing turbine speed. The wastegate is operated by a spring loaded diaphragm device (actuator assembly) that senses the pressure differential across the compressor. When boost reaches a set value about ambient pressure, the wastegate begins to bypass exhaust gas.

NOTE Any alteration to the air intake or exhaust system which upsets the air flow balance may result in serious damage to the turbocharged engine.

Operation

ELECTRONIC SPARK CONTROL

Turbocharged engines use a modified HEI system which is called electronic spark control (ESC). The ESC system is used to control engine detonation by automatically retarding ignition timing during periods of engine operation when detonation occurs.

The intake manifold transmits the vibrations caused by detonation to the sensor mounting location. The sensor detects the presence and intensity of detonation and feeds this information to the controller. The controller, which is mounted on the fan shroud, evaluates the sensor signal and sends a command signal to the distributor to adjust timing.

The HEI distributor has a modified electronic module which responds to signals from the controller. Electronic spark control is continually monitoring engine operation for detonation and retarding ignition timing up to 18 to 20° to minimize detonation levels, as necessary.

ENRICHMENT VACUUM REGULATOR

The power enrichment vacuum regulator (PEVR) is designed to control vacuum flow to the carburetor power piston on turbocharged V-6 engines. The PEVR regulates vacuum to the remote power enrichment port on the carburetor based on the manifold vacuum/pressure signal.

The PEVR has an input port and an output port. The vacuum input port is in the center of the PEVR. The vacuum output port is located on the perimeter of the PEVR. The manifold signal port extends into the intake manifold.

TURBOCHARGER OIL SUPPLY

An adequate supply of clean engine oil is essential to the proper operation of the turbocharger. The rotating assembly (turbine wheel, connecting shaft and compressor wheel) can obtain speeds of 130,000 to 140,000 rpm during boost. Interruption or contamination of the oil supply to the bearings in the center housing rotating assembly (CHRA) which support the rotating assembly can result in major turbocharger damage.

When changing the oil and oil filter on a turbocharged V-6 engine or performing any operation which results in

oil drainage or loss, use the following procedures before starting the engine.

1. Disconnect ignition switch connector (pink wire) from the HEI distributor.
2. Crank engine several times (not to exceed 30 seconds for each cranking interval) until oil light goes out.
3. Reconnect pink wire to the distributor. This procedure will aid the filling of the oil system.

NOTE Any time a basic engine bearing (main bearing, connecting rod bearing and camshaft bearing) has been damaged in a turbocharged V-6 engine, the oil and oil filter should be changed as a part of the repair procedure. In addition, the turbocharger should be flushed with clean engine oil to reduce the possibility of contamination.

Any time a center housing rotating assembly, or any part of a turbocharger assembly, which includes the center housing rotating assembly, is being replaced, the oil and oil filter should be changed as a part of the repair procedure.

Test Procedures

GENERAL PRECAUTIONS

Before starting any turbocharger unit repair procedure, several general precautions should be considered.

1. Clean area around turbocharger with non-caustic solution before removal of assembly.
2. When removing turbocharger assembly, take special care not to bend, nick or in any way damage compressor or turbine wheel blades. Any damage may result in rotating assembly imbalance, failure of center housing rotating assembly (CHRA) and failure of compressor and/or turbine housings.
3. Before disconnecting center housing rotating assembly from either compressor housing or turbine housing, scribe the components in order that they may be reassembled in the same relative position.
4. If silastic sealer, or equivalent, is found at any point in turbocharger disassembly (such as between center housing rotating assembly backplate and compressor housing), the area should be cleaned and sealed with an equivalent sealer during reassembly.

WASTEGATE/BOOST PRESSURE

1. Visually inspect wastegate-actuator mechanical linkage for damage.
2. Check hose from compressor housing to actuator assembly and return tubing from actuator to PCV tee.
3. Attach hand operated vacuum/pressure pump J-23738 in series with compound gage J-28474 to actuator assembly. Replace compressor housing to actuator assembly hose.
4. Apply pressure to actuator assembly. At approximately 9 psi (8.5 to 9.5 psi), the actuator rod end should move .015 inch, actuating the wastegate linkage. If not, replace the actuator assembly and check that opening calibration pressure is 9 psi. Crimp threads on actuator rod to maintain correct calibration.

5. Remove test equipment and reconnect compressor housing to actuator assembly hose.

6. An alternative method of checking wastegate operation is to perform a road test which measures boost pressure.

POWER ENRICHMENT VACUUM REGULATOR

1. Visually check the PEVR and attaching hoses for deterioration, cracking or other damage.

2. Tee one hose from manometer J-23951 between the yellow-striped input hose and the input port. Connect the other manometer hose directly to the output port of the PEVR.

3. Start the engine and let it idle. There should be no more than a 14″ H²O difference. If there is, replace the PEVR.

4. If the PEVR passes the preceding test and is still considered to be a possible problem source, remove the PEVR from the intake manifold.

5. Plug the intake manifold and connect the input and output hoses to the PEVR.

6. Tee compound gage J-28474 into the output hose of the PEVR.

7. Start the engine and let it idle. The compound gage reading from the output port should be 7.0 to 9.0″ Hg.

8. Apply 3 psi to the manifold signal port of the PEVR. The vacuum reading from the output port should be 1.4 to 2.6″ Hg. If there is difficulty in measuring this low level of vacuum output, an additional requirement can be used. Apply a minimum of 5 psi to the manifold signal port of the PEVR. There should be no vacuum output from the PEVR.

9. If the PEVR does not meet requirements 7 and 8, replace the PEVR.

TURBOCHARGER INTERNAL INSPECTION

1. Remove turbocharger exhaust outlet pipe from the elbow assembly. Using a mirror, observe movement of wastegate while manually operating actuator linkage. Replace elbow assembly if wastegate fails to open or close.

2. Remove turbocharger assembly from engine following removal procedure for center housing rotating assembly (CHRA). Omit the last step which involves separation of the center housing rotating assembly (CHRA) from the turbine housing.

ing gasket or O-ring. Tighten or replace as necessary.

4. Gently spin compressor wheel. If rotating assembly binds, replace CHRA.

5. Remove oil drain from CHRA. Check CHRA for sludging in oil drain area. Clean, if minor. Replace CHRA if severely sludged or coked.

6. Inspect compressor wheel area for oil leakage from CHRA. If leakage is present, replace CHRA.

7. If compressor wheel is damaged or severely coked replace CHRA.

8. If CHRA is being replaced, pre-lubricate with clean engine oil.

9. Inspect compressor housing (still attached to engine) and turbine housing. Replace either housing if gouged, nicked or distorted.

10. If CHRA is not being replaced, remove turbine housing from CHRA and check journal bearing radial clearance and thrust bearing axial clearance. Check the journal bearings for radial clearance as follows.

a. Attach a dial indicator with a two inch long, ¾ to 1 inch offset extension rod to the center housing such that the indicator plunger extends through the oil outlet port and contacts the shaft of the rotating assembly. If required, a dial indicator mounting adapter can be used.

b. Manually apply pressure equally and at the same time to both the compressor and turbine wheels as required to move the shaft away from the dial indicator plunger as far as it will go.

c. Set the dial indicator to zero.

d. Manually apply pressure equally and at the same time to both the compressor and turbine wheels to move the shaft toward the dial indicator plunger as far as it will go. Note the maximum value on the indicator dial. Make sure that the dial indicator reading noted is the maximum reading obtainable, which can be verified by rolling the wheels slightly in both directions while applying pressure.

e. Manually apply pressure equally and at the same time to the compressor and turbine wheels as required to move the shaft away from the dial indicator plunger as far as it will go. Note that the indicator pointer returns exactly to zero.

f. Repeat steps as required to make sure that the maximum clearance between the center housing bores and the shaft bearing diameters, as indicated by the maximum shaft travel, has been obtained.

g. If the maximum bearing radial clearance is less than 0.003 inch or greater than 0.006 inch, replace CHRA and inspect housings.

NOTE *Continued operation of a turbocharger having improper bearing radial clearance will result in severe damage to the compressor wheel and housing or to the turbine wheel and housing.*

11. Check for thrust bearing axial clearance as follows.

a. Mount a dial indicator at the turbine end of the turbocharger such that the dial indicator tip rests on the end of the turbine wheel.

b. Manually move the compressor wheel and turbine wheel assembly alternatively toward and away from the dial indicator plunger. Note the travel of the shaft in each direction, as shown on the dial indicator.

c. Repeat as required to make sure that the maximum clearance between the thrust bearing components has been obtained.

d. If the maximum thrust bearing axial clearance is less than 0.001 inch or greater than 0.003 inch, replace CHRA and inspect housings.

NOTE *Continued operation of a turbocharger having an improper amount of thrust bearing axial clearance will result in severe damage to the compressor wheel and housing or to the turbine wheel and housing.*

Turbocharger Components

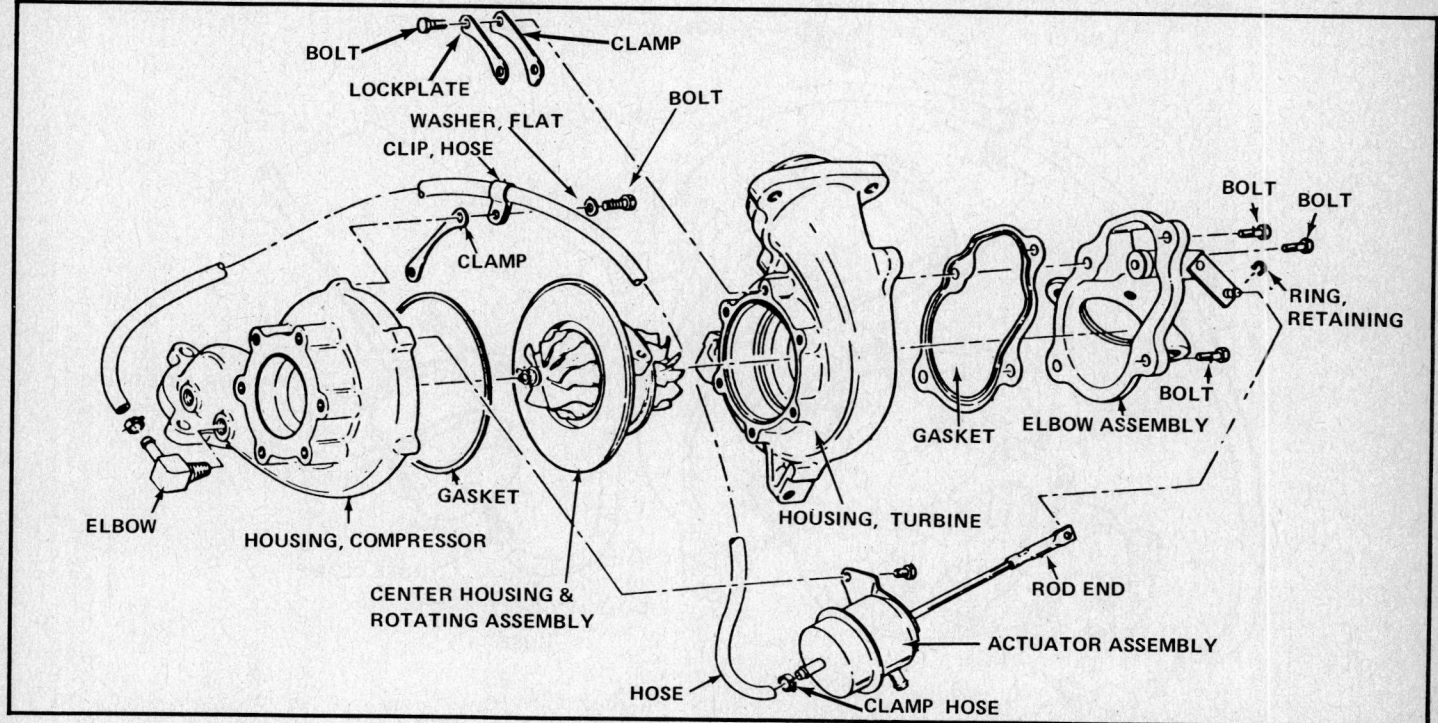

12. Install oil drain on CHRA.

13. Install turbocharger assembly to engine following the installation procedure for the center housing rotating assembly.

14. Before connecting turbocharger exhaust outlet pipe to elbow assembly, gently spin the turbine wheel to be certain that the rotating assembly (turbine wheel, connecting shaft and compressor wheel) does not bind.

ROAD TEST

1. Tee compound gage J-28474 into tubing between compressor housing and boost gage switches with sufficient length of hose to place gage in passenger compartment.

CHILTON CAUTION Determine that hose and compound gage are in proper operating condition to avoid possible leakage of air-fuel mixture into passenger compartment during road test.

2. Conditions and speed limits permitting, perform a zero to 40 to 50 mph wide open throttle acceleration. Boost pressure, as measured by the compound gage during road testing, should reach 9-10 psi. If not, replace actuator assembly and check for proper calibration. Actuator rod end should move .015″ at approximately 9 psi.

Component Service
WASTEGATE ACTUATOR

1. Disconnect hoses. Remove the clip attaching waste-gate linkage to actuator rod and remove mounting bolts.

2. Installation is the reverse of removal.

ELECTRONIC SPARK CONTROL DETONATION SENSOR

1. Squeeze sides of metal connector crosswire to wire from controller and gently pull straight up to remove connector. Do not pull up on the wire.

2. Unbolt and remove the sensor.

3. When installing sensor, torque to 14 ft. lbs. Do not use an impact tool, apply a side load to the sensor or attempt to repair the tapped hole in intake manifold.

ELBOW ASSEMBLY

1. Loosen turbocharger exhaust outlet pipe at the catalytic converter and disconnect it from the elbow assembly.

2. Remove the clip attaching wastegate linkage to actuator rod. Remove the bolts which mount the elbow to the turbine housing.

3. Installation is the reverse of removal.

TURBINE HOUSING AND ELBOW ASSEMBLY/CENTER HOUSING ROTATING ASSEMBLY

1. Disconnect turbocharger exhaust outlet pipe from the catalytic converter and the elbow assembly.

2. Disconnect turbocharger exhaust inlet pipe from the turbine housing and the exhaust manifold.

3. Remove bolts attaching turbine housing to bracket on intake manifold.

TURBOCHARGERS

GM V-6

Wastegate Actuator Attachments

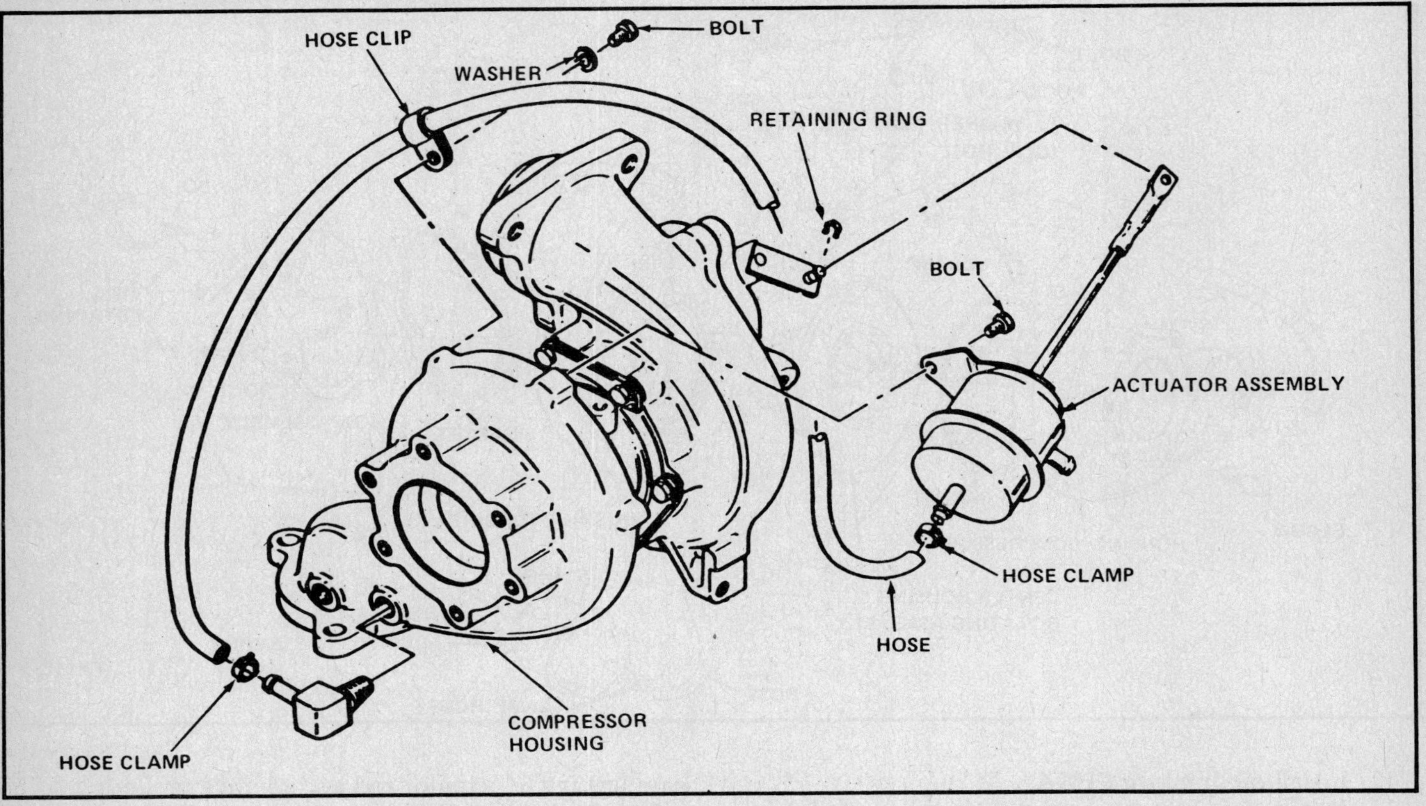

HOSE CLIP

WASHER

BOLT

RETAINING RING

BOLT

ACTUATOR ASSEMBLY

HOSE CLAMP

HOSE

COMPRESSOR HOUSING

HOSE CLAMP

Electronic Spark Control (ESC) Detonation Sensor

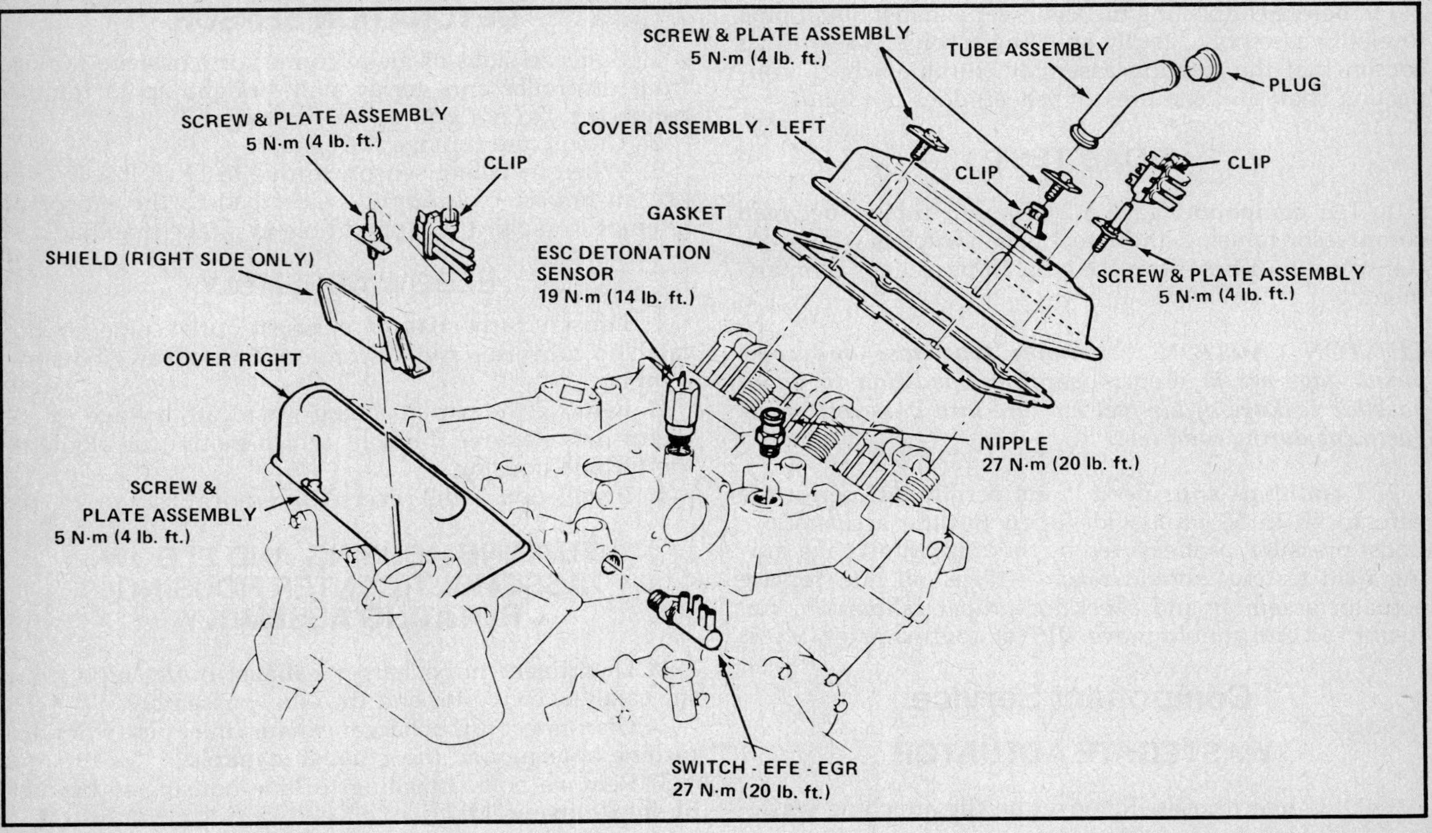

SCREW & PLATE ASSEMBLY
5 N·m (4 lb. ft.)

TUBE ASSEMBLY

PLUG

COVER ASSEMBLY - LEFT

CLIP

CLIP

SCREW & PLATE ASSEMBLY
5 N·m (4 lb. ft.)

CLIP

GASKET

SCREW & PLATE ASSEMBLY
5 N·m (4 lb. ft.)

SHIELD (RIGHT SIDE ONLY)

ESC DETONATION
SENSOR
19 N·m (14 lb. ft.)

COVER RIGHT

NIPPLE
27 N·m (20 lb. ft.)

SCREW &
PLATE ASSEMBLY
5 N·m (4 lb. ft.)

SWITCH - EFE - EGR
27 N·m (20 lb. ft.)

B108

Carburetor-to-plenum Mounting

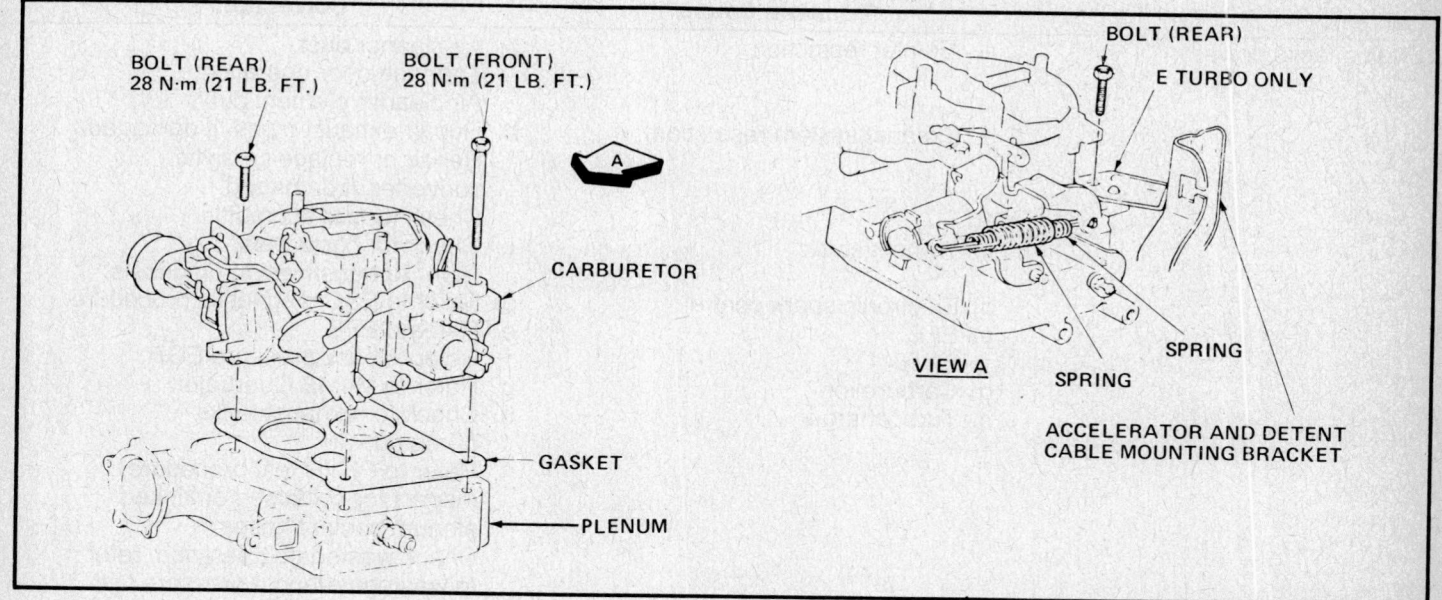

9. Remove bolts attaching turbine housing to bracket on intake manifold.
10. Remove bolts attaching EGR valve manifold to plenum. Loosen the bolts attaching the EGR valve manifold to the intake manifold.
11. Remove AIR bypass-to-pipe-to-check valve hose.
12. Remove bolts attaching compressor housing to intake manifold.
13. Remove turbocharger and actuator, still attached to carburetor and plenum, from the engine. Separate components as necessary.

14. Installation is the reverse of removal.

PLENUM

1. Use Turbocharger and Actuator Assembly procedure for plenum removal and replacement.

EGR VALVE MANIFOLD

1. Disconnect vacuum line and unbolt from EGR manifold, plenum and intake manifold.

TURBOCHARGER TROUBLESHOOTING

Problem	Possible Cause	Correction
Engine detonation	a. Electronic spark control	a. Refer to ESC diagnostic procedure.
	b. EGR	b. Refer to back pressure EGR.
	c. Carburetor or turbocharger	c. Correct air inlet restrictions. Air cleaner duct. Thermac door operation. Air cleaner dirty. Eliminate actuator overboost. Mechanical linkage jammed or blocked. Hose from compressor housing to actuator assembly or return hose from actuator to carburetor tee damaged or loose. Wastegate not operating, refer to wastegate-boost pressure test procedure. Service carburetor power system. Refer to PEVR test procedure. Refer to M4ME Quadrajet. Inspect turbocharger, refer to turbocharger internal inspection procedure.
	d. Other causes	d. Refer to naturally-aspirated engine diagnosis.

TURBOCHARGER TROUBLESHOOTING

Problem	Possible Cause	Correction
Engine lacks power	a. Air inlet restriction	a. Air cleaner duct. Thermac door operation. Air cleaner element dirty.
	b. Exhaust system restriction	b. Repair exhaust pipes, if damaged. Repair or replace catalytic converter, if damaged. Check for correct muffler.
	c. Transmission	c. Check for correct shifting. Refer to transmission diagnosis.
	d. Electronic spark control	d. Refer to ESC diagnostic procedure.
	e. EFE	e. Refer to EFE.
	f. EGR	f. Refer to back pressure EGR.
	g. Carburetion	g. Refer to M4ME Quadrajet.
	h. Turbocharger	h. Check for exhaust leaks or restrictions. Refer to PEVR test procedure. Inspect for collapsed or kinked plenum coolant hoses. Check wastegate operation, refer to wastegate-boost pressure test procedure. Refer to turbocharger internal inspection procedure.
	i. Other causes	i. Refer to naturally-aspirated engine diagnosis.
Engine surges	a. Electronic spark control	a. Refer to ESC diagnostic procedure.
	b. Carburetion	b. Refer to PEVR test procedure. Refer to M4ME Quadrajet.
	c. EGR	c. Refer to back pressure EGR.
	d. Turbocharger	d. Inspect turbocharger for loose bolts on compressor side of assembly, tighten.
	e. Other causes	e. Refer to naturally-aspirated engine diagnosis.
Excessive oil consumption or blue exhaust smoke	a. External turbocharger oil leaks	a. Inspect turbocharger oil inlet for proper connection. Inspect turbocharger oil drain hose for leaks or restriction.
	b. PCV	b. Refer to PCV.
	c. Other causes	c. Refer to naturally-aspirated engine diagnosis.
	d. Turbocharger	d. Refer to turbocharger internal inspection procedure.
Black exhaust smoke	a. Carburetion	a. Refer to PEVR test procedure. Refer to M4ME Quadrajet.
	b. Other causes	b. Refer to naturally-aspirated engine diagnosis.
Engine noise excessive	a. EFE	a. Refer to EFE.
	b. Exhaust system	b. Inspect for incorrect or loose mountings.
	c. AIR system	c. Refer to AIR system.
	d. Other causes	d. Refer to naturally-aspirated engine diagnosis.
	e. Turbocharger	e. Check for exhaust leaks. Inspect for restriction of turbocharger oil supply. Refer to turbocharger internal inspection procedure.

Troubleshooting Electronic Spark Control System

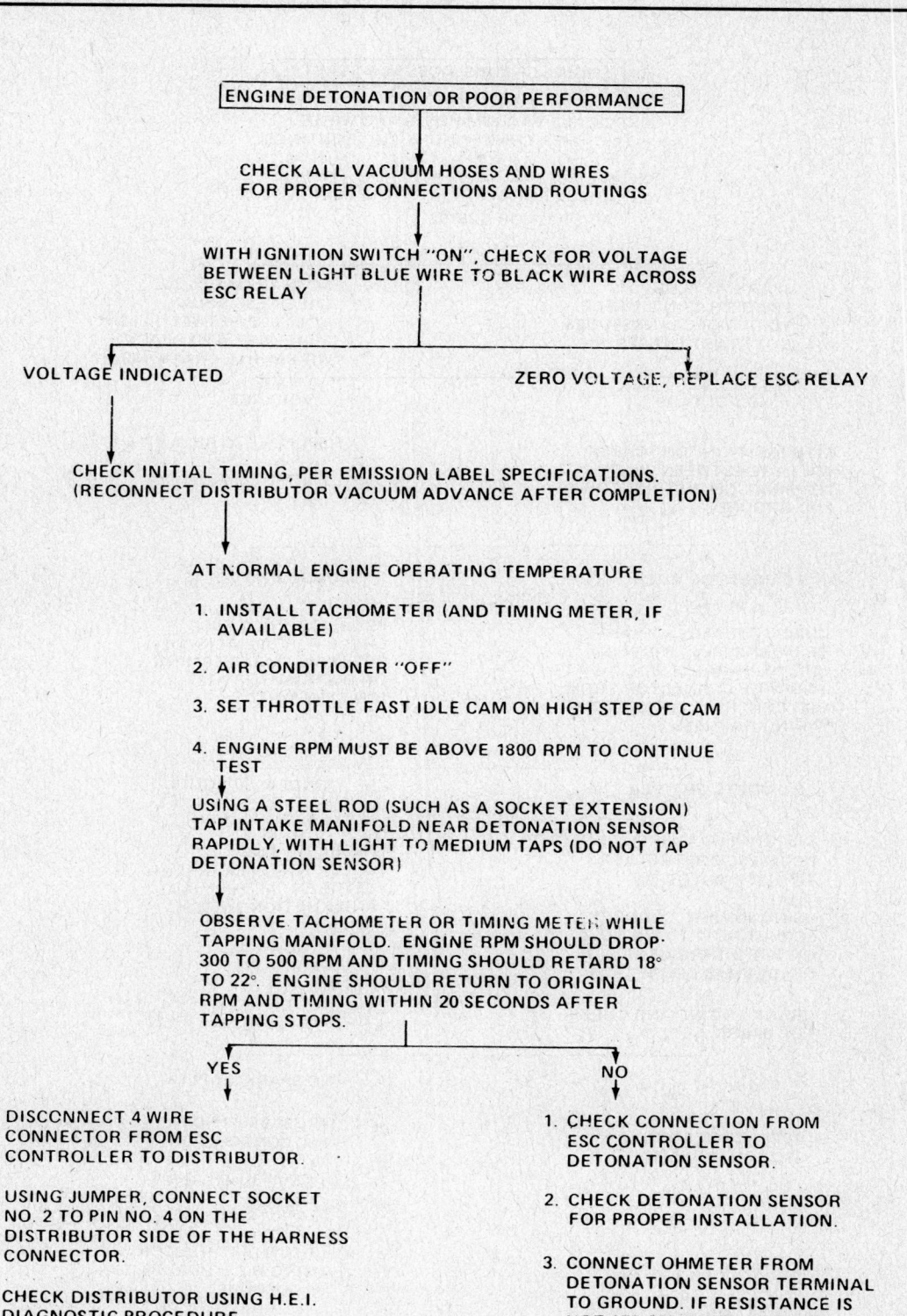

ENGINE DETONATION OR POOR PERFORMANCE

CHECK ALL VACUUM HOSES AND WIRES
FOR PROPER CONNECTIONS AND ROUTINGS

WITH IGNITION SWITCH "ON", CHECK FOR VOLTAGE
BETWEEN LIGHT BLUE WIRE TO BLACK WIRE ACROSS
ESC RELAY

VOLTAGE INDICATED   ZERO VOLTAGE, REPLACE ESC RELAY

CHECK INITIAL TIMING, PER EMISSION LABEL SPECIFICATIONS.
(RECONNECT DISTRIBUTOR VACUUM ADVANCE AFTER COMPLETION)

AT NORMAL ENGINE OPERATING TEMPERATURE

1. INSTALL TACHOMETER (AND TIMING METER, IF
   AVAILABLE)

2. AIR CONDITIONER "OFF"

3. SET THROTTLE FAST IDLE CAM ON HIGH STEP OF CAM

4. ENGINE RPM MUST BE ABOVE 1800 RPM TO CONTINUE
   TEST

USING A STEEL ROD (SUCH AS A SOCKET EXTENSION)
TAP INTAKE MANIFOLD NEAR DETONATION SENSOR
RAPIDLY, WITH LIGHT TO MEDIUM TAPS (DO NOT TAP
DETONATION SENSOR)

OBSERVE TACHOMETER OR TIMING METER WHILE
TAPPING MANIFOLD. ENGINE RPM SHOULD DROP
300 TO 500 RPM AND TIMING SHOULD RETARD 18°
TO 22°. ENGINE SHOULD RETURN TO ORIGINAL
RPM AND TIMING WITHIN 20 SECONDS AFTER
TAPPING STOPS.

YES   NO

1. DISCONNECT 4 WIRE
   CONNECTOR FROM ESC
   CONTROLLER TO DISTRIBUTOR.

2. USING JUMPER, CONNECT SOCKET
   NO. 2 TO PIN NO. 4 ON THE
   DISTRIBUTOR SIDE OF THE HARNESS
   CONNECTOR.

3. CHECK DISTRIBUTOR USING H.E.I.
   DIAGNOSTIC PROCEDURE.

4. AFTER DISTRIBUTOR REPAIR,
   REMOVE JUMPER AND RECONNECT
   ESC CONTROLLER.

1. CHECK CONNECTION FROM
   ESC CONTROLLER TO
   DETONATION SENSOR.

2. CHECK DETONATION SENSOR
   FOR PROPER INSTALLATION.

3. CONNECT OHMETER FROM
   DETONATION SENSOR TERMINAL
   TO GROUND. IF RESISTANCE IS
   NOT 175-375 OHMS, REPLACE
   DETONATION SENSOR.

4. IF STEPS 1-3 DO NOT CORRECT
   PROBLEM, REPLACE ESC
   CONTROLLER

TURBOCHARGERS

GM V-6

Troubleshooting Electronic Spark Control System

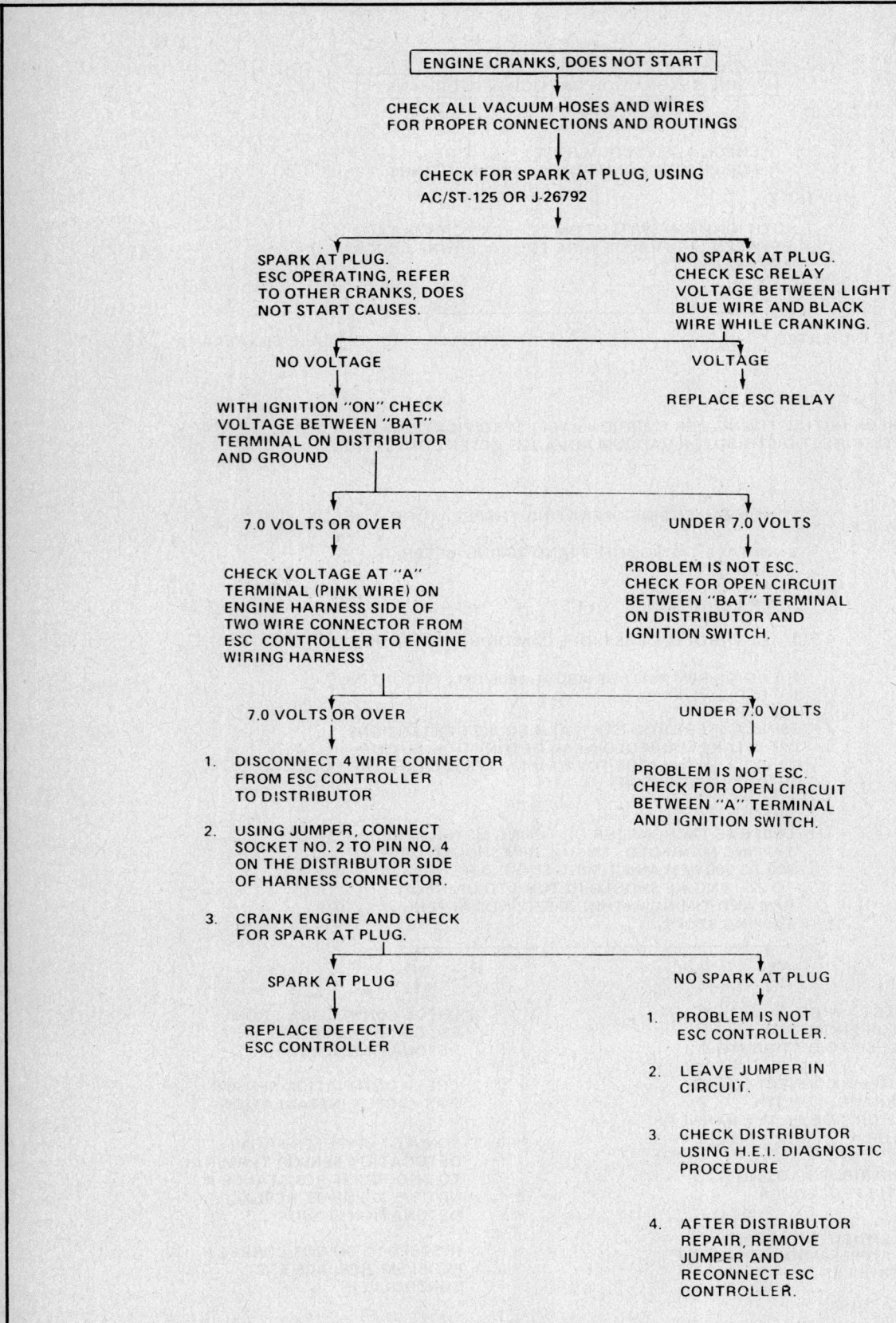

ENGINE CRANKS, DOES NOT START

CHECK ALL VACUUM HOSES AND WIRES
FOR PROPER CONNECTIONS AND ROUTINGS

CHECK FOR SPARK AT PLUG, USING
AC/ST-125 OR J-26792

SPARK AT PLUG.
ESC OPERATING, REFER
TO OTHER CRANKS, DOES
NOT START CAUSES.

NO SPARK AT PLUG.
CHECK ESC RELAY
VOLTAGE BETWEEN LIGHT
BLUE WIRE AND BLACK
WIRE WHILE CRANKING.

NO VOLTAGE

VOLTAGE

WITH IGNITION "ON" CHECK
VOLTAGE BETWEEN "BAT"
TERMINAL ON DISTRIBUTOR
AND GROUND

REPLACE ESC RELAY

7.0 VOLTS OR OVER

UNDER 7.0 VOLTS

CHECK VOLTAGE AT "A"
TERMINAL (PINK WIRE) ON
ENGINE HARNESS SIDE OF
TWO WIRE CONNECTOR FROM
ESC CONTROLLER TO ENGINE
WIRING HARNESS

PROBLEM IS NOT ESC.
CHECK FOR OPEN CIRCUIT
BETWEEN "BAT" TERMINAL
ON DISTRIBUTOR AND
IGNITION SWITCH.

7.0 VOLTS OR OVER

UNDER 7.0 VOLTS

1. DISCONNECT 4 WIRE CONNECTOR
FROM ESC CONTROLLER
TO DISTRIBUTOR

2. USING JUMPER, CONNECT
SOCKET NO. 2 TO PIN NO. 4
ON THE DISTRIBUTOR SIDE
OF HARNESS CONNECTOR.

3. CRANK ENGINE AND CHECK
FOR SPARK AT PLUG.

PROBLEM IS NOT ESC.
CHECK FOR OPEN CIRCUIT
BETWEEN "A" TERMINAL
AND IGNITION SWITCH.

SPARK AT PLUG

NO SPARK AT PLUG

REPLACE DEFECTIVE
ESC CONTROLLER

1. PROBLEM IS NOT
ESC CONTROLLER.

2. LEAVE JUMPER IN
CIRCUIT.

3. CHECK DISTRIBUTOR
USING H.E.I. DIAGNOSTIC
PROCEDURE

4. AFTER DISTRIBUTOR
REPAIR, REMOVE
JUMPER AND
RECONNECT ESC
CONTROLLER.

GM V-8 TURBOCHARGERS

General Description

A turbocharger is used to increase power on a demand basis. As the load on the engine is increased and the throttle is opened, more air-fuel mixture flows into the combustion chambers. As this increased flow is burned, a larger volume of higher energy exhaust gas enters the engine exhaust system and is directed through the turbocharger turbine housing. Some of this energy is used to increase the speed of the turbine wheel. The turbine wheel is connected by a shaft to the compressor wheel. The increased speed of the compressor wheel allows it to compress the air-fuel mixture it receives from the carburetor and delivers to the intake manifold. The resulting higher pressure in the intake manifold allows a denser charge to enter the combustion chambers. This denser charge can develop more power during the combustion cycle.

The intake manifold pressure (boost) is controlled to a correct maximum value by an exhaust bypass valve (wastegate). The valve allows a portion of the exhaust gas to bypass the turbine wheel, thus not increasing turbine speed. The wastegate is operated by a spring loaded diaphragm device (actuator assembly) that senses the pressure differential across the compressor. When boost reaches a set value above ambient pressure, the wastegate begins to bypass exhaust gas.

NOTE Any alteration to the air intake or exhaust system which upsets the air flow balance may result in serious damage to the turbocharged engine.

Operation

ELECTRONIC SPARK CONTROL

Turbocharged engines use a modified high energy ignition (HEI) system which is called electronic spark control (ESC). The ESC system is used to control engine detonation by automatically retarding ignition timing during periods of engine operation when detonation occurs.

The intake manifold transmits the vibrations caused by detonation to the sensor mounting location. The sensor detects the presence and intensity of detonation and feeds this information to the controller. The controller evaluates the sensor signal and sends a command signal to the distributor to adjust timing.

The HEI distributor has a modified electronic module which responds to signals from the controller. Electronic spark control is continually monitoring engine operation for detonation and retarding ignition timing up to 13 to 17° to minimize detonation levels.

TURBOCHARGER POWER ENRICHMENT VACUUM REGULATOR

The power enrichment vacuum regulator (PEVR) is designed to control vacuum flow to the carburetor power piston on turbocharged V-8 engines. The PEVR regulates vacuum to the remote power enrichment port on the carburetor based on the manifold vacuum/pressure signal.

The PEVR has an input port and an output port. The vacuum input port is in the center of the PEVR. The vacuum output port is located on the perimeter of the PEVR. The manifold signal port extends into the intake manifold.

TURBOCHARGER OIL SUPPLY

An adequate supply of clean engine oil is essential to the proper operation of the turbocharger. The rotating assembly (turbine wheel, connecting shaft and compressor wheel) can obtain speeds of 130,000 to 140,000 rpm during boost. Interruption or contamination of the oil supply to the bearings in the center housing rotating assembly (CHRA), which support the rotating assembly, can result in major turbocharger damage.

Test Procedures

GENERAL PRECAUTIONS

Before starting any turbocharger unit repair procedure, several general precautions should be considered.

1. Clean area around turbocharger with non-caustic solution before removal of assembly.
2. When removing turbocharger assembly, take special care not to bend, nick or in any way damage compressor or turbine wheel blades. Any damage may result in rotating assembly imbalance, failure of center housing rotating assembly (CHRA) and failure of compressor and/or turbine housings.
3. Before disconnecting center housing rotating assembly from either compressor housing or turbine housing, scribe the components so they can be reassembled in the same relative position.
4. When silastic sealer, or equivalent, is found at any point in turbocharger disassembly (such as between center housing rotating assembly back plate and compressor housing), the area should be cleaned and sealed with an equivalent sealer during reassembly.

NOTE Any time a basic engine bearing (main bearing, connecting rod bearing, camshaft bearing) has been damaged in a turbocharged V-8 engine, the oil and oil filter should be changed as a part of the repair procedure. In addition, the turbocharger should be flushed with clean engine oil to reduce the possibility of contamination.

Any time a center housing rotating assembly or any part of a turbocharger assembly which includes the center housing rotating assembly is being replaced, the oil and oil filter should be changed as part of the repair procedure.

TURBOCHARGERS

GM V-8

Electronic Spark Control (ESC) System

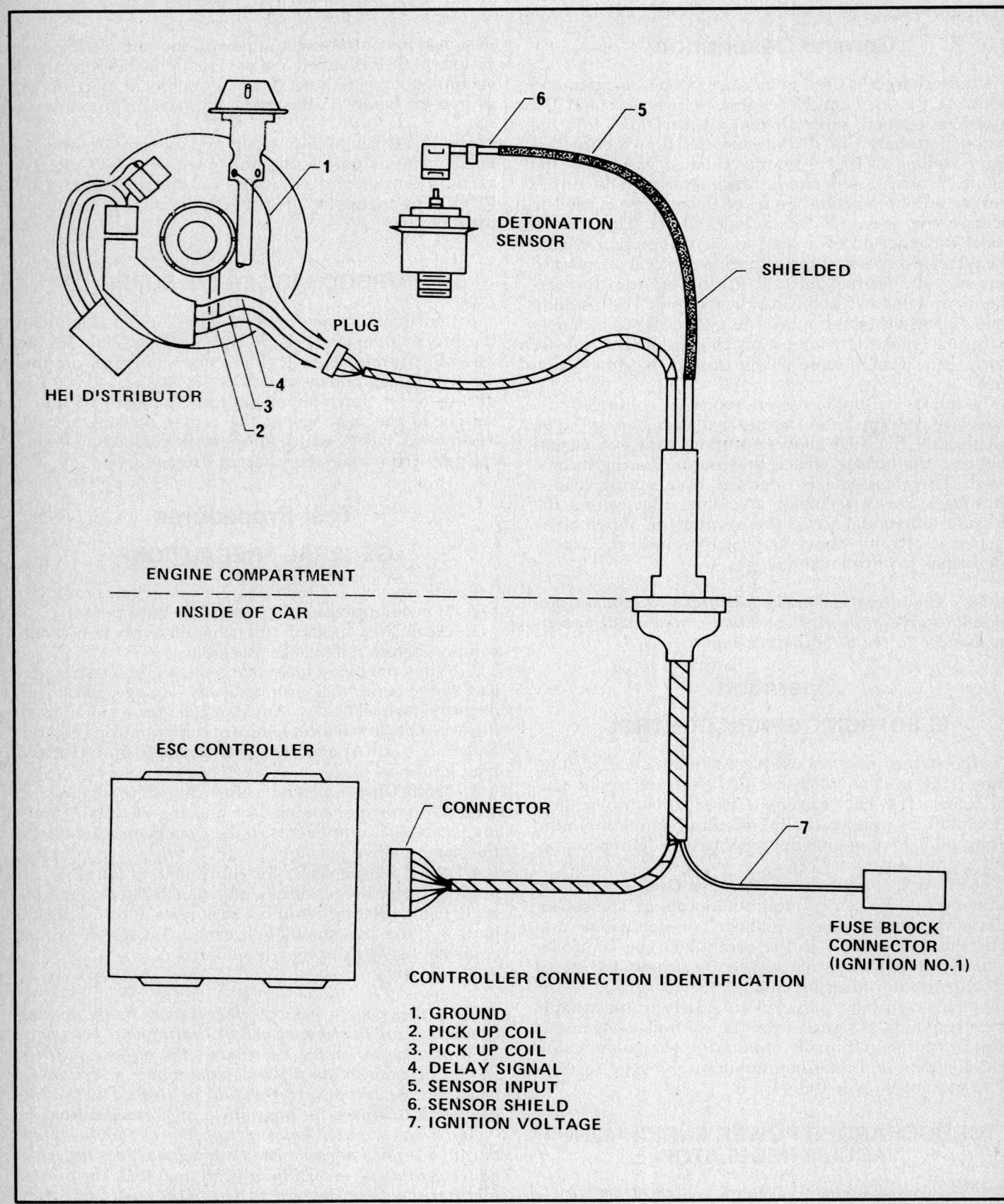

HEI DISTRIBUTOR

PLUG

DETONATION SENSOR

SHIELDED

ENGINE COMPARTMENT

INSIDE OF CAR

ESC CONTROLLER

CONNECTOR

FUSE BLOCK CONNECTOR (IGNITION NO.1)

CONTROLLER CONNECTION IDENTIFICATION

1. GROUND
2. PICK UP COIL
3. PICK UP COIL
4. DELAY SIGNAL
5. SENSOR INPUT
6. SENSOR SHIELD
7. IGNITION VOLTAGE

WASTEGATE/BOOST PRESSURE

1. Visually inspect wastegate-actuator mechanical linkage for damage.
2. Check hose from compressor housing to actuator assembly and diaphragm equalizer tubing from actuator to plenum.
3. Attach a hand-operated vacuum/pressure pump in series with component gage J-28474 to actuator assembly, replacing compressor housing to actuator assembly hose.
4. Apply pressure to actuator assembly. At approximately 9 psi (8.5 to 9.5 psi) the actuator rod end should move .015″, actuating the wastegate linkage. If not, replace the actuator assembly and check that opening calibration pressure is 9 psi. Crimp adjustment barrel on actuator rod to maintain correct calibration.
5. Remove test equipment and reconnect compressor housing to actuator assembly hose and clamps.
6. An alternative method of checking wastegate operation is to perform a road test which measures boost pressure.

POWER ENRICHMENT VACUUM REGULATOR

1. Visually check the PEVR and attaching hoses for deterioration, cracking or other damage. Replace as required.
2. Tee one hose from manometer J-23951 between the yellow-striped input hose and the input port. Connect the other manometer hose directly to the output port of the PEVR.
3. Start the engine and let it idle. There should be no more than a 14″ H_2O difference. If there is, replace the PEVR.
4. If the PEVR passes the preceding test and is still considered to be a possible problem source, remove the PEVR from the intake manifold.
5. Plug the intake manifold and connect the input and output hoses to the PEVR.
6. Tee compound gage J-28474 into the output hose and the PEVR.
7. Start the engine and let it idle. The compound gage reading from the output port should be 8.0 to 10.0″ Hg.
8. Apply 3 psi to the manifold signal port of the PEVR. The vacuum reading from the output port should be 1.4 to 2.6″ Hg. If there is difficulty in measuring this low level of vacuum output, an additional requirement can be used. Apply a minimum of 5 psi to the manifold signal port of the PEVR. There should be no vacuum output from the PEVR.
9. If the PEVR does not meet requirements 7 and 8, replace the PEVR.

TURBOCHARGER INTERNAL INSPECTION PROCEDURE

1. Remove turbocharger exhaust outlet pipe from the elbow assembly. Using a mirror, observe movement of wastegate while manually operating actuator linkage. Replace elbow assembly if wastegate fails to open or close. Inspect wastegate poppet valve for deterioration and warpage. Replace elbow assembly if poppet valve is damaged.
2. Remove turbocharger assembly from engine.
3. Check for loose backplate to CHRA bolts and missing gasket or O-ring. Tighten or replace as necessary.
4. Gently spin compressor wheel. If rotating assembly binds, replace CHRA.
5. Remove oil drain from CHRA. Check CHRA for sludging in oil drain area. Clean, if minor. Replace CHRA if severely sludged or coked.
6. Inspect compressor wheel area for oil leakage from CHRA. If leakage is present, replace CHRA.
7. If compressor wheel is damaged or severely cocked, replace CHRA.
8. If CHRA is being replaced, pre-lubricate with clean engine oil and proceed to step 9. If CHRA is not being replaced, proceed to step 10.
9. Inspect compressor housing (still attached to engine) and turbine housing. Replace either housing if gouged, nicked or distorted.
10. If CHRA is not being replaced, remove turbine housing from CHRA.

Journal Bearing Clearance Measurement

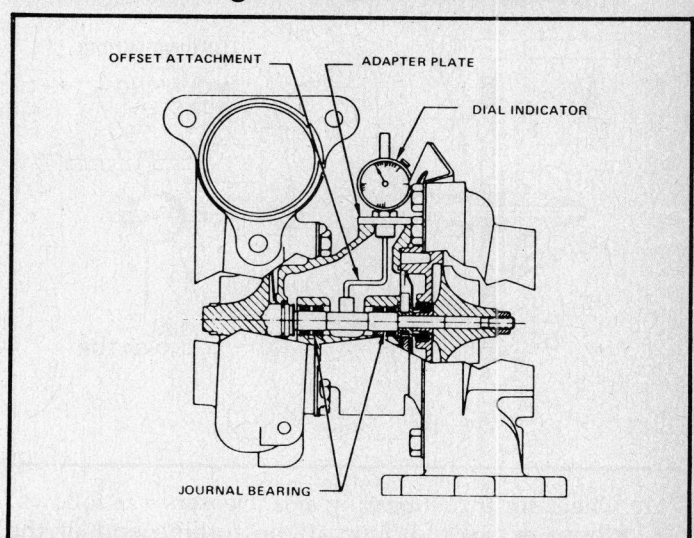

11. Check the journal bearings for radial clearance as follows.
a. Attach a dial indicator with a two inch long, ¾ to 1 inch offset extension rod to the center housing such that the indicator plunger extends through the oil outlet port and contacts the shaft of the rotating assembly.
b. Manually apply pressure equally and at the same time to both the compressor and turbine wheels as required to move the shaft away from the dial indicator plunger as far as it will go.
c. Set the dial indicator to zero.
d. Manually apply pressure equally and at the same time to both the compressor and turbine wheels to move the shaft toward the dial indicator plunger as far as it will go. Move the maximum value on the indicator dial.

NOTE   Make sure that the dial indicator reading noted is the maximum reading obtainable, which can be verified by rolling the wheels slightly in both directions while applying pressure.

e. Manually apply pressure equally and at the same time to the compressor and turbine wheels as required to move the shaft away from the dial indicator plunger as far as it will go. Note that the indicator pointer returns exactly to zero.

f. Repeat steps a. through f. as required to make sure that the maximum clearance between the center housing bores and the shaft bearing diameters, as indicated by the maximum shaft travel, has been obtained.

g. If the maximum bearing radial clearance is less than 0.003 inch or greater than 0.006 inch, replace CHRA and inspect housings as indicated in step 9.

NOTE   Continued operation of a turbocharger having improper bearing radial clearance will result in severe damage to the compressor wheel and housing or to the turbine wheel and housing.

Thrust Bearing Clearance Measurement

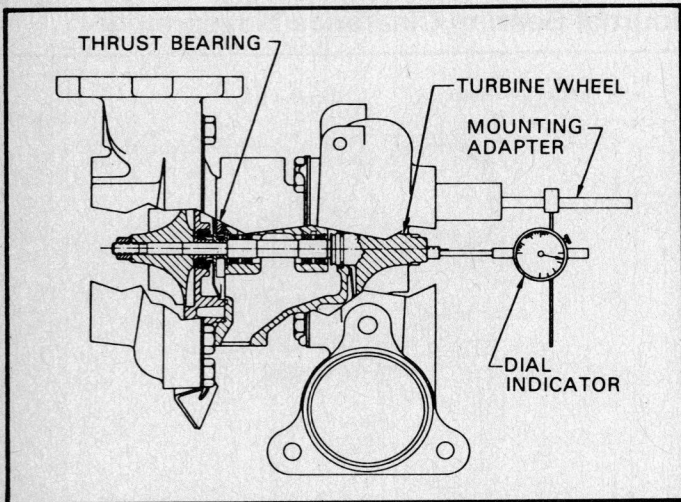

12. Check for thrust bearing axial clearance as follows.

a. Mount a dial indicator at the turbine end of the turbocharger such that the dial indicator tip rests on the end of the turbine wheel.

b. Manually move the compressor wheel and turbine wheel assembly alternately toward and away from the dial indicator plunger. Note the travel of the shaft in each direction, as shown on the dial indicator.

c. Repeat step b. as required to make sure that the maximum clearance between the thrust bearing components has been obtained.

d. If the maximum thrust bearing axial clearance is less than 0.001 inch or greater than 0.003 inch, replace CHRA and inspect housings as indicated in step 9.

NOTE   Continued operation of a turbocharger having an improper amount of thrust bearing axial clearance will result in severe damage to the compressor wheel and housing or to the turbine wheel and housing.

13. Install oil drain adapter and tube on CHRA.

14. Install turbocharger assembly to engine.

NOTE   Before connecting turbocharger exhaust outlet pipe to elbow assembly, gently spin the turbine wheel to be certain that the rotating assembly (turbine wheel, connecting shaft and compressor wheel) does not bind.

ROAD TEST

1. Remove ¼" pipe plug or vacuum switch located in the power enrichment adapter. Install a straight vacuum fitting and compound gauge tubing J-28474 into the power enrichment adapter, with sufficient length of hose to place gauge in passenger compartment.

CHILTON CAUTION   Determine that the hose and compound gage are in proper operating condition to avoid possible leakage of air-fuel mixture into the passenger compartment during road test.

2. Conditions and speed limits permitting, perform a zero to 40 or 50 mph wide open throttle acceleration. Boost pressure, as measured by the compound gage during road testing, should reach 9-10 psi. If not, replace actuator assembly and check for proper calibration. Actuator rod end should move .015" at approximately 9 psi, as detailed in the wastegate test procedure.

ESC Detonation Sensor

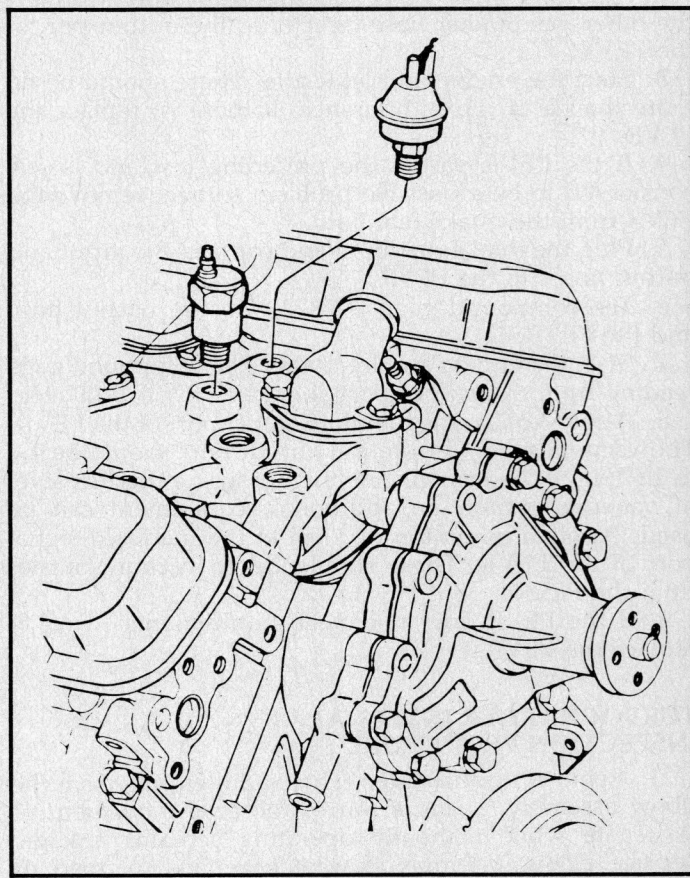

Component Service

ELECTRONIC SPARK CONTROL (ESC)— DETONATION SENSOR

1. Squeeze sides of metal connector crosswise to wire from controller and gently pull straight up to remove connector. Do not pull up on the wire.
2. Remove detonation sensor.
3. When installing, torque detonation sensor to 19 N•m (14 lb. ft.).

NOTE   Do not over-torque. Proper sensor torque is critical to the sensor performance. Do not use impact tool. Do not apply a side load to the detonation sensor. Do not attempt to repair tapped hole in intake manifold for detonation sensor.

4. Squeeze sides of metal connector crosswise to wire from controller and start straight down over detonation sensor terminal. Release sides of metal connector and push down until connector snaps into place.

WASTEGATE ACTUATOR ASSEMBLY

1. Disconnect hose clamp and two hoses from actuator assembly.
2. Remove retainer attaching wastegate linkage to actuator rod.
3. Remove two bolts attaching actuator assembly to compressor housing.
4. Installation is the reverse of removal.

ELBOW ASSEMBLY

NOTE   Whenever the elbow assembly is replaced, the wastegate actuator assembly must also be replaced with the adjustable type. Adjust as described in wastegate test procedure.

1. Detach turbocharger exhaust outlet pipe and catalytic converter at the intermediate pipe.
2. Disconnect turbocharger exhaust outlet pipe from elbow assembly.
3. Disconnect turbocharger inlet pipe at elbow assembly. Loosen at exhaust manifold and swing out of the way.
4. Remove retainer attaching wastegate linkage to actuator rod.
5. Remove elbow assembly support bracket bolts at elbow. Loosen bracket bolts at intake manifold and swing out of the way.
6. Remove six bolts attaching elbow assembly to turbine housing.
7. Installation is the reverse of removal.

CENTER HOUSING ROTATING ASSEMBLY

1. Remove elbow assembly.
2. Remove oil feed and return lines from housing.
3. Remove six bolts and three lockplates attaching turbine housing to CHRA.
4. Installation is the reverse of removal.

Elbow Assembly

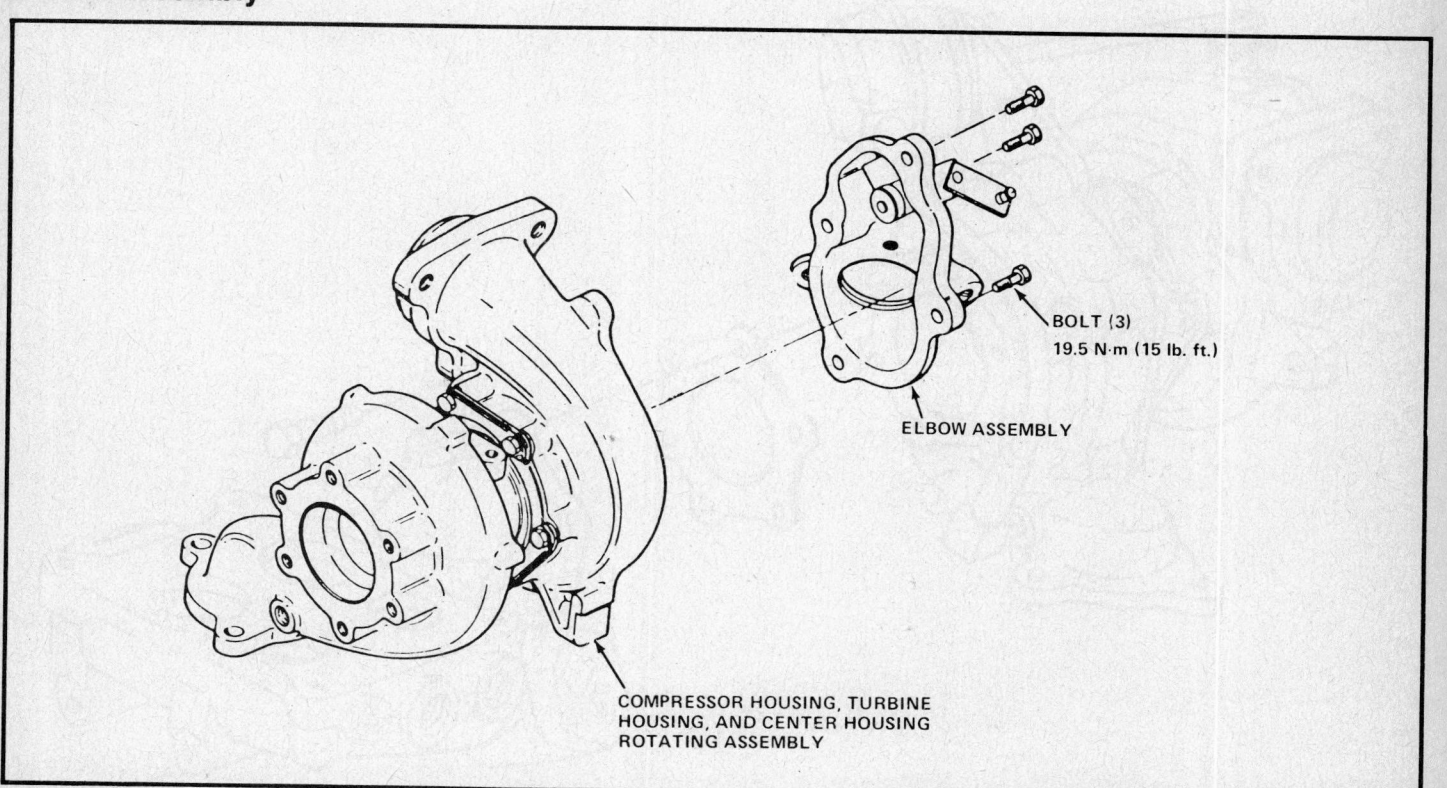

BOLT (3)
19.5 N·m (15 lb. ft.)

ELBOW ASSEMBLY

COMPRESSOR HOUSING, TURBINE HOUSING, AND CENTER HOUSING ROTATING ASSEMBLY

TURBOCHARGERS
GM V-8

Center Housing Rotating Assembly (CHRA)

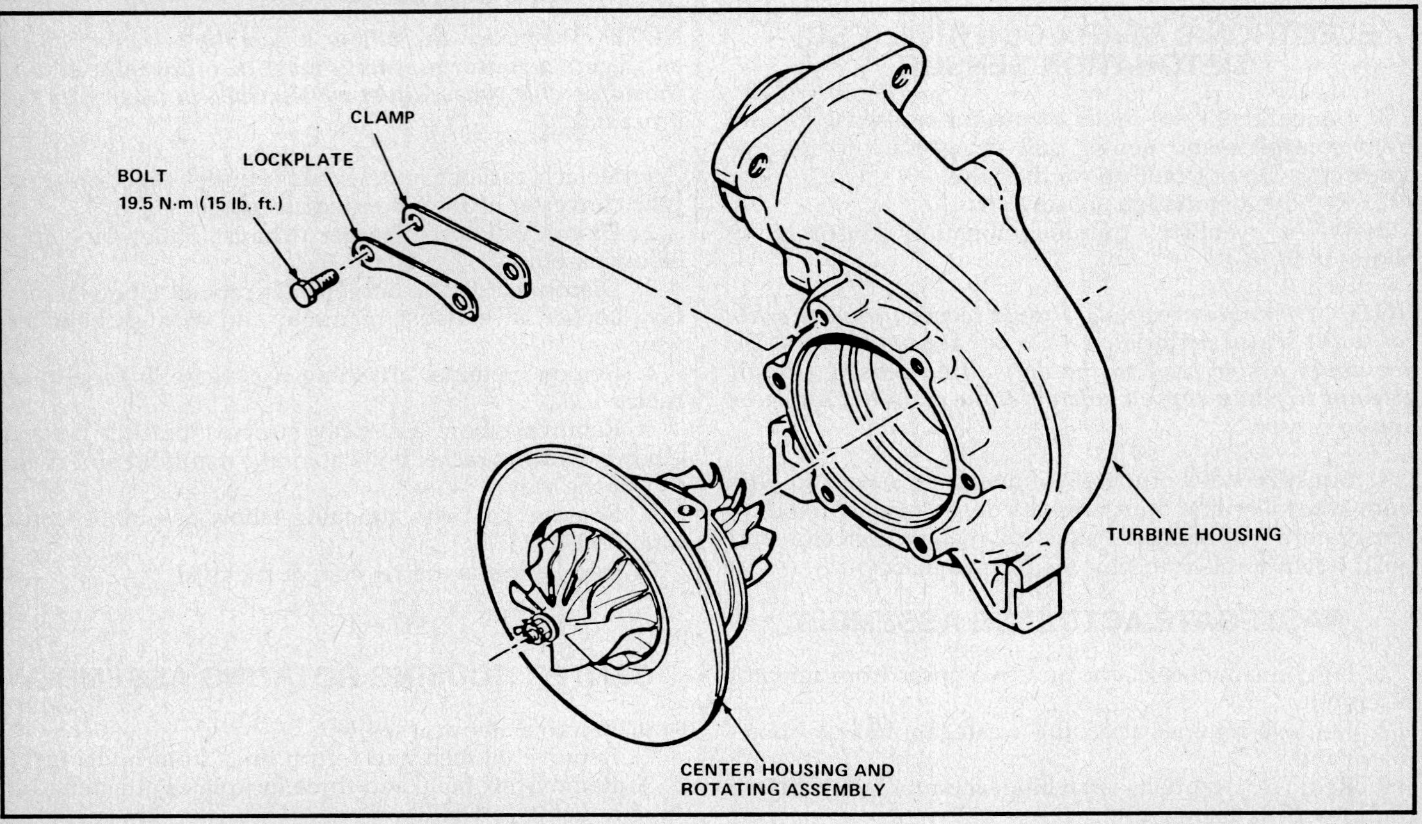

BOLT
19.5 N·m (15 lb. ft.)

LOCKPLATE

CLAMP

TURBINE HOUSING

CENTER HOUSING AND
ROTATING ASSEMBLY

Turbocharger-to-Plenum Mounting

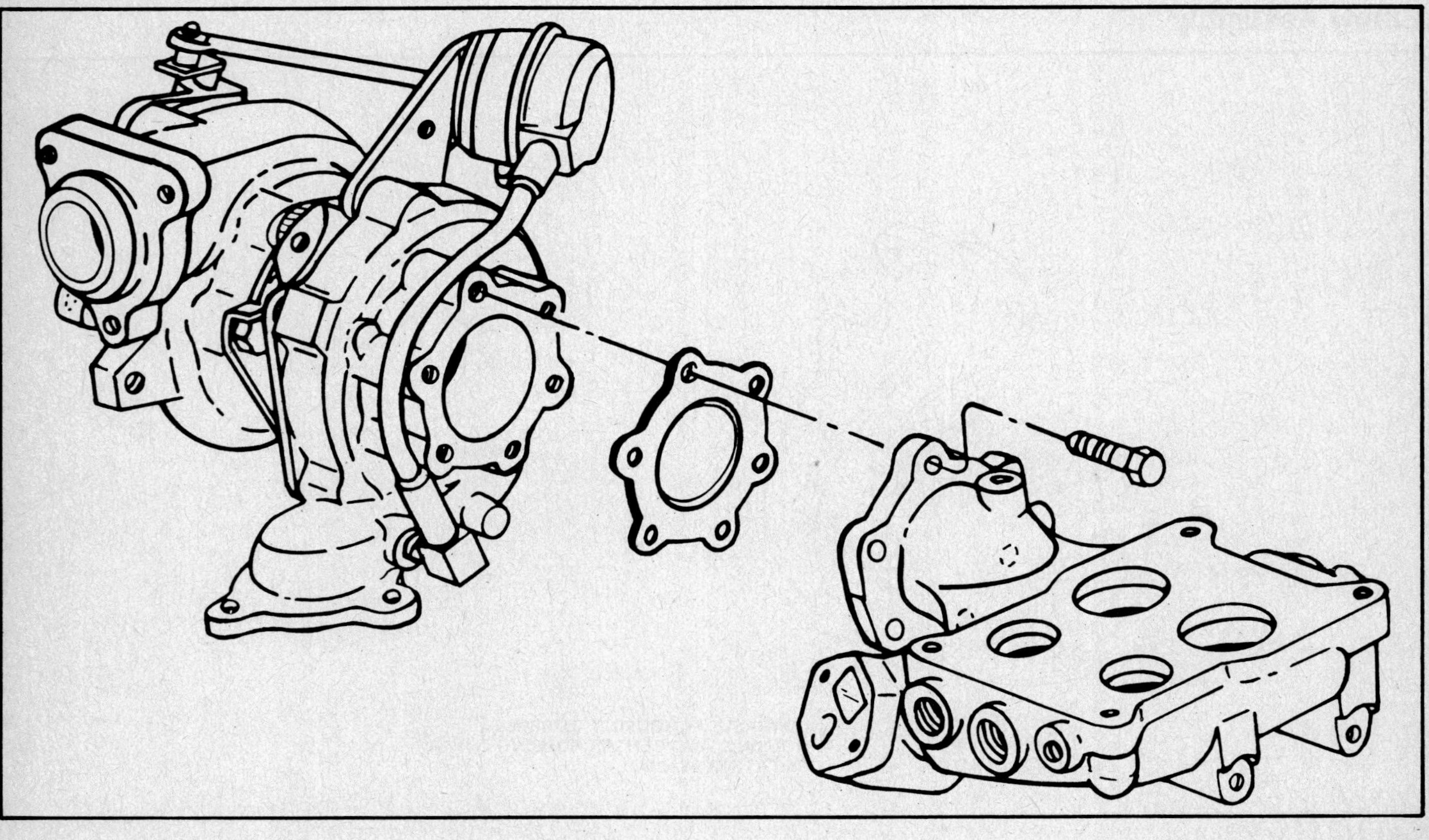

COMPRESSOR HOUSING

1. Remove turbo elbow assembly and CHRA.
2. Remove air cleaner.
3. Remove EGR valve and heat shield.
4. Remove six bolts attaching compressor housing to plenum.
5. Remove three bolts attaching compressor housing to intake manifold.
6. Installation is the reverse of removal.

TURBOCHARGER AND ACTUATOR ASSEMBLY

1. Disconnect turbocharger exhaust inlet pipe and exhaust outlet pipe at turbocharger.
2. Remove air cleaner.
3. Disconnect accelerator, cruise and detent linkages at carburetor.
4. Disconnect carburetor fuel line and necessary vacuum hoses.
5. Drain cooling system.
6. Disconnect coolant hoses at front and rear of plenum.
7. Disconnect EGR pipe at intake manifold fitting.
8. Remove two bolts attaching turbine housing to bracket on intake manifold.
9. Remove three bolts attaching compressor housing to intake manifold.
10. Remove turbocharger and actuator, still attached to carburetor and plenum assembly, from engine. Disconnect vacuum hoses as necessary.
11. Remove six bolts attaching turbocharger and actuator assembly to plenum and carburetor assembly.
12. Remove oil drain from center housing rotating assembly.
13. Installation is the reverse of removal.

PLENUM

1. Remove turbocharger and actuator assembly.
2. Remove two bolts, throttle bracket and two nuts attaching carburetor to plenum.
3. If replacing plenum, remove all necessary parts from plenum for transfer.
4. Installation is the reverse of removal.

EGR VALVE

1. Disconnect vacuum line to EGR valve.
2. Remove two bolts attaching EGR valve to plenum.
3. Installation is the reverse of removal.

Compressor Housing

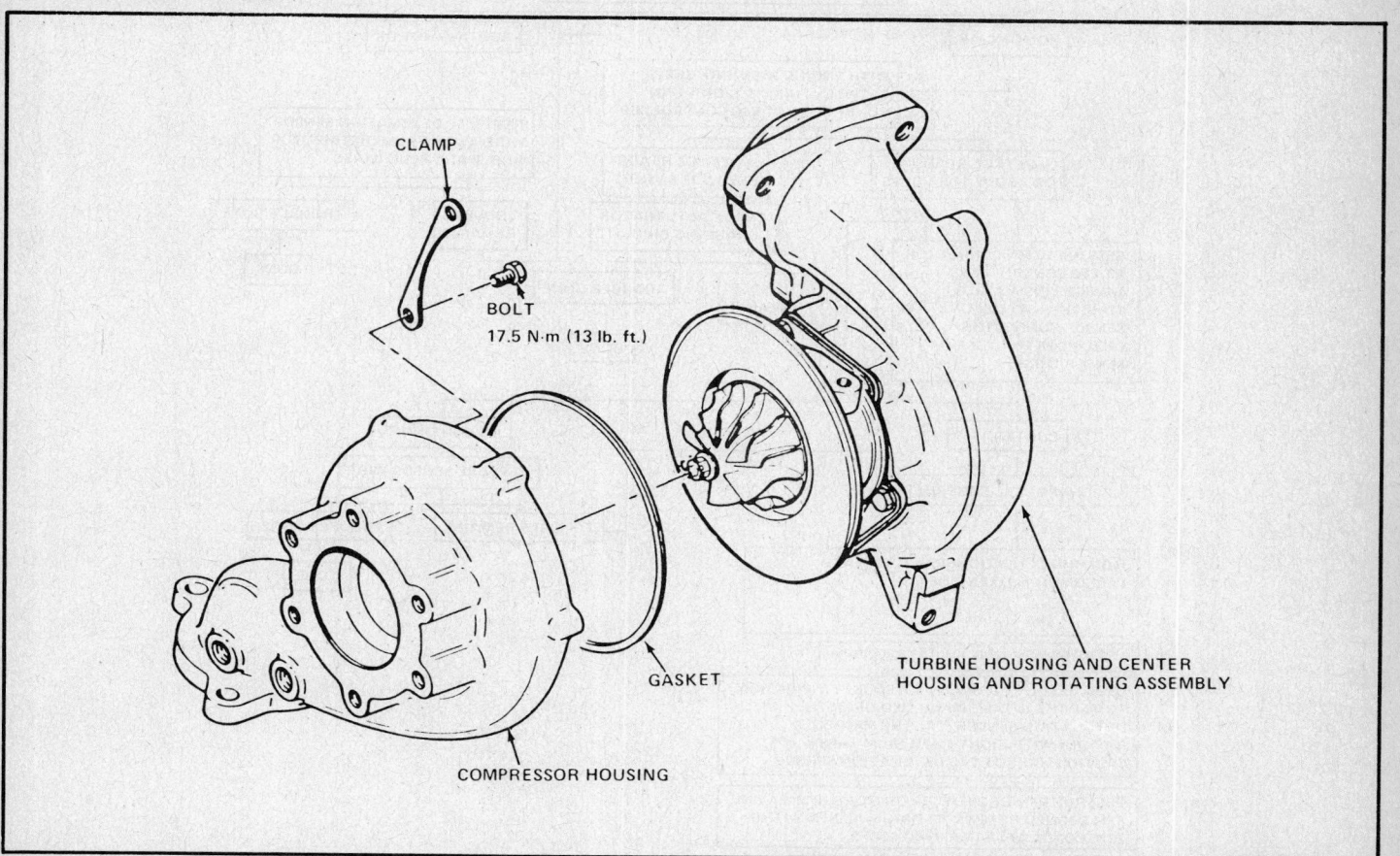

CLAMP

BOLT
17.5 N·m (13 lb. ft.)

GASKET

TURBINE HOUSING AND CENTER HOUSING AND ROTATING ASSEMBLY

COMPRESSOR HOUSING

Electronic Spark Control (ESC) System

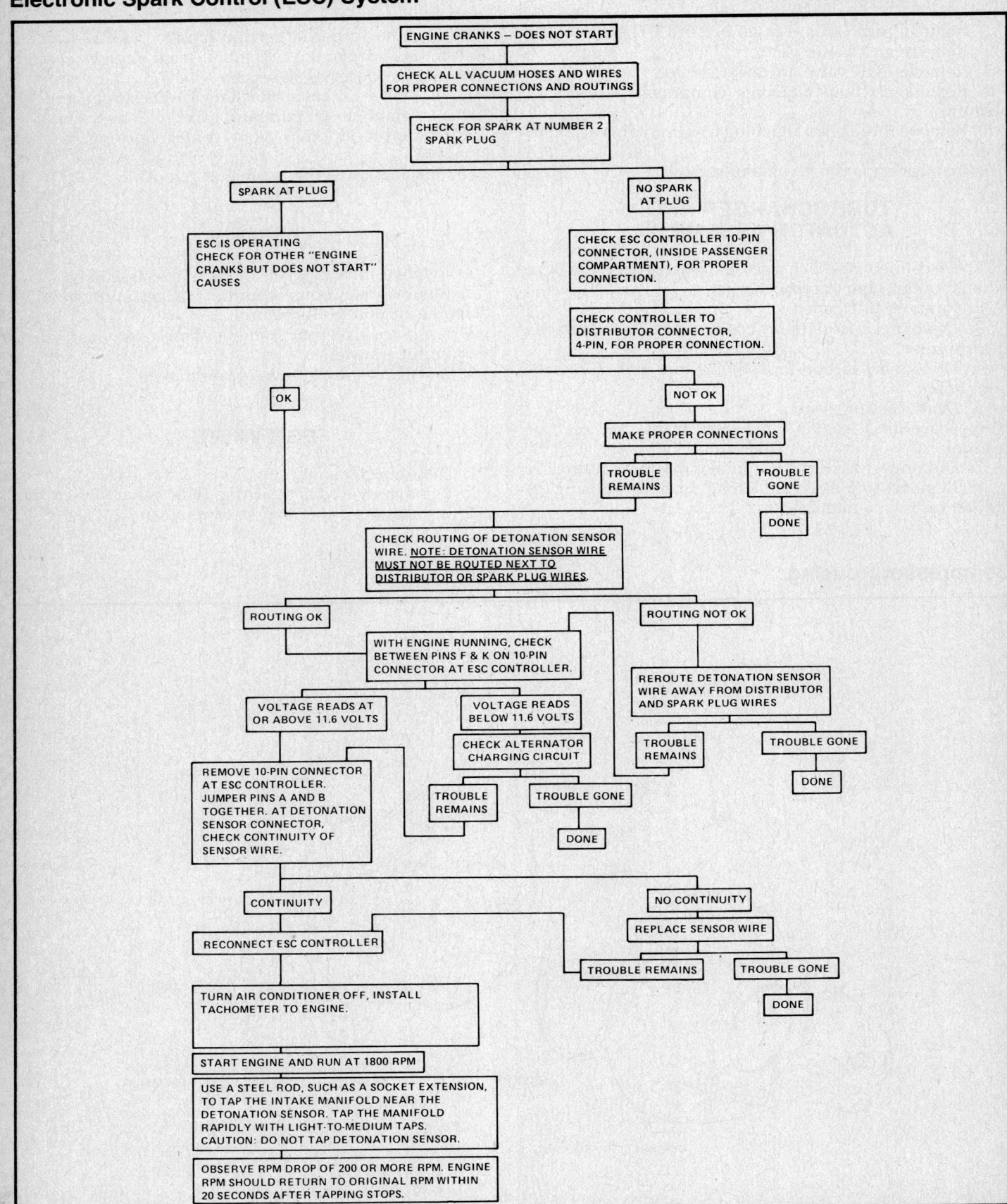

ENGINE CRANKS – DOES NOT START

CHECK ALL VACUUM HOSES AND WIRES FOR PROPER CONNECTIONS AND ROUTINGS

CHECK FOR SPARK AT NUMBER 2 SPARK PLUG

SPARK AT PLUG

ESC IS OPERATING
CHECK FOR OTHER "ENGINE CRANKS BUT DOES NOT START" CAUSES

NO SPARK AT PLUG

CHECK ESC CONTROLLER 10-PIN CONNECTOR, (INSIDE PASSENGER COMPARTMENT), FOR PROPER CONNECTION.

CHECK CONTROLLER TO DISTRIBUTOR CONNECTOR, 4-PIN, FOR PROPER CONNECTION.

OK

NOT OK

MAKE PROPER CONNECTIONS

TROUBLE REMAINS

TROUBLE GONE

DONE

CHECK ROUTING OF DETONATION SENSOR WIRE. NOTE: DETONATION SENSOR WIRE MUST NOT BE ROUTED NEXT TO DISTRIBUTOR OR SPARK PLUG WIRES.

ROUTING OK

WITH ENGINE RUNNING, CHECK BETWEEN PINS F & K ON 10-PIN CONNECTOR AT ESC CONTROLLER.

ROUTING NOT OK

REROUTE DETONATION SENSOR WIRE AWAY FROM DISTRIBUTOR AND SPARK PLUG WIRES

VOLTAGE READS AT OR ABOVE 11.6 VOLTS

VOLTAGE READS BELOW 11.6 VOLTS

CHECK ALTERNATOR CHARGING CIRCUIT

TROUBLE REMAINS

TROUBLE GONE

REMOVE 10-PIN CONNECTOR AT ESC CONTROLLER. JUMPER PINS A AND B TOGETHER. AT DETONATION SENSOR CONNECTOR, CHECK CONTINUITY OF SENSOR WIRE.

TROUBLE REMAINS

TROUBLE GONE

DONE

DONE

CONTINUITY

RECONNECT ESC CONTROLLER

NO CONTINUITY

REPLACE SENSOR WIRE

TROUBLE REMAINS

TROUBLE GONE

DONE

TURN AIR CONDITIONER OFF, INSTALL TACHOMETER TO ENGINE.

START ENGINE AND RUN AT 1800 RPM

USE A STEEL ROD, SUCH AS A SOCKET EXTENSION, TO TAP THE INTAKE MANIFOLD NEAR THE DETONATION SENSOR. TAP THE MANIFOLD RAPIDLY WITH LIGHT-TO-MEDIUM TAPS. CAUTION: DO NOT TAP DETONATION SENSOR.

OBSERVE RPM DROP OF 200 OR MORE RPM. ENGINE RPM SHOULD RETURN TO ORIGINAL RPM WITHIN 20 SECONDS AFTER TAPPING STOPS.

Electronic Spark Control (ESC) System

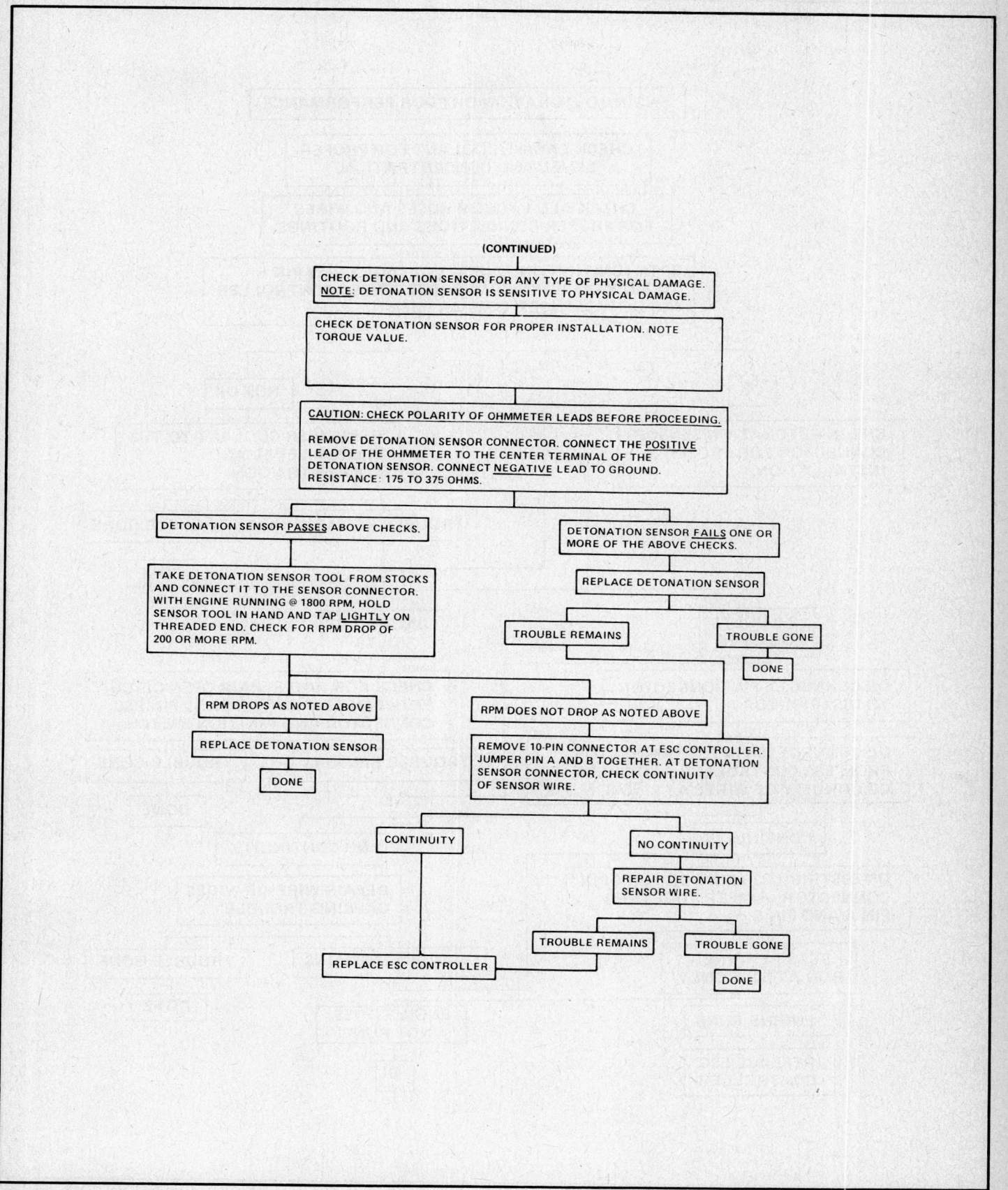

(CONTINUED)

CHECK DETONATION SENSOR FOR ANY TYPE OF PHYSICAL DAMAGE.
NOTE: DETONATION SENSOR IS SENSITIVE TO PHYSICAL DAMAGE.

CHECK DETONATION SENSOR FOR PROPER INSTALLATION. NOTE TORQUE VALUE.

CAUTION: CHECK POLARITY OF OHMMETER LEADS BEFORE PROCEEDING.

REMOVE DETONATION SENSOR CONNECTOR. CONNECT THE POSITIVE LEAD OF THE OHMMETER TO THE CENTER TERMINAL OF THE DETONATION SENSOR. CONNECT NEGATIVE LEAD TO GROUND. RESISTANCE: 175 TO 375 OHMS.

DETONATION SENSOR PASSES ABOVE CHECKS.

DETONATION SENSOR FAILS ONE OR MORE OF THE ABOVE CHECKS.

TAKE DETONATION SENSOR TOOL FROM STOCKS AND CONNECT IT TO THE SENSOR CONNECTOR. WITH ENGINE RUNNING @ 1800 RPM, HOLD SENSOR TOOL IN HAND AND TAP LIGHTLY ON THREADED END. CHECK FOR RPM DROP OF 200 OR MORE RPM.

REPLACE DETONATION SENSOR

TROUBLE REMAINS

TROUBLE GONE

DONE

RPM DROPS AS NOTED ABOVE

RPM DOES NOT DROP AS NOTED ABOVE

REPLACE DETONATION SENSOR

DONE

REMOVE 10-PIN CONNECTOR AT ESC CONTROLLER. JUMPER PIN A AND B TOGETHER. AT DETONATION SENSOR CONNECTOR, CHECK CONTINUITY OF SENSOR WIRE.

CONTINUITY

NO CONTINUITY

REPAIR DETONATION SENSOR WIRE.

TROUBLE REMAINS

TROUBLE GONE

DONE

REPLACE ESC CONTROLLER

Electronic Spark Control (ESC) System

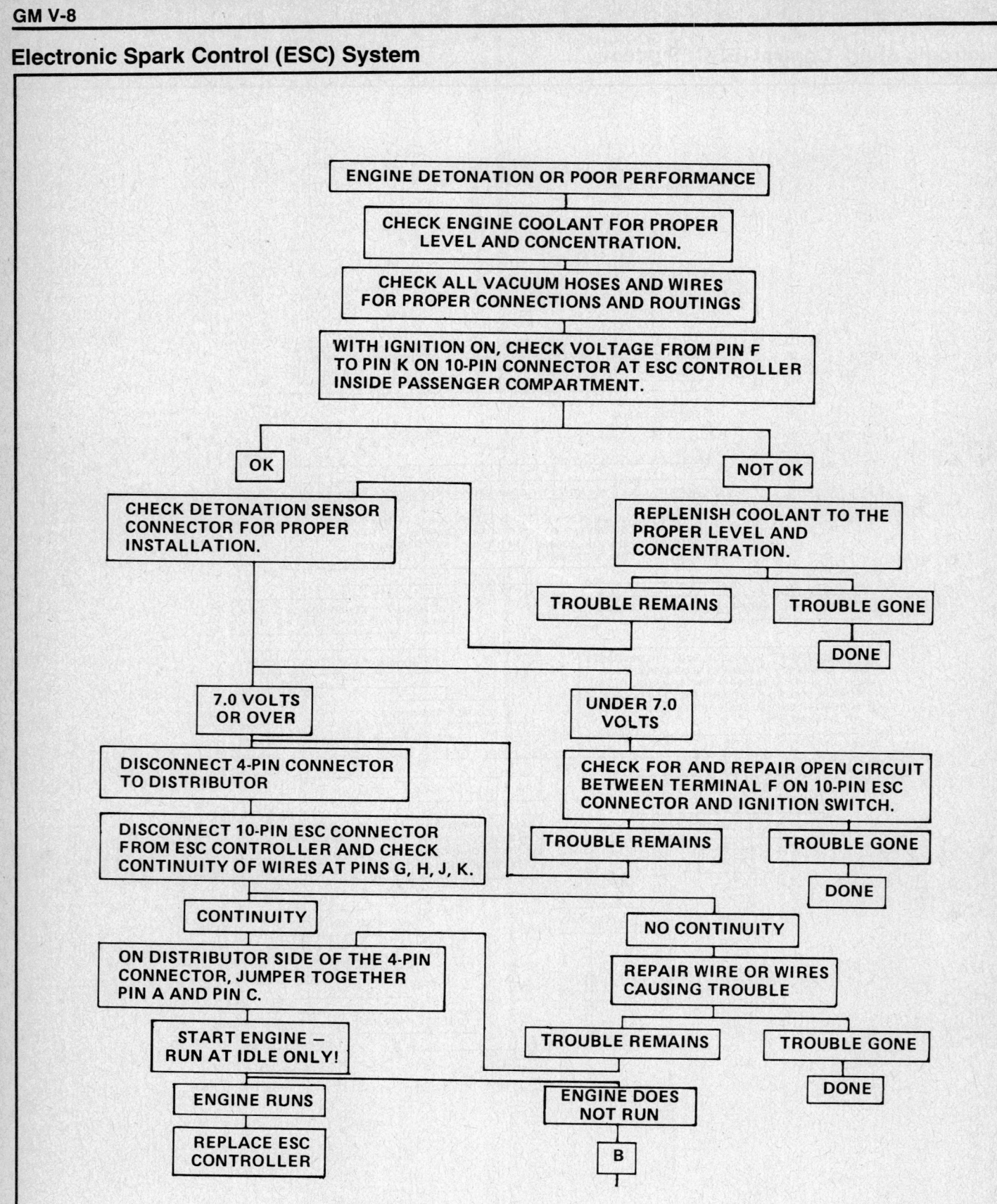

ENGINE DETONATION OR POOR PERFORMANCE

CHECK ENGINE COOLANT FOR PROPER LEVEL AND CONCENTRATION.

CHECK ALL VACUUM HOSES AND WIRES FOR PROPER CONNECTIONS AND ROUTINGS

WITH IGNITION ON, CHECK VOLTAGE FROM PIN F TO PIN K ON 10-PIN CONNECTOR AT ESC CONTROLLER INSIDE PASSENGER COMPARTMENT.

OK

NOT OK

CHECK DETONATION SENSOR CONNECTOR FOR PROPER INSTALLATION.

REPLENISH COOLANT TO THE PROPER LEVEL AND CONCENTRATION.

TROUBLE REMAINS

TROUBLE GONE

DONE

7.0 VOLTS OR OVER

UNDER 7.0 VOLTS

DISCONNECT 4-PIN CONNECTOR TO DISTRIBUTOR

CHECK FOR AND REPAIR OPEN CIRCUIT BETWEEN TERMINAL F ON 10-PIN ESC CONNECTOR AND IGNITION SWITCH.

DISCONNECT 10-PIN ESC CONNECTOR FROM ESC CONTROLLER AND CHECK CONTINUITY OF WIRES AT PINS G, H, J, K.

TROUBLE REMAINS

TROUBLE GONE

DONE

CONTINUITY

NO CONTINUITY

ON DISTRIBUTOR SIDE OF THE 4-PIN CONNECTOR, JUMPER TOGETHER PIN A AND PIN C.

REPAIR WIRE OR WIRES CAUSING TROUBLE

START ENGINE – RUN AT IDLE ONLY!

TROUBLE REMAINS

TROUBLE GONE

DONE

ENGINE RUNS

ENGINE DOES NOT RUN

REPLACE ESC CONTROLLER

B

Electronic Spark Control (ESC) System

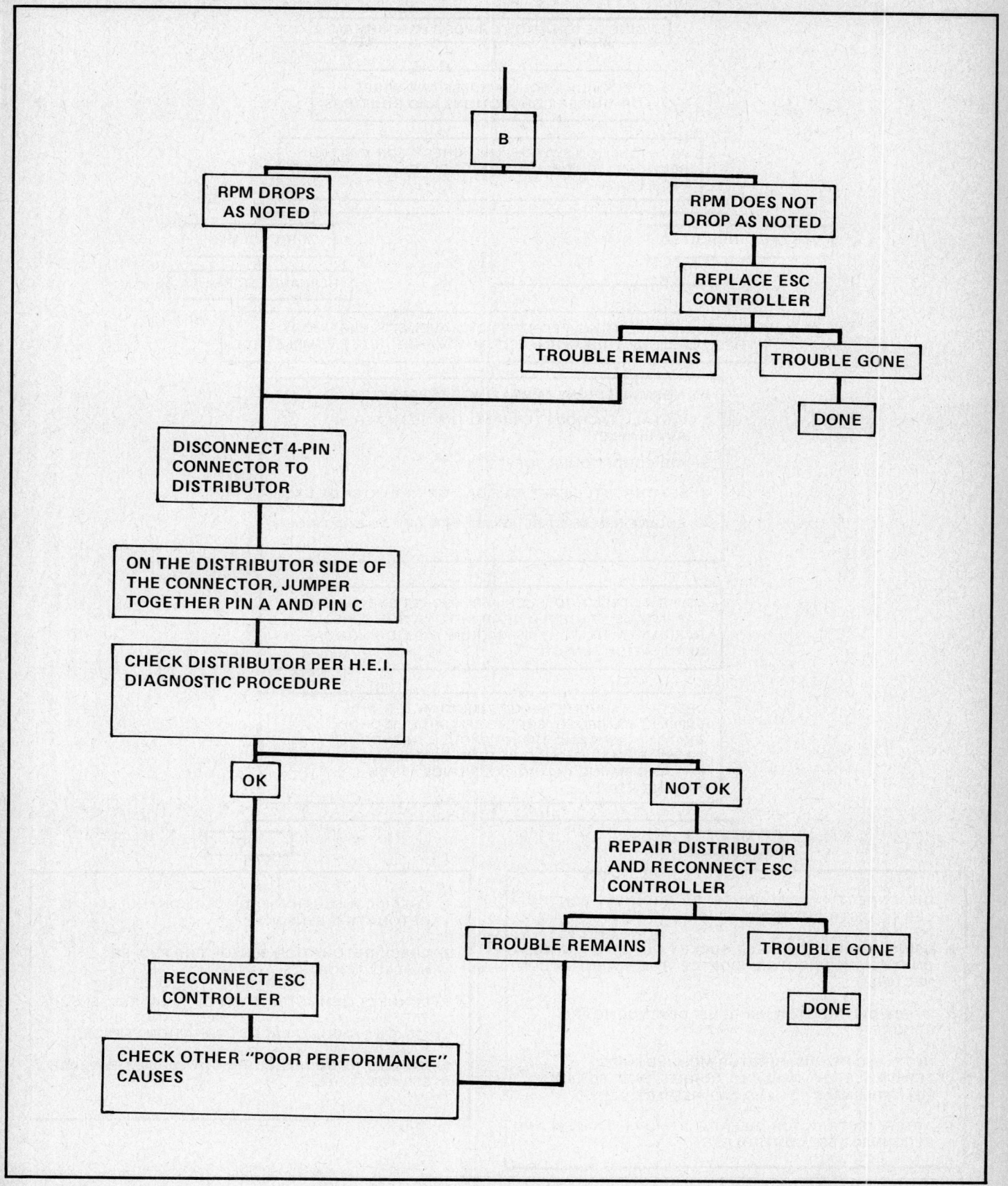

B

RPM DROPS AS NOTED

RPM DOES NOT DROP AS NOTED

REPLACE ESC CONTROLLER

TROUBLE REMAINS

TROUBLE GONE

DONE

DISCONNECT 4-PIN CONNECTOR TO DISTRIBUTOR

ON THE DISTRIBUTOR SIDE OF THE CONNECTOR, JUMPER TOGETHER PIN A AND PIN C

CHECK DISTRIBUTOR PER H.E.I. DIAGNOSTIC PROCEDURE

OK

NOT OK

REPAIR DISTRIBUTOR AND RECONNECT ESC CONTROLLER

TROUBLE REMAINS

TROUBLE GONE

DONE

RECONNECT ESC CONTROLLER

CHECK OTHER "POOR PERFORMANCE" CAUSES

TURBOCHARGERS

GM V-8

Electronic Spark Control (ESC) System

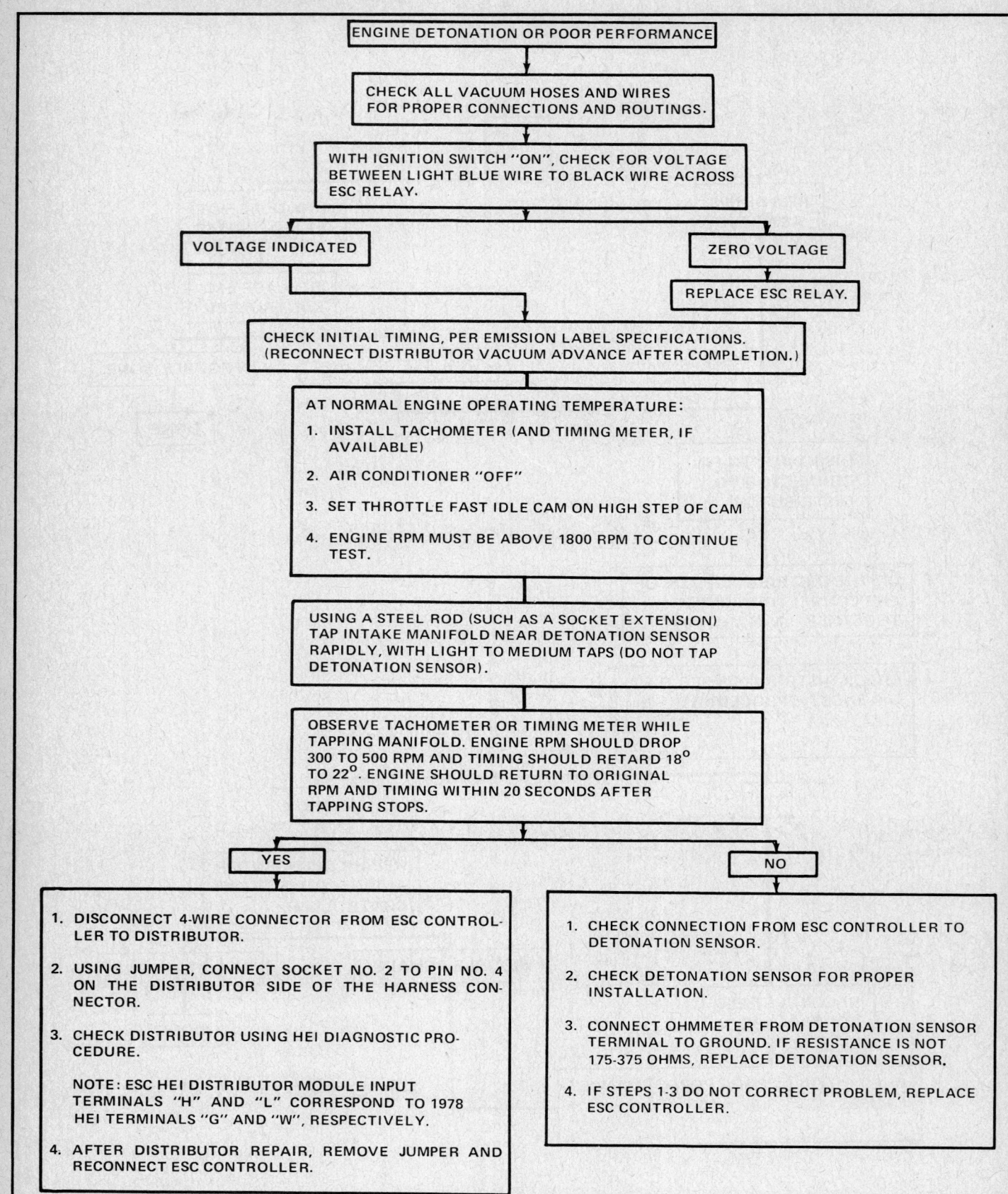

ENGINE DETONATION OR POOR PERFORMANCE

CHECK ALL VACUUM HOSES AND WIRES FOR PROPER CONNECTIONS AND ROUTINGS.

WITH IGNITION SWITCH "ON", CHECK FOR VOLTAGE BETWEEN LIGHT BLUE WIRE TO BLACK WIRE ACROSS ESC RELAY.

VOLTAGE INDICATED

ZERO VOLTAGE

REPLACE ESC RELAY.

CHECK INITIAL TIMING, PER EMISSION LABEL SPECIFICATIONS. (RECONNECT DISTRIBUTOR VACUUM ADVANCE AFTER COMPLETION.)

AT NORMAL ENGINE OPERATING TEMPERATURE:

1. INSTALL TACHOMETER (AND TIMING METER, IF AVAILABLE)

2. AIR CONDITIONER "OFF"

3. SET THROTTLE FAST IDLE CAM ON HIGH STEP OF CAM

4. ENGINE RPM MUST BE ABOVE 1800 RPM TO CONTINUE TEST.

USING A STEEL ROD (SUCH AS A SOCKET EXTENSION) TAP INTAKE MANIFOLD NEAR DETONATION SENSOR RAPIDLY, WITH LIGHT TO MEDIUM TAPS (DO NOT TAP DETONATION SENSOR).

OBSERVE TACHOMETER OR TIMING METER WHILE TAPPING MANIFOLD. ENGINE RPM SHOULD DROP 300 TO 500 RPM AND TIMING SHOULD RETARD 18° TO 22°. ENGINE SHOULD RETURN TO ORIGINAL RPM AND TIMING WITHIN 20 SECONDS AFTER TAPPING STOPS.

YES

NO

1. DISCONNECT 4-WIRE CONNECTOR FROM ESC CONTROLLER TO DISTRIBUTOR.

2. USING JUMPER, CONNECT SOCKET NO. 2 TO PIN NO. 4 ON THE DISTRIBUTOR SIDE OF THE HARNESS CONNECTOR.

3. CHECK DISTRIBUTOR USING HEI DIAGNOSTIC PROCEDURE.

   NOTE: ESC HEI DISTRIBUTOR MODULE INPUT TERMINALS "H" AND "L" CORRESPOND TO 1978 HEI TERMINALS "G" AND "W", RESPECTIVELY.

4. AFTER DISTRIBUTOR REPAIR, REMOVE JUMPER AND RECONNECT ESC CONTROLLER.

1. CHECK CONNECTION FROM ESC CONTROLLER TO DETONATION SENSOR.

2. CHECK DETONATION SENSOR FOR PROPER INSTALLATION.

3. CONNECT OHMMETER FROM DETONATION SENSOR TERMINAL TO GROUND. IF RESISTANCE IS NOT 175-375 OHMS, REPLACE DETONATION SENSOR.

4. IF STEPS 1-3 DO NOT CORRECT PROBLEM, REPLACE ESC CONTROLLER.

TURBOCHARGER TORQUE SPECIFICATIONS

Area	N•m	Lb. Ft.
Exhaust outlet pipe to elbow assembly	19	14
Elbow assembly to compressor housing	20	15
Exhaust inlet pipe to turbine housing	19	14
Exhaust inlet pipe to right manifold	19	14
Oil feed pipe to fitting (both ends)	10	7
Oil feed pipe fitting to CHRA	10	7
CHRA to turbine housing	20	15
CHRA backplate to compressor housing	18	13
Compressor housing to plenum	20	15
Compressor housing to intake manifold	37	27
Oil drain adapter to CHRA	27	20
Manifold to plenum	20	15
ESC detonation sensor to intake manifold	19	14
Carburetor to plenum support	17	13
Bracket to cylinder head	37	27
Plenum support bracket to plenum	28	21
PEVR to intake manifold	27	20
Turbine support bracket to intake manifold	20	15
Turbine housing bracket to turbine housing	20	15
Fuel line to carburetor	27	20
Oil drain tube to adapter	60	45
Power enrichment regulator adapter	27	20
Power enichment adapter to intake	27	20
EGR elbow fitting to manifold	20	15
Wastegate vacuum equalizer fitting to plenum	12	8
Plenum vacuum plug	20	15
Oil feed reducer to block	38	27
Oil feed connector fitting to reducer	10	7
Plenum water nipples	34	25
Plenum water plug	34	25
TVS to plenum	34	25

ENGINE CONTROLS

INDEX

AMERICAN MOTORS CORPORATION

General Description

Two different feedback systems are used with American Motors Corporation automobiles. The four cylinder engine uses General Motors' computer command system which controls ignition timing and carburetion. The six cylinder engine system controls only carburetion.

COMPUTERIZED EMISSION CONTROL SYSTEM (CEC)

This system is used with six cylinder AMC automobiles (except Eagle).

MICRO COMPUTER UNIT (MCU)

The MCU monitors the oxygen sensor voltage and, based upon the mode of operation, generates an output control signal for the carburetor stepper motor. If the system is in the closed loop mode of operation, the air-fuel mixture will vary according to the oxygen content in the exhaust gas and engine operation. If the system is in the open loop mode of operation, the air-fuel mixture will be based on a predetermined ratio that is dependent on engine rpm.

STEPPER MOTOR

The stepper motor controls the metering pins that vary the size of the air bleed orifices located in the carburetor

Computerized Engine Control—Six Cylinder

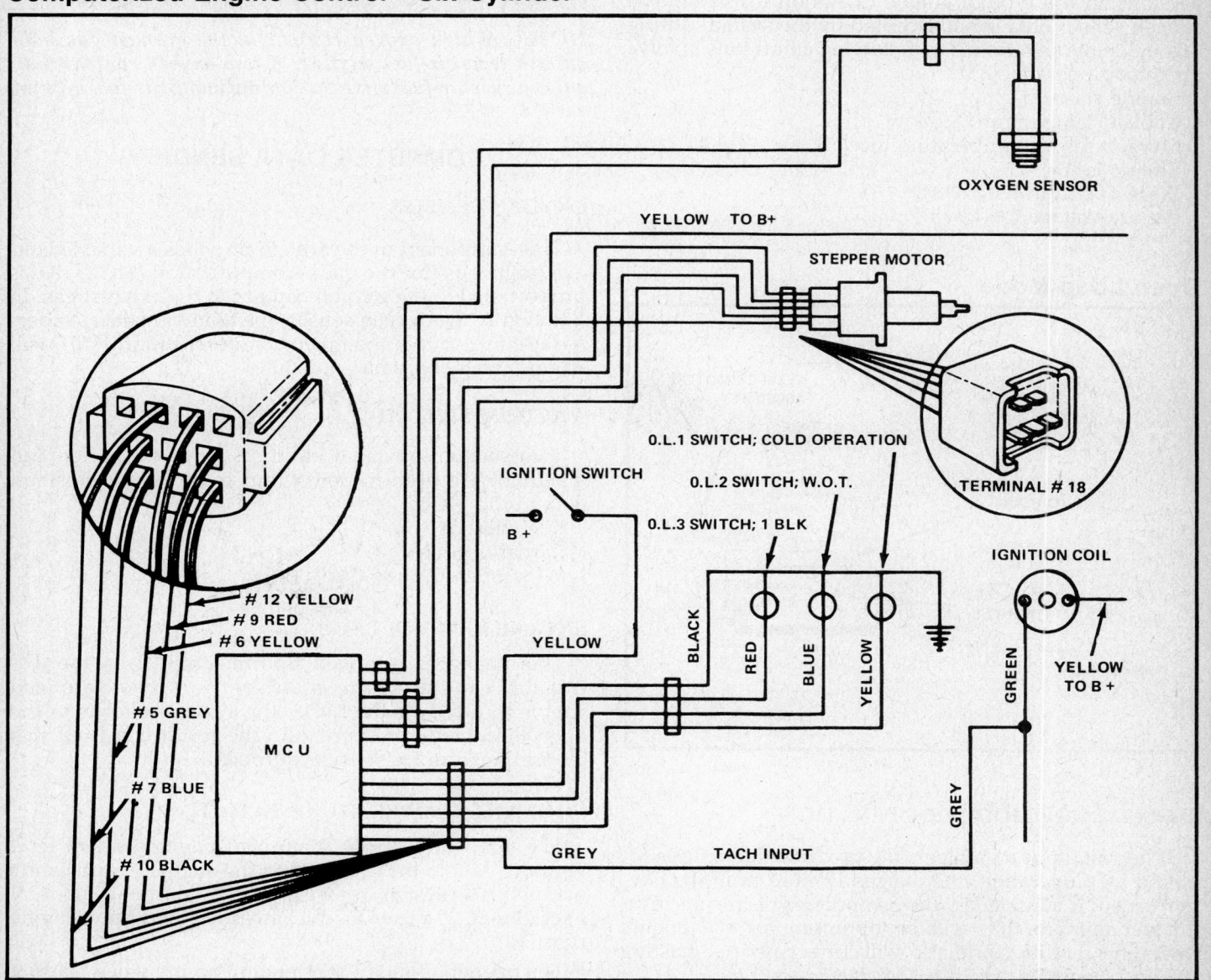

body. The motor moves the pins in and out of the orifices in steps according to the control signal generated by the MCU. The motor has a range of 100 steps, but the normal operating area is mid-range. When the metering pins are stepped in the direction of the orifices, the air-fuel mixture becomes richer; when stepped away from the orifices, the mixture becomes leaner.

SYSTEM OPERATION

There are two primary modes of operation for the feedback system, open loop and closed loop.

OPEN LOOP MODE OF OPERATION

The system will be in the open loop mode of operation (or a variation of it) whenever the engine operation conditions do not meet the programmed criteria for closed loop operation. During open loop operation, the air-fuel mixture is maintained at a programmed ratio that is dependent on the type of engine operation involved. The oxygen sensor data is not accepted by the system during this mode of operation. The following conditions involve open loop operation.

Engine start-up
Coolant temperature too low
Oxygen sensor temperature too low
Engine idling
Wide open throttle (WOT)
Battery voltage too low

Open Loop Mode

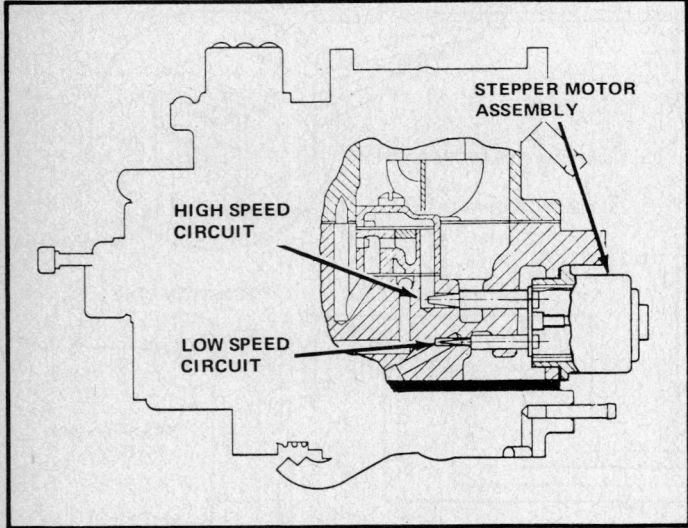

CLOSED LOOP MODE OF OPERATION

When all input data meets the programmed criteria for closed loop operation, the oxygen content from the oxygen sensor is accepted by the computer. This results in an air-fuel mixture that will be optimum for the engine operating condition and also will correct any pre-existing mixture condition which is too lean or too rich.

Closed Loop Mode

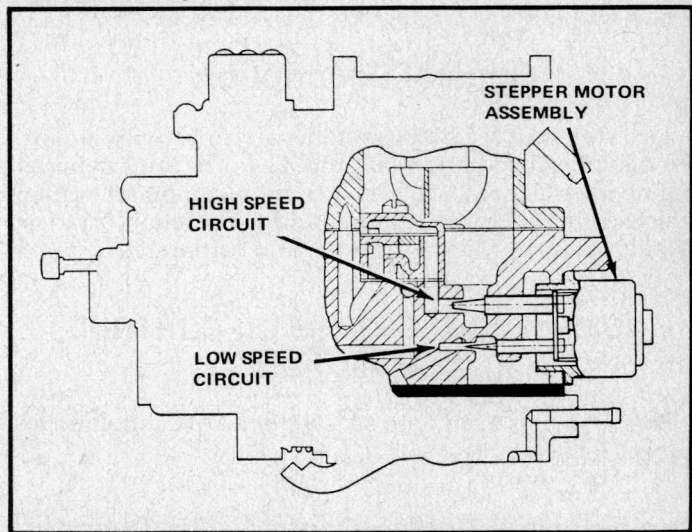

NOTE   A high oxygen content in the exhaust gas indicates a lean air-fuel mixture. A low oxygen content indicates a rich air-fuel mixture. The optimum air-fuel mixture ratio is 14.7:1.

COMPUTER DATA SENDERS

OXYGEN SENSOR

This component of the system provides a variable voltage (millivolts) for the micro computer unit (MCU) that is proportional to the oxygen content in the exhaust gas. In addition to the oxygen sensor, the following data senders are used to supply the micro computer unit (MCU) with engine operation data.

VACUUM SWITCH

Two vacuum-operated electrical switches (ported and manifold) are used to detect and send throttle position data to the MCU.

Idle (closed)
Partial throttle
Wide open throttle (WOT)

ENGINE RPM VOLTAGE

This voltage is supplied from a terminal on the distributor. Until a voltage equivalent to a predetermined rpm is received by the MCU, the system remains in the open loop mode of operation. The result is a fixed rich air-fuel mixture for starting purposes.

COOLANT TEMPERATURE SWITCH

The temperature switch supplies engine coolant temperature data to the MCU. Until the engine is sufficiently warmed, the system remains in the open loop mode of operation (i.e., a fixed air-fuel mixture based upon engine rpm).

The open loop mode of operation occurs when starting

the engine or the engine is cold, when the engine is idling, or when the engine is at wide open throttle (WOT). When any of these three conditions occur, the metering pins are driven to a predetermined programmed position for each condition. Because the positions are predetermined and no feedback relative to the results is accepted, this type of operation is referred to as open loop operation. The three open loop operations are characterized by the metering pins being driven to a position where they are stopped and remain stationary.

OPEN LOOP PRIORITIES

Each open loop operation has a specific metering pin position and, because more than one of the open loop triggering conditions can be present at one time, the MCU is programmed with a priority ranking for the operations. It complies with the input having the highest priority. The priorities are as follows.
1. Open loop 1, cold operation, starting engine
2. Open loop 2, wide open throttle (WOT)
3. Open loop 3, idle
4. Closed loop

OPEN LOOP PREDETERMINED POSITION VARIATION

An additional function of the MCU is to correct for a change in ambient conditions (high altitude). During closed loop operation, the MCU stores the amount and direction that the metering pins are driven to correct the oxygen content. If the movements are consistently to the same position, the MCU will vary all three open loop predetermined positions a corresponding amount. This function allows the open loop air-fuel mixture ratios to be tailored to the existing ambient condition during each uninterrupted use of the system.

CLOSED LOOP OPERATION

The CEC system controls the air-fuel ratio with movable air metering pins, visible from the top of the carburetor air horn, that are driven by a stepper motor. The stepper motor moves the metering pins in increments or small steps via electrical impulses generated by the MCU. The MCU causes the stepper motor to drive the metering pins to a richer or leaner position in reaction to the voltage input from the oxygen sensor.

The oxygen sensor voltage varies in reaction to changes in oxygen content present in the exhaust gas. Because the content of oxygen in the exhaust gas indicates the completeness of the combustion process, it is a reliable indicator of the air-fuel mixture that is entering the combustion chamber.

Because the oxygen sensor only senses oxygen, any air leak or malfunction between the carburetor and sensor may cause the sensor to provide an erroneous voltage output. This could be caused by a fouled spark plug, manifold air leak or malfunctioning secondary air check valve.

The engine operation characteristics never quite permit the MCU to compute a single metering pin position that constantly provides the optimum air-fuel mixture. Therefore, closed loop operation is characterized by constant movement of the metering pins because the MCU is forced constantly to make small corrections in the air-fuel mixture in an attempt to create a system null.

ENGINE DATA SENDERS

The other components of the CEC system are not actually involved in the fuel metering. They provide input data to the MCU to trigger either the open loop or closed loop operation.
1. The open loop 1 vacuum switch is colored yellow. It is controlled by manifold vacuum through a CTO switch and has a normally open (NO) electrical contact that is closed by 3 ± .5 in. Hg vacuum.
2. The open loop 2 vacuum switch is colored blue. It is controlled by manifold vacuum and has a normally closed (NC) electrical switch that is opened by 4 ± .5 in. Hg vacuum.
3. The open loop 3 vacuum switch is colored pink. It is controlled by carburetor ported vacuum and has a normally closed (NC) electrical switch that is opened by 3 ± .5 in. Hg vacuum.
4. The rpm voltage input is provided by a harness wire connected between the MCU and the negative terminal of the ignition coil.

NOTE   For the system to operate properly, all associated components and related systems must be intact and operational. This includes EGR valves, EGR related componentry, correct spark vacuum routing, etc.

INITIALIZATION (START-UP)

When the ignition system is turned off, the MCU is also turned off. It has no memory circuit for prior operation. As a result, it has an initialization function that is activated when the ignition is turned on.

The MC initialization function moves the metering pins to the predetermined starting position by first driving them all the way to the rich end stop and then driving them in the lean direction by a predetermined number of steps. No matter where they were before initialization, they will be at the predetermined position at the end of every initialization period.

Since open loop operation metering pin position is dependent on the initialization function, this function is the first operational check in the diagnostic procedure.

Diagnosing Computerized Engine Control

The steps in each check and test systematically evaluate each component that could cause the operational problem experienced. The "okay" or "not okay" result of the steps determine additional steps or repairs which are necessary.

After completing a repair, repeat the operational check to insure the problem is solved.

TEST EQUIPMENT

The equipment required to perform the checks and tests includes a tachometer, a hand vacuum pump and a digital volt-ohmmeter (DVOM) with a minimum ohms per volt of 10 meg-ohms.

CHILTON CAUTION   The use of a voltmeter with less than 10 meg-ohms per volt input impedance can destroy the oxygen sensor.

CHILTON CAUTION   Since it is necessary to look inside the carburetor with the engine running, observe the following precautions.

1. Shape a sheet of clear acrylic plastic at least .250 inches thick and 15 x 15 inches.

2. Secure the acrylic sheet with an air cleaner wing nut after the top of the air cleaner has been removed.

3. Wear eye protection whenever performing checks and tests.

4. When engine is operating, keep hands and arms clear of fan, drive pulleys and belts. Do not wear loose clothing. Do not stand in line with fan blades.

5. Do not stand in front of running car.

PRELIMINARY CHECKS

CHECK A: INITIALIZATION (START-UP)

1. Remove air cleaner cover.

NOTE   Metering pins operate in tandem. Only the upper pin is visible.

2. While observing metering pins by looking down into carburetor, turn ignition switch to "ON" position without starting the engine.

3. Metering pins should move fully toward front of automobile. Reverse direction and move partially back toward rear. Stop and remain stationary for approximately 40 seconds, and then move in either direction.

4. If okay, continue with step 7.

5. If not okay and pins do not move at all, perform Test 1.

6. If not okay and pins do not move at the end of 40 seconds, perform Test 2 starting with step 3.

Air Cleaner Cover

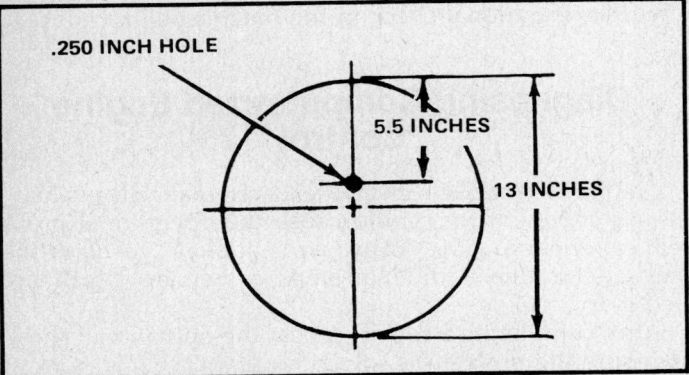

7. Turn ignition off.
8. Continue with Check B.

CHECK B: OPEN LOOP 1—COLD START AND OPERATION

This check should be performed with the coolant temperature below 100°F (38°C) to ensure the CTO diverts vacuum to the yellow vacuum switch. If the coolant temperature is above 100°F (38°C), cold operation may be simulated by removing the vacuum hose from the yellow vacuum switch and applying (and maintaining) a vacuum of 5 to 10 in. Hg to the switch.

1. Start engine and maintain engine rpm at 1500.

2. At the end of initialization period (approximately 40 seconds if cold, but may vary if hot), metering pins should not move. Release vacuum applied to yellow vacuum switch (disconnect vacuum hose or vacuum pump, if used). The metering pins should move.

3. If okay, perform Check C.

4. If not okay, perform Test 2.

CHECK C: OPEN LOOP 2—WIDE OPEN THROTTLE (WOT)

1. While observing metering pins with engine at idle below 800 rpm and no vacuum applied to yellow vacuum switch, disconnect vacuum hose connected to blue vacuum switch.

2. Metering pins should move toward front of automobile, stop and remain stationary.

3. If okay, continue with step 5.

4. If not okay, continue with step 7.

5. Reconnect vacuum hose to blue vacuum switch.

6. Continue with Check D.

7. Reconnect vacuum hose to blue vacuum switch.

8. Continue with Test 3.

CHECK D: OPEN LOOP 3—IDLE

1. Turn engine off. Have a helper restart and idle engine below 800 rpm.

2. Observe metering pins during initialization function.

3. At the end of initialization period, metering pins should move forward, stop and remain stationary.

4. If okay, perform Check E.

5. If not okay, perform Test 4.

CHECK E: CLOSED LOOP—WARM MID-RANGE

1. With no vacuum applied to yellow vacuum switch increase engine speed slowly to 2000 rpm while observing metering pins. Maintain 2000 rpm and determine if metering pins start moving and continue in incremental steps.

2. If okay, CEC system is functioning normally. Continue with step 5.

3. If not okay and metering pins do not move, perform Test 4.

Open and Closed Loop Modes of Operation

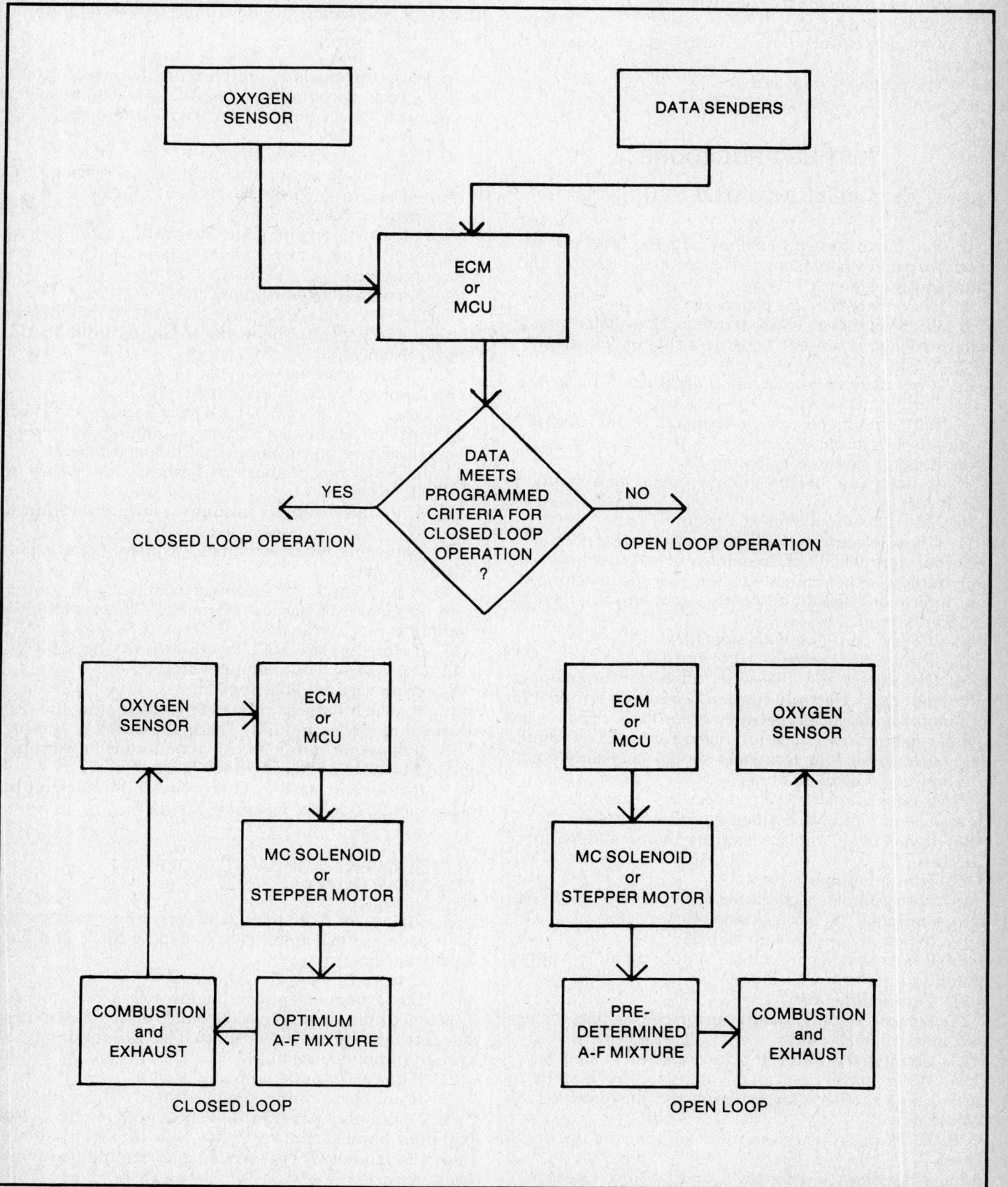

4. If not okay and metering pins move fully to either stop and remain stationary, perform Test 5.

5. Turn engine off.

6. Install carpet pulled down during test procedures, if required.

7. Connect all vacuum hoses.

8. Install air cleaner cover.

TESTING PROCEDURE

TEST 1: FAILURE TO INITIALIZE

1. Pull down forward edge of carpeting that extends up dash panel on passenger side to expose MCU and harness connectors.

2. Disconnect six-wire connector.

3. With voltmeter, check terminal 12 to determine if battery voltage is present at harness side of connector.

4. If okay, continue with step 6.

5. If not okay, repair circuit and perform Check A.

6. Turn ignition off.

7. With ohmmeter, check terminal 10 for electrical continuity to ground.

8. If okay, continue with step 10.

9. If not okay, repair ground circuit and perform Check A.

10. Disconnect four-wire connector.

11. Check electrical continuity between harness side connector terminal 12 of six-wire connector and each of four harness-side terminals of four-wire connector. All four indications should be nearly equal and between 50 and 95 ohms.

12. If okay, continue with step 17.

13. If not okay, continue with step 14.

14. Disconnect the five-wire connector on stepper motor and check electrical continuity between terminal 18 and motor housing and between other four terminals on stepper motor. Resistance to housing should be infinite. Resistance to all four terminals should be nearly equal and between 53 and 85 ohms.

15. If okay, repair wiring defect in harness between stepper motor and MCU, then perform Check A.

16. If not okay, replace stepper motor and perform Check A.

17. Turn ignition on.

18. With voltmeter, check for presence of battery voltage on terminal 18, harness side of connector.

19. If okay, continue with step 21.

20. If not okay, repair voltage supply circuit to stepper motor and perform Check A.

21. Turn ignition off.

22. Remove stepper motor, push metering pins further into motor. Install motor.

23. Connect the connector disconnected in step 14.

24. While observing metering pins, have ignition turned on and check for metering rod movement. Pins should move.

25. If okay, replace stepper motor and perform Check A.

26. If not okay, replace MCU and perform Check A.

TEST 2: LOOP 1—COLD START AND OPERATION

NOTE   *If an alternate vacuum source was used for Check B, start with step 4.*

1. With the coolant temperature less than 100°F (38°C), check vacuum hose to yellow vacuum switch for vacuum. A vacuum of 5 in. Hg or more should be indicated.

2. If okay, continue with step 4.

3. If not okay, repair vacuum leak or replace CTO valve and return to Check B.

4. Turn ignition off.

5. Pull down forward edge of carpeting extending up dash panel on passenger side to expose MCU and harness connectors.

6. Disconnect six-wire connector.

7. Check terminal 6 on harness connector for electrical continuity to ground. There should be no continuity (infinite resistance).

8. If okay, continue with step 13.

9. If not okay, continue with step 10.

10. Disconnect vacuum switch from harness and check feed wire (terminal 6) for electrical continuity to ground. There should be no continuity (infinite resistance).

11. If okay, repair short in harness and return to Check B.

12. If not okay, replace vacuum switch and return to Check B.

13. Apply and hold vacuum of 5 to 10 in. Hg to yellow vacuum switch.

14. Repeat check for electrical continuity to ground from terminal 6 of harness connector. There should be continuity.

15. If okay, replace MCU and return to Check B.

16. If not okay, continue with step 17.

17. With vacuum still applied, check yellow wire at vacuum switch harness connector (switch side) for electrical continuity to ground. There should be continuity.

18. If okay, reconnect six-wire connector. Repair open circuit in harness and return to Check B.

19. If not okay, reconnect six-wire connector and replace vacuum switch. Return to Check B.

TEST 3: OPEN LOOP 2—WIDE OPEN THROTTLE (WOT)

1. Pull down forward edge of carpeting extending up dash panel on passenger side to expose MCU and harness connector.

2. Disconnect six-wire connector.

3. Using ohmmeter with engine still at idle, test for electrical continuity to ground from terminal 7 on harness side of connector. There should be no continuity to ground (infinite resistance).

4. If okay, continue with step 9.

5. If not okay, continue with step 6.

6. Disconnect vacuum switches from engine compartment harness and test blue wire for electrical continuity to ground. There should be no continuity (infinite resistance).

7. If okay, repair short in harness and return to Check C.

8. If not okay, continue with step 15.

9. Disconnect and plug vacuum hose to blue vacuum switch and retest terminal 7 for continuity to ground. There should be continuity.

10. If okay, replace MCU and return to Check C.

11. If not okay, continue with step 12.

12. Disconnect blue vacuum switch from engine compartment harness and test blue wire for continuity to ground. There should be continuity.

13. If okay, repair open circuit in harness and return to Check C.

14. If not okay, replace switch and return to Check C.

15. Disconnect vacuum hose to blue vacuum switch and check for vacuum in hose. With engine still at idle, there should be vacuum.

16. If okay, replace blue vacuum switch. Reconnect harness and vacuum hose and return to Check C.

17. If not okay, repair vacuum leak. Reconnect harness and vacuum hose and return to Check C.

TEST 4: OPEN LOOP 3—IDLE AND CLOSED LOOP SWITCH-IN

1. Pull down forward edge of carpeting extending up dash panel on passenger side to expose MCU and harness connector.

2. Disconnect six-wire connector.

3. Check voltage at terminal 5 on harness side of connector. Voltage should be 7 volts ± 2 volts.

4. If okay, continue with step 6.

5. If not okay, repair harness wiring to coil and return to Check D.

6. Check for electrical continuity to ground from terminal 9 on harness side of connector with engine at idle. There should be continuity.

7. If okay, continue with step 15.

8. If not okay, continue with step 9.

9. Check for vacuum at pink vacuum switch. There should be no vacuum at idle.

10. If okay, continue with step 12.

11. If not okay, correct vacuum line routing or carburetor idle speed setting. Return to Check D.

12. Disconnect vacuum switch harness connector and check pink wire for electrical continuity to ground with no vacuum applied. There should be continuity.

13. If okay, repair open circuit in harness wiring and reconnect. Return to Check D.

14. If not okay, replace switch and reconnect harness. Return to Check D.

15. Increase engine speed to 1500 rpm and recheck continuity. There should be no continuity.

16. If okay, return engine to idle. Replace MCU and return to Check D.

17. If not okay, continue with step 18.

18. With engine still at 1500 rpm, check vacuum hose to pink vacuum switch for vacuum. There should be more than 5 in. Hg.

19. If okay, continue with step 21.

20. If not okay, return engine to idle. Repair vacuum hose routing and return to Check D.

21. Reconnect vacuum hose to pink switch.

22. Disconnect harness connection to vacuum switches.

23. With engine at 1500 rpm, check pink wire for electrical continuity to ground at switch. There should be no continuity (infinite resistance).

24. If okay, repair short circuit in harness wiring and reconnect. Return to Check D.

25. If not okay, replace switch and reconnect harness. Return to Check D.

TEST 5: CLOSED LOOP OPERATION

CHILTON CAUTION The use of a voltmeter with less than 10 meg-ohms per volt input impedance in this test will destroy the oxygen sensor. A digital volt-ohm meter must be used.

1. Turn engine off.

2. Remove air cleaner assembly and plug vacuum hoses.

3. Turn ignition to on for four seconds. Then turn off.

4. Disconnect stepper motor connector.

5. Disconnect oxygen sensor connector.

6. Using voltmeter with minimum of 10 meg-ohms per volt, connect positive (+) lead to pin 2 on oxygen sensor connector and negative (−) lead to pin 4. Set meter on 1-volt scale.

7. Start engine and warm up for four minutes.

8. Increase engine speed to 1200 rpm and hold while closing choke butterfly valve. Keep valve closed for one minute, while observing voltmeter. Turn engine off.

9. While choke was closed, voltmeter should have indicated minimum of 0.6 volts. Turn ignition switch off.

10. If okay, replace MCU and continue with step 19.

11. If not okay, continue with step 12.

12. Disconnect and plug hose leading to exhaust manifold air distribution check valve at manifold.

13. Start engine and warm up for one minute.

14. Close choke valve with engine at 1200 rpm and observe voltmeter. Turn engine off.

15. While choke was closed, voltmeter should have indicated 0.6 volts or more.

16. If okay, replace air distribution check valve and continue with step 18.

17. If not okay, replace oxygen sensor and continue with step 18.

18. Unplug and reconnect hose to air distribution check valve.

19. Connect oxygen sensor to harness.

20. Connect stepper motor connector.

21. Install air cleaner (without cover) and vacuum hoses.

22. Start engine and return to Check E.

NOTE   If, after completing Test 5 and returning to Check E, the problem persists, it is not in the CEC system. Any other engine associated system that can affect mixture, combustion efficiency or exhaust gas composition can be at fault. These systems include the following.

1. Basic carburetor adjustments
2. Mechanical engine operation (plugs, valves and rings)
3. Ignition
4. Gaskets (intake manifold, carburetor or base plate)
5. Loose vacuum hoses or fittings

Component Replacement

OXYGEN SENSOR

1. Disconnect two-wire plug.
2. Remove sensor from exhaust pipe.
3. Clean threads in pipe.
4. Coat replacement sensor threads with antiseize compound.
5. Tighten sensor to 31 foot-pounds (42 N•m) torque.

CHILTON CAUTION Ensure that wire terminal ends are properly seated in plug prior to connecting plug.

NOTE Do not push rubber boot down on sensor body beyond ½ inch above base.

NOTE Oxygen sensor pigtail wires cannot be spliced or soldered. If broken, replace sensor.

VACUUM SWITCHES

NOTE The vacuum switches are not serviced individually. The complete assembly must be replaced as a unit.

1. Remove vacuum switch and bracket assembly from left inside fender panel.

2. Install replacement vacuum switch and bracket.
3. Connect electrical plug and vacuum hoses.

COMPUTER

The computer unit is located in the passenger compartment beneath the dash panel on the right-hand side. Replace complete unit.

NOTE The ECM bracket is insulated from automobile ground. Do not ground bracket.

CHILTON CAUTION Ensure that the terminal ends are not forced out of position when connecting plug.

STEPPER MOTOR (CARBURETOR)

CHILTON CAUTION Avoid dropping metering pins and spring when removing motor.

1. Remove retaining screw and unit from carburetor.
2. Install replacement motor on carburetor with retaining screw. Tighten to 25 inch-pounds (2.8 N•m) torque.
3. Connect wire plug.
4. Install air cleaner.

COOLANT TEMPERATURE SWITCH

1. Disconnect electrical connector.
2. Remove switch.
3. Install replacement switch. Tighten to 72 inch-pounds (7 N•m) torque.

CADILLAC DIGITAL ELECTRONIC FUEL INJECTION

General Description

Digital electronic fuel injection consists of a pair of electrically actuated fuel metering valves which, when actuated, spray a calculated quantity of fuel into the engine intake manifold. These valves or injectors are mounted on the throttle body above the throttle blades with the metering tip pointed into the throttle throats. The injectors are normally actuated alternately.

Gasoline is supplied to the inlet of the injectors through the fuel lines and is maintained at a constant pressure across the injector inlets. When the solenoid-operated valves are energized, the injector ball valve moves to the full open position. Since the pressure differential across the valve is constant, the fuel quantity is changed by varying the time that the injector is held open.

The amount of air entering the engine is measured by monitoring the intake manifold absolute pressure (MAP), the intake manifold air temperature (MAT) and the engine speed (in rpm). This information allows the computer to compute the flow rate of air being inducted into the engine and, consequently, the flow rate of fuel required to achieve the desired air-fuel mixture for the particular engine operating condition.

The following abbreviations are used in this section.

TPS	throttle position sensor
ECM	electronic control module
ISC	idle speed control (includes idle speed motor and throttle switch)
HEI	high energy ignition

System Components

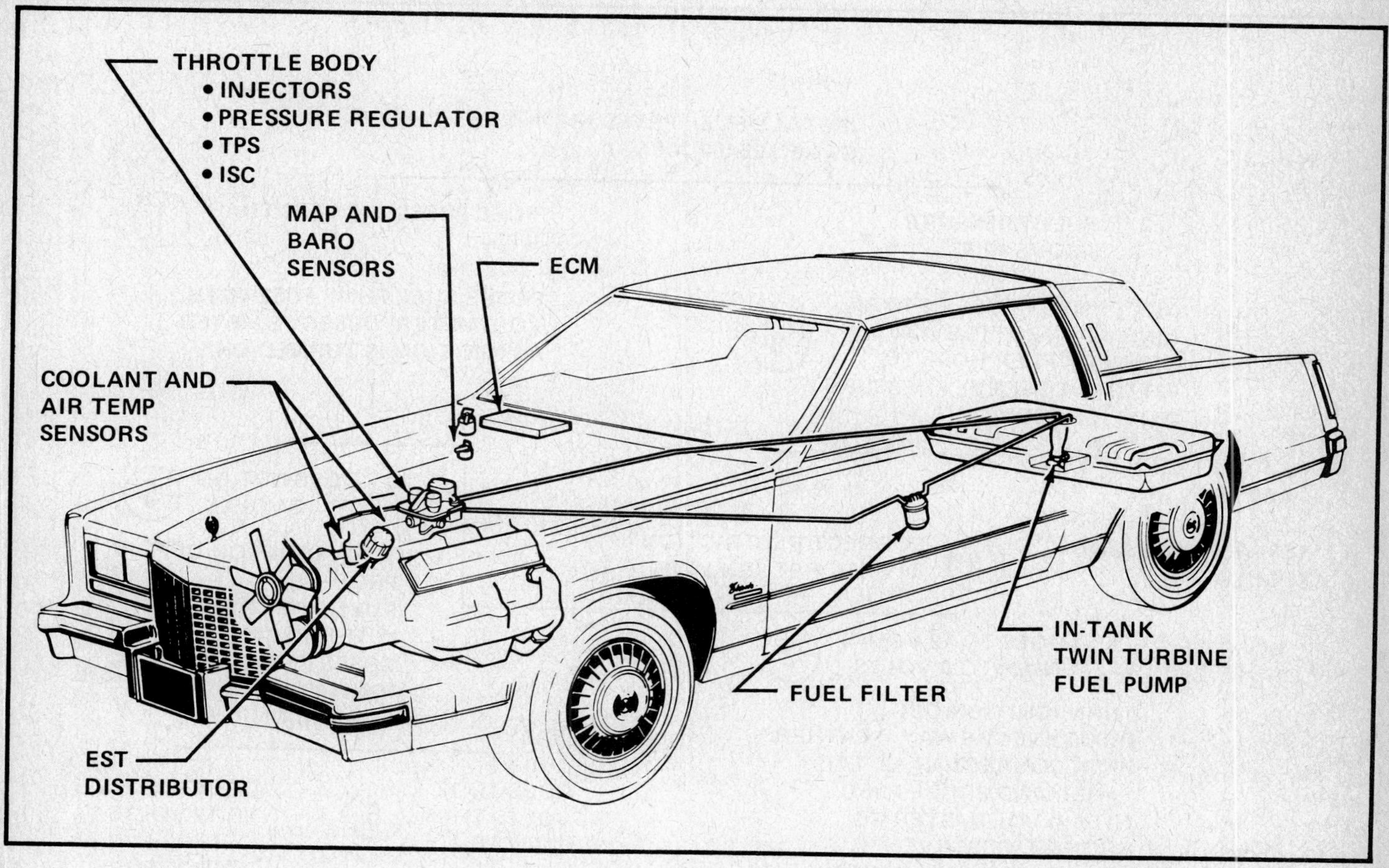

THROTTLE BODY
- INJECTORS
- PRESSURE REGULATOR
- TPS
- ISC

MAP AND BARO SENSORS

ECM

COOLANT AND AIR TEMP SENSORS

EST DISTRIBUTOR

FUEL FILTER

IN-TANK TWIN TURBINE FUEL PUMP

EST	electric spark timing
MAP	manifold absolute pressure (sensor)
BARO	barometric pressure (sensor)
ECC	electronic climate control
MAT	manifold air temperature (sensor)
CTS	coolant temperature sensor
MPG	miles per gallon (display panel)
EGR	exhaust gas recirculation

FUEL SUPPLY SYSTEM

The fuel supply system components provide fuel at the correct pressure for metering into the throttle bores by the injectors. The pressure regulator controls fuel pressure to a nominal 10.5 psi across the injectors. The fuel supply system is made up of a fuel tank mounted electric pump, a full-flow fuel filter mounted on the vehicle frame, a fuel pressure regulator integral with the throttle body, fuel supply and fuel return lines and two fuel injectors. The timing and amount of fuel supplied is controlled by the computer.

FUEL PUMP

An electric motor-driven twin turbine-type pump is integral with the fuel tank float unit. It provides fuel at a positive pressure to the throttle body and fuel pressure

regulator. The pump is specific for DEFI application and is not repairable. However, the pump may be serviced separately from the fuel gage unit.

Fuel pump operation is controlled by the fuel pump relay, located in the relay center. Operation of the relay is

Fuel Injector

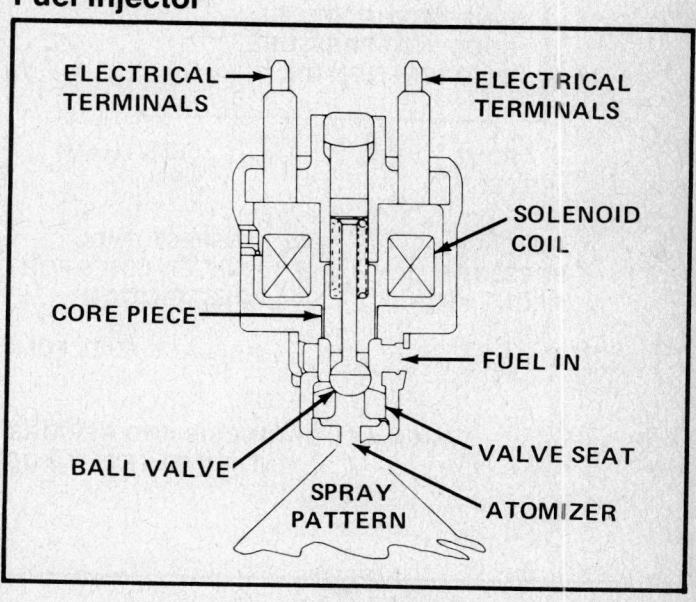

ELECTRICAL TERMINALS

ELECTRICAL TERMINALS

SOLENOID COIL

CORE PIECE

FUEL IN

BALL VALVE

VALVE SEAT

SPRAY PATTERN

ATOMIZER

Fuel Supply Diagnosis Chart

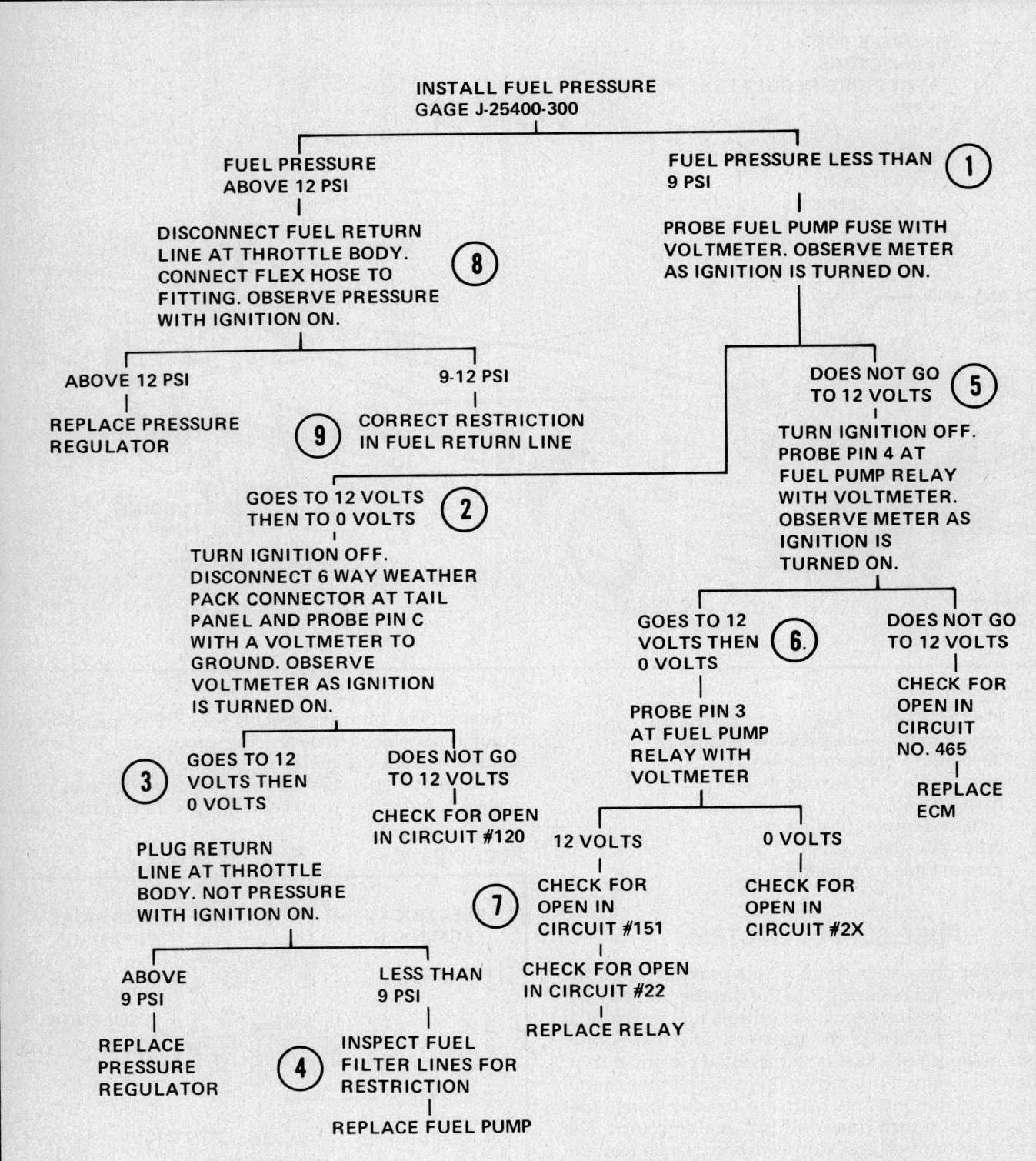

INSTALL FUEL PRESSURE GAGE J-25400-300

FUEL PRESSURE ABOVE 12 PSI

FUEL PRESSURE LESS THAN 9 PSI ①

DISCONNECT FUEL RETURN LINE AT THROTTLE BODY. CONNECT FLEX HOSE TO FITTING. OBSERVE PRESSURE WITH IGNITION ON. ⑧

PROBE FUEL PUMP FUSE WITH VOLTMETER. OBSERVE METER AS IGNITION IS TURNED ON.

ABOVE 12 PSI

REPLACE PRESSURE REGULATOR

⑨ 9-12 PSI CORRECT RESTRICTION IN FUEL RETURN LINE

DOES NOT GO TO 12 VOLTS ⑤

TURN IGNITION OFF. PROBE PIN 4 AT FUEL PUMP RELAY WITH VOLTMETER. OBSERVE METER AS IGNITION IS TURNED ON.

GOES TO 12 VOLTS THEN TO 0 VOLTS ②

TURN IGNITION OFF. DISCONNECT 6 WAY WEATHER PACK CONNECTOR AT TAIL PANEL AND PROBE PIN C WITH A VOLTMETER TO GROUND. OBSERVE VOLTMETER AS IGNITION IS TURNED ON.

GOES TO 12 VOLTS THEN 0 VOLTS ⑥.

DOES NOT GO TO 12 VOLTS

CHECK FOR OPEN IN CIRCUIT NO. 465

REPLACE ECM

PROBE PIN 3 AT FUEL PUMP RELAY WITH VOLTMETER

③ GOES TO 12 VOLTS THEN 0 VOLTS

DOES NOT GO TO 12 VOLTS

CHECK FOR OPEN IN CIRCUIT #120

PLUG RETURN LINE AT THROTTLE BODY. NOT PRESSURE WITH IGNITION ON.

12 VOLTS

⑦ CHECK FOR OPEN IN CIRCUIT #151

CHECK FOR OPEN IN CIRCUIT #22

REPLACE RELAY

0 VOLTS

CHECK FOR OPEN IN CIRCUIT #2X

ABOVE 9 PSI

REPLACE PRESSURE REGULATOR

LESS THAN 9 PSI

④ INSPECT FUEL FILTER LINES FOR RESTRICTION

REPLACE FUEL PUMP

WHEN ALL DIAGNOSIS AND REPAIRS ARE COMPLETED, CLEAR STORED CODES AND ROAD TEST VEHICLE. CHECK FOR NEW CODES.

Fuel Pressure Regulator

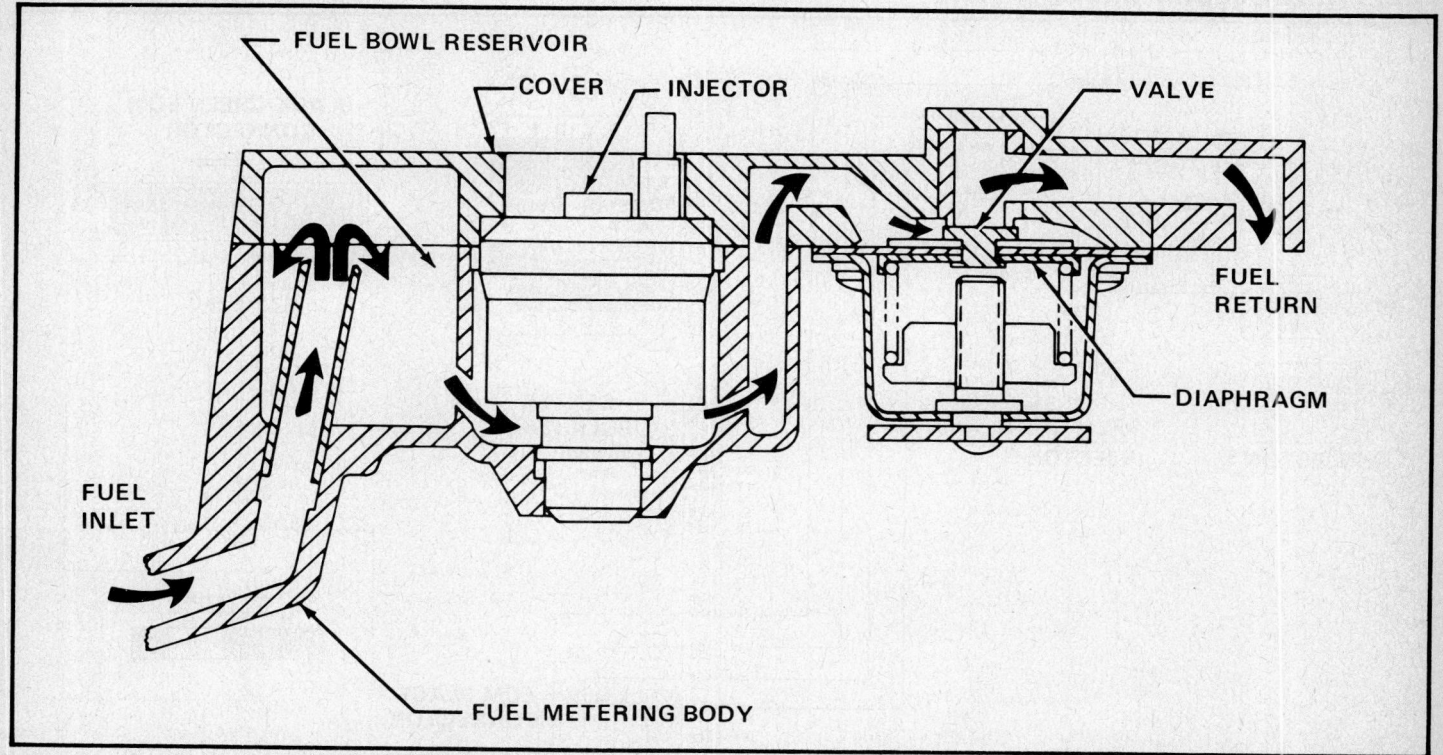

FUEL BOWL RESERVOIR — COVER — INJECTOR — VALVE — FUEL RETURN — DIAPHRAGM — FUEL INLET — FUEL METERING BODY

controlled by a signal from the computer. The fuel pump circuit is protected by a 10 amp fuse, located in the mini-fuse block. The computer turns the pump on with the ignition "ON" or "START." However, if the engine is not cranked within one second after the ignition is turned on, the computer signal is removed and the pump turns off.

Fuel is pumped from the fuel tank through the supply line and the filter to the throttle body and pressure regulator. The injectors supply fuel to the engine in precisely timed bursts as a result of electrical signals from the computer. Excess fuel is returned to the fuel tank through the fuel return line.

FUEL TANK

The fuel tank incorporates a reservoir directly below the sending unit-in-tank pump assembly. The "bathtub" shaped reservoir is used to ensure a constant supply of fuel for the in-tank pump even at low fuel level and severe maneuvering conditions.

Fuel System Diagnosis

1. Low or no fuel pressure diagnosis should begin by trying to determine if the fuel pump is operating or not. This is most easily accomplished by turning the ignition on and listening for the one second "run" of the fuel pump and the associated relay clicks. Since this may not be possible in some shops, the best test is to probe both sides of the fuel pump fuse in the mini-fuse block with a voltmeter. Observe the meter as the ignition is turned on.

It should go to battery voltage (12 volts) and then, after one second, to zero volts.

2. If the fuel pump circuit is operating properly, the computer signal and the relay are okay. The last connector in the fuel pump circuit is the six-way connector at the tail panel. The voltage actions seen at the fuse should be repeated. If not, there is an open in the circuit. Check the connectors and repair wiring as required. Individual sections of the wiring can be tested with an ohmmeter.

3. If the fuel pump signal is correct at the tail panel connector, a fuel delivery system situation exists. If the pump cannot be heard to run during the one second on period, the pump should be replaced. This observation is more easily made if a helper turns the ignition on as the technician listens at the fuel tank or filler neck area. If the fuel pump can be heard to run, disconnect the fuel return line at the throttle body and install a plug in the throttle body opening. This will effectively "dead head" the fuel pump and eliminate the pressure regulator. If the pump is able to produce above 9 psi under these conditions (with the ignition on), replace the fuel pressure regulator as it is controlling at too low pressure.

4. If the fuel pressure remains below 9 psi with the return line plugged, a restriction in the fuel supply line may exist. A blocked fuel line or fuel filter can be determined by visually inspecting the filter element and the fuel line routing for kinks, damage, etc. If lines and filter are okay, replace fuel pump.

5. If the voltage at the fuel pump fuse does not go to 12 volts, first inspect the fuse. If the fuse is okay, check the contacts at terminals 1 and 3 of the fuel pump relay connecting block. The contacts close when the relay coil is

Fuel Pump Injector Circuit

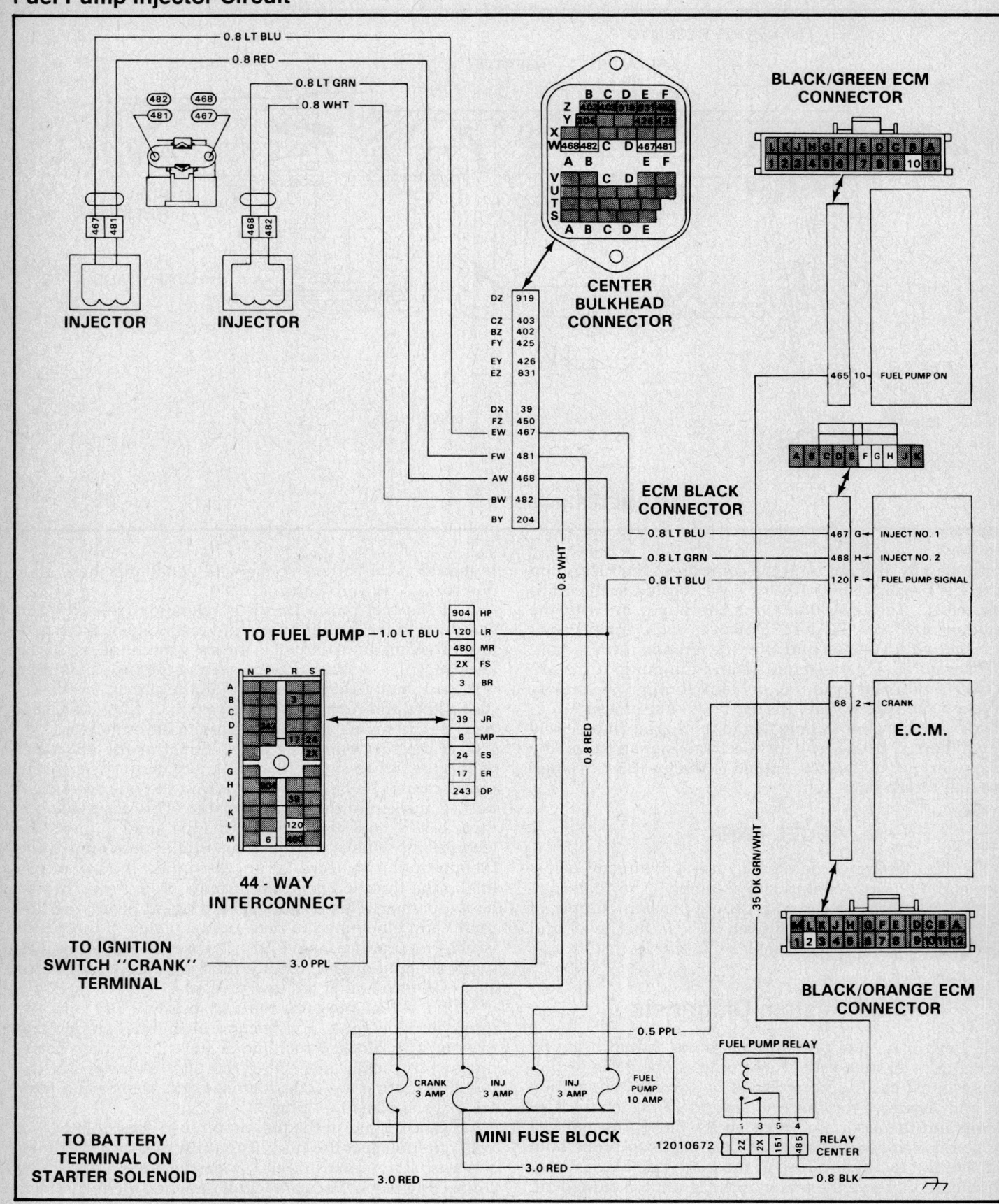

energized by the computer. Remove the relay. Probe the relay center socket, which corresponds to relay terminal 4, with a voltmeter.

After ignition has been off for at least 10 seconds, turn the ignition on. If the voltage does not go to 12 volts and back to zero, inspect for opens or shorts to ground. Checking for opens can be done with an ohmmeter connected to both ends of the circuit. If continuity is indicated (0 ohms), check for a short to ground by jumping one end to ground and probing the opposite end with an ohmmeter to ground. An infinite reading indicates the wire is not grounded and the circuit is OK. Replace the computer. If a short to ground in the circuit is found, the computer will be damaged. Replace the computer after repair.

6. If voltage at relay terminal 4 goes to 12 volts and then to zero, the computer is performing properly. Probe the relay center socket which corresponds to relay pin 3 with a voltmeter. Since this circuit comes directly from the battery terminal of the starter solenoid, it should be 12 volts at all times. If voltage is zero, inspect the circuit for open.

7. Twelve volts at pin 3 indicates that most of the relay's requirements are met. However, there are still two wiring circuits which could prevent proper relay operation. The computer signal has been proven okay. However, if the coil ground is open, the coil will not be energized. To check, probe the relay center socket which corresponds to relay pin 5, with an ohmmeter connected to ground. Continuity (0 ohms) indicates a good circuit. An infinite reading indicates an open. Repair wire as required.

The second circuit in which an open could occur, preventing the proper voltage at the fuse, is between the fuel pump relay terminal 1 and the mini-fuse block. This circuit can be checked by probing both ends with an ohmmeter. If the circuit has continuity as indicated by a zero ohms reading, replace fuel pump relay.

8. High fuel pressure is caused by either a malfunction of the pressure regulator or a restriction in the fuel return line. To determine which of these problems exists, disconnect the fuel return line at the throttle body and connect a suitable fitting to the throttle body to accept a length of flexible rubber fuel hose. Insert the open end of the hose into a suitable fuel container. Observe the fuel pressure as the ignition switch is turned on. If the fuel pressure remains above 12 psi, replace the pressure regulator as it is unable to regulate with no return restriction.

9. If the fuel pressure now falls into the correct pressure range of 9–12 psi, the restriction has been eliminated by bypassing the return system. A restricted fuel return line can be located by visually inspecting the line routing for kinks, damage, etc.

Diagnosing Poor Performance

1. Unsatisfactory engine performance complaints which are related to the digital electronic fuel injection system are caused either by improper fuel delivery or improper ignition advance (controlled by the computer).

To isolate the problem to one of these systems, remove the air cleaner and observe the injector spray pattern of both injectors at idle. The spray pattern should be compared to a proper injector spray pattern of a known good car.

2. Improper fuel delivery which affects both injectors is most likely a fuel delivery system problem. By switching injector connectors, it can be determined if the problem is the injector assembly or the signal to the injector. If the problem remains with the original injector, it is most likely an injector problem. Replace the injector. If the problem moves with the injector connector, an improper signal circuit is indicated. The injectors are powered through the 3 amp fuses in the mini-fuse block. The fuse block receives battery voltage from the starter solenoid battery terminal when the fuel pump relay is energized by the computer during crank or run. With the relay closed, the circuits apply 12 volts to the injector. The computer provides the ground to energize the solenoid.

3. Check the injector fuses by visually inspecting the fuse filament. If the fuses are okay there is a harness problem in the voltage feed or ground. The troubled circuit should be investigated. Check for opens with an ohmmeter. If harness checks okay, replace computer.

4. A blown injector fuse should be replaced. If it blows again, a short to ground is indicated. To check for this condition, connect ohmmeter between the red or white wire at the injector connector and ground (ignition off and computer disconnected). A low reading indicates a short circuit. Repair as required. If harness is okay, replace the computer.

5. A proper injector spray pattern indicates that improper ignition timing is the main DEFI component which can cause poor performance. Ground the "set timing" pigtail and check timing. It should be at the base (or initial) value of 10° BTDC (800 rpm or less). If not, reset to 10°.

6. Once it has been established that the ignition timing is using the proper reference signal, the system's ability to advance the spark must also be determined. Since the actual ignition advance produced is the result of other variables besides engine rpm and manifold vacuum, it is not possible to establish checkpoints. However, if the system does advance, the shape of the advance curve can be assumed to be correct, since it is determined by the electronic circuitry which was able to recognize that some advance was required and did respond to this information.

Disconnect the "set timing" jumper and check ignition timing. At normal idle, this should be approximately 20° to 30° BTDC.

7. If the ignition timing does not advance as a result of disconnecting the "set timing" jumper, a problem with the advance system is indicated. Since the computer selects and determines the spark advance curve, it is necessary to determine if the computer is operating properly or not.

During cranking, no spark advance is desired. The computer limits the advance to base timing by turning off the voltage signal. The pick-up coil pulse is used directly to turn the HEI module on. When the engine starts, the computer turns on the voltage in the circuit and the pick-up coil pulse is sent to the computer, modified by the computer and sent back to the module.

Whether the computer advances the timing or not depends upon whether it applied a voltage to the circuit or not (no voltage= base timing; voltage= electric spark timing). To check the circuit, disconnect the four-way connector at the distributor while the engine is idling. This will stop the engine. Probe the harness side pin C (not distributor side harness) with a voltmeter while the ignition switch remains on. If voltage is greater than 4 volts, refer to HEI diagnosis because the computer has signaled that EST should be used, but timing did not advance when checked.

8. Voltage less than 1 volt indicates that either the computer signal is not being produced or the circuit is open or shorted to the ground. To check for shorts, disconnect the black/green computer connector and probe harness pin D with an ohmmeter to ground (ignition off and distributor connector disconnected). A zero ohm reading indicates a short. Repair as required.

If the ohmmeter reads infinity, check for opens by jumping distributor connector pin C to ground. If the ohmmeter reading remains infinite, circuit is open. Repair as required. If the ohmmeter reads zero ohms, the circuit is okay.

Check MAT and coolant sensor circuits for an open between the splice and the computer. Attention should be focused on the bulk head and computer connectors. If the circuit is okay, substitute a new computer and observe performance.

9. The EGR system utilizes various controls in order to provide EGR gases only when they are needed for emission control. One of these controls is the EGR solenoid, with power feed from the ignition switch through the 20 amp fuse. Ground for the solenoid is provided by the computer. The computer provides this ground whenever the coolant temperature signal from the coolant sensor says the temperature is below 43°C (110°F). This energizes the solenoid and blocks the flow of vacuum to the EGR transducer thus preventing EGR operation at cold engine temperatures. Above 71°C (160°F), the solenoid ground is removed and the solenoid opens, allowing vacuum to the EGR valve. This vacuum signal is a ported vacuum which exists only off idle. This means that even on a warm engine, there is no EGR vacuum signal and no EGR flow at idle.

10. If EGR operation is okay, check to make sure that throttle valves open to wide open throttle when the accelerator pedal is wide open. If this is okay, the performance problem is not related to the DEFI system. If EGR problems are found, check hoses, etc.

Ignition Timing Adjustment

Ignition timing may be adjusted by either of two methods, with conventional strobe light timing equipment or with a probe-type timing advance meter.

1. Adjust distributor clamp nut to allow distributor to be turned by hand, but without excessive looseness.

2. Insert a timing light adapter between the number 1 spark plug and its lead wire. Avoid puncturing the boots or cable cover.

3. Connect a suitable timing light to the adapter. Make sure that timing marks and scribe marks are clean.

4. Disconnect and plug the EGR vacuum hose.

5. Connect tachometer to engine. Set parking brake securely and place transmission lever in Park position.

6. Start engine.

7. When engine is warmed up to normal operating temperature (upper radiator hose hot), connect a jumper wire between the "set timing" connector and ground.

NOTE   Timing ground wire is located on the driver's side valve cover.

8. Use a timing light to set the timing to proper specification as shown on emission label under hood on radiator support.

9. Tighten distributor clamp nut. Recheck timing to make sure it did not change.

10. Disconnect the tachometer and timing light. Remove adapter and jumper wire from engine. Replace EGR vacuum hose. Position hose clamps properly.

TIMING ADVANCE METER

1. Adjust distributor clamp nut to allow distributor to be turned by hand, but without excessive looseness.

2. Disconnect and plug EGR vacuum hose.

3. Connect power supply for timing meter to battery. Observe correct polarity.

4. Install ignition pick-up clip over number 1 spark plug wire. Be sure jaws are clean and locking button is pressed forward to close jaws firmly.

5. Install magnetic pick-up in receptacle of timing tab and press down firmly. Pick-up should be as close to pulley surface as possible without making contact.

6. Make sure that all leads to advance meter are out of the way of moving parts and exhaust manifold. Place transmission selector lever in Park position.

7. Turn power switch on and timing-advance to "TIMING" position.

8. Start the engine.

9. When engine is warmed up to normal operating temperature (upper radiator hose hot), connect a jumper wire between the "set timing" connector and ground.

NOTE   Wire located center of valve cover on driver's side of engine.

10. With the engine speed at idle, observe the engine degrees meter. Set timing to proper specifications according to emission label under hood on radiator support.

11. Tighten distributor clamp nut. Recheck timing to be sure that it did not change.

12. Replace EGR vacuum hose. Position hose clamps properly.

13. Disconnect timing advance meter connections from engine.

14. Remove ground wire from set timing connector.

Electrical Dignosis

ELECTRONIC CONTROL MODULE (ECM) OR COMPUTER

The electronic control module, (ECM) or computer provides all computation and controls for the DEFI system. Sensor inputs are fed into the computer from the various sensors. They are processed to produce the appropriate pulse duration for the injectors, the correct idle speed for the particular operating condition and the proper spark advance. Analog inputs from the sensors are converted to digital signals before processing. The computer assembly is mounted under the instrument panel and consists of various printed circuit boards mounted in a protective metal box.

The computer receives power from the vehicle battery. When the ignition is set to the "ON" or "CRANK" position, the following information is received from the sensors.

Engine coolant temperature
Intake manifold air temperature
Intake manifold absolute pressure
Barometric pressure
Engine speed
Throttle position
The following commands are transmitted by the ECM.
Electric fuel pump activation
Idle speed control
Spark advance control
Injection valve activation
EGR solenoid activation

The desired air-fuel mixture for various driving and atmospheric conditions are programmed into the computer. As signals are received from the sensors, the computer processes the signals and computes the engines fuel requirements. The computer issues commands to the injection valves to open for a specific time duration. The duration of the command pulses varies as the operating conditions change.

Electronic Control Module

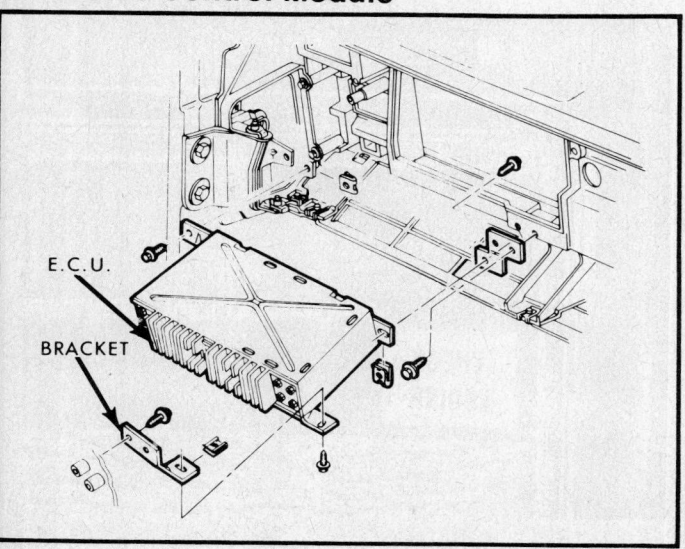

The digital electronic fuel injection system is activated when the ignition switch is turned to the "ON" position. The following events occur at this moment.
1. The computer receives the ignition "ON" signal.
2. The fuel pump is activated by the ECM. The pump will operate for approximately one second only, unless the engine is cranking or running.
3. All engine sensors are activated and begin transmitting signals to the computer.
4. The EGR solenoid is activated to block the vacuum signal to the EGR valve at coolant temperatures below 110°F.
5. The "CHECK ENGINE" and "COOLANT" lights are illuminated as a functional check of the bulb and circuit.
6. Operation of the fuel economy lamps begins.
The following events occur when the engine is started.
1. The fuel pump is activated for continuous operation.
2. The idle speed control motor will begin controlling idle speed, including fast idle speed, if the throttle switch is closed.
3. The spark advance shifts from base (bypass) timing to the computer programmed spark curve.
4. The fuel pressure regulator maintains the fuel pressure at 10.5 psi by returning excess fuel to the fuel tank.
5. The following sensor signals are continuously received and processed by the computer.
a. Engine coolant temperature
b. Intake manifold air temperature
c. Barometric pressure
d. Intake manifold absolute air pressure
e. Engine speed
f. Throttle position changes
6. The computer alternately grounds each injector, precisely controlling the opening and closing time (pulse width) to deliver fuel to the engine.

ECM FUNCTIONS
Fuel Delivery System

The computer's control of fuel delivery can be considered in three basic modes: cranking, part throttle and wide open throttle.

If the engine is determined to be in the cranking mode by the presence of a voltage in the cranking signal wire from the ignition switch, the starting fuel delivery consists of one long "prime" pulse from both injectors followed by a series of "starting" pulses until the cranking mode signal is no longer present.

In addition, there is a "clear flood" condition in which smaller alternating fuel pulses are delivered if the throttle is held wide open and cranking exceeds five seconds.

Once the engine is running, injector pulse width is then adjusted to account for operating conditions such as idle, part throttle, acceleration, deceleration and altitude.

For wide open throttle conditions, which are sensed by matching the manifold absolute pressure and barometric pressure sensor inputs, additional enrichment is provided.

Spark System

Engine ignition timing is controlled by the computer.

The two basic operating modes are cranking (or bypass) and normal engine operation.

When the engine is in the cranking/bypass mode, ignition timing occurs at a reference setting (distributor timing set point) regardless of other engine operating parameters. Under all other normal operating conditions, basic engine ignition timing is controlled by the computer and modified or added to, depending on particular conditions such as altitude and/or engine loading.

Idle Speed Control System

The idle speed control system is controlled by the computer. The system acts to control engine idle speed in three ways; as a normal idle (rpm) control, as a fast idle device and as a "dashpot" on decelerations and throttle closing.

The normal engine idle speed is programmed into the computer and no adjustments are possible. Under normal engine operating conditions, idle speed is maintained by monitoring idle speed in a closed loop fashion. To accomplish this loop, the computer periodically senses the engine idle speed and issues commands to the idle speed control to move the throttle stop to maintain the correct speed.

For engine starting, the throttle is either held open by the idle speed control for a longer (cold) or a shorter (hot) period to provide adequate engine warm-up prior to normal operation. When the engine is shut off, the throttle is opened by fully extending the idle speed control actuator to get ready for the next start.

Signal inputs for transmission gear, air conditioning compressor clutch (engaged or not engaged) and throttle (open or closed) are used to either increase or decrease throttle angle in response to these particular engine loadings.

ELECTRONIC SPARK TIMING (EST)

The EST type HEI distributor receives all spark timing information from the computer when the engine is running. The computer provides spark plug firing pulses based upon the various engine operating parameters. The electronic components for the electronic spark control system are integral with the computer.

IDLE SPEED CONTROL SYSTEM (ISC)

Vehicle idle speed is controlled by an electrically driven actuator (idle speed control) which changes the throttle angle by acting as a movable idle stop. Inputs to the ISC actuator motor come from the ECM and are determined by the idle speed required for the particular operating condition. The electronic components for the ISC system are integral with the ECM. An integral part of the ISC is the throttle switch. The position of the switch determines whether the ISC should control idle speed or not. When the switch is closed, as determined by the throttle lever resting upon the end of the ISC actuator, the ECM will issue the appropriate commands to move the idle speed control to provide the programmed idle speed. When the throttle lever moves off the idle speed control actuator

Electronic Spark Timing Distributor

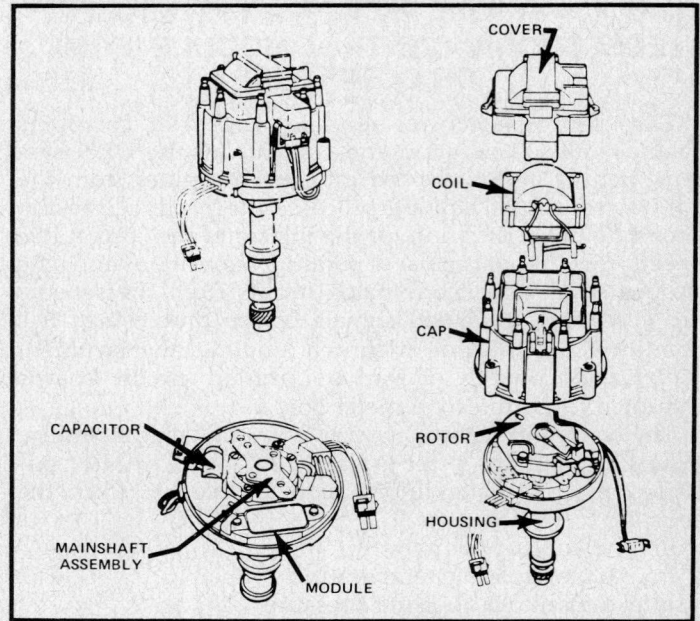

from idle, the throttle switch is opened. The computer then extends the actuator and stops sending idle speed commands and the driver controls the engine speed.

DIAGNOSTIC LIGHT

An amber dash-mounted "CHECK ENGINE" light, in the right-hand information center, is used to inform the driver of certain computer detected DEFI system malfunctions or abnormalities. These malfunctions may be related to the various sensors or to the computer itself. The light resets automatically when the fault clears. However, the computer stores the trouble code associated with the detected failure until the diagnostic system is cleared.

Check Engine Light

Diagnostic Functions

PRESS TO DISPLAY TROUBLE CODES

PRESS TO CLEAR TROUBLE CODES

DIAGNOSTIC DISPLAY

The dash-mounted digital display panel normally used for the electronic climate control (ECC) system, is used to display trouble codes stored in the computer when desired. Any codes that may be stored can be called up and/or cleared by properly exercising the ECC controls.

OPERATION WITH SYSTEM FAILURES

In the event the computer detects a system malfunction, the "CHECK ENGINE" light will be activated, the corresponding trouble code stored and substitute values to replace missing date may be made available for computations by the computer. This can be thought of as a "Fail Soft" operation. In this mode, driveability of the car may be poor under certain conditions and the diagnostic procedures should be exercised.

HOW TO ENTER DIAGNOSTIC MODE

To enter diagnostics, proceed as follows.
1. Turn ignition "ON".
2. Depress "OFF" and "WARMER" buttons on the ECC panel simultaneously and hold until ".." appears. "88" will then be displayed, which indicates the beginning of the diagnostic readout.
3. Trouble codes will be displayed on the digital ECC panel beginning with the lowest numbered code. Note that the test panel does not display when the system is in the diagnostic mode.

HOW TO CLEAR TROUBLE CODES

Trouble codes stored in the ECM's memory may be cleared (erased) by entering the diagnostic mode and then depressing the "OFF" and "HI" buttons simultaneously. Hold until "00" appears.

HOW TO EXIT DIAGNOSTIC MODE

To get out of the diagnostic mode, depress any of the ECC function keys (Auto, Econ, etc. except Rear Defog) or turn ignition switch off for 10 seconds. Trouble codes are not erased when this is done.

System Diagnosis

Illumination of the "CHECK ENGINE" light indicates that a malfunction has occured for which a trouble code has been stored and can be displayed on the ECC control panel. The malfunction may or may not result in abnormal engine operation. To determine which system(s) has malfunctioned, proceed as follows.
1. Turn ignition switch "O" for 5 seconds.
2. Depress the "OFF" and "WARMER" buttons on the electronic climate control panel simultaneously and hold until ".." appears.
3. Numerals "88" should then appear. The purpose of the "88" display is to check that all segments of the display are working. Diagnosis should not be attempted unless the entire "88" appears, as this could lead to misdiagnosis (Code 31 could be Code 34 with two segments of the display inoperative, etc.).
4. Trouble codes will then be displayed on the digital test panel as follows.
a. The lowest numbered code will be displayed for approximately three seconds.
b. Progressively higher codes, if present, will be displayed consecutively for three second intervals until the highest code present has been displayed.
c. "88" is again displayed.
d. Displays from steps a., b. and c. will be repeated a second time.
e. Displays from steps a. and b. will be repeated a third time.

f. Code 70 will then be displayed, which signals the beginning of the "switch tests" section.

g. Switch tests require some action on the part of the technician. This action is analyzed by the computer for proper operation.

SWITCH TESTS PROCEDURE

When all stored trouble codes have been displayed for the third time, the computer will automatically begin the switch tests. To perform these checks, proceed as follows.

1. Display of trouble Code 70 signals the beginning of this section. This code will continue to be displayed until the proper test action is taken. When ready to begin tests, depress service brake pedal. This begins the test sequence by displaying Code 71.

2. With Code 71 displayed, depress the service brake pedal again to test the brake light circuit. When this check is completed, the test program will automatically sequence to Code 72. If the test action is not performed within 10 seconds, the test program will automatically sequence to "72" and Code 71 will be stored in the computer memory as "not passed".

3. With Code 72 displayed, depress the throttle from idle to wide open throttle and release. This action allows the computer to analyze the operation of the throttle switch. When this check is completed, the test program will automatically sequence to Code 73. Again, if action is not taken within 10 seconds, a Code 72 will be stored as "not passed".

4. With Code 73 displayed, shift the transmission lever to Drive and then to Neutral. When this check is completed, the test program will automatically sequence to Code 74. This action must be taken within 10 seconds or a Code 73 will be set.

5. With Code 74 displayed, shift the transmission lever to Reverse and then to Park. Shift transmission within 10 seconds or a Code 74 will be set. When this check is completed, the test program will automatically sequence to Code 78.

6. With Code 78 displayed, depress the "AVERAGE" button on the test panel. When this check is completed, the test program will automatically sequence to Code 79. Again, this must be done within 10 seconds or a Code 78 will be set.

7. With Code 79 displayed, depress the "RESET" button on the test panel within 10 seconds to test the function of this switch. This is the end of the switch tests.

8. With the switch tests completed, the computer will now go back and display the switch test code(s) which did not test properly. Each code which did not pass the interrogation will be displayed beginning with the lowest number. This time through, the codes will not disappear until the tested component has been repaired and/or tested for proper operation.

9. Upon completion of the trouble code and switch test displays, the ECC panel will remain in the diagnostic mode and display "00" until an ECC mode is selected or the ignition is turned off.

10. Malfunctioning circuits should be analyzed.

"INTERMITTENT" CODES VS. "HARD FAILURE" CODES

Trouble codes stored in the ECM's memory at any time can be either of the following.

1. A code for malfunctions which are occurring now (a "HARD FAILURE"). This malfunction will cause illumination of the "CHECK ENGINE" light.

2. A code for any intermittent malfunctions which have occurred within the last 20 ignition switch cycles. These codes will not cause the "CHECK ENGINE" light to be on now.

Intermittent codes should be diagnosed by inspecting the connectors. During any diagnostic interrogation which displays more than one diagnostic code, it is necessary to determine which code is for the "HARD FAILURE" and which is the "INTERMITTENT." To make this determination, proceed as follows.

1. Enter diagnostics, read and record stored trouble codes.

2. Clear trouble codes.

3. Exit diagnostics by turning the ignition switch off for ten seconds.

4. Turn ignition on and wait 5 seconds, then start engine.

5. Accelerate the engine (to approximately 2000 rpm) for a few seconds.

6. Return to idle.

7. Shift transmission into Drive.

8. Shift to Park.

9. If the "CHECK ENGINE" light comes on, enter diagnostics. Read and record trouble codes. This will reveal only "HARD FAILURE" codes. If the light does not come on, then all stored codes are "INTERMITTENTS."

10. Begin diagnosis with lowest numbered code displayed.

ECM TROUBLE CODES

Trouble Code	Circuit Affected
00	All diagnostics complete
12	No tach signal
14	Shorted coolant sensor circuit
15	Open coolant sensor circuit
21	Shorted throttle position sensor circuit
22	Open throttle position sensor circuit
28	Shorted idle speed control circuit
29	Idle speed control circuit
30	Idle speed control circuit
31	Shorted MAP sensor circuit
32	Open MAP sensor circuit
33	MAP/BARO sensor correlation
34	MAP hose
35	Shorted BARO sensor circuit
36	Open BARO sensor circuit
37	Shorted MAP sensor circuit
38	Open MAT sensor circuit
55	ECM (computer)
56	ECM (computer)

SWITCH TEST CODES

Switch Code	Switch
71	Brake light switch
72	ISC throttle switch
73	Drive (ADL) switch
74	Backup lamp switch
78	MPG panel "AVG" switch
79	MPG panel "RESET" switch

Modulated Displacement Engine (1981 Models)

Modulated displacement is an electromechanical system, controlled by a microprocessor, that calls up four, six or eight engine cylinders depending on driving requirements.

The selective operation of four, six or eight cylinders is provided for by four engine valve selector units that are controlled through the use of a microprocessor (computer).

In each case, as the number of cylinders in operation is reduced, the engine is effectively converted from 6.0 liter displacement with all eight cylinders in use, to 4.5 liters with six cylinders operating, to a 3.0 liter engine with four cylinders providing power. By varying the size of the engine in this manner, significant reductions are made in the amount of internal work the engine has to do.

The system automatically actuates only the number of cylinders needed to satisfy the demand. In doing so, the mechanical efficiency of the engine is improved. Four, six or eight cylinder selection is entirely automatic and operates according to driving demands. A digital instrument panel display of "active cylinders" is standard as part of a new MPG Sentinel system. This system also provides a display of average and instantaneous miles per gallon and expected fuel range.

Service is limited to replacement. An electrical check can be done without removing the valve cover. Hook up a voltmeter and check voltage at the solenoid wire (engine running). Run the engine in all three modes, 8 cyl.- 6 cyl.-4 cyl. If there is full voltage at the actuation solenoid and the solenoid does not click, investigate the solenoid or the valve shifter.

CAUTION *If you chose to electrically test the valve shifter on the engine, it is important that both valves be in the closed position.*

OPERATION

During active operation, the fulcrum point is near the center of the rocker arm. As the cam reaches its high point, the valve is brought to an open position, allowing a fuel charge to enter the cylinder. During the inactive stage, the valve will not open because the selector is commanded to release the rocker arm pivot, allowing it to move upward. This in effect shifts the fulcrum point to the tip of the stationary valve. With the valve being held closed by its spring, the cylinder is rendered inactive.

Modulated Displacement Valve Operation

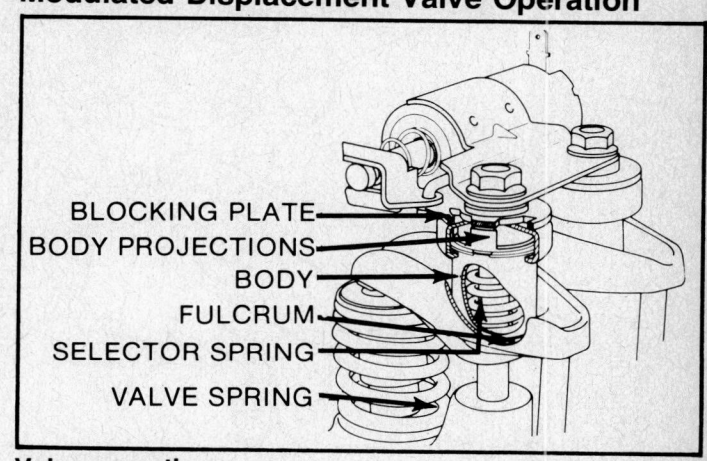

Valve operating

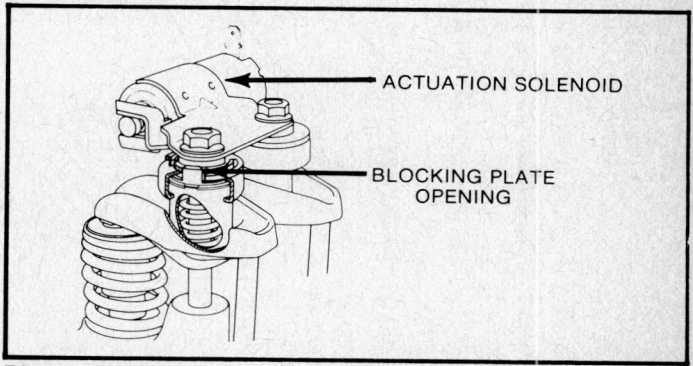

Pivot released

CHRYSLER COMBUSTION COMPUTERS

Introduction

COMBUSTION COMPUTER

The combustion computer is the heart of the entire system. It has the capability of controlling the air-fuel ratio and the ignition timing.

SENSORS

There are eight types of sensors which supply the combustion computer with the information needed to control air-fuel ratio and ignition timing.

Chrysler Combustion Computer System

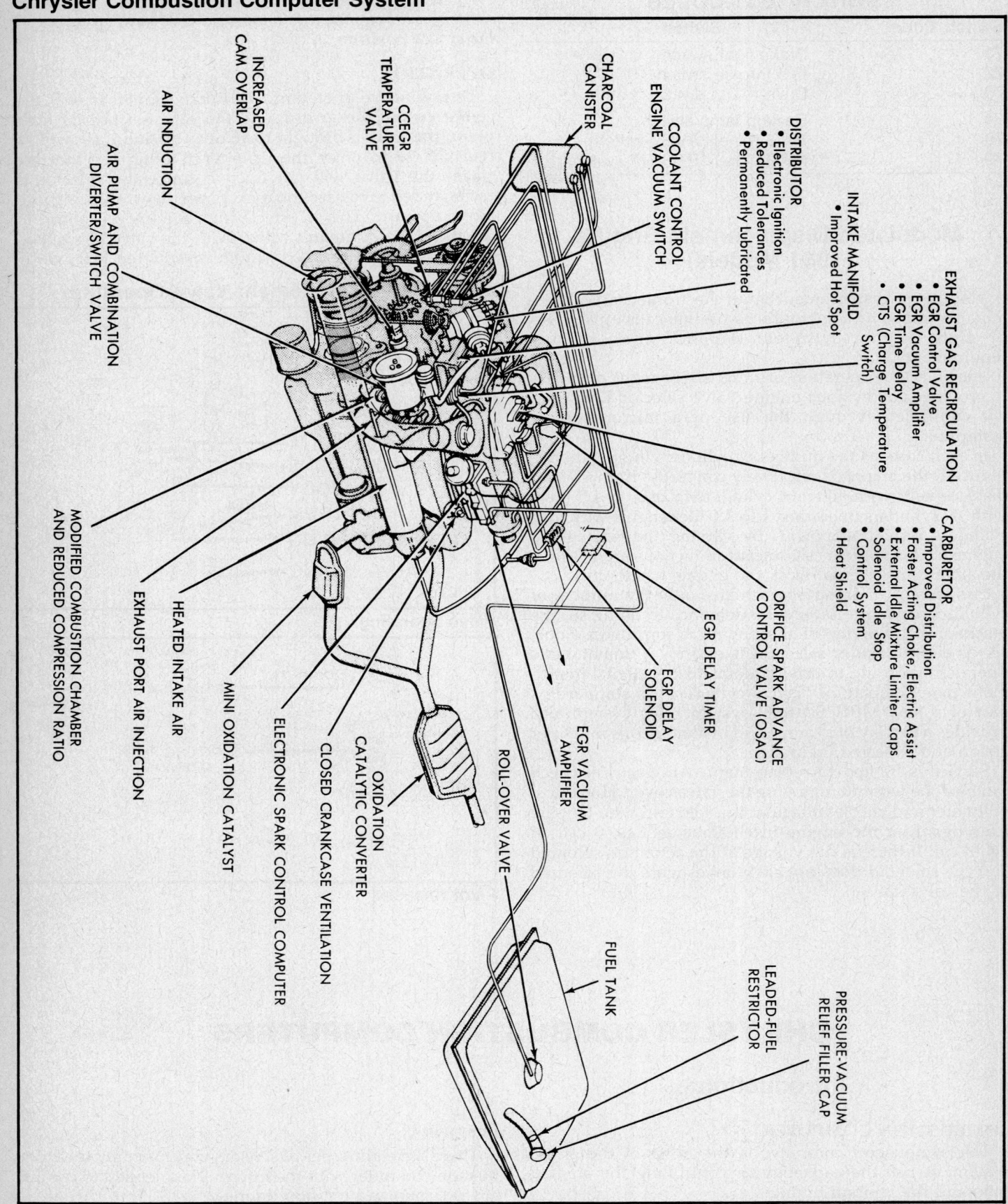

INCREASED
CAM OVERLAP

AIR INDUCTION

AIR PUMP AND COMBINATION
DIVERTER/SWITCH VALVE

CCEGR
TEMPERATURE
VALVE

COOLANT CONTROL
ENGINE VACUUM SWITCH

CHARCOAL
CANISTER

DISTRIBUTOR
• Electronic Ignition
• Reduced Tolerances
• Permanently Lubricated

INTAKE MANIFOLD
• Improved Hot Spot

EXHAUST GAS RECIRCULATION
• EGR Control Valve
• EGR Vacuum Amplifier
• EGR Time Delay
• CTS (Charge Temperature Switch)

CARBURETOR
• Improved Distribution
• Faster Acting Choke, Electric Assist
• External Idle Mixture Limiter Caps
• Solenoid Idle Stop
• Control System
• Heat Shield

ORIFICE SPARK ADVANCE
CONTROL VALVE (OSAC)

EGR DELAY TIMER

EGR DELAY
SOLENOID

EGR VACUUM
AMPLIFIER

ROLL-OVER VALVE

FUEL TANK

LEADED-FUEL
RESTRICTOR

PRESSURE-VACUUM
RELIEF FILLER CAP

CLOSED CRANKCASE VENTILATION

ELECTRONIC SPARK CONTROL COMPUTER

OXIDATION
CATALYTIC CONVERTER

MINI OXIDATION CATALYST

HEATED INTAKE AIR

EXHAUST PORT AIR INJECTION

MODIFIED COMBUSTION CHAMBER
AND REDUCED COMPRESSION RATIO

Combustion Computer

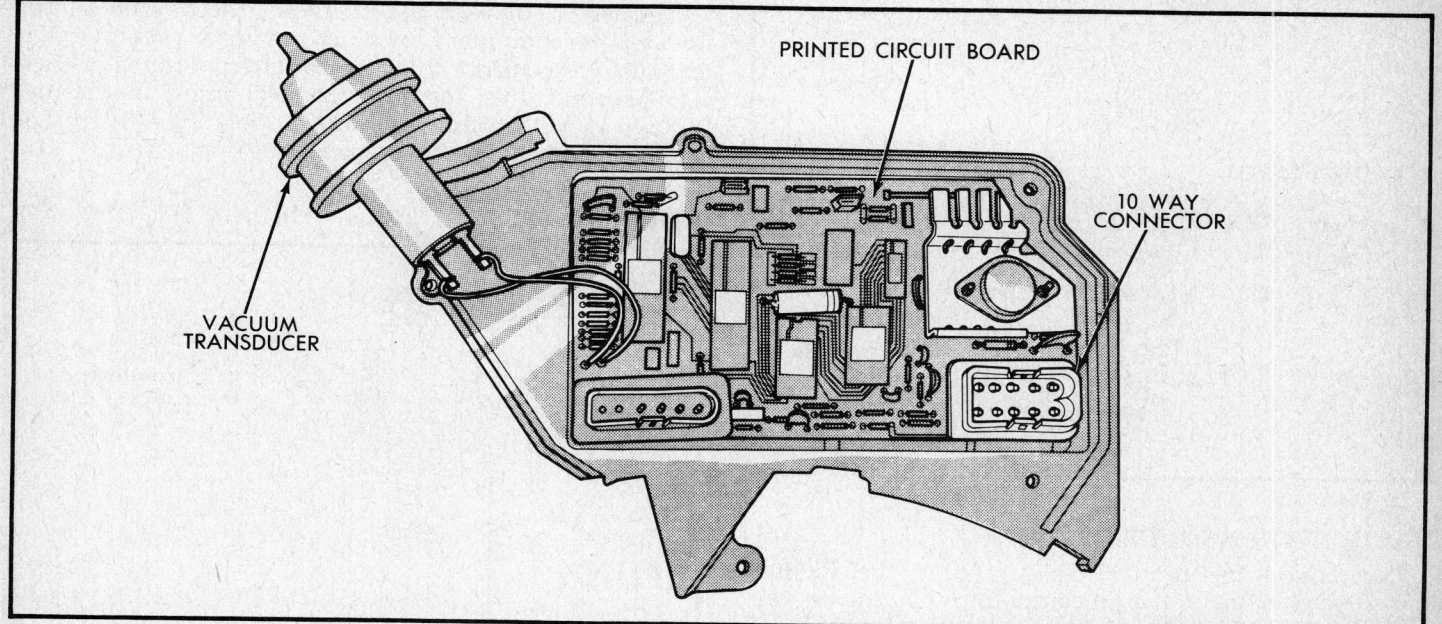

PICK-UP COILS

On four and six cylinder engines, the pick-up coil which is located in the distributor supplies the basic timing signal to the computer. From this signal, the computer can determine engine speed (rpm) and cranking mode.

Eight cylinder engines use two pick-up coils. The start pick-up coil supplies a signal to the computer which will cause the spark plugs to fire at a fixed amount of advance

during cranking only. The run pick-up coil functions like any other Chrysler type, except that its signal is not recognized during engine cranking.

Dual Pick-Up Distributor

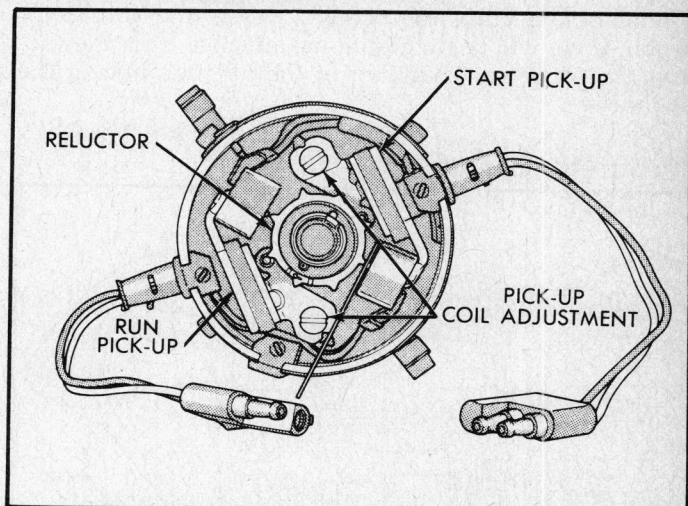

Single Pick-Up Distributor

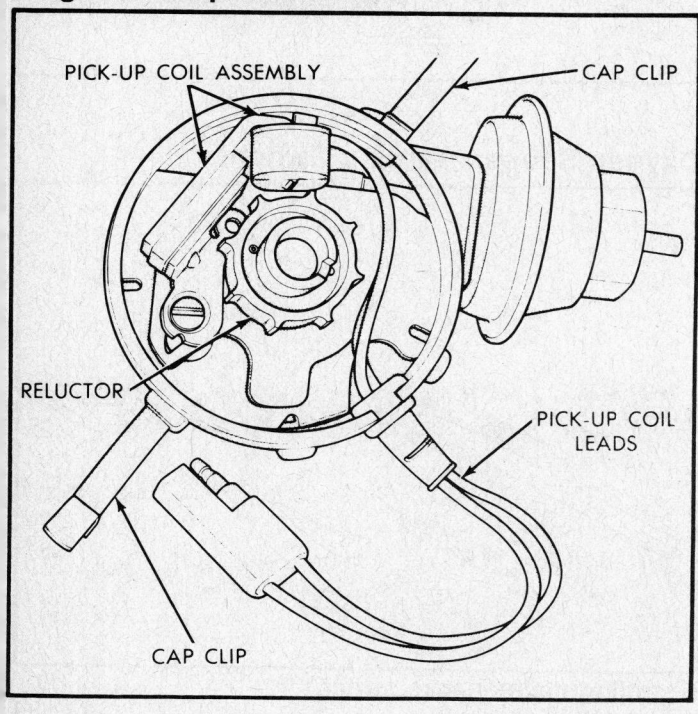

COOLANT SWITCH

The coolant switch supplies a signal to the computer when the engine coolant temperature is below 150°F. This information is required to prevent changing of the air-fuel ratio until the engine reaches operating temperature. When the engine temperature reaches 150°F, the computer will switch the air pump injection from upstream to downstream into the exhaust system and will allow the charcoal canister to purge.

1. Engine with 4145003 combustion computer 150°F
2. Engine with 4145088 combustion computer 98°F

ENGINE CONTROLS
CHRYSLER COMBUSTION COMPUTER

Coolant Switch

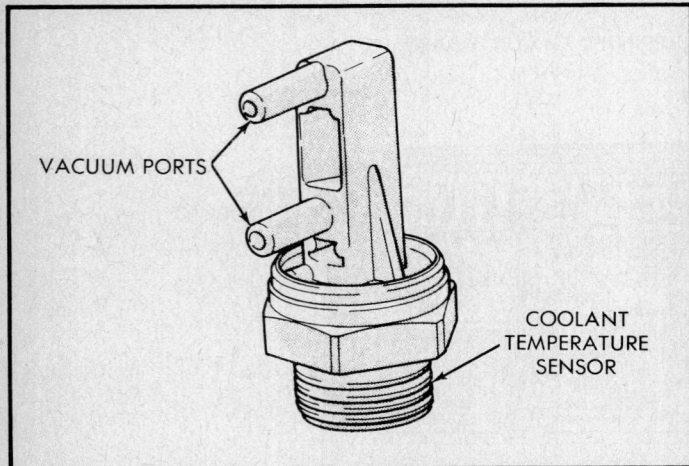

VACUUM PORTS

COOLANT TEMPERATURE SENSOR

VACUUM TRANSDUCER

Located on the combustion computer, the vacuum transducer's signal tells the computer what engine vacuum is. Engine vacuum is one of the factors that will determine how the computer will advance or retard ignition timing and change the air-fuel ratio of the carburetor.

CARBURETOR SWITCH

Located on the end of the idle stop, the carburetor switch tells the computer when the engine is at idle. Whenever the curb idle screw touches the carburetor switch, there will be no additional advance from the vacuum transducer or changing of the air-fuel ratio of the carburetor.

Carburetor Switch

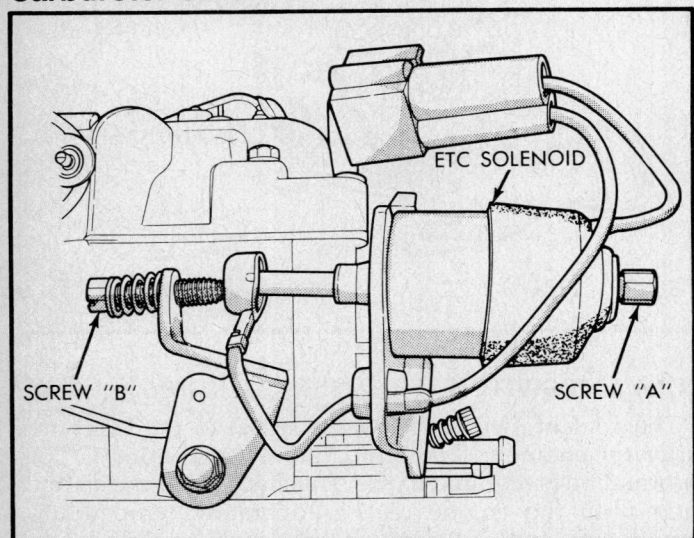

ETC SOLENOID

SCREW "B"

SCREW "A"

SPEED SENSOR

Additional amounts of ignition advance will be allowed by the computer in relationship to engine rpm.

OXYGEN SENSOR

Located in the exhaust manifold, the oxygen sensor will tell the computer how much oxygen is present in the exhaust gases. Since this amount is proportional to rich and lean mixtures, the computer will adjust the air-fuel ratio to a level which will maintain operating efficiency of the three-way catalyst system and engine.

Oxygen Sensor

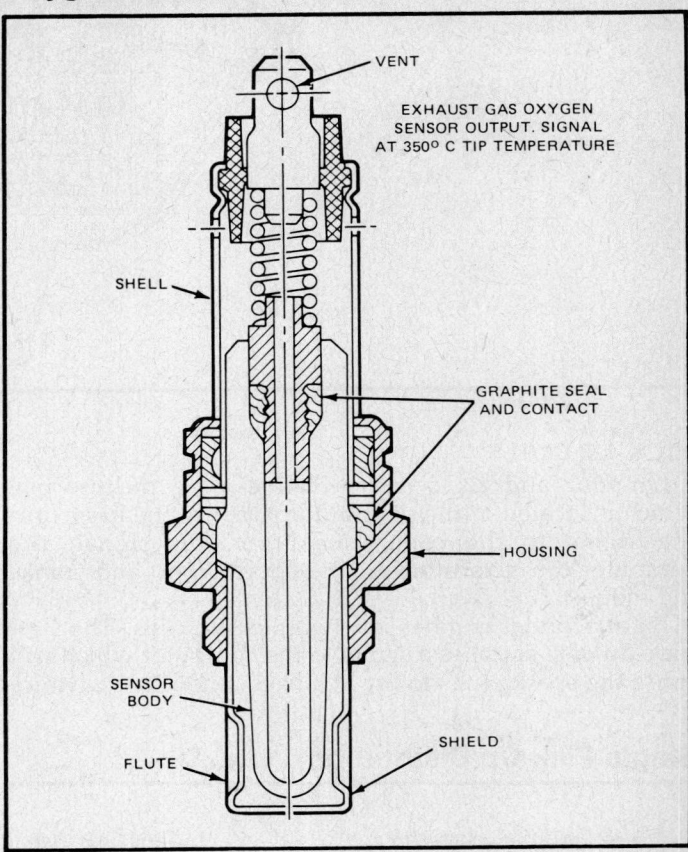

VENT

EXHAUST GAS OXYGEN SENSOR OUTPUT. SIGNAL AT 350° C TIP TEMPERATURE

SHELL

GRAPHITE SEAL AND CONTACT

HOUSING

SENSOR BODY

FLUTE

SHIELD

Oxygen Sensor Warning Switch

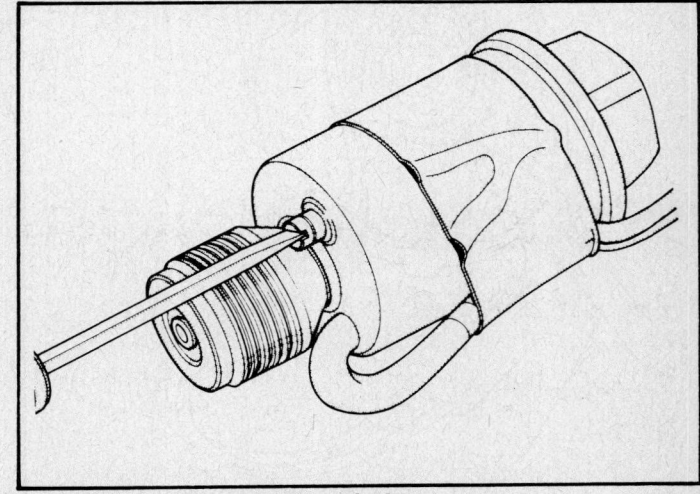

Resetting maintenance switch

DETONATION SENSOR

The detonation sensor tells the computer when detonation occurs, so that the computer will retard the ignition timing.

Detonation Sensor

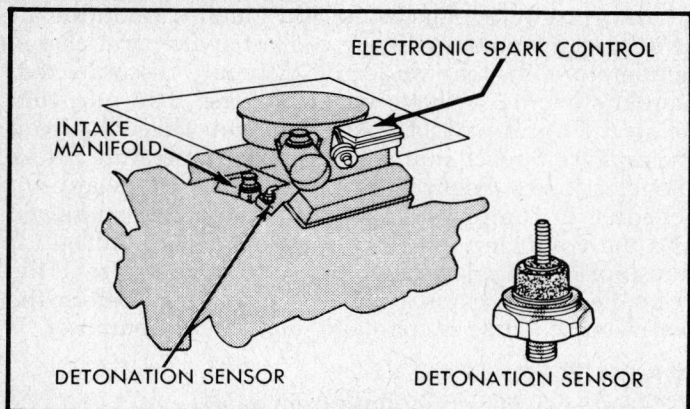

CHARGE TEMPERATURE SWITCH (CTS)— SIX AND EIGHT CYLINDER ONLY

The CTS will be closed when the intake charge (air-fuel mixture) temperature is below 60°F. When closed, the switch allows no EGR timer function or EGR valve operation. On eight cylinder engines, air injection will be switched upstream in the exhaust manifold.

The CTS will be open when the intake charge temperature is above approximately 60°F, thus allowing the EGR

Charge Temperature Switch

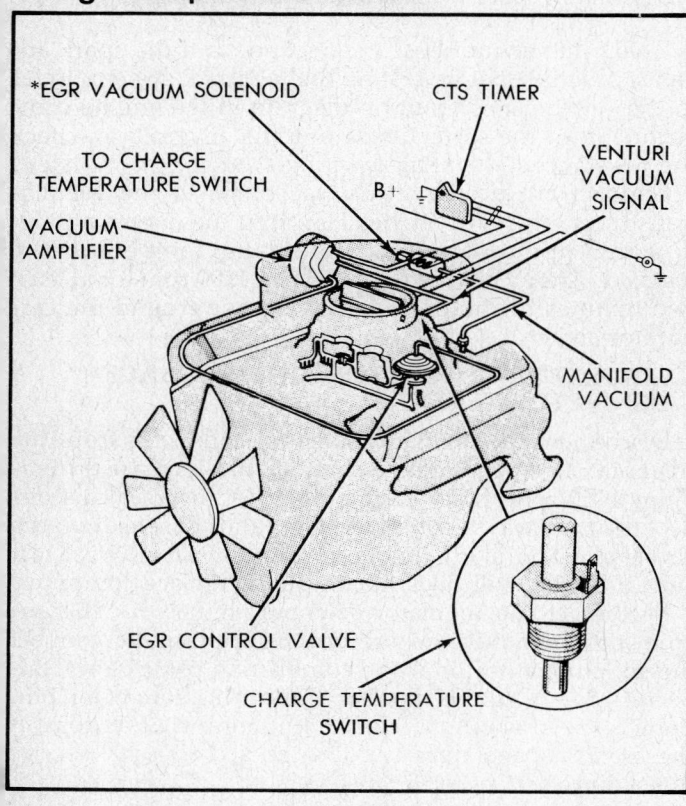

timer to time out and the EGR valve to operate. On eight cylinder engines, air injection will switch downstream into the exhaust system.

Diagnosing Combustion Computer Components

SYSTEM OPERATION

When the engine is started, a series of events occur within the computer. In order to diagnos system problems, it is better to take the ignition and fuel systems separately.

ELECTRONIC SPARK ADVANCE (ESA)

During cranking, an electrical signal from the distributor is fed into the computer. This signal will cause the computer to fire the spark plugs at a fixed amount of advance. Once the engine starts, the timing will be controlled by the computer, based on the information received from the various sensors.

The amount of spark advance is determined by two factors, engine speed and engine vacuum. However, where it happens depends on the following conditions.

1. Advance from vacuum will be given by the computer when the carburetor switch is open. The amount is programmed in the computer and is proportional to the amount of vacuum and rpm.

2. Advance from speed will be given by the computer when the carburetor switch is open and is programmed to engine rpm.

ELECTRONIC FEEDBACK CARBURETOR (EFC)

There are two operating modes in the carburetor feedback system. In the open loop mode, the air-fuel ratio is fixed by programmed information in the computer. In the closed loop mode, air-fuel ratio is varied by the computer, based on information supplied by the oxygen sensor.

When the system is cold, the system will be in open loop. During that time, the air-fuel ratio will be fixed at a richer level, allowing proper engine warm-up. Also during this period, air injection will be upstream in the exhaust manifold. Once the engine warms up, the air injection will be switched to downstream into the exhaust system. The system will operate in open loop at idle and closed loop off idle.

DIGITAL MICROPROCESSOR TESTING

1. Engine at operating temperature.
2. Remove and plug vacuum hose at vacuum transducer.
3. Connect an auxiliary vacuum supply to vacuum transducer and set in 14" of vacuum.
4. Raise engine speed to 2000 rpm, wait one minute and check specifications. Advance specifications are in addition to basic advance.

Four cylinder:	20–28° (manual)
	31–39° (auto)
Six cylinder:	10–18°
Eight cylinder:	15–23°

AIR SWITCH SYSTEM TESTING

VACUUM SUPPLY SYSTEM

1. Remove vacuum hose for air switching/divertor valve and connect a vacuum gauge to hose.
2. Start engine and observe vacuum reading on gauge.

Engine Cold

Engine vacuum should be present on gauge until engine coolant temperature is as follows.

Four cylinder:	
with manual transmission	98°
with automatic transmission	125°
Six cylinder:	150°
Eight cylinder:	
with 4145003 combustion computer	150°
with 4145088 combustion computer	98°

Charge temperature switch (CTS) must be open and fuel mixture temperature above 60°. When temperatures are reached, vacuum should drop to 0. If no vacuum is present on gauge, check as follows.

1. On four cylinder, check vacuum supply and coolant controlled engine vacuum switch (CCEVS).
2. On six and eight cylinder, check vacuum supply, air switching solenoid, coolant switch, wiring and connections to computer and charge temperature switch (CTS on eight cylinder only). If they are okay, then it is possible that the computer is bad and is preventing air switching.

Engine Warm

1. On four cylinder, no vacuum should be present on gauge. If there is, check coolant controlled engine vacuum switch (CCEVS).
2. On six cylinder, vacuum should be present for 100 seconds; on eight cylinder with 4145003 computer, for 25 seconds; and on eight cylinder with 4145088 computer, for 90 seconds. It should then drop to 0. If there is no vacuum, check vacuum supply, air switching solenoid, coolant switch, wiring and connections to computer and charge temperature switch (CTS on eight cylinder only) as follows. If they are okay, then it is possible that the computer is bad and is preventing air switching.

Connect a voltmeter to the light green wire on the air switching solenoid. With the coolant switch and charge temperature switch (on eight cylinder) disconnected, start the engine. Voltage should be less than one volt. Allow the warm-up schedule to time out. This will permit the catalyst to reach normal operating temperature before the electronics begin operation. When the warm-up schedule is completed, the solenoid will de-energized and the voltmeter will read charging system voltage. If not, replace the solenoid and repeat the procedure. If the voltmeter indicates charging system voltage before the warm-up schedule is complete, replace the computer.

AIR SWITCHING VALVE

1. Remove air supply hose from valve.
2. Remove vacuum hose from valve and install an auxiliary vacuum supply.
3. Start engine. Air should be blowing out of side port. Apply vacuum to valve. Air should now be blowing out of bottom port.

Electronic Feedback Carburetor Diagnosis

FOUR CYLINDER ENGINES

NOTE   Systems must be tested in order (1, 2, 3 and 4) and air switching system must be working properly.

Check all vacuum hose connections and the spark advance schedule before testing the feedback system. Refer to the vacuum hose routing diagram in the engine compartment for the correct hose routing. In addition, check the resistance in all related wiring.

Connect an auxiliary vacuum source to the vacuum transducer. Apply 10 inches Hg. Start the engine and let it warm up until normal operating temperature is reached. After a hot restart, maintain 1200 rpm for at least two minutes before proceeding. Do not ground the carburetor switch.

CARBURETOR REGULATOR AND FEEDBACK CARBURETOR TEST

Disconnect the regulator solenoid connector from the solenoid. Average engine speed should increase a minimum of 50 rpm. If the engine does not respond, disconnect the four-way tee from the temperature sensor on the air cleaner and allow engine to draw in air. Repeat test and, if engine still does not respond, replace computer.

Reconnect the regulator solenoid connector. The engine speed should slowly return to 1200 rpm. Disconnect the six-pin connector at the combustion computer. Connect a ground to the number 15 harness connector pin. Engine speed should decrease a minimum of 50 rpm. If the engine speed does not change accordingly, service the carburetor (check for air leaks).

Vacuum Solenoid/Regulator

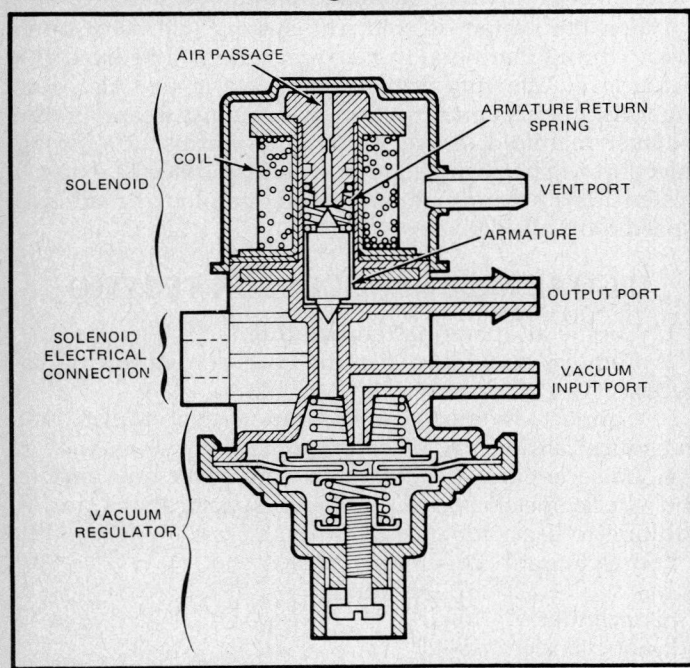

COOLANT SWITCH

With the engine cold, the coolant temperature switch should have continuity to ground. With the engine warmed up (water temperature greater than 150°F), the switch should be open.

COMBUSTION CONTROL COMPUTER TEST

With the engine hot, disconnect the coolant temperature switch. The carburetor switch must not be grounded. Maintain an engine speed of 1200 rpm. Separate the connector at the oxygen sensor and connect a jumper wire to the harness end. Connect the other end of the jumper to a good ground. An increase in engine speed should be observed and, after 15 seconds, return to original speed. If the engine does not respond, disconnect the four-way tee from the temperature sensor on the air cleaner and allow engine to draw in air. Repeat test and, if engine still does not respond, replace computer. Then connect the end of the jumper wire to battery voltage. The engine speed should decrease. If the computer fails the tests, replace it.

OXYGEN SENSOR TEST

The oxygen sensor should be changed every 30,000 miles. The feedback electronics must be working properly for the test. Run the engine at 1200 rpm with carburetor switch ungrounded. Connect a voltmeter to the solenoid output wire going to the carburetor.

Full Rich

Hold the choke blade(s) closed. During the next ten seconds, the voltage should decrease to less than three volts or less and maintain that level. If the engine does not respond, disconnect the four-way tee from the temperature sensor on the air cleaner and allow the engine to draw in air. Repeat test and if engine still does not respond, replace computer. If the sensor fails the test, replace it.

Full Lean

Disconnect the PCV system and/or the canister purge hose. During the next ten seconds, the voltage should be greater than nine volts. Voltage should then decrease to a slightly lower level and maintain this level until the vacuum hoses are reconnected. If the sensor fails the test, replace it.

SIX AND EIGHT CYLINDER ENGINES

NOTE *System must be tested in order 1, 2, 3 and 4. Air switching system must be working properly. Do not ground the carburetor switch.*

Run engine until normal operating temperature is reached. After restarting, maintain 1200 rpm for at least two minutes.

CARBURETOR OR VACUUM REGULATOR AND FEEDBACK CARBURETOR TEST
Six Cylinder Engines

First, check the vacuum regulator as follows. With a 0–5 inch Hg vacuum gauge teed into the vacuum reg-

ulator supply to the carburetor, separate the wiring connector from the regulator. With the engine running and no voltage applied to the regulator, vacuum to the carburetor should be 0 inches Hg (engine rpm should increase by at least 50). Use a jumper wire to supply battery voltage to one terminal of the regulator while grounding the other. Vacuum should now go to 5 inches Hg (engine rpm should decrease by at least 50). If the regulator does not operate properly, replace it. Repeat the test and, if the response is still incorrect, replace the carburetor.

Eight Cylinder Engines

Disconnect the regulator solenoid connector from the solenoid. Average engine speed should increase a minimum of 50 rpm. Reconnect the regulator solenoid connector. The engine speed should slowly return to 1200 rpm. Disconnect the six-pin connector at the combustion computer. Connect a ground to the number 15 harness connector pin. Engine speed should decrease a minimum of 50 rpm. If the engine speed does not change accordingly, service the carburetor.

COOLANT SWITCH TEST

When the engine is cold, resistance of the coolant switch should be less than 10 ohms. With the engine warmed up (water temperature greater than 150°F for computer 4145003, greater than 98° for computer 4145088), the switch should be open.

COMBUSTION CONTROL COMPUTER TEST

NOTE *Do not ground the idle stop switch. Use a sensitive tachometer.*

With the engine hot, disconnect the coolant temperature switch and charge temperature switch. Maintain an engine speed. Separate the connector at the oxygen sensor and connect a jumper wire to the harness end. Connect the other end of the jumper wire to a good ground. An increase in engine speed should be observed (minimum of 50 rpm). After 15 seconds, it should return to original speed. Now, connect the end of the jumper wire to battery voltage. The engine speed should decrease (minimum of 50 rpm). If the computer fails the tests, replace it.

DETONATION SENSOR TEST

1. Connect a variable timing light to the engine.
2. Start the engine and run it on the second highest step of the fast idle cam (at least 1200 rpm).
3. Tap lightly on the manifold near the sensor, with a small metal object such as a small hammer.
4. Using the timing light, look for a decrease in the spark advance. The amount of decrease in timing is directly proportional to the strength and frequency of the tapping.
5. If tapping the sensor does not retard the timing, trouble in the detonation circuit is indicated.

Ignition Timing Procedure

Ground the carburetor switch. Refer to timing specifications on engine decal.

IDLE SPEED ADJUSTMENT

NOTE   Idle mixture screws are set as sealed at the factory. If curb idle speed is not within tolerance after performing these adjustments, an improper mixture setting may be suspected. To correct this situation, make sure the oxygen feedback system is operating properly before disturbing idle adjustments.

Four Cylinder Engines

1. Ground carburetor switch with a jumper wire. Remove EGR hose at the valve and plug hose. Pull PCV valve from grommet and allow to draw in air. Disconnect canister purge hose at the carburetor and do not plug either hose or carburetor fitting. Run the cooling fan with a jumper wire.

2. Set parking brake. Start engine and allow it to reach operating temperature. If so equipped, turn speed control off.

3. Set curb idle speed as follows.

a. On non A/C manual transmissions, disconnect idle stop solenoid wire at connector and set throttle stop screw to 700 rpm. Reconnect wire and open throttle to set solenoid plunger. Set curb idle speed to 900 rpm using screw on solenoid.

b. On non A/C automatic transmissions, disconnect idle stop solenoid wire and set throttle stop screw to 700 rpm (in Park). Reconnect wire and open throttle to set solenoid plunger. Set curb idle speed to 900 rpm using screw on solenoid.

c. On A/C manual transmissions, remove curb idle screw from idle stop solenoid. With solenoid energized and compressor running, insert Allen wrench into solenoid and set to 850 rpm. Reinstall curb idle screw into solenoid and set curb idle speed to 900 rpm with A/C compressor off.

d. On A/C automatic transmissions, remove curb idle screw from idle stop solenoid. With solenoid energized, compressor running and transmission in Drive, insert Allen wrench into solenoid and set to 750 rpm. Turn compressor off and set transmission in Park. Reinstall curb idle screw into solenoid and set curb idle speed to 900 rpm.

4. Reconnect canister purge hose to carburetor. Reinstall PCV valve into grommet.

5. Remove top of air cleaner. Place fast idle speed screw on lowest step (step 3) of cam. Set speed to 1400 rpm (manual transmission) or 1700 rpm (automatic transmission).

6. Remove jumper wire from carburetor switch. Reconnect EGR hose.

Six Cylinder Engines

1. Ground carburetor switch with a jumper wire. Remove wire from coolant temperature switch and ground it with a jumper wire. This lead must be grounded before starting engine for proper setting.

2. Remove EGR hose at valve and plug hose. Remove PCV valve from valve cover and allow to draw in air. Remove canister control vacuum hose at carburetor and plug carburetor nipple. If so equipped, place cruise control switch in "OFF" position.

3. Start engine and allow it to reach operating temperature. If engine is already warmed up, wait two minutes before proceeding with adjustment.

4. To set solenoid energized speed, connect a jumper wire from the positive battery post to the solenoid lead wire in the three-way connector on the carburetor.

CHILTON CAUTION   Do not disconnect the three-way wiring connector that has the feed wire to solenoid to connect jumper wire from battery, just insert jumper into connector. Also, make sure jumper wire is not accidentally connected to curb switch wire in connector.

Open throttle slightly to energize solenoid. Remove curb idle speed screw from solenoid. Insert a 1/8" Allen wrench into solenoid and adjust energized speed to 900 rpm. Reinstall curb idle speed screw into solenoid. Turn screw until it seats and then back out 1/2 turn as a starting point to set curb idle.

5. Remove jumper wire from wiring connector. If engine stalls at any time, wait two minutes after restarting before resuming adjustment. Turn curb idle screw and set speed to 840 rpm.

6. Reconnect canister purge hose and reinstall PCV valve into valve cover. Remove air cleaner cover and place fast idle speed screw on the second highest step of the fast idle cam. Set speed to 2000 rpm. Return to idle.

7. Reinstall air cleaner cover. Remove jumper wire from carburetor switch. Reconnect wire to coolant switch and hose to EGR valve. Curb idle should be a nominal 750 rpm.

Eight Cylinder Engines

1. Ground carburetor switch with a jumper wire. Remove wire from coolant temperature switch and ground it with a jumper wire. This lead must be grounded before starting engine for proper setting.

2. Remove EGR hose at valve and plug hose. Remove PCV valve from valve cover and allow to draw in air. Remove canister control valve vacuum hose at carburetor and plug carburetor nipple.

3. Start engine and allow it to reach operating temperature. If engine is already warmed up, wait one minute before proceeding with adjustment.

4. To set solenoid energized speed, connect a jumper wire from the positive battery post to the solenoid lead wire in the four-way wiring connector on the carburetor.

CHILTON CAUTION   Do not disconnect the four-way connector that has the feed wire to solenoid to connect the jumper wire from battery, just insert jumper into connector. Also, make sure jumper wire is not accidentally connected to the carburetor switch wire in the connector.

5. If equipped with A/C, turn it on and disconnect compressor lead. Open throttle slightly to energize solenoid. Set energized speed to 950 rpm by turning the screw on the throttle shaft lever.

6. Remove jumper wire from wiring connector. Turn off A/C and reconnect lead to compressor. Set curb idle speed to 650 rpm using screw on back of solenoid.

7. Reconnect canister purge hose and reinstall PCV valve into valve cover. Remove air cleaner cover and place fast idle speed screw on the second highest step of the fast idle cam. Set speed to 1300 rpm. Return to idle.

8. Reinstall air cleaner cover. Remove jumper wire from carburetor switch. Reconnect wire to coolant switch and hose to EGR valve. Curb idle should be nominal 700 rpm.

GM COMPUTER COMMAND CONTROL SYSTEM

General Description

The computer command control is a system that controls emissions by close regulation of the air-fuel ratio and by the use of a three-way catalytic converter which lowers the level of oxides of nitrogen, hydrocarbons and carbon monoxide.

The essential components are an exhaust gas oxygen sensor (OS), an electronic control module (ECM), an electronically controlled air-fuel ratio carburetor and a three-way catalytic converter (ORC).

To maintain good idle and driveability under all conditions, input signals are used to modify the computer output signal. These input signals are supplied by the engine temperature sensor, the vacuum control switch (es), the throttle position switch (TPS), the distributor (engine speed), the manifold absolute pressure sensor (MAP) and the barometer pressure sensor (BARO).

Basic Cycle of Operation

LEAN MIXTURE O_2 IN EXHAUST GAS → LOW SENSOR VOLTAGE → ELECTRONIC CONTROL UNIT DE-ENERGIES CARBURETOR SOLENOID → CARBURETOR CONTROL ENRICHENS MIXTURE → LESS O_2 IN EXHAUST GAS → HIGH SENSOR VOLTAGE → ELECTRONIC CONTROL UNIT ENERGIZES CARBURETOR SOLENOID → CARBURETOR CONTROL "LEANS" MIXTURE → LEAN MIXTURE O_2 IN EXHAUST GAS

Typical C-4 System Air-Fuel Metering Control

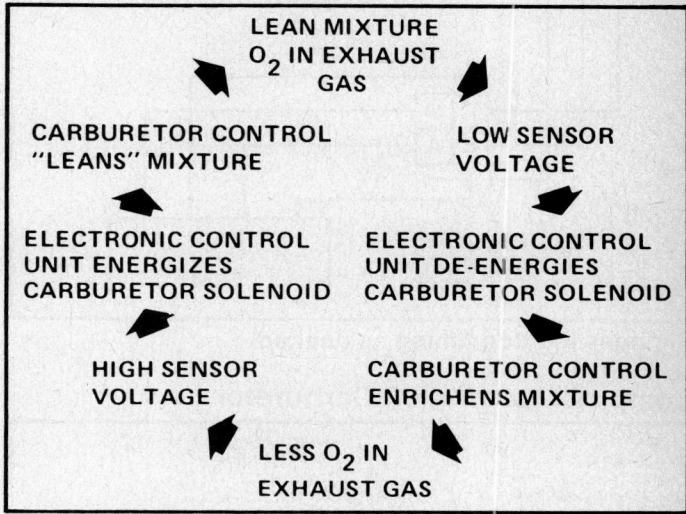

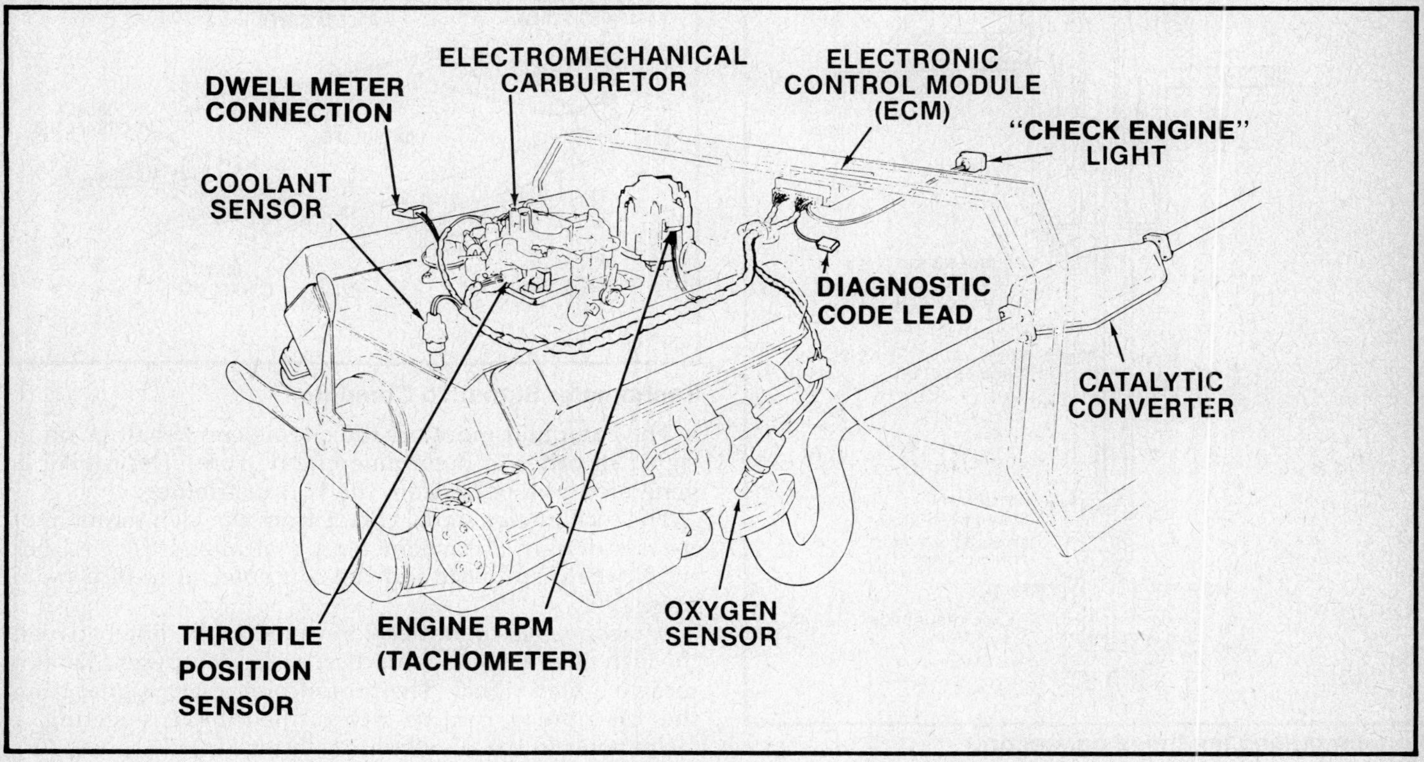

DWELL METER CONNECTION — ELECTROMECHANICAL CARBURETOR — ELECTRONIC CONTROL MODULE (ECM) — "CHECK ENGINE" LIGHT — COOLANT SENSOR — DIAGNOSTIC CODE LEAD — CATALYTIC CONVERTER — THROTTLE POSITION SENSOR — ENGINE RPM (TACHOMETER) — OXYGEN SENSOR

ENGINE CONTROLS

GM COMPUTER COMMAND CONTROL SYSTEM

Computer Controlled Distributor

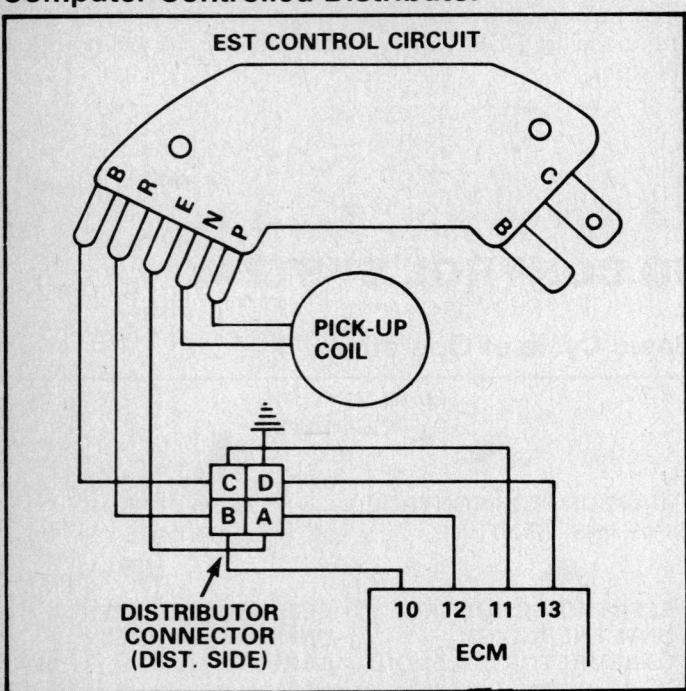

Changes ignition timing as needed

Computer Controlled Carburetor

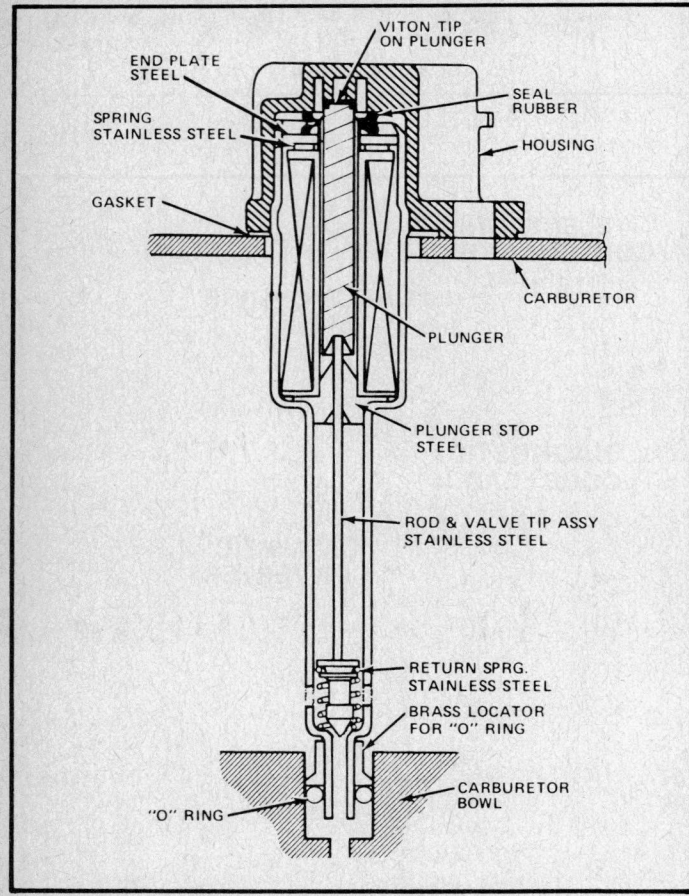

Plunger pulses ten times per second

System Components & Operation

ELECTRONIC CONTROL MODULE (ECM)

The electronic control module (ECM) monitors the voltage output of the oxygen sensor, along with information from other input signals, to generate a control signal to the carburetor solenoid. The control signal is continually cycling the solenoid between "ON" (lean command) and "OFF" (rich command). When the solenoid is on (energized), the solenoid pulls down a metering rod which reduces fuel flow. When the solenoid is off (de-energized), the spring-loaded metering rod returns to the up position and fuel flow increases. The amount of time on relative to time off is a function of the input voltage from the oxygen sensor.

On 3.8 liter V-6 engines, the ECM also controls the electronic spark timing system (EST). On 5.7 liter V-8 engines, the ECM also controls the electronic module retard (EMR) system. The EMR module has the capability of retarding the engine timing 10 degrees during certain engine operations to reduce the exhaust emissions.

During other engine operations, the module functions the same as a standard HEI module. The terminal "R" on the module is connected to the ECM and the retard is accomplished by an internal ground. The timing is retarded 10 degrees only when the engine coolant temperature is between 19°C (66°F) and 64°C (130°F), with the throttle opening position below 45% and the engine speed above 400 rpm.

Electronic Control Module (Computer)

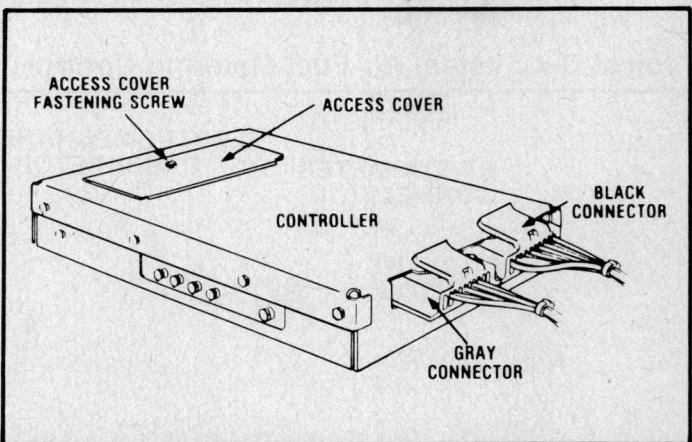

Tachometer Signal To Computer

The computer monitors the engine crankshaft position signal in order to determine engine rpm. This signal is generated as a pulse from the HEI distributor.

The tachometer signal comes from the tach terminal of the distributor. A tachometer signal filter is located between the distributor and the computer to reduce radio noise.

A tachometer cannot be connected in the line between the tach filter and the computer, or the computer may not receive a tach signal. The presence of a tach signal from the distributor can be determined by connecting a tachometer to the distributor tach terminal.

ENGINE COOLANT SENSOR

The coolant temperature sensor in the engine block sends the ECM information on engine temperature which can be used to vary the air-fuel ratio as the engine coolant temperature varies with time during a cold start. It also accomplishes various switching functions at different temperatures (EGR, EFE, etc.), provides a switch point for hot temperature light indication and varies spark advance.

The coolant temperature sensor has a connector which lets the ground return lead surround the signal lead. This design provides an interference shield to prevent high voltage in the area (such as spark plug leads) from affecting the sensor signal to the computer.

NOTE   The ground return wire goes to the computer which internally grounds the wire.

Coolant Sensor Assembly

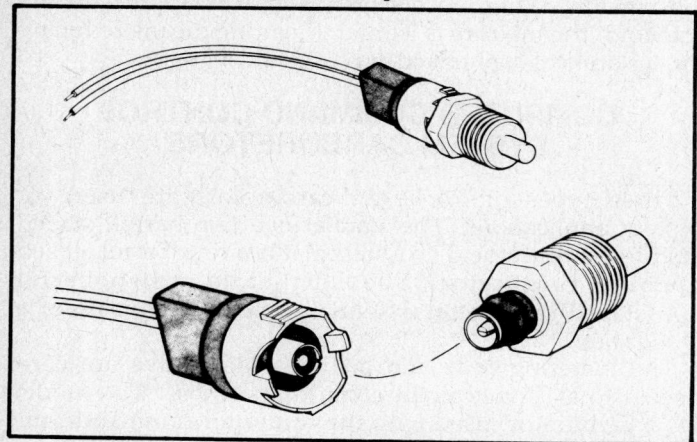

EXHAUST OXYGEN SENSOR

The oxygen sensor located in the exhaust manifold compares the oxygen content in the exhaust stream to the oxygen content in the outside air. This shows that there is a passage from the top of the oxygen sensor to the inner chamber which permits outside air to enter. When servicing the sensor, do not plug or restrict this air passage.

A rich exhaust stream is low in oxygen content and will cause the oxygen sensor to send a rich signal, approximately one volt, to the computer. A lean exhaust stream will result in a lean signal, less than half a volt, from the oxygen sensor to the computer.

As the sensor temperature increases during engine warm-up, the sensor voltage also increases. Because the minimum voltage required to operate this circuit is half a volt, the computer will not use the oxygen sensor signal until the sensor has reached 600°F.

Oxygen Sensor Service

An oxygen sensor maintenance reminder is provided in the instrument panel which indicates time for oxygen sensor replacement.

To reset the sensor warning flag, use the following procedure.

Exhaust Oxygen Sensor

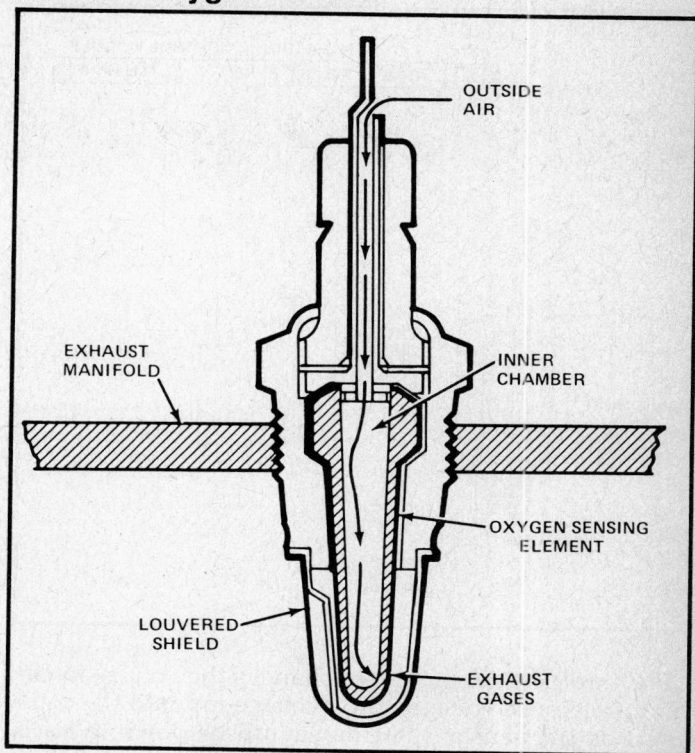

1. Remove the instrument cluster trim plate.
2. Using a pointed tool, apply a slight downward force to the detent on the flag outer rim until reset.
3. Reinstall instrument cluster trim plate.

Leaded fuel will coat the sensor tip, thus adversely effecting its operation.

A special anti-sieze compound is used on the oxygen sensor threads. The compound consists of a liquid graphite and glass beads. The graphite will tend to burn away, but the glass beads will remain, making the sensor easier to remove.

Although 18 ft. lbs. of torque are required to install the oxygen sensor, 70 ft. lbs. may be needed to remove it.

NOTE   Care must be taken when handling oxygen sensors in order to preserve their efficiency. The inline connector and louvered end must be kept free of grease and other contaminants. Cleaning solvents of any type must be avoided.

It is also important that care be taken when installing the oxygen sensor so that the silicone boot is in the correct position to insure proper oxygen operation and to avoid melting the boot.

THROTTLE POSITION SENSOR (TPS)

This sensor is located in the carburetor body and is actuated by the accelerator pump lever. The stem of the sensor projects up through the air horn, contacting the underside of the lever. As the throttle valves are opened, the pump lever presses down proportionately on the sensor, thus indicating throttle position.

ENGINE CONTROLS

Throttle Position Sensor

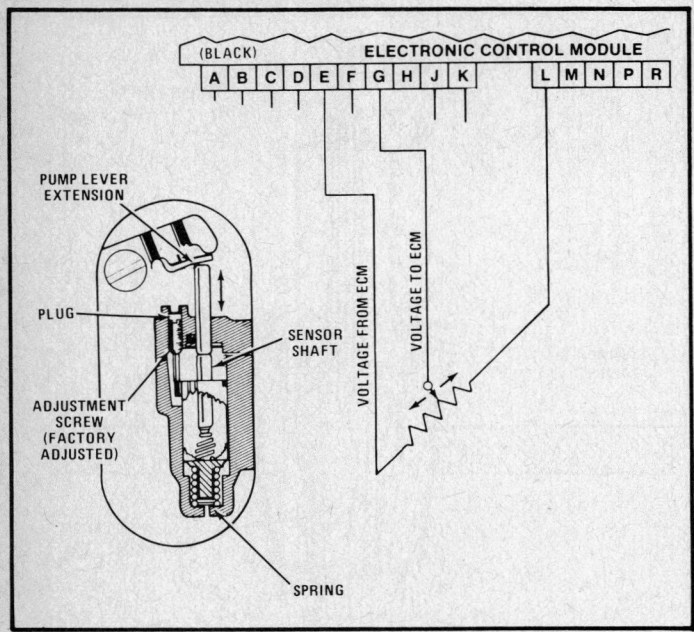

The throttle position sensor changes the voltage in circuit E (reference voltage) to G (voltage input to the computer) as the sensor shaft moves up or down. This is similar to the operation of the gas tank gauge sending unit, except that the throttle position sensor permits the computer to read throttle position.

BAROMETRIC PRESSURE SENSOR

The barometric pressure sensor provides a voltage to the computer to allow ambient pressure compensation of the controlled functions. This unit senses ambient barometric pressure and provides information to the computer on atmospheric pressure changes due to weather and/or altitude.

Typical Pressure Sensor

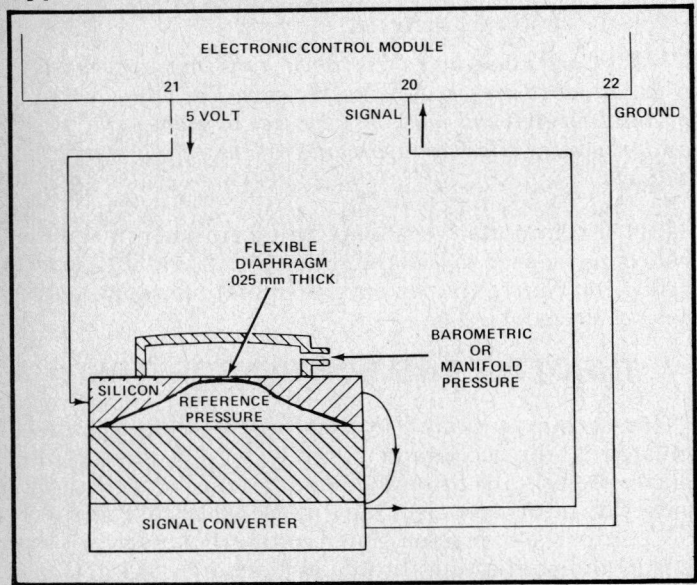

The computer uses this information to adjust the air-fuel ratio. The sensor is mounted under the instrument panel near the right-hand A/C outlet and is electronically connected to the computer. The atmospheric opening is covered by a foam filter.

MIXTURE CONTROL (M/C)

The mixture control solenoid actuates two spring-loaded rods, controlling fuel flow to the idle and main metering circuits of the carburetor. Energizing the solenoid lowers the metering rod into the main metering jet. This makes the air-fuel mixture in the Dualjet and Quadrajet carburetors leaner. The Varajet carburetor has a solenoid operated fuel control valve.

The mixture control solenoid changes the air-fuel ratio by allowing more or less fuel to flow through the carburetor. When no electrical signal is applied to the solenoid, maximum fuel flows to the idle and main metering circuits. When an electrical signal is applied to the solenoid, the mixture is leaned. (Leaning means reducing the amount of fuel mixed with the air.)

COMPUTER COMMAND CONTROL SYSTEM CARBURETORS

Three types of Rochester carburetors are used for system applications. The Varajet is a two barrel, staged opening carburetor. The Quadrajet is a four barrel staged opening carburetor. The Dualjet is a two barrel non-staged carburetor, essentially the primary side of a Quadrajet.

The metering rods and an idle bleed valve are connected to a 12 volt mixture control solenoid. The model E2SE carburetor, used with the computer command control system, is a controlled air-fuel ratio carburetor of a two barrel, two stage down-draft design with the primary bore smaller in size than the secondary bore. Air-fuel ratio control is accomplished with a solenoid controlled on/off fuel valve which supplements the preset flow of fuel which supplies the idle and main metering systems. The solenoid on/off cycle is controlled by a 12 volt signal from the computer. The solenoid also controls the amount of air bled into the idle system. The air bleed valve and fuel control valve work together so that the fuel valve is closed when the air bleed valve is open, resulting in a leaner air-fuel mixture. Enrichment occurs when the fuel valve is open and air bleed valve closed.

The Quadrajet-Dualjet arrangement is such that the level of metering is dependent on the positioning of rods in the orifices. The Varajet system is different in that it features a non-moving-part main system for lean mixtures and a supplemental system to provide for rich mixture.

AIR FLOW CONTROL SYSTEMS

Two types of air systems are used on computer command control engines, the pulse air injection reactor (PAIR) and the belt-driven air pump (AIR). Both types are controlled by the computer through solenoid valves. The PAIR system uses an on/off solenoid which is open dur-

Mixture Control Solenoid Circuit

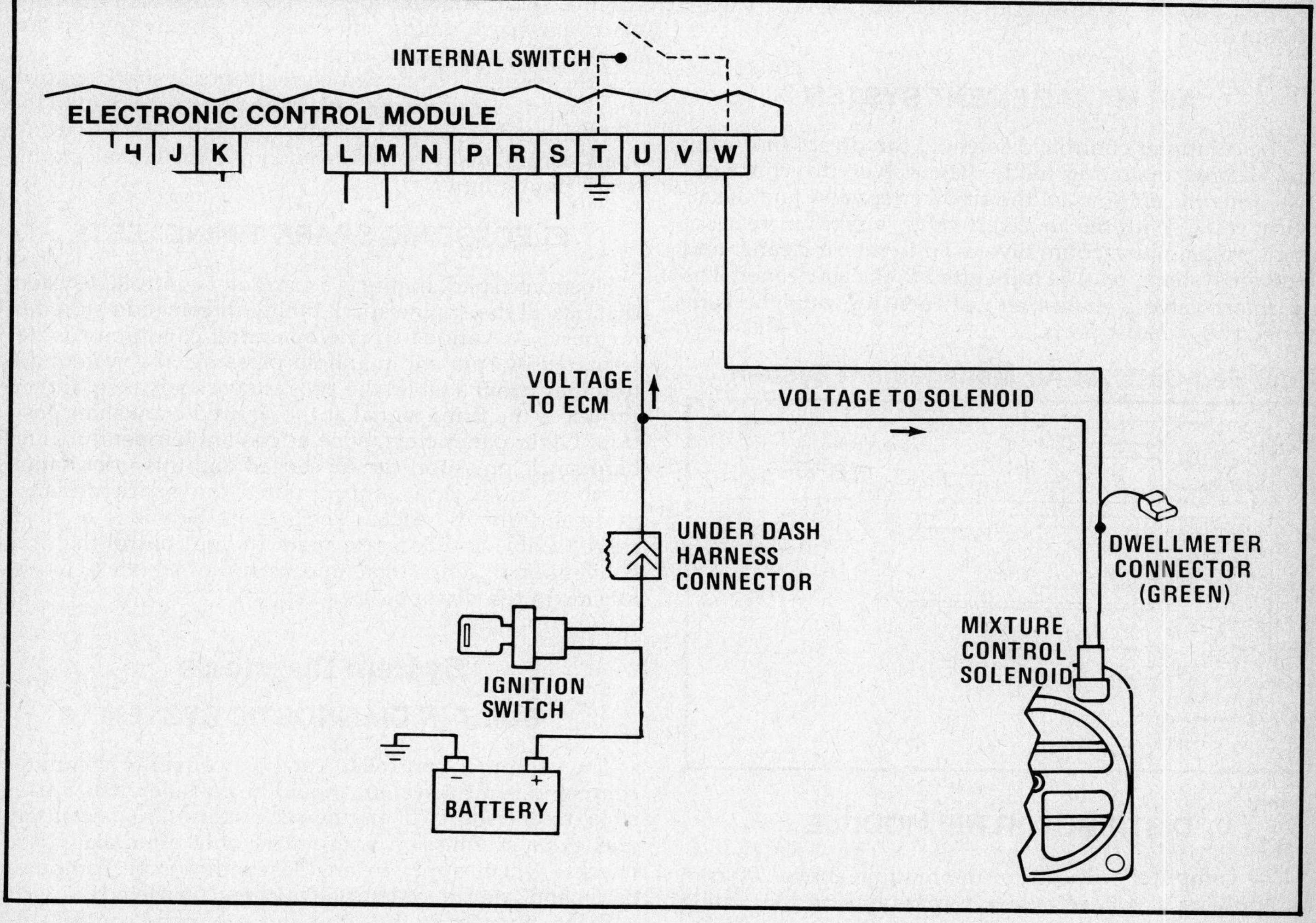

INTERNAL SWITCH

ELECTRONIC CONTROL MODULE

4 J K L M N P R S T U V W

VOLTAGE TO ECM

VOLTAGE TO SOLENOID

UNDER DASH HARNESS CONNECTOR

IGNITION SWITCH

BATTERY

DWELLMETER CONNECTOR (GREEN)

MIXTURE CONTROL SOLENOID

PAIR Solenoid

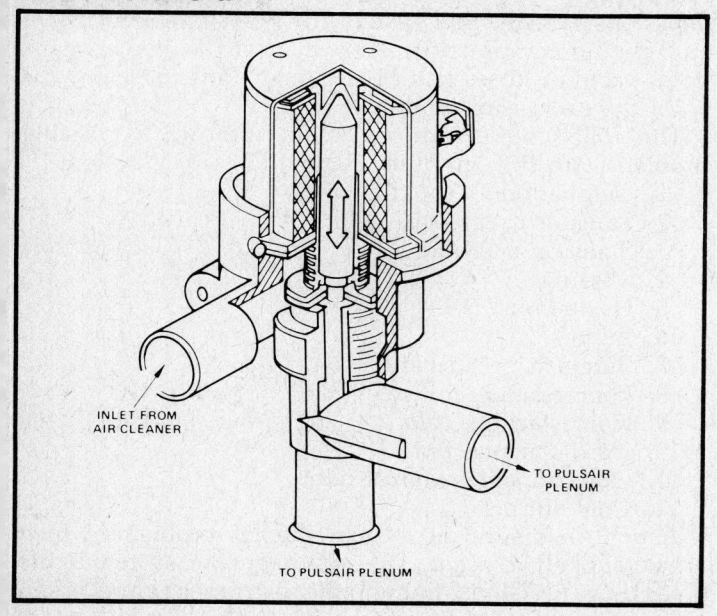

INLET FROM AIR CLEANER

TO PULSAIR PLENUM

TO PULSAIR PLENUM

Air Injection Schematic

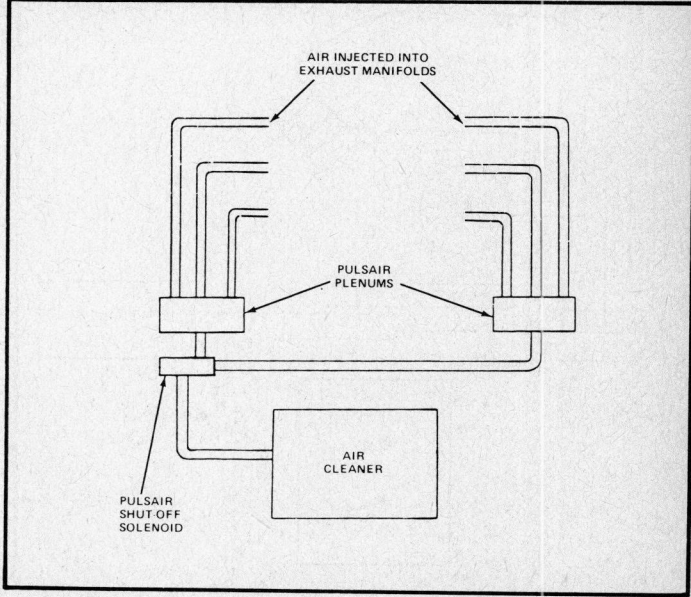

AIR INJECTED INTO EXHAUST MANIFOLDS

PULSAIR PLENUMS

AIR CLEANER

PULSAIR SHUT OFF SOLENOID

ing cold operation and wide open throttle (WOT). Air is injected into the exhaust ports when the solenoid valves are open.

AIR MANAGEMENT SYSTEM

The computer controlled solenoid can divert air during any desired operating mode. The valves diverting and switching the air flow are the air diverter valve and the air select valve. With the air divert valve, a rapid increase of engine manifold vacuum diverts air to the air cleaner and high air system pressure is diverted to the air cleaner. The air select valve switches air between the catalytic converter and exhaust ports.

Dual Bed Catalyst Air Management System

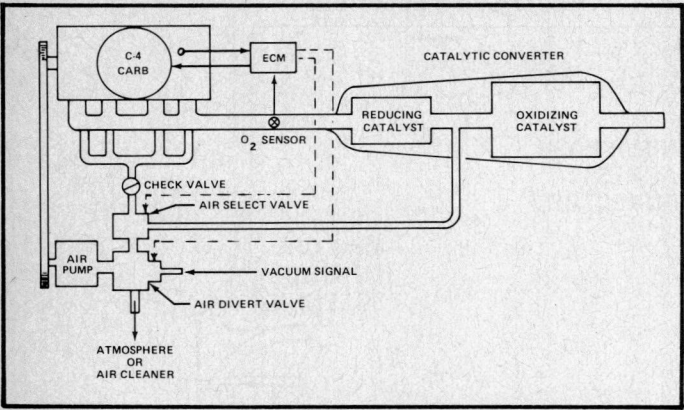

DISTRIBUTOR HEI MODULE

The computer will control the module above 200 rpm by applying a voltage to the by-pass line and signaling terminal E.

EST Control Circuit

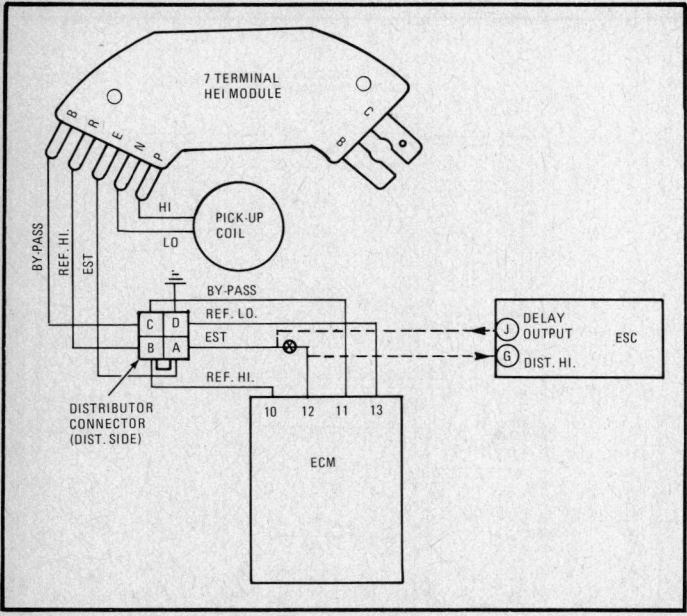

Current loss at terminals R or B will cause the distributor (HEI) module to take over. Loss of terminal E electronic spark timing will cause the engine to stop (assuming by-pass voltage is present).

If the engine is equipped with electronic spark control, the computer electronic spark timing line would go to the electronic spark control distributor high. The electronic spark control delay output would go to the HEI electronic spark timing input.

ELECTRONIC SPARK TIMING (EST)

Electronic spark timing is a computer controlled system that has all the engine spark timing information stored in memory. At various engine operating conditions as determined by rpm and manifold pressure, the system determines (from a table) the proper spark advance. It then produces the firing signal at the desired crankshaft position. Other parameters, such as coolant temperature and barometric pressure, can be sensed and this information used to modify, as appropriate, the spark advance number from the table. The system provides a much more flexible and accurate spark timing control than the conventional centrifugal and vacuum advance mechanisms in the distributor.

System Diagnosis
BUILT-IN DIAGNOSTIC SYSTEM

The computer controlled catalytic converter computer command control system should be considered as a possible trouble source of engine performance, fuel economy and exhaust emission complaints only after diagnostic checks, which apply to engines without the computer command control system, have been completed.

Before suspecting the computer command control system or any of its components as a trouble source, check the ignition system including the distributor, timing, spark plugs and wires. Check the air cleaner, evaporative emissions system, EFE system, PCV system, EGR valve and engine compression. Also inspect the intake manifold, vacuum hoses and hose connections for leaks. Inspect the carburetor mounting bolts.

The following symptoms could indicate a possible problem with the computer command control system.
1. Detonation
2. Stalls or rough idle, cold
3. Stalls or rough idle, hot
4. Missing
5. Hesitation
6. Surges
7. Sluggish performance
8. Poor gasoline mileage
9. Hard starting, cold
10. Hard starting, hot
11. Objectionable exhaust odor
12. Cuts out

A built-in diagnostic system catches problems which are most likely to occur. The self-diagnostic system lights a "CHECK ENGINE" light on the instrument panel when

Typical C-4 Non-Turbo Wiring Diagram

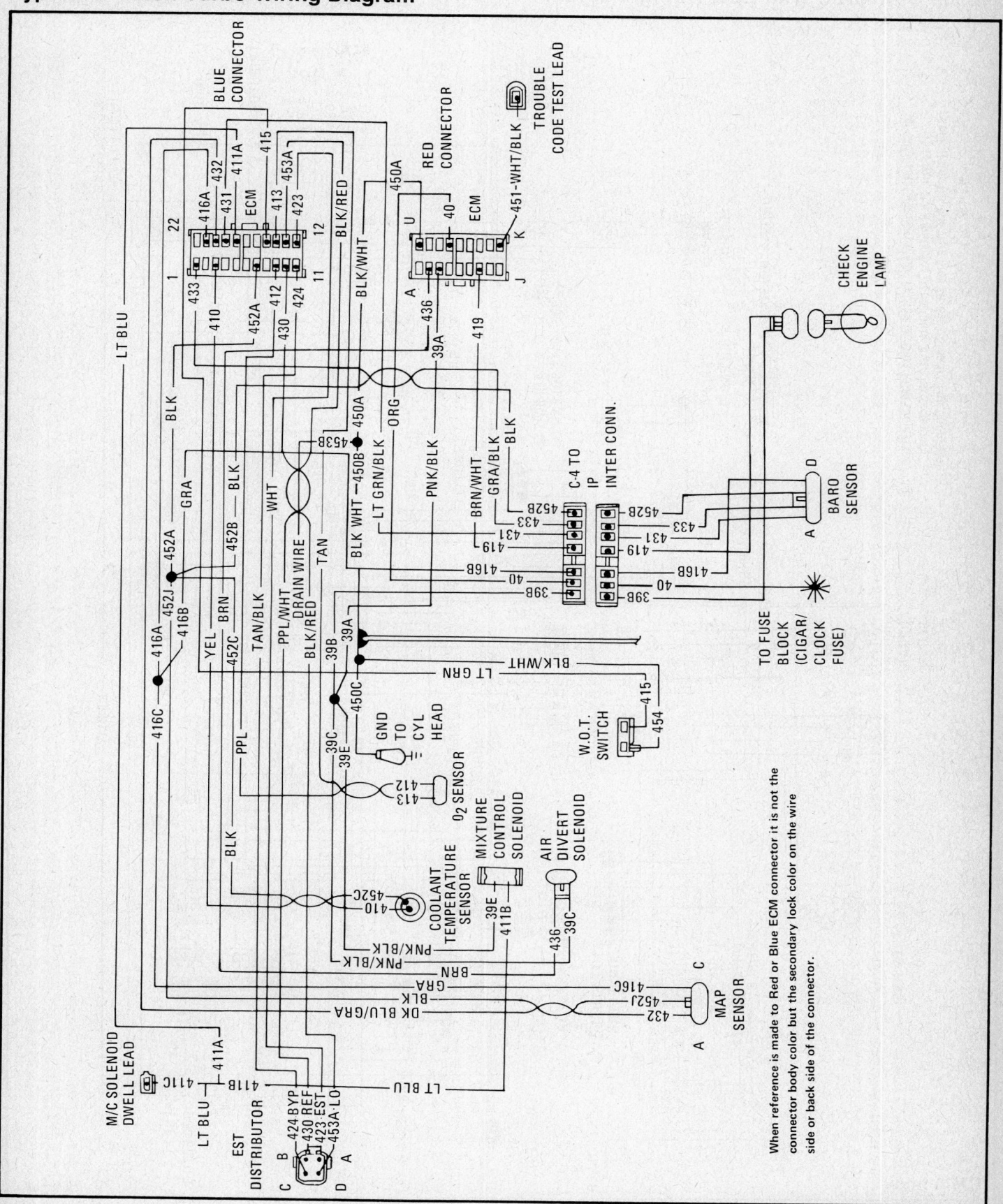

ENGINE CONTROLS
GM COMPUTER COMMAND CONTROL SYSTEM

Typical C-4 Turbo With ESC Wiring Diagram

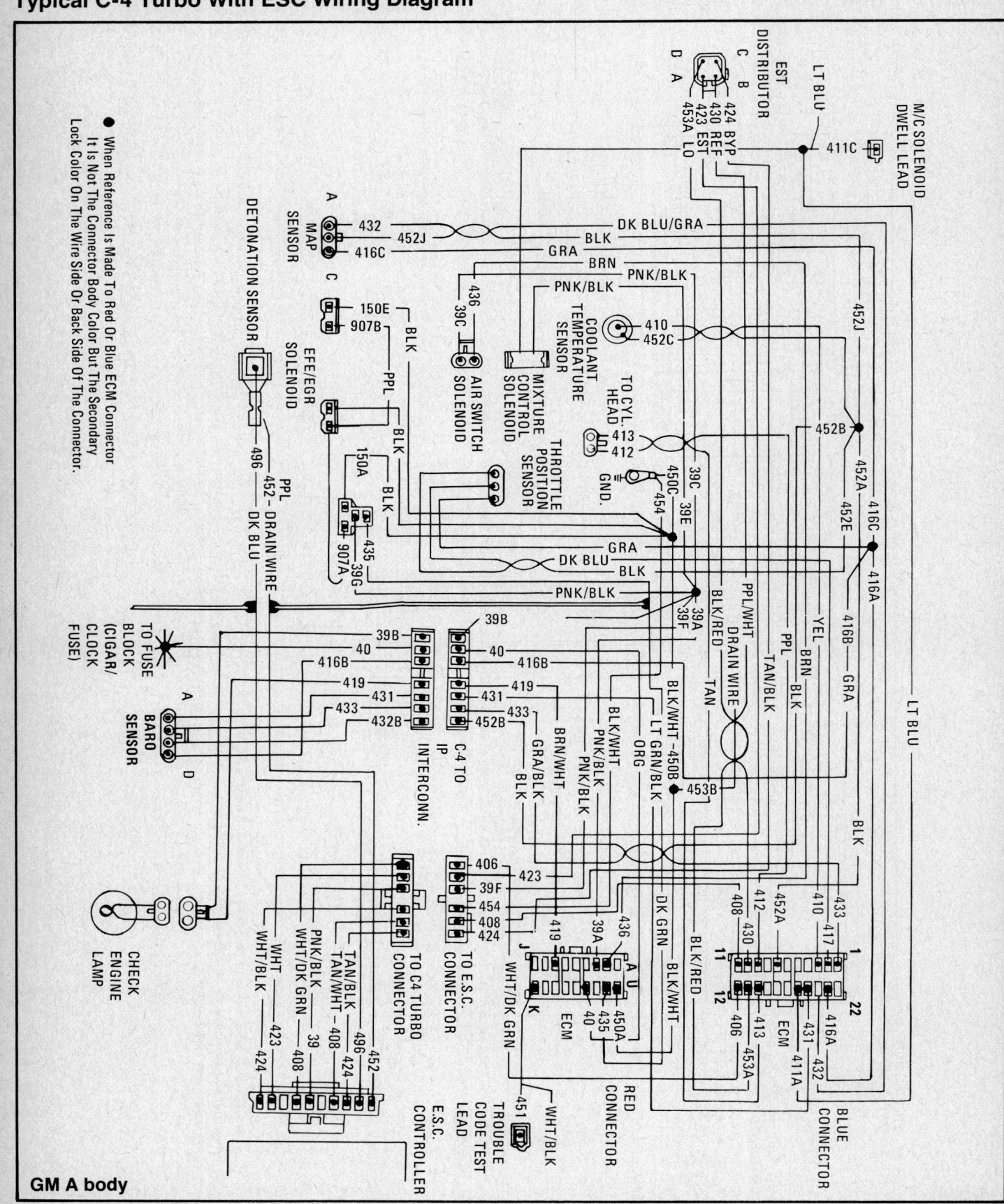

GM A body

Non-Turbocharged Functional Block Diagram

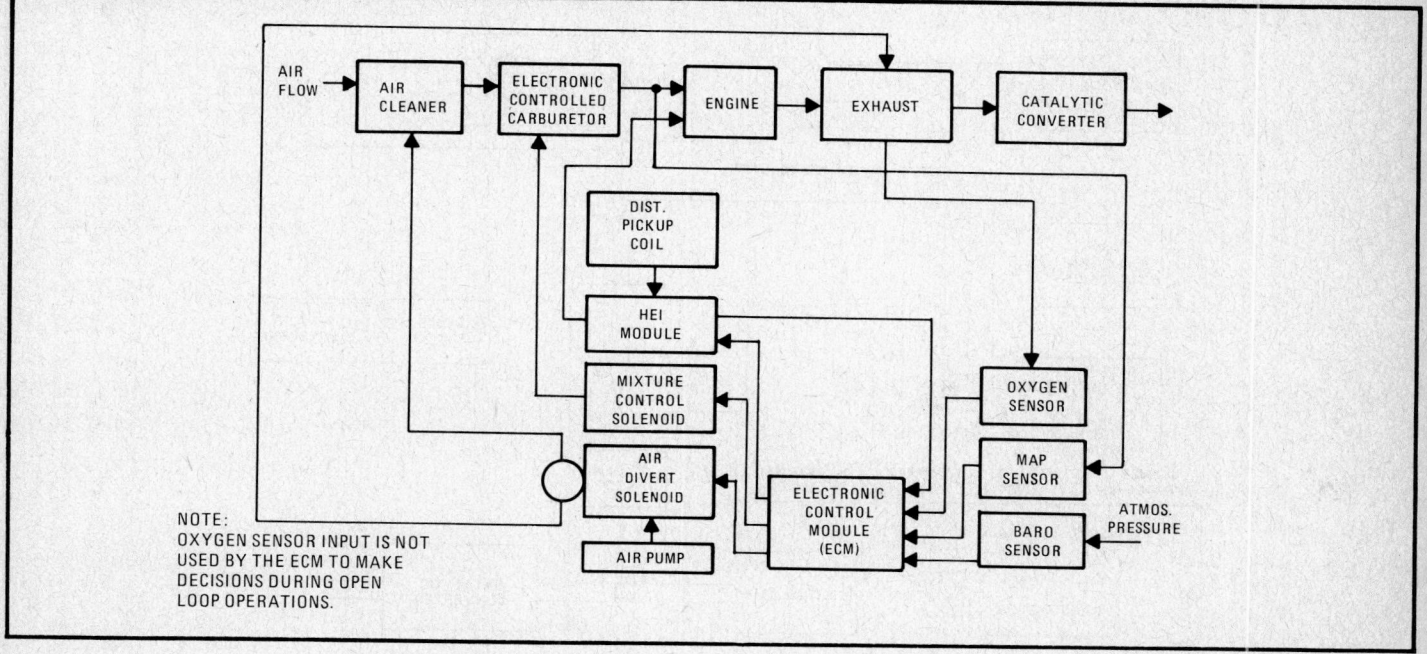

Turbocharged Functional Block Diagram

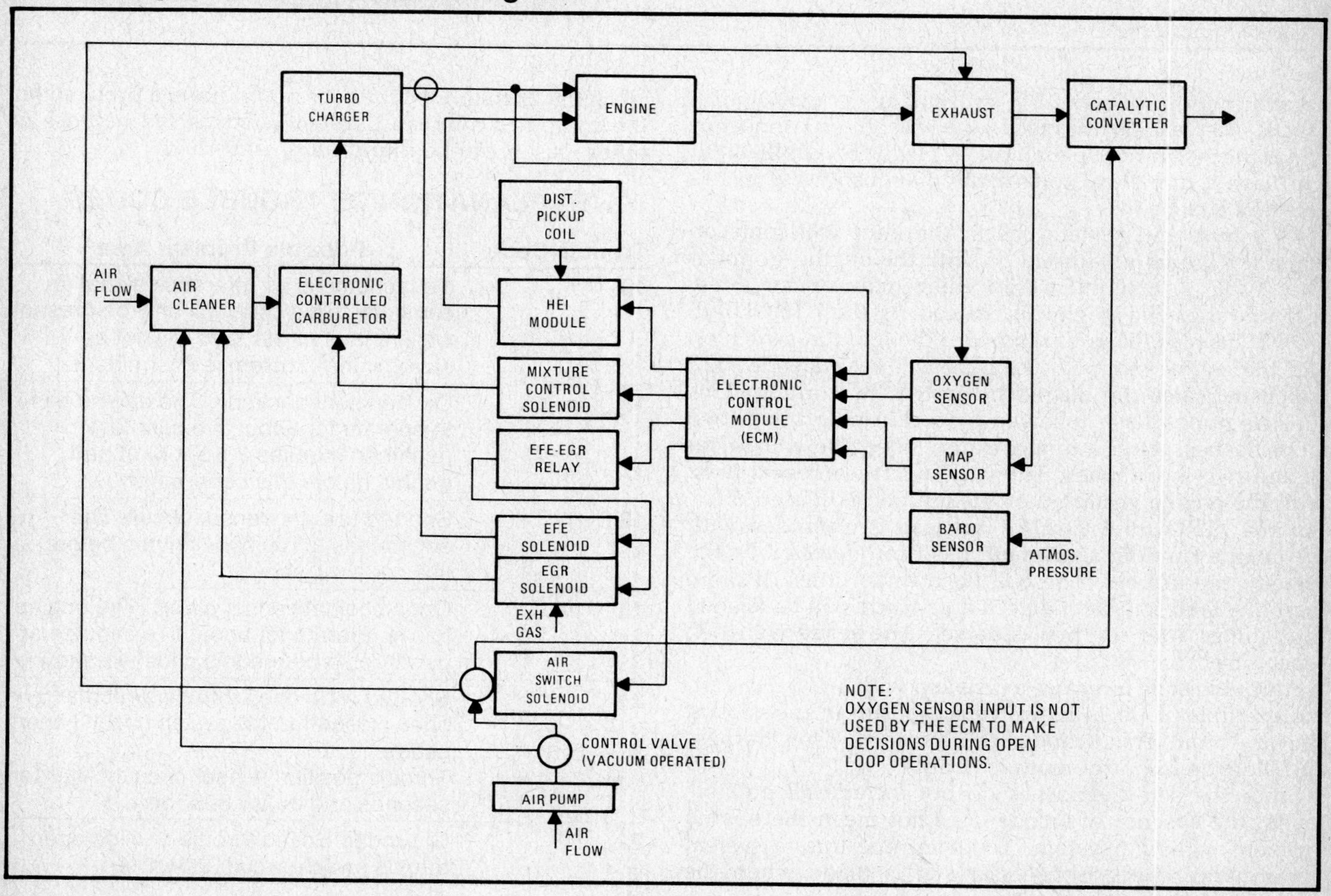

C-4 System Schematic

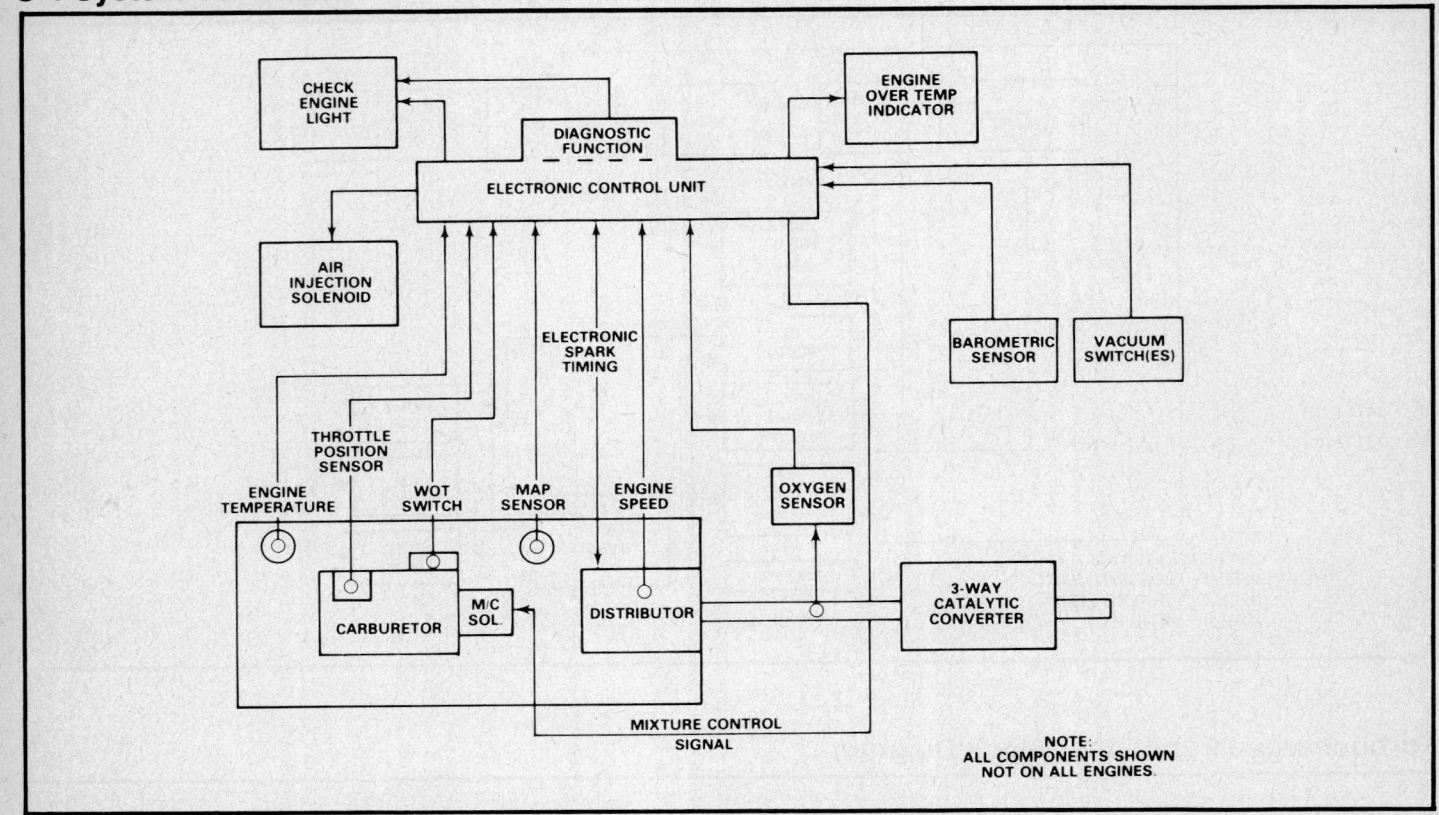

a malfunction occurs. By grounding a "TROUBLE CODE" test lead (white/black wire with green connector) under the instrument panel, the "CHECK ENGINE" light will flash a numerical code if the diagnostic system has detected a fault.

As a bulb and system check, the light will come on when the ignition is turned on with the engine stopped. The "CHECK ENGINE" light will remain on for a few seconds after the engine is started. If the "TROUBLE CODE" test lead is grounded with the ignition switch on and the engine stopped, the light will flash a code "12" which indicates the diagnostic system is working. This consists of one flash followed by a pause, and then two more flashes. After a longer pause, the code will be repeated two more times. The cycle will then repeat itself until the engine is started or the ignition is turned off.

If the "TROUBLE CODE" test lead is grounded with the engine running and a fault has been detected by the system, the trouble code will flash three times. If more than one fault has been detected, its code will be flashed three times after the first code set. The series will then repeat itself.

A trouble code indicates a problem with a given circuit. For example, code 14 indicates a problem in the coolant sensor circuit. This includes the coolant sensor, harness and electronic control module (ECM).

Since the self-diagnostics do not include all possible faults, the absence of a code does not mean there is no problem with the system. To determine this, a system performance check is necessary. It is made when the

"CHECK ENGINE" light does not indicate a problem but the computer command system is suspected because no other reason can be found for a complaint.

EXPLANATION OF TROUBLE CODES

Trouble Code	Possible Problem Area
12	No tachometer or reference signal to computer. This code will only be present while a fault exists, and will not be stored if the problem is intermittent.
13	Oxygen sensor circuit. The engine has to operate for about five minutes (eighteen minutes 3.8L V-6) at part throttle before this code will show.
13 & 14	Shorted coolant sensor circuit. The engine has to run two minutes before this code will show.
15	Open coolant sensor circuit. The engine has to operate for about five minutes at part throttle before this code will show.
21	Shorted wide open throttle switch and/or open closed-throttle switch circuit (when used). Throttle position sensor circuit. (After ten seconds and below 800 rpm).
22	Grounded closed throttle or wide open throttle switch circuit (2.5L L-4).

EXPLANATION OF TROUBLE CODES

Trouble Code	Possible Problem Area
21 & 22 (at same time)	Grounded wide open throttle switch circuit. (2.5L L-4).
23	Open or grounded carburetor solenoid circuit.
32	Barometric pressure sensor (BARO) output low.
32 & 55 (at same time)	Grounded +8V, V(REF) or faulty computer.
34	Manifold absolute pressure (MAP) sensor output high. (After ten seconds and below 800 rpm).
43	Throttle position sensor adjustment.
44	Lean oxygen sensor. Engine must be run for approximately five minutes in closed loop mode and part throttle at roadload (drive car) before this code will show.
45	Rich oxygen sensor. Engine must be run for approximately five minutes in closed loop mode and part throttle before this code will show.
44 & 45 (at same time)	Faulty oxygen sensor or open sensor low.
51	Faulty calibration unit (PROM), or improper PROM installaton.
52 & 53	"CHECK ENGINE" light off, intermittent computer problem. "CHECK ENGINE" light on, faulty computer (replace).
54	Faulty carburetor solenoid and/or computer.
55	Faulty oxygen sensor, open manifold absolute pressure sensor or computer (3.8 LV-6). Faulty throttle position sensor or computer (except 3.8 LV-6). Faulty computer (2.5L L-4).

C-4 Diagnostic Test Lead

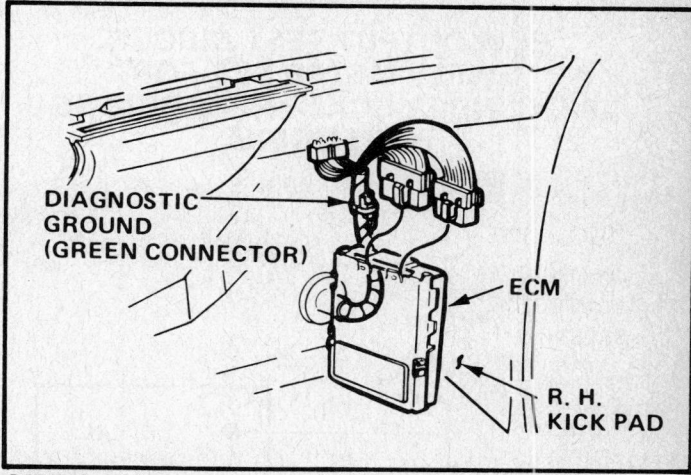

GM B body

DWELLMETER CHECK

The computer command system performance is checked by connecting a dwellmeter to the pigtail connector in the mixture control solenoid wiring harness. Dwell, used in computer command system performance diagnosis, is the time that the M/C solenoid is closed or energized. The dwellmeter will translate this time into degrees. The 6 cylinder 0 to 60° scale on the dwellmeter is used for this reading.

When a dwellmeter is connected to a contact point ignition system, it measures the amount of time the points are closed and converts that time to degrees of rotation. The ability of the dwellmeter to make this kind of conversion makes it an ideal tool to check the amount of time the computer internal switch is closed, thus energizing the mixture control solenoid. The only difference is that the degree scale on the meter is more like percent of solenoid time than degrees of dwell.

CHILTON CAUTION *Use care in connecting the dwellmeter and tachometer.*

Connect the positive clip lead of the dwellmeter to the mixture control solenoid pigtail connector. Attach the

C-4 Diagnostic Test Lead

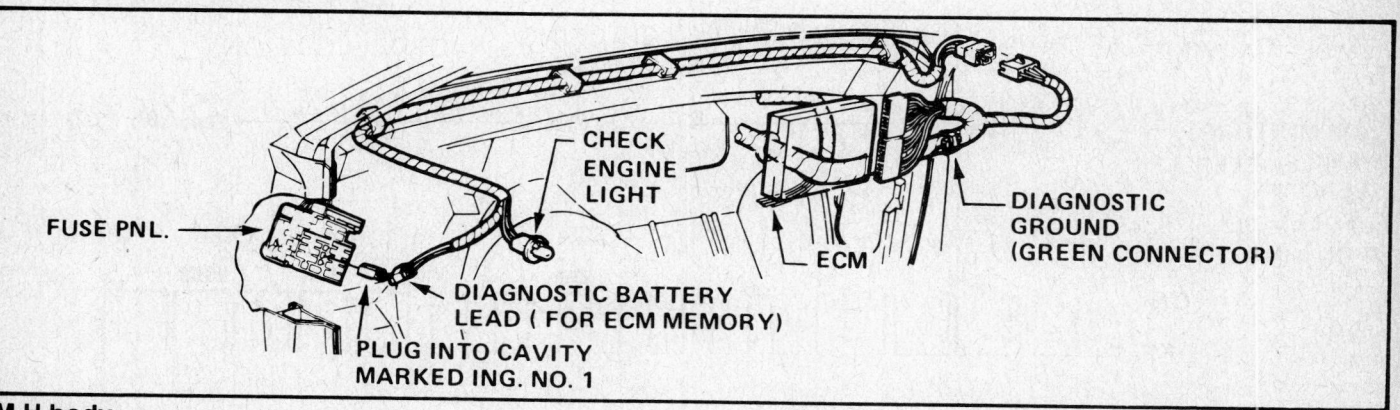

GM H body

Dwellmeter Hook-Up

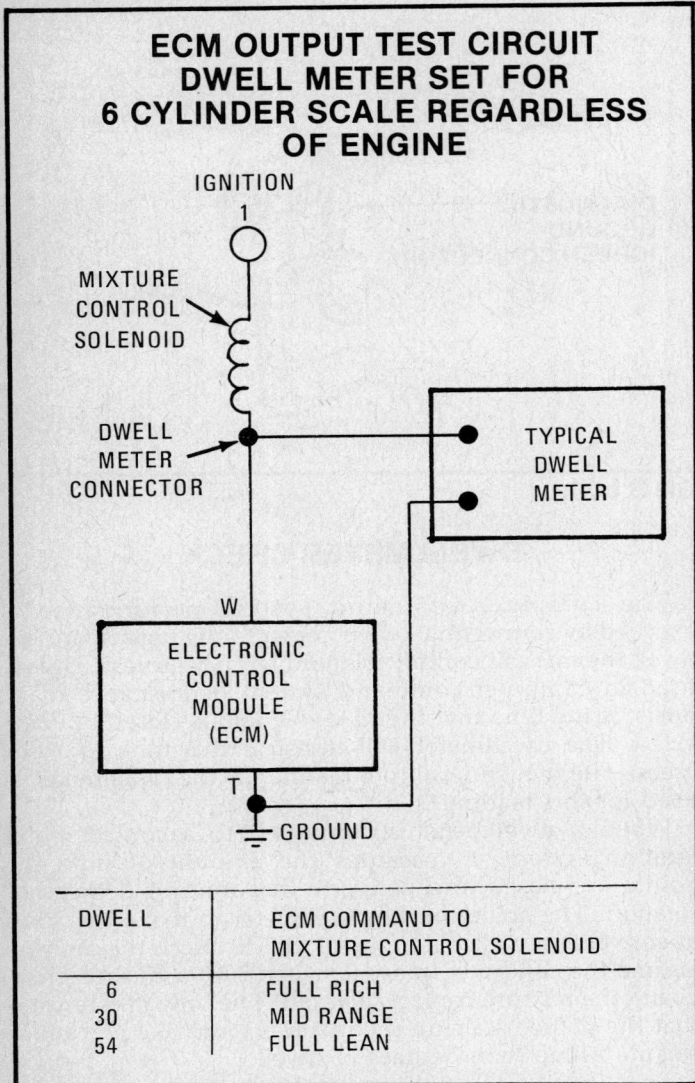

ECM OUTPUT TEST CIRCUIT DWELL METER SET FOR 6 CYLINDER SCALE REGARDLESS OF ENGINE

DWELL	ECM COMMAND TO MIXTURE CONTROL SOLENOID
6	FULL RICH
30	MID RANGE
54	FULL LEAN

Tachometer Connection

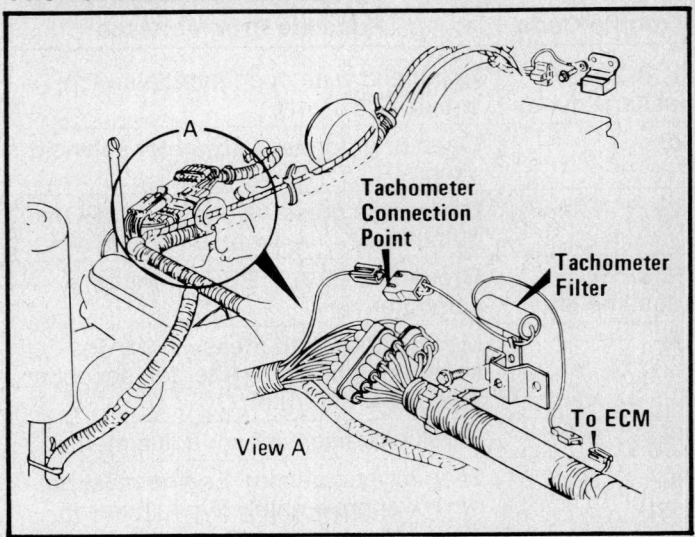

View A

other dwellmeter clip lead to the ground. Do not allow the clip leads to contact other conductive cables or hoses which could interfere with accurate readings. Most dwellmeters will work. However, if one causes a change in engine operation when connected to the mixture control lead, it should not be used.

A tachometer should be connected to the tachometer pigtail connector to provide engine rpm information. This information is used with the dwellmeter readings for diagnostic purposes. Care should be used in making this connection. Do not connect between the tach filter and the computer because the tach signal is much weaker at that point. Connecting a tachometer to this weak signal may prevent the signal from reaching the computer.

Dwellmeter Readings

The mixture control solenoid moves the metering rods up and down ten times per second. This frequency was

Analyzing Dwellmeter Readings

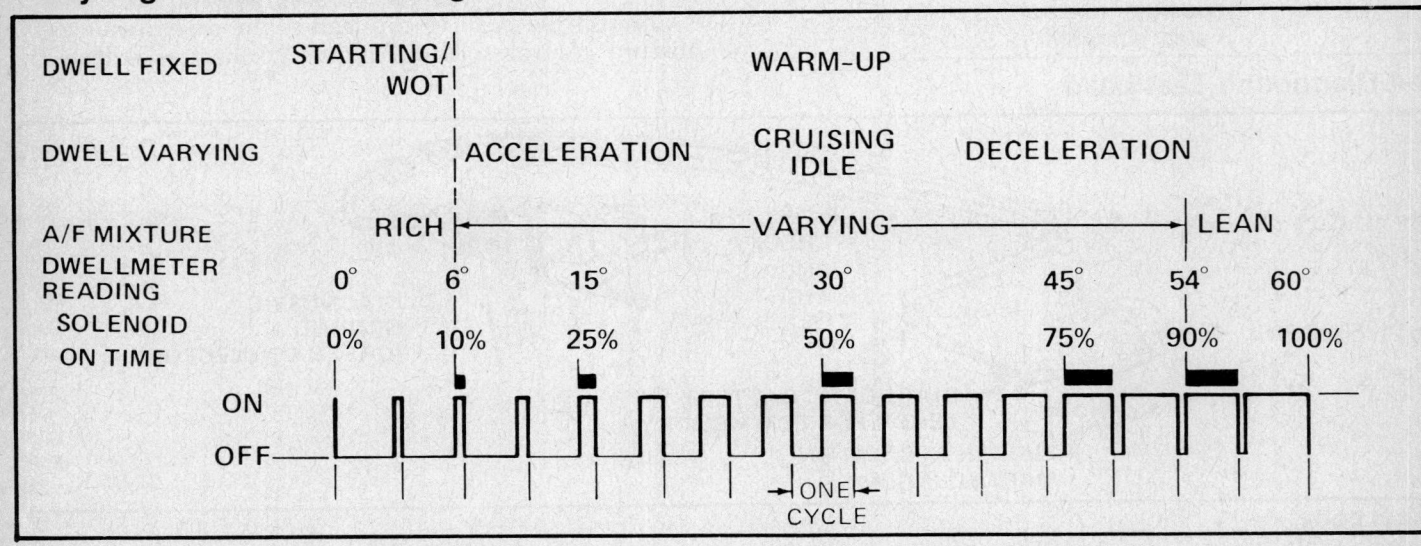

chosen to be slow enough to allow full stop to stop mixture control solenoid travel, but fast enough to prevent any undesirable influence on vehicle response.

On a normal operating engine, the dwell at both idle and part throttle reads somewhere between 10 and 50° and will vary. This means that the needle will continually move up and down the scale. The amount it moves does not matter, only the fact that it does move is important.

This is called closed loop operation, meaning that the dwell is being varied by the signal sent to the computer by an oxygen sensor in the exhaust manifold. Under certain operating conditions, such as wide open throttle (WOT) or a cold engine, the dwell will be a fixed value and the needle will be steady. This is called open loop, meaning that the oxygen sensor has no effect on the dwell.

TYPICAL SYSTEM PERFORMANCE SUMMARY

Engine Condition	Inputs to ECM	M/C Solenoid Operation	Dwellmeter Readings
Cranking	Tachometer less than 200 rpm	Solenoid off (rich mixture)	0°
Warm-up	Tach above 200 rpm 02 sensor under 600°F Coolant under 66°F Less than 10 seconds since starting [1]	Fixed command from ECM to M/C solenoid	Fixed reading between 10 and 50°
Warm operation idle and cruising	02 sensor above 600° Coolant above 66°F After 10 seconds have elapsed [1]	M/C solenoid controlled by 02 sensor information to ECM	Varying anywhere between 10 and 50° (faster with higher rpm)
Acceleration and deceleration	Throttle position sensor closed at idle Throttle position sensor partially open at part throttle Tachometer rpm M/C solenoid signal	Momentary programmed signal from ECM during period after change until 02 sensor corrects itself and resumes control of M/C solenoid	Momentary change cannot be read on dwellmeter, will be varying between changes
Wide open throttle	Throttle position sensor fully open	Very rich command to M/C solenoid	6°

[1] Time varies from 10 to 160 seconds, depending on engine and ECM

FORD FEEDBACK CARBURETOR

System Operation

The system is equipped to supply input signals to the microprocessor control unit module (MCU). These inputs originate from the exhaust gas oxygen sensor, cold temperature vacuum switch, idle tracking switch and the rpm tach input from the coil.

The MCU module continuously monitors the input signals and computes the correct operating mode for a given condition. Output signals from the MCU module are applied to control the vacuum solenoid regulator, thermactor bypass control solenoid and the thermactor diverter control solenoid (manual transmission only).

The primary function of the 2.3L MCU module is to control the vacuum regulator solenoid. The MCU module sends ten signals per second to the vacuum regulator

solenoid in a timed duty cycle. By varying the "ON" time to the "OFF" time of the cycle, the MCU module is able to maintain or change the air-fuel mixture.

The MCU module does not control ignition timing. The system uses a conventional distributor and coil.

OPERATING MODES

The MCU system has three operating modes. These modes are system initialization (start-up), open loop and closed loop.

System Initialization (Start-Up)

The MCU module will initialize when battery power is applied to the computer pior to engine cranking and again immediately with engine starting. During initialization, the duty cycle to the vacuum regulator

Microprocessor Control System

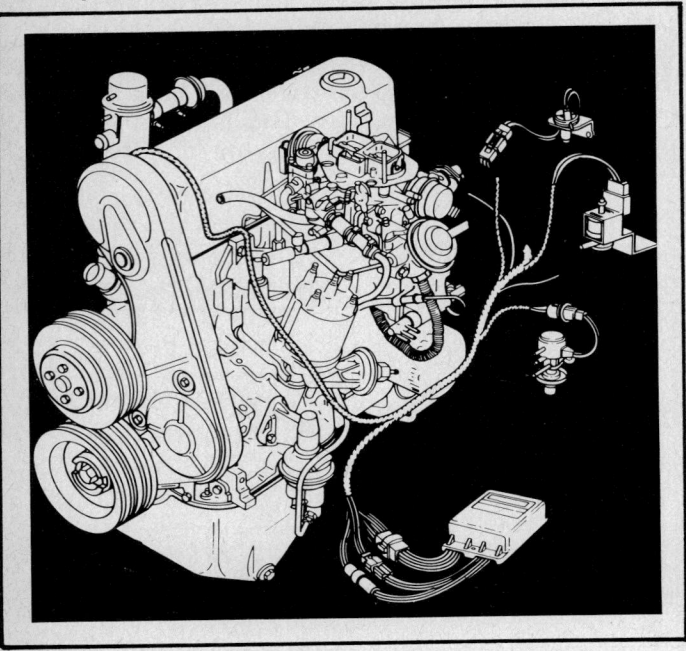

solenoid is maintained at 50%. After starting, initialization lasts for only a fraction of a second. Then, the MCU system goes into the open or closed loop.

Open Loop

The system is in the open loop mode when either the cold temperature vacuum switch or idle tracking switch is activated. In the open loop mode, the MCU module will control the duty cycle with "ON" time signals to the vacuum regulator solenoid. These will provide a calibrated air-fuel mixture.

Closed Loop

With the proper signals from the idle tracking switch and the cold temperature switch, the MCU module changes to the closed loop mode for close range monitoring and control of the air-fuel ratio. The exhaust gas oxygen sensor monitors the exhaust gas to determine if the engine is running rich or lean. This information is used by the MCU module to adjust the carburetor to the air-fuel ratio desired for the operating condition.

Signals from the MCU module, which produce carburetor adjustments, are calibrated. This provides a damping effect to minimize over-correction and abrupt changes.

System Components

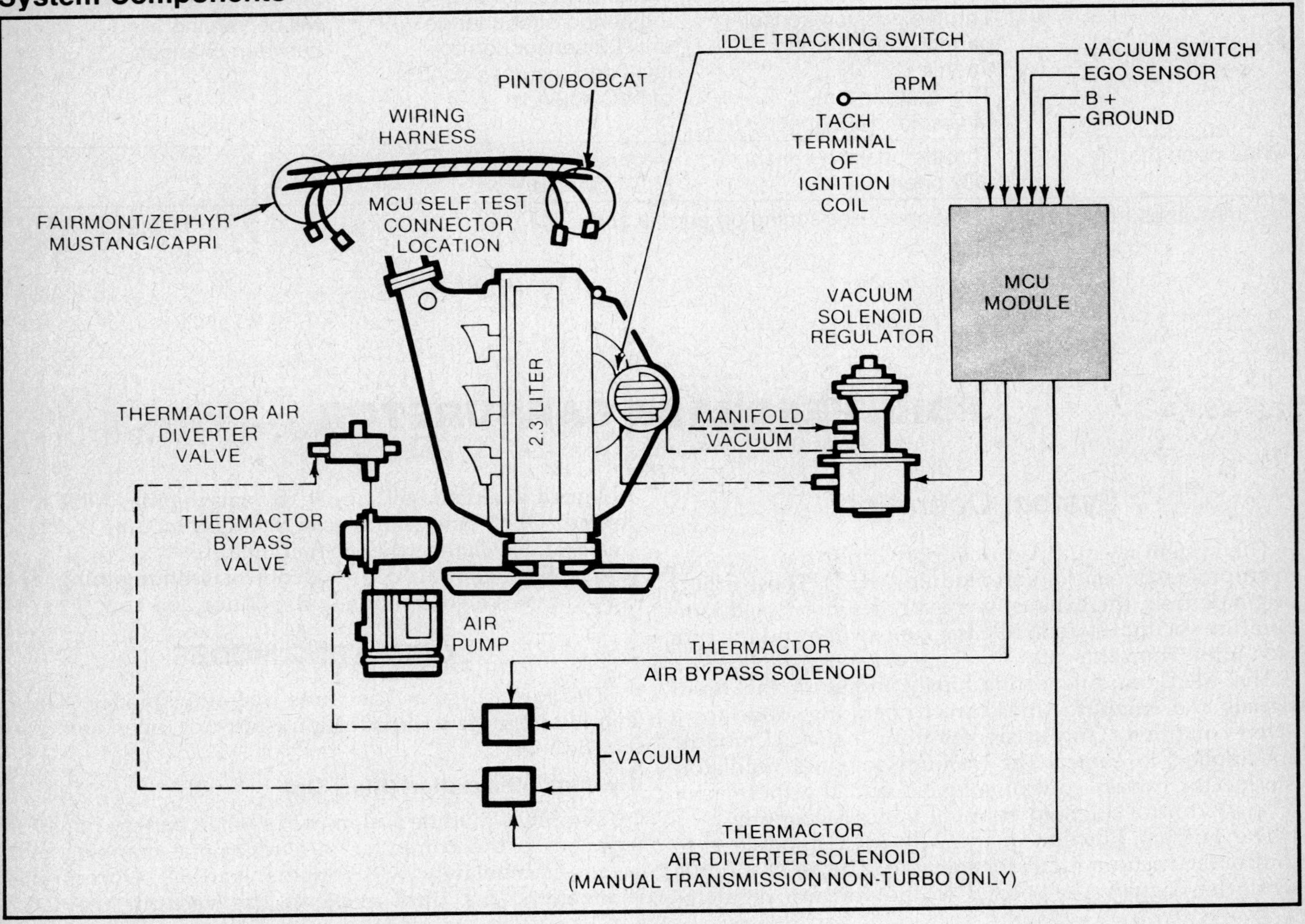

IDLE TRACKING SWITCH

VACUUM SWITCH
EGO SENSOR
B +
GROUND

PINTO/BOBCAT

RPM

WIRING
HARNESS

TACH
TERMINAL
OF
IGNITION
COIL

FAIRMONT/ZEPHYR
MUSTANG/CAPRI

MCU SELF TEST
CONNECTOR
LOCATION

MCU
MODULE

VACUUM
SOLENOID
REGULATOR

2.3 LITER

THERMACTOR AIR
DIVERTER
VALVE

MANIFOLD
VACUUM

THERMACTOR
BYPASS
VALVE

AIR
PUMP

THERMACTOR
AIR BYPASS SOLENOID

VACUUM

THERMACTOR
AIR DIVERTER SOLENOID
(MANUAL TRANSMISSION NON-TURBO ONLY)

System Components
MCU MODULE

The MCU is the brain of the system. It is a solid-state, programmed micro-computer. It takes the information inputs and uses its program to provide output control signals to the control solenoids. The MCU module receives its power from the battery through the ignition switch.

The module is located either in the engine compartment or under the instrument panel to the left of the steering column. It appears similar to an ignition switch module, but differences in the wiring connectors prevent interchangeability.

With the engine cold or at idle, the air-fuel ratio is at a preset level. When the engine is warm and off idle, the air-fuel mixture is adjusted by a signal from the exhaust gas oxygen sensor. These adjustments are made by an "ON-OFF" control signal from the module. For example, when the sensor signals a rich mixture, control "ON" time is increased, while "ON" time is decreased for a lean mixture.

MCU Control Module

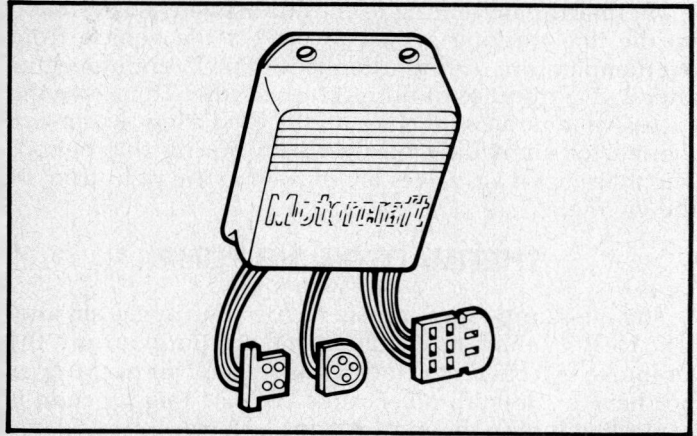

COLD TEMPERATURE VACUUM SWITCH

The cold temperature switch is a normally closed switch, with vacuum controlled through a ported vacuum switch (PVS). The MCU system will enter a closed loop

Cold Temperature Vacuum Switch

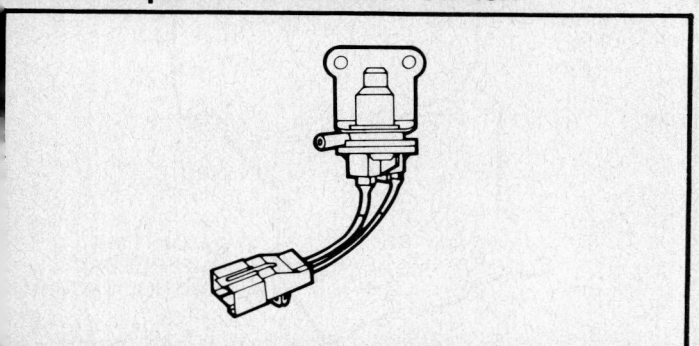

mode when the cold temperature switch is activated, provided the vehicle is operating at part throttle.

When the engine is cold, the PVS valve blocks vacuum from the cold temperature vacuum switch. The switch position provides a ground path as a signal to the control unit. When the engine is above 95°F, the PVS valve opens to allow ported vacuum to activate the normally closed switch. With the contacts opened, the ground path signal to the control unit is interrupted.

IDLE TRACKING SWITCH

The idle tracking switch is a limit switch used to detect the throttle in the idle position. It is normally closed but opens at closed throttle, sending the MCU system into an open loop mode. The idle tracking switch is mounted on the rear of the carburetor.

Idle Tracking Switch

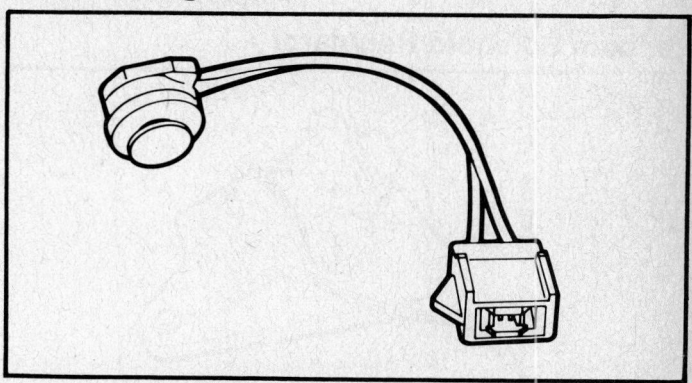

EXHAUST GAS OXYGEN SENSOR

The exhaust gas oxygen sensor is threaded into the exhaust manifold, directly in the path of the exhaust gas stream. The sensor provides information to the computer about the air-fuel ratio, indicated by the oxygen concentration in the exhaust gases.

Exhaust Gas Oxygen Sensor

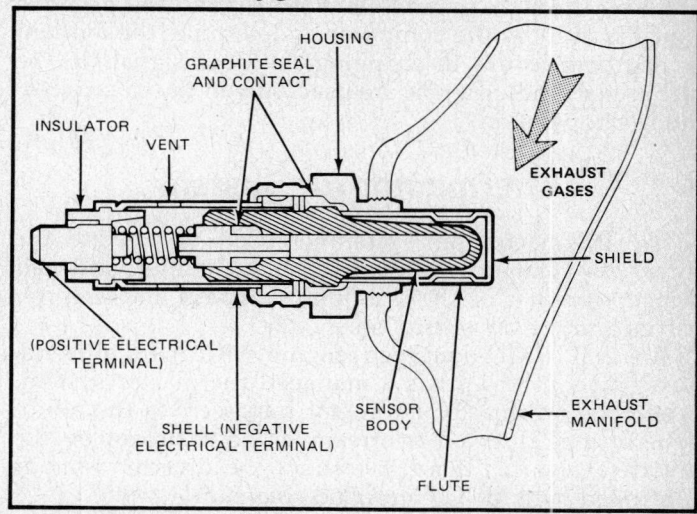

When it senses a rich mixture, the sensor generates a high voltage signal to the computer. A low voltage is generated when a lean mixture (high oxygen level in the exhaust) is sensed. The voltage signal is used by the MCU module for adjustment of the duty cycle during the closed loop mode of operation.

VACUUM SOLENOID REGULATOR

The vacuum solenoid regulator controls manifold vacuum which has been regulated to 5" Hg. This solenoid receives ten signals per second from the MCU module. The vacuum applied to the metering rod of the carburetor is controlled by varying the duty cycle ("ON-OFF" ratio of the MCU signal).

At 100% duty cycle, 5" Hg. vacuum is applied to the metering rod, producing a full lean condition. At 0% duty cycle, the metering rod diaphragm is vented to the atmosphere, producing a full rich condition.

Vacuum Solenoid Regulator

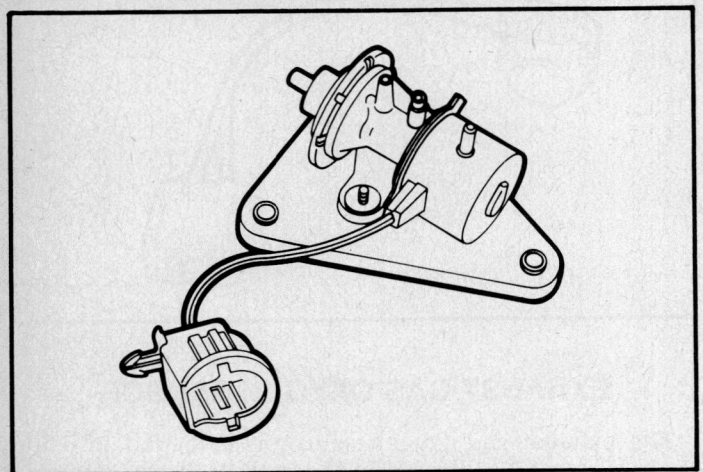

RPM INPUT TO THE MCU MODULE

The rpm signal to the computer is taken from the "tach" terminal of the ignition coil. This circuit is identified by the dark green-yellow dot wire. This negative signal is used by the computer to determine the amount of damping to use in changing the duty signals to the carburetor. These signals are used only in the closed loop mode of operation.

Thermactor Air System

The thermactor air system is used to operate the three-way catalytic converter system. The thermactor air system consists of the air pump, bypass and diverter valves and the air control solenoids.

The 2.3L MCU-equipped engine with manual transmission (non-turbo) has a managed thermactor system. When the thermactor air is not bypassed to the atmosphere, it is directed upstream or downstream by the diverter valve. In this application, the diverter valve is controlled by a MCU-controlled solenoid.

Thermactor Air System

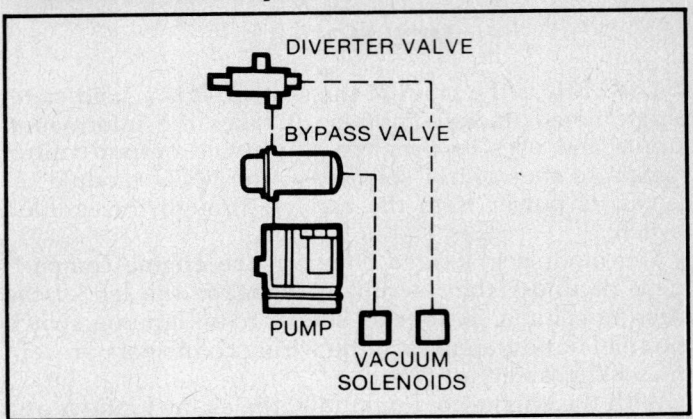

The automatic transmission and turbocharged 2.3L engine do not have an air diverter solenoid or a managed thermactor air system. Routing for the thermactor air is determined by engine performance, mode and operating temperature. The valves are pre-calibrated. During normal engine operation, thermactor air is directed downstream. This provides fresh air to the catalyst for the oxidation of HC and CO gases in the exhaust.

Thermactor air venting to the atmosphere is controlled by the idle tracking switch to protect the vehicle from overtemperature during extended idling. Venting begins after 2–2½ minutes of uninterrupted idle. To reduce the excessive amounts of HC and CO during warm-up, thermactor air is directed upstream during this period. The thermactor air valves are located at the right front of the engine.

THERMACTOR AIR PUMP

The air pump is an impeller-type centrifugal air filter fan. Heavier than air contaminants are thrown from the air intake by centrifugal force. This type of air pump does not have a pressure relief valve because this function is controlled by the thermactor bypass valve.

Thermactor Air Control Solenoids

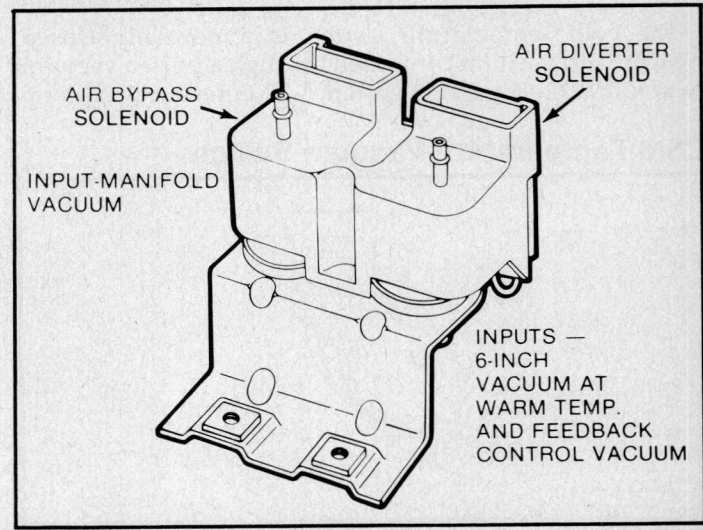

THERMACTOR BYPASS SOLENOID AND DIVERTER SOLENOID

The bypass valve operation and diverter valve operation for non-turbocharged engines with manual transmissions are controlled by the thermactor air control solenoids. The solenoids route vacuum in three possible directions: bypass, upstream or downstream.

In the bypass mode, air is vented to the atmosphere. In the upstream mode, air is injected into the exhaust manifold. In the downstream mode, air is directed into the three-way catalyst between the two catalyst stages.

Ignition System

A conventional ignition system is used with the MCU-equipped 2.3L engine. The ignition system includes the Duraspark® II coil and ignition module, and a conventional distributor. The MCU system does not control ignition timing. The primary function of the MCU system is the monitoring and adjustment of the air-fuel ratio. The two separate systems complement each other to produce performance in a wide range of operating conditions.

Fuel System

CARBURETOR CONTROL

Controlled vacuum from the vacuum regulator solenoid is channeled to the cavity above the metering rod diaphragm. With no vacuum present, the valve spring causes the valve to move to its lowest (richest) position, where maximum fuel can pass through the orifice. As vacuum is applied to the diaphragm, spring pressure is overcome and the metering rod rises, making the mixture leaner.

Electric Fuel Pump

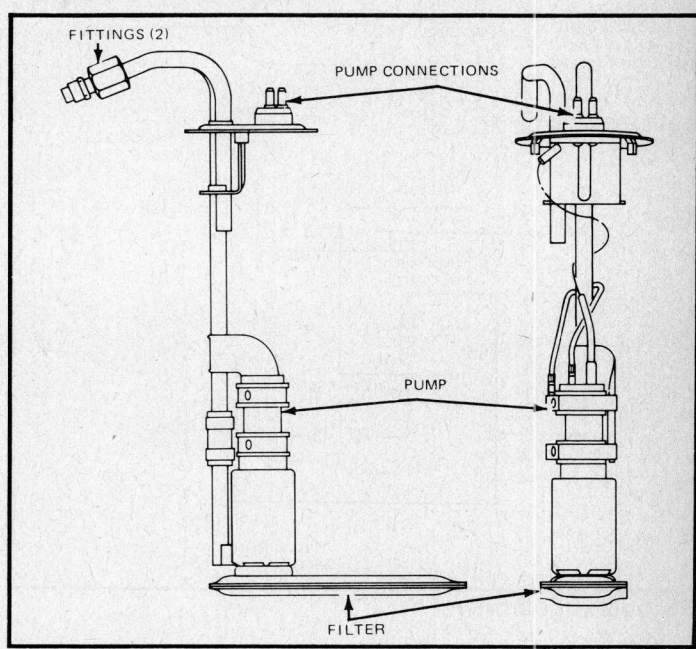

Fuel Metering System

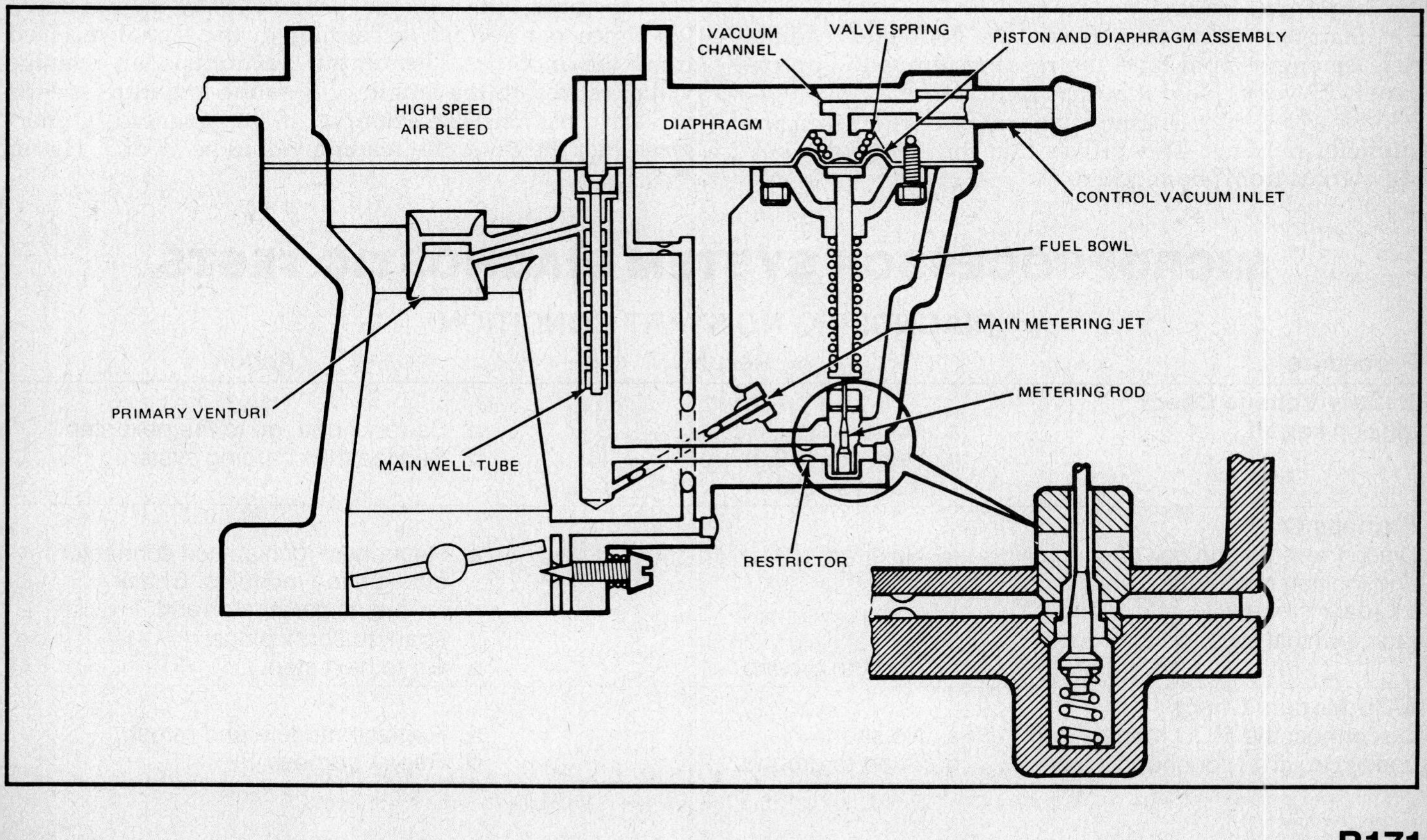

Electric Fuel Pump Wiring Diagram

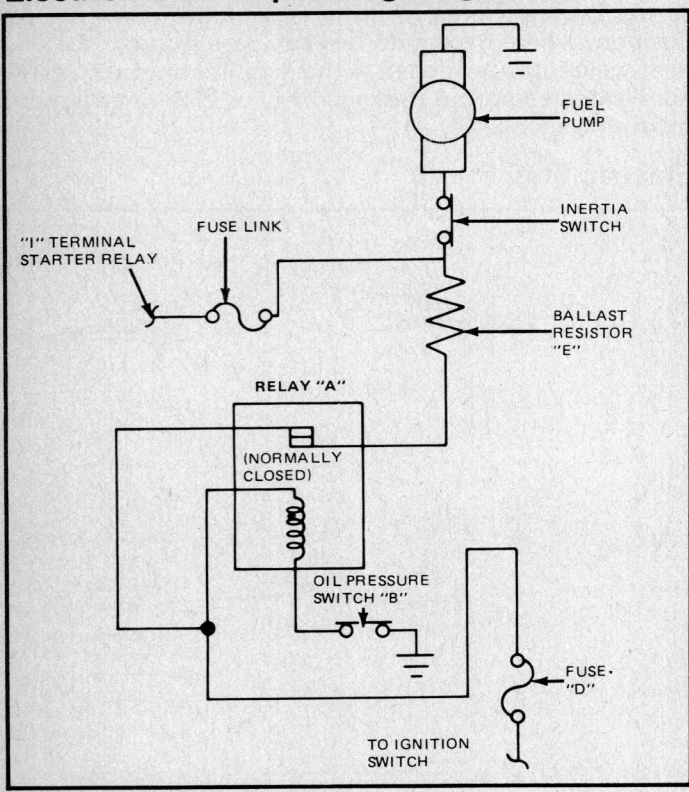

Turbocharged only

Solenoid Test With Engine Running

1. Connect a voltmeter to the vacuum solenoid at the regulator input lead.
2. Start the engine and observe the voltmeter reading. Increase engine rpm until the reading jumps to approximately 12 volts. Hold it at that rpm.
3. Slowly reduce engine rpm and check to see if the voltmeter pulsates. This proves that the solenoid is getting signals from the module.

The metering valve is calibrated so that the maximum vacuum signal supplied to the diaphragm by the regulator/solenoid (5" Hg.) raises the rod to its highest (leanest) position.

If the feedback fuel valve piston and diaphragm assembly is removed for any reason during servicing of the Holley Model 6500 carburetor, it is essential that this procedure is followed during reassembly to insure proper operation.

1. Apply one drop of Loctite® or equivalent to the threads in each of the three tapped retaining screw holes.
2. Position the feedback fuel diaphragm and piston assembly over the spring so that the attaching screw holes align with the tapped holes in the upper body (air horn). Make sure the diaphragm is properly installed. One end of the spring should be over the end of the adjustment screw, the other end centered within the cupped washer of the diaphragm and piston assembly.
3. Install and tighten the three retaining screws.

VACUUM SOLENOID/REGULATOR

The component that supplies the vacuum signal to the carburetor feedback valve is the vacuum solenoid/regulator. When current from the control module is applied to the solenoid coil, the armature moves upward until it rests on its upper seat. This blocks the atmospheric pressure passage and opens the vacuum passage to the output port. The output vacuum will now reach a constant 5" Hg. When current is removed from the coil, the armature moves downward until it rests against its lower seat. This opens the atmospheric passage and closes the vacuum passage, causing the output vacuum to drop to zero.

In operation, the armature actually cycles up and down ten times per second, according to the signal received from the module. The output vacuum is an average value, related to the length of time the armature spends in each position. For example, if the solenoid is energized half the time, the reading would be ½ of 5" Hg. or 2½" Hg.

MICROPROCESSOR SYSTEM DIAGNOSTIC TESTS

DIAGNOSING NO START CONDITION

Procedure	Result	Action
Battery Voltage Check Ignition key off.	a. 10-16 volts b. Less than 10, more than 16 volts	a. Battery good, go to the next step. b. Service the charging system.
Harness Check Disconnect ignition coil connector and ignition module. Check circuit 11 (dark green with yellow dot) tach terminal for short to ground.	a. No short b. Short to ground	a. Reconnect ignition coil connector and ignition modules. Check for fuel to carburetor and spark to spark plugs. b. Go to next step.
MCU Module Check Disconnect the MCU module and check circuit 11 for short to ground.	a. No short b. Short to ground	a. Replace module and retest. b. Repair harness.

MICROPROCESSOR SYSTEM DIAGNOSTIC TESTS

DIAGNOSING COLD ENGINE CONDITION
If condition occurs only when engine is cold, perform this test first

Procedure	Result	Action
Ported Vacuum Switch (PVS) (PVS) Check This test must be performed without starting the engine and with the PVS temperature below 80°F. Disconnect the hose from the cold temperature switch and leave disconnected. Remove the vacuum hose from the carburetor port. Apply vacuum to the hose.	a. Vacuum is held b. Vacuum is not held	a. PVS is good. b. Check for leaks. If there are no leaks, replace PVS and repeat vacuum test.

MCU SELF-TEST PROGRAM
Preliminary Testing

1. A routine pre-test can produce immediate results and help identify a service condition needing correction.
2. With the engine off, place transmission in Park or Neutral. Set the parking brake and block the wheels.
3. Turn off all accessories.
4. Check the vacuum hoses for tight connections.
5. Check the wiring harness, tach lead to coil and MCU components for bad connections and physical damage.
6. Start the engine and warm to operating temperature.
7. While engine is warming, check for vacuum leaks and for exhaust leaks around the exhaust manifold and the exhaust gas oxygen sensor.

MCU SELF-TEST PROGRAM
Test Preparations

1. Perform the PVS check and the preliminary checks first.
2. With the engine off, ground the brown single-pin connector. On Fairmont, Zephyr, Mustang, and Capri, this connector is located along the right side dash panel, engine side. On Pinto and Bobcat, it is located along the left side dash panel, engine side.
3. Connect voltmeter across the thermactor air bypass solenoid. Use the 0−15 volt scale.
4. Connect a tachometer to the engine.
5. System is now ready to test.

MCU Self-Test Connectors

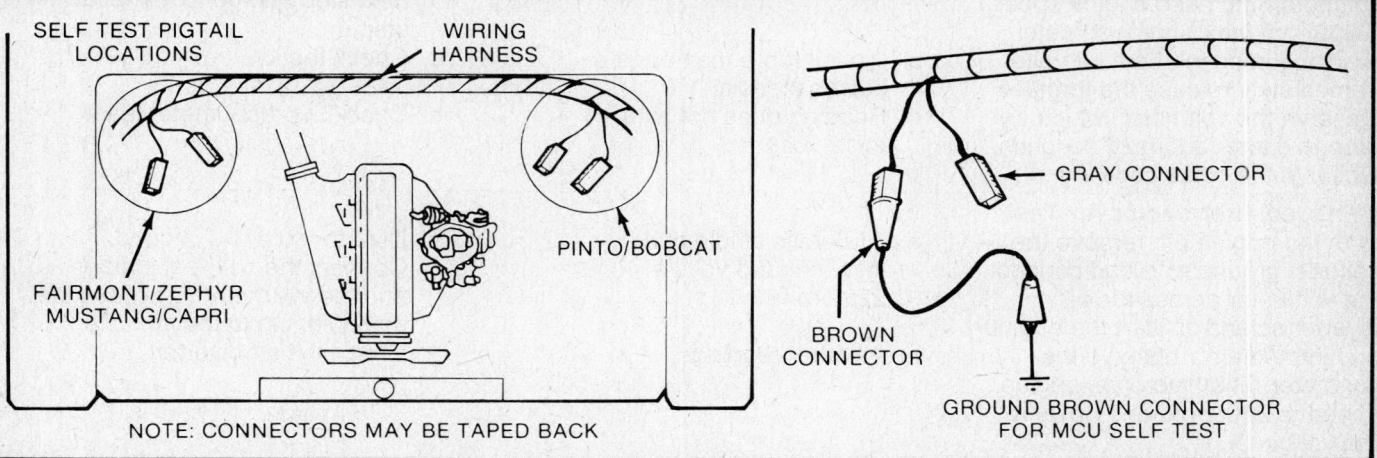

SELF TEST PIGTAIL LOCATIONS · WIRING HARNESS · FAIRMONT/ZEPHYR MUSTANG/CAPRI · PINTO/BOBCAT · GRAY CONNECTOR · BROWN CONNECTOR · GROUND BROWN CONNECTOR FOR MCU SELF TEST · NOTE: CONNECTORS MAY BE TAPED BACK

MICROPROCESSOR SYSTEM DIAGNOSTIC TEST

MCU SELF-TEST PROGRAM
Test Preparations

Procedure	Result	Action
Cold Temperature Vacuum Switch Check With the engine off, turn the ignition key to "RUN". Observe the voltmeter for a pulse code signal. Allow 5 seconds for signal to start after first pulse.	a. Pulses steadily b. One pulse c. Steady high or low reading	a. Switch is good. Go to next step. b. Check switch for continuity. c. Recheck jumper wire at brown test connector and ground. Check voltmeter connections. If same results, substitute a good switch.
Cold Temperature Vacuum Switch Check Disconnect vacuum hose from switch and apply 10″ Hg. vacuum to the switch. (If vacuum will not hold, check for leaks and replace switch if necessary.) Turn the ignition key to "RUN" and observe the voltmeter for pulse code signal.	a. One pulse b. Pulses steadily	a. Switch is good. Go to next step. b. Check switch for continuity.
Spark Port Vacuum Check Start the engine and run at 2500 to 2800 rpm. Check for vacuum at cold temperature vacuum switch. There should be greater than 5″ vacuum at the switch.	a. Vacuum at hose b. No vacuum at hose	a. Go to the next step. b. Check hoses, PVS and carburetor port for restriction, contamination, damage or vacuum leaks. Repair as needed and go to next step.

MCU SELF-TEST PROGRAM

Procedure	Result	Action
Idle Tracking Switch Check Turn the ignition key off and reconnect the hose to the cold temperature vacuum switch. Start the engine and observe the voltmeter. Increase engine speed (2800 rpm max.) until voltmeter reading jumps to about 12 volts. Immediately release the throttle. Observe the voltmeter, which will drop to 0 after about 20 seconds. Observe the pulse code signal.	a. One pulse b. Pulses more than once or pulses steadily c. Reading does not jump to 12 volts	a. Switch is good. On non-turbocharged engines with manual transmissions, go to the next step. On all others, skip the next step and go to the following step. b. Check the idle tracking switch. c. Check the tachometer lead.
Managed Thermactor Air Test With the engine off, remove the self-test ground wire and connect the voltmeter across the air diverter solenoid. Start the engine and immediately observe the voltmeter. Then increase engine speed to 2200 rpm and observe the voltmeter.	a. 11.5 volts at idle and less than 2.5 volts at 2200 rpm b. All other readings	a. Diverter solenoid is good. Connect the self-test jumper and the voltmeter to bypass the solenoid. Go to the next step. b. Check the air diverter.

MICROPROCESSOR SYSTEM DIAGNOSTIC TESTS

MCU SELF-TEST PROGRAM

Procedure	Result	Action
MCU System Running Test Turn the engine off and restart the engine. Observe the voltmeter. Increase engine speed until the meter jumps to about 12 volts and hold that engine speed. Observe the voltmeter and return the engine to idle when the reading drops to 0. Observe the pulse code signal.	a. Pulses steadily b. One pulse c. Two or three pulses	a. MCU sub-system is good. The test is completed, remove test equipment. b. Go to the idle tracking switch check. c. Go to the fuel control check.

FUEL CONTROL CHECK
Test Preparation and Preliminary Testing

1. Remove the grounding jumper wire from the brown self-test connector.
2. Inspect the choke plate for freedom of movement.
3. Recheck for vacuum leaks and burned or damaged wiring.
CHILTON CAUTION: Do not hold the throttle open with any device since this will activate the idle tracking switch.
4. Turn the ignition key to "RUN" with the engine off.
5. Listen or feel for clicking at the vacuum solenoid regulator.
6. If there is steady clicking, skip the first four steps of the fuel control test procedure.
7. If there is irregular clicking or no clicking at all, begin with the first step of the test procedure.

MCU Harness Connectors

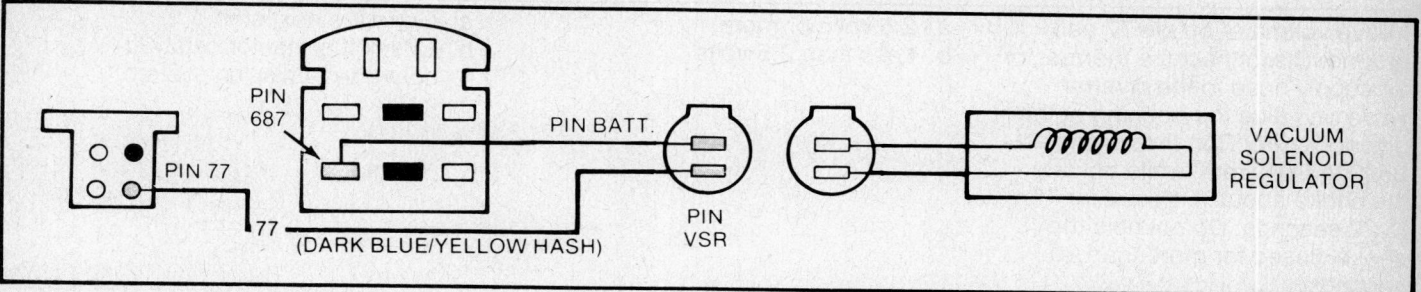

FUEL CONTROL CHECK

Procedure	Result	Action
Exhaust Gas Oxygen Sensor Test Check continuity from pin 77 to pin VSR.	a. Continuity b. No continuity	a. Check the harness. b. Repair open in circuit 77 (dark blue with yellow hash).
Check continuity from pin 77 to ground.	a. Continuity b. No continuity	a. Repair short in circuit 77. b. Go to the next step.
Check continuity from pin 687 to pin BATT.	a. Continuity b. No continuity	a. Go to the next step. b. Repair open in circuit 687 (gray with yellow stripe).
Measure vacuum solenoid regulator resistance. It should be 30 ohms.	a. 30 to 75 ohms b. Less than 30 or more than 75 ohms	a. Replace the MCU module. b. Replace the vacuum solenoid regulator.

MICROPROCESSOR SYSTEM DIAGNOSTIC TESTS

FUEL CONTROL CHECK

Procedure	Result	Action
Tee vacuum gauge into hose to feedback port of carburetor. Run engine at 2500 to 2800 rpm.	a. Less than 2.5" vacuum b. More than 2.5" vacuum	a. Skip the next two steps. b. Go to the next step.
Connect voltmeter from pin 77 to ground. Run the engine at 2500 to 2800 rpm.	a. 2.5 volts or more b. Less than 2.5 volts	a. Replace the vacuum solenoid regulator. b. Go to the next step.
Leave voltmeter between pin 77 and ground, and reconnect the vacuum hose. Unplug the exhaust gas oxygen sensor from the harness. Run the engine at 2500 to 2800 rpm.	a. 10 or more volts b. Less than 10 volts	a. Check stepper motor needle travel. b. Replace MCU module.
Connect voltmeter to pin 77 and ground. Run the engine at 2500 to 2800 rpm.	a. 10 or more volts b. Less than 10 volts	a. Skip the next step. b. Go to the next step.
Remove tee and attach the vacuum gauge directly to the hose from the center port of the vacuum solenoid regulator. Run the engine at idle speed.	a. 4" vacuum b. Less than 4" vacuum	a. Check the carburetor feedback system. b. Check the hose between the vacuum solenoid regulator and carburetor. Check the vacuum source to VSR and if less than 10", repair. If 10" or more, replace the vacuum solenoid regulator.
Leave voltmeter on pin 77 and ground. Disconnect the thermactor air supply hose to the diverter valve and plug the opening at the diverter valve. Run the engine at 2500 to 2800 rpm, while holding the choke about ¾ closed for 10 to 20 seconds. Do not hold the choke closed for more than 20 seconds.	a. 2.5 volts or more b. Less than 2.5 volts	a. Go to the next step. b. Check thermactor catalytic converter emission system.

Exhaust Gas Oxygen Sensor Circuit

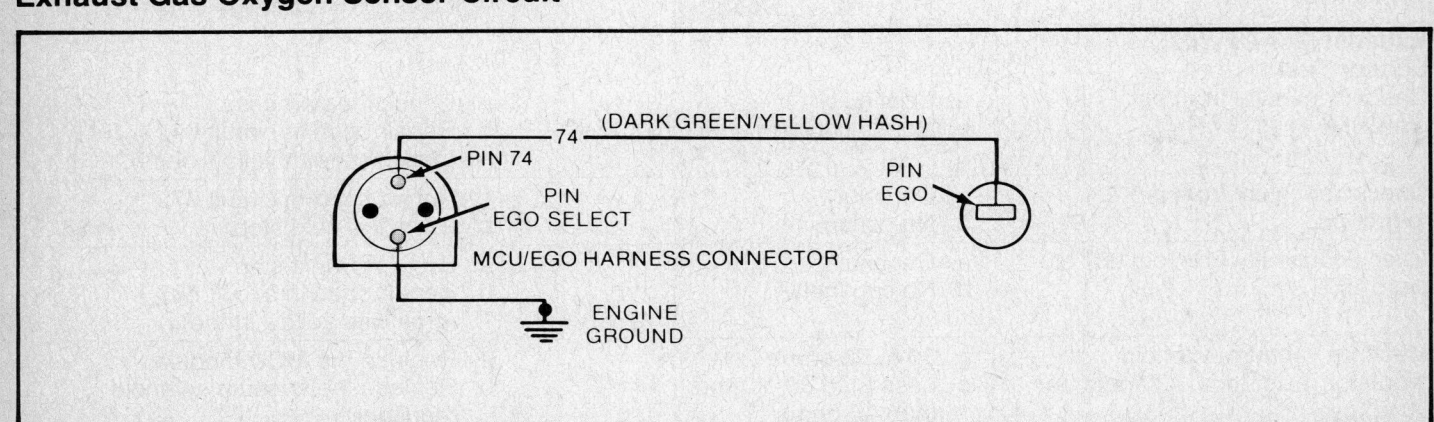

B176

MICROPROCESSOR SYSTEM DIAGNOSTIC TESTS

FUEL CONTROL CHECK

Procedure	Result	Action
Disconnect the exhaust gas oxygen sensor from the harness. Check continuity from pin 74 to pin EGO.	a. Continuity b. No continuity	a. Go to the next step. b. Repair open in circuit 94 (dark green with purple hash).
Check continuity from pin 74 to ground.	a. Continuity b. No continuity	a. Repair short in circuit 94. b. Go to the next step.
Check continuity from pin EGO to ground.	a. Continuity b. No continuity	a. Go to the next step. b. Repair open circuit.
Connect MCU to harness. Leave the voltmeter connected from pin 77 to ground and run the engine at idle. Carefully run a jumper from pin EGO to the positive terminal of the battery. Increase the engine speed to 2500 to 2800 rpm.	a. Less than 2.5 volts b. 2.5 volts or more	a. Replace the exhaust gas oxygen sensor. b. Replace the MCU module.

COLD TEMPERATURE VACUUM SWITCH CIRCUIT TESTS

Procedure	Result	Action
With the key off, check for continuity from pin 73 to ground.	a. Continuity b. No continuity	a. Replace the MCU module. b. Unplug the switch and ground wire 73 (orange with light blue hash) at the switch connector. If there is continuity, go to the next step. If there is no continuity, repair open in circuit 73.
With the key off, check for continuity from ground to pin B.	a. Continuity b. No continuity	a. Repair open in circuit 57 (black base). b. Replace cold temperature vacuum switch.
With the key off, apply 10″ vacuum to the cold temperature vacuum switch. Check for continuity from pin 73 to ground.	a. No continuity b. Continuity	a. Replace the MCU module. b. Unplug the switch. If there is still continuity, repair short in circuit 73. If there is no continuity, replace the switch.

Cold Temperature Vacuum Switch Circuit

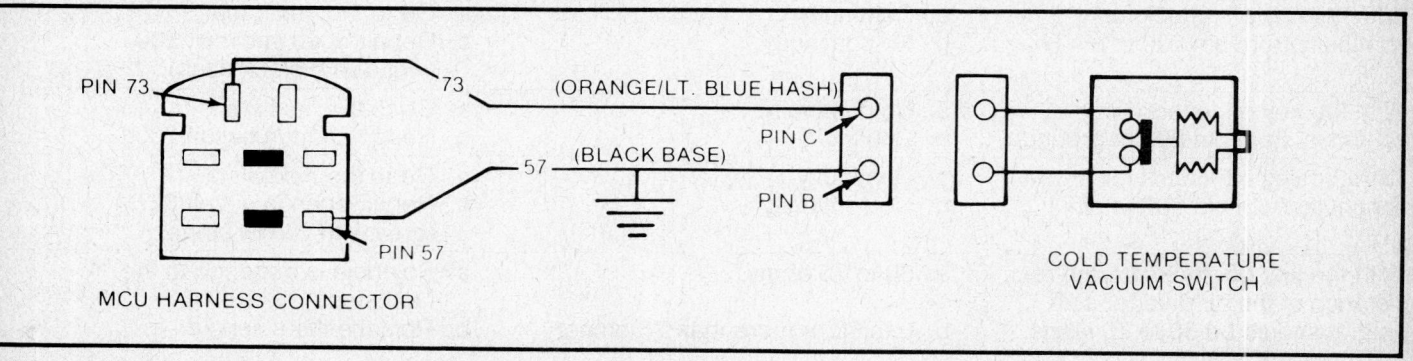

B177

MICROPROCESSOR SYSTEM DIAGNOSTIC TESTS

IDLE TRACKING SWITCH CIRCUIT TESTS

Procedure	Result	Action
CHILTON CAUTION: Before performing the following tests, be sure the idle tracking switch is in proper position for throttle at idle. The throttle arm should fully depress the switch.		
With the key off and the throttle closed, check for continuity from pin 189 to ground.	a. No continuity b. Continuity	a. Replace the MCU module. b. Unplug the idle tracking switch. If there is still continuity, repair short in wire 189 (light blue with pink dots). If there is no continuity, replace the switch.
With the key off and the throttle open, check for continuity from pin 189 to ground.	a. Continuity b. No continuity	a. Go to the last step. b. Unplug the switch and ground wire 189 at the connector. If there is continuity, go to the next step. If there is no continuity, repair open in wire 189.
With the key off, check for continuity from ground to pin A.	a. No continuity b. Continuity	a. Repair open in circuit 57 (black base). b. Replace the idle tracking switch.
With the key off, measure the resistance from pin 189 to pin 687. (Should be 120 ohms.)	a. 90 to 150 ohms b. Less than 90 or more than 150 ohms	a. Replace MCU module. b. Repair or replace harness resistor.

Idle Tracking Switch Circuit

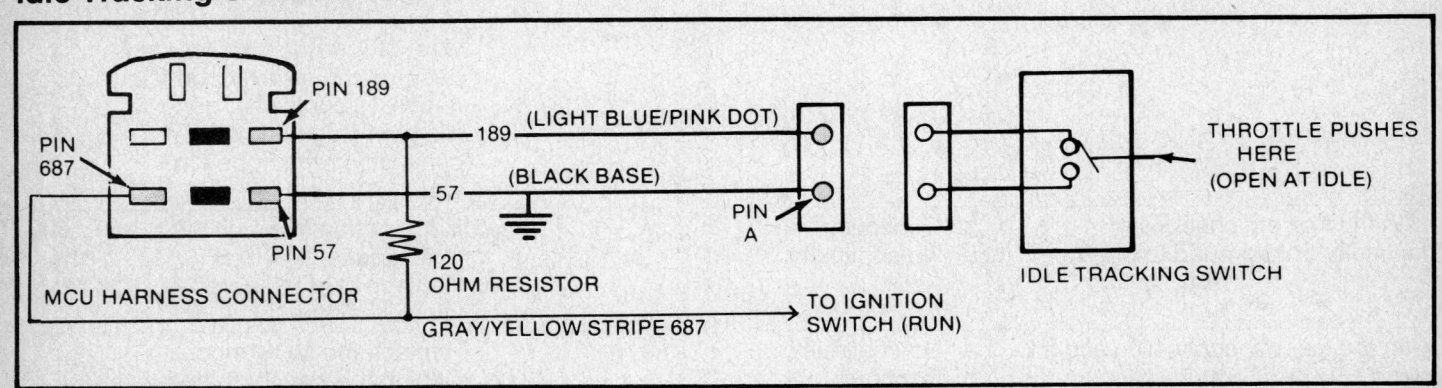

THERMACTOR AIR DIVERTER SOLENOID CIRCUIT TESTS

Procedure	Result	Action
With the key off, check for continuity from pin 200 to pin H.	a. Continuity b. No continuity	a. Go to the next step. b. Repair open in circuit 200 (white with black hash).
With the key off, check for continuity from pin 200 to ground.	a. No continuity b. Continuity	a. Go to the next step. b. Repair short in circuit 200.
With the key off, check for continuity from pin 687 to pin J.	a. Continuity b. No continuity	a. Go to the next step. b. Repair open in circuit 687 (gray with yellow stripe).
With the key off, measure the resistance of the air diverter solenoid. It should be 30 to 75 ohms.	a. 30 to 75 ohms. b. 0 to 30 or more than 75 ohms.	a. Solenoid is good, go to the next step. b. Replace the solenoid.

MICROPROCESSOR SYSTEM DIAGNOSTIC TESTS

THERMACTOR AIR DIVERTER SOLENOID CIRCUIT TESTS

Procedure	Result	Action
With the key off, check for continuity from pin 201 to ground.	a. No continuity b. Continuity	a. Go to the next step. b. Repair short in circuit 201.
CHILTON CAUTION: Before continuing with the following tests, be sure the idle tracking switch is in the proper position for throttle at idle. The throttle arm should fully depress the idle tracking switch. If not in the correct position, the idle tracking switch can cause air diverter solenoid circuit problems.		
With the key off and the throttle open, check for continuity from pin 189 to ground.	a. Continuity b. No continuity	a. Skip the next step and go to the following step. b. Unplug the idle tracking switch and ground wire 189 at the connector. If there is continuity, go back to the third step of this procedure. If there is no continuity, repair open in wire 189.
With the key off, check for continuity from ground to pin A.	a. No continuity b. Continuity	a. Repair open in circuit 57 (black). b. Replace idle tracking switch.
With the key off, measure the resistance from pin 189 to pin 687. It should be 120 ohms.	a. 90 to 150 ohms. b. Less than 90 or more than 150 ohms	a. Replace the MCU module. b. Repair or replace the harness resistor.

Air Diverter Solenoid Circuit

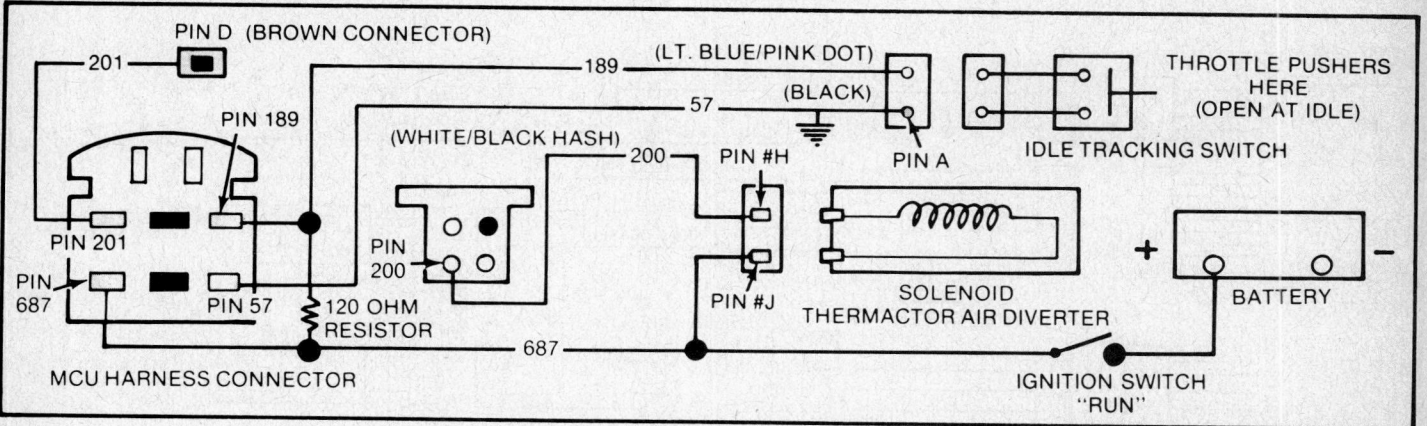

THERMACTOR AIR BY-PASS RESISTANCE TESTS

Procedure	Result	Action
With the key off, check for continuity from pin 201 to pin D.	a. Continuity b. No continuity	a. Go to the next step. b. Repair open in circuit 201 (brown connector, self-test trigger).
With the key off, check for continuity from pin 687 to the positive battery terminal.	a. Continuity b. No continuity	a. Go to the next step. b. Repair open in circuit 687 (gray with yellow stripe).
With the key off, check for continuity from pin 687 to pin E.	a. Continuity b. No continuity	a. Go to the next step. b. Repair open in circuit 687.
With the key off, check for continuity from pin 57 to ground.	a. Continuity b. No continuity	a. Go to the next step. b. Repair open in circuit 57 (black base).

MICROPROCESSOR SYSTEM DIAGNOSTIC TESTS

THERMACTOR AIR BY-PASS RESISTANCE TESTS

Procedure	Result	Action
With the key off, check for continuity from pin 190 to pin F.	a. Continuity b. No continuity	a. Go to the next step. b. Repair open in circuit 190 (white with red dot).
With the key off, check for continuity from pin 190 to ground.	a. No continuity b. Continuity	a. Go to the next step. b. Repair open in circuit 190.
With the key off, measure the resistance of the air by-pass solenoid.	a. 30 to 75 ohms b. 0 to 30 or more than 75 ohms	a. The solenoid is good, replace the MCU module. b. Replace the solenoid.

TACHOMETER LEAD TEST

Procedure	Result	Action
With the key off, check for continuity from pin 11 to the tach terminal.	a. Continuity b. No continuity	a. Wiring is good, replace the MCU module. b. Repair open in circuit 11 (dark green with yellow dot).

Feedback Carburetor Electrical Control Circuits

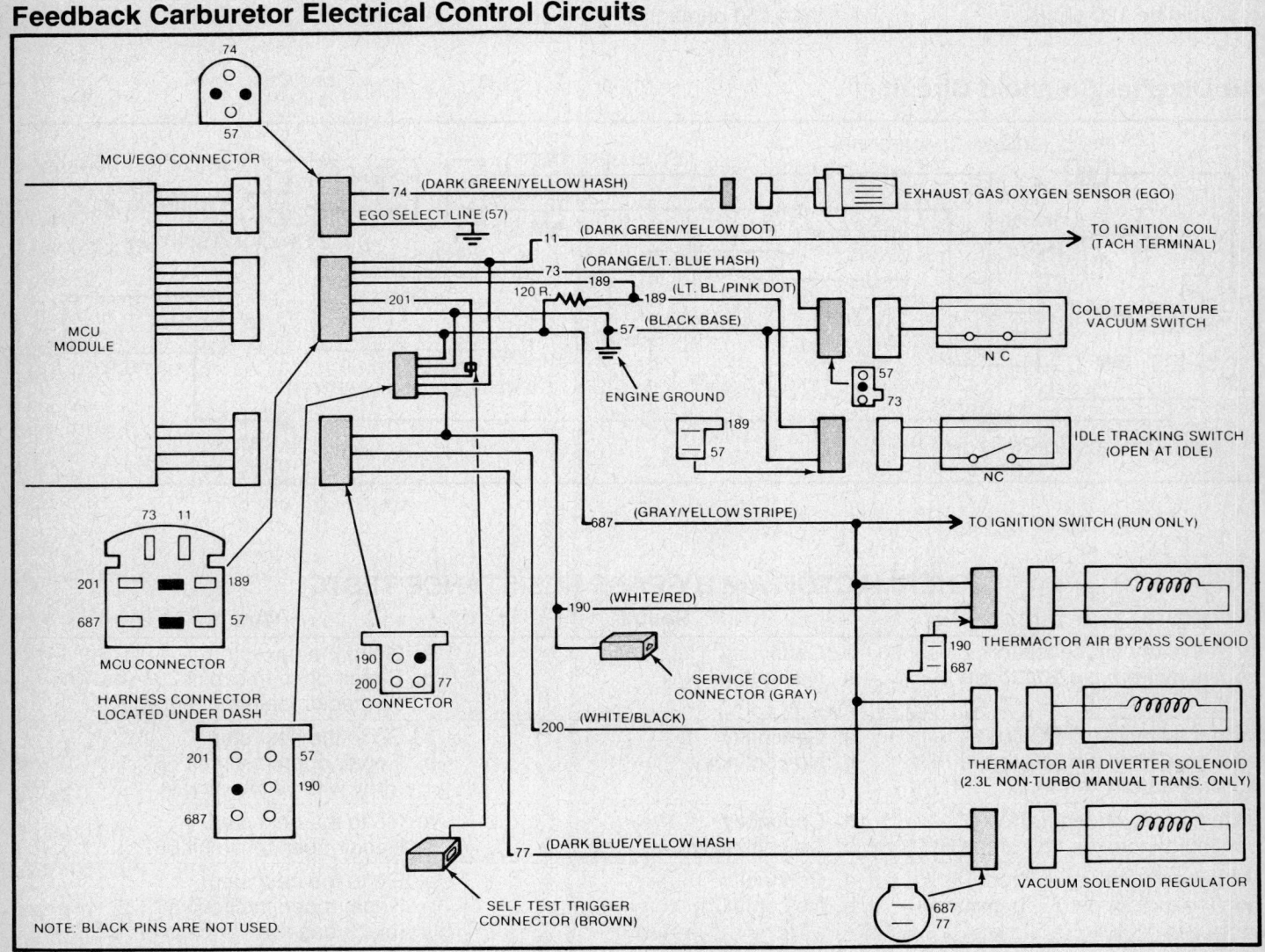

NOTE: BLACK PINS ARE NOT USED.

MCU Vacuum Schematics

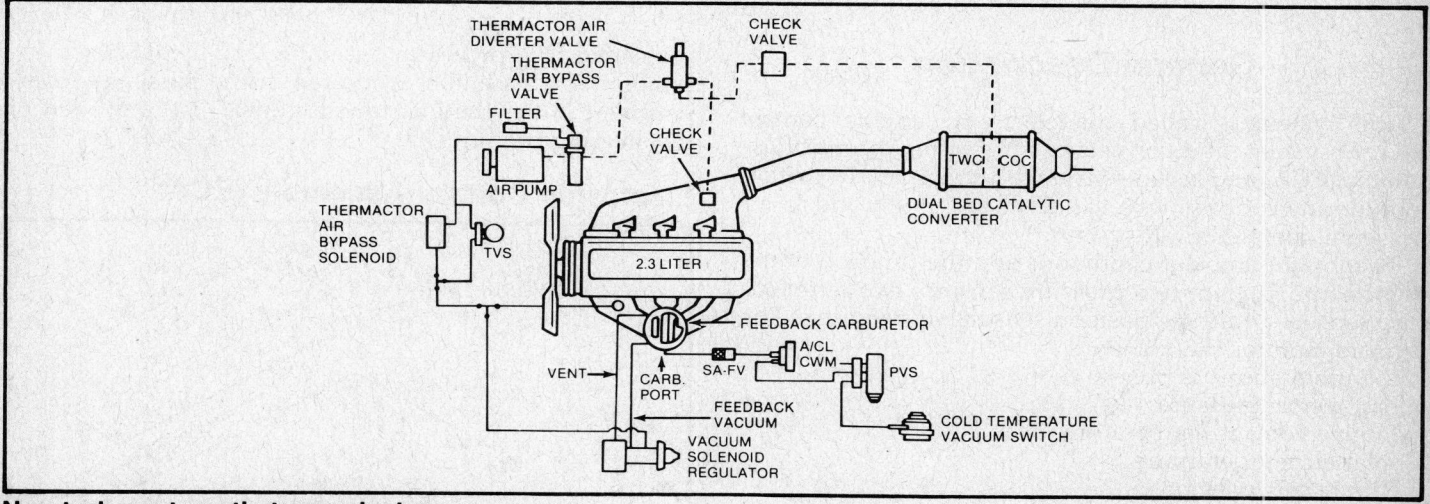

Non-turbo automatic transmission

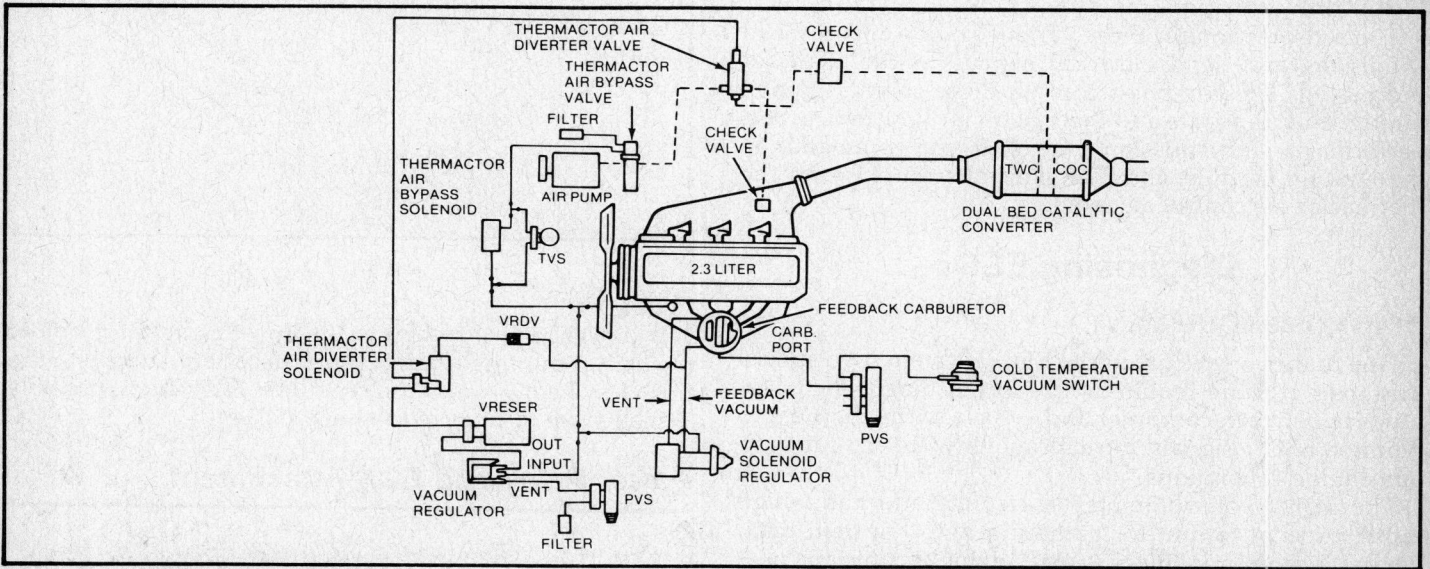

Non-turbo manual transmission

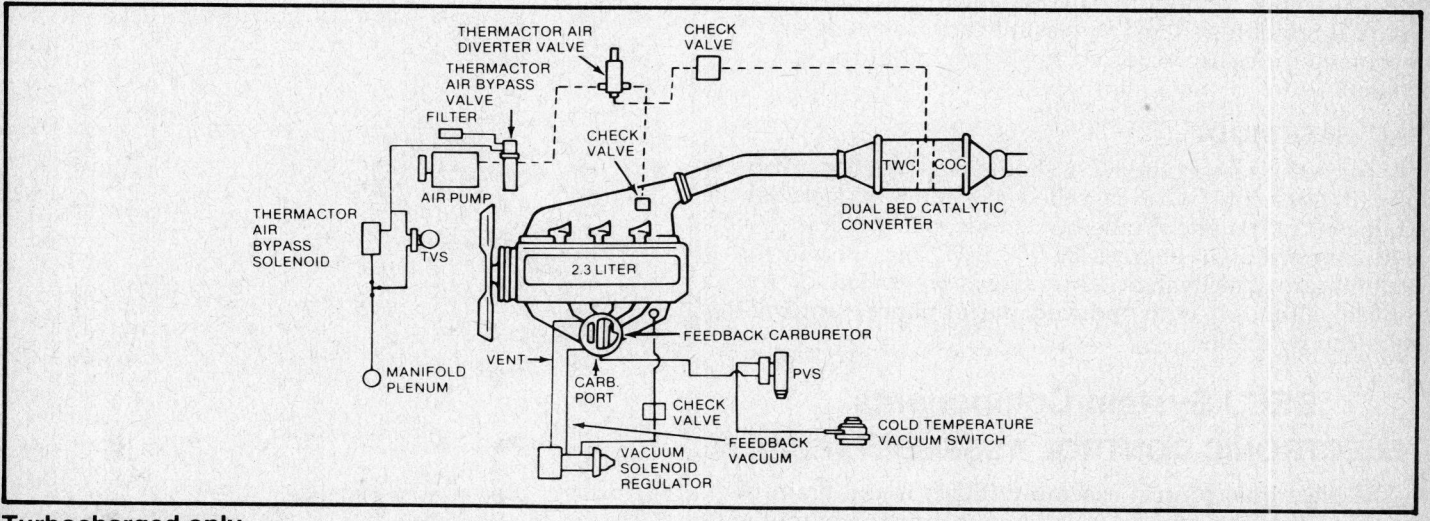

Turbocharged only

FORD ELECTRONIC ENGINE CONTROLS I

General Description

The system is called the electronic engine control (EEC I) system, and consists of an electronic control assembly (ECA) and seven sensors, a Dura Spark II ignition module and coil, a unique distributor assembly and an air pressure operated EGR system.

To monitor ambient conditions and the function of the vehicle and engine, two pressure sensors, two temperature sensors and three position sensors are required. The sensors monitor the following.

    Manifold absolute pressure
    Barometric pressure
    Engine coolant temperature
    Inlet air temperature
    Crankshaft position
    Throttle position
    EGR valve position

The sensors monitor these various engine and ambient conditions and send electrical signals to the ECA for processing. The computer computes the correct ignition timing, EGR flow rate and thermactor air flow for the best performance and emission control. It also commands to the ignition module, the EGR control solenoids and the thermactor air control solenoid.

Diagnosing EEC I

DIAGNOSIS EQUIPMENT

Due to the complexity of the EEC I system, two special diagnosis aids are required. The EEC I diagnostic tester plugs in between computer and vehicle wiring harness to monitor EEC I signals. Specifications will vary for various engine calibrations.

The digital volt-ohmmeter is accurate and has a high input impedance unit for gathering EEC I system data. Digital readout minimizes errors, giving technicians necessary accuracy for EEC diagnosis.

An advance timing light compatible with the Dura Spark II ignition system, a pressure/vacuum gauge and a tachometer are also required for diagnosis of the EEC I system.

FAIL-SAFE MODE

If for some reason the ECA should not function properly, it goes into what is called the limited operation strategy (LOS) mode. In the LOS mode, spark advance is held constant at 10 degrees BTDC. EGR and thermactor systems are deactivated. This allows operation of the vehicle, although with reduced performance, until repairs can be made.

EEC I System Components

ELECTRONIC CONTROL ASSEMBLY (ECA)

The electronic control assembly (ECA) is the brain of the EEC system, and is a solid-state, micro-computer consisting of a processor assembly and a calibration assembly. This assembly is located in the passenger compartment under the instrument panel, just to the left of the steering column.

Electronic Control Assembly (ECA)

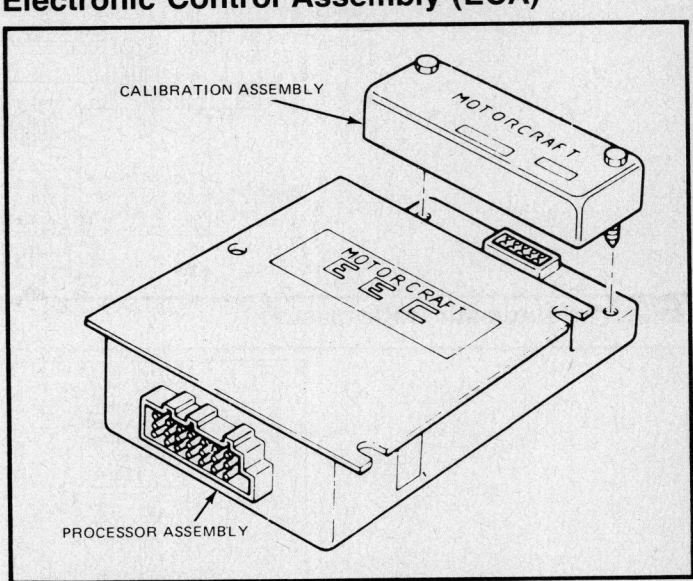

Power Relay

A power relay attached to the lower right hand side of the ECA mounting bracket supplies battery voltage to the EEC I system. It also protects the ECA from possible damage due to reversed voltage polarity.

Power Relay and ECA Attachment

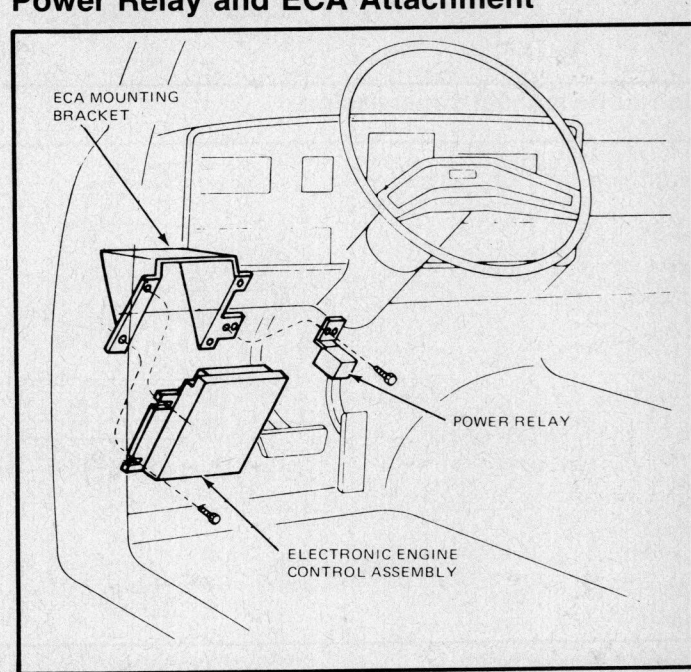

Typical EEC I System

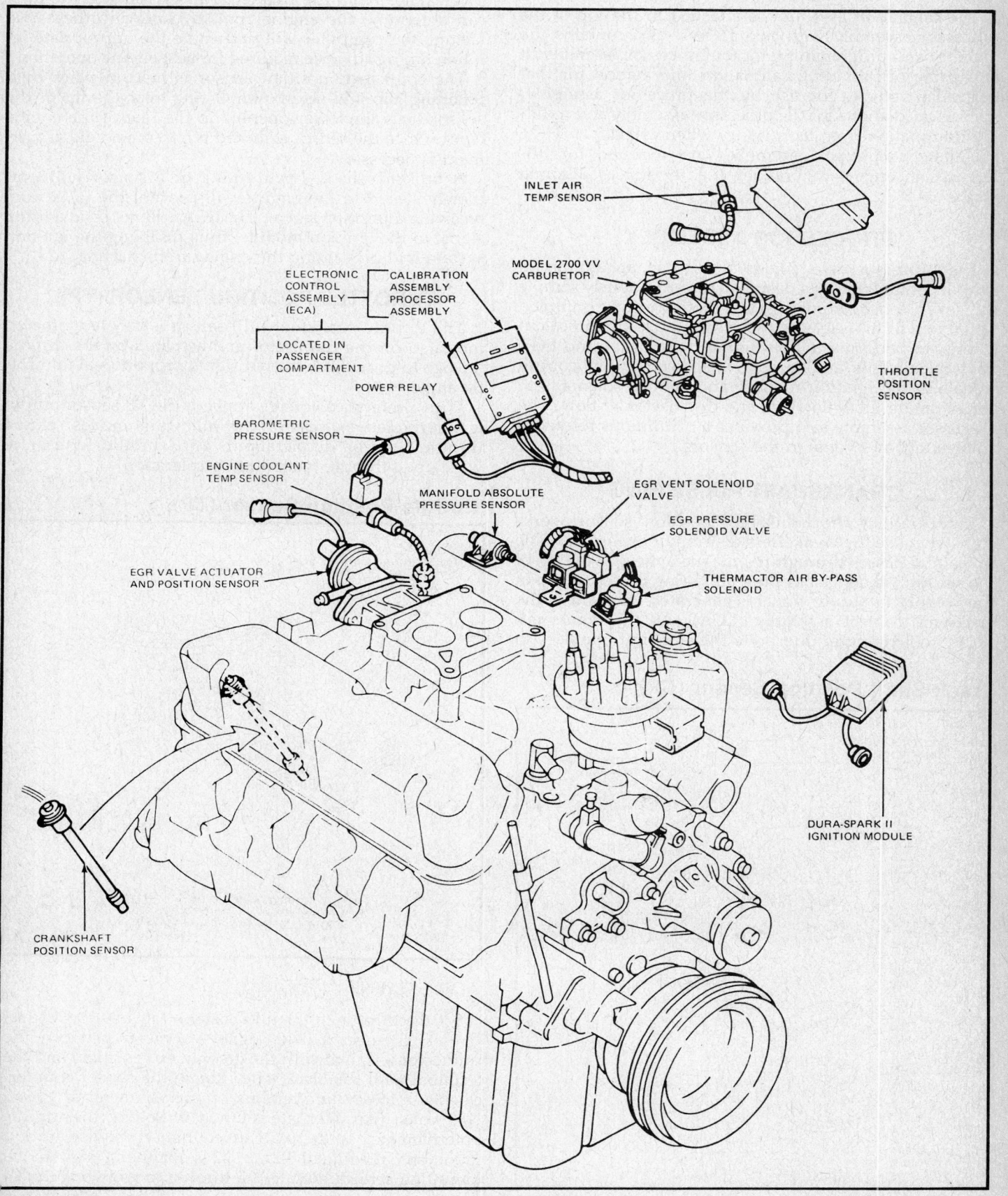

INLET AIR
TEMP SENSOR

MODEL 2700 VV
CARBURETOR

ELECTRONIC
CONTROL
ASSEMBLY
(ECA)

CALIBRATION
ASSEMBLY
PROCESSOR
ASSEMBLY

LOCATED IN
PASSENGER
COMPARTMENT

THROTTLE
POSITION
SENSOR

POWER RELAY

BAROMETRIC
PRESSURE SENSOR

ENGINE COOLANT
TEMP SENSOR

MANIFOLD ABSOLUTE
PRESSURE SENSOR

EGR VENT SOLENOID
VALVE

EGR PRESSURE
SOLENOID VALVE

EGR VALVE ACTUATOR
AND POSITION SENSOR

THERMACTOR AIR BY-PASS
SOLENOID

DURA-SPARK II
IGNITION MODULE

CRANKSHAFT
POSITION SENSOR

CALIBRATION ASSEMBLY

The calibration assembly is attached to the top of the processor assembly with two screws, and contains the memory and programming for the processor assembly. It is capable of providing calibration information for that particular vehicle, for use by the processor assembly, storing calculations for the processor assembly and recalling information from its memory when asked.

Unique calibration assemblies are required for differences in engine calibrations (i.e. 49 state, California etc.).

PROCESSOR ASSEMBLY

The processor assembly is housed in an aluminum case. It contains circuits designed to continuously sample the seven sensor input signals, to convert the sampled signal to a form usable by the computer section in calculations, to perform ignition timing, thermactor and EGR flow calculations and to send electrical output control signals to the ignition module and control solenoids to adjust timing, EGR flow rate and thermactor air flow. The processor assembly also provides a continuous reference voltage (about 9 volts) to the sensors.

CRANKSHAFT PULSE RING

In operation, the crankshaft position sensor works somewhat like the breakerless distributor pickup coil. The pulse ring passes through the magnetic field at the tip of the sensor. When a lobe of the pulse ring passes the tip of the sensor, an output signal is generated and sent to the electronic control assembly (ECA). As the crankshaft turns, the computer interprets the electrical impulses to determine the exact position of the crankshaft at any given time. From the frequency of the pulses, the ECA can determine the engine rpm. By knowing these two factors, the computer will determine the appropriate ignition timing advance required for best engine operation.

The crankshaft position sensor is held in place by a retaining clip and screw. An O-ring near the tip of the sensor seals the lower opening in the rear of the engine block. Once the sensor is locked in place, no field adjustment is necessary.

A broken sensor, open wiring or a sensor not completely seated in the engine will prevent the ECA from receiving a position signal. The ECA will not send a firing signal to the ignition module, thus disabling the ignition system and preventing the engine from starting.

THROTTLE POSITION SENSOR (TP)

The throttle positioner (TP) sensor is a potentiometer, mounted on the carburetor and actuated by the throttle linkage to provide an output signal proportional to throttle angle.

With a reference voltage applied, the TP sensor output is interpreted as one of the following modes, closed throttle (idle or deceleration), part throttle (cruise) or wide open throttle (maximum acceleration).

Crank Shaft Position Sensor (CP)

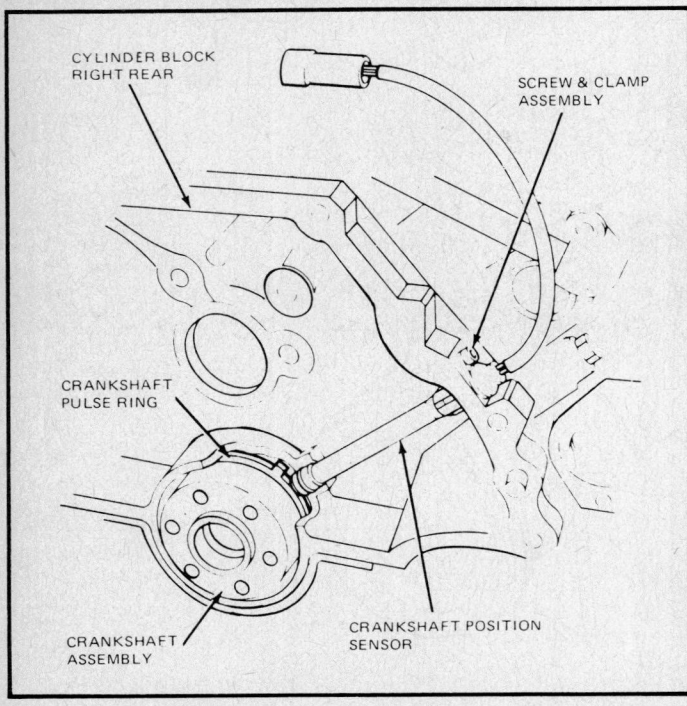

CYLINDER BLOCK
RIGHT REAR

SCREW & CLAMP
ASSEMBLY

CRANKSHAFT
PULSE RING

CRANKSHAFT
ASSEMBLY

CRANKSHAFT POSITION
SENSOR

Throttle Position Sensor (TP)

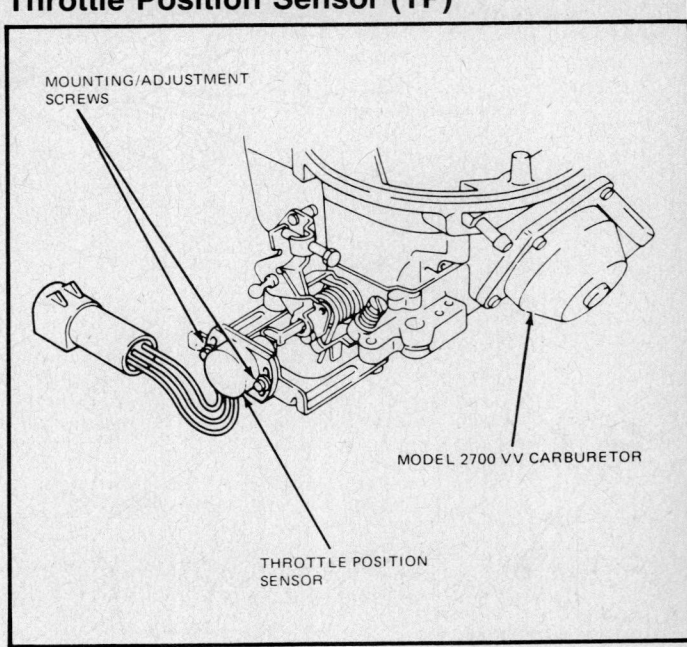

MOUNTING/ADJUSTMENT
SCREWS

MODEL 2700 VV CARBURETOR

THROTTLE POSITION
SENSOR

ADJUSTMENT

Set the throttle to the idle position (against the idle set screw). Connect a 0-10 digital voltmeter between the connector terminal with the green wire (positive) and the terminal with the black wire. Rotate the sensor counterclockwise to obtain a reading on the voltmeter of 1.89 ± .180 volts. (An alternate method of setting the throttle potentiometer is to rotate it counter-clockwise until a ratiometric reading of 0.21 ± .02 is obtained). Tighten the mounting screws. Rotate the throttle to wide open position and release. Recheck the sensor output at idle. Adjust as required.

As a final check, rotate the throttle to a wide open condition and release. The throttle must return to an idle condition unassisted. Reconnect to wire harness.

EGR System

COMPONENTS

The amount of EGR gas flow is controlled by the computer which utilizes air pressure from the thermactor system bypass valve to operate the EGR valve. When the EGR valve is open, exhaust gas from the exhaust manifold is allowed to flow into the intake manifold, becoming part of the combustion cycle and reducing NOx emissions.

EGR VALVE AND SENSOR ASSEMBLY

The EGR valve used with the EEC I system resembles the valve used with non-EEC I system applications, but is air pressure operated rather than vacuum operated. The EGR valve attaches to a spacer that mounts under the carburetor on the intake manifold. The valve controls the flow of gases through a tapered pintle valve and seat. A position sensor built into the valve provides an electrical signal to the ECA that indicates EGR valve position.

Unlike conventional system EGR valves, the EEC I system EGR valve is completely sealed, and no pintle valve movement can be seen when the valve is installed on the spacer. The valve and position sensor are serviced as a unit.

EGR Valve and Spacer

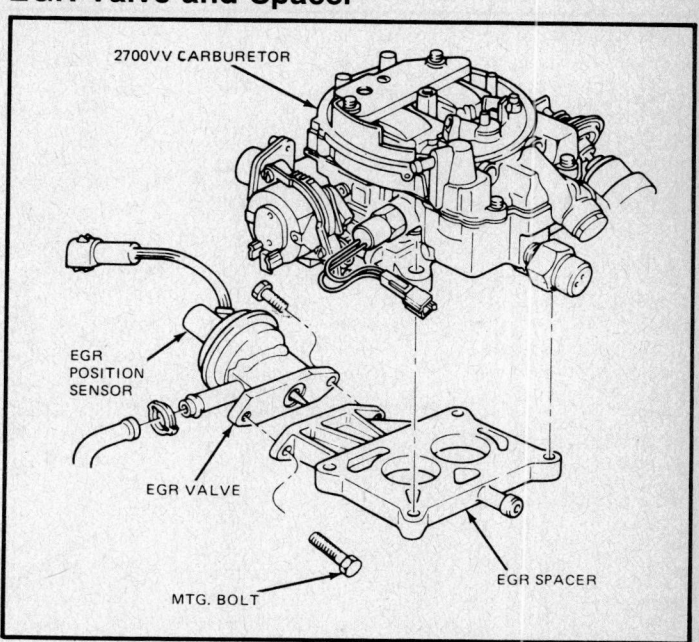

EGR COOLER ASSEMBLY

In order to provide improved flow characteristics, better engine operation and EGR valve durability, an external EGR gas cooler is used to reduce EGR gas temperature. The cooler assembly is mounted over the right valve cover and uses engine coolant to reduce the temperature of exhaust gases routed from the exhaust manifold to the EGR valve.

Air Operated EGR Valve

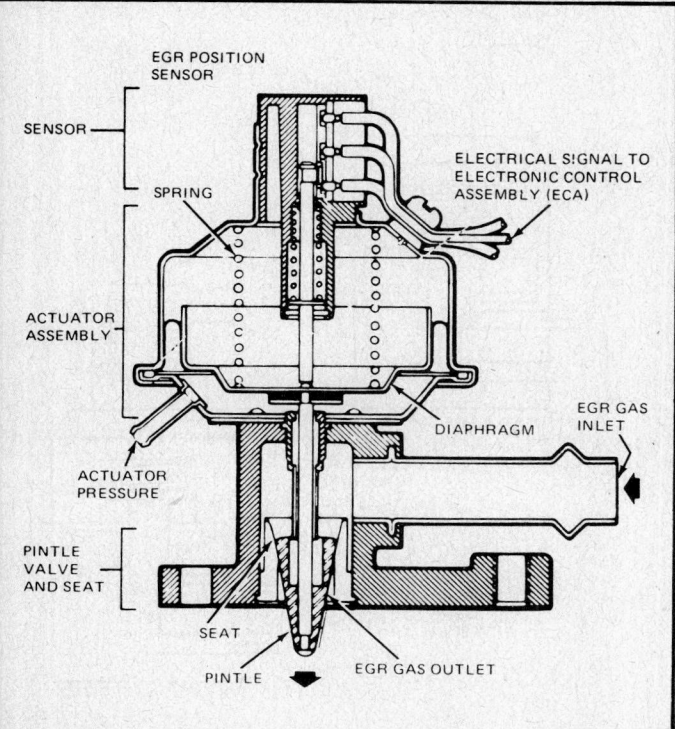

EGR Gas Cooler

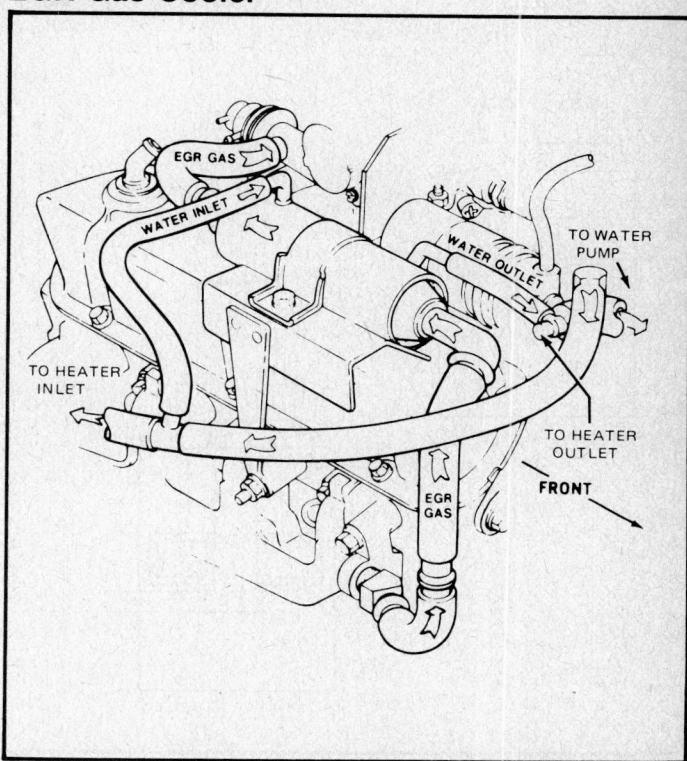

Dual EGR Control Solenoids

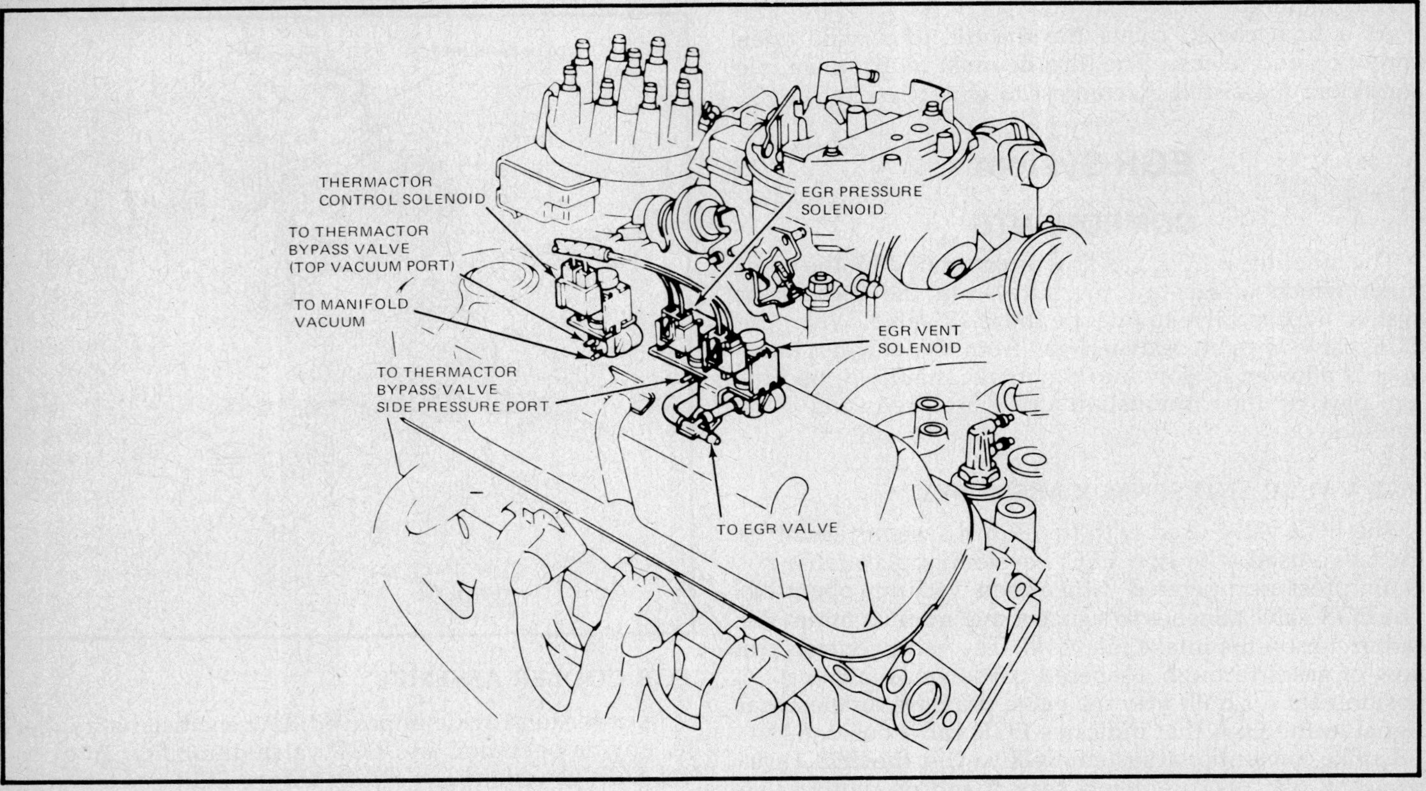

THERMACTOR
CONTROL SOLENOID

EGR PRESSURE
SOLENOID

TO THERMACTOR
BYPASS VALVE
(TOP VACUUM PORT)

TO MANIFOLD
VACUUM

EGR VENT
SOLENOID

TO THERMACTOR
BYPASS VALVE
SIDE PRESSURE PORT

TO EGR VALVE

Vent and Pressure Solenoids

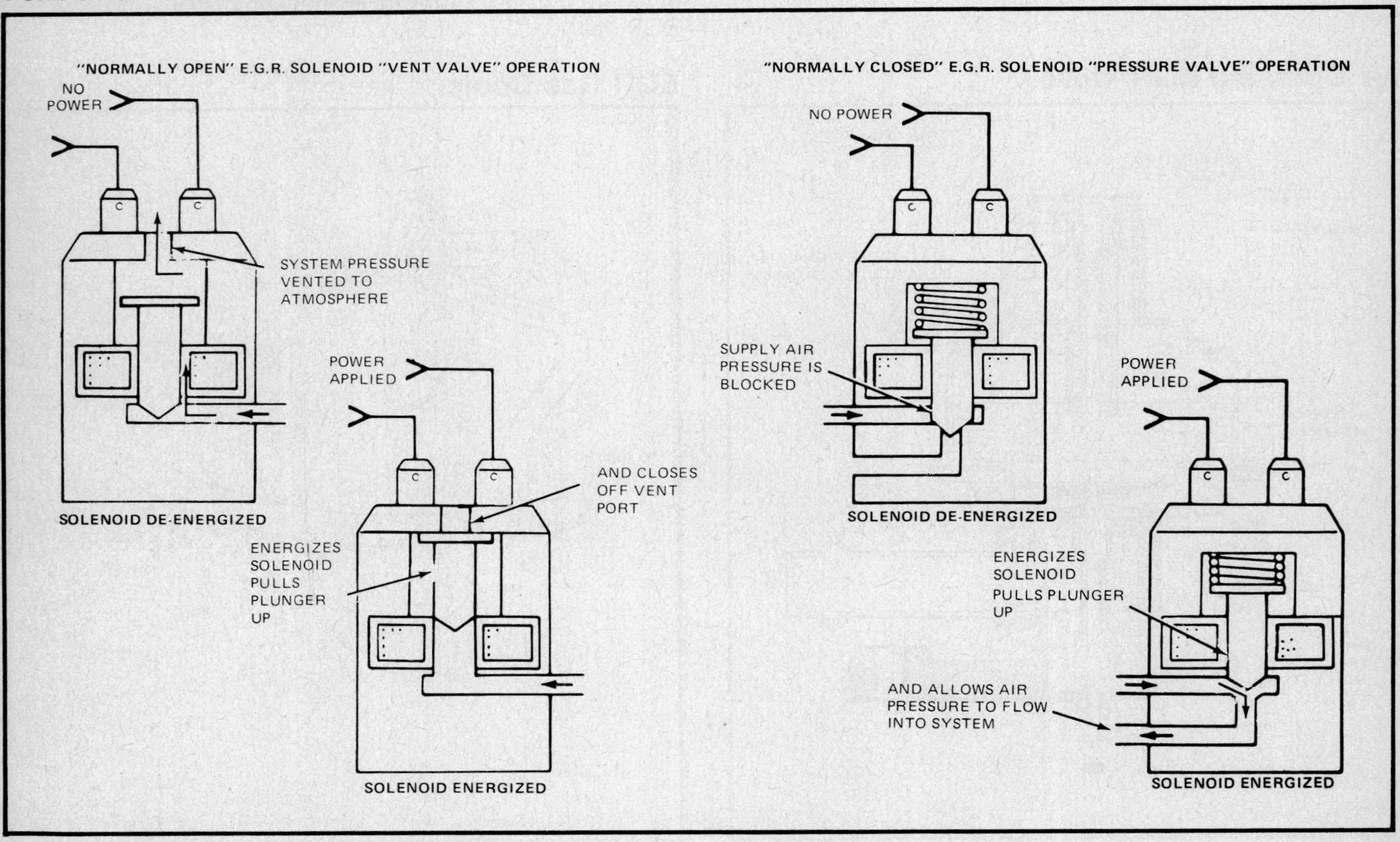

"NORMALLY OPEN" E.G.R. SOLENOID "VENT VALVE" OPERATION

NO POWER

SYSTEM PRESSURE
VENTED TO
ATMOSPHERE

SOLENOID DE-ENERGIZED

POWER
APPLIED

AND CLOSES
OFF VENT
PORT

ENERGIZES
SOLENOID
PULLS
PLUNGER
UP

SOLENOID ENERGIZED

"NORMALLY CLOSED" E.G.R. SOLENOID "PRESSURE VALVE" OPERATION

NO POWER

SUPPLY AIR
PRESSURE IS
BLOCKED

SOLENOID DE-ENERGIZED

POWER
APPLIED

ENERGIZES
SOLENOID
PULLS PLUNGER
UP

AND ALLOWS AIR
PRESSURE TO FLOW
INTO SYSTEM

SOLENOID ENERGIZED

DUAL EGR CONTROL SOLENOIDS

EGR valve movement is controlled by two solenoid valves mounted on a bracket above the left hand valve cover. To properly control the air pressure used to operate the EGR valve and to allow for application, hold and release of the air pressure requires two types of solenoid valve. The first is a vent valve which is normally open; that is, the outlet port is normally connected to the inlet port when the solenoid is not operated. The other is a pressure valve which is normally closed; that is, the outlet port is normally blocked when the solenoid is not operated.

OPERATION

The EGR valve is operated by air pressure supplied from the thermactor bypass valve. The pressure and vent solenoid valves work together under the direction of the computer to increase EGR flow by applying air pressure to the EGR valve, maintain EGR flow by trapping air pressure in the system and decrease EGR flow by venting system pressure to the atmosphere.

With data received from the various sensors, the computer determines the correct amount of EGR flow required, checks the position of the EGR valve pintle and decides if a change in position is required. In response to these calculations, the ECA puts the EGR system into one of the modes. The ECA samples and calculates these changes about 10 times each second for improved economy and driveability under all conditions.

MANIFOLD ABSOLUTE PRESSURE SENSOR (MAP)

The manifold absolute pressure (MAP) sensor is mounted on the left rocker arm cover and monitors the changes in intake manifold pressure which result from changes in engine load, speed and atmospheric pressure. (Manifold absolute pressure is defined as barometric pressure minus manifold vacuum). The MAP sensor contains a pressure-sensing element and electronic circuits that convert pressure sensed by the unit into an electric signal for the ECA. This signal is used by the ECA to determine part throttle spark advance and EGR flow rate.

BAROMETRIC PRESSURE SENSOR (BP)

The BP sensor is mounted on the engine compartment side of the dash panel and senses barometric pressure. The pressure is then converted into an electrical signal and fed to the ECA for computations. From this input, the ECA is able to determine EGR flow requirements, depending on the altitude at which the vehicle is being driven.

COOLANT TEMPERATURE SENSOR (ECT)

The engine coolant temperature sensor is installed in the rear of the intake manifold and converts engine coolant temperature into an electrical signal for the ECA to process. The sensor consists of a brass housing which contains a thermistor (variable resistor which decreases its resistance as the temperature rises) that measures engine temperature.

Manifold Absolute Pressure (MAP)

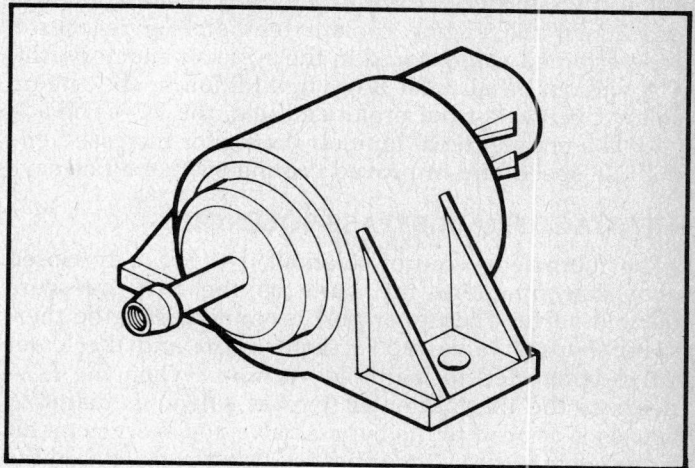

Barometric Pressure Sensor (BP)

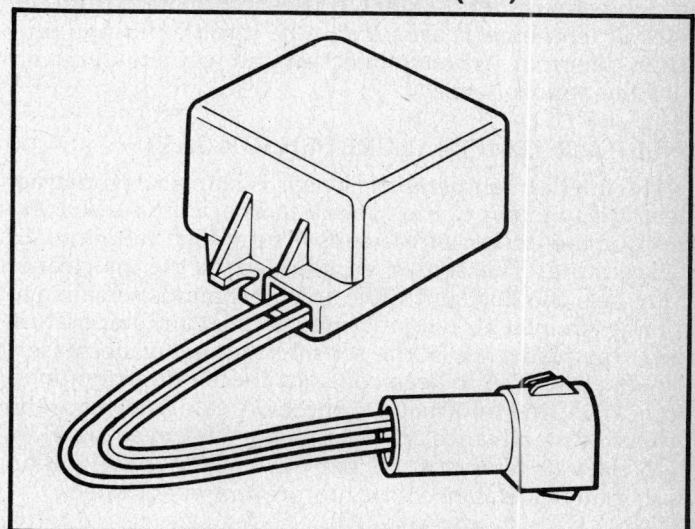

Coolant Temperature Sensor (ECT)

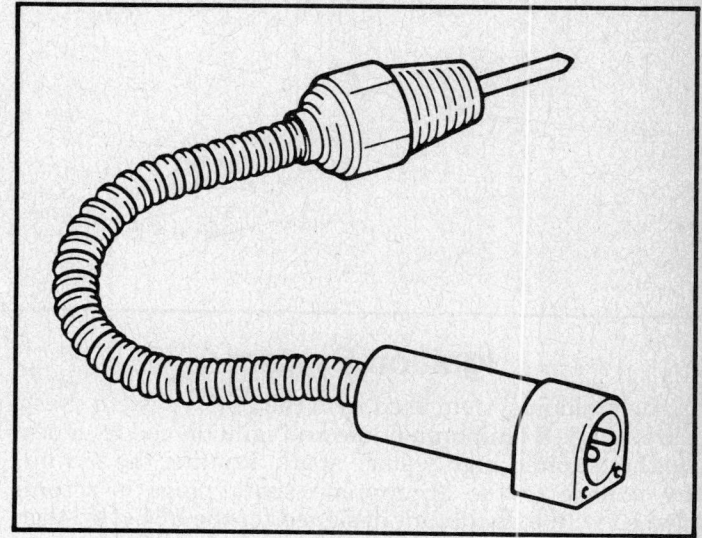

The coolant temperature sensor takes the place of the cooling PVS and EGR PVS used in the conventional system. When the engine coolant temperature reaches a predetermined value stored in the system's memory, the ECA will cut off all EGR flow. In addition, if the engine coolant overheats from prolonged idle, the ECA will advance the engine initial ignition timing for increased engine idle speed and improved cooling system efficiency.

THERMACTOR AIR BYPASS SOLENOID

The thermactor control solenoid is a normally closed valve that functions the same as the EGR pressure solenoid valve. The upper port is connected to the thermactor bypass valve top (actuator) port and the lower port is connected to manifold vacuum. When the ECA energizes the thermactor air bypass solenoid, manifold vacuum is applied to the bypass valve and thermactor air is injected into the cylinder head exhaust ports. When the ECA de-energizes the thermactor air bypass solenoid, the valve closes and the bypass valve dumps thermactor air into the atmosphere. The ECA uses information from the inlet air temperature sensor and the throttle position sensor to determine when to inject air and when to dump air into the atmosphere.

INLET AIR TEMPERATURE SENSOR (IAT)

The inlet air temperature sensor is similar in construction and function to the coolant temperature sensor, except for the design of the sensor tip which monitors air temperature. The sensor is mounted in the air cleaner body near the duct and valve assembly and is sensitive to changes in inlet air temperature. As inlet air temperature rises, the resistance of the sensing thermistor decreases, allowing the ECA to keep constant check on the temperature. With this information, the ECA can determine the proper spark advance and thermactor system air flow. At high inlet air temperatures the ECA will modify ignition timing advance as necessary to prevent spark knock.

Inlet Air Temperature Sensor (IAT)

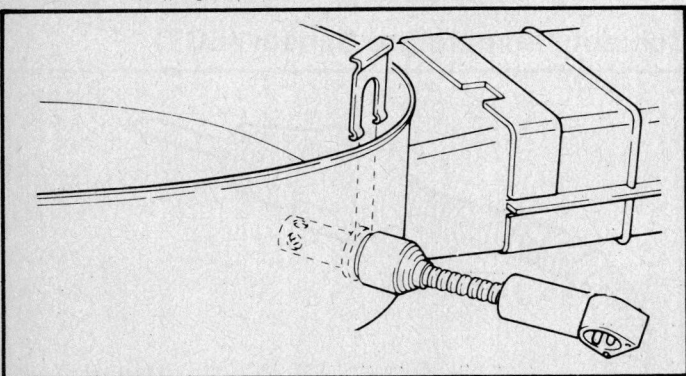

Ignition System

The ignition system used with the EEC I system uses a Dura Spark II ignition module and ignition coil to generate the required high voltage spark. Routing the secondary voltage to the appropriate spark plugs is accomplished with a distributor designed for the EEC I system.

DISTRIBUTOR

The EEC I distributor does not have conventional mechanical or vacuum advance mechanisms as do other Ford distributors. Instead, all ignition timing is controlled by the electronic control assembly (ECA), which is capable of firing the spark plug at any point from top dead center (TDC) to 60 degrees before top dead center (BTDC). This increased spark advance capability requires greater separation of adjacent distributor cap electrodes to prevent cross fire.

BI-LEVEL ROTOR AND DISTRIBUTOR CAP

The distributor rotor and cap electrodes have been designed to handle the additional advance capability, by using a two-level design. Both the rotor and cap have upper and lower electrode levels. As the rotor turns, one of the high-voltage electrode pick-up arms aligns with one spoke of the distributor cap center electrode plate. This allows high voltage to pass from the plate, through the rotor to a terminal on the distributor cap and out to the spark plug.

The numbers molded into the top of the cap are spark plug wire identification numbers. However, due to the unique construction of the distributor cap and rotor, the wires are not arranged in the cap in firing order.

NOTE Do not attempt to remove any silicone coating from the rotor lower electrode blades or from the distributor cap electrodes.

EEC I Distributor Cap and Rotor

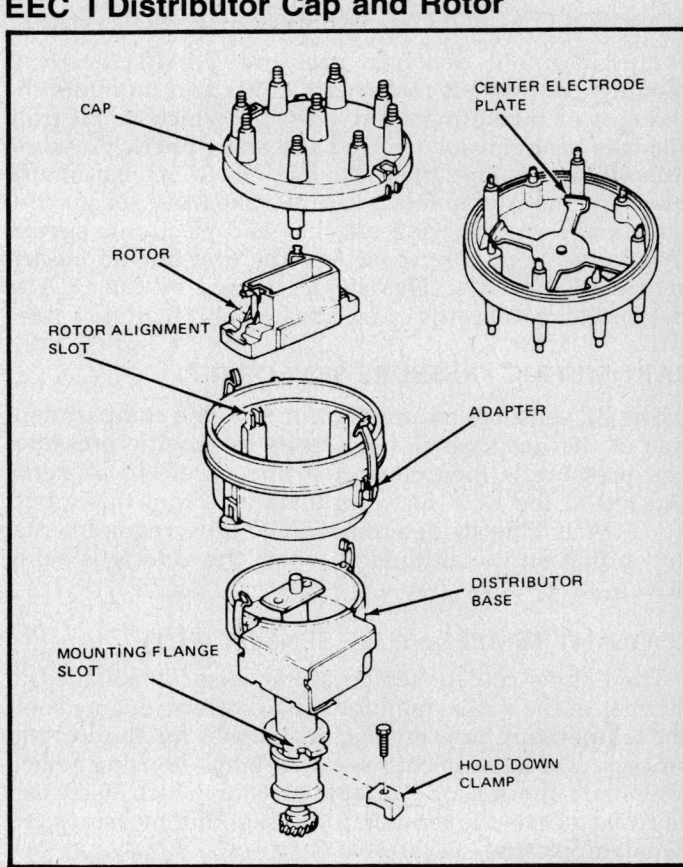

EEC I System Wiring Diagrams

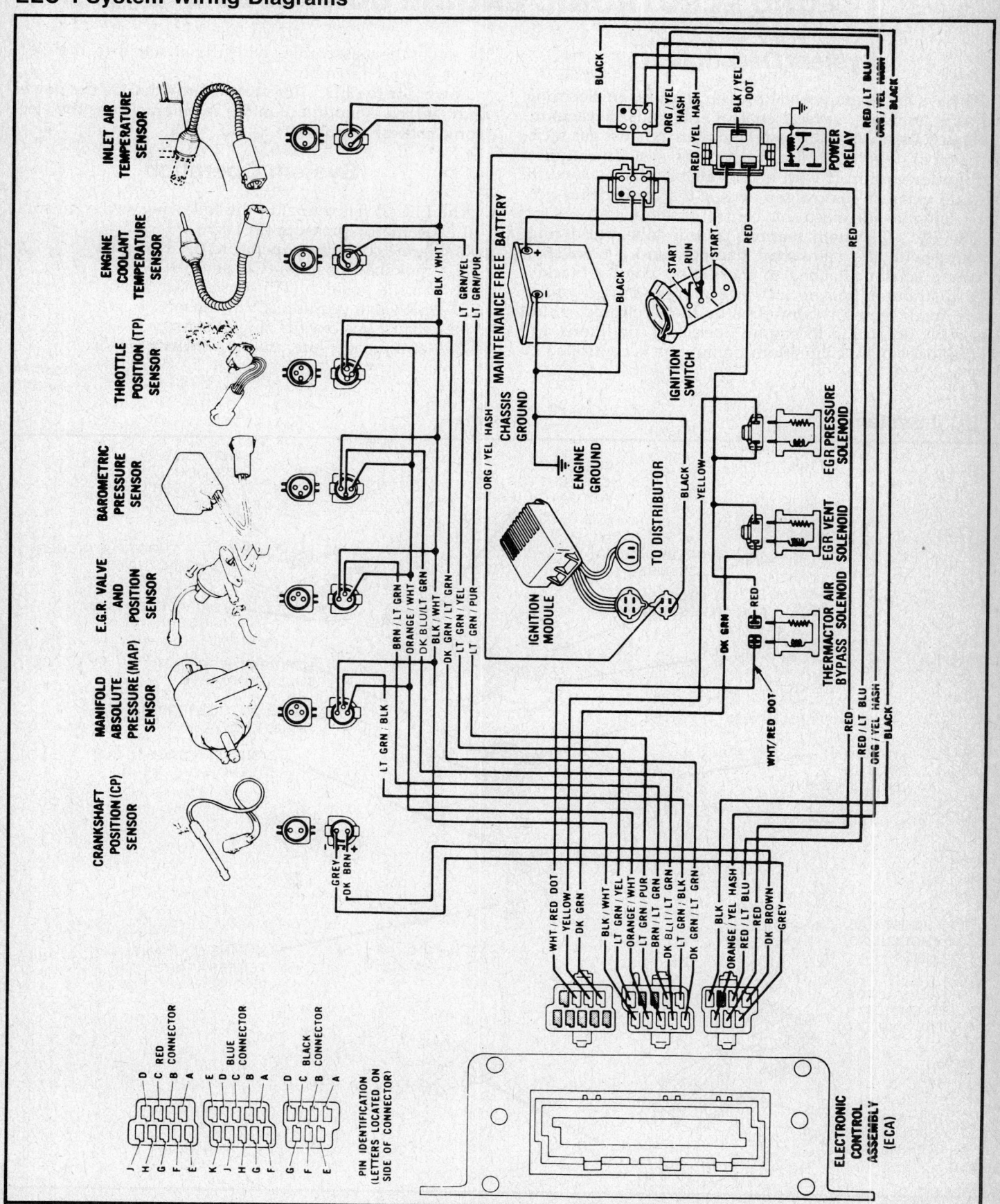

FORD ELECTRONIC ENGINE CONTROLS II

System Description

The system is composed of seven sensors, an electronic control assembly, several control solenoids, a vacuum-operated thermactor air system and an exhaust gas recirculation system (EGR). In addition, the system features a carburetor equipped with a controllable air-fuel mixture and an exhaust gas oxygen sensor that provides a rich/lean signal to the electronic control assembly.

The EEC II system features a four lobe pulse ring, integral with the crankshaft damper, and a crankshaft position sensor attached to the timing pointer bracket. The distributor has no advance or retard mechanism, since spark timing is controlled by the electronic control assembly according to engine operating conditions and individual vehicle calibration. Calibration is controlled by the calibration assembly, which is attached to the electronic control assembly.

Power for the EEC II system is provided by the power relay, which is mounted on the same bracket as the electronic control assembly.

System Operation

The EEC II has a total of the following seven sensors.
1. Barometric pressure (BP) sensor
2. Engine coolant temperature (ECT) sensor
3. Crankshaft position (CP) sensor
4. Throttle position (TP) sensor
5. EGR valve position (EVP) sensor
6. Exhaust gas oxygen (EGO) sensor
7. Manifold absolute pressure (MAP) sensor

EEC II System

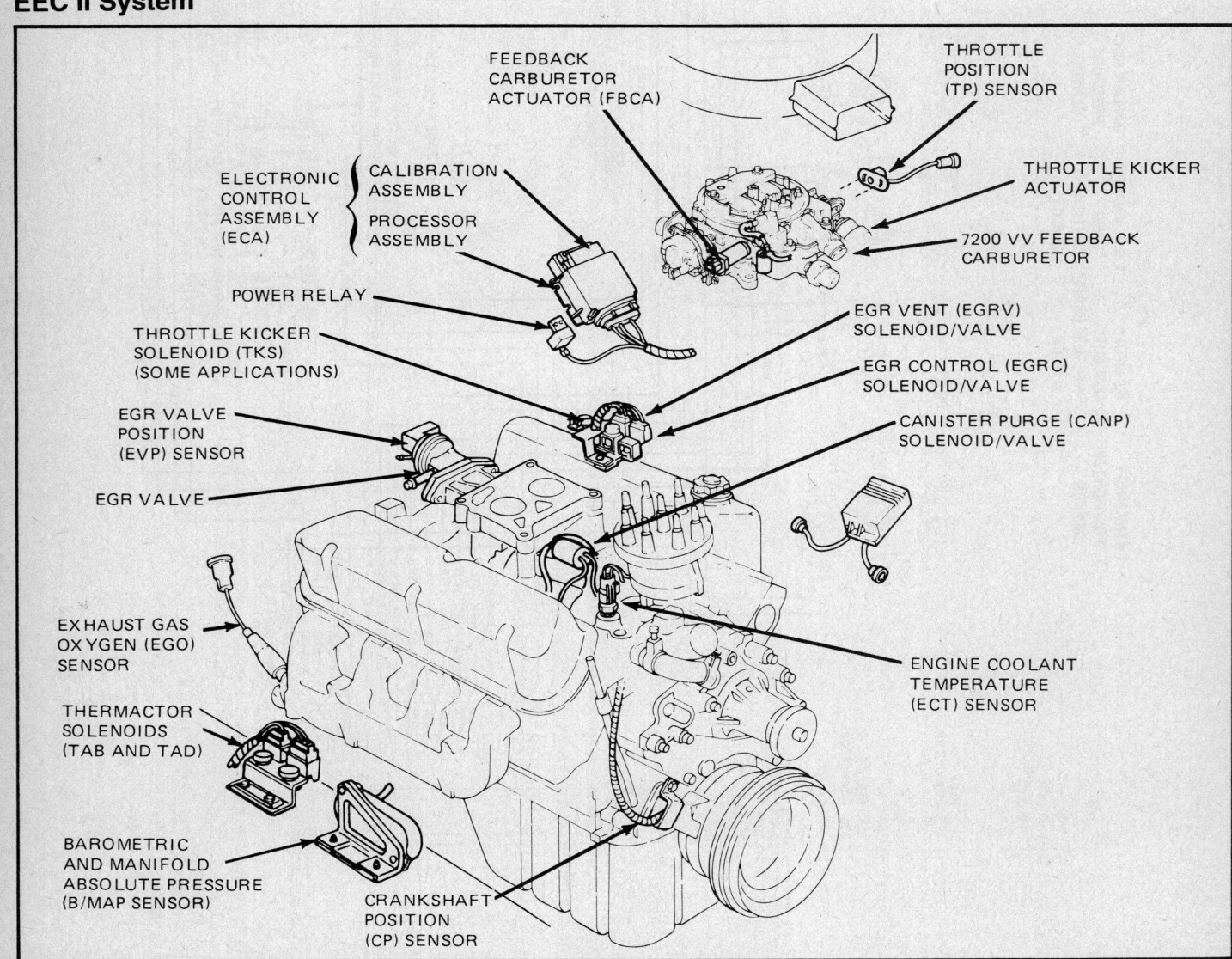

EEC II System Schematic

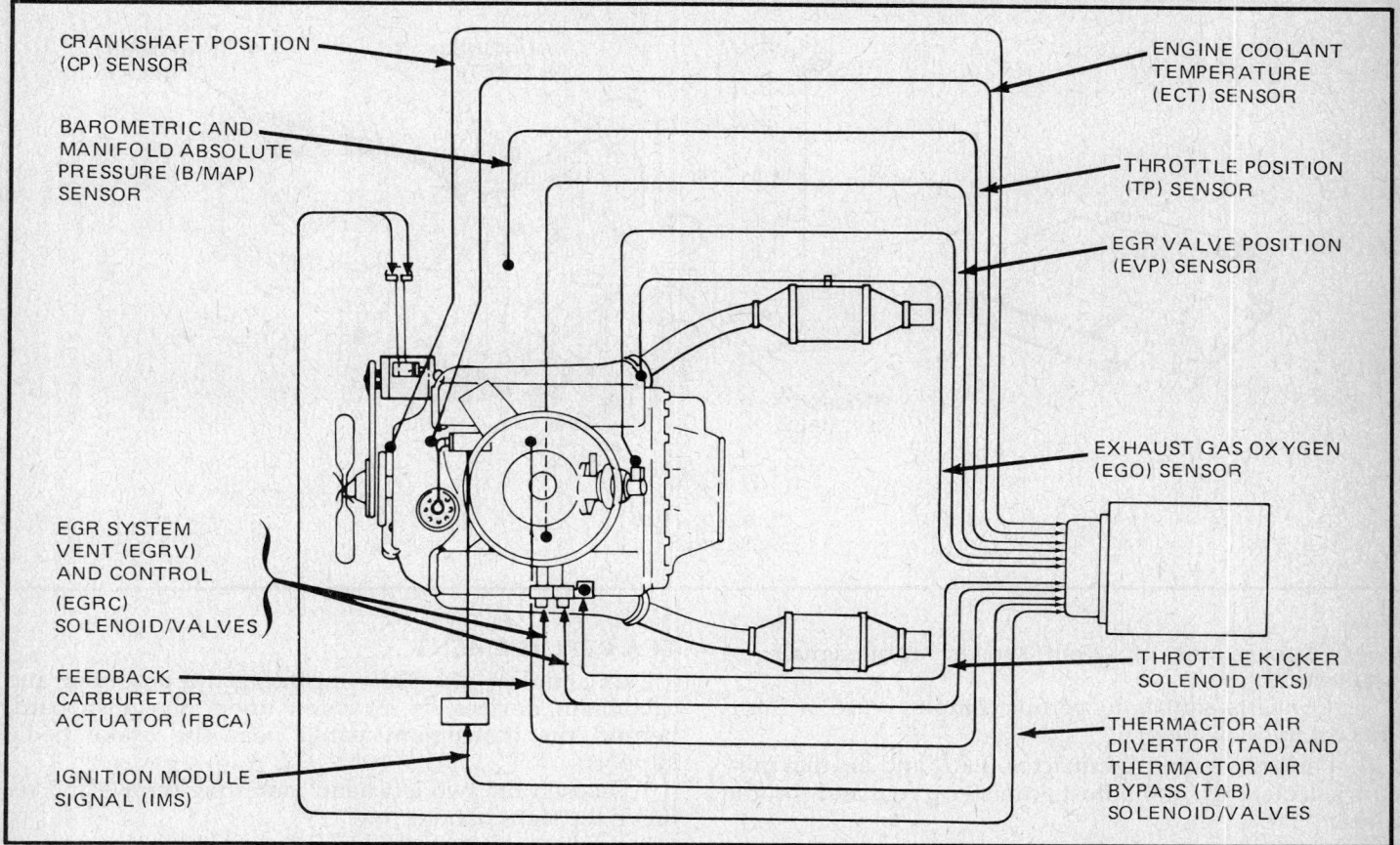

CRANKSHAFT POSITION (CP) SENSOR

BAROMETRIC AND MANIFOLD ABSOLUTE PRESSURE (B/MAP) SENSOR

EGR SYSTEM VENT (EGRV) AND CONTROL (EGRC) SOLENOID/VALVES

FEEDBACK CARBURETOR ACTUATOR (FBCA)

IGNITION MODULE SIGNAL (IMS)

ENGINE COOLANT TEMPERATURE (ECT) SENSOR

THROTTLE POSITION (TP) SENSOR

EGR VALVE POSITION (EVP) SENSOR

EXHAUST GAS OXYGEN (EGO) SENSOR

THROTTLE KICKER SOLENOID (TKS)

THERMACTOR AIR DIVERTOR (TAD) AND THERMACTOR AIR BYPASS (TAB) SOLENOID/VALVES

NOTE   MAP sensor and the BP sensor are contained in a single unit.

During engine starting and operation, the electronic control assembly (ECA) constantly monitors these sensors to determine the required timing advance, EGR flow rate, thermactor air mode and air-fuel ratio for any given instant of vehicle operation.

The ECA then sends output commands for the following.

1. Ignition module, for spark timing
2. Throttle kicker solenoid
3. EGR control solenoids
4. Canister purge solenoids
5. Feedback carburetor actuator (FBCA), to adjust air-fuel mixture
6. Thermactor solenoids, to direct thermactor air flow

The continuous adjustment of ignition timing, EGR flow rate, and air-fuel ratio results in optimum engine performance under all vehicle operating conditions.

FAIL-SAFE

If for some reason there is a failure in the ECA, the system goes into the limited operational strategy (LOS) mode. In this mode, the ECA commands are cut off and the engine operates with initial spark advance only, regardless of sensor input signals. The engine can be operated until repairs are made, but poor performance may be experienced as long as the system is in the LOS mode.

System Components

ELECTRONIC CONTROL ASSEMBLY (ECA)

The ECA consists of two parts, the processor assembly and the calibration assembly.

CALIBRATION ASSEMBLY

The calibration assembly is a memory storage device and is attached to the top of the processor assembly by two screws. It performs three functions.

1. Provides calibration information unique to the vehicle for use by the processor assembly.
2. Stores data calculated by the processor assembly.
3. Recalls appropriate data from the memory bank when required.

PROCESSOR ASSEMBLY

The processor assembly performs four important functions within a fraction of one second.

ENGINE CONTROLS

Electronic Control Assembly

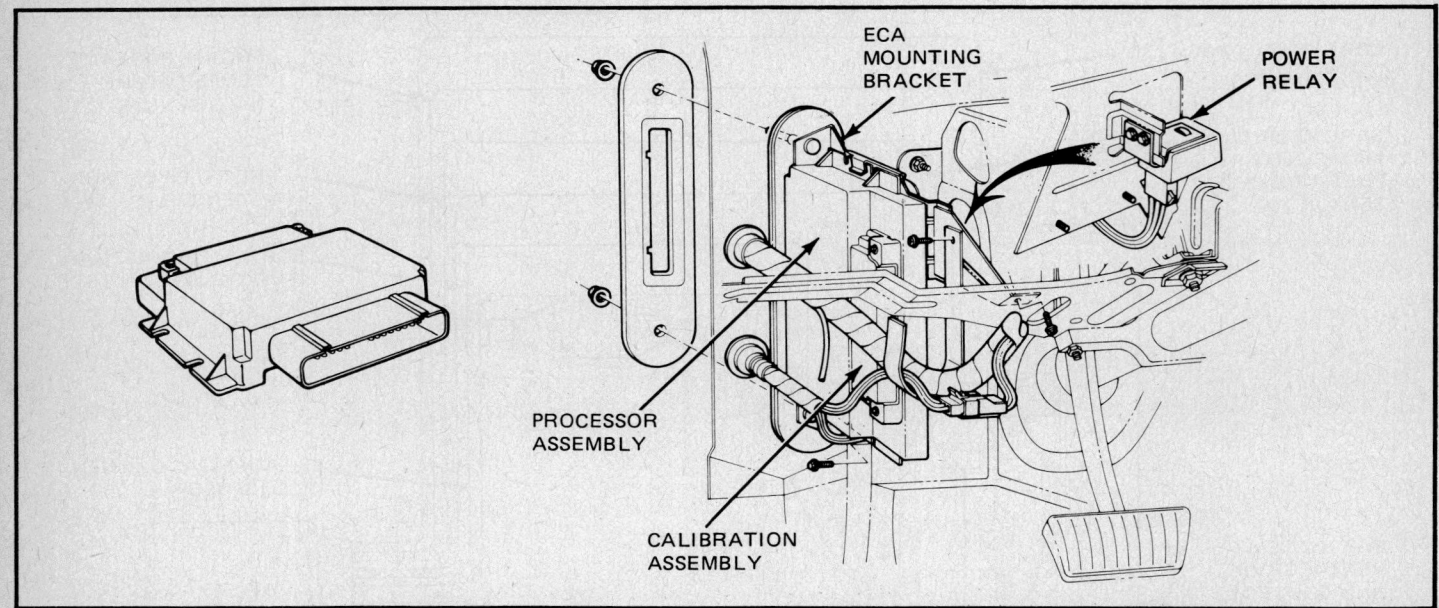

1. Chooses one of seven sensor input signals for analysis.
2. Converts signals to permit computer use of information in calculation.
3. Performs spark, thermactor, EGR and air-fuel mixture calculations, and adjusts canister purge and throttle kicker.
4. Sends electrical output control signals to the ignition module and control solenoids to adjust calibration timing, EGR flow rate, thermactor air mode, carburetor mixture, throttle kicker mode and canister purge mode.

The processor assembly compensates for such variables as altitude, engine rpm, ambient temperature, etc. It also contains a separate power supply which provides a continuous 8 to 10 volts to the sensors.

ECA REPLACEMENT

The complete assembly, including the processor and calibration devices, is mounted under the dashboard, behind the instrument panel near the brake pedal support.
1. Loosen the two left hand mounting screws and remove the right hand screw.
2. Slide the unit out away from the left hand mounting screws.
3. Disconnect the wiring harness connector, which can be tested from the engine compartment.

THROTTLE POSITION SENSOR

The throttle position sensor is a variable resistor control coupled to the carburetor throttle shaft, mounted on a

Throttle Position (TP) Sensor

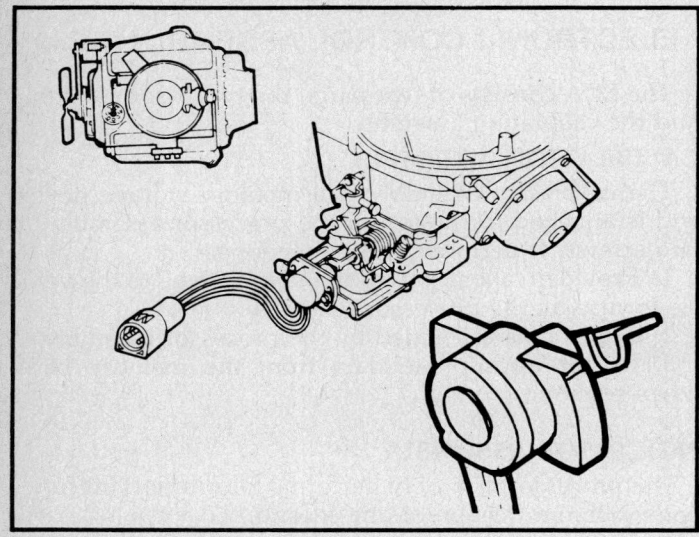

Engine Coolant Temperature (ECT) Sensor

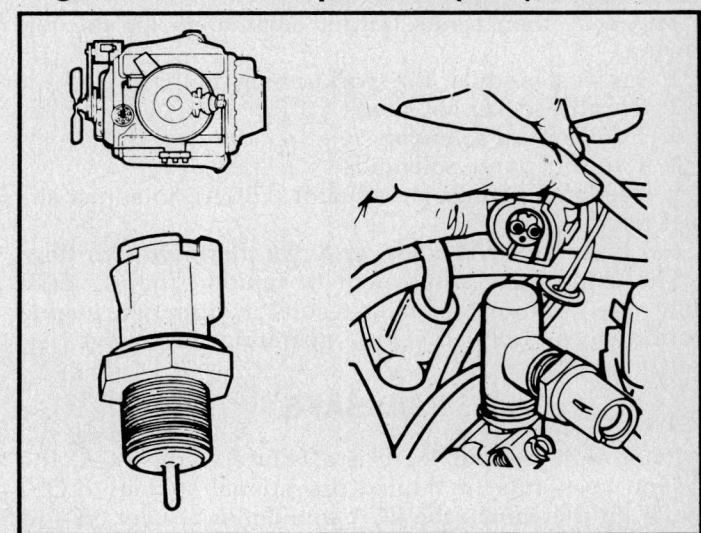

EGR Valve Position Sensor

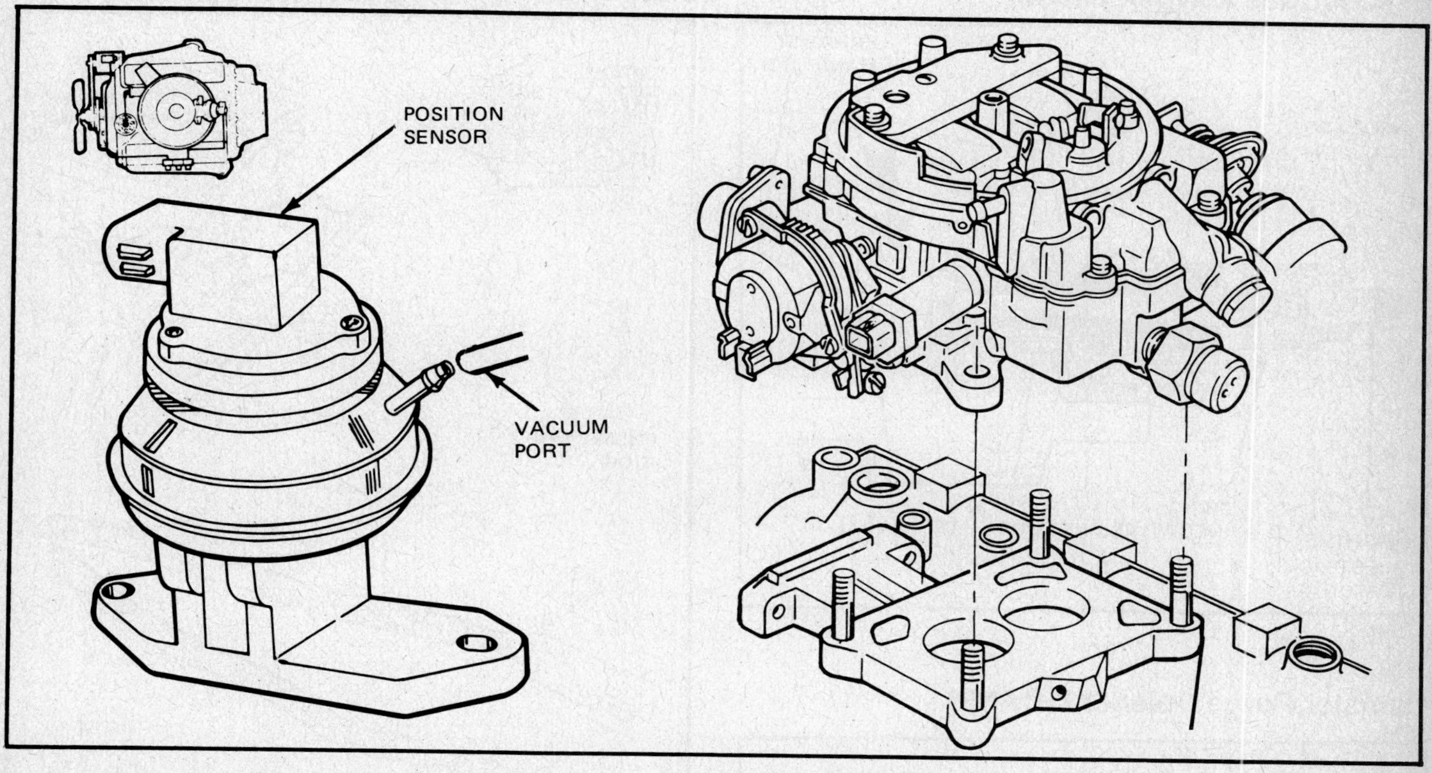

POSITION
SENSOR

VACUUM
PORT

special carburetor bracket. When reference voltage is applied, the developed signal is proportional to the throttle plate angle. This information is supplied to the ECA, indicating closed, part, or wide open throttle.

ADJUSTMENT

CHILTON CAUTION   Use only a digital-type voltmeter, as conventional meters are not sensitive enough to gather EEC II system data. Also, use of a standard 9-volt ohm-meter may damage the computer calibration unit or the EGR position sensor.

1. If sensor needs replacement, correct positioning is essential or false throttle angle information will be fed to the ECA.

2. Turn ignition to the run position with the engine off.
3. Adjust the sensor by loosening the mounting screws and turning the sensor until voltage is between 1.85 and 2.35. Tighten the screws to 8-10 in. lbs.

COOLANT TEMPERATURE SENSOR

The coolant temperature sensor consists of a thermistor in a brass housing with the integral harness connector extending from the body. It is mounted in the heater outlet fitting, in front of the intake manifold, near the left rocker arm cover. As the temperature rises in the cooling system, the resistance of the sensor decreases, sending a stronger signal to the ECA. This sensor replaces the cool-

Barometric Manifold Absolute Pressure (B/MAP) Sensor

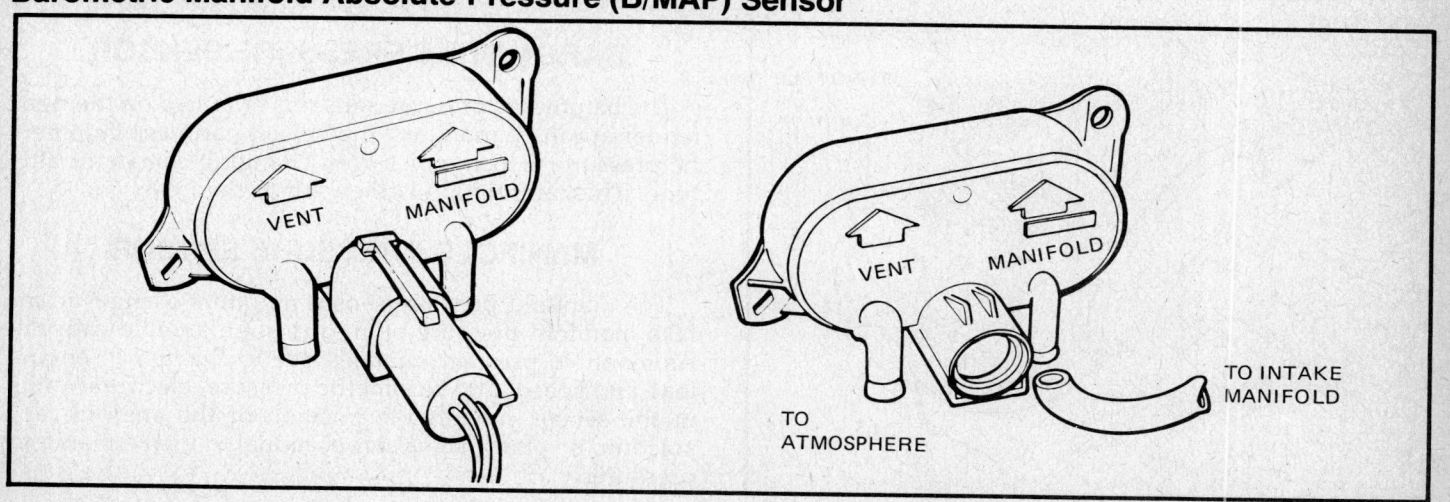

VENT   MANIFOLD

VENT   MANIFOLD

TO INTAKE
MANIFOLD

TO
ATMOSPHERE

ENGINE CONTROLS

Exhaust Gas Oxygen Sensor

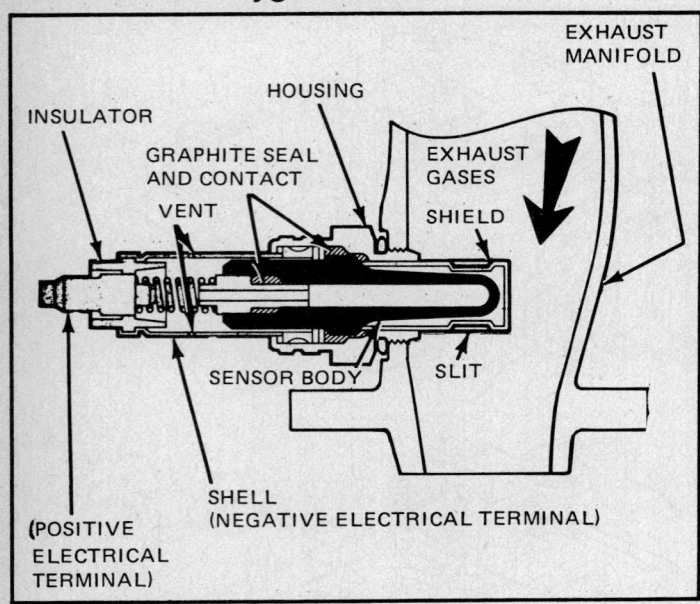

Canister Purge Solenoid (CANP)

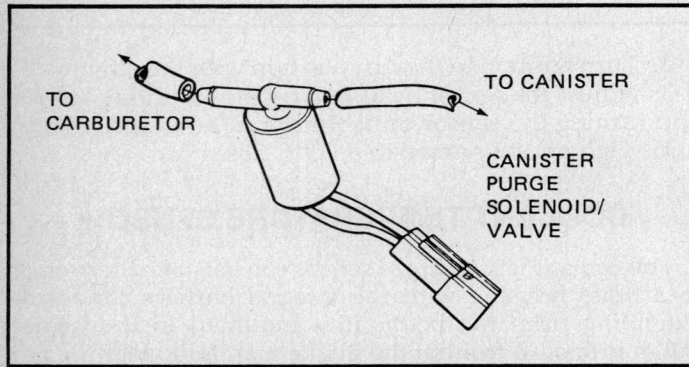

Throttle Kicker Solenoid and Actuator

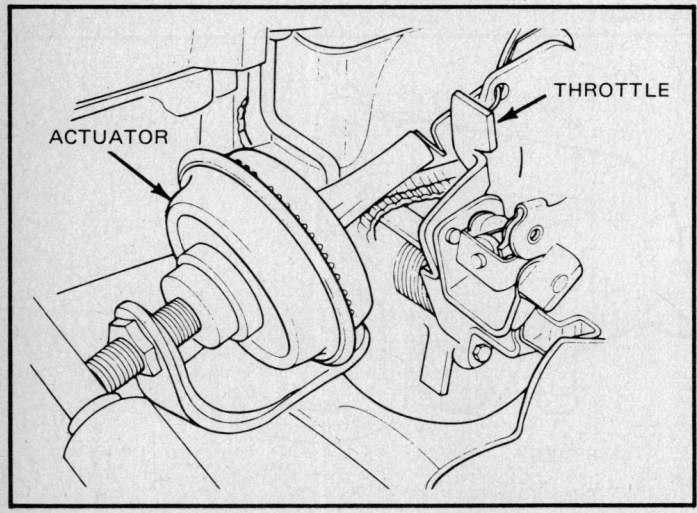

Crankshaft Position Sensor

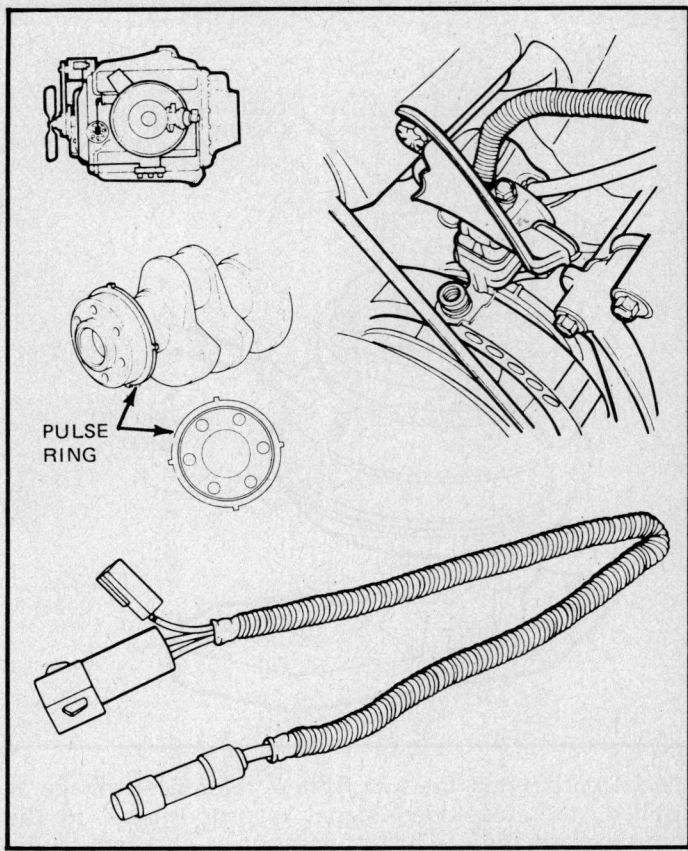

ant temperature switch and the EGR ported vacuum switch in vehicles not equipped with EEC II.

EGR VALVE POSITION SENSOR

The EGR valve position sensor is mounted on the EGR valve and measures the linear position the metering rod in the fixed orifice. The developed signal to the ECA varies with the amount of EGR valve opening.

NOTE   At higher altitudes, the EGR signal may be eliminated to maintain proper engine performance.

BAROMETRIC PRESSURE SENSOR

The barometric pressure sensor is mounted on the right fender apron. It monitors engine compartment barometric pressure, which varies with changing climate or altitude. This information is then fed to the ECA.

MANIFOLD PRESSURE SENSOR

The manifold pressure sensor monitors changes in intake manifold pressure by means of an aneroid capsule. As manifold pressure changes due to changes in engine load and speed, and barometric pressure, electronic units in the sensor convert the position of the aneroid capsule into a voltage signal proportional to intake manifold pressure.

Feedback Carburetor Actuator

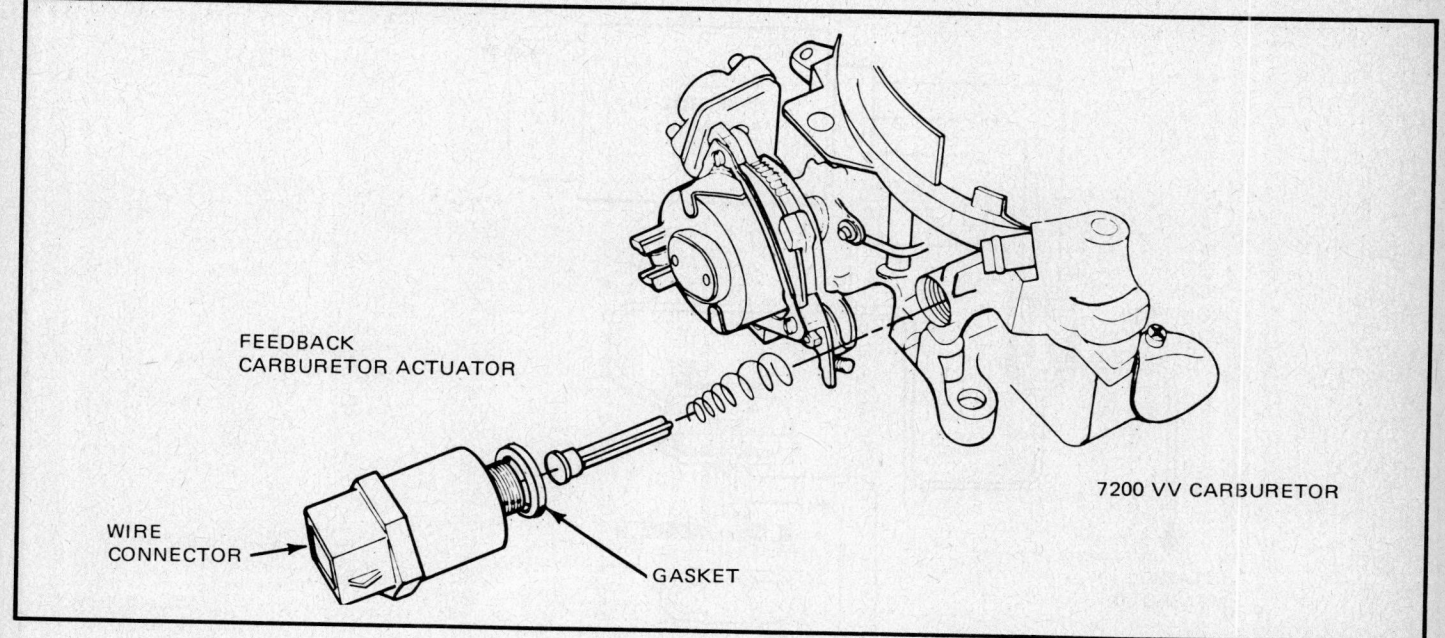

FEEDBACK
CARBURETOR ACTUATOR

7200 VV CARBURETOR

WIRE
CONNECTOR →

← GASKET

CRANKSHAFT POSITION SENSOR

The crankshaft position sensor is mounted on the front of the engine block and is held in place by a retaining clip and screw. The tip of the sensor contains an electromagnet, whose magnetic field is cut by the rotating lobes on the pulse ring. This action generates an output voltage to the ECA.

Positioning of the pulse ring is critical, since this determines basic engine timing. The pulse ring is a press fit on the crankshaft damper, and cannot be removed or adjusted. It is set for a basic timing of 10° BTDC.

EXHAUST GAS OXYGEN SENSOR

SENSOR OPERATION

1. The sensor shield covers the sensor body and protrudes into the stream of exhaust gases in the manifold.
2. Exhaust gases flow into the shield and contact the sensor body through slits in the shield.
3. Atmospheric pressure is admitted through a vent to the end of the sensor body opposite the exhaust gases.
4. The sensor body generates a voltage, due to pressure difference between vent air and oxygen in the exhaust gases.
   a. In a rich mixture, low oxygen pressure generates higher output voltage (0.6 volt or greater).
   b. In a lean mixture, high oxygen pressure generates a lower output voltage (0.2 volt or less).

CANISTER PURGE (CANP) SOLENOID

The canister purge solenoid is a combination valve/solenoid, located in the canister vent line. Operated by a signal from the ECA, it controls the flow of vapors during engine operating modes. Operation depends on calibration, but is also influenced by engine coolant temperature, engine rpm, the time since engine start-up and throttle position.

THROTTLE KICKER SOLENOID (TKS) AND ACTUATOR (TKA)

The vacuum-operated actuator which increases idle rpm, is energized when the solenoid receives a signal from the computer. Idle speed is increased during air conditioning system operation or when engine temperature is too high or too low.

FEEDBACK CARBURETOR ACTUATOR (FBCA)

The FBCA is a stepper motor mounted into the model 7200 VV carburetor. It has 120 steps, with a total range of .400" in and out. Setting of the air-fuel mixture is dependent on calibration of the computer, so the air-fuel ratio changes constantly due to sensor signals to the ECA.

EGR System

GENERAL DESCRIPTION

The EGR system is similar to those found on vehicles not equipped with EEC II. Opening and closing of the valve, which can not be seen when the EGR assembly is mounted on the engine, is controlled by the ECA signal to the EGR valve position sensor. When the EGR valve is open, it allows exhaust gases to be reburned in the engine, reducing the formation of nitrous oxides (NOx).

ENGINE CONTROLS

FORD ELECTRONIC ENGINE CONTROLS II

EGR System Used With EEC II

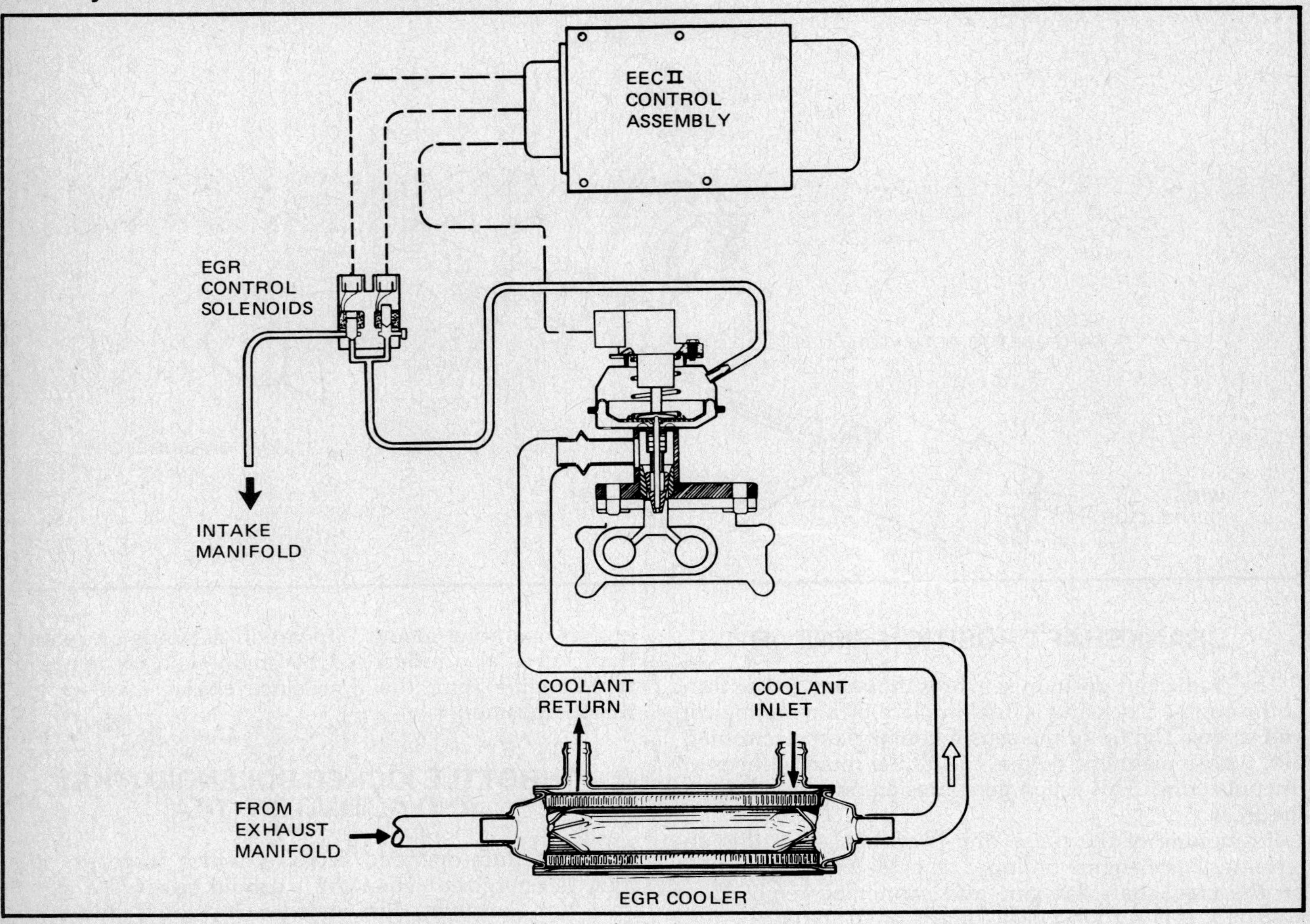

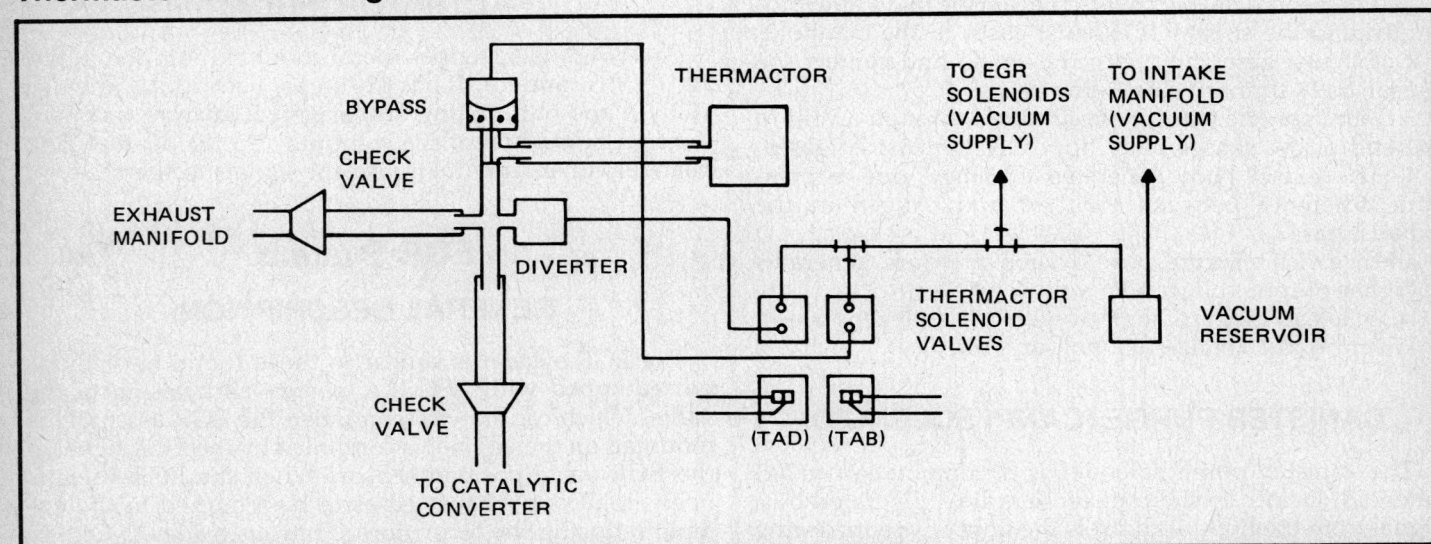

Thermactor Control Diagram

EGR Solenoid Valve Operation

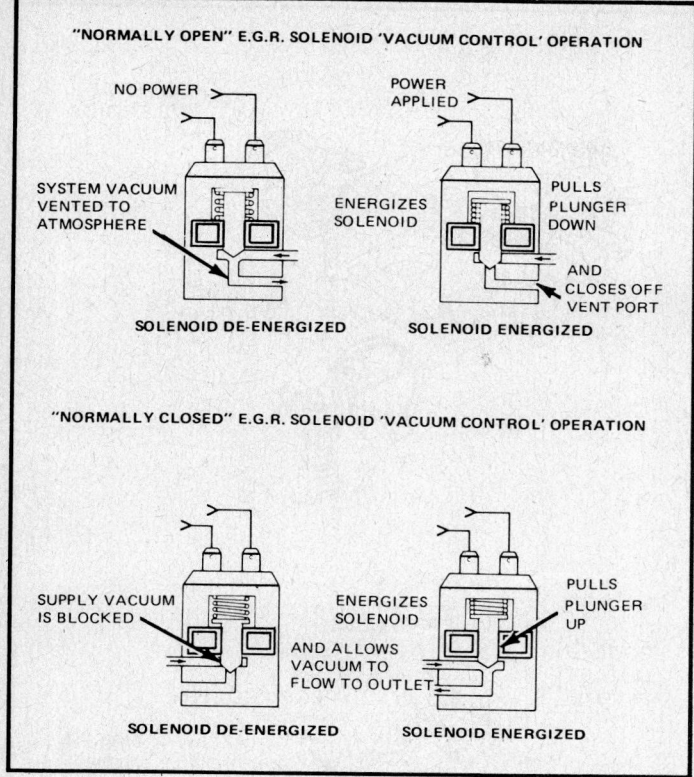

"NORMALLY OPEN" E.G.R. SOLENOID 'VACUUM CONTROL' OPERATION

NO POWER

SYSTEM VACUUM VENTED TO ATMOSPHERE

SOLENOID DE-ENERGIZED

POWER APPLIED

ENERGIZES SOLENOID

PULLS PLUNGER DOWN

AND CLOSES OFF VENT PORT

SOLENOID ENERGIZED

"NORMALLY CLOSED" E.G.R. SOLENOID 'VACUUM CONTROL' OPERATION

SUPPLY VACUUM IS BLOCKED

SOLENOID DE-ENERGIZED

ENERGIZES SOLENOID

AND ALLOWS VACUUM TO FLOW TO OUTLET

PULLS PLUNGER UP

SOLENOID ENERGIZED

Maintain EGR Flow System Operation

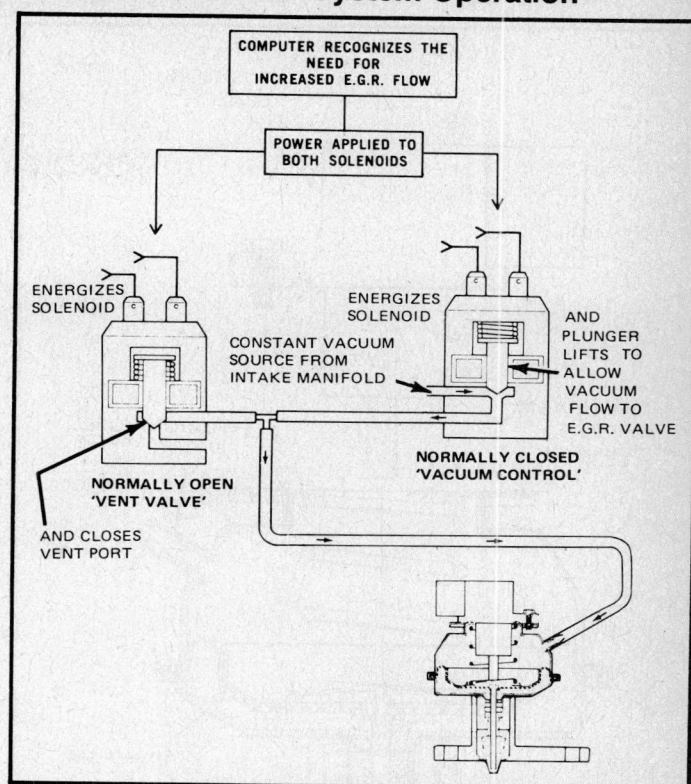

COMPUTER RECOGNIZES THE NEED FOR INCREASED E.G.R. FLOW

POWER APPLIED TO BOTH SOLENOIDS

ENERGIZES SOLENOID

ENERGIZES SOLENOID

CONSTANT VACUUM SOURCE FROM INTAKE MANIFOLD

AND PLUNGER LIFTS TO ALLOW VACUUM FLOW TO E.G.R. VALVE

NORMALLY OPEN 'VENT VALVE'

AND CLOSES VENT PORT

NORMALLY CLOSED 'VACUUM CONTROL'

Increase EGR Flow System Operation

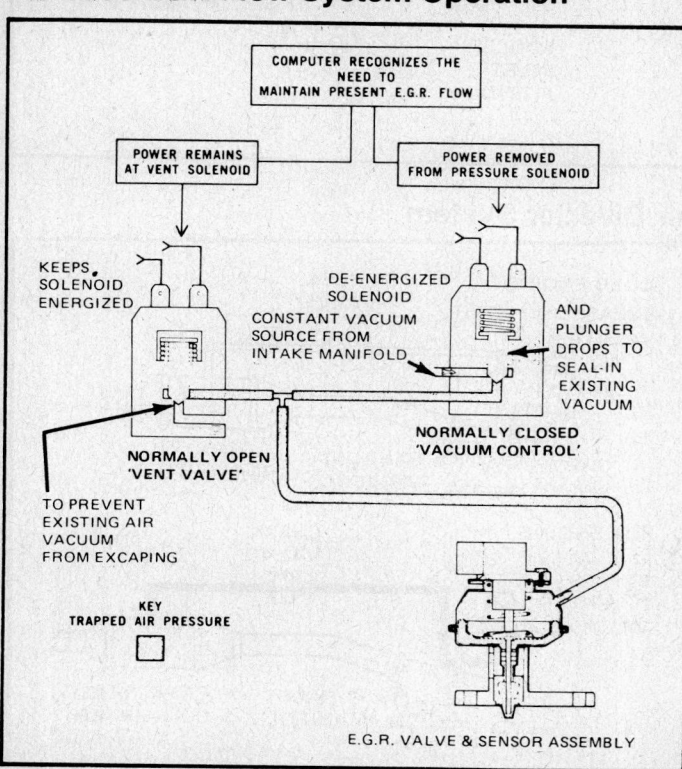

COMPUTER RECOGNIZES THE NEED TO MAINTAIN PRESENT E.G.R. FLOW

POWER REMAINS AT VENT SOLENOID

POWER REMOVED FROM PRESSURE SOLENOID

KEEPS SOLENOID ENERGIZED

DE-ENERGIZED SOLENOID

CONSTANT VACUUM SOURCE FROM INTAKE MANIFOLD

AND PLUNGER DROPS TO SEAL-IN EXISTING VACUUM

NORMALLY OPEN 'VENT VALVE'

NORMALLY CLOSED 'VACUUM CONTROL'

TO PREVENT EXISTING AIR VACUUM FROM EXCAPING

KEY
TRAPPED AIR PRESSURE

E.G.R. VALVE & SENSOR ASSEMBLY

Decrease EGR Flow System Operation

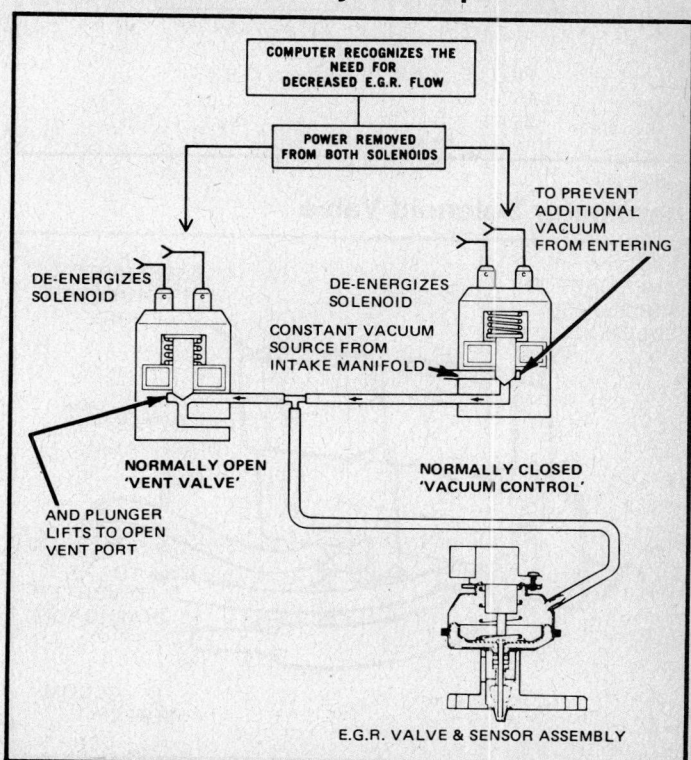

COMPUTER RECOGNIZES THE NEED FOR DECREASED E.G.R. FLOW

POWER REMOVED FROM BOTH SOLENOIDS

DE-ENERGIZES SOLENOID

DE-ENERGIZES SOLENOID

TO PREVENT ADDITIONAL VACUUM FROM ENTERING

CONSTANT VACUUM SOURCE FROM INTAKE MANIFOLD

NORMALLY OPEN 'VENT VALVE'

NORMALLY CLOSED 'VACUUM CONTROL'

AND PLUNGER LIFTS TO OPEN VENT PORT

E.G.R. VALVE & SENSOR ASSEMBLY

ENGINE CONTROLS

FORD ELECTRONIC ENGINE CONTROLS II

EGR Valve

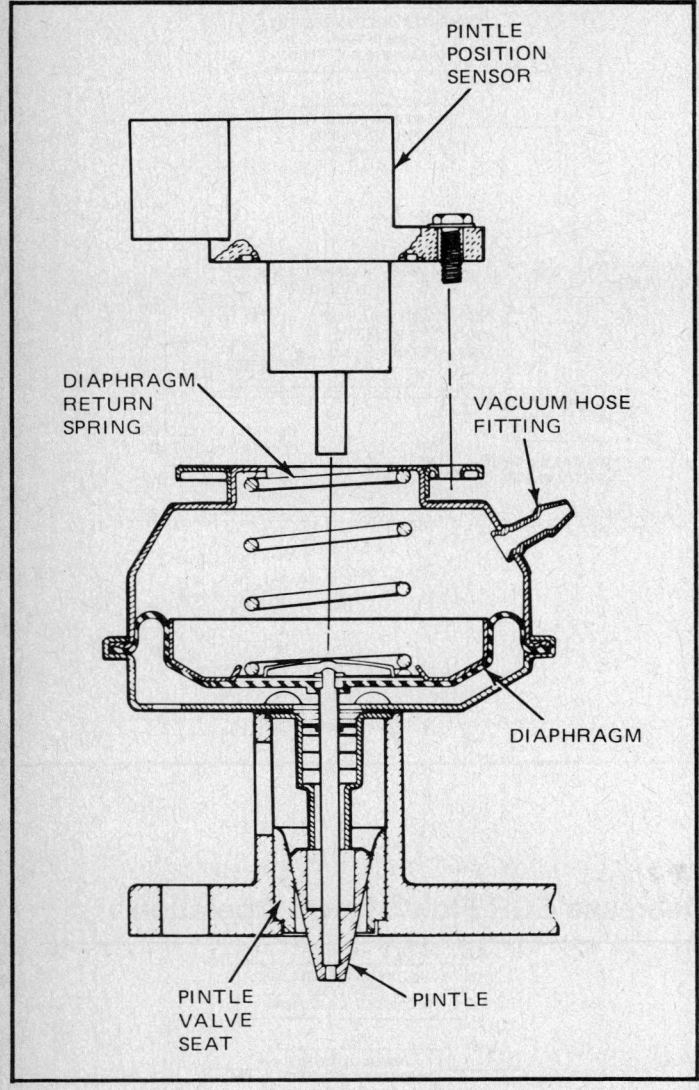

PINTLE POSITION SENSOR

DIAPHRAGM RETURN SPRING

VACUUM HOSE FITTING

DIAPHRAGM

PINTLE VALVE SEAT

PINTLE

EGR Cooler Assembly

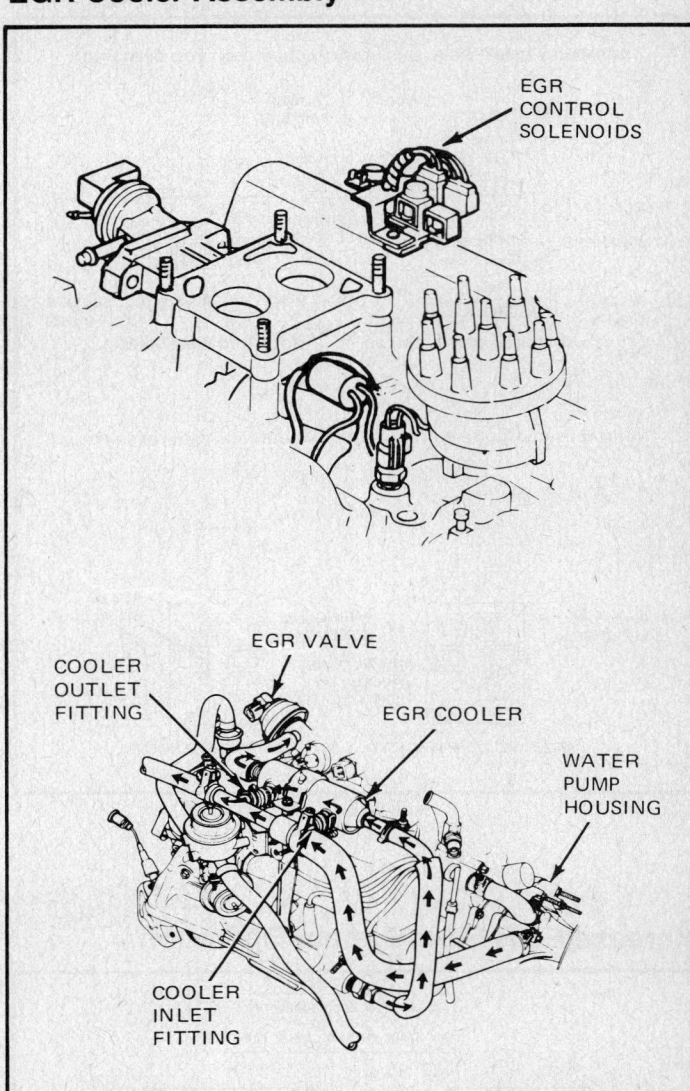

EGR CONTROL SOLENOIDS

COOLER OUTLET FITTING

EGR VALVE

EGR COOLER

WATER PUMP HOUSING

COOLER INLET FITTING

Thermactor Solenoid Valve

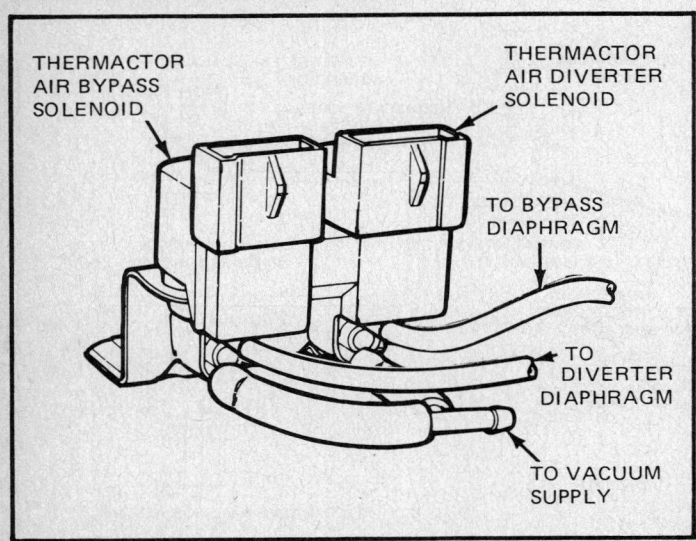

THERMACTOR AIR BYPASS SOLENOID

THERMACTOR AIR DIVERTER SOLENOID

TO BYPASS DIAPHRAGM

TO DIVERTER DIAPHRAGM

TO VACUUM SUPPLY

Air Diverter System

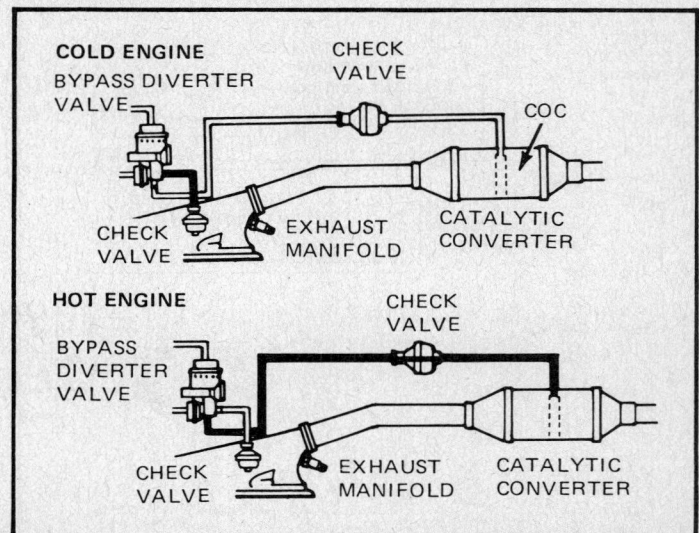

COLD ENGINE

BYPASS DIVERTER VALVE

CHECK VALVE

COC

CHECK VALVE

EXHAUST MANIFOLD

CATALYTIC CONVERTER

HOT ENGINE

BYPASS DIVERTER VALVE

CHECK VALVE

CHECK VALVE

EXHAUST MANIFOLD

CATALYTIC CONVERTER

COMPONENTS AND OPERATION

EGR VALVE AND SENSOR ASSEMBLY

The EGR valve and sensor assembly is made up of the pintle valve and seat assembly, the actuator diaphragm and housing assembly, and the EGR valve position sensor (EVP).

The EGR valve is operated by vacuum from the EGR control (EGRC) and EGR vacuum (EGRV) solenoid/valves. These solenoid/valves work together to apply vacuum to the EGR valve and increase EGR, to maintain vacuum and EGR, or to vent vacuum to the atmosphere and shut off EGR.

The vacuum from the control solenoid/valves pulls on the actuator diaphragm which is attached to the pintle valve. The pintle valve is tapered so that EGR flow is determined by its position.

The EGR valve position sensor monitors the position of the pintle valve and feeds this information to the ECA. The ECA then determines whether to increase, maintain or shut off EGR flow.

EGR COOLER ASSEMBLY

The EGR cooler assembly is a heat exchanger used with the electronic control assembly to provide improved flow characteristics and better engine operation. It uses engine coolant to cool exhaust gases passing from the exhaust manifold through the EGR valve to the intake manifold.

EGR CONTROL SOLENOIDS

The EGR control solenoids, mounted in a bracket above the left rocker arm cover, control actual vacuum to the EGR valve. Closest to the rear of the engine is the normally open EGR vacuum (EGRV) solenoid. Next to it is the normally closed EGR control (EGRC) solenoid.

Since the vacuum valve is normally open, its output port is open to the atmosphere in the de-energized mode, closed in the energized mode. The control valve is normally closed, so its output port is closed in the de-energized mode and open to system vacuum in the energized mode.

Thermactor Air System

COMPONENTS AND OPERATION

THERMACTOR AIR PUMP

The thermactor air pump is engine-driven and supplies air to the bypass/diverter valve. It is located on a bracket on the lower right front of the engine.

AIR BYPASS/DIVERTER VALVE

The bypass/diverter valve is used to route air in three directions. It routes air downstream to the catalytic converter mid-bed, upstream to the exhaust manifold and bypass to the atmosphere. Air routing is controlled by the ECA, depending on engine temperature, sensor input, calibration and the ECA program.

Normal operation of the system is as follows.
1. Upstream during engine start-up.
2. Downstream during engine operation.

3. Bypass after a certain time at closed-throttle operation, or if the EGO sensor inputs exceed a certain time period (for catalyst protection).
4. Bypass at wide open throttle.

Ignition System

Ignition systems for the EEC II equipped vehicles use a Duraspark® III ignition module and a Duraspark® II coil to generate a high voltage spark. Since the computer controls all ignition timing, there are no vacuum or centrifugal advance mechanisms in the ignition module. The only function of the distributor is to transmit high voltage from the coil to the correct spark plug.

BI-LEVEL ROTOR AND DISTRIBUTOR CAP

Since the EEC II system allows up to 36° distributor advance, the new design rotor and cap allow additional advance capability without crossfire.

The bi-level rotor and cap have two levels of secondary voltage distribution. As the rotor turns, one of the high voltage electrode pick-up arms aligns with one spoke of the distributor cap center electrode plate, allowing high voltage to be transmitted from the plate through the rotor, cap and plug wire. The correct firing order is 1-3-7-2-6-5-4-8.

NOTE *Engine firing order can not be read off the distributor cap.*

CHILTON CAUTION *Proper rotor alignment must be established to obtain maximum allowable spark advance without crossfiring to adjacent distributor cap electrodes.*

Air Bypass/Diverter Valve

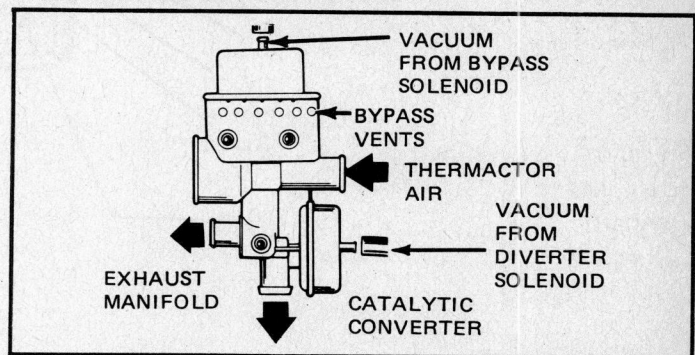

Dual-Bed Catalytic Converter

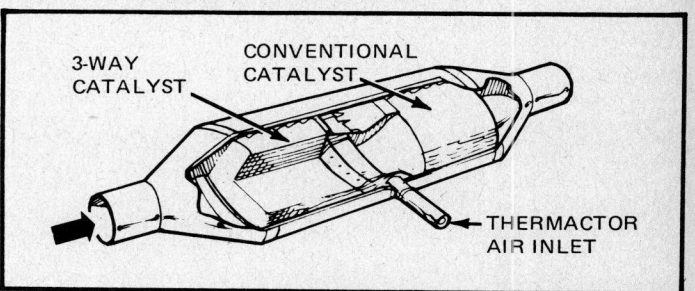

ENGINE CONTROLS

FORD ELECTRONIC ENGINE CONTROLS II

Electronic Control Assembly (ECA) 32-Pin Harness Connector

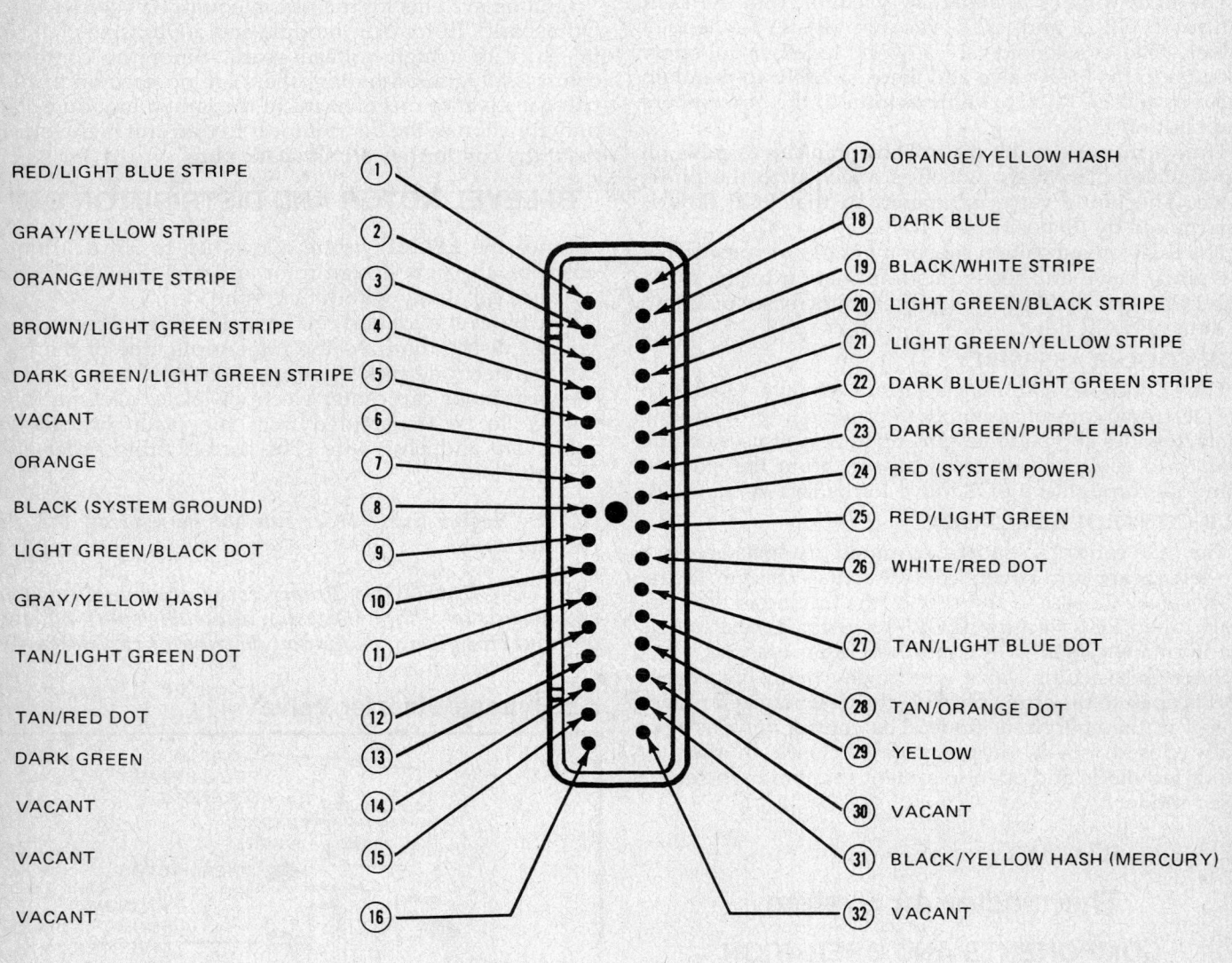

RED/LIGHT BLUE STRIPE — ①	⑰ — ORANGE/YELLOW HASH
GRAY/YELLOW STRIPE — ②	⑱ — DARK BLUE
ORANGE/WHITE STRIPE — ③	⑲ — BLACK/WHITE STRIPE
BROWN/LIGHT GREEN STRIPE — ④	⑳ — LIGHT GREEN/BLACK STRIPE
DARK GREEN/LIGHT GREEN STRIPE — ⑤	㉑ — LIGHT GREEN/YELLOW STRIPE
VACANT — ⑥	㉒ — DARK BLUE/LIGHT GREEN STRIPE
ORANGE — ⑦	㉓ — DARK GREEN/PURPLE HASH
BLACK (SYSTEM GROUND) — ⑧	㉔ — RED (SYSTEM POWER)
LIGHT GREEN/BLACK DOT — ⑨	㉕ — RED/LIGHT GREEN
GRAY/YELLOW HASH — ⑩	㉖ — WHITE/RED DOT
TAN/LIGHT GREEN DOT — ⑪	㉗ — TAN/LIGHT BLUE DOT
TAN/RED DOT — ⑫	㉘ — TAN/ORANGE DOT
DARK GREEN — ⑬	㉙ — YELLOW
VACANT — ⑭	㉚ — VACANT
VACANT — ⑮	㉛ — BLACK/YELLOW HASH (MERCURY)
VACANT — ⑯	㉜ — VACANT

EEC II Wiring Diagram

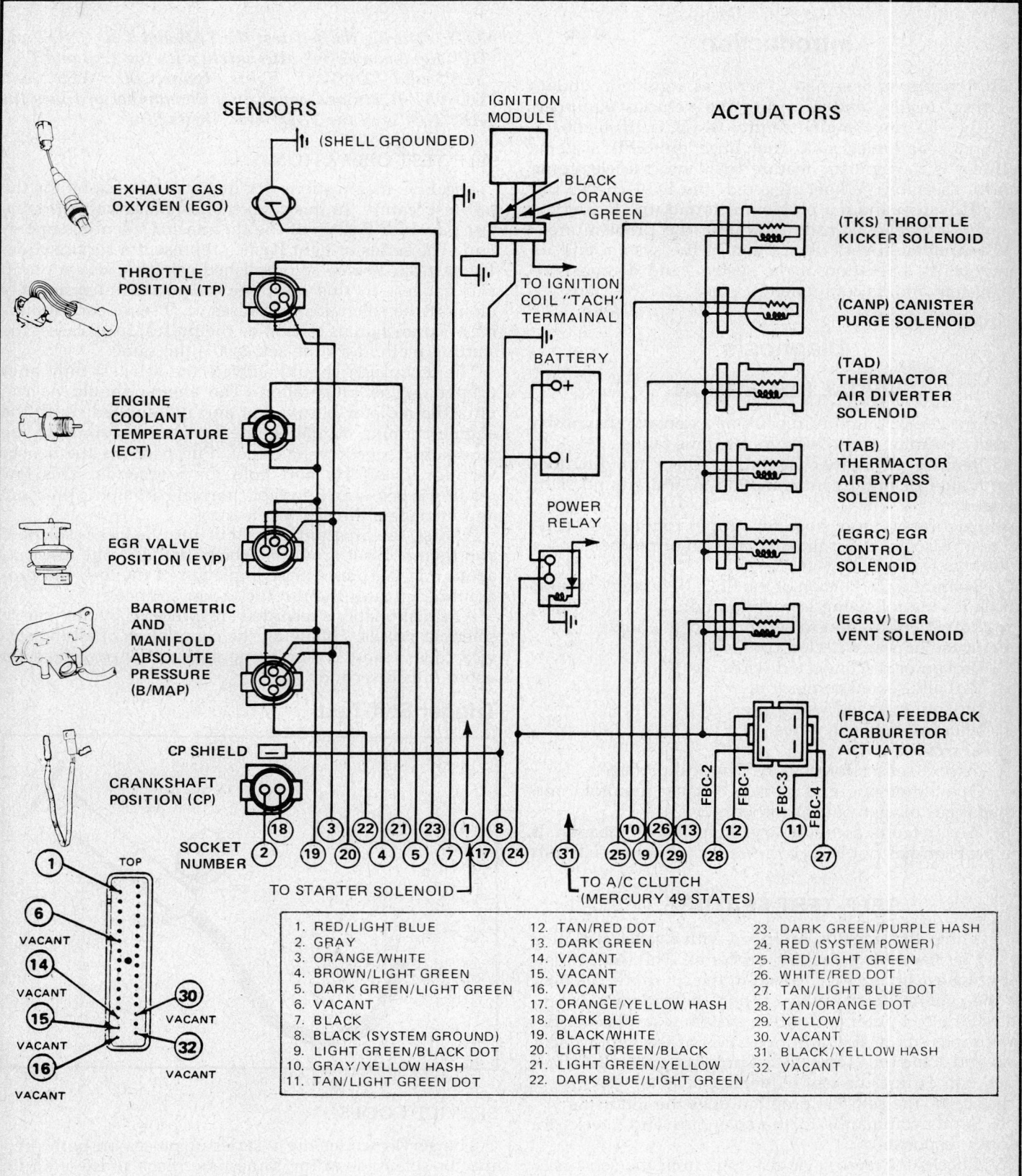

SENSORS   IGNITION MODULE   ACTUATORS

(SHELL GROUNDED)

EXHAUST GAS OXYGEN (EGO)

BLACK
ORANGE
GREEN

(TKS) THROTTLE KICKER SOLENOID

THROTTLE POSITION (TP)

TO IGNITION COIL "TACH" TERMAINAL

(CANP) CANISTER PURGE SOLENOID

BATTERY

(TAD) THERMACTOR AIR DIVERTER SOLENOID

ENGINE COOLANT TEMPERATURE (ECT)

(TAB) THERMACTOR AIR BYPASS SOLENOID

POWER RELAY

(EGRC) EGR CONTROL SOLENOID

EGR VALVE POSITION (EVP)

(EGRV) EGR VENT SOLENOID

BAROMETRIC AND MANIFOLD ABSOLUTE PRESSURE (B/MAP)

(FBCA) FEEDBACK CARBURETOR ACTUATOR

CP SHIELD

CRANKSHAFT POSITION (CP)

FBC-2 FBC-1 FBC-3 FBC-4

SOCKET NUMBER

TOP

VACANT
VACANT
VACANT
VACANT
VACANT
VACANT
VACANT

TO STARTER SOLENOID

TO A/C CLUTCH (MERCURY 49 STATES)

1. RED/LIGHT BLUE	12. TAN/RED DOT	23. DARK GREEN/PURPLE HASH
2. GRAY	13. DARK GREEN	24. RED (SYSTEM POWER)
3. ORANGE/WHITE	14. VACANT	25. RED/LIGHT GREEN
4. BROWN/LIGHT GREEN	15. VACANT	26. WHITE/RED DOT
5. DARK GREEN/LIGHT GREEN	16. VACANT	27. TAN/LIGHT BLUE DOT
6. VACANT	17. ORANGE/YELLOW HASH	28. TAN/ORANGE DOT
7. BLACK	18. DARK BLUE	29. YELLOW
8. BLACK (SYSTEM GROUND)	19. BLACK/WHITE	30. VACANT
9. LIGHT GREEN/BLACK DOT	20. LIGHT GREEN/BLACK	31. BLACK/YELLOW HASH
10. GRAY/YELLOW HASH	21. LIGHT GREEN/YELLOW	32. VACANT
11. TAN/LIGHT GREEN DOT	22. DARK BLUE/LIGHT GREEN	

FORD ELECTRONIC ENGINE CONTROLS III

Introduction

This chapter is designed to serve as a guide in understanding, testing and servicing the vehicles equipped with the electronic engine control III (ECC III) feedback carburetor and electronic fuel injection (EFI) system. Self-test is a diagnostic feature built into the electronic control assembly. When triggered, the ECA checks the EEC III system and if a problem is found, the technician is given a diagnostic code indicating the problem area.

This chapter covers description of the system and its components, operation of the system, and diagnosis of the system and its components.

Diagnosis

VISUAL INSPECTION

Before attempting any repairs or extensive diagnosis, visually examine the vehicle for obvious faults.

1. Remove air cleaner assembly. Check for dirt, foreign matter or other contamination in and around filter element.

2. Examine vacuum hose for proper routing and connection. Also check for broken, cracked or pinched hoses or fittings.

3. Examine each portion of the EEC III wiring harness. Check for the following at each location.
   a. Proper connection to sensors and solenoids
   b. Loose or disconnected connectors
   c. Broken or disconnected wires
   d. Partially seated connectors
   e. Broken or frayed wires
   f. Shorting between wires
   g. Corrosion

4. Inspect sensor for obvious physical damage.

5. Operate engine and inspect exhaust manifold and exhaust gas oxygen sensor for leaks.

6. Repair faults as necessary. Reinstall air cleaner. If the problem has not been corrected, proceed to self-test.

SELF-TEST FEATURE

The EEC III system is equipped with a self-test feature to aid in diagnosing possible problems. The self-test is a set of instructions programmed in the computer memory of the calibration assembly. When the program is activated, the computer performs a system test. This verifies the proper connection and operation of the various sensors and actuators. The self-test program controls vehicle operation during the test sequence.

Basically, the self-test program does the following.

1. Sends commands to the solenoids and checks for proper response.

2. Checks for reasonable readings from the sensors.

3. Produces numbered codes that inform the technician of a trouble area or of "all okay" operation.

NOTE   During the self-test the TAB and TAD "NO" and "UP" lights may blink alternately with the TAB and TAD "YES" and "DOWN" lights. Ignore the "YES" and "DOWN" lights and count only the number of times the TAB "NO" and the TAD "UP" lights blink.

SELF-TEST OPERATION

The EEC diagnostic tester includes provisions for the self-test feature. In this case, the technician monitors the test panel for flashes of the thermactor solenoids operation. The series of light flashes represent a service code. The test can also be accomplished using a vacuum pump and gauges. In this case, the technician must actually monitor the solenoids for pulses or observe corresponding vacuum signals caused by the pulses. In all cases, the starting method for the self-test is the same.

The technician should activate the self-test only after proper engine preparation. The engine should be run until the radiator hose is hot and pressurized. With the engine running at idle, connect a vacuum pump to the barometric sensor vent outlet. Pump down the sensor vacuum to 20" Hg and hold for 5 seconds. This low reading is below any possible normal barometric pressure and it triggers the self-test to start.

At first, the program pulses the throttle kicker solenoid and then holds it on during the entire test. The test lasts about one minute. After completion of the test, the program deactivates the throttle kicker solenoid.

Any malfunctions recorded are indicated by thermactor solenoid pulses. Following the completion of all the service codes, the canister purge solenoid is energized for about fifteen seconds.

Trigger Self-Test

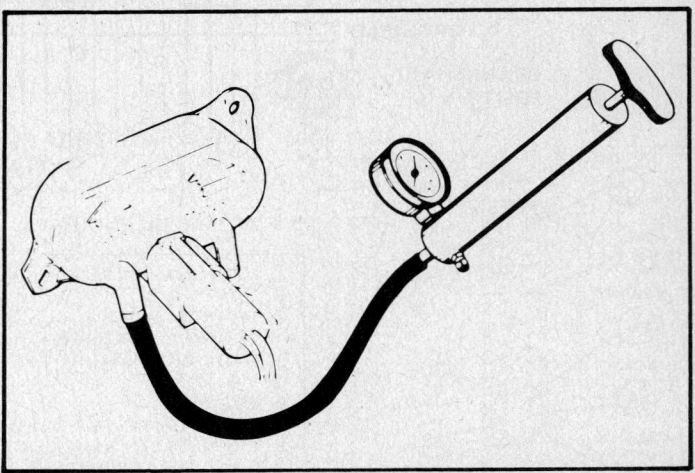

SERVICE CODES

The service codes are a series of pulses on both thermactor solenoids at the same time. Each pulse is on for one-half second and off for a one-half second. This sequence represents the number "one". The solenoids are off for a full second before starting the second digit of the code. In the case of the multiple service codes, the solenoids are off for five full seconds between two-digit codes. An example follows.

Service code 23 throttle position sensor, would follow this pattern.

1. one-half second on; one-half second off
2. one-half second on; one full second off (2)
3. one-half second on; one-half second off
4. one-half second on; one-half second off
5. one-half second on; five full seconds off (3)

– –	– – –	5 second	– – – – –
2	3	pause	4 1

Graphic illustration of code 23 followed by code 41

The vehicle remains in self-test for 15 seconds after completing the last code. It then returns to normal operation.

When beginning diagnosis, consider the final code first. In the above case of 23 then 41, begin with diagnosis of code 41–fuel control lean, and then continue with code 23–throttle position sensor.

Explanation of Code

Service codes are a series of pulses on both the thermactor air lights (TAB and TAD). The pulses form two-digit numbers. Each pulse is on for ½ second then off for ½ second for each count. A full second pause separates the digits, a 5-second pause separates service code numbers.

Code Number	Malfunction
11	EEC system okay
12	Engine rpm is out of specifications
21	Engine coolant temperature sensor (ECT) fault
22	Manifold absolute pressure sensor (MAP) fault
23	Throttle position sensor (TP) fault
31	EGR position sensor (EVP) fails to open
32	EGR position sensor (EVP) fails to close
41	Fuel control lean
42	Fuel control rich
43	Engine temperature reading below 120 deg. F
44	Thermactor air system (TAB and TAD) fault

System Description

EMISSION CONTROL SYSTEMS

The emission control system regulates specific emission control functions. Based on sensor voltage inputs, the computer calculates appropriate voltages to energize en-

Electronic Engine Control (EEC III) System Installation with Feed-Back carburetor

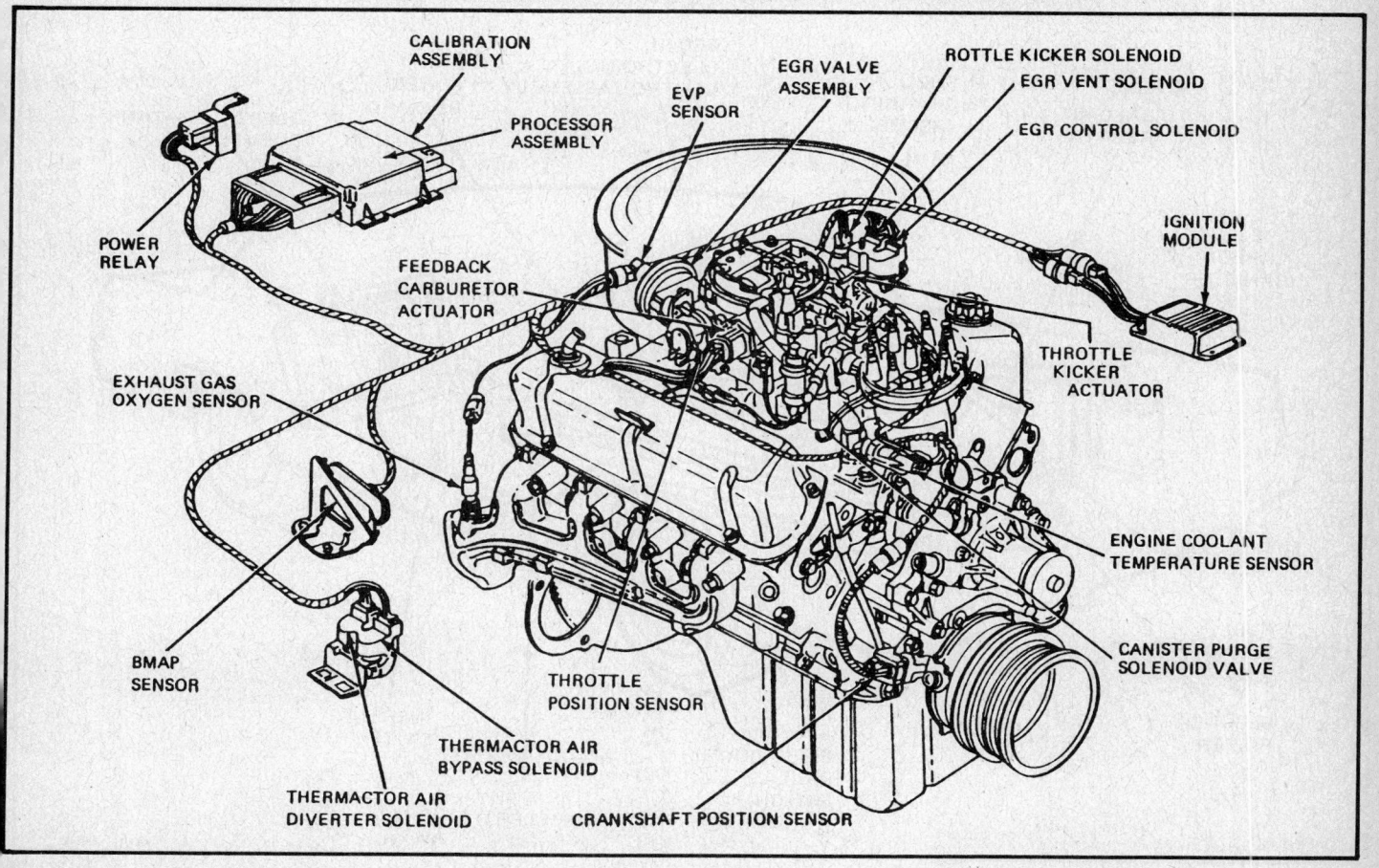

gine control solenoids or trigger the Dura Spark ignition module. The solenoids cause desired vacuum or air flow and the module controls the spark advance timing curve. As engine operating conditions vary, sensor voltages change and the computer recalculates input data into output voltages. In this manner, the computer directs the engine emission control systems to continuously control exhaust emission performance.

The EEC III system consists of two types of emission control systems, feedback carburetor and electronic throttle body fuel injection. Basically the two systems differ in the method of controlling air-fuel ratio.

The feedback carburetor contains an electronically controlled actuator which varies fuel mixture and uses a conventional fuel pump. The electronic fuel injection is an electric fuel pump which supplies high pressure fuel to a fuel charging assembly consisting of a throttle body and two electronically controlled fuel injectors.

Both systems include several engine sensors, an electronic control assembly, several control solenoids and a vacuum operated thermactor air system and exhaust gas recirculation (EGR). A four-lobe crankshaft pulse ring and crankshaft position sensor provide engine speed and location measurements. The distributor has no advance or retard mechanism. The control assembly determines timing depending on the engine operation conditions and individual vehicle calibration. A calibration assembly at-tached to the electronic control assembly contains specific calibration values for "tailored" engine performance. A power relay attached to the control assembly bracket, supplies system electrical power.

System Operation

The EEC III system uses the following sensors.
Throttle position sensor
Barometric pressure and manifold absolute pressure sensors, contained in a single housing
Engine coolant temperature sensor
Crankshaft position sensor
EGR valve position sensor
Exhaust gas oxygen sensor
Manifold charging temperature sensor, electronic fuel injection only
During engine starting and operation, the electronic control assembly constantly monitors these sensors to determine required timing advance, EGR flow rate, thermactor air mode and air-fuel ratio for any given instant of vehicle operation.

The electronic control assembly then sends output commands to the following.
Ignition module, for spark timing
Throttle kicker solenoid, if equipped

Electronic Fuel Injection (EFI) System Installation with Throttle Body Injection

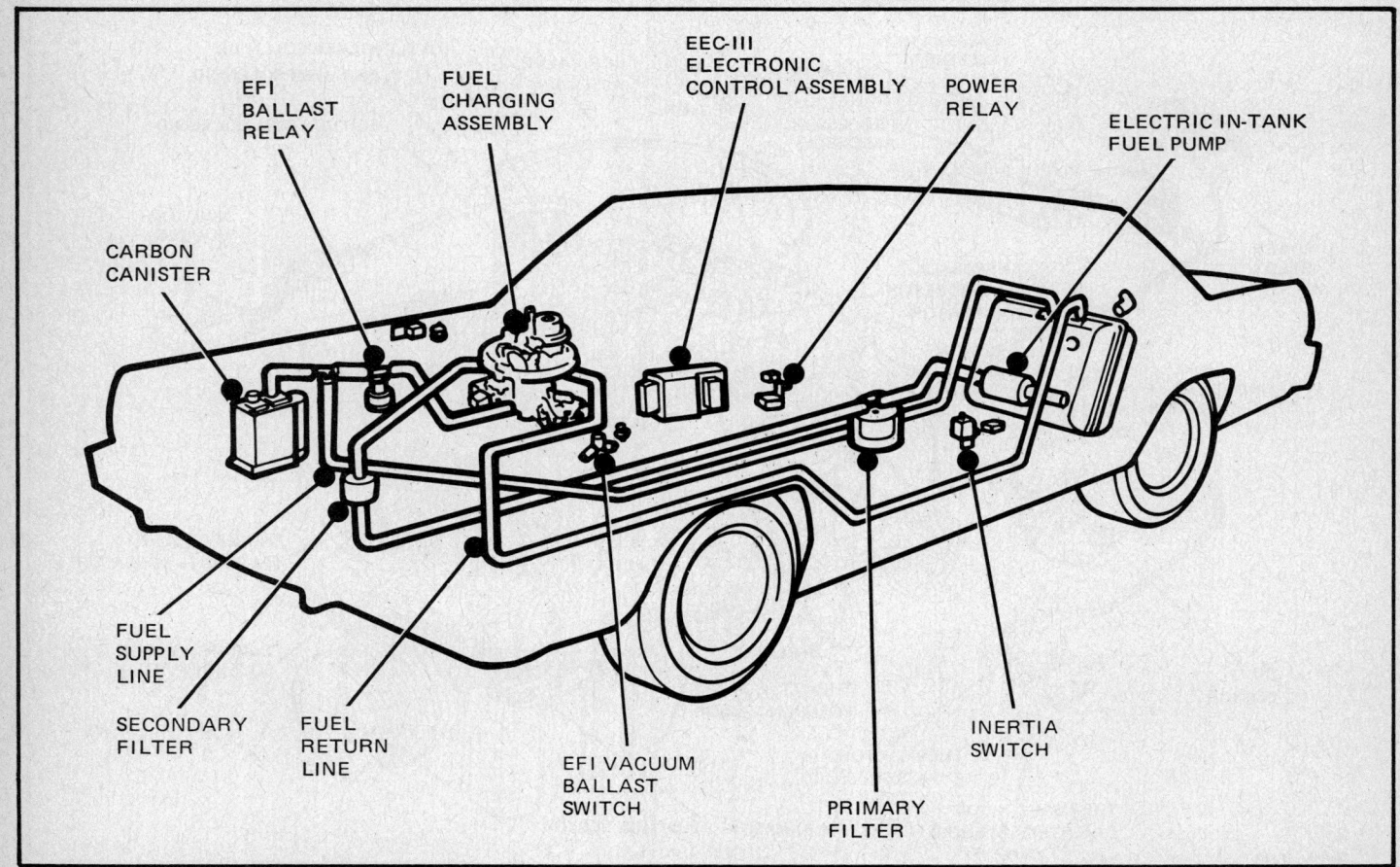

Electronic Engine Control System (EEC III)

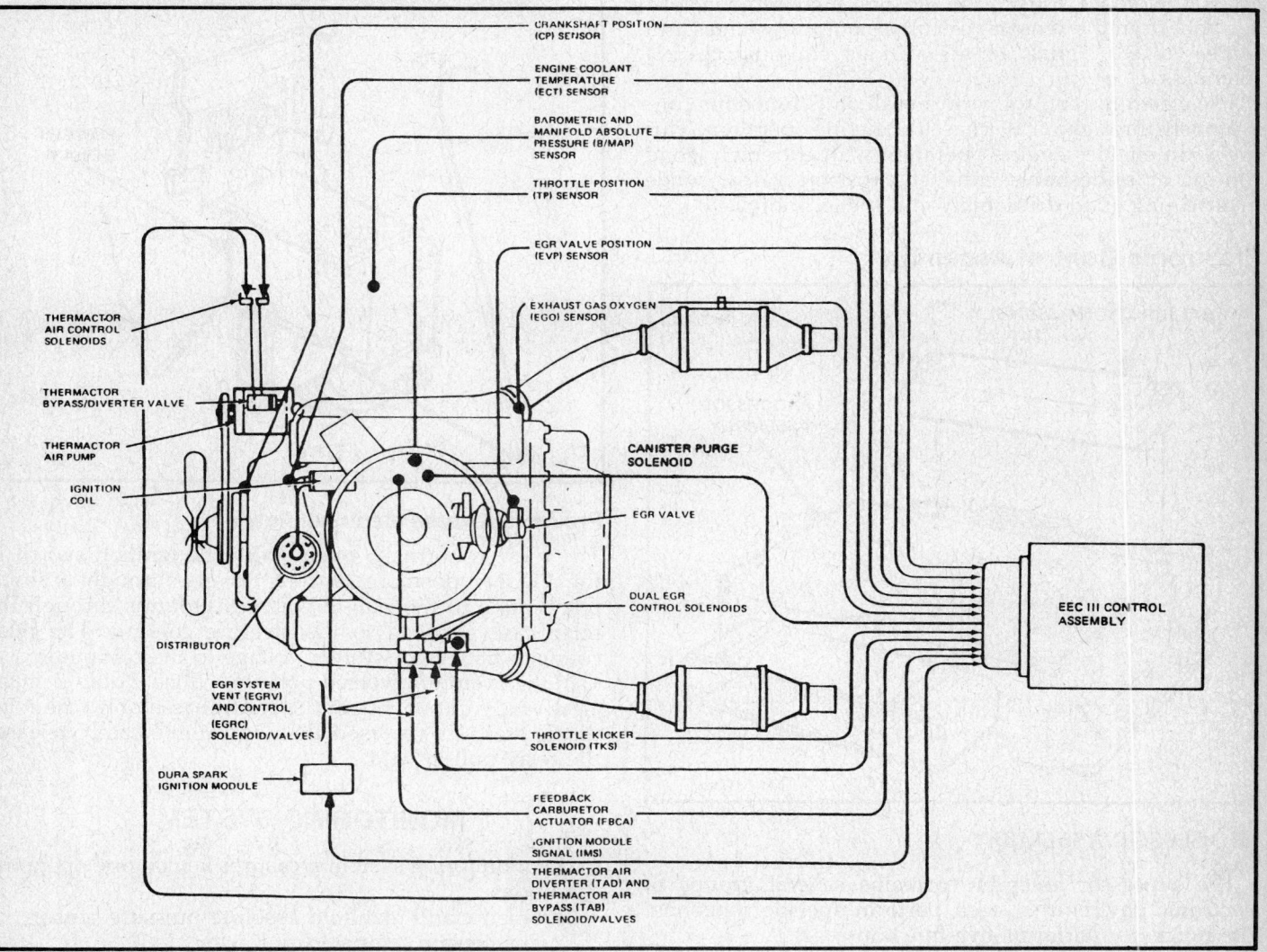

CRANKSHAFT POSITION (CP) SENSOR

ENGINE COOLANT TEMPERATURE (ECT) SENSOR

BAROMETRIC AND MANIFOLD ABSOLUTE PRESSURE (B/MAP) SENSOR

THROTTLE POSITION (TP) SENSOR

EGR VALVE POSITION (EVP) SENSOR

EXHAUST GAS OXYGEN (EGO) SENSOR

THERMACTOR AIR CONTROL SOLENOIDS

THERMACTOR BYPASS/DIVERTER VALVE

THERMACTOR AIR PUMP

IGNITION COIL

CANISTER PURGE SOLENOID

EGR VALVE

DUAL EGR CONTROL SOLENOIDS

EEC III CONTROL ASSEMBLY

DISTRIBUTOR

EGR SYSTEM VENT (EGRV) AND CONTROL (EGRC) SOLENOID/VALVES

DURA SPARK IGNITION MODULE

THROTTLE KICKER SOLENOID (TKS)

FEEDBACK CARBURETOR ACTUATOR (FBCA)

IGNITION MODULE SIGNAL (IMS)

THERMACTOR AIR DIVERTER (TAD) AND THERMACTOR AIR BYPASS (TAB) SOLENOID/VALVES

EGR control solenoids, to control EGR flow rate
Canister purge solenoid
Feedback carburetor actuator or fuel injectors, to adjust air-fuel mixture
Thermactor solenoids, to direct thermactor air flow
The continuous control and adjustment of ignition timing, EGR flow rate and air-fuel ratio results in optimum engine performance under all vehicle operating modes.

LOS MODE (FAIL SAFE)

If for some reason there is a failure in the electronic control assembly, the system goes into what's called the limited operational strategy (LOS) mode. In this mode, the electronic control assembly output commands are cut off, and the engine operates with a fixed 10° BTDC spark advance only, regardless of sensor input signals. The engine can be operated until repairs are made, but poor performance may be experienced as long as the system is in the limited operational strategy (LOS) mode.

System Components

SENSOR AND SOLENOID CONNECTORS

All other sensor and solenoid connectors in the EEC III system are the "pull apart" type that feature a release tab attached to the male side of the connector. This assures that proper contact between the sockets and pins in the connector will be maintained.

To disconnect these connectors, lift the tab on the side of the connector slightly to decrease its holding pressure and separate the two connector halves. To reconnect the connectors, simply align the two connector halves and press them together. The holding tab on the side of the connector is designed to provide pressure to hold the two halves together.

ELECTRONIC CONTROL ASSEMBLY

The electronic control assembly controls the various functions of the entire emission control system. A separate relay powers the assembly. The control unit delivers 8.1–9.9 reference volts to the sensors. It collects the voltage data from the sensors, calculates output voltages and sends voltage signals to the various emission control solenoids.

The electronic control performs all of its functions continuously throughout all phases of engine operation. This precision enables engine operation with extremely good control of undesirable exhaust emission gases, while maintaining good driveability and fuel economy.

Electronic Control Assembly

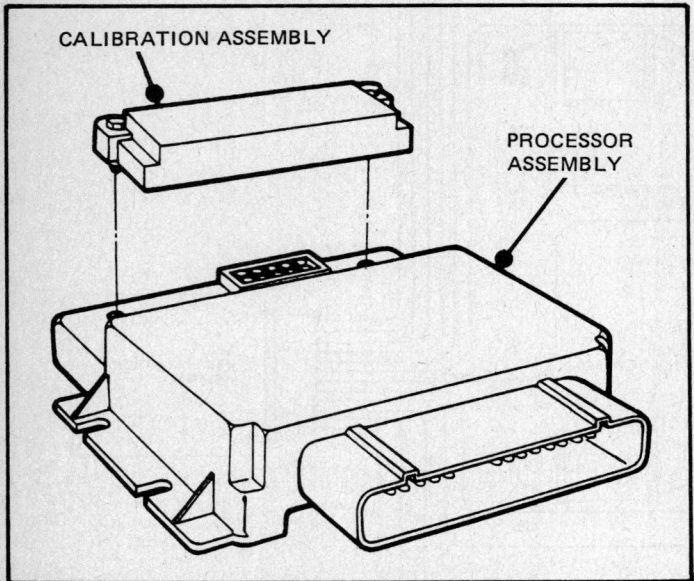

CALIBRATION ASSEMBLY

PROCESSOR ASSEMBLY

PROCESSOR ASSEMBLY

The processor assembly contains several groups of electronic devices that each perform specific functions. The processor performs five functions.
1. Analyzes sensor input voltages
2. Converts voltages to input for computer calculations
3. Selects operating strategy
4. Calculates spark, EGR flow, air-fuel ratio, canister purge, throttle kicker and other output voltage values
5. Dispatches voltage signals to the various emission control solenoids and ignition module to cause emissions control functions.

CALIBRATION ASSEMBLY

The calibration assembly is a memory storage device and is attached to top side of processor assembly. It performs two functions.
1. Provides calibration information unique to the vehicle for use by processor assembly.
2. Recalls appropriate data from memory bank, when required.

POWER RELAY

A separate electrical relay provides the source of EEC III current. From a common battery positive terminal, a fusible link carries voltage to one relay terminal.

Electronic Control Assembly Power Relay

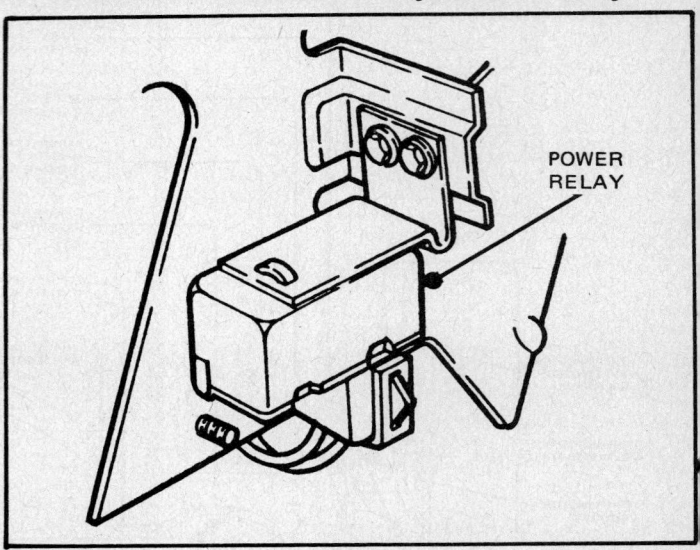

POWER RELAY

Prevents reverse electrical flow

The relay is normally open. With the ignition switch in the "RUN" position, current travels through a single relay diode to the pull-in coil and grounds through the relay case attached to the steering column. The relay connects battery or system voltage to the computer.

In the event of reversed polarity, which would damage electronic components in the control assembly, the relay diode prevents reversed flow and immediately releases the relay pull-in field.

MONITORING SYSTEM

The monitoring system measures key engine operating conditions.
Barometric and manifold absolute pressure sensor
Engine coolant temperature sensor
Throttle position sensor
Crankshaft position sensor
EGR valve pintle position sensor
Exhaust gas oxygen sensor
Manifold charging temperature sensor, electronic fuel injection only.
Each of these components senses a mechanical condition. It then converts it to an electrical voltage signal. The sensors provide the monitoring necessary to control the engine combustion process. The sensors react mechanically to pressure, temperature and position variations. They constantly adjust voltage signals to the electronic control assembly.

Barometric and Manifold Absolute Pressure Sensor

The barometric pressure and manifold absolute pressure sensor assembly contains two sensors. Each sensor converts a pressure into an electrical voltage. The assembly is mounted on the right fender apron.

The barometric pressure sensor reacts to normal atmospheric pressure. The computer uses this voltage to determine EGR flow requirements depending on the altitude at which the vehicles operate. The manifold absolute pressure sensor converts the manifold vacuum signal to an electrical voltage. The computer reads the voltages which indicate changes in engine load and atmospheric pressure. It reacts to control distributor spark advance at part throttle. It also controls EGR valve flow and air-fuel ratio.

Barometric and Manifold Absolute Pressure Sensor

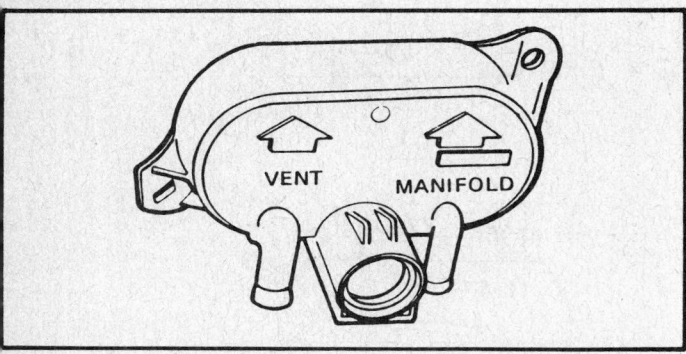

Exhaust Gas Oxygen Sensor

The exhaust gas oxygen sensor monitors the overall effectiveness of the engine exhaust emission control system. It does this by measuring the presence of oxygen in the exhaust gas. Unlike the other sensors in the monitor-

Exhaust Gas Oxygen Sensor

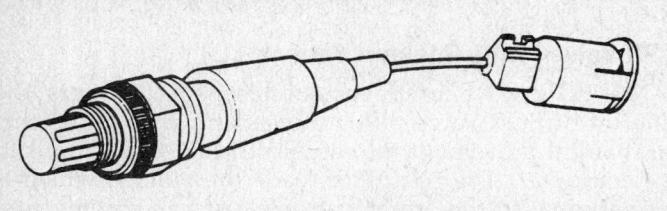

ing system which provide computer input about operating conditions, the exhaust gas oxygen sensor provides voltage data about engine operation output.

Engine Coolant Temperature Sensor

The engine coolant temperature sensor measures coolant temperature for the computer. The sensor threads into the heater water outlet at the front of the intake manifold.

Engine Coolant Temperature Sensor

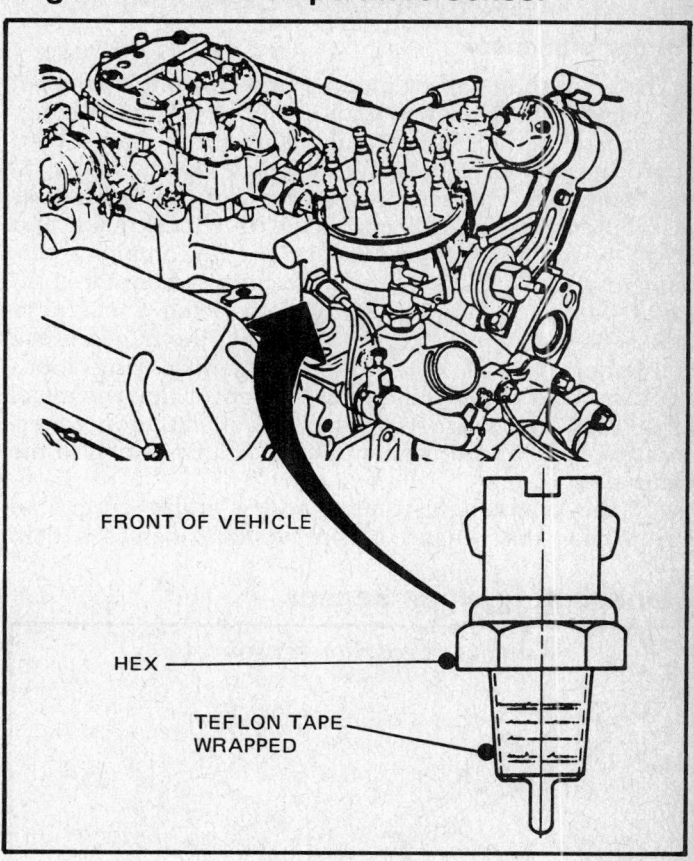

Exhaust Gas Oxygen Sensor

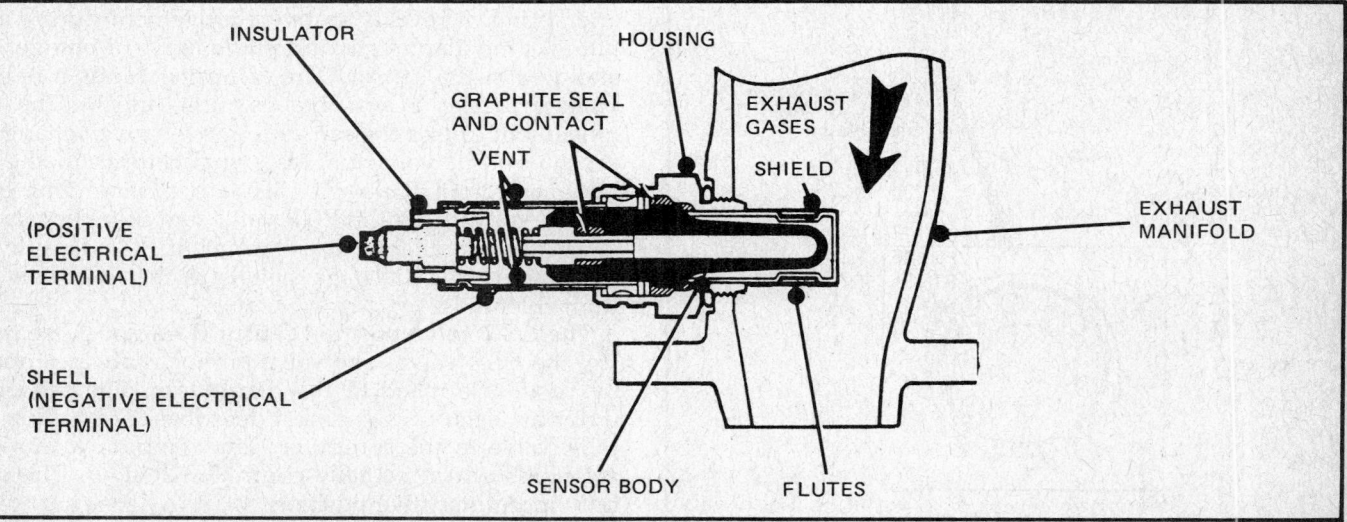

ENGINE CONTROLS

Crankshaft Pulse Ring

The pulse ring position establishes reference timing for the engine. The lobes positioned on the crankshaft align with the sensors at 10° in advance of TDC. This sets timing at 10° BTDC.

The crankshaft pulse ring is located on the crankshaft vibration damper inside hub. It is installed during manufacturing and cannot be removed or adjusted. The ring contains four lobes equally spaced at 90°. Since the crankshaft rotates twice for each distributor revolution, four lobes suffice for 8 cylinder operation.

Crankshaft Sensor

The crankshaft sensor mounts immediately in front of the cylinder block aligned with the crankshaft pulse ring. The sensor identifies the actual position of the crankshaft. It produces a corresponding electrical voltage signal to the computer. The sensor operates like the breakerless distributor pick-up coil and reluctor which make and break the ignition primary circuit. The tip contains a permanent magnet and wire coil. The current from the computer passes throught the coil, producing a magnetic field. The output wire carries voltage to the ECA. As the crankshaft rotates, the individual pulse ring lobes approach and finally align with the sensor tip. The metal lobe "cuts" the magnetic field. This interruption generates a voltage output signal of crankshaft position to the computer.

As the crankshaft rotates and a pulse ring lobe approaches the sensor, sensor voltage increases then

Crankshaft Position Sensor

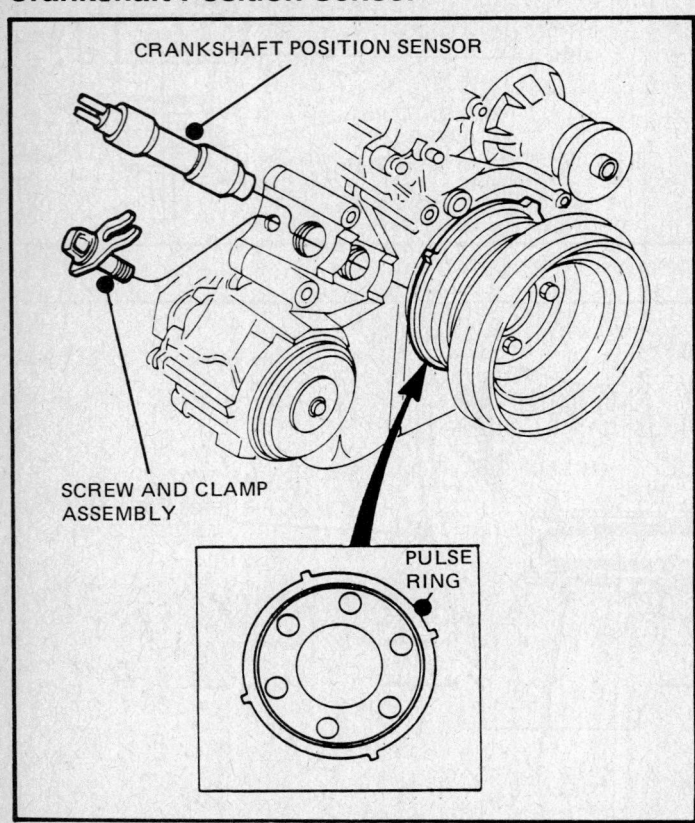

EGR Valve

sharply decreases and returns to base level. This occurs once each time a lobe cuts the sensor magnetic field. Crankshaft position sensor identifies the correct ignition firing. An inoperative sensor, connector or wiring harness will prevent engine starting.

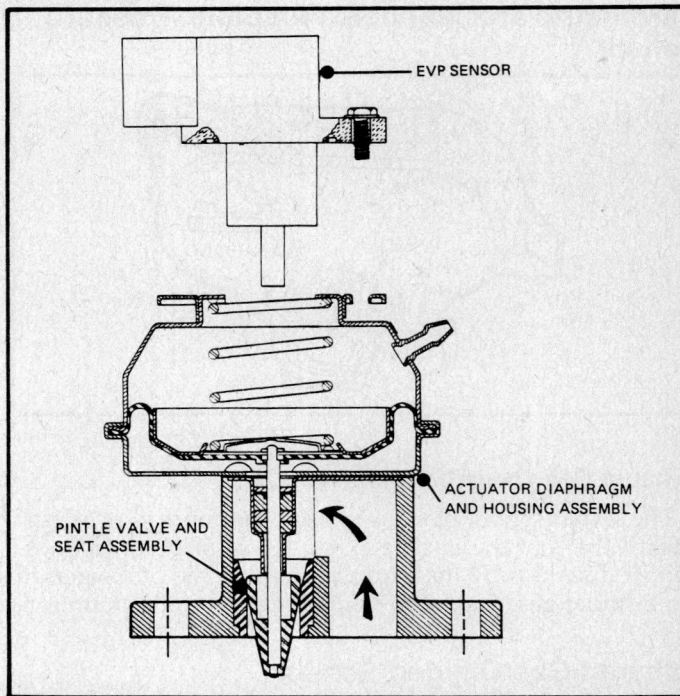

EGR Valve Pintle Position Sensor

The EGR valve pintle position sensor monitors the amount of EGR valve pintle movement. It converts this mechanical movement into an electrical voltage input to the computer. The computer reads the voltage which is proportional to the amount of exhaust gas flowing into the intake manifold. Basically, the computer measures EGR flow through the sensor signals.

The valve contains a completely enclosed diaphragm and spring. It reveals no pintle movement during operation. As the diaphragm and pintle move, a plunger operates within the sensor. The computer sends a reference voltage to the EGR valve position sensor. The pintle movement causes the sensor to move, which changes the sensor output voltage. This signal returns to the computer where EGR flow is calculated. Depending on the voltage input from the EGR valve and other sensors, the computer can change the amount of EGR flow by controlling electrical voltage signals to the EGR valve vacuum solenoids.

The EGR valve position sensor does not move or control the EGR valve. The valve pintle, as always, operates by vacuum applied to the diaphragm. The sensor produces an electrical signal that describes the position of the EGR valve to the computer. The computer controls the solenoids which actually control EGR flow. The sensor only monitors valve position.

Throttle Position Sensor

The throttle position sensor indicates driver demand through use of a potentiometer. A potentiometer is a variable resistor control. As the driver operates the accelerator and throttle shaft, the sensor delivers voltage signals depending on electrical resistance.

Three operating modes are sensed. They are closed throttle (idle or deceleration), part throttle (normal operation) and wide open throttle (maximum acceleration). The computer applies a set voltage to the sensor as a reference. It then classifies the output which depends on the resistance caused by one of the three modes. The ECA identifies driver demand and reacts to control spark advance, EGR flow, air-fuel ratio and thermactor air flow.

The throttle position sensor is mounted on a slotted bracket that provides proper adjustment if replaced. The sensor must be correctly positioned or the ECA will read erroneous information.

Throttle Sensor Adjustment

TP SENSOR

MOUNTING SCREWS

LOOSEN MOUNTING SCREWS — TURN SENSOR UNTIL READING IS BETWEEN 1.8 AND 2.4 — TIGHTEN MOUNTING SCREWS

1. Key on, engine off.
2. Verify throttle is off fast idle cam.
3. Remove vacuum hose from throttle kicker actuator.
4. Adjust sensor until voltmeter reads between 1.8 and 2.4 volts.

Throttle Position Sensor

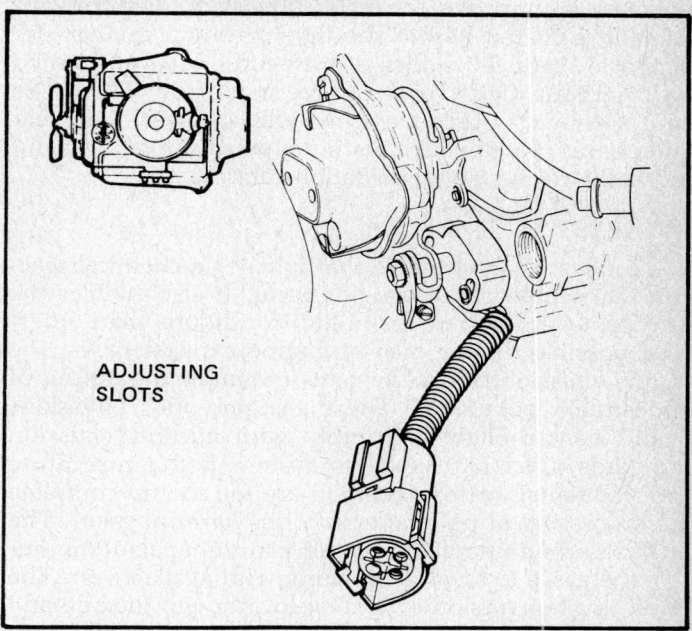

ADJUSTING SLOTS

CATALYTIC CONVERTER

The EEC III system contains a three-way catalyst for final processing of undesirable exhaust emission gases. The control assembly provides the precise control that enables use of the three-way catalyst. Without it, the lean mixtures required would not be possible and converter efficiency would drop.

The EEC III converter contains two catalysts. Each is a porous honeycomb construction coated with a catalytic

Dual Catalytic Converter

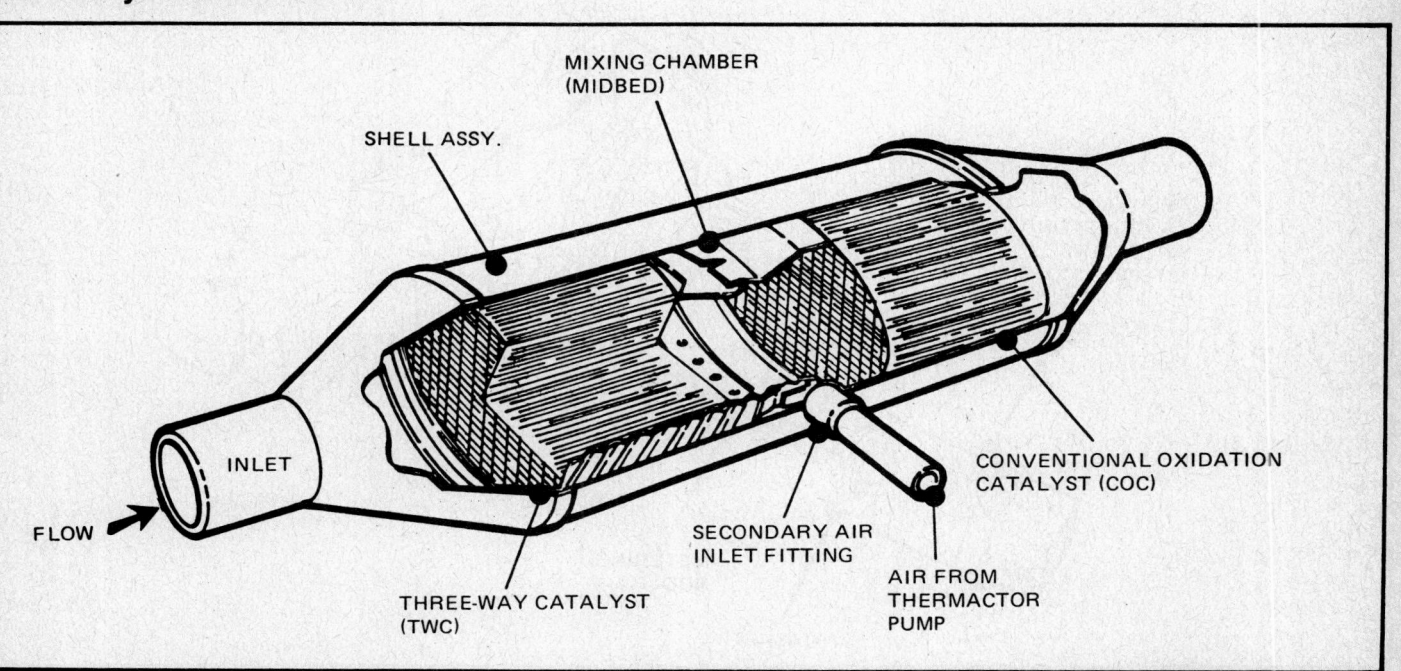

MIXING CHAMBER (MIDBED)

SHELL ASSY.

INLET

FLOW

CONVENTIONAL OXIDATION CATALYST (COC)

SECONDARY AIR INLET FITTING

AIR FROM THERMACTOR PUMP

THREE-WAY CATALYST (TWC)

material. The honeycomb shape maximizes available surface area to improve converter efficiency. The forward element is coated with a rhodium/platinum catalyst designed to "reduce" oxides of nitrogen (NOx), unburned hydrocarbons (HC), and carbon monoxide (CO). The front element is called a three-way catalyst. The rear converter is coated with a platinum/paladium catalyst and is called a conventional oxidation catalyst.

CATALYST

A catalyst is a substance that initiates a chemical reaction that would otherwise not occur. It also enables the reaction to proceed under milder conditions than otherwise possible. In the case of engine exhaust gases, the engine emission control systems minimize the output of undesirable pollutants. These "engine-out" emissions would be too high to comply with current emission standards. Once in the exhaust system, both temperature and additional air for oxidation are too low to complete the processing of pollutants into less harmful gases. The catalysts, rhodium/platinum and platinum/paladium, enable the gases to continue oxiding with available air. The result is a conversion of NOx into nitrogen dioxide and HC and CO into carbon dioxide and water. Some other gases also result in small concentrations.

Operation

Exhaust gases enter the converter and flow first through the three-way catalyst. They pass through a "midbed" of air injected from the thermactor air pump and into the oxidizing catalyst. The combined effect of the chemical reactions and mixing with air results in acceptable reduction of pollutants and exhaust air quality which complies with emission regulations.

Under some conditions when rich mixtures (such as cold enrichment and wide open throttle) could enter the converter, the thermactor air might result in overreaction and converter overheating. In these cases, thermactor air is redirected to treat exhaust gases at the manifold ports or bypassed to the atmosphere.

The exhaust gas oxygen sensor plays a key role in monitoring exhaust air quality. Combined with the computer control voltages, the complete system effectively controls undesirable pollutants under all engine operating conditions.

Feedback Carburetor
FEEDBACK CARBURETOR ACTUATOR

The feedback carburetor actuator consists of a solenoid stepper motor which controls a metering rod position. The metering rod varies the vacuum level applied to the carburetor fuel reservoir. The degree of pressure acting on the fuel affects how easily fuel leaves the main discharge tube. Control of this function then controls carburetor air-fuel ratio.

The computer sends a voltage signal that actuates the feedback motor. Based on voltage inputs from the exhaust gas oxygen sensor, barometric pressure and manifold absolute pressure sensors, etc., the electronic control assembly computes an output timed voltage to the feedback actuator. This achieves the desired air-fuel ratio.

The actuator stepper motor is mounted on the carburetor's right side. It contains 120 steps in a total linear travel range of 0.400 in. The computer sequentially energizes four separate armature windings to obtain the nec-

Feedback Carburetor Actuator

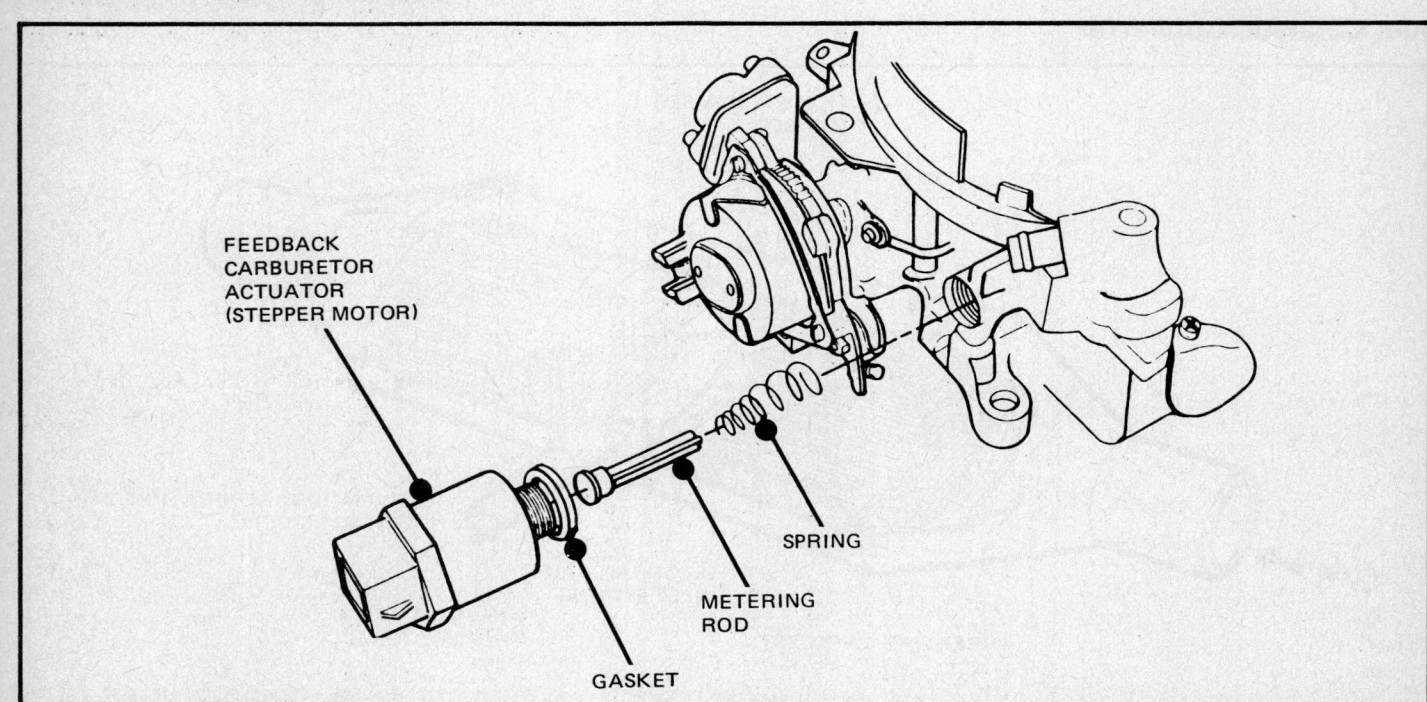

FEEDBACK CARBURETOR ACTUATOR (STEPPER MOTOR)

SPRING

METERING ROD

GASKET

essary vacuum metering rod position. The motor varies the position of this metering valve to achieve the desired effect. The extended position provides a rich air-fuel mixture. Admitting vacuum to the fuel chamber lowers the pressure above the fuel and results in a leaner air-fuel mixture.

During cranking and immediately after starting, the computer sets the feedback actuator to initial position, depending on calibration. As engine operation continues, the computer modulates the actuator, based on sensor voltage inputs.

Feedback Carburetor Actuator

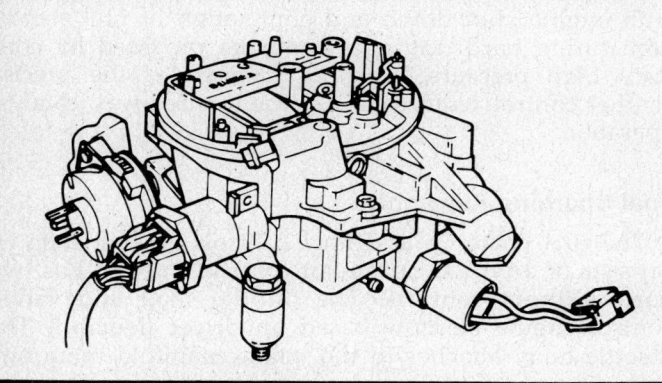

THROTTLE KICKER

A throttle kicker is used to control engine idle speed for different engine operations. The assembly includes a solenoid valve which controls the vacuum signal to a vacuum actuator. The computer provides the output voltage signal to operate the throttle kicker solenoid. When energized, the actuator diaphragm extends a carburetor throttle stop to increase engine idle speed.

The computer operates the solenoid for the following conditions.

1. Below specified temperature to improve warm-up idle performance
2. Above a specified temperature to increase engine cooling as needed
3. With the air conditioning unit on to improve idle quality while under additional compressor load
4. Above a specified altitude to improve idle quality

The thermactor bypass/diverter valve contains three outlet passages: downstream to the catalytic converter, upstream to the exhaust manifold and bypass to the atmosphere. During normal engine temperature, thermactor air is directed downstream to the catalyst. The computer controls the desired routing based on coolant temperature for a calibrated time and other sensor inputs. The ECA energizes the bypass solenoid when time at closed throttle exceeds a calibrated time value. If time between the EGO lean/rich sensor exceeds a set time value, it also bypasses. These two calibrated functions are intended to protect the catalytic converter from damage and/or for vehicle safety. The computer also energizes the bypass solenoid during wide open throttle.

Typical Throttle Kicker Actuator, Except Automatic Overdrive Transmission

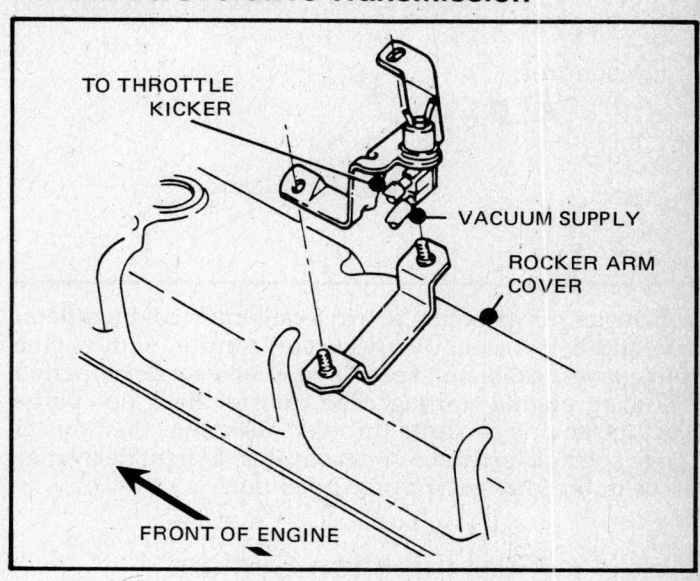

Vacuum Throttle Kicker

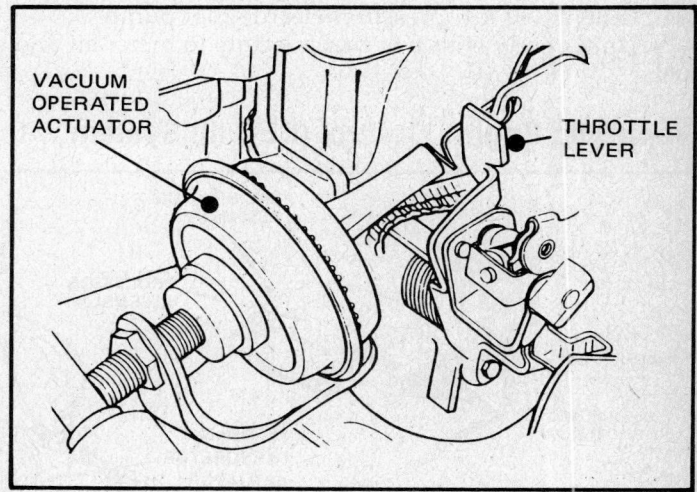

Thermactor Air Bypass and Diverter Solenoids

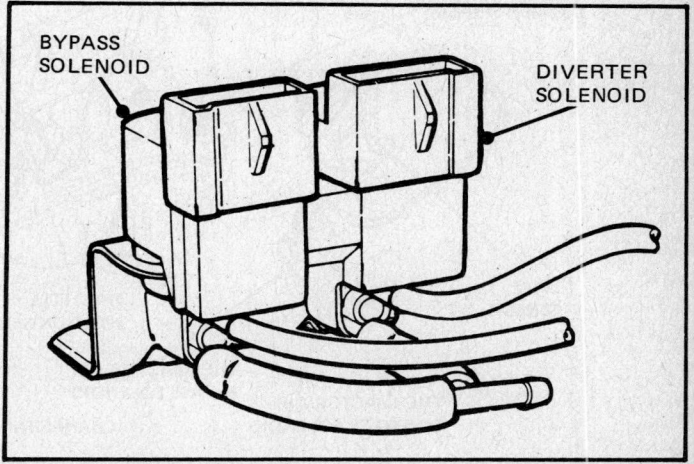

Canister Purge Solenoid

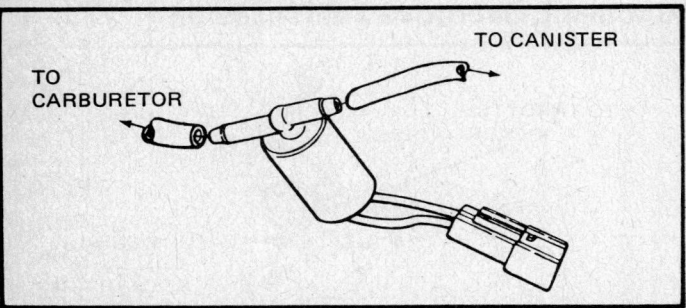

Canister purge occurs above a calibrated cold temperature and below a set overheat temperature, with engine rpm above a calibrated speed and after a set delay period following engine starting. The canister does not purge with the engine at closed throttle. Also, once the canister purge solenoid activates or deactivates, a slight delay may occur in the change of purge operation.

Fuel Injection System

COMPONENTS

1. In-tank (40 lbs. pressure) electric fuel pump
2. Upper body with two fuel injectors to meter air and fuel
3. Throttle body which houses the throttle, an electric bi-metal coil to control cold idle speed and an automatic kickdown motor
4. Primary and secondary fuel filters
5. Manifold charging temperature sensor
6. Necessary fuel supply and return lines

The electronic fuel injection system has several distinct advantages over conventional carburetion. It has improved fuel distribution, capability of fine tuning for altitude and temperature variations, fuel vapor formation and vapor lock largely eliminated due to high pressure in fuel system and reduced evaporative losses due to elimination of the fuel bowl. It also has elimination of engine run-on, since fuel flow immediately stops electrically with engine shut down and elimination of fuel starvation during hard driving maneuvers provided by constant high pressure injection. It provides the precise air-fuel control required for efficient three-way catalyst operation.

Fuel Charging Assembly

The fuel charging assembly controls air-fuel ratio. It consists of a typical carburetor throttle body. It has two bores without venturis. The throttle shaft and valves control engine air flow based on driver demand. The throttle body attaches to the intake manifold mounting pad.

Electronic Engine Control (EEC III) System with Carburetor

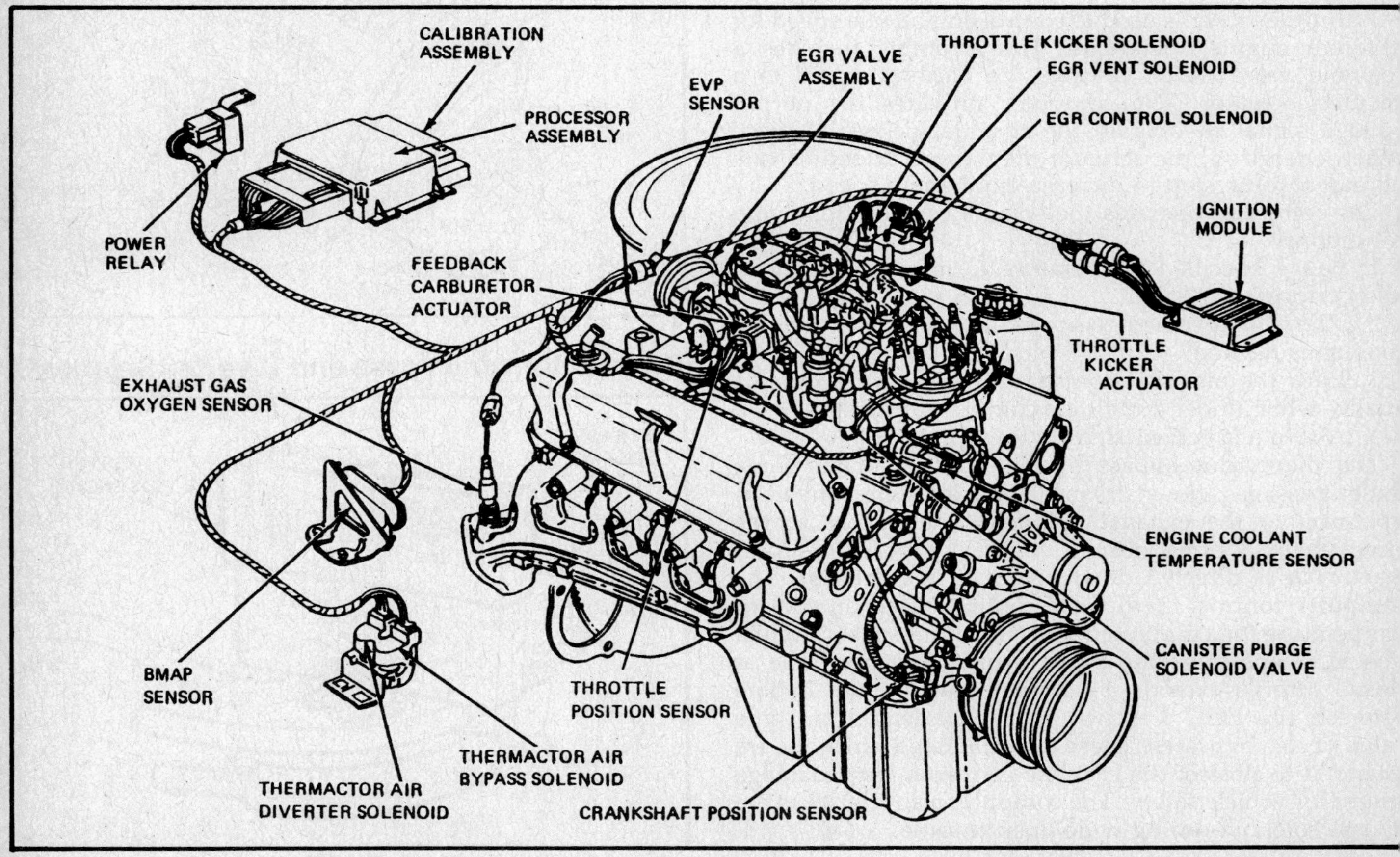

Electronic Fuel Injection Fuel Charging Assembly

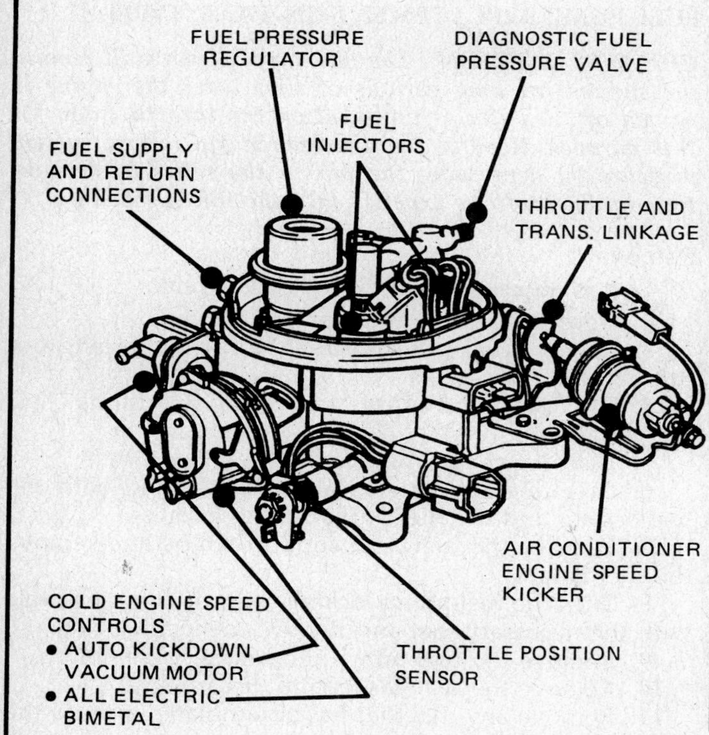

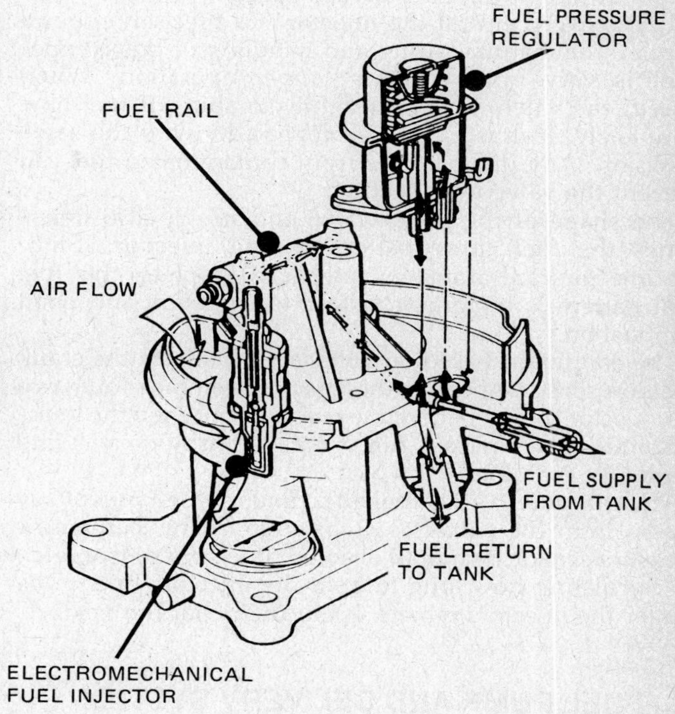

FUEL PRESSURE
REGULATOR

DIAGNOSTIC FUEL
PRESSURE VALVE

FUEL
INJECTORS

FUEL SUPPLY
AND RETURN
CONNECTIONS

THROTTLE AND
TRANS. LINKAGE

AIR CONDITIONER
ENGINE SPEED
KICKER

COLD ENGINE SPEED
CONTROLS
● AUTO KICKDOWN
  VACUUM MOTOR
● ALL ELECTRIC
  BIMETAL

THROTTLE POSITION
SENSOR

FUEL PRESSURE
REGULATOR

FUEL RAIL

AIR FLOW

FUEL SUPPLY
FROM TANK

FUEL RETURN
TO TANK

ELECTROMECHANICAL
FUEL INJECTOR

A throttle position sensor is attached to the throttle shaft. It includes a potentiometer (or rheostat) that electrically senses throttle opening. A throttle kicker solenoid fastens opposite the throttle position sensor. During air conditioning operation, the solenoid extends to slightly increase engine idle speed.

Cold engine speed is controlled by an automatic kickdown vacuum motor. There is also an all-electric, bimetal coil spring which controls cold idle speed. The bi-metal electric coil operates like a conventional carburetor choke coil, but the electronic fuel injection system uses no choke. Fuel enrichment for cold starts is controlled by the computer and injectors.

Fuel Pressure Regulator

The fuel pressure regulator controls critical injector fuel pressure. The regulator receives high pressure fuel from the electric fuel pump. It then adjusts the fuel to the desired pressure for uniform fuel injection. The regulator sets fuel pressure at 39 psi.

Fuel Rail

The fuel rail evenly distributes fuel to each injector. Its main purpose is to equalize the fuel flow. One end of the fuel rail contains a relief valve for testing fuel pressure during operation.

Fuel Injectors

The two identical fuel injectors are electro-mechanical devices. The electrical solenoid operates a pintle valve

Throttle Body Injector Assembly

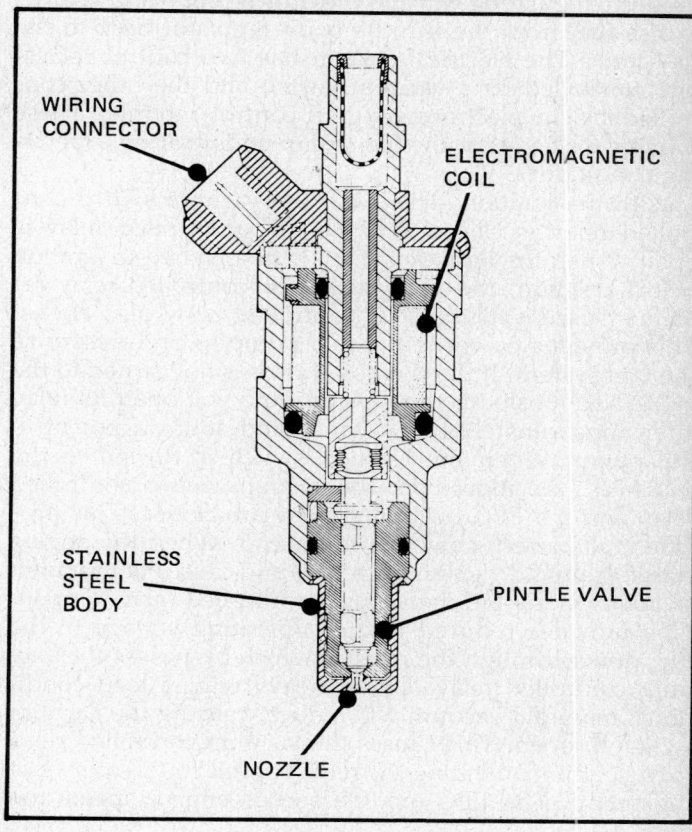

WIRING
CONNECTOR

ELECTROMAGNETIC
COIL

STAINLESS
STEEL
BODY

PINTLE VALVE

NOZZLE

ENGINE CONTROLS

which always travels the same distance from closed to open to closed. Injection is controlled by varying the length of time the pintle valve is open.

The delivery end of the injector is a precisely ground nozzle. The manufacturing and handling of this component is very important for proper operation. When closed, the valve must seal tightly to shut off fuel flow completely. It must seat itself repeatedly with the same precision. Any dirt particles from contaminated fuel can prevent the valve from seating.

The shape of the pintel valve and nozzle also determines the fuel spray pattern during injection. Since the injectors are atomizing fuel into droplets, this fuel mist pattern is important to fast vaporization and good combustion.

The computer, based on voltage inputs from the crank position sensor, operates the injector solenoids four (two per injector) times per engine revolution. When the injector pintle valve unseats, fuel is sprayed in a fine mist into the intake manifold.

The computer varies fuel enrichment based on voltage inputs from the exhaust gas oxygen sensor, barometric pressure sensor, manifold absolute pressure sensor, etc., by calculating how long to hold the injectors open. The longer the injectors remain open, the richer the mixture.

FUEL PUMP AND DELIVERY SYSTEM

An in-tank electric fuel pump is used on all vehicles equipped with electronic fuel injected (EFI) engines. The fuel system is a recirculating system that delivers fuel to a pressure regulating valve in the throttle body and returns excess fuel from the throttle body regulator back to the fuel tank. The electrical system has two control relays, one controlled by a vacuum switch and the other controlled by an electronic engine control module. These provide for power to the fuel pump under various operating conditions.

With the ignition switch off, the vacuum switch controlled relay is closed and the EEC controlled relay is open. When the ignition switch is first turned to ignition "ON" position, the vacuum switch controlled relay remains closed and the EEC controlled relay also closes. This provides power to the fuel pump to pre-pressurize the fuel system. If the ignition switch is not turned to the "CRANK" position, the EEC module will open its relay after approximately two seconds and shut off power to the pump. When the ignition switch is turned to the "CRANK" position, both the vacuum switch controlled relay and the EEC controlled relay are closed. This provides full battery power to the pump. When the engine starts, manifold vacuum increases and causes the vacuum switch to close and the vacuum controlled relay to open. This provides reduced normal operating voltage to the fuel pump through the resistor which by-passes the vacuum controlled relay. Under heavy engine load conditions, manifold vacuum will reduce, causing the vacuum switch to open. This causes the vacuum controlled relay to close, thus providing the return of full battery power to the pump. The EEC module senses engine speed and

shuts off the pump by opening the EEC controlled relay when the engine stops.

FUEL PUMP REPLACEMENT (IN-TANK TYPE)

CHILTON CAUTION *The fuel supply lines will remain pressurized for long periods of time after the engine is turned off. A valve is provided on the throttle body for this purpose. Remove the air cleaner and relieve system pressure by depressing the pin in the relief valve cautiously. Fuel will be expelled into the throttle body.*

Removal

1. It is necessary to remove the fuel tank.
2. Depressurize the fuel system.
3. Remove fuel from the fuel tank by pumping out through the filter tube.
4. Disconnect the supply and return line fittings and the vent line.
5. Disconnect and remove the fuel filler tube.
6. Disconnect the electrical connections to both the fuel sender and the fuel pump wiring harness.
7. Remove the fuel tank support straps and remove the fuel tank.
8. Turn the fuel pump locking ring counter-clockwise with the necessary tool and remove the locking ring.
9. Remove the fuel pump and bracket assembly.
10. Remove the seal gasket and discard.
11. Remove any dirt that has accumulated around the fuel pump attaching flange, to prevent it from entering the tank during removal and installation.

Electric Fuel Pump Installation

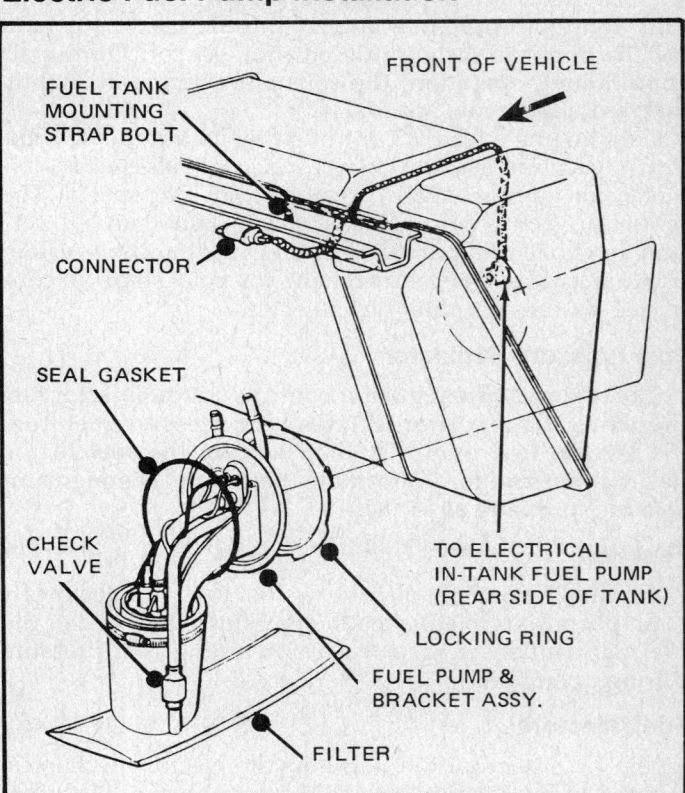

Installation

1. Put a light coating of heavy grease on a new seal ring to hold it in place during assembly. Install it in fuel tank ring groove.
2. Install the tank in the vehicle.
3. Install the electrical connector.
4. Install the fuel line fittings and tighten to 40-54 N•m (30-40 ft.-lbs.).
5. Install a minimum of 10 gallons of fuel and inspect for leaks.
6. Install pressure gauge on valve on throttle body and turn ignition key to "ON" position for 3 seconds. Turn ignition key off and back on for 3 seconds repeatedly, 5 to 10 times, until pressure gauge shows at least 35 psi. Reinspect for leaks at fittings.
7. Remove pressure gauge. Start engine and reinspect for leaks.

INERTIA SWITCH

In the event of a collision impact, the inertia switch will open, shutting off the fuel pump even if the engine does not stop. The engine will stop moments after the pump is shut off and cannot be restarted until after the inertia switch is reset manually. The inertia switch, located in the luggage compartment, must not be manually reset until after the complete fuel system is thoroughly inspected for damage or leaks.

FUEL LINES

The fuel pump delivers filtered fuel to the pressure regulator. It passes to the fuel rail and on to the injectors. The capacity of the fuel pump exceeds the amount of fuel injection. Therefore, a fuel return line is provided to carry surplus fuel back to the fuel tank. Evaporative fuel vapors are routed from the tank to the charcoal canister by a third fuel line.

FUEL FILTERS

The close tolerances of the injector pintle valve and seat require extreme cleanliness in fuel handling. For this reason, two fuel filters are used. The primary filter is mounted at the rear of the vehicle. It includes an underbody stone shield to prevent hazard damage. The secondary filter is attached in the engine compartment also in the fuel supply line. Regularly scheduled maintenance of filters is essential for proper system operation.

MANIFOLD CHARGING TEMPERATURE SENSOR (MCT)

This sensor is similar in construction to the engine coolant temperature (ECT) sensor, except it is packaged to improve sensor response time. The sensor is threaded into a cylinder runner on the intake manifold and provides the electronic fuel injection (EFI) fuel metering system with fuel and air mixture temperature. The MCT is used both as a density corrector for air flow calculations and to proportion the cold enrichment fuel flow.

Fuel Pump Inertia Switch

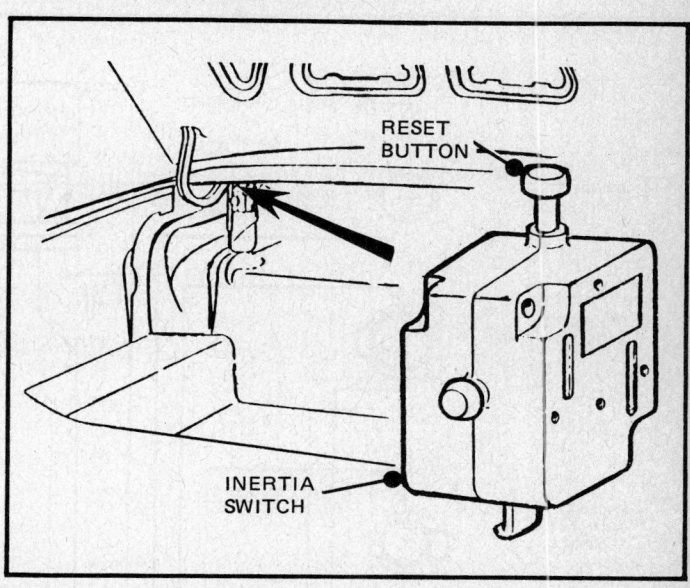

Electric Fuel Pump Wiring and Fuel Lines Routing Diagram

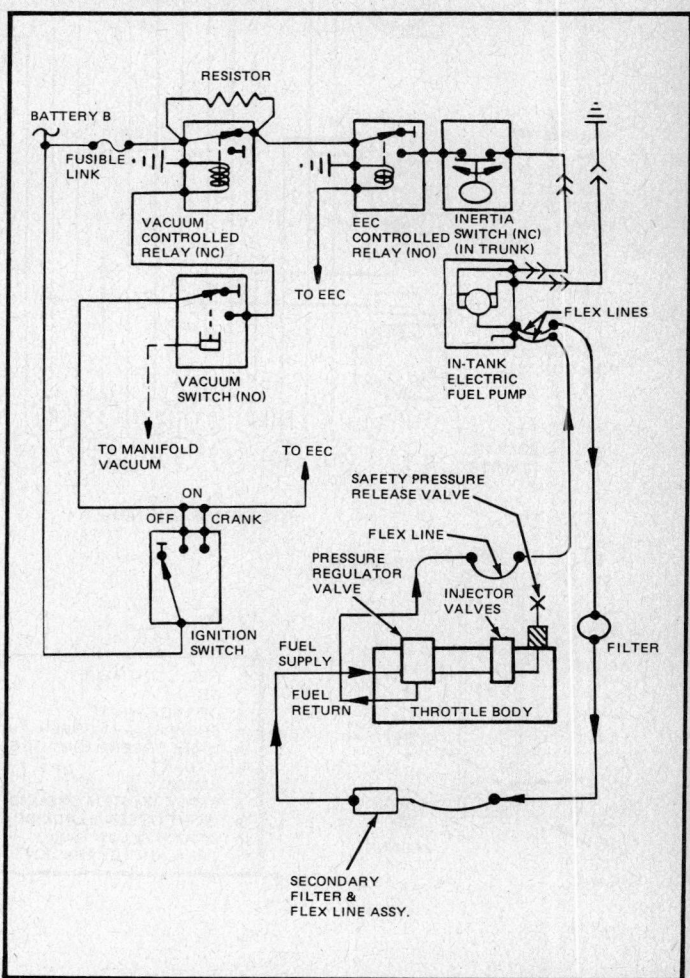

EEC III Wiring Diagram

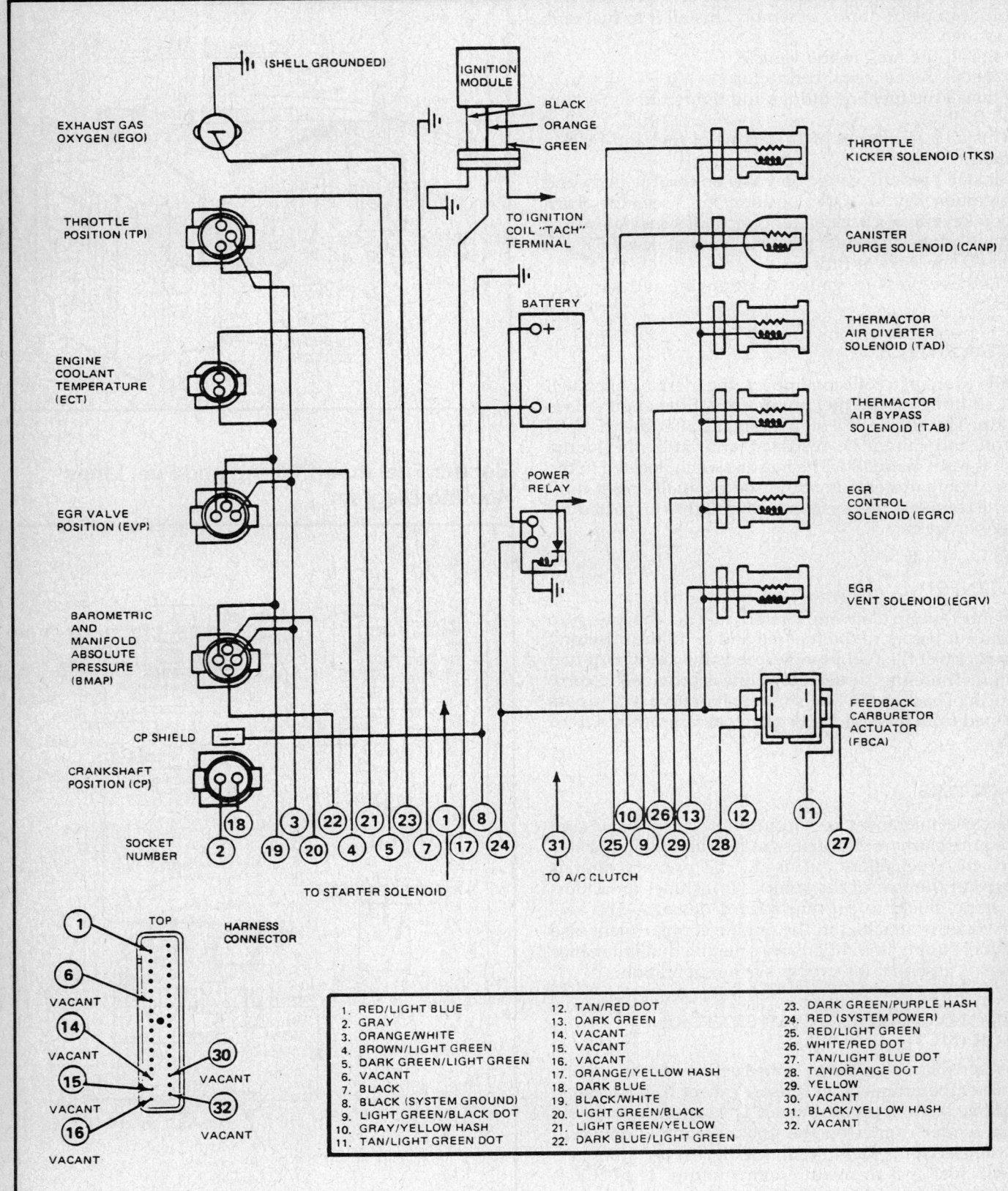

Electronic Fuel Injection Wiring Diagram

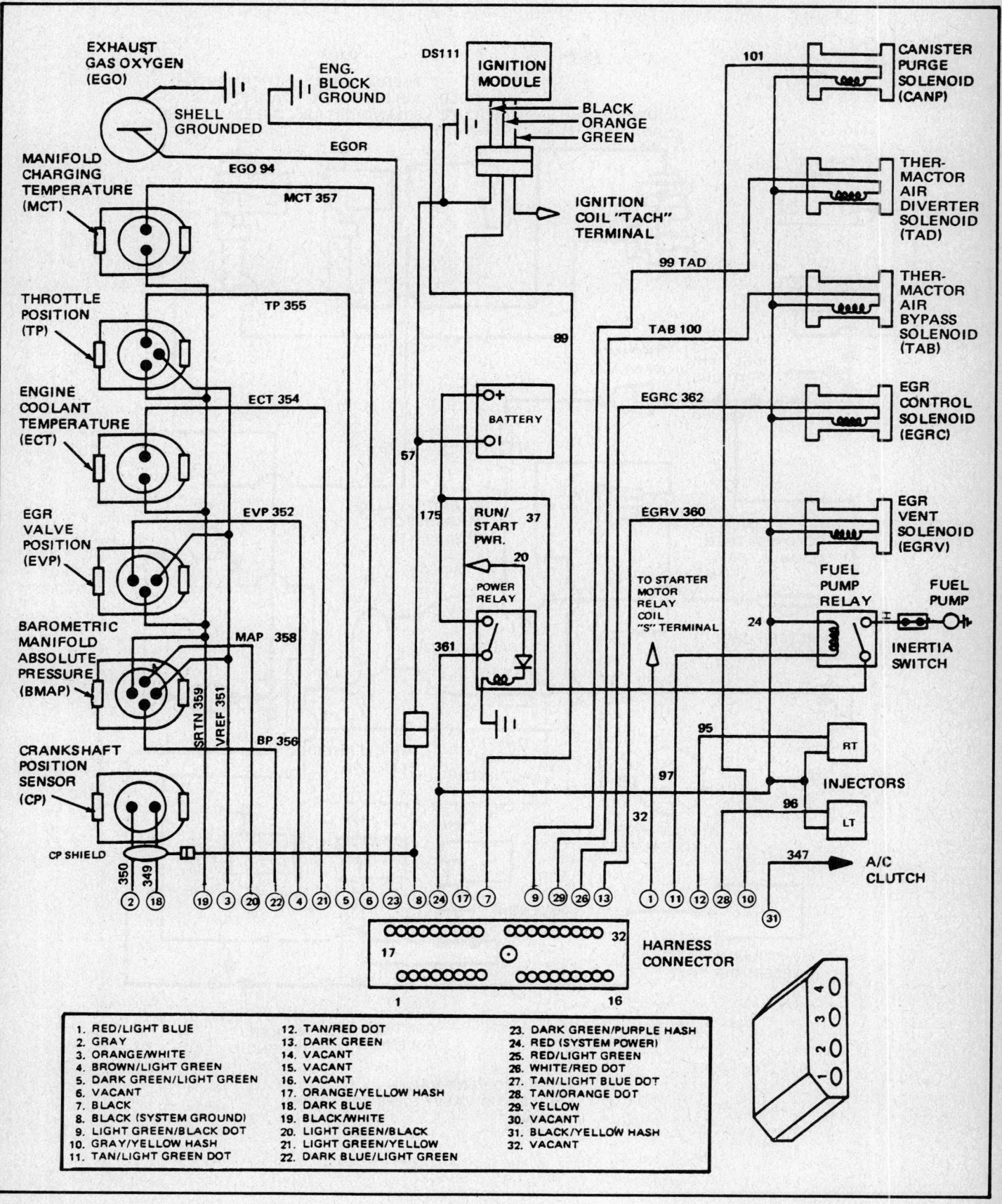

1. RED/LIGHT BLUE	12. TAN/RED DOT	23. DARK GREEN/PURPLE HASH
2. GRAY	13. DARK GREEN	24. RED (SYSTEM POWER)
3. ORANGE/WHITE	14. VACANT	25. RED/LIGHT GREEN
4. BROWN/LIGHT GREEN	15. VACANT	26. WHITE/RED DOT
5. DARK GREEN/LIGHT GREEN	16. VACANT	27. TAN/LIGHT BLUE DOT
6. VACANT	17. ORANGE/YELLOW HASH	28. TAN/ORANGE DOT
7. BLACK	18. DARK BLUE	29. YELLOW
8. BLACK (SYSTEM GROUND)	19. BLACK/WHITE	30. VACANT
9. LIGHT GREEN/BLACK DOT	20. LIGHT GREEN/BLACK	31. BLACK/YELLOW HASH
10. GRAY/YELLOW HASH	21. LIGHT GREEN/YELLOW	32. VACANT
11. TAN/LIGHT GREEN DOT	22. DARK BLUE/LIGHT GREEN	

ENGINE CONTROLS

FORD ELECTRONIC ENGINE CONTROLS III

Electronic Engine Control System (EEC III) Vacuum Schematic

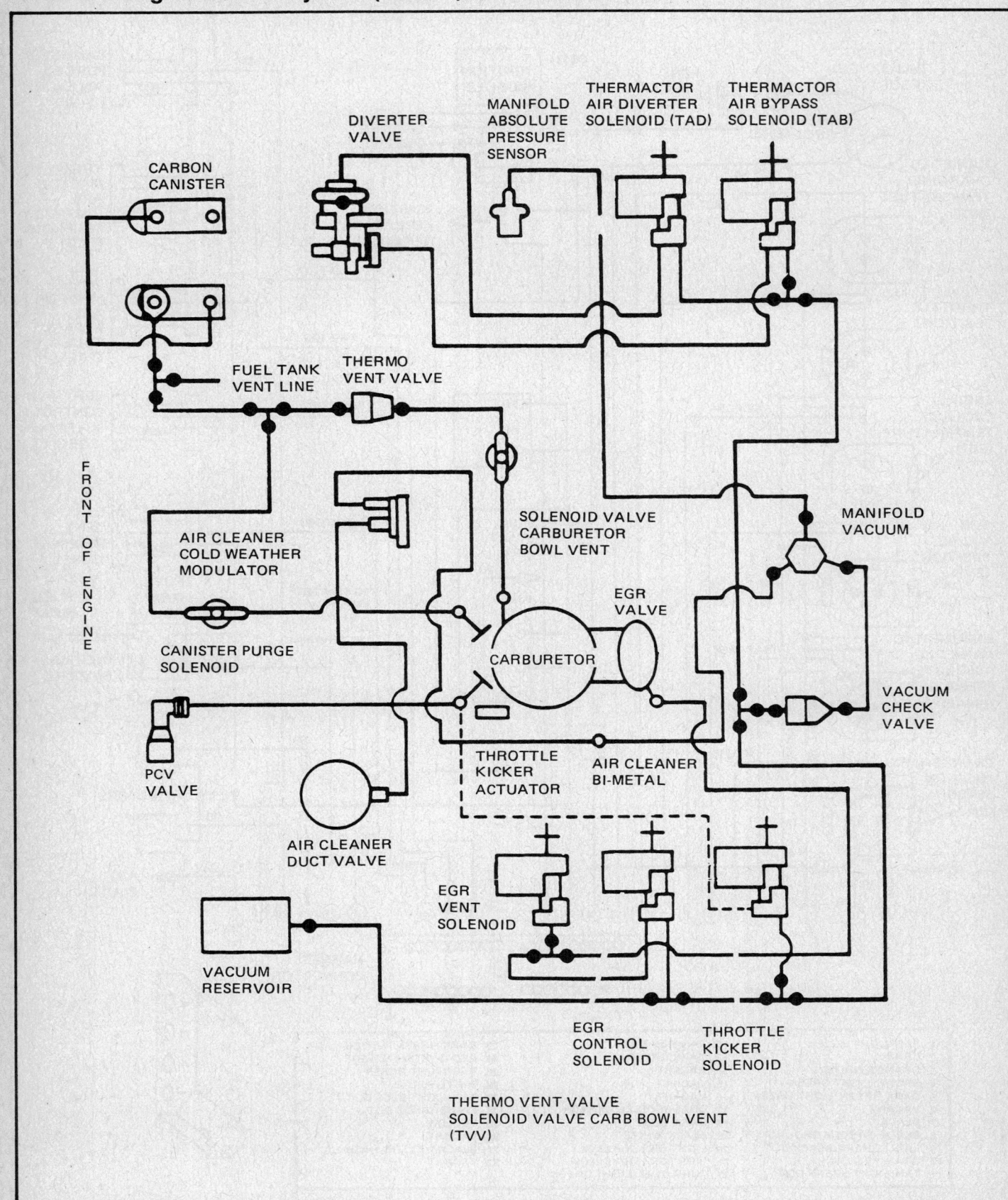

BENDIX FUEL INJECTION DIAGNOSIS

THE PROBLEM	THE CAUSE
Engine Cranks But Will Not Start|| Not Start	(NOTE: The following problems assume that the rest of the car electrical system is functioning properly.) 1. Blown 10 amp in-line fuel pump fuse located below instrument panel near ECU connectors.* 2. Open circuit in 12 purple wire between starter solenoid and ECU. 3. Open circuit in 18 dark green wire between generator "BAT" terminal and ECU (fusible link).* 4. Poor connection at ECU jumper harness (below instrument panel) or at ECU. 5. Poor connection at fuel pump jumper harness (below instrument panel near ECU), 14 dark green wire.* 6. Poor connection at engine coolant sensor or open circuit in sensor or wiring (cold engine only).** 7. Poor connection at distributor trigger (speed sensor). 8. Distributor trigger (speed sensor) stuck closed. 9. Malfunction in chassis-mounted pump. 10. Malfunction in throttle position switch (W.O.T. section shorted). To check, disconnect switch—engine should start. 11. Fuel flow restriction.
Hard Starting	1. Open engine coolant sensor (cold or partially warm engine only—starts ok hot).** 2. Malfunction in throttle position switch (W.O.T. section shorted). To check, disconnect switch—Engine should start normally. 3. Malfunction in chassis-mounted fuel pump. (Check valves leaking back). 4. Malfunction in pressure regulator.
Poor Fuel Economy	1. Disconnected or leaking MAP sensor hose. 2. Disconnected vacuum hose at fuel pressure regulator or at throttle body. 3. Malfunction of air or coolan sensor.***
Engine Stalls After Start	1. Open circuit in 12 black/yellow ignition signal wire between fuse block and ECU or poor connection at connector (12 black/yellow wire) located below instrument panel near ECU. 2. Poor connection at engine coolant sensor or open circuit in sensor or wiring (cold or warm engine only).**
Rough Idle	1. Disconnected, leaking or pinched MAP sensor hose. If plastic harness line requires replacement, replace entire EFI engine harness. 2. Poor connection at air or coolant sensor or open circuit in sensor or wiring (cold engine only).** 3. Poor connection at injection valve(s). 4. Shorted engine coolant sensor.*** 5. Speed sensor harness located to close to secondary ignition wires.
Prolonged Fast Idle	1. Poor connection at fast idle valve or open circuit in heating element. 2. Throttle position switch misadjusted. 3. Vacuum Leak.
No Fast Idle	1. Bent fast idle valve micro switch causing heater to malfunction and drive valve section down to locked closed position.
Engine Hesitates or Stumbles on Acceleration	1. Disconnected, leaking on pinched MAP sensor hose. If plastic harness line requires replacement, replace entire EFI engine harness. 2. Throttle position switch misadjusted. 3. Malfunction in throttle position switch. 4. Intermittent malfunction in distributor trigger (speed sensor). 5. Poor connection at 6 pin connector of ECU. 6. Poor connection at EGR solenoid or open solenoid (cold engine only).
Lack of High Speed Performance	1. Misadjusted throttle position switch (W.O.T. only). 2. Malfunction in throttle position switch. 3. Malfunction of chassis-mounted fuel pump. 4. Intermittent malfunction in distributor trigger (speed sensor). 5. Fuel filter blocked or restricted. 6. Open circuit in 12 purple wire between starter solenoid and ECU.

*To check, listen for chassis-mounted fuel pump "Whine" (one second only) as key is turned to "ON" position (not to "START" position).

**To check for an "open" circuit in an EFI temperature sensor, connect an ohmmeter to the sensor connector terminals. If the sensor resistance is greater than 1600 ohms, replace the sensor.

***To check for a "closed" (short) circuit in an EFI temperature sensor, connect an ohmmeter to the sensor connector terminals. If the sensor resistance is less than 700 ohms, replace the sensor.

FUEL INJECTION

BENDIX CLOSED LOOP TYPE

Theory of Operation

Electrical fuel Injection precisely controls the air/fuel mixture for combustion. This is accomplished by monitoring selected engine operating conditions, and electronically metering the fuel requirements to meet those conditions.

EFI basically involves electrically actuated fuel metering valves which, when actuated, spray a predetermined quantity of fuel into the engine.

This arrangement is commonly known as port injection. The injector opening is timed in accordance with the engine frequency so that the fuel charge is in place prior to the intake stroke for the cylinder.

Gasoline is supplied to the inlet of the injectors through the fuel rail at high enough pressure to obtain good fuel atomization and to prevent vapor formation in the fuel system. When the solenoid operated valves are energized the injector metering valve (pintle) moves to the full open position and since the pressure differential across the valve is constant, the fuel quantity is changed by varying the time that the injector is held open by the computer.

The injectors could be energized all at one time (called continuous injection) or one after the other in phase with the opening of each intake valve (called sequential injection) or they can be energized in groups.

The EFI System is a two-group system. In a two-group system, the eight injectors are divided into two groups of four each. Cylinders 1, 2, 7 and 8 form group 1 while group 2 consists of cylinders 3, 4, 5 and 6. All four injectors in a group are opened and closed simultaneously while the groups operate alternately.

The amount of air entering the engine is measured by monitoring the intake manifold absolute pressure, the inlet air temperature, and the engine speed (in rpm). This information, allows the electronic unit to compute the flow rate of air being inducted into the engine, and consequently, the flow rate of fuel required to achieve the desired air/fuel ratio for the particular engine operating condition. Each of the groups are activated once for every revolution of the camshaft and two revolutions of the crankshaft.

The input/output block diagram shown represents two group EFI system. In this system, the prevailing engine conditions are monitored with sensors and provide information to the Electronic Control Unit (ECU). The ECU converts the multi-variable input information into an injector pulse width which opens the injectors for the proper duration and at the proper time with respect to the cylinder firing sequence.

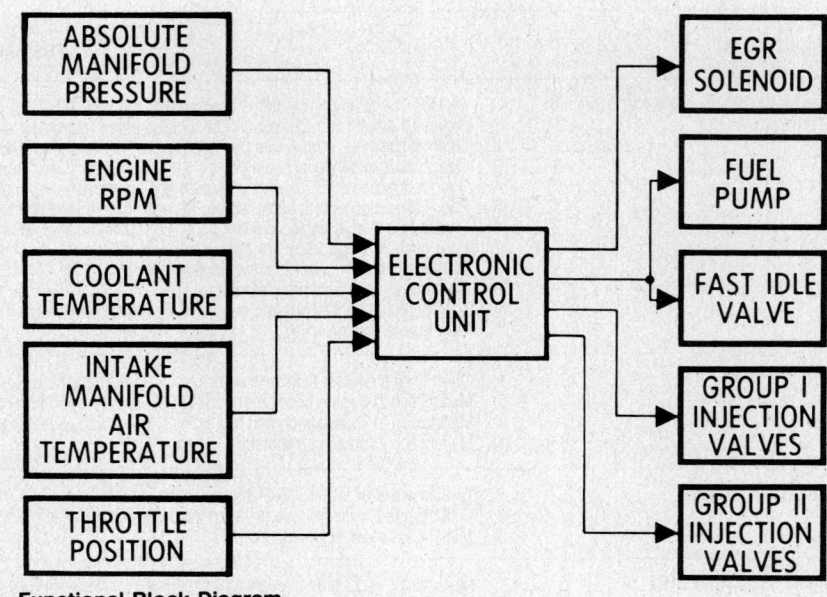

Functional Block Diagram

The object of the ECU is to calculate fuel requirements for the engine for various combinations of inputs from the sensors to determine an injector pulse width to provide accurate control of the air/fuel ratio.

Computer Input Diagram

Fuel Supply System

The fuel delivery system, includes an in-tank pump, a chassis-mounted constant-displacement fuel pump, a fuel filter, the fuel rails, one injector for each cylinder, a fuel pressure regulator, and supply and return lines. The fuel pumps are activated by the electronic control unit (ECU) when the ignition is turned on and the engine is cranking or operating. (If the engine stalls or if the starter is not engaged, the fuel pumps will deactivate in approximately one second.) Fuel is pumped from the fuel tank through the supply line and the filter to the fuel rails. The injectors supply fuel to the engine cylinders in precisely timed bursts as a result of electrical signals from the ECU. Excess fuel is returned to the fuel tank.

The fuel delivery system components are as follows:

Fuel Tank

The fuel tank incorporates a reservoir directly below the sending unit-in-tank pump assembly. The special shaped reservoir is used to insure a constant supply of fuel for the in-tank pump even at low fuel level and severe maneuvering conditions. The fuel returned to the tank by the fuel pressure regulator is directed into the reservoir as an additional means of keeping the pump intake below the fuel level.

Tank, Fuel Pump

Located inside the fuel tank and an integral part of the fuel gage tank unit, the in-tank pump, is used to supply fuel to the chassis-mounted pump.

Chassis-Mounted Fuel Pump

The Chassis-Mounted Fuel Pump, is a constant-displacement, roller-vane pump driven by a 12 volt motor. The pump incorporates a check valve to prevent backflow. This maintains fuel pressure when the pump is off. The pump has a flow rate of 33 gallons per hour under normal operating conditions (39 PSI). An internal relief valve provides over-pressure protection by opening at an excessive pressure.

Fuel Pressure Regulator

The Fuel Pressure Regulator contains an air chamber and fuel chamber separated by a spring-loaded diaphragm. The air chamber is connected by a rubber hose to the throttle body assembly. The pressure in this chamber is identical to the pressure of the intake manifold. The changing manifold pressure and the spring, control the action of the diaphragm valve, opening or closing an orifice in the fuel chamber. (Excess fuel is returned to the fuel tank.) This regulator, being connected to the fuel rail and intake manifold, maintains a constant 39 psi differential across the injectors.

Fuel Filter

The Fuel Filter, consists of a casing with an internal paper filter element capable of filtering foreign particles down to the 20 micron size. The filter element is a

Fuel injection components

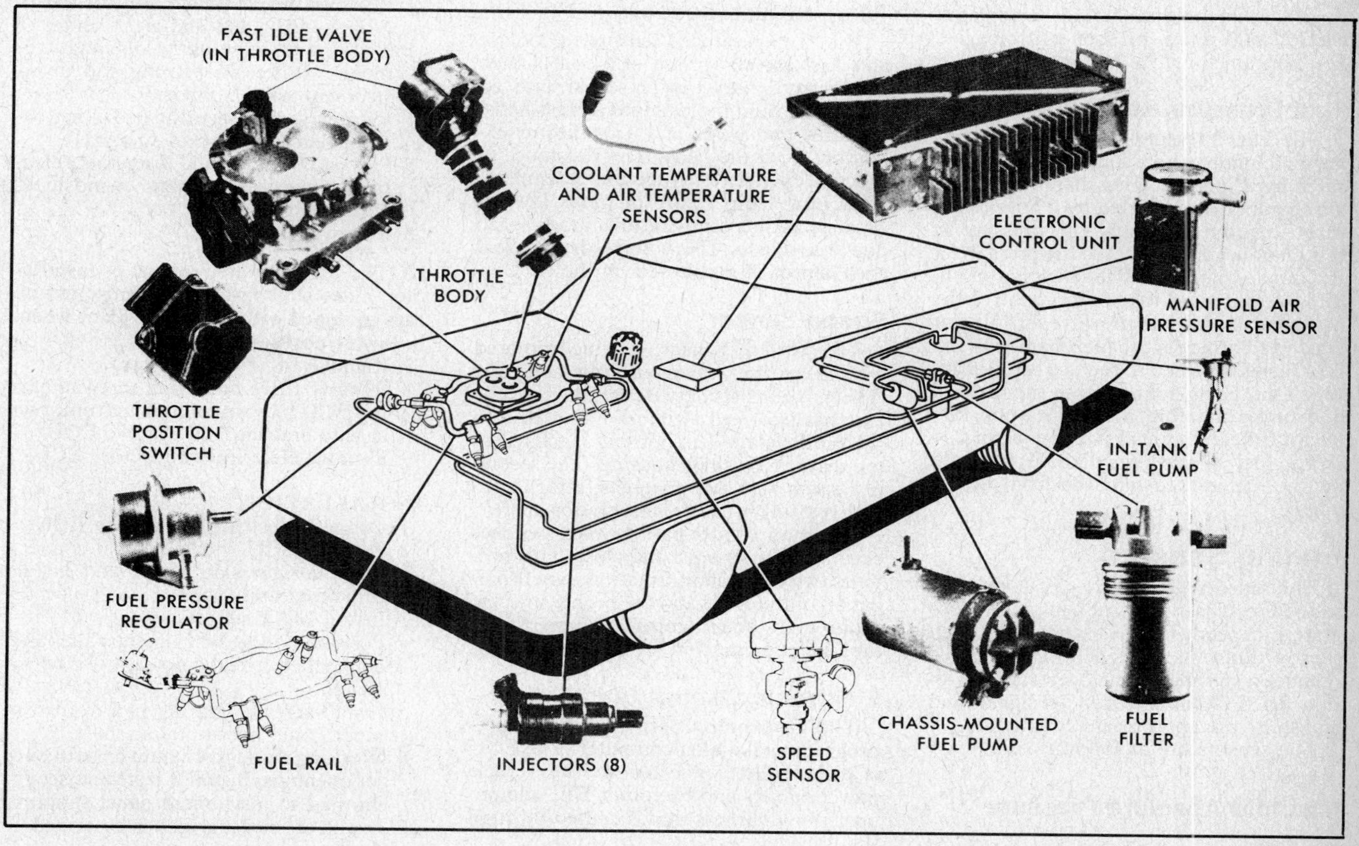

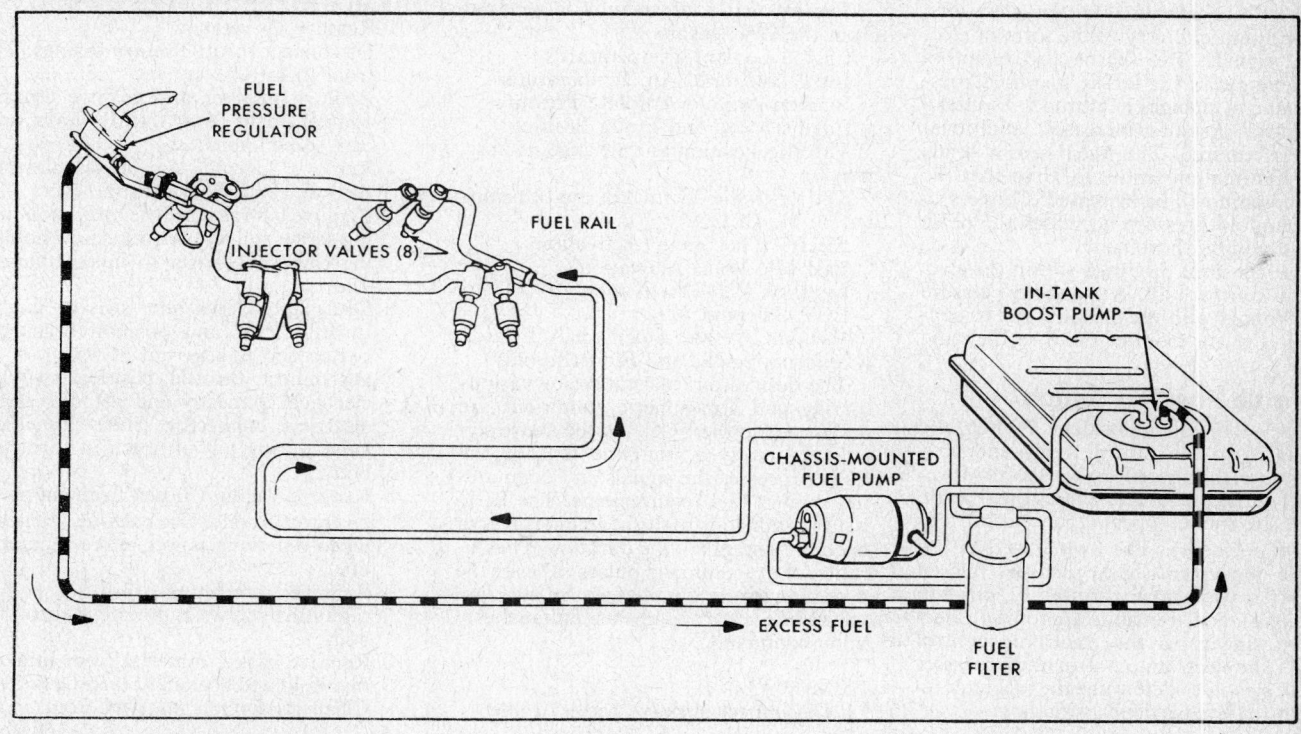

FAST IDLE VALVE (IN THROTTLE BODY)

COOLANT TEMPERATURE AND AIR TEMPERATURE SENSORS

ELECTRONIC CONTROL UNIT

THROTTLE BODY

MANIFOLD AIR PRESSURE SENSOR

THROTTLE POSITION SWITCH

IN-TANK FUEL PUMP

FUEL PRESSURE REGULATOR

FUEL RAIL

INJECTORS (8)

SPEED SENSOR

CHASSIS-MOUNTED FUEL PUMP

FUEL FILTER

Fuel delivery system

FUEL PRESSURE REGULATOR

FUEL RAIL

INJECTOR VALVES (8)

IN-TANK BOOST PUMP

CHASSIS-MOUNTED FUEL PUMP

EXCESS FUEL

FUEL FILTER

FUEL INJECTION

throwaway type and should be replaced each 22,500 miles, or sooner if clogged. See diagram for filter location.

Fuel Pressure Regulator

The Fuel Pressure Regulator contains an air chamber and fuel chamber separated by a spring-loaded diaphragm. The air chamber is connected by a hose to the throttle body assembly. The pressure in this chamber is identical to the pressure of the intake manifold. The changing manifold pressure and the spring, control the action of the diaphragm valve, opening or closing an orifice in the fuel chamber. (Excess fuel is returned to the fuel tank). This regulator, being connected to the fuel rail and intake manifold, maintains a constant 39 psi differential across the injectors.

The fuel pressure regulator is mounted on the fuel rail toward the front of the engine,

Engine Sensors

The sensors are electrically connected to the Electronic Control Unit and all operate independently of each other. Each sensor transmits a signal to the ECU, relating a specific engine operating condition. The ECU analyzes all the signals and transmits the appropriate commands.

The sensors are as follows:

Manifold Absolute Pressure Sensor

The Manifold Absolute Pressure (MAP) Sensor, monitors the changes in intake manifold pressure which result from engine load, speed and barometric pressure variations. These pressure changes are supplied to the electronic control unit circuitry in the form of electrical signals. The sensor also monitors the changes in the intake manifold pressure due to changes in altitude. As intake manifold pressure increases, additional fuel is required. The MAP sensor sends this information to the ECU so that the pulse width will be increased. Conversely as manifold pressure decreases the pulse width will be shortened.

The sensor is mounted within the electronic control unit. A manifold pressure line, routed with the engine harness, connects it to the front of the throttle body.

Throttle Position Switch

The Throttle Position Switch, is mounted to the throttle body and connected to the throttle valve shaft. Movement of the accelerator causes the throttle shaft to rotate (opening or closing the throttle blades). The switch senses the shaft movement and position (closed throttle, wide open throttle, or position changes), and transmits appropriate electrical signals to the electronic control unit. The electronic control unit processes these signals to determine the fuel requirement for the particular situation.

Temperature Sensors

The Temperature Sensors, (Coolant and Air) are comprised of a coil of high temperature nickel wire sealed into an epoxy case, and molded into a brass housing with two wires and a connector extending from the body. The resistance of the wire changes as a function of temperature. Low temperature provides low resistance and as temperatures increase, so does resistance. The voltage drop across each sensor is monitored by the ECU.

Speed Sensor

The Speed Sensor, is incorporated within the ignition distributor assembly (HEI). It consists of two components. The first has two reed switches mounted to a plastic housing. The housing is affixed to the distributor shaft housing. The second is a rotor with two magnets, attached to and rotating with the distributor shaft.

The rotor rotates past the reed switches causing them to open and close. This provides two types of information: synchronization of the ECU and the proper injector group with the intake valve timing (phasing); and engine rpm for fuel scheduling.

Electronic Control Unit

The Electronic Control Unit, is a pre-programmed analog computer. The ECU is electrically connected to the vehicle power supply and the other EFI components by a harness that is routed through the firewall.

The ECU receives power from the vehicle battery when the ignition is set to the ON or CRANK position. During cranking and engine operation, the following events occur.

The following information is received from the EFI sensors:

Engine Coolant Temperature
Intake Manifold Air Temperature
Intake Manifold Absolute Pressure
Engine Speed and Firing Position
Throttle Position and Change of Position

The following commands are transmitted by the ECU:

Electric Fuel Pump Activation
Fast Idle Valve Activation
Injection Valve Activation
EGR Solenoid Activation
Vacuum Retard Solenoid Activation
(California Seville and Eldorado only)

The desired air/fuel ratios for various driving and atmospheric conditions are designed into the ECU. As the above signals are received from the sensors, the ECU processes the signals and computes the engines fuel requirements. The ECU issues commands to the injection valves to open for a specific time duration. The duration of the command pulses varies as the operating conditions change. All injection valves in each group open simultaneously upon command.

REMOVAL

1 Disconnect negative battery cable.

2 Remove three climate control outlet grilles—right, left and right center.
3 Working through outlet openings, remove 3 fasteners securing pad to instrument panel support.
4 Remove screws securing pad to instrument panel horizontal support.
5 Pull pad outward and disconnect electrical connector from windshield wiper switch.
6 Remove pad.

NOTE: To facilitate removal or installation, place shift lever in lo range and on cars equipped with tilt wheel, place wheel in lowest position.

7 Remove MAP sensor hose.
8 Remove three mounting screws holding ECU in position (one in front, two at side bracket, and remove ECU.
9 Remove electrical connectors ECU.

INSTALLATION

1 Connect electrical harness to ECU.
2 Position ECU with electrical connectors on right side of car and install three mounting screws.
3 Install MAP sensor hose.
4 Position pad to instrument panel and connect electrical connector for wiper switch.
5 Install screws securing pad to instrument panel horizontal support.
6 Working through climate control outlet openings, install 3 fasteners securing pad to instrument panel support.
7 Install air outlet grilles as described in Section 1, Note.
8 Connect negative battery cable.

Throttle Body Assembly

REMOVAL

1 Remove air cleaner.
2 Disconnect throttle return springs (2) from throttle lever.
3 Remove retainer and remove cruise control chain from throttle lever on cars so equipped,
4 Remove "hairpin" clip and disconnect throttle cable from throttle lever.
5 Remove left rear throttle body mounting screw and remove one screw holding throttle bracket to intake manifold.
6 Disengage downshift switch from throttle lever and position bracket, switch and linkage out of way.
7 Disconnect throttle position switch electrical connector and fast idle valve electrical connector. Slide fast idle valve wiring out of notch in throttle body.
8 Remove vacuum hoses from nipples on throttle body. Use back-up wrench when removing power brake vacuum line.
9 Remove remaining throttle body mounting screws and remove throttle body,
10 Remove gasket material from intake manifold and bottom of throttle body. Clean all foreign material from area

around intake manifold throttle bores.

11 The following parts are not included in a new throttle body assembly and should be removed as necessary:
   a. Throttle position switch.
   b. Fast idle valve seat.
   c. Fast idle valve spring.
   d. Fast idle valve.
   e. Fast idle valve heater assembly.
   f. Power brake vacuum fitting.

INSTALLATION

1 Position a new throttle body gasket to intake manifold with identification tab on left.
2 Install throttle position switch to right side of throttle body as described in note 10b and adjust switch as described in note 20.
3 Position throttle body to intake manifold and loosely install both front and right rear mounting screws.
4 Move throttle linkage bracket into position over left rear mounting screw and install throttle body mounting screw.
5 Install one additional bracket mounting screw and torque screws 4 to 15 ft./lbs. Adjust transmission downshift.
6 Position throttle cable to throttle lever and secure with "hairpin" clip. Check for proper operation and wide-open-throttle.
7 Position cruise control chain to throttle lever and secure with clip on cars so equipped. Check for proper operation.
8 Install power brake vacuum fitting to rear of throttle body and tighten securely. Use back-up wrench.
9 Install throttle return springs (2) between throttle lever and pressure regulator bracket with open end of spring on outside of throttle lever.
10 Install vacuum hoses to appropriate nipples on throttle body as shown in. Actual hose routing is shown in.
11 Install fast idle valve.
12 Install air cleaner.

Throttle Position Switch

REMOVAL

1 Remove throttle body as described in note 8a.
2 Remove two mounting screws and remove switch from throttle body.

INSTALLATION

1 Install throttle position switch to right side of throttle body so that tab on switch engages flat on throttle shaft.
2 Install two mounting screws and tighten screws so that switch will still move but is not loose.
3 Adjust throttle position switch as described in note 20.
4 Install throttle body.

Fast Idle Valve

REMOVAL

1 Remove air cleaner and disconnect

electrical connector from fast idle valve heater.
2 Remove air cleaner stud.
3 To remove fast idle valve heater, push down and twist 90° counter clockwise.
4 Remove fast idle valve, spring and seat from position in throttle body.

INSTALLATION

1 Install fast idle valve seat, spring and valve in position in throttle body.
2 Position heater on top of fast idle valve and push down to compress spring. Care should be taken to avoid damaging micro-switch contact arm on bottom of heater housing.
3 Align tabs on fast idle valve heater with cut-out portion of throttle body and compress spring further.
4 Rotate heater 90° clockwise to secure in position.
5 Connect electrical connector.
6 Install air cleaner stud and air cleaner.

CHILTON CAUTION: *DO NOT LOOSEN FITTINGS UNTIL ALL PRECAUTIONS HAVE BEEN TAKEN TO RELIEVE PRESSURE. FUEL IN SYSTEM MAY BE UNDER HIGH PRESSURE WHICH COULD SPRAY OUT AND RESULT IN A FIRE HAZARD AND POSSIBLE PERSONAL INJURY.*

Injection Valve

REMOVAL

1 Remove front and rear fuel rails.
2 Remove electrical conduit from injector brackets 4 places each side.
3 Remove screws holding each injector bracket to intake manifold and remove brackets and grommets.
4 Disconnect electrical lead from all injectors on fuel rail being removed.
5 Remove fuel rail and injectors from engine as a unit. Some injectors will stick in fuel rail while others may remain in manifold.
6 Remove injectors from fuel rail and from intake manifold as required.
7 Injection valves are sealed by O-rings at both fuel rail and intake manifold. Remove and discard all used O-rings.

INSTALLATION

1 Lubricate and install a new O-ring on the fuel rail end of each injector.
2 Install injectors into fuel rail with electrical connector facing inboard.

NOTE: Fuel rails are specific for right and left sides of engine.

3 Lubricate and install a new O-ring into each injector port in the intake manifold.
4 Install fuel rail-injector assembly to intake manifold making sure that each injector is properly installed in manifold O-ring.
5 Install rubber grommets on fuel rail (flange down) and install injector brackets in position.
6 Secure each bracket with two screws.

7 Route electrical harness along bracket and secure to brackets—4 positions.
8 Connect injector leads as follows:
   Front cylinder—red/black wires
   Front-center cylinder—black/white wires
   Rear-center cylinder—black/white wires
   rear cylinder—red/black wires

NOTE: Injectors may be rotated to provide proper harness routing.

9 Repeat steps 1 thru 8 for opposite side if necessary.
10 Install front and rear fuel rails as described in note 9b and d.
11 Turn ignition ON and OFF several times to build up fuel rail pressure and check for fuel leaks.
12 Start engine and check for leaks.

NOTE: A "dry" fuel system on cars equipped with EFI may require a substantial cranking period.

Fuel Pressure Regulator

REMOVAL

1 Remove vacuum hose from nipple on top of pressure regulator.
2 Remove and discard clamps securing flexible fuel hose connecting regulator to fuel rail, Remove return line.
3 Remove one nut securing pressure regulator to bracket.

NOTE: This nut has metric threads

4 Work regulator off of flexible fuel hose and out of bracket.

INSTALLATION

1 Install new hose clamp over flexible fuel hose.
2 Position regulator to bracket and work flexible fuel hose to fuel rail over nipple on side of regulator. Secure to bracket with one nut.

NOTE: This nut has metric threads. Use the nut supplied with each new regulator or the nut removed in step 3a.

3 Connect return line to fitting on end of regulator.
4 Tighten clamps, securing flexible fuel hose to regulator.
5 Install vacuum hose to remaining nipple on pressure regulator.
6 A "dry" fuel system on cars with EFI may require a substantial cranking period before starting.

Fuel Rail

FRONT—REMOVAL

1 Remove and discard hose clamp securing pressure regulator hose to front fuel rail.
2 Using a back-up wrench at side rail fitting, remove flare nut from each end of fuel rail.
3 Disengage front rail from pressure regulator hose and remove from vehicle.

FUEL INJECTION

FRONT—INSTALLATION
1 Install new hose clamp over flexible hose.
2 Position front rail to pressure regulator hose and force hose over nipple.
3 Move rail into position and tighten flare nut into fitting on each side rail to *Use a back-up wrench to hold side rail fittings.* Do *not* use teflon tape on flare nuts.
4 Tighten hose clamp securing pressure regulator hose to rail.
5 Turn ignition ON and OFF several times to build up fuel rail pressure and check for fuel leaks.

REAR—REMOVAL
1 Using a back-up wrench on fuel rail, remove fuel inlet line from rear rail.
2 Using a back-up wrench on fuel rail, remove flare nut at each side rail and remove rear fuel rail.

REAR—INSTALLATION
1 Position rear fuel rail and thread flare nuts into side rails. Do *not* use teflon tape on flare nuts.
2 Thread fuel inlet line flare nut into rear rail. Do *not* use teflon tape on flare nut.
3 *Using a back-up wrench on fuel rail,* tighten flare nuts
4 Turn ignition ON and OFF several times to build up fuel rail pressure and check for fuel leaks.

SIDE—REMOVAL
Right or Left side fuel rail removal is the same as injector removal

Fuel Filter
The fuel filter element is replaced by unscrewing the bottom cover and removing the filter element. Replace element and gasket with AC type GF 157 or equivalent. Hand tighten bottom cover.

A "Dry" fuel system on cars equipped with EFI may require a substantial cranking period before starting.

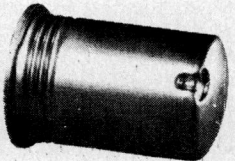

Fuel Filter Components

Chassis-Mounted Fuel Pump
The chassis-mounted pump is located forward of the rear wheel along the frame side rail.

REMOVAL
Peel back rubber boot and remove two nuts, one from each electrical terminal. Remove electrical leads.

NOTE: These nuts have metric threads.

INSTALLATION
1 Position fuel pump to mounting

bracket and secure with two screws with flat washers.

Fuel Tank
REMOVAL
1 Disconnect battery, open fuel tank filler door and disconnect sending unit feed wire (tan).

DRAIN FUEL (SIPHON)
1 Remove screw securing ground wire to cross member.
2 Disconnect fuel line, evaporative loss control system and return lines at front of tank.
3 Support tank with jack and wood block and remove one screw, each side, securing fuel tank support straps to body at front of tank.
4 Lower jack and fuel tank to a position where fuel pump lead may be removed.
5 Remove fuel tank.

REMOVE TANK FUEL PUMP
1 Remove fuel inlet and outlet hoses from nipples on pump.
2 Remove locknuts securing fuel gage tank unit and fuel pump feed wires to tank unit.
3 Position fuel tank sending unit remover and installer J-24187 on cam locking ring so that tool engages three tabs on ring.
4 Install ratchet and turn counter clockwise to disengage lock ring from fuel tank. Remove tool and lift gage-pump unit from tank.

INSTALLATION
1 Install gage-pump unit in fuel tank, using new gasket.
2 Install fuel tank sending unit remover and installer J-24187 so that it engages three tabs on cam locking ring.
3 Turn clockwise until locking ring is fully engaged in fuel tank.
4 Connect electrical leads to fuel gage and secure with locknut.

5 Position tank near underbody and attach fuel pump lead wire (14 green) to terminal marked "pump".
6 Move tank to underbody; position fuel tank support straps under tank and loosely install screws securing straps to body.
7 Secure ground wire to rear cross member.
8 Tighten tank strap screws until bottomed. Torque to 25 foot-pounds.
9 Connect fuel line, evaporative loss control system line and return line to

fittings at front of tank. Secure with new clamps.
10 Lower car.
11 With fuel filler door open, connect sending unit feed wire (tan).
12 Replace drained fuel in tank.
13 A "dry" fuel system on cars equipped with EFI may require a substantial cranking period before starting.

Air Temperature Sensor
REMOVAL
1 Locate air temperature sensor at right rear of intake manifold and disconnect sensor from car harness.
2 Remove sensor from intake manifold.

INSTALLATION
1 Apply a non-hardening sealer to threads of sensor and install sensor in intake manifold.
2 Tighten sensor to 15 foot-pounds.
3 Connect air temperature sensor connector to car harness.

Coolant Temperature Sensor
REMOVE
1 Drain radiator until coolant level is below level of cylinder heads.
2 Locate water temperature sensor in heater hose outlet at rear of right hand cylinder head, and disconnect sensor from car harness.
3 Remove sensor from position in heater hose.

INSTALLATION
1 Apply a non-hardening sealer to threads of sensor and install sensor in heater hose outlet fitting.
2 Tighten sensor to 15 foot-pounds.
3 Connect coolant temperature sensor connector to car harness.
4 Fill cooling system to proper level.

Distributor
REMOVAL
Distributor removal remains the same as for carbureted vehicles except the speed sensor (distributor trigger) electrical connector must be disconnected prior to removal.

Idle Speed
1 Disconnect parking brake hose at vacuum release cylinder and plug hose. Set parking brake and block wheels. Disconnect air leveling compressor hose at air cleaner and plug hose.
2 Connect tachometer, start and warm-up engine to operating temperature in park.
3 Place transmission selector lever in drive, turn air conditioning off.
4 Loosen lock nut on idle by-pass adjusting screw on front of throttle body.
5 Adjust idle by-pass adjusting screw to give 600 rpm.
6 Tighten lock nut on idle by-pass adjusting screw.
7 Shut off engine. Remove tachometer.
8 Reconnect all disconnected hoses.

Throttle Position Switch Adjustment

1 Loosen two throttle position switch mounting screws to permit rotation of the switch.
2 Hold the throttle valves in the idle position while performing step 3 and 4.
3 Turn the throttle position switch carefully counterclockwise until the end-stop has been reached.
4 Tighten throttle position switch mounting screws to 11 in./lbs.
5 Check to insure that throttle valves close to the throttle stop. If not, repeat steps 2, 3 and 4.

Ignition Timing and Idle Speed Adjustment
Strobe Light Timing

1 With engine at normal operating temperature, loosen distributor clamp nut to allow distributor to be turned by hand but without excessive looseness.
2 Disconnect vacuum advance unit hose and plug hose.
3 Disconnect parking brake vacuum hose at diaphragm and plug hose.
4 Disconnect ALC vacuum hose at air cleaner and plug hose.
5 Connect a suitable timing light to No. 1 or No. 4 ignition lead.

NOTE: If spark plug adapters are not available, disconnect No. 1 spark plug wire and connect timing light to wire. Time engine on seven cylinders. Do not force pins or wires thru spark plug nipple.

6 Connect tachometer to engine (use HEI terminal marked "Tach").
7 Set parking brake, start engine and place transmission selector lever in "Drive".

Idle Adjustment

8 Turn Air Conditioning to "OFF" position.
9 With idle speed at 600 RPM or less, observe timing light flashes on pulley in relation to notches on front cover. Set timing to specifications indicated on the engine tune up decal.
10 Tighten clamp nut and recheck timing to make sure that it did not change.
11 Connect vacuum hose to vacuum advance unit and adjust idle speed to 600 RPM with transmission in "Drive", by adjusting idle speed screw in front of throttle body.
12 Stop engine and disconnect timing light and tachometer. Reconnect all vacuum hoses.

Timing Advance Meter

1 With engine at normal operating temperature, loosen distributor clamp nut to allow distributor to be turned by hand but without excessive looseness.
2 Disconnect vacuum advance unit hose and plug hose.
3 Disconnect parking brake vacuum hose at diaphragm and plug hose.
4 Disconnect ALC vacuum hose at air cleaner and plug hose.
5 Connect power supply for timing meter to battery. Observe correct polarity.
6 Install ignition pick-up clip over No. 1 spark plug wire.

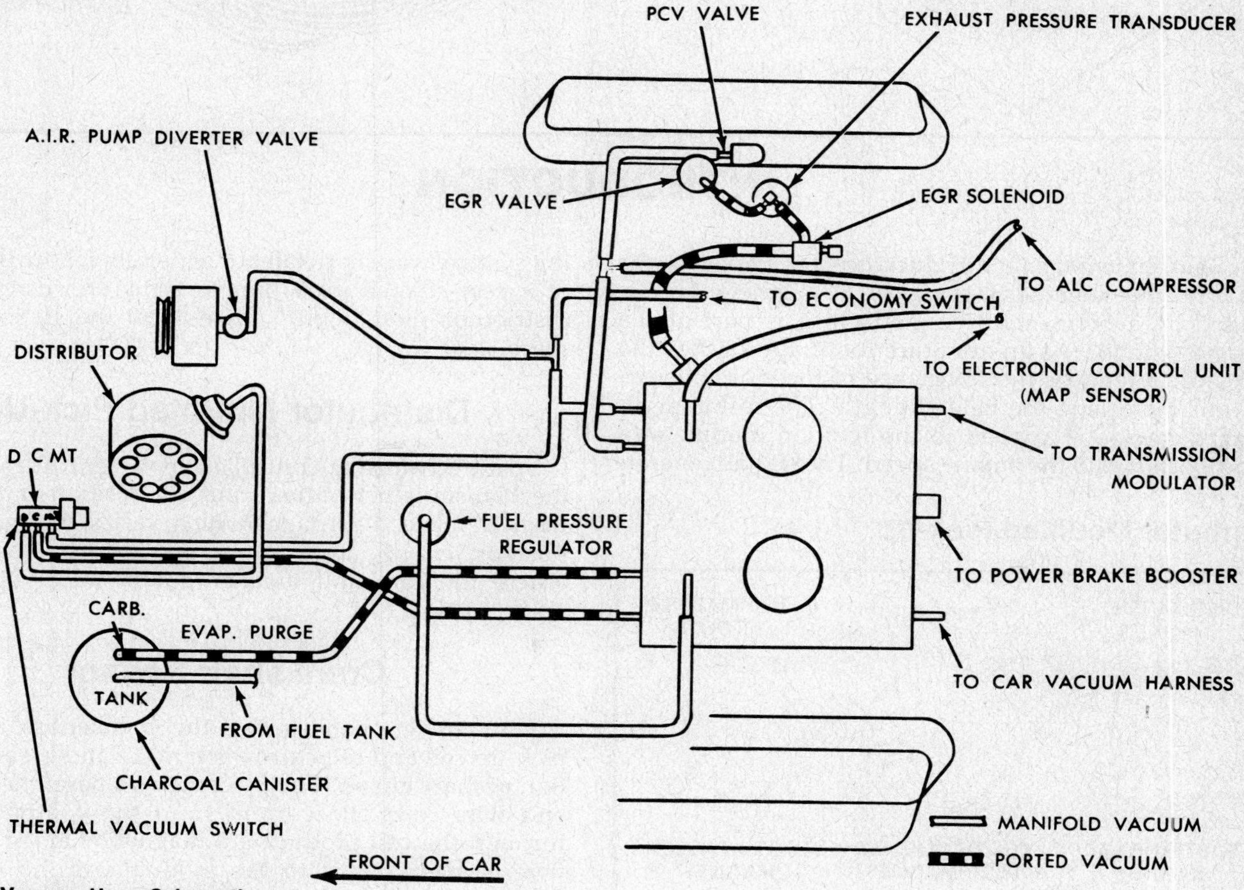

Vacuum Hose Schematic

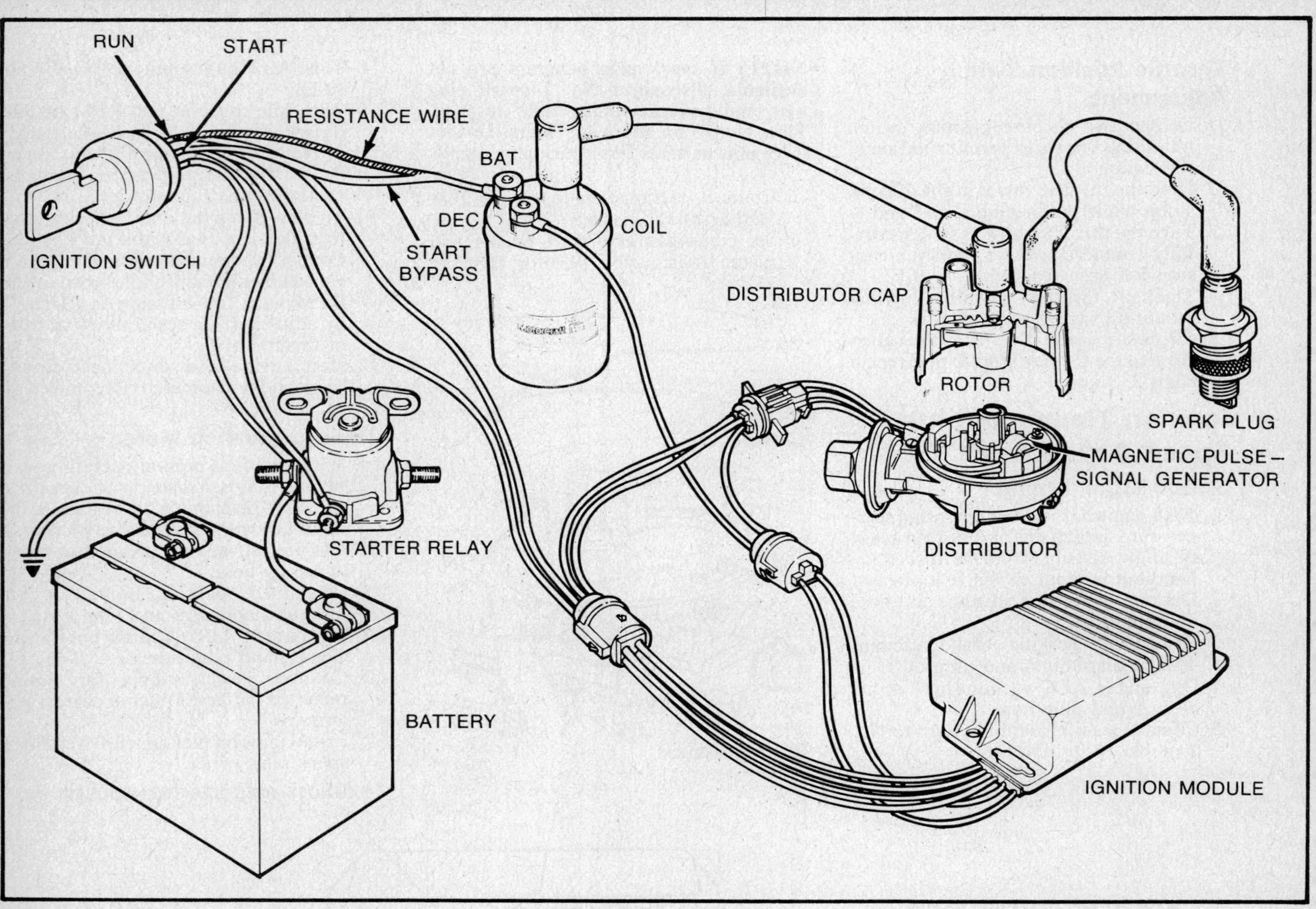

FORD SOLID STATE IGNITION

IGNITION SWITCH · RUN · START · RESISTANCE WIRE · START BYPASS · DEC · BAT · COIL · DISTRIBUTOR CAP · ROTOR · SPARK PLUG · MAGNETIC PULSE—SIGNAL GENERATOR · DISTRIBUTOR · STARTER RELAY · BATTERY · IGNITION MODULE

INTRODUCTION

All solid state magnetic inductance ignition systems operate on the same basic principle. A magnetic field is provided by a permanent magnet which is part of the pick-up assembly. As an armature tooth approaches the pole piece, it reduces the reluctance of the magnetic circuit, thus increasing the field strength. The resultant alternating voltage is applied to the ignition module at a rate proportional to the engine speed. The signal-generating systems vary in detail but generally follow the pattern of a gear-shaped iron rotor or armature, driven by the distributor shaft, which rotates past the stationary pole piece.

Distributor Mounted Pick-Up

Spark advance is controlled by a centrifugal advance mechanism which varies armature position and by a vacuum advance diaphragm which varies the pick-up coil position exactly as in prior conventional distributors where the cam and breaker points were repositioned respectively.

Crankshaft Sensor

The sensor operates like the breakerless distributor pick-up coil and reluctor which make and break the ignition primary circuit. The tip contains a permanent magnet and wire coil. The current from the computer passes through the coil producing a magnetic field. The output wire carries voltage to the module. As the crankshaft rotates, the individual pulse ring lobes approach and

Distributor Mounted Pick-Up

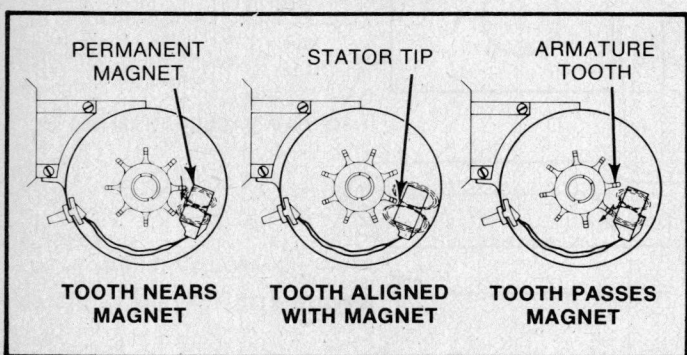

PERMANENT MAGNET · STATOR TIP · ARMATURE TOOTH

TOOTH NEARS MAGNET · **TOOTH ALIGNED WITH MAGNET** · **TOOTH PASSES MAGNET**

Crankshaft Position (Pick-Up Unit)

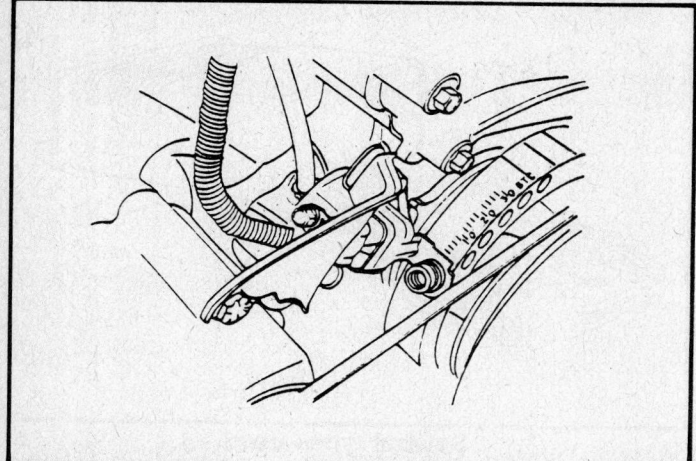

Conventional Distributor

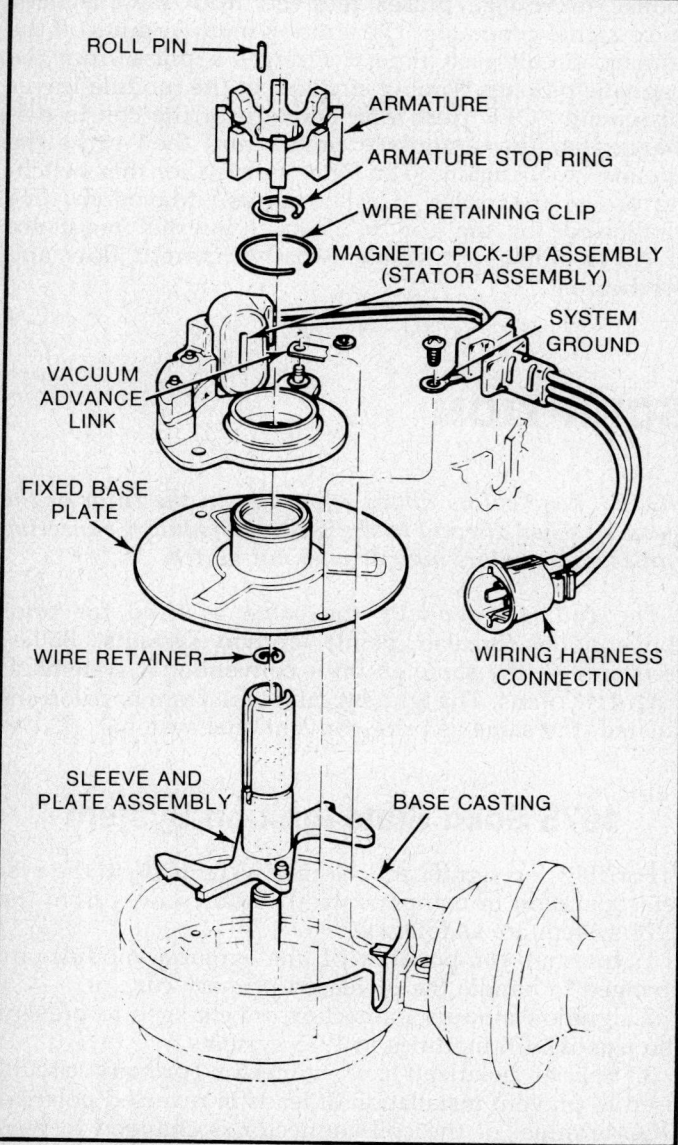

- ROLL PIN
- ARMATURE
- ARMATURE STOP RING
- WIRE RETAINING CLIP
- MAGNETIC PICK-UP ASSEMBLY (STATOR ASSEMBLY)
- SYSTEM GROUND
- VACUUM ADVANCE LINK
- FIXED BASE PLATE
- WIRE RETAINER
- WIRING HARNESS CONNECTION
- SLEEVE AND PLATE ASSEMBLY
- BASE CASTING

Electronic-Controlled Distributor

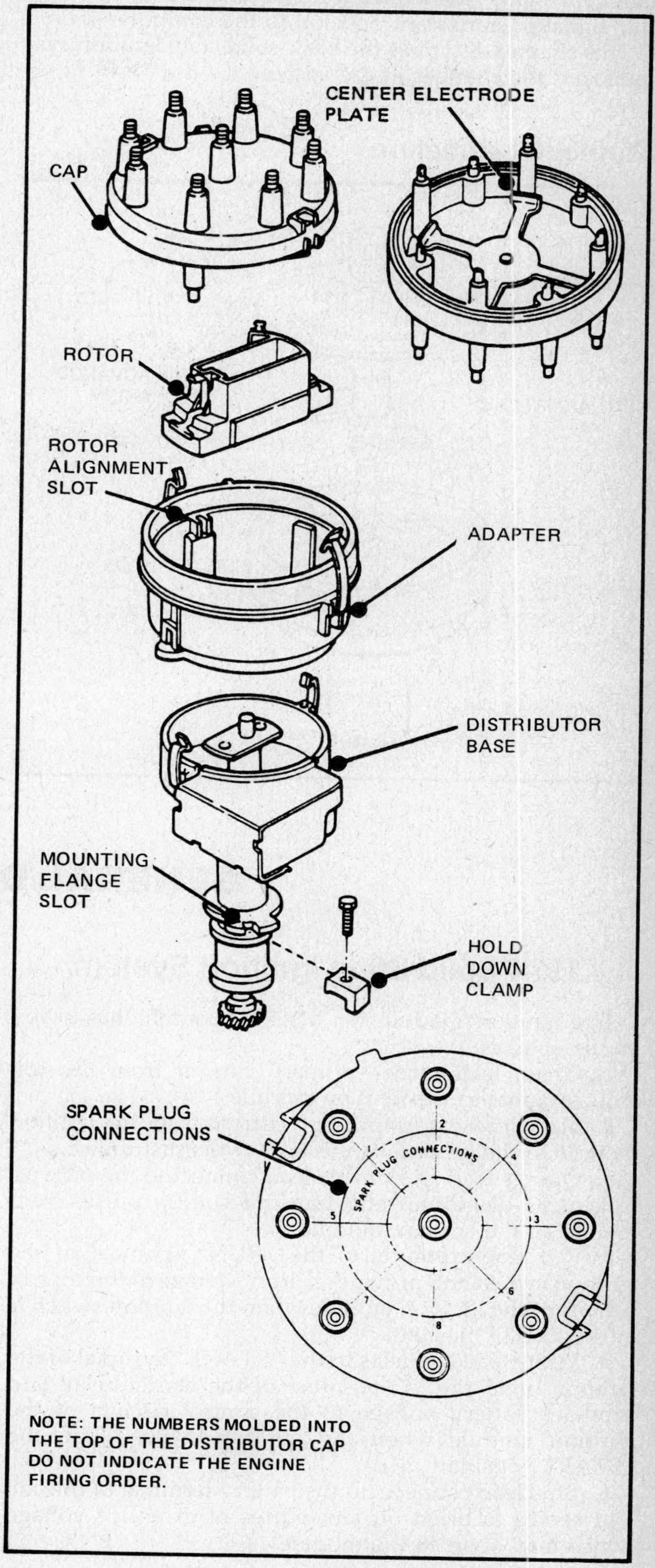

- CENTER ELECTRODE PLATE
- CAP
- ROTOR
- ROTOR ALIGNMENT SLOT
- ADAPTER
- DISTRIBUTOR BASE
- MOUNTING FLANGE SLOT
- HOLD DOWN CLAMP
- SPARK PLUG CONNECTIONS

SPARK PLUG CONNECTIONS

NOTE: THE NUMBERS MOLDED INTO THE TOP OF THE DISTRIBUTOR CAP DO NOT INDICATE THE ENGINE FIRING ORDER.

FORD SOLID STATE IGNITION

finally align with the sensor tip. The metal lobe "cuts" the magnetic field. This interruption generates a voltage output signal of crankshaft position to the computer.

This chapter describes the basic solid state ignition systems and the changes in the system.

Distributor Armature

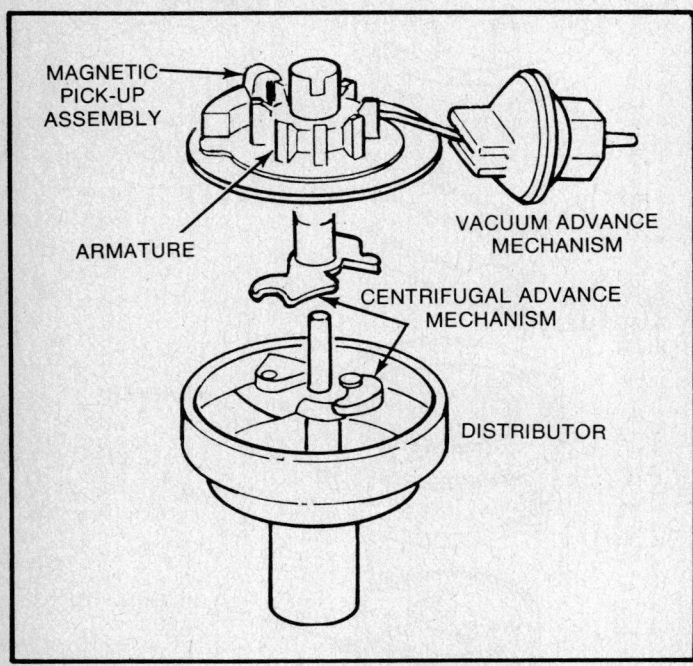

Ignition Module

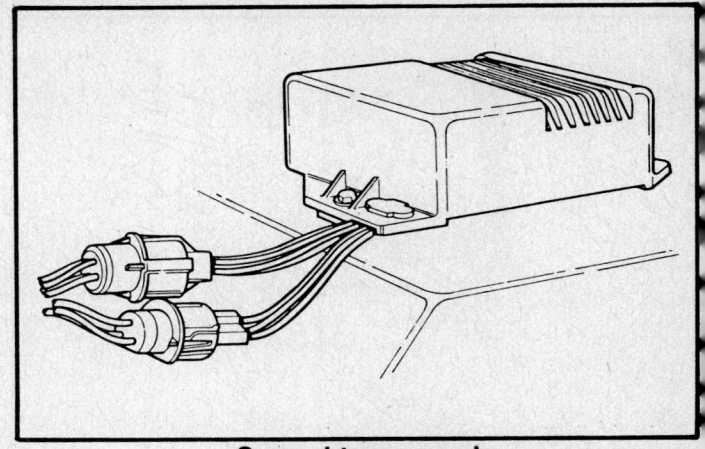

Several types used

The ignition module is simply an electronic switching circuit which turns the primary circuit off and on in response to voltage pulses received from the magnetic pulse-signal generator. The ignition module shuts off the primary circuit each time it receives a pulse from the magnetic pick-up. Timing circuitry in the module leaves this circuit "OFF" just long enough for the coil to discharge into the secondary circuit, and then turns the primary "ON" again. (The time intervals for this switching are in the order of milliseconds.) Maximum time is allowed for the coil to charge. Internal resistance of coil windings prevents excessive current flow and overheating.

GENERAL DESCRIPTION

1974 Solid State Ignition System

The ignition module for the 1974 system has seven electrical leads.

1. Green lead carries primary current from the coil DEC terminal to the ignition module.

2. Black lead carries primary current from the ignition module to the ground connection in the distributor.

3. Orange lead and purple lead connect to the pick-up coil in the distributor and transmit voltage pulses from the coil to the ignition module.

4. Red lead connects to the "RUN" terminal of the ignition switch and provides battery voltage to the control circuits of the ignition module when the ignition switch is in the "RUN" position.

5. White lead connects to the "START" terminal of the ignition or to the "I" terminal of the starter relay and provides battery voltage to the control circuits of the ignition module when the ignition switch is in the "START" position.

6. Blue lead connects to the battery terminal of the coil and serves to bleed off any pulses of excessive voltage which may occur in the module.

NOTE   Wire colors above refer only to the color of the leads attached directly to the ignition module. Connecting harness wire colors may or may not match.

The coil is essentially the same as used for prior conventional (breaker point) ignition systems. Ballast resistance is the same as prior conventional systems at 1.30–1.40 ohms. The ignition cables are 7mm hypalon-insulated, the same as prior conventional systems.

1975 Solid State Ignition System

For 1975, no significant changes were made to the system operation or components. The differences from the 1974 system are as follows.

1. Internal components of the ignition module are changed to handle the increased primary current.

2. Ignition module connectors are changed to prevent the use of 1974 modules in 1975 systems.

3. Special polarized coil connector (primary circuit) used to prevent installation of leads in reversed polarity. DEC terminal of the coil connector is changed to read

1974–75 System

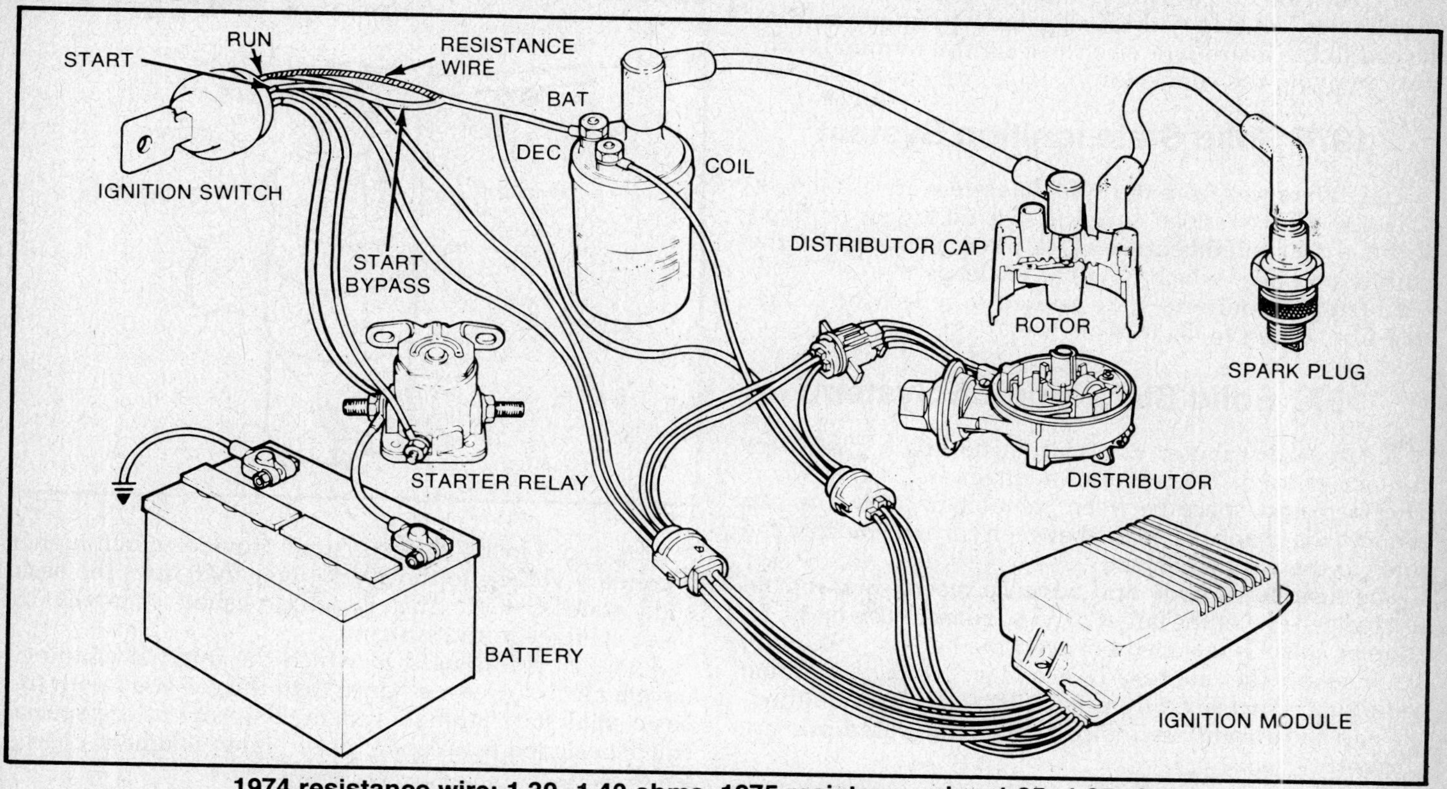

START RUN RESISTANCE WIRE BAT DEC COIL IGNITION SWITCH START BYPASS STARTER RELAY BATTERY DISTRIBUTOR CAP ROTOR SPARK PLUG DISTRIBUTOR IGNITION MODULE

1974 resistance wire: 1.30–1.40 ohms, 1975 resistance wire: 1.25–1.35 ohms

1976 System

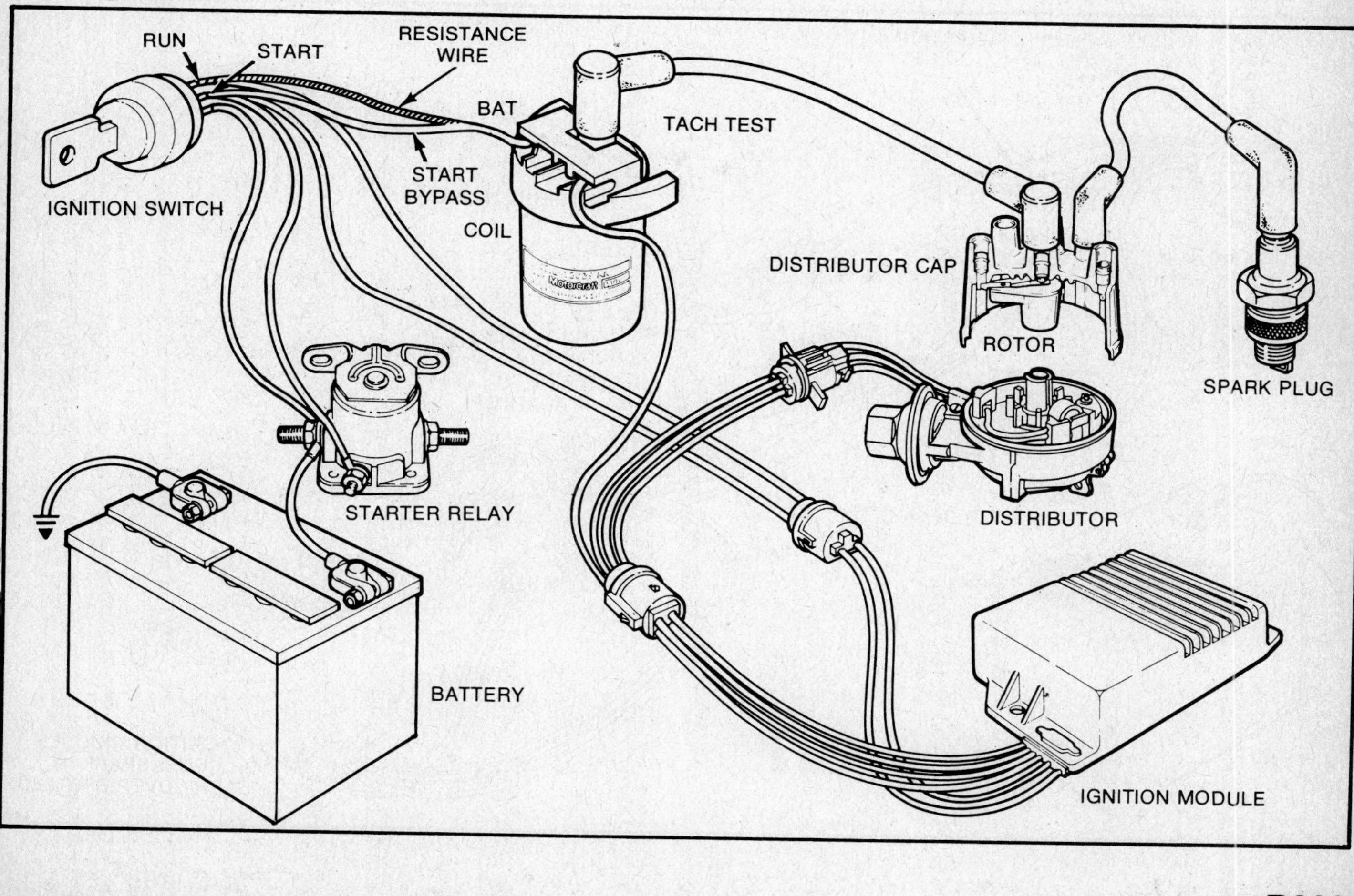

RUN START RESISTANCE WIRE BAT TACH TEST IGNITION SWITCH START BYPASS COIL STARTER RELAY BATTERY DISTRIBUTOR CAP ROTOR SPARK PLUG DISTRIBUTOR IGNITION MODULE

B229

FORD SOLID STATE IGNITION

"tach test" for 1975 systems. The new connector allows a tachometer test lead with an alligator-type clip to be connected to the distributor electronic control terminal without removing the connector.

1976 Solid State Ignition System

The differences from the 1974-75 system are as follows.
1. The blue overload shunt lead is no longer required and it is eliminated because of the internal changes in the ignition module, which now has six leads.
2. Ignition connectors are revised to reflect the reduction from seven to six leads.

1977 Solid State Ignition System

A larger distributor cap with male spark plug type contacts is used. This requires a longer and higher rotor. The increased space between cable contacts in the cap reduces the chance of arcing between contacts or from the rotor to the wrong contact.

The distributor body and advance mechanism remain unchanged. To fit the larger cap and rotor to this body, an adapter collar is installed between the body and the cap. To insulate the increased secondary voltage, ignition cable size is increased from 7mm to 8mm. Ignition module and coil are changed to handle the increased primary current.

Special Coil and Current Contr

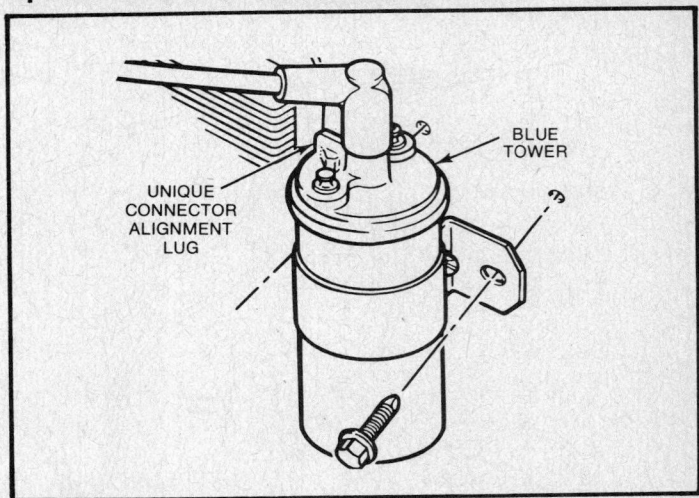

Introduced in 1977, this system provides much higher secondary voltage to the spark plugs than does the basic solid state system. This is accomplished primarily by three changes in the system.

A special coil is used in which the internal windings have a much lower resistance than the coil used with the basic solid state ignition system. The core of the special coil is designed to accept a much higher magnetic charge

1977 Duraspark II System

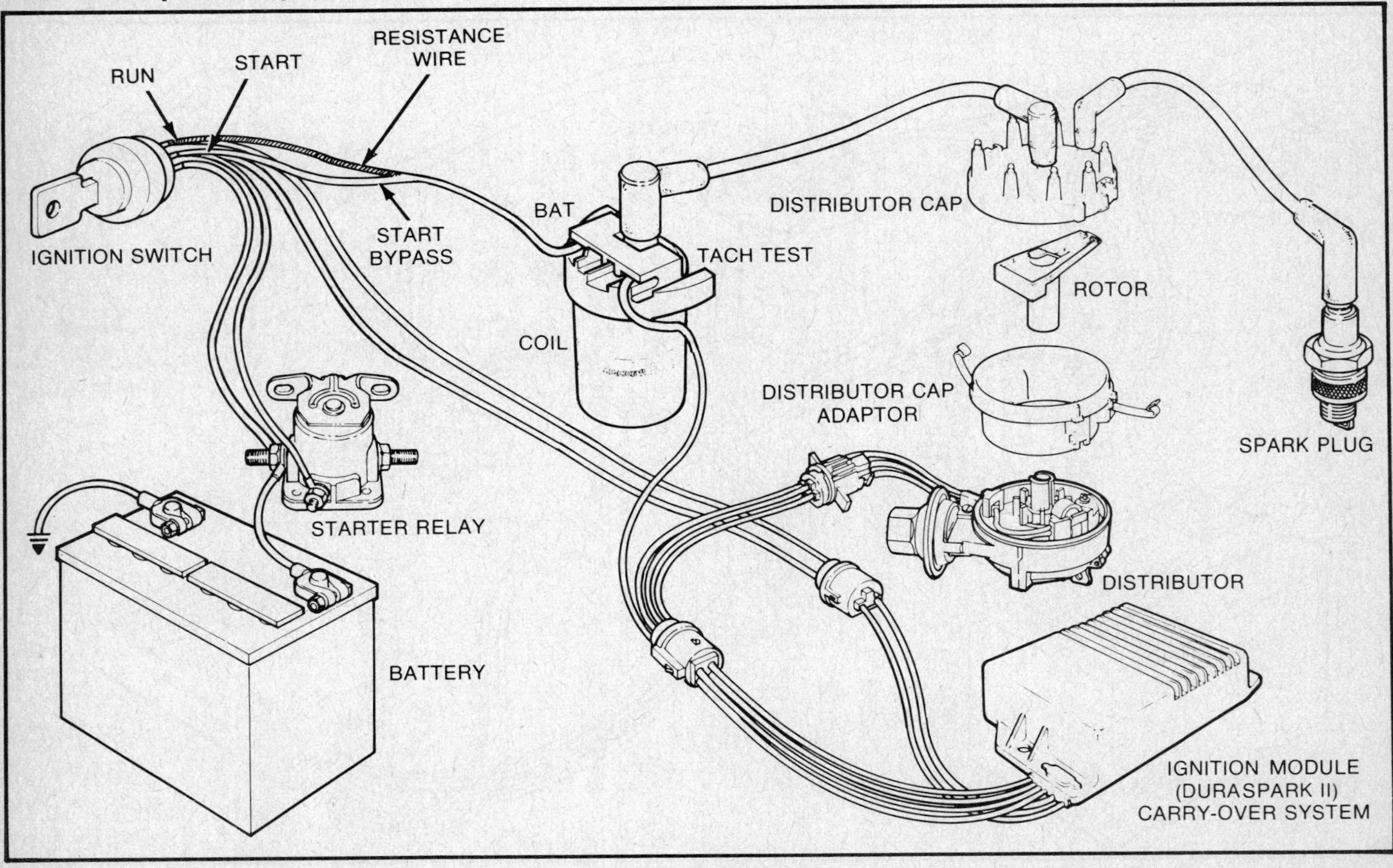

1977-79 Duraspark I System

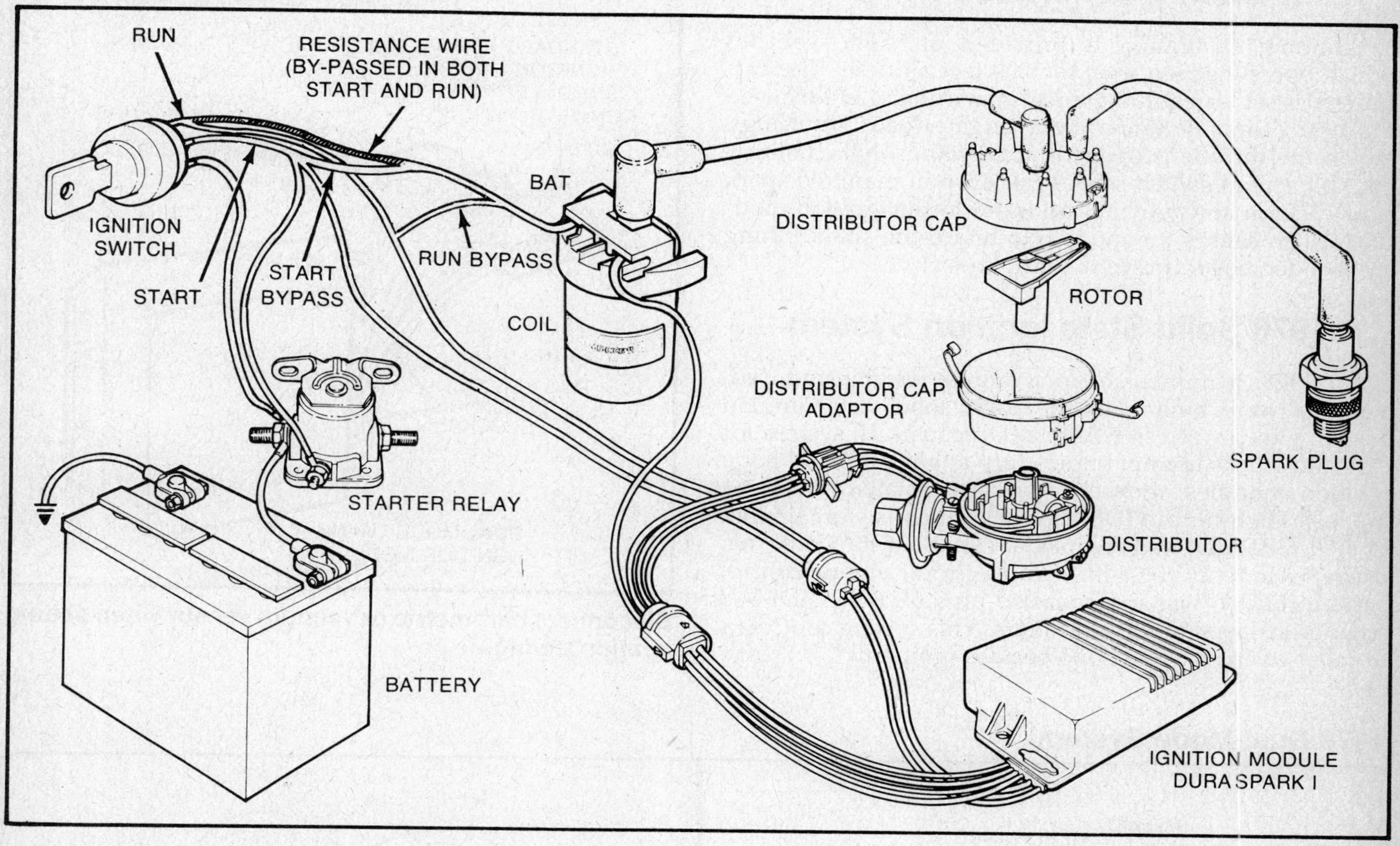

RUN

RESISTANCE WIRE
(BY-PASSED IN BOTH
START AND RUN)

BAT

DISTRIBUTOR CAP

IGNITION
SWITCH

RUN BYPASS

ROTOR

START
START
BYPASS

COIL

DISTRIBUTOR CAP
ADAPTOR

SPARK PLUG

STARTER RELAY

DISTRIBUTOR

BATTERY

SPARK PLUG

IGNITION MODULE
DURA SPARK I

from the increased current which flows through the low-resistance windings. This produces a substantially higher voltage to the spark plugs and allows the coil to reach "full charge" much more rapidly than previous systems. This coil has a unique alignment lug on the blue coil tower which prevents attachment of this coil into a basic solid state ignition system harness. Spark intensity is greatly increased, especially at higher engine rpm. If this coil were allowed to run with the same dwell control (maximum charging time) as the basic solid state systems, the coil would, at low engine rpm, overcharge and over-heat. For this reason, a "current-control" circuit is needed with this system.

"Current-control" circuitry shuts off the primary current if the engine stalls. The ignition switch must be turned to "START" to shift the module back into the operating mode. In appearance, this module is identical to the basic solid state ignition system module. It has the same six leads. However, the sealing block through which the leads enter the module is red in color. (The sealing block for the basic solid state system is blue.) The connector keyway on the high-output (Duraspark I) ignition module has been changed from the basic system, so that the modules of the two systems are not interchangeable.

There are two types of dual-mode ignition systems. One is for altitude compensation, the other for economy calibration. Both use the same ignition module.

Tachometer Connection

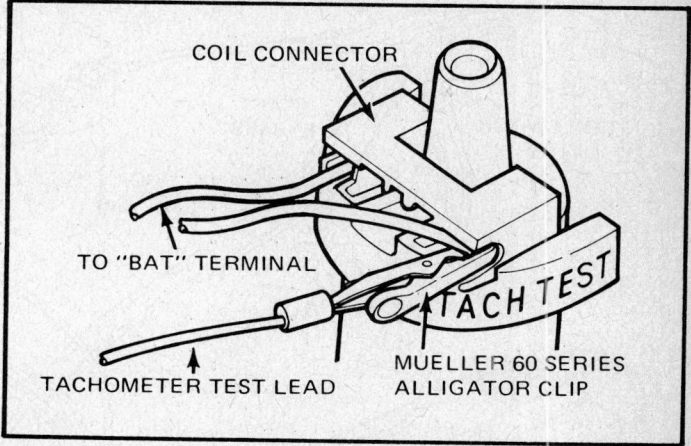

COIL CONNECTOR

TO "BAT" TERMINAL

ATTACH TEST

TACHOMETER TEST LEAD

MUELLER 60 SERIES
ALLIGATOR CLIP

Altitude Compensation System

Altitude compensation is provided on some vehicles which normally operate at altitudes above 4000 feet. The carburetor is set lean for operation at altitudes with nor-mal spark advance. Below the specified altitude, a barometric pressure switch provides an input signal to the ignition module, which causes the module to retard spark timing by 3–6 degrees to prevent spark knock.

FORD SOLID STATE IGNITION

Economy Calibration System

Economy calibration is provided on some vehicles which operate at sea level to 3000 feet altitude. The carburetor is set lean and the initial spark timing is advanced for best economy under light engine loads (cruising). When the throttle is opened (acceleration, hill climbing, etc.) a vacuum switch senses the drop in manifold/spark port vacuum and provides an input to the ignition module, which causes the module to retard the spark timing by 3–6 degrees to prevent spark knock.

1978 Solid State Ignition System

For 1978, a number of innovations were introduced. Vehicles were built with the basic solid state ignition system which was essentially a (Duraspark II) system for cars and trucks (except super-duty engines). Dual-mode ignition modules and sensors were installed on some models. High-output (Duraspark I) systems were limited to 5.0L (302 CID) V-8 engines in cars built for California usage, except on Versailles. An electronic engine control system (EEC I) was incorporated on 5.0L (302 CID) V-8 engines installed in Versailles cars. This system controls a number of engine functions besides ignition.

Dual-Mode Module

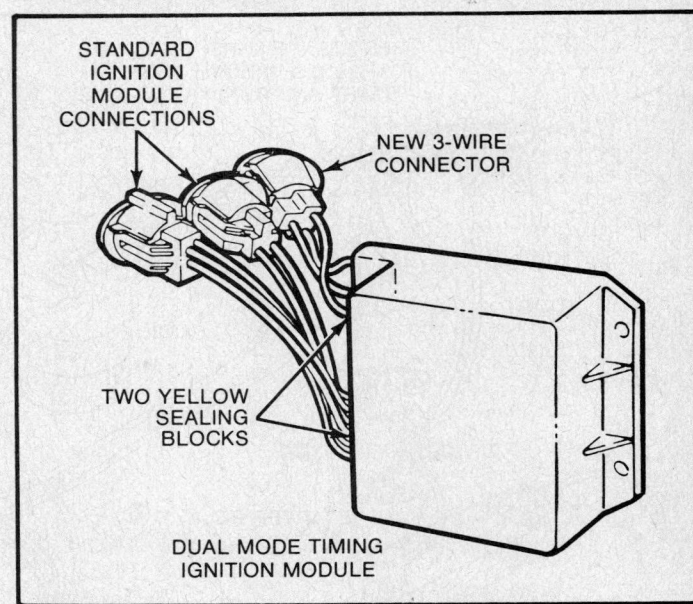

Disconnect barometric or vacuum sensor when setting ignition timing

1978 Dual-Mode System

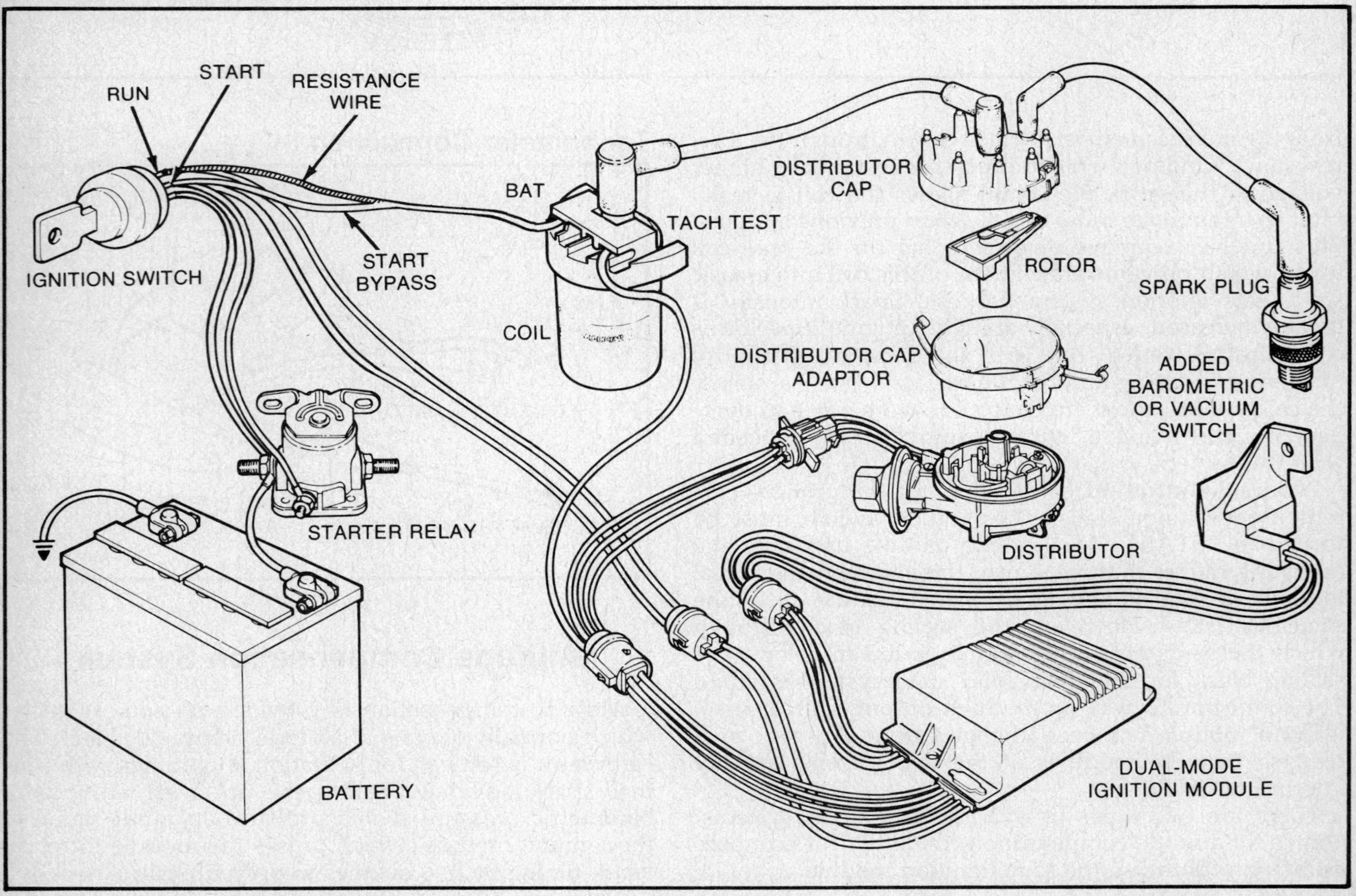

1979 Solid State Ignition System

For 1979, EEC I is continued on the 5.0L (302 CID) V-8 engines in Versailles except in California. Also, an expanded version, EEC II, is installed on Fords with the 5.8L (351W CID) V-8 engines built for use in California only and on Mercurys with the 5.8L (351W CID) V-8 engines built for all 50 states. The high-output (Dura-spark I) ignition system is used only on the 5.0L (302 CID) V-8 engines in cars built for California usage.

Non-turbocharged 2.3L engines with automatic transmission have a "cranking retard" circuit built into the ignition module. The retard feature is actuated only during engine crank by the slow rpm signal of the distributor magnetic pick-up. This signal actuates a circuit in the ignition module to retard ignition timing up to 18 degrees.

The ignition control module with cranking retard can be identified by the white sealing block and white 4-pin connector. The module is not functionally interchangeable with other ignition control modules.

NOTE Starting with some 1979 cars, emission control units are controlled by a computer.

The Systems are called EEC I, EEC II and EEC III. All EEC units use an electrical control (advance) distributor. EEC I uses a crankshaft positioner (pick-up) attached to the rear of the crankshaft. On EEC II and III, the pick-up unit is mounted on the front of the engine.

Cranking Retard Module

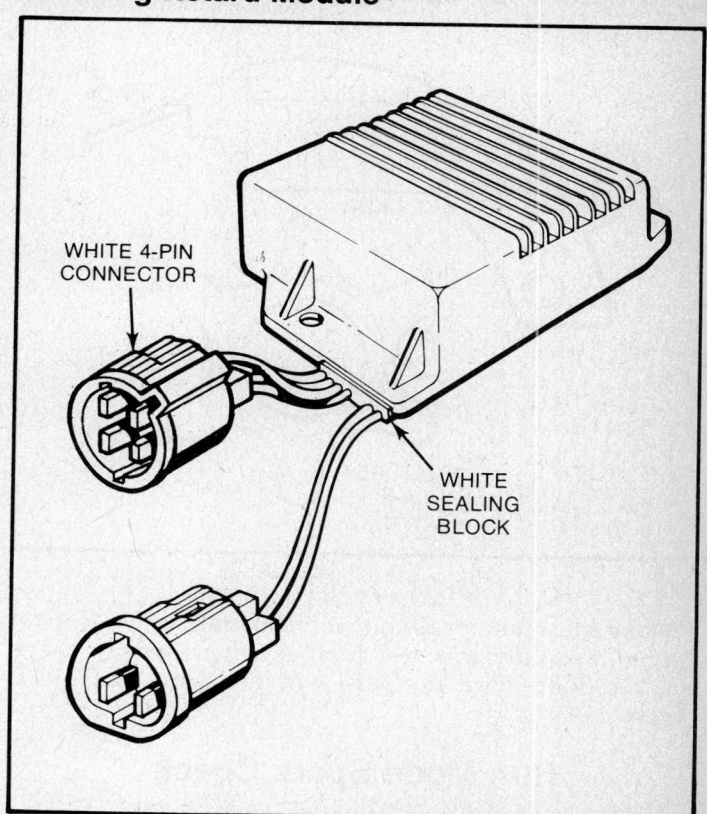

WHITE 4-PIN CONNECTOR

WHITE SEALING BLOCK

TROUBLESHOOTING

Many times a quick check can locate the cause of a problem without going into full system checkout. Included are checks which may isolate the cause of the problem. Just as with a conventional breaker point ignition system, the first step is to verify that the problem exists and then to make some preliminary checks to find out whether the problem is in the ignition system or somewhere else. The following procedures are intended to provide quick checks to identify and locate some of the more frequently encountered problems.

There is also the possibility that there is an intermittent problem in the module or the magnetic pick-up. Some intermittent problem checks are included at the end of these quick checks.

Preliminary Checks

1. Check battery for state of charge and for clean, tight battery terminal connections.
2. Inspect all wires and connectors for breaks, cuts, abrasions or burned spots. Repair or replace as necessary. Make sure all wires are connected correctly.
3. Unplug all connectors and inspect for corroded/burned contacts. Repair as necessary and plug connectors

back together. Do not remove the lubricant compound in connectors.
4. Check for loose or damaged spark plug or coil wires. If boots or nipples are removed on 8mm ignition wires, reline inside of each with new silicone di-electric compound.

Special Test Jumper

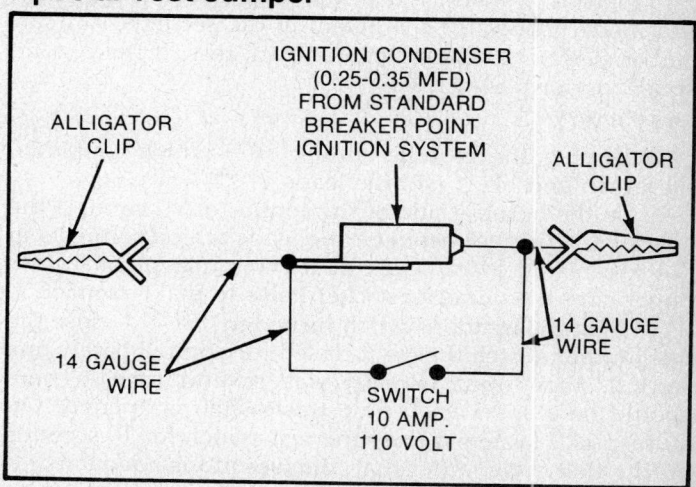

IGNITION CONDENSER (0.25-0.35 MFD) FROM STANDARD BREAKER POINT IGNITION SYSTEM

ALLIGATOR CLIP

ALLIGATOR CLIP

14 GAUGE WIRE

14 GAUGE WIRE

SWITCH 10 AMP. 110 VOLT

FORD SOLID STATE IGNITION

Distributor Pick-Up Alignment

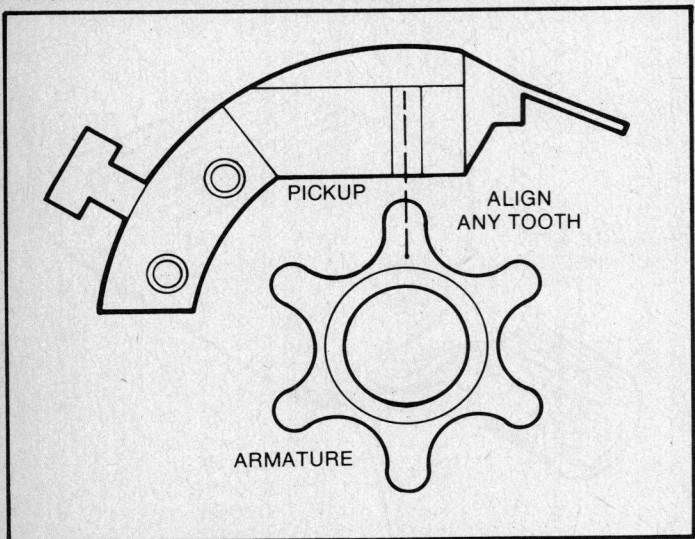

PICKUP ALIGN ANY TOOTH

ARMATURE

Make a test jumper as shown in illustration. It is important to use only this test jumper when making these checks. Solid wire jumpers will not work for quick checks.

Run Mode Spark Check

STEP ONE

1. Remove distributor cap and rotor from distributor.
2. Crank engine to align one tooth of armature with magnet in pick-up coil (ignition "OFF").
3. Remove coil wire from distributor cap.
a. 1977 and later, install a modified spark plug (side electrode removed) in the coil wire terminal and, using insulated pliers, hold the spark plug shell against the engine block.
b. 1976 and earlier, using insulated pliers, hold the coil wire terminal ¼ inch from engine block or head.
4. Turn the ignition switch to "RUN" and tap the distributor body with a screwdriver handle. There should be a spark at the spark plug or coil wire terminal.

If there is a spark, the primary circuit is okay in the run mode. Check for a problem in the secondary circuit and/or perform the start mode spark test. If there is no spark, perform Step Two.

STEP TWO

1. Unplug the module connector(s) which contain(s) the green and black module leads.
2. To the harness side of the connector(s), connect the special test jumper between the leads which connects to the green and black leads of the module pigtails. Use paper clips in connector socket holes to make contact.
3. With the ignition switch turned to "RUN," close the test jumper switch. Leave it closed for approximately one second, then open. Repeat this several times. There should be a spark each time this switch is opened. On Duraspark I systems, close the test switch for 10 seconds on the first cycle. After that, one second is adequate.

If there is no spark, the problem is most probably in the primary circuit through the ignition switch, coil, green lead, black lead or ground connection in the distributor. Perform Step Three.

If there is a spark, the primary circuit wiring and coil are probably okay. The problem is most probably in the distributor pick-up, the module bias power feed (red wire) or the module. Perform Step Six.

STEP THREE

1. Disconnect the test jumper lead from the black lead and connect to a good ground on the engine. Turn the test jumper switch "ON" and "OFF" several times as in step 2.
2. If there is no spark, the problem is most probably in the green lead, the coil or the coil feed circuit. Perform Step Five.

If there is a spark, the problem is most probably in the black lead or the ground connection in the distributor. Perform Step Four.

STEP FOUR

1. Connect an ohmmeter between the black lead and a good ground on the engine. With the meter on its lowest scale, there should be no measurable resistance in the circuit.
2. If there is resistance, check the ground connection in the distributor and the black lead from the module. Repair or replace as necessary. Remove the meter, plug in all the connectors and repeat Step One.

If there is no resistance, the primary ground wiring is okay. Perform Step Six.

STEP FIVE

1. Disconnect the test jumper from the green lead and the ground and connect it between the tach-test terminal of the coil and a good ground on the engine.
2. With the ignition switch turned to "RUN," turn the jumper switch on. Hold it on for approximately one second and turn it off as in Step Two. Repeat this several times. There should be a spark each time the switch is turned off.

If there is no spark, the problem is most probably in the coil or in the primary circuit through the ignition switch to the coil battery terminal.
a. Check the coil for internal shorts or opens and for primary resistance (Duraspark I—.7 ohm, Duraspark II—1.17 ohm) and secondary resistance (Duraspark I—7.3–8.2 k ohms, Duraspark II—7.7–9.3 k ohms). Replace the coil if necessary.
b. Check the coil power circuit for opens, shorts or high resistance. Repair as necessary. Remove test jumper, plug in connectors and recheck Step One.

If there is a spark, the coil and its feed circuit are most probably okay. The problem may be in the green lead between the coil and the module. Check for open or short and repair as necessary. Remove the test jumper. Plug in all connectors and repeat Step One.

STEP SIX

1. Connect a voltmeter between the orange and purple leads on the harness side of the module connectors.

CHILTON CAUTION   If the vehicle has a catalytic converter, disconnect the air supply line between the by-pass valve and the manifold before turning the engine with the ignition off. This will prevent damage to the catalytic converter. After testing, run the engine for at least 3 minutes before reconnecting the air supply line to clear excess fuel from the exhaust system.

NOTE   Do not use a voltmeter which is combined with a dwell-meter. Slight needle oscillations (½ volt) may not be detectable on this type of test unit.

2. Set the meter on its lowest scale and crank the engine. The meter needle should oscillate slightly (approximately ½ volt).

If the meter needle does not oscillate, check the circuit through magnetic pick-up (in the distributor) for open, shorts, shorts to ground and resistance. Resistance between the orange and purple leads should be 400–1000 ohms and between each lead and the ground should be more than 70 k ohms. Repair as necessary. Plug in all connectors and recheck Step One.

If the meter oscillates, the problem is most probably in the power feed to the module (red wire) or in the module itself. Perform Step Seven.

STEP SEVEN

1. Remove all meters and jumpers. Plug in all connectors.
2. Turn the ignition switch to "RUN" and measure voltage to engine ground at the following.
 a. Battery positive terminal, reading should be at least 12 volts.
 b. The red lead of the module. Use a straight pin to pierce the insulation of the lead and connect the voltmeter to the pin.
3. These two readings should be within 1 volt of each other.

If readings are not within one volt, check the circuit feeding power to the red lead for shorts, open, or high resistance. Repair as necessary and repeat Step One.

If readings are within one volt, the problem is probably in the module. Disconnect the module and connect a known-good module in its place. Repeat Step One. If this corrects the problem, reconnect the original module and recheck. If the problem returns, remove the old module and install the new one.

Start Mode Spark Test

STEP ONE

1. Remove the coil wire from the distributor cap.
 a. For 1977 and later, install the modified spark plug (side electrode removed) in the coil wire terminal. Using an insulated pliers, hold the spark plug shell against the engine block.
 b. 1976 and earlier, hold the coil wire terminal ¼ inch from the engine block or head using an insulated pliers.
2. Crank the engine (from the ignition switch).
If there is a good spark, the problem is probably in the

distributor cap, rotor, ignition cable(s) or spark plug(s).
If there is no spark, proceed to Step Two.

STEP TWO

1. Measure battery voltage and voltage at the white wire of the module (use a straight pin to pierce the wire) while cranking the engine.
2. These two readings should be within 1 volt of each other. If readings are not within one volt, check and repair the feed through the ignition switch to the white wire. Recheck for spark (Step One). If readings are within one volt, or if there is still no spark after the power feed to white wire is repaired, proceed to Step Three.

STEP THREE

1. Measure coil battery terminal voltage while cranking the engine (see catalytic converter caution).
2. The reading should be within 1 volt of battery voltage. If the reading is not within one volt, check and repair the feed through the ignition switch to the coil. Recheck for spark (Step One). If the reading is within one volt, the problem is probably in the ignition module. Plug in a known-good module and recheck for spark (Step One).

NOTE   If all the above steps check out okay, checks should be made of the fuel system and of the engine itself.

Testing for Intermittent Conditions

If the ignition system becomes operative in the course of performing these procedures and you have not made a repair, it is likely an intermittent connection or an intermittent ignition component has become functional. The following suggestions are offered.

With the engine running, attempt to recreate the problem by wiggling the wires at the coil, module, distributor and other harness connectors. Start first with the connections you might have already disturbed. Also check the ground connection in the distributor. Disconnecting and reconnecting connectors may also be helpful.

CHILTON CAUTION   Do not clean lubricant compound from connectors as it is required to prevent terminal corrosion.

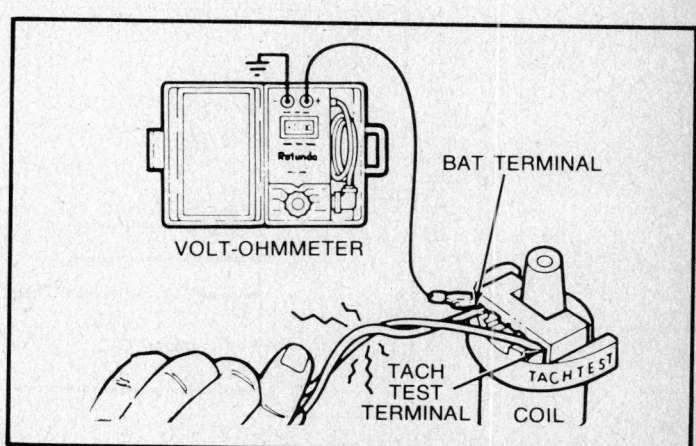

TESTING PICK-UP COIL

With the engine off, remove the distributor cap, rotor and adaptor if so equipped, and heat the stator pick-up coil by placing a 250-watt heat lamp approximately 1 to 2" from its top surface. Apply heat for 5 to 10 minutes while monitoring pick-up coil continuity between the parallel blades of the disconnected distributor connector. The resistance should be 400–1000 ohms. Tapping with a screwdriver handle may also be helpful. Reinstall the distributor cap. A reading less than 400 ohms would indicate a short, while an infinity reading would indicate an open.

Tap Pick-Up Coil

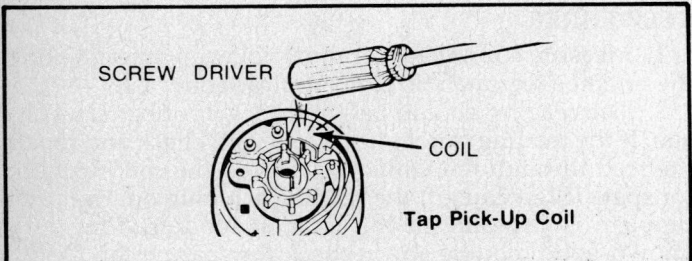

TESTING IGNITION MODULE

With the engine running, heat module by placing a 250-watt heat lamp approximately 1 to 2" from the top surface of the module. Tapping may also be helpful.

Heat Test

Heat Module

Duraspark Wiring Diagram

Typical Schematic — 1978

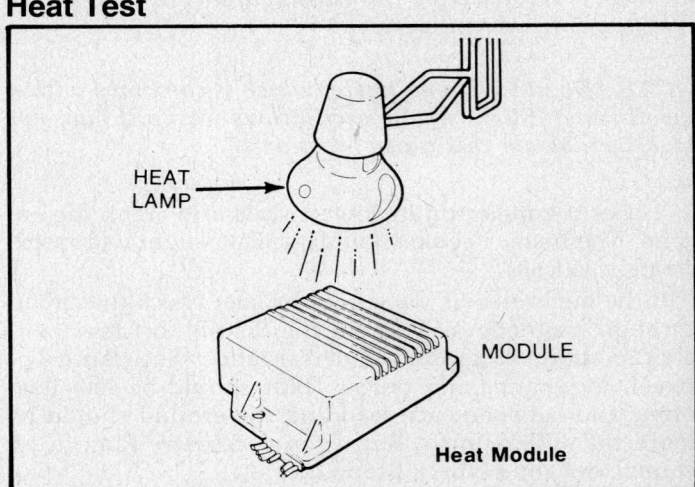

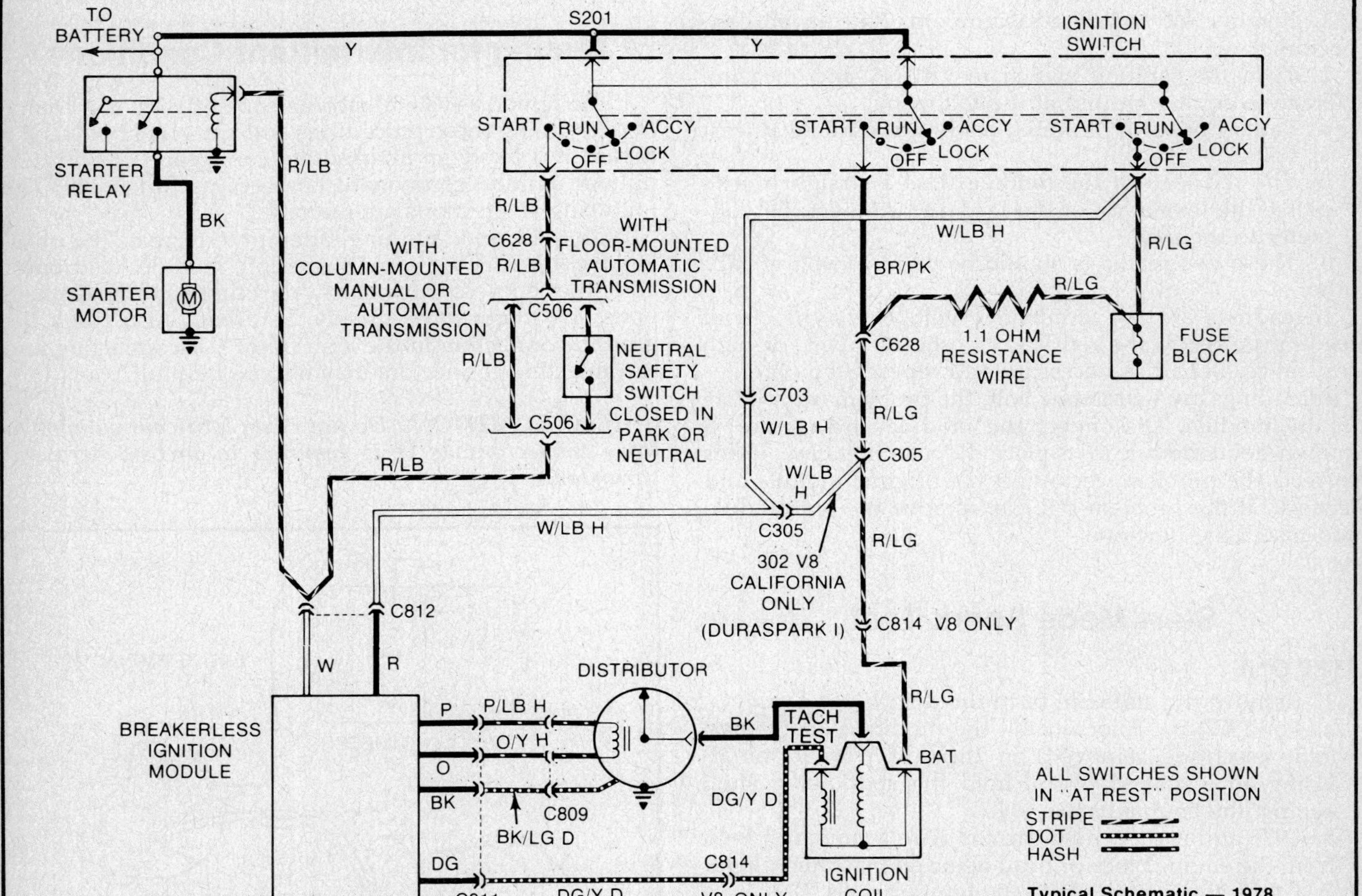

CHILTON CAUTION *The module temperature should not exceed 212 degrees F (boiling). After the first 10 minutes of heating, check the temperature by applying a few drops of water to the module housing. Repeat this check every two minutes until the water droplets boil. Avoid tapping the module to the extent that the housing is distorted.*

If this procedure results in ignition malfunction, substitute a known-good module. If the malfunction is corrected by the substitution validate that the original module is at fault by reconnecting it to the vehicle. A functional check of the original and known-good module can quickly be accomplished by using the run mode check.

Quick Checks for Duraspark I

The same quick checks that have been explained for basic solid state ignition can also be used for cars with Duraspark I with a few variations. The Duraspark I module has internal connections which shut off the primary circuit in the "RUN" mode when the engine stalls (no pulses coming from the pick-up coil). To perform the quick checks, it is necessary to by-pass these connections.

However, with these connections by-passed, the current flow in the primary circuit is so great that it will cause damage to both the ignition coil and the module unless it is controlled. To control primary current, install a ballast

Coil Wire Removal

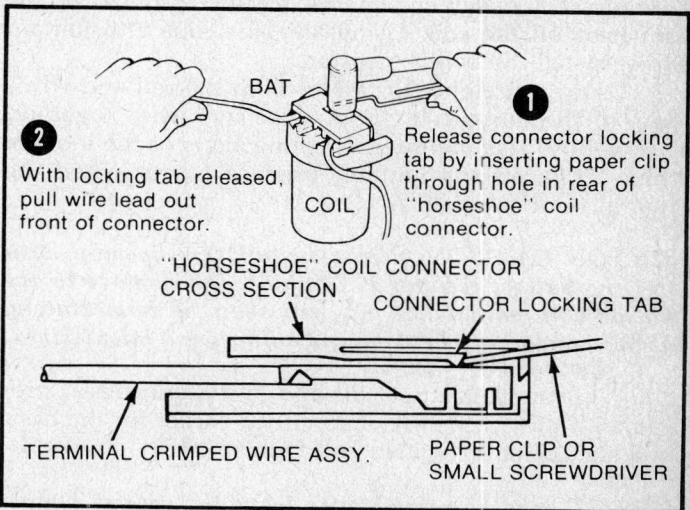

resistance in *series* with the primary circuit at the battery terminal of the ignition coil. (See Duraspark I Test Circuit.) Ford has such a resistor available as Motorcraft Part Number DY-36. A 1.3 ohm, 100 watt wire-wound power resistor can also be used.

CHILTON CAUTION *This resistor will become very hot during testing.*

Duraspark I System

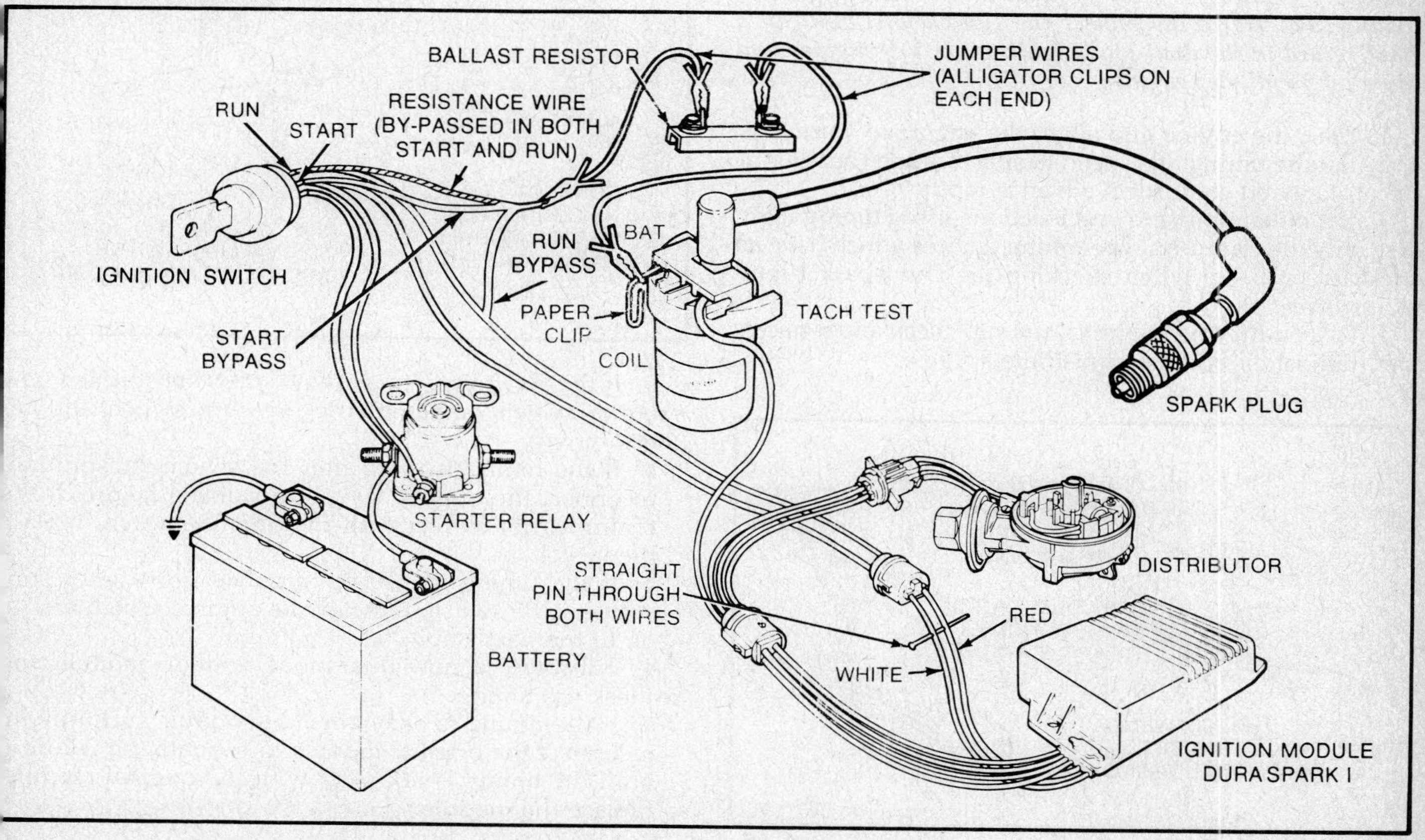

FORD SOLID STATE IGNITION

1. Release the battery terminal lead from the coil.
2. Insert a paper clip in the battery terminal of the connector on the coil. Using alligator clips and jumper wires, install the ballast resistor.
3. Using a straight pin, pierce both the red and white leads of the module to short these two leads together. This will by-pass the internal connections of the module which turns off the ignition primary circuit when the engine is not running.

CHILTON CAUTION Never install this by-pass until after the ballast resistor is in place. The damage to the ignition coil and module may not show up immediately, but the damage will be there and will cause a later failure.

4. With the ballast resistor and by-pass in place, proceed with the quick checks described earlier for the basic solid state ignition system and Duraspark II.

NOTE It may be necessary to leave the special jumper switch on for up to 10 seconds before turning it off to get a spark at the test spark plug.

Checking Timing

NOTE The following points must be considered when checking timing on conventional type distributors. For vehicles equipped with the dual-mode ignition module using either the ignition barometric pressure switch assembly or the vacuum switch, disconnect the 3-pin switch assembly connector from the dual-mode timing ignition module. Failure to disconnect the switch will build in a 3–6° retard in the dual-mode ignition on V-8 engines and more on 6 cylinder engines.

1. Start the engine and allow the engine to warm up.
2. Set the timing idle speed to specification (per engine decal) to avoid centrifugal advance input.
3. Set initial timing to specifications using timing light. Use only the clamp-on type timing devices which have an inductive pick-up when checking the Duraspark I ignition system.
4. After adjusting the initial timing, check and if necessary, adjust curb idle and fast idle speeds.

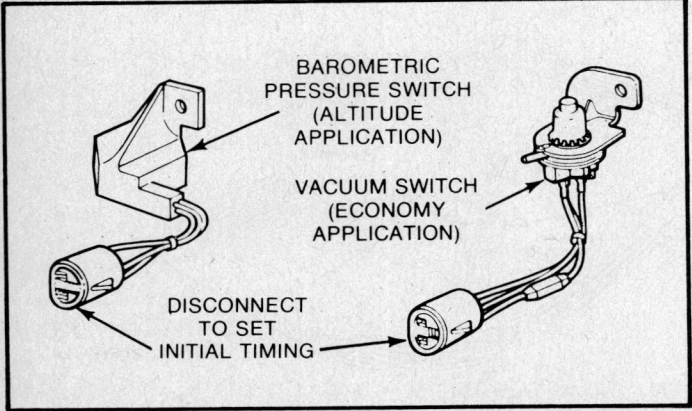

Checking Dual-Mode Ignition System (Functional Test)

Perform the initial timing. Then reconnect the 3-pin switch assembly connector to the module.

1. Vacuum switch applications: disconnect the vacuum line to the switch. Using an external vacuum source, apply vacuum to the switch and compare basic timing to the requirements.

Applied Vacuum	Basic Timing
Greater than 10 in. Hg.	Per specification
Between 6 and 10 in. Hg.	Per specification or per specification less 3–6°
Less than 6 in. Hg. or 0	Per specification less 3–6°

2. Barometric pressure switch applications

Elevation	Basic Timing
Below 2400 ft.	Per specification less 3–6°
2400 ft. to 4300 ft.	Per specification or per specification less 3–6°
Over 4300 ft.	Per specification

Barometric/Vacuum Modules

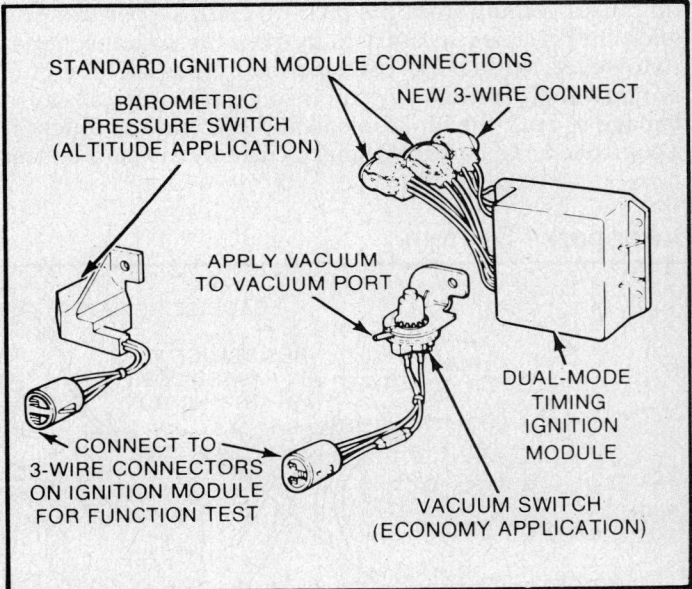

3. If these requirements are not met, substitute a new vacuum switch or barometric pressure switch and recheck timing.

a. If the timing is okay after the switch substitution, reconnect the original switch to validate failure. If the timing is not correct with the original switch, replace the switch.

b. If the timing is outside specified limits after substituting the switch, reinstall the original switch and go on to the next step.

4. Substitute a new dual-mode ignition module and recheck the timing.

a. If the timing is okay after the module substitution, reconnect the original module to validate the failure.

b. If the timing is not okay with the original module, replace the module.

Engine Operates Well at Idle But Not When RPM's Are Increased

1. Remove the distributor cap and inspect for the presence of the roll pin holding the armature on the distributor shaft. If the roll pin is missing, the armature may have rotated out of position relative to the distributor shaft, causing timing to be out of phase.

2. Check for the correct connection of the orange and purple wires between the distributor and the module. If the wires are reversed, the distributor timing is 22½ degrees out of phase.

3. If these checks are okay, perform further tests as described in the solid state ignition system.

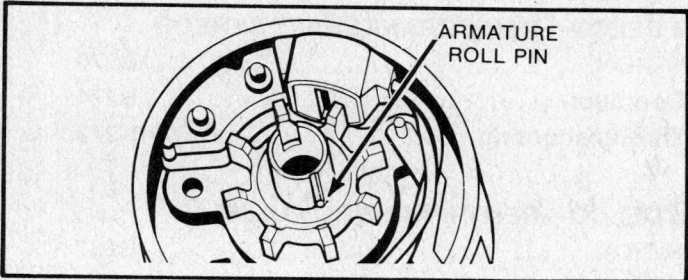

ARMATURE ROLL PIN

Engine Starts and Runs Okay But Quits as Normal Operating Temperature Is Reached

1. Run the engine until normal operating temperature is reached or until the engine quits, whichever occurs first.

2. While cranking the engine, check the voltage between the orange and purple wires at the ignition module. With the voltmeter at the lowest range, only a slight meter movement should be noted (approximately ½ volt).

3. With the ignition switch off, check the resistance between the purple and orange wires at the distributor. Resistance should be 400–1000 ohms.

4. Again with the ignition switch off, check the resistance between the purple wire at the distributor and ground and between the orange wire and ground. In each case, the resistance should be over 70,000 ohms.

If any of these measurements are not within specification, replace the magnetic pick-up assembly.

Engine Quits Intermittently with Complete Loss of Ignition

1. Check the primary circuit ground resistance at the ignition module connector (black wire). The resistance should be 0 ohms.

2. If the resistance is not 0 ohms, remove the distributor cap and inspect the attaching screw at the rubber plug where the wires enter the distributor housing. A loose or cross-threaded screw or a dirty/corroded connection at this screw can cause an intermittent high-resistance ground or a complete loss of ground.

Voltmeter Test

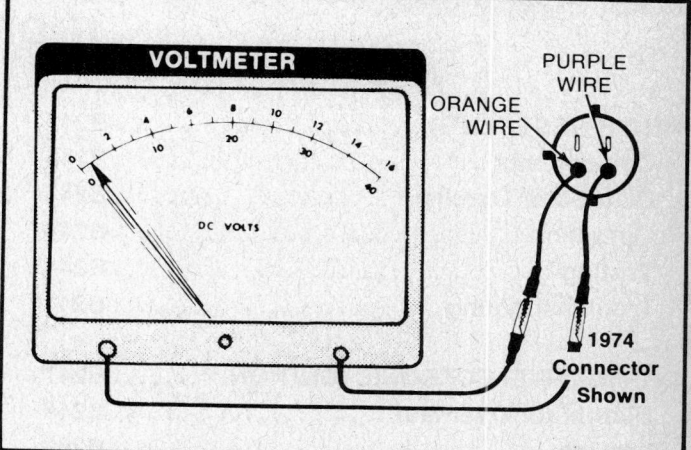

VOLTMETER

DC VOLTS

PURPLE WIRE

ORANGE WIRE

1974 Connector Shown

Ohmmeter Test

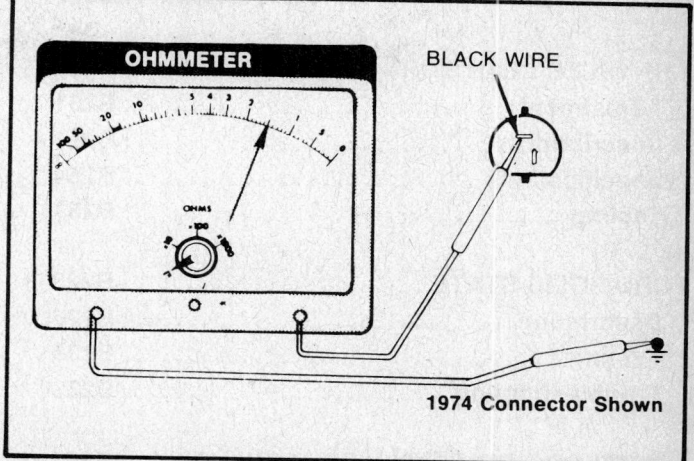

OHMMETER

OHMS

BLACK WIRE

1974 Connector Shown

Magnetic Pick-Up

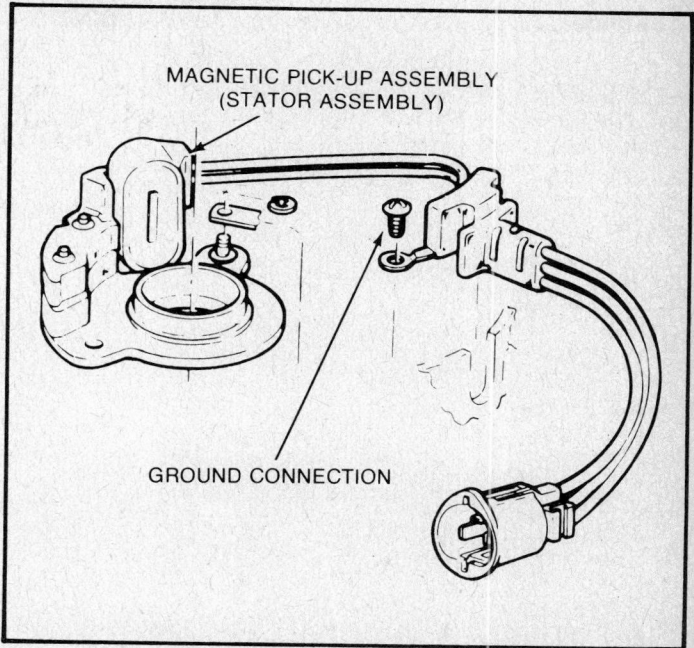

MAGNETIC PICK-UP ASSEMBLY (STATOR ASSEMBLY)

GROUND CONNECTION

ELECTRONIC IGNITIONS

INDEX

TROUBLESHOOTING
AMC PRESTOLITE IGNITION

The Condition	Possible Cause	Correction
Engine Fails to Start (No Spark at Plugs).	No voltage to ignition system.	Check battery, ignition switch and wiring. Repair as needed.
	Electronic ignition control ground lead open, loose or corroded.	Clean, tighten, or repair as needed.
	Primary wiring connectors not fully engaged.	Make sure connectors are clean and firmly seated.
	Coil open or shorted.	Test coil. Replace if faulty.
	Damaged trigger wheel or sensor	Replace damaged part.
	Electronic ignition control faulty.	Replace electronic ignition control.
Engine Backfires but Fails to Start.	Incorrect ignition timing.	Check timing. Adjust as needed.
	Moisture in distributor cap.	Dry cap and rotor.
	Distributor cap faulty (shorting out).	Check cap for loose terminals, cracks and dirt. Clean or replace as needed.
	Wires not in correct firing order.	Reconnect in proper firing order.
Engine Does Not Operate Smoothly and/or Engine Misfires at High Speed.	Spark plugs fouled or faulty.	Clean and regap plugs. Replace if needed.
	Spark plug cables faulty.	Check cables. Replace if needed.
	Spark advance system(s) faulty.	Check operation of advance system(s). Repair as needed.
Excessive Fuel Consumption.	Incorrect ignition timing.	Check timing. Adjust as needed.
	Spark advance system(s) faulty.	Check operation of advance system(s). Repair as needed.
Erratic Timing Advance.	Faulty vacuum advance assembly.	Check operation of advance diaphragm and replace if needed.
Basic Timing Not Affected by Vacuum. (Disconnected)	Misadjusted, weak or damaged mechanical advance springs.	Readjust or replace springs as needed.
	Worn distributor shaft bushings.	Check for worn bushings. Replace distributor.

TROUBLESHOOTING
AMC PRESTOLITE IGNITION

CHECK ALL CONNECTIONS BEFORE BEGINNING TEST

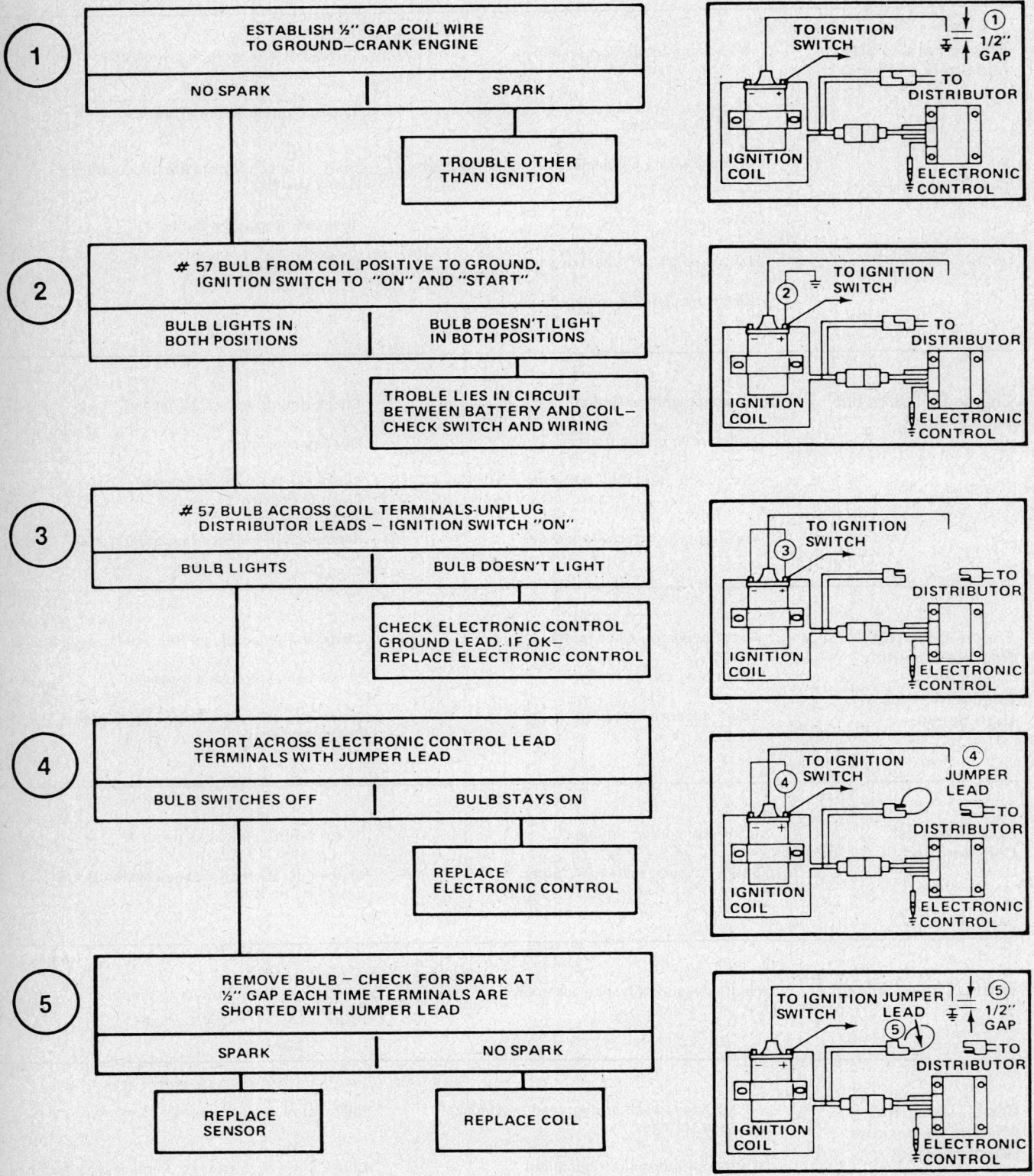

(1) ESTABLISH ½" GAP COIL WIRE TO GROUND—CRANK ENGINE

| NO SPARK | SPARK |

TROUBLE OTHER THAN IGNITION

(2) # 57 BULB FROM COIL POSITIVE TO GROUND. IGNITION SWITCH TO "ON" AND "START"

| BULB LIGHTS IN BOTH POSITIONS | BULB DOESN'T LIGHT IN BOTH POSITIONS |

TROBLE LIES IN CIRCUIT BETWEEN BATTERY AND COIL—CHECK SWITCH AND WIRING

(3) # 57 BULB ACROSS COIL TERMINALS-UNPLUG DISTRIBUTOR LEADS – IGNITION SWITCH "ON"

| BULB LIGHTS | BULB DOESN'T LIGHT |

CHECK ELECTRONIC CONTROL GROUND LEAD. IF OK— REPLACE ELECTRONIC CONTROL

(4) SHORT ACROSS ELECTRONIC CONTROL LEAD TERMINALS WITH JUMPER LEAD

| BULB SWITCHES OFF | BULB STAYS ON |

REPLACE ELECTRONIC CONTROL

(5) REMOVE BULB – CHECK FOR SPARK AT ½" GAP EACH TIME TERMINALS ARE SHORTED WITH JUMPER LEAD

| SPARK | NO SPARK |

REPLACE SENSOR

REPLACE COIL

AMC PRESTOLITE IGNITION

AMC Prestolite Breakerless Inductive Discharge (BID) Ignition System

The American Motors BID Ignition System consists of five major components: an electronic ignition control unit, an ignition coil, a distributor, high tension wires, and spark plugs.

Control Unit

The electronic control unit is a solid-state, moisture-resistant module. The component parts are permanently sealed in a potting material to resist vibration and environmental conditions. All connections are waterproof. The unit has built-in current regulation, reverse polarity protection and transient voltage protection.

Because the control unit has built-in current regulation, there is no resistance wire or ballast resistor used in the primary circuit. Battery voltage is present at the ignition coil positive terminal whenever the ignition key is in the ON or START position; therefore, there is no need for an ignition system bypass during cranking. The primary (low voltage) coil current is electronically regulated by the control unit. The control unit is not repairable and must be serviced as a unit.

Ignition Coil

The ignition coil is an oil-filled, hermetically-sealed unit (standard construction). Ignition coils do not require special service other than keeping terminals and connections clean and tight. For correct polarity, the coil positive terminal should be connected to the battery ignition feed.

The function of the ignition coil in the BID ignition system is to transform battery voltage in the primary winding to a high voltage for the secondary system.

When an ignition coil is suspected of being defective, it should be checked on the car. A coil may break down after it has reached operating temperature; it is important that the coil be at operating temperature when tests are made. Perform the test following the instructions of the Test Equipment Manufacturer.

Distributor

The distributor is conventional except that a sensor and trigger wheel replace the usual contact points, condenser, and distributor cam.

The distributor uses two spark advance systems (mechanical and vacuum) to establish the spark timing setting required for various engine speed and load conditions. The two systems operate independently, yet work together to provide proper spark advance.

The mechanical (centrifugal) advance system is built internally into the distributor and consists of two flyweights which pivot on long-life, low-friction bearings and are controlled by calibrated springs which tend to hold the weights in the no-advance position. The flyweights respond to changes in engine (distributor shaft) speed, and rotate the trigger wheel with respect to the distributor shaft to advance the spark as engine speed increases and retard the spark as engine speed decreases. Mechanical advance characteristics can be adjusted by bending the hardened spring tabs to alter the spring tension.

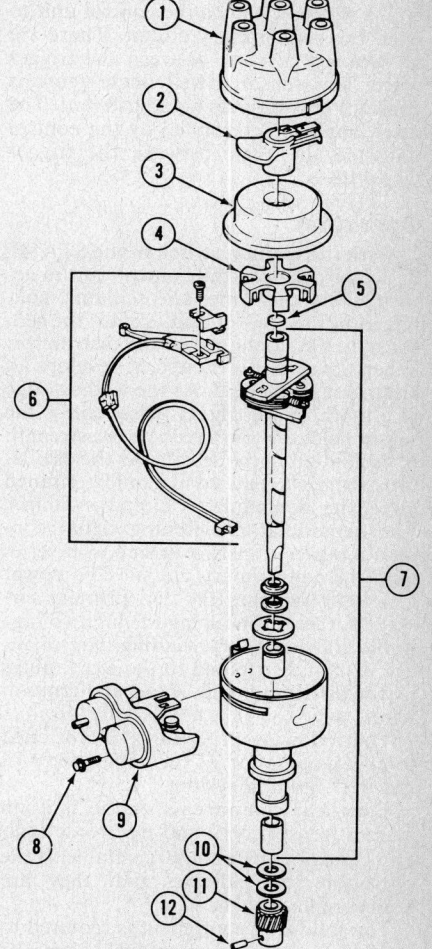

1. DISTRIBUTOR CAP
2. ROTOR
3. DUST SHIELD
4. TRIGGER WHEEL
5. FELT
6. SENSOR ASSEMBLY
7. HOUSING
8. VACUUM CONTROL SCREW
9. VACUUM CONTROL
10. SHIM
11. DRIVE GEAR
12. PIN

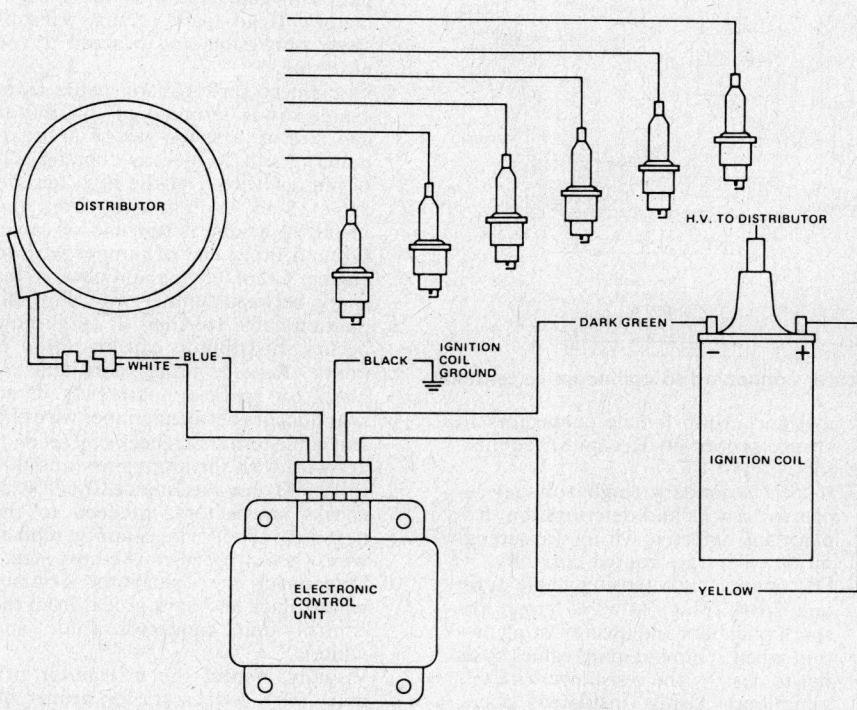

AMC Breakerless Inductive Discharge ignition system component schematic

AMC Breakerless Inductive Discharge ignition system distributor, exploded view

ELECTRONIC IGNITIONS

AMC PRESTOLITE IGNITION

The vacuum advance system incorporates a vacuum diaphragm unit which moves the distributor sensor in response to the changes in carburetor throttle bore vacuum.

Sensor/Trigger Wheel

The sensor (a component of the distributor) is a small coil, wound of fine wire, which received an alternating current signal from the electronic control unit.

The sensor develops an electromagnetic field which is used to detect the presence of metal. The sensor detects the edges of the metal in the teeth of trigger wheel. When a leading edge of a trigger wheel tooth aligns with the center of the sensor coil, a signal is sent to the control unit to open the coil primary circuit. There are no wearing surfaces between the trigger wheel and sensor, dwell angle remains constant and requires no adjustment. The dwell angle is determined by the control unit and the angle between the trigger wheel teeth.

Operation

With the ignition switch in the START or RUN position, the control unit is activated. At this time, an oscillator, contained in the control unit, excites the sensor which is contained in the distributor. When the sensor is excited, it develops an electromagnetic field. As the leading edge of a tooth of the trigger wheel enters the sensor field, the tooth reduces the strength of oscillation in the sensor. As the oscillator strength is reduced to a predetermined level, the demodulator circuit switches. The demodulator switching signal controls a power transistor which is in series with the coil primary circuit. The power transistor switches the coil primary circuit off, thereby inducing the high voltage in the coil secondary winding. High voltage is then distributed to the spark plugs by the distributor cap, rotor, and ignition wires.

The following procedures can be used to check operation of the components of the BID ignition system.

Electrical components of the ignition system (sensor, coil, and electronic ignition control unit) are not repairable. If the operation test indicates that they are faulty, replace them.

The following equipment is required to make this test: ohmmeter, DC voltmeter, jumper wire (12 to 18 inches long) with clip at each end, Tester (distributor sensor substitute) J-25331, insulated pliers (grippers) for handling high tension cables.

BID System Test

1 Test battery using DC voltmeter. Voltage should be 12 to 13 volts for a fully charged battery. If necessary charge or replace battery.
2 Inspect ignition primary (low voltage) circuit for loose or damaged wiring. Inspect connectors for proper fit. Spread male connector with punch or

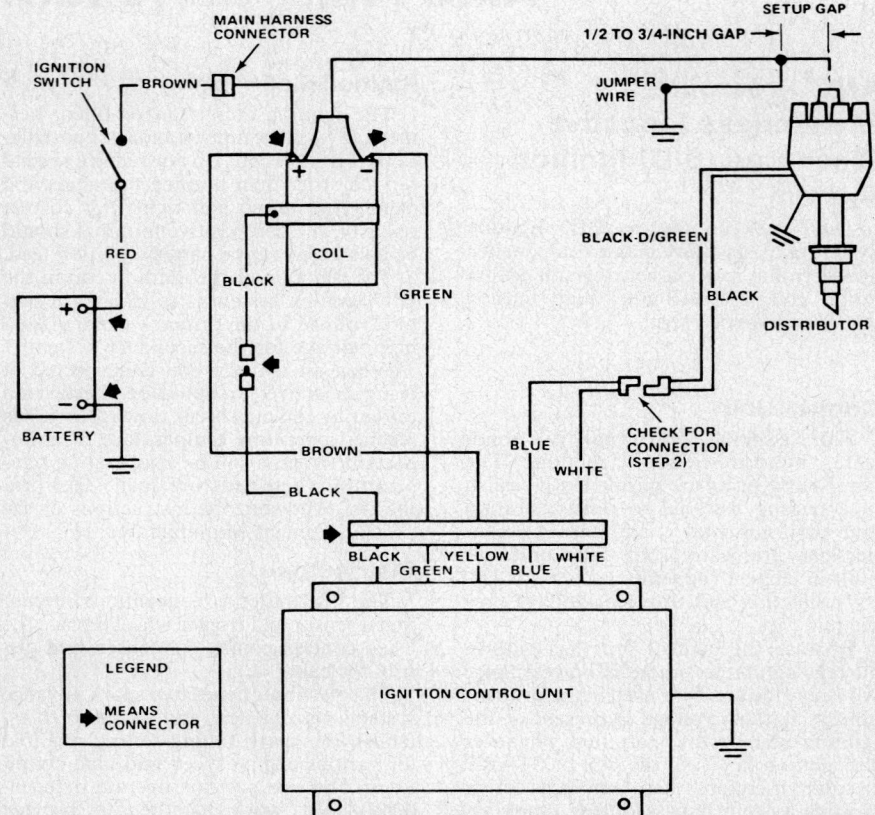

Checking the spark gap on AMC's Breakerless Inductive Discharge ignition system

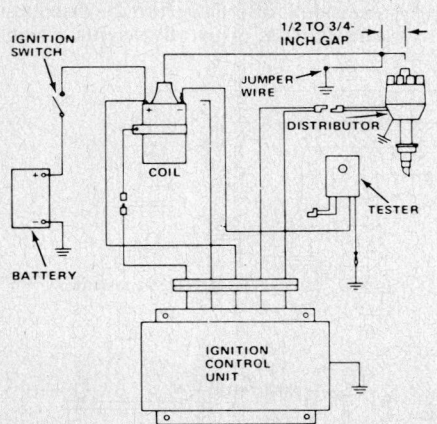

Tester connected to coil negative terminal

awl and crimp female connectors to ensure proper fit. Reconnect connectors.
3 Inspect secondary (high voltage) cables for cracks and deterioration. Replace any defective wiring. Be sure ignition cables are routed correctly.
4 Disconnect high tension cable from one spark plug. (always grasp the spark plug boot and use a twisting motion when removing plug cables so as not to destroy the resistance wire termination.) Using insulated pliers, hold plug cable to create approximately ½ to a ¾-inch gap between

cable terminal and engine. Crank engine and observe spark. If a spark jumps the gap, ignition system is satisfactory. If no spark occurs, reinstall spark plug cable and proceed to the next step.
5 Disconnect high tension cable from center tower terminal of distributor cap. Set up a spark gap of approximately ½ to ¾ inch by clipping end of jumper wire over the high tension cable ½ to ¾ inch away from the metal tip at distributor end of cable. Ground other end of jumper wire to engine. Crank engine and observe for spark between jumper wire clip and ignition cable terminal. If spark now occurs, distributor cap or rotor is faulty. Replace faulty part and recheck for spark at spark plug. If no spark occurs between jumper wire clip and cable terminal, check coil secondary wire with the ohmmeter for 5,000 to 10,000 ohms resistance. If coil wire checks satisfactory, proceed to the next step. If coil wire is faulty, replace wire, then proceed to the next step.
6 Disconnect the distributor primary wires (black and dark green) from the control unit connector (blue and white).
7 Visually inspect the distributor primary wire connectors for proper fit. Spread male connector with a punch or awl and slightly crimp the female

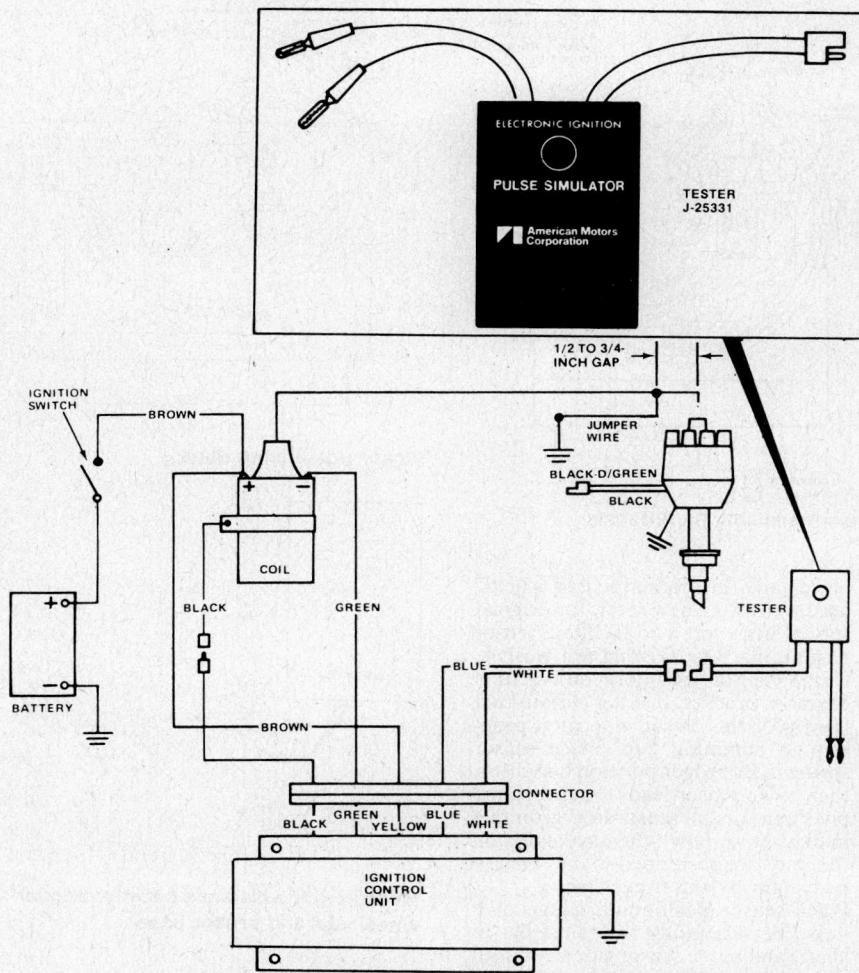

Tester connected into AMC's Breakerless Inductive Discharge ignition system

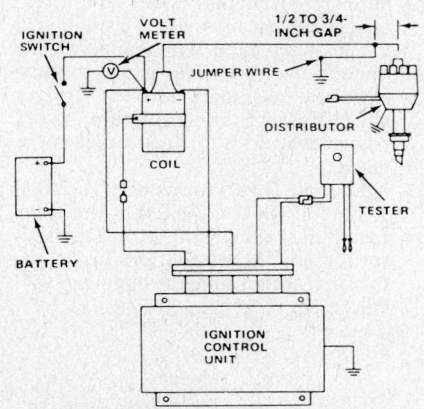

Voltmeter connected to coil positive terminal

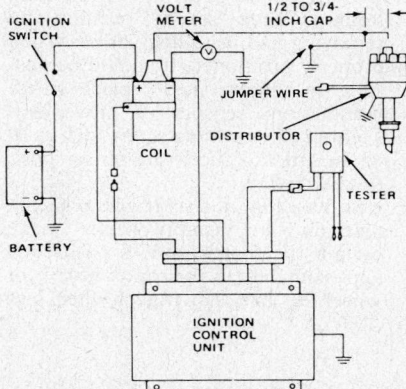

Voltmeter connected to coil negative terminal

connector to ensure proper fit.

8 Connect distributor primary wires to control unit connector and crank engine. Observe for spark between jumper wire clip and ignition cable terminal. If spark now jumps the gap, the ignition system is satisfactory. If no spark occurs between jumper wire

clip and cable terminal, proceed to the next step.

9 Disconnect the distributor primary wires (black and dark green) and plug Tester J)25331 into wire harness. Turn ignition switch on. Cycle test button and observe for spark between jumper wire clip and ignition cable

terminal. If spark occurs, distributor sensor unit is faulty and must be replaced. If no spark occurs, proceed to the next step.

10 Connect voltmeter between coil positive (+) terminal and ground. With ignition switch ON, voltmeter should read battery voltage. If voltage at coil positive terminal is noticeably lower than battery (through ignition switch) and the coil. Before proceeding, the resistance must be corrected. If voltage at coil positive terminal equals battery voltage, proceed to the next step.

11 Connect voltmeter between coil negative (−) terminal and ground. With ignition switch ON, voltage should read 5 to 8 volts. A reading under 5 volts or over 8 volts indicates a bad coil which must be replaced. If voltage is satisfactory, press button on tester and observe voltmeter. Voltage reading should increase to battery voltage (12 to 13 volts). Release button on tester. Voltage should drop to 5 to 8 volts. If voltage does not switch up and down, the electronic ignition control is faulty and must be replaced. If voltage switches up and down but there is no spark between jumper wire clip and ignition cable terminal, proceed to the next step.

12 Disconnect tester from control unit.

13 Turn off ignition switch. Remove wire from the negative terminal of the ignition coil.

14 Connect one clip lead from tester to negative terminal of ignition coil and the other clip lead to an engine ground.

15 Turn on ignition switch. Cycle test button.

16 Spark should jump the gap. If spark does not, test the ignition coil. The coil can be tested on any conventional coil tester or with an ohmmeter. (A coil tester is preferable as it will detect faults that an ohmmeter will not.) The coil primary resistance should be 1 to 2 ohms. Coil secondary resistance should be 8,000 to 12,000 ohms. Coil open-circuit output should exceed 20 kv. If the coil does not pass these tests, it must be replaced.

Distributor Disassembly

1 Place distributor in suitable holding device.

2 Remove rotor and dust shield.

3 Remove trigger wheel using a small gear puller. Be sure the puller jaws are gripping the inner shoulder of the trigger wheel or the trigger wheel may be damaged during removal. Use a thick flat washer or nut as a spacer. Do not press against the small center shaft.

4 Loosen sensor locking screw about three turns. The sensor locking screw has a tamper proof head design which requires a Special Driver Bit Tool J-25097. If a driver bit is not available, use a small needlenose pliers to re-

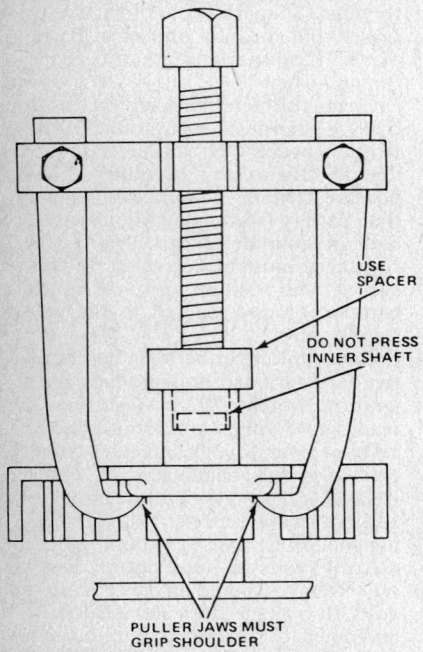

Trigger wheel removal with puller

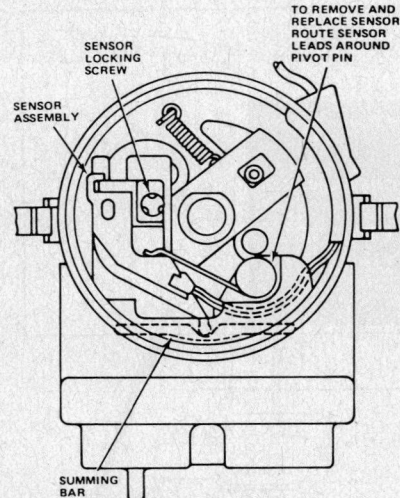

Sensor assembly R&R details

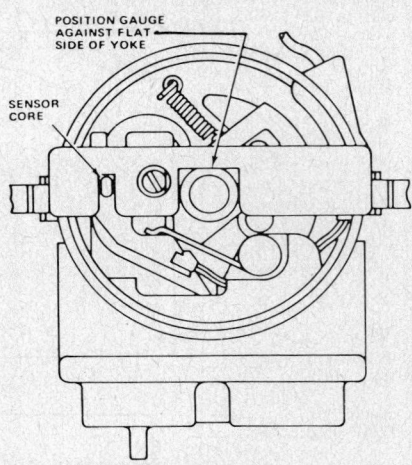

Sensor positioning details

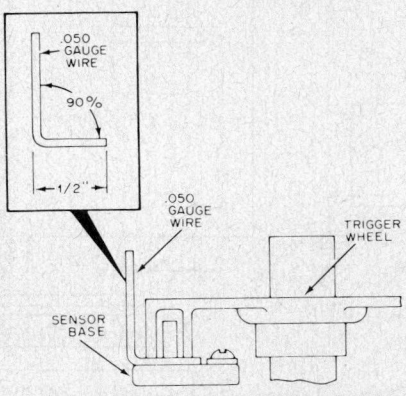

Measuring the distance between trigger wheel legs and sensor base

move screw. The service sensor has a standard slotted head screw.

Lift the sensor lead grommet out of the distributor bowl. Pull sensor leads out of the slot around sensor spring pivot pin. Lift and release sensor spring, making sure it clears the leads, then slide the sensor off bracket.

5 If the vacuum chamber is to be replaced, remove the retaining screw and slide the vacuum chamber out of the distributor. DO NOT remove the vacuum chamber unless replacement is required.

6 Clean dirt or grease off of the vacuum chamber bracket. Clean and dry sensor and bracket. The material used for sensor and vacuum chamber requires no lubrication.

7 With the vacuum chamber installed, assemble sensor, sensor guide, flat washer, and retaining screw. Install retaining screw only far enough to hold assembly together and be sure it does not project beyond the bottom of sensor.

8 If the vacuum chamber has been re-

placed and the original sensor is being used, substitute new screw for original special head screw to facilitate sensor positioning. Use existing flat washer.

9 Install sensor assembly on vacuum chamber bracket, making certain that the tip of the sensor is located properly in summing bar. Place sensor spring in its proper position on sensor, then route sensor leads around spring pivot pin. Install sensor lead grommet in distributor bowl, then make certain the leads are positioned so they cannot be caught by the trigger wheel.

10 Place sensor positioning gauge over yoke (be sure gauge is against flat of shaft) and move sensor sideways until the gauge can be positioned. With the gauge in place, use a small blade screwdriver to snug down retaining screw. Check sensor position by removing and installing gauge. When properly positioned, it should be possible to remove and replace gauge without any sensor side movement. Tighten the retaining screw to 5 to 10 oz.-in., then recheck the sensor position as before.

11 Remove gauge and set trigger wheel in place on yoke. Visually check to make certain the sensor core is positioned approximately in the center of trigger wheel legs and that trigger wheel legs

cannot touch sensor core.

12 Support distributor shaft and press trigger wheel onto yoke. Using).050 gauge wire, bend wire gauge to the dimension shown. Use gauge to measure the distance between trigger wheel legs and the sensor base. Install trigger wheel until it just touches the gauge.

13 Add about 3 to 5 drops of SAE 20 oil to the felt wick in the top of the yoke.

14 Install dust shield and rotor. Distributor is ready for installation. Install the distributor and time the engine to specification.

TROUBLESHOOTING
CHRYSLER TYPE IGNITION

CONDITION	POSSIBLE CAUSE	CORRECTION
ENGINE WILL NOT START (Fuel and Carburetion Known to be OK)	a) Dual Ballast	Check resistance of each section: Compensating resistance: .50-.60 ohms @ 70°-80°F Auxiliary Ballast: 4.75-5.75 ohms Replace if faulty. Check wire positions.
	b) Faulty Ignition Coil	Check for carbonized tower. Check primary and secondary resistances: Primary: 1.41-1.79 ohms @ 70°-80°F Secondary: 9,200-11,700 ohms @ 70°-80°F Check in coil tester.
	c) Faulty Pickup or Improper Pickup Air Gap	Check pickup coil resistance: 400-600 ohms Check pickup gap. .010 in. feeler gauge should not slip between pickup coil core and aligned reluctor blade. No evidence of pickup core striking reluctor blades should be visible. To reset gap, tighten pickup adjustment screw with a .008 in. feeler gauge held between pickup core and an aligned reluctor blade. After resetting gap, run distributor on test stand and apply vacuum advance, making sure that the pickup core does not strike the reluctor blades.
	d) Faulty Wiring	Visually inspect wiring for brittle insulation. Inspect connectors. Molded connectors should be inspected for rubber inside female terminals.
	e) Faulty Control Unit	Replace if all of the above checks are negative. Whenever the control unit or dual ballast is replaced, make sure the dual ballast wires are correctly inserted in the keyed molded connector.
ENGINE SURGES SEVERELY (Not Lean Carburetor	a) Wiring	Inspect for loose connection and/or broken conductors in harness.
	b) Faulty Pickup Leads	Disconnect vacuum advance. If surging stops, replace pickup.
	c) Ignition Coil	Check for intermittent primary.
ENGINE MISSES (Carburetion OK)	a) Spark Plugs b) Secondary Cable c) Ignition Coil d) Wiring e) Faulty Pickup Lead f) Control Unit	Check plugs. Clean and regap if necessary. Check cables with an ohmmeter, or observe secondary circuit performance with an oscilloscope. Check for cabonized tower. Check in coil tester. Check for loose or dirty connections. Disconnect vacuum advance. If miss stops, replace pickup. Replace if the above checks are negative.

CHRYSLER TYPE IGNITION

Chrysler Electronic Ignition

Testing Ignition

ALL CARS

To properly test the Electronic Ignition System, special testors should be used. But in the event they are not available, the system may be tested using a voltmeter with a 20,000 ohm/volt rating and an ohmmeter which uses a 1½ volt battery for its operation. Both meters should be in calibration. When Ignition System problems are suspected, the following procedure should be followed:

1 Visually inspect all secondary cables at the coil, distributor and spark plugs for cracks and tightness.
2 To check wiring harness and connections, check primary wire at the ignition coil and ballast resistor for tightness. If the above checks do not determine the problem, the following steps will determine if a component is faulty.
3 Check and note battery voltage reading using voltmeter. Battery voltage should be at least 12 volts.
4 Remove the multi-wiring connector from the control unit.

CHILTON CAUTION: *Whenever removing or installing the wiring harness connector to the control unit, the ignition switch must be in the "Off" position.*

5 Turn the ignition switch "On".
6 Connect the negative lead of a voltmeter to a good ground.
7 Connect the positive lead of the voltmeter to the wiring harness connector cavity #1. Available voltage at cavity #1 should be within 1 volt of battery voltage with all accessories off. If there is more than a 1 volt difference, the circuit must be checked between the battery and the connector.
8 Connect the positive lead of the voltmeter to the wiring harness connector cavity #2. Available voltage at cavity

ELECTRONIC IGNITIONS
CHRYSLER TYPE IGNITION

#2 should be within 1 volt of battery voltage with all accessories off. If there is more than a 1 volt difference, the circuit must be checked back to the battery.

9 Connect the positive lead of the voltmeter to the wiring harness connector cavity #3. Available voltage at cavity #3 should be within 1 volt of battery voltage with all accessories off. If there is more than a 1 volt difference, the circuit that must be checked back to the battery.

10 Turn ignition switch "Off".

11 To check distributor pickup coil connect an ohmmeter to wiring harness connector cavity #4 and #5. The ohmmeter resistance should be between 150 and 900 ohms.

 If the readings are higher or lower than specified, disconnect the dual lead connector coming from the distributor. Using the ohmmeter, check the resistance at the dual lead connector. If the reading is not between the prementioned resistance values, replace the pickup coil assembly in the distributor.

12 Connect one ohmmeter lead to a good ground and the other lead to either connector of the distributor. Ohmmeter should show an open circuit (infinity). If the ohmmeter does show a reading less than infinity the pick up coil in the distributor must be replaced.

13 To check electronic control unit ground circuit connect one ohmmeter lead to a good ground and the other lead to the control unit connector pin #5. The ohmmeter should show continuity between the ground and the connector pin. If continuity does not exist, tighten the bolts holding the control unit to the fire wall. Then recheck. If continuity does still not exist, control unit must be replaced.

14 Reconnect wiring harness at control unit and distributor.

NOTE: Whenever removing or installing the wiring harness connector to the control unit, the ignition switch must be in the "Off" position.

15 Check air gap between reluctor tooth and pick up coil. To set the gap refer to Air Gap Adjustment.

16 Check ignition secondary; remove the high voltage cable from the center tower of the distributor. Hold the cable approximately 3/16 inch from engine. Crank engine. If arcing does not occur, replace the control unit.

17 Crank the engine again. If arcing still does not occur, replace the ignition coil.

18 If a problem does not show up when making the voltage checks, coil resistance checks, or ground continuity checks it is likely the control unit or coil is faulty. It is unlikely that both units would fail simultaneously. However, before replacing the control unit

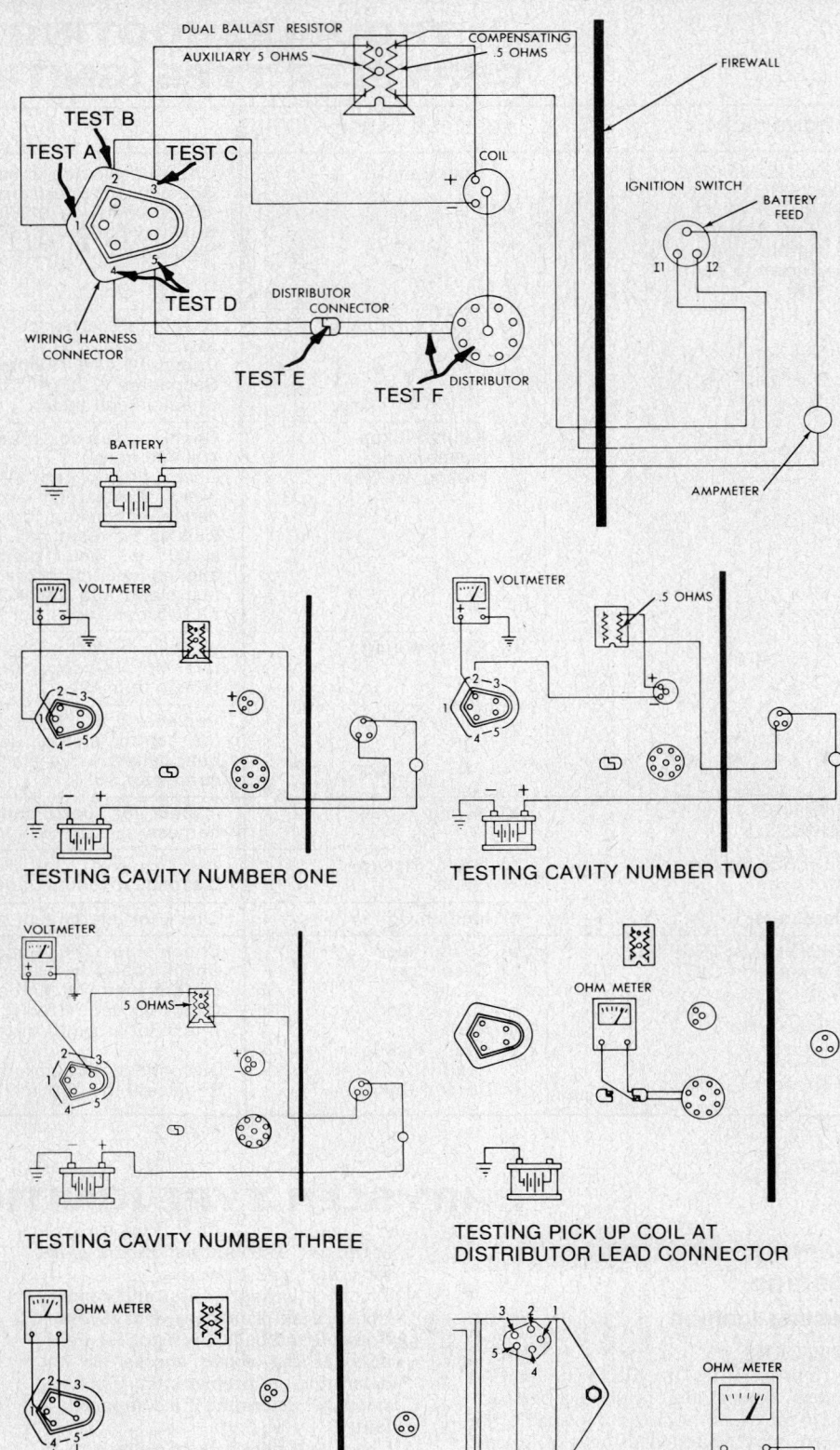

TESTING CAVITY NUMBER ONE

TESTING CAVITY NUMBER TWO

TESTING CAVITY NUMBER THREE

TESTING PICK UP COIL AT DISTRIBUTOR LEAD CONNECTOR

TESTING GROUND CIRCUIT

TESTING PICK UP COIL AT WIRING HARNESS CONNECTOR, CAVITIES FOUR AND FIVE

make sure no foreign matter is lodged in or blocking the female terminal cavities in the harness connector. If clear, try replacing control unit or coil to see which one restores secondary ignition voltage.

Servicing Procedures

Pick-Up Coil R&R

1 Remove the distributor.
2 Remove the two screws and lockwashers attaching the vacuum control unit to the distributor housing. Disconnect the arm and remove the vacuum unit.
3 Remove the reluctor by pulling it off with your fingers, or use two small screwdrivers to pry it off. Be careful not to distort or damage the teeth on the reluctor.
4 Remove the two screws and lockwashers attaching the lower plate to the housing and lift out the lower plate, upper plate, and pick-up coil as an assembly.
5 Remove the upper plate and pick-up coil assembly from the lower plate by depressing the retaining clip and moving it away from the mounting stud.
6 Remove the upper plate and pick-up coil assembly. The pick-up coil is not removable from the upper plate, and is serviced as an assembly. On early models, the coil was removable from the plate.
7 To install the pick-up coil assembly, put a little distributor cam lube on the upper plate pivot pin and lower plate support pins.
8 Position the upper plate pivot pin through the smallest hole in the lower plate.
9 Install the retaining clip. The upper plate must ride on the three support pins on the lower plate.
10 Install the lower plate, upper plate, and pickup coil assembly into the distributor and install screws.
11 Attach the vacuum advance arm to the pick-up plate, then install the vacuum unit attaching screws and washers.
12 Position the reluctor keeper pin in place on the reluctor sleeve, then slide the reluctor down the sleeve and press firmly into place.

Air Gap Adjustment

1 Align one reluctor tooth with the pick-up coil tooth.
2 Loosen the pick-up coil hold-down screw.
3 Insert a 0.008 in. nonmagnetic feeler gauge between the reluctor tooth and the pick-up coil tooth.
4 Adjust the air gap so that contact is made between the reluctor tooth, the feeler gauge, and the pick-up coil tooth.
5 Tighten the hold-down screw.
6 Remove the feeler gauge.

NOTE: No force should be required in removing the feeler gauge.

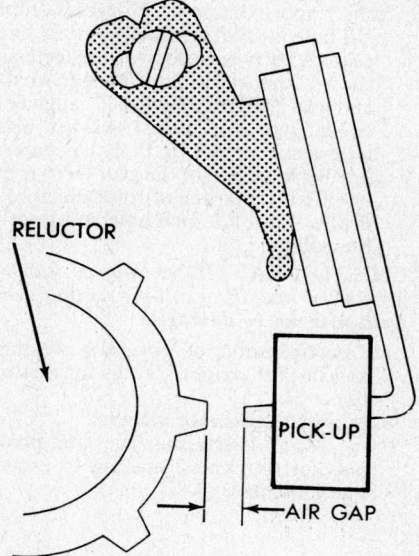

Air gap adjustment

7 A 0.010 in. feeler gauge should not fit into the air gap. Do not force the feeler gauge.

CHILTON CAUTION: *A 0.010 in. feeler gauge can be forced into the air gap. DO NOT FORCE THE FEELER GAUGE INTO THE AIR GAP.*

8 Apply vacuum to the vacuum unit and rotate the governor shaft. The pick-up pole should not hit the reluctor teeth. The gap is not properly adjusted if any hitting occurs. If hitting occurs on only one side of the reluctor, the distributor shaft is probably bent, and the governor and shaft assembly should be replaced.

Shaft and Bushing Wear Test

1 Remove distributor and rotor.
2 Clamp distributor is a vise equipped with soft jaws and apply only enough pressure to restrict any movement of the distributor during the test.
3 Attach a dial indicator to distributor housing so indicator plunger arm rests against reluctor.
4 Wiggle the shaft and read the total movement of the dial indicator plunger. If the movement exceeds .006 in. replace the housing or shaft.

Distributor Overhaul

1 Remove distributor rotor.
2 Remove the two screws and lockwashers attaching the vacuum control unit to distributor housing, disconnect the vacuum control arm from upper plate, and remove control.
3 Remove reluctor by prying up from the bottom of the reluctor with two screwdrivers. Be careful not to distort or damage the teeth on the reluctor.
4 Remove two screws and lockwashers attaching the lower plate to the housing and lift out the lower plate, upper

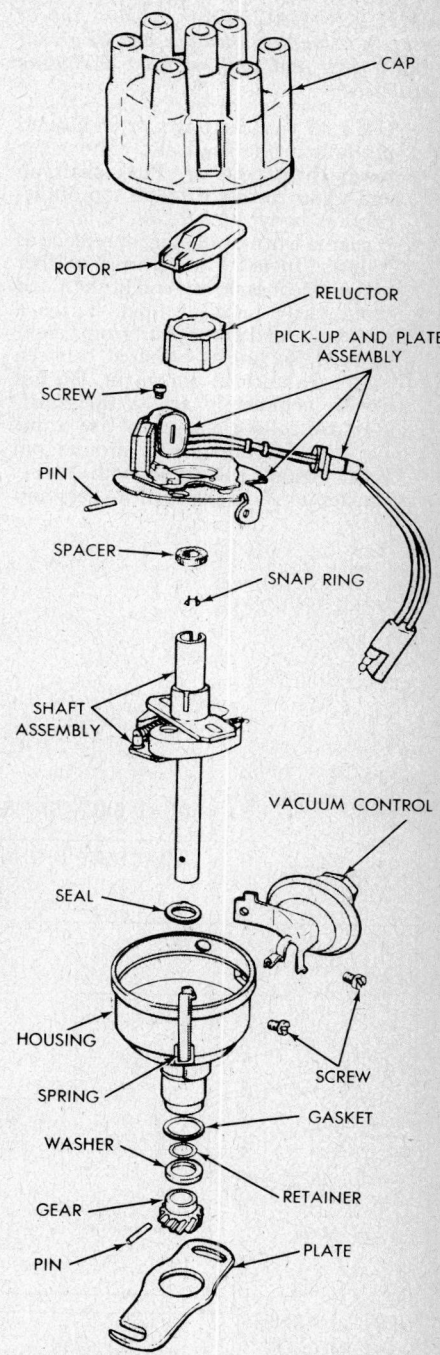

Chrysler electronic distributor

plate, and pick-up coil as an assembly. Distributor cap clamp springs are held in place by peened metal around the openings and should not be removed.
5 If the side play exceeds .006 inch in "Shaft and Bushing Wear Test", replace distributor housing assembly or shaft and governor assembly as follows: Remove distributor drive gear retaining pin and slide gear off end of shaft.

ELECTRONIC IGNITIONS

CHRYSLER TYPE IGNITION

CHILTON CAUTION: *Support hub of gear in a manner that pin can be driven out of gear and shaft without damaging gear teeth.*

Use a file to clean burrs, from around pin hole in the shaft and remove the lower thrust washer. Push shaft up and remove shaft through top of distributor body.

6 If gear is worn or damaged, replace as follows: Install lower thrust washer and old gear on lower end of shaft and temporarily install rollpin. Scribe a line on the end of the shaft from center to edge, so line is centered between two gear teeth as shown in. **Do not Scribe completely across the shaft.** Remove rollpin and gear. Use a fine file to clean burrs from around pin hole. Install new gear with thrust washer in place. Drill hole in gear and

shaft approximately 90 degrees from old hole in shaft and with scribed line centered between the two gear teeth as shown. Before drilling through shaft and gear, place a .007 feeler gauge between gear and thrust washer and after again observing that the centerline between two of the gear teeth is in line with centerline of rotor electrode drill a .124–.129 inch hole and install the rollpin.

CHILTON CAUTION: *Support hub of gear when installing roll-pin so that gear teeth will not be damaged.*

7 Test operation of governor weights and inspect weight springs for distortion.
8 Lubricate governor weights.
9 Inspect all bearing surfaces and pivot pins for roughness, binding or excessive looseness.

10 Lubricate and install upper thrust washer (or washers) on the shaft and slide the shaft into the distributor body.
11 Install lower plate, upper plate and pick-up coil assembly and install attaching screws.
12 Slide shaft into distributor body, then align scribe marks and install gear and rollpin.
13 Attach vacuum advance unit arm to the pick-up plate.
14 Install vacuum unit attaching screws and washers.
15 Position reluctor keeper pin into place on reluctor sleeve.
16 Slide reluctor down reluctor sleeve and press firmly into place.
17 Lubricate the felt pad in top of reluctor sleeve with 1 drop of light engine oil and install the rotor.

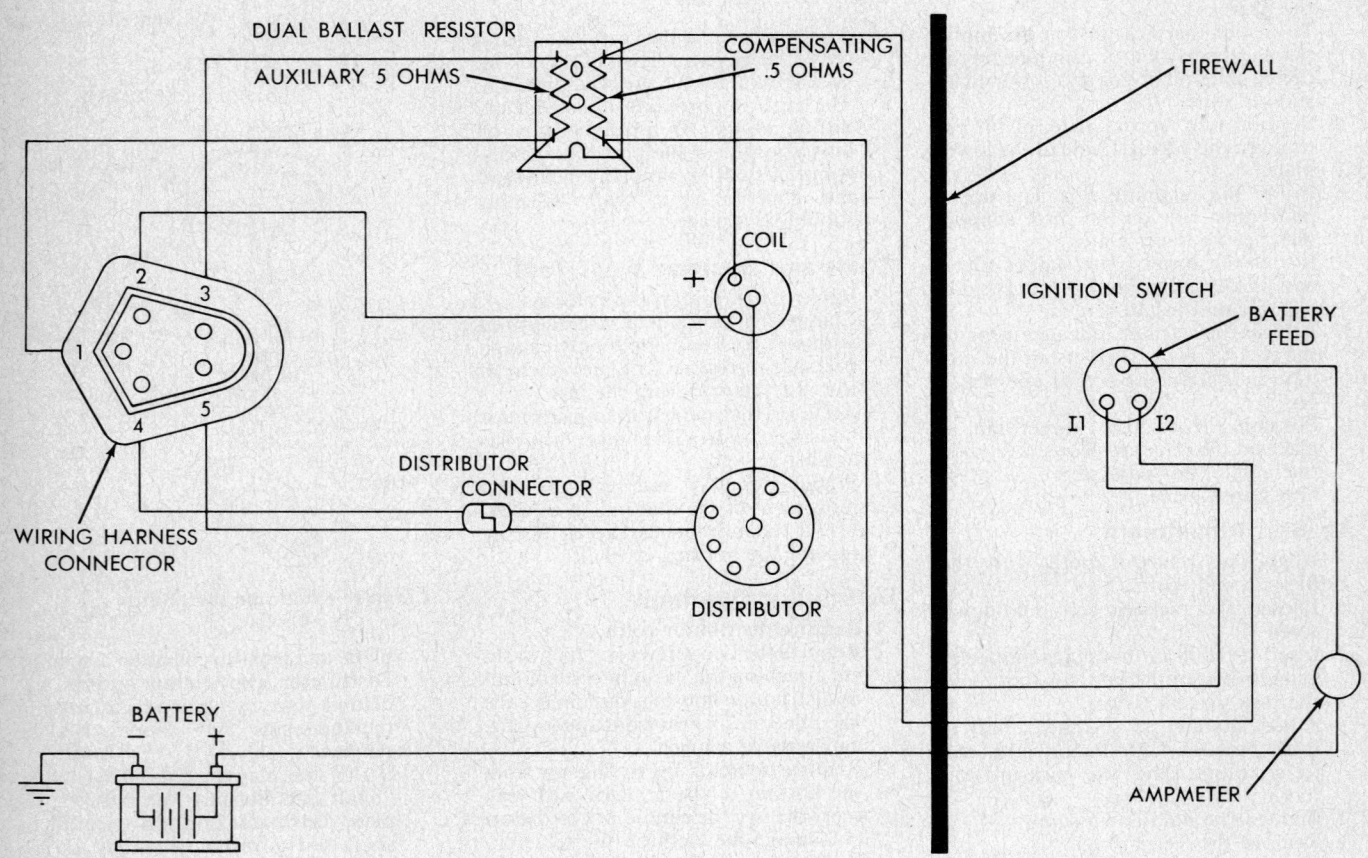

CHRYSLER LEAN BURN SYSTEM

Description

About the simplest computer to understand is the dial telephone.

As we lift the receiver we turn on the power. Each digit we dial is stored into the computer until we have dialed all our numbers. Then an impulse is routed, the number called and a phone bell rings.

Automotive computers are basically the same idea only they work much faster. The sensors are like phone push buttons. They send a message to the computer. Chrysler's Electronic Lean Burn system is a group of sensors which report engine conditions to a computer that controls ignition timing. The sensors monitor, and report changes in, engine speed, throttle position, manifold vacuum, coolant temperature, and, in pre-1978 models, intake air temperature. The sensors used are: run pickup coil, start pickup coil, throttle position transducer, coolant temperature sensor, vacuum transducer, carburetor switch sensor and air temperature sensor.

When the ignition switch is turned to the start position the start pickup coil signals the computer, and additional spark advance is provided during cranking to aid in engine starting. Immediately after the engine starts, the run pickup coil takes over signalling the computer. The computer will provide additional advance for the first minute the engine is operating, but during this period the advance will be slowly eliminated. With the engine running, and the engine coolant below 150°F., the coolant temperature sensor will signal the computer to prevent any additional spark advance. Normal system operation begins after the engine reaches normal operating temperature.

Under normal system operation, the run pickup coil sends a basic timing signal to the computer which creates the maximum timing advance for any engine speed. At the same time, input signals from the other sensors tell the computer how much total advance is necessary for optimum engine performance.

If either the computer or run pickup coil fail, the system will go into the "limp-in mode". In this condition the system is operating on the start pickup coil only, and poor fuel economy and performance can be expected.

The start pickup and run pickup coils are separate units in the 1977 and earlier models. In 1978 and later models, both coils are contained in a single unit.

Spark Control Computer

The spark control computer is the heart of the system. The unit consists of printed electronic circuitry and is serviced only by replacement. The computer simultaneously receives signals from all sensors, and advances or retards ignition timing based on this data. The advancing and retarding of the ignition timing is not based on a constant curve. The curves can be infinite and variable.

NOTE: Do not attempt to disassemble the spark control computer. Replace with a new unit if it fails.

Spark Control Computer Testing

To test only the computer without electronic diagnostic equipment, perform the "vacuum advance schedule", "speed advance schedule" and "failure to start" tests.

Run Pickup Coil

The run pickup coil is located in the distributor. It supplies the basic timing signal to the computer, and this signal instructs the computer to provide the maximum timing advance for any engine speed. This signal also tells the computer the engine speed and when each piston is coming up on its compression stroke. This coil functions during all engine operating conditions except starting. Wiring from the run pickup coil connects to the smaller of the two connectors, and the coil is mounted next to the distributor cap index tang.

Run Pickup Coil Testing

Connect one ohmmeter lead to ground, and with the other lead, check for continuity at each terminal of the leads going into the distributor. There should be no continuity. Replace the pickup coil if continuity exists.

Start Pickup Coil

The start pickup coil is located in the distributor and functions during engine cranking. It signals the spark control computer to provide more advance during cranking for easier engine starting.

This coil also functions in the "limp-in mode" where either the run pickup coil or spark control computer has failed. Extremely poor performance will be noted under this condition.

The air gap between the reluctor teeth and the metal core of the start pickup coil (.008 inch) is less than the air gap of the run pickup coil (.012 inch). The smaller air gap produces a stronger electrical impulse as the reluctor turns slowly during engine cranking.

Start Pickup Coil Testing

Connect one ohmmeter lead to ground, and with the other lead, check for continuity at each terminal of the leads going into the distributor. There should be no continuity. Replace the pickup coil if continuity exists.

Throttle Position Transducer

The transducer signal tells the computer the position and rate of change of the throttle plates. Additional spark advance is provided by the computer as the throttle plates open. More advance is provided for about one second if the throttle is opened quickly.

The throttle position transducer is a switch with an infinite number of positions. Inside the transducer coil is a moveable metallic core. Attached to this core is a spring steel wire with a small hook at one end. This hook attaches to a grooved pin which is part of the carburetor throttle lever. As the throttle is opened, the metallic core is pulled outward from inside the transducer housing. As the throttle opens and closes, this transducer varies a voltage signal which is sent to the spark control computer.

Throttle Position Transducer Testing

Turn ignition switch to the "Run" position, but do not start engine. Connect negative lead of a voltmeter to a good engine ground. With voltmeter positive lead, touch one terminal of throttle position transducer. While fully opening and closing carburetor throttle either transducer terminal should show approximately a 0.5 to 2.0 volt change. If this voltage change is not noted, either the transducer or spark control computer is bad. If a known good transducer produces the same results, replace the spark control computer.

Throttle Position Transducer Adjustment

1977 AND EARLIER
NOTE: Adjustment can only be made when the air temperature sensor inside the computer is below 135°F. If it is necessary to adjust transducer when engine is at operating temperature, the air temperature sensor will have to be cooled. This can be done with a suitable cooling agent used to rapidly lower the temperature of electronic components. These cooling agents are available at most electronic stores.

To cool the air temperature sensor, remove the top of the air cleaner, insert the spray nozzle of the cooling agent into the computer and spray the sensor for about fifteen seconds. If it takes longer than three or four minutes to adjust, *turn engine off* and recool air temperature sensor.

ELECTRONIC IGNITIONS
CHRYSLER LEAN BURN SYSTEM

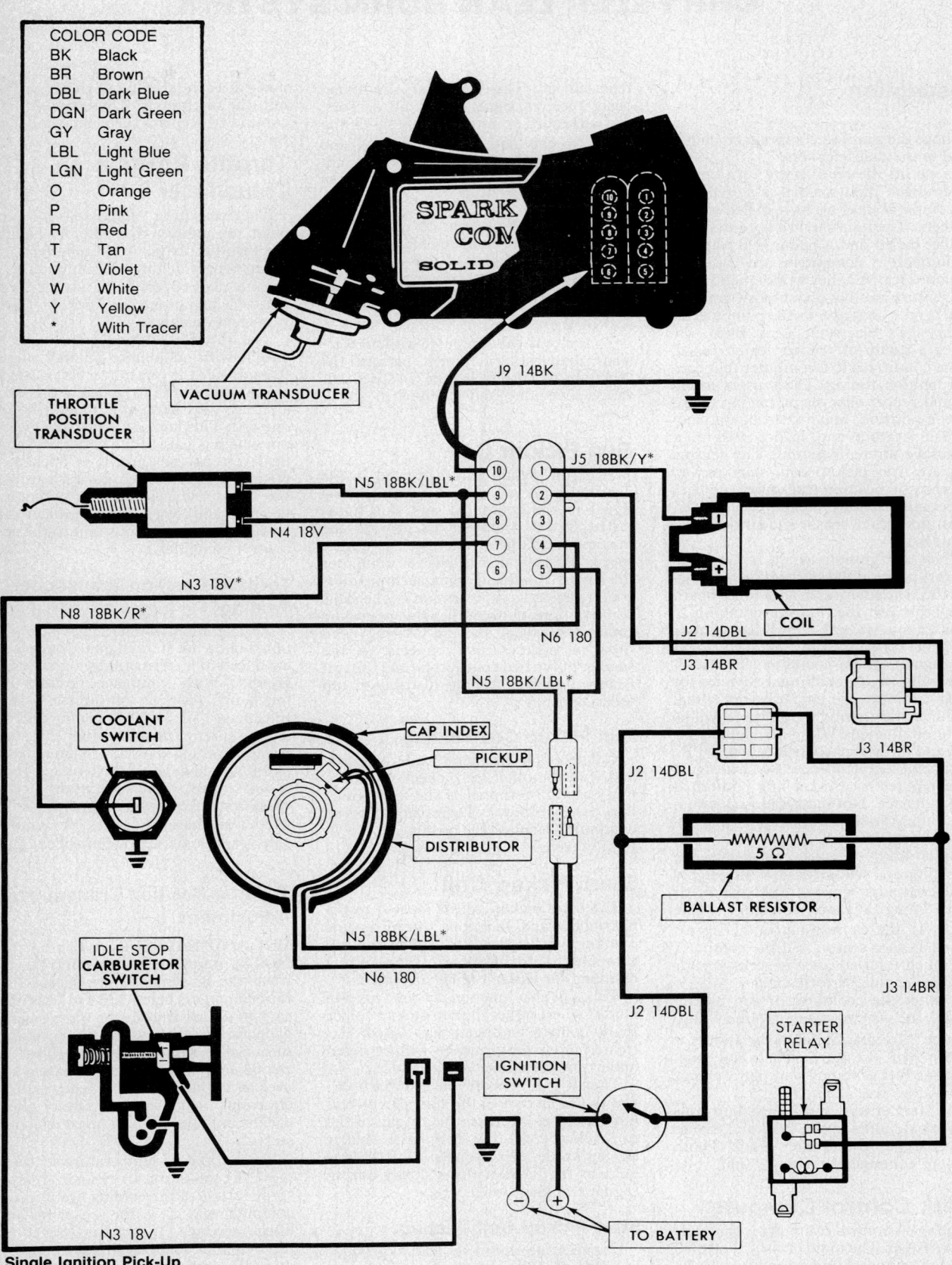

COLOR CODE
BK   Black
BR   Brown
DBL   Dark Blue
DGN   Dark Green
GY   Gray
LBL   Light Blue
LGN   Light Green
O   Orange
P   Pink
R   Red
T   Tan
V   Violet
W   White
Y   Yellow
*   With Tracer

VACUUM TRANSDUCER

THROTTLE
POSITION
TRANSDUCER

SPARK COM. SOLID

J9 14BK

J5 18BK/Y*

N5 18BK/LBL*

N4 18V

N3 18V*

N8 18BK/R*

COIL

N6 180

N5 18BK/LBL*

J2 14DBL

J3 14BR

J3 14BR

COOLANT
SWITCH

CAP INDEX

PICKUP

J2 14DBL

DISTRIBUTOR

N5 18BK/LBL*

5 Ω

BALLAST RESISTOR

IDLE STOP
CARBURETOR
SWITCH

N6 180

J2 14DBL

IGNITION
SWITCH

STARTER
RELAY

J3 14BR

N3 18V

TO BATTERY

Single Ignition Pick-Up

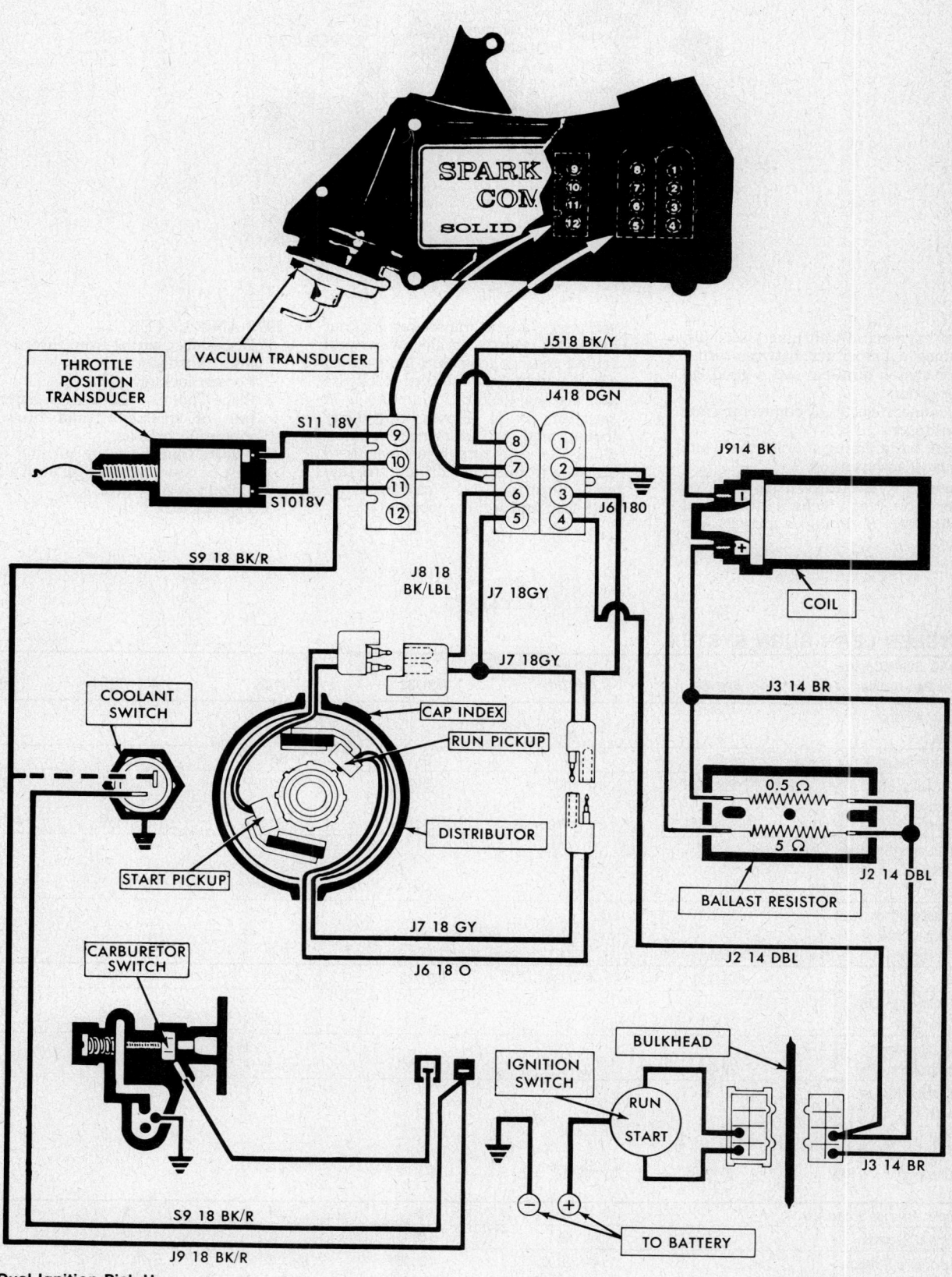

Dual Ignition Pick-Up

ELECTRONIC IGNITIONS
CHRYSLER LEAN BURN SYSTEM

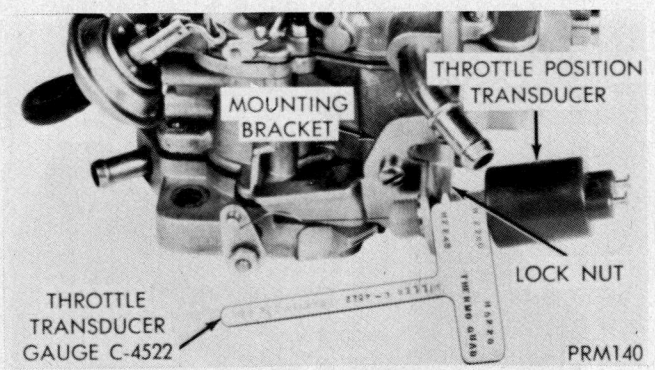

Throttle Position Transducer adjustment

1 Start engine and wait ninety seconds.
2 Connect a jumper wire between carburetor switch terminal and a good engine ground.
3 Disconnect electrical connector from transducer.
4 Check basic timing at crankshaft, and adjust if necessary.
5 Reconnect electrical connector to transducer and recheck timing at crankshaft. *If timing is greater than specified,* loosen transducer locknut and turn transducer clockwise until timing returns to within limits, then turn an additional half turn clockwise and tighten locknut. *If timing is at specified limits,* loosen transducer locknut and turn transducer counterclockwise until timing just begins to advance from specified limit. At that point, turn transducer clockwise one half turn and tighten locknut.

1978 AND LATER
1 Disconnect wiring from throttle position transducer.
2 Loosen locknut.
3 Place Tool C-4522 between outer portion of transducer and transducer mounting bracket.
4 Adjust transducer by turning clockwise or counterclockwise until a clearance fit is obtained.
5 Tighten lock nut.

CHRYSLER LEAN BURN SYSTEM

Custom I.C. Spark Control Computer Part Number	4091730	4091731	4091732	4091786	4091787	4091788
Spark Timer Advance Schedule	8°	8°	8°	8°	8°	8°
Delay Time in Seconds	60	60	60	60	60	60
Throttle Advance Schedule	7°-9°@100°F	4°-6°@100°F	5°-7°@100°F	5°-7°@100°F	5°-7°@100°F	7°-9°@100°F
Test Transducer Core Out 1 Inch	3°-6°@140°F	2°-4°@140°F	2°-5°@140°F	2°-4°@140°F	2°-4°@140°F	4°-6°@140°F
Vacuum Advance Schedule (A) Operating Vacuum Range	0"-12"	0"-14"	0"-14"	0"-15.5"	0"-10"	0"-14"
(B) Advance Off Idle (Carb Switch Isolated With Paper	None	7°-11°	None	5°-9°	None	7°-11°
	4091730	4091731	4091732	4091786	4091787	4091788
(C) Accumulation Time (In minutes)	8	8	8	7	8	8
(D) Advance After Accumulation Time	28°-32°	23°-27°	26°-30°	18°-22°	23°-27°	20°-24°
Speed Advance (Ground Carb Switch and Disconnect Throttle Transducer Before Checking) @2000 RPM	4°-8°	4°-8°	0°-3°	0°-1°	2°-5°	1°-5°
@4000 RPM	8°-12°	10°-14°	2°-6°	0°-2°	7°-11°	4°-8°
Spark Timer Advance Schedule		8°	8°	8°	8°	8°
Delay Time in Seconds		60	60	60	60	60
Throttle Advance Schedule		4°-6°@100°F	5°-7°@100°F	9°-11°@100°F	5°-7°@100°F	7°-9°@100°F
Test Transducer Core Out 1 Inch		1°-4°@140°F	2°-5°@140°F	5°-8°@140°F	2°-5°@140°F	4°-6°@140°F

CHRYSLER LEAN BURN SYSTEM

Custom I.C. Spark Control Computer Part Number	4091791	4091923	4091924	4091954	4091955
Vacuum Advance Schedule					
(A) Operating Vacuum Range	0"-12"	0"-14"	0"-14"	0"-15.5"	0"-14"
(B) Advance Off Idle (Carb Switch Isolated With Paper)	None	8°-12°	None	None	7°-11°
(C) Accumulation Time (In Minutes)	8	8	8	8	7
(D) Advance After Accumulation Time	20°-24°	24°-28°	21°-25°	18°-22°	20°-24°
Speed Advance (Ground Carb Switch and Disconnect Throttle Transducer Before Checking) @2000 RPM	7°-11°	1°-4°	10°-15°	0°-1°	1°-5°
@4000 RPM	8°-12°	6°-10°	16°-21°	0°-2°	4°-8°

Custom I.C. Spark Control Computer Part Number	4111012	4111013	4111014	4111015	4111159
Spark Timer Advance Schedule	8°	8°	8°	8°	8°
Delay Time in Seconds	60	60	60	60	60
Throttle Advance Schedule	0°	9°-11°@100°F	5°-7°@100°F	5°-7°@100°F	5°-7°@100°F
Test Transducer Core Out 1 Inch	0°	5°-8°@140°F	2°-5°@140°F	2°-5°@140°F	2°-5°@140°F
Vacuum Advance Schedule					
(A) Operating Vacuum Range	0"-15.5"	0"-14"	0"-12"	0"-14"	0"-15.5"
(B) Advance Off Idle (Carb Switch Isolated With Paper)	None	None	2°-6°	2°-6°	None
(C) Accumulation Time (In Minutes)	8	8	8	8	8
(D) Advance After Accumulation Time	18°-22°	21°-25°	18°-22°	18°-22°	18°-22°
Speed Advance (Ground Carb Switch and Disconnect Throttle Transducer Before Checking) @2000 RPM	4°-8°	10°-14°	8°-12°	8°-12°	0°-1°
@4000 RPM	6°-10°	16°-21°	12°-16°	12°-16°	0°-2°

Custom I.C. Spark Control Computer Part Number	4111169	4111170	4111172	4111217	4111218
Spark Timer Advance Schedule	None	None	None	8°	8°
Delay Time in Seconds	None	None	None	60	60
Throttle Advance Schedule	5°-7°@100°F	5°-7°@100°F	2°-5°@140°F	0°	0°
Test Transducer Core Out 1 Inch	5°-7°@100°F	2°-5°@140°F	2°-5°@140°F	0°	0°
Vacuum Advance Schedule					
(A) Operating Vacuum Range	0"-10"	0"-10"	0"-10"	4"-14"	4"-14"
(B) Advance Off Idle (Carb Switch Isolated With Paper)	5°-9°	5°-9°	5°-9°	6°-10°	2°-6°
(C) Accumulation Time (In Minutes)	8	8	8	7	7
(D) Advance After Accumulation Time	16°-20°	16°-20°	16°-20°	18°-22°	18°-22°
Speed Advance (Ground Carb Switch and Disconnect Throttle Transducer Before Checking) @2000 RPM	1°-5°	1°-5°	1°-5°	8°-12°	8°-12°
@4000 RPM	4°-8°	4°-8°	4°-8°	12°-16°	12°-16°

Coolant Temperature Sensor

The coolant temperature sensor is located on the water pump housing and supplies a signal to the spark control computer when the coolant temperature is below 150°F and above 225°F. The coolant switch is also wired into the vacuum transducer electrical circuit inside the computer. As a result there can be no additional advance from the vacuum transducer regardless of the level of intake manifold vacuum. Even with the curb-idle speed screw not touching the carburetor switch contact, the vacuum transducer circuit inside the computer remains grounded out by the coolant temperature switch whenever the temperature is below 150°F. Engine coolant temperature above 150°F opens the ground circuit inside the computer and the vacuum transducer input will then produce a signal anytime manifold vacuum is above zero and the carburetor switch contact is not touching the curb-idle speed screw.

Coolant Temperature Sensor Testing

Connect one ohmmeter lead to a good engine ground and connect the other ohmmeter lead to terminal of coolant temperature switch. Continuity should be present in a cold engine and an engine with coolant above 225°F. No continuity should be present between 150°F and 225 °F.

Vacuum Transducer

The vacuum transducer is located on the spark control computer. Its signal tells the computer what the manifold vacuum is. The amount of advance increases concurrently with manifold vacuum increases. To obtain the maximum advance for any vacuum reading the carburetor switch sensor must remain open for a specified amount of time. During that time the advance will build up at a slow rate. If the carburetor switch closes before the predetermined time period, the advance build-up at that time will be cancelled in the ignition system, but the computer will put it into memory and slowly return it to zero. If the switch reopens before the advance is returned to zero, the build up of advance starts at the point where the computer still has it in memory. If the switch is reopened after the advance is returned to zero, the build-up will start all over again.

Vacuum Transducer Testing

Other than testing the vacuum diaphragm the transducer is part of the spark control computer and both are serviced as an assembly.

Carburetor Switch Sensor

The carburetor switch sensor is located on the right side of the carburetor. Its signal tells the computer whether the engine is at idle or off idle. This is a two position switch. When on, it grounds the spark control computer preventing advance buildup. When off, it allows the computer to provide spark advance as dictated by the other sensors.

Carburetor Switch Sensor Testing

The switch should prevent timing from advancing more than two degrees beyond basic timing at idle.
1 Set basic timing.
2 If timing advances more than two degrees when grounding wire is removed from carburetor sensor switch, the switch must be replaced.

Air Temperature Sensor

The air temperature sensor is a thermistor inside the computer. It monitors intake air temperature, and the computer considers this additional data when programming ignition advance.

Basic Ignition Timing

NOTE: Engine should be at normal operating temperature to check basic timing.

1 Connect timing light to number one cylinder, and connect a tachometer.
2 Disconnect and plug vacuum hose at the spark control computer.
3 Connect a jumper wire between the carburetor switch sensor and a good ground.
4 Start the engine, wait ninety seconds and check and adjust timing. Basic timing advance should be within specifications on the underhood emission control/tune up label.
5 Unplug and reconnect the vacuum hose at spark control computer, and remove the jumper wire from the carburetor switch. Recheck timing, and, if it has advanced more than two degrees, replace the carburetor switch sensor.

Failure To Start Test

NOTE: Before proceeding with this test, confirm that the ignition system is at fault by checking for spark at the spark plugs.

1 Note battery voltage for later reference, and check that battery specific gravity is at least 1.220 temperature corrected.
2 Disconnect coolant temperature sensor.
3 Place a piece of paper between curb idle adjusting screw and carburetor switch.
4 Connect negative lead of a voltmeter to a good engine ground.
5 Turn ignition switch to "Run" position and measure voltage at carburetor switch terminal. If voltage is greater than five volts but less than ten volts proceed to step seven. If voltage is greater than ten volts, check to insure continuity between terminal ten of dual connector and ground on 1978 and later models. On 1977 and earlier models check for continuity between terminal two and ground. If carburetor switch voltage is less than five volts, turn ignition switch to "Off," and disconnect the dual connector from the spark control computer. Turn ignition switch back to "Run" and measure the voltage at terminal four on 1977 and earlier models. Measure voltage at terminal two on 1978 and later models. Measured voltage should be within one volt of previously noted battery voltage. If voltage is correct, proceed to step six; otherwise check the wiring between the terminal and the ignition switch for opens, shorts or poor connections.
6 Turn ignition switch to "Off," and disconnect single connector from spark control computer. Check with an ohmmeter for continuity between the carburetor switch terminal and terminal eleven (1977 and earlier models) or terminal seven (1978 and later models). If there is no continuity, check wiring between these two points for opens, shorts or poor connections. If continuity is noted, check for continuity between terminal two (1977 and earlier) or terminal ten (1978 and later) and ground. If there is no continuity check for opens or poor connections. Proceed to step seven if engine still fails to start.
7 Turn ignition switch to "Run" and, with voltmeter positive lead, measure voltage at terminals seven and eight (1977 and earlier) or terminal one (1978 and later). Voltage should be within one volt of previously noted battery voltage. If it is, proceed to step eight; if not proceed as follows:
   For terminal one—check wiring and connections between connector and ignition switch.
   For terminal seven—check wiring and connections between connector and ignition switch. Also check five ohm side of ballast resistor.
   For terminal eight—check wiring and connections between connector and ignition switch. Check primary windings of coil and ½ ohm side of ballast resistor.
8 Turn ignition switch to "Off" and measure resistance between terminals five and six (1977 and earlier) or terminals five and nine (1978 and later). Resistance should be between 150 and 900 ohms. If resistance is correct proceed to step nine. If resistance is not correct, disconnect pickup coil leads from distributor. Measure resistance at leads going into distributor. If resistance is between 150 and 900 ohms, there is an open, shorted or poor connection between distributor connector and spark control connector. If resistance is not correct, the start pickup coil is defective.
9 Connect one lead of ohmmeter to engine ground and with the other lead check for continuity at each terminal of lead going into the distributor. There should be no continuity. If continuity exists, replace start pickup coil.
10 Remove distributor cap and check air gaps of pickup coils. Adjust to correct specification.
11 Install distributor cap, reconnect all wiring and try to start engine. If engine fails to start, replace spark control computer.
12 If, after installing new computer, the engine still fails to start, reinstall original computer and repeat complete test procedure.

Start Up Advance Timing Test

1977 AND EARLIER
1 Connect an adjustable timing light.

2 Have helper start engine, snap throttle open and closed, and immediately place gear selector in drive.

3 Look at timing mark on crankshaft damper *immediately* after vehicle is in drive, and adjust timing light so the basic timing signal is seen at the timing plate. Observe timing for ninety seconds. The additional advance should slowly reduce to the basic timing signal after approximately one minute. If timing did not initially increase or did not return to basic, replace spark control computer. If it checked okay proceed to "Throttle Advance Schedule Test".

1978 AND LATER

1 Connect an adjustable timing light.

2 Connect a jumper wire between the carburetor switch and good ground.

3 Look at timing mark on crankshaft damper *immediately* after engine is started, and adjust timing light so basic signal is seen at the timing plate. Observe timing for ninety seconds. The additional advance should slowly reduce to the basic timing signal after approximately one minute. If timing did not initially increase or return to basic, replace spark control computer. If it checked okay proceed to "Throttle Advance Schedule Test".

Throttle Advance Schedule Test

NOTE: Before making this test, be sure the throttle position transducer is adjusted correctly.

1977 AND EARLIER

1 Place ignition switch in "Off" and disconnect single connector from spark control computer.

2 Measure resistance between terminals nine and ten. Resistance should be between fifty and ninety ohms. If resistance is correct, reconnect connector and proceed to step three. If resistance is not correct, remove connector from throttle position transducer terminals, and measure resistance at terminals. A reading between fifty and ninety ohms indicates an open, short or poor connection of the wires between terminals nine and ten and the transducer. If resistance is not within fifty to ninety ohms, replace the transducer.

3 Reconnect all wiring, and turn ignition switch to "Run," but do not start engine. Connect negative lead of a voltmeter to a good engine ground. With voltmeter positive lead, touch one terminal of the throttle position transducer. While opening throttle of carburetor all the way and then closing, watch voltmeter reading. Repeat with the other transducer terminal. Either terminal should show approximately a 0.5 to 2.0 volt change when throttle is opened and closed. If volt-age is correct, proceed to step four. If voltage is not correct, do not yet replace transducer because the spark control computer could be causing the malfunction. It will be necessary to proceed to step four to check this.

4 Position throttle linkage on fast idle cam, ground the carburetor switch with a jumper wire, disconnect electrical connector from throttle position transducer, and connect it to a known good transducer.

5 Move core of test transducer in so that it is fully bottomed, start engine, wait ninety seconds and move core out about one inch.

6 Adjust timing light so basic timing signal is seen at the timing plate. The meter on the timing light should show additional advance. Move core back into transducer, and timing should return to basic setting. If timing advanced and returned, proceed to step seven. If timing did not advance or return, replace spark control computer, and check transducer again with the new computer.

7 Return timing light meter to zero, and have a helper move transducer core in and out about one inch five or six times quickly while you are looking at timing marks. There should be additional advance of about seven to twelve degrees for about one second and then return to basic setting. Replace spark control computer if this does not occur. Also, if throttle position transducer failed in step three, replace it now.

1978 AND LATER

1 Place ignition switch in "Off" and disconnect single connector from spark control computer.

2 Measure resistance between terminals eight and nine. Resistance should be between sixty and ninety ohms. If resistance is correct, proceed to step three after replacing connector. If resistance is not correct, remove connector from throttle position transducer, and measure resistance at terminals. If this measurement shows sixty to ninety ohms, there is an open, short or poor connection between terminals eight and nine and the transducer. If resistance is not correct, replace throttle position transducer.

3 Position throttle linkage on fast idle cam, ground the carburetor switch with a jumper wire, disconnect wire from throttle position transducer, and connect to a known good transducer.

4 Move test transducer core in so that it is fully bottomed, start engine, wait ninety seconds, and move core out one inch.

5 Adjust timing light so the basic timing signal is seen at the timing plate. The meter on the light should show additional advance. Move core back into transducer, and timing should return to basic setting. If timing did not ad-vance or return, replace spark control computer.

6 Check throttle position transducer again with the new computer.

Vacuum Advance Schedule Test

1977 AND EARLIER

1 Connect an adjustable timing light to engine, and run until normal operating temperature is reached. Place transmission in neutral.

2 Place a piece of paper between carburetor switch and curb idle adjustment screw. Adjust timing light so basic timing signal is seen at the timing plate. The meter on the light should show additional advance as indicated under specifications. If advance is not within specifications, replace spark control computer. If advance is okay, allow engine to run at least nine minutes, making sure there is at least sixteen inches of vacuum at the vacuum transducer.

3 Adjust timing light so basic timing signal is seen at the timing plate. The timing light meter should show the additional advance as indicated by specifications. If advance is not within specifications, replace spark control computer. If advance is okay proceed to step four.

4 Remove paper from carburetor switch, and timing should return to basic signal. If timing does not return to basic, turn engine off and check the wire between terminal eleven and carburetor switch for opens, shorts and poor connections. If wiring checks okay, repeat test and, if timing will still not return to basic signal, replace spark control computer.

1978 AND LATER

1 Connect an adjustable timing light to engine, and run until normal operating temperature is reached. Place transmission in neutral.

2 Place a piece of paper between carburetor switch and curb idle adjustment screw. Adjust timing light so basic timing signal is seen at the timing plate. Let engine run at least nine minutes and make sure there is a minimum of sixteen inches of vacuum at the vacuum transducer. The timing light meter should show an additional amount of advance as indicated under the specifications. If advance is not within specifications, replace spark control computer.

3 Remove paper from carburetor switch, and timing should return to basic setting. If timing does not return to basic, turn engine off and check the wire between terminal seven and carburetor switch for shorts, opens or poor connections. If it checks out okay, repeat test and if timing still will not return to basic, replace the spark control computer.

ELECTRONIC SPARK IGNITION SYSTEM DIAGNOSIS

Engine Cranks But Will Not Run

NOTE: IF A TACHOMETER IS CONNECTED TO THE TACHOMETER TERMINAL, DISCONNECT IT BEFORE PROCEEDING WITH THE TEST.

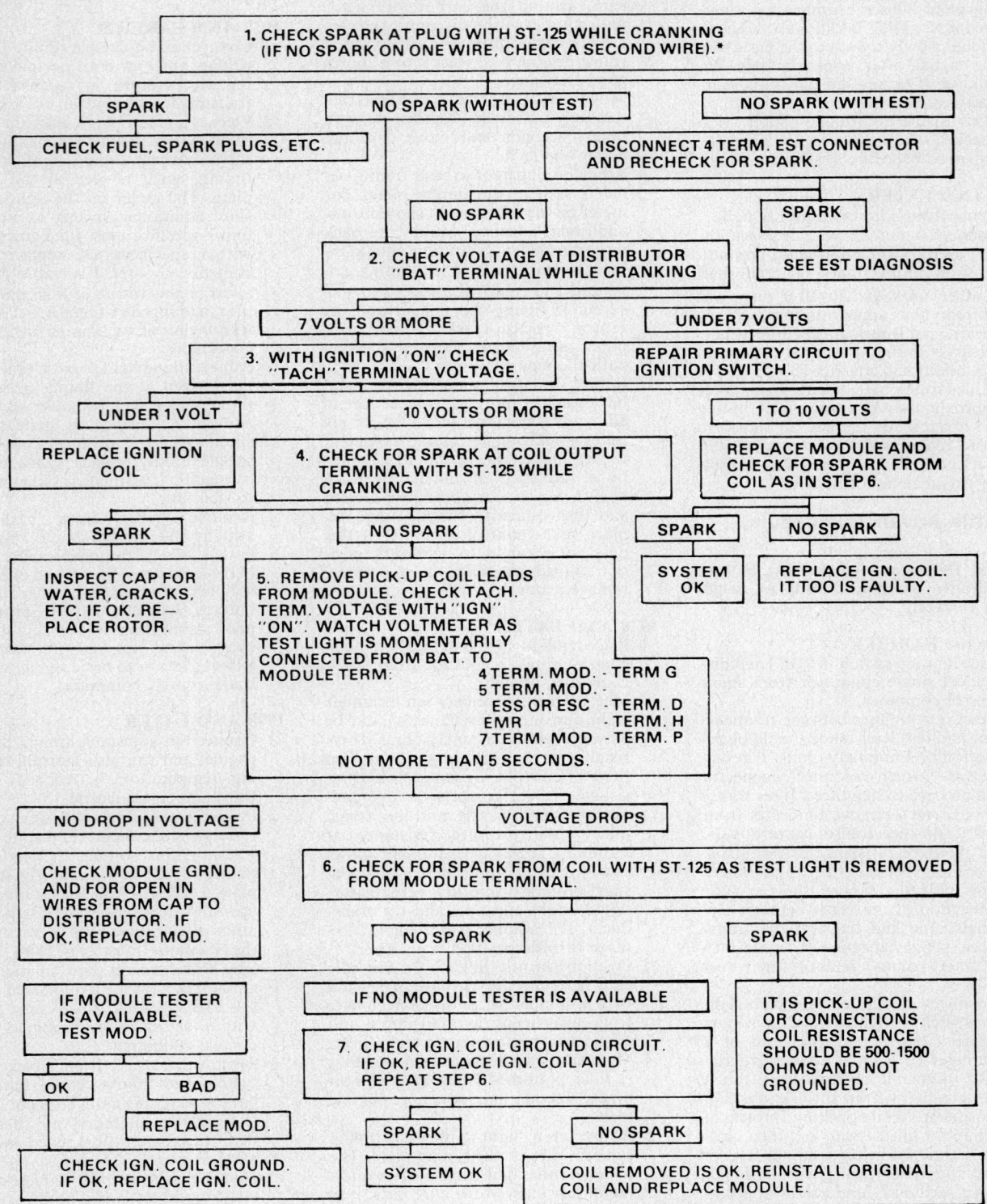

*SOME EST PROBLEMS WILL RESULT IN ONE OR TWO SPARKS WHEN CRANKING IS STARTED, THEN SPARK WILL STOP. THIS IS CONSIDERED A "NO SPARK" CONDITION.

GM DELCO-REMY ELECTRONIC SPARK TIMING SYSTEM

Distributor Disassembly and Test

COIL IN CAP DISTRIBUTOR

1. A 6-cyl. EST distributor with coil-in-cap is illustrated.
2. Detach the wiring connector from the cap, as shown.
3. Turn four latches and remove the cap and coil assembly from the lower housing.

Coil in Cap Distributor

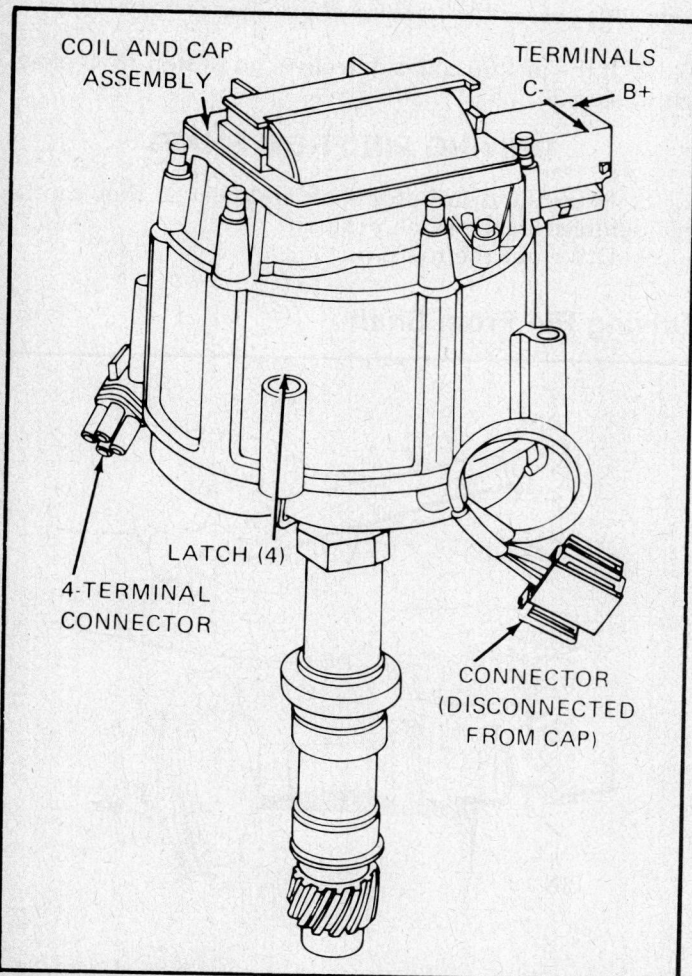

Steps 1 through 3

TESTING IGNITION COIL

4. Connect the ohmmeter, Test 1.
5. The reading should be zero or nearly zero. If not, replace the coil, step 8.
6. Connect the ohmmeter both ways, Test 2. Use the high scale. Replace the coil only if both readings are infinite, step 8.
7. If the coil is good, go to step 13.

Testing Ignition Coil

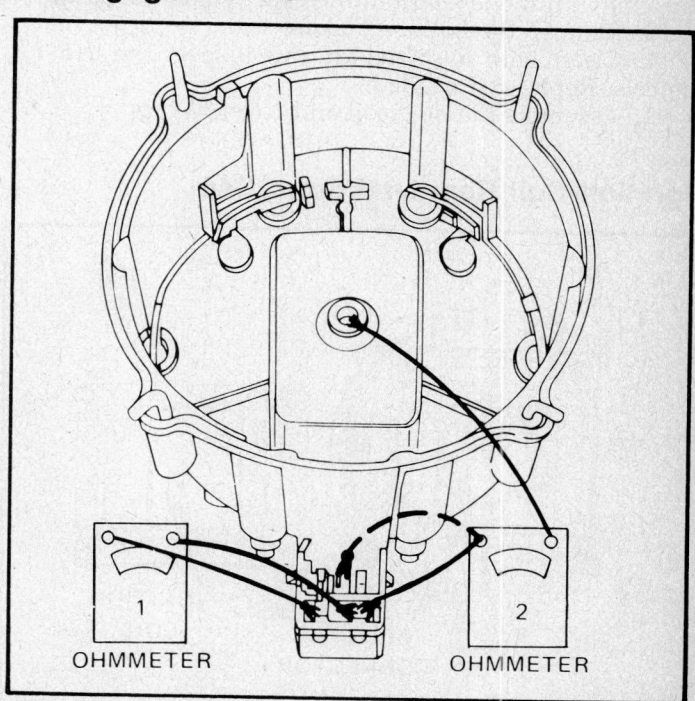

Steps 4 through 7

IGNITION COIL ATTACHING SCREWS

8. Remove the coil-cover attaching screws and lift off the cover.

Ignition Coil Attaching Screws

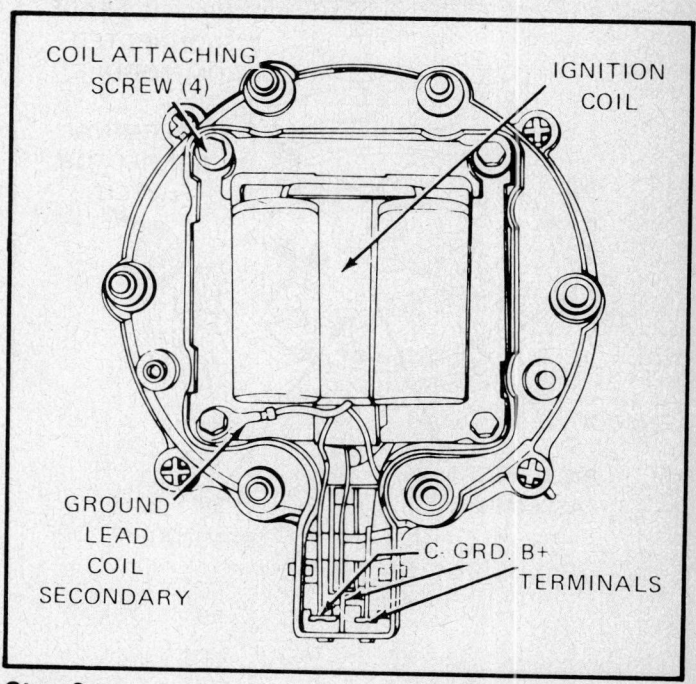

Step 8

IGNITION COIL REMOVED FROM CAP

9. Remove the ignition coil attaching screws and lift the coil with the leads from the cap.

10. Remove the ignition coil arc seal.

11. Clean with a soft cloth and inspect the cap for defects. Replace, if needed.

12. Assemble the new coil and cover to cap.

Ignition Coil Removed From Cap

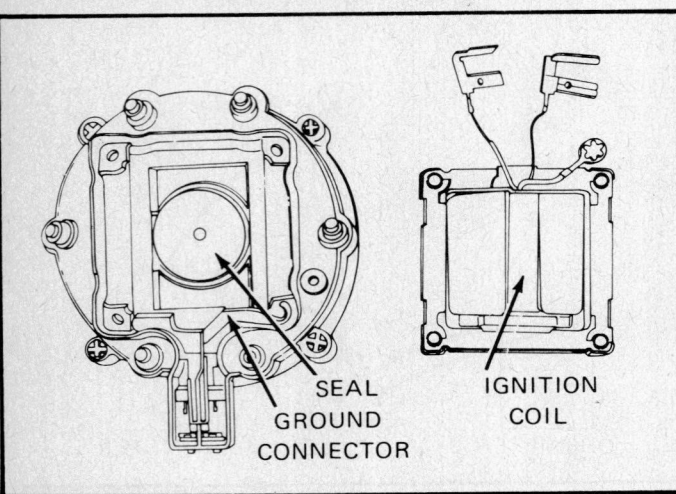

Steps 9 through 12

Testing Pickup Coil

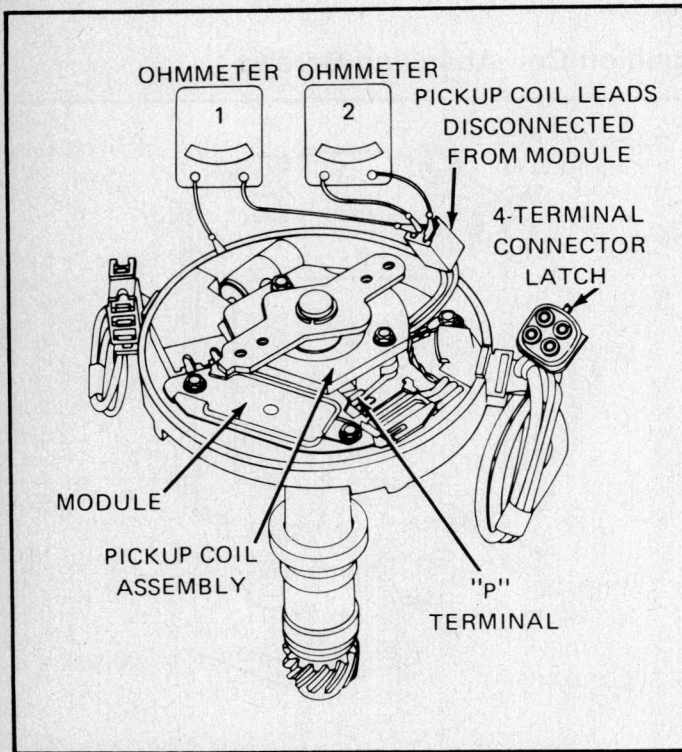

Steps 13 through 17

TESTING PICKUP COIL

13. On all distributors, remove the rotor and pickup coil leads from the module.

14. Connect the ohmmeter Test 1 and then Test 2.

15. If the vacuum unit is used, connect the vacuum source to the vacuum unit. Replace the unit if inoperative. Observe the ohmmeter throughout the vacuum range. Flex the leads by hand without vacuum to check for intermittent opens.

16. Test 1 should read infinite at all times.

Test 2 should read steady at one value within 500-1500 ohm range.

NOTE The ohmmeter may deflect if the operating vacuum unit causes the teeth to align. This is not a defect.

17. If the pickup coil is defective, go to step 18. If okay, go to step 23.

DRIVING PIN FROM SHAFT

18. Mark the distributor shaft and gear so they can be reassembled in the same position.

19. Drive out the roll pin.

Driving Pin From Shaft

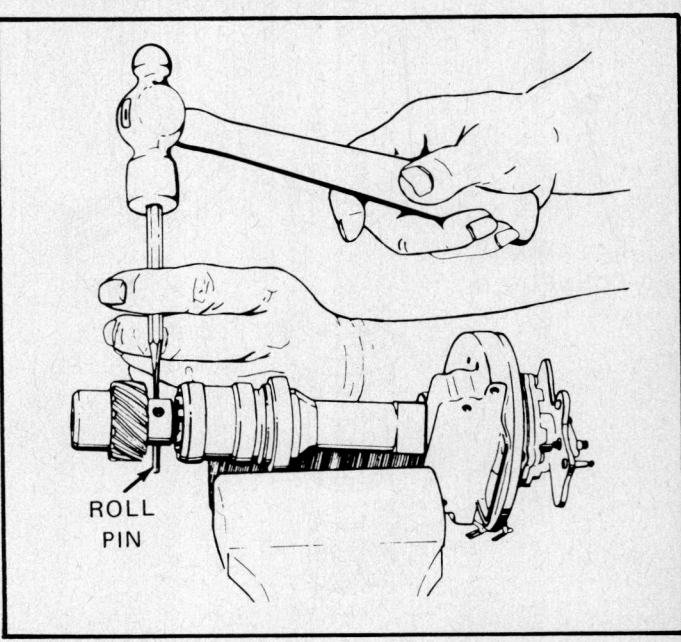

Steps 18 and 19

SHAFT ASSEMBLY REMOVED

20. Remove the gear and pull the shaft assembly from the distributor.

ALUMINUM NON-MAGNETIC SHIELD REMOVED

21. Remove the three attaching screws and remove the magnetic shield.

Shaft Assembly Removed

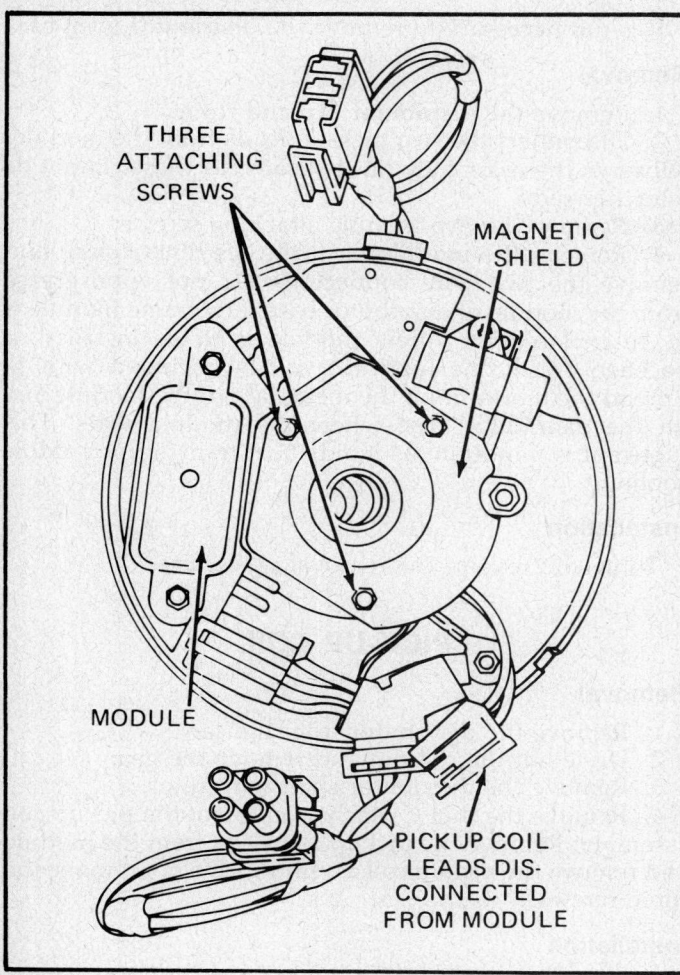

Step 20

Aluminum Non-Magnetic Shield Removed

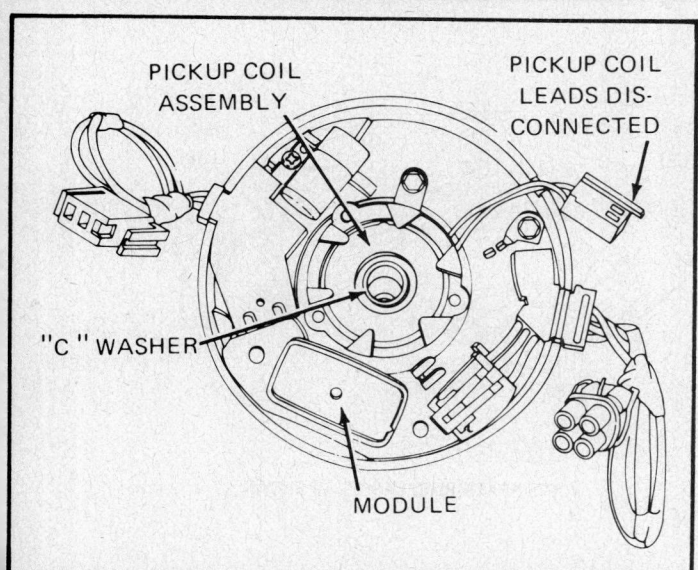

Step 21

PICKUP COIL REMOVED AND DISASSEMBLY

22. Remove the retaining ring. Remove the pickup coil magnet and pole piece.

Pickup Coil Removed and Disassembled

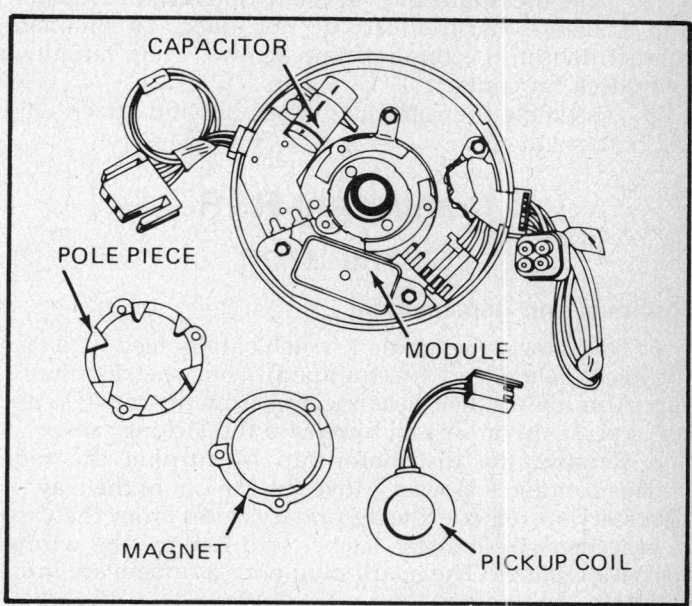

Step 22

MODULE REMOVED

23. Remove the two module attaching screws and the capacitor attaching screw. Lift the module, capacitor and harness assembly from the base.
24. Disconnect the wiring harness from the module.
25. Check the module with an approved module tester.

Module Removed

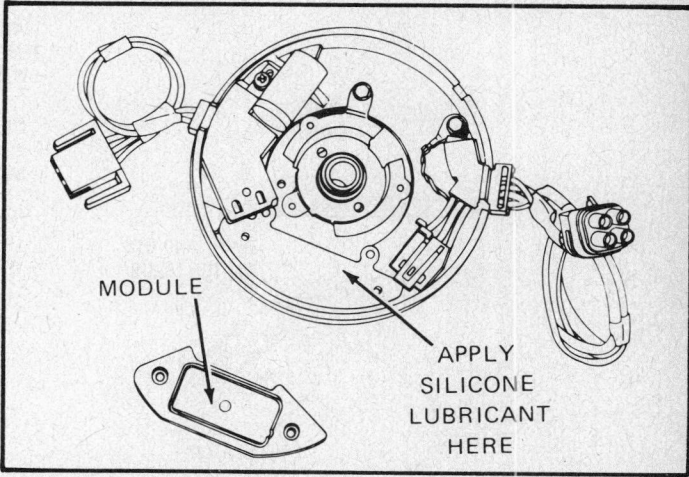

Steps 23 through 26

26. Install the module, wiring harness and capacitor assembly. Use silicone lubricant on the housing under the module.

INSTALL PICKUP COIL SHAFT ASSEMBLY AND CAP

27. Install the pickup coil assembly, shaft and gear.

28. Spin the shaft and, if used, operate the vacuum unit to insure that the teeth do not touch. To eliminate contact, loosen the three pickup screws. Then retighten and check for contact.

29. Assemble the rotor, cap assembly and attach wiring harness to cap.

Component R&R

DISTRIBUTOR

Removal and Replacement

1. Disconnect the ignition switch battery feed wire and the tachometer lead (if equipped) from the distributor cap. Also release the coil connectors from the cap. (Do not use a screwdriver or tool to release the locking tabs.)

2. Remove the distributor cap by turning the four latches counterclockwise. Move the cap out of the way. If necessary to remove the secondary wires from the cap, release the wire harness latches and remove the wiring harness retainer. The spark plug wire numbers are indicated on the retainer.

.3. Remove the distributor clamp screw and hold-down clamp.

4. Note the position of the rotor. Then pull the distributor up until the rotor just stops turning counterclockwise. Again note the position of the rotor. To insure correct timing of the distributor, the distributor must be installed with the rotor correctly positioned.

MODULE

It is not necessary to remove the distributor from car.

Removal

1. Remove the distributor cap and rotor.

2. Disconnect the two pick-up leads from the module. (Observe the color code on the leads, as these cannot be interchanged.)

3. Remove the two module attaching screws.

4. Remove the module from the distributor base and remove the two wire connectors. Do not wipe grease from the module of distributor base if the same module is to be replaced. If a new module is to be installed, a package of silicone lubricant will be included with it. Spread the lubricant on the metal face of the module and on the distributor base where the module seats. This lubricant is important as it aids heat transfer for module cooling.

Installation

To install, reverse the removal procedure.

PICK-UP COIL

Removal

1. Remove the distributor from the car.

2. Drive out the roll pin and remove the gear.

3. Remove the distributor shaft with rotor.

4. Remove the thin C-washer on top of the pickup coil assembly. Remove the pickup coil leads from the module and remove the pickup coil assembly. (Do not remove the three screws.)

Installation

To install, reverse the removal procedures.

Engine Wiring for VIN F and Y

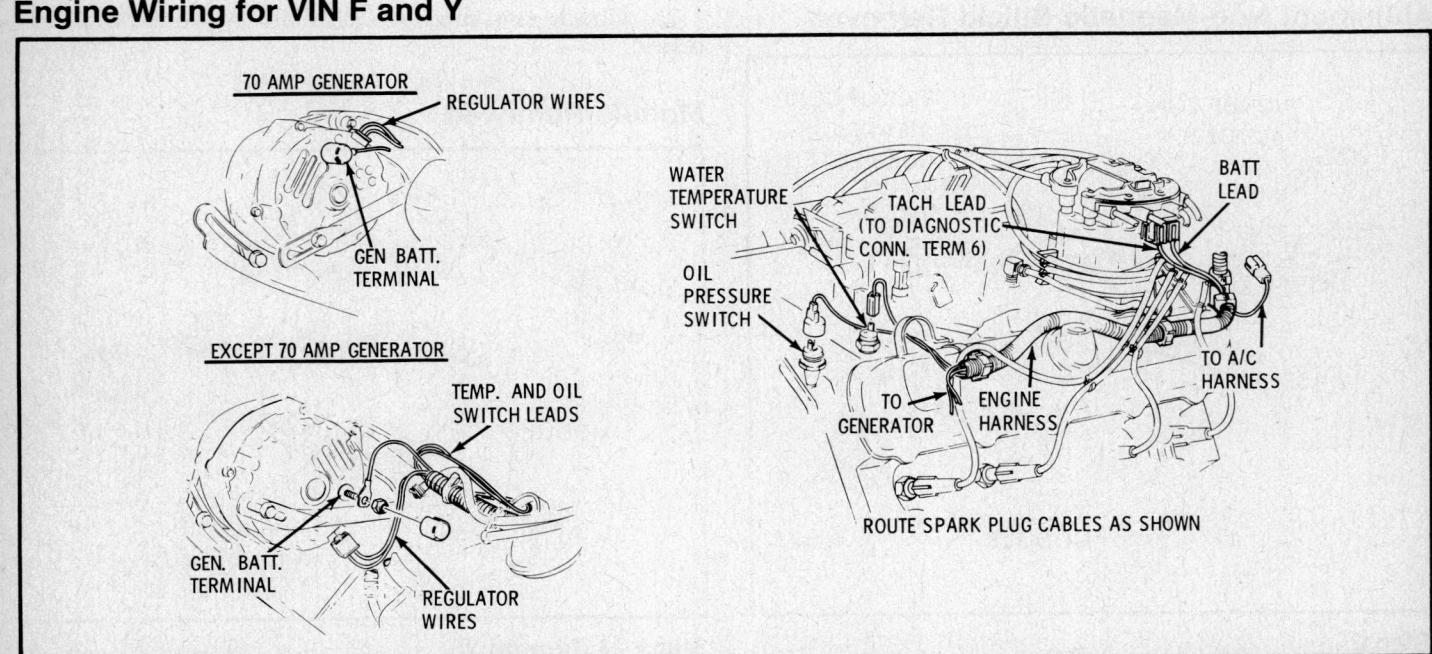

70 AMP GENERATOR — REGULATOR WIRES

GEN BATT. TERMINAL

EXCEPT 70 AMP GENERATOR

TEMP. AND OIL SWITCH LEADS

GEN. BATT. TERMINAL

REGULATOR WIRES

WATER TEMPERATURE SWITCH

OIL PRESSURE SWITCH

TACH LEAD (TO DIAGNOSTIC CONN. TERM 6)

BATT LEAD

TO GENERATOR

ENGINE HARNESS

TO A/C HARNESS

ROUTE SPARK PLUG CABLES AS SHOWN

Engine Electrical Diagnostic Connector

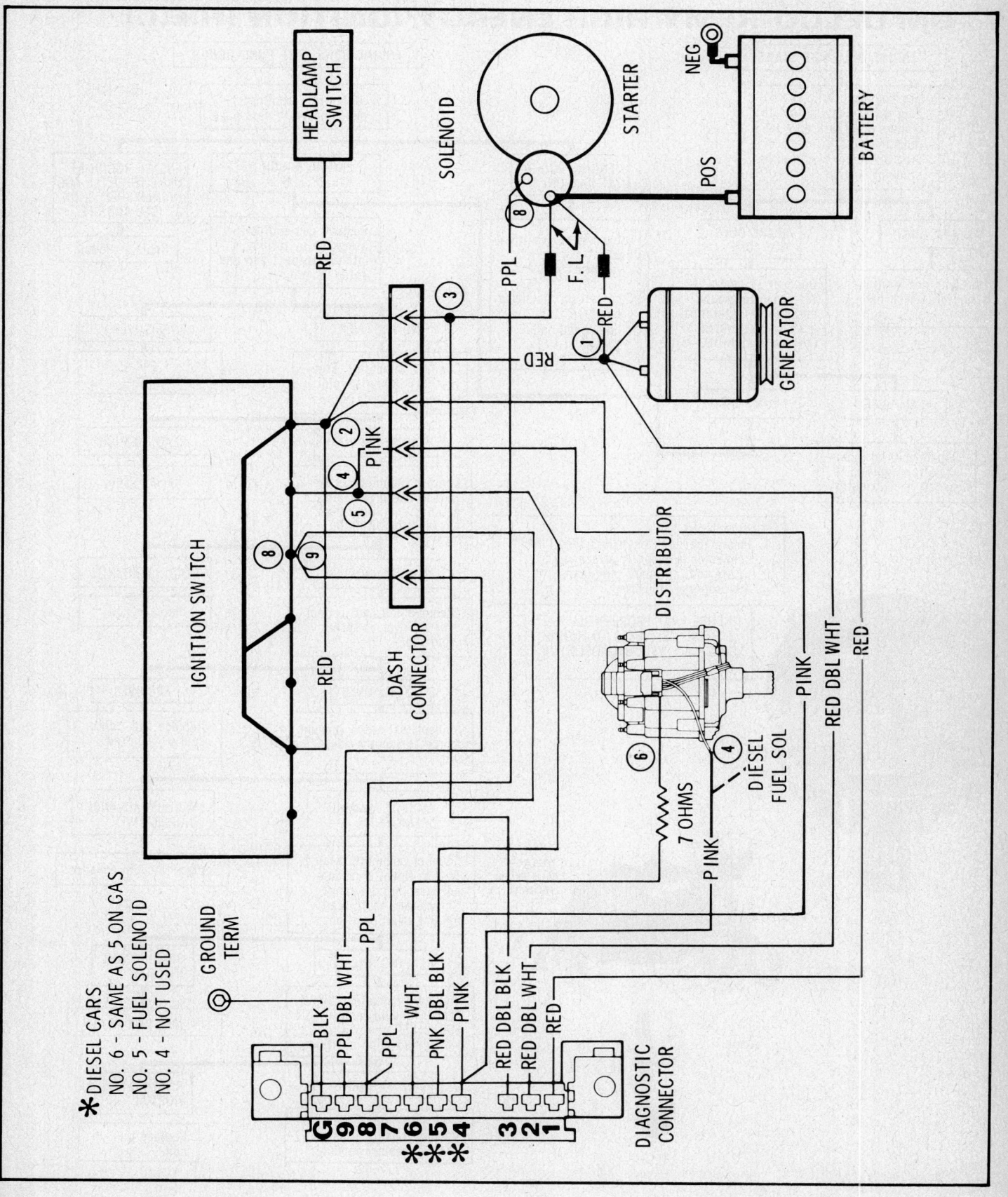

B263

TROUBLESHOOTING
GM DELCO-REMY HIGH ENERGY IGNITION (H.E.I.)

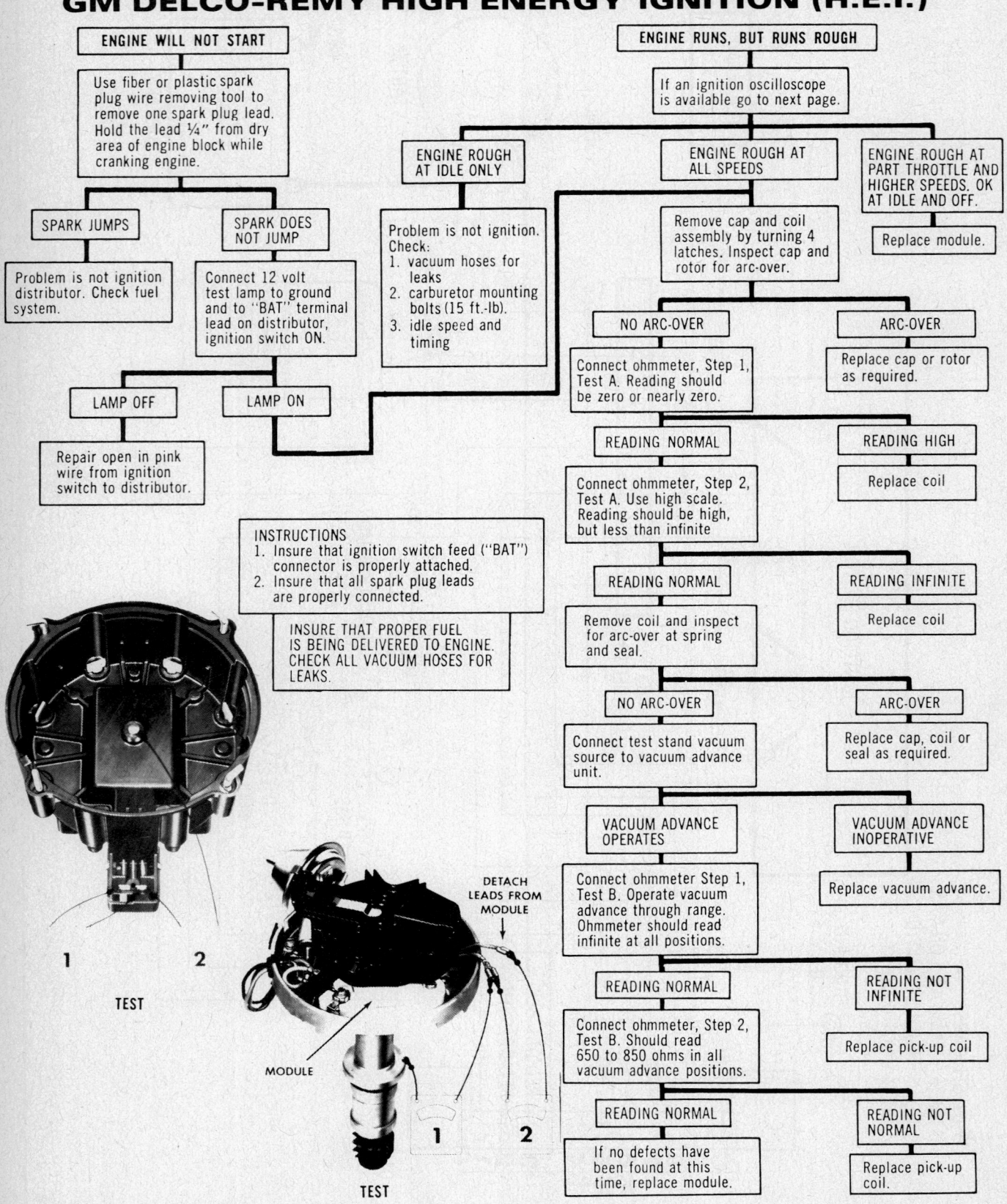

ENGINE WILL NOT START

Use fiber or plastic spark plug wire removing tool to remove one spark plug lead. Hold the lead ¼" from dry area of engine block while cranking engine.

SPARK JUMPS

Problem is not ignition distributor. Check fuel system.

SPARK DOES NOT JUMP

Connect 12 volt test lamp to ground and to "BAT" terminal lead on distributor, ignition switch ON.

LAMP OFF

Repair open in pink wire from ignition switch to distributor.

LAMP ON

INSTRUCTIONS
1. Insure that ignition switch feed ("BAT") connector is properly attached.
2. Insure that all spark plug leads are properly connected.

INSURE THAT PROPER FUEL IS BEING DELIVERED TO ENGINE. CHECK ALL VACUUM HOSES FOR LEAKS.

1 **2**

TEST

DETACH LEADS FROM MODULE

MODULE

1 **2**

TEST

ENGINE RUNS, BUT RUNS ROUGH

If an ignition oscilloscope is available go to next page.

ENGINE ROUGH AT IDLE ONLY

Problem is not ignition. Check:
1. vacuum hoses for leaks
2. carburetor mounting bolts (15 ft.-lb).
3. idle speed and timing

ENGINE ROUGH AT ALL SPEEDS

Remove cap and coil assembly by turning 4 latches. Inspect cap and rotor for arc-over.

ENGINE ROUGH AT PART THROTTLE AND HIGHER SPEEDS. OK AT IDLE AND OFF.

Replace module.

NO ARC-OVER

Connect ohmmeter, Step 1, Test A. Reading should be zero or nearly zero.

ARC-OVER

Replace cap or rotor as required.

READING NORMAL

Connect ohmmeter, Step 2, Test A. Use high scale. Reading should be high, but less than infinite

READING HIGH

Replace coil

READING NORMAL

Remove coil and inspect for arc-over at spring and seal.

READING INFINITE

Replace coil

NO ARC-OVER

Connect test stand vacuum source to vacuum advance unit.

ARC-OVER

Replace cap, coil or seal as required.

VACUUM ADVANCE OPERATES

Connect ohmmeter Step 1, Test B. Operate vacuum advance through range. Ohmmeter should read infinite at all positions.

VACUUM ADVANCE INOPERATIVE

Replace vacuum advance.

READING NORMAL

Connect ohmmeter, Step 2, Test B. Should read 650 to 850 ohms in all vacuum advance positions.

READING NOT INFINITE

Replace pick-up coil

READING NORMAL

If no defects have been found at this time, replace module.

READING NOT NORMAL

Replace pick-up coil.

GM DELCO-REMY HIGH ENERGY IGNITION (H.E.I.)

GM Delco-Remy High Energy Ignition (HEI)

OPERATION

The magnetic pick-up assembly located inside the distributor contains a permanent magnet, a pole piece with internal teeth, and a pick-up coil. When the teeth of the rotating timer core and pole piece align, an induced voltage in the pick-up coil signals the electronic module to open the coil primary circuit. As the primary current decreases, a high voltage is induced in the secondary windings of the ignition coil, directing a spark through the rotor and high voltage leads to fire the spark plugs. The dwell period is automatically controlled by the electronic module and is increased with increasing engine rpm. The HEI System features a longer spark duration which is instrumental in firing lean and EGR diluted fuel/air mixtures. The condenser (capacitor) located within the HEI distributor is provided for noise (static) suppression purposes only and is not a regularly replaced ignition system component.

Major Repair Procedures (Distributor in Engine)

IGNITION COIL REPLACEMENT

1. Disconnect the feed and module wire terminal connectors from the distributor cap.
2. Remove the ignition set retainer.
3. Remove the four coil cover-to-distributor cap screws and the coil cover.
4. Remove the four coil-to-distributor cap screws.
5. Using a blunt drift, press the coil wire spade terminals up out of distributor cap.
6. Lift the coil up out of the distributor cap.
7. Remove and clean the coil spring, rubber seal washer and coil cavity of the distributor cap.
8. Reverse the above procedures to install.

DISTRIBUTOR CAP REPLACEMENT

1. Remove the feed and module wire terminal connectors from the distributor cap.
2. Remove the retainer and spark plug wires from the cap.
3. Depress and release the four distributor cap-to-housing retainers and lift off the cap assembly.
4. Remove the four coil cover screws and cover.
5. Using a finger or a blunt drift, push the spade terminals up out of the distributor cap.
6. Remove all four coil screws and lift the coil, coil spring and rubber seal washer out of the cap coil cavity.

7. Using a new distributor cap, reverse the above procedures to assemble.

ROTOR REPLACEMENT

1. Disconnect the feed and module wire connectors from the distributor.
2. Depress and release the four distributor cap to housing retainers and lift off the cap assembly.
3. Remove the two rotor attaching screws and rotor.
4. Reverse the above procedure to install.

VACUUM ADVANCE REPLACEMENT

1. Remove the distributor cap and rotor as previously described.
2. Disconnect the vacuum hose from the vacuum advance unit.
3. Remove the two vacuum advance retaining screws, pull the advance unit outward, rotate and disengage the operating rod from its tang.
4. Reverse the above procedure to install.

MODULE REPLACEMENT

1. Remove the distributor cap and rotor as previously described.
2. Disconnect the harness connector and pick-up coil spade connectors from the module.
3. Remove the two screws and module from the distributor housing.
4. Coat the bottom of the new module with dielectric lubricant. Reverse the above procedure to install.

DISTRIBUTOR REMOVAL

1. Disconnect the ground cable from the battery.
2. Disconnect the feed and module terminal connectors from the distributor cap.
3. Disconnect the hose at the vacuum advance.

4. Depress and release the four distributor cap-to-housing retainers and lift off the cap assembly.
5. Using crayon or chalk, make locating marks on the rotor and module and on the distributor housing and engine for installation purposes.
6. Loosen and remove the distributor clamp bolt and clamp, and lift distributor out of the engine. Noting the relative position of the rotor and module alignment marks, make a second mark on the rotor to align it with the one mark on the module.

DISTRIBUTOR INSTALLATION

1. With a new O-ring on the distributor housing and the second mark on the rotor aligned with the mark on the module, install the distributor, taking care to align the mark on the housing with the one on the engine. It may be necessary to lift the distributor and turn the rotor slightly to align the gears and the oil pump driveshaft.
2. With the respective marks aligned, install the clamp and bolt finger-tight.
3. Install and secure the distributor cap.
4. Connect the feed and module connectors to the distributor cap.
5. Connect a timing light to the engine and plug the vacuum hose.
6. Connect the ground cable to the battery.
7. Start the engine and set the timing.
8. Turn the engine off and tighten the distributor clamp bolt. Disconnect the timing light and unplug and connect the hose to the vacuum advance.

Service Procedures (Distributor Removed)

DRIVEN GEAR REPLACEMENT

1. With the distributor removed, use a 1/8 in. pin punch and tap out the driven gear roll pin.
2. Hold the rotor end of shaft and rotate the driven gear to shear any burrs in the roll pin hole.

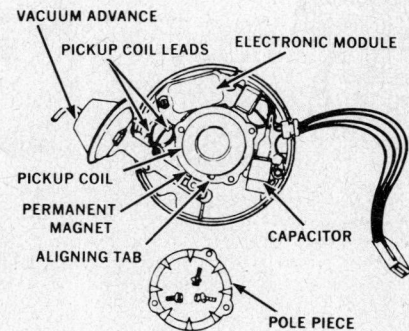

VACUUM ADVANCE
PICKUP COIL LEADS   ELECTRONIC MODULE
PICKUP COIL
PERMANENT MAGNET
ALIGNING TAB
CAPACITOR
POLE PIECE

1: pole piece removal

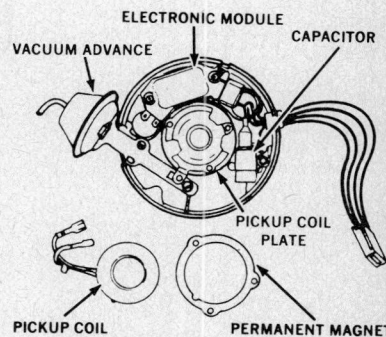

ELECTRONIC MODULE
VACUUM ADVANCE   CAPACITOR
PICKUP COIL PLATE
PICKUP COIL   PERMANENT MAGNET

2: coil & magnet removal

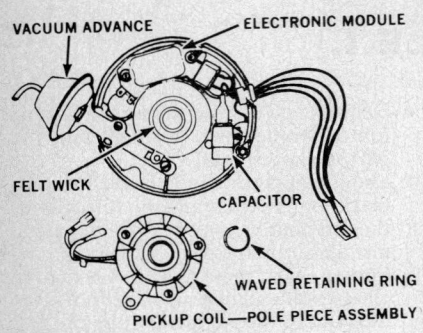

3: pick-up coil removal

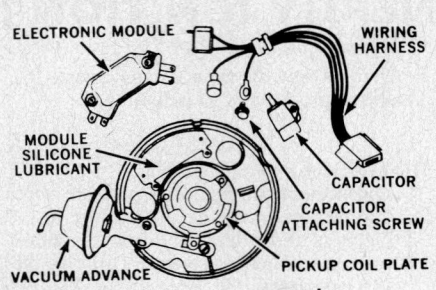

4: module & harness removal

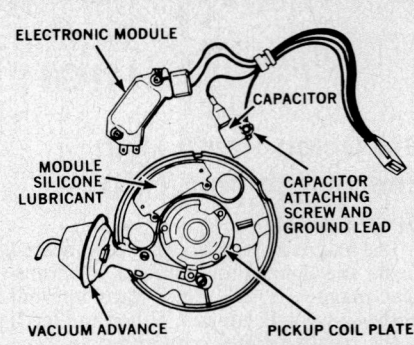

5: module & harness installation

3 Remove the driven gear from the shaft.
4 Reverse the above procedure to install.

MAINSHAFT REPLACEMENT
1 With the driven gear and rotor removed, gently pull the mainshaft out of the housing.

2 Remove the advance springs, weights and slide the weight base plate off the mainshaft.
3 Reverse the above procedure to install.

POLE PIECE, MAGNET OR PICK-UP COIL REPLACEMENT
1 With the mainshaft out of its housing, remove the three retaining screws,

pole piece and magnet and/or pick-up coil.
2 Reverse the removal procedure to install making sure that the pole piece teeth do not contact the timer core teeth by installing and rotating the mainshaft. Loosen the three screws and realign the pole piece as necessary.

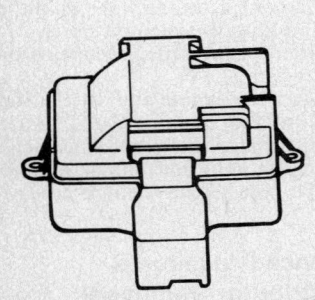

Coil Cover

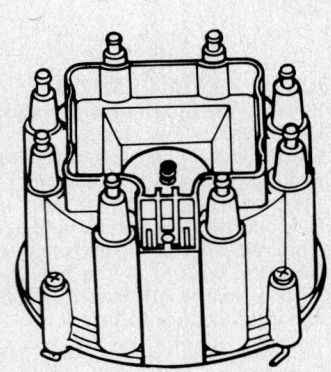

Cap

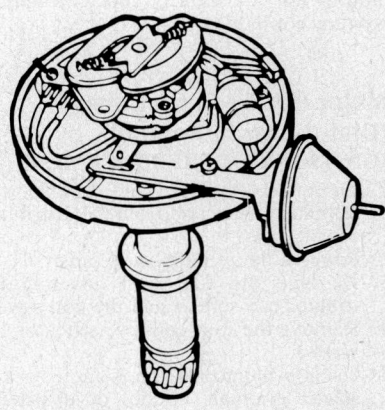

Distributor

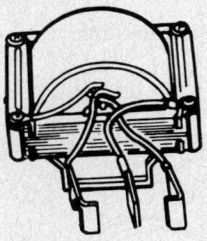

Coil

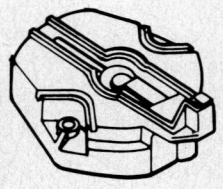

Rotor

TROUBLESHOOTING
GM DELCO-REMY MAGNETIC PULSE IGNITION

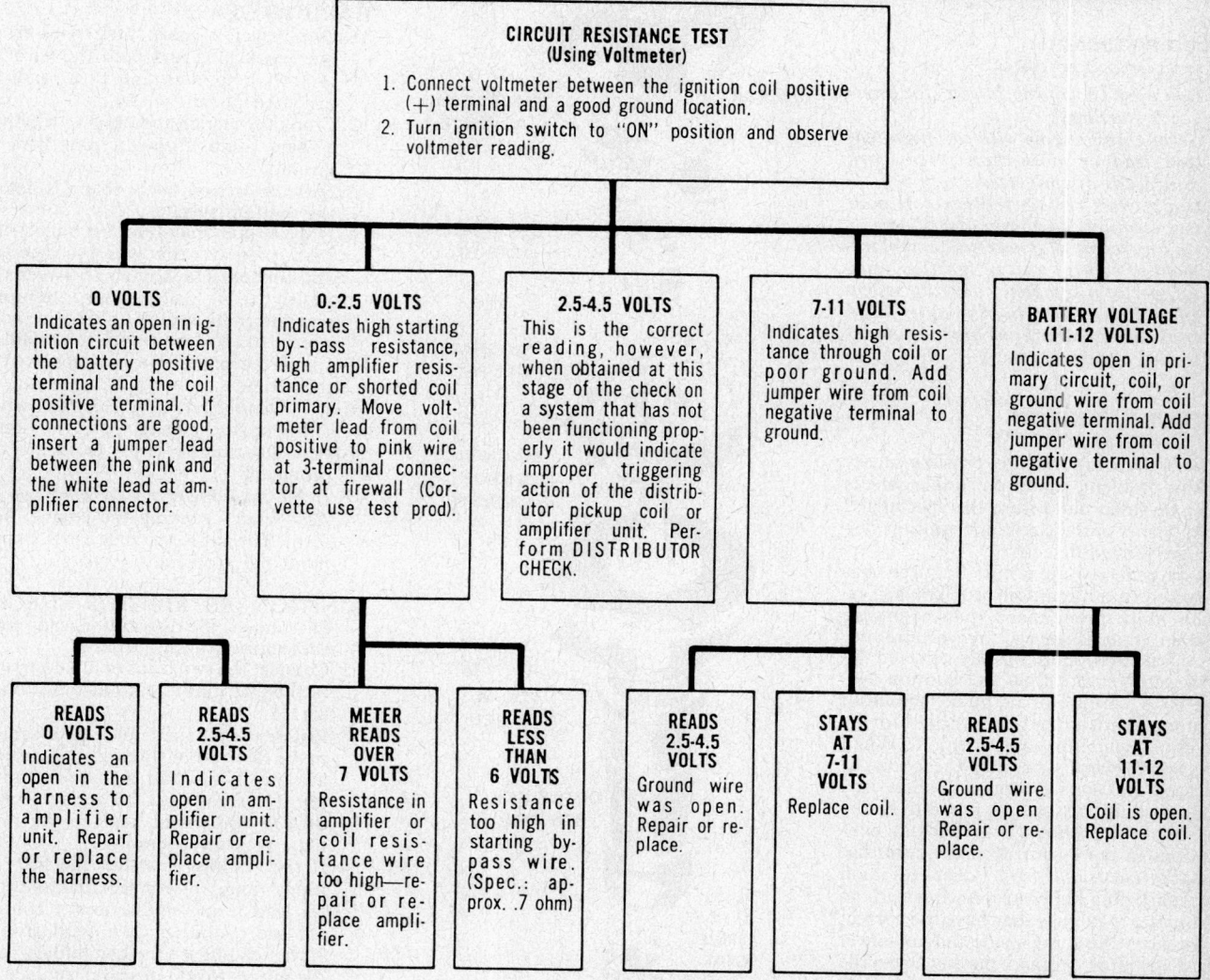

CIRCUIT RESISTANCE TEST
(Using Voltmeter)
1. Connect voltmeter between the ignition coil positive (+) terminal and a good ground location.
2. Turn ignition switch to "ON" position and observe voltmeter reading.

0 VOLTS
Indicates an open in ignition circuit between the battery positive terminal and the coil positive terminal. If connections are good, insert a jumper lead between the pink and the white lead at amplifier connector.

0.-2.5 VOLTS
Indicates high starting by-pass resistance, high amplifier resistance or shorted coil primary. Move voltmeter lead from coil positive to pink wire at 3-terminal connector at firewall (Corvette use test prod).

2.5-4.5 VOLTS
This is the correct reading, however, when obtained at this stage of the check on a system that has not been functioning properly it would indicate improper triggering action of the distributor pickup coil or amplifier unit. Perform DISTRIBUTOR CHECK.

7-11 VOLTS
Indicates high resistance through coil or poor ground. Add jumper wire from coil negative terminal to ground.

BATTERY VOLTAGE (11-12 VOLTS)
Indicates open in primary circuit, coil, or ground wire from coil negative terminal. Add jumper wire from coil negative terminal to ground.

READS 0 VOLTS
Indicates an open in the harness to amplifier unit. Repair or replace the harness.

READS 2.5-4.5 VOLTS
Indicates open in amplifier unit. Repair or replace amplifier.

METER READS OVER 7 VOLTS
Resistance in amplifier or coil resistance wire too high—repair or replace amplifier.

READS LESS THAN 6 VOLTS
Resistance too high in starting by-pass wire. (Spec.: approx. .7 ohm)

READS 2.5-4.5 VOLTS
Ground wire was open. Repair or replace.

STAYS AT 7-11 VOLTS
Replace coil.

READS 2.5-4.5 VOLTS
Ground wire was open. Repair or replace.

STAYS AT 11-12 VOLTS
Coil is open. Replace coil.

GM DELCO-REMY MAGNETIC PULSE IGNITION

GM Delco-Remy Magnetic Pulse Ignition System

OPERATION

The ignition primary circuit is connected from the battery, through the ignition switch, through the ignition pulse amplifier assembly, through the primary side of the ignition coil, and back to the amplifier housing where it is grounded externally. The secondary circuit is the same as in conventional ignition systems: the secondary side of the coil, the coil wire to the distributor, the rotor, the spark plug wires and the spark plugs.

The magnetic pulse distributor is also connected to the ignition pulse amplifier. As the distributor shaft rotates, the distributor rotating pole piece turns inside the stationary pole piece. As the rotating pole piece turns inside the stationary pole piece, the eight teeth on the rotating pole piece align with the eight teeth on the stationary pole piece eight times during each distributor revolution (two crankshaft revolutions since the distributor runs at one-half crankshaft speed). As the rotating pole piece teeth move close to, and align with, the teeth on the stationary pole piece, the magnetic rotating pole piece induces voltage into the magnetic pole piece through the stationary pole piece. This voltage pulse is sent to the ignition pulse amplifier from the magnetic pole piece. When the pulse enters the amplifier, it signals the ignition pulse amplifier to interrupt the ignition primary circuit. This causes the primary circuit to collapse and begins the induction of the magnetic lines of force from the primary side of the coil into the secondary side of the coil. This induction provides the required voltage to fire the spark plugs.

The advantages of this system are that the transistors in the ignition pulse amplifier can make and break the primary ignition circuit much faster than conventional ignition points. Higher primary voltage also can be utilized since this system can be made to handle higher voltage without adverse effects, whereas ignition breaker points cannot. The shorter switching time of this system allows longer coil primary circuit saturation time and longer induction time when the primary circuit collapses. This increased time allows the primary circuit to build up more current and the secondary circuit to discharge more current.

Troubleshooting
CHILTON CAUTIONS:
1 *Don't use 18 volts or 24 volts for emergency starting.*
2 *Never crank engine with coil high-tension lead or more than three spark plug leads disconnected.*
3 *Don't short circuit between coil positive terminal and ground.*
4 *On any repair that necessitates replacement of control unit or ignition resistor, perform complete charging system check before releasing the unit. Basic cause of trouble may be high or uncontrolled charging rate.*

ENGINE SURGE OR INTERMITTENT MISS
Since there are so many possible causes for this problem, all other possible defects must be ruled out before the specialized components of the electronic ignition system are judged defective.

As a general rule, a miss or surge that is caused by an ignition problem will be much more pronounced than a similar problem that is caused by carburetion. Also, carburetion is usually affected by temperature more than the ignition system is. A carburetor or intake manifold vacuum leak is often compensated for by the choke when the engine is cold. When the engine warms up and the choke is released, the engine surge will show up.

If the ignition system is found to be the source of the problem, first check all connections in the system to make sure that they are *clean and tight*. Check the coil and spark plug high-tension wires with an ohmmeter to be sure they have the correct resistance. Check the inside and outside of the distributor cap and the tower on the ignition coil for cracks which would allow the high voltage intended for the spark plugs to short to ground.

If none of the above checks uncovers a defective component, the distributor pickup coil leads may be reversed in the

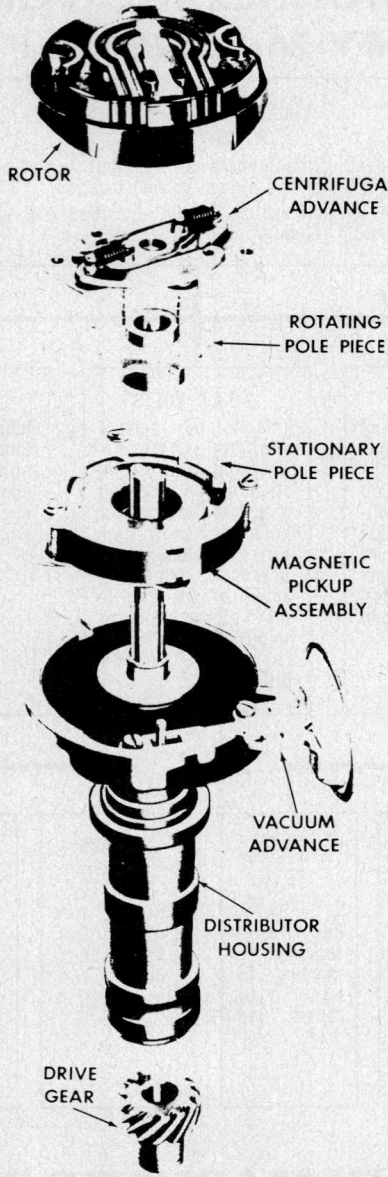

GM Delco-Remy Magnetic Pulse distributor and components

ROTOR

CENTRIFUGAL ADVANCE

ROTATING POLE PIECE

STATIONARY POLE PIECE

MAGNETIC PICKUP ASSEMBLY

VACUUM ADVANCE

DISTRIBUTOR HOUSING

DRIVE GEAR

connector, or the pick-up coil itself may have an intermittent open.

ENGINE WILL NOT START OR IS HARD TO START
1 Disconnect a spark plug wire from one spark plug and hold the wire ¼ in. from a good ground with a pair of insulated pliers.
2 Crank the engine and observe whether a spark jumps from the plug wire to ground.
3 *If spark occurs,* the problem is not in the ignition system.
4 *If spark does not occur,* reconnect the spark plug wire that was disconnected and connect a tachometer between the positive (+) coil primary terminal and the pink wire in the 3-wire connector to the ignition pulse amplifier.
5 Crank the engine over and observe the tachometer.
6 *If the tachometer needle deflects* while cranking the engine, perform "Ignition Distributor Test" to locate the problem.
7 *If the tachometer needle does not deflect* while cranking the engine, perform "Circuit Resistance Test" to pinpoint the problem.

IGNITION DISTRIBUTOR CHECK
1 Disconnect the distributor leads from the engine wiring harness.
2 Connect the two leads of an ohmmeter to the distributor leads at the connector.
3 Rotate the magnetic pick-up assembly in the distributor through full vacuum advance travel and read the ohmmeter. If the reading is not within a range of 500–700 ohms, replace the magnetic pick-up assembly.
4 If the reading is within the 500–700 ohms range, disconnect one ohmmeter lead from the distributor connector and connect it to a good ground. If the reading is less than infinity (needle moves to end of scale), replace the magnetic pick-up assembly.
5 If the reading is infinite, and there was no spark when the spark plug wire was disconnected from the plug, the amplifier is defective.

TROUBLESHOOTING
GM DELCO-REMY CRANKSHAFT SENSOR IGNITION

* Calibrated spark gap tool. If spark occurs, HEI output is OK.

ENGINE DOES NOT START (CRANKS OK - BATTERY 12 VOLTS OR MORE)

Check EST fuse in fuse panel

FUSE OK ← → FUSE BLOWN

* Check for spark at plug with AC/ST-125 or J-26792

Disconnect 3 wire connector near controller assembly. Install new fuse. Turn ignition on.

NO SPARK — SPARK IS OK

FUSE OK ← → FUSE BLOWS

Check distributor position and reference timing. If no trouble found, trouble is not ignition. Check fuel and plugs.

Locate and repair short circuit in red wire from connector on controller assembly to crankshaft sensor.

Locate and repair short circuit in pnk dbl blk wire from 3 wire connector through instrument panel harness to fuse panel.

Inspect crankshaft sensor, harness and disc for damage. Check sensor alignment and clearance at disc. Check ground screw (black wire) in distributor. If connection is OK, turn ignition key to "RUN" and check for battery voltage at locations listed below. Look at circuit diagram for wire connections when more information is needed.

1. Ignition wire (blk pnk str) at connector on distributor - 12 volts or more, OK. Less than 12 volts, check ignition wire from distributor to ignition switch for loose connections or open circuit, also check ignition switch.
2. Terminal J (2 wires, pnk and red) in connector at controller assembly - 12 volts or more, OK. Less than 12 volts, check pink wire for loose connection or open circuit from connector at controller to 3 wire connector near controller then pnk/dbl blk str wire through instrument panel harness to fuse panel. (See circuit diagram).
3. Tan wire in 2 wire connector near distributor. Do not disconnect. Voltage should be .5 to 2 volts while cranking.

VOLTAGES OK ← → VOLTAGE NOT OK

Check distributor cap, rotor, coil and module. Replace part that checks bad.

Check voltage at terminal C (tan wire) in connector at controller assembly. Voltage should be .5 to 2 volts while cranking.

VOLTAGE OK — VOLTAGE NOT OK

Check tan wire from controller assembly to 2 wire connector near distributor for loose connection or open circuit. Repair or replace as required.

Check voltage at terminal D (lt blu wire) in connector at controller assembly while cranking. Record reading then check voltage again with crankshaft sensor disconnected and placed so that it won't be damaged.

VOLTAGES NOT THE SAME (.5 to 2 VOLTS DIFFERENT) ← → SAME VOLTAGES

Replace controller assembly.

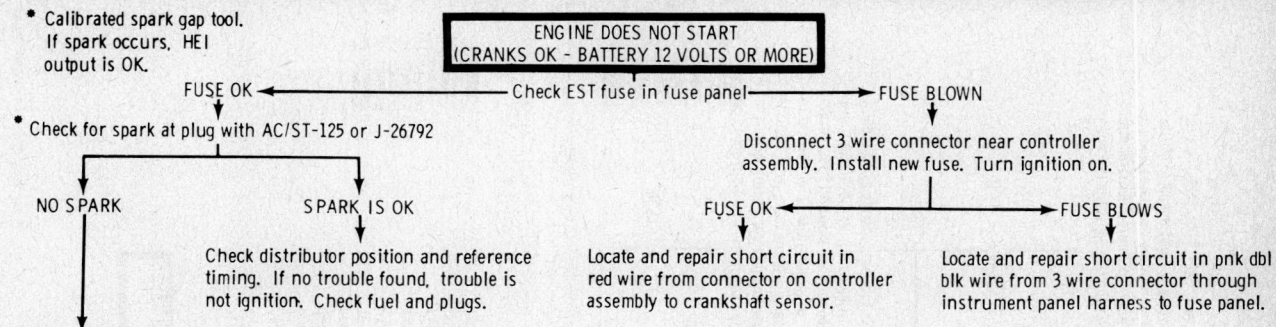

RED 12 VOLT — SLOT
SHIELD 0 VOLT
PPL 8-10 VOLTS — LT BLU 8-10 VOLTS

Turn ignition key to "RUN" and check voltage at 12 volt terminal and at shield terminal in crankshaft sensor harness connector.

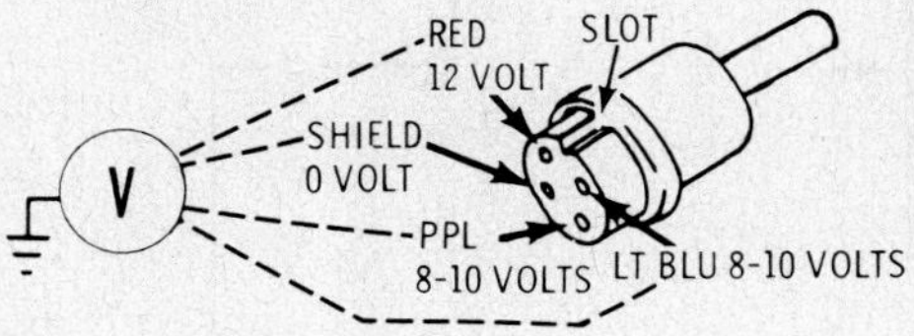

VOLTAGE OK (11V OR MORE) SHIELD, ZERO VOLTS ← → VOLTAGE NOT OK

Replace harness

Turn ignition key to "RUN" and check voltage at both 8-10 volt terminals.

VOLTAGES OK — VOLTAGE(S) NOT OK

Replace crankshaft sensor.

Check voltage at controller assembly connector with ignition key in "RUN". Reference 8-10 volts terminal D (lt blu), Position 8-10 volts terminal E (ppl).

VOLTAGE OK — VOLTAGE(S) NOT OK

Replace harness

Replace controller assembly.

B269

TROUBLESHOOTING
GM DELCO-REMY CRANKSHAFT SENSOR IGNITION

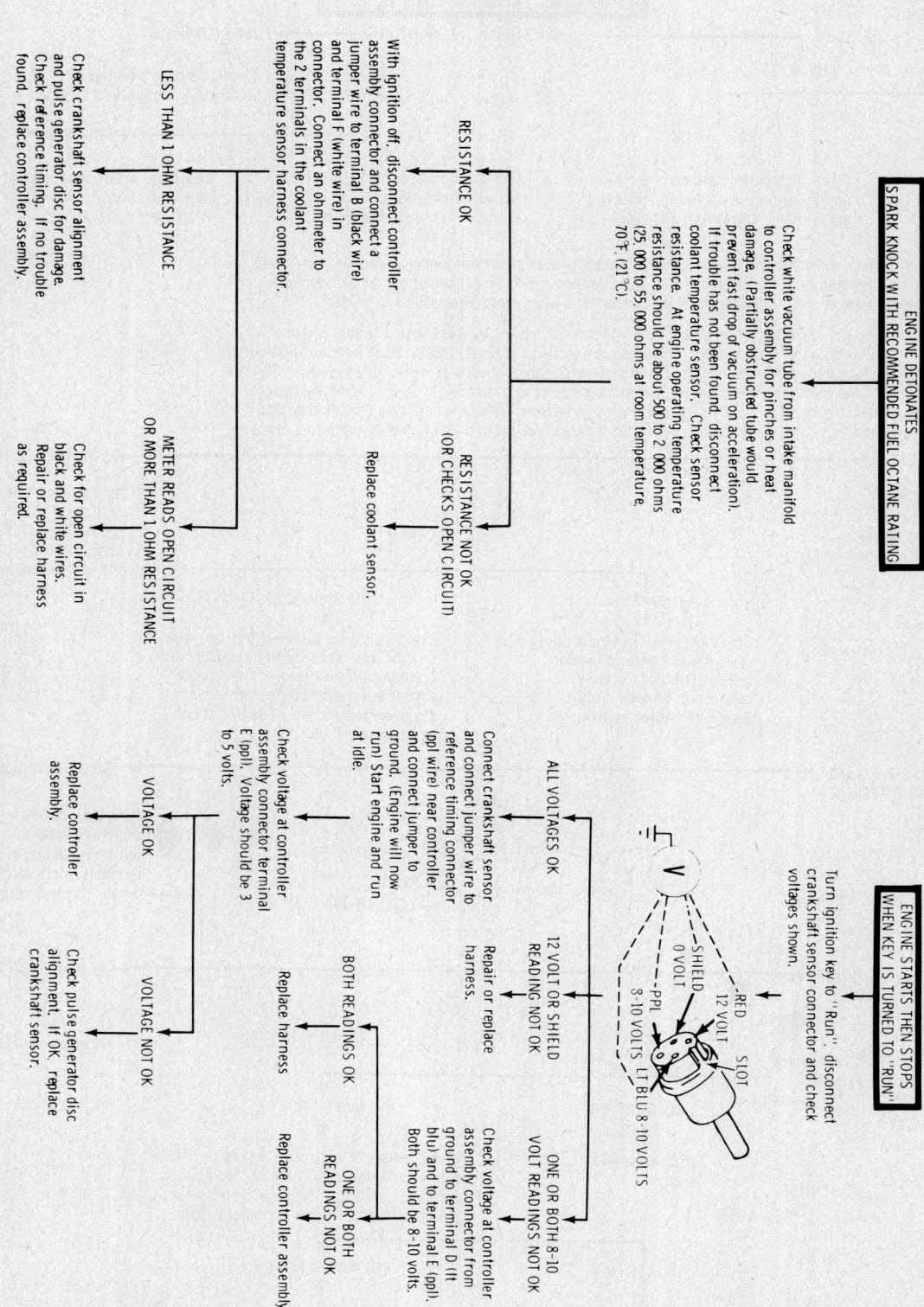

SPARK KNOCK WITH RECOMMENDED FUEL OCTANE RATING
ENGINE DETONATES

Check white vacuum tube from intake manifold to controller assembly for pinches or heat damage. (Partially obstructed tube would prevent fast drop of vacuum on acceleration). If trouble has not been found, disconnect coolant temperature sensor. Check sensor resistance. At engine operating temperature resistance should be about 500 to 2,000 ohms (25,000 to 55,000 ohms at room temperature. 70°F (21°C).

RESISTANCE OK

With ignition off, disconnect controller assembly connector and connect a jumper wire to terminal B (black wire) and terminal F (white wire) in connector. Connect an ohmmeter to the 2 terminals in the coolant temperature sensor harness connector.

RESISTANCE NOT OK (OR CHECKS OPEN CIRCUIT)

Replace coolant sensor.

LESS THAN 1 OHM RESISTANCE

Check crankshaft sensor alignment and pulse generator disc for damage. Check reference timing. If no trouble found, replace controller assembly.

METER READS OPEN CIRCUIT OR MORE THAN 1 OHM RESISTANCE

Check for open circuit in black and white wires. Repair or replace harness as required.

ENGINE STARTS THEN STOPS WHEN KEY IS TURNED TO "RUN"

Turn ignition key to "Run", disconnect crankshaft sensor connector and check voltages shown.

SHIELD 0 VOLT
RED 12 VOLT
PPL 8-10 VOLTS
LT BLU 8-10 VOLTS
SLOT

ALL VOLTAGES OK

Connect crankshaft sensor and connect jumper wire to reference timing connector (ppl wire) near controller and connect jumper to ground. (Engine will now run) Start engine and run at idle.

12 VOLT OR SHIELD READING NOT OK

Repair or replace harness.

ONE OR BOTH 8-10 VOLT READINGS NOT OK

Check voltage at controller assembly connector from ground to terminal D (lt blu) and to terminal E (ppl). Both should be 8-10 volts.

BOTH READINGS OK

Replace harness

ONE OR BOTH READINGS NOT OK

Replace controller assembly

Check voltage at controller assembly connector terminal E (ppl). Voltage should be 3 to 5 volts.

VOLTAGE OK

Replace controller assembly.

VOLTAGE NOT OK

Check pulse generator disc alignment. If OK, replace crankshaft sensor.

TROUBLESHOOTING
GM DELCO-REMY CRANKSHAFT SENSOR IGNITION

**HARD STARTING, ROUGH ENGINE, POOR PERFORMANCE
(BATTERY FULLY CHARGED)**

1. Check fuel system, choke, spark plugs and cables.
2. Make sure harness connections to distributor, coolant temperature sensor and controller assembly are good.
3. Inspect crankshaft sensor for alignment and clearance between sensor and pulse generator disc. (.045" to .055" top and bottom). Make sure harness and connector are good. Check disc for proper installation. Button on disc should be visible in hole in pulley.
4. Check all vacuum hoses for pinches, or disconnects. Check white vacuum tube from intake manifold to controller.
5. With engine at idle, transmission in park and parking brakes applied, connect voltmeter to ground and touch probe to ignition wire (blk-pnk str) in connector on distributor. Voltage should be 12 volts or more. If less, check for loose connection between distributor connector and ignition switch.

6. Connect voltmeter to ground and touch probe to terminal J in controller assembly connector (two wires, pink and red). Voltage should be 12 volts or more. If less, check for loose connection through instrument panel extension harness connector to fuse panel. (Refer to circuit diagram).
7. Remove distributor cap, check rotor and cap for signs of arcing. Check ground wire (screw) in distributor. Check module with J-24642. Check distributor position and reference timing.
    IF REFERENCE TIMING CANNOT BE SET to 20 degrees or if engine will not run at fast idle or timing light gives double flash causing timing mark to change position, replace crankshaft sensor.
8. If trouble has not been found, go to step 9.

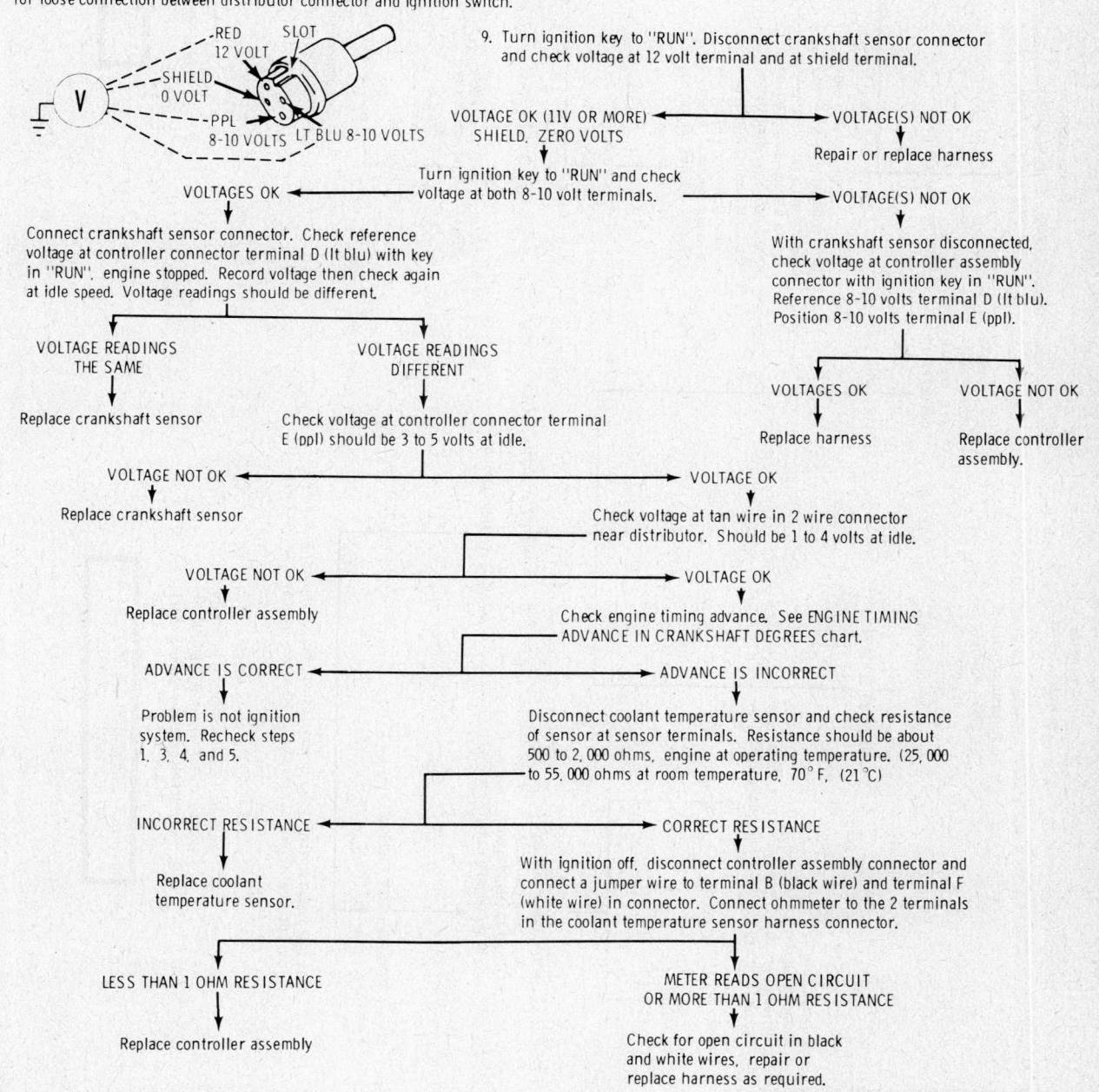

RED
12 VOLT
SLOT
SHIELD
0 VOLT
PPL
8-10 VOLTS
LT BLU 8-10 VOLTS

9. Turn ignition key to "RUN". Disconnect crankshaft sensor connector and check voltage at 12 volt terminal and at shield terminal.

VOLTAGE OK (11V OR MORE) ◄———————————————► VOLTAGE(S) NOT OK
SHIELD, ZERO VOLTS
Repair or replace harness

Turn ignition key to "RUN" and check voltage at both 8-10 volt terminals.

VOLTAGES OK ◄———————————————► VOLTAGE(S) NOT OK

Connect crankshaft sensor connector. Check reference voltage at controller connector terminal D (lt blu) with key in "RUN", engine stopped. Record voltage then check again at idle speed. Voltage readings should be different.

With crankshaft sensor disconnected, check voltage at controller assembly connector with ignition key in "RUN". Reference 8-10 volts terminal D (lt blu). Position 8-10 volts terminal E (ppl).

VOLTAGE READINGS THE SAME   VOLTAGE READINGS DIFFERENT

Replace crankshaft sensor

Check voltage at controller connector terminal E (ppl) should be 3 to 5 volts at idle.

VOLTAGES OK   VOLTAGE NOT OK

Replace harness   Replace controller assembly.

VOLTAGE NOT OK ◄———————————————► VOLTAGE OK

Replace crankshaft sensor

Check voltage at tan wire in 2 wire connector near distributor. Should be 1 to 4 volts at idle.

VOLTAGE NOT OK ◄———————————————► VOLTAGE OK

Replace controller assembly

Check engine timing advance. See ENGINE TIMING ADVANCE IN CRANKSHAFT DEGREES chart.

ADVANCE IS CORRECT   ADVANCE IS INCORRECT

Problem is not ignition system. Recheck steps 1, 3, 4, and 5.

Disconnect coolant temperature sensor and check resistance of sensor at sensor terminals. Resistance should be about 500 to 2,000 ohms, engine at operating temperature. (25,000 to 55,000 ohms at room temperature, 70°F, (21°C).

INCORRECT RESISTANCE ◄———————————————► CORRECT RESISTANCE

Replace coolant temperature sensor.

With ignition off, disconnect controller assembly connector and connect a jumper wire to terminal B (black wire) and terminal F (white wire) in connector. Connect ohmmeter to the 2 terminals in the coolant temperature sensor harness connector.

LESS THAN 1 OHM RESISTANCE   METER READS OPEN CIRCUIT OR MORE THAN 1 OHM RESISTANCE

Replace controller assembly

Check for open circuit in black and white wires, repair or replace harness as required.

ELECTRONIC IGNITIONS
GM DELCO-REMY CRANKSHAFT SENSOR IGNITION

TROUBLESHOOTING
GM DELCO-REMY CRANKSHAFT SENSOR IGNITION

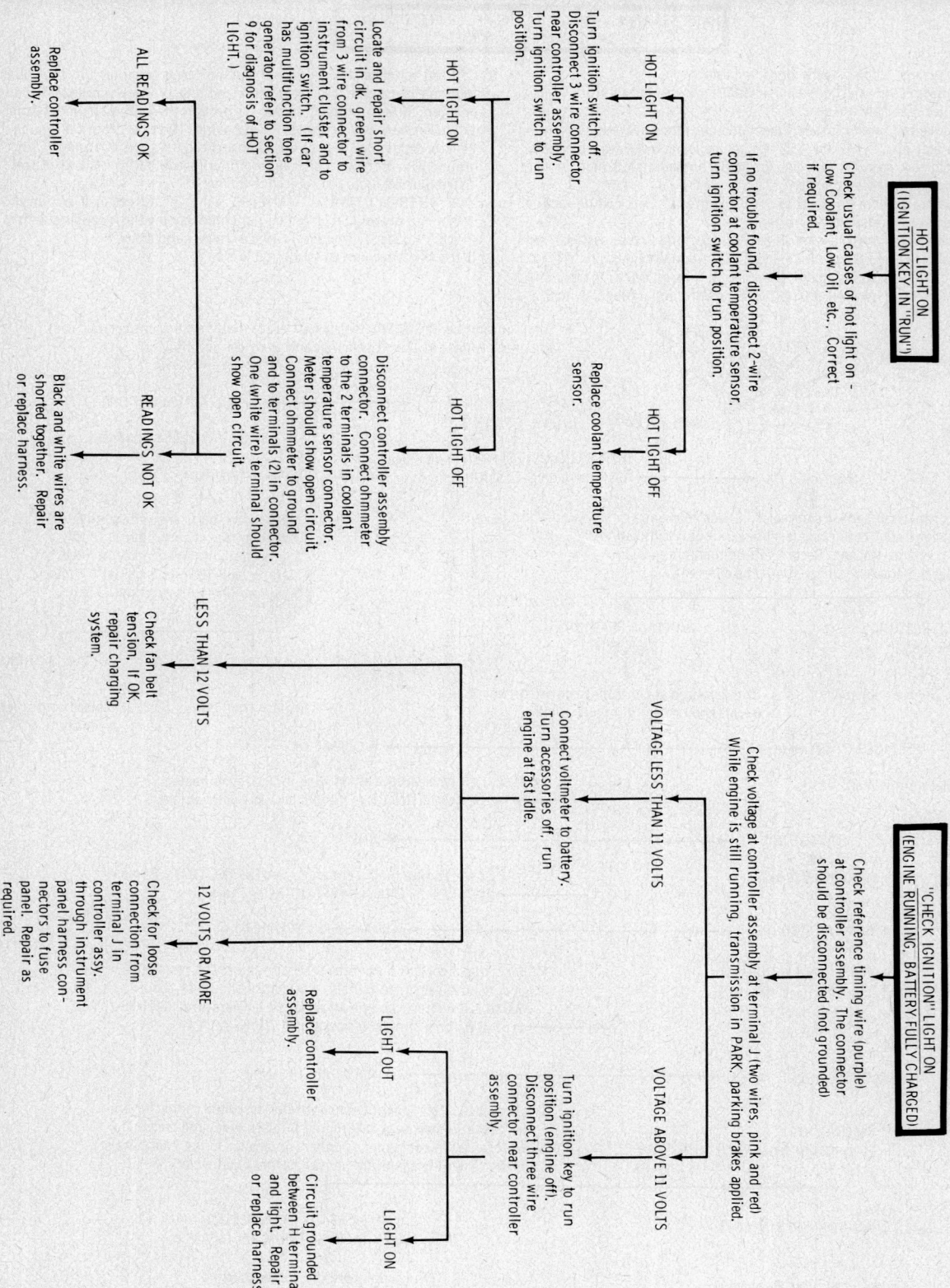

Hot Light and Check Ignition Light diagnosis

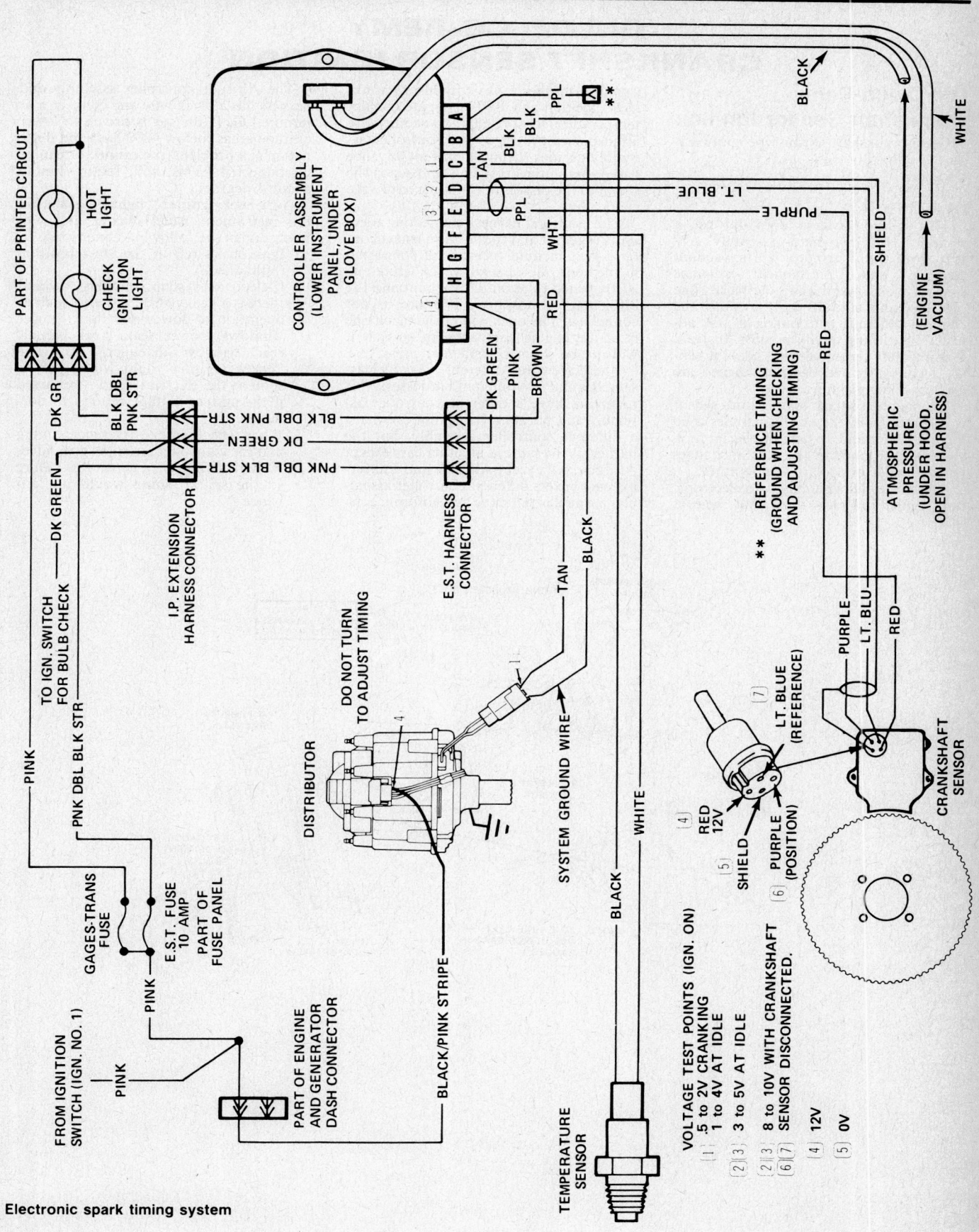

Electronic spark timing system

GM DELCO-REMY
CRANKSHFT SENSOR IGNITION

GM Delco-Remy Crankshaft Sensor Ignition

GM's crankshaft sensor type ignition is on the following cars:

Cadillac

Oldsmobile

OPERATION

This ignition system does not use a standard HEI distributor assembly. Absent from the distributor are a vacuum advance unit, mechanical advance weights pick up coil and pole piece. The cap, coil and module are the same, the rotor is different and timing is not adjusted by turning the distributor. Instead, a crankshaft sensor, engine coolant sensor, a controller and electrical harness are used to control timing.

The engine coolant temperature sensor is different from the on-off switches used in other cars and is part of the ignition system Resistance in the sensor changes with changes in coolant temperature.

The controller assembly is an electronic unit, under the glove box, that recieves signals from the crankshaft sensor (crankshaft position and RPM), engine coolant temperature sensor, engine vacuum and atmospheric pressure. The controller assembly decides the most efficient advance based on the sensor signals and sends the signal to the distributor module to fire the spark plugs.

The electrical harness connecting these units together and to the car harness contains two vacuum tubes, both connected to the controller assembly; the white one is connected to manifold vacuum and the black one (atmospheric pressure) is not connected. The open end of the black one is in the engine compartment so that it will not be open to inside car pressure.

There are three different controller assemblies and two different harnesses. Altitude cars have a different controller assembly and harness. California cars have a different controller assembly, but the harness is the same as all other cars except Altitude. All except Altitude and California cars have a different controller assembly; harness is the same as California cars.

The Altitude controller assembly and harness has a black wire and connector at terminal G. If the car is driven to lower altitude areas (below 4000 feet) and detonation is a problem, the connector can be disconnected. This will retard timing about 4 degrees.

A "Check Ignition" light is located in the instrument panel cluster and will light, under the following conditions:

1. Ignition switch in the start position (bulb check).
2. If electrical system voltage is low and there is a heavy electrical load such as operation of power door lock, power windows, power seat, cigar lighter, rear window defogger, etc. The "check ignition" light will go off as soon as the electrical load is removed if the system voltage returns to normal.
3. When checking the reference timing and the controller circuit is grounded.
4. If there should be a controller failure so the spark timing would not advance.

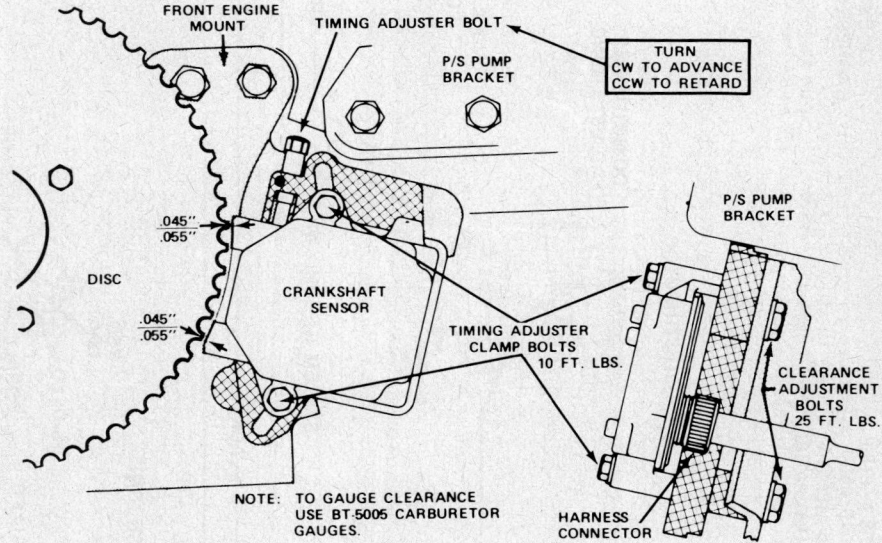

1977 TORONADO IGNITION SYSTEM

Description

The Toronado ignition system does not use a standard HEI distributor. The distributor does not have a vacuum advance unit, mechanical advance weights or pick up coil and pole piece. Although the cap, coil and module are the same, *the rotor is not and timing is not adjusted by turning the distributor.* This system uses a crankshaft sensor, engine coolant sensor, a controller and electrical harness.

The engine coolant temperature sensor is different from the on-off switches used in other cars. It is part of the ignition system and resistance in the sensor changes with changes in coolant temperature. (Resistance lowers when temperature rises.)

The controller assembly is an electronic unit, mounted under the glove box, that receives signals from the crankshaft sensor (crankshaft position and RPM), engine coolant temperature sensor, engine vacuum and atmospheric pressure. The controller assembly decides the most efficient advance based on the input signals

and sends the signal to the distributor module to fire the spark plugs.

The electrical harness connecting these units together and to the car harness contains two vacuum tubes. They both connect to the controller assembly; the white one is connected to manifold vacuum and the black one (atmospheric pressure) is not connected. The open end of the black one is in the engine compartment so that it will not be open to inside car pressure.

There are two different controller assemblies. The controller assembly used on California cars have different advance specifications.

A "Check Ignition" light is located in the Instrument Panel Cluster and will come on under the following conditions:

1 Ignition switch in the start position—bulb check.
2 If electrical system voltage is low and there is a heavy electrical load such as operation of power door lock, power windows, power seat, cigar lighter, rear window defogger, etc.

NOTE: The "check ignition" light will go off as soon as the electrical load is

removed if the system voltage returns to normal.

3 When checking the reference timing and the reference timing connector is grounded.
4 If there should be a controller failure so. the spark timing would not advance.

Adjusting Distributor Position

1 Remove ignition feed wire (black with pink stripe) from distributor to prevent arcing.
2 Remove distributor cap.
3 Turn engine with starter until rotor points toward rear of engine and number one piston is almost on T.D.C. (0 degrees on timing indicator).
4 Use a socket on crankshaft bolt head to turn crankshaft to 0 degrees.
5 White mark on side of rotor should be aligned with white pointer in distributor. If not, loosen distributor clamp bolt and turn distributor to align.
6 Tighten distributor clamp bolt. This is final distributor position.
7 Install distributor cap and wiring connectors.

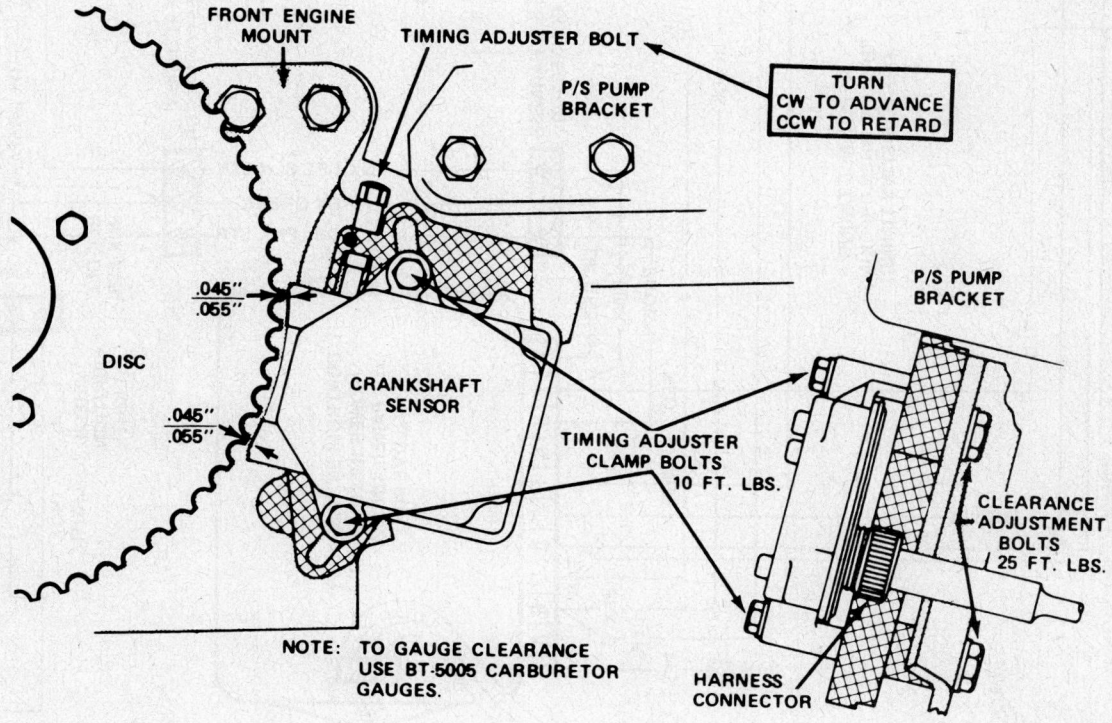

Crankshaft Timing Sensor

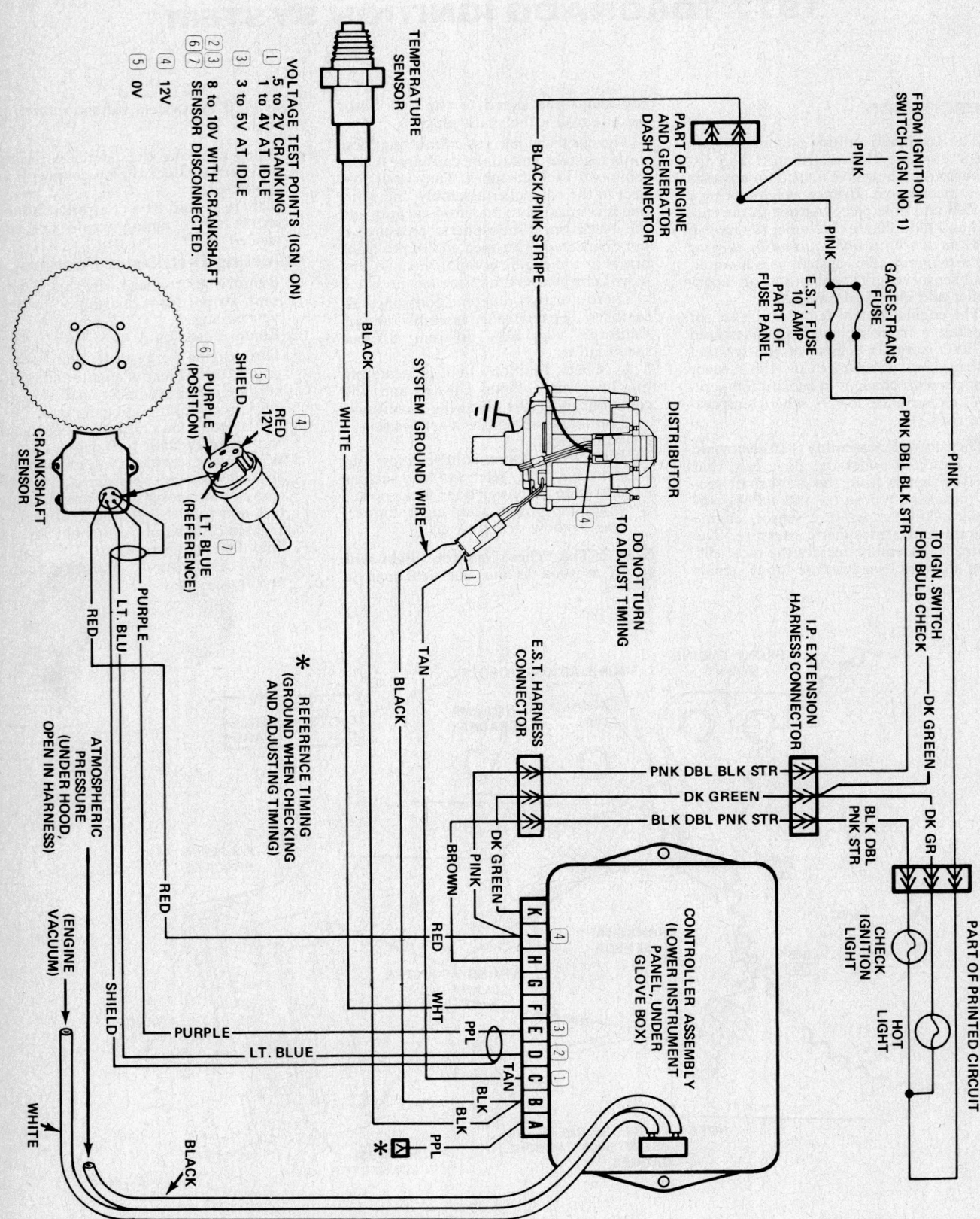

Ignition System Wiring—Toronado 1977

IGNITION SYSTEM DIAGNOSIS—TORONADO 1977

• Calibrated spark gap tool.
  If spark occurs, HEI
  output is OK.

ENGINE DOES NOT START
(CRANKS OK - BATTERY 12 VOLTS OR MORE)

FUSE OK ← Check EST fuse in fuse panel → FUSE BLOWN

• Check for spark at plug with AC/ST-125 or J-26792

Disconnect 3 wire connector near controller
assembly. Install new fuse. Turn ignition on.

NO SPARK   SPARK IS OK

FUSE OK ←   → FUSE BLOWS

Check distributor position and reference
timing. If no trouble found, trouble is
not ignition. Check fuel and plugs.

Locate and repair short circuit in
red wire from connector on controller
assembly to crankshaft sensor.

Locate and repair short circuit in pnk dbl
blk wire from 3 wire connector through
instrument panel harness to fuse panel.

Inspect crankshaft sensor, harness and disc for damage. Check sensor alignment and clearance at disc. Check ground
screw (black wire) in distributor. If connection is OK, turn ignition key to "RUN" and check for battery voltage at
locations listed below. Look at circuit diagram for wire connections when more information is needed.

1. Ignition wire (blk pnk str) at connector on distributor - 12 volts or more, OK. Less than 12 volts, check
   ignition wire from distributor to ignition switch for loose connections or open circuit, also check ignition switch.
2. Terminal J (2 wires, pnk and red) in connector at controller assembly - 12 volts or more, OK. Less than 12 volts,
   check pink wire for loose connection or open circuit from connector at controller to 3 wire connector near
   controller then pnk/dbl blk str wire through instrument panel harness to fuse panel. (See circuit diagram).
3. Tan wire in 2 wire connector near distributor. Do not disconnect. Voltage should be .5 to 2 volts while cranking.

VOLTAGES OK ←   → VOLTAGE NOT OK

Check distributor
cap, rotor, coil
and module. Replace
part that checks bad.

Check voltage at terminal
C (tan wire) in connector
at controller assembly.
Voltage should be .5 to 2
volts while cranking.

VOLTAGE OK   VOLTAGE NOT OK

Check tan wire from controller
assembly to 2 wire connector
near distributor for loose
connection or open circuit.
Repair or replace as required.

Check voltage at terminal D (lt blu wire)
in connector at controller assembly while
cranking. Record reading then check
voltage again with crankshaft sensor
disconnected and placed so that it won't
be damaged.

VOLTAGES NOT THE SAME ←   → SAME VOLTAGES
(.5 to 2 VOLTS DIFFERENT)

Replace controller assembly.

Turn ignition key to "RUN"
and check voltage at 12
volt terminal and at shield
terminal in crankshaft.
sensor harness connector.

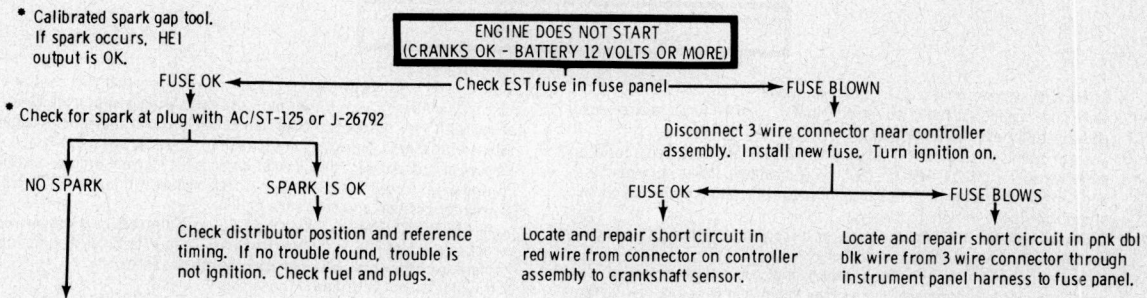

RED   SLOT
12 VOLT

SHIELD
0 VOLT

PPL
8-10 VOLTS   LT BLU 8-10 VOLTS

V

VOLTAGE OK (11V OR MORE) ←   → VOLTAGE NOT OK
SHIELD, ZERO VOLTS

Replace harness

Turn ignition key to "RUN" and check
voltage at both 8-10 volt terminals.

VOLTAGES OK   VOLTAGE(S) NOT OK

Replace crankshaft
sensor.

Check voltage at controller assembly
connector with ignition key in "RUN".
Reference 8-10 volts terminal D (lt
blu). Position 8-10 volts terminal E (ppl).

VOLTAGE OK   VOLTAGE(S) NOT OK

Replace harness

Replace controller
assembly.

IGNITION SYSTEM DIAGNOSIS—TORONADO 1977

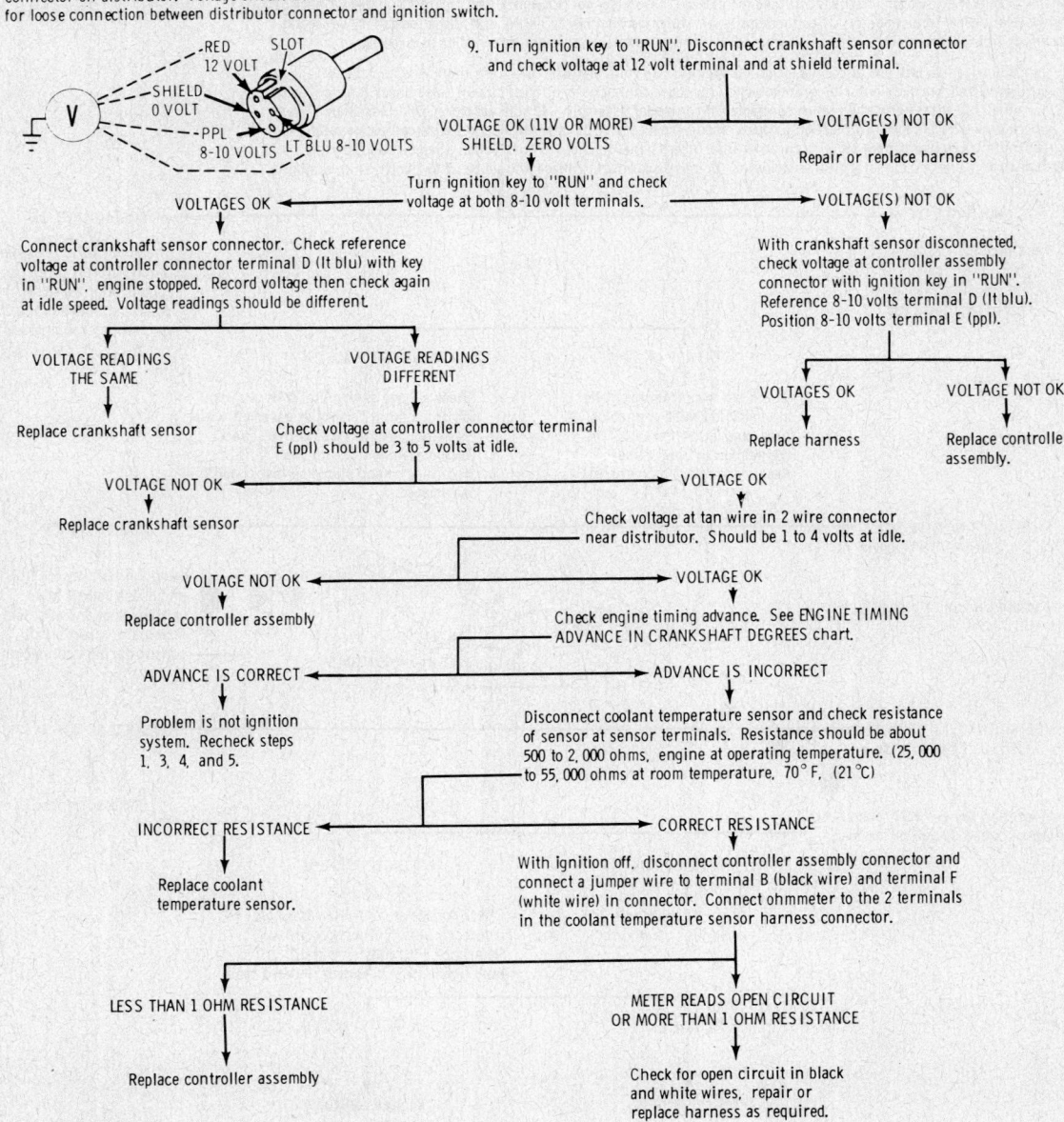

HARD STARTING, ROUGH ENGINE, POOR PERFORMANCE
(BATTERY FULLY CHARGED)

1. Check fuel system, choke, spark plugs and cables.
2. Make sure harness connections to distributor, coolant temperature sensor and controller assembly are good.
3. Inspect crankshaft sensor for alignment and clearance between sensor and pulse generator disc. (.045'' to .055'' top and bottom). Make sure harness and connector are good. Check disc for proper installation. Button on disc should be visible in hole in pulley.
4. Check all vacuum hoses for pinches, or disconnects. Check white vacuum tube from intake manifold to controller.
5. With engine at idle, transmission in park and parking brakes applied, connect voltmeter to ground and touch probe to ignition wire (blk-pnk str) in connector on distributor. Voltage should be 12 volts or more. If less, check for loose connection between distributor connector and ignition switch.
6. Connect voltmeter to ground and touch probe to terminal J in controller assembly connector (two wires, pink and red). Voltage should be 12 volts or more. If less, check for loose connection through instrument panel extension harness connector to fuse panel. (Refer to circuit diagram).
7. Remove distributor cap, check rotor and cap for signs of arcing. Check ground wire (screw) in distributor. Check module with J-24642. Check distributor position and reference timing.
   IF REFERENCE TIMING CANNOT BE SET to 20 degrees or if engine will not run at fast idle or timing light gives double flash causing timing mark to change position, replace crankshaft sensor.
8. If trouble has not been found, go to step 9.

9. Turn ignition key to "RUN". Disconnect crankshaft sensor connector and check voltage at 12 volt terminal and at shield terminal.

RED 12 VOLT   SLOT
SHIELD 0 VOLT
PPL 8-10 VOLTS   LT BLU 8-10 VOLTS

VOLTAGE OK (11V OR MORE) ◄
SHIELD, ZERO VOLTS

VOLTAGE(S) NOT OK ►
Repair or replace harness

Turn ignition key to "RUN" and check voltage at both 8-10 volt terminals.

VOLTAGES OK ◄

VOLTAGE(S) NOT OK ►

Connect crankshaft sensor connector. Check reference voltage at controller connector terminal D (lt blu) with key in "RUN", engine stopped. Record voltage then check again at idle speed. Voltage readings should be different.

With crankshaft sensor disconnected, check voltage at controller assembly connector with ignition key in "RUN". Reference 8-10 volts terminal D (lt blu). Position 8-10 volts terminal E (ppl).

VOLTAGE READINGS THE SAME   VOLTAGE READINGS DIFFERENT

VOLTAGES OK   VOLTAGE NOT OK

Replace crankshaft sensor   Check voltage at controller connector terminal E (ppl) should be 3 to 5 volts at idle.

Replace harness   Replace controller assembly.

VOLTAGE NOT OK   VOLTAGE OK
Replace crankshaft sensor

Check voltage at tan wire in 2 wire connector near distributor. Should be 1 to 4 volts at idle.

VOLTAGE NOT OK   VOLTAGE OK
Replace controller assembly

Check engine timing advance. See ENGINE TIMING ADVANCE IN CRANKSHAFT DEGREES chart.

ADVANCE IS CORRECT   ADVANCE IS INCORRECT

Problem is not ignition system. Recheck steps 1, 3, 4, and 5.

Disconnect coolant temperature sensor and check resistance of sensor at sensor terminals. Resistance should be about 500 to 2,000 ohms, engine at operating temperature. (25,000 to 55,000 ohms at room temperature, 70°F, (21°C)

INCORRECT RESISTANCE   CORRECT RESISTANCE

Replace coolant temperature sensor.

With ignition off, disconnect controller assembly connector and connect a jumper wire to terminal B (black wire) and terminal F (white wire) in connector. Connect ohmmeter to the 2 terminals in the coolant temperature sensor harness connector.

LESS THAN 1 OHM RESISTANCE   METER READS OPEN CIRCUIT OR MORE THAN 1 OHM RESISTANCE

Replace controller assembly   Check for open circuit in black and white wires, repair or replace harness as required.

IGNITION SYSTEM DIAGNOSIS—TORONADO 1977

IGNITION SYSTEM DIAGNOSIS-TORONADO CONTINUED

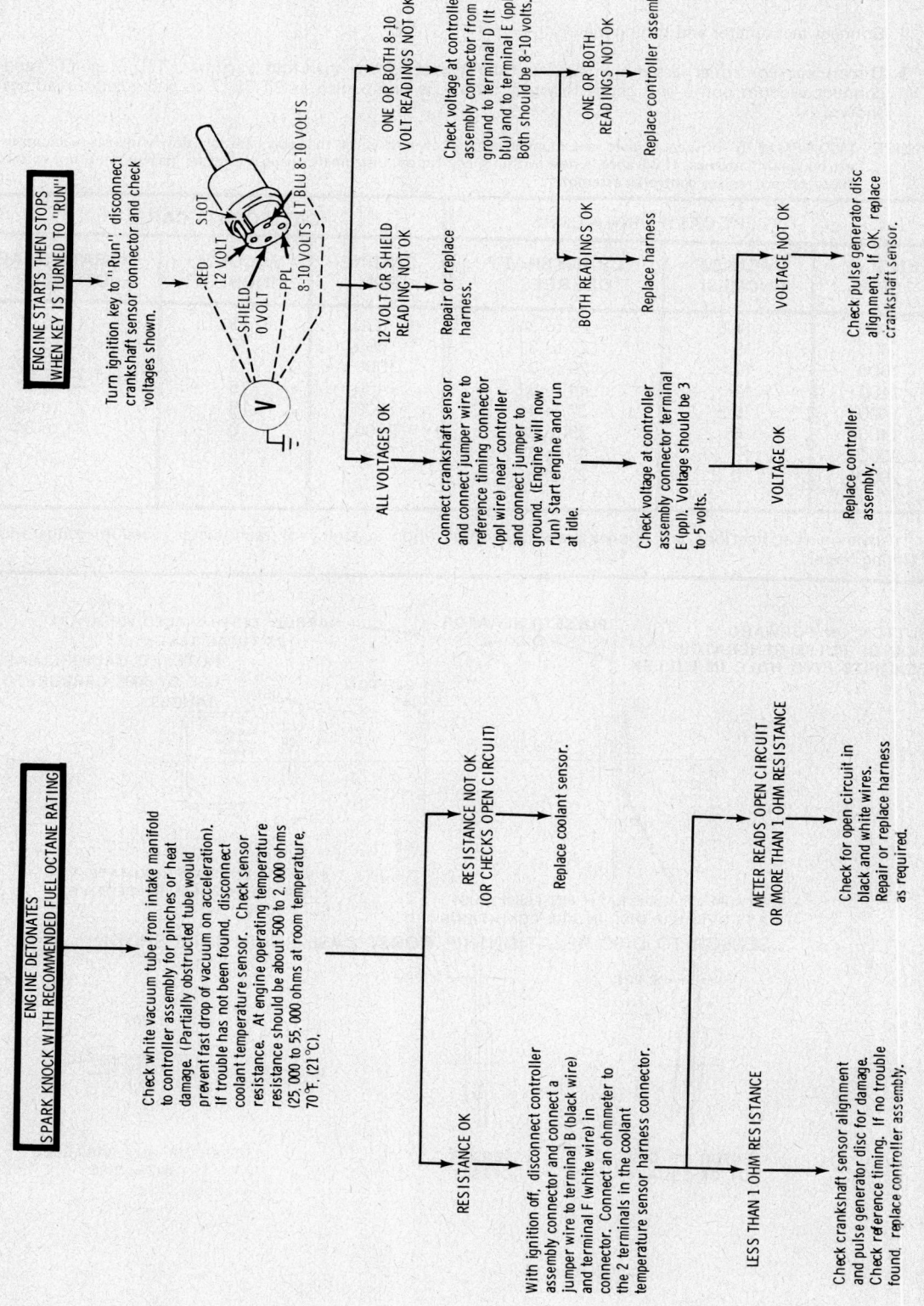

ENGINE STARTS THEN STOPS WHEN KEY IS TURNED TO "RUN"

Turn ignition key to "Run", disconnect crankshaft sensor connector and check voltages shown.

SLOT
RED 12 VOLT
SHIELD 0 VOLT
PPL 8-10 VOLTS LT BLU 8-10 VOLTS

ONE OR BOTH 8-10 VOLT READINGS NOT OK
Check voltage at controller assembly connector from ground to terminal D (lt blu) and to terminal E (ppl). Both should be 8-10 volts.

ONE OR BOTH READINGS NOT OK
Replace controller assembly.

BOTH READINGS OK
Replace harness.

12 VOLT OR SHIELD READING NOT OK
Repair or replace harness.

ALL VOLTAGES OK
Connect crankshaft sensor and connect jumper wire to reference timing connector (ppl wire) near controller and connect jumper to ground. (Engine will now run) Start engine and run at idle.

Check voltage at controller assembly connector terminal E (ppl). Voltage should be 3 to 5 volts.

VOLTAGE NOT OK
Check pulse generator disc alignment. If OK, replace crankshaft sensor.

VOLTAGE OK
Replace controller assembly.

ENGINE DETONATES
SPARK KNOCK WITH RECOMMENDED FUEL OCTANE RATING

Check white vacuum tube from intake manifold to controller assembly for pinches or heat damage. (Partially obstructed tube would prevent fast drop of vacuum on acceleration). If trouble has not been found, disconnect coolant temperature sensor. Check sensor resistance. At engine operating temperature resistance should be about 500 to 2,000 ohms (25,000 to 55,000 ohms at room temperature. 70°F. (21°C).

RESISTANCE NOT OK (OR CHECKS OPEN CIRCUIT)
Replace coolant sensor.

RESISTANCE OK
With ignition off, disconnect controller assembly connector and connect a jumper wire to terminal B (black wire) and terminal F (white wire) in connector. Connect an ohmmeter to the 2 terminals in the coolant temperature sensor harness connector.

METER READS OPEN CIRCUIT OR MORE THAN 1 OHM RESISTANCE
Check for open circuit in black and white wires. Repair or replace harness as required.

LESS THAN 1 OHM RESISTANCE
Check crankshaft sensor alignment and pulse generator disc for damage. Check reference timing. If no trouble found, replace controller assembly.

B279

IGNITION SYSTEM DIAGNOSIS—TORONADO 1977

1. Engine **MUST BE** at operating temperature.

2. Connect tachometer and timing meter.

3. Disconnect controller assembly vacuum tube (white) from manifold vacuum "T". Plug "T" and connect vacuum pump and gauge to white tube. Use pump such as BT-7517 to get vacuum readings shown.

NOTE: 1400 RPM at 15" of vacuum gives maximum advance. If advance is less than specification, slowly increase vacuum to get maximum advance. If advance is now within specification, instruments/gauges used are inaccurate. If not within specification, replace controller assembly.

EXCEPT CALIFORNIA CARS			CALIFORNIA CARS		
ENGINE RPM	VACUUM (INCHES)	*CRANKSHAFT DEGREES	ENGINE RPM	VACUUM (INCHES)	*CRANKSHAFT DEGREES
600	16.5	29 to 34	600	13.5	17 to 20
600	15	27 to 31	600	12	17 to 20
1000	12	29 to 37	1000	12	19 to 22
1400	15	44 to 61	1400	15	44 to 61
1400	10.5	37 to 41	2000	18	31 to 49
1400	6	25 to 35	2000	0	31 to 34
2000	18	44 to 53			
2000	0	28 to 31			

* Advance specifications are approximate depending upon accuracy of tachometer, vacuum gauge and timing meter.

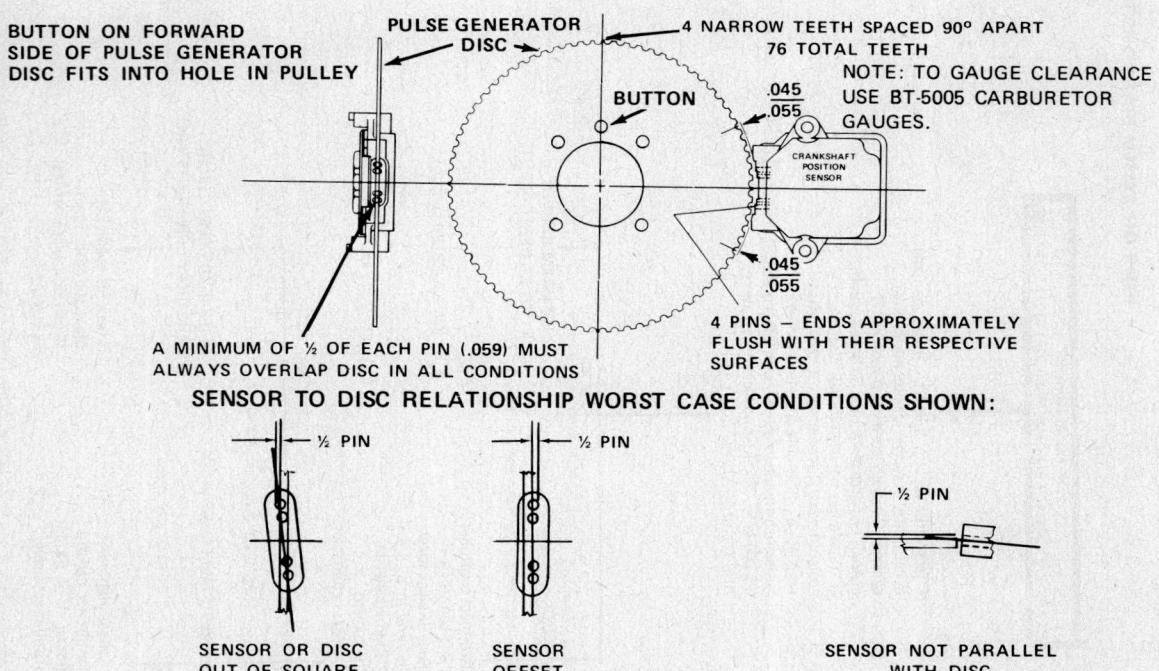

BUTTON ON FORWARD SIDE OF PULSE GENERATOR DISC FITS INTO HOLE IN PULLEY

PULSE GENERATOR DISC

4 NARROW TEETH SPACED 90° APART 76 TOTAL TEETH

BUTTON

NOTE: TO GAUGE CLEARANCE USE BT-5005 CARBURETOR GAUGES.

.045 .055

CRANKSHAFT POSITION SENSOR

.045 .055

A MINIMUM OF ½ OF EACH PIN (.059) MUST ALWAYS OVERLAP DISC IN ALL CONDITIONS

4 PINS — ENDS APPROXIMATELY FLUSH WITH THEIR RESPECTIVE SURFACES

SENSOR TO DISC RELATIONSHIP WORST CASE CONDITIONS SHOWN:

½ PIN

½ PIN

½ PIN

SENSOR OR DISC OUT OF SQUARE

SENSOR OFFSET

SENSOR NOT PARALLEL WITH DISC

8 Check reference timing.

Adjusting Ignition Timing (Magnetic probe timing meter preferred method of checking timing.)

1 With distributor adjusted to correct position, connect a jumper wire to

Reference Timing connector near controller assembly and ground other end of jumper.

2 With transmission in "Park", drive wheels blocked, and parking brake applied, start engine and run at slow idle. Timing should be at 20 degrees (Engine RPM does not affect timing, and "Check ignition" light will be on because of ground wire installed in Step 1.)

3 If timing is incorrect, stop engine, loosen timing adjuster clamp bolts and rotate timing adjuster bolt (clockwise to advance, counter-clockwise to retard). One complete turn equals about one degree.

4 Recheck timing and if OK, stop engine and tighten timing adjuster clamp bolts.

5 Remove ground wire

1978 TORONADO IGNITION SYSTEM

Description

The EST ignition system does not use a standard H.E.I. distributor. The distributor does not have a vacuum advance unit or mechanical advance weights. The rotor, ignition coil and pole piece are the same, but the pick-up coil and harness are different. There is a spark shield under the rotor to protect electronic circuits from false impulses. The system consists of the distributor, controller, temperature sensor and two separate harnesses.

The engine coolant temperature sensor is different from the on-off switches used in other cars. It is part of the ignition system and resistance in the sensor changes with changes in coolant temperature. (Resistance lowers when temperature rises.)

The controller is an electronic unit that receives signals from the distributor pick-up coil, engine vacuum and atmospheric pressure. It then decides the most efficient advance based on the input signals and sends a signal to the distributor module to fire the spark plug.

One of the electrical harnesses also contains the vacuum tube that connects to engine vacuum and to the controller in the car. The atmospheric pressure sensor in the controller is open to a port on top of the controller.

There are two different controllers. The controllers used on California cars have different advance specifications.

A "Check Ignition" light is located in the Instrument Panel Cluster and will come on under the following conditions:

1 Ignition switch in the start position—bulb check.

2 If electrical system voltage is low and there is a heavy electrical load such as operation of power door lock, power windows, power seat, cigar lighter, rear window defogger, etc.

NOTE: The "check ignition" light will go off as soon as the electrical load is removed if the system voltage returns to normal.

3 When checking the reference timing and the reference timing connector is grounded.

4 If there should be a controller failure so the spark timing would not advance. Light will be on because of ground wire installed in Step 1.

5 If timing is incorrect, loosen distributor clamp bolt. Turn distributor clockwise to advance, counterclockwise to retard. Tighten clamp bolt.

6 Remove jumper wire (installed in Step 1).

On-Car Service
Controller (Under glove box)
REMOVAL

1 Turn ignition off and disconnect connectors from controller.

2 Remove controller mounting bracket screws from lower edge of instrument panel.

3 Lower controller and disconnect vacuum connector and electrical connectors.

4 Remove controller to bracket screws and remove controller.

INSTALLATION

1 Position mounting bracket to controller so that electrical connectors will be down when bracket is installed in the car. Install bracket on controller, then install controller and bracket assembly.

2 Make sure ignition is off, then install connectors. Do not start engine until all mounting screws are tight.

ADJUSTING IGNITION TIMING (MAGNETIC PROBE TIMING METER PREFERRED METHOD OF CHECKING TIMING.)

1 Connect a jumper wire to Reference Timing connector near controller assembly and ground other end of jumper.

2 With transmission in "Park", drive wheels blocked, and parking brake applied, start engine and run at 1100 RPM. Timing should be 20 degrees at 1100 RPM (Exc. California—22 degrees at 1100 RPM). "Check ignition"

Temperature Sensor (Left rear of intake manifold)
REMOVAL AND INSTALLATION

1 Disconnect temperature sensor connector. (Press wide sides together to unlock tabs, then pull on harness and connector.)

2 Carefully turn radiator cap to release pressure on cooling system, then tighten cap.

3 Remove sensor.

4 Install new sensor, use thread sealer.

5 Install connector.

Vacuum Tube

If it is necessary to install a new vacuum tube, the tube must be placed inside the plastic conduit in the engine compartment. Connect the tube to the vacuum "T".

TO SET REFERENCE TIMING

1. CONNECT OPEN REFERENCE TIMING CONNECTOR (TAPED TO HARNESS) TO GROUND USING ABOUT A 2 FT. JUMPER WIRE.

2. CONNECT TIMING LIGHT OR METER AND TACHOMETER THEN START ENGINE. "CHECK IGNITION" LIGHT WILL BE ON IF GROUND WIRE WAS PROPERLY INSTALLED.

3. TIMING SHOULD BE 20 DEGREES AT 1100 RPM (CALIFORNIA 22 DEGREES AT 1100 RPM).

4. IF TIMING IS INCORRECT, LOOSEN DISTRIBUTOR CLAMP BOLT AND TURN DISTRIBUTOR TO ADJUST TIMING.

5. TIGHTEN DISTRIBUTOR CLAMP BOLT. REMOVE JUMPER WIRE. "CHECK IGNITION" LIGHT WILL GO OUT.

LOWER I.P. TIE-BAR
I.P. HARNESS EXTENSION
VACUUM TUBE AND CONNECTOR
IGNITION HARNESS ASM.
THE CONTROLLER ASSEMBLY IS LOCATED BELOW THE GLOVE BOX
REFERENCE TIMING CONNECTOR
CONTROLLER ASSEMBLY

Reference Timing Connector

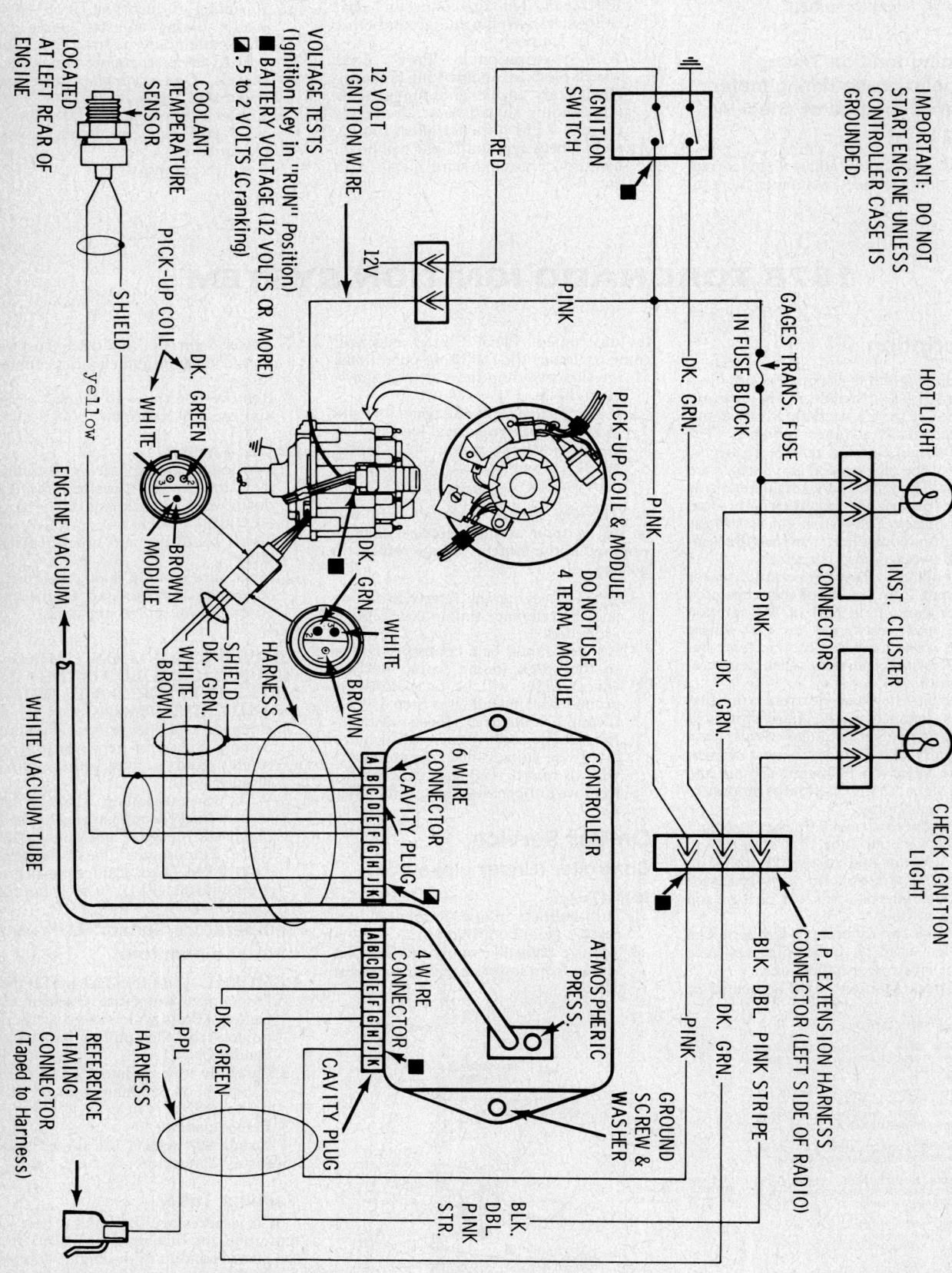

1978 Toronado Ignition System Wiring Diagram

IGNITION SYSTEM DIAGNOSIS—TORONADO 1978

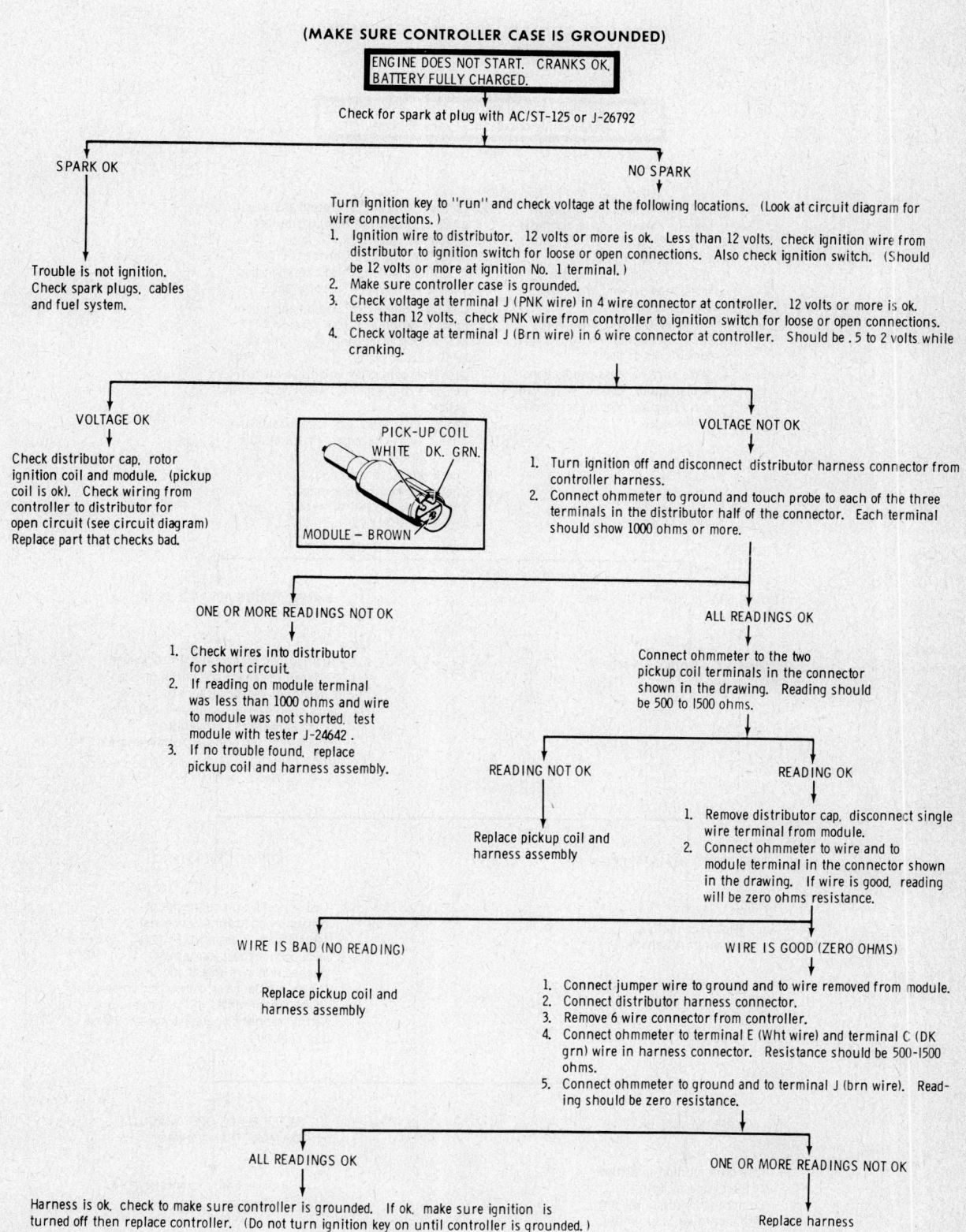

(MAKE SURE CONTROLLER CASE IS GROUNDED)

ENGINE DOES NOT START. CRANKS OK. BATTERY FULLY CHARGED.

Check for spark at plug with AC/ST-125 or J-26792

SPARK OK

Trouble is not ignition. Check spark plugs, cables and fuel system.

NO SPARK

Turn ignition key to "run" and check voltage at the following locations. (Look at circuit diagram for wire connections.)
1. Ignition wire to distributor. 12 volts or more is ok. Less than 12 volts, check ignition wire from distributor to ignition switch for loose or open connections. Also check ignition switch. (Should be 12 volts or more at ignition No. 1 terminal.)
2. Make sure controller case is grounded.
3. Check voltage at terminal J (PNK wire) in 4 wire connector at controller. 12 volts or more is ok. Less than 12 volts, check PNK wire from controller to ignition switch for loose or open connections.
4. Check voltage at terminal J (Brn wire) in 6 wire connector at controller. Should be .5 to 2 volts while cranking.

VOLTAGE OK

Check distributor cap, rotor ignition coil and module. (pickup coil is ok). Check wiring from controller to distributor for open circuit (see circuit diagram) Replace part that checks bad.

PICK-UP COIL
WHITE   DK. GRN.
MODULE – BROWN

VOLTAGE NOT OK

1. Turn ignition off and disconnect distributor harness connector from controller harness.
2. Connect ohmmeter to ground and touch probe to each of the three terminals in the distributor half of the connector. Each terminal should show 1000 ohms or more.

ONE OR MORE READINGS NOT OK

1. Check wires into distributor for short circuit.
2. If reading on module terminal was less than 1000 ohms and wire to module was not shorted, test module with tester J-24642.
3. If no trouble found, replace pickup coil and harness assembly.

ALL READINGS OK

Connect ohmmeter to the two pickup coil terminals in the connector shown in the drawing. Reading should be 500 to 1500 ohms.

READING NOT OK

Replace pickup coil and harness assembly

READING OK

1. Remove distributor cap, disconnect single wire terminal from module.
2. Connect ohmmeter to wire and to module terminal in the connector shown in the drawing. If wire is good, reading will be zero ohms resistance.

WIRE IS BAD (NO READING)

Replace pickup coil and harness assembly

WIRE IS GOOD (ZERO OHMS)

1. Connect jumper wire to ground and to wire removed from module.
2. Connect distributor harness connector.
3. Remove 6 wire connector from controller.
4. Connect ohmmeter to terminal E (Wht wire) and terminal C (DK grn) wire in harness connector. Resistance should be 500-1500 ohms.
5. Connect ohmmeter to ground and to terminal J (brn wire). Reading should be zero resistance.

ALL READINGS OK

Harness is ok, check to make sure controller is grounded. If ok, make sure ignition is turned off then replace controller. (Do not turn ignition key on until controller is grounded.)

ONE OR MORE READINGS NOT OK

Replace harness

IGNITION SYSTEM DIAGNOSIS—TORONADO 1978

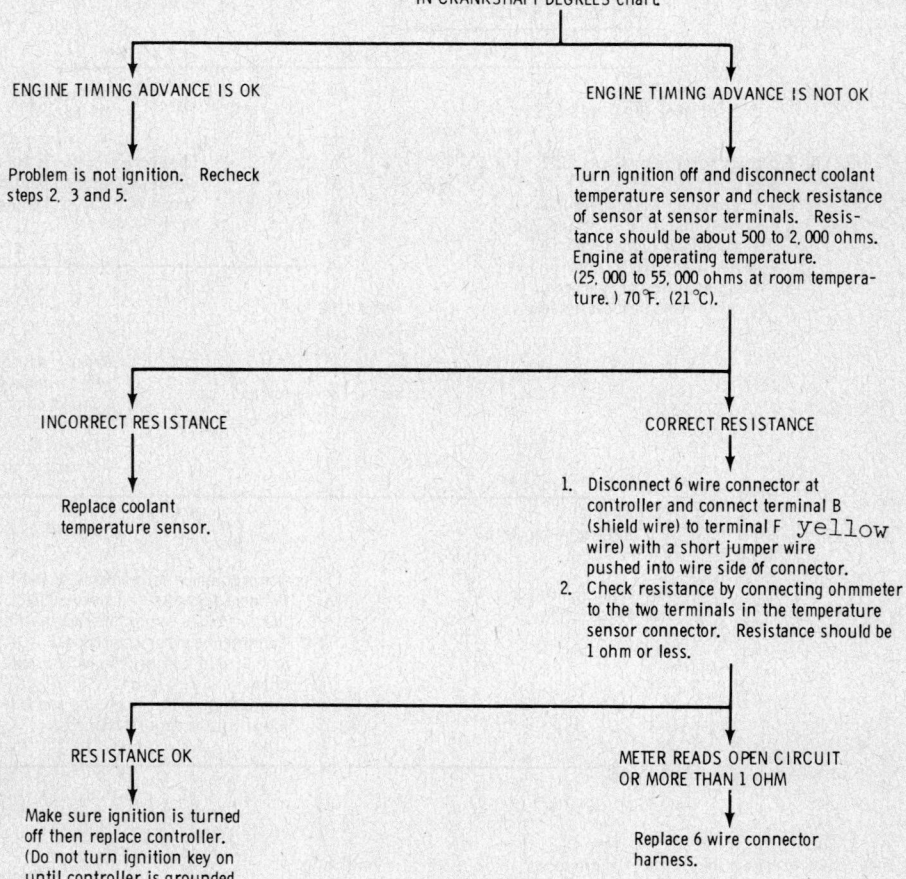

(MAKE SURE CONTROLLER CASE IS GROUNDED)

HARD STARTING, ROUGH ENGINE, POOR PERFORMANCE
(Battery fully charged - 12 Volts or more)

1. If CHECK IGNITION light is on (engine running), use diagnosis chart CHECK IGNITION LIGHT ON - ENGINE RUNNING.
2. If CHECK IGNITION light is off, check fuel system, choke, spark plugs and cables.
3. Check all vacuum hoses and white vacuum tube to controller for pinches or leaks.
4. Make sure harness connections to distributor, coolant sensor and controller are good and controller is grounded.

5. Connect voltmeter to ground and touch probe to ignition wire at distributor 12 volts or more is ok. If less, check ignition wire from distributor to ignition switch. Also check ignition switch. Refer to circuit diagram.
6. Connect voltmeter to ground and touch probe to terminal J (PNK wire) in 4 wire connector at controller. Should be 12 volts or more. If less, check PNK wire from controller to ignition switch for loose connections. Also check ignition switch.
7. Remove distributor cap, check rotor and cap for signs of arcing. Check module with J-24642.
8. Check reference timing.
9. Check engine timing advance. See ENGINE TIMING ADVANCE IN CRANKSHAFT DEGREES chart.

ENGINE TIMING ADVANCE IS OK

Problem is not ignition. Recheck steps 2, 3 and 5.

ENGINE TIMING ADVANCE IS NOT OK

Turn ignition off and disconnect coolant temperature sensor and check resistance of sensor at sensor terminals. Resistance should be about 500 to 2,000 ohms. Engine at operating temperature. (25,000 to 55,000 ohms at room temperature.) 70°F. (21°C).

INCORRECT RESISTANCE

Replace coolant temperature sensor.

CORRECT RESISTANCE

1. Disconnect 6 wire connector at controller and connect terminal B (shield wire) to terminal F yellow wire) with a short jumper wire pushed into wire side of connector.
2. Check resistance by connecting ohmmeter to the two terminals in the temperature sensor connector. Resistance should be 1 ohm or less.

RESISTANCE OK

Make sure ignition is turned off then replace controller. (Do not turn ignition key on until controller is grounded.)

METER READS OPEN CIRCUIT OR MORE THAN 1 OHM

Replace 6 wire connector harness.

IGNITION SYSTEM DIAGNOSIS—TORONADO 1978

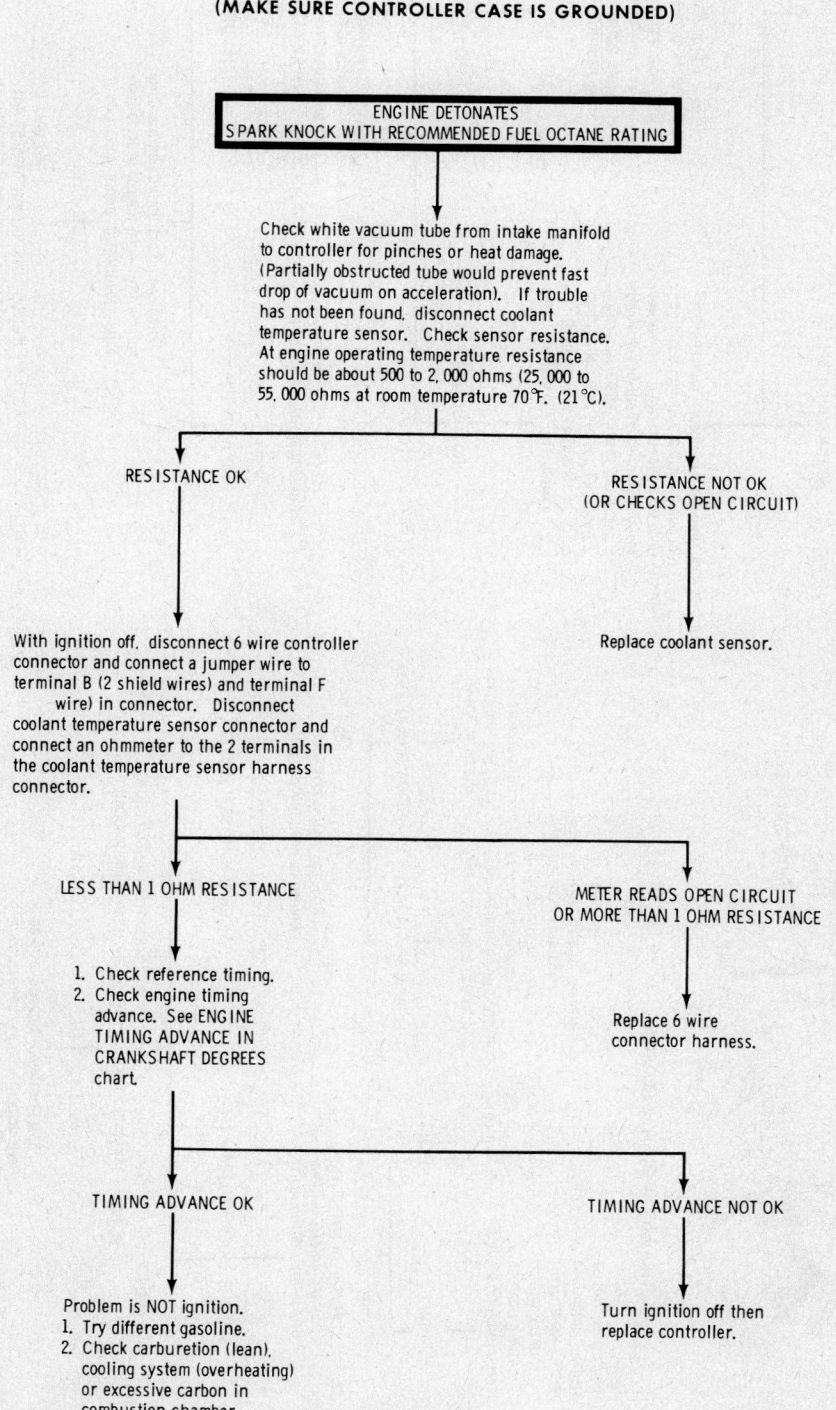

(MAKE SURE CONTROLLER CASE IS GROUNDED)

ENGINE DETONATES
SPARK KNOCK WITH RECOMMENDED FUEL OCTANE RATING

Check white vacuum tube from intake manifold to controller for pinches or heat damage. (Partially obstructed tube would prevent fast drop of vacuum on acceleration). If trouble has not been found, disconnect coolant temperature sensor. Check sensor resistance. At engine operating temperature resistance should be about 500 to 2,000 ohms (25,000 to 55,000 ohms at room temperature 70°F. (21°C).

RESISTANCE OK

RESISTANCE NOT OK
(OR CHECKS OPEN CIRCUIT)

With ignition off, disconnect 6 wire controller connector and connect a jumper wire to terminal B (2 shield wires) and terminal F wire) in connector. Disconnect coolant temperature sensor connector and connect an ohmmeter to the 2 terminals in the coolant temperature sensor harness connector.

Replace coolant sensor.

LESS THAN 1 OHM RESISTANCE

METER READS OPEN CIRCUIT
OR MORE THAN 1 OHM RESISTANCE

1. Check reference timing.
2. Check engine timing advance. See ENGINE TIMING ADVANCE IN CRANKSHAFT DEGREES chart.

Replace 6 wire connector harness.

TIMING ADVANCE OK

TIMING ADVANCE NOT OK

Problem is NOT ignition.
1. Try different gasoline.
2. Check carburetion (lean), cooling system (overheating) or excessive carbon in combustion chamber.

Turn ignition off then replace controller.

IGNITION SYSTEM DIAGNOSIS—TORONADO 1978

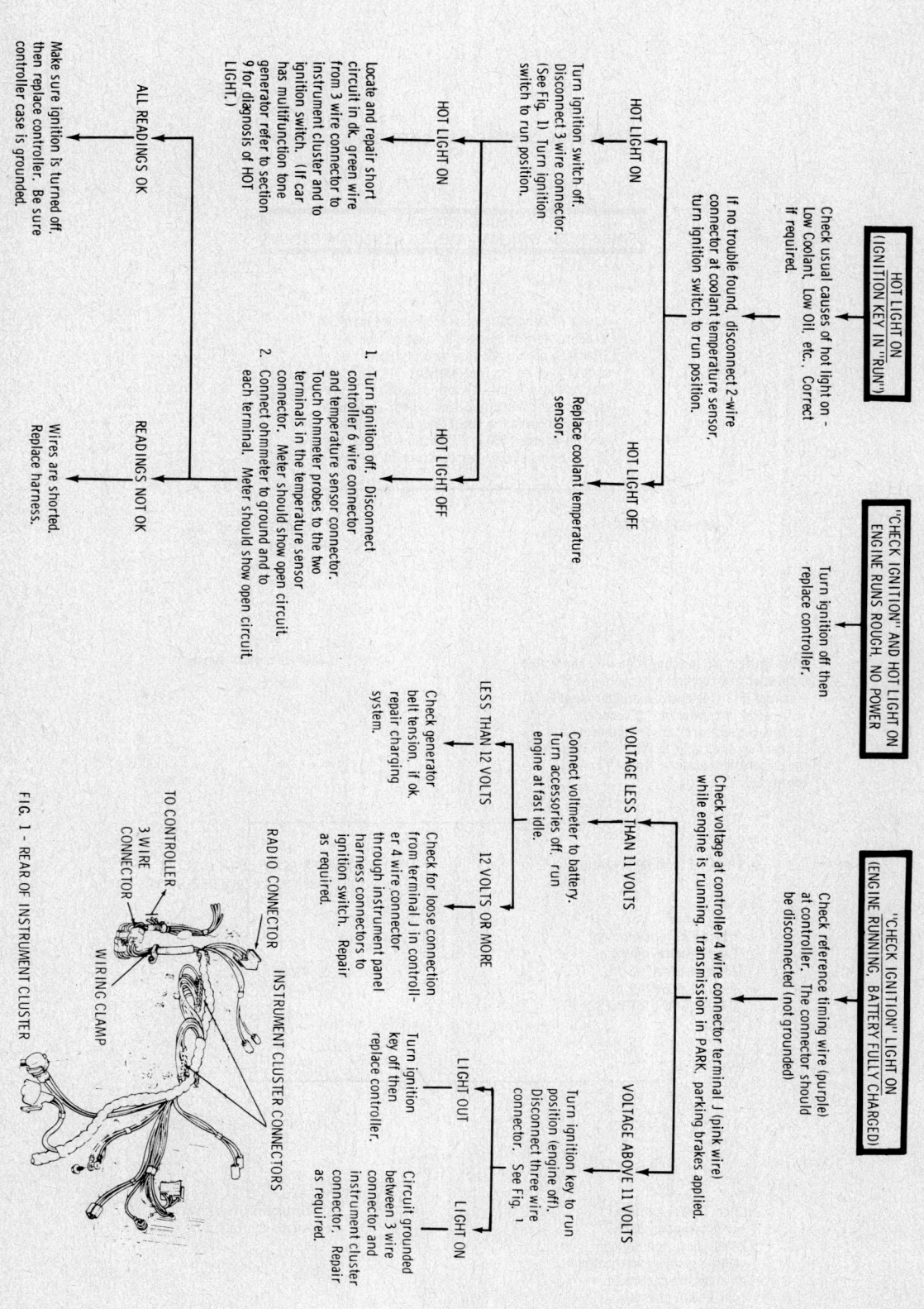

(MAKE SURE CONTROLLER CASE IS GROUNDED)

HOT LIGHT ON (IGNITION KEY IN "RUN")

Check usual causes of hot light on - Low Coolant, Low Oil, etc. Correct if required.

If no trouble found, disconnect 2-wire connector at coolant temperature sensor, turn ignition switch to run position.

HOT LIGHT ON — Turn ignition switch off. Disconnect 3 wire connector. (See Fig. 1) Turn ignition switch to run position.

HOT LIGHT ON — Turn ignition switch off, circuit in dk. green wire from 3 wire connector to instrument cluster and to ignition switch. (If car generator refer to section 9 for diagnosis of HOT LIGHT.)

locate and repair short

ALL READINGS OK

Make sure ignition is turned off, then replace controller. Be sure controller case is grounded.

HOT LIGHT OFF — Replace coolant temperature sensor.

HOT LIGHT OFF
1. Turn ignition switch off. Disconnect controller 6 wire connector and temperature sensor connector. Touch ohmmeter probes to the two terminals in the temperature sensor connector. Meter should show open circuit.
2. Connect ohmmeter to ground and to each terminal. Meter should show open circuit

READINGS NOT OK — Wires are shorted. Replace harness.

"CHECK IGNITION" AND HOT LIGHT ON ENGINE RUNS ROUGH, NO POWER

Turn ignition off then replace controller.

"CHECK IGNITION" LIGHT ON (ENGINE RUNNING, BATTERY FULLY CHARGED)

Check reference timing wire (purple) at controller. The connector should be disconnected (not grounded)

Check voltage at controller 4 wire connector terminal J (pink wire) while engine is running, transmission in PARK, parking brakes applied.

VOLTAGE LESS THAN 11 VOLTS
Connect voltmeter to battery. Turn accessories off, run engine at fast idle.

LESS THAN 12 VOLTS — Check generator belt tension. If ok, repair charging system.

12 VOLTS OR MORE — Check for loose connection from terminal J in controller 4 wire connector through instrument panel harness connectors to ignition switch. Repair as required.

VOLTAGE ABOVE 11 VOLTS
Turn ignition key to run position (engine off). Disconnect three wire connector. See Fig. 1

LIGHT OUT — Turn ignition key off then replace controller.

LIGHT ON — Circuit grounded between 3 wire connector and instrument cluster connector. Repair as required.

RADIO CONNECTOR

INSTRUMENT CLUSTER CONNECTORS

TO CONTROLLER 3 WIRE CONNECTOR

WIRING CLAMP

TO INSTRUMENT CLUSTER

FIG. 1 - REAR OF INSTRUMENT CLUSTER

1. Engine **MUST BE** at operating temperature and timing set to specification.

2. Connect tachometer and timing meter. Do not ground reference timing connector.

3. Disconnect controller assembly vacuum tube (white) from manifold vacuum "T". Plug "T" and connect vacuum pump and gage to white tube. Use pump such as BT-7517 to get vacuum readings shown.

NOTE: 1400 RPM at 15" of vacuum gives maximum advance. If advance is less than specification, slowly increase vacuum to get maximum advance. If advance is now within specification, instruments/gages used are inaccurate. If not within specification, replace controller.

EXCEPT CALIFORNIA CARS			CALIFORNIA CARS		
ENGINE RPM	VACUUM (INCHES)	*CRANKSHAFT DEGREES	ENGINE RPM	VACUUM (INCHES)	*CRANKSHAFT DEGREES
600	16.5	29 to 34	600	13.5	15 to 22
600	15	27 to 31	600	12	15 to 22
1000	12	32 to 35	1000	12	17 to 25
1400	15	49 to 62	1400	15	39 to 65
1400	10.5	38 to 40	2000	18	24 to 33
1400	6	27 to 35	2000	0	23 to 32
2000	18	44 to 47			
2000	0	29 to 31			

* Advance specifications are approximate depending upon accuracy of tachometer, vacuum gage and timing meter.

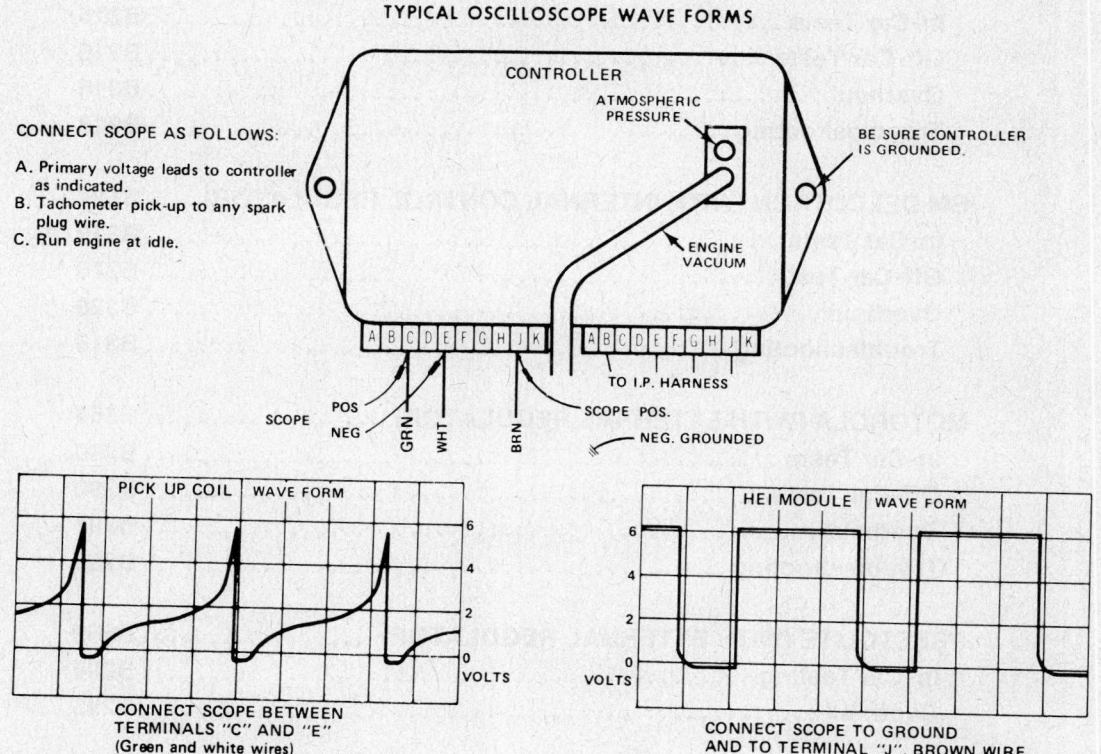

TYPICAL OSCILLOSCOPE WAVE FORMS

CONTROLLER

ATMOSPHERIC PRESSURE

BE SURE CONTROLLER IS GROUNDED.

ENGINE VACUUM

CONNECT SCOPE AS FOLLOWS:

A. Primary voltage leads to controller as indicated.
B. Tachometer pick-up to any spark plug wire.
C. Run engine at idle.

SCOPE   POS   GRN   WHT   BRN
         NEG

TO I.P. HARNESS
SCOPE POS.
NEG. GROUNDED

PICK UP COIL   WAVE FORM
6
4
2
0 VOLTS

CONNECT SCOPE BETWEEN TERMINALS "C" AND "E" (Green and white wires)

Engine Timing Advance in Crankshaft Degrees

HEI MODULE   WAVE FORM
6
4
2
0
VOLTS

CONNECT SCOPE TO GROUND AND TO TERMINAL "J". BROWN WIRE.

ALTERNATORS

INDEX

MOTOROLA ALTERNATOR
(WITH EXTERNAL REGULATOR)

Motorola Alternator

Charging System Precautions

To prevent damage to the alternator and regulator, the following precautionary measures must be taken when working with the electrical system.

1. Never reverse battery connections. Always check the battery polarity visually. This should be done before any connections are made to be sure that all of the connections correspond to the battery ground polarity of the truck.
2. Booster batteries for starting must be connected properly. Make sure that the positive cable of the booster battery is connected to the positive terminal of the battery that is getting the boost. The same applies to the negative cables.
3. Disconnect the battery cables before using a fast charger; the charger has a tendency to force current through the diodes in the opposite direction for which they were designed. This burns out the diodes.
4. Never use a fast charger as a booster for starting the vehicle.
5. Never disconnect the voltage regulator while the engine is running.
6. Do not the ground the alternator output terminal.
7. Do not operate the alternator on an open circuit with the field energized.
8. Do not attempt to polarize an alternator.

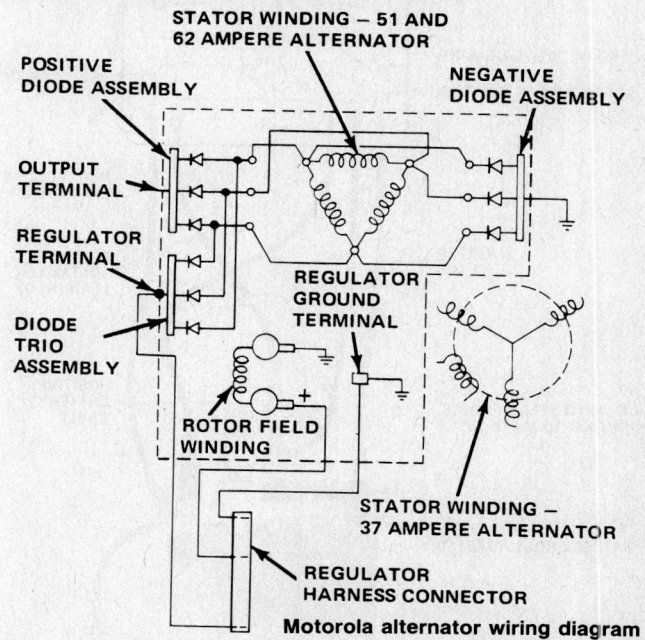

Motorola alternator wiring diagram

Charging System Operation

NOTE: If the current indicator is to give an accurate reading, the battery cables must be of the same gauge and length as the original equipment.

1. With the engine running and all electrical systems off, place a current indicator over the positive battery cable.
2. If a charge of about 5 amps is recorded, the charging system is working. If a draw of about 5 amps is recorded, the system is not working. If a draw is indicated, continue to the next testing procedure. If an overcharge of 10–15 amps is indicated, check for a faulty regulator, or a bad ground at either the regulator or the alternator.

Preliminary Charging System Inspection

NOTE: Before performing any tests on automotive charging systems, the following precautions should be taken to ensure the accuracy of the tests described in this section.

1. Check condition of the alternator belt; tighten if necessary.
2. Check that battery is fully charged and in good condition.
3. Clean the battery cable connections at the battery. Make sure that all connections are good. Disconnect the positive terminal only, and proceed to the next step.
4. With the key off, insert a test light

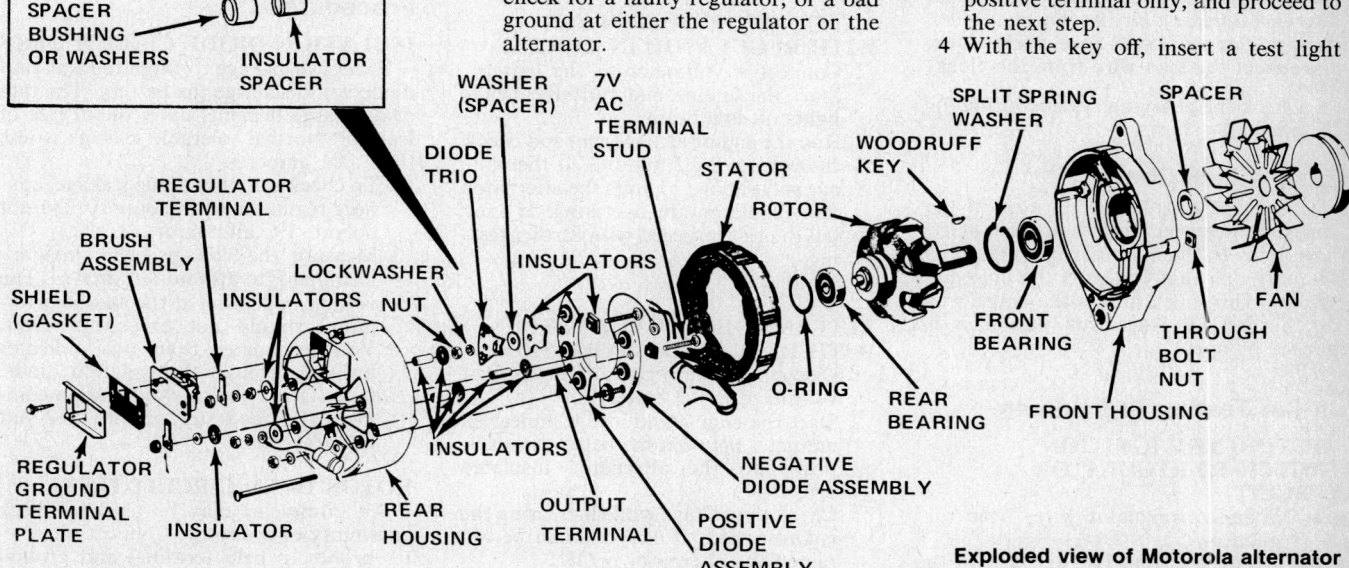

Exploded view of Motorola alternator

ALTERNATORS

MOTOROLA (WITH EXTERNAL REGULATOR)

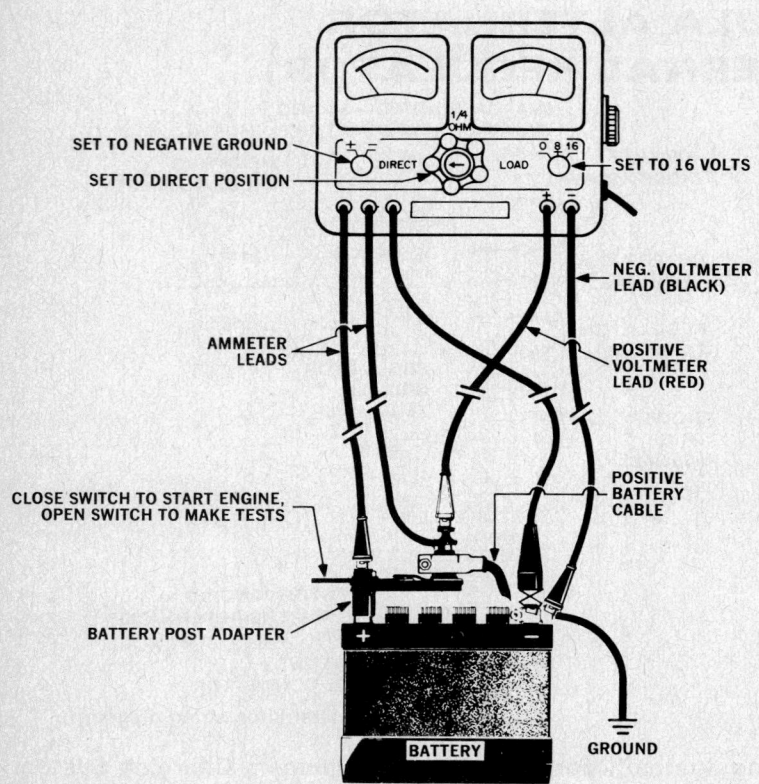

Charging system test connections

CHILTON CAUTION: *Do not exceed 16 volts or damage to the charging system may occur.*

4 If high voltage occurs with a good battery, and the regulator is grounded to the battery, the regulator is bad.

FIELD CURRENT DRAW TEST
1 With battery disconnected, disconnect the wires from the alternator output terminal and the alternator field terminal.
2 With a field rheostat in the open position, connect its leads to the disconnected alternator output wire and to the positive lead of the test ammeter.
3 Connect the negative ammeter lead to the alternator field terminal.
4 Connect the positive voltmeter lead to the alternator field terminal.
5 Connect the negative voltmeter lead to the alternator ground terminal.
6 Reconnect the battery.
7 Start the engine and run at fast idle.
8 Adjust field rheostat to closed position. Note the voltmeter and ammeter readings.
9 Adjust field rheostate control to the open position.
10 Compare the readings obtained in Step 8 with manufacturer's specifications.
11 If readings are zero, there is an indication of trouble in the field coil, or in the connections between field coil and slip ring.
12 If readings are low, there is probably trouble in the slip rings or brushes.
13 If readings are high, the field coil is probably shorted.
14 If readings are normal, on an alternator which failed to produce its rated output, the probable cause lies in the stator or diodes. Replace the alternator in this case.

between the battery positive terminal and the disconnected positive battery terminal clamp. If the test light comes on, there is a short in the electrical system of the car. The short must be repaired before proceeding. If the light fails to glow, reconnect the clamp and proceed to the next step.

NOTE: Alternators with transistorized regulators sometimes draw a slight current even when the key is turned off. To properly check these systems for a short, the regulator must be disconnected. Also, on cars equipped with an electric clock, disconnect the lead wire from the clock.

5 Check the charging system wiring for breaks or shorts.

Fusible Link Check
Check the fusible link located in the wiring between the battery terminal of the horn relay to the main wire harness. It is the only one that concerns the charging system. This link protects the entire wiring harness. Replace this link if it is burned or open.

In-Car Testing Procedures

TESTING THE IGNITION SWITCH-TO-REGULATOR CIRCUIT
1 Disconnect regulator wires from the regulator.
2 Turn on the key. Use a test light or

voltmeter to check for current between the voltage supply wire and ground. This wire is usually orange and has another wire connected to it, usually blue or orange with a tracer.
3 If current is present, this part of the system is OK. If no voltage is present, check for: broken or shorted wiring; a bad indicator bulb; a bad fuse in the fuse panel; or a bad connection at either the ignition switch or on the battery side of the starter relay.

ALTERNATOR OUTPUT TEST WITH REGULATOR IN CIRCUIT
1 Connect a voltmeter to the battery. Start the engine and turn the headlights on low beam.
2 Run the engine at 1000 rpm and check the voltage for 2 minutes. If the voltage stays above 13 volts the alternator and regulator are operating. If they fail the test, proceed with further testing.

ALTERNATOR OUTPUT TEST WITH REGULATOR BYPASSED
1 Disconnect the regulator. Connect a voltmeter to the battery.
2 Start the engine and idle. Connect an ammeter between the battery positive post and the alternator insulated brush.
3 Check the voltage while increasing the engine speed. If 16 volts can be obtained the alternator is OK.

Off-Car Bench Testing Procedures

ISOLATION DIODE CIRCUIT TEST
Excessive leakage through the isolation diode will discharge the battery. The rate of discharge depends upon the degree of leakage. Normal tolerable leakage is less than .001 amperes.
1 To check isolation diode leakage, connect regulator to the battery. Do not operate the alternator.
2 Measure the voltage from auxiliary terminal F to ground terminal G. The voltage appearing at the auxiliary terminal should not exceed 0.1 volt. Voltage greater than this indicates leakage through the isolation diode. Check the isolation diode with a commercial diode tester, or with a 12-volt DC test lamp.

ROTOR OPEN CIRCUIT TEST
An ohmmeter may be used to check continuity of the rotor. Connect ohmmeter probes to field terminal and ground

terminal (test points B and G). Resistance should be about 6 ohms. If resistance is high, field coil is open.

ISOLATION DIODE TEST
CHILTON CAUTION: *If a commercial diode tester is not available, use a 12-volt DC test lamp only, otherwise diodes may be damaged.*

Connect the test lamp to output terminal and auxiliary terminal. Then reverse the test probes. Test lamp should light in one direction only. If test lamp lights in both directions, the isolation diode is shorted. If lamp won't light in either direction, the diode is open.

ROTOR LEAKAGE TEST
This is a check of the field coil for leakage or shorts to rotor poles. An ohmmeter or test lamp (12V or 120V) may be used.
1 Remove the brush assembly to gain access to rotor slip rings.
2 Connect ohmmeter or test lamp probes to one of the slip rings and the ground terminal, points G and P.
Ohmmeter resistance should be infinite or test lamp should not light. If condition is contrary, leakage or a short exists between field coil and rotor.

Repeat test after rotor has been removed from the alternator to pinpoint findings.

OUT-OF-CIRCUIT STATOR LEAK TEST
Disassemble alternator and remove the rectifier-diode plates and stator as an assembly. An ohmmeter or 12-volt DC test lamp may be used.

Connect ohmmeter or test lamp probes to one of the rectifier diode terminals and to the stator test points N and Q. Resistance reading should be infinite (or the test light should not light). If result is contrary, high leakage or a short exists between stator winding and stator. In either case, stator should be replaced.

OUT-OF-CIRCUIT RECTIFIER DIODE TEST
If a commercial diode tester is not

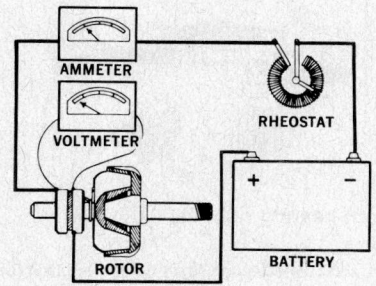
Rotor test connections

available, check the diodes with a 12-volt DC test lamp only.

CHILTON CAUTION: *When unsoldering the stator wires from the rectifier diode assembly, provide a heat sink to the diode terminal with a pair of longnosed pliers.*

Connect test lamp probes to diode terminal and diode plate stud. Reverse test lamp probes. The test light should light in one direction but not in the other. If the test lamp lights in both directions, the diode is shorted. If test lamp does not light in either direction, the diode is open. Test the remaining diodes of the assembly in the same manner. Replace entire assembly if one of the diodes is found to be bad.

NOTE: Starting in 1974, use a diode tester that draws a 1 amp (maximum) at 12 volts to test the diode trio, and a tester that draws 20 amps at 12 volts to test the rectifier diodes. Keep the test connections hooked up for at least two minutes.

STATOR COIL LEAK & CONTINUITY TEST
1 Separate winding ends. An ohmmeter or 12-volt DC test lamp may be used.
2 Connect one lead of the ohmmeter or test lamp to point 1. Connect the other test lead to point 2 and then to point 3. Ohmmeter reading should be infinite or the test lamp should not light.
3 Connect test leads to points 2 and 3. Ohmmeter reading should be infinete, or the test lamp should not light.

If the test results in Steps 2 or 3 above are contrary, excess leakage or a short exists between stator windings; replace the stator.
4 Check continuity by measuring the resistance of each winding in the stator with an ohmmeter, between test points, 1 to 1A, 2 to 2A and 3 to 3A. Resistance should be very low (about 0.1 ohm).

Never replace stator until all other components have been checked and proven satisfactory.

ALTERNATOR DISASSEMBLY
1 Remove the two self-tapping screws and the cover. Pull the brush assembly straight up to clear the locating pins; lift out the brush assembly.
2 Remove the two locknuts. Remove the isolation diode assembly from the rear housing.
3 Scribe a matchmark across the front housing, stator, and rear housing. Remove the four through bolts and nuts,

Alternator rear housing removal

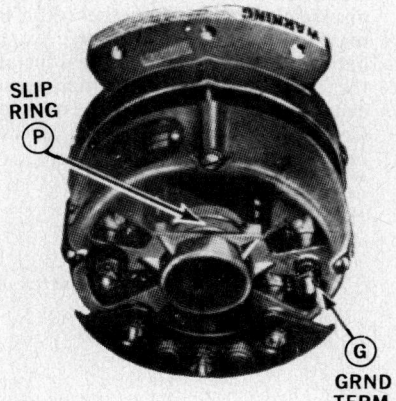
Rotor leakage test connections

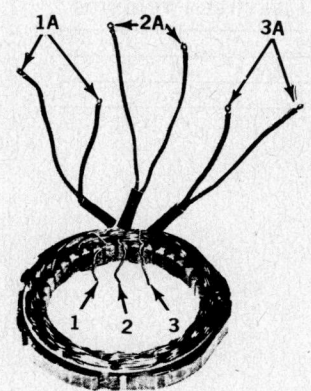
Stator coil test points

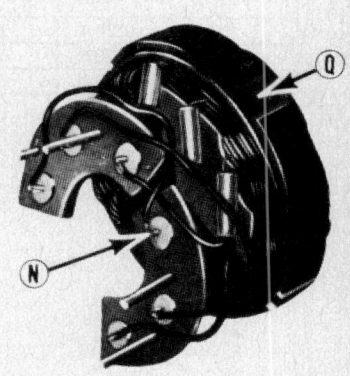
Stator leakage test connections

Split ring washer removal

Front bearing removal

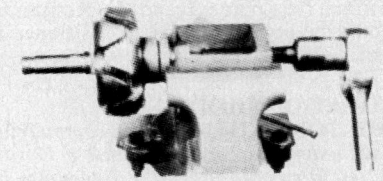

Rear bearing removal

then carefully separate the rear housing and stator from the front housing. Use two screwdrivers in the slots provided.

CHILTON CAUTION: *Do not insert screwdrivers deeper than 1/16 in., to avoid damaging stator winding.*

4 Remove the four locknuts and insulating washers that hold the stator and diode assembly. Separate the assembly from the rear housing. Avoid bending the stator wires—do not unsolder the wires without using pliers as a heat sink.

NOTE: There is no reason to remove the rotor from the front housing unless there is a defect in the field coil or front bearing. Front and rear bearings are lubricated for life and sealed. As a rule, they do not go bad unless the drive belt has been adjusted with too much tension. If the rotor must be removed, use a puller to remove the front drive pulley.

5 Next unseat the split-ring washer using long-nose pliers through the front housing to compress the washer while pulling on the rotor. Tap the rotor shaft lightly to remove the rotor and front bearing. Reach in and remove the split-ring washer. Bearings must be removed using a puller. New bearings must be pressed into place.

ALTERNATOR ASSEMBLY

1 Clean the bearing and the inside of the bearing hub in the front housing. Gently seat the bearing using a socket of appropriate size and a small hammer.
2 Insert the split-ring washer into the hub of the front housing and seat the washer in its groove. Be extremely careful doing this, because the bearing seal is easily damaged.
3 The front bearing now must be seated against the shoulder on the rotor shaft. Install the fan and pulley spacer, then the Woodruff key, fan and pulley. Using a 7/16 in. socket or equivalent tool to fit inside the rear bearing race, apply pressure to drive the bearing against the shoulder of the rotor shaft.
4 Assemble the front and rear housing assemblies by hand. Make certain that the rear bearing is properly seated in the rear housing hub and that the diode wires are not touching the rotor at any point.
5 Align the matchmarks made during disassembly. Now spin the rotor to make sure sufficient clearance exists between it and the diode wires. Install the through bolts and tighten them evenly, using only a hand wrench. Continue assembly in the reverse order of disassembly.

ALTERNATOR	LOAD	MAXIMUM VOLTAGE DROP	MAXIMUM VARIANCE BETWEEN WINDINGS
37	20A	7.2 – 8.2	.7
51	20A	5.5 – 6.5	.6
62	20A	6.7 – 7.2	.5

Stator load test

TROUBLESHOOTING PRESTOLITE ALTERNATOR (WITH EXTERNAL REGULATOR)

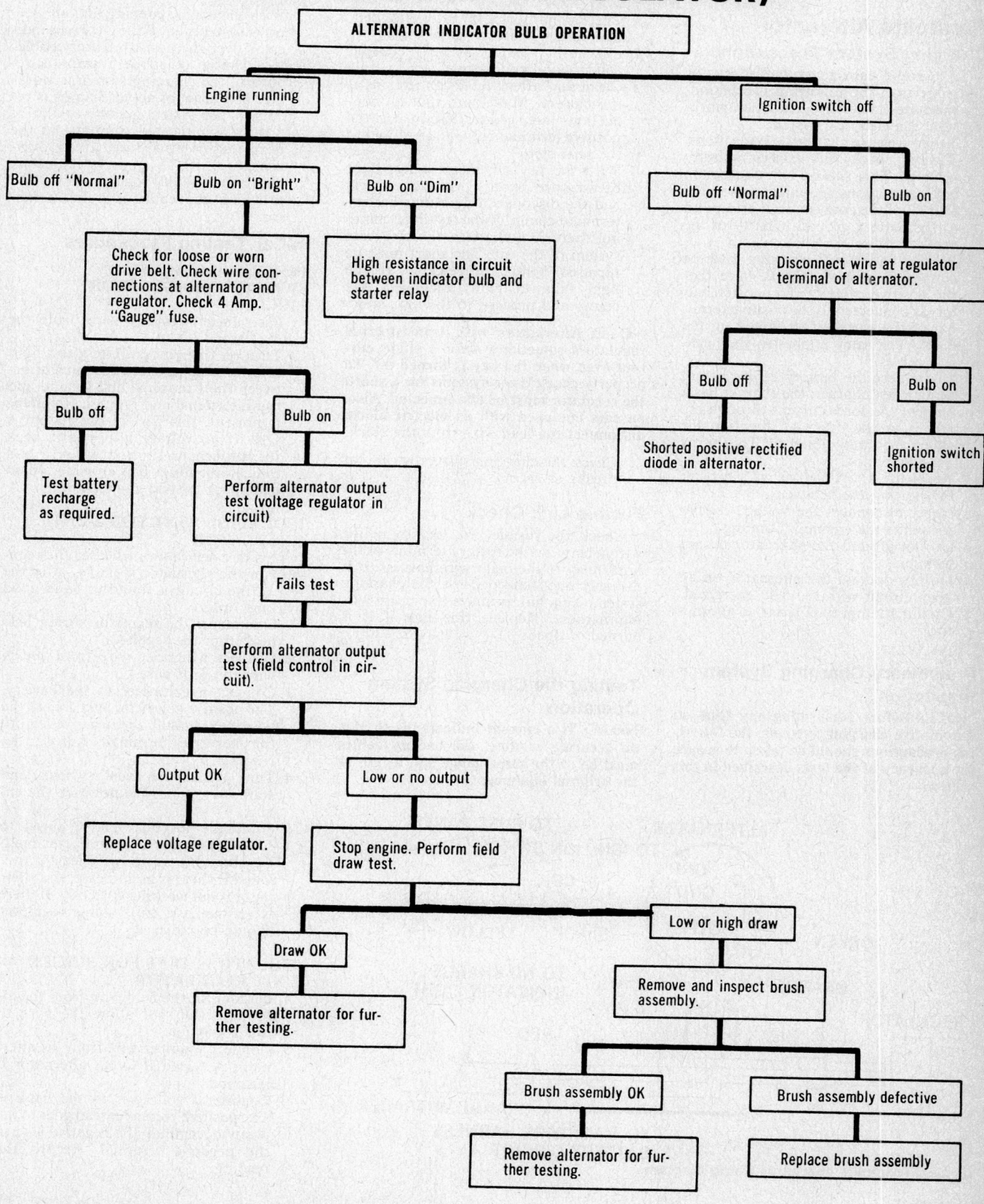

PRESTOLITE ALTERNATOR
(WITH EXTERNAL REGULATOR)

Prestolite Alternator
Charging System Precautions

To prevent damage to the alternator and regulator, the following precautionary measures must be taken when working with the electrical system.

1 Never reverse battery connections. Always check the battery polarity visually. This should be done before any connections are made to be sure that all of the connections correspond to the battery ground polarity of the truck.

2 Booster batteries for starting must be connected properly. Make sure that the positive cable of the booster battery is connected to the positive terminal of the battery that is getting the boost. The same applies to the negative cables.

3 Disconnect the battery cables before using a fast charger; the charger has a tendency to force current through the diodes in the opposite direction for which they were designed. This burns out the diodes.

4 Never use a fast charger as a booster for starting the vehicle.

5 Never disconnect the voltage regulator while the engine is running.

6 Do not ground the alternator output terminal.

7 Do not operate the alternator on an open circuit with the field energized.

8 Do not attempt to polarize an alternator.

Preliminary Charging System Inspection

NOTE: Before performing any tests on automotive charging systems, the following precautions should be taken to ensure the accuracy of the tests described in this section.

1 Check condition of the alternator belt; tighten if necessary.

2 Check that battery is fully charged and in good condition.

3 Clean the battery cable connections at the battery. Make sure that all connections are good. Disconnect the positive terminal only, and proceed to the next step.

4 With the key off, insert a test light between the battery positive terminal and the disconnected positive battery terminal clamp. If the test light comes on, there is a short in the electrical system of the car. The short must be repaired before proceeding. If the light fails to glow, reconnect the clamp and proceed to the next step.

NOTE: Alternators with transistorized regulators sometimes draw a slight current even when the key is turned off. To properly check these systems for a short, the regulator must be disconnected. Also, on cars equipped with an electric clock, disconnect the lead wire from the clock.

5 Check the charging system wiring for breaks or shorts.

Fusible Link Check

Check the fusible link located in the wiring between the battery terminal of the horn relay to the main wire harness. It is the only one that concerns the charging system. This link protects the entire wiring harness. Replace this link if it is burned or open.

Testing the Charging System Operation

NOTE: If a current indicator is to give an accurate reading, the battery cables must be of the same gauge and length as the original equipment.

1 With the engine running and all electrical systems off, place a current indicator over the positive battery cable.

2 If a charge of about 5 amps is recorded, the charging system is working. If a draw of about 5 amps is recorded, the system is not working. If a draw is indicated, continue to the next testing procedure. If an overcharge of 10–15 amps is indicated, check for a faulty regulator, or a bad ground at the regulator or the alternator.

In-Car Testing Procedures

TESTING THE IGNITION SWITCH-TO-REGULATOR CIRCUIT

1 Disconnect regulator wires from the regulator.

2 Turn on the ignition. Use a test light or voltmeter to check for current between the I terminal and ground and the L terminal and ground. If voltage is present, this part of the system is OK. If no voltage is present, check for: broken or shorted wires; a bad indicator bulb; a bad ammeter (if so equipped); or bad connections.

ISOLATION TEST FOR 2-UNIT REGULATOR

This test determines whether the regulator or the alternator is faulty, after the rest of the circuit is found to be in good working order.

1 Disconnect the regulator wiring harness from the regulator.

2 Connect a jumper wire from the A wire to the F wire.

3 Connect a voltmeter to the battery. The positive voltmeter lead goes to the positive terminal; the negative lead to the negative terminal. Record the reading.

4 Turn off all electrical systems and start the engine. Do not race the engine.

5 Gradually increase engine speed to 1500–2000 rpm. The voltmeter reading should increase by at least 1 to 2 volts. If there is no increase, the alternator is not working correctly. If there is an increase, the voltage regulator should be replaced.

ISOLATION TEST FOR SINGLE UNIT REGULATOR

1 Disconnect the field wire from the alternator. Do not allow the wire to touch ground.

2 Connect a jumper wire from the alternator A terminal to the alternator F terminal.

3 Connect a voltmeter to the battery. The positive voltmeter lead goes to the positive terminal; the negative lead to the negative terminal. Record the reading.

Typical Prestolite alternator wiring diagram

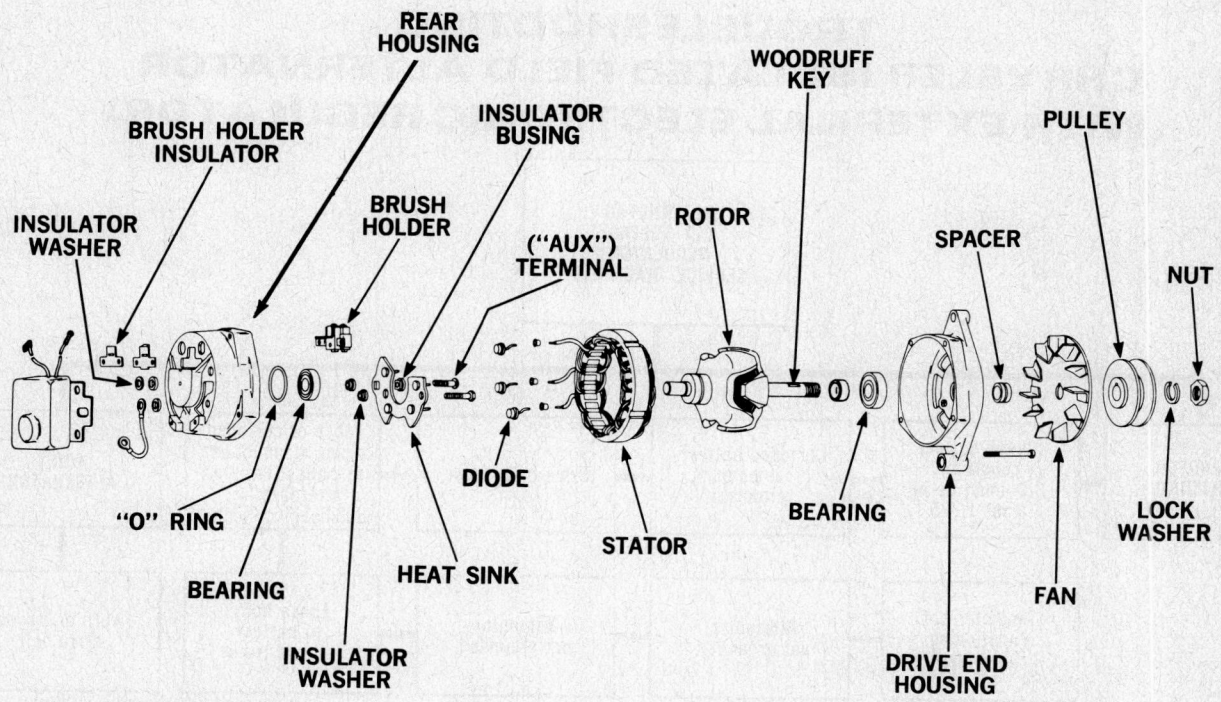

Prestolite alternator assembly

4 Turn off all electrical systems and start the engine. Do not race the engine.
5 Gradually increase engine speed to 1500–2000 rpm. The voltmeter reading should increase above the previously recorded battery voltage reading by at least 1 to 2 volts. If there is no increase, the alternator is not working correctly. If there is an increase, the voltage regulator should be replaced.

STATOR COIL TEST

1 Use a No. 57 bulb, connected in series with a 12-volt battery, as a test light. Touch one test lead to the connection of the three stator windings. Touch the other test lead to each stator lead that is connected to the diodes. If the bulb does not light, the winding is open.
2 To test for a grounded stator, use a 110-volt test lamp. First disconnect the diodes from the stator leads. Now touch one test lead to the stator core and the other test lead to each of the three stator leads. If the test lamp lights, the winding is grounded.

NOTE: If all other components are OK and alternator still does not work, it can be assumed that the stator windings are internally shorted. This type of short is impossible to detect by using the previous test. Diode tests are the same as for the Motorola alternator.

ALTERNATOR DISASSEMBLY

1 Remove the two brush mounting screws and cover. Tip the brush assembly away from the alternator and remove.
2 Matchmark the rear housing, stator and drive end housing. Remove the four retaining screws. The stator and rear housing are removed as a unit by tapping lightly with a fiber hammer to separate them from the front housing.
3 The rotor should not be removed unless it or the front bearing is defective. To remove the rotor under these conditions, first remove the pulley nut and pulley (using a two-jaw puller), next remove the fan, Woodruff key and spacer. The rotor is removed from the front housing by using a 3-jaw puller. (Such a puller is made by Snap-On Tool Corp.—part No. CG 253).
4 The front bearing is easily removed, after taking out the retaining ring, by pressing it out in a large vise. Use sockets to support the housing from the rear.

ALTERNATOR ASSEMBLY

1 Press the front bearing into the front housing. Make sure the dust seal faces the rotor. Install the bearing retaining snap-ring. Press the shoulder of the shaft against the inner bearing race using a tool that fits over the shaft and against the race. Install the spacer, Woodruff key, fan and pulley. Now install the lock-washer and pulley nut.
2 Install the diode heat sink, negative diodes and stator. Solder any stator to diode connections that were unsoldered. Use pliers as a heat sink to prevent overheating.
3 Install the rotor and front drive housing to stator and rear housing, aligning the matchmarks made during disassembly. Install the four retaining screws, then the brush holder assembly and retaining screws.
4 Make sure the stator leads and brush holder assembly clear the rotor and that the rotor can be spun by hand without binding.

TROUBLESHOOTING
CHRYSLER ISOLATED FIELD ALTERNATOR
(WITH EXTERNAL ELECTRONIC REGULATOR)

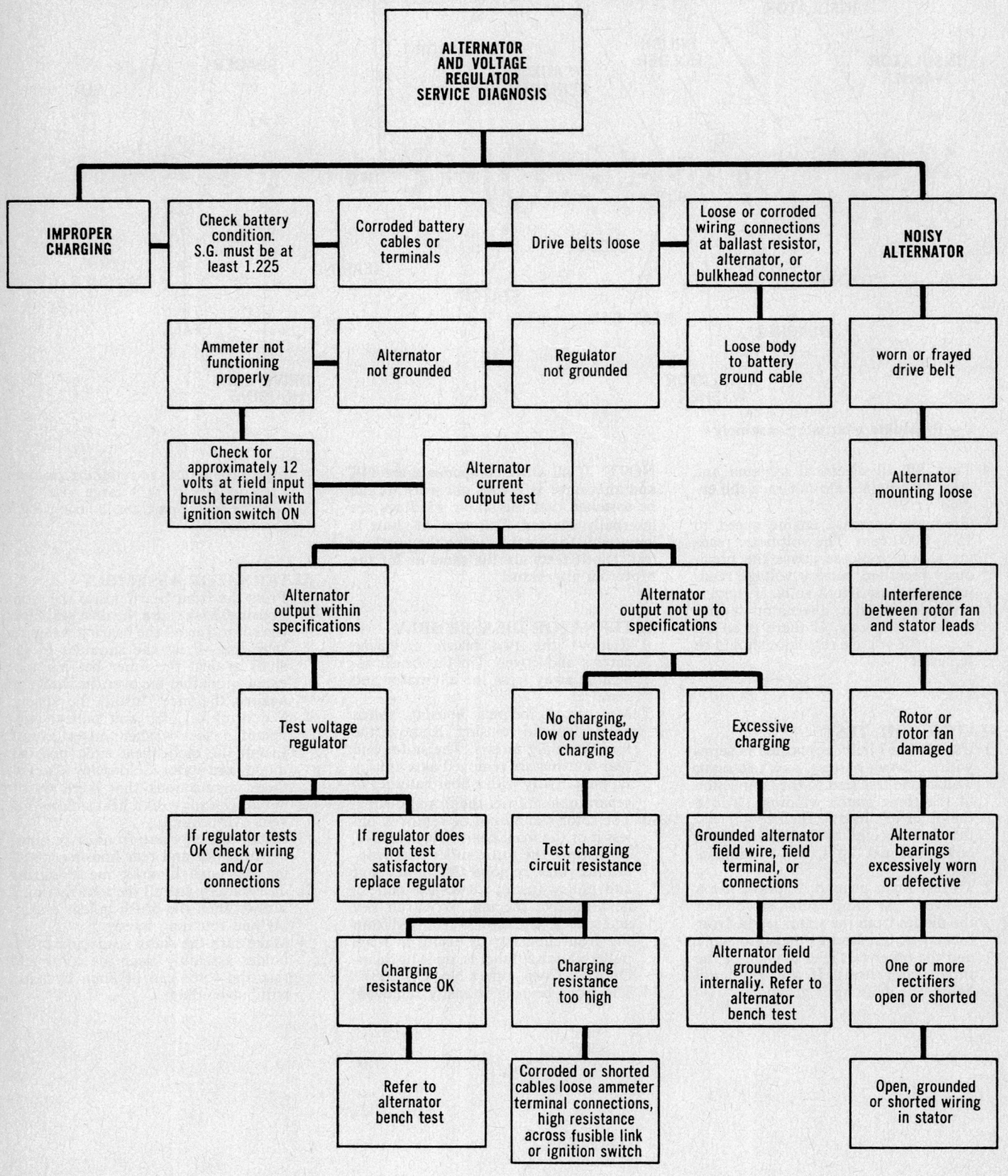

CHRYSLER ISOLATED FIELD ALTERNATOR
(WITH EXTERNAL ELECTRONIC REGULATOR)

Chrysler Isolated Field Alternator (& Electronic Regulator)

Charging System Precautions

To prevent damage to the alternator and regulator, the following precautionary measures must be taken when working with the electrical system.

1 Never reverse battery connections. Always check the battery polarity visually. This should be done before any connections are made to be sure that all of the connections correspond to the battery ground polarity of the truck.
2 Booster batteries for starting must be connected properly. Make sure that the positive cable of the booster battery is connected to the positive terminal of the battery that is getting the boost. The same applies to the negative cables.
3 Disconnect the battery cables before using a fast charger; the charger has a tendency to force current through the diodes in the opposite direction for which they were designed. This burns out the diodes.
4 Never use a fast charger as a booster for starting the vehicle.
5 Never disconnect the voltage regulator while the engine is running.
6 Do not ground the alternator output terminal.
7 Do not operate the alternator on an open circuit with the field energized.
8 Do not attempt to polarize the alternator.

Operation

The isolated field alternator is so-called because it has a field winding (rotor winding) that is not grounded in the alternator. Each end of the field winding is connected to an insulated terminal on the alternator. One of the field terminals is supplied with battery current whenever the ignition switch is on. The other field terminal connects to the electronic regulator, which provides a regulated ground to control the charging voltage.

Two types of isolated field alternators are used. The conventional alternator has six silicon rectifiers (diodes) to convert the A.C. generated current into D.C. output. A 100-ampere alternator is also available. It has twelve silicon rectifiers (diodes) and is recognizable by the double mounting ears on the front half of the housing.

Starting in 1975, a field-loads relay was added to the system on all except Valiant and Dart. It is mounted on the firewall, and shortens the wire from the battery to the regulator, so that the regulator is more responsive to battery condition. Also, the relay disconnects the heater-air conditioning blower motor, and the alternator regulator and field circuit during cranking, for better cold weather starting.

Fusible Links

Chrysler Corporation cars have a single fusible link which is connected between the starter relay and the junction block. Failure of this link will cause all electrical systems to stop functioning.

Testing the Charging System Operation

NOTE: If a current indicator is to give an accurate reading, the battery cables must be of the same gauge and length as the original equipment.

1 With the engine running and all electrical systems off, place a current indicator over the positive battery cable.
2 If a charge of about 5 amps is recorded, the charging system is working. If a draw of about 5 amps is recorded the system is not working. If a draw is indicated, proceed to the next testing procedure. If an overcharge of 10–15 amps is indicated, check for a faulty regulator.

CHRYSLER ISOLATED FIELD ALTERNATOR SPECIFICATIONS

Output Rating	Minimum Output
34 amp unit	36 amps
41 amp unit	40 amps
50 amp unit	47 amps
60 amp unit	57 amps
65 amp unit	62 amps
100 amp unit	72 amps

Current output is measured at:
All except 100 amp unit—1250 rpm & 15v
100 amp unit—900 rpm & 13v

ELECTRONIC VOLTAGE REGULATOR SPECIFICATIONS

Temperature measured ¼ in. from regulator	Voltage Range
−20°F	14.9 to 15.9
+80°F	13.9 to 14.6
+140°F	13.3 to 13.9
Above +140°F	Less than 13.6

In-Car Testing Procedures

IGNITION SWITCH-TO-REGULATOR CIRCUIT CHECK

1 Disconnect the regulator wires at the regulator.
2 Turn the key on; do not start the engine.

3 Using a voltmeter or test light, check for voltage across the I and F terminals. If there is current present, the circuit is good. If there is no current, check for bad connections, a bad ballast resistor, a bad ammeter, broken wires, bad ground at the alternator or voltage regulator, or a bad field-loads relay. Also, check for voltage from the I wire to ground; current should be present. Check for voltage from the F terminal to ground; current should not be present.

ISOLATION TEST

This test determines whether the regulator or alternator is bad, if everything else in the circuit was OK.

1 Disconnect, at the alternator, the wire that runs between one of the alternator field connections and the voltage regulator.
2 Run a jumper wire from the disconnected alternator terminal to ground.
3 Connect a voltmeter to the battery. The positive voltmeter lead connects to the positive battery terminal; the negative lead goes to the negative terminal. Record the reading.
4 Make sure that all electrical systems are turned off. Start the engine. Do not race the engine.
5 Gradually raise engine speed to 1500–2000 rpm. There should be an increase of 1 to 2 volts on the voltmeter. If this is true, the alternator is good and the voltage regulator should be repaired. If there is no voltage increase, the alternator is faulty.

NOTE: The following tests require the use of a carbon pile and an ammeter.

CHARGING CIRCUIT RESISTANCE TEST

1 Disconnect battery ground cable.
2 Disconnect the lead from the alternator output (BATT.) terminal.
3 Hook up an ammeter as follows:
   a. Connect the positive lead to the alternator output terminal
   b. Connect the negative lead to the lead just disconnected from the alternator output terminal
4 Hook up voltmeter as follows:
   a. Connect the positive voltmeter lead to the lead just disconnected from the alternator output terminal
   b. Connect the negative voltmeter lead to the positive battery post
5 Disconnect the green (regulator) lead from the alternator field (FLD.) terminal. The hot lead to the other FLD terminal must be left connected.
6 Connect a jumper wire between alternator field (regulator) terminal and ground.
7 Hook up a tachometer to the engine.

ALTERNATORS
CHRYSLER ISOLATED FIELD (WITH EXTERNAL ELECTRONIC REGULATOR)

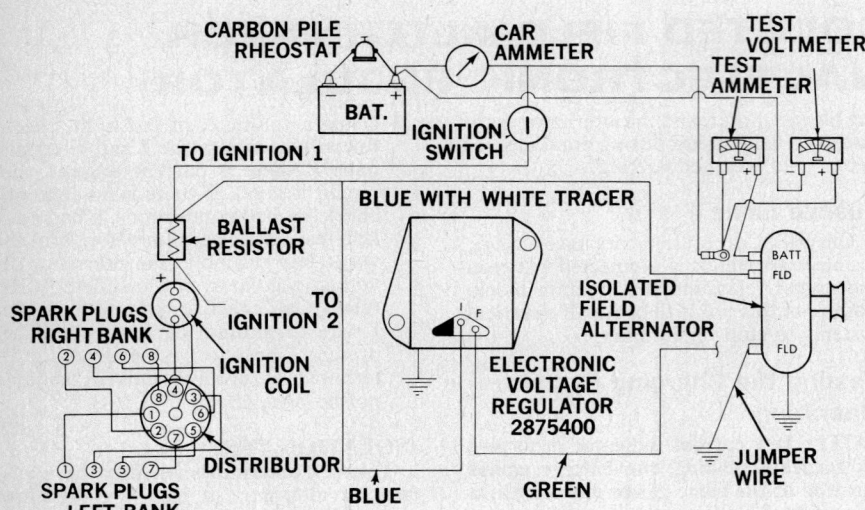

Check for charging circuit resistance

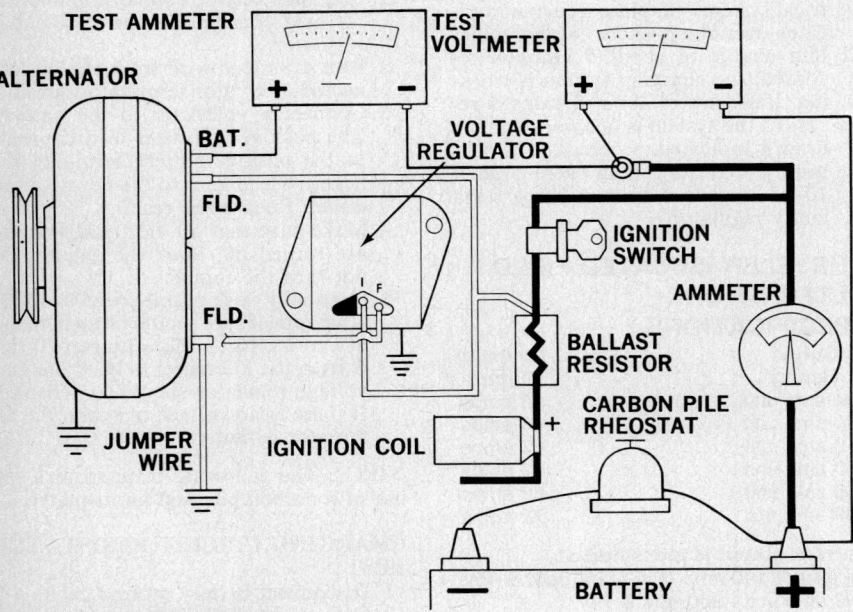

Checking alternator output

8 Connect the battery ground cable; connect carbon pile to battery terminals.

9 Start the engine; allow to idle.

10 Slowly adjust engine speed and carbon pile until the ammeter registers 20 amps.

11 The voltmeter reading will now show the voltage drop in the charging circuit. There should be not more than 0.7 volt drop.

12 If the voltage drop exceeds 0.7 volt, stop the engine, clean and tighten all circuit connections. Repeat the test.

CURRENT OUTPUT TEST

1 The ammeter, carbon pile, and field connection hookup should remain the same as for the circuit resistance test.

2 Connect the voltmeter negative lead to the battery negative post.

3 Move the positive voltmeter lead to the alternator BATT post.

4 Start engine and adjust speed to 1250 rpm.

CHILTON CAUTION: *Reduce engine speed to idle immediately after starting the engine. Adjust the carbon pile and engine speed incrementally until 1250 rpm is reached. (900 rpm on 100 amp alternator).*

5 Note voltmeter and ammeter readings. Maintain a 15 volt reading by adjusting the carbon pile control. (13 volts on 100 amp alternator)

6 Compare ammeter reading with manufacturer's specifications. The reading should be no less than specified.

7 If below specifications, internal trouble is indicated. Remove the alternator for further testing. On cars with a

field-loads relay (1975 and later, except Valiant and Dart) be sure the field-loads relay is okay before removing the alternator.

ELECTRONIC VOLTAGE REGULATOR TEST

1 Make sure battery terminals are clean and battery is charged. (Specific gravity of at least 1.200)

2 On all 1974 and 1975 and later Valiant, Dart, Aspen and Volare connect the positive lead of a test voltmeter to ignition Terminal #1 of the ballast resistor. (Blue or black wire)

NOTE: Don't remove the connector from the ballast resistor terminal.

On 1975 and later models except Aspen, Volare, Dart and Valiant connect the positive lead to the positive battery cable.

3 Connect the negative voltmeter lead to a good body ground.

4 Start engine and allow it to idle at 1250 rpm, all lights and accessories turned off. Voltage should be as follows:

Ambient Temp. ¼ in. from Regulator	Voltage
−20°F.	14.9–15.9
80°F.	13.9–14.6
140°F.	13.3–13.9
Above 140°F.	Less than 13.6

5 If the voltage is below specifications, check the following:
   a. Voltage regulator ground—check voltage drop between regulator base and ground
   b. Harness wiring—disconnect regulator plug (ign. switch off), then turn ign. switch on and check for battery voltage at the terminal with the blue and green leads. Wiring harness must be disconnected from the regulator when checking individual leads. If no voltage is present in either lead, the problem is in the car wiring, alternator field, or field-loads relay.

6 If Step 5 tests show no malfunctions, install a new regulator and repeat Step 4.

7 If voltage is above specifications (Step 4), or fluctuates, check the following:
   a. Ground between regulator and body, and between body and engine
   b. Ignition switch circuit between switch and regulator

8 If voltage is still more than ½ volt above specifications, install a new regulator and repeat Step 4.

FIELD-LOADS RELAY TEST

1 Disconnect the wiring harness on the regulator; connect the negative lead of a voltmeter to a good ground.

2 Turn the ignition switch to the ON position but do not start the engine.

3 With the positive lead from the voltmeter, measure the voltage from the wiring harness connector. The voltage should be the same as the battery voltage.

4 If battery voltage is measured at the harness connector, the relay is functioning. If battery voltage is not measured at the harness connector, check all wiring and connections in the circuit. If all the wiring and connectors check OK the relay is defective.

Off-Car Bench Testing Procedures

TESTING SILICON DIODE RECTIFIERS WITH OHMMETER

Dissassemble the alternator and remove the starter.

There are six diode rectifiers mounted in the back of the alternator. Three of them are marked with a plus (+), and three are marked with a minus (−). These marks indicate diode case polarity.

To test, set ohmmeter to its lowest range. If case is marked positive (+), place positive meter probe to case and negative probe to the diode lead. Meter should read between 4 and 10 ohms. Now, reverse leads of ohmmeter, connecting negative meter probe to positive case and positive meter probe to wire of rectifier. Set meter on a high range. Meter needle should move very little, if any (infinite reading.) Do this to all three positive diode rectifiers.

The three with minus (−) marks on their cases are checked the same way as above. Only now the negative ohmmeter probe is connected to the case for a reading of 4 to 10 ohms. Reverse leads as above for the other part to test.

If a reading of 4 to 10 ohms is obtained in one direction and no reading (infinity) is read on the ohmmeter in the other direction, diode rectifiers are good. If either infinity or a low resistance is obtained in both directions on a rectifier, it must be replaced.

If meter reads more than 10 ohms when ohmmeter positive probe is connected to positive on diode, and negative probe to negative, replace diode rectifier.

NOTE: With this test, it is necessary to determine the polarity of the ohmmeter probes. This can be done by connecting the ohmmeter to a DC voltmeter. The voltmeter will read up-scale when the positive probe of the ohmmeter is connected to the positive side of the voltmeter and the negative probe of the ohmmeter is connected to the negative side of the voltmeter.

ALTERNATE METHOD—TEST LIGHT

Be sure that all leads, including stator leads, to the diode rectifiers are disconnected.

To test rectifiers with plus (+) case, touch positive probe of tester to case and minus (−) probe to lead wire of rectifier.

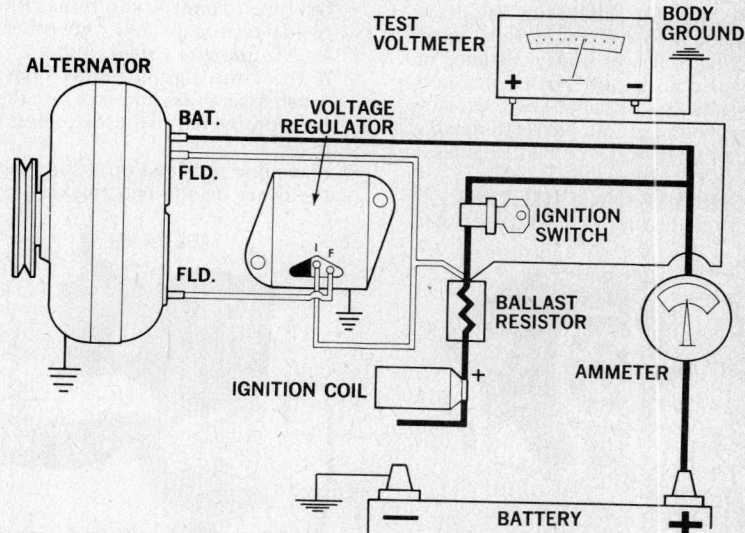

Checking electronic voltage regulator

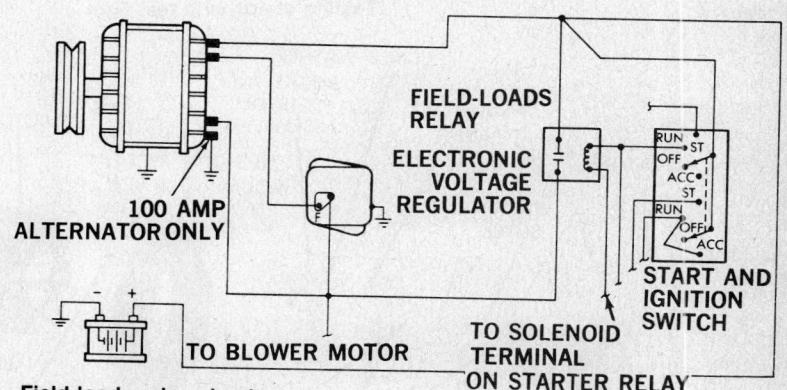

Field loads relay circuit

Diode test with test light

Bulb should light if rectifier is good. If bulb does not light, replace rectifier.

Now reverse tester probe connections to rectifier. Bulb should not light. If bulb does light, replace rectifier.

For testing minus (−) marked cases, follow above procedure, except that now bulb should light with negative probe of tester touching rectifier case and positive probe touching lead wire.

Rectifier is good if the bulb lights when

tester probes are connected one way, and does not light when tester connections are reversed.

Rectifier must be replaced if the bulb does not light either way. Also, replace rectifier if bulb lights both ways.

NOTE: The usual cause of an open or blown diode or rectifier is a defective capacitor or a battery that has been installed in reverse polarity. If the battery is installed properly and the diodes are open, test the capacitor.

Capacitor Specifications
Capacitor capacity:
· · · · · · · · 50 microfarad ± 20%

FIELD COIL DRAW

1 Connect a jumper between one FLD terminal and the positive terminal of a fully charged 12 volt battery.

2 Connect the positive lead of a test ammeter to the other field (FLD) terminal and the negative test lead to the negative battery terminal.

Slowly rotate the rotor by hand and observe the ammeter. The proper field coil draw is 4.5–6.5 amps at 12 volts.

ALTERNATORS

CHRYSLER ISOLATED FIELD (WITH EXTERNAL ELECTRONIC REGULATOR)

On the 100 amp. alternator the draw should be 4.75–6.0 amps. Low rotor coil draw indicates high resistance in the field coil circuit. High rotor coil draw indicates possible shorted rotor coil or grounded coil. No reading indicates an open rotor or bad brushes.

FIELD CIRCUIT GROUND TEST
1 Touch one test lead of a 110 volt AC test bulb to one of the alternator brush (field) terminals and the other test lead to the end shield.
2 If the lamp lights, remove the field brush assemblies and separate the end housing by removing the three thru-bolts.
3 Place one test lead on a slip ring and the other on the end shield.
4 If the lamp lights, the rotor assembly is grounded internally and must be replaced.
5 If the lamp does not light, the cause of the problem was a grounded brush.

STATOR TEST
1 Connect a test light between the stator frame and each stator lead, in sequence.
2 If the lamp lights the stator lead is grounded.
3 Press one test lead to one stator lead; and the other test lead to each of the remaining stator leads.
4 If the lamp does not light the stator is open.
5 If the stator checks either open or grounded replace it.

CURRENT OUTPUT TOO HIGH (NO CONTROL) CAUSED BY OPEN RECTIFIER OR OPEN PHASE
Perform rectifier open in all three phases). If the rectifier tests satisfactorily, inspect the stator connections before replacing the stator.

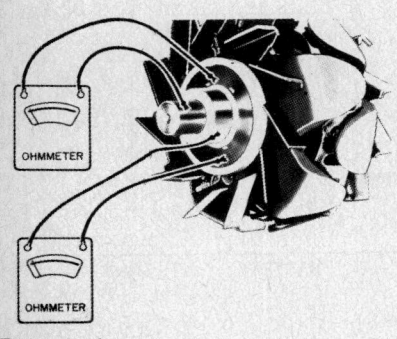

Rotor test

Testing stator with test light

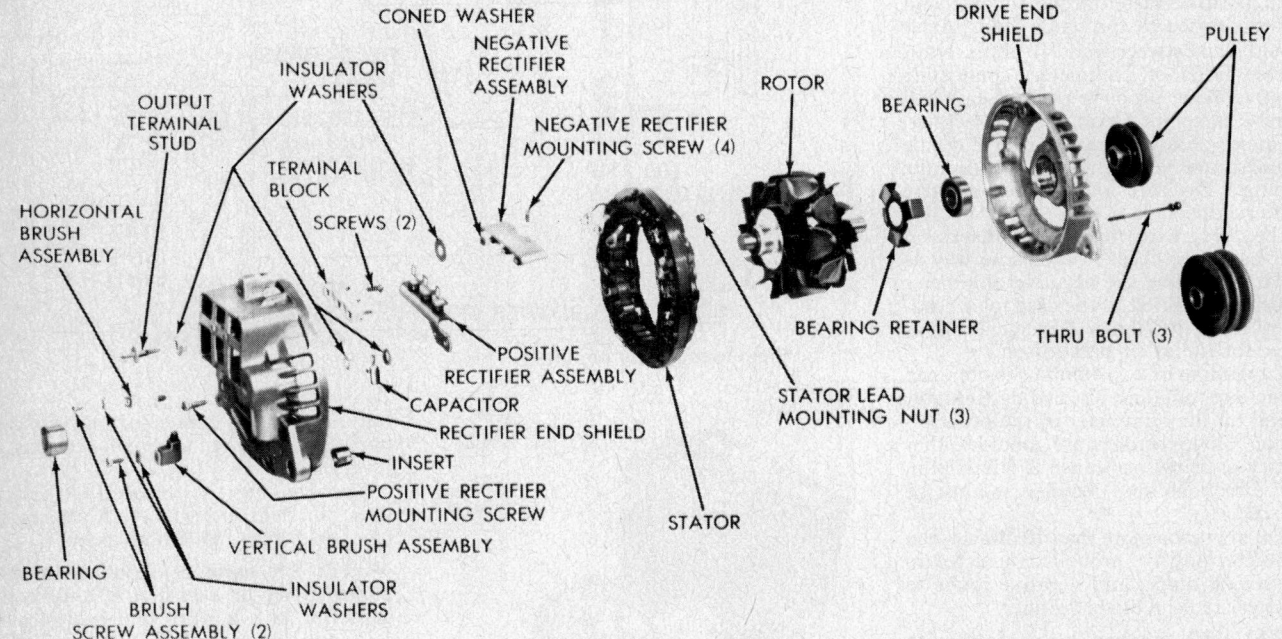

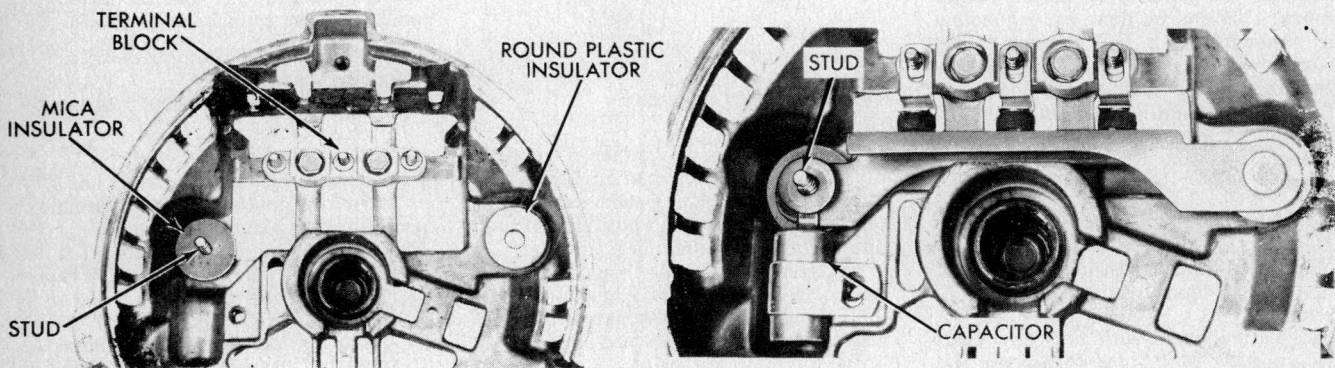

Chrysler Corp. alternator

LOW OUTPUT

(About 50% output accompanied with a growl-hum caused by a shorted phase or a shorted rectifier.)

Perform rectifier tests (rectifier open in all three phases). If the rectifiers are found to be within specifications, replace the stator assembly.

ROTOR TEST

1 To check for a grounded field coil, touch the test leads of an ohmmeter to each slip ring and the rotor shaft. The reading should be infinite. If the reading is zero or higher the rotor is grounded.
2 To check for an open field coil, connect the leads of an ohmmeter to the slip rings. The meter should read between 1½ and 2 ohms at room temperature. Resistance between 2½ and 3 ohms indicate a rotor that has been overheated, but is still usable. If the reading is above 3½ ohms it may be necessary to replace the rotor.
3 To check for a shorted field coil connect the leads from an ohmmeter to the slip rings. If the reading is below 1½ ohms the coil is shorted.

Overhaul Procedures

Alternator disassembly repair and assembly procedures are basically the same for all Chrysler alternators, including the Isolated Field type. Certain variations in design, or in-production modifications, could require slightly different procedures. These should be obvious upon inspection of the unit being serviced. An example of this is the newer type of isolated field alternator, which has two FLD terminals.

DISASSEMBLY

To prevent damage to the brush assemblies they should be removed before proceeding with disassembly of the alternator. The brushes are mounted in plastic holders that position the brushes against the slip rings.

1 Remove the retaining screw, flat washer, nylon washer and field terminal; carefully lift the plastic holder containing the spring and brush assembly from the end housing.

CHILTON CAUTION: *The stator is laminated. Do not burr the stator or end housings.*

2 Remove the through bolts. Pry between the stator and drive end housing with a thin blade screwdriver. Carefully separate the drive end housing, pulley and rotor assembly from the stator and rectifier housing assembly.
3 The pulley is an interference fit on the rotor shaft. Remove with a puller and special adapters.
4 Remove the three nuts and washers. While supporting the end frame, tap the rotor shaft with a plastic hammer

Alternator field brush removal

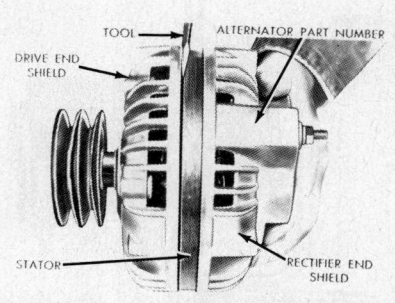
Separating drive end shield from stator

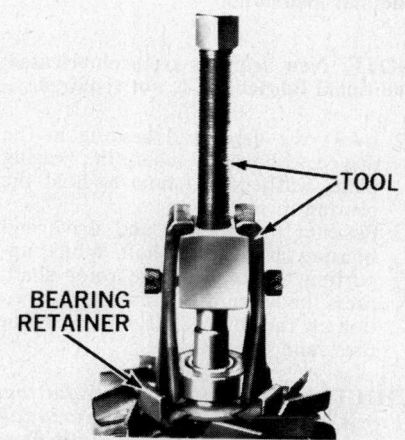
Removal of bearing from rotor shaft

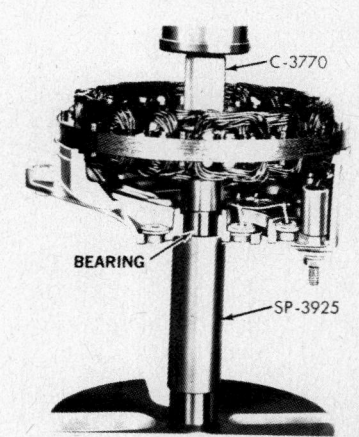
Removal of rectifier end shield bearing

and separate the rotor and end housing.
5 The drive end ball bearing is an interference fit with the rotor shaft. Remove the bearing with puller and adapters.

NOTE: Further dismantling of the rotor is not advisable, as the remainder of the rotor assembly is not serviced separately.

NOTE: The heat sink is also held in place by the terminal screw.

Now remove the insulator.

NOTE: Three positive rectifiers are pressed into the heat sink and three negative rectifiers in the end housing. When removing the rectifiers, it is necessary to support the end housing and/or heat sink to prevent damage to these castings.

CHILTON CAUTION: *Don't subject the diode rectifiers to unnecessary jolting. Heavy vibration or shock may ruin them.*

a. Cut rectifier wire at point of crimp
b. Support rectifier housing

NOTE: The factory tool is cut away and slotted to fit over the wires and around the bosses in the housing. Be sure that the bore of the tool completely surrounds the rectifier, then press the rectifier out of the housing.

NOTE: The roller bearing in the rectifier end frame is a press fit. To protect the end housing it is necessary to support the housing with a tool when pressing out the bearing.

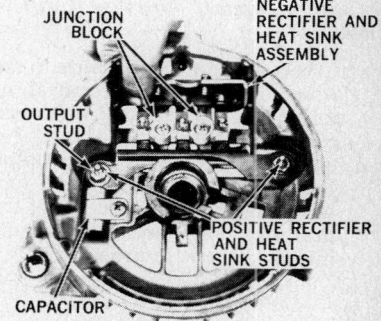
Heat sink & rectifier assembly removal

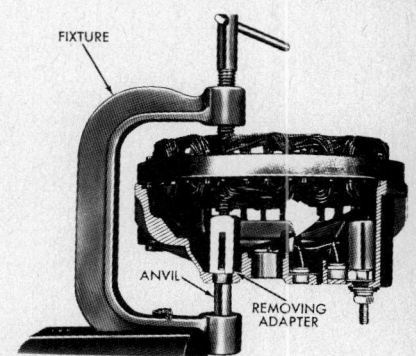
Rectifier removal

ALTERNATORS
CHRYSLER ISOLATED FIELD (WITH EXTERNAL ELECTRONIC REGULATOR)

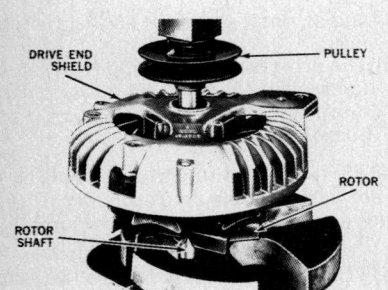

Alternator pulley installation

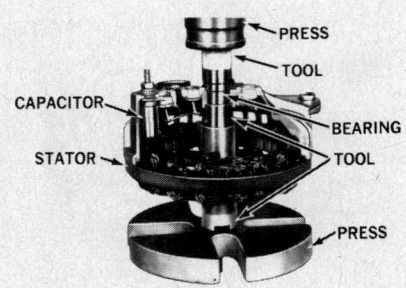

Rectifier end shield bearing installation

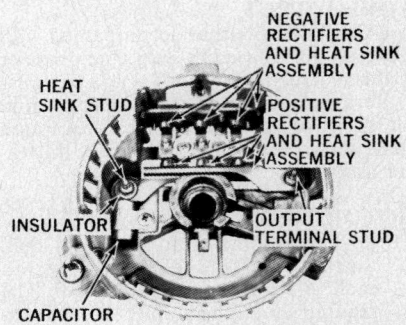

Rectifier installation

6 Remove rectifier and heat sink assemblies. Do this by removing two nuts securing positive rectifier and heat sink assembly to insulated terminals in end shield. Lift the assembly from the case. Loosen the four screws retaining the negative rectifier and heat sink to the end shield. Remove the two outer screws and lift the assembly from the case.

ASSEMBLY
1 On early models support the heat sink or rectifier end housing on circular plate.
   a. Check rectifier identification to be sure the correct rectifier is being used. The part numbers are stamped on the case of the rectifier. They are also marked, red for positive and black for negative.
   b. Start the new rectifier into the casting and press it in squarely.

CHILTON CAUTION: *Do not start rectifier with a hammer otherwise it will be ruined.*

   c. Crimp the new rectifier wire to the wires disconnected at removal, or solder (using a heat sink with rosin core solder)
   d. Support the end housing on tool so that the notch in the support tool will clear the raised section of the heat sink, then press the bearing into position with proper tool.

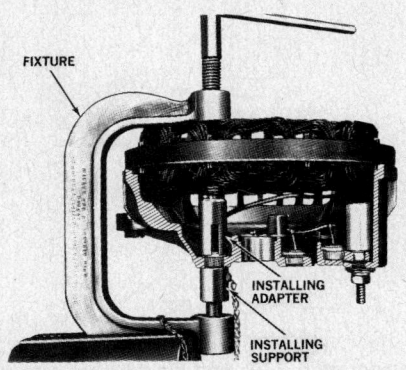

Rectifier installation

NOTE: New bearings are prelubricated; additional lubrication is not required.

2 Insert the drive end bearing in the drive end housing. Install the bearing plate, washers and nuts to hold the bearing in place.
3 Position the bearing and drive end housing on the rotor shaft. While supporting the base of the rotor shaft, press the bearing and housing in position on the rotor shaft with an arbor press and arbor tool.

CHILTON CAUTION: *Be careful that there is no cocking of the bearing at installation; otherwise damage will result. Press the bearing on the rotor shaft until the* bearing contacts the shoulder on the rotor shaft.

4 Install pulley on rotor shaft. Shaft of rotor must be supported so that all pressing force is on the pulley hub and rotor shaft.

NOTE: Do not exceed 6800 lbs. pressure. Pulley hub should just contact bearing inner race. Do not use a hammer.

5 Some alternators will be found to have the capacitor mounted internally. Be sure the heat sink insulator is in place.
6 Position the stator on the rectifier end housing. Be sure that all of the rectifier connectors and phase leads do not interfer with the rotor fan blades and that the capacitor lead (internally mounted) has clearance.
7 Position the rotor assembly in the rectifier end housing. Align the through bolt holes in the stator with both end housings.
8 Enter stator shaft in the rectifier end housing bearing; compress stator and both end housings manually and install through bolts, washers and nuts.
9 Install the insulated brush and terminal attaching screw.
10 Install the ground screw and attaching screw.
11 Rotate pulley slowly to be sure the rotor fan blades do not hit the rectifier and stator connectors.

TROUBLESHOOTING
FORD AUTOLITE/MOTORCRAFT ALTERNATOR
(WITH INTERNAL REGULATOR)

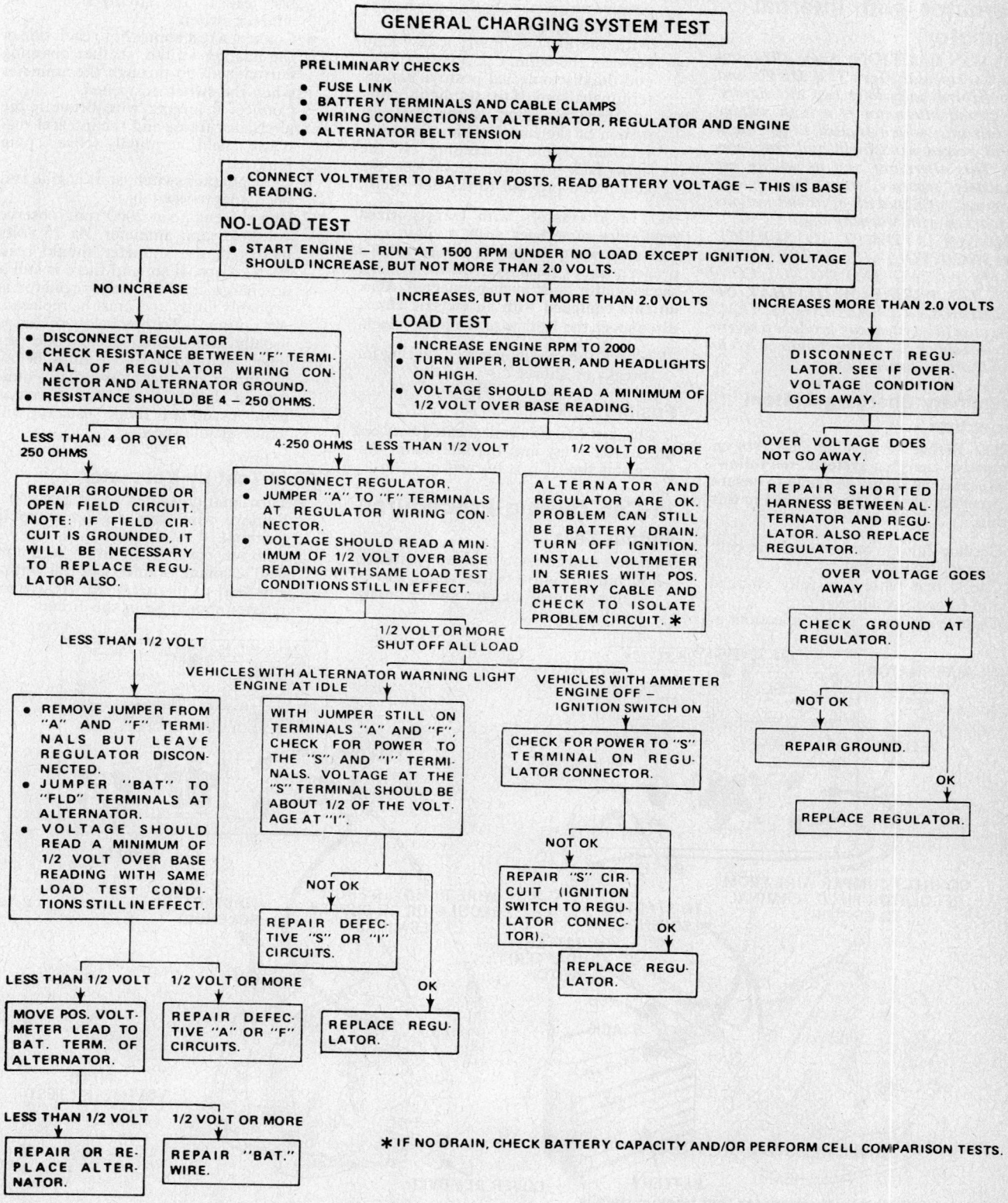

GENERAL CHARGING SYSTEM TEST

PRELIMINARY CHECKS
- FUSE LINK
- BATTERY TERMINALS AND CABLE CLAMPS
- WIRING CONNECTIONS AT ALTERNATOR, REGULATOR AND ENGINE
- ALTERNATOR BELT TENSION

- CONNECT VOLTMETER TO BATTERY POSTS. READ BATTERY VOLTAGE — THIS IS BASE READING.

NO-LOAD TEST
- START ENGINE — RUN AT 1500 RPM UNDER NO LOAD EXCEPT IGNITION. VOLTAGE SHOULD INCREASE, BUT NOT MORE THAN 2.0 VOLTS

NO INCREASE

INCREASES, BUT NOT MORE THAN 2.0 VOLTS

LOAD TEST

INCREASES MORE THAN 2.0 VOLTS

- DISCONNECT REGULATOR
- CHECK RESISTANCE BETWEEN "F" TERMINAL OF REGULATOR WIRING CONNECTOR AND ALTERNATOR GROUND.
- RESISTANCE SHOULD BE 4 – 250 OHMS.

- INCREASE ENGINE RPM TO 2000
- TURN WIPER, BLOWER, AND HEADLIGHTS ON HIGH.
- VOLTAGE SHOULD READ A MINIMUM OF 1/2 VOLT OVER BASE READING.

DISCONNECT REGULATOR. SEE IF OVERVOLTAGE CONDITION GOES AWAY.

LESS THAN 4 OR OVER 250 OHMS

4-250 OHMS

LESS THAN 1/2 VOLT

1/2 VOLT OR MORE

OVER VOLTAGE DOES NOT GO AWAY.

REPAIR GROUNDED OR OPEN FIELD CIRCUIT. NOTE: IF FIELD CIRCUIT IS GROUNDED, IT WILL BE NECESSARY TO REPLACE REGULATOR ALSO.

- DISCONNECT REGULATOR.
- JUMPER "A" TO "F" TERMINALS AT REGULATOR WIRING CONNECTOR.
- VOLTAGE SHOULD READ A MINIMUM OF 1/2 VOLT OVER BASE READING WITH SAME LOAD TEST CONDITIONS STILL IN EFFECT.

ALTERNATOR AND REGULATOR ARE OK. PROBLEM CAN STILL BE BATTERY DRAIN. TURN OFF IGNITION. INSTALL VOLTMETER IN SERIES WITH POS. BATTERY CABLE AND CHECK TO ISOLATE PROBLEM CIRCUIT. ✱

REPAIR SHORTED HARNESS BETWEEN ALTERNATOR AND REGULATOR. ALSO REPLACE REGULATOR.

OVER VOLTAGE GOES AWAY

CHECK GROUND AT REGULATOR.

LESS THAN 1/2 VOLT

1/2 VOLT OR MORE SHUT OFF ALL LOAD

VEHICLES WITH ALTERNATOR WARNING LIGHT ENGINE AT IDLE

VEHICLES WITH AMMETER ENGINE OFF — IGNITION SWITCH ON

NOT OK

- REMOVE JUMPER FROM "A" AND "F" TERMINALS BUT LEAVE REGULATOR DISCONNECTED.
- JUMPER "BAT" TO "FLD" TERMINALS AT ALTERNATOR.
- VOLTAGE SHOULD READ A MINIMUM OF 1/2 VOLT OVER BASE READING WITH SAME LOAD TEST CONDITIONS STILL IN EFFECT.

WITH JUMPER STILL ON TERMINALS "A" AND "F", CHECK FOR POWER TO THE "S" AND "I" TERMINALS. VOLTAGE AT THE "S" TERMINAL SHOULD BE ABOUT 1/2 OF THE VOLTAGE AT "I".

CHECK FOR POWER TO "S" TERMINAL ON REGULATOR CONNECTOR.

REPAIR GROUND.

OK

LESS THAN 1/2 VOLT

1/2 VOLT OR MORE

NOT OK

REPLACE REGULATOR.

MOVE POS. VOLTMETER LEAD TO BAT. TERM. OF ALTERNATOR.

REPAIR DEFECTIVE "A" OR "F" CIRCUITS.

REPAIR DEFECTIVE "S" OR "I" CIRCUITS.

REPAIR "S" CIRCUIT (IGNITION SWITCH TO REGULATOR CONNECTOR).

OK

OK

REPLACE REGULATOR.

LESS THAN 1/2 VOLT

1/2 VOLT OR MORE

REPLACE REGULATOR.

REPAIR OR REPLACE ALTERNATOR.

REPAIR "BAT." WIRE.

✱ IF NO DRAIN, CHECK BATTERY CAPACITY AND/OR PERFORM CELL COMPARISON TESTS.

FORD AUTOLITE/MOTORCRAFT ALTERNATOR (WITH INTERNAL REGULATOR)

Ford Autolite/Motorcraft Alternator (with Internal Regulator)

CHILTON CAUTION: *Some 1974 and later Continental Mark IVs, MKV's and Thunderbirds may have two alternators. The second alternator is a high voltage 120-volt unit which is used to operate a special heated windshield and rear window. This alternator and its wiring are completely separate from the regular charging system and all of its connections are marked with warning tags.*

DO NOT ATTEMPT TO SERVICE THE HIGH VOLTAGE ALTERNATOR OR ITS WIRING AND DO NOT CONFUSE ITS WIRING WITH THAT OF THE REGULAR CHARGING SYSTEM.

Because this system can produce a severe electrical shock, its service should be left to an authorized facility.

Preliminary Charging System Inspection

NOTE: Before performing any tests on automotive charging systems, the following precautions should be taken to ensure the accuracy of the tests described in this section.

1 Check condition of the alternator belt; tighten if necessary.
2 Check that battery is fully charged and in good condition.
3 Clean the battery cable connections at the battery. Make sure that all connections are good. Disconnect the positive terminal only, and proceed to the next step.
4 With the key off, insert a test light between the battery positive terminal and the disconnected positive battery terminal clamp. If the test light comes on, there is a short in the electrical system of the car. The short must be repaired before proceeding. If the light fails to glow, reconnect the clamp and proceed to the next step.

NOTE: Alternators with transistorized regulators sometimes draw a slight current even when the key is turned off. To properly check these systems for a short, the regulator must be disconnected. Also, on cars equipped with an electric clock, disconnect the lead wire from the clock.

5 Check the charging system wiring for breaks or shorts.

Fusible Links

Check the fusible link located between the starter relay and the alternator. Replace this link if it is burned or open.

In-Car Testing Procedures

Output Test

1 Place transmission in Neutral or Park.
2 Remove positive battery cable and install a battery adapter switch in the line.
3 Attach one lead of a test voltmeter to the negative battery post and the other test lead to the circuit side of the adapter switch.
4 Connect a test ammeter to each side of the adapter switch, so that charging current will go through the ammeter when the switch is opened.
5 Connect a jumper wire between the alternator frame and the integral regulator field terminal (cover plug removed).
6 Close adapter switch; start engine and open adapter switch.
7 Run the engine at 2000 rpm; observe voltmeter and ammeter. At 15 volts indicated, the ammeter should read 50–57 amps. If so, and there is still a no-charge condition, the regulator is probably faulty and must be replaced. An output 2–8 amps below 50 amps usually indicates an open diode rectifier; an output 10–15 amps below minimum specifications usually indicates a shorted diode. An alternator with a shorted diode usually will whine at idle speed.

Field Test by Voltmeter

1 Turn ignition switch to off position.
2 Remove wire from regulator supply terminal.
3 Remove cover plug from regulator field terminal. Connect one test voltmeter lead to this terminal. A ¼ ohm resistor should be in the circuit.

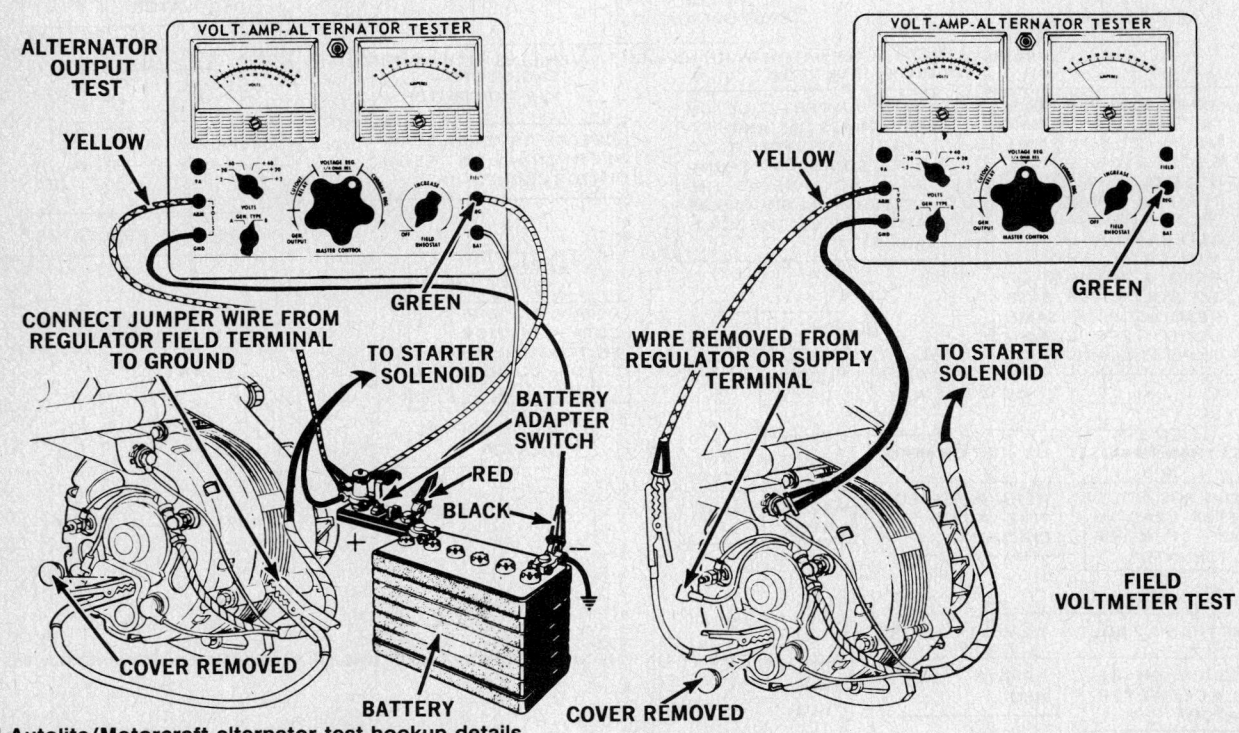

Ford Autolite/Motorcraft alternator test hookup details

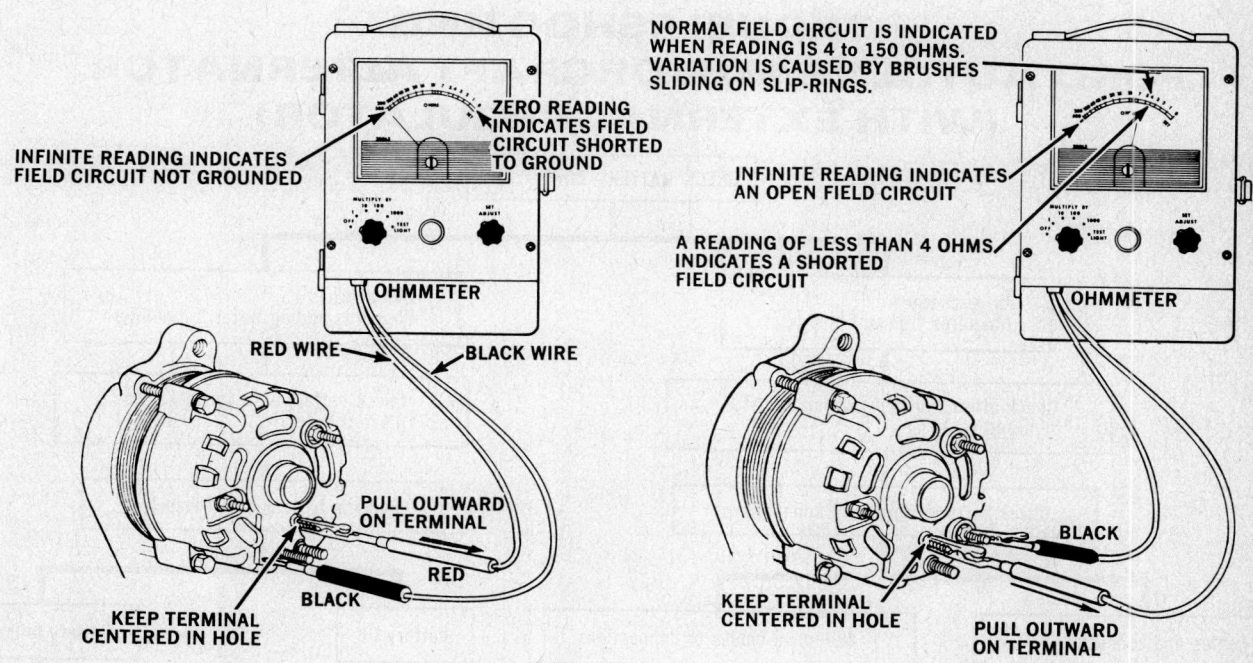

INFINITE READING INDICATES FIELD CIRCUIT NOT GROUNDED

ZERO READING INDICATES FIELD CIRCUIT SHORTED TO GROUND

NORMAL FIELD CIRCUIT IS INDICATED WHEN READING IS 4 to 150 OHMS. VARIATION IS CAUSED BY BRUSHES SLIDING ON SLIP-RINGS.

INFINITE READING INDICATES AN OPEN FIELD CIRCUIT

A READING OF LESS THAN 4 OHMS INDICATES A SHORTED FIELD CIRCUIT

OHMMETER

OHMMETER

RED WIRE — BLACK WIRE

PULL OUTWARD ON TERMINAL

RED

BLACK

BLACK

KEEP TERMINAL CENTERED IN HOLE

KEEP TERMINAL CENTERED IN HOLE

PULL OUTWARD ON TERMINAL

GROUNDED FIELD CIRCUIT TEST

SHORTED OR OPEN FIELD CIRCUIT TEST

Ohmmeter check hookup

4 Connect the other test voltmeter lead to a good engine ground.
5 The voltmeter should read 12 volts. If no voltage is present, the field circuit is open or grounded.
6 If voltmeter reads more than 1 volt, but still less than battery voltage, there is probably a partial ground in the alternator field circuit. The circuit should be checked with an ohmmeter.

Field Test by Ohmmeter

1 Disconnect battery ground cable; remove alternator from car.
2 Remove regulator from the alternator (covered later).
3 Make the ohmmeter tests as illustrated. If any of the tests indicates a field circuit problem, disassemble the alternator to further isolate the trouble.
   a. Contact each ohmmeter probe to a slip ring. Resistance should be 4–5 ohms. A higher reading indicates a damaged slip ring soldered connection or a broken wire. A lower reading indicates a shorted wire or slip ring assembly.

b. Contact one ohmmeter probe to a slip ring and the other probe to the rotor shaft. Any reading other than infinite ohms indicates a short to ground.
   If neither of these tests (a & b above) isolates the trouble, the brushes or brush assembly are the probable cause.

Voltage Limiter Test

1 Check the battery specific gravity. If it is not at least 1.230, charge the battery or install a charged battery for the test.
2 Make sure all lights and accessories are turned off, including such items as dome lights and radio.
3 Make the test connections as illustrated.
4 Place transmission in Neutral or Park; close battery adapter switch; start the engine.
5 Open the battery adapter switch and operate engine at 2000 rpm for 5 minutes. The voltmeter should read 13.–3–15.3 volts.
6 If voltage does not rise above 12 volts, perform a regulator supply voltage

test to determine whether or not the regulator is getting voltage from the battery. Before replacing a regulator, check the wiring of the entire charging system for shorts, opens, or high resistance connections.

Regulator Supply Voltage Test

The regulator is turned on by the application of battery voltage through a 10 ohm resistor wire. If the supply circuit is defective, the regulator will not function and the alternator will not put out current.

1 Connect a 12-volt test light or voltmeter between the regulator supply lead and ground.
2 Turn on the ignition switch. The test light should glow or the voltmeter indicate. If not, the supply circuit should be checked back to the battery, especially the resistance wire.

Overhaul

The overhaul procedures for this alternator are the same as for the Ford Autolite/Motorcraft Alternator with electromechanical regulator.

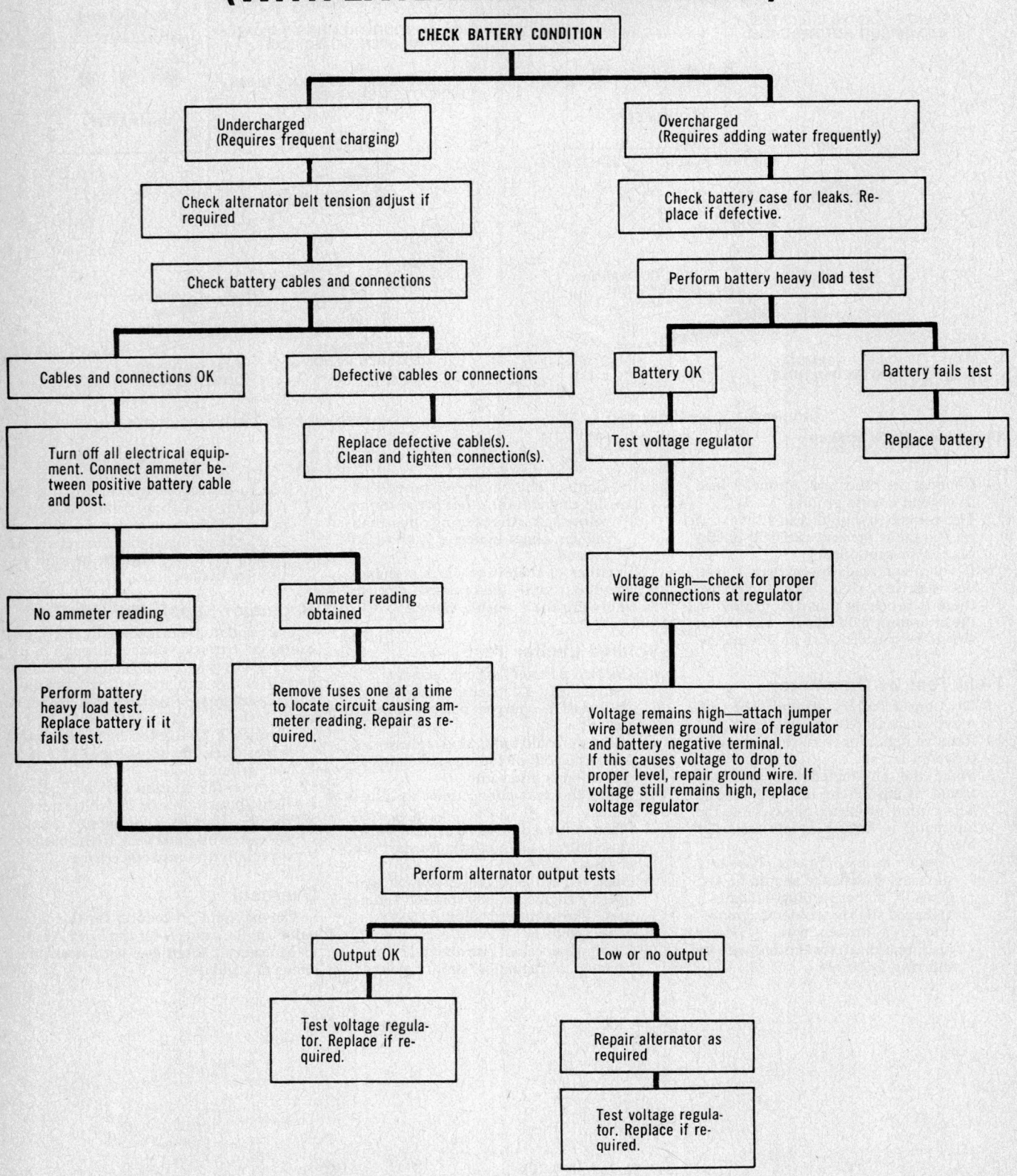

TROUBLESHOOTING
FORD AUTOLITE/MOTORCRAFT ALTERNATOR
(WITH EXTERNAL REGULATOR)

CHECK BATTERY CONDITION

Undercharged
(Requires frequent charging)

Overcharged
(Requires adding water frequently)

Check alternator belt tension adjust if required

Check battery case for leaks. Replace if defective.

Check battery cables and connections

Perform battery heavy load test

Cables and connections OK

Defective cables or connections

Battery OK

Battery fails test

Turn off all electrical equipment. Connect ammeter between positive battery cable and post.

Replace defective cable(s). Clean and tighten connection(s).

Test voltage regulator

Replace battery

No ammeter reading

Ammeter reading obtained

Voltage high—check for proper wire connections at regulator

Perform battery heavy load test. Replace battery if it fails test.

Remove fuses one at a time to locate circuit causing ammeter reading. Repair as required.

Voltage remains high—attach jumper wire between ground wire of regulator and battery negative terminal. If this causes voltage to drop to proper level, repair ground wire. If voltage still remains high, replace voltage regulator

Perform alternator output tests

Output OK

Low or no output

Test voltage regulator. Replace if required.

Repair alternator as required

Test voltage regulator. Replace if required.

FORD AUTOLITE/MOTORCRAFT ALTERNATOR (WITH EXTERNAL REGULATOR)

Ford Autolite/Motorcraft Alternator (with Electro-Mechanical Regulator)

Charging System Precautions

To prevent damage to the alternator and regulator, the following precautionary measures must be taken when working with the electrical system.

1 Never reverse battery connections. Always check the batter polarity visually. This should be done before any connections are made to be sure that all of the connections correspond to the battery ground polarity of the truck.
2 Booster batteries for starting must be connected properly. Make sure that the positive cable of the booster battery is connected to the positive terminal of the battery that is getting the boost. The same applies to the negative cables.
3 Disconnect the battery cables before using a fast charger; the charger has a tendency to force current through the diodes in the opposite direction for which they were designed. This burns out the diodes.
4 Never use a fast charger as a booster for starting the vehicle.
5 Never disconnect the voltage regulator while the engine is running.
6 Do not ground the alternator output terminal.
7 Do not operate the alternator on an open circuit with the field energized.
8 Do not attempt to polarize an alternator.

CHILTON CAUTION: *Some 1974 and later Continental Mark IVs and Thunderbirds may have two alternators. The second alternator is a high voltage 120-volt unit which is used to operate a special heated windshield and rear window. This alternator and its wiring are completely separate from the regular charging system. All of its connections are marked with warning tags.*

DO NOT ATTEMPT TO SERVICE THE HIGH VOLTAGE ALTERNATOR OR ITS WIRING AND DO NOT CONFUSE ITS WIRING WITH THAT OF THE REGULAR CHARGING SYSTEM.

Because this system can produce a severe electrical shock, its service should be left to an authorized facility.

Preliminary Charging System Inspection

NOTE: Before performing any tests on automotive charging systems, the following precautions should be taken to ensure the accuracy of the tests described in this section.

1 Check condition of the alternator belt; tighten if necessary.
2 Check that battery is fully charged and in good condition.
3 Clean the battery cable connections at the battery. Make sure that all connections are good. Disconnect the positive terminal only, and proceed to the next step.
4 With the key off, insert a test light between the battery positive terminal and the disconnected positive battery terminal clamp. If the test light comes on, there is a short in the electrical system of the car. The short must be repaired before proceeding. If the light fails to glow, reconnect the clamp and proceed to the next step.

NOTE: Alternators with transistorized regulators sometimes draw a slight current even when the key is turned off. To properly check these systems for a short, the regulator must be disconnected. Also, on cars equipped with an electric clock, disconnect the lead wire from the clock.

5 Check the charging system wiring for breaks or shorts.

Fusible Links

Check the fusible link located between the starter relay and the alternator. Replace this link if it is burned or open.

Charging System Operation

NOTE: If the current indicator is to give an accurate reading, the battery cables must be of the same gauge and length as the original equipment.

1 With the engine running, and all electrical systems turned off, place a current indicator over the positive battery cable.
2 If a charge of about 5 amps is recorded, the charging system is working. If a draw of about 5 amps is recorded, the system is not working. If a draw is indicated, continue to the next testing procedure. If an overcharge of 10–15 amps is indicated, check for a faulty regulator or a bad ground at the regulator or the alternator.

In-Car Testing Procedures

Testing the Ignition Switch-to-Regulator Circuit

1 Disconnect the regulator wiring harness from the regulator.
2 Turn the key to on. Use a test light or voltmeter to check for voltage between the I wire and ground. Check for voltage between the A wire and ground. If voltage is present at this part of the system the circuit is OK. If there is no voltage at the I wire, check

for a burned-out charge indicator bulb, a burned-out resistor, or a break or short in the wiring. If there is no voltage present at the A wire check for a bad connection at the starter relay or a break or short in the wire.

Isolation Test

This test determines whether the regulator or the alternator is faulty, after the rest of the circuit is found to be in good working order.

1 Disconnect the regulator wiring harness from the regulator.
2 Connect a jumper wire from the A wire to the F wire in the wiring harness plug.
3 Connect a voltmeter to the battery. The positive voltmeter lead goes to the positive terminal; the negative lead to the negative terminal. Record the reading on the voltmeter.
4 Turn off all electrical systems. Start the engine. Do not race the engine.
5 Gradually increase engine speed to 1500–2000 rpm. The voltmeter reading should increase above the previously recorded battery voltage reading by at least 1 to 2 volts. If there is no increase, the alternator is not working correctly. If there is an increase, the voltage regulator needs to be replaced.

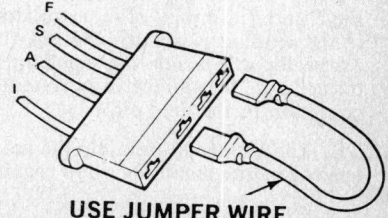

USE JUMPER WIRE TO CONNECT "A" AND "F" TERMINALS AT REGULATOR PLUG
Regulator jumper wire connections

Charging System Voltmeter Tests

TEST 1

These tests will determine if the charging system is operating properly.

1 Connect a voltmeter to the battery and a tachometer to the engine.
2 Check the battery voltage. Start the engine.
3 Run the engine at 1500 rpm and make sure that all electrical systems are switch off. The reading on the voltmeter should increase 1 to 2 volts above the first battery reading.
4 Increase engine speed to 2000 rpm and turn on the headlights, heater blower and/or A/C blower. The voltage should be a minimum of 0.5 volts above the first battery reading.

ALTERNATORS

FORD-AUTOLITE MOTORCRAFT (WITH EXTERNAL REGULATOR)

If the system checks out as described above it is operating properly. If not, proceed with the following tests.

TEST 2

1 If the voltage measured in Step 4 above, was more than 2 volts above battery voltage, turn engine off and check the ground for alternator and regulator. Check the voltage again.
2 If a higher voltage reading still exists, remove the wiring connector from regulator. Check the voltage again using the first test. If the high voltage condition is gone replace the regulator. Check the voltage again.
3 If high voltage is still present, even with the regulator connector removed, check for a short in the wiring between the alternator and the regulator. Test voltage again.

TEST 3

1 If the voltage was too low, check for voltage at the alternator BAT. terminal and the regulator plug A terminal. The reading should be the same as battery. If there is no voltage present check the wiring and repeat the voltage test.
2 If low voltage still exists, check the field circuit for a grounded condition by connecting an ohmmeter to the F terminal of the regulator plug and the battery ground. The ohmmeter reading should be between 4 to 250 ohms.
3 Check the regulator for a burned out wire by connecting an ohmmeter to the F and I terminals of the regulator. If the reading is about 10 ohms the connector wire inside the regulator is burned out. This indicates a grounded condition in the field circuit.

NOTE: The grounded field circuit must be repaired before installing a new regulator.

Field Circuit & Alternator Test

1 If the field circuit is OK, disconnect the regulator wiring plug at the regu-

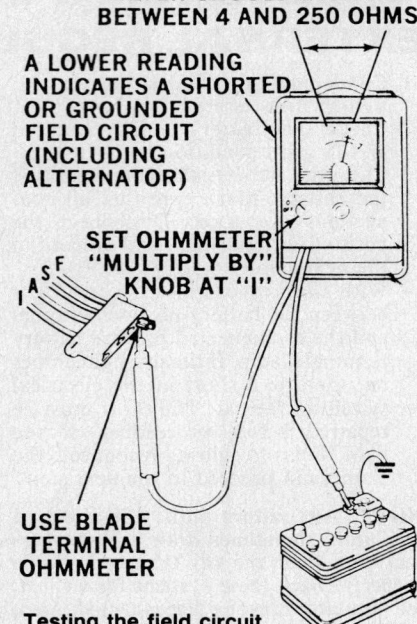

METER SHOULD INDICATE BETWEEN 4 AND 250 OHMS

A LOWER READING INDICATES A SHORTED OR GROUNDED FIELD CIRCUIT (INCLUDING ALTERNATOR)

SET OHMMETER "MULTIPLY BY" KNOB AT "I"

USE BLADE TERMINAL OHMMETER

Testing the field circuit

lator. Connect a jumper wire from the A to the F terminals on the regulator plug.
2 Repeat Charging System Voltmeter Test 1.
3 If Test 1 still indicates a problem of low voltage, remove the jumper wire from the regulator plug and leave the plug disconnected from the regulator. Connect a jumper wire to the FLD. and BAT. terminals on the alternator.
4 Repeat Charging System Voltmeter Test 1.
5 If Test 1 results are now satisfactory, repair the wiring harness from the alternator to the regulator. Then, remove the jumper wire at the alternator and connect the regulator wiring plug to the regulator.
6 Repeat Charging System Voltmeter Test 1 to be sure the charging system is operating normally.

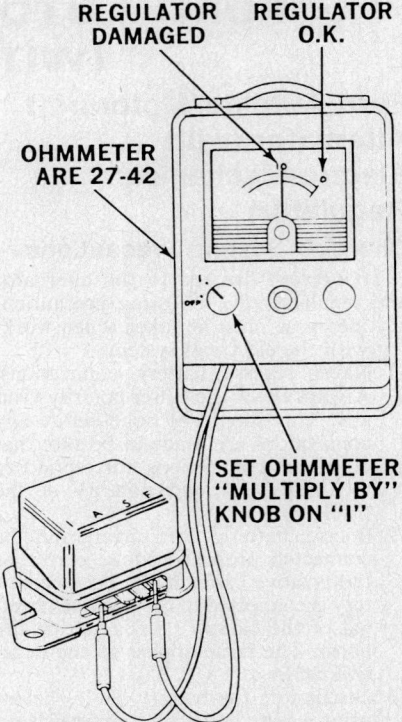

REGULATOR DAMAGED   REGULATOR O.K.

OHMMETER ARE 27-42

SET OHMMETER "MULTIPLY BY" KNOB ON "I"

Connections for burned out wire test

7 If the test results still indicate low voltage, repair or replace the alternator. With the jumper wire removed, connect the wiring to the alternator and regulator.
8 Repeat Charging System Voltmeter Test 1.

Regulator I&S Circuit Tests

S CIRCUIT WITH AMMETER

1 Connect the positive lead of the voltmeter to the S terminal of the regulator wiring plug. Turn the ignition switch to the on position. Do not start the engine.
2 The voltmeter reading should indicate battery voltage.
3 If there is no voltage, disconnect the positive voltmeter lead from the positive battery clamp and repair the S wire lead from the ignition switch to the regulator wiring plug.
4 Connect the positive voltmeter lead to the positive battery cable terminal and repeat Charging System Voltmeter Test 1 described above.

Off-Car Bench Testing Procedures

Field Current Draw Test

1 Connect a test ammeter between the alternator frame and the positive post of a 12-volt test battery.
2 Connect a jumper wire between the negative test battery post and the alternator field terminal.

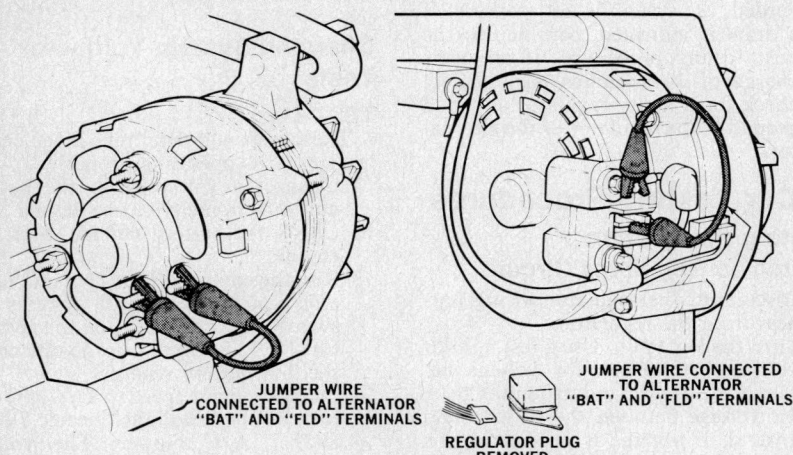

JUMPER WIRE CONNECTED TO ALTERNATOR "BAT" AND "FLD" TERMINALS

JUMPER WIRE CONNECTED TO ALTERNATOR "BAT" AND "FLD" TERMINALS

REGULATOR PLUG REMOVED FROM REGULATOR

Alternator jumper wire connections

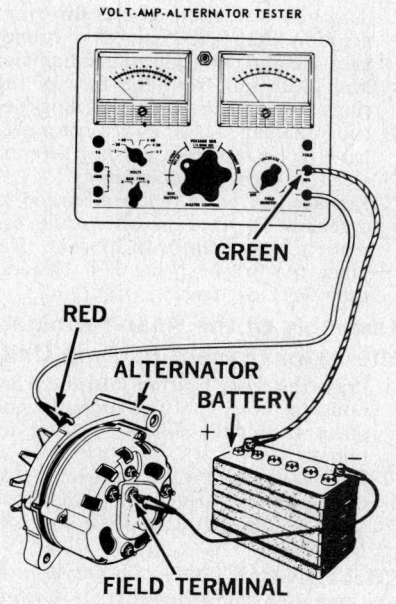

Connections for field current draw test

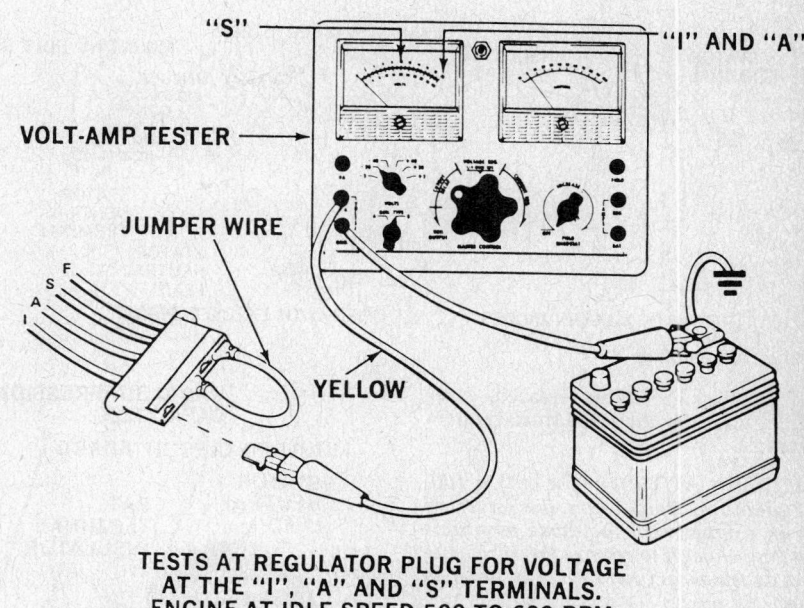

TESTS AT REGULATOR PLUG FOR VOLTAGE
AT THE "I", "A" AND "S" TERMINALS.
ENGINE AT IDLE SPEED 500 TO 600 RPM

Connections for regulator voltage plug test

3 Observe the ammeter:
  a. Little or no current flow indicates high brush resistance, open field windings, or high winding resistance.
  b. Current in excess of specifications (approximately 2.9 amps for most models) indicates shorted or grounded field windings, or brush leads touching.

NOTE: Sometimes the alternator produces current output at low engine speeds, but ceases to put out at higher speeds. This can be caused by centrifugal force expanding the rotor windings to the point where they short to ground. Place a test stand and check field current draw while spinning alternator.

Diode Tests

Disassemble the alternator. Disconnect diode assembly from stator and make tests as illustrated. To test one set of diodes, contact one ohmmeter probe to the diode plate and contact each of the three stator lead terminals with the other probe. Reverse the probes and repeat the test. All tests should show a reading of 60 ohms in one direction and infinite ohms in the other. If two high readings, or two low readings, are obtained after reversing probes the diode is faulty and must be replaced.

Stator Tests

Dissamble the stator from the alternator assembly and rectifiers. Connect test ohmmeter probes between each pair of stator leads. If the ohmmeter does not indicate equally between each pair of leads, the stator coil is open and must be replaced.

Connect test ohmmeter probes between one of the stator leads and the stator core. The ohmmeter should not show any reading. If it does show continuity, the stator winding is grounded and must be replaced.

Overhaul Procedures
Disassembly of the Rear-Terminal Alternator (Except 65 Amp Unit)

1 Mark both end housings with a scribe mark for assembly.
2 Remove the three housing through bolts.
3 Separate the front housing and rotor from the stator and rear housing.
4 Remove the nuts from the rectifier to rear housing mounting studs. Remove the rear housing.
5 Remove the brush holder mounting screws and the holder, brushes, springs, insulator, and terminal.
6 If replacement is necessary, press the bearing from the rear end housing, support housing on inner boss.

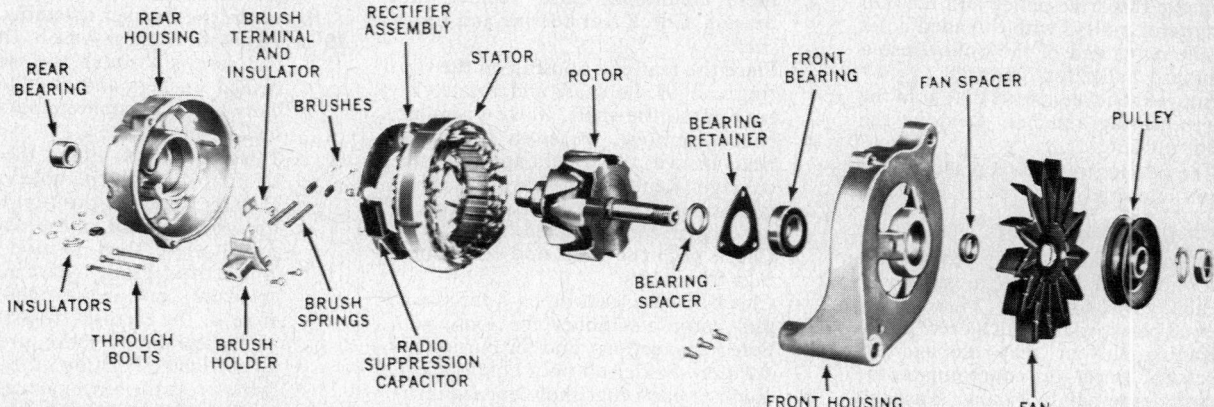

Ford Autolite/Motorcraft rear terminal alternator assembly

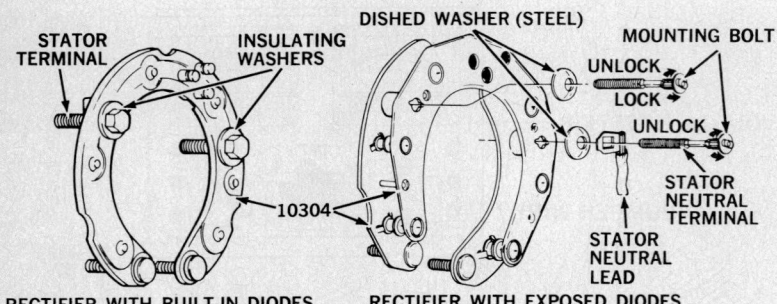

RECTIFIER WITH BUILT-IN DIODES   RECTIFIER WITH EXPOSED DIODES

Rectifier assemblies

7 If rectifiers are to be replaced, carefully unsolder the leads from the terminals.

CHILTON CAUTION: *Use only a 100-watt soldering iron. Leave the soldering iron in contact with the diode terminals only long enough to remove the wires. Use pliers as temporary heat sinks in order to protect the diodes.*

8 Various types of rectifier assembly circuit boards are installed in production of this model alternator. One type has the circuit board spaced away from the diode plates with the diodes exposed. Another type consists of a single circuit board with integral diodes. Still another has integral with an additional booster diode plate containing two diodes. This last type is used only on the 8-diode, 61-amp. 1974 Ford Autolite alternator. To disassemble, use the following procedures:

   a. **Exposed Diodes**—remove screws from the rectifier by rotating bolt heads ¼ turn clockwise to unlock; then unscrew them.

   b. **Integral Diodes**—press out the stator terminal screw, making sure not to twist it while doing this. Do not remove grounded screw.

   c. **Booster Diodes**—press out the stator terminal screw about ¼ in.; now remove the nut from the end of the screw and lift screw from circuit board, making sure not to twist it as it comes out.

9 Remove the drive pulley and fan. On alternator pulleys with threaded holes in the outer end of the pulley, use a standard puller for removal.

10 Remove the three screws that hold the front bearing retainer. Remove the front housing.

11 If the bearing is to be replaced, press from housing.

Cleaning & Inspection

1 The rotor, stator, diode rectifier assemblies, and bearings must not be cleaned with solvent. These parts should be wiped off with a clean cloth. Cleaning solvent may damage the electrical parts or contaminate the bearing internal lubricant. Wash all other parts in solvent and dry them.

2 Rotate the front bearing on the drive-

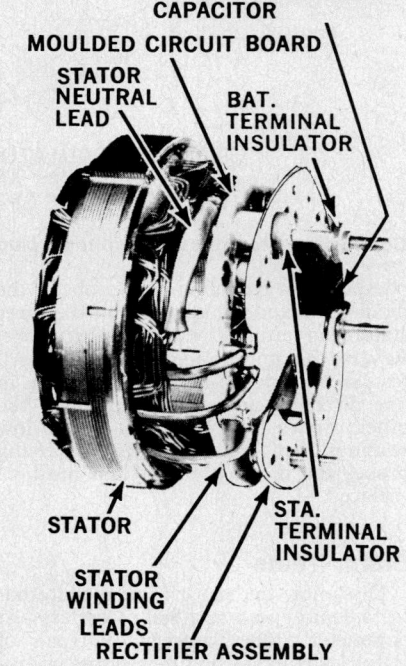

Stator lead connections

shaft. Check for any scraping noises, looseness or roughness that indicates the bearing is excessively worn. As the bearing is being rotated, look for excessive lubricant leakage. If any of these conditions exist, replace the bearing. Check rear bearing and rotor shaft.

3 Place the rear end housing on the slip ring end of the shaft and rotate the bearing on the shaft. Make a similar check for noise, looseness or roughness. Inspect the rollers and cage for damage. Replace the bearing if these conditions exist, or if the lubricant is missing or contaminated.

4 Check both the front and rear housings for cracks.

5 Check all wire leads on both the stator and rotor assemblies for loose soldered connections, and for burned insulation. Solder all poor connections. Replace parts that show burned insulation.

6 Check the slip ring for runout and for

damaged insulation. If the slip rings are more than 0.0005 in. out of round, take a light cut (minimum diameter limit 1.22 in.) from the face of the rings to true them. If the slip rings are badly damaged, the entire rotor will have to be replaced, as they are serviced as a complete assembly.

7 Replace any parts that are burned or cracked. Replace brushes that are worn to less than 5/16 in. long. Replace the brush spring if it has less than 7–12 oz. tension.

Assembly of the Rear-Terminal Alternator (Except 65 Amp Unit)

1 Press the front bearing into the front housing boss, putting pressure on outer race only. Install bearing retainer.

2 If the stop ring on the drive-shaft was damaged, install a new stop ring. Push the new ring onto the shaft and into the groove.

CHILTON CAUTION: *Do not open the stop ring with snap-ring pliers, as it will be rendered useless.*

3 Position the front bearing spacer on the driveshaft against the stop ring.

4 Place the front housing over the shaft, with the bearing positioned in the front housing cavity.

5 Install fan spacer, fan, pulley, lockwasher and retaining nut. Tighten nut to 60–100 ft./lbs. holding the drive shaft with an Allen key.

6 If rear bearing was removed, press a new one into rear housing.

7 Assemble brushes, springs, terminal and insulator in the brush holder; retract the brushes and insert a short length of ⅛ in. rod or stiff wire through the hole in the holder to hold brushes in the retracted position.

8 Position the brush holder assembly in the rear housing and install mounting screws. Position brush leads as illustrated to prevent shorting.

9 Wrap the three stator winding leads around the circuit board terminals and solder them using only rosin core solder and a 100-watt iron. Position the stator neutral lead eyelet on the stator terminal screw and install the screw in the rectifier assembly.

10 a. **Exposed Diodes**—insert the special screws through the wire lug, dished washers and circuit board. Turn ¼ turn counterclockwise to lock in place.

   b. **Integral Diodes**—insert the screws straight through the holes.

   c. **Booster Diodes**—position the stator wire terminal on the stator terminal screw, then position screw on rectifier. Place square insulator over the screw and into the square hole in the rectifier; rotate terminal screw until it locks; press it in fingertight. Position the stator wire; press the terminal screw into the rectifier and insulator with a vise.

NOTE: The dished washers are to be used on molded circuit boards only. Using these washers on a fiber board will result in a serious short circuit since only a flat insulating washer between the stator terminal and the board is used on fiber circuit boards.

11 Place the radio noise suppression condenser on the rectifier terminals. With molded circuit board, install the STA. and BAT. terminal insulators. With fiber circuit board, place the square stator terminal insulator in the square hole in the rectifier assembly, then position BAT. terminal insulator.
   Position the stator and rectifier assembly in the rear housing. Make sure that all terminal insulators are seated properly in the recesses. Position STA., BAT. and FLD. insulators on terminal bolts; install nuts.
12 Clean the rear bearing surface of the rotor shaft with a rag; position rear housing and stator assembly over rotor. Align matchmarks made during disassembly and install through bolts.
13 Remove brush retracting wire and place a dab of silicone sealer over the hole.

Disassembly of the Rear-Terminal 65-Amp Alternator

1 Remove the brush holder and cover assembly from the rear housing.
2 Scribe both end housings and the stator for reassembly.
3 Remove the three housing through bolts.
4 Separate the front housing and rotor from the stator and rear housing.
5 Remove the drive pulley nut, lockwasher, flat washer, pulley, fan, fan spacer and rotor from the front housing.
6 Remove the three screws that hold the front bearing retainer. Remove the retainer. If the bearing is damaged or has lost its lubricant, support the housing close to the bearing boss and press out the bearing.
7 Remove all the nut and washer assemblies and insulators from the stator and rectifier assembly.
8 If necessary, press the rear bearing from the housing, supporting the housing on the inner boss.
9 Unsolder the three stator leads from the rectifier assembly, and separate the stator from the assembly. Use a 200-watt soldering iron.

Cleaning and Inspection

   Nicks and scratches may be removed from the rotor slip rings by turning down the slip rings. Do not go beyond the minimum diameter limit of 1.22 in. If the slip rings are badly damaged, the entire rotor must be replaced. The rectifier also is serviced as an assembly.

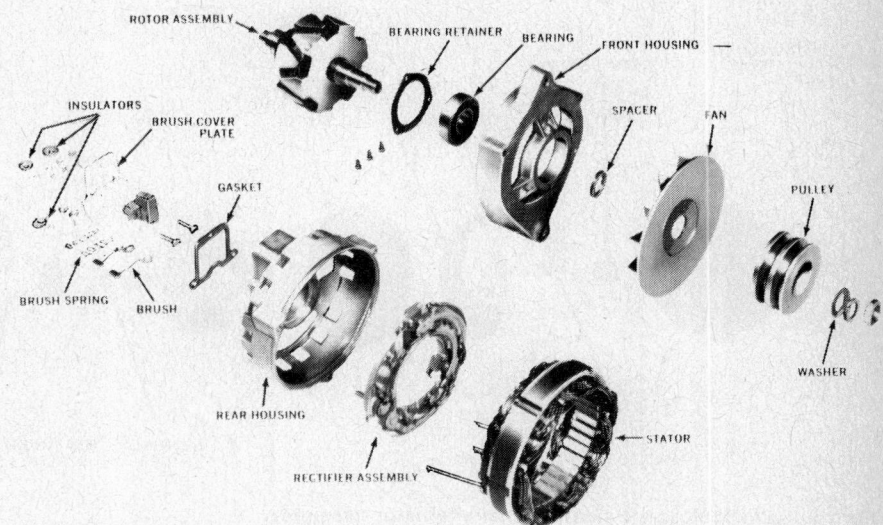

Ford Autolite/Motorcraft 65 amp rear terminal alternator assembly

Assembly of the Rear-Terminal 65-Amp Alternator

1 If the front bearing is being replaced, press the new bearing into the bearing boss. Put pressure on the outer race only. Install the bearing retainer and tighten the retainer screws until the tips of the retainer touch the housing.
2 Position the rectifier assembly to the stator. Wrap the three stator leads around the diode plate terminals. Solder them with a 200-watt soldering iron.
3 If the rear housing bearing was removed, press in a new bearing from the inside of the housing; put pressure on the outer race only.
4 Install the BAT.-GRD. insulator, and position the stator and rectifier assembly in the rear housing.
5 Install the STA. (purple) and BAT. (red) terminal insulators on the terminal bolts; install the nut and washer assemblies. Make certain that the shoulders on all insulators, both inside and outside of the housing, are seated properly before tightening the nuts.
6 Position the front housing over the rotor and install the fan spacer, fan, pulley, flat & lockwashers and nut on the rotor shaft.
7 Wipe the rear bearing surface of the rotor shaft with a clean rag.
8 Position the rotor with the front housing into the stator and rear housing assembly. Align the matchmarks made during disassembly. Seat the machined portion of the stator core into the step in both housings. Install through bolts.
9 If the field brushes have worn to less than ⅜ in., replace both brushes. Hold the brushes in position by inserting a stiff wire into the brush holder.
10 Position the brush holder assembly

Rectifier insulator installation

into the rear housing and install the three mounting screws. Remove the brush retracting wire and put a dab of silicone cement over the hole.

Disassembly of the Side Terminal Alternator

1 Matchmark both end housings and the stator to aid in assembly.
2 Remove the four housing through bolts. Separate the front housing rotor assembly from the rear housing stator assembly. Use the screwdriver slots provided for this purpose.

CHILTON CAUTION: *Do not separate the rear housing and stator at this point.*

3 Remove the drive pulley nut with a socket and an Allen wrench.
4 Withdraw the lockwasher, pulley, cooling fan, and spacer from the rotor shaft.
5 Pull the rotor shaft assembly out of the front housing. Take the spacer off the shaft.

ALTERNATORS
FORD-AUTOLITE MOTORCRAFT (WITH EXTERNAL REGULATOR)

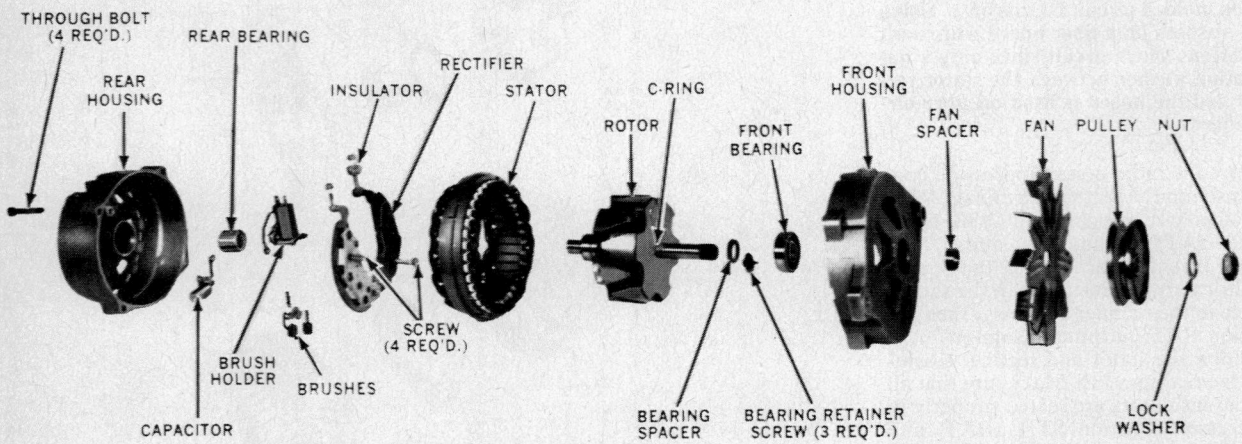

Ford Autolite/Motorcraft side terminal alternator assembly

6 Unfasten the three screws which secure the bearing to the front housing. Remove the bearing by pressing it out of the housing, while it is being supported close to the bearing boss.

NOTE: It is only necessary to remove the bearing if it is damaged or has lost its lubricant.

7 Use a 200-watt soldering iron to unsolder the three stator leads from the rectifier.

8 Remove the stator from the housing.

9 Use the 200-watt soldering iron to unsolder the brush holder lead from the rectifier.

10 Unfasten the screw which secures the capacitor lead to the rectifier.

11 Unfasten the four screws which secure the rectifier to the rear housing.

12 Remove the two terminal nuts, complete with insulators, from the outside of the housing.

13 Withdraw the rectifier assembly from the housing.

14 Unfasten the two brush holder securing screws and withdraw it, with brushes, from the housing. Clean off any sealer remaining on the housing or brush holder.

15 Remove the screw which secures the capacitor to the housing and remove the capacitor.

16 Remove the bearing from the rear housing, as necessary, in the same manner as detailed for the front bearing in Step 6.

Cleaning and Inspection

Do not clean the rotor, stator, or bearings in solvent; wipe them with a clean cloth. Inspect for damaged or worn parts, and replace as necessary.

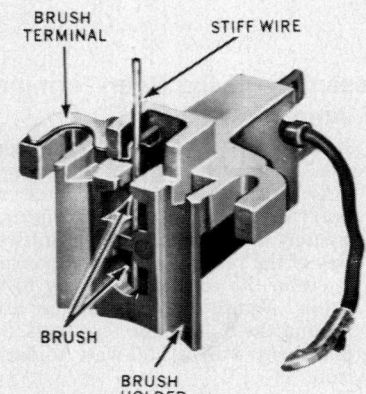

Brush holder assembly

Assembly of the Side Terminal Alternator

1 If it is to be replaced, press a new bearing into the front housing. Apply pressure to its outer race only.

2 Secure the bearing with it retaining screws.

3 Fit the inner spacer on the rotor shaft, then install the shaft through the front housing and bearing.

4 Place the spacer, fan pulley, and lockwasher on the front of the rotor shaft.

5 Tighten the retaining nut to 60–100 ft./lbs., while holding the shaft with an Allen wrench.

6 If it was to be replaced, press the new bearing in, from the inside of the rear housing, so that it is flush with the boss on its outer surface.

7 Place the brush terminal on the brush holder, and install the springs and brushes in the holder Temporarily retract the brushes with a piece of wire.

8 Place the brush holder in the rear housing and loosely secure it with its attaching screws. Slide the brush holder toward the shaft opening. Tighten the screws.

9 Secure the capacitor to the rear housing with its retaining screw.

10 Lay the two rectifier insulators over the two bosses on the rear housing. The insulator tabs fit into the recesses at the ends of the bosses.

CHILTON CAUTION: *Use of a hotter soldering gun will damage the rectifier.*

11 Position the insulator on the large terminal marked BAT. on the rectifier. Install the rectifier in the rear housing. Fit the external insulator over the BAT. terminal. Finger-tighten the nuts on the BAT. and GRD. terminals.

12 Loosely install the four rectifier securing screws.

13 First tighten the BAT. and GRD. terminal nuts and then tighten the rectifier securing screws.

14 Connect the capacitor lead to the rectifier and install its securing screws.

15 Push the end of the brush holder lead on the rectifier pin. Solder it using a 200-watt soldering iron.

16 Align the matchmarks made on the stator and rear housing during disassembly. Push the ends of the three stator leads over the pins on the rectifier. Solder them securely, using a 200-watt solder iron.

17 Assemble the front housing and rotor to the rear housing and stator, by aligning the matchmarks made during disassembly. Insert the through-bolts, tightening the two opposing bolts first and then the two remaining bolts.

18 Rotate the fan and pulley to check for any binding in the alternator.

19 Withdraw the wire inserted to keep the brushes retracted.

20 Seal the hole with a small amount of waterproof cement. Do not allow cement to run down the hole.

TROUBLESHOOTING
GM DELCOTRON ALTERNATOR
(WITH EXTERNAL REGULATOR)

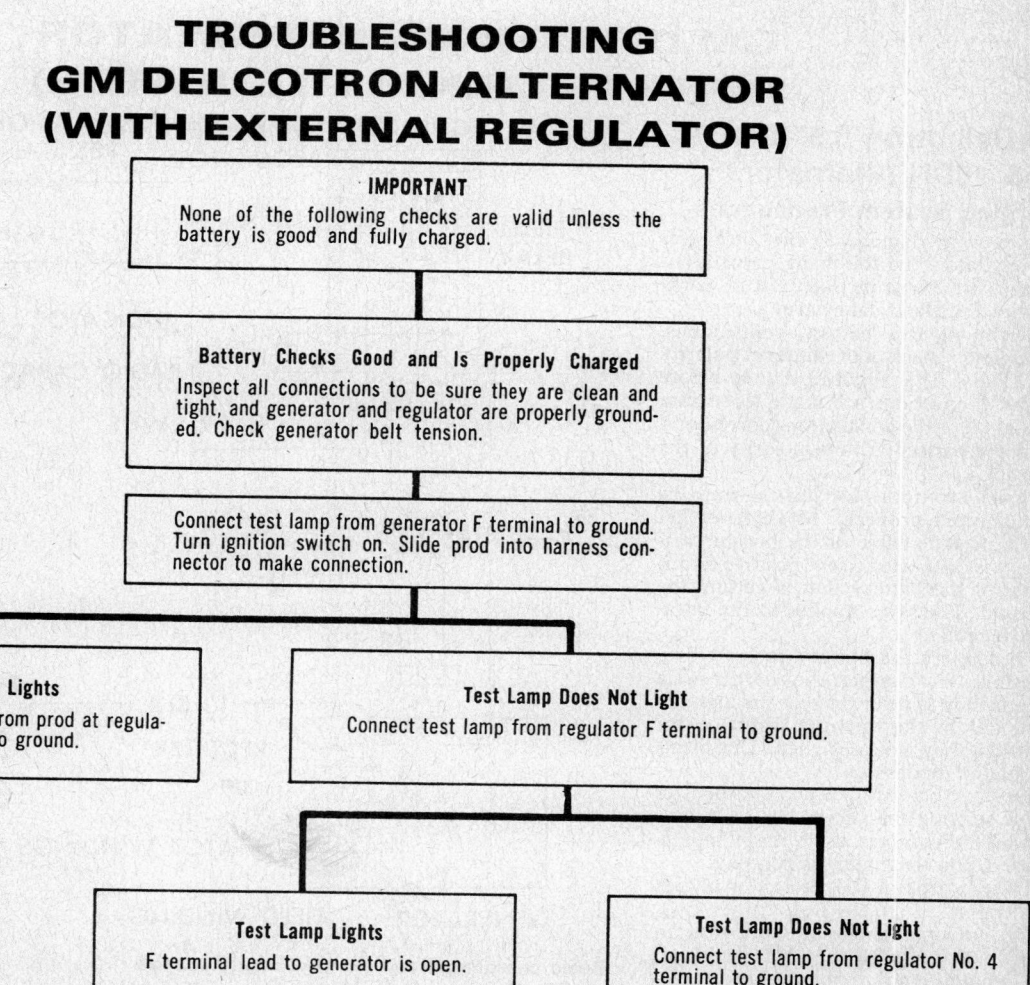

IMPORTANT
None of the following checks are valid unless the battery is good and fully charged.

Battery Checks Good and Is Properly Charged
Inspect all connections to be sure they are clean and tight, and generator and regulator are properly grounded. Check generator belt tension.

Connect test lamp from generator F terminal to ground. Turn ignition switch on. Slide prod into harness connector to make connection.

Test Lamp Lights
Connect test light from prod at regulator No. 3 terminal to ground.

Test Lamp Does Not Light
Connect test lamp from regulator F terminal to ground.

Test Lamp Lights
F terminal lead to generator is open.

Test Lamp Does Not Light
Connect test lamp from regulator No. 4 terminal to ground.

Test Lamp Lights
Replace voltage regulator.

Test Lamp Does Not Light
Lead from this terminal to ignition switch is open.

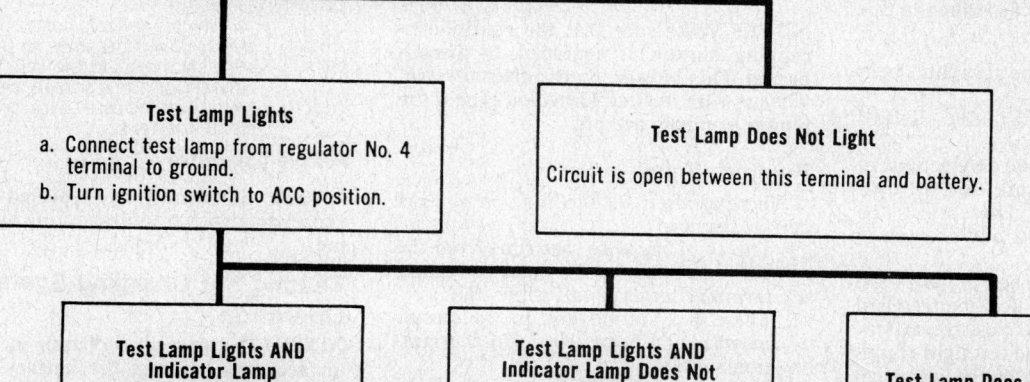

Test Lamp Lights
a. Connect test lamp from regulator No. 4 terminal to ground.
b. Turn ignition switch to ACC position.

Test Lamp Does Not Light
Circuit is open between this terminal and battery.

Test Lamp Lights AND Indicator Lamp Operates Normally

Go to generator output test.

Test Lamp Lights AND Indicator Lamp Does Not Go Off With Engine Running

Go to indicator lamp test No. 3

Test Lamp Does Not Light

Resistance wire to ACC terminal is open.

GM DELCOTRON ALTERNATOR
(WITH EXTERNAL REGULATOR)

GM Delcotron 5.5″ Series 1D & 10DN Alternators

Charging System Precautions

To prevent damage to the alternator and regulator, the following precautionary measures must be taken when working with the electrical system.

1 Never reverse battery connections. Always check the battery polarity visually. This should be done before any connections are made to be sure that all of the connections correspond to the battery ground polarity of the truck.
2 Booster batteries for starting must be connected properly. Make sure that the positive cable of the booster battery is connected to the positive terminal of the battery that is getting the boost. The same applies to the negative cables.
3 Disconnect the battery cables before using a fast charger; the charger has a tendency to force current through the diodes in the opposite direction for which they were designed. This burns out the diodes.
4 Never use a fast charger as a booster for starting the vehicle.
5 Never disconnect the voltage regulator while the engine is running.
6 Do not ground the alternator output terminal.
7 Do not operate the alternator on an open circuit with the field energized.
8 Do not attempt to polarize an alternator.

Preliminary Charging System Inspection

NOTE: Before performing any tests on automotive charging systems, the following precautions should be taken to ensure the accuracy of the tests described in this section.

1 Check condition of the alternator belt; tighten if necessary.
2 Check that battery is fully charged and in good condition.
3 Clean the battery cable connections at the battery. Make sure that all connections are good. Disconnect the positive terminal only, and proceed to the next step.
4 With the key off, insert a test light between the battery positive terminal and the disconnected positive battery terminal clamp. If the test light comes on, there is a short in the electrical system of the car. The short must be repaired before proceeding. If the light fails to glow, reconnect the clamp and proceed to the next step.

NOTE: Alternators with transistorized regulators sometimes draw a slight cur-

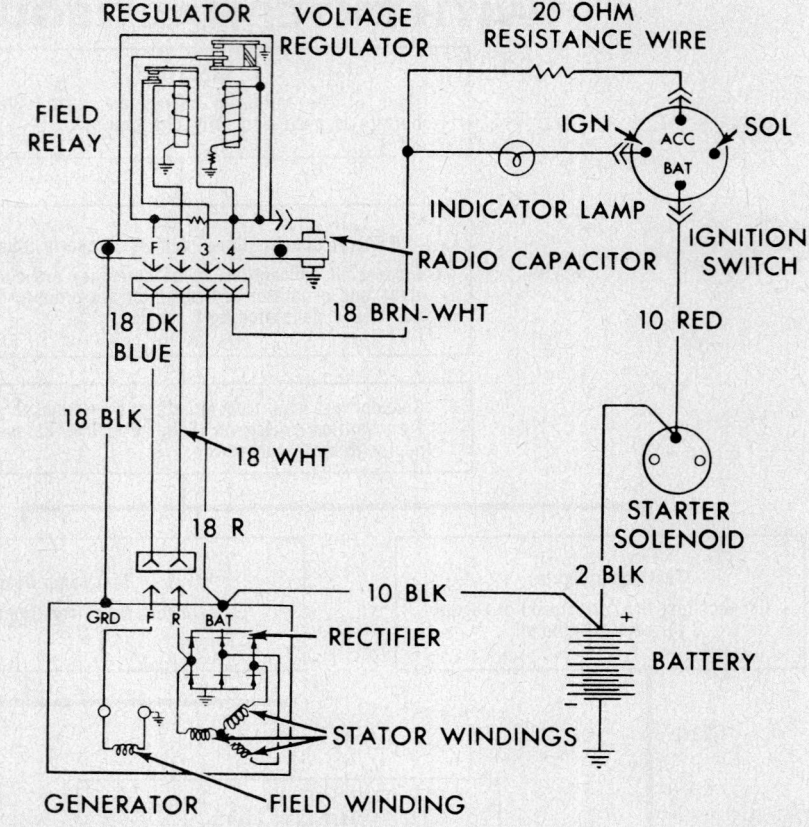

Basic charging circuit external regulator type

rent even when the key is turned off. To properly check these systems for a short, the regulator must be disconnected. Also, on cars equipped with an electric clock, disconnect the lead wire from the clock.

5 Check the charging system wiring for breaks or shorts.

NOTE: Make sure that the continuous-running blower, if equipped, is disconnected. This blower, unless disconnected, will run with the key turned on even if the blower controls are off.

Fusible Links

There are four fusible links on all GM cars. They are:

1 The 14 gauge wire that runs from the junction block to the positive battery terminal serves as a fusible link.
2 There is a second link in the circuit between the horn relay and the ignition switch.
3 A third link is in the wire running to the #3 voltage regulator terminal. It protects the regulator contacts and the alternator field circuit.
4 The fourth link is connected between the main junction block and the horn relay.

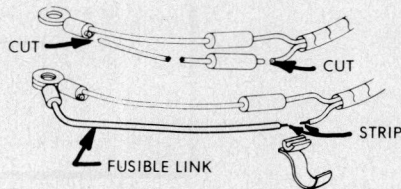

Fusible link repair

These links must be inspected before proceeding with troubleshooting and testing.

Testing the Charging System Operation

NOTE: If a current indicator is to give an accurate reading, the battery cables must be of the same gauge and length as the original equipment.

1 With the engine running and all electrical systems turned off, place a current indicator over the positive battery cable.

2 If a charge of about 5 amps is re-corded, the charging system is work-ing. If a draw of about 5 amp amps is recorded, the system is not working. If a draw is indicated, proceed with fur-ther testing. If an overcharge of 10–15 amps is indicated, check for a faulty regulator.

GM DELCOTRON 5.5″ SERIES 1D & 10DN ALTERNATOR SPECIFICATIONS

Output Rating	Minimum Output
37 amp unit	29 amps
42 amp unit	32 amps
55 amp unit	44 amps
61 amp unit	47 amps
63 amp unit	59 amps
*64 amp unit	55 amps

* Current output for the 64 amp unit is mea-sured at 2400 rpm
  Current output for all other units is mea-sured at 1500 rpm

VOLTAGE REGULATOR SPECIFICATIONS

Field Relay		Voltage Regulator	
closing voltage	point opening	voltage setting	point opening
1.5–3.2	.030″	13.8–14.8 at 85°F	.014″

ELECTRONIC REGULATOR SPECIFICATIONS

Voltage setting after
15 min. warmup . . . . 14v ± .3v

In-Car Testing Procedures

INDICATOR LIGHT CIRCUIT TEST

The indicator light is important in AC charging systems. It provides initial field excitation current to the alternator. The light goes out when the field relay closes. This relay applies battery current to both sides of the bulb. If the light does not go on when the key is turned: the bulb could be faulty; there could be an open circuit in the wiring; or a positive diode in the alter-nator could be shorted to ground.

1 Disconnect plug from regulator. Con-nect a test light between terminal #4 (in plug) and ground. Turn on ignition switch and observe the light. If light does not go on check bulb, socket or wiring between switch and regulator plug. If light goes on check regulator, wiring between regulator F terminal and alternator, or Delcotron itself.
2 Disconnect jumper wire at ground end and reconnect to F terminal in plug. Turn on ignition for a second and note light. If light goes on, the problem is in regulator. If light does not go on problem is in wire between F termi-nals (regulator and alternator).
3 Disconnect light at plug F terminal and reconnect the free end to F termi-nal at alternator. Turn on ignition switch for a second and note light. If

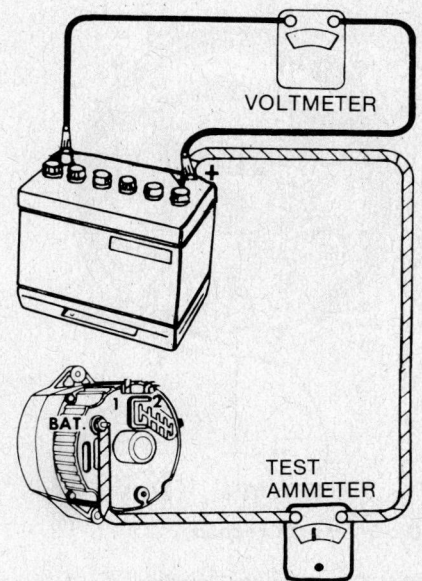

Voltmeter ammeter hook up

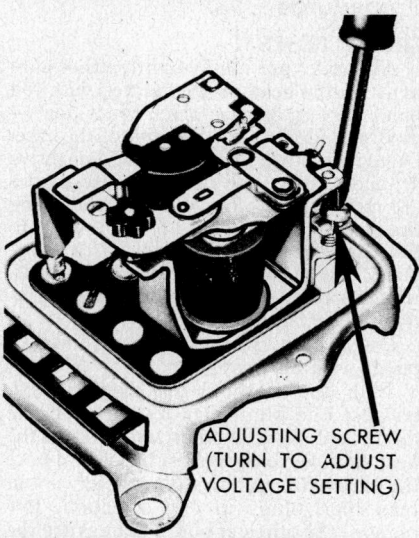

ADJUSTING SCREW
(TURN TO ADJUST
VOLTAGE SETTING)

Adjusting voltage regulator setting

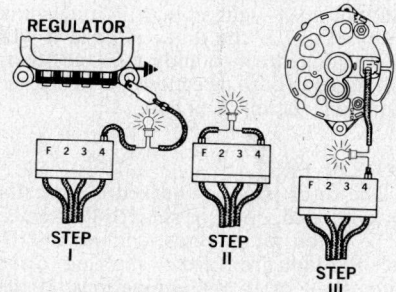

Testing indicator light circuit

light goes on, problem is an open cir-cuit in the wire connecting the regula-tor and alternator F terminals. If light does not go on, the alternator field windings are defective.
If the indicator light does not go out when engine is started, check for: loose

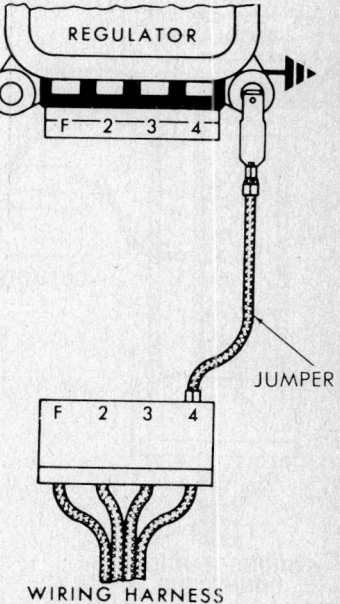

Testing indicator lamp circuit

drive belt; faulty alternator; open parallel resistance wire (usually shows up at idle).
If the light stays on with the key turned off, an alternator positive diode is shorted to ground.

ISOLATION TEST

1 Disconnect the wiring harness from the voltage regulator. With a jumper wire connect the F wire to the #3 wire in the wire harness plug.
2 Connect a voltmeter across the battery terminals, the positive voltmeter lead to the positive battery terminal; the negative lead to the negative terminal. Record the reading.
3 Start the engine. Do not race the en-gine.
4 Gradually raise engine speed to 1500–2000 rpm. The reading on the voltme-ter should increase 1 to 2 volts over the initial reading. If there is no in-crease in the reading, repair the alter-nator. If there is an increase in the voltmeter reading, replace the regula-tor.

FIELD RELAY TEST

1 Connect a voltmeter between the #2 terminal and the ground on the regu-lator.
2 Turn ignition switch on; do not start the engine. Voltmeter should read bat-tery voltage.
3 If voltmeter reads zero, check circuit connecting regulator terminal #2 and Delcotron R terminal. Start engine and run at 1500–2000 rpm. If voltage exceeds closing voltage (field realy), and light remains on, field relay is faulty and must be checked.

FIELD CIRCUIT RESISTANCE TESTING

The resistance wire is an integral part of

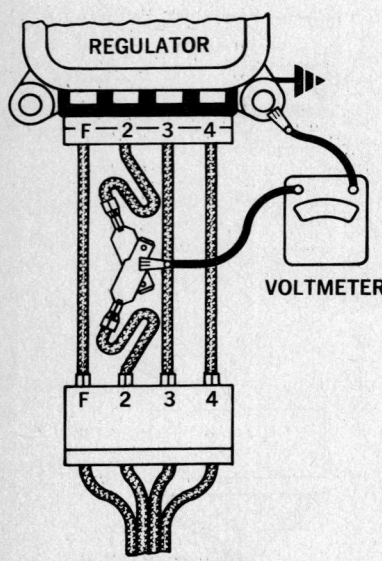

WIRING HARNESS CONNECTOR

Testing operation of field relay

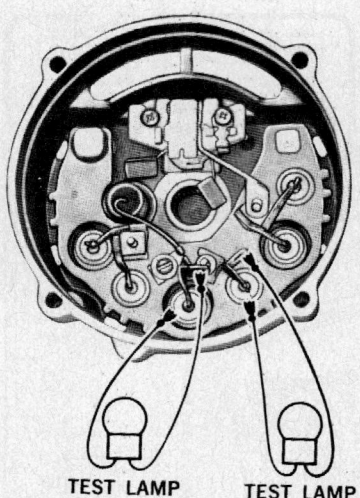

Diode test connections

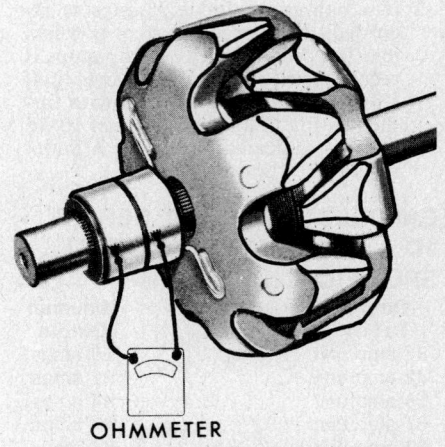

OHMMETER
(CHECK FOR SHORTS AND OPENS)

Checking rotor winding

the ignition wiring harness. The wire cannot be soldered; any connections must be made using crimp-type connectors. Resistance is 10 ohms, 6¼ watts.

1 Connect a voltmeter between the wiring harness terminal #4 and ground.
2 Turn on ignition switch, needle must indicate otherwise resistor is open.

CURRENT OUTPUT TEST

NOTE: Disconnect battery ground cable while making test connections, then reconnect cable after completing Step 5. Disconnect battery ground cable again before removing test set-up This test yields the same information as the isolation test but requires the use of an ammeter and a carbon pile.

1 Disconnect lead from BAT. terminal of Delcotron.
2 Hook an ammeter to the lead just disconnected, and to the BAT. terminal of the Delcotron.
3 Hook up the voltmeter leads to the BAT. terminal and a good ground on the alternator.
4 Disconnect the lead from the FR terminal of the Delcotron.
5 Hook up a jumper wire between BAT and F terminals of the Delcotron.
6 With a carbon pile load control hooked up to the battery posts, start the engine and set engine to 1500–2000 rpm, while adjusting carbon pile to obtain 14 volts.

CHILTON CAUTION: *Be careful not to exceed the recommended regulator voltage setting. This is controlled by the carbon pile load.*

7 Ammeter should read within 5 to 10 amps of rated output, as stamped on frame of each unit.

Off-Car Bench Testing Procedures

DIODE TESTS

All diodes are marked with either a + or − on the head or are marked with red paint for + diodes, black paint for − diodes to identify the polarity of the case. On a generator to be used with a negative ground system, the negative case diodes are mounted into the slip ring end fram; the positive case diodes are mounted into the insulated heat sink. Diodes with a negative case have positive polarity leads, whereas positive case diodes have negative polarity leads.

Diodes can be checked for shorts or opens with an ohmmeter.

With the stator leads disconnected, connect one ohmmeter test prod to the diode lead and the other test prod to the heat sink. Reverse the test prods and note the ohmmeter readings. The meter should read high ohms in one direction, low ohms in the other. If both readings are the same, either both high or both low, the diode is faulty and must be replaced. A 1½ volt test light also will indicate a faulty diode. If the diode is good it will light in one direction and not in the other. If it lights in both directions, or in neither direction, the diode is bad.

ROTOR TEST

The rotor may be checked electrically for grounded, open, or shorted field coils.

To check for grounds, connect a 110-volt test light from either slip ring to the rotor shaft or to the laminations. If the lamp lights, the field windings are grounded.

To check for opens, connect the leads of a 110-volt test light to each slip ring. If the lamp fails to light, the windings are open.

The windings are checked for short-circuits by connecting a battery and ammeter in series with the two slip rings. Note the ammeter reading.

An ammeter reading greater than 2.2 to 2.6 amps indicates shorted windings. The rotor assembly must be replaced if the windings are defective.

STATOR TEST

Stator windings may be checked for grounded, open, or shorted windings. If a 110-volt test lamp lights when connected from any stator lead to the stator frame, the windings are grounded. If the lamp fails to light when successively connected between each pair of stator leads, the windings are open.

A short circuit in the stator windings is difficult to locate without laboratory equipment, due to the low resistance of the windings. However, if all other electrical checks are normal and the generator fails to supply the rated output, shorted stator windings are indicated.

Adjustment Procedures

FIELD RELAY

Connect a voltmeter between #2 regulator terminal and ground. To adjust, connect a 50 ohm rheostat between wiring harness terminal #3 and regulator terminal #2, after disconnecting the spade lug on the end of the #2 regulator terminal wire. Connect a voltmeter between regulator terminal #2 and ground. Turn the resistor to 'open' position; turn off ignition switch; slowly decrease resistance until relay closes (noting at this point). Voltage can be adjusted by bending heel iron as illustrated.

Overhaul Procedures

DISASSEMBLY

1 Remove four bolts.
2 Separate drive end frame and rotor from stator assembly by prying with screwdriver. Note that seperation is between stator frame and drive end frame.
3 Place tape over slip ring end frame bearing to seal dirt.
4 Lightly clamp rotor in vise to remove shaft nut.

CHILTON CAUTION: *Do not distort rotor by overtightening vise.*

5 After nut removal, take off washer, pulley, fan and collar.
6 Separate drive end frame from rotor shaft.
7 Remove three stator lead attaching nuts and separate stator from end frame.
8 Remove screws, brushes and holder assembly.
9 Remove BAT., GND., and attaching screw terminals; then remove heat sink.

SLIP RING SERVICING & REPLACEMENT

Slip rings which are rough or out of round should be trued in a lathe to .001 in. maximum indicator reading. Remove only enough material to make the rings smooth and round. Finish with 400 grit or finer polishing cloth and blow away all dust.

Slip rings which must be replaced can be removed from the shaft with a gear puller, after the leads have been unsoldered. The new assembly should be pressed on with a sleeve which just fits over the shaft; this will apply all pressure to the inner slip ring collar and prevent damage to the outer slip ring. Only pure tin solder should be used when reconnecting field leads.

DIODE REPLACEMENT

1 Support end frame on a deep socket with a larger inside diameter than the diode outside diameter.
2 Carefully press out the diode with a brass drift and an arbor press, or a large bench vise. Be extremely careful so as not to distort the end frame.
3 Select a new diode (red or black), noting that the red (+) diodes go into the heat sink and the black (−) diodes into the end frame.
4 Support end frame on a flat, smooth surface around diode hole and carefully press the new diode into position. Diode must be square when starting or both diode and frame will be ruined.

BRUSH REPLACEMENT

The extent of brush wear can be determined by comparison with a new brush. If brushes are one-half worn, they should be replaced.

1 Remove brush holder assembly from end frame by removing two holder assembly screws.
2 Place springs and brushes in the holder and insert straight wire or pin into holes at bottom of holder to retain brushes.
3 Attach holder assembly onto end frame.

ASSEMBLY

1 Install stator assembly into slip ring end frame and locate diode connectors over the relay, diode and stator leads. Tighten terminal nuts.
2 Install rotor into drive end frame.
3 Install fan, spacer, puller washer and nut.
4 Install 5/16 in. Allen wrench into end of shaft to hold drive shaft; then tighten pulley nut to 40–50 ft./lbs. using a 15/16 in. crowsfoot wrench and torque wrench.
5 Assemble slip ring end frame and stator assembly to drive end frame and rotor.
6 Install four through bolts and tighten securely.

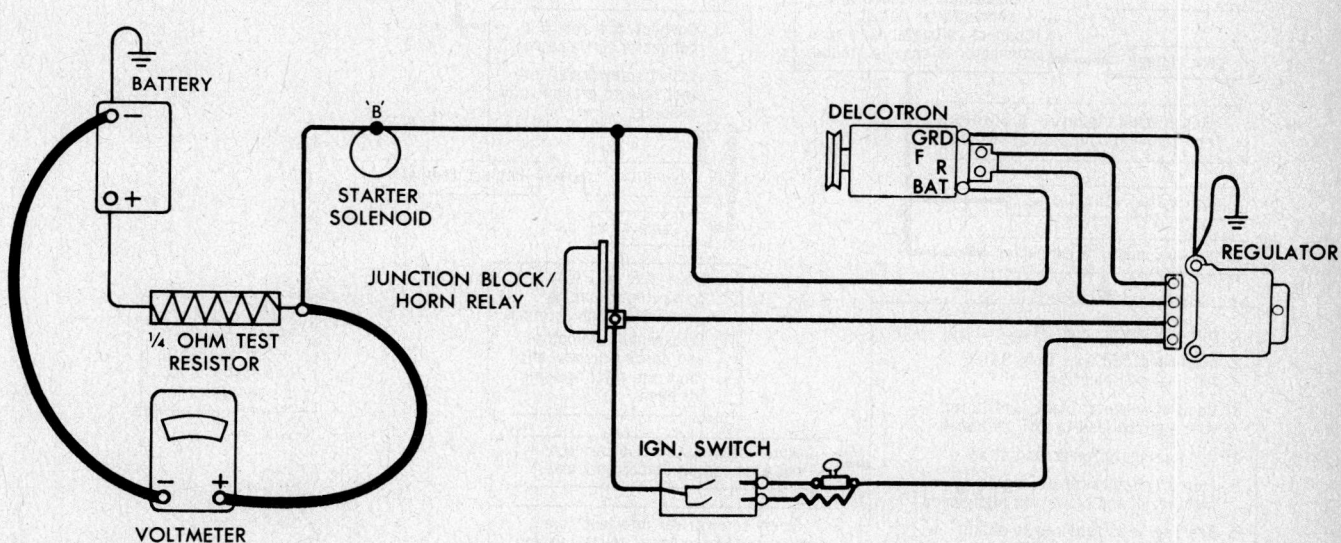

Voltage setting test connections

TROUBLESHOOTING
GM DELCOTRON ALTERNATOR
(WITH INTERNAL CONTROL REGULATOR)

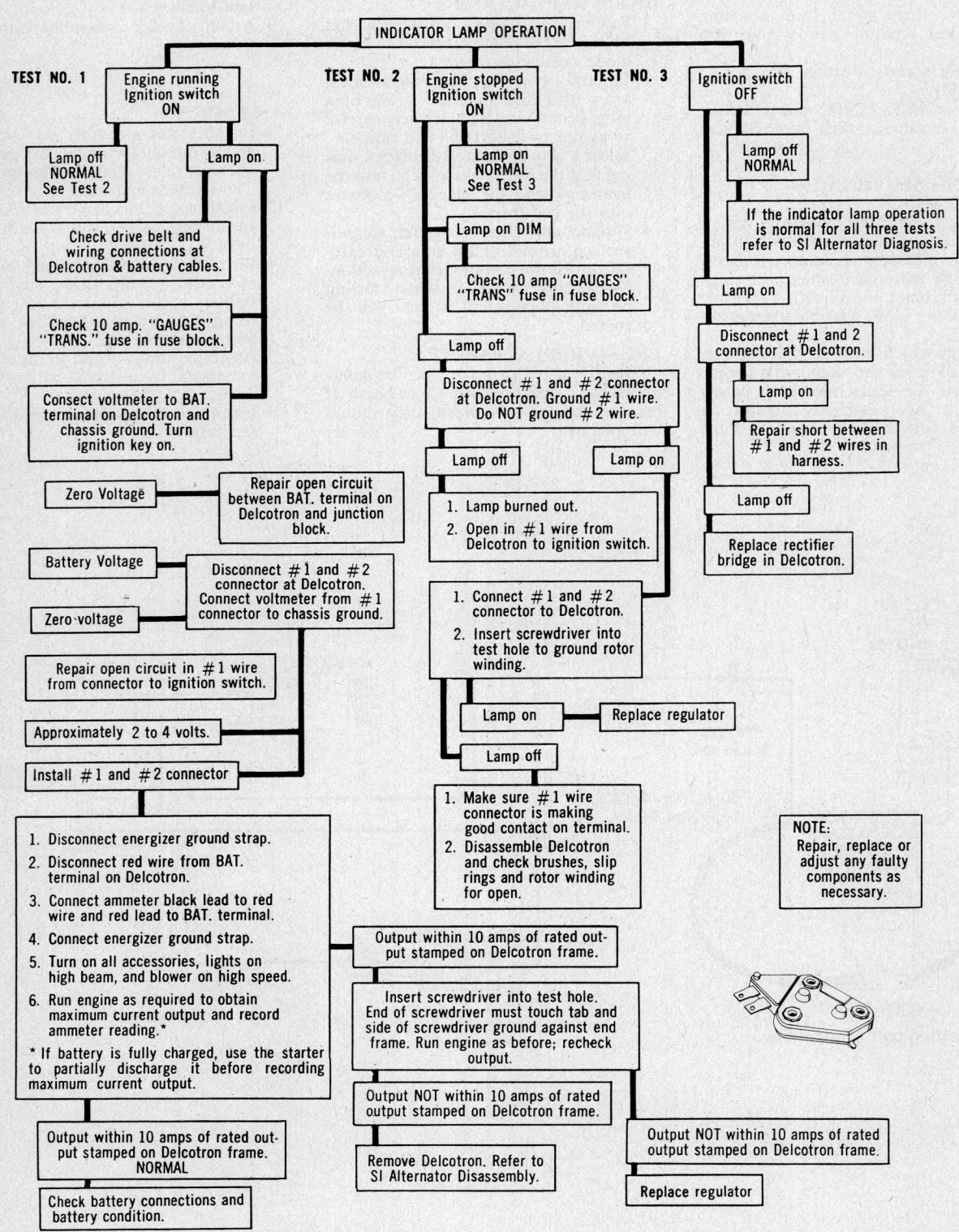

INDICATOR LAMP OPERATION

TEST NO. 1

Engine running Ignition switch ON

Lamp off NORMAL See Test 2

Lamp on

Check drive belt and wiring connections at Delcotron & battery cables.

Check 10 amp. "GAUGES" "TRANS." fuse in fuse block.

Consect voltmeter to BAT. terminal on Delcotron and chassis ground. Turn ignition key on.

Zero Voltage

Repair open circuit between BAT. terminal on Delcotron and junction block.

Battery Voltage

Zero voltage

Disconnect #1 and #2 connector at Delcotron. Connect voltmeter from #1 connector to chassis ground.

Repair open circuit in #1 wire from connector to ignition switch.

Approximately 2 to 4 volts.

Install #1 and #2 connector

1. Disconnect energizer ground strap.
2. Disconnect red wire from BAT. terminal on Delcotron.
3. Connect ammeter black lead to red wire and red lead to BAT. terminal.
4. Connect energizer ground strap.
5. Turn on all accessories, lights on high beam, and blower on high speed.
6. Run engine as required to obtain maximum current output and record ammeter reading.*

* If battery is fully charged, use the starter to partially discharge it before recording maximum current output.

Output within 10 amps of rated output stamped on Delcotron frame. NORMAL

Check battery connections and battery condition.

TEST NO. 2

Engine stopped Ignition switch ON

Lamp on NORMAL See Test 3

Lamp on DIM

Check 10 amp "GAUGES" "TRANS." fuse in fuse block.

Lamp off

Disconnect #1 and #2 connector at Delcotron. Ground #1 wire. Do NOT ground #2 wire.

Lamp off

Lamp on

1. Lamp burned out.
2. Open in #1 wire from Delcotron to ignition switch.

1. Connect #1 and #2 connector to Delcotron.
2. Insert screwdriver into test hole to ground rotor winding.

Lamp on → Replace regulator

Lamp off

1. Make sure #1 wire connector is making good contact on terminal.
2. Disassemble Delcotron and check brushes, slip rings and rotor winding for open.

Output within 10 amps of rated output stamped on Delcotron frame.

Insert screwdriver into test hole. End of screwdriver must touch tab and side of screwdriver ground against end frame. Run engine as before; recheck output.

Output NOT within 10 amps of rated output stamped on Delcotron frame.

Remove Delcotron. Refer to SI Alternator Disassembly.

TEST NO. 3

Ignition switch OFF

Lamp off NORMAL

If the indicator lamp operation is normal for all three tests refer to SI Alternator Diagnosis.

Lamp on

Disconnect #1 and 2 connector at Delcotron.

Lamp on

Repair short between #1 and #2 wires in harness.

Lamp off

Replace rectifier bridge in Delcotron.

Output NOT within 10 amps of rated output stamped on Delcotron frame.

Replace regulator

NOTE:
Repair, replace or adjust any faulty components as necessary.

GM DELCOTRON ALTERNATOR (WITH INTERNAL CONTROL REGULATOR)

GM Delcotron Series 10-SI Alternator (with Built-in Regulator)

Charging System Precautions

To prevent damage to the alternator and regulator, the following precautionary measures must be taken when working with the electrical system.

1 Never reverse battery connections. Always check the battery polarity visually. This should be done before any connections are made to be sure that all of the connections correspond to the battery ground polarity of the vehicle.
2 Booster batteries for starting must be connected properly. Make sure that the positive cable of the booster battery is connected to the positive terminal of the of the battery that is getting the boost. The same applies to the negative cables.
3 Disconnect the battery cables before using a fast charger; the charger has a tendency to force current through the diodes in the opposite direction for which they were designed. This burns out the diodes.
4 Never use a fast charger as a booster for starting the vehicle.
5 Never disconnect the voltage regulator while the engine is running.
6 Do not ground the alternator output terminal.
7 Do not operate the alternator on an open circuit with the field energized.
8 Do not attempt to polarize an alternator.

PRELIMINARY CHARGING SYSTEM INSPECTION

NOTE: Before performing any tests on automotive charging systems, the following precautions should be taken to ensure the accuracy of the tests described in this section.

1 Check condition of the alternator belt; tighten if necessary.
2 Check that battery is fully charged and in good condition.
3 Clean the battery cable connections at the battery. Make sure that all connections are good. Disconnect the positive terminal only, and proceed to the next step.
4 With the key off, insert a test light between the battery positive terminal and the disconnected positive battery terminal clamp. If the test light comes on, there is a short in the electrical system of the car. The short must be repaired before proceeding. If the light fails to glow, reconnect the clamp and proceed to the next step.

NOTE: Alternators with transistorized regulators sometimes draw a slight cur-

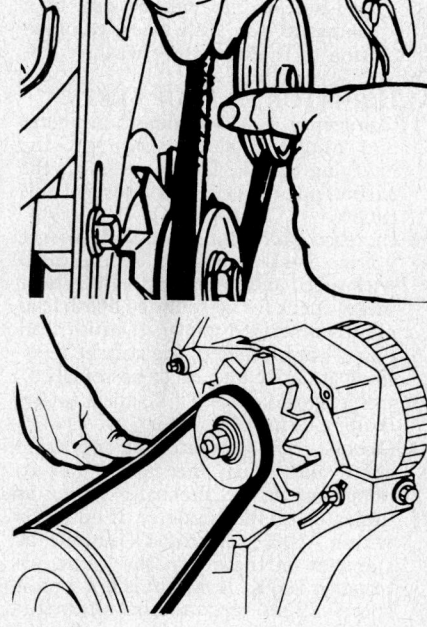

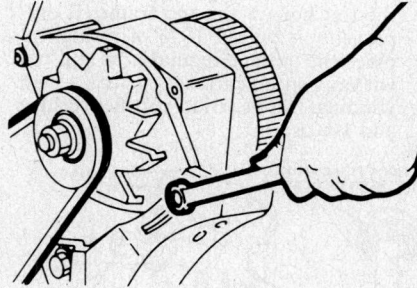

Alternator belt inspection

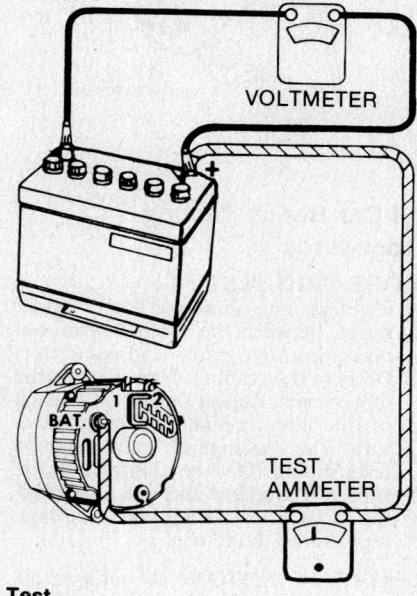

Test

rent even when the key is turned off. To properly check these systems for a short, the regulator must be disconnected. Also, on cars equipped with an electric clock, disconnect the lead wire from the clock.

5 Check the charging system wiring for breaks or shorts.

NOTE: Make sure that the continuous-running blower, if equipped, is disconnected. This blower, unless disconnected, will run with the key turned on even if the blower controls are off.

GM DELCOTRON SERIES 10-SI ALTERNATOR SPECIFICATIONS

Output Rating	Minimum Output
37 amp unit	32 amps
42 amp unit	37 amps
55 amp unit	50 amps
61 amp unit	55 amps
63 amp unit	58 amps
80 amp unit	74 amps

Current output for all units is measured at 5000 rpm.

ELECTRONIC REGULATOR SPECIFICATIONS

Voltage setting after 15 minute warmup . . . . $14v \pm .3v$

In-Car Testing Procedures

CHARGING SYSTEM TEST FOR LOW CHARGING RATE

After battery condition, drive belt tension, and wiring terminals and connections have been checked, charge the battery fully and perform the following test:

1 Connect a test voltmeter between the alternator BAT. terminal and ground; ignition switch on. Connect the voltmeter in turn to alternator terminals #1 and 2, the other voltmeter lead being grounded as before. A zero reading indicates an open circuit between the battery and each connection at the alternator. If this test discloses no faults in the wiring, proceed to Step 2.
2 Connect the test voltmeter to the alternator BAT. terminal (the other test lead to ground); start the engine; run at 1500–2000 rpm with all lights and electrical accessories turned on. If the voltmeter reads 12.8 volts or greater, the alternator is good and no further checks need be made. If the voltmeter reads less than 12.8 volts, ground the field winding by inserting a screwdriver into the test hole in the end frame.

CHILTON CAUTION: *Do not force tab more than ¾ in. into end frame.*

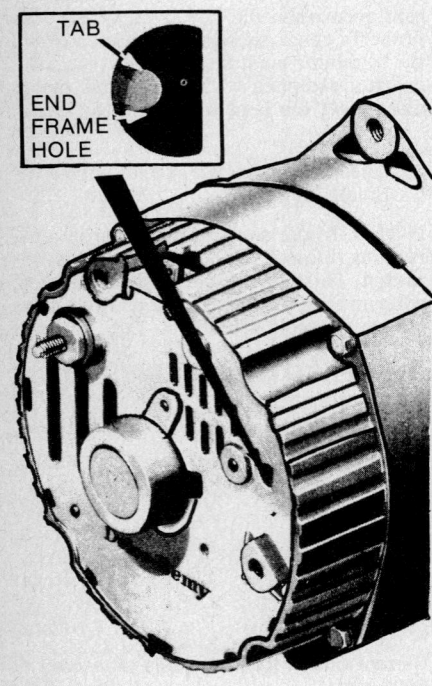

INSERT SCREWDRIVER
GROUND TAB TO
END FRAME

TAB

END
FRAME
HOLE

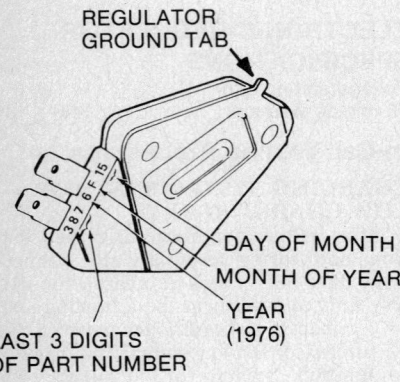

REGULATOR
GROUND TAB

LAST 3 DIGITS
OF PART NUMBER

DAY OF MONTH
MONTH OF YEAR
YEAR
(1976)

Test

a. If voltage increases to 13 volts or more, the regulator unit is defective.
b. If voltage does not increase significantly, generator is defective.

CHARGING SYSTEM TEST FOR HIGH CHARGING RATE

1 With the battery fully charged, connect a voltmeter between alternator terminal #2 and ground. If the reading is zero, #2 circuit from the battery is open.
2 If #2 circuit is OK, but an obvious overcharging condition still exists, proceed as follows:
   a. Remove the alternator and separate the end frames.
   b. Connect a low-range ohmmeter between the brush lead clip and the end frame, as illustrated in test 1;

then reverse the lead connections. If both readings are zero, either the brush lead clip is grounded or the regulator is defective. A grounded brush lead clip can be due to a damaged insulating sleeve or omission of the insulating washer.

ALTERNATOR OUTPUT TEST

1 Connect a test voltmeter, ammeter and 10-ohm 6-watt resistor into the charging circuit. Do not connect the carbon pile to the battery posts at this time.
2 Increase alternator speed and observe voltmeter—if voltage is uncontrolled with speed and increases to 16 volts or more, check for a grounded brush lead clip as described above. If brush lead clip is not grounded, the voltage regulator is faulty and must be replaced.
3 Connect the carbon pile load to the battery terminals.
4 Operate the alternator at moderate speed and adjust the carbon pile to obtain maximum alternator output as indicated on the ammeter. If output is within 10% of rated output as stamped on the alternator frame, alternator is OK. If output is not within specifications, ground the alternator field by inserting a screwdriver into the test hole in the end frame. If output now is within 10% of rating, replace the voltage regulator; if still not within specifications, check field winding, diode trio, rectifier bridge and stator.

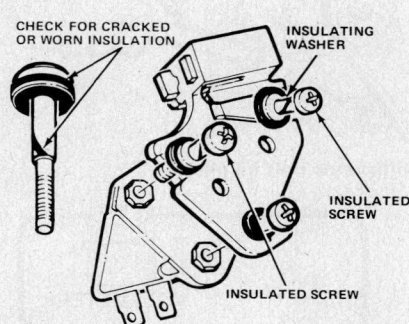

CHECK FOR CRACKED
OR WORN INSULATION

INSULATING
WASHER

INSULATED
SCREW

INSULATED SCREW

Test

Off-Car Bench Testing Procedures

DIODE TRIO TESTING

1 Connect an ohmmeter, on lowest range, between the single brush connector and one stator lead connector.
2 Observe the reading. Now reverse the meter leads. Repeat this test with each of the other two stator lead connectors. The readings on each of these tests should NOT be identical. There should be one low and one high reading for each test. If this is not the case, replace the diode trio.

CHILTON CAUTION: *Do not use high voltage on the diode trio.*

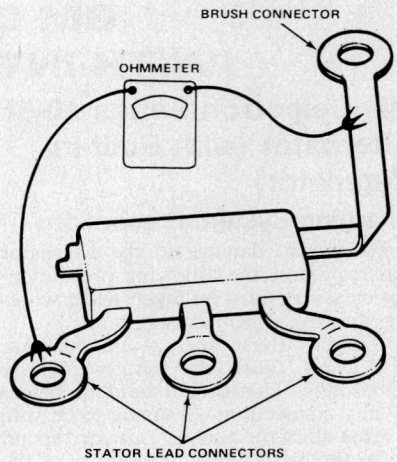

BRUSH CONNECTOR

OHMMETER

STATOR LEAD CONNECTORS

Test

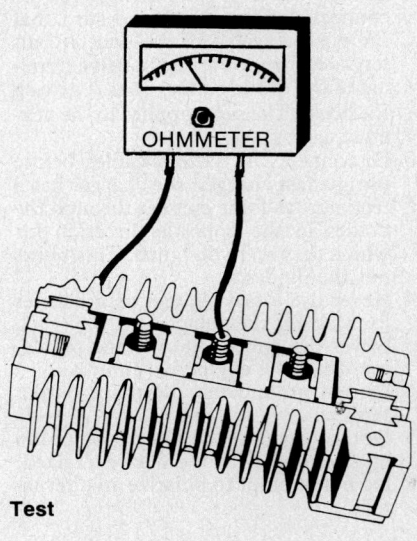

OHMMETER

Test

RECTIFIER BRIDGE TESTING

1 Connect an ohmmeter between the heat sink (ground) and the base of one of the three terminals. Take a reading. Reverse the meter leads and take a reading. If both readings are identical, the bridge is defective and must be replaced.
2 Repeat this test with the remaining two terminals. Then, repeat the test between the INSULATED heat sink (as opposed to the GROUNDED heat sink in previous test) and each of the three terminals. As before, if any two readings are identical, on reversing the meter leads, the rectifier bridge must be replaced.

ROTOR & STATOR TESTS

Overhaul Procedures

DISASSEMBLY & ASSEMBLY

1 Place alternator in a vise clamped by the mounting flange only.
2 Remove the four through bolts. Separate the slip ring end frame and stator assembly from the drive end and rotor

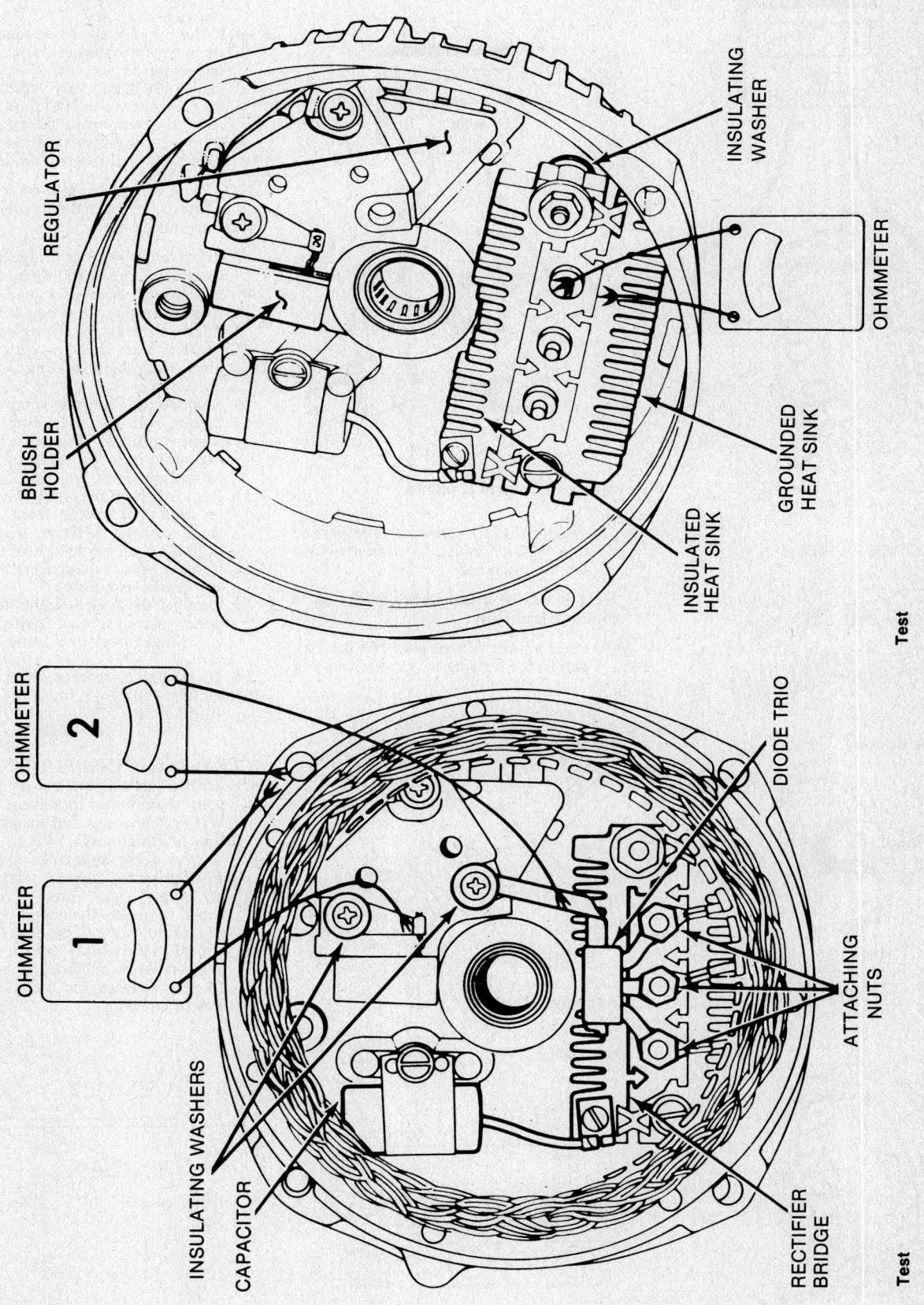

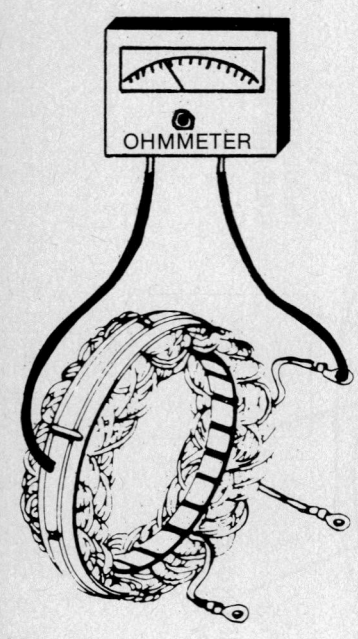

Test

RECTIFIER BRIDGE

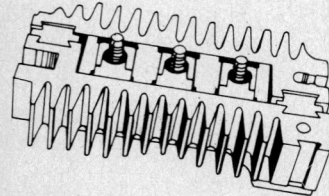

Rectifier Bridge

ROTOR

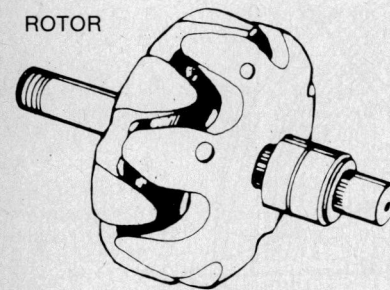

Rotor

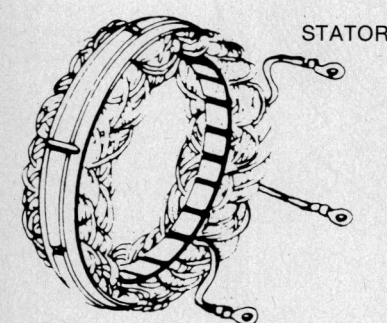

STATOR

Stator

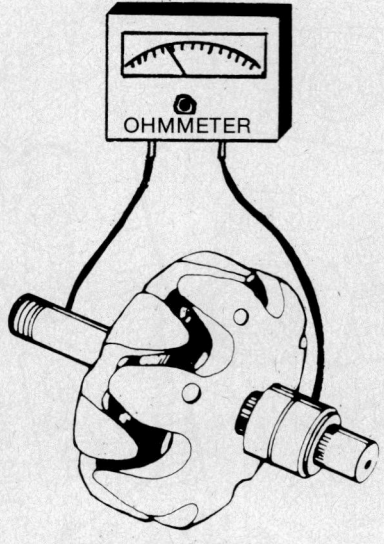

Check for shorts & opens

assembly. Use a screwdriver to pry the two sections apart, in slots provided for the purpose.

NOTE: Scribe matchmarks on the parts to aid in assembly.

3 Place a piece of tape over the slip ring end frame bearing to prevent entry of

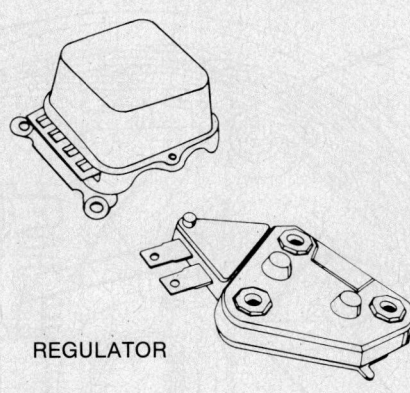

REGULATOR

Regulator

DIODE TRIO

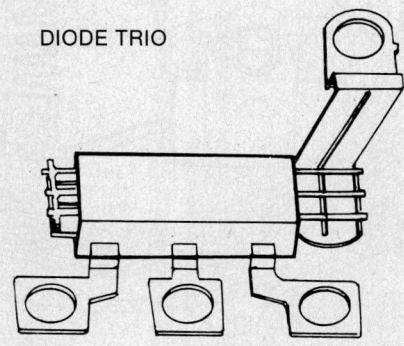

Diode Trio

dirt; also tape shaft at slip ring end to prevent scratches.

4 If the brushes are to be reused, clean them with trichloroethylene or carbon tetrachloride solvent. Use these solvents only in properly ventilated area.

5 Remove the stator lead nuts and separate the stator from the end frame.

6 Remove the screw that secures the diode trio and remove diode trio.

NOTE: at this point, test the rotor, rectifier bridge, stator and diode trio if these tests are necessary.

7 Remove the rectifier bridge holddown screw and the BAT. terminal screw. Disconnect condenser lead. Remove rectifier bridge from end frame.

8 Remove the two securing screws and brush holder and regulator assemblies. Note the insulating sleeves over the screws.

9 Remove the retaining screw and condenser from the end frame.

10 Remove the slip ring end frame bearing, if it is to be replaced. Use the procedure given later in this section.

11 Remove the pulley nut, washer, pulley, fan and spacer from the rotor shaft, using a 5/16 in. Allen key to hold the shaft while loosening the nut.

12 Remove rotor and spacers from drive end frame assembly.

13 Remove drive end frame bearing retainer plate, screws, plate, bearing, and slinger from end frame, if necessary.

14 To assemble, reverse order of disassembly. Pulley nut must be torqued to 40–50 ft./lbs.

CLEANING & INSPECTION

1 Clean all metal parts except stator and rotor assemblies, in solvent.

2 Wipe off bearings and inspect for pitting or roughness.

3 Inspect rotor slip rings for scoring. They may be cleaned with 400 grit sandpaper (not emery): rotate the rotor to make the rings concentric. Maximum out-of-true is 0.001 in. If slip rings are deeply scored, the entire rotor must be replaced as a unit.

4 Inspect brushes for wear; minimum length is ¼ in.

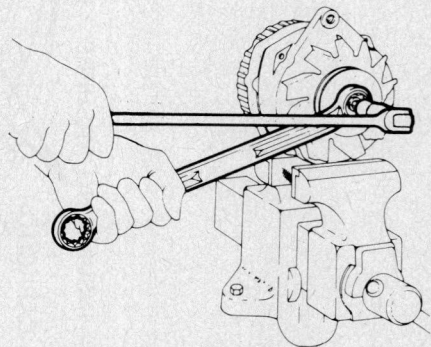

Pulley Removal

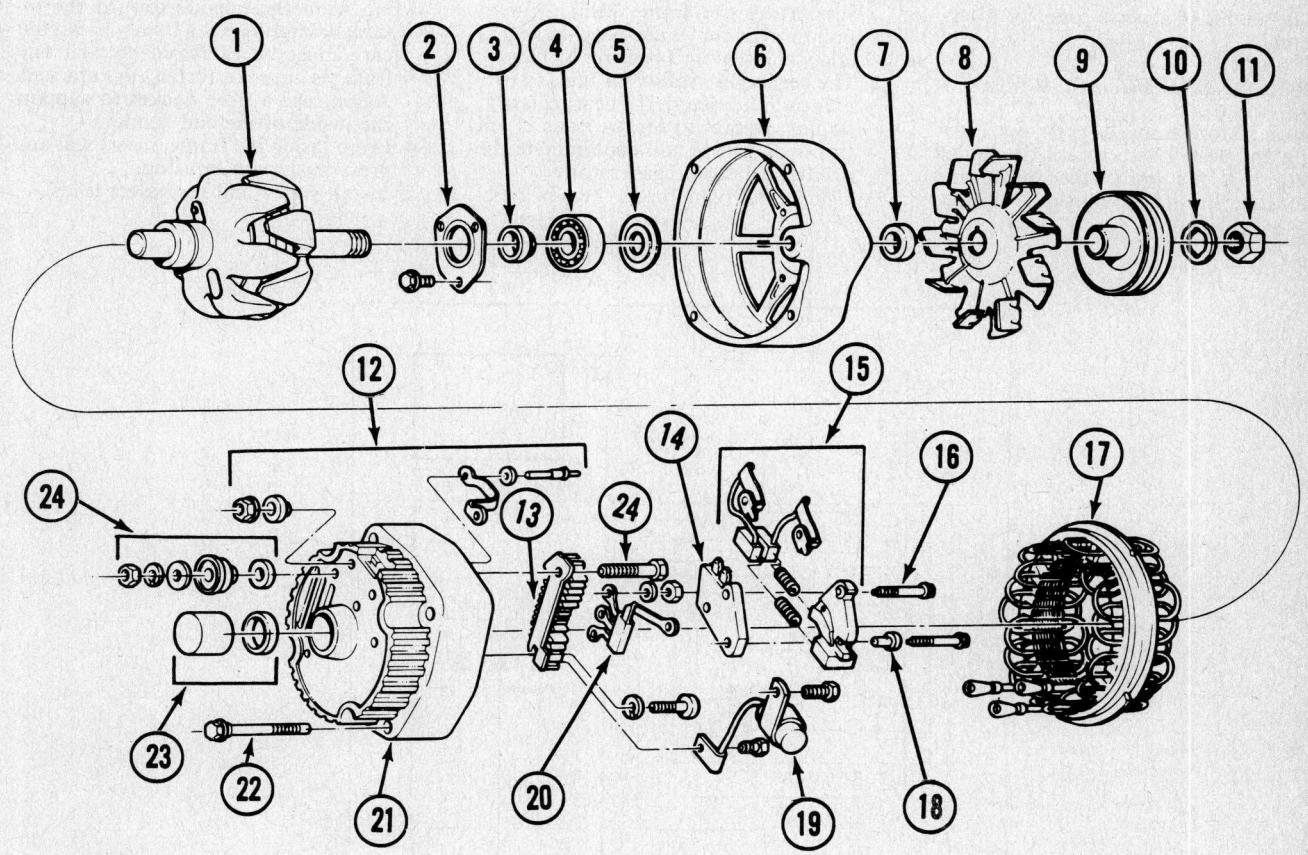

Delco Alternator

1. ROTOR
2. FRONT BEARING RETAINER
3. COLLAR (INNER)
4. BEARING
5. WASHER
6. FRONT HOUSING
7. COLLAR (OUTER)
8. FAN
9. PULLEY
10. LOCKWASHER
11. PULLEY NUT
12. TERMINAL ASSEMBLY
13. RECTIFIER BRIDGE
14. REGULATOR
15. BRUSH ASSEMBLY
16. SCREW
17. STATOR
18. INSULATING WASHER
19. CAPACITOR
20. DIODE TRIO
21. REAR HOUSING
22. THROUGH-BOLT
23. BEARING AND SEAL ASSEMBLY
24. TERMINAL ASSEMBLY

DIODE TRIO INITIAL TESTING
1 Before removing this unit, connect an ohmmeter between the brush lead clip and the end frame. The lowest reading scale should be used for this test.
2 After taking a reading, reverse the lead connections. If the meter reads zero, the brush lead clip is probably grounded, due to omission of the insulating sleeve or insulating washer.

DIODE TRIO REMOVAL
1 Remove the three nuts which secure the stator.
2 Remove stator.
3 Remove the screw which secures the diode trio lead clip, the remove diode trio.

NOTE: The position of the insulating washer on the screw is critical; make sure it is returned to the same position on reassembly.

RECTIFIER BRIDGE REMOVAL
1 Remove the attaching screw and the BAT. terminal screw.
2 Disconnect the condenser lead.
3 Remove the rectifier bridge.

NOTE: The insulator between the insulated heat sink and the end frame is extremely important to the operation of the unit. It must be replaced in exactly the same position on reassembly.

CHILTON CAUTION: *Do not use high voltage to test the rectifier bridge.*

BRUSH &/OR VOLTAGE REGULATOR R&R
1 Remove two brush holder screws and the stator lead-to-strap nut and washer, brush holder screws and one of the diode trio lead strap attaching screws.

NOTE: The insulating washers must be replaced in the same position on reassembly.

2 Remove brush holder and brushes. The voltage regulator may also be removed at this time if desired.
3 Brushes and brush springs must be free from corrosion, undamaged and completely free of oil or grease.
4 Insert spring and brushes into holder, noting whether they slide freely without binding. Insert wooden or plastic toothpick into bottom hole in holder to retain brushes.

NOTE: The brush holder is serviced as a unit; individual parts are not avaialable.

5 Reassemble in reverse order of disassembly.

SLIP RING END FRAME & SEAL R&R

1 With stator removed, press out bearing and seal. Use a socket or similar tool that fits inside the end frame housing. Press from outside to inside, supporting the frame inside with a hollow cylinder (large, deep socket) to allow the seal and bearing to pass.

2 The bearins are sealed for life and permanently lubricatd. If a bearing is dry, do not attempt to repack it, as it will throw off grease and contaminate the inside of the gene generator.

3 Using a flat plate, press the new bearing from the outside toward the inside. A large vise is a handy press, but care must be exercised so that end fram is not distorted or cracked. Again, use a deep socket to support the inside of the end frame.

4 From inside the frame, insert seal and press flush with housing.

5 Install stator and reconnect leads.

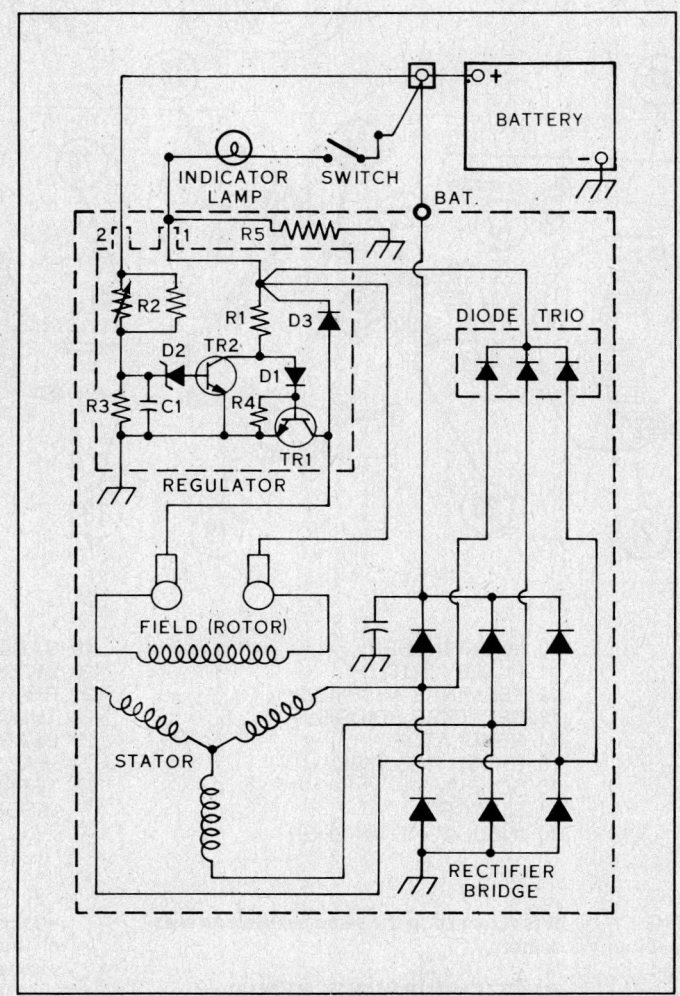

Circuit wiring—Delcotron integral regulator charging system

ELECTRICAL DIAGNOSIS

The Starter System

The cranking motor armature revolves at a relatively high speed to produce sufficient power to crank an engine. Since the cranking speed required to start the engine is comparatively slow, the cranking motor is equiped with a small drive pinion which meshes with the teeth of the flywheel ring gear resulting in a gear reduction. Although the gear reduction ratio varies on different applications, the cranking motor armature may revolve as many as 19 times for every revolution of the flywheel. This permits the cranking motor to develop relatively high armature speed and considerable power while cranking the engine at relatively low speed.

After the engine starts, its speed immediately increases and it soon may reach speeds as high as 1,000 rpm. If the cranking motor drive pinion remained in mesh with the flywheel, the cranking motor armature would be spun at 19,000 rpm (with 19-1 gear ratio). This speed may ruin the armature. To prevent this, the starter clutch will disengage the starter drive from the engine flywheel.

Troubleshooting the Cranking Circuit

After establishing that the starter solenoid is getting current from the key, and neither the starter safety switch or the seat belt system is causing an interruption of the flow of current to the starter solenoid, several checks, both visual and electrical, should be made in a defective cranking circuit to isolate trouble before removing any unit. Many times a component is removed from the vehicle only to find it is completely servicable after making reliable tests. Therefore, before removing a unit in a defective cranking system, the following checks should be made:

Battery Capacity

It is not enough for a battery to have a high no load voltage and to be in a charged condition. The battery must also be able to maintain a certain minimum voltage while it is delivering a heavy load to the starting motor. If the battery is not able to maintain this minimum voltage while cranking the starting motor, it does not have sufficient capacity to guarantee ignition. (See battery testing).

To make a capacity test, hook up a voltmeter. Connect the test leads direct to the battery posts (not to the cable connectors) turn on the lights, heater, etc. Remove the high tension cable from the distributor and ground it, or remove the electrical feed wire from the coil so the engine will not start. Close the starter switch for 30 seconds. (No longer.) Repeat the process two or three times but

REVERSE TEST LEADS
IF METER READS
BACKWARDS

Measuring battery capacity

TOUCH THE POST
NOT THE CABLE

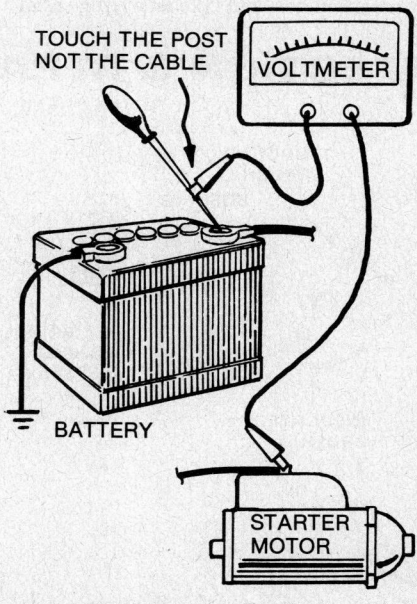

Testing circuit "battery to starter"

pause about 30 seconds between each test so as not to damage the starter motor by overheating. Observe batter voltage during the course of the test.

WIRING:

Inspect the wiring for frayed insulation or other damage. Replace any wiring that is damaged. Inspect all connections to the cranking motor, solenoid or magnetic switch, ignition switch or any other controll switch, and battery, including all ground connections. Clean and tighten all connections and wiring as required.

Starter Circuit (Battery Side)

Poor cranking speed may also be caused from poor connections in that portion of the starter circuit from the starter to the "hot side" of the battery. To measure the entire side of the circuit connect a voltmeter (3 amps). Before closing the starter switch the voltmeter should read zero. Close the switch, (run starter) and watch voltmeter very closely.

NOTE: You may have to turn meter prongs around to see total voltage drop. The meter reading should be as low as possible. If the meter shows .2 of a volt, there is excessive resistance in the circuit.

On starters where the switch is located right on the motor housing and where there is no access to an exposed starter terminal, remove the inspection band from the motor. Measure the loss in this type of circuit by connecting one test lead to the battery in the usual manner but by connecting the other test lead to one of the insulated brushes in the starting motor. When measuring for losses by this method, allow an extra .6 of a volt drop across the field winding.

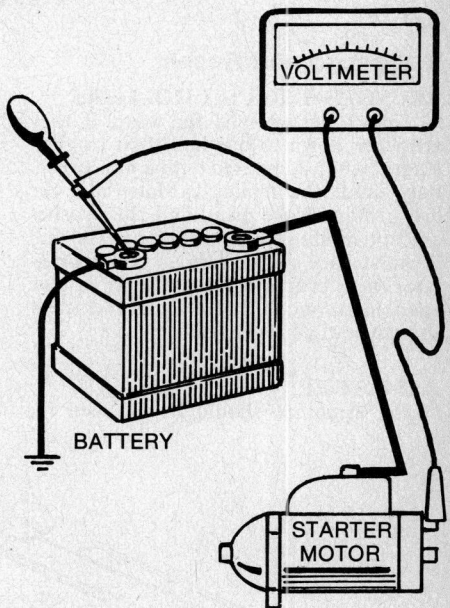

Testing starter for ground

Starter Circuit (Ground Side)

Connect the voltmeter leads as follows: Place one on the battery ground terminal post, not on the cable; and place the other to the starter motor housing, making sure of a good connection. Break through the paint, etc.

NOTE: Remove the coil wire or coil ignition wire to prevent engine from starting.

Close the starter switch and take a reading. If the pointer on the meter moves backwards, reverse the test leads.

In most cases the pointer will move only a small amount.

The amount it does move is the voltage "loss" or "drop" between the starter housing and the battery ground post. It should not exceed .4 of a volt. If the reading exceeds the allowable amount, determine the exact location of the loss.

Starter Motor Amperage Draw

Knowledge of the amount of current a starting motor draws often has some value in analyzing starting motor problems.

However, there are factors that defy giving a figure on starter amperage draw. Temperature, Oil Viscosity, Compression Ratio, etc.

To measure starter amperage draw, you should have a heavy duty 400 amp ammeter, in series with the starter positive battery cable.

Disconnect the coil wire or the coil electrical feed wire to prevent the engine from starting. Close the starter motor switch for 15 seconds and take an amperage reading.

Another way is the use of a starter current indicator. To measure starter cur-

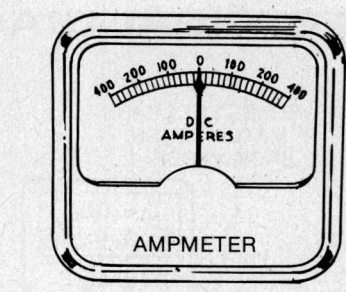

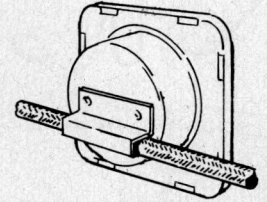

Starter current indicator

rent, place the yoke of the meter over the cable. Remove the ignition cable from the center of the distributor and ground it so the engine will not start. Then close the starter switch for 15 or 20 seconds. Observe the meter, and take an average read-

ing. (If the pointer moves backward reverse the position of the meter.)

Starting motors draw current in proportion to their speed. For instance, a motor running free on the bench may draw only 60 amperes. That same motor cranking a V-8 engine, might draw 60 amperes. If the oil in the crank case were heavy, it might draw 180 amperes. If the weather were cold and the oil extremely thick, it might draw 250 amperes. If the engine were locked so it could not turn, the starter might draw 500 amperes or as much as the battery could deliver.

High Amperage and Slow Cranking indicates: Stiff engine, friction in starter (worn bushings, dragging pole pieces, bent shaft, damaged drice), grounded starter armature, or grounded starter field.

CHILTON CAUTION: *Experience is the best teacher! One car! Starter problem!*

A.   Replaced battery.
B.   Replaced starter motor.
C.   Again, replaced starter motor.

Answer. A voltage drop test revealed that the starter ground mounted on the engine alternator bracket showed a high resistance. The alternator bracket was not completeing a good ground to the engine.

INSPECTION & REPAIR

Inspection and Repair

BRUSHES & BRUSH HOLDERS

Inspect the brushed for wear. If they are worn down to one-half their original length, when compared with a new brush, they should be replaced. Make sure the brush holders are clean and the brushes are not binding in the holders. The full brush surface should ride on the commutator with proper spring tension to give good, firm contact. Brush leads and screw should be tight and clean.

ARMATURE

The armature should be checked for

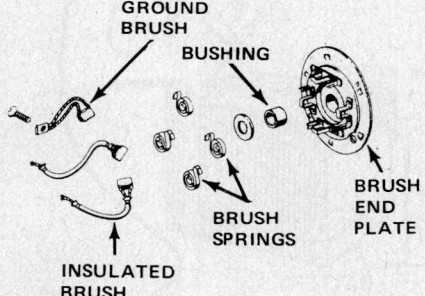

short circuits, opens, and grounds:

1   Short circuits are located by rotating the armature in a growler with a steel strip such as a hacksaw blade held on the armature. The steel strip will vibrate on the area of the short cricuit. Shorts between bars are sometimes produced by brush dust or copper between the bars. Undercutting the insulation will eliminate these shorts.

2   Opens may be located by inspecting the points where the conductors are joined to the commutator for loose connections. Poor connections cause arcing and burning of the commutator. If the bars are not badly burned,

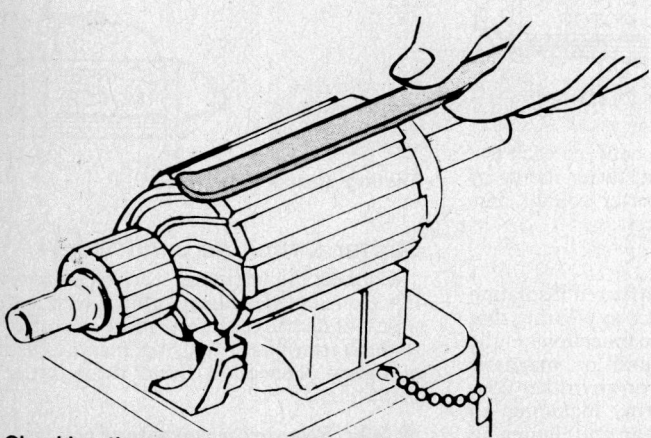

Checking the armature for short circuits

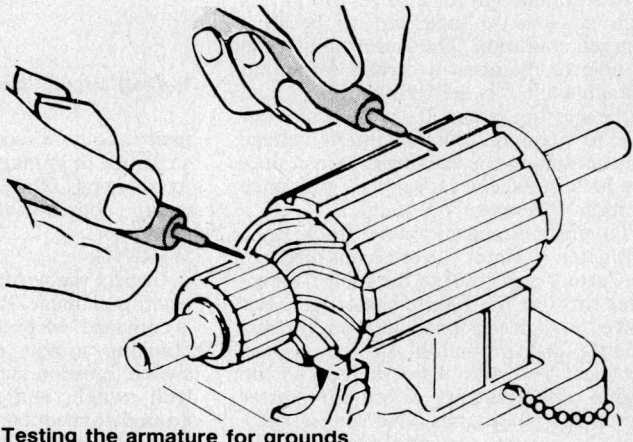

Testing the armature for grounds

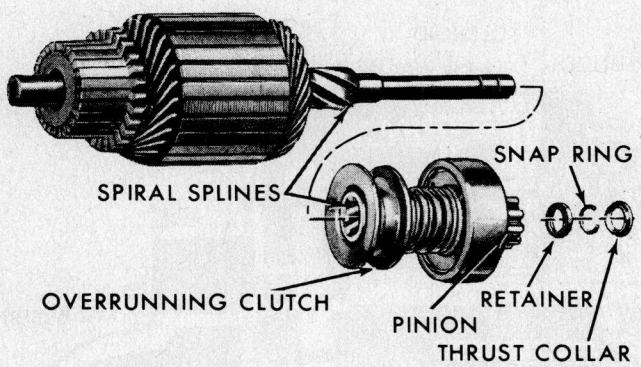

SPIRAL SPLINES

SNAP RING

OVERRUNNING CLUTCH

RETAINER

PINION

THRUST COLLAR

Starter armature assembly

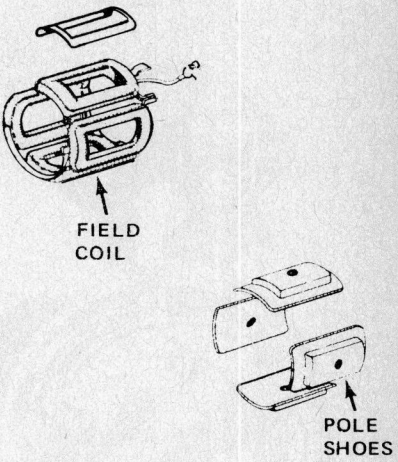

FIELD COIL

POLE SHOES

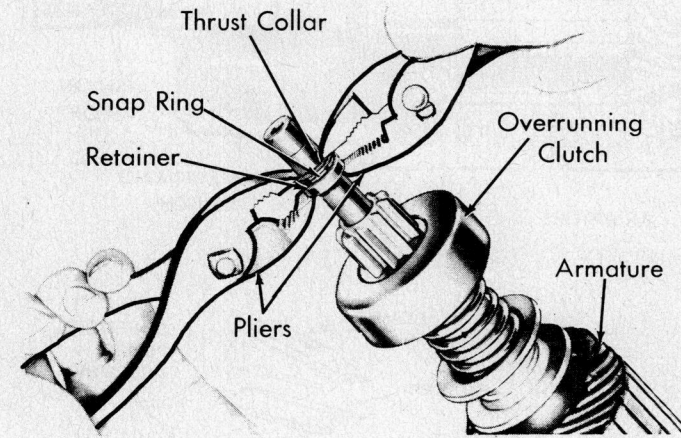

Thrust Collar

Snap Ring

Retainer

Overrunning Clutch

Pliers

Armature

Installing snap ring on retainer

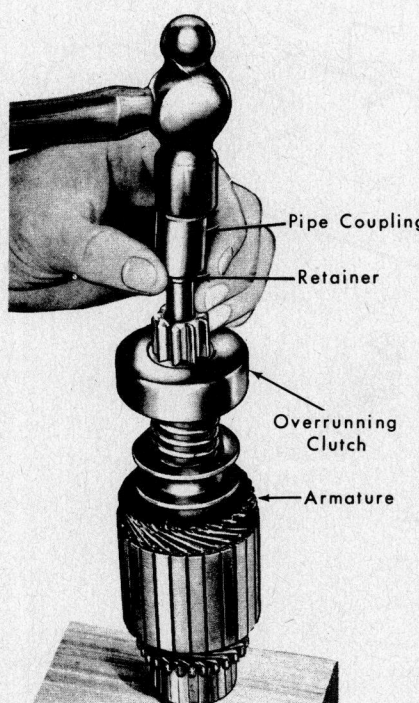

Pipe Coupling

Retainer

Overrunning Clutch

Armature

Removing overrunning clutch

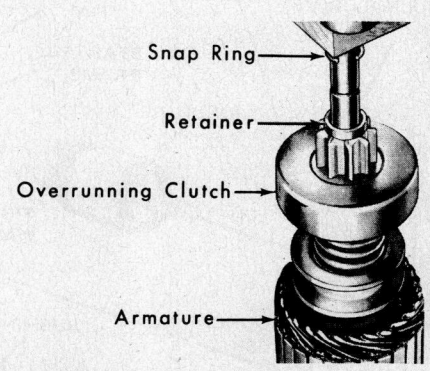

Snap Ring

Retainer

Overrunning Clutch

Armature

Installing snap ring on shaft

turned down and undercut as previously described.

FIELD COILS

The field coils should be checked for grounds and opens using a test lamp.

1 Grounds—Disconnect field coil ground connections. Connect one test prod to the field frame and the other to the field connector. If the lamp lights, the field coils are grounded and must be repaired or replaced.

2 Opens—Connect test lamp prods to ends of field coils. If lamp does not light, the field coils are open.

If the field coils need to be removed for repair or replacememt, a pole shoe spreader and pole shoe screwdriver should be used. Care should be exercised in replacing the field coils to prevent grounding or shorting them as they are tightened into place. Where the pole shoe has a long lip on one side, it shoul be assembled in the direction of armature rotation.

Renew Starter Drive Clutch Cover Running Clutch

Remove armature from starter motor,

1 Slide thrust collar off end of armature shaft.

2 Slide a 5/8" deep socket onto shaft so end of socket butts against edge of retainer.

3 Tap end of socket with hammer, driving retainer toward armature and off snap ring.

4 Remove snap ring from grove with spreader type pliers.

5 Slide clutch assembly from armature.

6 Install new clutch assembly from armature.

7 Install new clutch assemlby on shaft.

8 Slide retainer on shaft.

9 Force lock ring on shaft until it is seated in the groove.

10 Slide lock ring retainer over lock ring and press with pliers until it is firmly into position over lock ring.

11 Reassemble starter motor.

resolder the leads in the riser bars and turn the commutator down in a lathe. Then undercut the insulation between the commutator bars 1/32".

3 Grounds in the armature can be detected by the use of a test lamp (or ohmmeter). If the lamp lights when one test prod is placed on the commutator and the other test prod on the armature core or shaft, the armature is grounded. If the commutator is worn, dirty, out of round, or has high insulation, the commutator should be

STARTER MOTOR
STARTER MOTOR INSPECTION & REPAIR

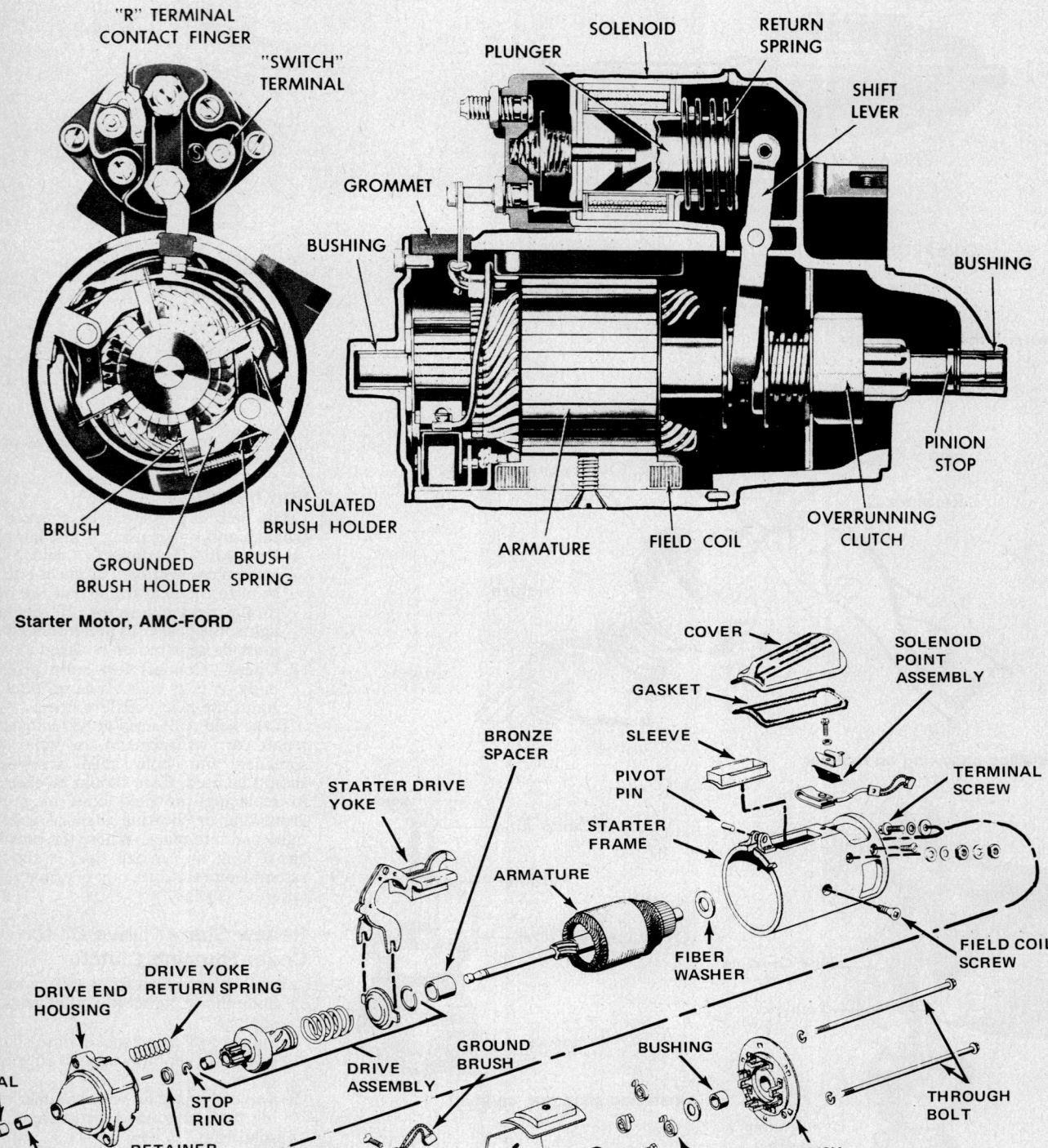

"R" TERMINAL
CONTACT FINGER

"SWITCH"
TERMINAL

BRUSH

GROUNDED
BRUSH HOLDER

BRUSH
SPRING

INSULATED
BRUSH HOLDER

Starter Motor, AMC-FORD

PLUNGER

SOLENOID

RETURN
SPRING

SHIFT
LEVER

GROMMET

BUSHING

BUSHING

PINION
STOP

ARMATURE

FIELD COIL

OVERRUNNING
CLUTCH

COVER

GASKET

SLEEVE

PIVOT
PIN

STARTER
FRAME

SOLENOID
POINT
ASSEMBLY

TERMINAL
SCREW

BRONZE
SPACER

STARTER DRIVE
YOKE

ARMATURE

FIELD COIL
SCREW

FIBER
WASHER

DRIVE YOKE
RETURN SPRING

DRIVE END
HOUSING

SEAL

BUSHING

STOP
RING

RETAINER

DRIVE
ASSEMBLY

GROUND
BRUSH

BUSHING

THROUGH
BOLT

BRUSH
END
PLATE

POLE
SHOES

BRUSH
SPRINGS

BUSHING
COVER
BAND

FIELD
COIL

INSULATED
BRUSH

Starter Motor-all GM cars

B328

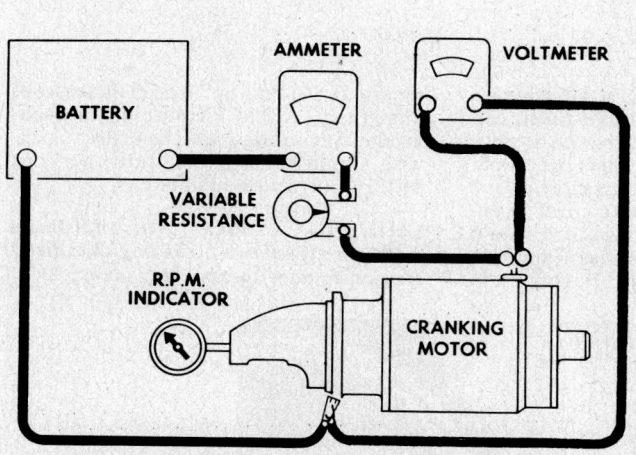

No load test hookup.

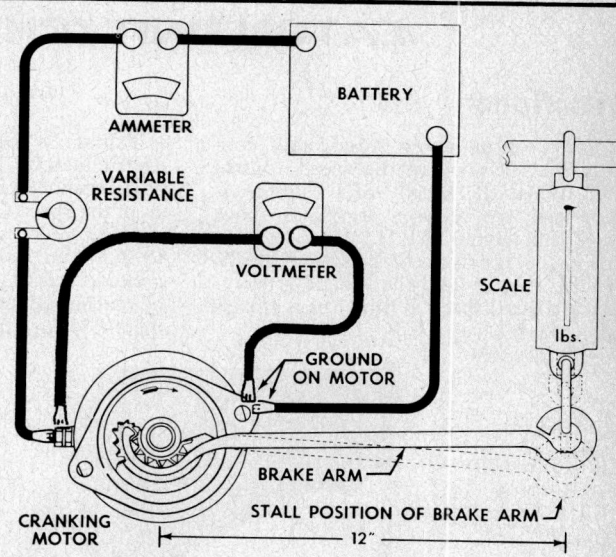

Lock torque test hookup.

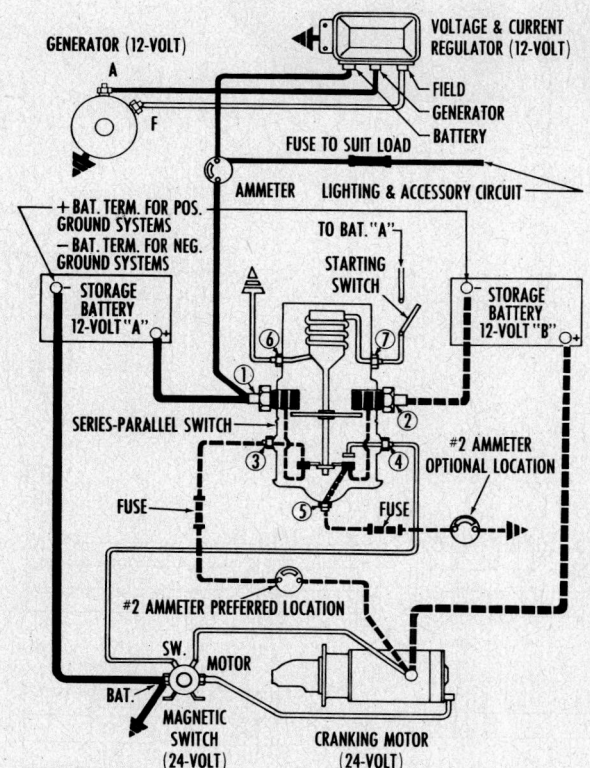

Circuit diagram of series-parallel system with switch completing parallel connections between batteries for normal operation of vehicle electrical equipment at 12 volts. The cranking motor is operated and controlled by a separately mounted magnetic switch.

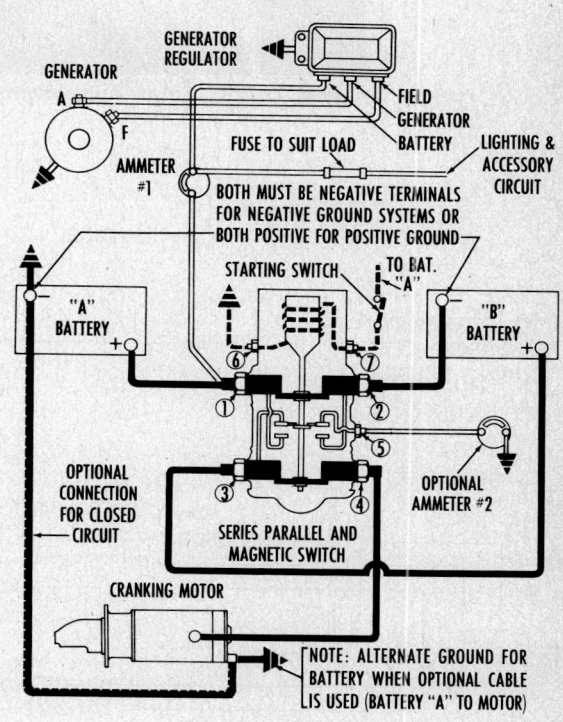

Circuit diagram of combination series-parallel and magnetic switch completing series connections between batteries for 24-volt cranking motor operation.

EATON UNIT (CHRYSLER PRODUCTS)

Description

The Lock-in Screw Adjustment controls the accuracy of the speed control unit. When the speed "SET" button is depressed and released at speeds above approximately 30 M.P.H.; the speed control system is activated, the system "locks in" and should hold the vehicle at virtually the same speed at which it is traveling.

This screw should never be adjusted indiscriminately. Need for adjustment can be determined only after accurate diagnosis of the Speed Control System operation.

If the speed "sags" (drops) more than 2 to 3 M.P.H. when speed control is activated, the lock-in adjusting screw should be turned counter-clockwise (approximately ¼ turn per one M.P.H. correction

required). If "Pull-up" (speed increase) of more than 2 to 3 M.P.H. occurs, the lock-in adjusting screw should be turned clockwise (approximately ¼ turn per one M.P.H. correction required.

CHILTON CAUTION: *This adjustment must not exceed two turns in either direction or damage to unit may occur.*

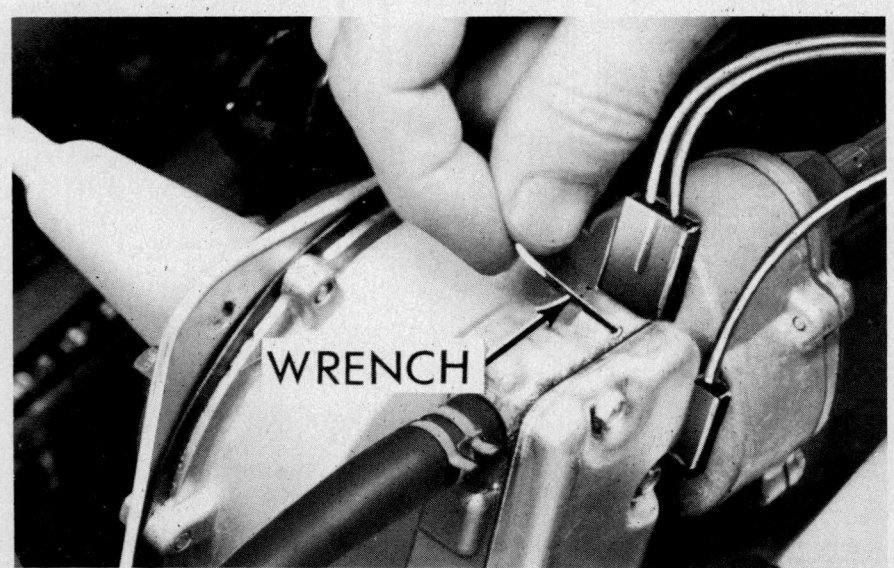

Speed, Locking Screw Adjustments

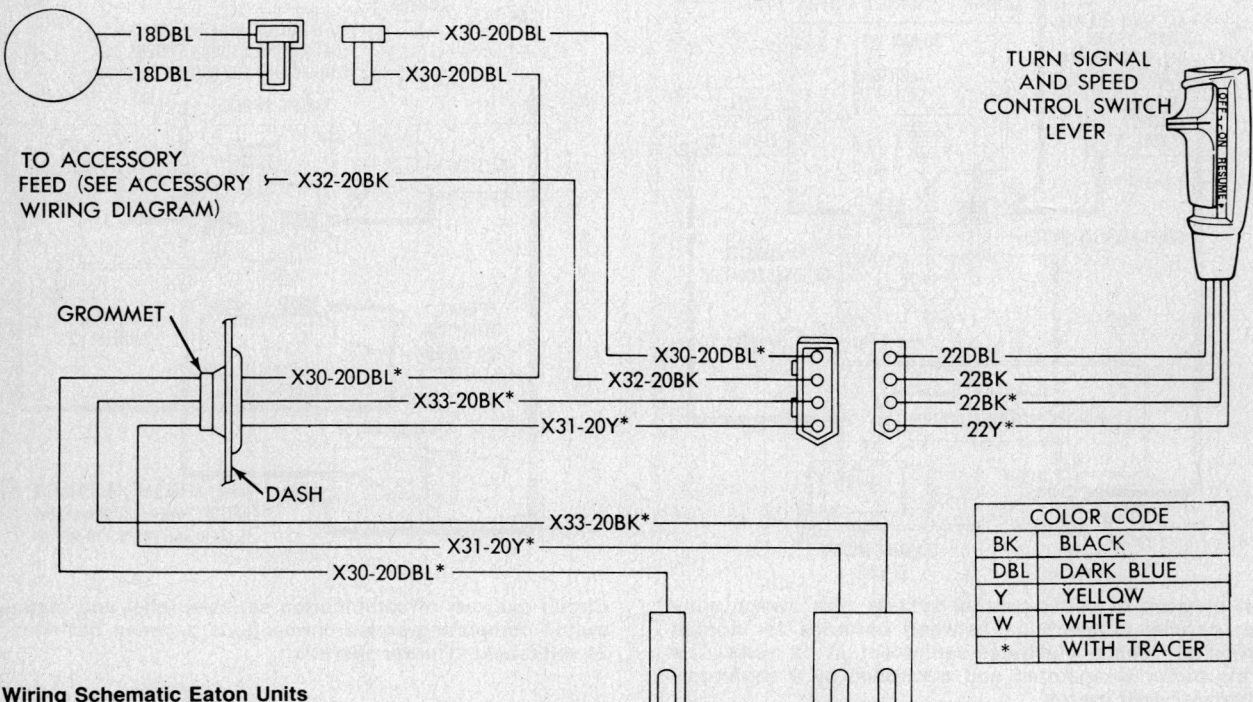

Wiring Schematic Eaton Units

COLOR CODE	
BK	BLACK
DBL	DARK BLUE
Y	YELLOW
W	WHITE
*	WITH TRACER

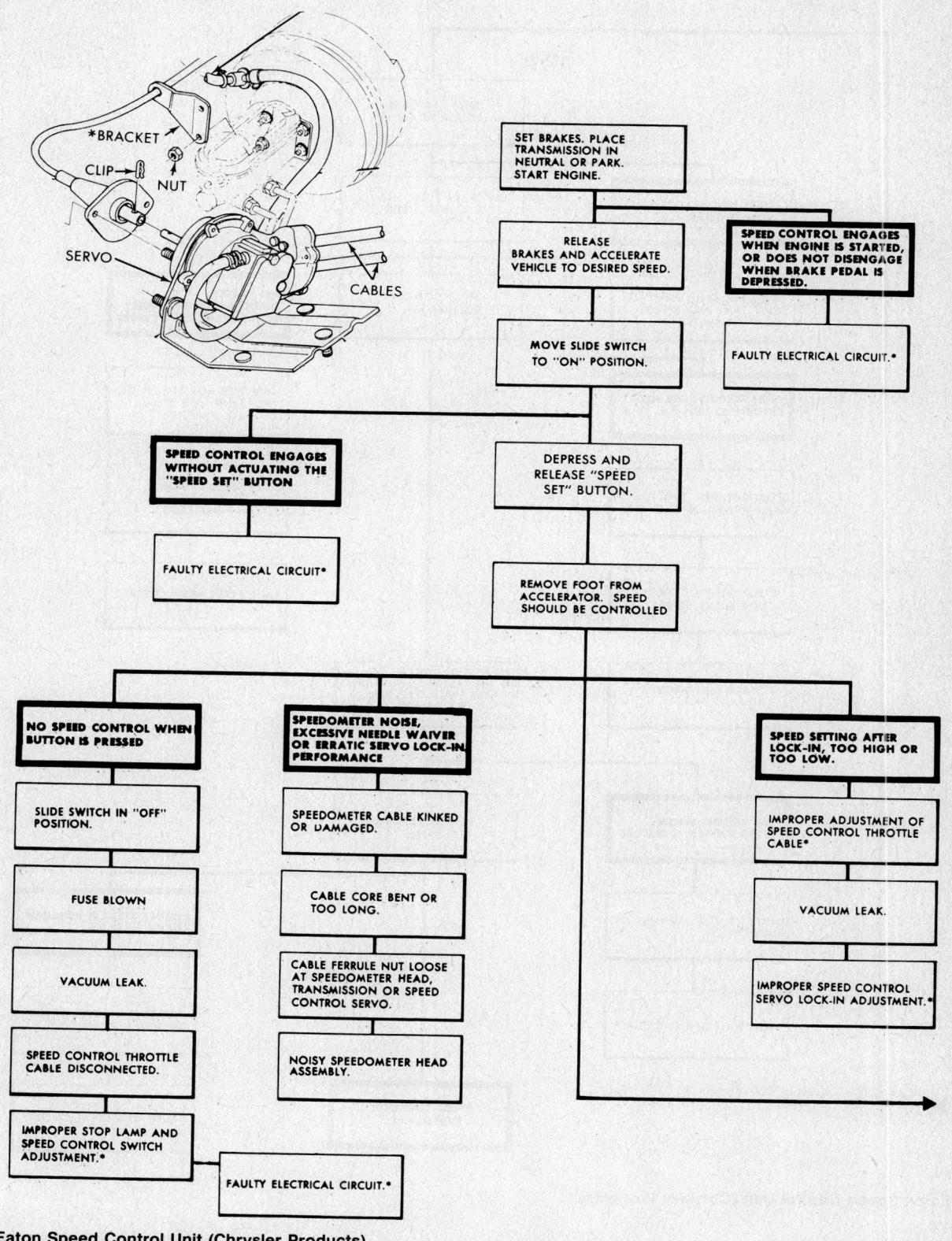

SET BRAKES. PLACE TRANSMISSION IN NEUTRAL OR PARK. START ENGINE.

RELEASE BRAKES AND ACCELERATE VEHICLE TO DESIRED SPEED.

SPEED CONTROL ENGAGES WHEN ENGINE IS STARTED, OR DOES NOT DISENGAGE WHEN BRAKE PEDAL IS DEPRESSED.

MOVE SLIDE SWITCH TO "ON" POSITION.

FAULTY ELECTRICAL CIRCUIT.*

SPEED CONTROL ENGAGES WITHOUT ACTUATING THE "SPEED SET" BUTTON

DEPRESS AND RELEASE "SPEED SET" BUTTON.

FAULTY ELECTRICAL CIRCUIT*

REMOVE FOOT FROM ACCELERATOR. SPEED SHOULD BE CONTROLLED

NO SPEED CONTROL WHEN BUTTON IS PRESSED

SPEEDOMETER NOISE, EXCESSIVE NEEDLE WAIVER OR ERRATIC SERVO LOCK-IN PERFORMANCE

SPEED SETTING AFTER LOCK-IN, TOO HIGH OR TOO LOW.

SLIDE SWITCH IN "OFF" POSITION.

SPEEDOMETER CABLE KINKED OR DAMAGED.

IMPROPER ADJUSTMENT OF SPEED CONTROL THROTTLE CABLE*

FUSE BLOWN

CABLE CORE BENT OR TOO LONG.

VACUUM LEAK.

VACUUM LEAK.

CABLE FERRULE NUT LOOSE AT SPEEDOMETER HEAD, TRANSMISSION OR SPEED CONTROL SERVO.

IMPROPER SPEED CONTROL SERVO LOCK-IN ADJUSTMENT.*

SPEED CONTROL THROTTLE CABLE DISCONNECTED.

NOISY SPEEDOMETER HEAD ASSEMBLY.

IMPROPER STOP LAMP AND SPEED CONTROL SWITCH ADJUSTMENT.*

FAULTY ELECTRICAL CIRCUIT.*

Eaton Speed Control Unit (Chrysler Products)

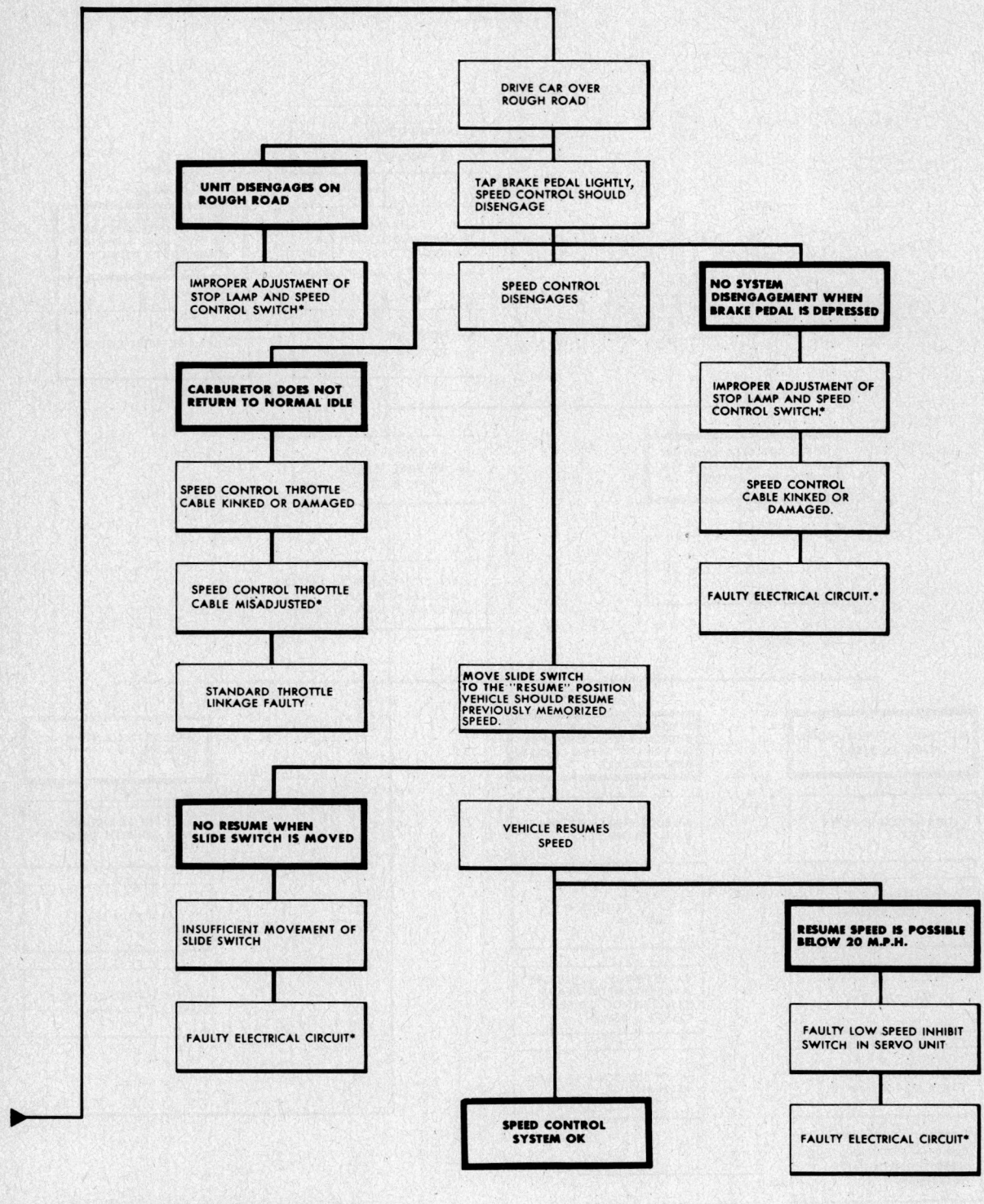

Eaton Speed Control Unit (Chrysler Products)

Speed Control Throttle Cable Adjustment

Optimum servo performance is obtained with a given amount of free play in the throttle control cable. To obtain proper free play, remove spring clip and insert a 1/16 inch diameter pin between forward end of slot in cable and carburetor linkage pin.

With choke in full open position and carburetor at curb idle, pull back on cable (toward dash panel) without moving carburetor linkage until all free play is removed. Tighten cable clamp nut to 45 inch-pounds, remove 1/16 inch diameter pin and install spring clip.

PERFECT CIRCLE ELECTRONIC TYPE DIAGNOSIS

Condition	Results	Remedy
Ignition switch "OFF", Speed Control "ON-OFF" switch "ON". Ground one lead of test light, touch other lead to each terminal in connector individually.	Light off, all terminals	None, system ok.
	Test light on at terminals 5, 7 and 14	Red wire connected to wrong power source. Use a "switched" power source at fuse block; "Hot" when ignition switch is "ON" and "Cold" when ignition switch is "OFF".
Ignition switch "ON", "ON-OFF" switch "ON". Ground one lead of test light, touch other lead to each terminal in connector individually.	Test light on at terminals 5, 7 and 14 only	None, system ok.
	No light on any terminal	Replace fuse, if blown. Connect red wire to ignition switched power source. Check ground connection, brown wire to light green wire (blue connector), or grounding terminal (green wire) at servo. Ground servo bracket.
Ignition switch "ON", "ON-OFF" switch "ON", push and hold "SET SPEED" button. Ground one lead of test light, touch other lead to terminal No. 14.	Test light off at terminal No. 14	None, system ok.
	Test light on at terminal No. 14	See engagement switch check.
Ignition switch "ON", "ON-OFF" switch "ON", push and hold slide switch to "RESUME" position. Ground one lead of test light, touch other lead to terminals No. 10 and No. 14 individually.	Test light on at terminal No. 10 and No. 14	None, system ok.
	No light at terminal No. 14 and/or No. 10	See engagement switch check.
Ignition switch "ON", "ON-OFF" switch "ON"; test light leads between terminals No. 5 and No. 13.	Test light on—push brake and test light goes off	None, system ok.
	Test light off	Adjust disengagement switch lever travel to get test light on; off when brake pedal is pushed.

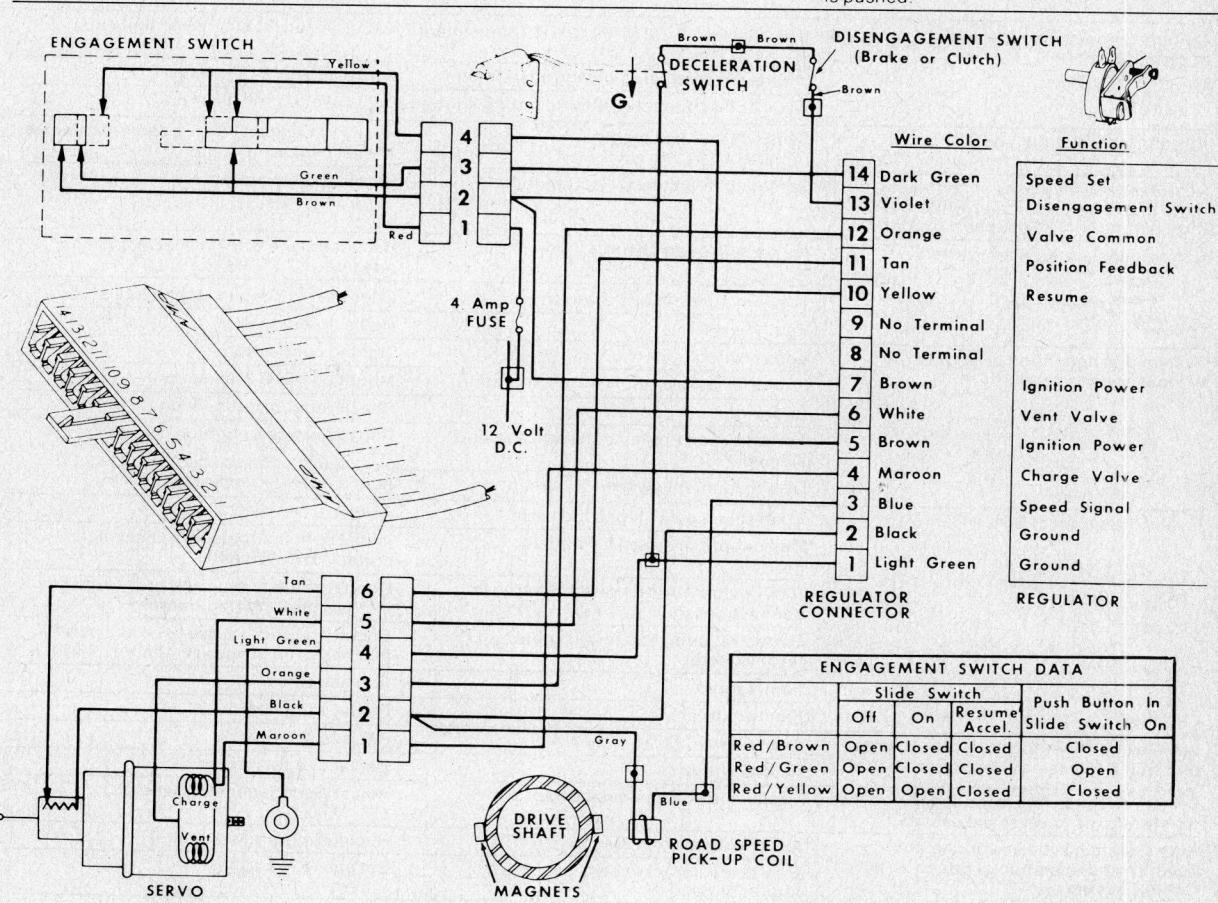

PERFECT CIRCLE ELECTRONIC TYPE DIAGNOSIS

Condition	Possible Cause	Remedy
In line fuse blown	Short or ground in Speed Control wiring harness	Perform electrical checks—Replace fuse with 5 amp max. fuse.
Does not engage, "ON-OFF" switch "ON"	No voltage on brown wire at regulator	Repair wiring harness or check for loose connections. Check disengagement switch adjustment. Instructions, "Disengagement Switch".
	Ported vacuum, restricted vacuum or no vacuum	Be sure vacuum connection is made to engine at a point that has continuous vacuum (below carburetor throttle plate)
	Vacuum leak	Repair leak
	Electrical	See "Electrical Checks"
	Faulty electrical or vacuum connections	Tighten connections
	Engagement switch inoperative	Replace engagement switch
	Speed pick up coil gap excessive or magnets not installed	Set gap to $^3/_4$" to $1^1/_4$". Instructions, "Road Speed Pick Up"
	Faulty regulator	Replace regulator
"Resume" feature inoperative	Bad ground connection	Check light green wire at servo for ground.
Does not disengage when brake is applied	Improper disengagement switch adjustment	Adjust disengagement switch. Instructions, "Disengagement Switch".
Re-engages when brake is released	Faulty disengagement switch (electrical)	Replace disengagement switch
	Faulty regulator	Replace regulator.
"Resume" feature does not cancel when ignition switch is turned off	Wrong power source, power supply is always on	Select correct power source—red wire of Speed Control wiring harness to 12 volts with ignition key to "On" or "Acc" position, no voltage when ignition key is in "Off" position
Carburetor does not return to normal idle	Improper Speed Control servo linkage adjustment	Adjust Speed Control servo linkage.
	Improper accelerator linkage adjustment	Adjust accelerator linkage
	Weak or disconnected throttle return spring	Replace or connect spring
Pulsating accelerator pedal	Sensitivity set too high	Rotate "Sensitivity Adj" counterclockwise & reset centering
Vehicle speed increases or decreases more than 2 miles per hour when making a setting with "Set Speed" button	Centering adjustment improperly set	Reset "Centering Adj."
Engine accelerates when started	No slack in bead chain	Recheck slack with throttle in hot idle position.
	Vacuum connections reversed on servo	Check servo vacuum connections.
	Faulty servo	Replace servo.
System disengages on level road without applying brake	Loose wiring connections	Tighten connections.
	Improper deceleration switch mounting	Mount on VERTICAL surface.
	Loose vacuum connections	Check vacuum connections.
	Servo linkage broken or throttle clamp slipped	Repair linkage or tighten clamps
	Disengagement switch adjustment	Adjust disengagement switch.
Erratic operation of Speed Control	Road speed pick up gap too large	Set gap to $^3/_4$" to $1^1/_4$".
	One or both drive shaft magnets inverted	Install both magnets with sheet metal surface to drive shaft.
	Pick up coil wires reversed at harness connections	Connect blue to blue and gray to gray. Instructions, "Wiring Harness".
	Ported vacuum (above carburetor throttle plate)	Engine vacuum source to be at a point that has continuous vacuum.
	Faulty servo	Replace servo.
	Faulty regulator	Replace regulator
Vehicle continues to accelerate after depressing & releasing "Set Speed" button	Faulty servo	Replace servo.
	Faulty regulator	Replace regulator.
System engages, but loses speed and then slowly returns to set speed selected	Vacuum leak at disengagement switch	Adjust disengagement switch.
After system has been working and used, erratic operation of Speed Control occurs	Missing drive shaft magnet(s)	Replace missing magnet(s).
	Pick up coil bracket bent, causing improper gap	Set gap to $^3/_4$" to $1^1/_4$".

PERFECT CIRCLE ELECTRONIC TYPE DIAGNOSIS

Test Terminal	Results	Remedy
Terminal No. 1 (Light Green)	Circuit closed	None, system ok.
	Circuit open	Check ¼" eyelet terminal to insure grounding. If eyelet is grounded and circuit still checks open check continuity from six-way connector to 14 pin edge card reg. connector, looking for broken wire, loose or broken terminal, terminal not locked into connector body (pushing out when plugging connector bodies together).
Terminal No. 2 (Black)	Circuit open	None, system ok.
	Circuit closed	Check black wire, tan wire, gray wire, and blue wire for worn thru insulation touching grounded portion of vehicle.
Terminal No. 3 (Blue)	Circuit open	None, system ok.
	Circuit closed	Make same checks as on circuit closed, terminal No. 2.
Terminal No. 4 (Maroon)	Circuit open	None, system ok.
	Circuit closed	Insure maroon, white or orange wires are not touching grounded portion of vehicle thru worn insulation on wires. (If Servo is shorted internally, this can be verified by performing step #3 of the service check of the Electronic Speed Control Servo).
Terminal No. 5 (Brown)	Circuit open	None, system ok.
	Circuit closed	Insure brown wires of main wiring harness, brown and green wires of Engagement Switch wiring harness or dark green wire of main wiring harness is not shorted to grounded portion of vehicle.
Terminal No. 6 (White)	Circuit open	None, system ok.
	Circuit closed	Same check procedure as listed for Terminal No. 4, circuit closed.
Terminal No. 7 (Brown)	Circuit open	None, system ok.
	Circuit closed	Same check procedure as listed for Terminal No. 5, circuit closed.
Terminal No. 8	No Terminal	
Terminal No. 9	No Terminal	
Terminal No. 10 (Yellow)	Circuit open	None, system ok.
	Circuit closed	Insure yellow wire of main wiring harness or yellow wire of Engagement Switch wiring harness has not shorted to grounded portion of vehicle.
Terminal No. 11 (Tan)	Circuit open	None, system ok.
	Circuit closed	Insure tan wires, black wires, gray wires or blue wires have not shorted to grounded portion of vehicle.
Terminal No. 12 (Orange)	Circuit open	None, system ok.
	Circuit closed	Same check procedure as listed for Terminal No. 4, circuit closed.
Terminal No. 13 (Violet)	Circuit open (open when brake pedal is depressed)	None, system ok.
	Circuit open	Check for broken wire or terminal at 14 pin edge card connector, bad splice where violet and brown wire of disengagement join, disengagement not adjusted so contacts will close, faulty disengagement switch—wires or terminals staked not making contact, bad splice of brown wire of disengagement switch to brown wire of deceleration switch, deceleration switch mounted in an improper way not allowing contact closing, or a bad deceleration switch (no continuity available), bad splice where brown wire of deceleration switch joins the light green wire of main wiring harness, check for broken wire or broken terminals, poor connections of terminals, insure six-way connector between servo harness and main wiring harness or ¼" eyelet is not grounded.
		If checks indicate closed circuit when brake pedal is depressed, disengagement switch is improperly mounted—check installation instructions for proper mounting.
Terminal No. 14 (Dark Green)	Circuit open	None, system ok.
	Circuit closed	Same check procedure as listed for Terminal No. 5, circuit closed.

NOTE:

If a grounded wire or bare wire is found in any of the checks, tape up the wire with electricians vinyl plastic tape or an equivalent substitute.

If terminal wire is broken, prepare wire and solder it.

You can obtain a new wiring harness, but a quick repair may put you back in service.

DELCO ELECTRONIC TYPE SPEED CONTROL TROUBLESHOOTING CHART

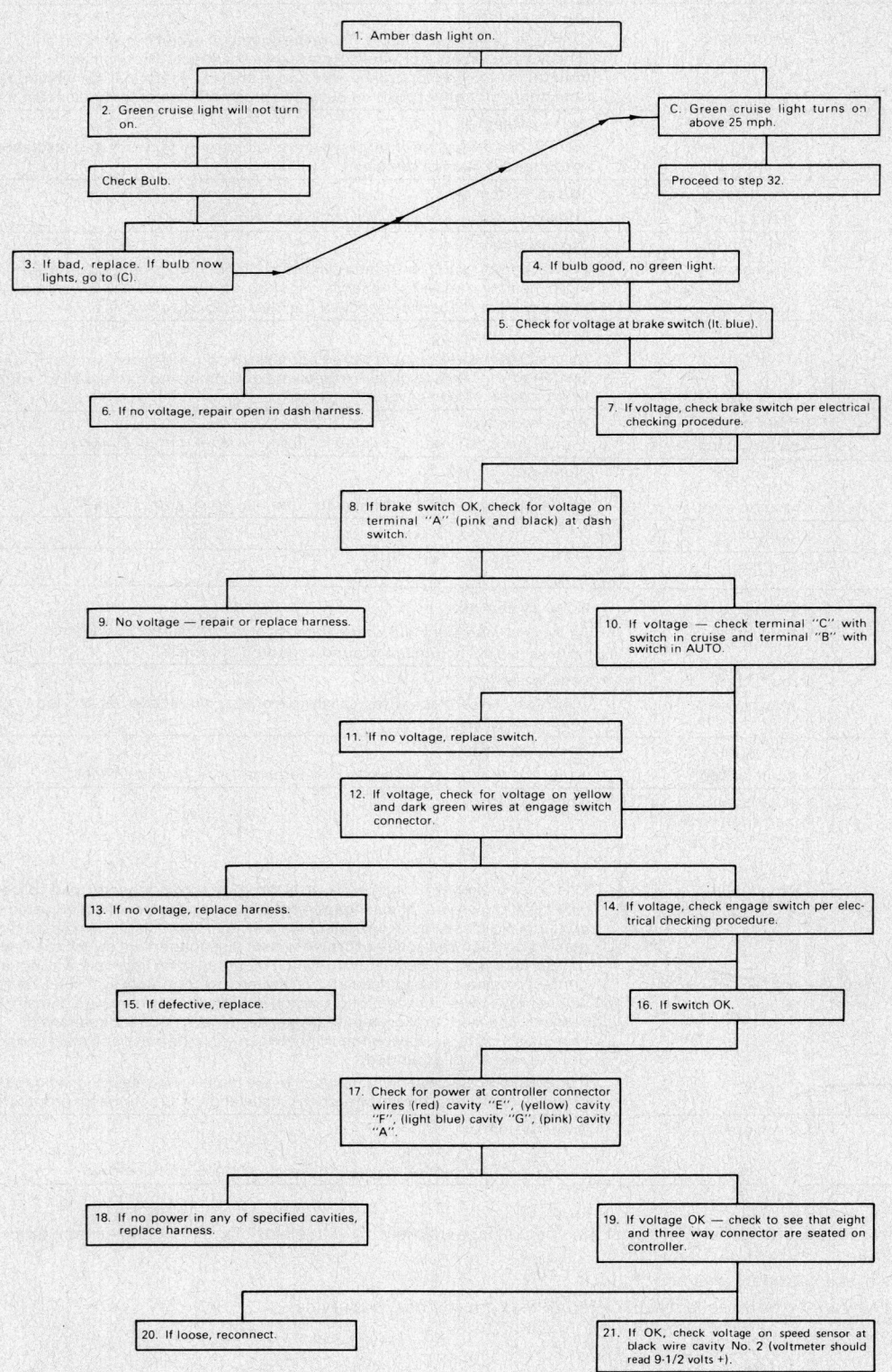

1. Amber dash light on.

2. Green cruise light will not turn on.

Check Bulb.

C. Green cruise light turns on above 25 mph.

Proceed to step 32.

3. If bad, replace. If bulb now lights, go to (C).

4. If bulb good, no green light.

5. Check for voltage at brake switch (lt. blue).

6. If no voltage, repair open in dash harness.

7. If voltage, check brake switch per electrical checking procedure.

8. If brake switch OK, check for voltage on terminal "A" (pink and black) at dash switch.

9. No voltage — repair or replace harness.

10. If voltage — check terminal "C" with switch in cruise and terminal "B" with switch in AUTO.

11. If no voltage, replace switch.

12. If voltage, check for voltage on yellow and dark green wires at engage switch connector.

13. If no voltage, replace harness.

14. If voltage, check engage switch per electrical checking procedure.

15. If defective, replace.

16. If switch OK.

17. Check for power at controller connector wires (red) cavity "E", (yellow) cavity "F", (light blue) cavity "G", (pink) cavity "A".

18. If no power in any of specified cavities, replace harness.

19. If voltage OK — check to see that eight and three way connector are seated on controller.

20. If loose, reconnect.

21. If OK, check voltage on speed sensor at black wire cavity No. 2 (voltmeter should read 9-1/2 volts +).

DELCO ELECTRONIC TYPE SPEED CONTROL TROUBLESHOOTING CHART

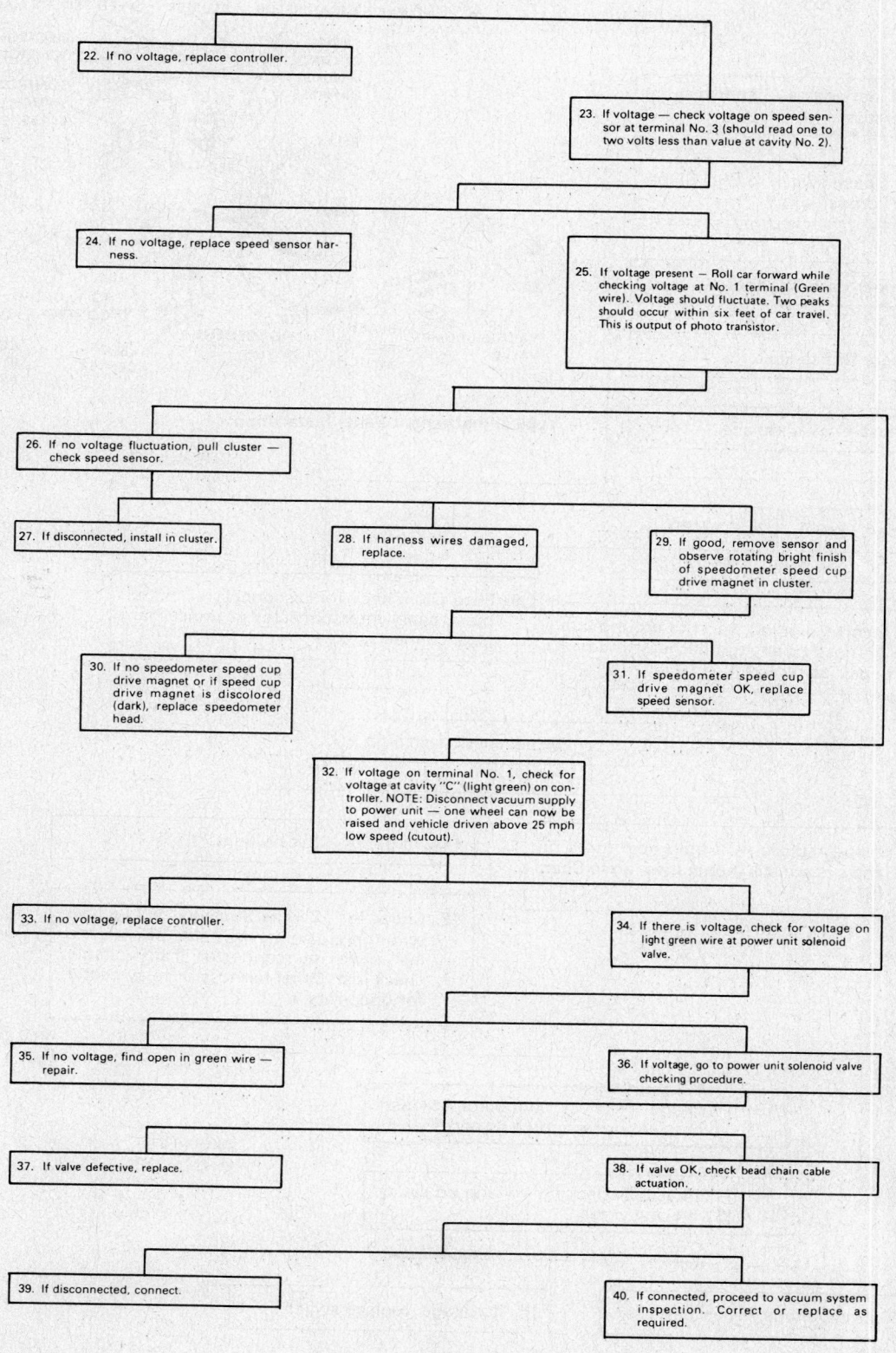

22. If no voltage, replace controller.

23. If voltage — check voltage on speed sensor at terminal No. 3 (should read one to two volts less than value at cavity No. 2).

24. If no voltage, replace speed sensor harness.

25. If voltage present — Roll car forward while checking voltage at No. 1 terminal (Green wire). Voltage should fluctuate. Two peaks should occur within six feet of car travel. This is output of photo transistor.

26. If no voltage fluctuation, pull cluster — check speed sensor.

27. If disconnected, install in cluster.

28. If harness wires damaged, replace.

29. If good, remove sensor and observe rotating bright finish of speedometer speed cup drive magnet in cluster.

30. If no speedometer speed cup drive magnet or if speed cup drive magnet is discolored (dark), replace speedometer head.

31. If speedometer speed cup drive magnet OK, replace speed sensor.

32. If voltage on terminal No. 1, check for voltage at cavity "C" (light green) on controller. NOTE: Disconnect vacuum supply to power unit — one wheel can now be raised and vehicle driven above 25 mph low speed (cutout).

33. If no voltage, replace controller.

34. If there is voltage, check for voltage on light green wire at power unit solenoid valve.

35. If no voltage, find open in green wire — repair.

36. If voltage, go to power unit solenoid valve checking procedure.

37. If valve defective, replace.

38. If valve OK, check bead chain cable actuation.

39. If disconnected, connect.

40. If connected, proceed to vacuum system inspection. Correct or replace as required.

DELCO ELECTRONIC TYPE SPEED CONTROL TROUBLESHOOTING CHART

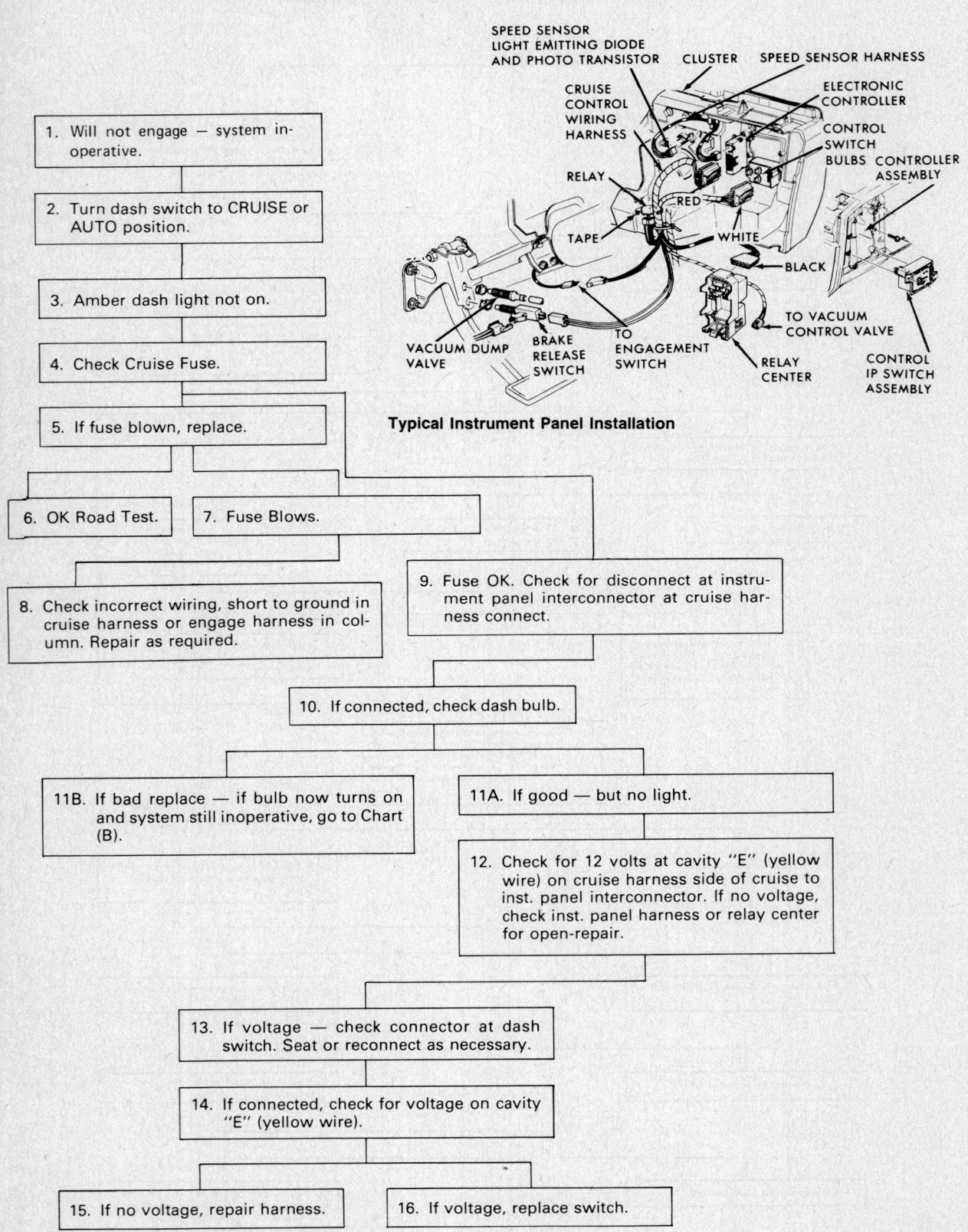

Typical Instrument Panel Installation

1. Will not engage — system inoperative.

2. Turn dash switch to CRUISE or AUTO position.

3. Amber dash light not on.

4. Check Cruise Fuse.

5. If fuse blown, replace.

6. OK Road Test.

7. Fuse Blows.

8. Check incorrect wiring, short to ground in cruise harness or engage harness in column. Repair as required.

9. Fuse OK. Check for disconnect at instrument panel interconnector at cruise harness connect.

10. If connected, check dash bulb.

11B. If bad replace — if bulb now turns on and system still inoperative, go to Chart (B).

11A. If good — but no light.

12. Check for 12 volts at cavity "E" (yellow wire) on cruise harness side of cruise to inst. panel interconnector. If no voltage, check inst. panel harness or relay center for open-repair.

13. If voltage — check connector at dash switch. Seat or reconnect as necessary.

14. If connected, check for voltage on cavity "E" (yellow wire).

15. If no voltage, repair harness.

16. If voltage, replace switch.

DELCO CRUISE MASTER MECHANICAL TYPE DIAGNOSIS

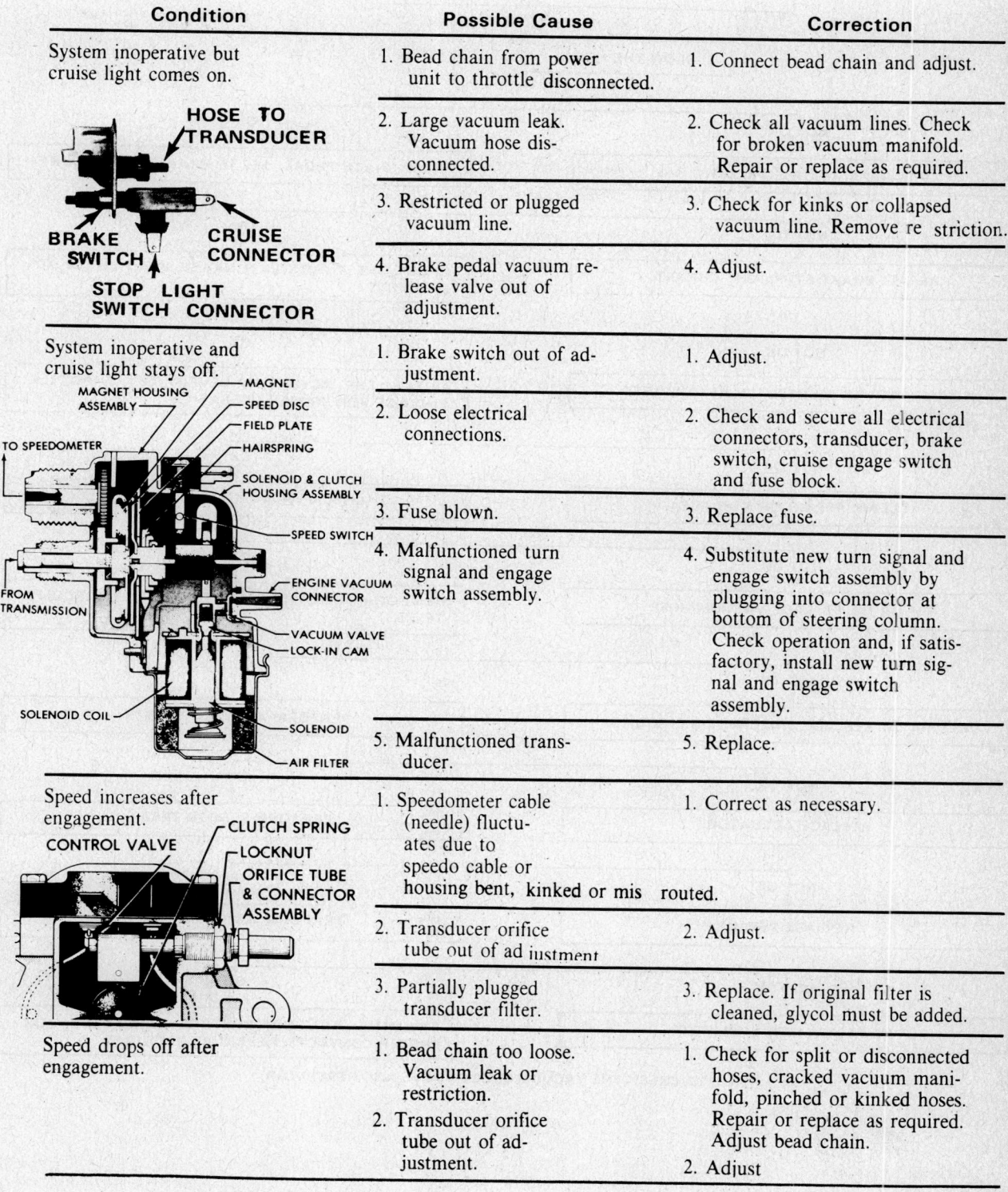

Condition	Possible Cause	Correction
System inoperative but cruise light comes on.	1. Bead chain from power unit to throttle disconnected.	1. Connect bead chain and adjust.
HOSE TO TRANSDUCER **BRAKE SWITCH** **CRUISE CONNECTOR** **STOP LIGHT SWITCH CONNECTOR**	2. Large vacuum leak. Vacuum hose disconnected.	2. Check all vacuum lines. Check for broken vacuum manifold. Repair or replace as required.
	3. Restricted or plugged vacuum line.	3. Check for kinks or collapsed vacuum line. Remove restriction.
	4. Brake pedal vacuum release valve out of adjustment.	4. Adjust.
System inoperative and cruise light stays off.	1. Brake switch out of adjustment.	1. Adjust.
MAGNET **MAGNET HOUSING ASSEMBLY** **SPEED DISC** **FIELD PLATE** **HAIRSPRING** **TO SPEEDOMETER** **SOLENOID & CLUTCH HOUSING ASSEMBLY** **SPEED SWITCH** **ENGINE VACUUM CONNECTOR** **FROM TRANSMISSION** **VACUUM VALVE** **LOCK-IN CAM** **SOLENOID COIL** **SOLENOID** **AIR FILTER**	2. Loose electrical connections.	2. Check and secure all electrical connectors, transducer, brake switch, cruise engage switch and fuse block.
	3. Fuse blown.	3. Replace fuse.
	4. Malfunctioned turn signal and engage switch assembly.	4. Substitute new turn signal and engage switch assembly by plugging into connector at bottom of steering column. Check operation and, if satisfactory, install new turn signal and engage switch assembly.
	5. Malfunctioned transducer.	5. Replace.
Speed increases after engagement.	1. Speedometer cable (needle) fluctuates due to speedo cable or housing bent, kinked or misrouted.	1. Correct as necessary.
CONTROL VALVE **CLUTCH SPRING** **LOCKNUT** **ORIFICE TUBE & CONNECTOR ASSEMBLY**	2. Transducer orifice tube out of adjustment	2. Adjust.
	3. Partially plugged transducer filter.	3. Replace. If original filter is cleaned, glycol must be added.
Speed drops off after engagement.	1. Bead chain too loose. Vacuum leak or restriction.	1. Check for split or disconnected hoses, cracked vacuum manifold, pinched or kinked hoses. Repair or replace as required. Adjust bead chain.
	2. Transducer orifice tube out of adjustment.	2. Adjust

FORD SPEED CONTROL DIAGNOSIS

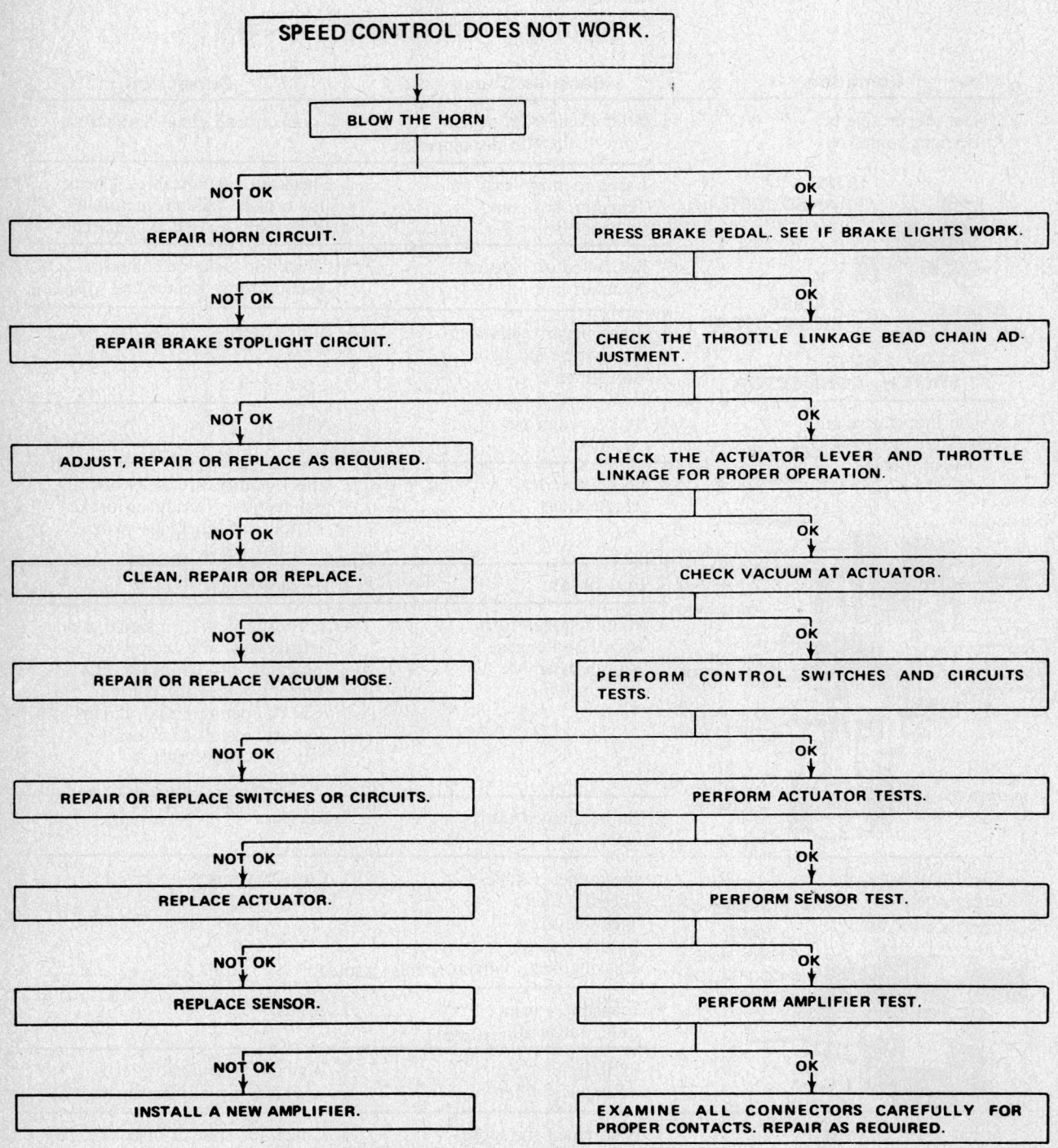

SPEED CONTROL DOES NOT WORK.

BLOW THE HORN

NOT OK — REPAIR HORN CIRCUIT.

OK — PRESS BRAKE PEDAL. SEE IF BRAKE LIGHTS WORK.

NOT OK — REPAIR BRAKE STOPLIGHT CIRCUIT.

OK — CHECK THE THROTTLE LINKAGE BEAD CHAIN ADJUSTMENT.

NOT OK — ADJUST, REPAIR OR REPLACE AS REQUIRED.

OK — CHECK THE ACTUATOR LEVER AND THROTTLE LINKAGE FOR PROPER OPERATION.

NOT OK — CLEAN, REPAIR OR REPLACE.

OK — CHECK VACUUM AT ACTUATOR.

NOT OK — REPAIR OR REPLACE VACUUM HOSE.

OK — PERFORM CONTROL SWITCHES AND CIRCUITS TESTS.

NOT OK — REPAIR OR REPLACE SWITCHES OR CIRCUITS.

OK — PERFORM ACTUATOR TESTS.

NOT OK — REPLACE ACTUATOR.

OK — PERFORM SENSOR TEST.

NOT OK — REPLACE SENSOR.

OK — PERFORM AMPLIFIER TEST.

NOT OK — INSTALL A NEW AMPLIFIER.

OK — EXAMINE ALL CONNECTORS CAREFULLY FOR PROPER CONTACTS. REPAIR AS REQUIRED.

* FOR 1973, CHECK THE VACUUM CHECK VALVE AND RESERVOIR.

FORD SPEED CONTROL DIAGNOSIS

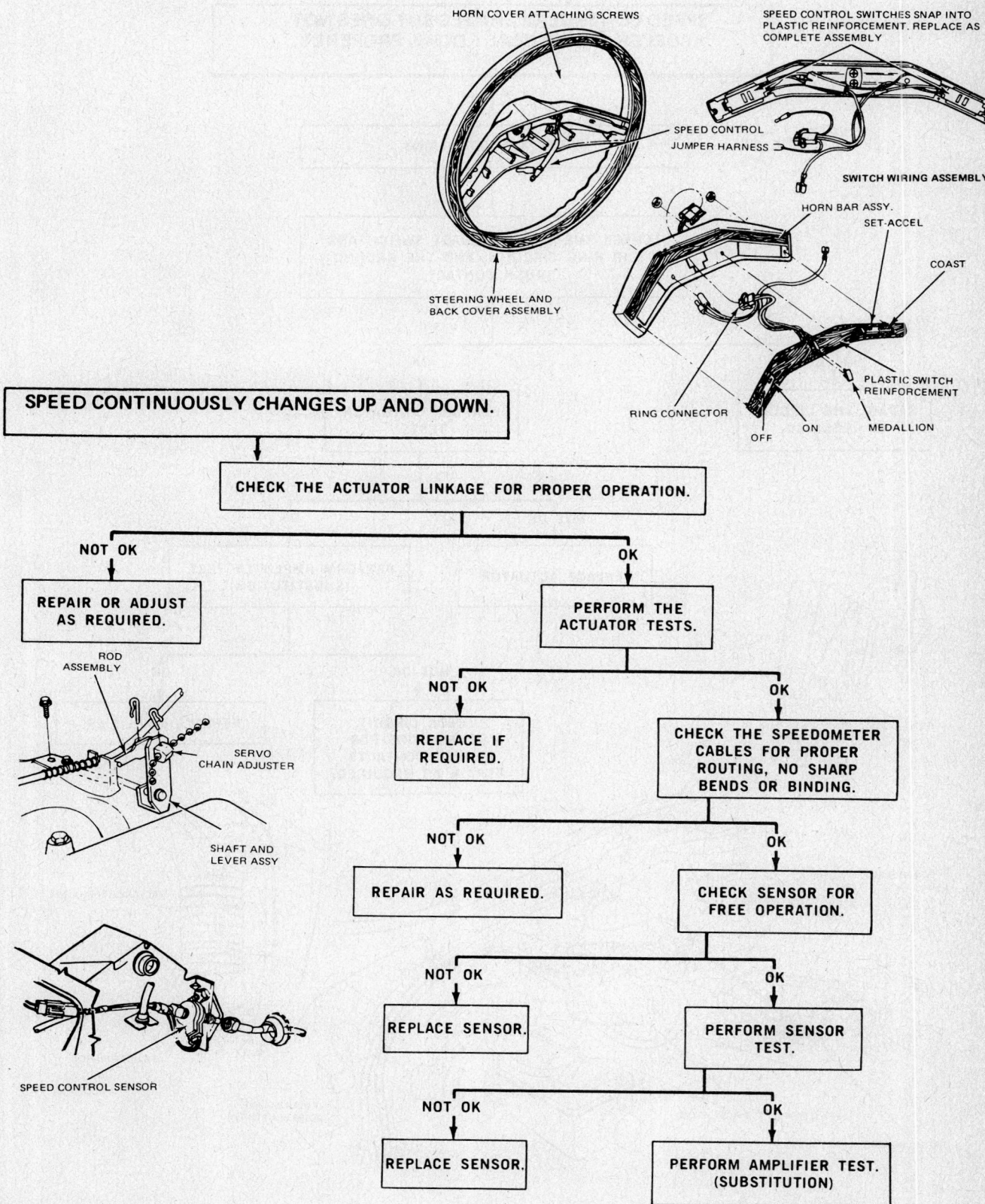

HORN COVER ATTACHING SCREWS

SPEED CONTROL SWITCHES SNAP INTO PLASTIC REINFORCEMENT. REPLACE AS COMPLETE ASSEMBLY

SPEED CONTROL JUMPER HARNESS

SWITCH WIRING ASSEMBLY

STEERING WHEEL AND BACK COVER ASSEMBLY

HORN BAR ASSY.

SET-ACCEL

COAST

RING CONNECTOR

OFF   ON   MEDALLION

PLASTIC SWITCH REINFORCEMENT

SPEED CONTINUOUSLY CHANGES UP AND DOWN.

CHECK THE ACTUATOR LINKAGE FOR PROPER OPERATION.

NOT OK

REPAIR OR ADJUST AS REQUIRED.

OK

PERFORM THE ACTUATOR TESTS.

ROD ASSEMBLY

SERVO CHAIN ADJUSTER

SHAFT AND LEVER ASSY

NOT OK

REPLACE IF REQUIRED.

OK

CHECK THE SPEEDOMETER CABLES FOR PROPER ROUTING, NO SHARP BENDS OR BINDING.

NOT OK

REPAIR AS REQUIRED.

OK

CHECK SENSOR FOR FREE OPERATION.

SPEED CONTROL SENSOR

NOT OK

REPLACE SENSOR.

OK

PERFORM SENSOR TEST.

NOT OK

REPLACE SENSOR.

OK

PERFORM AMPLIFIER TEST. (SUBSTITUTION)

B341

FORD SPEED CONTROL DIAGNOSIS

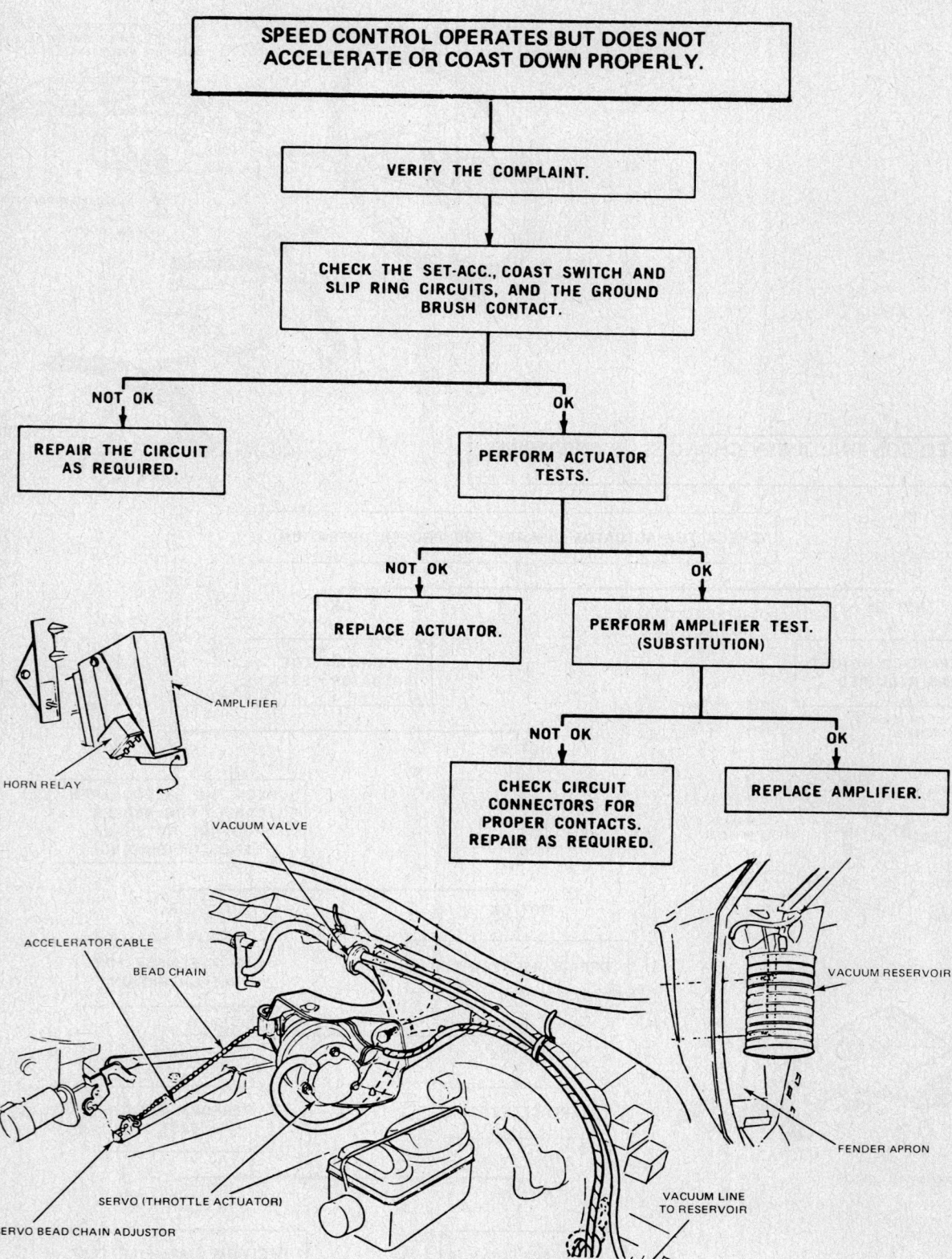

SPEED CONTROL OPERATES BUT DOES NOT ACCELERATE OR COAST DOWN PROPERLY.

VERIFY THE COMPLAINT.

CHECK THE SET-ACC., COAST SWITCH AND SLIP RING CIRCUITS, AND THE GROUND BRUSH CONTACT.

NOT OK

REPAIR THE CIRCUIT AS REQUIRED.

OK

PERFORM ACTUATOR TESTS.

NOT OK

REPLACE ACTUATOR.

OK

PERFORM AMPLIFIER TEST. (SUBSTITUTION)

NOT OK

CHECK CIRCUIT CONNECTORS FOR PROPER CONTACTS. REPAIR AS REQUIRED.

OK

REPLACE AMPLIFIER.

AMPLIFIER

HORN RELAY

VACUUM VALVE

ACCELERATOR CABLE

BEAD CHAIN

VACUUM RESERVOIR

FENDER APRON

SERVO (THROTTLE ACTUATOR)

SERVO BEAD CHAIN ADJUSTOR

VACUUM LINE TO RESERVOIR

FORD SPEED CONTROL DIAGNOSIS

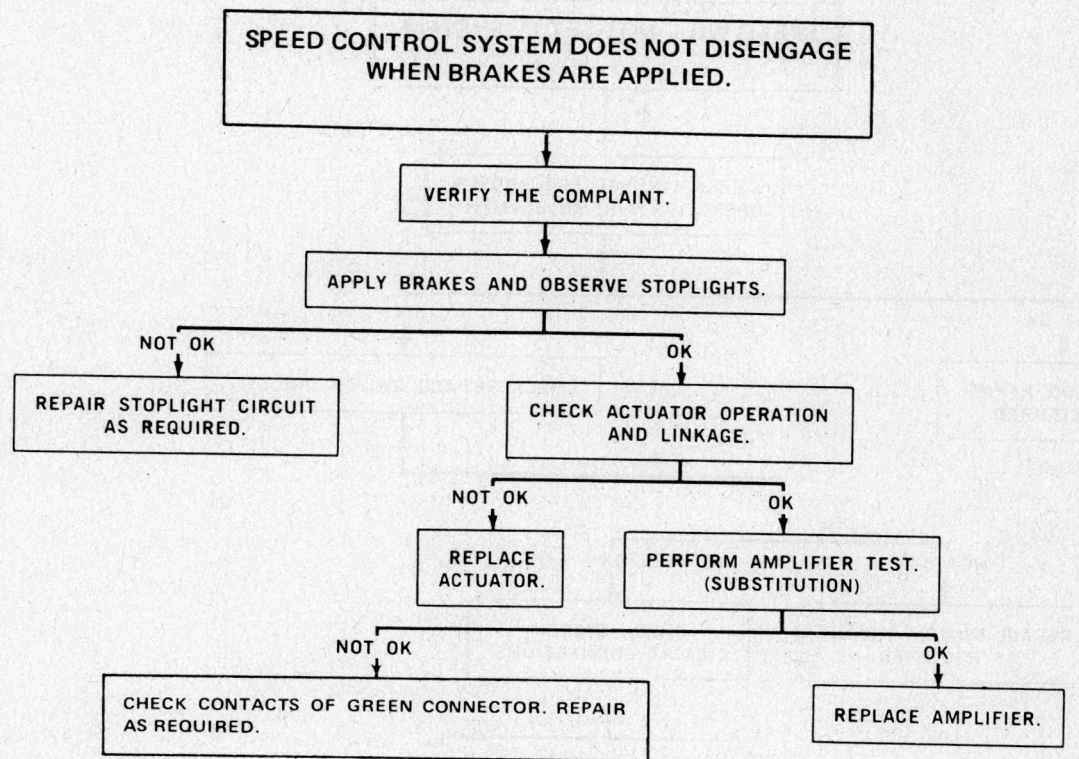

SPEED CONTROL SYSTEM DOES NOT DISENGAGE WHEN BRAKES ARE APPLIED.

VERIFY THE COMPLAINT.

APPLY BRAKES AND OBSERVE STOPLIGHTS.

NOT OK → REPAIR STOPLIGHT CIRCUIT AS REQUIRED.

OK → CHECK ACTUATOR OPERATION AND LINKAGE.

NOT OK → REPLACE ACTUATOR.

OK → PERFORM AMPLIFIER TEST. (SUBSTITUTION)

NOT OK → CHECK CONTACTS OF GREEN CONNECTOR. REPAIR AS REQUIRED.

OK → REPLACE AMPLIFIER.

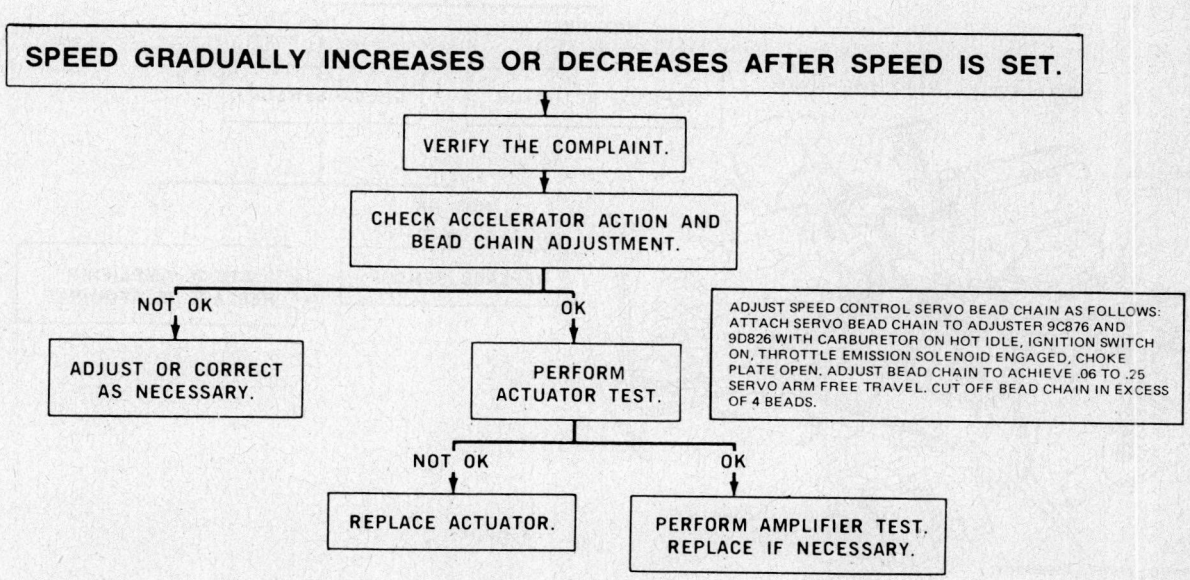

SPEED GRADUALLY INCREASES OR DECREASES AFTER SPEED IS SET.

VERIFY THE COMPLAINT.

CHECK ACCELERATOR ACTION AND BEAD CHAIN ADJUSTMENT.

NOT OK → ADJUST OR CORRECT AS NECESSARY.

OK → PERFORM ACTUATOR TEST.

NOT OK → REPLACE ACTUATOR.

OK → PERFORM AMPLIFIER TEST. REPLACE IF NECESSARY.

ADJUST SPEED CONTROL SERVO BEAD CHAIN AS FOLLOWS: ATTACH SERVO BEAD CHAIN TO ADJUSTER 9C876 AND 9D826 WITH CARBURETOR ON HOT IDLE, IGNITION SWITCH ON, THROTTLE EMISSION SOLENOID ENGAGED, CHOKE PLATE OPEN. ADJUST BEAD CHAIN TO ACHIEVE .06 TO .25 SERVO ARM FREE TRAVEL. CUT OFF BEAD CHAIN IN EXCESS OF 4 BEADS.

FORD SPEED CONTROL DIAGNOSIS

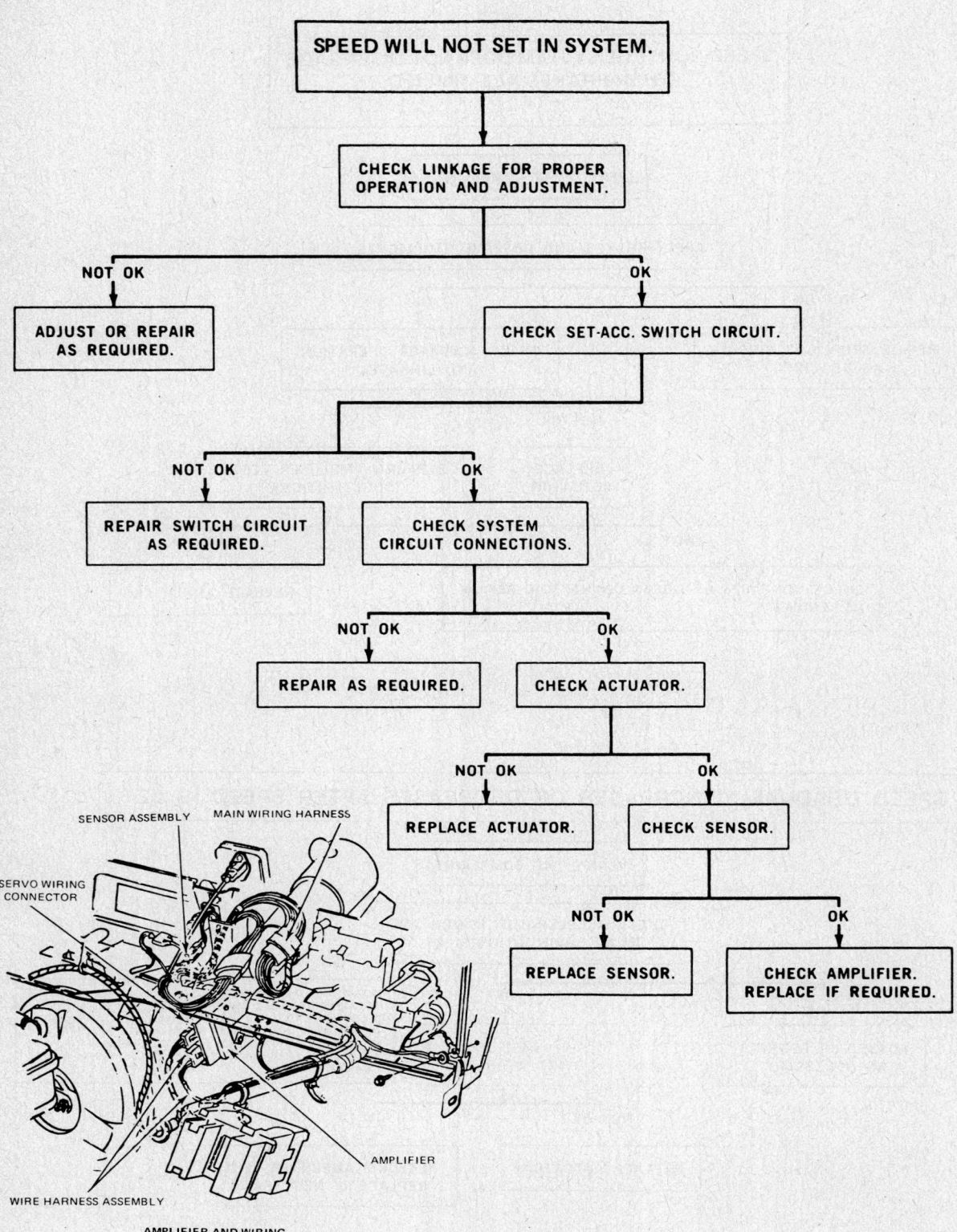

SPEED WILL NOT SET IN SYSTEM.

↓

CHECK LINKAGE FOR PROPER OPERATION AND ADJUSTMENT.

NOT OK → ADJUST OR REPAIR AS REQUIRED.

OK → CHECK SET-ACC. SWITCH CIRCUIT.

NOT OK → REPAIR SWITCH CIRCUIT AS REQUIRED.

OK → CHECK SYSTEM CIRCUIT CONNECTIONS.

NOT OK → REPAIR AS REQUIRED.

OK → CHECK ACTUATOR.

NOT OK → REPLACE ACTUATOR.

OK → CHECK SENSOR.

NOT OK → REPLACE SENSOR.

OK → CHECK AMPLIFIER. REPLACE IF REQUIRED.

SENSOR ASSEMBLY

MAIN WIRING HARNESS

SERVO WIRING CONNECTOR

AMPLIFIER

WIRE HARNESS ASSEMBLY

AMPLIFIER AND WIRING

GM GASOLINE ENGINES

INDEX

GASOLINE ENGINE

TROUBLESHOOTING GASOLINE ENGINE

CONDITION	CORRECTION
Dieseling	Make visual checks of the following for sticking: Carburetor, choke, and throttle linkage Fast idle cam Check and reset ignition timing, idle, RPM and check idle solenoid for proper operation. Refer to emission label. Remove carbon with top engine cleaner. Follow instructions on can.
Detonation	Check for obvious overheating problems: Low coolant Loose fan belt Restricted air flow, etc. Check ignition timing per emission control information label. Note: If timing is too early—speed up engine to see if timing mark moves. If not, check for stuck mechanical advance. Remove carbon with top engine cleaner or equivalent. Follow instructions on can. If condition still exists, suggest that owner try different gasoline.
Stalls or Rough Idle-Cold	With engine running, remove air cleaner cover and filter. Damper door in air cleaner snorkel should be closed when engine is cold. It may be necessary to place cold wet rag over sensor to close it if engine is too warm. If damper door does not close, apply vacuum directly to vacuum motor. If door closes, replace sensor. If door stays open, replace vacuum motor. Visually check the following: Hot air tube to air cleaner connection and condition of hot air stove. Vacuum hoses for splits, kinks and proper connections. Air leaks at carburetor mounting and intake manifold. Ignition wires for cracking, hardness and proper connections. Check the following for sticking:

CONDITION	CORRECTION
Stalls or Rough Idle-Cold	Carburetor, choke, and throttle linkage. Fast idle cam. Carburetor flooding. With engine running, visually check vacuum break linkage for movement while removing and reinstalling vacuum hose. If the linkage does not move and vacuum is at hose, replace vacuum break assembly. With engine off, check all choke adjustments. Check engine timing and idle speed. See emission control information label. Remove vacuum hose from EGR valve and connect an extra hose from any manifold vacuum source to valve. If RPM doesn't drop, valve is leaking. Check EFE valve. Disconnect EFE hose from tube and connect an extra vacuum hose from any manifold vacuum source to EFE tube. Observe actuator linkage for movement. If no movement, repair as necessary.
Stalls or Rough Idle-Hot	With engine running, remove air cleaner cover and filter. Damper door in air cleaner snorkel should be open. If closed and engine is hot, check temperature operation of sensor unit. Visually check the following: Vacuum hoses for splits, kinks and proper connections. Air leaks at carburetor mounting and intake manifold. Ignition wires for cracking, hardness and proper connections. Check engine timing and idle speed. See emission control information label. Check PCV valve for proper operation by placing finger over inlet hole in valve end several times. Valve should snap back. If not, replace valve. Remove vacuum hose from EGR valve and connect an

TROUBLESHOOTING
GASOLINE ENGINE

CONDITION	CORRECTION
Stalls or Rough Idle-Hot	extra hose from any manifold source to valve. If RPM doesn't drop, valve is leaking. Adjust carburetor idle speed and mixture screws. Refer to emission control information label for idle speed. Remove carbon with top engine cleaner or equivalent. Follow instructions on can. If idle is still rough, run a cylinder compression check.
Miss	Visually check the following: Vacuum hoses for splits, kinks and proper connections. Air leaks at carburetor mounting and intake manifold. Ignition wires for cracking, hardness and proper connections. Repair or replace as necessary. Disconnect air cleaner and EGR vacuum hoses and cap both vacuum sources. Remove one spark plug wire at a time with insulated pliers. If there is an RPM drop on all cylinders, go to rough idle (hot) diagnosis. If there is no RPM drop on one or more cylinders, remove spark plug(s) and check for: Cracks Wear Improper gap Burned Electrodes Heavy deposits Check spark plug wires by connecting ohmmeter to ends of each wire in question. If meter reads over 50,000 ohms, replace wire(s). Visually check distributor cap and rotor for moisture, dust, cracks, carbon track, burns, etc. Perform compression check on questionable cylinder(s). Remove rocker covers. Check for bent push rods, worn rocker arms, broken valve springs, worn camshaft lobes.
Hesitates	Visually check the following: Vacuum hoses for splits, kinks and proper connections. Air leaks at carburetor mounting and intake manifold. Check ignition wires for cracking, hardness and proper connections.

CONDITION	CORRECTION
Hesitates	NOTICE: COLD ENGINE ONLY. Check the following for sticking or faulty operation: Carburetor, choke, and throttle linkage. Fast idle cam. Check carburetor accelerator pump operation. With air cleaner removed and engine off, hold choke valve open and look for gas squirt in carburetor bore while moving thottle. If weak or no pump squirt, check and adjust the pump rod adjustment. If no pump squirt, remove carburetor air horn and repair pump system as necessary. Check float level adjustment before replacing air horn and pump rod assembly. Disconnect and plug vacuum advance hose, connect tachometer and timing light. Set ignition timing and idle speed to specs. on emission label. With engine running, remove air cleaner cover and filter. Damper door in air cleaner snorkel should be closed when engine is cold. It may be necessary to place cold wet rag over sensor to close if engine is too warm. If damper door does not close, apply vacuum directly to vacuum motor. If door closes, replace sensor. If door stays open, replace vacuum motor.
Surges	With engine running, remove air cleaner cover and filter. Damper door in air cleaner snorkel should be closed when engine is cold. It may be necessary to place cold wet rag over sensor to close if engine is too warm. If damper door does not close, apply vacuum directly to vacuum motor. If door closes, replace sensor. If door stays open, replace vacuum motor. Visually check the following: Vacuum hoses for splits, kinks and proper connections. Air leaks at carburetor mounting and intake manifold. Ignition wires for cracking,

TROUBLESHOOTING
GASOLINE ENGINE

CONDITION	CORRECTION
Surges	hardness and proper connections. Repair or replace as necessary. Check ignition timing per emission control information label. Vacuum advance hose should be disconnected and plugged. NOTICE: To check mechanical advance, observe timing marks. It should advance as throttle is opened and return to mark as throttle is closed. With engine off, remove vacuum hose from distributor vacuum advance. Connect vacuum pump and apply 15" vacuum. Vacuum should hold steady for 15 seconds. If vacuum drops, replace vacuum advance unit. Check carburetor fuel inlet filter. Replace if dirty or plugged. Test fuel pump by connecting hose from carburetor fuel feed line to a suitable container. Start engine and let idle for 15 seconds. Mechanical pump should supply ½ pint or more. If not, go to step 7. If OK, go to step 9. If electric pump supplies less than ½ pint, check fuel lines to tank for kinks or dirt. If OK, go to step 9. NOTICE: Check electric supply to pump. To check mechanical fuel pump, disconnect inlet hose at pump and connect a vacuum gauge. Crank or run engine until maximum vacuum is reached. If less than 12 inches, replace pump. If vacuum reading is 12 inches or more, go to step 8. Check fuel lines and hoses for splits, leaks or kinks by disconnecting each section of line and connect vacuum gauge. Crank or run engine until vacuum gauge peaks. Vacuum should be at least 12 inches. If fuel lines and pump check O.K., remove tank unit, replace strainer and clean fuel tank, if necessary. Remove spark plugs. Check for cracks, wear, improper gap, burned electrodes, heavy deposits. Repair or replace as necessary.

CONDITION	CORRECTION
Surges	Remove carburetor, clean and adjust.
Sluggish or Spongy	Remove air cleaner cover and check air filter for dirt or being plugged. Replace as necessary. With engine running, damper door in air cleaner snorkel should be closed when engine is cold. It may be necessary to place cold wet rag over sensor to close if engine is too warm. If damper door does not close, apply vacuum directly to vacuum motor. If door closes, replace sensor. If door stays open, replace vacuum motor. Check ignition timing per emission label. Disconnect and plug vacuum advance hose. NOTICE: To check mechanical advance, observe timing marks. It should advance as throttle is opened and return to mark as throttle is closed. Remove air cleaner and check for full throttle valve opening in carburetor by depressing accelerator pedal to floor; also check for full choke valve opening and free operating air valve (if equipped). Remove vacuum hose from EGR valve and connect an extra hose from any manifold vacuum source to valve. If RPM doesn't drop, valve is leaking. With engine off, remove vacuum hose from distributor vacuum advance. Connect vacuum pump and apply 15" vacuum. Vacuum should hold steady for 15 seconds. If vacuum drops, replace vacuum advance unit. Remove spark plugs. Check for cracks, wear, improper gap, burned electrodes, heavy deposits. Repair or replace as necessary. Remove carburetor air horn and check the following: Power piston for freeness Dirt in carburetor Float adjustment Metering rods Power valve(s)

TROUBLESHOOTING
GASOLINE ENGINE

CONDITION	CORRECTION	CONDITION	CORRECTION
Poor Gasoline Mileage	With engine running, remove air cleaner cover and filter. Check filter for dirt or being plugged. Damper door in air cleaner snorkel should be closed when engine is cold. It may be necessary to place cold wet rag over sensor to close it if engine is too warm. If damper door does not close, apply vacuum directly to vacuum motor. If door closes, replace sensor. If door stays open, replace vacuum motor. Visually check the following: Vacuum hoses for splits, kinks and proper connections. Air leaks at carburetor mounting and intake manifold. Ignition wires for cracking, hardness and proper connections. Check ignition timing per emission control information label. Disconnect and plug vacuum advance hose. NOTICE: To check mechanical advance, observe timing mark. It should advance as throttle is opened and return to mark as throttle is closed. Check carburetor choke linkage and settings. With engine off, remove vacuum hose from distributor vacuum advance. Connect vacuum pump and apply 15" vacuum. Vacuum should hold steady for 15 seconds. If vacuum drops, replace vacuum advance unit. Remove spark plugs, check for cracks, wear, improper gap, burned electrodes, heavy deposits. If in previous checks, adjustments have not been made that could improve mileage, remove carburetor air horn and check the following: Power piston for freeness Dirt in jets and metering passages Metering rods Power valve(s) Float adjustment Check P.E.V.R. hoses and operation of valve.	Cuts Out	Check ignition wires, boots, cap and coil for: Damage Deterioration Loose connections Carbon tracking Clean, tighten and/or replace defective parts as necessary. Connect secondary voltage output meter or scope to engine. Using insulated pliers, check output as each spark plug wire is removed, output voltage should read: 25 KV or above No arcing should occur If any reading is below specification or arcing occurs, with engine off, remove distributor cap and visually inspect for moisture, dust, cracks, burns, etc. Check distributor for: Worn shaft Bare or shorted wires Faulty pick up coil, module, ignition coil, and condenser. Remove spark plugs. Check for cracks, wear, improper gap, burned electrodes, heavy deposits. Check carburetor fuel inlet filter. Replace if dirty or plugged. Test fuel pump by connecting hose from carburetor fuel feed line to a suitable container. Start engine and let idle for 15 seconds. Mechanical pump should supply ½ pint or more. If not, go to step 7. If electric pump supplies less than ½ pint, check fuel lines to tank for kinks or dirt. If OK, go to step 8. NOTICE: Check electric supply to pump. To check mechanical fuel pump, disconnect inlet hose at pump and connect a vacuum gauge. Crank or run engine until maximum vacuum is reached. If less than 12 inches, replace pump. If vacuum reading is 12 inches or more, go to step 8. Check fuel lines and hoses for splits, leaks or kinks by disconnecting each section of line and connecting a vacuum gauge. Crank or run engine until vacuum gauge peaks.

TROUBLESHOOTING
GASOLINE ENGINE

CONDITION	CORRECTION	CONDITION	CORRECTION
Cuts Out	Vacuum should be at least 12 inches. If fuel pump and fuel lines check O.K., remove tank unit, replace strainer and clean fuel tank, if necessary.	Hard Starting-Cold (Engine Cranks O.K.)	and connect a vacuum gauge. Crank or run engine until maximum vacuum is reached. If less than 12 inches, replace pump. If more than 12 inches, go to step 8. Check fuel lines and hoses for splits, leaks or kinks by disconnecting each section of line and connect vacuum gauge. Crank or run engine until vacuum gauge peaks. Vacuum should be at least 12 inches. If fuel lines and pump check O.K., remove tank unit, replace strainer and clean fuel tank, if necessary.
Hard Starting-Cold (Engine Cranks O.K.)	Visually check the following: Vacuum hoses for splits, kinks and proper connections. Air leaks at carburetor mounting and intake manifold. Ignition wires for cracking, hardness, proper connections, and carbon tracking. Check ignition timing per emission control information label. NOTICE: If timing is too early—speed up engine to see if timing mark moves. If not, check for stuck mechanical advance. Check the following: Choke, throttle linkage and fast idle cam for sticking. Carburetor flooding. Connect secondary voltage output meter or scope to engine. Using insulated pliers, check output with spark plug wire removed. Output voltage should read 25 KV or above. If any reading is below specifications or arcing occurs, stop engine, remove distributor cap and visually inspect for moisture, dust, cracks, burns, etc. Check distributor for: Worn shaft Bare and shorted wires Faulty pick up coil, module, ignition coil and shorted condenser. Remove spark plugs. Check for cracks, wear, improper gap, burned electrodes, heavy deposits. Test fuel pump by connecting hose from carburetor fuel feed lines to a suitable container. Start engine and let idle for 15 seconds. Pump should supply ½ pint or more. If more than ½ pint, check filter in carburetor. Replace if necessary. If less than ½ pint, for mechanical pump go to step 7. Go to step 9 for electric pump. NOTICE: Check current to electric pump. Disconnect inlet hose at pump	Hard Starting-Hot (Engine Cranks O.K.)	Visually check the following: Vacuum hoses for splits, kinks and proper connections. Air leaks at carburetor mounting and intake manifold. Ignition wires for cracking, hardness, proper connections, and carbon tracking. Check ignition timing per emission control information label. NOTICE: If timing is too early—speed up engine to see if timing mark moves. If not, check for stuck mechanical advance. Check the following: Choke, throttle linkage and fast idle cam for sticking. Carburetor flooding. Connect secondary voltage output meter or scope to engine. Using insulated pliers, check output with spark plug wire removed. Output voltage should read 25 KV or above. If any reading is below specifications or arcing occurs, turn off engine, remove distributor cap and visually inspect for dust, cracks, burns, etc. Check distributor for: Worn shaft Bare and shorted wires Faulty pick up coil, module, ignition coil, and shorted condenser. Remove spark plugs. Check for cracks, wear, improper gap, burned electrodes, heavy deposits. Test fuel pump by connecting hose from carburetor fuel feed line to a suitable container.

TROUBLESHOOTING
GASOLINE ENGINE

CONDITION	CORRECTION	CONDITION	CORRECTION
Hard Starting-Hot (Engine Cranks O.K.)	Start engine and let idle for 15 seconds. Pump should supply ½ pint or more. If more than ½ pint, check filter in carburetor. Replace if necessary. If less than ½ pint, for mechanical pump go to step 7. Go to step 9 for electric pump. NOTICE: Check current to electric pump. Disconnect inlet hose at pump and connect a vacuum gauge. Crank or run engine until maximum vacuum is reached. If	Hard Starting-Hot (Engine Cranks O.K.)	less than 12 inches, replace pump. If more than 12 inches, go to step 8. Check fuel lines and hoses for splits, leaks or kinks by disconnecting each section of line and connect vacuum gauge. Crank or run engine until vacuum gauge peaks. Vacuum should be at least 12 inches. If fuel lines and pump check O.K., remove tank unit. replace strainer and clean fuel tank, if necessary.

Chevrolet-built 173 CID engine

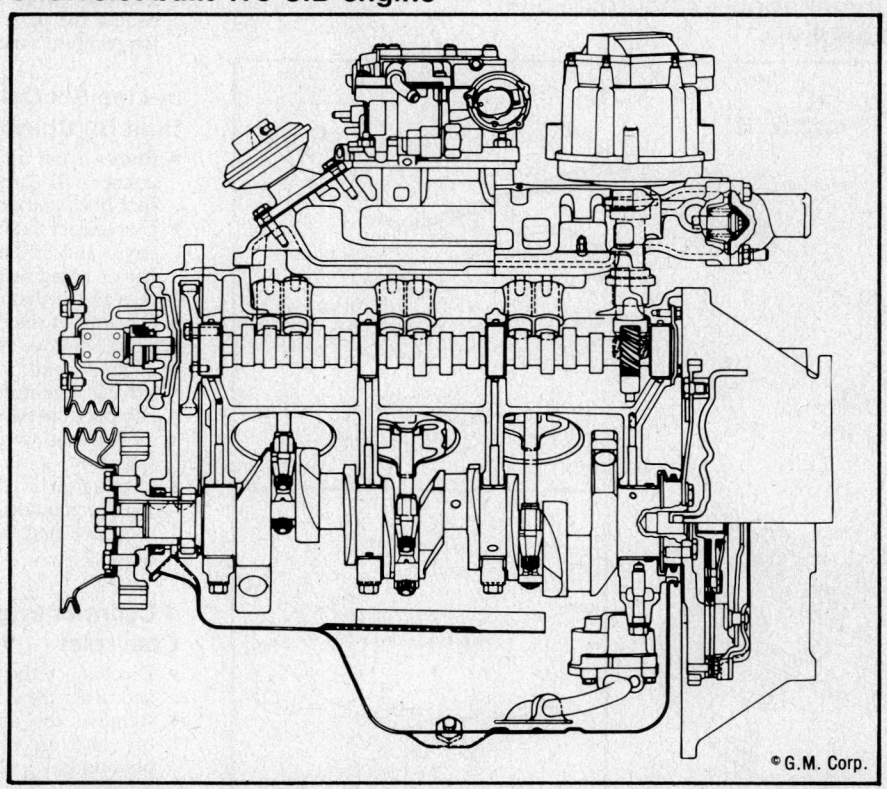

© G.M. Corp.

This completely new 60°V6 engine is tranverse-mounted in GM X Body cars

Intake manifold installation— 173 CID V6 engine

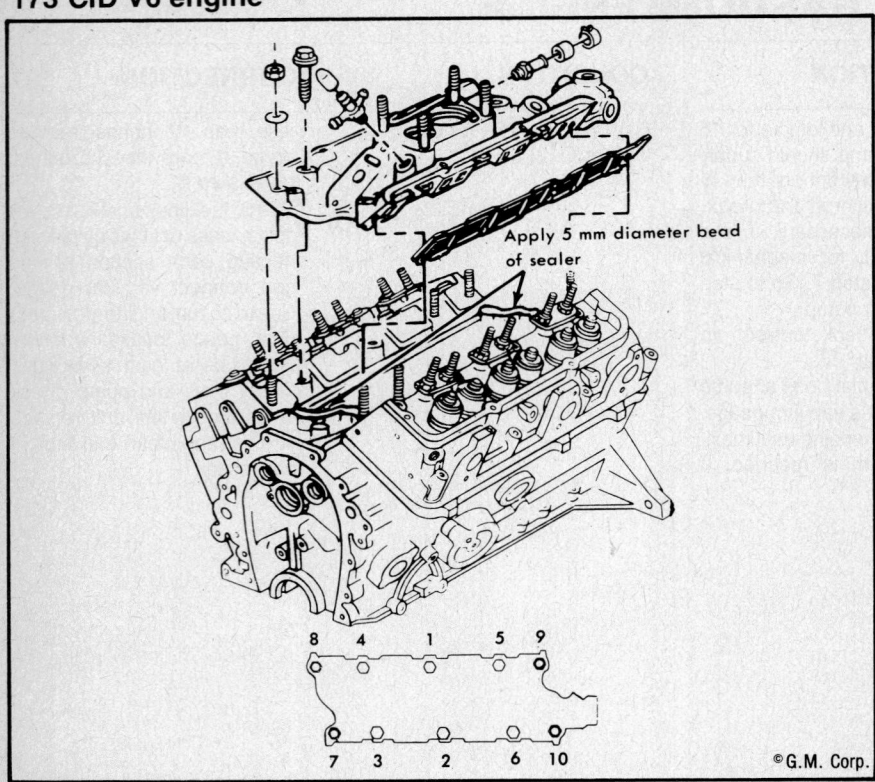

Apply 5 mm diameter bead of sealer

8 4 1 5 9

7 3 2 6 10

© G.M. Corp.

Intake manifold installation—Chevrolet-built 200 and 229 CID engines

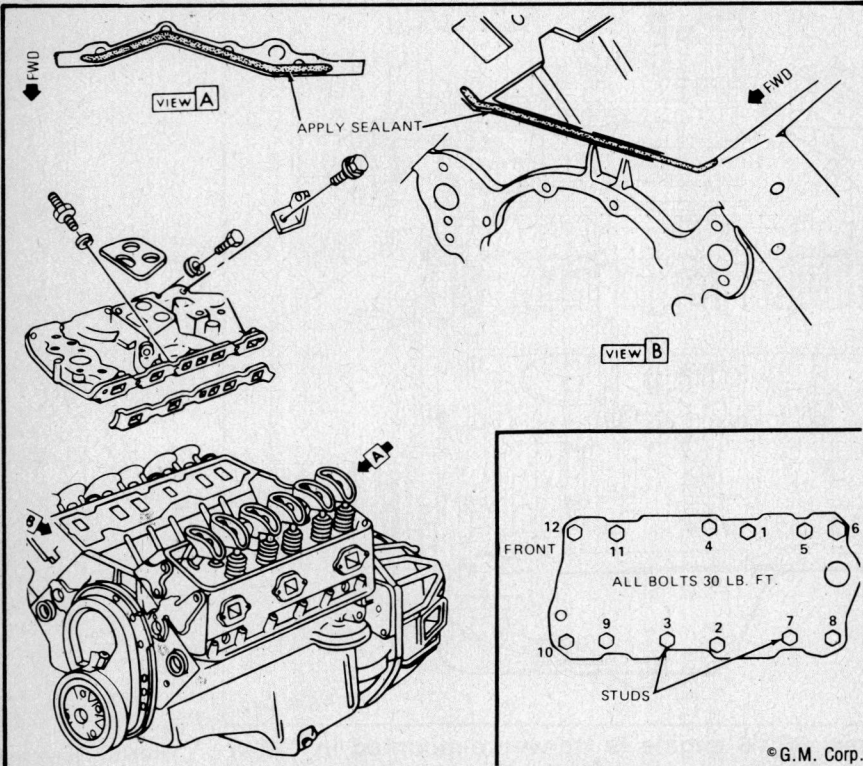

FWD

VIEW A

APPLY SEALANT

FWD

VIEW B

A

FRONT

12 11 4 1 5 6

ALL BOLTS 30 LB. FT.

9 3 2 7 8

10

STUDS

© G.M. Corp.

Intake Manifold

GM V8 and V6 Engines

NOTE: The carburetor and manifold are removed as a unit.

- Disconnect the negative battery cable, and remove the air filter housing.
- Drain the cooling system on all engines except 368, 425 and 500 Cadillacs.
- Disconnect or remove any of the following which apply to the vehicle being serviced:
  a. Distributor
  b. Ignition coil
  c. Attached radiator and heater hoses
  d. Carburetor and cruise control linkages
  e. Fuel and vacuum lines
  f. PCV system
  g. Oil filter tube
  h. Electrical connections such as coil wires, temperature sender, downshift switch, antidieseling solenoid and air conditioning compressor clutch
  i. Turbocharger plumbing and hardware
- Position power steering pump, alternator and air conditioning compressor out of the way if necessary.
- Remove attaching bolts and lift manifold.
- Installation is the reverse of removal. Tighten manifold bolts in prescribed sequence and torque to correct specifications.
- The new gasket may have to be cut to fit behind the push rods. Seal with a room temperature vulcanizing sealant.

In-Line Six Cylinder Engines Built By Chevrolet

- Remove the air filter housing and disconnect all carburetor control linkages, fuel lines and vacuum lines.
- Disconnect the P.C.V. hose at the rocker cover and any emission control plumbing or accessories necessary to gain access to the manifold.
- Disconnect the exhaust pipe at the manifold, remove the attaching bolts and clamps, and remove the intake and exhaust manifolds as an assembly.
- Separate the two manifolds by removing the bolt and two nuts at the center of the assembly.
- Installation is the reverse of removal. Tighten mounting bolts in the prescribed sequence and torque to correct specifications.

4 Cylinder Engines Built By Chevrolet

- Disconnect the negative battery cable, and drain the cooling system.
- Remove the air filter housing assembly and all related emission control plumbing.

Intake manifold and components—Oldsmobile-built engines

CHOKE HOT AIR PIPE

CHOKE CLEAN AIR PIPE

20 LB. FT. (27 N•m)

WATER TEMP SWITCH

17 LB. FT. (23 N•m)

40 LB. FT. (54 N•m)

WATER OUTLET

GASKET

ENGINE LIFTING STRAP

BY-PASS HOSE

25 LB. FT. (34 N•m)

THERMAL VACUUM SWITCH

CHOKE HEATER

E.G.R. VALVE

E.G.R. VALVE

THERMOSTAT

GASKET

35 LB. FT. (48 N•m)

GASKET

E.G.R. VALVE ADAPTER (CALIF.)

REAR SEAL

E.G.R. PORTS (UNDER CARB. PRIMARY BORES)

FRONT SEAL

E.G.R. PASSAGE

INTAKE MANIFOLD GASKET

INTAKE MANIFOLD CROSS SECTION

© G.M. Corp.

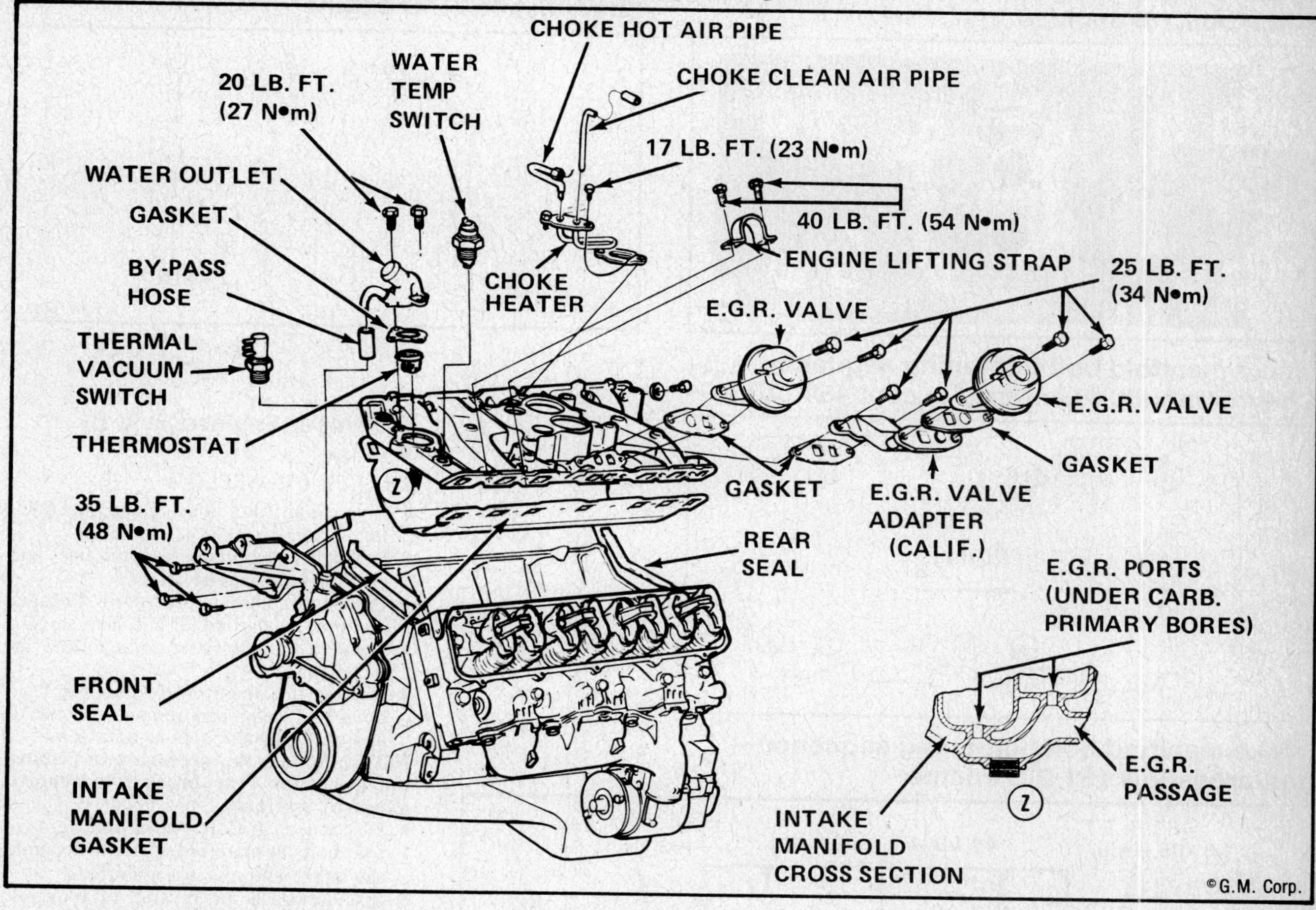

- Disconnect all carburetor control linkages, fuel lines and vacuum lines.
- Disconnect heater hose from manifold.
- Move the alternator aside to gain access to manifold bolt, and remove the power steering pump brace.
- Remove manifold mounting bolts and remove manifold.
- Installation is the reverse of removal. Tighten mounting bolts in the prescribed sequence and torque to correct specification.

Intake manifold bolt tightening sequence— Oldsmobile-built engines

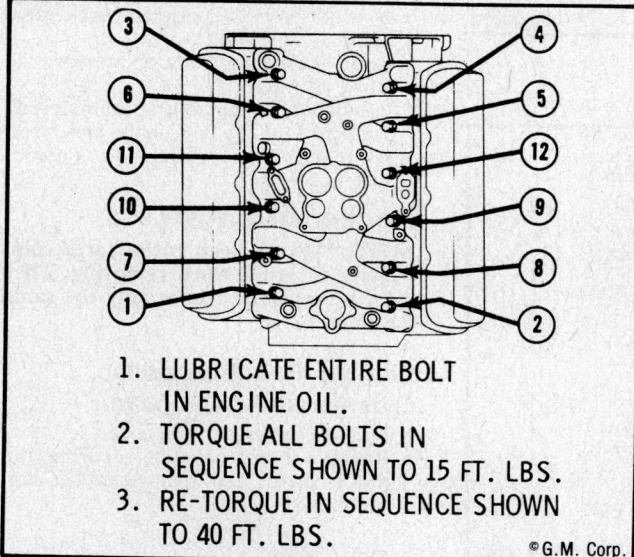

1. LUBRICATE ENTIRE BOLT IN ENGINE OIL.
2. TORQUE ALL BOLTS IN SEQUENCE SHOWN TO 15 FT. LBS.
3. RE-TORQUE IN SEQUENCE SHOWN TO 40 FT. LBS.

© G.M. Corp.

Intake manifold bolt tightening sequence— Buick-built V6 engines

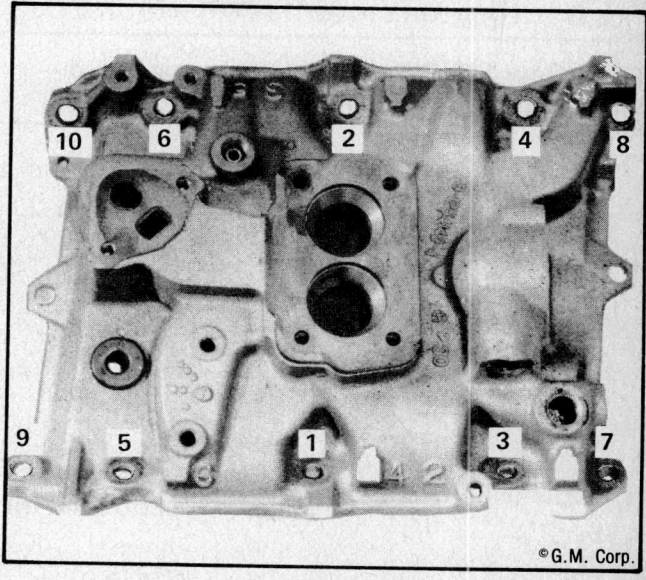

© G.M. Corp.

B353

GM GASOLINE ENGINES

Intake manifold bolt tightening sequence—
Buick-built V8 engines

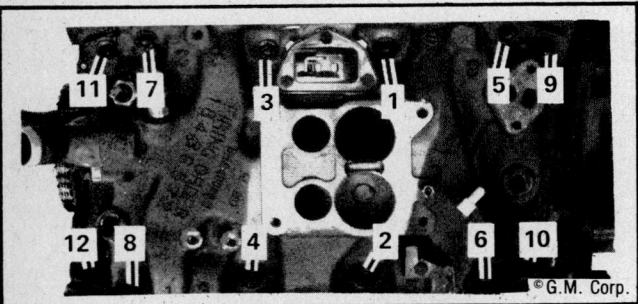

©G.M. Corp.

Intake manifold bolt tightening sequence—
Chevrolet 454 CID engine

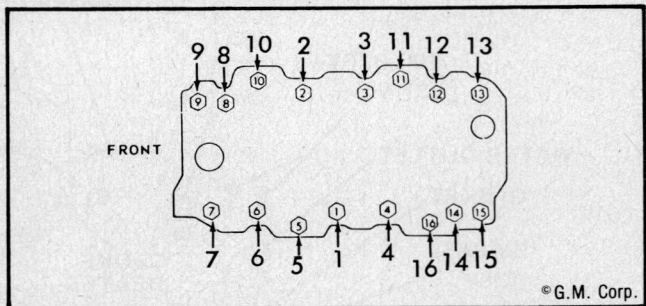

©G.M. Corp.

Intake manifold bolt tightening sequence—
Chevrolet-built V8 engines except 454 CID

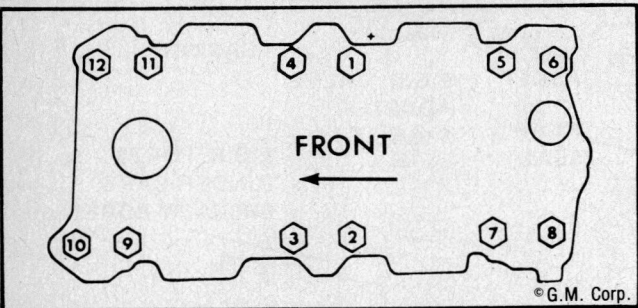

©G.M. Corp.

Intake manifold bolt tightening sequence—
non-crossflow 151 CID engine

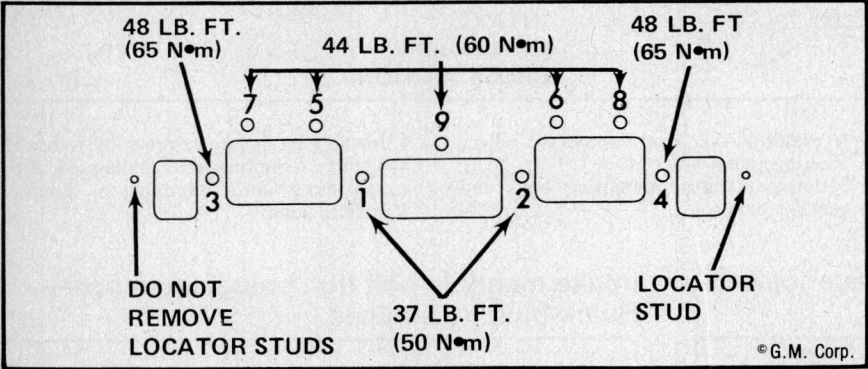

©G.M. Corp.

Crossflow 151 CID engine intake manifold
bolt tightening sequence

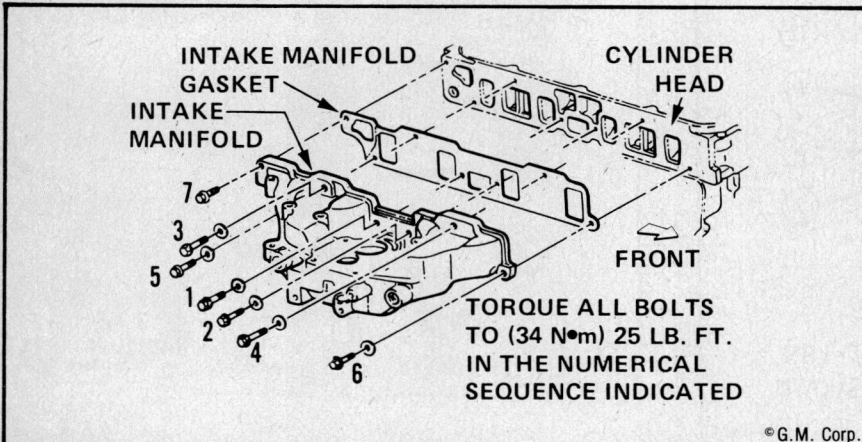

©G.M. Corp.

4 Cylinder Engines Built By Pontiac

EXCEPT CROSSFLOW
- Remove air filter housing and inlet ducting.
- Disconnect fuel lines, vacuum lines and electrical connectors.
- Disconnect carburetor control linkages and remove carburetor and heat shield.
- Remove exhaust pipe to manifold attachments.
- Remove the manifold to cylinder head bolts and nuts, and remove the intake and exhaust manifolds as an assembly.

NOTE: It may be necessary to remove the generator rear bracket to remove manifold assembly.

- Disconnect E.G.R. pipe and remove four bolts at manifold center to separate the intake and exhaust manifolds.
- Installation is the reverse of removal. Install a *new* gasket between intake and exhaust manifolds (perforated side toward intake manifold). Tighten in prescribed sequence and torque to correct specification.

CROSSFLOW
- Drain cooling system, and remove the carburetor.
- Disconnect manifold attachments such as heater hose and pulse air check valve bracket.
- Remove attaching bolts, and remove the intake manifold.
- Installation is the reverse of removal. Tighten mounting bolts in the prescribed sequence and torque to correct specification.

Rocker Arm R&R

NOTE: Always keep rocker arm components in order when removing. They must be reinstalled in exactly the same positions.

Engines Built By Cadillac, Oldsmobile And Pontiac
- Remove the rocker arm cover.
- Remove bolts or nuts securing the rocker arms, and remove rocker arm assemblies.

- Installation is the reverse of removal. Torque retaining nuts or bolts to the following specifications:
  Cadillac built engines . . . . . . 60 ft./lbs.
  Oldsmobile built engines . . . 25 ft./lbs.
  Pontiac built engines . . . . . . 20 ft./lbs.

Rocker arms in Cadillac-built engines

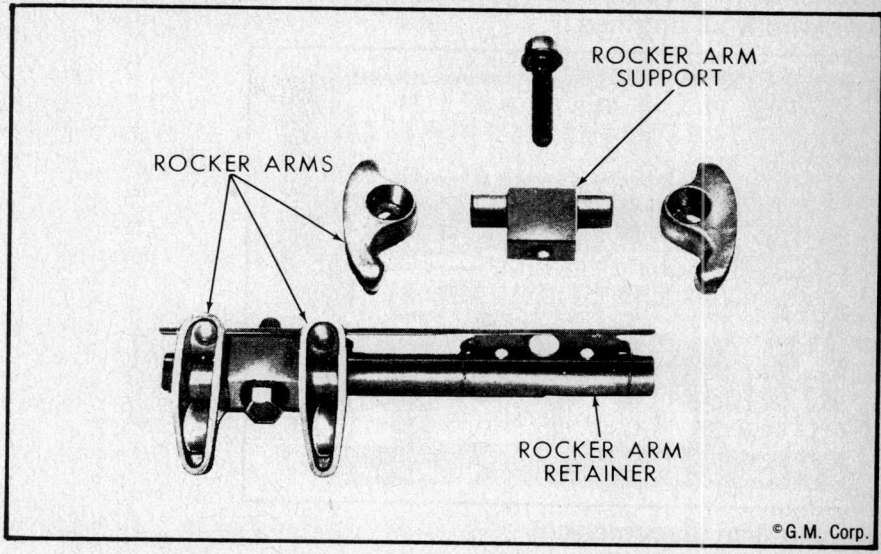

ROCKER ARM SUPPORT

ROCKER ARMS

ROCKER ARM RETAINER

© G.M. Corp.

Rocker arms and cylinder head—Oldsmobile-built engines

ROCKER ARM PIVOT

ROCKER ARM

28 FT. LBS.

PUSH ROD

VALVE LIFTER

130 FT. LBS.

CYLINDER HEAD

CYLINDER HEAD GASKET (PUT CONTRASTING COLOR STRIPE FACING UP)

© G.M. Corp.

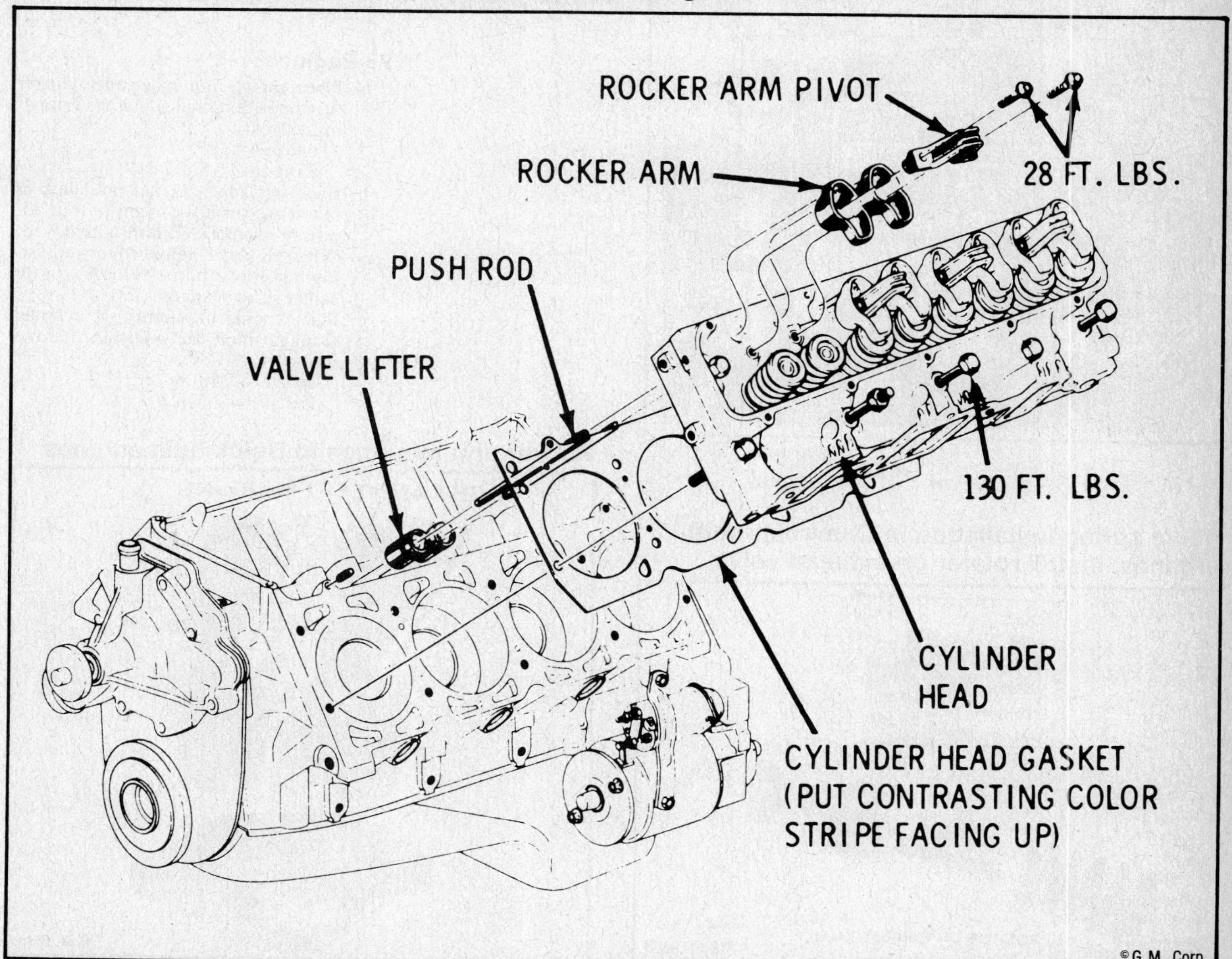

GM GASOLINE ENGINES

Rocker arm placement in Buick-built V8 engines

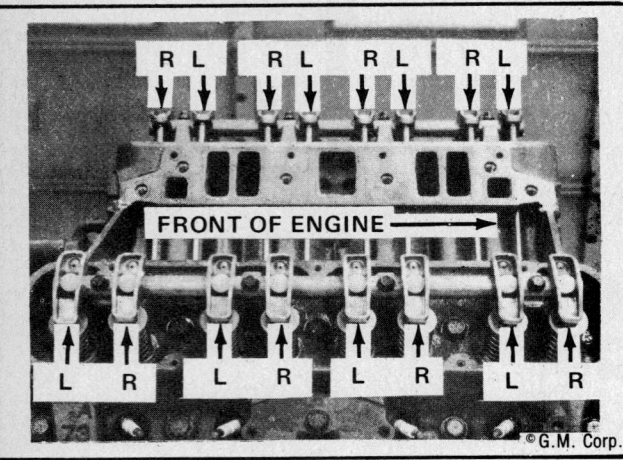

FRONT OF ENGINE →

© G.M. Corp.

Rocker arm placement in Buick-built V6 engines

← FRONT OF ENGINE

© G.M. Corp.

Valve spring installation in Chevrolet-built V8 engines. Install rotator on exhaust valve

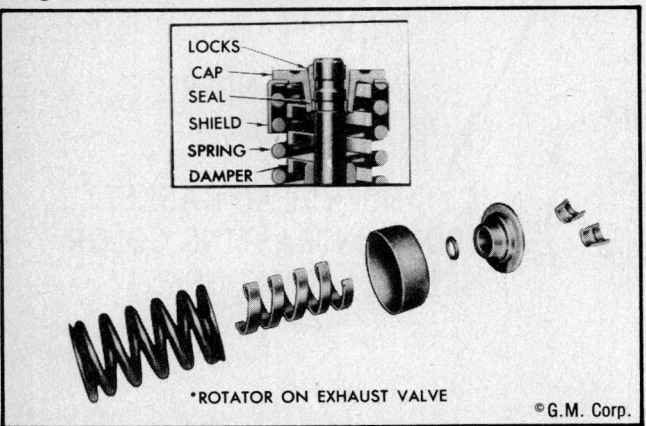

LOCKS
CAP
SEAL
SHIELD
SPRING
DAMPER

*ROTATOR ON EXHAUST VALVE

© G.M. Corp.

Engines Built By Buick

- Remove rocker arm cover.
- Remove rocker arm and shaft assembly to cylinder head bolts, and remove the shaft assembly.
- Pry out nylon rocker arm retainers to free rocker arms.
- Rocker arms must be installed on the shaft in the correct sequence when assembling. All rocker arms are stamped (R) right (L) left.
- Center each arm on the ¼" hole in the shaft and install new nylon rocker arm retainers.
- Install the rocker arm assembly and torque shaft assembly–to–cylinder head bolts to correct specifications.

Engines Built By Chevrolet

- Remove rocker arm cover.
- Remove rocker arm nuts, balls and rocker arms.
- Installation is the reverse of removal. Tighten each rocker arm nut until all lash is eliminated, and adjust when lifter is on base circle of camshaft lobe as follows:

V8 Engines

a. Place engine in number one cylinder firing position, and adjust the following valves:

    Intake—1,2,5,7

    Exhaust—1,3,4,8

b. Back out adjusting nut until lash is felt at the push rod, then turn in adjusting nut until all lash is removed. When all play is removed turn adjusting nut in one full additional turn (to center lifter plunger).

c. Place engine in number six cylinder firing position, and adjust the following valves:

    Intake—3,4,6,8

    Exhaust—2,5,6,8

Rocker arm markings in Buick-built engines

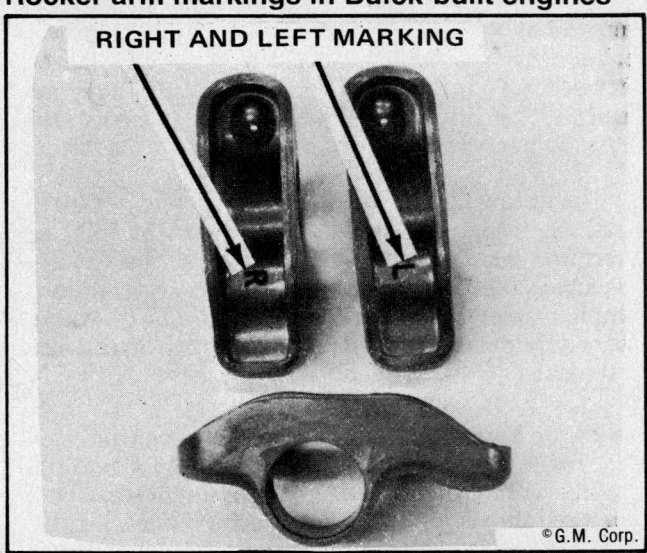

RIGHT AND LEFT MARKING

© G.M. Corp.

In-Line Six Cylinder Engines

   a. Place engine in number one cylinder firing position, and adjust the following valves:
      Intake—1,2,4
      Exhaust—1,3,5

   b. Back out adjusting nut until lash is felt at the push rod, then turn in adjusting nut until all lash is removed. When all play is removed turn adjusting nut in one full additional turn (to center lifter plunger).

   c. Place engine in number six cylinder firing position, and adjust the following valves:
      Intake—3,5,6
      Exhaust—2,4,6

V6 Engines

   a. Place engine in number one cylinder firing position, and adjust the following valves:

      Intake—1,2,3
      Exhaust—1,5,6

   b. Back out adjusting nut until lash is felt at the push rod, then turn in adjusting nut until all lash is removed. When all play is removed turn adjusting nut in one full additional turn (to center lifter plunger).

   c. Place engine in number six cylinder firing position, and adjust the following valves:
      Intake—4,5,6
      Exhaust—2,3,4

Four Cylinder 85 & 97.6 CID Engines Built By Chevrolet

- Remove camshaft cover.
- Depress valve spring with tool J-25477, and remove the rocker arm, guide and lash adjuster.
- Installation is the reverse of removal.

Valve Adjustment

Engines Built By Buick, Cadillac, Oldsmobile and Pontiac

Hydraulic valve lifters are used in all engines, and no adjustment is possible. Correct rocker arm retainer torque is essential to maintaining proper operating clearances.

V8 Engines Built By Chevrolet

- Remove rocker arm covers, and place engine in number one cylinder firing position. Perform adjustment procedure on the following valves:
    Intake—1,2,5,7
    Exhaust—1,3,4,8
- Adjustment procedure:
   a. Back out adjusting nut until lash is felt at the push rod, then turn in until all lash is removed. With play removed turn the adjusting nut in one full turn (to center lifter plunger).
- Place engine in number six firing position. Perform the adjustment procedure on the following valves:
    Intake—3,4,6,8
    Exhaust—2,5,6,7
- Install rocker arm covers.

Valve arrangement in 151 CID engine and all V8 engines built by Buick, Pontiac and Chevrolet except 454 CID

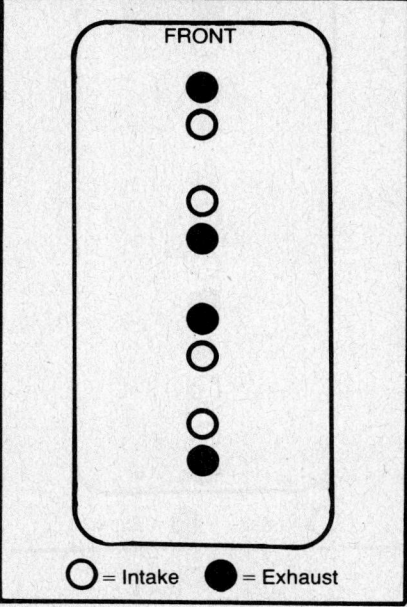

FRONT

○ = Intake   ● = Exhaust

Valve arrangement in Chevrolet-built four cylinder engines

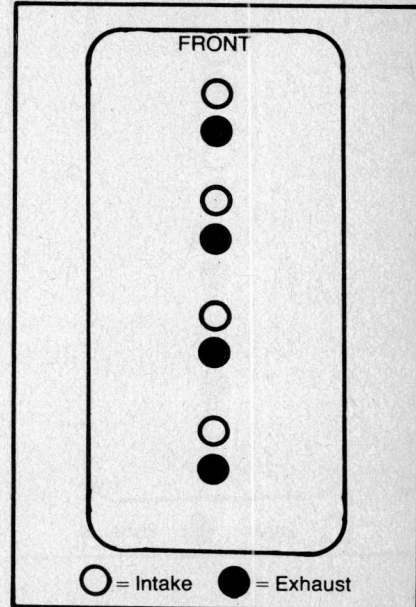

FRONT

○ = Intake   ● = Exhaust

Valve arrangement in Cadillac-built engines

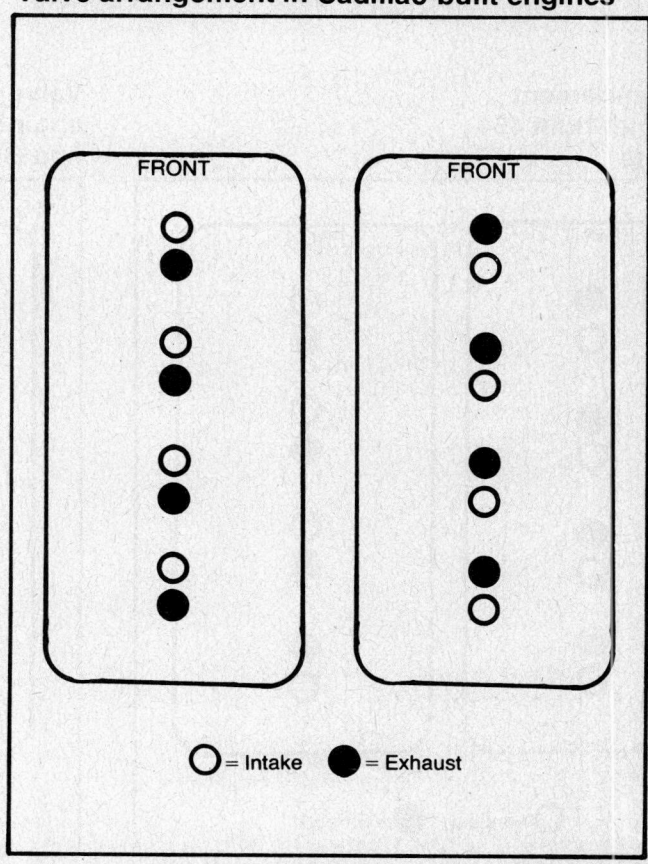

FRONT   FRONT

○ = Intake   ● = Exhaust

GM GASOLINE ENGINES

Valve arrangement in Oldsmobile-built engines

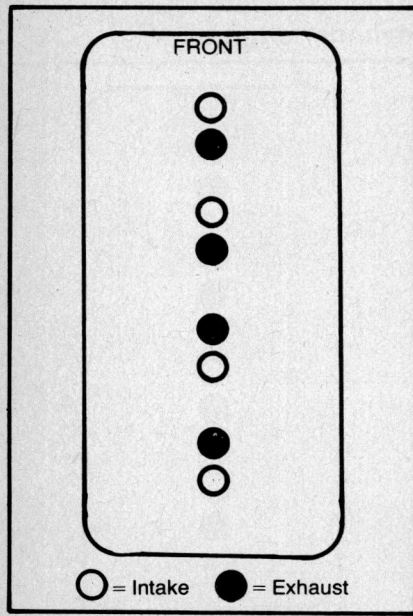

O = Intake ● = Exhaust

Valve arrangement in 250 CID, six cylinder engine

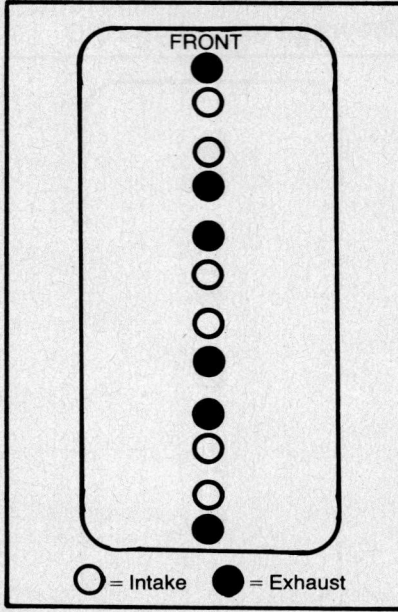

O = Intake ● = Exhaust

In-Line Six Cylinder Engines Built By Chevrolet

- Remove rocker arm cover, and place engine in the number one cylinder firing position. Perform adjustment procedures on the following valves:
  - Intake—1,2,4
  - Exhaust—1,3,5
- Adjustment procedure:
  a. Back out adjusting nut until lash is felt at the push rod, then turn in until all lash is removed. With play removed turn the adjusting nut in one full turn (to center lifter plunger).
- Place engine in number six firing position. Perform the adjustment procedure on the following valves:
  - Intake—3,5,6
  - Exhaust—2,4,6
- Install rocker arm cover.

V6 Engines Built By Chevrolet

a. Place engine in number one cylinder firing position, and adjust the following valves:
  - Intake—1,2,3
  - Exhaust—1,5,6
b. Back out adjusting nut until lash is felt at the push rod, then turn in adjusting nut until all lash is removed. When all play is removed turn adjusting nut in one full additional turn (to center lifter plunger).
c. Place engine in number six cylinder firing position, and adjust the following valves:
  - Intake—4,5,6
  - Exhaust—2,3,4

Valve arrangement in Chevrolet-built 454 CID engine

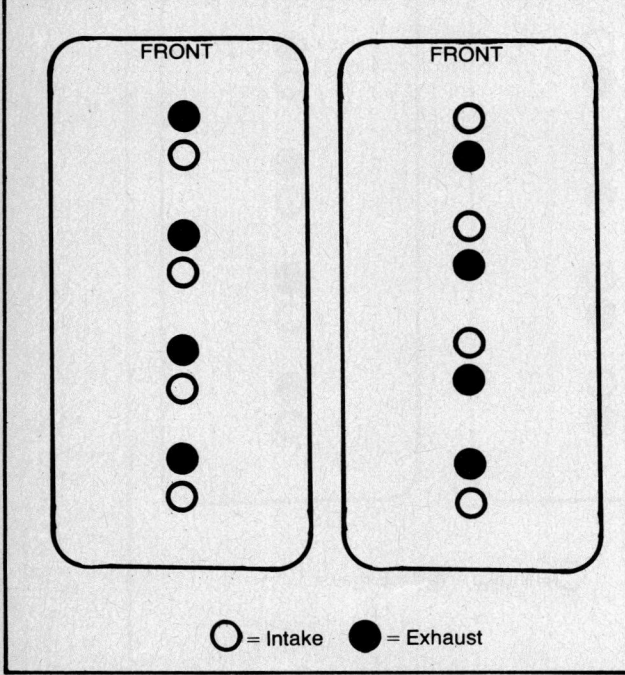

O = Intake ● = Exhaust

Valve arrangement in V6 engines built by Chevrolet and Buick

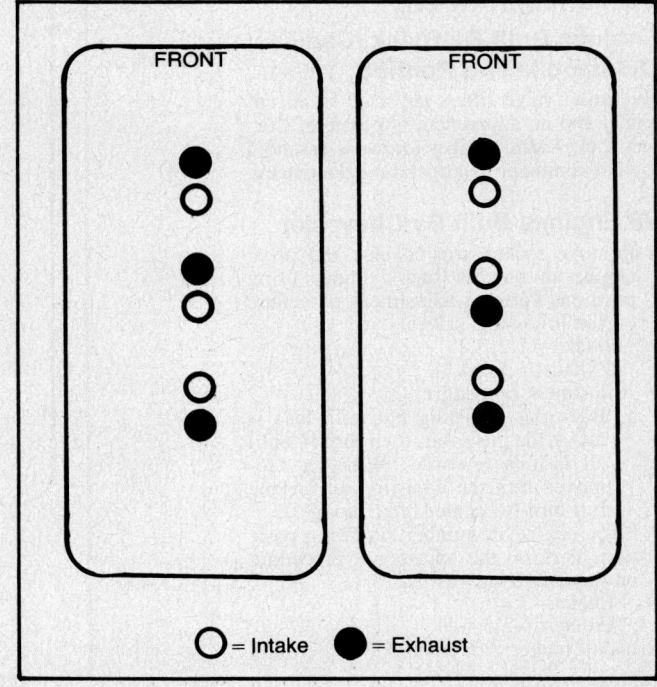

O = Intake ● = Exhaust

Four Cylinder 140 and 122 CID Engines Built By Chevrolet

NOTE: No adjustment is necessary on the 140 CID engine when used in 1976 and later model cars.

VALVE CLEARANCE SPECIFICATIONS

	140 CID	122 CID
Intake	.016 in. cold	.015 in. cold
Exhaust	.031 in. cold	.015 in. cold

- Remove camshaft cover.
- Place engine in number one cylinder firing position. Adjust the following valves:
    Intake—1,2
    Exhaust—1,3

NOTE: The valve adjusting screw is threaded in all areas exept the valve stem contact surface. It is mandatory that the adjusting screw be turned a complete revolution to maintain correct stem-to-screw relationship. The adjusting screw is turned clockwise to decrease lash, and each revolution will change lash by .003 inch.

- Place engine in number four cylinder firing position. Adjust the following valves:
    Intake—3,4
    Exhaust—2,4
- Install camshaft cover.
- Adjust engine idle speed if required.

Valve adjustment in 140 CID engine

© G.M. Corp.

Valve tappet and adjusting screw in 140 CID engine

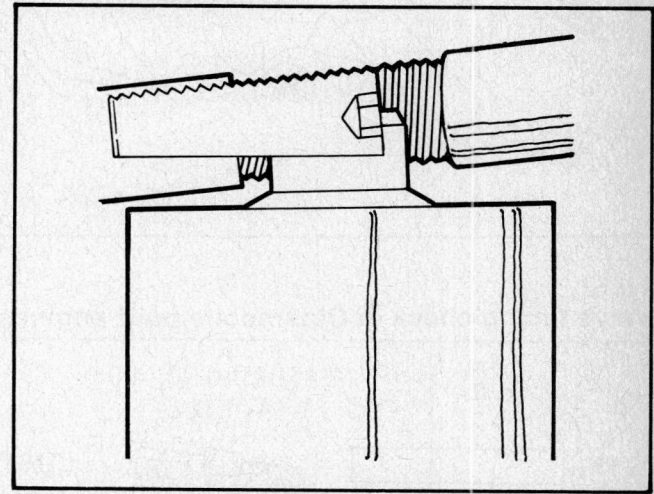

Valve and tappet arrangement in 140 CID engine

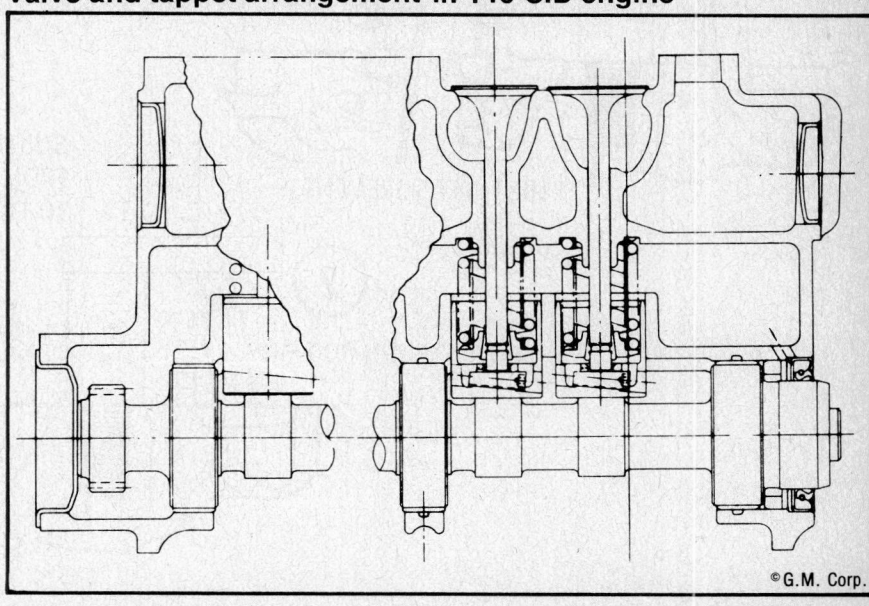

© G.M. Corp.

Removing valve lifter from V8 engine

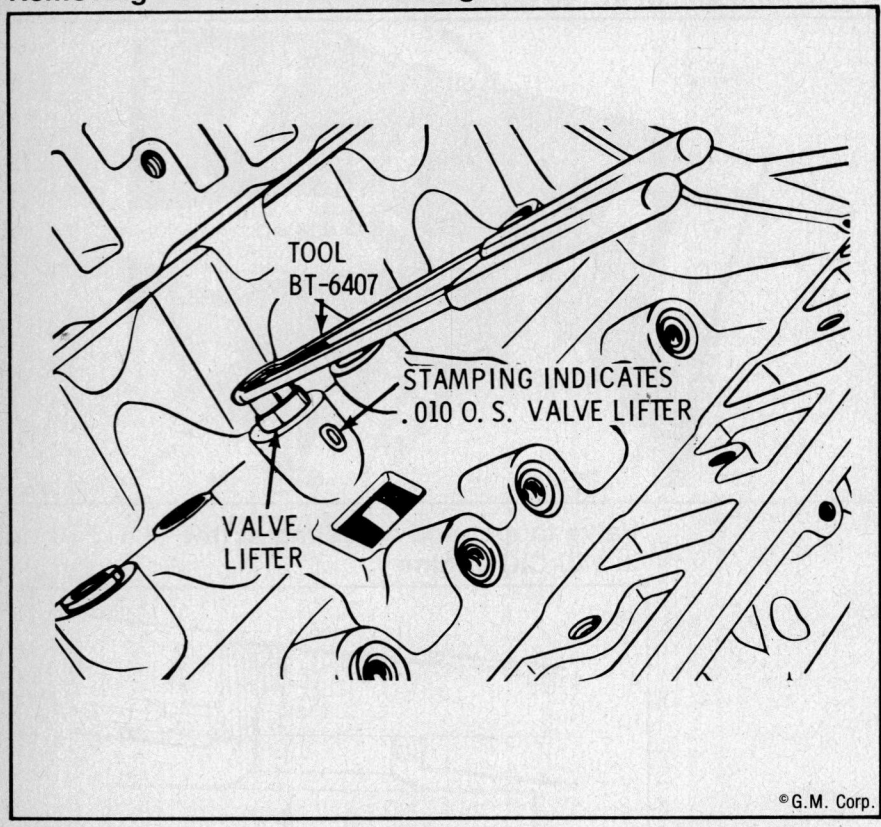

TOOL
BT-6407

STAMPING INDICATES
.010 O.S. VALVE LIFTER

VALVE
LIFTER

© G.M. Corp.

Hydraulic Valve Lifter R&R

NOTE: Replacement lifters are available in standard and .010 inch oversize. On oversize applications both lifter and bore are stamped with an "O."

G.M. V8 and V6 Engines

- Remove rocker arm covers, rocker arms and push rods.
- Remove intake manifold.
- Carefully lift hydraulic lifters out of bores.
- Installation is the reverse of removal. Tighten each rocker arm retainer with its lifter on the base circle of the cam.

NOTE: See "Rocker Arm R&R" for correct installation of rocker arm in Chevrolet built engines.

In-Line Six Cylinder Engines Built By Chevrolet and Four Cylinder Engines Built By Pontiac

- Remove rocker arm cover.
- Loosen rocker arms, and remove push rods.
- Remove distributor on six cylinder engines.
- Remove push rod covers.
- Carefully lift valve lifters out of their bores.
- Installation is the reverse of removal. See "Rocker Arm R&R" for correct installation of rocker arms.
- Adjust engine idle speed if required.

Valve timing check in Oldsmobile-built engines

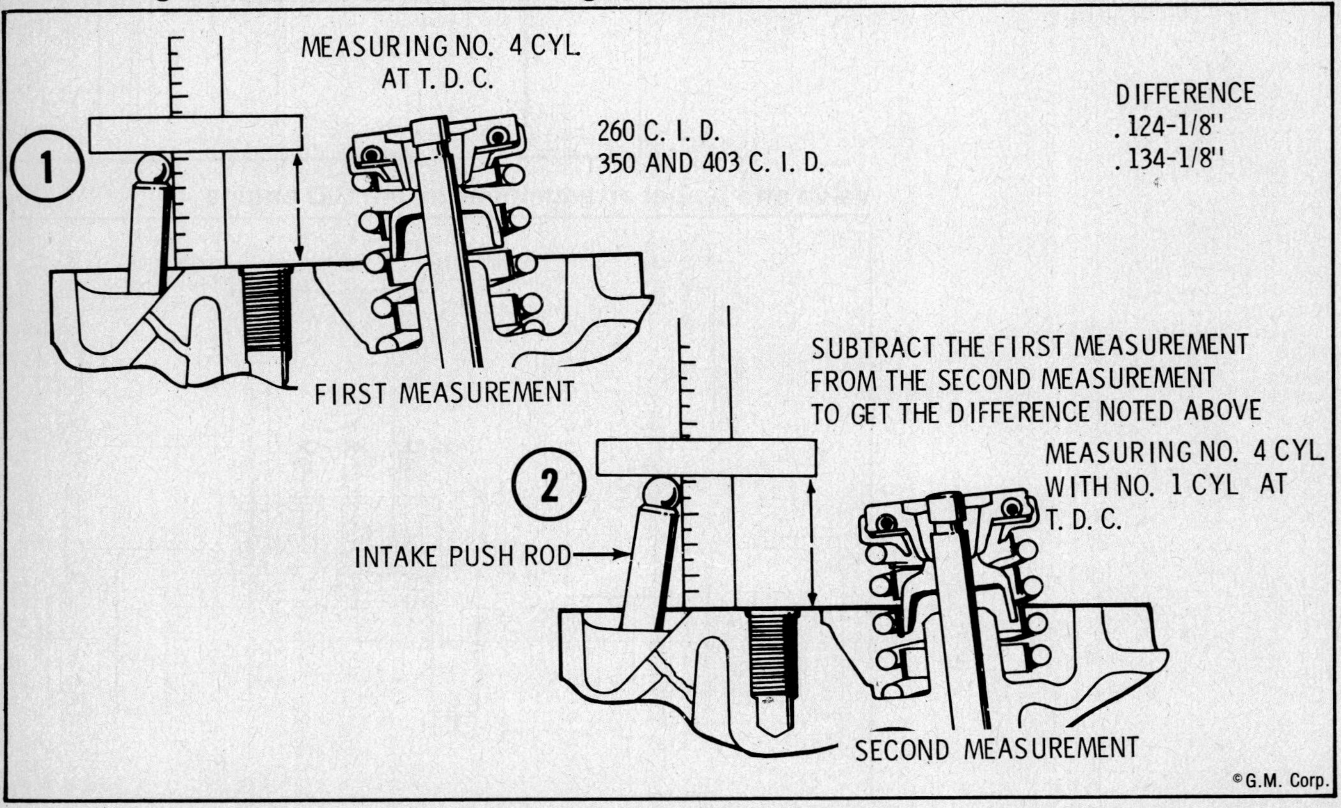

① MEASURING NO. 4 CYL. AT T.D.C.

260 C.I.D.
350 AND 403 C.I.D.

DIFFERENCE
.124-1/8"
.134-1/8"

FIRST MEASUREMENT

SUBTRACT THE FIRST MEASUREMENT FROM THE SECOND MEASUREMENT TO GET THE DIFFERENCE NOTED ABOVE

② INTAKE PUSH ROD

MEASURING NO. 4 CYL WITH NO. 1 CYL AT T.D.C.

SECOND MEASUREMENT

© G.M. Corp.

Four Cylinder Engines Built By Chevrolet

- Remove the camshaft.
- Release spring tension on the lifters and position the levers to one side.
- Lift each hydraulic lifter out of its bore.
- Installation is the reverse of removal.

Rocker Arm Stud

NOTE: When replacing threaded-in rocker arm studs on the Pontiac built 301 and 265 CID engines, drain the cooling system first, and use sealant on stud threads when installing.

Most GM engines use threaded-in rocker arm studs. When a press-fit stud requires replacement use this procedure.

- Remove old stud.
- Ream the hole to fit oversize stud.
- Coat press-fit area of new stud with hypoid axle lubricant, and install the new stud.

Cylinder Head R&R

Engines Built By Buick

- Drain cooling system and remove intake manifold.
- Place steering pump, alternator, air conditioning compressor and A.I.R. pump out of the way.
- On Apollo, Skylark, Omega, and Ventura disconnect exhaust crossover pipe and support, disconnect engine mounts, and raise engine so left cylinder head can be removed with exhaust manifold attached.
- On other models remove exhaust manifold retaining bolts.
- Remove rocker arms covers, rocker arm assemblies and push rods.
- Remove mounting bolts and remove cylinder head.
- Installation is the reverse of removal. On V6 engine place cylinder head gasket with the bead down toward the cylinder block, and use thread sealant on mounting bolts.

Engines Built By Cadillac

- Drain cooling system and remove intake manifold.
- Disconnect electrical and ground connections from cylinder head.
- Place steering pump, alternator and A.I.R. pump out of the way if necessary.
- Remove exhaust manifold.
- Remove rocker arm cover, rocker arm assemblies and push rods.
- Remove mounting bolts and remove cylinder head.
- Installation is the reverse of removal. Tighten cylinder head bolts to the correct torque starting in the center and working alternately toward both ends.

Cylinder head bolt tightening sequence— Buick-built V8 engines

© G.M. Corp.

Cylinder head bolt tightening sequence— Buick-built V6 engines

© G.M. Corp.

Cylinder head bolt placement in Cadillac-built engines

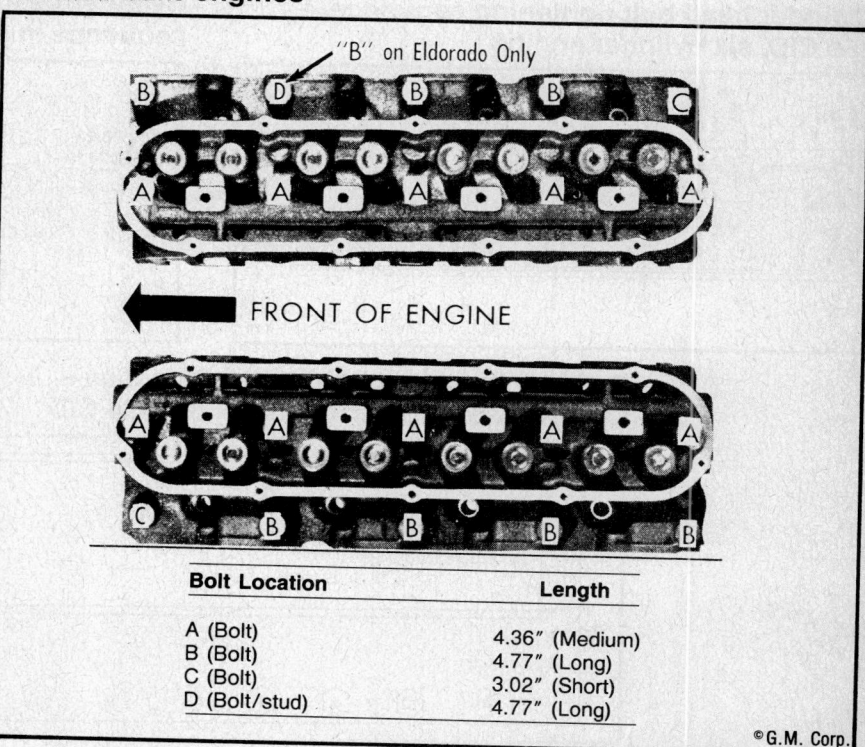

Bolt Location	Length
A (Bolt)	4.36″ (Medium)
B (Bolt)	4.77″ (Long)
C (Bolt)	3.02″ (Short)
D (Bolt/stud)	4.77″ (Long)

© G.M. Corp.

GM GASOLINE ENGINES

Cylinder head installation—173 CID V6 engine

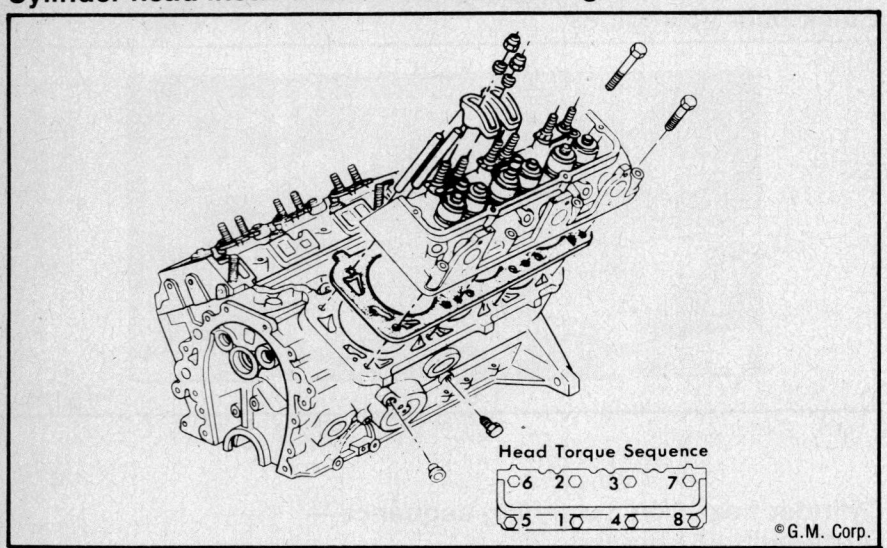

Head Torque Sequence

© G.M. Corp.

Six and Eight Cylinder Engines Built By Chevrolet

- Drain cooling system and remove intake manifold.
- Place alternator, air conditioning compressor, etc. out of the way.
- Remove exhaust manifold.
- Remove valve cover, loosen rocker arm assemblies and remove push rods.
- Remove cylinder head bolts and remove cylinder head.
- Installation is the reverse of removal. Install cylinder head gasket with bead up. Use no sealer on engines using composition steel-asbestos gasket.

Cylinder head bolt tightening sequence— Chevrolet-built 454 CID engine

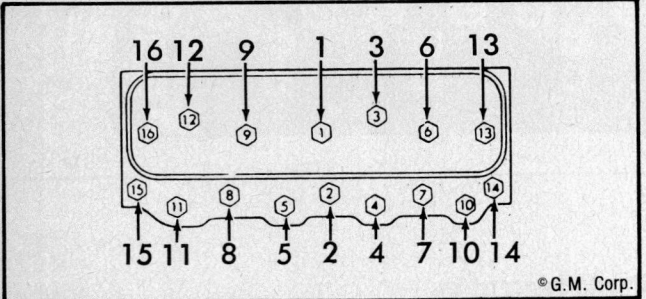

© G.M. Corp.

Cylinder head bolt tightening sequence— Chevrolet-built 200 and 229 CID engines

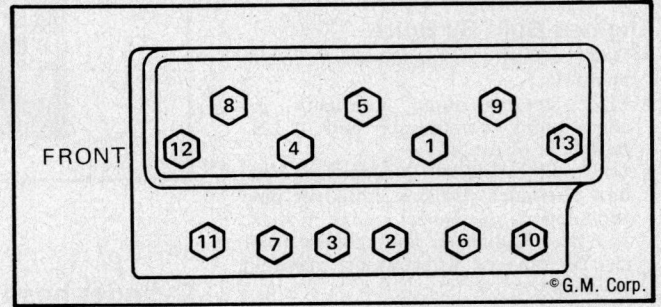

© G.M. Corp.

Cylinder head bolt tightening sequence— 250 CID, six cylinder engine

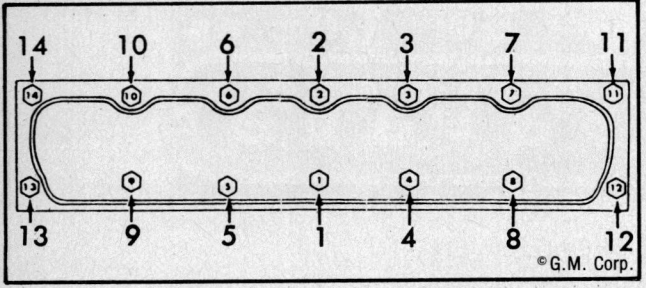

© G.M. Corp.

Cylinder head-to-exhaust manifold tightening sequence in six cylinder, 250 CID engine

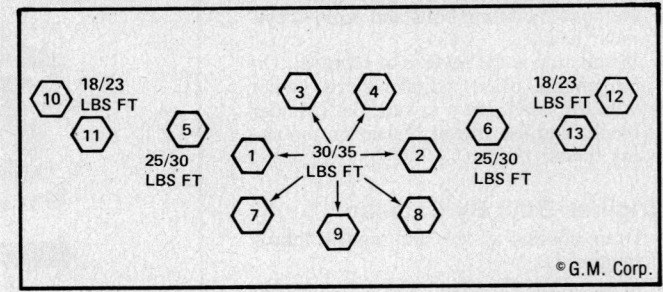

© G.M. Corp.

Cylinder head bolt tightening sequence— Chevrolet-built V8 engines except 454 CID

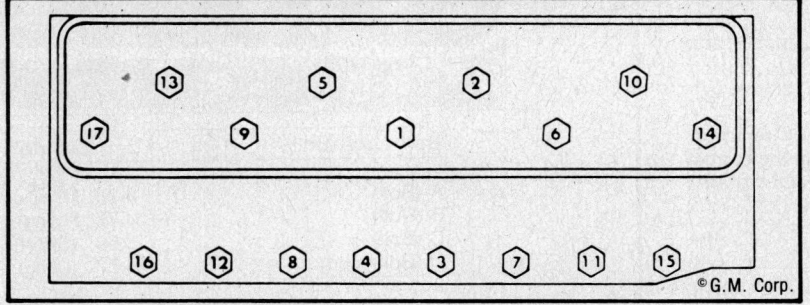

© G.M. Corp.

B362

Cylinder head bolt tightening sequence—140 CID engine

© G.M. Corp.

Cylinder head bolt tightening sequence—85 and 97.6 CID engines

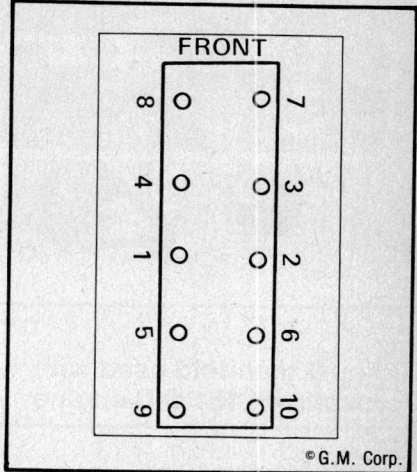

© G.M. Corp.

4 Cylinder Engines Built By Chevrolet

NOTE: Cylinder heads are removed with intake and exhaust manifold attached.

- Drain cooling system, and remove camshaft covers, engine front covers, timing belt (and camshaft timing sprocket on 140 CID engine).
- Disconnect exhaust pipe from manifold.

- Disconnect oil dipstick and any other components attached to the exhaust manifold.
- Disconnect carburetor linkages and fuel and vacuum lines. Do not remove the carburetor.
- Disconnect all electrical, vacuum and cooling system attachments to intake manifold and cylinder head.
- On 85 and 97.6 CID engines remove

cam cover to camshaft housing attaching studs, rocker arms, guides, valve lash adjusters and cam carrier.
- Remove cylinder head attaching bolts and remove cylinder head.
- Installation is the reverse of removal. Place smooth side of cylinder head gasket up, and on 140 CID engines place the longer mounting bolts on the manifold side.

140 CID engine cylinder head

© G.M. Corp.

GM GASOLINE ENGINES

Cylinder head bolt tightening sequence—Oldsmobile-built engines

© G.M. Corp.

Exhaust manifold used with "crossflow" 151 CID engine

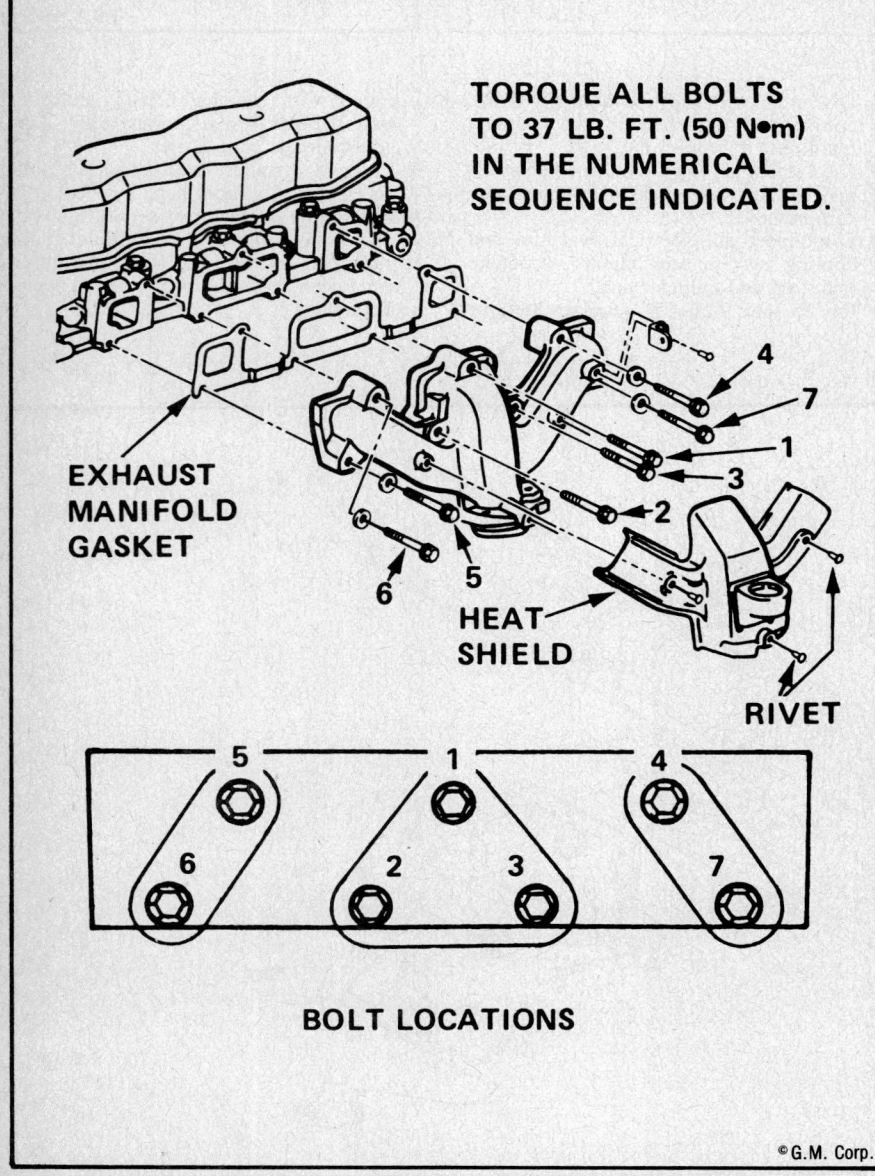

TORQUE ALL BOLTS TO 37 LB. FT. (50 N•m) IN THE NUMERICAL SEQUENCE INDICATED.

EXHAUST MANIFOLD GASKET

HEAT SHIELD

RIVET

BOLT LOCATIONS

© G.M. Corp.

Engines Built By Oldsmobile

- Drain the cooling system and remove the intake manifold.
- Remove exhaust manifold.
- Loosen or remove any accessory brackets that interfere, and remove rocker arm cover, rocker arms and push rods.
- Remove cylinder head bolts and remove cylinder head.
- Installation is the reverse of removal. Use no sealer on composition cylinder head gasket, and install with color stripe facing up. On 455 CID engine install cylinder head gasket with bead toward cylinder block.

Engines Built By Pontiac

- Drain cooling system and remove intake manifold.
- Disconnect exhaust pipe from manifold.

NOTE: Remove cylinder heads with exhaust manifolds attached except on 4 cylinder engine and left cylinder head of 455, HO, SD engines.

- Remove rocker arm covers, loosen or remove rocker arms and remove push rods.
- Remove cylinder head attaching bolts, and remove cylinder head.
- Installation is the reverse of removal. Use prescribed head bolt tightening sequence on 301 CID engine. On other engines begin tightening in the center and tighten alternately toward both ends. On 301 CID engines coat all cylinder head mounting bolts with thread sealant on threads and base of heads.

Cylinder head gasket identification in Oldsmobile-built engines

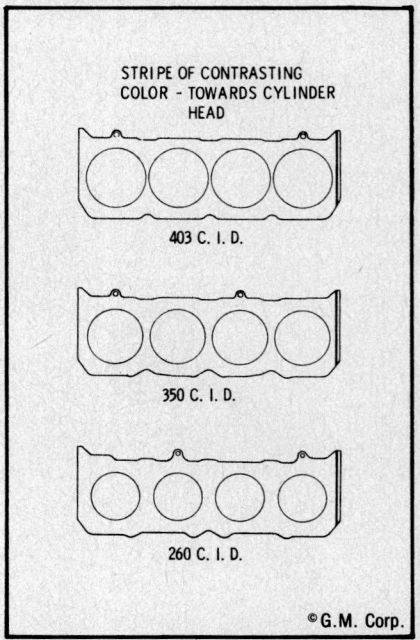

STRIPE OF CONTRASTING COLOR - TOWARDS CYLINDER HEAD

403 C. I. D.

350 C. I. D.

260 C. I. D.

© G.M. Corp.

Cylinder head bolt tightening sequence—151 CID engine

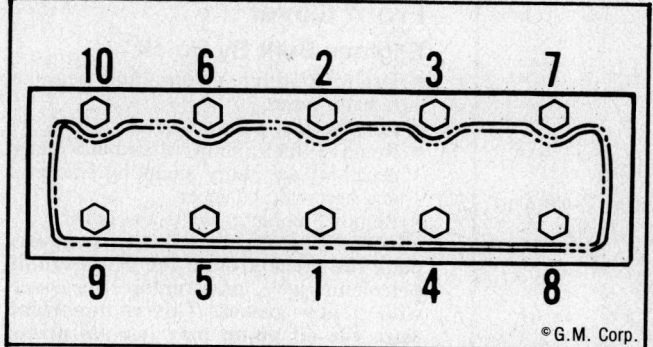

10
6
2
3
7
9
5
1
4
8
©G.M. Corp.

Cylinder head bolt tightening sequence—Pontiac-built V8 engines. Coat all bolts with sealer when installing

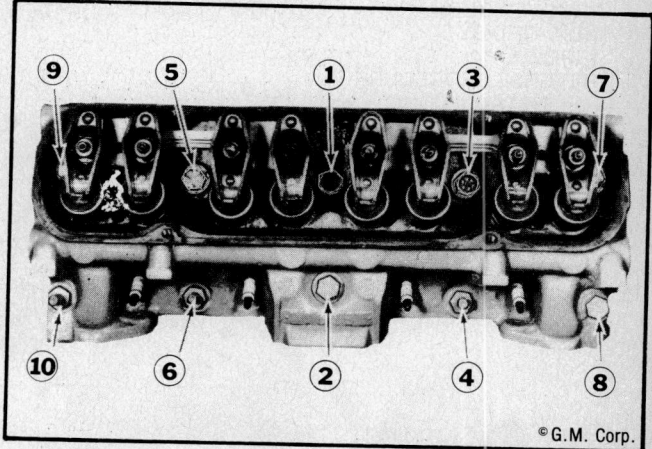

9
5
1
3
7
10
6
2
4
8
©G.M. Corp.

Cylinder head and attaching parts—non-crossflow 151 CID engine

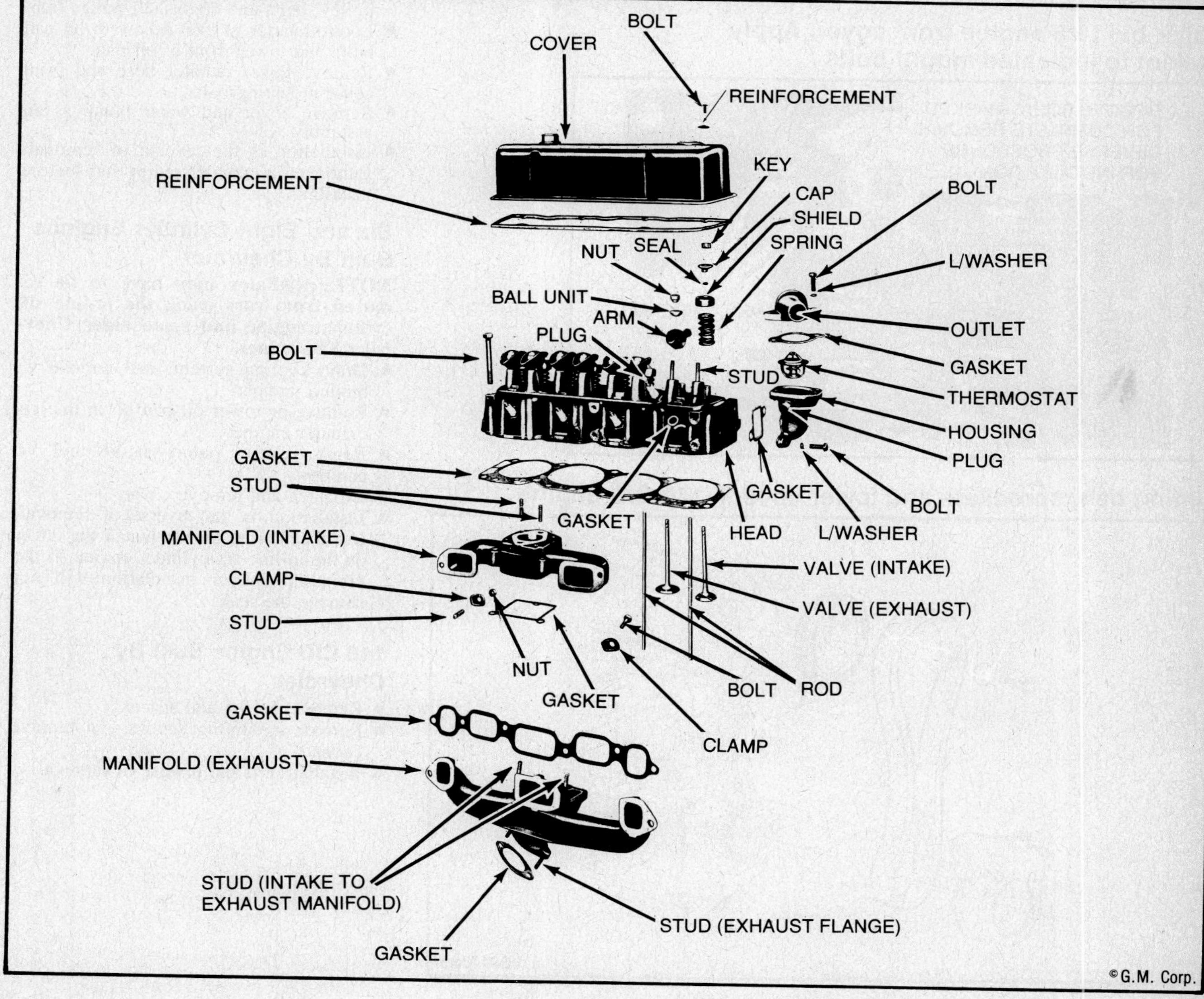

BOLT
COVER
REINFORCEMENT
KEY
REINFORCEMENT
CAP
SHIELD
BOLT
NUT
SEAL
SPRING
L/WASHER
BALL UNIT
ARM
OUTLET
PLUG
BOLT
GASKET
STUD
THERMOSTAT
HOUSING
GASKET
PLUG
STUD
GASKET
BOLT
GASKET
HEAD
L/WASHER
MANIFOLD (INTAKE)
VALVE (INTAKE)
CLAMP
VALVE (EXHAUST)
STUD
NUT
GASKET
BOLT
ROD
GASKET
CLAMP
MANIFOLD (EXHAUST)
STUD (INTAKE TO EXHAUST MANIFOLD)
STUD (EXHAUST FLANGE)
GASKET
©G.M. Corp.

GM GASOLINE ENGINES

Buick-built V6 engine front cover. Apply sealant to indicated mount bolts

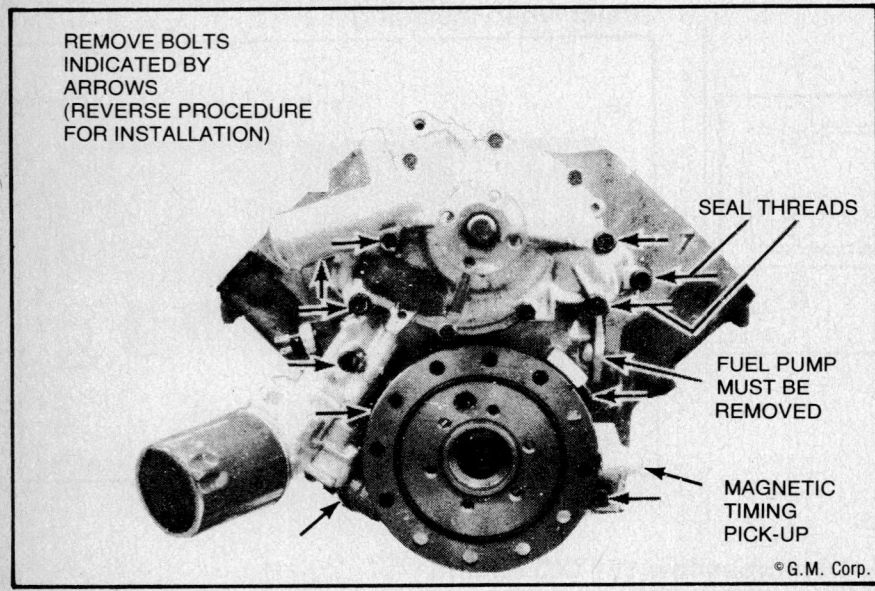

REMOVE BOLTS
INDICATED BY
ARROWS
(REVERSE PROCEDURE
FOR INSTALLATION)

SEAL THREADS

FUEL PUMP
MUST BE
REMOVED

MAGNETIC
TIMING
PICK-UP

© G.M. Corp.

Buick-built V8 engine front cover. Apply sealant to indicated mount bolts

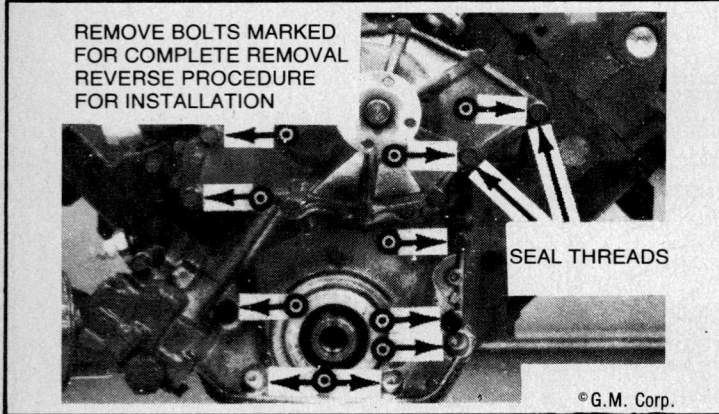

REMOVE BOLTS MARKED
FOR COMPLETE REMOVAL
REVERSE PROCEDURE
FOR INSTALLATION

SEAL THREADS

© G.M. Corp.

Timing belt, sprockets and lower cover—140 CID engine

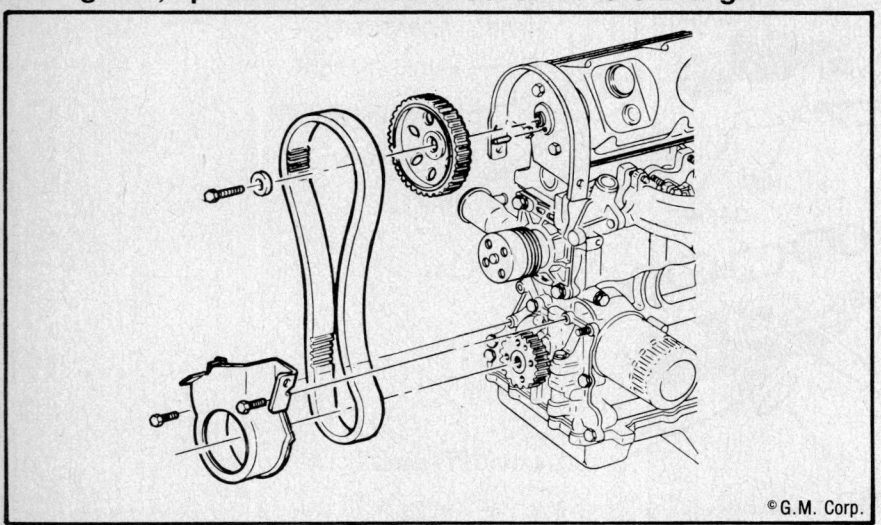

© G.M. Corp.

Front Cover

Engines Built By Buick

- Drain cooling system, and remove radiator hoses.
- Remove fan, pulleys and drive belts.
- Remove fuel pump, distributor, any necessary accessory mounting brackets, and harmonic balancer.
- Remove mounting bolts and cover.

NOTE: Remove the oil pump cover, pack the space around the gears full of petroleum jelly, and replace the cover with a new gasket. This is important since the oil pump may lose its prime whenever the pump, pump cover or timing chain cover is disturbed.

- Installation is the reverse of removal. Use thread sealant on mounting bolts shown in illustrations.

Engines Built By Cadillac

NOTE: 1974-75 Eldorado requires engine removal.

- Drain cooling system, and remove fan, pulley, belts and crankshaft pulley hub.
- Loosen starter to gain access to oil pan bolts and lower front of oil pan.
- Remove lower radiator hose and front cover mounting bolts.
- Remove cover and water pump as an assembly.
- Installation is the reverse of removal. Lubricate crankshaft pulley hub before installing.

Six and Eight Cylinder Engines Built By Chevrolet

NOTE: Radiator may have to be removed from cars using the in-line six cylinder engine and some older Chevrolet V8 engines.

- Drain cooling system, and remove vibration damper.
- Remove or lower oil pan on in-line six cylinder engines.
- Remove water pump on V8 and V6 engines.
- Unfasten and remove cover.
- Installation is the reverse of removal. Use a centering tool to install the cover on the in-line six cylinder engine so the vibration damper installation will not damage the seal.

140 CID Engine Built By Chevrolet

- Remove the fan and spacer.
- Remove mounting screws and remove cover.
- Installation is the reverse of removal.

Cadillac-built engine front cover attaching bolts

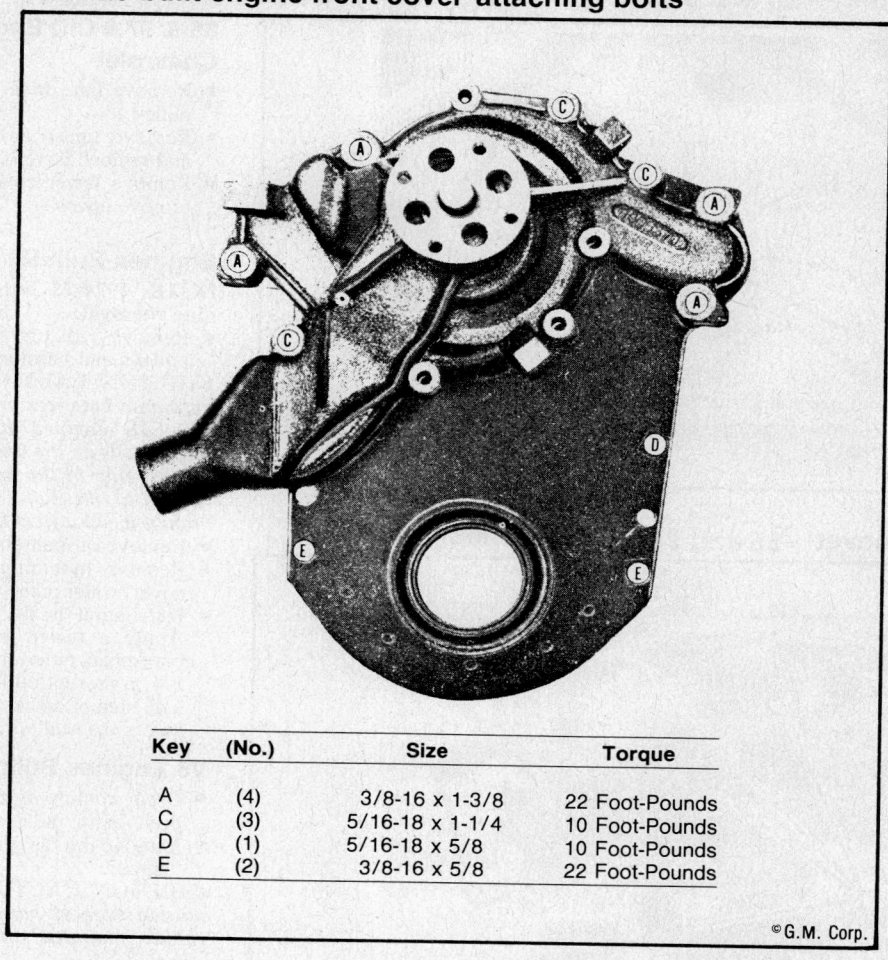

Key	(No.)	Size	Torque
A	(4)	3/8-16 x 1-3/8	22 Foot-Pounds
C	(3)	5/16-18 x 1-1/4	10 Foot-Pounds
D	(1)	5/16-18 x 5/8	10 Foot-Pounds
E	(2)	3/8-16 x 5/8	22 Foot-Pounds

© G.M. Corp.

Front cover installation—250 CID engine

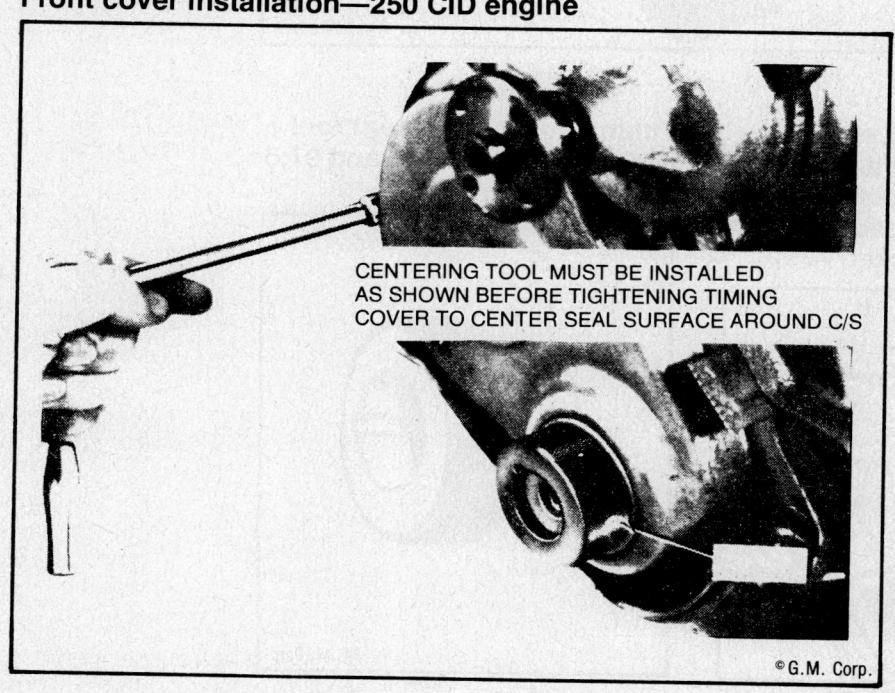

CENTERING TOOL MUST BE INSTALLED AS SHOWN BEFORE TIGHTENING TIMING COVER TO CENTER SEAL SURFACE AROUND C/S

© G.M. Corp.

GM GASOLINE ENGINES

Front cover mounting— 85 and 97.6 CID engines

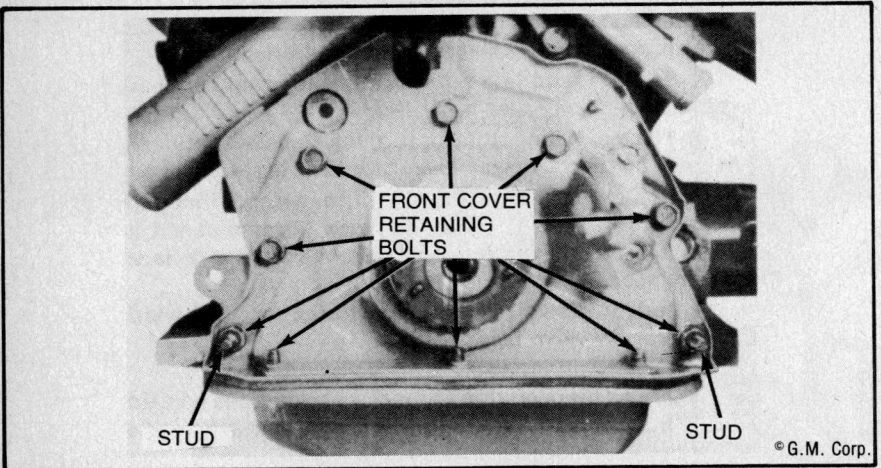

FRONT COVER RETAINING BOLTS

STUD   STUD

© G.M. Corp.

Timing belt front cover—85 and 97.6 CID engines

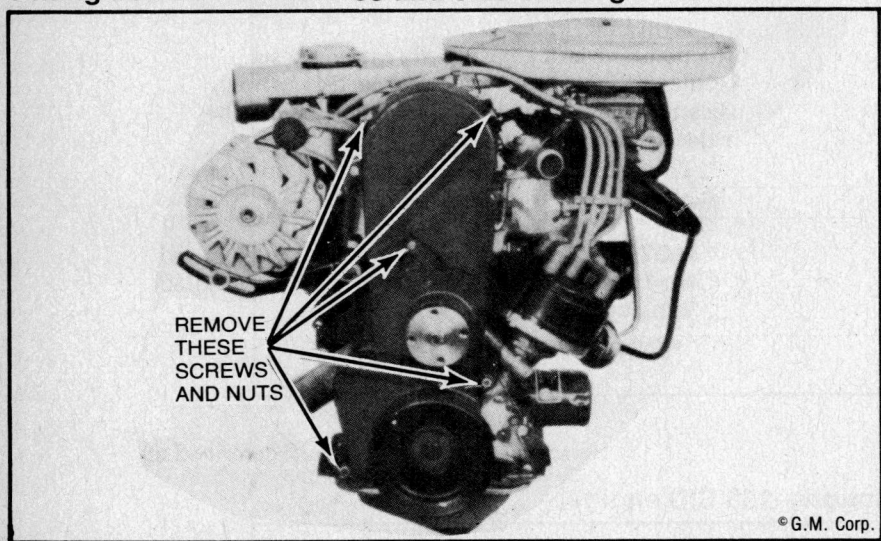

REMOVE THESE SCREWS AND NUTS

© G.M. Corp.

85 & 97.6 CID Engines Built By Chevrolet

- Remove fan, drive belts and crankshaft pulley.
- Remove upper cover retaining screws and remove cover.
- Remove lower cover retaining nut and remove cover.

Engines Built By Oldsmobile

NOTE: *1974-75 Toronado requires engine removal.*

- Remove radiator, all drive belts, fan, pulleys and harmonic balancer.

CHILTON CAUTION: *To remove the harmonic balancer on 307, 350, 403 and 455 CID engines do not use any tool which pulls on the outside of the hub. The outside ring of the balancer is bonded in rubber to the hub, and if the bond is broken it will affect engine timing.*

- Remove oil pan on 1974-75 engines.
- Remove mounting bolts, and remove cover, water pump and timing indicator.
- Installation is the reverse of removal. Apply a sealer to inside diameter of crankshaft pulley hub and to crankshaft key to prevent oil leakage, and coat outside area of crankshaft pulley hub which enters the seal with lubricant.

V8 Engines Built By Pontiac

- Drain cooling system and remove fan, drive belts, pulleys and water pump.
- Remove the fuel pump and the vibration damper.

CHILTON CAUTION: *Do not pry on outside edge of harmonic balancer. It is rubber mounted and balance could be affected.*

- Remove mounting bolts and remove cover.
- Installation is the reverse of removal.

In 85 and 97.6 CID engines, form a replacement front cover-to-oil pan gasket by cutting the front section from a new oil pan gasket

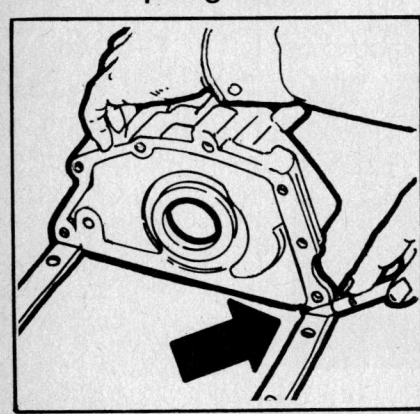

Timing cover alignment tool J-26434 used with 85 and 97.6 CID engines

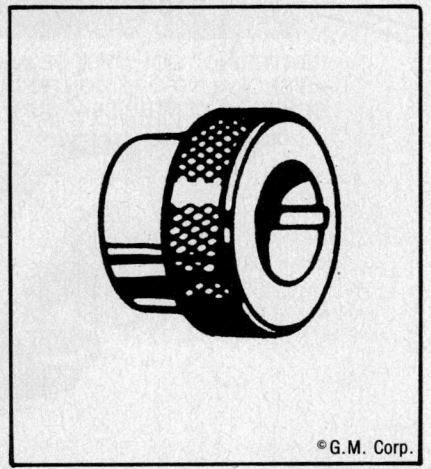

© G.M. Corp.

151 CID Engine Built By Pontiac
EXCEPT X BODY CARS
- Remove drive belts and crankshaft hub and pulleys.
- Remove cover mounting screws, cut the oil pan gasket and remove the cover.
- Installation is the reverse of removal. Apply silicone rubber to joint formed at oil pan and centering block. Use a centering tool to prevent seal damage when installing hub.

X BODY CARS
- The right fender inner splash shield must be removed, and the engine raised for front cover removal.
- Remove the right fender inner splash shield.
- Remove the pulley hub, alternator bracket and front engine mount-to-cradle nuts.
- Raise the engine, and remove the engine mount bracket.
- Remove the oil pan-to-front cover screws, and pull the cover forward enough to cut the front seal.
- Installation is the reverse of removal. Use a room temperature vulcanizing sealant on the joint formed at oil pan and centering block. Use a centering tool to prevent seal damage when installing the hub.

Front Cover Oil Seal
Remove the pulley and vibration damper and pry the seal out. Drive a new seal in with open end toward engine on all but Buick built engines. For engines built by Buick:
 a. Remove front cover.
 b. Drive out seal and shedder from the front toward rear of timing chain cover.
 c. Coil new packing around opening so ends are at top. Drive in shedder and stake in place at three locations.
 d. Size the packing by rotating a hammer handle around the packing until the balancer hub can be inserted through the opening.
 e. Install front cover.

EST crankshaft sensor mounting used in 1977 Toronado

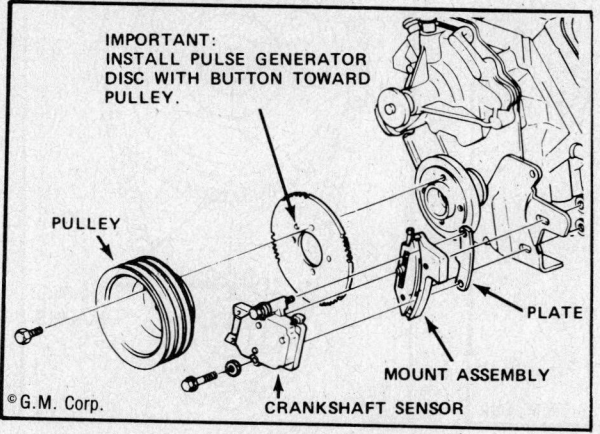

IMPORTANT:
INSTALL PULSE GENERATOR
DISC WITH BUTTON TOWARD
PULLEY.

PULLEY

PLATE

MOUNT ASSEMBLY

CRANKSHAFT SENSOR

© G.M. Corp.

Oldsmobile-built engine front cover

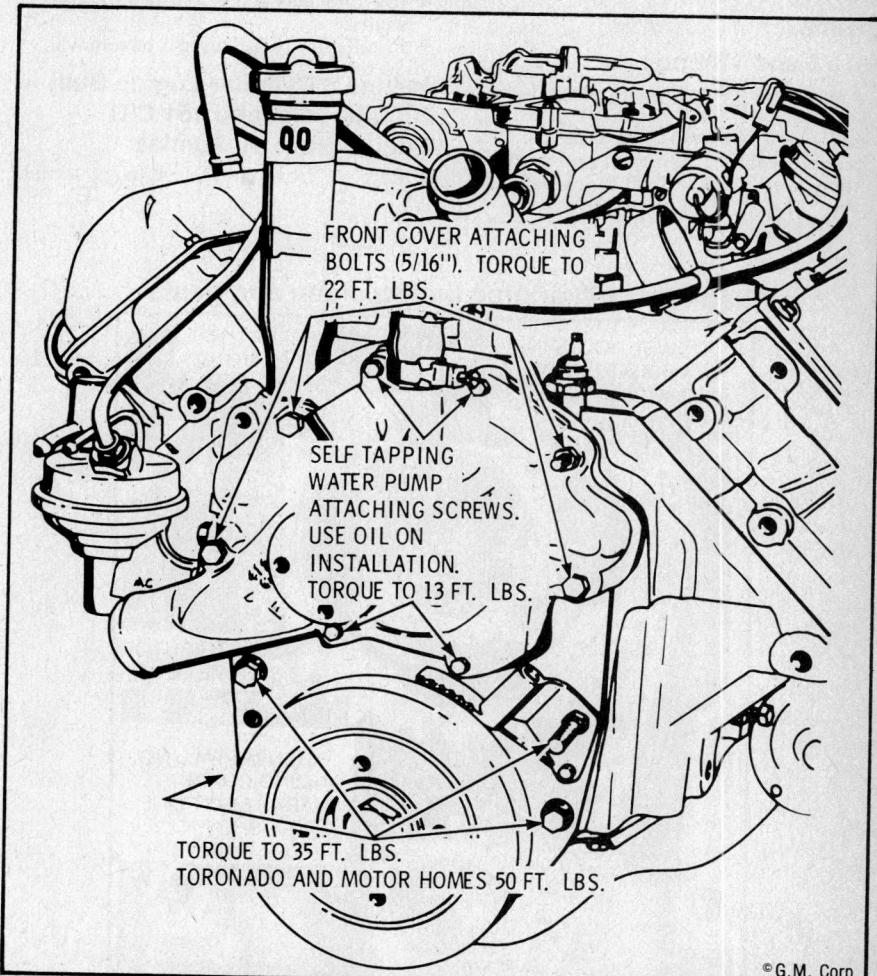

FRONT COVER ATTACHING
BOLTS (5/16"). TORQUE TO
22 FT. LBS.

SELF TAPPING
WATER PUMP
ATTACHING SCREWS.
USE OIL ON
INSTALLATION.
TORQUE TO 13 FT. LBS.

TORQUE TO 35 FT. LBS.
TORONADO AND MOTOR HOMES 50 FT. LBS.

© G.M. Corp.

Oldsmobile engine front cover installation

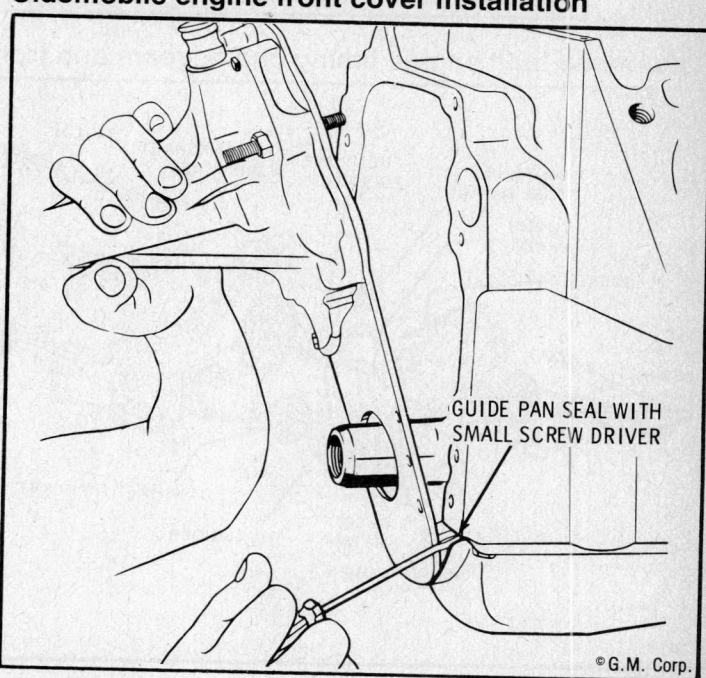

GUIDE PAN SEAL WITH
SMALL SCREW DRIVER

© G.M. Corp.

GM GASOLINE ENGINES

Timing Chain, Belt or Gears

GM V6 and V8 Engines

- Remove front cover and align timing marks.
- Remove distributor drive gear and fuel pump eccentric. Remove crankshaft oil slinger, and on 455 CID Buick built engine remove the oil pan.
- Pry sprockets and chain forward and off shafts.
- Installation is the reverse of removal.

In-Line 6 Cylinder Engine Built By Chevrolet and 151 CID Engine Built By Pontiac

- Remove front cover, and align timing marks.
- Remove camshaft and use a press to separate timing gear from camshaft.
- Use gear puller to remove crankshaft timing gear.
- Installation is the reverse of removal.

Cadillac-built engine timing chain and gears

DOWEL HOLES IN CAMSHAFT AND SPROCKET MUST LINE UP

FUEL PUMP ECCENTRIC

DISTRIBUTOR DRIVE GEAR

WHEN INSTALLING TIMING CHAIN, MARKS MUST LINE UP AS SHOWN

KEY

©G.M. Corp.

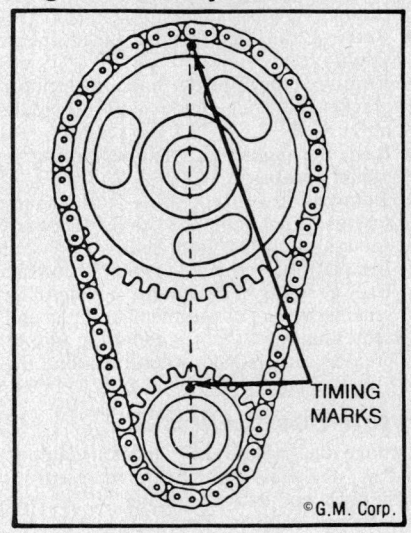

Timing marks aligned in V8 engines built by Pontiac

TIMING MARKS

©G.M. Corp.

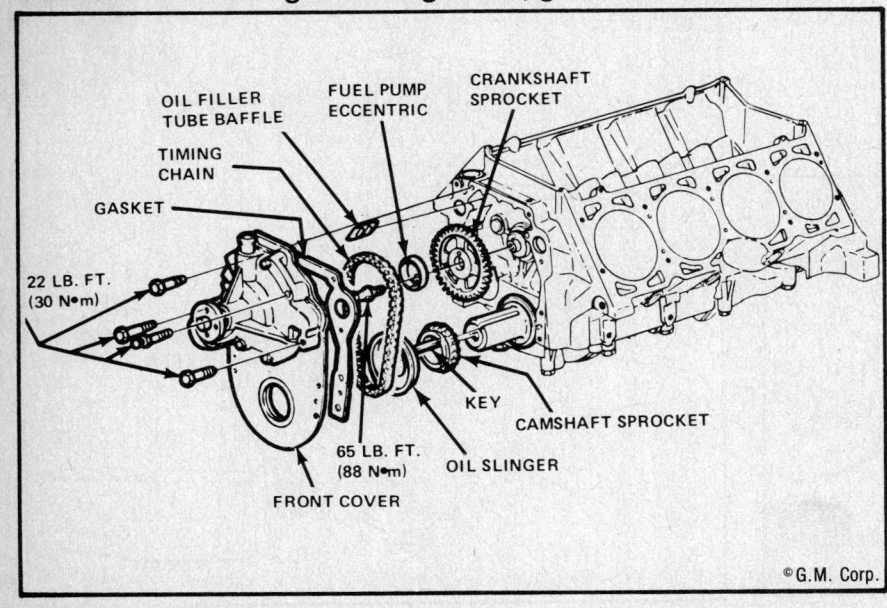

Oldsmobile-built engine timing chain, gears and front cover

OIL FILLER TUBE BAFFLE

FUEL PUMP ECCENTRIC

CRANKSHAFT SPROCKET

TIMING CHAIN

GASKET

22 LB. FT. (30 N•m)

65 LB. FT. (88 N•m)

FRONT COVER

OIL SLINGER

KEY

CAMSHAFT SPROCKET

©G.M. Corp.

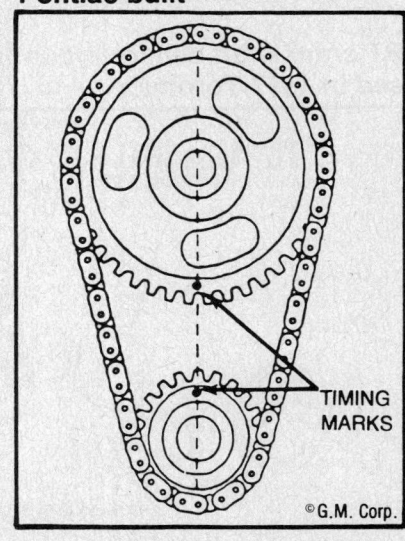

Timing marks aligned in all V6 and V8 engines except Pontiac-built

TIMING MARKS

©G.M. Corp.

Front cover sealing—173 CID, V6 engine

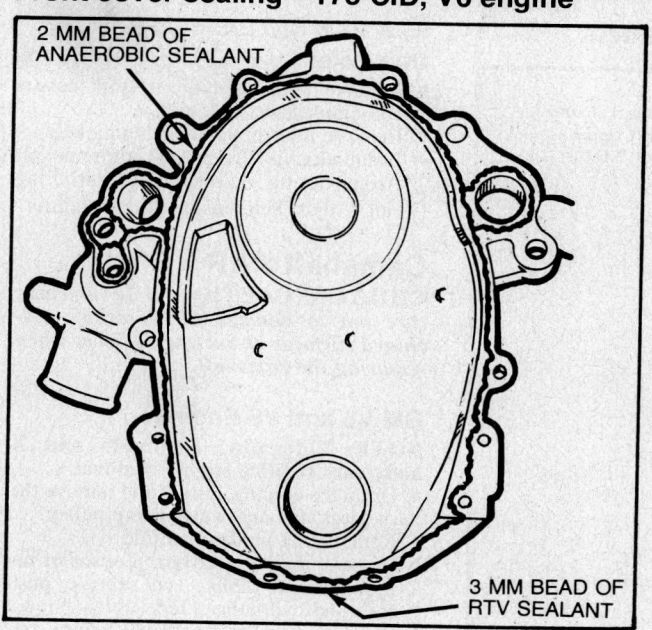

2 MM BEAD OF ANAEROBIC SEALANT

3 MM BEAD OF RTV SEALANT

Front cover, timing chain and gears in 173 CID, V6 engine

© G.M. Corp.

140 CID Engine Built By Chevrolet

NOTE: Tension can only be taken off the timing belt by loosening the water pump. Remove the water pump and use a new gasket when installing.

- Drain the cooling system. Remove engine front cover, accessory drive pulley and timing belt lower cover.
- Disconnect and remove water pump, and remove timing belt.
- Installation is the reverse of removal. Install belt with timing marks aligned. Use water pump position to place 75-140 lbs. of tension on the timing belt.

Timing marks aligned in 250 and 151 CID engines

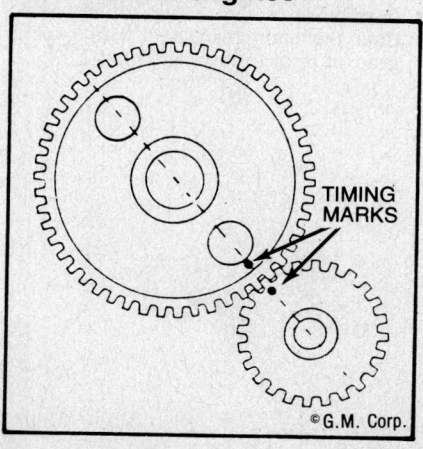

TIMING MARKS

© G.M. Corp.

Timing mark alignment—140 CID engine

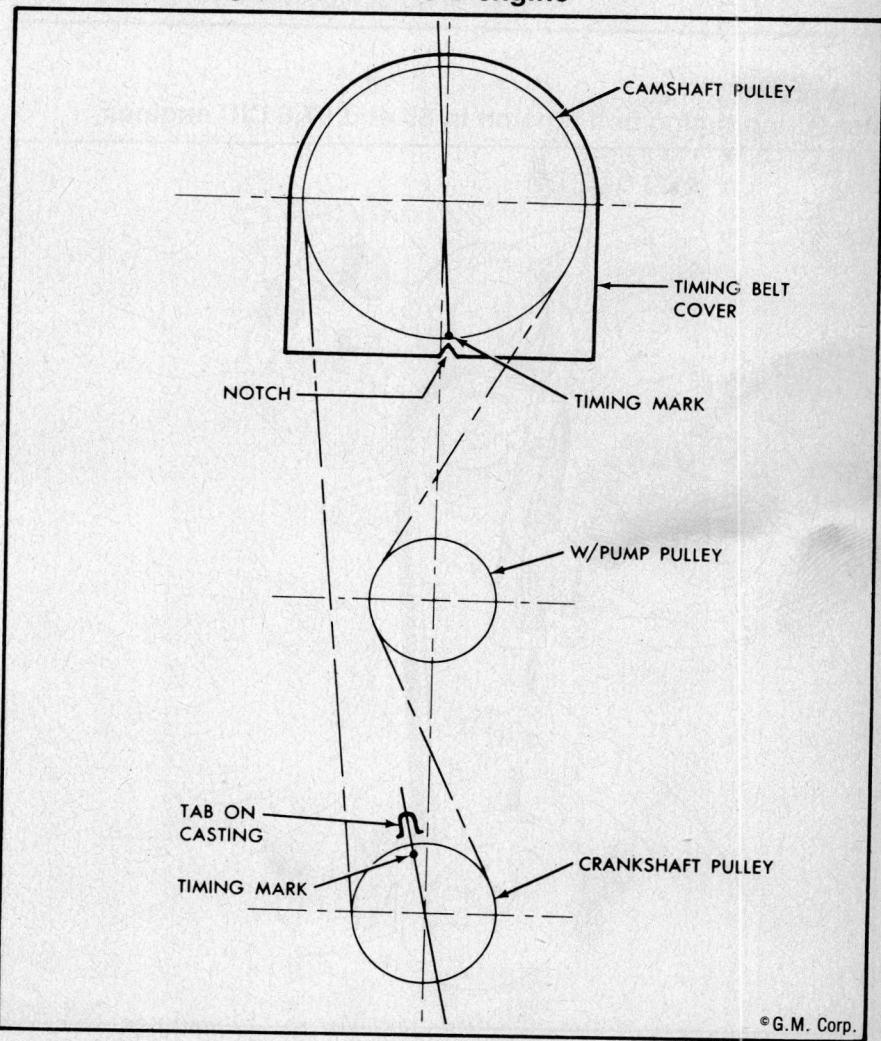

CAMSHAFT PULLEY

TIMING BELT COVER

NOTCH

TIMING MARK

W/PUMP PULLEY

TAB ON CASTING

TIMING MARK

CRANKSHAFT PULLEY

© G.M. Corp.

In 85 and 97.6 CID engines, place a ⅛ inch drill bit through the camshaft sprocket and rear cover for timing alignment

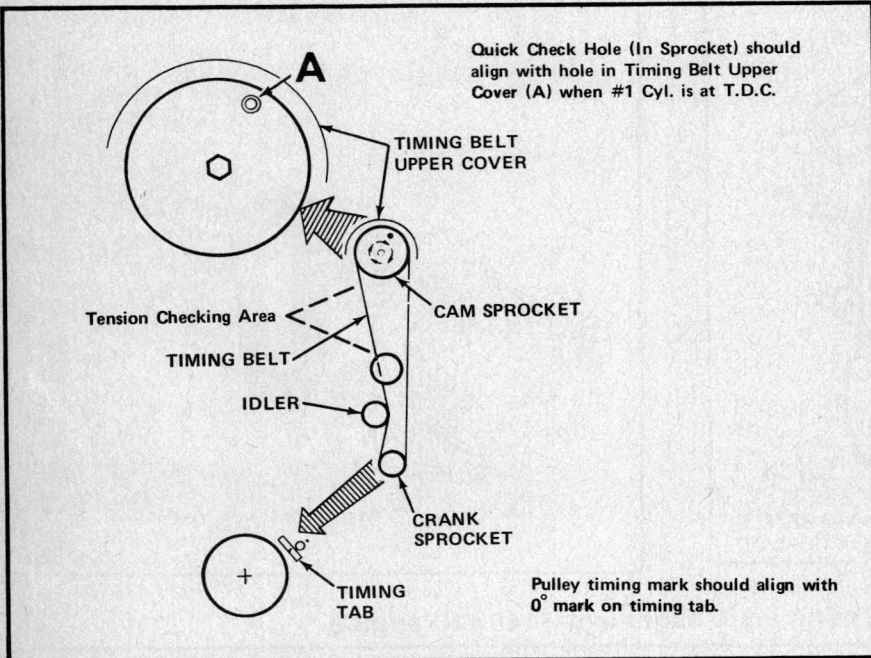

Quick Check Hole (In Sprocket) should align with hole in Timing Belt Upper Cover (A) when #1 Cyl. is at T.D.C.

TIMING BELT UPPER COVER

CAM SPROCKET

Tension Checking Area

TIMING BELT

IDLER

CRANK SPROCKET

TIMING TAB

Pulley timing mark should align with 0° mark on timing tab.

Measuring timing belt tension in 85 and 97.6 CID engines

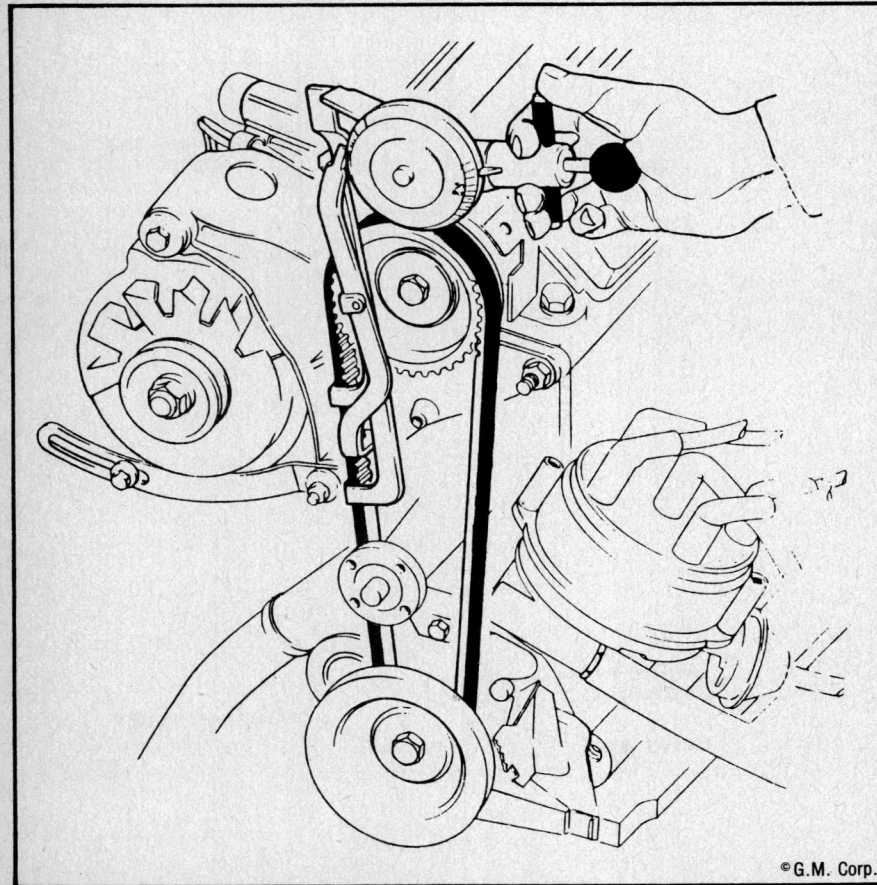

© G.M. Corp.

85 & 97.6 CID Engines Built By Chevrolet
- Remove upper and lower front covers and crankshaft drive pulley.
- Remove idler pulley and timing belt.
- Installation is the reverse of removal. Align timing marks before installing belt. Adjust belt tension after installing.

Camshaft R&R
CHILTON CAUTION: *Use extreme care not to damage the camshaft machined surfaces or bearing surfaces when removing the camshaft.*

GM V6 and V8 Engines
NOTE: Eldorado, Toronado and X body cars require engine removal.
- Drain the cooling system and remove the radiator, fan and water pump pulley.
- Remove the intake manifold.
- Remove the valve covers. Loosen or remove rocker arms, and remove push rods and hydraulic lifters.
- Remove distributor and fuel pump.
- Remove the harmonic balancer, water pump, timing chain cover, timing chain and sprocket.
- Slide the camshaft forward out of the bearing bores. It may be necessary on some cars to raise the engine slightly or remove the front grille-work for sufficient clearance.
- Installation is the reverse of removal. Coat the entire camshaft with hypoid gear oil prior to installation.

In-Line Six Cylinder Engine Built By Chevrolet
NOTE: The front grille-work must be removed and the engine raised to remove the camshaft with the engine in the vehicle, so it may be more convenient to remove the engine.
- Remove the valve cover and push rod covers. Loosen the rocker arms and remove the push rods and hydraulic lifters.
- Remove the fuel pump and distributor.
- Remove crankcase front cover.
- Remove the camshaft thrust plate bolts, and pull the gear and camshaft out through the front of the engine block.
- Installation is the reverse of removal. Coat the entire camshaft with hypoid gear oil prior to installation.

Four Cylinder 140 CID Engine Built By Chevrolet

NOTE: A special valve tappet depressing tool is necessary for camshaft removal.

- Remove the camshaft timing belt and sprocket.
- Remove the three screws securing the camshaft seal and retainer assembly and timing cover to the cylinder head.
- Inspect the seal, prying it out and replacing it if necessary.
- Remove the camshaft cover.
- Disconnect the fuel line at the carburetor.
- Remove:
  a. Idle solenoid from its bracket
  b. The choke coil, cover and rod assembly
  c. Ignition distributor
- Raise the vehicle on a hoist, disconnect the front engine mounts at the body attachment, raise the front of the engine and install wood blocks, about 1½ in. thick, between the engine mounts and the body.
- Install camshaft removal tool on the cylinder head to hold down the lifters so that the camshaft may be removed.
  a. Position the tool so that the attaching holes are aligned with the lower cam cover bolt holes and the tappet levers of the tool are aligned to depresss both valves of each cylinder.
  b. Back off the bolts in the bottom of the tool so that they are not contacting the bosses beneath the tool.
  c. Install the tool attaching bolts, tightening them securely.
  d. Tighten the bolts in the bottom of the cylinder head. Before depressing the tappets, rotate the crankshaft 90° clockwise from the timing mark on the tab. This assures that the pistons are not a TDC and will prevent valve-to-piston contact.
  Grease the ball end of the lever depressing bolts and tighten the bolts to depress the tappets.

NOTE: Torque the lever bolts to 10 ft./lbs. If more tightening is required, check to see that the tool is properly installed, then proceed cautiously to prevent damaging the depressing lever.

- Slide the camshaft forward until it clears the head.

NOTE: The camshaft bearings may be removed. It is not necessary to remove the camshaft end plug. Gently tap out the bearings, starting at the forward end. Tap out the rear bearing slowly into the distributor housing, being careful not to unseat the end plug. Crush the rear bearing to remove it from the distributor housing. Install, starting with the rear bearing. The oil holes in the bearings must align with the oil holes in the case. On the first two bearings the oil holes are at 11 o'clock (as seen from the front of the engine) and the oil groove in the number one bearing toward the front of the engine.

- Install the camshaft with the journals seated in the bores.
- With the car up on a hoist, raise the front of the engine and remove the wood blocks from the engine mounts.
- Install the front engine mounts, then lower the vehicle.
- Using a new gasket, install the timing belt upper cover and retainer plate and seal assembly. Tighten the retaining bolts to 15 ft./lbs.
- Using a dial indicator, measure the camshaft end-play. If it is not 0.004—0.012 in., select a camshaft retainer (according to cam locator thickness) which will provide more or less end-play as required.
- Remove the tappet depressing tool by first releasing the tappet depressing lever bolts, and then removing the tool attaching bolts.
- Install:
  a. Camshaft timing sprocket
  b. The timing belt
  c. Front engine cover
  d. Distributor
  e. Vehicle hood if removed
- Adjust the valve tappets.
- Install the camshaft cover.
- Install and adjust the carburetor choke coil, cover and rod assembly.
- Connect the carburetor fuel line.
- Install the idle solenoid to the bracket.
- Check and adjust the ignition timing.

Four Cylinder 85 & 97.6 CID Engines Built By Chevrolet

- Remove camshaft sprocket.
- Remove valve rocker arms.
- Remove heater assembly and set aside.
- Remove cam carrier rear cover.
- Remove camshaft thrust plate bolts, slide camshaft rearward slightly and remove thrust plate.
- Remove engine mount nuts and wire retainers.
- Raise engine using floor jack.
- Remove camshaft.
- Installation is the reverse of removal.

Four Cylinder 151 CID Engine Built By Pontiac

- Drain the cooling system and remove the radiator, fan and water pump pulley.
- Remove valve cover, loosen rocker arms and remove push rods. Remove push rod cover, and remove hydraulic valve lifters.
- Remove distributor and fuel pump.
- Remove hub and timing gear cover.
- Remove two camshaft thrust plate screws, and remove the camshaft and gear assembly by pulling it out through the front of the block.
- Installation is the reverse of removal. Coat the entire camshaft with hypoid gear oil before installing.

Camshaft removal tool used to depress tappets on 140 CID engine

J-23591

Oil pump installation—140 CID engine

© G.M. Corp.

Oil pump drive shaft—151 CID engine

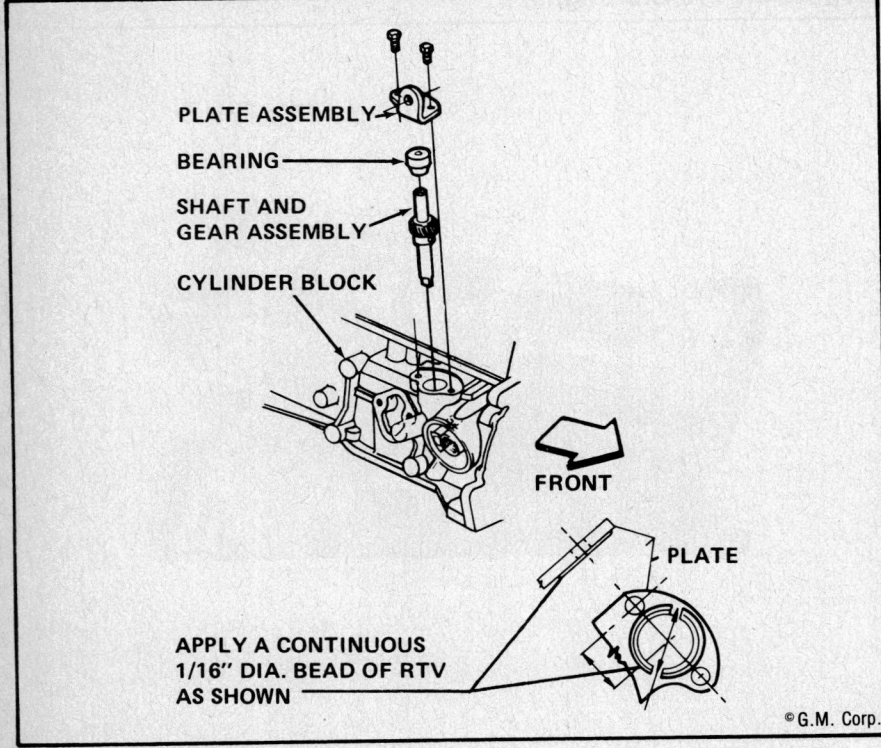

PLATE ASSEMBLY

BEARING

SHAFT AND
GEAR ASSEMBLY

CYLINDER BLOCK

FRONT

PLATE

APPLY A CONTINUOUS
1/16" DIA. BEAD OF RTV
AS SHOWN

© G.M. Corp.

Oil Pump R&R

Four Cylinder 140 CID Engine Built By Chevrolet

- Remove front engine cover, accessory drive pulley, timing belt, timing belt lower cover and crankshaft sprocket.
- Raise vehicle and drain oil.
- Remove oil pan and baffle.
- Remove oil pump bolts and the pump.
- Inspect for wear. (Gear and body are serviced as units)
- Check pressure regulator for free operation.
- When installing be sure pump drive Key is installed properly. Use anti-seize compound on threads of pump mounting bolts. Tighten to 15 ft./lbs. The stud is installed in the upper right (facing pump) and tightened to 30 ft./lbs.
- Install oil pan before tightening the timing cover bolts.

85 & 97.6 CID Engines Built By Chevrolet

- Remove coil bracket bolts and lay coil aside.
- Remove fuel pump, push rod, fuel pump gasket and distributor.
- Remove oil pan and oil pump.
- Replace oil pump and install in reverse order of removal.

NOTE: Make certain pilot on oil pump engages case.

Four Cylinder 151 CID Engine Built By Pontiac

- Drain oil and remove oil pan.
- Remove two flange mounting bolts and nut from main bearing cap bolt and remove pump and screen assembly.
- Inspect for wear (burrs or scoring).
- When installing align oil pump drive shaft to match with distributor tang.
- Install oil pump to block positioning flange over distributor lower bushing (use no gasket).
- Tighten bolts to 115 in./lb. (Oil pump should slide easily into place).
- Install oil pan using new gaskets and seals.

All GM V6 and V8 Engines

- Remove oil filter, and on Chevrolet, Pontiac except Ventura, Oldsmobile except Omega, Cadillac except Seville remove oil pan.
- Disconnect the lead from the oil pressure indicator switch in the fitter bypass valve cap (Oldsmobile V6 and 75-76 Omega V8 350).
- Unbolt the pump cover assembly from the timing chain cover (Oldsmobile & Buick).
- Remove pump attaching screws and carefully lower pump.

NOTE: On Cadillac except Seville remove screw nearest pressure regulator last.

- Slide driveshaft, drive gear and driven gear out of housing.
- Inspect for wear (burrs or scoring).
- Install pump in reverse order of removal and be sure to pack pump full with petroleum jelly (don't use grease).

CHILTON CAUTION: *Unless the pump is primed this way, it won't produce any oil pressure when the engine is started.*

Oil pump mounting in Oldsmobile-built engines

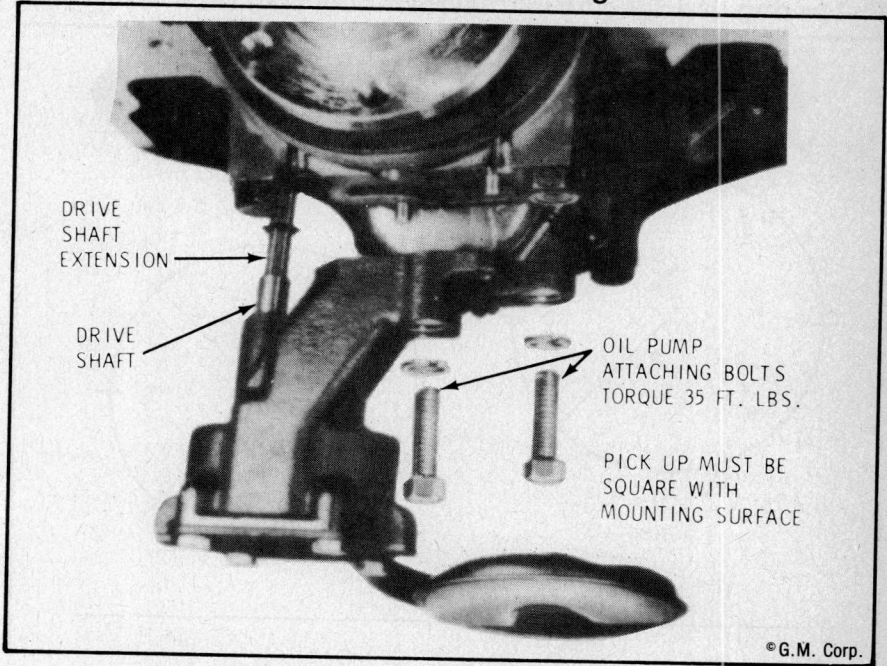

DRIVE SHAFT EXTENSION

DRIVE SHAFT

OIL PUMP ATTACHING BOLTS TORQUE 35 FT. LBS.

PICK UP MUST BE SQUARE WITH MOUNTING SURFACE

© G.M. Corp.

Oil pump mounting in Cadillac-built engines

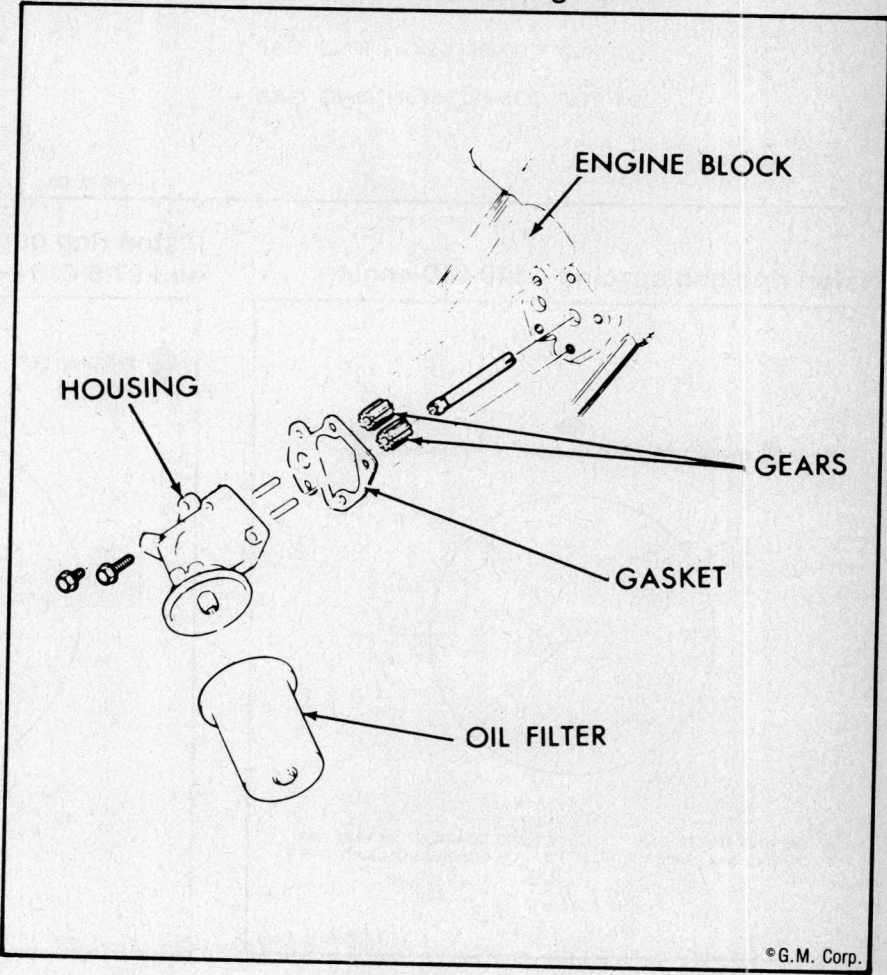

ENGINE BLOCK

HOUSING

GEARS

GASKET

OIL FILTER

© G.M. Corp.

GM GASOLINE ENGINES

Piston ring gap spacing in Chevrolet-built engines

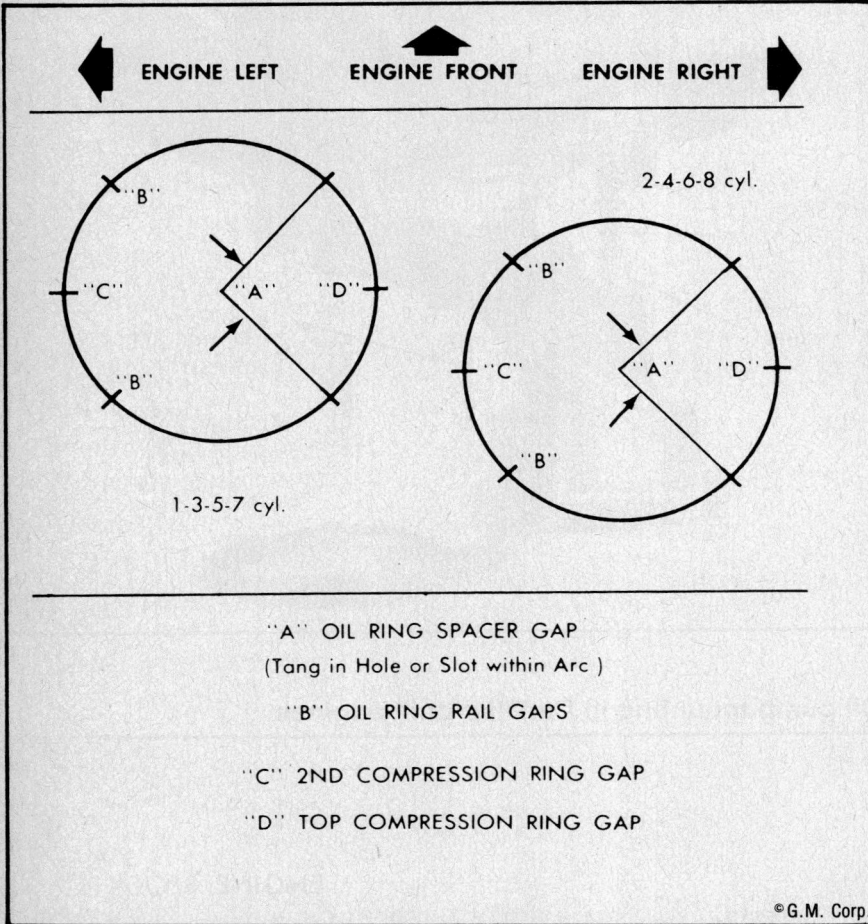

"A" OIL RING SPACER GAP

(Tang in Hole or Slot within Arc)

"B" OIL RING RAIL GAPS

"C" 2ND COMPRESSION RING GAP

"D" TOP COMPRESSION RING GAP

© G.M. Corp.

Piston and Connecting Rod R&R

All GM Engines

- Remove intake manifold, head or heads.
- Remove oil pan.
- Remove oil pump assembly if necessary.

NOTE: Stamp cylinder number on the machined surfaces of the bolt bosses of the connecting rod and cap for identification when reinstalling. If the pistons are to be removed from the connecting rod, mark cylinder number on piston with a silver pencil or quick drying paint for proper cylinder identification and cap to rod location. The right bank is numbered 2-4-6-V6's and 2-4-6-8-V8's, left bank 1-3-5-V6's and 1-3-5-7-V8's.

- Remove rod bearing cap and bearing.
- Install guide hose over threads of rod bolts to prevent damage to bearing journal and rod bolt threads.
- Remove rod and piston assemblies through the top of the cylinder bore.
- On reinstallation space ring gaps at equal intervals around piston circumference.
- Be sure to install piston in its original bore, pistons must have the piston notch and the "F" facing the front of the engine.
- Install ring compressor over rings on piston.
- Lower piston and rod assembly into bore until ring compressor contacts block.
- Using wooden handle of hammer push piston into bore while guiding rod onto journal.

Piston ring gap spacing—140 CID engine

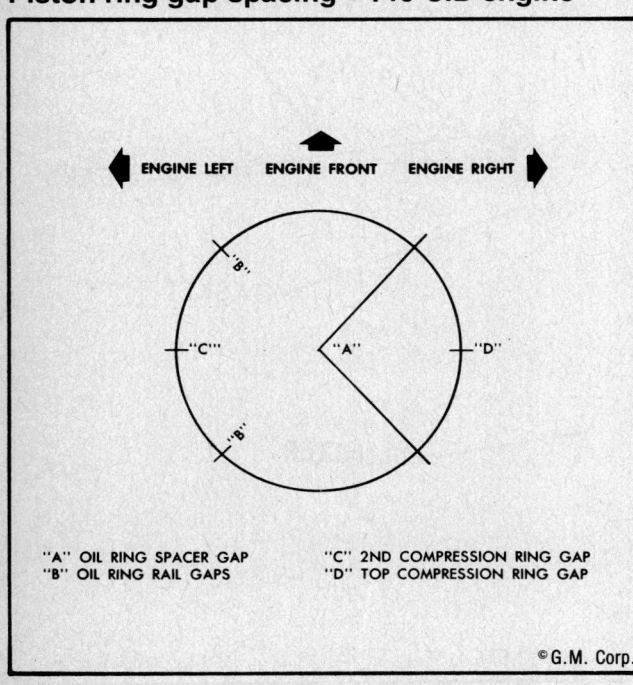

"A" OIL RING SPACER GAP
"B" OIL RING RAIL GAPS
"C" 2ND COMPRESSION RING GAP
"D" TOP COMPRESSION RING GAP

© G.M. Corp.

Piston ring gap spacing—85 and 97.6 CID engines

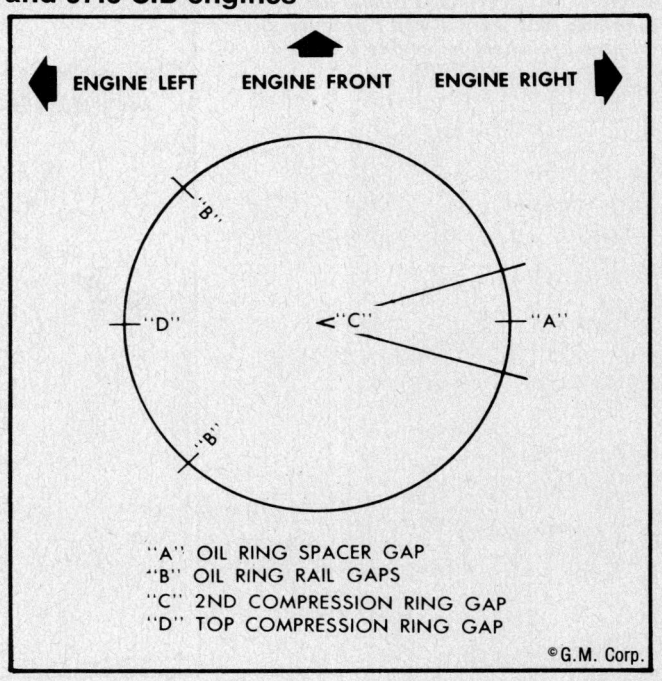

"A" OIL RING SPACER GAP
"B" OIL RING RAIL GAPS
"C" 2ND COMPRESSION RING GAP
"D" TOP COMPRESSION RING GAP

© G.M. Corp.

Piston and rod installation in Pontiac-built V8 engines

NOTE: NOTCH ON TOP OF PISTON FACES FRONT OF ENGINE, ALL MODELS

301 VIN CODE Y AND W NOTCHES ON RODS ALL FACE REARWARD

400 VIN CODE Z NOTCHES ON ROD FACE FORWARD ON RIGHT BANK AND REARWARD ON LEFT BANK

© G.M. Corp.

Piston ring gap positioning in Buick-built engines

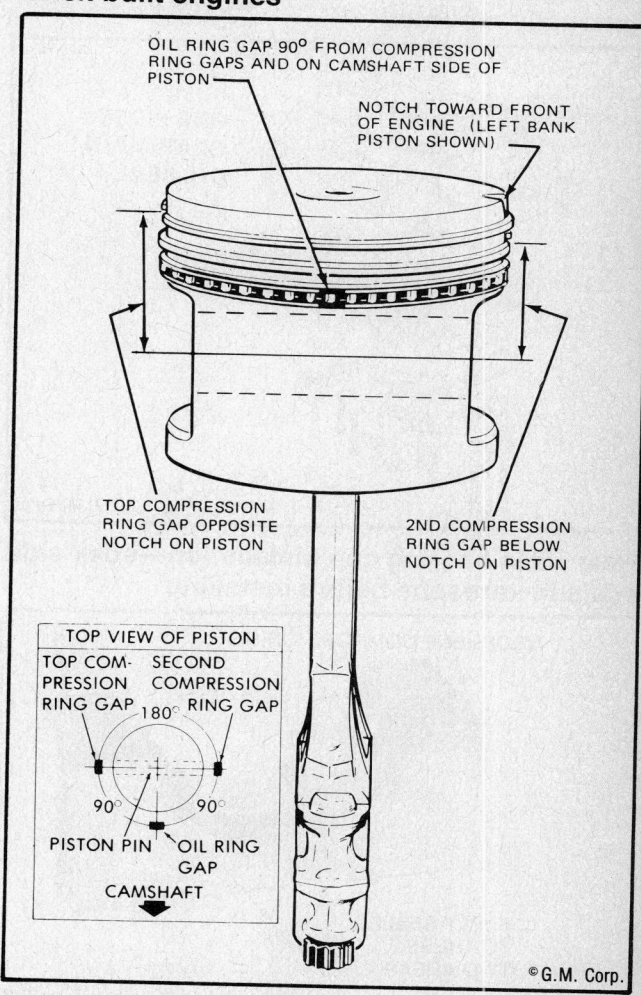

OIL RING GAP 90° FROM COMPRESSION RING GAPS AND ON CAMSHAFT SIDE OF PISTON

NOTCH TOWARD FRONT OF ENGINE (LEFT BANK PISTON SHOWN)

TOP COMPRESSION RING GAP OPPOSITE NOTCH ON PISTON

2ND COMPRESSION RING GAP BELOW NOTCH ON PISTON

TOP VIEW OF PISTON

TOP COMPRESSION RING GAP   SECOND COMPRESSION RING GAP

180°

90°   90°

PISTON PIN   OIL RING GAP

CAMSHAFT

© G.M. Corp.

Piston and rod installation in Buick-built V8 engines

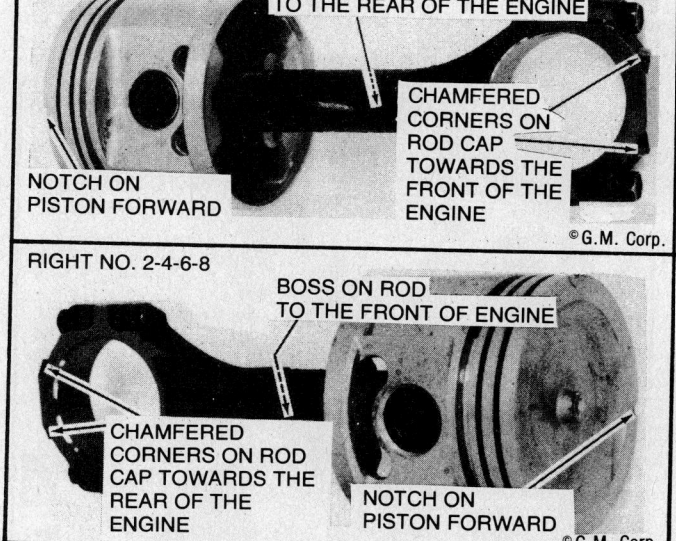

LEFT NO. 1-3-5-7

BOSS ON ROD TO THE REAR OF THE ENGINE

CHAMFERED CORNERS ON ROD CAP TOWARDS THE FRONT OF THE ENGINE

NOTCH ON PISTON FORWARD

© G.M. Corp.

RIGHT NO. 2-4-6-8

BOSS ON ROD TO THE FRONT OF ENGINE

CHAMFERED CORNERS ON ROD CAP TOWARDS THE REAR OF THE ENGINE

NOTCH ON PISTON FORWARD

© G.M. Corp.

Piston and rod installation in Buick-built V6 engines

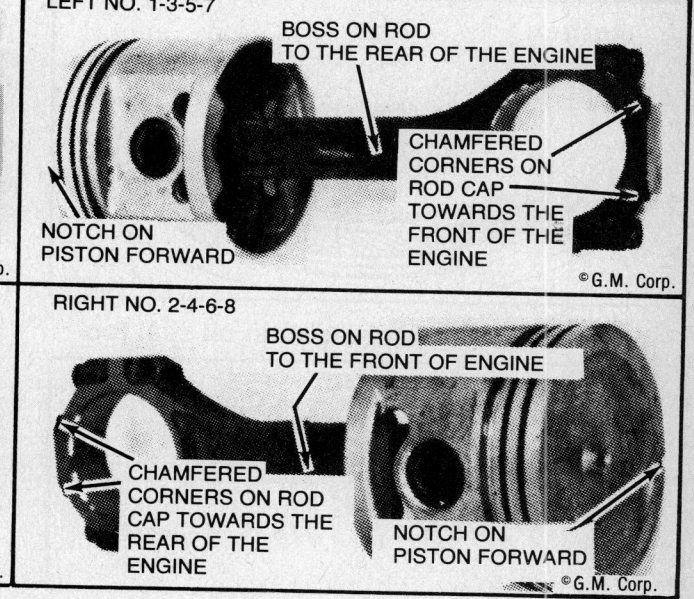

LEFT NO. 1-3-5-7

BOSS ON ROD TO THE REAR OF THE ENGINE

CHAMFERED CORNERS ON ROD CAP TOWARDS THE FRONT OF THE ENGINE

NOTCH ON PISTON FORWARD

© G.M. Corp.

RIGHT NO. 2-4-6-8

BOSS ON ROD TO THE FRONT OF ENGINE

CHAMFERED CORNERS ON ROD CAP TOWARDS THE REAR OF THE ENGINE

NOTCH ON PISTON FORWARD

© G.M. Corp.

Crankshaft rear oil seal used in "crossflow" 151 CID engine. The seal is externally mounted

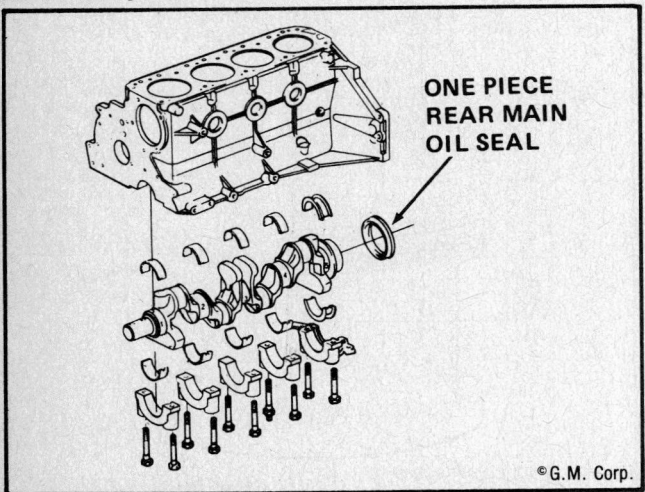

ONE PIECE REAR MAIN OIL SEAL

© G.M. Corp.

Rear main bearing cap installation—soak side seals in kerosene before installing

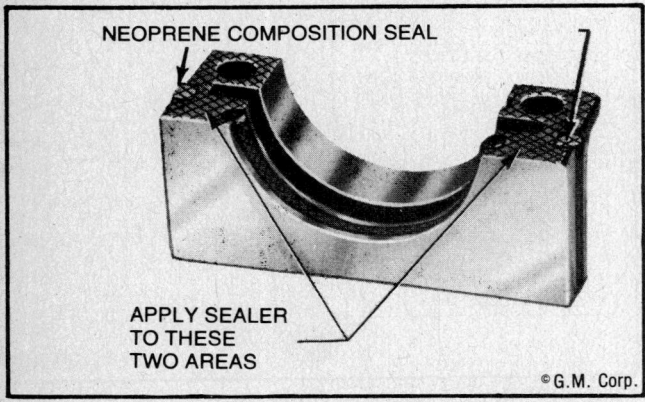

NEOPRENE COMPOSITION SEAL

APPLY SEALER TO THESE TWO AREAS

© G.M. Corp.

Crankshaft rear main oil seal used in engines not using braided fabric seal

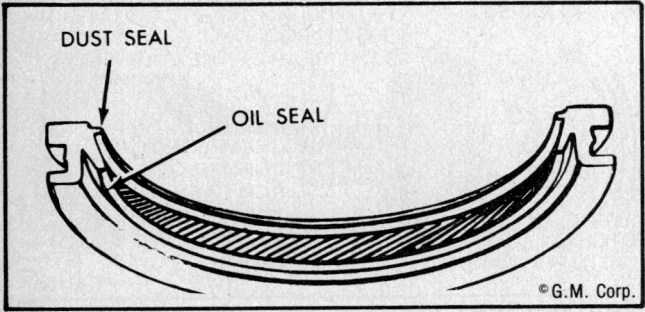

DUST SEAL

OIL SEAL

© G.M. Corp.

Fabricated crankshaft rear main oil seal tool

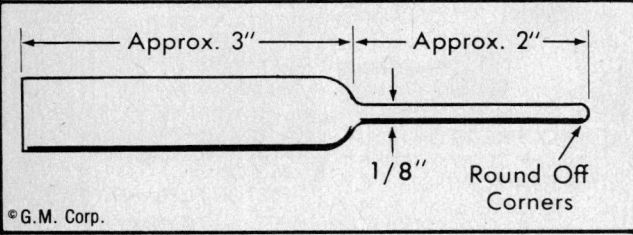

Approx. 3"   Approx. 2"

1/8"   Round Off Corners

© G.M. Corp.

Crankshaft Rear Main Oil Seal

NOTE: Chevette cars require engine removal for seal replacement. The four cylinder engine in "X" body cars uses a one-piece external seal.

All Except Engines Built By Buick, Oldsmobile and Pontiac

- The upper seal half can be replaced without removing the crankshaft.
- Use a blunt punch to tap the seal until it protrudes far enough to be pulled out with pliers.
- With the bearing cap loosely installed, move the crankshaft first to the rear and then to the front to position thrust surfaces (when installing).

Engines Built By Buick, Oldsmobile and Pontiac

- Braided fabric seals are used, and replacement requires crankshaft removal.
- To *repair* the seal upper half without removing the crankshaft, pack the old seal tightly up into its housing and fill in with cut sections from the old lower half seal.
- Soak new side seals in kerosene before installing, and apply room temperature vulcanizing sealant to bearing cap mating surfaces.

Crankshaft rear main bearing cap installation

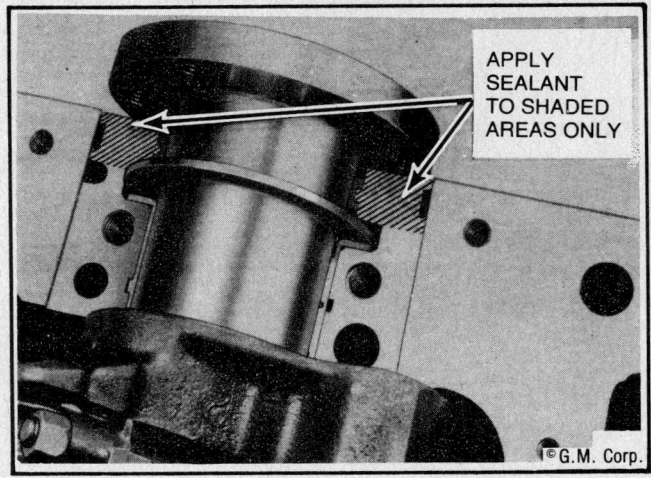

APPLY SEALANT TO SHADED AREAS ONLY

© G.M. Corp.

Braided fabric seal installation in rear bearing cap

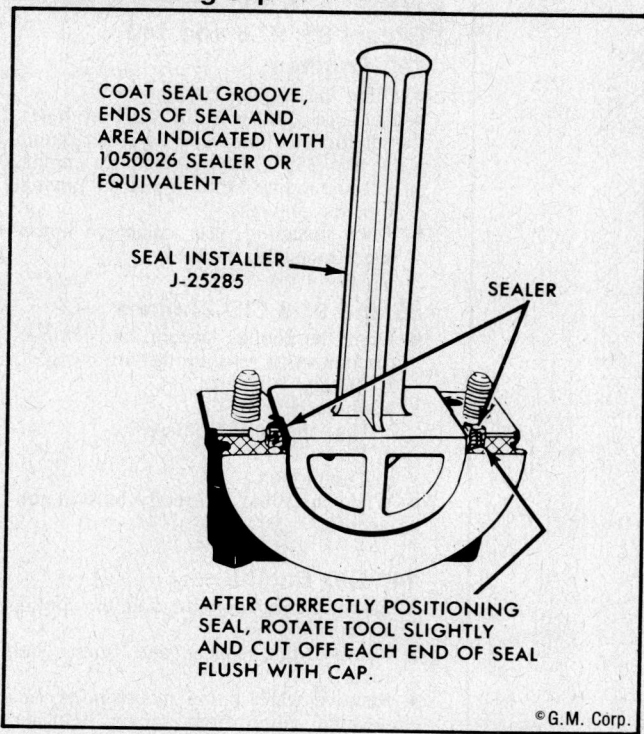

COAT SEAL GROOVE, ENDS OF SEAL AND AREA INDICATED WITH 1050026 SEALER OR EQUIVALENT

SEAL INSTALLER J-25285

SEALER

AFTER CORRECTLY POSITIONING SEAL, ROTATE TOOL SLIGHTLY AND CUT OFF EACH END OF SEAL FLUSH WITH CAP.

© G.M. Corp.

Braided fabric seal upper half installation

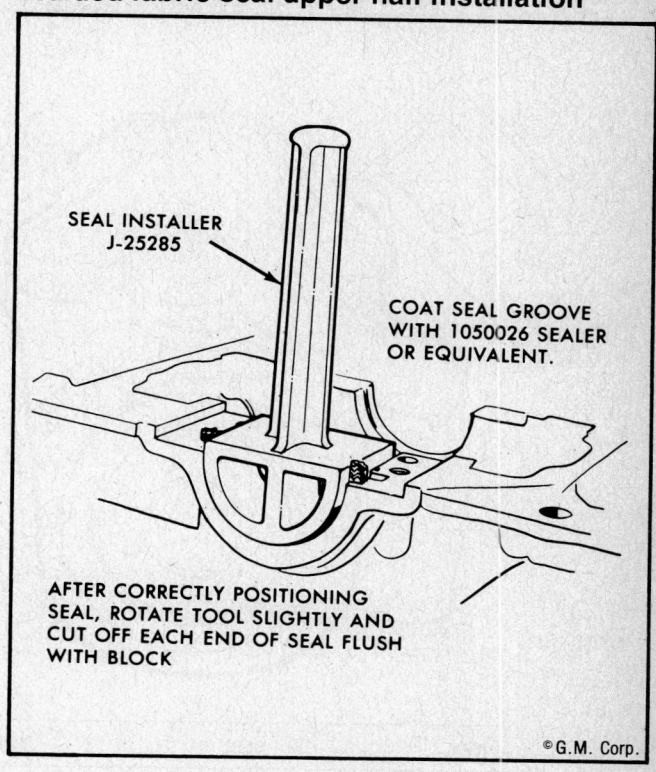

SEAL INSTALLER J-25285

COAT SEAL GROOVE WITH 1050026 SEALER OR EQUIVALENT.

AFTER CORRECTLY POSITIONING SEAL, ROTATE TOOL SLIGHTLY AND CUT OFF EACH END OF SEAL FLUSH WITH BLOCK

© G.M. Corp.

Packing crankshaft rear oil seal into housing to effect repair where braided fabric seal is used

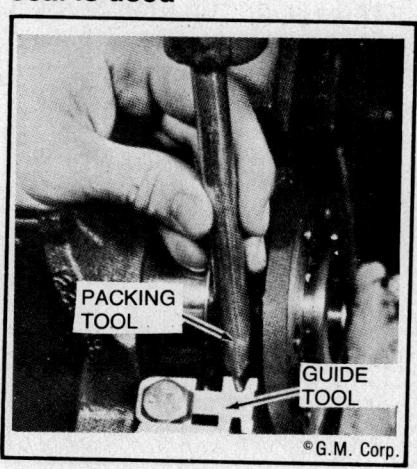

PACKING TOOL

GUIDE TOOL

© G.M. Corp.

Crankshaft installation—Oldsmobile-built engines

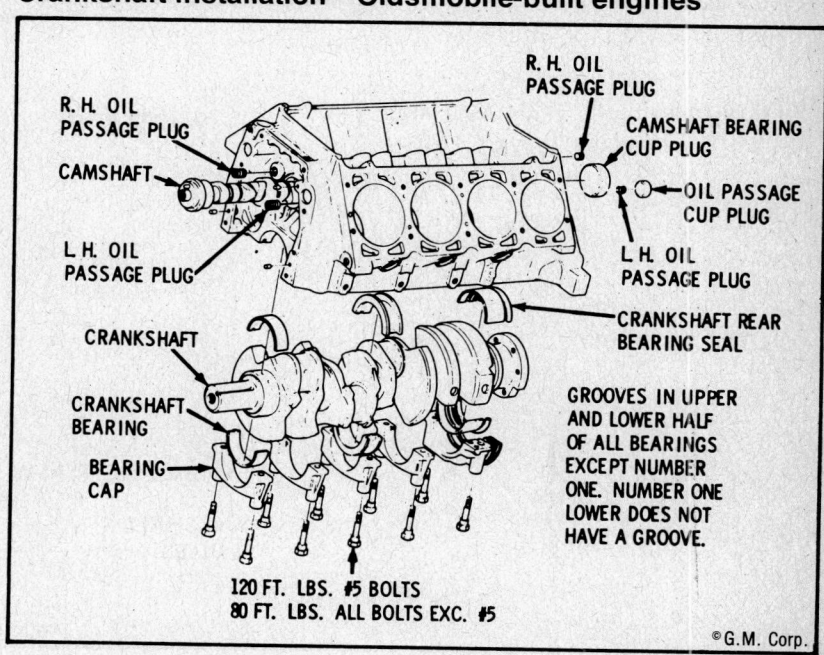

R. H. OIL PASSAGE PLUG

R. H. OIL PASSAGE PLUG

CAMSHAFT BEARING CUP PLUG

CAMSHAFT

OIL PASSAGE CUP PLUG

L. H. OIL PASSAGE PLUG

L. H. OIL PASSAGE PLUG

CRANKSHAFT REAR BEARING SEAL

CRANKSHAFT

CRANKSHAFT BEARING

BEARING CAP

GROOVES IN UPPER AND LOWER HALF OF ALL BEARINGS EXCEPT NUMBER ONE. NUMBER ONE LOWER DOES NOT HAVE A GROOVE.

120 FT. LBS. #5 BOLTS
80 FT. LBS. ALL BOLTS EXC. #5

© G.M. Corp.

GM GASOLINE ENGINES

Water pump mounting bolts in Oldsmobile-built engines

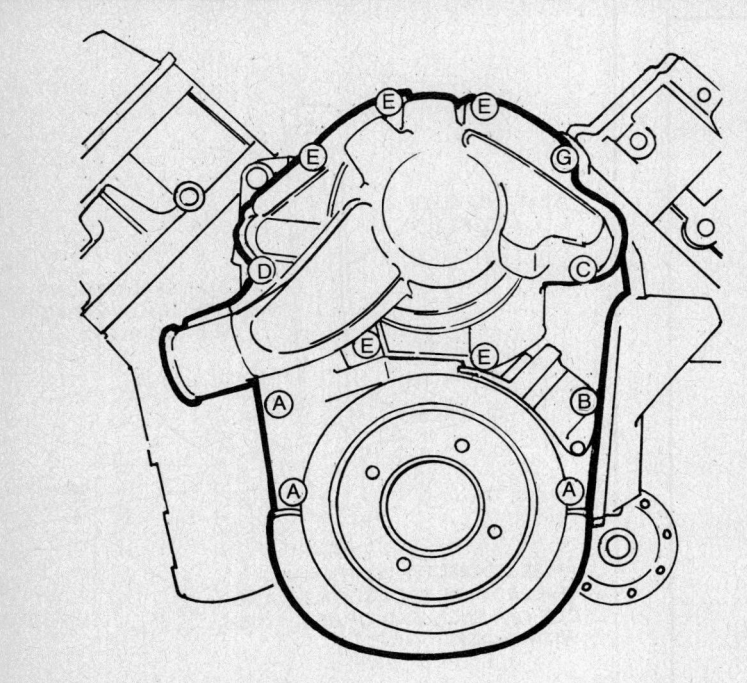

KEY	SIZE	TORQUE
A	3/8-16 x 3/4	35 ft.-lbs.
B	3/8-16 x 1 (stud head)	35 ft.-lbs.
C	5/16-18 x 1-1/2	22 ft.-lbs.
D	5/16-18 x 2-1/2	22 ft.-lbs.
G	5/16-18 x 1-1/2 (stud head)	22 ft.-lbs.

Fan-to-water pump mounting in Oldsmobile-built engines

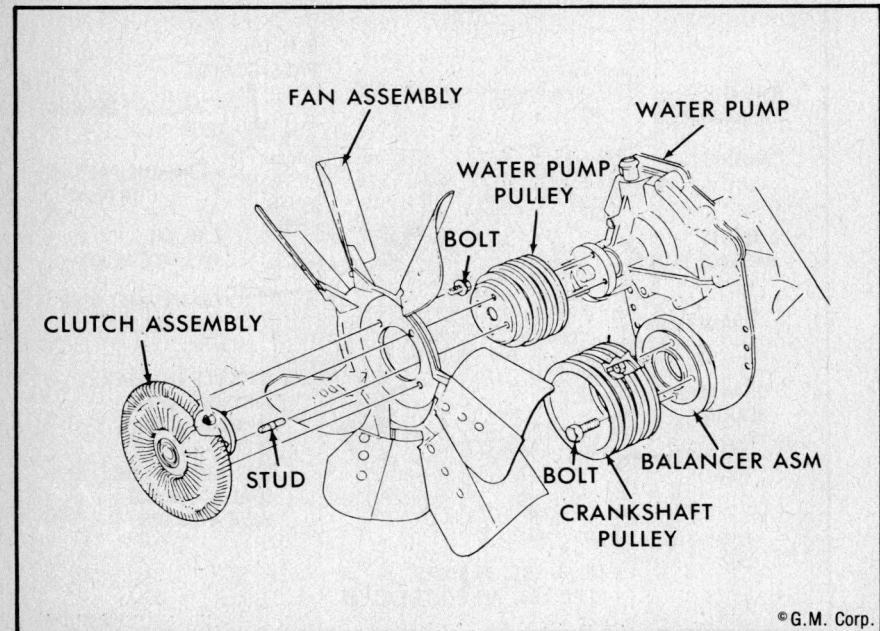

© G.M. Corp.

Water Pump

Except 85, 97.6 and 140 CID Engines
- Drain the cooling system.
- Remove fan shroud, drive belts, radiator, etc. for access to water pump.
- On the 250 CID, six cylinder engine, pull the pump straight out to prevent impeller damage.
- When installing, use sealant on appropriate mounting bolts.

85 and 97.6 CID Engines
- Drain the cooling system, and remove, disconnect or relocate the following:
  a. Battery
  b. Drive belts
  c. Fan, spacer and pulley
  d. Hoses
  e. Timing belt
- When installing, correctly tension timing belt.

140 CID Engine
- Disconnect battery and drain the cooling system.
- Remove fan, spacer and timing belt cover.
- Remove water pump mount bolts, and separate pump from timing belt and hoses.
- When installing, position water pump so it places 75-140 lbs. tension on the timing belt.

Water Pump

151 CID Engine

REMOVAL
1. Disconnect negative battery cable.
2. Remove accessory drive belts.
3. Remove water pump attaching bolts and remove pump.

INSTALLATION
If installing a new water pump, transfer pulley from old unit.

In Cadillac-built engines, use thread sealant on indicated water pump mounting bolts

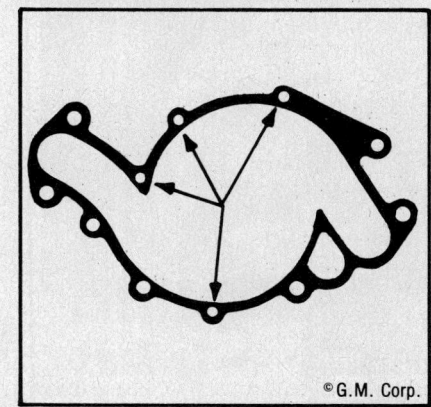

© G.M. Corp.

Water pump and fan installation in Cadillac-built engines

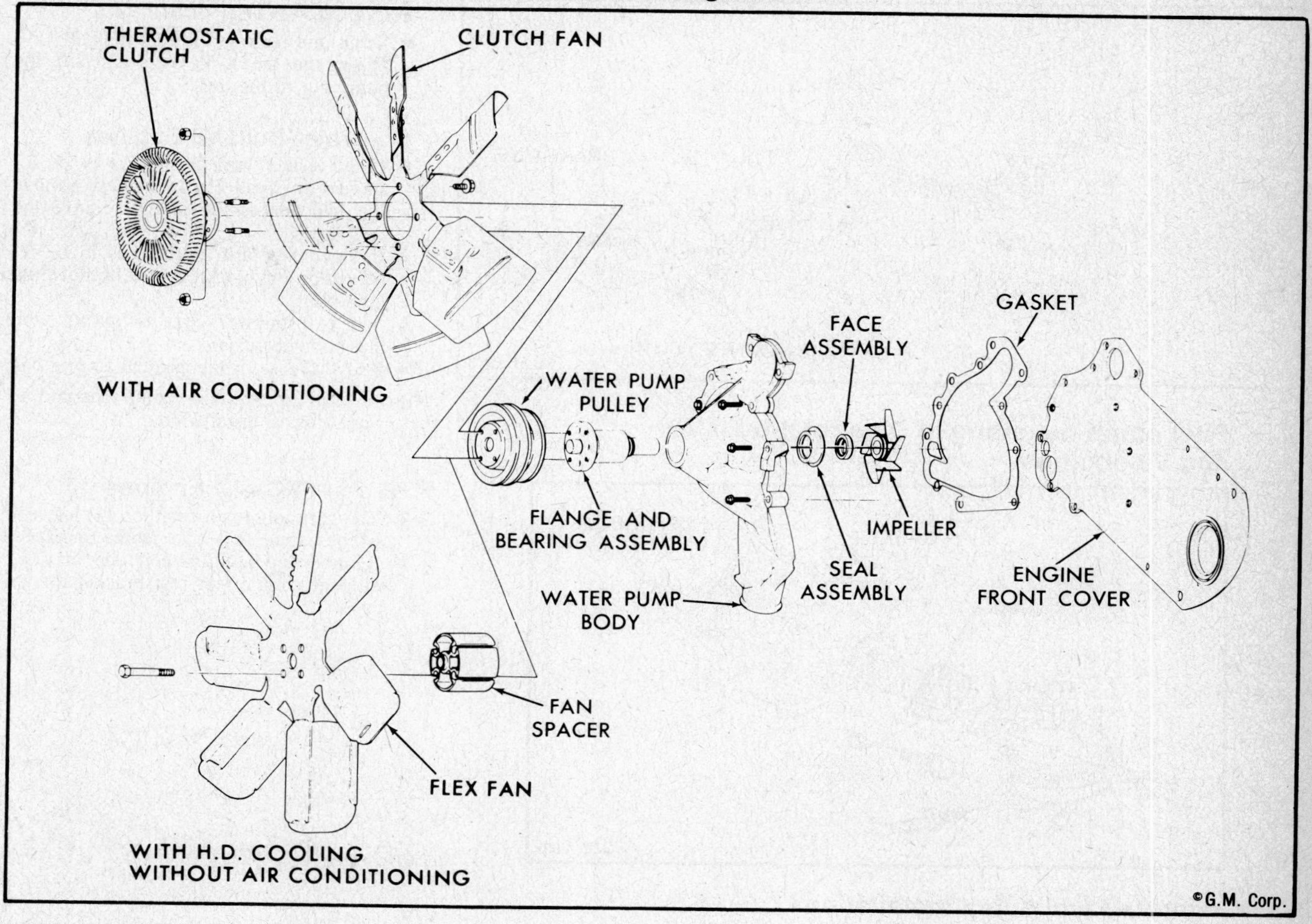

THERMOSTATIC CLUTCH

CLUTCH FAN

WITH AIR CONDITIONING

WATER PUMP PULLEY

FLANGE AND BEARING ASSEMBLY

WATER PUMP BODY

FACE ASSEMBLY

GASKET

IMPELLER

SEAL ASSEMBLY

ENGINE FRONT COVER

FAN SPACER

FLEX FAN

WITH H.D. COOLING WITHOUT AIR CONDITIONING

© G.M. Corp.

1. With sealing surfaces cleaned, place a 3 mm (⅛ in.) bead of sealant #1052289 or equivalent on the water pump sealing surface. While sealer is still wet, install pump and torque bolts to 25 N·m (6 lb.ft.).
2. Install accessory drive belts. Adjust to specification.
3. Connect negative battery cable.

173 CID Engine

NOTE: A special tool is necessary to hold the timing cover against the block (tool No. J-29167). This tool prevents the timing cover from moving when the pump attaching bolts are removed.

REMOVAL

1. Disconnect negative battery cable.
2. Drain cooling system and remove heater hose.
3. Remove water pump attaching bolts and nuts. Remove pump.

INSTALLATION

1. With the scaling surface cleaned, place a 2 mm (³/₃₂) in. bead of sealant.
2. Clean old sealant from the pump.
3. Coat bolt threads with pipe sealant.
4. Install the pump and torque the bolts.

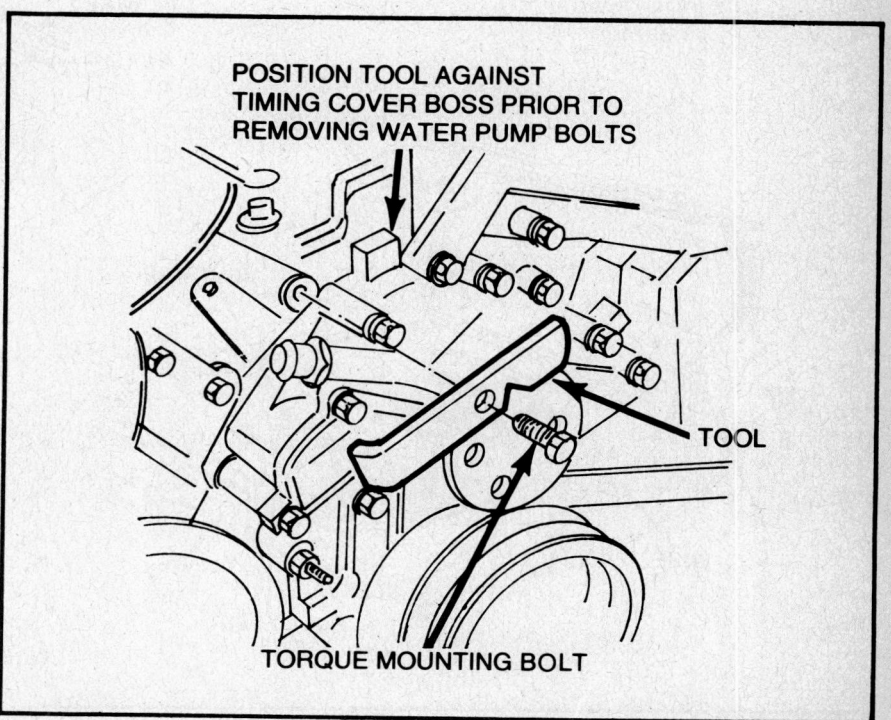

POSITION TOOL AGAINST TIMING COVER BOSS PRIOR TO REMOVING WATER PUMP BOLTS

TOOL

TORQUE MOUNTING BOLT

GM GASOLINE ENGINES

Chassis-mounted fuel pump installation

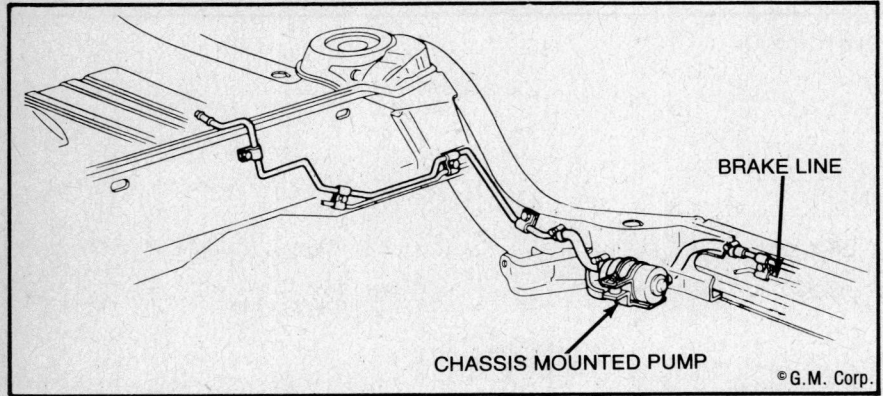

BRAKE LINE

CHASSIS MOUNTED PUMP

© G.M. Corp.

Fuel pump mounting in Chevrolet-built V6 and V8 engines

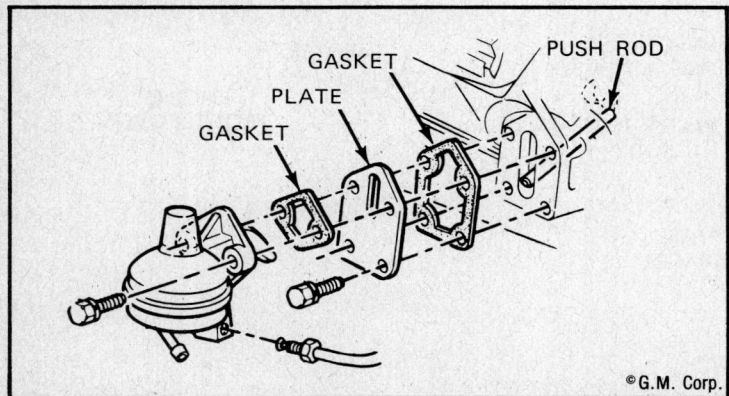

PUSH ROD

GASKET

PLATE

GASKET

© G.M. Corp.

TANK MOUNTED PUMP

- Drain and remove the fuel tank.
- Disengage the lock ring, and lift the pump out of the tank.

Chevrolet-Built V8 Engines

- If the rocker arm pushrod is to be removed on small block engines, remove the two adapter bolts and remove the adapter.
- If the rocker arm pushrod is to be removed on big block engines, remove the pipe plug.
- When installing, coat mounting bolt threads with sealer.
- Heavy grease or mechanical fingers can be used to hold the pump pushrod in place during installation.

85 and 97.6 CID Engines

- The fuel pump is located on the left side of the engine under the intake manifold.
- Remove the ignition coil and air conditioner compressor rear bracket for access.

Tank-mounted fuel pump installation

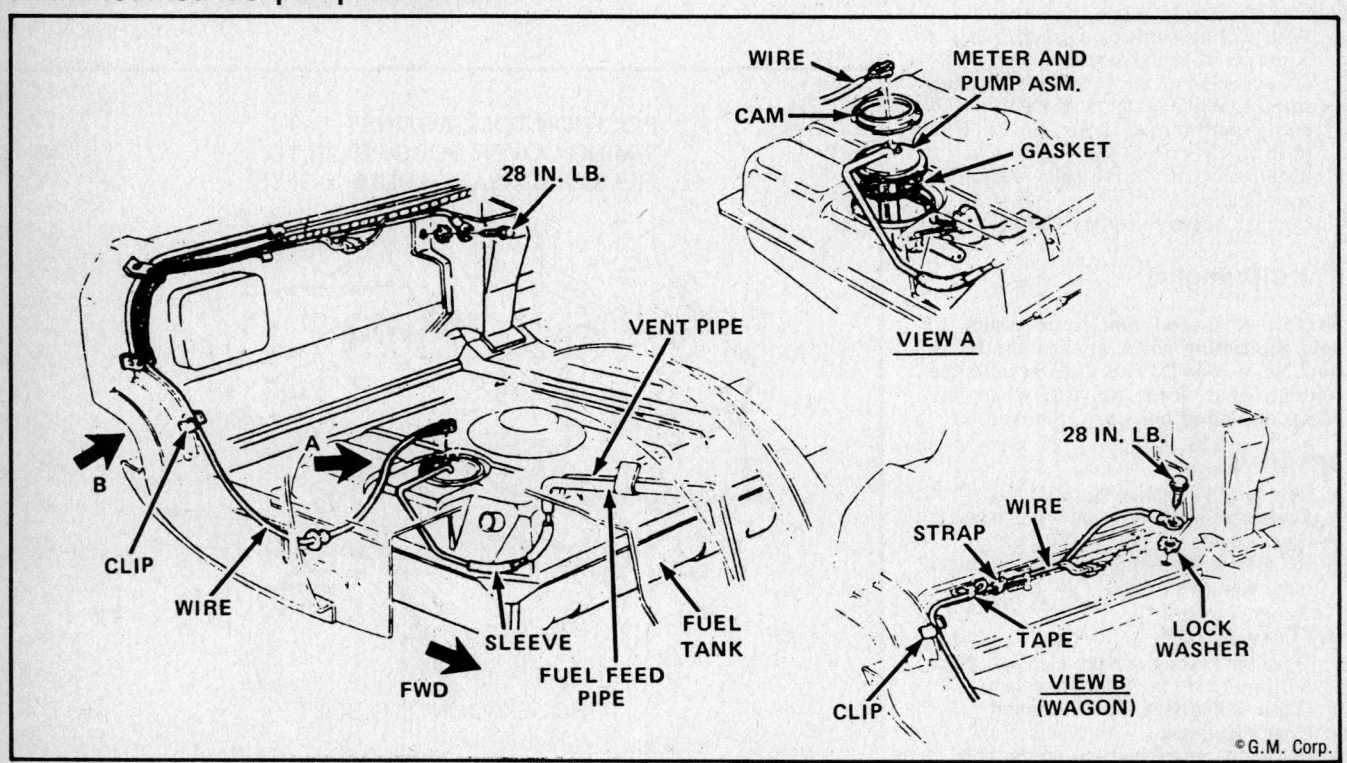

28 IN. LB.

VENT PIPE

WIRE

CAM

METER AND PUMP ASM.

GASKET

VIEW A

B

CLIP

WIRE

SLEEVE

FUEL FEED PIPE

FUEL TANK

FWD

A

28 IN. LB.

STRAP

WIRE

CLIP

TAPE

LOCK WASHER

VIEW B (WAGON)

© G.M. Corp.

OIL PAN AND ENGINE MOUNT SERVICES

Oil Pan Removal
Buick models except Skyhawk and 1980 X body all except 196, 231 and 250 CID engines
- Remove, disconnect or relocate anything necessary to facilitate engine raising and pan removal clearance such as fan shroud, starter exhaust plumbing, steering linkage, shift linkage, engine mounts, etc.
- On air conditioned vehicles, support the right side of the transmission when raising the engine to prevent cocking.
- On the 455 CID engine, remove the rear seal.
- Remove the flywheel cover and exhaust crossover pipe, and remove the oil pan.

Six Cylinder 250 CID Engine
NOTE: This removal procedure does not require engine removal, however, engine removal may require less effort.
- Remove radiator upper mounting panel or side mount bolts, and protect radiator from engine contact when the engine is raised.
- Remove, disconnect or relocate the following:
  a. Fuel line at pump
  b. Starter
  c. Flywheel or converter underpan
  d. Steering rod at idler lever
  e. Brake line-to-front crossmember
  f. Engine front mounts and left mount frame bracket
- With the torsional damper timing mark at six o'clock position, lower the oil pan by rolling it into the opening created by left engine mount removal.

V6 Engines
NOTE: Remove the engine from Riviera models.
- Remove the flywheel cover and exhaust crossover pipe, and remove the oil pan.

Cadillac
FRONT WHEEL DRIVE CARS
- Remove, disconnect or relocate the following:
  a. Starter
  b. Exhaust plumbing
  c. Idler arm support mounting screws from frame side member and lower support.
  d. Pitman arm at drag link
  e. Transmission lower cover
- Unbolt and remove oil pan.

Chevrolet Except Chevette, Monza, Vega and Citation
ALL EXCEPT 250 CID SIX CYLINDER AND BUICK BUILT V6 ENGINES
- With the Chevrolet-built engines in 1977 and later vehicles, remove, relocate or

disconnect the following:
  a. Oil dipstick tube
  b. Exhaust crossover pipe
  c. Converter housing cover
  d. Starter
- With the 1976 and earlier V8 engines except in Corvette, the engine must be raised. Remove, relocate or disconnect the following:
  a. Fan shroud
  b. Ignition distributor cap
  c. Exhaust plumbing
  d. Converter underpan
  e. Steering linkage
  f. Starter
- On the 454 CID engine in Chevelle, also raise the transmission rear end.
- In the Corvette it is necessary only to remove the oil dipstick tube and disconnect the steering linkage idler arm.

SIX CYLINDER 250 CID ENGINE
- Remove radiator upper mounting panel or side mount bolts, and protect radiator from engine movement when the engine is raised.
- Remove, relocate or disconnect the following:
  a. Fuel line at pump
  b. Starter
  c. Flywheel or converter underpan
  d. Steering rod at idler lever
  e. Brake line-to-front crossmember
  f. Engine front mounts and left mount frame bracket
- With the torsional damper timing mark at six o'clock position, lower the oil pan by rolling it into the opening created by left engine mount removal.

BUICK BUILT V6 ENGINES
- Remove the flywheel cover and exhaust crossover pipe, and remove the oil pan.

Chevette
- The engine must be raised to remove the oil pan.
- Remove, disconnect or relocate the following:
  a. Heater housing
  b. Radiator upper support and fan shroud
  c. Flywheel splash shield
  d. Rack and pinion-to-front crossmember bolts on manual transmission cars
- Raise the engine far enough to remove the oil pan.

Rear Wheel Drive Small Cars Except Chevette
FOUR CYLINDER ENGINES
- Support front of engine on all except 151 CID engine.
- Remove, disconnect or relocate any of the following necessary for oil pan removal clearance:
  a. Front and rear crossmember
  b. Idler arm
  c. Steering linkage pitman arm
  d. Exhaust pipe
  e. Starter
  f. Flywheel cover or converter underpan

Oil pan mounting in 151 CID engine

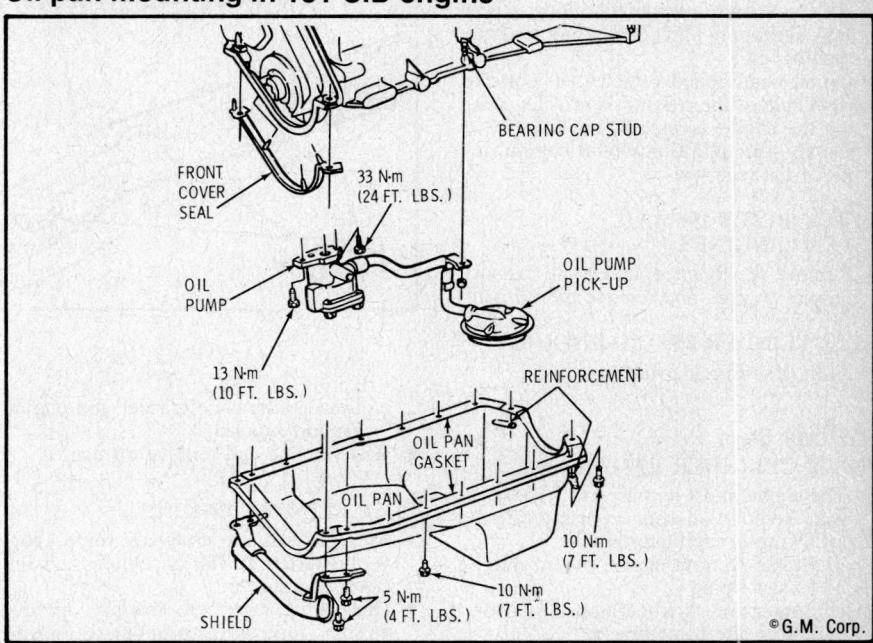

GM GASOLINE ENGINES

V6 AND V8 ENGINES

- Remove, disconnect or relocate any of the following necessary for oil pan removal clearance:
  a. Flywheel or converter cover
  b. Exhaust crossover pipe
  c. Steering idler arm
  d. Starter
- On V8 engines, support the front of the engine and remove the crossmember. (Scribe locating marks for installation reference.)

Oldsmobile Except Starfire and 1980 X Body

ALL EXCEPT 196, 231 AND 250 CID ENGINES

- Remove, disconnected or relocate anything necessary to facilitate engine raising and pan removal clearance such as fan shroud, starter, exhaust plumbing, steering linkage, shift linkage, engine mounts, vacuum pump, etc.
- On air conditioned cars, it may be necessary to support the right side of the transmission when raising the engine to prevent cocking.

V6 ENGINES

- Remove the flywheel cover and exhaust crossover pipe, and remove the oil pan.

SIX CYLINDER 250 CID ENGINE
NOTE: Use procedure listed under Buick.

Pontiac except Astre, Sunbird and 1980 X Body

ALL EXCEPT 196, 231 AND 250 CID ENGINES

- Remove, disconnect or relocate anything necessary to facilitate engine raising and pan removal clearance such as fan shroud, starter, exhaust plumbing, steering linkage, shift linkage, engine mounts, etc.
- On air conditioned vehicles, support the right side of the transmission when raising the engine to prevent cocking.
- On the 455 CID Buick-built engine, remove the rear seal.

BUICK-BUILT 196 AND 231 CID ENGINES

- Remove the flywheel cover and exhaust crossover pipe, and remove the oil pan.

SIX CYLINDER 250 CID ENGINE
NOTE: Use Buick procedure.

X Body Cars
FOUR CYLINDER ENGINE

- The engine must be raised to remove oil pan. Remove, disconnect or relocate the following to facilitate this:
  a. Cradle-to-front engine mount nuts
  b. Exhaust pipe
  c. Starter and flywheel housing cover
  d. Upper alternator bracket
  e. Lower alternator bracket and engine support bracket.
- Raise engine and remove oil pan.

SIX CYLINDER ENGINE

- Remove exhaust crossover pipe, converter/starter shield or clutch housing cover and starter.
- On manual transaxle models, remove engine mounting bracket-to-engine mount retaining nuts and raise front of engine far enough to facilitate oil pan removal.

Engine Mounts
Buick Except Skyhawk and 1980 X Body

- Support engine at forward edge of oil pan while changing a mount.

Oil pan mounting in Oldsmobile-built engines

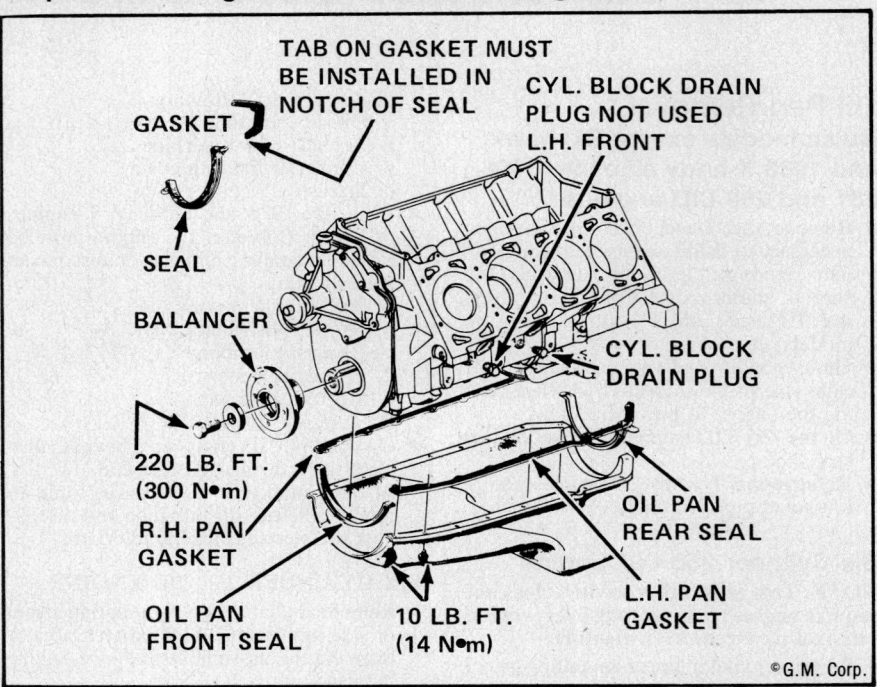

Front oil pan gasket sealing

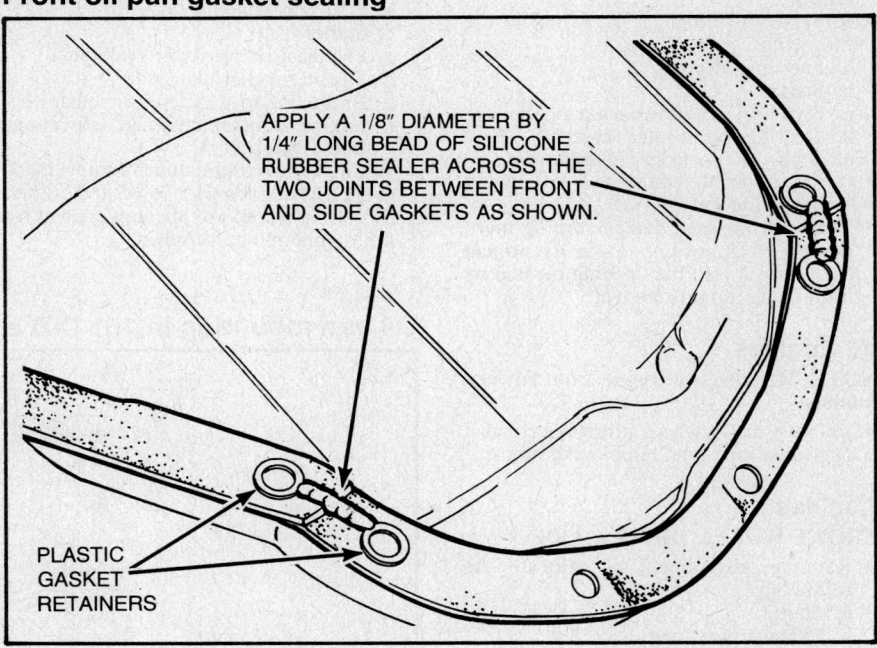

B384

Toronado and Eldorado engine mounts

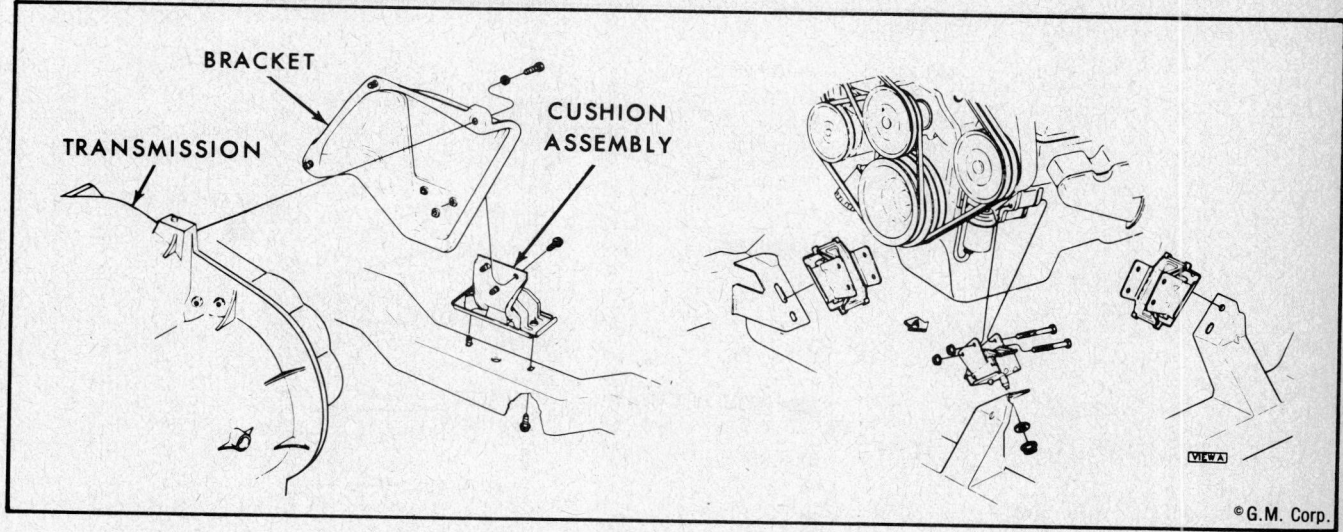

© G.M. Corp.

Cadillac
REAR WHEEL DRIVE MODELS
- Remove the radiator cover, wheelhouse struts and exhaust crossover pipe.
- Raise the engine to change the mount.

FRONT WHEEL DRIVE MODEL RIGHT MOUNT
- Remove the radiator cover.
- Remove the left and right engine mount nuts.
- Remove first the lower mounting bolt (from the rear), and then the upper mounting bolt.

- Raise the engine with a jack under the crankshaft pulley, and remove the mount.
- When raising the engine, watch for interference between the frame rail and right drive axle tripot housing. Such interference requires right drive axle removal. Also be cautious of the fuel lines which limit vertical movement.

FRONT WHEEL DRIVE MODEL LEFT MOUNT
- Remove the radiator cover.
- Disconnect transmission oil cooler lines from the final drive bracket.

- Remove the flex coupling shroud.
- Remove the cross bar mount securing bottom of final drive bracket to final drive. Remove bracket by tipping to rear and left of car.
- Raise engine and remove mount.

Chevrolet Except Chevette, Citation, Monza and Vega
- Raise the engine at either forward edge of oil pan or in the affected mount area.
- On some eight cylinder engines the fuel pump may have to be removed to change the right side mount.

Six cylinder, 250 CID engine mount installation

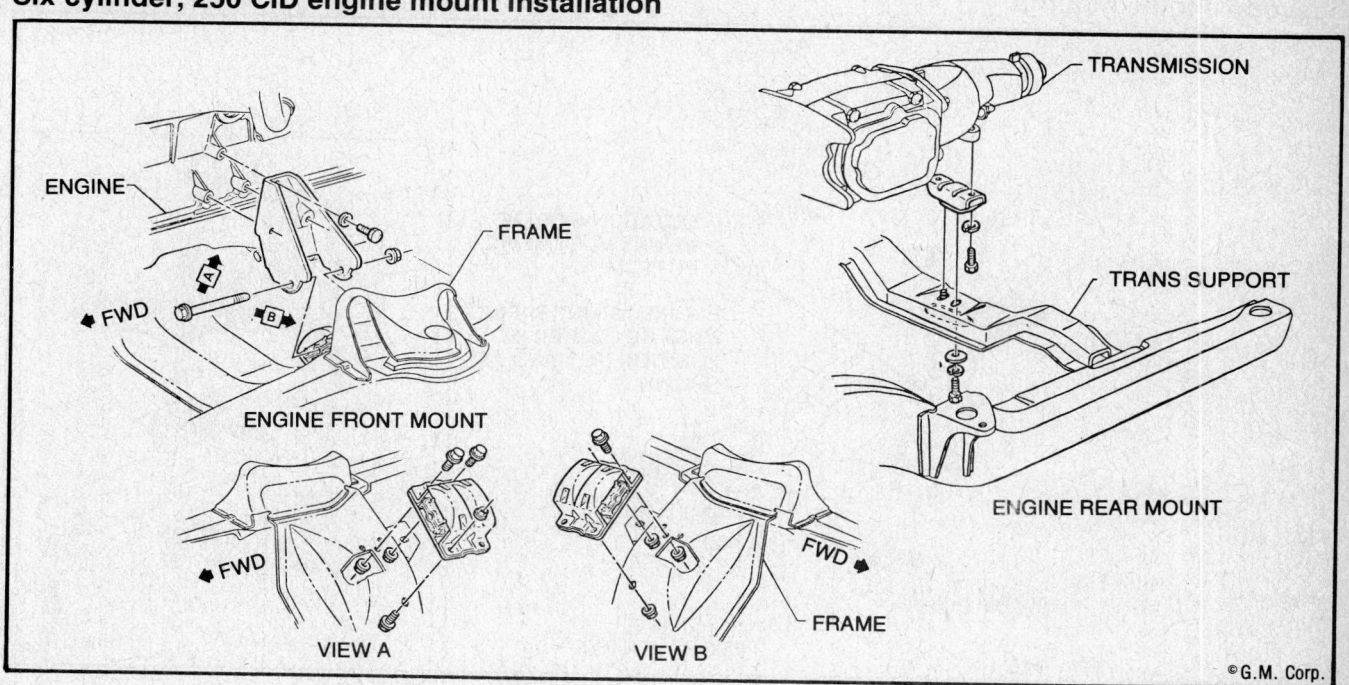

© G.M. Corp.

GM GASOLINE ENGINES

Engine and transmission mounts typical in V6 and V8 engines

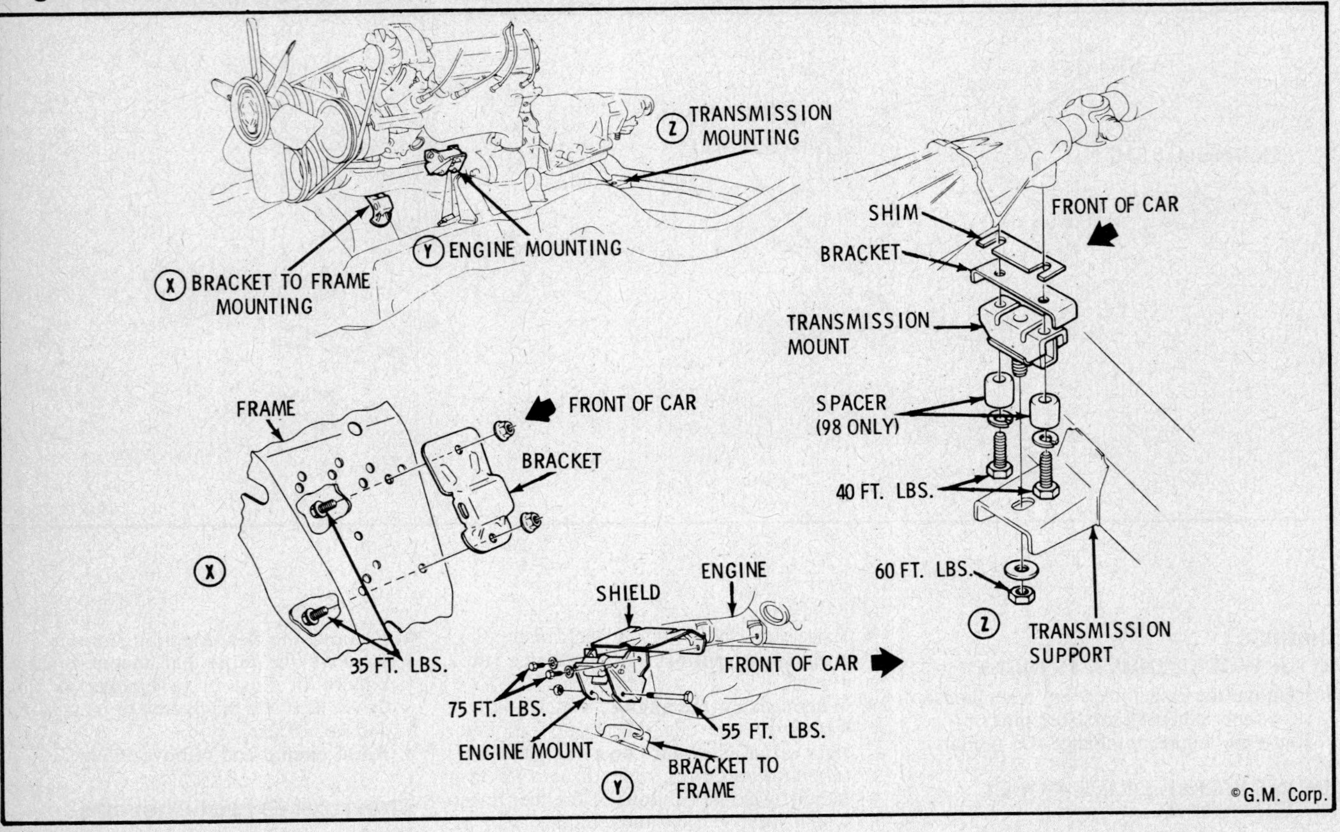

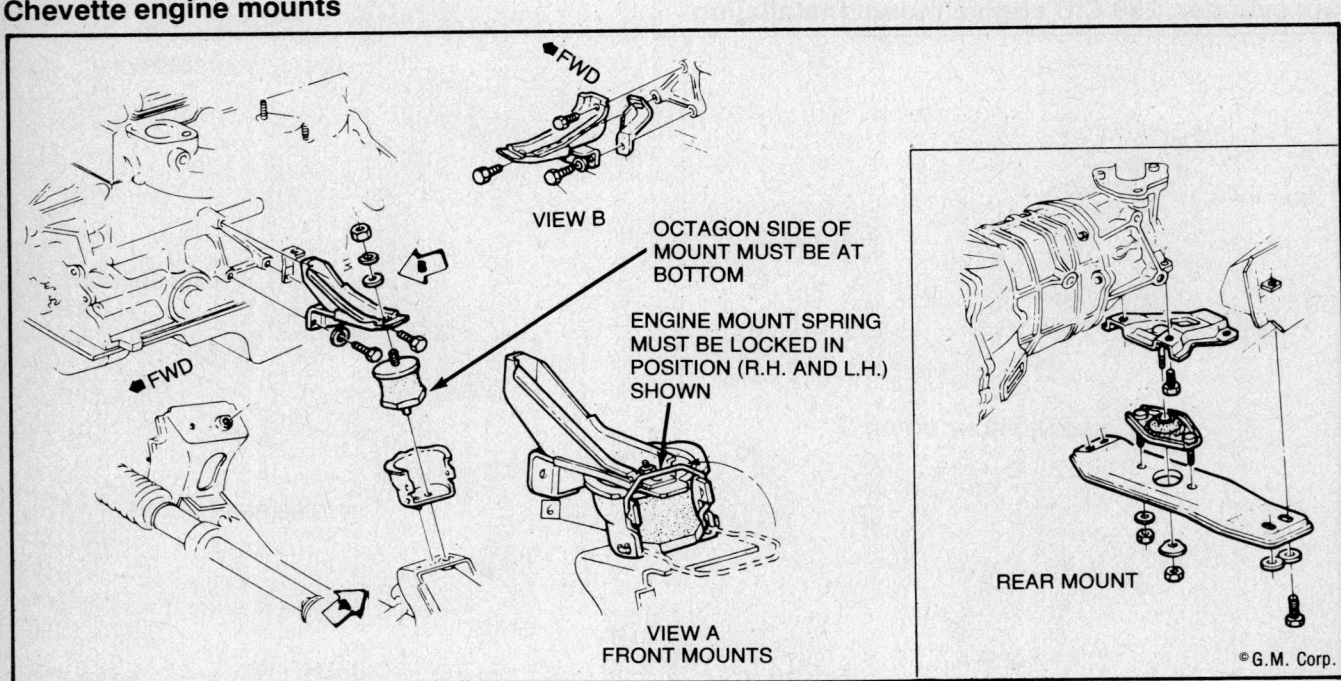

TRANSMISSION MOUNTING (Z)

X BRACKET TO FRAME MOUNTING

Y ENGINE MOUNTING

SHIM

BRACKET

FRONT OF CAR

TRANSMISSION MOUNT

SPACER (98 ONLY)

40 FT. LBS.

60 FT. LBS.

Z TRANSMISSION SUPPORT

FRAME

FRONT OF CAR

BRACKET

X

35 FT. LBS.

SHIELD

ENGINE

FRONT OF CAR

75 FT. LBS.

55 FT. LBS.

ENGINE MOUNT

BRACKET TO FRAME

Y

© G.M. Corp.

Chevette

FRONT

- Remove the heater and upper radiator support before raising engine far enough to remove the mount.

REAR

- Remove the crossmember-to-mount bolts, and support the transmission.

Chevette engine mounts

FWD

VIEW B

OCTAGON SIDE OF MOUNT MUST BE AT BOTTOM

ENGINE MOUNT SPRING MUST BE LOCKED IN POSITION (R.H. AND L.H.) SHOWN

FWD

VIEW A FRONT MOUNTS

REAR MOUNT

© G.M. Corp.

Engine front mount—140 CID engine

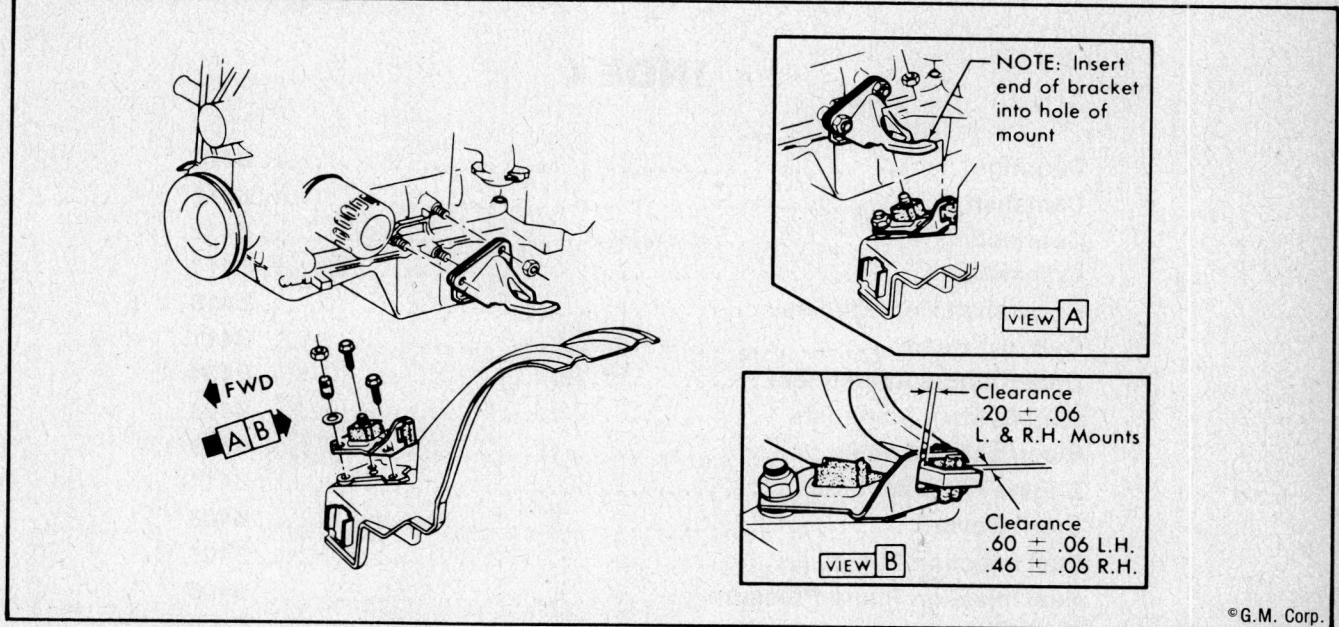

Rear Wheel Drive Small Cars Except Chevette

ALL EXCEPT 140 CID ENGINE

- Support engine in the area of the mount being changed, and separate the mount from its mounting bracket.

140 CID ENGINE

- Support the engine to take the weight off the front mounts. Remove the mount-to-engine bracket nut on the mount not being removed.
- It may be necessary to remove the starter brace or air conditioner compressor brace for clearance.

Oldsmobile Except Starfire

- Support the engine either in the area of the mount being changed or at the forward edge of the oil pan while changing a mount.

Pontiac Except Astre, Sunbird and 1980 X Body

NOTE: Use Oldsmobile procedure.

X Body Cars

FOUR CYLINDER ENGINE

- Remove chassis-to-mount attaching nuts.

- On air conditioned cars, remove forward torque reaction rod bolts at radiator support panel.
- Raise engine until mount is free of chassis.
- Remove two upper mount-to-engine support bracket nuts and remove mount.

SIX CYLINDER ENGINE

- Remove mount retaining nuts from below cradle mounting bracket.
- Raise front of engine and remove mount-to-engine bracket nuts, and remove mount.
- After installation, check transaxle mounts for correct alignment.

Engine rear mount—140 CID engine

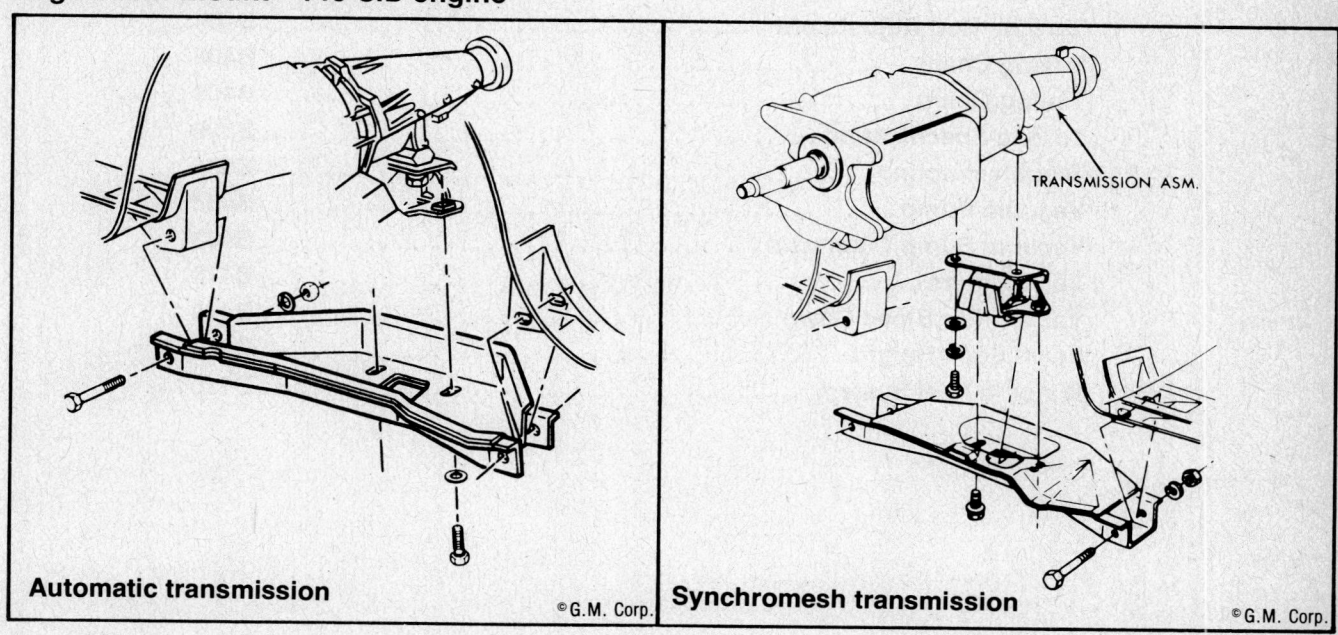

Automatic transmission   Synchromesh transmission

GM DIESEL ENGINES

INDEX

ENGINE SPECIFICATIONS

Engine VIN Code	Engine	Engine Mfg.	Tax H.P.	Horse-power @ rpm	Torque @ rpm (ft. lbs.)	Bore & Stroke (in.)	Comp. Ratio	Oil Capacity W/Filter Change	Fuel Pump Press. (psi)	Oil Press. @ 2000 rpm
N	350 (5.7L) V8	Olds.	52.7	125 @ 3600	225 @ 1600	4.057 x 3.385	22.5:1	6 qts.	5-6	30-45
V	262.5 (4.3L) V6	Olds.	39.2	NA	NA	4.057 x 3.385	21.6:1	6 qts.	5-6	30-45
T	262.5 (4.3L) V6	Olds.	39.2	NA	NA	4.057 x 3.385	21.6:1	6 qts.	5-6	30-45

CRANKSHAFT AND CONNECTING ROD SPECIFICATIONS

VIN Code	Engine	Engine Mounting	Bearing Number	Main Brg. Journal Diam.	Main Brg. Oil Clearance	Shaft End-Play	Thrust on No.	Journal Diameter	Oil Clearance	Side Clearance
				CRANKSHAFT				CONNECTING ROD		
N	350 (5.7L) V8	Longitudinal	1-4	2.9993-3.0003	.0005-.0021	.0035-.0135	3	2.1238-2.1248	.0005-.0026	.006-.020
			5	2.9993-3.0003	.0015-.0031					
V	262.5 (4.3L) V6	Longitudinal	1,2,4,5	2.9993-3.0003	①	.0030-.0135	3	2.2490-2.2510	.0005-.0026	.006-.020
			3	1.1985-1.2015	①					
T	262.5 (4.3L) V6	Transverse	1,2,4,5	2.9993-3.0003	①	.0035-.0135	3	2.2490-2.2510	.0005-.0026	.006-.020
			3	1.1985-1.2015	①					

① Main bearing clearance: no. 1, 2, and 3: .013-.053 mm (.0005-.0021 in.)
   no. 4 (rear): .051-.086 mm (.0020-.0034 in.)
Bearing shell width: no. 1 and 2: 24.638-24.892 mm (.970-.980 in.)
   no. 3: 30.302-30.353 mm (1.193-1.195 in.)
   no. 4: 32.26 mm (1.27 in.)

VALVE SPECIFICATIONS

VIN Code	Engine	Seat Angle (deg)	Face Angle (deg)	Spring Test Pressure (lbs. @ in.)	Spring Installed Height (in.)	STEM TO GUIDE CLEARANCE (in.) Intake	Exhaust	STEM DIAMETER (in.) Intake	Exhaust
N	350 (5.7L) V8	①	②	144-158 @ 1-3	1.67	.0010-.0027	.0015-.0032	.3425-.3432	.3425-.3427
V	262.5 (4.3L) V6	①	②	—	③	.0010-.0027	.0015-.0027	.3425-.3432	.3420-.3427
T	262.5 (3.4L) V6	①	②	—	③	.0010-.0027	.0015-.0035	.3425-.3432	.3420-.3427

① Intake 45°, exhaust 31°
② Intake 44°, exhaust 30°
③ Very critical, special tool (gauge) #B76428 or J-25289. If this measurement is less than .127 mm (.005 in.), a new valve should be installed. There must be a minimum of .762 mm (.030 in.) clearance between valve rotator and gauge. Failure to maintain this clearance will cause rocker arm and valve rotator interference.

GM DIESEL ENGINES

TORQUE SPECIFICATIONS
Readings in ft. lbs. (N•m)

VIN Code	Engine	Cylinder Head Bolts ①	Rod Bearing Nuts	Main Bearing Bolts	Crankshaft Pulley or Damper Bolt	Flywheel to Crankshaft Bolts	MANIFOLD ① Intake	MANIFOLD ① Exhaust
N	350 (5.7L) V8	130 (176)	42 (57)	120 (163)	200 (310)	60 (81)	40 (54)	25 (34)
V	262.5 (3.4L) V6	② ③	42 (57)	107 (145)	160 (217)	48 (65)	41 (55)	29 (39)
T	262.5 (4.3L) V6	③	42 (57)	107 (145)	160 (217)	48 (65)	—	—

① Clean and dip entire bolt in engine oil before tightening to obtain a correct torque reading.   ③ Use sealer on threads.
② Cylinder head bolts: Torque all bolts except 5, 6, 11, 12, 13 and 14 to 142 ft. lbs. (193 N•m).
    Torque bolts 5, 6, 11, 12, 13 and 14 to 59 ft. lbs. (80 N•m).

ENGINE TORQUE SPECIFICATIONS

Application	350 (5.7L) V8 VIN N Ft. Lbs.	350 (5.7L) V8 VIN N N•m	262.5 (4.3L) V6 VIN V LONGITUDINAL Ft. Lbs.	262.5 (4.3L) V6 VIN V LONGITUDINAL N•m	262.5 (4.3L) V6 VIN T TRANSVERSE Ft. Lbs.	262.5 (4.3L) V6 VIN T TRANSVERSE N•m
Fuel Pump						
Fuel pump to block bolt and nut	25	34	Electric		Electric	
Engine						
Controller (glow plug)	20	27	20	27	NA	NA
Injection pump attaching nuts	18	24	18	24		
Injection line nut to pump	25	34	35	48	35	48
Injection pump adapter bolts	25	34	22	30		
Injection line nut to nozzle	25	34	18	24	18	24
Injection pump fuel filter inlet line	20	27	20	27	20	17
Injection pump fuel filter outlet line	18	24	10	14	10	14
Injection pump fuel inlet line	20	27	20	27	20	27
Injection nozzle	25	34	25	34		
Glow plug	12	16	15	21		
Flywheel to converter	40	54	35	47	35	47
Flywheel to crankshaft	60	81	48	65	48	65
Oil pump to bearing cap bolts	35	47	18	24	18	24
Oil pump cover to pump bolts	8	11	8	11	8	11
Rocker arm pivot bolt to head	28	38	28	37		
Oil pan bolts	10	14	10	14	10	14
Oil pan drain plug	30	41	26	36	26	36
Crankshaft balancer to crankshaft bolt	200-310	271-420	160-350	217-475	160-350	217-475
Oil filter element to base	20	27	②	②	②	②
Oil filter assembly to cylinder block bolts	35	47	29	40	29	40
Oil cooler lines to oil filter base	12	16	29	40	29	40
Oil cooler lines to radiator	25	34	25	34	25	34
Front cover to cylinder block	35	47	41	55		
Fan driven pulley to hub bolts	20	27	20	27	20	27
Fan driving pulley to balancer bolts	20	27	20	27	20	27
Water pump to front cover bolts ③	13	18	21	28	NA	NA
Water outlet to manifold bolts	20	27	18	24	NA	NA
Engine mount to cylinder block bolts	75	102	37	50	37	50
Engine mount to frame mount	50	68	38	52	38	52
Starter to cylinder block bolts	35	47	20	27	20	27
Starter brace to cylinder block bolts	25	34	29	40	29	40
Starter brace to starter bolt	15	20	13	17	13	17
Vacuum pump clamp to cylinder block bolt	17	23	18	Belt Driven	—	Electric
Camshaft sprocket bolt	65	88	64	87	64	87

① Clean and dip entire bolt in engine oil before tightening to obtain a correct torque reading   ③ Dip bolts in sealer
② ⅔ turn after gasket contact

B390

Longitudinal V6 Diesel Engine

Transverse V6 Diesel Engine

GENERAL DESCRIPTION

Electrical System

The diesel engine electrical system has a controller which regulates glow plug temperature, preglow time, wait light and afterglow time. It also consists of a lamp control relay, glow plug relay, glow plugs, fast idle relay, fast idle solenoid and coolant temperature switch.

Eight glow plugs are used to heat the pre-chamber to aid in starting. They are 6 volt heaters that turn on when the ignition key is turned to the "RUN" position prior to starting the engine. They remain on a short time after starting, then automatically turn off.

The 12 volt sealed top batteries connected in parallel are required for the higher electrical load due to glow plugs and starter. The starter is larger and designed to crank the engine at least the 100 rpm required for starting. The two batteries, one on each side in the engine compartment, provide the required capacity and eliminate the need for a single double-size special battery.

A 12 volt alternator supplies charging current to both batteries at the same time. There are no switches or relays in the charging circuit.

The controller is located in the front water passage of the intake manifold. It senses coolant temperature and glow plug current to determine preglow and afterglow time periods. It also signals the lamp control relay to turn off the wait light.

The lamp control relay is located on the dash panel. It responds to the control signal to turn the wait lamp off, telling the driver the engine is ready to be started.

The fast idle solenoid is located on the dash panel. It feeds current to the fast idle solenoid when the engine is cold.

Located on the left rear of the intake manifold, the coolant temperature switch closes to complete the fast idle relay circuit. When the coolant temperature reaches about 120°F, the switch opens to reduce idle speed.

The glow plug relay is located on the right fender filler panel and is pulsed off and on by the controller to keep glow plug voltage at 6 volts.

Cooling System

Engine cooling is the same as used in the gasoline engine except the radiator tank has two oil coolers. One is connected to the transmission, the other one connects into the oil filter base.

Lubrication System

Oil pressure is provided by a gear-type oil pump driven off the camshaft and is bolted to the rear main bearing cap. Pressurized oil passes through the oil filter on the right side of the engine block and then to the oil cooler, located in the radiator. In case of a cooler line restriction, a bypass valve opens in the oil filter base at 12 psi.

The fuel injection pump is lubricated by engine oil through a passage at the top of the front camshaft bearing. Oil exits the shaft portion of the driven gear through an angled passage to the rear driven gear bearing.

The oil pressure sending switch is located on the left front oil gallery. It is designed to light the warning lamp when pressure drops to 2–6 psi.

The vacuum pump is also lubricated by engine oil. The drive for the vacuum pump also drives the oil pump.

Diesel Engine Glow Plug Identification

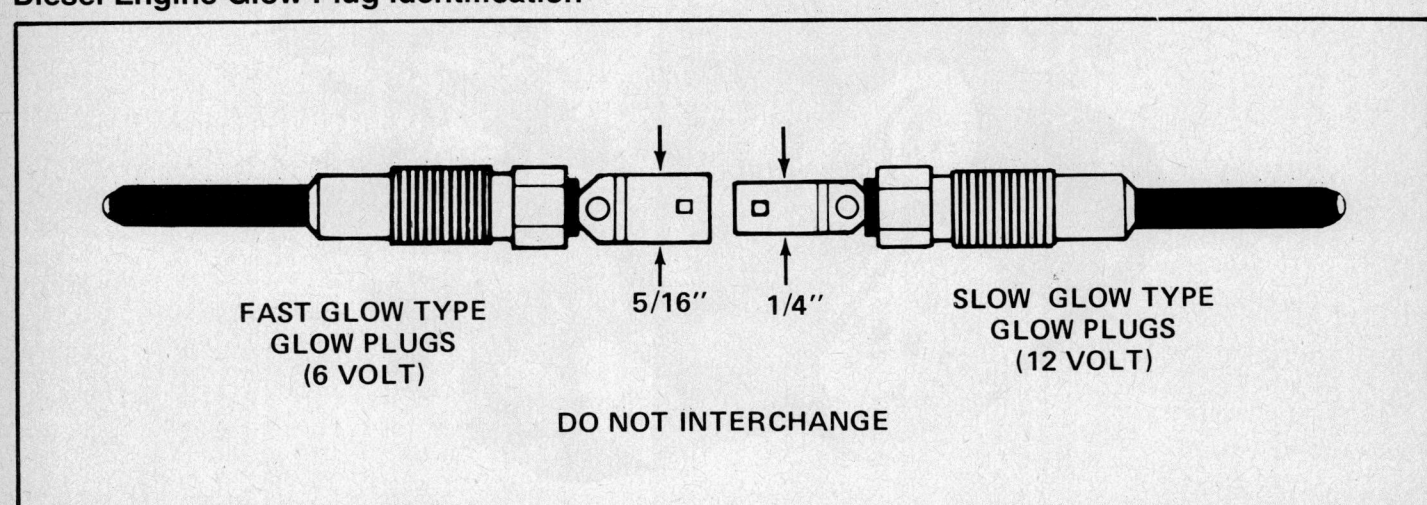

FAST GLOW TYPE GLOW PLUGS (6 VOLT)   5/16"   1/4"   SLOW GLOW TYPE GLOW PLUGS (12 VOLT)

DO NOT INTERCHANGE

Engine Lubrication

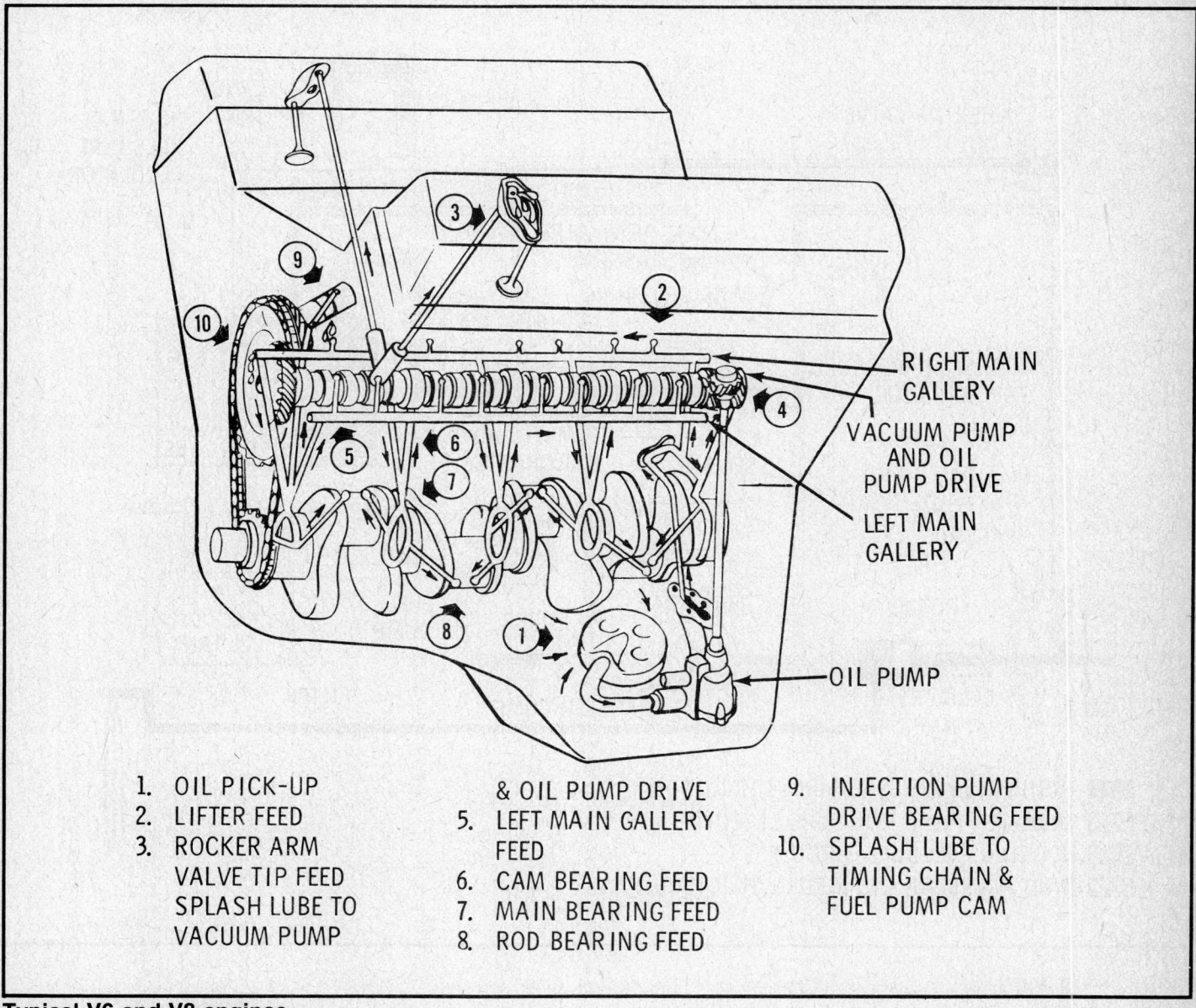

1. OIL PICK-UP
2. LIFTER FEED
3. ROCKER ARM VALVE TIP FEED SPLASH LUBE TO VACUUM PUMP
4. & OIL PUMP DRIVE
5. LEFT MAIN GALLERY FEED
6. CAM BEARING FEED
7. MAIN BEARING FEED
8. ROD BEARING FEED
9. INJECTION PUMP DRIVE BEARING FEED
10. SPLASH LUBE TO TIMING CHAIN & FUEL PUMP CAM

Typical V6 and V8 engines

Fuel System

The diesel fuel injection pump is gear driven off the camshaft and turns at camshaft speed. It is a high pressure rotary pump that injects a metered amount of fuel to each cylinder at the proper time. The eight high pressure delivery pipes from the pump to the injection nozzle in each cylinder are the same length to prevent any difference in timing, cylinder-to-cylinder.

The fuel injection pump provides the required timing advance under all operating conditions. Engine rpm is controlled by a rotary fuel metering valve. Pushing down on the accelerator pedal moves the throttle cable to open the metering valve and allow more fuel to be delivered. The injection pump also has a low pressure transfer pump to deliver fuel from the fuel line to the high pressure pump.

The fuel filter is located between the mechanical fuel pump and the injection pump. The diaphragm type mechanical fuel pump is mounted on the right side of the engine and driven by a cam on the crankshaft. The fuel tank is at the rear of the car, connected by fuel pipes and hoses to the mechanical fuel pump. Excess fuel returns from the fuel injection pump and injection nozzles to the fuel tank through pipes and hoses.

GM DIESEL ENGINES

Diesel Engine Fuel Circuit

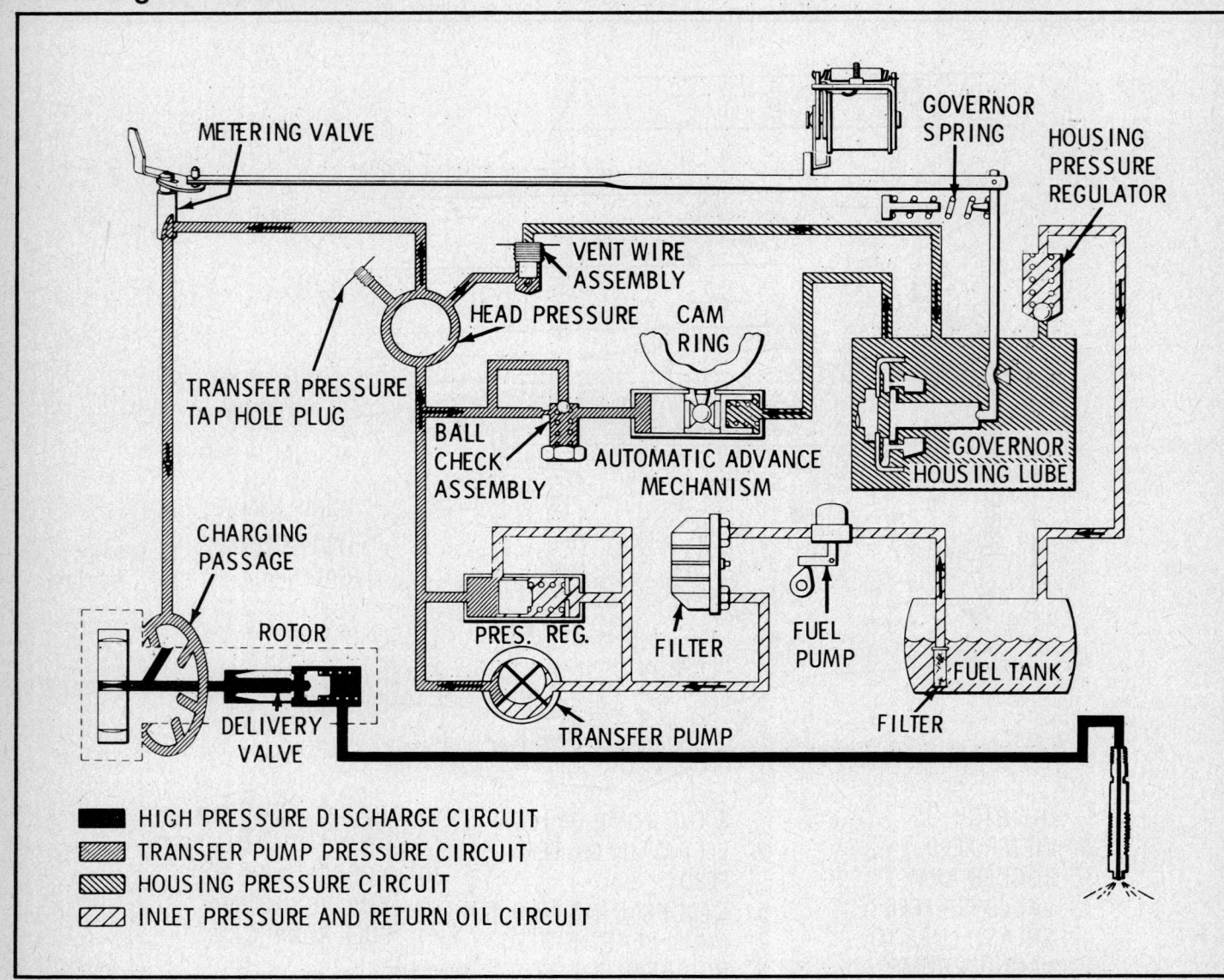

TROUBLESHOOTING ①
GM Diesel Engines

Condition	Cause	Correction
Engine will not crank	1. Loose or corroded battery cables	1. Check connections at batteries, engine block and starter solenoid.
	2. Discharged batteries	2. Check generator output and generator belt adjustment.
	3. Starter inoperative	3. Check voltage to starter and starter solenoid. If okay, remove starter for repair.
Engine cranks slowly, will not start (minimum engine cranking speed 100 rpm cold, 240 rpm hot)	1. Battery cable connections loose or corroded	1. Check connections at batteries, engine block and starter.
	2. Batteries undercharged	2. Check charging system.
	3. Wrong engine oil	3. Drain and refill with oil of recommended viscosity.

TROUBLESHOOTING ①
GM Diesel Engines

Condition	Cause	Correction
Engine cranks normally, will not start	1. Incorrect starting procedure	1. Use recommended starting procedure.
	2. No voltage to fuel solenoid	2. Connect a 12 volt test lamp from wire at injection pump solenoid to ground, turn ignition to "ON", lamp should light. If lamp lights, remove test light, connect and disconnect solenoid connector and listen for solenoid operation. If solenoid does not operate, remove injection pump for repair.
	3. Plugged fuel return system	3. Disconnect fuel return line at injection pump and route hose to a metal container. Connect a hose to the injection pump connection, route it to the metal container. Crank the engine, if it starts and runs, correct restriction in fuel return lines.
	4. No fuel to nozzles	4. Loosen injection line at a nozzle, do not disconnect. Use care to direct fuel away from sources of ignition. Wipe connection to be sure it is dry. Crank 5 seconds. Fuel should seep from injection line. Tighten connection. If fuel seeps, go to step 8.
	5. No fuel to injection pump	5. Remove line at inlet to injection pump fuel filter. Connect hose from line to metal container. Crank engine. If no fuel is discharged, test the engine fuel pump. (If fuel does not flow from pump outlet, go to step 6.) If the fuel pump is okay, check the injection pump fuel filter and, if plugged, replace it. If fuel filter and line to injection pump are okay, remove injection pump for repair.
	6. Restricted fuel tank filter	6. Remove fuel tank and check filter. Filter for diesel fuel is blue.
	7. Incorrect or contaminated fuel	7. Flush fuel system and install correct fuel.
	8. Pump timing incorrect	8. Make certain that pump timing mark is aligned with mark on adapter.
	9. Low compression	9. Check compression to determine cause.
Engine starts but will not continue to run at idle	1. Slow idle incorrectly adjusted	1. Adjust idle screw to specification.
	2. Fast idle solenoid inoperative	2. With engine cold, start engine; solenoid should move to hold injection pump lever in fast idle position.
	3. Restricted fuel return system	3. Disconnect fuel return line at injection pump and route hose to a metal container. Connect a hose to the injection pump connection, route it to the metal container. Crank the engine and allow it to idle. If engine idles normally, correct restriction in fuel return lines.
	4. Pump timing incorrect	4. Make certain that timing mark on injection pump is aligned with mark on adapter.
	5. Limited fuel to injection pump	5. Test the engine fuel pump, check fuel lines. Replace or repair as necessary.

TROUBLESHOOTING ①
GM Diesel Engines

Condition	Cause	Correction
Engine starts but will not continue to run at idle	6. Air in injection lines to nozzles	6. Loosen injection line at nozzle(s) and bleed air. Use care to direct fuel away from sources of ignition.
	7. Incorrect or contaminated fuel	7. Flush fuel system and install correct fuel.
	8. Injection pump malfunction	8. Remove injection pump for repair.
	9. Low compression	9. Check compression to determine cause.
	10. Fuel solenoid closes in run position	10. Ignition switch out of adjustment
Engine starts and idles rough without abnormal noise or smoke	1. Slow idle incorrectly adjusted	1. Adjust slow idle screw to specification.
	2. Injection line leaks	2. Wipe off injection lines and connections. Run engine and check for leaks. Correct leaks.
	3. Restricted fuel return system	3. Disconnect fuel return line at injection pump and route hose to a metal container. Connect a hose to the injection pump connection, route it to the metal container. Start the engine and allow it to idle. If engine idles normally, correct restriction in fuel return lines.
	4. Air in injection lines to nozzles	4. Loosen injection line at nozzle(s) and bleed air. Use care to direct fuel away from sources of ignition.
	5. Internal fuel leak at nozzle(s)	5. Disconnect fuel return system from nozzles on one bank at a time. Connect a hose to the injection pump fuel return line connection, route it to a metal container. Start engine and allow it to idle. Watch for normal fuel leakage at the nozzles. Replace any nozzle with excessive fuel leakage.
	6. Nozzle(s) malfunction	6. With engine running, loosen injection line fitting at each nozzle in turn. Use care to direct fuel away from sources of ignition. Each good nozzle should change engine idle quality when fuel is allowed to leak. It is possible for a nozzle to have an internal defect that allows too much fuel into the return fuel line. If this happens, the fuel delivery for the next nozzle in the firing order may be inadequate. This may result in a miss at idle. If a miss is isolated to a specific cylinder, it may be the previous nozzle in the firing order that contains a defect. If nozzle is found that does not change idle quality, it should be replaced.
	7. Incorrect or contaminated fuel	7. Flush fuel system and install correct fuel.
	8. Uneven fuel distribution to cylinders	8. Install new or reconditioned nozzles, one at a time, until condition is corrected as indicated by normal idle.
Engine starts and idles rough with excessive noise and/or smoke	1. Injection pump timing incorrect	1. Be sure timing mark on injection pump is aligned with mark on adapter.
	2. Air in injection lines to nozzles	2. Loosen injection line at nozzle(s) and bleed air. Use care to direct fuel away from sources of ignition.

TROUBLESHOOTING ①
GM Diesel Engines

Condition	Cause	Correction
Engine starts and idles rough with excessive noise and/or smoke	3. Nozzle(s) malfunction	3. With engine running, loosen injection line at each nozzle, one at a time. Use care to direct fuel away from sources of ignition. Each good nozzle should change engine idle quality when fuel is allowed to leak. If a nozzle is found that does not affect idle quality or changes noise and/or smoke, it should be replaced.
	4. High pressure lines incorrectly installed	4. Check routing of each line, correct as required. Firing order is 1-8-4-3-6-5-7-2.
Engine misfires above idle but idles correctly	1. Plugged fuel filter	1. Replace filter.
	2. Incorrect injection pump timing	2. Be sure that timing mark on injection pump and adapter are aligned.
	3. Incorrect or contaminated fuel	3. Flush fuel system and install correct fuel.
Engine will not return to idle	1. External linkage binding or misadjusted	1. Free up linkage. Adjust or replace as required.
	2. Internal injection pump malfunction	2. Remove injection pump for repair.
Fuel leaks on ground, no engine malfunction	1. Loose or broken fuel line or connection	1. Examine complete fuel system, including tank, lines, injection and fuel return lines. Determine source and cause of leak and repair.
	2. Injection pump internal seal leak	2. Remove injection pump for repair.
Noticeable loss of power	1. Restricted air intake	1. Check air cleaner element.
	2. Restricted or damaged exhaust system	2. Check system and replace as necessary.
	3. Plugged fuel filter	3. Replace filter.
	4. Plugged fuel tank vacuum vent in fuel cap	4. Remove fuel cap. If loud hissing noise is heard, vacuum vent in fuel cap is plugged. Replace cap. (Slight hissing sound is normal.)
	5. Pinched or otherwise restricted return system	5. Examine system for restriction and correct as required.
	6. Restricted fuel supply from fuel tank to injection pump	6. Examine fuel supply system to determine cause of restriction. Repair as required.
	7. Incorrect or contaminated fuel	7. Flush fuel system and install correct fuel.
	8. Restricted fuel tank filter	8. Remove fuel tank and check filter. Filter for diesel fuel is blue.
	9. External compression leaks	9. Check for compression leaks at all nozzles and glow plugs. If leak is found, tighten nozzle clamp or glow plug. If leak does not stop at a nozzle, remove it and install a new carbon stop seal and compression seal.
	10. Plugged nozzle(s)	10. Remove nozzles. Have them checked for plugging and repair or replace.
	11. Low compression	11. Check compression to determine cause.
Rap from one or more cylinders (sounds like rod bearing knock)	1. Air in fuel system	1. Check for air leaks in fuel line and correct.
	2. Air in high pressure line(s)	2. Loosen injection line at nozzle(s) and bleed air at each cylinder determined to be causing noise. Use care to direct fuel away from sources of ignition.

TROUBLESHOOTING ①
GM Diesel Engines

Condition	Cause	Correction
Rap from one or more cylinders (sounds like rod bearing knock)	3. Nozzle(s) sticking open or with very low nozzle opening pressure	3. Loosen injection lines at nozzles one at a time. Noise will stop or change when line is loosened at bad nozzle. Remove nozzle for repair.
Objectionable overall combustion noise over normal noise level with excessive black smoke	1. Timing not set to specification	1. Make certain that timing mark on injection pump is aligned with mark on adapter.
	2. Internal engine problem	2. Check for presence of an excessive amount of oil in the air crossover. If present, determine cause and correct.
	3. Injection pump housing pressure out of specifications	3. Check housing pressure. If incorrect, replace fuel return line connector assembly.
	4. Injection pump internal problem	4. Remove injection pump for repair.
Internal or external engine noise	1. Engine fuel pump, generator, water pump, valve train, vacuum pump, bearings, etc.	1. Repair or replace as necessary. If noise is internal, see diagnosis for "Rap from one or more cylinders" and "Engine starts and idles rough with excessive noise and/or smoke."
Engine overheats	1. Coolant system leak, oil cooler system leak or coolant recovery system not operating	1. Check for leaks and correct as required. Check coolant recovery jar, hose and radiator cap.
	2. Belt slipping or damaged	2. Replace or adjust as required.
	3. Thermostat stuck closed	3. Check and replace if required.
	4. Head gasket leaking	4. Check and repair as required.
Instrument panel oil warning lamp on at idle	1. Oil cooler or oil cooler line restricted	1. Remove restriction in cooler or cooler line.
	2. Oil pump pressure low	2. Check and repair oil pump.

① Diesel engine mechanical diagnosis such as noisy lifters, rod bearings, main bearings, valves, rings and pistons is the same as for gasoline engines. This diagnosis covers only those conditions that are different for diesel engines.

Vacuum Circuit—Toronado

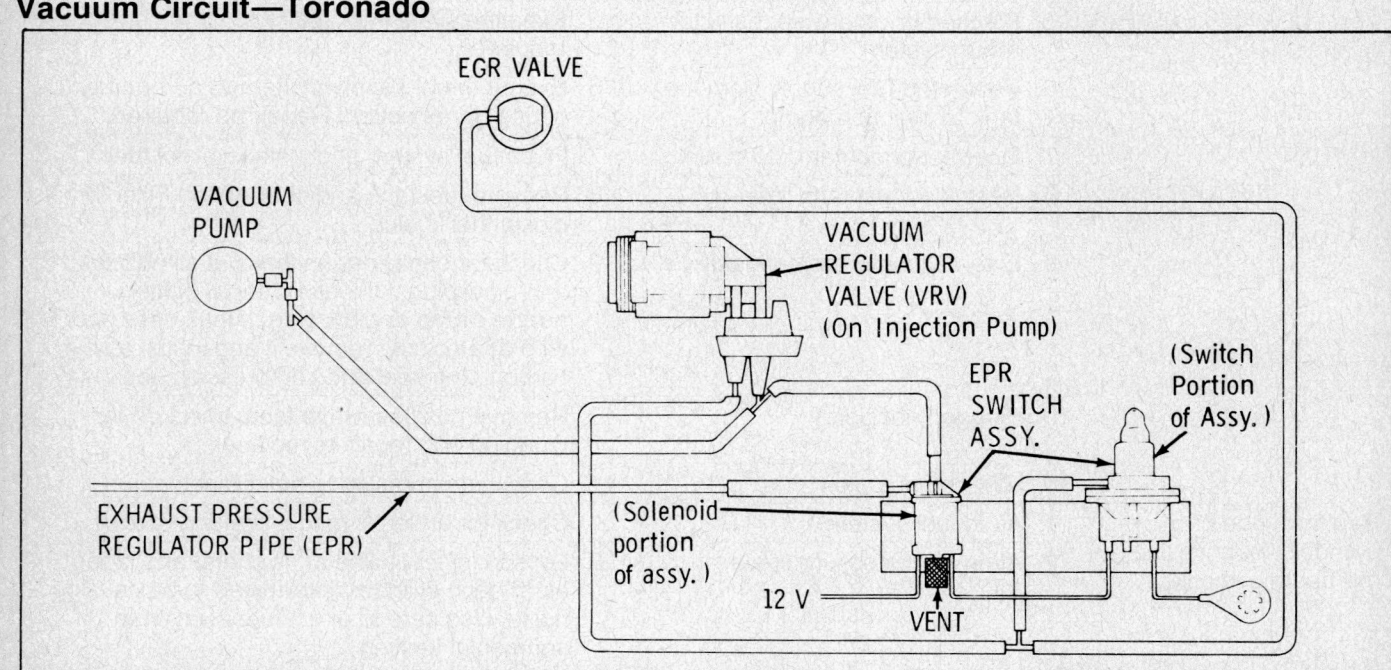

DIESEL ELECTRICAL SYSTEM DIAGNOSIS

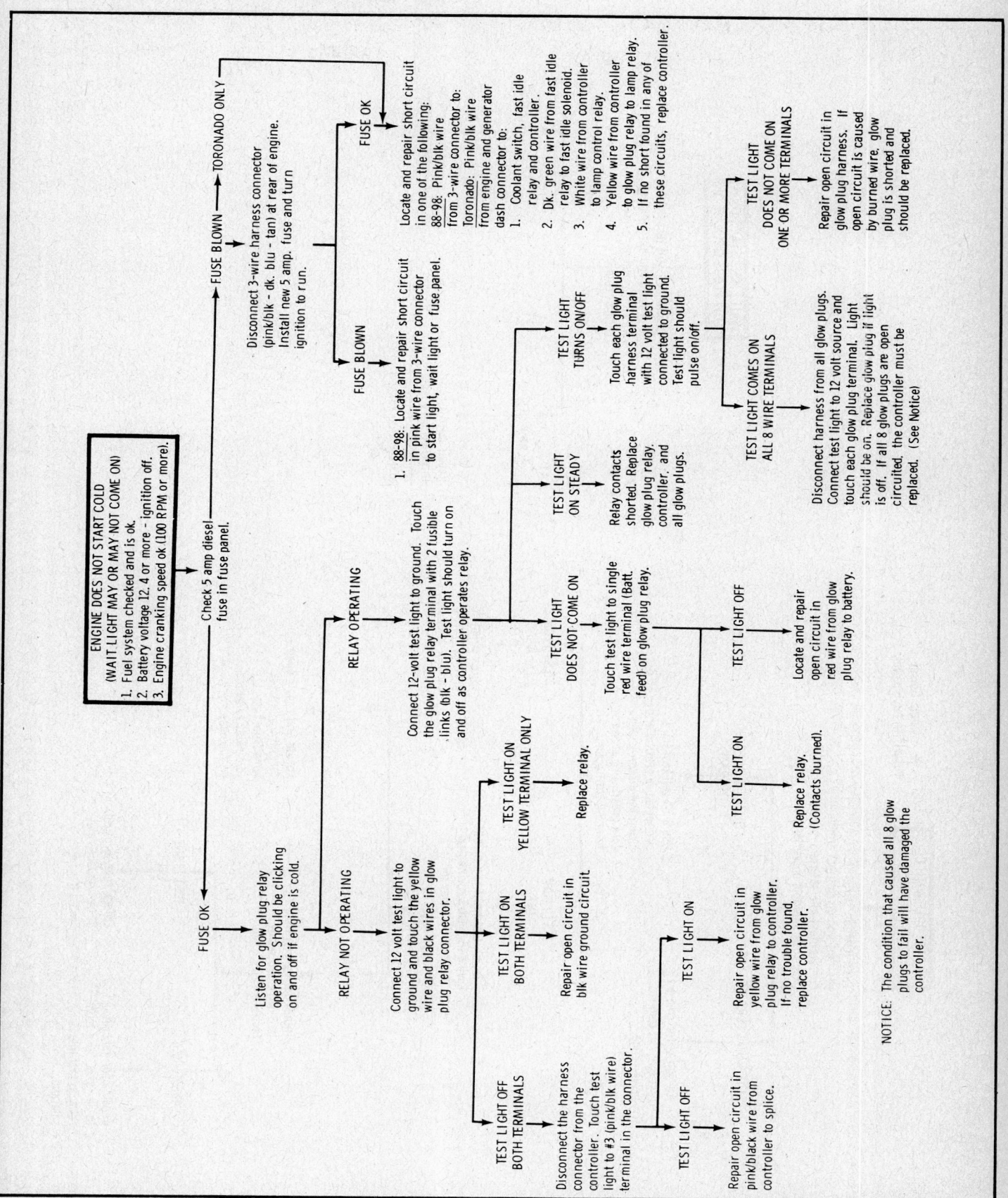

ENGINE DOES NOT START COLD
(WAIT LIGHT MAY OR MAY NOT COME ON)
1. Fuel system checked and is ok.
2. Battery voltage 12. 4 or more - ignition off.
3. Engine cranking speed ok (100 RPM or more).

Check 5 amp diesel fuse in fuse panel.

FUSE OK

Listen for glow plug relay operation. Should be clicking on and off if engine is cold.

RELAY NOT OPERATING

Connect 12 volt test light to ground and touch the yellow wire and black wires in glow plug relay connector.

TEST LIGHT OFF BOTH TERMINALS

Disconnect the harness connector from the controller. Touch test light to #3 (pink/blk wire) terminal in the connector.

TEST LIGHT OFF

Repair open circuit in pink/black wire from controller to splice.

TEST LIGHT ON

Repair open circuit in yellow wire from glow plug relay to controller. If no trouble found, replace controller.

TEST LIGHT ON BOTH TERMINALS

Repair open circuit in blk wire ground circuit.

TEST LIGHT ON YELLOW TERMINAL ONLY

Replace relay.

RELAY OPERATING

Connect 12-volt test light to ground. Touch the glow plug relay terminal with 2 fusible links (blk - blu). Test light should turn on and off as controller operates relay.

TEST LIGHT DOES NOT COME ON

Touch test light to single red wire terminal (Batt. feed) on glow plug relay.

TEST LIGHT OFF

Locate and repair open circuit in red wire from glow plug relay to battery.

TEST LIGHT ON

Replace relay. (Contacts burned).

TEST LIGHT ON STEADY

Relay contacts shorted. Replace glow plug relay, controller, and all glow plugs.

TEST LIGHT TURNS ON/OFF

Touch each glow plug harness terminal with 12 volt test light connected to ground. Test light should pulse on/off.

TEST LIGHT COMES ON ALL 8 WIRE TERMINALS

Disconnect harness from all glow plugs. Connect test light to 12 volt source and touch each glow plug terminal. Light should be on. Replace glow plug if light is off. If all 8 glow plugs are open circuited, the controller must be replaced. (See Notice)

TEST LIGHT DOES NOT COME ON ONE OR MORE TERMINALS

Repair open circuit in glow plug harness. If open circuit is caused by burned wire, glow plug is shorted and should be replaced.

FUSE BLOWN → TORONADO ONLY

Disconnect 3-wire harness connector (pink/blk - dk. blu - tan) at rear of engine. Install new 5 amp. fuse and turn ignition to run.

FUSE OK

Locate and repair short circuit in one of the following:
88-98: Pink/blk wire from 3-wire connector to:
Toronado: Pink/blk wire from engine and generator dash connector to:
1. Coolant switch, fast idle relay and controller.
2. Dk. green wire from fast idle relay to fast idle solenoid.
3. White wire from controller to lamp control relay.
4. Yellow wire from controller to glow plug relay to lamp relay.
5. If no short found in any of these circuits, replace controller.

FUSE BLOWN

1. 88-98: Locate and repair short circuit in pink wire from 3-wire connector to start light, wait light or fuse panel.

NOTICE: The condition that caused all 8 glow plugs to fail will have damaged the controller.

DIESEL ELECTRICAL SYSTEM DIAGNOSIS

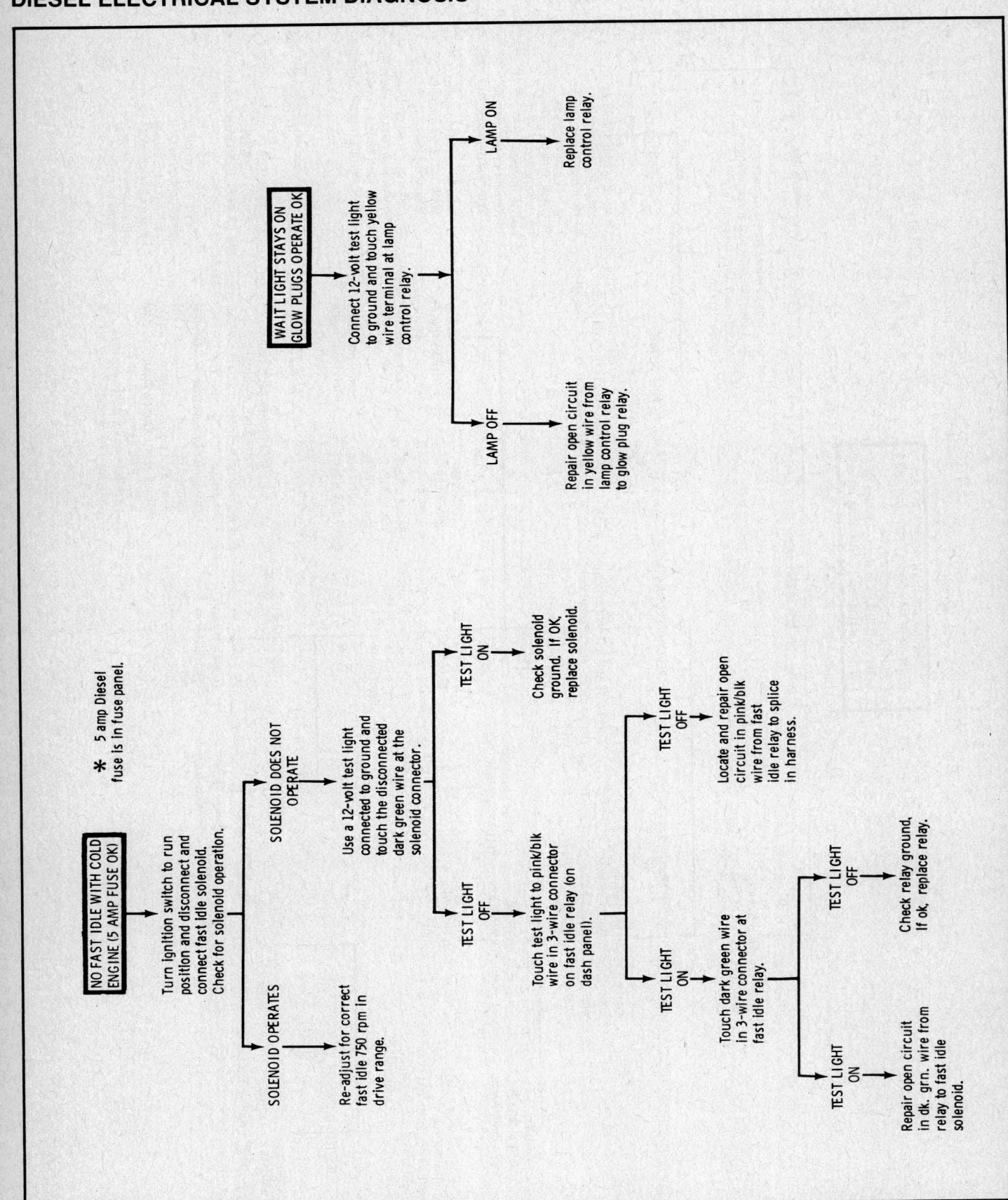

WAIT LIGHT STAYS ON GLOW PLUGS OPERATE OK

Connect 12-volt test light to ground and touch yellow wire terminal at lamp control relay.

- **LAMP ON** → Replace lamp control relay.
- **LAMP OFF** → Repair open circuit in yellow wire from lamp control relay to glow plug relay.

NO FAST IDLE WITH COLD ENGINE (5 AMP FUSE OK)

* 5 amp Diesel fuse is in fuse panel.

Turn ignition switch to run position and disconnect and connect fast idle solenoid. Check for solenoid operation.

- **SOLENOID OPERATES** → Re-adjust for correct fast idle 750 rpm in drive range.

- **SOLENOID DOES NOT OPERATE** → Use a 12-volt test light connected to ground and touch the disconnected dark green wire at the solenoid connector.

  - **TEST LIGHT ON** → Check solenoid ground. If OK, replace solenoid.

  - **TEST LIGHT OFF** → Touch test light to pink/blk wire in 3-wire connector on fast idle relay (on dash panel).

    - **TEST LIGHT OFF** → Locate and repair open circuit in pink/blk wire from fast idle relay to splice in harness.

    - **TEST LIGHT ON** → Touch dark green wire in 3-wire connector at fast idle relay.

      - **TEST LIGHT OFF** → Check relay ground, If ok, replace relay.

      - **TEST LIGHT ON** → Repair open circuit in dk. grn. wire from relay to fast idle solenoid.

DIESEL ELECTRICAL SYSTEM DIAGNOSIS

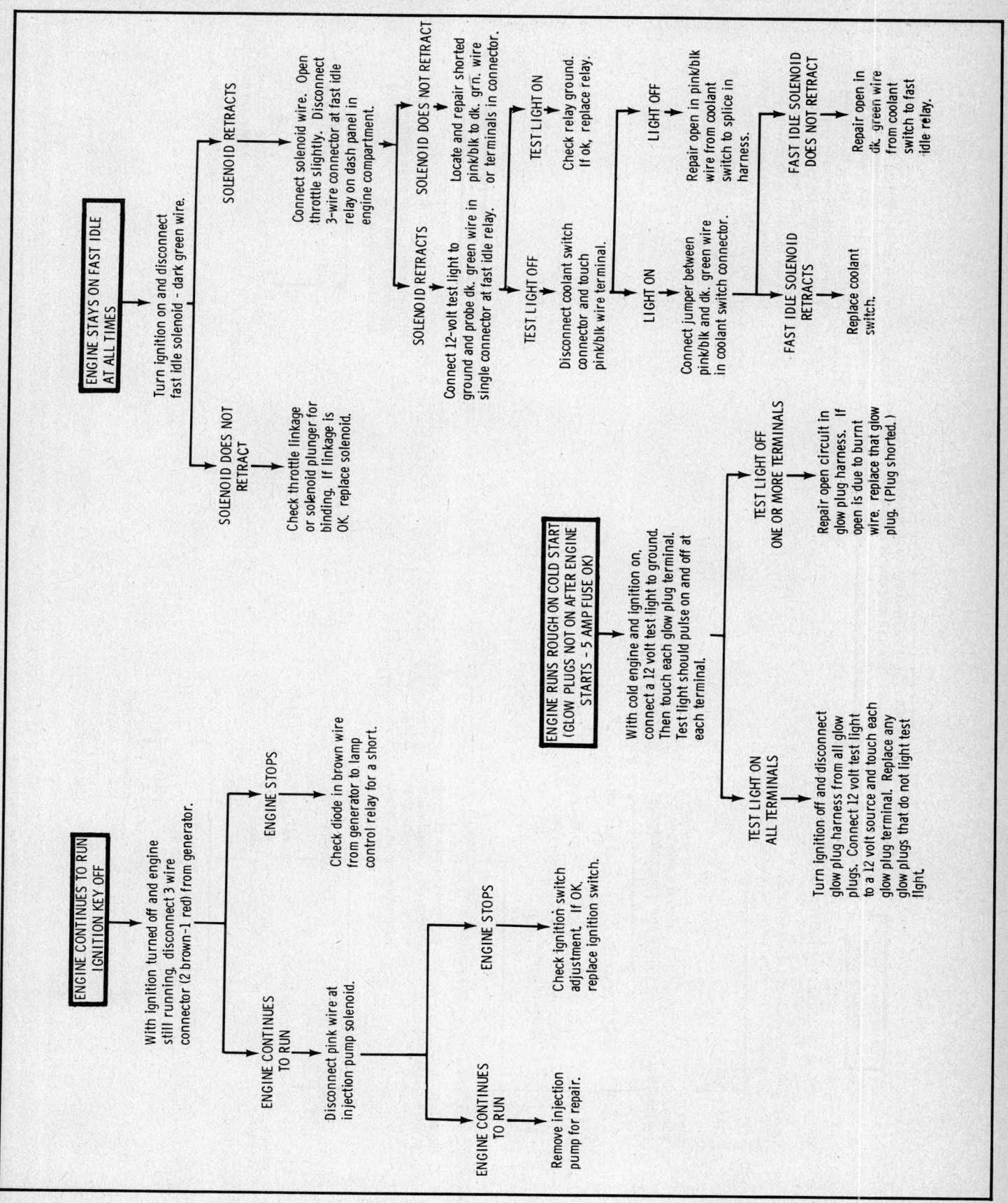

GM DIESEL ENGINES

DIESEL ELECTRICAL SYSTEM DIAGNOSIS

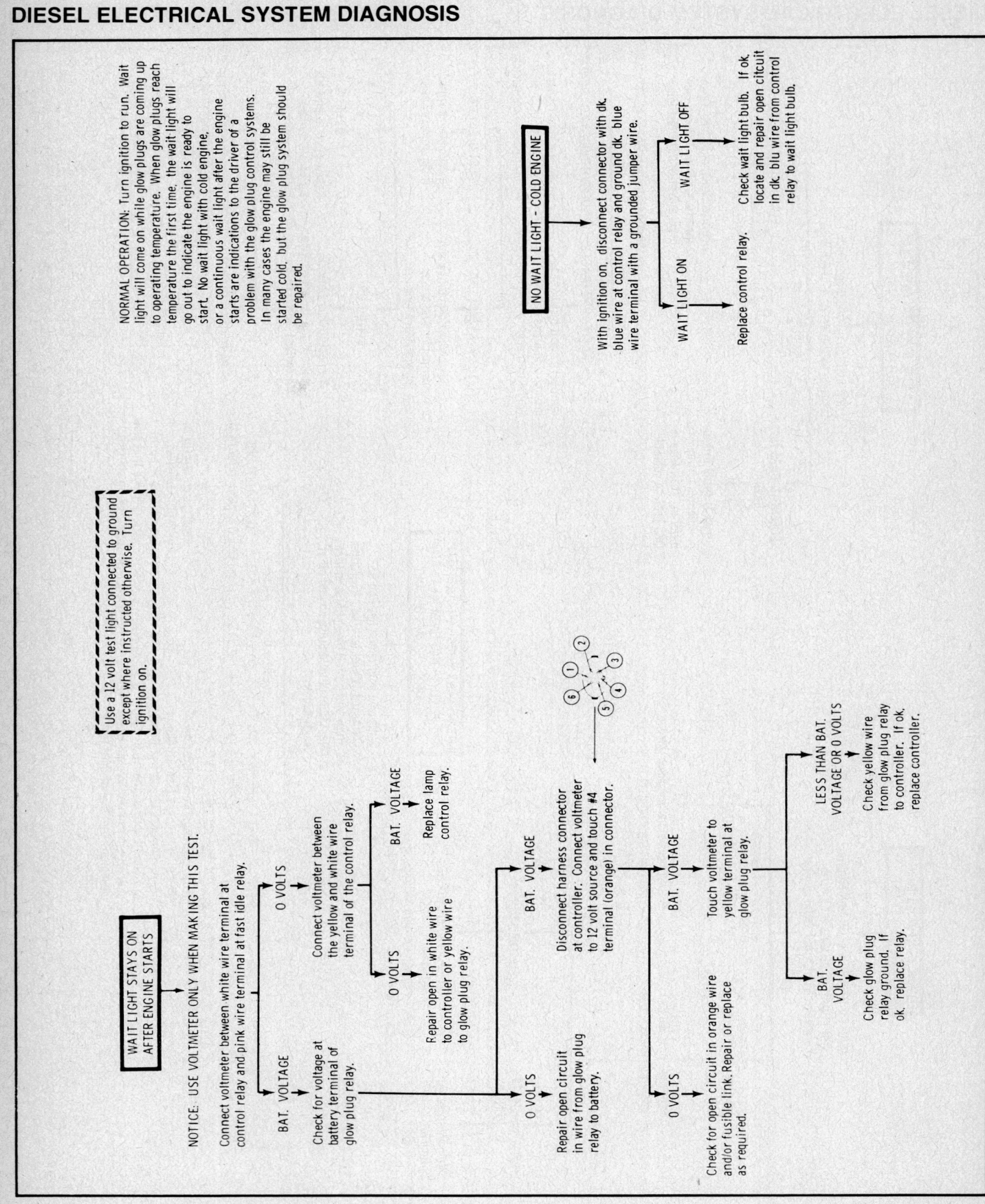

NORMAL OPERATION: Turn ignition to run. Wait light will come on while glow plugs are coming up to operating temperature. When glow plugs reach temperature the first time, the wait light will go out to indicate the engine is ready to start. No wait light with cold engine, or a continuous wait light after the engine starts are indications to the driver of a problem with the glow plug control systems. In many cases the engine may still be started cold, but the glow plug system should be repaired.

NO WAIT LIGHT - COLD ENGINE

With ignition on, disconnect connector with dk. blue wire at control relay and ground dk. blue wire terminal with a grounded jumper wire.

WAIT LIGHT OFF → Check wait light bulb. If ok. locate and repair open circuit in dk. blu wire from control relay to wait light bulb.

WAIT LIGHT ON → Replace control relay.

Use a 12 volt test light connected to ground except where instructed otherwise. Turn ignition on.

WAIT LIGHT STAYS ON AFTER ENGINE STARTS

NOTICE: USE VOLTMETER ONLY WHEN MAKING THIS TEST.

Connect voltmeter between white wire terminal at control relay and pink wire terminal at fast idle relay.

- **0 VOLTS** → Connect voltmeter between the yellow and white wire terminal of the control relay.
  - **BAT. VOLTAGE** → Replace lamp control relay.
  - **0 VOLTS** → Repair open in white wire to controller or yellow wire to glow plug relay.

- **BAT. VOLTAGE** → Check for voltage at battery terminal of glow plug relay.
  - **BAT. VOLTAGE** → Disconnect harness connector at controller. Connect voltmeter to 12 volt source and touch #4 terminal (orange) in connector.
  - **0 VOLTS** → Repair open circuit in wire from glow plug relay to battery.

Disconnect harness connector at controller. Connect voltmeter to 12 volt source and touch #4 terminal (orange) in connector.
- **BAT. VOLTAGE** → Touch voltmeter to yellow terminal at glow plug relay.
  - **BAT. VOLTAGE** → Check glow plug relay ground. If ok. replace relay.
  - **LESS THAN BAT. VOLTAGE OR 0 VOLTS** → Check yellow wire from glow plug relay to controller. If ok. replace controller.
- **0 VOLTS** → Check for open circuit in orange wire and/or fusible link. Repair or replace as required.

B402

EGR SYSTEM DIAGNOSIS

Condition	Cause	Correction
EGR valve will not open, no noticeable effect to driver	Binding or stuck EGR valve	Replace EGR valve
	No vacuum to EGR valve	Check EGR vacuum solenoid, EGR vacuum switch, vacuum regulator valve and vacuum pump for proper operation
EGR valve will not close, heavy smoke on acceleration	Binding or stuck EGR valve, check with engine off	Replace EGR valve
	Vacuum to EGR at W.O.T.	Check EGR vacuum solenoid (open when energized,) EGR vacuum switch (N.O. below preset vacuum) and vacuum regulator valve
EGR valve closes early, no noticeable effect to driver	Vacuum switch opening circuit above calibration (8 inches)	Replace vacuum switch
	Vacuum regulator valve misadjusted	Adjust vacuum regulator valve
EGR valve closes late, smoke on medium acceleration but not at W.O.T.	Vacuum switch opening circuit below calibration (8 inches)	Replace vacuum switch
	Vacuum regulator valve misadjusted	Adjust vacuum regulator valve
Loss of engine performance and smokey exhaust	Exhaust restriction	Replace restricted part
	Air cleaner filter element restricted	Replace air cleaner filter element

VACUUM PUMP DIAGNOSIS

Condition	Cause	Correction
Excessive or clattering noise	Loose screws between pump assembly and drive assembly	Tighten screws to specifications Replace O-ring Replace pump assembly
	Loose tube on pump assembly	Replace pump assembly
Hooting noise	Valves not functioning properly	Replace pump assembly
Pump assembly loose on drive assembly	Stripped threads	Replace pump assembly
Oil around end plug	Loose plug	Seat plug Replace drive assembly
Oil leaking out crimp	Bad crimp	Replace pump assembly
Vacuum gauge reading of 20 inches vacuum minimum with engine running. With engine off, vacuum level loss should not drop to 19 inches in less than 1½ seconds	Defective valves	Replace pump assembly
	Defective diaphragm	Replace pump assembly
	Worn push rod seal	Replace pump assembly
	Loose tube	Replace pump assembly

GM DIESEL ENGINES

SERVICE

Checking and Adjusting Fuel Timing

1. To check the timing, make sure the marks on the injection pump adapter and the injection pump flange are aligned.
2. To adjust timing, use tool J-26987 to loosen the three pump retaining nuts. Rotate the injection pump to align the marks and tighten the nuts to 35 ft. lb.
3. Adjust the throttle rod.

Throttle Rod Adjustment

1. Remove the clip from the cruise control rod and remove the rod from the bellcrank.

Timing Marks and Injection Pump Lines

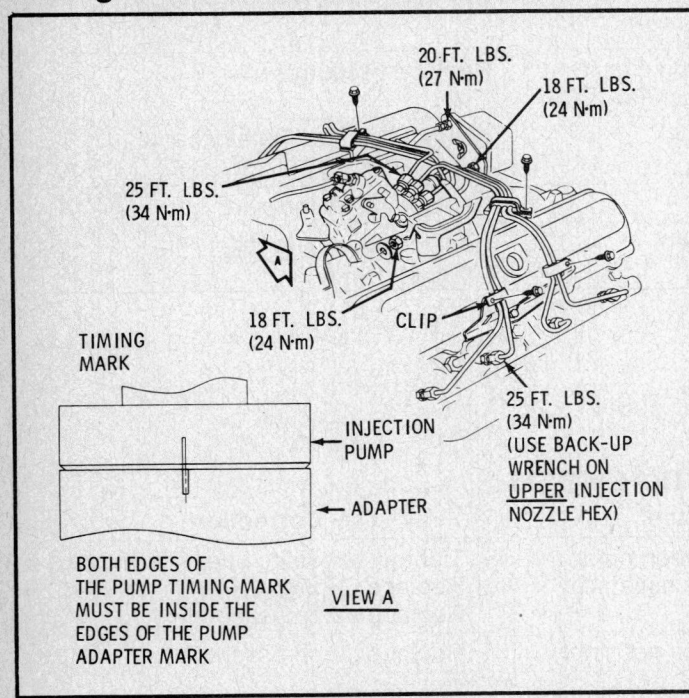

Injection Pump Assembly

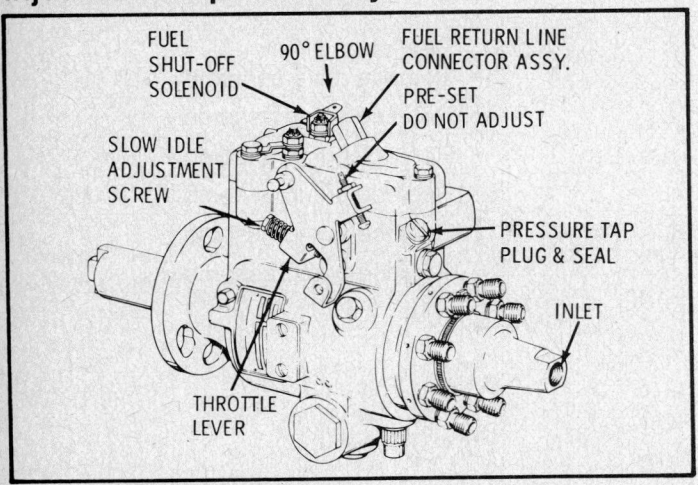

2. Remove the detent cable from the bellcrank.
3. Rotating the bellcrank to the full throttle stop, lengthen the throttle rod until the injection lever contacts the injection pump full throttle stop.

Detent Cable Adjustment

CHILTON CAUTION The throttle rod must be adjusted first.

1. Remove the throttle rod from the bellcrank and push the snap lock to the disengaged position.
2. Holding the bellcrank to the full throttle stop, push in the snap lock until it is flush with the cable end fitting.

Throttle and Cruise Control Linkage

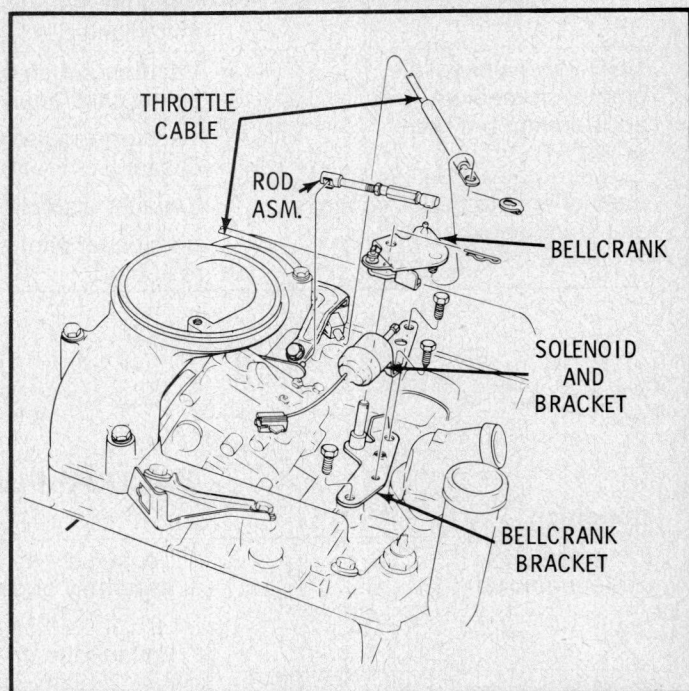

Throttle Linkage

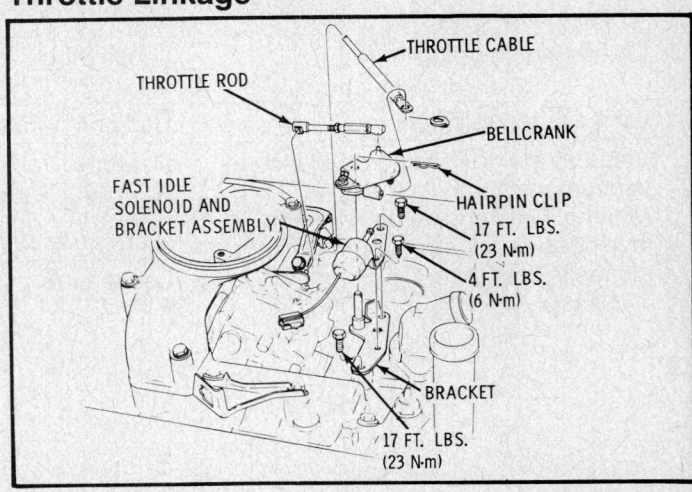

B404

Detent Cable Adjustment

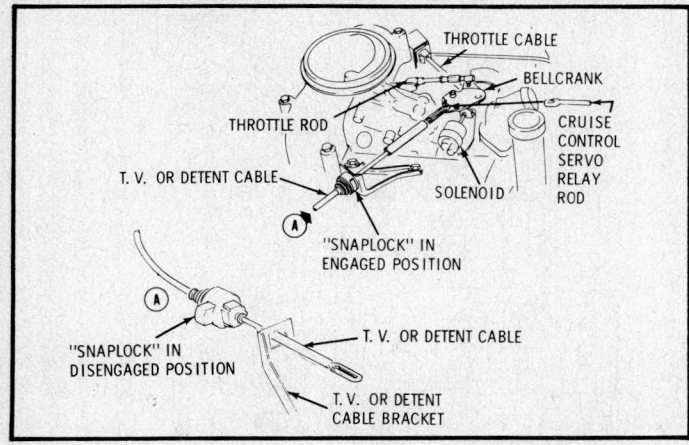

Adapter to Manifold Mounting

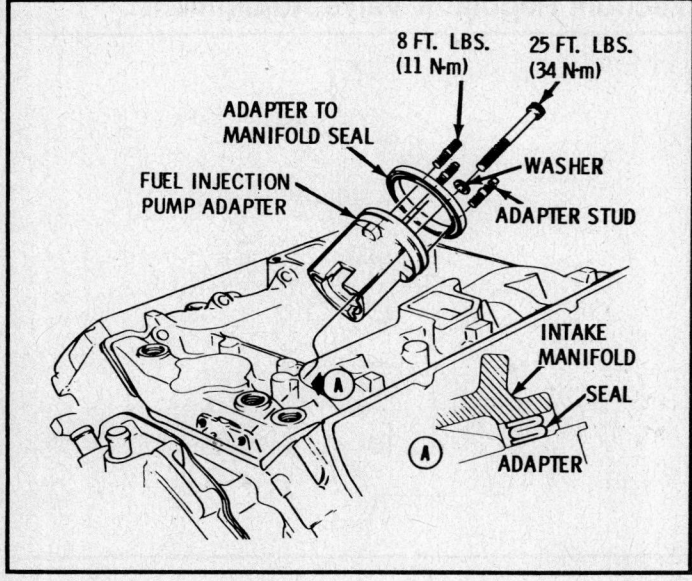

Adapter Seal Installation

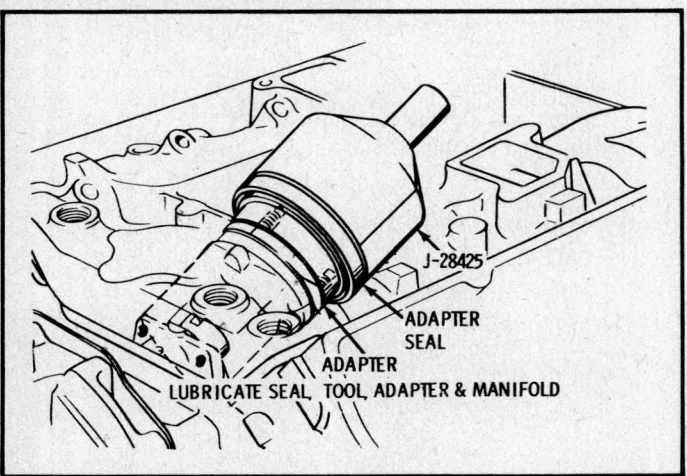

Checking Fuel Injection Pump Pressure

1. Remove the air crossover and the pressure tap plug from the injection pump.

2. Fuel pressure should be 8–12 psi at 1000 rpm with no more than 2 psi fluctuation.

3. If the pressure is incorrect, first replace the fuel return line connector assembly and recheck the pressure. If the pressure is still incorrect, the injection pump is defective.

Fuel Injection Pump Replacement

1. Remove, disconnect or relocate the following.
a. Air cleaner
b. Air crossover
c. Throttle rod, bellcrank, and cables
d. Fuel filter and fuel lines
e. Fuel return lines
f. Fuel injector pump lines at the nozzles
g. Pump mounting nuts

2. To install, position engine number one cylinder TDC and align the mark on the balancer with the zero mark on the indicator. Line up the offset tang on the pump drive-

Fuel Filter and Lines

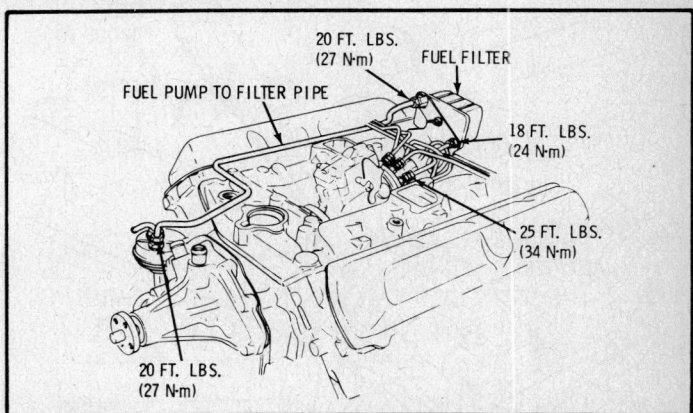

Pump Driven Gear Offset

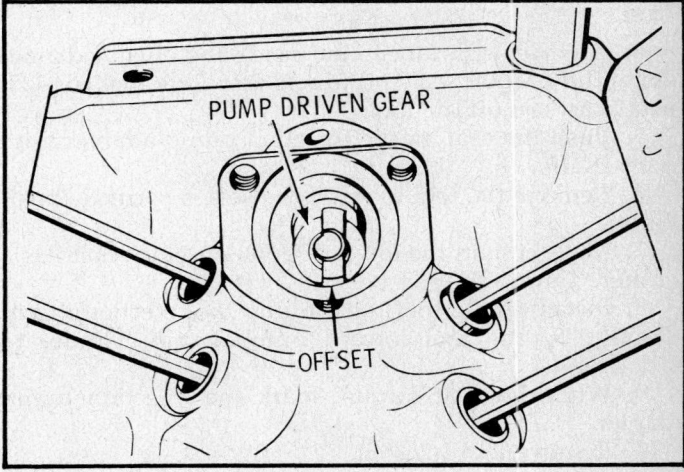

GM DIESEL ENGINES

shaft with the pump driven gear. Install the injector pump.

3. Connect injection pump lines, fuel supply lines, etc.

4. Align the injection pump line exactly with the line on the adapter. Torque the pump mounting nuts to correct specifications. Reinstall or reconnect all displaced components, cables, brackets, etc.

5. Start and run engine for two minutes, shut off for two minutes and restart. This will bleed air from the injection pump.

ESTABLISHING NEW TIMING MARK

1. File the previous timing mark off the injection pump adapter.

2. Position engine at number one cylinder top dead center, and align the mark on the balancer with the zero mark on the indicator. (The index is offset to the right when number one cylinder is at top dead center).

3. Apply chassis lube to the seal area on adapter, taper edge and seal area in the intake manifold. Install the adapter and leave loose.

Marking Injection Pump Adapter

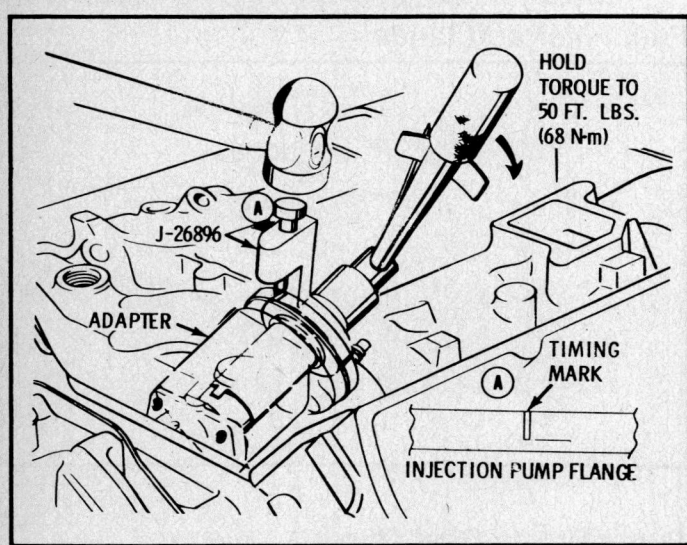

4. Apply chassis lube to the inside and outside diameters of the adapter seal and to seal installing tool J-28425. Install the seal on the tool.

5. Push the seal on the injection pump adapter with tool J-28245.

6. Remove the tool to see if the seal is correctly positioned.

7. Make certain the lower adapter-to-block bolt has a washer. Torque adapter bolts to 25 ft. lbs.

8. Install timing tool J-26896 into the injection pump adapter. Torque tool toward number one cylinder to 50 ft. lbs.

9. While holding torque, mark the injection pump adapter.

10. Remove tool J-26896.

Vacuum Regulator Valve Adjustment

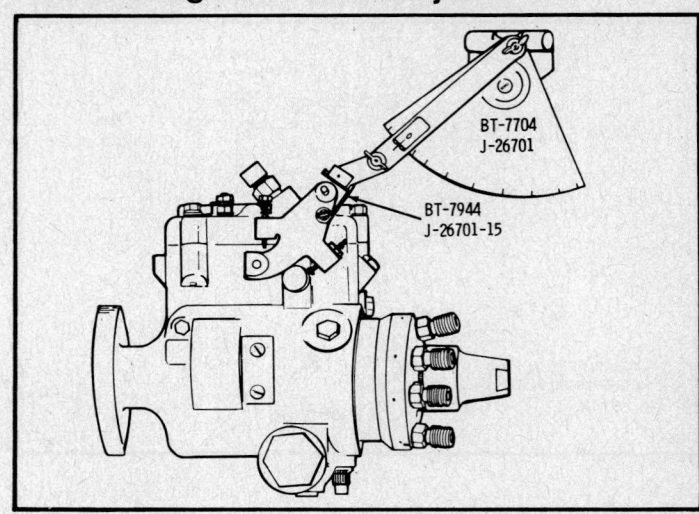

Vacuum Regulator Valve Adjustment

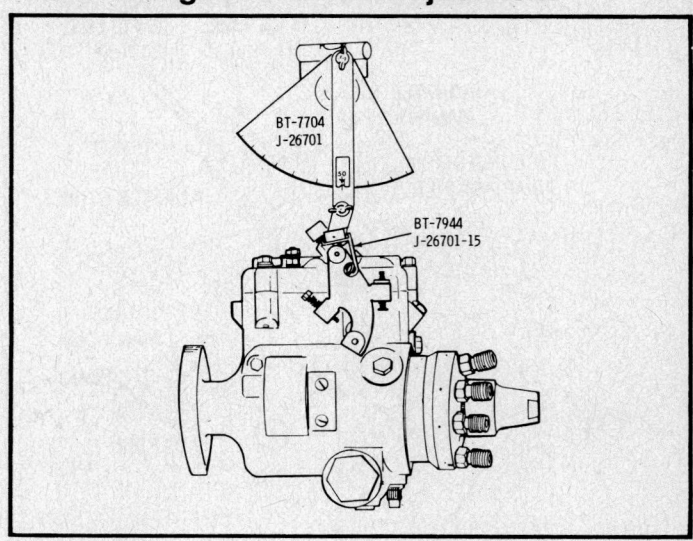

Vacuum Regulator Valve Adjustment

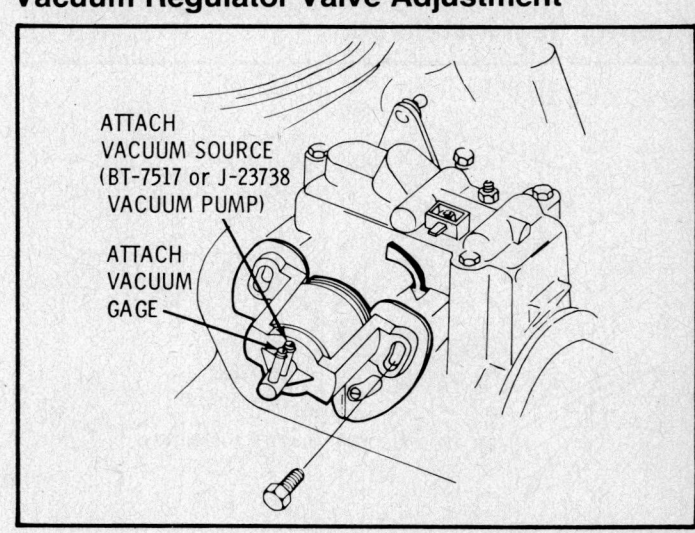

Vacuum Regulator Valve Adjustment

1. Note the location of the two vacuum hoses and remove the valve. (When installing, the valve must be adjusted.)

2. Remove the air crossover, disconnect the throttle rod from the throttle lever and loosen the vacuum regulator valve injection pump bolts.

3. Place the carburetor angle gauge adapter on the injection pump throttle lever. Place the angle gauge on the adapter.

4. Rotate the throttle lever to wide open throttle and set the angle gauge to zero degrees. Center the bubble in the level and reset the angle gauge to 50 degrees.

5. Rotate the throttle lever to center the bubble. Apply an outside vacuum source of 18–22 inches to the inboard port of the vacuum valve. Rotate the valve clockwise to obtain 7–8 inches of vacuum.

Vacuum Pump Overhaul

1. Remove the bracket holding the pump and remove the pump.

Vacuum Pump Removal and Overhaul—V8 Engine

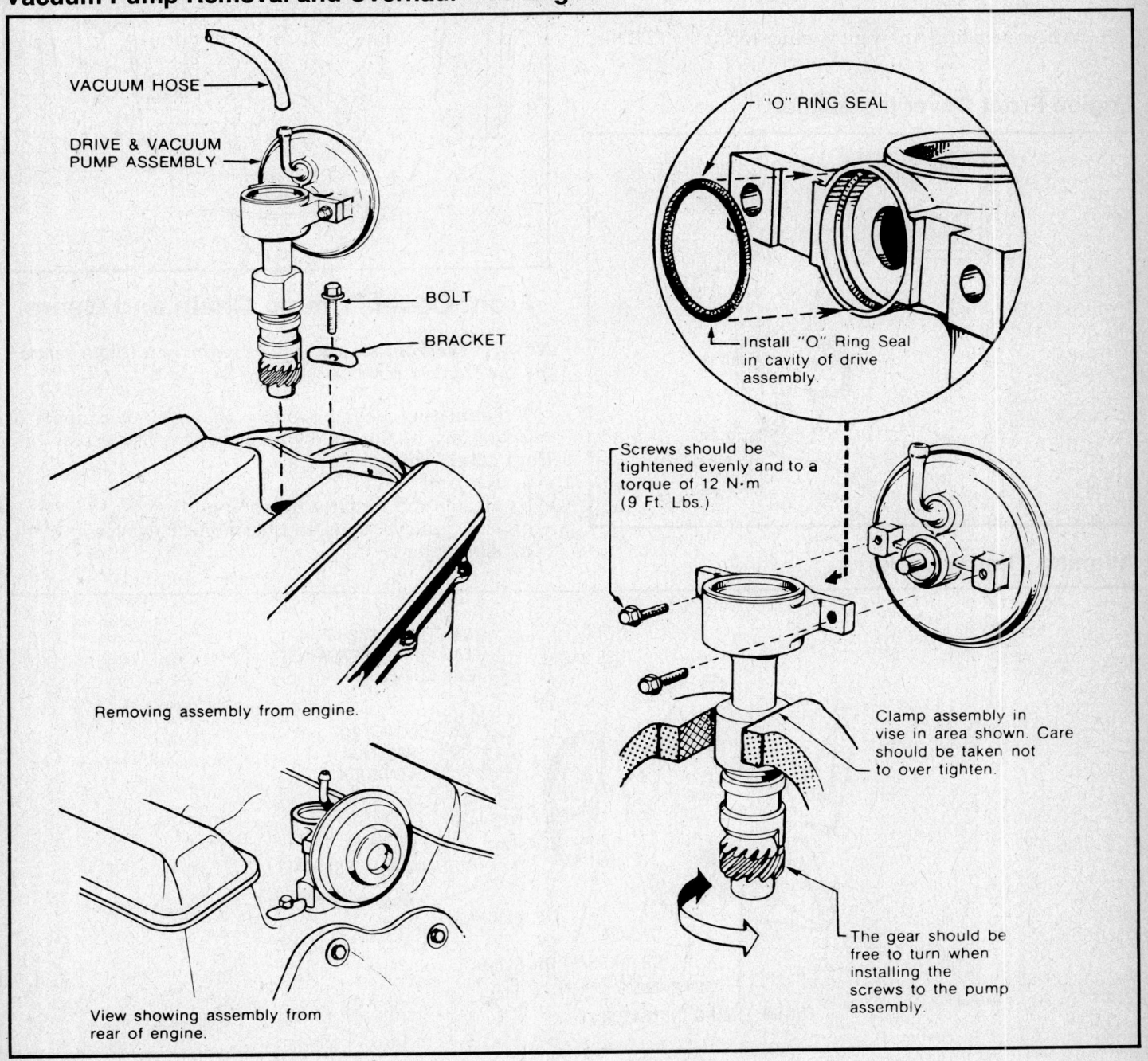

VACUUM HOSE

DRIVE & VACUUM PUMP ASSEMBLY

BOLT

BRACKET

Removing assembly from engine.

View showing assembly from rear of engine.

"O" RING SEAL

Install "O" Ring Seal in cavity of drive assembly.

Screws should be tightened evenly and to a torque of 12 N·m (9 Ft. Lbs.)

Clamp assembly in vise in area shown. Care should be taken not to over tighten.

The gear should be free to turn when installing the screws to the pump assembly.

GM DIESEL ENGINES

CHILTON CAUTION Do not run the engine with the vacuum pump removed, as the vacuum pump drives the oil pump.

2. Remove the vacuum diaphragm from the drive assembly and remove the O-ring seal.

3. Install a new O-ring seal on reassembly.

4. To install, insert the pump into the engine, making sure the pump and camshaft gears mesh.

Glow Plugs

CHILTON CAUTION Use extreme care when removing a burned out glow plug as the tip may break off. To remove a broken tip, the cylinder head must be removed.

1. When installing a new glow plug, torque to 12 ft. lb.

Engine Front Cover Installation

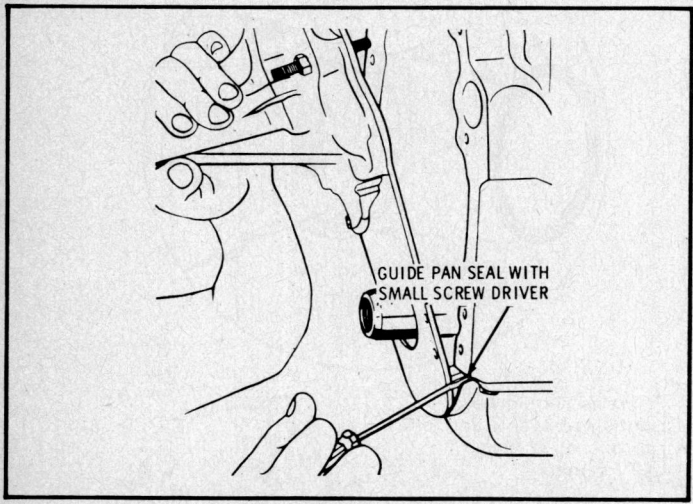

GUIDE PAN SEAL WITH SMALL SCREW DRIVER

Aligning Timing Marks

Front Cover Removal—V6 and V8 Engines

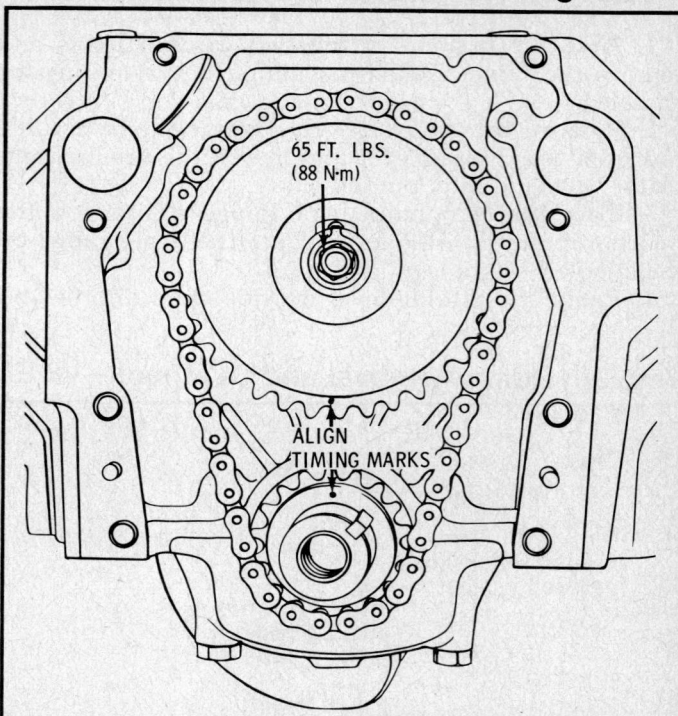

65 FT. LBS. (88 N·m)

ALIGN TIMING MARKS

Front Cover, Timing Chain and Gears

NOTE The front oil seal can be replaced without removing the front cover.

1. Drain the cooling system. Remove, disconnect or relocate any of the following necessary for access and front cover removal clearance.
   a. Radiator
   b. Heater and radiator hoses
   c. Fan, pulleys, belts and harmonic balancer
   d. Alternater

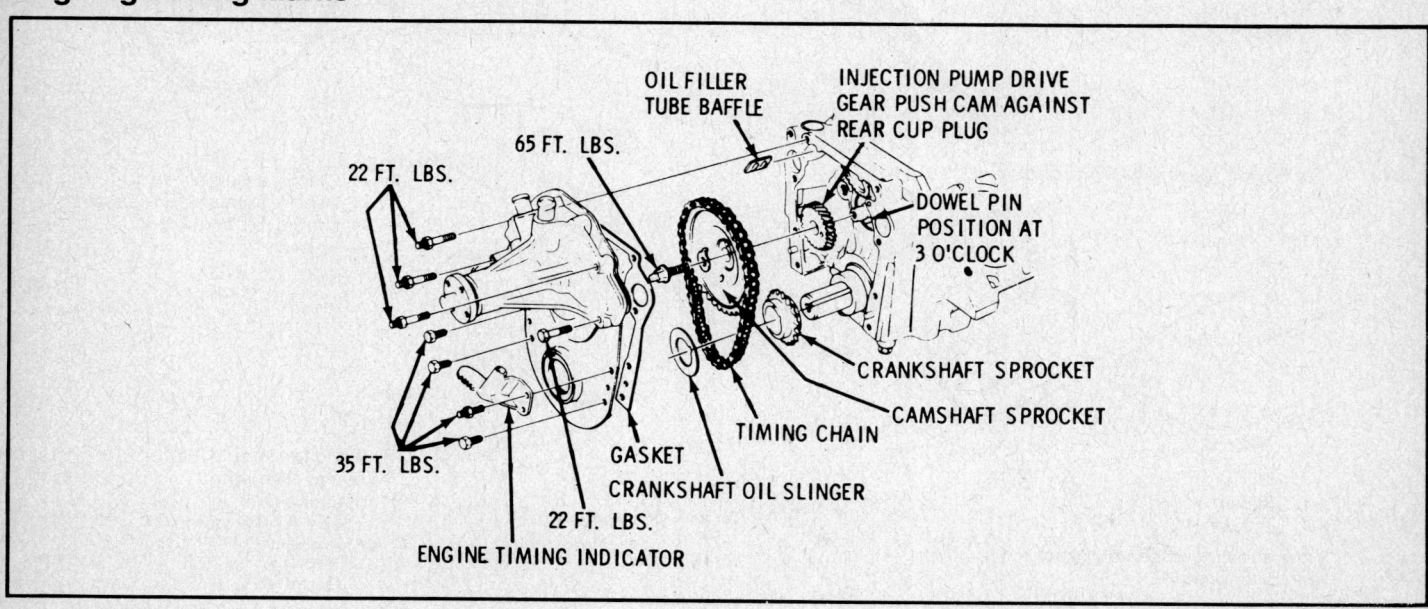

OIL FILLER TUBE BAFFLE

INJECTION PUMP DRIVE GEAR PUSH CAM AGAINST REAR CUP PLUG

65 FT. LBS.

22 FT. LBS.

DOWEL PIN POSITION AT 3 O'CLOCK

CRANKSHAFT SPROCKET

CAMSHAFT SPROCKET

TIMING CHAIN

35 FT. LBS.

GASKET

CRANKSHAFT OIL SLINGER

22 FT. LBS.

ENGINE TIMING INDICATOR

e. Emission control systems
f. Water pump
g. Fuel pump

NOTE When removing the harmonic balancer, do not pry on the outside edge. The outer ring is bonded in rubber to the hub, and engine timing could be affected if the bond is broken.

2. Remove front cover mounting bolts. Remove cover, timing indicator and water pump assembly.

3. Align timing marks and pry the sprockets forward off shafts.

4. When installing the front cover, use thread sealant on appropriate mounting bolts and room temperature vulcanizing sealer in the oil pan area and any other leak prone area.

Oil Pan Installation

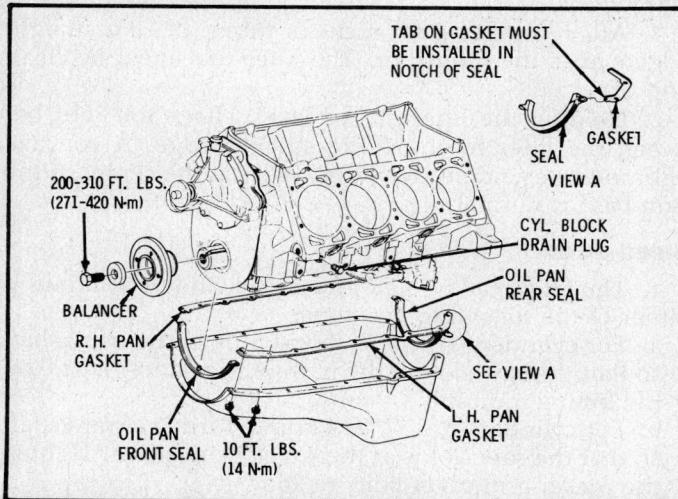

TAB ON GASKET MUST BE INSTALLED IN NOTCH OF SEAL

GASKET

SEAL

VIEW A

200-310 FT. LBS. (271-420 N·m)

CYL BLOCK DRAIN PLUG

OIL PAN REAR SEAL

BALANCER

R. H. PAN GASKET

SEE VIEW A

L. H. PAN GASKET

OIL PAN FRONT SEAL

10 FT. LBS. (14 N·m)

Intake Manifold Torque Sequence—V6 Engine

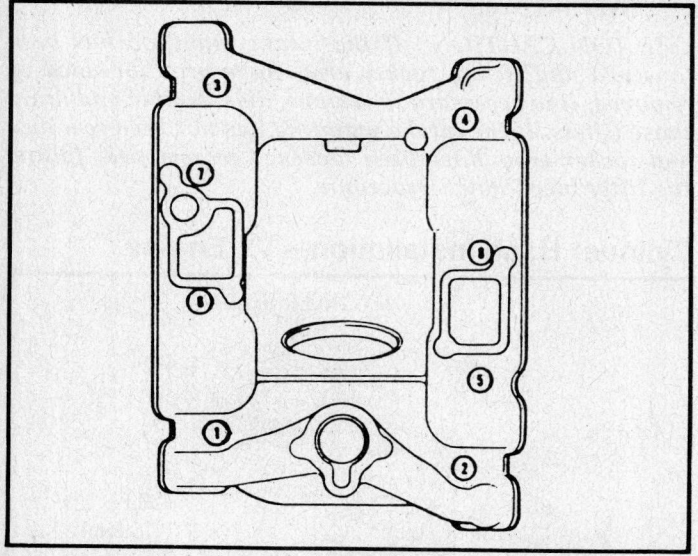

Oil Pump

1. Remove the oil pan and disconnect the oil pump from the rear main bearing cap.

Oil Pump Installation

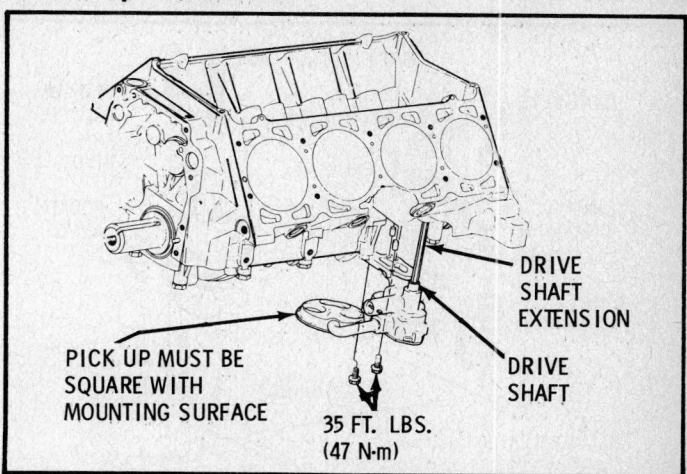

DRIVE SHAFT EXTENSION

DRIVE SHAFT

PICK UP MUST BE SQUARE WITH MOUNTING SURFACE

35 FT. LBS. (47 N·m)

2. To install, insert the drive shaft extension through the opening in the main bearing cap until the shaft meshes with the vacuum pump driven gear.

3. Position the pump onto the bearing cap and tighten the bolts to 35 ft. lbs.

Intake Manifold

1. Remove, disconnect, or relocate the following.
a. Air crossover assembly
b. Throttle linkage
c. Alternator and air conditioning brackets
d. Fuel line and filter
e. Injection and vacuum pumps
f. Injection pump adapter

2. On installation, apply sealant to both sides of gasket mating surfaces. The seals and mating surfaces must be dry, using RTV sealant only on each end of the seal.

Intake Manifold Bolt Torque Sequence—V8 Engine

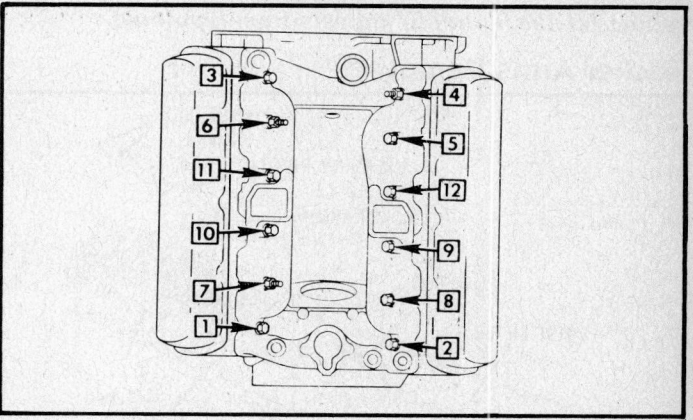

Rocker Arms

1. Remove the valve cover, rocker flanged bolts, pivot and rocker arms.

2. On installation, the valve lifters must be bled down before running the engine to prevent valve train damage.

GM DIESEL ENGINES

Cylinder Head—Exploded View

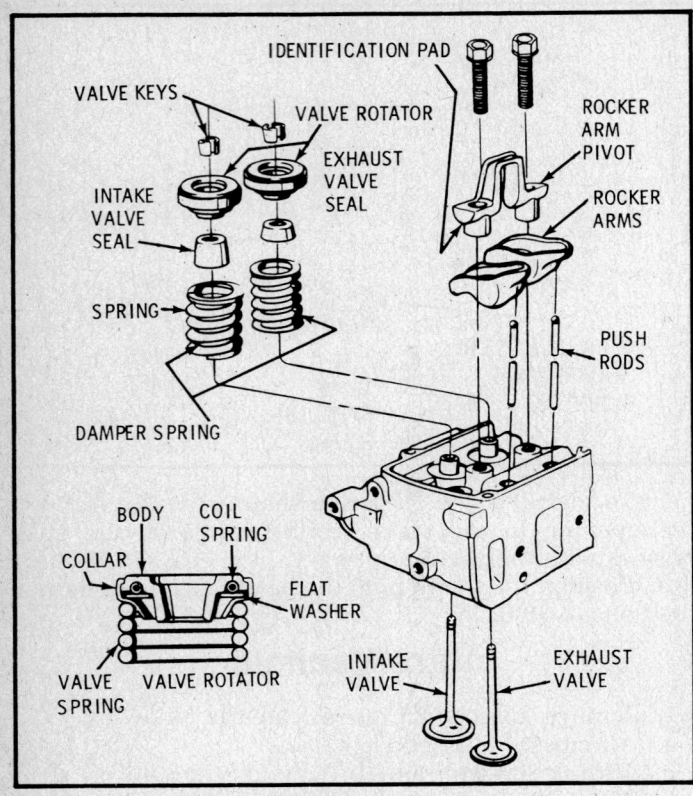

Valve Lifters

1. Keep all lifters in order for installation. On some lifters an "O" may be marked to indicate a .010" oversize.
2. Remove the intake manifold, valve cover, rocker arm assemblies and push rods.
3. Remove the valve lifters.

NOTE Beginning in 1981, roller bearing cam followers are used on all diesel engines. A spring steel insert is used to prevent the hydraulic tappets from revolving.

Rocker Arms Removal

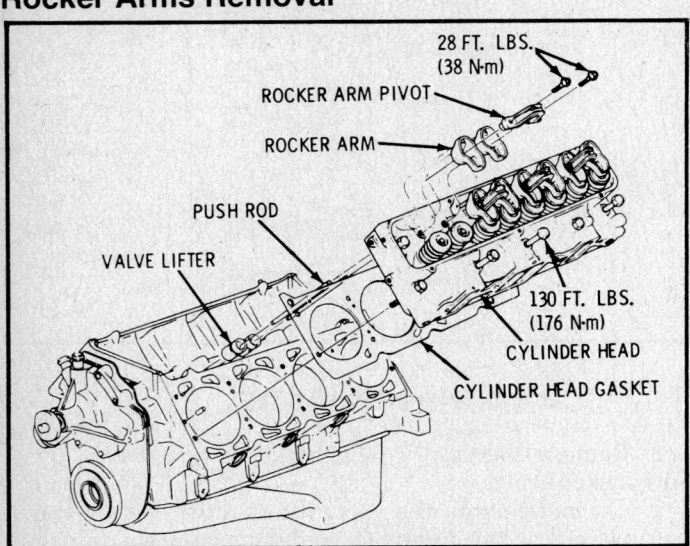

Hydraulic Roller Lifter

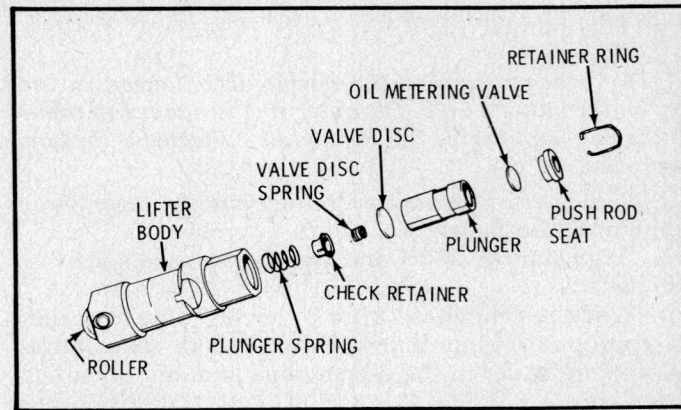

Inspection

1. After inspecting for nicks or burrs, place a straight edge across the lifter foot. The lifter foot must be clean and dry.
2. Holding the lifter at eye level, check for light between the lifter foot and the straight edge. A concave light indicates a defective lifter. Wear at the center of the cam base is normal.

Bleed-down

1. The lifters can be bled down six cylinders at a time in either of the following positions.
   a. For cylinders 3, 5, 7, 2, 4 and 8, turn the crankshaft so that the saw slot on the harmonic balancer is at 0 on the timing indicator.
   b. For cylinders 1, 3, 7, 2, 4 and 6, turn the crankshaft so that the saw slot is at the 4 o'clock position. Tighten the rocker arm pivot bolts to 28 ft. lb.
2. Allow the engine to sit 45 minutes in each position for the valve lifters to bleed down.

CHILTON CAUTION If the intake manifold has been loosened and if any rocker arms have been loosened or removed, it is necessary to remove, disassemble and drain those lifters. If the intake manifold has not been removed and rocker arms have been loosened or removed, follow the lifter bleed-down procedure.

Cylinder Head Installation—V8 Engine

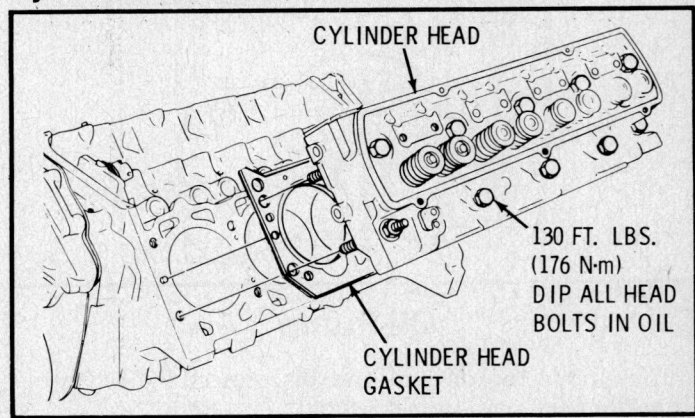

Cylinder Head

CHILTON CAUTION All damaged cylinder heads (warping, etc.) must be replaced, as close manufacturing tolerances do not permit machining.

Removal

1. To gain access to the head, it is necessary to remove the intake manifold, any accessory brackets which interfere, glow plug wiring, ground strap, exhaust manifold and the engine block drain plug.

2. Note the position of rocker arms and pivots and remove. Remove the push rods.

3. If it is necessary to remove the pre-chamber, remove the glow plug and injection nozzle. Tap them out with a blunt drift.

Cylinder Head Bolt Location

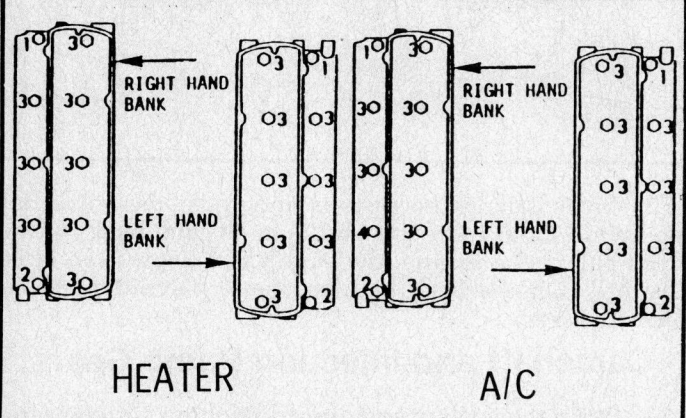

Installation

CHILTON CAUTION All new head gaskets are pre-coated with a special sealant. Applying additional sealant will cause leaks.

1. When installing heads on 1978–80 models, use new head bolts.

2. Tighten head bolts to the correct torque before installing rocker arms and pivots.

Six Cylinder Head Torque Sequence

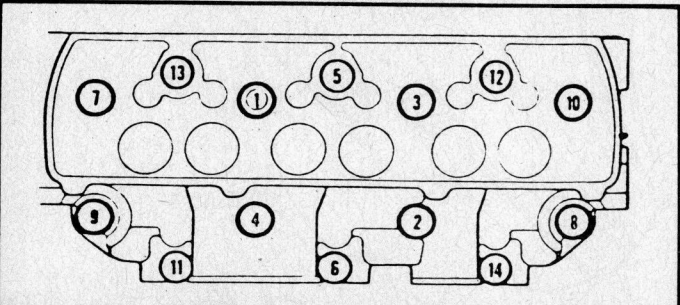

Torque all bolts except 5, 6, 11, 12, 13 and 14 to 193 N·m (142 ft. lbs.). Torque bolts 5, 6, 11, 12, 13 and 14 to 80 N·m (59 ft. lbs.).

Head Bolt Identification

PART NUMBER	LOCATION NUMBER	SIZE
22510580	1	1/2 - 13 x 3.10
22510582	2	1/2-13 x 3.10 stud end
22510579	3	1/2 - 13 x 4.30
22510585	4	1/2 - 13 x 4.30 stud end

Measuring Valve Stem Height

1. Measure the valve stem height after installing a new valve or grinding valves as follows.

a. Check the clearance between the gauge surface and the valve stem. If clearance is less than .015″, grind the valve using the Vee block attachment to obtain a smooth 90 end. Be certain to break the sharp edge on the valve tip. Check an original valve to determine chamfer.

b. After seating valve keys and rotators, regauge all valves (.015″ minimum) and check the rotator to gauge clearance (.030″ minimum). If any valve stem is less than .005″ above the rotator, replace the valve.

Measuring Rotator Height

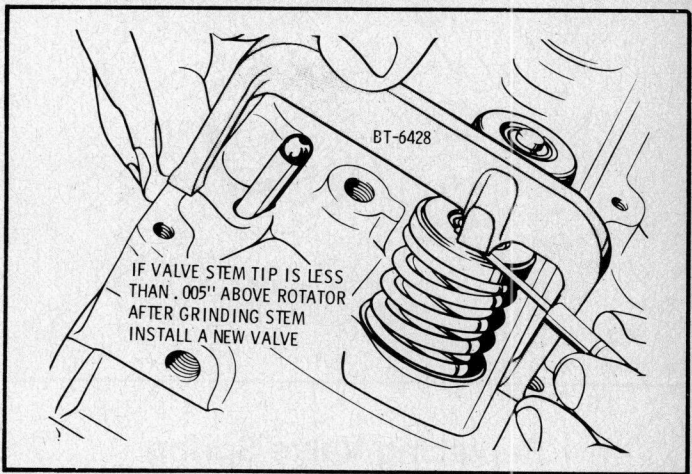

Eight Cylinder Head Torque Sequence

Valve Stem Wear

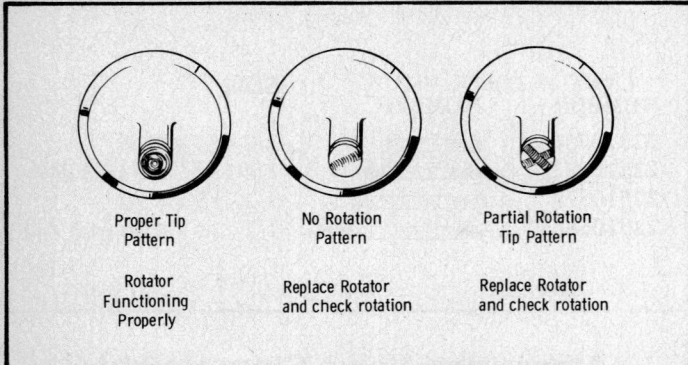

Proper Tip
Pattern

Rotator
Functioning
Properly

No Rotation
Pattern

Replace Rotator
and check rotation

Partial Rotation
Tip Pattern

Replace Rotator
and check rotation

Checking Valve Rotators

1. Apply a dab of paint across the rotator body and down the collar. Observe the rotator while running the engine at 1500 rpm. The body will seem to "walk" around the collar.

Measuring Valve Stem Height

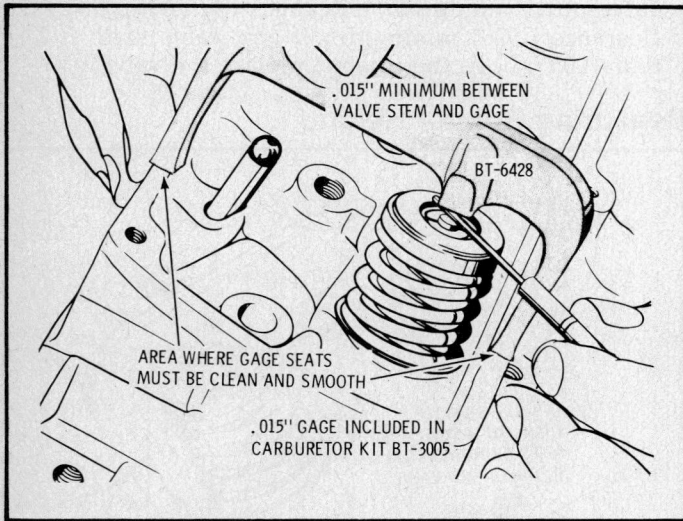

.015" MINIMUM BETWEEN
VALVE STEM AND GAGE

BT-6428

AREA WHERE GAGE SEATS
MUST BE CLEAN AND SMOOTH

.015" GAGE INCLUDED IN
CARBURETOR KIT BT-3005

Replacing Valve Spring (Head on engine)

1. Remove the rocker arm assembly and rotate the engine so that the piston is at TDC.
2. Compress the valve spring. Remove keys, rotators and springs.

Connecting Rods and Pistons

1. Connecting rods and pistons are removed through the top of the block after removing the cylinder head, oil pan and oil pump.

CHILTON CAUTION Install a guide hose over the connecting rod bolts to prevent damage to the threads.

Valve Spring Removal

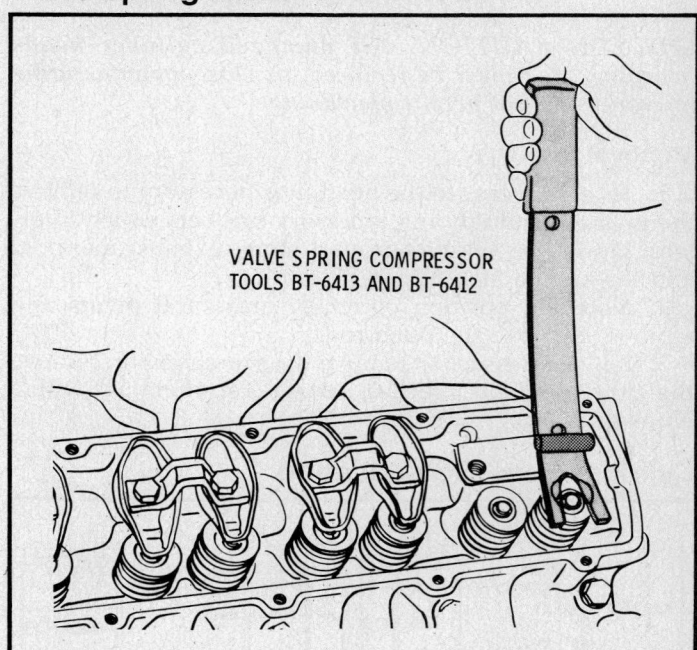

VALVE SPRING COMPRESSOR
TOOLS BT-6413 AND BT-6412

2. On installing the pistons and rods, the valve depressions should face the inside on all cylinders. On the front half of the engine, the large valve depression faces forward. On the back half, the large valve depression faces the rear.

Camshaft and Injection Pump Gears

1. Drain the cooling and air conditioning systems, and remove the radiator and condenser.

Connecting Rod Bolt Guide

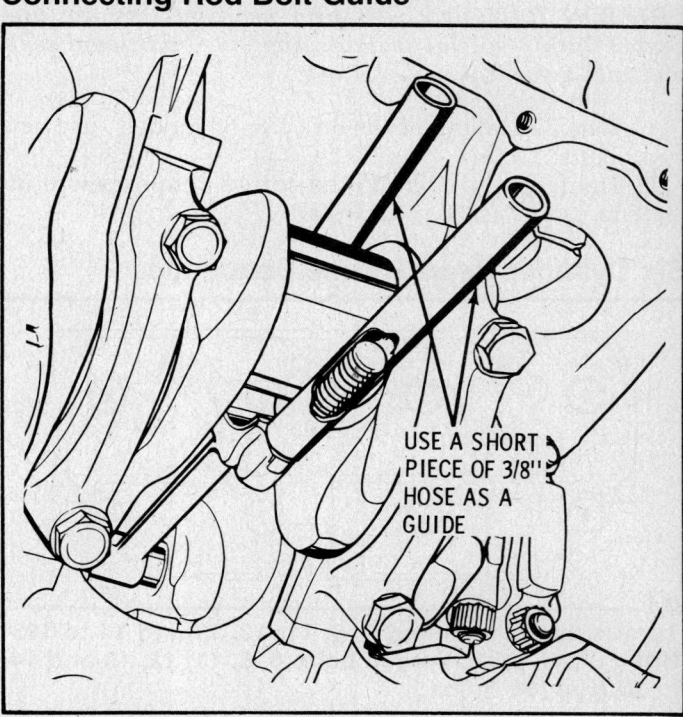

USE A SHORT
PIECE OF 3/8"
HOSE AS A
GUIDE

Rod Bearing Tang and Notch

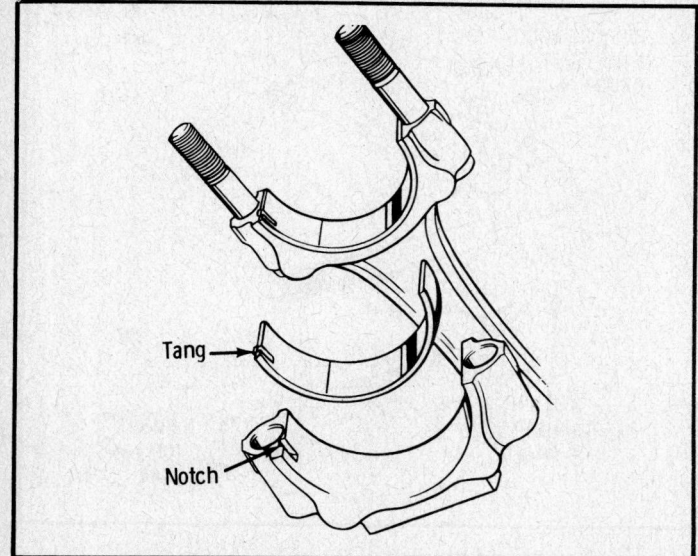

Tang

Notch

Injection Pump Driven Gear

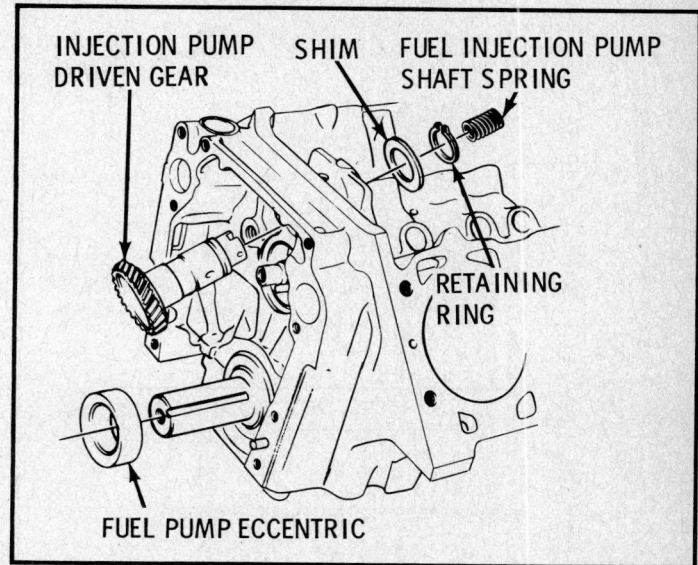

INJECTION PUMP DRIVEN GEAR   SHIM   FUEL INJECTION PUMP SHAFT SPRING

RETAINING RING

FUEL PUMP ECCENTRIC

2. Remove the intake manifold, injection pump, timing chain and sprocket.

3. Position the camshaft dowel pin at 3 o'clock. With the camshaft held rearward, remove the pump drive gear by sliding off the camshaft while rocking the pump driven gear.

4. Remove the injection pump adapter, snap ring and selective washer. Remove the pump driven gear.

5. Remove the camshaft through the front of the engine.

6. Before installing the camshaft, coat it with hypoid gear oil. Injection pump gears are to be replaced only in pairs.

7. A new timing mark must be made on the injection pump.

8. Install the injection pump driven gear, spring, shim and snap ring. Check the gear end play. If it is not within .002 to .006", replace the shim with the available oversize shims.

Correct Piston Installation

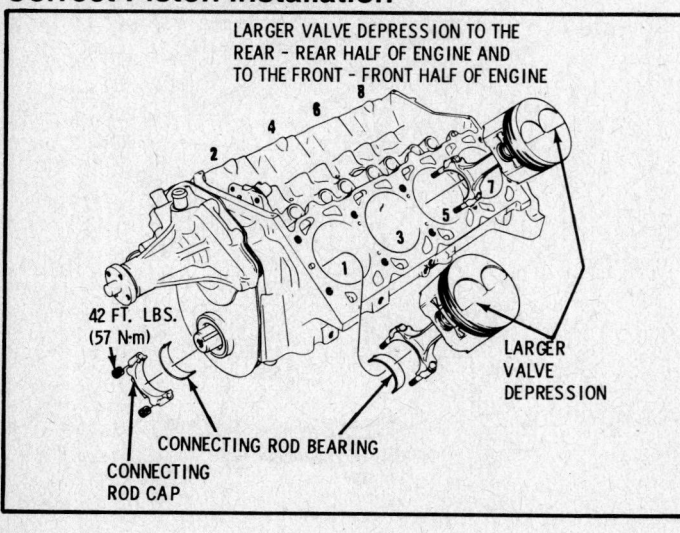

LARGER VALVE DEPRESSION TO THE REAR - REAR HALF OF ENGINE AND TO THE FRONT - FRONT HALF OF ENGINE

42 FT. LBS. (57 N·m)

CONNECTING ROD BEARING

CONNECTING ROD CAP

LARGER VALVE DEPRESSION

Rear Cam Bearing Installation

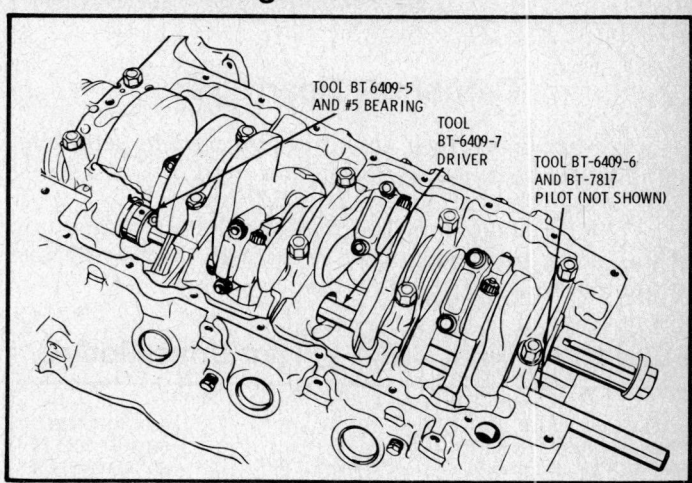

TOOL BT 6409-5 AND #5 BEARING

TOOL BT-6409-7 DRIVER

TOOL BT-6409-6 AND BT-7817 PILOT (NOT SHOWN)

Oil Hole Alignment Check

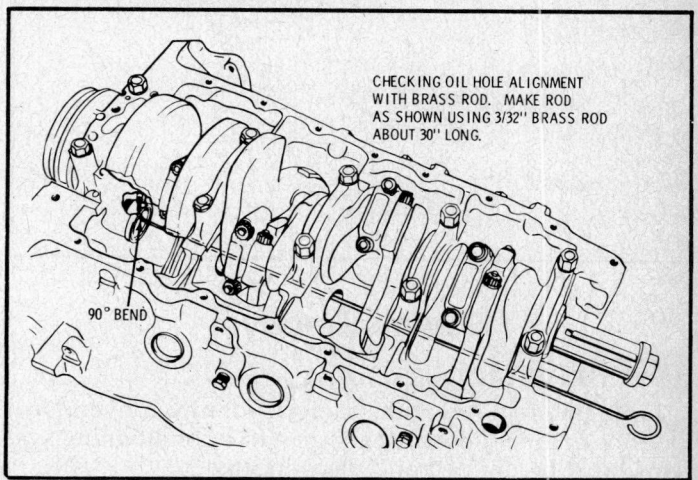

CHECKING OIL HOLE ALIGNMENT WITH BRASS ROD. MAKE ROD AS SHOWN USING 3/32'' BRASS ROD ABOUT 30'' LONG.

90° BEND

Front Cam Bearing Installation

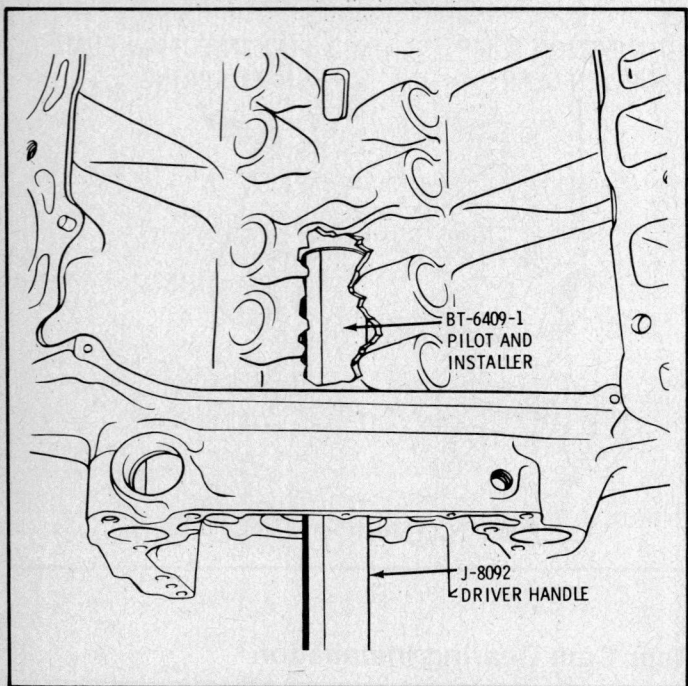

Camshaft Bearings

1. Camshaft bearings are to be replaced in sets only. Remove the bearings in order 1 through 5. On installation, install the bearings in order 5 through 1.

2. When installing the bearings and the injection pump bushings, be sure to align the holes with the oil passages in the block.

Supporting Final Drive—Front Drive Models

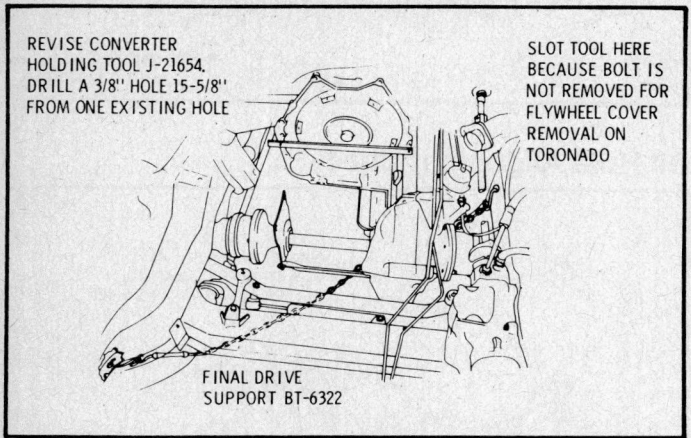

Engine Removal

REAR DRIVE MODELS

1. Engine removal is the same as for any conventional gasoline engine. Power steering and air conditioning systems must be drained and disconnected.

Output Shaft Alignment—Front Drive Models

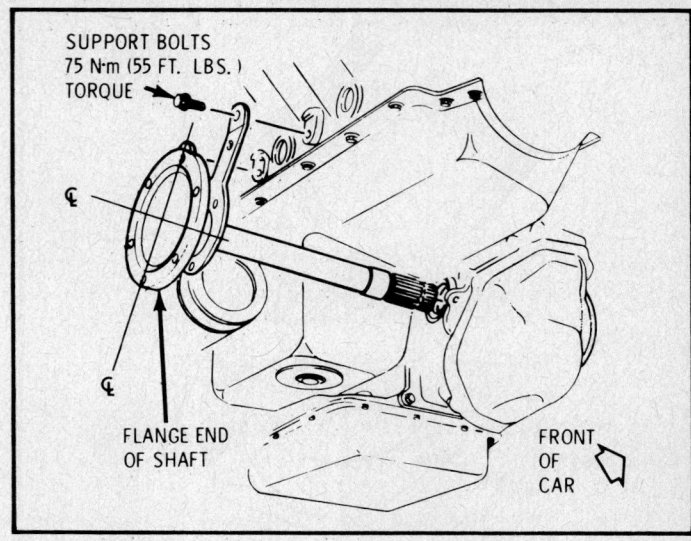

FRONT DRIVE MODELS

1. The power steering pump and air conditioning compressor brackets can be set aside for clearance without disconnecting any lines.

2. When disconnecting output shafts, scribe a line around the washers for installation reference.

3. Support the final unit with a chain before hoisting engine out of car.

Crankshaft

1. The crankshaft can be removed with the cylinder heads attached.

Crankshaft Removed from Engine

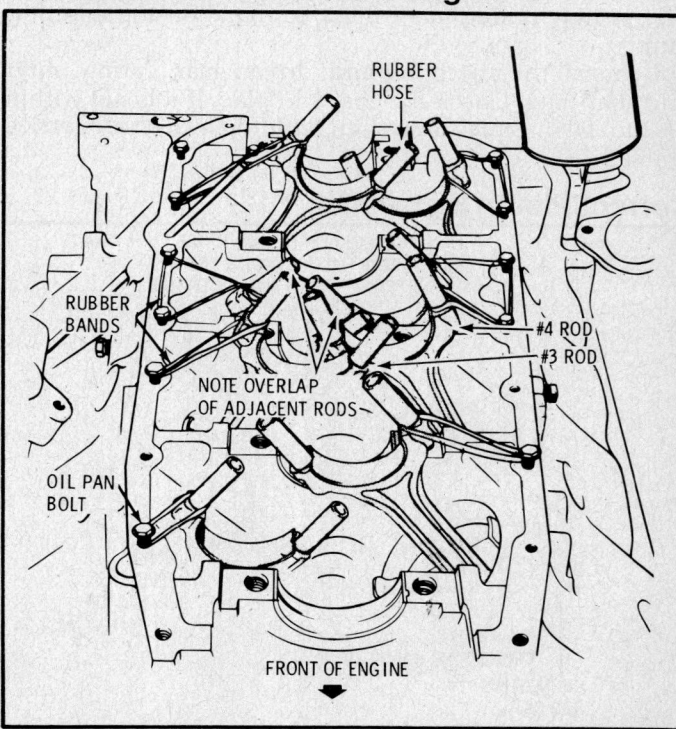

2. Mark the cylinder number of each main bearing cap for installation reference.

3. Note the position of the keyway in the crankshaft so it can be installed in the same position.

4. Attach rubber bands from oil pan bolts to connecting rods to prevent the pistons from moving when the crankshaft is removed.

Main Bearings

1. Each main bearing is marked with a part number and the amount undersize. It is possible to have different bearing sizes in the same engine.

2. Bearing shells are to be replaced only in sets.

Packing Oil Seal

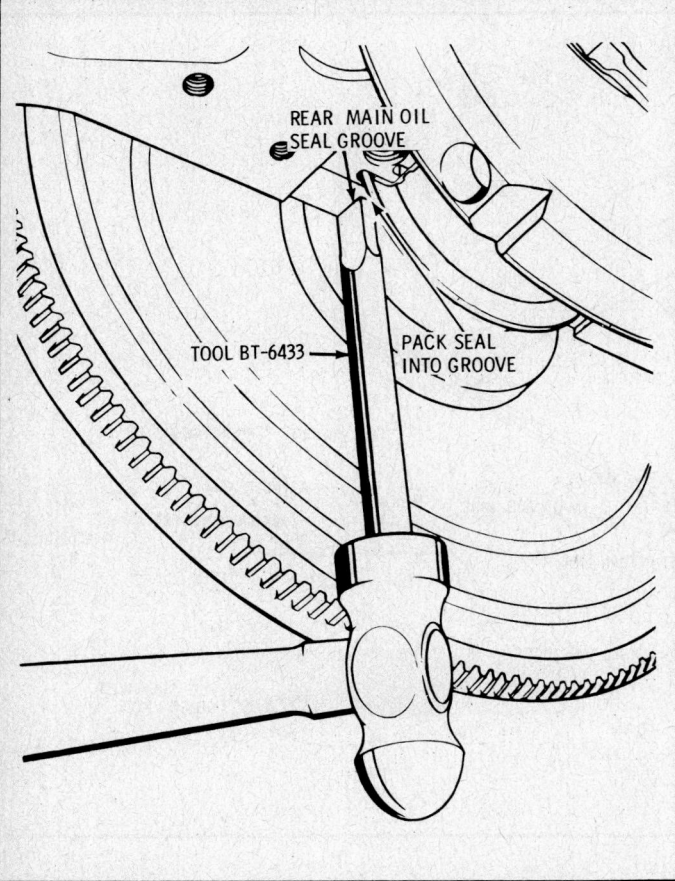

Rear Main Bearing Upper Seal

1. The rear main upper seal can be repaired without removing the crankshaft.

2. Remove rear main bearing cap and pack the old seal tightly into the groove.

3. Cut a length of old seal from the bearing cap. Coat it with sealer and pack the cut portion up into the block. Place a piece of shim stock between the seal and the crankshaft to protect the bearing surface before trimming.

Rear Oil Seal Installation

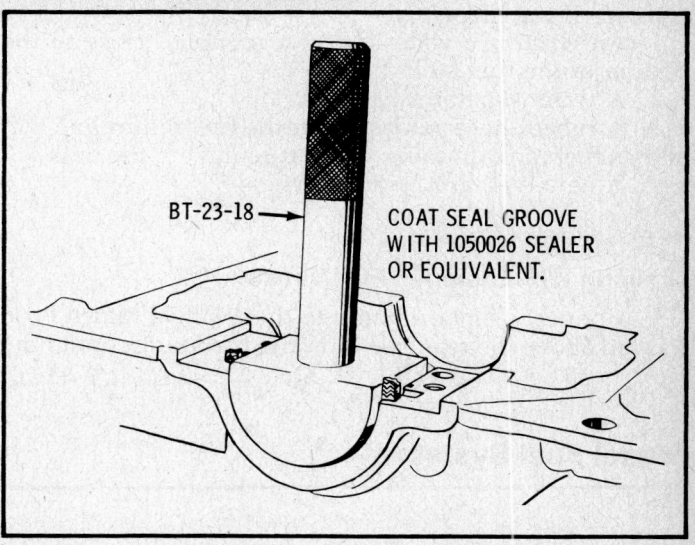

Rear Main Lower Seal

1. Remove the bearing cap and old seal. Pack the new seal into the bearing cap and install the bearing cap. Trim the seal flush with mating surface.

Water In Fuel (WIF) System

The WIF system consists of a revised fuel tank sending unit and a warning lamp on the dash panel which lights

Trimming New Seal

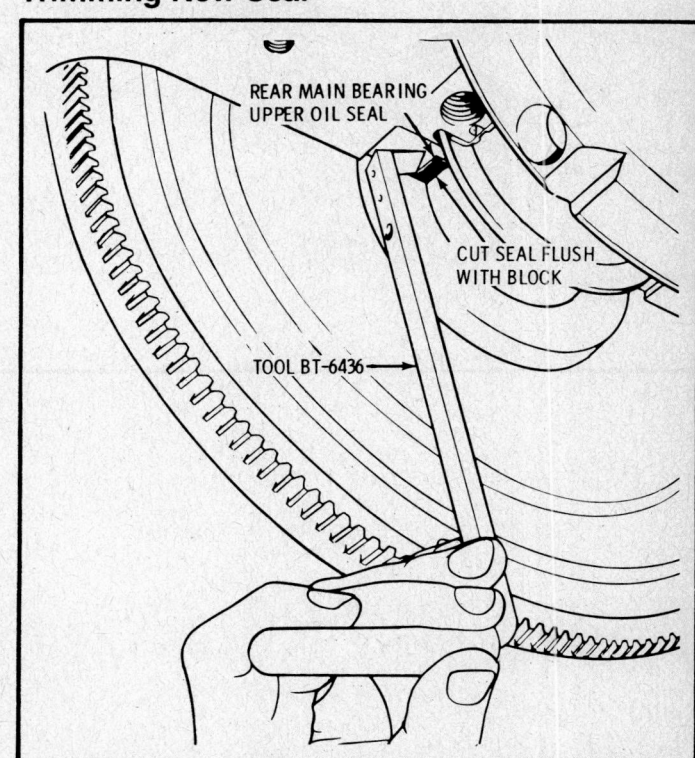

when there is water in the fuel tank. The sending unit consists of the following.

1. An electronic water detector mounted close to the bottom of the fuel tank
2. A water separator filter
3. A rubber hose extension on the fuel return line that allows fuel tank draining without removing the tank
4. A new fuel tank wiring harness

Draining WIF-Equipped Fuel Tanks

1. Connect a siphon pump to the 1/4" fuel return hose located above the rear axle or at the fuel pump under the hood. Continue siphoning until pure diesel fuel begins to drain.

CHILTON CAUTION   Remove the fuel filler cap before draining the tank.

Bench Testing the WIF Unit

1. Submerge the water sensing probe into a container of water and connect to a 12 volt source. Be sure to ground the water.
2. Connect a 12 volt, 2 candle power bulb into the positive wire. The bulb should light until the probe is removed from the water.

Diesel Fuel System

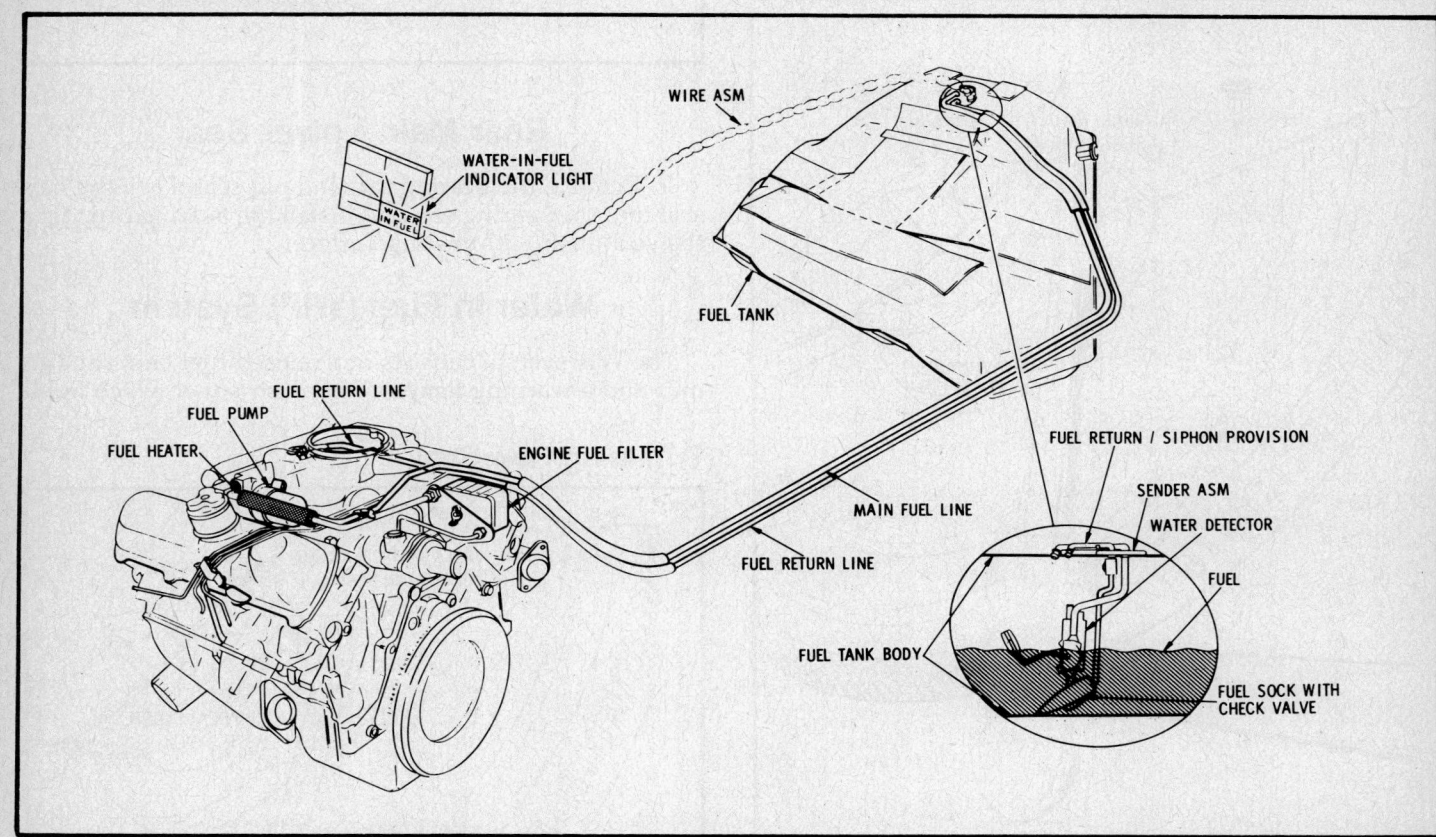

B416

ISUZU DIESEL ENGINE

INDEX

ENGINE DIAGNOSIS

Hard Starting

Difficulty will not be experienced in starting a diesel engine, provided sufficient power is supplied for cranking, compression pressure is sufficiently high, preheating system is operating normally and an appropriate volume of fuel is supplied. As an initial step for checking the cause of hard-starting, loosen pipe joint at nozzle side and see if the fuel is being supplied. In some instances, it may be necessary to check nozzle spray conditions and fuel injection timing. If these checks do not disclose any problems, measure the compression pressure to determine the condition of valves and piston rings.

If the engine starts but stalls suddenly and can not be restarted, presence of air in the fuel system is suspected. Engine startability is more or less affected by the environmental temperature conditions.

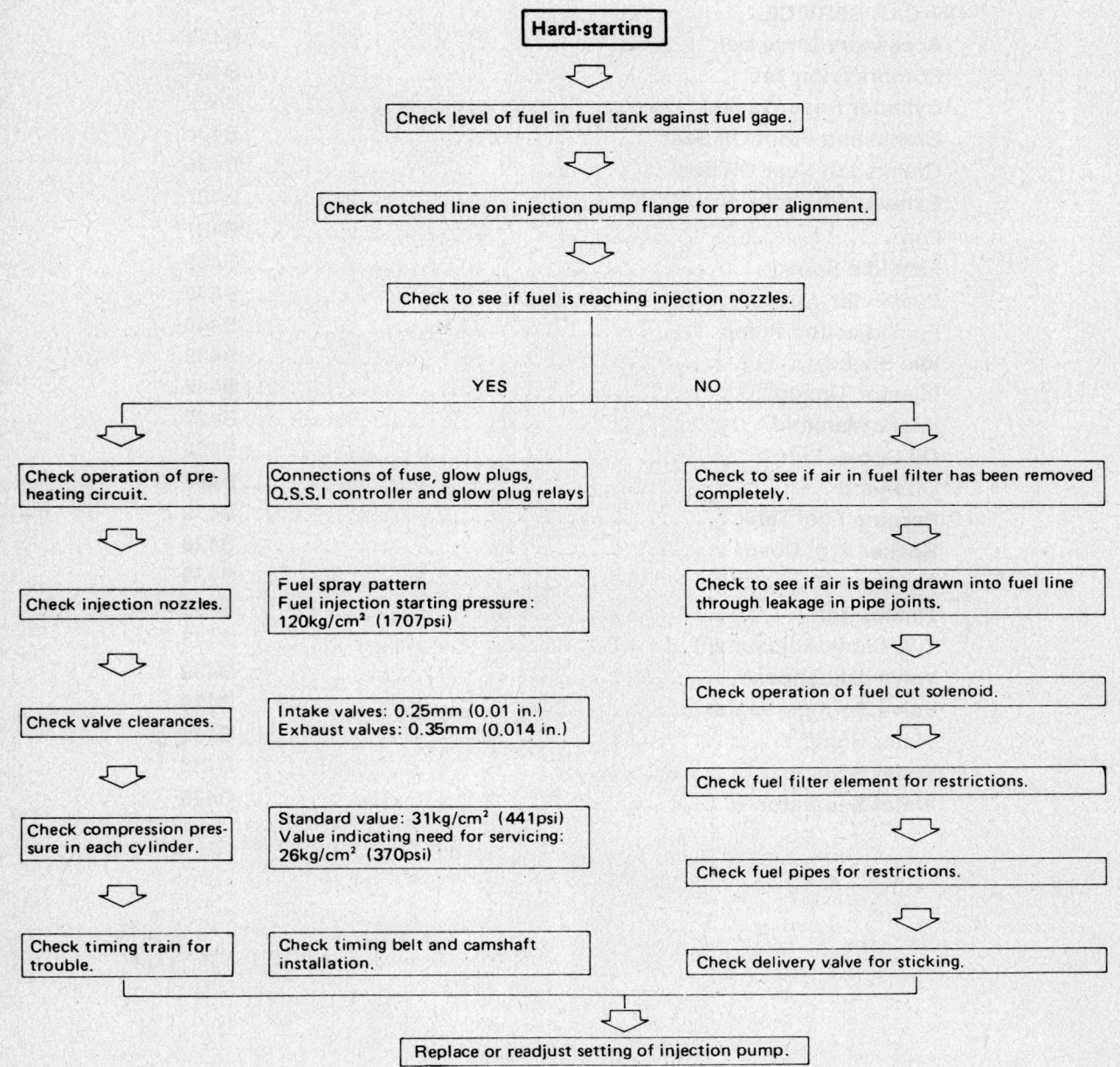

Engine Idling Rough

Rough engine idling can cause engine surging and sudden engine stalling at quick deceleration. If the engine operates normally at medium and high speeds, then check engine idling speed.

Engine hunting may be caused by too low an idling speed, rough plunger operation, over-tightened delivery valve holder, etc. If the engine stalls at quick deceleration, idling speed might have been set too low.

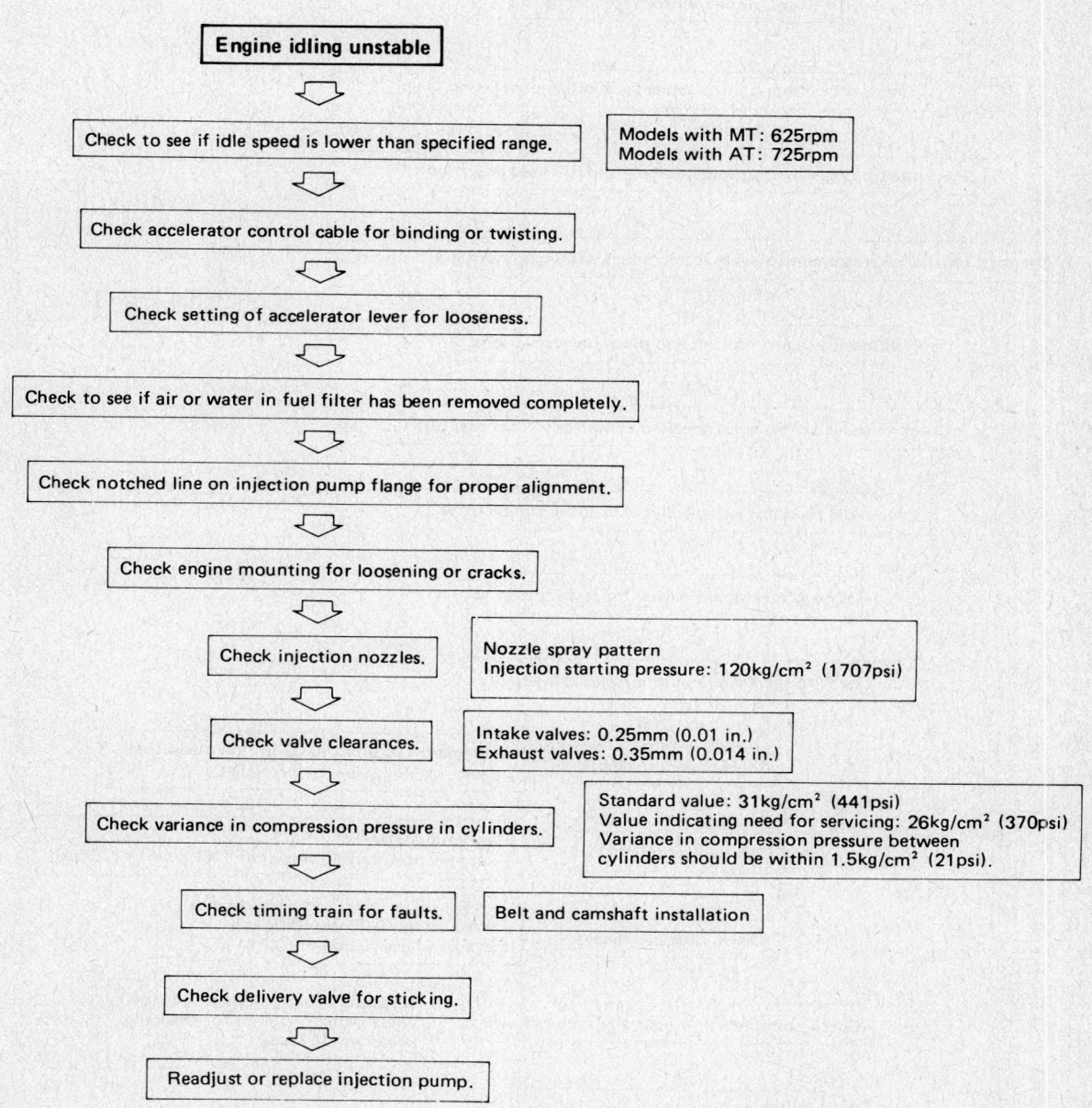

Lack of Engine Power

Lack of engine power may be caused by insufficient injection volume, insufficient volume of intake air, lowered compression pressure, etc. If the trouble is due to lack of volume fuel injection, check fuel filter element for restrictions and fuel system for presence of air. If the volume of intake air is insufficient, check air cleaner element for restrictions and exhaust pipes(s) for clogging.

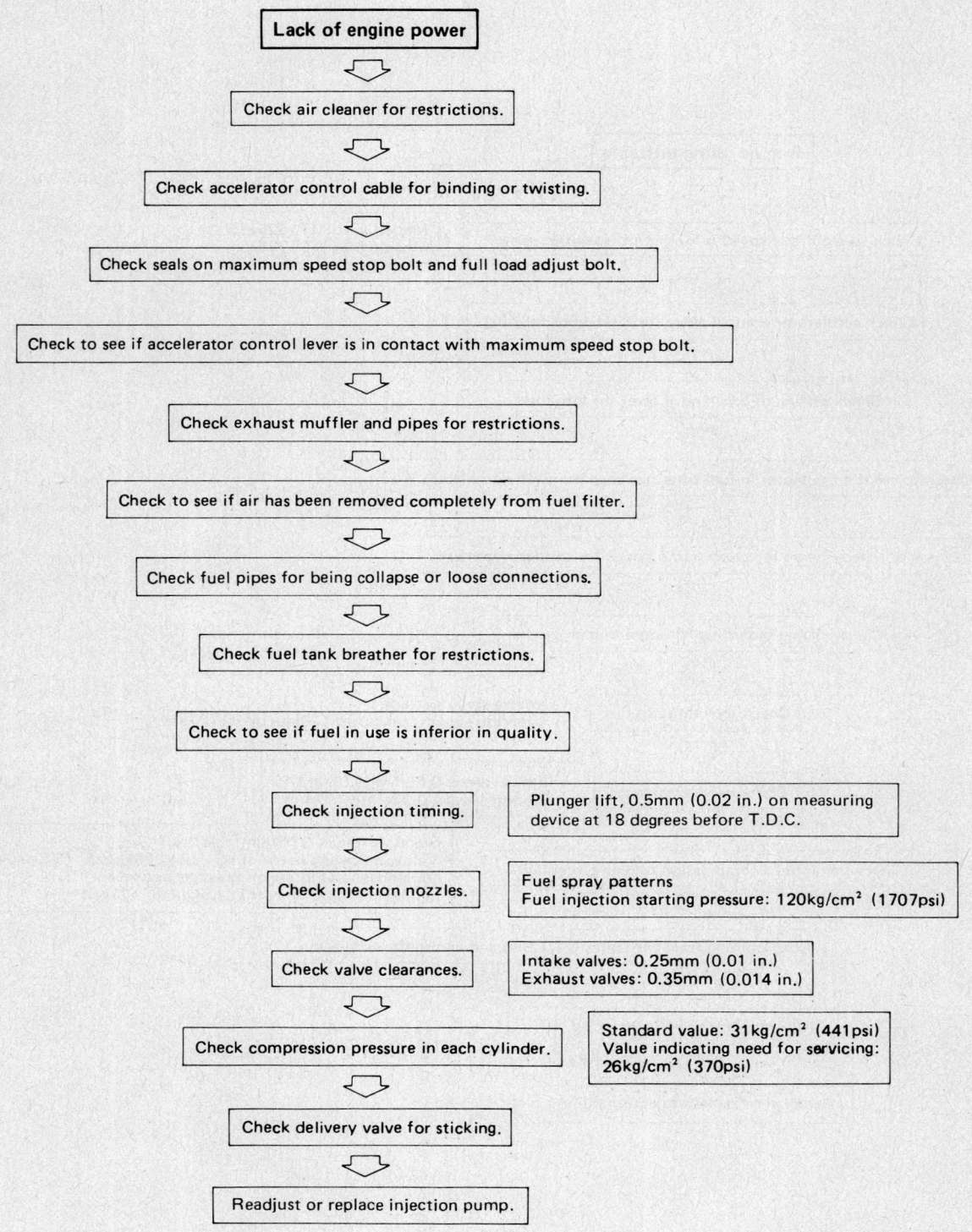

Dark or White Exhaust Smoke

A considerable amount of dark smoke in the exhaust gases is due to incomplete fuel combustion caused by excessive volume of fuel injection, insufficient volume of intake air, poor spray condition, excessively advanced injection timing, etc. To determine the cause, check seals on the injection pump, check compression pressure, condition of air cleaner and injection nozzle spray conditions. Then check fuel injection timing.

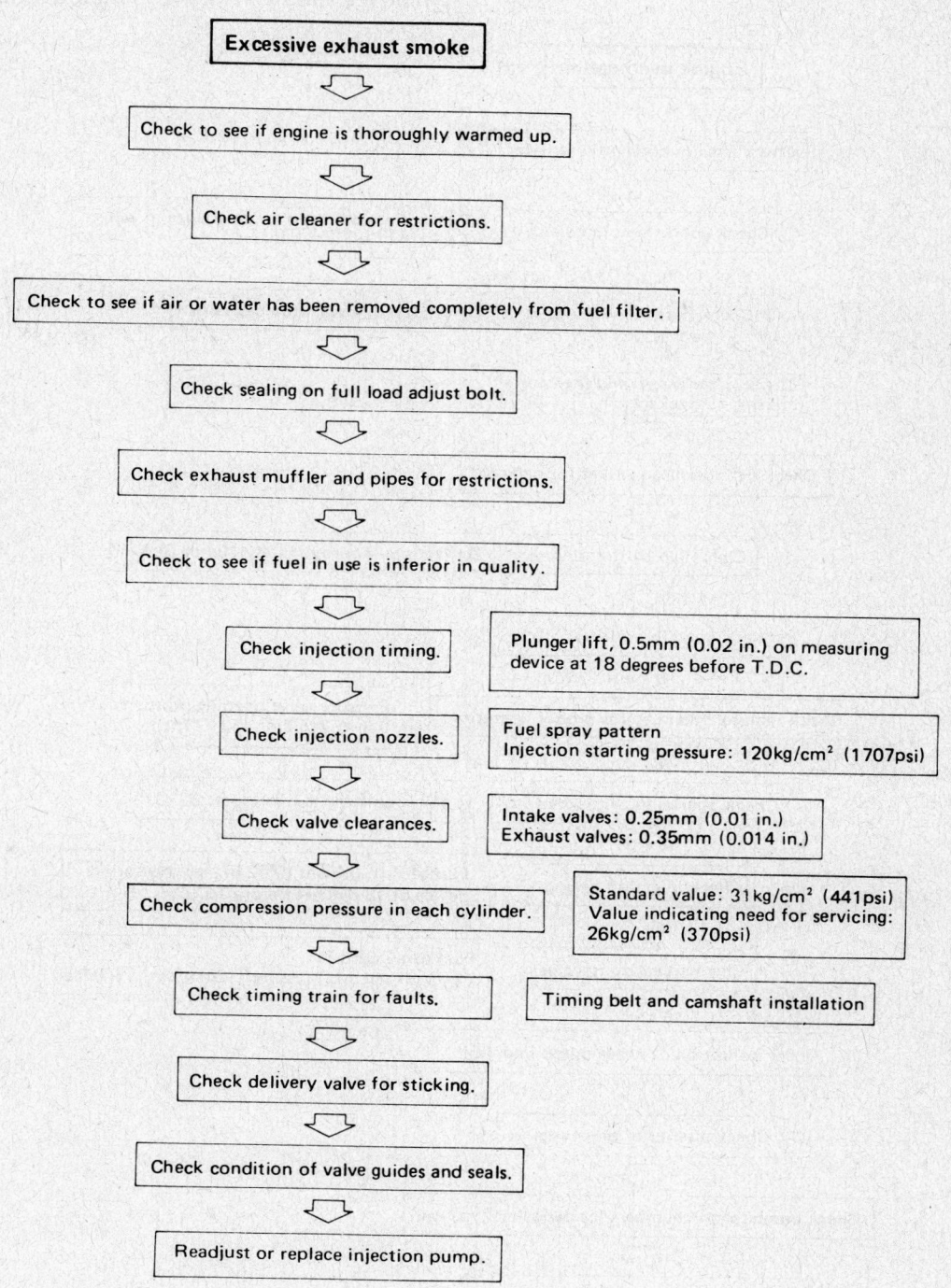

Engine Overheating

When locating the cause of engine overheating, it is necessary to find whether the engine is actually overheating or the temperature gage is giving a false indication. To determine the true cause, measure the temperature of engine coolant at the upper part of the radiator with the engine running. Compare the measured value with the reading of the temperature gage on the instrument panel to check the accuracy of gage indication. Then check the following causes, starting with the item which can be checked easily.

Common causes of engine overheating will be as follows when listed in sequence of frequency: Leakage of coolant from water pump, radiator and hoses and thermostat housing which causes a reduction in coolant level, defective themostat, formation of scales in water passages, etc. Leakage of gases into cooling water circuit due to defective gasket, excessive volume of fuel injection, incorrect injection timing, deposit of carbon within the combustion chambers are but some of the causes of engine overheating which are often overlooked.

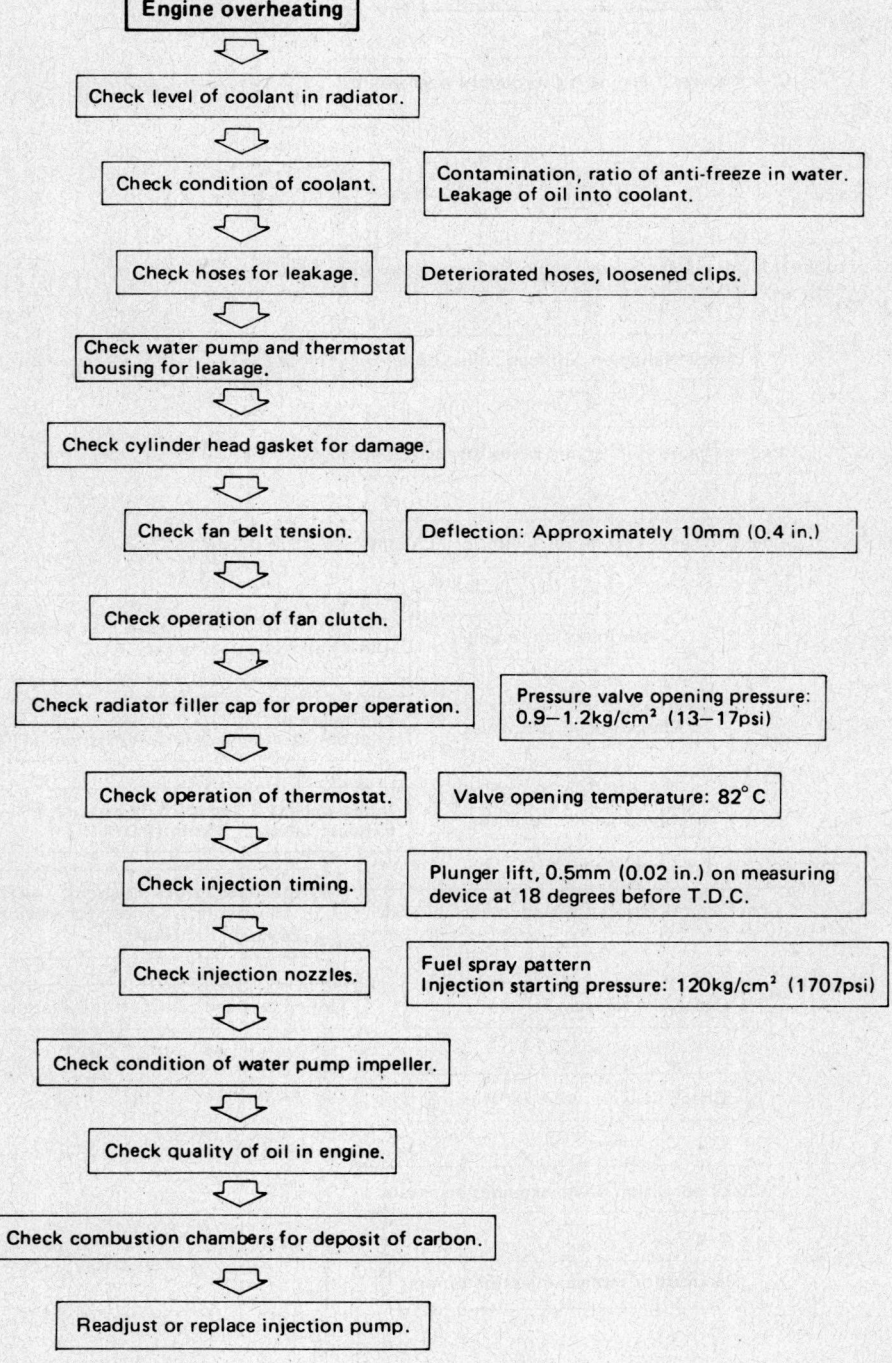

Engine Noisy

Abnormal noise of engine includes knocking sound, piston slap, etc. Engine may produce slight knocking immediately after starting which normally diminishes as the engine temperature increases. Engine knocking is a result of rapid fuel combustion caused by a delay in the injection timing. It is due mainly to excessively advanced fuel injection timing or deteriorated fuel spray conditions.

If engine produces a continuous noise, systematic checks are usually performed to determine the source of the noise. Noise from the auxiliaries such as generator, water pump, etc. can be shut-off by removing fan belt to make checks on the engine easier. If the engine produces slapping noise such as piston slap, piston pins and connecting-rod bearing noise, from which cylinder the noise comes can be checked by interrupting flow of fuel with the injection pipe joints loosened in sequence. Engine crank shaft noise can be diagnosed by moving the clutch pedal in and out, if noise is caused by crank shaft movement. Noise will change as the clutch is operated.

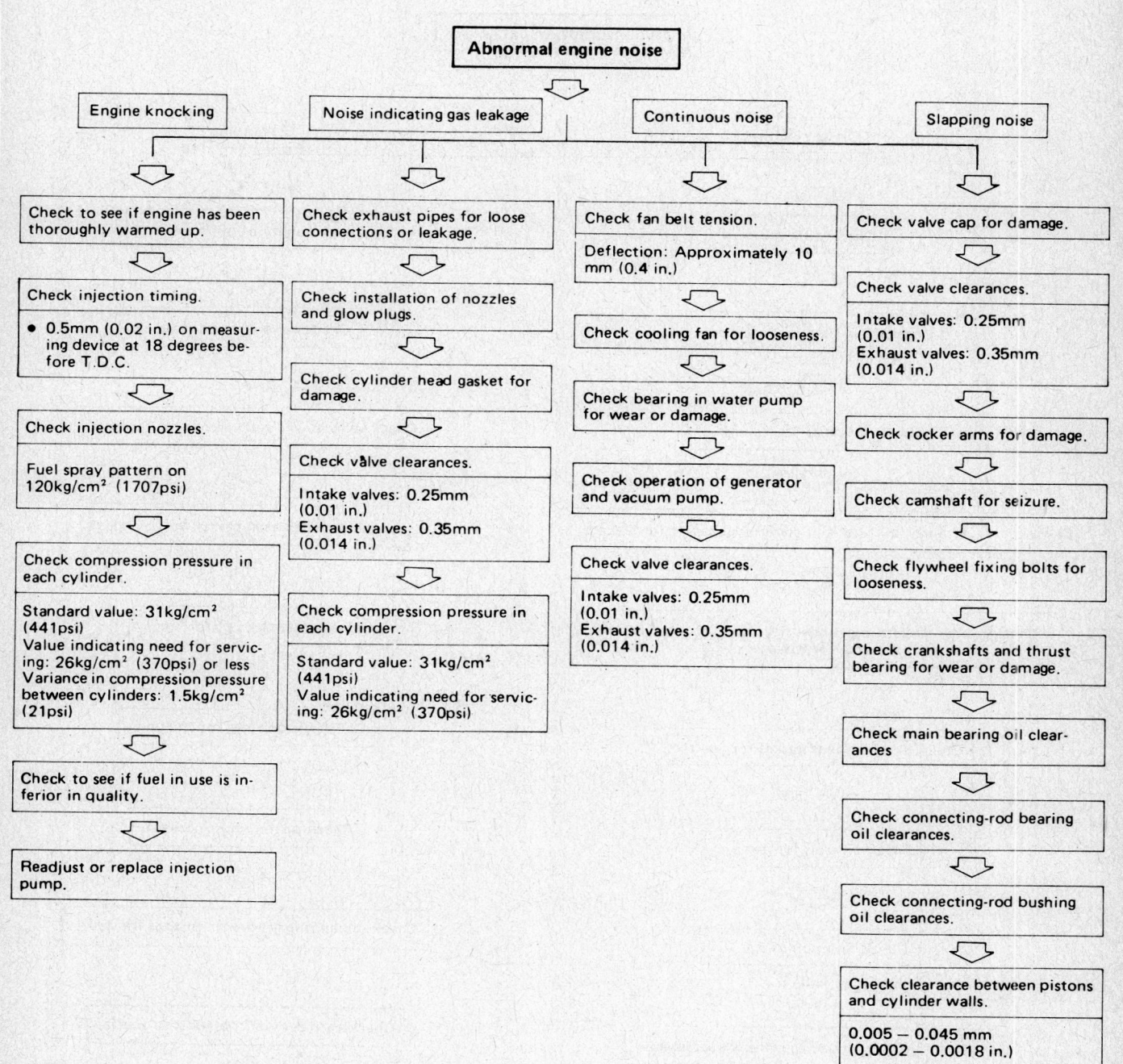

Excessive Engine Oil Consumption

Major causes of excessive oil consumption include oil leakage, oil burning and internal leakage of oil past the piston clearances, and external oil leakage can be detected with relative ease through visual checks. To find whether oil is burning or leaking past the piston clearances, start and let the engine idle for a few minutes. Then check with the cylinder head removed. Oil burning is indicated by the traces of oil around the circumference of pistons. A trace of oil is normally found around the valve head and deposit of carbon is localized to that area when internal oil leakage is present.

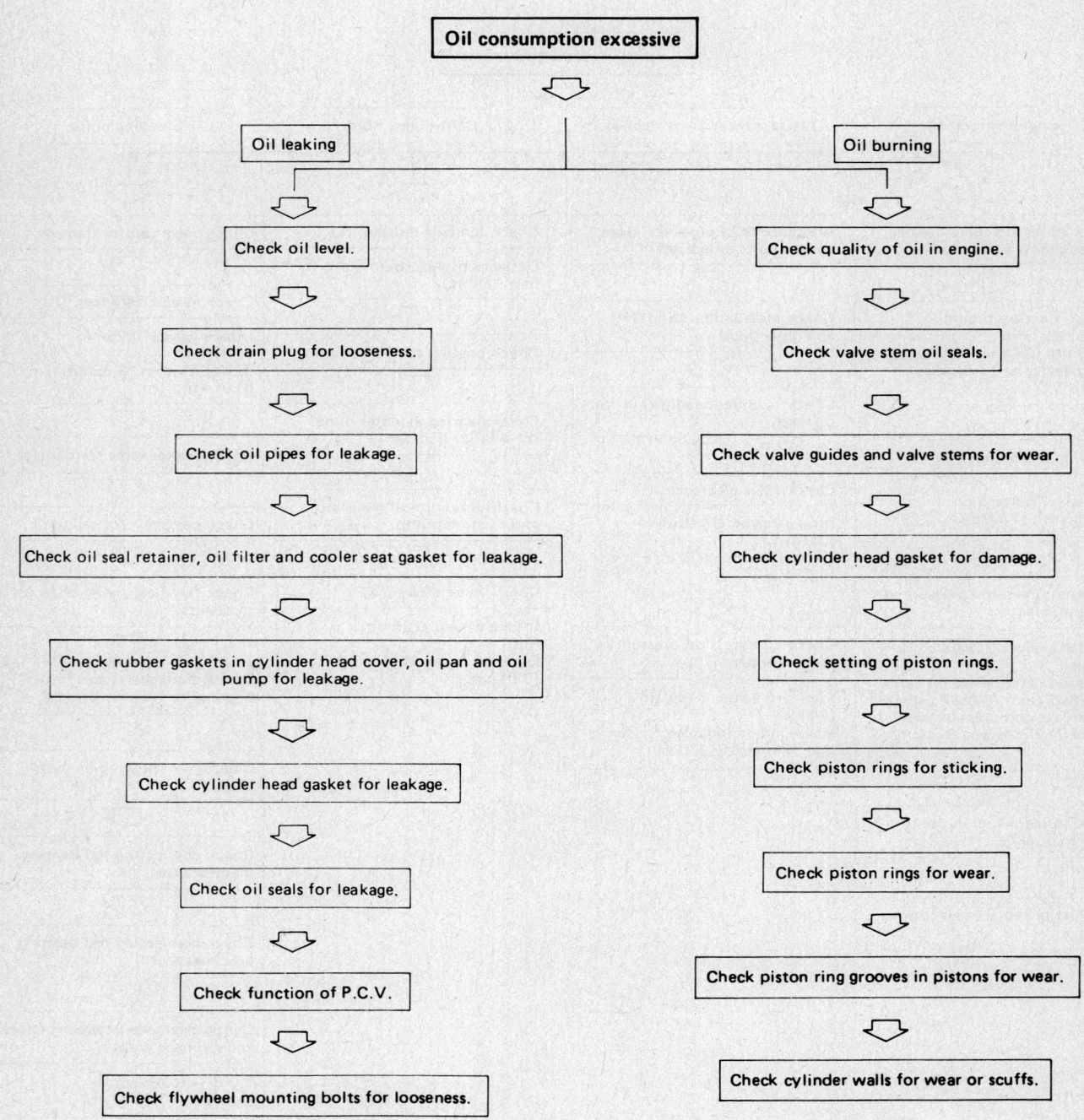

Excessive Fuel Consumption

It is necessary to find what rate of fuel consumption is registered under which driving conditions before following the diagnosis procedure since the fuel consumption varies greatly with the driving habits, load the vehicle carries and general condition of the roads and streets. As a first step, check the air cleaner and exhaust muffler for restrictions. Then check the compression pressure in the cylinders. Road test the vehicle to see if the engine operates normally, giving reasonable acceleration. If the results of the road test are satisfactory, trouble in the fuel system is suspected. To determine the condition of the fuel system, check fuel spray condition and injection starting pressure using a nozzle tester. Then measure the volume of fuel injection with an injection pump tester.

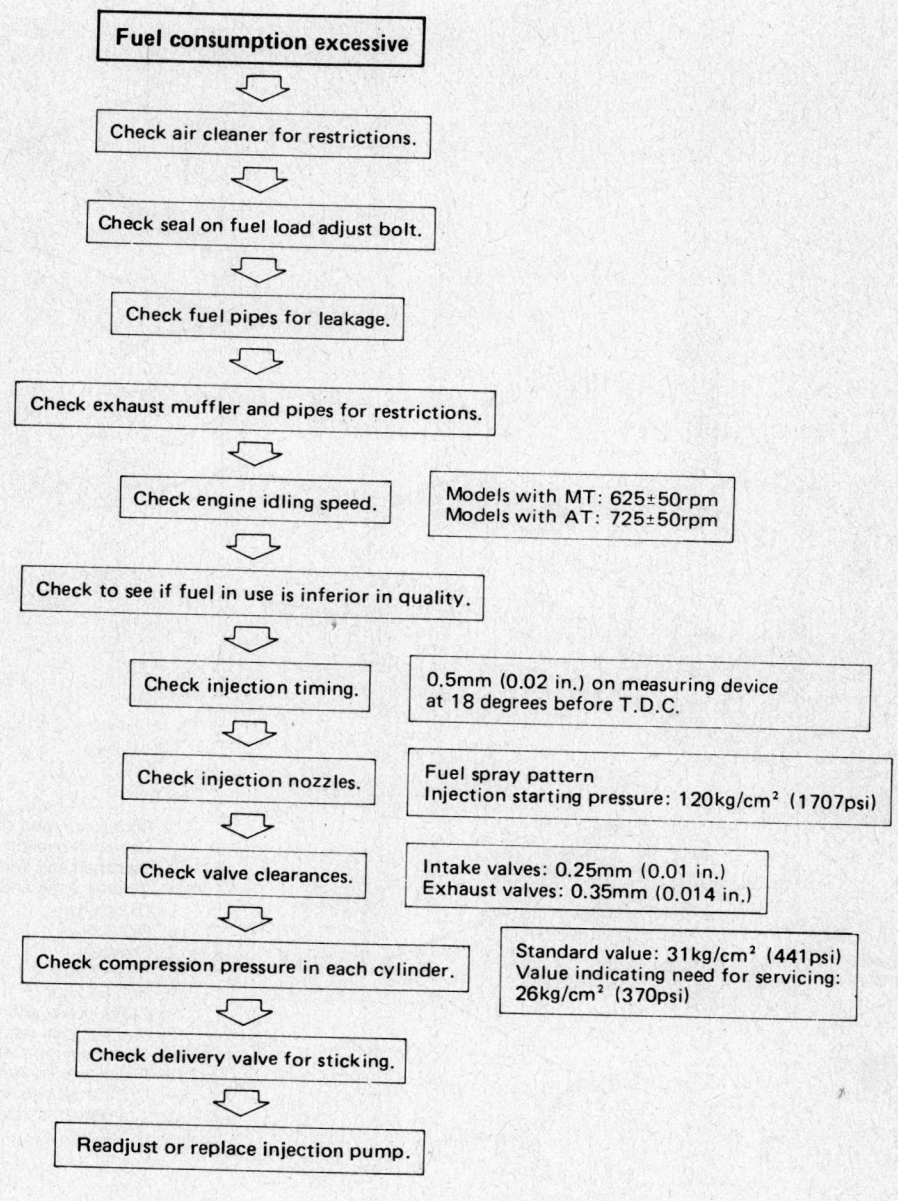

Fuel consumption excessive

Check air cleaner for restrictions.

Check seal on fuel load adjust bolt.

Check fuel pipes for leakage.

Check exhaust muffler and pipes for restrictions.

Check engine idling speed.
Models with MT: 625±50rpm
Models with AT: 725±50rpm

Check to see if fuel in use is inferior in quality.

Check injection timing.
0.5mm (0.02 in.) on measuring device at 18 degrees before T.D.C.

Check injection nozzles.
Fuel spray pattern
Injection starting pressure: 120kg/cm² (1707psi)

Check valve clearances.
Intake valves: 0.25mm (0.01 in.)
Exhaust valves: 0.35mm (0.014 in.)

Check compression pressure in each cylinder.
Standard value: 31kg/cm² (441psi)
Value indicating need for servicing: 26kg/cm² (370psi)

Check delivery valve for sticking.

Readjust or replace injection pump.

ENGINE DESCRIPTION

The diesel engine is a 1.8 liter 4 cylinder engine and a manual 5 speed transmission. The 3-speed automatic is offered as an option. The diesel is an in-line 4 cylinder 4 cycle water cooled engine. Bore and stroke are 3.31 and 3.23 inches. Piston displacement is 111 cubic inches. The compression ratio is 22 to 1.

Cylinder head and cylinder block are of cast iron and are the crossflow design. The engine has an overhead camshaft with direct acting rocker arms. Valve lash adjustment is obtained through lash adjusters on the opposite ends of the rocker arms. The camshaft and injection pump are driven by a cog belt.

Engine Components

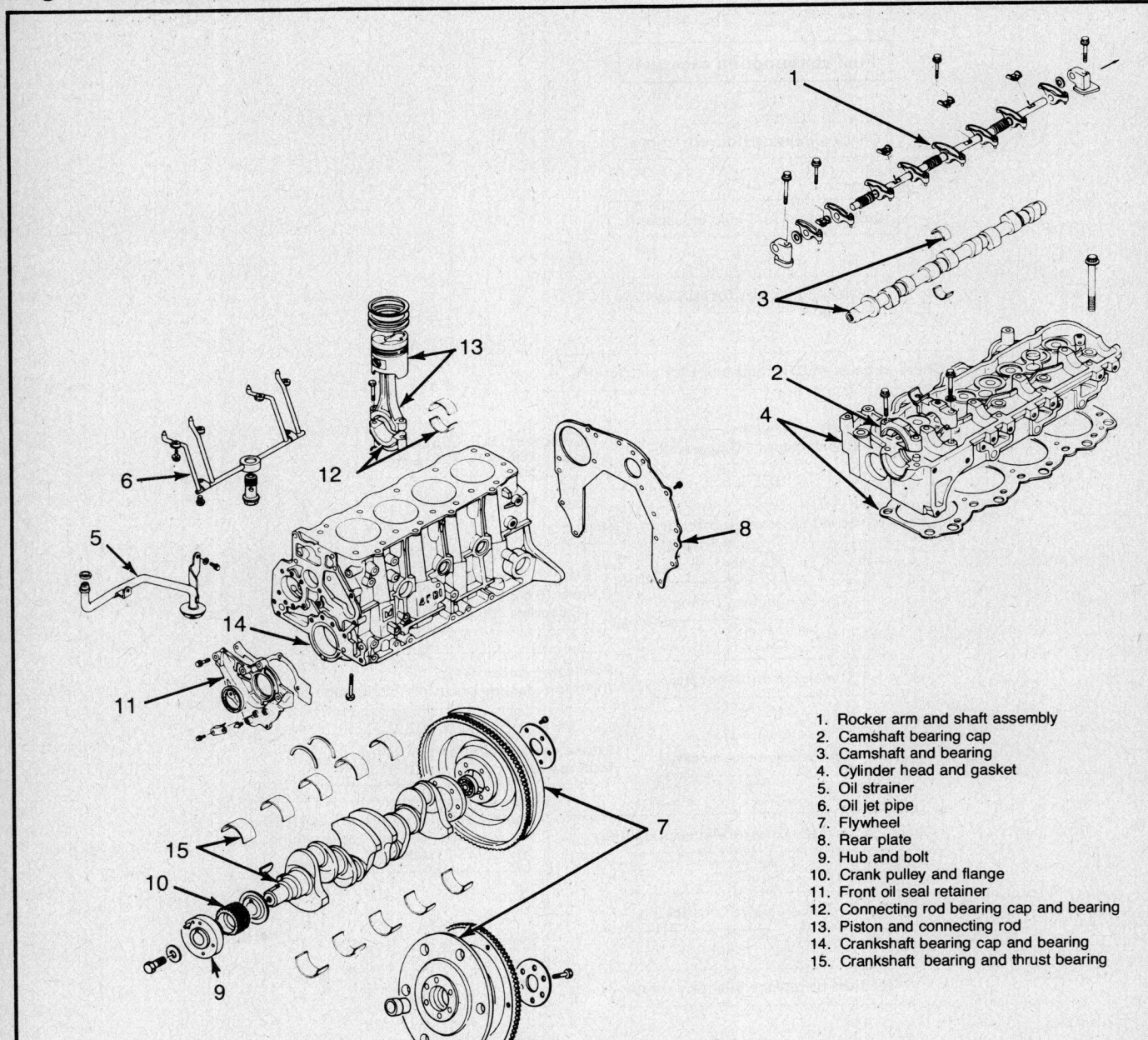

1. Rocker arm and shaft assembly
2. Camshaft bearing cap
3. Camshaft and bearing
4. Cylinder head and gasket
5. Oil strainer
6. Oil jet pipe
7. Flywheel
8. Rear plate
9. Hub and bolt
10. Crank pulley and flange
11. Front oil seal retainer
12. Connecting rod bearing cap and bearing
13. Piston and connecting rod
14. Crankshaft bearing cap and bearing
15. Crankshaft bearing and thrust bearing

ON CAR SERVICE

Compression Test

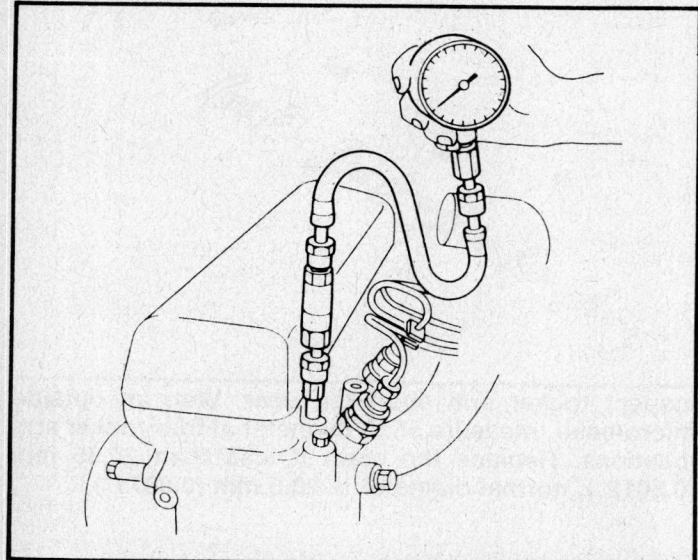

a time in a sequence starting with the inner bolts and working outward.

3. If equipped with power steering, adjust drive belt.

Intake Manifold

REMOVAL

1. Disconnect battery negative cable.
2. Disconnect fresh air hose and vent hose.
3. Remove fuel separator.
4. Disconnect electrical connectors and accelerator linkage and glow plug wires.
5. Remove injector lines at pump and injectors.
6. Remove injection line, hold down clamps and remove lines.
7. Remove glow plug line at head.
8. If equipped with power steering, remove belt and idler pulley and bracket.
9. Remove upper front dust cover.
10. Remove front cover bracket.
11. Remove intake manifold bolts.

INSTALLATION

The gasket surfaces on both the head and manifold

Compression Test

1. Start the engine and bring engine coolant temperature to 75-80°C (167°F-176°F).
2. Remove the following:
a. Sensing resistor
b. Glow plug connector
c. Glow plugs (4)
d. Fuel cust solenoid connector
e. Disconnect the fusible link wire of Q.S.S. (quick start and silent idling) at the connector.
3. Install adaptor J-29762 and compression gage.
4. Take measurement by engaging starter motor.
a. Standard: 31.0 (441) kg.cm (psi) at 200 rpm or more.
b. Limit: 26.0 (370) kg.cm (psi) at 200 rpm or less.

Exhaust Manifold

REMOVAL

1. Disconnect battery negative cable.
2. Raise vehicle.
3. Disconnect exhaust pipe from exhaust manifold.
4. Remove power steering belt.
5. Remove flex hose.
6. Remove power steering pump.
7. Remove manifold bolts.
8. Remove exhaust manifold.

INSTALLATION

The gasket surfaces on both the head and manifold must be clean of any foreign matter and free of nicks or heavy scratches.
1. Place new gasket on the mounting studs.
2. Reverse removal procedures. Tighten bolts a little at

Exhaust Manifold

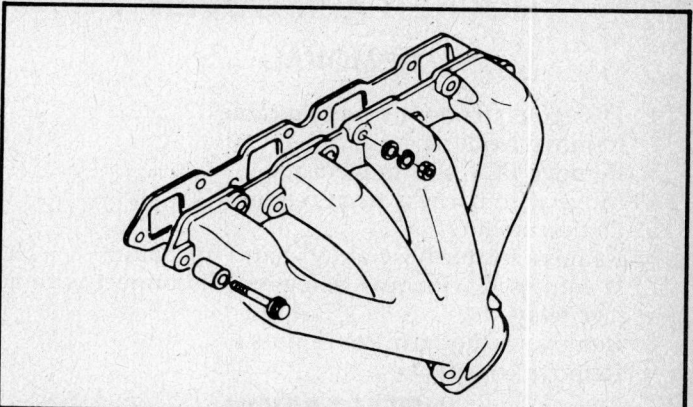

Intake Manifold

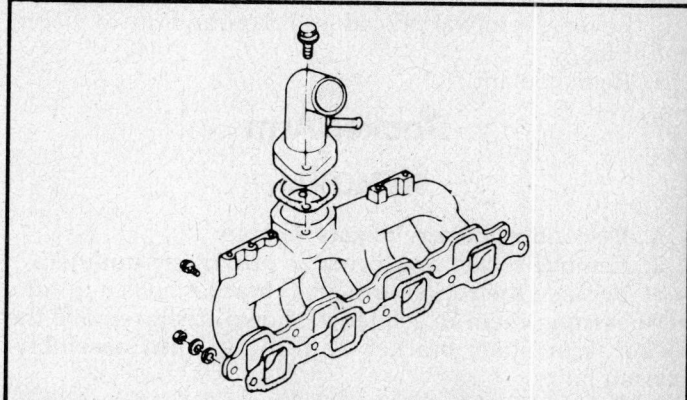

ISUZU DIESEL ENGINE
ON-CAR SERVICE

Rocker Arm Cover

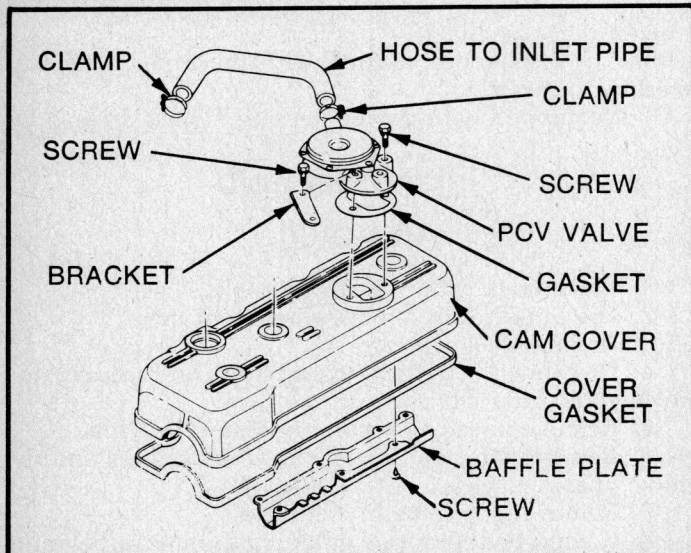

must be clean of any foreign material and free of nicks and heavy scratches.

1. Place a new gasket over the mounting studs.
2. Install the intake manifold.
3. Torque bolts to 40 N•m (30 ft.lbs.).
4. Reverse removal procedures.
5. If equipped with power steering, adjust drive belt.

ROCKER ARM COVER

REMOVAL

1. Disconnect battery negative cable.
2. Remove fresh air hose.
3. Remove PCV and move aside.
4. Move wire harness from retainers.
5. Drain coolant.
6. Remove heater hose at left hand insulator.
7. If equipped with rear defogger, disconnect wire at defogger relay.
8. Remove rocker arm cover nuts.
9. Remove cover.

INSTALLATION

1. Check gasket for damage, replace if necessary.
2. Reverse removal procedures. Torque nuts to 9 N•m (6-8 ft.lbs.).
3. Refill coolant.

Rocker Arm

REMOVAL

1. Disconnect battery negative cable.
2. Remove rocker arm cover as previously outlined.
3. Remove the rocker arm shaft bracket bolts and nuts by loosening them in sequence shown, then remove the rocker arm shaft bracket and rocker arm assembly. Loosen bolts.
4. Remove rocker arms.

Rocker Arms, Bracket and Shaft

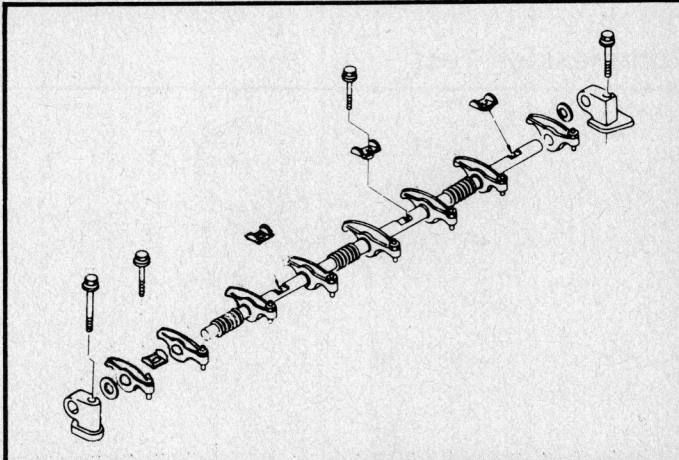

Inspect rocker arm shaft for wear. With an outside micrometer, measure shaft diameter at four rocker arm locations. Replace the shaft if less than 20.35 mm (0.8012″); normal diameter is 20.5 mm (0.8071″)

Bolt Sequence

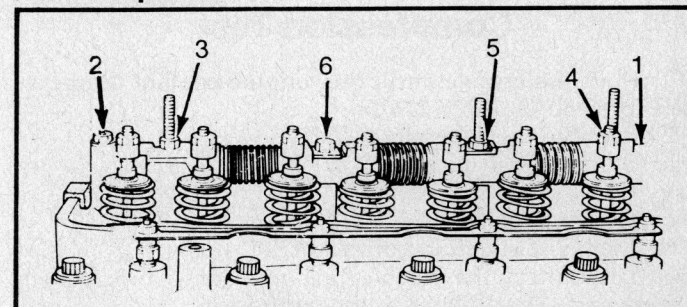

INSTALLATION

1. Apply a generous amount of clean engine oil to the rocker arm shaft, rocker arms and valve stem end caps.
2. Install the rocker arm shaft assembly and tighten the bolts in sequence as shown. Torque to 27 N•m (20 ft.lbs.).
3. Adjust valves as outlined later in this section.
4. Reinstall the cam cover.

Valve Springs and/or Valve Stem Oil Seal

REMOVAL

1. Remove rocker arm cover as previously outlined.
2. Remove rocker arm shaft and bracket assembly as previously outlined.
3. Rotate engine to TDC for cylinder being serviced.
4. Remove valve stem end caps.
5. Compress valve spring using tool J-29760. Remove valve collets and remove valve spring upper seat and valve springs.
6. Remove valve stem oil seal.

7. Remove valve spring lower seat.

INSTALLATION

1. Lubricate valve stem and valve spring lower seat with clean engine oil.

2. Install new seal over valve stem and onto valve guide. Check that projection on inner face of oil seal fits into the groove in the valve guide.

3. Install inner and outer springs and upper seat. Compress valve springs using Spring Compressing Tool J-29760 and install valve spring retainers. Remove tool and inspect to make sure retainers are fully seated in the valve stem groove.

4. Apply valve stem end caps with clean engine oil and install stem end caps.

5. Reinstall rocker arm shaft and bracket assembly.

Valve Adjustment

1. Check the rocker arm shaft bracket bolts and nuts for looseness. Torque to 27 N•m (20 ft.lbs.) before adjusting valves.

2. Rotate crank shaft until #1 or #4 cylinder is at TDC on compression stroke.

3. Select the valves to be adjusted. For each valve, insert feeler gage of specified thickness into the clearance

Valve Adjustment

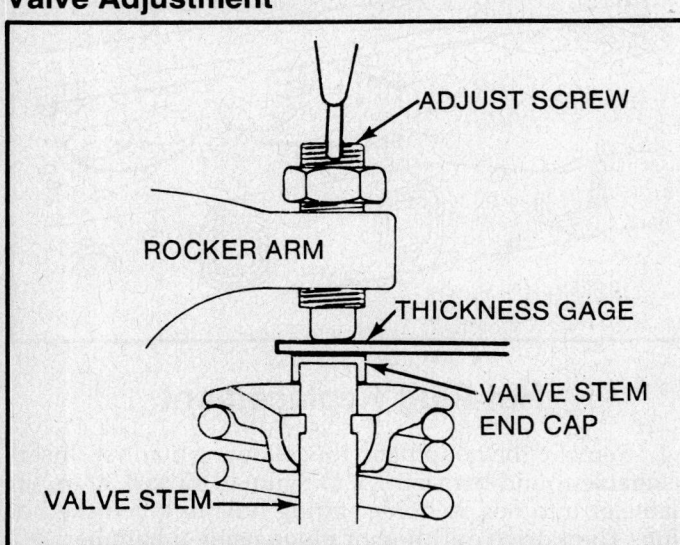

Intake valves: 0.01″ (0.25 mm)
Exhaust valves: 0.014″ (0.35 mm)

Adjustment Chart

CYLINDER NO.	1		2		3		4	
VALVES	I	E	I	E	I	E	I	E
STEP. 1	○	○	○			○		
STEP. 2				○	○		○	○

I : INTAKE VALVE
E : EXHAUST VALVE

Valve Spring Compressor

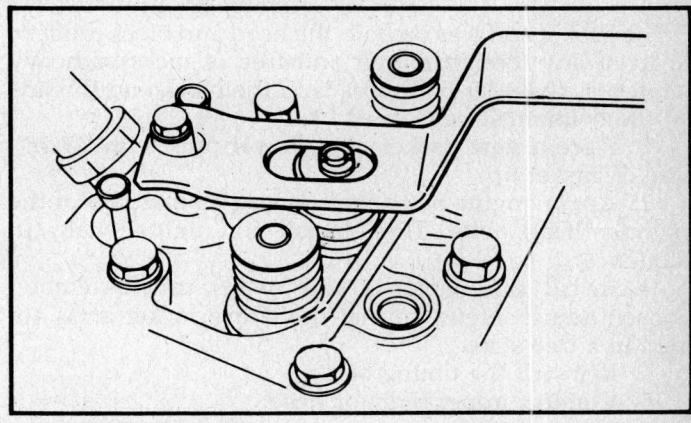

Valve Assembly

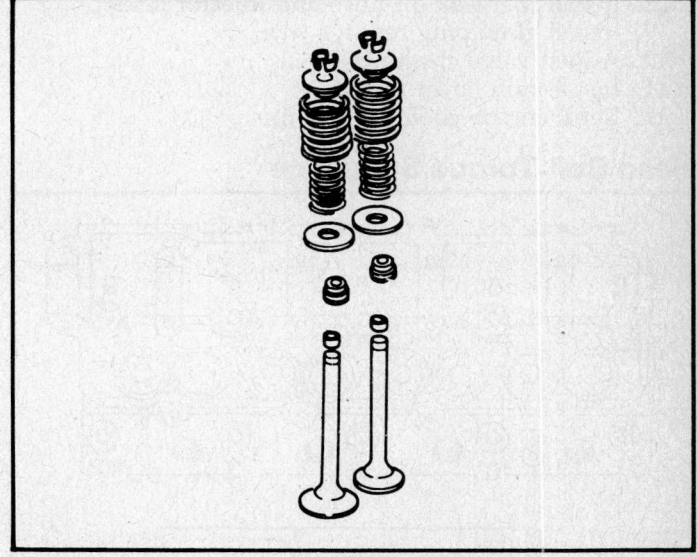

between the valve stem end and the rocker arm. Adjust as required.

4. Rotate crank shaft on revolution and adjust the remaining valves.

Cylinder Head and/or Gasket

REMOVAL

1. Disconnect battery negative cable.
2. Drain cooling system.
3. Remove cam cover.
4. Remove timing belt. It will not be necessary to remove lower cover and damper.
5. Remove camshaft.
6. Remove glow plug resistor wire.
7. Remove injector lines.
8. Remove fuel leak off hose.
9. Disconnect exhaust pipe at manifold.
10. Remove oil feed at rear of head.
11. Disconnect upper radiator hose.
12. Remove head bolts.
13. Remove head with intake and exhaust.

ISUZU DIESEL ENGINE

INSTALLATION

The gasket surfaces on both the head and block must be clean of any foreign matter and free of nicks or heavy scratches. Cylinder bolt threads in the block and threads on the bolts must be cleaned.

1. Place a new gasket over dowel pins with "TOP" side of gasket up.

2. Apply engine oil to threads and seating face of the cylinder head bolts. Then install and tighten bolts in sequence.

3. Install the camshaft and rocker arm assembly. Loosen adjust screws so that the entire rocker arms are held in a free state.

4. Reinstall the timing belt.

5. Connect upper radiator hose.

6. Connect oil feed at rear of head.

7. Connect exhaust pipe at manifold.

8. Install fuel leak off hose and injector lines.

9. Install glow plug resistor wire.

10. Adjust valve clearance.

11. Install cam cover.

12. Refill engine cooling system.

Head Bolt Torque Sequence

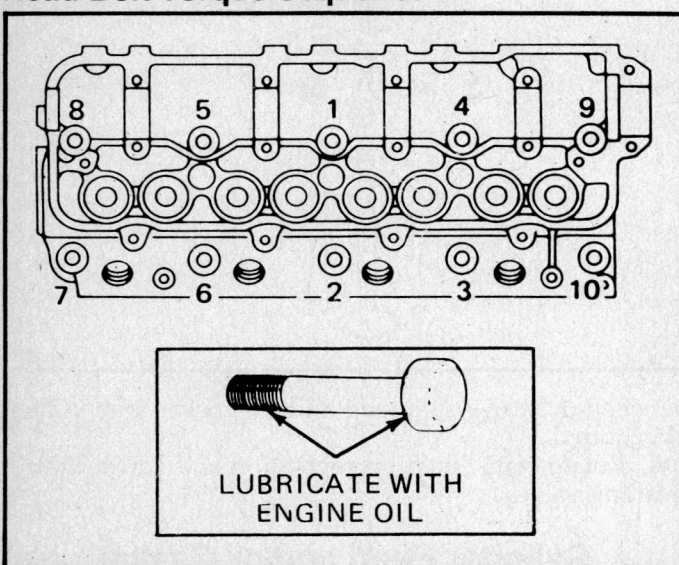

First pull: 21-36 lbs.
Second pull, old bolt: 90-105 lbs.
Second pull, new bolt: 83-98 lbs.

Distortion of Lower Surface

Check the lower face for distortion in directions diagonally and across the face as shown using a straight edge and a feeler gage. Correction is necessary if the amount of distortion is beyond the specified value.

Depression of Hot Plugs

Check the amount of depression of hot plugs no. 1 through no. 4 cylinders using a feeler gage, with a straight edge held against the hot plug face.

Head Distortion

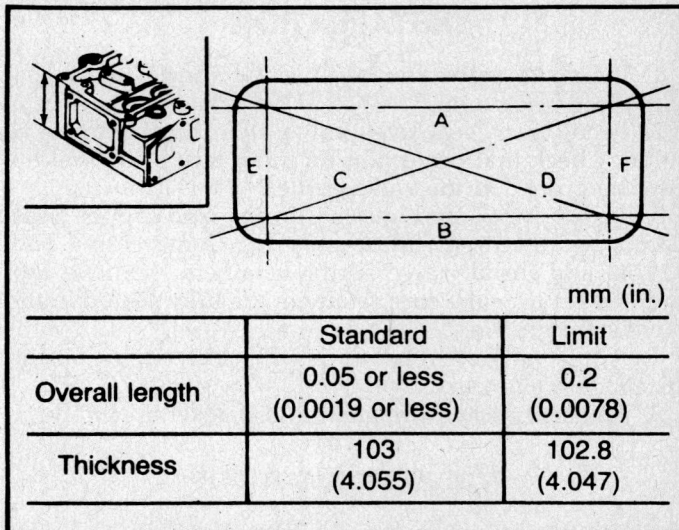

		mm (in.)
	Standard	Limit
Overall length	0.05 or less (0.0019 or less)	0.2 (0.0078)
Thickness	103 (4.055)	102.8 (4.047)

Depression of Hot Plug

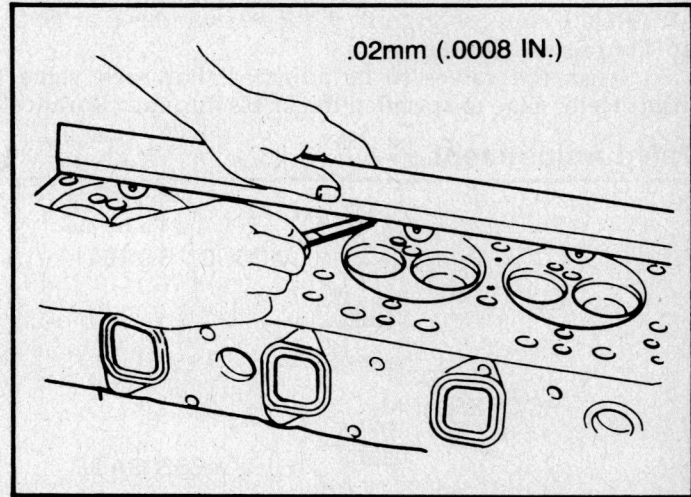

.02mm (.0008 IN.)

Hot Plug Replacement

1. Remove the hot plug in the following manner. Insert a suitable round bar sizing 3 to 5 mm (0.12 to 0.20 in.) in diameter into nozzle holder fitting hole to touch the hot plug. Then drive out the hot plugs using a hammer.

2. Install lock ball into groove in hot plug. Drive the hot plug into cylinder head by aligning lock ball in hot plug with groove in cylinder head.

3. Press the hot plug into position by applying 4500 to 5000 kg (9922.5 to 11250 lbs.) pressure using a bench press with a piece of metal fitted against the hot plug face for protection. After installation, grind the face of hot plug flush with the face of the cylinder head.

Valve Guide Replacement

1. Drive out the valve guide with tool J-26512 fitted against the valve guide from lower face of the cylinder head.

Driving Out Hot Plug

MATCH MARK

Hot Plug Replacement

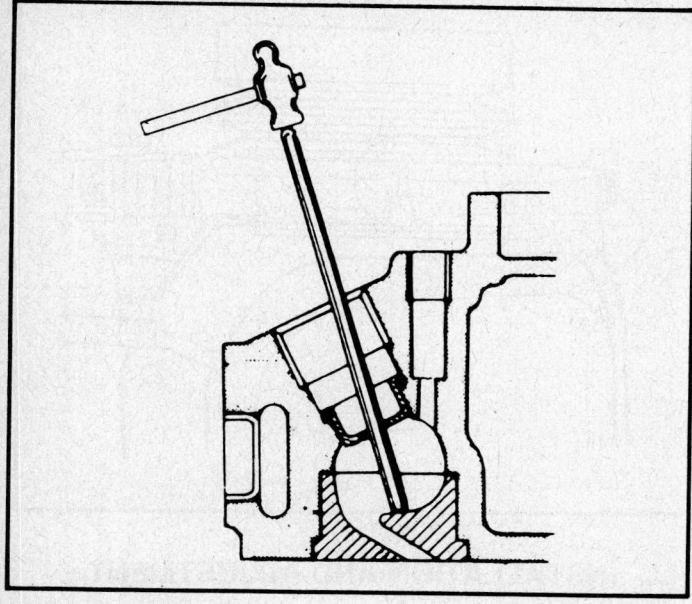

2. Apply engine oil to the outer circumference of the valve guide. Set the installer (J-26512) to the valve guide. Then drive the guide into position from the upper face of the cylinder head using a hammer. The valve guide should always be replaced together with the valve as a set.

Valve Seat Insert

Check valve seat contact width, condition of seat contact, scores, dents, etc. Check the amount of valve seat depression (from lower face of cylinder head to valve face) using a depth gage with a valve fitted into cylinder head.

Pressing in Hot Plug

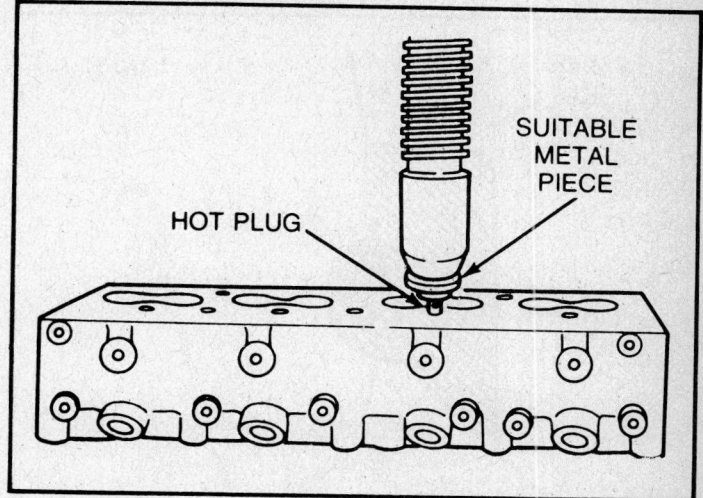

SUITABLE METAL PIECE

HOT PLUG

Valve Guide Removal

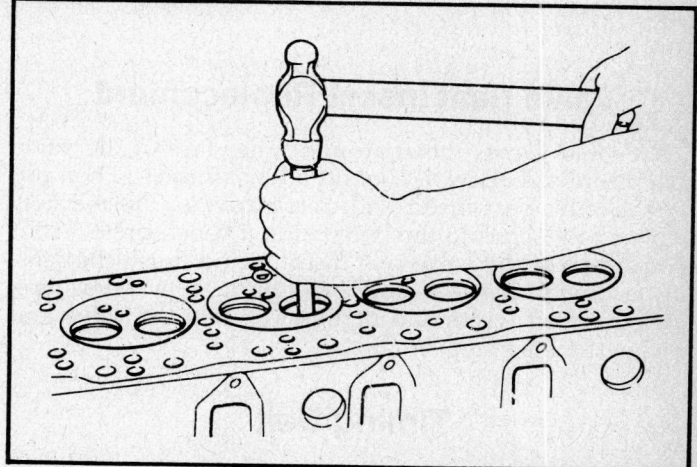

Valve Guide Installation

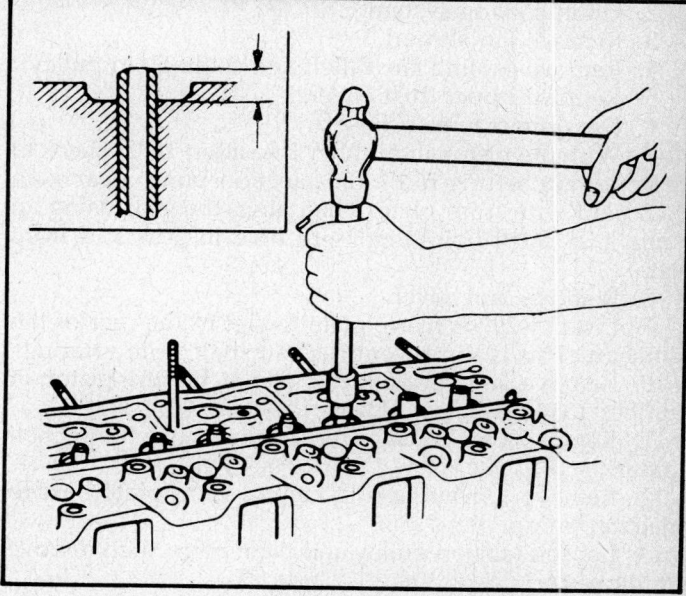

ISUZU DIESEL ENGINE
ON-CAR SERVICE

Valve Seat Insert Replacement

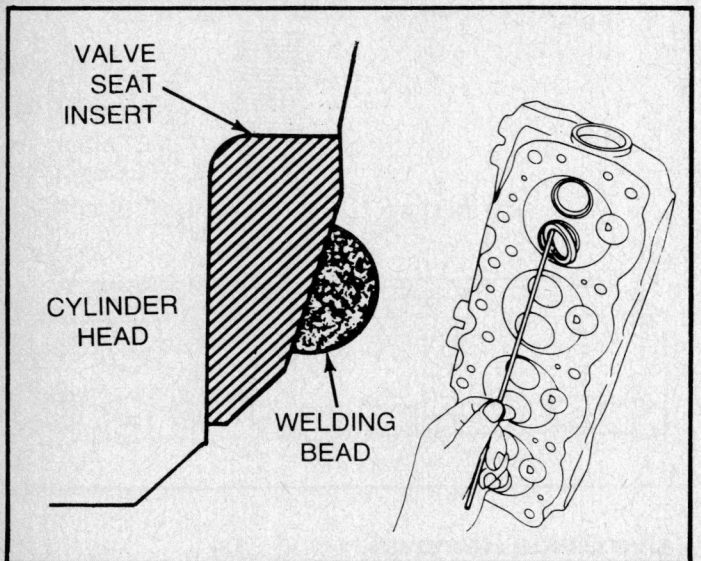

Upper and Lower Dust Cover

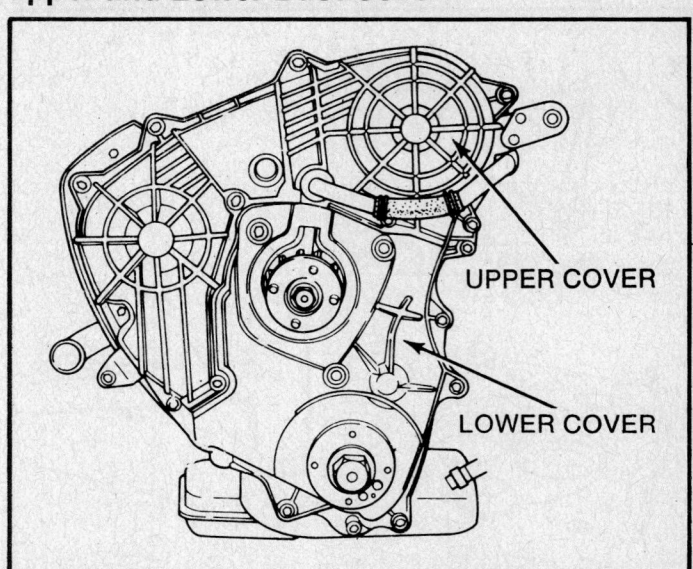

Valve Seat Insert Replacement

Arc-weld excess metal around inner face of the valve seat insert and allow to cool off a few minutes. Then pry off the valve seat insert with screwdrivers. Press a new valve seat insert into the bore using a bench press. After installation of the valve seat insert, grind finish the seating face with a seat grinder carefully noting the seating angle, contact width and depression. Lap the valve and seat as the final step.

Timing Belt

REMOVAL

1. Disconnect battery negative cable.
2. Drain cooling system.
3. Remove fan shroud.
4. Remove cooling fan V-Belt and cooling fan pulley.
5. Remove upper dust cover.
6. Disconnect bypass hose.
7. With the piston in number 1 position TDC, check to make certain setting mark on injection pump gear is in alignment with front plate. Then align the gear using an 8 mm 1.25 pitch bolt (alignment hole in gear and front plate).
8. Remove cam cover.
9. Install J-29761 fixing plate to slot in the rear of the camshaft. This is to prevent the camshaft from rotating.
10. Remove damper pulley. Check to be sure piston in number 1 cylinder is at TDC.
11. Remove lower dust cover. Then remove timing belt holder.
12. Remove tension spring behind front plate next to injection pump.
13. Loosen tension pulley and plate bolts, then remove timing belt.

Damper Pulley

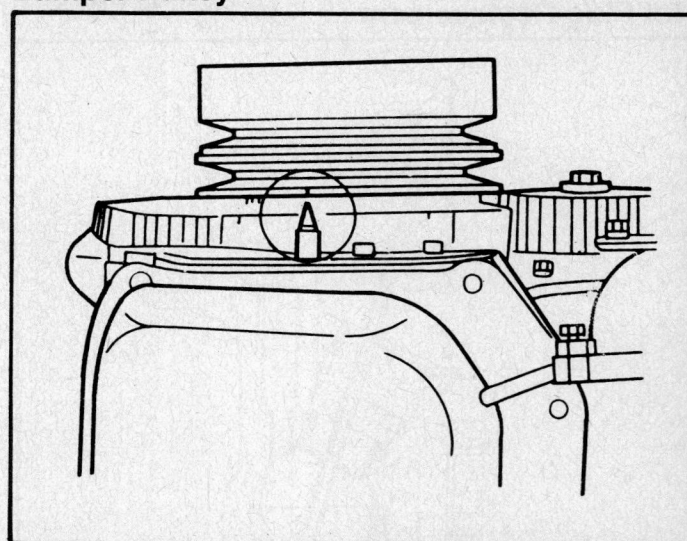

INSTALLATION AND ADJUSTMENT

1. Remove bolt attaching camshaft gear.
2. Install puller J-22888 and remove cam gear.
3. Reinstall cam gear loosely, so the gear can be turned smoothly by hand.
4. Install timing belt with the following noted:
a. Belt should be properly tensioned between pulleys.
b. Cogs on belt and pulley should be engaged properly.
c. Crank shaft should not be turned.
d. Concentrate belt looseness on tension pulley, depress tension pulley with finger and install tension spring.
5. Semi-tighten bolts in numerical sequence to prevent movement of tension pulley.

Injector Gear Setting Mark

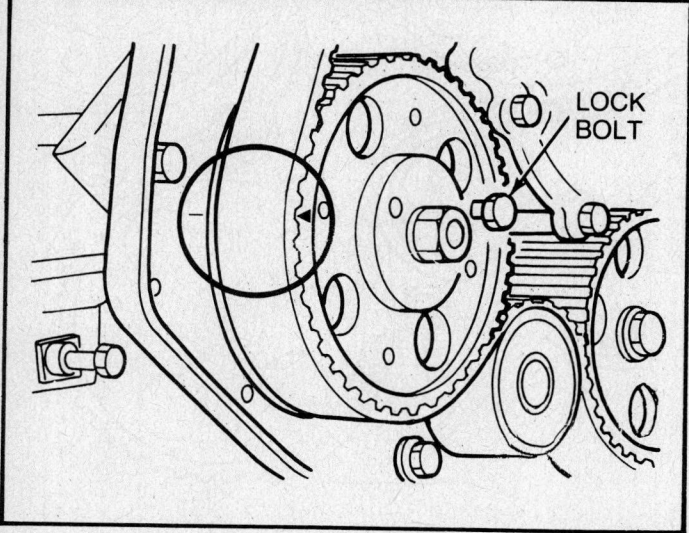

LOCK BOLT

Tension Spring

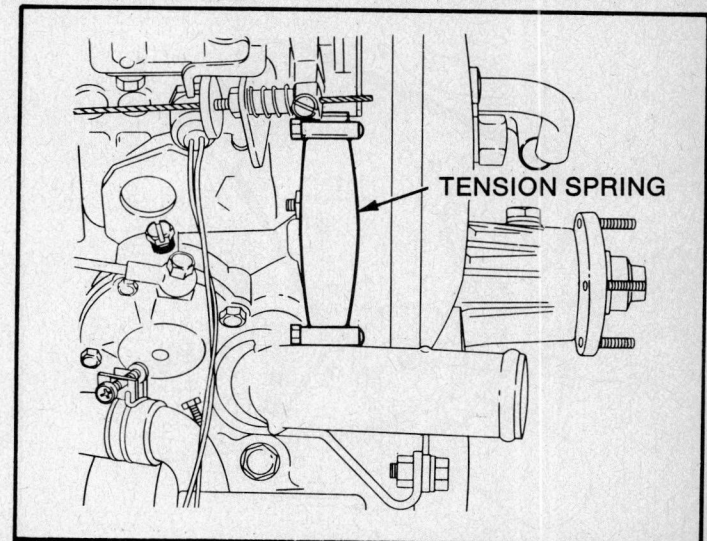

TENSION SPRING

6. Tighten camshaft pulley bolt to 60 N•m (45 ft.lbs.).
7. Remove injection pump gear lock bolt.
8. Remove fixing plate on end of camshaft.
9. Install damper pulley on hub and check that the piston in number 1 cylinder is at TDC. Do not turn the crank shaft in an attempt to make an adjustment.
10. Check to make certain that mark on injection pump pulley is in alignment with the mark on the plate.
11. Fixing plate should fit smoothly into slot at rear of camshaft, then remove the fixing plate.
12. Loosen tensioner pulley and plate bolts. Concentrate looseness of belt on tensioner, then tighten bolts in numerical sequence.

13. Belt tension should be checked at a point between the camshaft gear and the injection pump gear, using tool J-26486.
14. Remove damper pulley and install the belt holder in position away from the timing bolt.
15. Install the bypass hose.
16. Install the dust covers and torque bolts to 7 N•m (5 ft.lbs.).
17. Install the damper pulley.
18. Install the cooling fan, belt and fan pulley.
19. Install the fan shroud.
20. Refill coolant.

Camshaft Fixing Plate

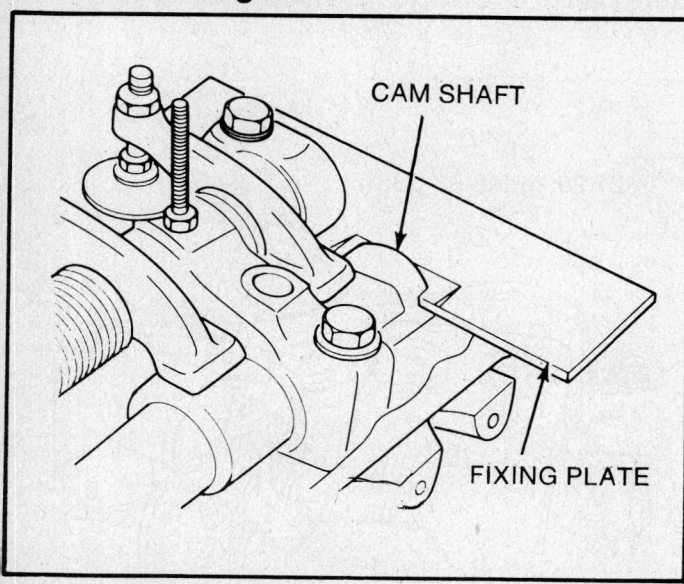

CAM SHAFT

FIXING PLATE

Timing Belt Holder

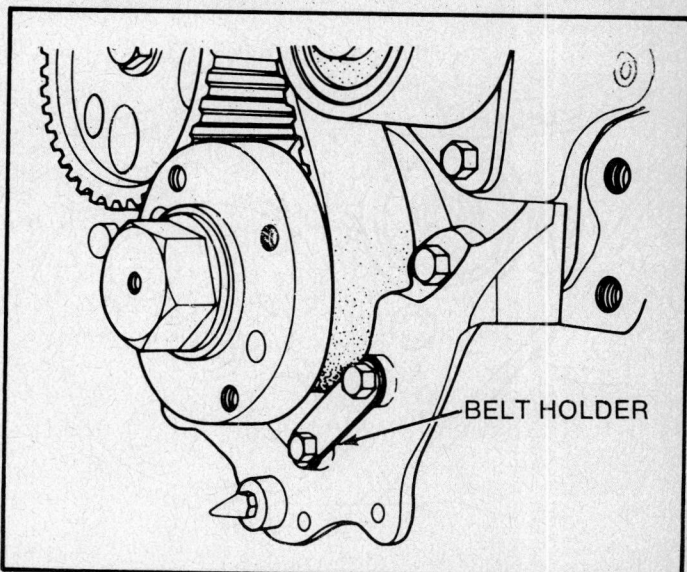

BELT HOLDER

ISUZU DIESEL ENGINE

ON-CAR SERVICE

Timing Belt Sequence

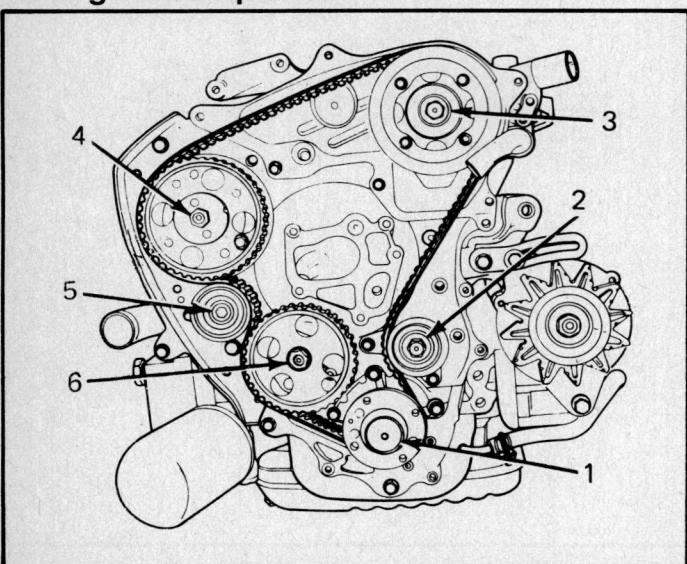

Tightening Bolts

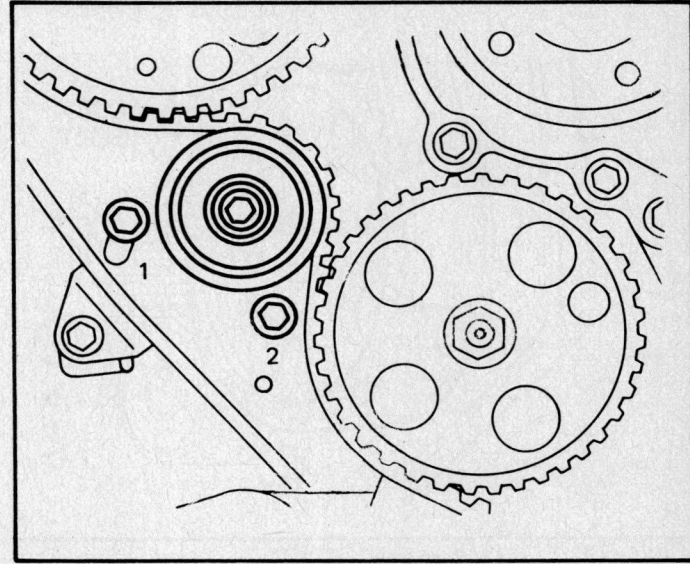

Crank Shaft Front Oil Seal

REMOVAL

1. Disconnect battery negative cable.
2. Drain coolant.
3. Remove radiator.
4. Remove timing belt.
5. Remove center bolt attaching hub and washer.
6. Using puller J-24420-A, remove hub from crank shaft.
7. Remove crank shaft gear from crank shaft using tool J-24420-A.
8. Pry out oil seal using a suitable tool.

INSTALLATION

1. Apply clean engine oil to lipped portion and fitting

face of front seal. Install the oil seal retainer using installer J-26587.
2. Install flange into crank shaft.
3. Align pulley groove with crank shaft key and install the crank shaft pulley on the crank shaft using installer J-26587.
4. Align hub groove with crank shaft key. Then install center bolt and torque to 150 N•m (110 ft.lbs.).
5. Reinstall the timing belt.

Oil Pump

REMOVAL

1. Remove timing belt.
2. Remove the 4 Allen bolts attaching oil pump. Remove the oil pump together with the pulley.

Tightening Tensioner

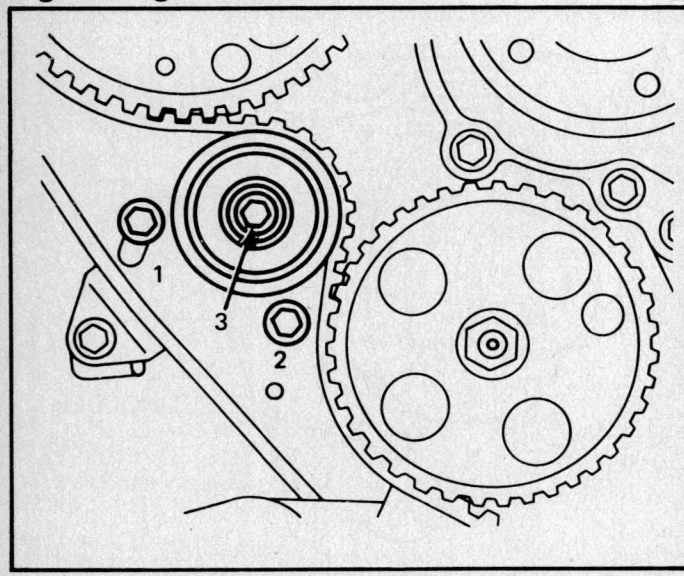

Belt Tension Check

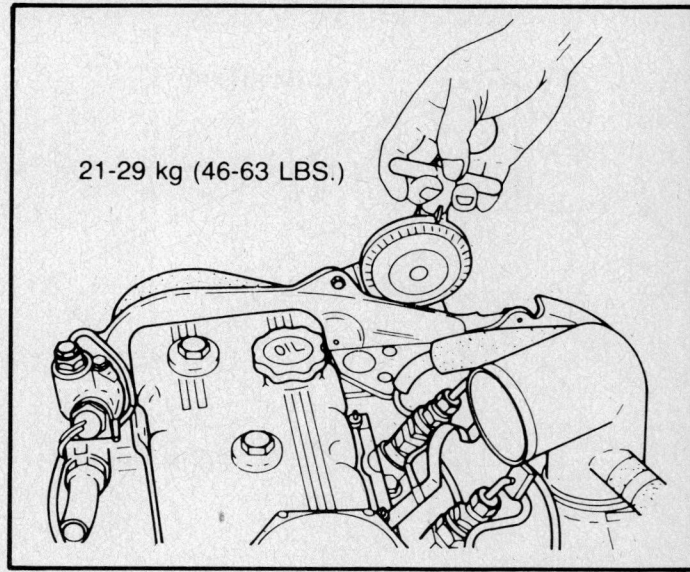

21-29 kg (46-63 LBS.)

Oil Pump Assembly

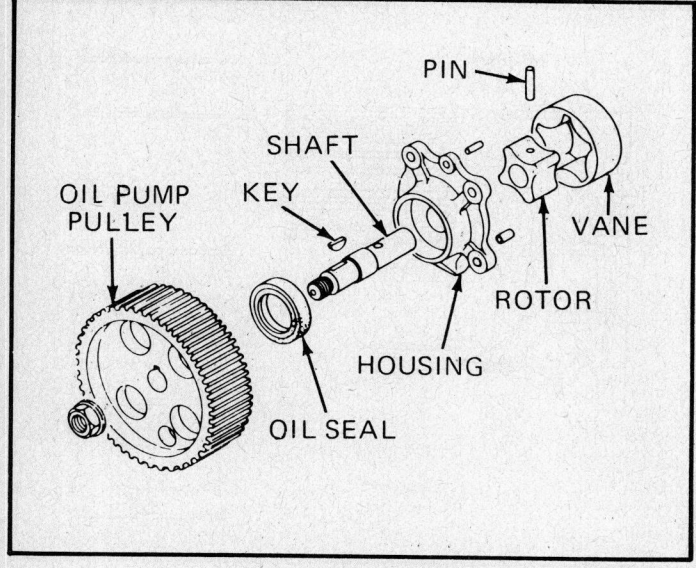

INSTALLATION

1. Apply a generous amount of new engine oil to the vane. Then install with the taper side turned to cylinder body.
2. Apply engine oil to the new O-ring and install it into the groove in the housing.
3. Install the rotor after applying engine oil and install the pump body together with pulley. Torque to 20 N•m (15 ft.lbs.).
4. Install timing belt.

Rear Main Oil Seal
REMOVAL

1. Remove transmission.
2. If equipped with manual transmission, remove clutch.

Oil Pan Removal

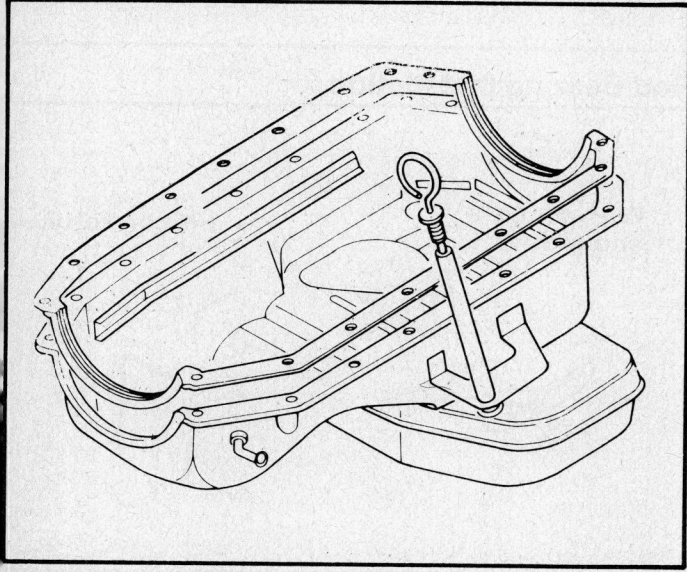

Crankshaft End Play

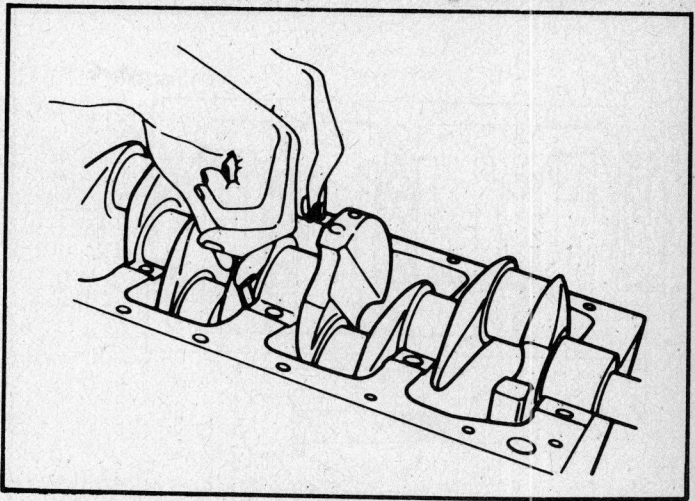

If clearance exceeds 0.0117-0.3 mm, replace thrust bearing

3. Remove flywheel.
4. Pry off the oil seal using a suitable tool.

INSTALLATION

1. Apply clean engine oil to lipped portion and fitting face of new oil seal. Install the oil seal into the No. 5 crank shaft bearing using installer J-29818.
2. Apply sealant to the threads of new bolts. Install flywheel and tighten bolts diagonal sequence. Torque to 55 N•m (40 ft.lbs.).
3. Reverse removal procedures.

Piston
INSTALLATION

1. The piston ring gaps should be set in position 180 degrees apart.

Main Bearing Installation

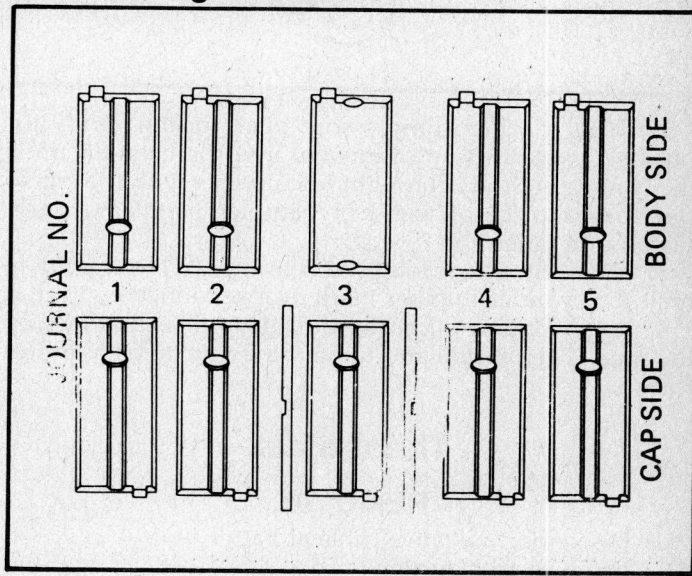

Bolt Torque Sequence

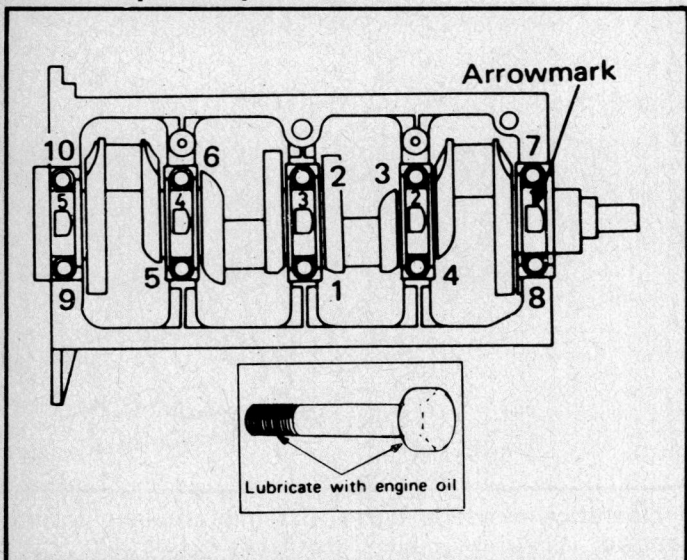

Main bearing torque: 75 lbs.

Piston and Connecting Rod Mark

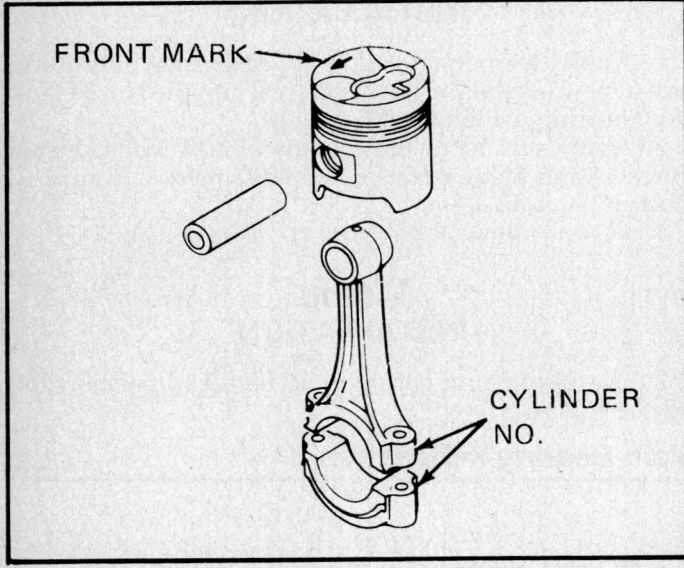

2. Using a ring compressor, push piston (with its notched mark to front of engine) into the cylinder until the connecting rod is brought into contact with the crank pin. Use a piece of wood or hammer handle to push piston into bore.

3. Install the connecting rod bearing cap by aligning it with the cylinder number mark on the connecting rod.

4. Apply engine oil to the threads and seating face of the nuts. Then install and tighten the nuts to 88 N•m (65 ft.lbs.).

Thermostat

REMOVAL

1. Disconnect negative cable at battery.
2. Drain cooling system.

Piston Rings

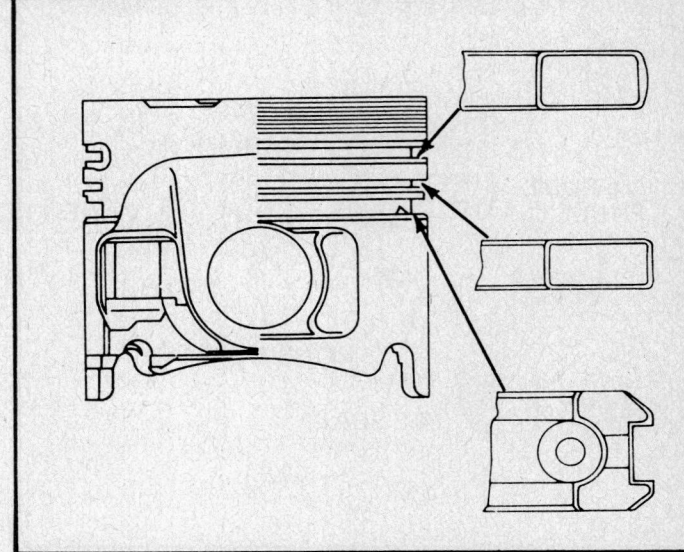

Bushing Replacement

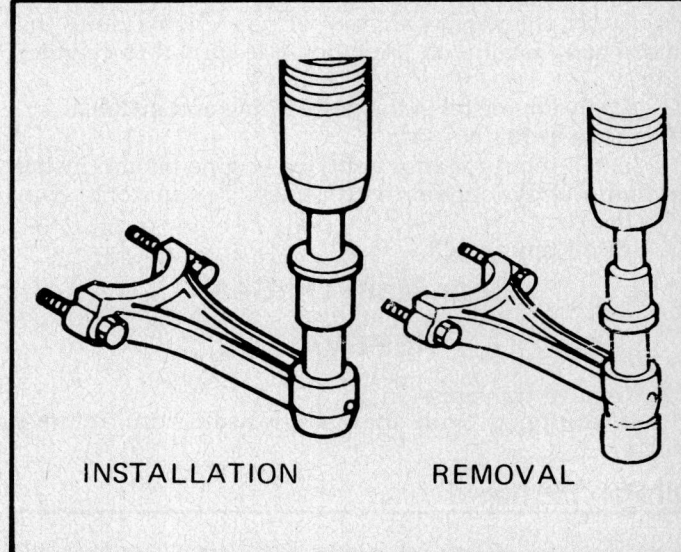

Rod Bearing Installation

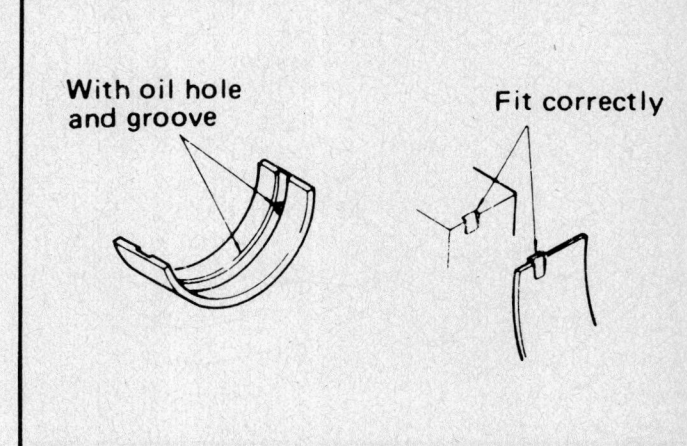

Installation of Bearing Cap

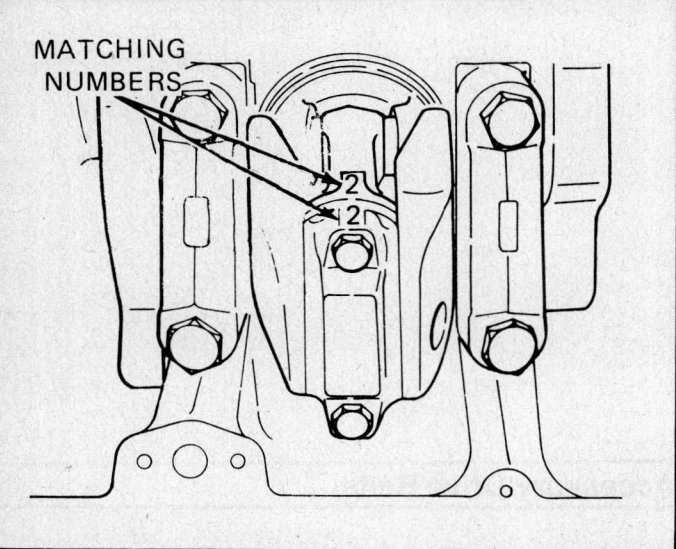

MATCHING NUMBERS

3. Remove water outlet to thermostat housing attaching bolts and remove thermostat.

INSTALLATION

1. Apply a thin coat of gasket adhesive to both surfaces of the outlet gasket before installation.
2. Place thermostat in housing and install water outlet. Torque bolts to 20 N•m (15 ft.lbs.).
3. Fill cooling system.
4. Connect negative cable at battery, start engine and check for leaks.

Fan

REMOVAL

1. Disconnect negative cable at battery.
2. Remove fan shroud.
3. Remove fan assembly.
4. Separate fan from clutch assembly.

INSTALLATION

1. Assemble fan to clutch.
2. Install fan assembly and torque to specifications.
3. Install fan shroud and torque to specifications.
4. Connect negative cable at battery.

Water Pump

REMOVAL

1. Disconnect negative cable at battery.
2. Drain cooling system.
3. Remove fan shroud, fan assembly and accessory drive belt.
4. Remove damper pulley.
5. Remove dust cover.
6. Remove by-pass hose at pump.

Fan Attachment

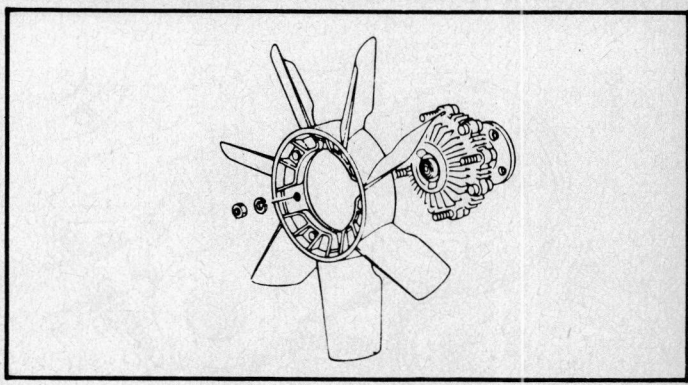

Coolant Flow Schematic

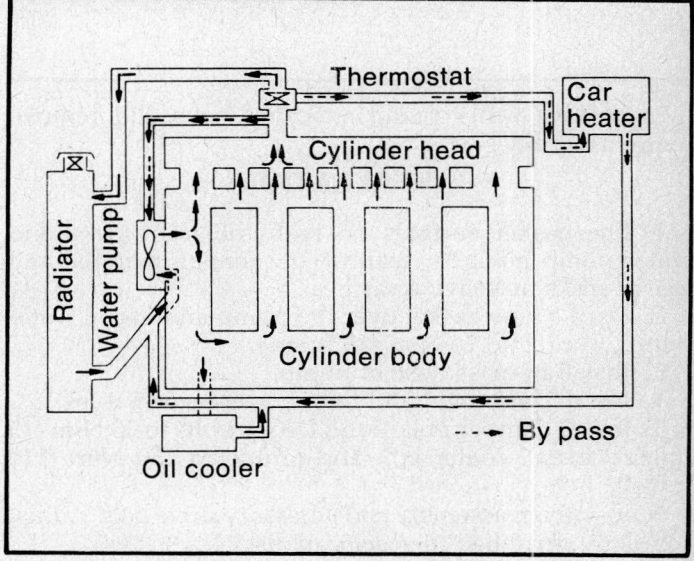

Thermostat Housing Assembly

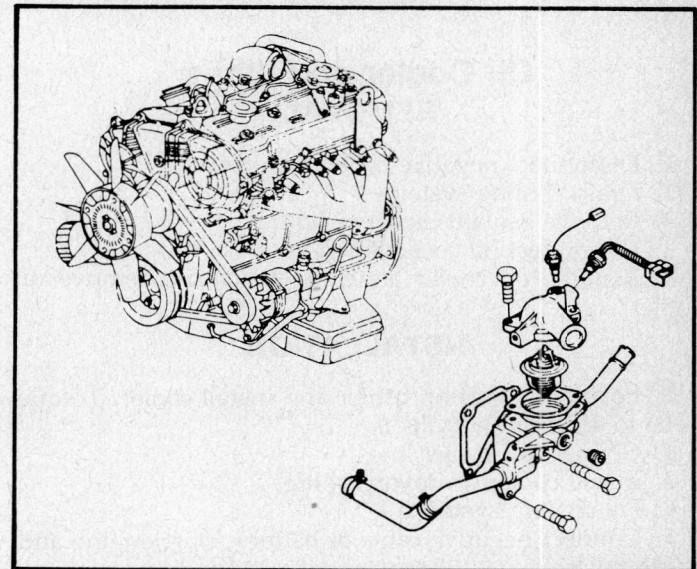

Water Pump Attaching Bolts

7. Remove water pump attaching bolts and remove pump assembly.

INSTALLATION

1. The gasket surfaces on both the front plate and water pump must be clean of any foreign material and free of nicks or heavy scratches.
2. Place a new gasket over the pump and install water pump. Torque to 20 N•m (15 ft.lbs.).
3. Install by-pass hose at pump.
4. Install dust cover and torque to 6 N•m (5 ft.lbs.).
5. Install damper pulley and torque bolts to 20 N•m (15 ft.lbs.). Install center bolt and torque to 150 N•m (110 ft.lbs.).
6. Install fan assembly and accessory drive belt. Adjust accessory drive belt to specifications.
7. Install fan shroud and torque to specifications.
8. Fill cooling system.
9. Connect negative cable at battery, start engine and check for leaks.

Oil Cooler and Lines
REMOVAL

1. Disconnect negative cable at battery.
2. Drain cooling system.
3. Remove coolant recovery bottle.
4. Disconnect oil cooler lines.
5. Remove oil cooler attaching bolts and remove oil cooler.

INSTALLATION

1. Position gasket on cooler and install cooler. Torque bolts to 45 N•m (35 ft.lbs.).
2. Connect oil cooler lines.
3. Install coolant recovery bottle.
4. Fill cooling system.
5. Connect negative cable at battery, start engine and check for leaks.

Oil Cooler Assembly

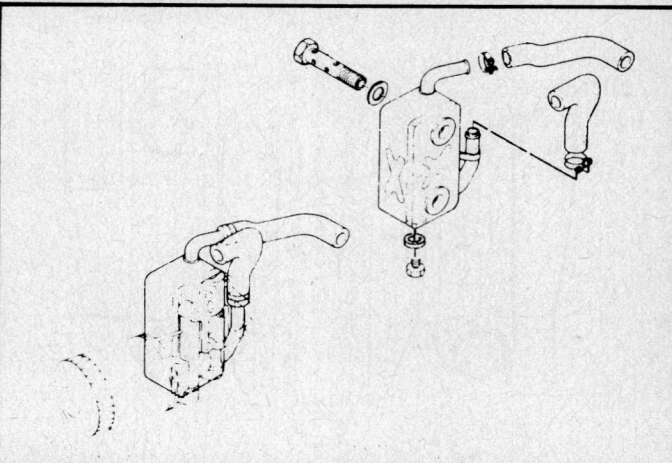

Accessory Drive Belts

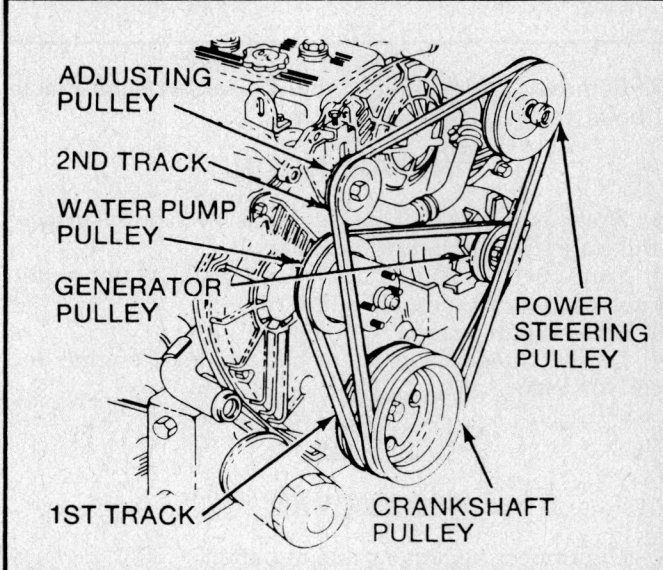

Generator Drive Belt Adjustment

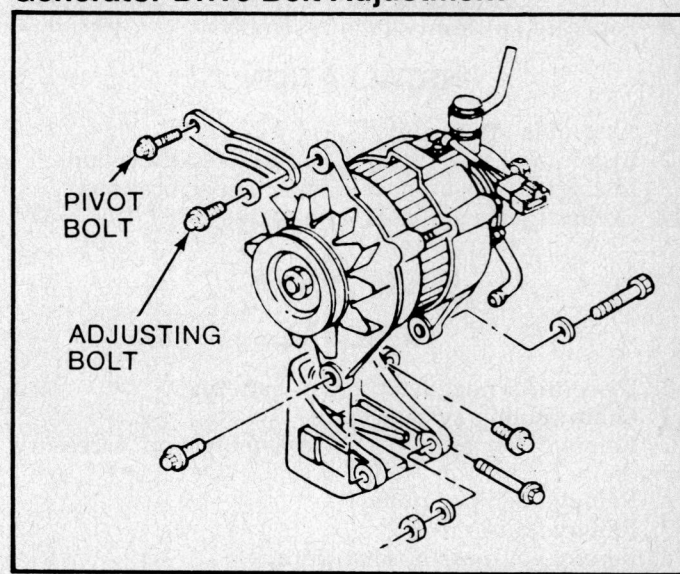

Accessory Drive Belts

Drive belt tension is important in maintaining proper operation of engine accessory drive systems and in extending the normal life of drive belts. When drive belts require replacement or adjustment, use belt tension tools.

Idle Speeds

Adjust idle speeds with engine at normal operating temperature and air cleaner installed.

BASE IDLE ADJUSTMENT

1. Set parking brake and block drive wheels.
2. Place transmission in neutral.
3. Connect tachometer.
4. Start engine and allow to run until at operating temperature.
5. Loosen lock nut on idle speed adjusting screw.
6. Turn adjusting to obtain speed specified on emission label.
7. Tighten lock nut.
8. Stop engine and disconnect tach.

FAST IDLE ADJUSTMENT

1. Set parking brake and block drive wheels.
2. Place transmission in neutral.
3. Connect tachometer.
4. Start engine and allow to run until at operating temperature.
5. Apply vacuum to the fast idle actuator.
6. Loosen lock nut on fast idle adjusting screw.
7. Adjust knurled nut to obtain speed specified on emission label.
8. Tighten lock nut.
9. Stop engine and disconnect tachometer.

Water Sensor

Refer to Fuel Filter.

Purging Fuel Tank

1. Remove fuel tank cap.
2. Disconnect fuel return hose from injector pump.
3. Connect a pump or siphon hose to the fuel return hose.
4. Operate pump or siphon until all water is removed from the fuel tank.
5. Remove pump or siphon and reinstall fuel return hose.
6. Replace fuel tank cap.

Water Separator

DRAINING

1. Place a container at the end of the vinyl hose beneath the drain plug on the water separator.

Base Idle Screw

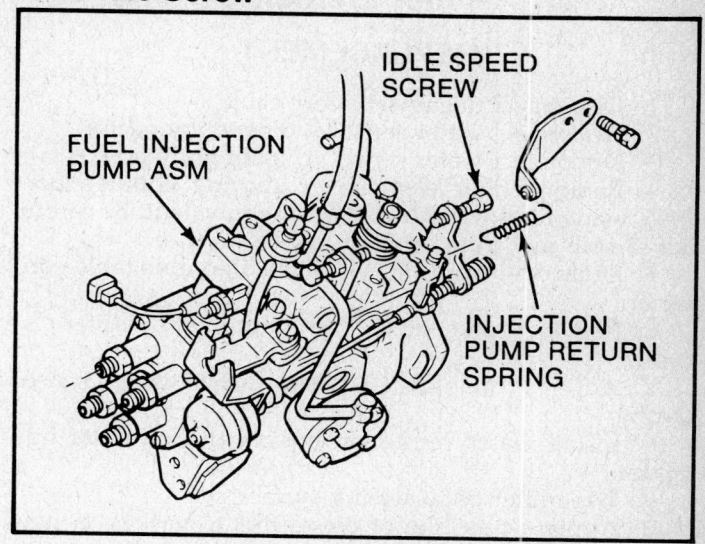

Fast Idle Screw

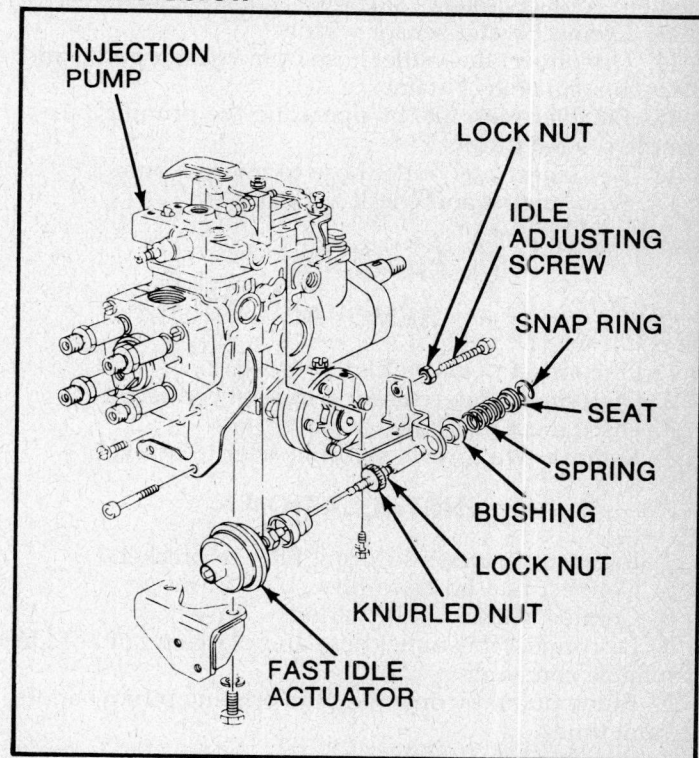

2. Open drain plug approximately 4 turns.
3. Operate the priming pump handle up and down about ten times or until all water is drained.
4. Close drain plug and again operate pump handle up and down several times.
5. Start the engine. Check for fuel leaks and that "Water in Fuel" indicator light has turned off.

Filter Element
REPLACEMENT

1. Disconnect negative battery cable.
2. Disconnect water sensor wiring at connector.
3. Disconnect water sensor to main body hose.
4. Remove filter element by turning counterclockwise, using filter wrench J-22700 or equivalent. Be careful not to spill fuel from element.
5. Drain fuel from filter element into a suitable container.
6. Remove water sensor from bottom of old filter element.
7. Apply a thin film of diesel fuel to water sensor O-ring.
8. Install water sensor on bottom of new filter and tighten.
9. Wipe filter body sealing surface clean.
10. Apply a thin film of diesel fuel to gasket on new filter element.
11. Install filter element and turn clockwise until gasket on element contacts sealing surface on main body.
12. Continue turning an additional ⅔ of a turn after element contacts sealing surface.
13. Connect water sensor wiring.
14. Disconnect fuel outlet hose from injector pump and place in a suitable container.
15. Fill filter with fuel by operating the priming pump handle several times.
16. Reconnect fuel outlet hose to injector pump.
17. Start engine and check for leaks.

Fuel Filter
REMOVAL

1. Disconnect negative battery cable.
2. Disconnect water sensor wiring at connector.
3. Disconnect fuel hoses at filter.
4. Remove two screws securing filter to bracket.

INSTALLATION

1. Install two screws securing filter to bracket.
2. Connect fuel hoses to filter.
3. Connect water sensor wiring.
4. Disconnect fuel outlet hose and place end of hose in a suitable container.
5. Prime pump by operating the priming pump handle several times.
6. Reconnect fuel outlet hose.
7. Connect negative battery cable.
8. Start engine and check for leaks.

Injection Pump
REMOVAL

1. Disconnect battery negative cable.
2. Drain cooling system.
3. Remove fan shroud.

Fuel Filter Assembly

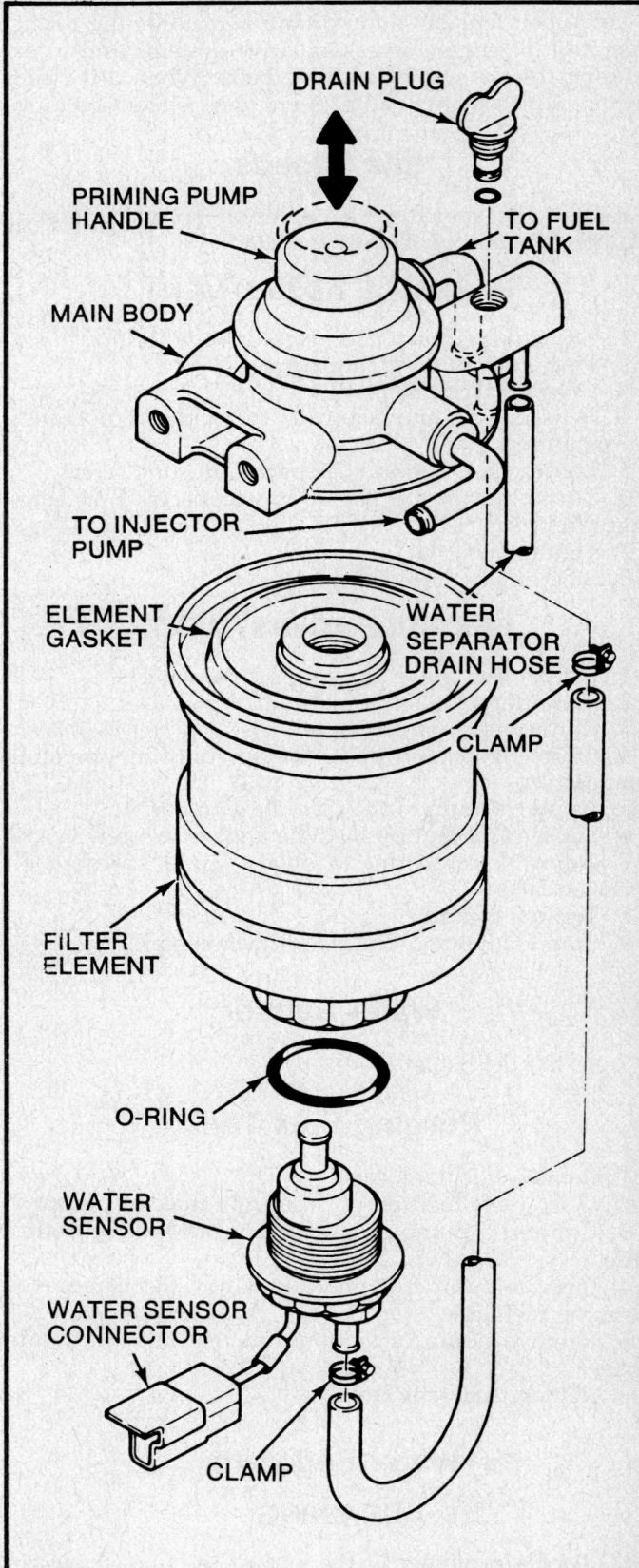

Rear Bracket Bolts

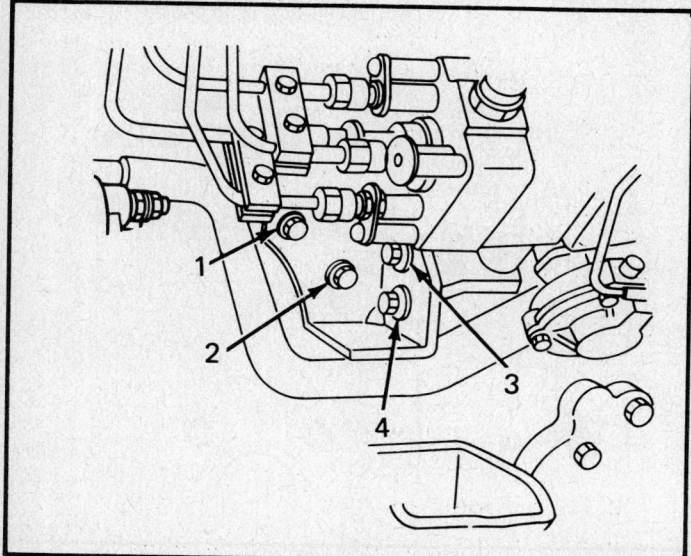

Alignment Mark

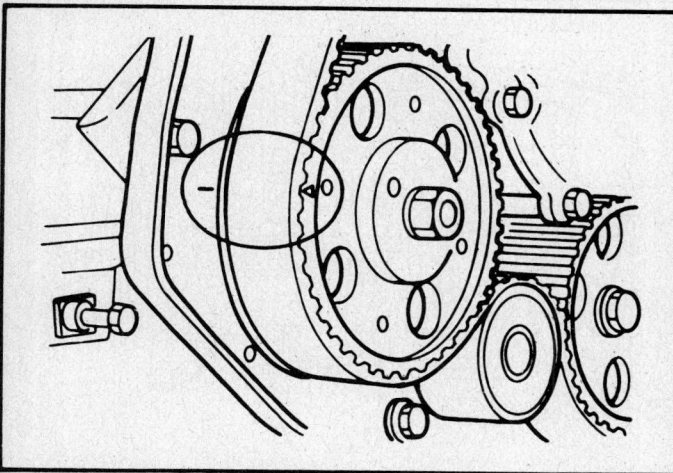

Tension Pulley Bolts

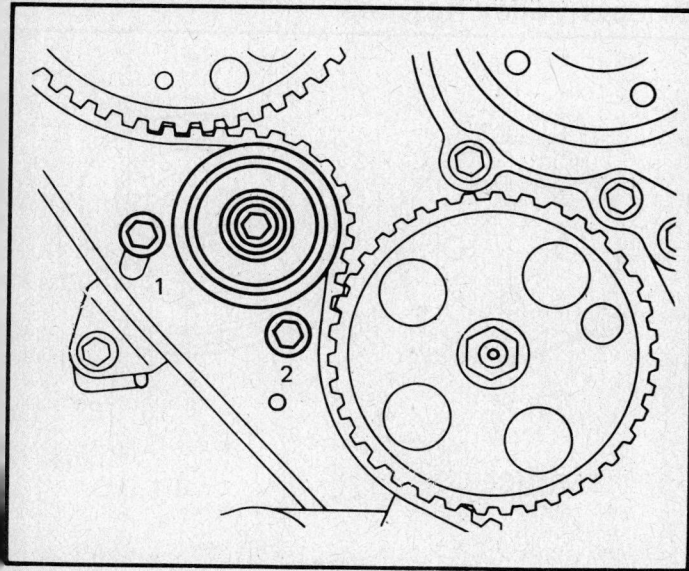

4. Remove radiator.
5. Remove coolant recovery bottle.
6. Remove upper dust cover.
7. Loosen tension pulley and plate bolt. Remove tension spring.
8. Remove the nut attaching the pump gear.
9. Remove injection pump gear using tool J-22888.
10. Disconnect necessary wires, hoses and cables. Use care so as not to spill fuel within the fuel hoses.
11. Remove fuel filter at bracket.
12. Remove injector lines at pump and nozzles and remove injector lines.
13. Remove 4 bolts attaching the pump rear bracket and remove the rear bracket.
14. Remove the nuts attaching the injection pump flange and remove the injection pump together with the fast idle device and return spring.

INSTALLATION AND ADJUSTMENTS

Timing Belt

1. Install the injection pump.
2. Tighten the 4 bolts in sequence. No clearance should be provided between the rear bracket and injection pump bracket.
3. Install the injection pump pulley by aligning it with the key groove. Align the mark on the gear with the mark on the front plate. Then tighten the nut using lock bolt (8 mm x 1.25) to prevent turning of pulley, torque nut to 60 N•m (45 ft.lbs.).
4. Remove cam cover.
5. With piston in number 1 position TDC, install J-29761 fixing plate to slot in the rear of camshaft. This is to prevent the camshaft from rotating.
6. Remove the bolt attaching camshaft gear.
7. Using puller J-22888, remove cam gear.
8. Re-install cam gear loosely so the gear can be turned smoothly by hand.
9. Install the timing belt with the following noted:
a. Belt should be properly tensioned between pulleys.
b. Cogs on belt and pulley should be engaged properly.
c. Crank shaft should not be turned.
d. Concentrate belt looseness on tension pulley. Depress tension pulley with finger and install tension spring.
10. Semi-tighten bolts in numerical sequence to prevent movement of tension pulley.
11. Tighten camshaft pulley bolt to 60 N•m (45 ft.lbs.).
12. Remove injection pump gear lock bolt.
13. Remove fixing plate on end of camshaft.
14. Check that piston is in number 1 TDC position. Do not turn the crank shaft in an attempt to make an adjustment.
15. Check to make certain that the mark on the injection pump pulley is in alignment with the mark on the plate.
16. Fixing plate should fit smoothly into slot at rear of camshaft, then remove the fixing plate.
17. Loosen tensioner pulley and plate bolts. Concen-

trate looseness or bolt on tensioner, then tighten bolts in numerical sequence as shown.

18. Belt tension should be checked at a point between the camshaft gear and the injection pump gear.

Injection Timing

1. Bring the piston in number 1 TDC or compression stroke by turning crank shaft as necessary.

2. With the upper cover removed, check the timing belt is properly tensioned and that the timing marks are aligned.

3. With the cam cover removed, check that the fixing plate fits smoothly into the slot at the rear end of the camshaft, then remove the fixing plate.

4. With the injection lines removed, remove the distributor head screw and washer.

5. Install the static timing gage J-29763, set lift approximately 1 mm (0.04 in.) from the plunger.

6. Bring the piston in number 1 cylinder to a point 45-60 degrees before TDC by turning the crank shaft. Then calibrate the dial indicator to zero. The damper pulley is provided with notched lines as illustrated in the drawing (Fig. 6A2-80). The damper pulley is provided with a total of 11 notch lines, (4 lines at one side, 7 lines at another area). The 4 lines are used for static timing.

7. Turn the crank shaft until the line (18°) on the damper pulley is brought into alignment with the pointer, then take reading of the dial indicator. Standard reading .5 mm (.02 in.). Turn the crank shaft in normal direction of rotation.

8. If the reading of the dial indicator deviates from the specified range, hold the crank shaft in position 18° before TDC and loosen two nuts on injection pump to a point where the dial indicator gives reading of .5 mm (0.02 in.), then tighten pump flange nuts.

9. Recheck dial indicator reading and readjust as necessary.

10. Install the distributor screw and washer into injection pump.

11. Install cam cover.

Bolt Tightening Sequence

Distributor Screw

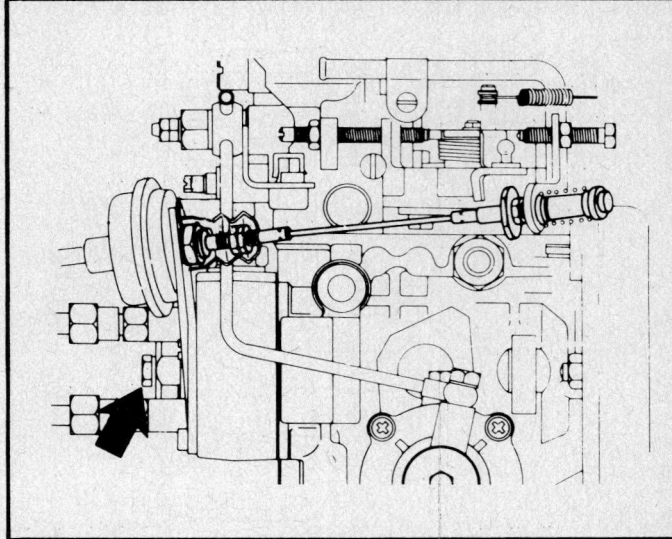

Static Timing Gauge

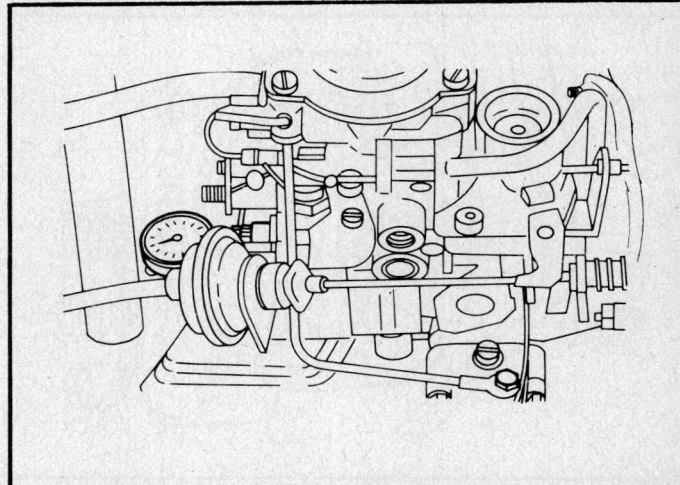

Damper Pulley Notches

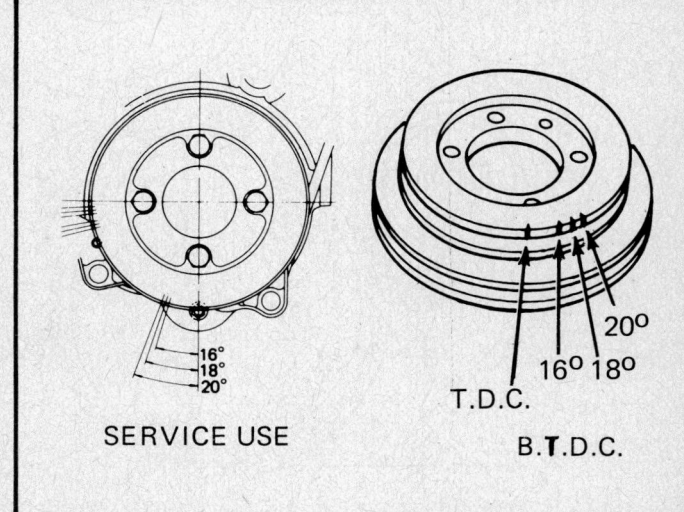

SERVICE USE

T.D.C.

B.T.D.C.

Calibrate Dial Indicator

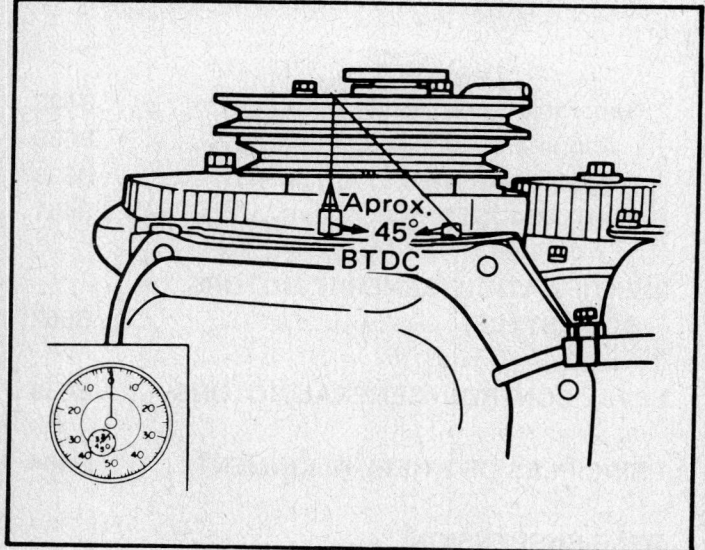

Static Timing Setting

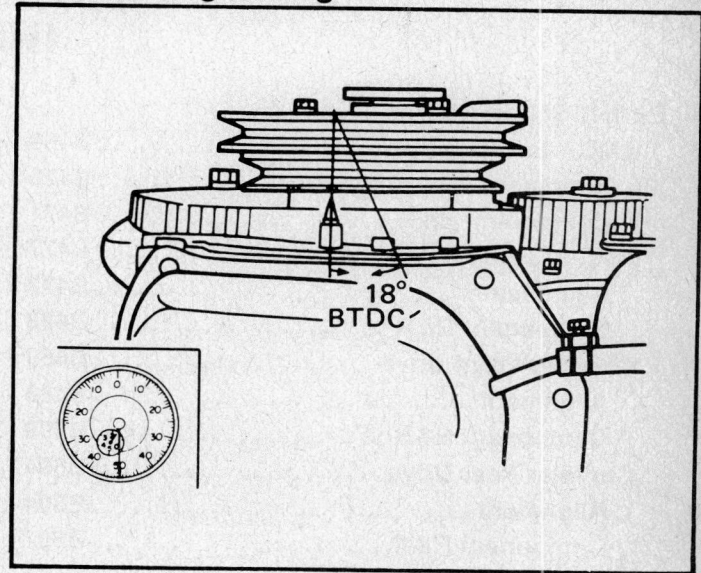

Adjusting the Pump

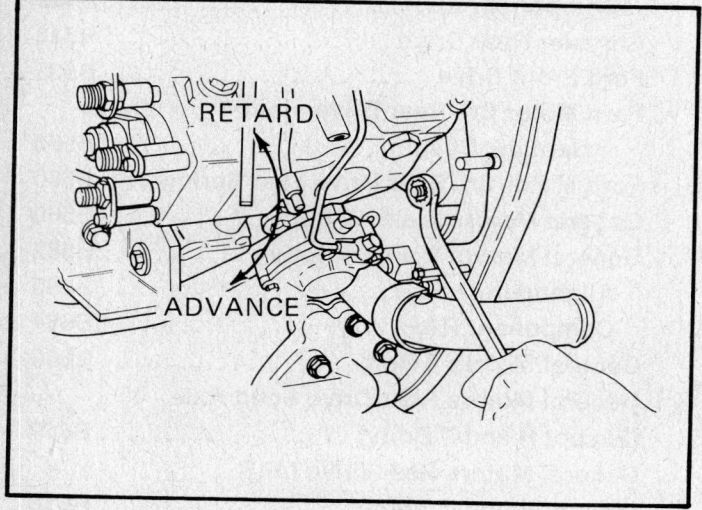

12. Install injection lines.
13. Install fuel filter.
14. Connect necessary wires and hoses.
15. Install the upper dust cover.
16. Install coolant and recovery bottle, radiator and fan shroud.
17. Adjust idle.

T.V. Cable

ADJUSTMENT PROCEDURE

1. After installation into transmission, install cable fitting into engine bracket.

CAUTION Slider must not ratchet through the fitting before or during assembly into bracket. Use the readjustment procedure to correct this condition.

2. Install cable terminal to fuel injection pump lever.
3. Open injection pump lever to "FULL THROTTLE STOP" position to automatically adjust slider on cable to correct setting.

CAUTION Lock tab must not be depressed during this operation.

4. Release injection pump lever.

READJUSTMENT PROCEDURE

In case readjustment is necessary because of inadvertent adjustment before or during assembly or for repair, perform the following:
1. Depress and hold metal lock tab.
2. Move slider back through fitting in direction away from carburetor lever until slider stops against fitting.
3. Release metal lock tab.
4. Repeat steps 2, 3 and 4 of adjustment procedure.

SUSPENSION
INDEX

MANUFACTURER'S SPECIFIED ALIGNMENT TOLERANCES

All vehicles should be set to the preferred specification when being realigned. The minimum and maximum settings specified are a guide to use when checking alignment. The manufacturers consider alignment within these tolerances acceptable for safe vehicle operation while still limiting abnormal tire wear.

AMERICAN MOTORS

Year	Model	Caster (Degrees) Min.	Pref.	Max.	Camber (Degrees) Min.	Pref.	Max.	Toe-In (Inches) Min.	Pref.	Max.	Toe-In (Millimeters) Min.	Pref.	Max.	Toe-Out on Turns (Degrees) Outside Wheel	Inside Wheel	Strg. Axis Incl. (Deg.)
76-77	Matador, Ambassador	1/2	1	1 1/2				1/16	1/8	3/16	1.6	3.2	4.8	22	25	7 3/4
	Left Wheel				1/8	3/8	5/8									
	Right Wheel				0	1/8	1/2									
76-77	Gremlin, Hornet	−1/2	0	1/2				1/16	1/8	3/16	1.6	3.2	4.8	22	25	7 3/4
	Left Wheel				1/8	3/8	5/8									
	Right Wheel				0	1/8	1/2									
76-77	Pacer	1/2	1	1 1/2				1/16	1/8	3/16	1.6	3.2	4.8	22	25	7 3/4
	Left Wheel				1/8	3/8	5/8									
	Right Wheel				0	1/8	1/2									
78	Pacer	1	2	3				1/16	1/8	3/16	1.6	3.2	4.8	22	25	7 3/4
	Left Wheel				1/8	3/8	5/8									
	Right Wheel				0	1/8	1/2									
78	Matador, AMX, Concord, Gremlin	0	1	2				1/16	1/8	3/16	1.6	3.2	4.8	22	25	7 3/4
	Left Wheel				1/8	3/8	5/8									
	Right Wheel				0	1/8	1/2									
79	AMX, Concord, Spirit	0	1	2 1/2	0	1/4	3/4	1/16	1/8	3/16	1.6	3.2	4.8	NA	38●	7 3/4
79-80	Pacer	1	2	3 1/2	0	1/4	3/4	1/16	1/8	3/16	1.6	3.2	4.8	NA	35●	7 3/4
80-82	Spirit, Concord, AMX	0	1	2 1/2				1/16	1/8	3/16	1.6	3.2	4.8	NA	38●	7 3/4
	Left Wheel				1/8	3/8	3/4									
	Right Wheel				−1/8	1/8	1/2									
80-82	Eagle ①	2	2 1/2	3	−1/8	3/8	5/8	1/16 (out)	1/8 (out)	3/16 (out)	1.6 (out)	3.2 (out)	4.8 (out)	NA	38●	11 27/32

① 1980 Eagle king pin inclination is 11 1/2°
● Wheels at full turning angle

CHRYSLER CORPORATION—CHRYSLER ① ② ③

Year	Model	Caster (Degrees) Min.	Pref.	Max.	Camber (Degrees) Min.	Pref.	Max.	Toe-In (Inches) Min.	Pref.	Max.	Toe-In (Millimeters) Min.	Pref.	Max.	Toe-Out on Turns (Degrees) Outside Wheel	Inside Wheel	Strg. Axis Incl. (Deg.)
76-79	Cordoba	−1/2	3/4	2				1/16	1/8	1/4	1.6	3.2	6.4	18	20	8
	Left Wheel				0	1/2	1									
	Right Wheel				−1/4	1/4	3/4									
77-79	LeBaron	1 1/2	2 1/2	3 3/4				1/16	1/8	1/4	1.6	3.2	6.4	18	20	8
	Left Wheel				0	1/2	1									
	Right Wheel				−1/4	1/4	3/4									
80-81	LeBaron	1 1/4	2 1/2	3 3/4	−1/4	1/2	1 1/4	0	1/8	5/16	0	3.2	8.0	18	20	8
82	LeBaron Front Drive	Fixed			−1/4	5/16	3/4	5/32 (out)	1/16 (out)	1/8 (in)	4.0 (out)	1.6 (out)	3.2 (in)	NA	NA	13 3/8
80-82	Cordoba	1 1/4	2 1/2	3 3/4	−1/4	1/2	1 1/4	0	1/8	5/16	0	3.2	8.0	18	20	8

SUSPENSION
SPECIFICATIONS

CHRYSLER CORPORATION—CHRYSLER ① ② ③

VEHICLE IDENTIFICATION		CASTER (Degrees)			CAMBER (Degrees)			TOE-IN (Inches)			TOE-IN (Millimeters)			TOE-OUT ON TURNS (Degrees)		Strg. Axis Incl. (Deg.)
Year	Model	Min.	Pref.	Max.	Min.	Pref.	Max.	Min.	Pref.	Max.	Min.	Pref.	Max.	Outside Wheel	Inside Wheel	
76	Newport, New Yorker	−½	¾	1¾				1/16	⅛	¼	1.6	3.2	6.4	18 5/16	20	9
	Left Wheel				0	½	1									
	Right Wheel				−¼	¼	¾									
77-78	Newport, New Yorker	−½	¾	2				1/16	⅛	¼	1.6	3.2	6.4	18 5/16	20	9
	Left Wheel				0	½	1									
	Right Wheel				−¼	¼	¾									
79	Newport, New Yorker	−½	¾	2				1/16	⅛	¼	1.6	3.2	6.4	18	20	8
	Left Wheel				0	½	1									
	Right Wheel				−¼	¼	¾									
80-82	Newport, New Yorker	−¼	1	2¼	−¼	½	1¼	0	⅛	5/16	0	3.2	8.0	18	20	8
81-82	Imperial	−¼	1	2¼	−¼	½	1¼	0	⅛	5/16	0	3.2	8.0	18	20	8

① Check vehicle suspension height before performing alignment. Suspension height tables follow alignment tolerance tables.
② Maximum left to right variation not to exceed 1¼° when checking alignment.
③ Engine must be running during toe adjustment of vehicles with power steering.

CHRYSLER CORPORATION—DODGE
Front Drive Cars ① ② ③

VEHICLE IDENTIFICATION		CASTER (Degrees)			CAMBER (Degrees)			TOE-IN (Inches)			TOE-IN (Millimeters)			TOE-OUT ON TURNS (Degrees)		Strg. Axis Incl. (Deg.)
Year	Model	Min.	Pref.	Max.	Min.	Pref.	Max.	Min.	Pref.	Max.	Min.	Pref.	Max.	Outside Wheel	Inside Wheel	
78-82	Omni, 024															
	Front		Fixed		−¼	5/16	¾	5/32 (out)	1/16 (out)	⅛ (in)	4.0 (out)	1.6 (out)	3.2 (in)	NA	NA	13⅜
	Rear		Fixed		−½	−1	−1½	5/32 (out)	3/32 (in)	11/32 (in)	4.0 (out)	2.4 (in)	8.7 (in)			
81-82	Aries															
	Front		Fixed		−¼	5/16	¾	5/32 (out)	1/16 (out)	⅛ (in)	4.0 (out)	1.6 (out)	3.2 (in)	NA	NA	13⅜
	Rear		Fixed		−1	−½	0	3/16 (out)	0	3/16 (in)	4.8 (out)	0	4.8 (in)			
1982	400															
	Front		Fixed		−¼	5/16	¾	5/32 (out)	1/16 (out)	⅛ (in)	4.0 (out)	1.6 (out)	3.2 (in)	NA	NA	13⅜
	Rear		Fixed		−1	−½	0	3/16 (out)	0	3/16 (in)	4.8 (out)	0	4.8 (in)			

① Suspension height tables follow alignment tolerance tables. Check vehicle suspension height before performing alignment.
② Maximum left to right variation in caster not to exceed 1¼° when checking alignment.
③ The engine must be running during toe adjustment of vehicles with power steering.

CHRYSLER CORPORATION—DODGE
Rear Drive Cars ① ② ③

Year	Model	Caster (Degrees) Min.	Pref.	Max.	Camber (Degrees) Min.	Pref.	Max.	Toe-In (Inches) Min.	Pref.	Max.	Toe-In (Millimeters) Min.	Pref.	Max.	Toe-Out on Turns (Degrees) Outside Wheel	Inside Wheel	Strg. Axis Incl. (Deg.)
76	Dart, Swinger, Challenger *W/Power Steering*	−1/2	3/4	1 3/4				1/16	1/8	1/4	1.6	3.2	6.4	18 1/2	20	7 1/2
	Left Wheel				0	1/2	1									
	Right Wheel				−1/4	1/4	3/4									
	W/Manual Steering	−1 3/4	−1/2	1/2				1/16	1/8	1/4	1.6	3.2	6.4	18 1/2	20	7 1/2
	Left Wheel				0	1/2	1									
	Right Wheel				−1/4	1/4	3/4									
76	Coronet, Charger *W/Power Steering*	−1/2	3/4	1 3/4				1/16	1/8	1/4	1.6	3.2	6.4	18	20	8
	Left Wheel				0	1/2	1									
	Right Wheel				−1/4	1/4	3/4									
	W/Manual Steering	−1 3/4	−1/2	1/2				1/16	1/8	1/4	1.6	3.2	6.4	18	20	8
	Left Wheel				0	1/2	1									
	Right Wheel				−1/4	1/4	3/4									
77-79	Diplomat	1 1/2	2 1/2	3 3/4				1/16	1/8	1/4	1.6	3.2	6.4	18	20	8
	Left Wheel				0	1/2	1									
	Right Wheel				−1/4	1/4	3/4									
77-79	Charger, Charger SE, Magnum XE, Monaco, Royal Monaco *W/Power Steering*	−1/2	3/4	2				1/16	1/8	1/4	1.6	3.2	6.4	18	20	8
	Left Wheel				0	1/2	1									
	Right Wheel				−1/4	1/4	3/4									
	W/Manual Steering	−1 3/4	−1/2	3/4				1/16	1/8	1/4	1.6	3.2	6.4	18	20	8
	Left Wheel				0	1/2	1									
	Right Wheel				−1/4	1/4	3/4									
76-79	Aspen	1 1/2	2 1/2	3 3/4				1/16	1/8	1/4	1.6	3.2	6.4	18	20	8
	Left Wheel				0	1/2	1									
	Right Wheel				−1/4	1/4	3/4									
80-82	Mirada	1 1/4	2 1/2	3 3/4	−1/4	1/2	1 1/4	0	1/8	5/16	0	3.2	8.0	18	20	8
80-82	Diplomat	1 1/4	2 1/2	3 3/4	−1/4	1/2	1 1/4	0	1/8	5/16	0	3.2	8.0	18	20	8
80	Aspen	1 1/4	2 1/2	3 3/4	−1/4	1/2	1 1/4	0	1/8	5/16	0	3.2		18	20	8
79	St. Regis	−1/2	3/4	2				1/16	1/8	1/4	1.6	3.2	6.4	18	20	8
	Left Wheel				0	1/2	1									
	Right Wheel				−1/4	1/4	3/4									
80-81	St. Regis	−1/4	1	2 1/4	−1/4	1/2	1 1/4	0	1/8	5/16	0	3.2	8.0	18	20	8

① Suspension height tables follow alignment tolerance tables. Check vehicle suspension height before performing alignment.
② Maximum left to right variation in caster not to exceed 1 1/4° when checking alignment.
③ The engine must be running during toe adjustment of vehicles with power steering.

SUSPENSION

SPECIFICATIONS

CHRYSLER CORPORATION—PLYMOUTH
Front Drive Cars ① ② ③

VEHICLE IDENTIFICATION		CASTER (Degrees)			CAMBER (Degrees)			TOE-IN (Inches)			TOE-IN (Millimeters)			TOE-OUT ON TURNS (Degrees)		Strg. Axis Incl. (Deg.)
Year	Model	Min.	Pref.	Max.	Min.	Pref.	Max.	Min.	Pref.	Max.	Min.	Pref.	Max.	Outside Wheel	Inside Wheel	
78-82	Horizon, TC3															
	Front Wheel		Fixed		−¼	5/16	¾	5/32 (out)	1/16 (out)	⅛ (in)	4.0 (out)	1.6 (out)	3.2 (in)	NA	NA	13⅜
	Rear Wheel		Fixed		−1½	−1	½	5/32 (out)	3/32 (in)	11/32 (in)	4.0 (out)	2.4 (in)	8.7 (in)			
81-82	Reliant															
	Front		Fixed		−¼	5/16	¾	5/32 (out)	1/16 (out)	⅛ (in)	4.0 (out)	1.6 (out)	3.2 (in)	NA	NA	13⅜
	Rear		Fixed		−1	−½	0	3/16 (out)	0 (in)	3/16 (in)	4.8 (out)	0 (in)	4.8 (in)			

① Check vehicle suspension height before performing alignment. Suspension height tables follow alignment tolerance tables.
② Maximum left to right variation in caster not to exceed 1¼° when checking alignment.
③ The engine must be running during toe adjustment of vehicles with power steering.

CHRYSLER CORPORATION—PLYMOUTH
Rear Drive Cars ① ② ③

VEHICLE IDENTIFICATION		CASTER (Degrees)			CAMBER (Degrees)			TOE-IN (Inches)			TOE-IN (Millimeters)			TOE-OUT ON TURNS (Degrees)		Strg. Axis Incl. (Deg.)
Year	Model	Min.	Pref.	Max.	Min.	Pref.	Max.	Min.	Pref.	Max.	Min.	Pref.	Max.	Outside Wheel	Inside Wheel	
76	Valiant, Duster															
	W/Power Steering	−½	¾	1¾				1/16	⅛	¼	1.6	3.2	6.4	18½	20	7½
	Left Wheel				0	½	1									
	Right Wheel				−¼	¼	¾									
	W/Manual Steering	−1¾	−½	½				1/16	⅛	¼	1.6	3.2	6.4	18½	20	7½
	Left Wheel				0	½	1									
	Right Wheel				−¼	¼	¾									
76	Fury															
	W/Power Steering	−½	¾	1¾				1/16	⅛	¼	1.6	3.2	6.4	18	20	8
	Left Wheel				0	½	1									
	Right Wheel				−¼	¼	¾									
	W/Manual Steering	−1¾	−½	½				1/16	⅛	¼	1.6	3.2	6.4	18	20	8
	Left Wheel				0	½	1									
	Right Wheel				−¼	¼	¾									
76	Gran Fury	−½	¾	1¾				1/16	⅛	¼	1.6	3.2	6.4	18 5/16	20	9
	Left Wheel				0	½	1									
	Right Wheel				−¼	¼	¾									
77-79	Volare	1½	2½	3¾				1/16	⅛	¼	1.6	3.2	6.4	18	20	8
	Left Wheel				0	½	1									
	Right Wheel				−¼	¼	¾									
77-78	Fury															
	W/Power Steering	−½	¾	2				1/16	⅛	½	1.6	3.2	6.4	18	20	8
	Left Wheel				0	½	1									
	Right Wheel				−¼	½	¾									
	W/Manual Steering	−1¾	−½	¾				1/16	⅛	¼	1.6	3.2	6.4	18	20	8
	Left Wheel				0	½	1									
	Right Wheel				−¼	¼	¾									

CHRYSLER CORPORATION—PLYMOUTH
Rear Drive Cars ① ② ③

Year	Model	CASTER (Degrees) Min.	Pref.	Max.	CAMBER (Degrees) Min.	Pref.	Max.	TOE-IN (Inches) Min.	Pref.	Max.	TOE-IN (Millimeters) Min.	Pref.	Max.	TOE-OUT ON TURNS (Degrees) Outside Wheel	Inside Wheel	Strg. Axis Incl. (Deg.)
77	Gran Fury	−½	¾	2				1/16	⅛	¼	1.6	3.2	6.4	18	20	9
	Left Wheel				0	½	1									
	Right Wheel				−¼	¼	¾									
80	Volare	1¼	2½	3¾	−¼	½	1¼	0	⅛	5/16	0	3.2	8.0	18	20	8
80-82	Gran Fury	−¼	1	2¼	−¼	½	1¼	0	⅛	5/16	0	3.2	8.0	18	20	8

① Check vehicle suspension height before performing alignment. Suspension height tables follow alignment tolerance tables.
② Maximum left to right variation in caster not to exceed 1¼° when checking alignment.
③ The engine must be running during toe adjustment of vehicles without power steering.

FORD MOTOR COMPANY—FORD
Front Drive Cars

Year	Model	CASTER (Degrees) Min.	Pref.	Max.	CAMBER (Degrees) Min.	Pref.	Max.	TOE-IN (Inches) Min.	Pref.	Max.	TOE-IN (Millimeters) Min.	Pref.	Max.	Toe-Out On Turns (Degrees)	Strg. Axis Incl. (Deg.)
81-82	Escort, Exp. ①	+.55	+1.30	+2.05				0.02 (in)	0.1 (out)	0.22 (out)	.07 (in)	2.4 (out)	5.6 (out)		
	Left Wheel				+1.40	+2.15	+2.90							19.97	14.64
	Right Wheel				−.95	+1.70	+2.45							17.07	15.09

① Caster measurement must be done for each wheel, regardless of equipment being used.

FORD MOTOR COMPANY—FORD
Rear Drive Cars

Year	Model	CASTER (Degrees) Min.	Pref.	Max.	CAMBER (Degrees) Min.	Pref.	Max.	TOE-IN (Inches) Min.	Pref.	Max.	TOE-IN (Millimeters) Min.	Pref.	Max.	TOE-OUT ON TURNS (Degrees) Outside Wheel	Inside Wheel	Strg. Axis Incl. (Deg.)
76	LTD ①	1¼	2	2¾				1/16	3/16	7/16	1.6	4.8	11.1	18¾	20	9¾
	Left Wheel				−¼	½	1¼									
	Right Wheel				−½	¼	1									
76	Thunderbird ①	3¼	4	4¾				1/16	3/16	7/16	1.6	4.8	11.1	18⅛	20	9
	Left Wheel				−¼	½	1¼									
	Right Wheel				−½	¼	1									
76	Granada ②	−1¼	−½	−¼	−½	¼	1	0	⅛	⅜	0	3.2	9.5			
	W/Power Steering													18 3/16	20	6¾
	W/Manual Steering													18 7/16	20	6¾
76	Maverick ②	−1¼	−½	¼	−½	¼	1	0	⅛	⅜	0	3.2	9.5			
	W/Power Steering													18⅛	20	6¾
	W/Manual Steering													18⅜	20	6¾

SUSPENSION

SPECIFICATIONS

FORD MOTOR COMPANY—FORD
Rear Drive Cars

VEHICLE IDENTIFICATION		CASTER (Degrees)			CAMBER (Degrees)			TOE-IN (Inches)			TOE-IN (Millimeters)			TOE-OUT ON TURNS (Degrees)		Strg. Axis Incl. (Deg.)
Year	Model	Min.	Pref.	Max.	Min.	Pref.	Max.	Min.	Pref.	Max.	Min.	Pref.	Max.	Outside Wheel	Inside Wheel	
76	Torino, Elite ①	3¼	4	4¾				0	⅛	⅜	0	3.2	9.5	18	20	9
	Left Wheel				−¼	½	1¼									
	Right Wheel				−½	¼	1									
76	Pinto Sedan ②	½	1¼	2	0	¾	1½	⅛	¼	⅜	3.2	6.4	9.5	18⅞	20	10
76	Pinto Wagon ②	¾	1½	2¼	0	¾	1½	⅛	¼	⅜	3.2	6.5	9.5	18⅞	20	10
76	Mustang ②	⅛	⅞	⅝	−¼	½	⅛¼	0	⅛	¼	0	3.2	6.4	18⅞	20	9¾
77	Maverick ②	−1¼	−½	¼	−½	¼	1	0	⅛	¼	0	3.2	6.4			6¾
	W/Power Steering													18⅛	20	
	W/Manual Steering													18⅜	20	
77-78	Pinto Sedan ②	¼	1	1¾	−¼	½	1¼	0	⅛	¼	0	3.2	6.4	18⅞	20	10
77-78	Pinto Wagon ②	−½	¼	1	−¼	½	1¼	0	⅛	¼	0	3.2	6.4	18⅞	20	10
77-78	LTD ①	1¼	2	2¾				1/16	3/16	5/16	1.6	4.8	8.0	18¾	20	9¾
	Left Wheel				−¼	½	1¼									
	Right Wheel				−½	¼	1									
77-78	Granada ②	−1¼	−½	¼	−½	¼	1	0	⅛	¼	0	3.2	6.4			6¾
	W/Power Steering													18³/₁₆	20	
	W/Manual Steering													18⁷/₁₆	20	
77-79	LTD II ①	3¼	4	4¾				0	⅛	¼	0	3.2	6.4	18	20	9
	Left Wheel				−¼	½	1¼									
	Right Wheel				−½	¼	1									
77-79	Thunderbird ①	3¼	4	4¾				0	⅛	¼	0	3.2	6.4	18	20	9½
	Left Wheel				−¼	½	1¼									
	Right Wheel				−½	¼	1									
78-79	Fairmont ①	⅛	⅞	1⅝	−⅜	⅜	1⅛	3/16	5/16	7/16	4.8	8.0	11.1	19¾	20	15¼
79	Pinto Wagon ②	−½	¼	1	−¼	½	1¼	0	⅛	¼	0	3.2	6.4	18⅞	20	10
79	LTD ②	2¼	3	3¾	−¼	½	1¼	1/16	3/16	5/16	1.6	4.8	8.0	18½	20	11³/₁₆
79-80	Mustang ②	¼	1	1¾	−½	¼	1	3/16	5/16	7/16	4.8	8.0	11.1	19¾	20	15¼
79-80	Pinto Sedan ②	¼	1	1¾	−¼	½	1¼	0	⅛	¼	0	3.2	6.4	18⅞	20	10
80	Pinto Wagon ②	−¾	¼	1¼	−¼	½	1¼	0	⅛	¼	0	3.2	6.4	18⅞	20	10
79-80	Granada ②	−1¼	−½	¼	−½	¼	1	0	⅛	¼	0	3.2	6.4			7½
	W/Power Steering													18³/₁₆	20	
	W/Manual Steering													18⁷/₁₆	20	
80	Thunderbird ①	⅛	1	1⅞	−½	⅜	1¼	⅛	¼	⅜	3.2	6.4	9.5	24²⁹/₃₂	20	9½
80	Fairmont Sedan ①	⅛	1	1⅞	−5/16	7/16	1³/₁₆	1/16	3/16	5/16	1.6	4.8	8.0	19¾	20	15¼
	Wagon ①	−⅛	¾	1⅝	−¼	½	1¼	1/16	3/16	5/16	1.6	4.8	8.0	19¾	20	15¼
80	LTD ②	2¼	3	3¾	−¼	½	1¼	1/16 (out)	1/16 (in)	3/16 (in)	1.6 (out)	1.6 (in)	4.8 (in)	18½	20	10⅞
	Left Wheel				1	1¾	2½							19³¹/₃₂	20	14²¹/₃₂
	Right Wheel				9/16	1¹/₃₂	2¹/₁₆							17¹/₃₂	20	15³/₃₂
80-81	LTD ②	2¼	3	3¾	−¼	½	1¼	1/16 (out)	1/16 (in)	3/16 (in)	1.6 (out)	1.6 (in)	4.8 (in)	18½	20	10³¹/₃₂
81-82	Mustang ②	¼	1	1¾	−½	¼	1	1/16	3/16	5/16	1.6	4.8	8.0	19²⁷/₃₂	20	15¹¹/₁₆

FORD MOTOR COMPANY—FORD
Rear Drive Cars

VEHICLE IDENTIFICATION		CASTER (Degrees)			CAMBER (Degrees)			TOE-IN (Inches)			TOE-IN (Millimeters)			TOE-OUT ON TURNS (Degrees)		Strg. Axis Incl. (Deg.)
Year	Model	Min.	Pref.	Max.	Min.	Pref.	Max.	Min.	Pref.	Max.	Min.	Pref.	Max.	Outside Wheel	Inside Wheel	
81-82	Thunderbird ②	$\frac{1}{8}$	1	$1\frac{7}{8}$	$-\frac{1}{2}$	$\frac{3}{8}$	$1\frac{1}{4}$	$\frac{1}{16}$	$\frac{3}{16}$	$\frac{5}{16}$	1.6	4.8	8.0	$19\frac{3}{4}$	20	$15\frac{23}{32}$
81-82	Fairmont															
	Sedan ②	$\frac{1}{8}$	1	$1\frac{7}{8}$	$-\frac{5}{16}$	$\frac{7}{16}$	$1\frac{3}{16}$	$\frac{1}{16}$	$\frac{3}{16}$	$\frac{5}{16}$	1.6	4.8	8.0	$19\frac{27}{32}$	20	$15\frac{23}{32}$
	Wagon ②	$-\frac{1}{8}$	$\frac{3}{4}$	$1\frac{5}{8}$	$-\frac{1}{4}$	$\frac{1}{2}$	$1\frac{1}{4}$	$\frac{1}{16}$	$\frac{3}{16}$	$\frac{5}{16}$	1.6	4.8	8.0	$19\frac{27}{32}$	20	$15\frac{23}{32}$
81-82	Granada ②	$\frac{1}{8}$	1	$1\frac{7}{8}$	$-\frac{5}{16}$	$\frac{7}{16}$	$1\frac{3}{16}$	$\frac{1}{16}$	$\frac{3}{16}$	$\frac{5}{16}$	1.6	4.8	8.0	$19\frac{27}{32}$	20	$15\frac{23}{32}$

① Maximum side to side variation; caster $\pm\frac{3}{4}°$, camber $-\frac{1}{2}°$ to $1°$.
② Maximum side to side variation; caster and camber $\pm\frac{3}{4}°$.

FORD MOTOR COMPANY—LINCOLN

VEHICLE IDENTIFICATION		CASTER (Degrees)			CAMBER (Degrees)			TOE-IN (Inches)			TOE-IN (Millimeters)			TOE-OUT ON TURNS (Degrees)		Strg. Axis Incl. (Deg.)
Year	Model	Min.	Pref.	Max.	Min.	Pref.	Max.	Min.	Pref.	Max.	Min.	Pref.	Max.	Outside Wheel	Inside Wheel	
76	Mark IV ①	$1\frac{1}{4}$	2	$2\frac{3}{4}$				$\frac{1}{16}$	$\frac{3}{16}$	$\frac{5}{16}$	1.6	4.8	8.0	$18\frac{1}{8}$	20	$9\frac{1}{2}$
	Left Wheel				$-\frac{1}{4}$	$\frac{1}{2}$	$1\frac{1}{4}$									
	Right Wheel				$-\frac{1}{2}$	$\frac{1}{4}$	1									
77	Mark V ①	$1\frac{1}{4}$	2	$2\frac{3}{4}$				$\frac{1}{16}$	$\frac{3}{16}$	$\frac{5}{16}$	1.6	4.8	8.0	$18\frac{1}{8}$	20	$9\frac{1}{2}$
	Left Wheel				$-\frac{1}{4}$	$\frac{1}{2}$	$1\frac{1}{4}$									
	Right Wheel				$-\frac{1}{2}$	$\frac{1}{4}$	1									
76-77	Continental ①	$1\frac{1}{4}$	2	$2\frac{3}{4}$				0	$\frac{1}{8}$	$\frac{3}{8}$	0	3.2	9.5	$18\frac{5}{32}$	20	$9\frac{1}{2}$
	Left Wheel				$-\frac{1}{4}$	$\frac{1}{2}$	$1\frac{1}{4}$									
	Right Wheel				$-\frac{1}{2}$	$\frac{1}{4}$	1									
78-79	Continental ①	$1\frac{1}{4}$	2	$2\frac{3}{4}$				0	$\frac{1}{8}$	$\frac{1}{4}$	0	3.2	6.4	$18\frac{1}{8}$	20	$9\frac{1}{2}$
	Left Wheel				$-\frac{1}{4}$	$\frac{1}{2}$	$1\frac{1}{4}$									
	Right Wheel				$-\frac{1}{2}$	$\frac{1}{4}$	1									
78-79	Mark V ①	$3\frac{1}{4}$	4	$4\frac{3}{4}$				$\frac{1}{16}$	$\frac{3}{16}$	$\frac{5}{16}$	1.6	4.8	8.0	$18\frac{1}{8}$	20	$9\frac{1}{2}$
	Left Wheel				$-\frac{1}{4}$	$\frac{1}{2}$	$1\frac{1}{4}$									
	Right Wheel				$-\frac{1}{2}$	$\frac{1}{4}$	1									
77-80	Versailles ②	$-1\frac{1}{4}$	$-\frac{1}{2}$	$\frac{1}{4}$	$-\frac{1}{2}$	$\frac{1}{4}$	1	0	$\frac{1}{8}$	$\frac{1}{4}$	0	3.2	6.4	$18\frac{3}{16}$	20	$6\frac{3}{4}$
80	Continental, Mark VI ②	$2\frac{1}{4}$	3	$3\frac{3}{4}$	$-\frac{1}{4}$	$\frac{1}{2}$	$1\frac{1}{4}$	$\frac{1}{16}$ (out)	$\frac{1}{16}$ (out)	$\frac{3}{16}$ (in)	1.6 (out)	1.6 (in)	4.8 (in)	$18\frac{1}{2}$	20	$10\frac{7}{8}$
81-82	Lincoln, Mark VI ②	$2\frac{1}{4}$	3	$3\frac{3}{4}$	$-\frac{1}{4}$	$\frac{1}{2}$	$1\frac{1}{4}$	$\frac{1}{16}$ (out)	$\frac{1}{16}$ (in)	$\frac{3}{16}$ (in)	1.6 (out)	1.6 (in)	4.8 (in)	$18\frac{1}{2}$	20	$11\frac{7}{8}$
82	Lincoln Continental	$-1\frac{1}{4}$	$-\frac{1}{2}$	$\frac{1}{4}$	$-\frac{1}{2}$	$\frac{1}{4}$	1	0	$\frac{1}{8}$	$\frac{1}{4}$	0	3.2	6.4	$18\frac{1}{8}$	20	$6\frac{3}{4}$

① Maximum side to side variation; caster $\pm\frac{3}{4}°$, camber $-\frac{1}{2}°$ to $1°$.
② Maximum side to side variation; caster and camber $\pm\frac{3}{4}°$.

SUSPENSION

SPECIFICATIONS

FORD MOTOR COMPANY—MERCURY
Front Drive Cars

VEHICLE IDENTIFICATION		CASTER (Degrees)			CAMBER (Degrees)			TOE-IN (Inches)			TOE-IN (Millimeters)			Toe-Out On Turns (Degrees)	Strg. Axis Incl. (Deg.)
Year	Model	Min.	Pref.	Max.	Min.	Pref.	Max.	Min.	Pref.	Max.	Min.	Pref.	Max.		
81-82	Lynx-LN7 ①	+.55	+1.30	+2.05				0.02 (in)	0.1 (out)	0.22 (out)	.07 (in)	2.4 (out)	5.6 (out)		
	Left Wheel				+1.40	+2.15	+2.90							19.97	14.64
	Right Wheel				+.95	+1.70	+2.45							17.07	15.09

① Caster measurement must be done for **each** wheel regardless of the equipment being used.

FORD MOTOR COMPANY—MERCURY
Rear Drive Cars

VEHICLE IDENTIFICATION		CASTER (Degrees)			CAMBER (Degrees)			TOE-IN (Inches)			TOE-IN (Millimeters)			TOE-OUT ON TURNS (Degrees)		Strg. Axis Incl. (Deg.)
Year	Model	Min.	Pref.	Max.	Min.	Pref.	Max.	Min.	Pref.	Max.	Min.	Pref.	Max.	Outside Wheel	Inside Wheel	
76	Bobcat Sedan ②	½	1¼	2	0	¾	1½	⅛	¼	⅜	3.2	6.4	9.5	18⅞	20	10
76	Bobcat Wagon ②	¾	1½	2¼	0	¾	1½	⅛	¼	⅜	3.2	6.4	9.5	18⅞	20	10
76	Cougar, Montego ①	3¼	4	4¾				0	⅛	⅜	0	3.2	9.5	18	20	9
	Left Wheel				−¼	½	1¼									
	Right Wheel				−½	¼	1									
76	Monarch ②	−1¼	−½	¼	−½	¼	1	0	⅛	⅜	0	3.2	9.5			
	W/Power Steering													18³⁄₁₆	20	6¾
	W/Manual Steering													18⁷⁄₁₆	20	6¾
77	Comet ②	−1¼	−½	¼	−½	¼	1	0	⅛	¼	0	3.2	6.4			
	W/Power Steering													18⅛	20	6¾
	W/Manual Steering													18⅜	20	6¾
77-79	Bobcat Sedan ②	¼	1	1¾	−¼	½	1¼	0	⅛	¼	0	3.2	6.4	18⅞	20	10
77-79	Bobcat Wagon ②	−½	¼	1	−¼	½	1¼	0	⅛	¼	0	3.2	6.4	18⅞	20	10
77-79	Cougar ①	3¼	4	4¾				0	⅛	¼	0	3.2	6.4	18	20	9
	Left Wheel				−¼	½	1¼									
	Right Wheel				−½	¼	1									
77-79	Monarch ②	−1¼	−1½	¼	−½	¼	1	0	⅛	⅜	0	3.2	9.5			
	W/Power Steering													18³⁄₁₆	20	6¾
	W/Manual Steering													18⁷⁄₁₆	20	6¾
77-78	Mercury ①	1¼	2	2¾				¹⁄₁₆	³⁄₁₆	⁵⁄₁₆	1.6	4.8	8.0	18¾	20	9½
	Left Wheel				−¼	½	1¼									
	Right Wheel				−½	¼	1									
78-79	Zephyr ①	⅛	⅞	1⅝	−⅜	⅜	1⅛	³⁄₁₆	⁵⁄₁₆	⁷⁄₁₆	4.8	8.0	11.1	19¾	20	15¼
79-80	Mercury ②	2¼	3	3¾	−¼	½	1¼	¹⁄₁₆ (out)	¹⁄₁₆ (in)	³⁄₁₆ (in)	1.6 (out)	1.6 (in)	4.8 (in)	18½	20	10⅞
79-80	Capri ②	¼	1	1¾	−½	¼	1	³⁄₁₆	⁵⁄₁₆	⁷⁄₁₆	4.8	8.0	11.1	19¾	20	15¼
80	Zephyr Sedan ①	⅛	1	1⅞	−⁵⁄₁₆	⁷⁄₁₆	1³⁄₁₆	¹⁄₁₆	³⁄₁₆	⁵⁄₁₆	1.6	4.8	8.0	19¾	20	15¼
80	Zephyr Wagon ①	−⅛	¾	⅝	−¼	½	1¼	¹⁄₁₆	³⁄₁₆	⁵⁄₁₆	1.6	4.8	8.0	19¾	20	15¼
80	Bobcat Sedan ②	¼	1	1¾	−¼	½	1¼	0	⅛	¼	0	3.2	6.4	18⅞	20	10

FORD MOTOR COMPANY—MERCURY
Rear Drive Cars

VEHICLE IDENTIFICATION		CASTER (Degrees)			CAMBER (Degrees)			TOE-IN (Inches)			TOE-IN (Millimeters)			TOE-OUT ON TURNS (Degrees)		Strg. Axis Incl. (Deg.)
Year	Model	Min.	Pref.	Max.	Min.	Pref.	Max.	Min.	Pref.	Max.	Min.	Pref.	Max.	Outside Wheel	Inside Wheel	
80	Bobcat Wagon ②	−¾	¼	1¼	−¼	½	1¼	0	⅛	¼	0	3.2	6.4	18⅞	20	10
80	Cougar ①	⅛	1	1⅞	−½	⅜	1¼	⅛	¼	⅜	3.2	6.4	9.5	24²⁹/₃₂	20	15⅜
80	Monarch ②	−1¼	−½	¼	−½	¼	1	0	⅛	¼	0	3.2	6.4			
	W/Power Steering													18³/₁₆	20	7½
	W/Manual Steering													18⁷/₁₆	20	7½
81-82	Mercury ②	2¼	3	3¾	−¼	½	1¼	¹/₁₆ (out)	¹/₁₆ (in)	³/₁₆ (in)	1.6 (out)	1.6 (in)	4.8 (in)	18½	20	10³¹/₃₂
81-82	Capri ②	¼	1	1¾	−½	¼	1	¹/₁₆ (out)	³/₁₆ (in)	⁵/₁₆ (in)	1.6	4.8	8.0	19²⁷/₃₂	20	15¹¹/₁₆
81-82	Cougar XR7 ②	⅛	1	1⅞	−½	⅜	1¼	¹/₁₆	³/₁₆	⁵/₁₆	1.6	4.8	8.0	19¾	20	15²³/₃₂
81-82	Cougar ②	⅛	1	1⅞	−⁵/₁₆	⁷/₁₆	1³/₁₆	¹/₁₆	³/₁₆	⁵/₁₆	1.6	4.8	8.0	19²⁷/₃₂	20	15²³/₃₂
81-82	Zephyr Sedan ②	⅛	1	1⅞	−⁵/₁₆	⁷/₁₆	1³/₁₆	¹/₁₆	³/₁₆	⁵/₁₆	1.6	4.8	8.0	19²⁷/₃₂	20	15²³/₃₂
81-82	Zephyr Wagon ②	−⅛	¾	1⅝	−¼	½	1¼	¹/₁₆	³/₁₆	⁵/₁₆	1.6	4.8	8.0	19²⁷/₃₂	20	15²³/₃₂

① Maximum side to side variation; caster ±¾°, camber −½° to 1°.
② Maximum side to side variation; caster and camber ±¾°.

GENERAL MOTORS CORPORATION—BUICK ①

VEHICLE IDENTIFICATION		CASTER (Degrees)			CAMBER (Degrees)			TOE-IN (Inches)			TOE-IN (Millimeters)			TOE-OUT ON TURNS (Degrees)		Strg. Axis Incl. (Deg.)
Year	Model	Min.	Pref.	Max.	Min.	Pref.	Max.	Min.	Pref.	Max.	Min.	Pref.	Max.	Outside Wheel	Inside Wheel	
76	Le Sabre, Electra, Riviera ②	½	1½	2½				¹/₁₆ (out)	¹/₁₆ (in)	³/₁₆ (in)	1.6 (out)	1.6 (in)	4.8 (in)	18½	20	9⁹/₁₆
	Left Wheel				¼	1	1¾									
	Right Wheel				−¼	½	1¼									
76	Estate Wagon	½	1½	2½				¹/₁₆ (out)	¹/₁₆ (in)	³/₁₆ (in)	1.6 (out)	1.6 (in)	4.8 (in)	18½	20	10¾
	Left Wheel				¼	1	1¾									
	Right Wheel				−¼	½	1¼									
76	Skylark				0	¾	1½	¹/₁₆ (out)	¹/₁₆ (in)	³/₁₆ (in)	1.6 (out)	1.6 (in)	4.8 (in)	NA	NA	10
	W/Power Steering	0	1	2												
	W/Manual Steering	−2	−1	0												
76	Century, Regal	1	2	3				¹/₁₆ (out)	¹/₁₆ (in)	³/₁₆ (in)	1.6 (out)	1.6 (in)	4.8 (in)			8
	Left Wheel				¼	1	1¾							18¹³/₁₆	20	
	Right Wheel				−¼	½	1¼							19³/₁₆	20	
77	Century Regal W/Radial Tires	1	2	3				¹/₁₆ (out)	¹/₁₆ (in)	³/₁₆ (in)	1.6 (out)	1.6 (in)	4.8 (in)	NA	NA	8
	W/Bias Tires	0	1	2												
	Left Wheel				¼	1	1¾									
	Right Wheel				−¼	½	1¼									

SUSPENSION
SPECIFICATIONS

GENERAL MOTORS CORPORATION—BUICK ①

VEHICLE IDENTIFICATION		CASTER (Degrees)			CAMBER (Degrees)			TOE-IN (Inches)			TOE-IN (Millimeters)			TOE-OUT ON TURNS (Degrees)		Strg. Axis Incl. (Deg.)
Year	Model	Min.	Pref.	Max.	Min.	Pref.	Max.	Min.	Pref.	Max.	Min.	Pref.	Max.	Outside Wheel	Inside Wheel	
77-79	Skylark				0	3/4	1 5/8	1/16	1/8	1/4	1.6	3.2	6.4	NA	NA	10
	W/Power Steering	0	1	2												
	W/Manual Steering	−2	−1	0												
76-80	Skyhawk	−1 3/4	−3/4	1/4	−1/2	1/4	1	1/16 (out)	1/16 (in)	3/16 (in)	4.8 (out)	1.6 (in)	1.6 (in)	NA	NA	8 1/2
77-82	Electra, Le Sabre	2	3	4	0	13/16	1 5/8	1/16	1/8	1/4	1.6	3.2	6.4	NA	NA	9 9/16
77-82	Estate Wagon	2	3	4	0	13/16	1 5/8	1/16	1/8	1/4	1.6	3.2	6.4	NA	NA	10 3/4
79-82	Riviera ②															
	Front	1 1/2	2 1/2	3 1/2	−13/16	0	13/16	1/8 (out)	0	1/8 (in)	3.2 (out)	0	3.2 (in)	NA	NA	11
	Rear		Fixed			Fixed		0	5/32	5/16	0	4.0	8.0			
80-82	Skylark	−2	0	2	0	1/2	1	0	3/32	3/16	0	2.5	5.0	NA	NA	14 1/2
78-82	Century, Regal				−5/16	1/2	1 5/16	1/16	1/8	1/4	1.6	3.2	6.4	NA	NA	8
	W/Power Steering	2	3	4												
	W/Manual Steering	0	1	2												

① Maximum side to side variation; caster and camber ½°
② Riviera F.W.D. trim height is measured from the edge of the wheel well opening directly over the center of the wheel to the floor.
1979 Front Suspension: 28½ in. (724 mm)
1979 Rear Suspension: 28 in (709 mm)
1980-81 Front Suspension: 28⅛ in. (726 mm)
1980-81 Rear Suspension: 27⁵/₁₆ (694 mm)

GENERAL MOTORS CORPORATION—CADILLAC ① ②

VEHICLE IDENTIFICATION		CASTER (Degrees)			CAMBER (Degrees)			TOE-IN (Inches)			TOE-IN (Millimeters)			TOE-OUT ON TURNS (Degrees)		Strg. Axis Incl. (Deg.)
Year	Model	Min.	Pref.	Max.	Min.	Pref.	Max.	Min.	Pref.	Max.	Min.	Pref.	Max.	Outside Wheel	Inside Wheel	
76	Seville	1	2	3				1/16 (out)	1/16 (in)	3/16 (in)	1.6 (out)	1.6 (in)	4.8 (in)	NA	NA	10 5/8
	Left Wheel				−1/4	1/2	1 1/4									
	Right Wheel				−1/2	1/4	1									
76	Cadillac except Eldorado, Seville and Fleetwood 75	−1	0	1				0	1/8	1/4	0	3.2	6.4	NA	NA	6
	Left Wheel				−3/4	0	3/4									
	Right Wheel				−1	−1/4	1/2									
76	Fleetwood 75	−2	−1	0				0	1/8	1/4	0	3.2	6.4	NA	NA	6
	Left Wheel				−3/4	0	3/4									
	Right Wheel				−1	−1/4	1/2									
76	Eldorado	−1	0	1				1/8 (out)	0	1/8 (in)	3.2 (out)	0	3.2 (in)	NA	NA	11
	Left Wheel				−3/4	0	3/4									
	Right Wheel				−1	−1/4	1/2									

GENERAL MOTORS CORPORATION—CADILLAC ① ②

VEHICLE IDENTIFICATION		CASTER (Degrees)			CAMBER (Degrees)			TOE-IN (Inches)			TOE-IN (Millimeters)			TOE-OUT ON TURNS (Degrees)		Strg. Axis Incl. (Deg.)
Year	Model	Min.	Pref.	Max.	Min.	Pref.	Max.	Min.	Pref.	Max.	Min.	Pref.	Max.	Outside Wheel	Inside Wheel	
77-79	Cadillac except Eldorado and Seville	2	3	4	−1/4	1/2	1 1/4	1/8 (out)	0	1/8 (in)	3.2 (out)	0	3.2 (in)	NA	NA	10^{19}/32
77-79	Seville	1	2	3	−3/4	0	3/4	1/16 (out)	1/16 (in)	3/16 (in)	1.6 (out)	1.6 (in)	4.8 (in)	NA	NA	10 5/8
79-82	Eldorado Front	1 1/2	2 1/2	3 1/2	−13/16	0	13/16	1/8 (out)	0	1/8 (in)	3.2 (out)	0	3.2 (in)	NA	NA	11
	Rear		Fixed			Fixed		0	5/32	5/16	0	4.0	8.0			
80-82	Seville Front	1 1/2	2 1/2	3 1/2	−13/16	0	13/16	1/8 (out)	0	1/8 (in)	3.2 (out)	0	3.2 (in)	NA	NA	11
	Rear		Fixed			Fixed		0	5/32	5/16	0	4.0	8.0			
80-82	Cadillac except Eldorado and Seville	2	3	4	−5/16	1/2	1 5/16	0	1/8	1/4	0	3.2	6.4	NA	NA	10^{19}/32
82	Cimarron	−2	0	2	+60°	±.50°		—	—	—		③		NA	NA	14

① Maximum side to side variation; after reset caster and camber 1 1/2°.
② Check suspension height before performing alignment. Suspension height tables follow alignment tolerance tables.
③ Toe (per wheel) .125° toe out ± 125°

GENERAL MOTORS CORPORATION—CHEVROLET
Front Drive Cars ①

VEHICLE IDENTIFICATION		CASTER (Degrees)			CAMBER (Degrees)			TOE-IN (Inches)			TOE-IN (Millimeters)			TOE-OUT ON TURNS (Degrees)		Strg. Axis Incl. (Deg.)
Year	Model	Min.	Pref.	Max.	Min.	Pref.	Max.	Min.	Pref.	Max.	Min.	Pref.	Max.	Outside Wheel	Inside Wheel	
80-82	Citation	−2	0	+2	0	1/2	1	0	3/32	3/16	0	2.5	5.0	NA	NA	14 1/2
82	Cavalier		Fixed		+.60°	±.50°			②			②		NA	NA	14
82	Celebrity	−2	0	2	0	1/2	1	0	3/32	3/16	0	2.5	5.0	NA	NA	14 1/2

① Maximum side to side variation; after reset caster and camber 1 1/2°.
② Toe (per wheel) .125°, toe out ± .125°

GENERAL MOTORS CORPORATION—CHEVROLET
Rear Drive Cars ①

VEHICLE IDENTIFICATION		CASTER (Degrees)			CAMBER (Degrees)			TOE-IN (Inches)			TOE-IN (Millimeters)			TOE-OUT ON TURNS (Degrees)		Strg. Axis Incl. (Deg.)
Year	Model	Min.	Pref.	Max.	Min.	Pref.	Max.	Min.	Pref.	Max.	Min.	Pref.	Max.	Outside Wheel	Inside Wheel	
76	Corvette W/Power Steering	1 1/4	2 1/4	3 1/4	0	3/4	1 1/2	1/8	1/4	3/8	3.2	6.4	9.5	NA	NA	7^{11}/16
	W/Manual Steering	0	1	2				1/8	1/4	3/8	3.2	6.4	9.5	NA	NA	7^{11}/16
	Rear				−1 1/8	−7/8	−5/8	1/32	1/16	3/32	0.8	1.6	2.4	NA	NA	

SUSPENSION
SPECIFICATIONS

GENERAL MOTORS CORPORATION—CHEVROLET
Rear Drive Cars ①

Year	Model	CASTER (Degrees) Min.	Pref.	Max.	CAMBER (Degrees) Min.	Pref.	Max.	TOE-IN (Inches) Min.	Pref.	Max.	TOE-IN (Millimeters) Min.	Pref.	Max.	TOE-OUT ON TURNS (Degrees) Outside Wheel	Inside Wheel	Strg. Axis Incl. (Deg.)
76	Monte Carlo	4	5	6				$1/16$ (out)	$1/16$ (in)	$3/16$ (in)	1.6 (out)	1.6 (in)	4.8 (in)	NA	NA	$9^{19}/32$
	Left Wheel				$1/4$	1	$1\frac{3}{4}$									
	Right Wheel				$-1/4$	$1/2$	$1\frac{1}{4}$									
76	Vega	$-1\frac{3}{4}$	$-\frac{3}{4}$	$1/4$	$-\frac{3}{4}$	$3/4$	$1\frac{1}{4}$	$3/16$ (out)	$1/16$ (out)	$1/16$ (in)	4.8 (out)	1.6 (in)	1.6 (in)	NA	NA	$8^{9}/16$
76	Camaro	0	1	2	$1/4$	1	$1\frac{3}{4}$	$1/16$ (out)	$1/16$ (in)	$3/16$ (in)	1.6 (out)	1.6 (in)	4.8 (in)	NA	NA	$10^{5}/32$
76	Nova				0	$3/4$	$1\frac{1}{2}$	$1/16$ (out)	$1/16$ (in)	$3/16$ (in)	1.6 (out)	1.6 (in)	4.8 (in)	NA	NA	10
	W/Power Steering	0	1	2												
	W/Manual Steering	-2	-1	0												
76	Chevette	$2\frac{1}{2}$	$4\frac{1}{2}$	$6\frac{1}{2}$	$-\frac{1}{2}$	$1/4$	1	$1/32$ (out)	$1/16$ (in)	$5/32$ (in)	0.8 (out)	1.6 (in)	4.0 (in)	NA	NA	$7^{9}/16$
76	Monza	$-1\frac{3}{4}$	$-\frac{3}{4}$	$1/4$	$-\frac{3}{4}$	$1/4$	$1\frac{1}{4}$	$3/16$ (out)	$1/16$ (out)	$1/16$ (in)	4.8 (out)	1.6 (out)	1.6 (in)	NA	NA	$8^{9}/16$
76	Chevrolet (full size)							$1/16$ (out)	$1/16$ (in)	$3/16$ (in)	1.6 (out)	1.6 (in)	4.8 (in)	NA	NA	10
	W/Radial Tires	$1/2$	$1\frac{1}{2}$	$2\frac{1}{4}$												
	W/Bias Tires	0	1	2												
	Left Wheel				$1/4$	1	$1\frac{3}{4}$									
	Right Wheel				$-1/4$	$1/2$	$1\frac{1}{4}$									
76	Chevelle, El Camino W/Power Steering	1	2	3				$1/16$ (out)	$1/16$ (in)	$3/16$ (in)	1.6 (out)	1.6 (in)	4.8 (in)	NA	NA	$9\frac{5}{8}$
	Left Wheel				$1/4$	1	$1\frac{3}{4}$									
	Right Wheel				$-1/4$	$1/2$	$1\frac{1}{4}$									
	W/Manual Steering	0	1	2				$1/16$ (out)	$1/16$ (in)	$3/16$ (in)	1.6 (out)	1.6 (in)	4.8 (in)	NA	NA	$9\frac{5}{8}$
	Left Wheel				$1/4$	1	$1\frac{3}{4}$									
	Right Wheel				$-1/4$	$1/2$	$1\frac{1}{4}$									
77	Nova				0	$13/16$	$1\frac{5}{8}$	$1/16$ (out)	$1/16$ (in)	$3/16$ (in)	1.6 (out)	1.6 (in)	4.8 (in)	NA	NA	10
	W/Power Steering	0	1	2												
	W/Manual Steering	-2	-1	0												
77	Vega	$-1^{13}/16$	$-^{13}/16$	$3/16$	$5/8$	$3/16$	1	$3/16$ (out)	$1/16$ (out)	$1/16$ (in)	4.8 (out)	1.6 (out)	1.6 (in)	NA	NA	$8^{9}/16$
77	Chevette	$2\frac{1}{2}$	$4\frac{1}{2}$	$6\frac{1}{2}$	$-\frac{1}{2}$	$3/16$	1	$1/32$ (out)	$1/16$ (in)	$5/32$ (in)	0.8 (out)	1.6 (in)	4.0 (in)	NA	NA	$7\frac{1}{2}$

GENERAL MOTORS CORPORATION—CHEVROLET
Rear Drive Cars ①

Year	Model	Caster (Degrees) Min.	Pref.	Max.	Camber (Degrees) Min.	Pref.	Max.	Toe-In (Inches) Min.	Pref.	Max.	Toe-In (Millimeters) Min.	Pref.	Max.	Toe-Out On Turns (Degrees) Outside Wheel	Inside Wheel	Strg. Axis Incl. (Deg.)
77	Chevelle, El Camino *W/Power Steering*							1/16 (out)	1/16 (in)	3/16 (in)	1.6 (out)	1.6 (in)	4.8 (in)	NA	NA	9 19/32
	W/Radial Tires	1	2	3												
	W/Bias Tires	0	1	2												
	Left Wheel				3/16	1	1 13/16									
	Right Wheel				−5/16	1/2	1 5/16									
	W/Manual Steering	0	1	2				1/16 (out)	1/16 (in)	3/16 (in)	1.6 (out)	1.6 (in)	4.8 (in)	NA	NA	9 19/32
	Left Wheel				3/16	1	1 13/16									
	Right Wheel				−5/16	1/2	1 5/16									
77	Monte Carlo	4	5	6				1/16 (out)	1/16 (in)	3/16 (in)	1.6 (out)	1.6 (in)	4.8 (in)	NA	NA	9 19/32
	Left Wheel				3/16	1	1 13/16									
	Right Wheel				−5/16	1/2	1 5/16									
77	Camaro	0	1	2	3/16	1	1 13/16	1/16 (out)	1/16 (in)	3/16 (in)	1.6 (out)	1.6 (in)	4.8 (in)	NA	NA	10 11/32
77-78	Corvette Front	1 1/4	2 1/4	3 1/4	0	3/4	1 1/2	1/8	1/4	3/8	3.2	6.4	9.5	NA	NA	7 11/16
	Rear				−1 1/8	−7/8	−5/8	1/32 (out)	0	1/32 (in)	0.8 (out)	0	0.8 (in)	NA	NA	
78-79	Camaro	0	1	2	3/16	1	1 13/16	1/16	1/8	1/4	1.6	3.2	6.4	NA	NA	10 3/64
78-79	Chevette	2 1/2	4 1/2	6 1/2	−1/2	3/16	7/8	0	3/32	7/32	0	2.5	5.5	NA	NA	7 1/2
78-79	Nova				0	13/16	1 5/8	0	1/8	1/4	1.6	3.2	6.4	NA	NA	10
	W/Power Steering	0	1	2												
	W/Manual Steering	−2	−1	0												
79	Corvette Front	1 1/4	2 1/4	3 1/4	0	3/4	1 1/2	1/8	1/4	3/8	3.2	6.4	9.5	NA	NA	7 11/16
	Rear				−1	−1/2	0	1/16	3/32	1/8	1.6	2.4	3.2	NA	NA	
77-80	Monza	−1 13/16	−13/16	3/16	−5/8	3/16	1	3/16	1/16	1/16	4.8	1.6	1.6	NA	NA	8 9/16
77-81	Chevrolet (full size)	2	3	4	0	13/16	1 5/8	1/16	1/8	1/4	1.6	3.2	6.4	NA	NA	9 25/32
78-82	Malibu, El Camino Monte Carlo				−5/16	1/2	1 5/16	1/16	1/8	1/4	1.6	3.2	6.4	NA	NA	7 7/8
	W/Power Steering	2	3	4												
	W/Manual Steering	0	1	2												
80-82	Corvette Front	1 1/4	2 1/4	3 1/4	0	3/4	1 1/2	1/8	1/4	3/8	3.2	6.4	9.5	NA	NA	7 11/16
	Rear				3/16	11/16	1 3/16	1/16	0	1/16	0	0.8	16			
80-82	Camaro	0	1	2	3/16	1	1 13/16	1/16	1/8	1/4	1.6	3.2	6.4	NA	NA	10 3/8
80-82	Chevette	2 1/2	4 1/2	6 1/2	−1/2	3/16	29/32	1/32 (out)	1/16 (in)	1/8 (in)	0.8 (out)	1.6 (in)	3.2 (in)	NA	NA	7 9/16

① Maximum side to side variation after reset caster and camber; All except Chevette 1/2°, Chevette 2°.

SUSPENSION
SPECIFICATIONS

GENERAL MOTORS CORPORATION—OLDSMOBILE
Front Drive Cars ①

VEHICLE IDENTIFICATION		CASTER (Degrees)			CAMBER (Degrees)			TOE-IN (Inches)			TOE-IN (Millimeters)			TOE-OUT ON TURNS (Degrees)		Strg. Axis Incl. (Deg.)
Year	Model	Min.	Pref.	Max.	Min.	Pref.	Max.	Min.	Pref.	Max.	Min.	Pref.	Max.	Outside Wheel	Inside Wheel	
80-81	Omega	−2	0	2	0	½	1	0	3/32	3/16	0	2.5	5.0	NA	NA	14½
82	Cutlass, Cierra	−2	0	2	0	½	1	0	3/32	3/16	0	2.5	5.0	NA	NA	14½

① Maximum side to side variation after reset; caster and camber ½°.

GENERAL MOTORS CORPORATION—OLDSMOBILE
Rear Drive Cars ①

VEHICLE IDENTIFICATION		CASTER (Degrees)			CAMBER (Degrees)			TOE-IN (Inches)			TOE-IN (Millimeters)			TOE-OUT ON TURNS (Degrees)		Strg. Axis Incl. (Deg.)
Year	Model	Min.	Pref.	Max.	Min.	Pref.	Max.	Min.	Pref.	Max.	Min.	Pref.	Max.	Outside Wheel	Inside Wheel	
76	88 & 98 Series	½	1½	2½				1/16 (out)	1/16 (in)	3/16 (in)	1.6 (out)	1.6 (in)	4.8 (in)	NA	NA	10½
	Left Wheel				¼	1	1¾									
	Right Wheel				−¼	½	1¾									
77	88 & 98 Series	2	3	4	0	¾	1½	0	1/8	¼	0	3.2	6.4	NA	NA	10½
76-77	Omega				0	¾	1½	1/16 (out)	1/16 (in)	3/16 (in)	1.6 (out)	1.6 (in)	4.8 (in)	NA	NA	10½
	W/Power Steering	0	1	2												
	W/Manual Steering	−2	−1	0												
76-77	Cutlass	1	2	3				1/16 (out)	1/16 (in)	3/16 (in)	1.6 (out)	1.6 (in)	4.8 (in)	NA	NA	10½
	Left Wheel				¼	1	1¾									
	Right Wheel				−¼	½	1¼									
76-77	Toronado ②	−1	0	1				1/8 (out)	0	1/8 (in)	3.2 (out)	0	3.2 (in)	NA	NA	11
	Left Wheel				−½	¼	1									
	Right Wheel				−1	−¼	−½									
78	Toronado ②	−1	0	1				1/8 (out)	0	1/8 (in)	3.2 (out)	0	3.2 (in)	NA	NA	11
	Left Wheel				−½	5/16	1									
	Right Wheel				−1	−5/16	½									
78-79	Omega				0	¾	1⅝	1/16	1/8	¼	1.6	3.2	6.4	NA	NA	10½
	W/Power Steering	0	1	2												
	W/Manual Steering	−2	−1	0												
76-80	Starfire	−1¾	−¾	¼	−½	¼	1	3/16 (out)	1/16 (out)	1/16 (in)	4.8 (out)	1.6 (out)	1.6 (in)	NA	NA	8½
79-81	Toronado ② Front	1½	2½	3½	13/16	0	13/16	1/8 (out)	0	1/8 (in)	3.2 (out)	0	3.2 (in)	NA	NA	11
	Rear		Fixed			Fixed		0	5/32	5/16	0	4.0	8.0			
78-81	88 & 98 Series	2	3	4	0	¾	1⅝	0	1/8	¼	0	3.2	6.4	NA	NA	10½

GENERAL MOTORS CORPORATION—OLDSMOBILE
Rear Drive Cars ①

VEHICLE IDENTIFICATION		CASTER (Degrees)			CAMBER (Degrees)			TOE-IN (Inches)			TOE-IN (Millimeters)			TOE-OUT ON TURNS (Degrees)		Strg. Axis Incl. (Deg.)
Year	Model	Min.	Pref.	Max.	Min.	Pref.	Max.	Min.	Pref.	Max.	Min.	Pref.	Max.	Outside Wheel	Inside Wheel	
78-82	Cutlass				−5/16	½	1 5/16	1/16	1/8	¼	1.6	3.2	6.4	NA	NA	7
	W/Power Steering	2	3	4												
	W/Manual Steering	0	1	2												

① Maximum side to side variation after reset; caster and camber ½°
② Toronado F.W.D. trim height is measured between the bottom of the rocker moulding to the floor. The measurement positions are:
79-82 at the front edge of the door and at 71″ (1775 mm) behind the front edge of the door.
76-78 at 6″ (152 mm) behind the front edge of the door, and at 66″ (1676 mm) behind the front edge of the door.
1976-78 Front Suspension: 9 in. (229 mm)
1976-78 Rear Suspension: 9¼ in. (235 mm)
1979-82 Front Suspension: 9½ in. (242 mm)
1979-82 Rear Suspension: 9½ in. (242 mm)
1976 maximum side to side, front to rear deviation: ½ in. (12.7 mm)
1977-81 maximum side to side, front to rear deviation: ¾ in. (19 mm)

GENERAL MOTORS CORPORATION—PONTIAC
Front Drive Cars ①

VEHICLE IDENTIFICATION		CASTER (Degrees)			CAMBER (Degrees)			TOE-IN (Inches)			TOE-IN (Millimeters)			TOE-OUT ON TURNS (Degrees)		Strg. Axis Incl. (Deg.)
Year	Model	Min.	Pref.	Max.	Min.	Pref.	Max.	Min.	Pref.	Max.	Min.	Pref.	Max.	Outside Wheel	Inside Wheel	
82	A6000	−2	0	2	0	½	1	0	3/32	3/16	0	2.5	5.0	NA	NA	14½
80-82	Phoenix	−2	0	2	0	½	1	0	3/32	3/16	0	2.5	5.0	NA	NA	14½
82	J2000	—	—	—	+.60° ±.50			②			②			NA	NA	NA

① Maximum side to side variation after reset, caster and camber ½°
② Toe (per wheel) .125°, toe out ±.125°

GENERAL MOTORS CORPORATION—PONTIAC
Rear Drive Cars ①

VEHICLE IDENTIFICATION		CASTER (Degrees)			CAMBER (Degrees)			TOE-IN (Inches)			TOE-IN (Millimeters)			TOE-OUT ON TURNS (Degrees)		Strg. Axis Incl. (Deg.)
Year	Model	Min.	Pref.	Max.	Min.	Pref.	Max.	Min.	Pref.	Max.	Min.	Pref.	Max.	Outside Wheel	Inside Wheel	
76	Catalina, Bonneville, Grandville, Brougham	½	1½	2½				1/16 (out)	1/16 (out)	3/16 (in)	1.6 (out)	1.6 (out)	4.8 (in)	NA	NA	8 9/16
	Left Wheel				¼	1	1¾									
	Right Wheel				−¼	½	1¼									
	W/Manual Steering	−2	−1	0												

SUSPENSION

SPECIFICATIONS

GENERAL MOTORS CORPORATION—PONTIAC
Rear Drive Cars ①

Year	Model	CASTER (Degrees) Min.	Pref.	Max.	CAMBER (Degrees) Min.	Pref.	Max.	TOE-IN (Inches) Min.	Pref.	Max.	TOE-IN (Millimeters) Min.	Pref.	Max.	TOE-OUT ON TURNS (Degrees) Outside Wheel	Inside Wheel	Strg. Axis Incl. (Deg.)
76	Grand Prix	2	3	4				1/16 (out)	1/16 (in)	3/16 (in)	1.6 (out)	1.6 (in)	4.8 (in)			10½
	Left Wheel				¼	1	1¾							19³/₁₆	20	
	Right Wheel				−¼	½	1¼							18⅜	20	
76	LeMans, Grand LeMans W/Power Steering	1	2	3				1/16 (out)	1/16 (in)	3/16 (in)	1.6 (out)	1.6 (in)	4.8 (in)	NA	NA	10⅜
	Left Wheel				¼	1	1¾							19³/₁₆	20	
	Right Wheel				−¼	½	1¼							18³/₁₆	20	
	W/Power Steering	0	1	2				1/16 (out)	1/16 (in)	3/16 (in)	1.6 (out)	1.6 (in)	4.8 (in)			10⅜
	Left Wheel				¼	1	1¾							19³/₁₆	20	
	Right Wheel				−¼	½	1¼							18³/₁₆	20	
76	Firebird	−1	0	1	¼	1	1¾	1/16 (out)	1/16 (in)	3/16 (in)	1.6 (out)	1.6 (in)	4.8 (in)	NA	NA	10⅜
76	Ventura				0	¾	1½	1/16 (out)	1/16 (in)	3/16 (in)	1.6 (out)	1.6 (in)	4.8 (in)	18½	20	10
	W/Power Steering	0	1	2												
76-77	Sunbird, Astre	−1¾	−¾	¼	−9/16	3/16	1	3/16 (out)	1/16 (out)	1/16 (in)	4.8 (out)	1.6 (out)	1.6 (in)	NA	NA	8⁹/₁₆
77	Catalina, Bonneville, Brougham, Grandville	2	3	4	0	¾	1⁹/₁₆	1/16 (in)	3/16 (in)	5/16 (in)	1.6	4.8	8.0	NA	NA	10⅜
76-77	Phoenix, Ventura				0	¾	1½	1/16 (out)	1/16 (in)	3/16 (in)	1.6 (out)	1.6 (in)	4.8 (in)	18½	20	10
	W/Power Steering	0	1	2												
	W/Manual Steering	−2	−1	0												
77	Grand Prix	4	5	6				1/16 (out)	1/16 (in)	3/16 (in)	1.6 (out)	1.6 (in)	4.8 (in)	NA	NA	10⅜
	Left Wheel				¼	1	1¾									
	Right Wheel				−¼	½	1¼									
77	LeMans, Grand LeMans W/Power Steering							1/16 (out)	1/16 (in)	3/16 (in)	1.6 (out)	1.6 (in)	4.8 (in)			10⅜
	W/Belted Tires	0	1	2												
	W/Radial Tires	1	2	3												
	Left Wheel				¼	1	1¾							19³/₁₆	20	
	Right Wheel				−¼	½	1¼							18³/₁₆	20	
	W/Manual Steering	0	1	2				1/16 (out)	1/16 (in)	3/16 (in)	1.6 (out)	1.6 (in)	4.8 (in)			10⅜
	Left Wheel				¼	1	1¾							19³/₁₆	20	
	Right Wheel				−¼	½	1¼							18³/₁₆	20	

GENERAL MOTORS CORPORATION—PONTIAC
Rear Drive Cars ①

Year	Model	CASTER (Degrees) Min.	Pref.	Max.	CAMBER (Degrees) Min.	Pref.	Max.	TOE-IN (Inches) Min.	Pref.	Max.	TOE-IN (Millimeters) Min.	Pref.	Max.	TOE-OUT ON TURNS (Degrees) Outside Wheel	Inside Wheel	Strg. Axis Incl. (Deg.)
77	Firebird	0	1	2	3/16	1	1¾	1/16 (out)	1/16 (in)	3/16 (in)	1.6 (out)	1.6 (in)	4.8 (in)	NA	NA	10⅜
78-79	Phoenix				0	13/16	1⅝	1/16	1/8	1/4	1.6	3.2	6.4	NA	NA	10
	W/Power Steering	0	1	2												
	W/Manual Steering	-2	-1	0												
78-79	Grand Prix				-5/16	1/2	1 5/16	1/16	1/8	1/4	1.6	3.2	6.4	NA	NA	8
	W/Power Steering	2	3	4												
	W/Manual Steering	0	1	2												
78-79	LeMans, Grand AM				-5/16	1/2	1 5/16	1/16	1/8	1/4	1.6	3.2	6.4	NA	NA	8
	W/Power Steering	2	3	4												
	W/Manual Steering	0	1	2												
78-80	Sunbird	-1 13/16	-13/16	3/16	-5/8	-3/16	1	3/16 (out)	1/16 (out)	1/16 (in)	4.8 (out)	1.6 (out)	1.6 (in)	NA	NA	8 9/16
78-82	Firebird	0	1	2	3/16	1	1 13/16	1/16	1/8	1/4	1.6	3.2	6.4	NA	NA	10⅜
78-82	Catalina, Bonneville	2	3	4	0	13/16	1⅝	1/16	1/8	1/4	1.6	3.2	6.4	NA	NA	10 19/32
80-82	Phoenix	-2	0	2	0	1/2	1	0	3/32	3/16	0	2.5	5.0	NA	NA	14½
80-82	Grand Prix and LeMans				5/16	1/8	1 5/16	1/16	1/8	1/4	1.6	3.2	6.4	NA	NA	8
	W/Manual Steering	0	1	2												
	W/Power Steering	2	3	4												
81-82	T-1000	2½	4½	6½	-1/2	3/16	29/32	1/32 (out)	1/16 (in)	1/8 (in)	0.8 (out)	1.6 (in)	3.2 (in)	NA	NA	7 9/16

① Maximum side to side variation after reset, caster and camber ½°

SUSPENSION HEIGHTS

CHRYSLER CORPORATION

Model	Year	Procedure	Inches	MM
Coronet and Fury Wagons	1976	D	11¼	285.6
Gran Fury, Monaco, Newport, New Yorker	1976	D	10⅛	257.2
Valiant, Dart	1976	D	10 15/16	277.8
Aspen, Volare	1976	C	10¼	280.4
Coronet, Fury, Charger SE, Cordoba except Coronet and Fury Wagons	1976	D	10¾	273.1
Monaco, Fury, Charger SE, Cordoba except Monaco and Fury Wagons	1977	D	10¾	273.1

SUSPENSION

CHRYSLER CORPORATION

Model	Year	Procedure	Inches	MM
Monaco and Fury Wagons	1977	D	11¼	285.6
Royal Monaco, Gran Fury, Newport, New Yorker	1977	D	10⅛	257.2
Aspen, Volare, Diplomat, LeBaron	1978	C	10¼	260.4
Monaco, Fury, Charger SE, Magnum XE, Cordoba except Monaco and Fury Wagons	1978	D	10¾	273.1
Monaco and Fury Wagons	1978	D	11¼	285.6
Newport, New Yorker	1978	D	10⅛	257.2
Aspen, Volare, Diplomat, Le Baron	1977	C	10¼	260.4
Aspen, Volare, Diplomat, Le Baron and Caravelle	1979	C	10¼	260.4
Newport, New Yorker, St. Regis Cordoba, Magnum XE	1979	D	10¾	273.1
Newport, New Yorker, St. Regis, Gran Fury	80-82	B	16¾ ± ¼	425.5 ± 6.4
Imperial	81-82	B	16¾ ± ¼	425.5 ± 6.4
Aspen, Volare, Diplomat, Le Baron, Caravelle, Mirada and Cordoba	80-82	A	12½ ± ¼	317.5 ± 6.4

NOTE: Before measuring or setting front suspension height, the vehicle should be devoid of cargo and passengers. The tire pressure should be set to specifications. The gasoline tank should be filled. If the gasoline tank cannot be filled, weight should be added to the rear of the vehicle to compensate for the missing gasoline. The front of the car must be jounced vigorously to eliminate friction effects before making car height measurements. The vehicle should be released at the bottom of the downward motion.

Chrysler Corporation Front Suspension Height Adjustment

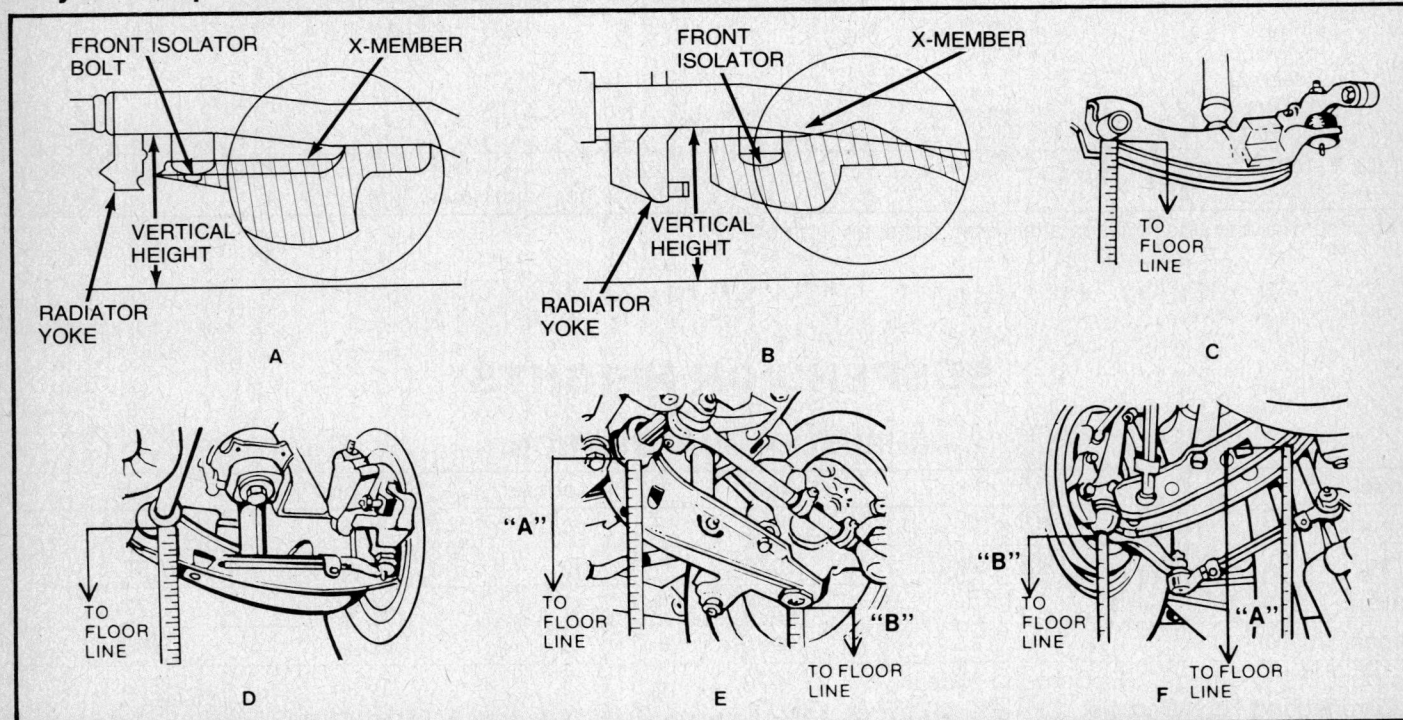

Front suspension height must be set to specifications before vehicle alignment is checked or reset. Maximum allowable height difference from side to side is ⅛ in.

PROCEDURE A—Vehicle resting on its tires. Measure from the head of the front suspension cross member front isolator bolt to the floor.

PROCEDURE B—Vehicle resting on its tires. Measure from the bottom of the front frame rail between the radiator yoke and the forward edge of the front suspension cross member to the floor line.

PROCEDURE C—Vehicle resting on its tires. Measure from the lowest point of the lower control arm inner pivot bushing to the floor line indicated by the lowest point of the front tires.

PROCEDURE D—Vehicle resting on its tires. Measure from the lowest point of the lower control arm torsion bar anchor at a point 1 inch from the rear face of the anchor to the floor line indicated by the lowest point of the front tires.

PROCEDURE E—Vehicle resting on its tires. Measure the distance from the lowest point of the front torsion bar anchor at the rear of the lower control arm flange to the floor line. Record as distance "A". Measure from the lowest point of the ball joint housing to the floor line and record as distance "B". Subtract distance "B" from distance "A". Answer must equal measurement shown in table or adjustment is required. Measure one side at a time.

PROCEDURE F—Vehicle resting on its tires. Measure the distance from the lowest point of the lower control arm adjusting blade to the floor line. Record as distance "A". Measure the distance from the lowest point of the steering knuckle arm at its center line and record as distance "B". Subtract distance "B" from distance "A". Answer must equal measurement shown in table or adjustment is required. Measure one side at a time.

CADILLAC

Model and Year	Front Suspension		Rear Suspension	
	Inches	MM	Inches	MM
Brougham				
76	$3^{7}/_{8}$-$4^{5}/_{8}$	98-118	$4^{7}/_{8}$-$5^{5}/_{8}$	124-143
77-79	$1^{7}/_{8}$-$2^{5}/_{8}$	48-67	$5^{3}/_{8}$-$6^{1}/_{8}$	137-161
80-82 W/ALC (Gas)	$1^{11}/_{16}$-$2^{1}/_{2}$	43-63	$4^{3}/_{4}$-$5^{17}/_{32}$	120-140
80-82 W/O ALC (Diesel)	$1^{7}/_{8}$-$2^{5}/_{8}$	47-67	$5^{5}/_{16}$-$6^{5}/_{64}$	134-154
80-82 W/O ALC (Gas)	$1^{13}/_{16}$-$2^{12}/_{32}$	45-65	$5^{9}/_{32}$-$6^{1}/_{16}$	134-154
DeVille, Calais				
76 W/O ALC	$3^{15}/_{16}$-$4^{11}/_{16}$	100-119	$5^{3}/_{8}$-$6^{1}/_{8}$	137-161
76 W/ALC	$3^{15}/_{16}$-$4^{11}/_{16}$	100-119	$4^{7}/_{8}$-$5^{5}/_{8}$	124-143
77-79 W/O ALC	$2^{1}/_{8}$-$2^{7}/_{8}$	54-73	$5^{3}/_{4}$-$6^{1}/_{2}$	146-170
77-79 W/ALC	$2^{1}/_{8}$-$2^{7}/_{8}$	54-73	$5^{3}/_{4}$-$6^{1}/_{2}$	146-170
80-82 W/ALC (Diesel)	$1^{3}/_{4}$-$2^{9}/_{16}$	45-65	$4^{25}/_{32}$-$5^{9}/_{16}$	121-141
80-82 W/ALC (Gas)	$1^{11}/_{16}$-$2^{1}/_{2}$	43-63	$4^{3}/_{4}$-$5^{17}/_{32}$	120-140
80-82 W/O ALC (Diesel)	$1^{7}/_{8}$-$2^{5}/_{8}$	46-66	$5^{1}/_{8}$-$5^{15}/_{16}$	130-150
80-82 W/O ALC (Gas)	$1^{13}/_{16}$-$2^{12}/_{32}$	45-65	$5^{7}/_{64}$-$5^{29}/_{32}$	129-140
Seville				
76 W/ALC Disconnected	$1^{3}/_{4}$-$2^{1}/_{2}$	44-63	$3^{1}/_{8}$-$3^{7}/_{8}$	79-98
76 W/ALC Connected	$1^{3}/_{4}$-$2^{1}/_{2}$	44-63	$3^{1}/_{2}$-$4^{1}/_{4}$	89-107
77-79 W/ALC Disconnected	$2^{1}/_{2}$	63	$3^{1}/_{2}$	89
77-79 W/ALC Connected	$2^{1}/_{2}$	63	$3^{7}/_{8}$	98
80-82 (Diesel)	$5^{1}/_{4}$-$6^{1}/_{32}$	133-153	5-$5^{25}/_{32}$	127-147
80-82 (Gas)	$5^{1}/_{4}$-$6^{1}/_{32}$	133-153	$5^{1}/_{16}$-$5^{13}/_{16}$	128-148
Fleetwood Limo				
78-79 W/ALC Disconnected	$1^{13}/_{16}$-$2^{5}/_{8}$	46-76	$5^{3}/_{8}$-$6^{1}/_{8}$	136-156
80-82 W/ALC	$2^{1}/_{8}$-$2^{29}/_{32}$	54-74	$5^{9}/_{32}$-$5^{1}/_{16}$	134-154
Fleetwood Formal				
78-79 W/ALC Disconnected	$1^{13}/_{16}$-$2^{5}/_{8}$	46-76	$5^{3}/_{8}$-$6^{1}/_{8}$	136-156
80-82 W/ALC	$1^{59}/_{64}$-$2^{23}/_{32}$	49-69	$5^{1}/_{8}$-$5^{15}/_{16}$	130-150
Commercial Chassis				
78-79 W/ALC Disconnected	$1^{13}/_{16}$-$2^{5}/_{8}$	46-76	$5^{3}/_{8}$-$6^{1}/_{8}$	136-156
80-82	$2^{21}/_{64}$-$3^{7}/_{64}$	59-79	$6^{3}/_{16}$-$6^{31}/_{32}$	157-177
Eldorado				
76	$8^{3}/_{16}$-$8^{7}/_{16}$	208-214	$4^{13}/_{16}$-$5^{9}/_{16}$	122-141
77-78	$8^{1}/_{4}$-$8^{1}/_{2}$	209-216	$4^{13}/_{16}$-$5^{9}/_{16}$	122-141
79	$5^{21}/_{32}$-$6^{13}/_{32}$	148-168	$5^{1}/_{2}$-$5^{7}/_{8}$	129-149
80-82 (Diesel)	$5^{1}/_{4}$-$6^{1}/_{32}$	133-153	$4^{31}/_{32}$-$5^{3}/_{4}$	126-146
80-82 (Gas)	$5^{1}/_{4}$-$5^{1}/_{32}$	133-153	5-$5^{25}/_{32}$	127-147

ALC = Automatic Load Control

B463

SUSPENSION
PRINCIPLES OF WHEEL ALIGNMENT

Cadillac Suspension Height Adjustment

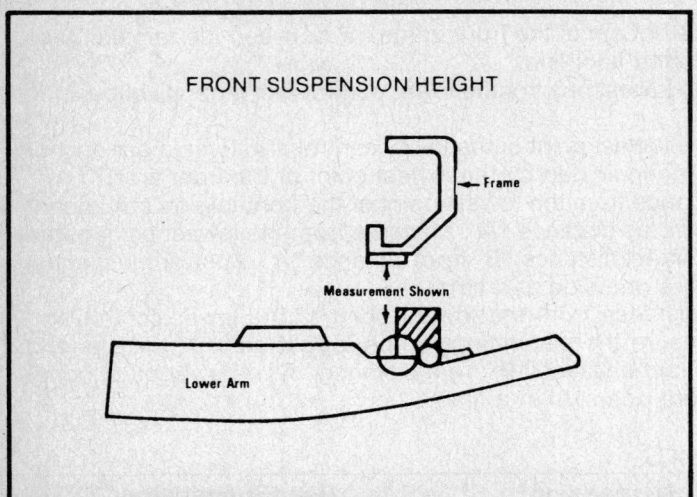

1976 models except Eldorado and Seville

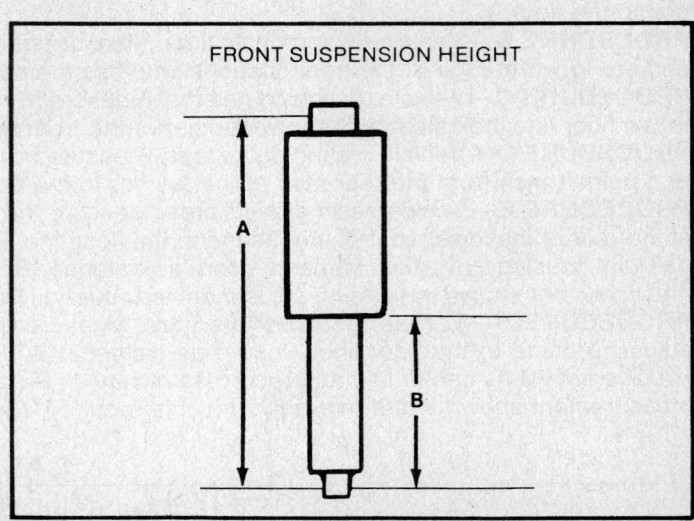

1976-82 Eldorado and 1980-82 Seville

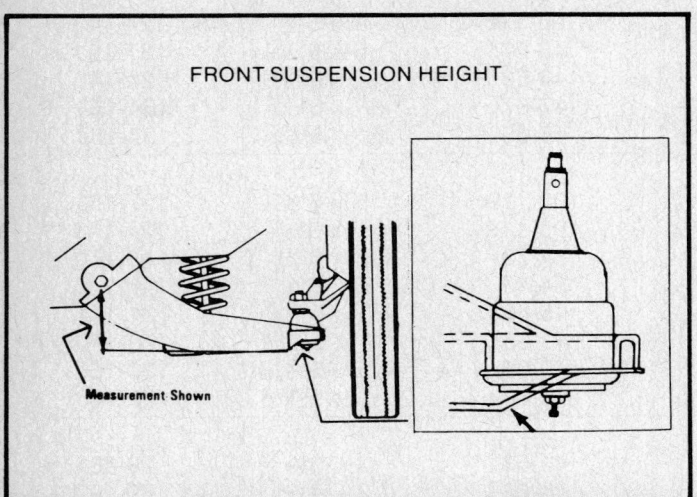

1977-82 models except Eldorado and 1980-82 Seville

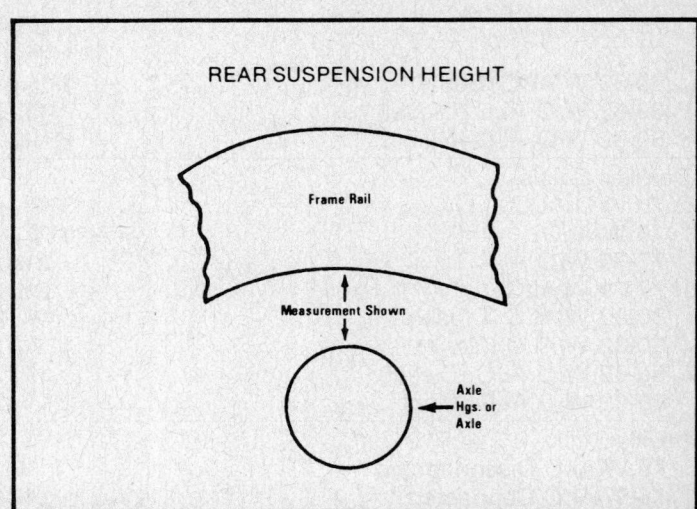

All models

PRINCIPLES OF WHEEL ALIGNMENT

Introduction

The term *wheel alignment* is well known, but it might be better understood as *motion balance*, because correct vehicle alignment involves balancing all of the forces created by friction, gravity, centrifugal force and momentum, while a vehicle is in motion.

A correct alignment job will make a vehicle run smoother, have better road-holding characteristics, have better steerability, and operate with more stability while running in a straight line and around curves. It also eliminates unnecessary road friction, which causes abnormal tire wear and decreases fuel mileage.

Wheel alignment is more than just the simple tracking of front and rear wheels to insure that they roll freely on a straight-ahead course. Front end alignment must also be maintained during turns and other steering maneuvers even though the road surface and other irregularities can cause the wheels to move up and down almost constantly. In addition to steering control, front end alignment also provides directional stability which helps the driver hold a straight course without making continuous steering corrections. Ideally, only very light pressure on the steering wheel should be enough to keep the vehicle headed on a straight course. However, a slight resistance (light turning load) is needed to help stabilize steering control. In effect, this resistance helps give the driver something to turn against, thus reducing the tendency to over-control.

In the past, caster, camber and toe were all adjustable. However, with the introduction of the MacPherson type of front suspension and its modified versions, caster adjustment can only be accomplished by bending the suspension. Camber is adjustable on some types, but not on others. This does not mean that these angles are not important. Proper setting of both caster and camber are absolutely essential to good stability, easy steering control and maximum tire life.

With the introduction of small front drive cars, the rear suspension now becomes a service item. Some rear axles have alignment adjustments, some do not. See each type axle in their respective sections.

SUSPENSION DIAGNOSIS

SYMPTOM	PROBABLE CAUSE
Excessive tire wear on outside shoulder	Excessive positive camber
Excessive tire wear on inside shoulder	Excessive negative camber
Excessive tire wear on both shoulders	Rounding curves at high speeds Underinflated tires
Saw-tooth tire wear	Too much toe-in or toe-out
One tire wears more than the other	Improper camber Defective brakes Defective shock absorber
Tire treads cupped or dished	Out-of-round tires Out-of-balance condition Defective shock absorber
Front wheels shimmy	Defective idler arm bushing Out-of-round tires Out-of-balance condition Excessive positive caster Uneven caster
Vehicle vibrates	Defective tires One or more of all 4 tires out-of-round One or more of all 4 tires out-of-balance Driveshaft bent Driveshaft sprayed with undercoating
Car tends to wander either to the right or left	Improper toe setting Looseness in steering system or ball joints Uneven caster Tire pull
Vehicle swerves or pulls to side when applying brakes	Uneven caster Brakes need adjustment Out-of-round brake drum Defective brakes Underinflated tire
Car tends to pull either to the right or left when taking hands off steering wheel	Improper camber Unequal caster Tires worn unevenly Tire pressure unequal
Car is hard to steer	Tires underinflated Power steering defective Too much positive caster Steering system too tight or binding
Steering has excessive play or looseness	Loose wheel bearings Loose ball joints Loose bushings Loose idler arm Loose steering gear assembly Worn steering gear or steering gear bearings

What Is Toe?

Toe-in is the amount, in fractions of an inch, that the wheels are closer together at the extreme front of the tire than they are at the rear. If the wheels are farther apart at the front, they toe-out.

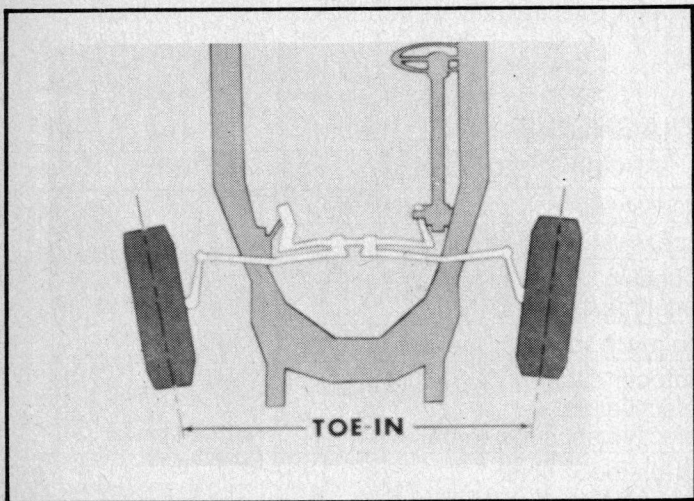

ZERO RUNNING TOE

When the vehicle is moving, zero toe provides parallel rolling of the two front wheels. This stabilizes steering and reduces sideslipping and tire wear to a minimum. To obtain a running toe of zero for average driving, it is usually necessary to provide a small amount of toe-in when the vehicle is at rest. This offsets small deflections due to rolling resistance and brake applications which tend to toe the wheels outward. When a vehicle is rolling forward a force is set up which compresses the tie-rod and the tie-rod ends. This lets the wheels spread outward at the front. Very little looseness in the steering linkage will allow wheels set at recommended toe-in actually to toe-out under running conditions.

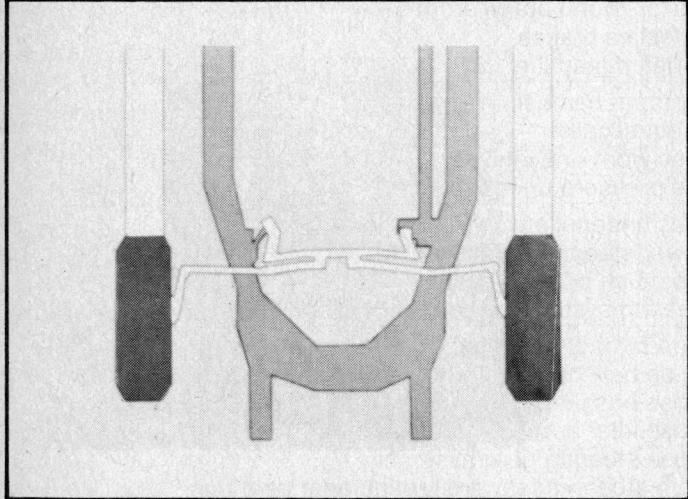

It has been common to talk about toe-in. However, many front drive cars require toe-out settings.

The foregoing explanation of the forces at work trying to change toe when the car is rolling helps explain why it is important to set toe to the preferred specification. It also explains the futility of trying to obtain zero running toe on a car having loose steering tie-rod ends.

CAUTION Tie-rod ball ends are designed to allow complete freedom of movement without binding. However, because each rod has two tie-rod ends, both of them must be centered exactly to avoid binding and interference when the wheels move up and down or are turned.

What Is Caster?

Caster is defined as the angle, when viewed from the side, between the steering axis and the vertical. It is simply a new name that describes what used to be known as the "kingpin axis." Caster is positive when the top of the axis is inclined rearward and negative when it is inclined forward.

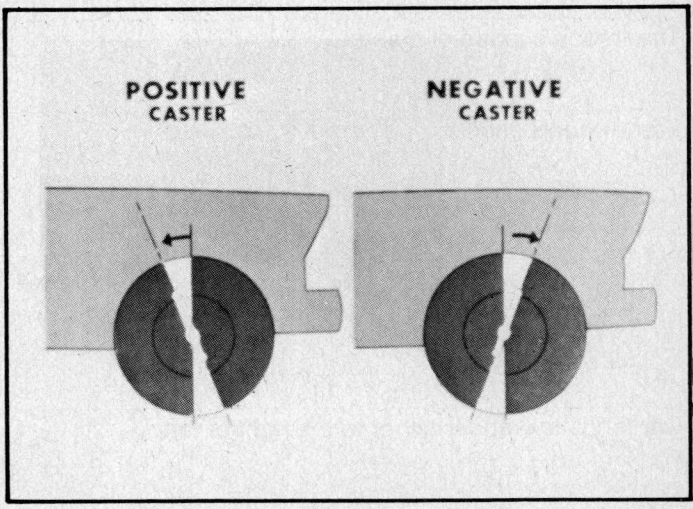

EFFECT OF CASTER ON STEERING

The mechanic's creeper illustrates the principle and effect of caster on steering geometry. When force is applied to the creeper, the casters turn on their pivots until the caster wheels are in line with the force applied and the wheels are then trailing behind the pivot point. The same principle applies to the front wheel of a car. If the steering axis pivot is tilted backward at the top the projected axis contacts the road ahead of the point of tire contact. This produces the same effect as the creeper's caster. The pivot axis pulls the wheel behind it, adding to the car's directional stability.

As the positive caster angle is increased, the effort required to turn and hold the car from a straight-ahead course is increased. The tendency of the front wheels to straighten out rapidly when leaving a turn is also increased.

NOTE   Although the caster angle tends to cause the car body and frame to lift when the wheels are turned, this is a very minor factor in the stability and returnability of present-day cars. There are two reasons for this: first, caster angles are so small that the lift is negligible; second, the higher rolling resistance of today's low-pressure tires produces far more directional stability from the caster effect than did smaller high-pressure tires used in the past.

On a power steering car too much positive caster indirectly can cause low-speed shimmy, increased road shock and high-speed wander. Unequal caster—either positive or negative—between the wheels is also undesirable. If all other factors are equal, a car will lead or drift toward the side with the least amount of caster. Unequal caster can also produce some braking problems. A considerable difference between the caster angles of the left and right wheels will cause the car to pull sharply toward the side with least caster. The worst possible situation exists when there is negative caster at one wheel and positive caster on the other. Under these conditions the wheel with negative caster tries to turn outward and the car pulls toward the side with negative caster when brakes are applied.

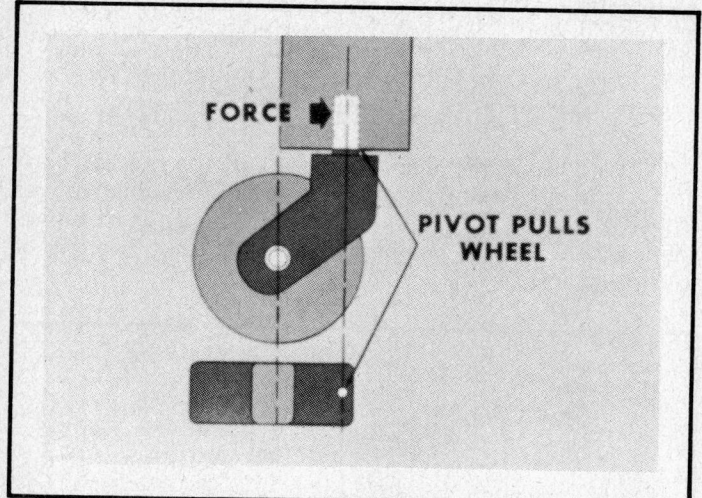

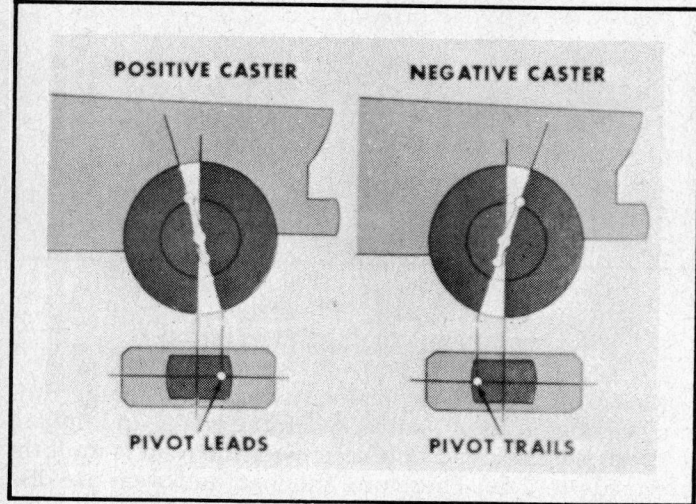

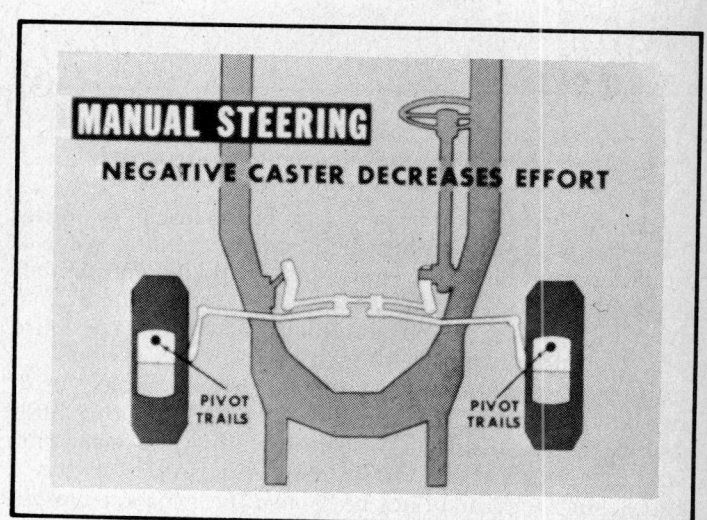

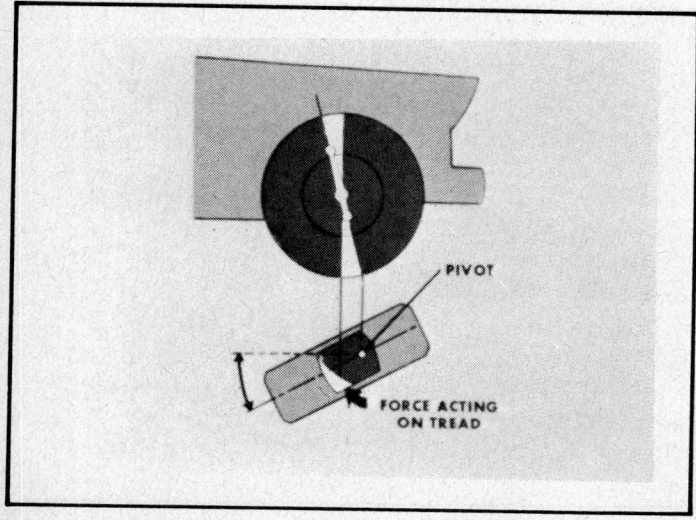

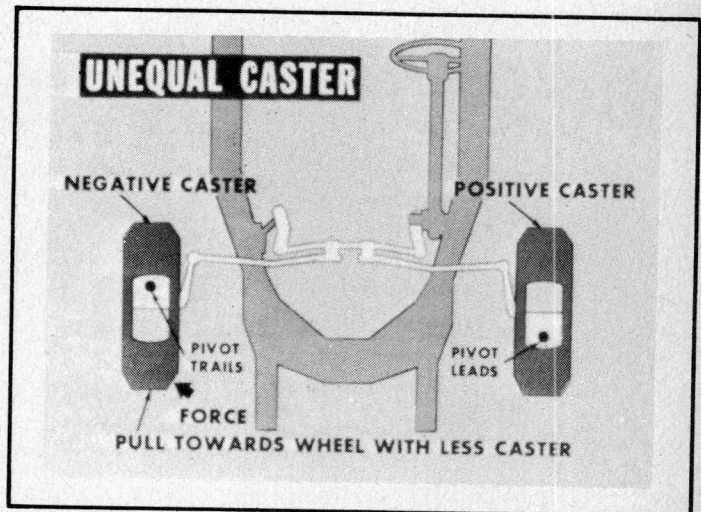

What Is Camber?

Camber is the amount, in degrees, that the wheel is inclined from the vertical as viewed from the front of the car. If the top of the wheel leans away from the car, the camber is positive. If the top of the wheel leans toward the car, the camber is negative.

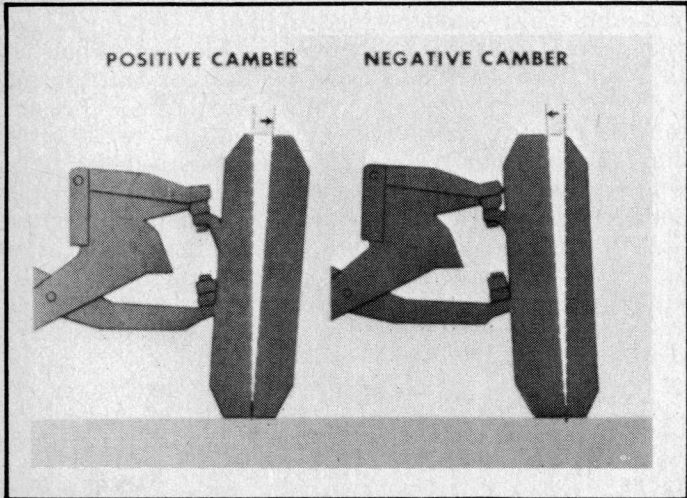

EFFECTS OF INCORRECT CAMBER

Too much positive camber causes tire wear at the outer shoulder; too much negative camber causes tire wear at the inner shoulder. However, you should also remember that rounding turns at high speeds also causes the tires to show more wear at the shoulders. Therefore such tire wear may not always be caused by incorrect camber.

Similarly, continuous high-speed driving on curves to the right and left will produce wear at the inner and outer shoulders of both tires. This often results in a wear pattern that looks very much like underinflation wear. Again, such wear may not be caused by incorrect camber and will not be corrected by adjusting the camber.

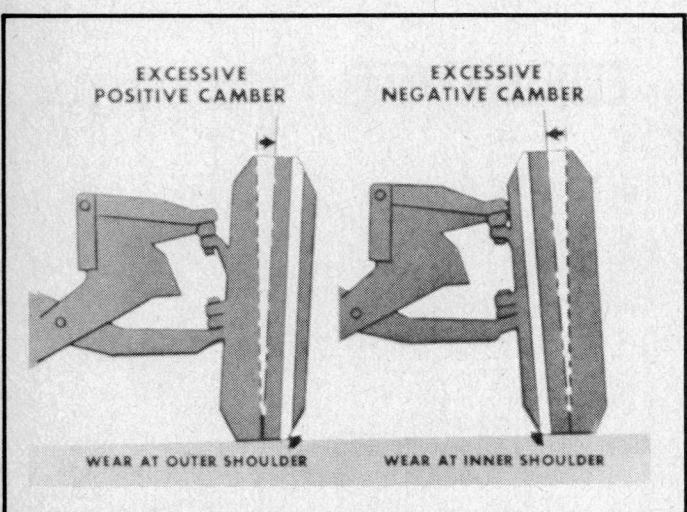

Under all driving conditions, the best average running camber is obtained when camber is adjusted to specifications. Deviation from specifications can cause hard steering, unstable steering and wander. Unequal camber can contribute to a low-speed shimmy condition.

CAMBER ANGLES CHANGE WITH VERTICAL WHEEL MOVEMENT

When a front wheel moves upward (or the car body and frame moves downward), the top of the wheel moves inward, producing negative camber. The upward movement of the wheel is usually called jounce motion or jounce travel.

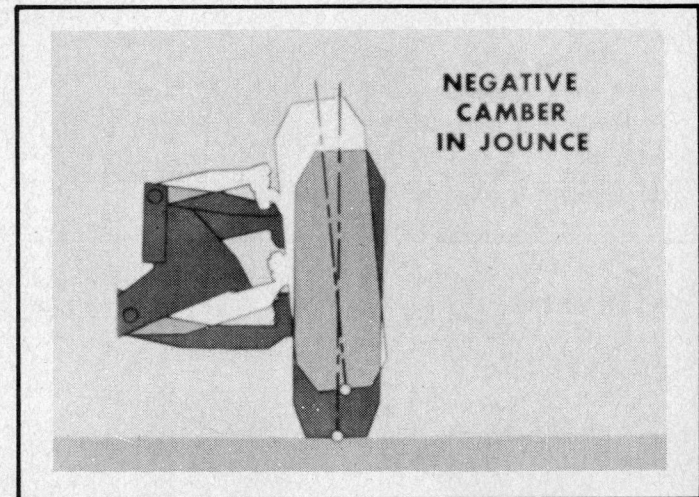

ZERO RUNNING CAMBER

Maximum tire life is obtained when the average running camber is zero. That is, when the wheel and tire are vertical, the tire tread in contact with the road is uniform from side-to-side. Therefore, the load and wear are distributed equally over the entire tread.

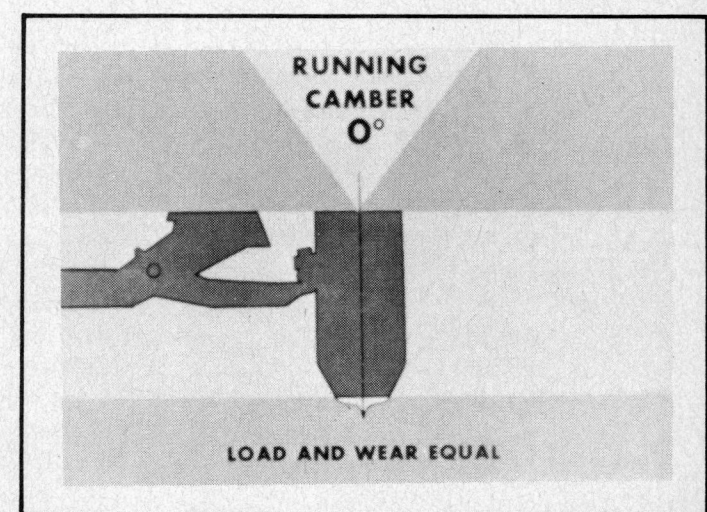

CAMBER ON TURNS

When a car goes into a turn at high speeds, centrifugal force causes a significant weight shift toward the outside wheel. The body and frame moves downward, producing negative camber at the outside wheel. At the same time, weight is reduced at the inside wheel and the body and frame tries to lift. This movement produces little camber change or a small amount of positive camber at the inside wheel.

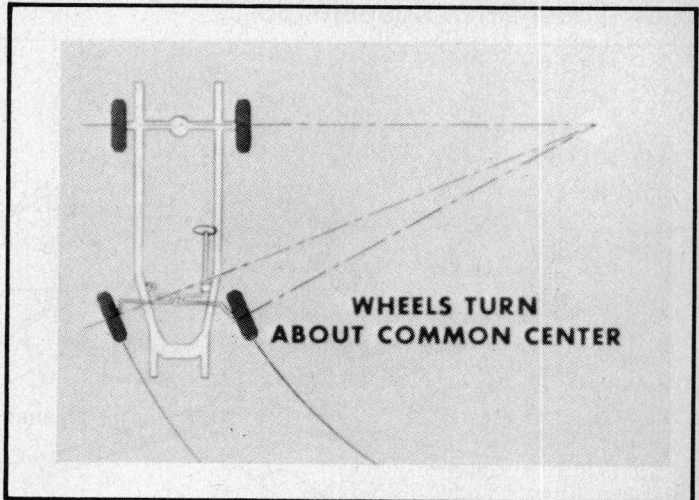

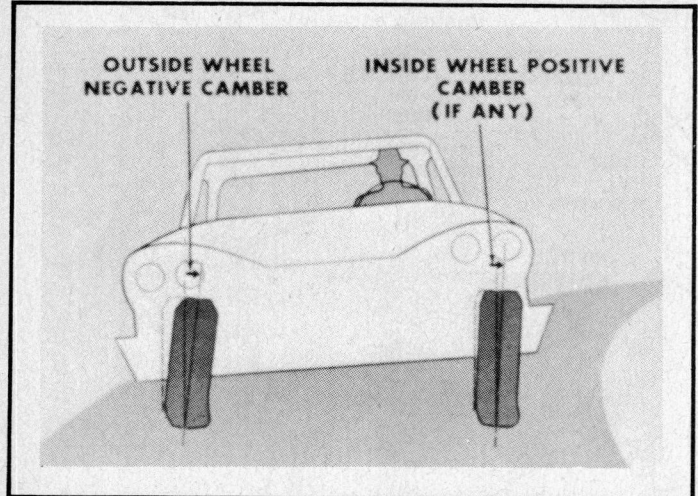

The negative camber at the outside wheel has the very desirable effect of bracing the tire tread against sideslip. The combination of negative camber and increased tractive force (more weight on outside wheel) minimizes tire slip and increases cornering stability. Similarly, zero camber or a small amount of positive camber at the inside wheel helps minimize tire slip at this point.

Toe-out On Turns

Toe-out on turns is an important non-adjustable measurement that should be checked after all other steering geometry angles are measured and adjusted to their straight-ahead specifications. When the wheels are turned, a fifth angle becomes important. This is commonly referred to as toe-out on turns.

In theory, all four car wheels should turn about the same center to minimize sideslipping of the tires. Since both rear wheels are connected by a solid axle, the front wheels should turn in circles whose centerlines intersect the centerline of the rear axle. Actually, all four tires slip

because of centrifugal force when rounding a corner at any speed greater than a brisk walk. As a result, the real turning center is considerably ahead of the true centerline of the rear axle.

When the wheels are turned to the left, both steering arm tie-rods move the same distance. However, the left arm is moving through that part of its travel where a small amount of movement results in turning the wheel a great deal. The right steering arm end is moving through a part of its travel that produces less turning of the wheel for the same amount of tie-rod movement. The fact that the inside wheel is forced to turn more than the outside wheel produces the necessary toe-out on turns.

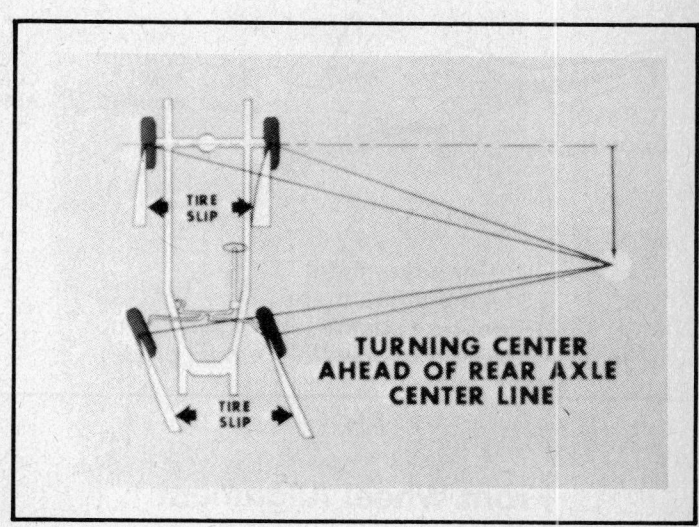

FRONT SUSPENSION—AMC EXCEPT PACER

Except for two types of steering knuckles, service procedures for both two wheel drive and four wheel drive vehicles are very similar. On two wheel drive cars, ball joints can be replaced in a conventional manner. On four wheel drive models, the complete control arm must be replaced.

SUSPENSION

Four Wheel Drive Suspension

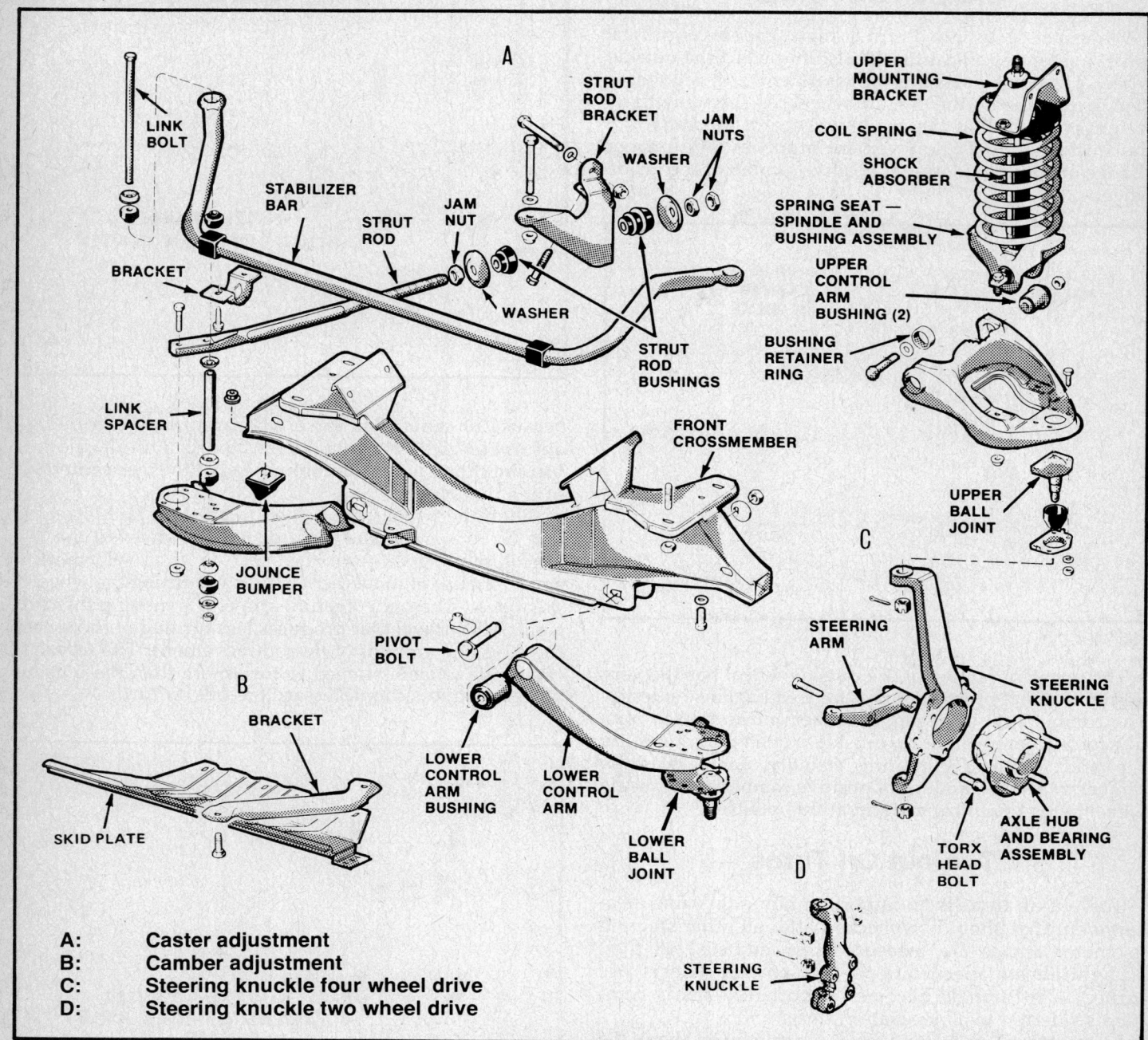

A: Caster adjustment
B: Camber adjustment
C: Steering knuckle four wheel drive
D: Steering knuckle two wheel drive

Front Wheel Alignment

Front wheel alignment, or steering geometry, refers to the various angles assumed by the components which form the front wheel turning mechanism. There are three adjustable alignment angles which are caster, camber, and toe-in.

Caster describes the forward or rearward tilt (from vertical) of the steering knuckle. Tilting the top of the knuckle rearward provides positive caster. Tilting the top of the knuckle forward provides negative caster. Caster is a directional stability angle which enables the front wheels to return to a straight-ahead position after turns.

Adjust caster by loosening the strut rod jamnut and turning the rod adjusting nuts in or out to move the lower control arm forward or rearward to obtain the desired caster angle. Tighten adjusting nuts to 65 foot-pounds (88 N•m) torque and jamnut to 75 foot-pounds (102 N•m) torque when adjustment is completed.

Camber describes the inward or outward tilt of the wheel relative to the center of the automobile. An inward tilt of the top of the wheel produces negative camber. An

Two Wheel Drive Suspension

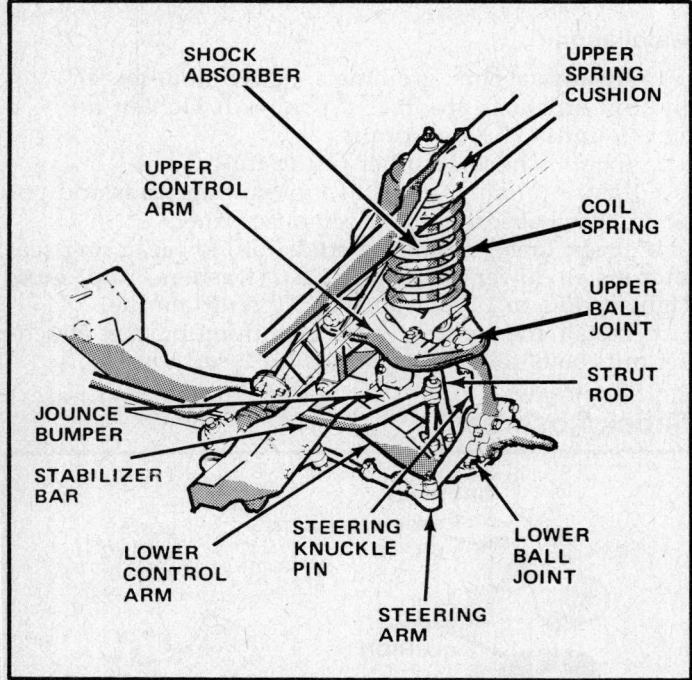

outward tilt produces positive camber. Camber greatly affects tire wear. Incorrect camber will cause abnormal wear on the tire outside or inside edge.

Adjust camber by turning lower control arm inner pivot bolt eccentric. Tighten pivot bolt locknuts to 110 foot-pounds (149 N•m) torque after completing camber adjustment.

Toe-in is a condition that exists when the measured distance at the front of each tire is less than the distance at the rear of the tires. When the distance at the front is less than the rear, the tires are toed-in. Toe-in compensates for normal steering play and causes the tires to roll in a straight-ahead manner. Incorrect toe-in will wear the tires to a feathered edge.

Adjust toe-in by turning tie rod adjuster tubes in or out to shorten or lengthen tie rods to obtain desired toe-in. Place front wheels in straight-ahead position and center steering wheel and gear. Turn tie rod adjusting tubes equally in opposite directions to obtain desired toe-in setting. If steering wheel spoke position was disturbed during toe-in adjustment, correct spoke position by turning toe rod tubes equally in same direction until desired position is obtained.

Front Wheel Bearings

TWO WHEEL DRIVE

When repacking and adjusting front wheel bearings, use an EP-type, lithium base wheel bearing lubricant. Pack the bearings with a generous amount of lubricant and place extra lubricant in the rotor hub cavity between the bearings. Always use a new grease seal during assembly.

When inspecting, replacing, or repacking bearings, be sure the inner cones of the bearings are free to creep on the spindle. The bearings are designed to creep to allow a constantly changing load contact between the cones and the rollers. Polishing and applying lubricant to the spindle will permit this movement and prevent rust formation.

Adjustment

1. Raise and support front of automobile.
2. Remove hub cap, grease cap and O-ring, cotter pin and nutlock.
3. On automobiles with styled wheels, remove wheel and hub cap. Install wheel.

Front Wheel Bearing—Two Wheel Drive

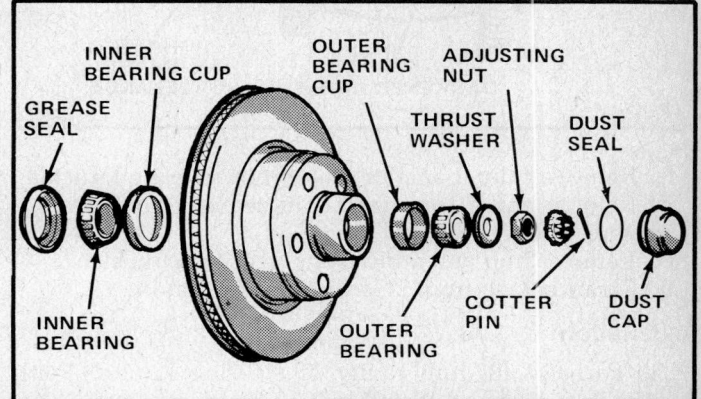

4. Tighten spindle nut to 25 foot-pounds (34 N•m) torque while rotating wheel to seat bearings.
5. Loosen spindle nut ⅓-turn. While rotating wheel, tighten spindle nut to 6 inch-pounds (0.7 N•m) torque.
6. Install nutlock on spindle nut so cotter pin holes in nutlock and spindle are aligned.
7. Install replacement cotter pin, grease cap and hub cap.
8. On automobiles with styled wheels, remove wheel, install hub cap and install wheel.

FOUR WHEEL DRIVE

Adjustment

Four wheel drive models have a unique front axle hub and bearing assembly. The assembly is sealed and does not require lubrication, periodic maintenance, or adjustment. The hub has ball bearings which seat in races machined directly into the hub. There are darkened areas surrounding the bearing race areas of the hub. These darkened areas are from a heat treatment process, are normal, and should not be mistaken for a problem condition.

Removal

1. Remove wheel, caliper and rotor.
2. Remove bolts attaching axle shaft flange to halfshaft.
3. Remove cotter pin, nut lock and axle hub nut.
4. Remove halfshaft.
5. Remove steering arm from steering knuckle.

Axle Hub Assembly—Eagle

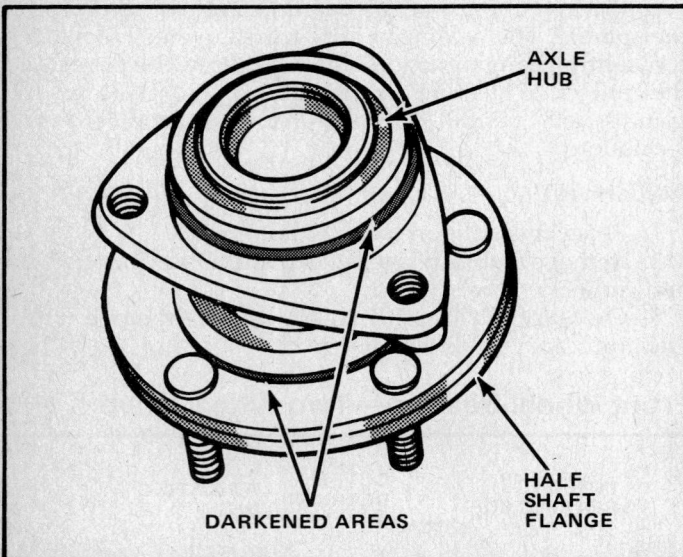

6. Remove caliper anchor plate from steering knuckle.
7. Remove three Torx head bolts retaining hub assembly using tool set J-25359.
8. Remove hub assembly from steering knuckle.
9. Clean grease from steering knuckle cavity.

Installation

1. Partially fill hub cavity of steering knuckle with chassis lubricant and install hub assembly.
2. Tighten hub Torx head bolts to 75 foot-pounds (102 N•m) torque.
3. Install caliper anchor plate and plate retaining bolts.
4. Tighten caliper anchor plate retaining bolts to 100 foot-pounds (136 N•m) torque.
5. Install steering arm bolts.
6. Tighten steering arm bolts to 100 foot-pounds (136 N•m) torque.
7. Install halfshaft. Install axle flange-to-shaft bolts and install hub nut.
8. Tighten halfshaft-to-flange bolts to 45 foot-pounds (61 N•m) torque.
9. Tighten hub nut to 175 foot-pounds (237 N•m) torque.
10. Install nut lock and cotter pin.
11. Install rotor, caliper and wheel.

Shock Absorber
ALL MODELS

Removal

1. Remove lower retaining nuts, washers and grommets.
2. Remove upper mounting bracket bolts/nuts from wheelhouse panel.
3. Remove upper bracket and shock absorber from wheelhouse panel.

4. Remove upper retaining nut from shock absorber and remove upper bracket from shock absorber.

Installation

1. Install washers, grommets, upper mounting bracket and nut on shock absorber if removed. Tighten nut to 8 foot-pounds (11 N•m) torque.
2. Extend shock absorber piston fully.
3. Install grommets on lower mounting studs and position shock absorber in wheelhouse panel.
4. Insert lower mounting studs into lower spring seat and install lower grommets, flat washers, and nuts. Tighten nuts to 15 foot-pounds (20 N•m) torque.
5. Install and tighten upper mounting bracket attaching nuts/bolts to 20 foot-pounds (27 N•m) torque.

Shock Absorber

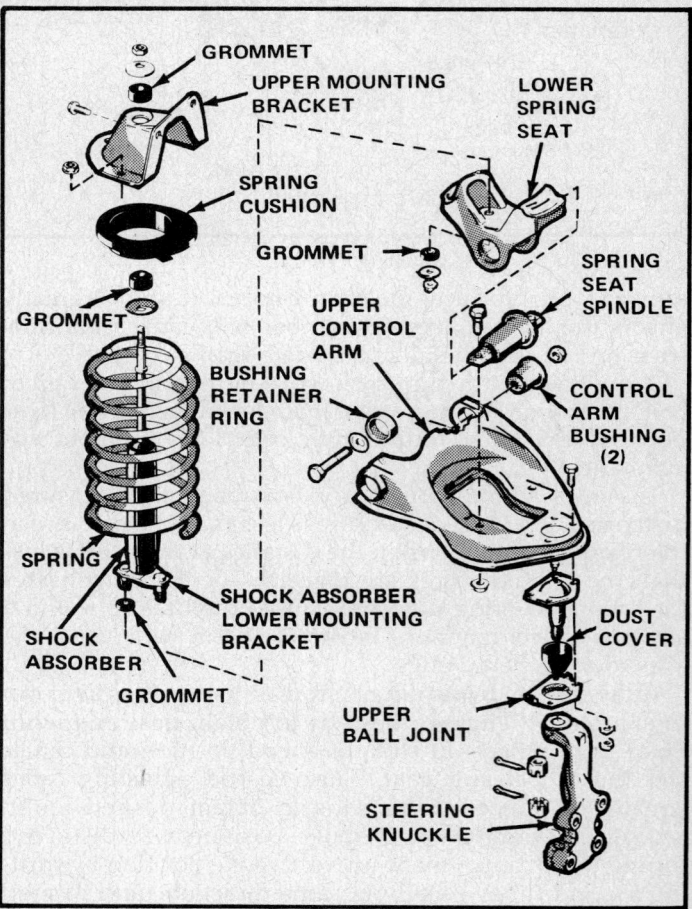

Upper Ball Joint
TWO WHEEL DRIVE

Inspection

1. Remove upper ball joint lubrication plug and install a dial indicator gauge through the lubrication hole so that you can measure the up and down movement of the ball joint socket.

Upper Ball Joint—Typical

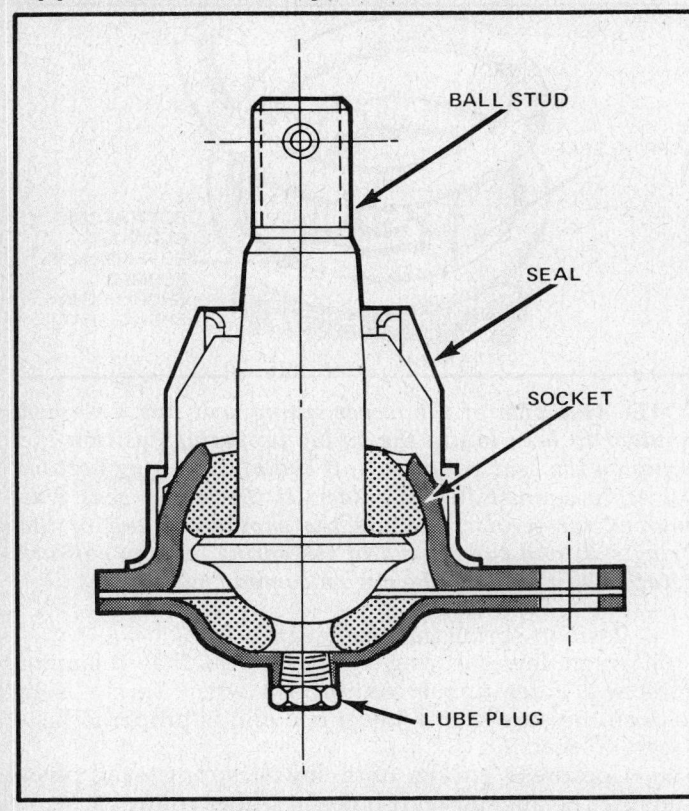

2. Place a pry bar under tire to load ball joint and raise tire several times to seat gauge tool pin.

3. Pry tire upward to load ball joint and record gauge reading; then release tire to unload ball joint and record gauge reading. Perform this operation several times to ensure accuracy.

4. The difference between load/no-load readings represents ball joint clearance. If clearance is more than 0.080-inch (2.03 mm), ball joint should be replaced.

Replacement

1. Install 2x4x5-inch (5.1x10.1x12.7 cm) wood block on frame side sill and under upper control arm.

Installing Wood Block

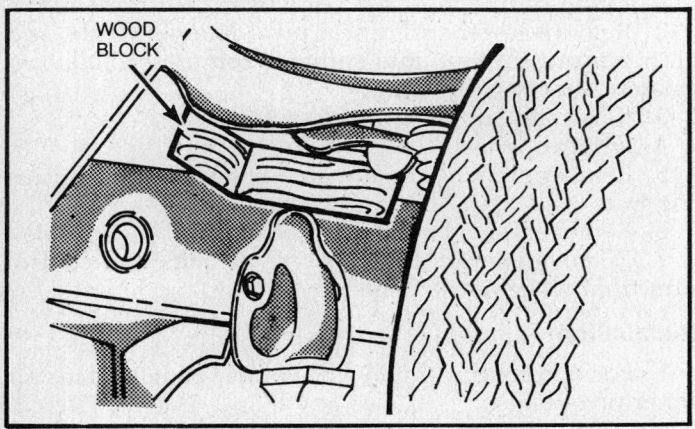

2. Raise and support front of car.

3. Remove wheel, caliper, and rotor.

4. Remove ball stud cotter pin and retaining nut.

5. Install ball joint remover and loosen ball stud in steering knuckle. Do not remove tool at this time.

6. Place support stand under lower control arm.

7. Remove heads from ball joint attaching rivets using chisel or grinding tool.

8. Drive rivets out of ball joint and control arm using hammer and punch.

9. Disengage ball joint from control arm.

10. Remove tool from ball joint stud and remove ball joint from steering knuckle.

11. Position replacement ball joint in control arm and align bolt holes.

12. Install ball joint attaching bolts (supplied in ball joint replacement kits) and tighten nuts to 25 foot-pounds (34 N•m) torque.

13. Install steering knuckle and retaining nut on ball joint stud. Tighten nut to 75 foot-pounds (102 N•m) torque and install a new cotter pin.

14. Install rotor, caliper and wheel.

FOUR WHEEL DRIVE

Inspection

Inspection procedures are the same as for two wheel drive models.

Replacement

If a ball joint is worn (upper or lower) the complete arm assembly must be replaced. Do not attempt to service the ball joint separately.

Lower Ball Joint
TWO WHEEL DRIVE

Inspection

1. Raise and support front of automobile.

2. Move lower portion of wheel and tire alternately toward and away from center of automobile. Perform this operation several times.

3. Lower ball joint is spring-equipped and preloaded in its socket at all times to minimize looseness and compensate for wear. If lower joint exhibits any lateral movement (shake), ball joint should be replaced.

Replacement

1. Install 2x4x5-inch (5.1x10.1x12.7 cm) wood block on frame side sill and under upper control arm.

2. Raise and support front of automobile.

3. Remove wheel, caliper, and rotor.

4. Disconnect strut rod at lower control arm.

5. Disconnect steering arm from steering knuckle.

6. Remove ball stud cotter pin and retaining nut.

7. Install ball joint removal tool and loosen ball stud in steering knuckle. Do not remove tool at this time.

8. Place support stand under lower control arm.

9. Remove heads from ball joint attaching rivets using chisel or grinding tool.

10. Drive rivets out of ball joint and control arm using punch.

11. Disengage ball joint from control arm.

12. Remove ball joint from steering knuckle.

13. Position replacement ball joint on control arm and align bolt holes.

14. Install but do not tighten attaching bolts supplied in replacement ball joint kit.

15. Attach strut rod to lower control arm. Tighten rod attaching bolts to 75 foot-pounds (102 N•m) torque.

16. Tighten ball joint attaching bolts to 25 foot-pounds (34 N•m) torque.

17. Apply chassis grease to steering stops.

18. Install ball joint stud in steering knuckle.

19. Install retaining nut on ball stud. Tighten nut to 75 foot-pounds (102 N•m) torque and install replacement cotter pin.

20. Install steering arm on steering knuckle.

21. Install rotor, caliper, and wheel.

FOUR WHEEL DRIVE

Inspection and Replacement

See the upper ball joint inspection and replacement procedures for four wheel drive models.

Coil Spring

ALL MODELS

Identification

A plastic identification tag which has the spring part number printed on it is attached to each coil spring. Whenever a spring must be replaced, refer to this part number when ordering a replacement spring.

Removal

1. Remove shock absorbers and mounting brackets.

2. Install spring compressor and compress spring approximately 1 inch (25.4 mm).

3. Remove lower spring seat pivot bolt retaining nuts.

4. Raise front of automobile until control arms are free of lower spring seat.

5. Remove wheel.

6. Pull lower spring seat away from automobile, and guide lower spring seat out and over upper control arm.

7. Remove spring compressor tool and remove lower retainer, spring seat, and spring.

CAUTION Do not use impact wrench to turn the compression nut. An impact wrench will place unnecessary stress on the compressor tool bolt threads which could result in thread damage or bolt breakage.

Installation

1. Install spring compressor tool.

2. Install spring upper cushion on top coil of spring. Tape cushion in place to retain it.

3. Install spring in lower spring seat.

Lower Spring Seat Position

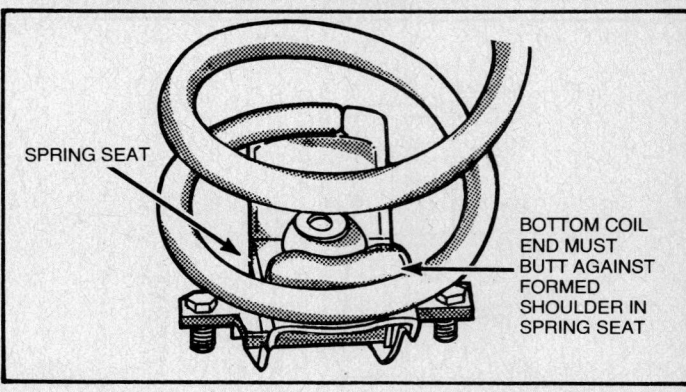

SPRING SEAT

BOTTOM COIL END MUST BUTT AGAINST FORMED SHOULDER IN SPRING SEAT

NOTE One side of the lower spring seat has a formed shoulder to help locate the spring properly. Position the spring on the seat so the cut-off end of the spring bottom coil seats against this shoulder. If the spring seat was removed for service, be sure the shouldered end of the spring seat and cut-off end of the spring bottom coil are installed so they face the engine compartment.

4. Position spring in upper seat.

5. Align lower spring seat pivot so that retaining studs will enter upper control arm when spring is in position. Be sure spring lower coil end is properly positioned on seat.

6. Compress spring until lower spring seat pivot studs can be aligned with holes in upper control arm.

7. Turn compression nut counterclockwise and guide spring seat pivot studs into control arm.

8. Install wheel.

9. Remove supports and lower automobile.

10. Install and tighten lower spring seat pivot retaining nuts to 35 foot-pounds (47 N•m) torque.

11. Remove spring compressor tool.

12. Install shock absorber and mounting bracket.

Upper Control Arm

ALL MODELS

Removal

1. Remove shock absorber and mounting bracket. Install spring compressor tool.

2. Remove lower spring seat pivot retaining nuts, and turn compressor tool until spring is compressed approximately 2 inches (5.03 cm).

3. Raise and support front of automobile.

4. Remove wheel.

5. Remove upper ball joint stud cotter pin and retaining nut.

6. Remove upper ball joint stud from steering knuckle.

7. Remove control arm inner pivot bolts and control arm from wheelhouse panel.

Installation

1. Position control arm in wheelhouse panel and install inner pivot bolts.

CAUTION Do not tighten the pivot bolts until the automobile is resting on the wheels as ride height may be affected.

2. Install steering knuckle and retaining nut on ball joint stud. Tighten nut to 75 foot-pounds (102 N•m) torque and install a new cotter pin.

3. Turn spring compressor tool compression nut and guide spring seat pivot studs into control arm.

Lower Control Arm
TWO WHEEL DRIVE

Removal

1. Raise and support front of automobile.
2. Remove wheel, caliper, and rotor.
3. Disconnect steering arm from steering knuckle.
4. Remove lower ball joint stud cotter pin and retaining nut.
5. Remove ball stud from steering knuckle.
6. Disconnect stabilizer bar from control arm, if equipped.
7. Disconnect strut rod from control arm.
8. Remove inner pivot bolt and remove control arm from crossmember.

Installation

1. Position control arm in crossmember and install inner pivot bolt.

Lower Control Arm Components— Spirit–AMX–Concord

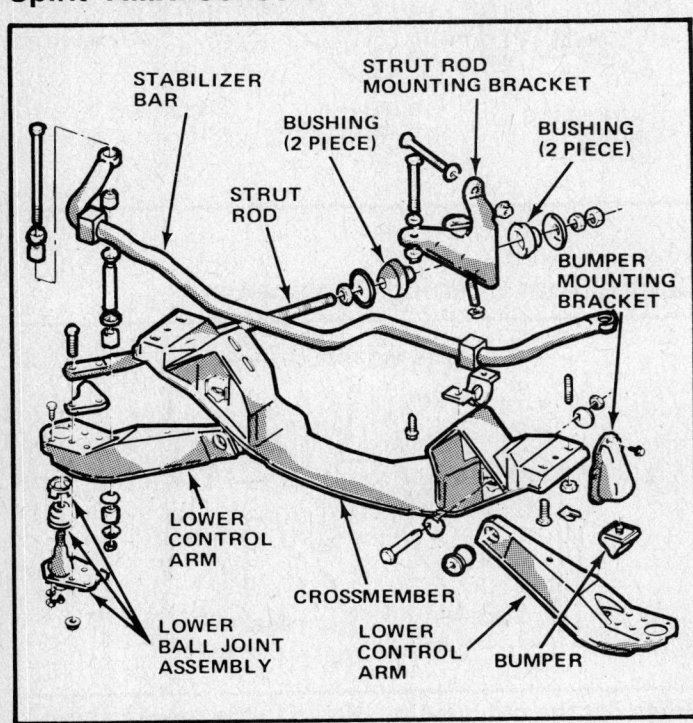

CAUTION *Do not tighten the inner pivot bolt until the automobile weight is supported by the wheels as ride height may be affected.*

2. Install steering knuckle and retaining nut on ball joint stud. Tighten nut to 75 foot-pounds (102 N•m) torque and install replacement cotter pin.

3. Connect strut rod to control arm. Tighten bolts to 75 foot-pounds (102 N•m) torque.

4. Connect stabilizer bar to control arm, if equipped. Tighten bolts to 7 foot-pounds (9 N•m) torque.

5. Connect steering arm to steering knuckle.

6. Install rotor, caliper and wheel.

7. Place a jack under control arm. Raise jack to compress spring slightly and tighten control arm inner pivot bolt to 110 foot-pounds (149 N•m) torque.

FOUR WHEEL DRIVE

Removal

1. Remove cotter pin, nut lock and hub nut.
2. Raise and support front of automobile.
3. Remove wheel, caliper and rotor.
4. Remove lower ball joint cotter pin and retaining nut.
5. Remove ball stud from steering knuckle.
6. Remove halfshaft flange bolts.
7. Remove halfshaft.
8. Remove bolts attaching strut rod to control arm.
9. Disconnect stabilizer bar from control arm.
10. Remove inner pivot bolt and remove control arm.

Installation

1. Position control arm in crossmember and install inner pivot bolt.

CAUTION *Do not tighten the inner pivot bolt until the automobile weight is supported by the wheels as ride height may be affected.*

2. Insert ball stud in steering knuckle and install retaining nut on ball joint stud. Tighten nut to 75 foot-pounds (102 N•m) torque and install replacement cotter pin.

3. Connect stabilizer bar to control arm. Tighten lock nut to 7 foot-pounds (9 N•m) torque.

4. Connect strut rod to control arm. Tighten bolts to 75 foot-pounds (102 N•m) torque.

5. Install halfshaft-to-axle flange bolts.

6. Tighten flange bolts to 45 foot-pounds (61 N•m) torque.

NOTE If control arm is worn or bushing is not tight when installed, control arm must be replaced.

Steering Knuckle and Spindle
TWO WHEEL DRIVE

Removal

1. Raise and support front of automobile.

2. Remove wheel, caliper, and rotor.

3. Remove caliper anchor plate, adapter, steering spindle, and steering arm from knuckle.

4. Remove upper and lower ball joint stud cotter pins and retaining nuts.

5. Remove ball joint studs from steering knuckle.

Installation

1. Install steering knuckle and retaining nuts on ball joint studs. Tighten nuts to 75 foot-pounds (102 N•m) torque and install new cotter pins.

2. Install steering arm, spindle, caliper anchor plate, and adapter. Tighten bolts to 55 foot-pounds (75 N•m) torque.

3. Install rotor, caliper, and wheel.

FOUR WHEEL DRIVE

Removal

1. Remove cotter pin, nut lock and hub nut.
2. Remove wheel, caliper and rotor.
3. Remove halfshaft-to-axle flange bolts.
4. Remove halfshaft.
5. Remove steering arm from steering knuckle.
6. Remove caliper anchor plate from steering knuckle.
7. Remove three Torx head attaching bolts retaining front wheel hub assembly.
8. Remove hub assembly from knuckle.
9. Remove rear hub seal from steering knuckle using small pry bar.
10. Remove upper and lower ball joint stud cotter pins and retaining nuts.
11. Remove ball joint studs from steering knuckle using a strike tool to loosen and remove studs from knuckle.

Installation

1. Install steering knuckle and ball joint retaining nuts on ball joint studs. Tighten nuts to 75 foot-pounds (102 N•m) torque and install new cotter pins.
2. Install hub rear seal.
3. Partially fill hub cavity of steering knuckle with chassis lubricant and install hub assembly in knuckle.
4. Tighten hub Torx head bolts to 75 foot-pounds (102 N•m) torque.
5. Install caliper anchor plate and retaining bolts.
6. Tighten caliper anchor plate bolts to 100 foot-pounds (136 N•m) torque.
7. Install steering arm and bolts.
8. Tighten steering arm bolts to 100 foot-pounds (136 N•m) torque.
9. Install halfshaft and shaft-to-axle flange bolts.
10. Tighten halfshaft-to-axle flange bolts to 45 foot-pounds (61 N•m) torque.
11. Install rotor, caliper and hub nut.
12. Install wheel.
13. Lower automobile.
14. Tighten hub nut to 180 foot-pounds (244 N•m) torque. Install nut lock and a new cotter pin.

Strut Rod and Bushing

ALL MODELS

Replacement

1. Raise and support front of automobile.
2. Remove jamnut and caster adjustment nut from strut rod.
3. Disconnect strut rod from lower control arm and remove rod, bushings, and washers.
4. On automobiles with one-piece bushing, lubricate the bushing with soapy water and install.

NOTE   A special tool is required to press the one-piece bushing in and out of the mounting bracket.

Strut Rod Bushings

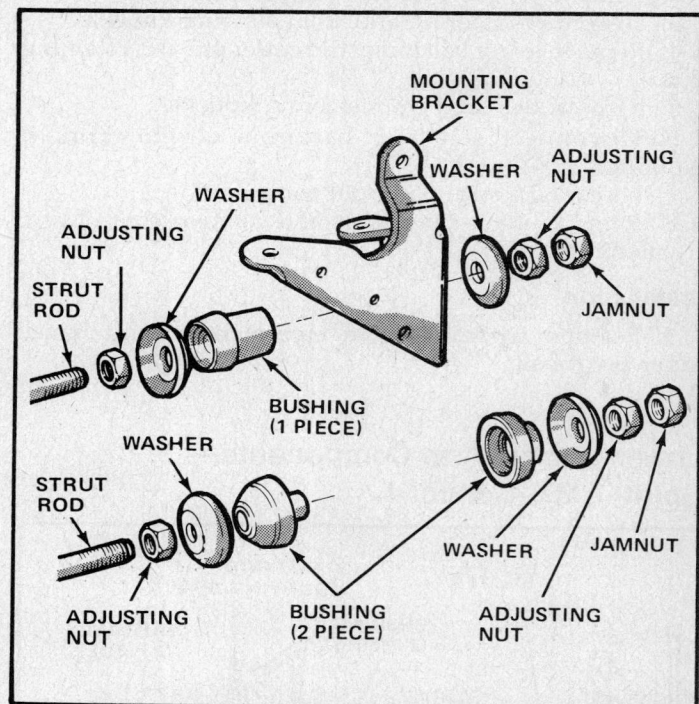

Control Arm Bushing Replacement

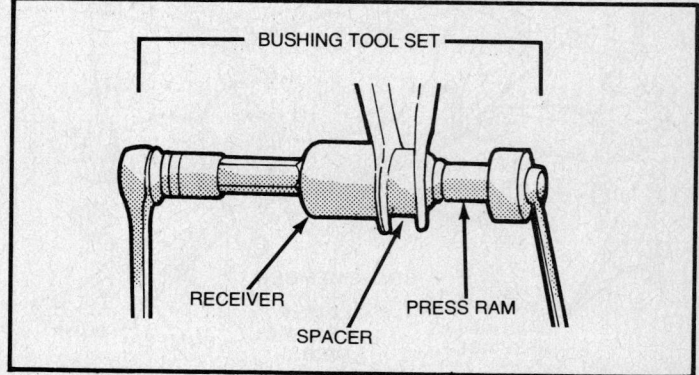

Press out the old bushing. Press in the new bushing.

FRONT SUSPENSION—AMC PACER

Front Wheel Alignment

Front wheel alignment, or steering geometry, refers to the various angles assumed by the components which form the front wheel turning mechanism. There are three adjustable alignment angles which are caster, camber, and toe-in.

Caster describes the forward or rearward tilt (from vertical) of the steering knuckle. Tilting the top of the knuckle rearward provides positive caster. Tilting the top of the knuckle forward provides negative caster. Caster is a directional stability angle which enables the front wheels to return to a straight-ahead position after turns.

Caster is adjusted by turning only the rear pivot bolt eccentric. After adjustment, tighten the pivot bolt locknut to 95 foot-pounds torque.

Camber describes the inward or outward tilt of the wheel relative to the center of the automobile. An inward

Front Suspension—Pacer

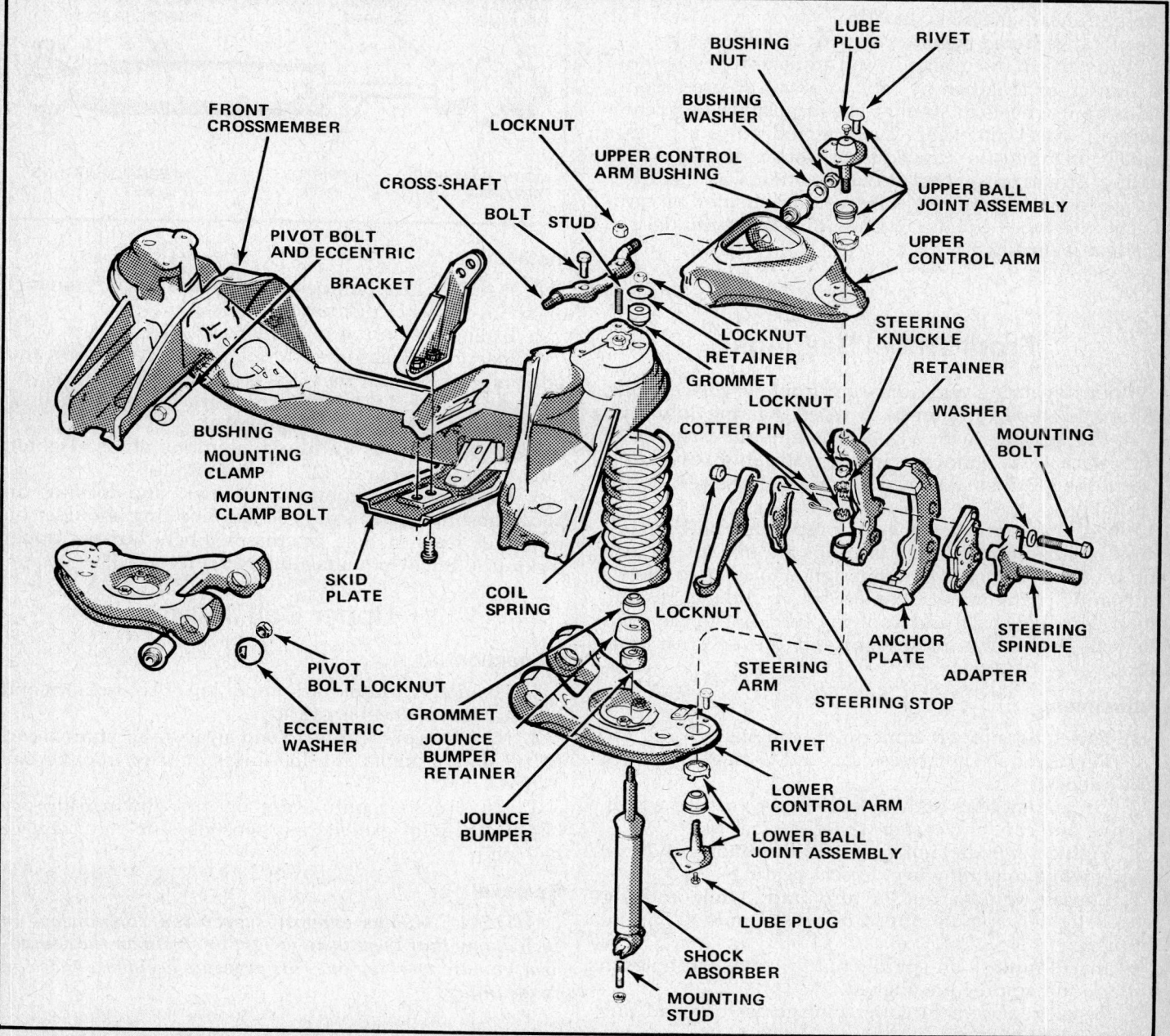

Caster/camber adjustments (A): Adjust camber first by moving both eccentric washers. Then adjust caster by moving rear eccentric only.

tilt of the top of the wheel produces negative camber. An outward tilt produces positive camber. Camber greatly affects tire wear. Incorrect camber will cause abnormal wear on the tire outside or inside edge.

Camber is adjusted by turning both the front or both front and rear lower control arm pivot bolt eccentrics as necessary to obtain the desired camber angle. After adjustment, tighten the pivot bolt locknuts to 95 foot-pounds torque.

Toe-in is a condition that exists when the measured distance at the front of each tire is less than the distance at the rear of the tires. When the distance at front is less than the rear, the tires are toed-in. Toe-in compensates for normal steering play and causes the tires to roll in a straight-ahead manner. Incorrect toe-in will wear the tires to a feathered edge.

Adjust toe-in by turning tie rod adjuster tubes in or out to shorten or lengthen tie rods to obtain desired toe-in. Place front wheels in straight-ahead position and center steering wheel and gear. Turn tie rod adjusting tubes equally in opposite directions to obtain desired toe-in setting. If steering wheel spoke position was disturbed during toe-in adjustment, correct spoke position by turning tie rod tubes equally in same direction until desired position is obtained.

Front Wheel Bearings

When repacking and adjusting front wheel bearings, use an EP-type, lithium base wheel bearing lubricant. Pack the bearings with a generous amount of lubricant and place extra lubricant in the rotor hub cavity between the bearings. Always use a new grease seal during assembly.

When inspecting, replacing, or repacking bearings, be sure the inner cones of the bearings are free to creep on the spindle. The bearings are designed to creep to allow a constantly changing load contact between the cones and the rollers. Polishing and applying lubricant to the spindle will permit this movement and prevent rust from forming.

Adjustment

1. Raise and support front of automobile.
2. Remove hub cap, grease cap and O-ring, cotter pin and nutlock.
3. On automobiles with styled wheels, remove wheel, remove hub cap, and install wheel.
4. Tighten spindle nut to 25 foot-pounds (34 N•m) torque while rotating wheel to seat bearings.
5. Loosen spindle nut 1/3-turn and, while rotating wheel, tighten spindle nut to 6 inch-pounds (0.7 N•m) torque.
6. Install nutlock on spindle nut so cotter pin holes in nutlock and spindle are aligned.
7. Install replacement cotter pin, grease cap and hub cap.
8. On automobiles with styled wheels, remove wheel, install hub cap and install wheel.

Shock Absorber

Removal

1. Remove shock absorber upper locknut, retainer, and grommet.
2. Remove locknuts from shock absorber lower mounting studs and remove shock absorber.
3. Remove lower grommet and jounce bumper retainer from shock absorber piston rod.

Front Shock Absorber Assembly

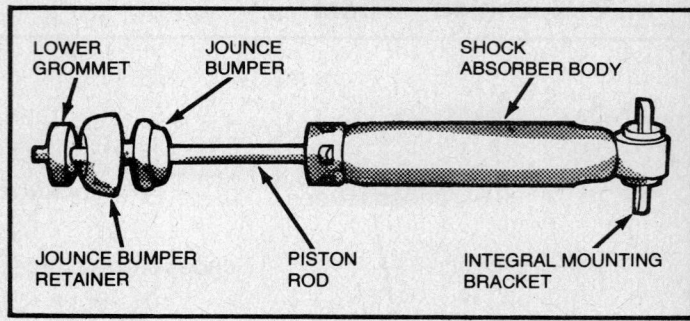

Installation

1. Install jounce bumper retainer and lower grommet on shock absorber piston rod.
2. Extend piston rod to full length.
3. Insert shock absorber through lower control arm and position shock absorber lower mounting bracket on mounting studs. Be sure piston rod is positioned in mounting hole in front crossmember.
4. Install locknuts on lower mounting studs. Tighten nuts to 20 foot-pounds (27.1 N•m) torque.
5. Install upper grommet, retainer, and locknut on shock absorber piston rod. Be sure locating shoulder on grommet seats in hole in crossmember. Tighten upper locknut to 8 foot-pounds (10.8 N•m) torque.

Upper Ball Joint

Inspection

1. Position hydraulic jack under lower control arm and raise car until wheel is off floor.
2. Move top of tire toward and away from center of car. If ball joint exhibits any looseness or play, replace ball joint.
3. Move upper control arm up and down using pry bar. If ball joint exhibits any looseness or play, replace ball joint.

Removal

CAUTION Always support suspension components in such a way that there is no weight or strain on the component you are working on. This prevents accidents that can cause injury.

1. Remove wheel and tire assembly.
2. Remove cotter pin and retaining nut from upper ball joint stud.

Upper and Lower Ball Joints

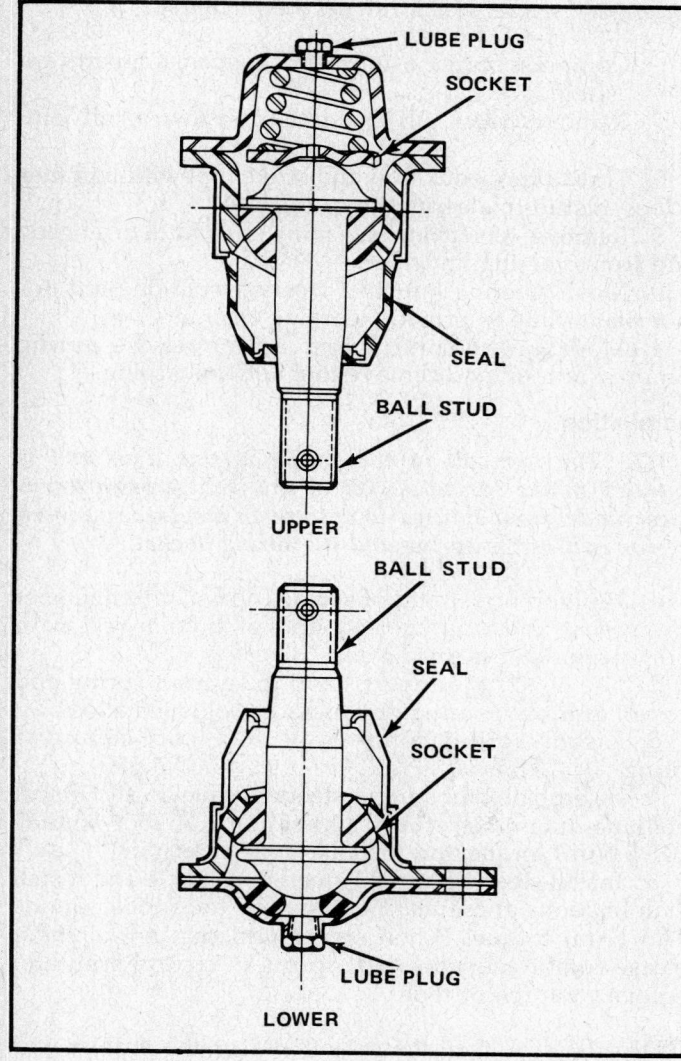

3. Raise and support lower control arm with a hydraulic jack.

4. Engage upper ball joint stud in steering knuckle and install retaining nut. Tighten nut to 75 foot-pounds (101.6 N•m) torque and install retainer and a new cotter pin.

5. Install wheel and tire assembly.

Lower Ball Joint

Inspection

1. Position car on level surface.
2. Remove lube plug from lower ball joint.
3. Fabricate checking tool from a 2- to 3-inch (5.08 to 7.62 cm) length of stiff wire or thin rod.
4. Insert tool into lubrication plug hole until it contacts ball stud. Accurately mark tool with knife or scriber where it is aligned with outer edge of lube plug hole. Distance from the ball stud to outer edge of lubrication plug hole is ball joint clearance.
5. Carefully measure distance from end of tool to mark made in step 4. If distance measured is less than 7/16 inch (11.1 mm) ball joint is serviceable. However, if distance is 7/16 inch (11.1 mm) or more, ball joint should be replaced.

Removal

1. Remove wheel, tire, caliper, and rotor.
2. Remove bolts attaching steering arm to steering knuckle and move steering arm aside.
3. Disconnect stabilizer bar link bolt at lower control arm, if equipped.
4. Support lower control arm with a jack.
5. Remove cotter pin and retaining nut from lower ball joint stud.
6. Thread ball joint removal tool on to the ball stud; lower the hydraulic jack.
7. Strike tool with hammer to loosen ball stud in knuckle.
8. Raise lower control arm with a jack. Unthread removal tool from ball joint stud and remove ball joint from steering knuckle.
9. Move steering knuckle, steering spindle, adapter, and anchor plate aside to provide working clearance.
10. Remove heads from ball joint attaching rivets using grinder or chisel.
11. Drive rivets out of ball joint and arm using punch.
12. Remove ball joint.

Installation

1. Position replacement ball joint in lower control arm.
2. Install ball joint attaching bolts and nuts supplied in replacement ball joint kit and tighten bolts to 25 foot-pounds (33.9 N•m) torque.

NOTE   Install the replacement ball joint attaching bolts from the underside of the control arm. The nuts should be on top.

3. Remove wire supporting steering knuckle, steering spindle, adapter, and anchor plate.
4. Engage ball joint stud in steering knuckle and install

3. Position a jack under lower control arm and raise arm approximately 1 inch (2.54 cm).
4. Thread ball joint removal tool on ball stud.
5. Remove heads from rivets attaching ball joint to control arm using grinder or chisel.
6. Drive rivets out of ball joint and arm using punch.
7. Lower jack slightly and strike ball joint removal tool with hammer to loosen stud in steering knuckle.
8. Remove tool from ball stud and remove ball joint from knuckle.

Installation

1. Position replacement ball joint in upper control arm.
2. Install ball joint-to-control arm attaching bolts and nuts supplied in replacement ball joint kit and tighten nuts to 25 foot-pounds (33.9 N•m) torque.

NOTE   Install the replacement ball joint attaching bolts from the underside of the control arm. The nuts should be on top.

retaining nut on ball stud. Tighten nut to 75 foot-pounds (101.6 N•m) torque and install replacement cotter pin.

5. Install steering arm on steering knuckle and install retaining bolts. Tighten bolts to 55 foot-pounds (74.5 N•m) torque.

6. Connect stabilizer bar link bolt to lower control arm, if equipped. Tighten nut to 7 foot-pounds (9.4 N•m) torque.

7. Install caliper, rotor, and wheel and tire assembly.

8. Remove supports and jack.

9. Check and adjust front wheel alignment if necessary.

Coil Spring

Removal

1. Remove shock absorber.

2. Disconnect stabilizer bar link bolt at lower control arm, if equipped.

3. Remove wheel, tire, caliper and rotor.

4. Remove bolts attaching steering arm to steering knuckle and move steering arm aside.

5. Install spring compressor tool.

Coil Spring Removal

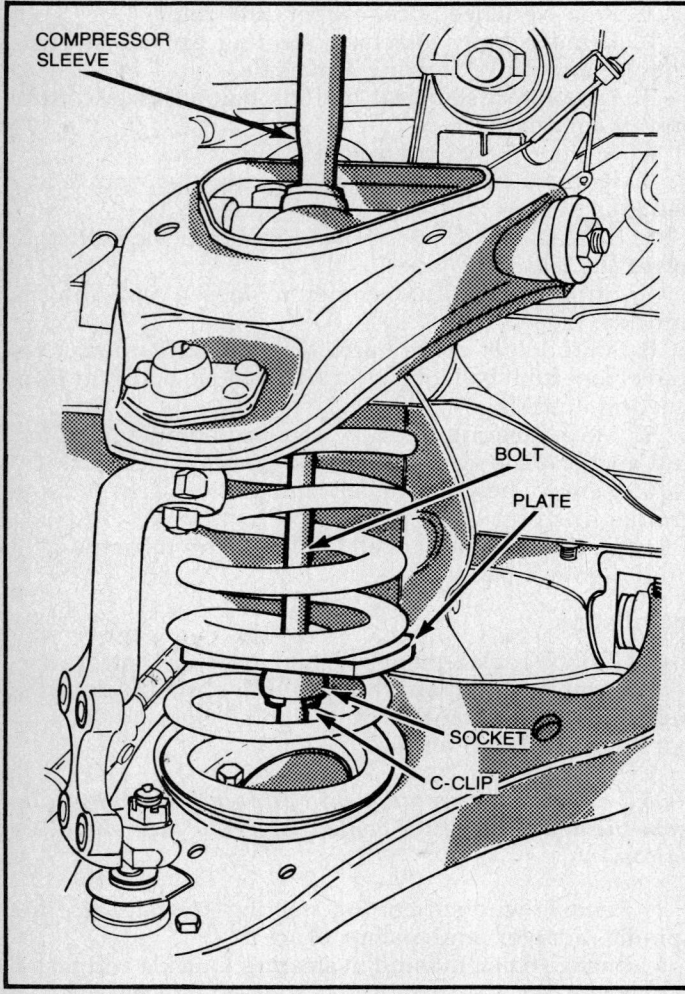

CAUTION Do not use an impact wrench to turn the compressor sleeve. Use a ratchet handle only.

6. Compress spring evenly until suspension parts are free of strain.

7. Remove cotter pin and nut from lower ball joint stud.

8. Thread tool onto stud and strike tool with hammer to loosen stud in steering knuckle.

9. Remove tool from ball joint stud and disengage stud from steering knuckle.

10. Move steering knuckle, steering spindle, and anchor plate aside to provide working clearance.

11. Move lower control arm aside, release spring compressor tool, and remove tool and coil spring.

Installation

NOTE The top coil of the spring is flat. This end is installed in the spring pocket of the front crossmember. Pacer model front springs do not use an insulator between the top coil of the spring and the spring pocket.

1. Position upper end of spring in front crossmember spring seat and align cut-off end of bottom coil with formed shoulder in spring seat.

2. Use a jack or support stand to support spring and control arm until spring compressor tool is installed.

3. Install spring compressor tool and compress spring.

4. Insert ball joint stud in steering knuckle and install retaining nut on ball stud. Tighten nut to 75 foot-pounds (101.6 N•m) torque and install a new cotter pin.

5. Install steering arm on steering knuckle and install retaining bolts and nuts. Tighten bolts to 55 foot-pounds (74.5 N•m) torque. When spring and seat are aligned, release compressor tool, seat spring in control arm, and remove compressor tool.

NOTE Be sure that the cut-off end of the bottom coil seats against the formed shoulder in the control arm spring seat.

6. Install shock absorber. Tighten lower mounting stud locknuts to 20 foot-pounds (27.1 N•m) torque.

7. Connect stabilizer bar link bolt to lower control arm. Tighten locknut to 7 ft.-lbs. (9.4 N•m) torque.

8. Install rotor, wheel, and tire.

9. Remove supports and lower car.

10. Install shock absorber upper grommet, retainer, and locknut. Be sure locating shoulder on grommet seats in hole in front crossmember. Tighten upper locknut on shock absorber to 8 foot-pounds (10.8 N•m) torque.

Upper Control Arm

Removal

1. Raise and support front of car.

2. Remove wheel and tire assembly.

3. Remove cotter pin, retaining nut, and locknut from upper ball joint stud.

4. Thread tool on stud and strike tool with hammer to loosen stud in steering knuckle.

5. Support lower control arm and rotor using hydraulic jack.

6. Remove tool from ball joint stud and disengage stud from steering knuckle.

Upper Control Arm Removal and Installation

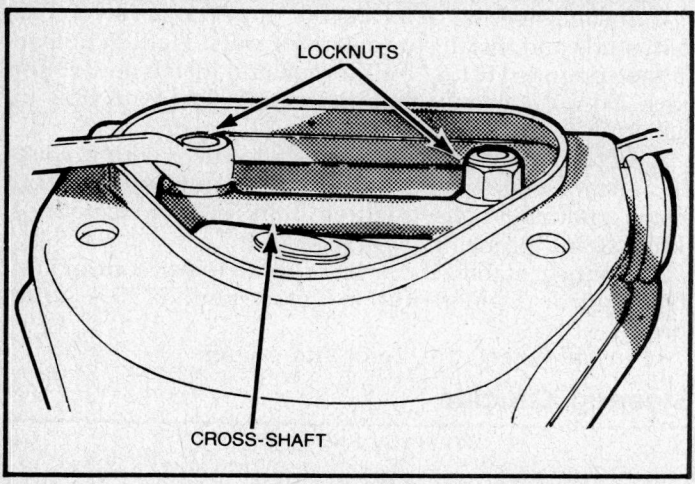

LOCKNUTS

CROSS-SHAFT

7. Remove retaining stud locknuts attaching cross-shaft to front crossmember and remove upper control arm assembly.

BUSHING REPLACEMENT

A special C-clamp tool is required to remove and install upper control arm bushings.

Upper Control Arm Bushing Removal

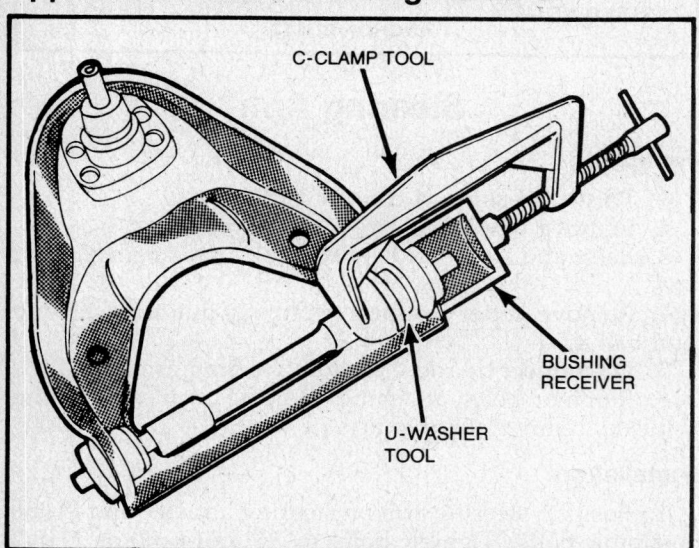

C-CLAMP TOOL

BUSHING RECEIVER

U-WASHER TOOL

Installation

1. Position upper control arm assembly on crossmember and install locknuts. Tighten locknuts to 80 foot-pounds (108.4 N•m) torque.

2. Insert upper ball joint stud in steering knuckle.

Raise lower control using hydraulic jack to ease installation and relieve spring tension on upper ball joint.

3. Install locknut on upper ball joint stud. Tighten nut to 75 foot-pounds (101.6 N•m) torque and install nut retainer and replacement cotter pin. Do not loosen nut to align slots in nut with hole in ball stud.

4. Tighten cross-shaft bushing nuts to 60 foot-pounds (81.3 N•m) torque.

Lower Control Arm

Removal

1. Remove shock absorber.

2. Disconnect stabilizer bar link bolt at lower control arm.

3. Remove wheel tire, caliper, and rotor.

4. Remove bolts attaching steering arm to steering knuckle and move steering arm aside.

5. Install spring compressor and compress spring evenly until all strain is off lower control arm.

6. Remove cotter pin and nut from lower ball joint stud.

7. Thread tool on stud and strike tool with hammer to loosen stud in steering knuckle.

8. Remove tool from ball joint stud and disengage stud from steering knuckle.

9. Move steering knuckle, steering spindle, adapter, and anchor plate aside to provide working clearance.

10. Remove two pivot bolts attaching lower control arm to front crossmember and remove lower control arm.

Lower Control Arm Removal

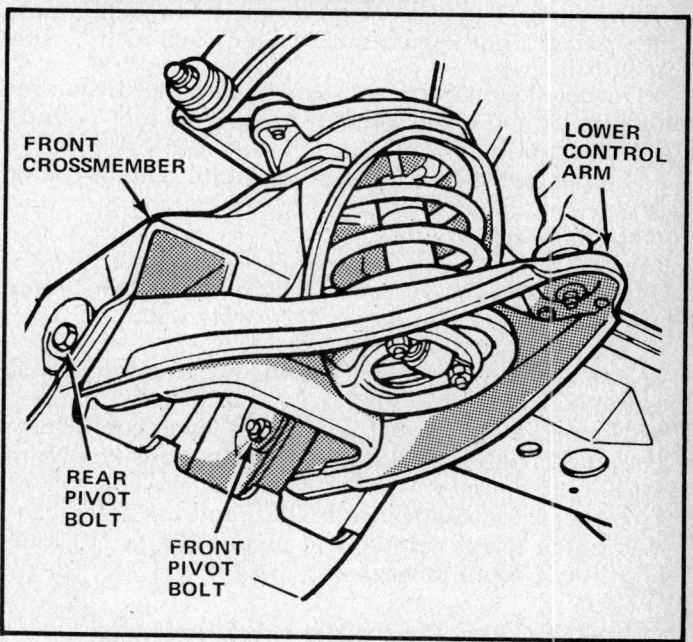

FRONT CROSSMEMBER

LOWER CONTROL ARM

REAR PIVOT BOLT

FRONT PIVOT BOLT

CAUTION When loosening/tightening the pivot bolts, take care to avoid damaging the steering protective boots. If the boots are cut or torn, the inner tie rod assemblies will be exposed to dirt, road splash, and other debris resulting in premature wear.

SUSPENSION

Lower Control Arm Rear Bushing Installation

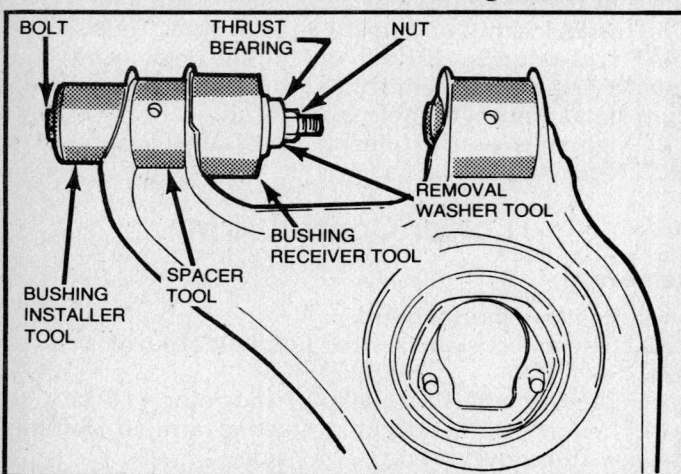

BUSHING REPLACEMENT

Do not attempt to remove the bushings without using the spacer tools, to avoid damaging the control arm.

NOTE The thrust washer and nut are part of bolt assembly.

Installation

1. Position lower control arm in front crossmember and install pivot bolts and locknuts. Tighten locknuts securely but not completely.

2. Insert lower control arm ball joint stud in steering knuckle and install retaining nut on ball stud. Tighten nut to 75 foot-pounds (101.6 N·m) torque and install a new cotter pin. Do not loosen nut to align slots in nut with hole in ball stud.

3. Install steering arm on steering knuckle. Install retaining bolts and nuts. Tighten bolts to 55 foot-pounds (74.5 N·m) torque.

4. Loosen spring compressor tool until bottom coil of spring rests in control arm. Align bottom coil of spring and spring seat in control arm.

NOTE The cut-off end of the bottom coil must seat against the formed shoulder in the spring seat.

5. Install shock absorber. Tighten lower mounting stud locknuts to 20 foot-pounds (27.1 N·m) torque.

6. Connect stabilizer bar link bolt to lower control arm if equipped. Tighten locknut to 7 foot-pounds (9.4 N·m) torque.

7. Install rotor, caliper, and wheel and tire assembly.

8. Tighten lower control arm pivot bolts to 110 foot-pounds (49.1 N·m) torque.

Steering Knuckle and Spindle

Removal

1. Remove wheel, tire, caliper and rotor.

2. Remove bolts attaching steering arm, steering stop, steering spindle, anchor plate, and adapter to steering knuckle and remove these components.

3. Disconnect stabilizer bar link bolt at lower control arm. Support lower control arm using a jack.

4. Remove cotter pins and retaining nuts from upper and lower ball joint studs. Disengage ball joint studs from steering knuckle.

5. Remove steering knuckle.

Installation

1. Install steering knuckle on upper and lower ball joint studs and install stud retaining nuts. Tighten nuts to 75 foot-pounds (101.6 N·m) torque and install new cotter pins. Do not loosen nuts to align nut slots with hole in ball studs.

2. Position steering stop, steering arm, steering spindle, anchor plate, and adapter on steering knuckle and install retaining bolts. Tighten bolts to 85 foot-pounds (115.2 N·m) torque.

3. Connect stabilizer bar link bolt to lower control arm if equipped. Tighten nut to 7 foot-pounds (9.4 N·m) torque.

4. Install wheel, tire, rotor and caliper.

Steering Knuckle

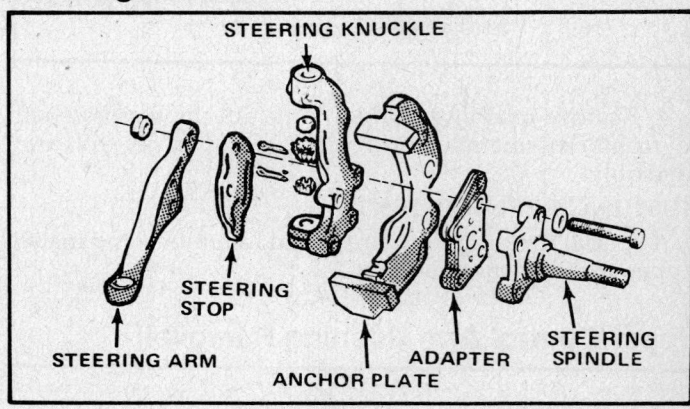

Steering Arm

Removal

1. Raise and support front of car.

2. Remove wheel and tire, caliper and rotor.

3. Raise and support lower control arm using hydraulic jack.

4. Remove cotter pin and retaining nut from tie rod end ball stud.

5. Disconnect tie rod end from steering arm.

6. Remove bolts attaching steering arm to steering knuckle; remove steering arm.

Installation

1. Position steering arm on steering knuckle and install retaining bolts. Tighten bolts to 85 foot-pounds (115.2 N·m) torque.

2. Insert tie rod end ball stud in steering arm (from bottom) and install retaining nut. Tighten nut to 50 foot-pounds (67.7 N·m) torque and install replacement cotter pin.

3. Install rotor, caliper, and wheel and tire.

4. Remove supports and hydraulic jack and lower car.

REAR SUSPENSION—AMC

Shock Absorber

Removal

1. Raise and support rear of automobile and support axle assembly with hydraulic jack.

NOTE Support the suspension in such a way that no strain is on shock absorber.

2. Remove locknut, retainer, and grommet which attach shock absorber lower mounting stud to spring plate.

3. Compress shock absorber by hand and disengage lower mounting stud from spring plate.

4. Remove bolts and lockwashers attaching shock absorber upper mounting bracket to underbody panel and remove shock absorber.

5. Remove locknut, retainer, and grommet which attach mounting bracket to shock absorber upper mounting stud and remove bracket.

6. Remove remaining grommets and retainers from shock absorber upper and lower mounting studs.

Installation

1. Install retainer and grommet on shock absorber mounting stud. Be sure locating shoulder on grommet faces end of mounting stud.

2. Install mounting bracket on shock absorber upper mounting stud with flat side of bracket facing underbody panel.

3. install second grommet on mounting stud and install retainer and locknut. Tighten locknut to 8 foot-pounds (11 N•m) torque.

NOTE Be sure the locating shoulders on the grommets are centered in the mounting bracket hole before tightening the locknut.

4. Position assembled mounting bracket and shock absorber on mounting studs in underbody panel. Install lockwashers and bolts. Tighten bolts to 28 foot-pounds (38 N•m) torque on Pacers and 15 foot-pounds (20 N•m) torque on all other models.

Rear Suspension Components

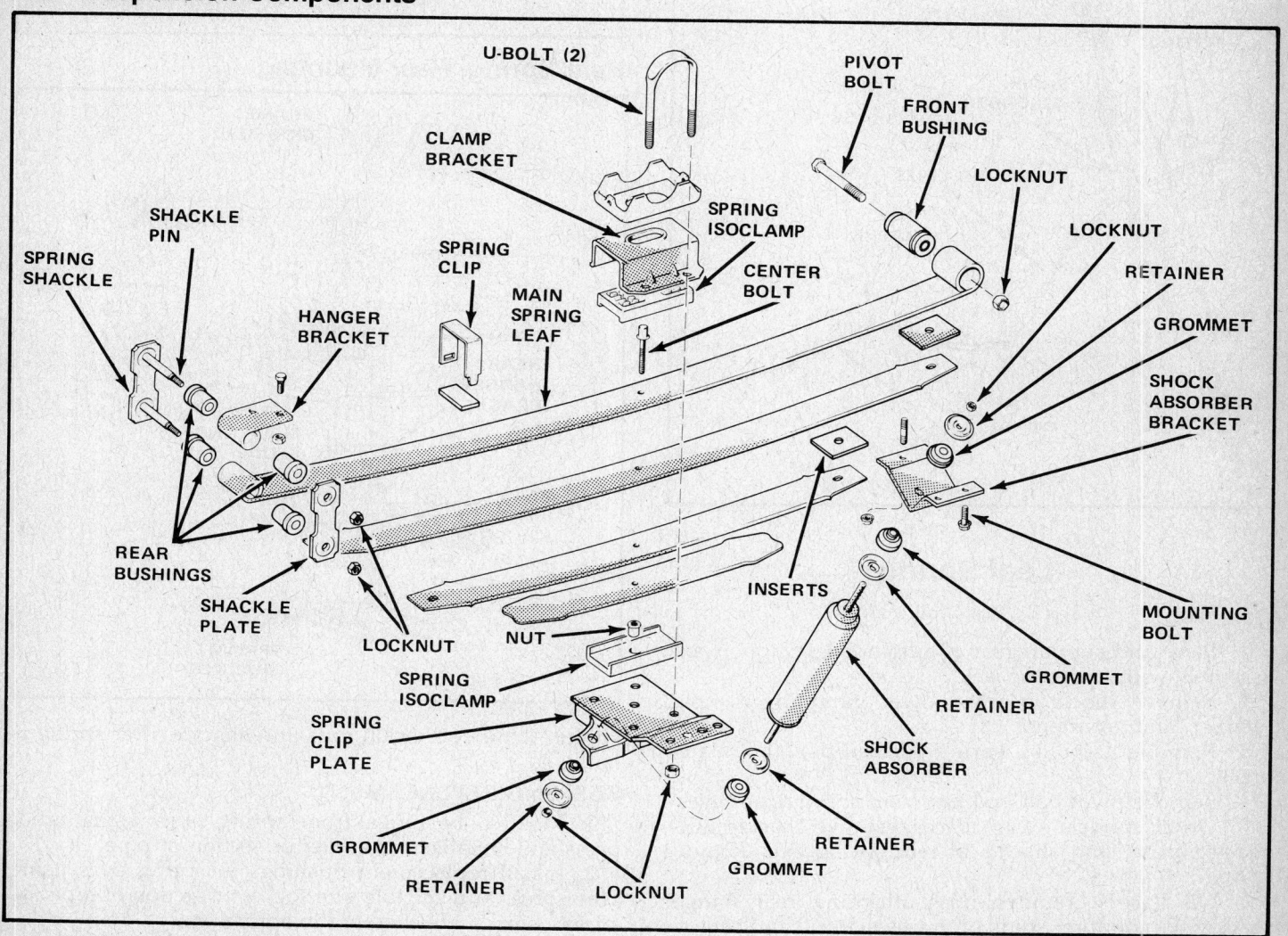

NOTE   If an adjustable shock absorber is being installed, adjust the ride control setting as necessary before connecting the shock to the spring clip plate.

5. Engage shock absorber lower mounting stud in spring clip plate.

6. Install second grommet with shoulder of grommet facing spring tie plate and install retainer and locknut. Tighten locknut to 8 foot-pounds (11 N•m) torque.

Air Shock Inflation Procedure

Do not inflate air shocks until after the automobile has been loaded or had a trailer attached. If the shocks are inflated before loading, the combined force of initial inflation and load weight could exceed shock absorber internal pressure limits and cause damage.

Air Shock System—Spirit and AMX

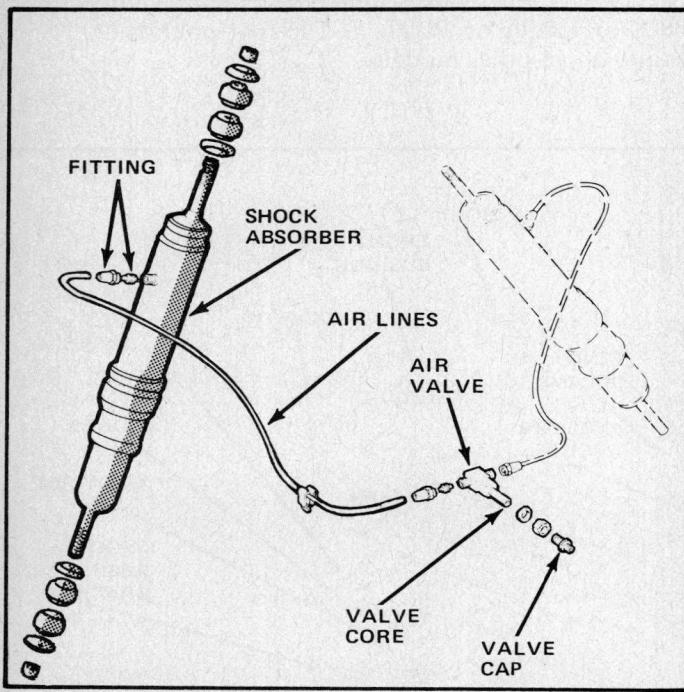

Leaf Spring

Removal

1. Raise and support rear of automobile. Support axle assembly with hydraulic jack.

2. Remove shock absorber lower mounting locknut, retainer, and grommet.

3. Remove U-bolts, spring isoclamps, and clamp bracket.

4. Remove pivot bolt and nut from spring front eye.

5. On all models except Pacer, remove shackle nuts, shackle plate, and shackle at rear spring eye. Remove spring.

6. On Pacers, remove nuts attaching rear hanger bracket to mounting studs on frame side sill and remove

Spring to Frame Mounting—Pacer

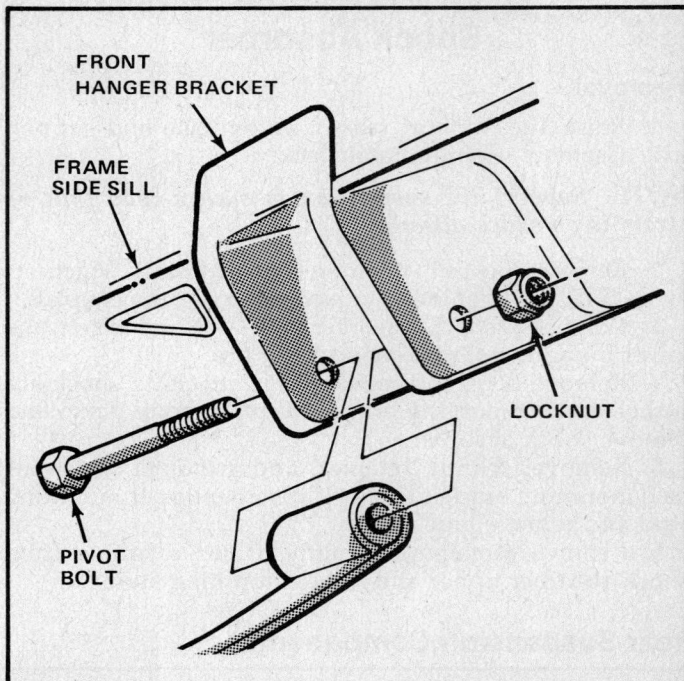

Rear Spring, Rear Mounting

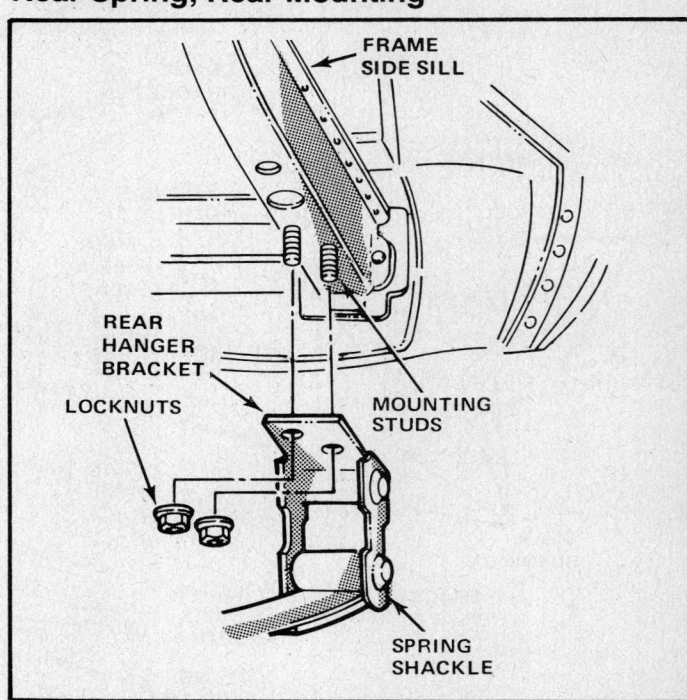

spring. Remove shackle nuts and shackle after spring is removed.

BUSHING REPLACEMENT

1. Remove bushings from spring eyes using arbor press and suitable size socket or section of pipe.

2. Install replacement bushings in spring eyes using arbor press and suitable size socket or section of pipe. Be sure bushings are centered in spring eyes.

Installation

1. On all models except Pacer, insert shackle pins into spring rear eye and rear hanger.

2. On Pacers, assemble rear hanger bracket and shackle and install in spring rear eye.

3. On Pacers, position rear hanger bracket on frame side sill and install mounting stud nuts. Tighten nuts to 45 foot-pounds (61 N•m) torque.

4. On all models, position front spring eye in front hanger and install pivot bolt and pivot bolt locknut. Tighten locknut to 110 foot-pounds (149 N•m) torque.

5. Install shackle plate and locknuts on shackle pins. Tighten locknuts to 30 foot-pounds (41 N•m) torque.

6. Install clamp bracket, spring isoclamps, spring plate, and U-bolts.

7. Engage shock lower mounting stud in spring plate and install grommet, retainer, and locknut. Tighten nut to 8 foot-pounds (11 N•m) torque.

Stabilizer Bar

Removal

1. Remove nuts and grommets attaching stabilizer bar to connecting links.

2. Remove bolts attaching stabilizer bar mounting clamps to spring clip plates.

3. Remove stabilizer bar.

Installation

1. Position stabilizer bar and mounting clamps on spring clip plates and install clamp bolts finger tight.

2. Install stabilizer bar on connecting links and install grommets and locknuts.

3. Tighten connecting link locknuts to 7 foot-pounds (9 N•m) torque and tighten stabilizer mounting clamp bolts to 25 foot-pounds (34 N•m) torque.

Automatic Load Leveling System Operation

The load leveling system automatically adjusts the rear height with changes in vehicle loading.

COMPRESSOR

The compressor assembly is a positive displacement single piston air pump powered by a 12 volt permanent magnet motor. The compressor head casting contains piston, intake and exhaust valves plus a solenoid operated exhaust valve which releases air from the system when energized.

NOTE   The compressor is not a serviceable item. If diagnosis indicates the compressor has malfunctioned, replace the compressor as an assembly only. Do not attempt to repair it.

RAISING THE AUTOMOBILE

When weight is added to the rear of the car, the body is forced downward which causes the height sensor actuating arm to rotate upward. This action causes the height sensor to electrically start the internal time delay circuit.

Rear Stabilizer Bar

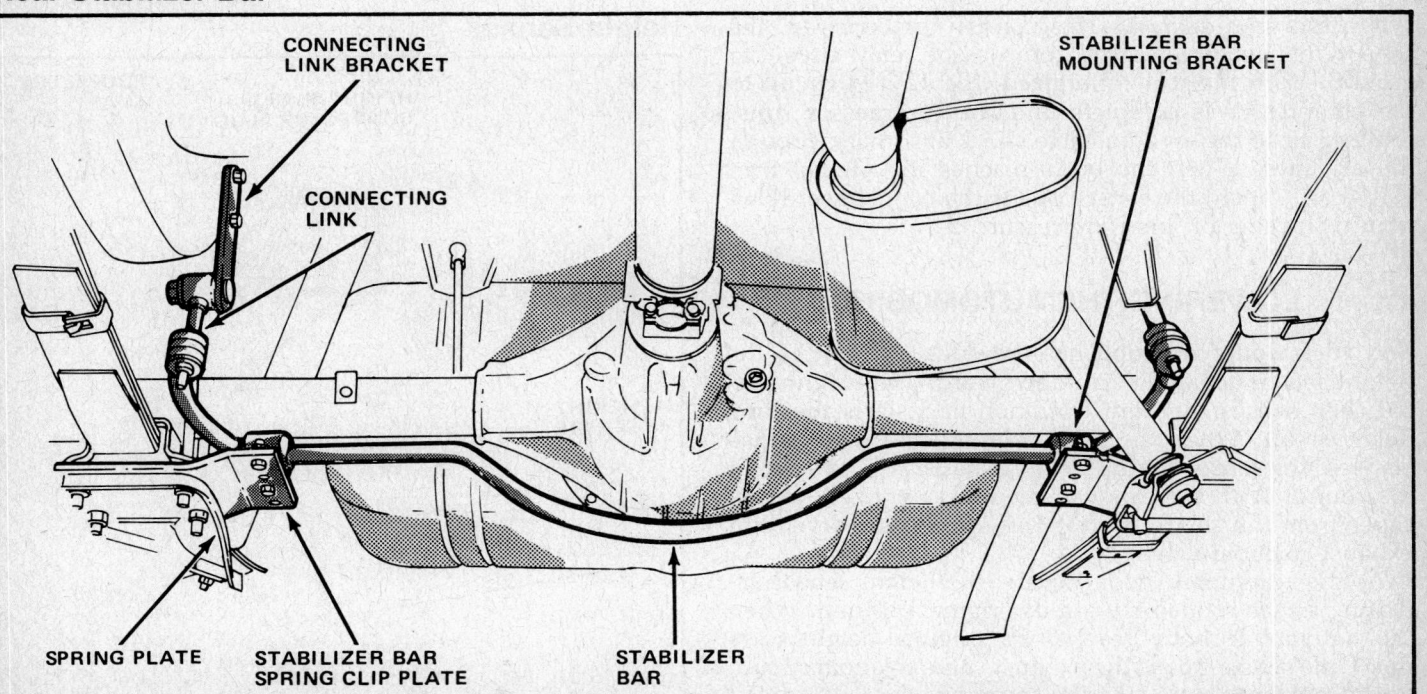

CONNECTING LINK BRACKET

STABILIZER BAR MOUNTING BRACKET

CONNECTING LINK

SPRING PLATE   STABILIZER BAR SPRING CLIP PLATE   STABILIZER BAR

SUSPENSION

Automatic Load Leveling System

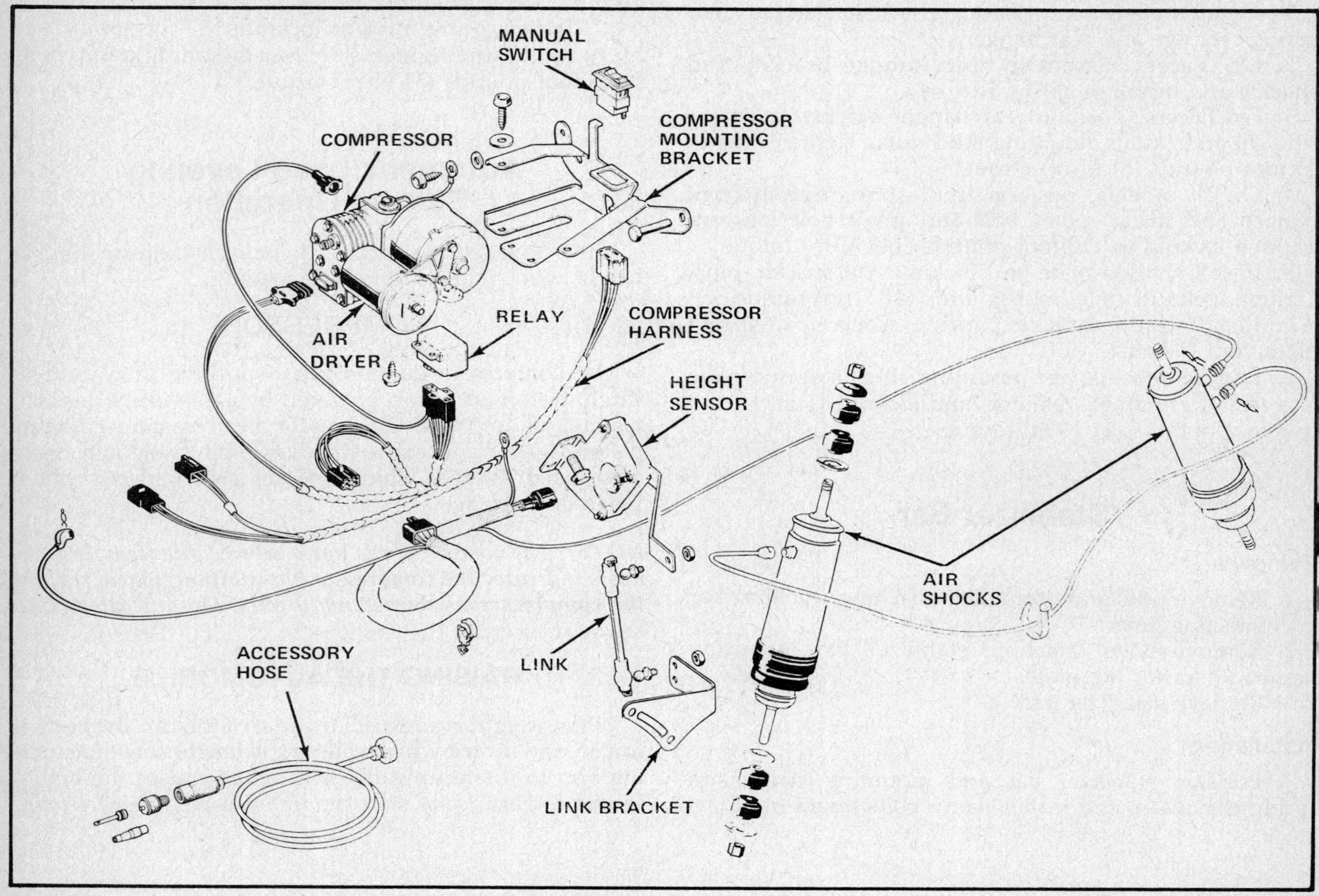

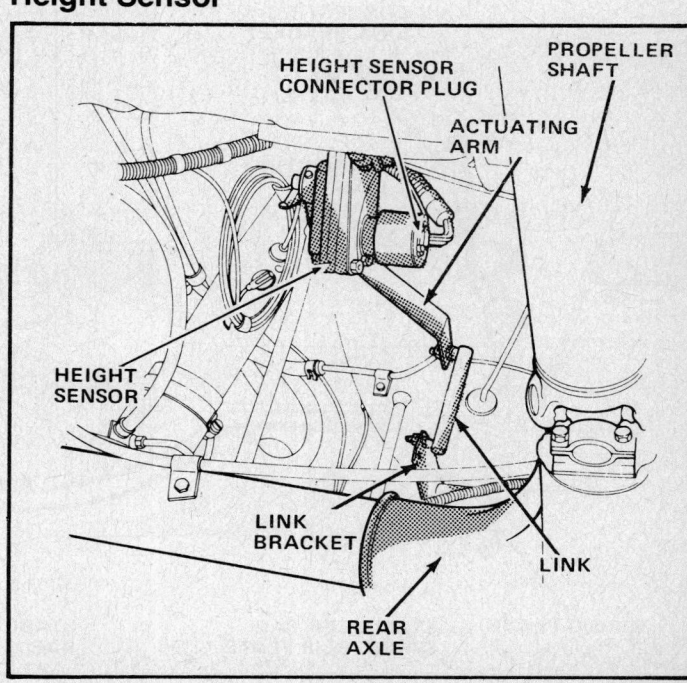

When the time delay (7–15 seconds) has occurred, the sensor then completes the compressor relay circuit to ground. With the relay energized, the 12V(+) circuit to the compressor is complete and the compressor runs, sending air to the air adjustable shock absorbers through the air lines. When the body reaches its original trim height (±¾ incn) the sensor opens the compressor relay circuit, shutting off the compressor.

LOWERING THE AUTOMOBILE

A High Body condition has the effect of rotating the height sensor actuating arm downward. The height sensor then senses the high condition and starts the time delay circuit. When the time delay (7–15 seconds) has elapsed, the sensor completes the exhaust solenoid circuit to ground. With the exhaust solenoid energized, air escapes from the shocks exiting through the air dryer and exhaust solenoid valve.

As the automobile body lowers, the height sensor actuating arm is rotated toward its original position. When the automobile body reaches its original height (±¾ inch), the sensor opens the exhaust valve solenoid circuit, which prevents more air from escaping.

Height Sensor

A minimum air pressure of 7–14 psi is maintained on the automobile. The minimum pressure provides improved ride characteristics when the automobile has a minimum load. The compressor relief valve is designed to operate at 120–150 psi. See the Diagnosis Chart for troubleshooting procedures.

HEIGHT SENSOR

Removal

1. Disconnect connector plug from sensor.

2. Disconnect link from sensor actuating arm.
3. Remove bolts attaching height sensor to underbody and remove sensor.

Installation

1. Position height sensor on underbody and install sensor attaching bolts.
2. Connect sensor actuating arm to link.
3. Connect wiring harness connector plug to height sensor.

Compressor Draw Test

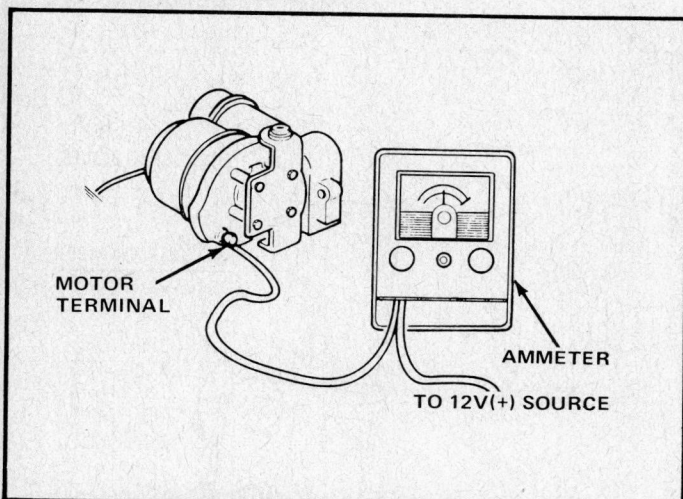

MOTOR TERMINAL

AMMETER

TO 12V(+) SOURCE

Current draw should not exceed 14 amps.

Compressor Pressure Test

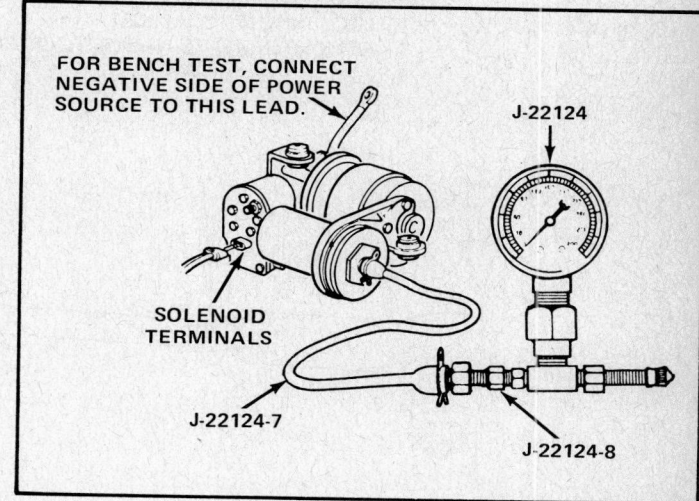

FOR BENCH TEST, CONNECT NEGATIVE SIDE OF POWER SOURCE TO THIS LEAD.

J-22124

SOLENOID TERMINALS

J-22124-7

J-22124-8

Wiring Diagram—Automatic Load Leveling System

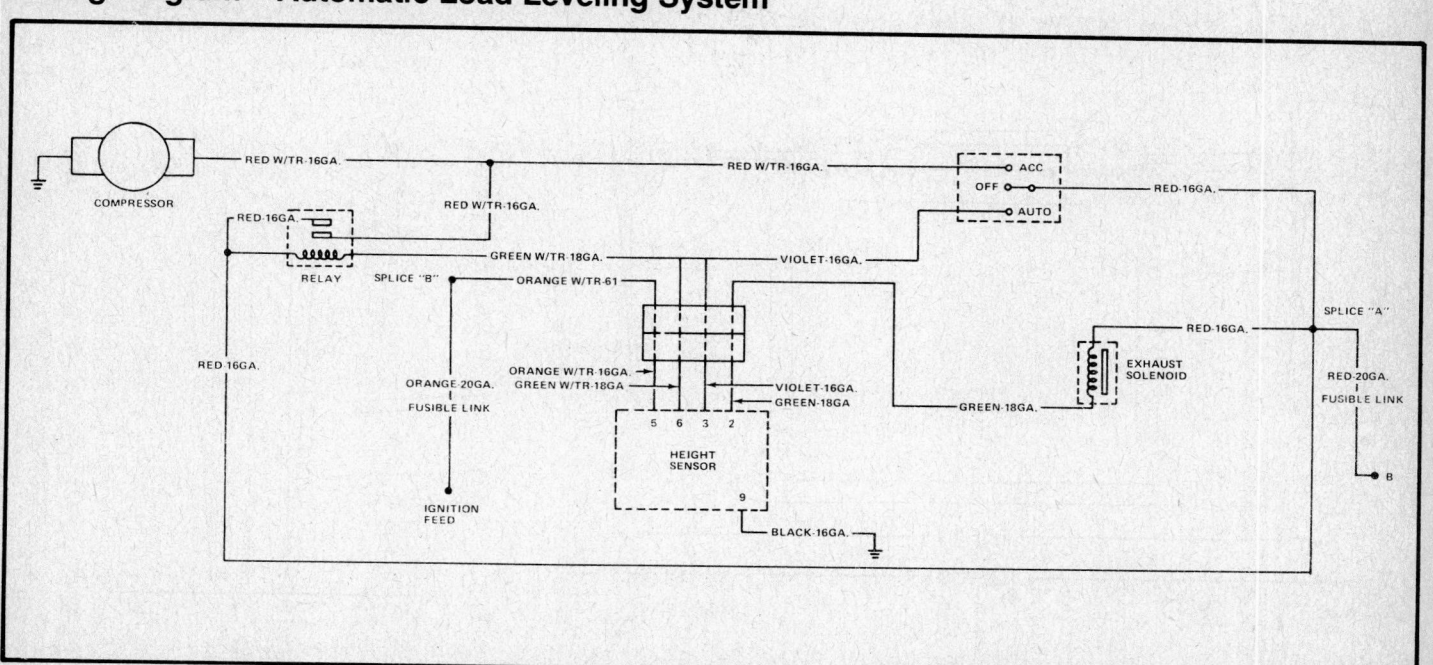

FRONT SUSPENSION—CHRYSLER FRONT DRIVE

Alignment

PRE-ALIGNMENT CHECK

There are six factors which are the foundation to front wheel alignment: Height, caster, camber, toe-in, steering axis inclination and toe-out on turns. Of these six basic factors, only camber and toe are mechanically adjustable.

1. Before any attempt is made to change or correct the wheel alignment, inspection and necessary corrections must be made on those parts which influence the steering of the vehicle.

2. Check and inflate tires to recommended pressures.

3. Check front wheel and tire assembly for radial runout.

4. Check struts (shock absorbers) for extra-stiff, notchy, or spongy operation.

5. Front suspension should be checked only after vehicle has the recommended tire pressures, full tank of fuel, no passenger or luggage compartment load and is on a level floor or alignment rack.

Front Suspension

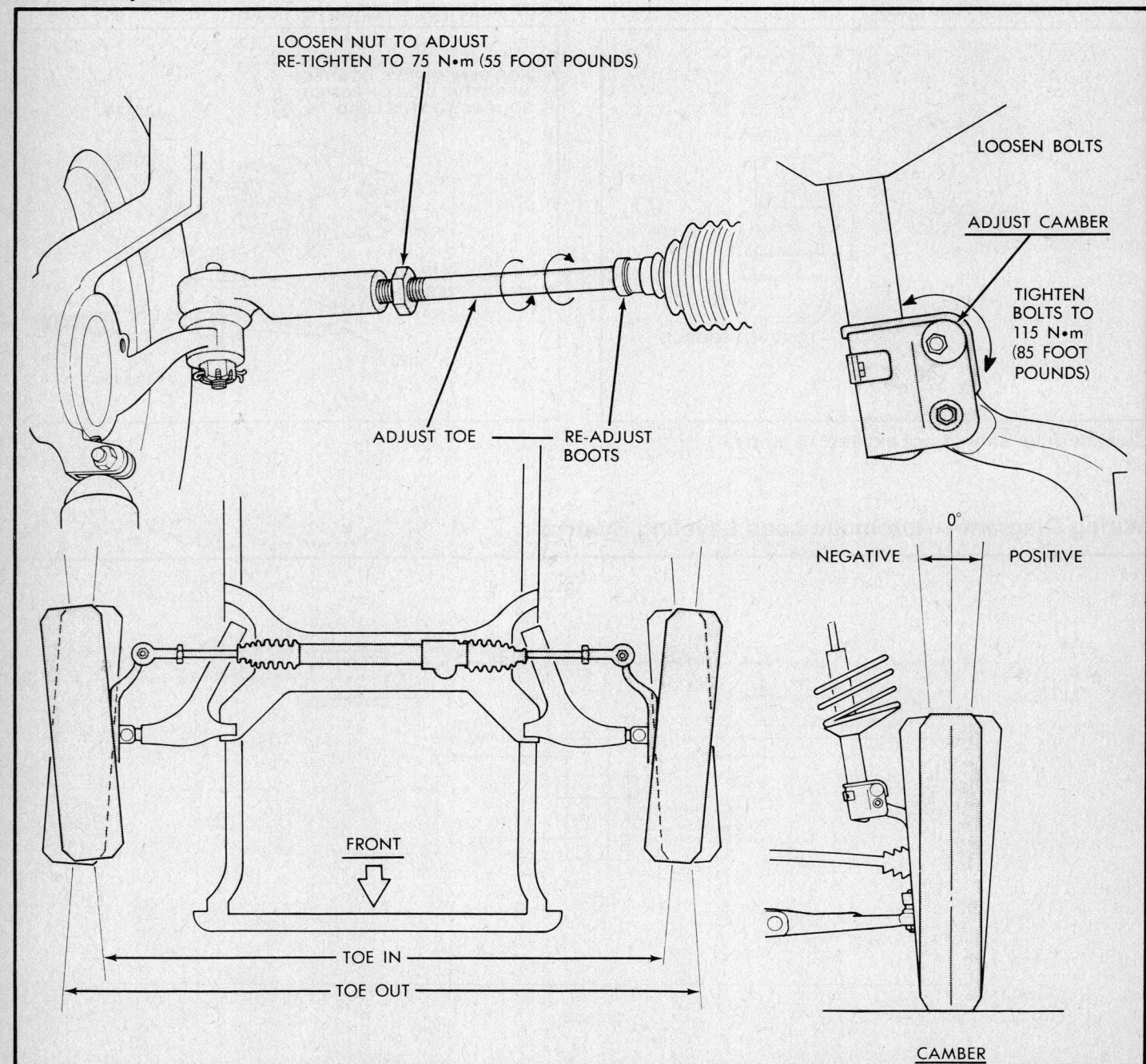

Steering Knuckle

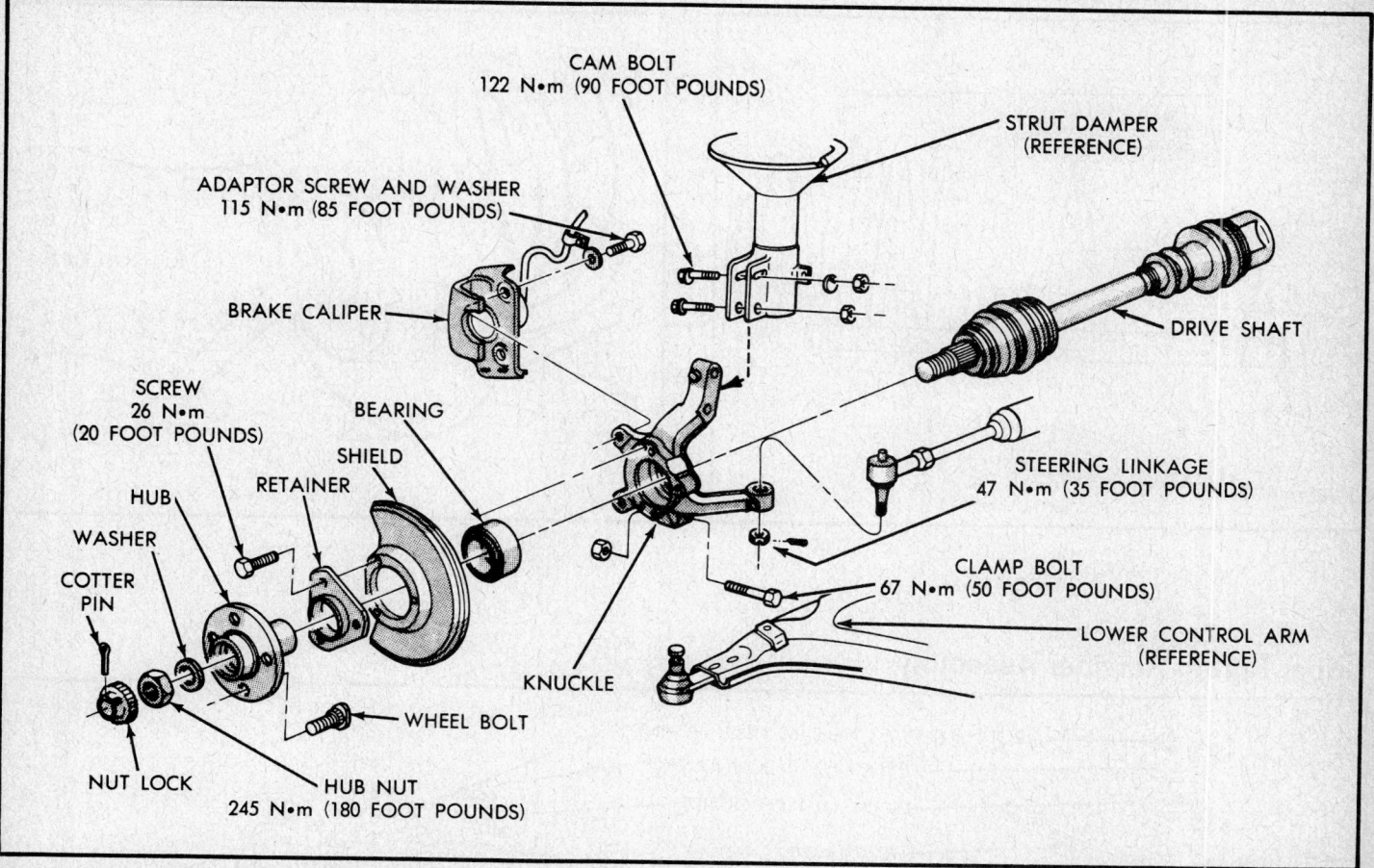

CAM BOLT
122 N•m (90 FOOT POUNDS)

STRUT DAMPER
(REFERENCE)

ADAPTOR SCREW AND WASHER
115 N•m (85 FOOT POUNDS)

BRAKE CALIPER

DRIVE SHAFT

SCREW
26 N•m
(20 FOOT POUNDS)

BEARING

SHIELD

RETAINER

HUB

WASHER

COTTER
PIN

KNUCKLE

STEERING LINKAGE
47 N•m (35 FOOT POUNDS)

CLAMP BOLT
67 N•m (50 FOOT POUNDS)

LOWER CONTROL ARM
(REFERENCE)

WHEEL BOLT

NUT LOCK

HUB NUT
245 N•m (180 FOOT POUNDS)

6. To obtain accurate reading, vehicle should be jounced in the following manner just prior to taking measurement. Grasp bumpers at center (rear bumper first) and jounce up and down several times. Always release bumpers at bottom of down cycle after jouncing both rear and front ends an equal number of times.

Camber Adjustment

1. Loosen cam and through bolts (each side).
2. Rotate upper cam bolt to move upper (knuckle and) wheel in or out to specified camber.
3. Tighten bolts to 115 N•m (85 foot-pounds).

Toe Adjustment

1. Center steering wheel and hold with steering wheel clamp.
2. Loosen tie rod locknuts. Rotate rods to align toe to specifications.

Front Wheel Bearings

The vehicle is equipped with permanently sealed front wheel bearings. There is no periodic lubrication, maintenance, or adjustment recommended for these units.

Service repair or replacement of front drive bearing, hub, brake dust shield or knuckle will require assembly removal from the vehicle.

Strut Damper Assembly

Removal

1. Remove wheel and tire assembly.
2. Remove cam adjusting bolt, through bolt and brake hose-to-damper bracket retaining screw.
3. Remove strut damper-to-fender shield mounting nut washer assemblies.

DISASSEMBLY

1. Compress coil with spring compressor tool.
2. Hold strut rod while loosening strut rod nut. Remove nut.
3. Remove retainers and bushings.
4. Remove coil spring.

NOTE   Mark spring for replacement in original position.

5. Check retainers for cracks or distortion.
6. Check bearings for binding. Check that they contain an adequate supply of lubricant.

ASSEMBLY

1. Reassemble and hold strut rod while tightening rod nut to 81 N•m (55 foot-pounds).

NOTE   Perform step 1 before releasing spring compressor tool.

SUSPENSION

Compressing Coil Spring

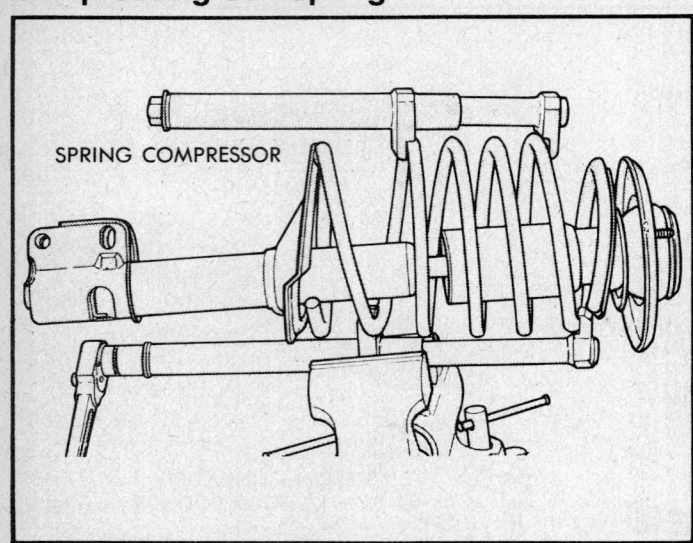

SPRING COMPRESSOR

Loosening Strut Rod Nut

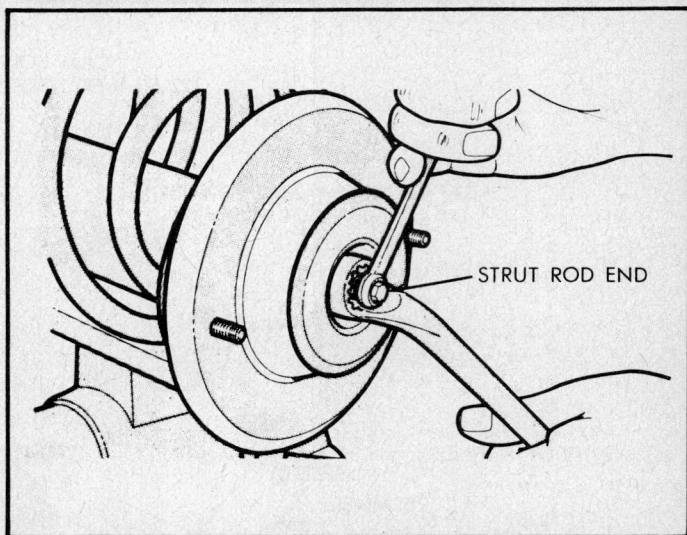

STRUT ROD END

Upper Spring Retainer Assembly

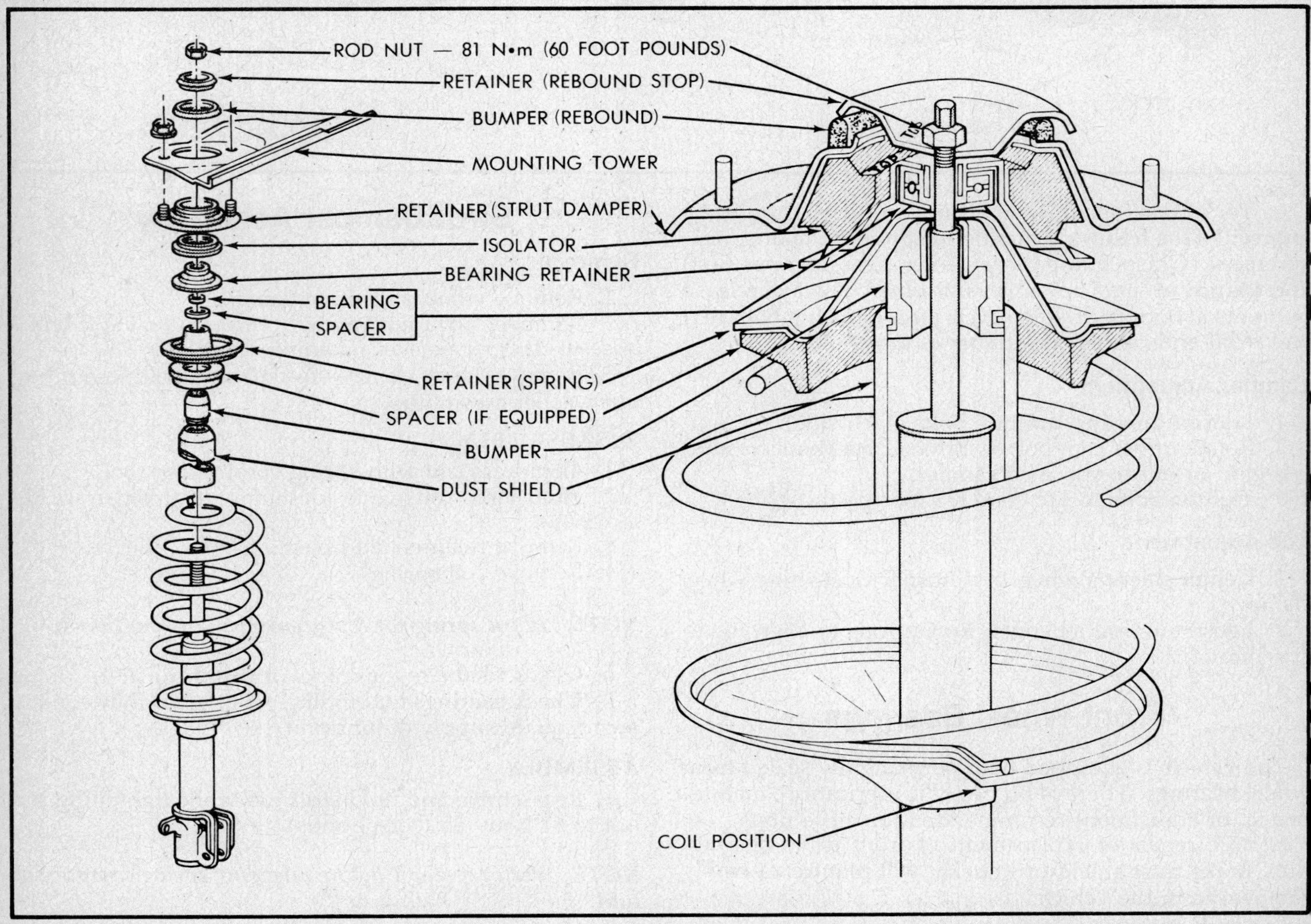

ROD NUT — 81 N•m (60 FOOT POUNDS)
RETAINER (REBOUND STOP)
BUMPER (REBOUND)
MOUNTING TOWER
RETAINER (STRUT DAMPER)
ISOLATOR
BEARING RETAINER
BEARING
SPACER
RETAINER (SPRING)
SPACER (IF EQUIPPED)
BUMPER
DUST SHIELD

COIL POSITION

Strut Assembly

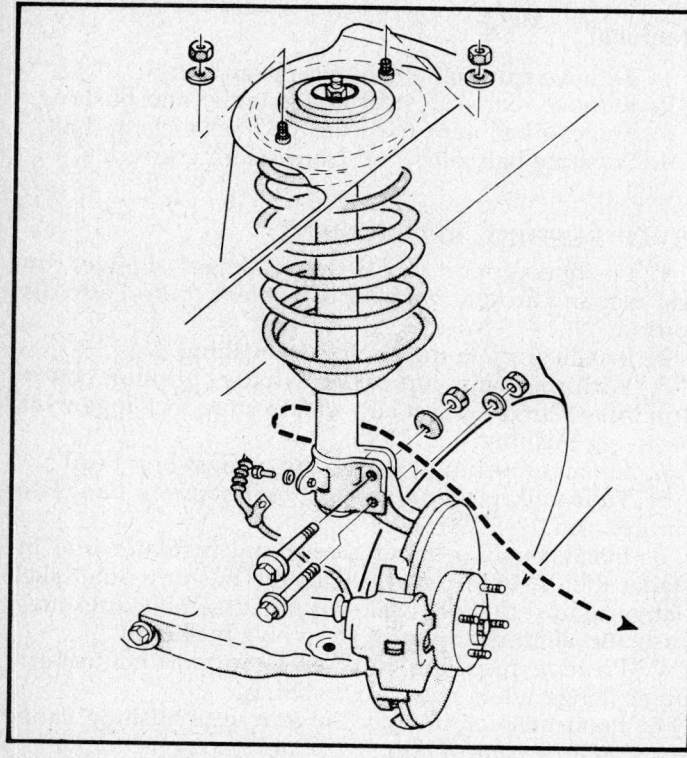

2. Release spring compressor tool.

NOTE Springs are rated separately for each side of vehicle depending on optional equipment and type of service.

During reassembly of spring to strut damper, ensure that coil end is seated in strut damper spring seat recess.

Installation

1. Install unit into fender reinforcement and install retaining nut and washer assemblies. Torque to 20 N•m (27 foot-pounds).
2. Position knuckle leg into strut and install upper (cam) and lower through bolts.
3. Attach brake hose retainer to damper; tighten screw to 12 N•m (10 foot-pounds).
4. Index cam bolt to original mark and tighten bolts to 115 N•m (85 foot-pounds) torque.
5. Install wheel and tire assembly. Tighten wheel nuts to 108 N•m (80 foot-pounds).

Ball Joints

Inspection

With the weight of the vehicle resting on the road wheels, grasp the grease fitting and attempt to move it. No mechanical assistance or added force is necessary. If the ball joint is worn, the grease fitting will move easily. If movement is noted, replacement of the ball joint is recommended.

Checking Ball Joint Wear

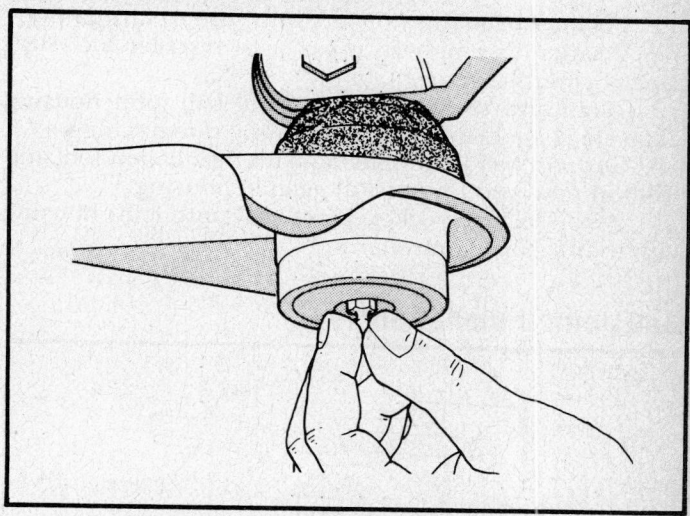

Ball Joint Removal

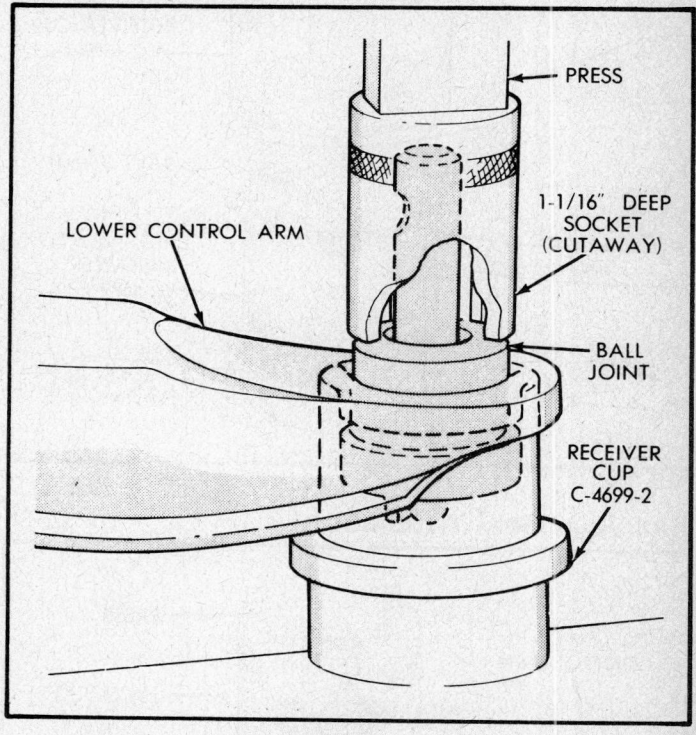

Removal

CAUTION Pulling steering knuckle out from center will separate inner universal joint. Support strut so that a swing away is impossible.

1. Pry off seal.
2. Position receiving cup tool to support lower control arm while receiving ball joint assembly.
3. Install 1¹/₁₆ inch deep socket over stud and against joint upper housing.
4. Press to remove joint assembly from arm.

SUSPENSION

FRONT SUSPENSION-CHRYSLER FRONT DRIVE

Installation

1. Position ball joint housing into control arm cavity.
2. Position assembly in press with installer tool supporting control arm.
3. Align and press assembly until ball joint housing ledge stops against control arm cavity down flange.
4. Support ball joint housing with installation tool and position new seal (over stud) against housing.
5. With 1½ inch socket, press seal onto joint housing with seat against control arm.

Ball Joint Installation

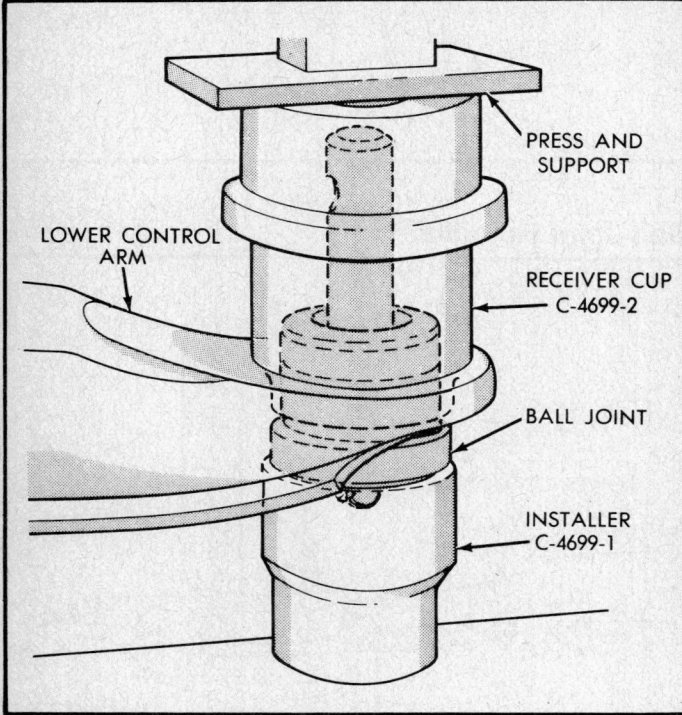

Ball Joint Seal Installation

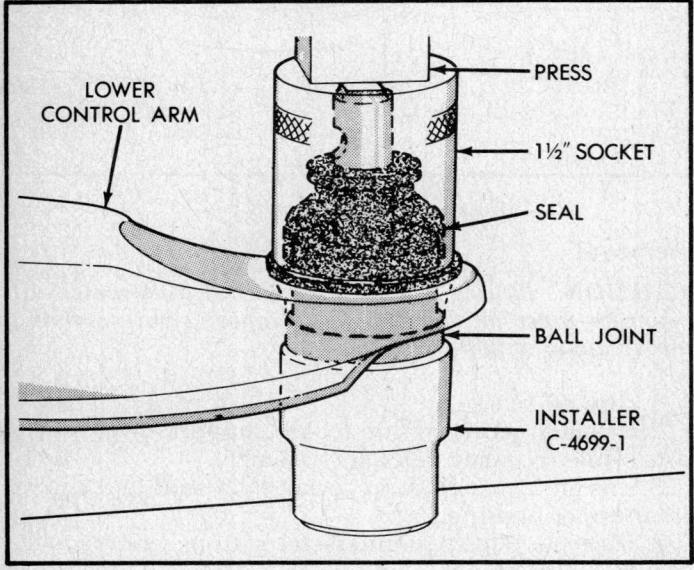

Lower Control Arm

Removal

1. Remove front inner pivot through bolt.
2. Remove rear stub strut nut, retainer and bushing.
3. Remove ball joint-to-steering knuckle clamp bolt.
4. Separate ball joint stud from steering knuckle.

PIVOT BUSHING REPLACMENT

1. Position support tool between flanges of lower control arm and around bushing to prevent control arm distortion.
2. Install ½ x 2½ inch bolt into bushing.
3. With receiving cup on press base, position control arm inner flange against cup wall to support flange while receiving bushing.
4. Remove bushing by pressing against bolt head.
5. To install, position support tool between flanges of control arm.
6. Install bushing inner sleeve and insulator into installer tool C-4699-1 cavity with the bushing outer shell flange against the tool wall. Position assembly onto press base and align control arm to receive bushing.
7. Position receiving cup tool to support control arm outer flange while receiving bushing.
8. Press bushing into control arm until bushing flange seats against control arm.

Pivot Bushing Removal

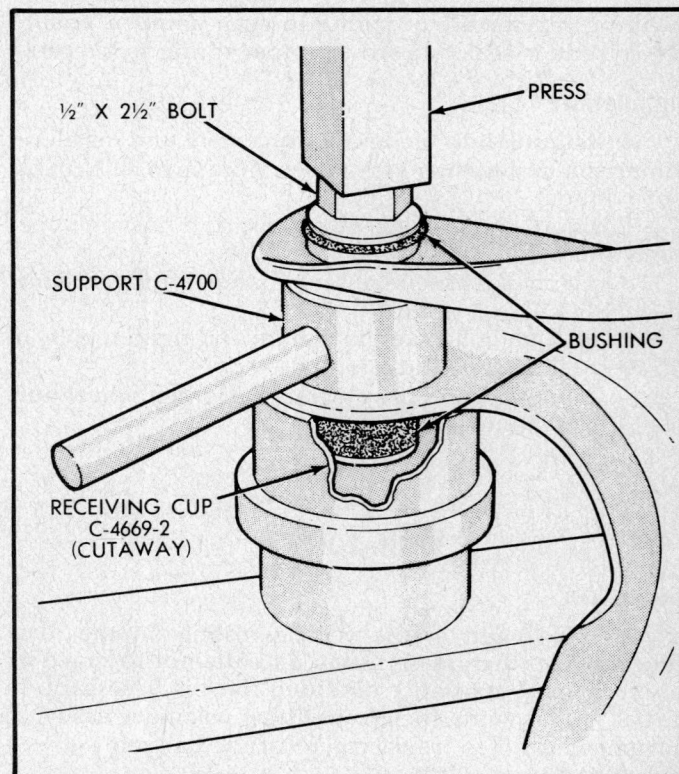

Ball Joint Replacement

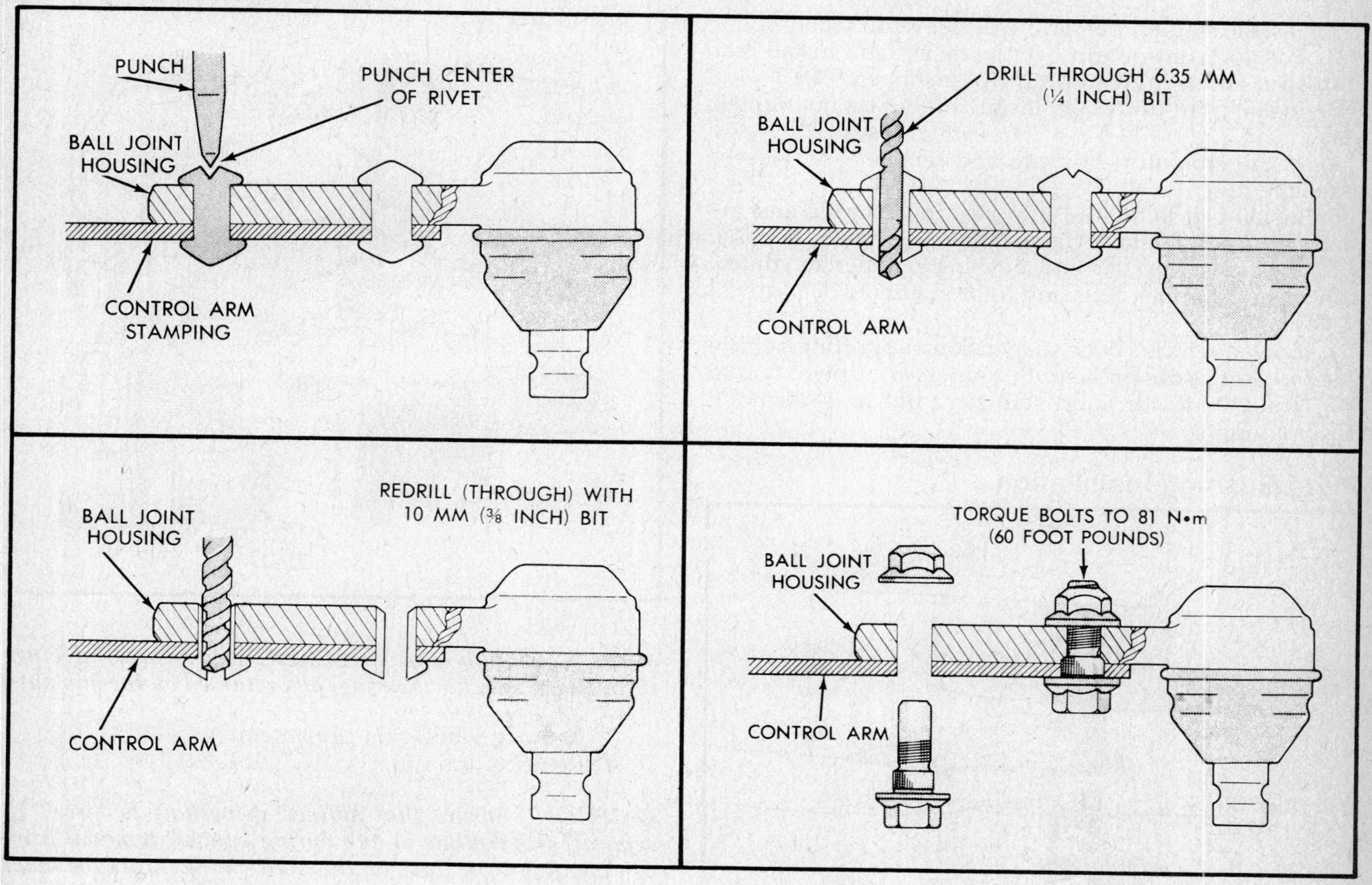

PUNCH

PUNCH CENTER OF RIVET

BALL JOINT HOUSING

CONTROL ARM STAMPING

DRILL THROUGH 6.35 MM (¼ INCH) BIT

BALL JOINT HOUSING

CONTROL ARM

REDRILL (THROUGH) WITH 10 MM (⅜ INCH) BIT

BALL JOINT HOUSING

CONTROL ARM

TORQUE BOLTS TO 81 N•m (60 FOOT POUNDS)

BALL JOINT HOUSING

CONTROL ARM

Lower Control Arm

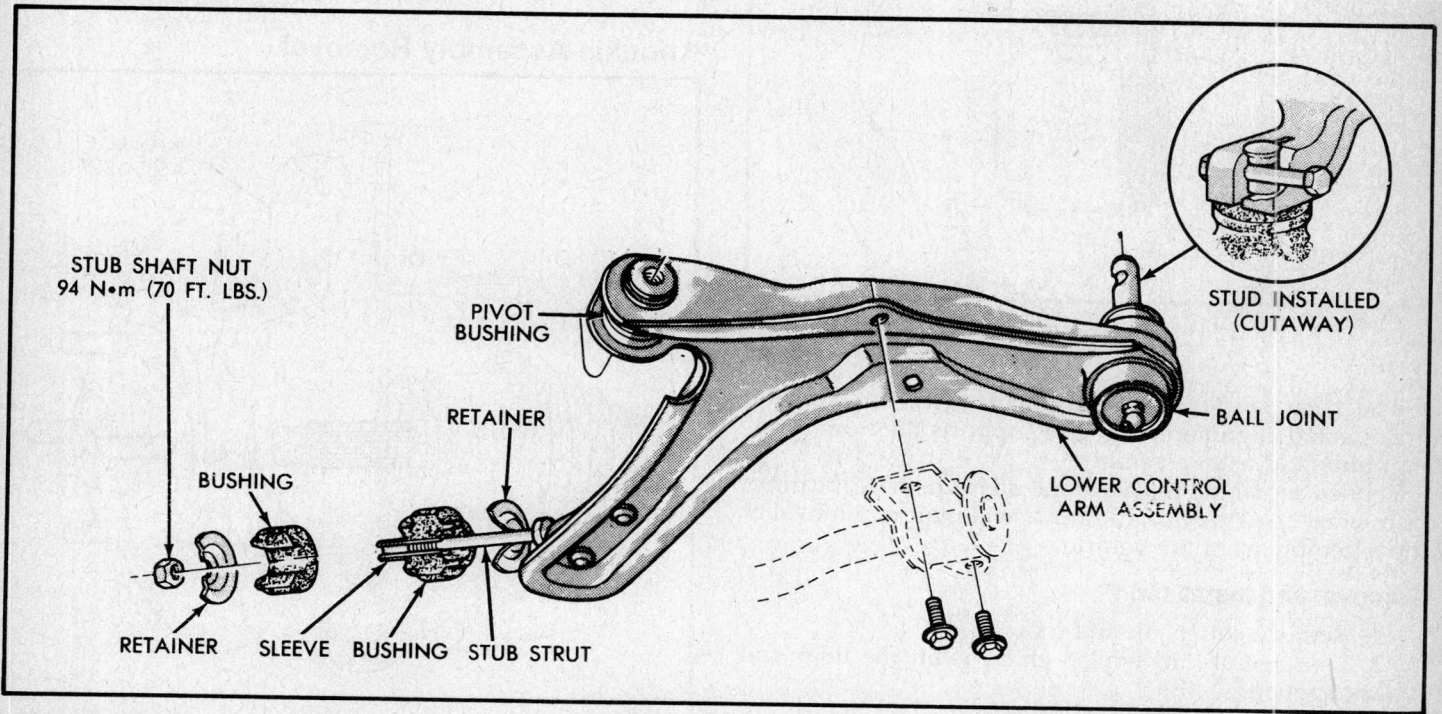

STUB SHAFT NUT 94 N•m (70 FT. LBS.)

PIVOT BUSHING

RETAINER

BUSHING

RETAINER   SLEEVE   BUSHING   STUB STRUT

STUD INSTALLED (CUTAWAY)

BALL JOINT

LOWER CONTROL ARM ASSEMBLY

SUSPENSION

FRONT SUSPENSION-CHRYSLER FRONT DRIVE

Installation

1. Install retainer, bushing and sleeve on stub strut.
2. Position control arm over sway bar and install rear stub strut and front pivot into crossmember.
3. Install front pivot bolt; install nut but do not tighten yet.
4. Install stub strut bushing and retainer and loosely assemble nut.
5. Install ball joint stud into steering knuckle and install clamp bolt. Tighten clamp bolt to 67 N•m (50 ft.-lbs.).
6. Position sway bar end bushing retainer to control arm. Install retainer bolts and tighten nuts to 30 N•m (22 ft.-lbs.).
7. Lower vehicle. With suspension supporting vehicle (control arm at design height), tighten front pivot bolt to 142 N•m (105 ft.-lbs.) and stub strut nut to 94 N•m (70 ft.-lbs.) torque.

Pivot Bushing Installation

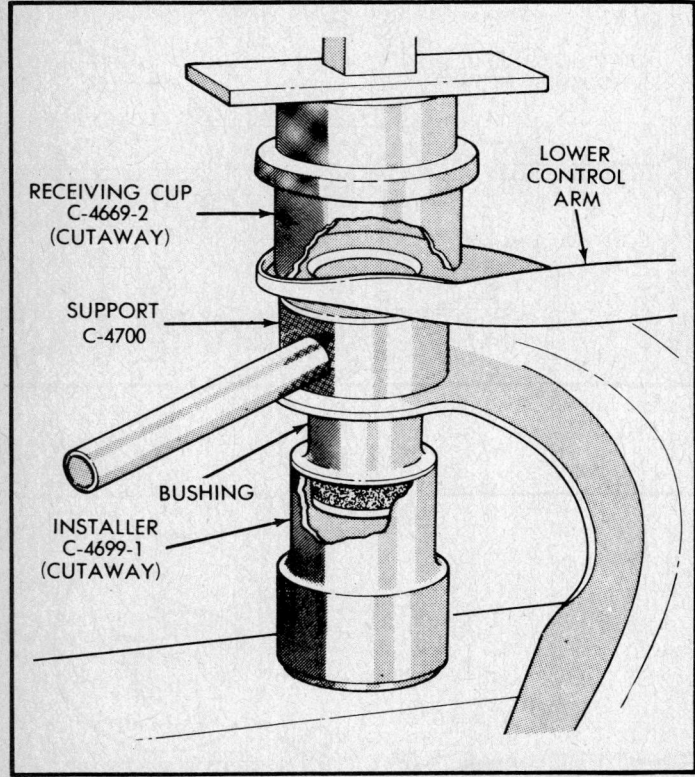

RECEIVING CUP
C-4669-2
(CUTAWAY)

SUPPORT
C-4700

BUSHING

INSTALLER
C-4699-1
(CUTAWAY)

LOWER
CONTROL
ARM

Knuckle

The front suspension knuckle provides for steering, braking and alignment, and also supports the front (driving) hub (and axle) assembly.

Service repair or replacement of front drive bearing, hub, brake dust shield or knuckle will require removal of the assembly from the vehicle.

Removal and Installation

1. Remove cotter pin and lock.
2. Loosen hub nut while vehicle is on the floor and brakes applied.

Steering Knuckle and Bearing

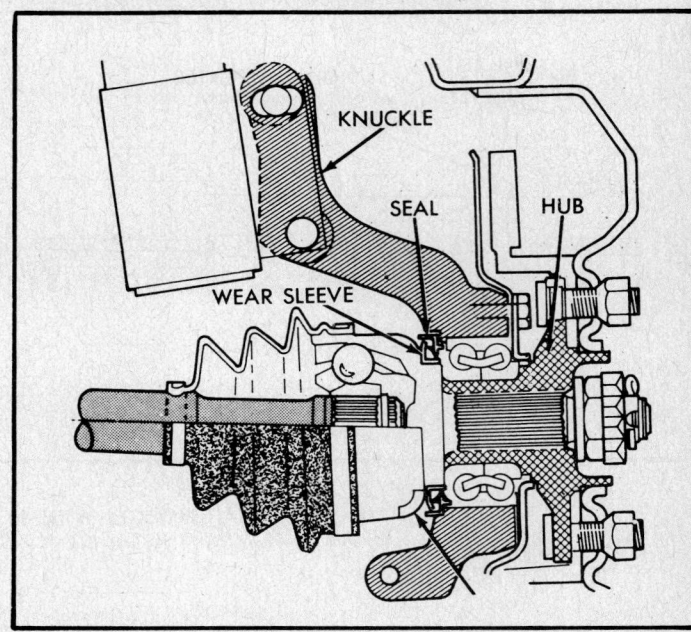

KNUCKLE

SEAL   HUB

WEAR SLEEVE

NOTE The hub and driveshaft are splined together through the knuckle (bearing) and retained by the hub nut.

3. Remove wheel and tire assembly.
4. Remove hub nut.

CAUTION Ensure that splined driveshaft is "free" to separate from spline in hub during knuckle removal from vehicle. A pulling force on the shaft can separate the inner universal joint. Tap lightly with soft brass punch if required.

Knuckle Assembly Removal

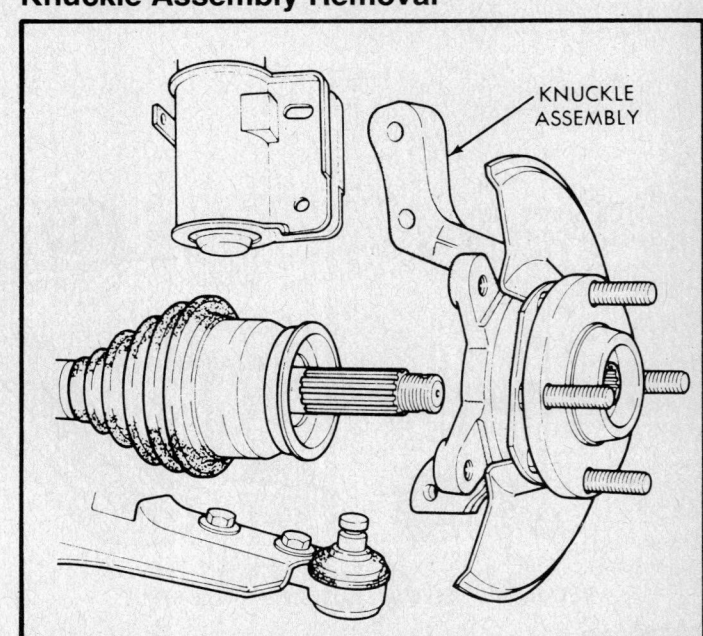

KNUCKLE
ASSEMBLY

Front Suspension Knuckle

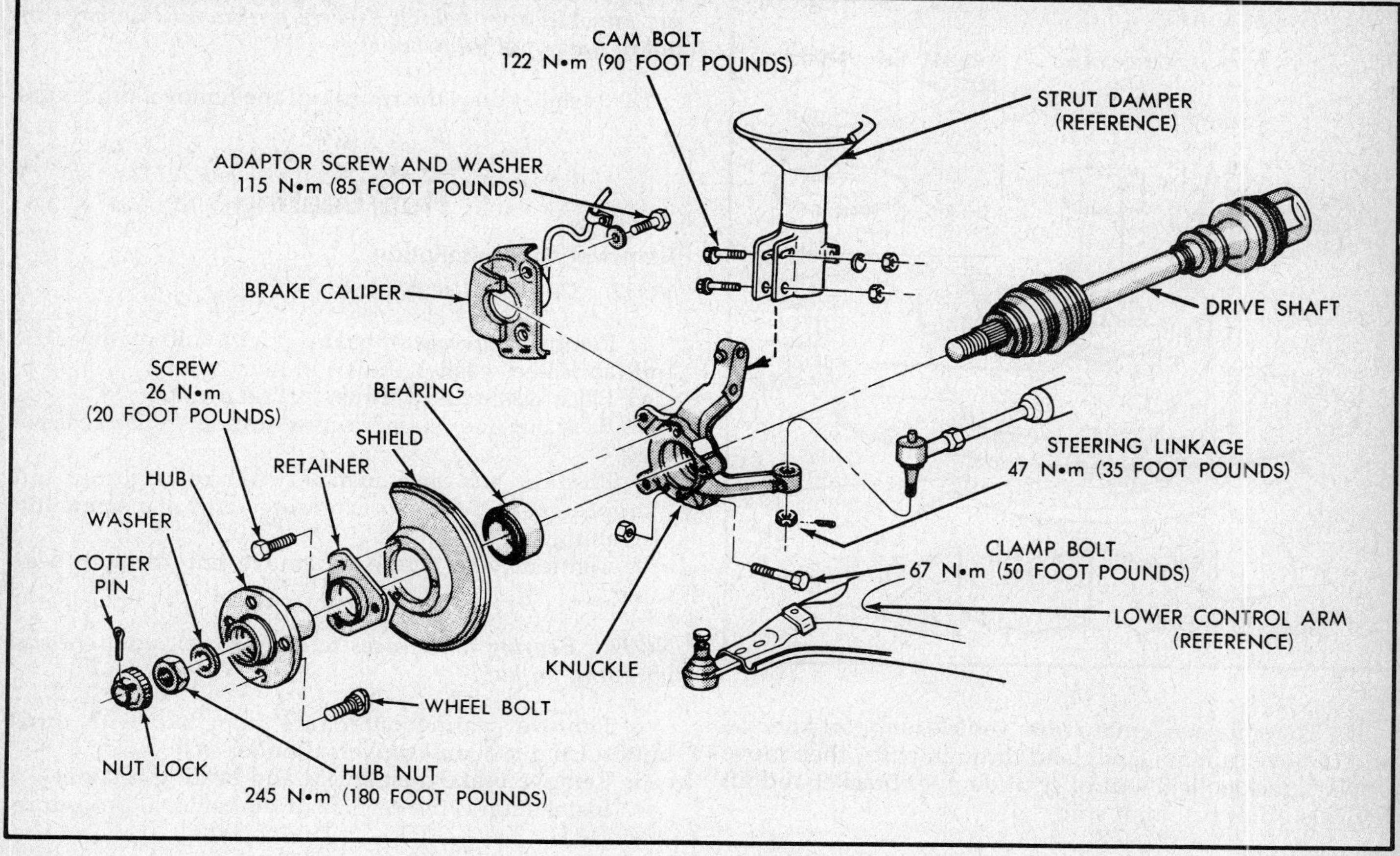

CAM BOLT
122 N•m (90 FOOT POUNDS)

STRUT DAMPER
(REFERENCE)

ADAPTOR SCREW AND WASHER
115 N•m (85 FOOT POUNDS)

BRAKE CALIPER

DRIVE SHAFT

SCREW
26 N•m
(20 FOOT POUNDS)

BEARING

SHIELD

STEERING LINKAGE
47 N•m (35 FOOT POUNDS)

HUB

RETAINER

WASHER

CLAMP BOLT
67 N•m (50 FOOT POUNDS)

COTTER
PIN

LOWER CONTROL ARM
(REFERENCE)

KNUCKLE

WHEEL BOLT

NUT LOCK

HUB NUT
245 N•m (180 FOOT POUNDS)

5. Disconnect tie rod end from steering arm.
6. Disconnect brake hose retainer from strut damper.
7. Remove clamp bolt securing ball joint stud into steering knuckle. Remove brake caliper adaptor screw and washer assemblies.

8. Support caliper with wire hook. Do not allow assembly to hang by brake hose.
9. Remove braking disc (rotor).
10. Mark camber position on upper cam adjusting bolt. Loosen both bolts.

Outboard Inner Race Removal

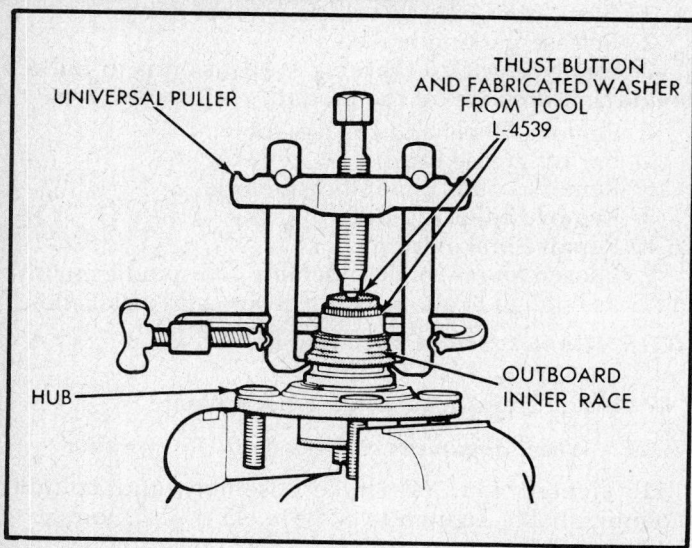

UNIVERSAL PULLER

THUST BUTTON
AND FABRICATED WASHER
FROM TOOL
L-4539

HUB

OUTBOARD
INNER RACE

Press Bearing Out of Knuckle

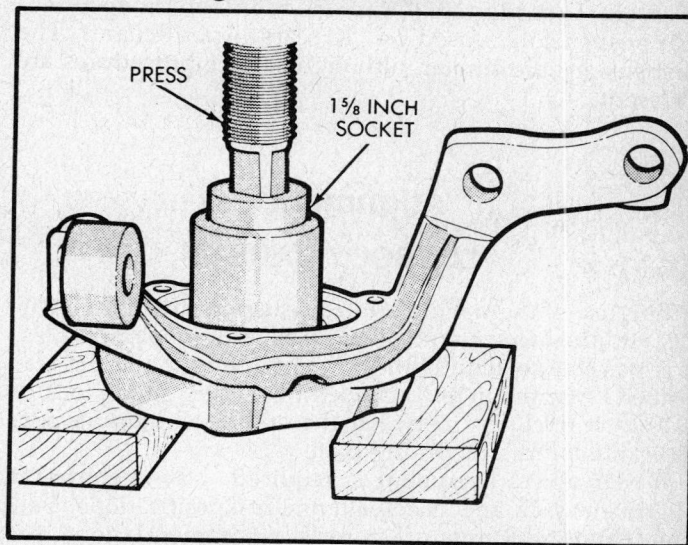

PRESS

1⅝ INCH
SOCKET

Hub Removal

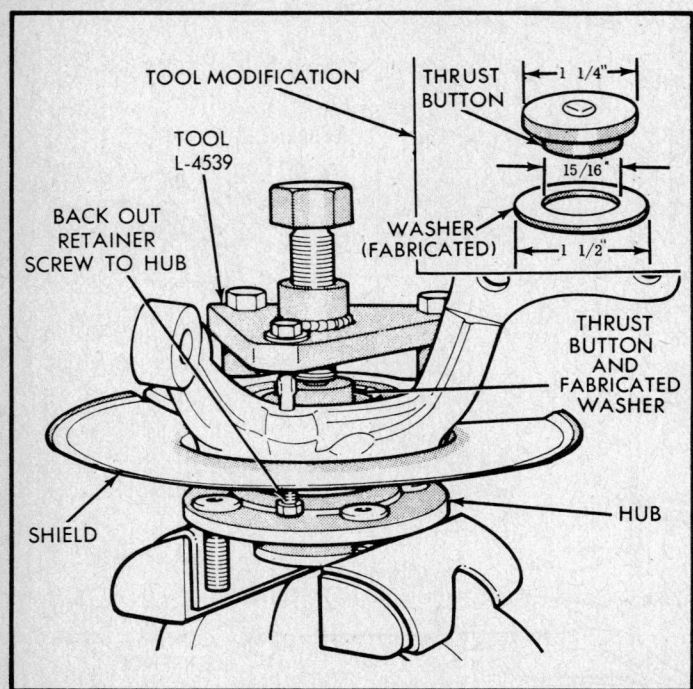

TOOL MODIFICATION

TOOL L-4539

THRUST BUTTON

1 1/4"

15/16"

BACK OUT RETAINER SCREW TO HUB

WASHER (FABRICATED)

1 1/2"

THRUST BUTTON AND FABRICATED WASHER

SHIELD

HUB

11. To remove assembly from vehicle, support knuckle and remove cam adjusting and through bolts, then move upper knuckle "leg" out of strut damper bracket and lift knuckle off of ball joint stud.

CAUTION   Support driveshaft during knuckle removal. Do not allow driveshaft to "hang" after separating steering knuckle from vehicle (severe angles will damage inboard universal joint boot).

12. Installation is the reverse of the removal procedure.

Hub/Bearing

Removal and Installation
NOTE   Do not reuse bearing.

1. Remove hub (out of bearing) with hub remover tool and fabricated washer shown in illustration.
   a. Place washer and thrust button on hub.
   b. Back out one retainer screw-to-hub, as far as it will go.
   c. Position tool and install two screws firmly into tapped brake adaption extensions and one screw into retaining screw threads.
   d. Tighten press screw to remove hub through bearing.

NOTE   Bearing inner races will separate; outboard race will stay on hub.

2. Remove bearing outer race from hub with thrust button from tool and universal puller.
3. Remove brake dust shield and bearing retainer.
4. Installation is the reverse of the removal procedure.

REAR SUSPENSION—CHRYSLER FRONT DRIVE

Introduction

Chrysler front drive cars have two types of rear suspension systems. A semi-independent rear suspension is used on "L" body cars (Omni-Horizon); an independent rear suspension is used on "K" cars (Aries/Reliant). The suspensions are similar, although service procedures are different.

Alignment

"L" BODY CARS

Because of the trailing arm rear suspension of the vehicle, and the incorporation of stub axles or wheel spindles, it is possible to align both the camber and toe of the rear wheels. Alignment is controlled by adding shim stock of .010-inch thickness between the spindle mounting surface and spindle mounting plate.

If rear wheel alignment is required, place vehicle on alignment rack and check alignment specifications. Follow equipment manufacturer's recommendations for their equipment. Maintain rear alignment within Chrysler corporation recommendations.

Installation of Rear Alignment Shims

1. Block front tires so vehicle will not move.
2. Release parking brake.
3. Hoist vehicle so that rear suspension is in full rebound and tires are off the ground.
4. Remove wheel and tire assembly.
5. Pry off grease cap.
6. Remove cotter pin and castle lock.
7. Remove adjusting nut.
8. Remove brake drum.
9. Loosen four (4) brake assembly and spindle mounting bolts enough to allow clearance for shim installation.

NOTE   Do not remove mounting bolts.

10. Install shims for desired wheel change.

NOTE   Wheel alignment changes by 0° 18' per shim.

11. Tighten four (4) brake assembly and spindle mounting bolts. Tighten to 60 N•m (45 ft.-lbs.) torque.
12. Install brake drum.

L Body Rear Suspension—Horizon/Omni

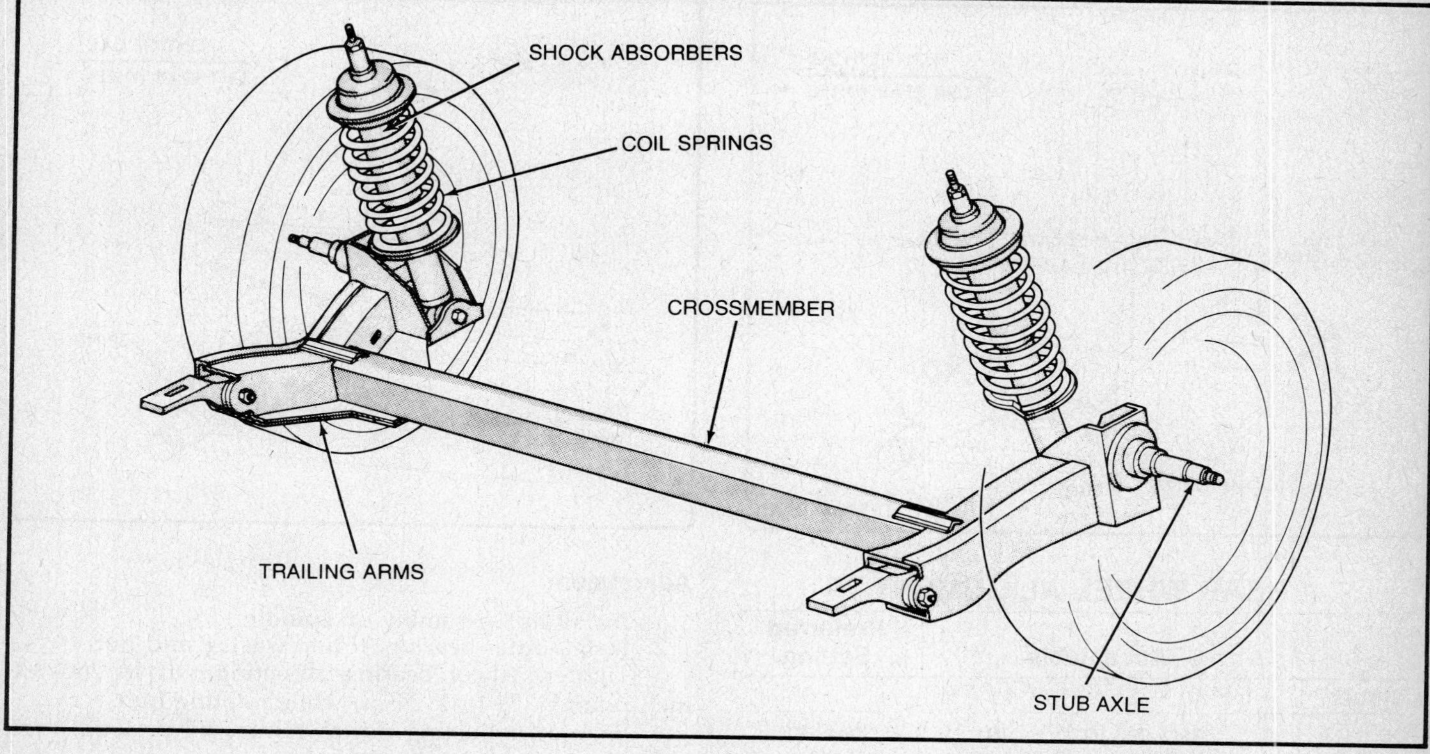

SHOCK ABSORBERS

COIL SPRINGS

CROSSMEMBER

TRAILING ARMS

STUB AXLE

13. Install washer and nut. Tighten adjusting nut to 27–34 N·m (240–300 in.-lbs.) while rotating wheel. Back off adjusting nut with wrench to completely release bearing preload. Finger-tighten adjusting nut.

14. Position nut lock with one pair of slots in line with cotter pin hole. Install cotter pin. The end play should be .025–.076 mm (.001–.003 in.). Clean and install grease cap.

15. Install wheel and tire assembly. Tighten wheel nuts to 108 N·m (80 ft.-lbs.) torque.

16. Lower vehicle.

17. Recheck alignment specifications.

Shim Installation for Toe In

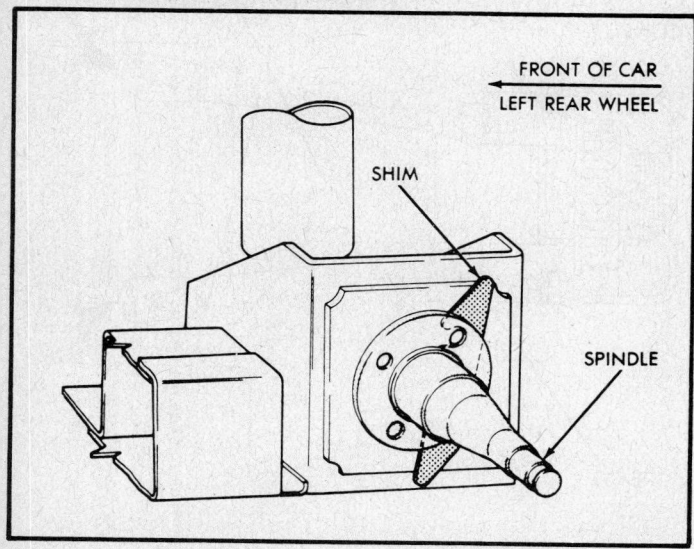

FRONT OF CAR

LEFT REAR WHEEL

SHIM

SPINDLE

Shim Installation for Negative Camber

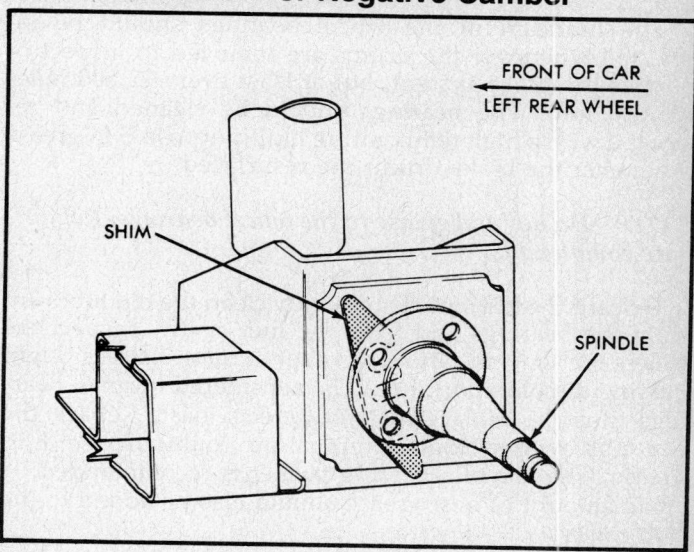

FRONT OF CAR

LEFT REAR WHEEL

SHIM

SPINDLE

SUSPENSION
REAR SUSPENSION-CHRYSLER FRONT DRIVE

Shim Installation for Toe Out

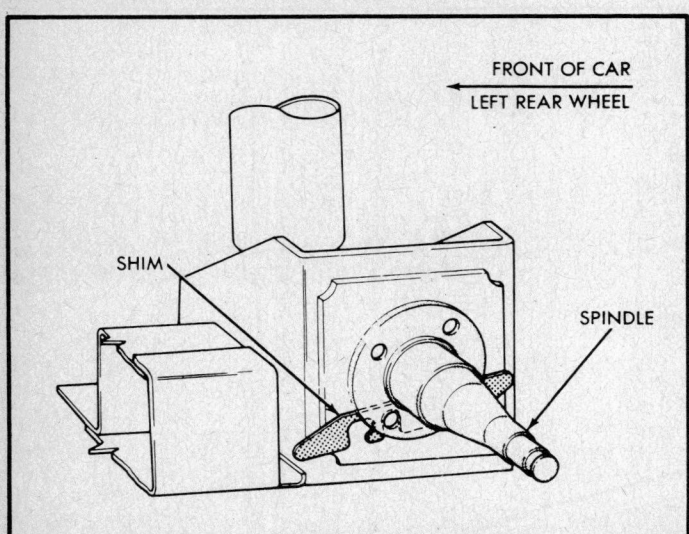

Shim Installation for Positive Camber

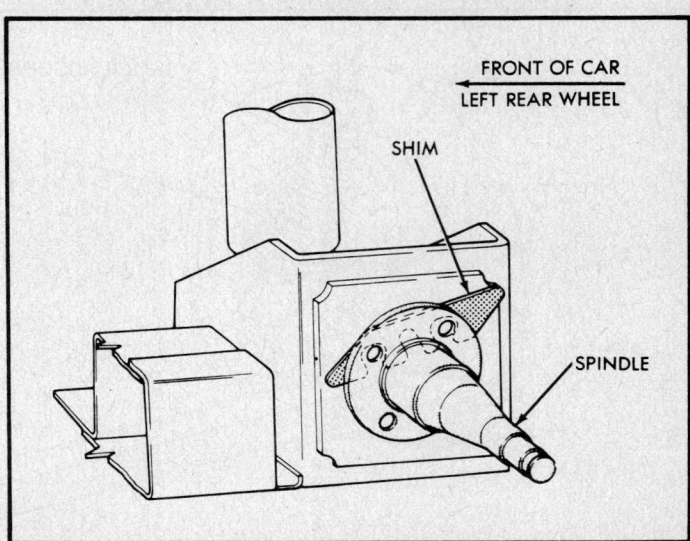

REAR WHEEL ALIGNMENT

	Acceptable	Preferred Setting
Camber	−1.5° to −.5° (−1½° to −½°)	−1.0°
Toe	5/32″ out to 11/32″ in 0.3° out to 0.7° in	3/32″ in 0.2° in

"K" BODY CARS

Camber and toe alignment of (stub) axle is adjustable; see specifications. Alignment adjustment, if required, is made by adding shims between the spindle and mounting plate.

Wheel Bearings
"L" BODY CARS

Lubrication

The lubricant in the wheel bearings should be inspected whenever the drums are removed to inspect or service the brake system, but at least every 22,500 miles (36,000 km). The bearings should be cleaned and re-packed with a high temperature multipurpose E.P. grease whenever the brake drums are resurfaced.

NOTE   Do not add grease to the wheel bearings. Relubricate completely.

Discard the old seal. Thoroughly clean the old lubricant from the bearings and from the hub cavity. Inspect the rollers for signs of pitting or other surface distress. Light bearing discoloration should be considered normal. Bearings must be replaced if any defects exist. Repack the bearings with a high temperature multipurpose E.P. grease. The use of a bearing packer is recommended. A small amount of new grease should also be added to the hub cavity.

Adjustment

1. Install hub assembly on spindle.
2. Install outer bearing, thrust washer and nut.
3. Tighten wheel bearing adjusting nut to 240–300 inch-pounds (31 to 38 N•m) while rotating hub.
4. Back off adjusting nut to release all preload, then tighten adjusting nut finger-tight.
5. Position lock on nut with one pair of slots in line with cotter pin hole. Install cotter pin.
6. Install grease cap and wheel and tire assemblies.

Wheel Bearing Lubrication

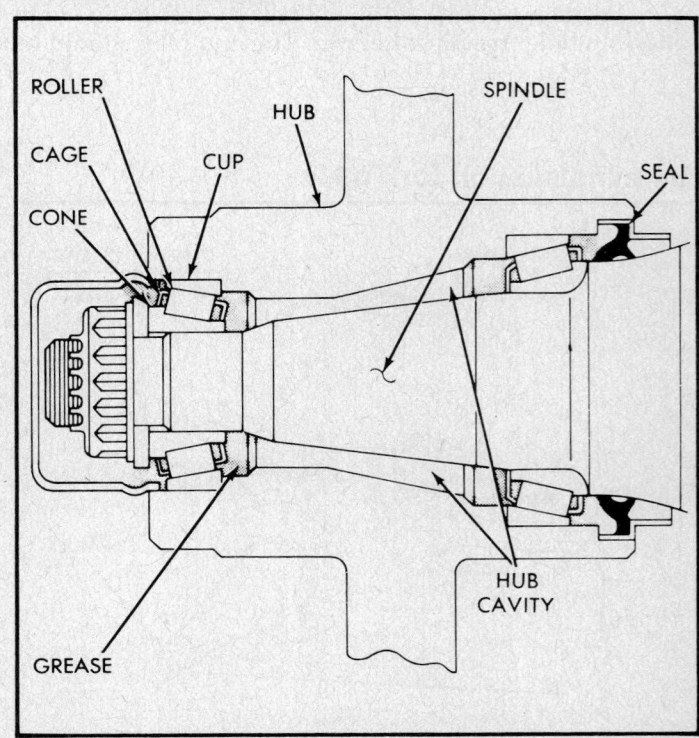

Rear Wheel Bearing

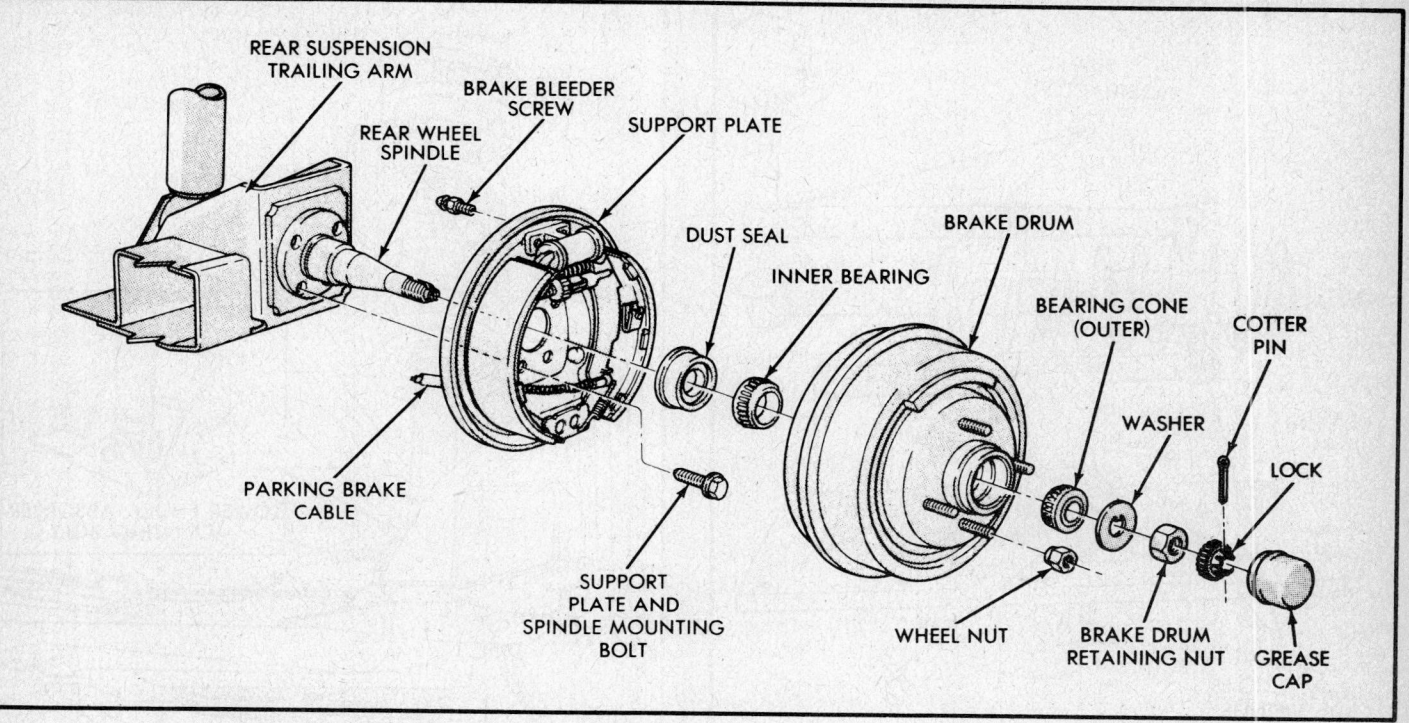

REAR SUSPENSION TRAILING ARM — BRAKE BLEEDER SCREW — REAR WHEEL SPINDLE — SUPPORT PLATE — DUST SEAL — INNER BEARING — BRAKE DRUM — BEARING CONE (OUTER) — COTTER PIN — WASHER — LOCK — PARKING BRAKE CABLE — SUPPORT PLATE AND SPINDLE MOUNTING BOLT — WHEEL NUT — BRAKE DRUM RETAINING NUT — GREASE CAP

"K" BODY CARS

Lubrication

The lubricant in the rear wheel bearings should be inspected whenever the drums are removed to inspect or service the brake system, or at least every 48,000 kilometres (30,000 miles). Bearings should be cleaned and repacked with a high temperature multipurpose E.P. grease whenever the brake drums are resurfaced.

NOTE Do not add grease to the wheel bearings. Relubricate completely.

Discard the old seal. Thoroughly clean the old lubricant from the bearings and from the hub cavity.

Inspect the rollers for signs of pitting or other surface distress. Light bearing discoloration should be considered normal. Bearings must be replaced if any defects exist. Repack the bearings with a high temperature multipurpose E.P. grease. Use of a bearing packer is also recommended. A small amount of new grease should also be added to the hub cavity.

Adjustment

1. Tighten adjusting nut to 27–34 N•m (240–300 in.-lbs.) torque, while rotating wheel.
2. Stop rotation and back off adjusting nut with wrench to completely release bearing preload.
3. Finger-tighten adjusting nut.
4. Position nut lock with one pair of slots in line with cotter pin hole.
5. Install cotter pin.

6. The end-play should be .025–.076 mm (.001–.003 in.).
7. Clean and install grease cap.
8. Install wheel and tire assembly.

Shock Absorber and Coil Spring Assembly
"L" BODY CARS

Removal

1. Locate upper shock absorber mounting nut protective cap inside of vehicle at upper rear wheel well area. (On two-door models, remove lower rear quarter trim panel.)
2. Unsnap cap. Use care to retain sound isolation material inside cap.
3. Remove upper shock absorber mounting nut, isolator retainer, and upper isolator. Remove lower shock absorber mounting bolt.
4. Remove shock absorber and coil spring assembly from trailing arm bracket. The shock absorber and coil spring assembly should now be free of vehicle.
5. Place coil spring compressor tool on coil spring and place in vise.

CAUTION Always grip 4 or 5 coils of spring in retractors. Never extend retractors beyond 9¼ inches.

6. Tighten spring retractors *evenly* until pressure is relieved from upper spring seat.
7. Hold flat at end of shock rod. Loosen retaining nut.

Retract Coil Spring

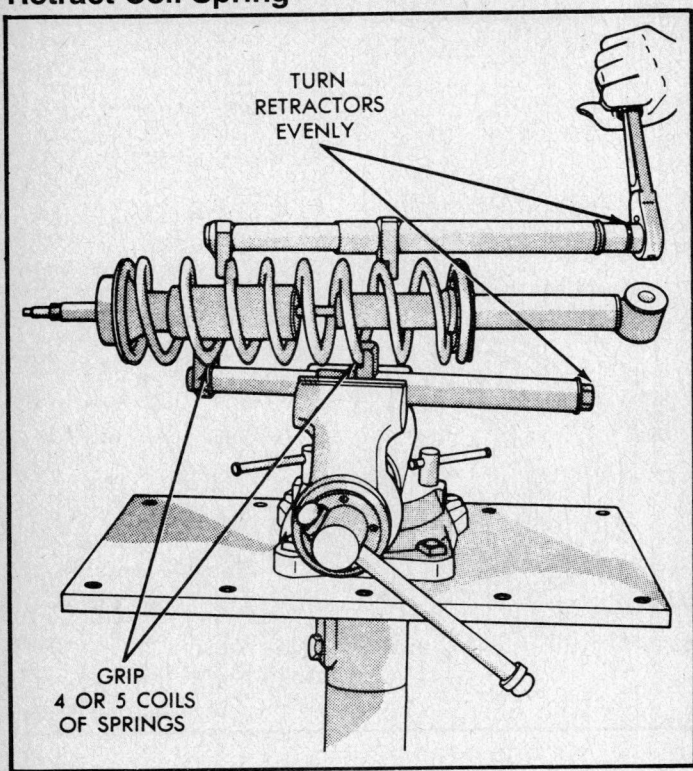

CAUTION *Be very careful when loosening retaining nut. If coil spring is not compressed enough, serious injury could occur when retaining nut is loosened.*

8. Remove lower isolator, shock rod sleeve, and upper spring seat.

9. Carefully remove shock absorber from coil spring.

Installation

1. Install lower spring seat on shock absorber. Orient seat recess to centerline of lower bushing.

2. Install dust shield and jounce bumper on shock absorber.

3. Carefully slip the unit inside the coil spring. Install upper spring seat. Make sure that the leveled surface on both spring seats are in position against the ends of the coil spring.

4. Install sleeve on shock rod. Install retaining nut on end of shock rod. Tighten retaining nut to 27 N•m (20 ft.-lbs.) torque.

5. Carefully loosen both coil spring retractors *evenly* and remove retractors from unit.

6. Install lower end of unit in trailing arm bracket. Insert bolt. Finger-tighten only. Make sure that upper end of unit is in proper hole at top of wheel well.

7. Tighten lower shock absorber bolt to 55 N•m (40 ft.-lbs.) torque.

8. Install upper isolator, isolator retainer, and upper mounting nut. Hold shock absorber rod end and tighten nut to 27 N•m (20 ft.-lbs.) torque.

9. Install sound isolation material and snap protective cap on securely.

Lower Shock Absorber Mounting Bolt

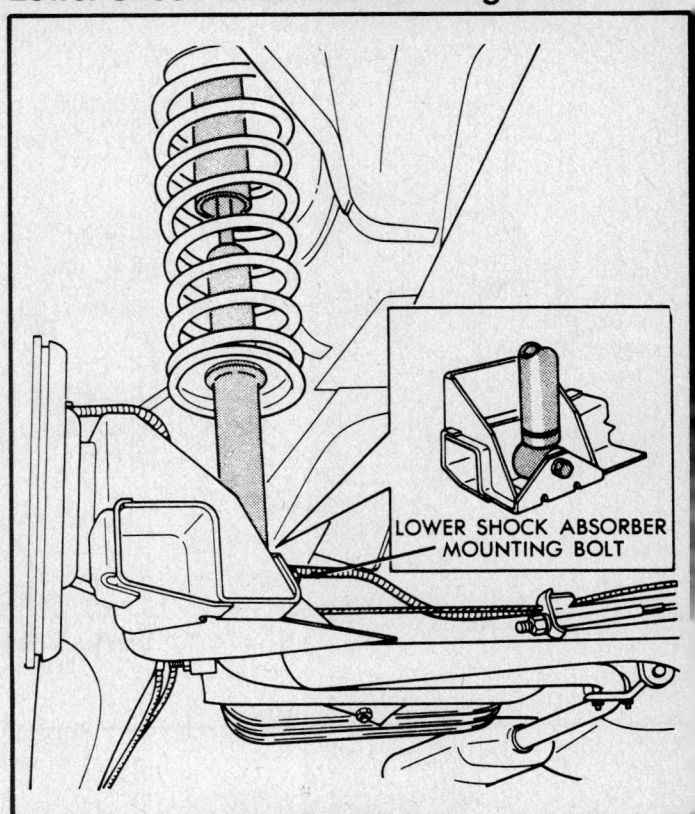

Loosen Retaining Nut

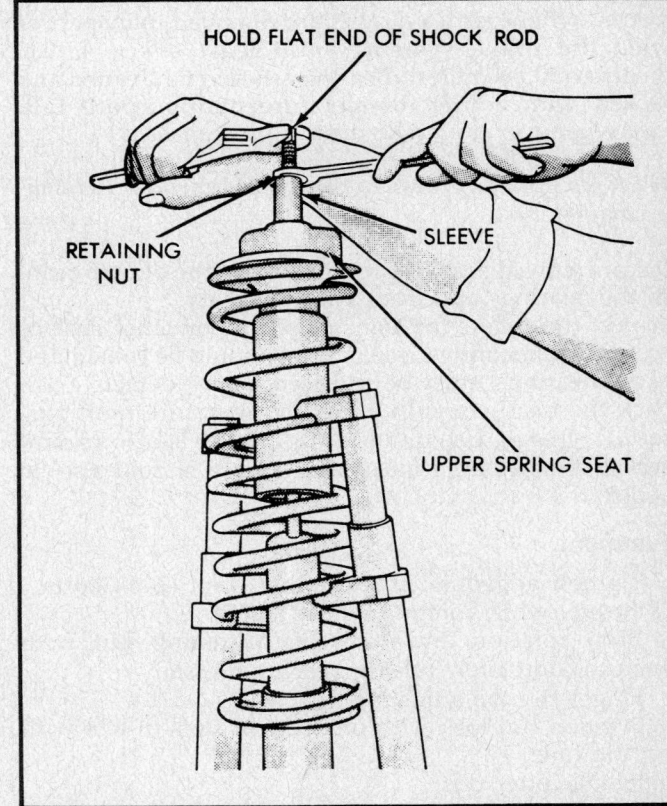

Upper Shock Absorber Mounting

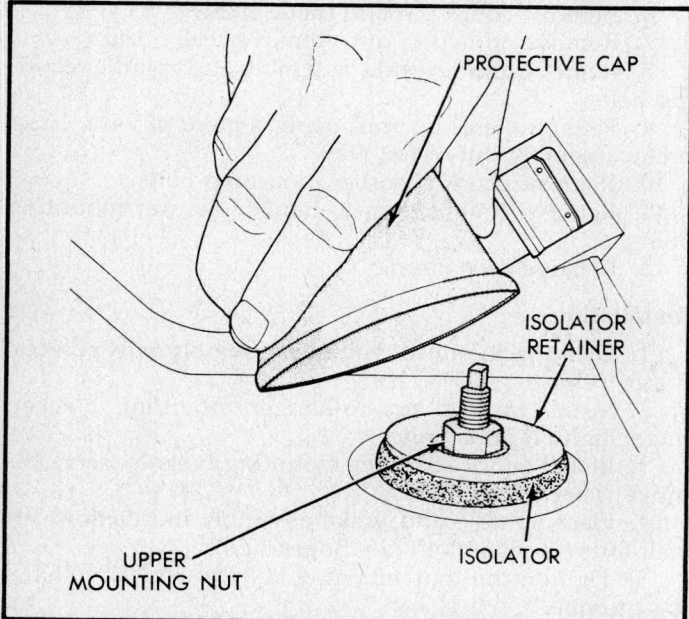

PROTECTIVE CAP

ISOLATOR RETAINER

UPPER MOUNTING NUT

ISOLATOR

Shock Absorbers

"K" BODY CARS

Removal

1. Support axle and remove wheel and tire assembly.
2. Remove upper and lower shock absorber fasteners and remove shock absorbers.

Installation

1. Position shock absorber and install fasteners; loosely assemble lower fastener. Tighten upper fastener to 54 N•m (40 foot-pounds).
2. Install wheel and tire assembly, tighten wheel stud nuts to 108 N•m (80 foot-pounds). Lower vehicle to ground.
3. With suspension supporting vehicle, tighten lower shock absorber fastener to 54 N•m (40 ft.-lbs.).

Coil Springs and Jounce Bumper

"K" BODY CARS

Removal

1. Lift vehicle.
2. Support axle assembly and remove both lower shock absorber attaching bolts.
3. Lower axle assembly until spring and spring upper isolator can be removed (do not stretch brake hose).
4. Remove two screws holding jounce bumper assembly to rail. Remove jounce bumper assembly.

Installation

1. Position jounce bumper to rail. Install and tighten attaching screws to 7 N•m (70 in.-lbs.).

2. Install isolator over jounce bumper and install spring.
3. Raise axle and loosely assemble both shock absorber-to-axle screws. Remove axle support and lower vehicle.
4. With suspension supporting vehicle, tighten both shock absorber attaching screws to 54 N•m (40 ft.-lbs.).

Rear Axle Assembly

"L" BODY CARS ONLY

Removal

NOTE *Support the car on the rear crossmember; let the axle hang down.*

1. Remove wheel and tire assembly.
2. Remove brake fittings and retaining clips holding flexible brake line.
3. Remove parking brake cable adjusting connection nut.
4. Release both parking brake cables from brackets by slipping ball-end of cables through brake connectors. Pull parking brake cable through bracket.

Rear Wheel Components

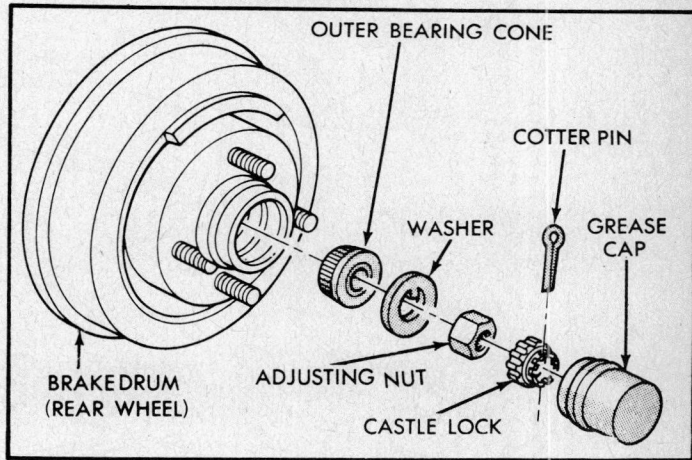

OUTER BEARING CONE

COTTER PIN

WASHER

GREASE CAP

BRAKE DRUM (REAR WHEEL)

ADJUSTING NUT

CASTLE LOCK

Brake Assembly and Spindle

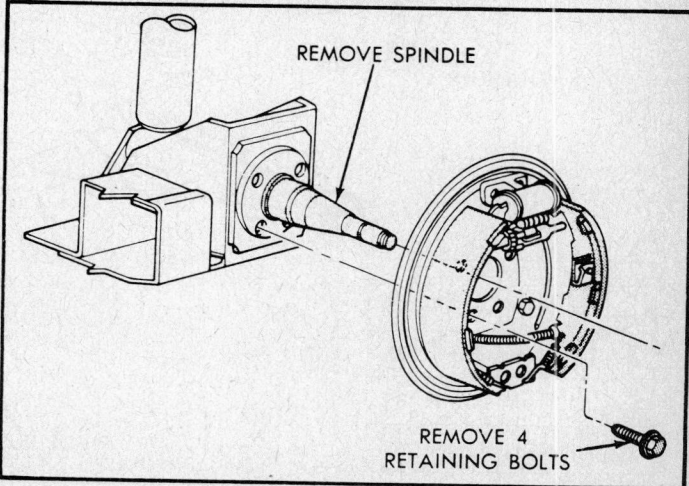

REMOVE SPINDLE

REMOVE 4 RETAINING BOLTS

SUSPENSION

REAR SUSPENSION-CHRYSLER FRONT DRIVE

K Car Trailing Arms Removal

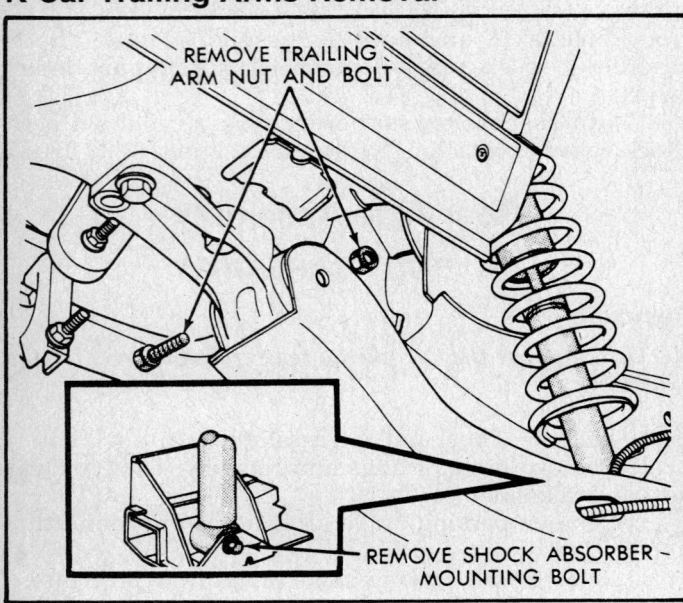

REMOVE TRAILING ARM NUT AND BOLT

REMOVE SHOCK ABSORBER MOUNTING BOLT

5. Pry off grease cap.
6. Remove cotter pin and castle lock.
7. Remove adjusting nut. Remove brake drum.
8. Remove four (4) brake assembly and spindle retaining bolts.
9. Set spindle aside and, using a piece of wire, hang brake assembly out of the way.
10. Remove shock absorber mounting bolts.
11. Remove trailing arm-to-hanger bracket mounting bolt.
12. Remove axle assembly.

Installation

1. Using jacks, raise rear axle assembly into position under vehicle.
2. Install trailing arm-to-hanger mounting bracket; finger-tighten bolts only.
3. Install shock absorber mounting bolts loosely. Remove jacks.
4. Place spindle and brake assembly in position. Install four (4) retaining bolts finger-tight.
5. Tighten the four retaining bolts to 60 N•m (45 ft.-lbs.) torque.

K Car Flex Arm Rear Suspension

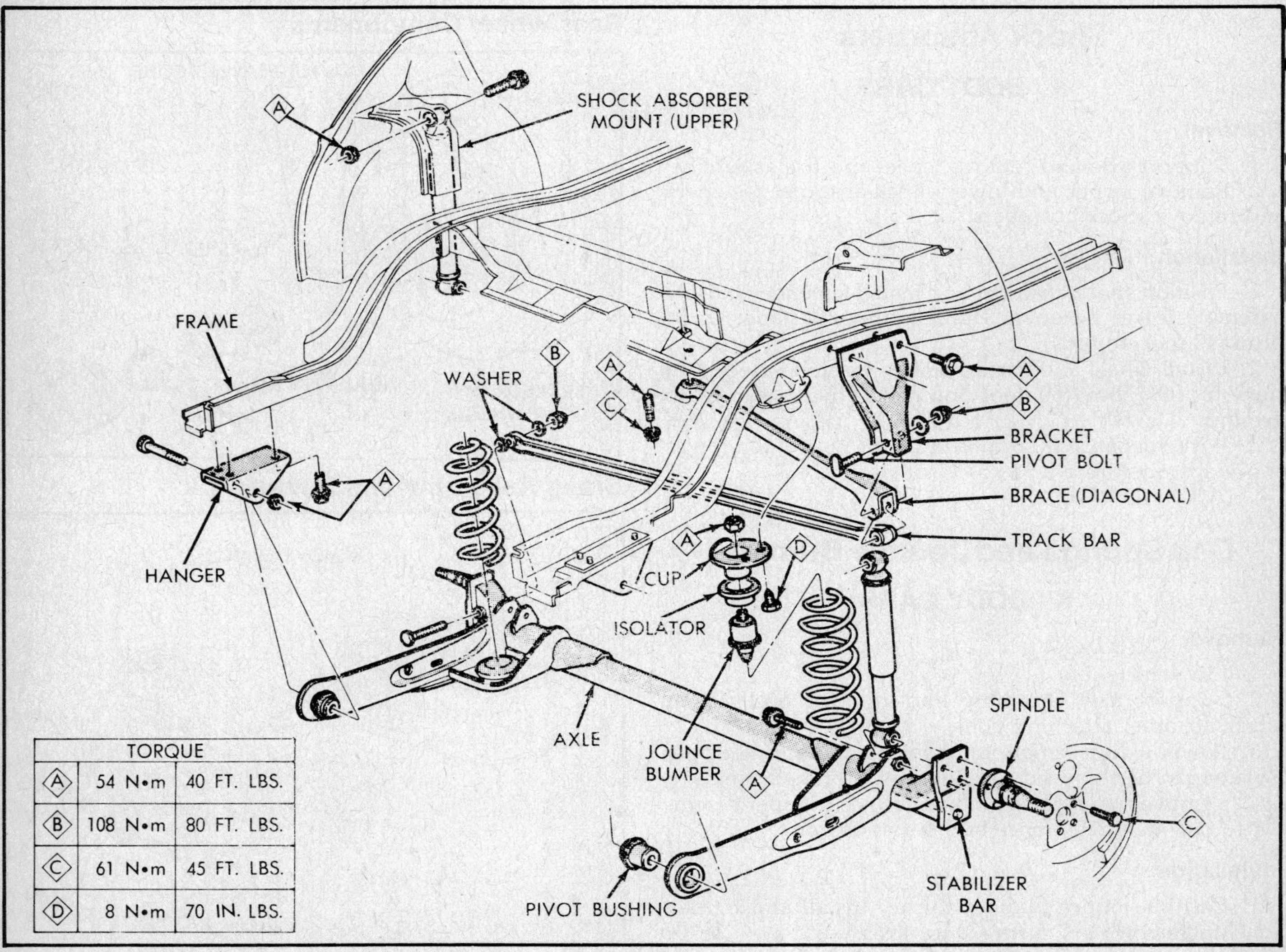

SHOCK ABSORBER MOUNT (UPPER)

FRAME

WASHER

HANGER

BRACKET
PIVOT BOLT
BRACE (DIAGONAL)
TRACK BAR

CUP
ISOLATOR
AXLE
JOUNCE BUMPER
SPINDLE

PIVOT BUSHING
STABILIZER BAR

TORQUE		
Ⓐ	54 N•m	40 FT. LBS.
Ⓑ	108 N•m	80 FT. LBS.
Ⓒ	61 N•m	45 FT. LBS.
Ⓓ	8 N•m	70 IN. LBS.

K Car Flex Arm Rear Suspension

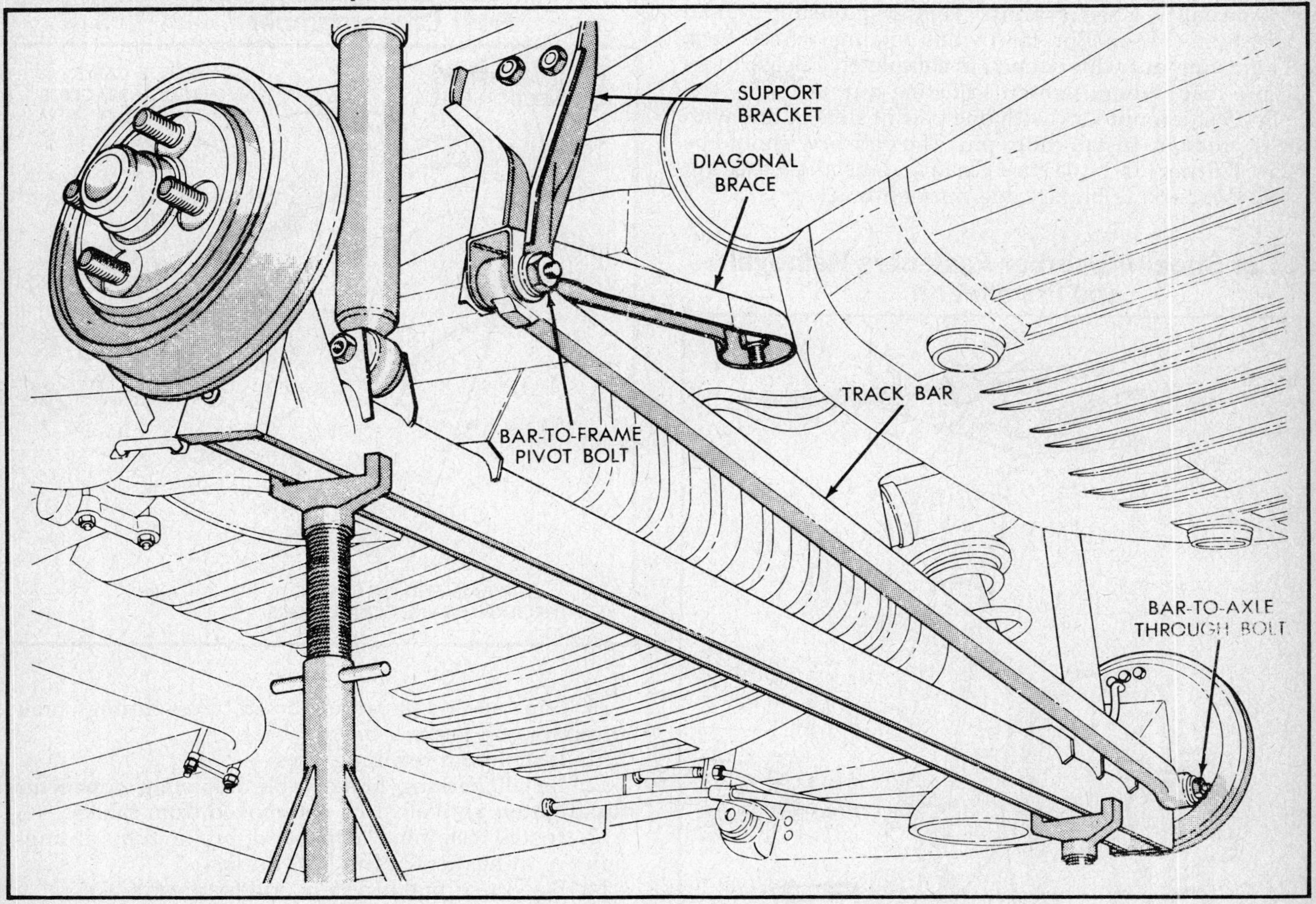

SUPPORT BRACKET

DIAGONAL BRACE

TRACK BAR

BAR-TO-FRAME PIVOT BOLT

BAR-TO-AXLE THROUGH BOLT

K Car Spring and Jounce Bumper

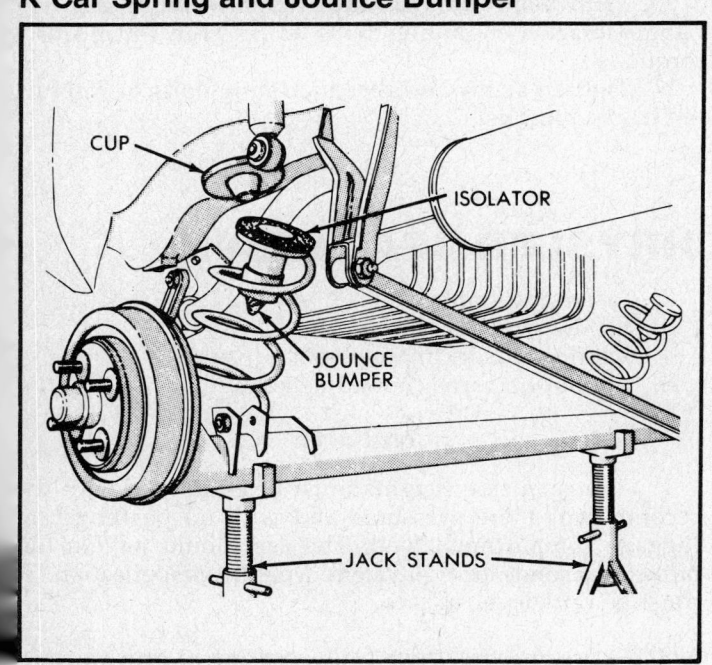

CUP

ISOLATOR

JOUNCE BUMPER

JACK STANDS

Rear Wheel Bearing Assembly

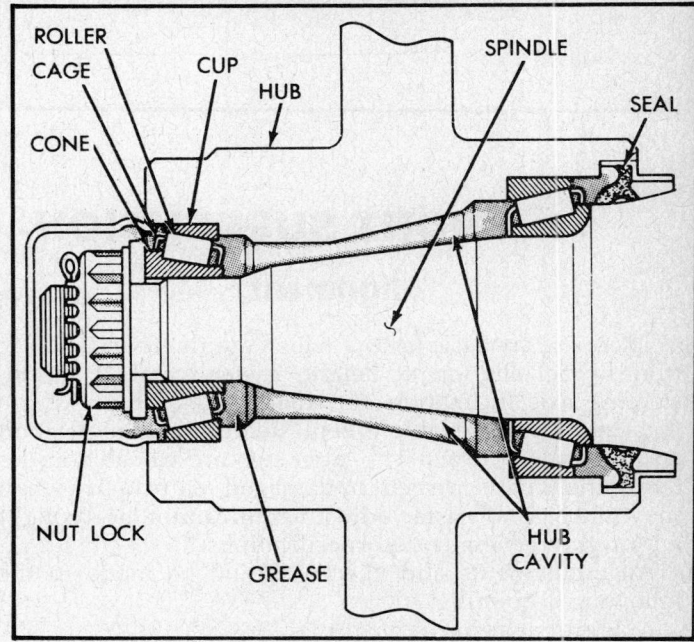

ROLLER CAGE

CUP

HUB

SPINDLE

SEAL

CONE

NUT LOCK

GREASE

HUB CAVITY

6. Install brake drum.

7. Install washer and nut. Tighten adjusting nut to 27–34 N•m (240–300 in.-lbs.) while rotating wheel. Back off adjusting nut with wrench to completely release bearing pre-load. Finger-tighten adjusting nut.

8. Position nut lock with one pair of slots in line with cotter pin hole. Install cotter pin. The end-play should be .025–.076 mm (.001–.003 in). Clean and install grease cap.

9. Put parking brake cable through bracket.

K Car Shock Absorber Fasteners Removal and Installation

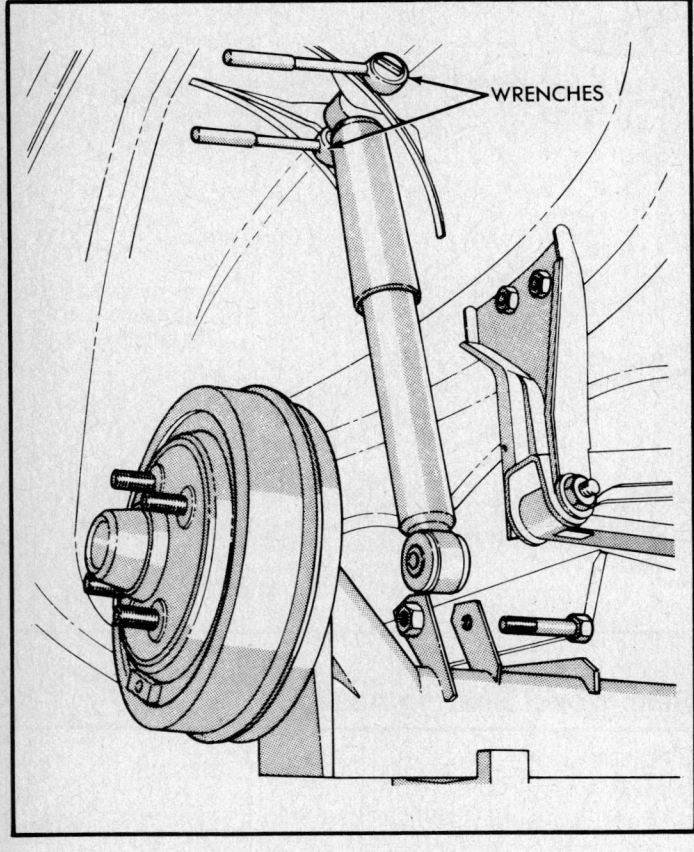

WRENCHES

Disassemble Parking Brake Cables at Rear Crossmember

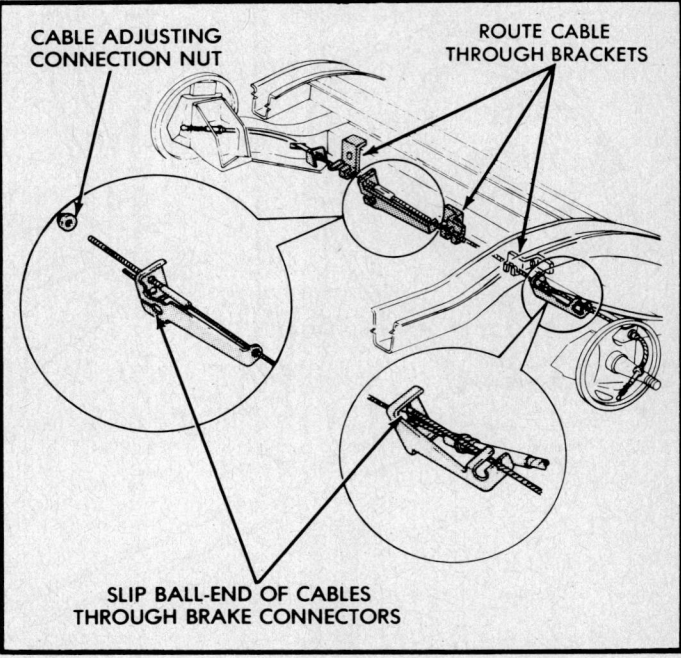

CABLE ADJUSTING CONNECTION NUT

ROUTE CABLE THROUGH BRACKETS

SLIP BALL-END OF CABLES THROUGH BRAKE CONNECTORS

10. Slip ball-end of parking brake cables through brake connectors on parking brake bracket.

11. Install both retaining clips.

12. Install parking brake cable adjusting connection nut. Tighten until all slack is removed from cables.

13. Install retaining clips and brake tube fittings. Tighten fittings to 12 N•m (110 in.-lbs.).

14. Bleed rear brake system and readjust brakes.

15. Install wheel and tire assembly. Tighten wheel nuts to 108 N•m (80 ft.-lbs.) torque.

16. With vehicle on ground, tighten trailing arm-to-hanger bracket mounting bolts to 55 N•m (40 ft.-lbs.) torque.

17. Tighten shock absorber mounting bolts to 55 N•m (40 ft.-lbs.) torque.

FRONT SUSPENSION—CHRYSLER REAR DRIVE

Alignment

There are six basic factors which are the foundation to front wheel alignment: height, caster, camber, toe-in, steering axis inclination and toe-out on turns. All are mechanically adjustable except steering axis inclination and toe-out on turns. The latter two are valuable in determining if parts are bent or damaged, particularly when the camber and caster adjustments cannot be brought within the recommended specifications.

All adjustments and checks should be made in the following sequence.

1. Front suspension height
2. Caster and camber
3. Toe-in
4. Steering axis inclination (not adjustable)
5. Toe-out on turns (not adjustable)

HEIGHT

Front suspension heights must be measured with the recommended tire pressures and with no passenger or luggage compartment load. The car should have a full tank of gasoline or equivalent weight compensation. It must be on a level surface.

NOTE See Specifications for measurement procedures.

Transverse Torsion Bar Suspension

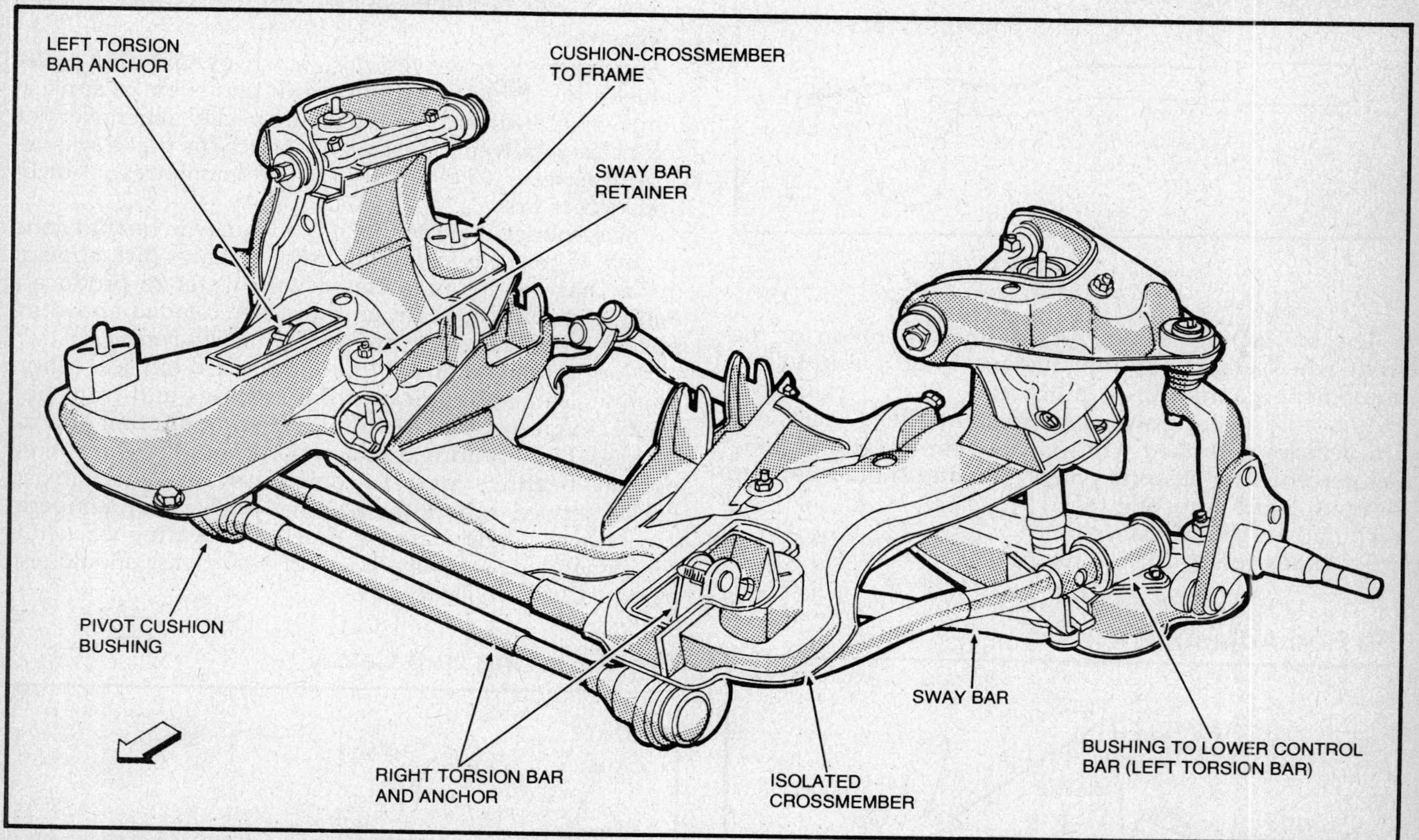

LEFT TORSION
BAR ANCHOR

CUSHION-CROSSMEMBER
TO FRAME

SWAY BAR
RETAINER

PIVOT CUSHION
BUSHING

RIGHT TORSION BAR
AND ANCHOR

ISOLATED
CROSSMEMBER

SWAY BAR

BUSHING TO LOWER CONTROL
BAR (LEFT TORSION BAR)

Front suspension for carlines H, N, F, G and B

CAMBER AND CASTER

1. Prepare vehicle for measuring wheel alignment.
2. Determine initial camber and caster readings to confirm variance to specifications before loosening pivot bar bolts.
3. Remove foreign material from exposed threads of pivot bar bolts.
4. Loosen nuts slightly holding pivot (caster/camber) bar. Slightly loosening the pivot bar nuts will allow the upper control arm to be repositioned without slipping to end of adjustment slots.
5. Position claw of tool on pivot bar and pin of tool into holes provided in tower or bracket. Make adjustments by moving pivot bar in or out. Adjust as follows:

Camber: Move both ends of upper control arm in or out exactly equal amounts. Camber settings should be held as close as possible to "preferred" setting.

Caster: Moving one end of the bar will change caster (and camber). To preserve camber while adjusting caster, move each end of the upper control arm pivot bar exactly equal amounts in opposite directions. For example, to increase positive caster move front of pivot bar away from engine, then move rear of pivot bar towards engine an equal amount. Caster should be held as nearly equal as possible on **both** wheels.

Tighten pivot bar holding bolts to specified torque, as follows:
All except Chrysler—150 ft.-lbs. (203 N•m)
Chrysler—175 ft.-lbs. (237 N•m)

Caster/Camber Adjustment

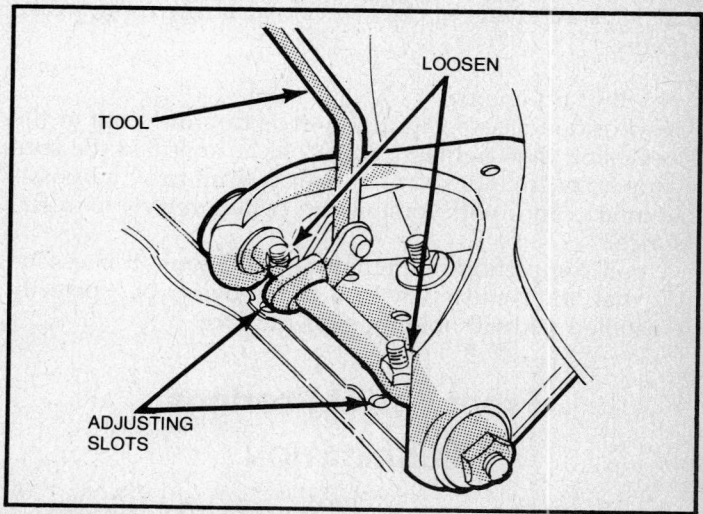

TOOL

LOOSEN

ADJUSTING
SLOTS

Loosen pivot bolt nuts

Caster/Camber Tool

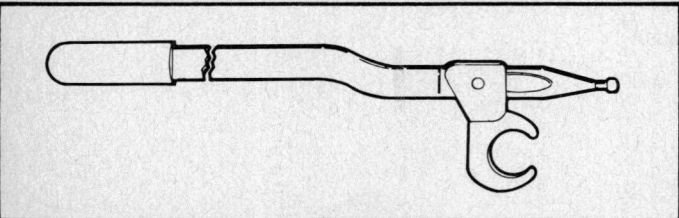

TOE

The toe setting should be the final operation of the front wheel alignment adjustments. In all cases, follow equipment manufacturers procedure.

1. Secure steering wheel in "straight-ahead" position. On vehicles equipped with power steering, start engine before centering steering wheel. (Engine should be kept running while adjusting toe).
2. Loosen tie rod clamp bolts.
3. Adjust toe by turning tie rod sleeves.

Tie Rod Adjustment

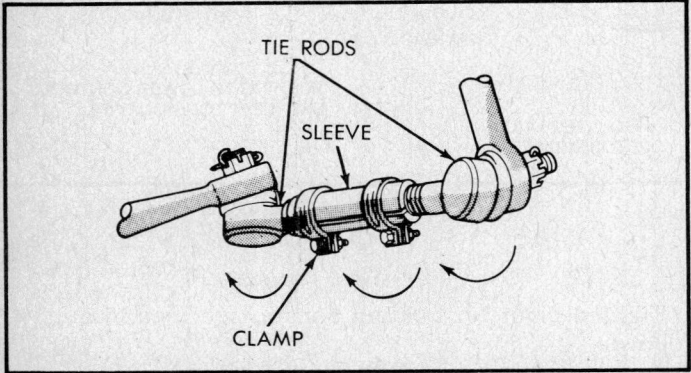

NOTE To avoid a binding condition in either tie rod assembly, rotate both tie rod ends in direction of sleeve travel during adjustment. This will ensure that both ends will be in the center of their travel when tightening sleeve clamps.

4. Shut off engine.
5. Position sleeve clamps so ends do not locate in the sleeve slot, then tighten clamp bolts as specified. Be sure clamp bolts are indexed at or near bottom to avoid possible interference with torsion bars when vehicle is in full jounce.

Upon completion of alignment operations, it is essential that the splash shields, if removed, be correctly reinstalled with all holding clips in place.

Front Wheel Bearings
LUBRICATION

Under normal service the lubricant in front wheel bearings should be inspected whenever brake drums or disc brake rotors are removed to inspect or service the brake system, but at least every 30,000 miles (48 000 kilometres).

For severe service vehicles, (such as taxi and police vehicles involving frequent or continuous brake application) wheel bearings should be inspected whenever the rotors are removed to inspect or service the brake system, or at least every 9,000 miles (14 000 kilometres), whichever occurs first.

Check lubricant to see that it is adequate in quantity and quality. If grease is low in quantity, contains dirt, appears dry or has been contaminated with water to produce a milky appearance, bearings should be cleaned and completely repacked. *Never add grease to wheel bearings.*

When relubrication is required, discard old seal. Thoroughly clean old lubricant from bearings and from hub cavity. Inspect rollers for signs of pitting or other surface distress. Light bearing discoloration should be considered normal. Bearings must be replaced if any defects exist. For all service, repack the bearings with a high temperature wheel bearing grease. Use of a bearing packer is recommended. A small amount of new grease should also be added to hub cavity.

Front Bearing Hub Cavity

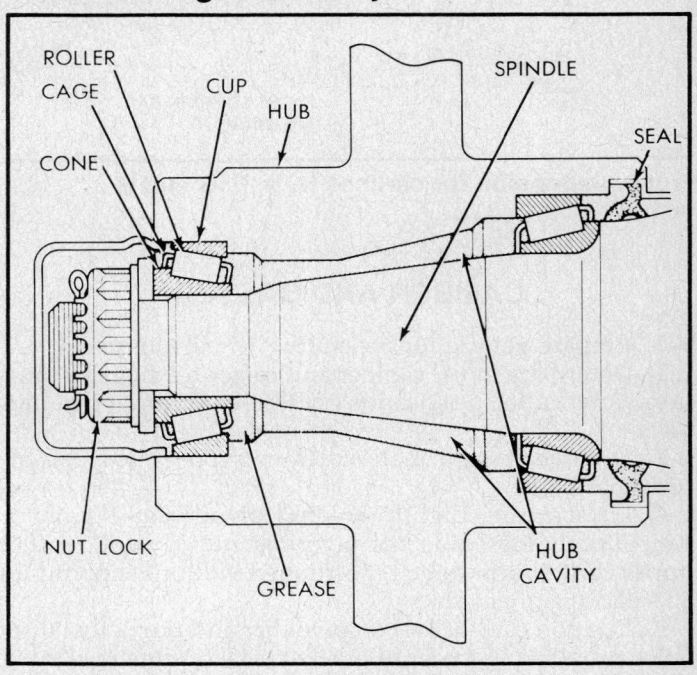

Adjustment

1. Tighten adjusting nut to 240–300 inch-pounds (27 to 34 N•m) while rotating wheel. Stop rotation and back off adjusting nut with wrench to completely release bearing pre-load. Next, finger-tighten adjusting nut. Position nut lock with one pair of slots in line with cotter pin hole. Install cotter pin. The resulting adjustment should be .0001–.003 inch end play.
2. Clean and install grease cap. Install wheel and tire assembly.

Removal

1. In the event the bearing cup is found defective during inspection, remove grease cap, cotter pin, nut lock and bearing adjusting nut.
2. Remove the disc brake sliding caliper retaining clips and anti-rattle springs.
3. Slowly slide caliper housing assembly up and away from brake disc and support caliper housing on steering knuckle arm. Do not let caliper housing hang by brake hose, as possible brake hose damage may result.
4. Remove thrust washer and outer bearing cone.
5. Slide wheel hub and disc assembly off the spindle.
6. Carefully drive out inner seal and remove bearing cone with ¾ inch diameter non-metallic rod.

Installation

1. Using a bearing drive tool, install new cone. Care must be taken to fully seat new cup against shoulder of hub.
2. Force lubricant between all bearing cone rollers or repack using a suitable bearing packer. A small amount of grease should be added to hub cavity.
3. Install inner cone and a new seal with lip of seal facing inward. Position seal flush with end of hub. The seal flange may be damaged if proper tool is not used.
4. Clean spindle and apply a light coating of wheel bearing lubricant over polished surfaces.
5. Install hub and braking disc assembly on spindle

and install outer bearing cone, thrust washer and adjusting nut. Refer to bearing adjustment procedure.
6. Slowly slide caliper housing assembly down on brake disc assembly into position on adaptor. Install caliper retaining clips and anti-rattle springs. Tighten to 180 inch-pounds (20 N•m).
7. Install tire and wheel.

Shock Absorbers

Removal

NOTE To remove the front shock absorbers on all models, you may find it more convenient to remove the tire and wheel assembly and perform the removal from under the fender.

1. Loosen and remove nut and retainer from upper end of shock absorber piston rod.
2. Raise car so wheels are clear of floor and remove lower attachment.
3. Compress shock absorber completely by pushing upward. Remove from vehicle by pulling down and out of upper shock absorber mounting bushing.
4. Check appearance of upper shock absorber mounting bushing. If it appears worn, damaged or deteriorated, remove bushing by first pressing out inner sleeve with a

Front Shock Absorbers—Transverse Torsion Bar Suspension

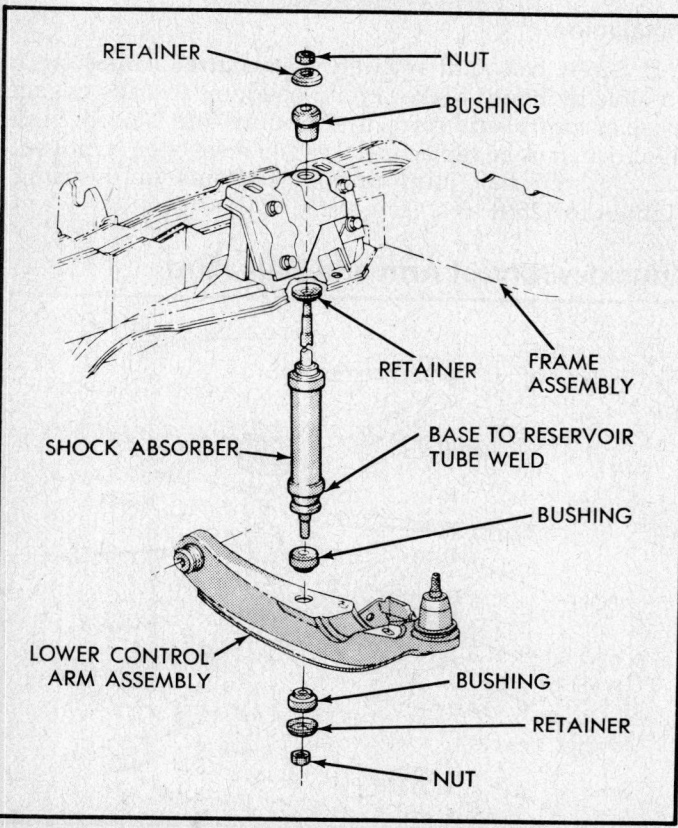

Front Shock Absorber—Conventional Torsion Bar Suspension

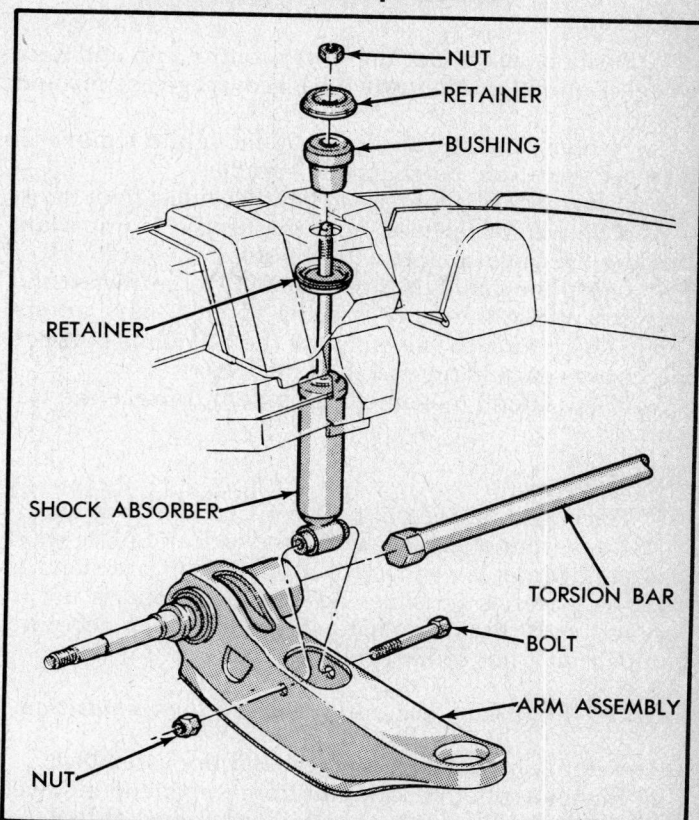

B507

suitable tool then prying out or cutting out the rubber bushing. (This bushing will take some set after it has been in service and must be replaced once it has been removed.)

Installation

1. To install upper rubber bushing, remove inner steel sleeve and immerse bushing in water (do not use oil) and with a twisting motion, start bushing into hole of upper mounting bracket. Tap into position with a hammer. Reinstall steel inner sleeve in bushing.

2. Test and expel air from shock absorber. Compress to its shortest length. Install upper bushing lower retainer and insert rod through upper bushing. Install upper retainer and nut; tighten to 25 foot-pounds (34 N•m).

NOTE In each case, install all retainers with the concave side in contact with the rubber.

3. Position and align lower eye of shock absorber with that of lower control arm mounting holes. Install shock absorber and tighten nut to 50 ft.-lbs. (68 N•m) on bolt-and-nut-type. On suspensions with removal bushings, tighten retainer nut to 35 ft.-lbs. (47 N•m) with full weight of vehicle on the wheels.

NOTE When tightening retaining nut, be sure to grip shock absorber at the base area below the weld to avoid reservoir damage.

Upper Ball Joint

Inspection

1. Position jack under the lower control arm and raise wheel clear of floor. Remove wheel cover, grease cap and cotter pin.

2. Tighten bearing adjusting nut enough to remove all play between hub, bearings and spindle.

3. Lower jack to allow tire to lightly contact floor (most of vehicle weight relieved from the tire). It is important that the tire have contact with the floor.

4. Grasp the top of the tire and apply force inward and outward. While this force is being applied, have an observer check for any movement at the ball joints between the upper control arm and the knuckle.

5. If any lateral movement is evident, replace the ball joint.

Removal

1. Place ignition switch in Off or Unlocked position.

2. Raise front of vehicle with hand jack and place short jack stand under lower control arm. Position jack stand as close to wheel as possible. Be sure jack stand is not in contact with brake splash shield. Rubber rebound bumper must not contact frame.

CAUTION Torsion bar will remain in loaded position.

3. Remove wheel cover, wheel and tire assembly.

4. Remove cotter pin and nut from upper end of lower ball joint to facilitate use of ball joint removal of tool.

Ball Joint Stud Removal—Typical

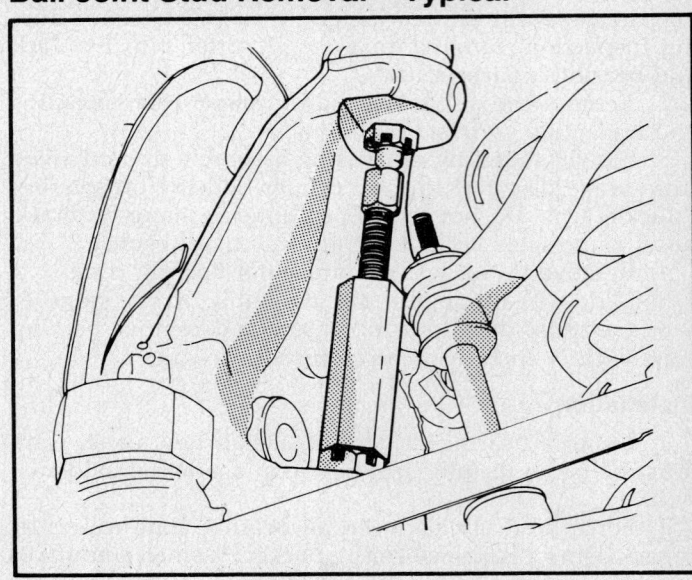

5. Slide tool on lower ball joint stud allowing tool to rest on knuckle arm. Set tool securely against upper stud.

6. Tighten tool to apply pressure to upper stud and strike knuckle sharply with hammer to loosen stud. Do not attempt to force stud out only with tool.

7. After removing tool, disengage upper ball joint from knuckle. Support knuckle and brake assembly to prevent damage to brake hose or lower ball joint.

8. Remove upper ball joint.

Installation

1. Screw ball joint squarely into control arm as far as possible by hand. Make certain ball joint threads engage those of control arm correctly if original arm is used: Seals should always be replaced once they have been removed.

2. Tighten ball joint until it bottoms on housing. Tighten to 125 ft.-lbs. (180 N•m)

Knuckle Control Arm and Ball Joint

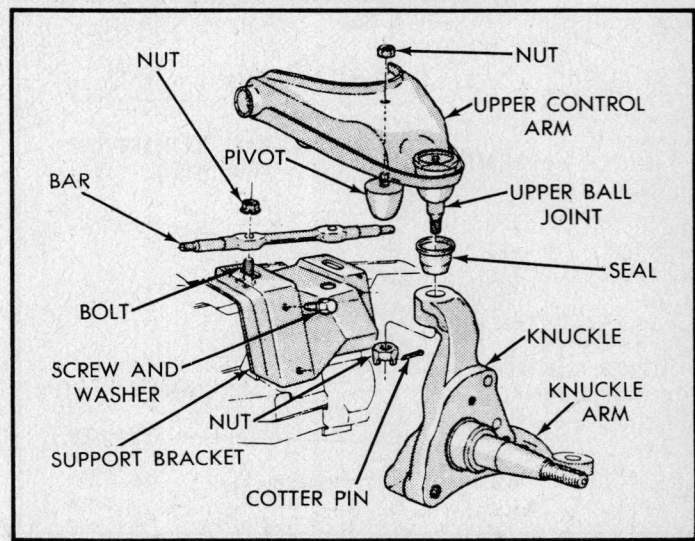

3. Position new seal over ball joint stud and install using tool adapter. Make sure seal is seated on ball joint housing.

4. Position upper ball joint stud in steering knuckle and install nut. Tighten nut to 100 ft.-lbs. (136 N•m).

5. Install lower ball joint stud nut and tighten to 100 ft.-lbs. (136 N•m). Install cotter pin and lubricate upper ball joint.

6. Torsion bar will remain in loaded position.

7. Install wheel and tire assembly with wheel cover.

Lower Ball Joint

Inspection

1. Raise the front of vehicle and install safety floor stands under both lower control arms as far outboard as possible. The upper control arms must not contact the rubber rebound bumpers.

2. With the weight of vehicle on the control arm, install dial indicator and clamp assembly to lower control arm.

3. Position dial indicator plunger tip against knuckle arm and zero dial indicator.

4. Measure axial travel of the knuckle arm with respect to the control arm, by raising and lowering the wheel using a pry bar under the center of the tire.

5. If during measurement you find the axial travel of the control arm is .030 inches (0.76 mm) or more, relative to the knuckle arm, the ball joint should be replaced.

Removal

1. Place ignition switch in Off or Unlocked position.

2. Raise vehicle on hoist to place front suspension in rebound. Place jack stands under front frame for additional support.

3. Remove wheel cover, wheel and tire assembly.

4. Remove brake caliper and support with wire hook. Do not hang caliper by brake hose alone.

5. Remove hub and rotor assembly and splash shield. Disconnect shock absorber at lower control arm.

6. Unwind torsion bar.

7. Remove upper and lower ball joint stud cotter pins and nuts. Slide tool over upper stud until tool rests on steering knuckle.

8. Turn threaded portion of tool, locking it securely against lower stud. Tighten tool enough to place lower ball joint stud under pressure, then strike steering knuckle arm sharply with a hammer to loosen stud. Do not attempt to force stud out of knuckle with tool alone.

9. Use tool to press ball joint out of lower control arm.

Installation

1. Press new ball joint into lower control arm assembly.

2. Place a new seal over ball joint with adapter tool. Press retainer portion of seal down on ball joint housing until it is securely locked in position.

3. Insert ball joint stud into opening in knuckle arm and install stud retaining nuts; tighten as specified. Install cotter pins and lubricate ball joint.

4. Place a load on torsion bar by turning adjusting bolt clockwise.

Lower Control Arm and Ball Joint

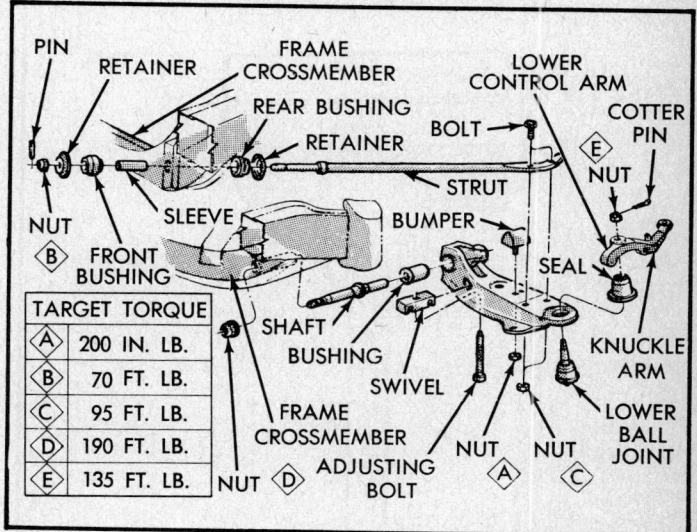

TARGET TORQUE	
A	200 IN. LB.
B	70 FT. LB.
C	95 FT. LB.
D	190 FT. LB.
E	135 FT. LB.

5. Install wheel, tire and brake assembly and adjust front wheel bearing.

6. Lower vehicle to floor. Adjust front suspension heights.

Torsion Bars (Straight-Type)

Straight torsion bars have a hex formed on each end. One hex end is installed in the lower control arm anchor, the opposite end is anchored in the frame or body crossmember.

Torsion bars are identified for use by length and thickness (depending on carline, body, engine, etc.), and are not interchangeable side for side. The bars are marked either right or left by the letter "R" or "L" stamped on one end of the bar.

Removal

1. Lift vehicle on hoist to place front suspension in rebound.

2. Release load from torsion bar by turning the anchor adjusting bolt in lower control arm counterclockwise.

Straight Torsion Bar

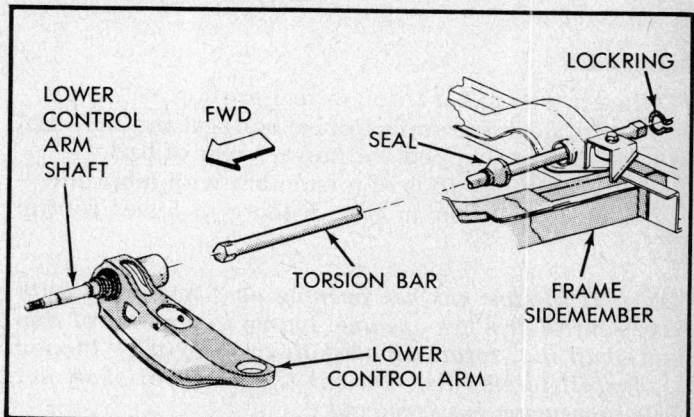

Drive Tool

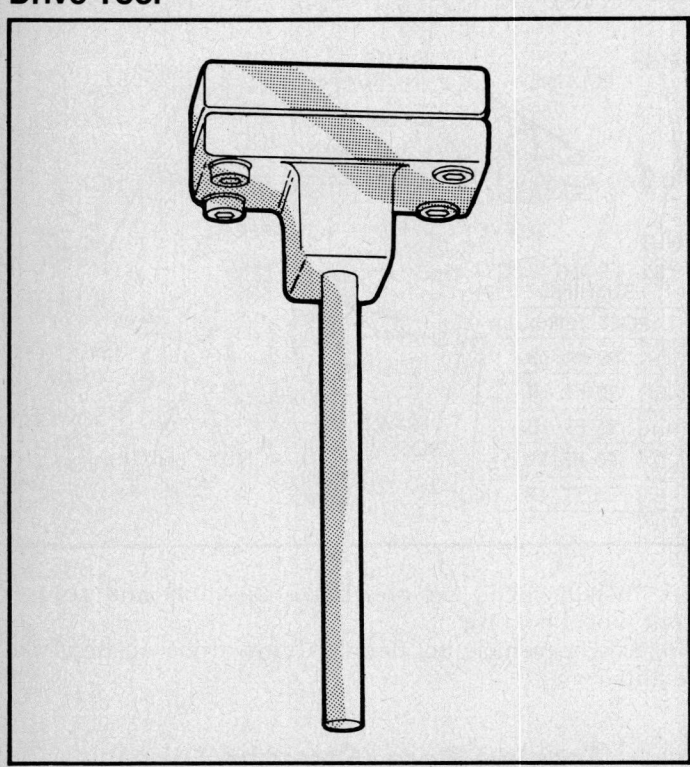

3. Remove lock ring from anchor at rear of bar. Install drive tool to remove torsion bar. (If necessary, remove transmission torque shaft to provide clearance.) Place tool toward rear of bar to allow sufficient room for striking pad of tool. Do not apply heat to torsion bar, front anchor or rear anchor.

4. Remove tool and slide bar out through rear anchor. Do not damage balloon seal when removing bar.

Inspection

1. Inspect torsion bar and seal for damage; replace if damaged.

2. Remove all foreign matter from hex opening(s) in anchors and from hex end(s) of torsion bar.

3. Inspect torsion bar adjusting bolt and swivel and replace if there is corrosion or other damage. Lubricate for easy installation.

Installation

1. Insert torsion bar through rear anchor.

2. Lubricate inside surface of balloon seal and slide seal over torsion bar (cupped end toward rear of bar).

3. Coat both hex ends of torsion bar with lubricant.

4. Slide torsion bar in hex opening of lower control arm.

NOTE If torsion bar hex opening does not index with lower control arm hex opening, loosen lower control arm pivot shaft nut, rotate pivot shaft to index with torsion bar. Install torsion bar. Do not tighten pivot shaft nut while suspension is in rebound.

5. Install lock ring, making sure it is seated in its groove.

6. Pack rear anchor openings at lock ring area and area under seals with lubricant. Position lip of seal in groove of anchor.

7. Turn adjusting bolt clockwise to place a load on torsion bar.

8. Lower vehicle to floor and tighten pivot shaft nut to 145 foot-pounds (197 N•m).

9. Adjust front suspension height.

Torsion Bars (Transverse-Type)

Torsion bars are formed with an angle for transverse mounting. Each bar is hex shaped on the anchor end with a replaceable torsion bar-to-lower control arm bushing on the opposite end and a pivot cushion bushing (permanently attached) midway on the bar creating right and left hand asemblies.

Torsion Bars, Transverse Mounting

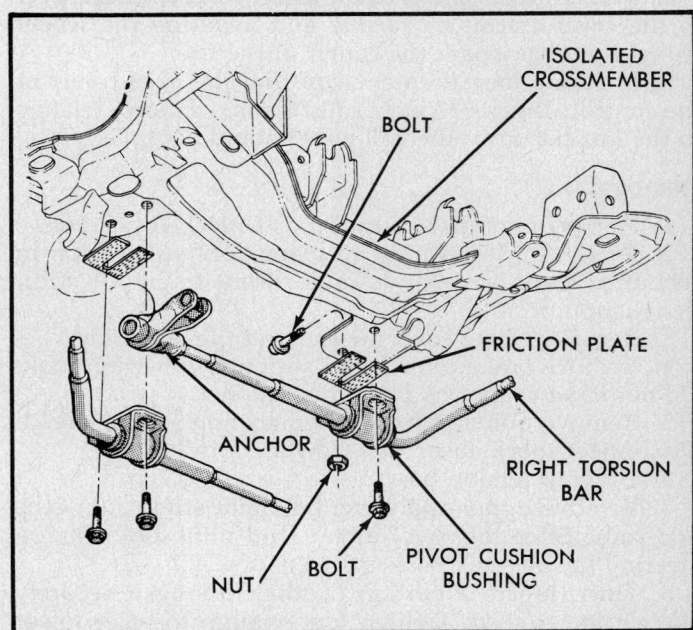

The hex end of the bar is anchored in the crossmember (opposite the affected wheel), extends parallel to the front crossmember, through the pivot cushion bushing (also attached to the crossmember), turns, and attaches to the lower control arm through the torsion bar to lower control arm bushing.

Removal

1. Raise car on hoist and support vehicle so that front suspension is in full rebound position.

2. Release load on **both** torsion bars by turning anchor adjusting bolts in frame crossmember counterclockwise. Remove anchor adjusting bolt on torsion bar to be removed.

Transverse Torsion Bar Front Suspension

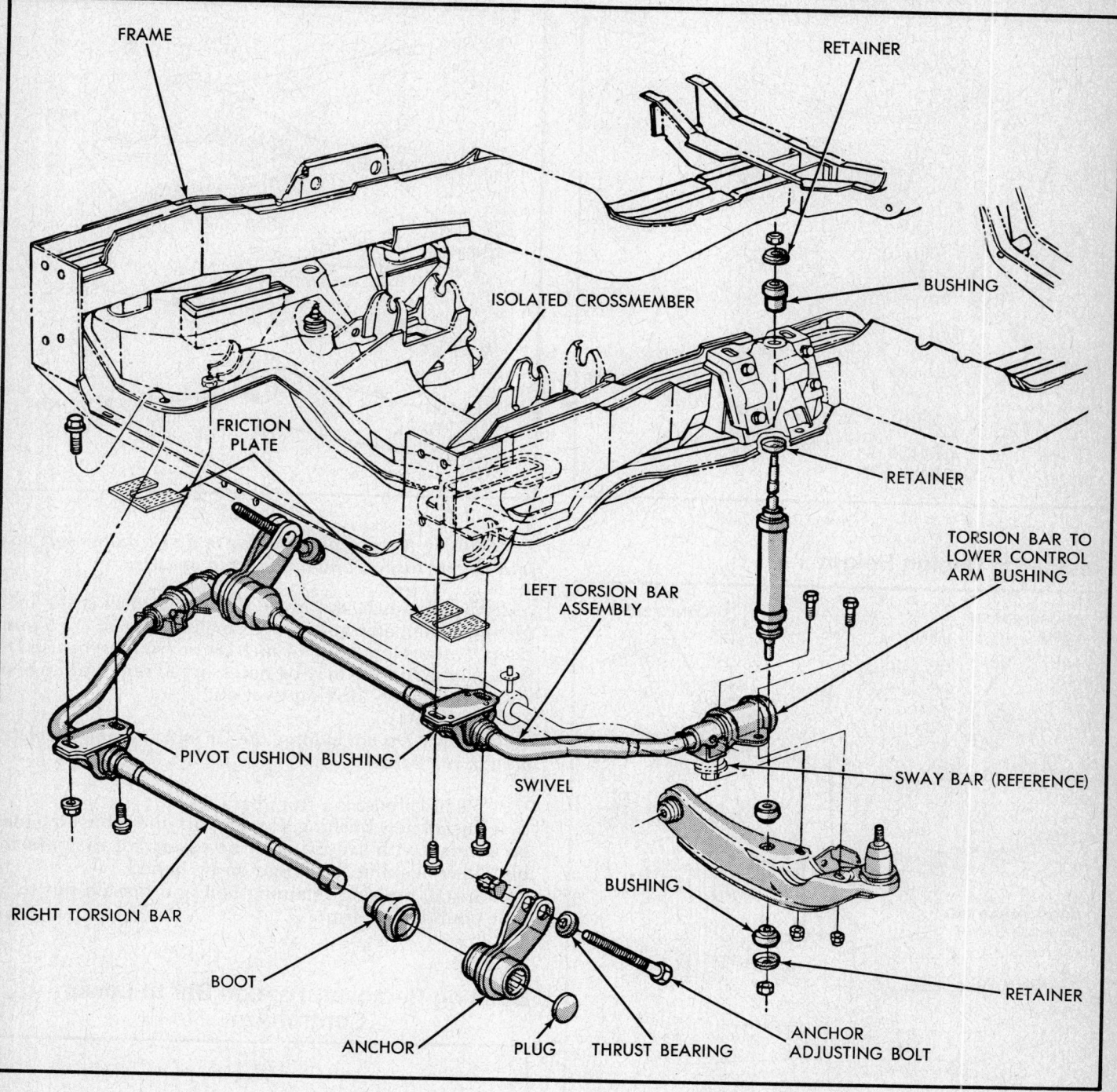

3. Raise lower control arms until clearance between crossmember ledge (at jounce bumper) and torsion bar end bushing is 2⅞ inches (63.0 mm). Support lower control arms at this design height (equal to three passenger position with vehicle on ground). This is necessary to align sway bar and lower control arm attaching points for disassembly and component re-alignment and attachment during reassembly.

4. Remove sway bar-to-control arm attaching bolt and retainers.

5. Remove two bolts attaching torsion bar end bushing to lower control arm.

6. Remove two bolts attaching torsion bar pivot cushion bushing to crossmember, and remove torsion bar and anchor assembly from crossmember.

7. Carefully separate anchor from torsion bar.

SUSPENSION
FRONT SUSPENSION-CHRYSLER REAR DRIVE

Transverse Torsion Bar Anchor Bolt

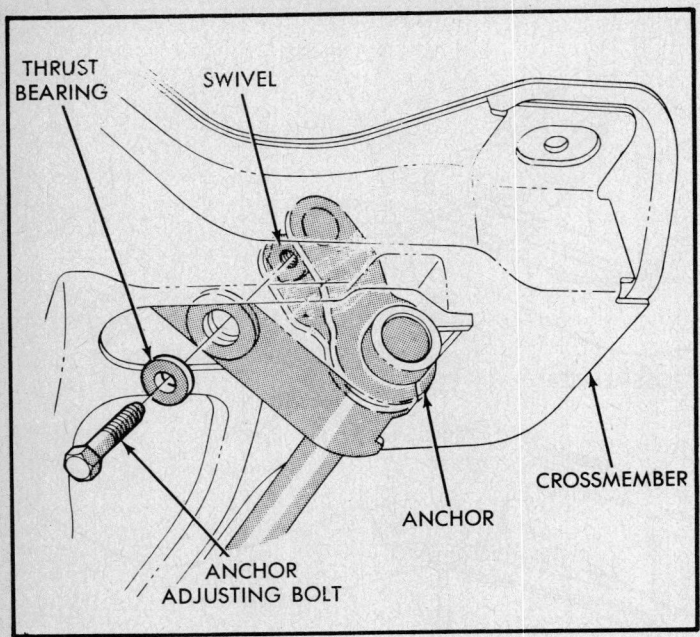

Transverse Bar Lower Control Arm Mounting

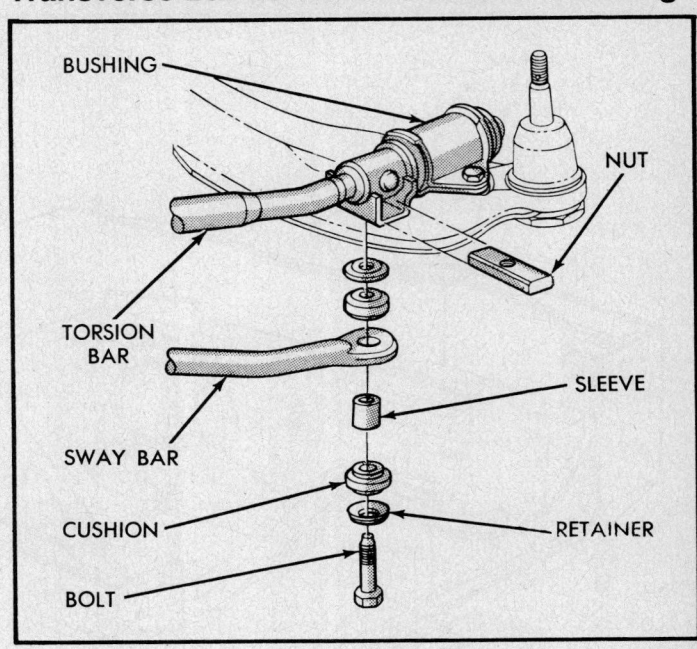

Measuring Design Height

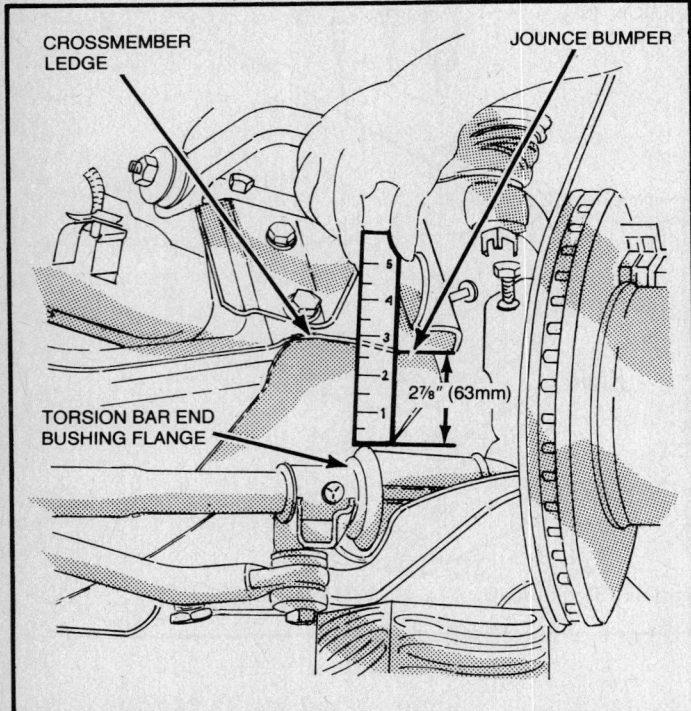

CAUTION   Never clamp the bar in a vise unless soft vise jaw inserts (brass, aluminum, etc.) are used.

2. Centerpunch the rivet head and drill a ⅜ inch (9.5 mm) diameter hole approximately ½ inch (12.5 mm) deep. A short length of ⁵/₁₆ inch (8mm) rod can be used to remove the rivet. It may be necessary to remove flange of rivet head before driving rivet out.

CAUTION   Do not enlarge the ⁷/₁₆ inch (11 mm) diameter hole in the bar.

3. Remove bushing from bar.
4. Install new bushing. Rough area under bushing may be cleaned with sandpaper if necessary for easy assembly. New bushing should go on by hand.
5. Install bushing retaining bolt and tighten nut to 50 foot-pounds (68 N•m).

Bushing Removal, Torsion Bar to Lower Control Arm

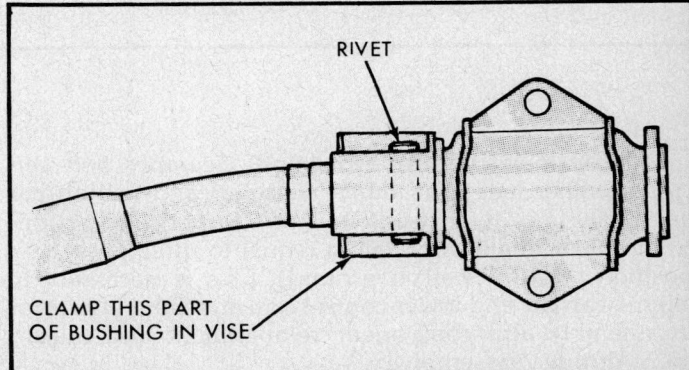

TORSION BAR-TO-LOWER CONTROL ARM BUSHING REPLACEMENT

Service replacement bars include pivot cushion bushing and torsion bar to lower control arm bushing.

1. Clamp assembly in vise with rivet head up (hex end of bar down).

B512

Inspection

1. Inspect seal for damage, replace if damaged.
2. Inspect bushing-to-lower control arm and pivot cushion bushing.

NOTE Inspect seals on cushion bushing for cuts, tears or severe deterioration that may allow moisture under cushion. If corrosion is evident, the torsion bar assembly should be replaced.

3. Remove all foreign matter from hex opening(s) in anchors and from hex end(s) of torsion bar.
4. Inspect torsion bar adjusting bolt and swivel and replace if there is any sign of corrosion or other damage. Lubricate for easy installation.

Installation

1. Carefully slide balloon seal over end of torsion bar (cupped end toward hex).
2. Coat hex end of torsion bar with lubricant.
3. Install torsion bar hex end into anchor bracket. With torsion bar in a horizontal position, the ears of the anchor bracket should be positioned nearly straight up. Position swivel into anchor bracket ears.
4. Place bushing end of bar into position on top of lower control arm. Then, install anchor bracket assembly into crossmember anchor retainer and install anchor adjusting bearing and bolt.
5. Attach pivot cushion bushing to crossmember with two bolt and washer assemblies. Leave bolt and washer assemblies loose enough to install friction plates.
6. With lower control arms at "design height," install two bolt and nut assemblies attaching torsion bar bushing to lower control arm. Tighten to 70 foot-pounds (95 N•m).
7. Ensure that torsion bar anchor bracket is fully seated in crossmember. Install friction plates between crossmember and pivot cushion bushing with open end of slot to rear and bottomed out on mounting bolt. Tighten cushion bushing bolts to 85 foot-pounds (115 N•m).
8. Position balloon seal over anchor bracket.

Torsion Bar Anchor Assembly

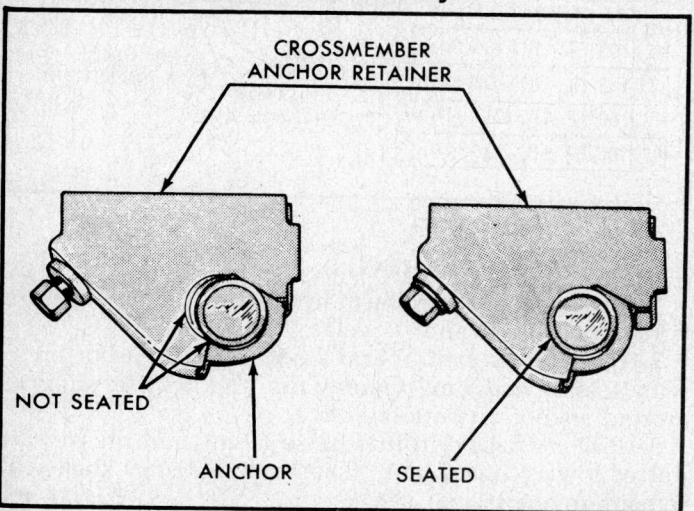

CROSSMEMBER ANCHOR RETAINER

NOT SEATED

ANCHOR   SEATED

9. Reinstall bolt, through sway bar, retainer cushions and sleeve, and attach to lower control arm end bushing. Tighten bolt to 50 foot-pounds (68 N•m).
10. Load torsion bar by turning anchor adjusting bolt clockwise.
11. Lower vehicle and adjust torsion bar height to specifications.

Upper Control Arm

Removal

1. Place ignition switch in Off or Unlocked position.
2. Raise front of vehicle with hand jack and remove wheel cover, wheel and tire assembly.
3. Position short jack stand under lower control arm near splash shield and lower hand jack. Observe that jack stand does not contact shield and rebound bumpers are under no load.
4. On some models, remove brake caliper and set aside to provide clearance for ball joint remover tool.
5. Remove cotter pin and nut from upper and lower ball joints to facilitate use of tool to free ball joint.
6. Slide spreader tool over lower ball joint stud to allow tool to rest on steering knuckle arm. Tighten tool to apply pressure to upper ball joint stud and strike steering knuckle boss sharply with hammer to loosen stud. Do not attempt to force stud out of knuckle with tool alone.
7. After removing tool, support brake and knuckle assembly to prevent damage to brake hose or lower ball joint, then disengage upper ball joint from knuckle.
8. From under hood, remove engine splash shield to expose upper control arm pivot bar.

Spreader Tool

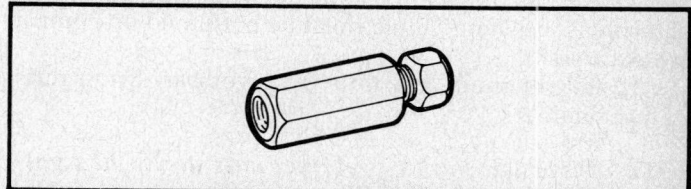

Knuckle and Control Arm

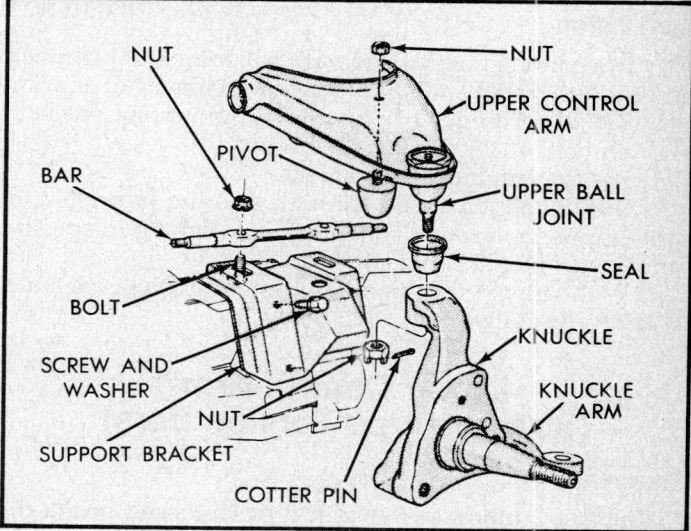

NUT   NUT

UPPER CONTROL ARM

PIVOT

BAR   UPPER BALL JOINT

SEAL

BOLT

KNUCKLE

SCREW AND WASHER

KNUCKLE ARM

NUT

SUPPORT BRACKET

COTTER PIN

SUSPENSION

9. Scribe a line on support bracket along inboard edge of pivot bar (to re-establish suspension alignment during reassembly).

10. Remove pivot bolts or nuts and lift upper control arm with ball joint and pivot bar assembly from bracket.

DISASSEMBLY (BUSHINGS)

1. Place upper control arm in vise and remove pivot bar nuts and bushing retainers.

2. Bolt support tool C-4253-1 to pivot bar.

3. Place puller tool C-4253-2 over end of pivot bar and reinstall nut. Snug bolts against arm.

4. Screw bolts equally until bushing is free in arm and remove tool and bushing.

Upper Control Arm Bushing Tool

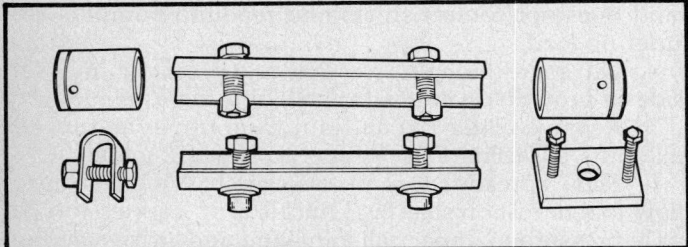

ASSEMBLY (BUSHINGS)

1. With control arm in vise, put pivot bar in arm and attach support bracket spacer tool.

2. Slip bushings over each end of pivot bar and pilot into holes in arm.

3. Install bushing cups over both bushings and press bushings together until both bushings are fully seated in arm. Pound bushings in place at the same time or use an arbor press. Bushing flange must be bottomed on control arm extrusion.

4. Install retainers and nuts on pivot bar. Snug nuts against retainers.

NOTE Pivot bar bushing retainer nuts are to be tightened to specifications AFTER suspension (upper control arm) is at design height.

Installation

1. Place upper control arm with ball joint and pivot bar on bracket. Install and snug attaching bolts against arm.

2. Set inboard edge of pivot bar on mounting bracket. Tighten bolts to 150 ft.-lbs. (204 N•m).

3. Replace engine splash shield.

4. Install ball joint stud through steering knuckle and install upper and lower ball joint nuts, tighten to specifications and install cotter pins.

5. With vehicle at design height tighten pivot bar nuts to 110 ft.-lbs. (150 N•m).

Lower Control Arm (Straight-Type Torsion Bars)

Removal

1. Place ignition switch in Off or Unlocked position.

2. Remove rebound bumper.

3. Raise vehicle on hoist to place front suspension in rebound. Place jack stands under front frame for additional support.

4. Remove wheel cover, wheel and tire assembly.

5. Remove brake caliper and set aside. Do not hang caliper by brake hose alone. Disconnect shock absorber lower bolt.

6. Remove hub and rotor assembly, splash shield and lower shock mounting nut. Remove bolt and nut.

7. Remove two (2) strut bar attaching bolts from lower control arm.

8. Remove automatic transmission gear shift torque shaft assembly if required for tool clearance.

9. Measure torsion bar anchor bolt depth into lower control arm before unwinding torsion bar. Unwind bar.

10. Remove torsion bar.

11. Separate lower ball joint from knuckle arm.

12. Remove lower control arm shaft nut from control arm shaft and push out shaft from frame crossmember. Strike threaded end of shaft with soft hammer to loosen if necessary. Remove lower control arm and shaft as an assembly from the vehicle.

13. In the event the shaft bushing indicates wear or deterioration, replacement is recommended.

Lower Control Arm Transverse Suspension

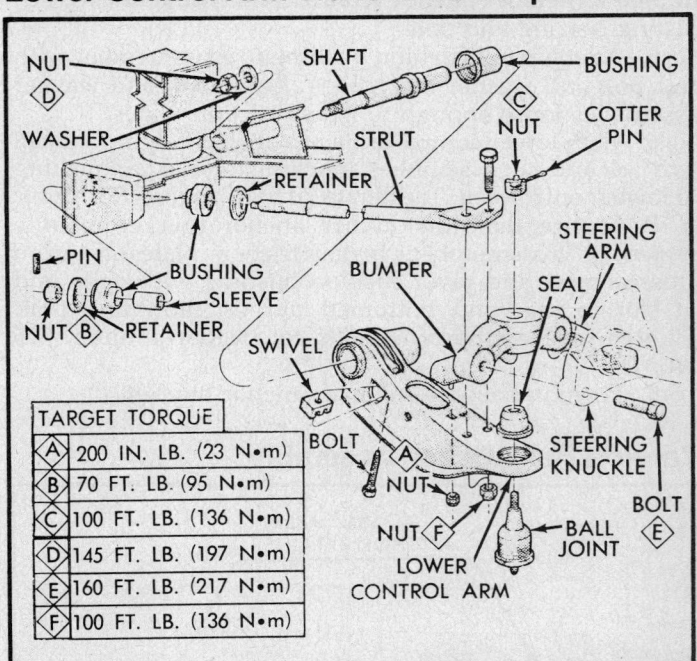

TARGET TORQUE	
Ⓐ	200 IN. LB. (23 N•m)
Ⓑ	70 FT. LB. (95 N•m)
Ⓒ	100 FT. LB. (136 N•m)
Ⓓ	145 FT. LB. (197 N•m)
Ⓔ	160 FT. LB. (217 N•m)
Ⓕ	100 FT. LB. (136 N•m)

DISASSEMBLY (BUSHINGS)

1. Place lower control arm in vise and remove torsion bar adjusting bolt and swivel.

2. Place lower control arm assembly in an arbor press with torsion bar hex opening up and with a support around anchor on bottom end.

3. Place a brass drift into hex opening and press shaft out of lower control arm. The bushing inner shell will remain on shaft.

4. Cut and remove rubber portion of bushing from control arm or shaft. Remove bushing outer shell by cutting with a chisel. Use care not to cut into control arm.

5. Remove bushing inner shell with pivot shaft.

ASSEMBLY (BUSHINGS)

1. Position new bushing on shaft (flange end of bushing first). Press shaft into inner sleeve until bushing seats on shoulder of shaft.

2. Press shaft and bushing assembly into lower control arm using an arbor press.

3. Install torsion bar adjusting bolt and swivel.

Installation

1. Position lower control arm with shaft in crossmember. Install lower control arm shaft nut and finger-tighten nut.

2. Position lower ball joint stud into knuckle arm and tighten nut to 100 ft.-lbs. (136 N•m).

3. Install torsion bar into lower control arm.

4. Replace transmission gear shaft torque shaft if removed.

5. Position strut bar with two attaching bolts to lower control arm. Tighten to 100 foot-pounds (136 N•m).

6. Attach brake splash shield and secure lower shock mounting bolt to lower control arm.

7. Attach hub and rotor and install brake caliper.

8. Install wheel and tire assembly.

9. Lower vehicle to floor and adjust front suspension heights. Tighten lower control arm pivot shaft nut to 145 foot-pounds (197 N•m). Install rebound bumper and tighten to 200 in.-lbs. (23 N•m).

10. Adjust wheel alignment.

Straight Torsion Bar Suspension

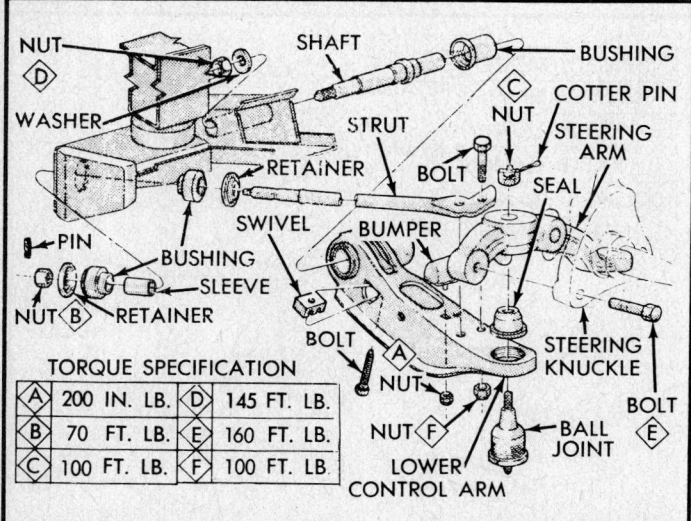

TORQUE SPECIFICATION			
A	200 IN. LB.	D	145 FT. LB.
B	70 FT. LB.	E	160 FT. LB.
C	100 FT. LB.	F	100 FT. LB.

Lower Control Arm (Transverse-Type Torsion Bars)

Removal

1. Raise car on hoist and remove wheel and tire assembly.

Lower Bushing Remover Tool

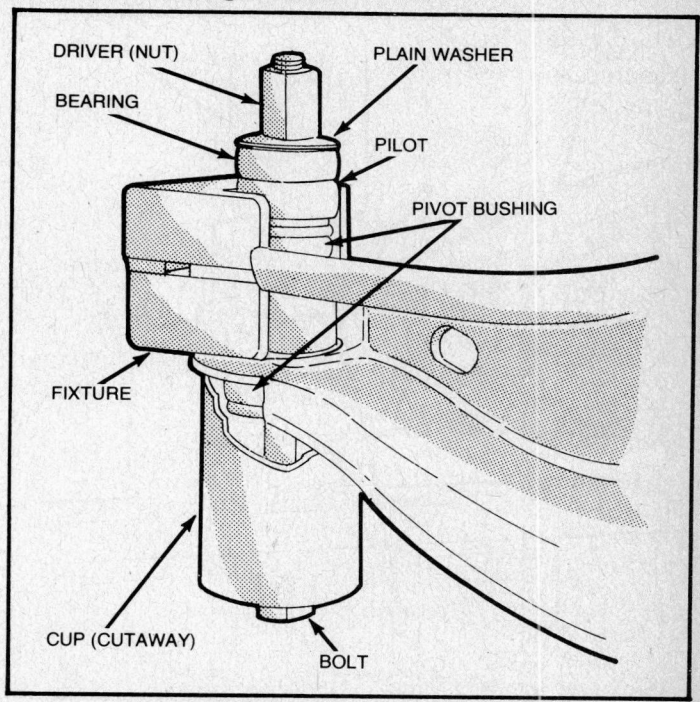

2. Remove brake caliper retaining screws, clips and anti-rattle springs and remove caliper from adaptor and support caliper assembly on wire hook. (Do not hang caliper by brake hose.)

3. Remove hub and rotor assembly and splash shield.

4. Remove shock absorber lower nut, retainer and insulator.

5. Release load on both torsion bars by turning anchor adjusting bolts counterclockwise. Releasing both torsion bars is required because of sway bar reaction from the opposite torsion bar.

6. Raise lower control arm until clearance between crossmember ledge (at jounce bumper) and torsion bar to lower control arm bushing is 2⅞ inches (73mm). Support control arm at this "design height" and remove two bolts attaching torsion bar end bushing to lower control arm.

7. Separate lower ball joint from knuckle arm.

8. Remove lower control arm pivot bolt and lower control arm.

DISASSEMBLY (BUSHINGS)

1. Place lower control arm in vise and install bushing removal tool.

2. Place support fixture between flanges of control arm and around bushing. Proper fixture position is required to prevent control arm distortion during bushing removal.

3. Position cup over flanged bushing end with bolt through cup and bushing.

4. Install pilot, thrust washer, plain washer and nut on through bolt.

5. Press bushing out of lower control arm by holding bolt on cup end while turning nut on pilot end.

SUSPENSION
FRONT SUSPENSION-CHRYSLER REAR DRIVE

Lower Control Arm Bushing Installation

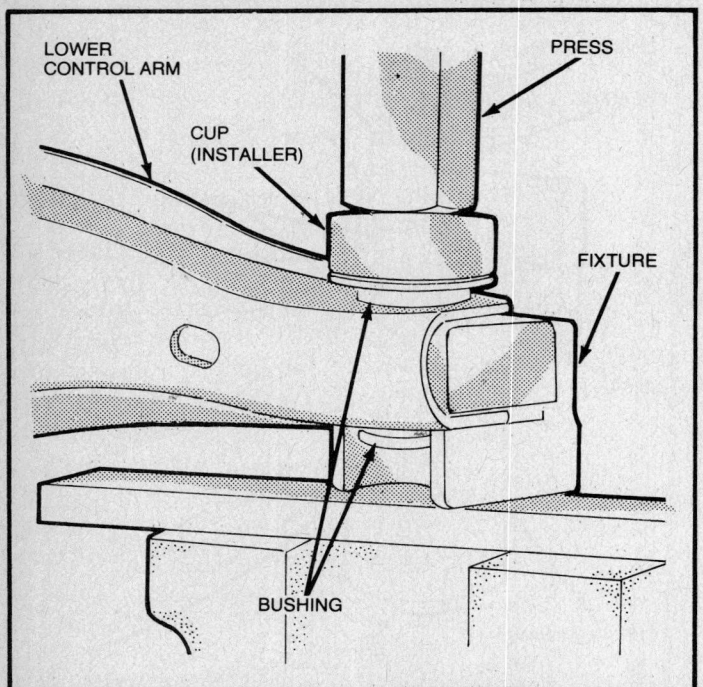

ASSEMBLY (BUSHINGS)

1. Place support fixture on lower control arm flanges and position assembly on base of suitable press. Proper fixture position is required to prevent control arm distortion during bushing installation.

2. Position flange end of new bushing into cup squarely and press bushing into control arm until bushing flange seats on arm.

Installation

1. Position lower control arm in crossmember, install pivot bolt and finger-tighten flanged nut.

2. Position lower ball joint stud into steering knuckle arm and tighten nut to 100 foot-pounds (136 N•m). Insert cotter key.

3. Install torsion bar into lower control arm.

4. Load torsion bar by returning torsion bar adjusting bolt depth to original position before removal.

5. Position strut bar with two attaching bolts to lower control arm. Tighten to 100 foot-pounds (136 N•m).

6. Attach brake splash shield and secure lower shock mounting bolt to lower control arm.

7. Attach hub and rotor and install brake caliper.

8. Install wheel and tire assembly.

9. Lower vehicle to floor and adjust front suspension heights. Tighten lower control arm pivot shaft nut to 145 foot-pounds (197 N•m). Install rebound bumper and tighten to 200 in.-lbs. (23 N•m).

10. Adjust wheel alignment.

Steering Knuckle Arm

Removal

1. Place ignition switch in Off or Unlocked position.

2. Remove rebound bumper.

3. Raise vehicle on hoist to place front suspension in rebound. Use jack stands under front frame for additional support.

4. Remove wheel cover, wheel and tire assembly.

5. Remove brake caliper and hang out of way with wire hook during this operation to prevent damage to brake hose.

6. Remove hub and brake disc assembly.

7. Remove brake splash shield from steering knuckle.

8. Unload torsion bars, by turning anchor adjusting bolt counterclockwise.

9. Disconnect tie rod from steering knuckle arm by removing cotter pin and nut. Use care not to damage seals.

Tie Rod End Puller

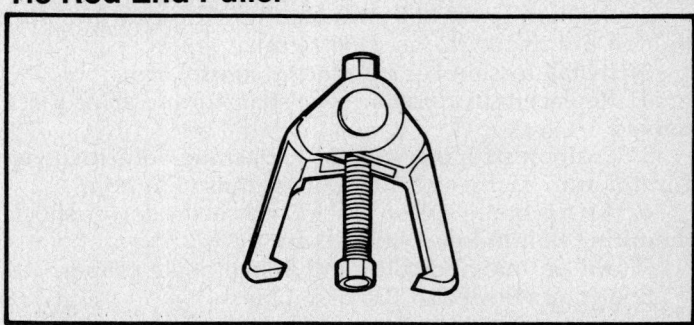

10. Remove lower ball joint stud from knuckle arm.

11. Separate knuckle arm from steering knuckle by removing two (2) nuts and two (2) attaching bolts.

12. Remove steering knuckle arm.

Upper Control Arm

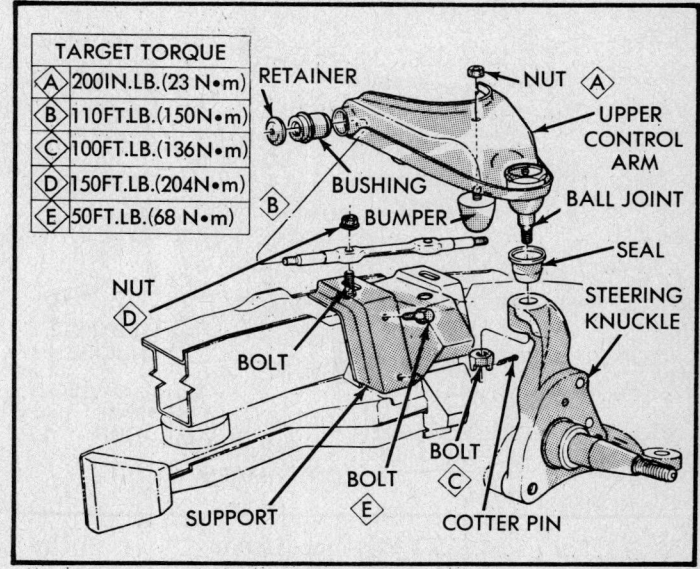

TARGET TORQUE	
A	200 IN.LB. (23 N•m)
B	110 FT.LB. (150 N•m)
C	100 FT.LB. (136 N•m)
D	150 FT.LB. (204 N•m)
E	50 FT.LB. (68 N•m)

Installation

1. Attach steering knuckle arm to knuckle and install two bolts and nuts. Tighten to 160 ft.-lbs. (217 N•m).

2. Attach lower ball joint stud to knuckle arm. Tighten nut to 100 foot-pounds (136 N•m) and install cotter key.

3. Attach tie rod end to steering knuckle arm and inside nut. Tighten to 40 ft.-lbs. (54 N•m) and install cotter pin.

4. Load torsion bar by turning adjusting bolt on lower control arm clockwise.

5. Install brake splash shield onto steering knuckle.

6. Install hub and disc assembly. Adjust wheel bearings. Install caliper.

7. Install wheel and tire assembly and attach wheel cover.

8. Lower vehicle to floor, adjust front suspension heights and wheel alignment as necessary.

Sway Bar (Straight-Type Torsion Bar)

Removal

1. Place ignition switch in Off or Unlocked position.

2. Raise car on hoist to place front suspension in rebound.

3. Remove wheel cover, wheel and tire assembly.

4. Remove nut and bolt on each end of bar attaching sway bar to strut clamp. Remove nut and bolt from both sway bar link straps to free sway bar from links.

5. Remove sway bar by pulling unit out through frame crossmember openings in direction of area where wheel has been removed.

6. In the event strut cushions and sway bar bushings show excessive wear or deterioration of rubber, replacement is recommended.

Sway Bar—Straight Type Torsion Bar

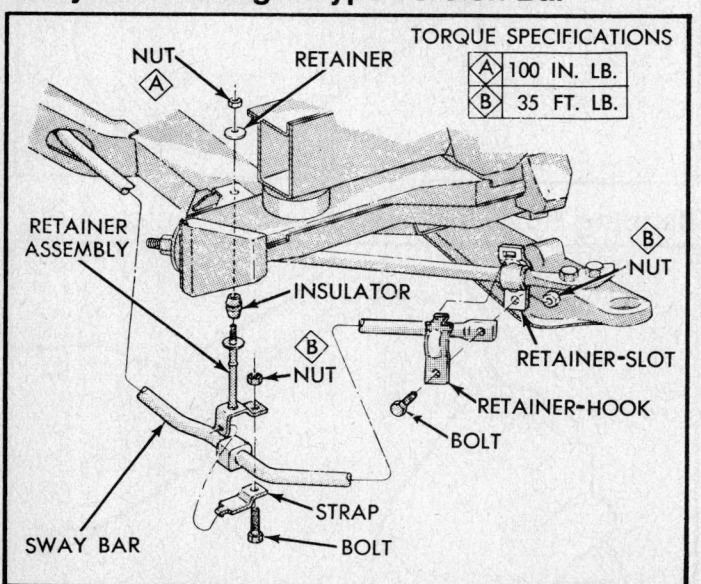

Installation

1. On side where wheel assembly has been removed, install sway bar with center offset in downward position. (Color code on bar is always on driver's side.)

2. Attach sway bar with bolt and nut to strut retainer clamp on each end of bar and tighten to 35 foot-pounds (47 N•m).

3. Lower vehicle to floor and attach both sway bar frame link straps. Tighten to 35 ft.-lbs. (47 N•m).

Sway Bar (Transverse-Type Torsion Bar)

Removal

1. Raise car on hoist.

NOTE Sway bar-to-lower control arm attaching points are aligned ONLY when lower control arms are at "design height" (equal to three passenger position with vehicle on ground). If frame contact or twin post hoist is used, release load on torsion bar by turning adjuster bolts counterclockwise. Raise lower control arms until clearance between crossmember ledge (at jounce bumper) and torsion bar to lower control arm bushing is 2⅞ inches (73 mm). Support lower control arms with jack stand during sway bar removal and installation.

2. With lower control arms supported as described in note above, remove sway bar-to-torsion bar bushing attaching bolts, retainers, cushions and sleeves.

3. Remove retainer assembly strap bolts and retainer straps. Remove sway bar.

4. Inspect cushions and bushings for excessive wear or deterioration and replace if required.

Installation

1. Position sway bar bushings against retainers and install retainer straps. Loosely assemble retainer bolts.

2. Reinstall bolt through sway bar retainer, cushions and sleeve, and attach to torsion bar lower control arm bushing. Tighten bolt to 50 foot-pounds (68 N•m) torque.

3. Tighten sway bar retainer and strap bolts to 30 foot-pounds (41 N•m).

4. Load torsion bar by turning anchor adjusting bolt in crossmember clockwise.

5. Lower vehicle and adjust torsion bar height to specifications.

Sway Bar—Transverse Type Torsion Bar

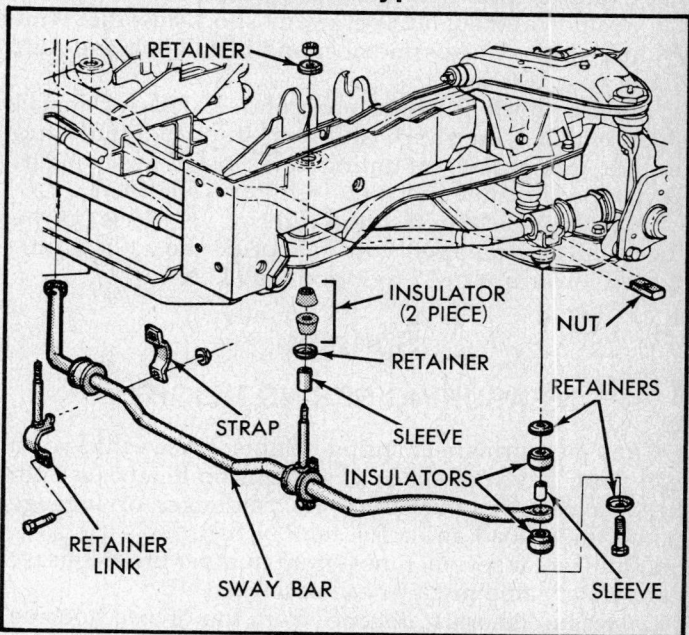

REAR SUSPENSION—CHRYSLER REAR DRIVE

Shock Absorber

Removal

1. Raise axle to relieve load on shock absorber.
2. Remove shock absorber lower end, as follows: Loosen and remove nut, retainer and bushing from spring plate. *When loosening retaining nut grip shock absorber at the base (below the base to reservoir tube weld) to avoid reservoir damage.*
3. Loosen and remove nut and bolt from upper shock absorber mounting, and remove shock absorber.

Expelling Air From New Shock Absorber

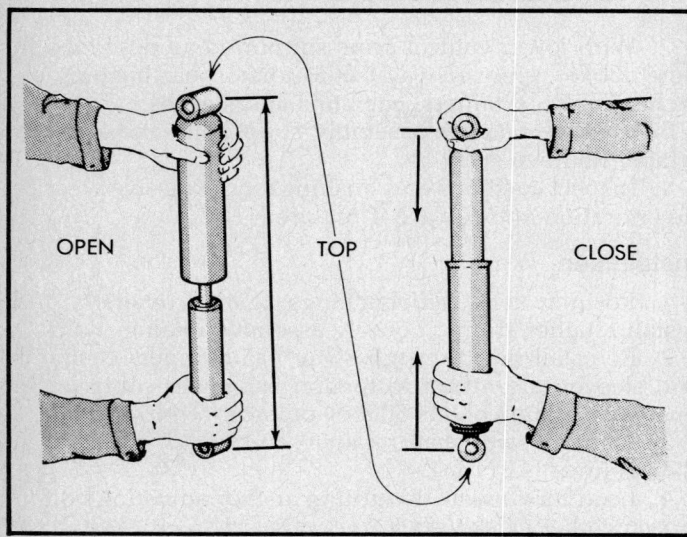

Installation

1. Expel air from new shock absorber.
2. Position and align upper eye of shock absorber with mounting holes in crossmember and install bolt and nut. Do not fully tighten.
3. Install shock absorber lower end, as follows: Install upper bushing on shock absorber stud and pull stud through spring plate mounting hole. Install lower bushing, cupped washer and nut. Tighten as specified.
4. Lower vehicle until full weight of vehicle is on the wheels. Tighten upper nut 70 foot-pounds (95 N•m). Tighten lower nut to 35 foot-pounds (47 N•m).

Springs

MEASURING SPRING HEIGHT

When measuring rear spring heights, place vehicle on a level floor, have correct front suspension height on both sides, correct tire pressures, no passenger or luggage compartment load and a full tank of fuel.

1. Jounce car several times (front bumper first). Release bumpers at same point in each cycle.
2. Measure shortest distance from top of axle housing to the rail at side of rear axle bumper strap (at rear of bumper).
3. Measure both right and left sides.

If these measurements vary by more than ¾ inch (side to side), it is an indication that one of the rear springs may need replacing.

Removal

1. Using floor stands under axle assembly, raise axle assembly to relieve weight on rear spring.
2. Disconnect rear shock absorber at spring plate. Lower axle assembly, permitting rear springs to hang free. (On vehicles so equipped, disconnect rear sway bar links.)

Pivot Bushing Removal and Installation

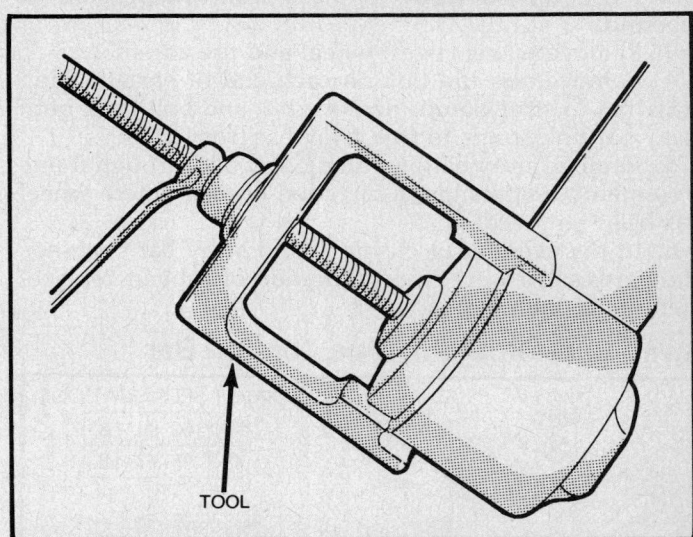

Bending Bushing Flanges

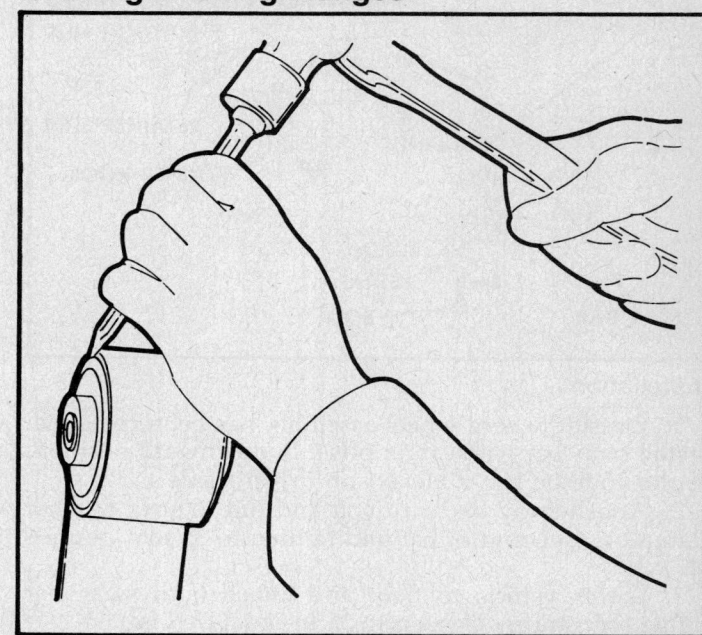

3. Loosen and remove U-bolt nuts and remove U-bolts and spring plate.

4. Loosen and remove the nuts holding front spring hanger to body mounting bracket.

5. Loosen and remove rear spring hanger bolts and let spring drop far enough to pull front spring hanger bolts out of body mounting bracket holes.

6. Loosen and remove front pivot bolt from front spring hanger.

7. Loosen and remove shackle nuts and remove shackle from rear spring.

BUSHING REPLACMENT

It is recommended that the spring assembly be removed from the vehicle for bushing replacement on the bench.

Rear Suspension Cars With Transverse Front Suspension

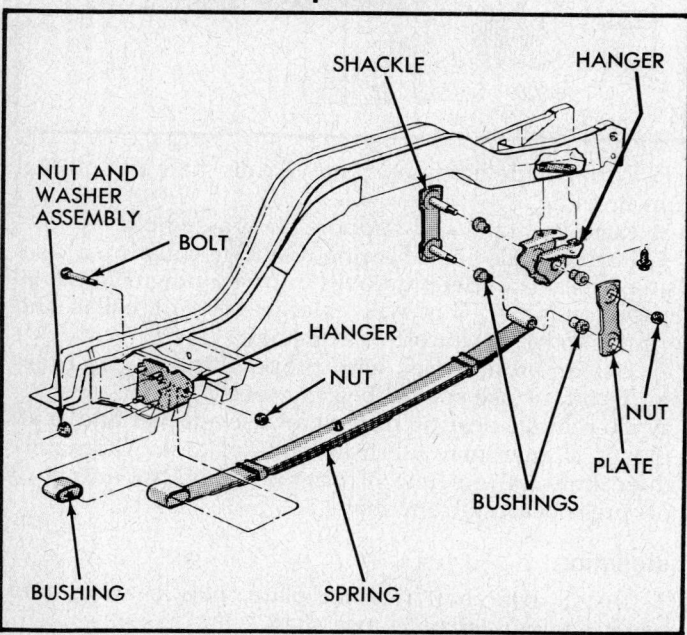

Rear Suspension Cars With Straight Torsion Bar Suspension

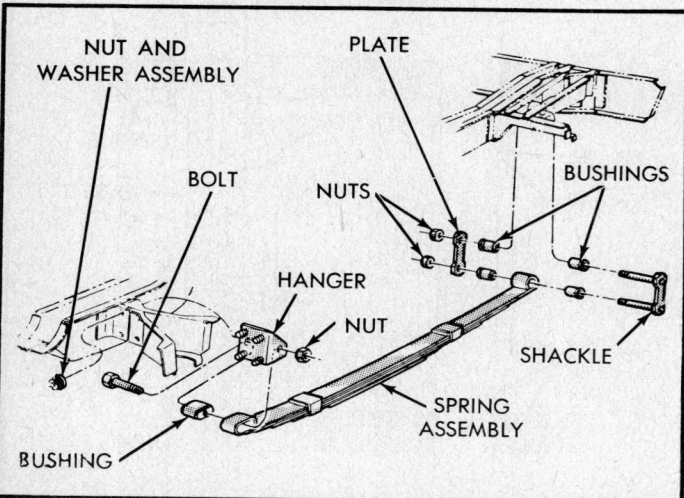

Rear Shock Absorbers

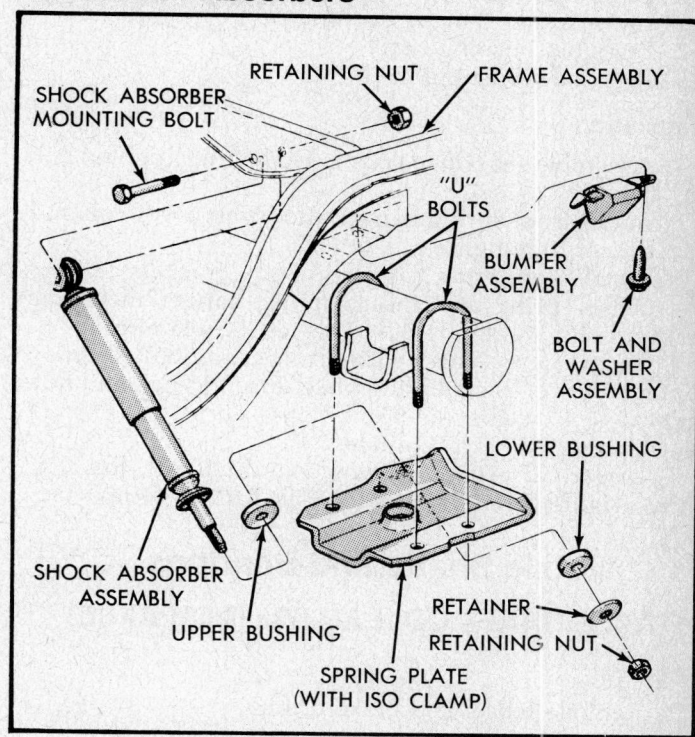

Rear Spring Isolators

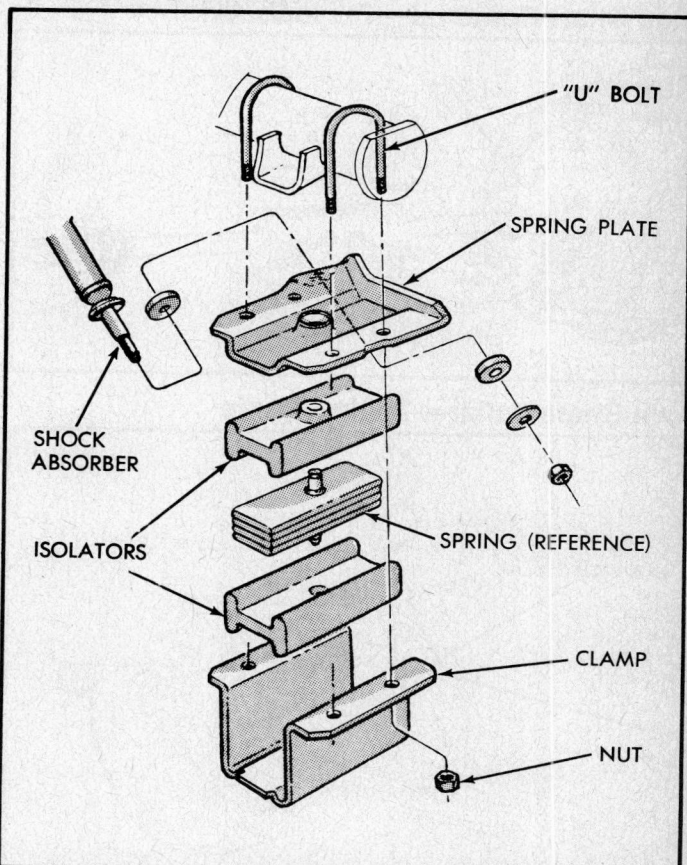

1. Bend two locking tabs away from spring eye on opposite side and remove bushing.
2. Press old bushing out.
3. Press new bushing in.

Installation

1. Assemble shackle to spring. Do not fully tighten bolt nut.
2. Install front spring hanger and insert pivot bolt and nut; do not fully tighten.
3. Install rear spring hanger-to-body bracket.
4. Raise spring and insert spring hanger mounting bracket bolts. tighten to 30–35 ft.-lbs. (42–46 N•m).
5. Align axle assembly with spring center bolt. Position center bolt over lower spring plate. Insert U-bolt and nut. Tighten to 45 ft.-lbs. (60 N•m).
6. Connect shock absorbers.
7. Lower car. Tighten pivot bolts to 105 ft.-lbs. (142 N•m). Tighten shackle nuts to 35 ft.-lbs. (46 N•m).

Axle Shafts and Bearings

AXLE SHAFT COLLAR (7¼ INCH AXLE)

Removal

1. Remove wheel and brake drum.
2. Disconnect brake lines at wheel cylinders.
3. Using access hole in axle shaft flange, remove retainer nuts.

Axle Shaft Removal—7¼ Inch Axle

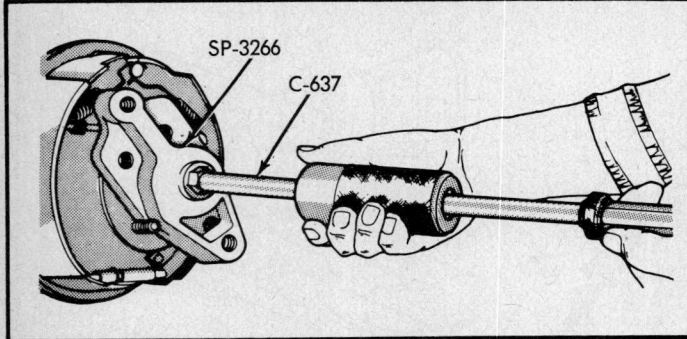

Axle Shaft Collar—7¼ Inch Axle

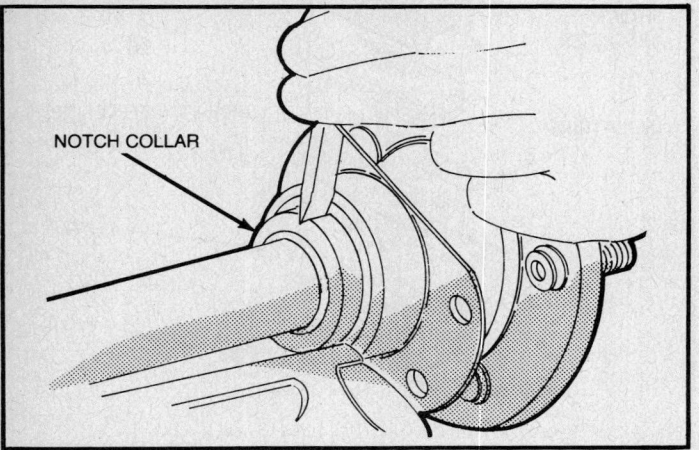

Axle Shaft Bearing Removal—7¼ Inch Axle

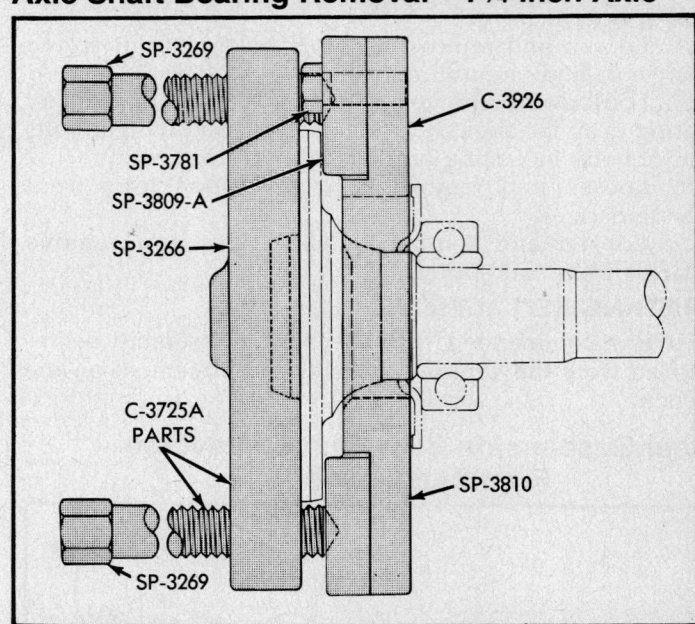

4. With a slide hammer, remove axle shaft and oil seal from housing.
5. Remove brake and support plate assembly.
6. Position axle shaft bearing retaining collar on a vise. Using a chisel cut deep grooves into retaining collar at 90 degree intervals. This will enlarge bore of collar and permit it to be driven off of axle shaft.
7. Use an arbor press, with proper supports, to press bearing off; or use special bearing tools.
8. To remove bearing from shaft use adapter and shaft remover. Generously lubricate bolts of tool. Alternately tighten bolts of tool 1 to 3 turns (to prevent binding of tool) press bearing from shaft.

Installation

1. Install axle shaft retainer plate, new bearing, and bearing retainer collar on axle shaft.

Rear Axle Shaft Bearing Installation— 7¼ Inch Axle

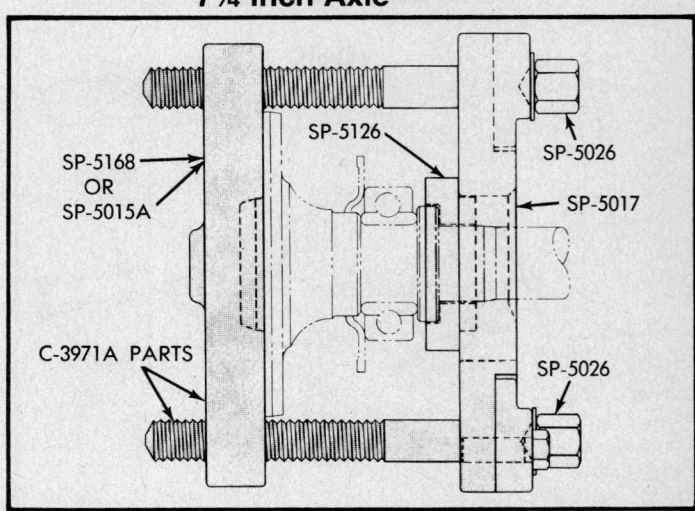

2. Install bearing, retainer collar, and adapter. Alternately tighten bolts of tool 1 to 3 turns (to prevent binding of tool), press them onto shaft.

3. The axle drive shaft bearing and oil seal bores at both ends of housing should be smooth and free of rust and corrosion. This also applies to the brake support plate and housing and flange face area. Install new axle shaft oil seals in axle housing.

Axle Shaft Oil Seal Installation—7¼ Inch Axle

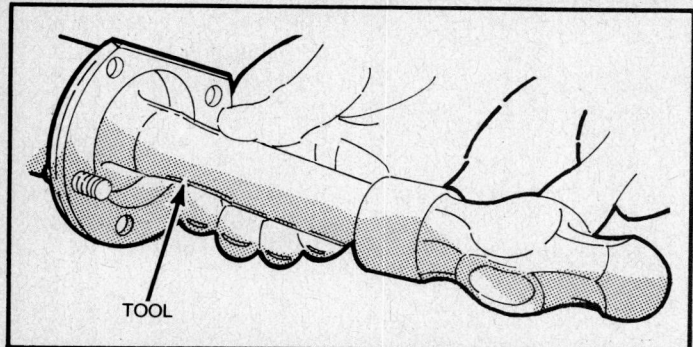

4. Apply a light film of multi-purpose lubricant on outside diameter of bearing to prevent rust and corrosion.

5. Install a new gasket on studs of axle housing and position brake support plate and brake assembly on axle housing studs, followed by outer gasket.

6. Carefully slide axle shaft assembly through oil seal and engage splines in differential side gear.

7. Tap end of axle shaft lightly with a non-metallic mallet to position axle shaft bearing in housing bearing bore. Position retainer plate over axle housing studs. Install retainer nuts and tighten to 35 foot-pounds (47 N•m).

8. Install brake drum, retainer clips, wheel and tire assembly. Tighten wheel nuts to 85 foot-pounds (115 N•m)

8¼ INCH AND 9¼ INCH AXLES

CAUTION Under no circumstances should rear axle bearing cones, cups, bores or journals be subjected to heating with a torch, beating with a hammer or any other abnormal abuse, as permanent damage may result.

Removal

1. Remove wheel cover and wheel and tire assembly. Remove brake drum.

2. Loosen housing cover and drain lubricant from rear axle. Remove cover.

3. Turn differential case to make differential pinion shaft lock screw accessible and remove lock screw and pinion shaft.

4. Push axle shafts toward center of vehicle and remove the "C" washers from recessed groove of axle shaft.

5. Remove axle shaft from housing being careful not to damage the straight roller-type axle shaft bearing which will remain in the rear axle housing.

6. Inspect the axle shaft bearing surfaces for signs of brinnelling, spalling or pitting. If any of these conditions

Axle Shaft C Washer Locks Removal and Installation—8¼ and 9¼ Inch Axle

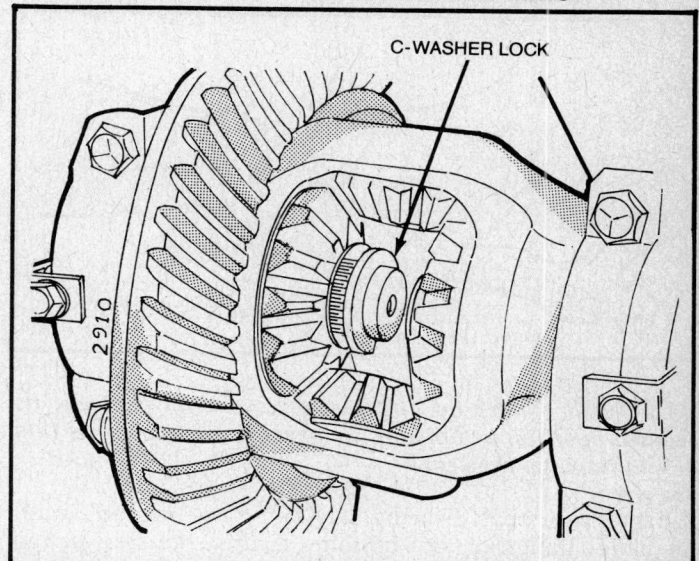

are present both the shaft and the bearing should be replaced. The normal bearing contact on the shaft will be a dull gray and may appear lightly dented.

7. Remove axle shaft seal from housing bore. Using a slide hammer motion, remove axle shaft bearing. If axle shaft and bearing show no signs of distress, they can be reinstalled along with a new axle shaft seal. Never reuse an axle shaft seal.

Axle Shaft Bearing Removal— 8¼ and 9¼ Inch Axle

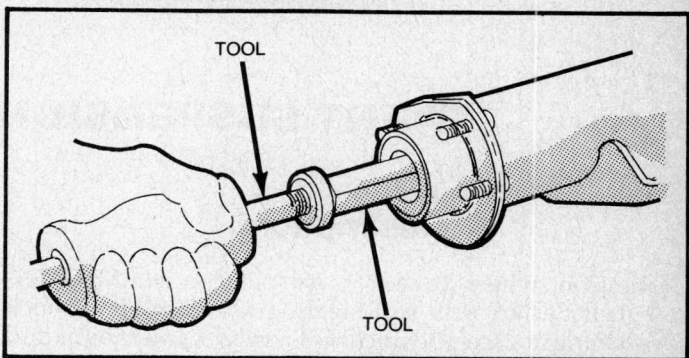

CAUTION Inspect housing bearing shoulder for burrs, and remove any if present; otherwise bearing could be cocked during installation.

Installation

1. Wipe axle shaft bearing cavity of axle housing clean. The axle shaft oil seal bores at both ends of housing should be smooth and free of rust and corrosion. This also applies to brake support plate and housing flange face surface.

2. Insert axle shaft bearing into cavity making sure it bottoms against the shoulder and is not cocked in bore.

Axle Shaft Oil Seal Installation— 8¼ and 9¼ Inch Axle

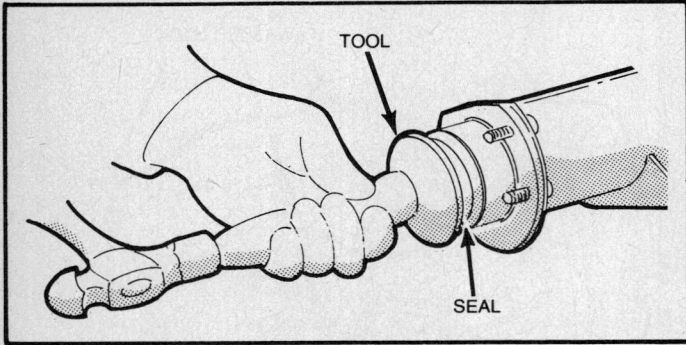

CAUTION   Under no circumstances should the seal be used to position or bottom the bearing in its bore as this would damage the seal.

Install axle shaft bearing seal using special tool, until the outer flange of tool bottoms against housing flange face. This positions the seal to the proper depth beyond the end of the flange face.

3. Lubricate bearing and seal area of axle shaft, slide axle shaft into place being careful that splines of shaft do not damage oil seal and properly engage with splines of differential side gears.

4. With axle shaft in place, install the "C" washers in recessed grooves of axle shaft, and pull outward on shaft so the "C" washers seat in the counterbore of differential side gear.

5. Install differential pinion shaft through case and pinions, aligning hole in shaft with lock screw hole. Install lock screw and tighten to 100 inch-pounds (11 N•m).

6. Clean up mating surfaces, and apply a ¹⁄₁₆ inch to ³⁄₃₂ inch bead of silicone rubber sealant along the bolt circle of the cover. Allow sealant to cure.

Rear Axle Housing Cover

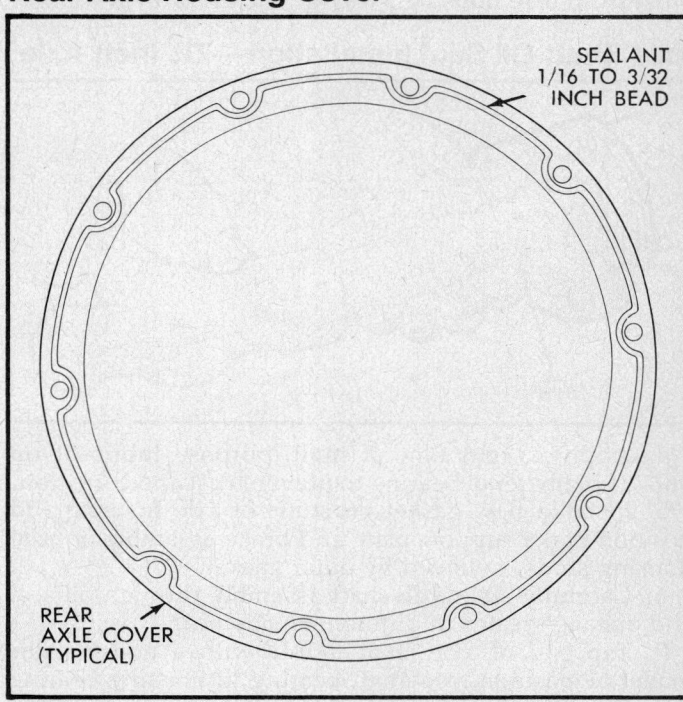

FRONT SUSPENSION—FORD FRONT DRIVE

Description

The front wheel drive front suspension is a MacPherson strut design with cast steering knuckles. The shock absorber strut assembly includes a rubber top mount and a coil spring insulator, mounted on the shock strut.

The entire strut assembly is attached at the top by two bolts, which retain the top mount of the strut to the body side apron. The lower end of the assembly is attached to the steering knuckle. A pinch joint is designed into the knuckle. A forged lower arm assembly is attached to the underbody side apron and steering knuckle. A stabilizer bar connects the outer end of lower arm to the engine mount bracket. The drive shaft outer stub shaft and wheel hub are attached inside the steering knuckle hub by a pressed fit of mating splines. The assembly is secured by a staked nut on the end of the stub shaft. The hub rotates on two non-adjustable tapered roller bearings which seat against cups in the steering knuckle.

Wheel Alignment
TOE

Toe is the difference in distance between the front and the rear of front wheels.

1. Start the engine (power steering only) and move the steering wheel back and forth several times until it is in the straight ahead or centered position.

2. Turn the engine off (power steering only) and lock the steering wheel in place using a steering wheel holder. Loosen and slide off small outer clamp from boot prior to starting toe adjustment to prevent boot from twisting.

3. Adjust left and right tie rods until each wheel has one-half of the desired total toe specification.

NOTE   When jam nuts are loosened for toe adjustment, the nuts must be tightened to specifications. Attach boot clamp after setting is completed and make sure boot is not twisted.

Front Wheel Drive Suspension

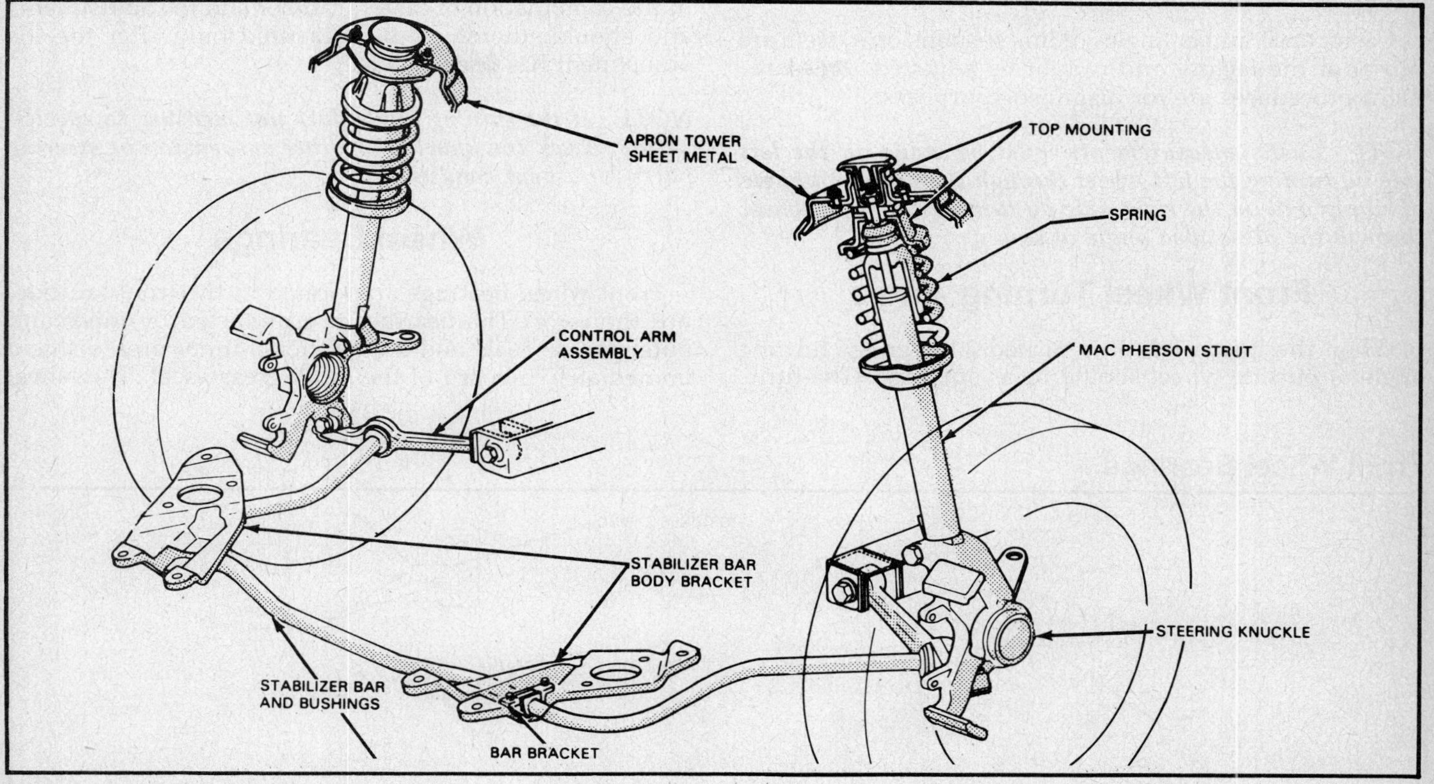

APRON TOWER
SHEET METAL

TOP MOUNTING

SPRING

CONTROL ARM
ASSEMBLY

MAC PHERSON STRUT

STABILIZER BAR
BODY BRACKET

STEERING KNUCKLE

STABILIZER BAR
AND BUSHINGS

BAR BRACKET

Tie Rod Adjustment

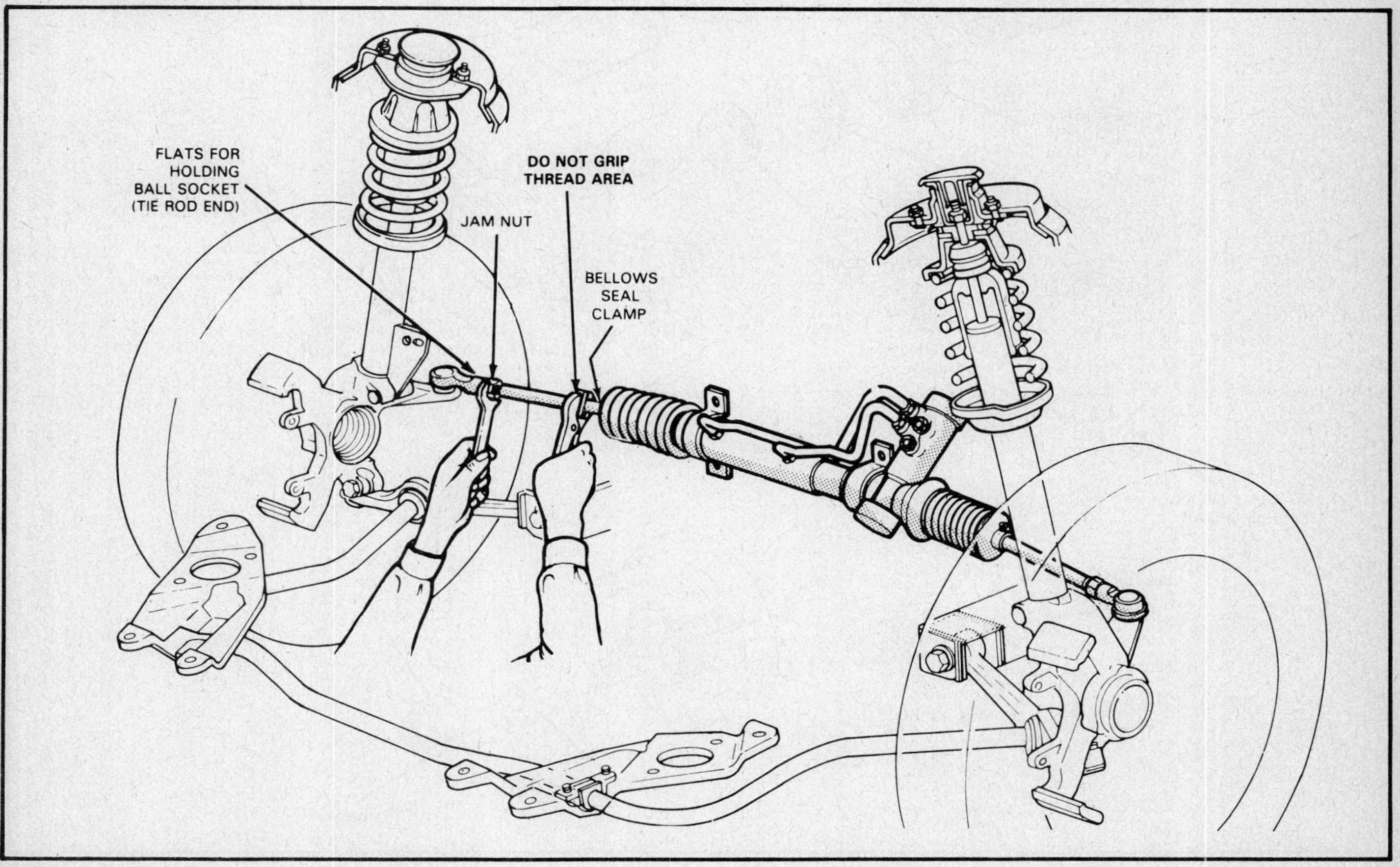

FLATS FOR
HOLDING
BALL SOCKET
(TIE ROD END)

DO NOT GRIP
THREAD AREA

JAM NUT

BELLOWS
SEAL
CLAMP

Caster and Camber

Caster and camber angles of this suspension system are preset at the factory and cannot be adjusted. Measurement procedures are for diagnostic purposes.

NOTE   Caster measurements must be made on the left side by turning the left wheel through the presribed angle of sweep and on the right side by turning the right wheel through the prescribed angle of sweep.

Front Wheel Turning Angle

When the inside wheel is turned 20 degrees, turning angle of outside wheel should be as specified. The turning angle cannot be adjusted directly, because it is a result of the combination of caster, camber and toe adjustments and should, therefore, be measured only after the toe adjustment has been made.

NOTE   If the turning angle does not measure to specification, check the knuckle or other suspension or steering parts for a bent condition.

Wheel Bearings

Front wheel bearings are located in the front knuckle, not the rotor. The bearings are protected by inner and outer grease seals and an additional inner grease shield immediately inboard of the inner grease seal. The wheel

Front Wheel Bearings

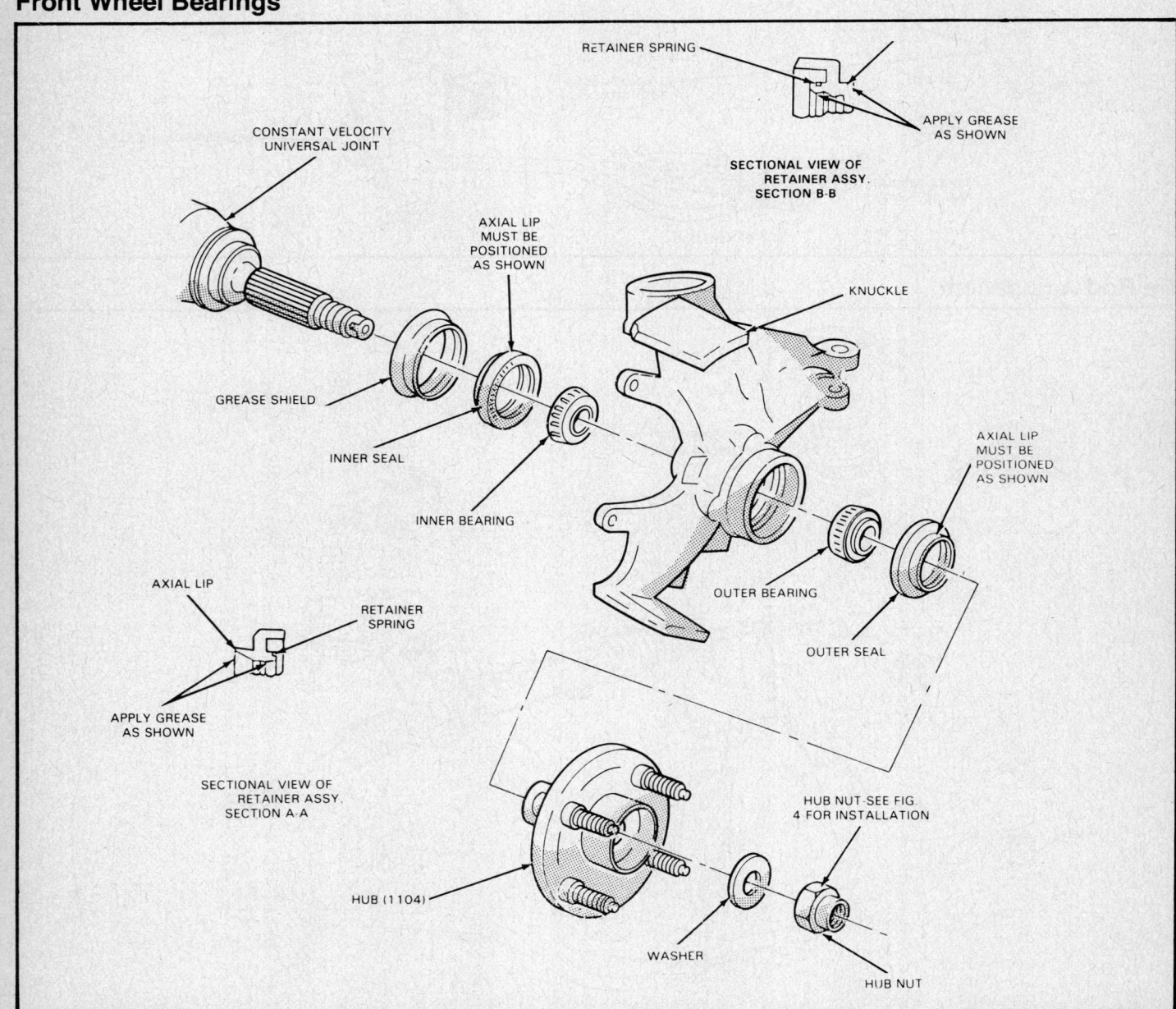

hub is installed with an interference fit to the constant velocity universal joint outer race shaft. The hub nut and washer are installed and tightened to 240–270 N•m (180–200 ft.-lbs.). The rotor fits loosely on the hub assembly and is secured when the wheel and wheel nuts are installed.

Adjustment

The front wheel bearings have a set-right design that requires no scheduled maintenance. The bearing design relies on component stack-up and deformation/torque at asembly to determine bearing setting. Therefore, bearings cannot be adjusted. In addition to maintaining bearing adjustment, the hub nut torque of 240–270 N•m (180–200 ft.-lbs.) restricts bearing/hub relative movement and maintains axial position of the hub. Due to the importance of the hub nut torque/tension relationship, certain precautions must be taken during service.

1. The hub nut must be replaced with a new nut whenever the nut is backed off or removed after the nut has been staked. Never re-use the nut.

2. The hub nut must not be backed off after reaching the required torque of 240–270 N•m (180–200 ft.-lbs.) during installation.

3. The hub nut collar must be staked into the outboard constant velocity joint slot with the proper tool to make sure the required torque is maintained during vehicle operation. The nut collar must not split or crack when staked. If the collar splits or cracks, the nut must be replaced.

4. Impact type tools must not be used to tighten the hub nut or bearing damage will result.

5. The hub and constant velocity joint splines have an interference fit requiring special tools for removal and assembly. The hub nut must not be used to accomplish assembly.

6. To remove the hub nut, apply sufficient torque to the nut to overcome the prevailing torque feature of the crimp in the nut collar. Do not use tools such as a screwdriver or chisel to remove the crimp.

Front Hub

Removal

1. Remove hub retaining nut and washer by applyng sufficient torque to the nut to overcome prevailing torque feature of the crimp in nut collar. Do not use tools such as a screwdriver or chisel to remove the crimp or use an impact-type tool to remove the hub nut. The hub nut must be discarded after removal.

2. Remove brake caliper. Do not remove caliper pins from the caliper assembly. Lift caliper off the rotor and hang it free of the rotor. Do not allow caliper assembly to hang from the brake hose. Support caliper assembly.

3. Remove rotor from hub by pulling it outboard off the hub bolts.

4. Install hub remover/installer tool, T81P-1104-A with T81P-1104-C and adaptors T81P-1104-B and remove the hub. If outer bearing is seized on the hub, use a puller to remove the bearing. Be careful not to damage bearing if it is being re-used and not to raise burrs on the hub journal

Hub Removal

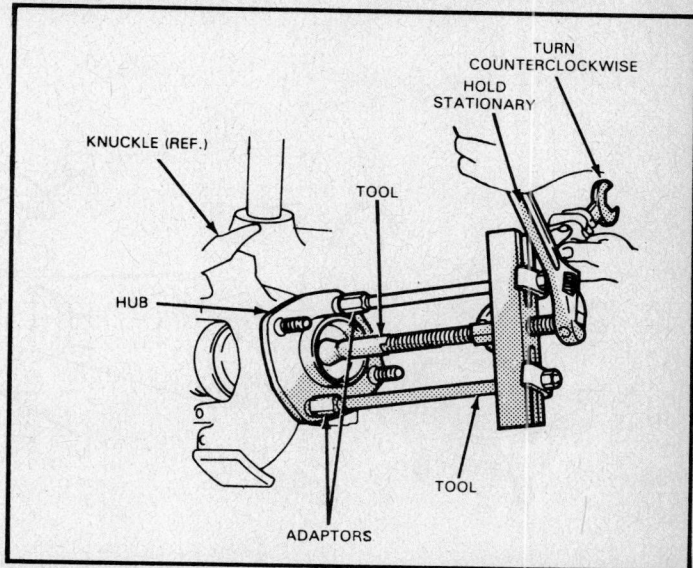

Remove hub from constant velocity universal joint splined stub shaft as shown.

diameter. If bearings are being re-used, carefully inspect both bearing cone and rollers, bearing cups and lubrication for any signs of damage or contamination. If damage or contamination exists, replace all bearing components including cups and seals. In the event the bearings are acceptable, clean and repack bearing components. Inner and outer grease retainers and hub nut must be replaced whenever bearings are inspected.

5. Remove front suspension knuckle.

Wheel Bearing and Caliper Assembly

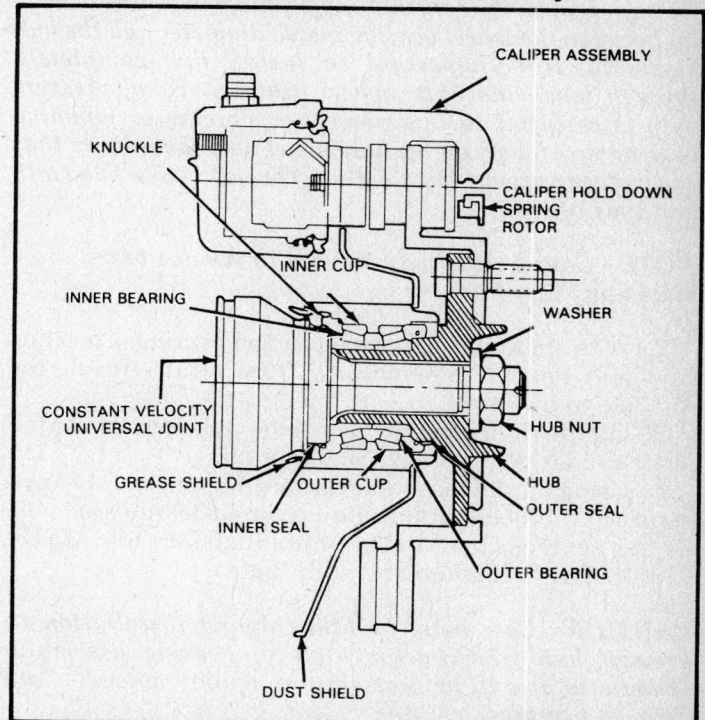

SUSPENSION

Hub Installation

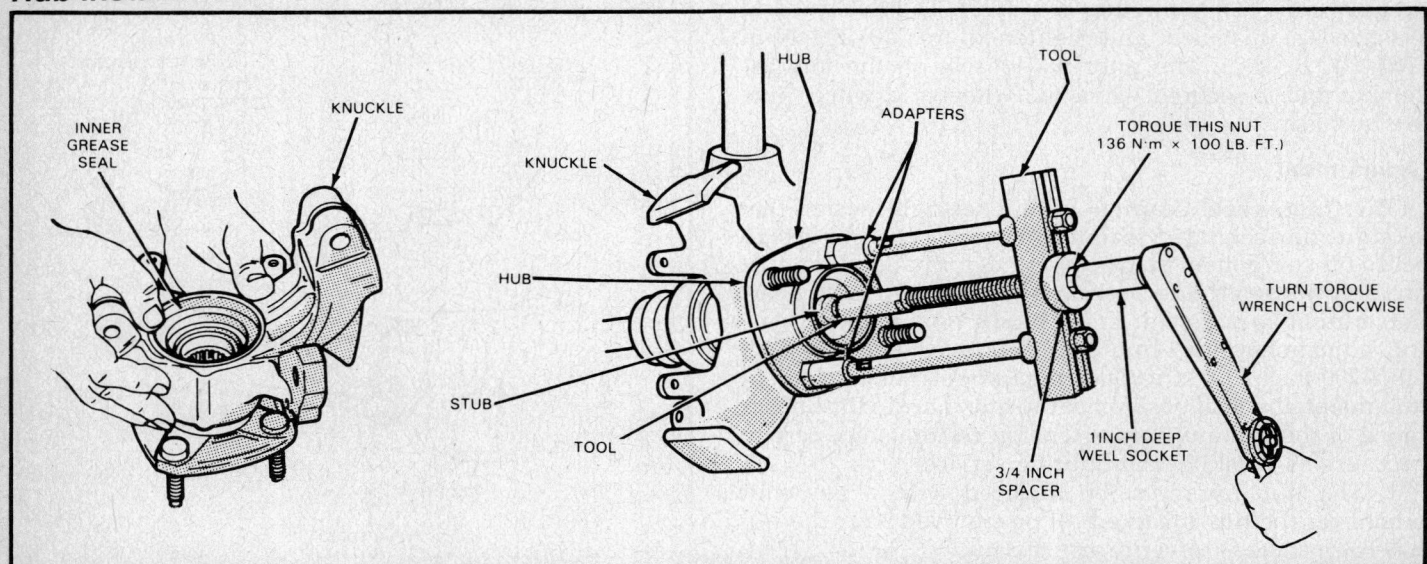

Step 1: Install hub to knuckle after bearing installation. Knuckle must be positioned as shown and hub must be inserted through bearings using hand pressure only. **Step 2:** Install hub to constant velocity universal joint splined stub shaft. Tighten tool nut to 150 N·m (110 lb-ft) using torque wrench to seat hub.

Installation

1. Place front knuckle and bearing assembly in a vise so that the inner knuckle bore faces upward (to prevent inner bearing from falling out of the knuckle). Start hub into outer knuckle bore and push the hub by hand through outer and inner wheel bearings as far as possible.

CAUTION Prior to assembly, remove burrs, nicks, score marks, foreign material (rust, dirt, etc.) from hub bearing journal. Due to the very close tolerance 0.0121 mm (0.0005 in) between the wheel bearing inside diameter and the hub assembly, it is important to install hub completely through inner and outer wheel bearings. Hand pressure only is essential to this procedure. Forcing or jamming bearing race (cone) on the hub barrel will cause burrs that can prevent proper installation. Do not strike hub with any type of tool.

NOTE Crocus cloth may be used to remove burrs, score marks and rust from the hub barrel.

2. With the hub fully seated in the bearings, position hub and knuckle assembly to front strut. Attach the knuckle to the strut.
3. Lightly lubricate the constant velocity joint stub shaft splines using S.A.E. 30 motor oil.
4. Using hand pressure only, insert splines of the constant velocity joint stub shaft into knuckle/hub assembly as far as possible. Install hub installer tool T81P-1104-C-B-A to the hub and stub shaft.

CAUTION Care must be taken during installation to prevent hub from backing out of bearing assembly. Otherwise, it will be necessary to again reassemble hub through bearings.

Hub Nut Installation

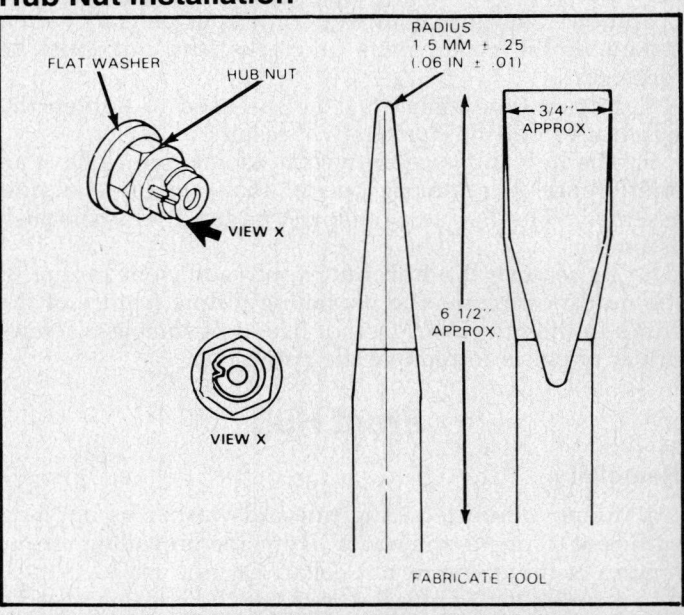

Tighten nut to 240–270 N·m (180–200 lb-ft) after hub is seated, using special hub installer tool T81P-1104-A. Do not use impact wrench for removal or installation of hub nut. After nut is torqued, deform nut collar into slot of driveshaft using tool as indicated. The nut must not split or crack when staked. If nut is split or cracked after staking, it must be removed and replaced with new unused nut. Removing or moving a hub nut after staking requires the nut be replaced with a new nut. The staking tool can be fabricated from an existed hardened chisel. The correct radius on the chisel tip will prevent improper staking. Do not attempt to stake with a sharp edged tool.

5. Tighten hub installer tool to 163 N•m (120 ft.-lbs.) torque to make sure that the hub is fully seated. Remove tool and install washer and hub nut. Tighten the hub nut finger tight.

6. Install disc brake rotor and brake caliper.

7. Lower vehicle and block wheels to prevent rolling.

8. Tighten wheel nuts to 109–142 N•m (80–105 ft.-lbs.) torque.

Strut, Spring and Upper Mount

Removal

1. Raise front of vehicle and place jack stands under frame jack pads, rearward of the wheels.

2. Remove tire and wheel assembly.

3. Remove brake line flex hose clip from strut.

4. Place a floor jack under lower control arm and raise strut as far as possible without lifting vehicle.

5. Install spring compressor tool by placing top jaw on second coil from top and bottom jaw so as to grip a total of five coils. Compress spring until there is about ⅛ inch between any two coils.

CAUTION   Use hand wrenches (no impact wrenches).

6. Using a pry bar slightly spread knuckle-to-strut pinch joint.

7. Place a piece of wood, 2 inches by 4 inches, and 7½ inches long, against shoulder on the knuckle. Using a

Separate Shock Absorber Strut From Knuckle

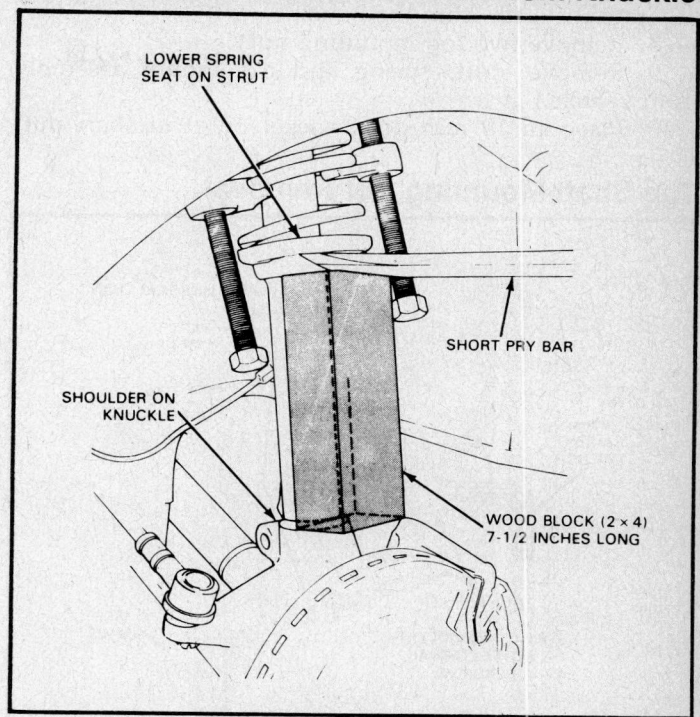

Raise Strut But Not Vehicle

Position Spring Compressor Tool

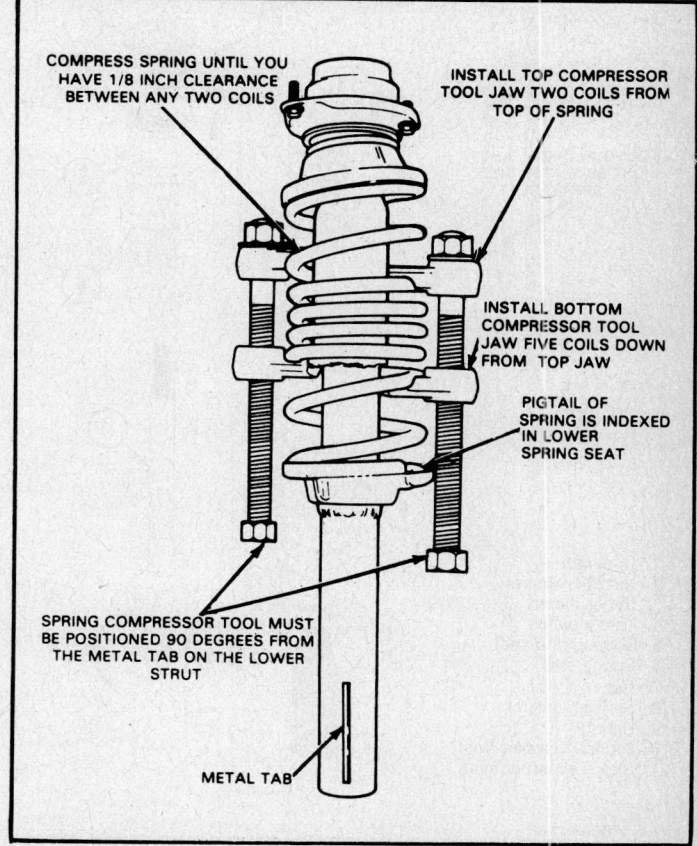

SUSPENSION

FRONT SUSPENSION-FORD FRONT DRIVE

short pry bar between wood block and lower spring seat, separate the strut from the knuckle.

8. Remove two top mounting nuts.

9. Remove strut, spring and top mount assembly from vehicle.

10. Place an 18 mm deep socket on strut shaft nut.

Top Shaft Mounting Nut Removal

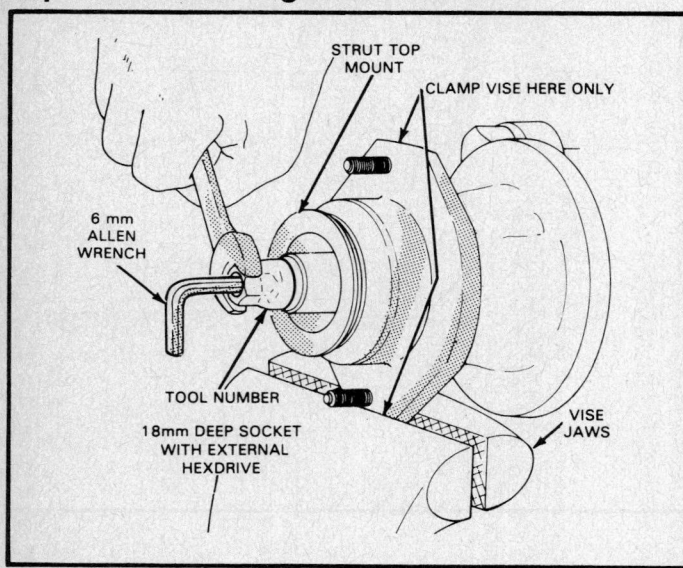

Top Mount Components

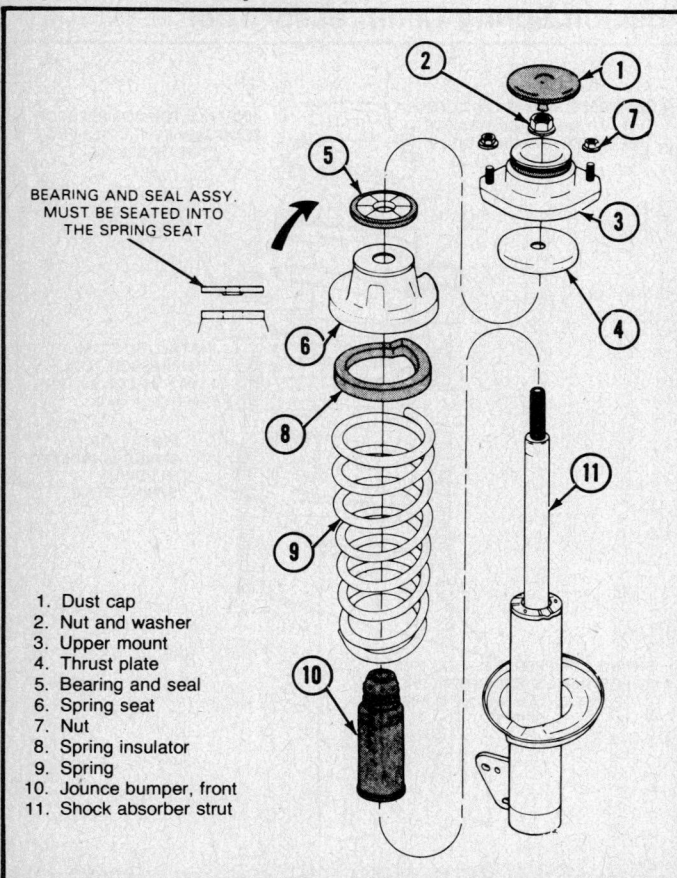

1. Dust cap
2. Nut and washer
3. Upper mount
4. Thrust plate
5. Bearing and seal
6. Spring seat
7. Nut
8. Spring insulator
9. Spring
10. Jounce bumper, front
11. Shock absorber strut

Insert a 6 mm allen wrench into shaft end and then clamp mount into a vise. Remove top shaft mounting nut from shaft while holding allen wrench with vise grips or a suitable extension.

11. Remove strut top mount components and spring.

Installation

1. Position compressed spring in lower spring seat. Be sure that:

   a. Pigtail of spring is indexed in seat.

   b. Spring compressor tool is positioned 90 degrees from metal tab on lower part of strut.

2. Using a new nut, assemble top mount components to strut.

CAUTION Be sure that the correct assembly sequence and proper positioning of bearing and seal assembly is followed. If bearing and seal assembly is out of position, damage to bearing will result.

3. Tighten shaft nut to torque of 65–85 N•m (48–62.5 ft.-lbs.).

4. Install strut, spring, upper mount and spring compressor into the vehicle as an assembly.

5. Position two top mounts attaching studs through holes in apron and start two new nuts. Do not tighten nuts at this time.

6. Install strut into steering knuckle pinch joint.

7. Install a new pinch bolt in the steering knuckle and tighten to torque of 90–110 N•m (68–81 ft.-lbs.).

8. Tighten two upper mount attaching nuts to torque of 30–40 N•m (22–29 ft.-lbs.).

Compressing Spring

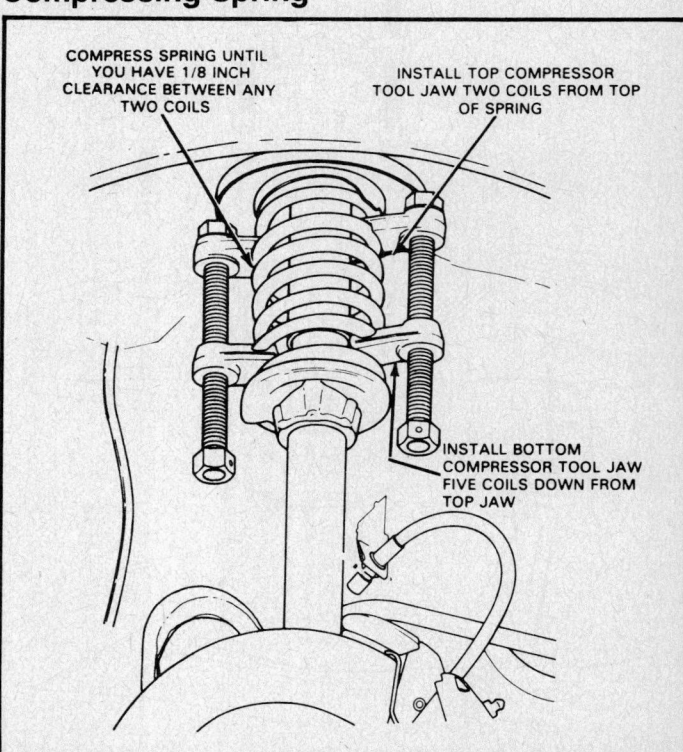

9. Remove spring compressor from the vehicle. As the compressor is loosened, be sure spring ends are indexed in upper and lower spring seats.
10. Install brake line flex hose clip to strut.
11. Install tire and wheel assembly.
12. Remove jack stands and lower vehicle.

Steering Knuckle

Removal

1. Raise vehicle on a hoist.
2. Remove tire and wheel assembly.
3. Remove cotter pin from the tie rod end stud and remove slotted nut.

4. Remove tie rod end from knuckle.
5. Remove the brake caliper.
6. Remove the hub from the driveshaft.
7. Remove lower arm-to-steering knuckle pinch bolt and nut. (A drift punch may be used to remove production bolt.) Using a screwdriver, slightly spread the knuckle-to-lower arm pinch joint and remove lower arm from steering knuckle.

NOTE *Be sure steering column is in unlocked position, and do not use a hammer to separate ball joint from knuckle.*

8. Remove shock absorber strut-to-steering knuckle

Steering Knuckle

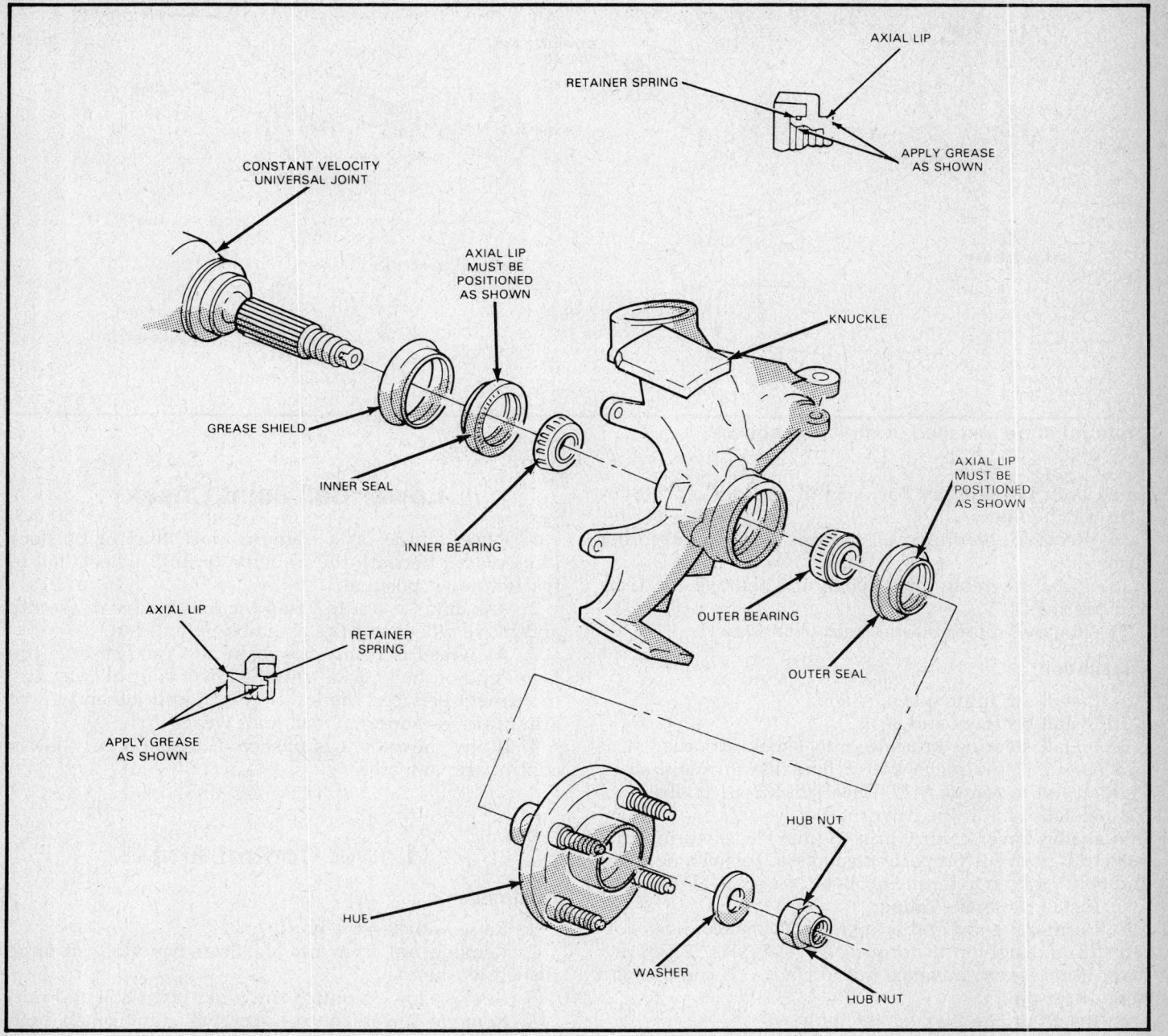

Front Suspension Fasteners

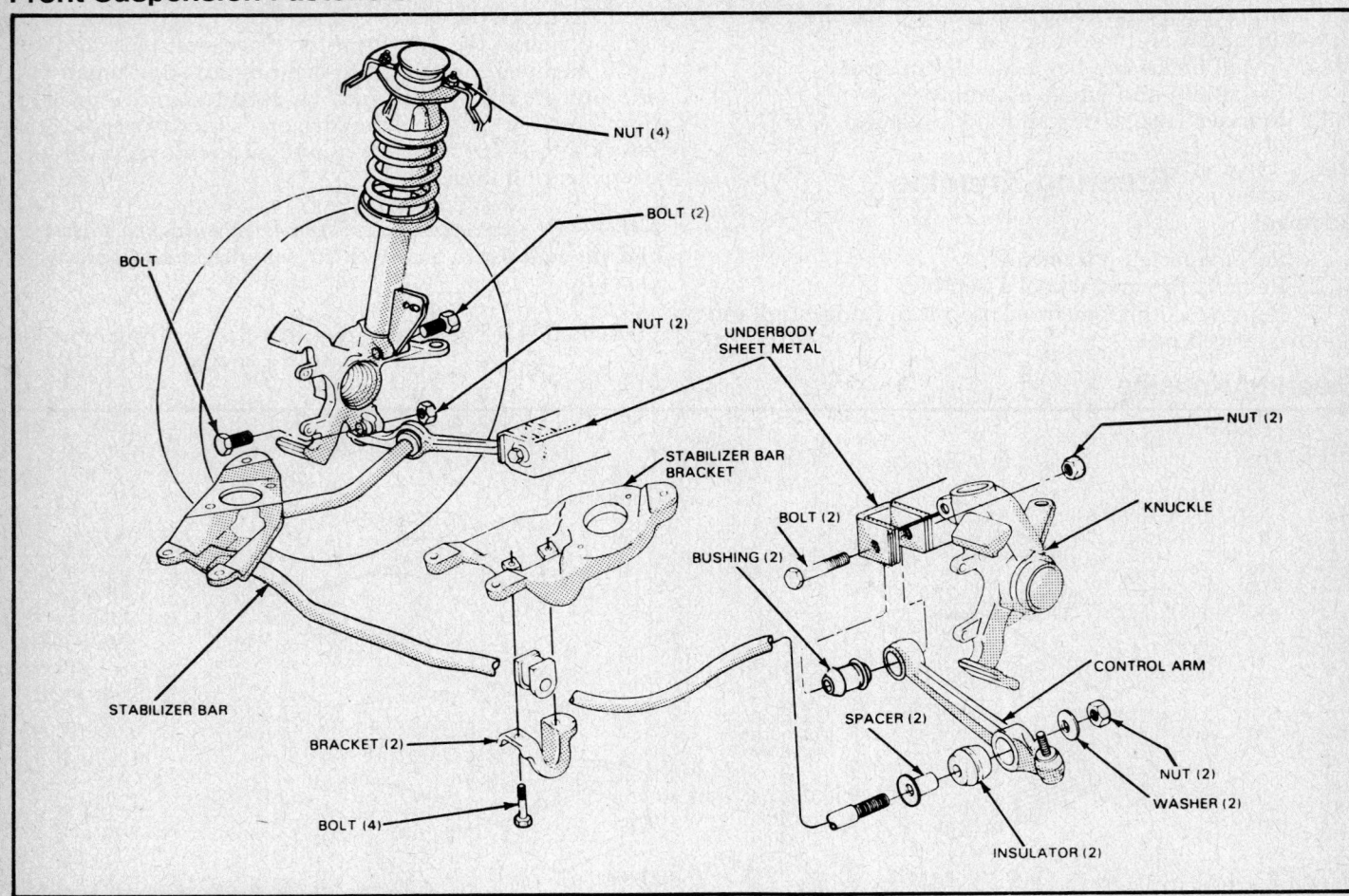

Bolts must be installed in direction shown.

pinch bolt. Using a pry bar, slightly spread knuckle-to-strut pinch joint.

9. Remove steering knuckle from the shock absorber strut.

10. Place assembly on a bench and remove the seals and bearings.

11. Remove rotor splash shield from knuckle.

Installation

1. Install the rotor splash shield.

2. Install bearings and seals.

3. Install steering knuckle onto shock absorber strut and install a new pinch bolt in knuckle to retain strut. Tighten nut to torque of 90–110 N•m (66–81 ft.-lbs.).

4. Install hub on the driveshaft.

5. Install lower control arm to knuckle, ensuring that ball stud groove is properly positioned. Install a new nut and bolt. Tighten to torque of 50–60 N•m (37–44 ft.-lbs.).

6. Install the brake caliper.

7. Position tie rod end into knuckle, install a new slotted nut and tighten to torque of 31–47 N•m (23–35 ft.-lbs.). If necessary, advance nut to align slot and install a new cotter pin.

8. Install tire and wheel assembly.

Lower Ball Joint Check

1. Raise vehicle on a frame contact hoist or by floor jacks placed beneath the underbody until wheels fall to the full down position.

2. Ask an assistant to grasp the lower edge of the tire and move wheel and tire assembly in and out.

3. As wheel is being moved in and out, observe the lower end of the knuckle and the lower control arm. Any movement between the lower end of knuckle and lower arm indicates abnormal ball joint wear.

4. If any movement is observed, install a new lower control arm assembly.

Lower Control Arm

Removal

1. Raise vehicle on a hoist.

2. Remove nut from the stabilizer bar. Pull off large dished washer.

3. Remove lower control arm inner pivot bolt and nut.

4. Remove lower control arm ball joint pinch bolt.

Checking Lower Ball Joint

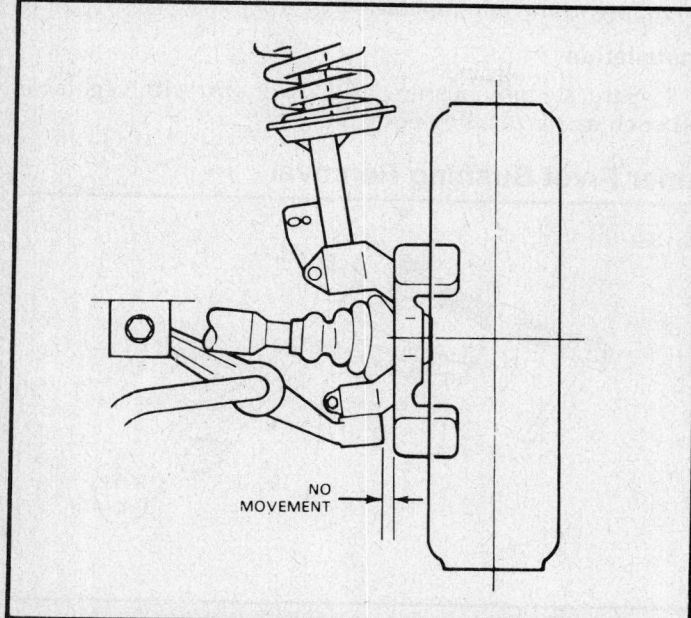

As wheel is being moved in and out, observe the lower end of the knuckle and the lower control arm. Any movement between lower end of the knuckle and the lower arm indicates abnormal ball joint wear.

Slightly spread the knuckle pinch joint and separate control arm from the steering knuckle. A drift punch may be used to remove the bolt.

NOTE   Be sure steering column is in unlocked position, and do not use a hammer to separate ball joint from knuckle.

Installation

1. Assemble lower control arm ball joint stud to the steering knuckle, insuring that the ball stud groove is properly positioned.
2. Insert a new pinch bolt and nut. Tighten nut to torque of 50–60 N•m (37–44 ft.-lbs.).
3. Position lower control arm onto stabilizer bar and then position lower control arm to the inner underbody mounting. Install a new nut and bolt. Tighten bolt to torque of 60–75 N•m (44–55.3 ft.-lbs.).
4. Assemble stabilizer bar, dished washer and a new nut to stabilizer bar. Tighten nut to torque of 80–100 N•m (59–73 ft.-lbs.).

Stabilizer Bar and/or Insulators

Removal

1. Raise vehicle.
2. Remove nut from stabilizer bar at each lower control arm and pull off large dished washer.
3. Remove stabilizer bar insulator mounting bracket bolts and remove stabilizer bar assembly.
4. Cut worn insulators from bar.

Stabilizer Bar Components

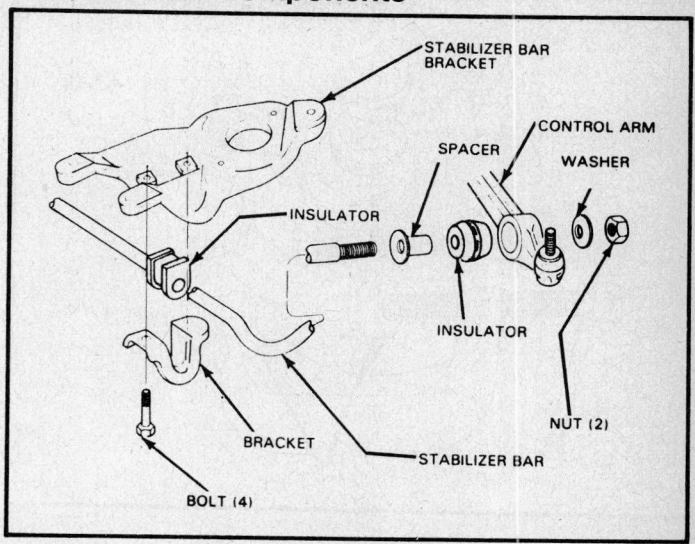

Installation

1. Coat bar and insulators with tire mounting lubricant or soapy water. Slide new insulators onto bar and position in approximate final location.
2. Install washer spacers onto bar ends and push mounting brackets over insulators.
3. Insert ends of bar into lower control arms. Using new bolts, attach bar and insulator mounting brackets to body. Tighten to 68–81 N•m (50–60 ft.-lbs.).
4. Using new nuts and original dished washers, attach bar to lower control arms. Tighten nuts to 80–100 N•m (59–73 ft.-lbs.).

Stabilizer Bar-to-Control Arm Insulator

Removal

1. Raise vehicle on a hoist.
2. Remove stabilizer bar-to-control arm nut and dished washer.
3. Remove control arm inner pivot nut and bolt and pull arm down from the underbody and away from stabilizer bar.
4. Using Tool T81P-5493-A and T74P-3044-A1, remove old insulator bushing from the control arm.

Installation

1. Saturate new insulator bushing and lower arm with vegetable oil such as Mazola® oil or an equivalent oil.

NOTE   Use only vegetable oil. Any mineral- or petroleum-based oil or brake fluid will deteriorate the rubber bushing.

2. Using Tool T81P-5493-A and T74P-3044-A1, install new insulator bushing in lower control arm by tightening the C-clamp very slowly until bushing pops in place.

Stabilizer Bar Bushing Removal

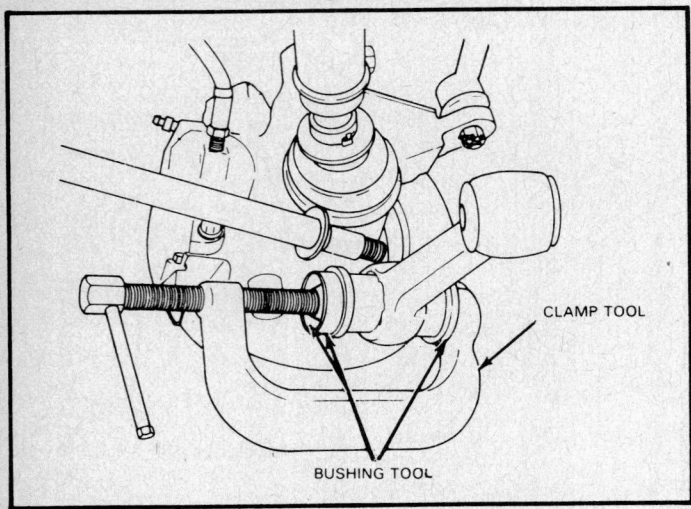

Stabilizer Bar Bushing Installation

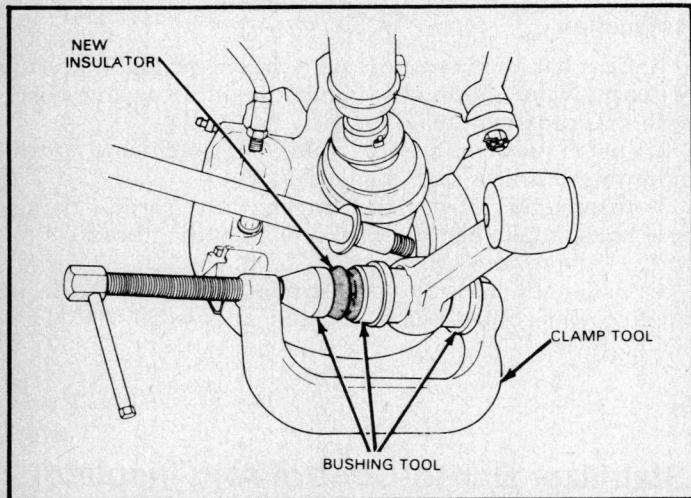

Lower Arm Inner Pivot Bushing

Removal

1. Raise vehicle on a hoist.
2. Remove stabilizer bar to control arm nut and dished washer.
3. Remove control arm inner pivot nut and bolt and pull arm down from underbody and away from stabilizer bar.
4. Using a sharp knife, carefully cut away retaining lip of bushing prior to its removal.
5. Using Tool T81P-5493-B and T74P-3044-A1, remove old bushing from control arm.

NOTE This operation can be done in vehicle without removing arm from knuckle.

Installation

1. Saturate new bushing and lower arm with vegetable oil such as Mazola® or equivalent.

Inner Pivot Bushing Removal

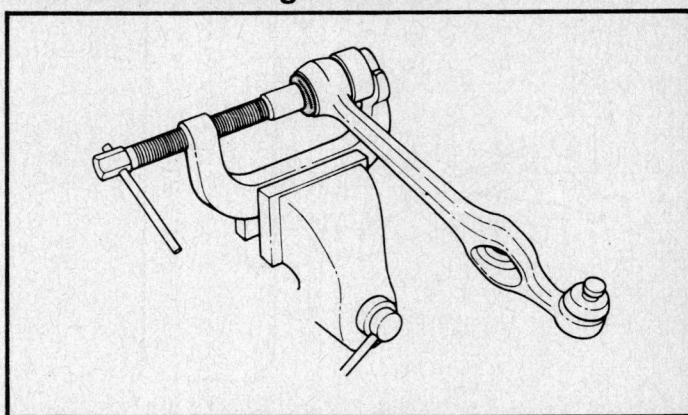

NOTE Use only vegetable oil. Any mineral- or petroleum-based oil or brake fluid will deteriorate the rubber bushing.

2. Using Tool T81P-5493-B and T74P-3044-A1, install new bushing in lower control arm.
3. Position control arm onto stabilizer bar. Be sure washer spacer is in place.
4. Position control arm to underbody and install a new nut and bolt. Tighten bolt to torque of 60–75 N•m (44–55.3 ft.-lbs.).
5. Install a new nut and the original dished washer on stabilizer bar. Tighten nut to torque of 80–100 N•m (59–73 ft.-lbs.).

Inner Pivot Bushing Installation

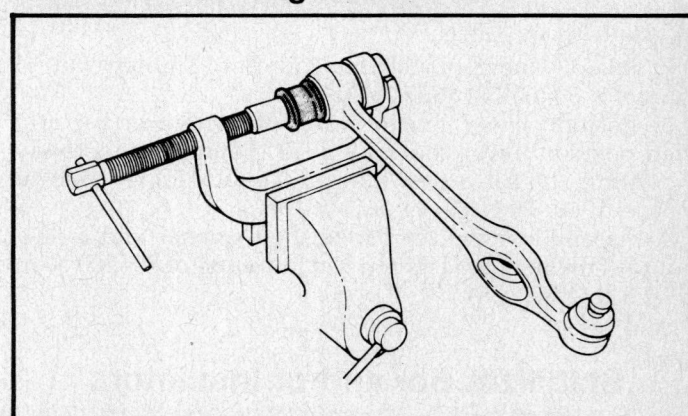

REAR SUSPENSION—FORD FRONT DRIVE

Wheel Bearings

Adjustment

Tighten adjusting nut "A" to 23–24 N•m (17–25 ft.-lbs.) while rotating hub and drum assembly. Back off adjusting nut approximately 100 degrees. Position nut retainer "B" over adjusting nut so slots are in line with cotter pin hole without rotating adjusting nut. Install cotter pin.

NOTE *The spindle has a prevailing torque feature that prevents adjusting the nut by hand.*

Component Replacement

The following applies regarding components that are replaced individually or as an assembly.
● The shock absorber strut upper mounting is separately serviceable.

Independent Rear Suspension

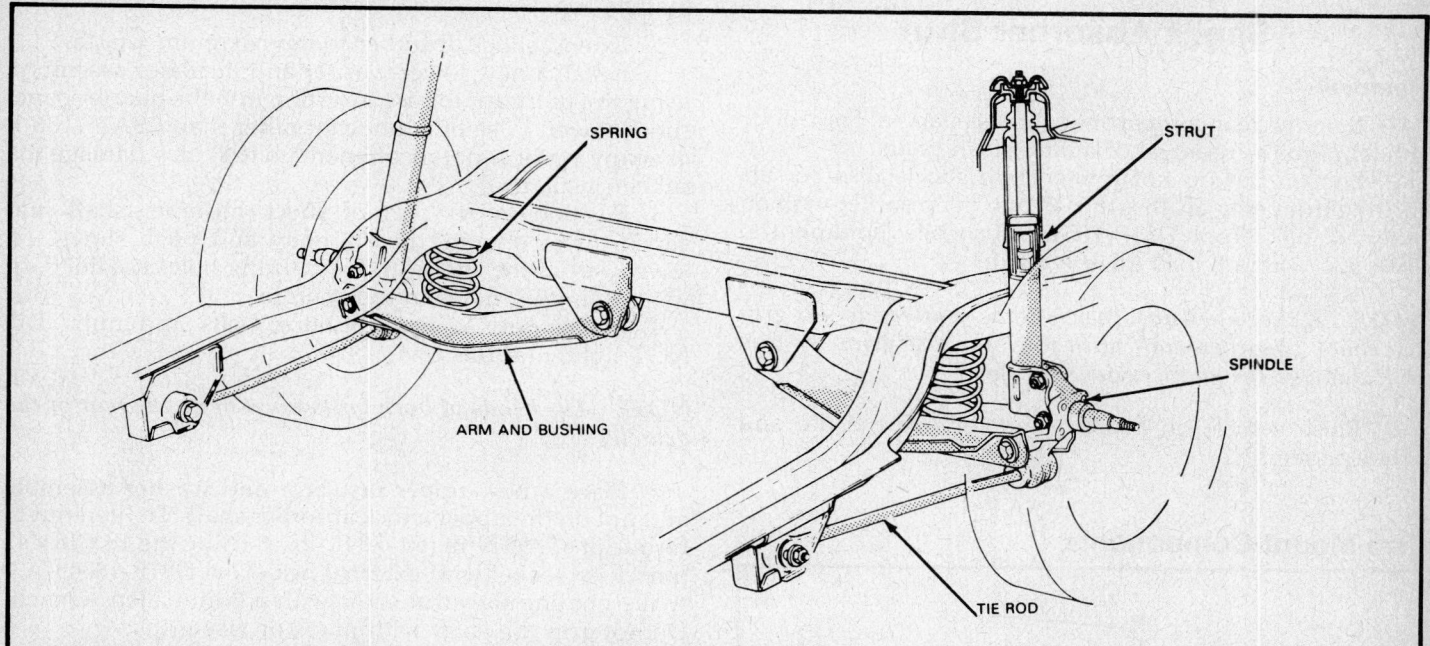

Rear Bearing

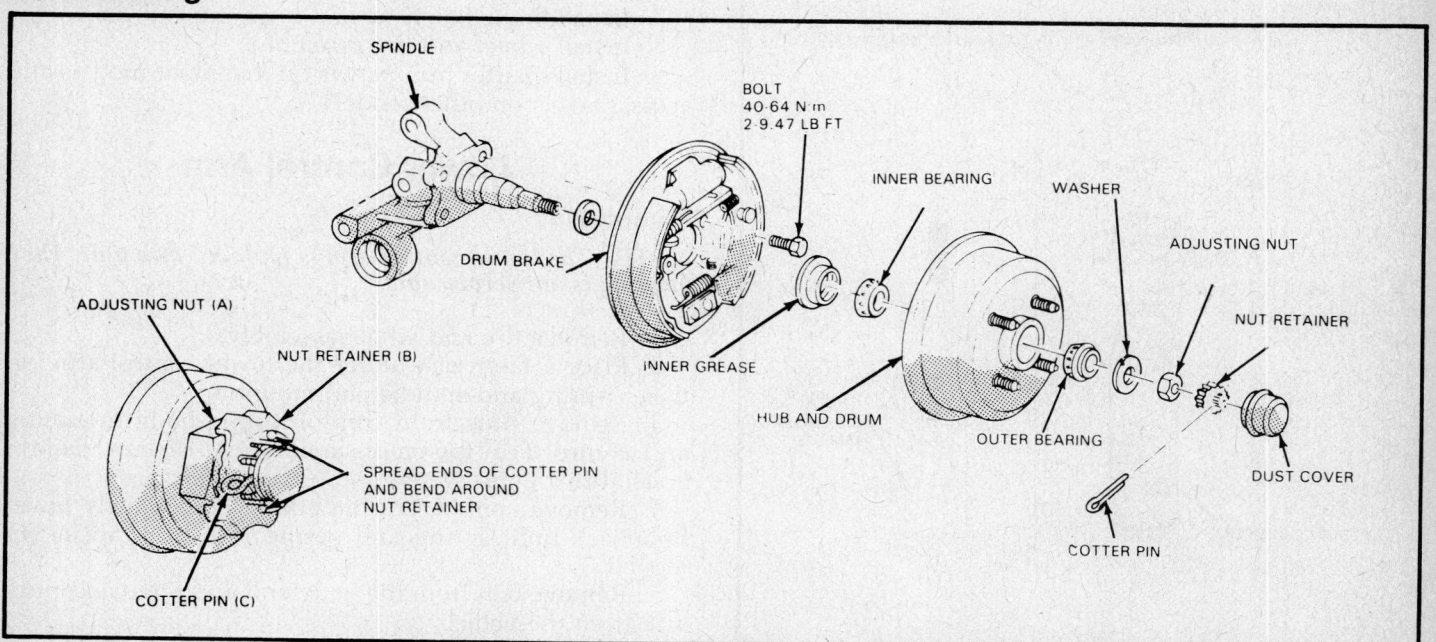

- The shock absorber strut is not repairable and must be replaced as an assembly.
- Lower control arm bushings are not serviceable. They must be replaced with a lower control arm and bushing assembly.
- Tie-rod bushings can be serviced separately at both the forward and rearward locations. However, if the tie-rod requires replacement, new bushings must be installed in the spindle at the same time.
- Coil springs are serviceable. If a rear coil spring is replaced, the upper spring insulator must also be replaced.

Shock Absorber Strut

Removal

1. Remove rear compartment access panels. Four-door model requires removal of quarter trim panel.

2. Loosen but do not remove top shock absorber attaching nut using an 18 x 18 x 43 mm deep socket with an external hex (Tool D81P-18045-A3) while holding the strut rod with a 6 mm Allen wrench.

NOTE   If the shock absorber is to be re-used, do not grip the shock absorber shaft with pliers or vise grips, as this will damage the shaft surface finish.

3. Raise vehicle on a hoist, and remove the tire and wheel assembly.

Top Mount Components

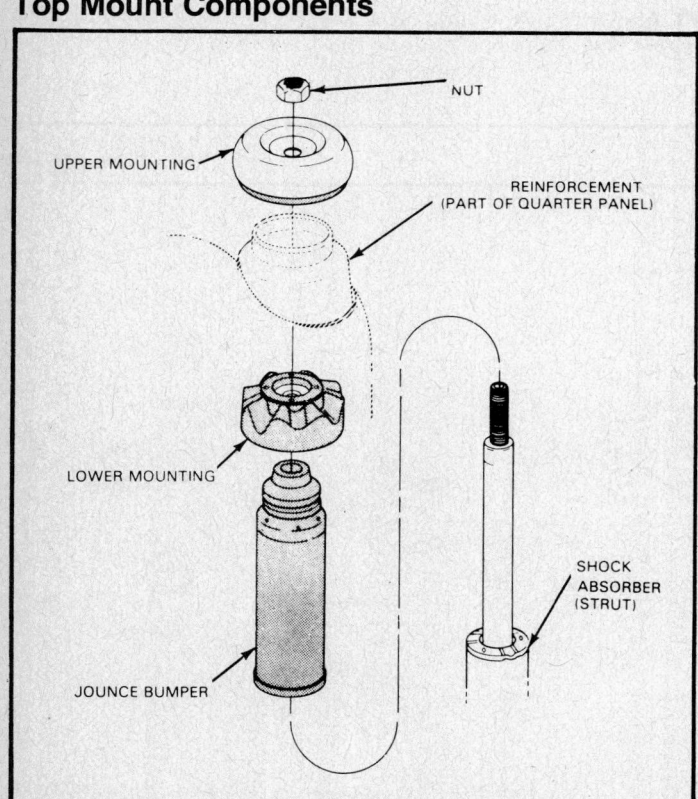

NUT

UPPER MOUNTING

REINFORCEMENT
(PART OF QUARTER PANEL)

LOWER MOUNTING

SHOCK
ABSORBER
(STRUT)

JOUNCE BUMPER

NOTE   If a frame contact hoist is used, support the lower control arm with a floor jack. If a twin post hoist is used, support the body with floor jacks on lifting pads forward of the tie-rod body bracket.

4. Remove clip retaining the brake flexible hose to the rear shock and carefully move hose aside.

5. Loosen two nuts and bolts retaining shock to the spindle. DO NOT remove bolts at this time.

6. Remove top mounting nut, washer and rubber insulator.

7. Remove two bottom mounting bolts and remove the shock from the vehicle.

Installation

1. Extend shock absorber to its maximum length.

2. Install a new lower washer and insulator assembly, using tire lubricant to ease insertion into the quarter panel shock tower. (Use of a lubricant other than ESA-M1B6-B or soapy water is not recommended as it may damage the rubber insulator.)

3. Position upper part of shock absorber shaft into shock tower opening in the body and push slowly on lower part of the shock until mounting holes are lined up with mounting holes in the spindle.

4. Install new lower mounting bolts and nuts. DO NOT tighten at this time.

NOTE   The heads of both bolts must be to the rear of the vehicle.

5. Place a new upper insulator and washer assembly and nut on the upper shock absorber shaft. Tighten nut to torque of 81–95 N•m (60–70 ft.-lbs.), using the 18 x 18 x 43 mm deep socket with external hex (Tool D81P-18045-A3) while holding the strut shaft with a 6 mm allen wrench. Do not grip the shaft with pliers or vise grips.

6. Tighten two lower mounting bolts to torque of 122–135 N•m (90–100 ft.-lbs.).

7. Install brake flex hose and retaining clip.

8. Install wheel and tire assembly.

9. Install quarter trim panels on four-door models and access panels on other models.

Lower Control Arm

Removal

NOTE   The lower control arm is replaced as a unit. The bushing is not serviceable.

1. Remove tire and wheel assembly.

2. Place a floor jack under the lower control arm between spring and spindle end mounting.

3. Remove nuts from control arm-to-body mounting and control arm-to-spindle mounting. Do not remove bolts at this time.

4. Remove spindle end mounting bolt. Slowly lower floor jack until spring and spring insulator can be removed.

5. Remove bolt from the body end and remove control arm from the vehicle.

Rear Suspension Fasteners

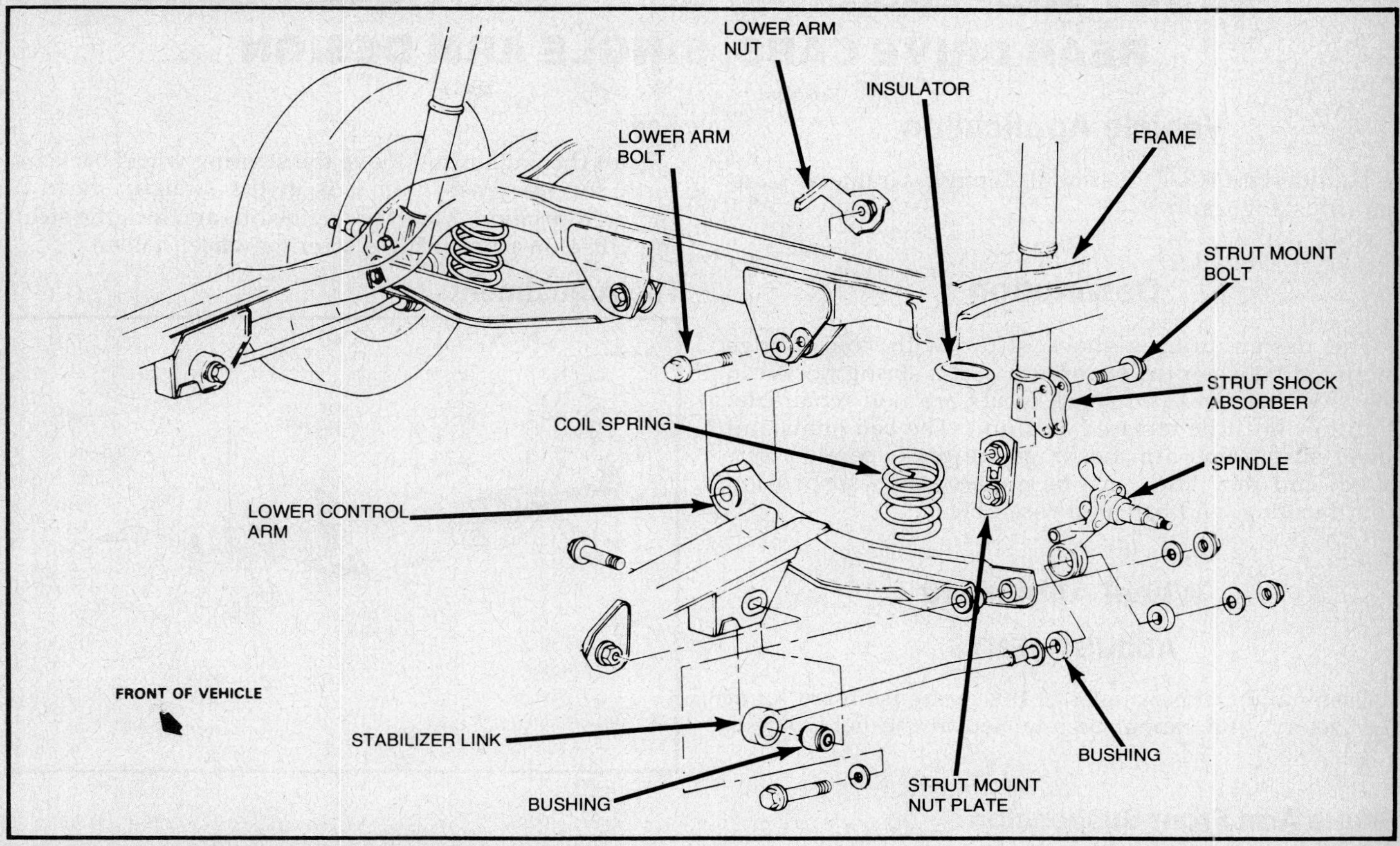

LOWER ARM NUT

INSULATOR

FRAME

LOWER ARM BOLT

STRUT MOUNT BOLT

STRUT SHOCK ABSORBER

SPINDLE

COIL SPRING

LOWER CONTROL ARM

BUSHING

FRONT OF VEHICLE

STABILIZER LINK

BUSHING

STRUT MOUNT NUT PLATE

All bolts must be installed in direction shown.

Installation

1. Attach lower control arm to body bracket using a new bolt and a new nut. DO NOT tighten at this time. Install this bolt with bolt head to the front of the vehicle.

2. Place spring in spring pocket in lower control arm. Be sure the spring pigtail is in the proper index in lower control arm and the insulator is at the top of spring, properly seated and indexed. Insulator must be placed on the spring before spring is placed in position.

3. Using a floor jack, raise lower control arm until it comes in line with mounting hole in the spindle.

4. Install lower control arm to spindle using a new nut, new bolt and new washers. DO NOT tighten at this time. Install this bolt with the bolt head to the front of the vehicle.

5. Using a floor jack, raise lower control arm to its curb height.

6. Tighten control arm-to-spindle bolt to torque of 122–135 N•m (90–100 ft.-lbs.).

Position Floor Jack Under Control Arm

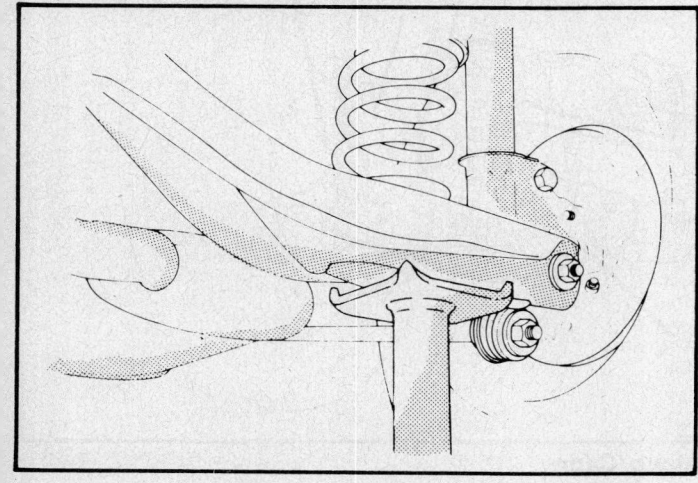

Snap In Insulator

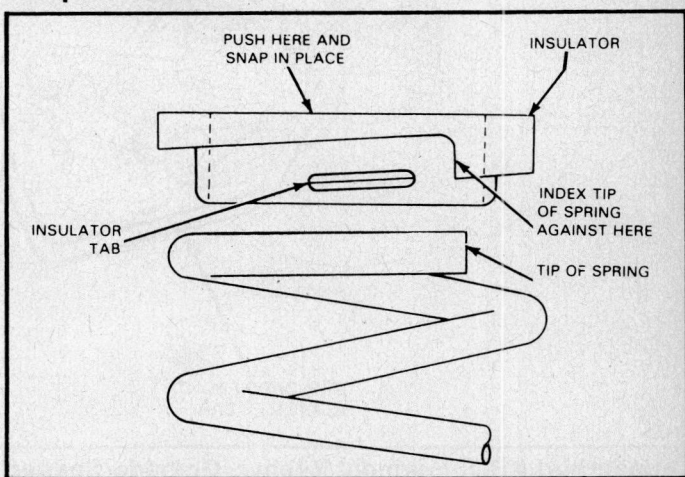

PUSH HERE AND SNAP IN PLACE

INSULATOR

INSULATOR TAB

INDEX TIP OF SPRING AGAINST HERE

TIP OF SPRING

FRONT SUSPENSION—FORD, LINCOLN, MERCURY REAR DRIVE CARS, SINGLE ARM DESIGN

Vehicle Application

Thunderbird/XR-7, Fairmont/Zephyr, Granada/Cougar, Mustang/Capri.

Description

The design utilizes shock struts with coil springs mounted between the lower arm and a spring pocket in the crossmember. The shock struts are non-repairable, and they must be replaced as a unit. The ball joints and lower suspension arm bushings are not separately serviced, and they also must be replaced as a suspension arm, bushing, and ball joint assembly.

Wheel Alignment

ADJUSTMENTS

Caster and camber angles of this suspension are set at the factory, and cannot be adjusted in the field. Toe is adjustable.

Toe

Start the engine and move the steering wheel back and forth several times until it is in the straight ahead or centered position. Turn the engine off, and lock the steering wheel in place using a steering wheel holder.

Toe Adjustment

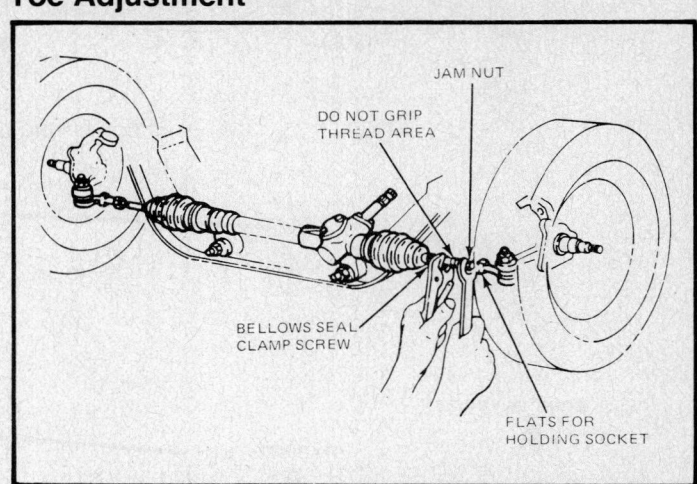

Single Arm Front Suspension

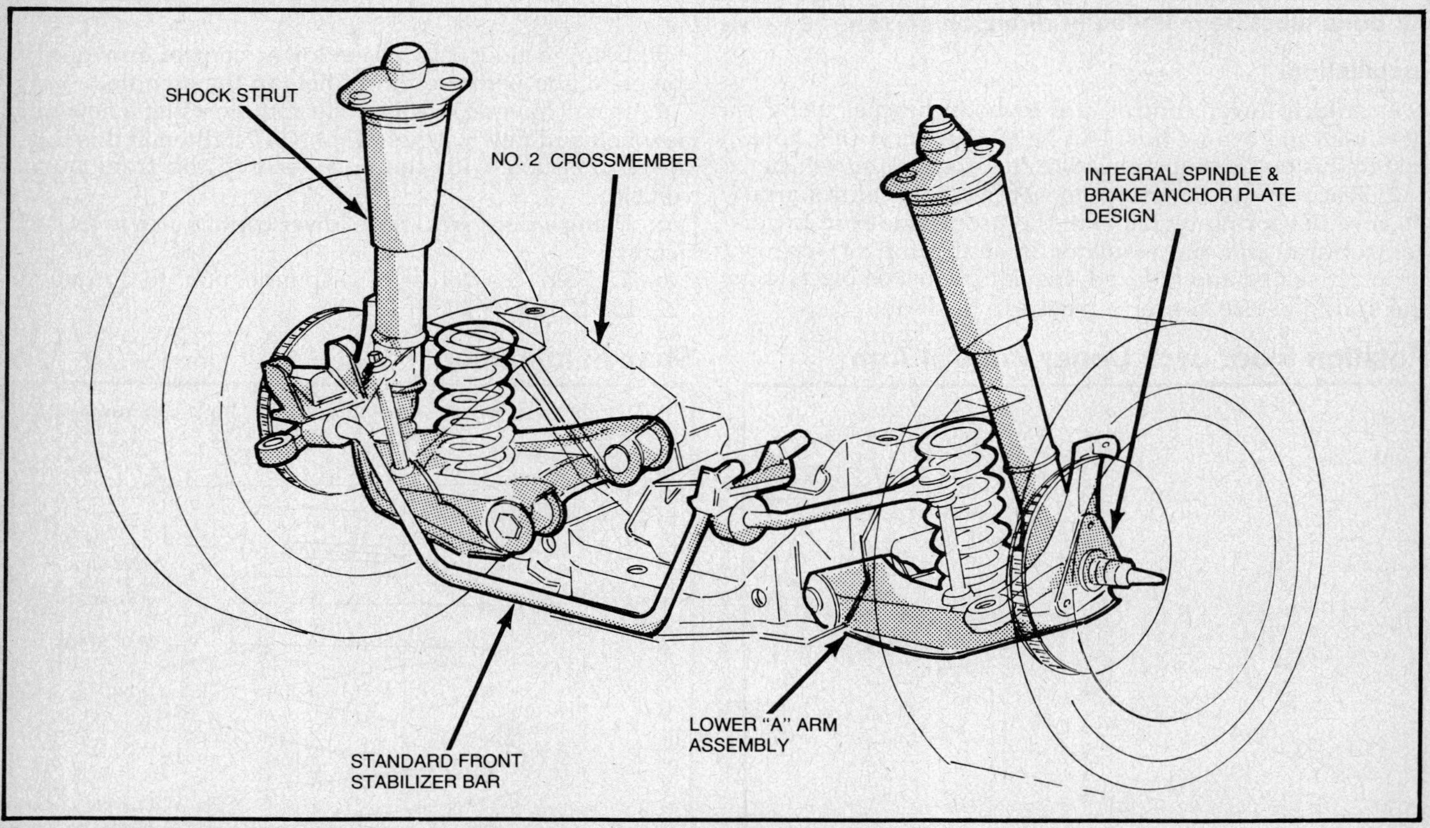

Thunderbird/XR-7, Fairmont/Zephyr, Granada/Cougar, Mustang/Capri

Adjust the left and right spindle connecting rod sleeves until each wheel has one-half of the desired total toe specification.

NOTE For all vehicles, whenever the jam nuts are loosened for toe adjustment, the nuts must be retightened to 48–67 N•m (35–50 ft.-lbs.).

Wheel Bearings

REPLACEMENT AND LUBRICATION

1. Raise the vehicle until the tire clears the floor, and remove wheel from hub and rotor.
2. Remove the caliper from the spindle, and wire it to the underbody to prevent damage to the brake hose.
3. Remove the grease cap from the hub. Remove the cotter pin, nut lock, adjusting nut, and flatwasher from the spindle. Remove the outer bearing cone and roller assembly.
4. Pull the hub and rotor assembly off the spindle.
5. Using tool 1175-AC or equivalent, remove and discard the grease retainer. Remove the inner bearing cone and roller assembly from the hub.
6. Clean the inner and outer bearing cups with solvent. Inspect the cups for scratches, pits, excessive wear, and other damage. If the cups are worn or damaged, replace.

Adjustment

If the wheel is loose on the spindle or does not rotate freely, adjust the front wheel bearings as follows:
1. Raise the vehicle until the tire clears the floor.
2. Remove the wheel cover. Remove the grease cap from the hub.
3. Wipe the excess grease from the end of the spindle. Remove the cotter pin and nut lock.
4. Loosen the adjusting nut three turns. Rock the wheel, hub, and rotor assembly in and out several times to push the shoe and linings away from the rotor.
5. While rotating the wheel, hub, and rotor assembly, tighten the adjusting nut to 23–34 N•m (17–25 ft.-lbs.), to seat the bearings.
6. Loosen the adjusting nut one-half turn, then re-tighten 1.1–1.7 N•m (10–15 in.-lbs.), using a torque wrench.

Front Wheel Bearing Adjustment

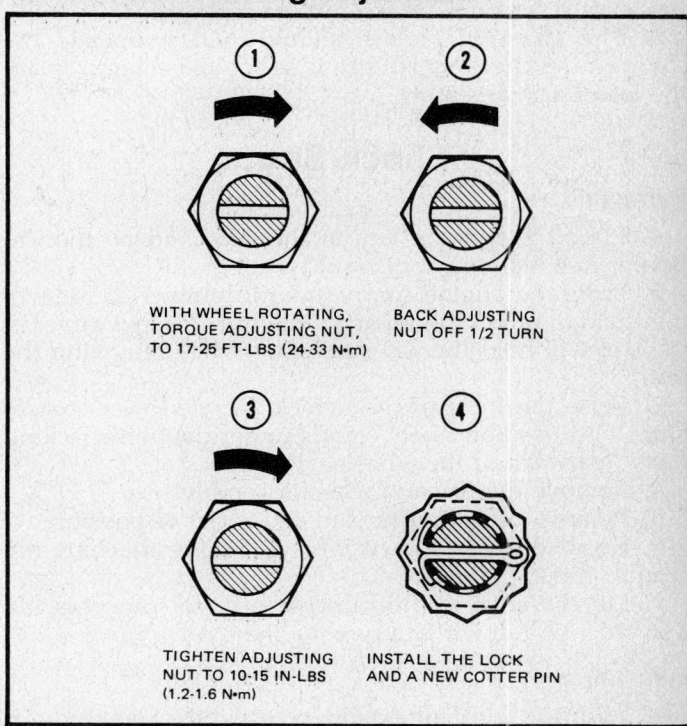

① WITH WHEEL ROTATING, TORQUE ADJUSTING NUT, TO 17-25 FT-LBS (24-33 N•m)

② BACK ADJUSTING NUT OFF 1/2 TURN

③ TIGHTEN ADJUSTING NUT TO 10-15 IN-LBS (1.2-1.6 N•m)

④ INSTALL THE LOCK AND A NEW COTTER PIN

7. Place the nut lock on the adjusting nut, so the castellations on the lock are in line with the cotter pin hole in the spindle.
8. Install a new cotter pin, and bend the ends around the castellated flange of the nut lock.
9. Check front wheel rotation. If the wheel rotates properly, reinstall the grease cap and wheel cover. If rotation is noisy or rough, follow the inspection, lubrication, and replacement procedures.
10. Before driving the vehicle, pump the brake pedal several times to restore normal brake pedal travel.

Lower Ball Joint

Inspection

1. Support the vehicle in normal driving position with both ball joints loaded.

Checking Lower Ball Joint—Fairmont/Zephyr, Mustang/Capri

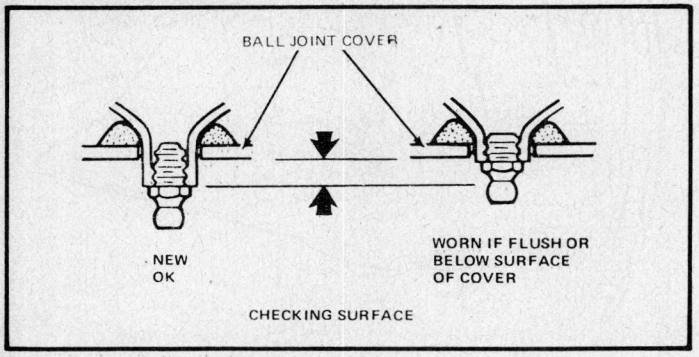

BALL JOINT COVER

NEW OK

WORN IF FLUSH OR BELOW SURFACE OF COVER

CHECKING SURFACE

Checking Lower Ball Joint—Thunderbird/XR-7, Granada/Cougar

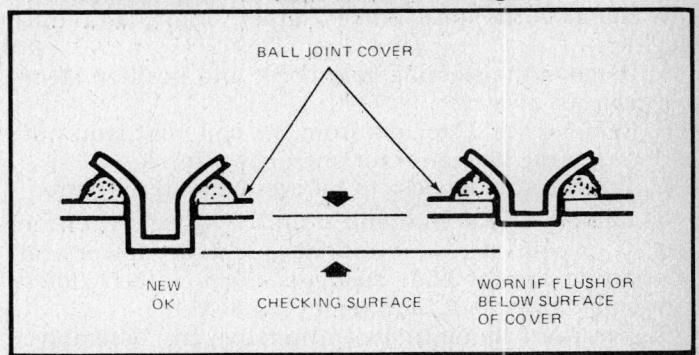

BALL JOINT COVER

NEW OK

CHECKING SURFACE

WORN IF FLUSH OR BELOW SURFACE OF COVER

2. Wipe the wear indicator and ball joint cover checking surface, so they are free of dirt and grease.

3. The checking surface should project outside the cover. If the checking surface is inside the cover, replace the lower arm assembly.

Shock/Strut

Removal

1. Place the ignition key in the unlocked position to permit free movement of front wheels.

2. From the engine compartment, remove the one 16 mm strut to upper mount attaching nut. A screwdriver in the slot will hold the rod stationary while removing the nut.

3. Raise the front of the vehicle by the lower control arms, and position safety stands under the frame jacking pads, rearward of the wheels.

4. Remove the tire and wheel assembly.

5. Remove brake caliper and rotate out of position.

6. Remove the two lower nuts and bolts attaching the strut to the spindle.

7. Lift the strut up from the spindle to compress the rod, then pull down and remove the strut.

Installation

1. With the rod half extended, place the rod through the upper mount, and hand start with a new 16 mm nut, engaging as many nut threads as possible.

2. Extend the strut, and position into the spindle.

3. Install two new lower mounting bolts, and hand start nuts.

4. Tighten the new 16 mm strut to upper mount attaching nut, inside the engine compartment to 81–102 N•m (60–75 ft.-lbs.). A screwdriver in the slot will hold the rod stationary while the nut is being tightened.

5. Remove the suspension load from the lower control arms by lowering the hoist, and tighten the lower mounting nuts to 203–244 N•m (150–180 ft.-lbs.).

Lower Suspension Arm

Removal

1. Raise the front of the vehicle, and position safety stands under both sides at the jack pads just behind the lower arms.

2. Remove the wheel and tire assembly.

3. Disconnect the stabilizer bar link from the lower arm.

4. Remove the disc brake caliper, rotor, and dust shield.

5. Remove the steering gear bolts, and position steering gear out of way.

6. Remove the cotter pin from the ball joint stud nut, and loosen the ball joint nut one or two turns.

7. Tap the spindle boss to relieve the stud pressure.

8. Remove the tie-rod end from the spindle with tool 3290-C or equivalent. Place floor jack under lower arm, supporting arm at both bushings. Remove both lower arm bolts, lower jack, and remove coil spring.

9. Remove ball joint nut, and remove arm assembly.

Installation

1. Place the new arm assembly into spindle, and tighten ball joint nut to 108–163 N•m (80–120 ft.-lbs.). Install a new cotter pin.

2. Position the coil spring in the upper spring pocket. Be sure the insulator is on top of the spring and the lower end (pigtail) is properly positioned (between two holes) in the depression of the lower arm.

3. Carefully raise the lower arm with the floor jack until the bushings are properly positioned in the cross-member.

4. Install the lower arm bolts and nut (finger-tight only).

5. Install the steering gear bolts, and tighten to 122–136 N•m (90–100 ft.-lbs.).

6. Connect the tie-rod end, and install the nut. Tighten to 47–64 N•m (35–41 ft.-lbs.)

7. Connect the stabilizer link bolt and nut. Tighten to 11–16 N•m (8–12 ft.-lbs.).

8. Install the brake dust shield, rotor, and caliper.

9. Install the wheel and tire assembly.

10. Remove the safety stands, and lower the vehicle. After the vehicle has been lowered to the floor and the vehicle is at curb height, tighten the lower arm nuts to 271–298 N•m (200–220 ft.-lbs.).

Spring

Removal

1. Raise the front of the vehicle, and position safety stands under both sides at the jack pads just back of the lower arms. Remove the wheel and tire assembly.

2. Disconnect the stabilizer bar link from the lower bar.

Spring Compressor Tool in Position Showing Marks on Spring Where Upper and Lower Plates Are Located

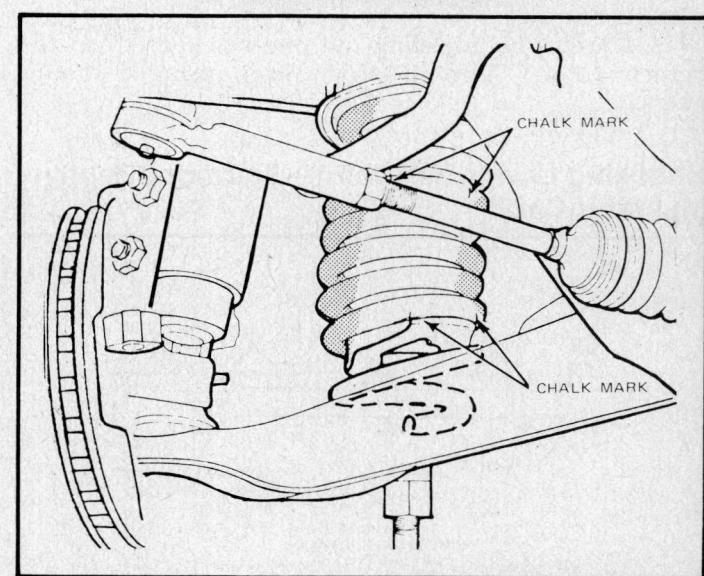

Coil Spring Removal Tool

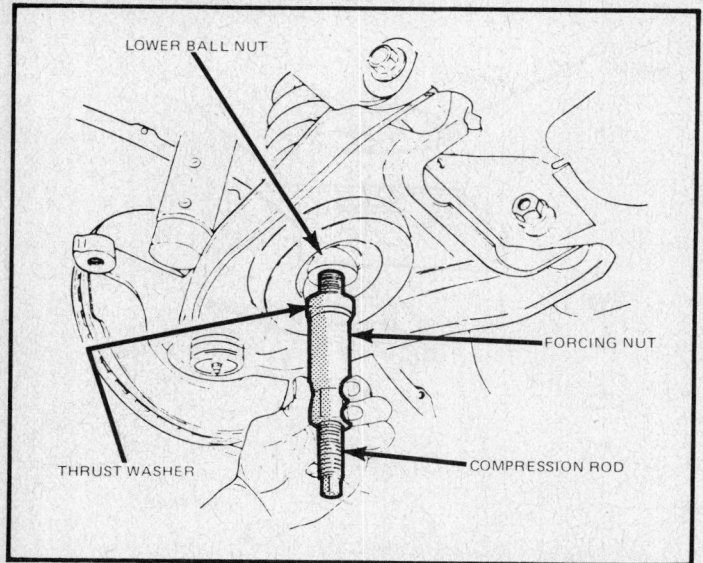

Spring Compressed for Removal

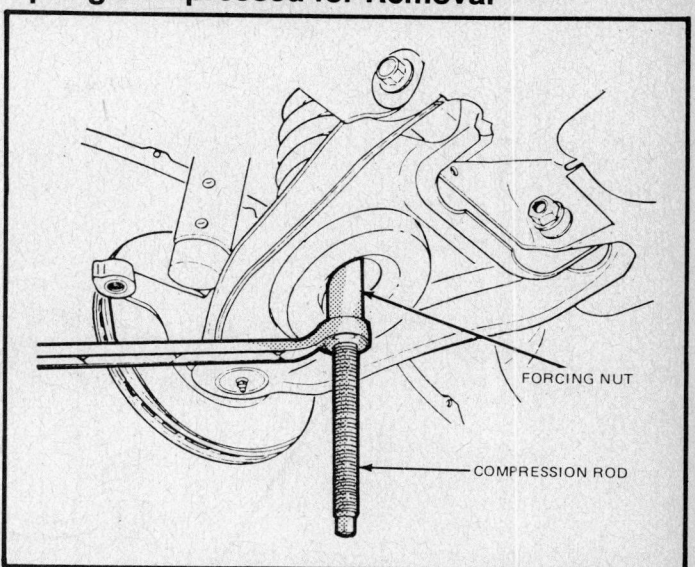

3. Remove the steering gear bolts, and move the steering gear out of the way.

4. Disconnect the tie rod from the steering spindle.

5. Using the spring compressor tool D78P-5310-A or equivalent, install one plate with the pivot ball seat down into the coils of the spring. Rotate the plate, so that it is fully seated into the lower suspension arm spring seat.

6. Install the other plate with the pivot ball seat up into the coils of the spring. Insert the ball nut through the coils of the spring, so it rests in the upper plate.

7. Insert compression rod into the opening in the lower arm through the lower and upper plate. Install upper ball nut on the rod, and return the securing pin.

NOTE   This pin can only be inserted one way into the upper ball nut because of a stepped hole design.

8. With the upper ball nut secured, turn the upper plate, so it walks up the coil until it contacts the upper spring seat.

9. Install the lower ball nut, thrust bearing and forcing nut on the compression rod.

10. Rotate the nut until the spring is compressed enough, so it is free in its seat.

11. Remove the two lower control arm pivot bolts and nuts and disengage the lower arm from the frame crossmember. Remove the spring assembly.

12. If a new spring is to be installed, mark the position of the upper and lower plates on the spring with chalk. Measure the compressed length of the spring as well as the amount of spring curvature to assist in the compression and installation of a new spring.

13. Loosen the nut to relieve spring tension, and remove the tools from the spring.

Installation

1. Assemble the spring compressor tool and locate tool through spring.

2. Before compressing the coil spring, be sure the upper ball nut securing pin is inserted properly.

3. Compress the coil spring.

4. Position the coil spring assembly into the lower arm.

NOTE   Be sure that the lower end (pigtail) of the coil spring is properly positioned between the two holes in the lower arm spring pocket depression.

5. Install coil spring. Reverse removal procedures.

Spindle Assembly

Removal

1. Raise the front of the vehicle, and position safety stands under both sides at the jacking pads just behind the lower arms.

2. Remove the wheel and tire assembly.

3. Remove the brake caliper, rotor, and dust shield.

4. Remove the stabilizer link from the lower arm assembly.

5. Remove the tie-rod end from the spindle.

6. Remove the cotter pin from the ball joint stud nut, and loosen the ball joint nut one or two turns.

CAUTION   Do not remove the nut from the ball joint stud at this time.

7. Tap the spindle boss to relieve the stud pressure.

8. Place a floor jack under the lower arm, compress the coil spring and remove the stud nut.

9. Remove the two bolts and nuts attaching the spindle to the shock strut. Compress the shock strut until working clearance is obtained.

10. Remove the spindle assembly.

Installation

1. Place the spindle on the ball joint stud, and install the stud nut. Do not tighten at this time.

SUSPENSION

FRONT SUSPENSION-FORD MOTOR CO., SINGLE ARM DESIGN

Single Arm Front Suspension

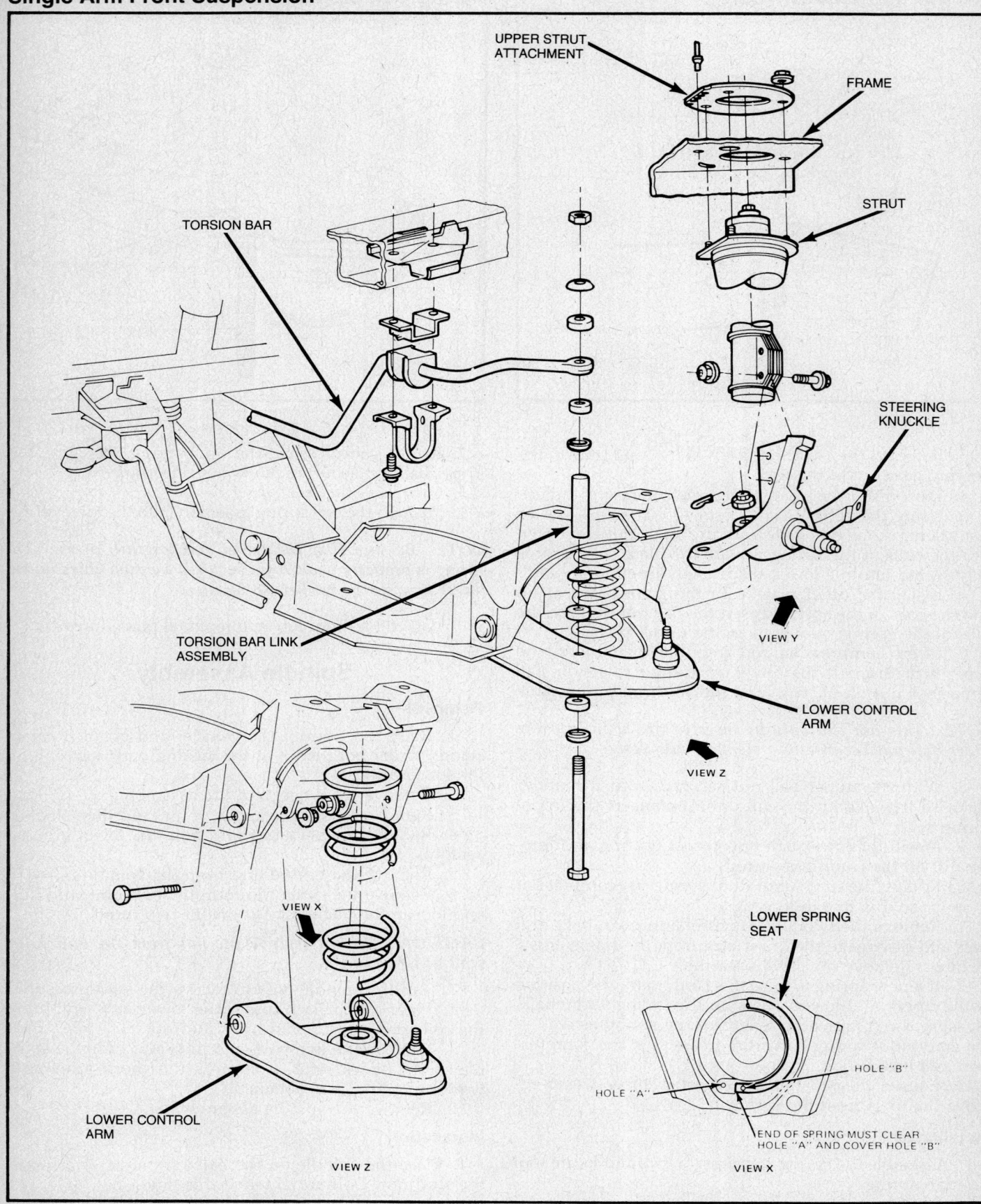

UPPER STRUT ATTACHMENT

FRAME

STRUT

TORSION BAR

STEERING KNUCKLE

VIEW Y

TORSION BAR LINK ASSEMBLY

LOWER CONTROL ARM

VIEW Z

LOWER SPRING SEAT

LOWER CONTROL ARM

VIEW X

HOLE "B"

HOLE "A"

END OF SPRING MUST CLEAR HOLE "A" AND COVER HOLE "B"

VIEW Z

VIEW X

2. Lower the shock strut until the attaching holes are in line with the holes in the spindle. Install two new bolts and nuts.

3. Tighten the ball joint stud nut to 108–163 N•m (80–120 ft.-lbs.), and install a new cotter pin.

4. Tighten the shock strut-to-spindle attaching nuts to 203–244 N•m (150–180 ft.-lbs.).

5. Lower the floor jack from under the suspension arm, and remove the jack.

6. Install the stabilizer link and tighten the attaching bolt and nut to 11–16 N•m (8–12 ft.-lbs.).

7. Attach the tie-rod end, and tighten the retaining nut to 47–64 N•m (35–47 ft.-lbs.).

8. Install the disc brake dust shield, rotor, and caliper.

9. Install the wheel and tire assembly.

Stabilizer Bar Link Insulators

Removal

To replace the link insulators on each stabilizer link, use the following procedure:

1. Raise the vehicle on a hoist.

2. Remove the nut, washer, and insulator from the upper end of the stabilizer bar attaching link bolt.

3. Remove the bolt and the remaining washers, insulators, and spacer.

Installation

1. Install the stabilizer bar link insulators by reversing the above steps.

2. Tighten the attaching nuts to 11–16 N•m (8–12 ft.-lbs.).

Stabilizer Bar and/or Insulator

Removal

1. Raise the vehicle on a hoist.

2. Disconnect the stabilizer from each stabilizer link and both stabilizer insulator attaching clamps. Remove the stabilizer bar assembly.

3. Cut the worn insulators and plastic sleeves from the stabilizer bar.

Installation

1. Coat the necessary parts of the stabilizer bar with D9AZ-19583-A or an equivalent lubricant; install new plastic sleeves with the flange inboard, and slide insulators onto the stabilizer bar and over sleeves. Be sure the insulator is fully seated against the flange.

2. Using a new nut and bolt, secure each end of the stabilizer bar to the lower suspension arm. Tighten these nuts to 11–16 N•m (8–12 ft.-lbs.).

3. Using new fasteners, clamp the stabilizer bar to the attaching brackets on the side rail. Tighten these bolts to 27–33 N•m (20–25 ft.-lbs.).

FRONT SUSPENSION—FORD, LINCOLN, MERCURY REAR DRIVE CARS, SPRING ON UPPER ARM DESIGN

Vehicle Application

Comet, Granada through 1980, Maverick, Monarch, Versailles

Wheel Alignment

ADJUSTMENTS

NOTE Two types of control arms are used on front suspensions with the spring on upper arm. Type "A"—both caster and camber are controlled by adjustments on the lower control arm. Type "B"—both caster and camber are controlled by adjustments on the upper control arm.

TYPE A ADJUSTMENTS ON LOWER ARM

Caster

Caster is controlled by the front suspension strut. To obtain positive caster, loosen the strut rear nut and tighten the strut front nut against the bushing. To obtain negative caster, loosen the strut front nut and tighten the strut rear nut against the bushing.

Camber

Camber is controlled by the eccentric cam located at the lower arm attachment to the side rail. To adjust the camber, loosen the camber adjustment bolt nut at the rear of the body bracket. Spread the body bracket at the camber adjustment bolt area just enough to permit lateral travel of the arm when the adjustment bolt is turned.

Caster and Camber Adjustment

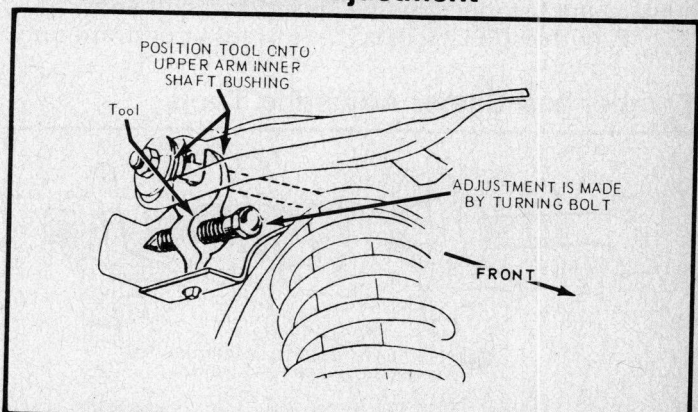

Front Suspension—Granada/Monarch, Versailles Similar

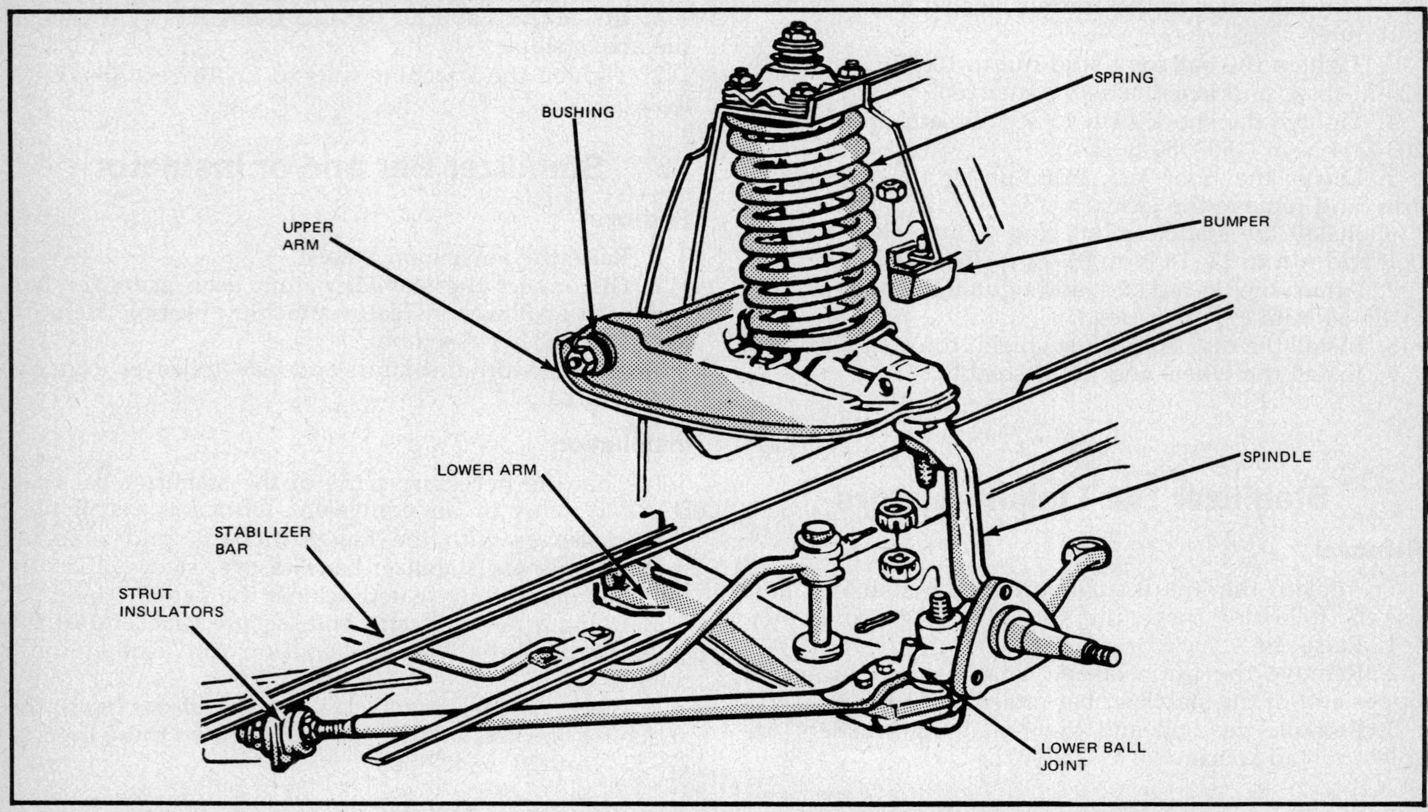

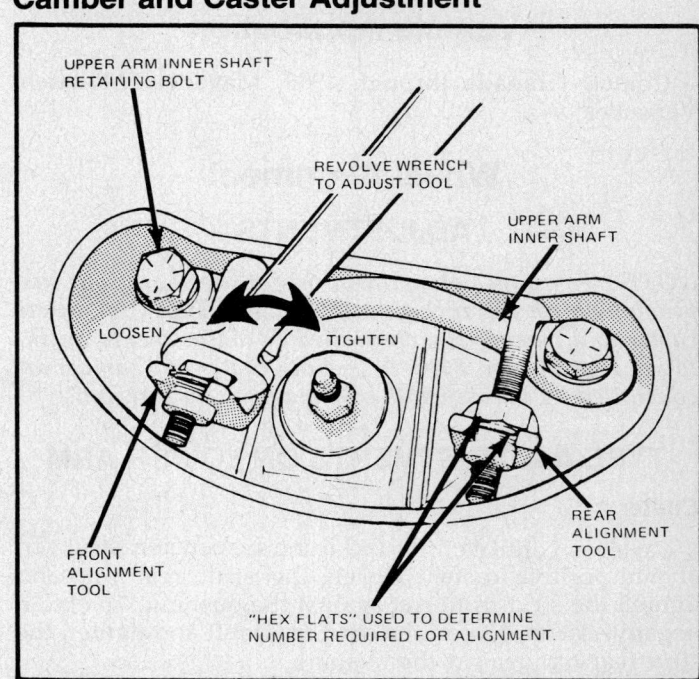

Ball joints must not be replaced. Upper or lower suspension arms should be replaced as a unit.

Rotate the bolt and eccentric as required to increase or decrease camber.

After the caster and camber have been adjusted to specification, torque the lower arm eccentric bolt nut and the strut front nut to specification.

TYPE B ADJUSTMENTS ON UPPER ARM

1. Working from inside the front wheel housing, install the special service tool T74P-3000, one at each end of the upper arm inner shaft. Turn special tool bolts inward until the bolt ends contact the body metal.

2. Loosen the two upper arm inner shaft-to-body attaching nuts. The upper arm inner shaft will then move inboard until stopped by the special tool bolt ends.

3. Turn the special tool bolt(s) inward or outward until caster and camber are within specifications. Tightening the special tool bolts forces the arm outward; loosening the adjustment bolts on the special tool permits the arm and inner shaft to move inboard due to weight force.

Camber and Caster Adjustment

Camber and Caster Adjusting Tools

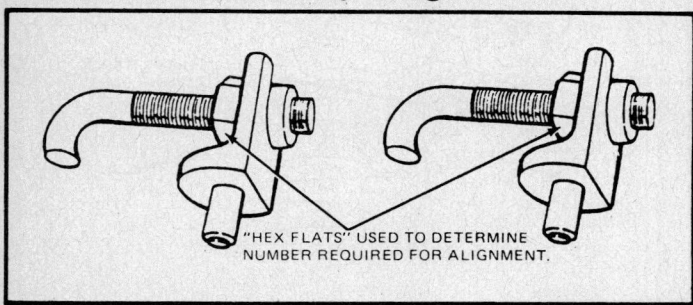

4. When caster and camber specifications are attained, tighten the upper arm inner shaft-to-body attaching nuts to (95–120 ft.-lbs.). 129–162 N•m.

5. Loosen the special tool bolts and remove tools.

TOE (ALL MODELS)

Start the engine and move the steering wheel back and forth several times until it is in the straight ahead or centered position. Turn the engine off and lock the steering wheel in place using a steering wheel holder.

Adjust the left and right spindle connecting rod sleeves until each wheel has one-half of the desired total toe specification.

Left-hand Sleeve

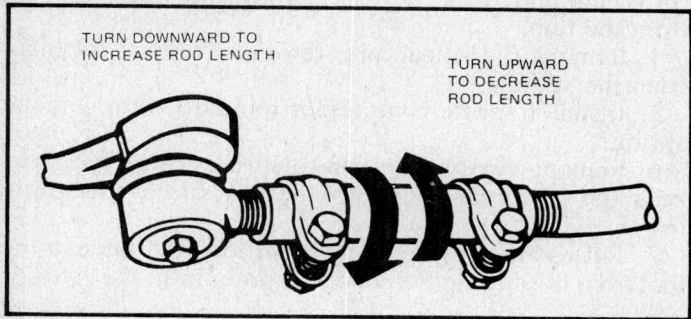

Right-hand Sleeve

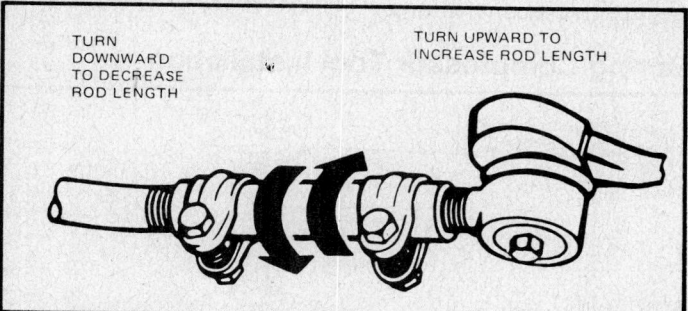

Front Wheel Bearing Adjustment

If the wheel is loose on the spindle or does not rotate freely, adjust the front wheel bearings as follows.

1. Raise the vehicle until the tire clears the floor.

2. Remove the wheel cover. Remove the grease cap from the hub.

3. Wipe the excess grease from the end of the spindle. Remove the cotter pin and nut lock.

4. Loosen the adjusting nut three turns. Rock the wheel, hub, and rotor assembly in and out several times to push the shoe and linings away from the rotor.

5. While rotating the wheel, hub and rotor assembly, tighten the adjusting nut to 23–34 N•m (17–25 ft.-lbs.), to seat the bearings.

6. Loosen the adjusting nut one-half turn, then re-tighten 1.1–1.7 N•m (10–15 in.-lbs.), using a torque wrench.

7. Place the nut lock on the adjusting nut so the castellations on the lock are in line with the cotter pin hole in the spindle.

8. Install a new cotter pin and bend the ends around the castellated flange of the nut lock.

9. Check front wheel rotation. If the wheel rotates properly, reinstall the grease cap and wheel cover. If rotation is noisy or rough, inspect, lubricate and replace.

10. Before driving the vehicle, pump the brake pedal several times to restore normal brake pedal travel.

Front Wheel Grease Seal Bearing

REPLACEMENT AND LUBRICATION

1. Raise the vehicle until the tire clears the floor. Remove wheel from hub and rotor.

2. Remove the caliper from the spindle and wire it to the underbody to prevent damage to the brake hose.

3. Remove the grease cap from the hub. Remove the cotter pin, nut lock, adjusting nut and flatwasher from the spindle. Remove the outer bearing cone and roller assembly.

4. Pull the hub and rotor assembly off the spindle.

5. Using tool 1175-AC or equivalent, remove and discard the grease retainer. Remove the inner bearing cone and roller assembly from the hub.

6. Clean the inner and outer bearing cups with solvent. Inspect the cups for scratches, pits, excessive wear and other damage. If the cups are worn or damaged, remove them with tools D80L-927-A and T77F-1102-A or equivalent and replace them.

Shock Absorber

Removal

1. Raise the hood and remove three shock absorber upper mounting bracket-to-spring tower attaching nuts. Position wood blocks.

Shock Absorber Upper Attachment

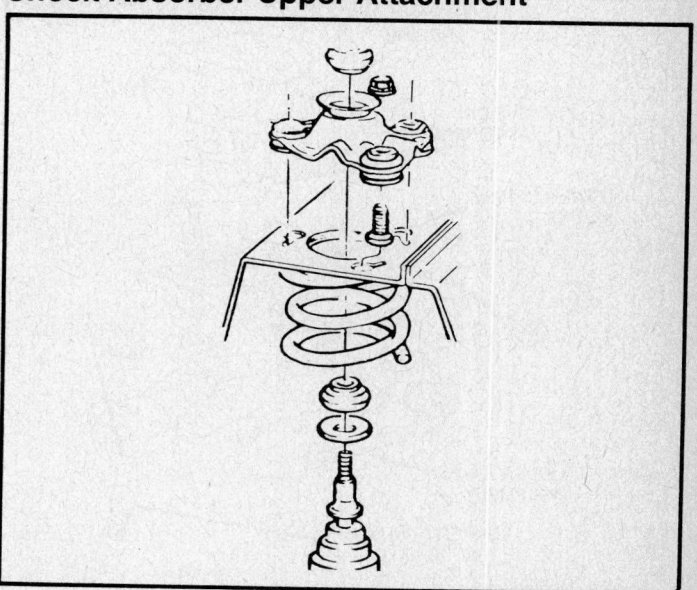

SUSPENSION

Position of Wood Block

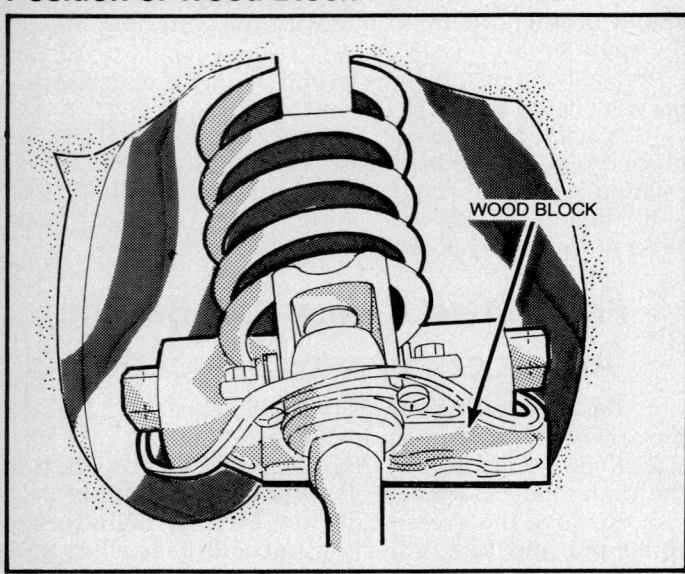

2. Raise the front of the vehicle and place safety stands under the lower arms.

3. Remove the shock absorber lower attaching nuts, washers and insulators.

4. Lift the shock absorber and upper bracket from the spring tower and remove the bracket from the shock absorber. Remove the insulators from the lower attaching studs.

Installation

1. Install the upper mounting bracket on the shock absorber and torque to specification. Install the insulators on the lower attaching studs.

2. Position the shock absorber and upper mounting bracket in the spring tower, making sure the shock absorber lower studs are in the pivot plate holes.

Shock Absorber Lower Attachment

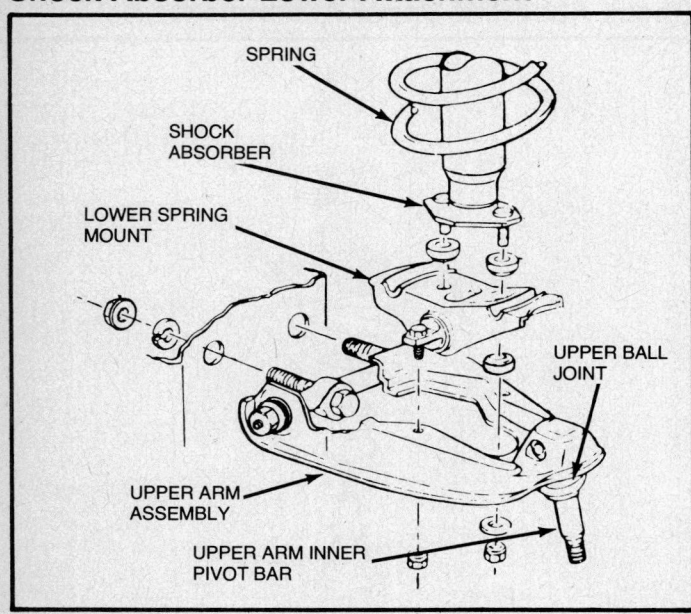

3. Install the two nuts on the shock absorber lower studs, and torque to specification.

4. Install the three shock absorber upper mounting bracket-to-spring tower attaching nuts, and torque to specification. Remove the safety stands and lower the vehicle. Remove wood blocks.

Front Spring

Removal

1. Remove the shock absorber and upper mounting bracket as an assembly. Position wood blocks.

2. Raise the vehicle on a hoist, install safety stands, and remove the wheel cover or hub cap.

3. Remove the grease cap from the hub. Remove the cotter pin, nut lock, adjusting nut, and outer bearing from the hub.

4. Remove the wheel, tire, rotor and caliper assembly from the spindle.

5. Install a spring compressor tool and compress the spring.

6. Remove two upper arm-to-spring tower attaching nuts and swing the upper arm outboard from the spring tower.

7. Release the spring compressor tool and remove the tool from the spring. Remove the spring from the vehicle.

Installation

1. Place the spring upper insulator on the spring and secure in place with tape.

Spring Compressor Tool Installation

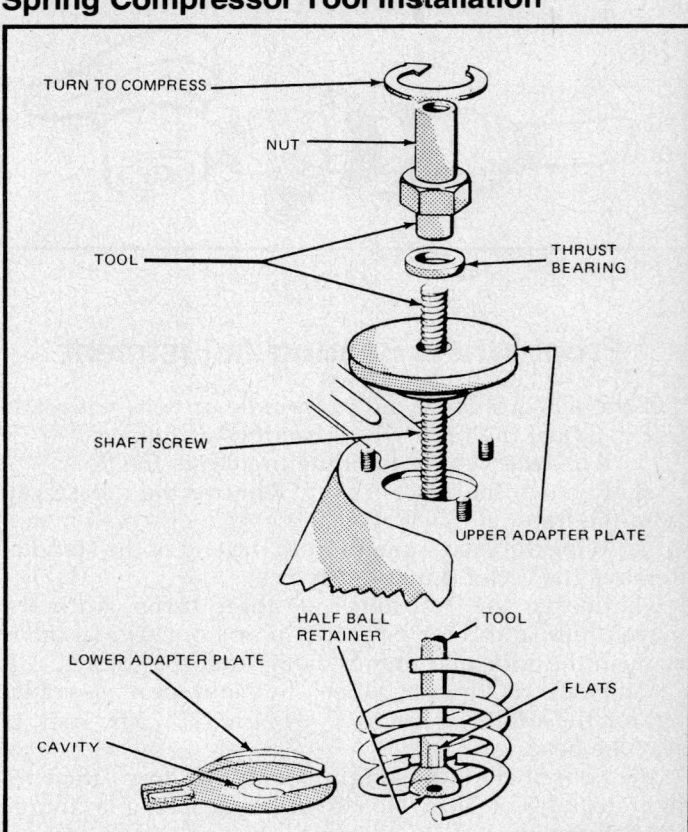

2. Position the spring in the spring tower. Install the spring compressor and compress the spring.

3. Swing the upper arm inward and insert the bolts through the holes in the side of the spring tower. Install the attaching nuts and lockwasher and torque them to specification.

4. Release the spring pressure and guide the spring into the upper arm spring seat.

NOTE   The end of the spring must be no more than ½ inch from the tab on the spring seat.

5. Remove the spring compressor and position the wheel, tire, and hub and drum on the spindle.

6. Install the bearing, washer, adjusting nut, and lock nut. Adjust the wheel bearing. Install the cotter pin, grease cap, and hub cap or wheel cover.

7. Lower the vehicle and install the shock absorber and upper mounting bracket. Remove wood blocks.

Lower Arm

Removal

1. Position wood blocks.

2. Raise the vehicle, position safety stands, and remove the wheel and tire.

3. Remove the stabilizer bar and link attaching nut. Disconnect the bar from the link and remove the link bolt.

4. Remove the strut-to-lower arm attaching nuts and bolts.

5. Remove the cotter pin from the lower ball joint stud nut.

Lower Arm Attachment

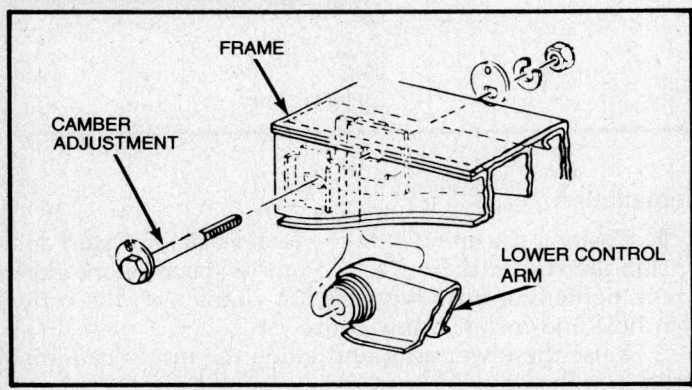

CAMBER ADJUSTMENT

FRAME

LOWER CONTROL ARM

6. Loosen the lower ball joint stud nut one to two turns.

NOTE   Do not remove the nut from the stud at this time.

7. Install tools T71P-3006-A and T60K-3006-A between upper and lower ball joint studs, against ends of studs, not nuts.

8. With a wrench, turn the adapter screw until the tool places the stud under compression. Tap the spindle near the lower stud with a hammer to loosen the stud in the spindle.

NOTE   Do not loosen the stud from the spindle with tool pressure only.

9. Remove the nut from the lower ball joint stud and lower the arm.

10. Remove the lower arm to underbody cam bolt, nut, and lock washer. Remove the lower arm.

Installation

1. Position the lower arm to the underbody bracket and install the cam bolt, lock washer, and nut loosely.

2. Raise the lower arm, guide the lower ball joint stud into the spindle bore, and install the stud attaching nut loosely.

3. Install the stabilizer link bolt, washer, bushings, and spacer. Connect the stabilizer bar to the link. Install the attaching nut and torque to specification.

4. Position the strut to the lower arm. Install the attaching bolts and nuts, and torque to specification.

5. Torque the lower ball joint stud nut to specification, continue to tighten the nut until the next slot aligns with the cotter pin hole, and install a new cotter pin.

6. While holding the head of the bolt with a wrench, torque the lower arm-to-underbody pivot bolt and nut to specification.

7. Remove the safety stands and lower the vehicle.

8. Remove the wood blocks.

9. Adjust caster, camber, and toe to specification.

Upper Arm

NOTE   Upper arm shaft and bushing may not be disassembled on these vehicles. The entire upper arm assembly must be replaced as a unit.

Removal

1. Position wood blocks. Raise the vehicle, position safety stands under the frame and lower the vehicle slightly.

Upper Arm Attachment

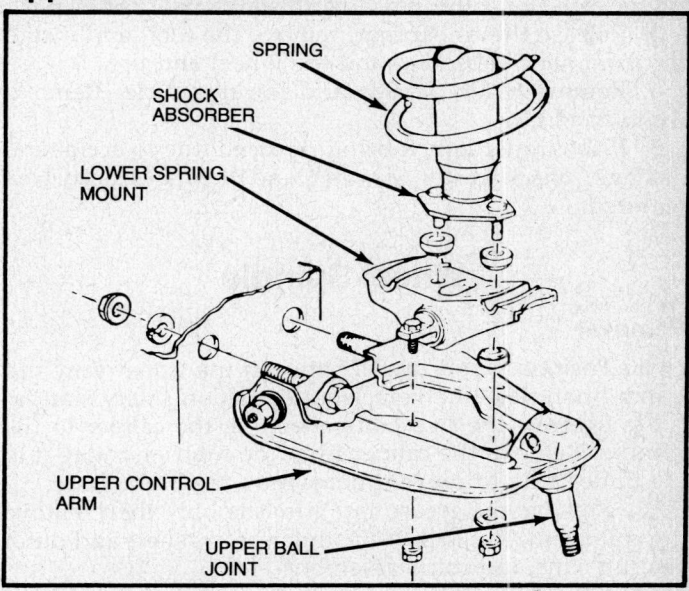

SPRING

SHOCK ABSORBER

LOWER SPRING MOUNT

UPPER CONTROL ARM

UPPER BALL JOINT

2. Remove the wheel and tire.

3. Remove the shock absorber lower attaching nuts and washers.

4. Remove the shock absorber upper mounting bracket attaching nuts and remove the shock absorber and bracket as an assembly. On all 8-cylinder vehicles, remove the air cleaner to obtain access for tool installation.

5. Install the spring compressor tool and compress the spring.

6. Position a safety stand under the lower arm.

7. Remove the cotter pin from the nut on the upper ball joint stud, and loosen the nut one or two turns.

NOTE   Do not remove the nut from the stud at this time.

8. Position the appropriate ball joint remover tool between the upper and lower ball joint studs. The tool should seat firmly against the ends of both studs and not against the stud nuts.

9. Turn the tool with a wrench until the tool places the studs under considerable compression, then hit the spindle sharply near the upper stud with a hammer to break the stud loose in the spindle.

NOTE   Do not loosen the stud in the spindle with tool pressure only.

10. Remove the nut from the upper stud and lift the stud out of the spindle.

11. Remove the upper arm inner shaft attaching nuts from the engine compartment and remove the upper arm.

Installation

1. Position the upper arm and spring seat assembly to the spring tower and install the nuts on the two inner shaft attaching bolts. Torque the nuts to specification.

2. Position the upper ball joint stud in the top of the wheel spindle, and install the stud nut. Torque the nut to specification, and continue to tighten it until the next slot aligns with the cotter pin hole. Install a new cotter pin.

3. Release the coil spring, remove the tool, and install the front shock absorber and the wheel and tire.

4. Remove safety stands and lower vehicle. Remove wood blocks.

5. If the upper arm is being replaced due to accidental damage, check caster, camber and tow and adjust as required.

Wheel Spindle

Removal

1. Position wood blocks between the upper arm and frame, then raise the vehicle and position safety stands.

2. Remove the two bolts attaching the caliper to the spindle. Remove the caliper from the rotor and wire it to the underbody to prevent damage to the brake hose.

3. Remove the grease cap from the hub, then remove the cotter pin, nut lock, adjusting nut, washer, and outer bearing cone and roller assembly.

4. Pull the hub and rotor assembly off the wheel spindle.

5. Remove the three caliper shield attaching bolts and remove the shield.

6. Disconnect the spindle connecting rod (tie-rod) end from the spindle arm.

7. Remove the cotter pins from both ball joint stud nuts, and loosen the nuts one or two turns.

NOTE   Do not remove the nuts from the studs at this time.

8. Position the appropriate ball joint remover tool between the upper and lower ball joint studs. The tool should seat firmly against the ends of both studs and not against the stud nuts.

9. Turn the tool with a wrench until the tool places the studs under considerable tension, and, with a hammer, hit the spindle near the studs to break them loose in the spindle.

NOTE   Do not loosen the studs in the spindle with tool pressure alone.

10. Position a floor jack under the lower arm.

11. Remove the upper and lower ball joint stud nuts, lower the jack and remove the spindle.

Spindle Attachments

SPINDLE

Installation

1. Position the spindle on the lower ball joint stud and install the stud nut. Torque the nut to specificaton. Continue tightening until the next slot aligns with the cotter pin hole and install a new cotter pin.

2. Raise the lower arm, and guide the upper ball joint stud into the spindle. Install the stud nut.

3. Torque the nut to specifications and install a new cotter pin. Remove the floor jack.

4. Connect the spindle connecting rod (tie-rod) end to the spindle arm and install the attaching nut. Torque the nut to specification and install a new cotter pin.

5. Position the caliper splash shield to the spindle and install the attaching bolts and nuts. Torque the nuts and bolts to specification.

6. Install the hub and rotor on the spindle. Position the caliper to the rotor and spindle and install the attaching bolts. Torque the bolts to specification. Install the wheel and tire on the hub and adjust the wheel bearing.

7. Install the hub cap or wheel cover.

Strut-To-Frame Attachment

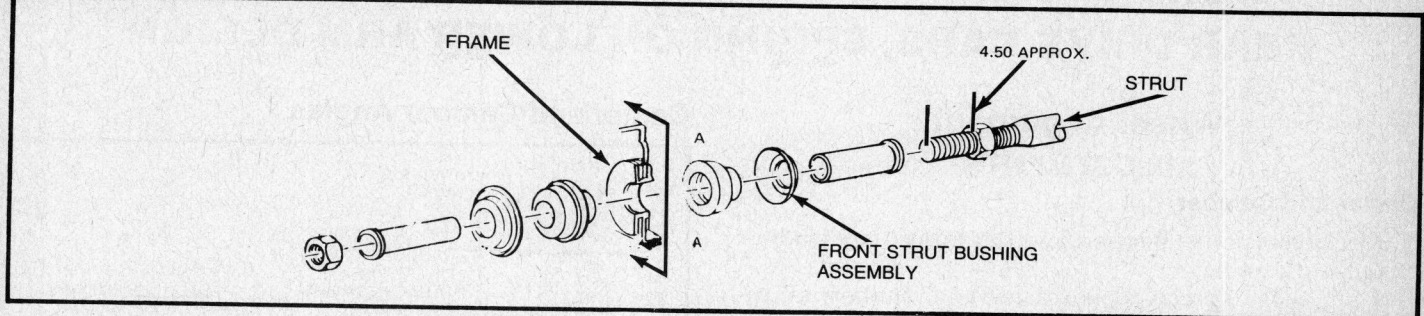

8. Remove the safety stands, and lower the vehicle.

9. Remove the wood blocks from between the upper arm and frame. Check and adjust caster, camber and tow as required.

Stabilizer Bar End Bushing

Removal

To replace the end bushings on each stabilizer link, use the following procedure:

1. Raise the vehicle on a hoist.
2. Remove the nut, washer, and insulator from the lower end of the stabilizer bar attaching bolt.
3. Remove the bolt and the remaining washers, insulators, and the spacer.

Installation

1. Assemble a cup washer and a new insulator on the bolt.
2. Insert the bolt through the stabilizer bar, then install a new insulator and cup washer.
3. Install the spacer, cup washer, and another new insulator on the bolt.
4. Insert the bolt through the lower arm and install a new insulator and cup washer. Install and torque the attaching nut to specification.

Lower Arm Strut and/or Insulators

Removal

1. Position wood blocks under the upper arm.
2. Raise the vehicle, position safety stands.
3. Remove the nut from the front of the strut.
4. Remove the two nuts attaching the strut to the lower arm. Tap the strut upward to loosen the bolt serrations in the lower arm. Remove the strut.
5. With two pry bars approximately 18 inches long, one at each side at the rear of the front washer, pry it forward to separate the inner sleeve from the outer

sleeve. Remove insulators, washers, inner and outer sleeves from the No. 1 crossmember.

Installation

1. Install outer sleeve, rear washer (large I.D.) and rear insulator bushing on the forward end of the strut rod.
2. Position the strut into the crossmember and to the lower suspension arm. Install the strut-to-arm attaching bolts and nuts, and torque them to specification.
3. Install the forward insulator washer (small ID), inner sleeve, and adjustment nut on the forward end of the strut.

NOTE Remove ¼ inch from the inner sleeve prior to assembly.

4. Remove the safety stands, and lower the vehicle. Remove the wood blocks from under the upper arm.
5. Adjust the caster and camber to specification.

Strut and Stabilizer Attachment to Lower Arm

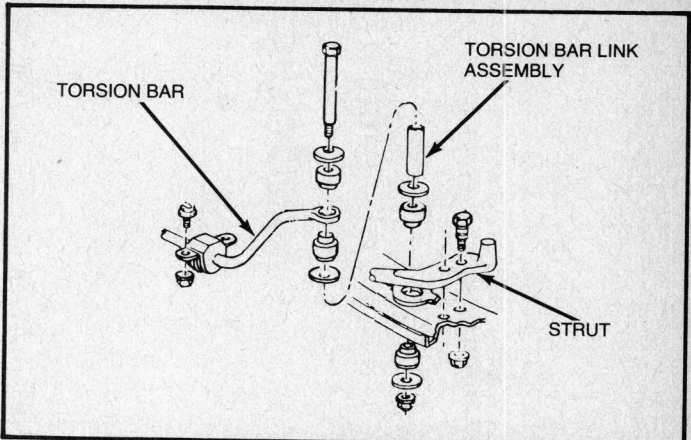

Bolt must be installed with head up. Do not press into hole. Bolt head must be held from turning when tightening nut.

FRONT SUSPENSION—FORD, LINCOLN, MERCURY REAR DRIVE CARS, SPRING ON LOWER ARM DESIGN

Wheel Alignment
ADJUSTMENTS

Caster and Camber

Special tools must be used in order to accurately adjust caster and camber.

Using these special tools, caster and camber adjustments are made in a single operation.

1. Check suspension with the front wheels in the straight-ahead position. Run the engine so that the power steering control valve will be in the center (neutral) position (if equipped).

2. Check caster and camber and record the readings.

3. Compare camber and caster readings with specifications to determine if adjustment is required to bring vehicle to nominal setting.

4. If adjustment is required, insert alignment tools into frame holes and "snug" the tool hooks finger-tight against the upper arm inner shaft. Then tighten hex nut of each alignment tool 1 additional "hex flat."

Caster and Camber Angles

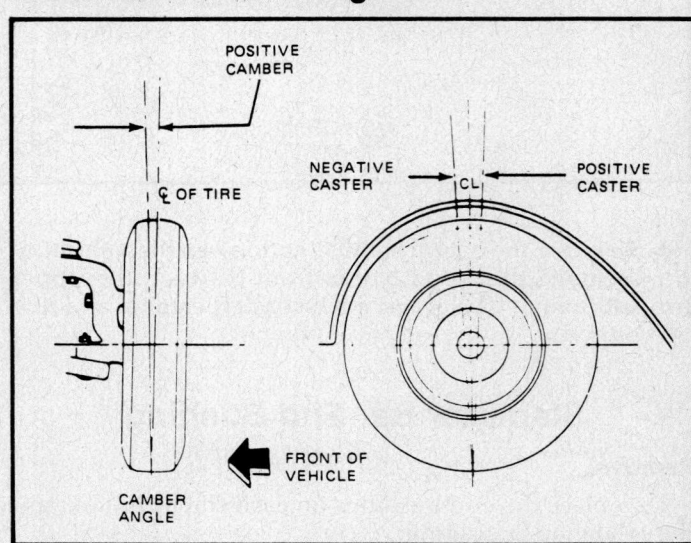

Strut Bar Suspension

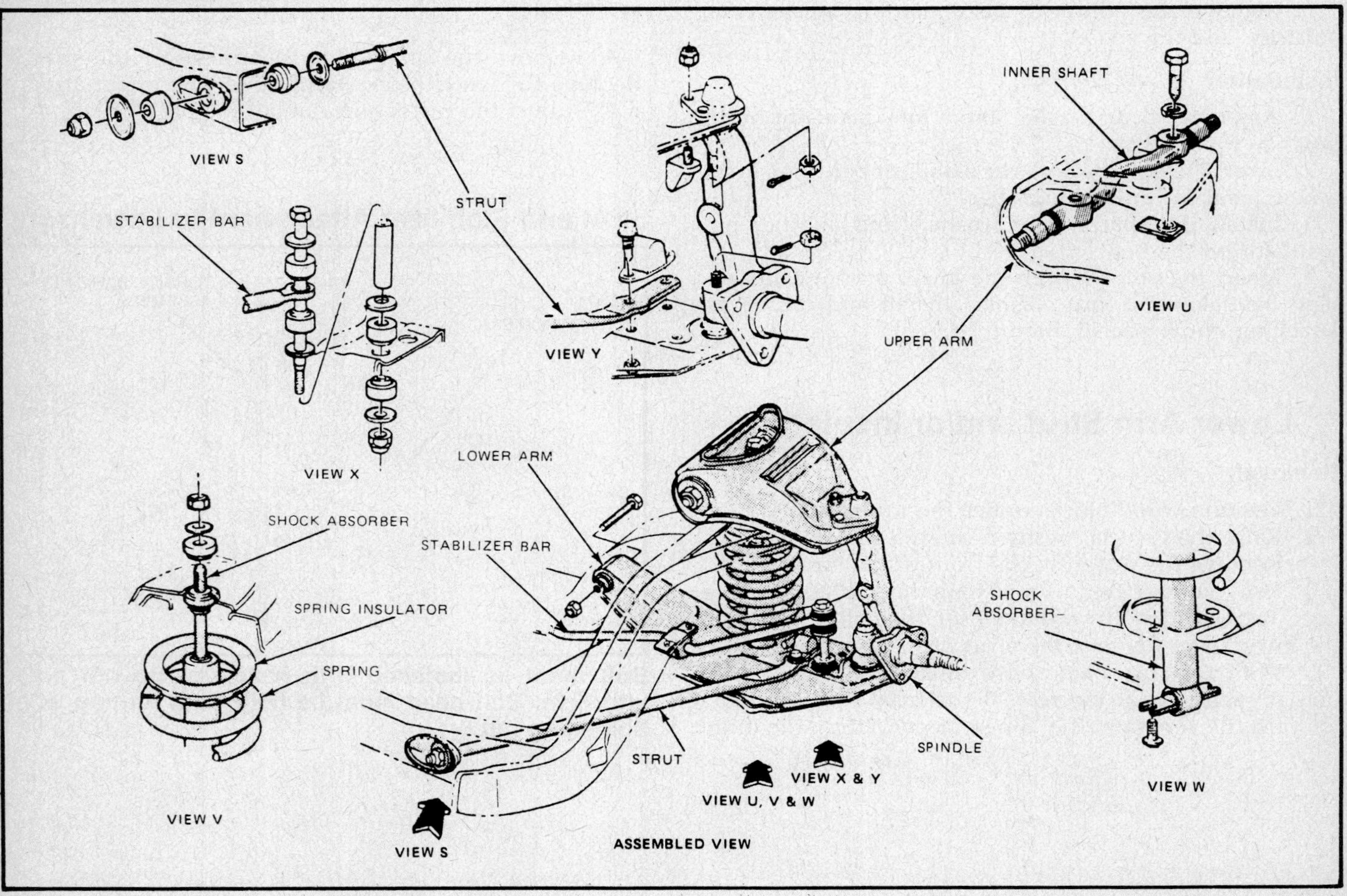

5. Loosen upper arm inner shaft-to-frame attaching bolts so that lockwashers on bolts are unloaded. Then firmly tap bolt heads to assure loosening of the lower assemblies.

6. Adjust camber and caster on each wheel.

7. Torque upper arm inner shaft-to-frame attaching bolts to 136–190 N•m (100–140 ft.-lbs.). It is not necessary to recheck caster and camber after this adjustment procedure is performed.

8. Check toe-in and steering wheel spoke position and adjust both (as required) at the same time.

Toe and Steering Wheel Spoke Position

After adjusting caster and camber, check the steering wheel spoke position with the front wheels in straight-ahead position. If the spokes are not in their normal position, they can be properly adjusted while toe is being adjusted.

1. Loosen the two clamp bolts on each spindle connecting rod sleeve.

2. Adjust toe. If the steering wheel spokes are in their normal position, lengthen or shorten both rods equally to obtain correct toe.

3. If the steering wheel spokes are not in their normal position, make the necessary rod adjustments to obtain correct toe and steering wheel spoke alignment.

4. When toe and the steering wheel spoke position are both correct, lubricate clamp, bolts, and nuts and tighten the clamp bolts on both connecting rod sleeves and specification. The sleeve position should not be changed when the clamp bolts are tightened for proper clamp bolt orientation.

Camber and Caster Adjusting Tools

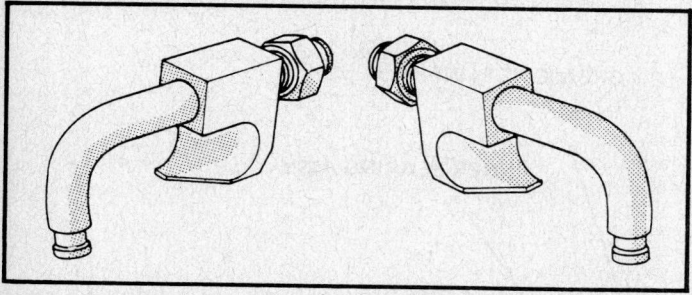

Special Tools for Camber and Caster Adjustment

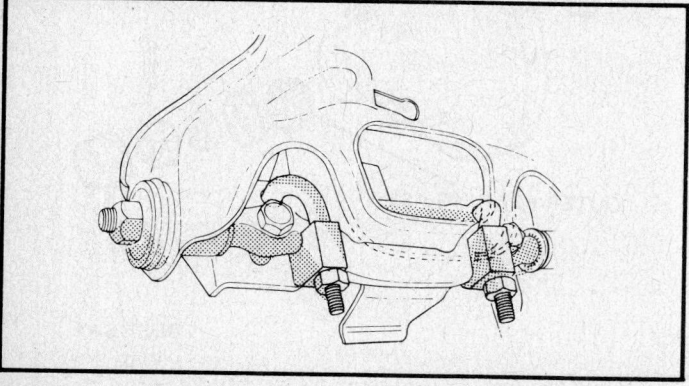

Spindle Connecting Rod Adjustment

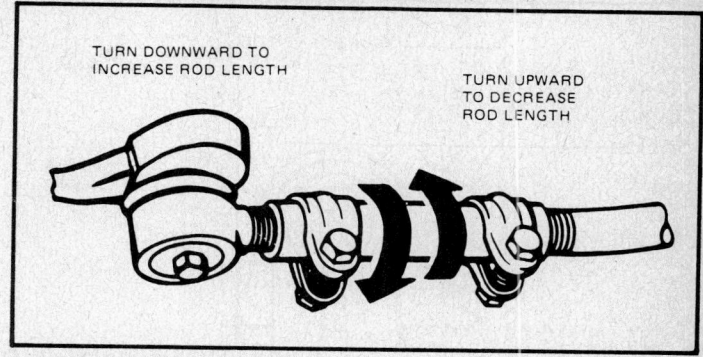

Left-hand sleeve

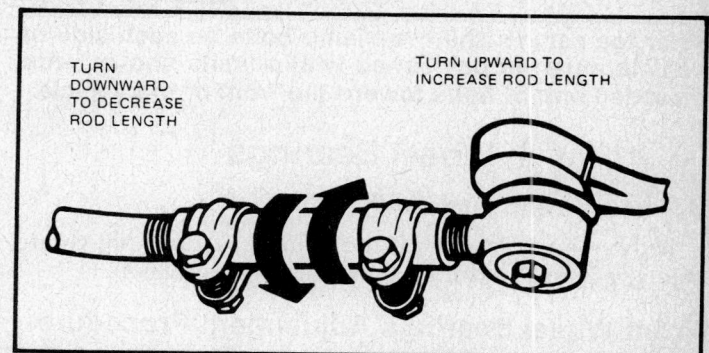

Right-hand sleeve

Steering Wheel Spoke Alignment

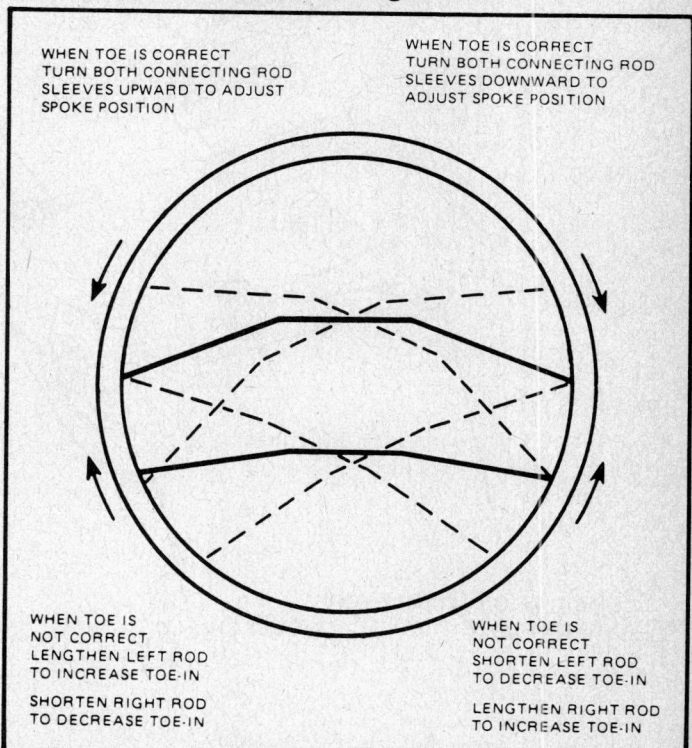

Adjust both rods equally to maintain normal spoke position.

SUSPENSION

FRONT SUSPENSION-FORD MOTOR CO. REAR DRIVE, SPRING ON LOWER ARM

Positioning Clamp Bolts

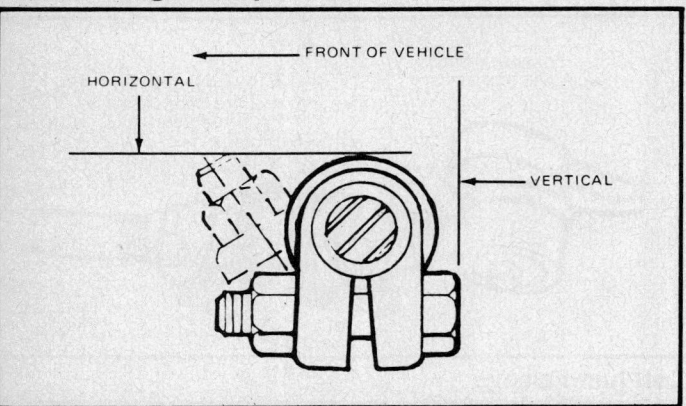

After toe setting, the two clamp bolts on each side of vehicle must be positioned within limits shown, with threaded end of bolts toward the front of the vehicle.

Wheel Bearings

Adjustment and Inspection

If the wheel is loose on the spindle or does not rotate freely, adjust the front wheel bearings as follows:

Front Wheel Bearings Adjustment Procedure

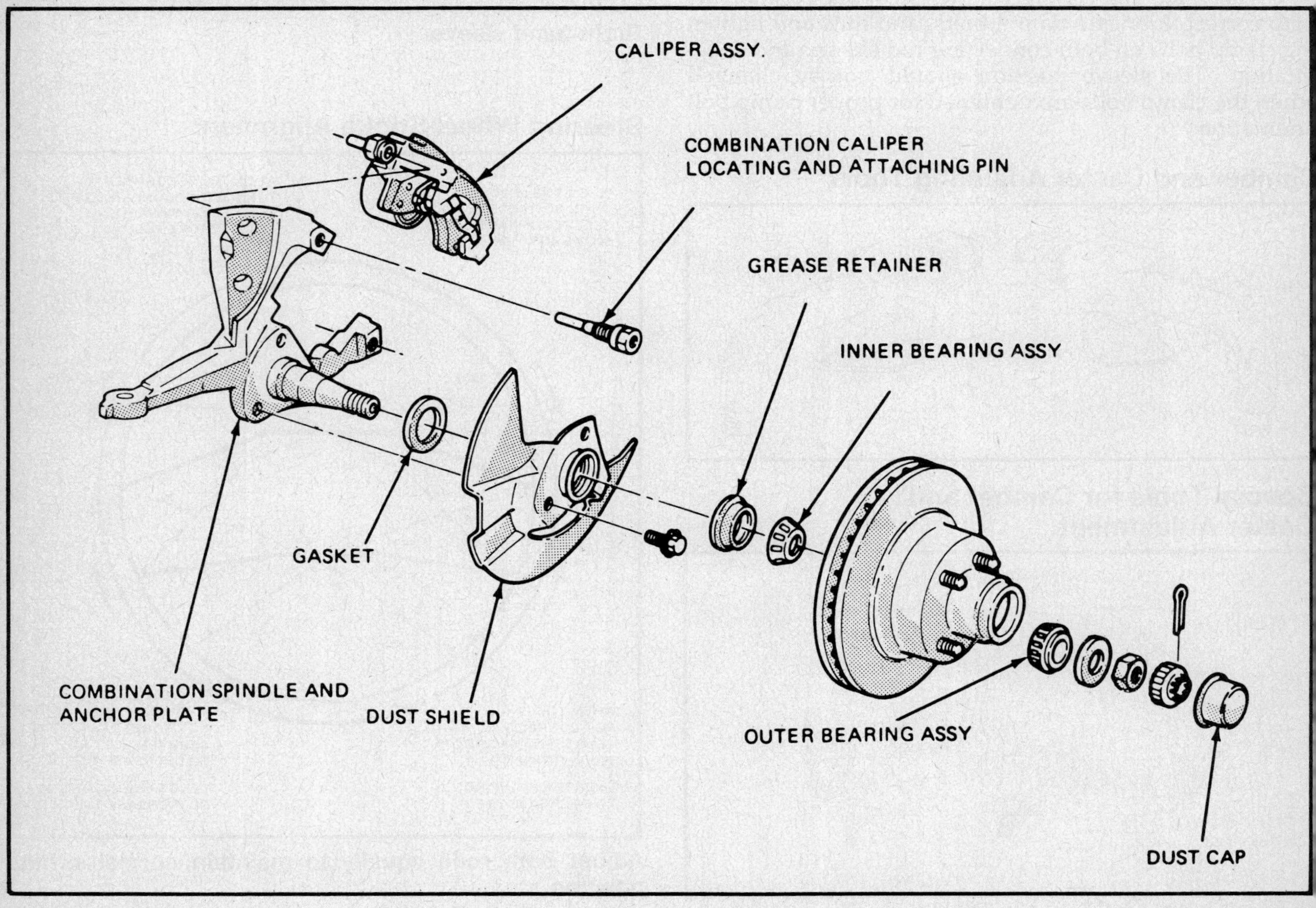

1. Raise the vehicle until the tire clears the floor.
2. Remove the wheel cover. Remove the grease cap from the hub.
3. Wipe the excess grease from the end of the spindle. Remove the cotter pin and nut lock.
4. Loosen the adjusting nut three turns and rock the wheel, hub and rotor assembly in and out several times to push the shoe and linings away from the rotor.
5. While rotating the wheel, hub and rotor assembly, torque the adjusting nut to 24–33 N•m (17–25 ft.-lbs.) to seat the bearings.
6. Loosen the adjusting nut one-half turn, then re-tighten to 1.2–1.6 N•m (10–15 in.-lbs.) using a torque wrench.
7. Place the nut lock on the adjusting nut so the castellations on the lock are in line with the cotter pin hole in the spindle.
8. Install a new cotter pin and bend the ends around the castellated flange of the nut lock.
9. Check front wheel rotation. If the wheel rotates properly, reinstall the grease cap and wheel cover. If rotation is noisy or rough, remove wheel hub and check for bearing problems.
10. Before driving the vehicle, pump the brake pedal several times to restore normal brake pedal travel.

CALIPER ASSY.

COMBINATION CALIPER
LOCATING AND ATTACHING PIN

GREASE RETAINER

INNER BEARING ASSY

GASKET

COMBINATION SPINDLE AND
ANCHOR PLATE

DUST SHIELD

OUTER BEARING ASSY

DUST CAP

Front Wheel Bearing Adjustment

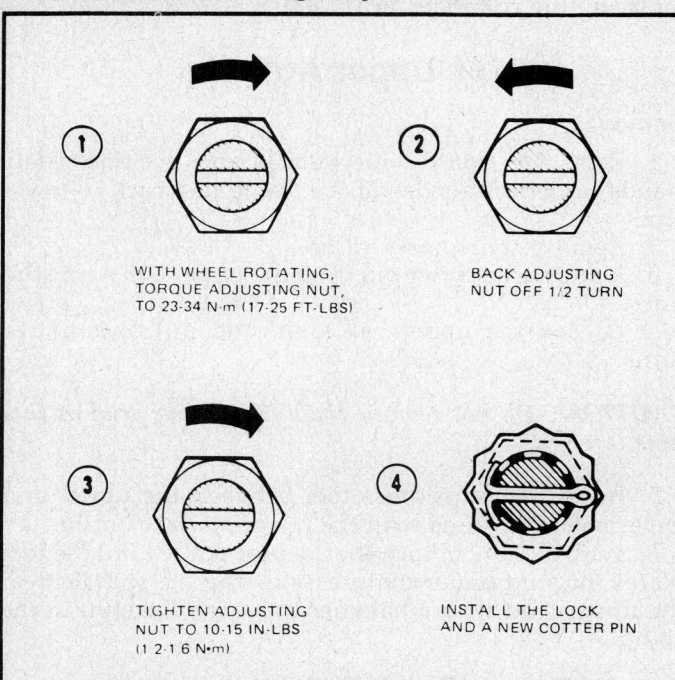

① WITH WHEEL ROTATING, TORQUE ADJUSTING NUT, TO 23-34 N·m (17-25 FT·LBS)

② BACK ADJUSTING NUT OFF 1/2 TURN

③ TIGHTEN ADJUSTING NUT TO 10-15 IN·LBS (1.2-1.6 N·m)

④ INSTALL THE LOCK AND A NEW COTTER PIN

Front Wheel Grease Seal Bearing

Replacement and Lubrication

1. Raise the vehicle until the tire clears the floor. Remove wheel from hub and rotor.
2. Remove the caliper from the spindle and wire it to the underbody to prevent damage to the brake hose.
3. Remove the grease cap from the hub. Remove the cotter pin, nut lock, adjusting nut and flatwasher from the spindle. Remove the outer bearing cone and roller assembly.
4. Pull the hub and rotor assembly off the spindle.
5. Using tool 1175-AC or equivalent, remove and discard the grease retainer. Remove the inner bearing cone and roller assembly from the hub.
6. Clean the inner and outer bearing cups with solvent. Inspect the cups for scratches, pits, excessive wear, and other damage. If the cups are worn or damaged, remove them with tools D80L-927-A and T77F-1102-A or equivalent and replace them.

Shock Absorber

Removal

1. Remove the nut, washer, and bushing from the shock absorber upper end.
2. Remove the two thread-cutting screws attaching the shock absorber to the lower arm and remove the shock absorber. Lightly wire brush the shock studs to free of rust, oil or corrosion.

Installation

1. Place a washer and bushing on the shock absorber top stud and position the shock absorber inside the front spring. Install the thread-cutting screws and torque to specifications. If the threads in the lower arm become stripped or damaged, the removed thread cutting screws should be re-used, along with $5/16$-18 lock nuts. Torque to the same specifications as when thread cutting screws are secured directly to the lower arm.
2. Remove the safety stands and lower the vehicle.
3. Place a bushing and washer on the shock absorber top stud and install nut.

Spring

Removal

1. Raise the vehicle. Remove the wheel and tire assembly.
2. Disconnect the stabilizer bar link from the lower arm.
3. Remove the two bolts attaching the shock absorber to the lower arm assembly.
4. Remove the upper nut, retainer and grommet from the shock absorber and remove the shock.
5. Remove the steering center link from the pitman arm.
6. Support the vehicle with safety stands under the jacking pads and lower the hoist for working room.
7. Using the spring compressor tool, install one plate with the pivot ball seat facing downward into the coils of the spring. Rotate the plate so that it is flush with the upper surface of the lower arm.

Coil Spring Removal

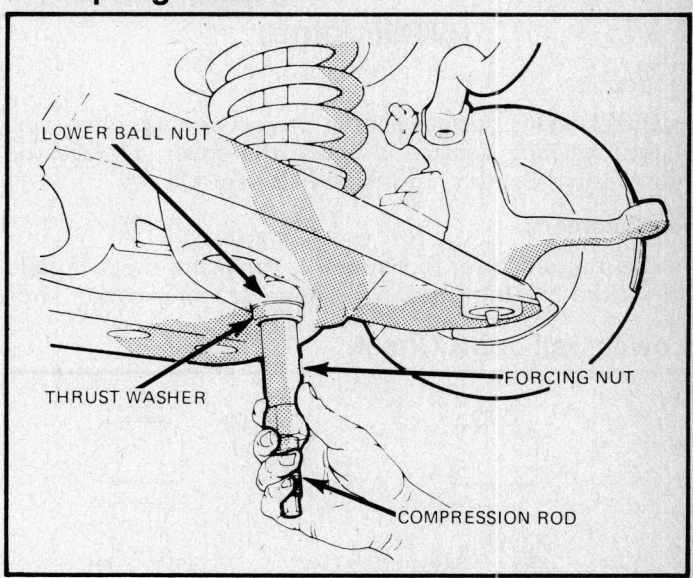

LOWER BALL NUT

THRUST WASHER

FORCING NUT

COMPRESSION ROD

8. Install the other plate with the pivot ball seat facing upward into the coils of the spring. Insert the upper ball nut through the coils of the spring so that nut rests in the upper plate.
9. Insert the compression rod into the opening in the lower arm, through the upper and lower plate and upper ball nut. Insert the securing pin through the upper ball nut and compression rod.

NOTE   This pin can only be inserted one way into the upper ball nut because of a stepped hole design.

10. With the upper ball nut secured, turn the upper plate so that it walks up the coil until it contacts the upper spring seat, then back off one half turn.

11. Install the lower ball nut and thrust washer on the compression rod, and screw on the forcing nut.

12. Tighten the forcing nut until the spring is compressed enough so that it is free in its seat.

13. Remove the two lower arm pivot bolts and disengage the lower arm from the frame crossmember; remove the spring assembly.

14. If a new spring is to be installed, mark the position of the upper and lower plates on the spring with chalk, and measure the compressed length of the spring and amount of spring curvature to assist in compression and installation of a new spring.

15. Loosen the forcing nut to relieve spring tension and remove the tools from the spring.

Installation

1. Assemble the spring compressor and locate in the same position as indicated in step 14 of Spring Removal.

2. Before compressing the coil spring, be sure that the upper ball nut securing pin is inserted properly.

3. Compress the coil spring until the spring height reaches the dimension obtained in step 14 of Spring Removal.

4. Position the coil spring assembly into the lower arm.

5. To install coil spring, reverse removal procedures.

Ball Joints

Inspection

The checking surface should project outside the cover. If the checking surface is inside the cover, replace the lower arm assembly, or install ball joint kit.

Replacement

The manufacturer recommends replacing the complete arm if the ball joint is worn. However, aftermarket sup-

Lower Ball Joint Check

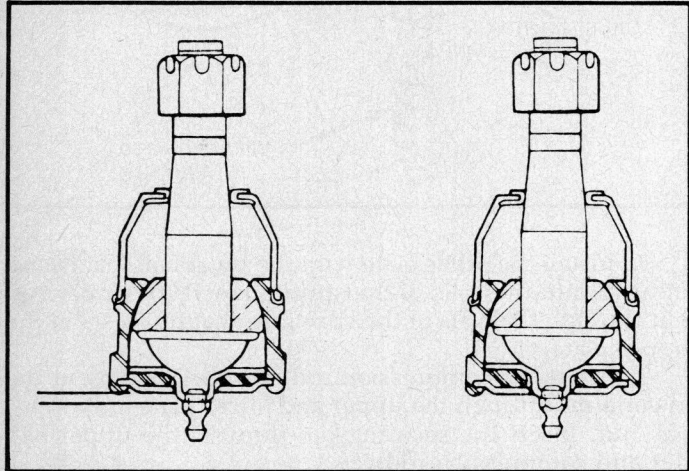

pliers sell ball joint kits to replace worn ball joints without replacing the complete arm.

Upper Arm

Removal

1. Raise the front of the vehicle and position safety stands under both sides of the frame just back of lower arm.

2. Remove the wheel and tire.

3. Remove the cotter pin from the upper ball joint stud nut.

4. Loosen the upper ball joint stud nut one or two turns.

CAUTION   Do not remove the nut from the stud at this time.

5. Insert ball joint press tool between the upper and lower ball joint studs with the adapter screw on top.

6. With a wrench, turn the adapter screw until the tool places the stud under compression. Tap the spindle near the upper stud with a hammer to loosen the stud in the spindle.

Special Tool to Break Ball Joint Loose

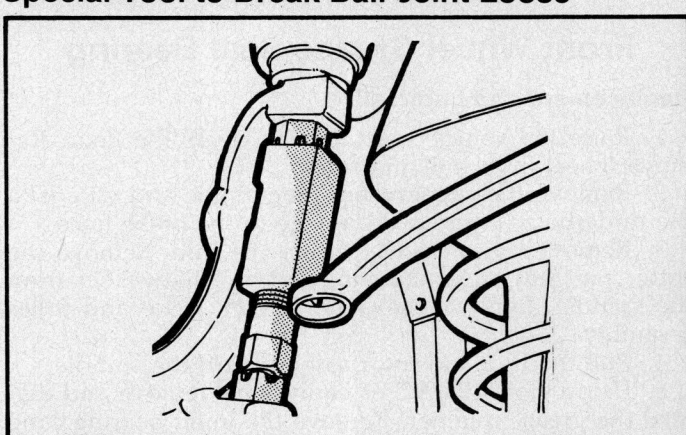

The tool should be seated firmly against the ends of both studs and not against the nuts or lower stud cotter pin.

NOTE   Do not loosen the stud from the spindle with tool pressure only. Do not contact the boot seal with the hammer.

7. Remove the tool from between the ball joint studs and place a floor jack under the lower arm.

8. Remove the upper arm attaching bolts, and remove the upper arm assembly.

Installation

1. Transfer the bumper from the old arm to the new arm.

2. Position the upper arm in new shaft to the frame bracket, and install the two attaching bolts and washers to a snug fit.

3. Connect the upper ball joint stud to the spindle and install the attaching nut. Torque the nut to specification and continue to tighten the nut until the cotter pin hole in the stud is in line with the nut slots, then install the cotter pin.

4. Install the wheel and tire and adjust the wheel bearing.

5. Remove the safety stands and lower the front of the vehicle.

6. Adjust caster, camber and toe-in to specification.

Upper Arm Bushings

Removal (With Arm Removed)

1. Remove the nuts and washer from both ends of the upper arm shaft.

NOTE Use the existing C-clamp tool part number T74P-3044-A-1 or equivalent and adapters to remove the bushings.

2. Position the shaft and new bushings to the upper arm and install the bushings and shaft to the upper arm.

Upper Arm Bushing Removal

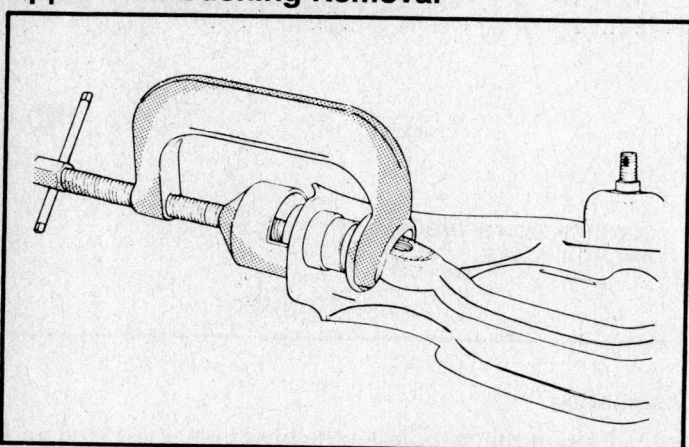

Upper Arm Bushing Installation

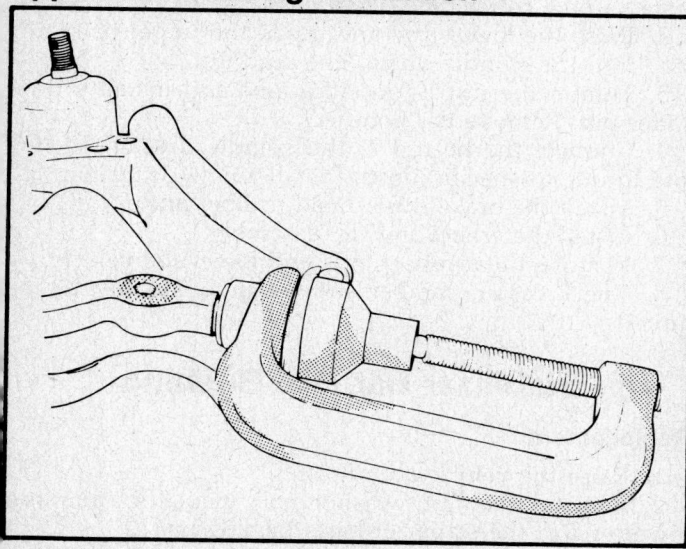

NOTE The front bushing is a larger diameter than the rear, requiring that adapter part number T79P-3044-A2 or equivalent, is used when installing rear bushing.

3. Make certain that the inner shaft is positioned so that the serrated side contacts the frame.

4. Install an inner washer, rear bushing only, and two outer washers and new nuts on each end of the inner shaft. Torque to specification.

Lower Arm

Removal

1. Raise the front of the vehicle and position safety stands under both sides of the frame just back of the lower arms.

2. Remove the wheel and tire.

3. Remove brake caliper and rotor, and dust shield as outlined in brake section.

4. Remove the shock absorber.

5. Disconnect the stabilizer bar link from the lower arm.

6. Disconnect the steering center link from the pitman arm.

7. Remove the cotter pin from the lower ball joint nut.

8. Loosen the lower ball joint stud nut one or two turns.

Front Spring and Lower Control Arm Removal

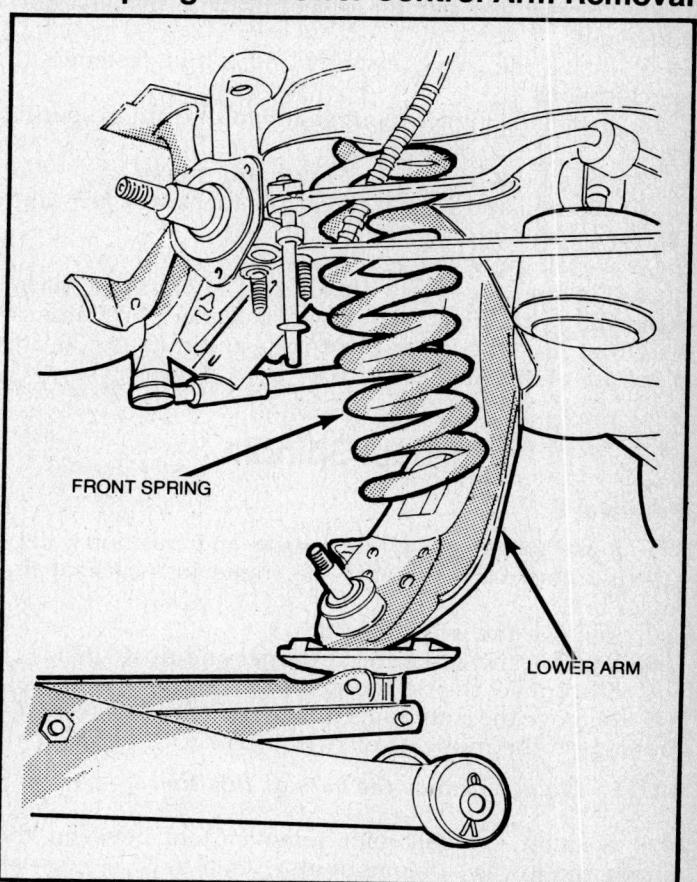

FRONT SPRING

LOWER ARM

9. Install ball joint press tool between the upper and lower ball joint studs.

10. Install the coil spring compression tools outlined in "Spring Removal" and remove the spring.

11. Remove the ball joint nut, and remove arm assembly.

12. With a wrench, turn the adapter screw until the tool places the stud under compression. Tap the spindle near the lower stud with a hammer to loosen the stud in the spindle.

13. Remove the ball joint press tool.

14. Place a floor jack under the lower arm.

15. Gently lower the arm until all tension is relieved.

16. Remove lower arm center bolt and remove arm.

Installation

1. Position the arm assembly ball joint stud into the spindle and install the nut. Torque to specification and install a new cotter pin.

2. Position the coil spring into the upper spring pocket; raise the lower arm and align the holes in the arm with the holes in the crossmember. Install bolts and nuts. Do not tighten at this time.

NOTE *Be sure that the pigtail of the lower coil of the spring is in the proper location of the seat of the lower arm, between the two holes.*

3. Remove the spring compressor tool.

4. Connect the steering center link at the pitman arm, install the nut and tighten to specification. Install a new cotter pin.

5. Install the shock absorber and torque fasteners to specifications.

6. Install the jounce bumper and torque nut to specification.

7. Install the dust shield, rotor and caliper.

8. Position the stabilizer link to the lower arm and install the bolt and attaching nut.

9. Install the wheel and tire.

10. Remove the safety stands and lower the vehicle. After the vehicle has been lowered to floor and at curb height, torque the lower pivot bolts and nuts to 136–189 N•m (100–140 ft.-lbs.).

Wheel Spindle

Removal

1. Raise the front of the vehicle and position safety stands under both sides of the frame just back of the lower arm.

2. Remove the wheel and tire.

3. Remove the brake rotor, caliper and dust shield.

4. Disconnect the tie-rod end from the spindle.

5. Remove the cotter pins from both ball joint stud nuts and loosen the nuts one or two turns.

NOTE *Do not remove the nuts at this time.*

6. Position the ball joint remover tool between the upper and lower ball joint studs.

7. Turn the tool with a wrench until the tool places the studs under compression. With a hammer, sharply hit the spindle near the studs to break it loose in the spindle.

8. Position a floor jack under the lower arm at the lower ball joint area.

9. Remove the upper and lower ball joint stud nuts, lower the jack *carefully* and remove the spindle.

Spindle Mounting

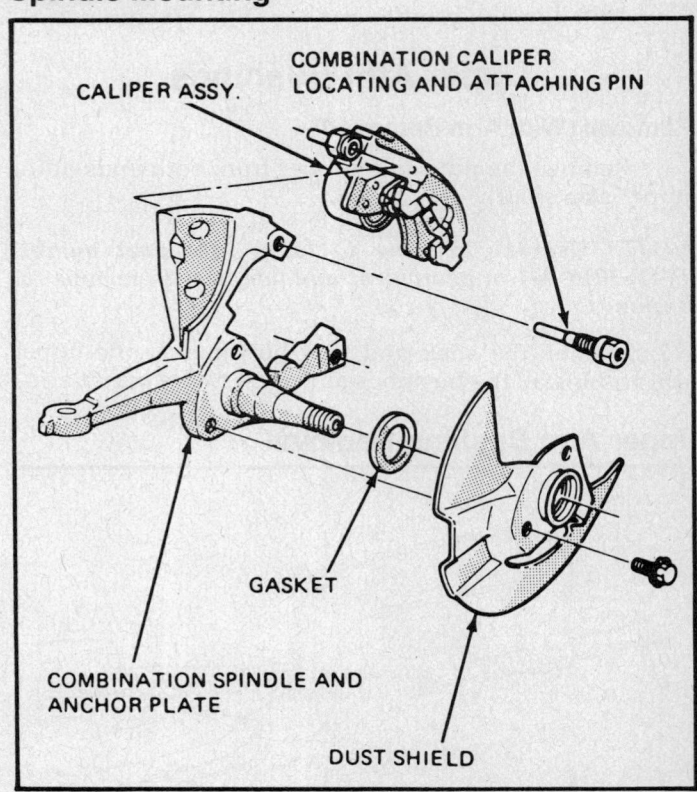

CALIPER ASSY.

COMBINATION CALIPER LOCATING AND ATTACHING PIN

GASKET

COMBINATION SPINDLE AND ANCHOR PLATE

DUST SHIELD

Installation

1. Position the spindle on the lower ball joint stud and install the stud nut. Torque the nut to specification and install a new cotter pin.

2. Raise the lower arm and guide the upper ball joint stud into the spindle. Install the stud nut.

3. Torque the nut to specifications and install a new cotter pin. Remove the floor jack.

4. Connect the tie-rod to the spindle. Install the nut and torque to specifications. Install a new cotter pin.

5. Install the brake dust shield, caliper and rotor.

6. Install the wheel and tire assembly.

7. Remove the safety stands and lower the vehicle.

8. Check caster, camber and toe-in and adjust as required.

Stabilizer Bar End Bushing

Replacement

1. Raise the vehicle on a hoist.

2. Remove the nut, washer and insulator from the lower end of the stabilizer bar attaching bolt.

3. Remove the bolt and the remaining washers, insulators, and the spacer.

4. Assemble a cup washer and new insulator on the bolt.

5. Insert the bolt through the stabilizer bar, then install new insulator and cup washer.

6. Install the spacer, cup washer, and another new insulator on the bolt.

7. Insert the bolt through the lower arm and install a new insulator and cup washer. Install and torque the attaching nut to specification.

Stabilizer Bar and/or Insulator

Removal

1. Raise the vehicle on a hoist, and place jack stands under the lower arm.

2. Disconnect the stabilizer from each stabilizer link and both stabilizer insulator attaching clamps. Remove the stabilizer bar assembly.

3. Cut the worn insulators from the stabilizer bar.

Installation

1. Coat the necessary parts of the stabilizer bar with Ruglyde or an equivalent lubricant; slide insulators onto the stabilizer bar.

2. Using a new nut and bolt, secure each end of the stabilizer bar to the lower suspension arm, making sure the bolt head is at the bottom. Tighten nuts to 9–16 N•m (6–12 ft.-lbs.).

3. Using new fasteners, clamp the stabilizer bar to the attaching brackets on the side rail. Tighten bolts to 19–35 N•m (14–26 ft.-lbs.).

REAR SUSPENSION—FORD, LINCOLN, MERCURY REAR DRIVE CARS, FOUR-BAR LINK DESIGN

Shock Absorber

Removal

1. Remove the attaching nut, washer, and insulator from the shock absorber's upper stud.

2. Raise the vehicle on a hoist, and support the rear axle.

3. From underneath the vehicle, compress the shock absorber to clear it from the hole in the upper shock tower.

4. Remove the lower shock absorber bolt, washer, and nut from the axle bracket.

5. Remove the shock absorber.

Protective Cover Installation— Thunderbird/XR-7

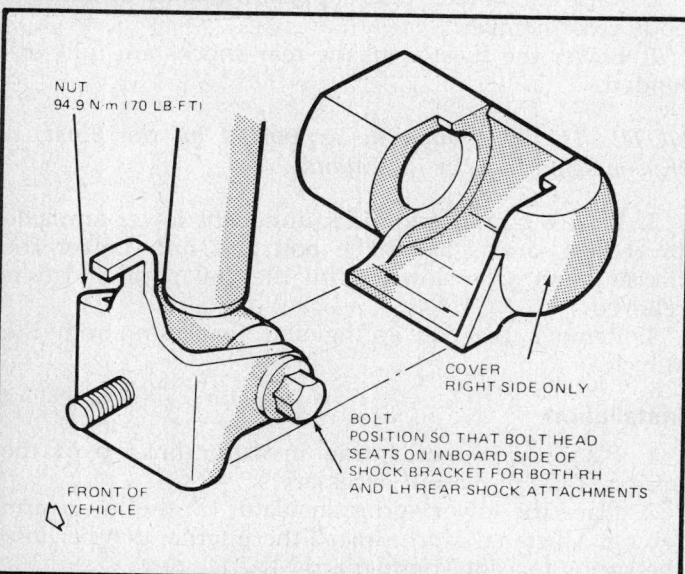

NUT
94.9 N·m (70 LB·FT)

COVER
RIGHT SIDE ONLY

BOLT
POSITION SO THAT BOLT HEAD
SEATS ON INBOARD SIDE OF
SHOCK BRACKET FOR BOTH RH
AND LH REAR SHOCK ATTACHMENTS

FRONT OF
VEHICLE

Rear Shock Lower Installation— Fairmont/Zephyr, Mustang/Capri, Granada/Cougar

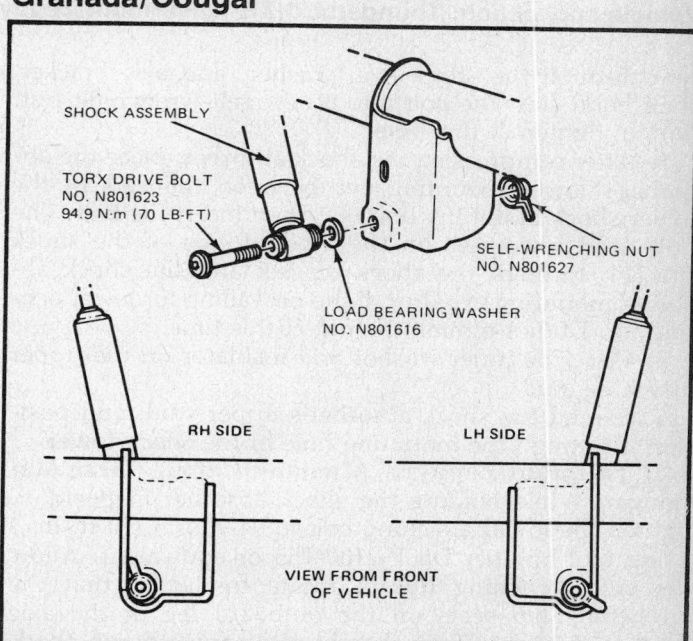

SHOCK ASSEMBLY

TORX DRIVE BOLT
NO. N801623
94.9 N·m (70 LB·FT)

SELF-WRENCHING NUT
NO. N801627

LOAD BEARING WASHER
NO. N801616

RH SIDE

LH SIDE

VIEW FROM FRONT
OF VEHICLE

Allow the self-wrenching nut to rotate freely, so that the wrenching tab seats on the outboard leg of the axle bracket. Do not restrain the nut using any other method.

Installation

1. Expel all air from the new shock absorber.

2. Compress the shock absorber and position the shock's mounting eye to the axle bracket mounting hole. Place a new load bearing washer between the shock eye and axle bracket. Install a new Torx drive bolt or equiva-

Four-Bar Link Coil Rear Suspension

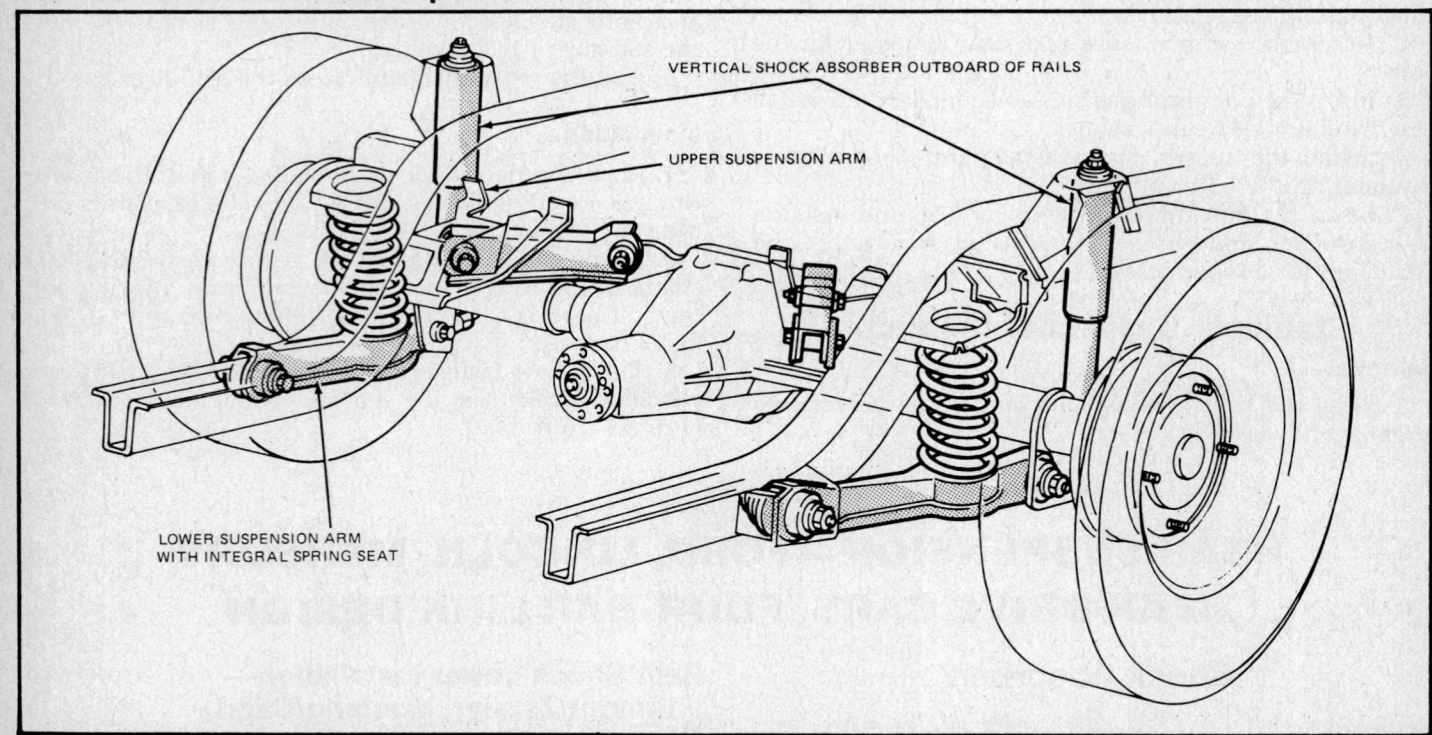

VERTICAL SHOCK ABSORBER OUTBOARD OF RAILS

UPPER SUSPENSION ARM

LOWER SUSPENSION ARM
WITH INTEGRAL SPRING SEAT

Vehicle application: Thunderbird/XR-7, Fairmont/Zephyr, Granada/Cougar, Mustang/Capri.

lent through the shock eye, washer, and axle bracket, then hand start the bolt into a new self-wrenching nut. Do not tighten at this time.

3. After compressing the shock absorber, place the absorber's lower mounting eye between the ears of the lower shock mounting bracket. Then insert the bolt. The bolt head must seat on the inboard side of the shock bracket, through the shock bracket and the shock absorber mounting eye. Install the prevailing torque attaching nut. Do not tighten the nut at this time.

4. Place the inner washer and insulator on the upper attaching stud.

5. Extend the shock absorber's upper stud, and position it through the mounting hole in the shock tower.

6. **Fairmont/Zephyr, Mustang/Capri, Granada/Cougar:** While holding the shock absorber in position, tighten the lower attaching bolt to 94.9 N•m (70 ft.-lbs.) using tool number D80P-2100-T55 or equivalent. Allow the self-wrenching nut to rotate freely, so that the wrenching tab seats on the outboard leg of the axle bracket. Do not restrain the nut using any other method.

7. **Thunderbird/XR-7:** While holding the shock absorber in position, tighten the lower shock cross bolt to 94.9 N•m (70 ft.-lbs.).

8. **Thunderbird/XR-7:** Install the protective cover (only one is required) to the right hand shock absorber. This is done by inserting the bolt point and nut into the cover's open end, sliding the cover over the shock bracket, and snapping the closed end of the cover over the bolt head. Properly installed, the cover will completely conceal the bolt point, nut, and bolt head. The rounded or closed end of the cover should be pointing inboard.

9. Lower the vehicle. Install the insulator, outer washer, and a new nut to the upper shock stud, and tighten. Install the rubber cap on the shock stud. Install the inside panel trim covers.

Spring

Removal

NOTE If vehicle is equipped with a rear stabilizer bar, remove the bar.

1. Raise the vehicle and support the body at the rear body crossmember.

2. Lower the hoist until the rear shocks are fully extended.

NOTE The axle must be supported by the hoist, a transmission jack, or jack stands.

3. Place a transmission jack under the lower arm axle pivot bolt, and remove the bolt and nut. Lower the transmission jack slowly until the coil spring load is relieved.

4. Remove the coil spring and insulators from the vehicle.

Installation

1. Place the upper spring insulator on top of the spring. Tape in place if necessary.

2. Place the lower spring insulator on the lower arm (except Mustang/Capri). Install the internal damper into the spring (except Thunderbird/XR-7.)

3. Position the coil spring on the lower arm spring seat, so that the pigtail on the lower arm is at the rear of the vehicle and pointing toward the left hand side of the vehicle. Slowly raise the transmission jack until the arm is in position. Insert a new rear pivot bolt and nut with the nut facing outwards. Do not tighten at this time.

4. Lower the transmission jack. Raise the axle to curb height. Tighten the lower arm pivot bolt to 135 N•m (100 ft.-lbs.).

5. If vehicle was equipped with a rear stabilizer bar, install bar.

6. Remove crossmember supports, and lower the vehicle.

Lower Arm

Removal

1. Raise the vehicle and support body at the rear body crossmember.

2. Lower the hoist until the rear shocks are fully extended.

NOTE   The axle must be supported by the hoist, a jack, or stands.

3. Place the transmission jack under the lower arm rear pivot bolt, and remove the bolt and nut.

4. Lower the jack slowly until the coil spring can be removed.

5. Remove the lower arm front pivot bolt and nut, and remove the lower arm assembly.

Installation

1. Position the lower arm assembly into the front arm bracket, and insert a new front pivot bolt and nut with nut facing outwards. Do not tighten at this time.

2. Install coil spring. Holding the spring in position, use the jack under the rear of the lower arm. Raise the jack until the arm is in position. Insert a new rear pivot bolt and nut with nut facing outwards. Do not tighten at this time.

3. Lower the jack. Raise the axle with the hoist to curb height. Tighten the lower arm front bolt and the rear pivot bolt heads to 135 N•m (100 ft.-lbs.).

4. If vehicle is equipped with a rear stabilizer bar, install bar.

5. Remove crossmember supports, and lower vehicle.

Upper Arm and Axle Bushing

Replacement

1. Remove upper arm rear pivot bolt and nut.

2. Remove front pivot bolt and nut. Remove upper arm from vehicle.

Rear Suspension—Thunderbird/XR-7

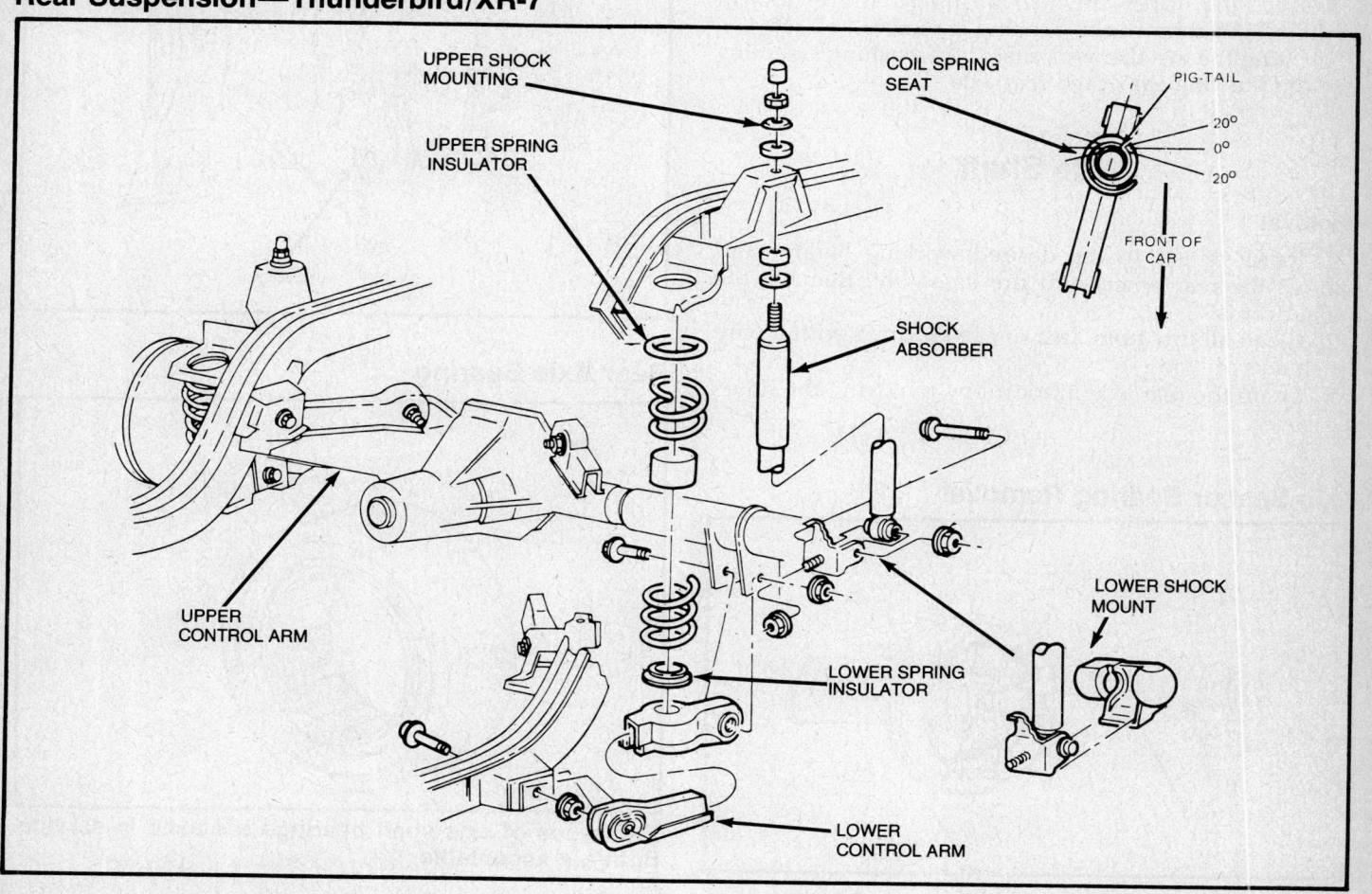

B557

Bushing Removal and Installation

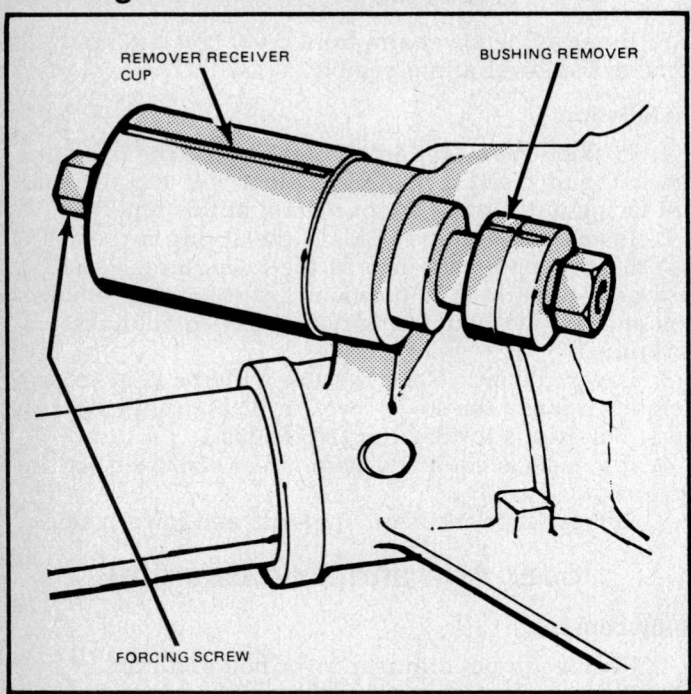

Differential Pinion Shaft and Lock Bolt

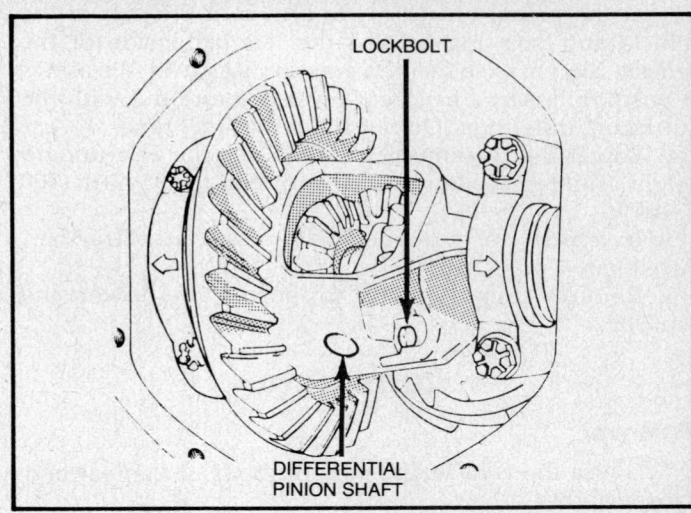

3. Place the upper arm rear bushing remover tool in position, and remove the bushing assembly.

4. Using the installer tool, install the bushing assembly into the bushing ear of the rear axle.

Axle Shaft

Removal

1. Raise vehicle to the desired working height, and remove the rear wheel and tire assembly. Remove the brake drums.

2. Clean all dirt from area of carrier cover with a wire brush and/or cloth.

3. Drain the rear axle lubricant by removing the housing cover.

C-Locks and Axle Shafts Removal and Installation

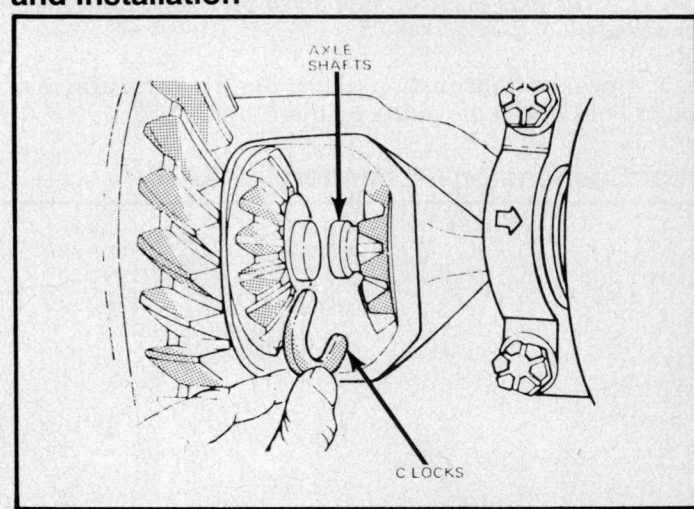

Axle Seal or Bearing Removal

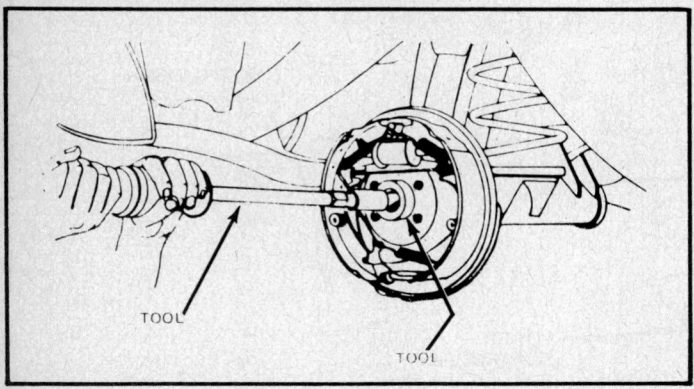

Rear Axle Bearing

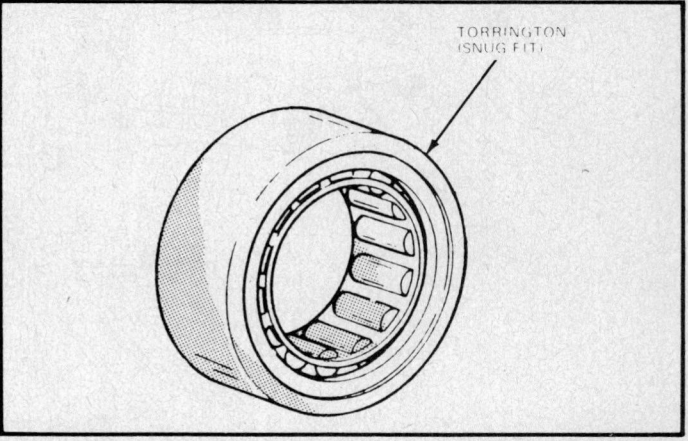

Two types of axle shaft bearings are used in service. Both are acceptable.

4. Remove differential pinion shaft lock screw and differential pinion shaft.

5. Push flanged end of the axle shafts toward the center of the vehicle and remove the C-lock from the button end of the axle shaft.

Gasket Installation

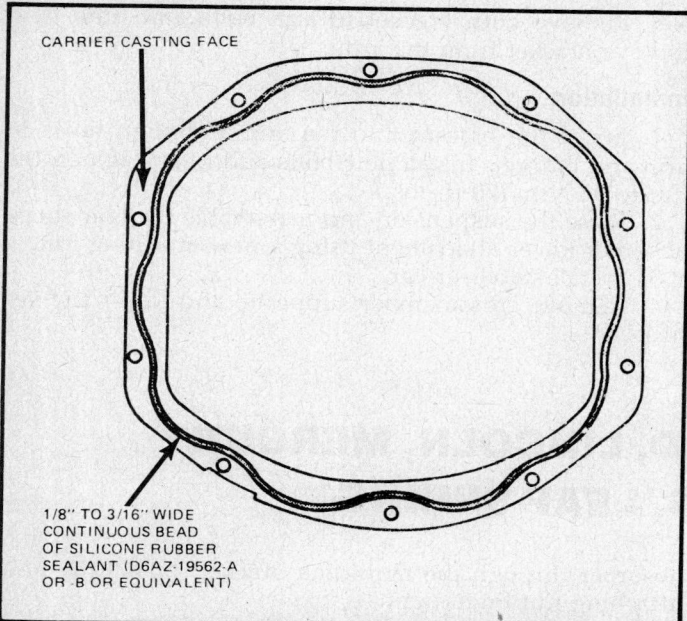

CARRIER CASTING FACE

1/8" TO 3/16" WIDE CONTINUOUS BEAD OF SILICONE RUBBER SEALANT (D6AZ-19562-A OR -B OR EQUIVALENT)

Cover assembly must be installed within 15 minutes of application of the silicone or new sealant must be reapplied. Gasket surface of housing and carrier must be free of oil.

Rear Stabilizer Bar Installation

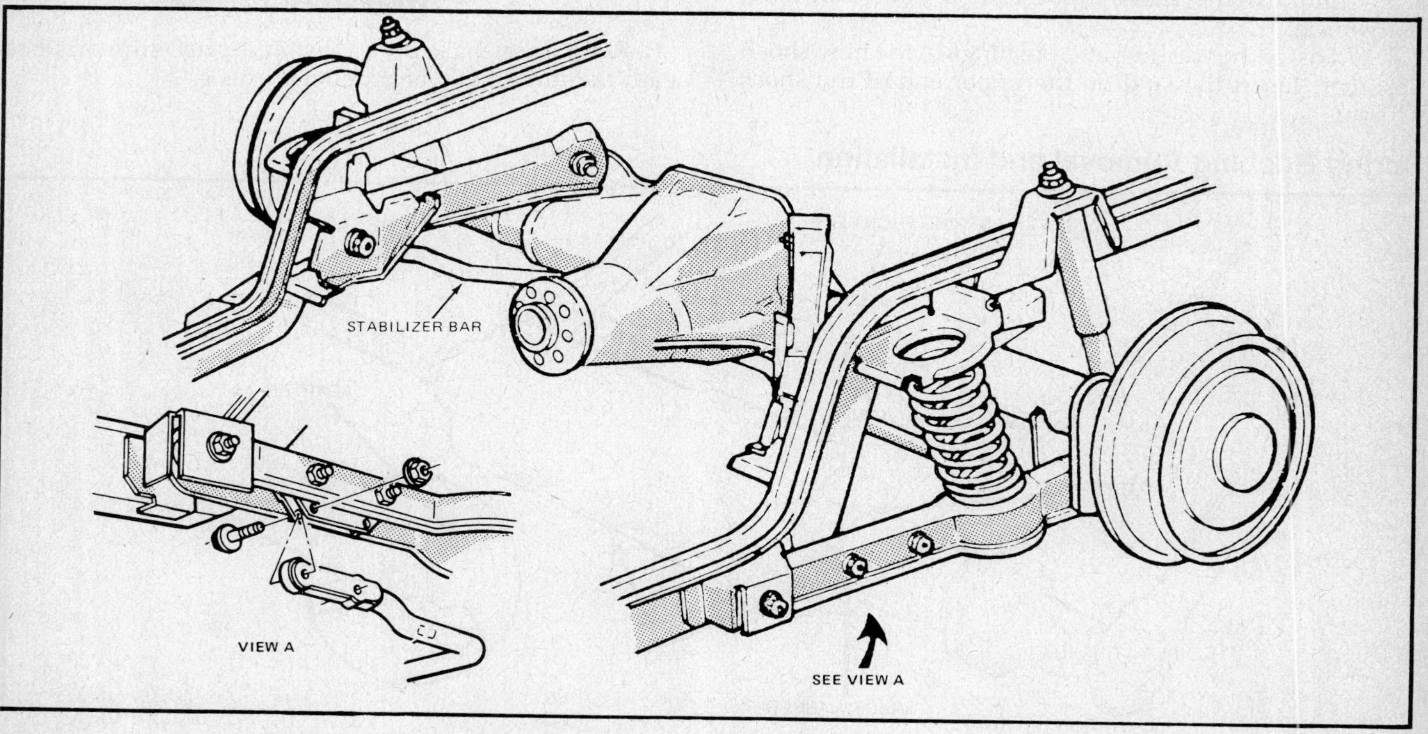

Installation

CAUTION   Care must be taken so as not to let the axle shaft splines damage the oil seal or bearing assembly.

1. Carefully slide the axle shaft into the axle housing, without damaging bearing or seal assembly. Start the splines into the side gear and push firmly until the button end of the axle shaft can be seen in the differential case.

2. Install the C-lock on the button end of the axle shaft splines, then push the shaft outboard until the shaft splines engage and the C-lock seats in the counterbore of the differential side gear.

3. Position the differential pinion shaft through the case and pinion gears, aligning the hole in the shaft with the lock screw hole. Install lock screw and torque to proper specifications.

4. Using silicone sealant No. D6AZ-19562-B (or equivalent), install cover and torque bolts to proper specification.

CAUTION   Make sure machined surfaces on both cover and carrier are clean before installing the new silicone sealant. Inside of axle must be covered when cleaning the machined surface to prevent axle contamination. Torque the cover bolts in a crosswise pattern to insure uniform draw on cover.

Stabilizer Bar

Removal

1. Raise vehicle on hoist.
2. Remove four bolts attaching stabilizer bar to brackets in lower arms.
3. Remove stabilizer bar from vehicle.

STABILIZER BAR

VIEW A

SEE VIEW A

SUSPENSION

REAR SUSPENSION-FORD MOTOR CO., REAR DRIVE, LEAF SPRING

Installation

NOTE Make sure bar is not installed upside down. A color code is provided on stabilizer bar (passenger side only) as an aid for proper orientation.

1. Align four holes in stablizer bar with holes in brackets in lower arms.
2. Install four new bolts, and tighten nuts to 27 N•m (20 ft.-lbs.).
3. Visually inspect installation to insure adequate clearance between stabilizer bar and lower arm.

Stabilizer Bar Brackets

Removal

1. Raise vehicle on hoist, and support body at rear crossmember.
2. Remove stabilizer bar.

3. Disconnect the shock absorbers at the lower shock bracket.
4. Slowly lower the suspension until the front bracket-to-arm bolt clears the body side rail.

NOTE Do not stress the brake hose when lowering the suspension.

5. Remove both bracket to arm bolts and nuts, and remove bracket from the arm.

Installation

1. Insert the bracket into the arm and align holes in arm and bracket. Install new bolts and nuts. Tighten the nut to 94 N•m (70 ft.-lbs.).
2. Raise the suspension and reassemble the rear shock absorber lower attachment using a new attaching nut.
3. Install stabilizer bar.
4. Remove crossmember supports, and lower the vehicle.

REAR SUSPENSION—FORD, LINCOLN, MERCURY REAR DRIVE CARS, LEAF SPRING

Rear Shock Absorber

REMOVAL AND INSTALLATION

1. Remove the lower end of the shock absorber from the U-bolt plate.
2. Remove the nut that fastens the upper end of the shock absorber to the mounting bracket.
3. Compress the shock absorber and remove it from the vehicle.
4. Transfer the washers and bushings to the new shock absorber. Insert the stud on the upper end of the shock

absorber through the mounting bracket. Install the new attaching nut fingertight.
5. Compress the shock absorber and assemble the lower end to the U-bolt plate together with the washers and bushings. Tighten the new attaching nut.

Rear Spring

REMOVAL

1. Raise the vehicle on a hoist and place supports beneath the underbody and under the axle.

Spring Bushing Removal and Installation

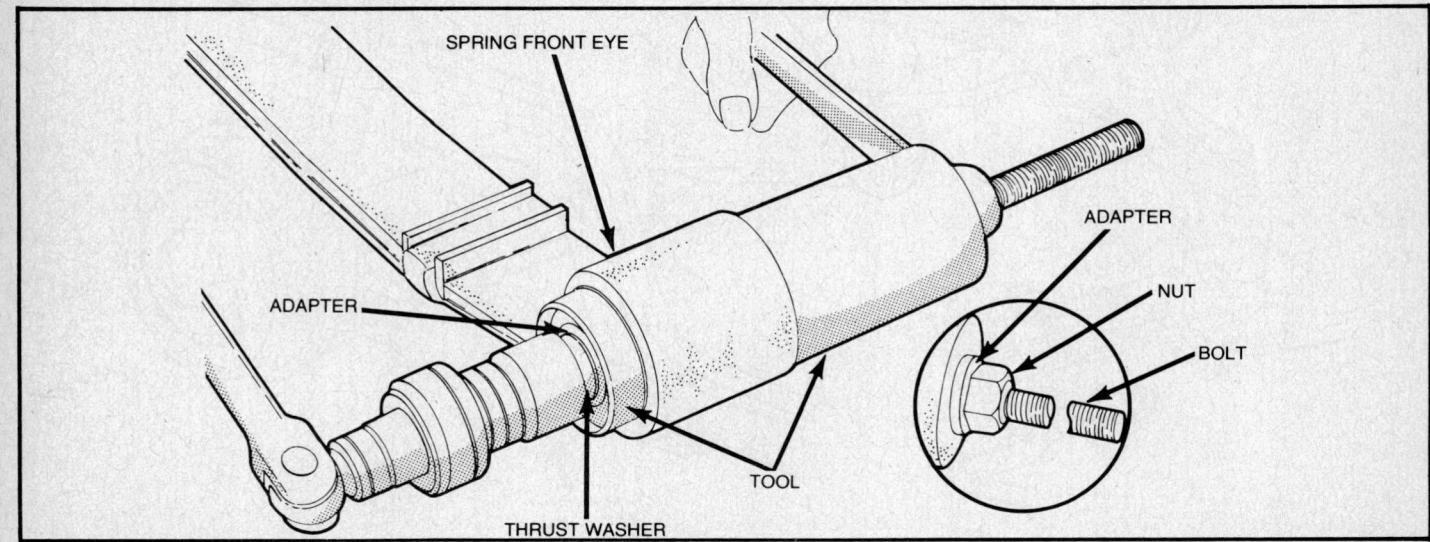

Leaf Springs Rear Suspension

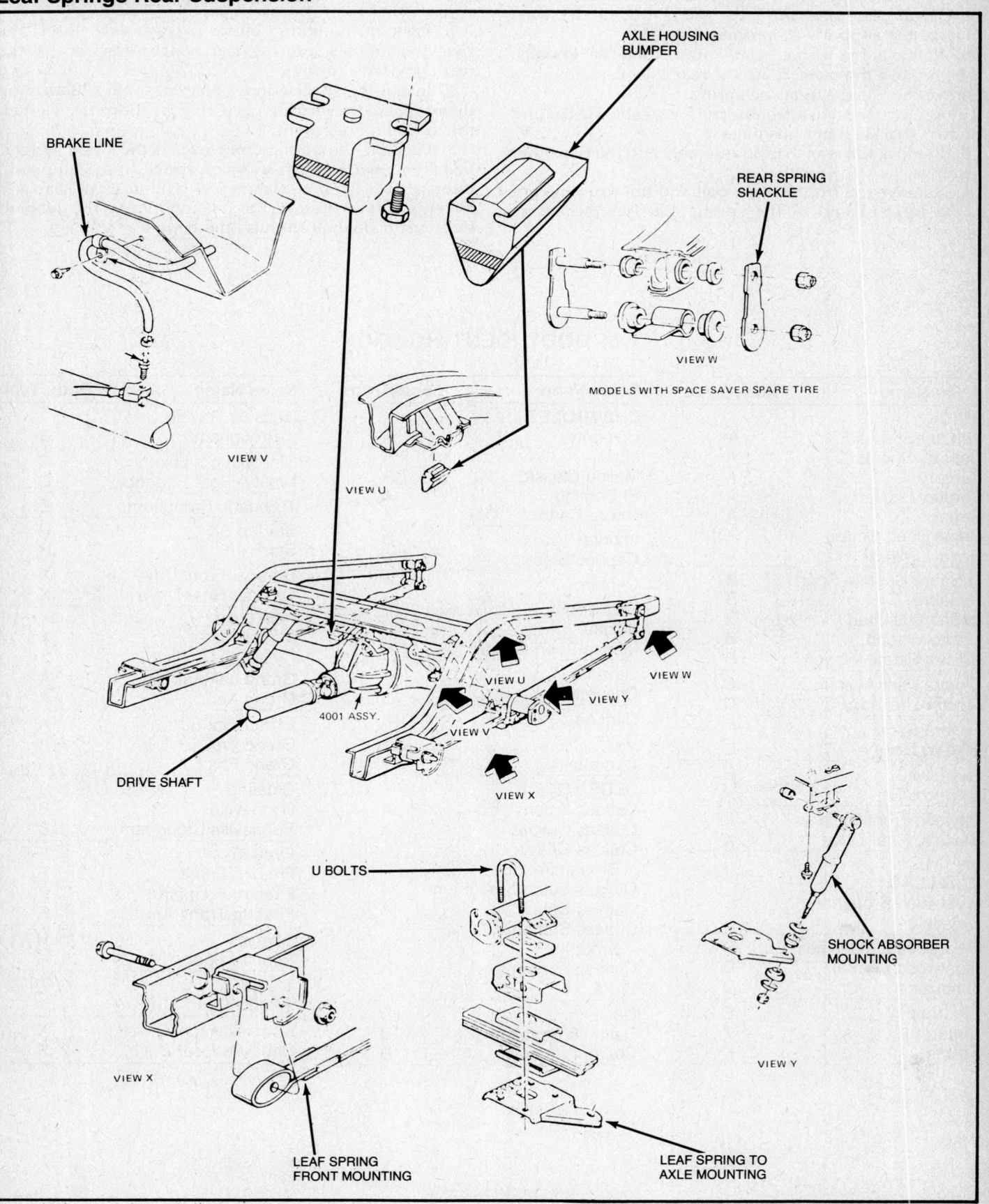

BRAKE LINE

AXLE HOUSING BUMPER

REAR SPRING SHACKLE

VIEW W

MODELS WITH SPACE SAVER SPARE TIRE

VIEW V

VIEW U

VIEW U

VIEW W

VIEW Y

4001 ASSY.

VIEW V

DRIVE SHAFT

VIEW X

SHOCK ABSORBER MOUNTING

U BOLTS

VIEW X

VIEW Y

LEAF SPRING FRONT MOUNTING

LEAF SPRING TO AXLE MOUNTING

B561

SUSPENSION

REAR SUSPENSION-FORD MOTOR CO., REAR DRIVE, LEAF SPRING

2. Disconnect the lower end of the shock absorber from the U-bolt plate and push the shock out of the way. Remove the supports from under the axle.

3. Remove the U-bolt plate nuts from the U-bolts. Then remove the plate. Raise the rear axle just enough to remove the weight from the spring.

4. Remove the two attaching nuts, rear shackle bar and the two shackle inner bushings.

5. Remove the rear shackle assembly and the two outer bushings.

6. Remove the front hanger bolt and nut from the eye at the forward end of the spring. Lift out the spring assembly.

INSTALLATION

1. Position the spring under the rear axle. Insert the shackle assembly into the rear hanger bracket and the rear eye of the spring.

2. Install the shackle inner bushings, after lubricating them. Install the shackle plate and the locknuts. Tighten the locknuts fingertight.

3. Position the spring front eye in the front hanger. Install retainer and insulators on spring (if so equipped). Lubricate isoclamp insulators with a lubricant or soap and water solution prior to installation. From the inboard side, insert the bolt through the hanger.

GM BODY IDENTIFICATION

Sales Name	Body Type	Sales Name	Body Type	Sales Name	Body Type
BUICK		**CHEVROLET**		Delta 88 Royale	
Century Special	A	Celebrity	A	Brougham	B
Century Sport	A	Malibu	A	Ninety-Eight Luxury	C
Century	A	Malibu Classic	A	Ninety-Eight Regency	C
Century Limited	A	El Camino	A	Toronado Brougham	E
Regal	A	Monte Carlo	A		
Regal Sport Coupe	A	Impala	B	Starfire SX	H
Regal Limited	A	Caprice Classic	B	Starfire	H
LeSabre Custom Sport	B	Camaro	F	Omega, Front Drive	X
LeSabre	B	Berlinetta	F	Omega, Rear Drive	X
LeSabre Limited	B	Monza	H	**PONTIAC**	
Estate Wagon	B	Monza Sport Coupe	H	A6000	A
Electra Estate Wagon	B	Cavalier	J	LeMans	A
Electra Park Avenue	C	Chevette	T	Grand LeMans	A
Electra Limited	C	Citation	X	Grand Am	A
Riviera Sport	E	Nova	X	Grand Prix SJ	A
Riviera Luxury	E	Corvette	Y	Grand Prix	A
Skyhawk	H	**OLDSMOBILE**		Grand Prix LJ	A
Skyhawk S	H	Cutlass Salon	A	Catalina	B
Skylark, Front Drive	X	Cutlass Cruiser	A	Bonneville	B
Skylark, Rear Drive	X	Cutlass Cruiser		Bonneville Brougham	B
		Brougham	A	Firebird	F
CADILLAC		Cutlass Salon Brougham	A	Firebird Esprit	F
Fleetwood Brougham	C	Cutlass Calais	A	Firebird Formula	F
DeVille	C	Cutlass Supreme		Firebird Trans Am	F
Fleetwood Limousine	D	Brougham	A	Sunbird	H
Fleetwood Formal	D	Cutlass Supreme	A	Sunbird Sport	H
Limousine	D	Ciera	A	T 1000	T
Eldorado	E	Delta 88	B	J 2000	J
Cimarron	J	Delta 88 Royale	B	Phoenix, Front Drive	X
Seville	K	Custom Cruiser	B	Phoenix, Rear Drive	X

FRONT SUSPENSION—GENERAL MOTORS A AND X BODY CARS

Wheel Alignment

Front alignment consists of the camber adjustment and toe setting. The caster setting is built into the vehicle with no provisions for adjustment.

Two bolts clamp the lower end of the MacPherson strut assembly to the upper arm of the steering knuckle. The lower of the two bolts has an eccentric washer at the head providing the camber adjustment. These special high tensile bolts with the loose nuts are torqued to 270 N•m (210 ft.-lbs.). The camber setting is plus .5 degree with a ± .5 degree tolerance.

The toe adjustment is conventional, with adjusting sleeves at the tie rod ends held in place with locking jam nuts. The toe setting is plus .1 degree with a tolerance of ± .1 degree.

Wheel Bearings

The front wheel bearing is a double row ball bearing design. It is a prelubricated sealed bearing and requires no regular maintenance. The bearing is a loose fit in the steering knuckle. The drive axle outer joint shaft is a splined fit through the bearing. The hub nut and washer are used to pre-load the bearing.

Knuckle-Strut Mounting

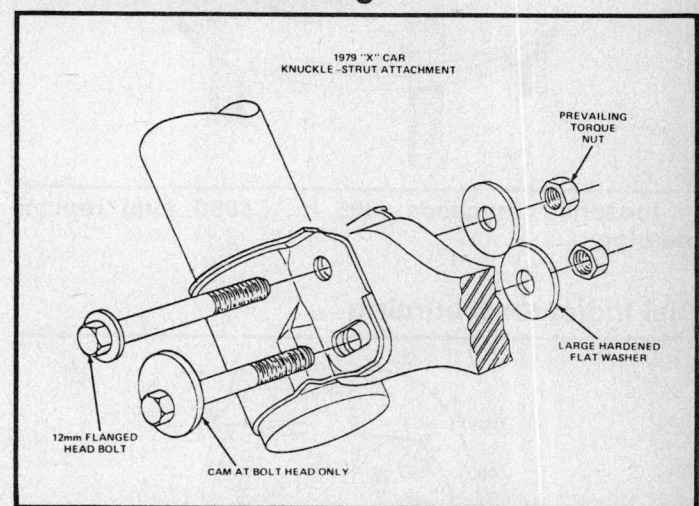

1979 "X" CAR KNUCKLE-STRUT ATTACHMENT

PREVAILING TORQUE NUT

LARGE HARDENED FLAT WASHER

12mm FLANGED HEAD BOLT

CAM AT BOLT HEAD ONLY

Front Suspension

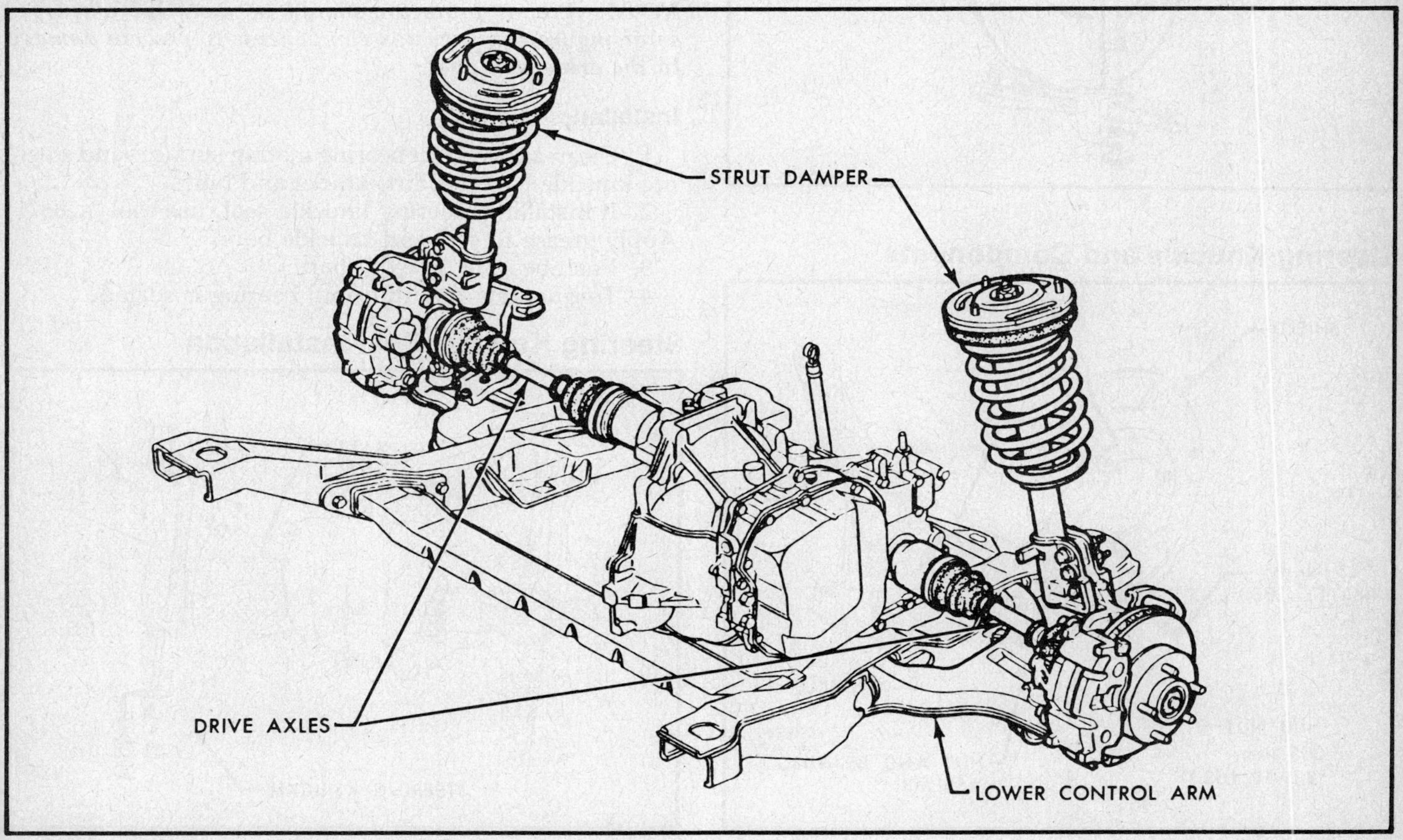

STRUT DAMPER

DRIVE AXLES

LOWER CONTROL ARM

Front Wheel Bearing

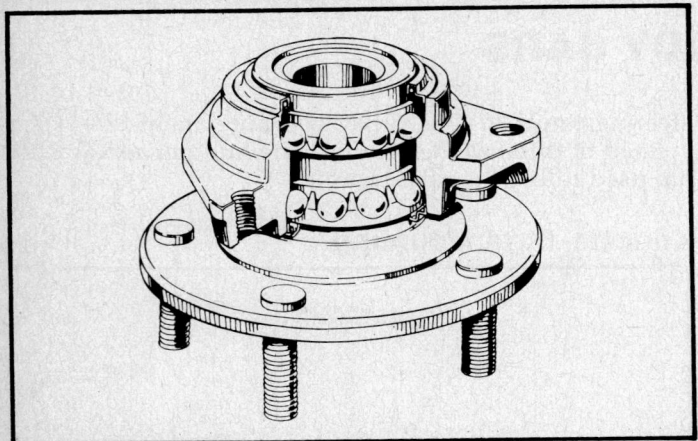

If looseness exceeds .005 in. (.5080 mm) replace bearing.

Dial Indicator Mounting

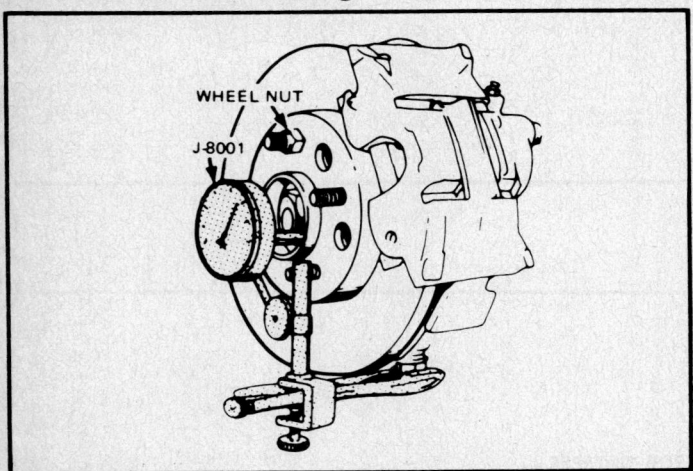

Steering Knuckle and Components

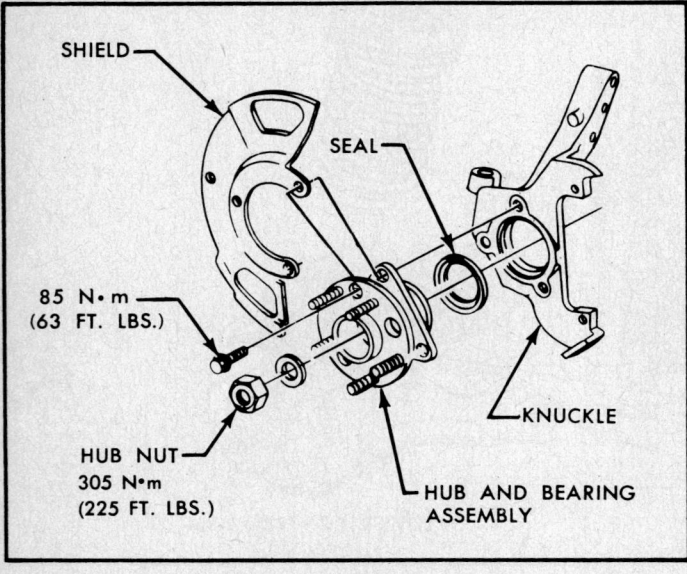

Axle Drive Cover

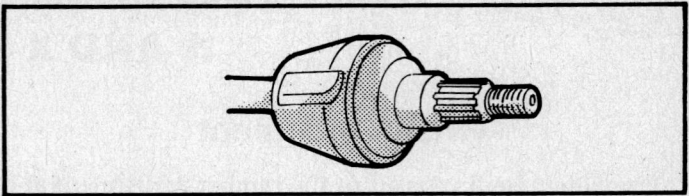

DIAGNOSIS

Check for proper drive axle nut torque, 250 N•m. Clean threads, remove nut, install new nut and torque to proper specification. Free the shoes from the disc or remove calipers. Reinstall two wheel nuts to secure disc to bearing. Mount dial indicator. Grasp disc and use a push-pull movement. Do not rock disc as this will give a false reading. If looseness exceeds .5080 mm (.005") replace bearing.

Removal

1. Break hub nut.
2. Raise car and remove wheel.
3. Remove hub nut and discard.
4. Remove brake caliper.
5. Remove three hub and bearing attaching bolts. If old bearing is being re-used, mark attaching bolts and corresponding holes for installation.
6. Install tool J-28733 and remove bearing. If excessive corrosion is present make sure bearing is loose in knuckle before using tool J-28733.

NOTE   A boot protector should be installed whenever servicing front suspension components to prevent damage to the drive axle boot.

Installation

1. Clean and inspect bearing mating surfaces and steering knuckle bore for dirt, knicks and burrs.
2. If installing steering knuckle seal, use tool J-28671. Apply grease to seal and knuckle bore.
3. Push bearing on axle shaft.
4. Torque new hub nut until bearing is seated.

Steering Knuckle Seal Installation

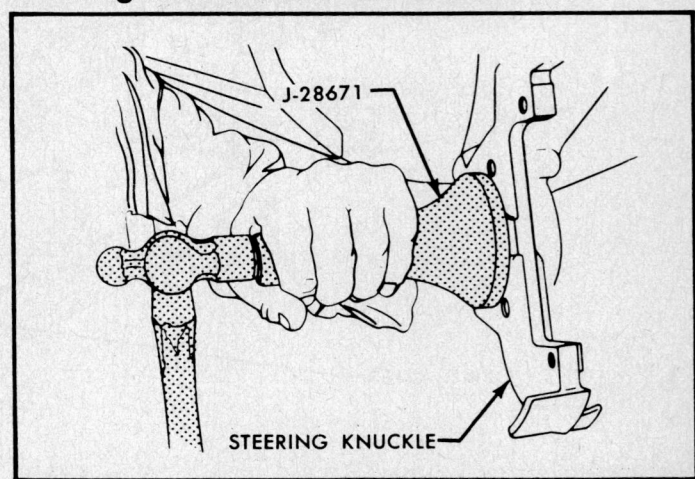

5. Install brake caliper.
6. Lower car.
7. Apply final torque to hub nut, 215 ft.-lbs. (305 N•m).

TORQUES

Top strut nut—68 ft.-lbs. (90 N•m)
Top mount nuts—18 ft.-lbs. (24 N•m)
Lower strut bolts—140 ft.-lbs. (190 N•m)

MacPherson Strut

Removal

1. Support the car so that there is no weight on the lower control arm.

MacPherson Strut

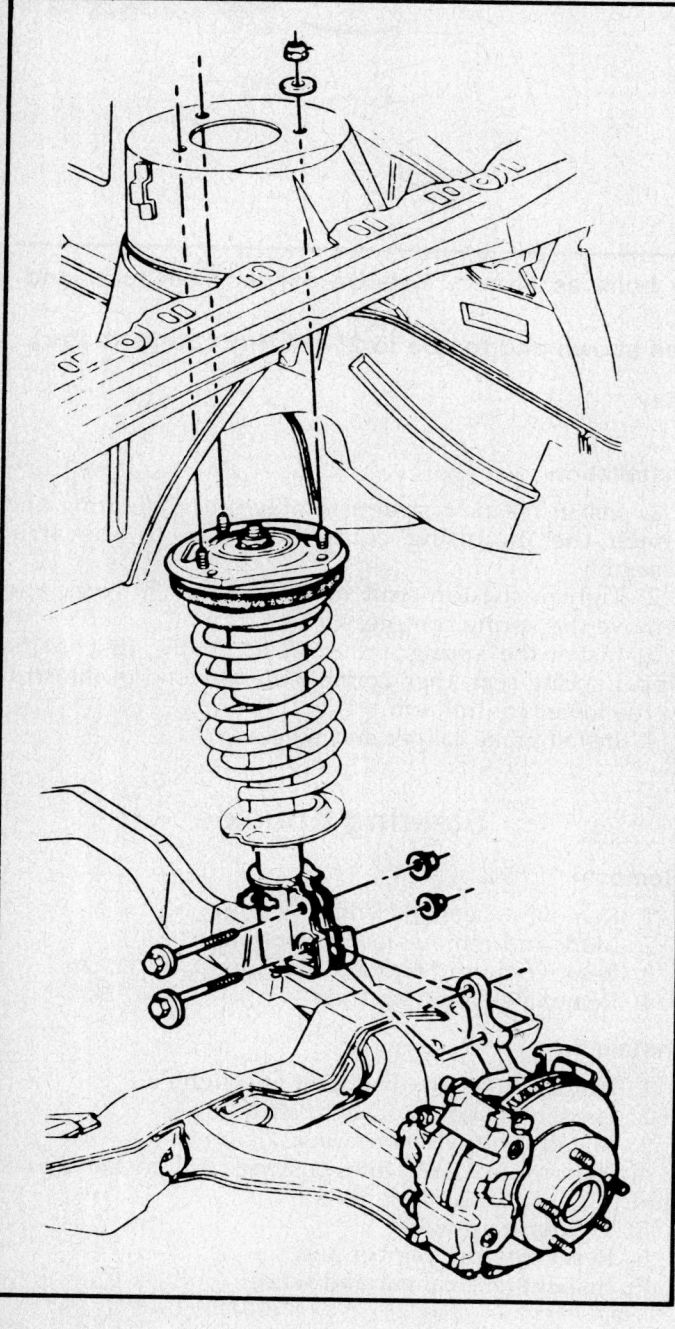

2. Remove wheel.
3. Clean up and mark the camber adjusting cam.
4. Remove the brake hose clip.
5. Remove the top three bolts from the lower strut bolts.
6. Remove the strut assembly, and take a sample to work bench.

CAUTION A reliable spring compressor tool is essential to disassemble and assemble strut bumper to avoid personal injury.

7. Compress spring with compressor until there is no pressure on the upper spring seat.

CAUTION Do not compress spring until it bottoms.

8. Remove the top nut from the strut shaft and remove the bumper shaft and the top mounting assembly.
9. Remove the spring from the strut assembly.

Lower Strut Bolts

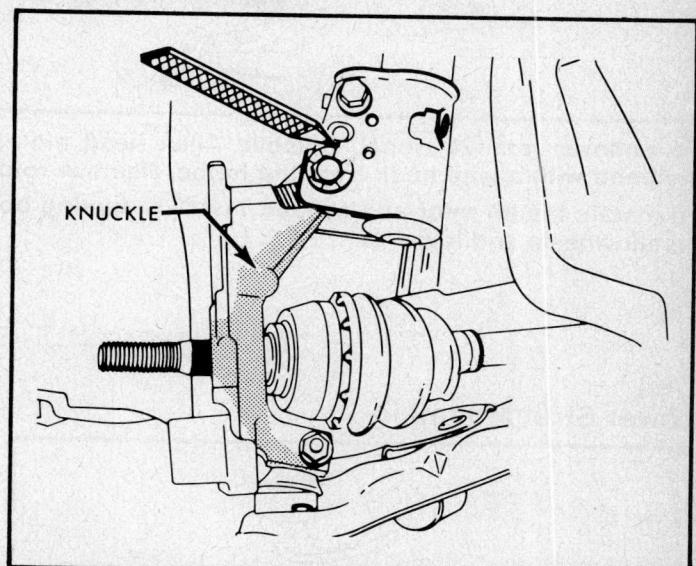

Upper Strut Mounting

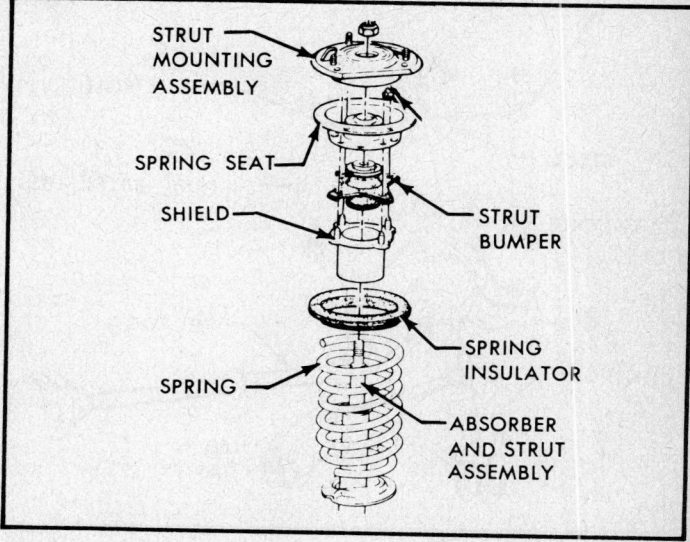

SUSPENSION

Brake Caliper Assembly

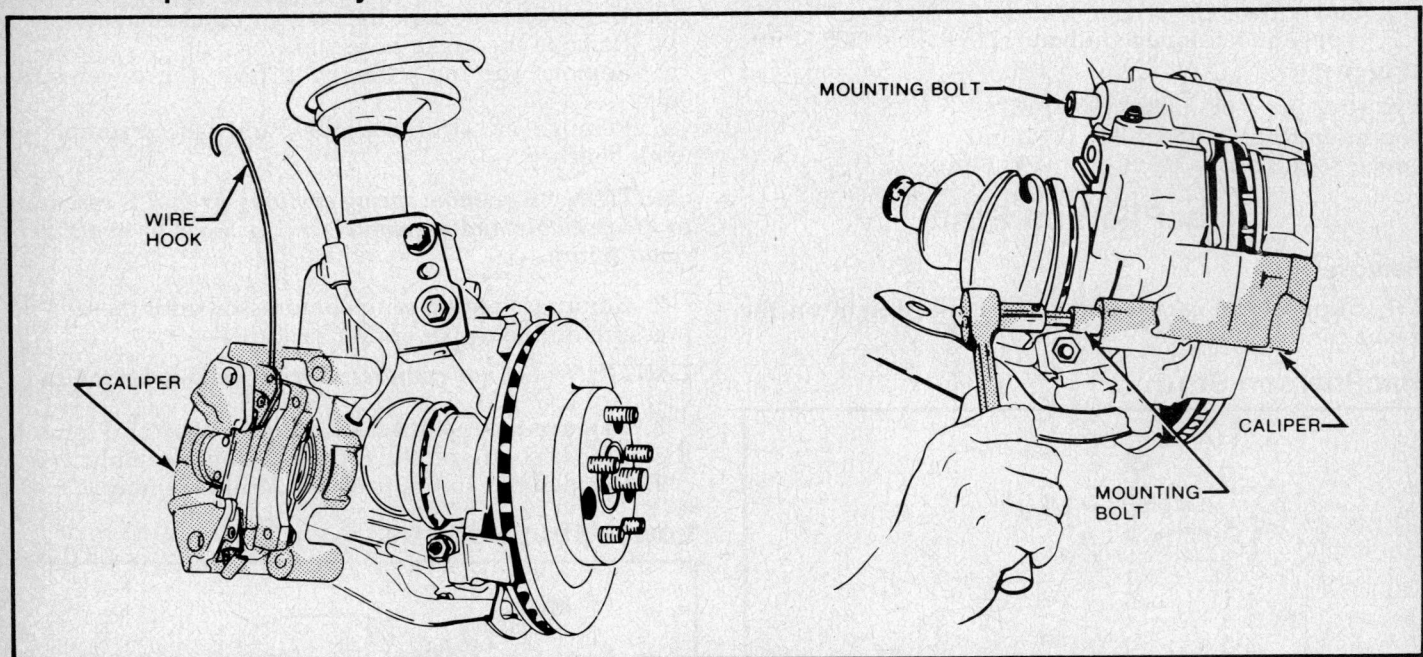

To remove: remove wheel. Remove Allen head mounting bolts as shown. Remove caliper from rotor and suspend with a wire hook from the frame. Remove rotor.

To install: install rotor and caliper. Install mounting bolts as shown and torque to 28–47 N•m (21–35 ft. lbs.). Install wheels and lower car.

Lower Strut Mounting

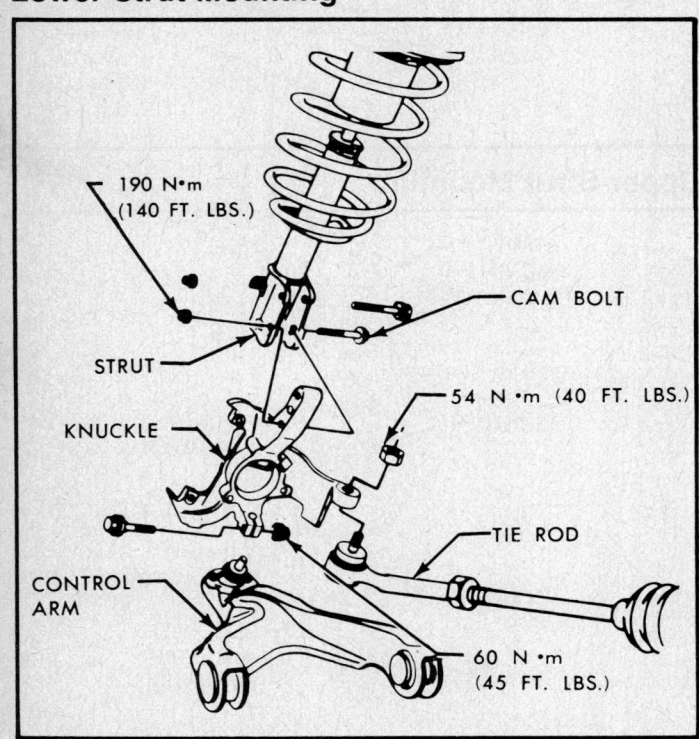

Installation

1. Install the new strut assembly into the spring and attach the mounting components on to the strut assembly.
2. Tighten the top strut nut 68 ft.-lbs. (90 N•m) and remove the spring compressor.
3. Install the spring and strut assembly, first in the upper spring seat, then connect the low end of the strut to the lower control arm.
4. Install brake caliper and wheel.

Steering Knuckle

Removal

1. Remove wheel and wheel bearing.
2. Mark and remove lower strut bolts.
3. Remove tie-rod end and ball joint.
4. Remove steering knuckle.

Installation

1. Install knuckle to ball joint and tighten.
2. Loosely install knuckle to strut.
3. Install front wheel bearing.
4. Jack control arm into position and install tie-rod end.
5. Tighten cam bolts.
6. Reset steering camber and toe.
7. Install brake caliper and wheel.

Ball Joint Removal and Installation

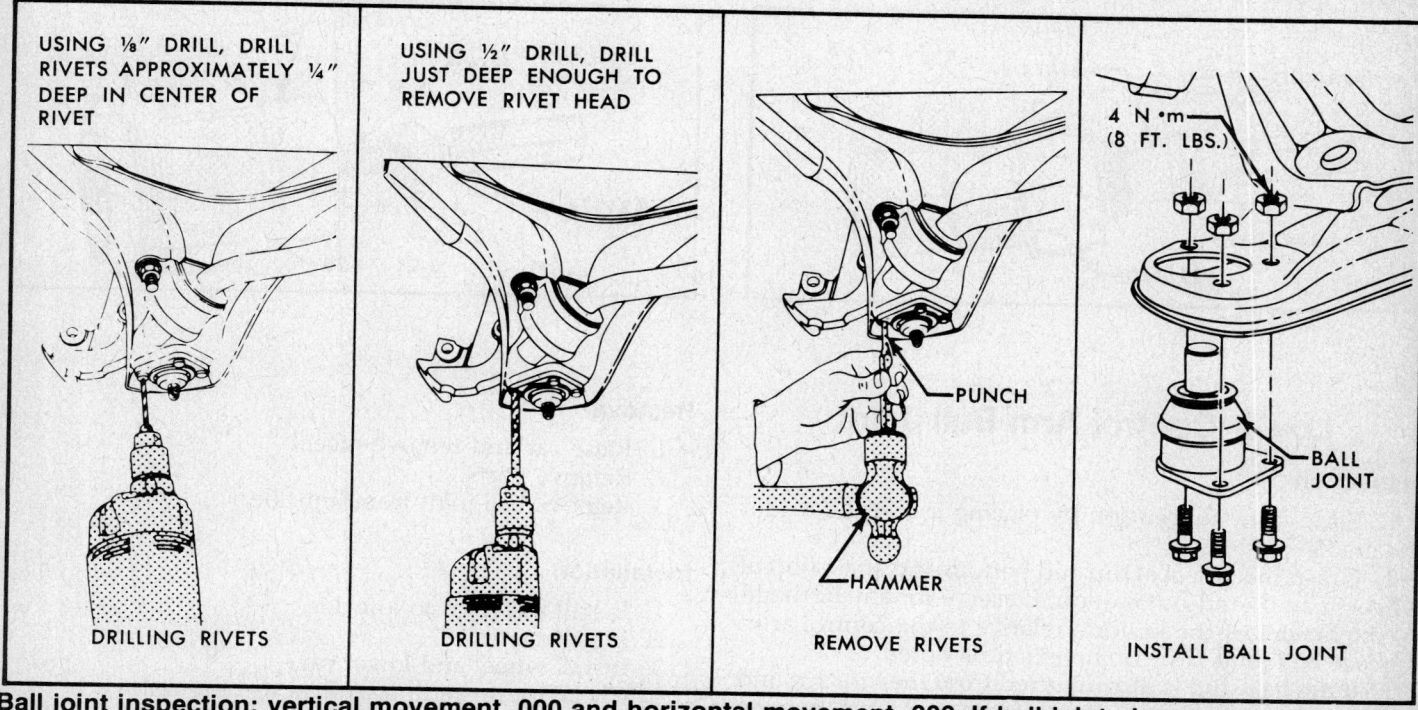

USING ⅛" DRILL, DRILL RIVETS APPROXIMATELY ¼" DEEP IN CENTER OF RIVET	USING ½" DRILL, DRILL JUST DEEP ENOUGH TO REMOVE RIVET HEAD		
DRILLING RIVETS	DRILLING RIVETS	REMOVE RIVETS	INSTALL BALL JOINT

PUNCH

HAMMER

4 N•m (8 FT. LBS.)

BALL JOINT

Ball joint inspection: vertical movement .000 and horizontal movement .000. If ball joint shows any movement replace. It is not necessary to remove control arm to replace joint.

Lower Control Arm and/or Bushings

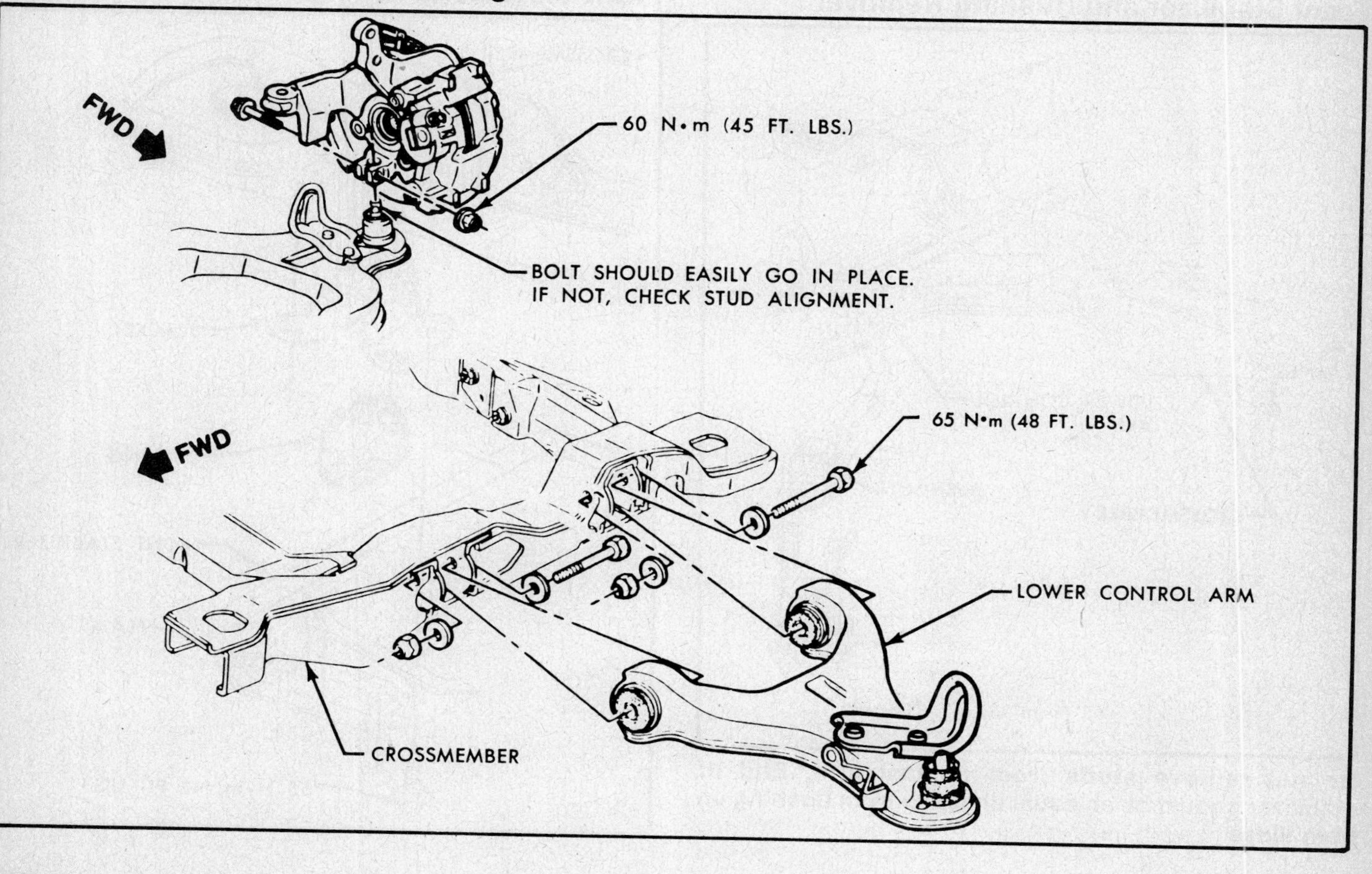

FWD

60 N•m (45 FT. LBS.)

BOLT SHOULD EASILY GO IN PLACE. IF NOT, CHECK STUD ALIGNMENT.

FWD

65 N•m (48 FT. LBS.)

LOWER CONTROL ARM

CROSSMEMBER

SUSPENSION

Lower Control Arm Bushing Removal

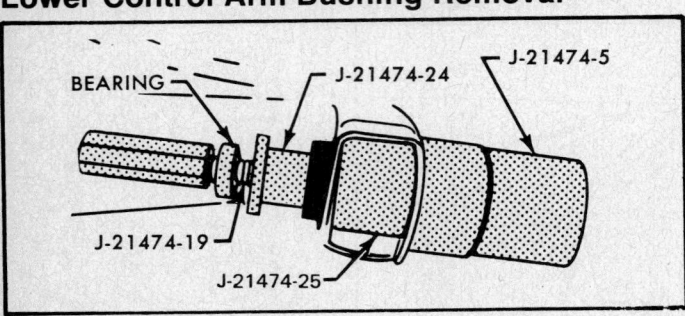

Lower Control Arm Bushing Installation

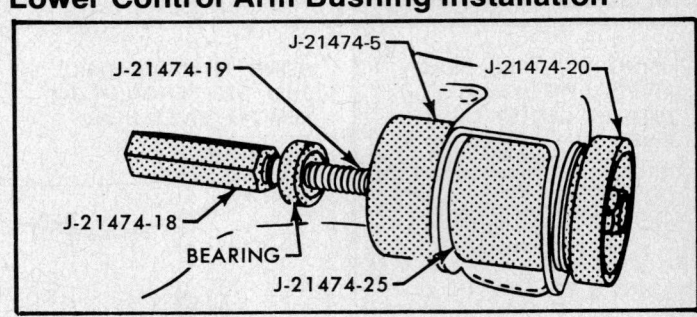

Lower Control Arm Ball Joint

Inspection

1. Raise front suspension by placing jack or lift under the cradle.

2. Grasp the wheel at top and bottom and shake top of wheel in an in-and-out motion. Observe for any horizontal movement of the knuckle relative to the control arm. Replace ball joint if such movement is noted.

3. If the ball stud is disconnected from the knuckle and any looseness is detected, or if the ball stud can be twisted in its socket using finger pressure, replace the ball joint.

Removal

1. Raise car and remove wheel.
2. Remove parts.
3. Remove ball joint from knuckle.

Installation

1. Install ball joint to knuckle.
2. Install parts.
3. Install wheel and lower car.
4. Check toe-in setting. Adjust as required.

Front Stabilizer and Bushing Removal

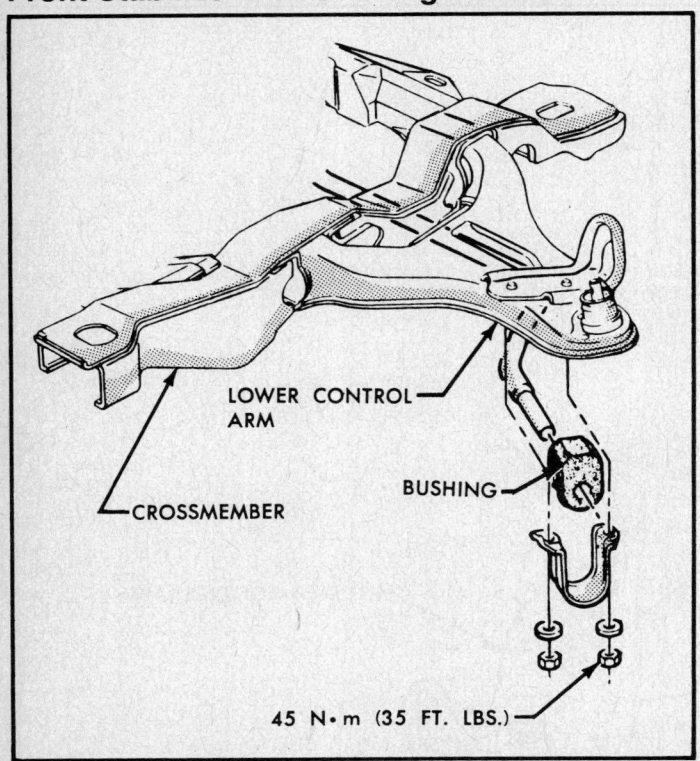

45 N·m (35 FT. LBS.)

Do not remove studs from control arm. End of stabilizer should be an equal distance from bushing on both sides.

Front Stabilizer Bushings

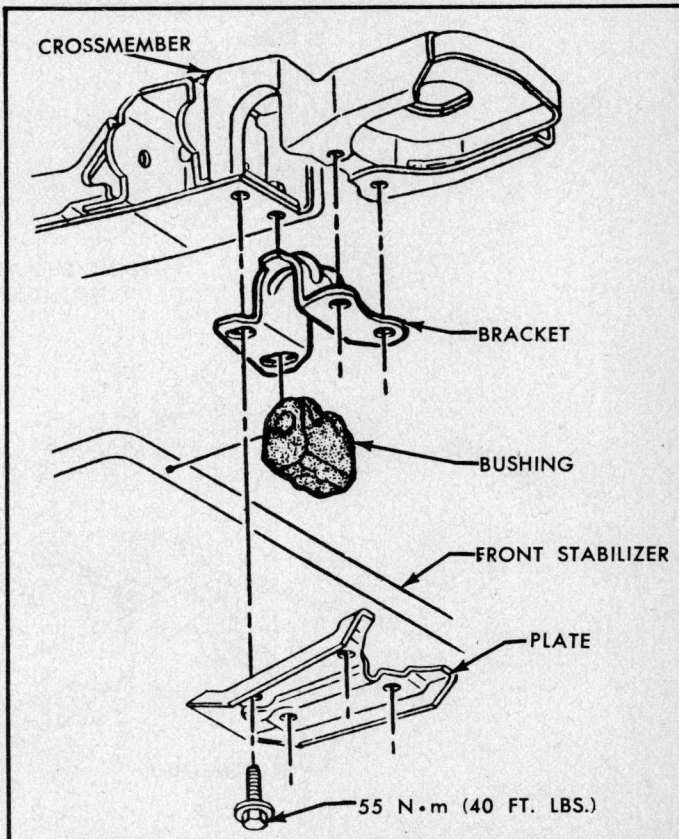

55 N·m (40 FT. LBS.)

REAR SUSPENSION—GENERAL MOTORS
A AND X BODY CARS

Wheel Bearings

The rear wheel bearing is a double row ball bearing. It is pre-lubricated and sealed at the factory. The bolt on bearing should be replaced if the looseness excedes recommendations.

Removal

1. Remove wheel and brake drum.

NOTE   Do not hammer on brake drum as damage to the bearing could result.

2. Remove four hub and bearing assembly-to-rear axle attaching bolts and remove hub and bearing assembly from axle.

NOTE   If the studs must be removed from the hub, do not remove with a hammer as damage to bearing will result.

Installation

1. Install hub and bearing assembly to rear axle. Tighten bolts to 55 N•m (35 ft.-lbs.).

Mounting Dial Indicator on Brakes

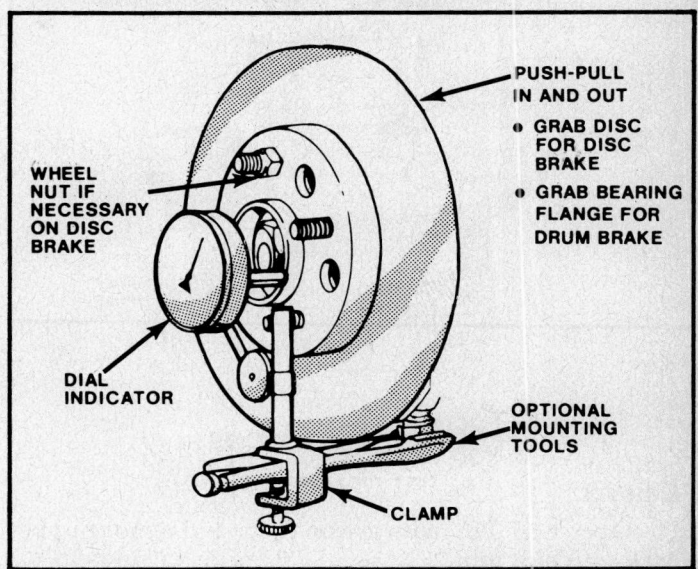

PUSH-PULL IN AND OUT
- GRAB DISC FOR DISC BRAKE
- GRAB BEARING FLANGE FOR DRUM BRAKE

WHEEL NUT IF NECESSARY ON DISC BRAKE

DIAL INDICATOR

OPTIONAL MOUNTING TOOLS

CLAMP

Replace if looseness exceeds .005 in. (.5080 N•m).

Rear Suspension

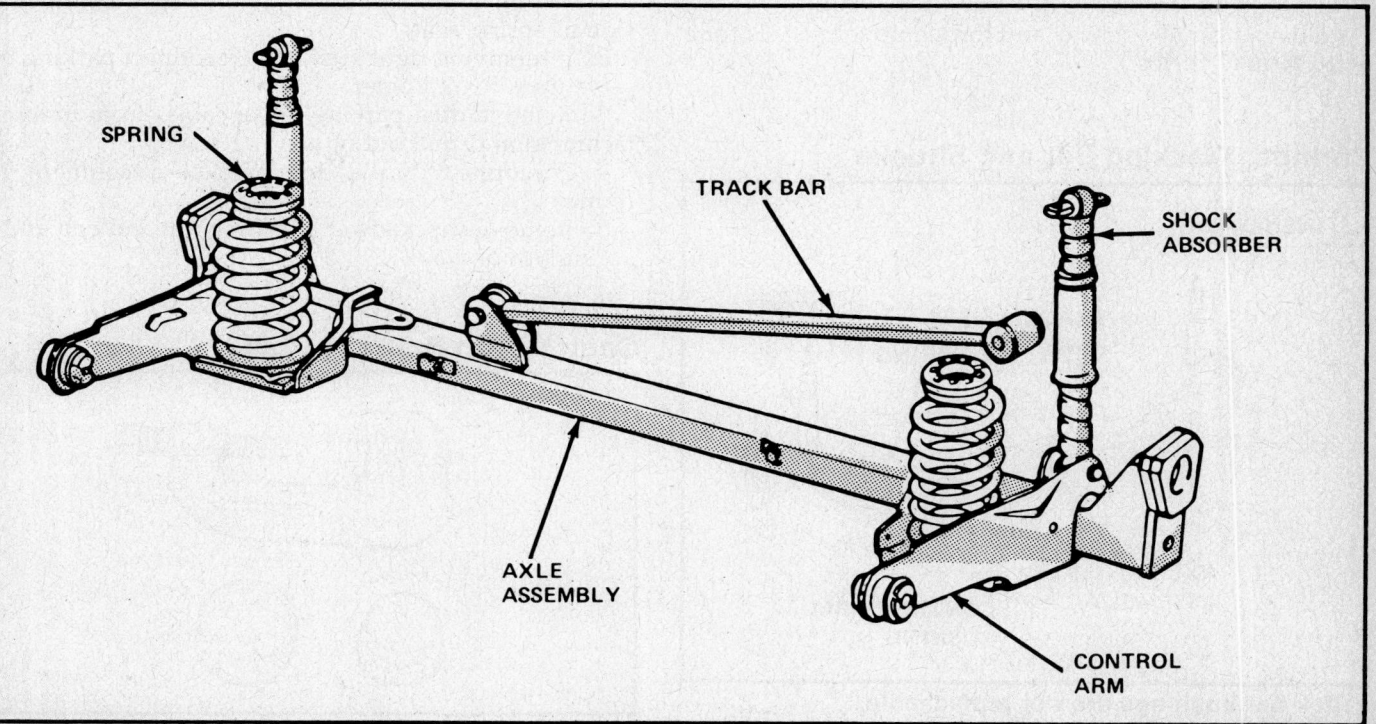

SPRING

TRACK BAR

SHOCK ABSORBER

AXLE ASSEMBLY

CONTROL ARM

SUSPENSION

Bolt-on Wheel Bearings

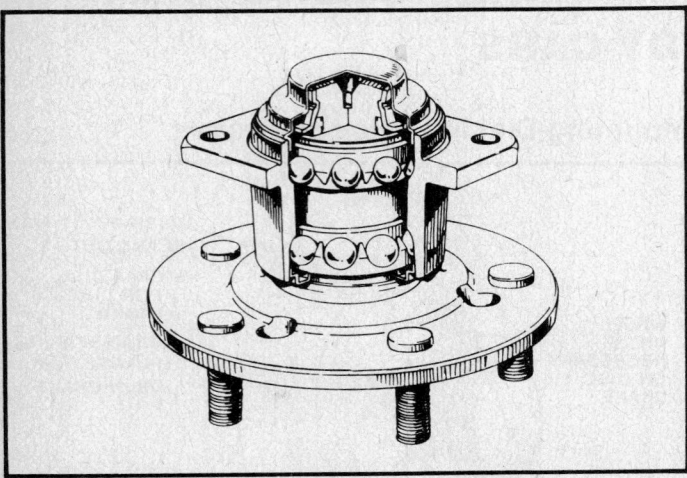

Shock Absorber

Removal

1. Open deck lid, remove trim cover and remove upper shock attaching nut.
2. Raise car on hoist and support rear axle assembly.
3. Remove lower attaching bolt and nut and remove shock.

Installation

1. Install shock at lower attachment, feed bolt through holes and loosely install nut.
2. Lower car enough to guide upper stud through body opening and install nut loosely.
4. Torque lower nut to 47 N•m (34 ft.-lbs.).
4. Lower car all the way and torque upper nut. Torque to 10 N•m (7 ft.-lbs.).

Springs, Tracking Bar and Shocks

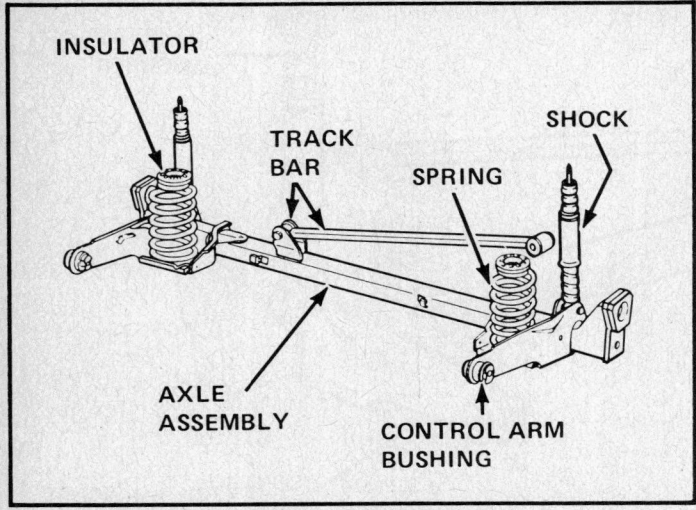

INSULATOR

TRACK BAR

SPRING

SHOCK

AXLE ASSEMBLY

CONTROL ARM BUSHING

Track bar bushings are not replaceable.

Track Bar

Removal

1. Raise car on hoist and support rear axle.
2. Remove nut and bolt at both the axle and body attachments and remove track bar.

Installation

1. Position track bar in left hand reinforcement and loosely install bolt and nut. The open side of the bar and nut must face rearward.
2. Place other end of track bar in body reinforcement and install bolt and nut (nut must be at the rear of reinforcement of both attachments). Torque nut at axle bracket to 45 N•m (33 ft.-lbs.) and torque nut at body reinforcement to 47 N•m (34 ft.-lbs.).

Spring

Removal and Installation

NOTE   Do not use a twin-post type hoist. The swing arc tendency of the rear axle when some fasteners are removed may cause it to slip from the hoist.

1. Raise the car. Support the rear axle while removing the brake line brackets, the track bar and the shock absorber lower mounts.
2. Lower rear axle and remove springs.
3. When installing, position springs correctly.

Control Arm Bushing

Removal

1. Raise car on hoist and support rear axle under front side of spring seat.
2. If removing right bushing, disconnect parking brake cable from hook guide.
3. Remove dual parking brake cables from bracket attachment and pull out of way.
4. Disconnect brake line bracket attachment from frame.
5. Remove shock lower attaching nut and bolt and pull spring out of way.

Control Arm Bushing Tool

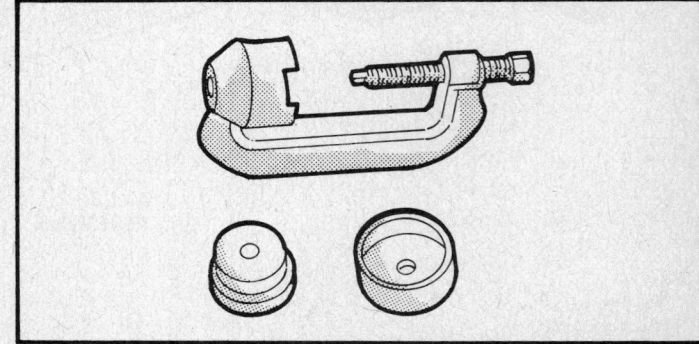

Rear Suspension

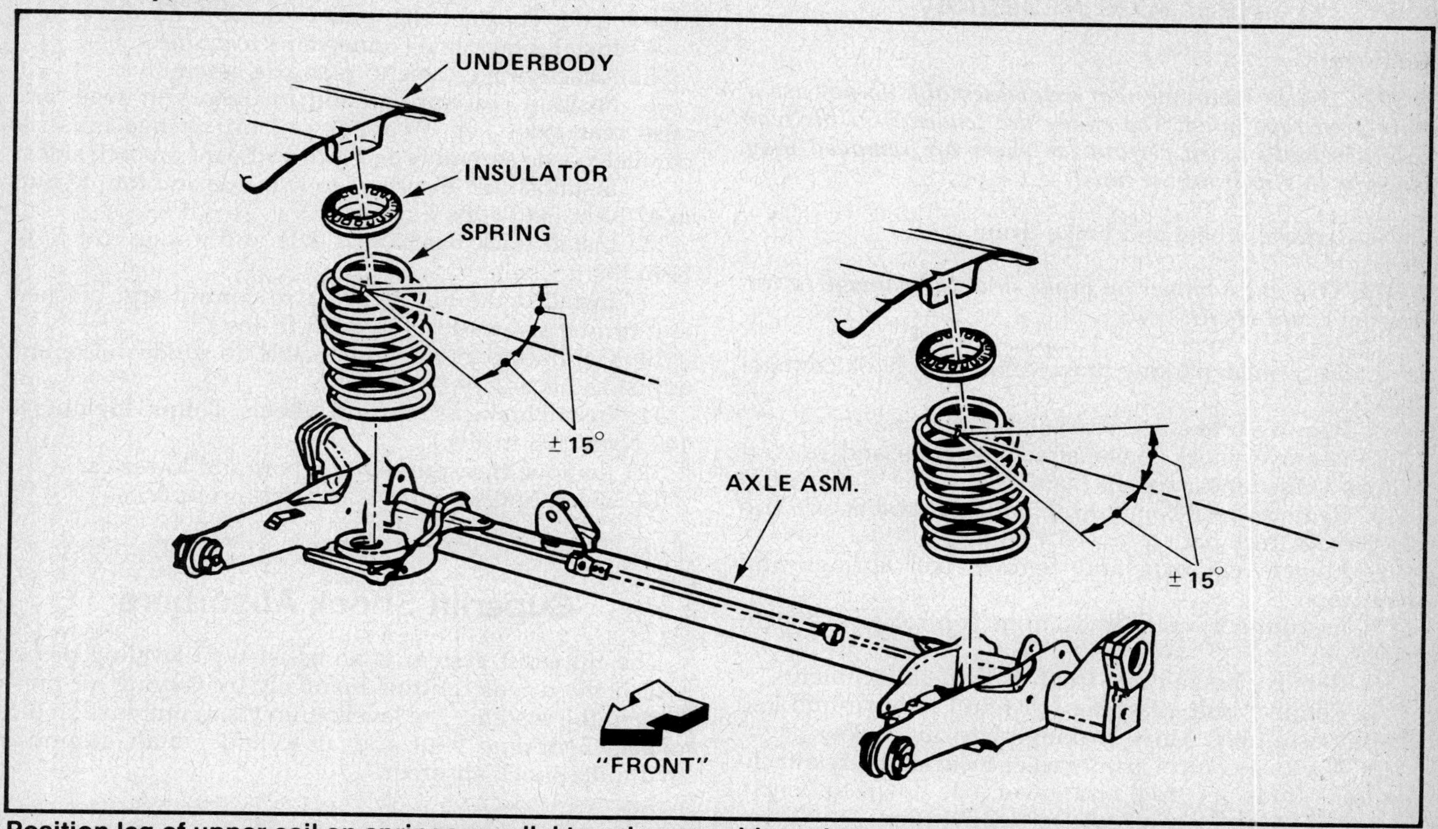

UNDERBODY

INSULATOR

SPRING

± 15°

AXLE ASM.

± 15°

"FRONT"

Position leg of upper coil on springs parallel to axle assembly and towards left-hand side of vehicle within limits shown. When removing rear springs, do not use a twin-post type hoist. The swing arc tendency of the rear axle assembly when certain fasteners are removed may cause it to slip from the hoist. Perform operation on floor if necessary.

6. Remove four control arm bracket-to-underbody attaching bolts and allow control arm to rotate downward.

7. Remove nut and bolt from bracket attachment and remove bracket.

8. Press bushing out of control arm.

Installation

1. Press bushing into control arm.

NOTE Cut-outs on rubber portion of bushing must face front and rear.

2. Install bracket to control arm and torque nut to 47 N•m (34 ft.-lbs.). Bracket must be at a 45-degree angle.

3. Raise control arm into position and install four control arm bracket-to-underbody attaching bolts. Torque to 27 N•m (20 ft.-lbs.).

4. Replace spring and insulator and install shock lower attaching nut and bolt. Torque nut to 47 N•m (34 ft.-lbs.).

5. Install brake line bracket to frame and torque screw to 11 N•m (8 ft.-lbs.).

6. On right side only, reconnect brake cables to bracket, and reinstall brake cable to hook. Adjust cable as necessary.

Rear Wheel Stud Removal

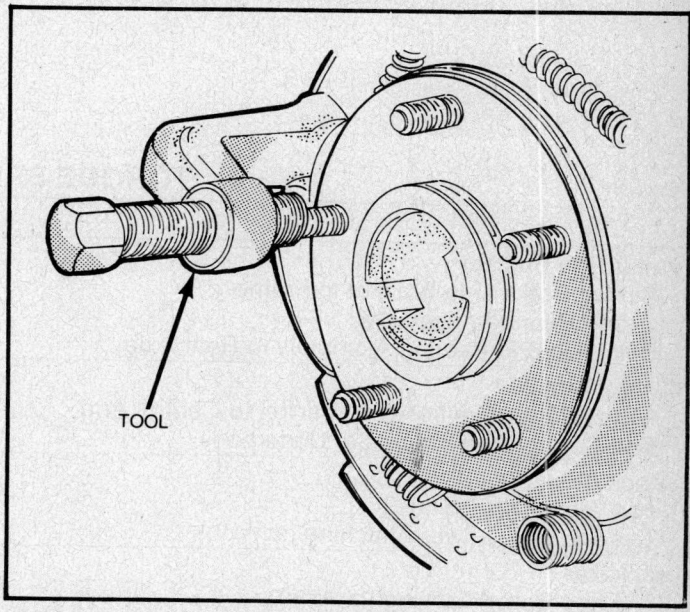

TOOL

Press stud out. Do not hammer.

Rear Axle Assembly

Removal

NOTE When removing rear axle assembly, do not use a twin-post type hoist. The swing arc tendency of the rear axle assembly when certain fasteners are removed may cause it to slip from the hoist.

1. Remove wheel and brake drum.

NOTE Do not hammer on brake drum as damage to the bearing could result.

2. Disconnect parking brake cable from hook connection.
3. Remove brake line brackets from frame.
4. Remove shock lower attaching bolts and nuts at axle and disconnect shocks from axle.
5. Remove track bar attaching nut and bolt at axle and disconnect track bar.
6. Lower rear axle and remove coil springs and insulators.
7. Disconnect brake lines from control arm attachments.
8. Remove brake cable from rear axle attachments.
9. Remove hub attaching bolts and remove hub and bearing assembly. Move backing plate out of way.
10. Remove control arm bracket-to-underbody attaching bolts (four per side) and lower axle down to bench. This may require two people to steady axle.
11. Remove control arm brackets from control arms.

Installation

1. Install control arm brackets to control arms. Torque nuts to 47 N•m (34 ft.-lbs.). Brackets must be at a 45-degree angle.
2. Place axle assembly on transmission jack and raise into position. Attach control arms to underbody with four bolts per side. Torque bolts to 27 N•m (20 ft.-lbs.).

3. Install backing plate and hub and bearing assembly to rear axle. Torque bolts to 55 N•m (35 ft.-lbs.).
4. Install brake line connections to frame.
5. Attach brake cable to rear axle assembly.
6. Position coil springs and insulators in seats and raise rear axle. Leg of upper coil on springs must be parallel to axle assembly and face outboard on both sides.
7. Install shock absorbers to rear axle and torque nuts to 47 N•m (34 ft.-lbs.).
8. Install track bar to rear axle and torque nut to 45 N•m (33 ft.-lbs.).
9. Install brake line brackets to control arm brackets and torque screws to 11 N•m (8 ft.-lbs.).
10. Connect parking brake cable to guide hook and adjust as necessary.
11. Install brake drums and wheels. Torque lug nuts to 140 N•m (103 ft.-lbs.).
12. Remove transmission support and lower car.
13. Bleed brake system and refill reservoir.

Superlift Shock Absorbers

The Superlift system is an assist-type leveling device which the driver controls manually by varying air pressure in the system. The leveling unit is a combination of a pliable neoprene boot and air cylinder built around a hydraulic shock absorber.

PRECAUTIONS

To insure satisfactory functioning of the Superlift system, observe the following precautions:
- Maintain a minimum of 70 kPa (10 psi) for best ride characteristics with an empty car.
- Vary pressure up to a maximum of 620 kPa (90 psi) to level the car with loads.

TORQUE SPECIFICATIONS

	N•m	Ft. Lbs.
Brake Line Bracket		
Screw, Brake Line Bracket to Frame	11	8
Hub and Bearing Assembly		
Bolt, Hub and Bearing Assembly to Rear Axle	100	74
Control Arm		
Nut and Bolt, Control Arm Bracket to Control Arm	70	52
Bolt Control Arm Bracket to Underbody	38	28
Shock Absorber		
Nut, Upper Attaching	10	7
Nut and Bolt, Lower Attaching (at Axle)	47	34
Track Bar		
Nut and Bolt, Attaching (at Axle)	45	33
Nut and Bolt, Attaching (at Underbody Reinforcement)	47	34

DIAGNOSIS AND TESTING

Condition	Cause	Correction
Superlift System loses air pressure	a. Broken or cracked line.	a. Inflate system to approximately 90 psi and inspect lines for evidence of escaping air. If lines are leaking, repair as needed.
	b. Loose connections or leaking valve core.	b. Apply a solution of soap and water to all connections and valve core. If air bubbles appear, repair leak.
	c. Fill valve leaking.	c. Detach valve assembly from car with air pressure retained inside valve and immerse assembly in water. If air bubbles appear, repair leak.
	d. Superlifts leaking.	d. Remove Superlifts from car and immerse in water with air pressure applied to Superlift. If air bubbles appear, Superlift is leaking and should be replaced.
Superlift System noisy when car is driven	a. Loose upper or lower mounting. b. Rubber mounting bushings worn or cracked. c. Internal failure of Superlift.	a. Inspect and tighten all connections. b. Replace Superlift shock. c. Road test car after above steps have been performed. If noise is still present, replace Superlift shocks.

FRONT SUSPENSION—GENERAL MOTORS E AND K SERIES

General Description

The front suspension consists of control arms, stabilizer bar, shock absorber and a right and left torsion bar. Torsion bars are used instead of the conventional coil springs. The front end of the torsion bar is attached to the lower control arm. The rear of the torsion bar is mounted into an adjustable arm at the torsion bar crossmember. The trim height of the car is controlled by this adjustment.

Wheel Alignment

HEIGHT ADJUSTMENT (TORSION BAR SUSPENSION MODELS)

The standing height must be checked, and adjusted if necessary, before performing the front end alignment procedure. The standing height is controlled by the adjustment setting of the torsion bar adjusting bolt.

Clockwise rotation of the bolt increases the front height; counterclockwise decreases the front height.

Car must be on a level surface, gas tank full, or a compensating weight added, front seat all the way to the rear, and front and rear tires inflated to the proper pressures. Doors, hood and trunk must be closed and no passengers or additional weight should be in car or trunk.

These tolerances are production specifications on bumper height. If there is more than 1 inch (25 mm) difference, side to side, at the wheel well opening, corrective measures may need to be implemented on a case by case basis. These are curb height dimensions which include a full tank of fuel.

CAMBER AND CASTER ADJUSTMENTS

These adjustments can be made either from under car or under hood, as desired. If under hood approach is used, however, be sure to recheck alignment after all operations are completed. Change in weight distribution caused by opened hood is sufficient to disturb final alignment settings.

1. Loosen nuts on upper suspension arm front and rear cam bolts.
2. Note camber reading and rotate front bolt to correct for ½ of incorrect reading or as near as possible.
3. Rotate rear cam bolt to bring camber reading to 0°.

NOTE   Do not use a socket to adjust rear cam bolt on left side as brake pipes could be damaged. An offset box end wrench is recommended at this adjustment point.

4. Tighten front and rear bolts and check caster. If

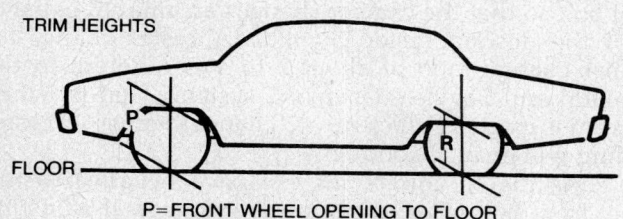

TRIM HEIGHTS

FLOOR

P=FRONT WHEEL OPENING TO FLOOR
R=REAR WHEEL OPENING TO FLOOR

	Trim	Height	Tolerance
FRONT (P)	mm	726	+32
	Inches	28.6	+1.25
REAR (R)	mm	694	+32
	Inches	27.3	+1.25

SUSPENSION

Front Suspension

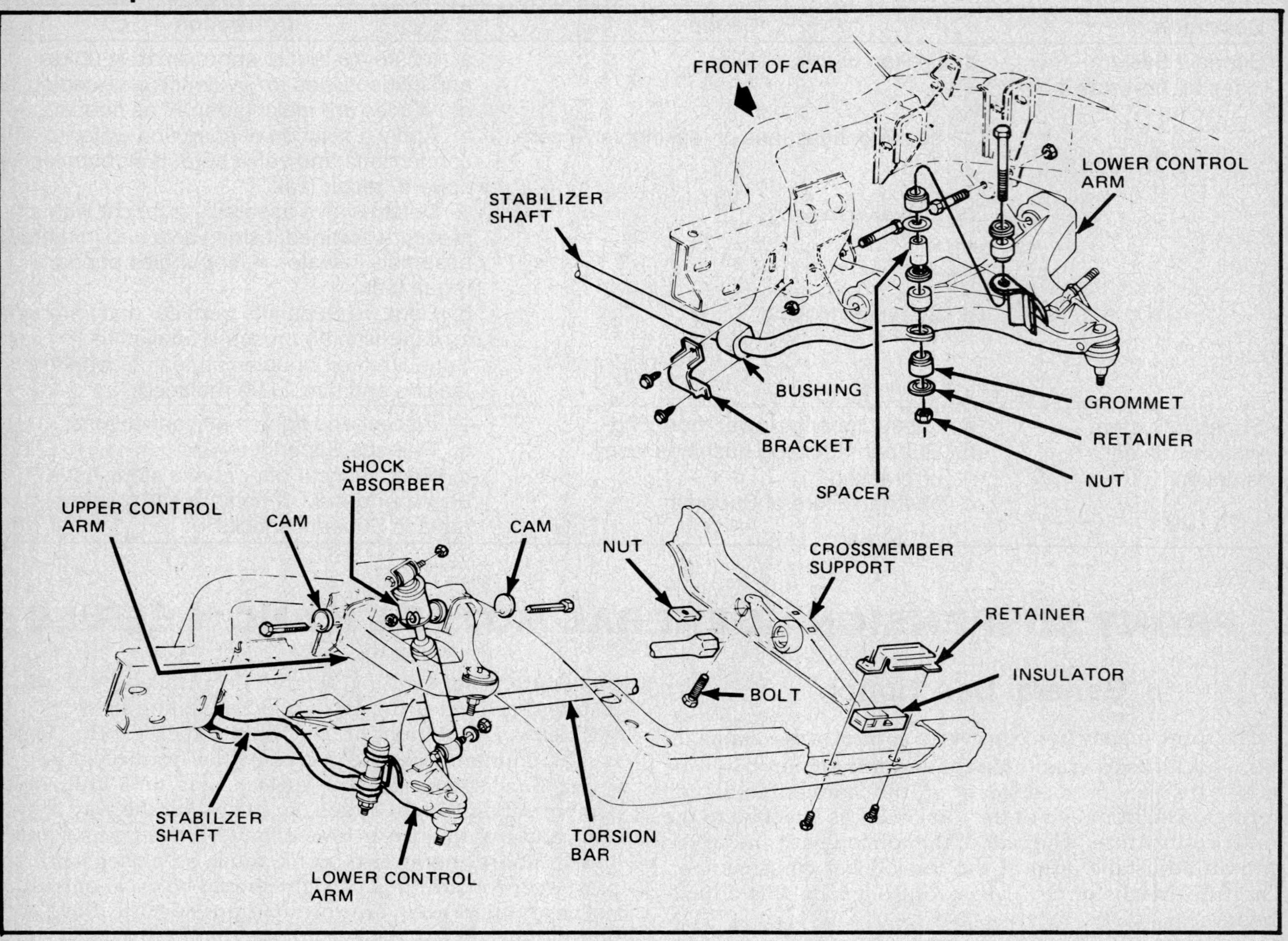

FRONT OF CAR

STABILIZER SHAFT

LOWER CONTROL ARM

BUSHING

BRACKET

GROMMET

RETAINER

NUT

SPACER

UPPER CONTROL ARM

SHOCK ABSORBER

CAM

CAM

NUT

CROSSMEMBER SUPPORT

RETAINER

INSULATOR

BOLT

STABILZER SHAFT

LOWER CONTROL ARM

TORSION BAR

Caster/Camber Adjustments

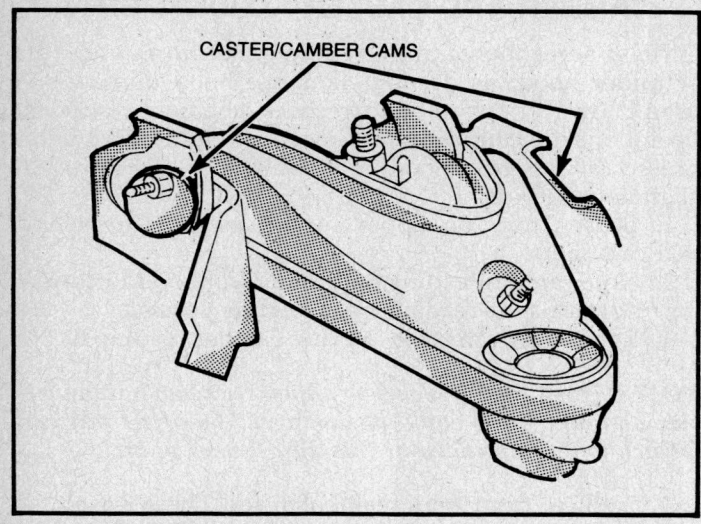

CASTER/CAMBER CAMS

caster requires adjustment, proceed with step 5; if not, move to step 8.

5. Loosen front and rear cam bolt nuts.

6. Using camber scale on alignment equipment, rotate front bolt so that the camber changes an amount equal to ¼ of the desired caster change. (A caster change-to-camber change ratio of about 2 to 1 is inherent to the Eldorado and Seville suspension system. That is, when one cam is rotated sufficiently to change camber 1°, caster reading will change about 2°.)

If adjusting to correct for excessive negative caster, rotate front bolt to increase positive camber. If adjusting to correct for excessive positive caster, rotate front bolt to increase negative camber.

7. Rotate the rear bolt until camber setting returns to its corrected position (step 3).

8. Tighten upper suspension arm cam nuts to 130 N•m (95 ft.-lbs.). Hold head of bolt securely; any movement of the cam will affect final setting and will require a recheck of the camber and caster adjustments.

TOE ADJUSTMENT

Before checking toe-in, make certain that the intermediate rod height is correct.

Toe-in is adjusted by turning the tie-rod adjuster tubes at the outer ends of each tie-rod after loosening clamp bolts. The readings should be taken only when the front wheels are in a straight ahead position so that the steering gear is on its high spot.

1. Center steering wheel, raise car, and check wheel runout.

2. Loosen tie-rod adjuster nuts and adjust tie-rods to obtain proper toe setting.

3. Position tie-rod adjuster clamps so that openings of clamps are facing up. Interference with front suspension components could occur while turning if clamps are facing down.

E Series Tie Rod Clamp and Sleeve Positioning

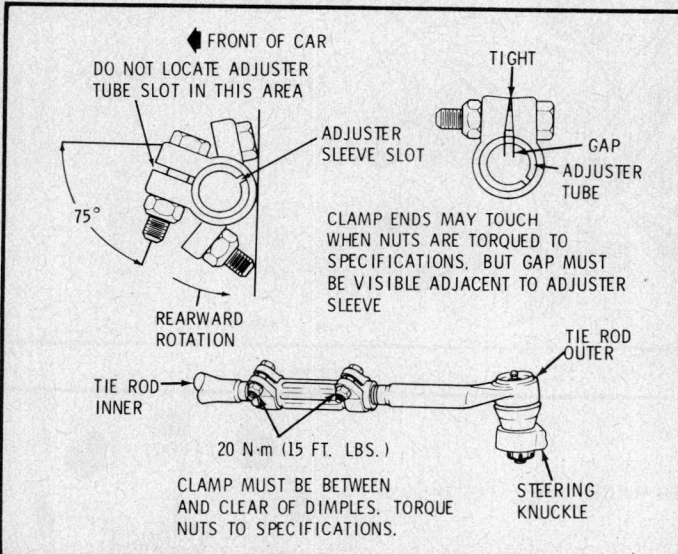

Bolts must be installed in direction shown. Rotate both inner and outer tie rod housings rearward to the limit of ball joint travel before tightening clamps. With this same rearward rotation, all bolt centerlines must be between angles shown after tightening clamps.

Wheel Bearings (Tapered Roller Bearings)

LUBRICATION

For normal application, clean and repack front wheel bearings with a high melting point wheel bearing lubricant at each front brake lining replacement or 30,000 miles (48 000 km), whichever comes first. For heavy duty application, clean and repack front wheel bearings at each front brake lining replacement or 15,000 miles (24 000 km) whichever comes first. Use wheel bearing lubricant; "long fiber" or "viscous" type lubricant should not be used. Do not mix wheel bearing lubricants. Be sure to thoroughly clean bearings and hubs of all old lubricant before repackaging.

NOTE Tapered roller bearings have a slightly loose feel when properly adjusted. They must never be overtightened (pre-loaded) or severe bearing damage may result.

Adjustment

The proper functioning of the front suspension cannot be maintained unless the front wheel tapered roller bearings are correctly adjusted. Cones must be a slip fit on the spindle and the inside diameter of cones should be lubricated to insure that the cones will creep. Spindle nut must be a free-running fit on threads.

1. Remove cotter pin from spindle and spindle nut.

2. Tighten the spindle nut to 16 N•m (12 ft.-lbs.) while turning the wheel assembly forward by hand to fully seat the bearings. This will remove any grease or burrs which could cause excessive wheel bearing play later.

3. Back off the nut to the "just loose" position.

4. Hand tighten the spindle nut. Loosen spindle nut until either hole in the spindle lines up with a slot in the nut (not more than ½ flat).

Bearing Adjustment

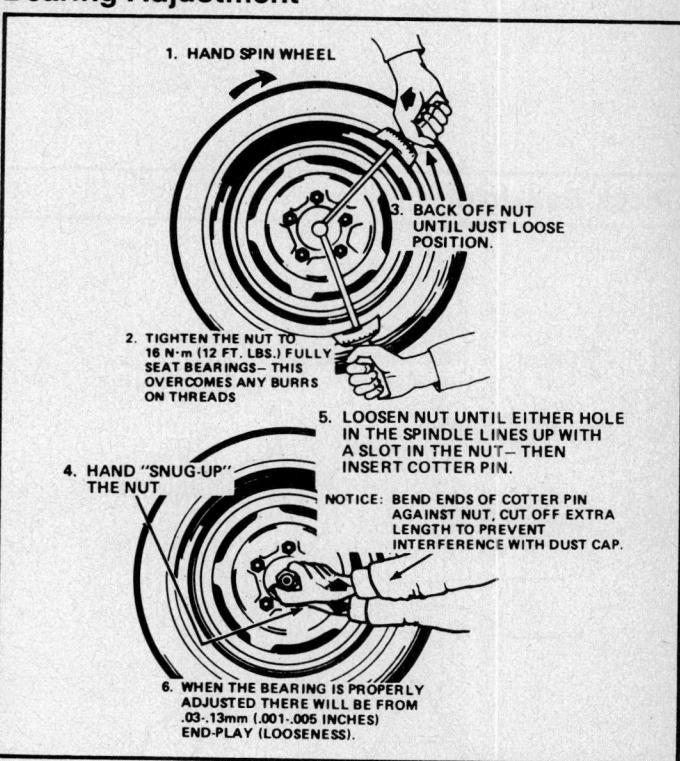

5. Install new cotter pin. Bend the ends of the cotter pin against nut. Cut off extra length to ensure ends will not interfere with the dust cap.

6. Measure the looseness in the hub assembly. There will be from .03 to .13 mm (.001 to .005 inches) end play when properly adjusted.

7. Install dust cap on hub.

SUSPENSION

Wheel Bearings (Bolt On-Type Bearings)

Starting in 1979, the E and K Series have front and rear sealed wheel bearings. The bearings are pre-adjusted and require no lubrication maintenance or adjustment. There are darkened areas on the bearing assembly. These darkened areas are from a heat treatment process and do not require bearing replacement.

Sealed Wheel Bearing

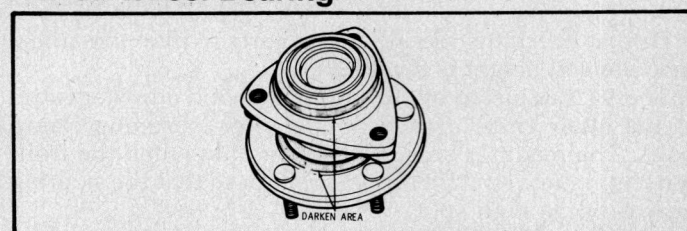

DARKEN AREA

Shock Absorber Removal and Installation

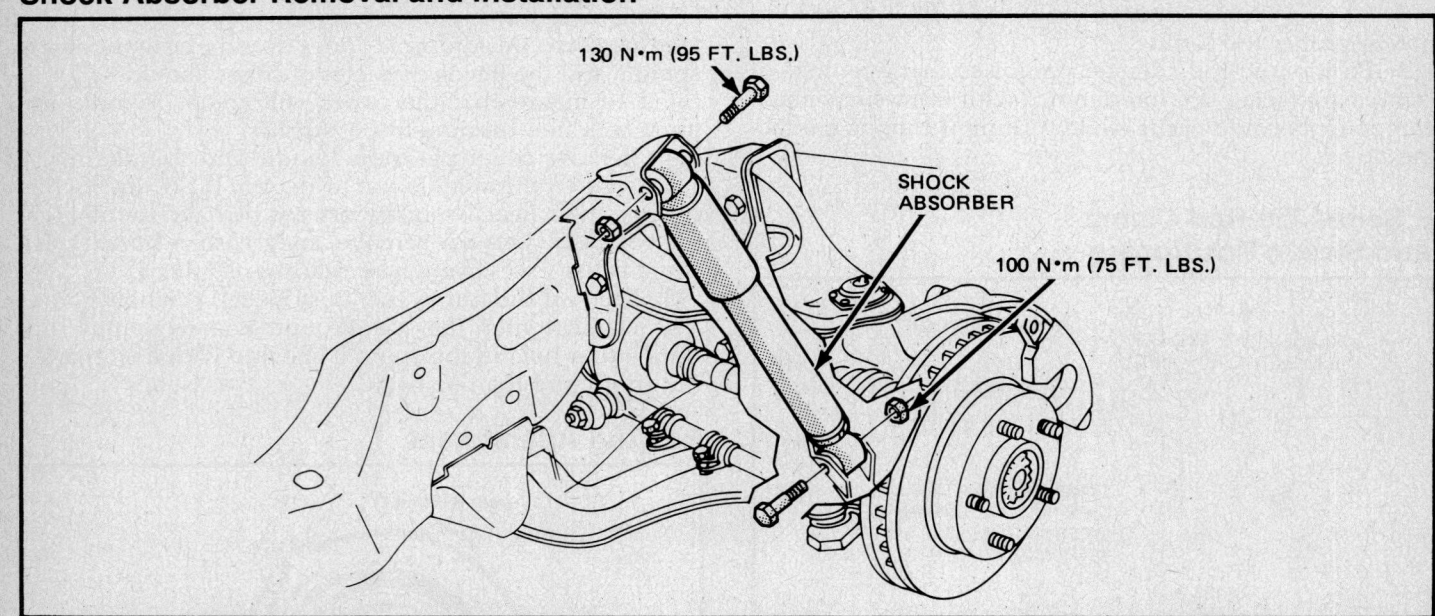

130 N•m (95 FT. LBS.)

SHOCK ABSORBER

100 N•m (75 FT. LBS.)

Check Ball Joint

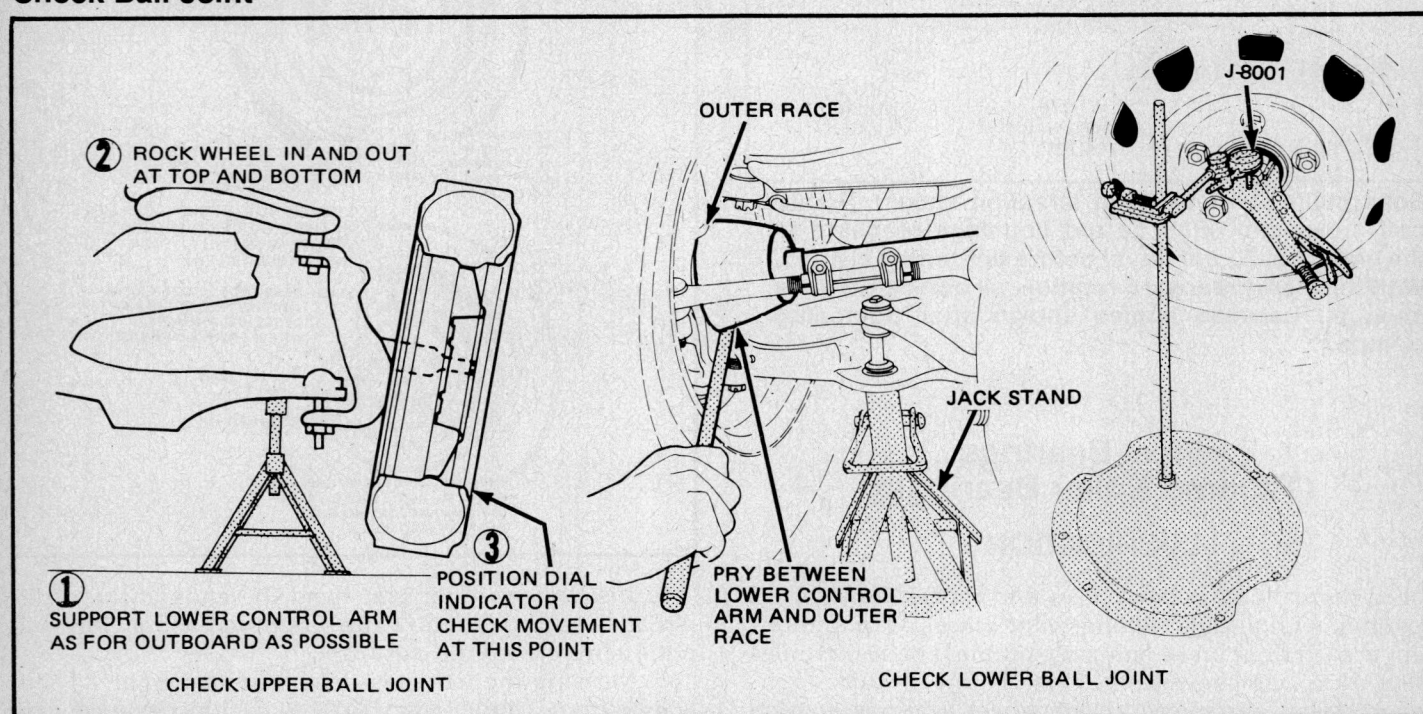

② ROCK WHEEL IN AND OUT AT TOP AND BOTTOM

① SUPPORT LOWER CONTROL ARM AS FOR OUTBOARD AS POSSIBLE

③ POSITION DIAL INDICATOR TO CHECK MOVEMENT AT THIS POINT

CHECK UPPER BALL JOINT

OUTER RACE

PRY BETWEEN LOWER CONTROL ARM AND OUTER RACE

JACK STAND

J-8001

CHECK LOWER BALL JOINT

Check ball joint as shown. If dial indicator reading exceeds 3.2 mm (.125 in.) or if ball stud is disconnected from knuckle and any looseness is detected or ball stud can be twisted in its socket with fingers, replace ball joint.

Bolt on Sealed Wheel Bearing Diagnosis

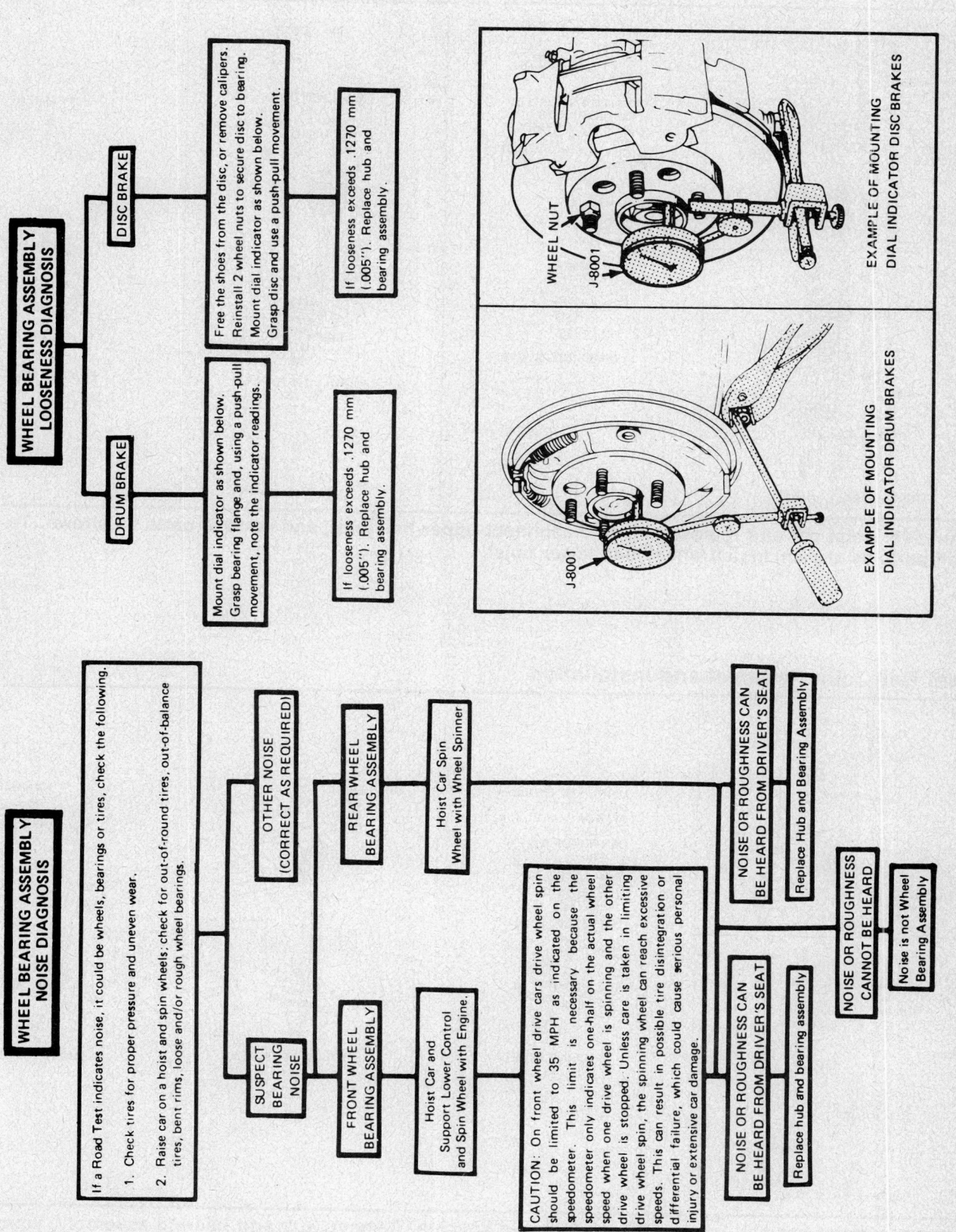

WHEEL BEARING ASSEMBLY LOOSENESS DIAGNOSIS

DISC BRAKE

Free the shoes from the disc, or remove calipers. Reinstall 2 wheel nuts to secure disc to bearing. Mount dial indicator as shown below. Grasp disc and use a push-pull movement.

If looseness exceeds .1270 mm (.005"). Replace hub and bearing assembly.

DRUM BRAKE

Mount dial indicator as shown below. Grasp bearing flange and, using a push-pull movement, note the indicator readings.

If looseness exceeds .1270 mm (.005"). Replace hub and bearing assembly.

WHEEL NUT

J-8001

EXAMPLE OF MOUNTING
DIAL INDICATOR DISC BRAKES

J-8001

EXAMPLE OF MOUNTING
DIAL INDICATOR DRUM BRAKES

WHEEL BEARING ASSEMBLY NOISE DIAGNOSIS

If a Road Test indicates noise, it could be wheels, bearings or tires, check the following.

1. Check tires for proper pressure and uneven wear.
2. Raise car on a hoist and spin wheels; check for out-of-round tires, out-of-balance tires, bent rims, loose and/or rough wheel bearings.

OTHER NOISE
(CORRECT AS REQUIRED)

REAR WHEEL BEARING ASSEMBLY

Hoist Car Spin Wheel with Wheel Spinner

SUSPECT BEARING NOISE

FRONT WHEEL BEARING ASSEMBLY

Hoist Car and Support Lower Control and Spin Wheel with Engine.

CAUTION: On front wheel drive cars drive wheel spin should be limited to 35 MPH as indicated on the speedometer. This limit is necessary because the speedometer only indicates one-half on the actual wheel speed when one drive wheel is spinning and the other drive wheel is stopped. Unless care is taken in limiting drive wheel spin, the spinning wheel can reach excessive speeds. This can result in possible tire disintegration or differential failure, which could cause serious personal injury or extensive car damage.

NOISE OR ROUGHNESS CAN BE HEARD FROM DRIVER'S SEAT

Replace Hub and Bearing Assembly

NOISE OR ROUGHNESS CANNOT BE HEARD

Noise is not Wheel Bearing Assembly

NOISE OR ROUGHNESS CAN BE HEARD FROM DRIVER'S SEAT

Replace hub and bearing assembly

SUSPENSION

Upper Ball Joint Removal and Installation

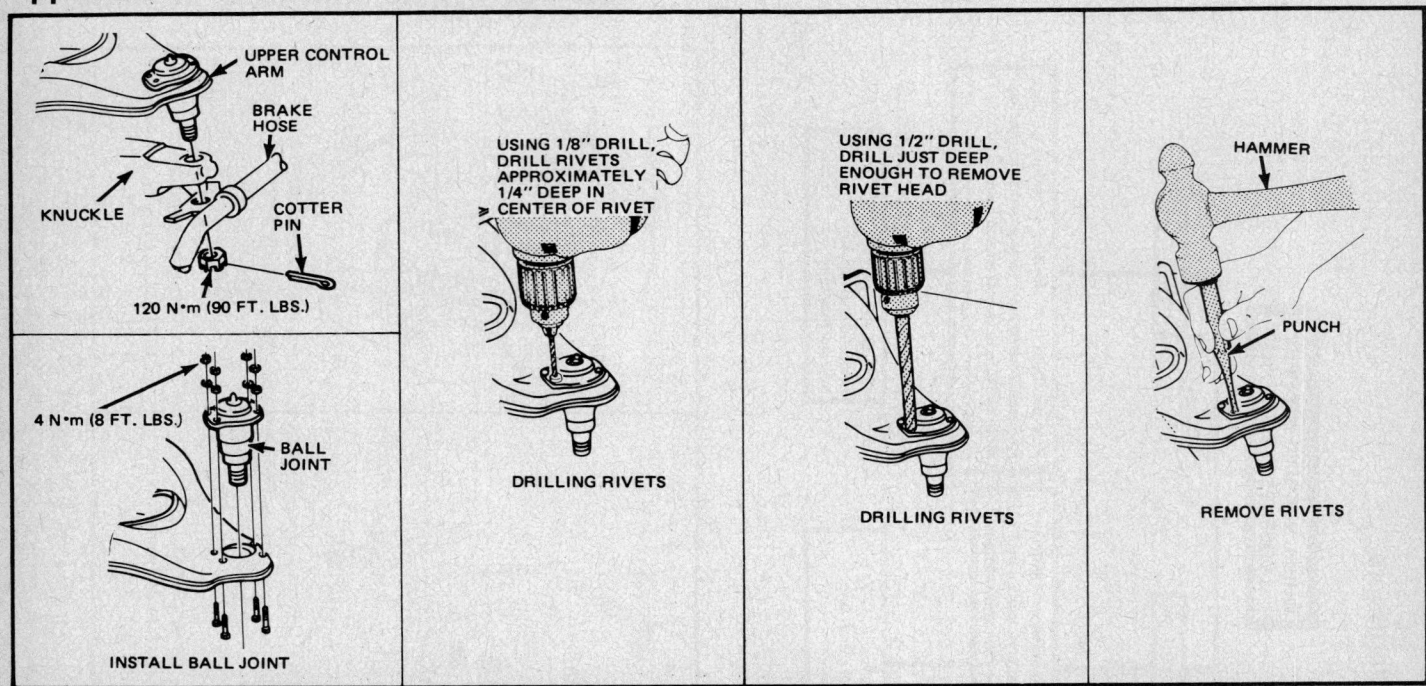

To remove: hoist car and remove wheel, disconnect upper ball joint, and remove parts as shown. To install: install parts as shown, install wheel, and lower hoist.

Lower Ball Joint Removal and Installation

To remove: hoist car and remove wheel. Remove knuckle. Remove hub and bearing assembly, knuckle and knuckle seal. Remove parts as shown. To install: install parts as shown. Install steering knuckle. Install hub and bearing assembly, knuckle and knuckle seal. Install wheel and lower hoist.

Upper Control Arm and/or Bushings Removal and Installation

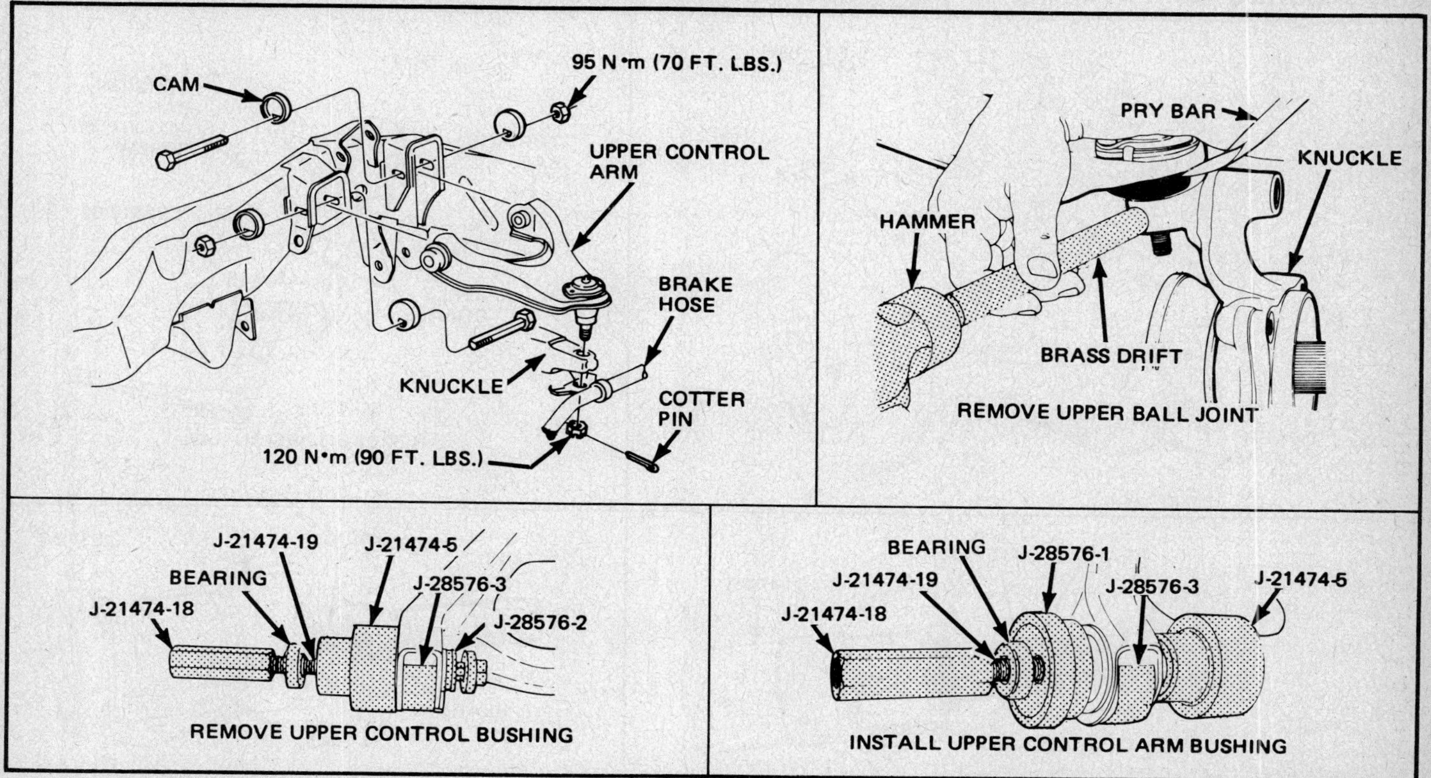

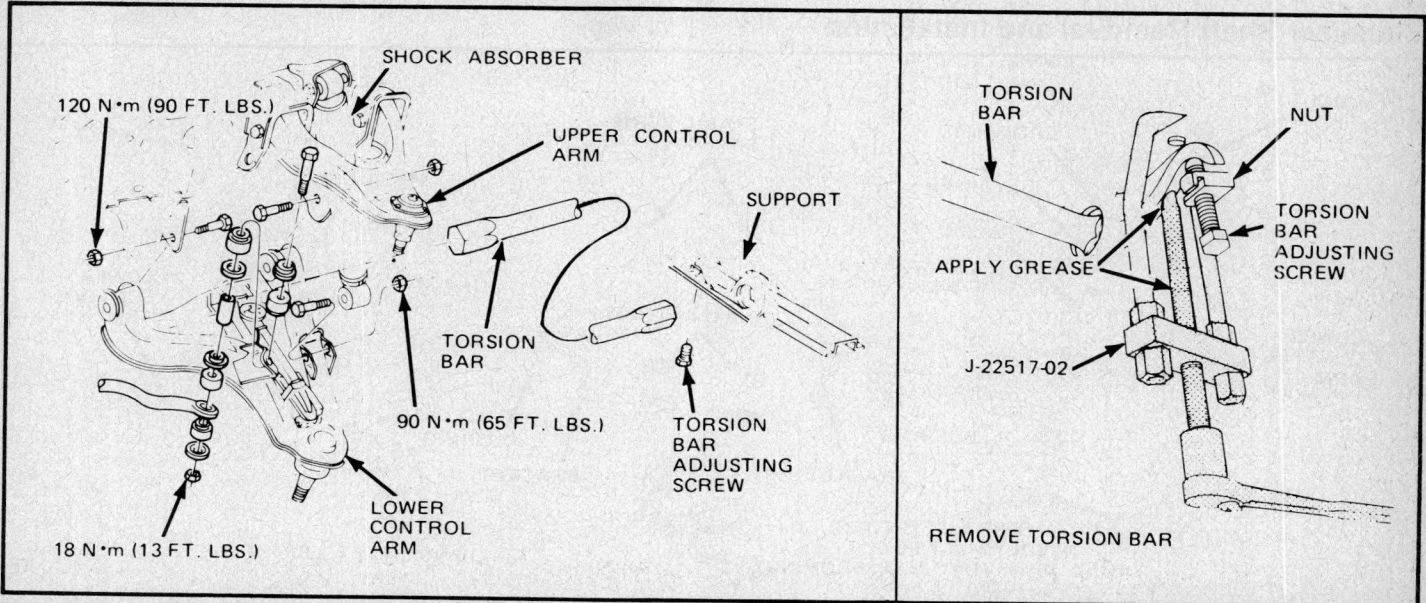

To remove: hoist car, remove wheel and remove parts as shown. To install: install parts as shown. Install wheel and lower hoist. Check alignment and adjust as necessary.

Lower Control Arm Removal and Installation

To remove: hoist car and remove wheel, remove knuckle, and remove parts as shown. To install: install parts as shown. Install knuckle, install wheel and lower hoist. Adjust trim height.

B579

Lower Control Arm Bushing Removal and Installation

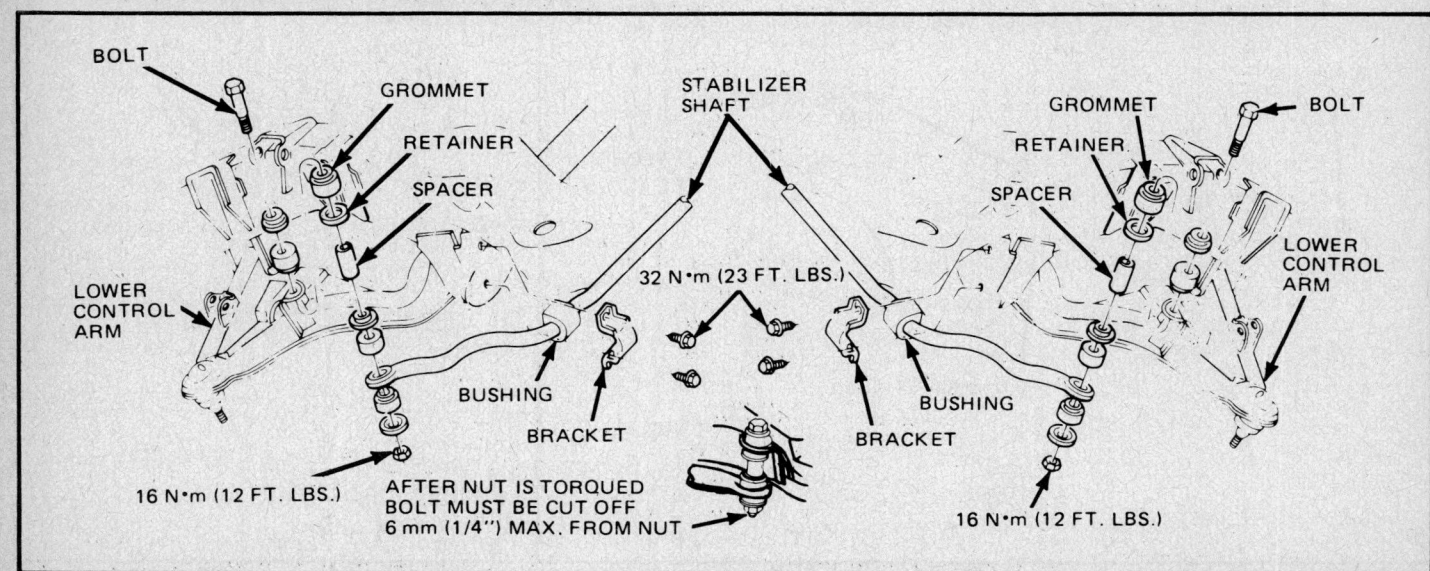

120 N·m (90 FT. LBS.)

LOWER CONTROL ARM

TORSION BAR

NUT

TORSION BAR ADJUSTING SCREW

J-22517-02

APPLY GREASE

REMOVE TORSION BAR

BEARING — J-21474-19
J-21474-18
J-21474-2
J-21474-5
J-28575-3
REMOVE LOWER CONTROL ARM BUSHING

J-21474-18
J-21474-19
J-28575-1
J-28575-2
BEARING
J-28575-3
INSTALL LOWER CONTROL ARM BUSHING

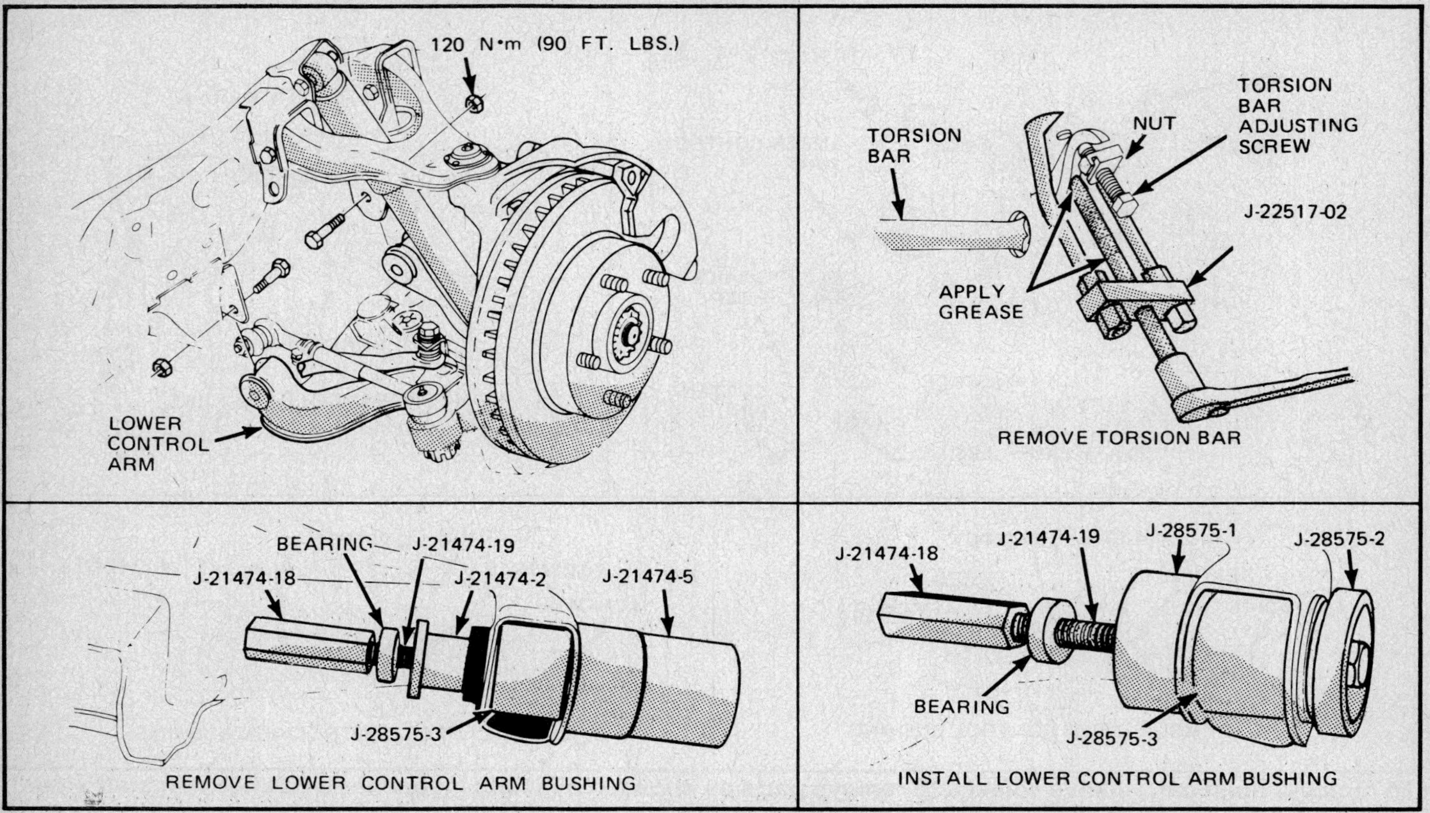

To remove: hoist car, place floor stands under frame, and then remove wheel. Remove parts as shown. To install: install parts as shown. Raise front hoist under lower control arm and remove floor stands. Install wheel and lower hoist. Adjust trim height.

Stabilizer Shaft Removal and Installation

BOLT

GROMMET

RETAINER

SPACER

LOWER CONTROL ARM

STABILIZER SHAFT

32 N·m (23 FT. LBS.)

GROMMET

RETAINER

SPACER

BOLT

LOWER CONTROL ARM

BUSHING

BRACKET

BUSHING

BRACKET

16 N·m (12 FT. LBS.)

AFTER NUT IS TORQUED BOLT MUST BE CUT OFF 6 mm (1/4") MAX. FROM NUT

16 N·m (12 FT. LBS.)

To remove: hoist car and remove parts as shown. To install: install parts as shown and lower hoist.

Torsion Bar and/or Support Removal and Installation

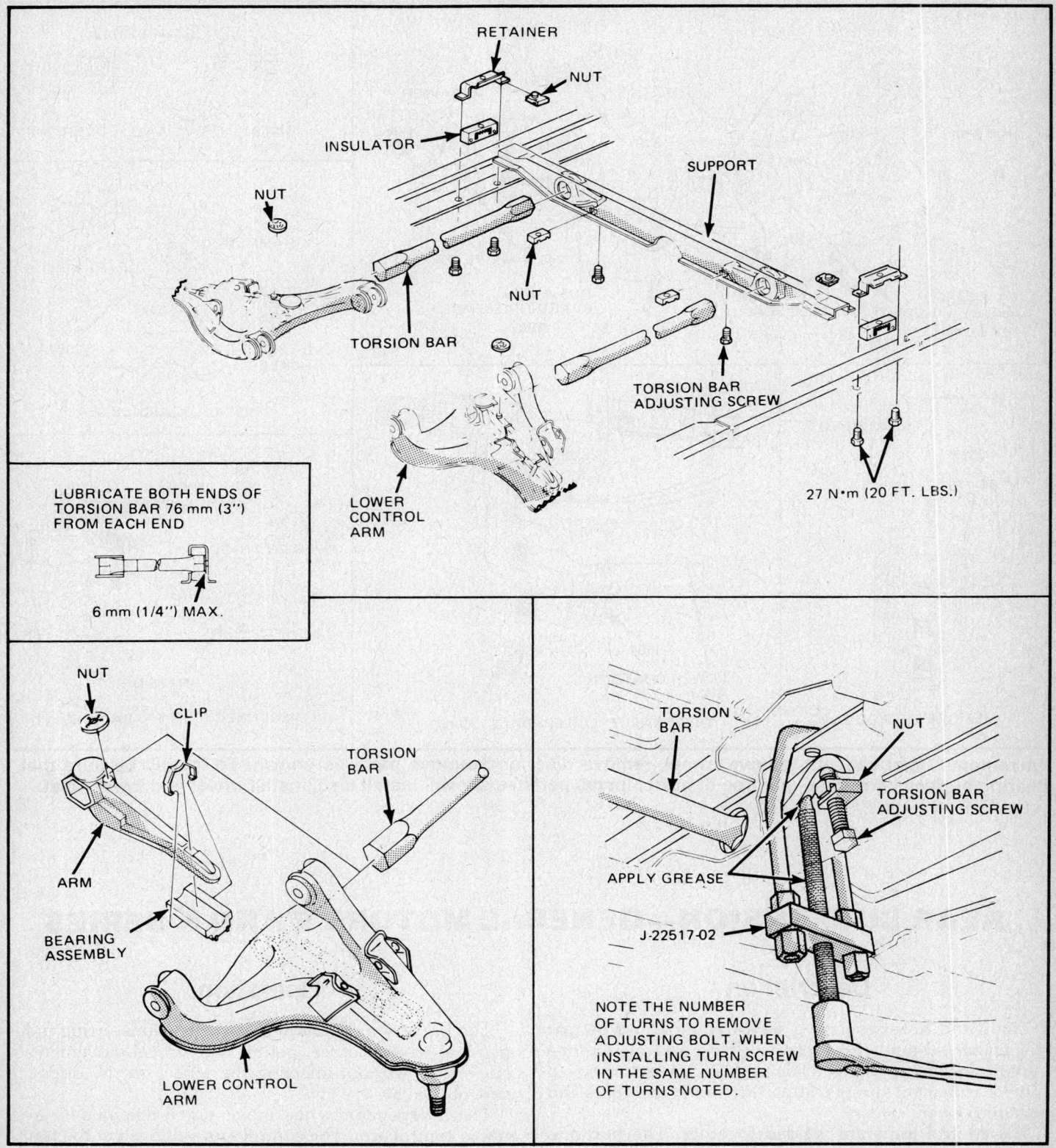

RETAINER

NUT

INSULATOR

SUPPORT

NUT

TORSION BAR

NUT

TORSION BAR ADJUSTING SCREW

LOWER CONTROL ARM

27 N•m (20 FT. LBS.)

LUBRICATE BOTH ENDS OF TORSION BAR 76 mm (3'') FROM EACH END

6 mm (1/4'') MAX.

NUT

CLIP

TORSION BAR

ARM

BEARING ASSEMBLY

LOWER CONTROL ARM

TORSION BAR

NUT

TORSION BAR ADJUSTING SCREW

APPLY GREASE

J-22517-02

NOTE THE NUMBER OF TURNS TO REMOVE ADJUSTING BOLT. WHEN INSTALLING TURN SCREW IN THE SAME NUMBER OF TURNS NOTED.

To remove: hoist car and remove parts as shown. To remove torsion bar(s) only: remove torsion bar adjusting screw as shown. Slide torsion bar forward in lower control arm until torsion bar clears support. Then pull down on bar and remove from control arm. To install: install parts as shown. Lower hoist and adjust trim height.

Hub and Bearing Assembly, Knuckle and Knuckle Seal Removal and Installation

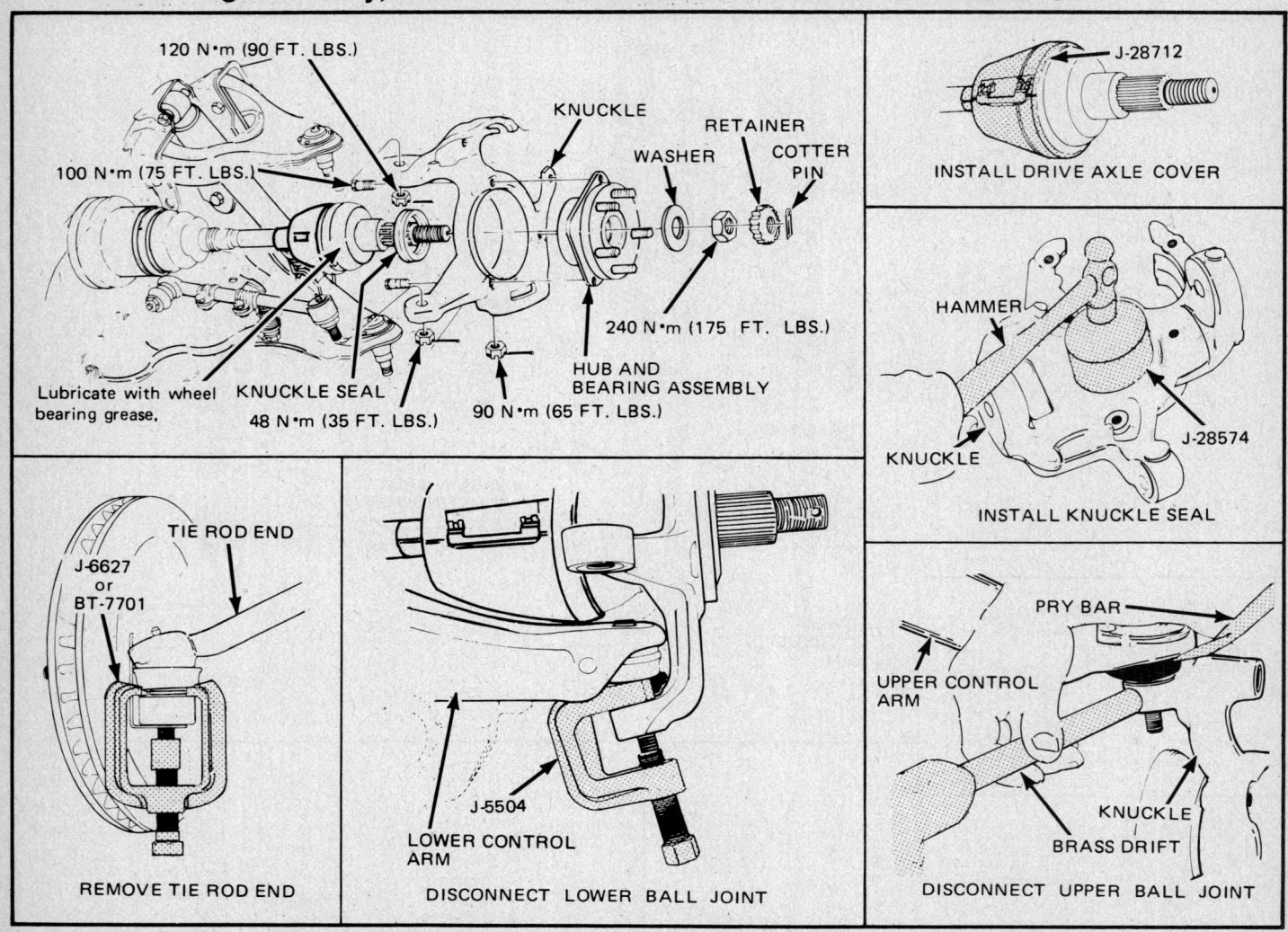

To remove: hoist car and remove wheel, remove disc, and remove parts as shown. To install: be sure that bearing surfaces are clean and free of burrs. Install parts as shown. Install disc, install wheel and lower hoist.

REAR SUSPENSION—GENERAL MOTORS E AND K SERIES

Description

The E and K Series have a semi-trailing arm-type rear suspension system with a relatively long control arm for a minimum camber change. The system consists of boxed control arms, coil springs, super-lift shock absorbers and a stabilizer bar.

The control arms are welded together. The hub and bearing attachment plane is machined for precise suspension alignment.

The hub and wheel bearing is a unit assembly which eliminates the need for wheel bearing adjustments and does not require periodic maintenance.

Operation

The left and right rear wheel suspensions, being independent of each other, permit the vertical movement of one wheel without affecting the wheel on the opposite side of the car.

This independent wheel movement is obtained by an A frame control arm. The control arm is hinged at the frame to provide the up and down movement of the wheel. The solid stabilizer bar forces the wheel to travel in through a controlled arc.

The control arm also carries the rear brake mounting bracket and hub and bearing assembly.

Rear Suspension

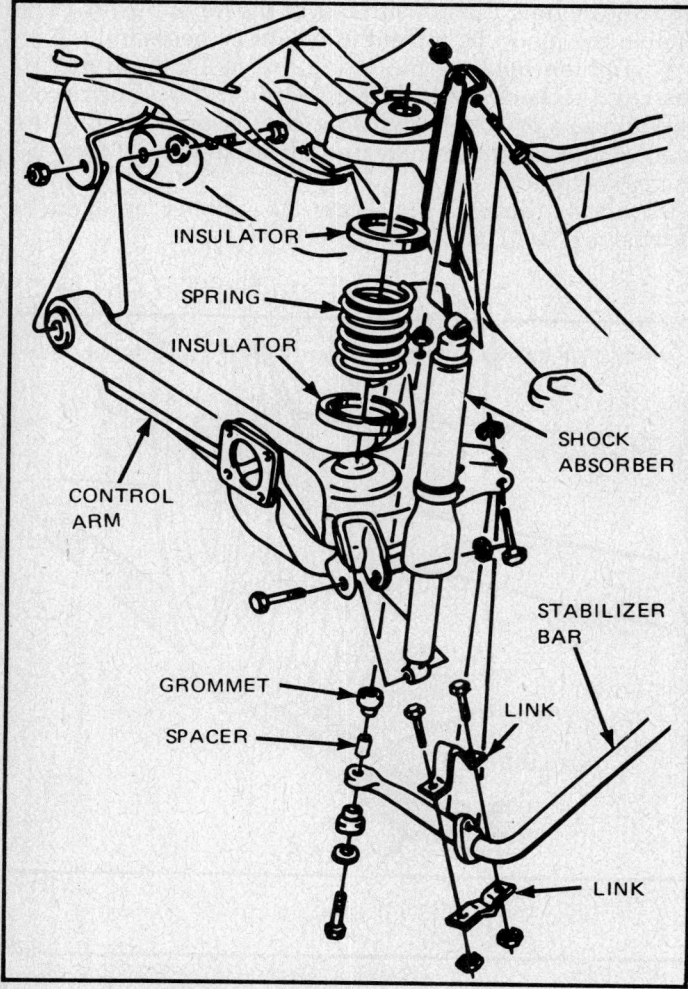

Shock Absorber Removal and Installation

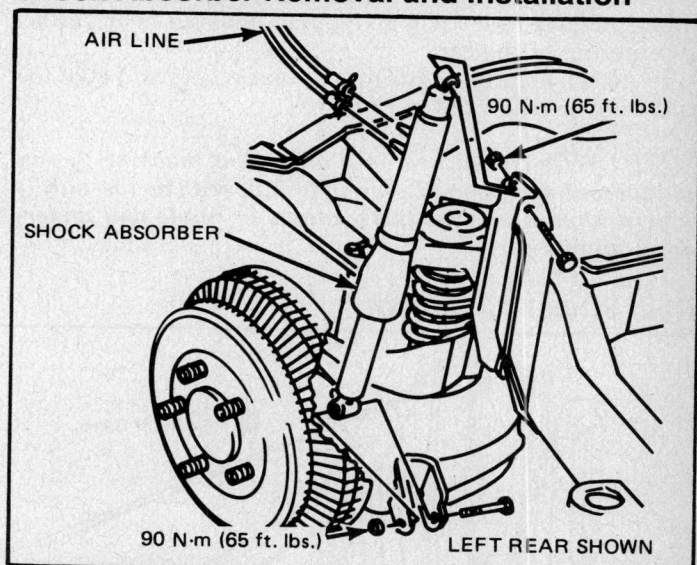

90 N·m (65 ft. lbs.)

90 N·m (65 ft. lbs.)

LEFT REAR SHOWN

To remove: hoist car and support control arm, remove parts as shown. To install: install parts as shown, remove support and lower hoist.

ALIGNMENT

Satisfactory operation may occur over a wide range of rear wheel alignment settings. Nevertheless, should settings vary beyond certain tolerances, readjustment of alignment is advisable. The specifications stated in column 1 of the charts should be used as guidelines.

These specifications provide an acceptable all-around operating range in that they prevent abnormal tire wear caused by wheel alignment.

In the event the actual settings are beyond the specifications set forth in column 1 or 2 (whichever is applicable), or whenever for other reasons the alignment is being reset, the factory recommends that the specifications given in column 3 of the charts be used.

Rear wheel alignment should be checked and adjusted as necessary in the following procedure.

1. Check front and rear trim heights.
2. Check electronic level control for proper operation.
3. Using an alignment machine, use one of the following procedures.

Preferred method

a. If machine does not have guide line, place tape on floor from wheel plate to rear of car to use as a guide for lining up car on machine.

b. Back car onto alignment machine placing rear wheel on wheel plates.

c. Place a straightedge at same rib of tire at front and rear and measure distance from inside edge of straight edge and edge of guide line. The measurement from the guide line to the straight edge must be greater at the rear tire by 16 mm (5/8 in.) ± 6 mm (1/4 in.).

Alternate method

a. Place a one inch tape on the floor along the right-hand side of the center line between the wheel plates of the alignment machine.

b. Back car onto alignment machine making sure car is as straight as possible.

Rear Wheel Alignment Diagnosis

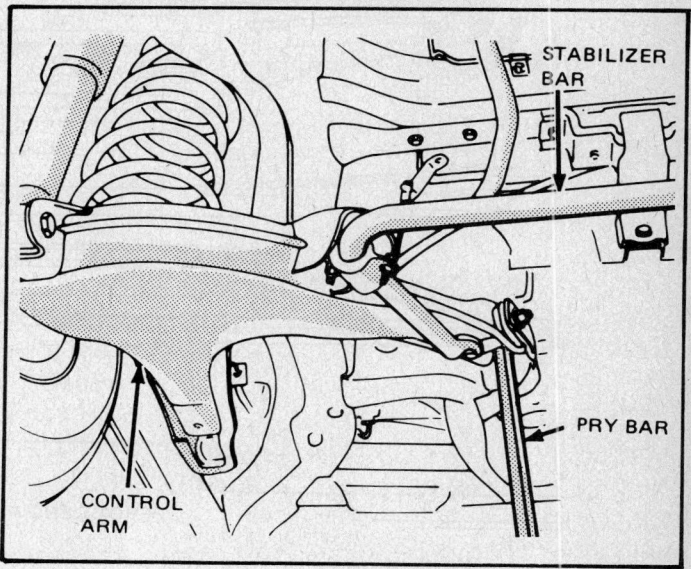

SUSPENSION

REAR SUSPENSION-GENERAL MOTORS E AND K BODY

c. Hanging plumbs on the front and rear crossmembers at gage holes will give guide lines for near perfect centering of the car.

4. Attach alignment mirrors to rear wheel and take toe and camber readings.

NOTE With car backed onto alignment machine, toe-in and toe-out are reversed. Toe-in will be read as toe-out. It is very important that the readings be made and understood properly.

5. Toe adjustments are made at the inner pivot bushings. Loosening the nut and bolt at the inner bushing will enable the toe to be moved in or out as necesary.

6. Tighten bushing mounting nut to 135 N•m (97 ft.-lbs.) and recheck toe for correct setting. It may be necessary to use a pry bar to move the control arm. Moving the control arm rearward increases toe-in; moving it forward increases toe-out.

7. Check camber. There are no camber adjustment provisions; see Diagnosis.

Rear Wheel Alignment

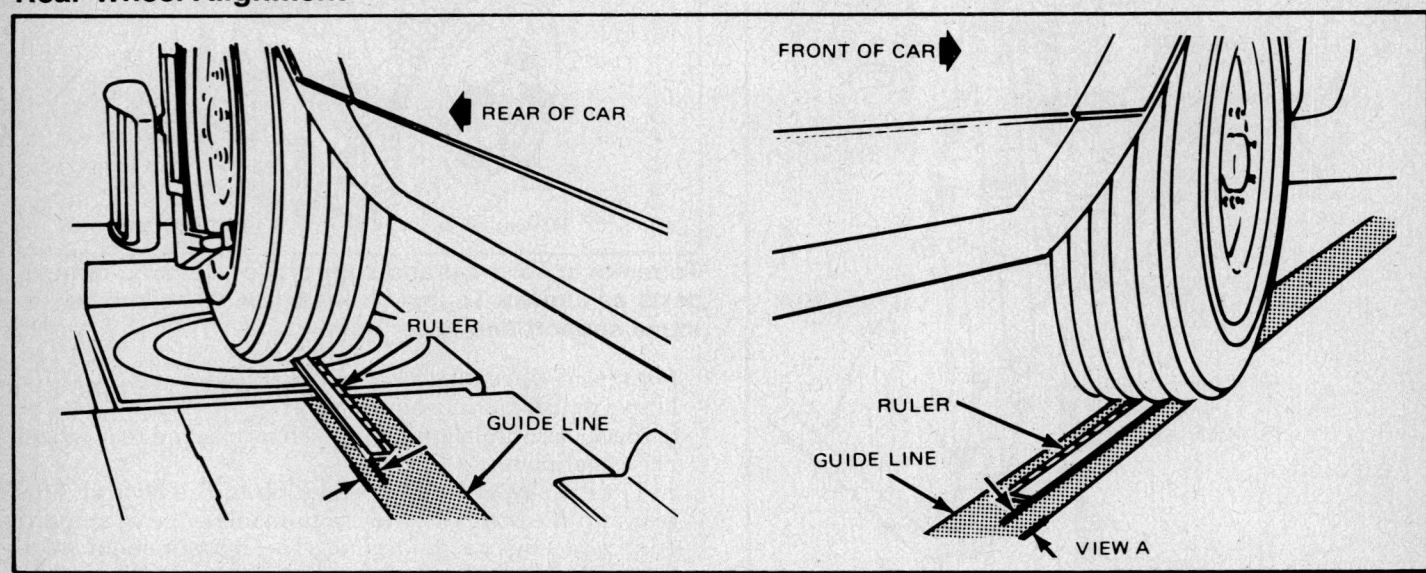

Rear Wheel Alignment

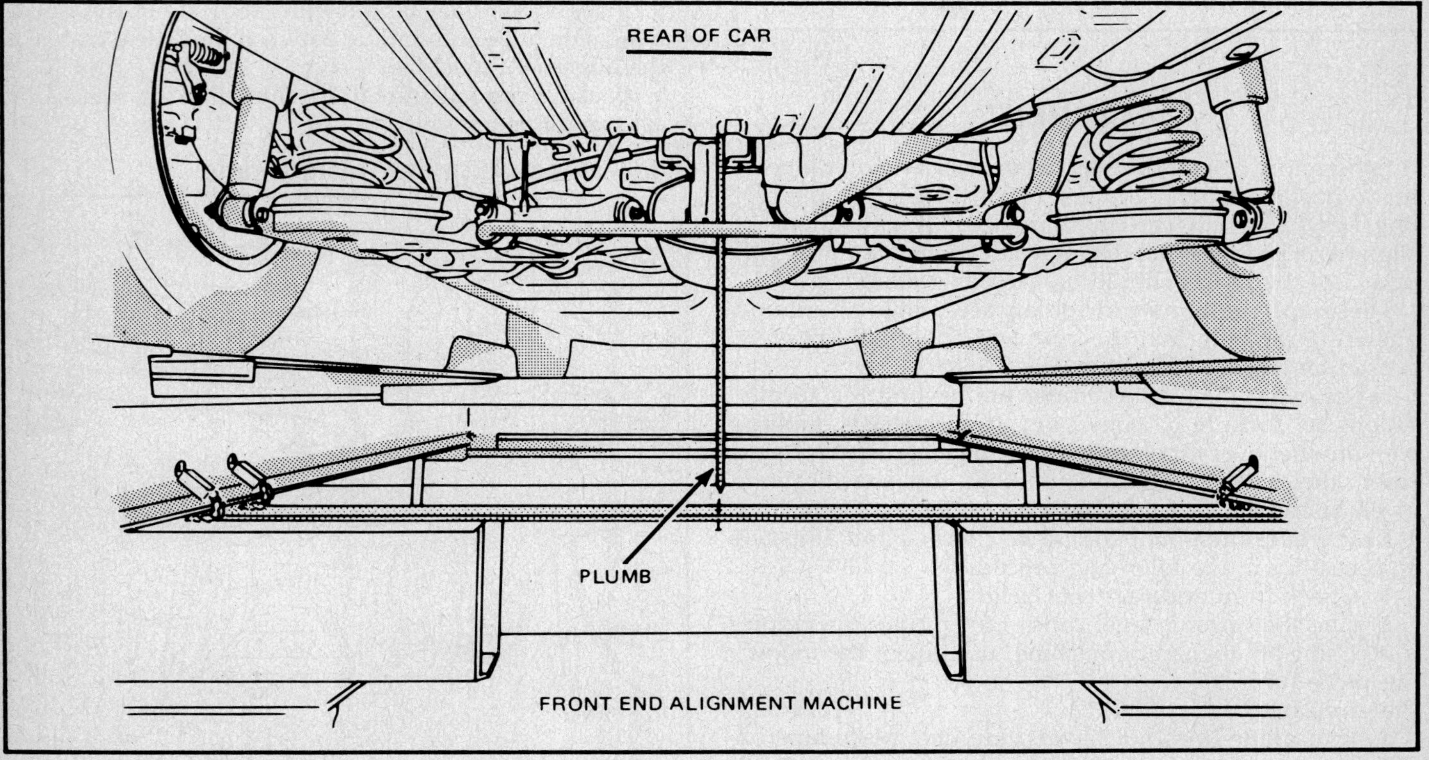

Rear Suspension Components

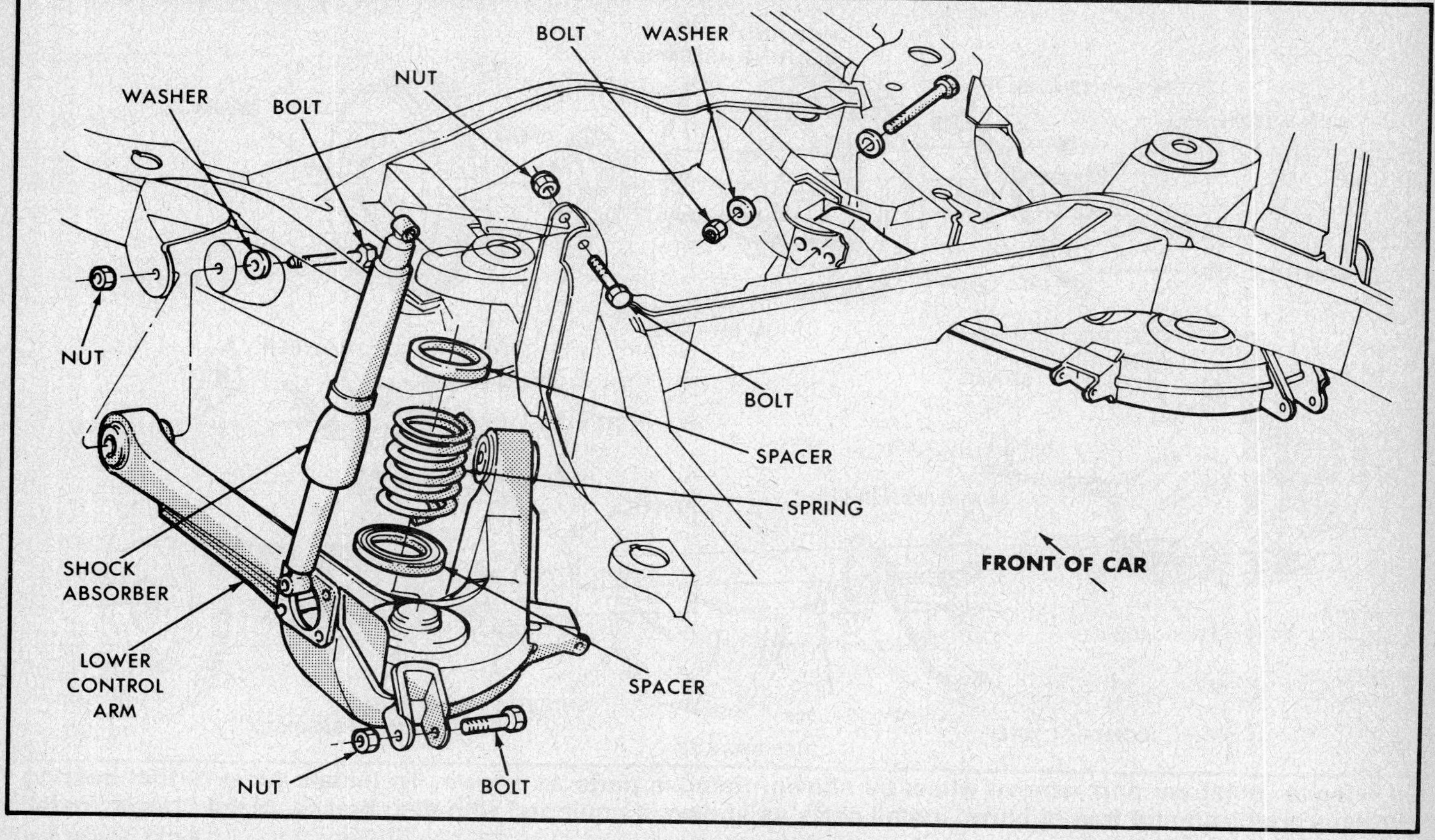

WASHER

BOLT

NUT

BOLT WASHER

WASHER

BOLT

NUT

BOLT

SPACER

SPRING

SHOCK ABSORBER

LOWER CONTROL ARM

SPACER

FRONT OF CAR

NUT

BOLT

Stabilizer Bar and/or Bushing Removal and Installation

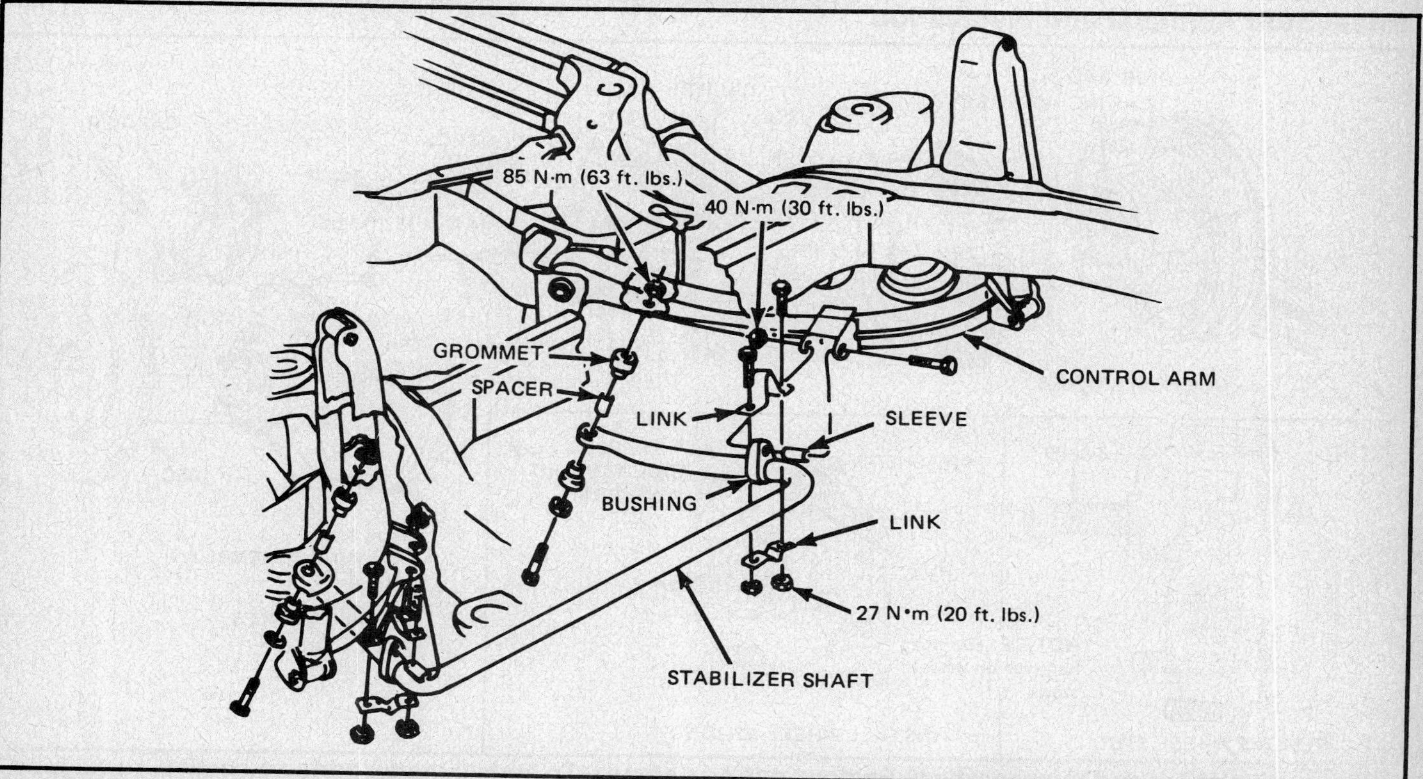

85 N·m (63 ft. lbs.)

40 N·m (30 ft. lbs.)

GROMMET

SPACER

LINK

SLEEVE

CONTROL ARM

BUSHING

LINK

27 N·m (20 ft. lbs.)

STABILIZER SHAFT

To remove: hoist car and remove parts as shown. To install: install parts as shown, and lower hoist.

B585

SUSPENSION

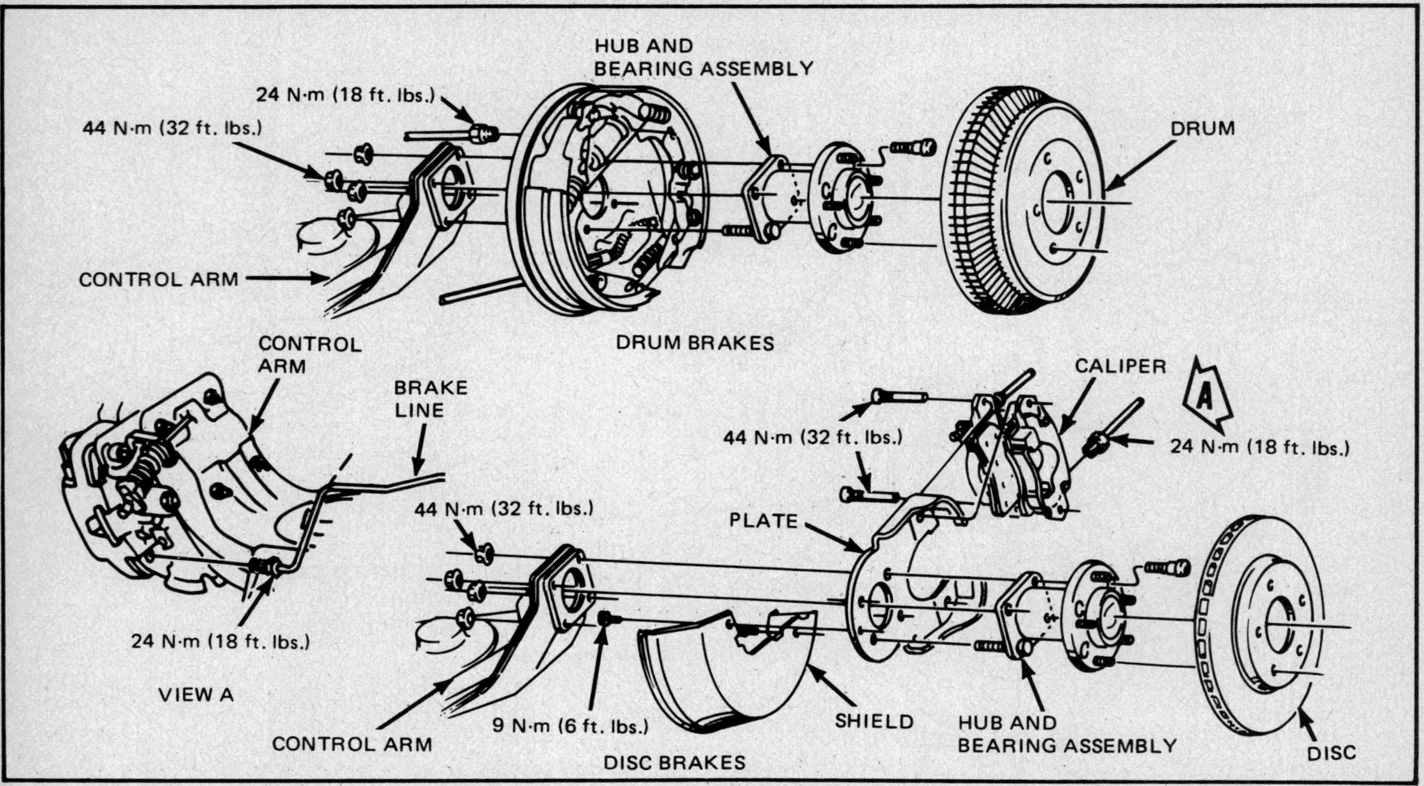

Hub and Bearing Assembly Removal and Installation

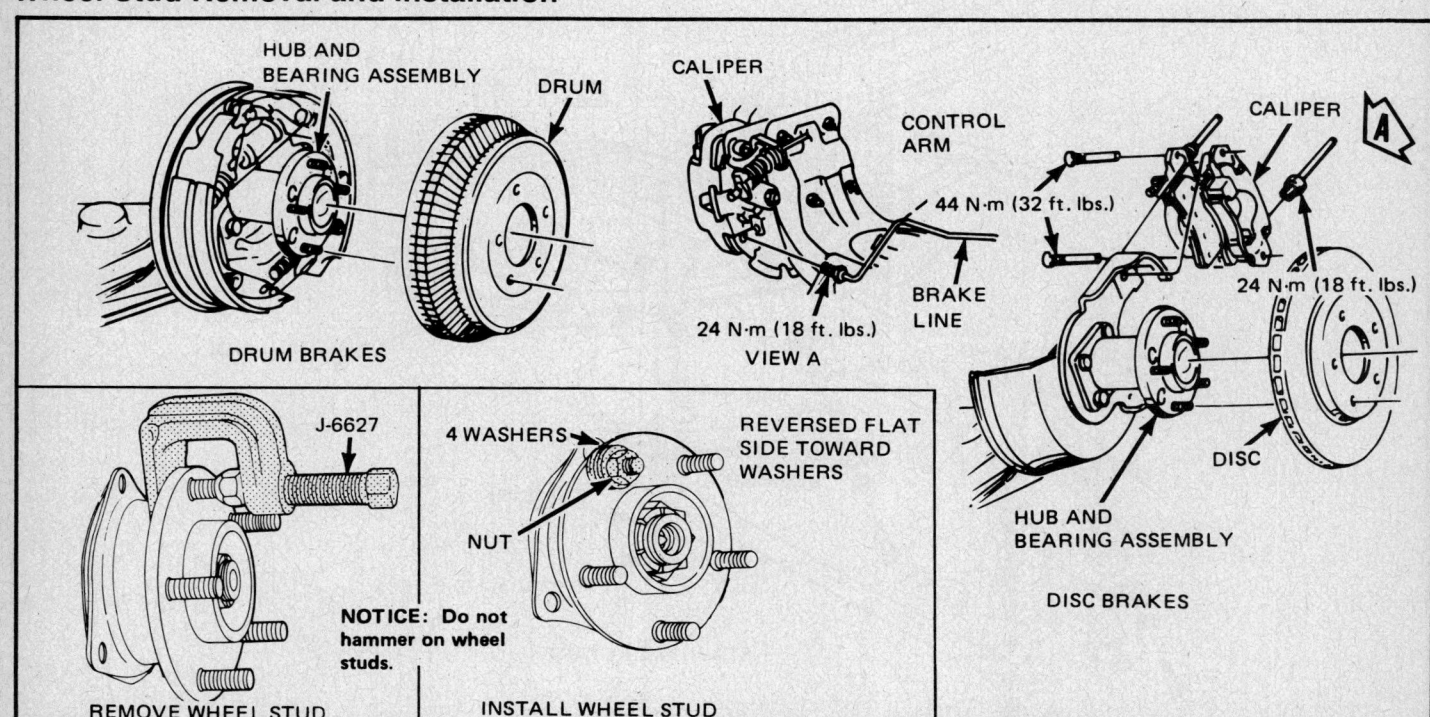

To remove: hoist car and remove wheel as shown. Remove parts as shown. To install: be sure that bearing surfaces are clean and free of burrs. Install parts as shown. If equipped with disc brakes, bleed brakes. Install wheel and lower hoist.

Wheel Stud Removal and Installation

To remove: hoist car and remove wheel. Remove parts as shown. To install: install parts as shown. If equipped with disc brakes, bleed brakes. Install wheel and lower hoist.

Rear Control Arm, Spring and/or Bushing Removal and Installation

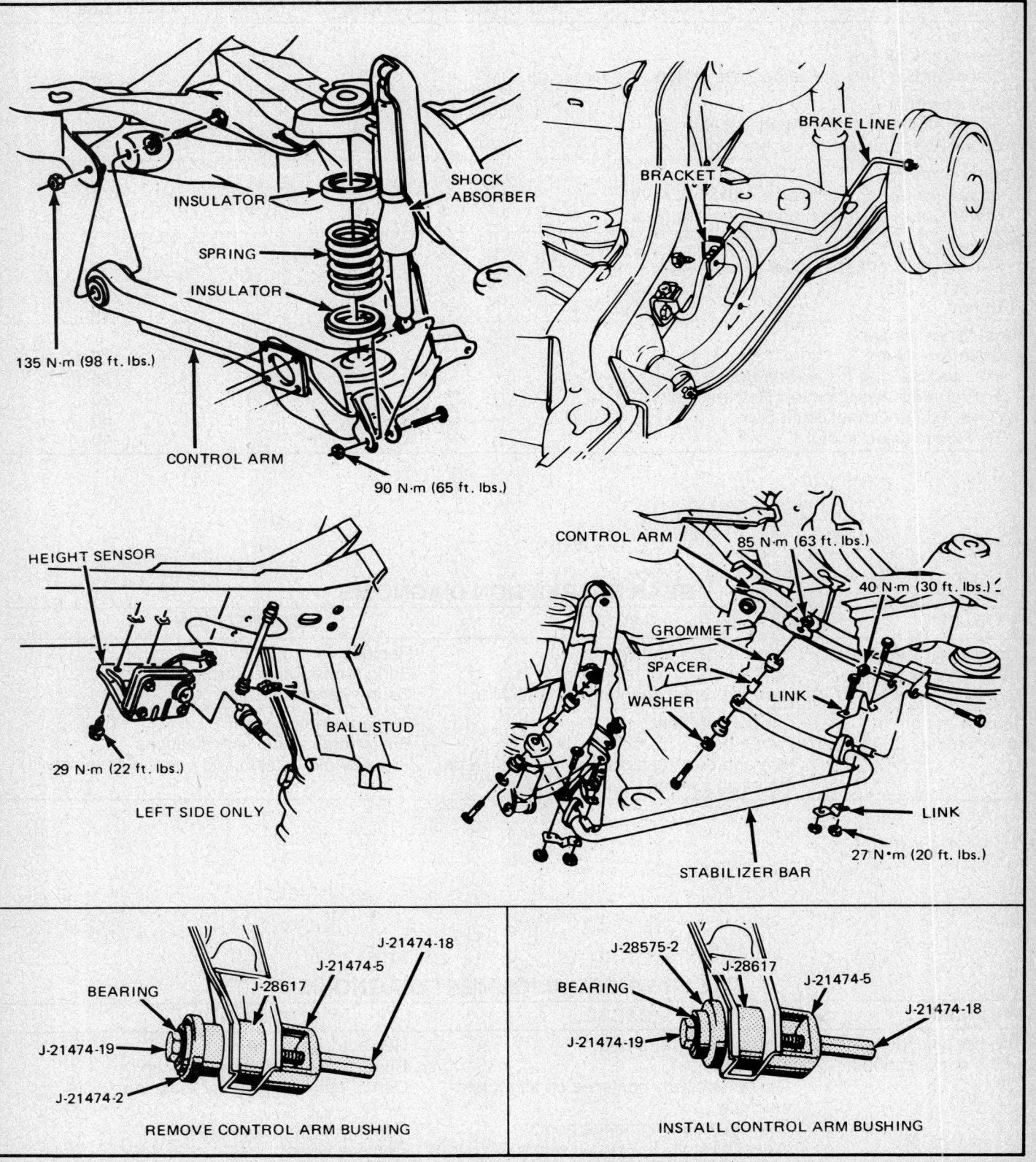

135 N·m (98 ft. lbs.)

INSULATOR

SHOCK ABSORBER

SPRING

INSULATOR

CONTROL ARM

90 N·m (65 ft. lbs.)

BRACKET

BRAKE LINE

HEIGHT SENSOR

BALL STUD

29 N·m (22 ft. lbs.)

LEFT SIDE ONLY

CONTROL ARM

85 N·m (63 ft. lbs.)

40 N·m (30 ft. lbs.)

GROMMET

SPACER

WASHER

LINK

LINK

27 N·m (20 ft. lbs.)

STABILIZER BAR

BEARING

J-28617

J-21474-18

J-21474-5

J-21474-19

J-21474-2

REMOVE CONTROL ARM BUSHING

J-28575-2

J-28617

BEARING

J-21474-5

J-21474-19

J-21474-18

INSTALL CONTROL ARM BUSHING

To remove: hoist car and remove wheel. Remove hub and bearing assembly. Remove parts as shown. To install: Install parts as shown. Install hub and bearing assembly. Bleed brakes. Install wheel and lower hoist.

B587

SUSPENSION

TORQUE SPECIFICATIONS

	N·m	Ft.Lbs.
Stabilizer		
Stabilizer Link Nut	18	13
Stabilizer Bar Brkt. to Frame Bolts & Nuts	33	24
Shock Absorber		
Shock Absorber Upper Attaching Nut	130	95
Shock Absorber to Control Arm Bolts	100	75
Control Arms		
Upper Control Arm to Frame Attaching Nuts	95	70
Lower Control Arm to Frame Attaching Nuts	120	90
Ball Joints		
Service Ball Joints to Upper Control Arm	11	8
Lower	90	65
Upper	120	90
Front Wheel Drive		
Drive Axle Nut	240	175
Hub and Bearing to Knuckle Bolts	100	75
Torsion Bar Crossmember Retainer Bolts	27	20
Drive Axle to Output Shaft Bolts	80	60
Tie Rod to Knuckle Nut	54	40

REAR SUSPENSION DIAGNOSIS

PROBLEM	CAUSE	CORRECTION
Toe not adjustable within specifications	Lower control arm bent Frame bent Car not properly centered on machine	Replace control arm Bring frame within specification Center car on machine
Camber out of specification	Control arm bent Frame bent Hub and bearing assembly not seated on mounting surface	Replace control arm Bring frame within specifications Properly mount Hub and bearing assembly

REAR WHEEL ALIGNMENT DIAGNOSIS

PROBLEM	CAUSE	CORRECTION
Toe not adjustable within specifications	Lower control arm bent Frame bent Car not properly centered on alignment machine Bearing mounting flange bent Wheel bent	Replace control arm Bring frame within specification Center car on alignment machine Replace bearing assembly Replace wheel
Camber out of specification	Control arm bent Frame bent Spindle-bearing	Replace control arm Bring frame within specifications Properly mount

REAR WHEEL ALIGNMENT

	Specifications for Diagnosis for Warranty Repair or Customer Paid Service	Specifications for Periodic Motor Vehicle Inspection	Specification for Alignment Resetting
Camber (measure only)	$-1.3°$ to $+0.3°$	$-1.5°$ to $+0.5°$	Refer to Rear Suspension Diagnosis
Toe-in per wheel	$0.00°$ to $+0.30°$ (0" to $+^5/_{32}$")	$-0.25°$ to $+0.55°$ ($-^1/_8$" to $+^9/_{32}$")	$+0.15° \pm 0.15°$ ($+^3/_{32}$" $\pm^3/_{32}$")
Toe-in both wheels	$0.00°$ to $+0.60°$ (0" to $+^5/_{16}$")	$-0.50°$ to $+1.10°$ ($-^1/_4$" to $+^9/_{16}$")	$+0.30° \pm 0.30°$ ($+^5/_{32}$" $\pm^5/_{32}$")

NOTE: It is important that toe-in be measured per wheel. If equipment is not available to measure each wheel, measure toe-in both wheels. When resetting be sure that toe-in on each wheel is the same.

CAUTION: With car backed onto alignment machine, toe-in and toe-out are reversed. Toe-in will be read as toe-out. It is very important that the readings be made and understood properly.

FRONT SUSPENSION—GENERAL MOTORS J BODY CARS

Description

The front suspension is a MacPherson strut design. The lower control arms pivot from the lower side rails. Rubber bushings are used for the lower control arm pivots. The upper end of the strut is isolated by a rubber mount which contains a non-serviceable bearing for wheel turning. The tie-rods connect to the steering arm on the strut, just below the spring seat. The lower end of the wheel steering knuckle pivots on a ball stud for wheel turning. The ball stud is riveted in the lower control arm and is fastened to the steering knuckle with a castellated nut and cotter pin.

Wheel Alignment

TOE

Toe is controlled by the tie-rod position. To adjust toe setting, loosen the clamp bolts at the outer end of the tie rod. Rotate adjuster to align toe to specifications. Tighten bolts to 20 N•m (15 ft.-lbs.).

Adjustment

1. Loosen clamp bolts at outer tie-rod.
2. Square the vehicle.
3. Rotate adjuster to set toe to specifications.
4. Tighten clamp bolts.

CAMBER

In special circumstances when camber adjustment becomes necessary, refer to the following procedure for instructions on modifying the front suspension strut assembly.

Toe Adjustment

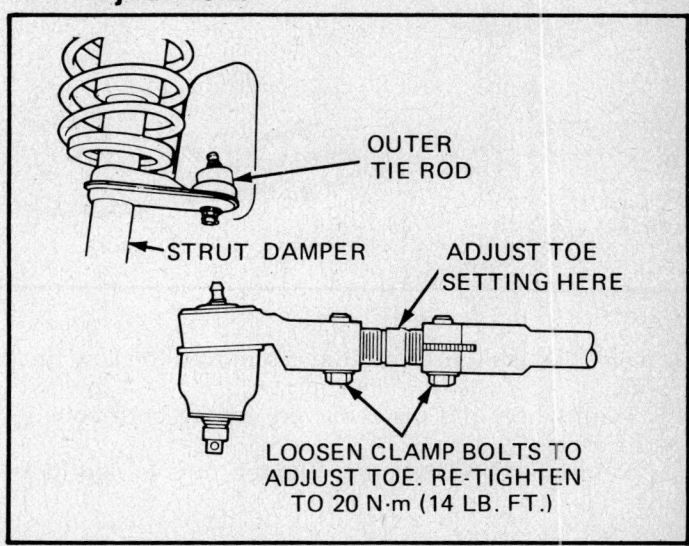

OUTER TIE ROD

STRUT DAMPER

ADJUST TOE SETTING HERE

LOOSEN CLAMP BOLTS TO ADJUST TOE. RE-TIGHTEN TO 20 N·m (14 LB. FT.)

Adjustment

1. Position the car on the alignment equipment. Follow the manufacturer's instructions to obtain the camber reading.

2. Use appropriate extensions to reach around both sides of the tire. Loosen both strut-to-knuckle bolts just enough to allow movement between the strut and the knuckle. Remove tools.

3. Grasp the top of the tire firmly, and move the tire inboard or outboard until the correct camber reading is obtained.

4. Carefully reach around the tire with appropriate extensions and tighten both bolts enough to hold the correct

Front Suspension

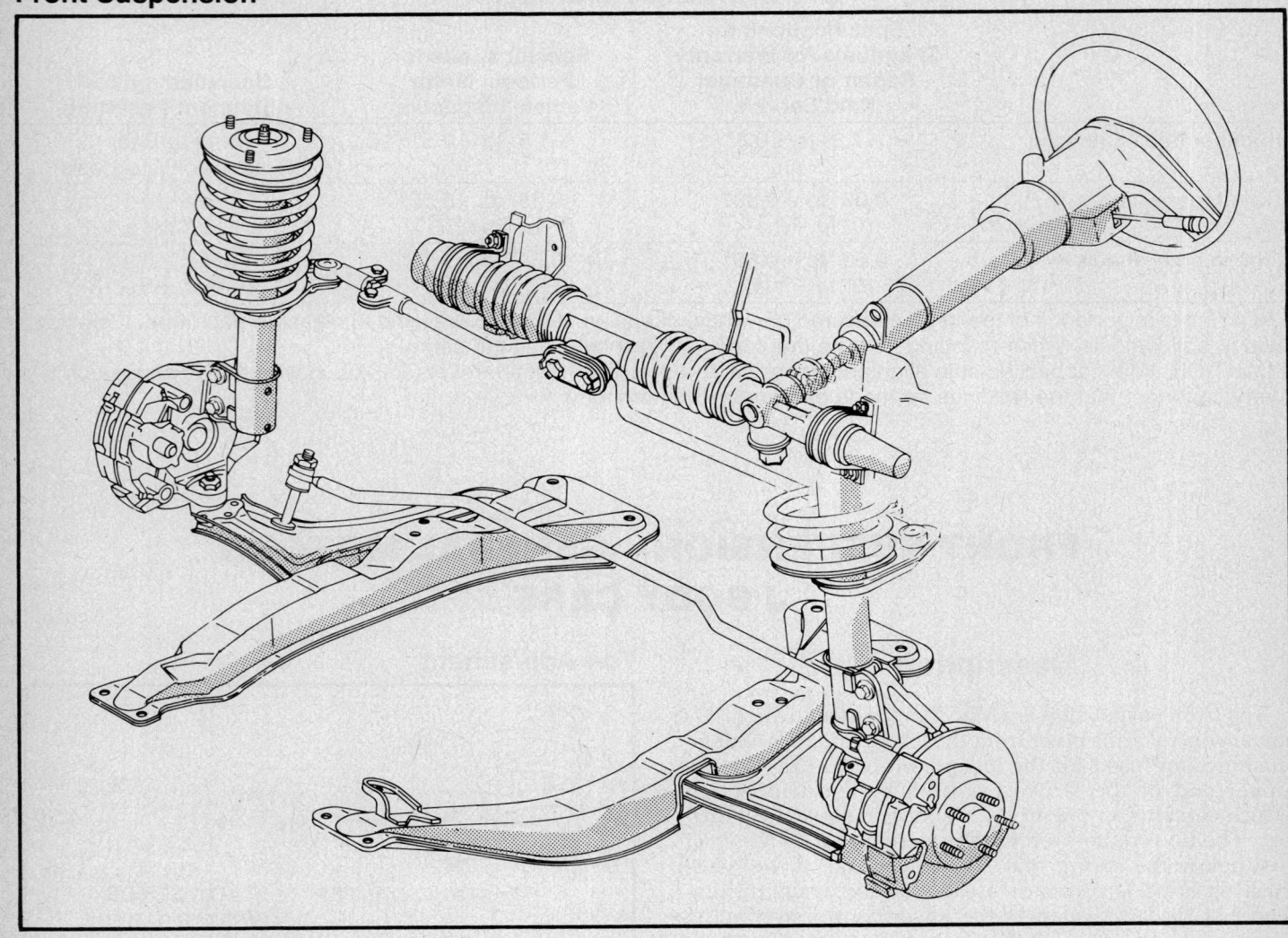

camber while the wheel and tire is removed to allow final torque.

5. With wheel and tire removed, torque both bolts to specifications.

6. Reinstall wheel and tire. Tighten nuts to specifications.

MacPherson Strut

Removal

1. Raise hood and disconnect upper strut-to-body nuts.

2. Hoist car, allowing front suspension to hang free.

3. Remove wheel and tire.

4. Install drive axle cover.

5. Disconnect tie-rod from strut.

6. Remove both strut-to-knuckle bolts.

7. Remove strut.

Installation

1. Install strut by reversing removal steps 1–6.

2. Place flats on both mounting bolts in a horizontal position.

3. Torque all fasteners to specifications.

STRUT MODIFICATION (Only for adjustment of camber setting)

1. Place strut in vise. (It is not necessary to remove the strut from the car. Filling can be accomplished by disconnecting strut from knuckle.)

2. File the holes in outer flanges to enlarge the bottom holes until they match the slots in the inner flanges.

STRUT DISASSEMBLY

1. Mount strut compressor in vise.

2. Place strut assembly in bottom adapter of compressor and install J 26584-86 (make sure adapter captures strut and that locating pins are engaged).

3. Rotate strut assembly to align top mounting assembly lip with strut compressor support notch.

4. Insert *both* J 26584-88 top adapters *between* the top mounting assembly and the top spring seat. Position top adapters so that the split line is in the 9 o'clock–3 o'clock position.

5. Using a ratchet with 1-inch socket, turn compressor forcing screw clockwise until top support flange contacts the J 26584-88 top adapters. Continue turning the screw, compressing the strut spring approximately ½ inch (four complete turns).

NOTE   Never bottom spring or strut damper rod.

6. The top nut can now be removed from the strut damper shaft and the top mounting assembly (containing bearing) can be lifted off the strut assembly.

7. Turn strut compressor forcing screw counterclockwise until the strut spring tension is relieved. Remove top adapters, bottom adapter, then remove components.

STRUT ASSEMBLY

CAUTION   Never place a hard tool such as pliers or a screwdriver against the polished surface of the damper shaft. The shaft can be held up from the top end with your fingers, or with the extension, to prevent it from receding into the strut assembly, while the spring is being compressed.

1. Clamp strut compressor body J 26584 in vise.

2. Place strut assembly in bottom adapter of compressor and install J 26584-86 (make sure adapter captures strut and locating pins are engaged).

3. Rotate strut assembly until mounting flange is facing out, directly opposite the compressor forcing screw.

Strut Damper Removal and Installation

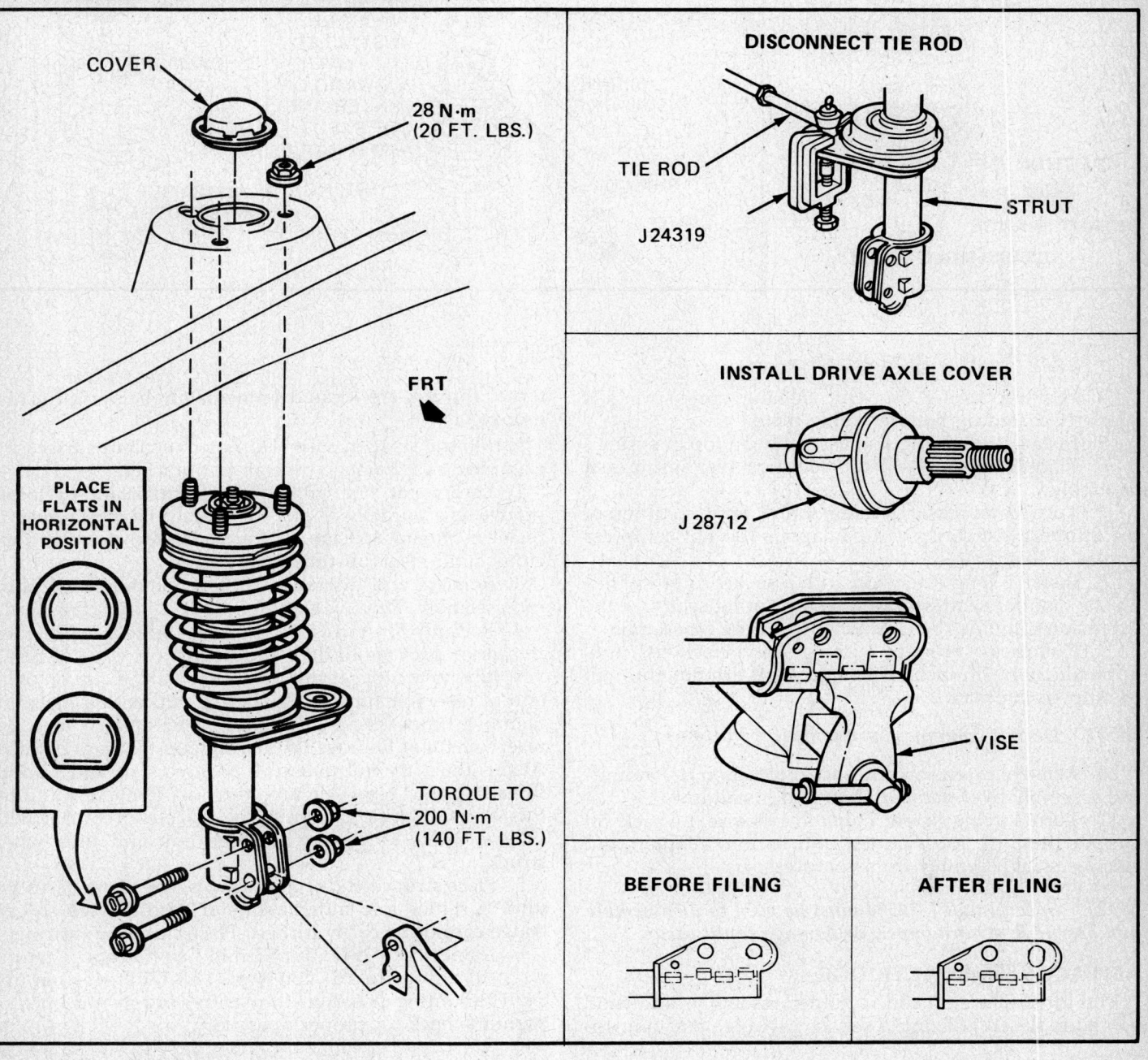

Disassembly and Reassembly of Strut Assembly

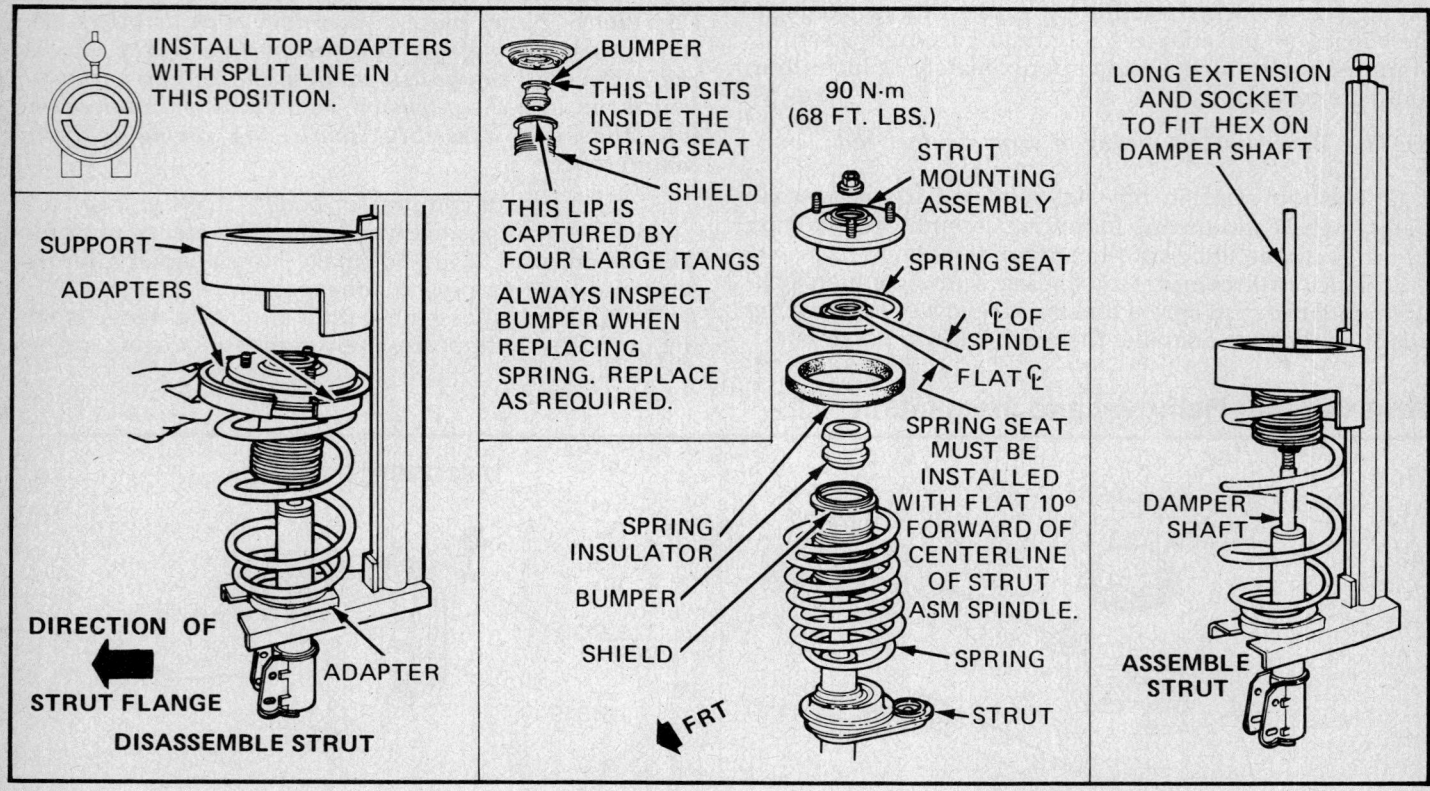

4. Position spring on strut making sure spring is properly seated on bottom spring plate.

5. Install strut spring seat assembly on top of spring.

6. Place *both* J 26584-88 top adapters over spring seat assembly.

7. Turn compressor forcing screw until compressor top support just contacts top adapters (do not compress spring at this time).

8. Install a long extension with a socket to fit the hex on the damper shaft through the top spring seat. Use the extension to guide the components during reassembly.

9. Compress spring by turning screw clockwise until approximately 1½ inch of damper shaft extends through the top spring plate.

NOTE   Do not compress spring until it bottoms.

10. Remove extension and socket, position top mounting assembly over damper shaft and install nut.

11. Turn forcing screw counterclockwise to back off support, remove top adapters and bottom adapter, and remove strut assembly from compressor.

NOTE   Special tool J-26584 must be used to disassemble and assemble strut damper, or damage could occur.

REPLACE STRUT CARTRIDGE

The internal piston rod, cylinder assembly, and fluid can be replaced utilizing a service cartridge and nut. In-ternal threads are located immediately below a cut line groove.

1. Mount strut in vise. Do not overclamp! Excessive clamping may damage tube and/or bracket.

2. Locate cut line groove. It is important to locate groove as accurately as possible because mislocation will result in thread damage. Cut around groove with a pipe cutter until reservoir tube is completely cut through.

3. Remove and discard end cap, cylinder, and piston rod assembly. Remove strut from vise and discard fluid.

4. Reclamp strut in vise. A flaring cup tool is provided in service package to flare and deburr cut edge of reservoir tube to accept service nut. Place flaring cup on open end of reservoir tube. Strike flaring cup with a mallet or hammer until flaring cup's flat outer surface rests on reservoir tube. Remove the flaring cup tool and discard. At this time, try nut to assure positive start and smooth threading into reservoir tube threads. Remove nut after this check. Flaring cup must be placed in contact with tube so there is no gap between cup and tube when struck.

5. Place strut cartridge in reservoir tube. Turn cartridge until it settles into indentations at base of tube so cartridge cannot be easily turned. Place nut over cartridge.

6. Using tool J 29778 for 53 mm hex nut and a torque wrench, tighten to 190–230 N·m (140–170 ft.-lbs.) in up-right mounting position. Stroke the piston rod once or twice to check for proper operation.

Strut Cartridge Replacement

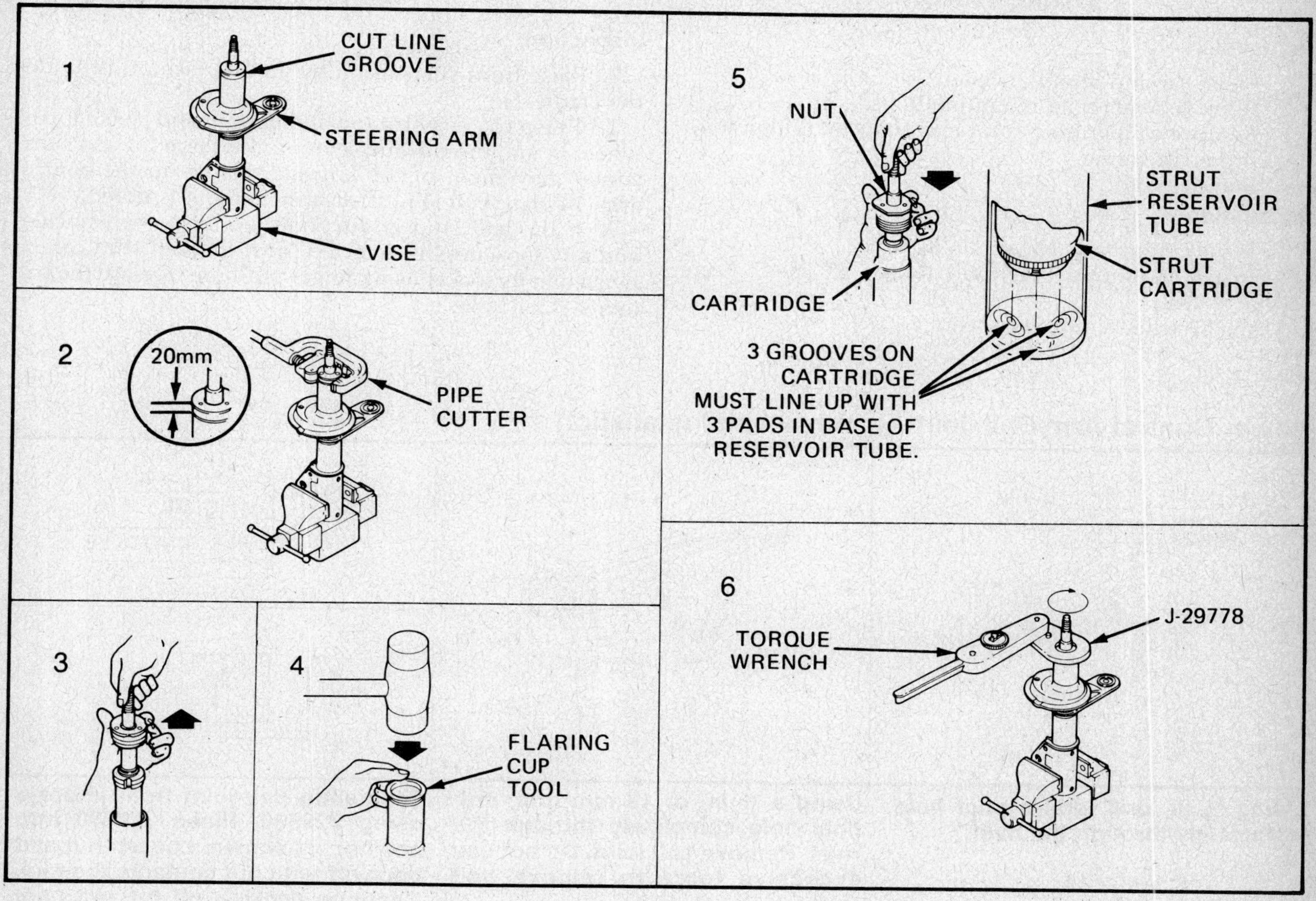

1

CUT LINE GROOVE

STEERING ARM

VISE

2

20mm

PIPE CUTTER

3

4

FLARING CUP TOOL

5

NUT

CARTRIDGE

STRUT RESERVOIR TUBE

STRUT CARTRIDGE

3 GROOVES ON CARTRIDGE MUST LINE UP WITH 3 PADS IN BASE OF RESERVOIR TUBE.

6

TORQUE WRENCH

J-29778

Caliper Removal and Installation

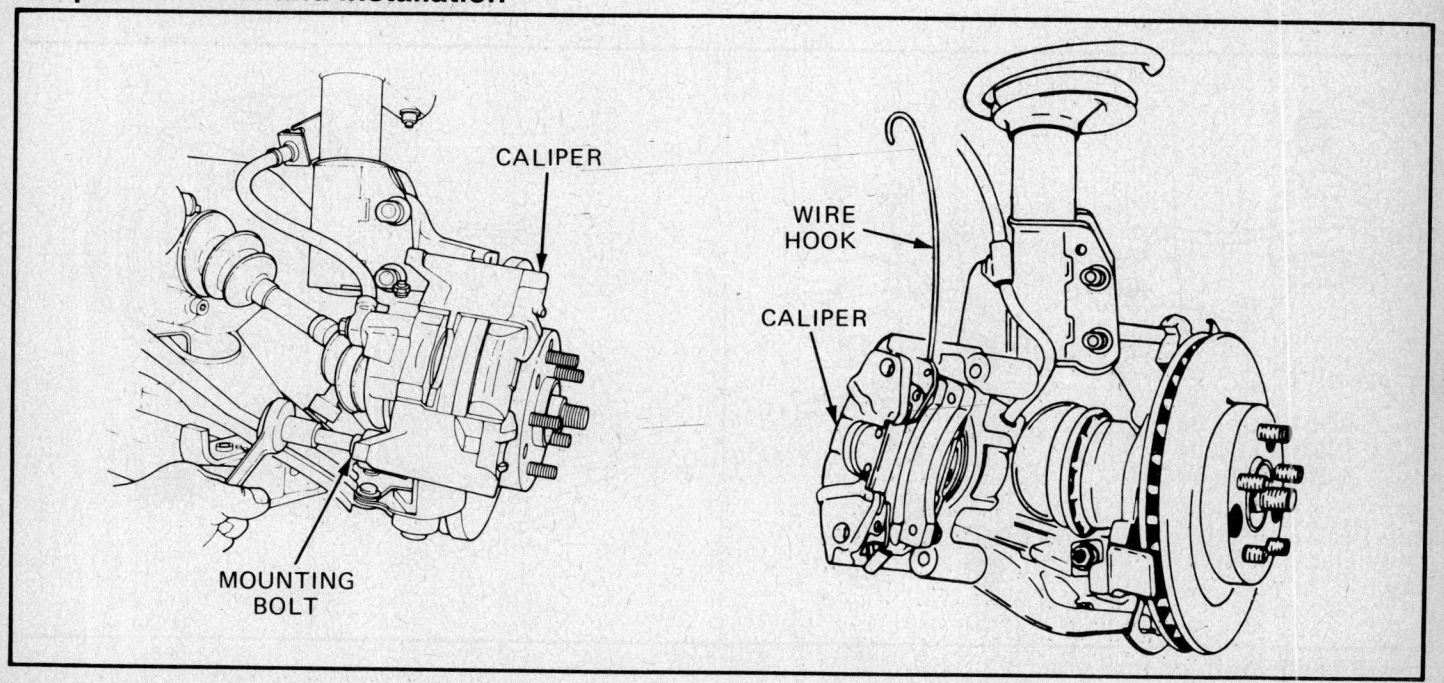

CALIPER

WIRE HOOK

CALIPER

MOUNTING BOLT

SUSPENSION

Brake Rotor

Removal

1. Hoist car and remove wheel.
2. Remove allen head mounting bolts.
3. Remove caliper from rotor and suspend with a wire hook from the frame.
4. Remove rotor.

Installation

1. Install rotor and caliper.
2. Install mounting bolts and torque to 28–47 N•m (21–35 ft.-lbs.).
3. Install wheels and lower car.

Ball Joints

Inspection

1. Raise front suspension by placing jack or lift under the cradle.
2. Grasp the wheel at top and bottom and shake top of wheel in an "in-and-out" motion. Observe for any horizontal movement of the knuckle relative to the control arm. Replace ball joint if such movement is noted.
3. If the ball stud is disconnected from the knuckle, and any looseness is detected, or if the ball stud can be twisted in its socket using finger pressure, replace the ball joint.

Lower Control Arm Ball Joint Removal and Installation

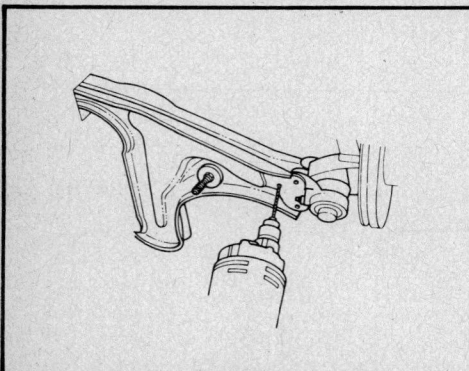

Using ⅛ in. drill, drill a pilot hole completely through the rivet.

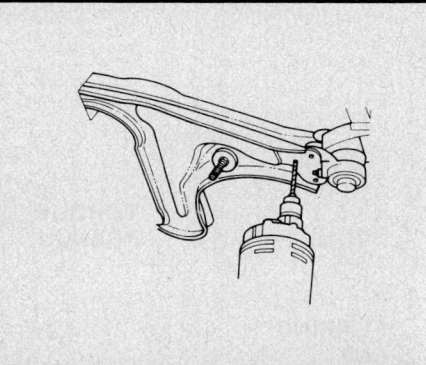

Using a ½ in. or 13 mm drill, drill final hole completely through the rivet. Remove ball joint. Do not use excessive force to remove ball joint.

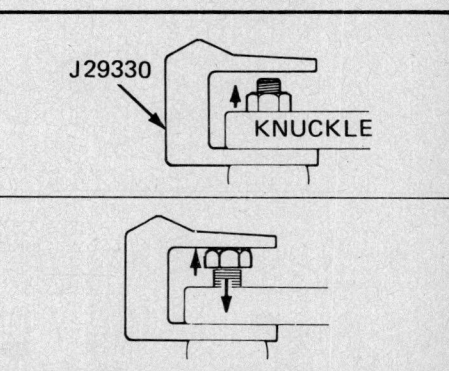

Separating ball joint from knuckle using J29330. Place J29330 into position as shown. Loosen nut and back off until nut contacts the tool. Continue backing off the nut until the nut forces the ball stud out of the knuckle.

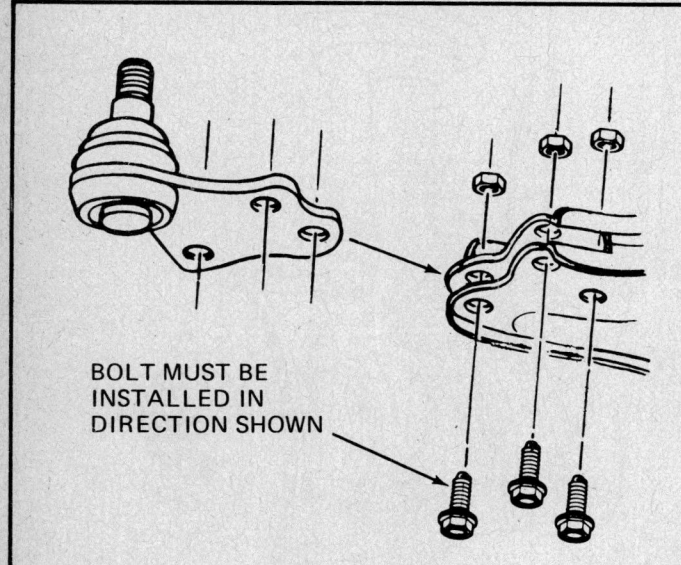

Install ball joint to control arm.

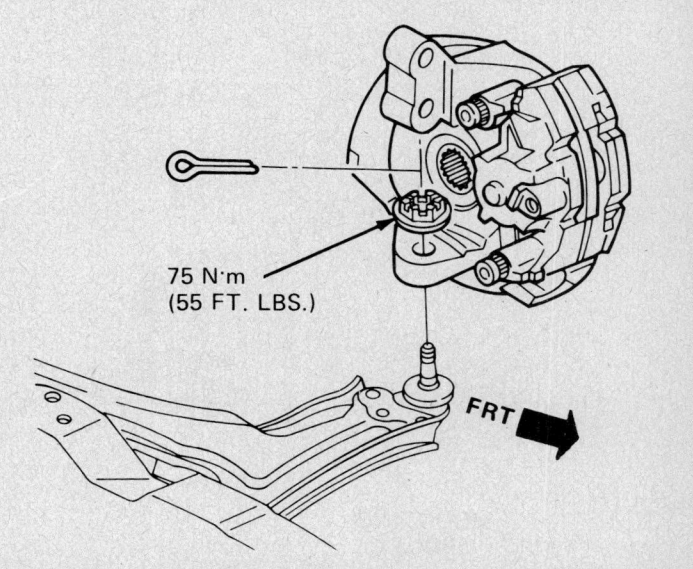

Removal

1. Raise car and remove wheel and tire.
2. If no countersink is found on the lower side of the rivets, carefully locate the center of the rivet body and mark with a punch.

3. Use the proper sequence to drill out rivets.
4. Use tool J 29330 to separate joint from knuckle.
5. Disconnect stabilizer from control arm.
6. Remove ball joint.

Lower Control Arm Support and Bushings Removal and Installation

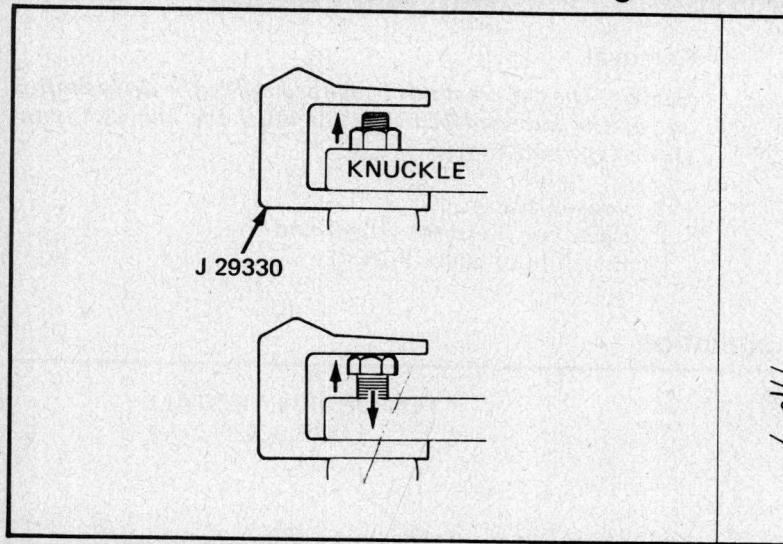

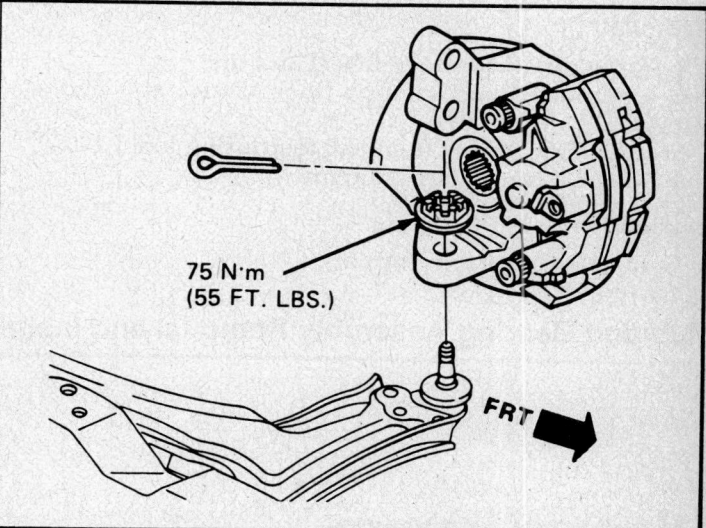

Place J29330 into position as shown. Loosen nut and back off until the nut contacts the tool. Continue backing off the nut until the nut forces the ball stud out of the knuckle.

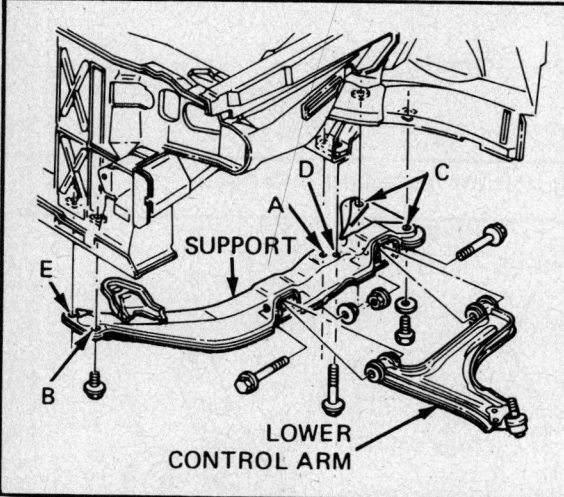

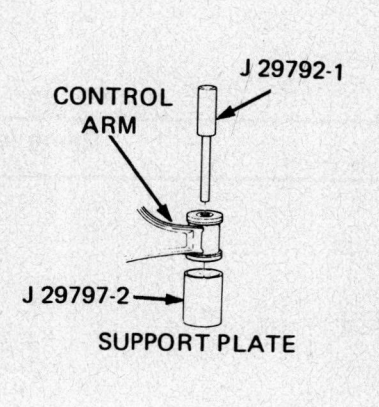

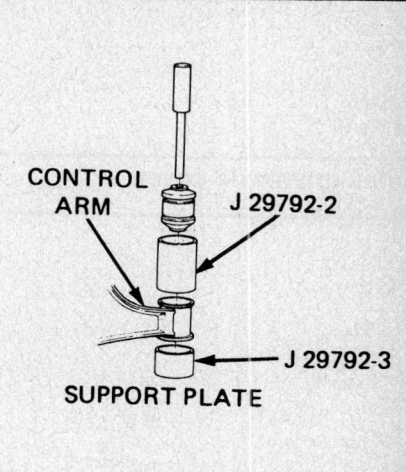

Front suspension support assembly attaching bolt/screw sequence: loosely install center bolt into hole (A). Loosely install tie bar bolt into outboard hole (B). Install both rear bolts into holes (C). Torque rear bolts. Install bolt into center hole (D), then torque. Torque bolt in hole (A). Install bolt into front hole (D), then torque. Torque bolt in hole (A). Install bolt into front hole (E), then torque. Torque bolt in hole (B). Torque support-to-body bolts 90 N·m (63 ft. lbs.) and LCA pivot bolts 95 N·m (67 ft. lbs.).

To remove, insert J29792-1 into bushing, support control arm on J29792-2. Press as shown.

To install, support control arm on J29792-3. Place bushing into J29792-2 and press bushing into control arm using J29792-1. Lubricate bushing.

SUSPENSION
FRONT SUSPENSION-GENERAL MOTORS J BODY

Installation

1. Install new ball joint using three bolts.
2. Reverse removal steps 1–5 to install. Tighten all fasteners to specifications.
3. Check toe setting. Adjust as required.

Control Arm

Removal

1. Raise car and remove wheel and tire.
2. Disconnect stabilizer bar from control arm and/or support.
3. Separate knuckle from ball joint using tool J 29330.
4. Remove control arm/support.

Installation

1. Install control arm/support.

2. When installing support, install the center bolts first.
3. Install ball joint to knuckle.
4. Install wheel and tire.
5. Lower car. Check toe seating, adjust as required.

Hub and Bearing

Removal

NOTE   The car must not be moved while the driveshaft is out of the hub-and-bearing, nor until the hub nut is installed to final torque.

1. Loosen hub nut.
2. Raise car. Remove wheel and tire.
3. Install boot cover J-28712.

Hub and Bearing Assembly Removal and Installation

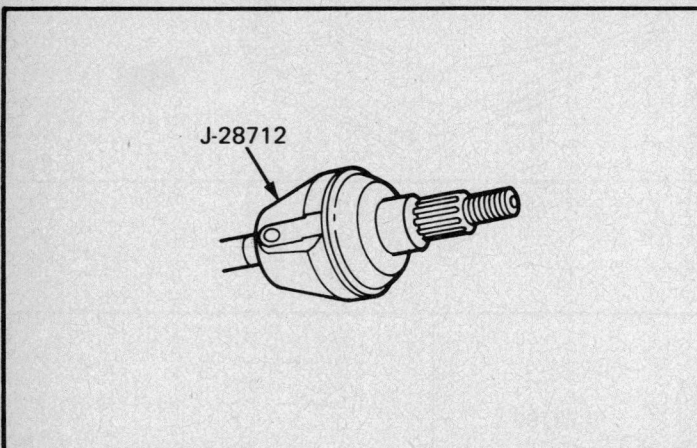

Install drive axle cover

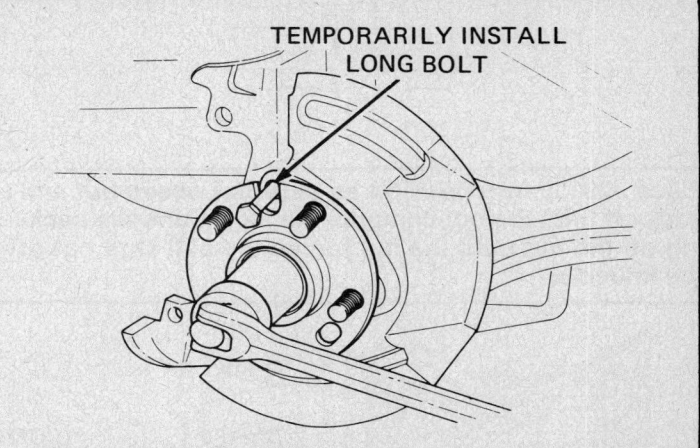

Using long bolt for installing hub nut

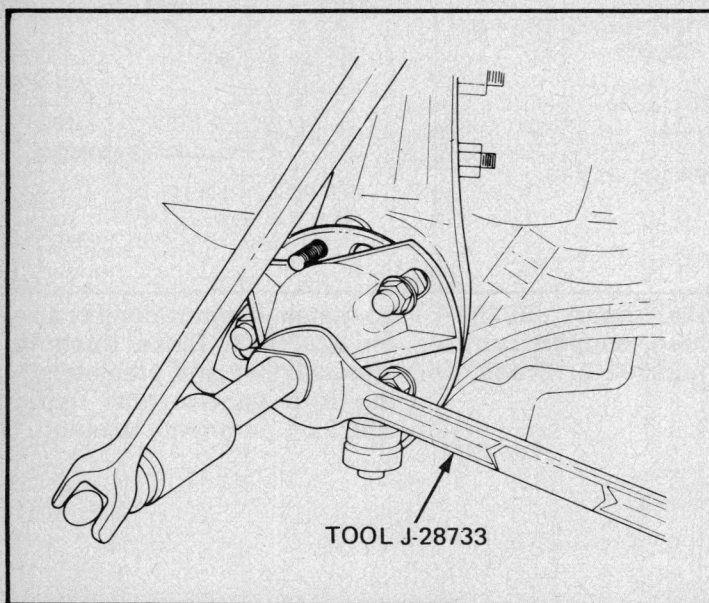

Remove hub and bearing assembly

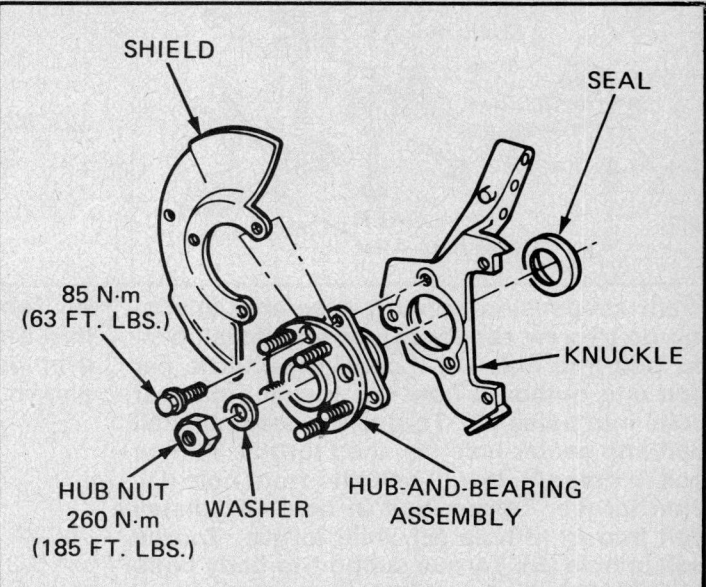

B596

Knuckle Removal and Installation

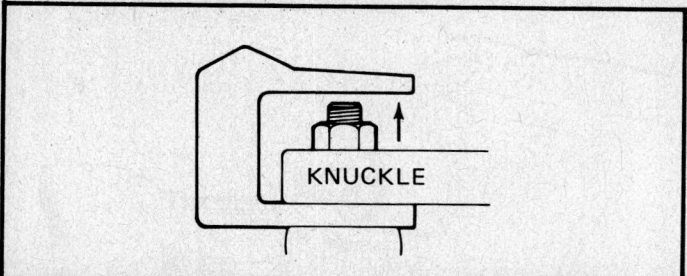

Place J29330 into position as shown. Loosen nut and back off until the nut contacts the tool.

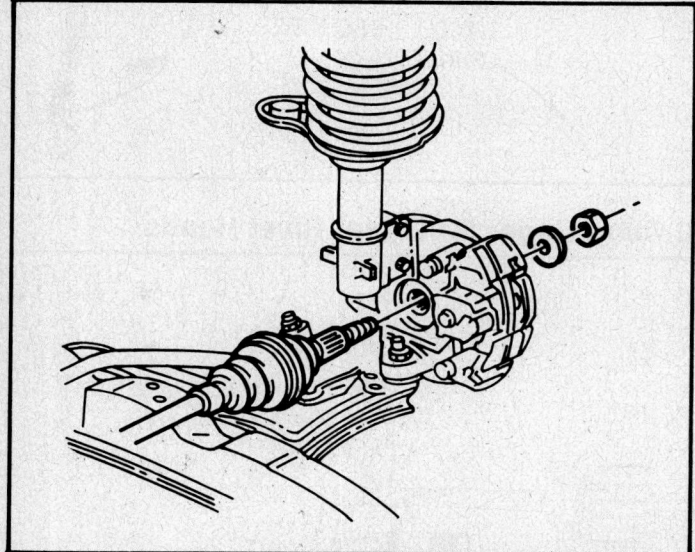

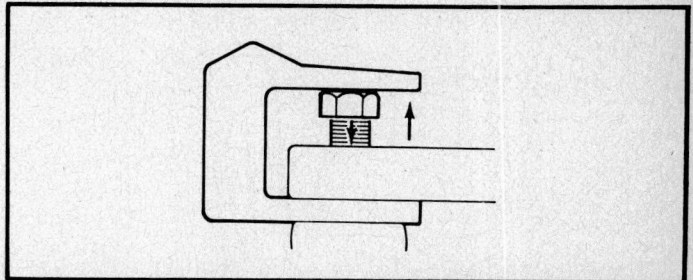

Continue backing off the nut until the nut forces the ball stud out of the knuckle.

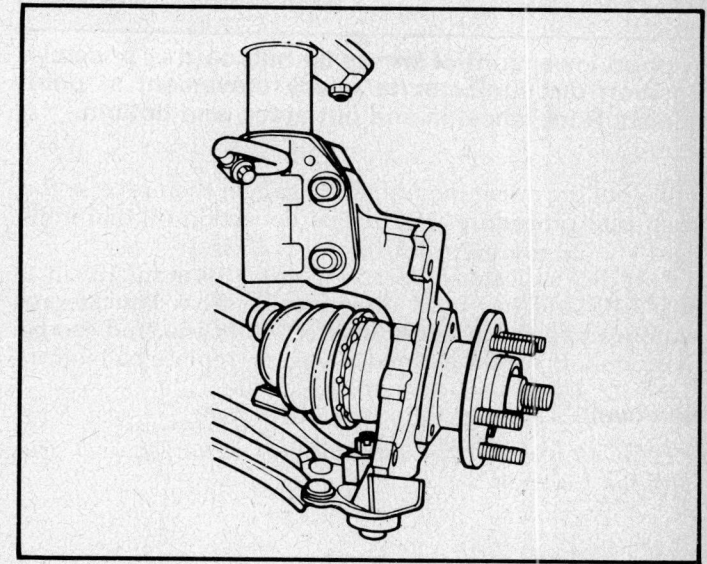

4. Remove hub nut.

5. Remove caliper and rotor.

6. Remove hub-and-bearing mounting bolts. Remove shield. If bearing assembly is to be re-used, mark attaching bolt and corresponding hole for installation in the same position.

7. Install tool J-28733, and turn bolt to press the hub-and-bearing assembly off of the drive shaft. If excessive corrosion is present, make sure the hub-and-bearing is loose in the knuckle before using J-28733.

8. If installing a new bearing assembly, replace the steering knuckle seal, using tool J-22388.

Installation

1. Clean and inspect bearing mating surfaces and steering knuckle bore for dirt, knicks and burrs.

2. If installing knuckle seal, apply grease to seal and to bore of knuckle.

3. Replace parts in reverse order of removal. When attaching hub-and-bearing mounting bolts, use one long bolt to extend through cut-out. This will serve as a reaction point to allow enough torque on hub nut to seat axle shaft into bearing. After tightening hub nut to 100 N•m

(70 ft.-lbs.), remove long bolt and replace with normal bolt.

4. Lower car. Apply final torque to hub nut, 260 N•m (185 ft.-lbs.).

Steering Knuckle

Removal

1. Hoist car. Remove wheel and tire.

2. Remove front wheel hub-and-bearing.

3. Disconnect ball joint from knuckle, using tool J-29330.

4. Remove both strut-to-knuckle mounting bolts. Remove steering knuckle.

Installation

1. Install both strut-to-knuckle mounting bolts loosely.

2. Install knuckle to ball joint. Torque ball joint nut to 75 N•m (55 ft.-lbs.). Install cotter pin.

3. Tighten mounting bolts to 200 N•m (140 ft.-lbs.).

4. Install remaining components.

SUSPENSION

FRONT SUSPENSION-GENERAL MOTORS J BODY

Upper Ball Joint Check

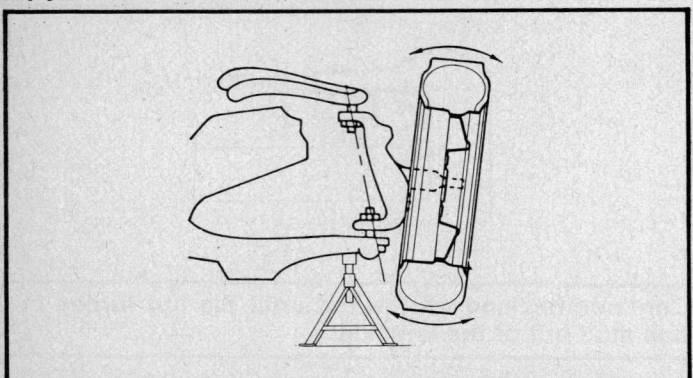

Support lower control arm as far outboard as possible. Position dial indicator to check movement at point shown. Rock wheel in and out at top and bottom.

while pulling out at the top. Read gauge, then reverse the push-pull procedure. Horizontal deflection on dial indicator should not exceed 3.18 mm (1.25 in.).

4. If dial indicator reading exceeds 3.18 mm (.125 in.), or if ball stud has been disconnected from knuckle assembly and any looseness is detected, or the stud can be twisted in its socket with your fingers, replace ball joint.

Removal

1. Raise front of car and support lower control arm with floor stands.

Disconnecting Upper Ball Joint

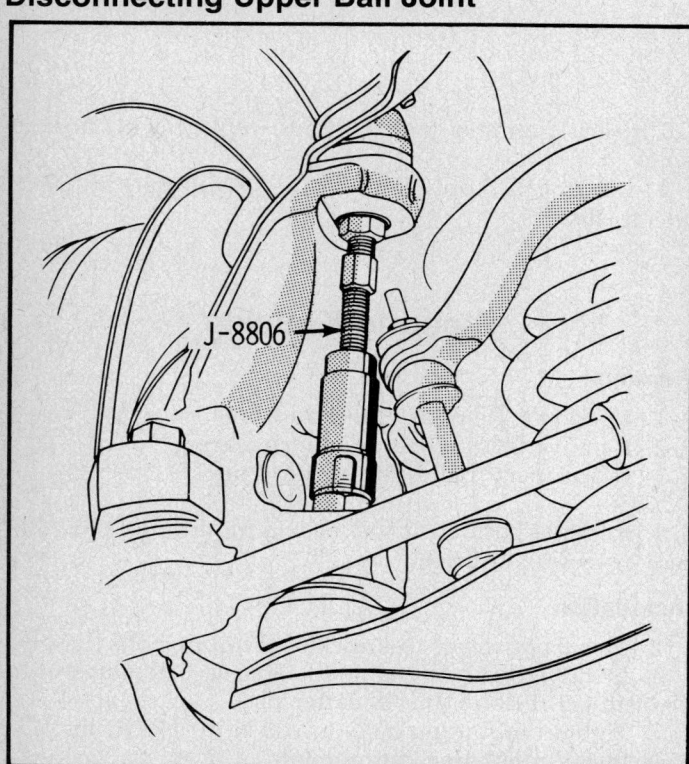

J-8806

Drilling Upper Ball Joint Rivet

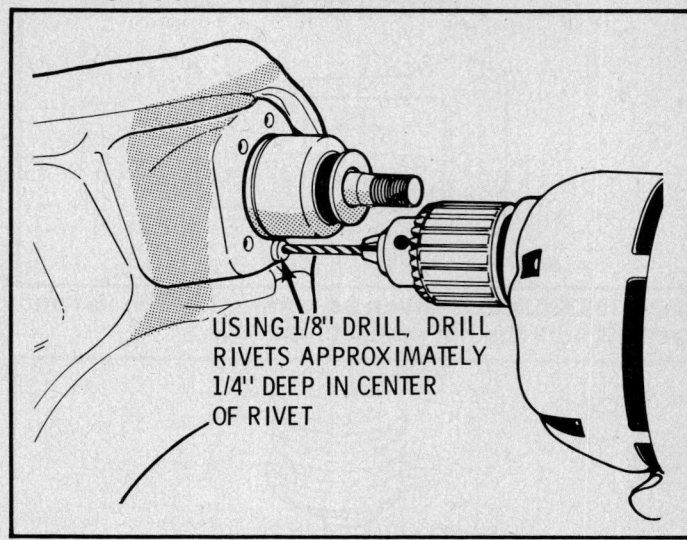

USING 1/8" DRILL, DRILL RIVETS APPROXIMATELY 1/4" DEEP IN CENTER OF RIVET

Drilling Upper Ball Joint Rivet Heads

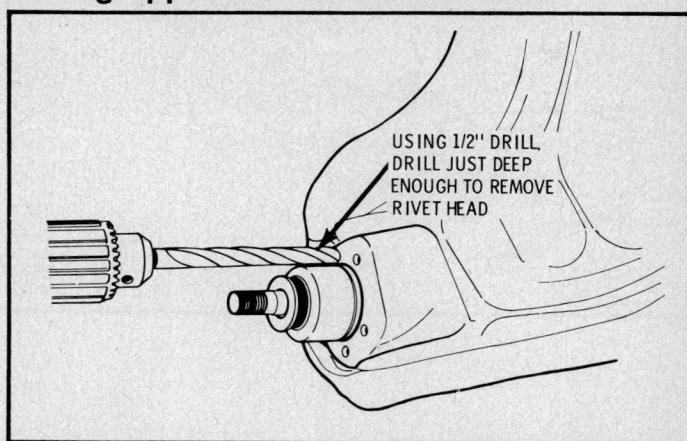

USING 1/2" DRILL, DRILL JUST DEEP ENOUGH TO REMOVE RIVET HEAD

Upper Ball Joint Removal

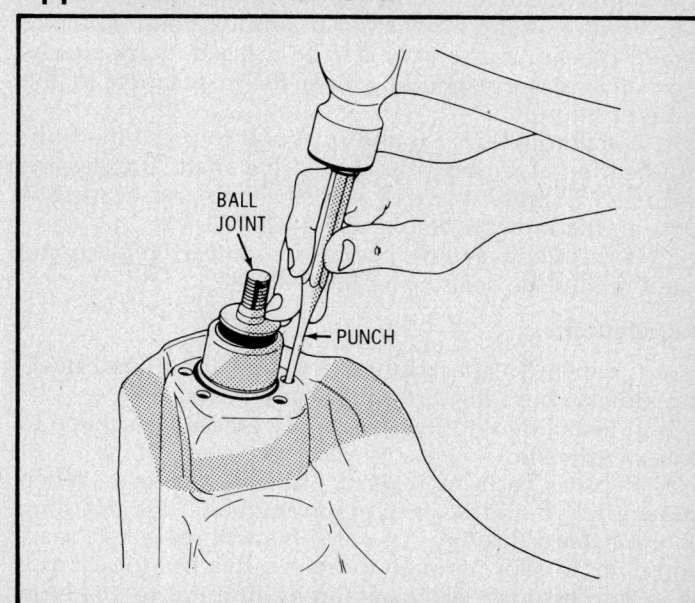

BALL JOINT

PUNCH

Lower Ball Joint Wear Indicator

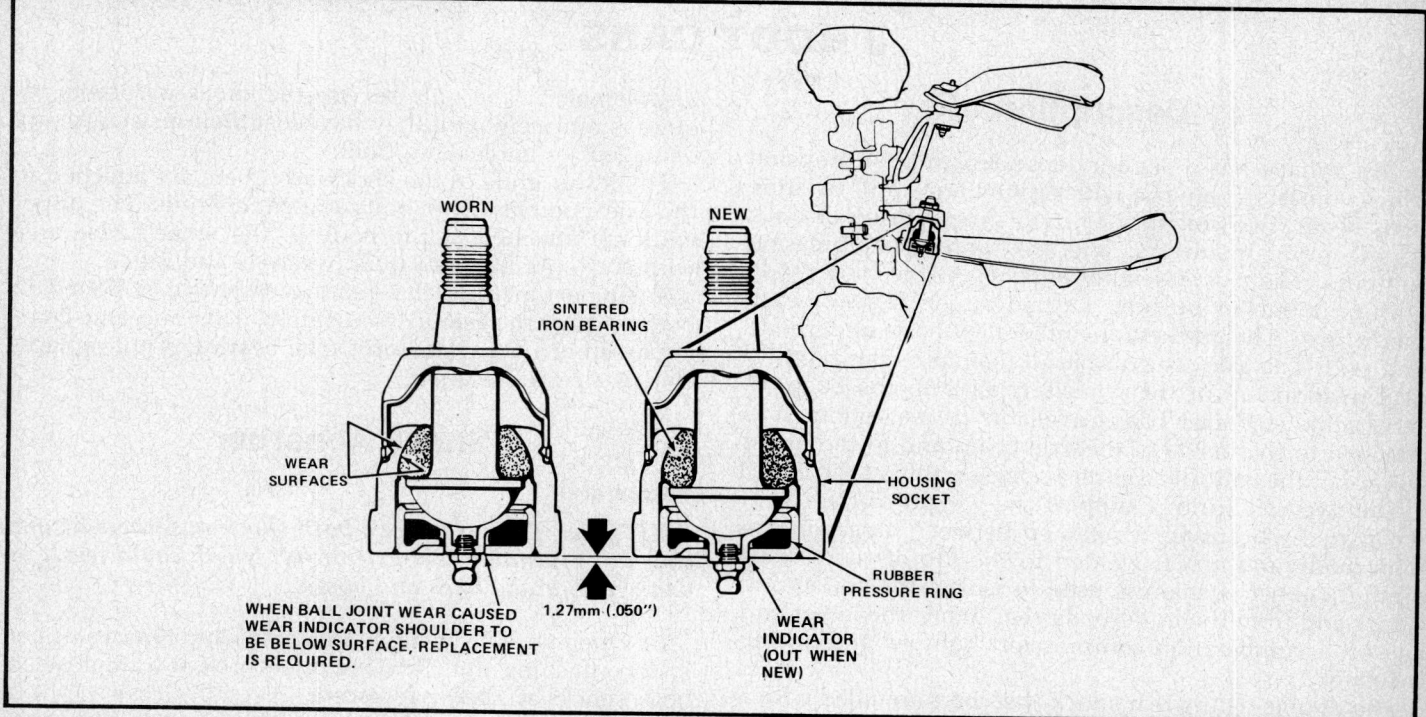

WORN

NEW

SINTERED IRON BEARING

WEAR SURFACES

HOUSING SOCKET

WHEN BALL JOINT WEAR CAUSED WEAR INDICATOR SHOULDER TO BE BELOW SURFACE, REPLACEMENT IS REQUIRED.

1.27mm (.050")

RUBBER PRESSURE RING

WEAR INDICATOR (OUT WHEN NEW)

CAUTION   Floor jack or stand must remain under control arm spring seat during removal and installation to retain spring and control arm in position.

Since the weight of the car is used to relieve spring tension on the upper control arm, the floor stands must be positioned between the spring seats and ball joints of the lower control arms for maximum leverage.

2. Remove wheel, then loosen the upper ball joint from the steering knuckle as follows:

a. Remove upper ball joint nut and install push tool.

b. Apply pressure on stud by expanding the tool until the stud breaks loose.

3. Remove tool and upper ball joint nut, then pull stud from knuckle. Support the knuckle assembly to prevent weight of the assembly from damaging the brake hose.

4. With control arm in the raised position, drill four rivets ¼ in. deep using a ⅛ in. diameter drill.

5. Drill off rivet heads using a ½ in. diameter drill.

6. Punch out rivets using a small punch, and remove ball joint.

Installation

1. Position new ball joint in control arm and install the four attaching bolts. Torque nuts to 11 N•m (8 ft.-lbs.).

2. Connect ball joint to steering knuckle. Torque nut to 40 N•m (30 ft.-lbs.).

Lower Ball Joint

Inspection

Car must be supported by the wheels so weight of car will properly load the ball joints.

The lower ball joint is inspected for wear by visual observation alone. Wear is indicated by the protrusion of the 12.7 mm (½ in.) diameter nipple into which the grease fitting is threaded. This round nipple projects 1.27 mm (.050 in.) beyond the surface of the ball joint cover on a new, unworn joint. Normal wear will result in the surface of this nipple retreating very slowly inward.

Disconnecting Lower Ball Joint

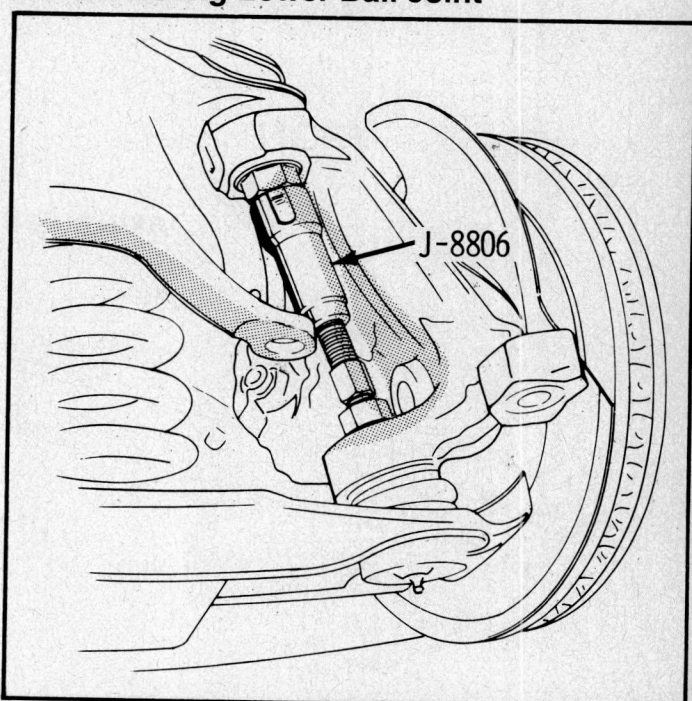

J-8806

REAR SUSPENSION—GENERAL MOTORS J BODY CARS

Description

This vehicle has a semi-independent rear suspension which consists of an axle with trailing arms and twisting cross beam, two coil springs, two shock absorbers, two upper spring insulators, and two spring compression bumpers. The axle assembly attaches to the underbody through a rubber bushing located at the front of each control arm. The brackets are integral with the underbody side rails. The axle structure itself maintains the geometrical relationship of the wheels relative to the body. A serviceable stabilizer bar is available as an option. It is attached to the inside of the axle beam and to the lower surface of the control arms as a subassembly of the axle.

The two coil springs support the weight of the car in the rear. Each spring is retained between a seat in the underbody and a seat welded to the top of the control arm. A rubber cushion is used to isolate the coil spring upper end from the underbody seat, while the lower end sits on a combination compression bumper and spring insulator.

The double-acting rear shock absorbers are filled with a calibrated amount of fluid, and sealed during production. They are non-adjustable, non-refillable, and cannot be disassembled. The only service the shock absorbers require is replacement if they have lost their resistance, are damaged, or are leaking fluid.

The lower ends of the shock absorbers are attached to the axle assembly, with bolts and paddle nuts. The upper ends are attached to the body in the wheelhouse area with conventional insulators, washers and nuts.

A single unit hub-and-bearing assembly is bolted to both ends of the rear axle assembly. This hub-and-bearing assembly is a sealed unit. The bearing is not replaceable as a separate unit.

Shock Absorber

Removal

CAUTION   Do not remove both shock absorbers at one time as suspending rear axle at full length could result in damage to brake lines and hoses.

1. Open deck lid, remove trim cover and remove upper shock attaching nut. Remove one shock at a time when both shocks are being replaced.
2. Raise vehicle on hoist and support rear axle assembly. When lifting vehicle with body hoist it will be

Shock Insulator

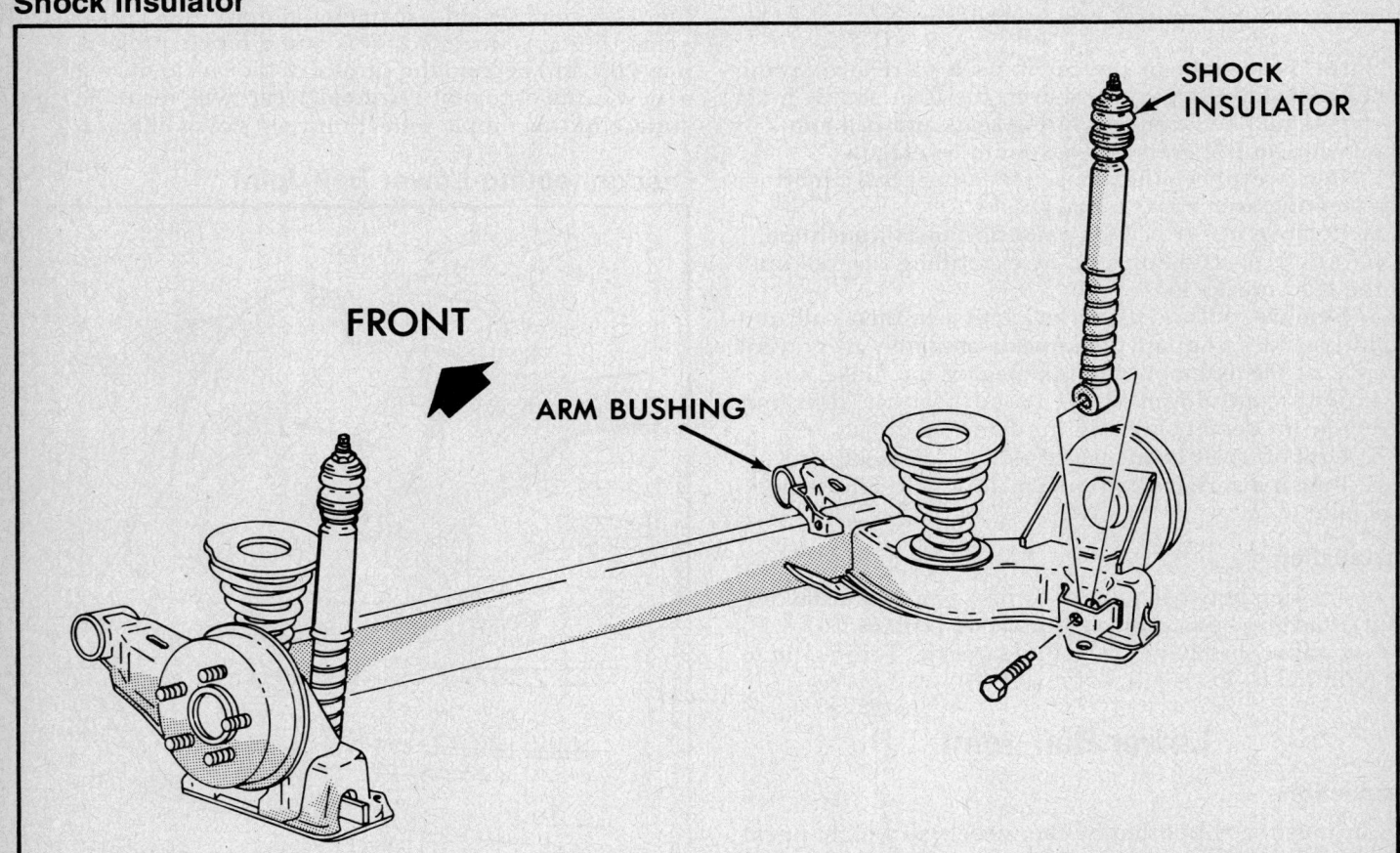

Shock Absorber and Stabilizer Bar Attachment

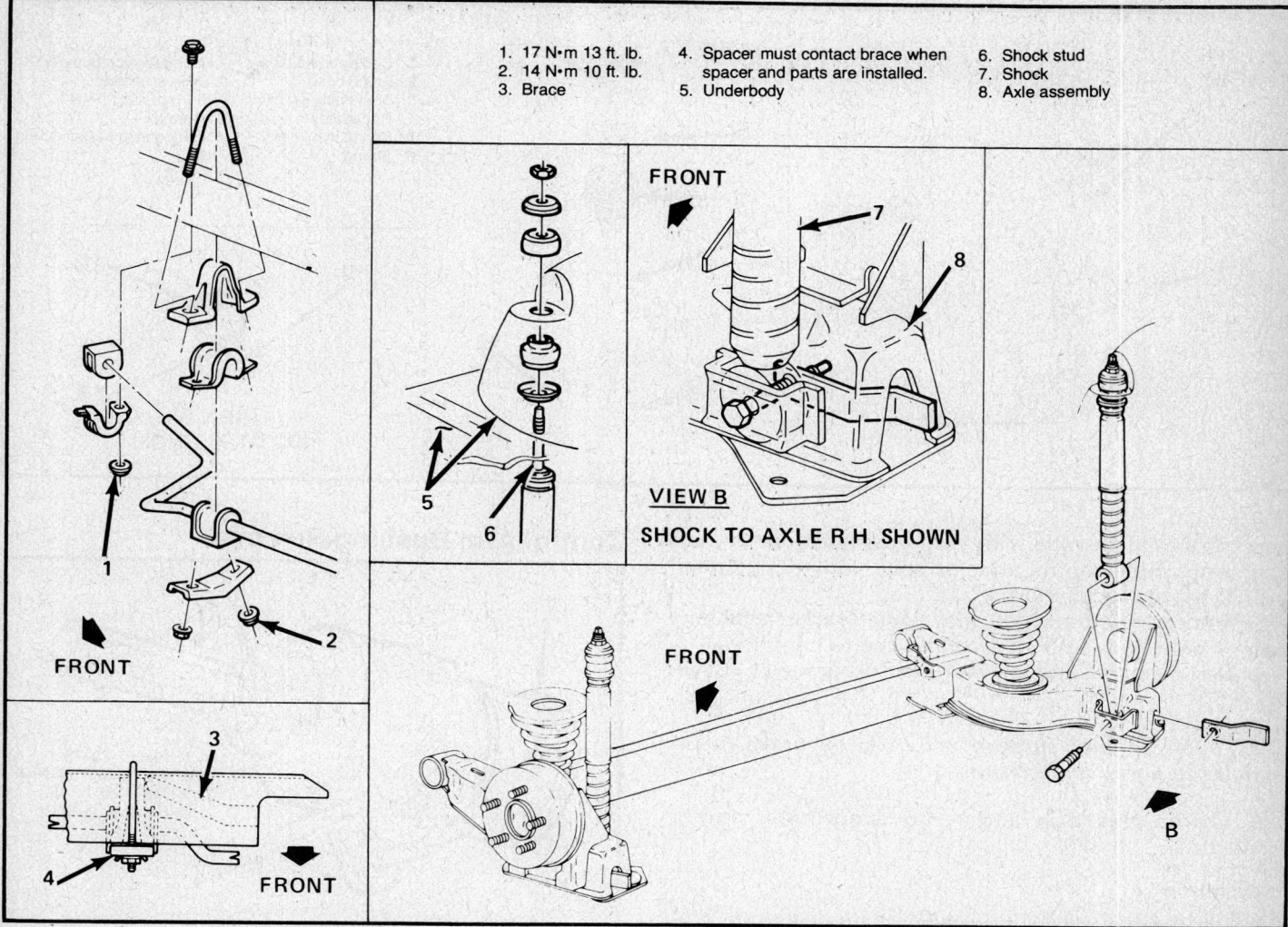

1. 17 N•m 13 ft. lb.
2. 14 N•m 10 ft. lb.
3. Brace
4. Spacer must contact brace when spacer and parts are installed.
5. Underbody
6. Shock stud
7. Shock
8. Axle assembly

VIEW B
SHOCK TO AXLE R.H. SHOWN

necessary to support rear axle with adjustable jack stands. When lifting vehicle with suspension hoist care should be taken to align axle on the hoist prior to lifting.

3. Remove lower attaching bolt and nut and remove shock.

Installation

1. Install shock absorbers at lower attachment, feed bolt through holes and loosely install paddle nut.
2. Lower vehicle enough to guide upper stud through body opening and install nut loosely.
3. Torque lower bolt to 55 N•m (41 ft.-lbs.).
4. Remove axle support and lower car all the way and torque upper nut. Torque to 17 N•m (13 ft.-lbs.).
5. Replace rear trim cover.

Stabilizer Bar

Removal

1. Raise vehicle on host and support body with jack stands.
2. Remove nuts and bolts at both the axle and control arm attachments and remove bracket, insulator and stabilizer bar.

Installation

1. Install U-bolts, upper clamp, spacer and insulator in trailing axle. Position stabilizer bar in insulators and loosely install lower clamp and nuts.
2. Attach the end of stabilizer bar to control arms and torque all nuts to 17 N•m (13 ft.-lbs.).
3. Torque axle attaching nut to 14 N•m (10 ft.-lbs.).
4. Lower vehicle and remove from hoist.

Springs and Insulators

Removal

CAUTION When removing rear springs do not use a twin-post type hoist. The swing arc tendency of the rear axle assembly when certain fasteners are removed may cause it to slip from the hoist. Perform operation on floor is necessary.

1. Raise vehicle using frame contact type hoist if possible and support rear control arms with jack stands. If

Coil Spring and Brake Line Bracket Attachment

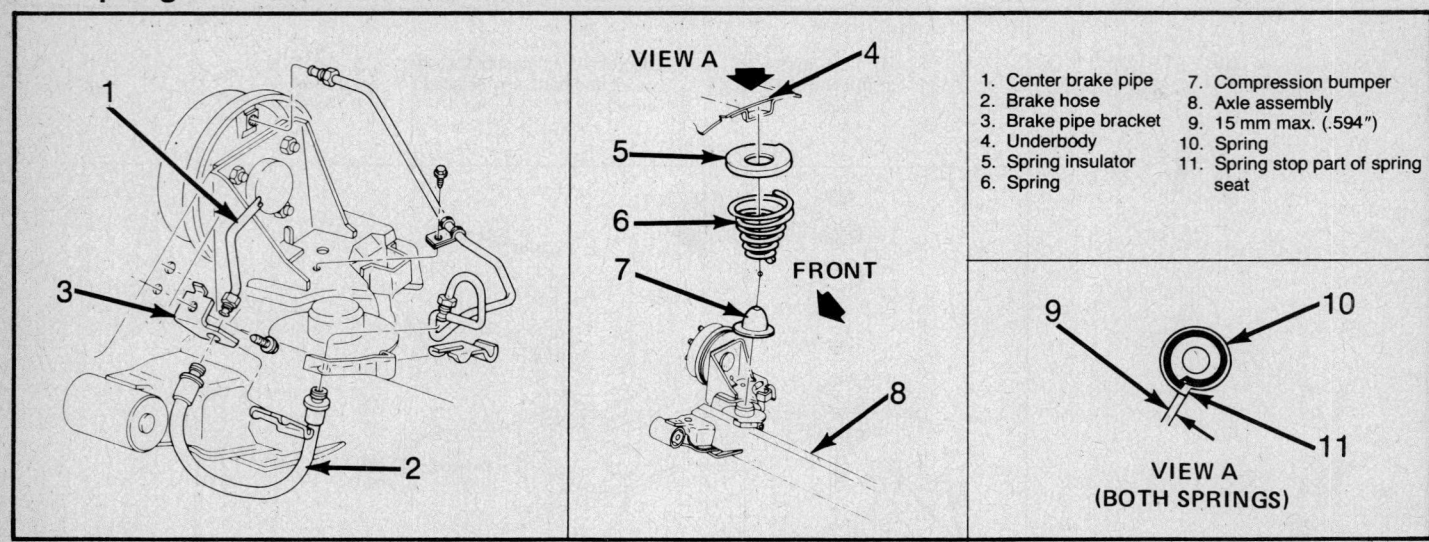

1. Center brake pipe	7. Compression bumper
2. Brake hose	8. Axle assembly
3. Brake pipe bracket	9. 15 mm max. (.594")
4. Underbody	10. Spring
5. Spring insulator	11. Spring stop part of spring
6. Spring	seat

necessary to lift vehicle with twin post hoist, lift by tires and support the control arms or body with jack stands.

2. Remove wheel and tire assembly.

3. Remove right and left brake line bracket attaching screws from body and allow brake line to hang free.

4. Remove right and left shock absorber lower attaching bolts.

CAUTION Do not suspend rear axle by brake hoses. Damage to hoses could result.

5. Lower rear axle and remove spring(s) and/or insulator(s).

Installation

1. Position springs and insulators in seats and raise axle. The ends of the upper coil on the spring must be positioned in the seat of the body. Prior to installing spring it will be necessary to install upper insulators to the body with adhesive to keep it in position while raising the axle assembly and springs.

2. Connect shocks to rear axle and torque bolts to 55 N•m (41 ft.-lbs.). It will be necessary to bring the axle assembly to standing height prior to torquing bolts on the shocks.

3. Install brake line brackets to body and torque screws to 11 N•m (8 ft.-lbs.).

4. Install wheel and tire assembly. Torque lug nuts to 140 N•m (102 ft.-lbs.).

5. Remove jack stands and lower vehicle.

Control Arm Bushing

Removal

1. Raise vehicle on hoist.

2. Remove wheel and tire assembly and support body with jack stands.

3. If removing right bushing, disconnect brake line from body. If left bushing is being removed, disconnect

Control Arm Bushing Removal

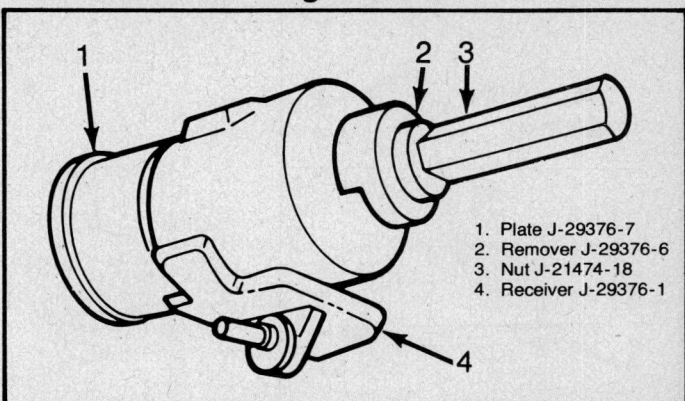

1. Plate J-29376-7
2. Remover J-29376-6
3. Nut J-21474-18
4. Receiver J-29376-1

brake line bracket from body, and parking brake cable from hook guide on the body. Replace only one bushing at a time.

4. Remove nut, bolt and washer from the control arm and bracket attachment, and rotate control arm downward.

5. Remove bushing as follows:

a. Install J 29376-1 on control arm over bushing and tighten attaching nuts until tool is securely in place.

b. Install J 21474-19 bolt through plate J 29376-7 and install into J 29376-1 receiver.

c. Place J 29376-6 remover into position on bushing and install nut J 21474-18 onto J 21474-19 bolt.

d. Remove bushing from control arm by turning bolt.

Installation

1. Install bushing on bolt and position into housing. Align bushing installer J 29376-4 arrow with arrow on receiver for proper indexing of bushing.

2. Install nut J 21474-18 onto bolt J 21474-19.

3. Press bushing into control arm by turning bolt. When bushing is in proper position the end flange will be flush against the face of the control arm.

Control Arm Bushing Installation

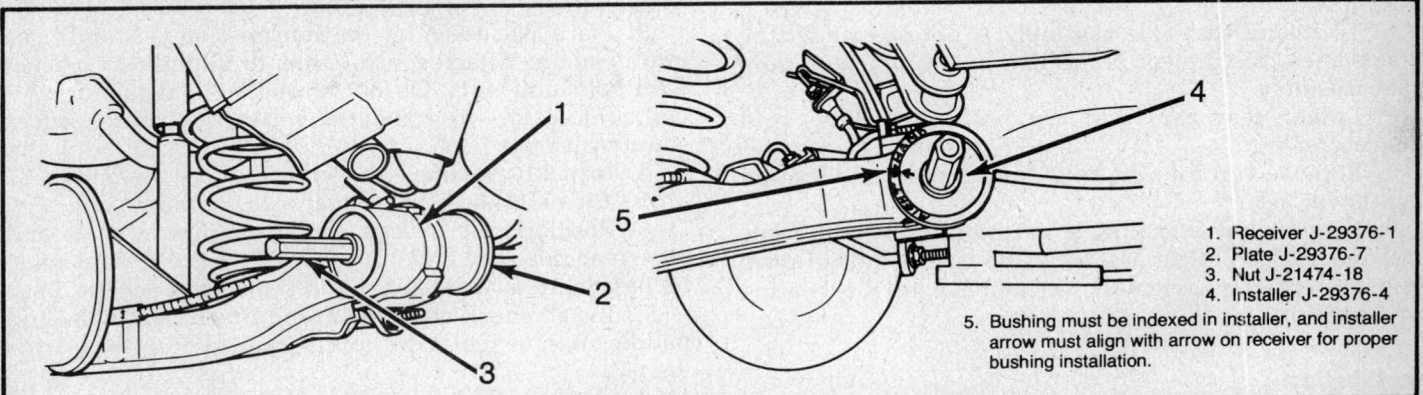

1. Receiver J-29376-1
2. Plate J-29376-7
3. Nut J-21474-18
4. Installer J-29376-4
5. Bushing must be indexed in installer, and installer arrow must align with arrow on receiver for proper bushing installation.

4. Use a screw type jack stand to position control arm into bracket and install bolt and nut. Do not torque bolt at this time. It will be necessary to torque the bolt of the control arm with vehicle at standing height.

5. Install brake line bracket to frame and torque screw to 11 N•m (8 ft.-lbs.).

6. If left side was disconnected, reconnect brake cables to bracket, and reinstall brake cable to hook. Adjust cable as necessary.

7. While supporting vehicle at standing height, tighten control arm bolt to 90 N•m (67 ft.-lbs.).

8. Remove jack stands and install wheel assembly and lower vehicle from hoist.

Hub and Bearing

Removal

1. Raise vehicle on hoist.
2. Remove wheel and tire assembly and brake drum.

CAUTION Do not hammer on brake drum as damage to the assembly could result.

3. Remove hub-and-bearing assembly-to-rear axle attaching bolts and remove hub and bearing assembly from axle. The top rear attaching bolt will not clear the brake shoe when removing the hub-and-bearing assembly. Partially remove hub-and-bearing assembly prior to removing this bolt.

Hub and Bearing Assembly

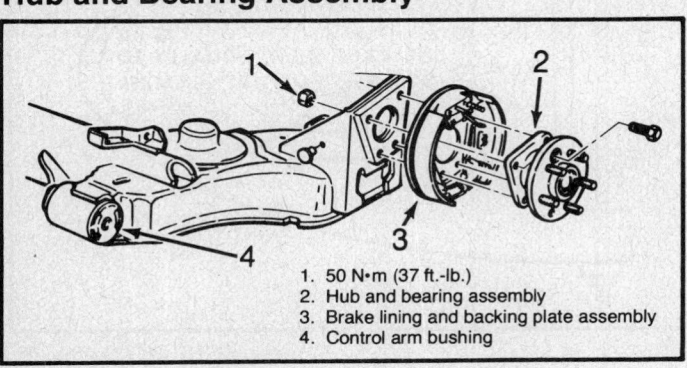

1. 50 N•m (37 ft.-lb.)
2. Hub and bearing assembly
3. Brake lining and backing plate assembly
4. Control arm bushing

Installation

1. Position top rear attaching bolt in hub-and-bearing assembly prior to the installation in the axle assembly.

2. Install remaining bolts and nuts. Torque bolts to 52 N•m (39 ft.-lbs.).

3. Install brake drum, and wheel and tire assembly. Torque lug nuts to 140 N•m (103 ft.-lbs.).

4. Lower vehicle and remove from hoist.

Wheel Stud Removal

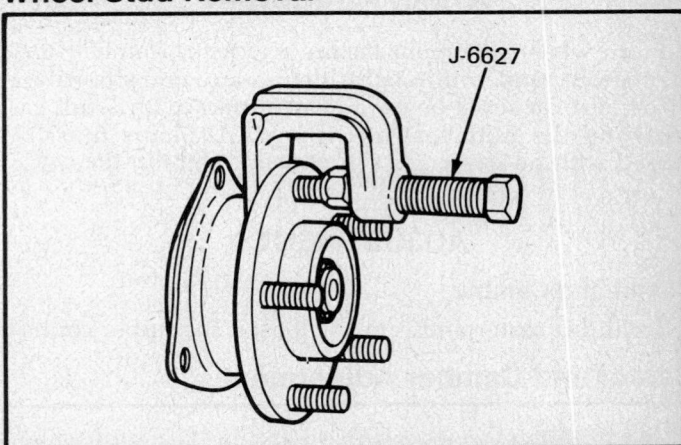

J-6627

Do not remove stud with hammer, as damage to bearing will result.

Rear Axle Assembly

Removal

1. Raise vehicle on hoist and support assembly with jack stands under the control arms.

2. Remove stabilizer bar from axle assembly, if so equipped.

3. Remove wheel and tire assembly and brake drum.

CAUTION Do not hammer on brake drum as damage to the bearing could result.

4. Remove shock absorber lower attaching bolts and paddle nuts at axle and disconnect shocks from control arm.

SUSPENSION

5. Disconnect parking brake cable from the axle assembly.

6. To insure that axle assembly is not suspended by brake lines, disconnect brake line at the brackets from axle assembly.

7. Lower rear axle and remove coil springs and insulators.

8. Remove control arm bolts from underbody bracket and lower axle.

9. Remove hub attaching bolts and remove hub, bearing and backing plate assembly. Be careful not to drop hub and bearing assembly, as damage to the bearing could result.

Installation

1. Install backing plate, and hub-and-bearing assembly to rear axle. Hold nuts and torque bolts to 52 N•m (39 ft.-lbs.).

2. Install stabilizer bar, if so equipped, by attaching nut and bolts to axle assembly and at the end to the control arms.

3. Place axle assembly on transmission jack and raise into position. Attach control arms to underbody bracket with bolts and nuts. Do not torque bolts at this time. It will be necessary to torque the bolt of the control arm at standing height.

4. Install brake line connections to axle assembly.

5. Attach brake cable to rear axle assembly.

6. Position coil springs and insulators in seats and raise rear axle. The end of upper coil on the springs must be parallel to axle assembly and seated in pocket.

7. Install shock absorber lower attachment bolts and paddle nuts to rear axle, torque bolt to 55 N•m (41 ft.-lbs.).

8. Connect parking brake cable to guide hook and adjust as necessary.

9. Install brake drums, wheels and tire assembly. Torque lug nuts to 140 N•m (103 ft.-lbs.).

10. Bleed brake system and refill reservoir.

FRONT SUSPENSION—GENERAL MOTORS REAR DRIVE EXCEPT H AND T BODY CARS

Wheel Alignment

Front wheel alignment factors are caster, camber, toe-in, toe-out, and trim height. Before any corrections are made, the car must be on a level surface with a full gas tank and the front seat to the rear. All doors must be closed with no passengers or excess weight in the car.

ADJUSTMENTS

Caster and Camber

To adjust caster and camber, loosen the upper control arm shaft-to-frame nuts, add or subtract shims as required, and retorque nuts.

A normal shim pack will leave at least two threads of the bolt exposed beyond the nut. The difference between front and rear shim packs must not exceed .40 inches.

If these requirements cannot be met in order to reach specifications, check for damaged control arms and related parts. Always tighten the nut on the thinner shim pack first, for improved shaft-to-frame clamping force and torque retention.

Toe-In

Toe-in can be increased or decreased by changing the

Caster and Camber Adjustment

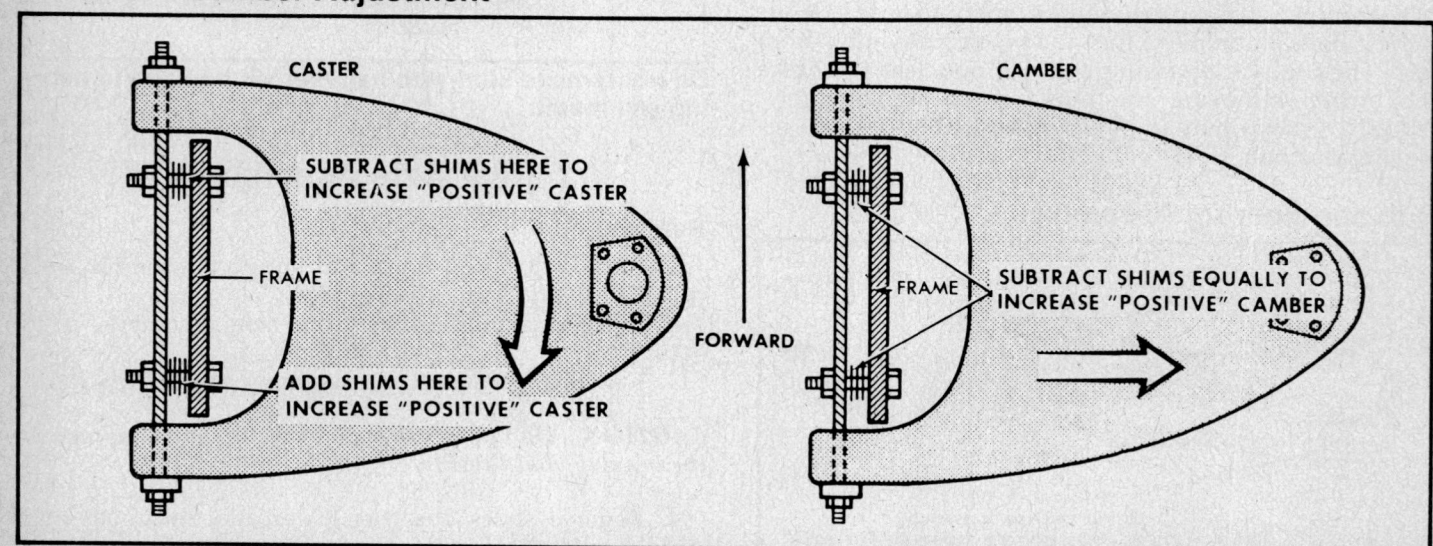

Pivot shaft inboard of frame

Front Suspension

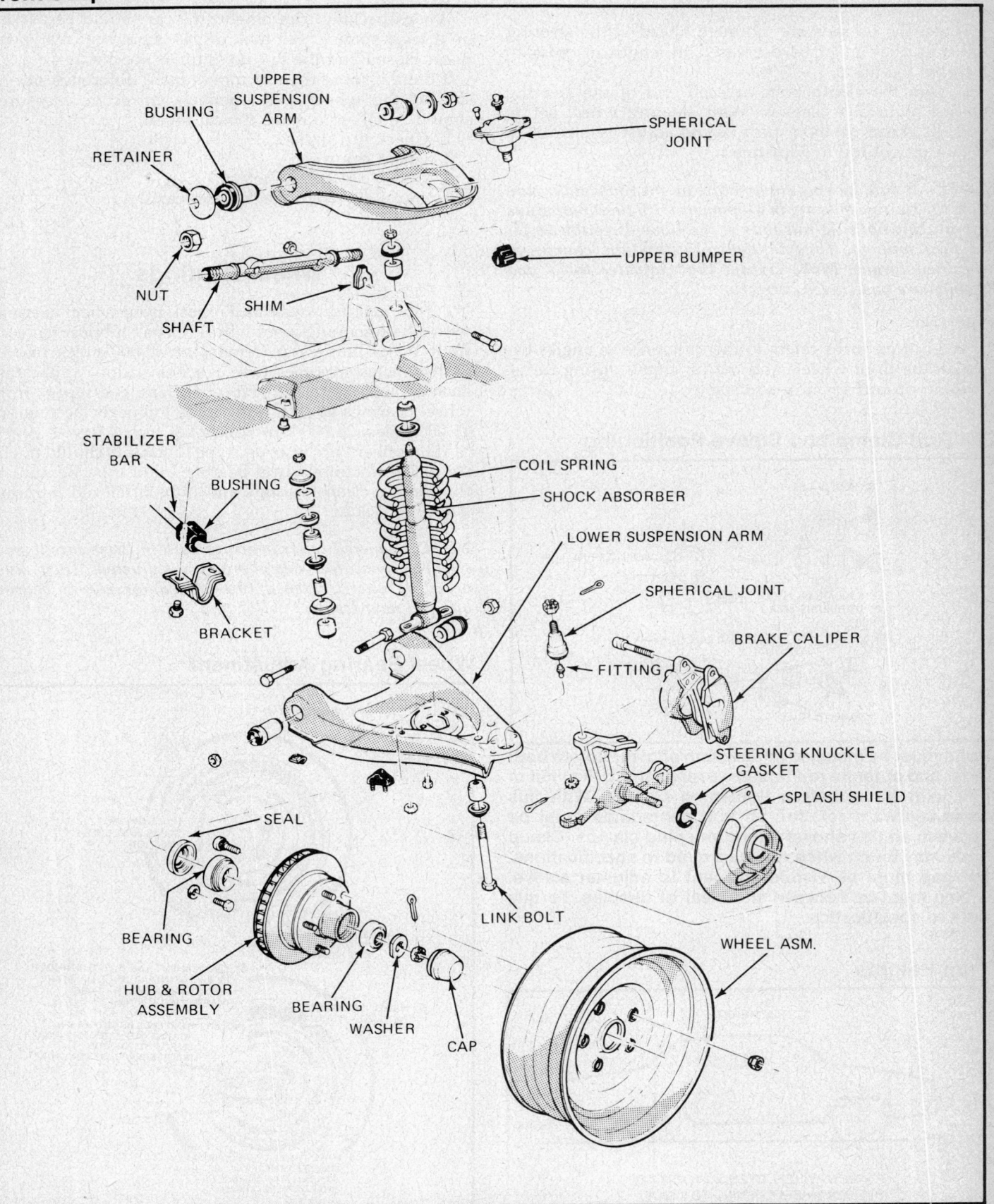

length of the tie-rods. A threaded sleeve is provided for this purpose.

When the tie-rods are mounted ahead of the steering knuckle, they must be decreased in length in order to increase toe-in.

Loosen the clamp bolts at each end of the steering tie-rod adjustable sleeves. With steering wheel set in straight ahead position, turn tie-rod adjusting sleeves to obtain proper toe-in adjustment.

NOTE   Before locking clamp bolts on the rods, make sure that the tie-rod ends are in alignment with their ball studs by rotating both tie-rod ends in the same direction as far as they will go. Then tighten adjuster tube clamps to specified torque. Make certain that adjuster tubes and clamps are positioned correctly.

Toe-Out

Toe-out on turns refers to the difference in angles between the front wheels and the car frame during turns. Toe-out on turns is non-adjustable.

Tie Rod Clamp and Sleeve Positioning

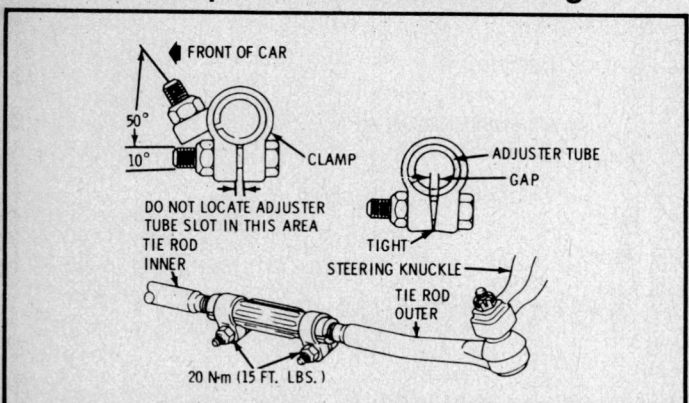

Bolts must be installed in direction shown. Rotate both inner and outer tie rod housings rearward to the limit of ball joint travel before tightening clamps. With this same rearward rotation all bolt centerlines must be between angles shown after tightening clamps. Clamp ends may touch when nut is torqued to specifications, but gap must be visible adjacent to adjuster sleeve. Clamp must be between and clear of dimples. Torque nuts to specification.

Trim Heights

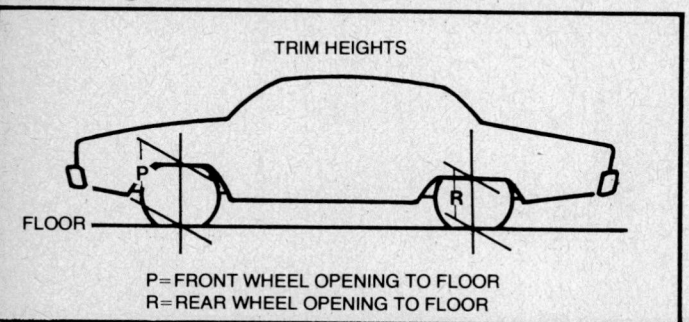

Trim Height

When checking trim height, the car should be parked on a level surface, full tank of gas, front seat rearward, doors closed and the tire pressure as specified.

If there is more than 24 mm (1 inch) difference side to side at the wheel well opening, corrective measures should be taken to make the car level.

1. Check tire sizes.
2. Check tire wear.
3. Check coil spring height.
4. Check for worn suspension parts.

Wheel Bearings

For normal use, clean and repack front wheel bearings with a high melting point wheel bearing lubricant at each front brake lining replacement or 30,000 miles (48,000 km), whichever comes first. For heavy duty application such as police cars and taxi cabs, clean and repack front wheel bearings at each front brake lining replacement or 15,000 miles (24,000 km) whichever comes first.

"Long fiber" or "viscous" type lubricants should not be used. Do not mix wheel bearing lubricants. Be sure to thoroughly clean bearings and hubs of all old lubricant before repacking.

NOTE   Tapered roller bearings used in these cars have a slightly loose feel when properly adjusted. They must never be over-tightened (pre-loaded) or severe bearing damage may result.

Wheel Bearing Adjustment

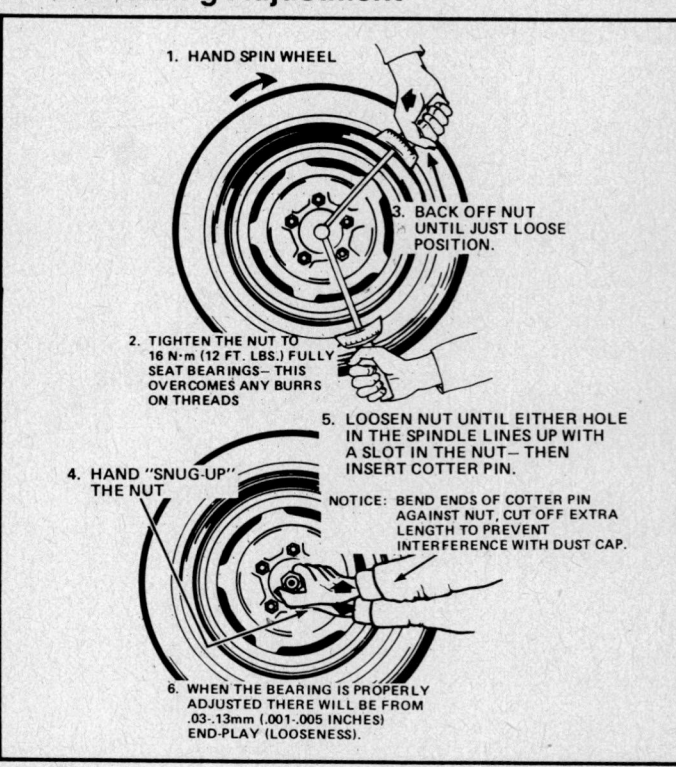

Front Wheel Components

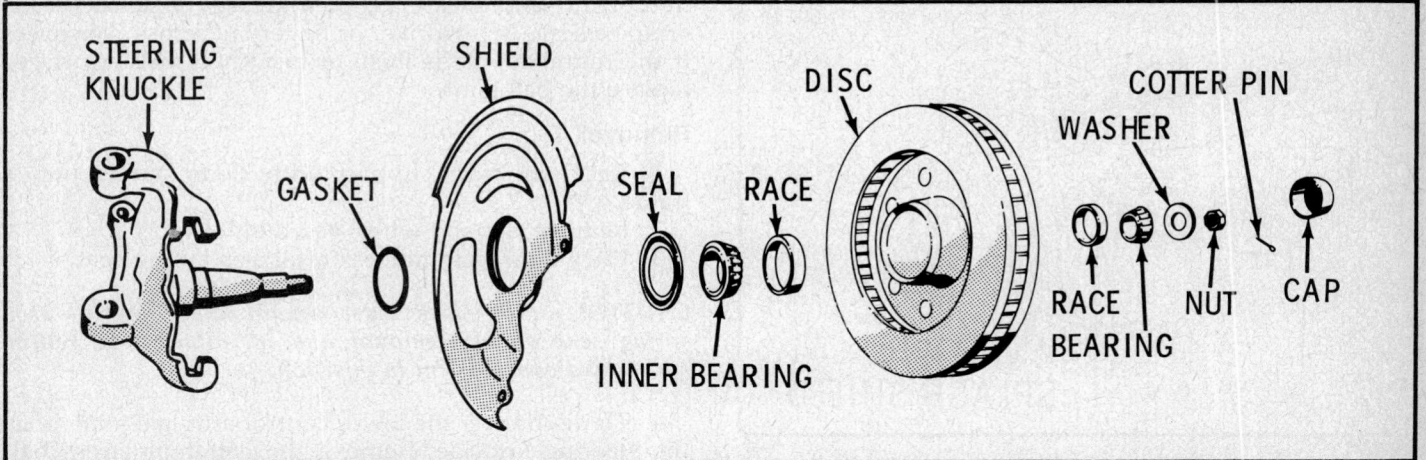

Adjustment

The proper functioning of the front suspension cannot be maintained unless the front wheel taper roller bearings are correctly adjusted. Cones must be a slip fit on the spindle and the inside diameter of cones should be lubricated to insure that the cones will creep. Spindle nut must be a free-running fit on threads.

1. Remove dust cap from hub.
2. Remove cotter pin from spindle and spindle nut.
3. Tighten the spindle nut to 16 N•m (12 ft.-lbs.) while turning the wheel assembly forward by hand to fully seat the bearings. This will remove any grease or burrs which could cause excessive wheel bearing play later.
4. Back off the nut to the "just loose" position.
5. Hand-tighten the spindle nut. Loosen spindle nut until either hole in the spindle lines up with a slot in the nut (not more than ½ flat).
6. Install new cotter pin. Bend the ends of the cotter pin against nut. Cut off extra length to ensure ends will not interfere with the dust cap.
7. Measure the looseness in the hub assembly. There will be from .03 to .13 mm (.001 to .005 inches) end-play when properly adjusted.
8. Install dust cap on hub.

Shock Absorbers

Removal

1. Raise car on hoist, and with an open end wrench hold the shock absorber upper stem from turning. Remove the upper stem retaining nut, retainer and rubber grommet.
2. Remove the two bolts retaining the lower shock absorber pivot to the lower control arm and pull the shock absorber assembly out from the bottom.

Installation

1. With the lower retainer and rubber grommet in place over the upper stem, install the shock absorber (fully extended) up through the lower control arm and spring so that the upper stem passes through the mounting hole in the upper control arm frame bracket.

Shock Absorber Attachment

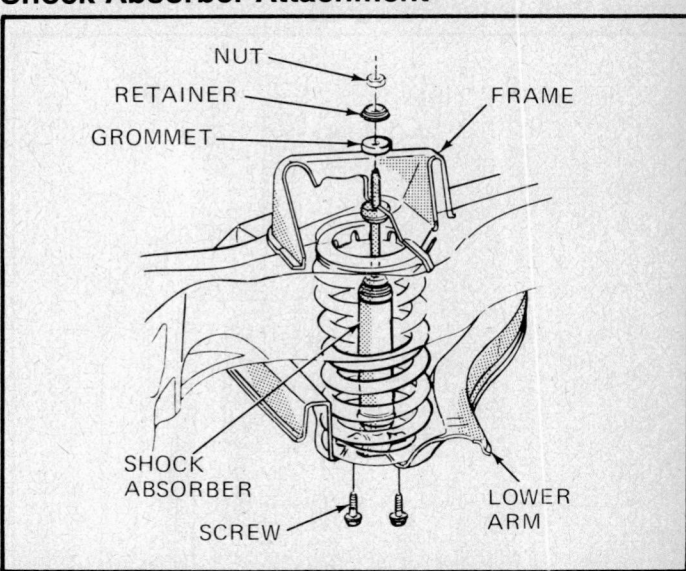

Upper nut torque is 19 N•m (14 ft. lbs.). Lower studs torque is 30 N•m (22 ft. lbs.).

2. Install the upper rubber grommet, retainer and attaching nut over the shock absorber upper stem.
3. With an open end wrench, hold the upper stem from turning and tighten the retaining nut.
4. Install the retainers attaching the shock absorber lower pivot to the lower control arm, torque and lower car to floor.

Upper Ball Joint

Inspection

1. Raise the car and position floor stands under the left and right lower control arm as near as possible to each lower ball joint. Car must be stable and should not rock on the floor stands. Upper control arm bumper must not contact frame.
2. Position dial indicator against the wheel rim.
3. Grasp front wheel and push in on bottom of tire

SUSPENSION

Guiding Lower Control Arm Past Shield

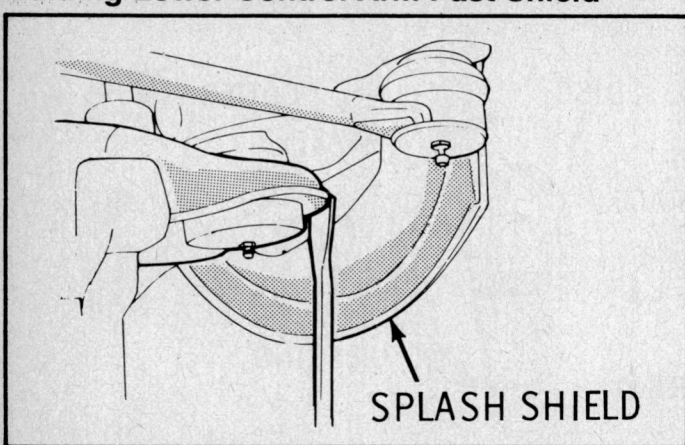

SPLASH SHIELD

Lower Ball Joint Removal

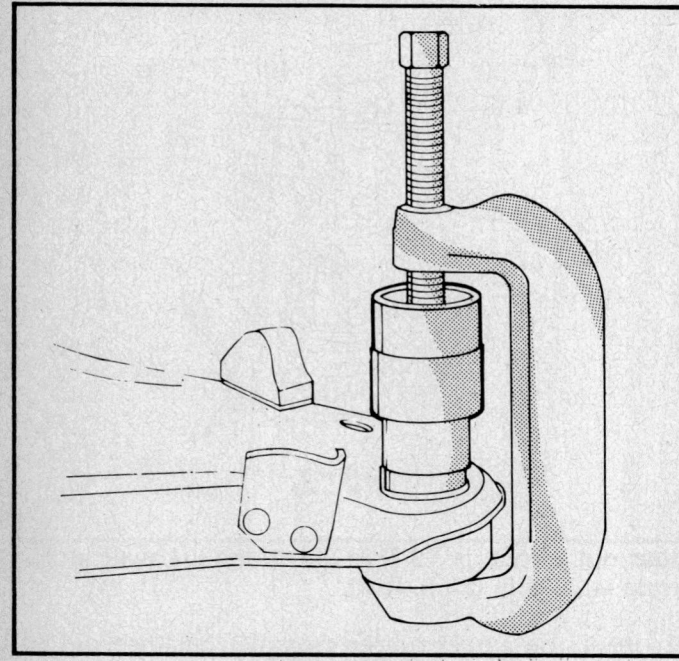

To inspect for wear, wipe the grease fitting and nipple free of dirt and grease as for a grease job. Observe or scrape a scale, screwdriver or fingernail across the cover. If the round nipple is flush or inside the cover surface, replace the ball joint.

Removal

1. Raise the car, support with floor stands under frame.
2. Remove tire and wheel assembly.
3. Place floor jack under control arm spring seat.

CAUTION Floor jack must remain under control arm spring seat during removal and installation to retain spring and control arm in position.

4. To disconnect the lower control arm ball joint from the steering knuckle. Remove the cotter pin from ball joint stud and remove stud nut. Tool J-8806 can be used to break the ball joint loose from knuckle after stud breaks loose.
5. Guide lower control arm out of opening in splash shield with a putty knife or similar tool.
6. Block knuckle assembly out of the way by placing a wooden block between frame and upper control arm.
7. Remove ball joint seal by prying off retainer with a pry bar or driving off with a chisel.
8. Remove grease fittings and install special tool to remove lower ball joint from lower control arm.

Coil Spring

Removal

1. Place transmission in neutral so steering wheel is unlocked.
2. Clean shock upper threads; oil, then remove nut, washer, and grommet.
3. Hoist car. Remove wheel and tire.
4. Remove stabilizer link nut, grommets washers, and bolt.
5. Support car with floor stands.
6. Remove shock.
7. Install coil spring tool. Make sure tool is fully seated into lower control arm spring seat.

Coil Spring Tool

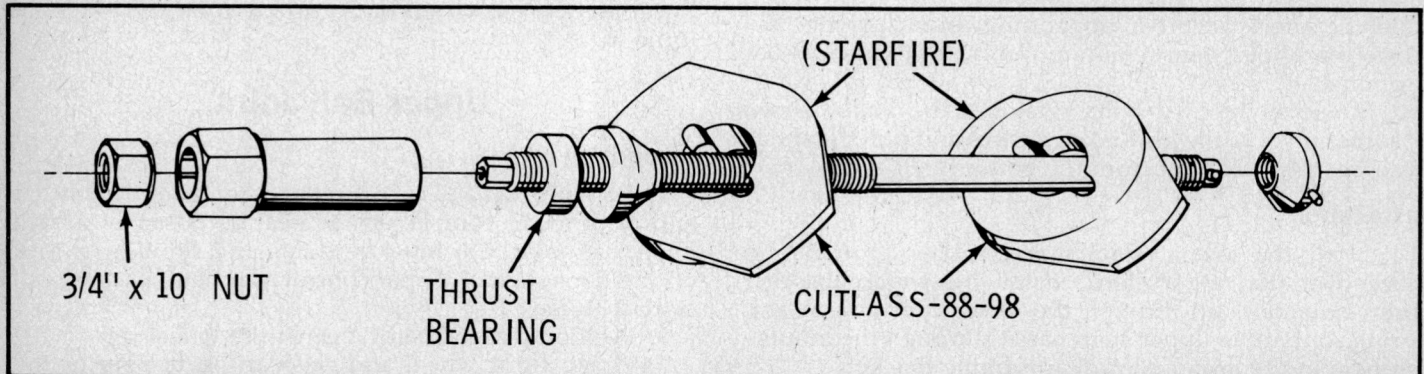

3/4'' x 10 NUT   THRUST BEARING   (STARFIRE)   CUTLASS-88-98

Compressed Coil Spring

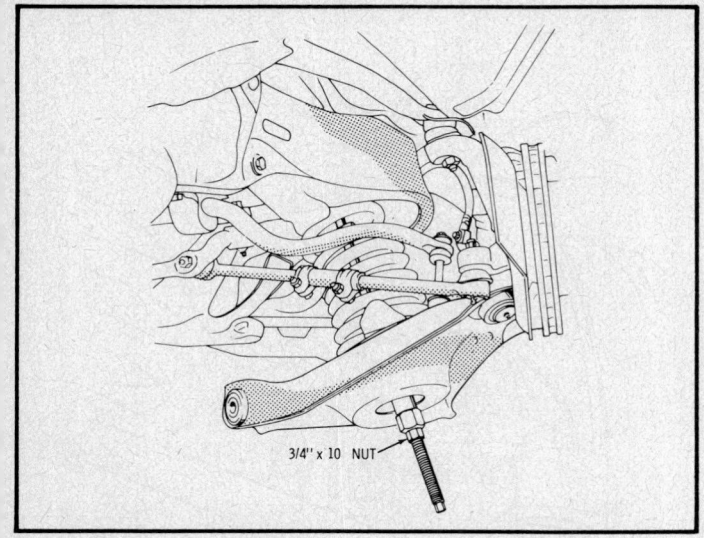

3/4'' x 10 NUT

8. Rotate nut until spring is compressed enough so that it is free in its seat.

9. Remove the two lower control arm pivot bolts and disengage lower control arm from frame. Rotate arm with spring rearward and remove spring from arm.

Spring Compressed On Bench

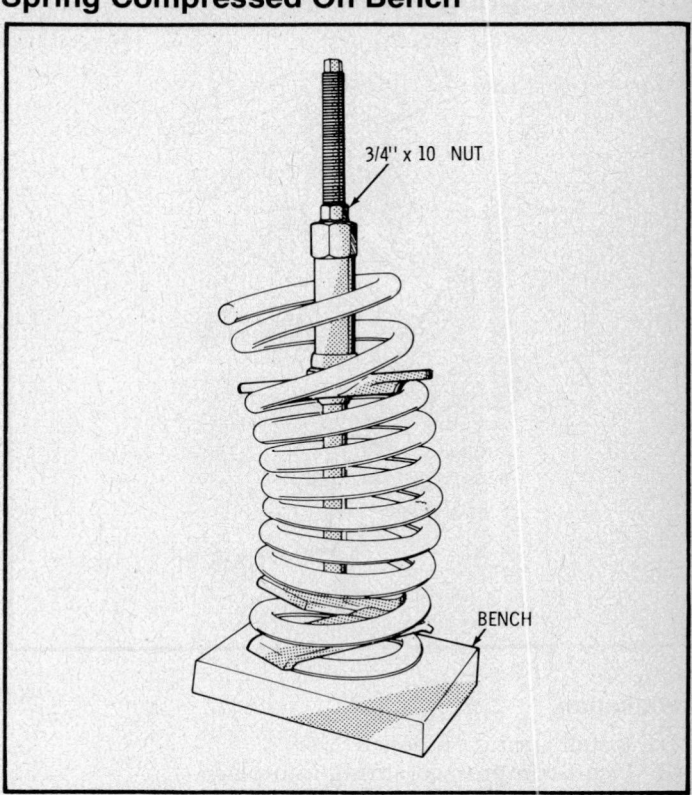

3/4'' x 10 NUT

BENCH

Coil Spring Positioning

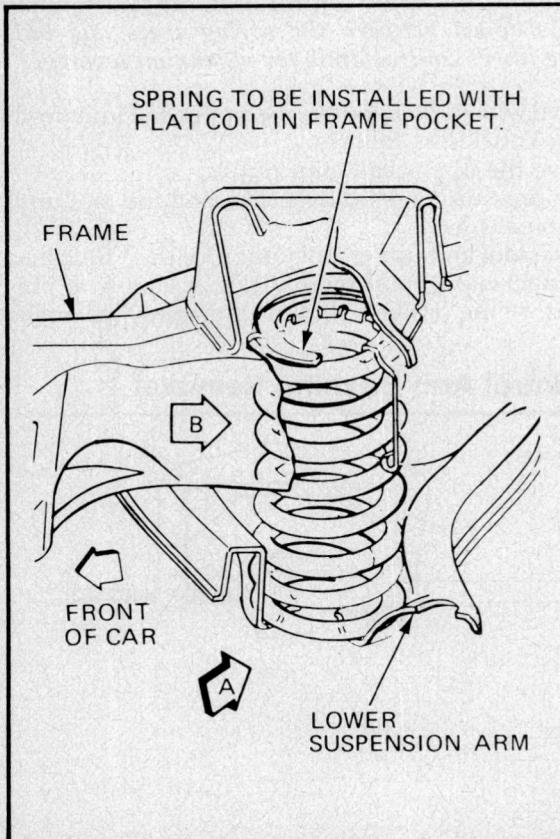

SPRING TO BE INSTALLED WITH FLAT COIL IN FRAME POCKET.

FRAME

B

FRONT OF CAR

A

LOWER SUSPENSION ARM

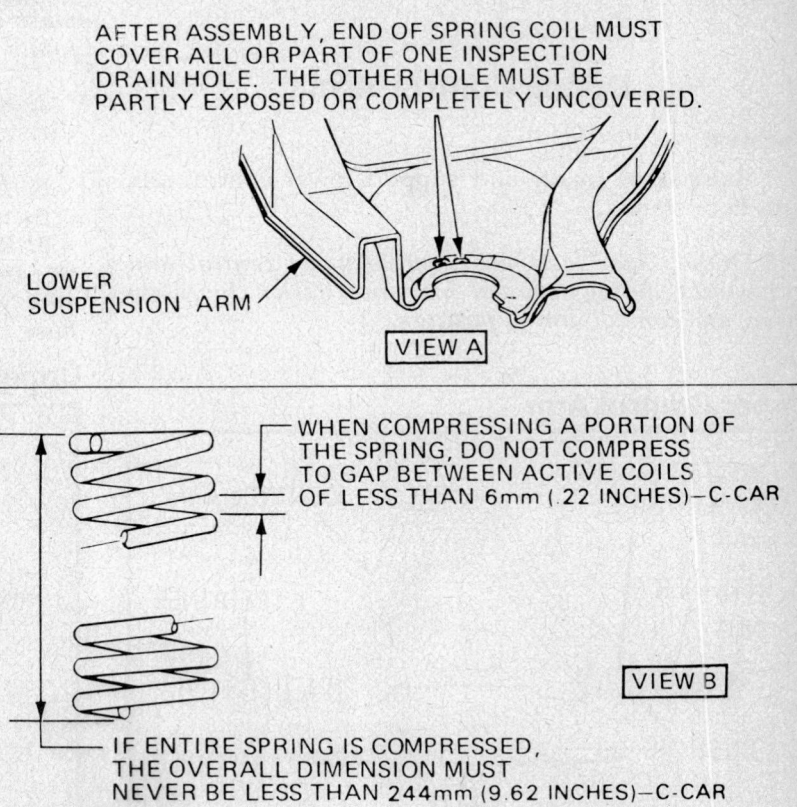

AFTER ASSEMBLY, END OF SPRING COIL MUST COVER ALL OR PART OF ONE INSPECTION DRAIN HOLE. THE OTHER HOLE MUST BE PARTLY EXPOSED OR COMPLETELY UNCOVERED.

LOWER SUSPENSION ARM

VIEW A

WHEN COMPRESSING A PORTION OF THE SPRING, DO NOT COMPRESS TO GAP BETWEEN ACTIVE COILS OF LESS THAN 6mm (.22 INCHES)—C-CAR

VIEW B

IF ENTIRE SPRING IS COMPRESSED, THE OVERALL DIMENSION MUST NEVER BE LESS THAN 244mm (9.62 INCHES)—C-CAR

SUSPENSION

Front Coil Spring Removal

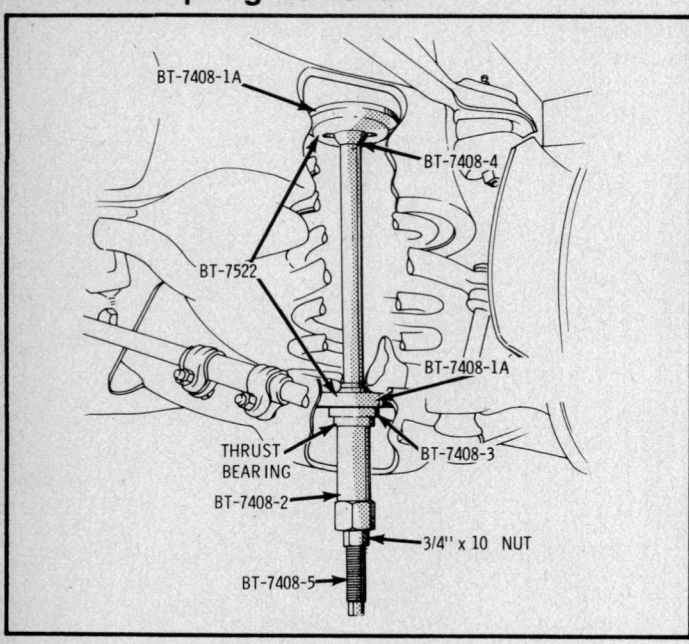

Installation

1. Install spring on bench.
2. Insert compressed spring into place.
3. Twist spring into proper position.
4. Carefully lift lower control arm and attach the lower control arm pivot bolts. Tighten nuts to 120 N•m (90 ft.-lbs.).

Upper Control Arm

Removal

1. Raise front of car and support lower control arm with floor stands.

CAUTION Floor jack must remain under control arm spring seat during removal and installation to retain spring and control arm in position.

Upper Control Arm

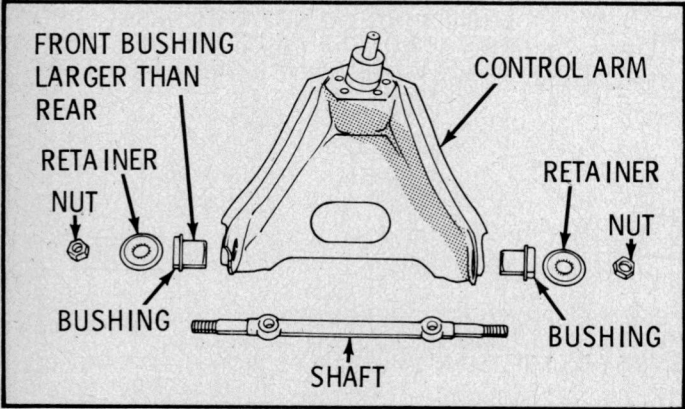

Disconnecting Upper Ball Joint

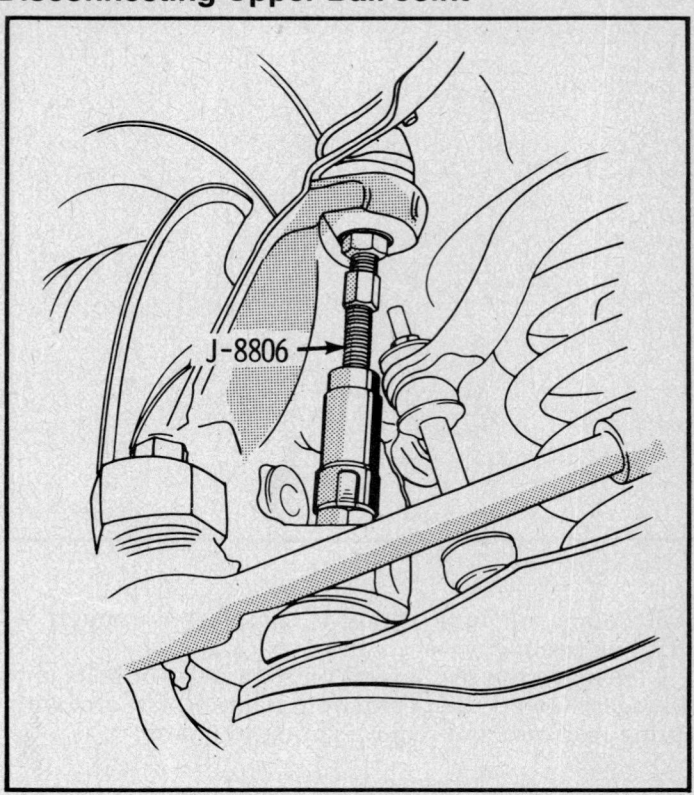

NOTE Since the weight of the car is used to relieve spring tension on the upper control arm, the floor stands must be positioned between the spring seats and ball joints of the lower control arms for maximum leverage.

2. Remove wheel, then loosen the upper ball joint from the steering knuckle as follows:
   a. Remove the upper ball joint nut.
   b. Apply pressure on stud by expanding the tool until the stud breaks loose.
3. Remove tool and upper ball joint nut, then pull stud free from knuckle. Support the knuckle assembly to prevent weight of the assembly from damaging the brake hose.

Upper Control Arm Bushing Removal

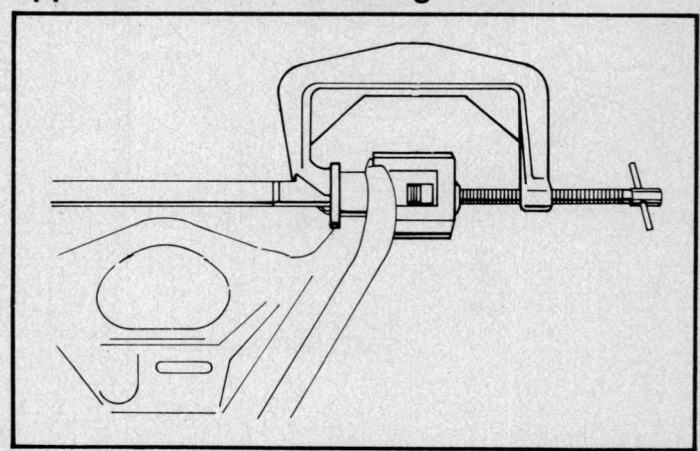

4. Remove the upper control arm attaching bolts to allow clearance to remove upper control arm assembly.

5. Remove upper control arm from the car.

PIVOT SHAFT BUSHING REPLACEMENT

1. Remove upper control arm assembly from the car.

2. Remove nuts from ends of pivot shaft.

3. Position control arm assembly and tools and push bushing out of control arm.

4. To install bushings, place pivot shaft in control arm and push new bushing into control arm and over end of pivot.

Lower Control Arm

Removal

1. Place transmission in neutral so steering wheel is unlocked.

2. Clean shock upper threads; oil, then remove nut, bolt, washer and grommet.

3. Hoist car. Remove wheel and tire.

4. Remove stabilizer link nut, grommets washers, and bolt.

5. Support car with floor stands and lower hoist. Remove shock.

6. Loosen the lower ball joint nut and use tool J-8806. Apply pressure on stud by expanding the tool until the stud breaks loose.

7. Install spring compressor in through front spring. Compress spring until all tension is off lower control arm.

8. Remove pivot bolts and ball joint.

9. Remove complete control arm.

Lower Control Arm Bushings

Steering Knuckle

It is recommended that the car be raised and supported so that the front coil spring remains compressed, yet the wheel and steering knuckle assembly remain accessible.

If a frame hoist is used, support the lower suspension arm with an adjustable jack stand to retain spring in the curb height position.

Removal

1. Raise car on hoist and support lower suspension arm.

Front Bushing Removal

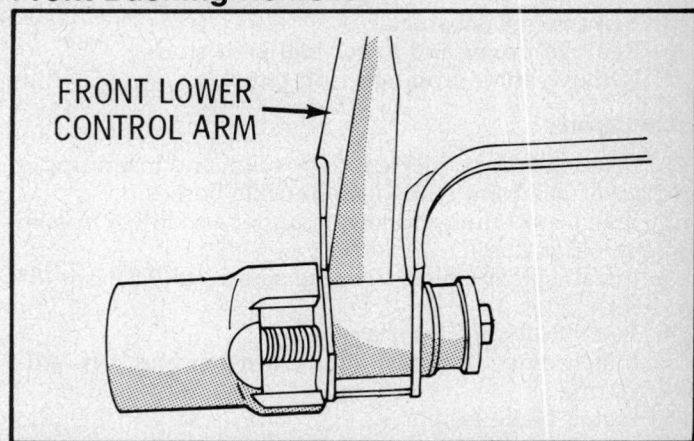

Press out old bushing. Press in new bushing

Rear Bushing Removal

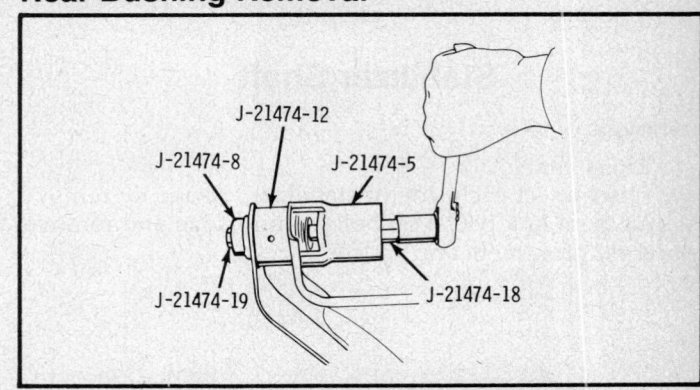

Press out old bushing. Press in new bushing

Steering Knuckle and Hub Assembly

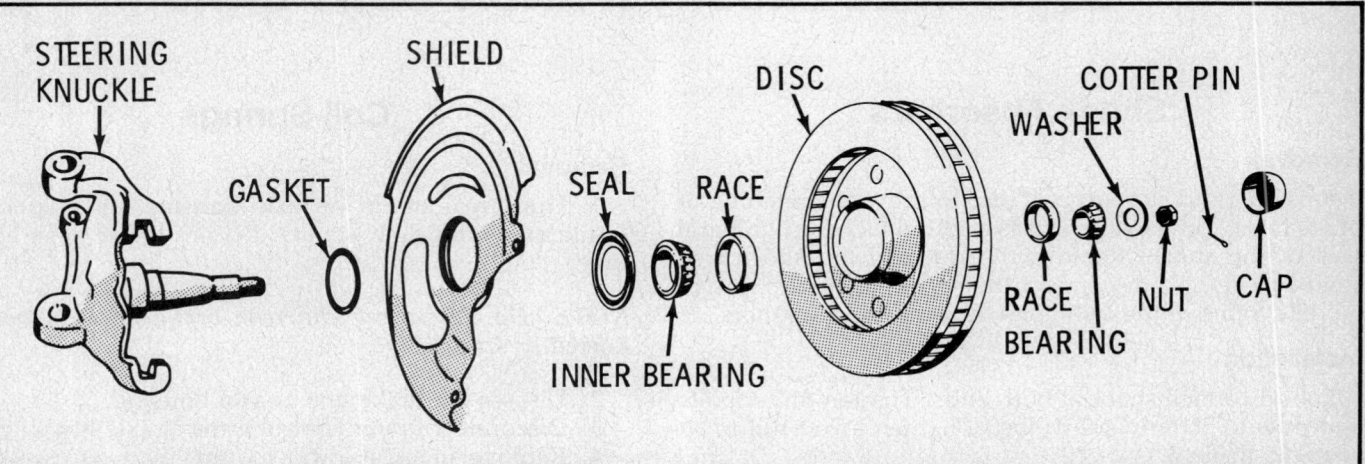

2. Remove wheel and tire assembly.

3. Remove tie-rod end from steering knuckle.

4. Remove brake caliper and hub and rotor assembly. Use a piece of wire to attach caliper to upper suspension arm.

NOTE Never allow caliper to hang from brake hose, as hose may be damaged.

5. Remove splash shield.

6. Remove upper and lower ball joint studs.

7. Remove studs from steering knuckle.

Installation

1. Place steering knuckle into position and insert upper and lower ball joint studs into knuckle bosses.

2. Install stud nuts and torque upper and lower nuts to 55 N•m (40 ft.-lbs.).

3. Install splash shield. Torque screws to 9.5 N•m (85 in.-lbs.).

4. Install hub and rotor assembly.

5. Install outer bearing, spindle washer and nut. Adjust bearing.

6. Install brake caliper.

7. Install wheel and tire assembly. Tighten nuts to 140 N•m (100 ft.-lbs.).

8. Lower car to floor.

9. Check front wheel alignment.

Stabilizer Shaft

Removal

1. Hoist car.

2. Disconnect each side of stabilizer linkage by removing nut from link bolt. Pull bolt from linkage and remove retainers, grommets and spacer.

3. Remove bracket-to-frame or body bolts and remove stabilizer shaft, rubber bushings and brackets. Some models require a special tool to remove stabilizer shaft bolt.

Installation

To replace, reverse sequence of operations, being sure to install with the identification forming on the right side of the car. The rubber bushings should be positioned squarely in the brackets with the slit in the bushings facing the front of car. Torque stabilizer link nut to 18 N•m (13 ft.-lbs.) and bracket bolts to 33 N•m (24 ft.-lbs.).

Stabilizer Shaft

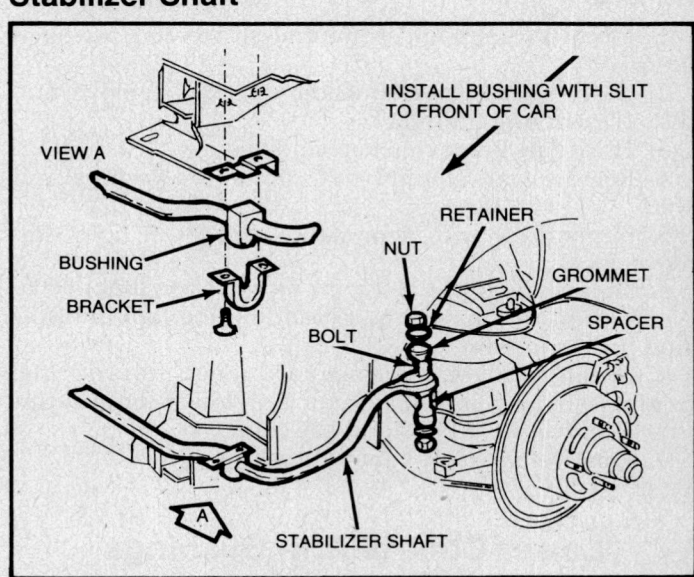

REAR SUSPENSION—GENERAL MOTORS REAR DRIVE SOLID AXLE EXCEPT H AND T BODY CARS

Shock Absorbers

Removal

Raise car and support rear axle to prevent stretching of brake hose. The lower end has a stud which is an integral part of the shock. Remove the nut and tap shock free from bracket. To disconnect the shock at the top, on all models, remove the two bolts, nuts and lockwashers.

Installation

Loosely attach shock at both ends. Tighten upper bolts and nuts to 26 N•m (20 ft.-lbs.). Tighten lower nut to 90 N•m (65 ft.-lbs.).

Coil Springs

Removal

1. Hoist rear of car on axle housing and support at frame rails with floor stands. Do not lower hoist at this time.

NOTE Do not allow the rear brake hose to become kinked or stretched.

2. Disconnect brake line at axle housing.

3. Disconnect upper control arms at axle housing.

4. Remove shock at lower mount.

Rear Suspension

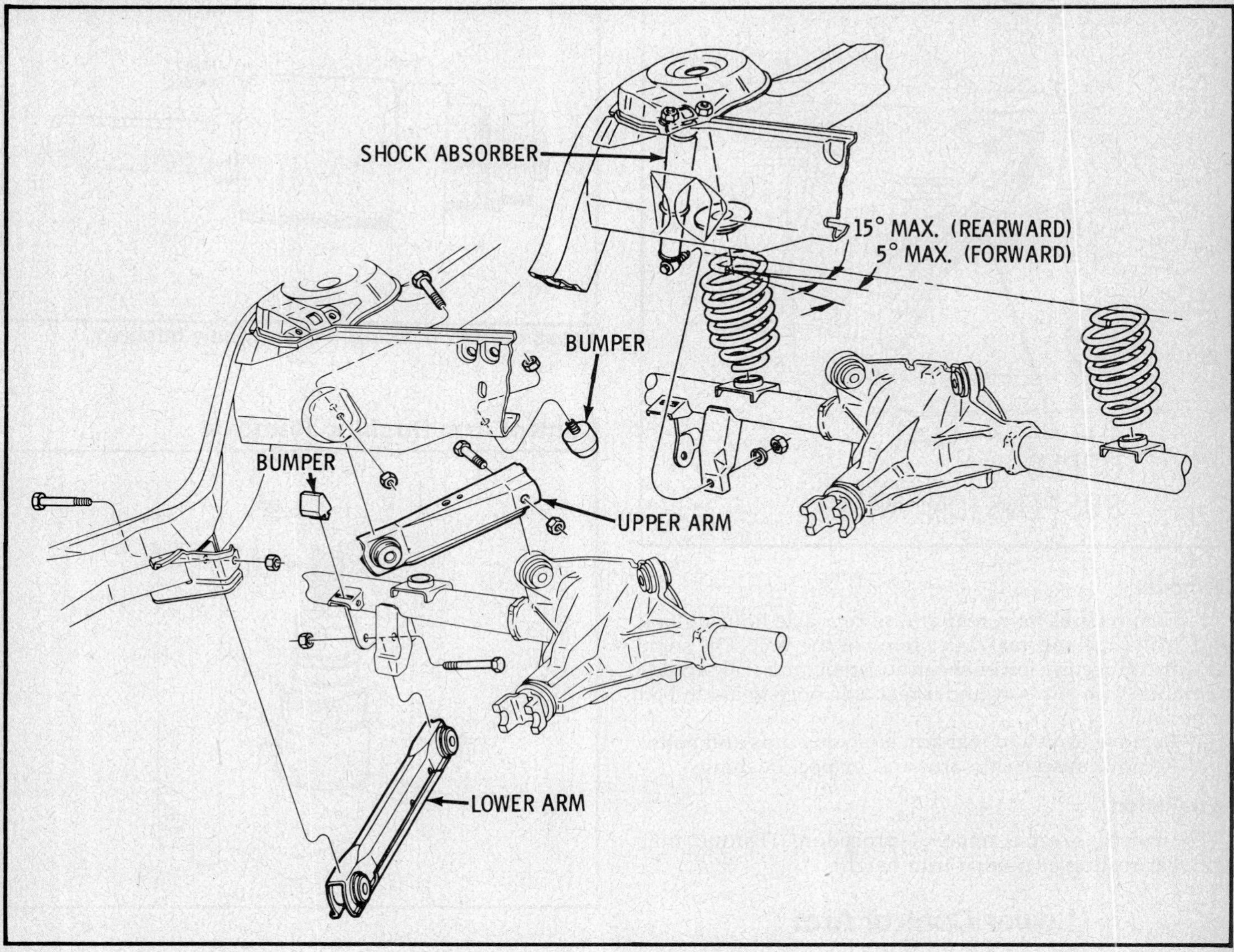

SHOCK ABSORBER

15° MAX. (REARWARD)
5° MAX. (FORWARD)

BUMPER

BUMPER

UPPER ARM

LOWER ARM

Coil Spring Mounting

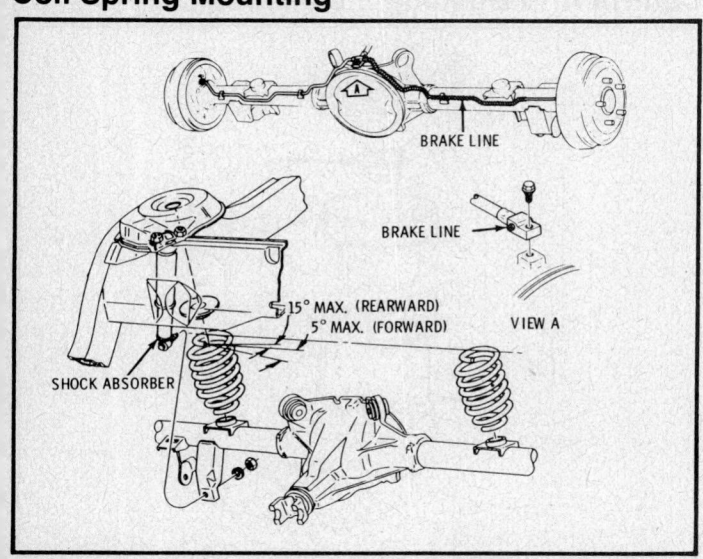

BRAKE LINE

BRAKE LINE

VIEW A

15° MAX. (REARWARD)
5° MAX. (FORWARD)

SHOCK ABSORBER

5. Lower hoist at rear axle.
6. Remove spring.

Installation

1. Install coil spring.
2. Raise hoist at rear axle.
3. Install shock at lower mount.
4. Install upper control arm bolts at axle housing.
5. Connect brake line at axle housing.
6. Remove jack stands and lower car.

Upper Control Arm

CAUTION   If both control arms are to be replaced, remove and replace one control arm at a time to prevent the axle from rolling or slipping sideways. This might occur with both upper control arms removed, making replacement difficult.

SUSPENSION
REAR SUSPENSION-GM REAR DRIVE SOLID AXLE (EXCEPT H AND T BODY)

Typical Upper Control Arm

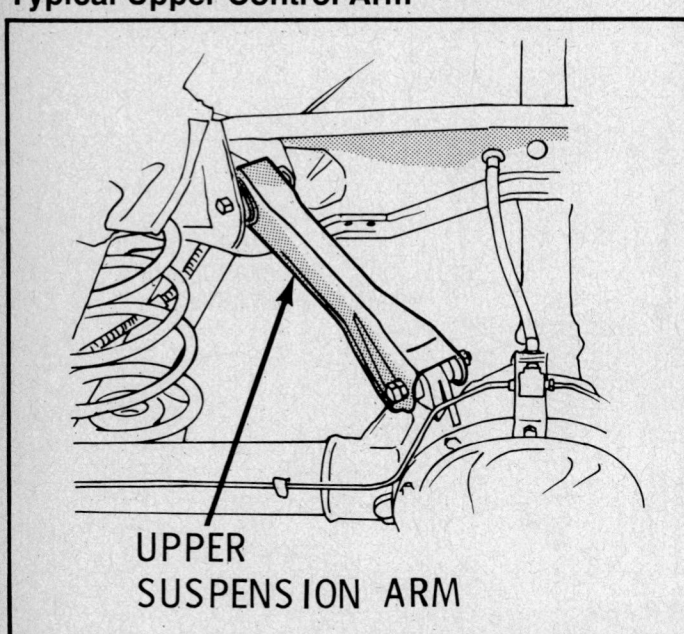

UPPER SUSPENSION ARM

Removal

1. Remove nut from rear arm to rear axle housing bolt and while rocking rear axle, remove the bolt. On some cars disconnecting lower shock absorber stud will provide clearance. Use support under rear axle nose to aid in bolt removal.
2. Remove front and rear arm attaching nuts and bolts.
3. Remove suspension arm and inspect bushings.

Installation

To install, reverse removal procedure. Torque nuts with car resting at normal trim height.

Lower Control Arm

CAUTION   If both control arms are to be replaced, remove and replace one control arm at a time to prevent the axle from rolling or slipping sideways. This might occur with both lower control arms removed, making replacement difficult.

Removal

1. Raise car and support under axle housing.
2. Remove rear arm-to-axle housing bracket bolt.

Differential Housing Bushings

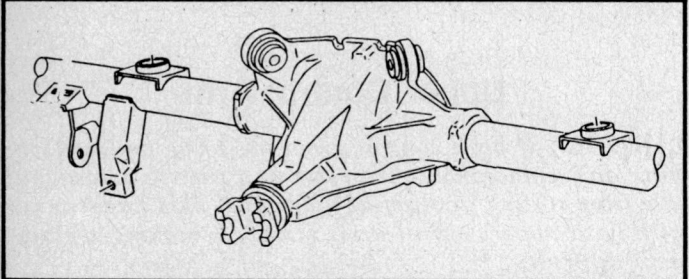

Bushing Removal (Rear Axle Housing)

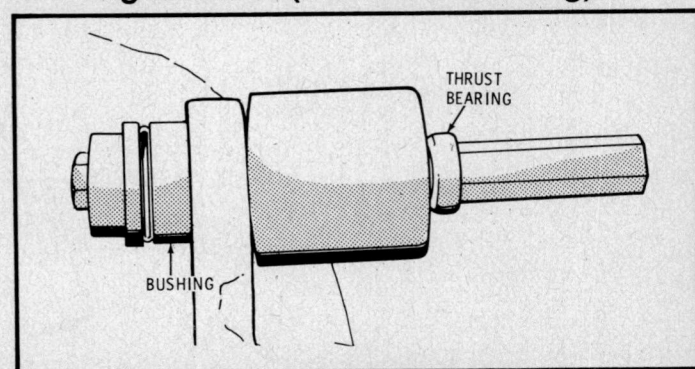

Press out old bushing. Press in new bushing.

Control Arm Bushing Removal

Control Arm Bushing Installation

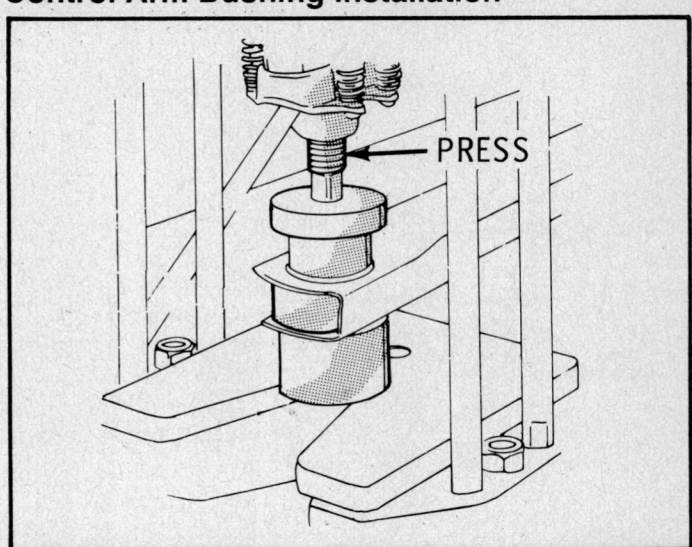

3. Remove front arm-to-bracket bolts and remove lower control arm.

Installation

To replace arm, reverse the removal sequence of operations. Torque arm attaching nuts with the weight of the car on the rear springs.

Leaf Spring

Removal

1. Raise vehicle on hoist. Support vehicle so axle can be raised and lowered.
2. Raise axle assembly so that all tension is removed from spring.
3. Disconnect shock absorber lower attaching mount.
4. Loosen the spring front eye-to-bracket retaining bolt.
5. Remove the screws securing the spring front bracket to the underbody.
6. Lower axle assembly sufficiently to permit access to spring front bracket and remove bracket from spring.
7. The spring eye bushing can be replaced without completely removing the spring from the vehicle.
8. Pry parking brake cable out of the retainer bracket mounted on the spring mounted plate.
9. Remove lower spring plate-to-axle bracket retaining nuts.

10. Remove upper and lower rubber spring pads and spring plate.
11. Support spring, then remove lower bolt from spring rear shackle. Separate shackle and withdraw spring from vehicle.
12. Remove rear spring shackle upper bolt and withdraw shackle bushings from frame.

Installation

1. Position spring front mounting bracket to spring front eye. Spring attaching bolt must be installed so that head of bolt is toward center of vehicle.
2. Position spring shackle upper bushings in frame. Position shackles to bushings and loosely install bolt and nut.
3. Install bushing halves in spring rear eye, place spring in shackles and loosely install shackle lower bolt and nut. When installing spring, make sure spring is positioned so that parking brake cable is on underside of spring.
4. Raise front end of spring and position bracket to underbody. Guide spring into position so that it will index in the axle bracket and also make sure that the tab on spring bracket is indexed in slot provided in the underbody.
5. Loosely install spring-to-underbody bracket.
6. Position spring upper cushion between spring and axle bracket so that spring cushion ribs align with axle bracket locating ribs.

Leaf Spring Rear Suspension

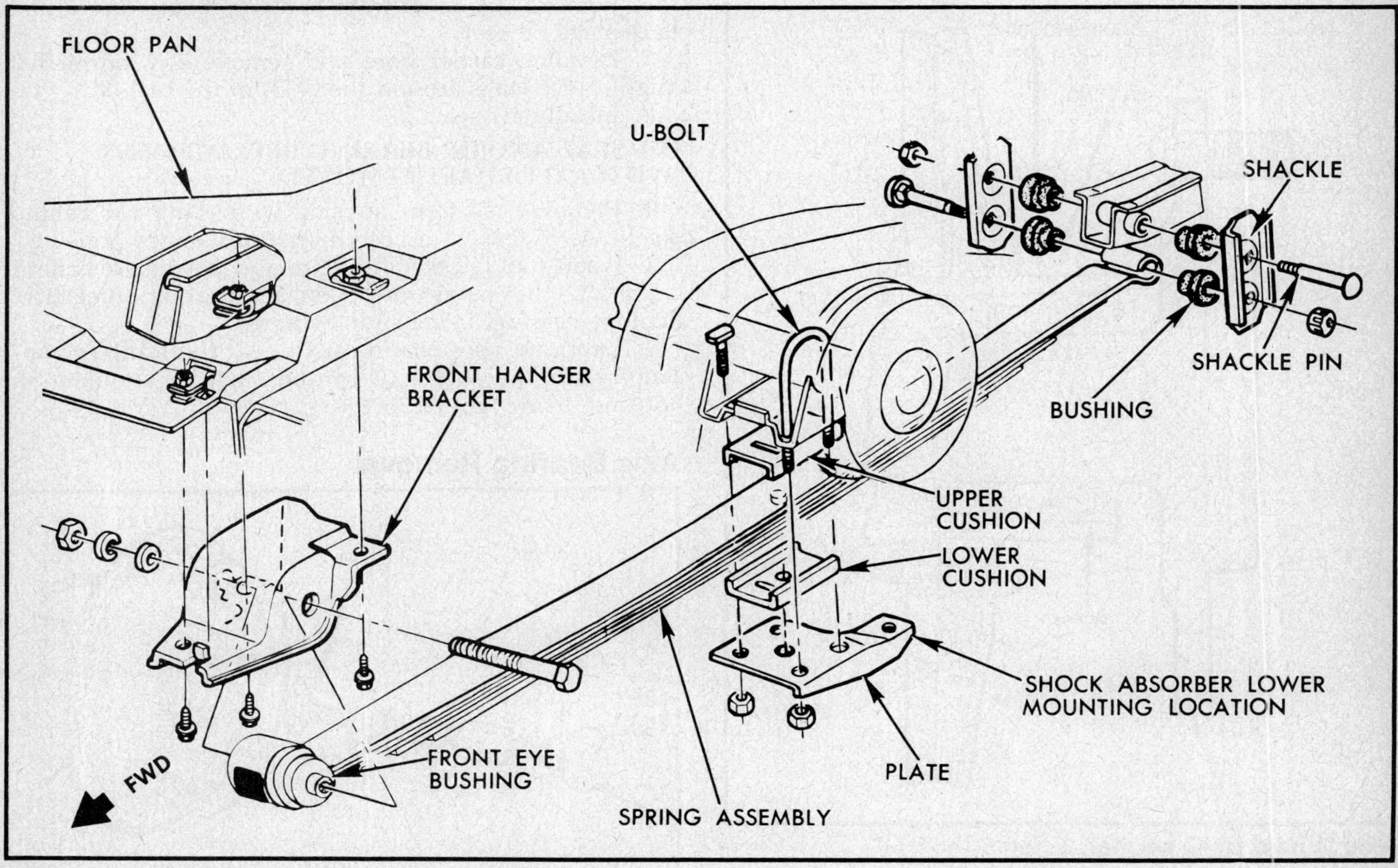

B615

SUSPENSION

REAR SUSPENSION-GM REAR DRIVE SOLID AXLE (EXCEPT H AND T BODY)

7. Place lower spring cushion on spring so that cushion is indexed on locating dowel. Upper cushion and lower cushion will be aligned if installation is correct.

8. Place lower mounting plate over locating dowel on spring lower pad and loosely install retaining nuts.

9. If new mounting plate was installed, transfer parking brake cable retaining bracket to new plate.

10. Attach shock absorber to spring mounting plate.

11. Position parking brake cable in retaining bracket and securely clamp bracket to retain cable.

12. Tighten all affected parts with vehicle weight on suspension components.

Rear Axle Bearing

Two types of bearings are used in the GM A, B, and C type rear suspension.
Type A axle shafts are retained by a C lock.
Type B axle shafts are retained with an outer retainer plate.

AXLE SHAFT TYPE A

Removal

1. Raise car and remove wheel and brake drum.
2. Clean all dirt from area of carrier cover.
3. Drain lubricant from carrier by removing cover.

Type A Axle Bearing

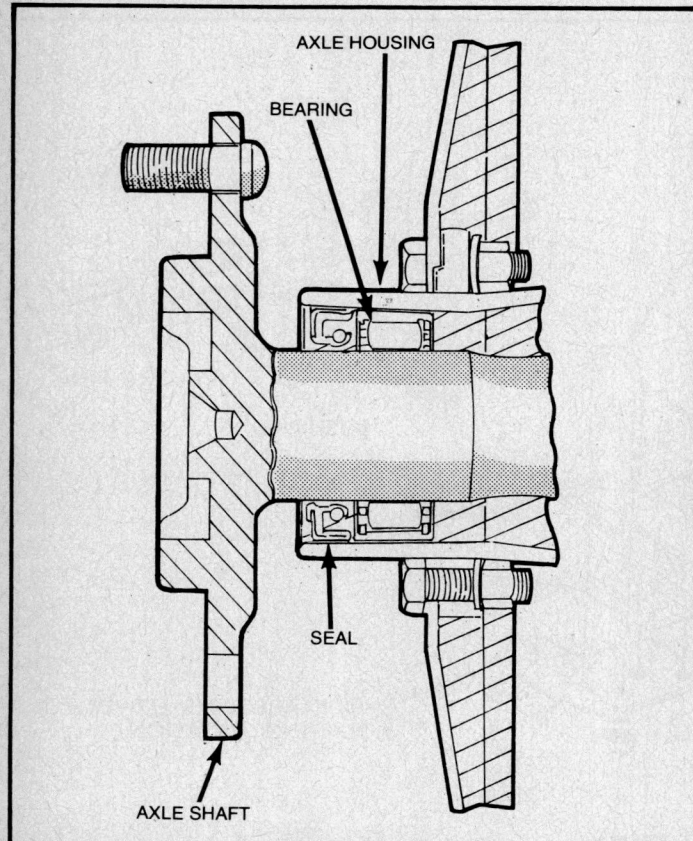

Axle is held by C washer.

Type B Axle Bearing

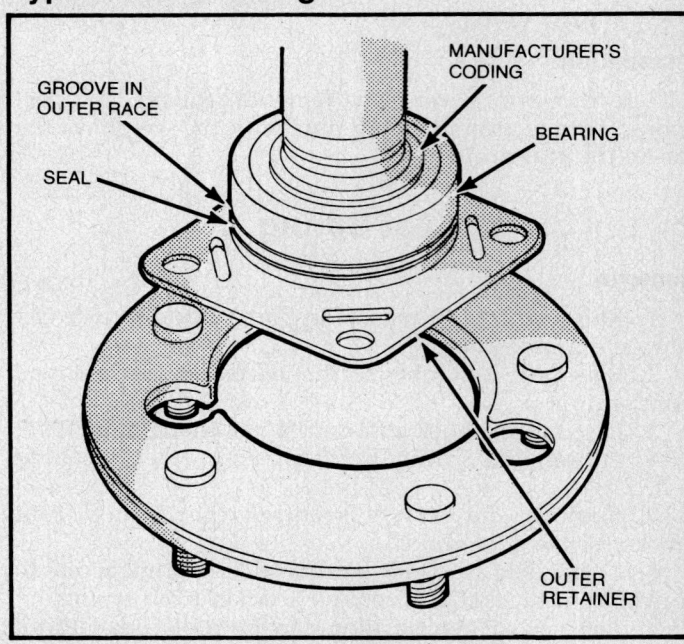

Axle bearing is held by outer plate.

4. Remove the rear axle pinion shaft lock screw and the rear axle pinion shaft.

5. Push flanged end of axle shaft toward center of car and remove C lock from button end of shaft.

6. Remove axle shaft from housing, being careful not to damage oil seal.

7. Examine carrier bore and remove any burrs that might cause leaks around the O.D. of the seal.

8. Install new seal.

OIL SEAL AND/OR BEARING REPLACEMENT (WITH AXLE SHAFT REMOVED)

1. Remove seal from housing with a pry bar behind steel case of seal, being careful not to damage housing.

2. Insert tool J-23689 into bore and position it behind bearing so that tangs on tool engage bearing outer race. Remove bearing, using slide hammer.

3. Lubricate new bearing with gear lubricant and install bearing so that tool bottoms against shoulder in housing, using tool J-23690.

Axle Bearing Removal

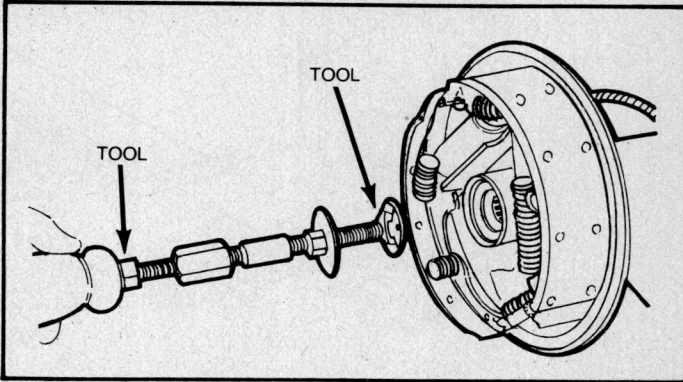

Pinion Shaft Lock Bolt

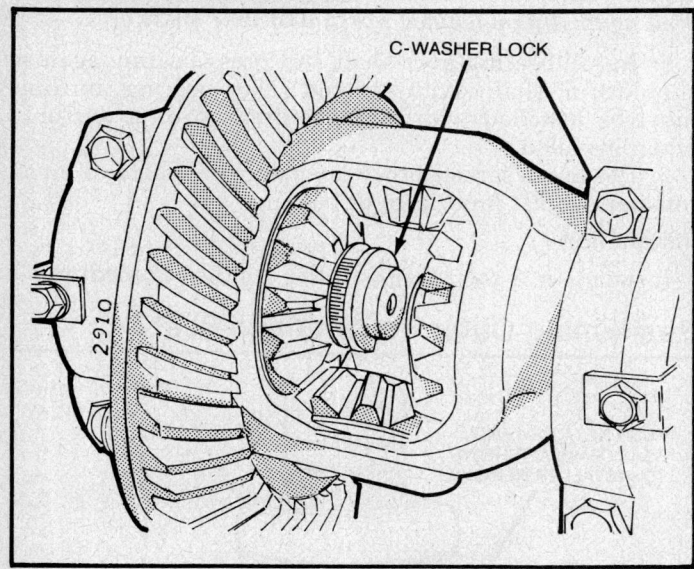

C-WASHER LOCK

4. Lubricate seal lips with gear lubricant. Position seal on tool J-21128 and position seal into housing bore. Tap seal into place so that it is flush with axle tube.

Installation

1. Slide axle shaft into place.

NOTE Exercise care that splines on end of shaft do not damage oil seal and that they engage with splines of rear axle side gear.

2. Install axle shaft C lock on button end of axle shaft and push shaft outward so that shaft lock seats in counterbore of rear axle side gear.
3. Position rear axle pinion shaft through case and pinions, aligning hole in shaft with lock screw hole. Install lock screw and torque to 27 N•m (20 ft.-lbs.).
4. Using a new gasket, install carrier cover and torque bolts to 27 N•m (20 ft.-lbs.).
5. Fill axle with lubricant to a level within 9.5 mm (3/8 in.) of filler hole.
6. Install brake drum and wheel.
7. Lower car and test operation of axle.

AXLE SHAFT TYPE B

Removal

1. Remove wheel and brake drum.
2. Remove nuts holding retainer to backing plate. Pull retainer clear of bolts and reinstall two lower nuts finger-tight to hold backing plate in position.
3. Pull out axle shaft.

AXLE BEARING AND SEAL REPLACEMENT

Replacement of bearing will require a new seal and inner and outer retainers. Replacement of seal only will not require a new bearing but will require inner and outer retainers.

Axle Shaft Bearing Installer

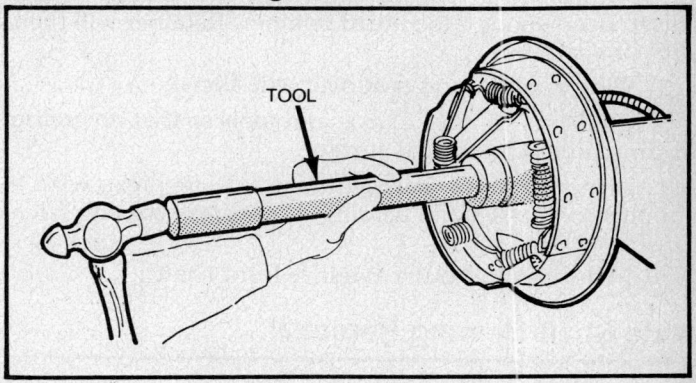

TOOL

Axle Shaft Removal

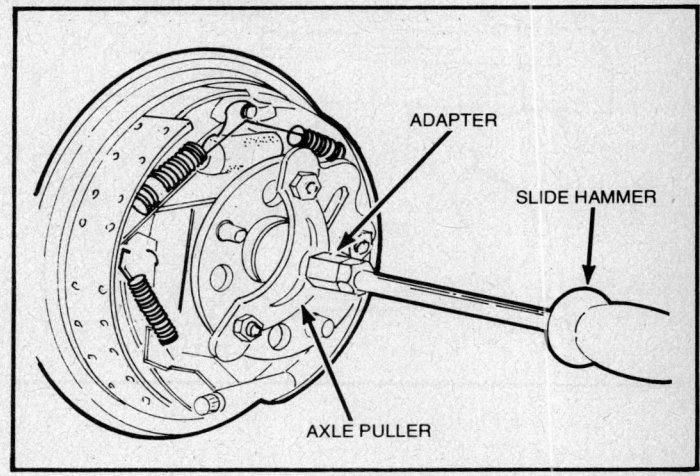

ADAPTER

SLIDE HAMMER

AXLE PULLER

Cutting Bearing Retainer

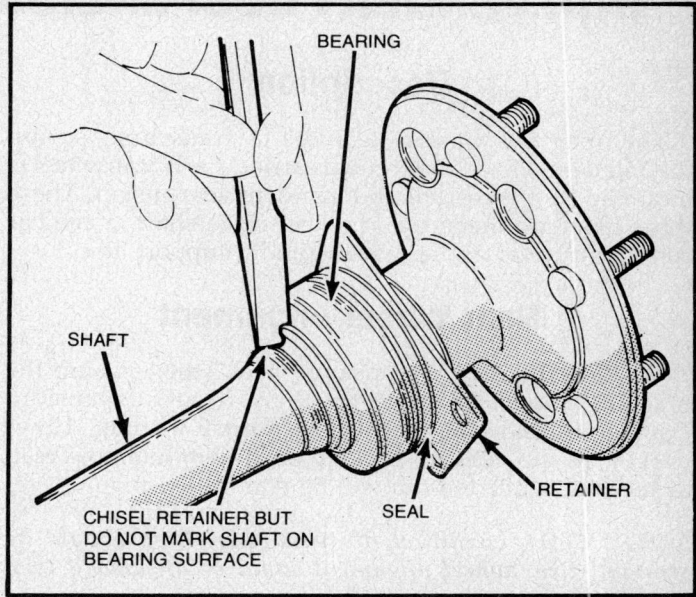

BEARING

SHAFT

CHISEL RETAINER BUT
DO NOT MARK SHAFT ON
BEARING SURFACE

SEAL

RETAINER

B617

1. Nick bearing retainer (inner) in two places with a chisel, deep enough to spread retainer. Retainer will then slip off shaft.

2. Slide retainer and seal over axle flange.

3. Clean seal surface of axle and tools so that no grease or dirt could scratch seal surface.

4. Using an arbor press, mount axle in press with a support tool under the bearing, then press bearing from axle.

5. Slide seal and outer retainer from shaft.

NOTE Care must be exercised so that seal is not damaged against unmachined portion of axle shaft.

6. Install bearing over shaft and press bearing against shoulder of shaft. With tapered roller bearing, bearing must be installed with manufacturer's coding readable when installed.

7. Position a service inner retainer over shaft and press retainer against inner race of bearing.

Installation

Installation is the reverse of the removal procedure.

Axle Shaft Bearing Removal

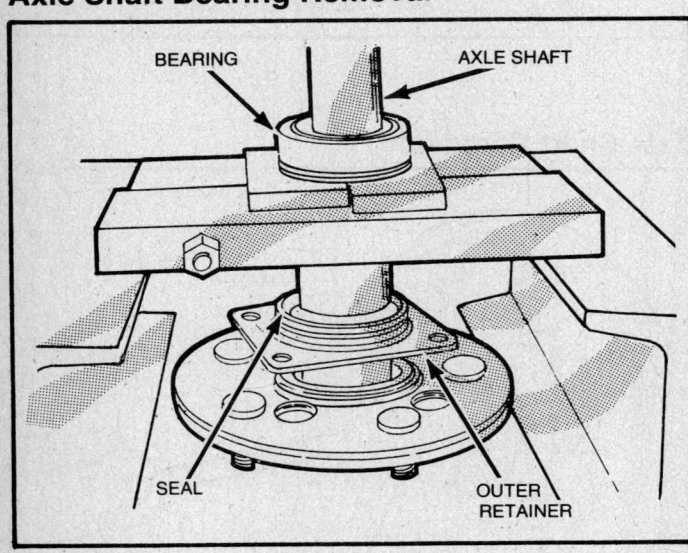

Positioning Outer Retainer and Seal

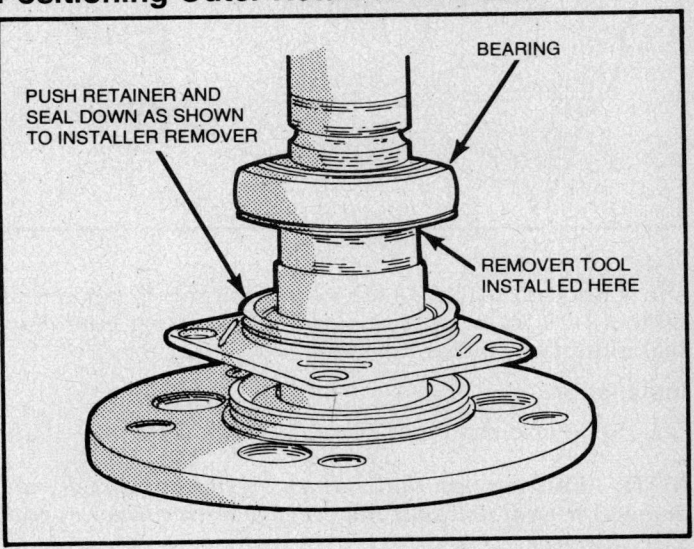

REAR SUSPENSION—GENERAL MOTORS REAR DRIVE INDEPENDENT SUSPENSION EXCEPT H AND T BODY CARS

Description

The rear suspension features a transverse spring mounted on a fixed differential carrier. Each rear wheel is mounted by a three-link independent suspension. These three links are made up of wheel drive shaft, a camber control strut rod and a wheel spindle support arm.

Rear Wheel Alignment

To align the rear suspension, "back" the car onto the machine normally used to align front suspension. Camber will now be read in the normal manner. However, with the vehicle "backed" in, toe-in will now read as toe-out, while toe-out will be read as toe-in.

NOTE Check condition of strut rods. They should be straight. Rear wheel alignment could be affected if they are bent.

REAR WHEEL ALIGNMENT

Camber	0° ± ½°
Toe-in (Per Wheel)	.06° ± .06°

NOTE: Each wheel must be adjusted independently.

CAMBER

Wheel camber angle is obtained by adjusting the eccentric cam and bolt assembly located at the inboard mounting of the strut rod. Place rear wheels on alignment machine and determine camber angle. To adjust, loosen cam bolt nut and rotate cam and bolt assembly until specified camber is reached. Tighten nut securely and torque to specifications.

TOE-IN

Wheel toe-in is adjusted by inserting shims of varying thickness inside the frame side member on both sides o

Rear Wheel Camber Adjustment

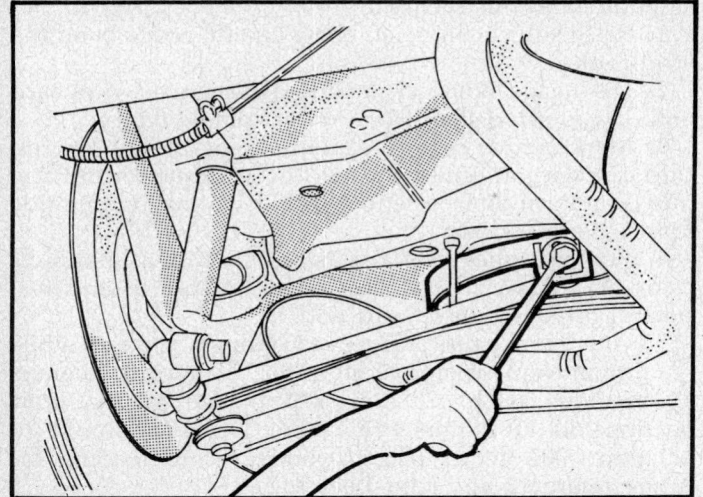

Toe-in Adjusting Shim Location

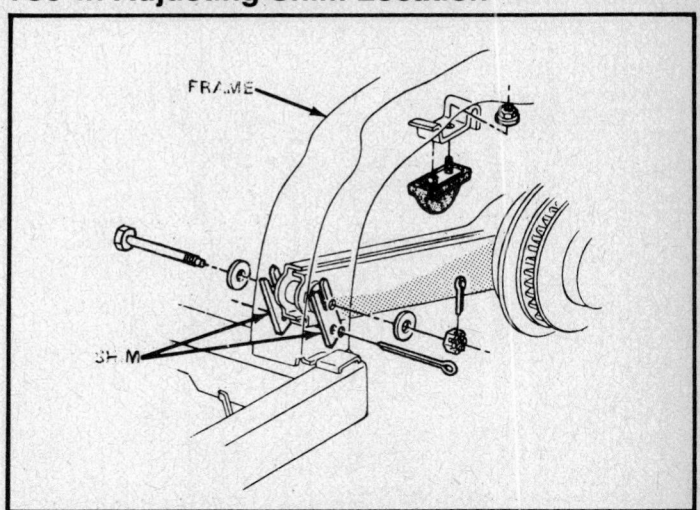

the torque control arm pivot bushing. Shims are available in thickness of .40 mm (1/64 in.), 79 mm (1/32 in.), 3.18 mm (1/8 in.) and 6.35 mm (1/4 in.).

To adjust toe-in, loosen torque control arm pivot bolt. Remove cotter pin retaining shims and remove shims. Position torque control arm to obtain specified toe-in. Shim the gap toward vehicle centerline between torque control arm bushing and frame side inner wall. Do not use thicker shim than necessary, and do not use undue force when shimming inner side of torque control arm. To do so may cause toe setting to change.

Shim outboard gap as necessary to obtain solid stackup between torque control arm bushing and inner wall of

frame side member. After correct shim stack has been selected, install cotter pin (with loop outboard) through shims. Torque nut to specifications, and install cotter pin. If specified torque does not permit cotter pin insertion, tighten nut to next flat.

Wheel Bearing
END-PLAY CHECK

The tapered-roller spindle bearings should have end play of .003 to .20 mm (.001 in. to .008 in.). During

Corvette Independent Rear Suspension

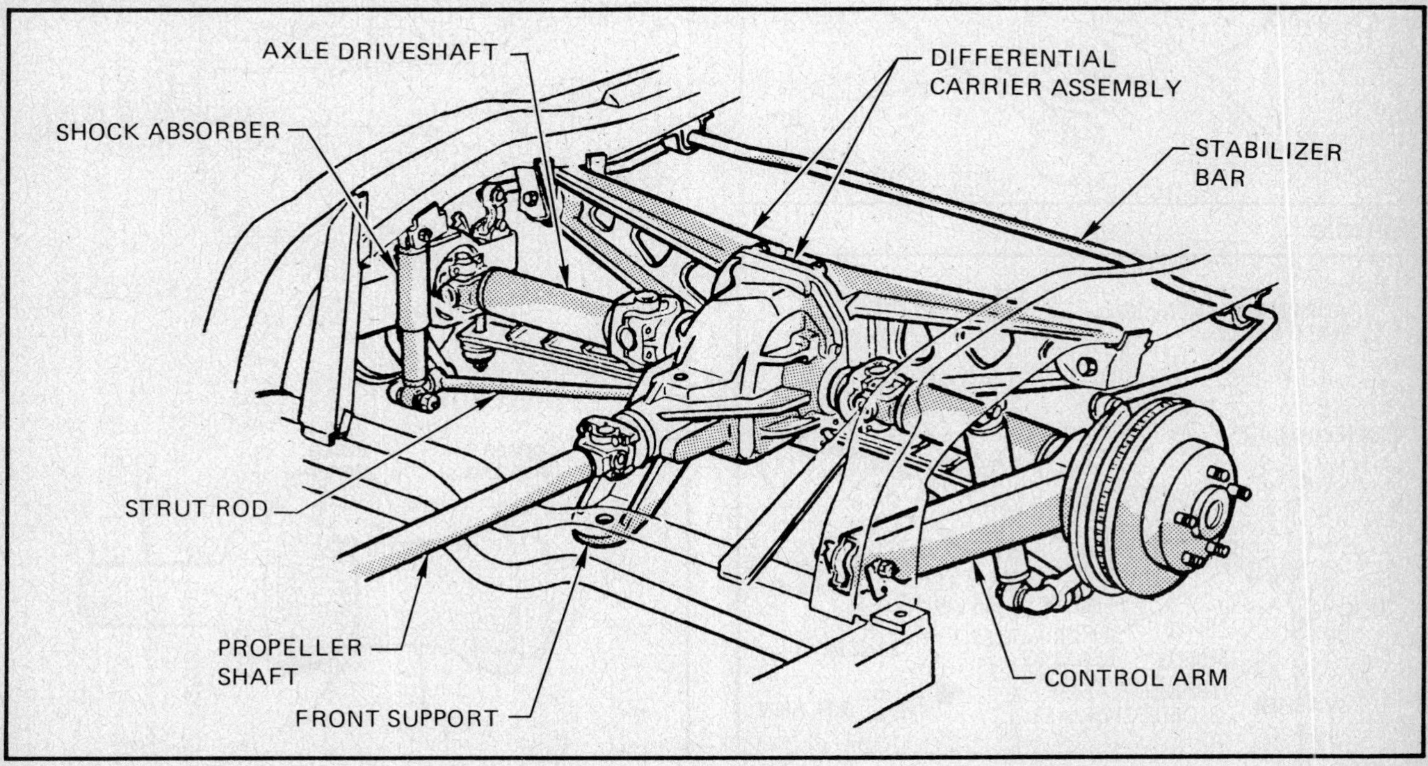

Spindle Bearing End Play Check

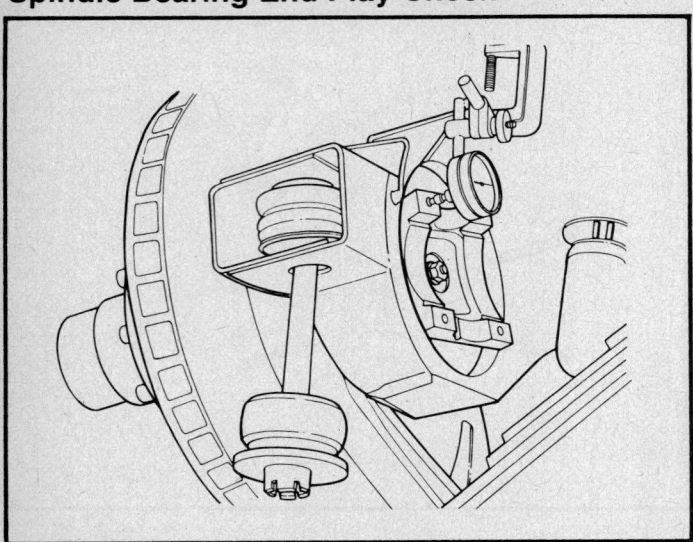

inspection, check end play and, when necessary, adjust as outlined in this section.

1. Raise vehicle on hoist, being careful not to bend the strut rods.

2. Disengage bolt lock tabs and disconnect outboard end of axle drive shaft from wheel spindle flange.

3. Mark camber cam in relation to bracket. Loosen and turn camber bolt until strut rod forces torque control arm outward. Position loose end of axle drive shaft to one side for access to spindle.

4. Remove wheel and tire assembly. Mount dial indicator on torque control arm adjacent surface and rest pointer on flange or spindle end.

5. Grasp brake disc and move axially (in and out) while reading movement on dial indicator. If end movement is within the .003 to .20 mm (.001 in. to .008 in.) limit, bearings do not require adjustment. If not within .003 to .20 mm (.001 in. to .008 in.) limit, record reading for future reference and adjust bearings.

Drive Spindle Removal

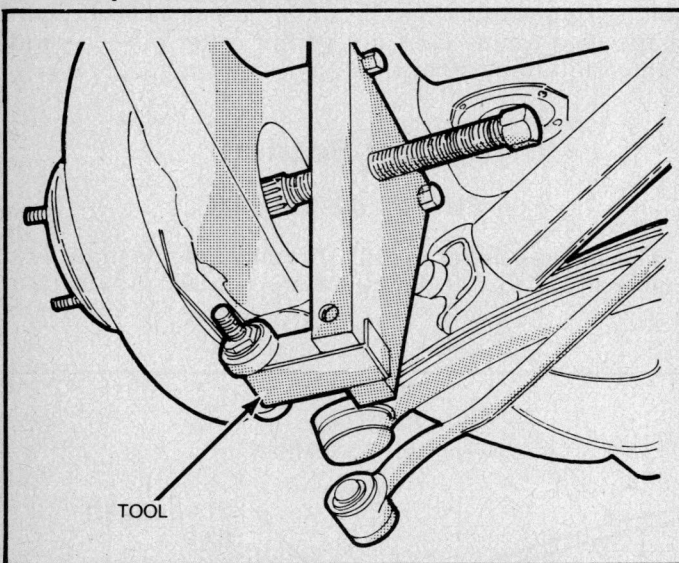

Spindle Removal

1. Apply parking brake to prevent spindle from turning and remove cotter pin and nut from spindle.

2. Release parking brake and remove drive spindle flange from splined end of spindle. It may be necessary to use tool J-8614-01 to remove flange from spindle.

3. Remove brake caliper.

Spindle

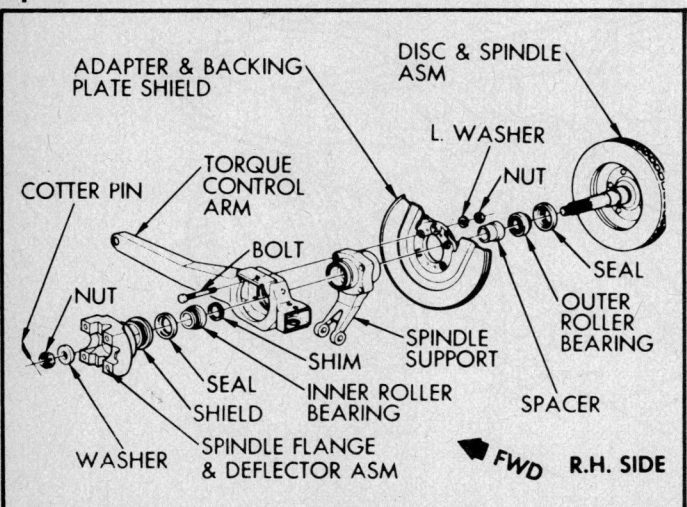

Sectional View of Spindle

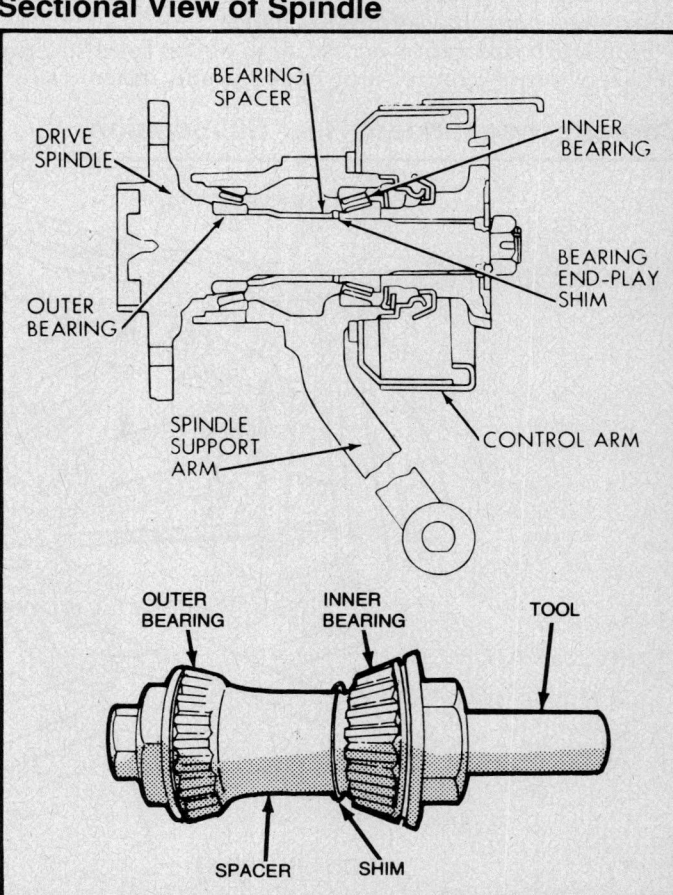

4. Install thread protector J-21859-1 over spindle threads. Remove drive spindle from spindle support, using tool J-22602.

When using tool J-22602 to remove drive spindle, make sure puller plate is positioned vertically in the torque control arm before applying pressure to the puller screw.

5. When the spindle is removed, the outer bearing will remain on the spindle. The inner bearing, tubular spacer, end-play adjustment shim and both outer races will remain in the spindle support.

6. Remove bearing, spacer and shim. Record shim thickness for later use.

Bearing Replacement and Adjustment, and Spindle Installation

1. With the spindle assembly on a bench, place the two halves of J-24489-1 into position between the outer bearing and the oil seal.

2. Mount J-8433-1 to J-24489-1 and draw bearing off spindle.

3. Remove outer oil seal from spindle shaft and inspect for damage. Replace if necessary.

4. Remove the outer races from the spindle support and install new ones, using J-7817 for reinstallation.

5. Pack new bearings with EPB-2 bearing lubricant, or equivalent.

6. Check bearing end play as measured in step 5 of Wheel Bearing End Play Check. Use the same adjusting shim thickness as the original. If end play was *not* within limits, use the following steps to determine the proper shim thickness:

a. If end play was greater than .20 mm (.008 in.), it will be necessary to reduce shim thickness to bring end play within limits.

b. For example, if end-play reading was .33 mm (.013 in.), and the shim measured 3.66 mm (.144 in.), you will have to decrease the shim thickness. Reducing the shim by .25 mm (.010 in.), from 3.66 to 3.40 mm (.144 to .134 in.), will also reduce end play by .25 mm (.010 in.), from .33 to .08 mm (.013 to .003 in.).

c. If no end play was found on inspection, add .08 mm (.003 in.) to the original shim as a starting point.

7. To check bearing end-play before final installation, use J-24626 as follows:

a. Mount the outer bearing onto the large shoulder, with the large end of the bearing against the flange.

b. Place the tubular spacer, with the large end against the outer bearing, and the shim selected in step 6 onto J-24626.

c. Place the tool into position in the spindle support and install inner bearing, large washer and nut.

d. Tighten nut to 140 N•m (100 ft.-lbs.) to simulate actual installed conditions.

e. Mount a dial indicator and check bearing end-play.

f. Alter shim thickness as necessary to obtain end-play from .03 to .20 mm (.001 to .008 in.). Shims are available in thicknesses from 2.46 to 3.68 mm (.097 to .145 in.).

g. Remove J-24626 from spindle support.

8. Install outer bearing into outer race. Install outer oil seal into bore of spindle support, making sure it is firmly seated.

9. Carefully install spindle assembly through the outer oil seal (being careful not to dislodge seal from the bore) and through the outer bearing.

10. Place the tubular spacer and the shim selected in step 7 onto the spindle shaft.

11. Place the inner bearing onto the spindle shaft.

12. Thread tool J-24490-1 onto the spindle shaft, then install sleeve J-24490-2, and washer and nut. Tighten nut against sleeve. Spindle shaft will now be drawn through the bearings to its final installed position.

13. Remove J-24490-1 and J-24490-2.

14. Position drive flange over spindle, making sure flange is aligned with spindle splines. Install washer and nut on spindle, then tighten nut to specifications and install cotter pin. If specified torque does not permit cotter pin insertion, tighten nut to next flat.

15. Install caliper onto disc.

16. Install axle drive shaft, wheel and tire assembly, adjust camber cam to original position and torque all components to specifications.

Spindle Support

Removal

1. Remove wheel spindle as outlined previously.
2. Disconnect parking brake cable from actuating lever.
3. Remove four nuts securing spindle support to torque control arm and withdraw brake backing plate. Position it out of the way.
4. Disconnect shock absorber lower eye from strut rod mounting shaft. It may be necessary to support spring outer end before disconnecting shock absorber, as shock absorber has internal rebound control.
5. Remove cotter pin and nut from strut rod mounting shaft, then pull shaft from support and strut rod.
6. Separate support from torque control arm.

Installation

1. Position support over torque arm bolts with strut rod fork toward center of vehicle and downward.
2. Place backing plate in position; install four nuts and torque to specifications.
3. Install strut rod and shock absorber mounting shaft onto support arm. Install shock absorber. Torque to specifications.
4. Connect parking brake cable to actuating lever.
5. Install drive spindle assembly.

Shock Absorber

Removal

1. Raise vehicle on hoist.
2. Disconnect shock absorber upper mounting bolt.
3. Remove lower mounting nut and lock washer.
4. Slide shock upper eye out of frame bracket and pull lower eye and rubber grommets off strut and mounting shaft.
5. Inspect grommets and shock absorber upper eye for excessive wear.

SUSPENSION

Shock Absorber Mounting

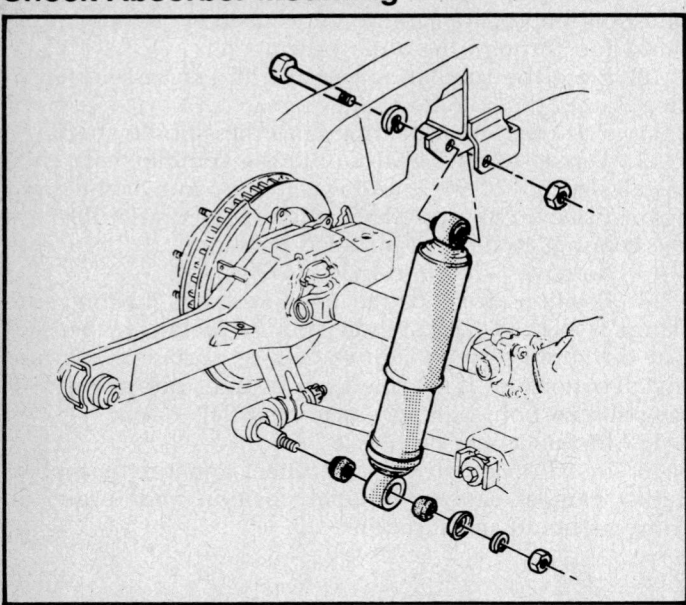

Installation

1. Slide upper mounting eye into frame mounting bracket and install bolt, lock washer and nut.
2. Place rubber grommet, shock lower eye, inboard grommet, washers and nut over strut rod shaft. Install washer with curve pointing inboard (away from grommet).
3. Torque nuts to specifications.
4. Lower vehicle and remove from hoist.

Strut Rod and Bracket

Removal

1. Raise vehicle on hoist.
2. Disconnect shock absorber lower eye from strut rod shaft.
3. Remove strut rod shaft cotter pin and nut. Withdraw shaft by pulling toward front of vehicle.
4. Mark relative position of camber adjusting cam and bracket, so they may be reassembled in same location.

Marking Camber Cam and Bracket

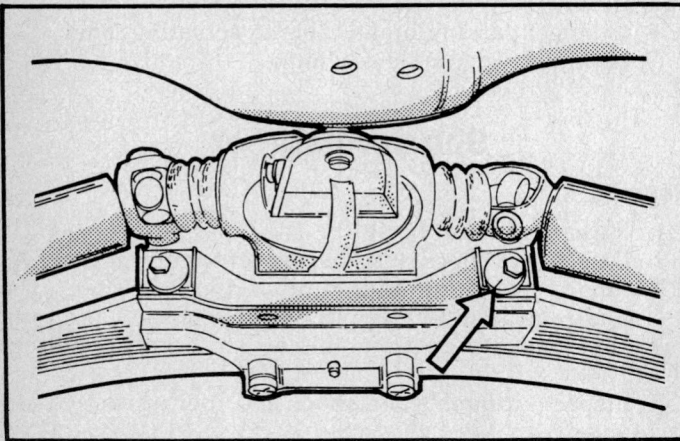

Strut Rod Mounting

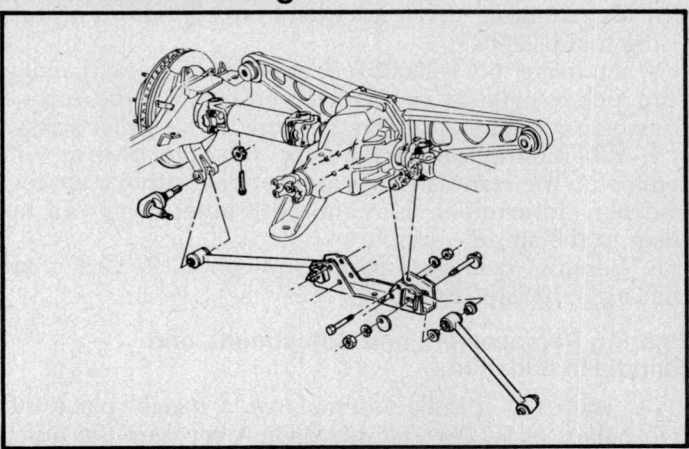

Install strut with outboard end angled forward

5. Loosen camber bolt and nut. Remove four bolts, lock washers and flat washers securing strut rod bracket to carrier and lower bracket.
6. Remove cam bolt nut and cam and bolt assembly. Pull strut down out of bracket and remove bushing caps.
7. Inspect strut rod bushings for wear and replace where necessary.

Installation

1. Place bushing caps over inboard bushing and slide rod into bracket. Install cam and bolt assembly and adjust cam to line up with mark on bracket. Tighten nut but do not torque at this point.
2. Raise bracket and assemble to carrier lower mounting surface. Be sure both flat washer and lock washer are between bolt and bracket. Torque bolts to specifications.
3. Raise outboard end of strut rod into spindle support fork and insert strut rod shaft into fork so that flat on shaft lines up with corresponding flat in spindle fork. Install retaining nut, but do not torque.
4. Place shock absorber lower eye and bushing over strut shaft, install washer and nut and torque to specifications.
5. With weight on wheels torque camber cam nut and strut rod shaft nut to specifications. Then install cotter pin through rod bolt.
6. Check rear wheel camber and adjust where necessary.
7. Lower vehicle and remove from hoist.

Transverse Spring

Removal

1. Raise vehicle on hoist allowing axle to hang. Remove wheels and tires.
2. Install a C clamp on spring approximately 23 cm. (9 in.) from one end. Tighten securely.
3. Place adjustable lifting device under spring with lifting pad of jack inboard of link bolt near the C clamp. Place a suitable piece of wood between jack pad and C clamp screw. The C clamp is merely acting as a stop so the jack will not slip when the spring is released. The

Clamp Plate Removal

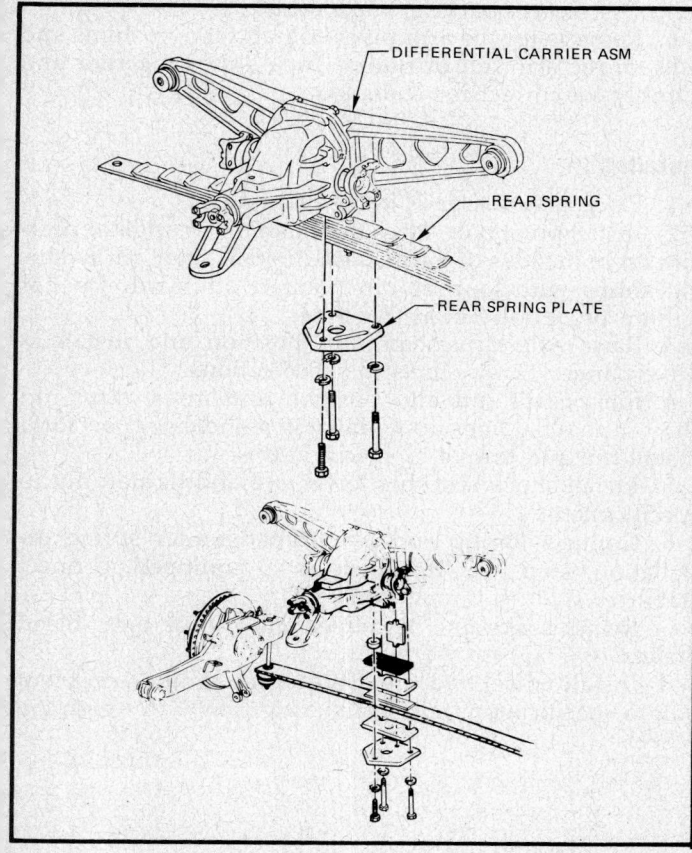

wood block is used to protect the clamp threads from distortion due to contact with the jack pad.

4. Raise jack until all load is off link. Remove link cotter key and link nut. Remove cushion. Do not grip shank of spring link bolt with Vise Grips. Use new bolt if the bolt surface is scored or damaged.

5. Carefully lower jack until spring tension is released.

6. Repeat steps 2-5 for other side.

7. Remove four bolts and washers securing spring center clamp plate.

Transverse Spring Mounting

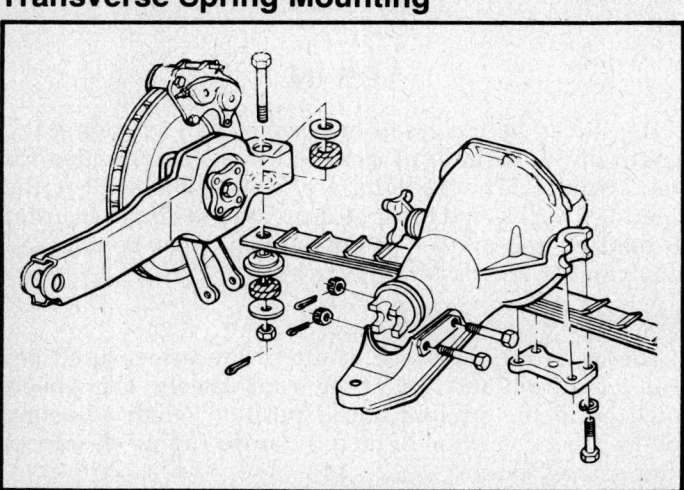

8. Slide spring out from under vehicle.

Installation

1. Place spring on carrier cover mounting surface, indexing center bolt head with hole in cover.

2. Place center clamp plate in position and install bolts and washers. Snug bolts to position spring and torque to specifications.

3. Install C clamp as in step 2 of removal procedure.

4. Place adjustable lifting device inboard of link bolt near C clamp. Add wooden block as in step 3 of removal procedure.

5. Raise spring outer end until spring is nearly flat, aligning torque arm with spring end.

6. install new attaching parts. Whenever servicing spring or removing spring attaching parts, always install new link bolts, rubber cushions, retainers, nuts and cotter pins.

7. Lower jack making sure cushions remain indexed in retainers. Remove C clamp.

8. Remove jack and repeat for other side.

9. Place vehicle weight on wheels and torque center clamp bolts to specifications.

Torque Control Arm

Removal

1. Disconnect spring on side torque arm is to be removed. Follow steps 1–5 of the spring removal procedure. If vehicle is so equipped, disconnect stabilizer shaft from torque arm.

2. Remove shock absorber lower eye from strut rod shaft.

3. Disconnect and remove strut rod shaft and swing strut rod down.

4. Remove four bolts securing axle drive shaft to spindle flange and disconnect driveshaft. It may be necessary to force torque arm outboard to provide clearance to lower driveshaft.

Torque Control Arm

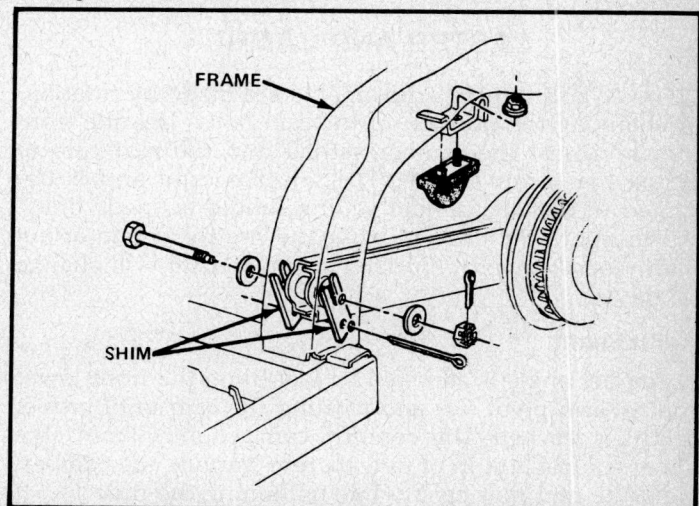

Stabilizer Shaft Installation

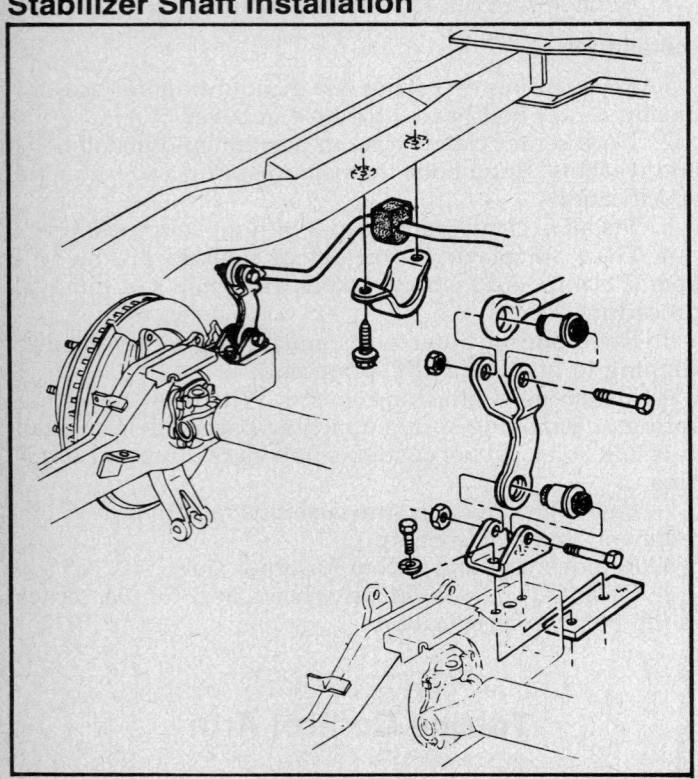

5. Disconnect brake line at caliper and from torque arm. Disconnect parking brake cable.

6. Remove torque arm pivot bolt and toe-in shims and pull torque arm out of frame. Tape shims together and identify for correct reinstallation.

Installation

1. Place torque arm in frame opening.

2. Install pivot bolt. Place toe-in shims in original position on both sides of torque arm. Install cotter pin retaining shims with loop of pin pointed outboard. Do not tighten pivot bolt nut at this time.

3. Raise axle driveshaft into position and install to drive flange. Torque bolts to specifications.

4. Raise strut rod into position and insert strut rod shaft so that flat lines up with flat in spindle support fork. Install nut and torque to specifications.

5. Install shock absorber lower eye and tighten nut to specifications.

6. Connect spring end as outlined under spring installation, step 3–6. If vehicle is so equipped, connect stabilizer shaft to torque arm.

7. Install brake line at caliper and torque arm. Bleed brakes.

8. Install wheel and tire. Torque the torque arm pivot bolt to specifications and install cotter pin with weight on wheels.

FRONT SUSPENSION— GENERAL MOTORS REAR DRIVE H BODY

Wheel Alignment

Front end alignment consists of three adjustments which should be done in order: camber (first), caster (second), toe-in (third).

CASTER AND CAMBER

Caster and camber adjustments are made by rotating, or changing the position of the cam bolts. Use the front cam to adjust the camber setting and the rear cam to adjust the caster setting. The lower control arm is designed so that the camber setting should be made first.

The front cam tends to move the control arm in or out with respect to the vehicle. This movement will change camber.

Adjustment

Camber angle is adjusted by loosening the front lower control arm pivot nut and rotating the cam until proper setting is reached. This eccentric cam action will move the lower control arm in or out, thereby varying the camber. Hold the cam bolt head while tightening the nut.

Caster angle is adjusted by loosening the rear lower control arm pivot nut and rotating the cam until proper setting is reached. This eccentric cam action will tend to move the lower control arm fore or aft thereby varying the caster. Hold the cam bolt head while tightening the nut. Recheck camber after setting caster.

TOE-IN

Toe-in can be increased or decreased by changing the length of the tie rods. A threaded sleeve is provided for this purpose. The tie rods are mounted ahead of the steering knuckle and must be decreased in length in order to increase toe-in. Toe-in adjustment must be checked after camber and caster adjustment.

Adjustment

Toe-in is the difference in the distance measured between the front and rear of the front wheels. The wheels must be in the straight ahead position when adjusting toe-in. Check position of tie rod clamps (frame clearance) after setting toe-in.

Front Suspension

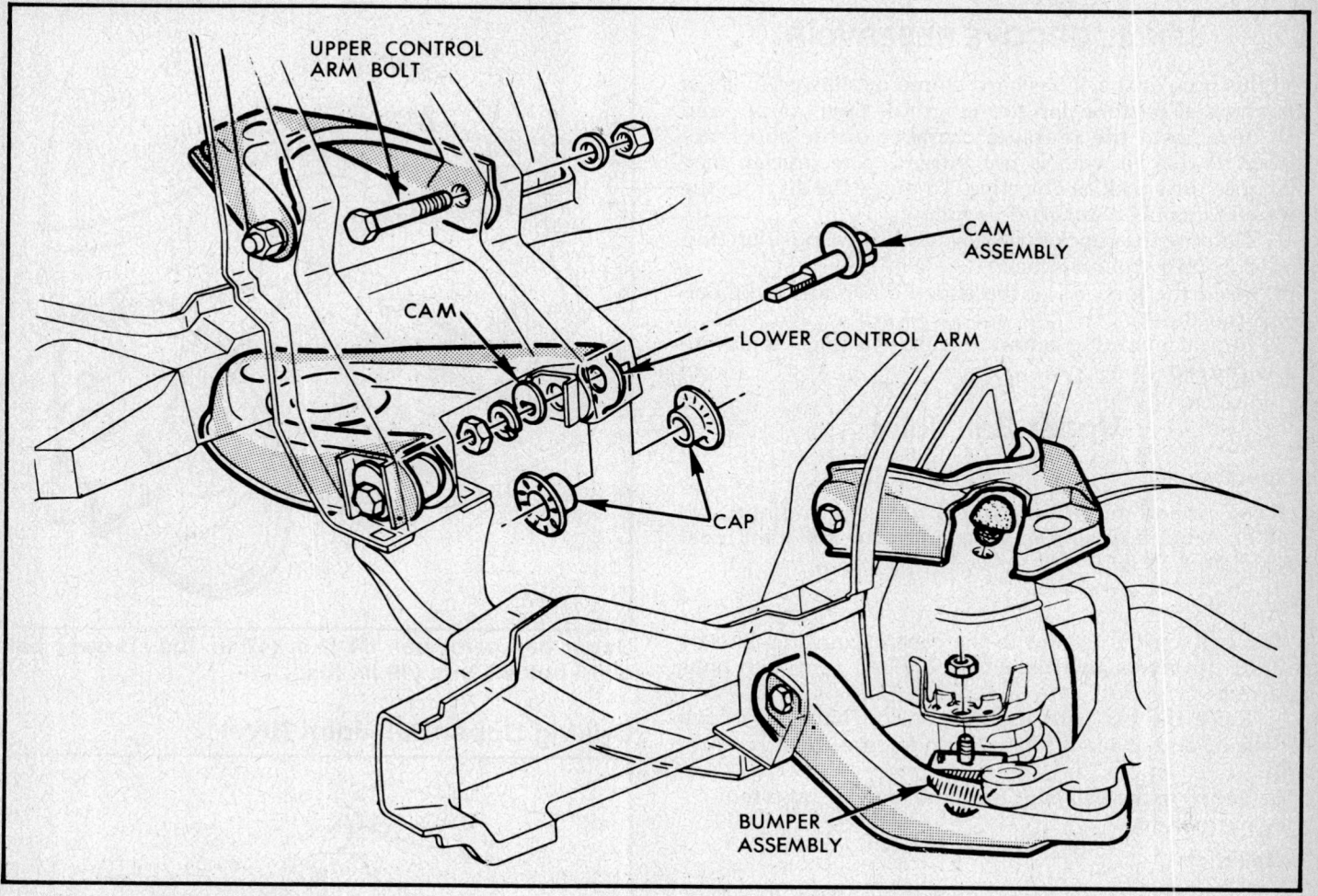

UPPER CONTROL ARM BOLT

CAM ASSEMBLY

CAM

LOWER CONTROL ARM

CAP

CAP

BUMPER ASSEMBLY

Wheel Bearings

NOTE Tapered roller bearings are used on all series vehicles and they have a slightly loose feel when properly adjusted. A design feature of front wheel tapered roller bearings is that they must never be pre-loaded. Damage can result from pre-loading.

Cones must be a slip fit on the spindle and the inside diameter of cones should be lubricated to insure that the cones will creep. Spindle nut must be a free-running fit on threads.

Inspection

1. Raise vehicle and support at front lower control arm.
2. Spin wheel to check for unusual noise or roughness.
3. If bearings are noisy, tight, or excessively loose, they should be cleaned, inspected and relubricated prior to adjustment.

To check for tight or loose bearings, grip the tire at the top and bottom and move the wheel assembly in and out on the spindle. Measure movement of hub assembly. If movement is less than .001 in. or greater than .005 in., adjust bearings.

Adjustment

1. Remove hub cap or wheel disc from wheel.
2. Remove dust cap from hub.
3. Remove cotter pin from spindle and spindle nut.
4. Tighten the spindle nut to 12 ft.-lbs. while turning the wheel assembly forward by hand to fully seat the bearings. This will remove any grease or burrs which could cause excessive wheel bearing play later.
5. Back off the nut to the "just loose" position.
6. Hand tighten the spindle nut. Loosen spindle nut until either hole in the spindle lines up with a slot in the nut. (Not more than ½ flat).
7. Install new cotter pin. Bend the ends of the cotter pin against nut, cut off extra length to ensure ends will not interfere with the dust cap.
8. Measure the looseness in the hub assembly. There will be from .001 to .005 inches end play when properly adjusted.
9. Install dust cap on hub.
10. Replace the wheel cover or hub cap.

Shock Absorber

SPIRAL GROOVE RESERVOIR

If this type of shock has been stored or allowed to lay in a horizontal position for any length of time, an air void will develop in the pressure chamber of the shock absorber. If this air void is not purged, a technician may diagnose the shock as defective. To purge the air from the pressure chamber, proceed as follows:

1. Holding the shock in its normal vertical position (top end up), fully extend shock.
2. Hold the top end of the shock down and fully collapse the shock.
3. Repeat pumping action at least five times to assure air is purged.

Upper Ball Joint

Inspection

Raise car and move front wheel vertically and horizontally by hand. if there is any free play, the ball joint must be replaced.

Removal

The ball joint is riveted to the control arm. Replace by drilling out rivets and installing new ball joint with bolts and nuts.

1. Raise the car with the suspension hanging in full rebound, and place a support under the lower control arm.
2. Separate the ball joint from the knuckle, and remove the control arm.

Installation

1. Install ball joint into control arm with nuts and bolts.
2. Install control arm.
3. Install ball joint stud to knuckle. Install a new cotter pin.

Shock Absorber

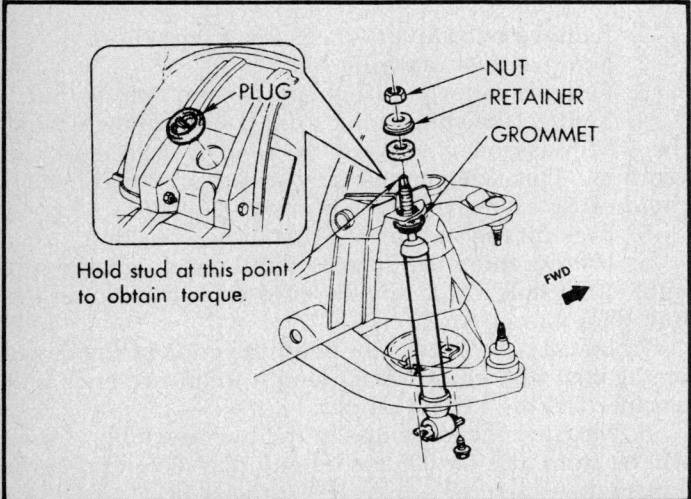

Lower studs 59 N·m (43 in. lbs.). Top nut 10 N·m (7 in. lbs.).

Ball Joint Replacement

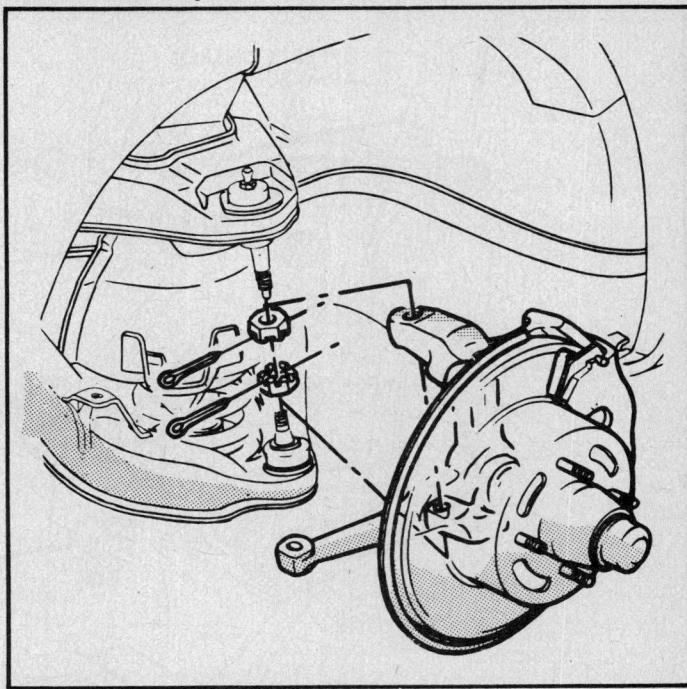

Upper ball pivot bolt 64 N·m (47 in. lbs.). Lower ball pivot bolt 66 N·m (49 in. lbs.).

Drilling Upper Ball Joint Rivet

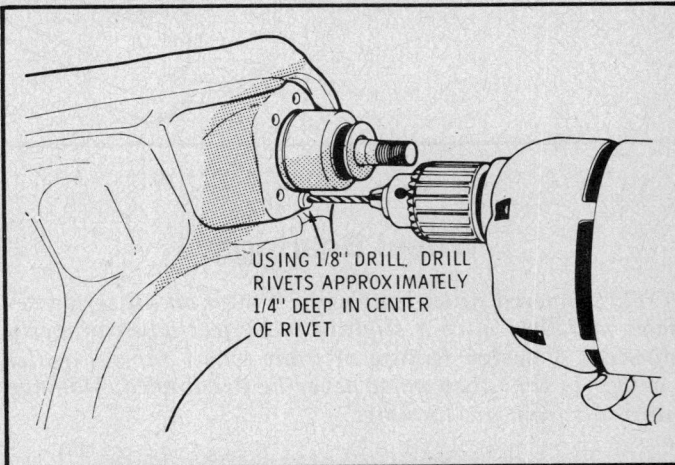

USING 1/8" DRILL, DRILL RIVETS APPROXIMATELY 1/4" DEEP IN CENTER OF RIVET

Using ⅛ in. drill, drill rivets approximately ¼ in. deep in center of rivet. Using ½ in. drill, drill just deep enough to remove rivet head.

Lower Ball Joint

Inspection

Wear indicators are incorporated in the lower ball joints.

Removal and Installation

The ball joint is a press fit in the control arm.
1. Raise the car with the suspension hanging in full

Built-in Wear Indicator for Lower Ball Joint

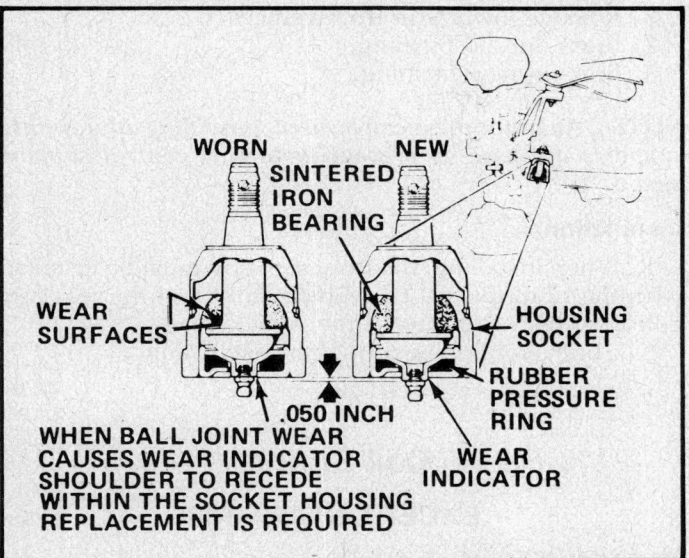

WORN   NEW   SINTERED IRON BEARING

WEAR SURFACES

HOUSING SOCKET

RUBBER PRESSURE RING

WEAR INDICATOR

.050 INCH

WHEN BALL JOINT WEAR CAUSES WEAR INDICATOR SHOULDER TO RECEDE WITHIN THE SOCKET HOUSING REPLACEMENT IS REQUIRED

rebound, and support the lower control arm at the outer end.

2. Free the ball joint from the knuckle, and press it out of the control arm.

Lower Control Arm

Removal

1. Raise the vehicle with suspension hanging in full rebound. Remove the shock absorber and coil spring and separate the ball joint from the knuckle.

2. Remove the inner pivot cam nuts and bolts after marking them for installation reference.

Press Out Ball Joint Stud

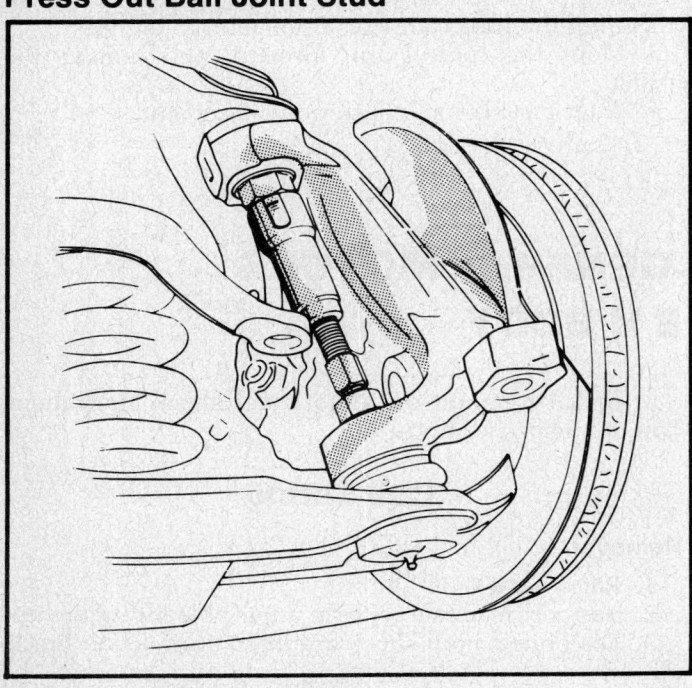

Front Coil Spring Positioning

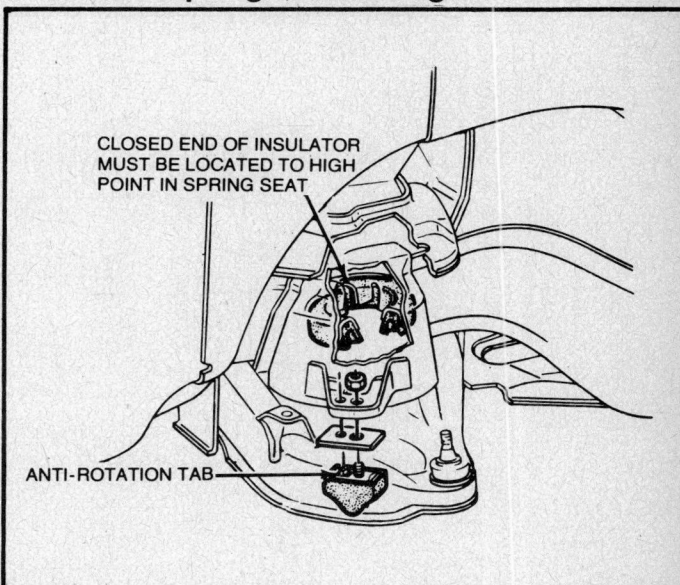

CLOSED END OF INSULATOR MUST BE LOCATED TO HIGH POINT IN SPRING SEAT

ANTI-ROTATION TAB

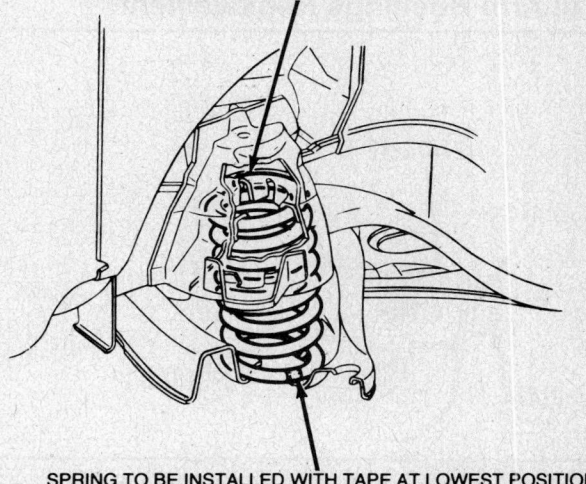

HELIX END OF SPRING (TOP) MUST BE SEATED IN UPPER SPRING SEAT. VISUALLY CHECK THROUGH SHOCK HOLE IN LOWER CONTROL ARM

SPRING TO BE INSTALLED WITH TAPE AT LOWEST POSITION. TOP OF SPRING IS COILED HELICAL AND BOTTOM OF SPRING IS COILED FLAT WITH A GRIPPER NOTCH NEAR END OF THE WIRE

WHEN A PORTION OF THE ACTIVE COILS ARE COMPRESSED, THE COIL-TO-COIL GAP MUST NEVER BE LESS THAN .44 IN. THE FIRST ¾ TURN OF COIL ON EACH END IS NOT ACTIVE

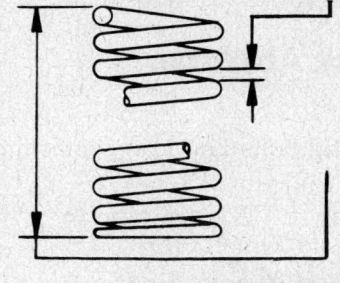

WHEN ENTIRE SPRING IS COMPRESSED, THE OVERALL DIMENSION MUST NEVER BE LESS THAN 7.30 IN.

Lower Ball Joint Installation

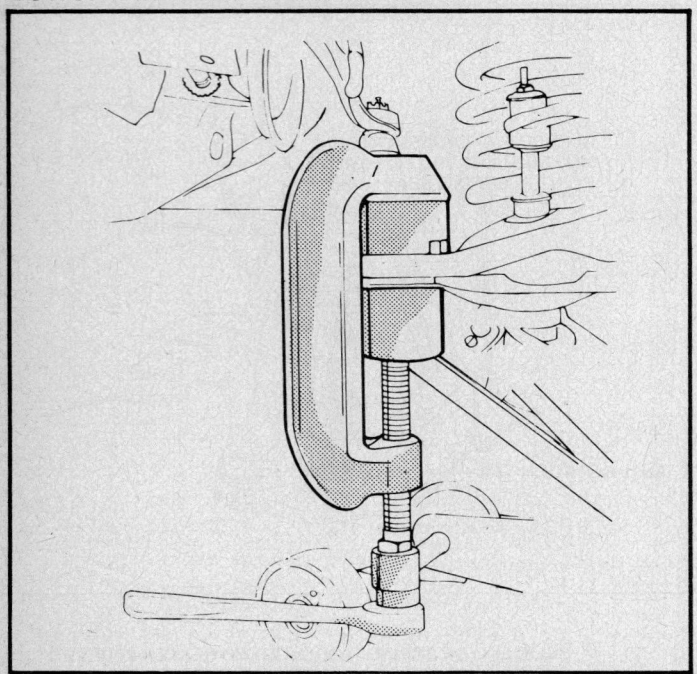

Control Arm Bushings Replacement

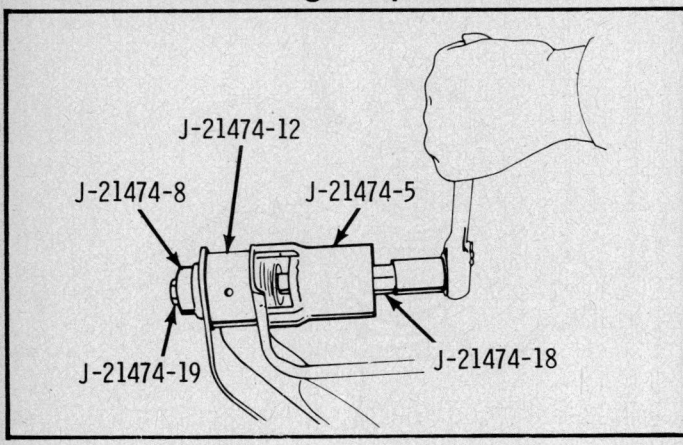

BUSHING REPLACEMENT

1. Remove lower arm from vehicle.
2. Press out old bushing.
3. Press in new bushing.

NOTE   An arbor press can be used, providing appropriate supports are used to prevent distorting control support ams.

Installation

1. When installing, the front cam bolt must be installed with the head toward the vehicle front and the rear cam bolt with the head toward the vehicle rear.
2. Check front alignment after installation.

Coil Spring
EXCEPT STARFIRE

Removal

1. Remove the shock absorber and stabilizer bar, and raise the vehicle with suspension hanging in full rebound.
2. Support the lower control arm with a jack, separate the ball joint and tie-rod end from the knuckle, and lower the control arm until the spring can be removed.

STARFIRE

Removal

NOTE   A spring compressor is required for coil spring removal.

1. Remove the shock absorber and stabilizer, and raise the vehicle.
2. Compress spring, remove lower control arm pivot bolts after marking cams for installation reference.
3. Move the control arm forward, and remove the spring.
4. After installation, check front alignment.

REAR SUSPENSION—GENERAL MOTORS REAR DRIVE H BODY

Rear Shock Absorber

Removal

1. Remove upper attaching bolts and lower attaching bolt and nut.
2. Remove shock absorber.

installation

1. Place shock into installed position and install upper retaining bolts. Torque to specifications.

2. Install bolt and nut onto lower shock attachment. Torque to specifications.

Coil Spring

Removal

1. Raise vehicle on a hoist.
2. Support rear axle with an adjustable lifting device.
3. Disconnect both shock absorbers from lower brackets.

Torque Arm Suspension

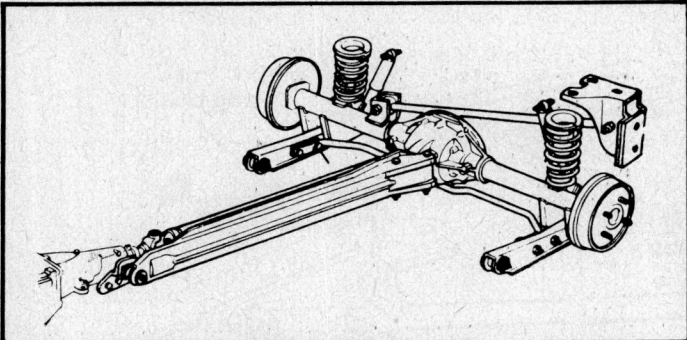

4. Lower the axle and remove the springs, insulators, and retainer/bumper assemblies. One or both springs may be removed. When lowering the axle, do not stretch the brake hose running from frame to axle.

Installation

1. Install retainer/bumper assembly onto top of spring. Place the insulator onto the retainer.
2. Raise the axle into the proper position, being sure the spring assembly is properly oriented to the underbody.
3. Reconnect the shock absorbers and torque to specifications.

Tie-Rod

Replacement

A tie-rod is mounted to the rear of the axle. It is important to use shims to position the axle assembly so that

Rear Shock Mounting

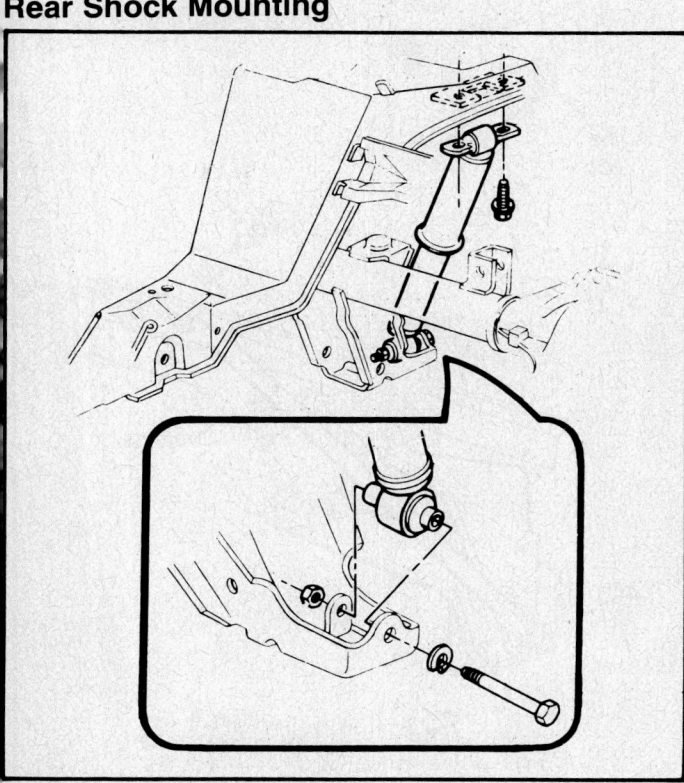

Coil Springs

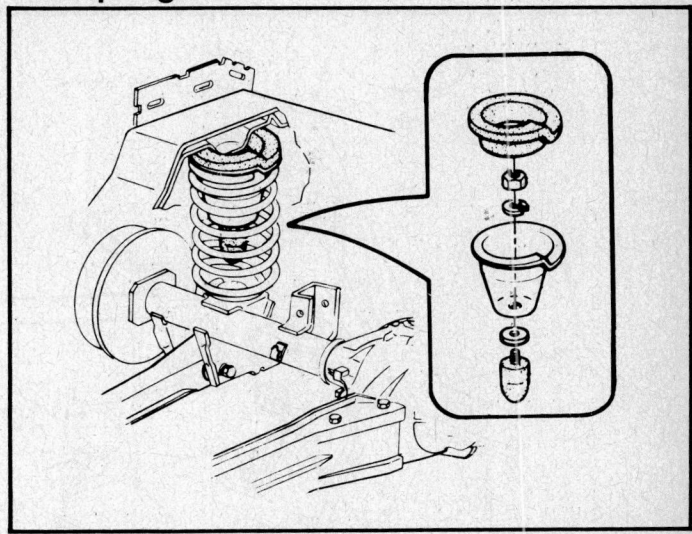

equal clearances exist between tire and wheelhouse on each side of the vehicle.
1. Raise vehicle on a hoist, and support the rear axle.
2. Remove bolt at underbody end of track rod.
3. Remove bolt at axle bracket.
4. Remove tie-rod from vehicle.
5. Place new tie-rod into position and install bolt at each bracket.

Axle Shaft

Removal

1. Raise vehicle on hoist. Remove wheel and tire assembly and brake drum.
2. Clean all dirt from area of carrier cover.
3. Drain lubricant from carrier by removing cover.
4. Unscrew differential pinion shaft lock screw and remove the differential pinion shaft.
5. Push flanged end of axle shaft toward center of vehicle and remove C lock from bottom end of shaft.
6. Remove axle shaft from housing, being careful not to damage oil seal.

OIL SEAL AND/OR BEARING REPLACEMENT

1. If replacing seal only, remove the oil seal by using the button end of the axle shaft. Insert the button end of the shaft behind the steel case of the oil seal, then pry seal out of bore being careful not to damage housing.
2. When removing bearings, insert tool into bore so that tool head grasps behind bearing. Slide washer against seal, or bearing, and turn nut against washer. Attach slide hammer and remove bearing.
3. Lubricate new bearing with hypoid lubricant and install into tube. Make sure tool contacts end of axle tube to insure that bearing is at proper depth.
4. Lubricate cavity between the seal lips with a high melting point wheel bearing lubricant; position seal on tool. Position seal in axle housing bore, tap seal in bore flush with end of housing.

Rear Suspension Tie Rod

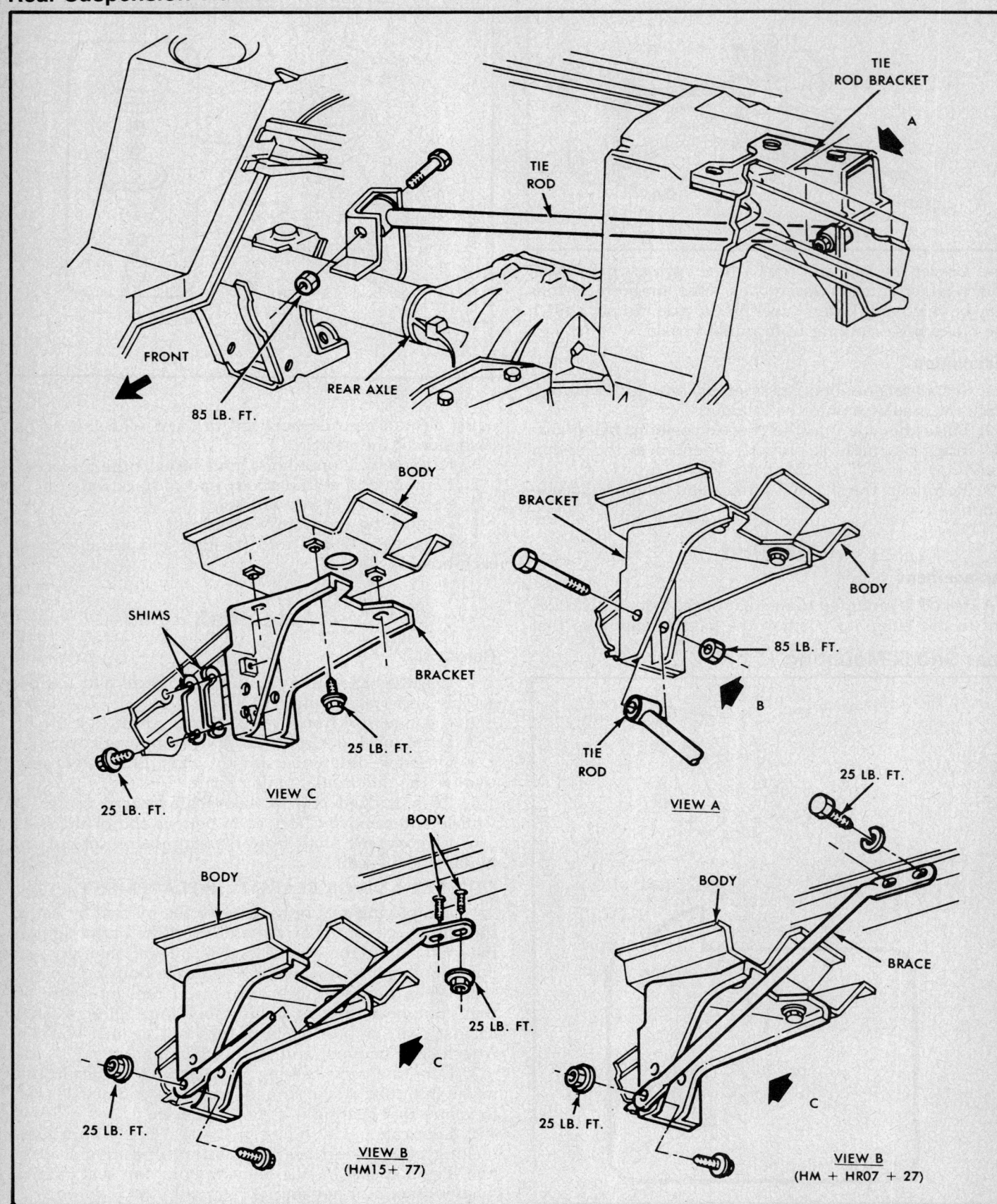

Axle Shaft Bearing and Seal

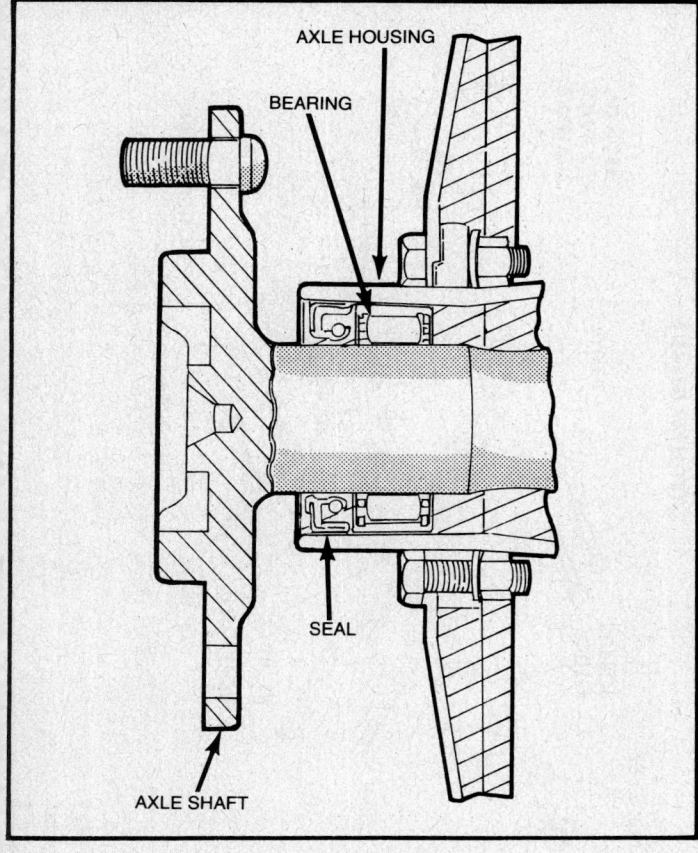

5. Install axle shaft, brake drum and wheel and tire assembly.

6. Bleed and adjust brakes.

Installation

1. Slide axle shaft into place.

CAUTION   Exercise care that splines on end of shaft do not damage oil seal and that they engage with splines of differential side gear.

Wheel Bearing and Oil Seal Removal

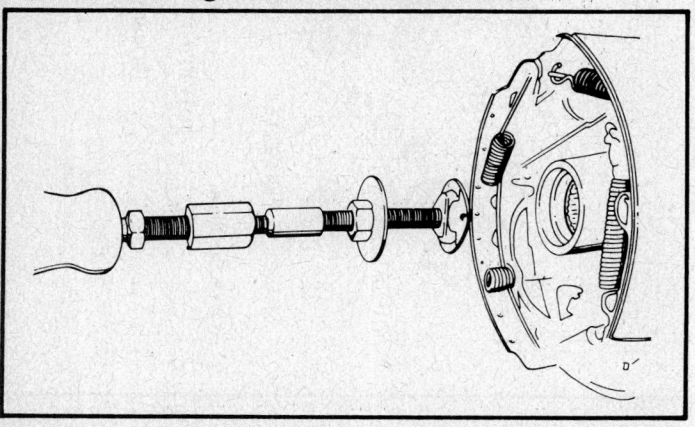

2. Install axle shaft C lock on button end of axle shaft and push shaft outward so that shaft lock seats in counterbore of differential side gear.

3. Position differential pinion shaft through case and pinions, aligning hole in shaft with lock screw hole. Install lock screw.

4. using a new gasket, install carrier cover and torque bolts to 20 ft.-lbs. Make sure both gasket surfaces on carrier and cover are clean before installing new gasket. Torque carrier cover bolts in a crosswise pattern to ensure uniform draw on cover gasket.

5. Fill axle with lubricant to level even with bottom of filler hole.

6. Install brake drum and wheel and tire assembly.

7. Lower vehicle and remove from hoist.

Wheel Bearing Installation

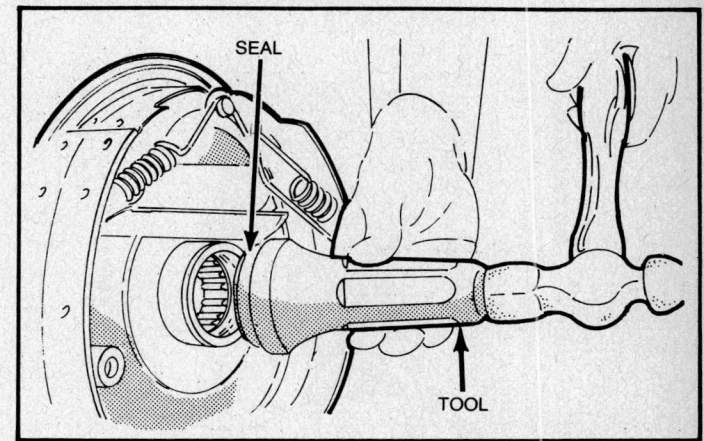

Torque Arm Attachments

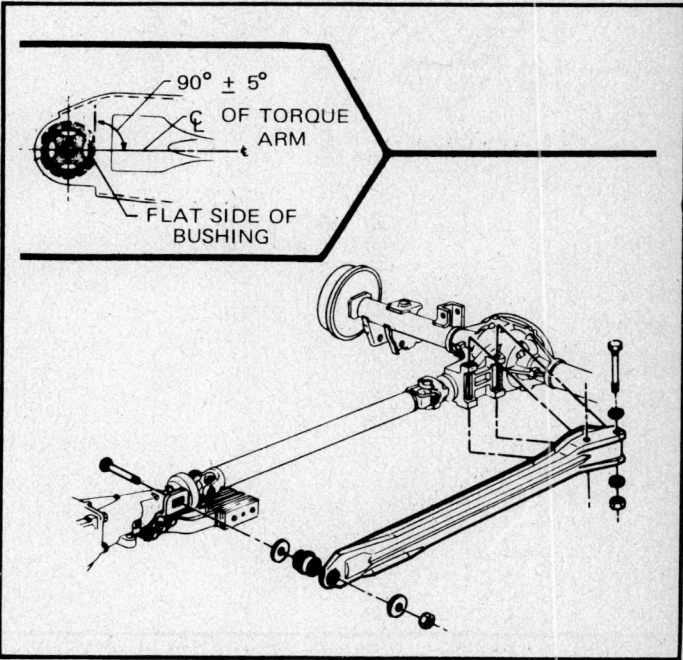

Torque Arm to Support Attachment

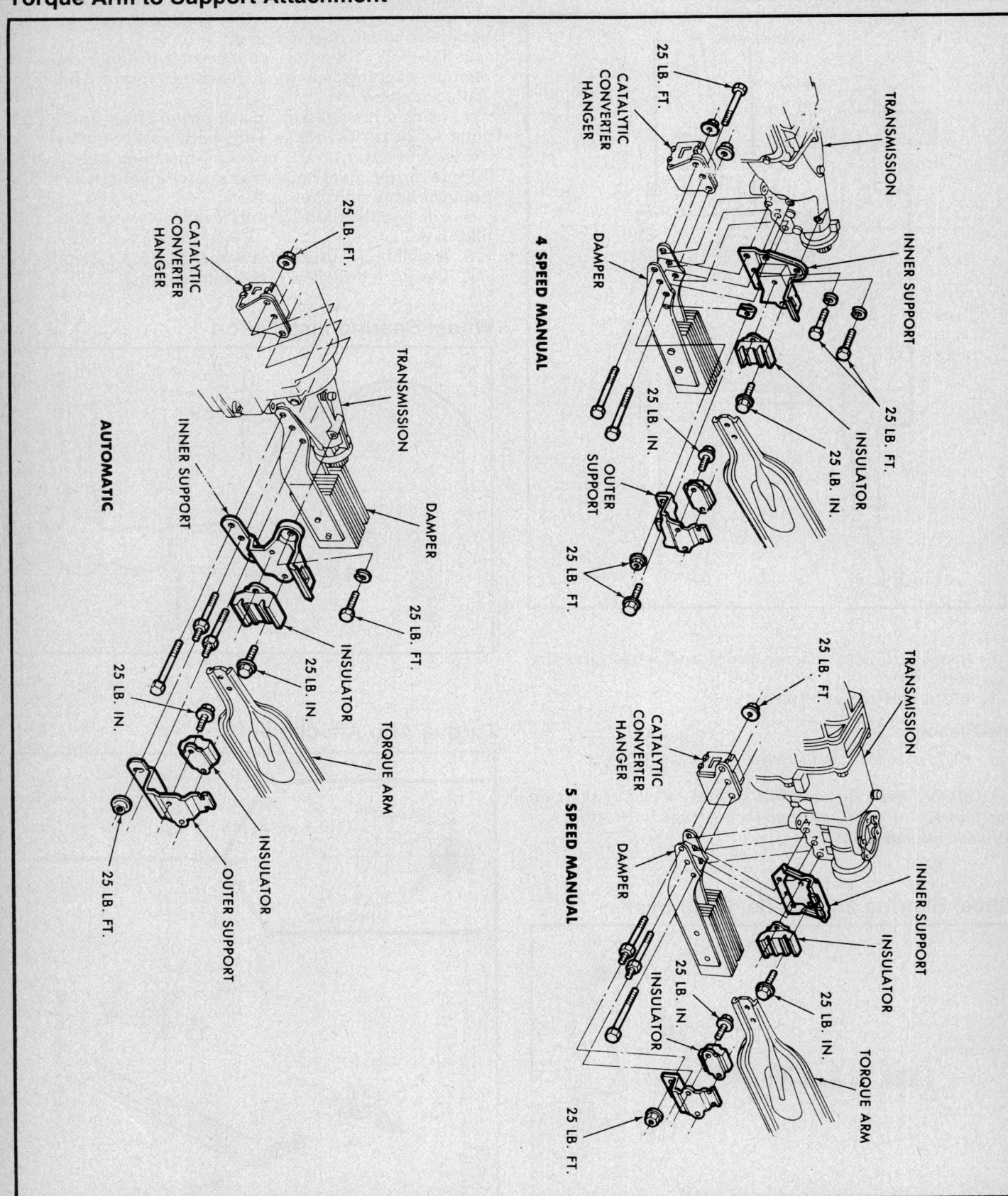

FRONT SUSPENSION—GENERAL MOTORS REAR DRIVE T BODY

Wheel Alignment

CAMBER

Camber angle can be increased approximately one degree. Remove the upper ball joint, rotate it one-half turn and reinstall it with the flat of the upper flange on the inboard side of the control arm.

Camber Adjustment

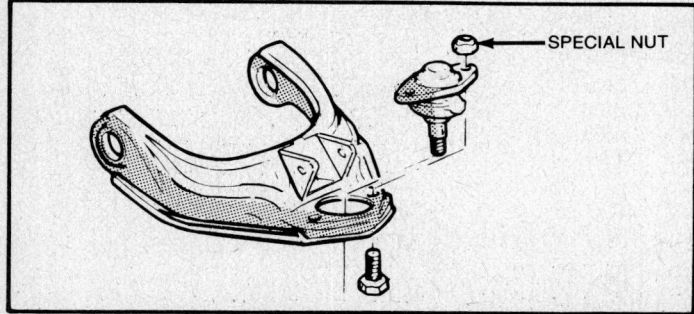

To increase camber, disconnect upper ball joint and rotate 180° to position "flat" of flange inboard. Then reconnect ball joint.

CASTER

Shims placed between the upper control arm and legs control caster. Always use two washers totalling 12 mm thickness, placing one washer at each end of the locating tube.

TOE

Adjust by changing tie-rod position. Loosen the nuts at the steering knuckle end of the tie rod and the rubber cover at the other end. Rotate tie-rod to change adjustment.

Wheel Bearings

NOTE Tapered roller bearings are used on all series vehicles and they have a slightly loose feel when properly adjusted. A design feature of front wheel tapered roller bearings is that they must never be pre-loaded. Damage can result from pre-loading.

The proper functioning of the front suspension cannot be maintained unless the front wheel taper roller bearings are correctly adjusted. Cones must be a slip fit on the spindle and the inside diameter of cones should be lubricated to insure that the cones will creep. Spindle nut must be a free-running fit on threads.

Inspection

1. Raise vehicle and support at front lower control arm.
2. Spin wheel to check for unusual noise or roughness.

3. If bearings are noisy, tight, or excessively loose, they should be cleaned, inspected, and relubricated prior to final adjustment. If it is necessary to inspect bearings, movement should be from 0.025 mm to 0.127 mm (.001–.005 in.). If movement is not in this range, adjust bearings.

Adjustment

1. Remove hub cap or wheel disc from wheel.
2. Remove dust cap from hub.
3. Remove cotter pin from spindle and spindle nut.
4. Tighten the spindle nut to 16 N•m (12 ft.-lbs.) while turning the wheel assembly forward by hand to fully seat the bearings. This will remove any grease or burrs which could cause excessive wheel bearing play later.
5. Back off the nut to the "just loose" position.
6. Hand-tighten the spindle nut. Loosen spindle nut until either hole in the spindle lines up with a slot in the nut (not more than ½ flat).
7. Install new cotter pin. Bend the ends of the cotter pin against nut, cut off extra length to ensure ends will not interfere with the dust cap.
8. Measure the looseness in the hub assembly. There will be from 0.025 to 0.127 mm (.001 to .005 in.) end-play when properly adjusted.
9. Install dust cap on hub.
10. Replace the wheel cover or hub cap.

Shock Absorbers

Removal

1. Hold the shock absorber upper stem and remove the nut, upper retainer and rubber grommet.

Front Shock Absorber

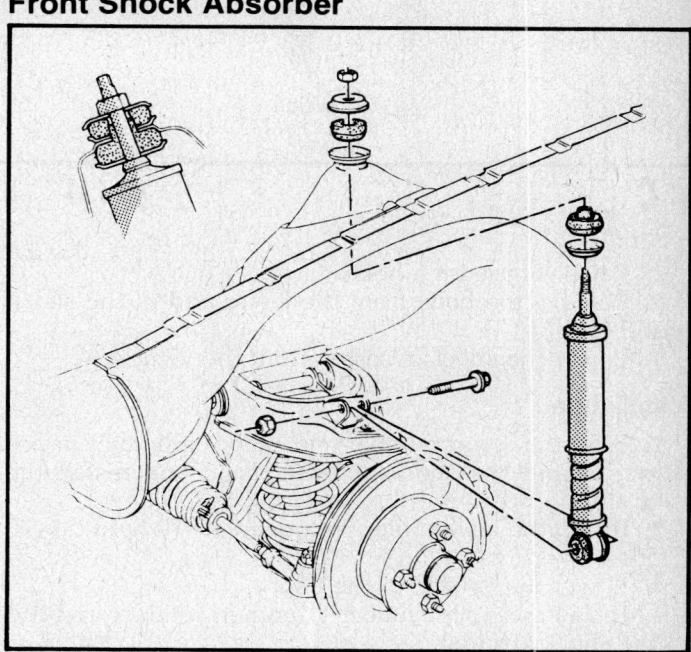

Front Suspension

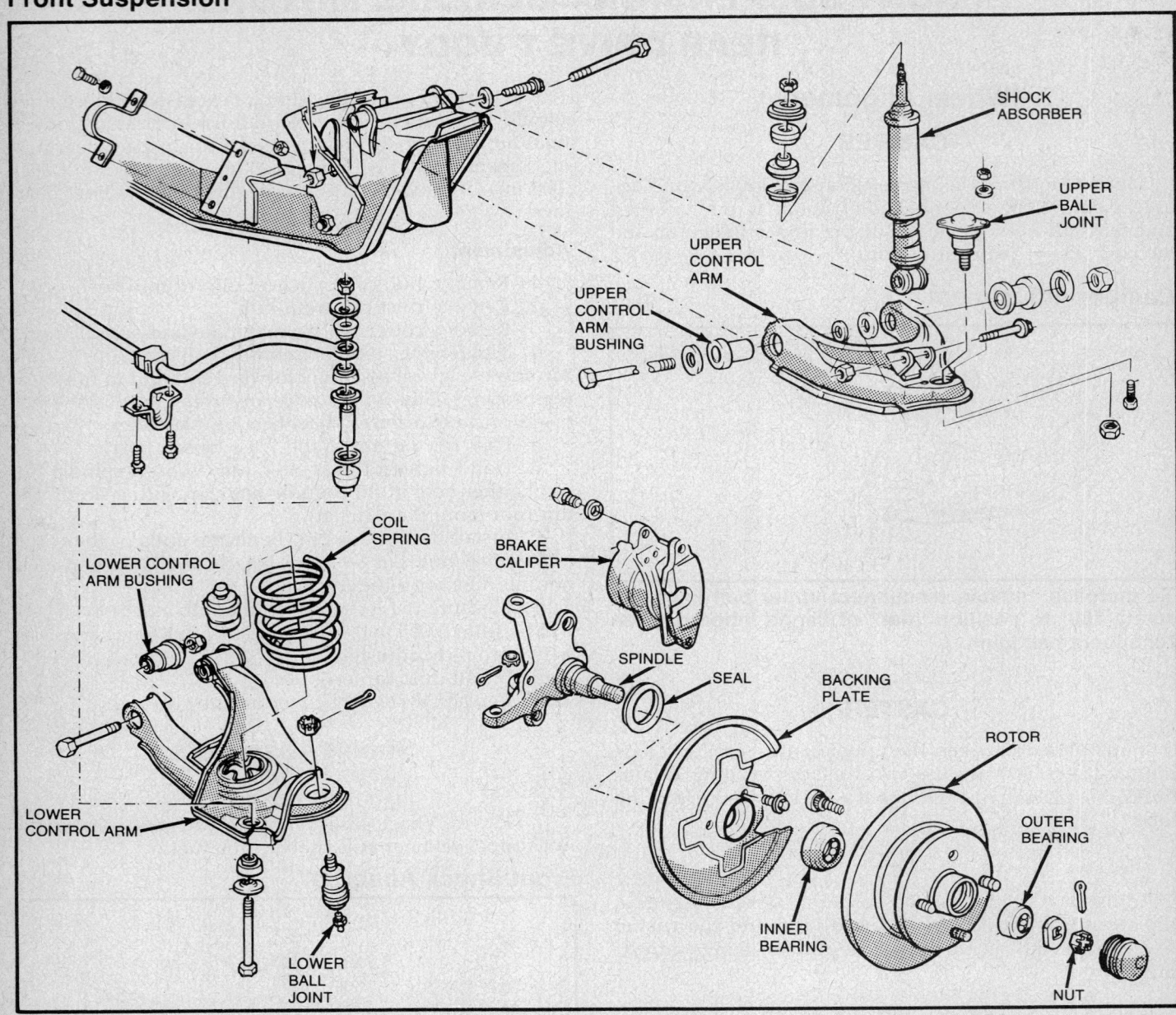

2. Raise vehicle on a hoist.

3. Remove the bolts from the lower end of the shock absorber.

4. Lower the shock absorber from the vehicle.

Installation

1. With the lower retainer and rubber grommet in position, extend the shock absorber stem and install the stem through the wheelhouse opening.

2. Install the lower bolts. Torque to 48–70 N•m (35–50 ft.-lbs.).

3. Lower the vehicle to the floor.

4. Install the upper rubber grommet, retainer and nut to the shock absorber stem.

5. Hold the stem and tighten the nut to 7–13 N•m (60–120 in.-lbs.). Torque is obtained by running nut to unthreaded portion of stud.

Upper Ball Joint

Removal

1. Raise the vehicle on a hoist.

2. Remove the tire and wheel assembly.

3. Support the lower control arm with a floor jack.

4. Remove upper ball stud nut. Reinstall nut finger-tight.

5. Install spreader tool and push stud loose from knuckle.

Ball Joint Tool

6. Remove tool and remove nut from ball stud.

7. Remove two nuts and bolts attaching ball joint to upper control arm, then remove ball joint.

Installation

Inspect the tapered hole in the steering knuckle. Remove any dirt and if any out-of-roundness, deformation, or damage is noted, the knuckle *must* be replaced.

1. Install bolts and nuts attaching ball joint to upper control arm, then mate the upper control arm ball stud to the steering knuckle. The ball joint studs use a special nut which *must be discarded* whenever loosened and removed. On reassembly, use a standard nut to draw the ball joint into position on the knuckle. Torque the standard nut to 30 N•m (22 ft.-lbs.), then remove that nut and *install a new special nut* for final installation.

2. Install the ball stud nut and torque to 39–49 N•m (29–36 ft.-lbs.).

3. Install the tire and wheel assembly.

Lower Ball Joint

Removal

1. Raise vehicle on hoist.
2. Remove the tire and wheel assembly.
3. Support the lower control arm with a hydraulic floor jack.
4. Remove lower ball stud nut, then reinstall nut finger-tight.

Removal of Ball Joints From Knuckle

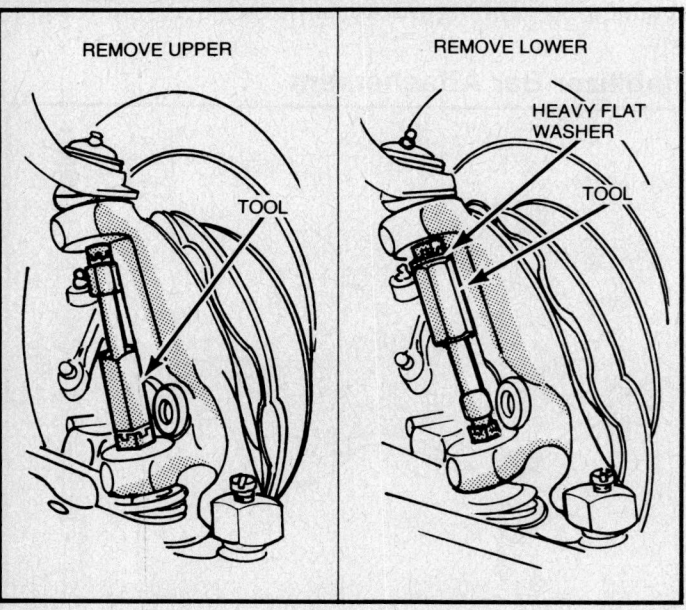

5. Install spreader tool and push the ball joint stud until it is free of the steering knuckle.
6. Remove tool and remove nut from ball stud.
7. Remove ball joint from lower control arm.

Installation

Inspect the tapered hole in the steering knuckle. Remove any dirt and if any out-of-roundness, deformation, or damage is noted, the knuckle *must* be replaced.

1. Mate the ball stud through the lower control arm and into the steering knuckle. The ball joint studs use a special nut which *must be discarded* whenever loosened and removed. On reassembly, use a standard nut to draw the ball joint into position on the knuckle. Torque the standard nut then remove that nut and *install a new special nut* for final installation.

2. Install the ball stud nut and torque to 56–73 N•m (41–54 ft.-lbs.).

3. Install the tire and wheel assembly.

Front Spring/Lower Control Arm

Removal

1. Remove wheel and tire assembly.
2. Disconnect stabilizer from lower control arm. Disconnect tie-rod from steering knuckle.
3. Support lower control arm with a jack.
4. Remove the nut from the lower ball joint. Install spreader tool and push the ball joint stud loose in the steering knuckle.
5. Swing the knuckle-and-hub out of the way, and attach securely with wire.
6. Loosen lower control arm pivot bolts.
7. Install chain through coil spring as a safety precaution.

CAUTION   The coil spring is under load. Be sure to install a chain and to slowly lower the jack.

8. Slowly lower the jack.

Correct Spring Position

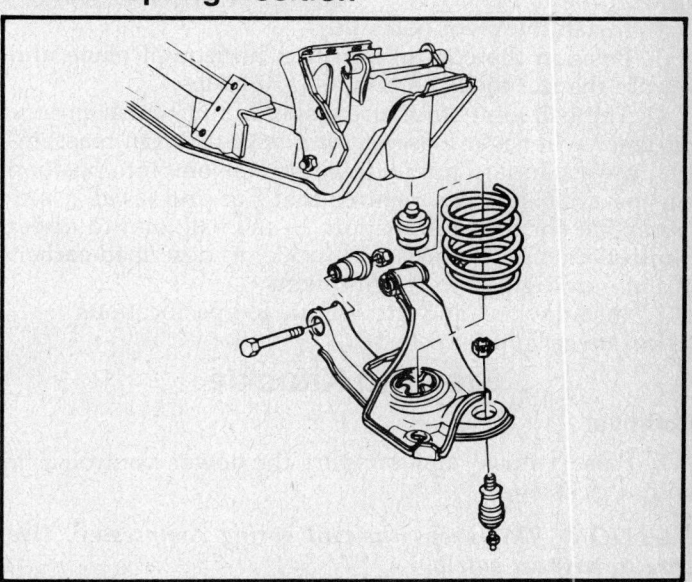

9. When the spring is extended as far as possible, use a prybar to carefully lift the spring over the lower control arm seat. Remove the spring.

10. Remove pivot bolts, and then remove lower control arm.

Installation

1. Install lower control arm and pivot bolts to underbody brackets.

2. Position spring and install spring into upper pocket. Use tape to hold insulator onto spring.

3. Install spring lower end onto lower control arm. It may be necessary to have an assistant help you compress the spring far enough to slide it over the raised area of the lower control arm seat.

4. Use a jack to raise the lower control arm and compress the coil spring.

5. The ball joint studs use a special nut which *must be discarded* whenever loosened and removed. On reassembly, use a standard nut to draw the ball joint into position on the knuckle, then remove that nut and *install a new special nut* for final installation. Install the ball joint through the lower control arm and into the steering knuckle. Install nut to ball joint stud and torque to 56–73 N•m (41–53 ft.-lbs.).

6. Connect stabilizer bar and tie-rod. Install wheel and tire assembly. Torque to specifications.

Upper Control Arm

Removal

1. Raise vehicle on a hoist.

2. Remove the tire and wheel assembly.

3. Support the lower control arm with a floor jack.

4. Remove upper ball joint from steering knuckle.

5. Remove control arm pivot bolts and remove control arm from vehicle.

Installation

1. Install upper control arm and pivot bolt to vehicle. The inner pivot bolt must be installed with the bolt head toward the front.

2. Install the pivot bolt nut.

3. Position the control arm in a horizontal plane and torque the nut to 59–68 N•m (43–50 ft.-lbs.)

4. The ball joint studs use a special nut which *must be discarded* whenever loosened and removed. On reassembly, use a standard nut to draw the ball joint into position on the knuckle, then remove that nut and *install a new special nut* for final installation. Install ball joint to upper control arm and to steering knuckle, as described earlier. Install nut; tighten to specifications.

5. Install wheel and tire; torque to specifications.

6. Lower vehicle to floor.

Steering Knuckle

Removal

1. Raise vehicle and support the lower control arm with a jackstand.

CAUTION This keeps the coil spring compressed. Use care to support safely.

2. Remove the tire and wheel assembly.

3. Remove the disc brake caliper. Do not allow the caliper to hang by the brake hose. Insert a piece of wood between the shoes to hold the piston in the caliper bore. The block of wood should be about the same thickness as the brake disc.

4. Remove the hub and disc.

5. Remove the splash shield.

6. Remove the tie-rod end from the steering knuckle.

7. Loosen both ball stud nuts. Using a spreader tool, push both the upper and lower ball studs from the steering knuckle.

8. Remove ball stud nuts and remove the steering knuckle.

Installation

1. Place steering knuckle in position and insert the upper and lower ball studs into knuckle bosses.

2. The ball joint studs use a special nut which *must be discarded* whenever loosened and removed. On reassembly, use a standard nut to draw the ball joint into position on the knuckle. Torque the standard nut then remove that nut and *install a new special nut* for final installation. Install ball stud nuts and tighten to specifications.

Stabilizer Bar

Removal

1. Raise the vehicle on a hoist.

2. Remove stabilizer bar nut and bolt from lower control arm.

3. Remove stabilizer bar bracket from body.

Installation

1. Hold stabilizer bar in place and install the body bushings and brackets.

2. Install the retainers, grommets and spacers to the lower control arm and install nuts.

3. Lower the vehicle to the floor.

4. Torque nut to 16–24 N•m (12–18 ft.-lbs.). Torque is obtained by running nut to unthreaded portion of link bolt.

Stabilizer Bar Attachement

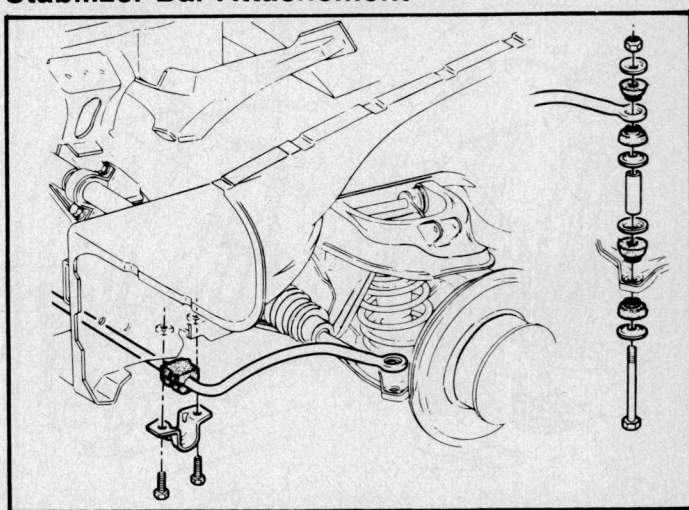

REAR SUSPENSION—GENERAL MOTORS REAR DRIVE T BODY

Rear Suspension

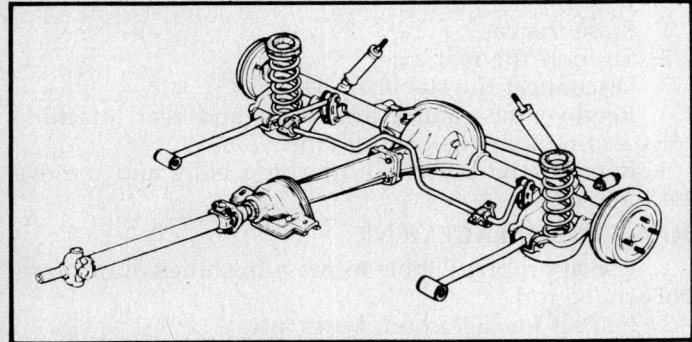

Rear Shock Absorber

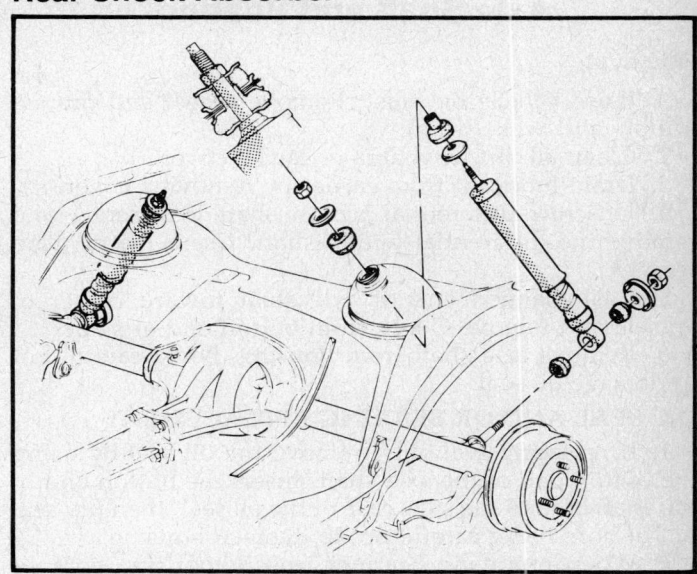

Shock Absorber

Removal

1. Support rear axle assembly.
2. Remove upper attaching bolts and lower attaching bolt and nut.
3. Remove shock absorber.

Installation

1. Install retainer and rubber grommet onto shock.
2. Place shock into installed position and install upper retaining bolts. Torque to specifications.
3. Install bolt and nut onto lower shock attachment. Torque to specifications.
4. Lower vehicle and remove from hoist.

Coil Spring

Removal

1. Raise vehicle on hoist.
2. Support rear axle with an adjustable lifting device.
3. Disconnect both shock absorbers from lower brackets.
4. Disconnect rear axle extension bracket.

CAUTION Be sure to use caution when disconnecting extension assembly. Be sure to support assembly safely.

5. Lower axle and remove springs and spring insulators. One or both springs may be removed at this point.

CAUTION When lowering axle, do not stretch brake hose running from frame to axle or damage to the brake line may result.

Installation

1. Install insulators on top and bottom of springs then position spring between upper and lower seats.

Coil Springs

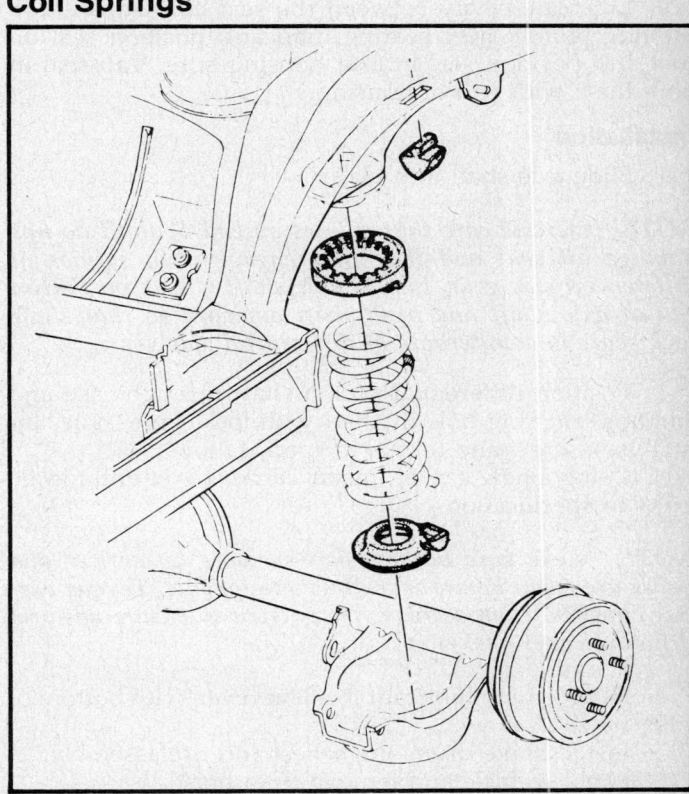

2. Raise axle and reconnect shock absorbers. Torque nut to specifications.

3. Remove lifting device from axle.

4. Lower vehicle and remove from hoist.

Axle Shaft and Bearing

Removal

1. Raise vehicle on hoist. Remove wheel and tire assembly and brake drum.

2. Clean all dirt from area of carrier cover.

3. Drain lubricant from carrier by removing cover.

4. Unscrew differential pinion shaft lock screw and remove the differential pinion shaft. Use a metric allen wrench.

5. Push flanged end of axle shaft toward center of vehicle and remove C lock from button end of shaft.

6. Remove axle shaft from housing, being careful not to damage oil seal.

OIL SEAL AND/OR BEARING REPLACEMENT

1. If replacing seal only, remove the oil seal by using the button end of the axle shaft. Insert the button end of the shaft behind the steel case of the oil seal, then pry seal out of bore being careful not to damage housing.

2. When removing bearings, insert tool into bore so that tool head grasps behind bearing. Slide washer against seal, or bearing, and turn nut against washer. Attach slide hammer and remove bearing.

3. Lubricate new bearing with hypoid lubricant and install into tube. Make sure tool contacts end of axle tube to insure that bearing is at proper depth.

4. Lubricate cavity between the seal lips with a high melting point wheel bearing lubricant; position seal on tool and position seal in axle housing bore. Tap seal in bore flush with end of housing.

Installation

1. Slide axle shaft into place.

NOTE Exercise care that splines on end of shaft do not damage oil seal and that they engage with splines of differential side gear. Install axle shaft C lock on button end of axle shaft and push shaft outward so that shaft lock seats in counterbore of differential side gear.

2. Position differential pinion shaft through case and pinions, aligning hole in shaft with lock screw hole. Install lock screw and torque to specifications.

3. Using a new gasket, install carrier cover and torque bolts to specifications.

NOTE Make sure both gasket surfaces on carrier and cover are clean before installing new gasket. Torque carrier cover bolts in a crosswise pattern to ensure uniform draw on cover gasket.

4. Fill axle with lubricant to a level even with bottom of filler hole.

5. Install brake drum and wheel and tire assembly.

6. Lower vehicle and remove from hoist.

Lower Control Arm and Tie-Rod

Removal

CAUTION If both control arms are to be replaced, remove and replace one control arm at a time to prevent the axle from rolling or slipping sideways.

1. Raise the car.

2. Support the rear axle.

3. Disconnect the stabilizer bar.

4. Remove the control arm front and rear attaching bolts and remove the control arm.

5. Remove the track rod attaching bolts and remove the track rod.

BUSHING REPLACEMENT

1. Use appropriate tools to press bushings out of control arm/tie rod.

2. Inspect for distortion, burrs, etc.

3. Press bushing into place.

Installation

1. Place control arm into position and install front and rear bolts. Torque to specifications.

2. Place tie-rod into position; torque bolts to specifications. Car must be at curb height when tightening pivot bolts. Tighten pivot bolts to 45 N•m (33 ft.-lbs.).

3. Reattach stabilizer bar.

Lower Control Arm and Tie Rod

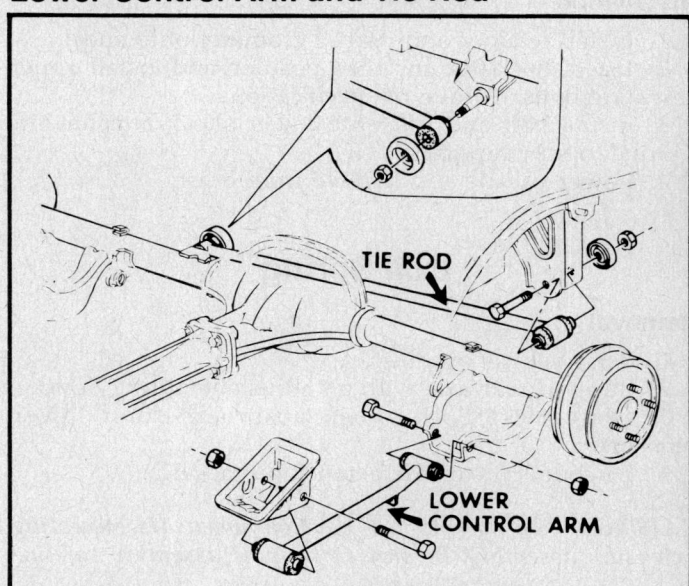

Stabilizer Bar

Removal

1. Raise vehicle on hoist.

2. Remove bolts securing brackets to body and link to axle and remove bar.

Installation

1. Place stabilizer into position. Install bolts and nuts. Torque to 20 N•m (15 ft.-lbs.).

GENERAL MOTORS ELECTRONIC LEVEL CONTROL

Description

The electronic level control (ELC) system automatically adjusts the rear height with varying car loads. The system is activated when weight is added to, or removed from, the rear of the car.

COMPONENTS

The electronic level control system consists of the following components:
1. Compressor
2. Air adjustable shock absorbers
3. Electronic height sensor
4. Compressor relay (two with E series)
5. Exhaust solenoid
6. Air dryer
7. Wiring and air tubing
8. Pressure regulator (E series only)

The E and K series front drive cars (torsion bar front suspension) have a pressure limiter valve added to the system. This valve is located in the engine compartment in the pressure line which runs from the compressor to the shocks. The limiter allows a maximum of 85 psi (586 kPa) ± 5 psi (34 kPa) to reach the rear shocks.

Head Cover Tightening Sequence

Torque bolts to 4 N·m (36 in.-lbs.)

Compressor Assembly

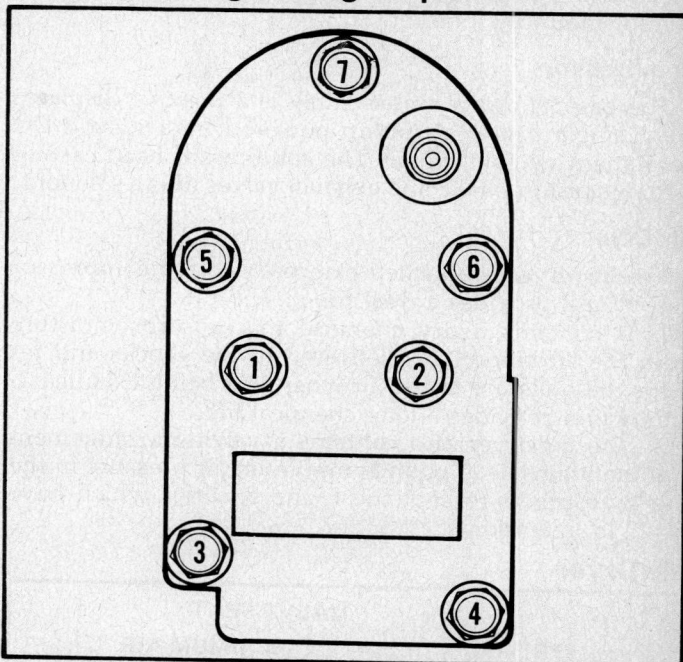

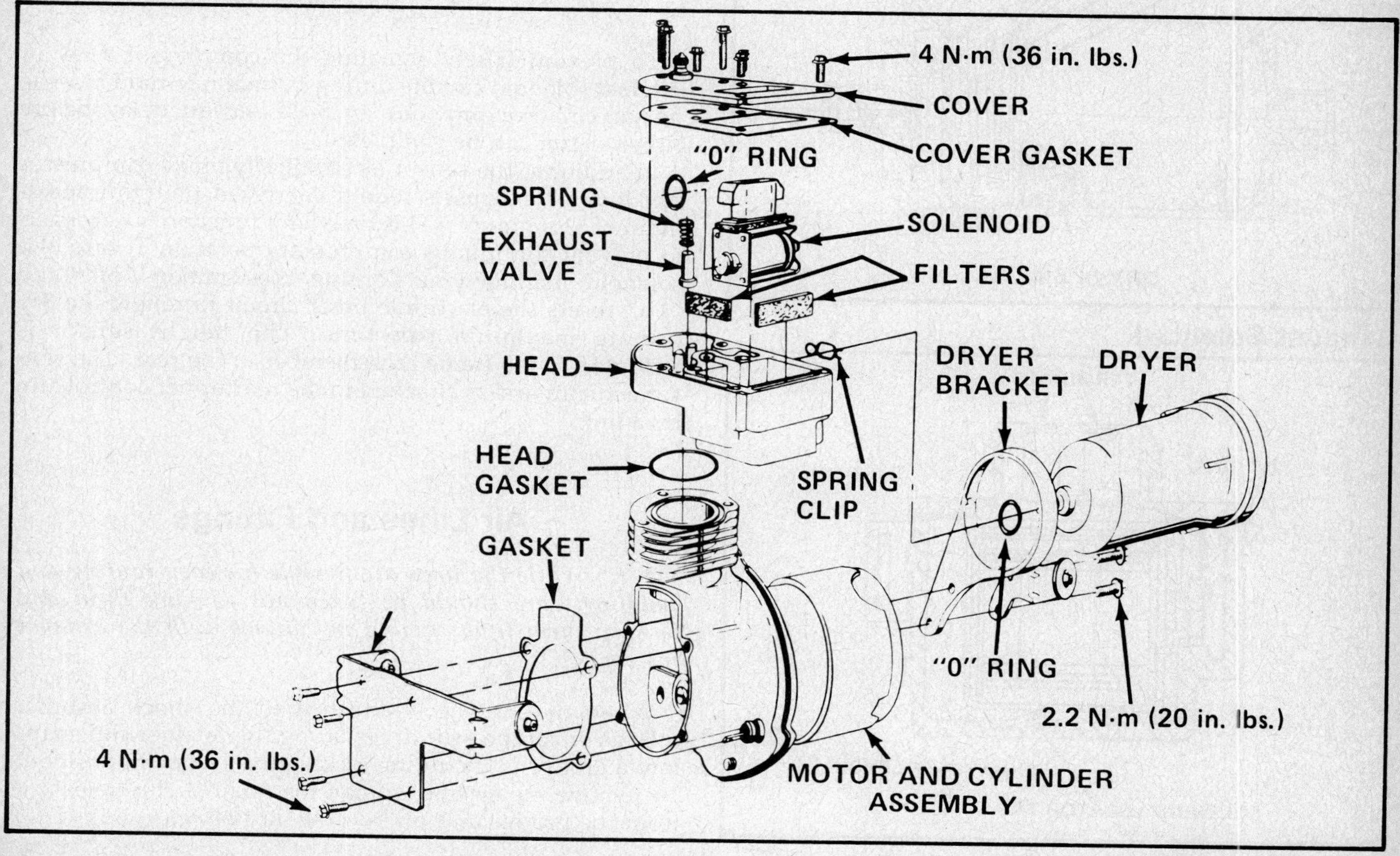

4 N·m (36 in. lbs.)
COVER
COVER GASKET
"0" RING
SPRING
EXHAUST VALVE
SOLENOID
FILTERS
HEAD
DRYER BRACKET
DRYER
HEAD GASKET
SPRING CLIP
GASKET
"0" RING
2.2 N·m (20 in. lbs.)
4 N·m (36 in. lbs.)
MOTOR AND CYLINDER ASSEMBLY

B639

Compressor Relay

This relay is a single pole single throw type that completes the 12V(+) circuit to the compressor motor when energized. The compressor relay is located on the compressor mounting bracket.

Compressor

The basic compressor assembly is a positive displacement single piston air pump powered by a 12 volt DC permanent magnet motor. The compressor head casting contains piston intake and exhaust valves plus a solenoid.

Air Dryer

The air dryer is attached externally to the compressor output and provides a dual function.

1. It contains a dry chemical that absorbs moisture from the air before it is delivered to the shocks and returns the moisture to the air when it is being exhausted. This action provides a long chemical life.

2. The air dryer also contains a valving arrangement that maintains 8–15 pounds minimum air pressure in the shock absorbers (except the E and K series which have 14–20 lb. retention.

Air Dryer

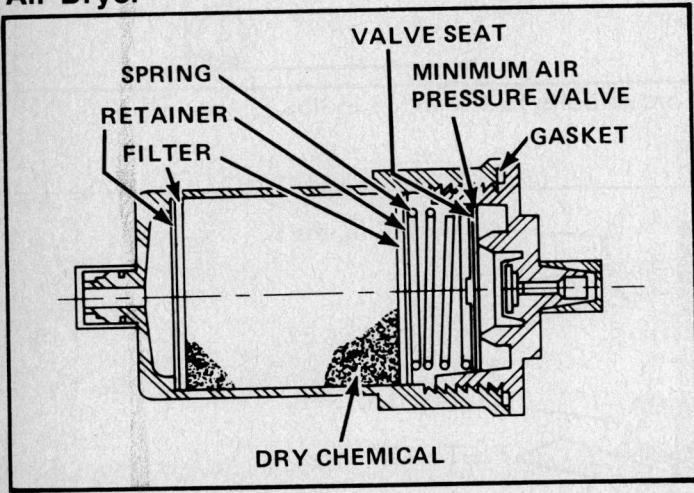

Exhaust Solenoid

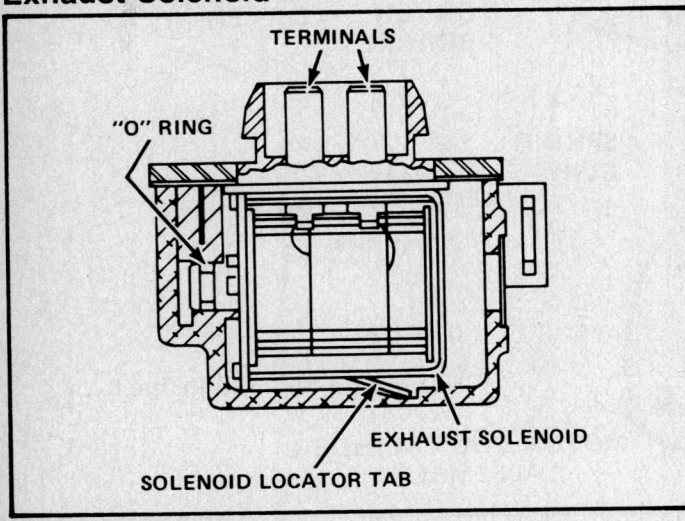

Exhaust Solenoid

The exhaust solenoid is located in the compressor head assembly and provides two functions.

1. It exhausts air from the system when energized. The height sensor controls this function.

2. It acts as a blow off valve to limit maximum pressure output of the compressor.

Height Sensor

The height sensor is an electronic device that controls two basic circuits.

1. Compressor relay coil ground circuit.

2. Exhaust solenoid coil ground circuit.

Height Sensor

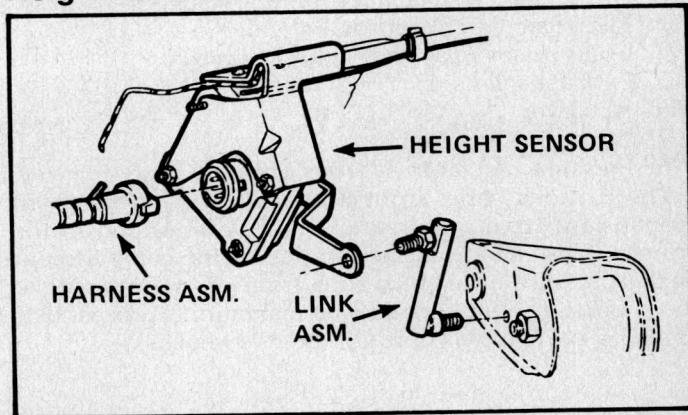

To prevent falsely actuating the compressor relay or exhaust solenoid circuits during normal ride motions, the sensor circuitry provides an 8–14 second delay before either circuit can be completed.

In addition, the sensor electronically limits compressor run time or exhaust solenoid energized time to a maximum of 3½ minutes. This time limit function is necessary to prevent continuous compressor operation in case of a solenoid malfunction. Turning the ignition "off" and "on" resets the electronic timer circuit to renew the 3½ minute maximum run time. The height sensor is mounted to the frame crossmember in the rear. The sensor actuator arm is attached to the rear upper control arm by a link.

Air Lines and Fittings

NOTE While the lines are flexible for easy routing and handling, care should be taken not to kink them and to keep them from coming in contact with the exhaust system.

When the air line is attached to the shock absorber fittings or compressor dryer fitting the retainer clip snaps into a groove in the fitting locking the air line in position. To remove the air line, spread the retainer clip, release it from the groove and pull on the air line.

Airline Retainer Clip

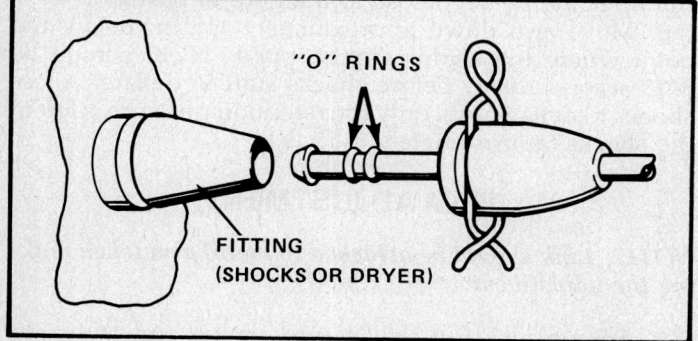

System Operation Check

NOTE When certain tests require raising the car on a hoist, the hoist should support the rear wheels or axle housing. When a frame type hoist is used, two additional jack stands should be used to support the rear axle housing in its normal curb weight position.

1. Select a suitable location at rear wheelhouse opening and measure distance to floor.
2. Start engine momentarily. Leave switch "ON".
3. Apply load to rear of car (two people or approximately 300–350 pounds).
   a. There should be 8–14 second delay before compressor turns on and the car begins to raise.
   b. Car should raise to within ¾ in. (19 mm) of measurement made in step 1 by the time the compressor shuts off. If car does not raise, refer to the diagnosis chart.

NOTE Failure of car to return to within ¾ in. (19 mm) of unloaded dimension can be caused by unusually heavy loading in the trunk which exceeds the capacity of the system. If this type of loading is encountered, remove it and repeat test.

4. Remove load applied in step 3.
   a. There should be 8–14 second delay before car begins to lower.
   b. Car should lower to within ¾ in. (19 mm) of measurement made in step 1 in less than 3½ minutes.

Compressor/Dryer Performance Test

COMPRESSOR CURRENT DRAW, PRESSURE OUTPUT AND LEAK DOWN TEST

1. Disconnect wiring from compressor motor and exhaust solenoid terminals.
2. Disconnect existing pressure line from dryer and attach pressure gauge to dryer fitting.
3. Connect ammeter to 12V source and to compressor.
   a. Current draw should NOT exceed 14 amp.

b. When gauge reads 110–120 psi SHUT COMPRESSOR OFF and observe if pressure leaks down.

IMPORTANT If compressor is permitted to run until it reaches its maximum output pressure, the solenoid exhaust valve will act as a relief valve. The resulting leak down when compressor is shut off will indicate a false leak.

c. Leak down pressure should not drop below 90 psi when compressor is shut off.

RESIDUAL AIR CHECK

1. Remove air line from dryer fitting and attach it to gauge. Attach gauge air line to dryer fitting.
2. Turn ignition "ON" and perform system check, to inflate shocks.
3. Turn ignition "OFF" and deflate system through compressor service valve. Gauge should read 8–15 psi after system is deflated.

COMPRESSOR/DRYER DIAGNOSIS CHART

Malfunction	Correction
1. Current draw exceeds 14 amps.	1. Replace motor cylinder assembly.
2. Compressor Inoperative.	2. Replace motor cylinder assembly.
3. Pressure build up OK but leaks down below 90 psi before holding steady.	3. Replace solenoid exhaust valve assembly.
4. Compressor pressure leaks down to 0 psi.	4. Leak test compressor/dryer assembly.
5. Compressor output less than 110 psi and current draw normal.	5. Perform compressor/dryer leak test. If no leak is found, replace motor/cylinder assembly.

Height Sensor Operational Check/Adjustment

OPERATIONAL CHECK

1. Turn ignition switch "ON" and raise car on hoist. If frame hoist is used, rear wheels or axle must be supported. Jacks should be adjusted upward until axle housing and/or wheels reach trim/curb weight position.
2. Compare neutral position of the height sensor metal arm with position of sensor arm being tested. (Shocks should have minimum air pressure.) If neutral position varies more than 3–4° check for correct sensor and/or link, sensor mounting bolts tight, sensor mounting bracket not bent. Make necessary corrections as required.
3. Disconnect link from height sensor arm.
4. Disconnect and reconnect wiring to height sensor to assure resetting the sensor time limit function. Failure to do this can result in erroneous diagnosis.

SUSPENSION
GENERAL MOTORS ELECTRONIC LEVEL CONTROL

5. Move sensor metal arm upward approximately 1½–2 in. above neutral position. There should be 8–15 seconds delay before compressor turns "ON." As soon as shocks noticeably inflate move sensor arm down slowly

Height Sensor Operation Check

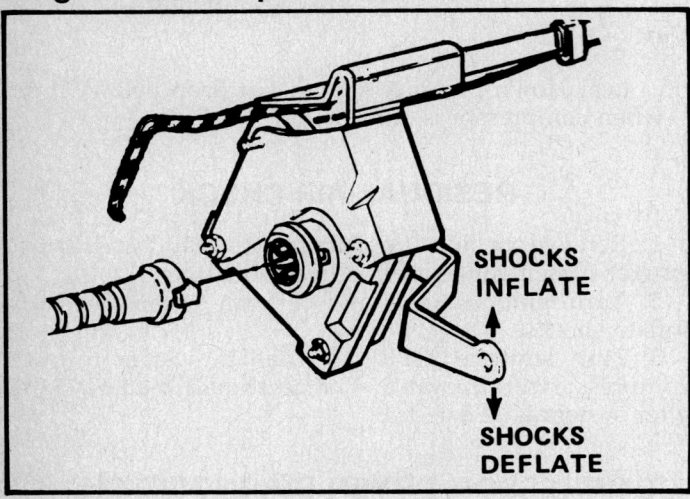

SHOCKS INFLATE

SHOCKS DEFLATE

and note arm position where compressor stops. This position should be very close to the neutral position.

6. Move arm down approximately 1½ in. below the point where the compressor stopped. There should be 8–15 seconds delay before shocks start to deflate. Allow shocks to deflate until only the retention pressure is left in the shocks (approximately 8–15 lbs.).

TRIM ADJUSTMENT

NOTE   Link should be attached to metal arm when making the adjustment.

1. Loosen lock nut that secures metal arm to height sensor plastic arm.
2. To increase car trim height move white plastic actuator arm upward and tighten lock nut.

NOTE   If all adjustment is used up, check trim height.

3. To lower car trim height, follow step 1 and move plastic arm down.
4. If adjustment cannot be made, check for correct height sensor.

Rear Drive

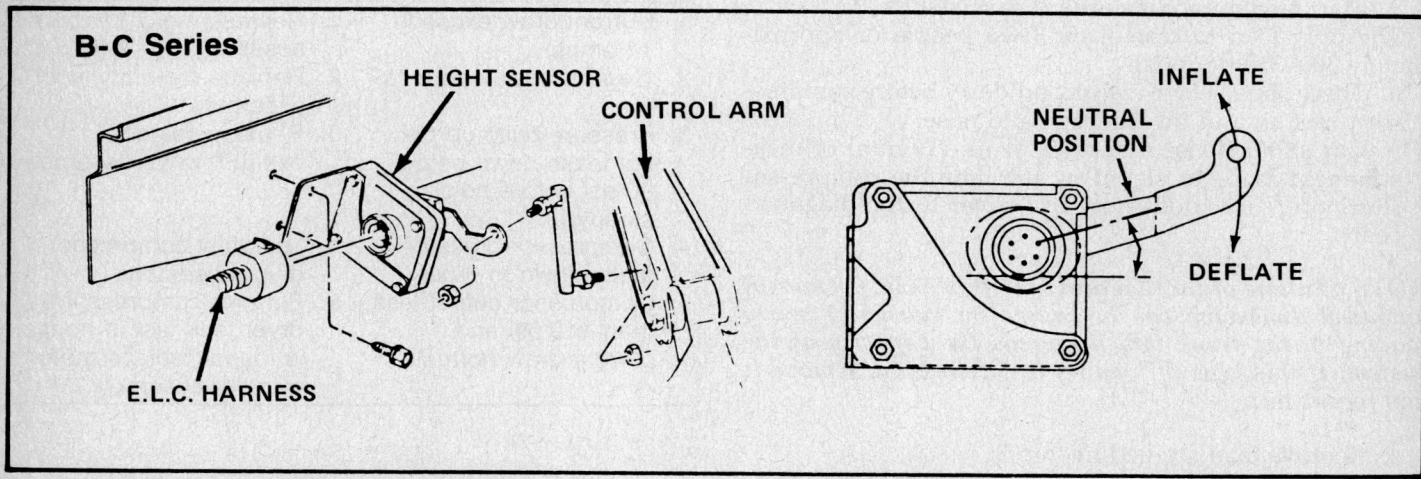

B-C Series

HEIGHT SENSOR   **CONTROL ARM**

E.L.C. HARNESS

INFLATE   **NEUTRAL POSITION**   **DEFLATE**

Neutral position may vary from 3 to 5°

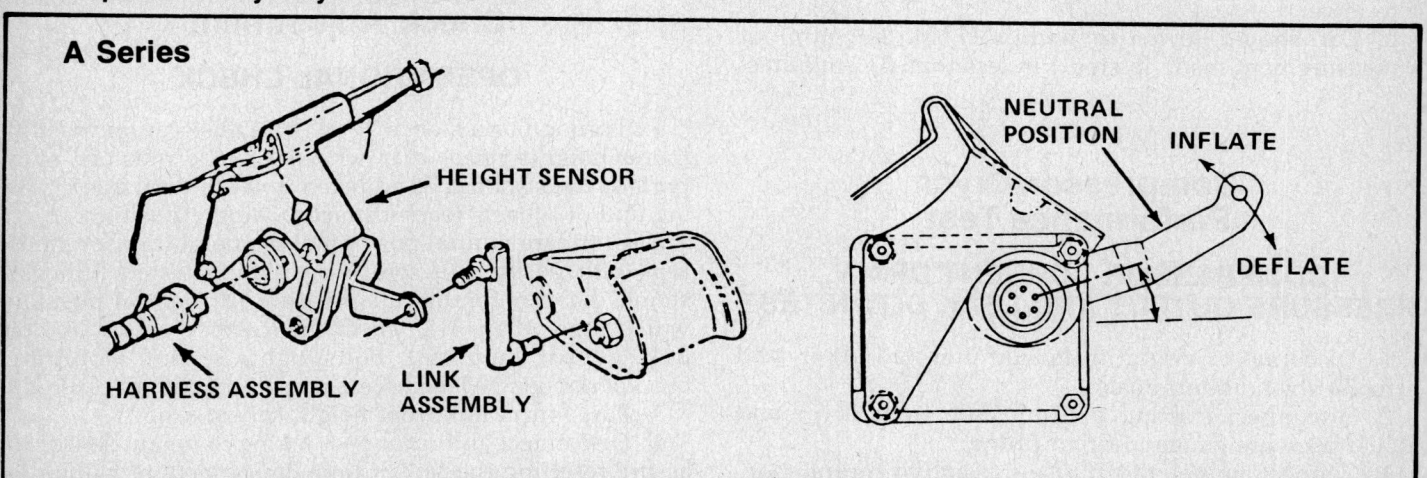

A Series

HEIGHT SENSOR

HARNESS ASSEMBLY   **LINK ASSEMBLY**

NEUTRAL POSITION   **INFLATE**   **DEFLATE**

Neutral position may vary from 3 to 5°

Front Drive

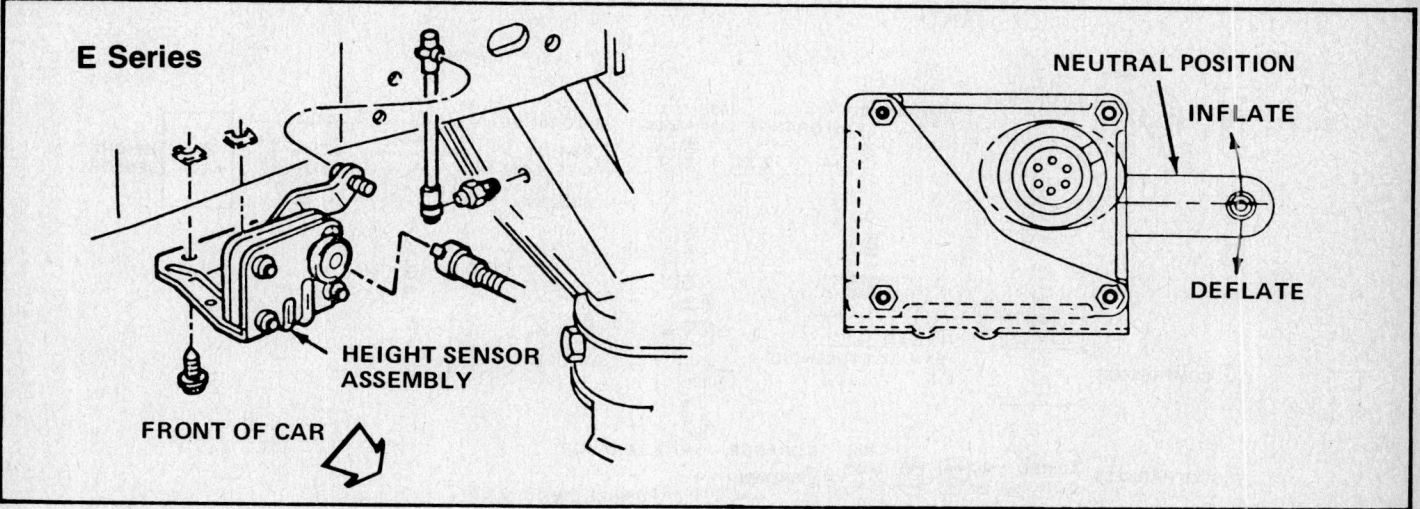

Compressor and Bracket

Removal

1. Remove negative battery cable.
2. Deflate system through service valve.
3. Disconnect high pressure line at air dryer by revolving spring clip 90° while holding connector end and removing tube assembly.
4. Remove two relay-to-compressor bracket screws and allow relay to hang to one side.
5. Remove support bracket screws.
6. Remove two radiator support to compressor bracket screws.
7. Disconnect solenoid and motor connectors.
8. Remove compressor and bracket assembly.
9. Remove three compressor mounting bracket screws then remove bracket.
10. If replacing compressor assembly remove dryer, dryer bracket, and compressor cylinder housing bracket and gasket.

Installation

1. If compressor was replaced install dryer and bracket and torque to 2.2 N•m (20 in.-lbs.)
2. Install mounting brackets to compressor assembly and torque screws to 4 N•m (36 in.-lbs.).
3. Connect solenoid and motor connectors.
4. Install two radiator support to compressor bracket screws and torque to 6 N•m (48 in.-lbs.).
5. Install support bracket screws and torque to 10 N•m (7 ft.-lbs.).
6. Install two compressor relay attaching screws.
7. Rotate clip on high pressure line until clip snaps in groove, then connect high pressure line at air dryer.
8. Cycle ignition switch and test for system operation and leaks at air dryer.

Air Dryer

Removal

1. Deflate system through service valve.

Height Sensor Adjustment

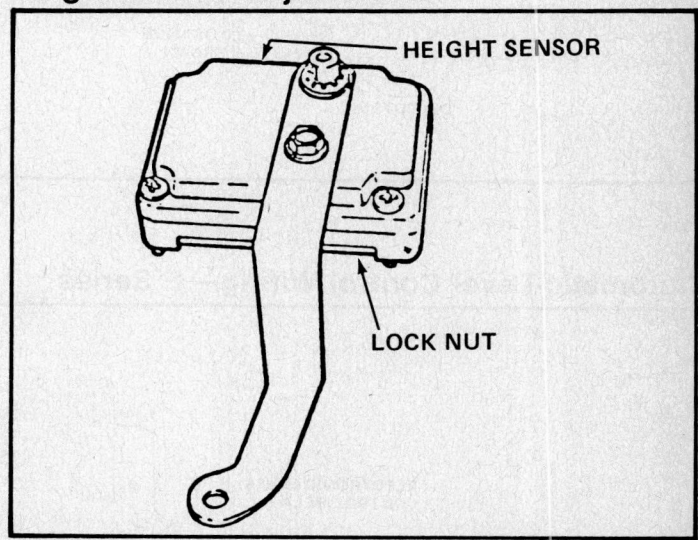

Height sensor adjustment 1° = ¼" at bumper. Adjustment of 5° total.

2. Disconnect high pressure line at air dryer by revolving spring clip and removing tube assembly.
3. Disconnect air dryer from compressor by revolving spring clip and sliding air dryer assembly away from compressor head through its bracket. Remove "O" ring from compressor head.

Installation

Lubricate dryer O-ring with Vaseline or equivalent before installing dryer in head casting.
1. Reverse removal procedure.
2. Check for leaks.

Air Line Repair

The air lines used on the superlift shock absorbers and the electronic level control systems can be repaired by splicing in a coupling at the leaking area.

Automatic Level Control Wiring—Except E Series

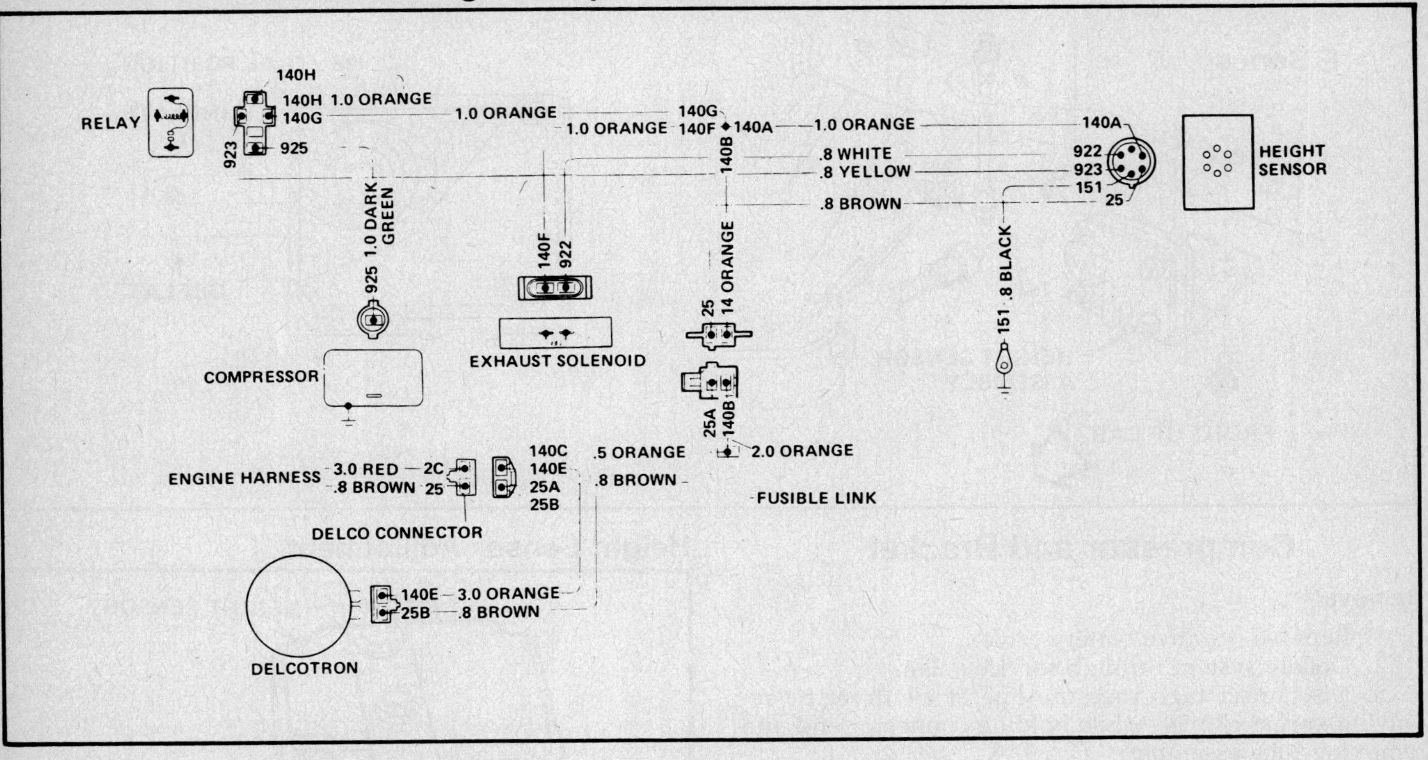

RELAY

140H
140H 1.0 ORANGE
140G
923 925
1.0 ORANGE
1.0 ORANGE 140G
140F 140A
1.0 ORANGE
140A
.8 WHITE
.8 YELLOW
.8 BROWN
140B
922
923
151
25

HEIGHT SENSOR

925 1.0 DARK GREEN

140F
922

25
14 ORANGE

151 .8 BLACK

COMPRESSOR

EXHAUST SOLENOID

25A
140B

ENGINE HARNESS
3.0 RED — 2C
.8 BROWN 25
140C
140E
25A
25B
.5 ORANGE
.8 BROWN
2.0 ORANGE

FUSIBLE LINK

DELCO CONNECTOR

140E 3.0 ORANGE
25B .8 BROWN

DELCOTRON

Automatic Level Control Wiring—E Series

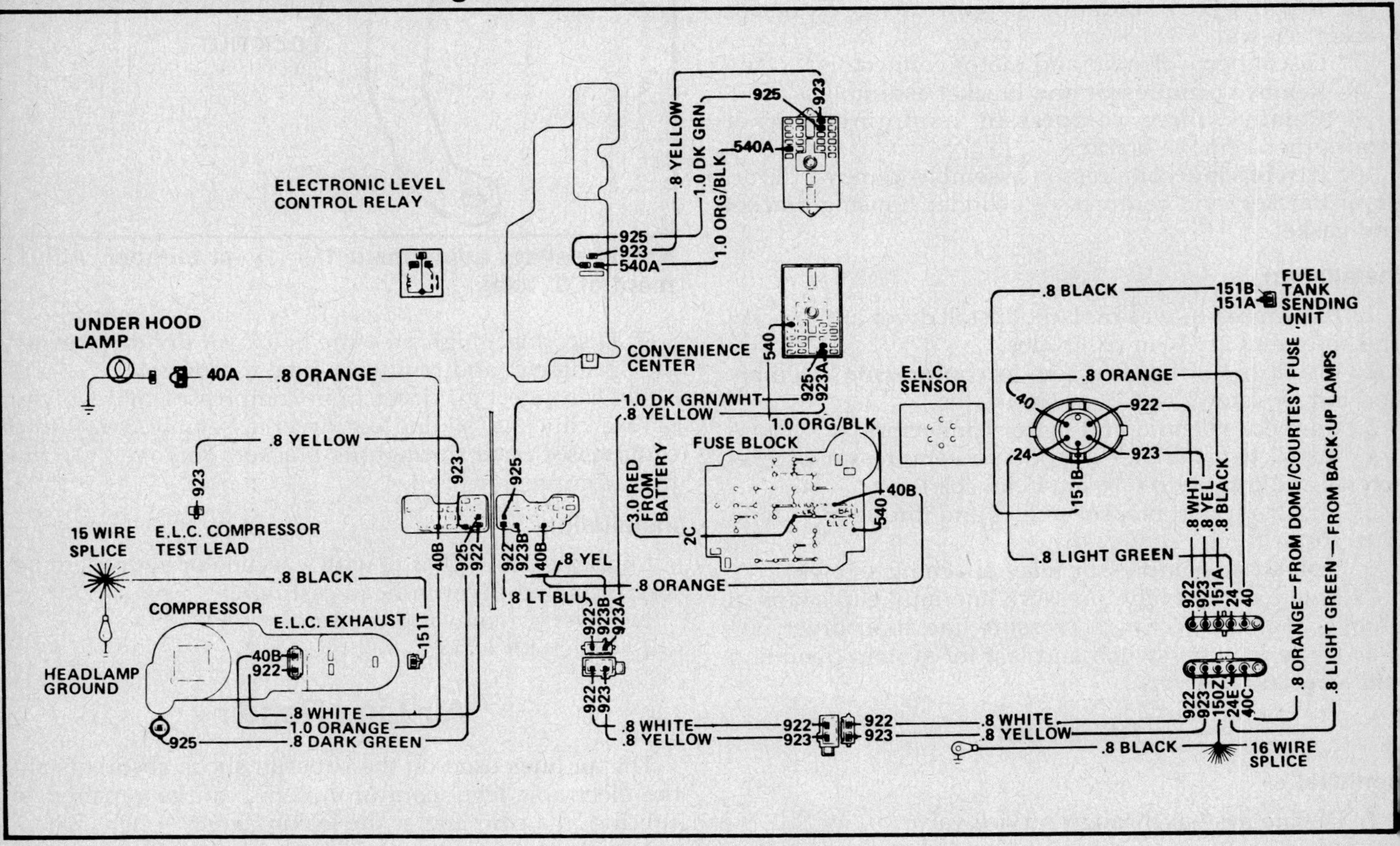

ELECTRONIC LEVEL CONTROL RELAY

.8 YELLOW
1.0 DK GRN
1.0 ORG/BLK
925
923
540A

UNDER HOOD LAMP

40A .8 ORANGE

923
925
540A

CONVENIENCE CENTER

540

.8 YELLOW
923

16 WIRE SPLICE
E.L.C. COMPRESSOR TEST LEAD

.8 BLACK

HEADLAMP GROUND

COMPRESSOR

E.L.C. EXHAUST

40B
922
151T

40B 925 922
923B
40B
.8 YEL
.8 LT BLU

1.0 DK GRN/WHT
.8 YELLOW
1.0 ORG/BLK

3.0 RED FROM BATTERY
2C

FUSE BLOCK

40B
540

.8 ORANGE

922
923A
925
923A

E.L.C. SENSOR

.8 BLACK
.8 ORANGE

40
24

151B
151A

FUEL TANK SENDING UNIT

922
923
151B

.8 LIGHT GREEN

.8 WHT
.8 YEL
.8 BLACK

922
923
151A
24E
40

922
923
150Z
24E
40C

.8 ORANGE—FROM DOME/COURTESY FUSE
.8 LIGHT GREEN—FROM BACK-UP LAMPS

.8 WHITE
1.0 ORANGE
.8 DARK GREEN
925

922
923A
923

.8 WHITE
.8 YELLOW

922
923

.8 WHITE
.8 YELLOW

.8 BLACK
16 WIRE SPLICE

MANUAL STEERING
POWER STEERING

INDEX

AMC MANUAL RACK & PINION-PACER

Manual Rack and Pinion Steering Gear

PACER

DESCRIPTION

The manual steering gear rack and pinion design combines the steering gear and steering linkage into one compact assembly.

STEERING GEAR INSPECTION

1 After removing assembly from car, place in a vise using protective jaws.

CHILTON CAUTION: *Do not clamp any part of tube in vise clamp housing only in vise.*

2 Cut and remove large diameter boot clamp on housing end of gear, and slide boot away from housing end of gear.
3 Turn flexible coupling to expose as many rack teeth as possible.
4 Clean and check rack teeth for signs of chipped, cracked, broken, excessive

wear or tooth flaking.
5 If any of these signs appear the gear assembly must be replaced.

NOTE: Do not replace steering gear if rack teeth have machining marks on them or appear excessively bright or shiny. These are normal conditions.

6 If teeth are in good condition, remove flexible coupling pinch bolt and separate coupling from pinion shaft.
7 Remove adjuster plug.
8 Remove pinion shaft from housing by pulling up and rotating counterclockwise.
9 Clean and inspect pinion shaft, if teeth are chipped cracked broken or excessively worn, steering gear assembly must be replaced.

DISASSEMBLY

1 Remove contraction plug from housing, using ¼ inch diameter brass rod, insert rod through upper and lower pinion bushings and tap on rod to dislodge plug.

2 Remove lower pinion bushing and preload spring from housing using brass rod.
3 Move rack to center position in tube housing.
4 Install pinion shaft and adjuster plug in housing, hand tighten adjuster plug.
5 Loosen adjuster tube clamp nuts and remove adjuster tubes and tie rod assemblies from inner tie rods.

NOTE: Mark position of adjuster tubes on inner tie rods for assembly reference.

6 Mark location of breather tube on tube and housing assembly. Boots and breather tube must be installed in same position to ensure proper sealing.
7 Cut and remove all boot clamps and remove boots.
8 Remove breather tube and shock dampener rings.
9 Clamp inner tie rod housing in vise and loosen jam nut.

Pacer manual rack and pinion

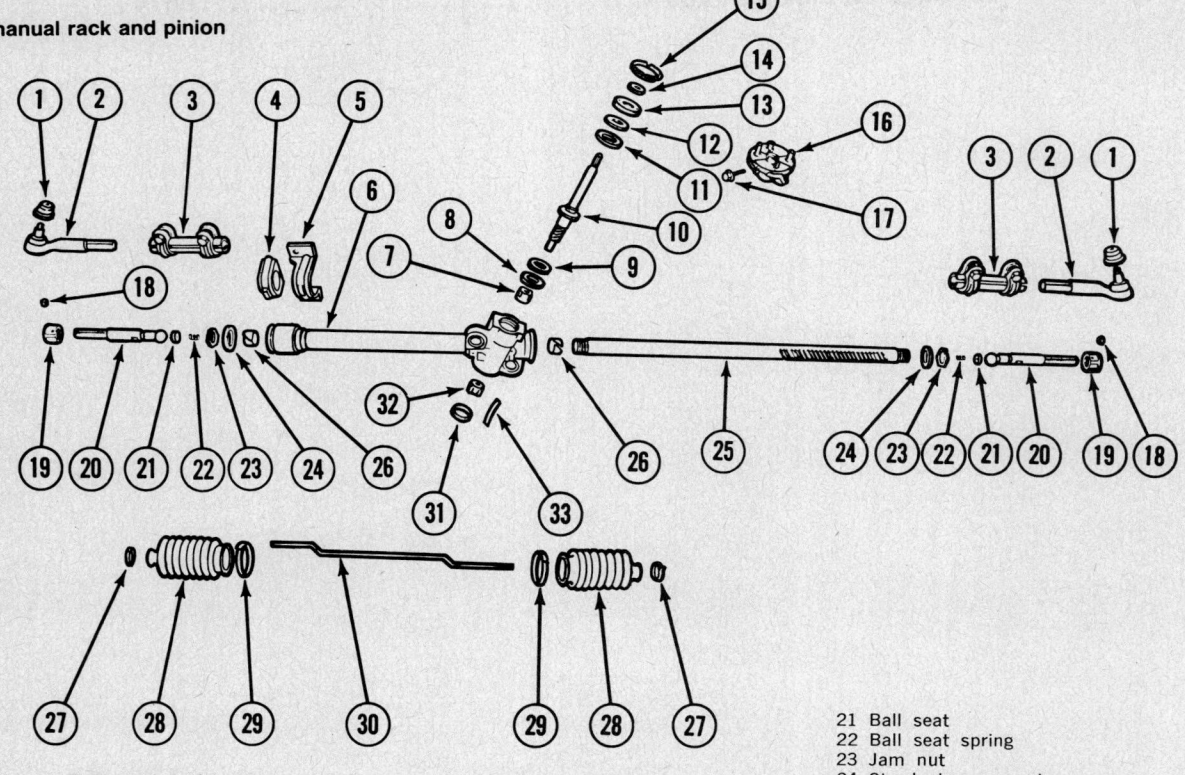

1 Tie rod seal	11 Upper thrust bearing	21 Ball seat
2 Tie rod end	12 Upper thrust bearing race	22 Ball seat spring
3 Adjuster tube	13 Adjuster plug	23 Jam nut
4 Mounting grommet	14 Pinion shaft seal	24 Shock dampener ring
5 Mounting clamp	15 Adjuster plug locknut	25 Steering rack
6 Tube and housing assembly	16 Flexible coupling	26 Rack bushing
7 Upper pinion bushing	17 Pinch bolt	27 Boot retainer
8 Lower thrust bearing race	18 Set screw	28 Boot
9 Lower thrust bearing	19 Tie rod housing	29 Boot clamp
10 Pinion shaft	20 Inner tie rod	30 Breather tube
		31 Contraction plug
		32 Lower pinion bushing
		33 Preload spring

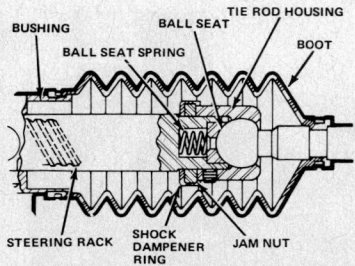

Removing the tie rod housing and inner tie rod

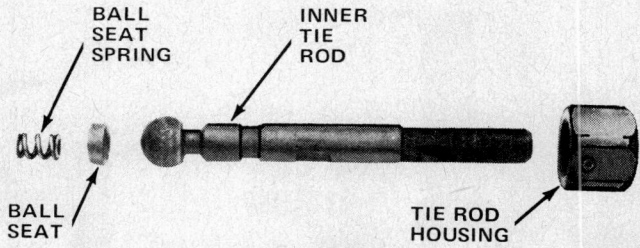

Exploded view of inner tie rod assembly

CHILTON CAUTION: *Tie rod housing must be held securely when loosening or tightening jamnut to prevent damage to internal components of steering gear.*

10 Loosen tie rod housing set-screws and remove inner tie rod housing, ball seats, springs, jam nuts and shock dampener rings from rack.

11 Remove adjuster plug and pinion shaft from housing.

12 Remove pinion shaft from housing by pulling upward and rotating counterclockwise. Remove lower thrust bearing and race.

13 Remove upper pinion bushing from housing with fingers.

14 Pull steering rack from tube and housing assembly.

15 Remove rack bushings by slipping knife blade under bushings, use needlenose pliers and pull straight out.

16 Remove pinion shaft seal by threading adjuster plug into housing and prying seal out with screwdriver.

ASSEMBLY

1 Install a new pinion shaft seal in the adjuster plug using a suitable sized socket. Press the seal in until it is flush with the face of the adjuster plug. Do not press on the lip of the seal.

2 Replace the rack bushings, if removed. Compress the leading end and force them into the housing or tube opening. Once they are past the lip of the tube or housing, the bushing will snap back to its original shape.

3 Coat the rack teeth with lithium based chassis grease and install the rack in the housing. Install the upper pinion bushing in the housing.

4 Lubricate the pinion shaft lower race and thrust bearing with the same type grease and install the race and thrust bearing in the housing with the flanged edge of the race facing up.

5 Center the steering rack in the housing. Set the distance between the end of the steering rack and the inner lip of the housing at 4 in.

6 Start the pinion shaft into the housing and rack with the flat on the splined end of the pinion shaft at about the 10 o'clock position. Turn the pinion shaft counterclockwise and push down until the pinion shaft race is bottomed on the thrust bearing.

7 Reset the distance between the end of

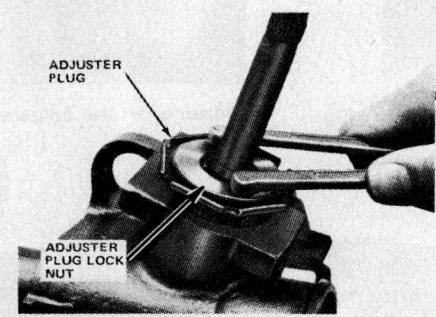

Removing the adjuster plug

Removing the upper pinion shaft bushing

the rack and the housing (step 5). The flat on the pinion shaft should be at the 3 o'clock position now. Be sure the pinion race is bottomed in the housing. If the flat on the pinion shaft is not at the 3 o'clock position with the rack set at 4 in., start over again at step 4.

NOTE: The rack must be centered, oth-

erwise, the steering wheel travel from left to right will be unequal.

8 Install the adjuster plug using a spanner type tool that fits in the two holes in the top of the plug. Tighten the plug until it bottoms. Mark the adjuster plug and housing at a spanner hole. Back off the adjuster plug (counterclockwise) until the hole marked is 3/16 in. to 1/4 in. past (counterclockwise) the reference mark made on the housing. Install and tighten the locknut to 50 ft./lbs.

9 Turn the assembly over and mount it in a vise. Fill the space around the pinion shaft with the same type of grease (step 3). Do not overfill because the pinion bushing and spring have to be installed yet.

10 Install the preload spring in the housing with the center hump of the spring bearing against the housing. Allow the spring to extend about 1/4 in. from the end of the housing.

11 Hold the top of the preload spring against the housing with needlenose pliers and install the busing in the housing with the chamfered end facing downward.

12 Seat the contraction plug in the housing using a brass rod or a suitable size socket.

13 Install the shock dampener rings on each end of the steering rack with the open ends facing out and install both jamnuts.

14 Liberally apply some lithium based chassis lubricant to all of the inner tie rod assembly wear surfaces. Pack the tie rod housings with the same type grease.

15 Assemble and install the inner tie rod assemblies to the rack. Tighten the tie

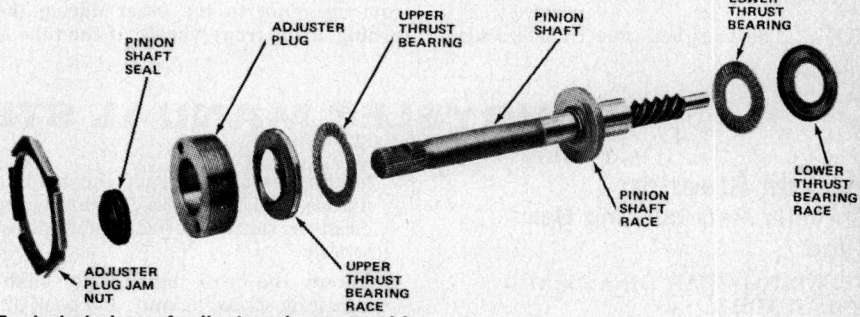

Exploded view of adjuster plug assembly

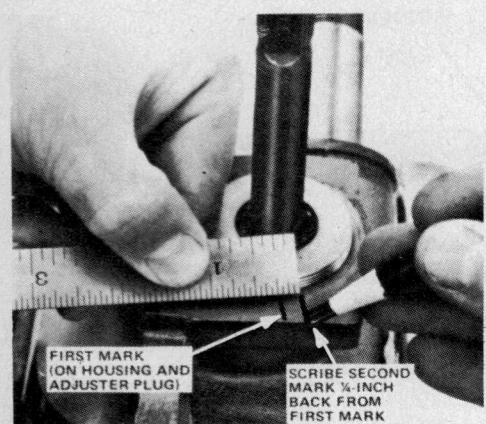

FIRST MARK (ON HOUSING AND ADJUSTER PLUG)

SCRIBE SECOND MARK ¼-INCH BACK FROM FIRST MARK

Marking the housing for adjustment of the adjusting plug

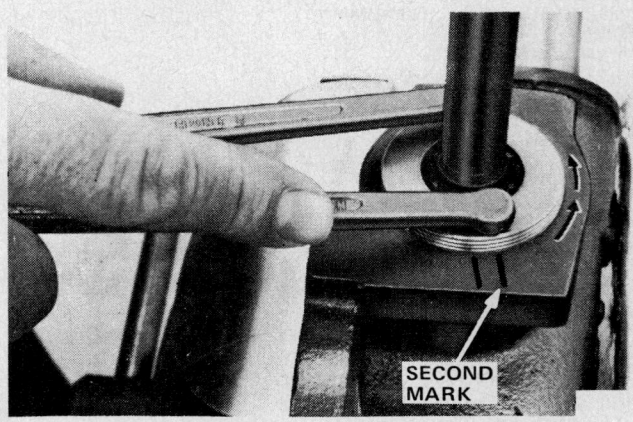

SECOND MARK

Backing off the adjuster plug to the proper adjustment

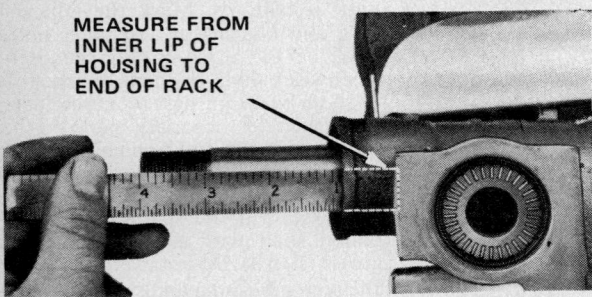

MEASURE FROM INNER LIP OF HOUSING TO END OF RACK

Centering the steering rack in the tube and housing

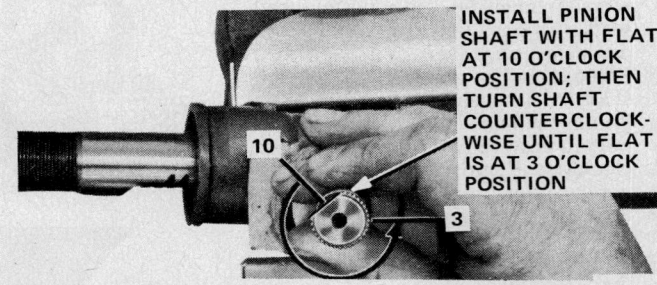

INSTALL PINION SHAFT WITH FLAT AT 10 O'CLOCK POSITION; THEN TURN SHAFT COUNTERCLOCKWISE UNTIL FLAT IS AT 3 O'CLOCK POSITION

10

3

Installing the pinion shaft and engaging the rack

rod housing to 75 in./lbs. while rocking the inner tie rod to relieve grease lock, loosen ½ turn and retighten the housing to 50 in./lbs.

16 Tighten the housing setscrews to 60 in./lbs.

17 Clamp the tie rod housings in the vise and tighten the jamnuts to 100 ft./lbs. using a crow-foot adapter on the end of a torque wrench.

18 Slip the shock dampener rings over the jamnuts.

19 Install the mounting clamp and grommet on the tube using the alignment marks made during disassembly.

20 Install the boot on the mounting bracket side of the tube and housing in position so that the hole in the boot aligns with the hole in the mounting grommet. Slide the short end of the tube through the grommet and boot breather tube holes. The long end of the tube lies against the tube and housing.

NOTE: The breather tube transfers air

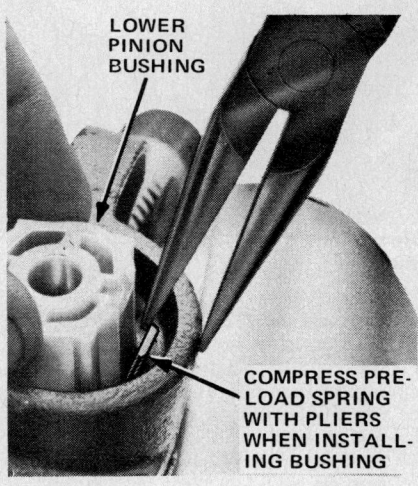

LOWER PINION BUSHING

COMPRESS PRELOAD SPRING WITH PLIERS WHEN INSTALLING BUSHING

Installing the lower pinion pushing

from one boot to the other during the turning of the front wheels. If the tube is

blocked in any way, dust and water could be drawn into the inner tie rod assemblies.

21 Install the opposite side boot with the hole in the boot aligned with the breather tube. The boot lip must fit into the housing flange to seat the tube.

22 Slide the small outer collars of the boots over the inner tie rod grooves. Install the small diameter boot clamps on the boots and tighten the clamps.

23 Install the adjuster tubes and tie rod ends on the inner tie rods. Align the tubes and tie rods using the marks made during disassembly. At least 3 threads should be visible at both ends of the adjuster tubes. The number of threads per side should not differ by more than 3.

24 Install the flexible coupling on the pinion shaft, flat to flat, and install the pinch bolt. Tighten the pinch bolt to 30 ft./lbs.

25 Install the steering gear in the car and check the toe-in adjustment.

CHRYSLER MANUAL STEERING

Manual Steering
Chrysler Recirculating Ball Type
STEERING GEAR DISASSEMBLY & ASSEMBLY

1 Attach the steering gear assembly to a holding fixture and put the holding fixture in a bench vise. Thoroughly clean the outside surface before disassembly.

2 Loosen the cross-shaft (sector shaft) adjusting screw locknut, and back out the adjusting screw about two turns to relieve the mesh load between the ball nut rack and the sector gear teeth. Remove the cross-shaft seal as given in the procedure for cross-shaft seal replacement.

3 Position the steering gear worm shaft in a straight ahead position.

TROUBLESHOOTING CHRYSLER MANUAL STEERING

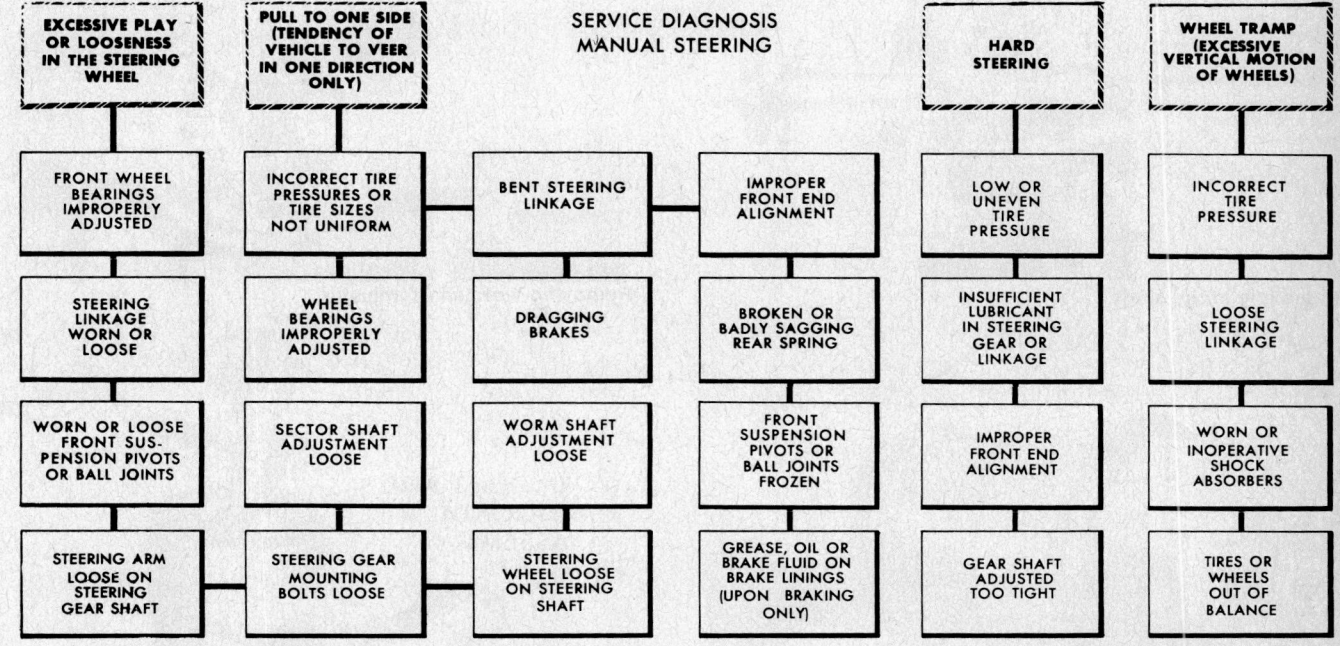

SERVICE DIAGNOSIS MANUAL STEERING

EXCESSIVE PLAY OR LOOSENESS IN THE STEERING WHEEL	PULL TO ONE SIDE (TENDENCY OF VEHICLE TO VEER IN ONE DIRECTION ONLY)			HARD STEERING	WHEEL TRAMP (EXCESSIVE VERTICAL MOTION OF WHEELS)
FRONT WHEEL BEARINGS IMPROPERLY ADJUSTED	INCORRECT TIRE PRESSURES OR TIRE SIZES NOT UNIFORM	BENT STEERING LINKAGE	IMPROPER FRONT END ALIGNMENT	LOW OR UNEVEN TIRE PRESSURE	INCORRECT TIRE PRESSURE
STEERING LINKAGE WORN OR LOOSE	WHEEL BEARINGS IMPROPERLY ADJUSTED	DRAGGING BRAKES	BROKEN OR BADLY SAGGING REAR SPRING	INSUFFICIENT LUBRICANT IN STEERING GEAR OR LINKAGE	LOOSE STEERING LINKAGE
WORN OR LOOSE FRONT SUSPENSION PIVOTS OR BALL JOINTS	SECTOR SHAFT ADJUSTMENT LOOSE	WORM SHAFT ADJUSTMENT LOOSE	FRONT SUSPENSION PIVOTS OR BALL JOINTS FROZEN	IMPROPER FRONT END ALIGNMENT	WORN OR INOPERATIVE SHOCK ABSORBERS
STEERING ARM LOOSE ON STEERING GEAR SHAFT	STEERING GEAR MOUNTING BOLTS LOOSE	STEERING WHEEL LOOSE ON STEERING SHAFT	GREASE, OIL OR BRAKE FLUID ON BRAKE LININGS (UPON BRAKING ONLY)	GEAR SHAFT ADJUSTED TOO TIGHT	TIRES OR WHEELS OUT OF BALANCE

4 Remove the attaching bolts from the cross-shaft cover and slowly remove the cross-shaft while sliding arbor tool into the housing. Remove the locknut from the adjusting screw and remove the screw from the cover by turning screw clockwise. Slide the adjustment screw and its shim out of the slot in the end of the cross-shaft.

5 Loosen the worm shaft bearing adjuster locknut with a brass drift (punch) and remove the locknut. Hold the worm shaft teady while unscrewing the adjuster. Slide the worm adjuster off the shaft.

CHILTON CAUTION: *Handle the adjuster carefully to avoid damaging the aluminum threads. Also, do not run the*

ball nut down to either end of the worm shaft to avoid damaging the ball guides.

6 Carefully remove the worm shaft and ball nut assembly. This assembly is serviced as a complete assembly only and is not to be disassembled or the ball return guides removed or disturbed.

7 Remove the cross-shaft needle bearing by placing the gear housing in an arbor press; insert tool in the lower end of the housing and press both bearings through the housing. The cross-shaft cover assembly, including a needle bearing or bushing, is serviced as an assembly.

8 Remove the worm shaft oil seal from the worm shaft bearing adjuster by in-

serting a blunt punch behind the seal and tapping alternately on each side of the seal until it is driven out of the adjuster.

9 Remove the worm shaft upper bearing cup in the same manner as that given in step 8. *Be careful not to cock the bearing cup and distort the adjuster counter bore.*

10 Remove the lower cup if necessary by placing the locking head jaws of remover tool C-3868 behind the bearing cup and expanding the remover head by pressing down on the center plunger of the tool. Pull the bearing cup out by turning the remover screw clockwise while holding the center screw steady.

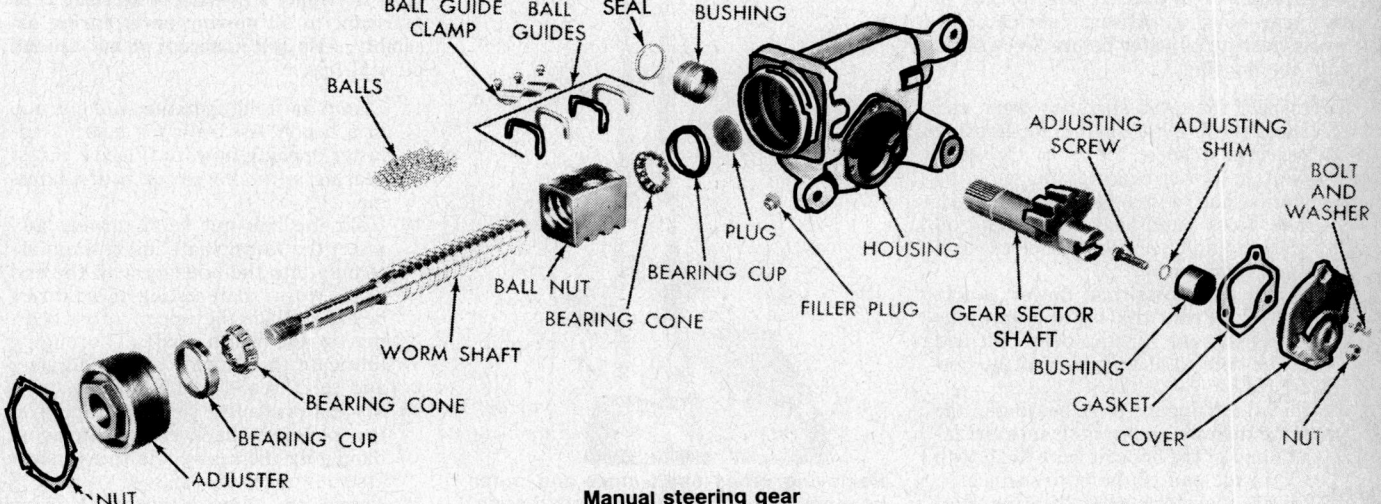

Manual steering gear

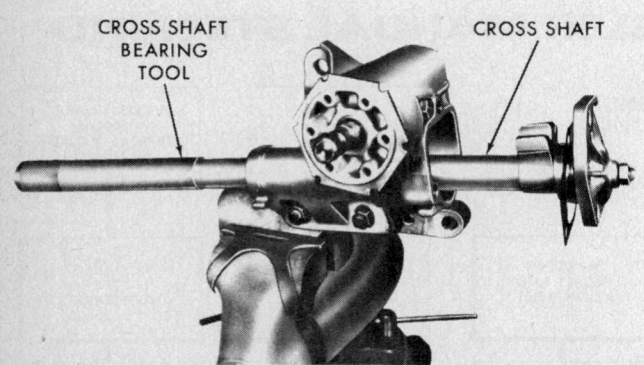

Removing cross shaft

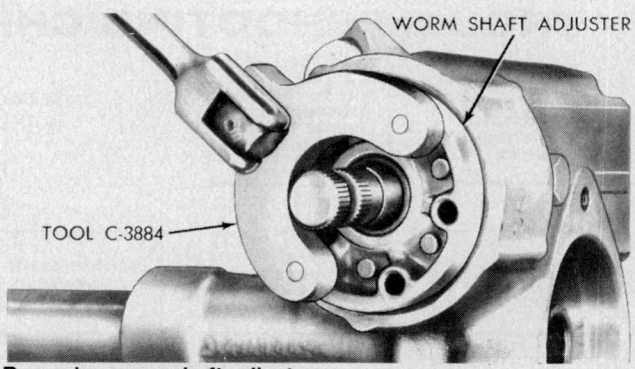

Removing wormshaft adjuster

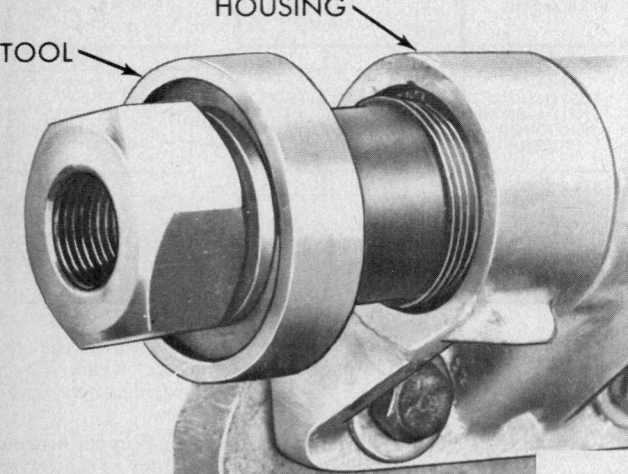

Removing cross shaft oil seal

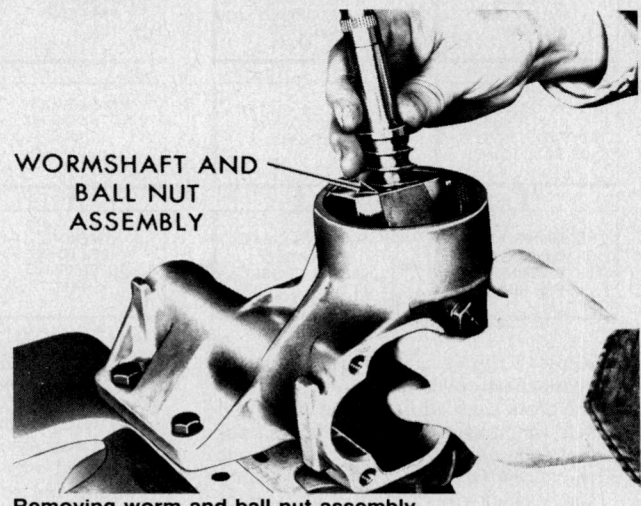

Removing worm and ball nut assembly

11 Wash all parts in clean solvent and dry thoroughly. Inspect all parts for wear, scoring, pitting, etc. Test operation of the worm shaft and ball nut assembly. If ball nut does not travel smoothly and freely on the worm shaft or if there is binding, replace the assembly.

NOTE: Extreme care must be taken when handling the aluminum worm bearing adjuster to avoid thread damage. Also, be careful not to damage the threads in the gear housing. Always lubricate the worm bearing adjuster before screwing it into the housing.

12 Inspect the cross-shaft for wear and check the fit of the shaft in the housing bearings. Inspect the fit of the shaft pilot in cover bearing. Be sure the worm shaft is not bent or damaged. The cross shaft and wormshaft oil seals should be replaced when the unit is reassembled.

13 Install the cross-shaft lower needle bearing. Press the bearing into the housing about 7/16 in. below the end of the bore to leave space for the new oil seal.

14 Install the upper needle bearing in the same manner and press it into the inside end of the housing bore flush with the inside end of the bore surface.

15 Install the worm shaft bearing cups (upper and lower) by placing them and their spacers in the adjuster nut and in the housing. Then press them

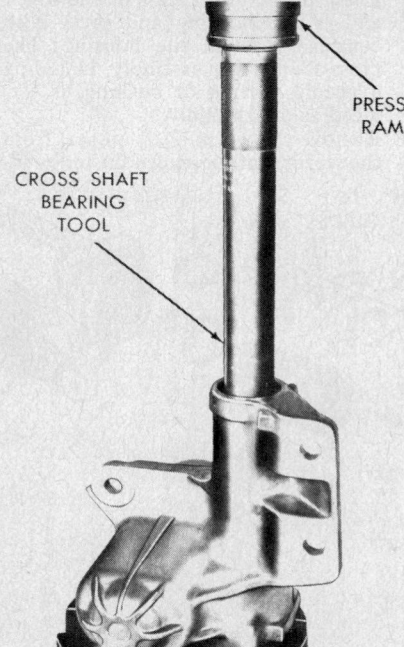

Removing cross shaft inner and outer bearings from Chrysler manual steering

into place.

16 Install the worm shaft oil seal by placing them and their spacers in the adjuster nut and press them into place.

17 Install the worm shaft oil seal by placing the seal in the worm shaft adjuster with the metal seal retainer up. Drive the seal into place with a suitable sleeve until it is just below the end of the bore in the adjuster.

NOTE: Apply a coating of steering gear lubricant to all moving parts during assembly. Also, put lubricant on and around oil seal lips.

18 Clamp the holding fixture and housing in a bench vise with the bearing adjuster opening upward. Place a thrust bearing in the lower cup in the housing.

19 Hold the ball nut from turning and insert the worm shaft and ball nut assembly into the housing with the end of the worm shaft resting in the thrust bearing. Place the upper thrust bearing on the worm shaft. Thoroughly lubricate the threads on the adjuster and the threads in the housing.

20 Place a protective sleeve of tape over the splines on the worm shaft to avoid damaging the seal. Slide the adjuster assembly over the shaft.

21 Thread the adjuster into the housing

and, with Tool wrench C-3884 and the splined nut set, tighten the adjuster to 50 ft./lbs. while rotating the worm shaft to seat the bearings.

22 Loosen the adjuster so no bearing preload exists. Tighten the adjuster for a worm shaft bearing preload of 1⅛ to 4½ in./lbs. Tighten the bearing adjuster locknut and recheck the preload.

23 Before installing the cross-shaft, pack the worm shaft cavities in the housing above and below the ball nut with steering gear lubricant. A good grade of multi-purpose lubricant may be used if steering gear lubricant is not available. *Do not use gear oil.* Pack enough lubricant into the worm cavities to cover the worm.

24 Slide the cross-shaft adjusting screw and shim into the slot in the end of the shaft. Check the end clearance for no more than 0.004 in. clearance. If the clearance is not within the limit, remove old shim and install a new shim, available in three different thicknesses, to get the proper clearance.

25 Start the cross-shaft and adjuster screw into the bearing in the housing cover. Using a screwdriver through the hole in the cover, turn the screw counterclockwise to pull the shaft into the cover. Install the adjusting screw locknut, but do not tighten at this time.

26 Rotate the worm shaft to center the ball nut.

27 Place a new gasket on the housing cover and install the cross-shaft and cover assembly into the steering gear housing. *Be sure to coat the cross-shaft and sector teeth with steering gear lubricant before installing the cross-shaft in the housing.* Allow some lash between the cross-shaft sector teeth and the ball nut rack. Install and tighten the cover bolts to 25 ft./lbs.

28 Place the cross-shaft seal on the cross-shaft with the lip of the seal facing the housing. Press the seal in place.

29 Turn the worm shaft about ¼ turn away from the center of the high spot position. Using a torque wrench and a ¾ in. socket on the worm shaft spline, check the torque needed to rotate the shaft through the high spot. The reading should be between 8 and 11 in./lbs. Readjust the cross-shaft adjusting screw until the proper reading is obtained. Tighten the locknut to 35 ft./lbs. and recheck cross-shaft torque.

CROSS-SHAFT OIL SEAL REPLACEMENT

1 Remove the steering gear arm retaining nut and lockwasher.
2 Remove seal with a seal puller or other appropriate tool.
3 Place a new oil seal onto the splines of the cross-shaft with the lip of the seal facing the housing.

4 Remove the tool, and install the steering gear arm, lockwasher, and retaining nut. Tighten the nut to 180 ft./lbs. torque.

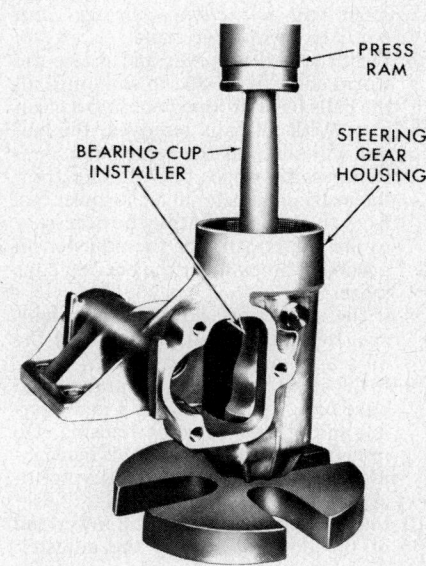

Installing lower bearing cup

Installing upper bearing cup

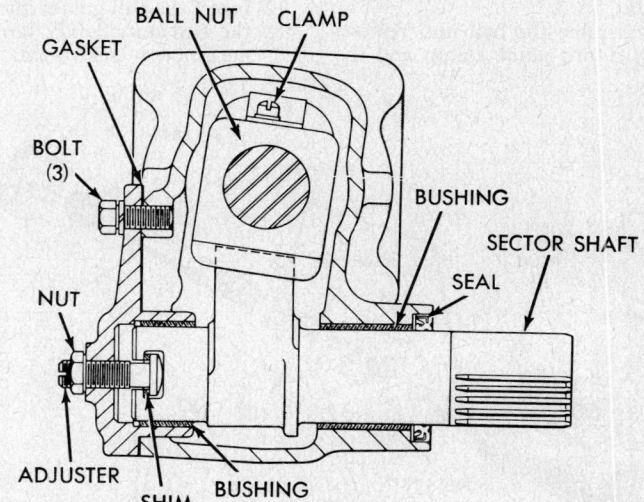

Sector shaft-sectional view

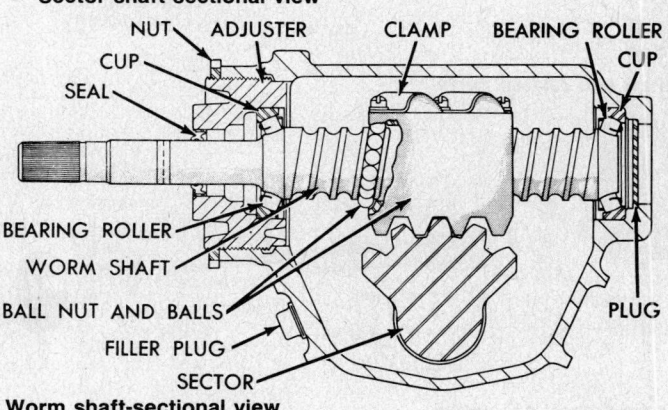

Worm shaft-sectional view

FORD RECIRCULATING BALL TYPE

Manual Steering
Ford Recirculating Ball Type

FORD MOTOR CO. ALL CARS (EXCEPT FORD MUSTANG II, PINTO AND MERCURY BOBCAT)

Steering Gear Disassembly & Assembly

1 Rotate the steering shaft to the center position.
2 Remove the sector shaft adjusting screw locknut and the housing cover bolts and remove the sector shaft with the cover. Remove the cover from the shaft by turning the screw clockwise. *Keep the shim with the screw.*
3 Loosen the worm bearing adjuster locknut and remove the adjuster assembly and wormshaft upper bearing.
4 Carefully pull the wormshaft and ball nut from the housing, and remove the wormshaft lower bearing. *Do not run the ball nut to either end of the worm gear to prevent damaging the ball return guides. Disassemble the ball nut only if there are signs of binding or tightness.*
5 To disassemble the ball nut, remove the ball return guide clamp and the ball return guides from the ball nut. *Keep ball nut clamp side up until ready to remove the balls.*
6 Turn the ball nut over and rotate the worm shaft from side to side until all the balls have dropped out into a clean pan. With all balls removed, the ball nut will slide off the wormshaft.
7 Remove the upper bearing cup from the bearing adjuster and the lower cup from the housing. It may be necessary to tap the housing or the adjuster on a wooden block to jar the bearing cups loose.
8 If the inspection shows bearing damage, the sector shaft bearing and the oil seal should be pressed out.
9 If the sector shaft bearing and oil seal have been removed, press a new bearing and oil seal into the housing. Do not clean, wash, or soak seals in cleaning solvent. Apply steering gear lubricant to the housing and seals.
10 Install a bearing cup in the lower end of the housing and in the adjuster. This is a clearance fit not a press fit.
11 Install a new seal in the bearing adjuster if the old seal was removed.
12 Insert the ball guides into the holes in the ball nut, lightly tapping them if necessary to seat them.
13 Insert half of the balls into the hole in the top of each ball guide. If necessary, rotate the shaft slightly to distribute the balls evenly in the circuit.
14 Install the ball guide clamp, tightening the screws to 42–70 in./lbs. for Maverick and Comet, and 18–42 in./lbs. on larger models. Check that the wormshaft rotates freely.
15 Coat the threads of the steering shaft bearing adjuster, the housing cover bolts, and the sector adjusting screw with a suitable oil-resistant sealing compound. Do not apply sealer to female threads. *Do not get sealer on the steering shaft bearings.*
16 Coat the worm bearings, sector shaft bearings, and gear teeth with steering gear lubricant.
17 Clamp the housing in a vise, with the sector shaft axis horizontal, and place the wormshaft lower bearing in its cup. Place the wormshaft and ball nut assemblies in the housing.
18 Position the wormshaft upper bearing on top of the worm gear and install the wormshaft bearing adjuster, adjuster nut, and the bearing cup. Leave the nut loose.
19 Adjust the worm bearing preload according to the instructions given earlier.
20 Position the sector adjusting screw and adjuster shim, and check for a clearance of not more than 0.002 in.

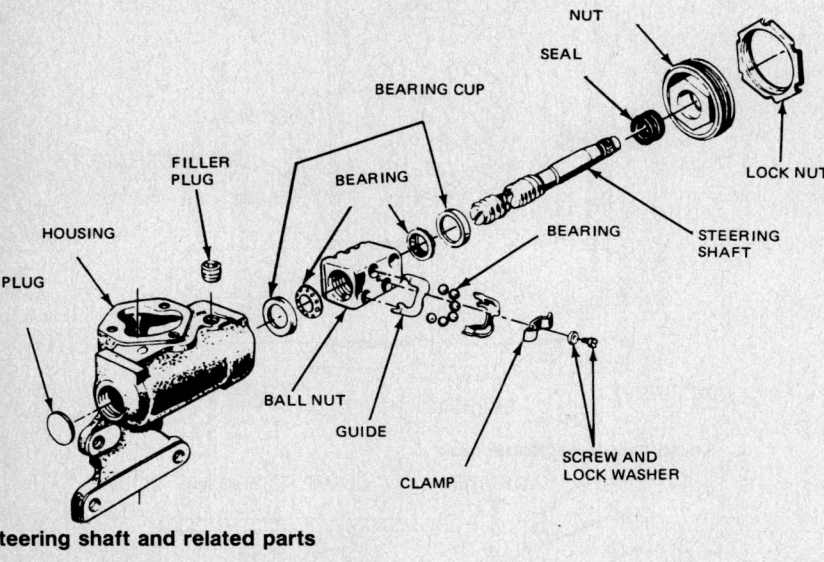

Steering shaft and related parts

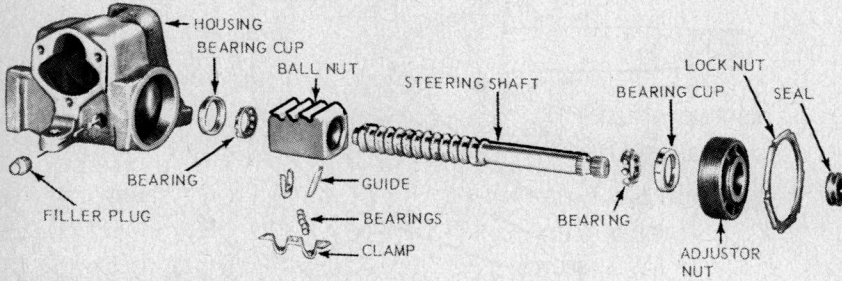

Typical steering shaft assembly

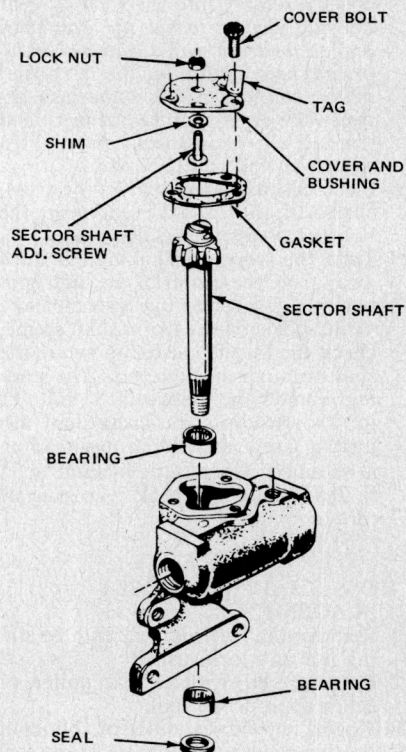

Sector shaft and housing

between the screw head and the end of the sector shaft. If the clearance exceeds 0.002 in., add enough shims to reduce the clearance to under 0.002 in. clearance.

21 Start the sector shaft adjusting screw into the housing cover. Install a new gasket on the cover.

22 Rotate the steering shaft until the ball nut teeth mesh with the sector gear teeth, tilting the housing so the ball will tip toward the housing cover opening.

23 Lubricate the sector shaft journal and install the sector shaft and cover. With the cover moved to one side, fill the gear with steering gear lubricant. Push the cover and the sector shaft into place, and install the two top housing bolts. Do not tighten the bolts until checking to see that there is some lash between the ball nut and the sector gear teeth. Hold or push the cover away from the ball nut and tighten the bolts to 17–25 ft./lbs. on Maverick and Comet, and 30–40 ft./lbs. on

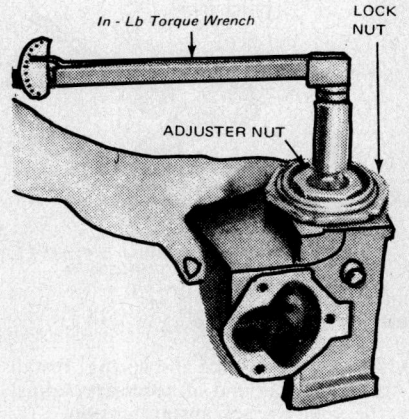

Checking steering shaft bearing preload

larger models.

24 Loosely install the sector shaft adjusting screw locknut and adjust the sector shaft mesh load as given earlier. Tighten the adjusting screw locknut.

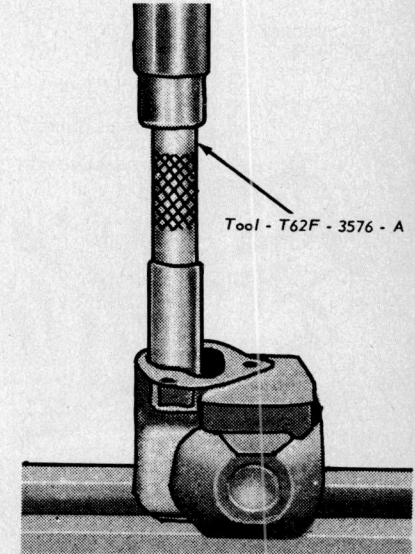

Tool - T62F - 3576 - A

Removing oil seal and bearing

FORD/AMC MANUAL RACK & PINION TYPE

Manual Rack and Pinion Type

FORD MUSTANG II, PINTO MERCURY BOBCAT

Disassembly

1 Clean exterior of gear and place in a bench-mounted holding fixture.
2 Remove the yoke cover, shims, gasket, yoke spring and yoke.
3 Remove tie rods and sockets from the ends of the rack by:
   a. remove tie rod ends and jam nuts.

   b. remove four bellows clamps, drain the lubricant and remove the bellows.
   c. a special tool is available for drilling the lock pin. Install the tool on the ball socket. Position the fixture so that the pin in the ball socket is lined up with the drill guide.
   d. drill out the lock pin.
   e. remove the tie rods and ball sockets.
4 Move the rack to either lock and note the position of the flat on the input

shaft.
5 Remove the pinion cover bolts, pinion cover, gasket, shaft, spacer, shims and upper bearing.
6 Remove the rack from the housing.
7 Remove the lower bearing through the pinion shaft bore.

Assembly

1 Install the lower bearing in the bottom of the housing.
2 Install the rack in the housing.

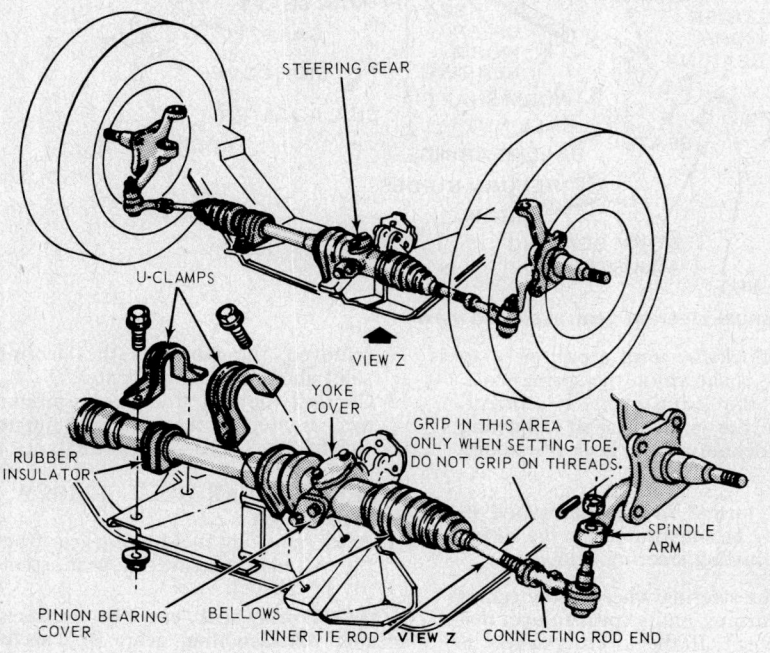

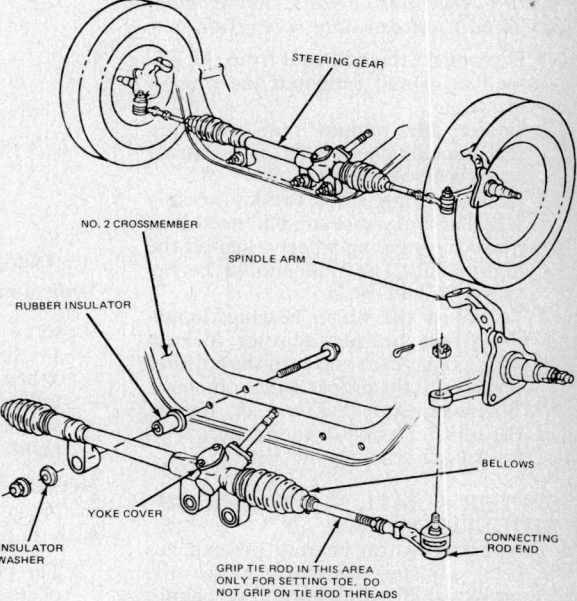

Manual rack and pinion steering linkage

MANUAL STEERING
GM SAGINAW RECIRCULATING BALL TYPE

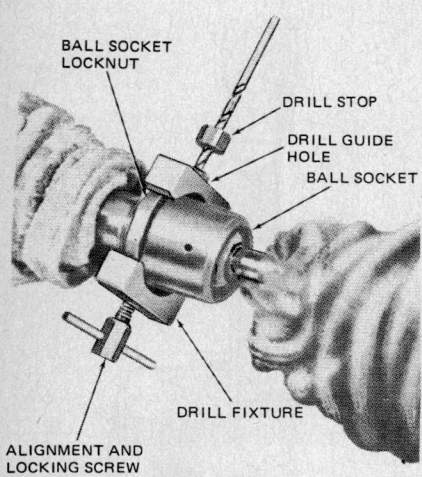

Drilling out retaining pin

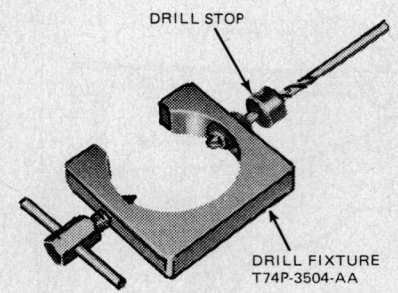

Setting holding fixture

3 Install the pinion shaft making sure the pinion shaft gear end is engaged in the lower bearing ID.

4 Install the upper bearing, shims, spacer, gasket and pinion cover. Torque cover bolts to 15–20 ft./lbs.

5 Assemble the yoke and spring. Install a new gasket and, if necessary, adjust the yoke-to-rack spring tension.

6 Assemble the shim pack and cover.

7 Coat the cover bolts with sealant and torque to 15–20 ft./lbs.

8 Install a new spring in rack end and assemble ball socket to tie rod.

9 Install a new inner thrust bearing in the ball socket.

10 Apply lubricant to the spring, thrust bearing, tie rod ball and ball socket.

11 Thread the ball joint locknut on the rack end.

12 Thread the ball socket onto the rack until the tie rod movement stiffens.

13 Rotate tie rod about 10 times to check movement.

14 Install tie rod ends.

15 Place hook of pull scale through hole in threaded area of the ball joint. With the tie rod in mid-position, parallel to the rack adjust the position of the ball socket on the rack until the pull effort is 4–6 lbs. Secure the unit by torquing the ball socket lock nut to 35–40 ft./lbs.

16 Install the drill fixture on the ball socket. Drill a hole on the line of contact between the lock nut and the ball socket.

NOTE: A new hole must be drilled even if the halves of the old hole align. A total of only two drilled holes are allowed on one end of the rack.

17 Insert the retaining pin flush in the drilled hole. Stake the pin. Clean rack and housing bores.

18 Install bellows and clamps. Add seven ounces of lubricant (Spec. M2E105-B) to either bellows.

19 Install jam nuts.

GM SAGINAW RECIRCULATING BALL TYPE

Manual Steering
G.M. Saginaw
Recirculating Ball Type

A.M.C CARS EXCEPT PACER,

ALL G.M. CORP. CARS

WORM BEARING PRELOAD ADJUSTMENT

CHILTON CAUTION: *Do not turn steering wheel hard against stops as damage to ball nut assembly may result.*

1 Disconnect the ball stud from the pitman arm, and retighten the pitman arm nut.

2 Loosen the pitman shaft adjusting screw locknut and back off adjusting screw a few turns.

3 Attach spring scale to the steering wheel and measure the pull needed to move the steering wheel when off the high point. The pull should be between ⅛ and ⅜ lb.

4 To adjust the worm bearing, loosen the worm bearing adjuster locknut with a brass drift and turn the adjuster screw until the proper pull is obtained. When adjustment is correct, tighten the adjuster locknut, and recheck with the spring scale again.

SECTOR & BALL NUT BACKLASH ADJUSTMENT

1 After the worm bearing preload has been adjusted correctly, loosen the pitman shaft adjusting screw locknut and turn the pitman shaft adjusting

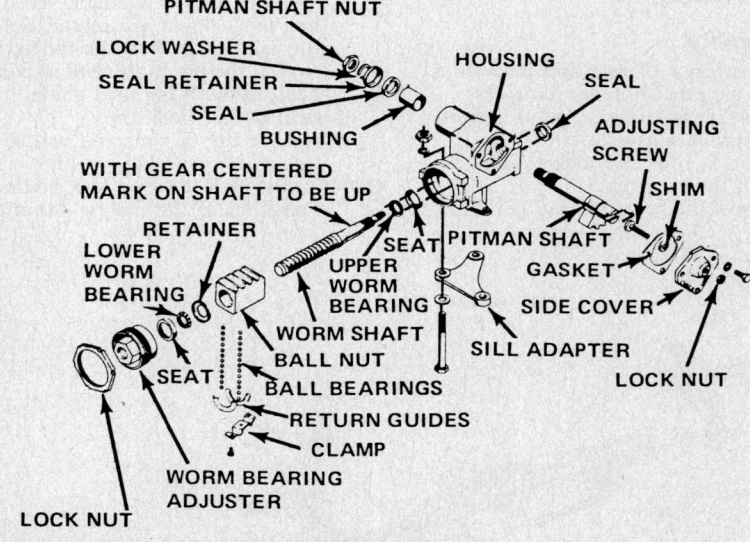

Typical manual steering gear exploded view

screw clockwise until a pull of ¾ to 1⅛ lbs. is shown on the spring scale. When the adjustment is correct, tighten the pitman shaft adjusting screw locknut and recheck the adjustment.

NOTE: A torque wrench calibrated in in./lbs. may be substituted for the spring scale in adjusting steering gear.

2 Turn the steering wheel to the center of its turning limits (pitman arm disconnected). If the steering wheel is

removed, the mark on the steering shaft should be at top center.

3 Connect the ball stud to the pitman arm, tightening the attaching nut to 115 ft./lbs. (Vega—93 ft./lbs.).

STEERING GEAR DISASSEMBLY & ASSEMBLY

1 After removing the steering gear from the car, place the steering gear assembly in a bench vise.

NOTE: Worm seal may be replaced without disassembling gear. Be careful

TROUBLESHOOTING GM MANUAL STEERING

CONDITION	POSSIBLE CAUSE	CORRECTION
Hard or Erratic Steering	(1) Incorrect tire pressure	(1) Inflate tires to recommended pressures
	(2) Insufficient or incorrect lubrication	(2) Lubricate as required (refer to Maintenance Section
	(3) Suspension, or steering linkage parts damaged or misaligned	(3) Repair or replace parts as necessary
	(4) Improper front wheel alignment	(4) Adjust incorrect wheel alignment angles
	(5) Incorrect steering gear adjustment	(5) Adjust steering gear
	(6) Sagging springs	(6) Replace springs
Play or Looseness in Steering	(1) Steering wheel loose	(1) Inspect shaft splines and repair as necessary. Tighten attaching nut and stake in place
	(2) Steering linkage or attaching parts loose or worn	(2) Tighten, adjust, or replace faulty components
	(3) Pitman arm loose	(3) Inspect shaft splines and repair as necessary. Tighten attaching nut and stake in place
	(4) Steering gear attaching bolts loose	(4) Tighten bolts
	(5) Loose or worn wheel bearings	(5) Adjust or replace bearings
	(6) Steering gear adjustment incorrect or parts badly worn	(6) Adjust gear or replace defective parts
Wheel Shimmy or Tramp	(1) Improper tire pressure	(1) Inflate tires to recommended pressures
	(2) Wheels, tires, or brake rotors or drums out-of-balance or out-of-round	(2) Inspect and replace out-of-balance parts
	(3) Inoperative, worn, or loose shock absorbers or mounting parts	(3) Repair or replace shocks or mountings
	(4) Loose or worn steering or suspension parts	(4) Tighten or replace as necessary
	(5) Loose or worn wheel bearings	(5) Adjust or replace bearings
	(6) Incorrect steering gear adjustments	(6) Adjust steering gear
	(7) Incorrect front wheel alignment	(7) Correct front wheel alignment
Tire Wear	(1) Improper tire pressure	(1) Inflate tires to recommended pressures
	(2) Failure to rotate tires	(2) Rotate tires
	(3) Brakes grabbing	(3) Adjust or repair brakes
	(4) Incorrect front wheel alignment	(4) Align incorrect angles
	(5) Broken or damaged steering and suspension parts	(5) Repair or replace defective parts
	(6) Wheel runout	(6) Replace faulty wheel
	(7) Excessive speed on turns	(7) Make driver aware of condition
Car Leads to One Side	(1) Improper tire pressures	(1) Inflate tires to recommended pressures
	(2) Front tires with uneven tread depth, wear pattern, or different cord design (i.e., one bias ply and one belted tire on front wheels)	(2) Install tires of same cord construction and reasonably even tread depth and wear pattern
	(3) Incorrect front wheel alignment	(3) Align incorrect angles
	(4) Brakes dragging	(4) Adjust or repair brakes
	(5) Pulling due to uneven tire construction	(5) Replace faulty tire

not to damage shaft or housing when removing seal.

2 Rotate the worm shaft until it is centered with the mark facing upward. Remove three cover attaching screws and the adjusting screw locknut. Remove the cover and gasket by turning adjusting screw clockwise through the cover.

3 Remove the adjusting screw with its shim from the slot in the end of the pitman shaft. Remove the pitman shaft from the housing being careful not to damage the seal in the housing.

4 Loosen the worm bearing adjuster locknut with a brass drift and remove the adjuster and bearing. Remove the bearing retainer with a screwdriver.

5 Remove the worm and shaft assembly with the ball nut assembly and bearing. Remove the ball nut return guide clamp by removing screws. Remove the guides, turn ball nut over, and remove the steel balls by rotating the shaft from side to side. After all steel balls have been removed, take the ball nut off the worm shaft.

B655

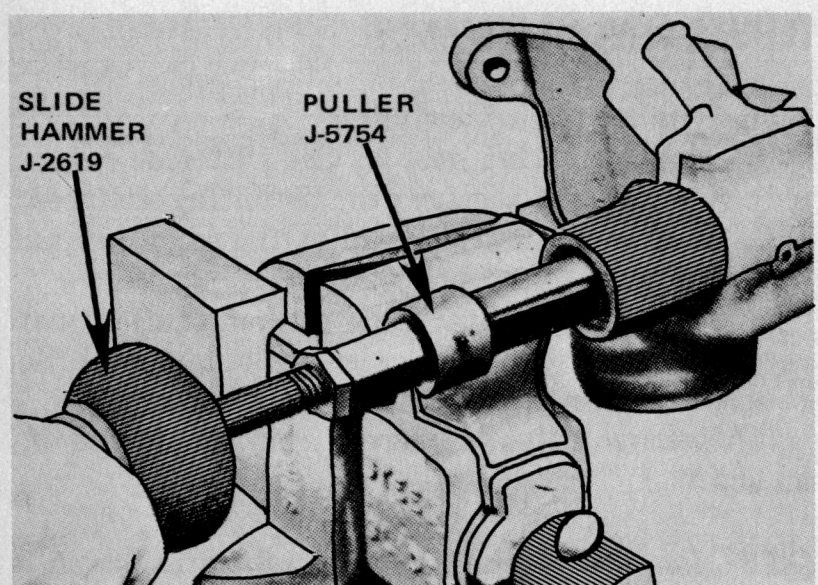

Pitman shaft bushing removal

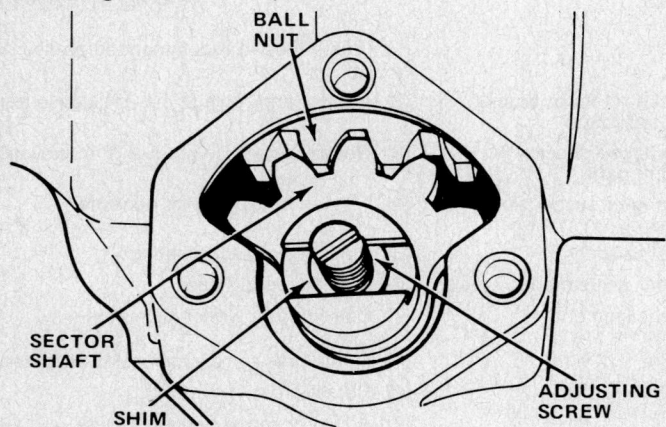

Pitman shaft and ball nut position

shaft. Install the steel balls in the return guides and the ball nut, placing an equal number in each circuit of the ball nut. Install the return guide clamp and screws.

CHILTON CAUTION: *Do not rotate the worm shaft while installing the steel balls since the balls may enter the crossover passage between the circuits, causing incorrect operation of the ball nut.*

13 Place bearing on shaft above the worm gear, center ball nut on worm gear; then, slide the steering shaft, bearing, and ball nut into the housing. *Do not damage the steering shaft seal in the housing.*
14 Place the bearing in the worm adjuster, install the bearing retainer, and install the adjuster and locknut on the housing, tightening it just enough to hold the bearing in place.
15 Install the pitman shaft adjusting screw and selective shim in the pitman shaft. Be sure there is no more than 0.002 in. of end play of the screw in the slot. If the end-play is more than 0.002 in., install a new selective shim to get the proper clearance. Shims are available in four thicknesses: 0.063 in., 0.065 in., 0.067 in., and 0.069 in.
16 Install the pitman shaft and adjusting screw with the sector and ball nut positioned as shown.
17 Install the cover and gasket on the adjusting screw, turning screw counterclockwise until it extends through the cover from 5/8 to 3/4 in. Install the cover attaching screws and torque to 35 ft./lbs. (Vega—18 ft./lbs.).
18 Tighten the pitman shaft adjusting screw so that the teeth on the shaft and the ball nut engage but do not bind. Final adjustment must be made later.
19 Wrap the pitman shaft splines with tape to protect the seal and install the seal.
20 Fill steering gear with a good quality steering gear lubricant. Turn the steering gear from one extreme to the other to make sure it does not bind. *Do not allow the ball nut to strike the ends of the ball races on the worm gear to avoid damaging the ball return guides.*
21 Install the steering gear as described previously. Perform the final adjustments on the worm bearing preload and the sector and ball nut backlash adjustments.

6 Clean all parts in solvent. Inspect all bearings, bearing cups, bushings, seals, worm groove, and gear teeth for signs of wear, scoring, pitting, etc. If the pitman shaft bushings or seal, steering shaft seal, or upper and lower bearing cups need replacement, see the replacement procedures given below.
7 Remove the pitman shaft seal with a screwdriver or punch. If there is leakage around the threads of the bearing adjuster, apply a non-hardening sealer.
8 Remove faulty bushings from the pitman shaft with Puller and Slide Hammer. Install new bushings, seating the inner end of the bushing flush with the inside surface of the housing.
9 Remove the steering shaft seal with a punch or screwdriver. Tap new seal in place, using a section of tubing to seat the seal.
10 Remove the upper or lower bearing cup from the worm bearing adjuster or steering gear housing using Puller and Slide Hammer. Install the new bearing cups.
11 Lubricate all seals, bushings, and bearings before installing into the steering gear assembly.
12 Position the ball nut on the worm

GM MANUAL RACK & PINION-CHEVETTE

Rack & Pinion—Chevette

DISASSEMBLY
1 Position assembly in vise, clamping

housing near center. Use soft jaws to prevent damage to housing.
2 Loosen jam nuts. Remove outer tie rod.

CHILTON CAUTION: *Hold housing while loosening nuts so as not to damage internal gear components.*

3 Remove inner boot clamp by cutting.

Remove the outer clamp by relieving tension in clamp. Remove boot by pulling. Repeat procedure for other end.

4 Position rack in soft jaw vise, and remove inner tie rod assemblies (both ends).

CHILTON CAUTION: *To prevent internal gear damage when removing housing, turn housing counterclockwise until assembly separates from rack.*

5 Remove adjuster plug locknut, adjuster plug, and spring.
6 Remove rack bearing from housing.
7 Clean surface at seal. Pierce seal at one of the two round spots on surface. Pry out seal.
8 Using snap ring pliers, remove retaining ring from bore.
9 Position end of shaft in soft jaw vise. Tap housing to separate pinion assembly from housing.

CHILTON CAUTION: *With pinion separated, rack may slide from housing and be damaged.*

10 Remove rack from housing.
11 The rack and pinion assembly is now disassembled. Clean all components, except inner tie rod assemblies, with an approved solvent. Air dry and inspect. Replace any seals which are cut or badly worn. If the pinion seal is removed, it must be replaced.

NOTE: Check major wear areas for cracking, chipping, etc. Replace as required.

MOUNTING GROMMETS

Do not remove grommets unless replacement is required. Replace both grommets if either requires replacement.
Cut through grommet and remove.
Lube inside of seals lightly with chassis lube. Start with left seal first and force it past the right side (smaller inside diameter) boss. Start right hand grommet and seat. Remove housing from vise and slide grommet to left hand mounting. Assemble grommet to housing.

GUIDE BUSHINGS

No attempt to replace the guide bushing should be made unless it is damaged or broken. If this occurs, replace the housing.

RACK BUSHING

The rack bushing should only be replaced if evidence of heavy wear is observed.
Remove retaining ring. Using a suitable size socket and extension, drive the bushing out of the housing. If a puller is available, position fingers of puller behind bushing and remove bushing using slide hammer.
Using a suitable size socket, press new rack bushing into housing until it bottoms. Install retaining ring.

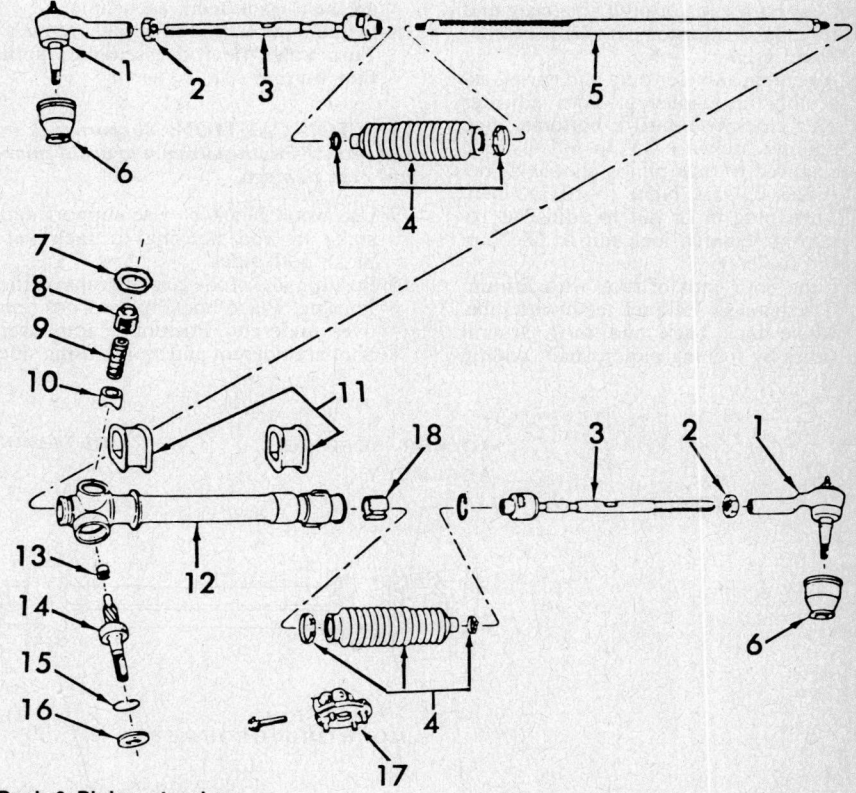

Rack & Pinion steering

1. TIE ROD ASSEMBLY (OUTER)
2. JAM NUT
3. TIE ROD ASSEMBLY (INNER)
4. BOOT SERVICE PACKAGE
5. RACK (STEERING)
6. SEAL (TIE ROD)
7. NUT (ADJUSTER PLUG)
8. ADJUSTER PLUG
9. SPRING (ADJUSTER)
10. BEARING (STEERING RACK)
11. GROMMET
12. HOUSING ASSEMBLY
13. BEARING ASSEMBLY (PINION ROLLER)
14. PINION & BEARING ASSEMBLY
15. RETAINING RING
16. SEAL (PINION)
17. FLANGE ASSEMBLY
18. BUSHING

ROLLER BEARING ASSEMBLY

Check condition of pinion pilot. If scored or badly worn, replace pinion and roller bearing assembly.
Press or tap out bearing using drift and press or hammer.
Using a suitable size socket, press or drive new bearing into housing until it bottoms.

BEARING & PINION ASSEMBLY

Inspect roller bearing pilot, pinion teeth, and rotor bearing assembly. If pilot is scored, teeth are chipped, or is loose on pinion shaft, the bearing and pinion assembly should be replaced.

INNER TIE RODS

The inner tie rod assemblies cannot be serviced. If the pivot is loose, replace the tie rod assembly. If the joint rocking or turning torque exceeds 17 N/m (150 in./lbs.), replace the inner tie rod assembly.

ASSEMBLY

1 Install rack with teeth facing pinion into housing. The flat on the teeth should be parallel with pinion shaft. Measure and set 68.5 mm (2.70 in.) from lip of housing to end of rack.

NOTE: Insert pinion with flat at 75° from vertical. Tap on pinion shaft with soft hammer until pinion seats. Reset 68.5 mm (2.70 in.) dimension of rack position. Flat should now be vertical. If flat is at plus or minus 30° from vertical, restart procedure.

CHILTON CAUTION: *Rack must be centered as described. If not, the steering wheel cannot travel fully, causing unequal turning radii.*

2 Install retaining ring using tool J-4245. Beveled edge of retaining ring should be up.
3 Liberally coat top of pinion bearing with anhydrous calcium grease, then seat pinion seal flush with housing. Seal can be seated by tapping on alternate sides with hammer.
4 Install rack bearing. Coat bearing with lithium based grease.

MANUAL STEERING

GM MANUAL RACK & PINION—CHEVETTE

5 Coat both ends of preload spring and threads of adjuster plug with lithium based grease.

6 Assemble adjuster plug and spring assembly into housing. Turn adjuster plug clockwise until it bottoms, then counterclockwise 45° to 60°. Torque required to turn pinion should be between 0.9–1.1 N/m (8–10 in./lbs.). Turn plug in or out to adjust as required. Tighten lock nut to 68 N/m (50 ft./lbs.).

7 Lube both ends of rack with lithium based grease. Fill rack teeth with lube. Move rack back and forth several times by turning pinion shaft, adding grease to rack teeth each time.

8 Install inner tie rod assemblies to rack. Turn inner tie rod assemblies until they bottom out.

CHILTON CAUTION: *Support rack in vise or with another wrench to avoid internal gear damage.*

9 Use wood block or vise support and stake tie rod housing to rack flat. Stake both sides.

10 Position one of the large clamps on the housing. Place boot lip into position over undercut. Position clamp over boot at undercut and secure using side cutter type pliers or tool J-22610.

11 Slip end of boot into rod undercut. Do not assemble clamp over boot until toe adjustment is made. Straighten boots if twisted before assembling clamps.

12 Thread jam nuts (both sides) onto tie rods.

13 Thread on tie rod ends. Do not tighten jam nuts until toe adjustment is made. Then tighten to 67 N/m (50 ft./lbs.).

14 Slip on coupling assembly. Flat on inside diameter of coupling mates with flat on pinion shaft. Install pinch bolt, but do not tighten until vehicle installation, then tighten to 41 N/m (30 ft./lbs.).

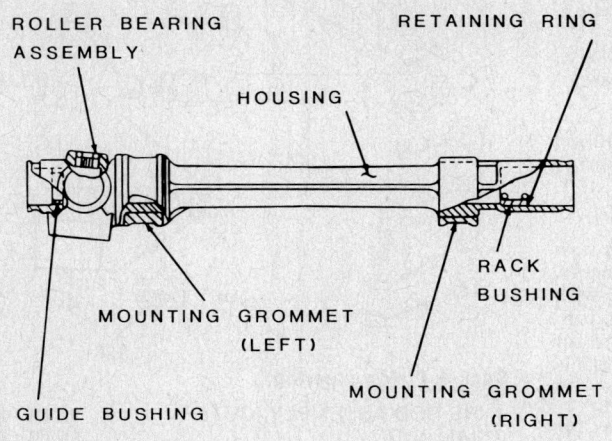

Housing Assembly

Rack and Pinion Steering		
Inner Tie Rod Rocking or Turning Torque		
(Not to Exceed)	5 N·m	(45 in. lbs.)
Tie Rod Jam Nuts	68 N·m	(50 ft. lbs.)
Pinion Turning Torque	0.7 to 1.5 N·m	(6 - 13 in. lbs.)
Adjuster Plug Lock Nut	68 N·m	(50 ft. lbs.)
Rack and Pinion Assembly Clamp Bolts	19 N·m	(14 ft. lbs.)
Steering Column		
Flexible Coupling Pinch Bolt	41 N·m	(30 ft. lbs.)
Intermediate Shaft to Flexible Coupling Bolts	24 N·m	(18 ft. lbs.)
Steering Column to Dash Cover Screws	2 N·m	(18 in. lbs.)
Column to Toe Pan Screw	27 N·m	(20 ft. lbs.)
Column to I.P. Bracket Bolts	30 N·m	(22 ft. lbs.)
Column Bracket to I.P. Nuts	27 N·m	(20 ft. lbs.)
Column Shroud to Housing Screws	2 N·m	(18 in. lbs.)
Column Housing & Shroud to Jacket	7 N·m	(60 in. lbs.)
Ignition Switch to Jacket Screws	4 N·m	(35 in. lbs.)
Turn Signal Switch Screws	4 N·m	(35 in. lbs.)

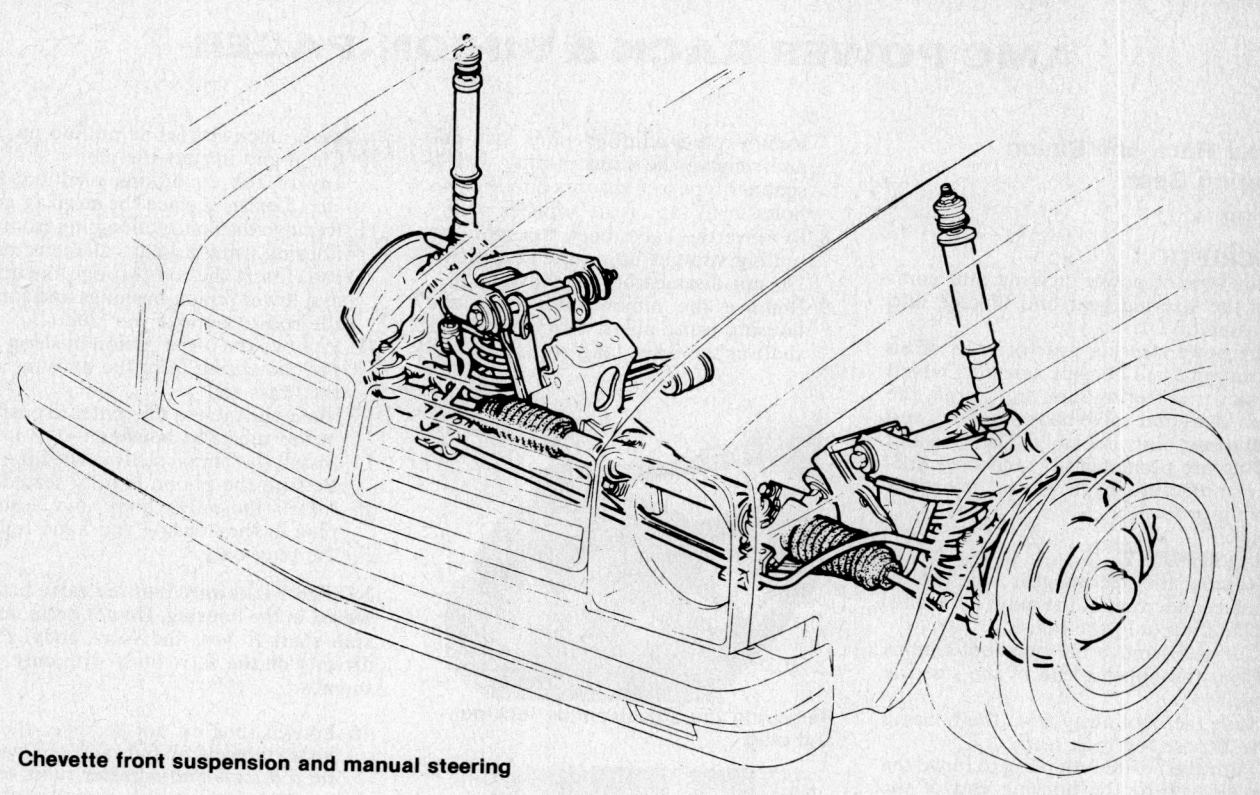

Chevette front suspension and manual steering

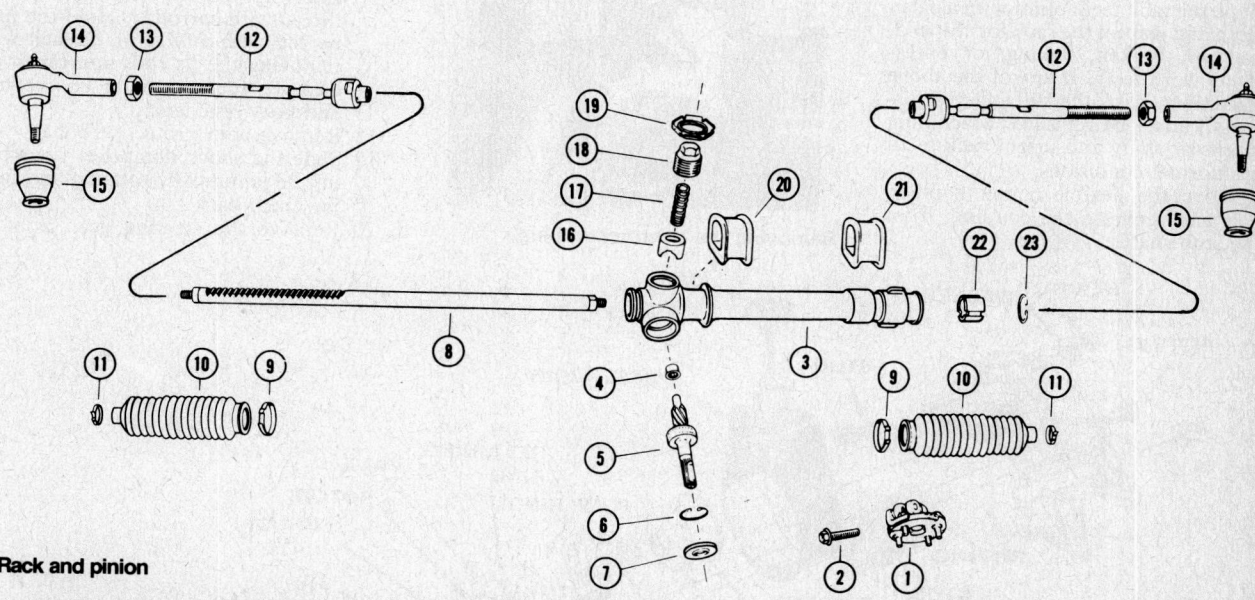

Rack and pinion

1 — FLANGE ASSY, COUPLING & STRG.
2 — BOLT, PINCH
3 — HOUSING ASSY, RACK & PINION
4 — BEARING ASSY, ROLLER
5 — PINION ASSY, BEARING &
6 — RING, RETAINING
7 — SEAL, STEERING PINION
8 — RACK, STEERING

9 — CLAMP, BOOT
10 — BOOT
11 — CLAMP, BOOT
12 — ROD ASSY, INNER TIE
13 — NUT, JAM
14 — ROD ASSY, OUTER TIE
15 — SEAL, TIE ROD
16 — BEARING, RACK

17 — SPRING, ADJUSTER
18 — PLUG, ADJUSTER
19 — NUT, ADJUSTER PLUG LOCK
20 — GROMMET, GEAR MOUNTING (LH)
21 — GROMMET, GEAR MOUNTING (RH)
22 — BUSHING, RACK
23 — RING, RETAINING

AMC POWER RACK & PINION-PACER

Power Rack and Pinion Steering Gear

PACER

DESCRIPTION

This type of power steering unit combines the steering gear and linkage into one assembly.

The powersteering gear consists of an internal tube and housing assembly which contains the steering rack and piston, the pinion shaft and valve body assembly and the adjuster plug assembly. The tube and housing are permanently connected during manufacture by a plastic injection-bonding process.

DISASSEMBLY

1 Remove the steering gear from the vehicle and mount the unit in a vise, clamping only the housing.
2 Cut and remove the two boot clamps from the housing end of the steering gear.
3 Slide the boot away from the housing to expose the rack teeth.
4 Turn the flexible coupling to move the rack toward the housing end of the steering gear and expose as many teeth as possible.
5 Wipe the rack teeth clean with a clean cloth and inspect the rack for chipped, cracked, broken, flaking, or excessively worn teeth. If any of the above conditions exist, the steering gear assembly must be replaced. Machining marks or shiny and bright rack teeth are normal conditions.
6 Remove the flexible coupling pinch bolt and separate the coupling from the stub shaft.

7 Remove the adjuster plug lock-nut and remove the adjuster plug with a spanner type tool that fits into the two holes in to top of the adjuster plug.
8 Remove the valve body assembly by pulling straight up on the stub shaft. Do not disassemble the valve body.
9 Remove the pinion shaft from the housing using pliers. Grip the pinion shaft at the drive tang and rotate the

Removing the adjuster plug lock-nut and plug

Removing the contraction plug

shaft clockwise while pulling up.
10 Clean and inspect the pinion shaft. If any of the conditions mentioned in step 5 exist, replace the steering gear.
11 Remove the contraction plug from the housing using a ¼ in. diameter brass rod. Insert the rod through the upper and lower pinion bushings and tap on the rod to remove the plug.
12 Remove the lower pinion bushing and preload spring from the housing with the brass rod.
13 Move the rack to the centered position in the tube and housing.
14 Install the pinion shaft in the housing. Be sure the pinion is fully seated.
15 Install the valve body and adjuster plug in the housing and hand tighten the plug only.

NOTE: Make sure that the valve body is seated in the housing. Do not press on the stub shaft to seat the valve body. Press directly on the valve body with only your thumbs.

16 Loosen, but do not remove, the adjuster tube clamp nuts and remove the tie rod ends and adjuster tubes as assemblies. Mark the position of the tubes and tie rods for reference during assembly. Use penetrating oil if the threads are corroded. Hold the inner tie rod with a 9/16 in. wrench while removing the tie rods and tubes.
17 Remove the remaining boot clamps and boot retainers.
18 Remove both protective boots.
19 Slide the shock dampener rings back off the jamnuts by rotating and pushing them back.
20 Remove the steering gear from the

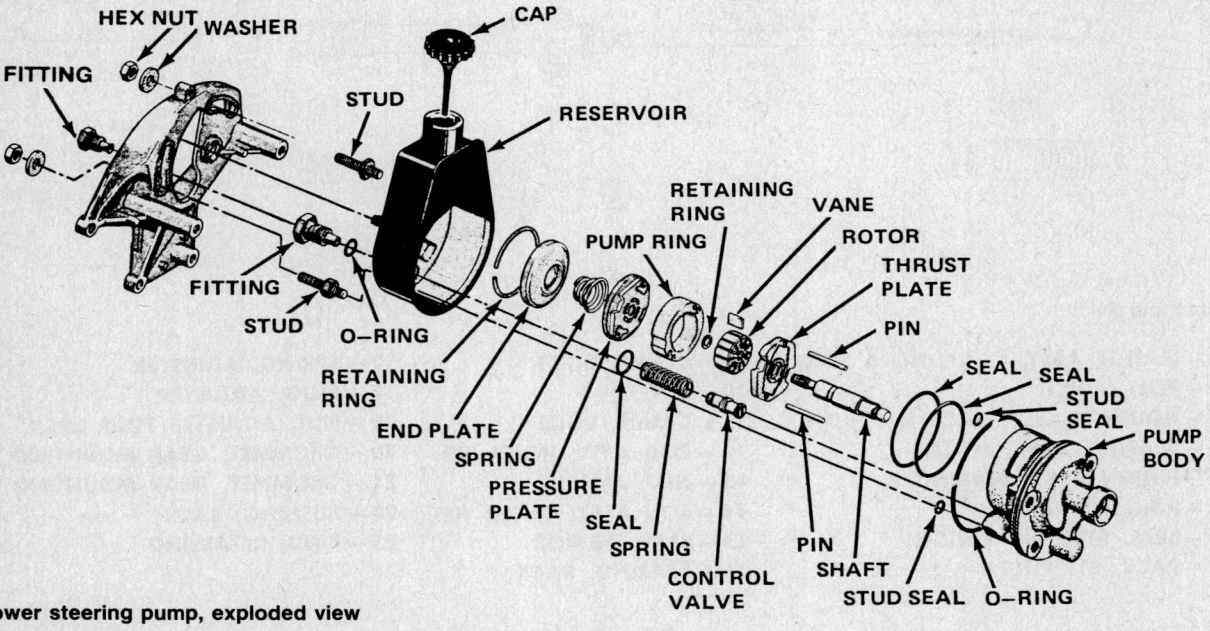

AMC power steering pump, exploded view

1 Flexible coupling-to-intermediate shaft attaching bolt
2 Lockwasher
3 Nut
4 Pinch bolt
5 Flexible coupling
6 Adjuster plug locknut
7 Adjuster plug assembly
8 Adjuster plug O-ring
9 Oil lines
10 Valve body seal rings
11 Valve body O-rings
12 Valve body
13 Spool valve damper O-ring
14 Spool valve
15 Torsion bar bushing
16 Torsion bar seal ring
17 Torsion bar
18 Drive pin
19 Stub shaft
20 Drive pin
21 Power steering hoses
22 Mounting bolt
23 Washer
24 Preload spring
25 Grommet
26 Bushing
27 Steering linkage
28 Rack bushing
29 Grommet
30 Washer
31 Nut
32 Steering rack
33 Rack piston
34 Bulkhead O-ring
35 Bulkhead retaining ring
36 Jam nut
37 Ball seat
38 Inner tie rod
39 Inner tie rod housing
40 Boot clamp

41 Boot
42 Adjuster tube clamp bolt
43 Adjuster tube clamp
44 Adjuster tube
45 Tie rod end
46 Lube plug
47 Tie rod end seal
48 Tie rod end nut
49 Cotter pin
50 Adjuster tube clamp nut
51 Boot clamp
52 Tie rod housing set screw
53 Ball seat spring
54 Shock dampener ring
55 Bulkhead seals
56 Bulkhead
57 Breather tube
58 Rack piston seal ring
59 Contraction plug
60 Lower pinion bushing
61 Housing
62 Nut
63 Washer
64 Grommet
65 Plastic injection ring
66 Locating bushing
67 Plastic injection ring
68 Mounting clamp
69 Bolt
70 Mounting clip
71 Mounting grommet
72 Inner rack seal
73 Tube and power cylinder
74 Upper pinion bushing
75 Pinion shaft seal
76 Support washer
77 Conical thrust bearing race
78 Thrust bearing
79 Drive pin
80 Shaft cap
81 Torsion bar bushing

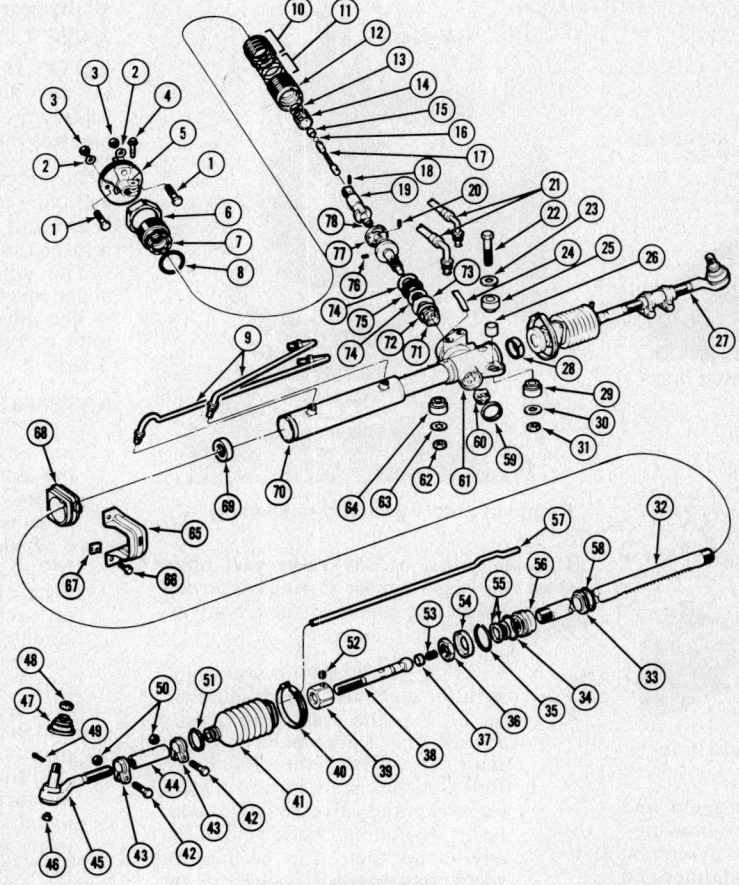

Pacer power rack and pinion steering gear, exploded view

vise, and clamp the inner tie rod housing. Loosen the jamnut using 1½ in. wrench. Loosen the jamnut at the opposite end of the rack also.

NOTE: The inner tie rod housings must be held in a vise while loosening the jamnuts to prevent damage to the rack, pinion, stub shaft and valve body.

21 Loosen but do not remove the set screw in each inner tie rod housing.
22 Reposition the steering gear in the vise as before, and remove the inner tie rod housings, inner tie rods, ball seats, ball seat springs, jamnuts, and shock dampener rings.
23 Remove the adjuster plug. Pull straight up and out on the stub shaft and remove the assembly.
24 Remove the pinion shaft from the housing with a pair of pliers. Grip the pinion shaft at the drive tang and rotate the shaft clockwise while pulling upward to remove the pinion shaft.
25 Remove the pinion thrust bearing conical thrust bearing races, and support washer from the housing with either your fingers, an external-type snap ring pliers, or a magnet.
26 Mark the position of the breather tube, mounting clamp and grommet on each end of the tube and housing for reference during assembly. The

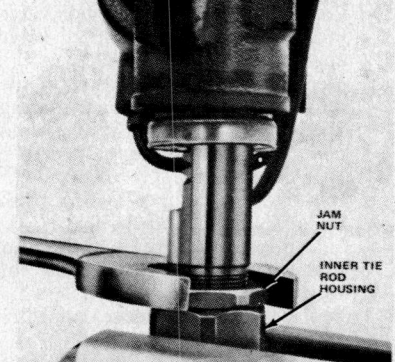

Loosening the inner tie rod housing jamnuts

breather tube, grommet and mounting clamp must be reassembled in their original positions to ensure proper seating and sealing.
27 Remove the breather tube and the grommet and mounting clamp by pulling and twisting at the same time.
28 Remove the bulkhead retaining ring from the end of the tube by inserting a pin punch through the access hole in the end of the tube to force the retaining ring out of its groove. Then, place the blade of a screwdriver behind the ring and pry it out.

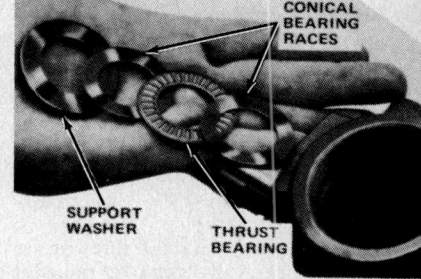

Removal of thrust bearing and races

NOTE: Be careful not to scratch the bore of the tube when removing the retaining ring. Remove any scratches with crocus cloth.

29 Pull the steering rack and bulkhead out of the tube and housing assembly.

NOTE: Do not remove the steering rack unless a new inner rack seal is available as the seal is rendered useless when the rack is removed. As the rack is removed, the rack piston will force the bulkhead out of the tube at the same time.

30 Remove the bulkhead from the steering rack.
31 Remove the plastic rack bushing from the housing. Insert a knife blade under the bushing and pry up. Grasp the

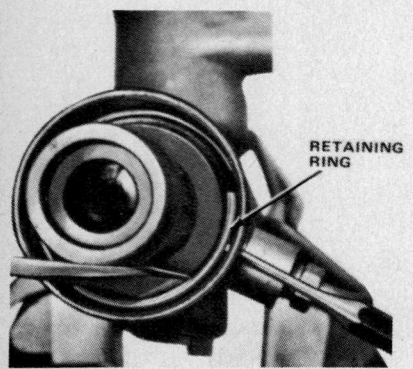

Removing the bulkhead retaining ring

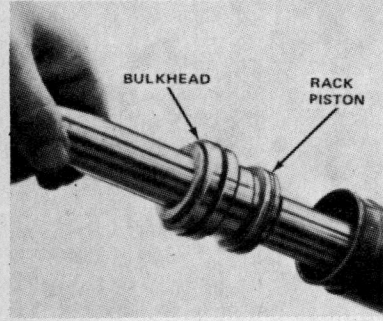

Removing the steering rack and bulkhead

bushing with a needlenose pliers and pull the bushing out of the housing.

32 Remove the inner rack seal by driving it out of the tube with a hammer and a brass rod 12 to 14 in. long.

33 Turn the steering gear over in the vise and remove the upper pinion bushing and pinion shaft seal with a ⅝ in. socket and extension. When the bushing separates from the housing, it will force the seal out also.

34 Remove the outer O-ring and two inner lip-type seals from the bulkhead. Note their positions for correct reassembly.

35 Using the blade of a small screwdriver or knife, carefully remove the seal from the rack piston. Be careful not to scratch the piston.

36 To disassemble the adjuster plug:
  a. Remove the thrust bearing retainer with a screwdriver and discard the retainer. Be careful not to damage the needle bearing bore.
  b. Remove the thrust bearing spacer, bearing, and bearing races.
  c. Remove the adjuster plug O-ring seal and discard the seal.
  d. Remove the stub shaft seal retaining ring with snap ring pliers.
  e. Remove the stub shaft dust seal and oil seal by prying them out with a small screwdriver.
  f. Remove the needle bearing.

37 To disassemble the valve body and stub shaft assembly:

NOTE: Do not disassemble the valve for any other reason than to replace the seals.

Removing the valve body assembly

If replacement of any valve part other than the seal rings or O-rings is necessary, replace the complete valve body assembly.

  a. Hold the valve body in your hand with the stub shaft pointing downward. Tap the stub shaft lightly against the workbench until the shaft cap is free of the valve body.
  b. Pull the stub shaft until the shaft cap clears the valve body by about ¼ in. Do not pull the stub shaft out any further than ¼ in. because the spool may become cocked in the body.
  c. Carefully remove the spool valve locating pin from the spool valve and remove the stub shaft.
  d. Remove the spool valve from the valve body by pushing and rotating the valve. If the valve becomes cocked, carefully align the valve, then remove it.
  e. Remove the damper O-ring from the spool valve and discard it.
  f. Carefully cut and remove the four seal rings and O-rings from the valve body.

38 To replace the housing hose connector seats:

NOTE: The hose connector seats do not need to be replaced unless they are damaged and/or do not provide proper sealing.

  a. Insert a no. 4 screw extractor into the seat and turn counterclockwise to remove the seat.
  b. Install a new seat by driving it into place with a brass rod. Be sure the seat is bottomed in the housing and is not cocked.

39 Wash all of the parts, except the rubber boots and nylon bushings in a suitable solvent and dry them with compressed air. Make sure you do not wash off the alignment marks for the breather tube and mounting clamp.

40 Inspect all of the parts for the conditions mentioned in step 4a.

NOTE: If the tube and housing or steering rack and pinion shaft need replacing, replace the complete steering gear assembly, less the steering linkage components.

Bushings, thrust bearings, steering linkage components, the breather tube and boots, and the flexible coupling can all be replaced individually.

The adjuster plug assembly components can be replaced separately.

The valve body and stub shaft assembly must be replaced as a unit if found to be defective.

ASSEMBLY

1 Install the split-type nylon rack bushing in the housing. Compress the leading edge of the bushing with your fingers and insert it into the housing. The bushing will snap into place once it is past the lip of the housing.

2 Install the inner rack seal on the steering rack by first cutting a 2½ in. × 4 in. section of a manila envelope or similar cardboard-type paper. Form the paper over the rack teeth. The paper will protect the seal from the rack teeth during installation. Dip the seal in power steering fluid and slide it over the rack and onto the paper. Install the seal on the rack with the seal lip facing the rack piston and the metal surface of the seal facing away from the rack piston. Remove the paper protector when the seal is over the rack teeth.

3 Lightly coat the outside diameter of the inner rack seal and bulkhead retaining ring groove in the tube with chassis grease.

4 Coat the rack teeth liberally with lithium base chassis lubricant.

5 Dip the rack piston seal ring in power steering fluid and install the seal ring on the rack piston. Be careful not to overstretch or twist the seal ring when installing it.

6 Carefully insert the steering rack into the tube. Push the steering rack into the tube as far as possible so that the rack piston will start the inner rack seal into its seat in the end of the tube. Bottom the seal in its seat. Install the upper pinion bushing with the chamfered side down, and start the pinion shaft seal, with the seal lip facing the bore, into the seat in the housing.

7 Place the support washer on top of the pinion shaft seal.

8 Using a 1¼ in. socket with an extension, lightly tap on the support washer until the pinion shaft seal and support washer are fully seated in the housing.

9 Lubricate the pinion shaft thrust bearing and races with petroleum jelly and install them on the pinion shaft. The bearing is installed between the two races.

10 Position the rack teeth parallel to the housing bore and set the end of the

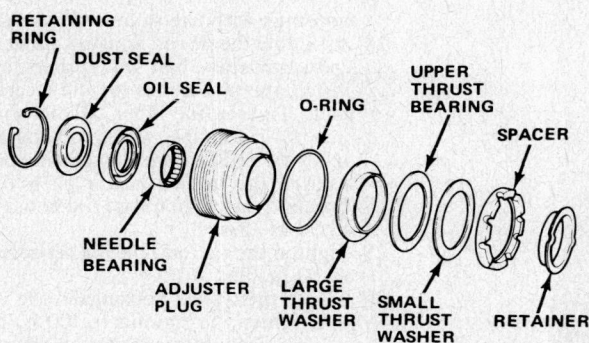

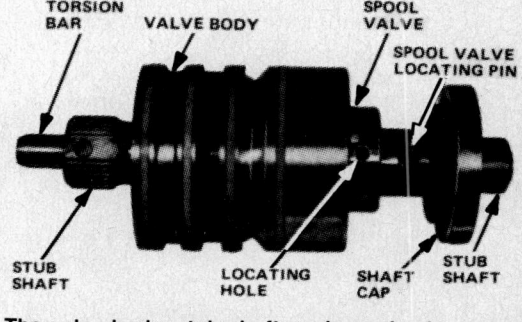

Exploded view of the pinion shaft and adjuster plug assemblies

The valve body, stub shaft, and spool valve assembly

rack 4 in. from the machined inner face of the housing.

11 Install the pinion shaft into the housing bore with the drive pin located between the 3 and 4 o'clock position. Push the pinion down until it bottoms in the housing.

12 Center the steering rack to the 4 in. setting. With the rack centered, the pinion shaft drive pin should now be located at the 12 o'clock position. If the drive pin is positioned incorrectly either at the 11 o'clock or 1 o'clock position, remove the pinion shaft and start over again at step 10.

13 Assemble the valve body and stub shaft in the following manner:

a. If the valve body O-rings and teflon rings were removed, install new O-rings in the oil ring grooves and lubricate them with power steering fluid.

b. Lubricate the 4 teflon seal rings with power steering fluid and install them in the grooves over the O-rings. Do not be concerned if the teflon rings appear to be distorted; the heat of the fluid during operation will straighten them.

c. Lubricate the spool valve dampener O-ring with power steering fluid and install it over the spool valve.

d. Lubricate the spool valve and valve body with power steering fluid and slide the spool valve into the valve body. Rotate the spool valve while pushing it into the valve body. Push the spool valve on through the body until the shaft pin hole is visible from the opposite end. The spool valve should be flush with the shaft cap end of the valve body.

e. Lubricate the stub shaft assembly with power steering fluid and carefully install it into the spool valve until the shaft pin can be placed into the spool valve.

f. Align the notch in the shaft cap with the pin in the valve body and press the spool valve and shaft assembly into the valve body. Make sure that the notch in the shaft cap mates with the valve body pin.

14 Align the notch in the valve body with

Centering the steering rack

Installing the stub shaft in the valve body

the drive pin in the pinion shaft and install the valve body in the housing. Be sure the drive lugs on the pinion shaft fully engage the slots in the stub shaft. When the valve body is correctly installed, the fluid return hole in the housing will be exposed. If the hole is not visible, either the pinion shaft is not seated, the spool valve locating pins are misaligned, or the valve body stub shaft locating pins are misaligned.

NOTE: Do not press on the stub shaft to seat the valve body. Press only with your thumbs directly on the valve body.

15 Assemble the adjuster plug components as follows:

a. If you are replacing the needle

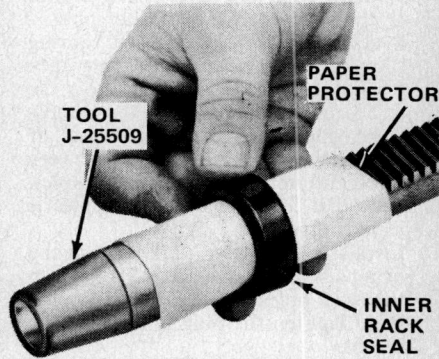

Installing the inner rack seal

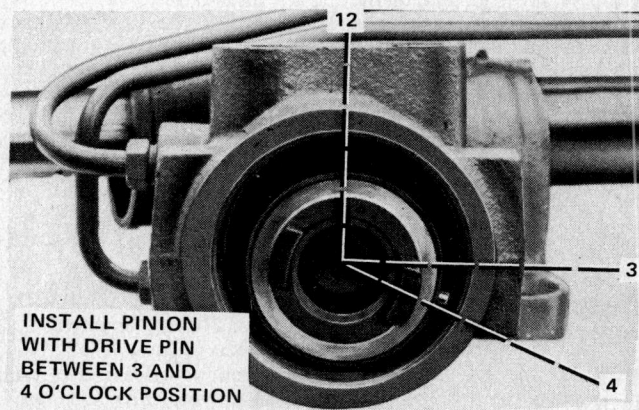

INSTALL PINION WITH DRIVE PIN BETWEEN 3 AND 4 O'CLOCK POSITION

Centering the pinion shaft in relation to the rack

Backing off the adjuster plug to the proper adjustment

bearing, drive the new bearing into the plug bore with a soft drift until it bottoms. The bearing identification number faces up.

b. Lubricate the new stub shaft oil seal and install the seal far enough to allow clearance for the dust seal and retaining ring.

c. Lubricate the new dust seal and install it in the plug with the identification number facing outward.

d. Install the retaining snap ring with snap ring pliers.

e. Lubricate the new O-ring seal with petroleum jelly and install it into the groove on the adjuster plug.

f. Assemble the large thrust bearing race, bearing, small bearing race and spacer on the plug. Press the bearing retainer into the needle bearing bore with a brass or wooden driver tool, being very careful not to damage the dimples. Radial location of the dimples is not important.

16 Install the adjuster plug in housing using a spanner type tool that fits into the two holes on the adjuster plug face. Tighten the plug until it is fully seated.

17 Adjust the thrust bearing preload by first measuring back (counterclockwise) 3/16 to 1/4 in. from one of the adjuster plug holes and making a mark. Back the adjuster plug off (counterclockwise) so that the hole used for reference is opposite the mark. Install the adjuster plug locknut and tighten it to 80 ft./lbs.

18 Install the O-ring and lip-type seals in the bulkhead. The lips of the seals must face the interior of the tube.

19 Slide the bulkhead into the tube and bottom it against the counterbore in the tube by tapping it with a brass rod.

20 Install the bulkhead retaining ring. The opening in the ring should be 1/4 in. away from the access hole in the tube.

21 Turn the steering gear over in the vise and place some lithium base chassis grease in the housing bore. Do not overfill.

22 Install the preload spring in the housing with the center hump of the spring against the housing. The end of the spring must enter the upper pinion bushing. Allow about 1/4 in. of spring to extend past the end of the housing.

23 Hold the preload spring against the housing with needlenose pliers, and install the lower pinion bushing. The chamfered end of the bushing faces inward toward the pinion shaft. Tap lightly on the spring and bushing until they are both seated.

24 Install the contraction plug in the housing and seat it using a brass rod or suitable size socket.

25 Install the mounting clamp and grommet on the tube. Position them according to the marks made during disassembly.

26 Install the shock dampener ring on each end of the steering rack with the open end facing out. Thread the jamnuts on the rack fully.

27 Liberally apply lithium base chassis grease to all wear surfaces of the inner tie rod assembly. Pack the tie rod

housings with the same type grease.

28 Assemble the tie rod housing, inner tie rods, ball seats, ball seat springs, and install the assemblies on the steering rack. Tighten the inner tie rod housings to 75 in./lbs. while rocking the inner tie rods to prevent grease lock. Loosen the tie rod housings 1/2 of a turn and retighten the tie rod housings to 50 in./lbs.

29 Tighten the tie rod housing set-screws to 60 in./lbs.

30 Clamp the tie rod housings in the vise and tighten the jamnuts to 100 ft./lbs. using a crow-foot adapter on the end of a torque wrench.

31 Slide the shock dampener rings over the jamnuts.

32 Install the mounting clamp and grommet on the tube end of the steering gear. Align the notch in the clamp with the oil line fitting boss in the tube.

33 Install the breather tube. Make sure the breather tube is not blocked in any way. The breather tube transfers air from one boot to the other during steering operation. Dust and air could be drawn into the inner tie rod assemblies if the tube is blocked.

34 Install the boot on the mounting bracket side of the tube and housing. Align the hole in the boot with the hole in the mounting grommet and breather tube. Install the boot clamp, but do not tighten it.

35 Install the opposite boot with the hole in the boot aligned with the breather tube. The boot lip must fit over the collar of the housing to seat the tube.

36 Slide the small ends of the boots over the inner tie rod undercuts and secure the boot with the small boot clamps. Tighten the clamps.

37 Secure the large end of the boot to the housing end of the steering gear. Fit the clamp over the groove in the boot with the clamp ear 3/4 in. from the tube. Compress the clamp.

38 Install the adjuster tubes and tie rod ends on the inner tie rods using the alignment marks you made during disassembly. At least 3 threads should be visible at both ends of the adjuster tubes. The difference in the number of threads on each side should be no more than 3.

39 Install the flexible coupling on the stub shaft, flat to flat. Install the pinch bolt and tighten it to 30 ft./lbs.

40 Install the steering gear and compress the boot clamps.

CHRYSLER POWER STEERING

Power Steering
Chrysler Full-Time Constant Control Type
RECONDITIONING

1 Drain gear by turning worm shaft from limit to limit with oil connections held downward. Thoroughly clean outside.

2 Remove valve body attaching screws, body and three O-rings.

3 Remove pivot lever and spring. Pry

under spherical head with a screwdriver.

CHILTON CAUTION: *Use care not to collapse slotted end of valve lever as this will destroy bearing tolerances of the spherical head.*

TROUBLESHOOTING CHRYSLER POWER STEERING

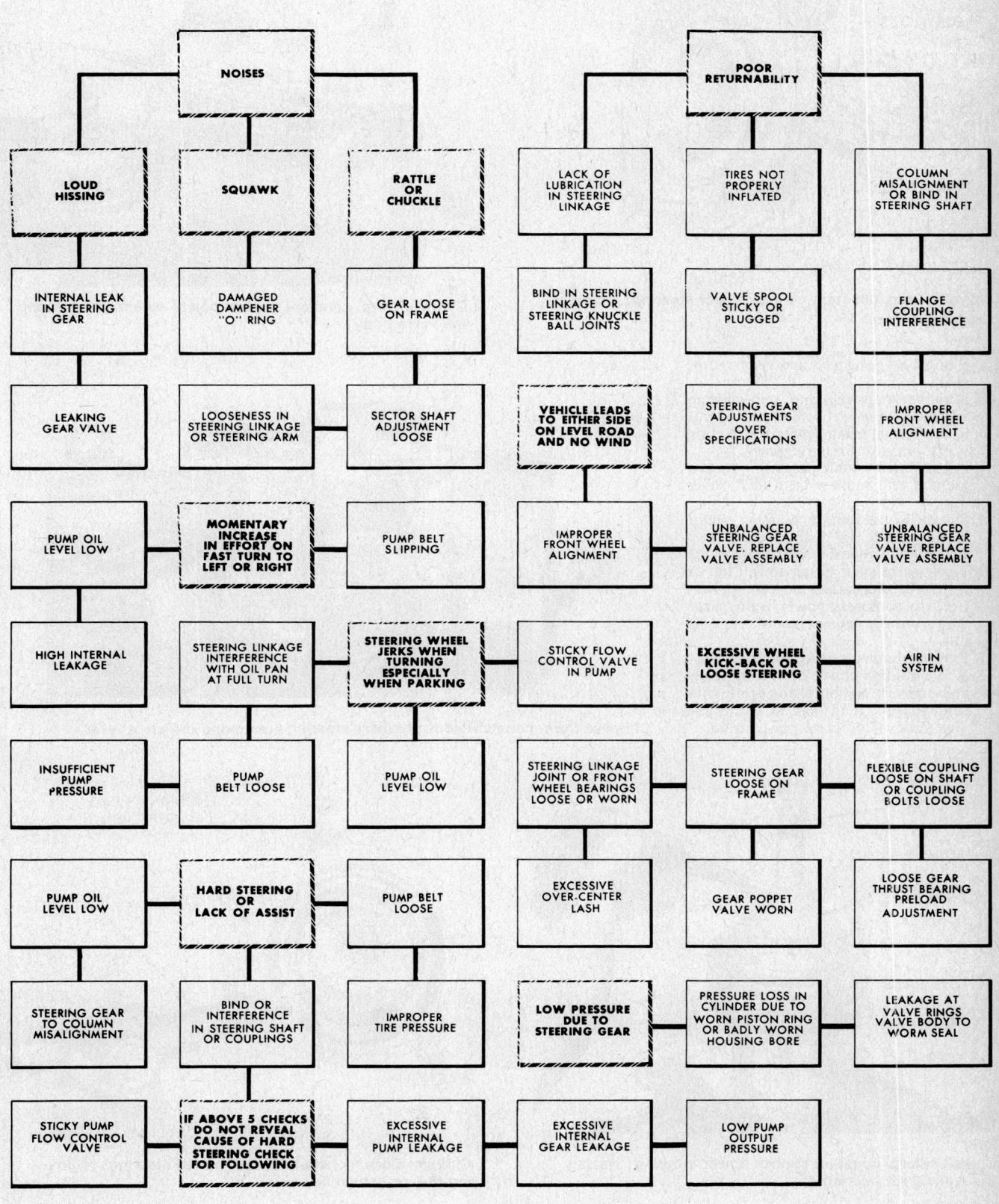

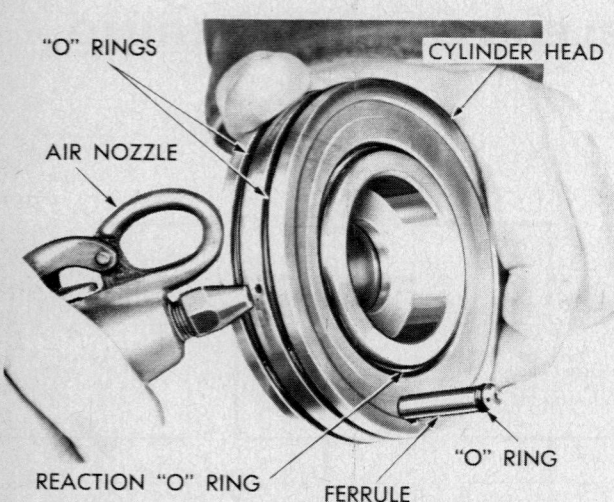

Chrysler Corp. constant control power steering: removing the reaction seal

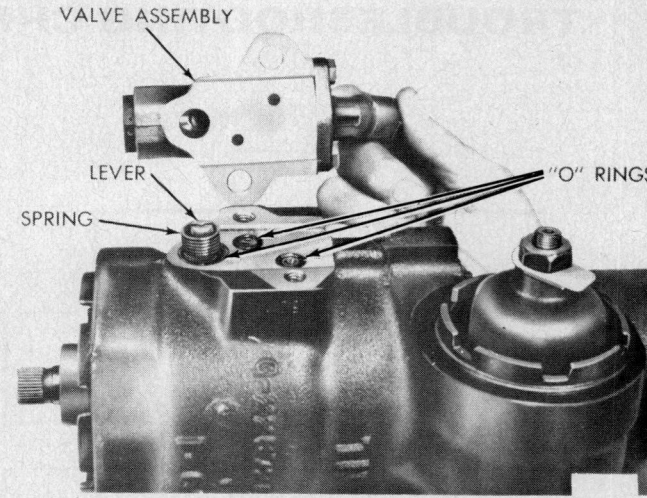

Chrysler Corp. constant control power steering: removing the valve body

4 Remove steering gear arm from sector shaft.

5 Remove snap-ring and seal backup washer.

6 Remove seal, using proper tool to prevent damage to relative parts.

7 Loosen gear shaft adjusting screw locknut and remove gear shaft cover nut.

8 Rotate wormshaft to position sector teeth at center of piston travel.

9 Loosen power train retaining nut.

10 Turn worm shaft either to full left or full right (depending on car application) to compress power train parts. Then remove power train retaining nut.

11 Remove housing head tang washer.

12 While holding power train completely compressed, pry on piston teeth with screwdriver, using shaft as a fulcrum, and remove complete power train.

Chrysler Corp. constant control power steering: removing the pivot lever

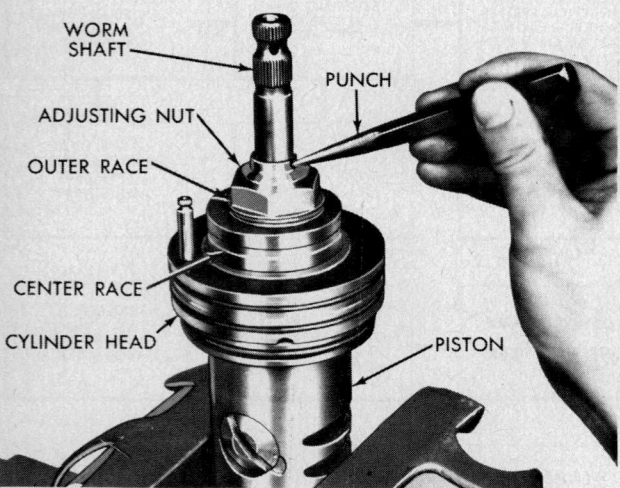

Chrysler Corp. constant control power steering: staking the wormshaft bearing nut

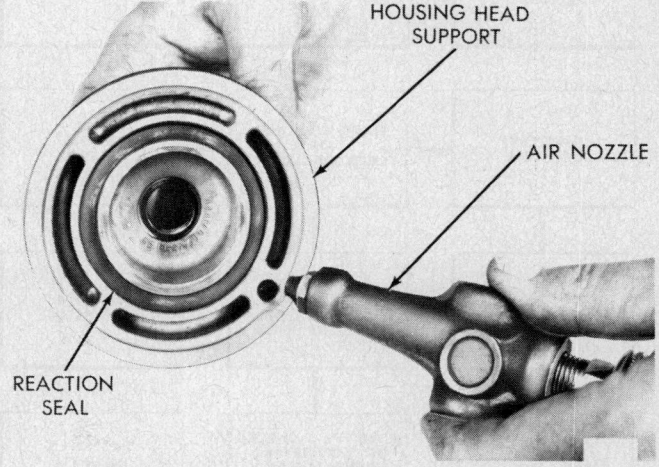

Chrysler Corp. constant control power steering: removing the lower reaction seal

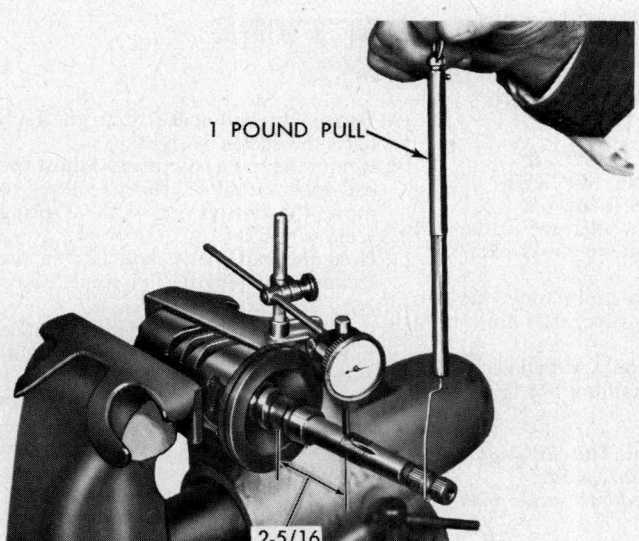

Chrysler Corp. constant control power steering : checking wormshaft side play

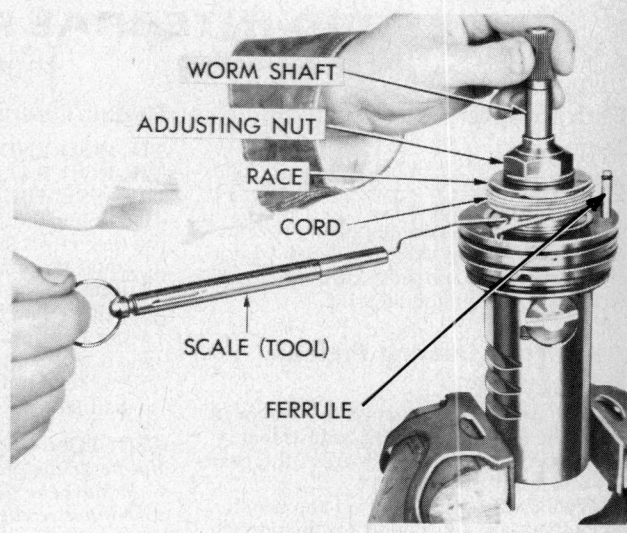

Chrysler Corp. constant control power steering : testing the center bearing preload

CHILTON CAUTION: *Maintain close contact between cylinder head, center race and spacer assembly and the housing head. This will eliminate the possibility of reactor rings becoming disengaged from their grooves in cylinder and housing head. It will prohibit center spacer from separating from center race and cocking in the housing. This could make it impossible to remove the power train without damaging involved parts.*

13 Place power train in soft-jawed vise in vertical position. The worm bearing rollers will fall out. Use of arbor tool will hold roller when the housing is removed.
14 Raise housing head until wormshaft oil shaft just clears the top of wormshaft and position arbor tool on top of shaft and into seal. With arbor in position, pull up on housing head until arbor is positioned in bearing. Remove when the housing is removed.
15 Remove large O-ring from housing head groove.
16 Remove reaction seal from groove in face of head with air pressure directed into ferrule chamber.
17 Remove reactor spring, reactor ring, worm balancing ring and spacer.
18 While holding wormshaft from turning, turn nut with enough force to release staked portions from knurled section and remove nut.
19 Remove upper thrust bearing race (thin) and upper thrust bearing.
20 Remove center bearing race.
21 Remove lower thrust bearing and lower thrust bearing race (thick).
22 Remove lower reaction ring and reaction spring.
23 Remove cylinder head assembly.
24 Remove O-rings from outer grooves in head.
25 Remove reaction O-ring from groove

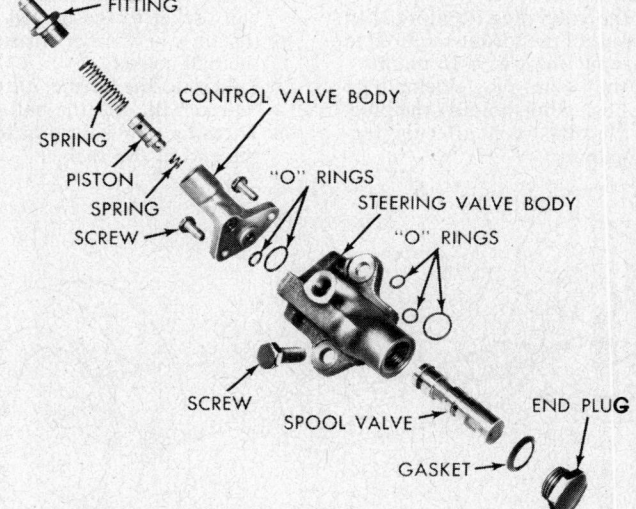

Chrysler Corp. constant control power steering: valve body exploded view

in face of cylinder head. Use air pressure in oil hole located between O-ring grooves.
26 Remove snap-ring, sleeve and rectangular oil seal from cylinder head counterbore.
27 Test wormshaft operation. Not more than 2 in./lbs. should be required to turn it through its entire travel, and with a 15 ft./lbs. side load.

NOTE: The worm and piston is serviced as a complete assembly and should not be disassembled.

28 Shaft side play should not exceed 0.-008 in. under light pull applied 2 5/16 in. from piston flange.

29 Assemble in reverse of above, noting proper adjustments and preload requirements following.
30 When cover nut in installed, tighten to 20 ft./lbs. torque.
31 Valve mounting screws should be tightened to 200 in./lbs. torque.
32 With hoses connected, system bled, and engine idling roughly, center valve unit until not self-steering. Tap on head of valve body attaching screws to move valve body up, and tap on end plug to move valve body down.
33 With steering gear on center, tighten gear shaft adjusting screw until lash just disappears.
34 Continue to tighten ⅜ to ½ turn and tighten locknut to 50 ft./lbs.

FORD INTEGRAL RACK & PINION TYPE

Ford Integral Rack & Pinion Type

FORD MUSTANG II & PINTO MERCURY BOBCAT

This system was developed to provide a power steering system for Ford Motor Company sub-compact cars equipped with rack and pinion steering.

Rack Yoke Bearing Preload Adjustment

The steering gear must be removed from the car to make this adjustment.
1 Remove the fluid lines from the gear and drain the fluid.
2 Fasten the unit down on the bench.
3 Attach an inch pound torque wrench to the input shaft.
4 Loosen the yoke plug locknut.
5 Attach an inch pound torque wrench to the yoke plug. Tighten the plug to 45–50 in./lbs. with the rack at the center of travel.
6 Back off the yoke plug no more than 45 degrees until the torque required to turn the input shaft is 7–15 in./lbs.
7 Tighten the yoke plug locknut to 44–66 ft./lbs., while holding the plug.
8 Recheck the adjustment after tightening the locknut.

Repair Operations

TIE-ROD ENDS, BELLOWS, & TIE-ROD BALL JOINT SOCKET DISASSEMBLY & ASSEMBLY

1 Loosen the jam nuts adjacent to the tie-rod sockets. Remove the sockets and jam nuts.
2 Remove the 4 clamps and remove the bellows and breather tube, after draining the fluid.
3 To remove the tie-rod and ball sockets, drill out the retaining pin in the ball socket.

CHILTON CAUTION: *This hole must not be drilled deeper than ⅜ in.*
Remove the tie-rod and ball socket with a spanner wrench.

4 Remove the locknut, inner thrust bearing, and rack spring from the recess in the end of the rack.
   To assemble:
5 Install a new rack spring in the recess in the end of the rack. Assemble the ball socket to the tie-rod.
6 Install a new inner thrust bearing in the ball socket.
7 Lubricate the spring, thrust bearing, tie-rod ball, and the ball socket.
8 Thread a new ball joint locknut onto the end of the rack.

9 Thread the ball socket onto the rack until the socket is tight.
10 Rotate the rod a few times. Adjust the ball socket until the effort required to move the tie-rod end with a spring scale is 4–6 lbs.
11 Hold the ball socket and tighten the locknut to 25–35 ft./lbs. Repeat Step 10.
12 Drill a new hole, similar to that made in Step 3. It must not enter the notches of the locknut.
13 Install the retaining pin and stake it in place.
14 Install the bellows and the breather tube. Install new clamps. Put 2½ oz. of lubricant into each bellows.
15 Install the jam nuts and tie-rod sockets on the outer ends of the tie-rods.

INPUT SHAFT & VALVE ASSEMBLY, DISASSEMBLY & ASSEMBLY

1 Remove the fluid lines. Remove the flare gaskets from the ports.
2 Loosen the yoke plug locknut and yoke plug to relieve the rack preload.
3 Remove the pinion bearing plug.
4 Hold the input shaft and remove the pinion bearing locknut.
5 Remove the 3 bolts holding the valve housing to the gear unit. Move the rack to the left stop. Mark the relationship of the input shaft to the valve housing for reinstallation. Carefully work the input shaft and valve assembly out of the gear housing.
6 Remove the pinion bearing from the gear housing with a slide hammer. Remove the bearing-to-gear housing and

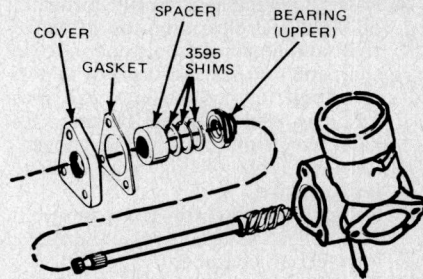

Pinion bearing cover and shim arrangement

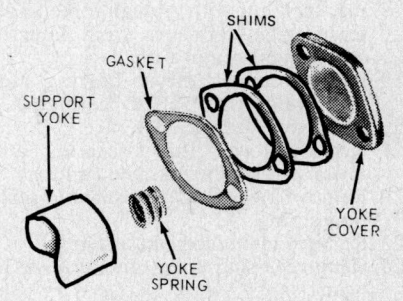

Support yoke arrangement

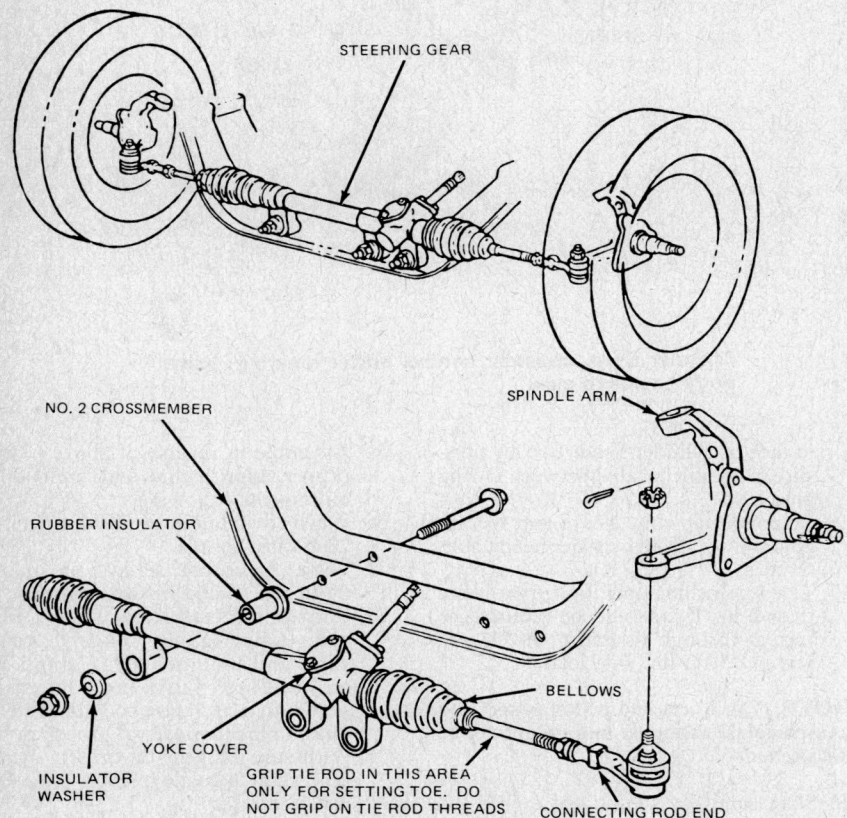

Ford integral rack & pinion steering system

valve housing-to-gear housing O-rings.

7 Remove the input shaft oil seal from the gear housing.

8 Slide the valve housing over the splined end of the input shaft to remove.

9 Remove the input shaft O-rings, being extremely careful not to damage the lands and grooves.

10 Remove the input shaft needle thrust bearing and the two thrust washers from the inside of the valve housing.

11 Use a slide hammer to remove the input shaft support bearing from the valve housing. Remove the input shaft oil seal also.

12 Pry the input shaft dust seal from the valve housing with a small sharp chisel.

To assemble:

13 Press the input shaft oil seal into the valve housing with a finger. Make sure that the lip faces in and that the seal bottoms in the bore.

14 Fill the input shaft dust seal bore with lubricant and install the dust seal.

15 Lubricate the input shaft support bearing with power steering fluid and install it in the valve housing. Avoid contact with the oil seal.

16 Install the 4 O-rings in the grooves on the valve.

17 Lubricate the two thrust washers and the needle thrust bearing with power steering fluid. Place a thrust washer on each side of the bearing and install over the input shaft.

18 Lubricate the O-rings and valve with power steering fluid. Insert the unit over the valve bore of the housing and push it through until it bottoms and the full spline passes through the dust seal.

19 Install the valve housing to gear housing O-ring on the flange protruding from the gear housing.

20 Use your fingers to install an input shaft oil seal in the gear housing. Make sure that the lip faces the input shaft and valve assembly.

21 Install the pinion bearing in the lower gear housing. Install an O-ring around the bearing adjacent to the gear housing.

22 Move the rack to the left stop. Install the input shaft and valve assembly in the gear housing bore. Align the marks made in Step 5.

23 Install the bolts holding the valve housing to the gear housing. Torque to 12–15 ft./lbs.

24 Install the pinion bearing locknut on the pinion shaft. Drill a hole in a spare pinion bearing plug large enough to insert a 9/26 in. socket. Thread the plug into the housing bore and tighten to hold the bearing firmly. Hold the input shaft and torque the pinion bearing locknut to 44–66 ft./lbs. Make sure that the rack is away from the stop while doing this. Remove the drilled bearing plug.

25 Install the pinion bearing plug. Torque it to 60–100 ft./lbs. Stake the plug in place.

26 Install the 4 small flare nuts in the pressure line fittings. Install the pressure lines.

27 Install the tube bracket with the tabs in the slots on the gear housing.

28 Install the yoke plug locknut. Make the rack yoke bearing preload adjustment described earlier, then torque the locknut to 44–66 ft./lbs.

CHILTON CAUTION: *When the front wheels of the vehicle are suspended completely off the ground, do not turn the wheels quickly or forcefully from lock to lock. This could cause a build-up of hydraulic pressure within the steering gear which could damage or blow out the bellows.*

BENDIX LINKAGE TYPE (FORD)

Power Steering
Bendix Linkage Type

FORD TORINO
MERCURY MONTEGO
FORD MAVERICK
MERCURY COMET
FORD GRANADA
MERCURY MONARCH

The Bendix linkage-type power steering system is a hydraulically controlled linkage-type, composed of an integral pump and fluid reservoir, a control valve, a power cylinder, connecting fluid lines, and the steering linkage. The hydraulic pump, which is driven by a belt turned by the engine, draws fluid from the reservoir and provides fluid pressure through hoses to the control valve and the power cylinder. There is a pressure relief valve to limit the pressures within the steering system to a safe level. After the fluid has passed from the pump to the control valve and the power cylinder, it returns to the reservoir.

The Bendix linkage-type steering system when used in Ford-built cars is called the Ford Non-Integral Power Steering System.

Control Valve Disassembly & Assembly

1 Clean the outside of the control valve of dirt and fluid.

2 Remove the centering spring cap from the valve housing. The control valve should be put in a soft-faced bench vise during disassembly. Clamp the control valve around the sleeve flange only, to avoid damaging the housing, spool, or sleeve.

3 Remove the nut from the end of the valve spool bolt. Remove the washers, spacer, centering spring, adapter, and the bushing from the bolt and valve housing.

4 Remove the two bolts holding the valve housing and the sleeve together. Separate the valve housing and the sleeve.

5 Remove the plug from the sleeve. Push the valve spool out of the centering spring end of the valve housing, and remove the seal from the spool.

6 Remove the spacer, bushing, and seal from the sleeve end.

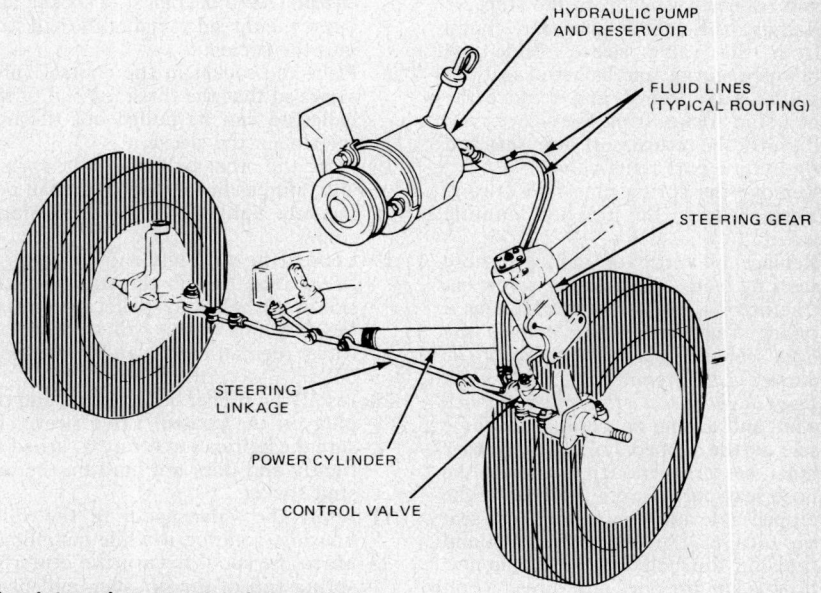

Non-integral power steering system

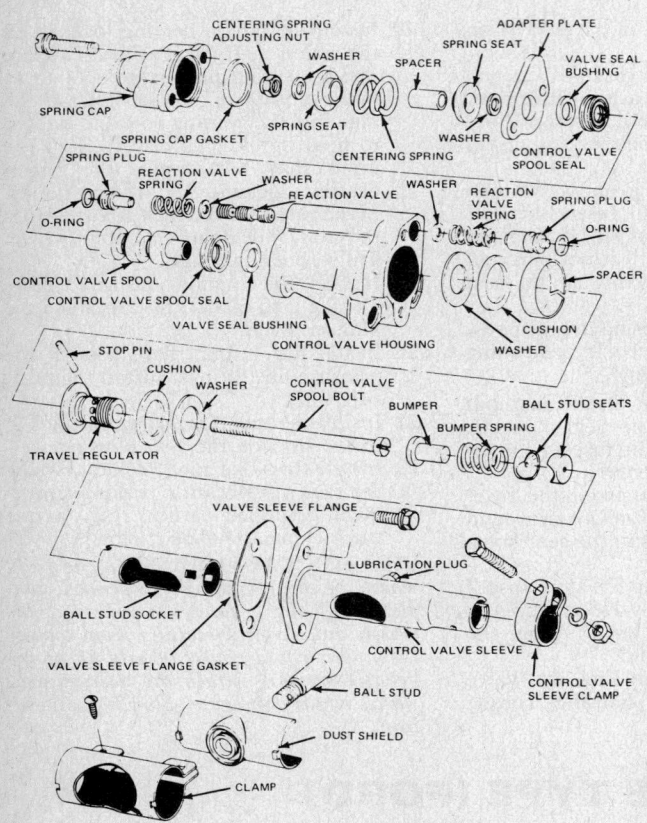

Control valve disassembled Maverick/Comet

Control valve disassembled Granada/Monarch

7 Drive the stop-pin out of the travel regulator stop with a punch and hammer. *Pull the head of the valve spool bolt tightly against the travel regulator stop before driving out the pin.*

8 Turn the travel regulator stop counterclockwise in the valve sleeve to remove the stop from the sleeve.

9 Remove the valve spool bolt, spacer, and rubber washer from the stop.

10 Remove the rubber boot and clamp from the valve sleeve. Slide the bumper, spring, and ball stud seat out of the valve sleeve, and remove the ball stud socket from the sleeve.

11 Remove the return port hose seat and the return port relief valve.

12 Remove the spring plug and O-ring. Then, remove the reaction limiting valve.

13 Replace all worn or damaged hose seats by using an Easy-Out screw extractor or a bolt of proper size as a puller. Tap the existing hole in the hose seat, using a starting tap of the correct size. *Remove all metal chips from the hose seat after tapping.* Place a nut and washer on a bolt of the same size as the tapped hole. The washer must be large enough to cover the hose seat port. Insert the bolt in the tapped hole and remove the hose seat by turning the nut clockwise and drawing the bolt out. Install a new hose seal in the port, and thread a bolt of the correct size in the port. Tighten

the bolt enough to bottom the seal in the port.

14 Coat all parts of the control valve assembly, except the seals, with power steering fluid. Use grease on the seals.

15 Install the reaction limiting valve, spring, and plug. Install the return port relief valve and the hose seat.

16 Insert one of the ball stud seats (flat end first) into the ball stud socket, and insert the threaded end of the ball stud into the socket.

17 Place the socket in the control valve sleeve so that the threaded end of the ball stud can be pulled out through the slot in the sleeve.

18 Place the other ball stud seat, spring, and bumper in the socket. Install and securely tighten the travel regulator stop.

19 Loosen the stop just enough to align the nearest hole in the stop with the slot in the ball stud socket, and install the stop pin in the ball stud socket, travel regulator stop, and valve spool bolt.

20 Install the rubber boot, clamp, and the plug on the control valve sleeve. Be sure the lubrication fitting is turned on tightly and does not bind on the ball stud socket.

21 Insert the valve spool in the valve housing, rotating it while installing.

22 Move the spool toward the centering spring end of the housing, and place the small seal, bushing, and spacer in

the sleeve end of the housing.

23 Press the valve spool against the inner lip of the seal and, at the same time, guide the lip of the seal over the spool with a small screwdriver. *Do not nick or scratch the seal or spool during installation.*

24 Place the sleeve end of the housing on a flat surface so that the seal, bushing, and spacer are at the bottom end, and push down the valve spool until it stops.

25 Carefully install the spool seal and bushing in the centering spring end of the housing. Press the seal against the end of the spool, guiding the seal over the spool with a small screwdriver. *Do not nick or scratch the seal or the spool during installation.*

26 Pick up the housing, and slide the spool back and forth to check for free movement.

27 Place the body gasket and valve sleeve on the housing so that the ball stud is on the same side of the housing as the ports for the two power cylinder lines. Install the two bolts in the sleeve, and torque them to the proper specification.

28 Place the adapter on the centering spring end of the housing, and install the bushing, washers, spacers, and centering spring on the valve spool bolt.

29 Compress the centering spring, and install the nut on the bolt. Tighten the

nut snug (90–100 in./lbs.); then, loosen it not more than ¼ turn. *Do not overtighten, to avoid breaking the stop-pin at the travel regulator stop.*

30 Move the ball stud back and forth to check for free movement.

31 Lubricate the two cap attaching bolts. Install the centering spring cap on the valve housing, and tighten the two cap bolts to the proper torque.

32 Install the nut on the ball stud so that the valve can be put in a vise. Then, push forward on the cap end of the valve to check the valve spool for free movement.

33 Turn the valve around in the vise, and push forward on the sleeve end to check for free movement.

Power Cylinder Seal R&R

1 Clamp the power cylinder in a vise, and remove the snap-ring from the end of the cylinder. *Do not distort or crack the cylinder in the vise.*

2 Pull the piston rod out all the way to remove the scraper, bushing, and seals. If the seals cannot be removed in this manner, remove them by carefully prying them out of the cylinder with a sharp pick. *Do not damage the shaft or seal seat.*

3 Coat the new seals with power steering fluid and place the parts on the piston rod, which should be lubricated.

4 Push the rod in all the way, and install the parts in the cylinder with a deep socket slightly smaller than the cylinder opening.

GM SAGINAW ROTARY TYPE

POWER STEERING
G.M. Saginaw Rotary Type

The power cylinder is an integral part of the gear housing. A double-acting piston allows oil pressure to be applied to either side of the piston. The one-piece piston and power rack is meshed to the sector shaft.

The hydraulic control valve is composed of a sleeve and valve spool. The spool is held in the neutral position by the torsion bar and spool actuator. Twisting of the torsion bar moves the valve spool, allowing oil pressure to be directed to either side of the power piston, depending on the directional rotation of the steering wheel, to give power assist.

On many American Motors cars a modified version of the G.M. system provides variable ratio steering for easier and safer control. The steering gear ratio will vary from a high ratio of about 16:1 while steering straight ahead to a lower gear ratio of about 12.4:1 while making a full turn to either side.

Repair Operations
ADJUSTER PLUG & ROTARY VALVE REMOVAL

1 Thoroughly clean exterior of gear assembly. Drain by holding valve ports down and rotating worm back and forth through entire travel.

2 Place gear in vise.

3 Loosen adjuster plug locknut with punch. Remove adjuster plug.

4 Remove rotary valve assembly by grasping stub shaft and pulling it out.

ADJUSTER PLUG DISASSEMBLY

1 Remove upper thrust bearing retainer with screwdriver. Be careful not to damage bearing bore. Discard retainer. Remove spacer, upper bearing and races.

2 Remove and discard adjuster plug O-ring.

3 Remove stub shaft seal retaining ring (Truarc pliers will help) and remove and discard dust seal.

4 Remove stub shaft seal by prying out with screwdriver and discard.

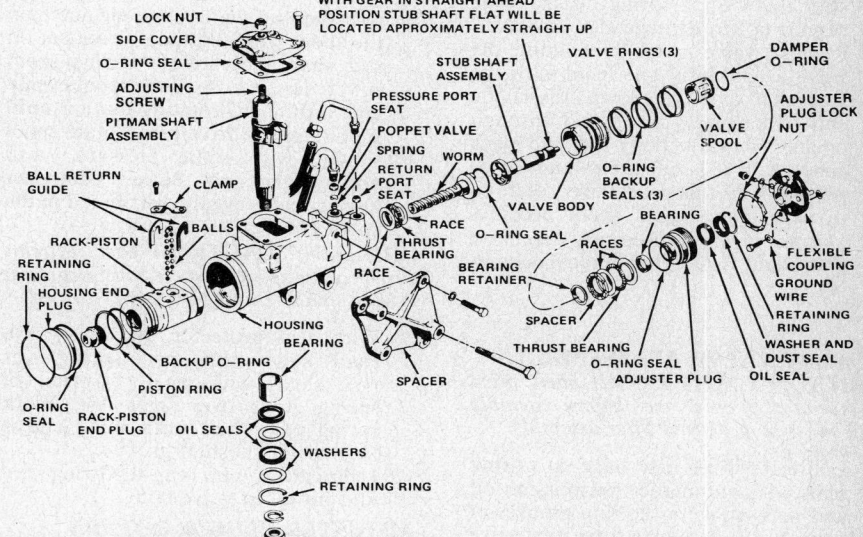

Typical power steering gear, exploded view

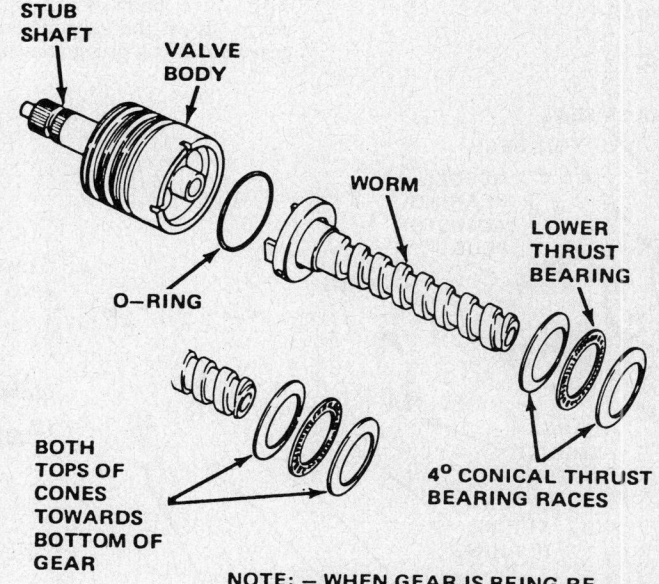

Steering gear stub shaft and wormshaft assembly

5 Examine needle bearing and, if required, remove same by pressing from thrust bearing end.

6 Inspect thrust bearing spacer, bearing rollers and races.

7 Reassemble in reverse of above.

ROTARY VALVE DISASSEMBLY

Repairs are seldom needed. Do not disassemble unless absolutely necessary. If the O-ring seal on valve spool dampener needs replacement, perform this portion of operation only.

1 Remove cap-to-worm O-ring seal and discard.

2 Remove valve spool spring by prying on small coil with small screw driver to work spring onto bearing surface of stub shaft. Slide spring off shaft. Be careful not to damage shaft surface.

3 Remove valve spool by holding the valve assembly in one hand with the stub shaft pointing down. Insert the end of pencil or wood rod through opening in valve body cap and push spool until it is out far enough to be removed. In this procedure, rotate to prevent jamming. If spool becomes jammed it may be necessary to remove stub shaft, torsion bar and cap assembly.

ROTARY VALVE REASSEMBLY

CHILTON CAUTION: *All parts must be free of dirt, chips, etc., before assembly and must be protected after assembly.*

1 Lubricate three new back-up O-ring seals with automatic transmission oil and reassemble in the ring grooves of valve body. Assemble three new valve body rings in the grooves over the O-ring seals by carefully slipping over the valve body.

NOTE: If the valve body rings seem loose or twisted in the grooves, the heat of the oil during operation will cause them to straighten.

2 Lubricate a new dampener O-ring with automatic transmission oil and install in valve spool groove.

3 Assemble stub shaft torsion bar and cap assembly in the valve body, aligning the groove in the valve cap with the pin in the valve body. Tap lightly with soft hammer until cap is against valve body shoulder. Valve body pin must be in the cap groove. Hold parts together during the remainder of assembly.

4 Lubricate spool. With notch in spool toward valve body, slide the spool over the stub shaft. Align the notch on the spool with the spool drive pin on stub shaft and carefully engage spool in valve body bore. Push spool evenly and with slight rotating motion until spool reaches drive pin. Rotate spool slowly, with some pressure, until notch engages pin. Be sure dampener O-ring seal is evenly distributed in the spool groove.

CHILTON CAUTION: *Use extreme care because spool-to-valve body clearance is very small. Damage is easily caused.*

5 With seal protector tool over stub shaft, slide valve spool spring over stub shaft, with small diameter of spring going over shaft last. Work spring onto shaft until small coil is located in stubshaft groove.

6 Lubricate a new cap-to-O-ring seal and install in valve body.

ADJUSTER PLUG & ROTARY VALVE INSTALLATION

1 Align narrow pin slot on valve body with valve body drive pin on the worm. Insert the valve assembly into gear housing by pressing against valve body with finger tips. Do not press on stub shaft or torsion bar. The return hole in the gear housing should be fully visible when properly assembled.

CHILTON CAUTION: *Do not press on stub shaft as this may cause shaft and cap to pull out of valve body, allowing the spool dampener O-ring seal to slip into valve body oil grooves.*

2 With protector over end of stub shaft, install adjuster plug assembly snugly into gear housing then back plug off approximately one-eighth turn. Install plug locknut but do not tighten. Adjust preload as described in the adjustment section.

3 After adjustment, tighten lock-nut.

PITMAN SHAFT REMOVAL & INSTALLATION

1 Completely drain the gear assembly and thoroughly clean the outside.

2 Place gear in vise.

3 Rotate stub shaft until pitman shaft gear is in center position. Remove side cover retaining bolts.

4 Tap end of pitman shaft with soft hammer and slide shaft out of housing.

5 Remove and discard side cover O-ring seal.

6 The seals, washers, retainers and bearings may now be removed and examined.

7 Examine all parts for wear or damage and replace as required.

8 Install in reverse of above. Make proper adjustment as described in adjustment section.

RACK-PISTON NUT & WORM ASSEMBLY REMOVAL

1 Completely drain the gear assembly and thoroughly clean the outside.

2 Remove pitman shaft assembly, previously described.

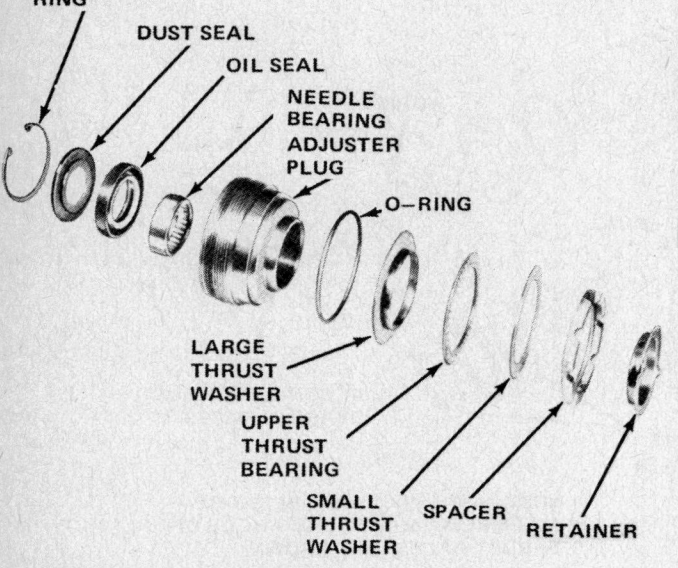

RETAINING RING
DUST SEAL
OIL SEAL
NEEDLE BEARING
ADJUSTER PLUG
O-RING
LARGE THRUST WASHER
UPPER THRUST BEARING
SMALL THRUST WASHER
SPACER
RETAINER

Adjuster plug assembly sequence

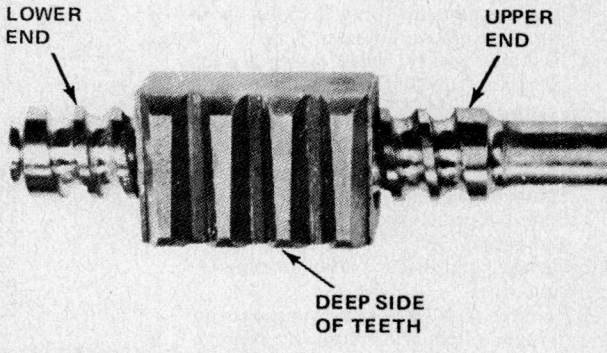

LOWER END
UPPER END
DEEP SIDE OF TEETH

Installation of ball nut or shaft

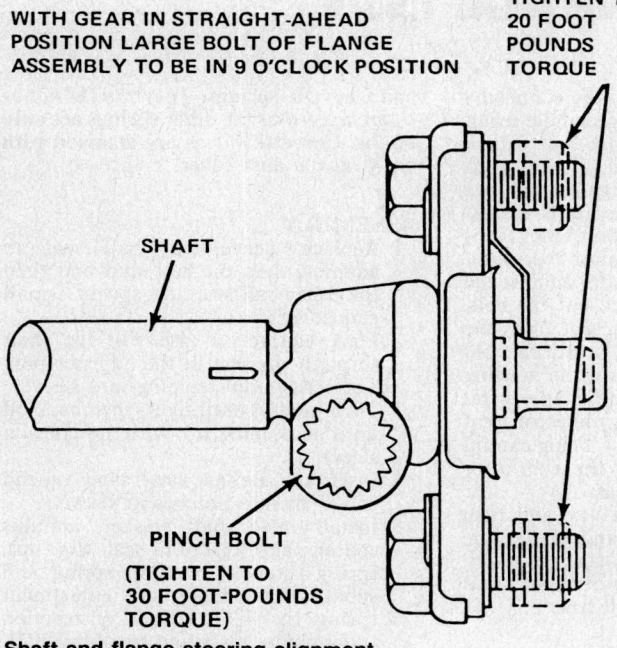

WITH GEAR IN STRAIGHT-AHEAD POSITION LARGE BOLT OF FLANGE ASSEMBLY TO BE IN 9 O'CLOCK POSITION

TIGHTEN TO 20 FOOT POUNDS TORQUE

SHAFT

PINCH BOLT (TIGHTEN TO 30 FOOT-POUNDS TORQUE)

Shaft and flange steering alignment

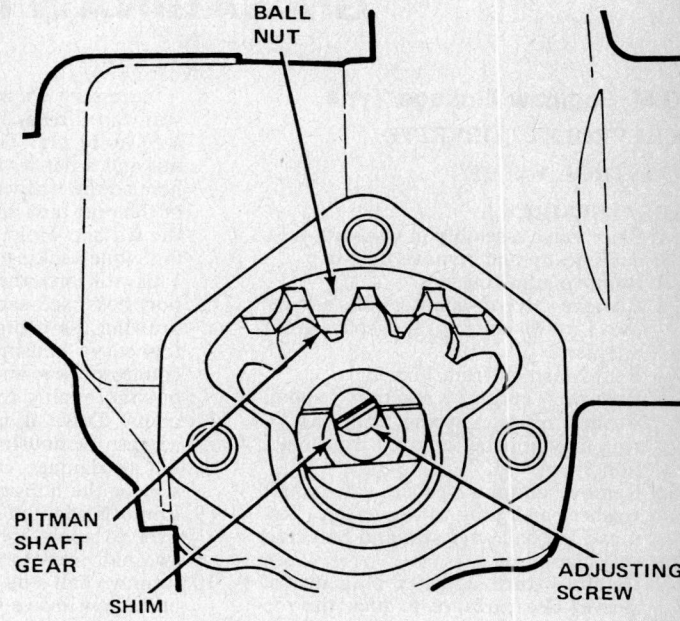

BALL NUT

PITMAN SHAFT GEAR

SHIM

ADJUSTING SCREW

Position of pitman shaft and ball nut

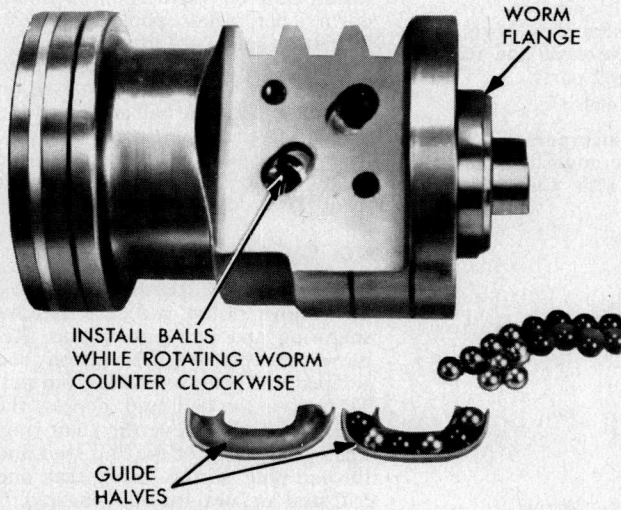

WORM FLANGE

INSTALL BALLS WHILE ROTATING WORM COUNTER CLOCKWISE

GUIDE HALVES

Installing balls in the rack piston

"O" RING

SPOOL VALVE

TEFLON RINGS (3)

"O" RINGS (3) - INSTALLED UNDER TEFLON RINGS

VALVE BODY

STUB SHAFT

"O" RING

Exploded view of the valve body and shaft assembly

3 Rotate housing end plug retaining ring so that one end of ring is over hole in gear housing. Spring one end of ring so screw-driver can be inserted to lift out ring.
4 Rotate stub shaft to full left turn position to force end plug out of housing.
5 Remove and discard housing end plug O-ring seal.
6 Remove rack-piston nut end plug with ½ in. square drive.
7 Insert tool in end of worm. Turn stub shaft so that rack-piston nut will go into tool and remove rack-piston nut from gear housing.
8 Remove adjuster plug and rotary valve assemblies as previously described.

9 Remove worm and lower thrust bearing and races.
10 Remove cap-to-O-ring seal and discard.

RACK-PISTON NUT & WORM DISASSEMBLY AND REASSEMBLY
1 Remove and discard piston ring and back-up O-ring on rack-piston nut.
2 Remove ball guide clamp and return guide.
3 Place nut on clean cloth and remove ball retaining tool. Make sure all balls are removed.
4 Inspect all parts for wear, nicks, scoring or burrs. If worm or rack-piston nut need replacing, both must be re-

placed as a matched pair.
5 In assembling, reverse the above.

NOTE: When assembling, alternate black and white balls, and install guide and clamp. Packing with grease helps in holding during assembly. When new balls are used, various sizes are available and a selection must be made to secure proper torque when making the high point adjustment.

RACK-PISTON NUT & WORM ASSEMBLY INSTALLATION
1 Install in reverse of removal procedure.
2 In all cases use new O-ring seals.
3 Make adjustments as described in that section.

GM SAGINAW LINKAGE TYPE

G.M. Saginaw Linkage Type

CHEVROLET CORVETTE

CONTROL VALVE

DISASSEMBLY

1 Place valve assembly in vise with dust cap end up and remove dust cap.
2 Remove adjusting nut.
3 Remove valve-to-adapter bolts and remove valve housing and spool from adapter.
4 Remove spool from housing.
5 Remove spring, reaction spool, washer, reaction spring, and seal. O-ring may now be removed from reaction spool.
6 Remove annulus spacer, valve shaft washer, and plug-to-sleeve key. Remove the ball stud seal and ball stud seal clamp.
7 Carefully turn adjuster plug out of sleeve. Use care not to nick the top surface.

8 If necessary to replace a connector seat, tap threads in center hole using a 5/16–18 tap. Thread a bolt with a nut and a flat washer into the tapped hole so the washer is against the face of the port boss and the nut is against the washer. Hold the bolt from turning while backing the nut off the bolt. This will force the washer against the port boss face and back out the bolt, drawing the connector seat from the top cover housing. Discard the old connector seat and clean the housing out thoroughly to remove any metal chips. Drive a new connector seat against the housing seat, being careful not to damage either the connector seat or the housing seat.
9 Remove adapter from vise and turn over to allow spring and one of the two ball seats to drop out.
10 Remove ball stud with other ball seat and allow sleeve to fall free.

INSPECTION

1 Wash all parts in clean, non-toxic solvent and blow dry with air.
2 Inspect all parts for scratches, burrs, distortion, or excessive wear and replace worn or damaged parts.
3 Replace all seals and gaskets.

NOTE: Corvette valves incorporate a 55 lb. centering spring which might be inadvertently interchanged with Chevrolet,

and Chevelle springs. *They should not be interchanged* as the other springs are only 30 lbs. Corvette valves are stamped with an X on the dust cover.

ASSEMBLY

1 Replace sleeve and ball seat in adapter, then the ball stud and then the other ball seat and spring. (small end down)
2 Place adapter in vise. Put the shaft through the seat in the adjuster plug and screw adjuster plug into sleeve.
3 Turn plug in until tight, then back off until slot lines up with notches in sleeve.
4 Insert key. Be sure small tangs on end of key fit into notches in sleeve.
5 Install valve shaft washer, annulus spacer, and reaction seal (lip up), spring retainer, reaction spring and spool, then washer and adjustment spring. Install O-ring seal on reaction spool before installing spool on shaft. Install washer with chamfer up.
6 Install seal on valve spool with lip down. Then install spool, being careful not to jam spool in housing.
7 Install housing with spool onto adapter. The side ports should be on the same side as the ball stud. Bolt the housing to the adapter.
8 Depress the valve spool and turn the locknut into the shaft about four turns. Use a clean wrench or socket.

Power Cylinder

DISASSEMBLY & REASSEMBLY

1 To remove piston rod seal, remove snap-ring and pull out on rod. Remove back-up washer, piston rod scraper, and piston rod seal from rod.
2 To remove the ball stud, depress the end plug and remove the snap ring. Push on the end of the ball stud and the end plug, spring, spring seat, and ball stud and seal may be removed. If the ball seat is to be replaced, it must be pressed out.
3 Reverse disassembly procedure. Be sure snap-ring is properly seated.

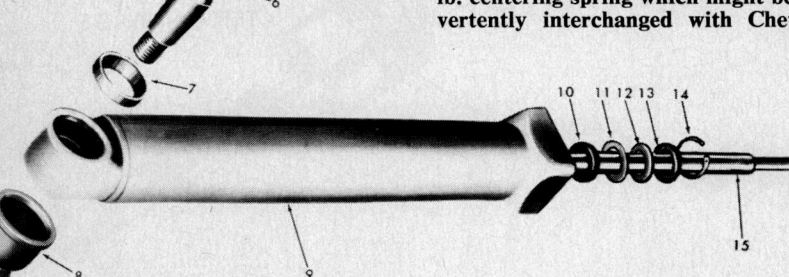

Corvette power cylinder

1. Snap Ring	6. Ball Stud	11. Backup Washer
2. End Plug and Lube Fitting	7. Ball Seat	12. Scraper Element
3. "O" Ring	8. Ball Stud Seal	13. Piston Rod Scraper
4. Spring	9. Piston Body	14. Snap Ring
5. Spring Seat	10. Piston Rod Seal	15. Piston Rod

GM/AMC SAGINAW ROTARY TYPE

Power Steering

G.M. Saginaw Rotary Type

ALL A.M.C. EXCEPT PACER

ALL G.M. CORP. CARS (EXCEPT CHEVROLET CORVETTE)

The G.M. Saginaw rotary type power steering gear is designed with all components in one housing.

The power cylinder is an integral part of the gear housing. A double-acting pis-

ton allows oil pressure to be applied to either side of the piston. The one-piece piston and power rack is meshed to the sector shaft.

The hydraulic control valve is composed of a sleeve and valve spool. The spool is held in the neutral position by the torsion bar and spool actuator. Twisting of the torsion bar moves the valve spool, allowing oil pressure to be directed to either side of the power piston, depending on the directional rotation of the steering

wheel, to give power assist.

On many General Motors cars a modified version of the system provides variable ratio steering for easier and safer control. The steering gear ratio will vary from a high ratio of about 16:1 while steering straight ahead to a lower gear ratio of about 12.4:1 while making a full turn to either side.

CHECKING STEERING EFFORT

Run the engine to attain normal operat-

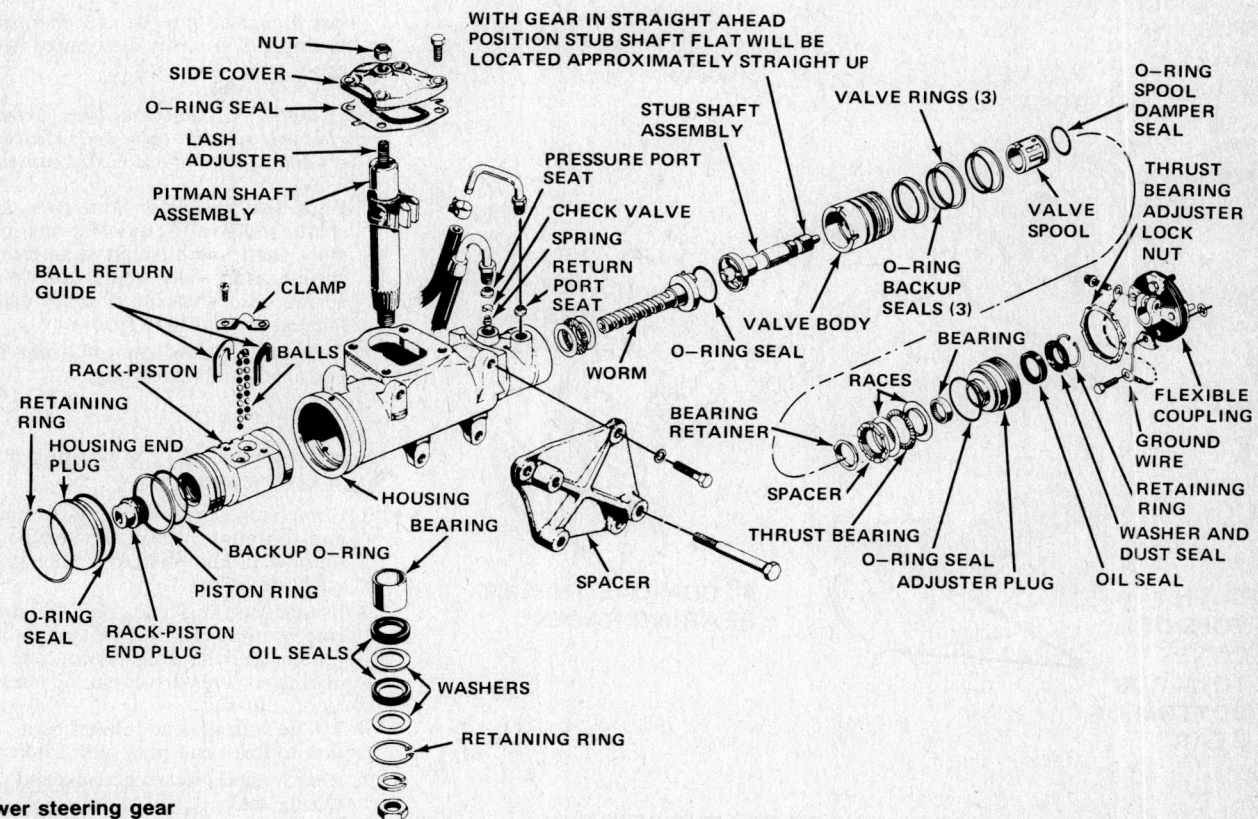

Power steering gear

ing temperatures. With the wheels on a dry floor, hook a pull scale to the spoke of the steering wheel at the outer edge. The effort required to turn the steering wheel should be 3½–5 lbs. If the pull is not within these limits, check the hydraulic pressure.

PRESSURE TEST
To check the hydraulic pressure, disconnect the pressure hose from the gear. Now connect the pressure gauge between the pressure hose from the pump and the steering gear housing. Run the engine to attain normal operating temperatures, then turn the wheel to a full right and a full left turn to the wheel stops.

Hold the wheel in this position only long enough to obtain an accurate reading.

The pressure gauge reading should be within the limits specified. If the pressure reading is less than the minimum pressure needed for proper operation, close the valve at the gauge and see if the reading increases. If the pressure is still low, the pump is defective and needs repair. If the pressure reading is at or near the minimum reading, the pump is normal and needs only an adjustment of the power steering gear or power assist control valve.

WORM BEARING PRELOAD & SECTOR MESH ADJUSTMENTS
Disconnect the Pitman arm from the sector shaft, then back off on the sector

shaft adjusting screw on the sector shaft cover.

Center the steering on the high point, then attach a pull scale to the spoke of the steering wheel at the outer edge. The pull required to keep the wheel moving for one complete turn should be ½–2/3 lbs.

If the pull is not within these limits, loosen the thrust bearing locknut and tighten or back off on the valve sleeve adjuster locknut to bring the preload within limits. Tighten the thrust bearing locknut and recheck the preload.

Slowly rotate the steering wheel several times, then center the steering on the high point. Now, turn the sector shaft adjusting screw until a steering wheel pull of 1–1½ lbs. is required to move the worm through the center point. Tighten the sector shaft adjusting screw locknut and recheck the sector mesh adjustment.

Install the pitman arm and draw the arm into position with the nut.

ADJUSTER PLUG & ROTARY VALVE REMOVAL
1 Thoroughly clean exterior of gear assembly. Drain by holding valve ports down and rotating worm back and forth through entire travel.
2 Place gear in vise.
3 Loosen adjuster plug locknut with punch. Remove adjuster plug.
4 Remove rotary valve assembly by grasping stub shaft and pulling it out.

ADJUSTER PLUG DISASSEMBLY
1 Remove upper thrust bearing retainer with screwdriver. Be careful not to damage bearing bore. Discard retainer. Remove spacer, upper bearing and races.
2 Remove and discard adjuster plug O-ring.
3 Remove stub shaft seal retaining ring (Truarc pliers will help) and remove and discard dust seal.
4 Remove stub shaft seal by prying out with screwdriver and discard.
5 Examine needle bearing and, if required, remove same by pressing from thrust bearing end.
6 Inspect thrust bearing spacer, bearing rollers and races.
7 Reassemble in reverse of above.

ROTARY VALVE DISASSEMBLY
Repairs are seldom needed. Do not disassemble unless absolutely necessary.

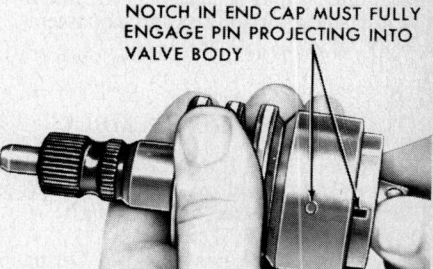

Installing the stub shaft assembly

GM/AMC SAGINAW ROTARY TYPE

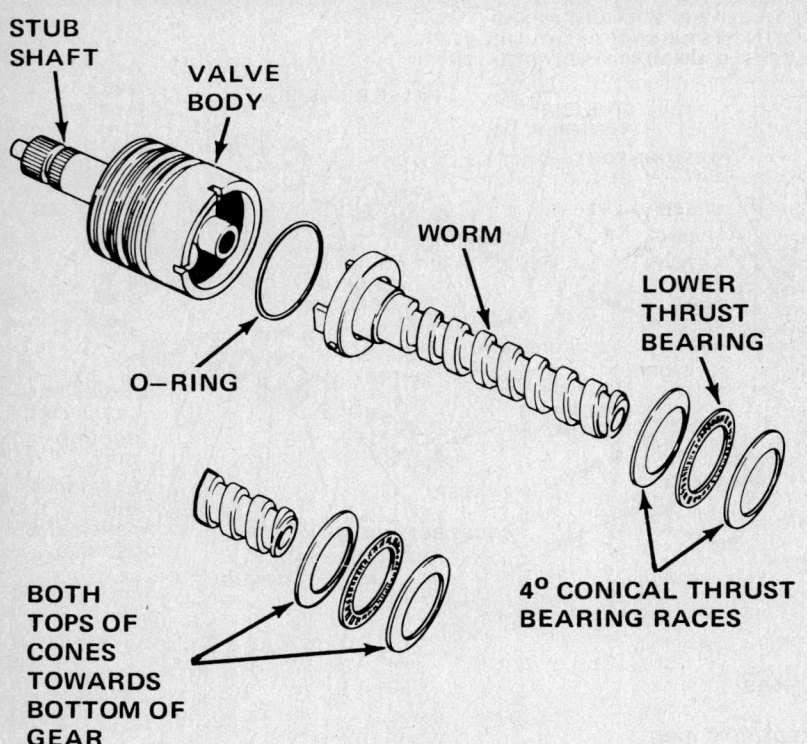

STUB SHAFT

VALVE BODY

WORM

LOWER THRUST BEARING

O—RING

BOTH TOPS OF CONES TOWARDS BOTTOM OF GEAR

4° CONICAL THRUST BEARING RACES

NOTE: — WHEN GEAR IS BEING RE—ASSEMBLED, MAKE SURE ANGLE OF THRUST RACES IS AS SHOWN.

Correct installation of thrust bearing races

If the O-ring seal on valve spool dampener needs replacement, perform this portion of operation only.

1 Remove cap-to-worm O-ring seal and discard.
2 Remove valve spool spring by prying on small coil with small screwdriver to work spring onto bearing surface of stub shaft. Slide spring off shaft. Be careful not to damage shaft surface.
3 Remove valve spool by holding the valve assembly in one hand with the stub shaft pointing down. Insert the end of pencil or wood rod through opening in valve body cap and push spool until it is out far enough to be removed. In this procedure, rotate to prevent jamming. If spool becomes jammed it may be necessary to remove stub shaft, torsion bar and cap assembly.

ROTARY VALVE REASSEMBLY

CHILTON CAUTION: *All parts must be free of dirt, chips, etc., before assembly and must be protected after assembly.*

1 Lubricate three new back-up O-ring seals with automatic transmission oil and reassemble in the ring grooves of valve body. Assemble three new valve body rings in the grooves over the O-ring seals by carefully slipping over the valve body.

NOTE: If the valve body rings seem loose or twisted in the grooves, the heat of the oil during operation will cause them to straighten.

2 Lubricate a new dampener O-ring with automatic transmission oil and install in valve spool groove.
3 Assemble stub shaft torsion bar and cap assembly in the valve body, aligning the groove in the valve cap with the pin in the valve body. Tap lightly with soft hammer until cap is against valve body shoulder. Valve body pin must be in the cap groove. Hold parts together during the remainder of assembly.
4 Lubricate spool. With notch in spool toward valve body, slide the spool over the stub shaft. Align the notch on the spool with the spool drive pin on stub shaft and carefully engage spool in valve body bore. Push spool evenly and with slight rotating motion until spool reaches drive pin. Rotate spool slowly, with some pressure, until

notch engages pin. Be sure dampener O-ring seal is evenly distributed in the spool groove.

CHILTON CAUTION: *Use extreme care because spool-to-valve body clearance is very small. Damage is easily caused.*

5 With seal protector tool over stub shaft, slide valve spool spring over stub shaft, with small diameter of spring going over shaft last. Work spring onto shaft until small coil is located in studshaft groove.
6 Lubricate a new cap-to-O-ring seal and install in valve body.

RACK-PISTON NUT & WORM ASSEMBLY REMOVAL

1 Completely drain the gear assembly and thoroughly clean the outside.
2 Remove pitman shaft assembly, previously described.
3 Rotate housing end plug retaining ring so that one end of ring is over hole in gear housing. Spring one end of ring so screwdriver can be inserted to lift out ring.
4 Rotate stub shaft to full left turn position to force end plug out of housing.
5 Remove and discard housing end plug O-ring seal.
6 Remove rack-piston nut end plug with ½ in. square drive.
7 Insert tool in end of worm. Turn stub shaft so that rack-piston nut will go into tool and remove rack-piston nut from gear housing.
8 Remove adjuster plug and rotary valve assemblies as previously described.
9 Remove worm and lower thrust bearing and races.
10 Remove cap-to-O-ring seal and discard.

RACK-PISTON NUT & WORM DISASSEMBLY & REASSEMBLY

1 Remove and discard piston ring and back-up O-ring on rack-piston nut.
2 Remove ball guide clamp and return guide.
3 Place nut on clean cloth and remove ball retaining tool. Make sure all balls are removed.
4 Inspect all parts for wear, nicks, scoring or burrs. If worm or rack-piston nut need replacing, both must be replaced as a matched pair.
5 In assembling, reverse the above.

NOTE: When assembling, alternate black and white balls, and install guide and clamp. Packing with grease helps in holding during assembly. When new balls are used, various sizes are available and a selection must be made to secure proper torque when making the high point adjustment.

MANUAL TRANSMISSIONS

INDEX

AMC HR1 FOUR SPEED

Transmission Disassembly

CHILTON CAUTION: Except for the fill plug, all threaded holes and bolts used in the model HR1 transmission are metric sizes. Do not attempt to substitute a different thread-type bolt if the original ones are lost.

1 Pull the throwout lever straight out of the lever opening in the clutch housing to disengage the lever retaining clip from the pivot ball stud.
2 Slide the throwout lever and bearing off the front bearing cap. Remove the lever and bearing as an assembly.
3 Remove the bolts attaching the clutch housing to the transmission. Remove the clutch housing.
4 Remove the dynamic absorber from the extension housing.
5 Remove the transmission support cushion adapter bracket from the extension housing.
6 Remove the backup lamp switch from the extension housing.
7 Remove the bolts attaching the top cover to the transmission case. Then remove the top cover and gasket.
8 Remove the detent plug using a hex wrench. Remove the detent spring and detent plunger.
9 Remove the access plug at the rear of the case using a punch and hammer.
10 Remove the interlock plate retaining pin using a 5/16-diameter rod inserted through the access plug hole. Remove the interlock plate.
11 Remove the selector arm roll pin using a 40 mm (5/32) pin punch.
12 Tap the forward end of the shift rail until the rail displaces the large plug at the rear of the extension housing. Remove the shift rail from the rear of the housing.
13 Remove the selector arm, interlock plate and shift forks from the case.

NOTE: Before removing the interlock plate, note the location and assembled position of the plate, selector arm and shift forks for assembly reference.

14 Remove the bolts attaching the front bearing cap to the case. Remove the bearing cap and bearing cap O-ring. Discard the O-ring.
15 Remove the front bearing cap oil seal. Pry the seal from the cap.

NOTE: If seal removal proves difficult, partially collapse the metal wall of the seal using a small, sharp chisel. However, do not gouge or nick the seal bore.

16 Remove the front bearing retaining and locating snap rings from the clutch shaft and front bearing.
17 Install bearing remover J-8157-01 on the front bearing. Install puller J-25132 and puller bolts J-26827 on the clutch shaft and bearing remover tool. Remove the front bearing.
18 Remove the bolts attaching the extension housing to the transmission case. Tap the housing with a plastic-tipped hammer to loosen it from the case.
19 Remove the clutch shaft from the front of the case.
20 Remove the extension housing and output shaft gear train assembly from the rear of the case. Do not allow the third-fourth synchronizer sleeve to separate from the hub during removal.
21 Remove the shift rail oil seal from the seal counterbore at the rear of the case. Pry the seal out of the counterbore.
22 Remove the main shaft pilot roller bearing from the clutch shaft bore or from the output shaft pilot bearing hub.
23 Remove the reverse idler gearshaft using slide hammer J-7004-1 and shaft remover J-26856. Thread the shaft remover into the reverse idler shaft and thread the slide hammer bolt into the shaft remover. Remove the reverse idler shaft.
24 Remove the reverse idler gear and gear spacer from the case. Note the position of the spacer for assembly reference.
25 Remove the countershaft using countershaft loading tool J-26826.
26 Remove the shift fork from the reverse lever. Note the position of the fork for assembly reference.
27 Remove the spring clip that retains the reverse lever on the lever pivot shaft. Remove the reverse lever and lever spring. Note the spring position for assembly reference.
28 Remove the countershaft gear and loading tool as an assembly. Remove the loading tool and remove the 38 needle bearings and 4 bearing retainers.

CHILTON CAUTION: There are two thick and two thin bearing retainers. Note the position of these parts for assembly reference. In addition, there are short and long countershaft needle bearings. Also note the position of these parts for assembly reference.

29 Remove the countershaft gear thrust washers.

OUTPUT SHAFT GEAR TRAIN DISASSEMBLY

1 Remove the fourth gear blocking ring from the third-fourth synchronizer.
2 Remove the output shaft rear snap ring using a needlenose pliers.

NOTE: The snap ring is positioned in a groove machined in the extension housing bore. To unseat the snap ring, first com- press it using the needlenose pliers. Then, slide it toward the first gear until it clears the extension housing.

3 Remove the extension housing from the bearing by tapping the end of the output shaft with a plastic-tipped hammer.
4 Remove the output shaft front snap ring. Discard the snap ring.
5 Remove the third-fourth synchronizer. Mark the hub and sleeve for assembly reference. Then separate the sleeve from the hub. Remove the synchronizer inserts and insert springs.
6 Remove the third gear and blocking ring.
7 Remove the second gear snap ring, second gear and the blocking ring.
8 Unseat the rear bearing snap ring using a snap ring pliers having 45 angle tips. Slide the snap ring toward the speedometer drive gear.
9 Remove the first gear, first gear spacer, rear bearing and speedometer gear as an assembly using bearing remover J-8157-01 and an arbor press. Position the bearing remover against the forward face of first gear. Do not allow the first gear blocking ring to become caught between the remover tool and gear.
10 Remove the first gear blocking ring.
11 Mark the first-second synchronizer sleeve and hub for assembly reference. Remove the sleeve from the hub. Remove the inserts and insert springs.

CHILTON CAUTION: Do not attempt to remove the first-second synchronizer from the output shaft. The hub and shaft are serviced as an assembly only.

12 Remove the extension housing oil seal using tool J-26829 and slide hammer J-7004-1.

Transmission Assembly

OUTPUT SHAFT GEAR TRAIN ASSEMBLY

1 Install the rear bearing in the extension housing bore. Use a plastic-tipped hammer to install the bearing. Be sure the bearing is fully seated in the housing bearing bore.
2 Select the thickest possible output shaft rear snap ring that fits in the snap ring groove of the extension housing. Then remove the snap ring.

NOTE: The output shaft rear snap ring is a selective-type, available in varying thickness increments. Trial-fit the snap rings until the desired thickness snap ring is obtained.

3 Remove the rear bearing from the extension housing using a long punch or ratchet handle extension.

Component identification

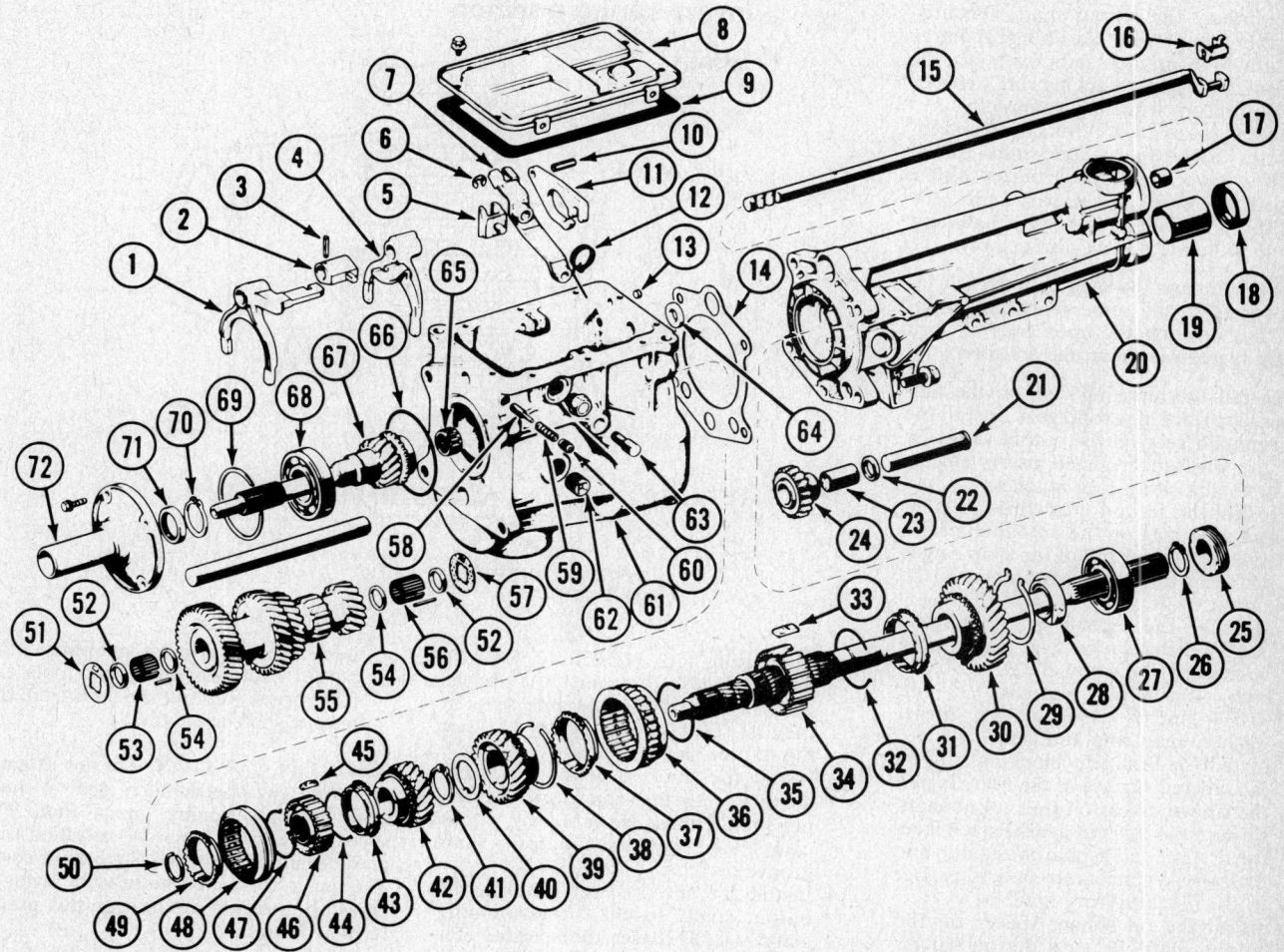

1. THIRD-FOURTH SHIFT FORK
2. SELECTOR ARM
3. SELECTOR ARM ROLL PIN
4. FIRST-SECOND SHIFT FORK
5. REVERSE LEVER SHIFT FORK
6. REVERSE LEVER SPRING CLIP
7. REVERSE LEVER
8. TOP COVER
9. TOP COVER GASKET
10. INTERLOCK PLATE RETAINING PIN
11. INTERLOCK PLATE
12. REVERSE LEVER SPRING
13. INTERLOCK RETAINING PIN ACCESS PLUG
14. EXTENSION HOUSING GASKET
15. SHIFT RAIL
16. SHIFT RAIL INSERT
17. SHIFT RAIL BUSHING (NYLON)
18. EXTENSION HOUSING SEAL
19. EXTENSION HOUSING BUSHING (SERVICED AS PART OF HOUSING)
20. EXTENSION HOUSING
21. REVERSE IDLER GEAR SHAFT
22. REVERSE IDLER GEAR SPACER
23. REVERSE IDLER GEAR BUSHING (SERVICED AS PART OF GEAR)
24. REVERSE IDLER GEAR
25. SPEEDOMETER GEAR
26. REAR BEARING SNAP RING
27. REAR BEARING

28. OIL SLINGER/SPACER
29. OUTPUT SHAFT REAR SNAP RING
30. FIRST GEAR
31. FIRST GEAR BLOCKING RING
32. FIRST-SECOND SYNCHRONIZER INSERT SPRING
33. FIRST-SECOND SYNCHRONIZER INSERT (3)
34. OUTPUT SHAFT AND FIRST-SECOND SYNCHRONIZER HUB ASSEMBLY (SERVICED AS ASSEMBLY ONLY)
35. FIRST-SECOND SYNCHRONIZER INSERT SPRING
36. FIRST-SECOND SYNCHRONIZER SLEEVE
37. SECOND GEAR BLOCKING RING
38. SECOND GEAR STOP RING (INSTALLED ON GEAR)
39. SECOND GEAR
40. SECOND GEAR SPACER
41. SECOND GEAR SNAP RING
42. THIRD GEAR
43. THIRD GEAR BLOCKING RING
44. THIRD-FOURTH SYNCHRONIZER INSERT SPRING
45. THIRD-FOURTH SYNCHRONIZER INSERT (3)
46. THIRD-FOURTH SYNCHRONIZER HUB
47. THIRD-FOURTH SYNCHRONIZER INSERT SPRING
48. THIRD-FOURTH SYNCHRONIZER SLEEVE
49. FOURTH GEAR BLOCKING RING

50. OUTPUT SHAFT FRONT SNAP RING
51. COUNTERSHAFT THRUST WASHER (METAL FACE)
52. COUNTERSHAFT BEARING RETAINER (THICK)
53. COUNTERSHAFT FRONT BEARINGS (SHORT-19 REQD.)
54. COUNTERSHAFT BEARING RETAINER (THIN)
55. COUNTERSHAFT GEAR
56. COUNTERSHAFT REAR BEARINGS (LONG-19 REQD.)
57. COUNTERSHAFT THRUST WASHER (METAL FACE)
58. DETENT PLUNGER
59. DETENT SPRING
60. DETENT PLUG
61. TRANSMISSION CASE
62. FILL PLUG
63. REVERSE LEVER PIVOT (SERVICED AS PART OF CASE)
64. SHIFT RAIL OIL SEAL
65. CLUTCH SHAFT ROLLER BEARING
66. FRONT BEARING CAP O-RING
67. CLUTCH SHAFT
68. FRONT BEARING
69. FRONT BEARING LOCATING SNAP RING
70. FRONT BEARING RETAINING SNAP RING
71. FRONT BEARING CAP OIL SEAL
72. FRONT BEARING CAP

4 Lubricate the output shaft, synchronizer components and all gear bores with transmission lubricant. Lubricate the tapered blocking ring surfaces of all gears with petroleum jelly.

5 Install the synchronizer spring and inserts in the first-second hub. Install the first-second synchronizer sleeve over the hub and inserts. Index the hub to the sleeve using the alignment marks made during disassembly.

NOTE: **Engage the tang end of each insert spring in the same synchronizer insert, but position the open ends of each spring face away from one another.**

6 Install the blocking ring on the tapered surface of second gear. Install the ring and gear on the output shaft. Be sure the synchronizer inserts engage in the blocking ring notches.

7 Install the second gear thrust washer and snap ring on the output shaft. Be sure the tabbed end of the snap ring is seated in the groove machined in the output shaft.

8 Measure the second gear end play using a feeler gauge. End play should be 0.10 to 0.35 mm (0.004 to 0.014 inch). If end play exceeds 0.35 mm (0.014 inch), replace the thrust washer, snap ring and gear.

9 Install the first gear blocking ring on the tapered surface of the gear. Install the ring and gear on the output shaft. Be sure the tapered gear surface faces the first-second synchronizer hub and that the synchronizer inserts engage in the blocking ring notches.

10 Install the oil slinger spacer on the output shaft. Be sure the oil slinger grooves face the first gear and the flat surface of the slinger spacer faces away from the gear.

11 Install the output shaft rear snap ring, selected in step two, on the output shaft. Position the snap ring over the oil slinger spacer and against first gear.

12 Install the rear bearing on the output

Insert spring position

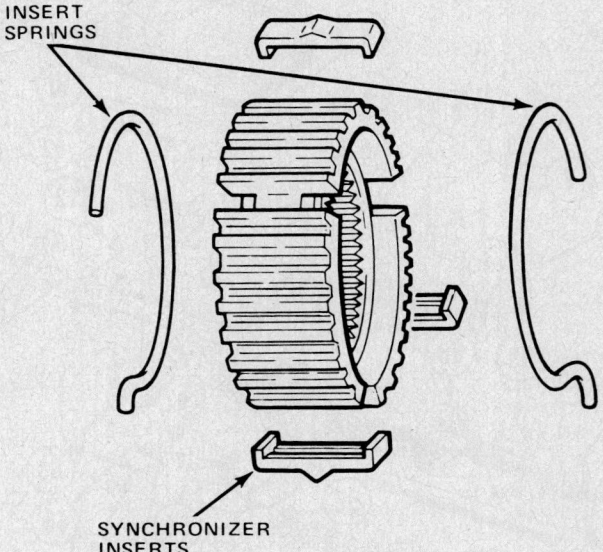

INSERT SPRINGS

SYNCHRONIZER INSERTS

Oil slinger/spacer location

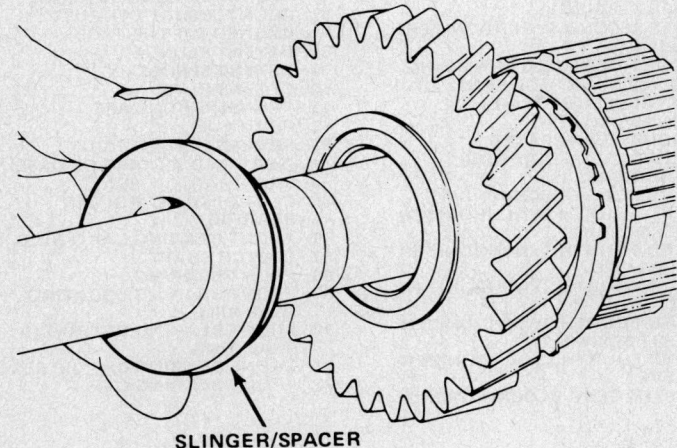

SLINGER/SPACER

shaft using tool J-25678-01. Be sure the bearing seats against the slinger spacer and that the first gear seats in the first-second synchronizer hub (on the output shaft).

13 Install the thickest possible replacement rear bearing snap ring in the output shaft groove. Be sure snap ring is completely seated in output shaft groove.

14 Install the speedometer gear on the output shaft. Install the positioning gauge J-26832 over the speedometer gear.

15 Mount the output shaft assembly in an arbor press.

16 Place rear bearing installer tool J-25678-01 over the output shaft and onto the positioning gauge tool.

17 Press the speedometer gear onto the output shaft until the positioning gauge contacts the rear bearing. Then

release the arbor press and remove the output shaft assembly and tools the from press. Remove the tools from the output shaft assembly.

CHILTON CAUTION: Do not attempt to install the speedometer gear without using the positioning gauge tool. The speedometer gear must be installed to a predetermined depth on the output shaft. The gauge tool must be used in order to correctly position the gear to this predetermined depth.

18 Install third gear on the output shaft. Install the blocking ring on the tapered surface of the gear.

19 Assemble the third-fourth synchronizer hub, sleeve, inserts and insert springs. Index the hub to the sleeve using the alignment marks made during disassembly.

NOTE: **Engage the tang end of each insert spring in the same synchronizer insert, but position the open ends of the springs so they face away from one another.**

20 Install the third-fourth synchronizer assembly on the output shaft. Install the output shaft front snap ring.

21 Measure the third-fourth synchronizer end play using a feeler gauge. End play should be 0.10 to 0.35 mm (0.004 to 0.014 inch). If end play exceeds 0.35 mm (0.014 inch), replace snap ring and synchronizer hub and sleeve.

22 Insert the assembled output shaft and gear train into the extension housing. Tap the front end of the output shaft with a plastic hammer to seat the rear bearing in the extension housing.

23 Compress the output shaft rear snap ring using a needlenose pliers. Install

the snap ring in the extension housing snap ring groove. Be sure the snap ring is completely seated.

TRANSMISSION CASE COMPONENTS ASSEMBLY

1 Lubricate all components with transmission lubricant, except where noted otherwise.
2 Insert countershaft loading tool J-26826 into the countershaft gear bore.
3 Coat the countershaft needle bearings and bearing retainers with petroleum jelly.
4 Install a thin bearing retainer in the needle bearing bores in each end of the countershaft gear.
5 Install 19 long needle bearings in the bore at the rear of the countershaft gear.
6 Install 19 short needle bearings in the bore at the front of the countershaft gear.
7 Install a thick bearing retainer in each countershaft gear bore over the ends of the needle bearings.
8 Coat the replacement countershaft gear thrust washers with petroleum jelly.
9 Position the thrust washer over the bearing bore at the front of the countershaft gear. Push the loading tool toward the front of the gear and through the thrust washer. The loading tool should extend only far enough to hold the washer in position.
10 Align the locating tab on the countershaft gear front thrust washer with the locating notch in the case. Install the gear in case. Be sure the washer tab and case notch are aligned to avoid mispositioning the washer.
11 Align the thrust washer and loading tool with the front countershaft bore in the case. Push the loading tool into the case front bore just enough to hold the thrust washer and countershaft gear in position.
12 Turn the case on end so the case rear bearing bore is now facing upward.
13 Align the locating tab on the countershaft gear rear thrust washer with the locating notch in the case. Install the thrust washer between the gear and case.
14 Align the countershaft gear rear bore, case rear bore and rear thrust washer. Insert the countershaft through the case bore and thrust washer and into the rear bore of the countershaft gear.
15 Turn the case back to the original position and complete the installation of the countershaft.

NOTE: Be sure the step machined in the rear end of the countershaft is in a horizontal position and that the lower step is facing downward.

16 Measure the countershaft gear end play using a feeler gauge. End play should be 0.15 to 0.45 mm (0.006 to 0.018 inch). If end play exceeds 0.45

Countershaft-to-extention housing alignment

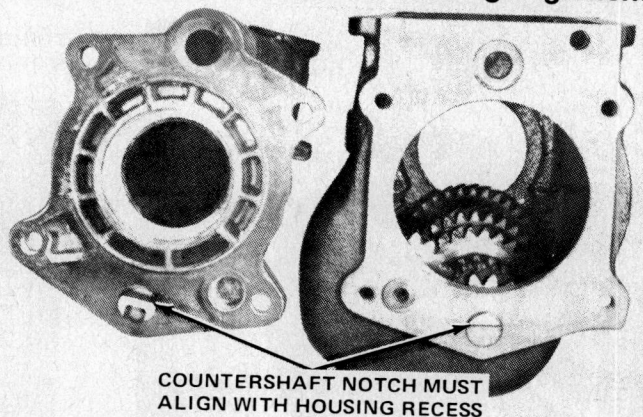

COUNTERSHAFT NOTCH MUST ALIGN WITH HOUSING RECESS

mm (0.018 inch), replace the thrust washers.
17 Install the reverse lever fork in the reverse lever.
18 Install the reverse lever and spring on the pivot shaft in the case. Then install the lever retaining spring clip.
19 Position the reverse idler gear and gear spacer in the case. Be sure the spacer is positioned between the idler gear and the rear of the case. Also be sure the reverse lever fork engages the idler gear.
20 Position the reverse idler gear and spacer, then install the idler gear shaft from the rear of the case. Be sure the reverse lever fork remains engaged with the gear during shaft installation.
21 Install the replacement shift rail oil seal in the counterbore at the rear of the case. Use a suitable size socket to install the seal.
22 Coat the output shaft pilot bearing with petroleum jelly. Install the bearing in the clutch shaft bore.
23 Install the blocking ring on the tapered surface of the clutch shaft and insert the shaft into the case.

24 Install the replacement gasket on the extension housing.
25 Insert the output shaft into the case and install the clutch shaft on the output shaft. Be sure the output shaft pilot hub is fully engaged in the clutch shaft pilot bearing.
26 Coat the extension housing bolts with non-hardening sealer.
27 Align the clutch and output shafts in the case. Install the extension housing bolts finger tight only.

CHILTON CAUTION: Be sure the notch in the end of the countershaft is aligned with the recess in the extension housing before installing the housing attaching bolts. If the notch and recess are not aligned, the housing will not seat against the case properly, resulting in lubricant leaks or a cracked housing.

28 Install the front bearing on the clutch shaft and into the case using front bearing installer J-5590.
29 Install the front bearing retaining and locating snap rings.
30 Install the replacement oil seal in the

Reverse gear components assembled

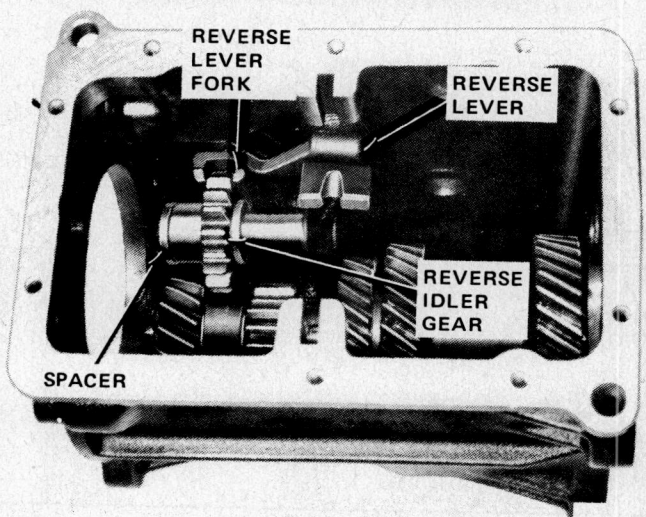

REVERSE LEVER FORK

REVERSE LEVER

REVERSE IDLER GEAR

SPACER

Reverse lever, spring clip and spring position

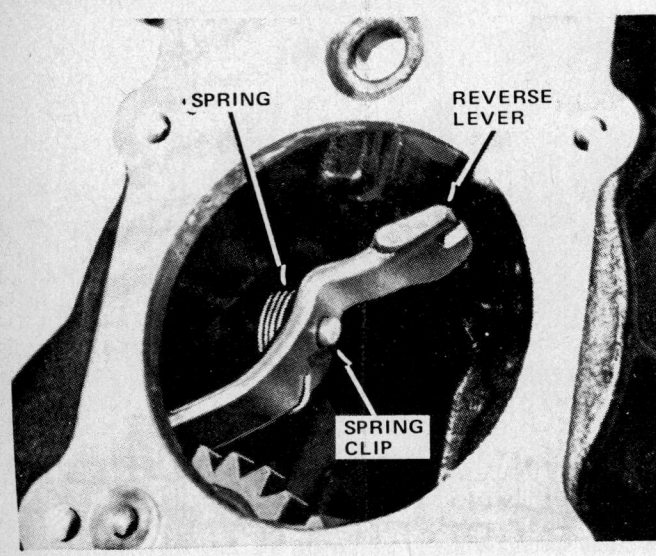

Shift mechanism components assembled

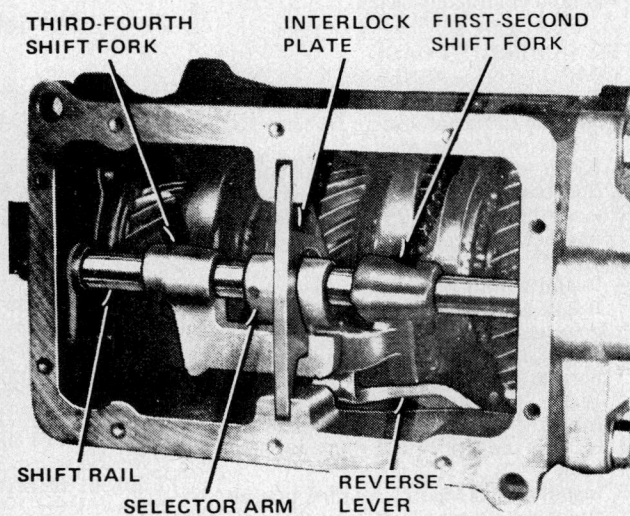

front bearing cap using tool J-26540.

31 Position the replacement front bearing cap O-ring on the case and install the front bearing cap.

32 Install the shift forks in the synchronizer sleeves.

33 Position the interlock plate in the case. Then install the replacement retaining pin.

34 Lubricate the shift rail with transmission lubricant and install the shift rail.

35 Slide the shift rail into the case and through the first-second shift fork and interlock plate.

36 Install the selector arm on the shift rail. Slide the rail through the third-fourth shift fork and into the case front bore.

37 Install the selector arm roll pin in the arm and shift rail. Be sure the pin is flush with the surface of the selector arm.

38 Install the detent plunger, spring and plug in the case.

39 Tighten the front bearing cap bolts.

40 Tighten the extension housing bolts.

41 Install the replacement access plugs in the shift rail bore in the extension

housing and in the interlock plate retaining pin access hole in the case.

42 Install the replacement extension housing oil seal using tool J-26830.

43 Pour 1.13 liters (2.4 pints) of transmission lubricant in the case. Install the replacement top cover gasket and top cover. Then tighten the cover bolts.

44 Install the dynamic absorber and rear support adapter bracket on the extension housing.

45 Install the clutch housing, throwout lever and throwout bearing. Tighten the clutch housing-to-case bolts.

Shifter components

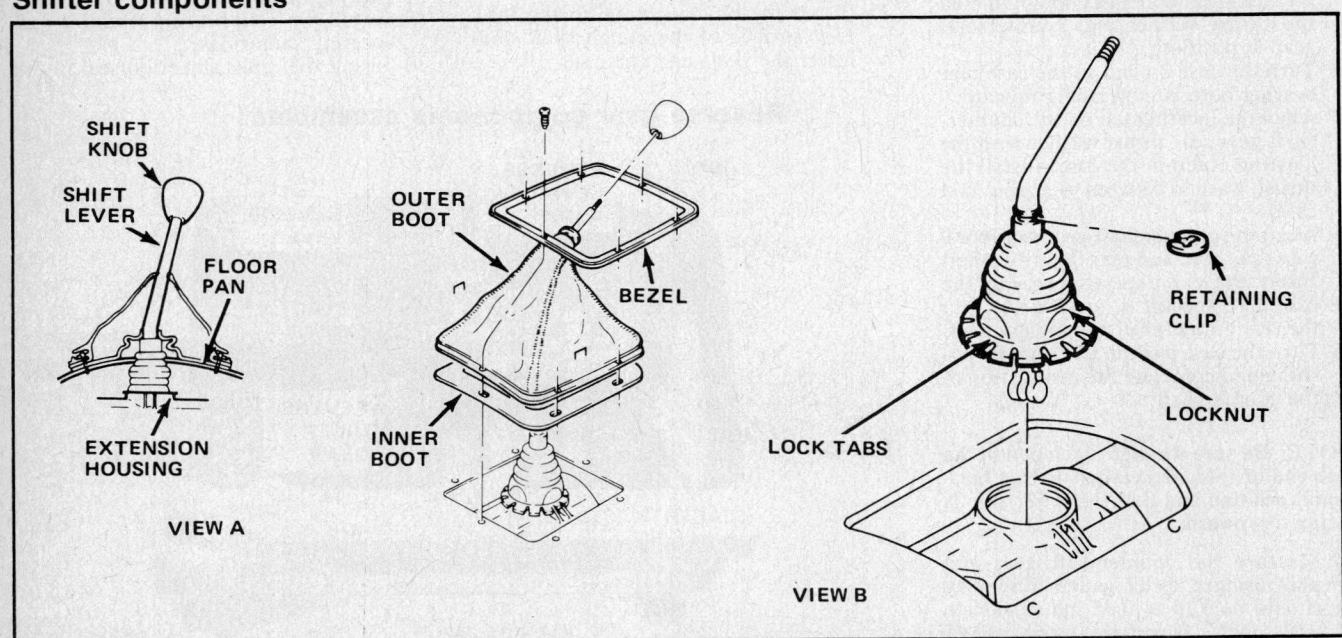

TORQUE SPECIFICATIONS①

	USA (ft. lbs.)		Metric (N·m)	
	Service Set-To Torque②	In-Use Recheck Torque③	Service Set-To Torque②	In-Use Recheck Torque③
Extension housing-to-case bolts	9	8–10	12	11–14
Fill plug	12	10–16	16	14–22
Detent plug	13	12–14	18	16–19
Front bearing cap bolt	9	8–10	12	11–14
Top cover-to-case bolt	9	8–10	12	11–14
Backup lamp switch	18	15–20	24	20–27
Clutch housing-to-case bolts	54	51–57	73	69–77
Clutch housing-to-engine bolts	54	46–62	73	62–84
Starter motor and housing nuts	33	28–38	45	38–51

① All torque values given in foot-pounds and newton-meters with dry fits, unless otherwise specified
② Service set-to torques should be used when assembling components.
③ Service In-use recheck torques should be used for checking a pre-torqued item

TRANSMISSION SPECIFICATIONS

Transmission model	HR1
Application	4 cylinder engine only
Transmission type	4-speed manual, fully synchronized, constant mesh, with internal shift mechanism (floor shift only)
Lubricant capacity	1.13 liters (2.4 pints U.S. measure)
Lubricants	
In service	SAE 80W-90 or SAE 90 gear lubricant, API Grade GL-4
During overhaul	Prelubricate all thrust washers, needle and roller bearings and gear tapered surfaces with petroleum jelly, all other components with SAE 80W-90 or SAE 90 gear lubricant

Gear Ratios	49 State/Cal.	High Alt.
First	3.65:1	3.98:1
Second	1.97:1	2.14:1
Third	1.37:1	1.42:1
Fourth	1.00:1	1.00:1
Reverse	3.66:1	3.99:1

End Play Tolerance	Inch	Mm
Countershaft gear	0.006–0.018	2.591–4.57
Second gear	0.004–0.014	0.102–0.356
Output shaft (measured at third-fourth synchronizer).	0.004–0.014	0.102–0.356

AMC 150T & FORD 3.03 3 SPEED

Disassembly

1 Remove the case cover.
2 Remove the extension housing from the transmission case. Remove a long spring which retains the detent plug in the case. Remove the detent plug with a small magnet.
3 Remove the front bearing retainer from the case.
4 Working through the filler plug hole, drive the roll pin out of the case and countershaft with a small punch.
5 With a dummy shaft, push the countershaft out of the rear of the case until the countershaft cluster gear can be lowered to the bottom of the case. Remove the countershaft from the rear of the case.
6 Remove the snap-ring. Lift the input gear and shaft from the front of the case. Press the shaft out of the bearing.
7 Remove the snap-ring that holds the speedometer gear onto the shaft. Slide the speedometer gear off the output shaft. Remove the speedometer gear lockball.
8 Remove the snap-ring that holds the output shaft bearing on the shaft. With a puller, remove the bearing from both the case and shaft.
9 Place both shaft levers in the neutral position.
10 Remove the set screw that holds the detent springs and plugs in the case. Remove a detent spring and plug from the case.
11 Remove the set screw that holds the first and reverse shift fork to the shift rail. Slide first and reverse shift rail out through the rear of the case.
12 Rotate the first and reverse shift fork upward, then lift it from the case.
13 Remove the set screw that holds the second and third shift fork to the shift rail. Rotate the shift rail 90°.
14 With a magnet, lift the interlock plug from the case.
15 Tap on the inner end of the second and third shift rail to remove the expansion plug. Remove the shift rail.
16 Remove second and third detent plug and spring from the detent bore.
17 Rotate the second and third shift fork upward, then lift it from the case.
18 Lift the output shaft out through the top of the case.
19 From the front bearing opening, drive the reverse idler shaft out through the rear of the case.
20 Lift the reverse idler gear and two thrust washers from the case.
21 Lift the countershaft gear and thrust washers from the case.
22 Remove the countershaft-to-case retaining pin and any needle bearings which may have fallen into the case.
23 Remove the shift levers and shafts from the case. Discard the O-rings.
24 Remove the snap-ring from the front of the output shaft. Slide the synchronizer and the second speed gear from the shaft.
25 Remove the next snap-ring and thrust washer from the output shaft, then slide the first gear and blocking ring off the shaft.
26 Remove the next snap-ring from the output shaft. Press off the first-reverse synchronizer hub from the shaft.
27 Remove the dummy shaft, 50 bearing rollers and the two retainer washers from the countershaft gear.
28 Disassemble the synchronizers.

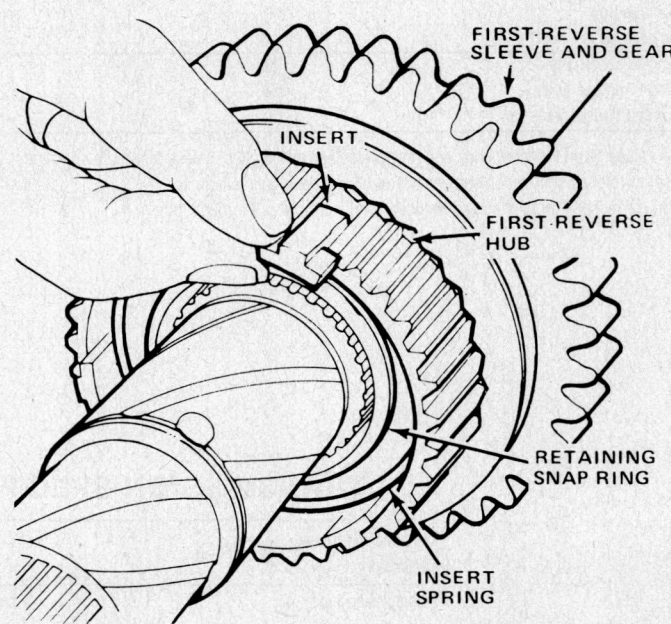

Installing retaining snap ring in first-reverse hub

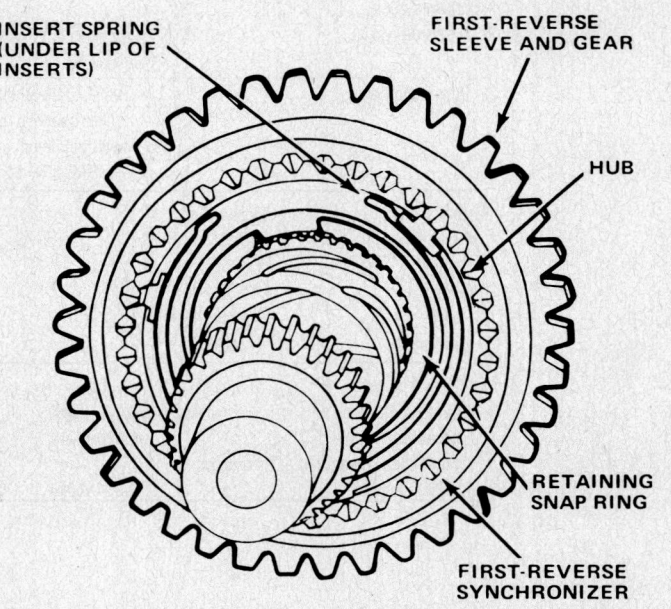

Snap ring and insert spring osition—first-reverse hub

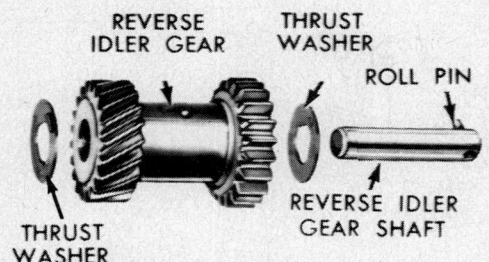

AMC 150T 3-speed: reverse idler shaft assembly

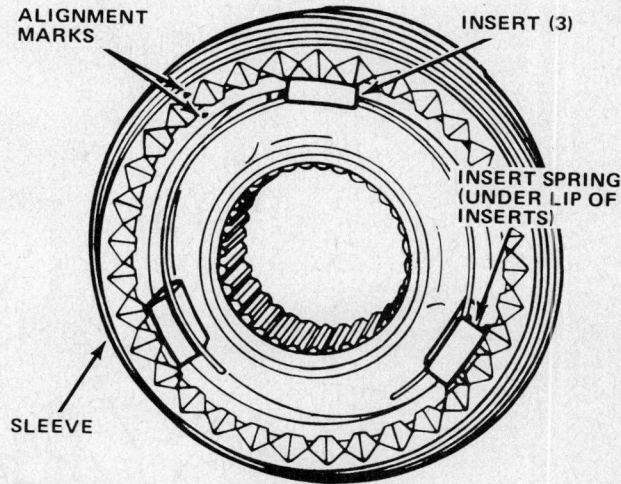

Second-third synchronizer assembly

Assembly

1 Coat the bore in each end of the countershaft gear with grease. Hold the dummy shaft in the gear. Install 25 bearing rollers and a retainer washer in each end of the gear. Install the countershaft gear, thrust washers and dummy shaft in the case. End-play is controlled with variable thickness thrust washers to .004–.018 in. Let the gear cluster assembly lie in the bottom of the case.

2 Install the idler gear, thrust washers and shaft in the case. Make sure that the thrust washer with the flat side, is at the web end and that the spur gear is toward the rear of the case. Idler gear end-play should be .004–.018 in.

3 Install an insert spring into the groove of the first and reverse synchronizer hub. Be sure that the spring covers all insert grooves. Start the hub in the sleeve. Align mating marks. Position the three inserts in the hub. Be sure the small end is over the spring and that the shoulder is on the inside of the hub. Slide the sleeve and reverse gear onto the hub until the detent is engaged. Install the other insert spring in the front of the hub to hold the inserts against it.

4 Install one insert spring into a groove of the second-third synchronizer hub. Align marks on the hub and sleeve. Start the hub into the sleeve. Place the three inserts on top of the retaining spring and push the assembly together. Install the remaining insert spring, so that the spring ends cover the same slots as do the other spring. Do not stagger the springs. Place a

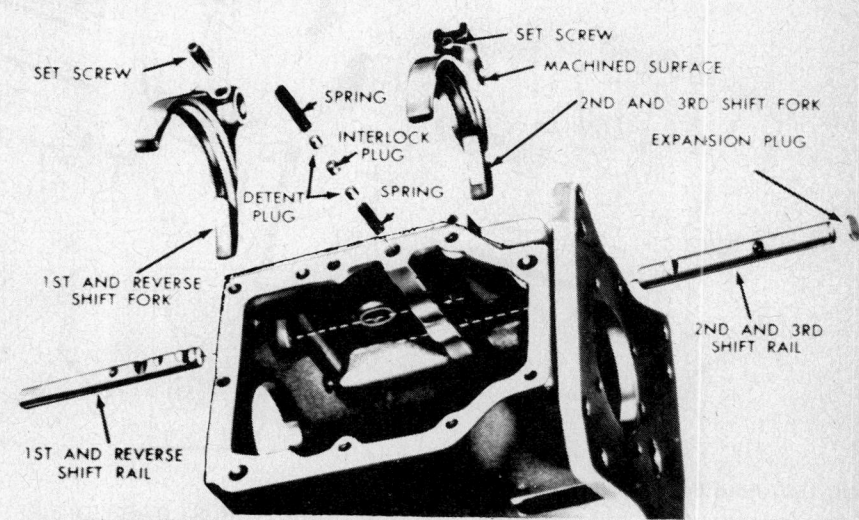

3-speed: shift rail and shifter forks assembly detail

synchronizer blocking ring in each end of the synchronizer sleeve.

5 Lubricate the output shaft splines and machined surfaces with transmission lubricant.

6 Press the first and reverse synchronizer hub onto the output shaft. The teeth end of the gear face toward the rear end of the shaft. Secure it with the snap-ring.

7 Place the blocking ring on the tapered machined surface of the first gear.

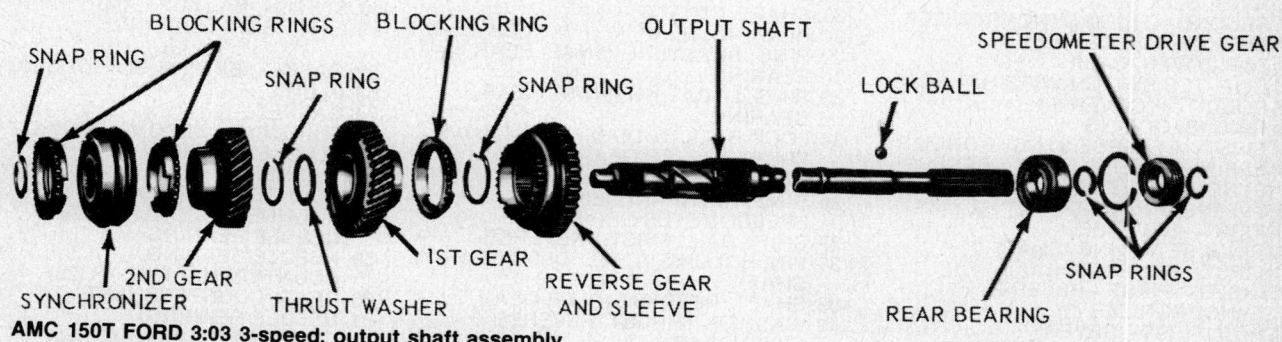

AMC 150T FORD 3:03 3-speed; output shaft assembly

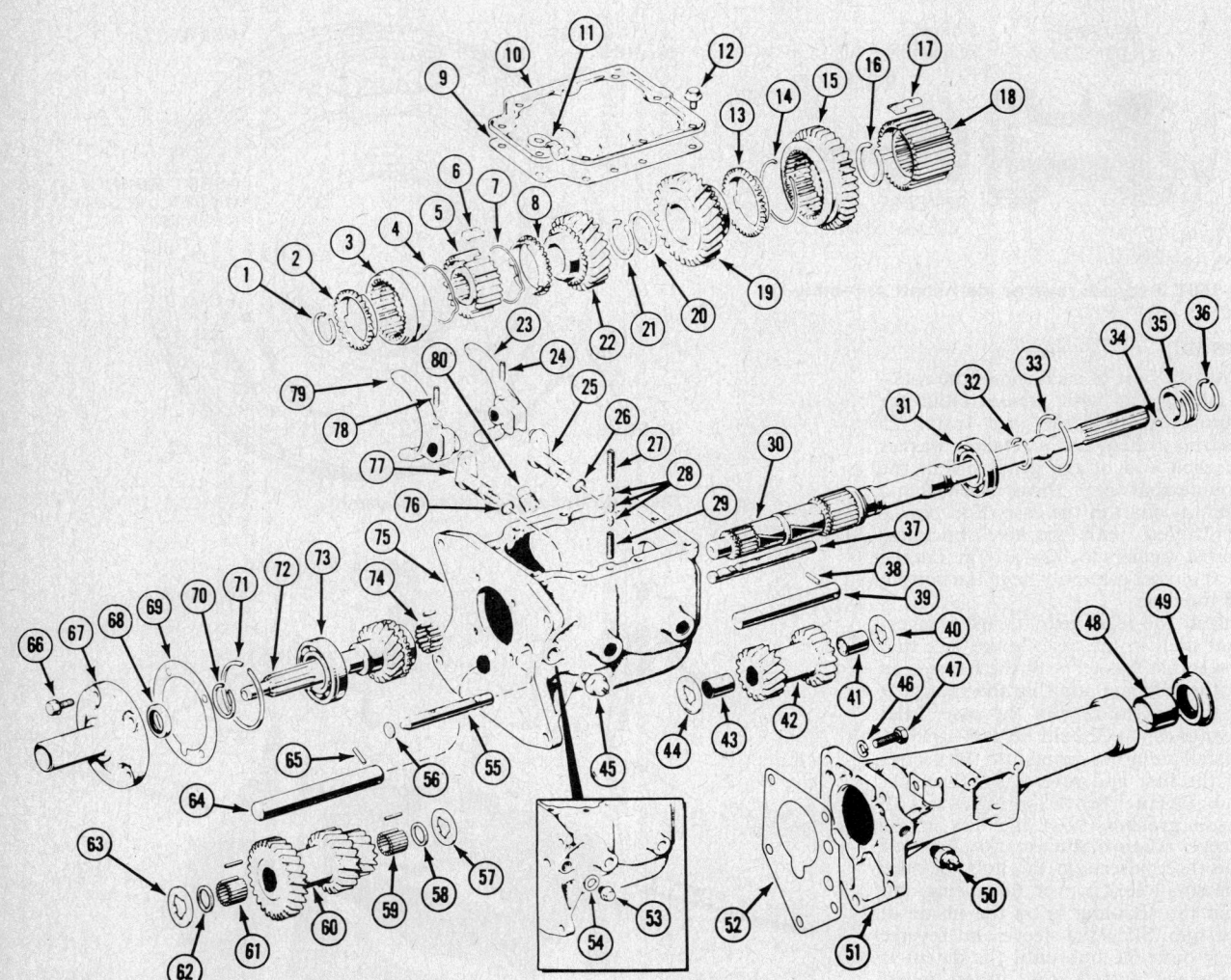

AMC 150T Ford design 3:03 3 Speed

1. RING, RETAINING (SNAP) OUTPUT SHAFT
2. RING, BLOCKING, SECOND—THIRD SYNCHRONIZER
3. SLEEVE, SECOND—THIRD SYNCHRONIZER
4. SPRING, INSERT, SECOND—THIRD SYNCHRONIZER
5. HUB, SECOND—THIRD
6. INSERT, SECOND—THIRD SYNCHRONIZER
7. SPRING, INSERT, SECOND—THIRD SYNCHRONIZER
8. RING, BLOCKING, SECOND—THIRD SYNCHRONIZER
9. GASKET, TOP COVER
10. TOP COVER, CASE
11. CLIP, TCS SWITCH WIRE HARNESS
12. BOLT, TOP COVER (9)
13. RING, BLOCKING, FIRST—REVERSE SYNCHRONIZER
14. SPRING, INSERT, FIRST—REVERSE SYNCHRONIZER
15. SLEEVE AND GEAR, FIRST—REVERSE
16. RING, RETAINING (SNAP) FIRST—REVERSE HUB
17. INSERT, FIRST—REVERSE SYNCHRONIZER (3)
18. HUB, FIRST—REVERSE
19. GEAR, FIRST

20. WASHER, THRUST (TABBED) FIRST GEAR
21. RING, RETAINING (SNAP) FIRST GEAR
22. GEAR, SECOND
23. FORK, FIRST—REVERSE SHIFT
24. SETSCREW, FIRST—REVERSE SHIFT FORK
25. SHAFT, SHIFTER FORK
26. O-RING, SHIFTER SHAFT
27. SPRING, UPPER DETENT (LONG)
28. PLUGS, GEAR SHIFT DETENT AND INTERLOCK (3)
29. SPRING, LOWER DETENT (SHORT)
30. SHAFT, OUTPUT
31. BEARING, REAR
32. RING, RETAINING (SNAP) REAR BEARING
33. RING, LOCATING (SNAP) REAR BEARING
34. LOCK BALL, ¼ DIAMETER—SPEEDOMETER GEAR
35. GEAR, SPEEDOMETER DRIVE
36. RING, RETAINING (SNAP) SPEEDOMETER DRIVE GEAR
37. SHIFT RAIL, FIRST—REVERSE
38. PIN, ROLL, REVERSE IDLER GEAR SHAFT
39. SHAFT, REVERSE IDLER GEAR
40. WASHER, THRUST, REVERSE IDLER GEAR.

41. BUSHING, REVERSE IDLER GEAR (INCLUDED WITH GEAR)
42. GEAR, REVERSE IDLER
43. BUSHING, REVERSE IDLER GEAR (INCLUDED WITH GEAR)
44. WASHER, THRUST, REVERSE IDLER GEAR
45. SWITCH, TCS
46. LOCKWASHER, EXTENSION HOUSING BOLT (5)
47. BOLT, EXTENSION HOUSING (5)
48. BUSHING, EXTENSION HOUSING (INCLUDED WITH HOUSING)
49. SEAL, OIL, EXTENSION HOUSING
50. SWITCH, BACKUP LAMP
51. EXTENSION HOUSING
52. GASKET, EXTENSION HOUSING
53. PLUG
54. GASKET
55. SHIFT RAIL, SECOND—THIRD
56. PLUG, EXPANSION
57. WASHER, THRUST, COUNTERSHAFT GEAR
58. RETAINER, COUNTERSHAFT NEEDLE BEARING
59. NEEDLE BEARING, COUNTERSHAFT GEAR (25)
60. GEAR, COUNTERSHAFT
61. NEEDLE BEARING, COUNTERSHAFT GEAR (25)

62. RETAINER, COUNTERSHAFT NEEDLE BEARING
63. WASHER, THRUST, COUNTERSHAFT GEAR
64. COUNTERSHAFT
65. PIN, ROLL, COUNTERSHAFT
66. BOLT, FRONT BEARING CAP (4)
67. CAP, FRONT BEARING
68. OIL SEAL, FRONT BEARING CAP

69. GASKET, FRONT BEARING CAP
70. RING, RETAINING (SNAP), FRONT BEARING TO CLUTCH SHAFT
71. RING, LOCATING (SNAP), FRONT BEARING
72. SHAFT, CLUTCH
73. BEARING, FRONT
74. BEARINGS, CLUTCH SHAFT ROLLER.

75. CASE, TRANSMISSION
76. O-RING, SHIFTER SHAFT
77. SHAFT, SHIFT FORK
78. SETSCREW, SECOND—THIRD SHIFT FORK
79. FORK, SECOND—THIRD SHIFT
80. PLUG, TRANSMISSION FILL

8 Slide the first gear onto the output shaft. The blocking ring faces the rear of the shaft. Rotate the gear to engage the three notches in the blocking ring with the synchronizer inserts. Secure the first gear with the thrust washer and snap-ring.

9 Slide the blocking ring onto the tapered, machined surface of the second gear. Slide the second gear, with blocking ring and the second and third gear synchronizer, onto the mainshaft. The tapered machined surface of the second gear must be toward the front of the shaft. Secure the synchronizer with a snap-ring.

10 Install new O-rings onto the two shift lever shafts. Lubricate the shafts with transmission fluid and install them into the case. Secure each shift lever onto its shaft.

11 Coat the bore of the input shaft with a light coat of grease. Install the 15 bearing rollers into the bore.

12 Position the output shaft assembly in the case.

13 Place a detent plug spring and a plug in the case. Place a second and third-speed shift fork in the synchronizer groove. Rotate the fork into position and install the second and third-speed

shift rail. Move the rail inward until the detent plug engages the forward notch (second). Secure the fork to the shaft with a set screw. Move the synchronizer to the neutral position.

14 Install the interlock plug in the case.

15 Place first and reverse shift fork in the groove of the first and reverse synchronizer. Rotate the fork into position and install the first and reverse shift rail. Move the rail inward until the center notch is aligned with the detent bore. Secure the fork to the shaft with a set screw. Install the remaining detent plug and spring. Secure the detent spring with the slotted head set screw. Tighten set screw until the head is flush with the case.

16 Install a new expansion plug in the case front.

17 Install the input shaft and gear in the front of the case.

18 Place front bearing retainer (with new gasket in place) on the case. The oil return groove faces bottom. Torque attaching screws to 30 ft./lbs.

19 Install the large snap-ring on the rear bearing. Place the bearing on the output shaft, with the snap-ring end toward the rear of the shaft. Press bear-

ing into place and secure with a snap-ring.

20 Hold the speedometer drive gear lock ball in the detent and slide the speedometer gear into place. Secure the gear with a snap-ring.

21 Lift the countershaft gear cluster up into place. Enter the countershaft at the rear of the case; push the dummy shaft out of the gear and transmission case. Before the countershaft is completely in place, align the roll pin hole in the shaft with the hole in the case.

22 From the filler hole, install a roll pin into the case and countershaft.

23 Install filler and drain plugs in the case.

24 Coat a new extension housing gasket with sealer and install it on the case.

25 Apply sealer to attaching screws and secure extension housing to the case. Torque the screws to 42 to 50 ft./lbs.

26 With transmission in gear, pour lubricant over the entire gear train while rotating the input or output shaft.

27 Install the transmission cover. Torque the nine attaching screws to 14–19 ft./lbs.

28 Check operation of transmission in all of the gear positions.

AMC 150T OVERDRIVE

AMC: Overdrive Transmission

Applications

The AMC Overdrive transmission unit is used on Gremlin and Hornet cars with the AMC 150T 3-speed gearbox. The following information details repair procedures for the AMC Overdrive unit.

Disassembly

1 Remove solenoid valve with wrench tool J-25304. Do not remove solenoid by turning body with pliers or similar tools; the solenoid could be damaged.

2 Remove self-locking nuts that attach clutch piston apply bars to thrust bearing cover pins. Discard nuts.

3 Remove nuts, lockwashers, and copper gaskets from main case-to-rear case studs. Separate main case assembly from rear case assembly.

NOTE: Copper gaskets are used under top two stud nuts. Note location of these gaskets for correct assembly.

4 Remove loose clutch return springs

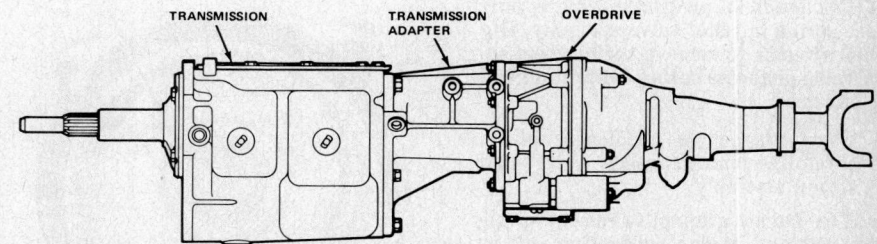

AMC 150T transmission, adapter & overdrive unit components

from main case. Remove clutch brake ring and gaskets from main case.

NOTE: Do not pry on clutch brake ring to remove it from main case. If brake ring is stuck, tap it lightly with plastic mallet to loosen.

5 Remove oil pan, oil pan gasket, oil pan filter and main case pressure plug from main case. Discard oil pan gasket.

6 Remove pressure filter plug from main case with spanner tool J-25305. Remove pressure filter and aluminum washer.

7 Remove pump body plug with spanner tool J-25305. Remove non-return valve ball seat spring, check ball, and valve seat. Remove O-ring from plug.

8 Using pliers, carefully remove clutch apply pistons from bores in main case. Remove O-rings from pistons. Discard O-rings.

NOTE: Do not remove lubrication relief plug, spring, or ball from main case.

9 Remove pump body and assembled pump plunger and pump strap as follows:
a. Push pump body upward until unseated in main case bore.

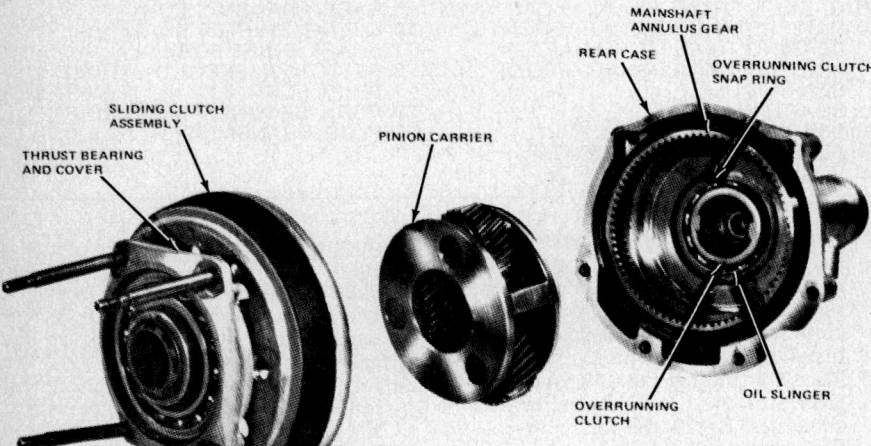

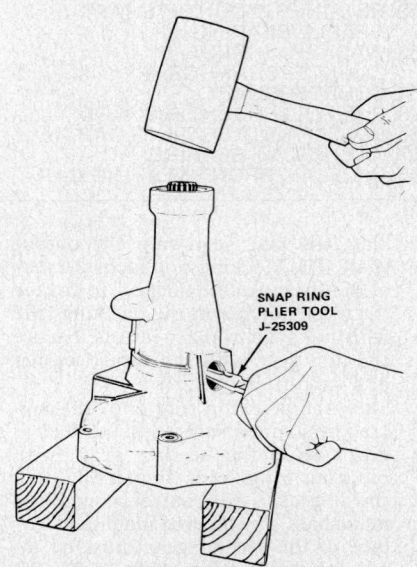

AMC Overdrive: sliding clutch & pinion carrier assembly

b. Carefully slide pump plunger out of pump body. Do not cock piston in body during removal.

c. Remove body from main case bore.

NOTE: Pump body has flat machined on one side. This flat aligns with oil feed hole and slot in main case bore. Note location of both for correct assembly.

d. Remove drive cam and key from pump strap. DO NOT disassemble pump strap and pump plunger. They are serviced as an assembly only.

10 Remove relief valve piston plug with spanner tool J-25305. Remove relief valve piston and relief valve residual pressure spring. Discard O-ring on plug.

NOTE: Residual pressure spring is only loose spring in relief valve assembly. DO NOT attempt to remove spring from relief valve piston as spring calibration will be impaired.

11 Using magnet or needlenose pliers, carefully remove relief valve and spring assembly.

NOTE: Do not attempt to remove spring from valve as spring calibration will be impaired.

12 Remove relief valve sleeve and relief valve body with tool J-25307 as follows:

a. Insert hooked end of tool into bore in relief valve body at bottom of case bore and under relief valve sleeve.

b. Insert tool through bore completely. Hook end of tool over inner edge of valve body. Slide barrel of tool downward to secure hook end of tool, and exert firm, steady pull on tool handle. Tool will remove valve body and sleeve together.

NOTE: Do not attempt to jerk valve and

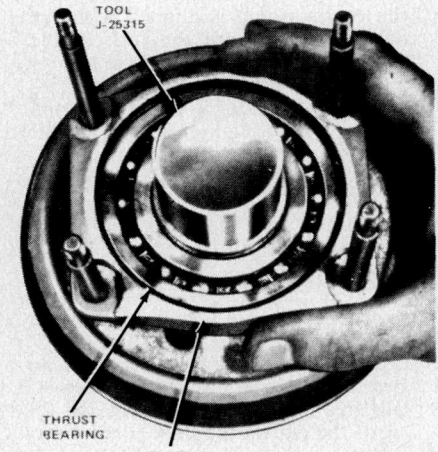

AMC Overdrive: driving the clutch hub from the bearing & cover

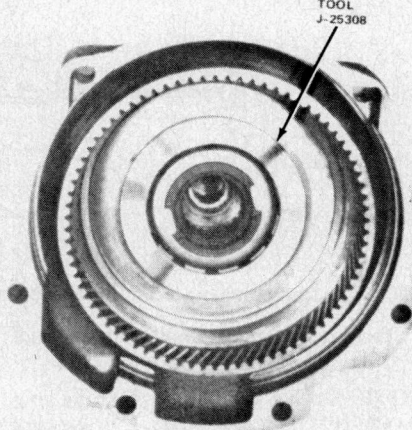

AMC Overdrive: overrunning clutch removal or installation with special tool

sleeve out of case bore as both parts could be damaged.

c. Remove O-rings from valve body, sleeve, and plug. Discard O-rings.

13 Remove sliding clutch, sun gear, and thrust bearing cover assembly from main shaft annulus gear in rear case.

Mainshaft removal procedure

Remove pinion carrier assembly from main shaft annulus gear.

14 Remove sun gear snap ring and sliding clutch ring lock. Push sun gear out of sliding clutch hub.

15 Separate thrust bearing and cover from sliding clutch hub with installer-remover tool J-25315 as follows:

a. Insert tool into sliding clutch hub.

b. Hand-support thrust bearing cover and tap on end of remover tool to drive clutch hub from thrust bearing.

16 Remove thrust bearing snap ring, with small screwdriver or pointed tool. Press bearing from cover using arbor press. Do not remove thrust bearing cover bolts.

17 Remove overrunning clutch snap ring and remove brass oil slinger.

18 Insert overrunning clutch remover-installer tool J-25308 into bore in main shaft annulus gear. Hold tool in position, reach through tool with finger or with relief valve body remover tool J-25307. Pull overrunning clutch into tool, and remove tool and overrunning clutch as an assembly. Remove main shaft thrust washer from recess in main shaft annulus gear. Remove overrunning clutch from tool and disassemble.

19 Remove expansion plug from rear case by driving punch or chisel into plug and prying out of case.

20 Remove main shaft annulus gear as follows:

a. Position rear case on two wood blocks. Allow sufficient space between blocks for main shaft annulus gear to pass through.

b. Expand main shaft bearing snap ring, accessible through expansion plug hole, with snap ring plier tool J-25309. Tap end of main shaft with mallet to drive main shaft out of rear case.

21 Place torque adapter tool J-25312 onto spline end of main shaft to hold main shaft. Remove drive gear locknut with remover-installer tool J-25311. Remove speedometer drive gear tab washer and speedometer drive gear. Remove main shaft bearing using bearing remover tool J-8157 and arbor press.

22 Pry rear case oil seal out of case with screwdriver. Remove main shaft bearing snap ring from machined groove in rear case.

NOTE: *DO NOT* remove disc washer or rear bushing from rear case. These components are not serviceable items. They are available only as part of the rear case.

Cleaning

Wash all parts, except sliding clutch, in a clean solvent. Do not use caustic cleaning agents on any part.

Dry all parts, except solenoid valve and sliding clutch, with filtered compressed air. Be sure to direct compressed air into all oil passages in the main case and main shaft to remove any remaining debris, foreign material, or cleaning solvent.

To clean the valve portion of the solenoid valve, immerse the valve portion up to the threads in solvent or kerosene. Allow to soak until clean, then air dry on a clean, lint-free shop cloth.

Do not attempt to clean the sliding clutch in any type of solvent. Solvent cleaning may loosen the friction material or reduce its holding ability. To clean the sliding clutch, simply wipe it off with a clean, lint-free cloth.

Inspection

Inspect overdrive components as follows:

MAIN CASE
Check for:
1 Cracks in case or in valve or piston bores
2 Nicks, scratches, grooves or warpage in mating surfaces and in valve piston bores
3 Worn, stripped or broken threads on plugs and in valve bores
4 Worn, stripped or broken threads on studs
5 Loose lubrication valve plug and/or blocked oil passages or control orifice

REAR CASE
Check for:
1 Cracks in case or in main shaft bearing snap ring groove
2 Nicks, scratches, or warpage in mating surface
3 Worn, stripped, or broken threads in stud holes
4 Worn or loose rear bushing or disc washer

PUMP, VALVES, PISTONS
Check for:
1 Scratches, nicks, burrs, excessive

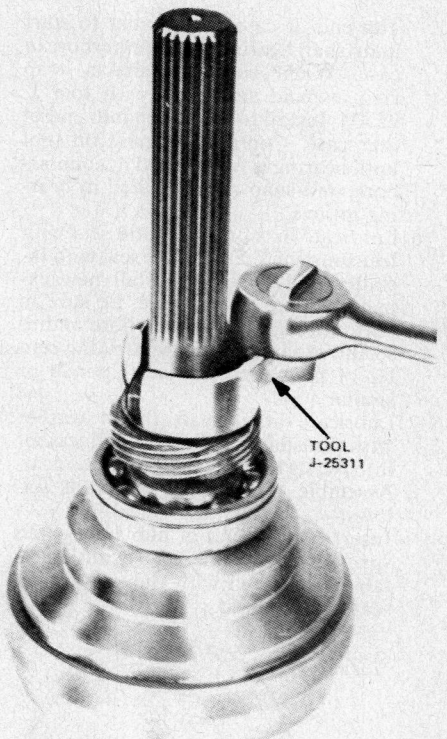

Speedometer gear locknut removal with special tool

wear, pitting, or corrosion of any pump or valve component
2 Weak, broken, or distorted relief valve springs
3 Torn, distorted, or plugged oil pan, and pressure filters
4 Cracked or warped coil pan
5 Check clutch apply pistons for nicks, scratches, and excessive wear
6 Check piston bores for wear, grooves, burrs, and cracks

CLUTCH BRAKE RING
Check for:
1 Worn, grooved, distorted, or burned clutch surfaces
2 Cracks in brake ring or at stud holes

SLIDING CLUTCH, THRUST BEARING, COVER
Check for:
1 Worn, burned, loose, or peeling friction material
2 Cracks in clutch hub or friction surface
3 Worn, rough, broken bearings and races in thrust bearing
4 Cracks, warpage, or worn thrust bolt splines in thrust bearing cover
5 Worn, broken, stipped threads on thrust bolts
6 Worn splines on thrust bolts (bolts rotate freely in cover)
7 Weak, broken or distorted clutch return springs

MAINSHAFT, PINION CARIER, SUN GEAR
Check for:
1 Loose or worn bushing in annulus gear bore
2 Chipped, worn, broken teeth in annulus gear
3 Worn, broken, chipped splines on sun gear and main shaft
4 Bent or distorted main shaft
5 Plugged lubrication oil holes in main shaft
6 Worn, burned, rough clutch surface on annulus gear
7 Cracks in main shaft or sun gear
8 Loose worn pins in pinion carrier
9 Cracked, worn, chipped teeth on pinion gears
10 Loose oil catcher on pinion carrier
11 Rough, broken worn mainshaft bearing

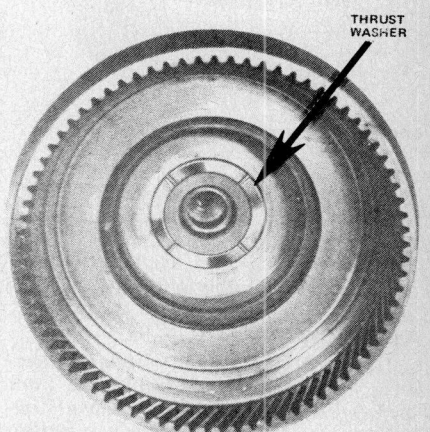

Mainshaft thrust washer location

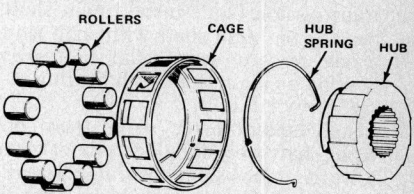

Overrunning clutch components

OVERRUNNING CLUTCH
Check for:
1 Cracked or worn hub and rollers
2 Broken or distorted spring, cracked, bent, or broken cage
3 Worn thrust washer
4 Worn clutch race in annulus gear bore
5 Cracked clutch hub
6 Worn splines in clutch hub

Component Service

All overdrive components are serviced individually except for the following which are serviced as assemblies:
1 Main shaft support bushing: included in main shaft—annulus gear assembly only.
2 Disc washer and rear case bushing: included in rear case assembly only.

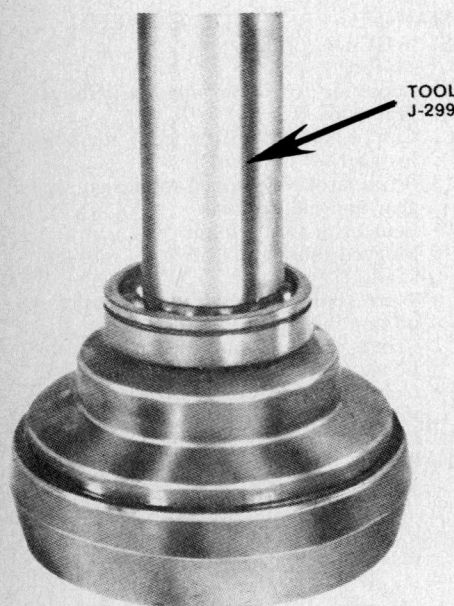

Mainshaft bearing installation

3 Overrunning clutch assembly.
4 Pump plunger, pump strap, and pump plunger pin.
5 Relief valve springs: available with relief valve assembly only.

Assembly

CHILTON CAUTION: *Assemble overdrive only on thoroughly cleaned work surface. Dirt or foreign material could impair operation after overdrive is installed.*

1 Lubricate main shaft bearing with transmission fluid. Install main shaft bearing on main shaft with snap ring groove toward rear of main shaft. Seat bearing on main shaft with bearing installer tool J-2995.
2 Install speedometer drive gear on main shaft with shoulder side of gear toward main shaft bearing. Install new speedometer drive gear washer on top of gear with washer tab located in main shaft slot. Install speedometer drive gear locknut (finger-tighten only)
3 Place torque adapter tool J-25312 on spline end of main shaft. Place installer tool J-25311 on speedometer drive gear locknut. While holding locknut with tool J-25311 and ratchet handle, insert a torque wrench into adapter tool J-25312 and tighten locknut to 55 ft./lbs. torque. Bend speedometer drive gear washer up against locknut in two places to further secure locknut.
4 Install new main shaft bearing snap ring in machined groove in rear case. Position snap ring so butt ends are accessible through expansion plug hole in case.
5 Place main shaft in upright position and lower rear case onto main shaft.

Tap end of case with mallet to start main shaft bearing into counterbore in case. When bearing contacts snap ring, expand snap ring with tool J-25309. Install tool J-25306 into end of rear case. Continue tapping on tool until bearing is fully seated in counterbore, and snap ring is seated in bearing groove.
6 Lubricate lip of rear case oil seal with transmission fluid. Install seal with installer tool J-25306. Install new expansion plug in rear case. Be sure to bottom oil seal in counterbore and to secure expansion plug by striking center of plug with flat-faced punch or similar tool.
7 Lubricate main shaft thrust washer with transmission fluid. Install washer into recess in main shaft annulus gear.
8 Assemble overrunning clutch as follows:
Insert hooked end of hub spring into spring locating hole in case until cage tabs are aligned with hub slots, then seat cage on hub.

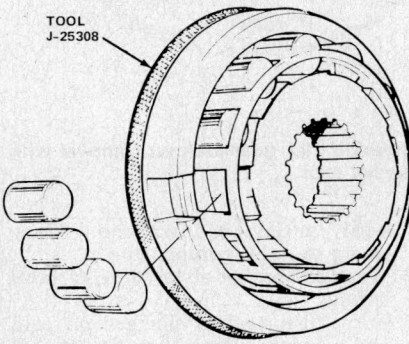

Clutch roller installation

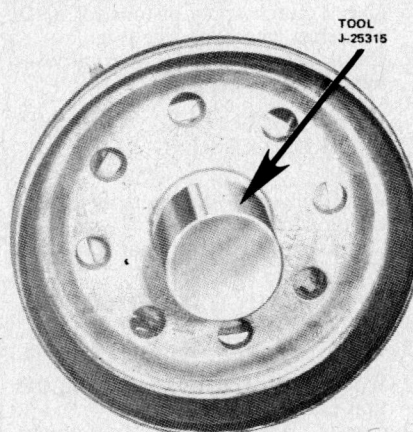

Installing clutch hub in the thrust bearing and cover

9 Place assembled cage and hub into overrunning clutch installer tool J-25308 with open end of cage facing out. Feed clutch rollers into cage slots through gate in tool J-25308. Turn cage in clockwise direction when installing rollers.
10 Lubricate overrunning clutch assem-

bly with transmission fluid and install in bore of main shaft annulus gear. Remove tool J-25308 and install brass oil slinger, with shoulder facing out. Install overrunning clutch snap ring. Be sure snap ring is fully seated in its groove.
11 Lubricate pinion carrier assembly with transmission fluid and install in main shaft annulus gear.
12 Press thrust bearing into thrust bearing cover using arbor press and install thrust bearing snap ring. Lubricate bearing with transmission fluid.
13 Install thrust bearing and cover assembly onto sliding clutch hub as follows:
   a. Positiion thrust bearing and cover assembly clutch hub. Tap cover with mallet to start bearing onto hub.
   b. Turn assembly over and hand support thrust bearing cover. Insert installer-remover tool J-25315 into clutch hub and drive hub into thrust bearing.
14 Install sun gear into sliding clutch hub. Install sliding clutch ring lock (sharp edge facing up) and sun gear snap ring. Be sure ring lock and snap ring are fully seated.
15 Install sliding clutch assembly onto main shaft annulus gear while engaging sun gear in pinion gears. Be sure sliding clutch is seated on annulus and sun gear is fully engaged in pinion gears.

NOTE: Rotating main shaft while engaging sun gear will ease installation.

16 Lubricate clutch apply pistons with transmission fluid. Install new O-ring seals. Install pistons in main case bores with counterbored end of pistons facing out.
17 Lubricate all relief valve assembly components with transmission fluid and install new O-ring seals on relief valve body, relief valve sleeve, and relief valve piston plug.
18 Install relief valve assembly as follows.
   a. Insert relief valve body into main case bore.
   b. Align oil hole in relief valve sleeve with oil hole in bore and insert sleeve.

NOTE: End of sleeve containing O-ring facing up.

   c. Push sleeve firmly into bore to seat sleeve and valve body.
   d. Install relief valve and spring assembly in relief valve body. And install relief valve residual pressure spring in relief valve and spring assembly.
   e. Install relief valve piston in relief valve sleeve and install relief valve piston plug. Tighten plug to 16 foot-pounds torque using torque wrench and spanner tool J-25305.
19 Install pressure filter into main case bore. Place new aluminum washer on

pressure filter plug and install plug. Tighten plug to 16 foot-pounds torque with torque wrench and spanner tool J-25305.

20 Lubricate pump plunger assembly, pump body, and non-return valve seat with transmission fluid. Install new O-ring seals on pump body and pump plug.

21 Install pump plunger, pump body, and non-return valve components as follows:

   a. Align flat on pump body with oil hole in main case bore and insert pump body halfway into bore.

   b. Carefully insert pump plunger into pump body then push pump body completely into main case bore until seated. Do not allow plunger to cock in pump body during installation.

   c. Install non-return valve seat on top of pump body with seat for check ball facing up. Place non-return valve check ball into valve seat.

   d. Place non-return valve ball seat spring in pump body plug and install plug and spring. Take care that spring or ball are not dislodged when plug is installed. Tighten plug to 16 foot-pounds with torque wrench and spanner tool J-25305.

22 Install main case pressure plug and gasket, oil pan filter, new oil pan gasket, and oil pump cover on main case. Tighten pan bolts to 6 foot-pounds torque and pressure plug to 13 foot-pounds torque.

23 Mount rear case assembly upright in soft jawed vise. Do not overtighten vise on aluminum rear case. Install new clutch return springs on thrust bearing cover bolts.

24 Install first clutch brake ring gasket on rear case. Install clutch brake ring into rear case with tapered surface of brake ring facing rear of case. Install second new clutch brake ring gasket on brake ring. Be sure gaskets and brake ring are aligned with stud holes in rear case.

25 Apply light coat of sealer to main

Pump body alignment detail

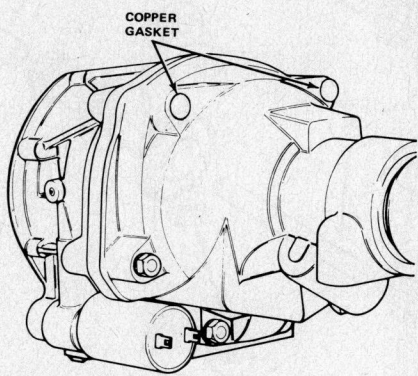

Copper gasket location

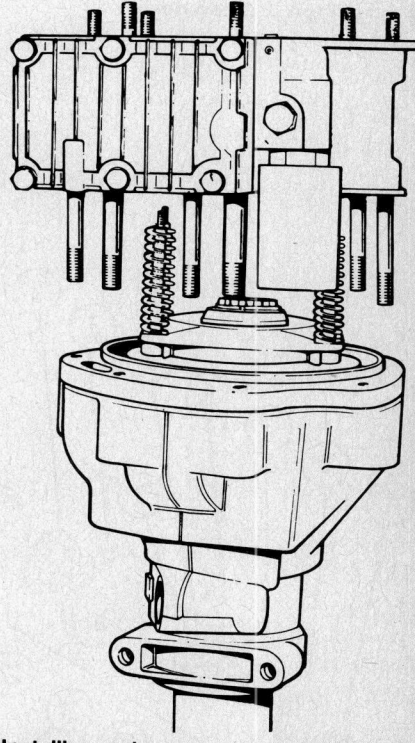

Installing main case on the rear case

case-to-rear case studs. Position main case assembly over rear case assembly, align studs, and lower main case assembly onto rear case assembly. As main case assembly is being lowered, align thrust bearing cover bolts with bolt holes in main case.

26 Install six nuts, four lockwashers, and two copper gaskets on main case-to-rear case studs. Copper gaskets are installed on top two studs. Tighten nuts progressively to avoid cocking main case or rear case. Both components

are under clutch return spring pressure. Tighten nuts to 11 foot-pounds torque.

27 Install clutch apply bars on thrust bearing cover bolts and secure with new locknuts. Tighten nuts to 8 foot-pounds torque.

28 Install solenoid valve using wrench tool J-25304. Tighten solenoid valve securely but do not overtighten.

29 Lubricate new drive cam with transmission fluid and install cam and new drive key on transmission output shaft. Secure with snap ring.

30 Pour approximately one pint of transmission fluid into oil pan through access hole in front of main case. Install overdrive.

WARNER T14A & T15A 3 SPEED

Warner T14A & T15A, 3-Speed Units

Transmission Disassembly

1 Separate the transfer case by removing the five capscrews.

2 Remove the cover and gasket. Disassemble the floorshift housing cover by removing the shift rails, poppet balls, springs, and shift forks.

3 Remove the nut, flat washer, transfer case drive gear, adaptor, and spacer.

4 Remove the main drive gear bearing retainer and gasket.

5 Remove the main drive gear and mainshaft bearing snap-rings.

6 Pull out the main drive gear and mainshaft bearings.

7 Remove the main drive gear.

8 Remove the mainshaft assembly through the cover opening.

9 On remote-shift models, remove the roll pins from the lever shafts and housing. From inside the case, slide the levers and interlock assembly out. Remove the forks and lever assemblies.

10 Remove the lockplate from the slots in the reverse idler shaft and countershaft.

11 Drive the countershaft out to the rear with a dummy shaft. Remove the

Warner T15A 3 Speed detail

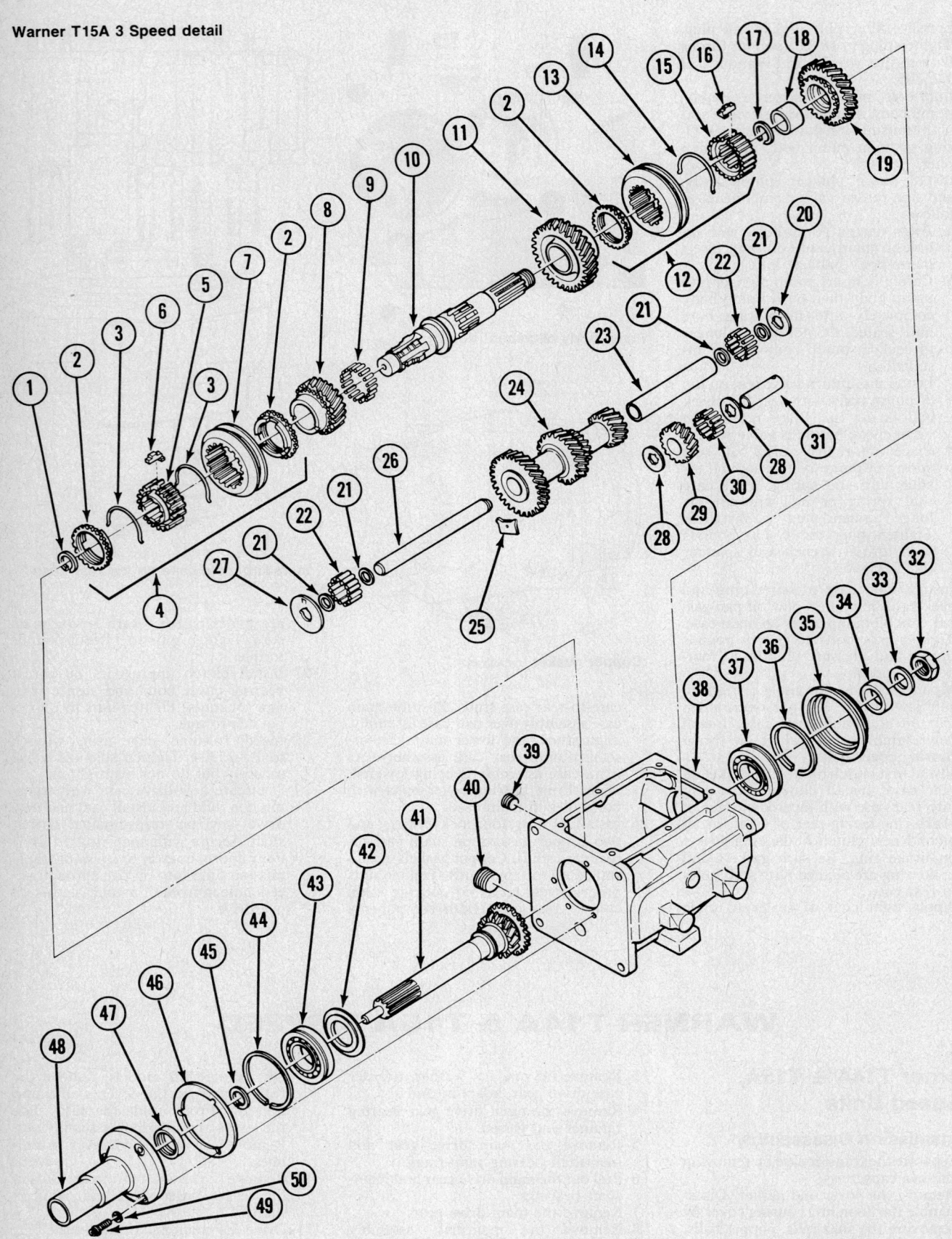

1. SECOND-THIRD SYNCHRONIZER SNAP RING
2. BLOCKING RINGS (3)
3. SYNCHRONIZER SPRINGS (2)
4. SECOND-THIRD SYNCHRONIZER ASSEMBLY
5. SECOND-THIRD CLUTCH HUB
6. SECOND-THIRD SHIFTING PLATE (3)
7. SECOND-THIRD CLUTCH SLEEVE
8. SECOND GEAR
9. MAINSHAFT PILOT BEARING ROLLERS (21)
10. MAINSHAFT
11. FIRST GEAR
12. FIRST GEAR SYNCHRONIZER ASSEMBLY
13. FIRST-REVERSE CLUTCH SLEEVE
14. SYNCHRONIZER SPRING (1)
15. FIRST GEAR CLUTCH HUB
16. FIRST GEAR SHIFTING PLATE (3)
17. FIRST GEAR SNAP RING
18. REVERSE GEAR BUSHING (INCLUDED WITH REVERSE GEAR)
19. REVERSE GEAR
20. COUNTERSHAFT GEAR THRUST WASHER (REAR)
21. COUNTERSHAFT GEAR BEARING WASHER (4)
22. COUNTERSHAFT GEAR BEARING ROLLERS (44)
23. COUNTERSHAFT GEAR BEARING SPACER
24. COUNTERSHAFT GEAR
25. COUNTERSHAFT-REVERSE IDLER SHAFT LOCKPLATE
26. COUNTERSHAFT
27. COUNTERSHAFT GEAR THRUST WASHER (FRONT)
28. REVERSE IDLER GEAR THRUST WASHER (2)
29. REVERSE IDLER GEAR
30. REVERSE IDLER GEAR BEARING ROLLERS
31. REVERSE IDLER GEAR SHAFT
32. MAINSHAFT LOCKNUT
33. MAINSHAFT WASHER
34. MAINSHAFT BEARING SPACER
35. REAR BEARING ADAPTER
36. REAR BEARING LOCK RING
37. REAR BEARING
38. TRANSMISSION CASE
39. FILL PLUG
40. DRAIN PLUG
41. CLUTCH SHAFT
42. FRONT BEARING RETAINER
43. FRONT BEARING
44. FRONT BEARING LOCK RING
45. FRONT BEARING SNAP RING
46. FRONT BEARING CAP GASKET
47. FRONT BEARING CAP OIL SEAL
48. FRONT BEARING CAP
49. FRONT BEARING CAP BOLT
50. LOCKWASHER

countergear and the two thrust washers. Remove the spacer washers, rollers, and spacer from the gear.

12 Drive the reverse idler shaft out to the rear. Remove the gear, washers, and roller bearings.

13 Remove the clutch hub snap-ring and the second-third synchronizer assembly.

14 Remove second and reverse gears.

15 Remove the clutch hub snap-ring and the low synchronizer assembly.

16 Remove low gear.

Synchronizer Disassembly & Assembly

1 Remove the springs. The low synchronizer has only one spring; second-third, two.

2 Mark the sleeve and hub before separating.

3 Remove the hub.

4 Remove the three shifter plates from hub.

5 Inspect all parts for wear.

6 Assemble in the reverse order of disassembly. On the second-third unit, make sure that the spring openings are 120° from each other, with spring tension opposed.

NOTE: If a synchronizer assembly is replaced on a floor-shift unit, the shift fork operating the synchronizer being replaced must have the letter A just under the shaft hole on the side opposite the pin.

Inspection

1 Wash all parts in solvent.

2 Air dry.

3 Check the case bearing and shaft bores. Check for cracks or burrs.

4 Check all gears and bronze blocking rings for cracks, and chipped, worn, or cracked teeth. If any gears are replaced, also replace the meshing gears.

5 Check all bearings and bushings for wear or damage.

6 Check to see that the synchronizer sleeves slide freely on the clutch hubs.

Transmission Assembly

1 Place the reverse idler gear with the dummy shaft, roller bearing, and thrust washers in the case. Install the reverse idler shaft.

2 Assemble the countershaft center spacer, four bearing spacers, and bearing rollers in the countershaft gear.

3 Install the large countergear thrust washer in front of case. Position the small thrust washer on the countergear hub with the lip facing the groove in the case. Holding the countergear in position, push in the countershaft from the rear.

4 Install the lockplate in the slots of the reverse idler shaft and the countershaft.

5 Install to mainshaft:

   a. low gear.
   b. bronze blocking ring.
   c. low synchronizer assembly.
   d. largest snap-ring that fits in groove.
   e. second gear.
   f. bronze blocking ring.
   g. second-third synchronizer assembly.
   h. largest snap-ring that fits in groove.
   i. reverse gear.

6 Install the mainshaft assembly through the top of the case.

7 Install the bronze blocking ring to the second-third synchronizer assembly.

8 On remote-shift units, install new O-rings on the shifter lever shafts and install the shafts into the case.

NOTE: T-15 interlock levers are marked as to location. T-14 levers have no marks and are interchangeable.

9 Depress the interlock lever while installing the shift fork into the shift lever and synchronizer clutch sleeve. Install the poppet spring. Install the tapered pins securing the shafts in the case.

10 Install the main drive gear roller bearings.

11 Install the main drive gear and oil slinger into the case with cut-away portion of the gear toward the countergear. Install the main drive gear to the mainshaft.

12 Using the bearing installer and thrust yoke tool, install the main drive gear and mainshaft bearings. Drive the bearings into position. The thrust yoke is needed to prevent damage to the synchronizer clutch.

13 Install the main drive gear and mainshaft bearing snap-rings. The main shaft bearing snap-ring is 0.010 in. thicker than the main drive gear bearing snap-ring.

14 Install the mainshaft rear bearing adaptor, spacer, transfer case drive gear, flat washer, and nut. Torque the nut to 130–170 ft./lbs.

15 Replace the main drive gear bearing retainer oil seal. Install the retainer and gasket. Align the oil drain holes in the retainer and gasket.

16 Install the case cover gasket. On remote-shift units, install the cover gasket with the vent holes to the left side.

17 Position the gear train and floor-shift assembly in neutral. Insert the shifter forks into the clutch sleeves. Install and torque the bolts to 8–15 ft./lbs.

WARNER T14 & T15 3 SPEED

Warner T14 & T15, 3-Speed Units

Transmission Disassembly

1 Remove cover, front bearing cap, gasket, and two front bearing snap rings.
2 Align notch in clutch shaft third gear with countergear. Remove clutch shaft and front bearing. A puller may be needed.
3 Pull off front bearing.
4 Remove extension housing and gasket. Using oil seal remover and slide hammer, remove extension housing oil seal. Remove extension housing bushing. Install new bushing. Align oil groove with housing slot.
5 Remove snap-ring, speedometer drive gear, and locating ball.
6 Remove two rear bearing snap-rings. Pull off rear bearing.

Shift fork removal

7 Move mainshaft aside. Remove both shift forks.
8 Push front synchronizer toward rear. Tilt front of mainshaft up and out through top of case.
9 If necessary, remove the transmission controlled spark switch assembly.
10 Drive out roll pins. Push shift shafts into case. Remove shift shafts and detent assembly.
11 Drive out roll pins. Push shift shafts into case. Remove shift shafts and detent assembly.
12 Tap reverse idler shaft and countershaft rearward. Remove shaft lockplate. Drive reverse idler shaft from case. Use dummy shaft to drive out countershaft.

Mainshaft Disassembly

1 From front of shaft, remove front snap-ring, second-third synchro-clutch assembly, and second gear.
2 From rear of shaft, remove reverse gear, rear snap-ring, rear synchro-clutch assembly, and low gear.

Inspection

1 Check gears for worn, chipped, or cracked teeth. Check fit to mainshaft.
2 Check bearings for smoothness and excessive play.
3 Check roller bearings for wear or damage.

Warner T-14 Shift forks pushed to one side of the case

4 Slide synchro-clutch and friction rings on gear cones and clutch shaft. Replace rings if taper is worn or pitted. There should be no play between hub and shaft splines.
5 Check case for cracks or damaged bearing bores.

Mainshaft Assembly

1 Install low gear and friction ring. Install friction ring hub to the rear.
2 Install low synchro-gear into synchro-collar. Deep end of gear faces low gear. Install synchro-plates (dogs) and retainer ring with large end of plates toward low gear.
3 Place synchro-clutch assembly on mainshaft with synchro-collar groove toward low gear. Install the thickest snap-ring that will fit in groove.
4 Measure clearance between first gear and collar on mainshaft. The clearance should be .003–.012 in. for the T-14; .003–.014 in. for the T-15.
5 Place second gear and the friction ring on the front of the mainshaft. The

gear hub and ring face forward. Place second synchro-gear into synchro-collar. Deep end of gear faces rear of shaft.
6 Hold synchro-clutch assembly with one synchro-plate, or dog, in 12 o'clock position. Install tang of retainer ring into the dog at 12 o'clock. Install ring clockwise. On opposite side, start with the same dog and install ring clockwise.
7 Place second synchro assembly on shaft with deep end to rear. Install the thickest snap-ring that will fit into the groove.
8 Measure clearance between second gear and collar on mainshaft. It must be .003–.018 in.
9 Install reverse gear on rear of mainshaft.

Transmission Assembly

1 Install dummy shaft in countergear. Install spacer washers and roller bearings.
2 Place countergear in case. Align thrust washers at each end. Insert countershaft.
3 Insert rollers in reverse idler gear. Hold rollers with petroleum jelly. Place gear in case. Position thrust washers. Insert shaft. Install shaft lockplate.
4 Insert shifter shafts in case. Position low-reverse lever to inside of case. Locate notches on top of levers to rear of case stud. Align shift detent assembly with shifter shafts and case stud. Push detent assembly and shifter shafts into place. Install shaft roll pins.
5 If removed, install the transmission controlled spark switch.
6 Place front synchronizer in second shift position. Place mainshaft assembly in case to one side.
7 Pull detent levers up. Place shift forks in shifting assembly.
8 Install mainshaft pilot end support in case. Install front bearing cap. Drive rear bearing on thickest rear bearing snap-ring with a 1¼ × 17 in. pipe. Install support and bearing cap.
9 Install locating ball, speedometer drive gear, and snap-ring.
10 Press front bearing onto clutch shaft.
11 Place rollers in clutch shaft. Hold with petroleum jelly.
12 Place friction ring on mainshaft. Slide clutch shaft into position from front.
13 Install thickest front bearing snap-ring that will fit in groove, gasket and cap. Align cap lubrication hole with hole in case.
14 Install extension housing. Install oil seal. Install shift lever, gaskets, and cover.

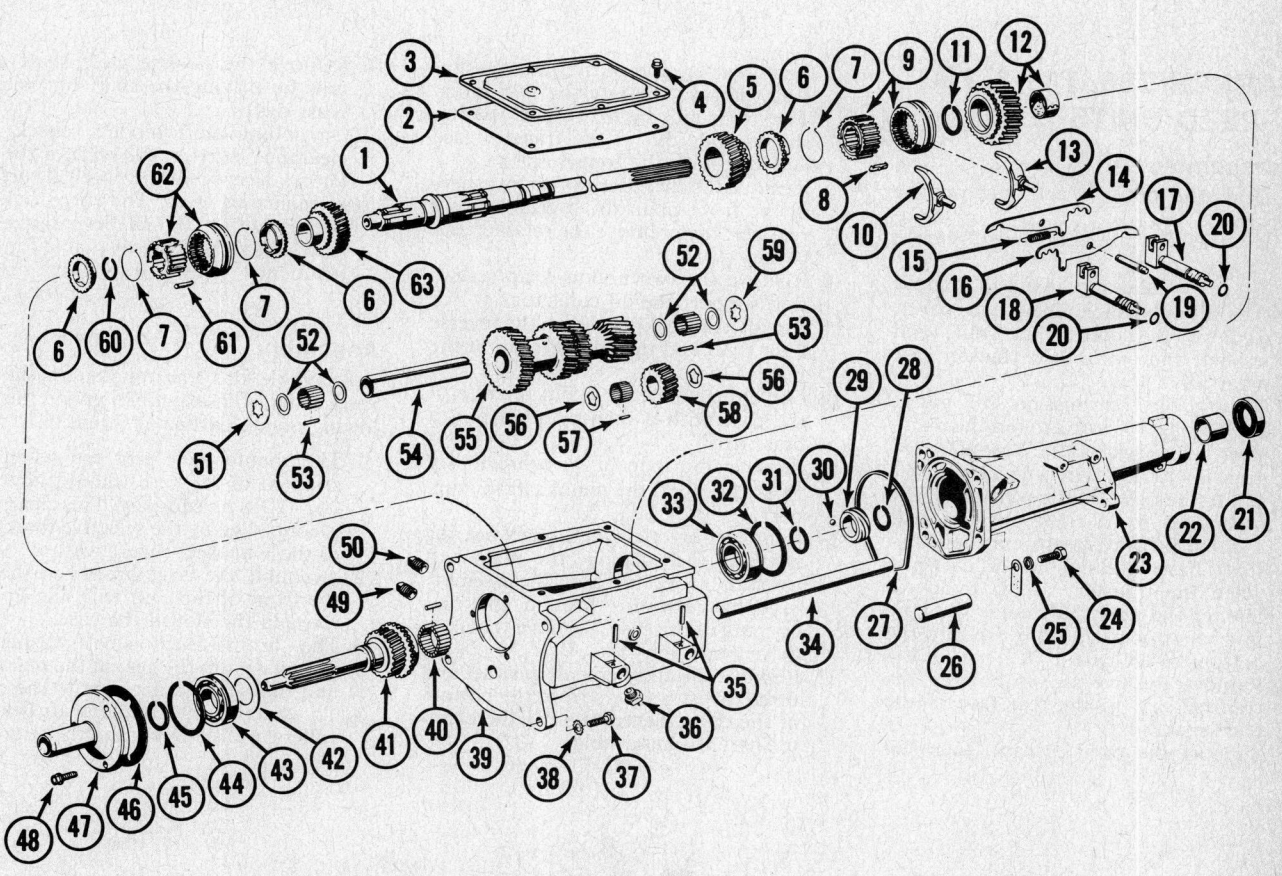

Warner T-14 or T-15 typical exploded view

1. SPLINE SHAFT
2. GASKET
3. CASE COVER
4. BOLT
5. FIRST GEAR
6. CLUTCH FRICTION RING SET
7. SHAFT PLATE RETAINING SPRING
8. CLUTCH SHAFT FIRST AND REVERSE PLATE
9. FIRST AND REVERSE CLUTCH ASSEMBLY
10. SHIFTER SECOND AND HIGH FORK
11. CLUTCH FIRST AND REVERSE GEAR SNAP RING
12. REVERSE GEAR
13. SHIFTER FIRST AND REVERSE R FORK
14. SHIFTER INTERLOCK FIRST AND REVERSE LEVER
15. SPEED FINDER INTERLOCK POPPET SPRING
16. SHIFTER INTERLOCK SECOND AND THIRD LEVER
17. SHIFTER FORK FIRST AND REVERSE SHAFT
18. SHIFTER FORK SECOND AND THIRD SHAFT

19. SHIFTER FORK INTERLOCK LEVER PIVOT PIN
20. SHIFTER FORK SHAFT SEAL
21. REAR BEARING CAP OIL SEAL
22. REAR BEARING CAP BUSHING
23. REAR BEARING CAP
24. BOLT
25. LOCK WASHER
26. IDLER GEAR SHAFT
27. REAR BEARING CAP GASKET
28. SPEEDOMETER DRIVE GEAR RING
29. SPEEDOMETER DRIVE GEAR
30. SPEEDOMETER DRIVE GEAR BALL
31. REAR BALL BEARING LOCKRING
32. REAR BALL BEARING LOCKRING
33. REAR BALL BEARING
34. COUNTERSHAFT
35. SHIFTER FORK RETAINING PIN
36. SOLENOID CONTROL SWITCH
37. BOLT
38. LOCK WASHER
39. CASE
40. SPLINE SHAFT PILOT BEARING ROLLER
41. CLUTCH SHAFT
42. FRONT BALL BEARING WASHER
43. FRONT BALL BEARING
44. FRONT BALL BEARING LOCKRING

45. FRONT BALL BEARING SNAP RING
46. GASKET
47. FRONT BEARING GAP
48. BOLT
49. DRAIN PLUG
50. FILLER PIPE PLUG
51. FRONT COUNTERSHAFT GEAR THRUST WASHER
52. COUNTERSHAFT GEAR BEARING ROLLER WASHER
53. COUNTERSHAFT GEAR BEARING ROLLER
54. COUNTERSHAFT GEAR ROLLER BEARING SPACER
55. COUNTERSHAFT GEAR
56. REVERSE IDLER GEAR BEARING ROLLER WASHER
57. REVERSE IDLER GEAR BEARING ROLLER
58. REVERSE IDLER GEAR
59. REAR COUNTERSHAFT THRUST WASHER (LESS LIP)
60. CLUTCH SECOND AND THIRD SNAP RING
61. CLUTCH SHAFT SECOND AND THIRD PLATE
62. SECOND AND THIRD CLUTCH ASSEMBLY
63. SECOND GEAR

WARNER T86-T89-T90 3 SPEED

WARNER T86, T89 & T90, 3-SPEED UNITS

Disassembly

1 Drain the lubricant and flush out the case.
2 If a transfer case is involved, remove its rear power.
3 If a power take-off is involved, remove the shift unit which replaces the cover.
4 Remove the cotter pin, nut, and washer, and remove the transfer case main drive gear.
5 Remove the transmission shift cover.
6 Loop a piece of wire around the mainshaft just back of the second-speed gear. Twist the wire and attach one end to the right front cover screw, the other end to the left cover screw. Tighten the wire to prevent the mainshaft from pulling out of the case when the transfer case is removed. Should the mainshaft come out, the synchronizer parts will drop into the bottom of the case.
7 Remove the five screws holding the transfer case to the rear face of the transmission.
8 Support the transfer case, then tap lightly on the end of the transmission mainshaft to separate the two units. The transmission mainshaft bearing should slide out of the transfer case and stay with the transmission.
9 Remove the three screws and washers in the front main drive gear bearing retainer, then remove the retainer and gasket.
10 Remove the two hollow-head screws that support the oil collector.
11 Remove the lockplate from the reverse idler shaft and the countershaft at the rear of the case.
12 Drive the countershaft out the rear of the case with a dummy shaft and a brass drift.
13 Remove the loop of wire previously twisted around the mainshaft for support.
14 Remove the mainshaft rear bearing adaptor, then remove the mainshaft assembly from the case. The assembly may be removed through the rear opening of the case. Remove the main drive gear.
15 Remove the countershaft gear set and three thrust washers from the bottom of the case, then dismantle the countershaft gear assembly.
16 Remove the reverse idler shaft and gear by driving the shaft out with a brass drift.
17 On column-shift models, check the clearance between the ends of the interlock sleeve and the notched surface of each shift lever. The correct clearance is 0.001–0.007 in. Several sizes of interlock sleeves are available for adjustment.

Assembly

Assemble the transmission in the reverse order of disassembly, giving the following points particular attention.

1 The countershaft gear set, when assembled in the case, should have 0.012–0.018 in. end-play. This clearance is controlled by the selective thickness of the rear steel thrust washer.
2 Assemble the large bronze washer at the front of the case with the lip entered in the slot in the case.
3 The bronze-faced steel washer is placed next to the gear at the rear end, and the steel washer next to the case.
4 To assemble the countershaft bearing rollers, use a dummy shaft. Use grease

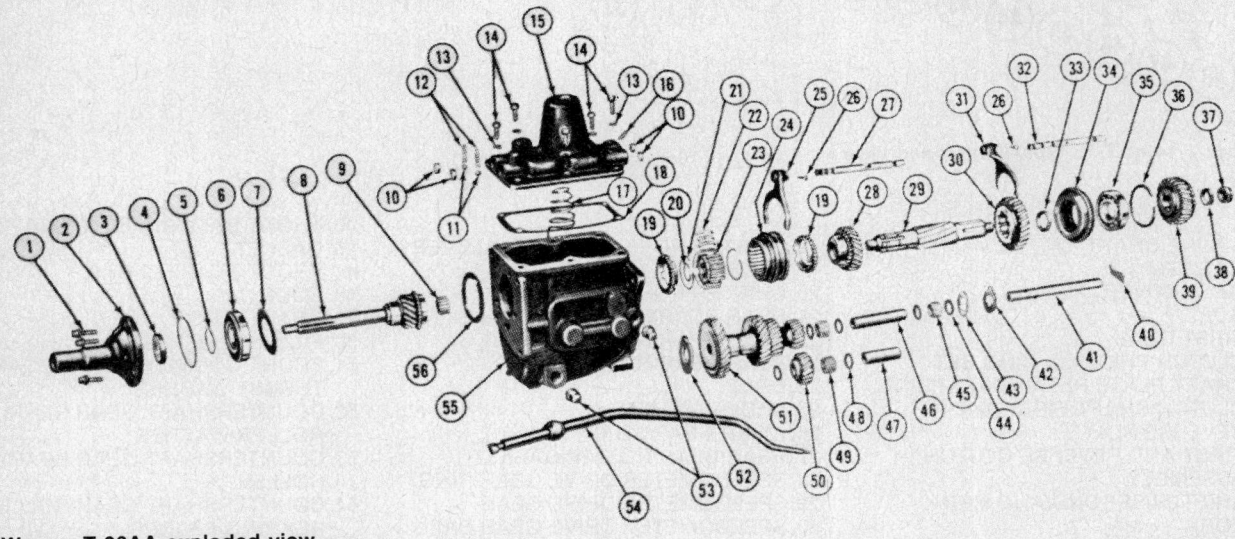

Warner T-86AA exploded view

1. BEARING RETAINER SCREWS
2. MAIN DRIVE GEAR BEARING RETAINER
3. BEARING RETAINER OIL SEAL
4. BEARING SNAP RING
5. MAIN DRIVE GEAR SNAP RING
6. MAIN DRIVE GEAR BEARING
7. FRONT BEARING OIL RETAINING WASHER
8. MAIN DRIVE GEAR
9. PILOT ROLLER BEARING
10. SHIFT RAIL CAP
11. POPPET BALL
12. POPPET SPRING
13. LOCK WASHER
14. SHIFT HOUSING BOLT
15. CONTROL HOUSING
16. INTERLOCK PLUNGER
17. SHIFT LEVER SPRING
18. SHIFT TOWER GASKET
19. BLOCKING RING
20. CLUTCH HUB SNAP RING
21. SYNCHRONIZER SPRING
22. SYNCHRONIZER PLATE
23. CLUTCH HUB
24. CLUTCH SLEEVE
25. HIGH AND INTERMEDIATE CLUTCH FORK
26. SHIFT FORK PIN
27. HIGH AND INTERMEDIATE SHIFT RAIL
28. SECOND SPEED GEAR
29. MAIN SHAFT
30. LOW AND REVERSE SLIDING GEAR
31. LOW AND REVERSE SHIFT FORK
32. LOW AND REVERSE SHIFT RAIL
33. BEARING SPACER
34. REAR BEARING ADAPTER
35. REAR BEARING
36. REAR BEARING SNAP RING
37. NUT
38. WASHER
39. TRANSFER CASE DRIVE GEAR
40. LOCK PLATE
41. COUNTERSHAFT
42. REAR COUNTERSHAFT THRUST WASHER (STEEL)
43. REAR COUNTERSHAFT THRUST WASHER (BRONZE)
44. COUNTERSHAFT BEARING WASHER
45. COUNTERSHAFT BEARING
46. COUNTERSHAFT CENTER BEARING SPACER
47. REVERSE IDLER GEAR SHAFT
48. REVERSE IDLER GEAR BEARING WASHER
49. REVERSE IDLER GEAR ROLLER BEARINGS
50. REVERSE IDLER GEAR
51. COUNTERSHAFT GEAR
52. COUNTERSHAFT FRONT THRUST WASHER
53. PLUG
54. SHIFT LEVER
55. TRANSMISSION CASE
56. RETAINER GASKET

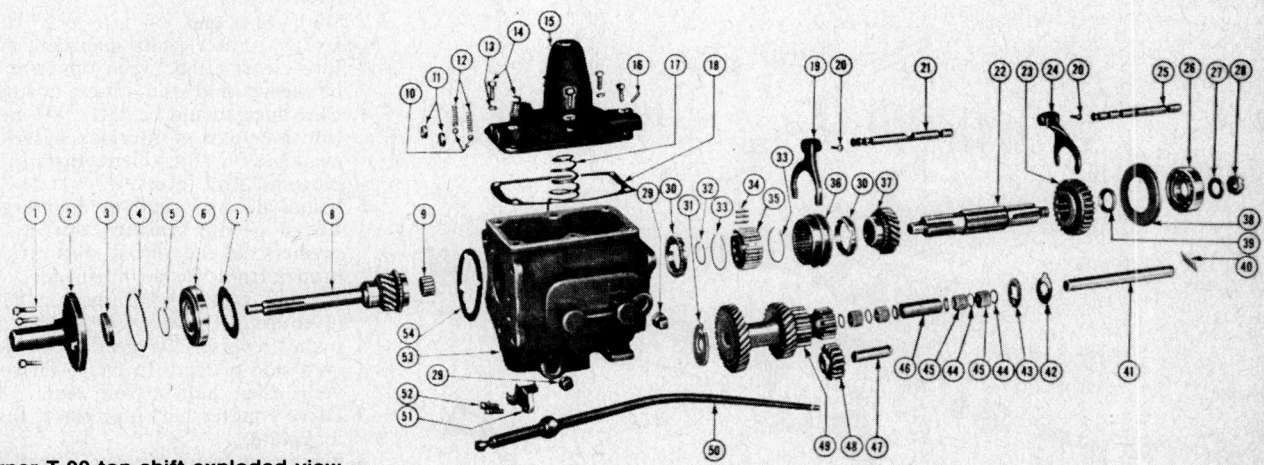

Warner T-90 top shift exploded view

1. BEARING RETAINER BOLT
2. BEARING RETAINER
3. BEARING RETAINER OIL SEAL
4. BEARING SNAP RING
5. MAIN DRIVE GEAR SNAP RING
6. MAIN DRIVE GEAR BEARING
7. FRONT BEARING WASHER
8. MAIN DRIVE GEAR
9. PILOT ROLLER BEARING
10. POPPET BALL
11. SHIFT RAIL CAP
12. POPPET SPRING
13. LOCKWASHER
14. SHIFT HOUSING BOLT
15. CONTROL HOUSING
16. INTERLOCK PLUNGER
17. SHIFT LEVER SPRING
18. SHIFT TOWER GASKET
19. HIGH AND INTERMEDIATE SHIFT FORK
20. SHIFT FORK PIN

21. HIGH AND INTERMEDIATE SHIFT RAIL
22. MAIN SHAFT
23. SLIDING GEAR
24. LOW AND REVERSE SHIFT FORK
25. LOW AND REVERSE SHIFT RAIL
26. REAR BEARING
27. MAIN SHAFT WASHER
28. MAIN SHAFT NUT
29. FILLER PLUG
30. BLOCKING RING
31. FRONT COUNTERSHAFT THRUST WASHER
32. CLUTCH HUB SNAP RING
33. SYNCHRONIZER SPRING
34. SYNCHRONIZER PLATE
35. CLUTCH HUB
36. CLUTCH SLEEVE
37. SECOND SPEED GEAR
38. REAR BEARING ADAPTER
39. BEARING SPACER

40. LOCK PLATE
41. COUNTERSHAFT
42. REAR COUNTERSHAFT THRUST WASHER
43. REAR COUNTERSHAFT THRUST WASHER
44. COUNTERSHAFT BEARING WASHER
45. COUNTERSHAFT BEARING
46. COUNTERSHAFT BEARING SPACER
47. REVERSE GEAR SHAFT
48. REVERSE IDLER GEAR
49. COUNTERSHAFT GEAR SET
50. SHIFT LEVER
51. OIL COLLECTOR*
52. OIL COLLECTOR SCREW*
53. TRANSMISSION CASE
54. BEARING RETAINER GASKET

*REMOVED ON LATER MODELS.

and a loading sleeve to facilitate reassembly of the countershaft gear components.

5 In assembling the mainshaft gears, low and reverse gear is installed with the shift shoe groove toward the front.
6 In assembling the synchronizer unit, install the two springs in the high and intermediate clutch hub with spring tension opposed. Place the right, lipped end of a spring in the slot of the

hub and place the spring in the hub. Turn the hub around and make the same installation with the other spring, starting with the same slot. Install the three synchronizer shifting plates into the three slots in the hub, with the smooth sides of the plates out. Hold the plate in position and slip the second and direct clutch sleeve over the hub, with the long beveled edge toward the long part of the

clutch hub. Install the completed assembly onto the mainshaft with the beveled edge of the clutch sleeve toward the front end of the shaft.

7 When installing the mainshaft, be sure the bearing rollers are in place in the pilot bore of the clutch gear.
8 Be sure that the countershaft and reverse idler shaft lockplate are in position and completely recessed into the indents of the transfer case.

WARNER T96 3 SPEED

Warner T96, 3-Speed

Disassembly

1 Remove top cover.
2 Remove front bearing cap, clutch shaft snap-ring, and bearing lockring.
3 Use a bearing puller and a thrust yoke to remove front bearing.
4 Remove oil slinger.
5 Remove extension housing. Replace rear bearing oil seal and extension housing bushing if necessary.
6 Remove speedometer drive gear, and retaining ball.
7 Move mainshaft assembly to rear ½ in. Lower front of clutch shaft and raise rear of countergear. Remove clutch shaft.
8 Check 21 roller bearings inside rear of clutch shaft for wear, pitting, or scoring.

9 Remove second-third shifter fork. Tilt mainshaft to remove synchro-clutch snap-ring.
10 Remove synchro-clutch, second gear, and low and reverse gear.
11 Remove low-reverse shifter fork.
12 Remove mainshaft and rear bearing from rear of case. Press rear bearing from shaft.
13 Remove reverse idler shaft and countershaft lockplate.
14 Drive countershaft out to rear with a dummy shaft. Lower dummy shaft and countergear to bottom of case.
15 Drive reverse idler shaft out to rear. Remove gear. Remove countergear.
16 Note position of reverse idler shaft thrust washers; check for wear or damage.
17 Remove outer shift levers and shifter shaft lockpin. Remove shifter shafts

from inside case. Remove two interlock ball bearings. Remove interlock sleeve, pin, and spring. Remove shifter shaft O-rings.

Inspection

1 Wash all parts in solvent.
2 Air dry.

GEARS & MAINSHAFT

1 Check for worn, cracked, or chipped teeth.
2 Check fit of gears to mainshaft. If gears are replaced, replace the gear with which they mesh.

BEARINGS

1 Check for cracked races.
2 Check for worn or scored balls.

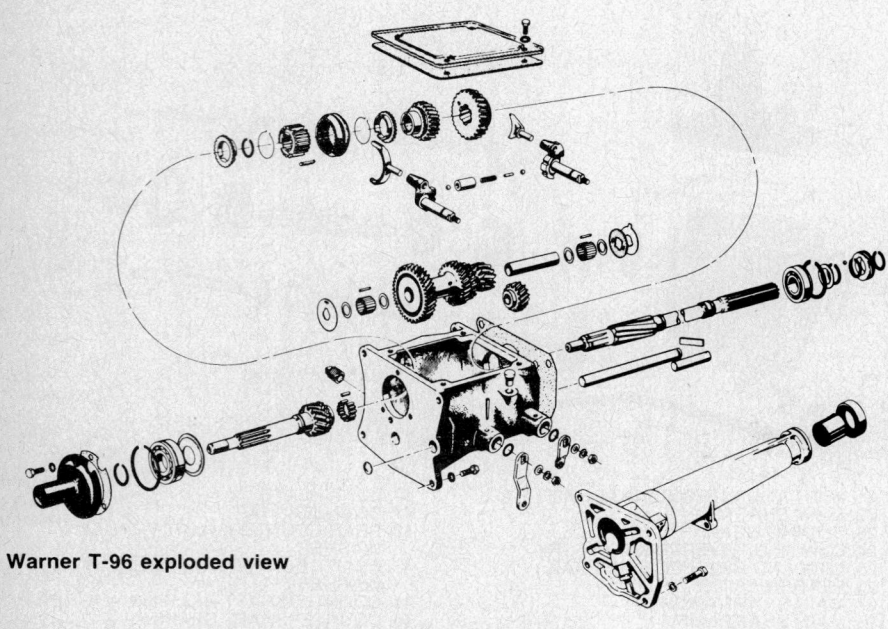

Warner T-96 exploded view

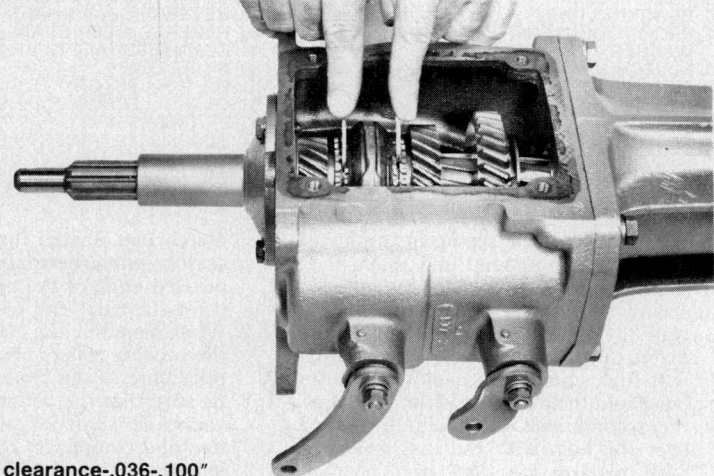

Gauging side clearance-.036-.100"

SYNCHRO-CLUTCH & FRICTION RINGS

1. Slide rings on cones of second gear and clutch shaft.
2. Replace rings if there is excessive wear or a pitted condition on the taper.

CASE

1. Check for evidence of bearings turning in their bores.
2. Check for cracks.

Assembly

1. Install new shift shaft O-rings.
2. Install low-reverse shift shaft interlock sleeve, ball bearing, and spring.
3. Install second-third shift shaft. Place second ball bearing in position.
4. Place shifter mechanism in any gear.

With one end of interlock sleeve against shifter shaft quadrant, measure clearance between opposite end of sleeve and the other quadrant. Clearance should be .001–.007 in. Selective lengths of interlock sleeves are available for adjustment. Install lockpins and shift levers.

5. Install dummy shaft in countergear. Install needle bearings, spacer, and washers. Install thrust washers. The bronze front washer must index with the case. Install countergear assembly in bottom of case.
6. Install reverse idler gear with chamfered side of teeth to front. Drive reverse idler shaft in from rear.
7. Drive countershaft into place. Install lockplate.
8. Press rear bearing on mainshaft. Install snap-rings. Place mainshaft in case.
9. Install shifter forks. Install first-reverse sliding gear, second gear, and synchro-clutch assembly, hub forward.
10. Install thickest mainshaft front snap-ring that will fit in groove.
11. There should be .003–.010 in. clearance between second gear and the mainshaft shoulder, with the synchro-clutch hub pressed against the snap-ring.
12. Hold the 21 clutch shaft bearings in place with petroleum jelly. Install front friction ring and clutch shaft on mainshaft.
13. Install the mainshaft rear bearing, align the shifter forks and gears. Guide the mainshaft into the clutch shaft.
14. Install the thickest rear mainshaft snap-ring that will fit in the groove.
15. Install retaining ball, speedometer drive gear, and snap-ring.
16. Install extension housing with a new oil seal.
17. Place oil slinger on clutch shaft with concave side to rear. Install front bearing using thrust yoke. Install thickest snap-ring that will fit in the groove.
18. Install bearing cap and a new gasket.
19. Check clearance of synchro-clutch friction rings. Both clearances should be .036–.100 in.
20. Check transmission operation in all gears. Install the case cover and gasket.

WARNER T10 4 SPEED

Warner T10, 4-Speed

Disassembly

1. Remove the side cover and shift controls.
2. Remove front bearing retainer and gasket.
3. Remove output shaft companion flange.
4. Drive lockpin up from reverse shifter lever boss. Pull shift-shaft out about ⅛ in. to disengage shifter fork from reverse gear.
5. Tap the extension (with soft hammer) rearward. When idler gear shaft is out as far as it will go, move extension to the left so the reverse fork clears the reverse gear. Remove extension and gasket.
6. Remove rear bearing snap-ring from mainshaft.

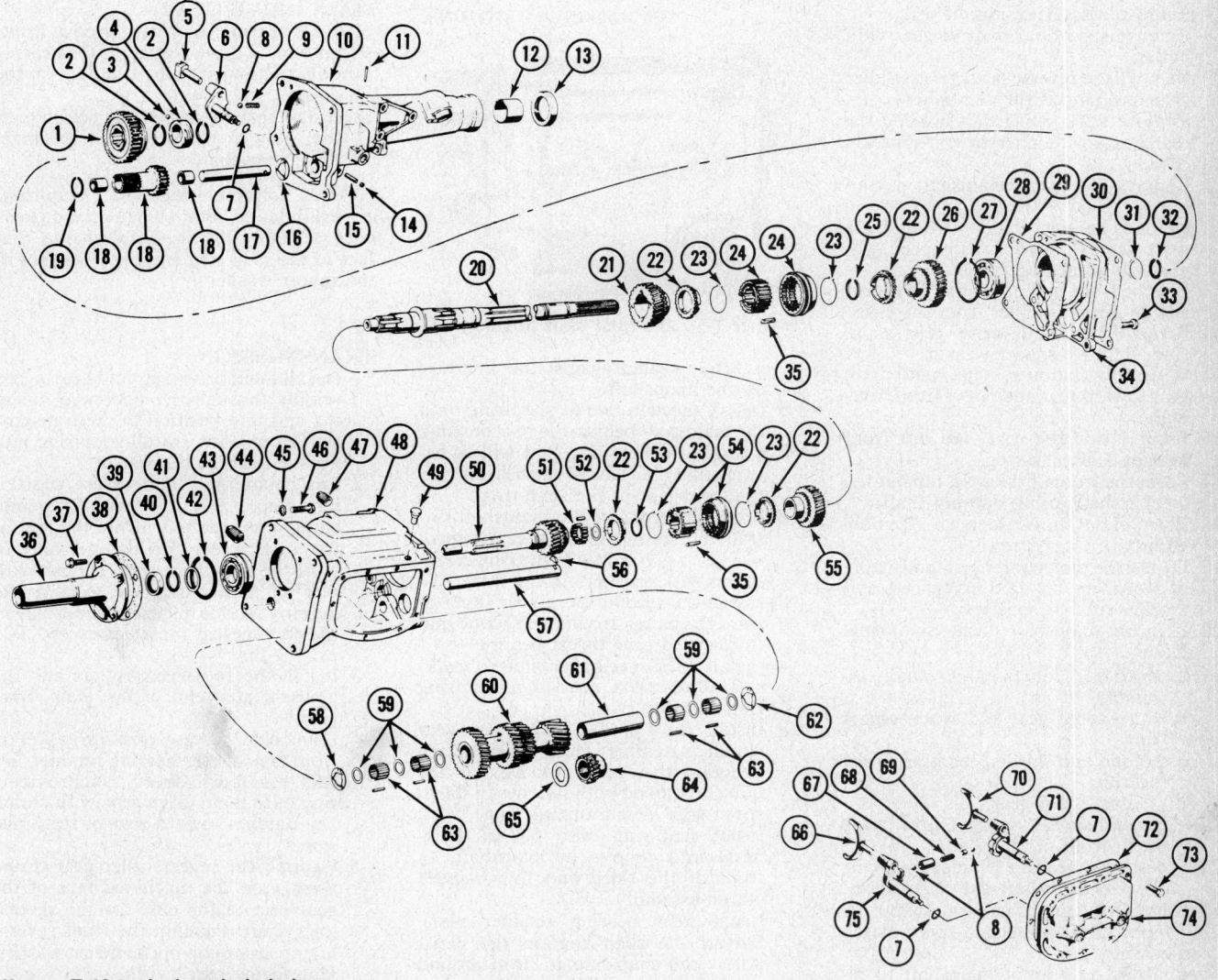

Warner T-10 typical exploded view

1. REVERSE GEAR
2. SPEEDOMETER DRIVE GEAR RING
3. SPEEDOMETER DRIVE GEAR BALL
4. SPEEDOMETER DRIVE GEAR
5. SHIFTER REVERSE FORK
6. SHIFTER FORK REVERSE SHAFT
7. SHIFTER FORK SHAFT SEAL
8. SPEED FINDER INTERLOCK POPPET
9. SPEED FINDER INTERLOCK POPPET REVERSE SPRING
10. REVERSE GEAR HOUSING
11. SHIFTER FORK SHAFT RETAINING PIN
12. REVERSE GEAR HOUSING BUSHING
13. REVERSE GEAR HOUSING SEAL
14. IDLER GEAR SHAFT PIN ACCESS PLUG
15. IDLER GEAR SHAFT RETAINING PIN
16. IDLER GEAR SHAFT THRUST WASHER
17. IDLER GEAR SHAFT
18. REVERSE IDLER GEAR AND BUSHINGS
19. REVERSE IDLER REAR SNAP RING
20. SPLINE SHAFT
21. SECOND GEAR
22. CLUTCH FRICTION RING SET
23. SHAFT PLATE RETAINING SPRING
24. FIRST AND SECOND GEAR CLUTCH ASSEMBLY
25. FIRST AND SECOND SNAP RING
26. FIRST GEAR
27. REAR BALL BEARING LOCKRING
28. REAR BALL BEARING
29. GASKET

30. GASKET
31. REAR BALL BEARING WASHER
32. REAR BALL BEARING LOCKRING
33. BOLT
34. REVERSE GEAR HOUSING ADAPTER
35. CLUTCH SHAFT PLATE
36. FRONT BEARING CAP
37. BOLT
38. FRONT BEARING CAP SHIM
39. FRONT BEARING OIL SEAL
40. FRONT BALL BEARING SNAP RING
41. FRONT BALL BEARING WASHER
42. FRONT BALL BEARING LOCKRING
43. FRONT BALL BEARING
44. DRAIN PLUG
45. LOCK WASHER
46. BOLT
47. FILLER PLUG
48. CASE
49. CASE BREATHER
50. CLUTCH SHAFT
51. SPLINE SHAFT PILOT BEARING ROLLER
52. SPLINE SHAFT PILOT BEARING ROLLER SPACER
53. THIRD AND FOURTH GEAR SNAP RING
54. THIRD AND FOURTH GEAR CLUTCH ASSEMBLY
55. THIRD GEAR
56. KEY
57. COUNTERSHAFT
58. FRONT COUNTERSHAFT GEAR THRUST WASHER

59. COUNTERSHAFT GEAR BEARING ROLLER WASHER
60. COUNTERSHAFT GEAR
61. COUNTERSHAFT GEAR ROLLER BEARING SPACER
62. REAR COUNTERSHAFT GEAR THRUST WASHER (LESS LIP)
63. COUNTERSHAFT GEAR BEARING ROLLER
64. REVERSE IDLER GEAR
65. REVERSE IDLER GEAR THRUST WASHER
66. SHIFTER THIRD AND FOURTH GEAR FORK
67. SPEED FINDER INTERLOCK SLEEVE
68. SPEED FINDER INTERLOCK POPPET SPRING
69. SPEED FINDER INTERLOCK PIN
70. SHIFTER FIRST AND SECOND GEAR FORK
71. SHIFTER FORK FIRST AND SECOND GEAR SHAFT
72. GASKET
73. BOLT
74. COVER
75. SHIFTER FORK THIRD AND FOURTH GEAR SHAFT

7 Remove case extension oil seal.

8 Remove speedometer drive gear with puller.

9 Remove the reverse gear, reverse idler gear and tanged thrust washer.

10 Remove self-locking bolt holding the rear bearing retainer to transmission case.

11 Remove the entire mainshaft assembly.

12 Unload bearing rollers from main drive gear. Remove fourth-speed synchronizer blocking ring.

13 Lift the front half of reverse idler gear and its thrust washer from the case.

14 Remove the main drive gear snapring. Remove spacer washer.

15 With soft hammer, tap main drive gear toward rear and out of front bearing.

16 From inside the case, tap out front bearing and snap-ring.

17 From the front of the case, tap out the countershaft, using dummy shaft.

18 Then lift out the countergear assembly with both tanged washers.

19 Dismantle the countergear, consisting of 80 rollers, six .050 in. spacers and a roller tubular spacer.

20 Remove mainshaft front snap-ring. Slide:
   a. third and fourth-speed clutch assembly
   b. third-speed gear and synchronizer ring
   c. second and third-speed gear thrust bearing
   d. second-speed gear
   e. second-speed synchronizer ring from front of mainshaft

21 Spread rear bearing retainer snap-ring and press mainshaft out of retainer.

22 Remove the mainshaft rear snap-ring.

23 Support first and second-speed clutch assembly
   a. Press on rear of mainshaft to remove:
   b. shaft from rear bearing
   c. first-speed gear, and synchromesh ring
   d. first and second-speed clutch sliding sleeve
   e. first-speed gear bushing

Assembly
MAINSHAFT

1 From the rear of the mainshaft, assemble first and second-speed clutch assembly to mainshaft (sliding clutch sleeve taper toward the rear, hub to the front). Press the first-speed gear bushing onto the shaft.

2 Install first-speed gear synchronizing ring. Align notches in ring with keys in hub.

3 Install first-speed gear (hub toward front) and the first-speed gear thrust washer. Grooves in the washer face first-speed gear.

4 Press on the rear bearing, with the snap-ring groove toward the front of the transmission. Be sure the bearing

SECOND GEAR POSITION

Warner T-10 2nd gear shift position

is firmly seated against the shoulder on the mainshaft.

5 Install the selective fit snap-ring onto the mainshaft behind the rear bearing. Use the thickest ring that will fit between the rear face of the bearing and the front face of the snap-ring.

6 From the front of the mainshaft, install the second-speed gear synchronizing ring. Notches in the ring correspond with the keys in the hub.

7 Install the second-speed gear (hub toward the back). Install the second and third-speed gear thrust bearing.

8 Install third-speed gear (hub to front) and third-speed gear synchronizing ring (notches front).

9 Install third and fourth-speed gear clutch assembly (hub and sliding sleeve) with taper front. Keys in the hub correspond with notches in third-speed gear synchronizing ring.

10 Install snap-ring (.086–.088 in. thickness) into groove in mainshaft, in front of the third and fourth-speed clutch assembly.

11 Install rear bearing retainer plate. Spread the snap-ring on the plate. Allow the snap-ring to drop around the rear bearing. Press on the end of the mainshaft until the snap-ring engages the groove in the rear bearing.

12 Install reverse gear (shift collar to the rear).

13 Press speedometer drive gear onto the mainshaft. Position the speedometer gear to get a measurement of 4½ in. from the center of the gear to the flat surface of the rear bearing retainer.

14 Install special snap-ring into the groove at the rear of the mainshaft.

COUNTERGEAR

1 Install countergear dummy and tubular roller bearing spacer into the countergear.

2 Using heavy grease to hold the rollers, install 20 bearing rollers in either end of the countergear, two spacers, 20 more rollers, then one spacer. Install the same combination of rollers and spacers in the other end of the countergear.

3 Set the countergear assembly in the bottom of the transmission case. Tanged thrust washers should be in their proper position.

MAIN DRIVE GEAR

1 Press bearing (snap-ring groove front) onto main drive gear until the bearing fully seats against the shoulder on the gear.

2 Install spacer washer and selective fit snap-ring in the groove in the main drive gear shaft.

NOTE: Variable thickness snap-rings are available to obtain a prescribed clearance of .000–.005 in. between the rear face of the snap ring and the front face of the spacer washer.

TRANSMISSION

1 Install main drive gear and bearing assembly through the side cover opening and into position in the transmission front bore. Install snap-ring into groove in front bearing.

2 Lift countergear and thrust washers into place. Install Woodruff key into end of countershaft. From the rear of the case, press the countershaft in until the end of the shaft is flush with rear of transmission case and the dummy shaft is displaced. End-play in the countergear must not exceed .025 in.

3 Install the 14 bearing rollers into the grease-coated end of the main drive gear.

4 Using heavy grease, position gasket on front face of rear bearing retainer. Install the fourth-speed synchronizing ring onto main drive gear with clutch key notches toward rear of transmission.

5 Position the reverse idler gear thrust washer on the machined face of the gear cast in the case for the reverse idler shaft. Position the front reverse idler gear on top of the thrust washer. Hub facing rear.

6 Lower the mainshaft assembly into the case. The notches of the fourth-speed synchronizing ring correspond to the keys in the clutch assembly.

7 Install self-locking bolt, holding the rear bearing retainer to the transmission case. Torque to 20–30 ft./lbs.

8 From the rear of the case, insert the rear reverse idler gear, engaging the splines with the portion of the gear within the case.

9 Grease gasket, and place in position on the rear face of the rear bearing retainer.

10 Install remaining tanged thrust washer into place on reverse idler shaft. The tang on the thrust washer fits in the notch in the idler thrust face of the extension.

11 Place the two clutches in neutral position.

12 Pull reverse shifter shaft to left side of extension. Rotate shaft to bring reverse fork to extreme forward position in extension. Line up forward and reverse idler gears.

13 Start the extension onto the transmis-

sion case by inserting reverse idler shaft through reverse idler gears. Push in on shifter until shift fork engages reverse gear shift collar. When the fork engages, rotate the shifter shaft to move reverse gear rearward. This will allow the extension to slide onto the transmission case.

14 Install three extension and retainer-to-case attaching bolts. Torque to 35–45 ft./lbs. Install two extension-to-

retainer attaching bolts Torque to 20–30 ft./lbs. Use sealer on the lower, right attaching bolt.

15 Adjust reverse shift shaft. Groove in shaft lines up with hole in boss. Drive in lockpin from top of boss.

16 Install the main drive gear bearing retainer and gasket. Align oil well with the oil outlet hole. Install four sealer-coated attaching bolts. Torque to 15–20 ft./lbs.

17 Install a shift fork into each clutch sleeve.

18 With both clutches in neutral, install side cover gasket and lower side cover into place.

19 Install attaching bolts. Torque to 10–20 ft./lbs. Use sealer on the lower right bolt.

20 Install first and second, and third and fourth shift levers, lock-washers and nuts.

WARNER T18 4 SPEED

WARNER T18, 4-SPEED
Disassembly

1 Remove the transmission transfer case adaptor plate and gasket.
2 Remove the transmission control housing assembly.
3 Mark the two blocking rings, third and high synchronizing gear, and third and high synchronizing sleeve. Also mark the blocking ring, low and second synchronizing gear, and low and second synchronizer sleeve.
4 Slide the low-speed gear toward the rear of the transmission case.
5 Disengage the reverse gearshift arm from the reverse idler gear and remove the reverse gearshift arm from the reverse mounting pin.
6 Move the low-speed gear back into neutral position.
7 Remove the rear bearing retainer. Remove the snap-ring from the main drive pinion (clutch shaft) and the outer race of the drive pinion ball bearing.
8 Remove the main drive pinion ball bearing and oil slinger.
9 Remove the snap-ring from the outer bearing race of the transmission mainshaft ball bearing, then, with a bearing puller, pull the bearing.
10 Separate the mainshaft assembly from the main drive pinion.
11 Lift the mainshaft assembly from the case.
12 Remove the main drive pinion from the case.
13 Remove the mainshaft pilot rollers from the drive pinion.
14 Mark the relation between the synchronizer gears and splines on the mainshaft.
15 Disassemble the mainshaft by removing the snap-ring holding the third and high synchronizer assembly onto the mainshaft.
16 Remove the snap-ring holding the second-speed synchronizer onto the mainshaft.
17 Slide the second-speed synchronizer and second-speed gear from the mainshaft.
18 Remove the two remaining snap-rings, spacer, and thrust washer from the mainshaft.

19 Remove the two large lockrings and push the synchronizer gear out of the sleeve.
20 If the second-speed synchronizer assembly is to be disassembled, wrap the assembly in a cloth to prevent losing the lock balls and springs. Push the

gear out of the sleeve in a direction opposite the shift fork groove. Remove the cloth and lift the balls, springs, and plates out of the gear.
21 Remove the lockplate for the countershaft and the reverse idler gear shaft.
22 With a pry bar in the slot of the re-

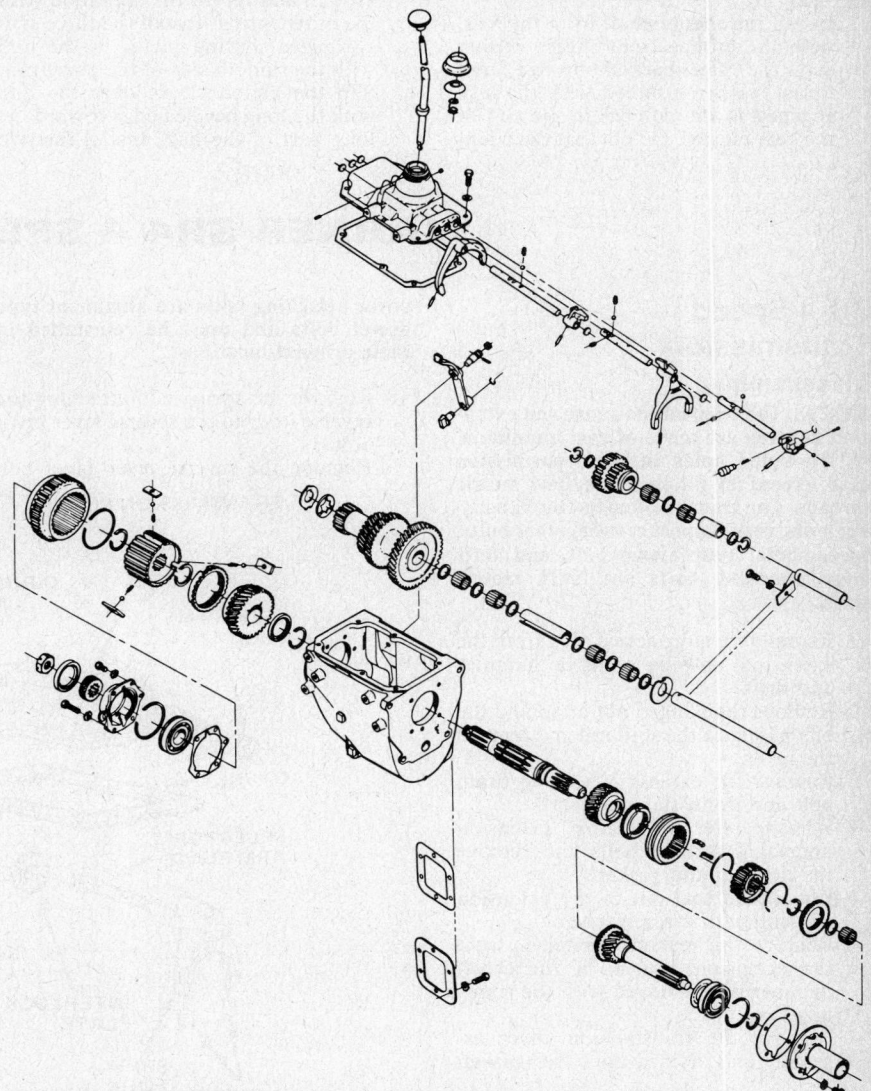

Warner T-18 4-speed manual transmission assembly, exploded view

verse idler gear shaft, loosen the shaft. Slip the reverse idler shaft out of the housing and gear. Lift the reverse idler gear from the case.

23 To remove the countershaft, use a dummy shaft, (1⅛ × 9.850 in.) to displace the countergear and keep the countergear components intact. After the countershaft has been pushed entirely out of the countergear and case, remove the gear.

24 Completely disassemble the countergear assembly.

25 To disassemble the reverse idler gear assembly, remove one of the snaprings and tap out the washer, both sets of bearing rollers, center spacer, and sleeve. Remove the remaining snapring.

Assembly

Assemble in the reverse order of disassembly. Pay particular attention to the following:

1 Install the countershaft from the rear, with the bronze front thrust washer and the steel-backed bronze rear thrust washer installed with the lugs engaged in the notches in the end of the gear cluster. Do not seat the coun-

tershaft until the reverse idler gear and shaft have been installed.

2 Install the reverse idler shaft until the lockplate slot is adjacent to the countershaft slot. Insert the lock-plate and tap the shafts together.

3 Assemble the second-speed synchronizer by installing the low-second hub into low-second gear. Install the retaining ring in the gear. Slide the hub out of the gear until the holes in the hub are clear of the gear. Install the shifter plates and springs. Push the hub back into the gear. Push a shifter plate toward the center of the gear while installing the ball. Repeat for the other two balls. Push the hub into the gear until the balls snap into position.

4 Assemble the third-fourth synchronizer by installing the springs with the tension opposed. Place the right, lipped end of one spring in a hub slot. Place the spring in hub. Turn the hub around and repeat the operation with the other spring. Install the three synchronizer shifting plates in the hub with the smooth side of the plates out. Slip the clutch sleeve over the hub with the long beveled edge toward the long part of the hub. Install the two

blocking rings.

5 Assemble the mainshaft, placing the threaded end up. Install the snap-ring and thrust washer with the recessed side covering the snap-ring. Install the bearing rollers around the shaft and hold them with a rubber band. Install the spacer. Install the second gear, tapered shoulder up. Install the snapring and blocking ring. Install the second-speed synchronizer and snapring. Install third gear, tapered shoulder to front. Install the thirdfourth synchronizer assembly and snap-ring.

6 Install the main drive gear assembly and bearings in front of the case and mainshaft assembly through the top of the case. Temporarily install the bearing retainer.

7 Install the mainshaft bearing snapring; press the bearing into the case. Remove the bearing retainer. Install the oil slinger and snap-ring. Press the main drive gear bearing into the case. Use the thickest snap-ring that will fit in the groove.

8 Measure the space between the main drive gear bearing retainer and the case. Install a gasket 0.003–0.005 in. thicker than this measurement.

WARNER SR4 4 SPEED

SR 4-Speed Transmission

Disassembly

NOTE: The transmission case and extension housing are made of cast aluminum. All threaded holes in the transmission case, except the fill plug hole, have metric threads. The transmission-to-clutch housing bolts, rear support crossmember bolts, speedometer gear clamp bolt, and shift lever attaching bolts are NOT metric sizes.

1 Remove the large access plug from the extension housing using a hammer and drift.

2 Remove the flanged nut attaching the offset lever to the shift rail and remove the lever.

3 Remove the extension housing drain bolt and drain the lubricant.

4 Remove the remaining extension housing attaching bolts and remove the housing and gasket.

5 Pry the oil seal out of the extension housing with a screwdriver.

6 Remove the rear crossmember from the extension housing if the crossmember was removed with the transmission.

7 Remove the transmission cover assembly and discard the cover gasket.

NOTE: The right rear and front left (looking from the rear, down from the top)

cover attaching bolts are alignment type dowel bolts and must be reinstalled in their original locations.

8 Remove the spring clip attaching the reverse lever to the reverse lever pivot bolt.

9 Remove the reverse lever pivot bolt

and remove the reverse lever and fork as an assembly.

10 Punch alignment marks in the front bearing cap and transmission case for reference during assembly and remove the bearing cap and gasket. Throw away the gasket.

11 Remove the speedometer gear snap-

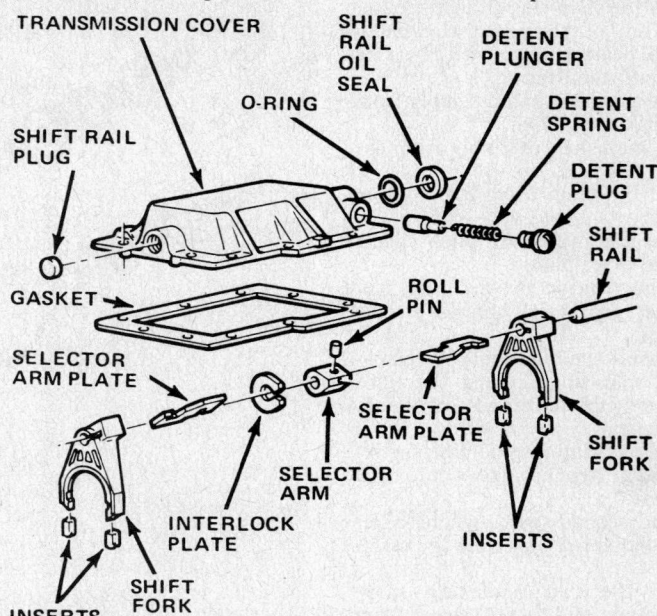

Exploded view of the SR4 4-Speed cover and shift mechanism

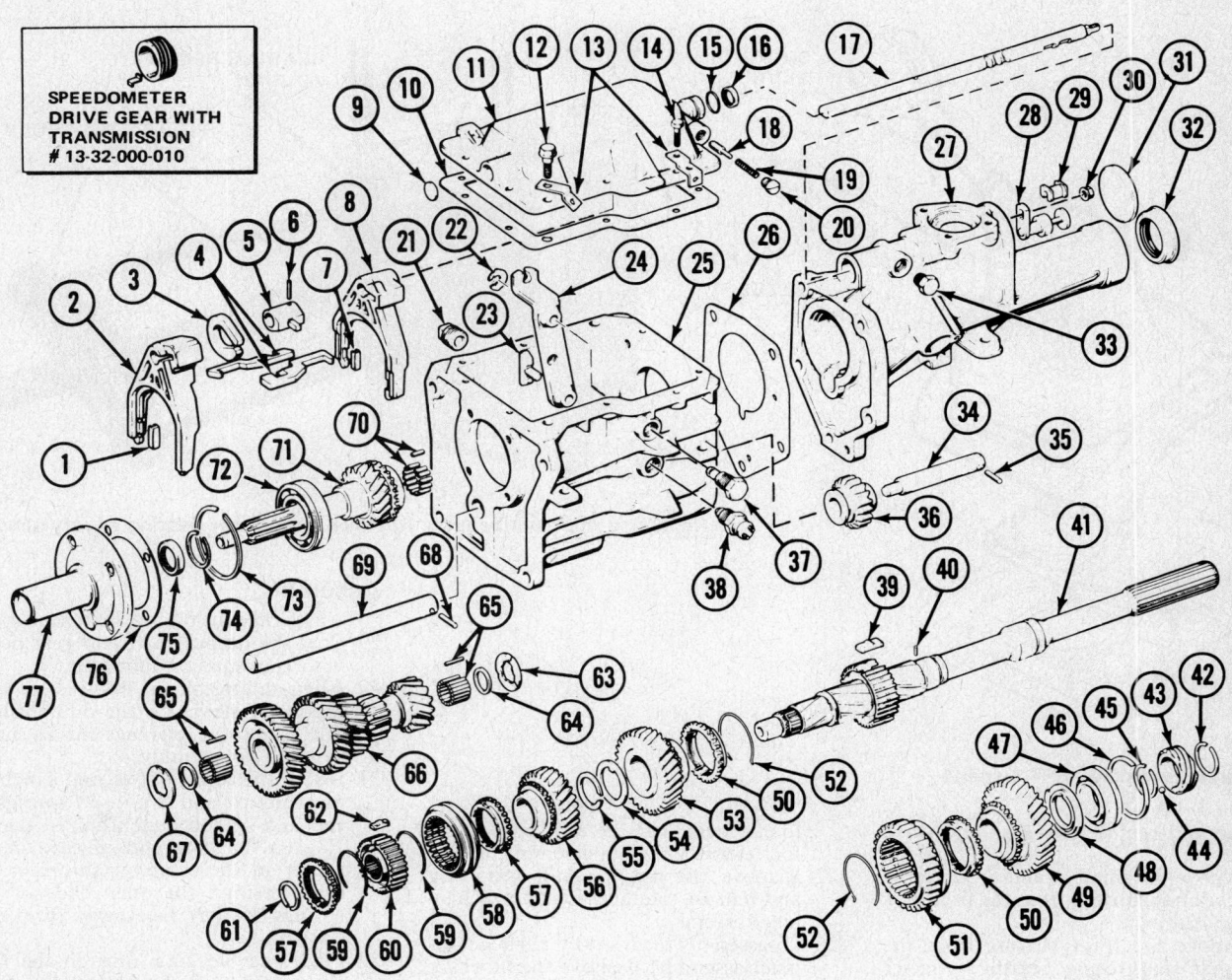

SPEEDOMETER
DRIVE GEAR WITH
TRANSMISSION
13-32-000-010

Exploded view of the SR4 4-Speed Transmission

1. Third-fourth shift fork insert (2)
2. Third-fourth shift fork
3. Interlock plate
4. Selector arm plate (2)
5. Selector arm
6. Selector arm roll pin
7. First-second shift fork insert (2)
8. First-second shift fork
9. Shift rail plug
10. Transmission cover gasket
11. Transmission cover
12. Transmission cover dowel bolt (2)
13. Clip
14. Transmission cover bolt (8)
15. Shift rail O-ring seal
16. Shift rail oil seal
17. Shift rail
18. Detent plunger
19. Detent spring
20. Detent plug
21. Fill plug
22. Reverse lever pivot bolt spring clip
23. Reverse lever fork
24. Reverse lever
25. Transmission case
26. Extension housing gasket
27. Extension housing
28. Offset lever

29. Offset lever insert
30. Offset lever retaining nut
31. Access plug
32. Extension housing oil seal
33. Threaded plug
34. Reverse idler shaft
35. Reverse idler shaft roll pin
36. Reverse idler gear
37. Reverse lever pivot bolt
38. Backup lamp switch
39. First-second synchronizer insert (3)
40. First gear roll pin
41. Output shaft and hub assembly
42. Speedometer gear snap ring
43. Speedometer gear
44. Speedometer gear drive ball
45. Rear bearing retaining snap ring
46. Rear bearing locating snap ring
47. Rear bearing
48. First gear thrust washer
49. First gear
50. First-second synchronizer blocking ring (2)
51. First-second synchronizer sleeve
52. First-second synchronizer insert spring (2)
53. Second gear
54. Second gear thrust washer (tabbed)

55. Second gear snap ring
56. Third gear
57. Third-fourth synchronizer blocking ring (2)
58. Third-fourth synchronizer sleeve
59. Third-fourth synchronizer insert spring (2)
60. Third-fourth synchronizer hub
61. Output shaft snap ring
62. Third-fourth synchronizer insert (3)
63. Countershaft gear rear thrust washer (metal)
64. Countershaft needle bearing retainer (2)
65. Countershaft needle bearing (50)
66. Countershaft gear
67. Countershaft gear front thrust washer (plastic)
68. Countershaft roll pin
69. Countershaft
70. Clutchshaft roller bearings (15)
71. Clutchshaft
72. Front bearing
73. Front bearing locating snap ring
74. Front bearing retaining snap ring
75. Front bearing cap oil seal
76. Front bearing cap gasket
77. Front bearing cap

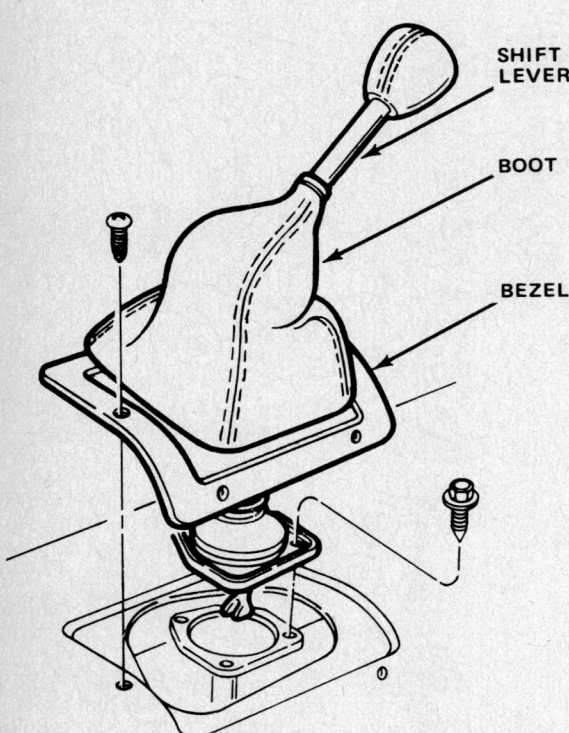

Floorshift assembly—SR4 4-speed

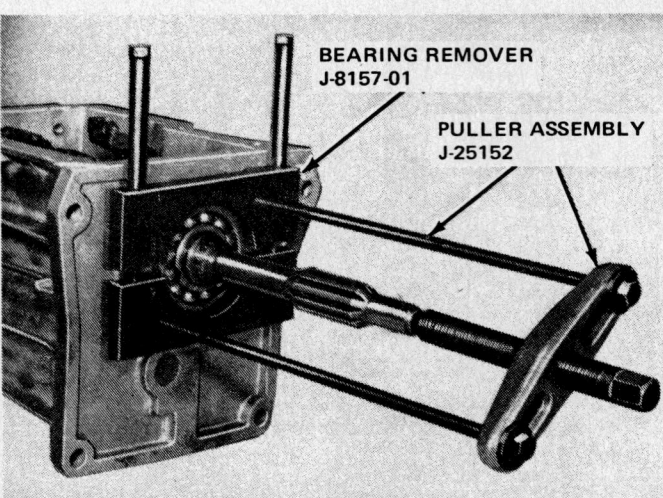

Removing the front bearing. Removal of the rear bearing is very similar

ring and remove the gear and drive ball.

12 Remove the small retaining and large locating snap-rings from the front and rear bearings.

13 Remove the front bearing from the clutch shaft using bearing remover tool #J-8157–01 with a puller and sufficiently long threaded stock with nuts and washers.

14 Remove the clutch shaft assembly from the case.

15 Remove the rear bearing from the output shaft using the same setup used to remove the front bearing.

16 Remove the output shaft and gear train as an assembly. Be careful not to allow the first-second or third-fourth gear synchronizer sleeves to separate from the hub during removal.

17 Push the reverse idler gear shaft out the rear of the case and remove the shaft and reverse idler gear.

18 Drive the countershaft out the rear of the case with a hammer and large drift.

19 Remove the countershaft gear thrust washers and any clutch shaft pilot bearings that fell into the case during disassembly. Note that the front countershaft gear thrust washer is plastic and the rear washer is metal.

20 Remove the needle bearing retainers and the 50 countershaft needle bearings from the countershaft gear.

To disassemble the output shaft gear train:

21 Scribe alignment marks on the third-

fourth synchronizer hub and sleeve for reference during assembly.

22 Remove the output shaft snap-ring and remove the third-fourth synchronizer assembly.

23 Disassembly the third-fourth synchronizer assembly. Remove the blocking rings, insert springs and inserts and separate the sleeve from the hub.

24 Remove third gear.

25 Remove second gear retaining snap-ring, remove the tabbed thrust washer anb remove the second gear and blocking ring.

26 Remove the first gear thrust washer and first gear rollpin from the rear of the output shaft, using a pair of wire cutters to remove the rollpin.

NOTE: The slide of the thrust washer with the oil groove and rollpin locating slot must face first gear when assembled.

27 Remove the first gear and blocking ring.

28 Scribe alignment marks on the first-second sleeve and output shaft hub for reference during assembly and remove the insert spring and inserts retaining the sleeve. Remove the sleeve from the output shaft hub.

CHILTON CAUTION: *Do not attempt to remove the first-second-reverse hub from the output shaft because the hub and shaft are assembled and machined as a matched set during manufacture to insure they both have the same center of rotation.*

Assembly

To assemble the output shaft gear train:

29 Coat the output shaft and gear bores with transmission lubricant.

30 Align and install the first-second synchronizer sleeve on the output shaft hub using the reference marks made prior to disassembly.

31 Install the three first-second synchronizer inserts and two insert springs in the first-second synchronizer sleeve. Engage the tang end of each insert spring in the same synchronizer insert. Position the open ends of the springs so they face away from one another.

32 Place the blocking ring on the first gear and install the gear and ring on the output shaft. Make sure the synchronizer inserts engage the notches in the first gear blocking ring.

33 Install the first gear rollpin in the output shaft.

34 Place the blocking ring on the second gear and install the gear and ring on the output shaft. Make sure the synchronizer inserts engage the notches in the second gear blocking ring.

35 Install the second gear thrust washer and snap-ring on the output shaft. Make sure the sharp edge of the washer faces outward and the tab is engaged in the output shaft notch.

36 Measure the second gear end-play with a feeler gauge between the gear and the thrust washer. End-play should be 0.004–0.014 in. If the end-play is excessive, replace the thrust washer and snap-ring and check the synchronizer hub for excessive wear.

NOTE: If any output shaft gear is replaced, the countershaft gear must also be replaced to maintain proper gear mesh and prevent gear noise.

37 Place the blockin ring on the third gear and install the gear and ring on the output shaft.

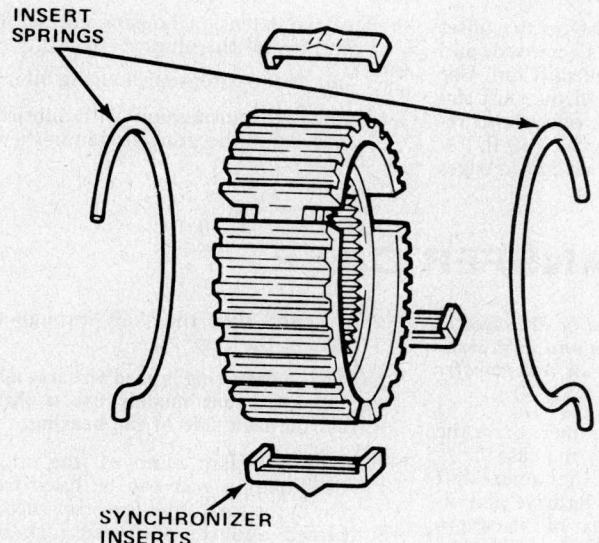

INSERT SPRINGS

SYNCHRONIZER INSERTS

Arrangement and installation of the synchronizer insert springs. Third-fourth and first-second synchronizer insert spring assembly and installation are the same

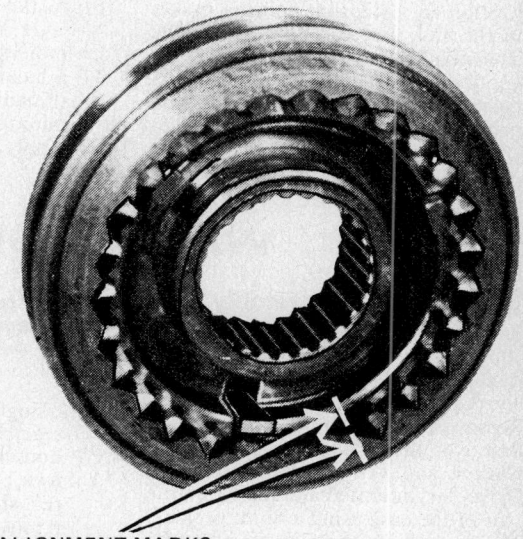

ALIGNMENT MARKS

Marking 3rd-4th synchronizer assembly—SR4 4-speed

38 Align and install the third-fourth synchronizer sleeve on the third-fourth synchronizer hub using the reference marks made during disassembly.

39 Install the three third-fourth synchronizer inserts and the two insert springs in the third-fourth synchronizer sleeve. Engage the tang end of each insert spring in the same synchronizer but position the open ends of the springs so they face away from one another.

40 Install the assembled third-fourth synchronizer on the output shaft with the machined groove in the synchronizer facing forward and install the output shaft snap-ring. Be sure the synchronizer inserts engage the notches in the third gear blocking rings.

41 Measure the output shaft end-play with a feeler gauge inserted between the snap-ring and the third-fourth synchronizer hub. End-play should be 0.004–0.014 in. If the end-play is excessive, replace the snap-ring and inspect the synchronizer hub for wear on the thrust faces.

NOTE: Remember that if any output shaft gear is replaced, the countershaft gear must also be replaced to maintain proper gear mesh and prevent gear noise.

To assemble the transmission case:

42 Coat the countershaft gear thrust wahers with petroleum jelly and position them in the case. The plastic washer is placed at the front of the case and the metal one at the rear.

43 Lubricate the 50 countershaft gear needle bearings with petroleum jelly and install the bearings in the bearing bores at the front and rear of the gear. Install the needle bearing retainers.

44 Position the assembled countershaft gear in the case and install the countershaft from the rear of the case. Make sure the thrust washers are not displaced during the installation of the countershaft and gear.

45 Position the reverse idle gear in the case with the shift lever groove facing toward the front of the case and install the reverse idler shaft from the rear of the case.

46 Install the output shaft and gear train in the case, Be careful not to disturb the position of the synchronizer assemblies during installation.

47 Install the fourth gear blocking ring in the third-fourth synchronizer sleeve. Make sure the synchronizer inserts engage the notches in the blocking ring.

48 Coat the pilot roller bearing bore of the clitch shaft with petroleum jelly and install the 15 roller bearings, Install the clutch shaft in the case and engage it with the third-fourth synchronizer sleeve and blocking ring.

49 Position the front bearing onto the clutch shaft. Position the output shaft first gear against the rear of the case. Align the bearing with the bearing bore in the case and drive the bearing completely onto the clutch shaft and into the case using a length of pipe with an inside diameter slightly larger than the outside diameter of the clutch shaft and a hammer.

NOTE: In order to tell the front and rear bearings apart, the rear bearing race has a notch, while the front bearing race has not.

50 Install the front bearing retaining and locating snap-rings.

51 Install the front bearing cap oil in the front bearing cap.

52 Install the front bearing cap gasket and cap. Make sure the groove in the cap and the cutout in the gasket are aligned with the oil hole in the case. Coat the bearing cap attaching bolts with sealant (non-hardening) and tighten them to 13 ft./lbs.

53 Make sure the first gear thrust washer is correctly installed and is engaged on the first gear rollpin, then, install the rear bearing using the same technique used to install the front bearing.

54 Install the retaining and locating snap rings on the rear bearing.

55 Install the speedometer gear drive ball in the output shaft and install the speedometer gear and snap-ring.

56 Position the reverse lever in the case. Apply non-hardening sealant to the threads of the reverse lever pivot bolt and partially install the bolt in the case. Mount the reverse lever on the pivot bolt and install the spring clip. Tighten the pivot bolt to 20 ft/lbs. Make sure the reverse lever fork is engaged in the reverse idler gear.

57 Rotate the clutch shaft and output shaft gears. If the blocking rings tend to stick on the gear cones, release the rings by gently prying them off the gear cones with a screwdriver.

58 Place the reverse lever in the Neutral position and install the transmission cover gasket and cover assembly on the case. With non-hardening sealant applied to the threads of the cover retaining bolts, install the bolts and alternately and evenly tighten them to 10 ft/lbs.

NOTE: Make sure the two cover dowel bolts are installed in their original positions; right rear and front left corners, looking from the rear and down from the top.

59 Position the extension housing gasket on the case and carefully install the extension housing.

60 Apply non-hardening sealer to the extension housing attaching bolts and install the bolts, tightening them to 23 ft/lbs.

61 Install the nylon insert on the offset lever, if the insert was removed, and mount the lever on the shift rail. Use a locking compound on the shift rail threads and install the offset lever retaining nut, tightening it to 10 ft/lbs.

62 Apply non-hardening sealant to edges of the extension housing access plug and install the plug.

63 Install the extension housing oil seal.

64 Fill the transmission with lubricant and install the transmission in the vehicle.

WARNER SR4 TRANSFER CASE

Transfer Case Disassembly

The transfer case can be disassembled as follows:

1 Remove the rear bearing cap assembly.

2 Remove the bottom cover.

3 Remove the lockplate bolt, lockwasher, and lock plate.

4 Drive the intermediate shaft out the rear of the case using a dummy shaft. This tool allows the two sets of needle bearings and three spacers to remain in position as the shaft is withdrawn. The aligner should be centered in the intermediate gear assembly to avoid interference from the thrust washers.

5 Remove the intermediate gear through the bottom of the case.

6 Remove the front output shaft yoke. Remove the felt oil seal, the oil seal gasket and front oil seal.

7 Remove the rear cover.

CHILTON CAUTION: *When removing the rear cover, care should be exercised to avoid damaging the gasket and shim separating the cover plate from the transfer case.*

8 Using a soft-faced hammer, drive the rear bearing cup from the case.

9 Loosen and remove the inner shift fork bolt. Tap the underdrive and direct shift rail to the rear of the case to remove the shift rail cap. Tap the inner rail out the front of the case. The main gear and inner shift fork can then be removed.

NOTE: Front refers to the transmission side of the transfer case.

10 Remove the shift rail housing assembly from the case and outer shift rail.

11 Wedge the front bearing cone and roller assembly from its seat on the output shaft. Drive the front bearing cone out of the case. Loosen the snap-ring and slide the shaft through the rear of the case.

NOTE: A snap-ring is used on early models only. Current models use a thrust washer on each side of the bearing.

12 With the shaft removed, the output shaft sliding gear can be lifted from the outer fork. The fork can then be turned and the shift rail fork bolt removed.

Transfer Case Assembly

NOTE: Design changes have been incorporated in the mainshaft, intermediate, and output shaft gears on silent type transfer cases. These late design gears are not interchangeable with early type gears. Should replacement be required, individual gears should be replaced with the identifying numbers on each.

1 Slide the front-wheel drive shift rail partially into the case. Place the front-

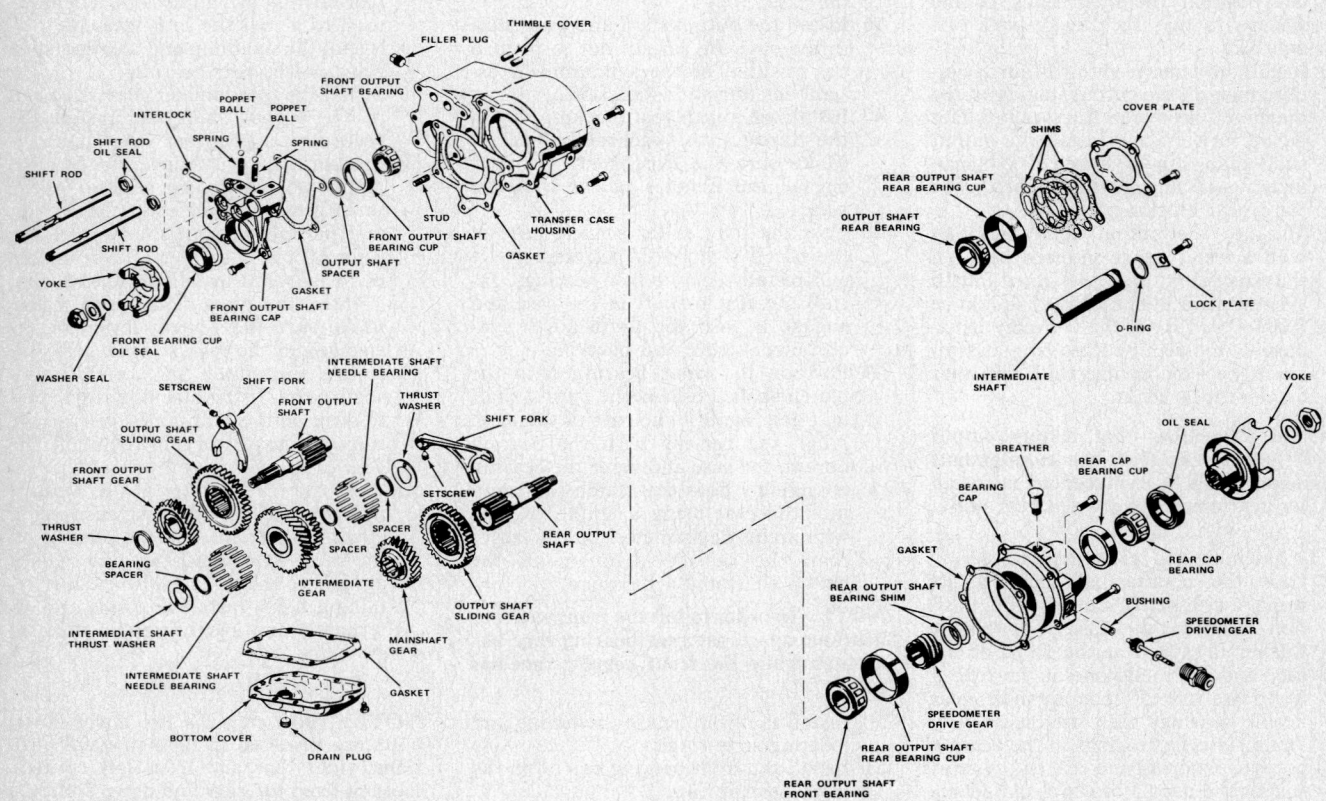

Model 20 transfer case exploded view

wheel drive shift fork on the rail with the shift rod fork bolt hole aligned with the countersunk hole on the rail. Replace the shift rail fork bolt and torque to 12–15 ft./lbs. Replace the safety wire.

2 Place the front-wheel drive shift fork in the proper position in the case. Set the front output shaft sliding gear in the shift fork with the gear facing the front of the transfer case.

3 Install the rear cone and roller on the front output shaft.

4 Hold the output shaft gear in place and insert the output shaft.

5 Install the thrust washer and snap-ring.

NOTE: A snap-ring is used on early models only. Current models use a thrust washer on each side of the bearing.

6 Install the front cone and roller on the front output shaft.

7 Install the front and rear bearing cup.

8 Install the shift rail housing gasket, shift rail housing, lockwashers, and bolts, and torque to 28–30 ft./lbs.

9 Replace the rear cover shim set, rear cover plate, lockwashers, and bolts (28–32 ft./lbs.).

10 Check the output shaft bearing adjustment using a dial indicator. Position the shaft in the extreme rear position. Set the dial indicator on zero, and pry the output shaft forward. A reading of 0.001–0.003 in. should be obtained. This clearance can be altered by changing the rear cover shims. Shims for this adjustment are available as follows: 0.003 in., 0.010 in., 0.031 in.

11 Position the outer shift rail so it will allow the shift rail interlocks to enter the detents in the rod as the inner shift rail is inserted in the shift rod housing.

12 Start the inner drive shift rail into the case along with its shift fork. Place the mainshaft gear on the fork with the gear facing the front of the transfer case. Push the shift rail into the case and through the fork until the countersunk hole on the rod aligns with the

shift fork bolt hole. Replace the bolt and torque to 12–15 ft./lbs.

13 Place the thrust washers, with the tang aligned to the groove, in the case. The rear thrust washer can be held in place by just starting the intermediate shaft into the case. The front thrust washer can be held with heavy grease.

14 Position the intermediate gear in the case. Using a soft-faced hammer, drive the intermediate shaft into the intermediate gear. Install the intermediate shaft lockplate, lockwasher, and bolt. Torque to 12–15 ft./lbs.

15 Install the rear bearing cap assembly. Torque the long bolt and four short bolts 28–32 ft./lbs.

16 Tap the shift rail cups about ⅜ in. into the case.

17 Install the lower cover gasket, the lower cover, lockwashers, and bolts (torque to 12–15 ft./lbs.).

18 Replace the oil seal gasket and felt oil seal.

19 Install the front and rear propeller shaft yokes (225–250 ft./lbs.).

WARNER SR4 (WITH QUATRA-TRAC)

Quadra-Trac Rear Case Cover R&R

Most Quadra-Trac components can be serviced without removing the complete unit from the vehicle. To gain access to the rear output shaft, drive sprocket and thrust washer, chain, differential and needle bearing, or the diaphragm control system, just the rear cover has to be removed.

1 Lift and support the vehicle.

2 If the vehicle is equipped with a reduction unit, continue on to the next step for the reduction unit removal procedure. If the vehicle is not equipped with a reduction unit, proceed to Step 7.

3 Loosen all the bolts that attach the reduction unit to the transfer case cover.

4 Move the reduction unit backward just enough to allow the oil to drain

from the unit.

5 Loosen the cable retaining bolt at the shift control lever. Loosen the cable clamp bolt and remove the control cable from the clamp bracket and control lever.

6 When the oil has drained, remove the bolts which hold the reduction unit to the transfer case cover. Move the reduction unit rearward to clear the transmission output shaft and pinion

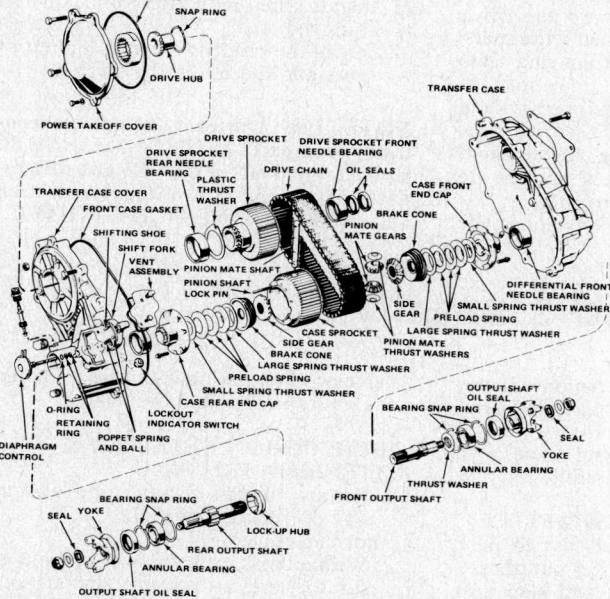

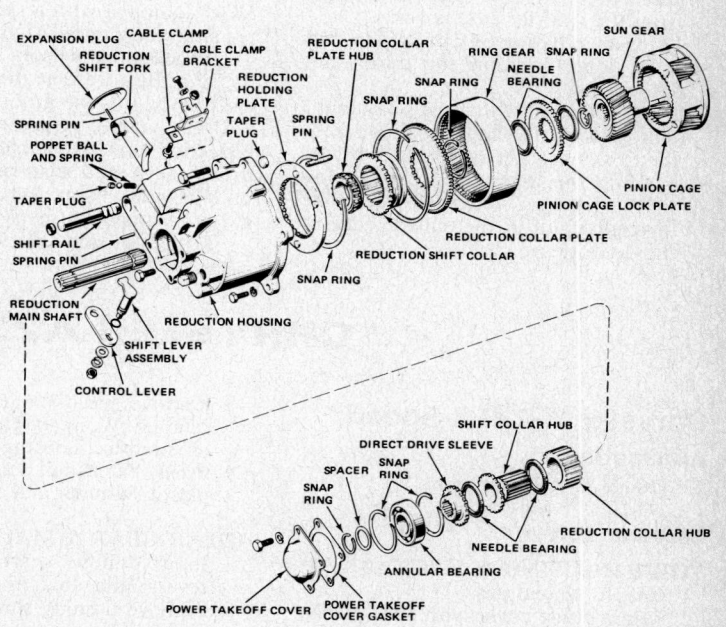

Quadra Trac lower unit, exploded view

MANUAL TRANSMISSIONS

cage which is attached to the transfer case drive sprocket. The pinion cage will remain with the transfer case assembly.

NOTE: The pinion cage should not be removed if the transfer case cover assembly is to be removed, but may be removed for inspection or replacement if the transfer case cover assembly is to remain in the vehicle. Removal of the pinion cage involves only removing the snap-ring which holds the cage to the sprocket and sliding the cage backward.

7 Remove the transfer case drain plug and allow the unit to drain.
8 Mark the rear output shaft yoke and universal joint to provide an alignment reference during reassembly. Disconnect the rear propeller shaft front universal joint from the transfer case rear yoke.
9 Mark the diaphragm control vacuum hoses for identification during reassembly, then disconnect them. Remove the lock-up indicator switch wire and the speedometer cable. Remove the indicator switch.
10 Disconnect the parking brake cable guide from the pivot on the right frame side.
11 Remove the bolts which attach the case cover assembly to the case (front housing). Carefully slide the cover assembly backward off the front output shaft and the transmission output shaft.
12 To disassemble the unit, remove the rear output shaft yoke.
13 If the unit is *not* equipped with a reduction unit, remove the power take-off cover from the rear of the transfer case cover. Remove the sealing ring from the transfer case cover.
14 Using a piece of wood 2 in. × 4 in. and 6 in. long, position the cover and sprocket.
15 If *not* equipped with a reduction unit, remove the drive hub and sleeve from the drive sprocket rear splines by expanding the internal snap-ring. The ring expanding tabs are accessible through a slot in the outside edge of the drive sleeve.

If equipped with a reduction unit, remove the pinion cage snap-ring and carrier. Lift the case cover from the drive sprocket and differential. The cover, rear output shaft, bearings and seal, drive sprocket rear needle bearing, and lock-up hub can now be serviced without any further disassembly of other components.
16 Slide the drive sprocket toward the differential unit and remove the chain. The differential unit may now be serviced without any further disassembly of other components.

Quadra-Trac Assembly and Rear Case Cover Installation

1 Position the drive sprocket on a block of wood 2 in. × 4 in. and 6 in. long.
2 Place the differential assembly about 2 in. from the drive sprocket with the front end of the differential on the bench.
3 Position the drive chain around the drive sprocket and the differential assembly. Be sure that the chain is properly engaged with the sprocket and differential teeth and that the slack is removed from the chain.
4 Insert the rear output shaft into the differential.
5 Shift the lock-up hub rearward in the case cover. Lubricate the drive sprocket thrust washer and insert it in position on the case cover.
6 Carefully align the case cover and position it onto the drive sprocket and differential. The output shaft may have to be slightly rotated to align it with the lock-up hub. Be sure that the drive sprocket thrust washer stays positioned correctly.
7 If equipped with a reduction unit, install the pinion cage onto the drive sprocket rear splines. Install the snap-ring. Be sure that the snap-ring seats properly in the groove.

If the vehicle is *not* equipped with a reduction unit, assemble the drive hub, drive sleeve, and snap-ring. Install them onto the drive sprocket rear splines. Be sure the snap-ring seats properly.
8 Rotate the drive sleeve or pinion cage

to be sure the drive sprocket thrust washer did not come out of position. No binding should be present.
9 If *not* equipped with a reduction unit, install the power take-off sealing ring and cover and tighten the screws.
10 Install the speedometer gear on the rear output shaft.
11 Install the rear output shaft oil seal and the rear yoke and nut. Tighten the nut.
12 Clean the front oil seal gasket groove. Install the seal.
13 Install two ⅜ in.-16 × 2 in. long pilot studs into the transfer case front cover housing.
14 Insert the oil tube into the case bore at the front output shaft bearing boss. Insert a 6 in. length of 5/16 in. rod into the tube. The rod will be used as a pilot to align the tube with the case cover.
15 Lift the cover assembly and align the tube pilot with the hole in the cover. Move the assembly forward over the pilot studs.
16 Move the cover assembly forward to mesh with the front output shaft and transmission output shaft. It may be necessary to rotate the rear output shaft slightly to allow the two sets of splines to engage.
17 When the cover is evenly touching the front half of the case, remove the pilot studs and install the rear cover attaching bolts. Tighten the bolts alternately and evenly.
18 Install the Lock-Out indicator switch and connect the Lock-Out switch wire, diaphragm control vacuum hoses, and the speedometer cable.
19 Install the rear drive shaft.
20 Install the parking brake cable guide to the pivot on the right frame side.
21 Install the reduction unit, if so equipped.
22 Install the proper type and amount of lubricant and lower the vehicle.

NOTE: Use lubricant blend: concentrate, Jeep part #8123004-8oz. SAE 30 non-detergent motor oil—4.5 pts. with reduction unit, 3.5 pts. without reduction unit. THERE IS NO SUBSTITUTE!

CHRYSLER A230 3 SPEED

Chrysler A-230 3-Speed
Applications
All Dodge & Plymouth cars

Disassembly
SHIFT HOUSING & MECHANISM
1 Shift to second gear.
2 Remove side cover with shift mechanism.
If shaft O-ring seals need replacement:
3 Pull shift forks out of shafts.

3 Remove speedometer pinion adapter retainer. Work adapter and pinion out of extension housing.
4 Break extension housing loose with plastic hammer and carefully remove.

IDLER GEAR & MAINSHAFT
1 Insert dummy shaft in case to push reverse idler shaft and key out of case.
2 Remove dummy shaft and idler gear together to prevent losing rollers.
3 Remove both tanged idler gear thrust washers.

4 Remove operating levers from shafts.
5 Deburr shafts. Remove shafts.

DRIVE PINION RETAINER & EXTENSION HOUSING
1 Remove pinion retainer and gasket. Pry off retainer oil seal.
For clearance:
2 With a brass drift, tap drive pinion as far forward as possible. Rotate cut away part of second gear next to countershaft gear. Shift second-third synchronizer sleeve forward.

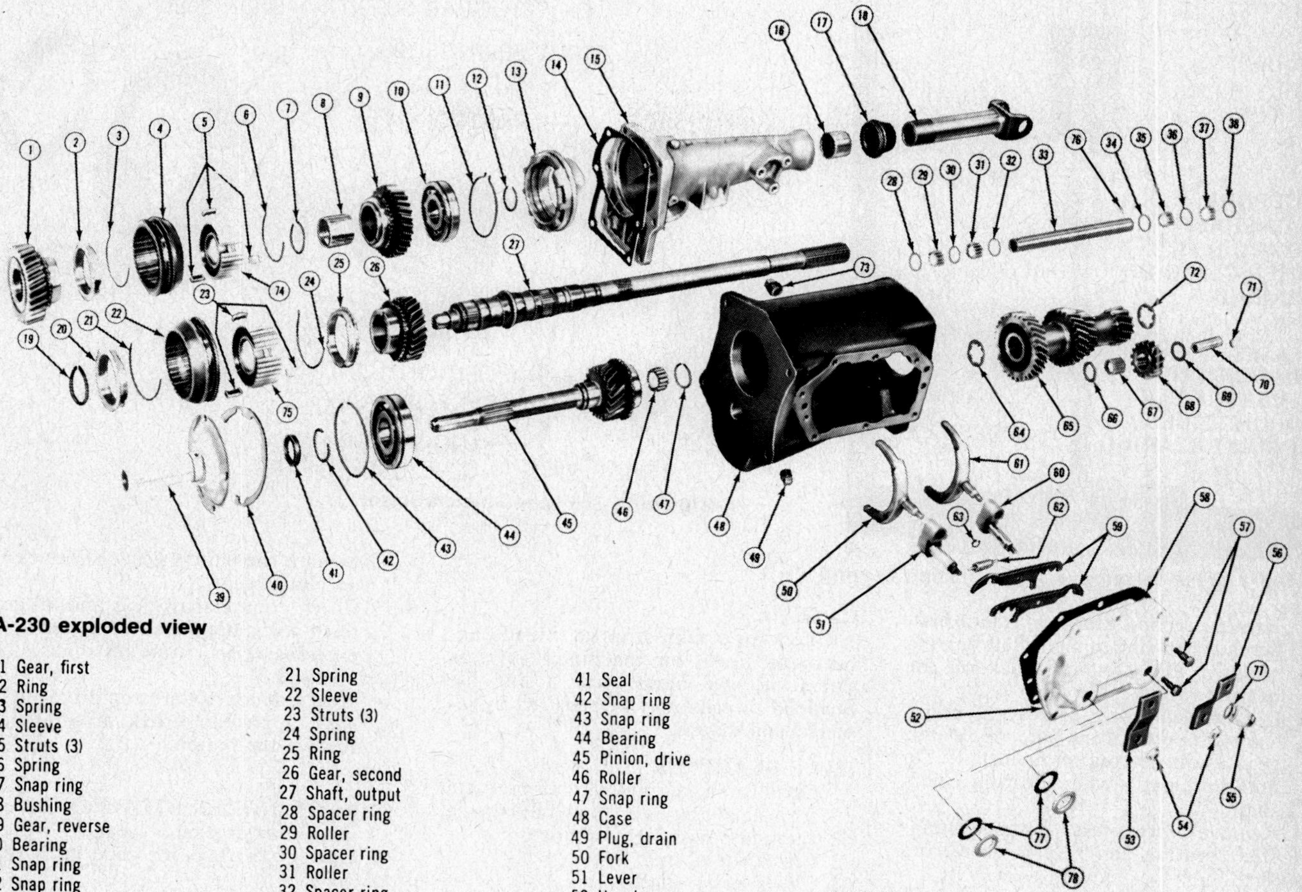

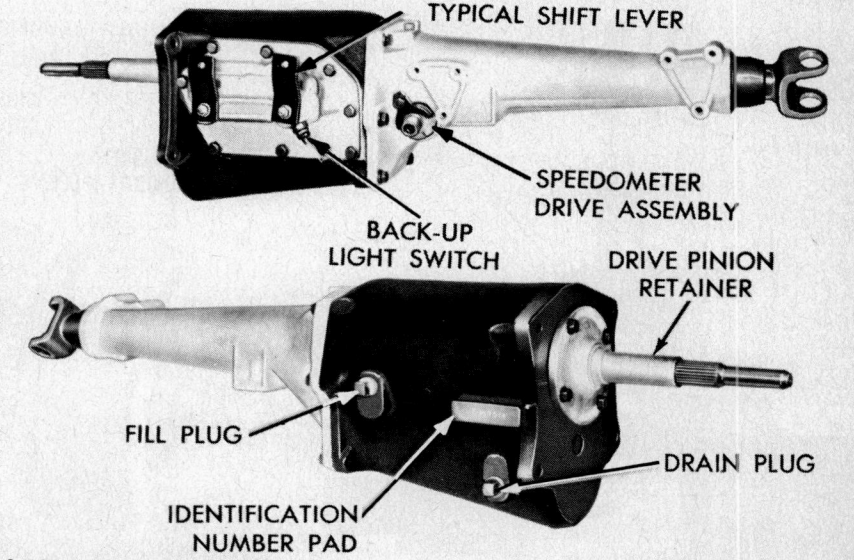

A-230 exploded view

1 Gear, first	21 Spring	41 Seal
2 Ring	22 Sleeve	42 Snap ring
3 Spring	23 Struts (3)	43 Snap ring
4 Sleeve	24 Spring	44 Bearing
5 Struts (3)	25 Ring	45 Pinion, drive
6 Spring	26 Gear, second	46 Roller
7 Snap ring	27 Shaft, output	47 Snap ring
8 Bushing	28 Spacer ring	48 Case
9 Gear, reverse	29 Roller	49 Plug, drain
10 Bearing	30 Spacer ring	50 Fork
11 Snap ring	31 Roller	51 Lever
12 Snap ring	32 Spacer ring	52 Housing
13 Retainer	33 Countershaft	53 Lever
14 Gasket	34 Spacer ring	54 Nut, locking
15 Extension	35 Roller	55 Switch
16 Bushing	36 Spacer ring	56 Lever
17 Seal	37 Roller	57 Bolt
18 Yoke	38 Spacer ring	58 Gasket
19 Snap ring	39 Retainer	59 Lever, interlock
20 Ring	40 Gasket	60 Lever

61 Fork	70 Shaft
62 Spring	71 Key
63 Snap ring	72 Washer
64 Washer	73 Plug, filler
65 Gear, countershaft	74 Gear, clutch
66 Washer	75 Gear, clutch
67 Roller	76 Key
68 Gear, idler	77 "O" rings (2)
69 Washer	78 "O" ring retainers (2)

4 Remove mainshaft assembly through rear of case.

COUNTERSHAFT GEAR & DRIVE PINION

1 Using a mallet and dummy shaft, tap the countershaft rearward enough to remove key. Drive countershaft out of case. Maintain contact between countershaft and dummy shaft so that washers will not drop out.
2 Lower countershaft gear to bottom of case.
3 Remove snap-ring from pinion bearing outer race (outside front of case).
4 Drive pinion shaft into case with plastic hammer. Remove assembly through rear of case.
5 If bearing is to be replaced, remove snap-ring and press off bearing.
6 Lift countershaft gear and dummy shaft out through rear of case.

MAINSHAFT

1 Remove snap-ring and second gear stop ring from front end of mainshaft.

A-230 3 speed transmission

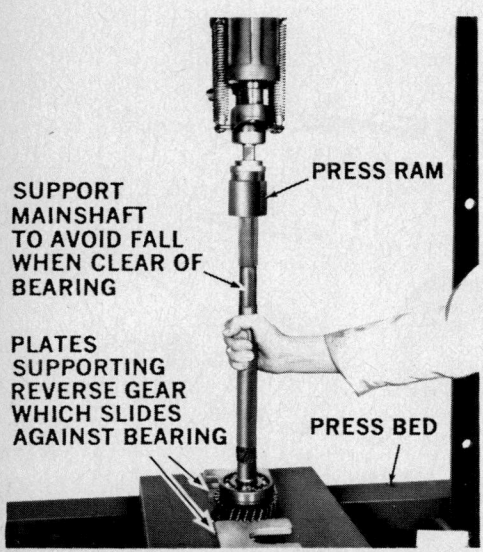

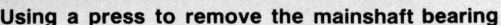

Using a press to remove the mainshaft bearing

SUPPORT MAINSHAFT TO AVOID FALL WHEN CLEAR OF BEARING

PRESS RAM

PLATES SUPPORTING REVERSE GEAR WHICH SLIDES AGAINST BEARING

PRESS BED

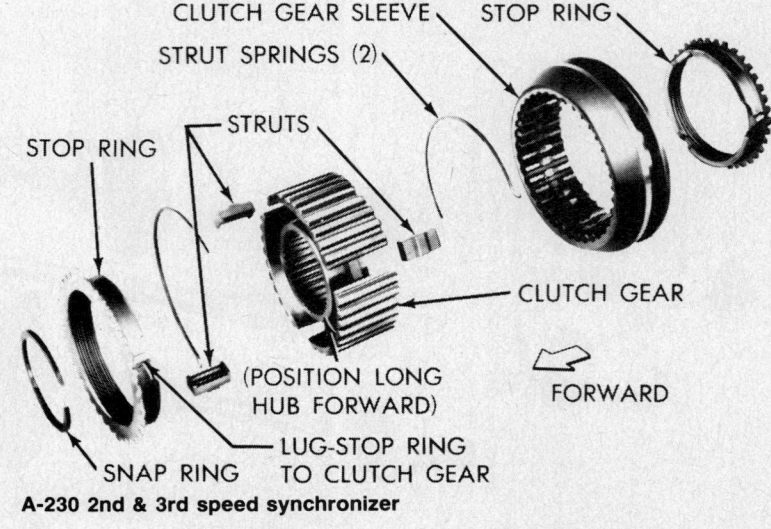

CLUTCH GEAR SLEEVE | STOP RING
STRUT SPRINGS (2)
STOP RING | STRUTS
CLUTCH GEAR
(POSITION LONG HUB FORWARD)
FORWARD
SNAP RING
LUG-STOP RING TO CLUTCH GEAR

A-230 2nd & 3rd speed synchronizer

Remove second gear from mainshaft.
2 Spread snap-ring in mainshaft bearing retainer. Slide retainer back off the bearing race.
3 Remove snap-ring at rear of mainshaft. Support front side of reverse gear. Press bearing off mainshaft. Do not drop parts when bearing clears shaft.
4 Remove from press. Remove mainshaft bearing and reverse gear from shaft.
5 Remove snap-ring from rear of shaft. Slide first-reverse synchronizer assembly off splines and remove rearward. Remove stop-ring and first gear through the rear.

Inspection
1 Clean all parts with solvent.
2 Dry with compressed air.

CASE
Check for cracks, stripped threads, and burrs or nicks on machined surfaces. Dress off any burrs with a fine file. Stripped threads may be repaired by use of Helicoil inserts.

BALL BEARINGS
1 Do not spin bearings with air pressure; turn slowly by hand to avoid damage.
2 Lubricate with light engine oil.
3 Check for pitting.
4 Check fit on shafts.

NEEDLE BEARINGS
1 Check rollers for flats.
2 Check roller spacers for wear.

GEARS
1 Check gear splines on synchronizer clutch gears and stop-rings for chipping or worn teeth.

2 Be sure the clutch sleeve slides easily on clutch gear.
3 Check countershaft gear and all gear teeth for chipping, broken teeth, or excessive wear. Stone off small nicks or burrs.
4 If oil seal contact area on drive pinion shaft is pitted, rusted, or scratched, replace the pinion.

SYNCHRONIZER STOP RINGS
1 Check for cracks or wear.
2 Check new rings for good fit on gear cones.

MAINSHAFT
1 Check mainshaft gear and bearing mating surfaces for excessive wear.
2 Check snap-rings for burred edges. Remove burrs with a fine file.
3 Check synchronizer clutch gear splines on shaft for burrs.

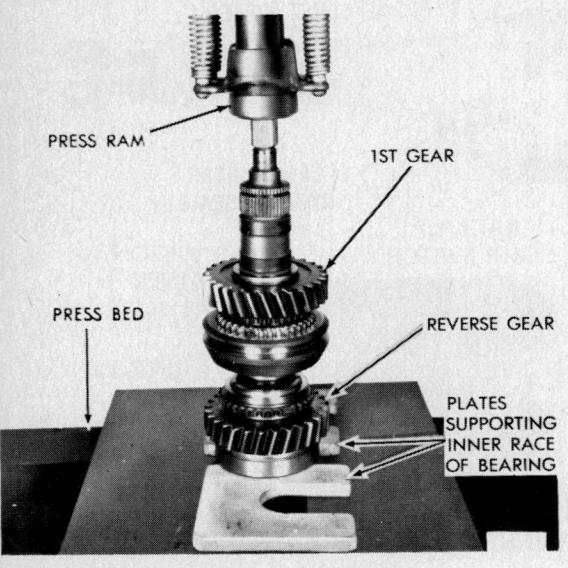

A-230 mainshaft bearing installation

PRESS RAM

PRESS BED

1ST GEAR

REVERSE GEAR

PLATES SUPPORTING INNER RACE OF BEARING

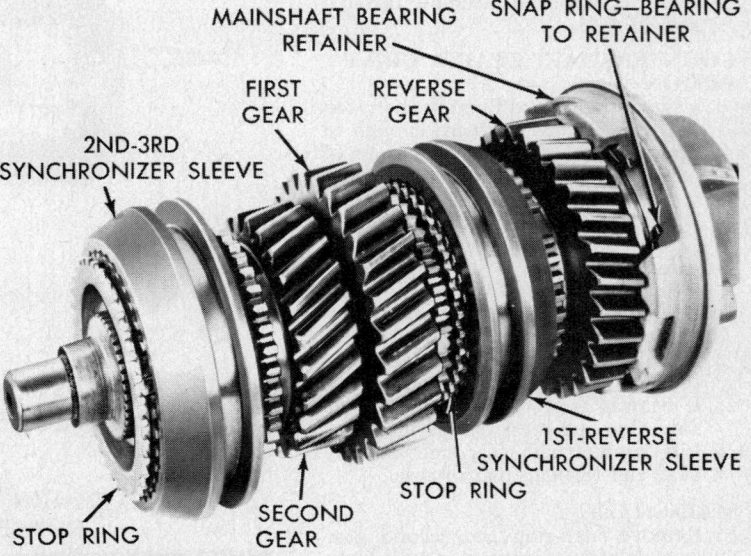

A-230 mainshaft assembly

MAINSHAFT BEARING RETAINER
SNAP RING—BEARING TO RETAINER
FIRST GEAR
REVERSE GEAR
2ND-3RD SYNCHRONIZER SLEEVE
1ST-REVERSE SYNCHRONIZER SLEEVE
STOP RING
STOP RING | SECOND GEAR

Assembly

COUNTERSHAFT GEAR

1 Slide dummy shaft into countershaft gear.
2 Slide one roller thrust washer over dummy shaft and into gear, followed by 22 greased rollers.
3 Repeat Step 2, adding one roller thrust washer on end.
4 Repeat steps 2 and 3 at other end of countershaft gear. There is a total of 88 rollers and 6 thrust washers.
5 Place greased front thrust washer on dummy shaft against gear with tangs forward.
6 Grease rear thrust washer and stick it in place in the case, with tangs rearward. Place countershaft gear assembly in bottom of transmission case until drive pinion is installed.

PINION GEAR

1 Press new bearing on pinion shaft with snap-ring groove forward. Install new snap-ring.
2 Install 15 rollers and retaining ring in drive pinion gear.
3 Install drive pinion and bearing assembly into case.
4 Install the countershaft gear assembly by positioning it and thrust washers so countershaft can be tapped into position. Keep the countershaft against the dummy shaft to keep parts from falling between them. Install key in countershaft.
5 Tap drive pinion forward for clearance.

MAINSHAFT

1 Place a stop-ring flat on the bench. Place a clutch gear and a sleeve on top. Drop the struts in their slots and snap in a strut spring. Place the tang inside one strut. Turn the assembly over and install second strut spring. Place tang in a different strut.
2 Slide first gear and stop-ring over rear of mainshaft and against thrust flange between first and second gears on shaft.
3 Slide first-reverse synchronizer assembly over rear of mainshaft. Index hub slots to first gear stop-ring lugs.
4 Install first-reverse synchronizer clutch gear snap-ring on mainshaft.
5 Slide reverse gear and mainshaft bearing into place. Press bearing on shaft, supporting inner race of bearing. Be sure snap-ring groove on outer race is forward.
6 Install bearing retaining snap-ring on mainshaft. Spread snap-ring in retainer groove and slide it over the bearing. Seat ring in groove.
7 Place second gear over front of mainshaft with thrust surface against flange.
8 Install stop-ring and second-third synchronizer assembly against second gear. Install second-third synchronizer clutch gear snap-ring on shaft.
9 Move second-third synchronizer sleeve forward as far as possible. Install front stop-ring, inside the sleeve with lugs indexed to struts. Coat the stop-ring with grease to hold it in position.
10 Rotate cut-out on second gear toward countershaft gear to provide clearance.
11 Insert mainshaft assembly into case. Tilt assembly to clear cluster gears and insert pilot rollers in drive pinion gear. If assembly is correct, the bearing retainer will bottom to the case without force. If not, check for a misplaced strut, pinion roller, or stop-ring.

REVERSE IDLER GEAR

1 Place dummy shaft into idler gear. Insert 22 greased rollers.
2 Position reverse idler thrust washers in case with grease.
3 Position idler gear and dummy shaft in case. Install idler shaft and key.

EXTENSION HOUSING

1 Remove extension housing yoke seal. Drive bushing out from inside housing.
2 Align oil hole in bushing with oil slot in housing. Drive bushing into place. Drive new seal into housing.
3 Install extension housing and gasket to hold mainshaft and bearing retainer in place.

DRIVE PINION BEARING RETAINER

1 Install outer snap-ring on drive pinion bearing. Tap assembly back until snap-ring contacts case.
2 Install a new seal in retainer bore.
3 Position main drive pinion bearing retainer and gasket on front of case.

Coat threads with sealing compound, install bolts, torque to 30 ft./lbs.

GEARSHIFT MECHANISM & HOUSING

1 If removed, place two interlock levers on pivot pin. Spring hangers are offset toward each other. Spring installs in a straight line. Place E-clip on pivot pin.
2 Grease and install new O-ring seals on both shift shafts. Grease housing bores. Push each shaft into its bore.
3 Install spring on interlock lever hangers.
4 Rotate each shift shaft fork bore to vertical position. Install shift forks through bores and under both interlock levers.
5 Position second-third synchronizer sleeve in second gear position. Position first-reverse synchronizer sleeve in neutral position. Place shift forks in the same positions.
6 Install gasket and gearshift mechanism. The bolt with the extra long shoulder must be installed at the center rear of the case. Torque bolts to 15 ft./lbs.
7 Install speedometer drive pinion gear and adapter. Range number on adapter, which represents the number of teeth on the gear, should be in 6 o'clock position.

EXHAUST EMISSION CONTROL SYSTEM SWITCH

Some models have a switch in the shift cover, adjacent to the 2–3 shift lever. It is actuated by a flat on the 2–3 shift lever, when in third gear. If vehicle is not equipped with Emission System, a plug is installed in the mounting hole. Torque the switch or plug to 15 ft./lbs.

SYNCHRONIZER SLEEVES MOVED FORWARD

POSITION CUT AWAY AREA ON 2ND GEAR NEXT TO CLUSTER GEAR FOR CLEARANCE

IDLER SHAFT

COUNTERSHAFT

A-230 position 2nd & 3rd gear and shift sleeves for clearance

CHRYSLER A250 & A903 3 SPEED

Chrysler A-250 & A-903 3-Speed Units

These units are virtually identical and service and repair procedures for both types are the same.

Disassembly

1. Remove output shaft yoke.
2. Remove the bolts that attach the extension housing to the transmission case. Remove the housing.
3. Remove extension housing oil seal.
4. Remove the transmission case cover. Measure synchronizer float with feeler gauges. This measurement is taken between the end of a synchronizer pin and the opposite synchronizer outer ring. This measurement should be .060–.117 in.
5. Remove the attaching bolts and remove the main drive pinion bearing retainer. Then grasp the pinion shaft and pull the assembly out of the case.

CHILTON CAUTION: *Be careful not to bind the inner synchronizer ring on the drive pinion clutch teeth.*

6. Remove the snap-ring that locks the main drive pinion bearing onto the pinion shaft. Remove the bearing washer, press the shaft out of the bearing and remove the oil slinger.
7. Remove the snap-ring from the pilot bearing in the end of the drive pinion and remove the 14 rollers.
8. With the transmission in reverse, remove the outer center bearing snap-ring. Partially remove the mainshaft.
9. Cock the mainshaft. Remove the clutch sleeve, the outer synchronizer rings, the front inner ring and the second-third shift box.
10. Remove clutch gear retaining snap ring. Slide the clutch gear off the end of the mainshaft.
11. Slide the second-speed gear, stop-ring and synchronizer spring off the mainshaft.
12. Remove the low and reverse sliding gear and shift fork, as the mainshaft is completely withdrawn from the case.
13. Check cluster gear end-play. End-play should be .005–.022 in. This measurement will determine thrust washer value at reassembly.
14. Drive the countershaft rearward, removing key, and out of the case.
15. Lift the gear cluster and thrust washers out of the case. Remove the needle bearings, (22 each end) and spacer from the cluster.
16. Drive the reverse idler shaft toward the rear and out of the case. Remove key.
17. Lift the reverse idler gear, thrust washers and 22 needle bearings out of the case.
18. Remove gearshift operating levers from their respective shafts. On an A-250 transmission, remove the tapered pins retaining the shift shafts to the case with a hammer and an 1/8 in. punch. Drive out the front pin to the front and the rear pin to the rear.
19. Drive out tapered retaining pin from either of the two lever shafts. Withdraw the shaft from inside the transmission case. (The detent balls are springloaded. The balls will fall to the bottom of the case.)
20. Remove the interlock sleeve, spring, pin and both balls from the case. Drive out the remaining tapered pin. Slide the lever shaft out of the transmission.
21. Remove the lever shaft seals and discard them.

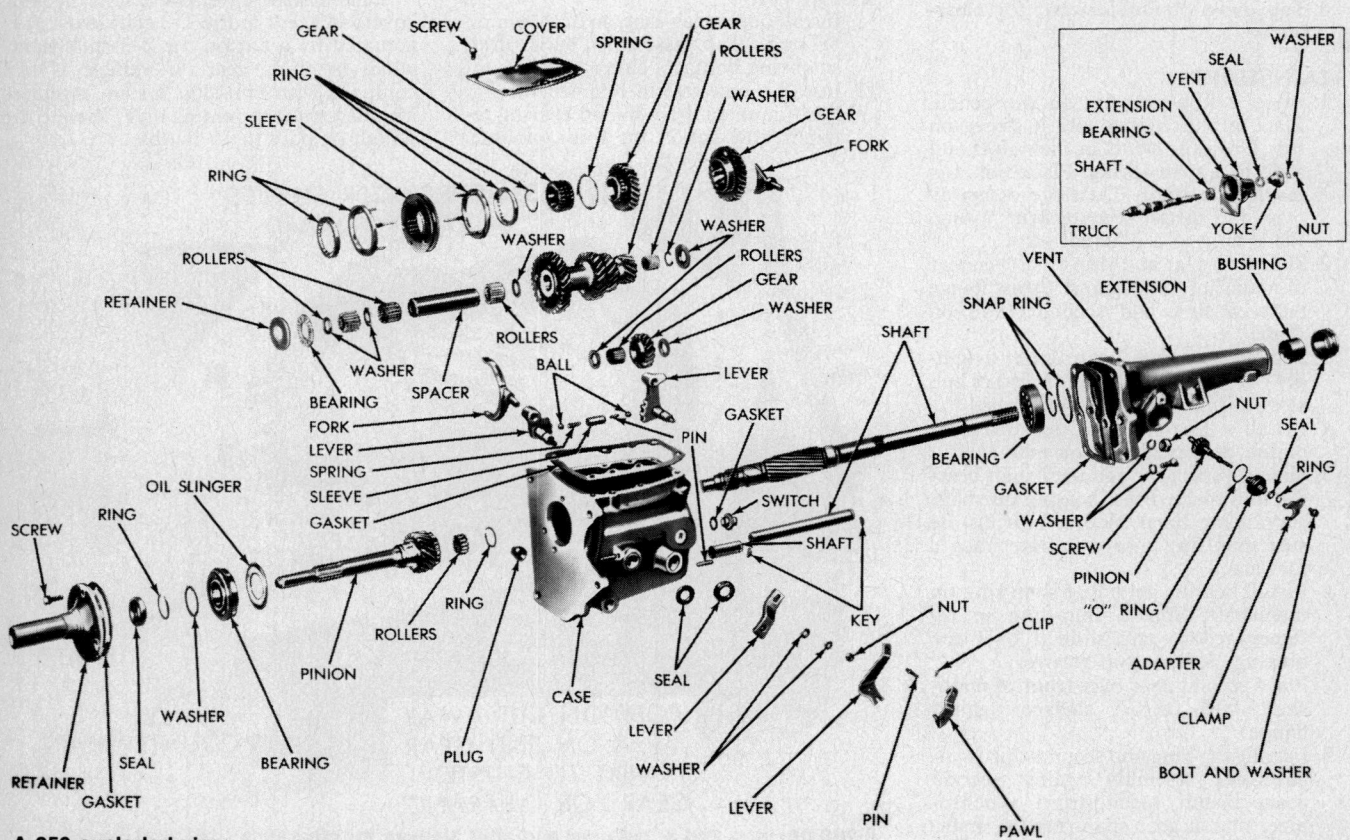

A-250 exploded view

Assembly

1. Install two new shift lever shaft seals in the case.
2. Carefully insert low and reverse lever shaft into the rear of the case, through the seal and into position. Lock with a tapered pin. Turn lever until the center detent is in line with the interlock bore.
3. Slide the interlock sleeve in its bore in the case, followed by one of the interlock balls. Install interlock spring and pin.
4. Place the remaining interlock ball on top of the interlock spring.
5. Depress the interlock ball and at the same time install the second and high lever shaft into the fully seated position. Align the center detent with the detent ball. Secure the shaft with the remaining tapered pin.
6. Install the operating levers and secure to the shafts with nuts. Torque the nuts to 18 ft./lbs.

COUNTERSHAFT (CLUSTER) GEAR

1. Slide the dummy shaft and tubular spacer into the bore of the counter-gear.
2. Grease and install 22 bearing rollers into each end of the countergear bore in the area around the arbor. Install the bearing retaining rings at each end of the gear, covering the bearings. If countershaft gear end-play measured over .022 in. at disassembly, install new thrust washers.
3. Install a thrust washer at each end of the countergear and over the arbor. Install the countergear assembly in the case. The tabs on the thrust washers slide into the grooves in the case.

REVERSE IDLER GEAR

1. Coat the bore of the reverse idler gear with grease. Slide dummy shaft into the bore. Install 22 bearing rollers in the bore and around the dummy shaft.
2. Install a new thrust washer at each end of the gear and over the arbor.
3. With the beveled end of the teeth forward, slide the gear into position in the case. Install the reverse idler shaft

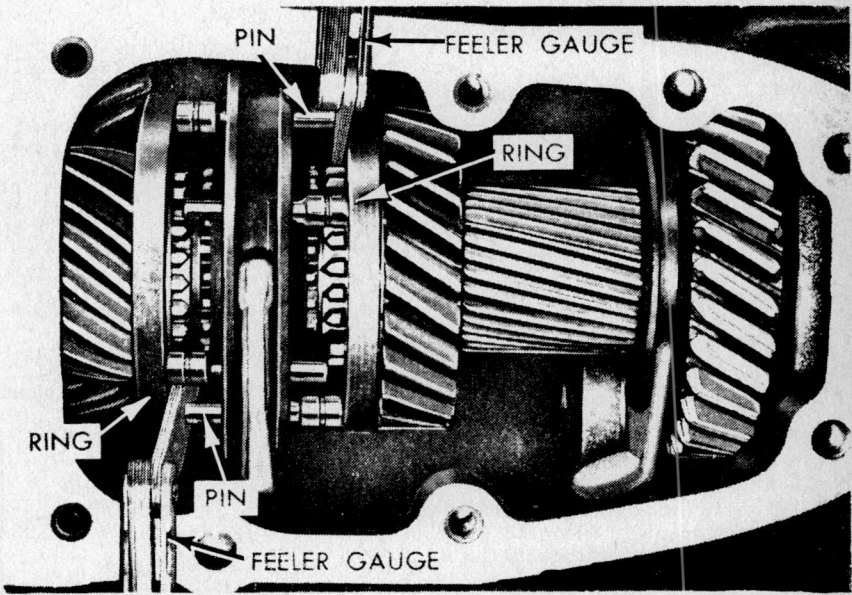

Measuring Synchronizer "Float".

in its bore in the rear of the case. Install Woodruff key and align with the keyway in the case.
4. Align the idler gear with the shaft, then drive the shaft into the case and gear until the key seats in recess.

MAINSHAFT

1. Install rear bearing on mainshaft and install selective fit snap-ring.
2. Hold low and reverse sliding gear in position with shift fork. Insert mainshaft with rear bearing through rear of case and into the sliding gear. Both shift forks are offset toward rear of the case.
3. Place synchronizer spreader ring, and then rear stop ring, on synchronizer splines of second speed gear. Install second speed gear on mainshaft, with shims if required. Shims should be installed to correct excessive synchronizer float. If synchronizer float is below minimum, as measured on disassembly, shorten all six synchronizer pins.

4. Install synchronizer clutch gear on mainshaft. Install snap-ring.
5. Install second and direct fork in lever shaft with offset toward rear of transmission. Hold synchronizer clutch gear sleeve and two outer rings together, with pins in holes in clutch gear sleeve. Engage second and direct fork with clutch gear sleeve.
6. While holding synchronizer parts and fork in position, slide mainshaft forward. Synchronizer clutch gear fits into clutch gear sleeve and mainshaft rear bearing into the case bore. Synchronizer parts must be correctly positioned before mainshaft is positioned.
7. Hold synchronizer parts in position; tap mainshaft forward until rear bearing bottoms in the case bore.
8. Install mainshaft rear bearing selective fit snap-ring into groove in case bore.

DRIVE PINION (CLUTCH SHAFT)

1. Slide the oil slinger over the pinion

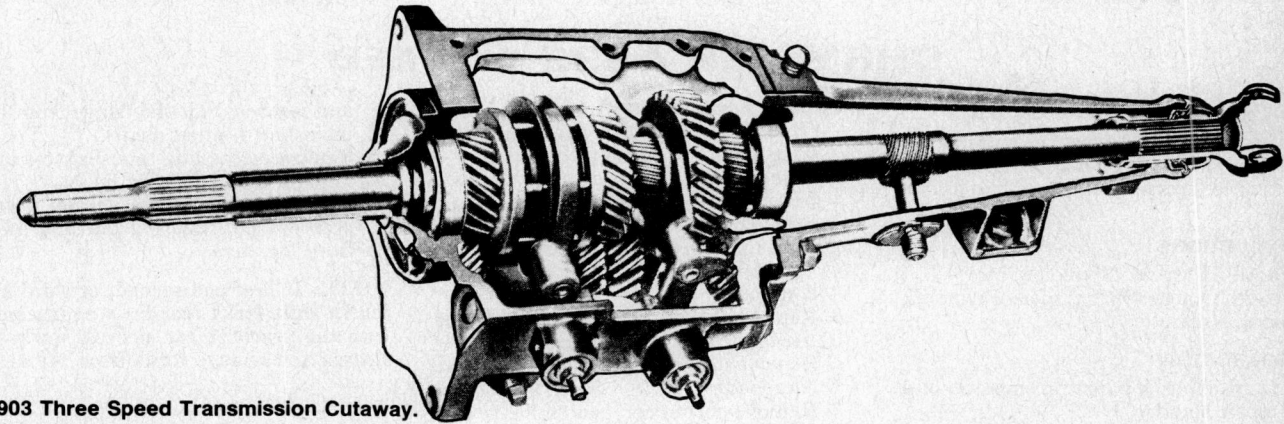

A-903 Three Speed Transmission Cutaway.

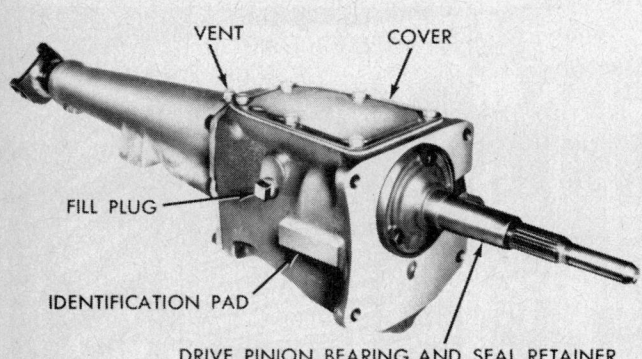

A-250 3 speed transmission

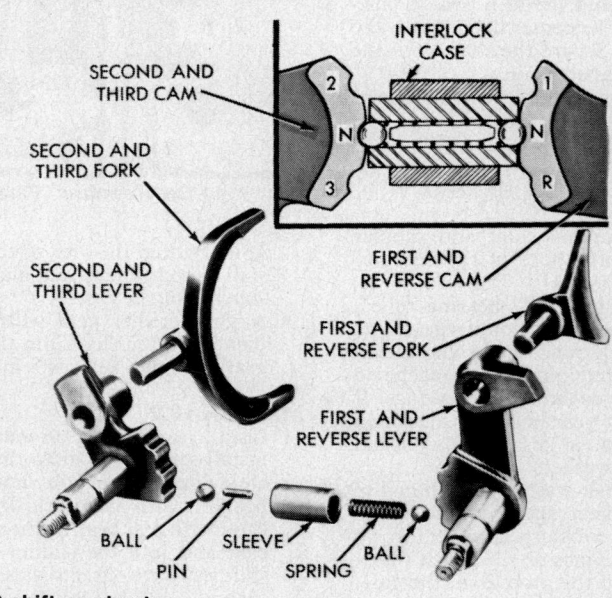

A-250 synchronizer

A-250 shift mechanism

shaft and down against the gear.

2 Slide the bearing over the pinion shaft (ring groove away from the gear), then press to a firm seat against the oil slinger and gear.

3 Install the keyed washer, then the snap-ring. Four thicknesses of snap-ring are available to eliminate end-play. Install the large snap-ring onto the race of the ball bearing.

4 Install 14 greased bearing rollers in the bore of the pinion shaft gear. Install bearing roller retaining ring in the pinion gear bore.

5 Install third gear outer stop-ring and third gear inner stop-ring onto the mainshaft. Guide the drive pinion through the front of the case and engage the inner stop-ring with the clutch teeth. Seat the bearing so the large snap-ring is hard against the case.

6 Install a new seal in the pinion bearing retainer.

7 Install the gasket on the retainer and install with attaching bolts torqued to 30 ft./lbs.

EXTENSION HOUSING

1 Install a new rear mainshaft bushing, and a new oil seal.

2 Protect the oil seal with thimble-type seal protector. With gasket attached, slide the extension housing over the mainshaft and down against the case. Torque bolts to 50 ft./lb.

3 Install flange assembly and secure with new washer and nut. Torque the nut to 140 ft./lbs.

4 Grease the cover gasket. Install gasket on cover. Torque attaching bolts to 12 ft./lbs.

5 Install drain plug and back-up light switch (if so equipped). Tighten securely. Refill transmission to proper level.

EXHAUST EMISSION CONTROL SWITCH

Some models have a switch mounted above the 2–3 shift lever, for emission control. In the absence of a switch a plug is substituted. Torque the plug or switch to 15 ft./lbs.

CHRYSLER A833 4 SPEED

Chrysler A-833 4-Speed

This unit varies somewhat with car application. However, illustrations and repair procedures may be considered as typical.

Applications

1974 All Dodge & Plymouth cars
1975–79 Dodge Dart Aspen, Plymouth Valiant, Volaré

Disassembly

1 If available, mount transmission in a repair stand.

2 Disconnect gearshift control rods from the shift control levers and the transmission operating levers.

3 Remove the two gearshift control housing mounting bolts.

4 Remove gearshift control housing from the transmission extension housing or mounting bracket (if so equipped).

5 Remove the gearshift control housing the bracket (if so equipped).

6 Remove back-up light switch (if so equipped).

7 Remove output companion flange nut and washer. Pull the flange from the mainshaft (output shaft).

8 Remove gearshift housing-to-transmission case attaching bolts.

9 With all levers in the neutral detent position, pull housing out and away from the case.

NOTE: If first and second, or third and fourth shift forks remain in engagement with the synchronizer sleeves, work the sleeves and remove forks from the case.

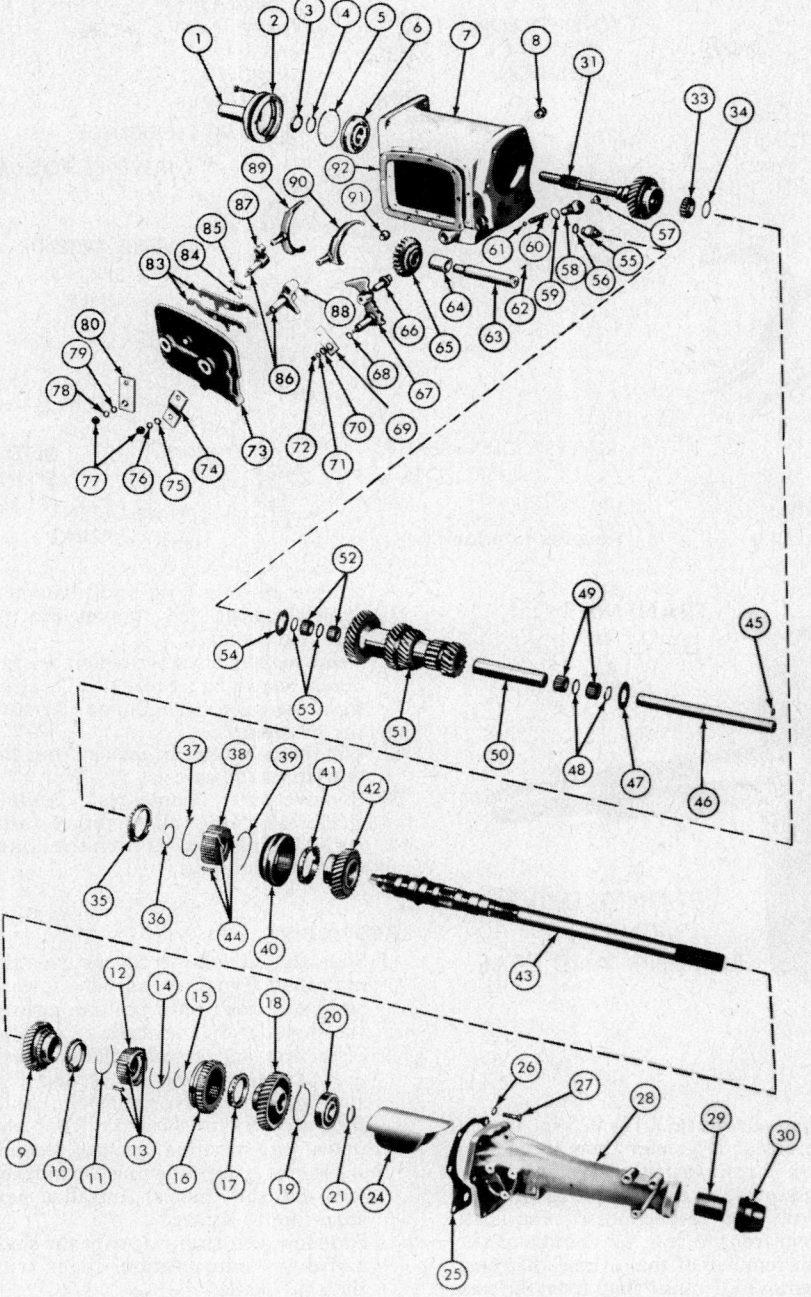

1 Bearing retainer
2 Bearing retainer gasket
3 Bearing retainer oil seal
4 Inner bearing snap-ring
5 Outer bearing snap-ring
6 Pinion bearing
7 Transmission case
8 Filler plug
9 2nd speed gear
10 Stop ring
11 Shift strut springs
12 Clutch gear
13 Shift struts (3)
14 Shift strut spring
15 Snap-ring
16 1st and 2nd clutch sleeve gear
17 Stop ring
18 1st speed gear
19 Bearing retainer ring
20 Rear bearing
21 Snap-ring
24 Baffle
25 Case to extension housing gasket
26 Lockwasher
27 Bolt
28 Extension housing
29 Mainshaft yoke bushing
30 Oil seal
31 Main drive pinion
33 Needle bearing
34 Snap-ring
35 Stop ring
36 Snap-ring
37 Shift strut spring
38 Clutch gear
39 Shift strut spring
40 Clutch sleeve
41 Stop ring
42 3rd speed gear
43 Mainshaft (output)
44 Shift struts (3)
45 Woodruff key
46 Countershaft
47 Gear thrustwasher (1)
48 Needle roller bearing thrustwasher
49 Needle bearing rollers
50 Bearing spacer
51 Countershaft gear (cluster)
52 Needle bearing rollers
53 Needle roller bearing thrustwasher
54 Gear thrustwasher (1)
55 Backup light switch
56 Backup light switch gasket
57 Plug
58 Reverse detent ball spring retainer
59 Gasket
60 Reverse detent ball spring
61 Reverse detent ball
62 Woodruff key
63 Reverse idler gear shaft
64 Reverse idler gear bushing
65 Reverse idler gear
66 Reverse shifter fork
67 Reverse lever
68 Reverse lever shaft oil seal
69 Reverse operating lever
70 Flatwasher
71 Lockwasher
72 Nut
73 Gearshift control housing
74 1st and 2nd operating lever
75 Flatwasher
76 Lockwasher lever
77 Lever nut
78 Lever lockwasher
79 Lever flatwasher
80 3rd and 4th operating lever
81 Switch
82 Gasket
83 Interlock lever (2)
84 E-ring
85 Spring
86 Oil seal (2)
87 3rd anl 4th lever
88 1st and 2nd lever
89 3rd and 4th speed fork
90 1st and 2nd speed fork
91 Drain plug
92 Shift control housing gasket

A-833 exploded view

10 Remove nuts, lock washers and flat washers that hold first-second, and third-fourth-speed shift operating levers to the shafts.
11 Disengage shift levers from the flats on the shafts. Remove levers.
12 Remove gearshift lever shafts out of the housing. Allow detent balls to fall free. Remove seals and discard.
13 Slide interlock sleeve, interlock pin and spring from the housing.
14 Remove main drive pinion bearing retainer attaching bolts. Slide retainer and gasket from the main drive shaft. Remove the pinion oil seal.
15 Remove the attaching bolts that hold the tailshaft extension housing to the transmission case.
16 Slide the third-fourth synchronizer sleeve slightly forward. Slide the reverse idler gear to the center of its shaft. Using a soft hammer, tap rearward on the extension housing. Slide housing and mainshaft assembly out and away from the case.
17 Remove the snap-ring that holds the third-fourth synchronizer clutch gear and sleeve. Slide third-fourth synchronizer assembly from the end of the mainshaft.
18 Slide third speed gear and stop-ring from the mainshaft.

NOTE: Do not separate third-fourth-speed synchronizer clutch gear, sleeve, shift plates or spring unless replacement is required.

19 With long-nose pliers, compress the snap-ring that retains the mainshaft

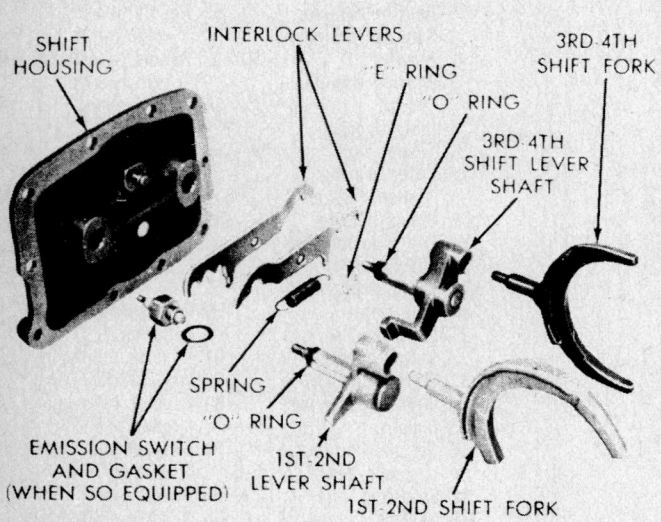

SHIFT HOUSING — INTERLOCK LEVERS — "E" RING — "O" RING — 3RD-4TH SHIFT FORK — 3RD-4TH SHIFT LEVER SHAFT — SPRING — "O" RING — EMISSION SWITCH AND GASKET (WHEN SO EQUIPPED) — 1ST-2ND LEVER SHAFT — 1ST-2ND SHIFT FORK

Shift Housing Detail

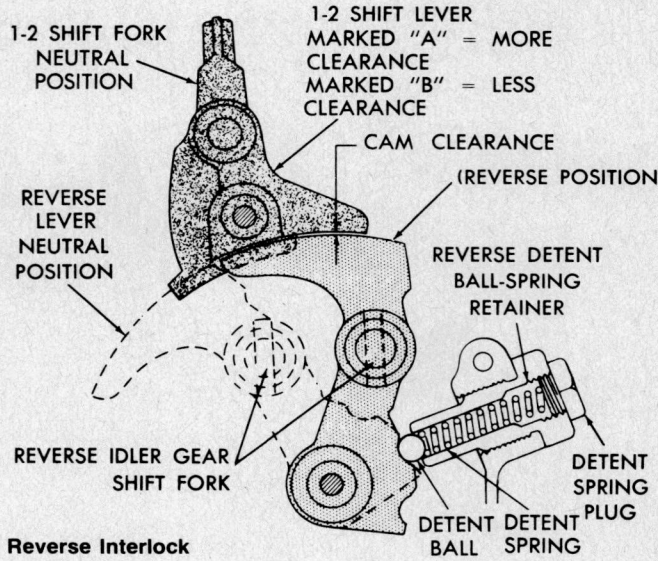

1-2 SHIFT FORK NEUTRAL POSITION — 1-2 SHIFT LEVER MARKED "A" = MORE CLEARANCE MARKED "B" = LESS CLEARANCE — CAM CLEARANCE (REVERSE POSITION) — REVERSE LEVER NEUTRAL POSITION — REVERSE DETENT BALL-SPRING RETAINER — REVERSE IDLER GEAR SHIFT FORK — DETENT BALL — DETENT SPRING — DETENT SPRING PLUG

Reverse Interlock

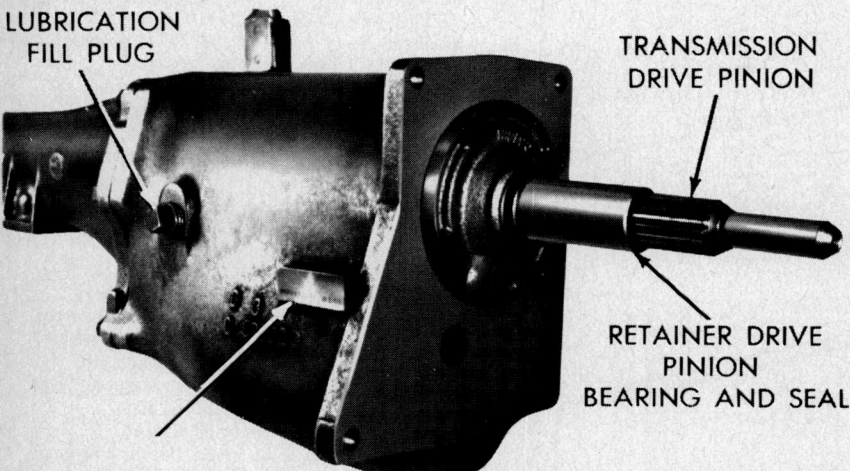

LUBRICATION FILL PLUG — TRANSMISSION DRIVE PINION — RETAINER DRIVE PINION BEARING AND SEAL

A-833 4 speed transmission

center bearing in the extension housing.

20 With snap-ring compressed, pull the mainshaft assembly and bearing out of the extension housing.

21 Remove and discard extension housing rear oil seal.

22 Remove rear bearing from the mainshaft with an arbor press.

23 Remove the snap-ring that holds the mainshaft bearing onto the shaft.

24 Remove mainshaft bearing, retainer ring, first-speed gear, and first-speed stop-ring.

25 Remove the snap-ring that holds the first and second clutch sleeve gear and clutch to the mainshaft.

26 Slide the first and second clutch sleeve gear and clutch from the mainshaft.

NOTE: Do not dismantle the clutch unless inspection reveals need for parts replacement.

27 With a feeler gauge, measure countershaft gear end-play. This measurement should be .015–.025 in. If measurement is greater than specified, a new thrust washer of desirable thickness must be installed at assembly.

28 Drive the reverse idler gear shaft, from front to rear, far enough to permit removal of the reverse idler gear.

29 Remove idler gear shaft from the case. Remove the Woodruff key from the shaft.

30 Remove reverse gearshift lever detent spring retainer, gasket, plug and detent ball spring from the rear of the case.

31 Push the reverse gearshift lever shaft into the case, and remove. Lift the detent ball from the bottom of the case.

32 Remove the shift fork from the shaft and detent plate.

33 Using a countershaft dummy, drive the countershaft from the gear and case. Allow the countergear and dummy assembly to rest on the bottom of the case.

34 Remove the main drive pinion bearing outer snap-ring. With a soft hammer, drive the main drive pinion into the case and remove.

35 Remove the main drive pinion bearing outer snap-ring. Press the bearing from the main drive pinion. Remove the oil slinger.

36 Lift the countergear cluster from the bottom of the case.

37 Remove the countergear dummy shaft, 76 bearing rollers, thrust washers and tubular spacer from the center of the countergear.

Assembly

1 Slide the second-speed gear over the mainshaft (synchronizer cone toward rear) and down into position against the shoulder on the shaft.

2 Slide first and second clutch sleeve gear assembly (including second gear stop-ring) over the mainshaft. Shift fork groove is toward the front and down into position against second-speed gear, (stop-ring must be indexed with the shift plates). Install a new snap-ring to secure.

3 Slide low gear stop-ring over the shaft and down into position. Index with the shift plates.

4 Slide first-speed gear, (synchronizer cone toward clutch sleeve gear) over the mainshaft and down into position against the clutch sleeve gear.

5 Install the mainshaft bearing retainer ring. Install the mainshaft center bearing. Press the bearing down into position. Install new snap-ring.

6 Slide the rear bearing over the mainshaft and drive, or press, into position.

7 Install partially assembled mainshaft into the extension housing. Engage the retaining ring in the slot in the extension housing. Compress the retaining ring. At the same time, seat the mainshaft in the extension housing.

8 Slide third-speed gear over the mainshaft, synchronizer cone forward, followed by third gear stop-ring.

9 Install third and fourth-speed synchronizer clutch gear assembly onto the mainshaft (shift fork groove toward rear) down against third-speed gear. Index the rear stop-ring with the clutch shift plates.

10 Install retaining snap-ring. Using heavy grease, position the front stop-ring over the clutch gear. Index the ring slots with the shift plates.

NOTE: If above indexing of the stop-rings and the positioning of the gears and clutches is ignored at this point, damage will most likely result when mating the extension housing to the transmission case.

11 Grease the bore of the countergear at each end. Install the roller bearing tubular spacer (centered). Insert the countergear dummy shaft.

12 Grease each bearing roller. Install 19 bearing rollers at each end of the gear. Install a flat spacer onto each end of the dummy shaft and into the gear, followed by 19 more bearing rollers and a spacer ring into each end of the countergear.

13 Grease the tanged thrust washers. Install them, one over each end of the dummy shaft, with the tangs toward the case (away from the gear).

14 Lay the countergear assembly into the bottom of the case.

15 Slide the bearing oil slinger over the main drive pinion shaft. Press the main drive pinion bearing on the pinion shaft. Outer snap-ring groove is toward the front). Seat bearing all the way against shoulder on gear.

16 Install a new inner snap-ring into the bearing retainer groove of the shaft.

17 Install the outer snap-ring into the main drive pinion bearing. Insert and tap the main drive pinion and bearing assembly into the front of the case.

18 Start the countershaft into its bore at the rear of the case. Raise the countergear cluster assembly until the gear bore is aligned with the countershaft bore in the case. (Be sure the thrust washer tangs are in place in the case recesses.)

19 Press the countershaft into the countergear, washer and bearings assembly. Install Woodruff key into countershaft. Continue pressing the countershaft and key into its bore and recess.

NOTE: Countergear end-play should not exceed .029 in.

20 Install a new oil seal onto the reverse gearshift lever shaft.

21 Lubricate and carefully install the lever shaft into the bore in the case. Insert reverse fork into the lever.

22 Install reverse shift detent ball and spring retainer gasket and retainer. Tighten securely.

23 Start reverse idler gear shaft into the end of the case. Press in far enough to position the reverse idler gear on the protruding end of the shaft. At the same time, engage the shifter groove with the reverse shift fork.

24 Properly position reverse idler gear. Install Woodruff key into the sliding gear shaft. Finish seating the shaft and key flush with the end of the case.

25 Grease, then position a new gasket on the end of the extension housing.

26 Center reverse sliding gear on its shaft. Carefully insert the mainshaft assembly into the case. Index third and fourth-speed stop-rings and shifter plates.)

27 Move third and fourth-speed clutch sleeve slightly toward the front. Align the end of the mainshaft with the main drive pinion. Push in on the extension housing assembly until it is entirely seated against the rear of the case.

28 Install extension-to-case attaching bolts and torque to 50 ft./lbs.

29 Install back-up light switch (if so equipped).

30 Move reverse sliding gear ahead to neutral position.

31 Slide interlock sleeve into position in the gearshift housing. Lubricate and slide a new seal over a shifter shaft and down into its groove.

32 Install the gearshift lever shaft into position in the housing. Install the gearshift operating lever onto the flats of the shaft, (lever pointing up). Install flat washer, lockwasher and nut. Tighten securely.

33 Place a detent ball in the sleeve, followed by the poppet spring and interlock pin.

34 Lubricate and slide a new seal over the other shifter shaft and down into its groove.

35 Push the shaft into position in the housing. Install the operating lever onto the flats of the shaft (lever pointing up). Install flat washer, lockwasher and nut. Tighten securely.

36 Place remaining detent ball on the poppet spring. Compress the ball and spring with a small screwdriver. Push the shafts in until seated. Turn the shafts until the balls drop into the neutral position detent.

37 Place transmission on its side, gearshift cover opening up.

38 Install a shift fork onto each synchronizer sleeve collar. With both sleeves in neutral position, install the shift housing and new gasket.

39 Install attaching bolts and tighten to 12 ft./lbs. (The center bolt on each side of the cover is a pilot bolt and should be installed first.)

40 Lubricate and install a new oil seal in the main drive pinion retainer bore. Install the retainer and gasket. Install attaching bolts, torqued to 15–20 ft./lbs.

41 Install gearshift control and rod assembly on the extension housing. Secure rods with washers and clips.

42 Install output companion flange, washer and nut. Torque to 175 ft./lbs.

CHRYSLER A833 4 SPEED (WITH OVERDRIVE)

Chrysler Overdrive
4-Speed

Starting 1976, there is an overdrive four speed available as an option on some models. This transmission is similar in design to the A-833 Chrysler four speed but repair procedures are different.

Applications
1974–76 Dart & Valiant
1977–80 Aspen & Volare

Disassembly

1 If available, mount transmission in a repair stand.

2 Disconnect gearshift control rods from the shift control levers and the transmission operating levers.

3 Remove the two gearshift control housing mounting bolts.

4 Remove gearshift control housing from the transmission extension housing or mounting bracket (if so equipped).

5 Remove the gearshift control housing mounting bracket bolts, then, remove the bracket (if so equipped).

6 Remove back-up light switch (if so equipped).

7 Remove output companion flange nut and washer, then pull the flange from the mainshaft (output shaft).

8 Remove gearshift housing-to-transmission case attaching bolts.

9 With all levers in the neutral detent position, pull housing out and away from the case.

NOTE: If first and second, or third and fourth shift forks remain in engagement with the synchronizer sleeves, work the sleeves and remove forks from the case.

10 Remove nuts, lock washers and flat washers that hold first-second, and third-fourth-speed shift operating levers to the shafts.

11 Disengage shift levers from the flats on the shafts and remove levers. Remove the E-ring on the overdrive four speed.

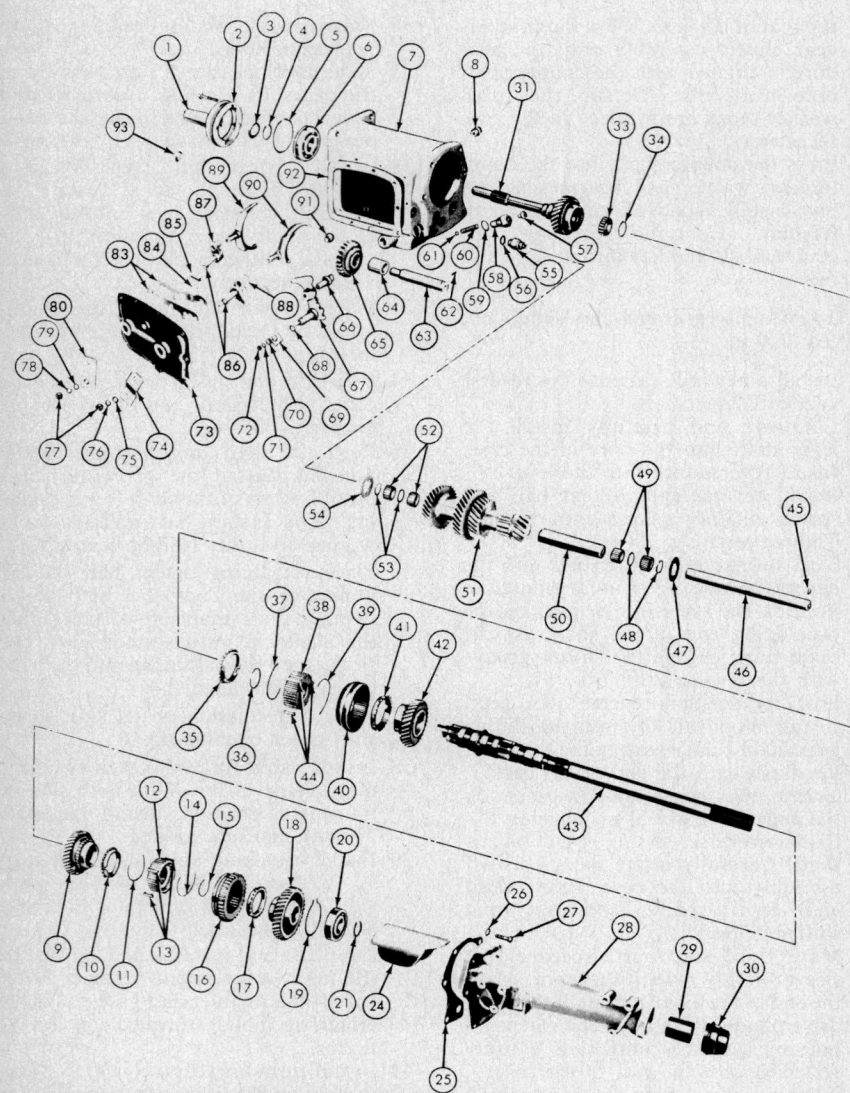

Exploded view of Chrysler Corp. overdrive 4-speed

1. Bearing Retainer
2. Bearing Retainer Gasket
3. Bearing Retainer Oil Seal
4. Snap-ring, Bearing (Inner)
5. Snap-ring, Bearing (Outer)
6. Pinion Bearing
7. Transmission Case
8. Filler plug
9. Gear, 2nd speed
10. Snap-ring
11. Shift strut springs
12. Clutch gear
13. Shift struts (3)
14. Shift strut spring
15. Snap-ring
16. 1st and 2nd clutch sleeve gear
17. Stop-ring
18. 1st speed gear
19. Bearing retainer ring
20. Rear bearing
21. Snap-ring
24. Baffle
25. Gasket, case to extension housing
26. Lockwasher
27. Bolt
28. Extension housing
29. Mainshaft yoke bushing
30. Oil seal
31. Main drive pinion
33. Needle bearing rollers

34. Snap-ring
35. Stop-ring
36. Snap-ring
37. Shift strut spring
38. Clutch gear
39. Shift strut spring
40. Clutch sleeve
41. Stop-ring
42. OD gear
43. Mainshaft (output)
44. Shift struts (3)
45. Woodruff key
46. Countershaft
47. Thrustwasher,
48. Spacer-ring needle roller bearing
49. Needle bearing rollers
50. Bearing spacer
51. Countershaft gear (Cluster)
52. Needle bearing rollers
53. Spacer ring needle roller bearing
54. Thrustwasher,
55. Backup light switch
56. Backup light switch gasket
57. Plug
58. Retainer, reverse detent ball spring
59. Gasket
60. Spring, reverse detent ball
61. Ball, reverse detent
62. Woodruff key
63. Reverse idler gear shaft
64. Bushing, reverse idler gear
65. Gear, reverse idler
66. Fork, reverse shifter
67. Reverse lever
68. Oil seal, reverse lever shaft
69. Reverse operating lever
70. Flatwasher
71. Lockwasher
72. Nut
73. Gearshift control housing
74. 1st and 2nd operating lever
75. Flatwasher
76. Lockwasher lever
77. Nut
78. Lockwasher
79. Flatwasher
80. 3rd and OD operating lever
83. Interlock Lever (2)
84. "E" ring
85. Spring
86. Oil seal (2)
87. 3rd and OD lever
88. 1st and 2nd lever
89. 3rd and OD speed fork
90. 1st and 2nd speed fork
91. Drain plug
92. Gasket
93. Expansion plug

12 Remove the bolt and retainer holding the speedometer pinion adapter in the extension housing, then remove the pinion adapter.

13 Remove the bolts attaching the extension housing to the transmission case.

14 Rotate the extension housing on the output shaft to expose the rear of the countershaft. Install one bolt to hold the extension in place.

15 Drill a hole in the countershaft extension plug at the front of the case.

16 Reaching through this hole, push the countershaft to the rear to expose the Woodruff key; when exposed, remove it. Push the countershaft forward against the expansion plug, and using a brass drift, tap the countershaft forward until the expansion plug is removed.

17 Using a countershaft arbor, push the

countershaft out the rear of the case, but don't let the countershaft out the rear of the case, and don't let the countershaft washers fall out of position. Lower the cluster gear to the bottom of the transmission case.

18 Remove the bolt and rotate the extension back to the normal position.

19 Remove the drive pinion attaching bolts and slide the retainer and gasket from the pinion shaft, then pry the pinion or seal from the retainer. When installing the new seal, don't nick or scratch the seal bore in the retainer or the surface on which the seal bottoms.

20 Using a brass drift, tap the pinion and bearing assembly forward and remove through the front of the case.

21 Slide the third and overdrive synchronizer sleeve slightly forward, slide the reverse idler gear to the center of its shaft, and tap the extension housing rearward. Slide the housing and mainshaft assembly out and away from the case.

22 Remove the snap ring holding the third and overdrive synchronizer clutch gear and sleeve assembly to the mainshaft, then remove the synchronizer assembly.

23 Slide the overdrive gear and stop ring off the mainshaft. Using pair of long nose pliers, compress the snap ring holding the mainshaft bearing in the extension housing. With it compressed, pull the mainshaft assembly and bearing out of the extension housing.

24 Remove the snap ring holding the mainshaft on the shaft. The bearing is removed by inserting steel plates on

the front side of the first speed gear, then pressing the mainshaft through the bearing being careful not to damage the gear teeth.

25 Remove the bearing, retainer ring, first speed gear and stop ring from the shaft.

26 Remove the first and second clutch gear and sleeve assembly from the mainshaft.

27 Remove the drive pinion bearing inner snap ring, then using an arbor press, remove the bearing. Remove the snap ring and bearing rollers from the cavity in the drive pinion.

28 Remove the countershaft gear from the bottom of the case, then remove the arbor, needle bearings, thrust washers and spacers from the center of the countershaft gear.

29 Remove the reverse gearshift lever detent spring retainer, gasket, plug, and detent ball spring from the rear of the case.

30 The reverse idler gear shaft is a tight fit in the case and will have to be pressed out.

31 If there is oil leakage visible around the reverse gearshift lever shaft, push the lever shaft in and remove it from the case. Remove the detent ball from the bottom of the transmission case and remove the shift fork from the shaft and detent plate.

Assembly

Follow the first four steps only if you removed the reverse shaft in the disassembly procedure.

1 Install a new oil seal O-ring on the lever shaft and coat the shaft with

grease; insert it into its bore and install the reverse fork in the lever.

2 Install the reverse detent spring and gasket and torque to 50 ft. lbs; insert the ball and spring and install the plug and gasket which are torqued to 24 ft. lbs.

3 Place the reverse idler gear shaft in position in the end of the case and drive it in far enough to position the reverse idler gear on the protruding end of the shaft with the fork slot toward the rear. While doing this, engage the slot with the reverse shift fork.

4 With the reverse idler gear correctly positioned, drive the reverse gear shaft into the case far enough to install the woodruff key. Drive the shaft in flush with the end of the transmission case. Install the back-up light switch and gasket.

COUNTERSHAFT GEAR AND DRIVE PINION

5 Coat the inside bore of the countershaft gear with a thin film of grease and install the roller bearing spacer with an arbor, into the gear; center the spacer and arbor.

6 Install the roller bearings and a spacer ring on each end.

7 Replace worn thrust washers; coat the new ones with grease and install them over the arbor with the tang side toward the case boss.

8 Install the countershaft assembly into the case and allow the gear assembly to sit on the bottom of the case so that the thrust washers won't come out of position.

9 Press the drive pinion bearing on the pinion shaft. Make sure the outer snap ring groove is toward the front and the bearing is seated against the shoulder on the gear.

10 Install a new snap ring on the shaft to hold the bearing in place; make sure the snap ring is seated and that there is minimum end play.

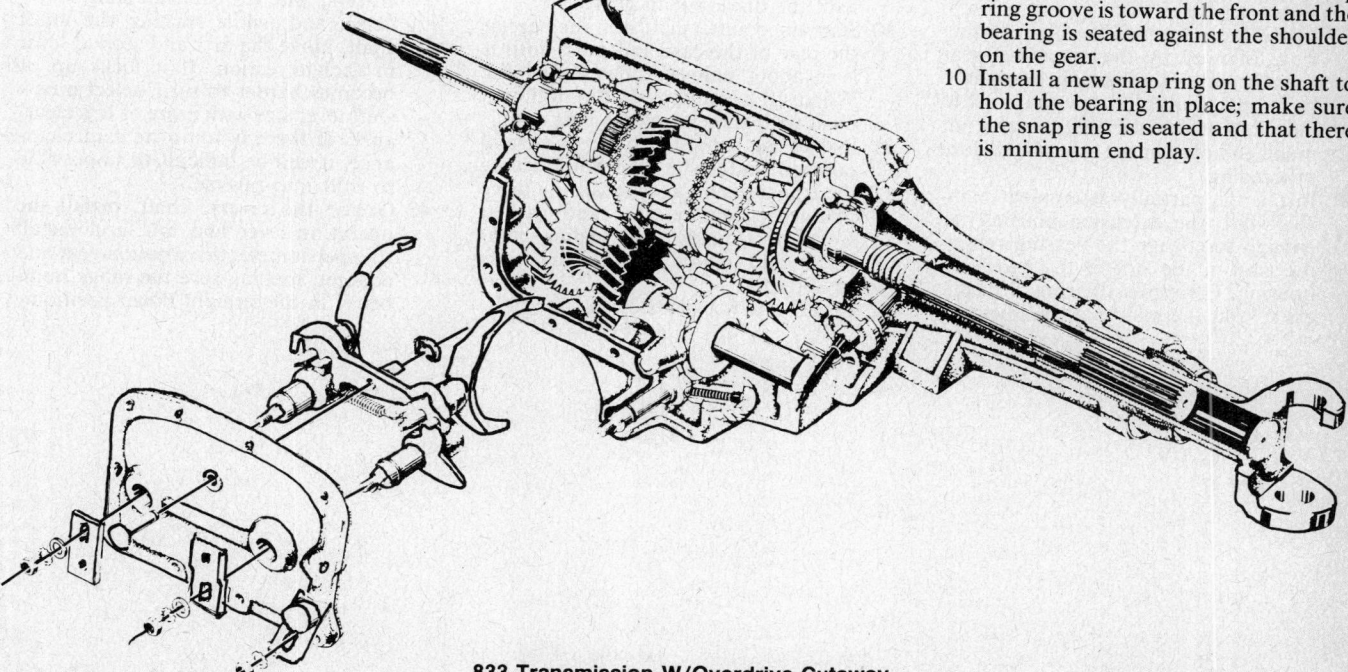

833 Transmission W/Overdrive Cutaway

11 Place the pinion shaft in a soft-jawed vise and install the roller bearings in the cavity of the shaft. Coat them with grease and install the retaining ring.

12 Install a new oil seal in the bore.

EXTENSION HOUSING BUSHING

13 Remove the yoke seal from the extension housing.

14 Drive out the old bushing and slide in a new one, aligning the oil hole in the bushing with the slot in the housing.

15 Place a new seal in the opening of the extension housing and then drive the bushing into place.

MAINSHAFT

Assemble the synchronizer as follows:

16 Place a stop ring flat on a bench followed by the clutch gear and sleeve; drop the struts in their sleeves and snap in a strut spring placing the tang inside one strut. Install the second strut spring tang in a different strut after turning the assembly over.

17 Slide the second speed gear over the mainshaft with the synchronizer cone toward the rear and down against the shoulder on the shaft.

18 Slide the first and second gear synchronizer assembly including stop rings with lugs indexed in the hub slots, over the mainshaft down against the second gear cone and hold it there with a new snap ring. Slide the next snap ring over the shaft and index the lugs into the clutch hub slots.

19 Slide the first speed gear with the synchronizer cone toward the clutch sleeve just installed over the mainshaft and into position against the clutch sleeve gear.

20 Install the mainshaft bearing retaining ring followed by the mainshaft rear bearing; press the bearing down into position and install a new snap ring to secure it. Make sure that there is not much end play in the assembly before proceeding.

21 Install the partially assembled mainshaft into the extension housing far enough to engage the bearing retaining ring in the slot in the extension housing. Compress the ring with pliers so that the mainshaft ball bearing can move in and bottom against its thrust shoulder in the extension housing. Release the ring and make sure that it is seated.

22 Slide the overdrive gear over the mainshaft with the synchronizer cone toward the front followed by the gears' snap ring.

23 Install the third-overdrive gear synchronizer clutch gear assembly on the mainshaft against the overdrive gear. Make sure to index the rear stop ring with the clutch gear struts.

24 Install the snap ring and position the front stop ring over the clutch gear again lining up the ring lugs with the struts; coat a new extension gasket with grease and place it in position.

25 Slide the reverse idler gear to the center of its shaft and move the third-overdrive synchronizer as far forward as possible without losing the struts.

26 Insert the mainshaft assembly in the case tilting it as necessary. Place the third-overdrive sleeve in the neutral detent.

27 Rotate the extension on the mainshaft to expose the rear of the countershaft and install one bolt to hold it in position.

28 Install the drive pinion and bearing assembly through the front of the case and position it in the front bore. Install the outer snap ring in the bearing groove and tap lightly into place. If it doesn't bottom easily, check to see if a strut, pinion roller or stop ring is out of position.

29 Turn the transmission upside down while holding the countershaft gear to prevent damage. Then lower the countershaft gear assembly into position making sure that the teeth mesh with the drive pinion gear.

30 Start the countershaft into the bore at the rear of the case and push until it is in about halfway; then install the Woodruff key and push it in until it is flush with the end of the rear case.

31 Rotate the extension back to normal position and install the bolts; rotate the transmission and install the drive pinion bearing retainer and gasket. Coat the threads with sealing compound and tighten the attaching bolts to 30 ft lbs.

32 Install a new expansion in its bore.

GEARSHIFT HOUSING AND MECHANISM

33 Install the interlock levers on the pivot pin and secure with the E-ring. Install the spring with a pair of pliers.

34 Grease and install new O-ring seals on both shift shafts; grease the housing bores and push the shafts through.

35 Install the operating levers and tighten the retaining nuts to 18 ft/lbs; make sure the third-overdrive lever points down.

36 Rotate each shift shaft fork bore straight up and install the third-overdrive shift fork in its bore and under both interlock levers.

37 Position both synchronizer sleeves in neutral and place the first and second gear shift fork in the groove of the first and second gear synchronizer sleeve. Turn the transmission on its right side and place the gearshift housing gasket in place holding it there with grease.

38 As the shift housing is lowered in place, guide the third-overdrive shift fork into its synchronizer groove then lead the shaft of the first and second shift fork into its bore in the first and second shift lever.

39 Raise the interlock lever with a screwdriver to allow the first and second shift fork to slip under the levers. The shift housing will now seat against the case.

40 Install the bolts lightly and shift through all the gears to check for proper operation.

41 The reverse shift lever and the first and second gear shift lever have cam surfaces which mate in reverse position to lock the first and second lever, the fork and synchronizer in the neutral position. To check for proper operation, put the transmission in reverse, and, while turning the input shaft, move the first and second lever in each direction. If it locks up or becomes harder to turn, select a new shift lever size with more or less clearance. If there is too little cam clearance, it will be difficult or impossible to shift into reverse.

42 Grease the reverse shaft, install the operating lever and nut, and install the speedometer drive pinion gear and adapter, making sure the range number is in the straight down position.

CHRYSLER A-412 MANUAL TRANSAXLE

Chrysler A-412 Manual Transaxle

Gear reduction, ratio selection and differential functions are combined in a single unit. The transaxle assembly is housed in a two piece magnesium case. One piece is the transmission housing and the other piece is the clutch and differential assembly housing.

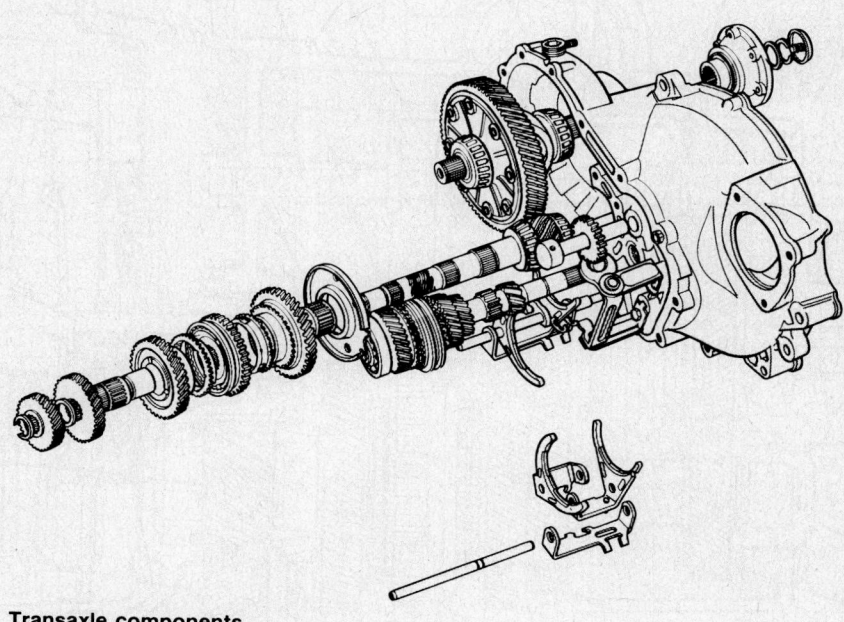

Transaxle components

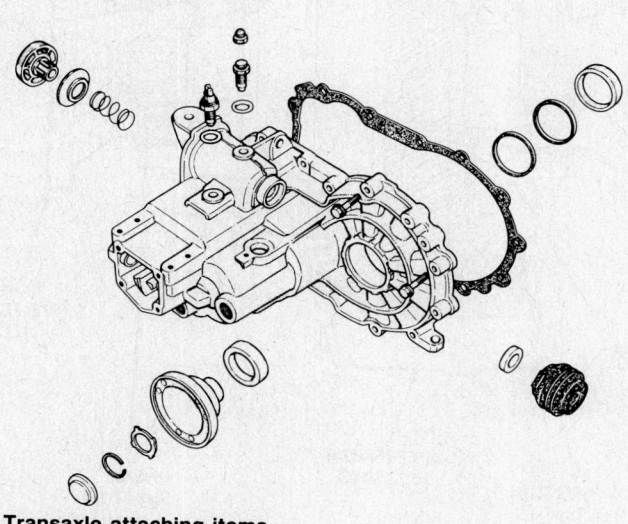

Transaxle attaching items

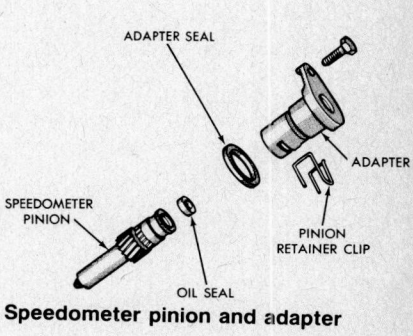

Speedometer pinion and adapter

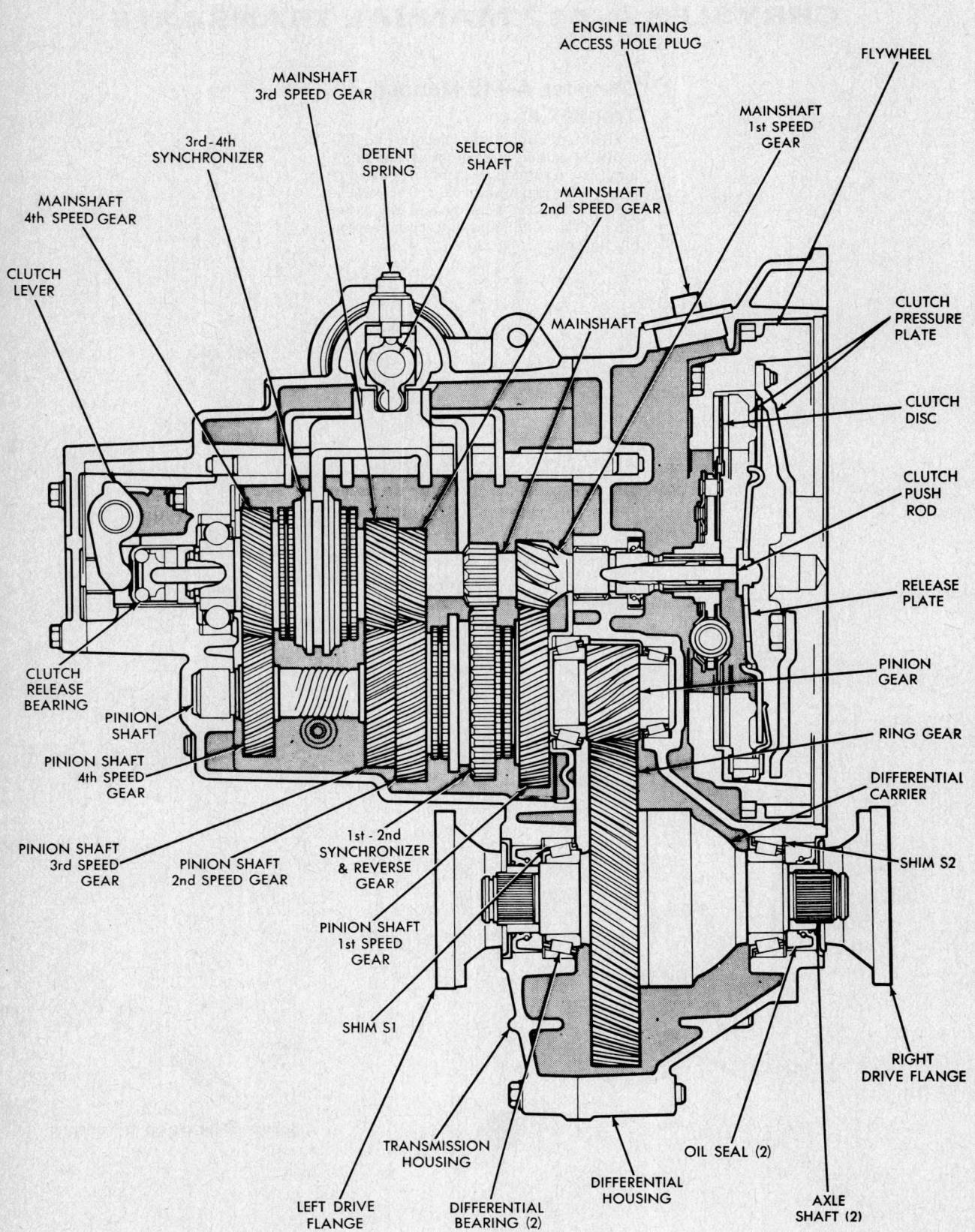

Chrysler A-412 manual transaxle

Disassembly

1 Remove the clutch push rod.
2 Remove the drive flange dust plug, snap ring, cone washer drive flange and drive flange oil seal.
3 Remove the selector shaft cover, push out the selector shaft and remove the selector shaft oil seal.
4 Remove the mainshaft bearing retaining nut rubber plugs, and remove the clutch release bearing end cover. While removing, hold the clutch release lever in upward position to avoid loading end cover and damaging case threads.
5 Remove the release bearing and the sleeve.
6 Remove the circlips from the torque shaft, and remove the clutch torque shaft, return spring and release lever. Remove the torque shaft oil seals.
7 Remove the mainshaft bearing retainer nuts. The three studs and clips will drop into the case.
8 Remove the case attaching bolts, the reverse idler shaft set screw and the back-up light switch. Remove the transmission case, and mark the shims for installation reference.
9 Remove the reverse shift fork supports and remove the reverse shift fork.
10 Remove the mainshaft assembly and pinion shaft fourth speed gear.
11 Disassemble the mainshaft by removing the bearing and fourth speed gear, the third-fourth synchronizer and third speed gear and needle bearing.

NOTE: **Synchronizers are serviced as an assembly.**

12 Remove the shift rail "E" clips, and remove the shift forks assembly.
13 Remove the clutch push rod seal and bushing assembly.
14 On the pinion shaft, remove the snap ring, third speed gear, second speed gear and needle bearing.
15 Remove the reverse gear idler shaft.
16 Complete pinion shaft disassembly by removing the first-second gears synchronizer, the second speed gear sleeve, the first gear stop ring and the first speed gear. The inner sleeve for second speed gear and the first speed gear are removed together.

NOTE: **Before installing the puller to remove the synchronizer, remove the plastic thrust button, and install Tool L-4443-4 or equivalent in the pinion shaft. The pinion shaft bearing retainer is notched in two places for puller jaws.**

17 Remove the pinion shaft retainer and first gear thrust washer, and remove the pinion shaft.

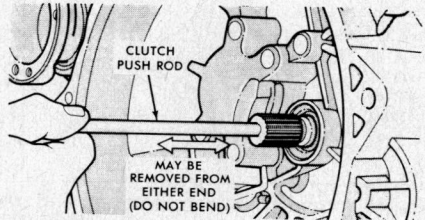

Clutch push rod

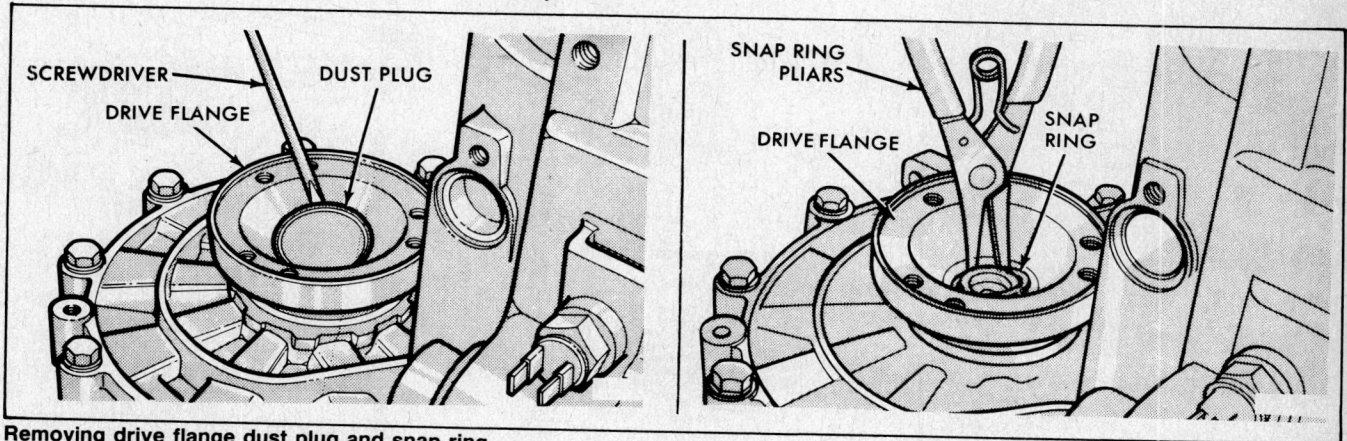

Removing drive flange dust plug and snap ring

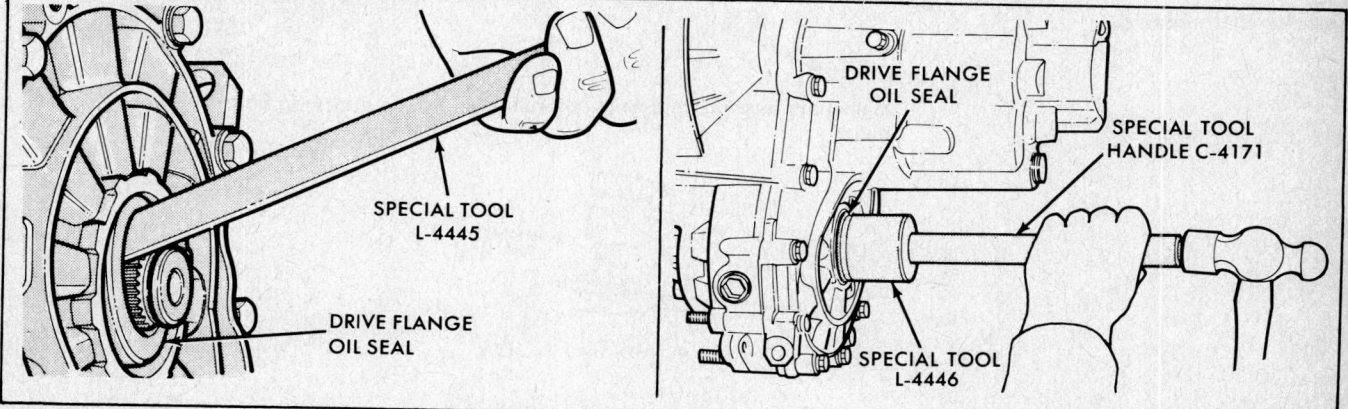

Drive flange oil seal replacement

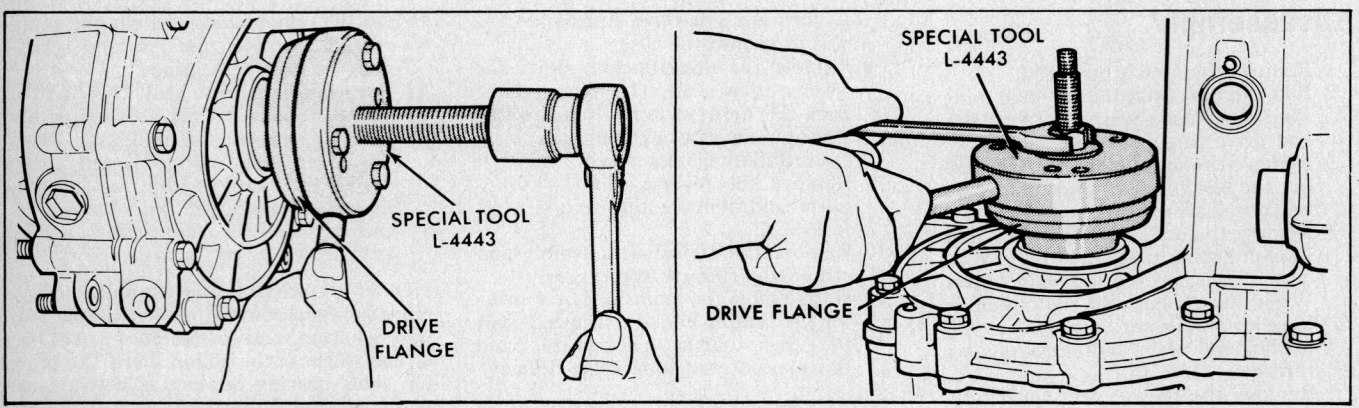

Drive flange removal and installation

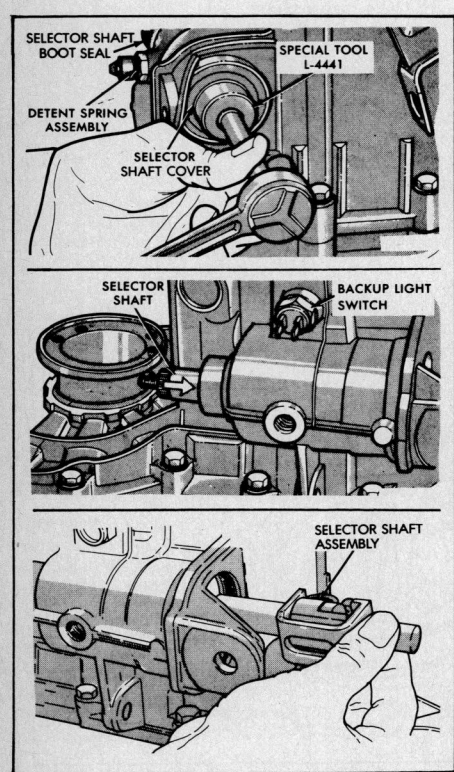

Selector shaft removal

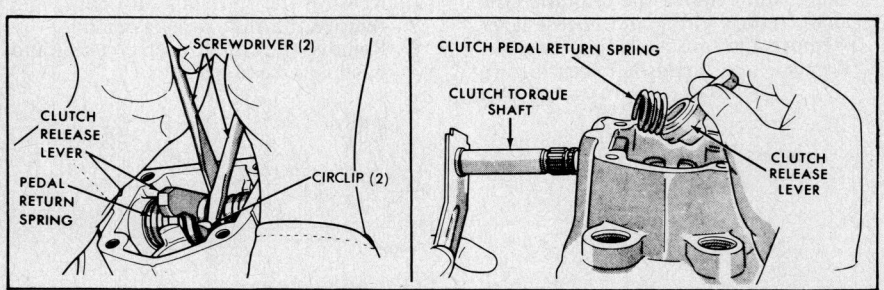

Clutch torque shaft, return spring and release lever removal

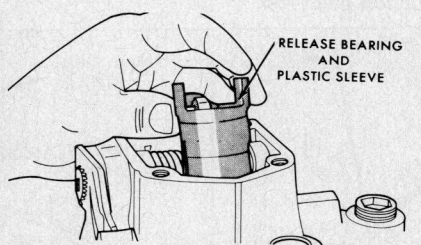

Removing release bearing and sleeve

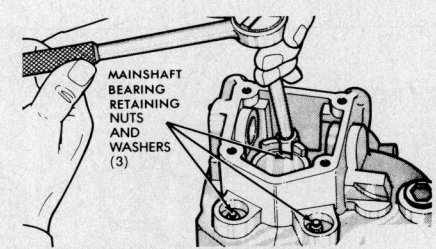

Mainshaft bearing and retainer nuts

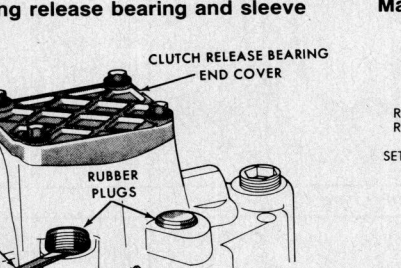

Mainshaft bearing retaining nut rubber plugs

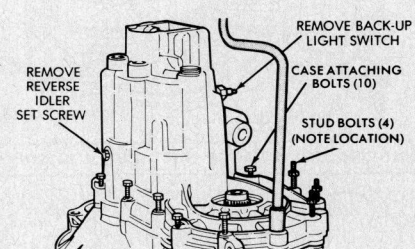

Case attaching bolts

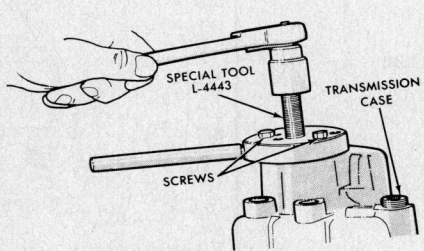

Transmission case removal

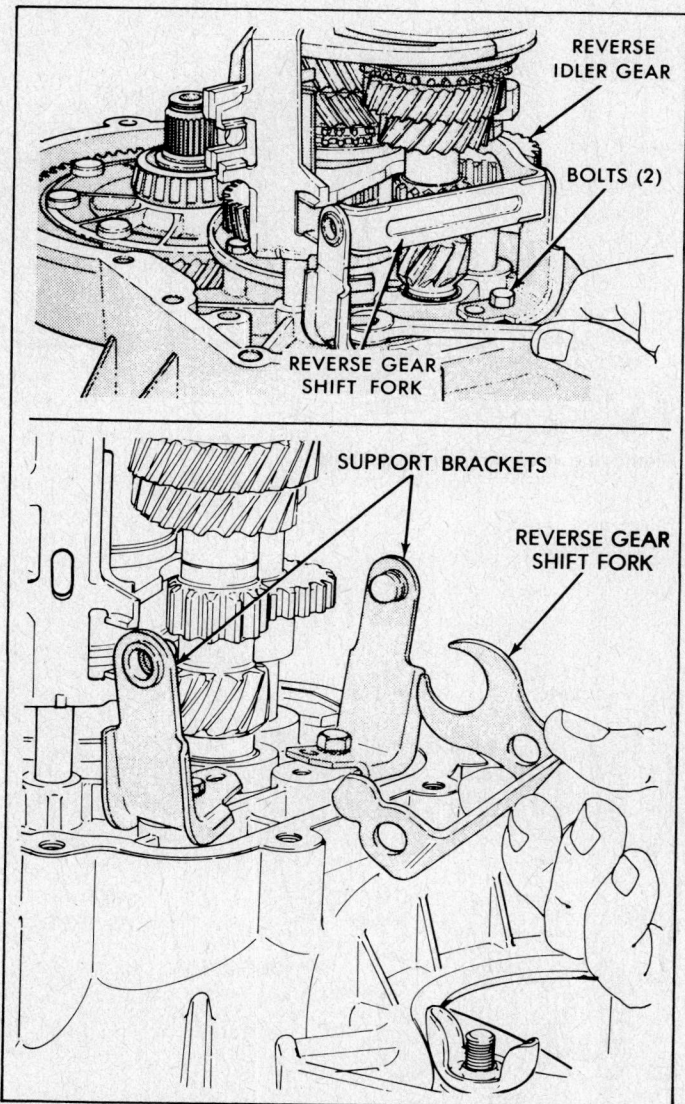

REVERSE IDLER GEAR

BOLTS (2)

REVERSE GEAR SHIFT FORK

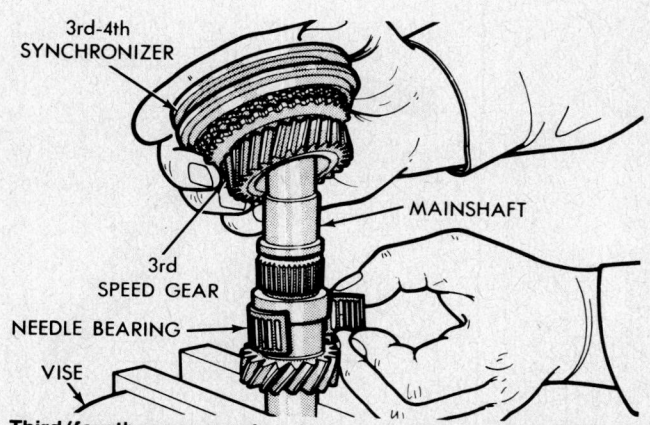

SUPPORT BRACKETS

REVERSE GEAR SHIFT FORK

Reverse shift fork removal

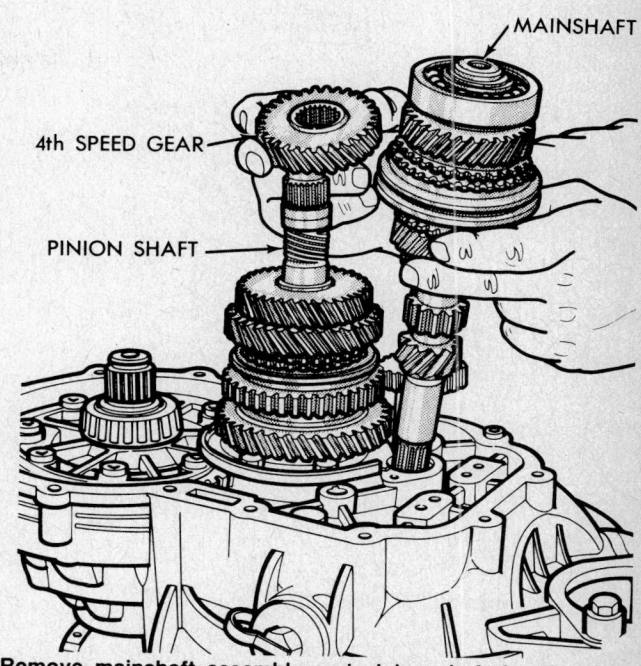

MAINSHAFT

4th SPEED GEAR

PINION SHAFT

Remove mainshaft assembly and pinion shaft fourth speed gear

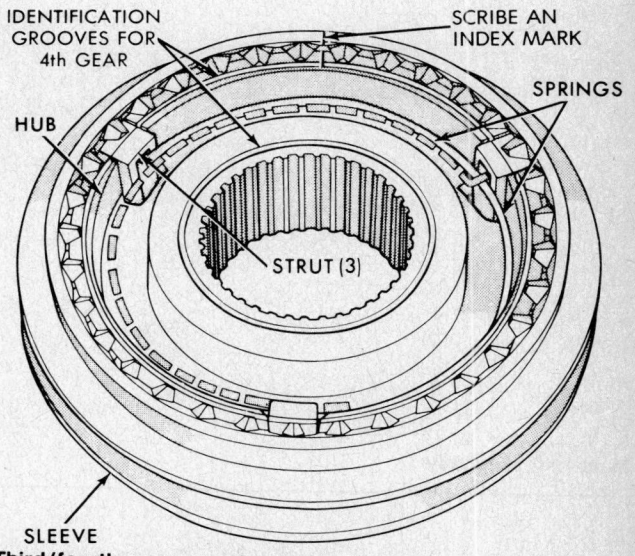

IDENTIFICATION GROOVES FOR 4th GEAR

SCRIBE AN INDEX MARK

SPRINGS

HUB

STRUT (3)

SLEEVE

Third/fourth gears synchronizer

3rd-4th SYNCHRONIZER

MAINSHAFT

3rd SPEED GEAR

NEEDLE BEARING

VISE

Third/fourth gears synchronizer and third speed gear and needle bearing on mainshaft

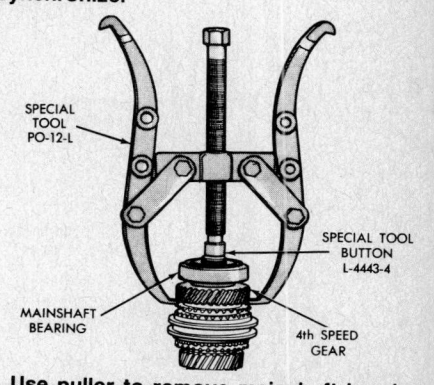

SPECIAL TOOL PO-12-L

SPECIAL TOOL BUTTON L-4443-4

MAINSHAFT BEARING

4th SPEED GEAR

Use puller to remove mainshaft bearing and mainshaft fourth speed gear

MANUAL TRANSMISSIONS
CHRYSLER A-412 MANUAL TRANSAXLE

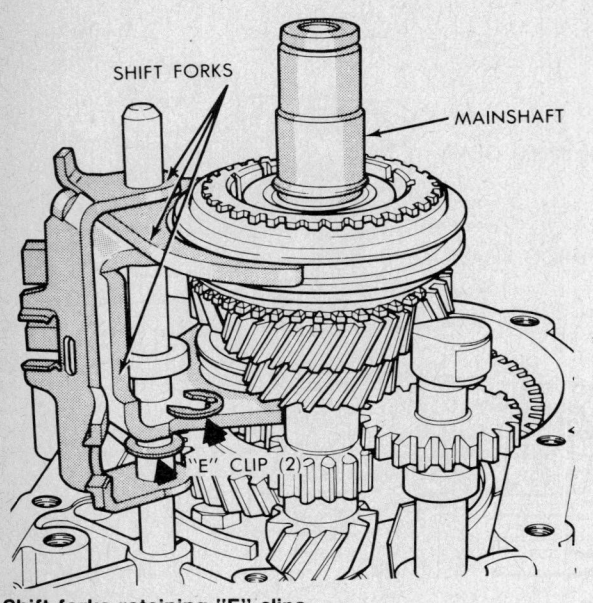

Shift forks retaining "E" clips

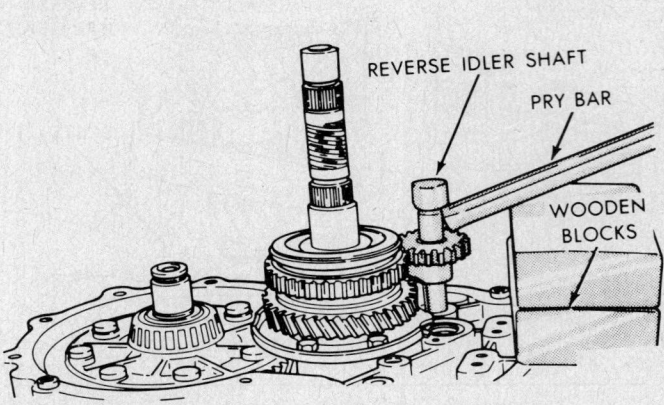

Removing reverse gear idler shaft

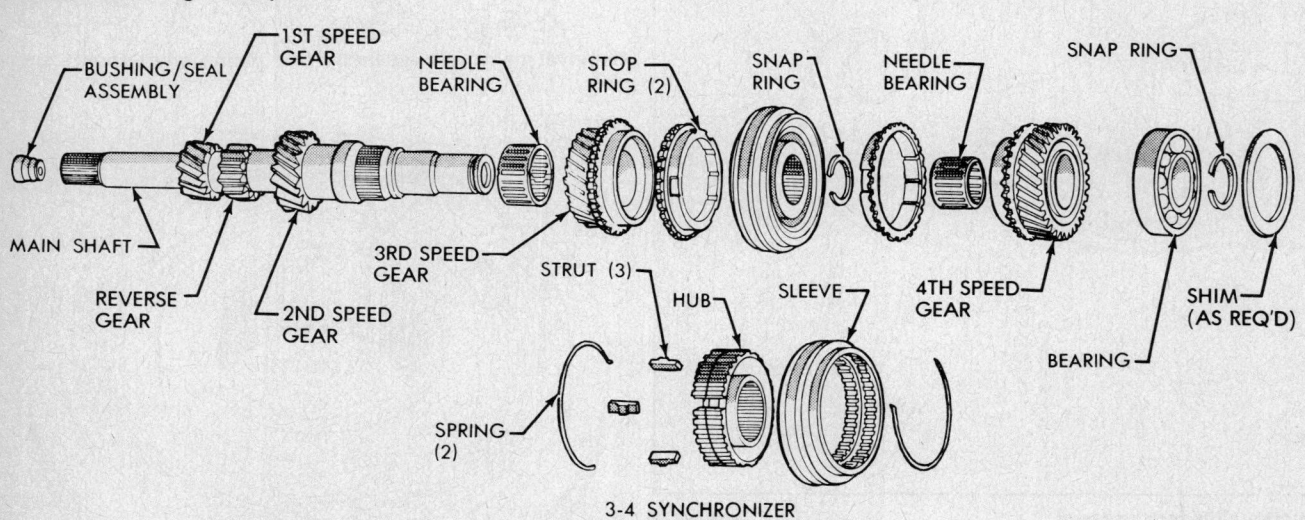

Mainshaft assembly

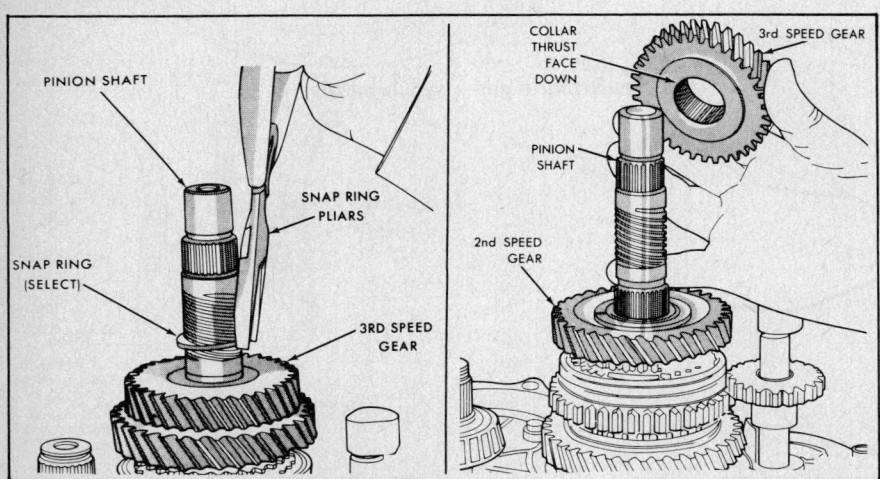

Removing snap ring and third speed gear

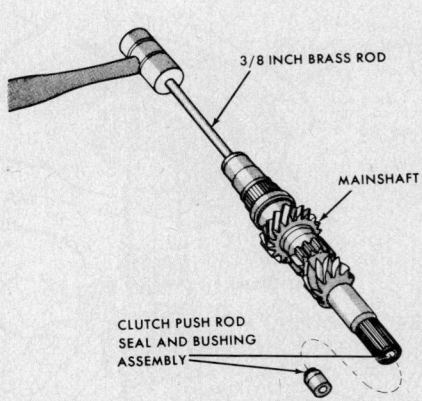

Removing clutch push rod seal and bushing assembly

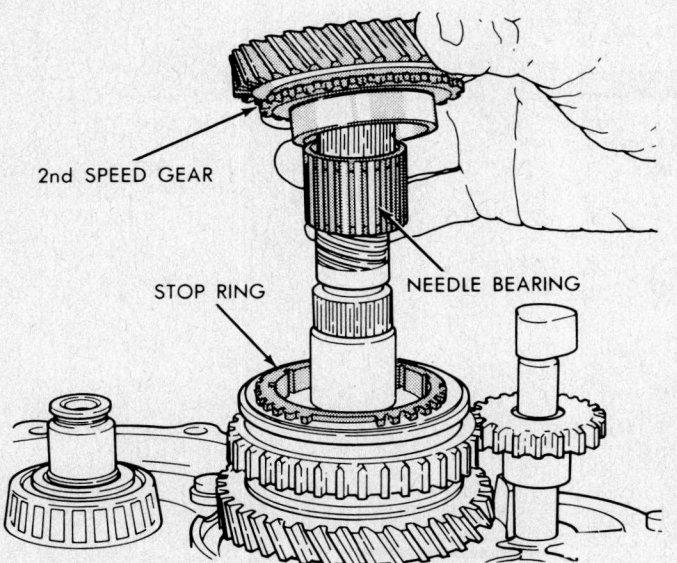

2nd SPEED GEAR

STOP RING

NEEDLE BEARING

Removing second speed gear and needle bearing from pinion shaft

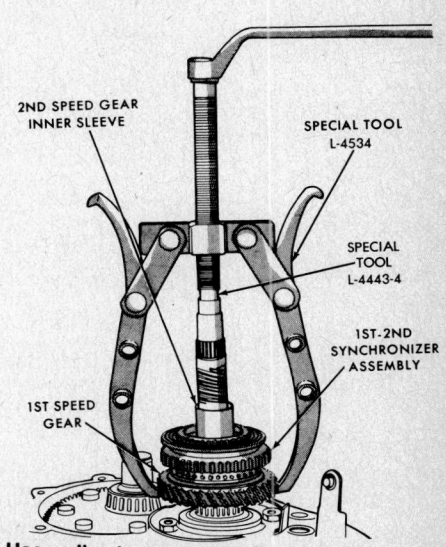

2ND SPEED GEAR INNER SLEEVE

SPECIAL TOOL L-4534

SPECIAL TOOL L-4443-4

1ST-2ND SYNCHRONIZER ASSEMBLY

1ST SPEED GEAR

Use puller to remove first/second gears synchronizer from pinion shaft

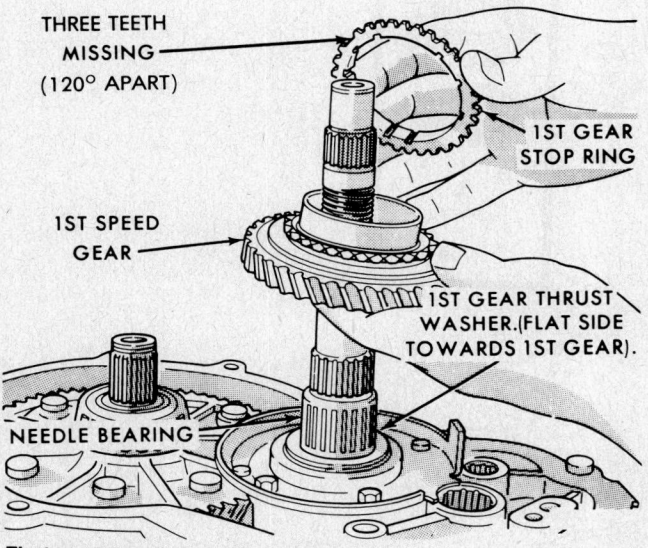

THREE TEETH MISSING (120° APART)

1ST GEAR STOP RING

1ST SPEED GEAR

1ST GEAR THRUST WASHER.(FLAT SIDE TOWARDS 1ST GEAR).

NEEDLE BEARING

First speed gear and needle bearing

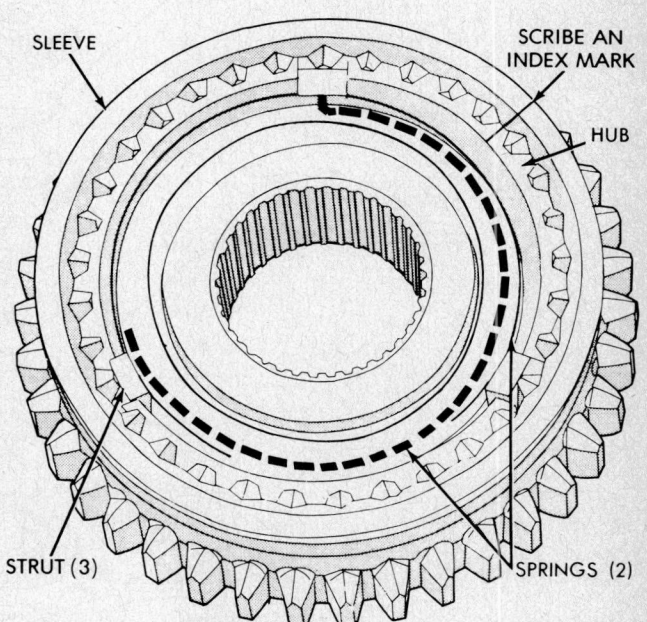

SLEEVE

SCRIBE AN INDEX MARK

HUB

STRUT (3)

SPRINGS (2)

First/second gears synchronizer. Scribe index mark for assembly reference

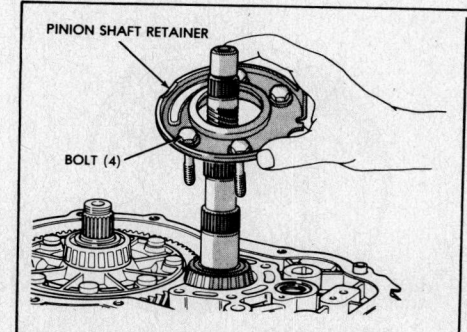

PINION SHAFT RETAINER

BOLT (4)

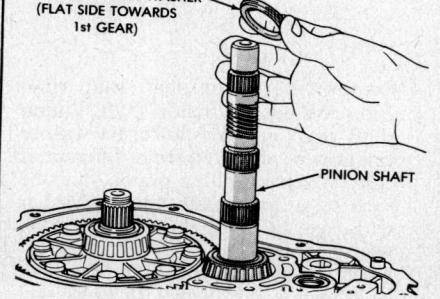

1st GEAR THRUST WASHER (FLAT SIDE TOWARDS 1st GEAR)

PINION SHAFT

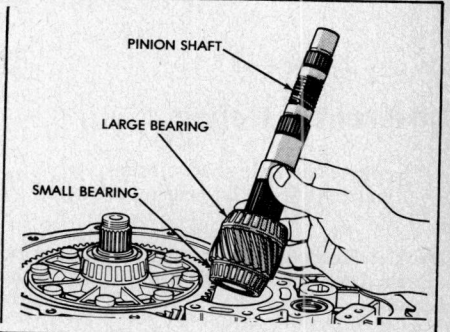

PINION SHAFT

LARGE BEARING

SMALL BEARING

Pinion shaft removal

B727

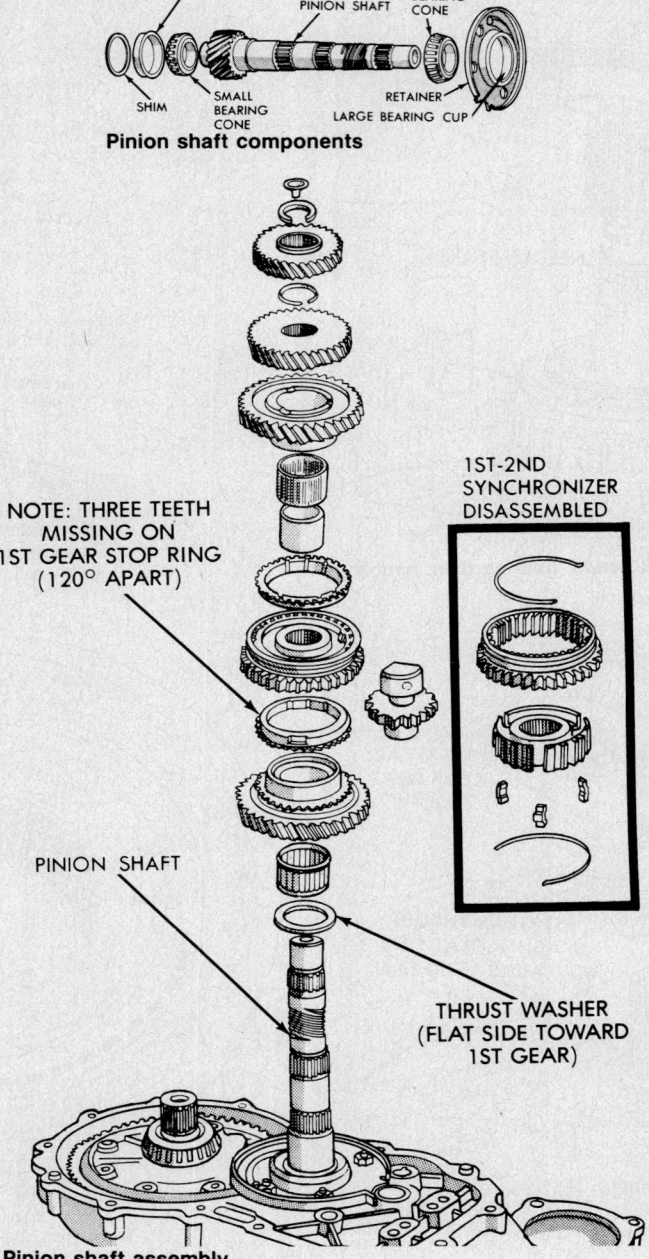

SMALL BEARING CUP   PINION SHAFT   LARGE BEARING CONE

SHIM   SMALL BEARING CONE   RETAINER   LARGE BEARING CUP

Pinion shaft components

NOTE: THREE TEETH MISSING ON 1ST GEAR STOP RING (120° APART)

1ST-2ND SYNCHRONIZER DISASSEMBLED

PINION SHAFT

THRUST WASHER (FLAT SIDE TOWARD 1ST GEAR)

Pinion shaft assembly

Differential Repair

1 Remove the axle shaft circlips.
2 Remove differential bearing cone and cup.

NOTE: Bearing cones and cups are matched sets and must be replaced as assemblies.

3 Remove the side gears.

4 Remove the pinion shaft snap ring, and drive out the pinion shaft. Pinion shaft gears and plastic thrust washer can now be removed from differential case. When installing pinion shaft be sure to align plastic thrust washer with case to avoid damage to thrust washer holes.
5 Drill out the ring gear rivets. The new ring gear is installed with bolts and nuts.

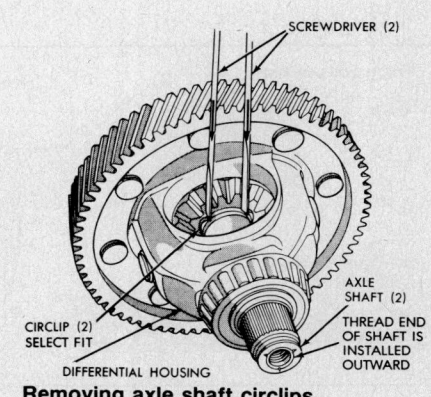

SCREWDRIVER (2)

AXLE SHAFT (2)

THREAD END OF SHAFT IS INSTALLED OUTWARD

CIRCLIP (2) SELECT FIT

DIFFERENTIAL HOUSING

Removing axle shaft circlips

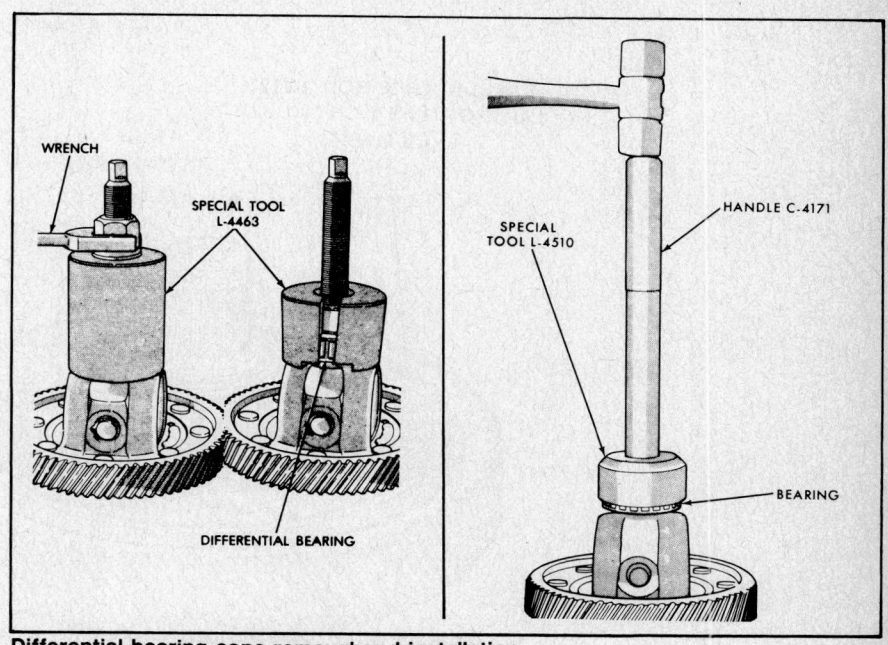

Differential bearing cone removal and installation

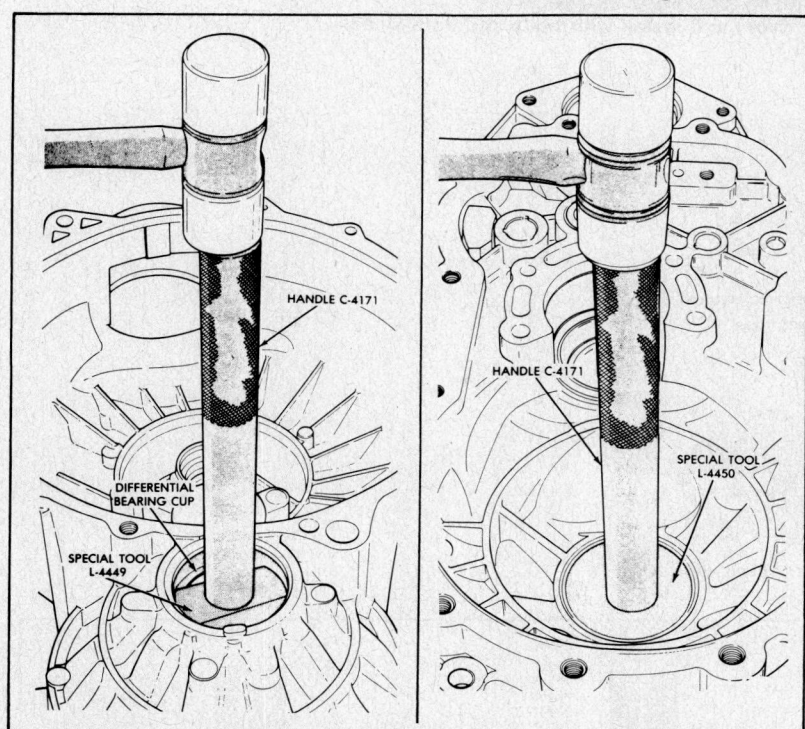

Differential bearing cup removal and installation

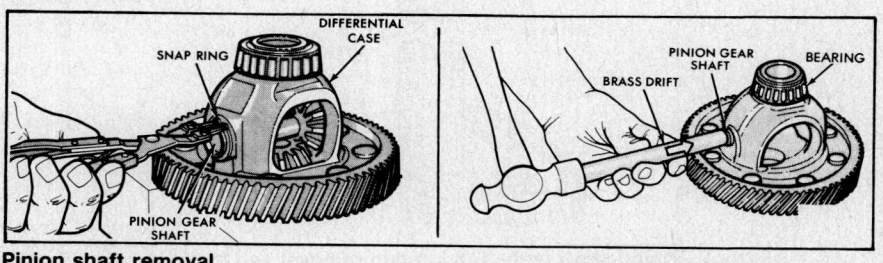

Pinion shaft removal

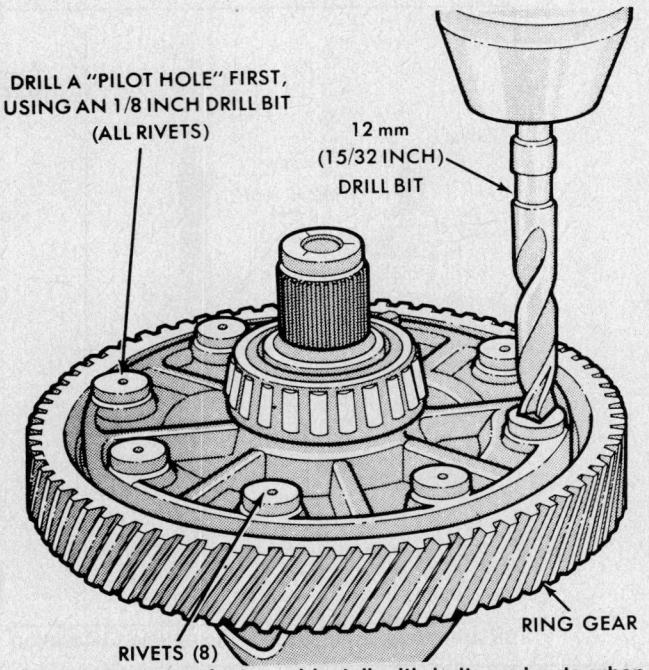

DRILL A "PILOT HOLE" FIRST, USING AN 1/8 INCH DRILL BIT (ALL RIVETS)

12 mm (15/32 INCH) DRILL BIT

RING GEAR

RIVETS (8)

Drill out ring gear rivets and install with bolts and nuts when replacing ring gear

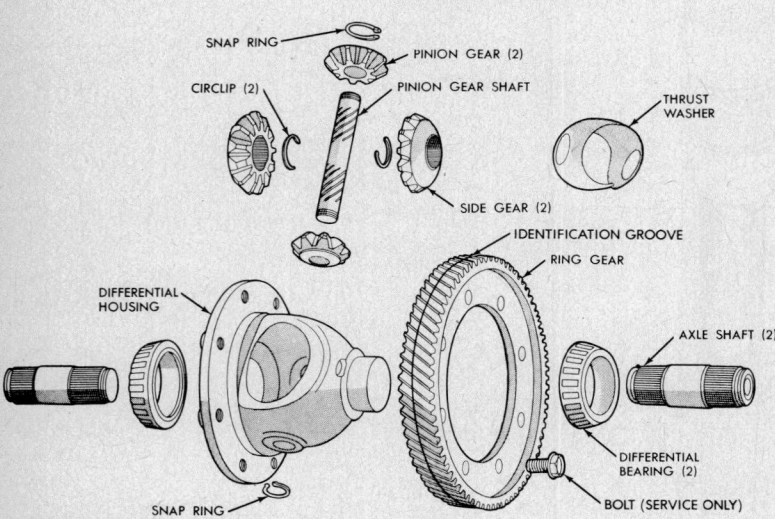

SNAP RING

CIRCLIP (2)

PINION GEAR (2)

PINION GEAR SHAFT

THRUST WASHER

SIDE GEAR (2)

IDENTIFICATION GROOVE

RING GEAR

DIFFERENTIAL HOUSING

AXLE SHAFT (2)

DIFFERENTIAL BEARING (2)

BOLT (SERVICE ONLY)

SNAP RING

Differential components

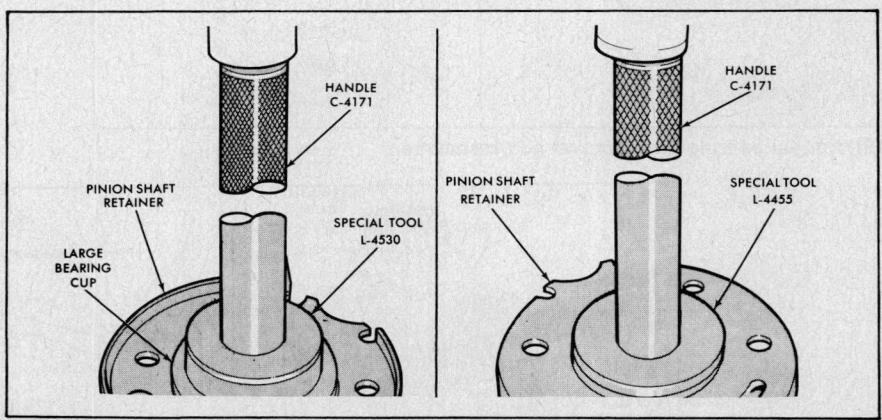

HANDLE C-4171

HANDLE C-4171

PINION SHAFT RETAINER

LARGE BEARING CUP

SPECIAL TOOL L-4530

PINION SHAFT RETAINER

SPECIAL TOOL L-4455

Pinion shaft large bearing cup removal and installation

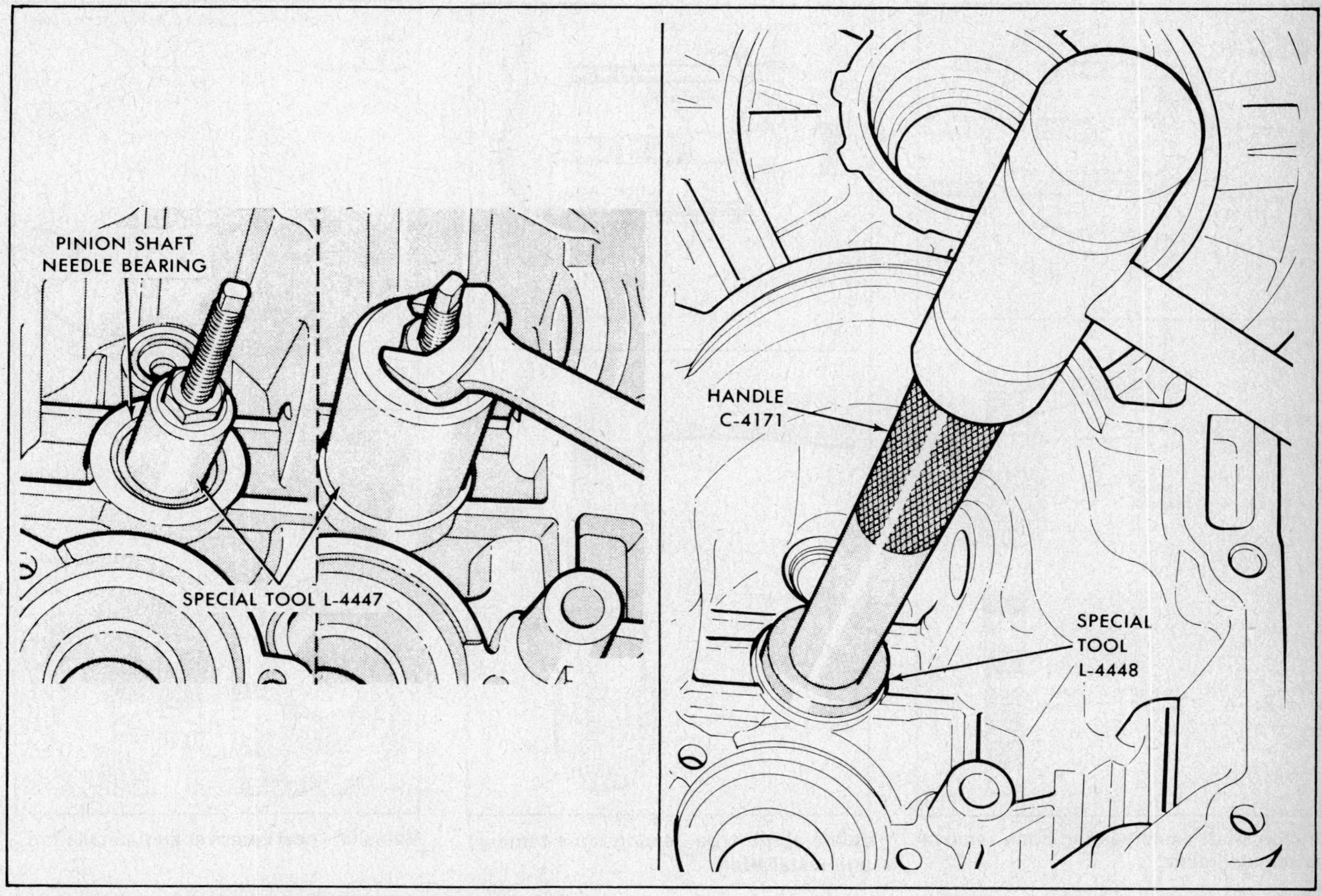

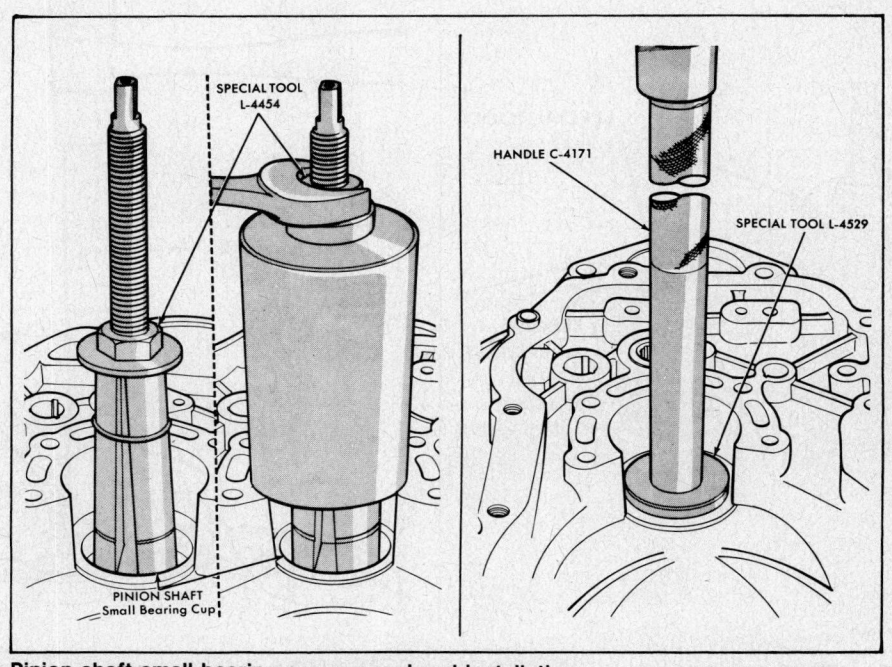

Pinion shaft needle bearing removal and installation

Pinion shaft small bearing cup removal and installation

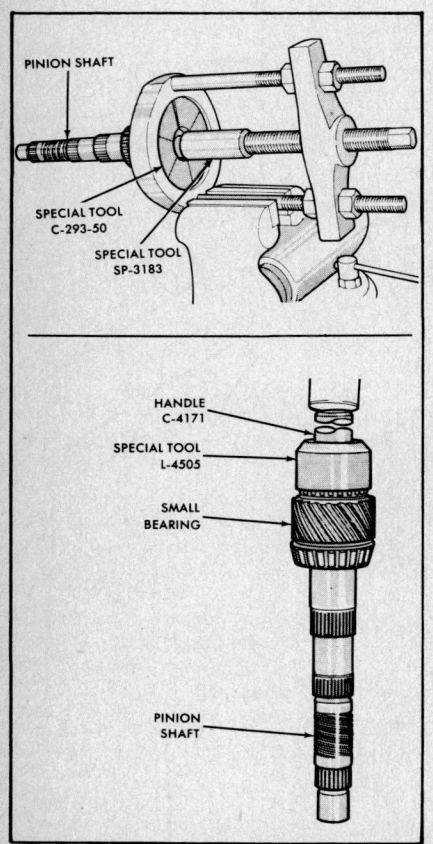

Pinion shaft small bearing cone removal and installation

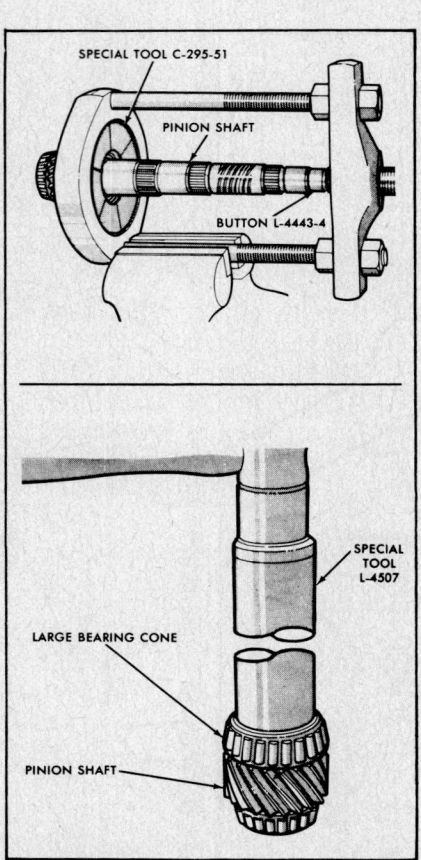

Pinion shaft large bearing cone removal and installation

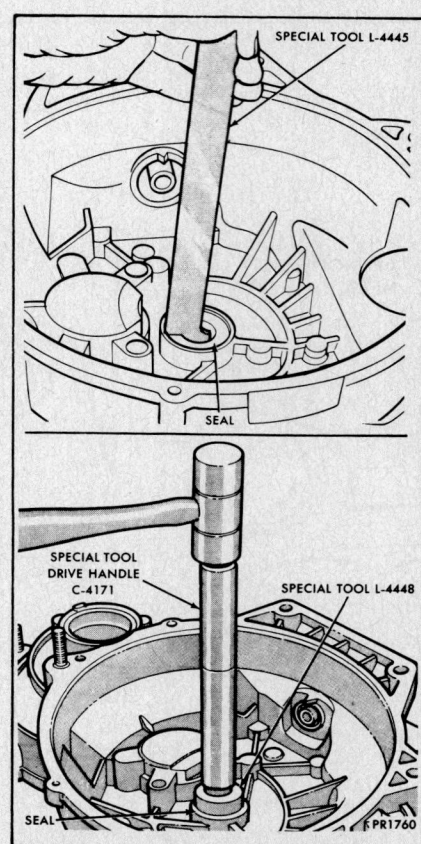

Mainshaft seal removal and installation

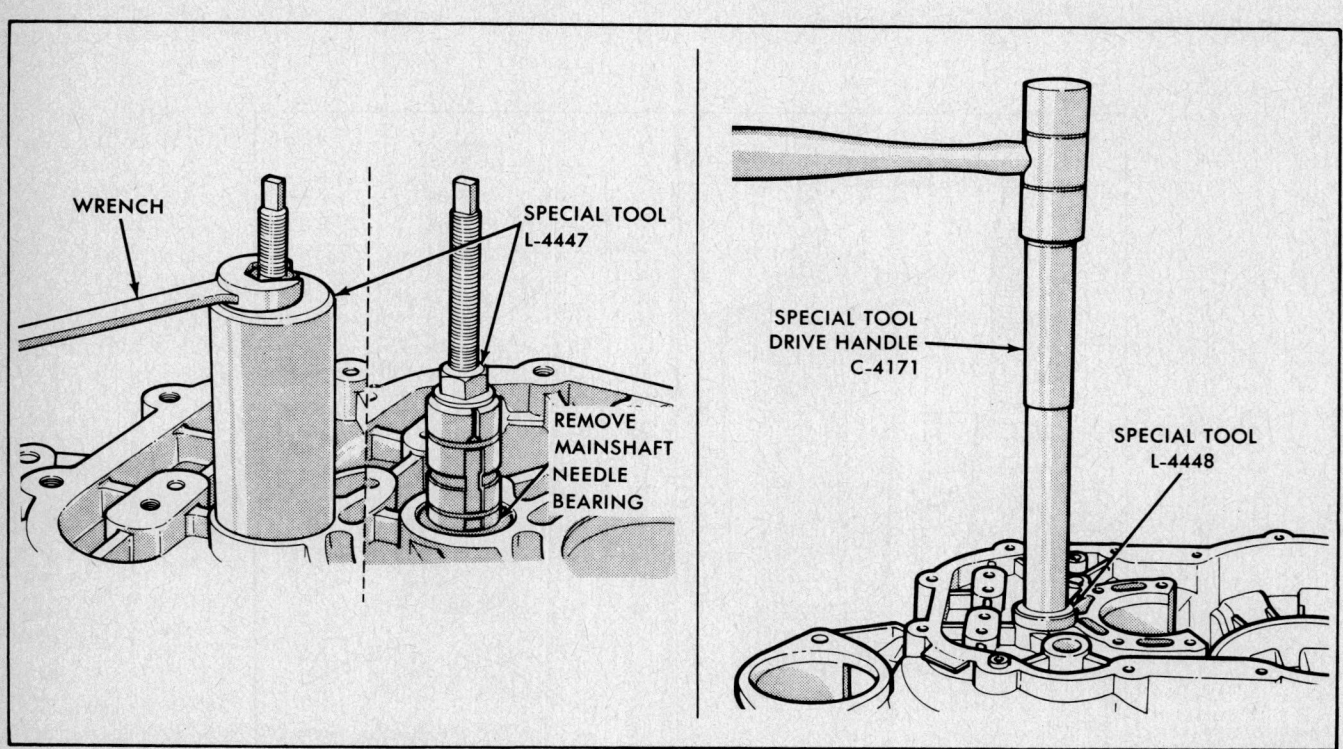

Mainshaft needle bearing removal and installation

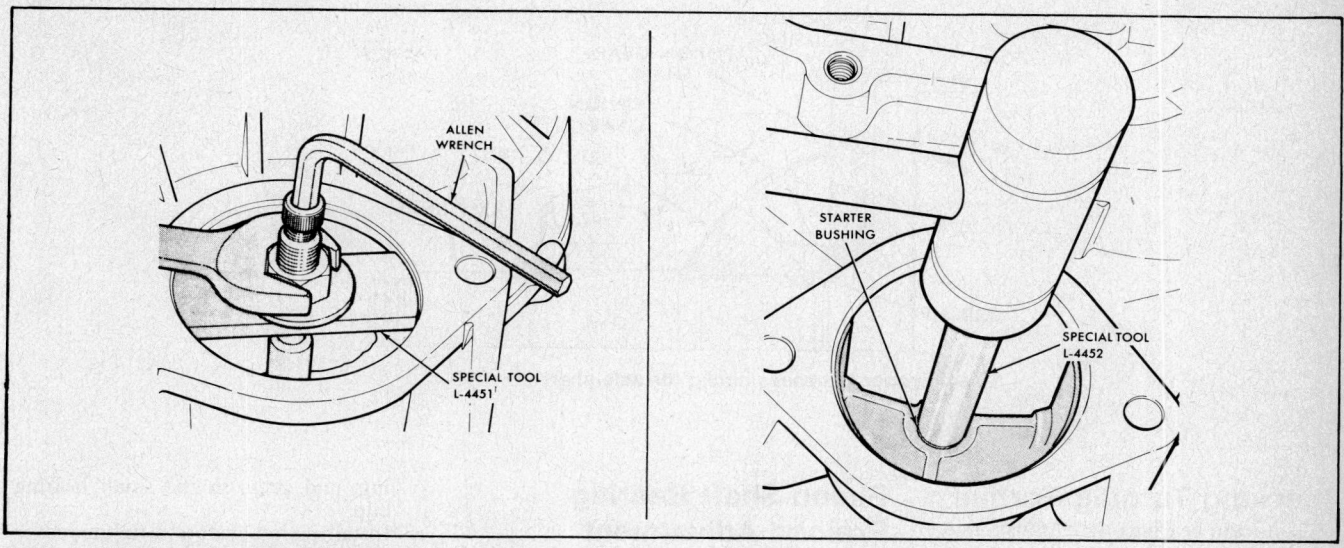

Starter bushing removal and installation

Differential Bearing Preload Adjusting

NOTE: Differential Bearing Preload adjustment is necessary after replacement of the transmission case, clutch housing, differential case or differential bearings.

1 Install cup of bearing (opposite ring gear) with shim S2 in clutch/differential housing. Shim S2 is always 1 mm. (.039 inch) thick.
2 Install outer race on ring gear side without shim S1 in transmission housing.

3 Install differential in its housing.
4 Place transmission housing in position with gasket and tighten five bolts to 14 ft./lbs.
5 Install a dial indicator, and move the differential up and down for measurement reading.

NOTE: Do not turn differential when measuring because bearings will settle and give incorrect reading.

6 Correct bearing preload is obtained by adding a constant figure (0.40 mm.) (.015 inch) to measured reading. For example:

	mm.	inch
Measured reading	0.90	.035
Plus preload (constant figure)	0.40	.015
Shim Thickness (S1) =	1.30	.050

7 Remove the transmission case, and drive out the outer bearing cup.
8 Insert selected shim S1; the thickest shim first. Shims are available in sizes ranging from 0.15 mm (.006 inch) to 0.80 mm (.031 inch).
9 Drive in bearing cup and install transmission housing with gasket and tighten. Before installing transmission housing, remove one axle shaft to check turning torques.

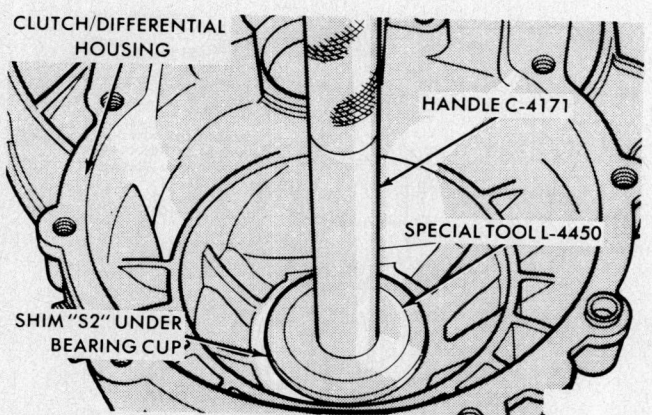

Placing shim S2 under bearing cup for differential bearing preload adjusting

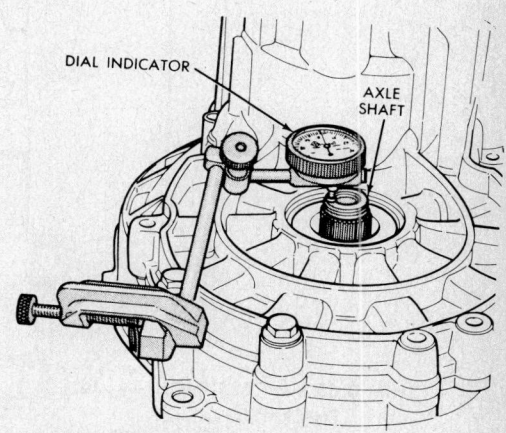

Checking differential end play

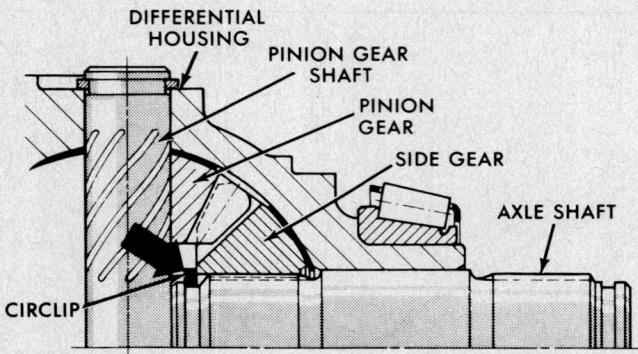

Select proper thickness circlip for axle shaft

Checking Turning Torque

1 Lubricate bearings with transmission oil, and check for the following turning torque:
New bearings—10.4 to 21.7 inch-pounds
Used bearings—minimum 2.7 inch-pounds

Pinion Shaft Bearing Preload Adjustment

1 If clutch housing, ring and pinion gears or differential bearing are changed, it is necessary to adjust preload on pinion shaft bearing.
2 Place a 0.65 mm shim in bearing housing, and press in the small bearing cup.
3 Install pinion shaft and tighten cover nuts to 14 foot-pounds.
4 Mount a dial gauge and move pinion shaft up and down for measurement reading. Do not turn pinion shaft when measuring because bearings will settle and give incorrect measurement.
5 Specified bearing preload is obtained by adding a constant figure (0.20 mm) to measured reading and shim thickness (0.65 mm).
For example:

Shim installed	0.65 mm (.025 inch)
Measured reading	0.30 mm (.012 inch)
Preload (constant figure)	0.20 mm (.008 inch)
Shim	= 1.15 mm

Shims are available in sizes from 0.65 mm (.025 inch) to 1.40 mm (.055 inch).
6 Remove ball bearing retainer, pinion shaft and small bearing cup and 0.65 mm shim. Install correct shim.

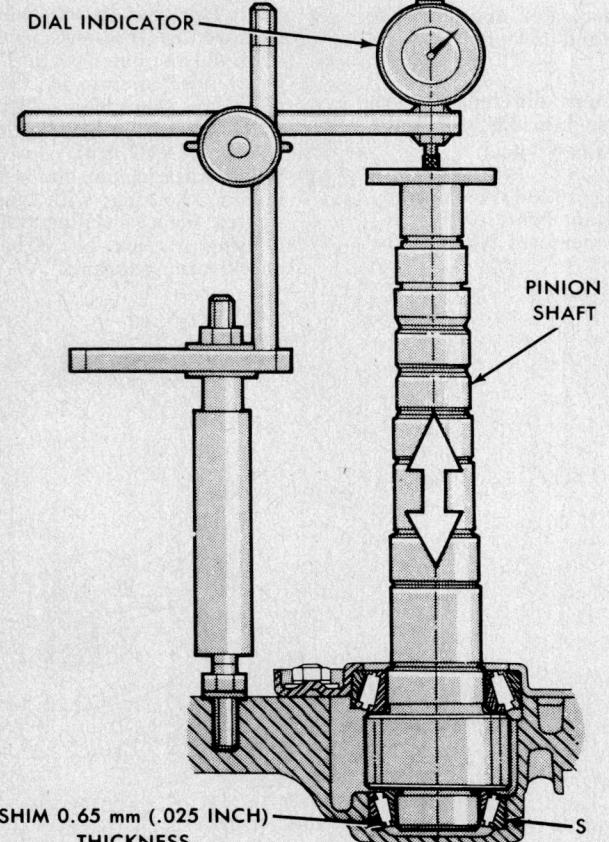

Measuring shim thickness for pinion shaft bearing preload

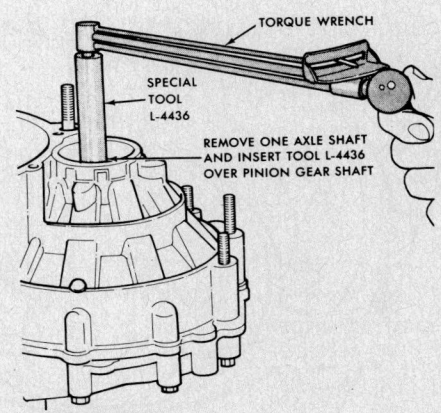

Checking turning torque

Transaxle Assembly

1 Install the pinion shaft.
2 Install first gear thrust washer flat side up, and install pinion shaft retainer.
3 Install first gear and stop ring and first/second gears synchronizer. The lowest thrust collar on the hub must go toward second gear. Install the sleeve with reverse teeth nearest first gear. Slots in synchronizer ring must be aligned with struts in first/second gears synchronizer assembly to avoid damage to stop ring on assembly.
4 Install second gear bearing race.
5 Install and correctly align reverse idler gear shaft.
6 Install needle bearing and second speed gear.
7 Install third speed gear. Select and install a retaining snap ring which will provide 0.00 to less than 0.1mm (.000 to less than .004 inch) end play.
8 Install the mainshaft and third/fourth gears synchronizer assembly.
9 Install fourth speed gear mainshaft needle bearing and mainshaft fourth speed gear.
10 Install fourth speed gear and snap ring on pinion shaft.
11 Use Tool L-4442 to correctly adjust mainshaft position to specifications.
12 Adjust mainshaft end play only if transmission case, clutch housing or main shaft has been changed.
13 Install shift forks and "E" clips.
14 Install reverse shift fork and support brackets.
15 Use guide pins to install transmission case on clutch housing. Be sure pinion shaft is aligned with pinion shaft needle bearing in transmission case.
16 Install mainshaft bearing snap ring.
17 Install reverse idler shaft bolt and install selector shaft assembly.
18 Install mainshaft bearing retainer and washer.
19 Install clutch torque shaft, return spring, release lever and circlips.
20 Install release bearing and sleeve.
21 Install the clutch release bearing end cover and mainshaft bearing retaining nut rubber plug.
22 Install selector shaft cover.
23 Install back-up light switch.
24 Install and adjust detent plunger:
   a. Loosen lock nut.
   b. Tighten adjusting sleeve until gap can be seen between lock ring and adjusting sleeve.
   c. Loosen adjusting sleeve ¼ turn.
   d. Hold adjusting sleeve in this position and tighten lock nut.
25 Install the clutch push rod and the selector shaft boot seal.

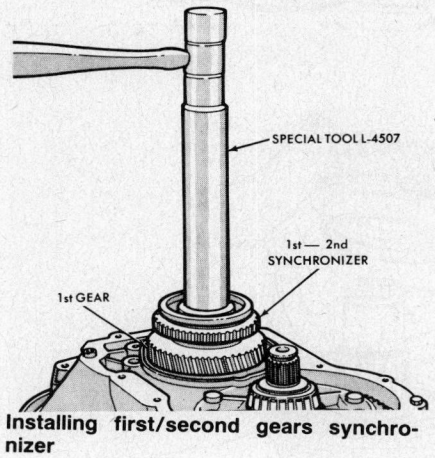

Installing first/second gears synchronizer

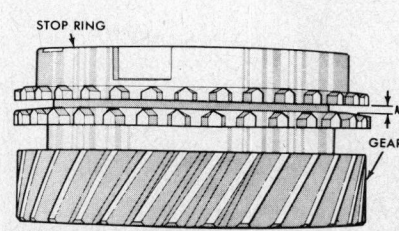

WEAR LIMIT: A = 0.5 mm (.019 INCH)
First gear stop ring wear limit

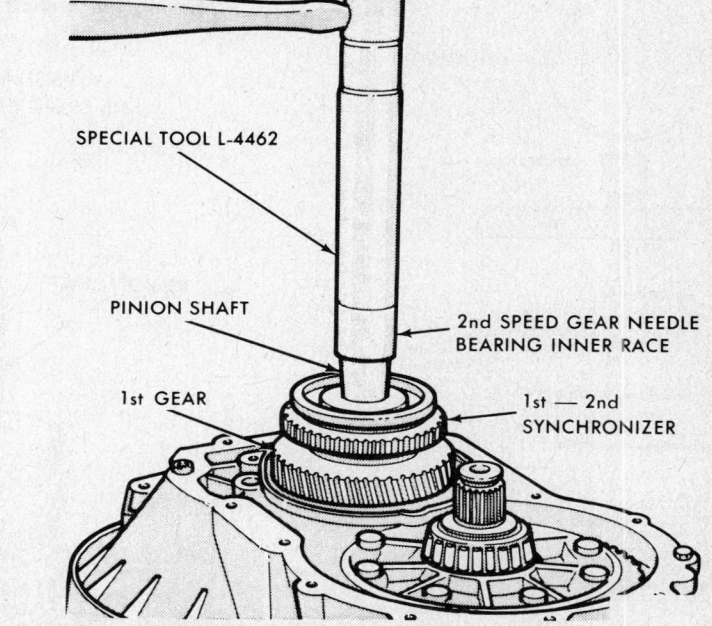

Installing second gear bearing race

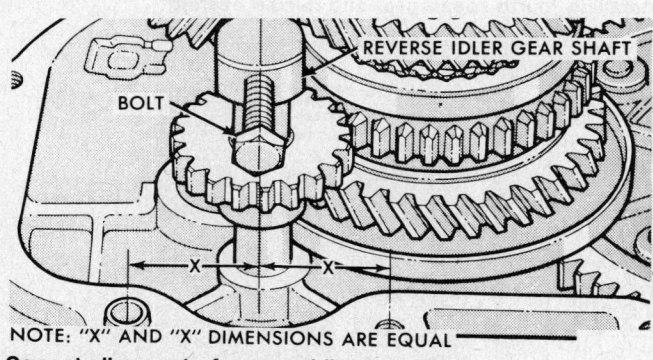
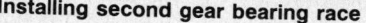

NOTE: "X" AND "X" DIMENSIONS ARE EQUAL
Correct alignment of reverse idler gear shaft

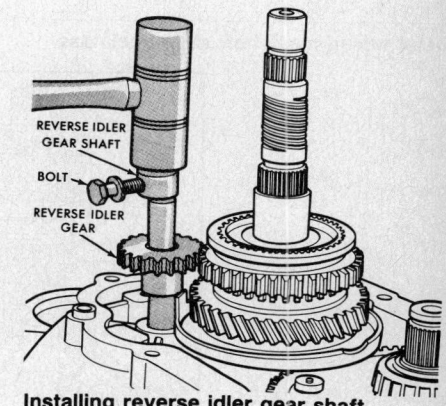

Installing reverse idler gear shaft

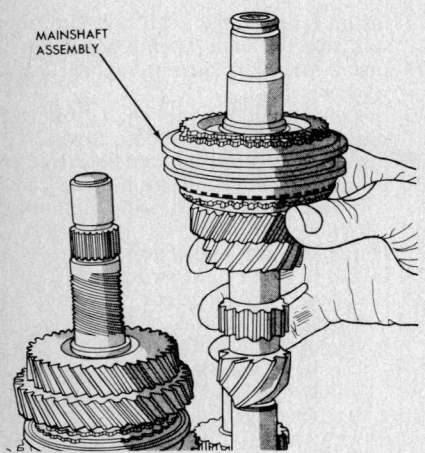

Installing mainshaft assembly

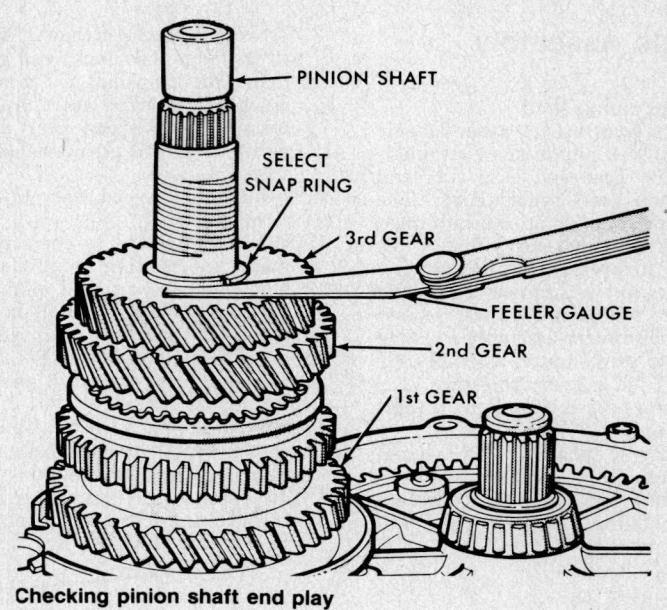

Checking pinion shaft end play

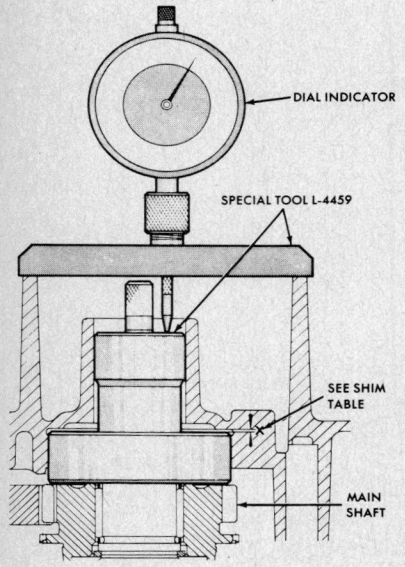

Shim table

Play "x" Millimetre	Inch	Shim Thickness Millimetre	Inch
.00 to 0.46	.000 to .018	—	—
.47 to 0.75	.019 to .029	.30	.012
.76 to 1.04	.030 to .041	.60	.024
1.05 to 1.45	.042 to .057	.90	.035

Determining mainshaft shim thickness

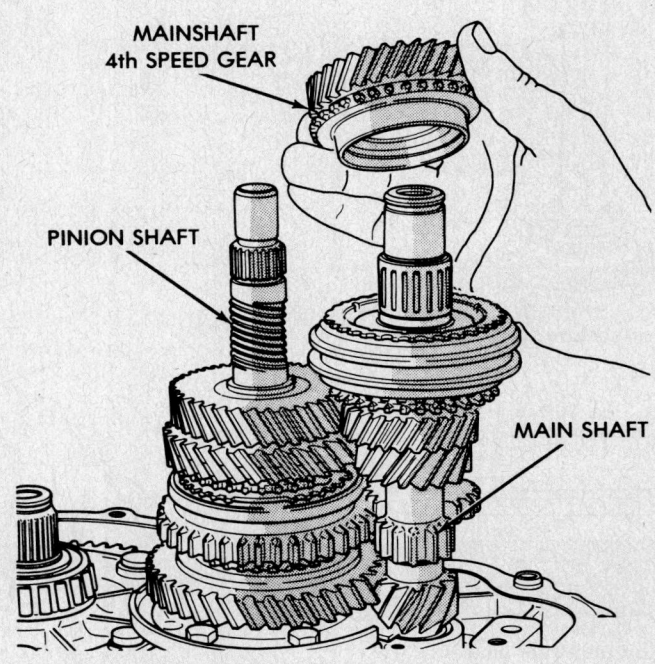

Installing fourth speed gear and needle bearing

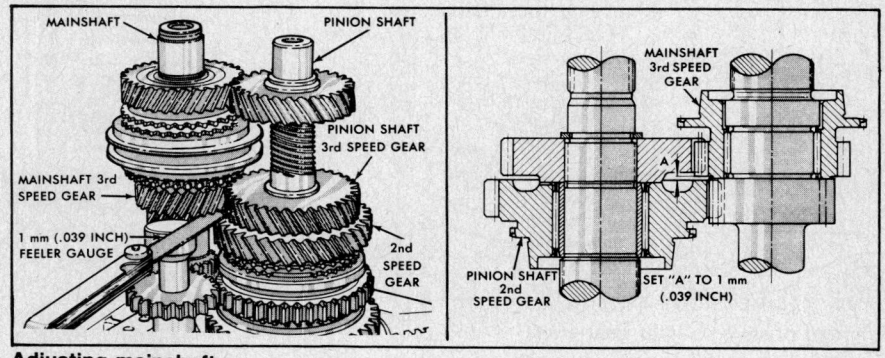

Adjusting mainshaft

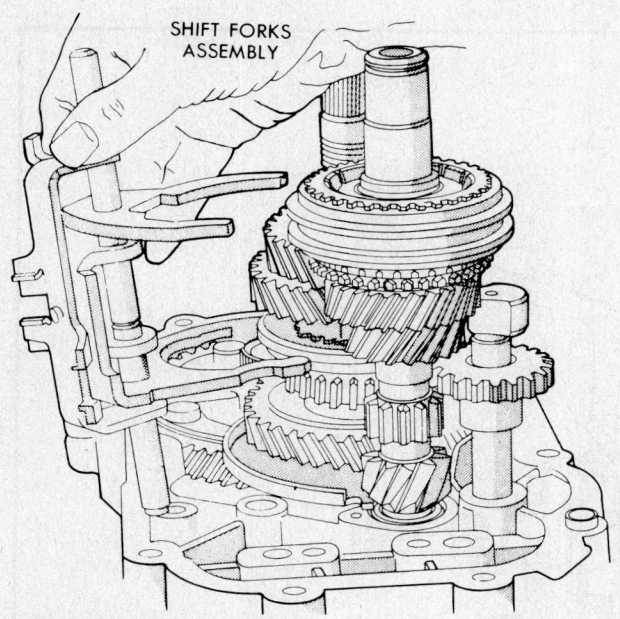

Installing shift forks assembly

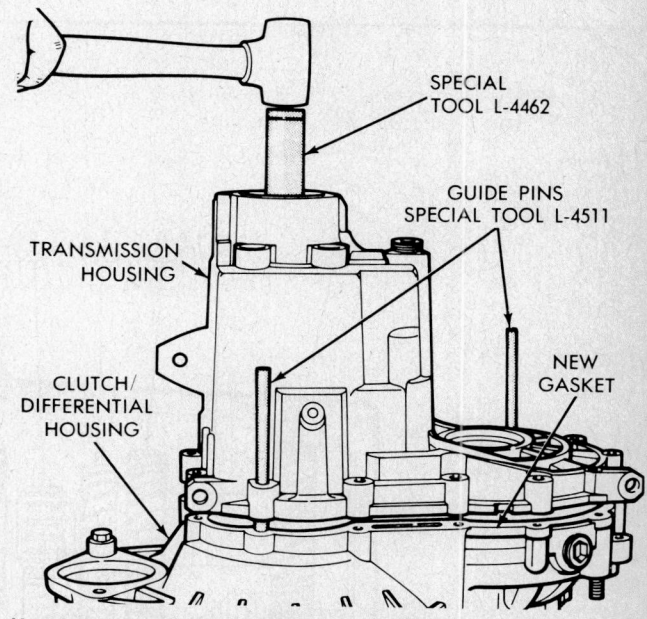

Use guide pins to install transmission case on clutch housing

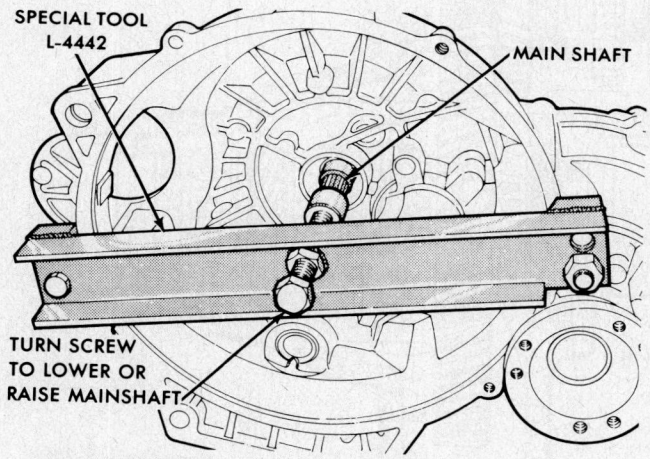

Adjusting mainshaft position

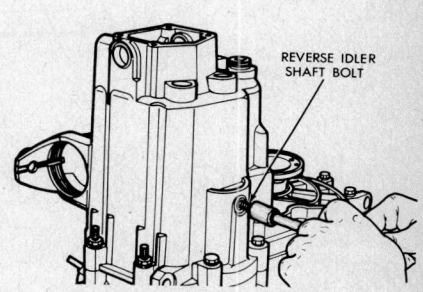

Installing reverse idler shaft bolt

A-412 MANUAL TRANSAXLE TORQUE SPECIFICATIONS

Clutch Housing Case Bolt	250 in/lbs
Clutch Housing Case Stud	250 in/lbs
Release Bearing End Cover Screw	105 in/lbs
Back-up Light Switch	144 in/lbs
Electronic Timing Probe Retainer	80 in/lbs
Gearshift Selector Shaft Cover	35 ft/lbs
Gearshift Detent Body Lock Nut	175 in/lbs
Drain Plug	175 in/lbs
Fill Plug	175 in/lbs
Pinion Shaft Bearing Retainer Bolt	175 in/lbs
Mainshaft Ball Bearing Retaining Nut	29 ft/lbs
Reverse Idler Shaft Set Screw	155 in/lbs
Reverse Idler Fork Bracket—Clutch Housing Screw	175 in/lbs
	105 in/lbs

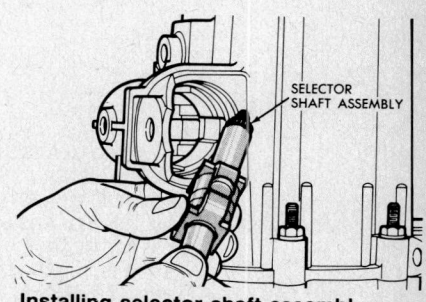

Installing selector shaft assembly

MTX transaxle

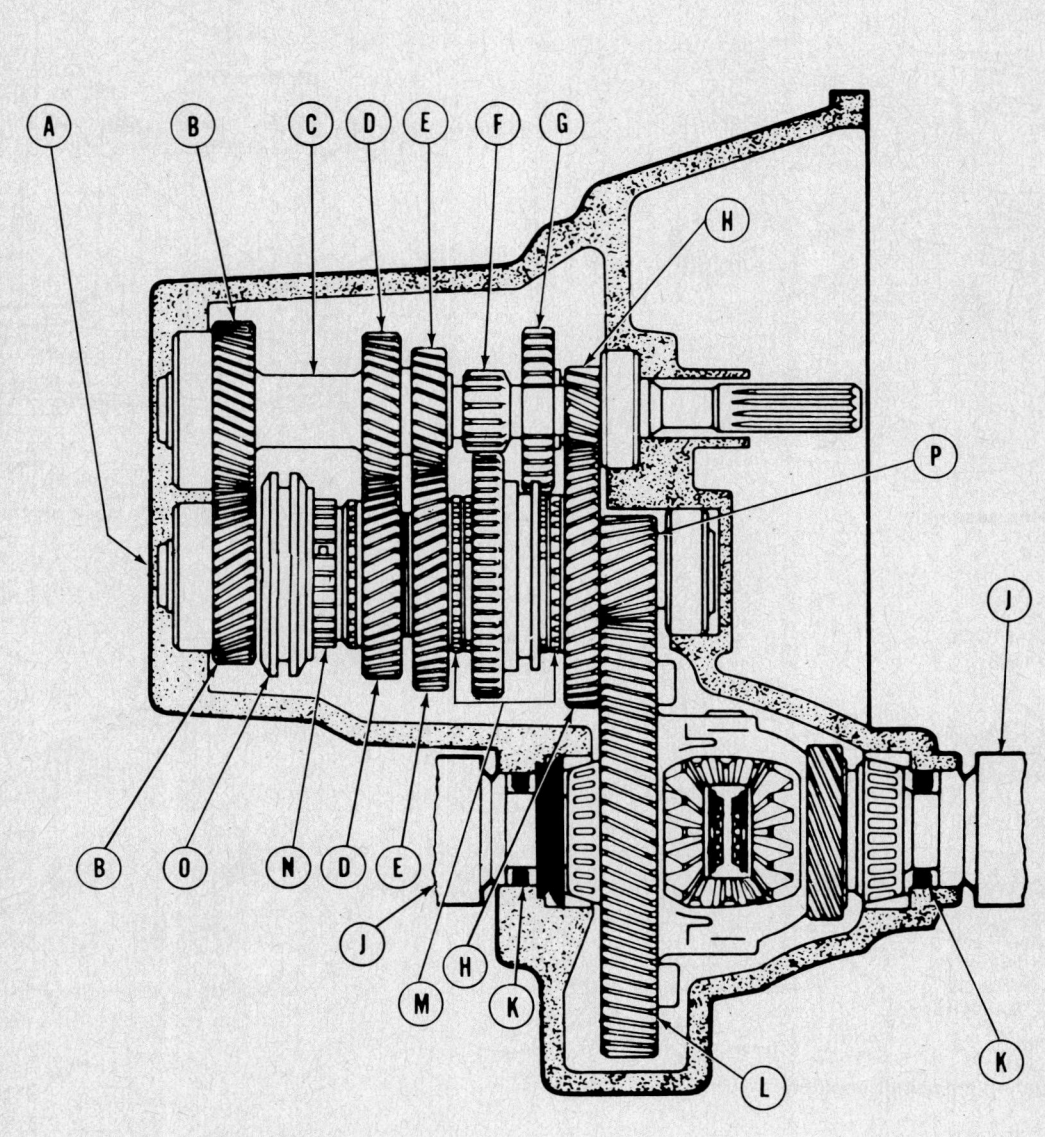

A. MAINSHAFT
B. 4TH SPEED GEARS
C. INPUT CLUSTER
D. 3RD SPEED GEARS
E. 2ND SPEED GEARS
F. RESERSE GEAR
G. REVERSE IDLER GEAR
H. 1ST SPEED GEARS

J. HALF SHAFTS
K. DIFFERENTIAL OIL SEALS
L. DIFFERENTIAL RING GEAR
M. 1ST/2ND SPEED SYNCHRONIZER
   BLOCKER RINGS
N. 3RD/4TH SPEED SYNCHRONIZER HUB
O. 3RD/4TH SPEED SYNCHRONIZER SLEEVE
P. PINION GEAR

MTX Transaxle

Gear Set Removal

1. Shift the transaxle into Neutral using a drift in the input shift shaft hole. Pull or push the shaft into the center detent position.
2. Remove the two shipping plugs (T81P-1177-B or equivalent) from the transaxle and drain the transmission fluid.

NOTE: Place the transaxle on a bench with the clutch housing face down to facilitate draining and service.

3. Remove the reverse idler shaft retaining bolt.
4. Remove the detent plunger retaining screw. Then using a magnet, remove the detent spring and the detent plunger.

NOTE: Label these parts, as they appear similar to the input shift shaft plunger and spring contained in the clutch case.

5. Remove the shift fork interlock sleeve retaining pin (19mm socket).
6. Remove the clutch housing-to-transmission case attaching bolts.
7. Tap the transmission case with a plastic tipped hammer to break the seal between the case halves.

NOTE: Do not insert pry bars or screwdrivers between case halves. Be careful not to drop out the tapered roller bearing cups or shims from the transmission case housing.

8. Remove the case magnet.
9. Remove the reverse idler shaft and reverse idler gear by lifting the shaft straight upward.
10. Remove the set screw from the shift lever assembly with a 4mm Allen wrench.

11. With a pair of pliers, rotate the shift lever shaft 90 degrees to disengage the reverse inhibitor plunger from the detent notch in the shift lever shaft. Slide the shaft toward the differential (away from the expansion plug in the clutch housing) and remove the shift lever assembly.

NOTE: With a 4.05:1 final drive ratio, the differential assembly will have to be tilted slightly to allow the shift lever shaft to slide far enough for removal of the shift lever assembly.

12. Lift the differential and final drive gear assembly from the clutch housing case.
13. Remove the main shaft assembly, input cluster shaft assembly, and main shift control shaft assembly as one unit.

MTX transaxle

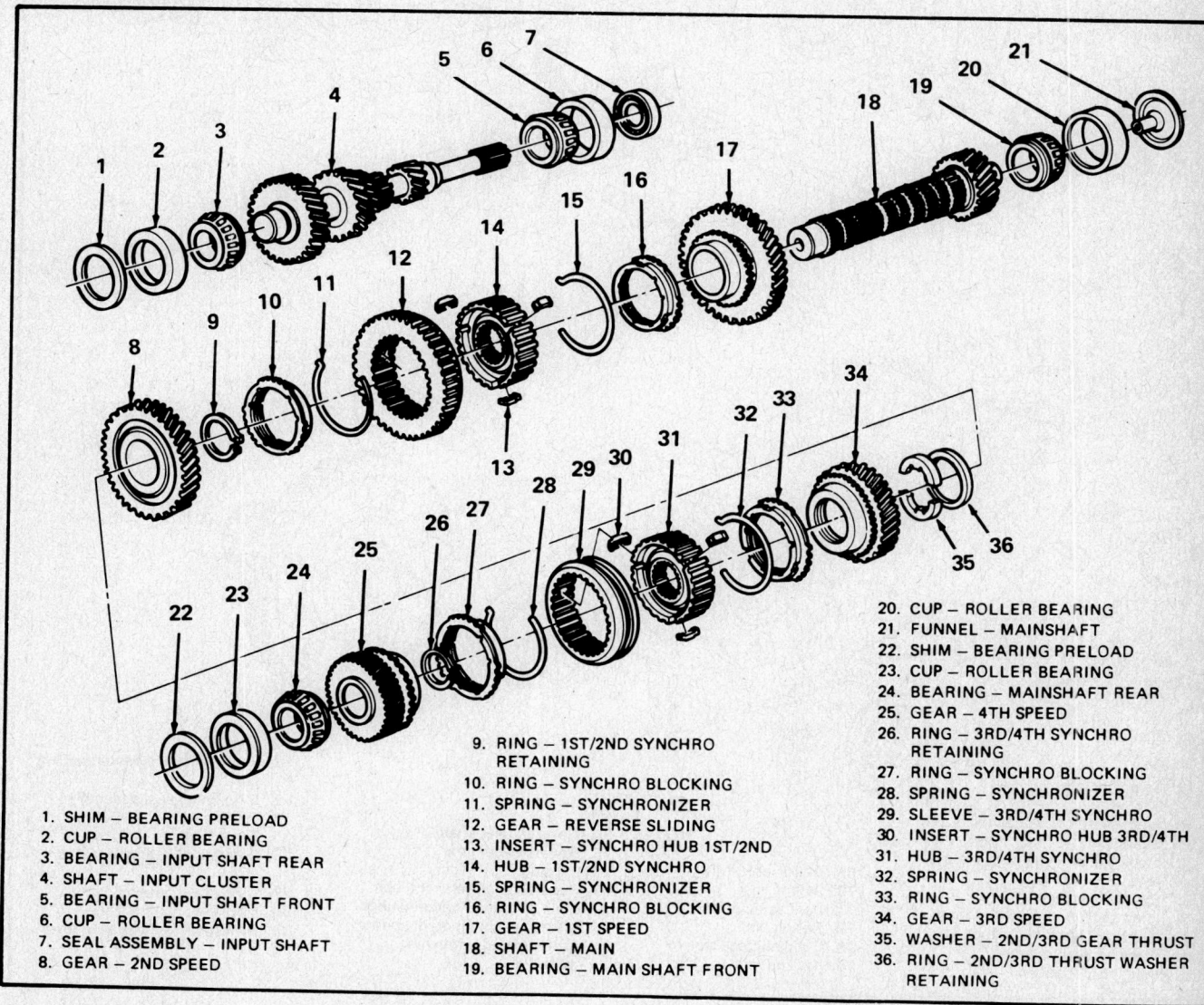

1. SHIM – BEARING PRELOAD
2. CUP – ROLLER BEARING
3. BEARING – INPUT SHAFT REAR
4. SHAFT – INPUT CLUSTER
5. BEARING – INPUT SHAFT FRONT
6. CUP – ROLLER BEARING
7. SEAL ASSEMBLY – INPUT SHAFT
8. GEAR – 2ND SPEED
9. RING – 1ST/2ND SYNCHRO RETAINING
10. RING – SYNCHRO BLOCKING
11. SPRING – SYNCHRONIZER
12. GEAR – REVERSE SLIDING
13. INSERT – SYNCHRO HUB 1ST/2ND
14. HUB – 1ST/2ND SYNCHRO
15. SPRING – SYNCHRONIZER
16. RING – SYNCHRO BLOCKING
17. GEAR – 1ST SPEED
18. SHAFT – MAIN
19. BEARING – MAIN SHAFT FRONT
20. CUP – ROLLER BEARING
21. FUNNEL – MAINSHAFT
22. SHIM – BEARING PRELOAD
23. CUP – ROLLER BEARING
24. BEARING – MAINSHAFT REAR
25. GEAR – 4TH SPEED
26. RING – 3RD/4TH SYNCHRO RETAINING
27. RING – SYNCHRO BLOCKING
28. SPRING – SYNCHRONIZER
29. SLEEVE – 3RD/4TH SYNCHRO
30. INSERT – SYNCHRO HUB 3RD/4TH
31. HUB – 3RD/4TH SYNCHRO
32. SPRING – SYNCHRONIZER
33. RING – SYNCHRO BLOCKING
34. GEAR – 3RD SPEED
35. WASHER – 2ND/3RD GEAR THRUST
36. RING – 2ND/3RD THRUST WASHER RETAINING

MTX transaxle

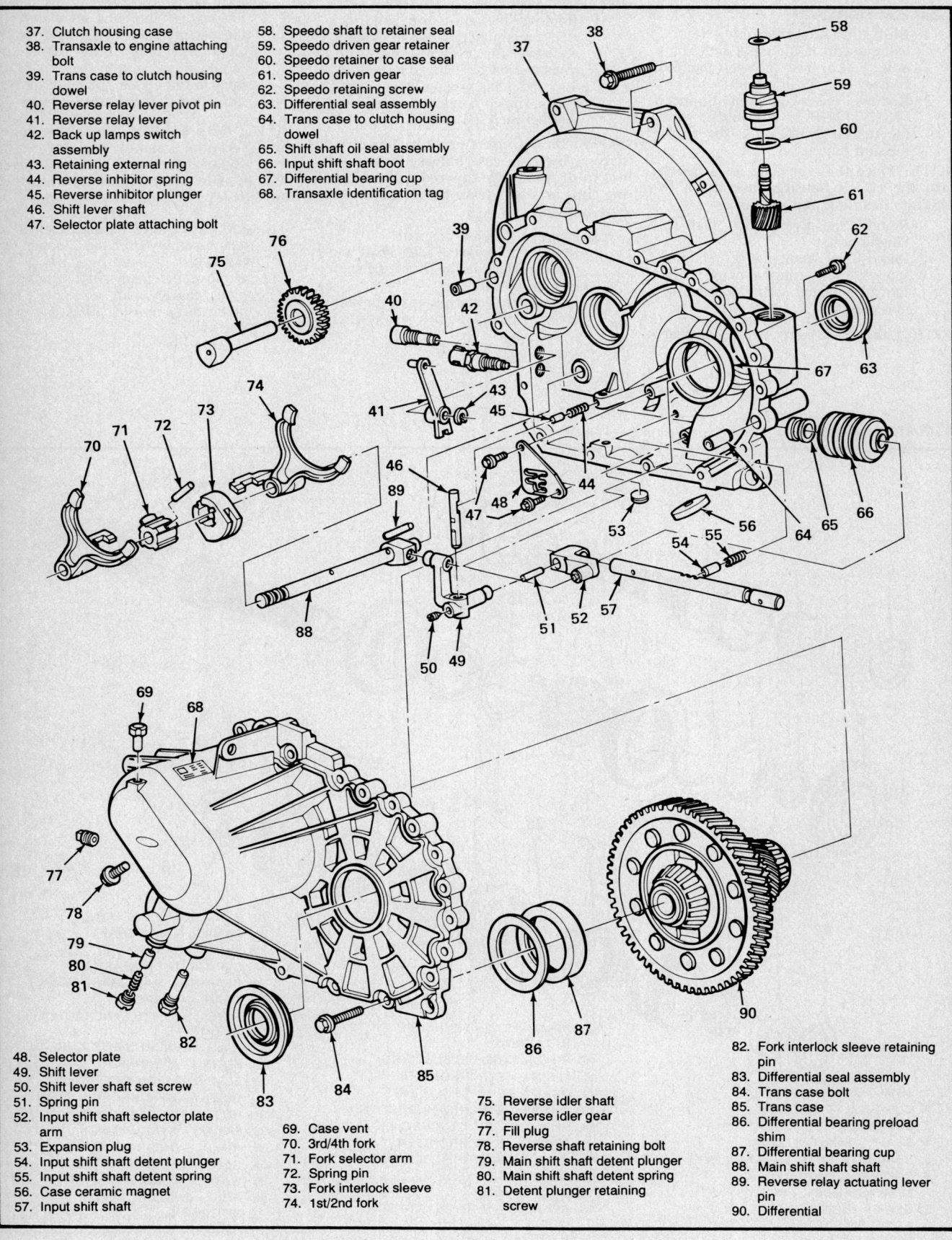

37. Clutch housing case
38. Transaxle to engine attaching bolt
39. Trans case to clutch housing dowel
40. Reverse relay lever pivot pin
41. Reverse relay lever
42. Back up lamps switch assembly
43. Retaining external ring
44. Reverse inhibitor spring
45. Reverse inhibitor plunger
46. Shift lever shaft
47. Selector plate attaching bolt

58. Speedo shaft to retainer seal
59. Speedo driven gear retainer
60. Speedo retainer to case seal
61. Speedo driven gear
62. Speedo retaining screw
63. Differential seal assembly
64. Trans case to clutch housing dowel
65. Shift shaft oil seal assembly
66. Input shift shaft boot
67. Differential bearing cup
68. Transaxle identification tag

48. Selector plate
49. Shift lever
50. Shift lever shaft set screw
51. Spring pin
52. Input shift shaft selector plate arm
53. Expansion plug
54. Input shift shaft detent plunger
55. Input shift shaft detent spring
56. Case ceramic magnet
57. Input shift shaft

69. Case vent
70. 3rd/4th fork
71. Fork selector arm
72. Spring pin
73. Fork interlock sleeve
74. 1st/2nd fork

75. Reverse idler shaft
76. Reverse idler gear
77. Fill plug
78. Reverse shaft retaining bolt
79. Main shift shaft detent plunger
80. Main shift shaft detent spring
81. Detent plunger retaining screw

82. Fork interlock sleeve retaining pin
83. Differential seal assembly
84. Trans case bolt
85. Trans case
86. Differential bearing preload shim
87. Differential bearing cup
88. Main shift shaft shaft
89. Reverse relay actuating lever pin
90. Differential

Main shaft assembly

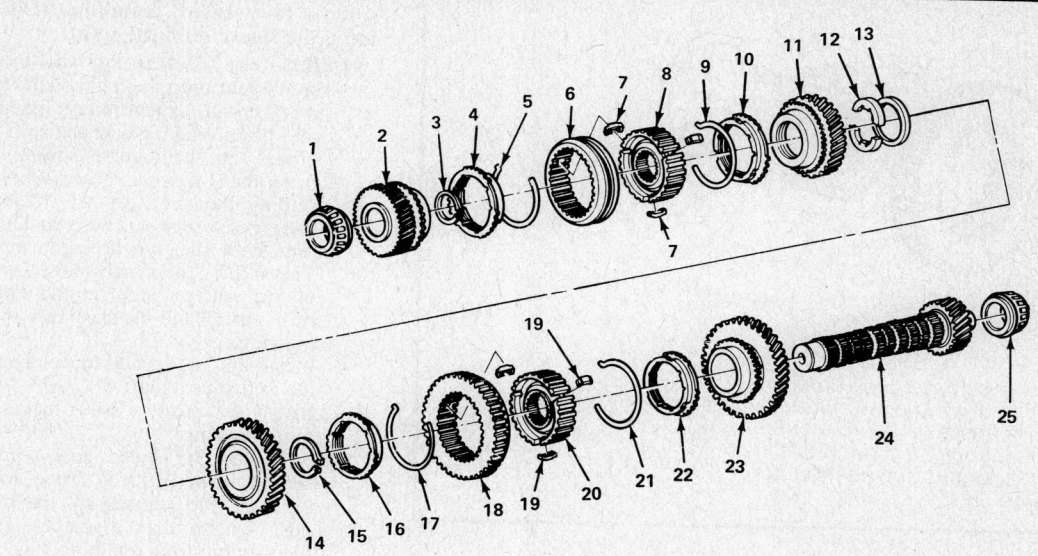

1. BEARING -- MAINSHAFT REAR
2. GEAR -- 4TH SPEED
3. RING -- 3RD/4TH SYNCHRO RETAINING
4. RING -- SYNCHRO BLOCKING
5. SPRING -- SYNCHRONIZER
6. SLEEVE -- 3RD/4TH SYNCHRO
7. INSERT -- SYNCHRO HUB 3RD/4TH
8. HUB -- 3RD/4TH SYNCHRO
9. SPRING -- SYNCHRONIZER
10. RING -- SYNCHRO BLOCKING
11. GEAR -- 3RD SPEED
12. WASHER -- 2ND/3RD GEAR THRUST
13. RING -- 2ND/3RD THRUST WASHER RETAINING
14. GEAR -- 2ND SPEED
15. RING -- 1ST/2ND SYNCHRO RETAINING
16. RING -- SYNCHRO BLOCKING
17. SPRING -- SYNCHRONIZER
18. GEAR -- REVERSE SLIDING
19. INSERT -- SYNCHRO HUB 1ST/2ND
20. HUB -- 1ST/2ND SYNCHRO
21. SPRING -- SYNCHRONIZER
22. RING -- SYNCHRO BLOCKING
23. GEAR -- 1ST SPEED
24. SHAFT -- MAIN
25. BEARING -- MAIN SHAFT FRONT

Main Shaft

Disassembly

1. Remove the tapered roller bearing from the pinion end of the main shaft using puller (D79L-4621-A or equivalent) and an arbor press.

NOTE: This bearing does not have to be removed to disassemble the main shaft, only to replace if damaged.

2. Remove the bearing on the 4th gear end of the shaft.

    Label the bearing for proper installation.

3. Remove the 4th speed gear and synchronizer blocker ring.

4. Remove the 3rd/4th synchronizer retaining ring.

    Slide the 3rd/4th gear synchronizer assembly, blocker ring, and 3rd speed gear from the shaft.

5. Remove the 2nd/3rd thrust washer retaining ring and the two-piece 2nd/3rd gear thrust washer.

6. Remove the 2nd speed gear and blocker ring.

7. Remove the 1st/2nd synchronizer retaining ring.

    Slide the 1st/2nd synchronizer assembly, blocking ring and 1st speed gear off the shaft.

Synchronizer

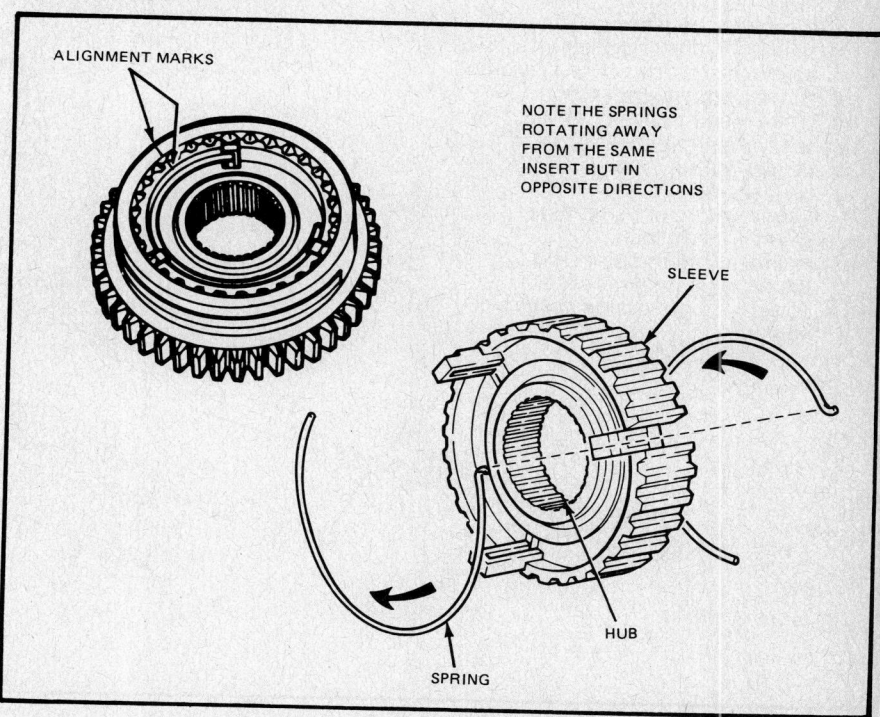

ALIGNMENT MARKS

NOTE THE SPRINGS ROTATING AWAY FROM THE SAME INSERT BUT IN OPPOSITE DIRECTIONS

SLEEVE

HUB

SPRING

Synchronizer gear

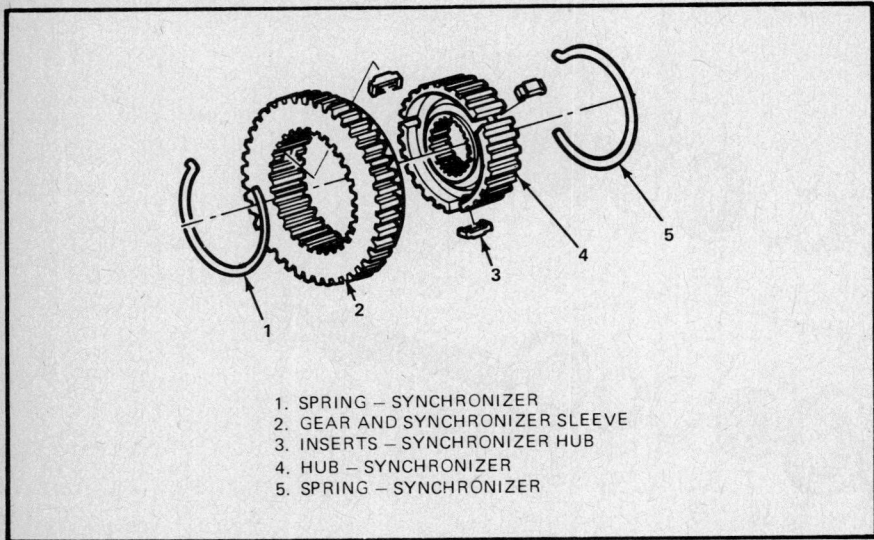

1. SPRING — SYNCHRONIZER
2. GEAR AND SYNCHRONIZER SLEEVE
3. INSERTS — SYNCHRONIZER HUB
4. HUB — SYNCHRONIZER
5. SPRING — SYNCHRONIZER

NOTE: When assembling synchronizers, notice that the sleeve and the hub have an extremely close fit and must be held square to prevent jamming. (Do not force the sleeve onto the hub).

1. Slide the blocker ring and the 1st speed gear onto the main shaft. Slide the 1st/2nd synchronizer assembly into place, making sure the shift fork groove on the reverse sliding gear faces the 1st speed gear. When installing the synchronizer, align the three grooves in the 1st gear blocker ring with the synchronizer inserts. This allows the synchronizer assembly to seat properly in the blocker ring. Install the synchronizer retaining ring.
2. Install the 2nd speed blocker ring and the 2nd speed gear.
3. Install the thrust washer halves and retaining ring.
4. Slide the 3rd speed gear onto the shaft followed by the 3rd gear synchronizer blocker ring and the 3rd/4th gear synchronizer assembly. Install the synchronizer retaining ring.
5. Install the 4th gear blocking ring and the 4th speed gear.
6. Install the bearing on the 4th gear end of the shaft using a 1 1/16 inch socket and an arbor press. Install the bearing on the pinion end of the shaft in a similar manner.

Assembly

In assembling synchronizers some points must be noted. The index marks must be aligned. Place the tab on the synchronizer spring into the groove of one of the inserts and snap the spring into place. Place the tab of the other spring into the same insert (on the other side of the synchronizer assembly), and rotate the spring in the opposite direction and snap into place.

Internal shift linkage

1. CASE — CLUTCH HOUSING
2. PIN — REVERSE RELAY LEVER PIVOT
3. LEVER — REVERSE RELAY
4. SWITCH ASSEMBLY — BACK UP LAMPS
5. RING — EXTERNAL RETAINING
6. PLUNGER — REVERSE INHIBITOR
7. SPRING — REVERSE INHIBITOR
8. BOLTS — SELECTOR PLATE ATTACHING
9. PLATE — CONTROL SELECTOR
10. SHAFT — SHIFT LEVER
11. SCREW — SHIFT LEVER SHAFT SET
12. LEVER — SHIFT
13. PIN — SPRING
14. ARM — INPUT SHIFT SHAFT SELECTOR PLATE
15. SHAFT — INPUT SHIFT
16. PLUNGER — INPUT SHIFT SHAFT DETENT
17. SPRING — INPUT SHAFT DETENT
18. DOWEL — TRANSMISSION CASE TO CLUTCH HOUSING
19. SEAL ASSEMBLY — SHIFT CONTROL SHAFT OIL
20. BOOT — SHIFT CONTROL SHAFT
21. SHAFT — MAIN SHIFT CONTROL
22. FORK — 3rd/4th
23. ARM — FORK SELECTOR
24. PIN — SPRING
25. SLEEVE — FORK INTERLOCK
26. FORK — 1st/2nd

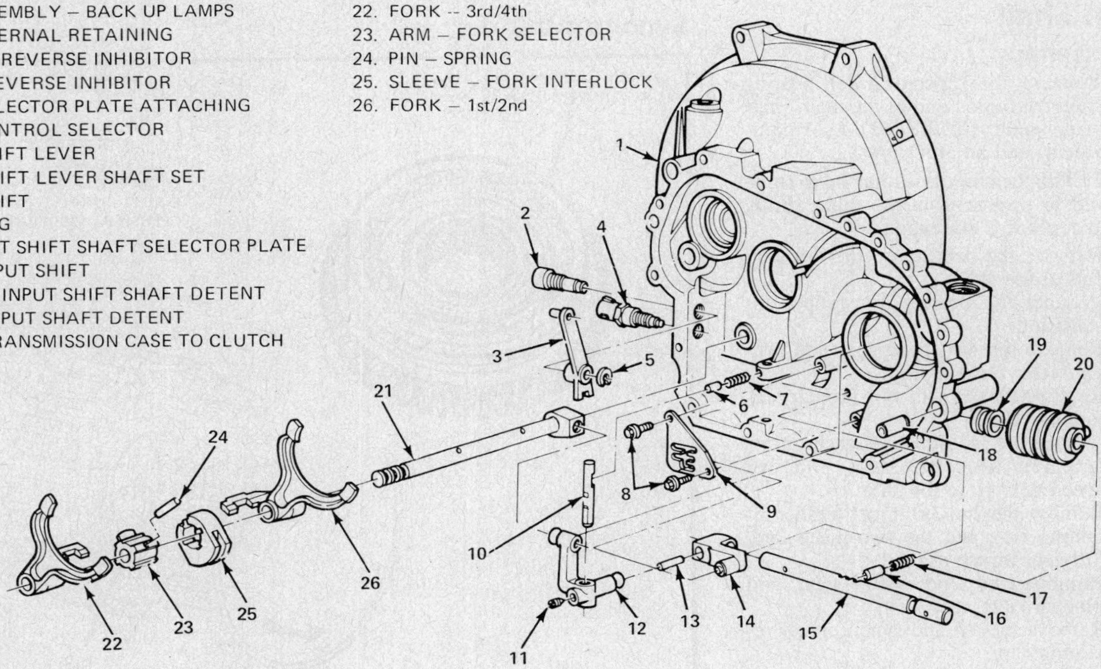

NOTE: Make sure bearings are seated against shoulder of main shaft.

Gear Set

Installation

1. Place the differential and the final drive gear assembly into the clutch housing case.
2. Position the main shift control shaft assembly so that the shift forks engage their respective slots in the synchronizer sleeves on the main shaft assembly.
3. Bring the main shaft assembly into mesh with the input cluster shaft assembly. Holding the three shafts (input cluster shaft, main shaft, and the main shift control shaft) in their respective working positions, lower them into their working bores in the clutch housing case as one unit.

NOTE: Be careful not to damage the input shaft oil seal or main shaft oil funnel.

4. Position the shift lever assembly in its working position (with one shift lever pin located in the socket of the input shift shaft selector plate arm assembly and the other in the socket of the main shift control shaft block). Slide the shift lever shaft through the shift lever and into its bore in the clutch housing. Rotate the shift lever shaft so the reverse inhibitor notch faces the reverse inhibitor plunger.
5. Position the shift lever shaft so the setscrew hole on the shaft aligns with the hole in the shift lever. Install the setscrew and tighten to specifications.

NOTE: Before tightening, position the shift lever on the shaft to make sure the setscrew is centered in the shaft center drilled hole.

6. Verify that the selector pin is in the neutral gate of the control selector plate and the finger of the fork selector arm is partially engaged with the 1st/2nd fork and partially with the 3rd/4th fork.
7. Place the reverse idler gear groove in engagement with the pin at the end of the reverse relay lever, and slide the shaft through the gear and into its bore. Align the retaining screw hole in the reverse idler shaft with the hole in the case. This will allow proper alignment between the reverse idler shaft retaining screw hole in the transmission case when the case is placed over this assembly.
8. Install the magnet in its pocket in the clutch housing case.
9. Apply a $1/16$ inch wide bead of sealer. Carefully lower the transmission case over the clutch housing case and move gently until the shift control shaft, mainshaft, and the input cluster shaft align with their respective bores in the transmission case. Gently slide the transmission case over the dowels and flush onto the clutch housing case, checking that the case does not bind on the magnet.
10. Install the transmission case-to-clutch housing bolts and tighten to specifications.

Preload Shims

Preload on the input cluster shaft and mainshaft bearings is maintained by shims. These preload shims are located behind the bearing cups in the transmission case.

If the bearing cups are removed from the case for any reason, it is very important to keep the bearing cup and its matching shim together. It is also very important to label the bearing cups as they are removed from the transmission case or clutch housing. Maintaining the proper bearing cup to shim relationship and proper bearing cup labeling will ensure the correct bearing preload when the transaxle is assembled.

A replacement bearing preload shim will be provided for service and should be installed in place of the original shim as outlined in the Service Shim Chart.

SERVICE SHIM CHART

Parts Replaced	SHIMS REPLACED WITH SERVICE SHIM	
	Input Cluster Shaft	Mainshaft
1 input cluster bearing	Yes	No
2 input cluster bearings	Yes	No
1 input cluster bearing 1 mainshaft bearing	Yes	Yes
2 mainshaft bearings 2 input cluster bearings	Yes	Yes
1 mainshaft bearing	No	Yes
2 mainshaft bearings	No	Yes
Clutch housing	Yes	Yes
Transmission housing	Yes	Yes

NOTE: The shims must be installed only under the bearing cups at the trans. case end of both the input and outputshafts.

NOTE: The use of nominal thickness service shim eliminates the need for gaging bearing clearances prior to reassembly. While this method produces wider variations of bearing settings than are present in factory assembled units, the extreem possible settings have been tested and found to be acceptable.

When repairs require the use of the service shim (see Service Shim Chart), discard the original shim. Do not use more than one shim per shaft. Ifparts are replaced other than the parts listed in the Service Shim Chart, then the original shims should be re-used.

A-460 MANUAL TRANSAXLE

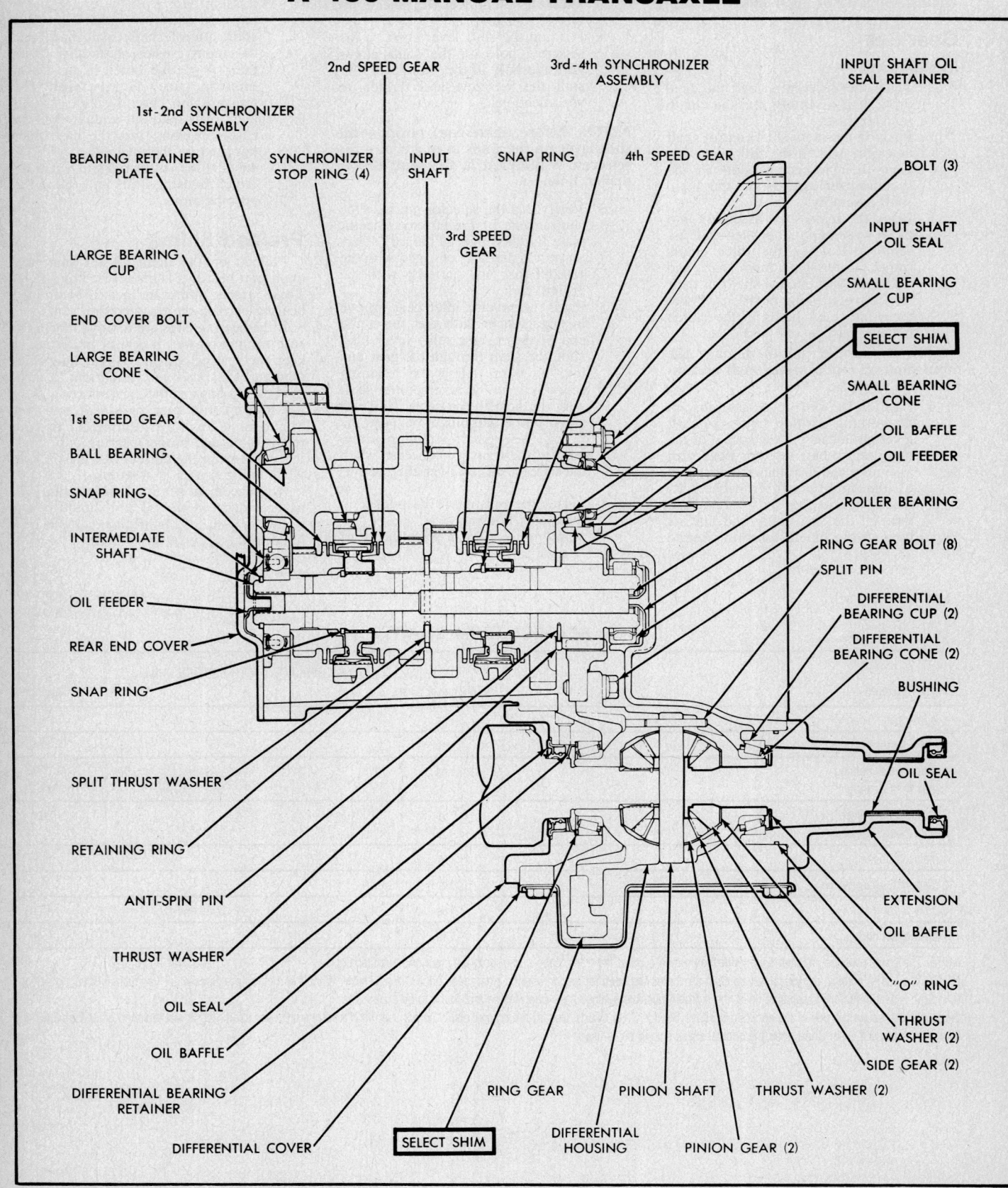

Cutaway view

Disassembly and Assembly

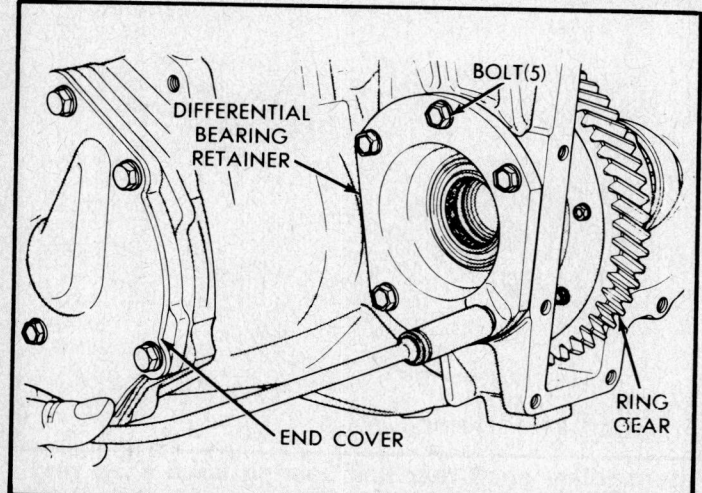

Differential bearing retainer bolts removal or installation

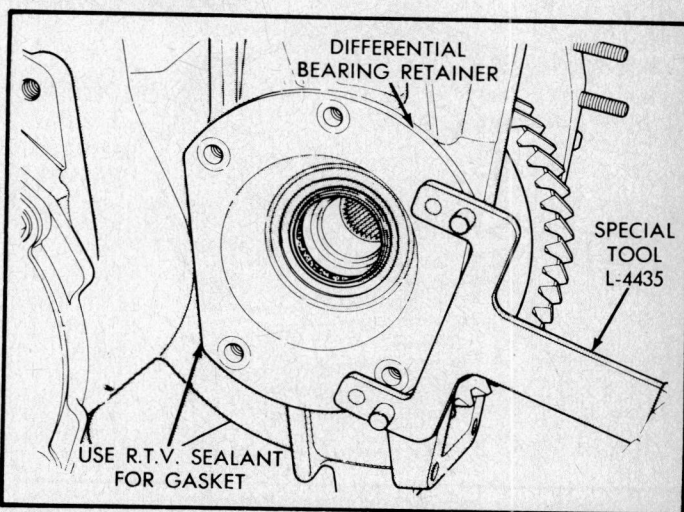

Using tool L-4435, rotate differential bearing retainer to remove or install

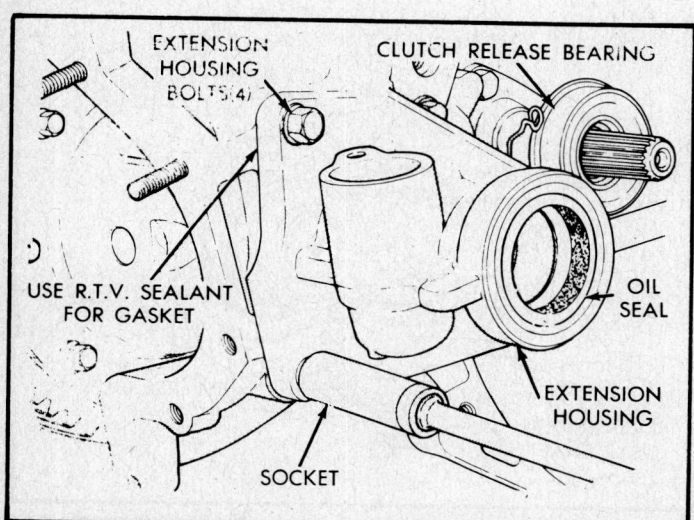

Extension housing bolts removal or installation

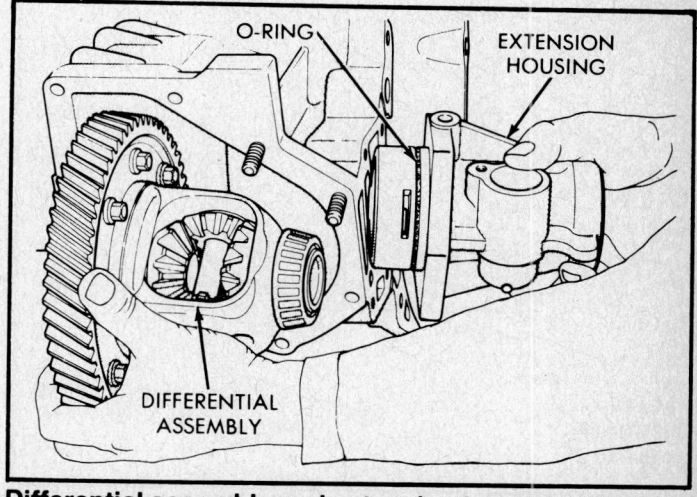

Differential assembly and extension housing removal or installation

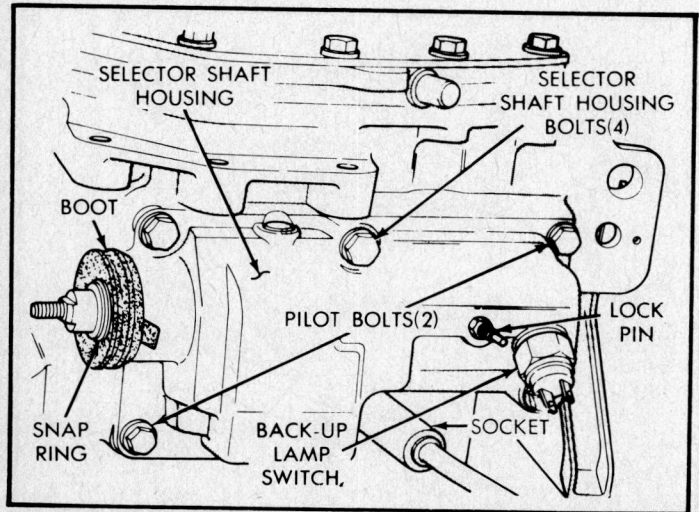

Selector shaft housing removal or installation

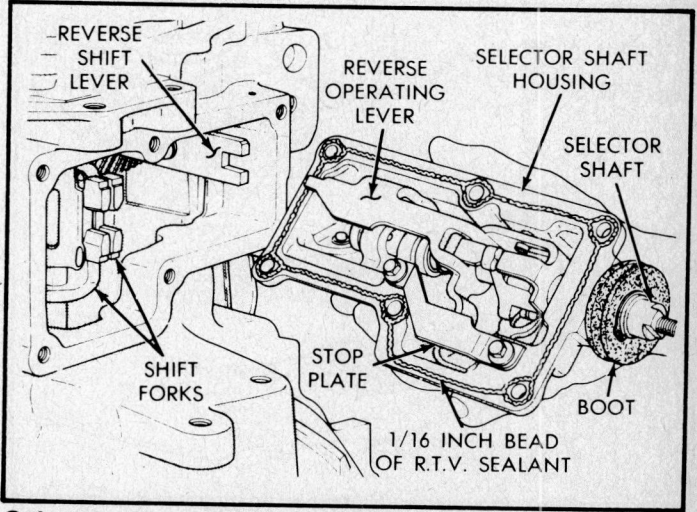

Selector shaft housing assembly removed

B745

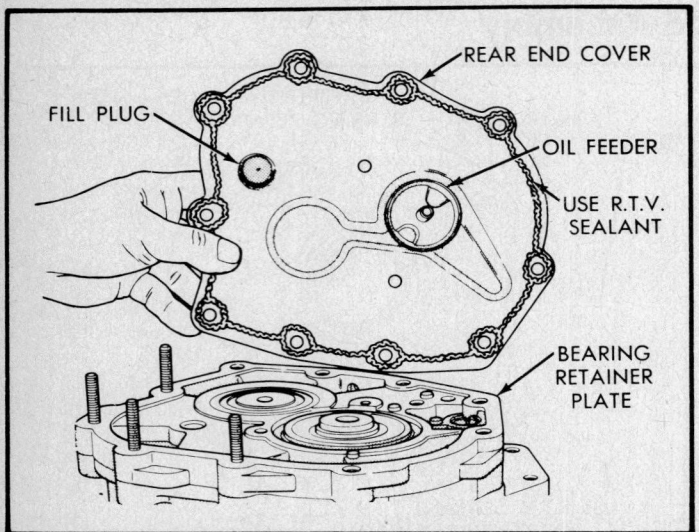

Rear end cover removal or installation

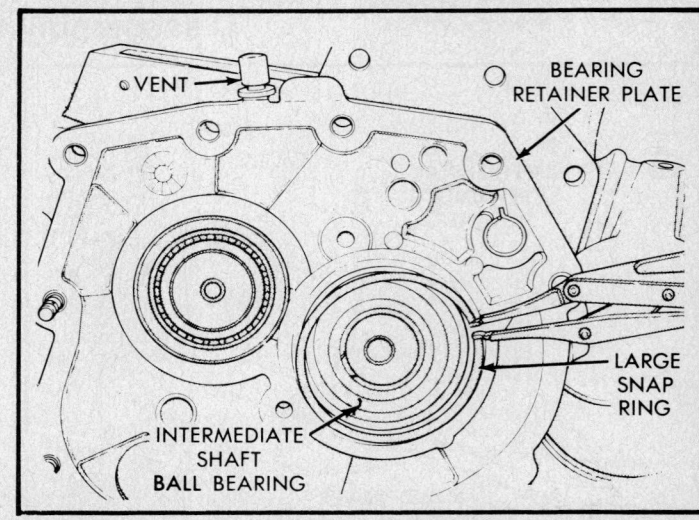

Intermediate shaft rear ball bearing large snap ring removal or installation

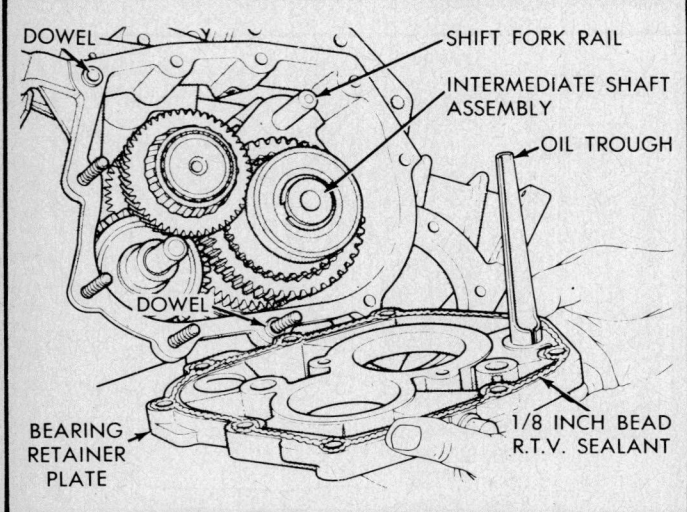

Bearing retainer plate removal or installation

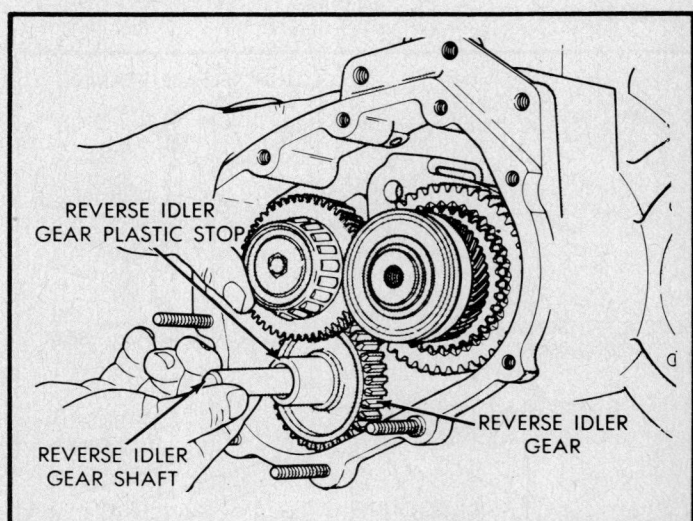

Reverse idler gear shaft and gear removal or installation

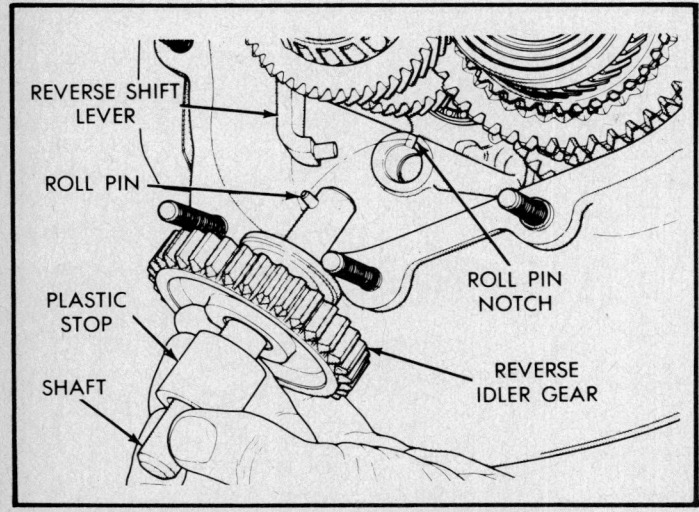

Reverse idler gear, shaft and plastic stop

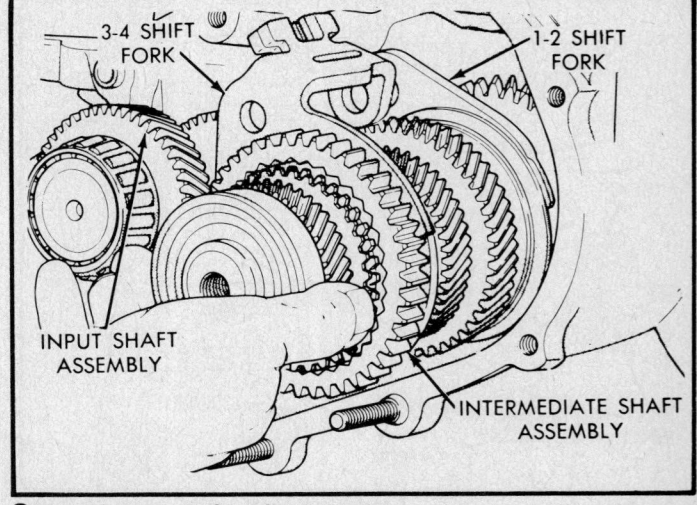

Gearset removal or installation

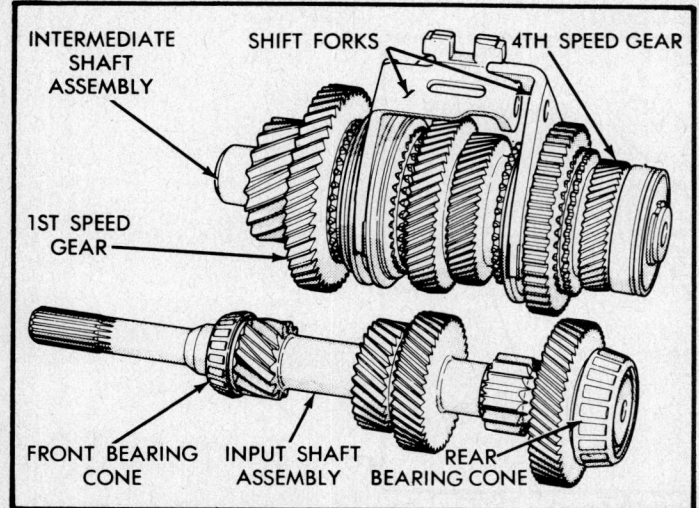

Gearset removed

INTERMEDIATE SHAFT ASSEMBLY

SHIFT FORKS

4TH SPEED GEAR

1ST SPEED GEAR

FRONT BEARING CONE

INPUT SHAFT ASSEMBLY

REAR BEARING CONE

Shift forks and pads

SHIFT FORKS

SHIFT FORK PADS

SHIFT FORK PADS

Clutch Release Bearing

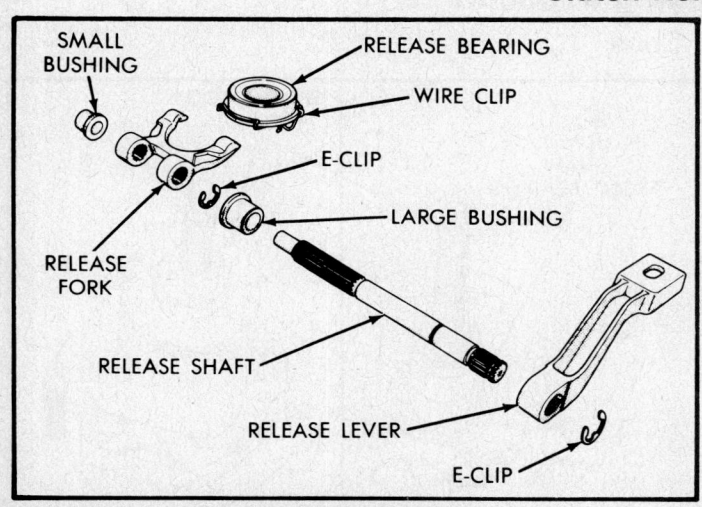

Clutch release shaft components

SMALL BUSHING

RELEASE BEARING

WIRE CLIP

E-CLIP

LARGE BUSHING

RELEASE FORK

RELEASE SHAFT

RELEASE LEVER

E-CLIP

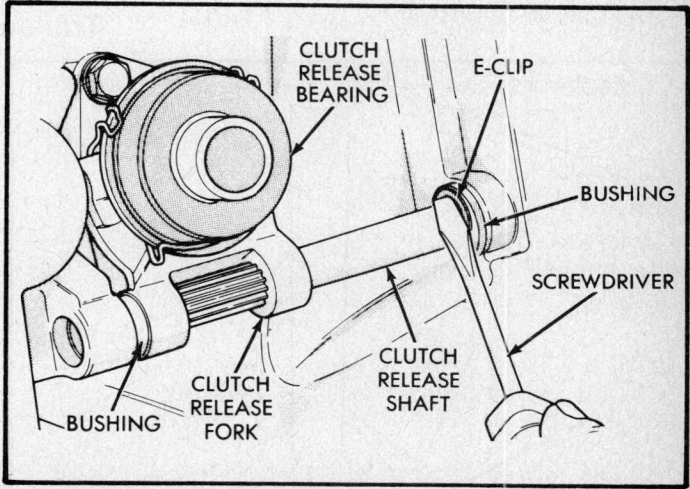

Retaining E-clip removal or installation

CLUTCH RELEASE BEARING

E-CLIP

BUSHING

SCREWDRIVER

CLUTCH RELEASE SHAFT

CLUTCH RELEASE FORK

BUSHING

Input Shaft Oil Seal

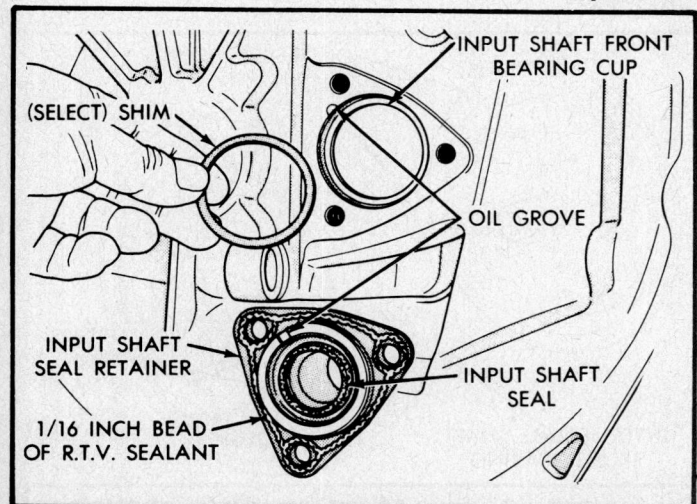

Input shaft seal retainer removal or installation

(SELECT) SHIM

INPUT SHAFT FRONT BEARING CUP

OIL GROVE

INPUT SHAFT SEAL RETAINER

INPUT SHAFT SEAL

1/16 INCH BEAD OF R.T.V. SEALANT

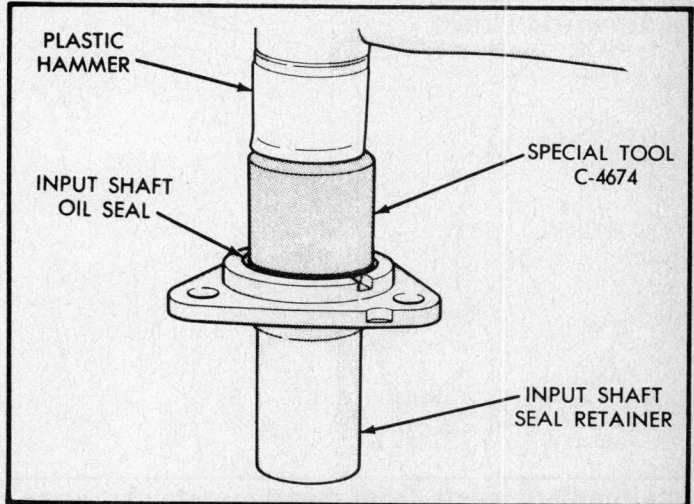

New input shaft oil seal installation

PLASTIC HAMMER

INPUT SHAFT OIL SEAL

SPECIAL TOOL C-4674

INPUT SHAFT SEAL RETAINER

B747

Reverse Shift Lever

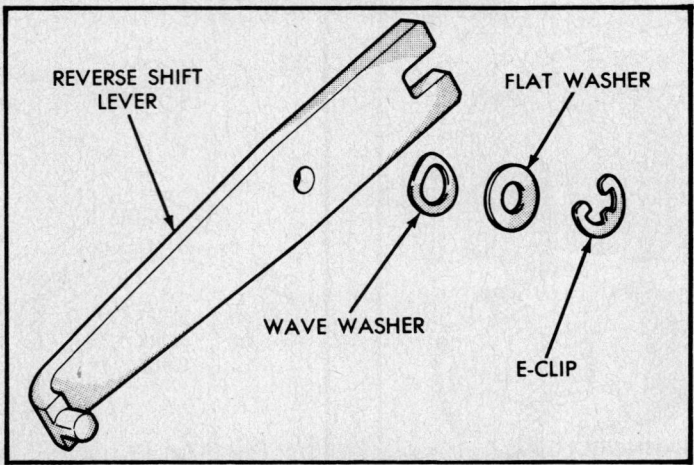

Disassembled view of reverse shift lever

Subassembly Rebuilding Procedures
Transaxle Case

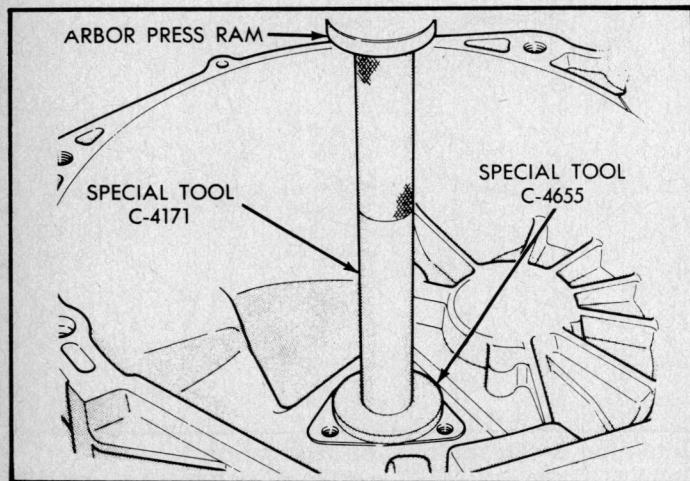

Input shaft front bearing cup installation

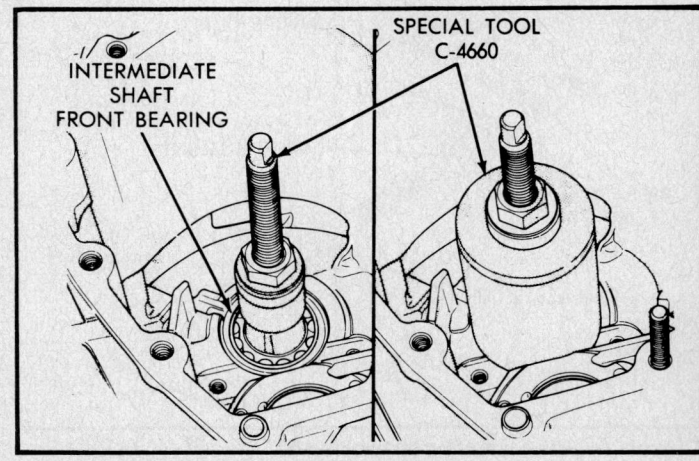

Intermediate shaft front bearing removal

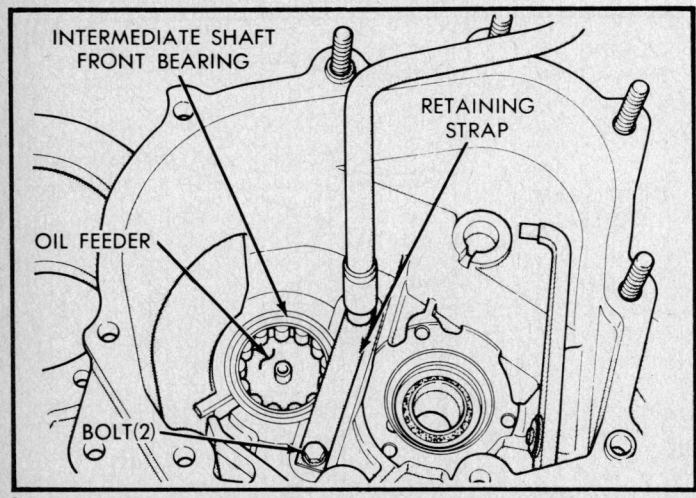

Intermediate shaft front bearing retainer strap removal or installation

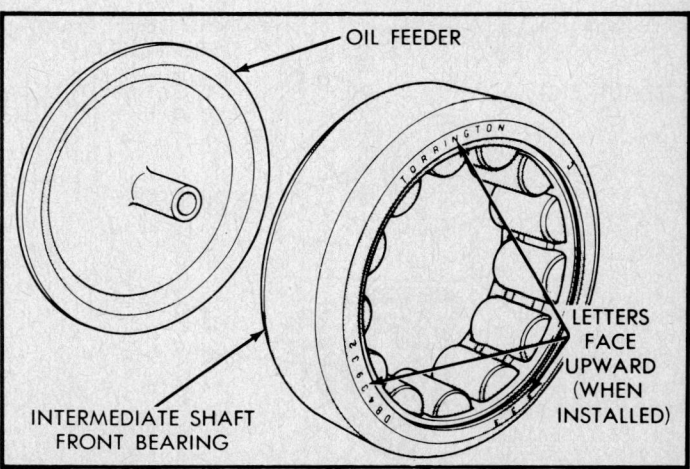

Disassembled view of intermediate shaft front bearing and oil feeder

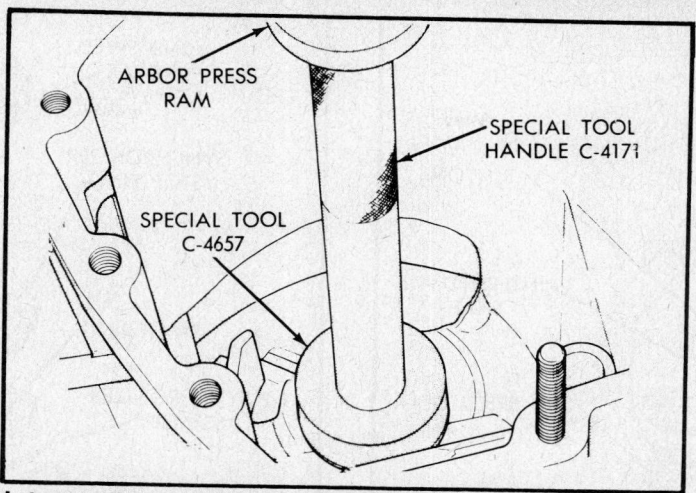

Intermediate shaft front bearing installation

INTERMEDIATE SHAFT ASSEMBLY

The 1-2 and 3-4 shift forks and synchronizer stop rings are interchangeable. However, if parts are to be reused, reassemble them in their original position. When assembling the intermediate shaft, make sure all gears turn freely and have a minimum of .076 mm (.003 inch) end play.

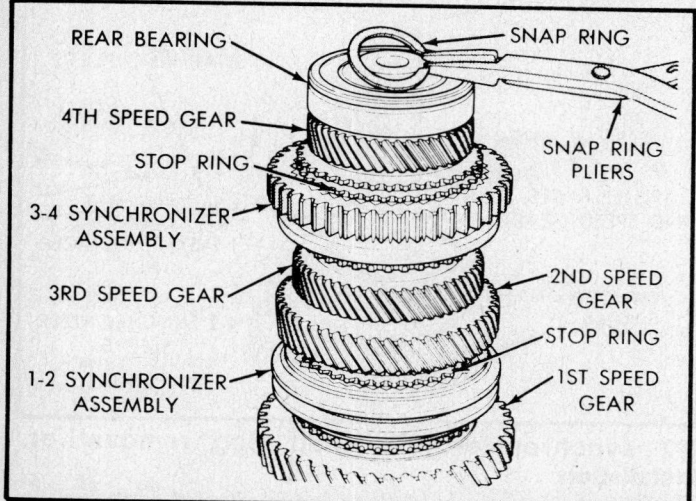

Intermediate shaft rear bearing snap ring removal or installation

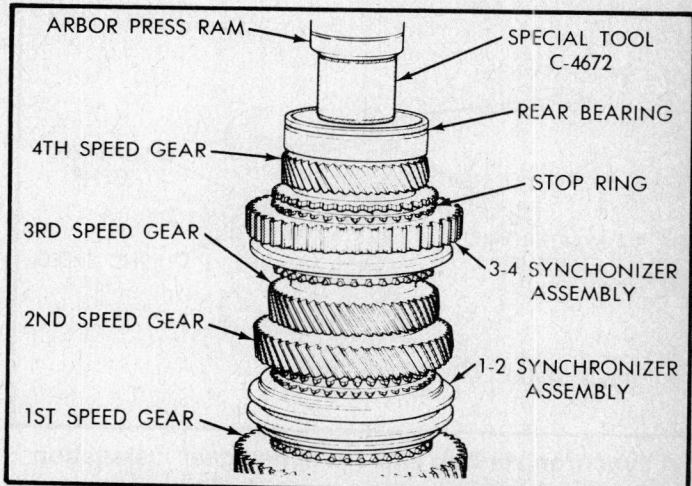

Intermediate shaft rear bearing installation

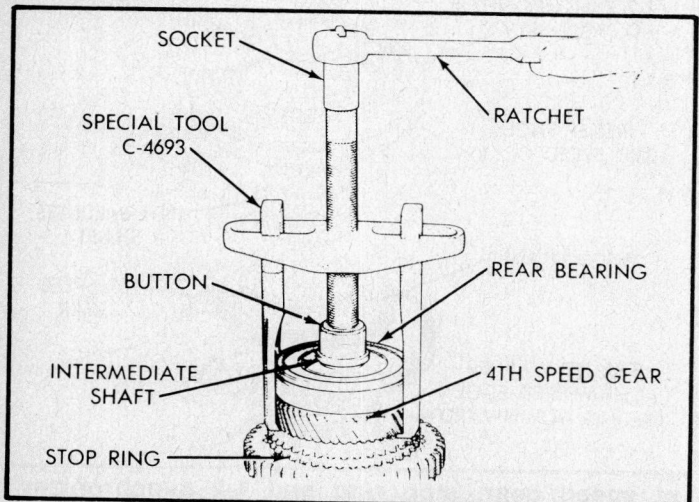

Intermediate shaft rear bearing removal

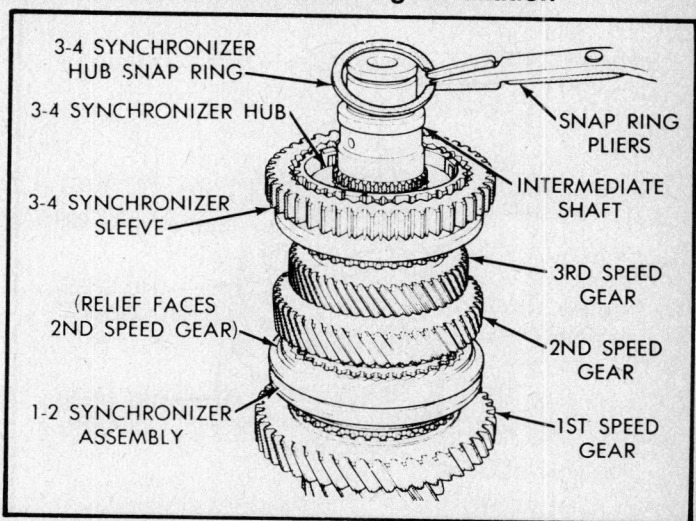

3-4 synchronizer hub snap ring removal or installation

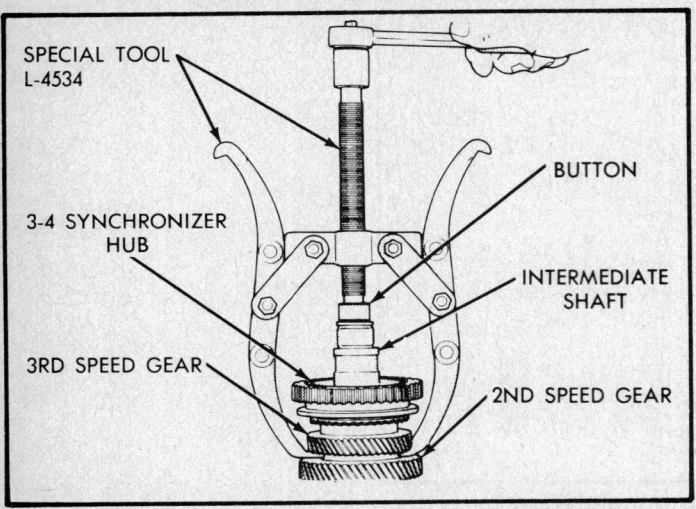

3-4 synchronizer hub and 3rd speed gear removal

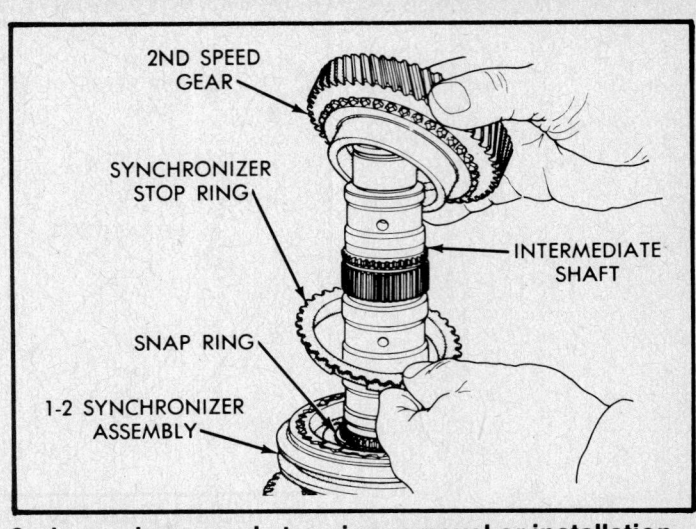

2nd speed gear and stop ring removal or installation

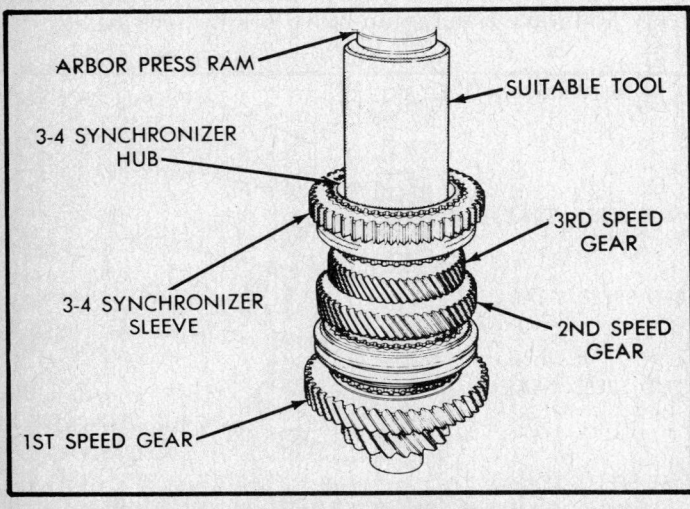

3-4 synchronizer hub and 3rd speed gear installation

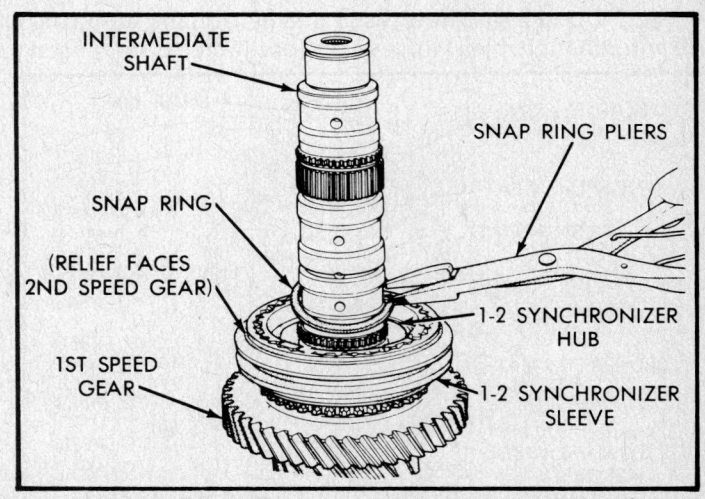

1-2 synchronizer hub snap ring removal or installation

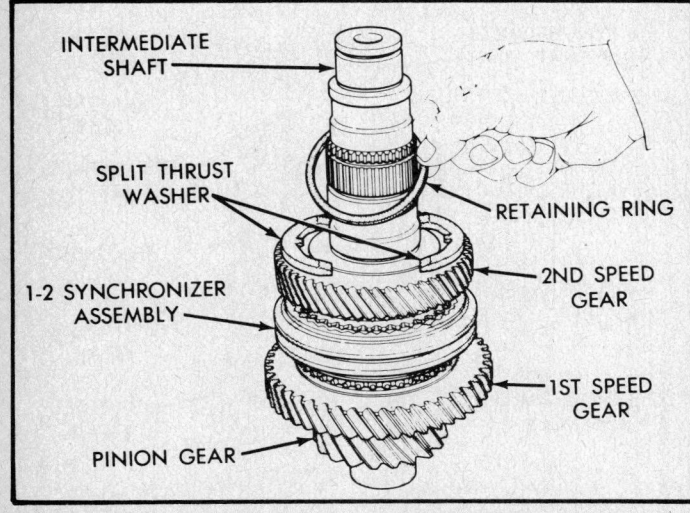

Retaining ring and split thrust washer removal or installation

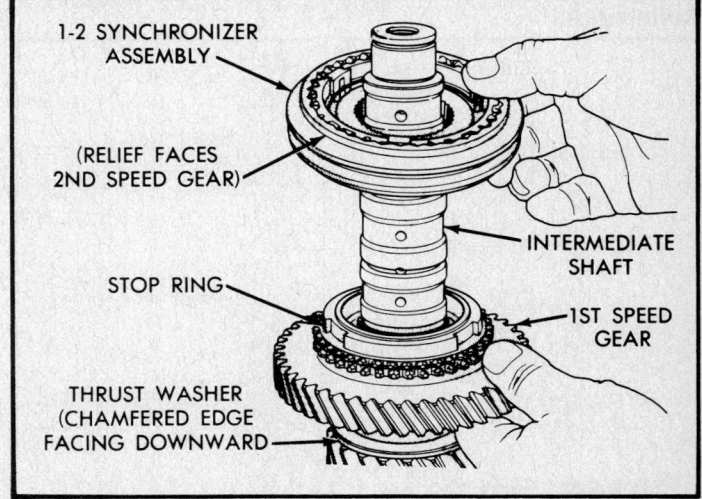

1st speed gear, stop ring and 1-2 synchronizer assembly removal or installation

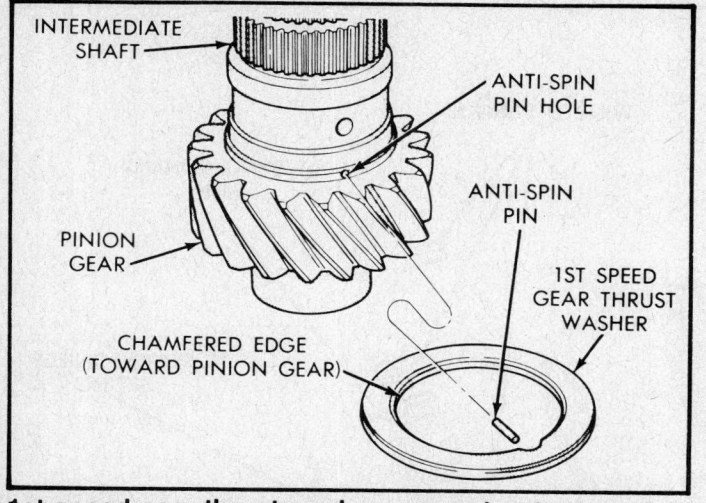

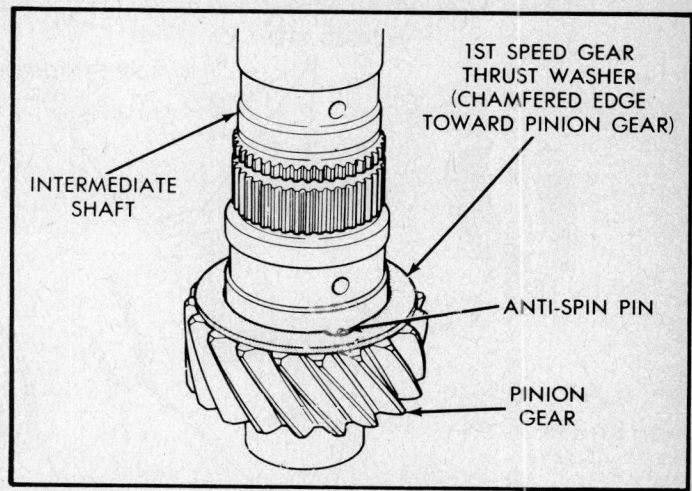

1st speed gear thrust washer removal or installation

1st speed gear thrust washer installation

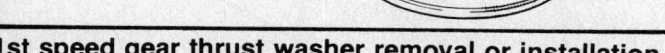

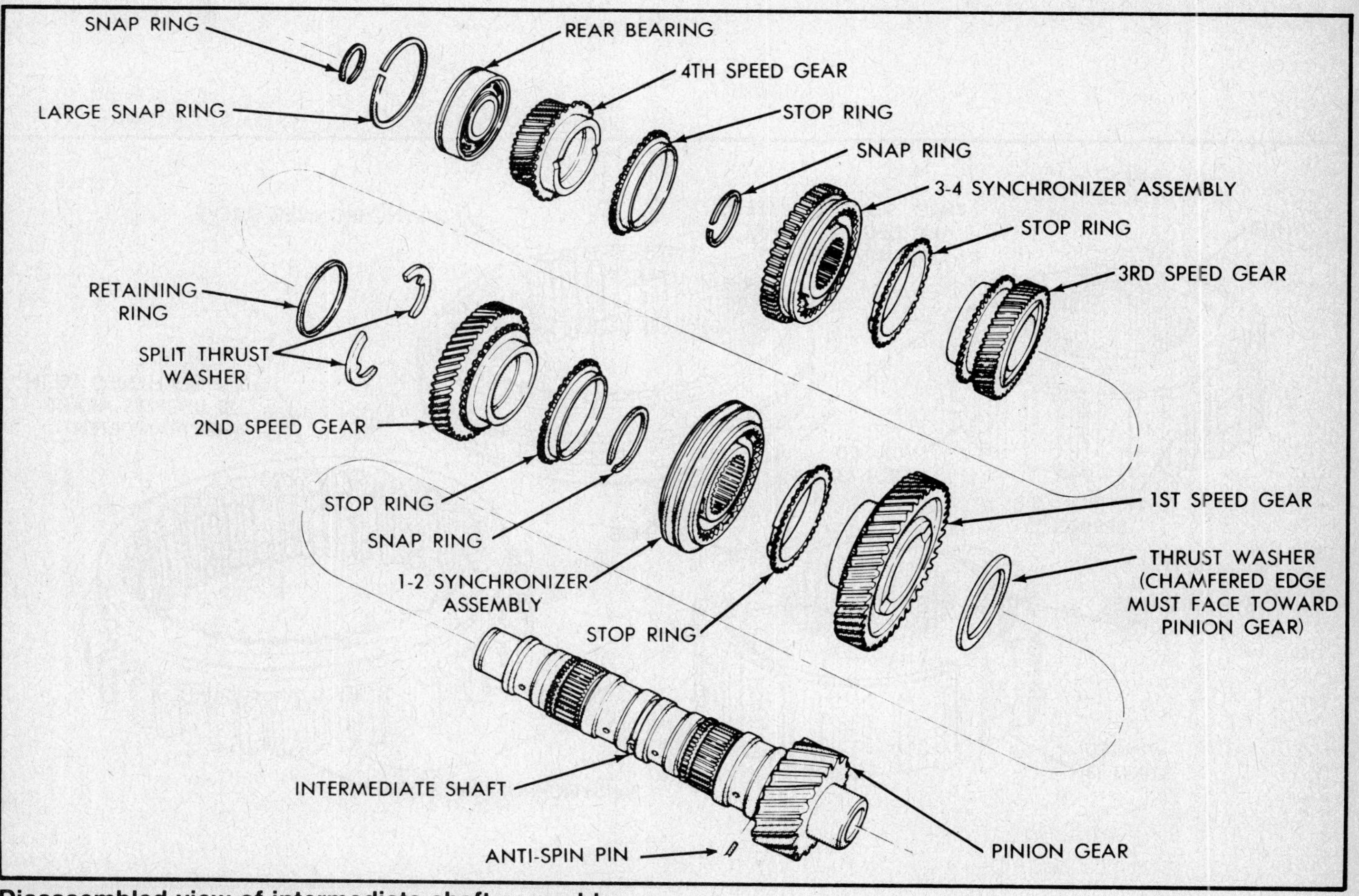

Disassembled view of intermediate shaft assembly

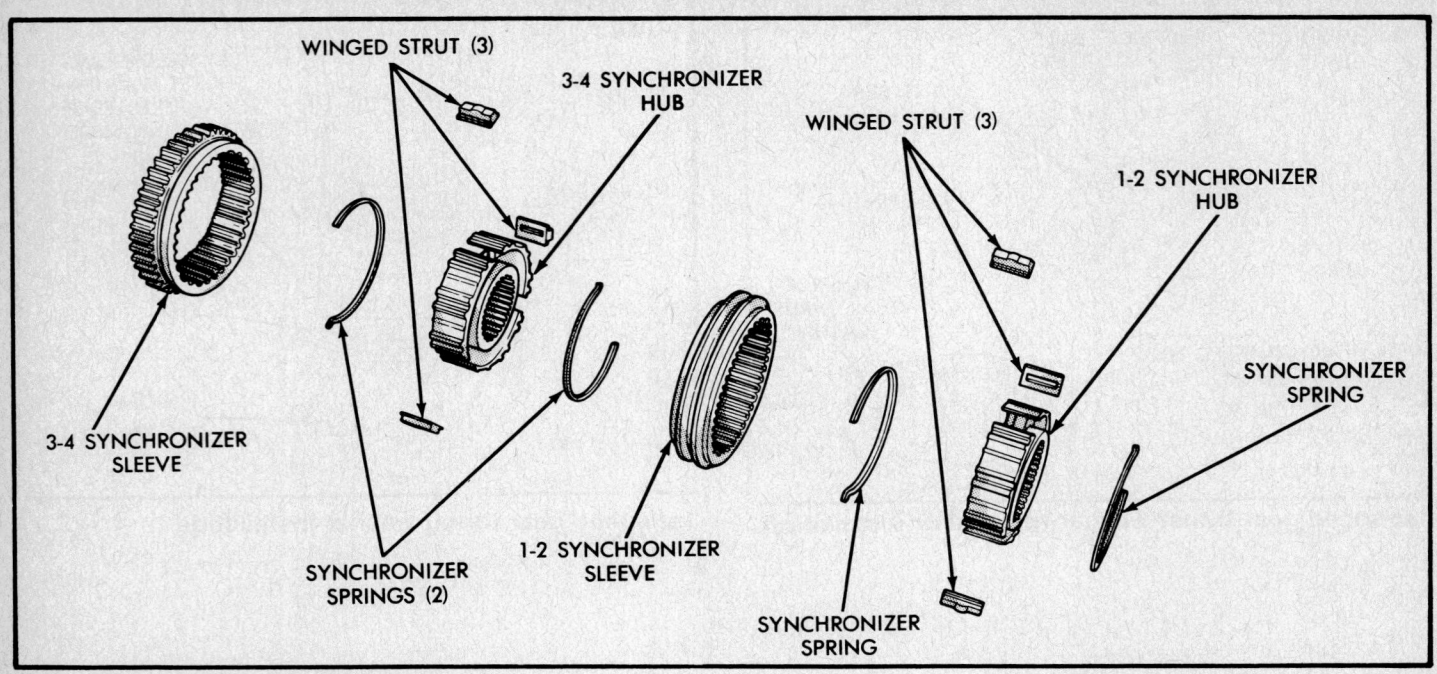

WINGED STRUT (3)

3-4 SYNCHRONIZER HUB

WINGED STRUT (3)

1-2 SYNCHRONIZER HUB

SYNCHRONIZER SPRING

3-4 SYNCHRONIZER SLEEVE

SYNCHRONIZER SPRINGS (2)

1-2 SYNCHRONIZER SLEEVE

SYNCHRONIZER SPRING

Disassembled view of synchronizers

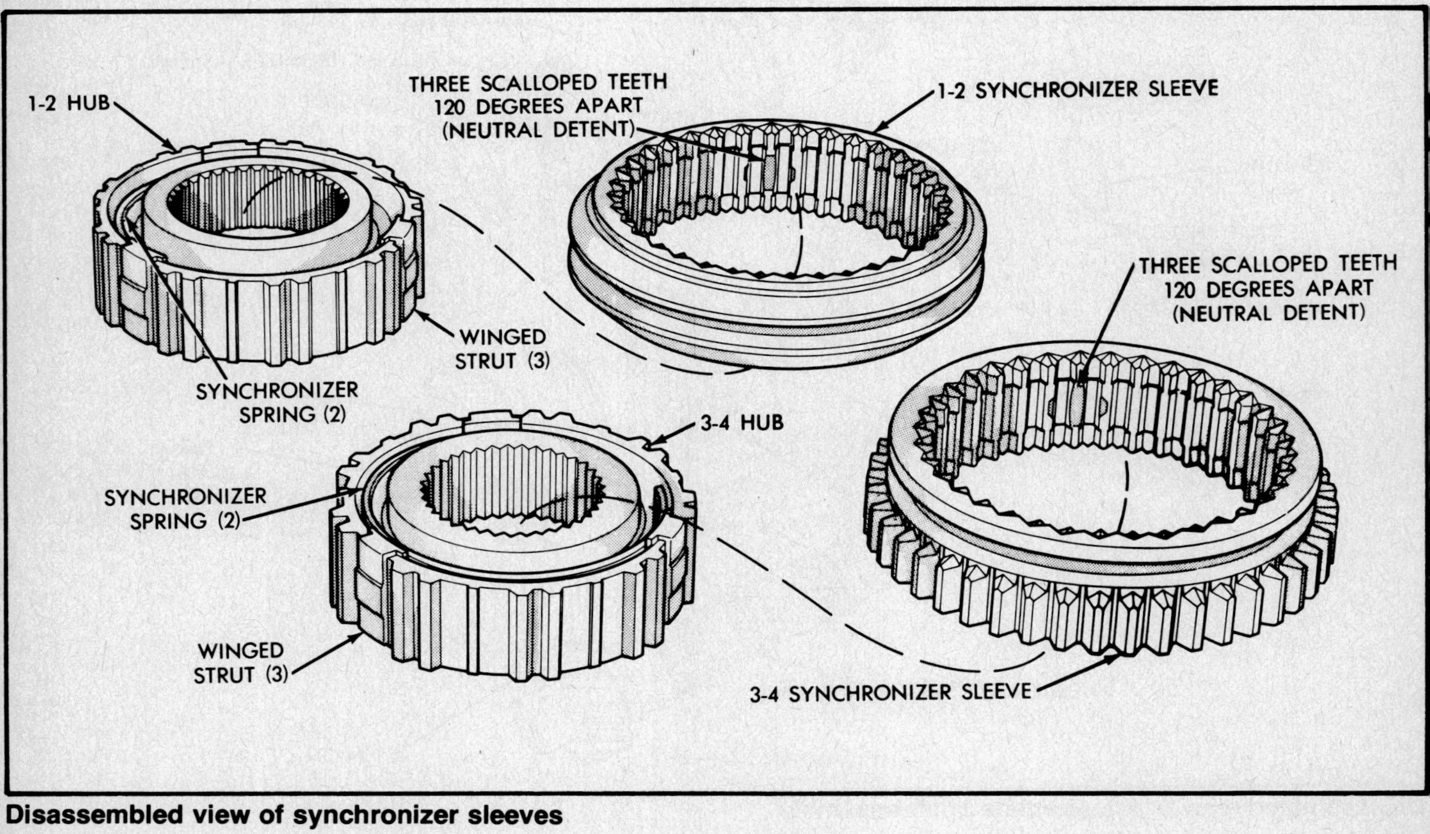

1-2 HUB

THREE SCALLOPED TEETH 120 DEGREES APART (NEUTRAL DETENT)

1-2 SYNCHRONIZER SLEEVE

WINGED STRUT (3)

SYNCHRONIZER SPRING (2)

THREE SCALLOPED TEETH 120 DEGREES APART (NEUTRAL DETENT)

SYNCHRONIZER SPRING (2)

3-4 HUB

WINGED STRUT (3)

3-4 SYNCHRONIZER SLEEVE

Disassembled view of synchronizer sleeves

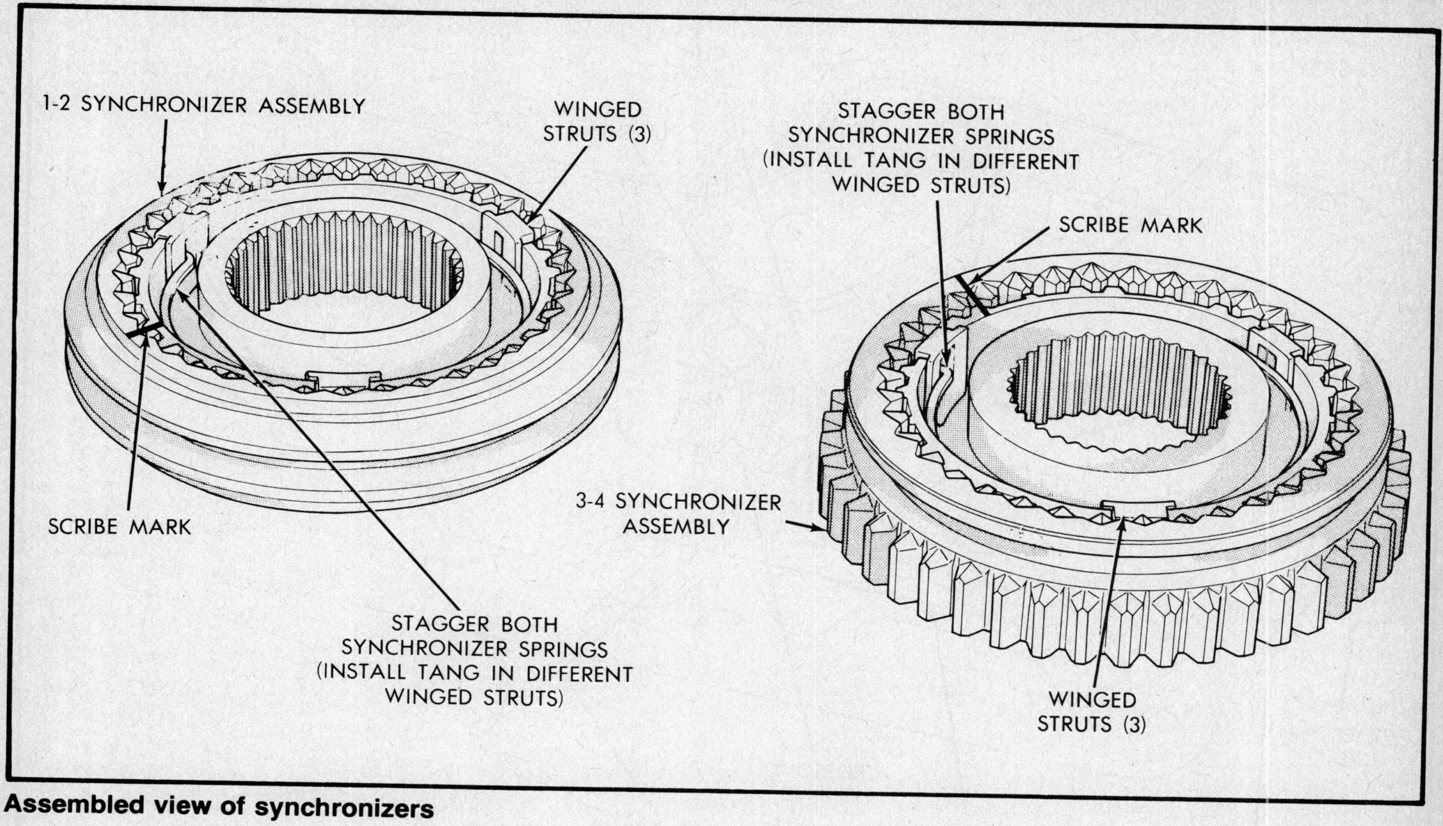

1-2 SYNCHRONIZER ASSEMBLY

WINGED STRUTS (3)

STAGGER BOTH SYNCHRONIZER SPRINGS (INSTALL TANG IN DIFFERENT WINGED STRUTS)

SCRIBE MARK

SCRIBE MARK

3-4 SYNCHRONIZER ASSEMBLY

STAGGER BOTH SYNCHRONIZER SPRINGS (INSTALL TANG IN DIFFERENT WINGED STRUTS)

WINGED STRUTS (3)

Assembled view of synchronizers

Selector Shaft Housing
(Boot and Snap Ring Removed)

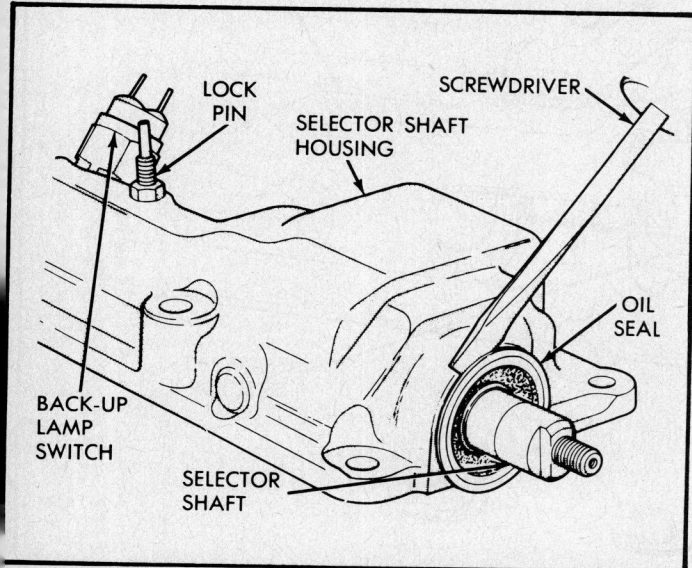

LOCK PIN

SCREWDRIVER

SELECTOR SHAFT HOUSING

OIL SEAL

BACK-UP LAMP SWITCH

SELECTOR SHAFT

Selector shaft oil seal installation

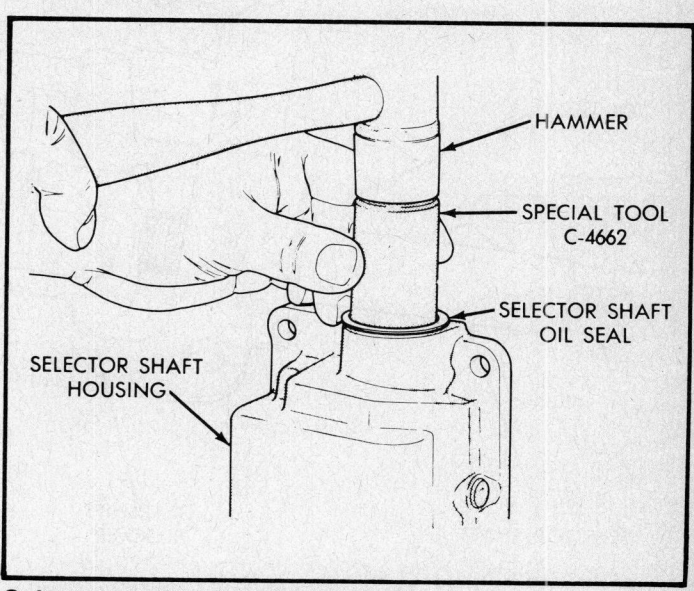

HAMMER

SPECIAL TOOL C-4662

SELECTOR SHAFT OIL SEAL

SELECTOR SHAFT HOUSING

Selector shaft oil seal installation

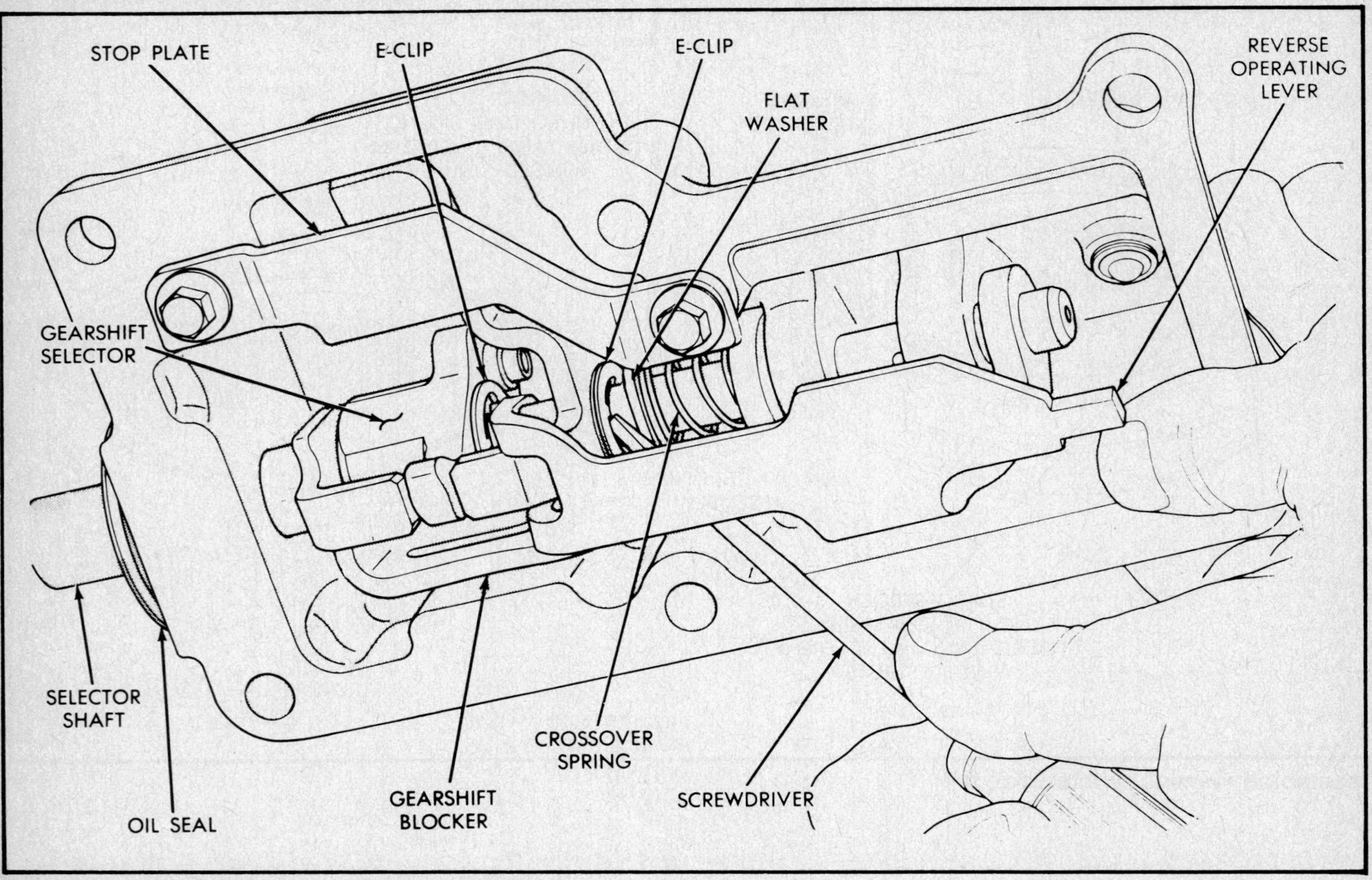

STOP PLATE E-CLIP E-CLIP FLAT WASHER REVERSE OPERATING LEVER

GEARSHIFT SELECTOR

SELECTOR SHAFT

OIL SEAL GEARSHIFT BLOCKER CROSSOVER SPRING SCREWDRIVER

Selector shaft E-clips removal or installation

STOP PLATE SCREWS REVERSE OPERATING LEVER

OIL SEAL

GEARSHIFT SELECTOR

E-CLIPS

SELECTOR SHAFT GEARSHIFT BLOCKER

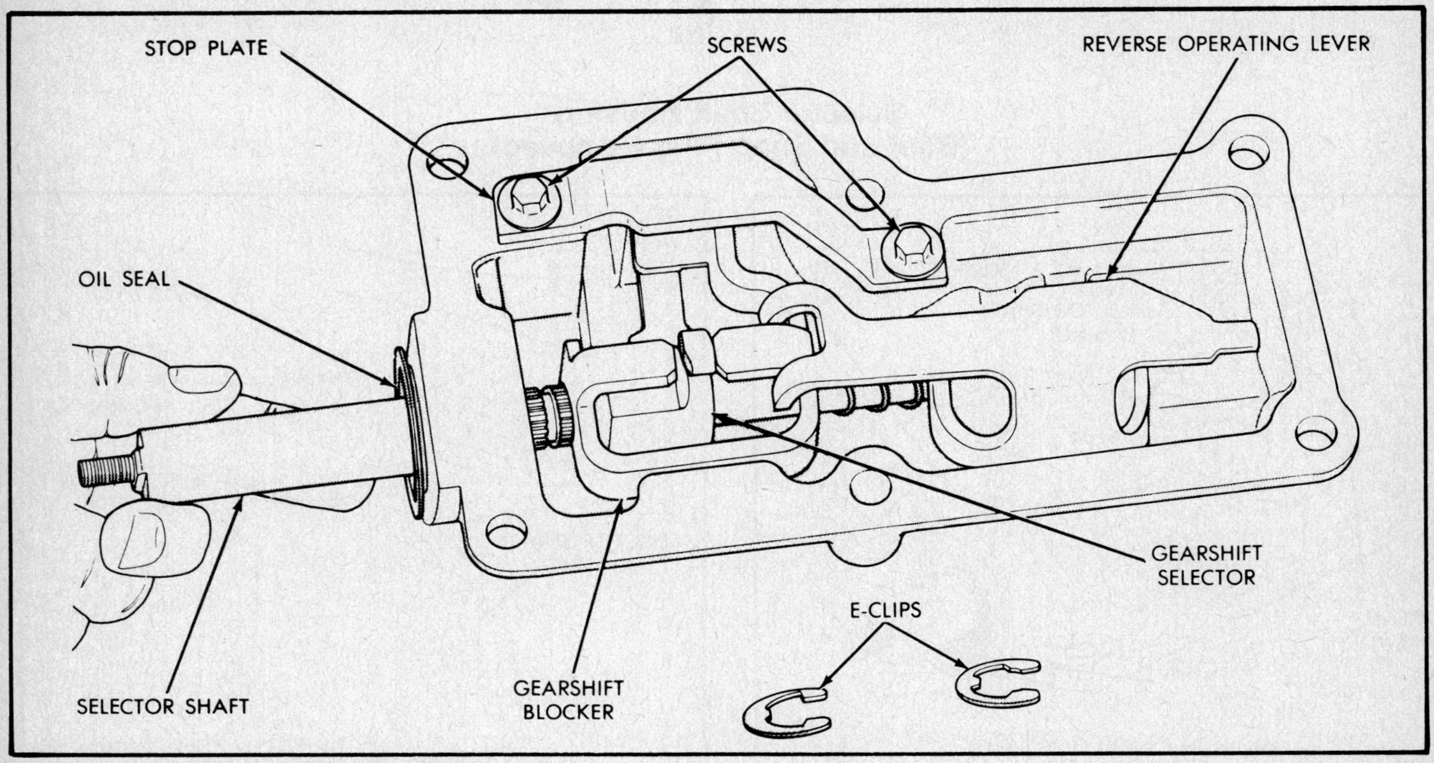

Selector shaft removal or installation

B754

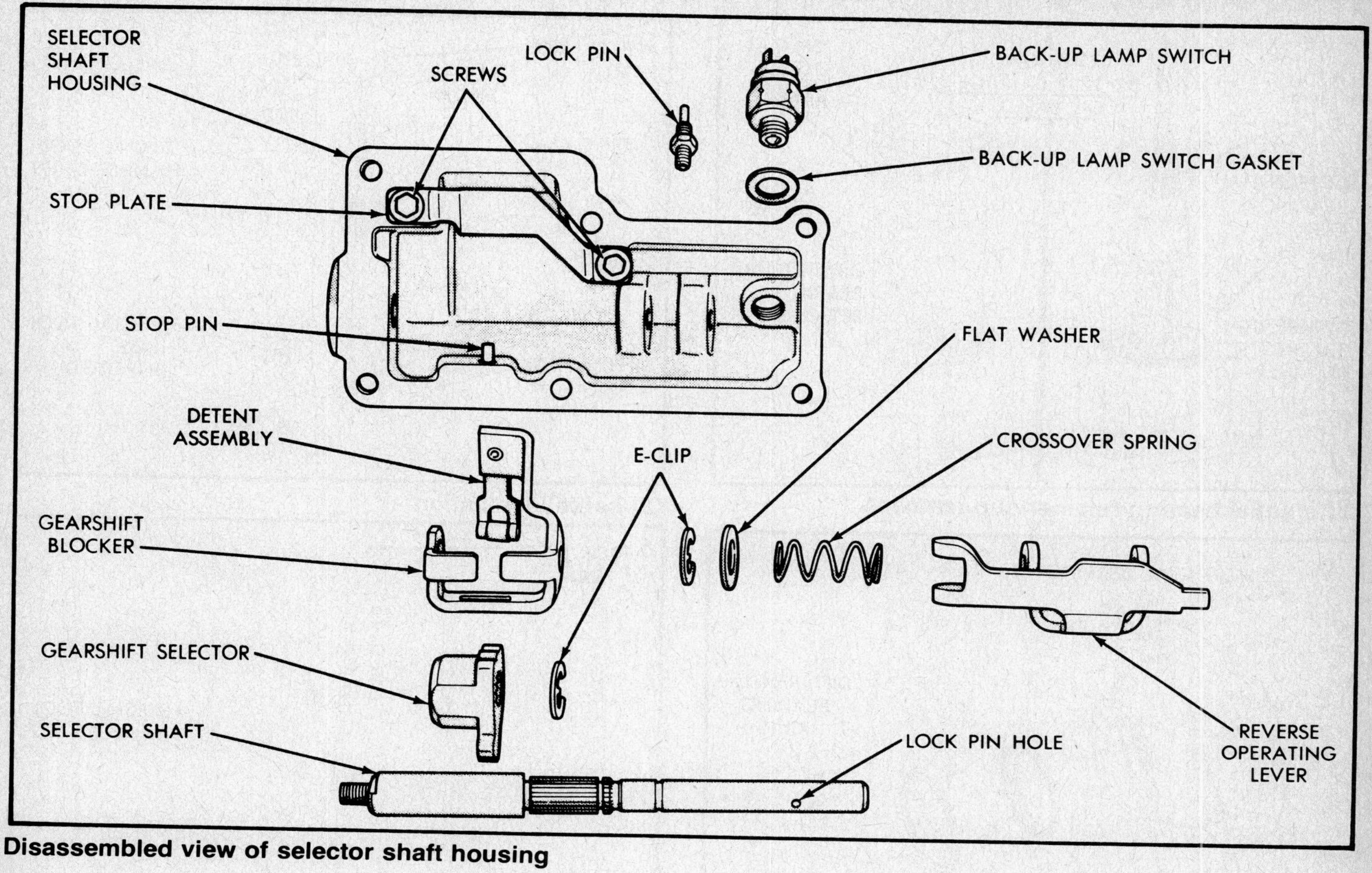

SELECTOR SHAFT HOUSING

SCREWS

LOCK PIN

BACK-UP LAMP SWITCH

BACK-UP LAMP SWITCH GASKET

STOP PLATE

STOP PIN

FLAT WASHER

DETENT ASSEMBLY

E-CLIP

CROSSOVER SPRING

GEARSHIFT BLOCKER

GEARSHIFT SELECTOR

SELECTOR SHAFT

LOCK PIN HOLE

REVERSE OPERATING LEVER

Disassembled view of selector shaft housing

Differential Bearing Retainer

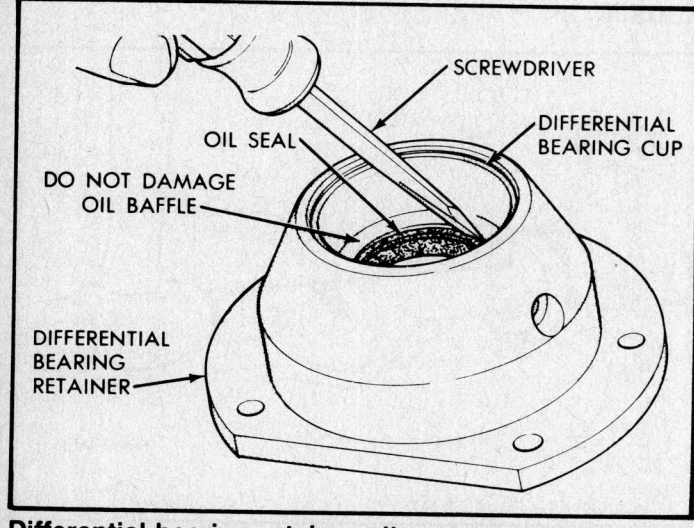

SCREWDRIVER

OIL SEAL

DIFFERENTIAL BEARING CUP

DO NOT DAMAGE OIL BAFFLE

DIFFERENTIAL BEARING RETAINER

Differential bearing retainer oil seal removal

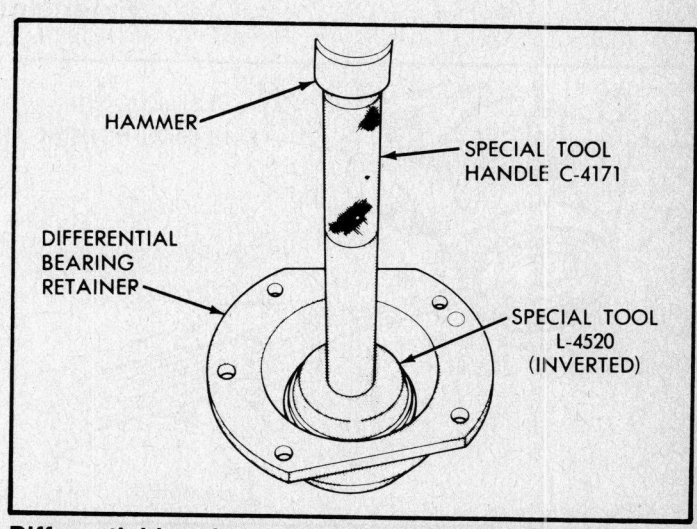

HAMMER

SPECIAL TOOL HANDLE C-4171

DIFFERENTIAL BEARING RETAINER

SPECIAL TOOL L-4520 (INVERTED)

Differential bearing retainer oil seal installation

B755

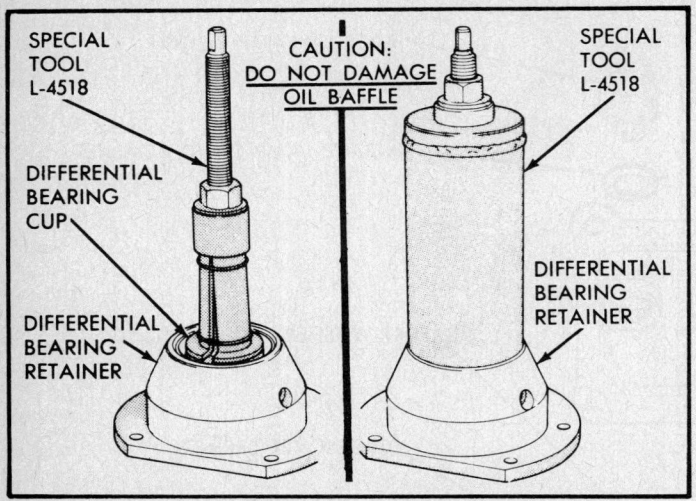

Differential bearing retainer cup removal

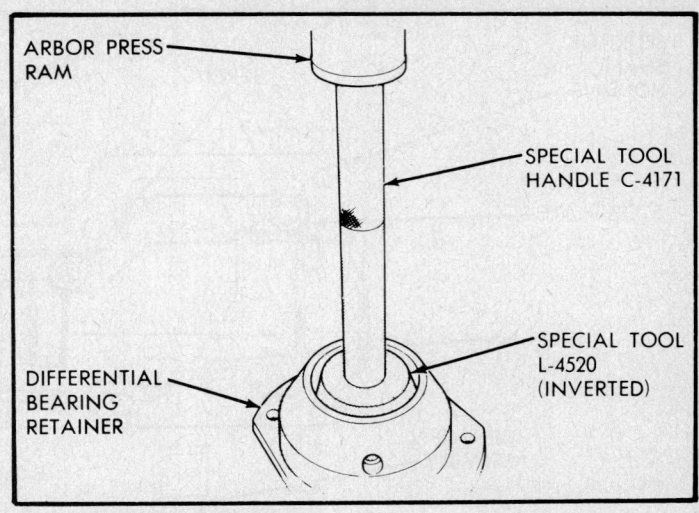

Oil baffle installation

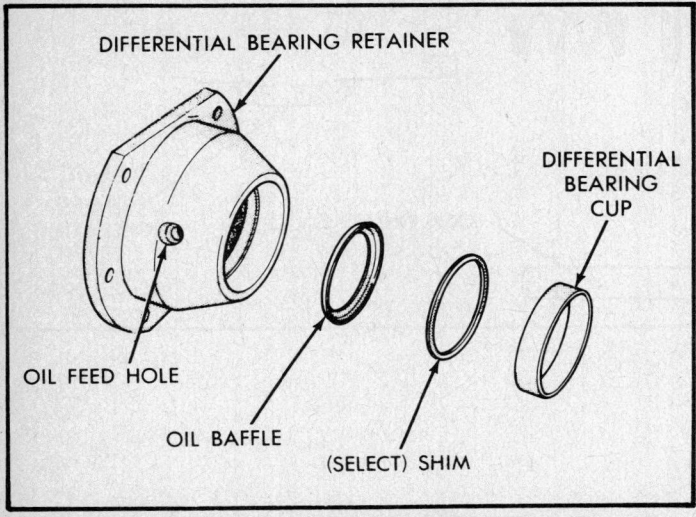

Disassembled view of differential bearing retainer

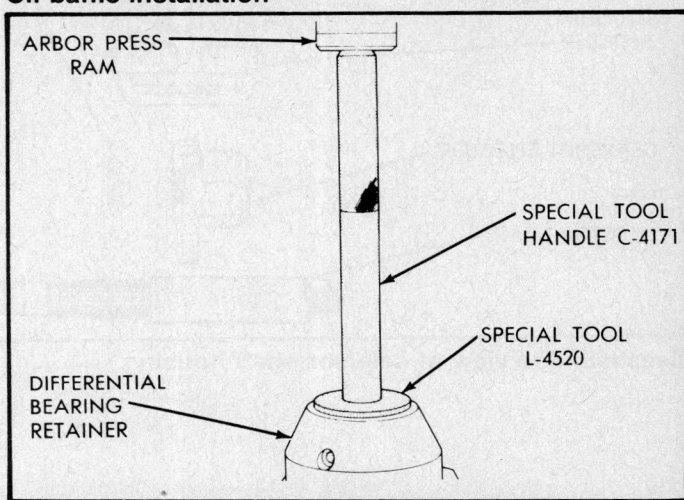

Insert select shim and differential bearing retainer cup

Extension Housing

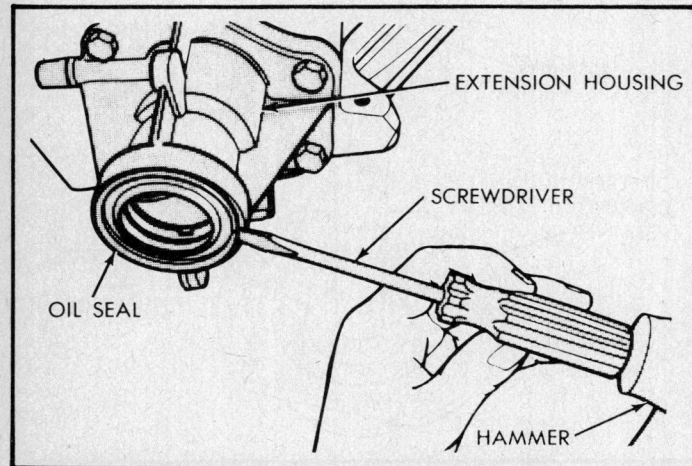

Extension housing oil seal removal

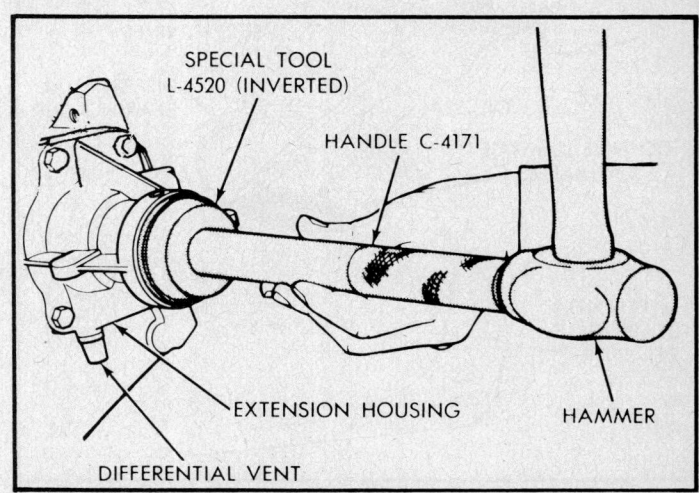

Extension housing oil seal installation

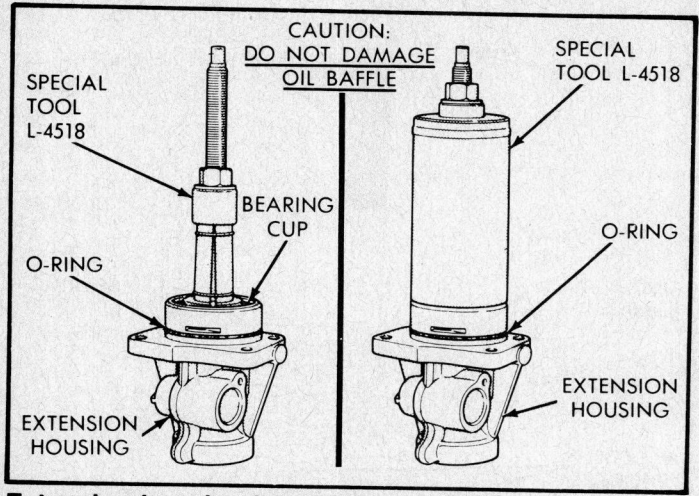

Extension housing bearing cup removal

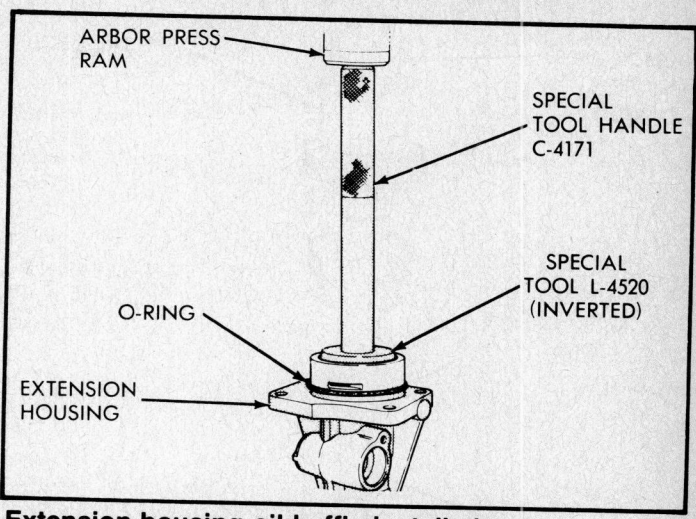

Extension housing oil baffle installation

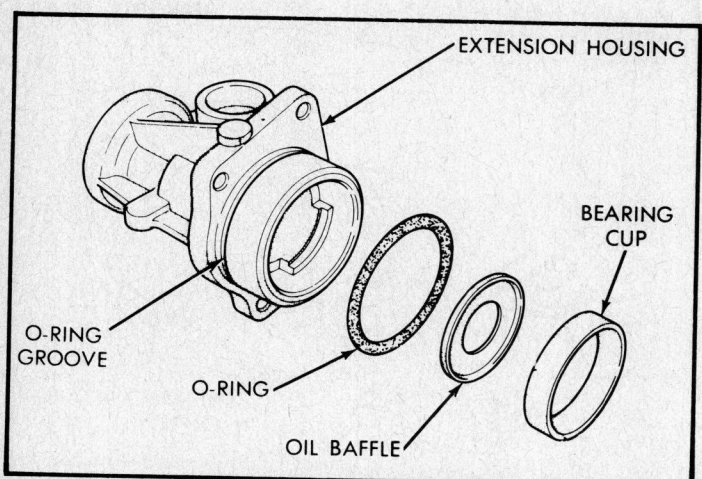

Disassembled view of extension housing

INPUT SHAFT

Shim thickness calculation need only be done if any of the following parts are replaced:
1. Transaxle case
2. Input shaft seal retainer
3. Bearing retainer plate
4. Rear end cover
5. Input shaft
6. Input shaft bearings

Refer to Bearing Adjustment Procedure to determine the proper shim thickness for correct bearing preload and proper bearing turning torque.

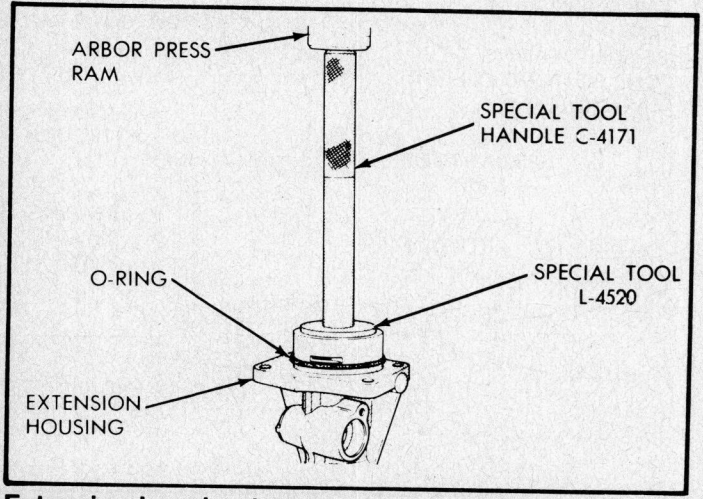

Extension housing bearing cup installation

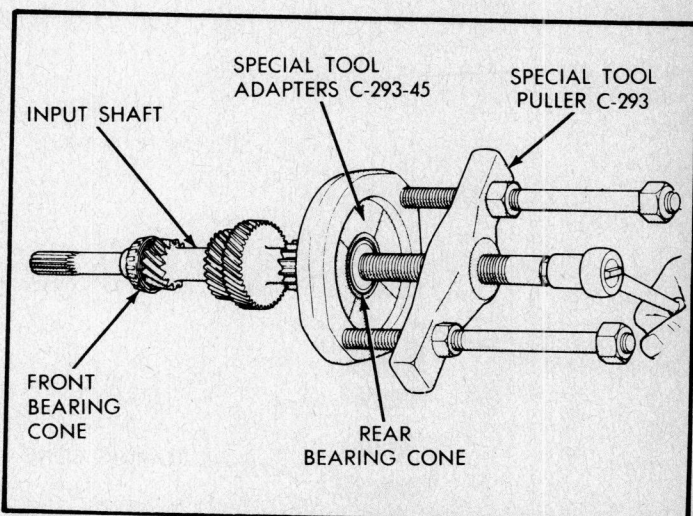

Input shaft rear bearing cone removal

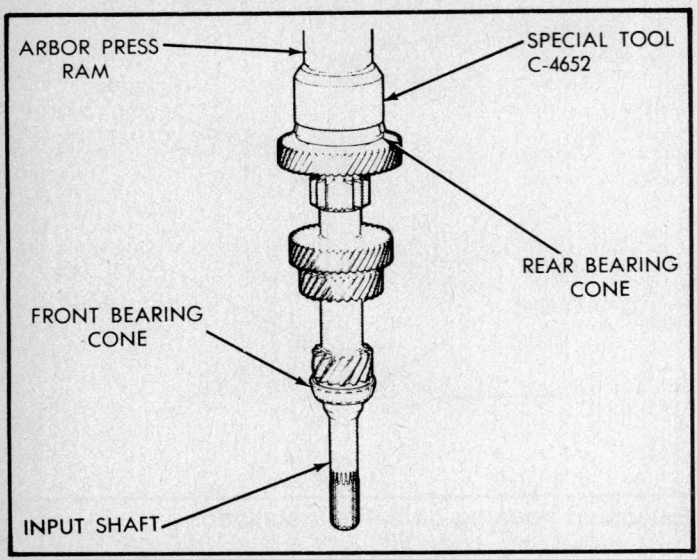

Input shaft rear bearing cone installation

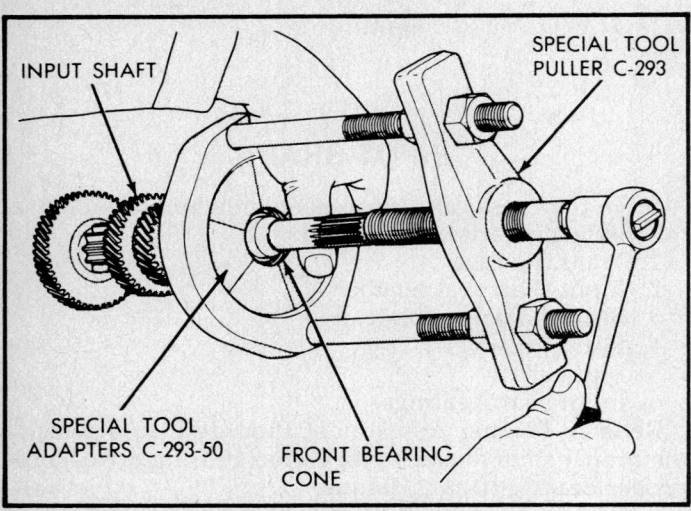

Input shaft front bearing cone removal

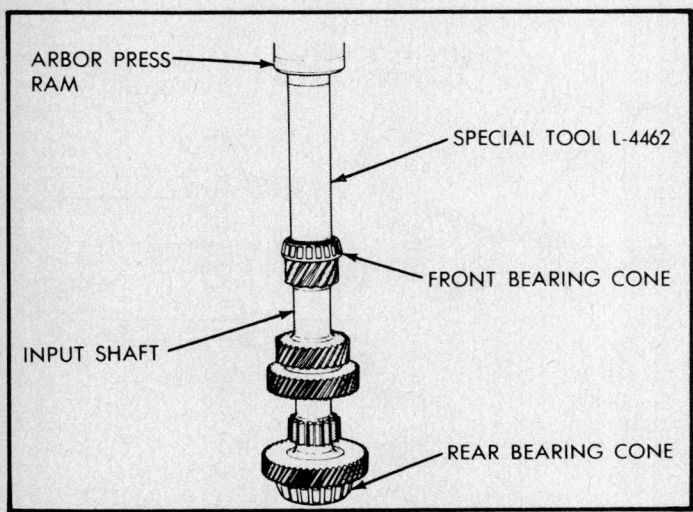

Input shaft front bearing cone installation

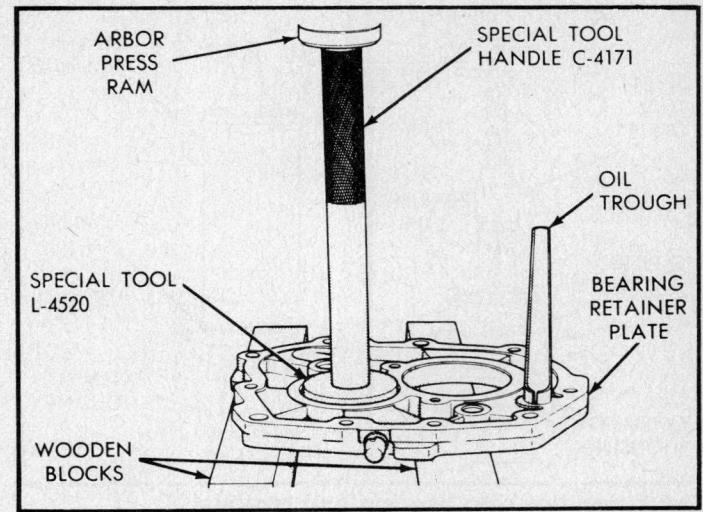

Input shaft rear bearing cup removal

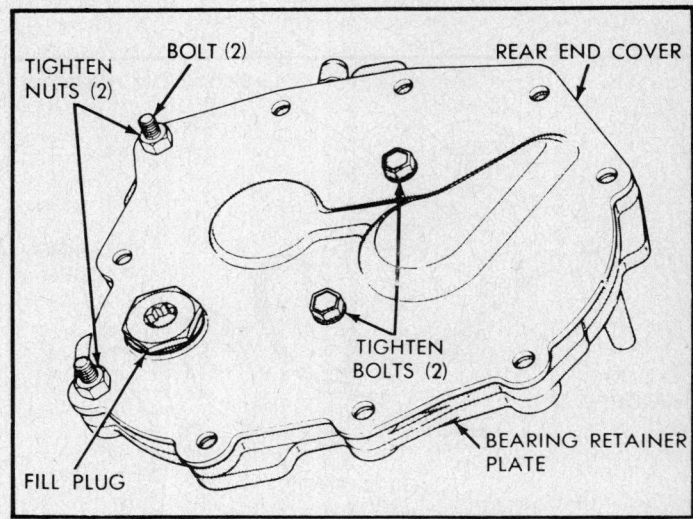

Bolt rear end cover on before installing input shaft rear bearing cup

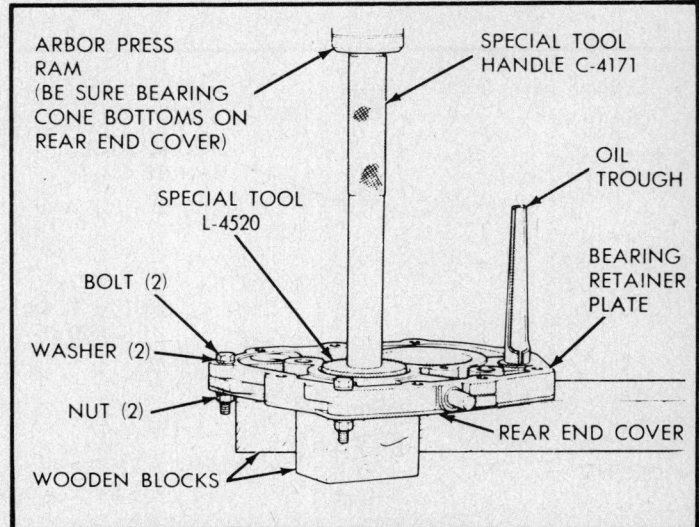

Input shaft rear bearing cup installation

DIFFERENTIAL

Shim thickness calculation need only be done if any of the following parts are replaced:
1. Transaxle case
2. Differential bearing retainer
3. Extension housing
4. Differential case
5. Differential bearings

Refer to Bearing Adjustment Procedure to determine the proper shim thickness for correct bearing preload and proper bearing turning torque.

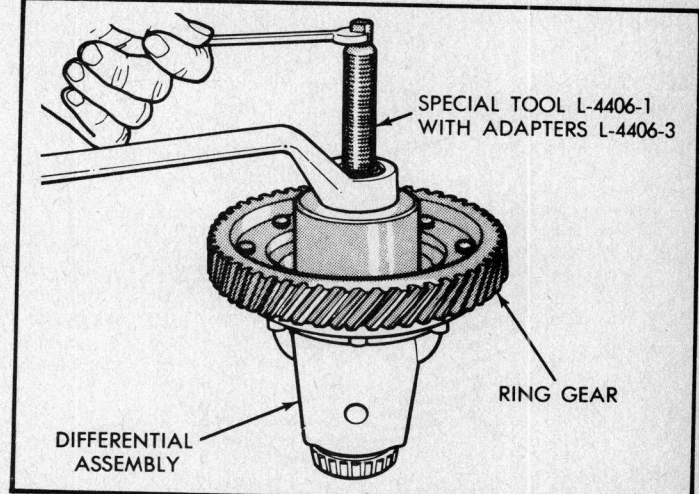

Differential bearing cone removal

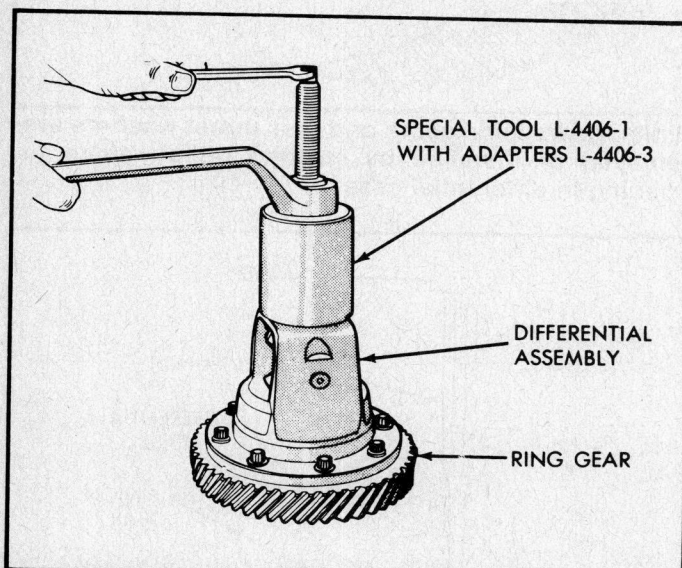

Differential bearing cone removal

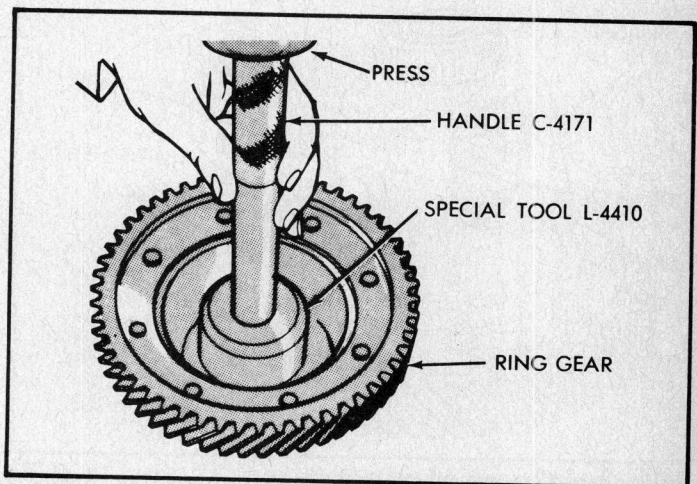

Differential bearing cone installation

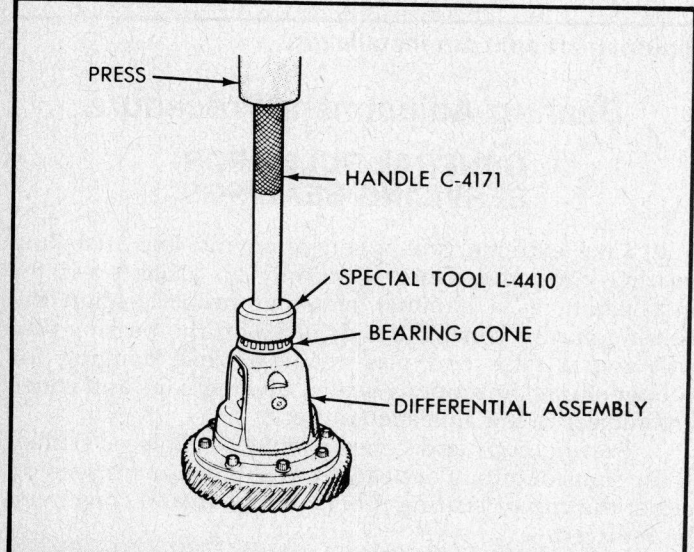

Differential bearing cone installation

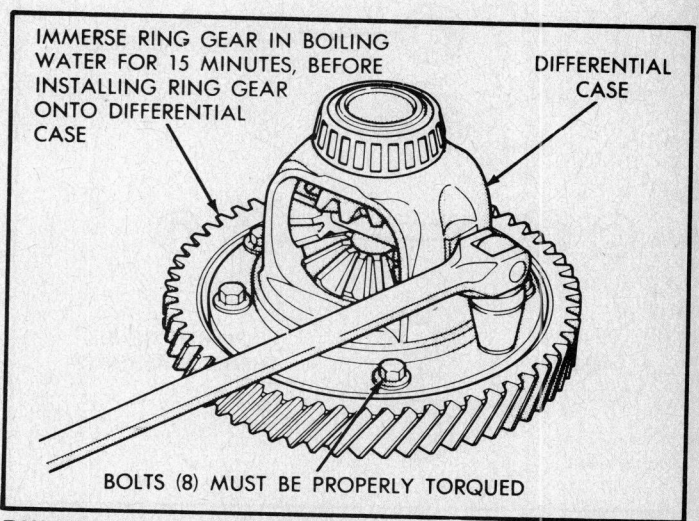

Differential ring gear bolts and ring gear removal or installation

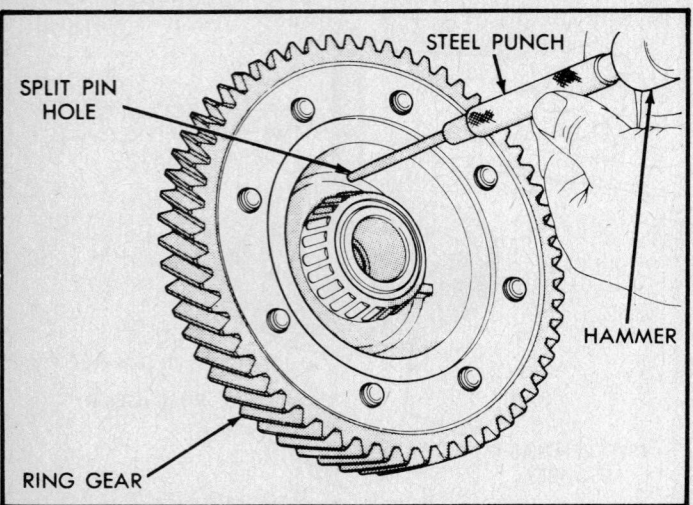

Pinion shaft split pin removal

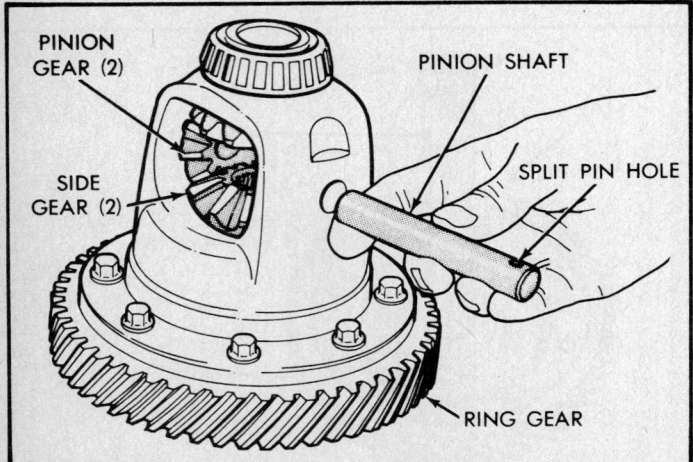

Pinion shaft removal or installation

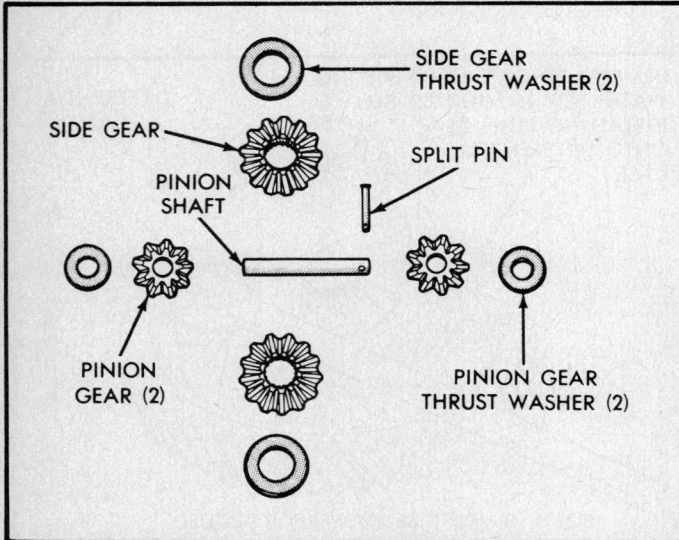

Disassembled view of differential gears, thrust washers and pinion shaft

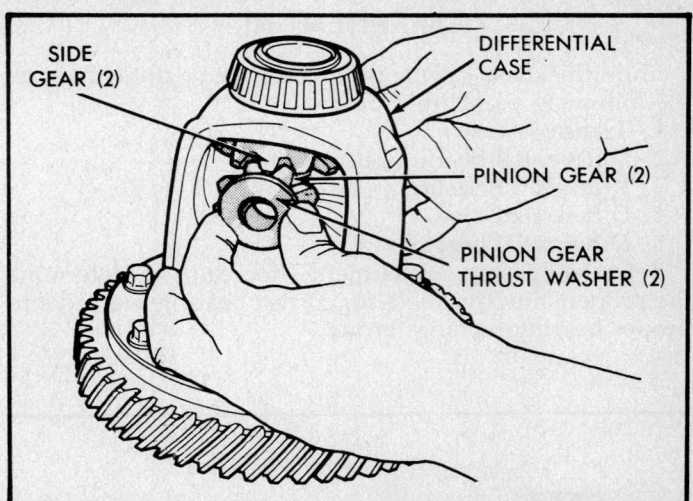

Pinion gears, side gears and four thrust washers are removed or installed by rotating pinion gears to opening in differential case

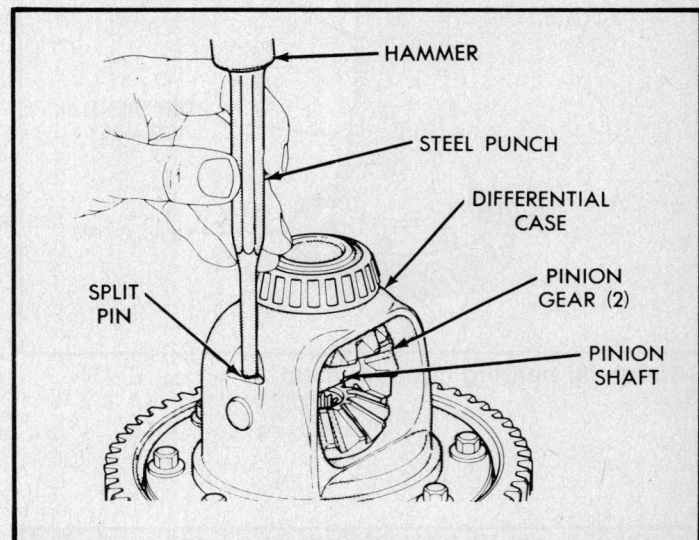

Pinion shaft split pin installation

Bearing Adjustment Procedure

GENERAL RULES FOR SERVICING BEARINGS

1. Take extreme care when removing and installing bearing cups and cones. Use only an arbor press for installation, as a hammer may not properly align the bearing cup or cone. Burrs or nicks on the bearing seat will give a false end play reading while gauging for proper shims. Improperly seated bearing cups and cones are subject to low mileage failure.

2. Bearing cups and cones should be replaced if they show signs of pitting or heat distress. If distress is seen on either the cup or bearing rollers, both cup and cone must be replaced.

3. Bearing end play and drag torque specifications *must be maintained* to avoid premature bearing failures.

Used (orginal) bearing may lose up to 50% of the original drag torque after break-in.

NOTE All bearing adjustments must be made with no other component interference or gear inter-mesh.

4. Replace bearings as a pair. For example, if one differential bearing is defective, replace both differential bearings. If one input shaft bearing is defective, replace both input shaft bearings.

5. Bearing cones *must not* be reused if removed.

6. Turning torque readings should be obtained while smoothly rotating in either direction (breakaway reading is not indicative of the true turning torque).

7. Replace the oil baffle, if damaged.

Input Shaft Bearing Preload Adjustment

1. Using tool L-4656 with handle C-4171, press the input shaft front bearing cup slightly forward in the case. Then, using tool L-4655 with handle C-4171, press the bearing cup back into the case, from the front to properly position the bearing cup before checking the input shaft end play (see input shaft front bearing cup replacement procedure in Subassembly Rebuilding Procedures section).

NOTE This step is not necessary if tool L-4655 was previously used to install the input shaft front bearing cup in the case and no input shaft (select) shim has been installed since pressing the cup into the case.

2. Select a gauging shim which will give 0.025 to 0.254 mm (.001 to .010 inch) end play.

NOTE Measure the original shim from the input shaft seal retainer and select a shim 0.254 mm (.010 inch) thinner than the original for the gauging shim.

3. Install the gauging shim on the bearing cup and install the input shaft seal retainer.

CAUTION The input shaft seal retainer is used to draw the input shaft front bearing cup the proper distance into the case bore during this step.

Alternately tighten the input shaft seal retainer bolts until the input shaft seal retainer is bottomed against the case. Tighten the bolts to 28 N•m (21 ft.lbs.)

4. Oil the input shaft bearings with A.T.F. and install the input shaft in the case. Install the bearing retainer plate with the input shaft rear bearing cup pressed in and the end cover installed. Tighten all bolts and nuts to 28 N•m (21 ft. lbs.)

5. Position the dial indicator to check the input shaft end play. Apply moderate load, by hand, to the input shaft splines. Push toward the rear while rotating the input shaft back and forth a number of times to settle out the bearings. Zero the dial indicator. Pull the input shaft toward the front while rotating the input shaft back and forth a number of times to settle out the bearings. Record the end play.

6. The shim required for proper bearing preload is the total of the gauging shim thickness, plus end play, plus (constant) preload of 0.076 mm (.003 inch). Combine shims, if necessary, to obtain a shim within .04 mm (.0016 inch) of the required shim (see Input Shaft Shim Chart for proper shim [s]).

7. Remove the input shaft seal retainer and gauging shim. Install the shim(s) selected in step 6 and reinstall the input shaft seal retainer with a 1/16 inch bead of R.T.V. sealant.

CAUTION Keep R.T.V. sealant out of the oil slot.

Observe the Caution in step 3. Tighten the input shaft seal retainer bolts to 28 N•m (21 ft.lbs.).

8. Using special tool L-4508 and an inch-pound torque wrench, check the input shaft turning torque. The turning torque should be 1 to 5 in.lbs. for new bearings or a minimum of 1 in.lb. for used bearings. If the turning torque is too high, install a .04 mm (.0016 inch) thinner shim. If the turning torque is too low, install a .04 mm (.0016 inch) thicker shim.

CAUTION Step 1 must be repeated every time a thinner shim is installed. This will assure that the input shaft front bearing cup is pressed the proper distance into the case.

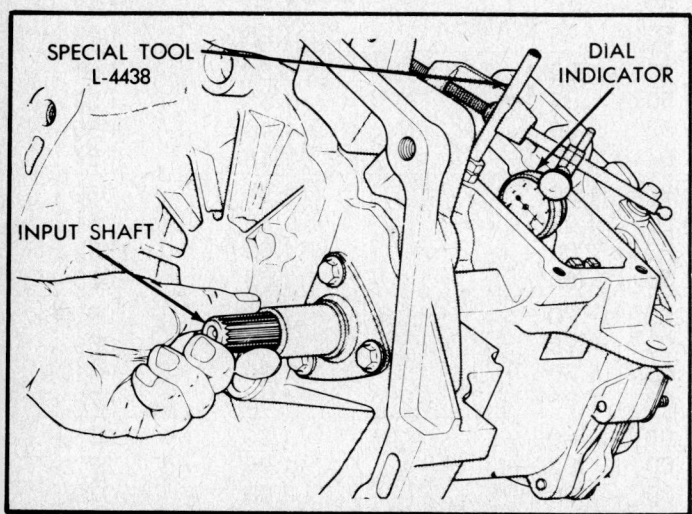

Checking input shaft bearing end play to determine shim thickness

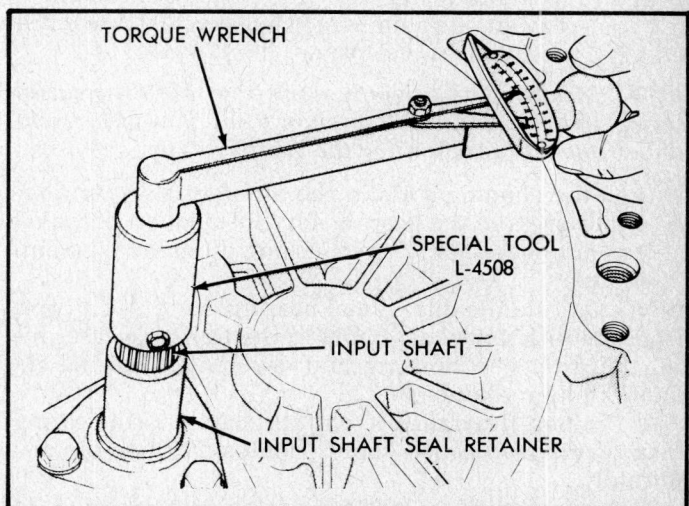

Checking input shaft bearing turning torque

9. Recheck the input shaft turning torque. Repeat step 8 until the proper bearing turning torque is obtained. Observe CAUTION in step 8.

INPUT SHAFT SHIM CHART

MM	MM	Inch
.66		.026
.70		.028
.74		.029
.78		.031
.82		.032
.86		.034
.90		.035
.94		.037
.98		.039
1.02		.040
1.06		.042
1.10		.043
1.14		.045
1.18		.046
1.22		.048
1.26		.050
1.30		.051
1.34		.053
1.36	(.66 + .70)	.054
1.40	(.66 + .74)	.055
1.44	(.70 + .74)	.057
1.48	(.70 + .78)	.059
1.52	(.74 + .78)	.060
1.56	(.74 + .82)	.061
1.60	(.78 + .82)	.063
1.64	(.78 + .86)	.065
1.68	(.82 + .86)	.066

Differential Bearing Preload Adjustment

1. Remove the bearing cup and existing shim from the differential bearing retainer. (See Differential Bearing Retainer in Subassembly Rebuilding Procedures section).

2. Select a gauging shim which will give 0.025 to 0.254 mm (.001 to .010 inch) end play.

NOTE Measure the original shim from the differential bearing retainer and select a shim 0.381 mm (.015 inch) thinner than the original for the gauging shim.

Install the gauging shim in the differential bearing retainer and press in the bearing cup. Installation of the oil baffle is not necessary when checking differential assembly end play.

3. Lubricate the differential bearings with A.T.F. and install the differential assembly in the transaxle case. Install the extension housing and differential bearing retainer. Tighten the bolts to 28 N•m (21 ft.lbs.).

4. Position the transaxle with the bell housing facing down on the workbench with C-clamps. Position the dial indicator.

5. Apply a medium load to the ring gear, by hand, in the downward direction while rolling the differential assembly back and forth a number of times to settle the

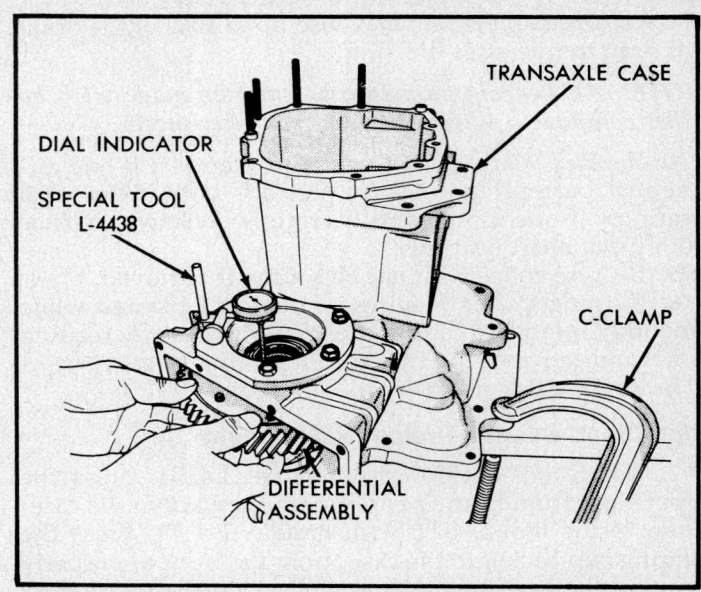

Checking differential bearing end play to determine shim thickness

DIFFERENTIAL BEARING SHIM CHART

Required Shim Combination (mm)		Total Thickness (mm)	(Inch)
.50		.50	.020
.75		.75	.030
.80		.80	.032
.85		.85	.034
.90		.90	.035
.95		.95	.037
1.00		1.00	.039
1.05		1.05	.041
.50 +	.60	1.10	.043
.50 +	.65	1.15	.045
.50 +	.70	1.20	.047
.50 +	.75	1.25	.049
.50 +	.80	1.30	.051
.50 +	.85	1.35	.053
.50 +	.90	1.40	.055
.50 +	.95	1.45	.057
.50 + 1.00		1.50	.059
.50 + 1.05		1.55	.061
1.00 +	.60	1.60	.063
1.00 +	.65	1.65	.065
1.00 +	.70	1.70	.067
1.00 +	.75	1.75	.069
1.00 +	.80	1.80	.071
1.00 +	.85	1.85	.073
1.00 +	.90	1.90	.075
1.00 +	.95	1.95	.077
1.00 + 1.00		2.00	.079
1.00 + 1.05		2.05	.081
1.05 + 1.05		2.10	.083

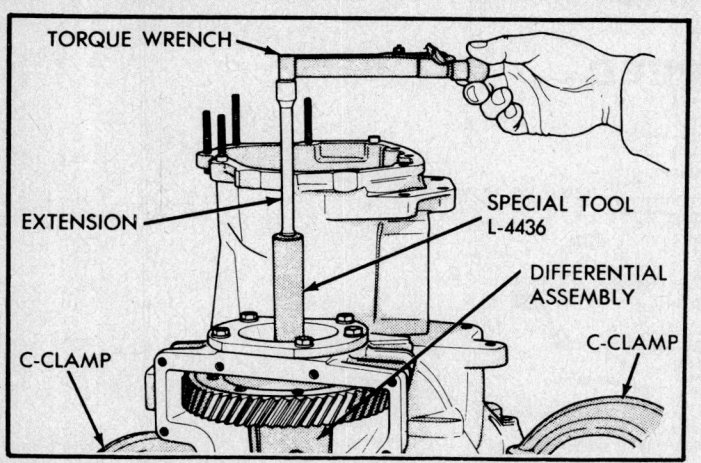

Checking differential bearing turning torque

bearings. Zero the dial indicator. To obtain end play readings, apply a medium load upward by hand while rolling the differential assembly back and forth a number of times to settle out the bearings. Record the end play.

6. The shim required for proper bearing preload is the total of the gauging shim thickness, plus end play, plus (constant) preload of 0.254 mm (.010 inch). Combine shims, if necessary, to obtain a shim within .05 mm (.002 inch) of the shim[s]).

7. Remove the differential bearing retainer. Remove the bearing cup and gauging shim. Properly install the oil baffle. Be sure the oil baffle is not damaged. Install the shim(s) selected in step 6 and press the bearing cup into the differential bearing retainer.

8. Using a 1/16 inch bead of R.T.V. sealant for gaskets, install the differential bearing retainer and extension housing. Tighten the bolts to 28 N•m (21 ft.lbs.).

9. Using special tool L-4436 and an inch-pound torque wrench, check the turning torque of the differential assembly. The turning torque should be 9 to 14 in.lbs. for new bearings or a minimum of 6 in.lbs. for used bearings. If the turning torque is too high, install a .05 mm (.002 inch) thinner shim. If the turning torque is too low, install a .05 mm (.002 inch) thicker shim.

10. Recheck the turning torque. Repeat step 9 until the proper turning torque is obtained.

TIGHTENING REFERENCE

A-460 Manual Transaxle	Grade x Thread Size	TORQUE Newton-Meters	TORQUE Foot-Pounds
Gearshift housing to case bolt	9.8 x M8 x 1.25	28	21
Gearshift operating lever attaching nut	9.8 x M8 x 1.25 x 6H	30	22
Fork stop plate to gearshift housing bolt	9.8 x M6 x 1.0	7	9
Shift linkage adjusting pin	9.8 x M6 x 1.0 x 6G	7	9
Dust covers to case screw (2.2L engine)	10.9 x N6 x 1.0	7	9
Dust cover (upper) to case screw (1.7L engine)	9.8 x M6 x 1.0	7	9
Dust cover (lower) to case bolt (1.7L engine)	9.8 x M6 x 1.0	7	9
Strut to block bolt	10.9 x M12 x 1.75	95	70
Strut to case bolt	10.9 x M12 x 1.75	95	70
Flywheel to crankshaft bolt (2.2L engine)	12.9 x M10 x 1.5	81	60
Flywheel to crankcase bolt (1.7L engine)	12.9 x M10 x 1.0	81	60
Clutch pressure plate to flywheel bolt	9.8 x M8 x 1.25	28	21
Case to block bolt	9.8 x M12 x 1.75	95	70
Mount to block and case bolt	9.8 x M12 x 1.75	95	70
Impact bracket to case stud nut	M8 x 1.25 x 6H	28	21
Anti-rotational strut bracket to stud nut	M8 x 1.25	23	17
Differential ring gear bolt	12.9 x M10 x 1.25	95	70
Differential bearing retainer bolt	9.8 x M8 x 1.25	28	21
Differential extension bolt	9.8 x M8 x 1.25	28	21
Differential oil pan screw and washer	9.8 x M8 x 1.25	19	14
Differential oil pan stud nut	M8 x 1.25 x 6H	19	14
Fill plug	M22 x 1.5	33	24
Intermediate shaft bearing strap screw	9.8 x M6 x 1.0	7	9
Input shaft seal retainer bolt	9.8 x M8 x 1.25	28	21
Steel end cover to case bolt	9.8 x M8 x 1.25	28	21
Steel end cover to bearing retainer bolt	9.8 x M8 x 1.25	28	21
Steel end cover to case stud nut	M8 x 1.25 x 6H	28	21

FORD 4 SPEED

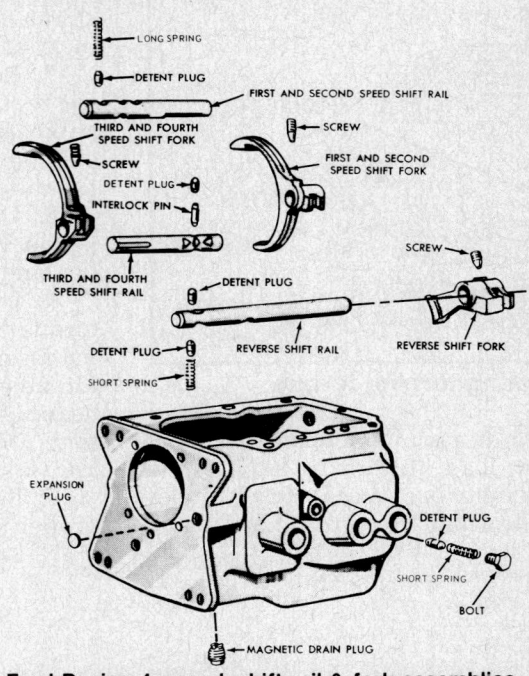

MANUAL TRANSMISSION APPLICATION CHART

Ford Design 3 sp.	1974 Torino, Monteego
	1974–77 Maverick
	1974–77 Comet
	1975–80 Granada, Monarch
71WG 4 sp.	Pinto
72WG 4 sp.	1974 Pinto
RAD 4 sp.	1974–80 Mustang
74 WT 4 sp.	1974 Pinto
75 WT 4 sp.	1975–79 Pinto, Bobcat

Ford Design 4–speed: shift rail & fork assemblies

Ford 4-Speed

Disassembly

1 Remove retaining clips and flat washers from the shift rods at the levers.
2 Remove shift linkage control bracket attaching screws. Remove shift linkage and control bracket.
3 Remove cover attaching screws. Lift cover and gasket from the case.
4 Remove extension housing attaching screws. Then, remove extension housing and gasket.
5 Remove input shaft bearing retainer attaching screws. Then, slide retainer from the input shaft.
6 Working a dummy shaft in from the front of the case, drive the countershaft out the rear of the case. Let the countergear assembly lie in the bottom of the case.
7 Locate first-second-speed gear shift lever in neutral. Locate third fourth-speed gear shift lever in third-speed position.
8 Remove the lockbolt that holds the third-fourth-speed shift rail detent spring and plug the left side of the case. Remove spring and plug with a magnet.
9 Remove the detent mechanism set screw from top of case. Then, remove the detent spring and plug with a small magnet.
10 Remove attaching screw from the third-fourth-speed shift fork. Tap lightly on the inner end of the shift rail to remove the expansion plug from front of case. Withdraw the third-fourth-speed shift rail from the front. (Do not lose the interlock pin from rail.)
11 Remove attaching screw from the first and second-speed shift fork. Slide the first-second shift rail from the rear of case.
12 Remove the interlock and detent plugs from the top of the case with a magnet.
13 Remove the snap-ring or disengage retainer that holds the speedometer drive gear to the output shaft. Slide the gear from the shaft. Remove speedometer gear drive ball.
14 Remove the snap-ring used to hold the output shaft bearing to the shaft. Remove output shaft bearing.
15 Remove the input shaft bearing and blocking ring from the front of the case.
16 Move output shaft to the right side of case. Maneuver the forks to permit lifting them from the case.
17 Support first-speed gear to prevent it sliding from the shaft. Lift output shaft from the case.
18 Remove reverse gear shift fork attaching screw. Rotate the reverse shift rail 90°. Slide the shift rail out the rear of the case. Lift out the reverse shift fork.
19 Remove the reverse detent plug and spring from the case with a magnet.
20 Using a dummy shaft, remove the reverse idler shaft from the case.
21 Lift reverse idler gear and thrust washers from the case. Be careful not to drop the bearing rollers or the dummy from the gear.
22 Lift the countergear, thrust washers, rollers and dummy shaft assembly from the case.
23 Remove the snap-ring from the front of the output shaft. Slide the third-fourth synchronizer blocking ring and the third-speed gear from the shaft.
24 Remove the next snap-ring and the second-speed gear thrust washer from the shaft. Slide the second-speed gear and the blocking ring from the shaft.
25 Remove the snap-ring. Slide the first-second synchronizer, blocking ring and the first-speed gear from the shaft.
26 Remove the thrust washer from rear of the shaft.

Unit Repairs

CAM & SHAFT SEALS
1 Remove attaching nut and washers from each shift lever. Remove the three levers.
2 Remove the three cams and shafts from inside the case.
3 Replace the old O-rings with new ones that have been well-lubricated.
4 Slide each cam and shaft into its respective bore in the transmission.
5 Install the levers and secure them with their respective washers and nuts.

INPUT SHAFT BEARING
1 Remove the snap-ring that holds the bearing to the shaft.
2 Press the shaft gear from the bearing.
3 Press a new bearing onto the input shaft.
4 Secure the bearing with a snap-ring.

SYNCHRONIZERS
1 Push the synchronizer hub from each synchronizer sleeve.
2 Separate the inserts and springs from the hubs. Do not mix parts of the first-second with parts of third-fourth synchronizers.
3 To assemble, position the hub in the sleeve. Be sure the alignment marks are properly indexed.
4 Place the three inserts into place on the hub. Install the insert springs so that the irregular surface (hump) is seated in one of the inserts. Do not stagger the springs.

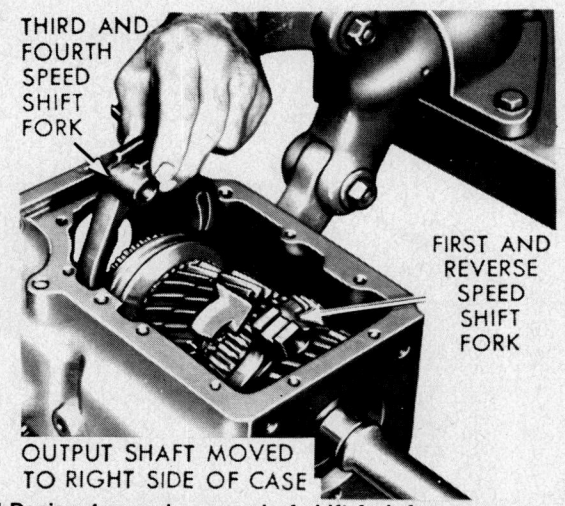

Ford Design 4–speed: removal of shift fork from case

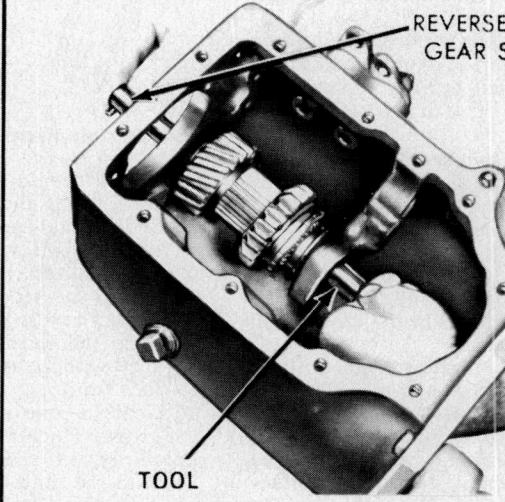

Ford Design 4–speed: rotating reverse shift rail

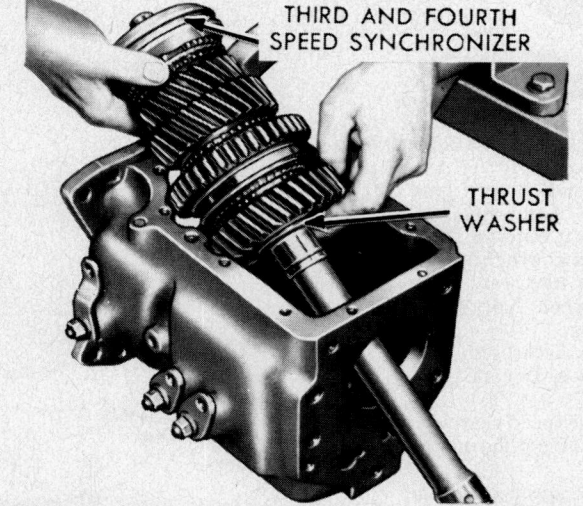

Ford Design 4–speed: removing or installing output shaft assembly

Ford Design 4–speed: removing reverse idler gear shaft

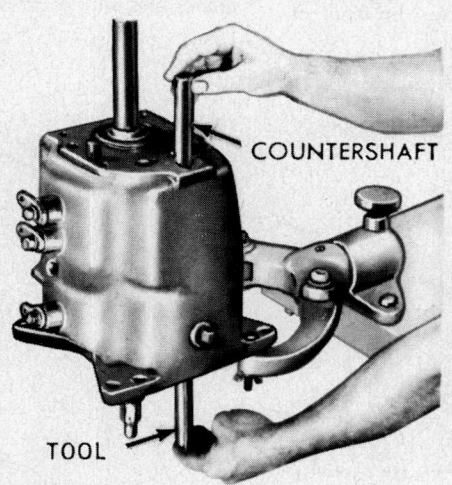

Ford Design 4–speed: installing countershaft

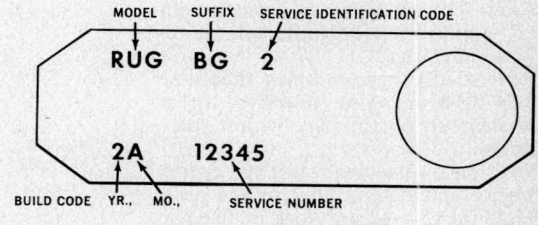

Ford Design 4–speed: ID tag

COUNTERSHAFT GEAR

1 Dismantle the countershaft gear assembly.
2 Assemble the gear by coating each end of the countershaft gear bore with grease.
3 Install dummy shaft in the gear. Install 21 bearing rollers and a retainer washer in each end of the gear.

REVERSE IDLER GEAR

1 Dismantle reverse idler gear.
2 Assemble reverse idler gear by coating the bore in each end of reverse idler gear with grease.
3 Hold the dummy shaft in the gear and install the 22 bearing rollers and the retainer washer into each end of the gear.
4 Install the reverse idler sliding gear on the splines of the reverse idler gear. Be sure the shift fork groove is toward the front.

INPUT SHAFT SEAL

1 Remove the seal from the input shaft bearing retainer.
2 Coat the sealing surface of a new seal with lubricant. Press the new seal into the input shaft bearing retainer.

Assembly

1 Grease the countershaft gear thrust surfaces in the case. Position a thrust washer at each end of the case.
2 Position the countershaft gear, dummy shaft, and roller bearings in the case.
3 Align the gear bore and thrust washers with the bores in the case. Install the countershaft.
4 With the case in a horizontal position, countershaft gear end-play should be from .004–.018 in. Use thrust washers to obtain play within these limits.
5 After establishing correct end-play, place the dummy shaft in the countershaft gear. Allow the gear assembly to remain on the bottom of the case.
6 Grease the reverse idler gear thrust surfaces in the case, and position the two thrust washers.
7 Position the reverse idler gear, sliding gear, dummy, etc. in place. Make sure that the shift fork groove in the sliding gear is toward the front.
8 Align the gear bore and thrust washers with the case bores. Install the reverse idler shaft.
9 Reverse idler gear end-play should be .004–.018 in. Use selective thrust washers to obtain play within these limits.
10 Position reverse gear shift rail detent spring and detent plug in the case. Hold the reverse shift fork in place on the reverse idler sliding gear. Install the shift rail from the rear of the case. Lock the fork to the rail with the Allen head set screws.
11 Install the first-second synchronizer onto the output shaft. The first and reverse synchronizer hub are a press

fit and should be installed with gear teeth facing the rear of the shaft.
12 Slide second-speed gear onto the front of the shaft with the synchronizer coned surface toward the rear.
13 Install the second-speed gear thrust washer and snap-ring.
14 Slide the third-speed gear onto the shaft with the synchronizer coned surface front.
15 Coat the cone of third-speed gear with grease. Place a blocking ring on the third-speed gear.
16 Slide the third-fourth speed gear synchronizer onto the shaft. Be sure that the inserts in the synchronizer engage the notches in the blocking ring. Install the snap-ring onto the front of the output shaft.
17 Coat the cone of second-speed gear with grease. Position the blocking ring on the gear.
18 Slide the first-second speed synchro-

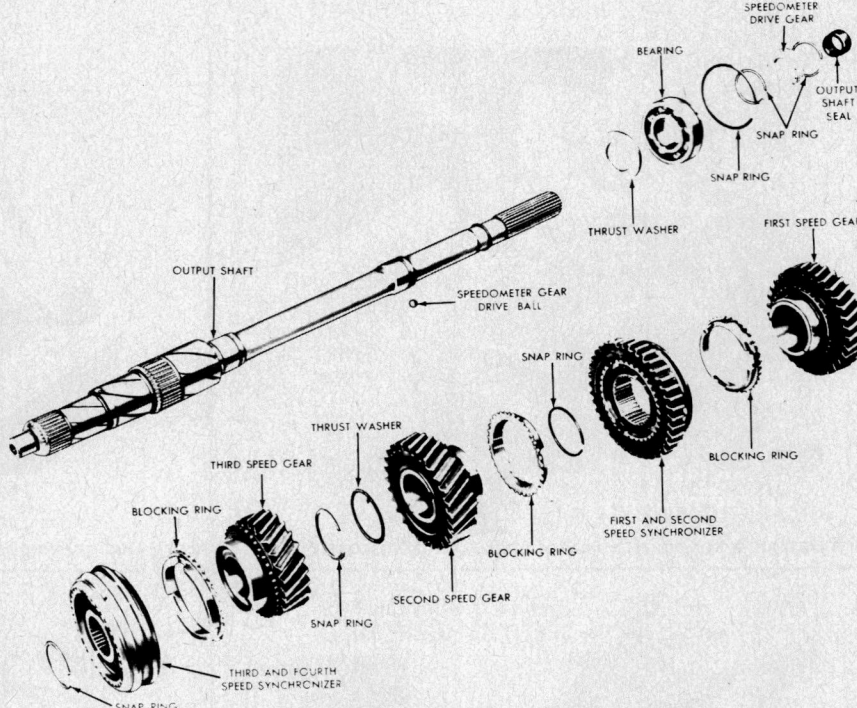

Ford Design 4–speed: output shaft components disassembled

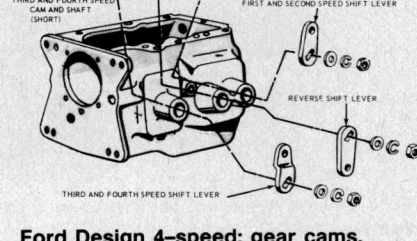

Ford Design 4–speed: gear cams, shafts and shift lever component detail

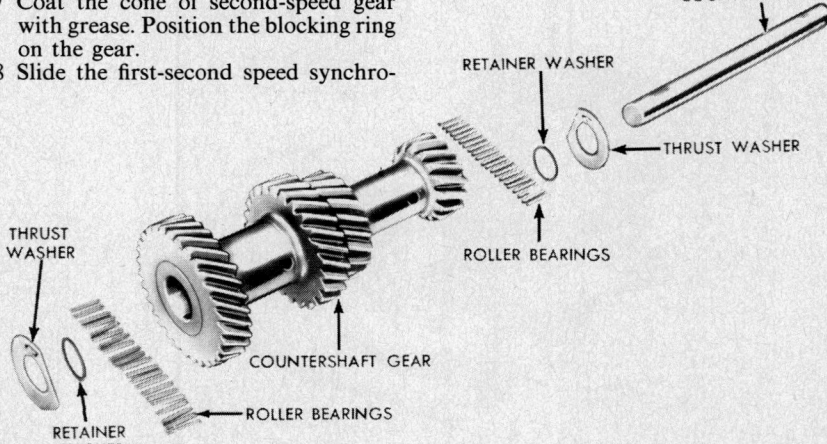

Ford Design 4–speed: countershaft gear disassembled

Ford Design 4–speed: reverse idler gear disassembled

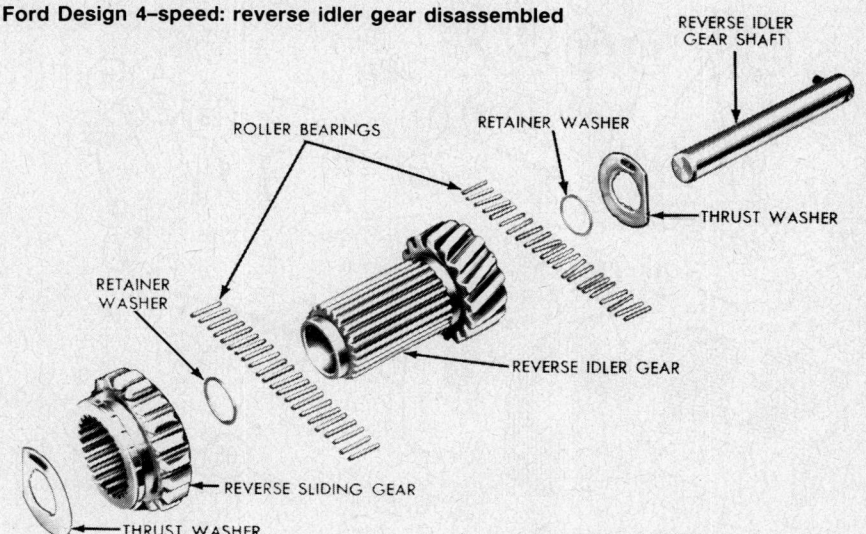

nizer onto the rear of the output shaft. Be sure that the inserts engage the notches in the blocking ring. The shift fork groove is toward the rear.

19 Coat the coned surface of first-speed gear with grease and position the blocking ring on it.

20 Slide the first-speed gear onto the rear of the output shaft. Be sure that the notches in the blocker ring engage the synchronizer inserts.

21 Install heavy thrust washer onto the rear of the output shaft.

22 Lower the output shaft assembly into the case.

23 Position the first-second speed shift fork and the third-fourth-speed shift fork in place on their respective gears. Rotate them into place.

24 Place a detent plug in the detent bore. Place the reverse shift rail into neutral position.

25 Coat the third-fourth-speed shift rail

interlock pin with grease. Position it in the shift rail.

26 Align the third-fourth speed shift fork with the shift rail bores and slide the shift rail into place. Be sure that the three detents are facing the outside of the case. Place the front synchronizer into third-fourth-speed position. Install the set screw into the third-fourth-speed shift fork. Move the synchronizer to neutral position. Install the third-fourth-speed shift rail detent plug, spring and bolt into the left side of the transmission case. Place the interlock plug (tapered ends) in the detent bore.

27 Align first-second-speed shift fork with the case bores. Slide the shift rail into place. Lock the fork with the set screw. Install the detent plug and spring into the detent bore. Thread the set screw into the case until the head is flush with the case.

28 Coat the input gear bore with a small amount of grease. Then install the 15 bearing rollers.

29 Place the input shaft gear in the case. Be sure that the output shaft pilot enters the roller bearing of the input shaft gear.

30 With a new gasket on the input bearing retainer, dip attaching bolts in sealer, install bolts and torque to 30–36 ft./lbs.

31 Install the output shaft bearing. Install the snap-ring to hold the bearing.

32 Position the speedometer gear drive ball in the output shaft. Slide the speedometer drive gear into place. Secure gear with snap-ring.

33 Align the countershaft gear bore and thrust washers with the bore in the case. Install the countershaft.

34 With a new gasket in place, install and secure the extension housing. Dip the extension housing screws in sealer. Torque screws to 42–50 ft./lbs.

35 Install the filler plug (torque 10–20 ft./lbs.) and the drain plug (torque 20–30 ft./lbs.), the drain plug is magnetic.

36 Pour in four pints of mild E.P. gear oil over the entire gear train while rotating the input shaft.

37 Place each shift fork in all positions to make sure they function properly.

38 With a new cover gasket in place, install the cover. Dip attaching screws in sealer. Torque screws to 14–19 ft./lbs.

39 Coat the third-fourth speed shift rail plug bore with sealer. Install a new plug.

40 Secure each shift rod to its respective lever with a spring washer, flat washer and retaining pin.

41 Position the shift linkage control bracket to the extension housing. Install and torque the attaching screws to 12–15 ft./lbs.

FORD RAD-B & RAD-C 4 SPEED

Ford Type RAD-B & RAD-C 4-Speed Units

NOTE: Both these gearboxes are assembled with metric fasteners.

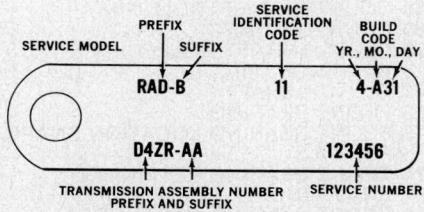

Ford RAD 4–speed: ID tag

Transmission Disassembly

1 Drain the lubricant by removing the lower extension housing bolt.

2 Drive the access plug from the rear of the extension housing. Remove the offset lever assembly.

3 Remove the extension from the case and discard the old gasket.

4 Remove the cover, shifter fork, shift rod assembly, and discard the old cover gasket.

5 Remove the front bearing retainer and gasket.

6 Remove the pivot and the reverse lever assembly.

7 Support the countershaft gear with a wire hook. To remove the countershaft, insert a dummy shaft in from the front of the case until the cluster gear falls to the bottom of the case. Then, remove the countershaft from the rear of the case. Lower the countershaft gear to the bottom of the case.

8 Remove the input shaft from the front of the case.

9 Remove the snap-ring securing the speedometer drive gear on the output shaft. Slide the gear off. Remove the lock ball from the shaft.

10 Remove the snap-ring retaining the output shaft bearing on the shaft. Use the outer snap-ring to pull the output shaft bearing from the shaft and case. Remove the snap-ring from the bearing. Carefully lift the output shaft and gear train assembly from the top of the case.

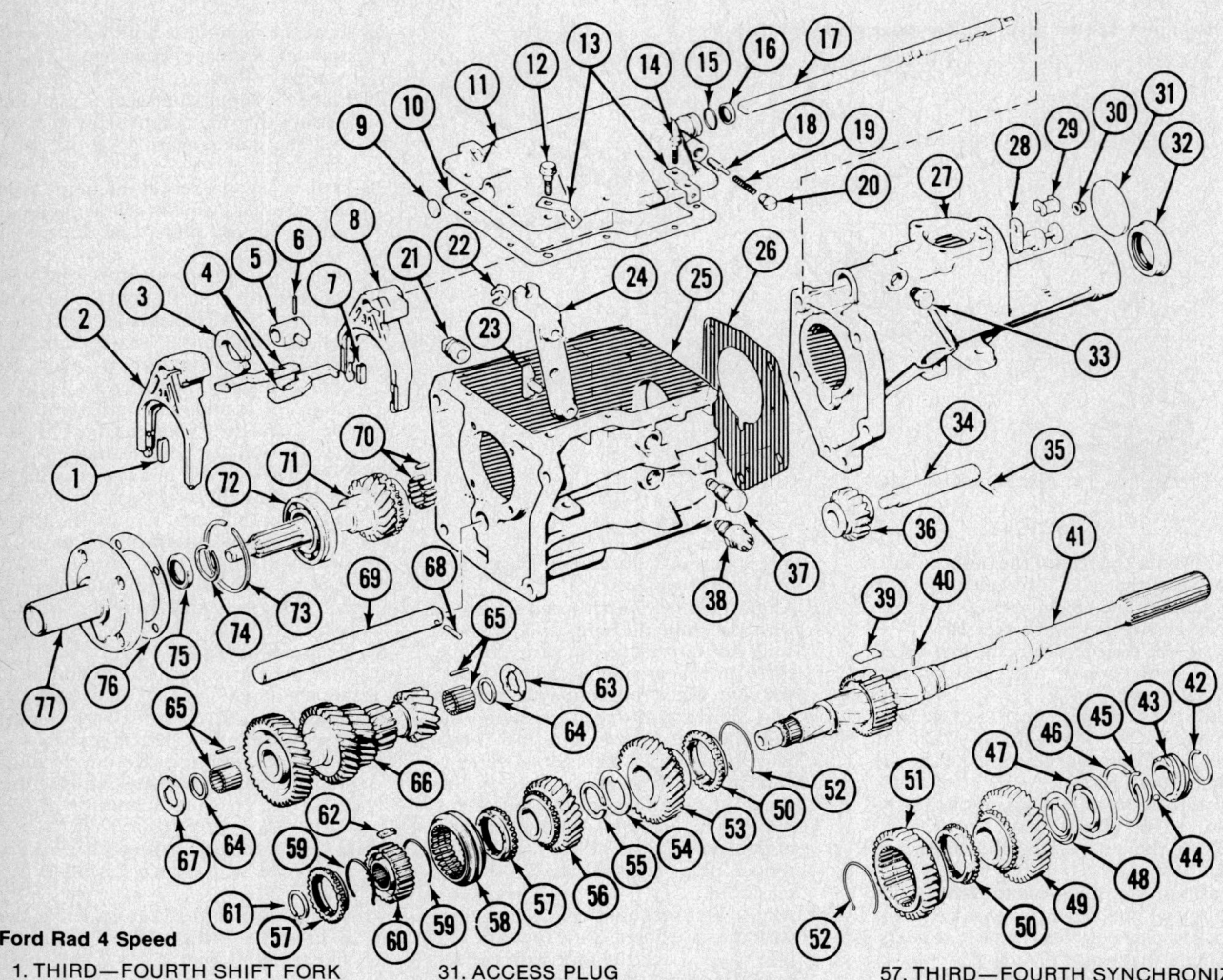

Ford Rad 4 Speed

1. THIRD—FOURTH SHIFT FORK INSERT
2. THIRD—FOURTH SHIFT FORK
3. SELECTOR INTERLOCK PLATE
4. SELECTOR ARM PLATE (2)
5. SELECTOR ARM
6. SELECTOR ARM ROLL PIN
7. FIRST—SECOND SHIFT FORK INSERT
8. FIRST—SECOND SHIFT FORK
9. SHIFT RAIL PLUG
10. TRANSMISSION COVER GASKET
11. TRANSMISSION COVER
12. TRANSMISSION COVER DOWEL BOLT (2)
13. CLIP
14. TRANSMISSION COVER BOLT (8)
15. SHIFT RAIL O-RING SEAL
16. SHIFT RAIL OIL SEAL
17. SHIFT RAIL
18. DETENT PLUNGER
19. DETENT SPRING
20. DETENT PLUNG
21. FILL PLUG
22. REVERSE LEVER PIVOT BOLT C-CLIP
23. REVERSE LEVER FORK
24. REVERSE LEVER
25. TRANSMISSION CASE
26. EXTENSION HOUSING GASKET
27. EXTENSION HOUSING
28. OFFSET LEVER
29. OFFSET LEVER INSERT
30. OFFSET LEVER RETAINING NUT

31. ACCESS PLUG
32. EXTENSION HOUSING OIL SEAL
33. THREADED PLUG
34. REVERSE IDLER SHAFT
35. REVERSE IDLER SHAFT ROLL PIN
36. REVERSE IDLER GEAR
37. REVERSE LEVER PIVOT BOLT
38. BACKUP LAMP SWITCH
39. FIRST—SECOND SYNCHRONIZER INSERT (3)
40. FIRST GEAR ROLL PIN
41. OUTPUT SHAFT AND HUB ASSEMBLY
42. SPEEDOMETER GEAR SNAP RING
43. SPEEDOMETER GEAR
44. SPEEDOMETER GEAR DRIVE BALL
45. REAR BEARING RETAINING SNAP RING
46. REAR BEARING LOCATING SNAP RING
47. REAR BEARING
48. FIRST GEAR THRUST WASHER
49. FIRST GEAR
50. FIRST—SECOND SYNCHRONIZER BLOCKING RING (2)
51. FIRST—REVERSE SLEEVE AND GEAR
52. FIRST—SECOND SYNCHRONIZER INSERT SPRING (2)
53. SECOND GEAR
54. SECOND GEAR THRUST WASHER (TABBED)
55. SECOND GEAR SNAP RING
56. THIRD GEAR

57. THIRD—FOURTH SYNCHRONIZER BLOCKING RING (2)
58. THIRD—FOURTH SYNCHRONIZER SLEEVE
59. THIRD—FOURTH SYNCHRONIZER INSERT SPRING (2)
60. THIRD—FOURTH SYNCHRONIZER HUB
61. OUTPUT SHAFT SNAP RING
62. THIRD—FOURTH SYNCHRONIZER INSERT (3)
63. COUNTERSHAFT GEAR REAR THRUST WASHER (METAL)
64. COUNTERSHAFT NEEDLE BEARING RETAINER (2)
65. COUNTERSHAFT NEEDLE BEARING (50)
66. COUNTERSHAFT GEAR
67. COUNTERSHAFT GEAR FRONT THRUST WASHER (PLASTIC)
68. COUNTERSHAFT ROLL PIN
69. COUNTERSHAFT
70. CLUTCH SHAFT ROLLER BEARINGS (15)
71. CLUTCH SHAFT
72. FRONT BEARING
73. FRONT BEARING LOCATION SNAP RING
74. FRONT BEARING RETAINING SNAP RING
75. FRONT BEARING CAP OIL SEAL
76. FRONT BEARING CAP GASKET
77. FRONT BEARING CAP

11 Slide out the reverse idler gear shaft through the rear of the case. Remove reverse gear.

12 Remove the cluster gear and dummy shaft assembly from the bottom of the case. Remove the cluster gear thrust washers.

13 Clean and inspect all parts. If the back-up light switch was damaged, remove it at this time.

Component Disassembly

COVER ASSEMBLY

1 Remove the detent screw, spring and plunger.

2 Pull the shifter shaft rod rearward, rotating it counterclockwise.

3 Remove the spring pin retaining the manual selector and interlock to the shifter shaft.

4 Remove the shifter shaft from the cover taking care not to damage the seal.

5 Remove the manual selector and interlock plate.

6 Remove the first and second speed shifter fork. Remove the third and fourth speed shifter fork.

7 Clean and inspect all parts. Replace the shifter shaft seal and welch plug, if damaged.

OUTPUT SHAFT

1 Scribe alignment marks on the synchronizer and blocker rings. Remove the snap-rings from the front of the output shaft. Slide the third and fourth speed synchronizer assembly, blocker rings and third gear off the shaft.

2 Remove the next snap-ring and the second gear thrust washer from the shaft. Slide second gear and the blocker ring off the shaft. Do not lose the sliding gear from the first and second speed synchronizer assembly. The first and second speed synchronizer hub cannot be removed from the output shaft.

3 Remove the first gear thrust washer (oil slinger) from the rear of the output shaft. Remove the spring pin re-

taining first gear onto the shaft.

4 Slide first gear off the output shaft. Remove the first speed blocker ring. Take care not to lose the sliding gear from the first and second speed synchronizer assembly.

5 Clean and inspect all parts.

COUNTERSHAFT GEAR BEARING REPLACEMENT

1 Remove the dummy shaft, bearing retainer washers and needle bearings from the countershaft gear. Clean and inspect the parts.

2 Coat the bore at each end of the countershaft gear with grease to retain the needle bearings.

3 While holding the dummy shaft in the gear, install the needle bearings and retainer washers in each end of the gear.

INPUT SHAFT BEARING REPLACEMENT

1 Remove the roller bearings from the input shaft.

2 Remove the snap-ring retaining the input shaft bearing. Press the input shaft out of the bearing. Clean and inspect all parts.

3 Press the input shaft bearing onto the input shaft. The snap-ring groove faces the front of the shaft. Install a new snap-ring to retain the bearing on the shaft.

4 Lightly coat the bore of the input shaft with grease.

NOTE: If a thick film of grease, such as wheel bearing grease, is applied to the shaft, the lubrication holes may become clogged. This prevents transmission oil from reaching the bearings. Premature bearing failure will result.

5 Install the roller bearings in the bore.

SYNCHRONIZER REPLACEMENT

1 Scribe alignment marks on the hub and sleeve of the synchronizer.

2 Push the synchronizer sleeve from each synchronizer hub.

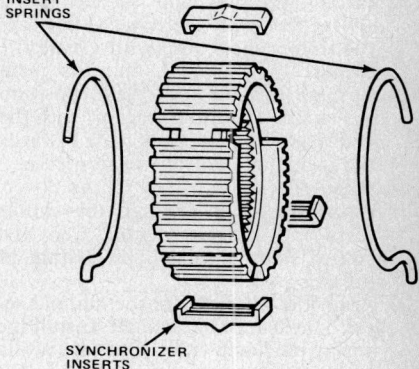

INSERT SPRINGS

SYNCHRONIZER INSERTS

NOTE: The first and second speed synchronizer hub cannot be removed from the output shaft.

3 Separate the inserts and insert springs from the hubs. Do not mix the parts of the first and second speed synchronizer with those of the third and fourth speed synchronizer. Clean and inspect all parts.

4 Position the sleeve on the hub. Align the marks scribed prior to disassembly are aligned.

5 Position the 3 inserts on the hub. Install the insert springs, taking care to seat the bent tab in one of the inserts. The springs must face in opposite directions.

Component Assembly

OUTPUT SHAFT

1 Place a blocker ring on the cone of first gear. Slide the gear and ring assembly onto the output shaft. Make sure that the inserts in the synchronizer engage in the blocker ring notches.

2 Install the spring pin retaining first gear to the output shaft.

3 Install a blocker ring on the cone of second gear. Slide the gear and ring assembly onto the output shaft. Make sure that the inserts in the synchronizer engage in the blocker ring notches.

4 Install the second gear thrust washer and new snap-ring on the shaft.

5 Install a blocker ring on the cone of third gear. Slide the gear and ring assembly onto the output shaft. Install the third and fourth speed synchronizer. Make sure that the inserts in the synchronizer engage in the blocker ring notches.

6 Install a new third and fourth gear synchronizer snap-ring.

7 Place the first gear thrust washer (oil slinger) on the shaft and on the spring pin retaining first gear.

CHILTON CAUTION: *The oil grooves must be positioned against the gear.*

COVER ASSEMBLY

1 Install the third and fourth speed shifter fork into the cover.

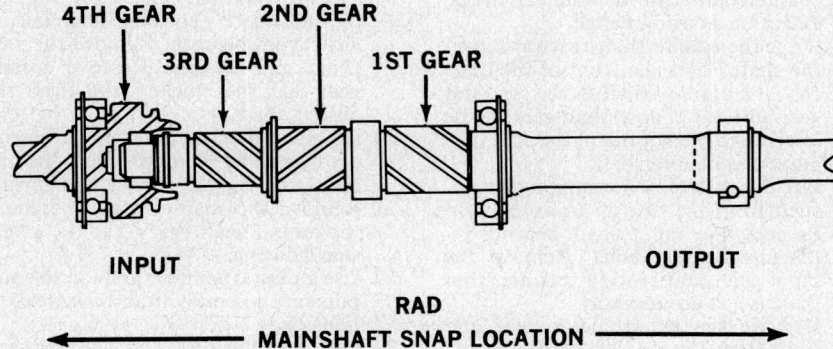

4TH GEAR **2ND GEAR**

3RD GEAR **1ST GEAR**

INPUT **OUTPUT**

RAD

◄—— **MAINSHAFT SNAP LOCATION** ——►

SNAP-RING LOCATIONS

Ford RAD 4–speed: mainshaft snap ring locations

2 Install the first and second speed shifter fork into the cover. Lubricate the shifter shaft bore with grease.

3 Install the manual selector arm through the interlock plate. Position the two pieces into the cover, with the wide leg of the interlock plate towards the inside of the transmission case.

4 Align the shifter shaft in the cover. Insert the shaft through the shifter forks and manual selector. Coat the shifter shaft with a light coating of grease.

5 Align the pin holes in the manual selector arm and shifter shaft. Install the spring pin flush with the surface of the selector arm.

6 Install the detent plunger, spring, and plug. Tighten the plug to 8–12 ft./lbs.

7 Check the operation of the shift forks in each gear position.

Transmission Assembly

1 Position the reverse idler gear and shaft in place.

2 Coat the surfaces of the countershaft thrust washer with a thin film of grease and position in the case. Position the cluster gear assembly in the bottom of the case.

3 Position the output shaft assembly into the case through the cover open-ing. With the snap-ring groove facing rearward, place the rear bearing on the output shaft. Place the transmission in the vertical position and install the bearing. Position the first gear thrust washer on the roll pin carefully, holding it tightly during bearing installation. Install the rear bearing snap-rings.

4 Return the transmission to the horizontal position. Install the input shaft and blocker ring through the front of the case. Make sure that the blocker ring notches engage the synchronizer insert.

5 Install the front bearing retainer using a new gasket. Apply gasket sealer to the bolt threads and tighten to 11–15 ft./lbs.

6 Place the transmission in the vertical position. Align the countershaft gear bore and thrust washers with the bore in the case. Install the countershaft from the rear of the case.

7 Install the reverse idler gear lever assembly, taking care to insert the fork in the reverse idler gear groove.

8 Apply gasket sealer to the reverse lever pivot bolt threads and install the bolt. Align the lever on the pivot bolt and torque the bolt to 15–25 ft./lbs. Install the reverse lever retaining spring clip to the reverse gear pivot bolt. Tilt the transmission forward and pour a light coating of gear lube over the gear train.

9 Using a new cover gasket, install the cover assembly. Install the bolts and wiring clips and tighten to 7–10 ft./lbs.

NOTE: The two shouldered locating bolts must be installed first.

Position the shift rail into first or third gear position.

10 Insert the speedometer drive gear lock ball into its hole. While holding the ball, slide the speedometer drive gear into place and secure it with a new snap-ring.

11 Using a new gasket, install the extension housing to the case. Using gasket sealer on the bolts, tighten them to 18–27 ft./lbs. Take care not to damage the extension yoke seal.

12 Install the offset lever assembly onto the shift shaft, securing the assembly with a nut and flat washer. Tighten to 14–20 ft./lbs.

13 Insert the gearshift lever into place. Check its operation in each gear position.

14 Install the access plug into the rear of the extension housing, using a soft mallet.

FORD AD or AE (GERMAN) 4 SPEED

Ford AD or AE German Design 4 Speed

German Design

NOTE: This transmission is assembled with metric fasteners.

NOTE: Cars equipped with this transmission are identified by a transmission ID code suffix of AD or AE. The transmission ID code appears on a tag located under the left extension housing-to-case bolt.

Transmission Disassembly

1 Remove the clutch release bearing and detach the clutch housing.

2 Remove the cover and gasket from the case.

3 Remove the threaded plug, spring and shift rail detent plunger from the front of the case.

4 Drive the access plug from the rear of the case. Drive the interlock retaining pin from the case. Remove the interlock plate.

5 Remove the roll pin from the selector lever arm.

6 Tap the front end of the shift rail to displace the plug at the rear of the extension housing. Remove the shift rail from the rear of the extension housing.

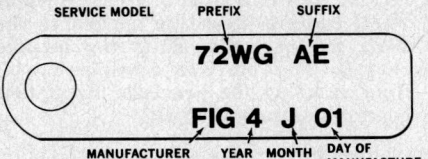

SERVICE MODEL   PREFIX   SUFFIX

72WG AE

FIG 4 J 01

MANUFACTURER   YEAR   MONTH   DAY OF MANUFACTURE

Ford (German) 4–speed: ID tag

7 Remove the selector arm and shift fork from the case.

8 Remove the extension housing attaching bolts. Loosen the extension housing. Rotate the housing to align the countershaft with the cutaway in the extension housing flange.

9 Drive the countershaft rearward until the shaft clears the front of the case. Install a dummy shaft in the case and gear until the countershaft gear can be lowered to the bottom of the case. Remove the countershaft.

10 Lift the extension housing and mainshaft from the case as an assembly.

11 Remove the input shaft bearing retainer attaching bolts. Remove the input shaft and bearing retainer from the case as an assembly.

12 Remove the reverse idler gear and shaft from the rear of the case.

13 Remove the bearing retainers, bearings, dummy shaft and spacer from the countershaft gear.

14 Remove the pilot bearing and bearing retainer from the input shaft gear.

15 Do not remove the ball bearing from the input shaft unless replacement is necessary.

16 Pry the input shaft seal out of the bearing retainer.

17 Lift the fourth gear blocker ring from the front of the output shaft.

18 Remove the snap-ring from the forward end of the output shaft.

19 Support third gear on press plates and place the output shaft and extension housing in a press. Press the output shaft out of the third-fourth speed synchronizer and third gear. Support the extension housing and output shaft from beneath. Remove the snapring and washer. Remove second gear and the blocker ring from the output shaft.

20 Disassemble the synchronizer assembly by pulling the sleeve from the hub and removing the inserts and spring.

21 Remove the snap-ring which retains the output shaft bearing to the extension housing.

22 Use a plastic hammer and tap the output shaft assembly from the extension housing.

23 Position press plates behind first gear. Place the assembly in a press. The first and second speed synchronizer are serviced as an assembly. No attempt

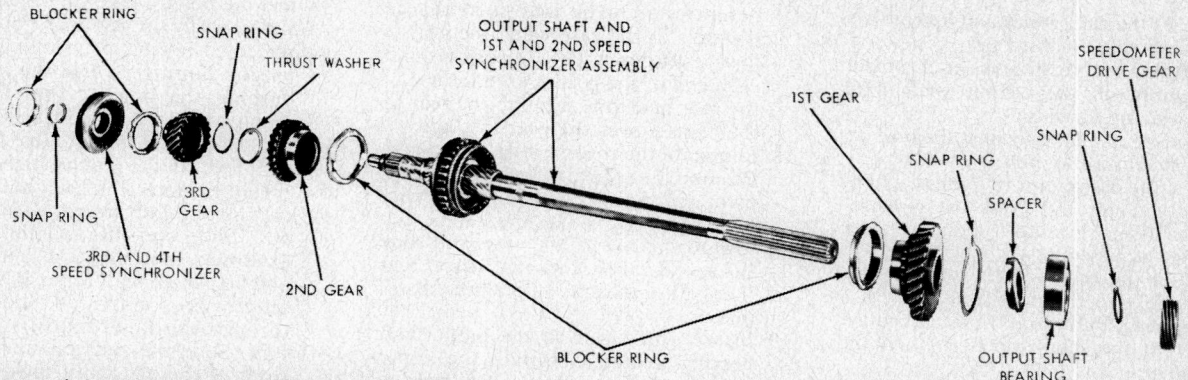

Ford (German) 4–speed: output shaft disassembled

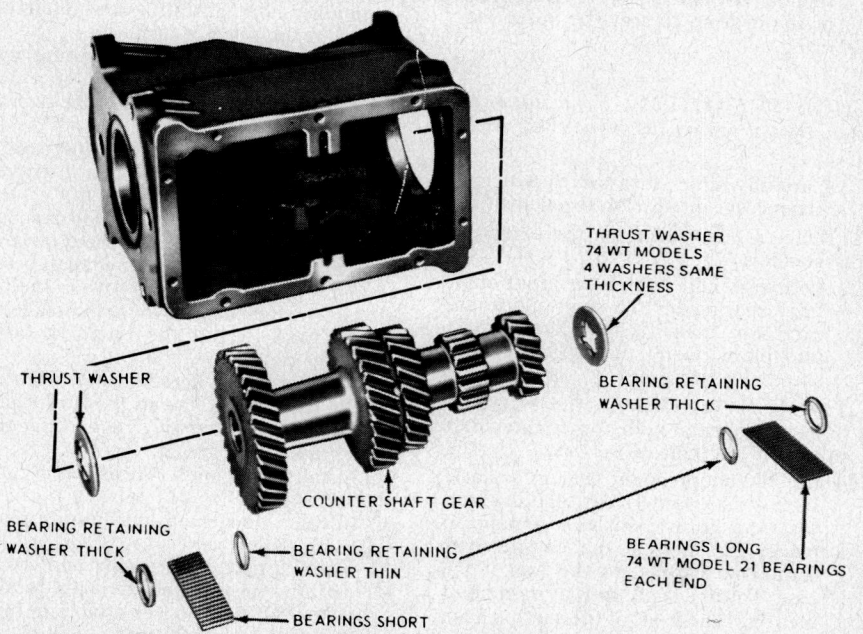

Ford (German) 4–speed: countershaft gear disassembled

should be made to separate the hub from the shaft. The only serviceable parts are the springs and inserts. If the hub or sleeve is worn, the shaft and synchronizer must be replaced as an assembly.

24 Drive the shift rail bushing from the rear of the extension housing, using a 9/16 in. socket. Do not remove serviceable bushings.

25 Pry the shift rail seal from the rear of the case.

26 Remove the remaining shaft linkage from the case. Do not remove the seat belt sensing switch unless it is damaged.

Transmission Assembly

1 Install a new shift rail seal in the rear of the case.

2 If the shift rail bushing was removed, drive a new one into position with a 9/16 in. socket.

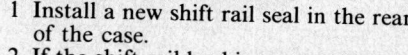

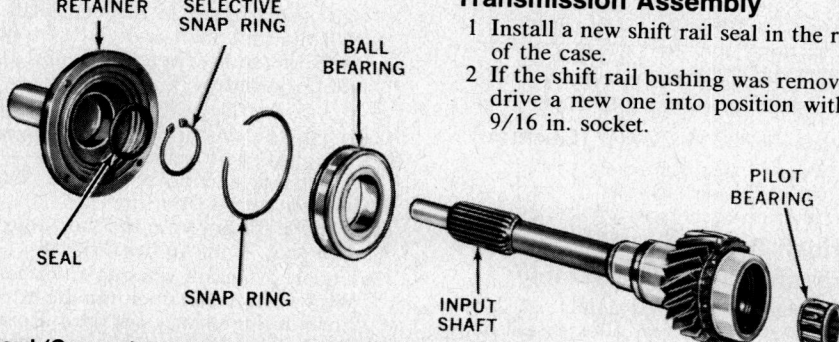

Ford (German) 4–speed: input shaft disassembled

3 Slide the synchronizer hub over the shaft. Make sure that the shift fork groove is toward the front of the shaft. The sleeve and hub are select fit and must be assembled with the etch marks in the same relative locations. Locate an insert in each of three slots in the hub. Oil all parts, and install an insert spring inside the sleeve. The spring tab must locate in a section of an insert. Fit the other spring to the opposite face. Locate the tab in the same insert. Both springs should be in the same rotational direction. The tab end of one spring should be aligned with the tab of the spring on the opposite side.

4 Assemble a blocker ring on the first gear side of the first-second synchronizer. Lubricate the cone surface of first gear and all out-put shaft gear journals. Slide the cone surface onto the output shaft. The cone surface should engage the blocker ring.

5 Position the spacer on the output shaft, larger diameter rearward.

6 Install the thickest possible snap-ring (selected from the chart). Position the output shaft bearing on the shaft. Press the bearing into place. Secure the bearing with the snap-ring.

Part No.	Thickness Identification
D1FZ-7030-A	0.0679-Color Coded—Copper
D1FZ-7030-B	0.0689-Letter—W
D1FZ-7030-C	0.0699-Letter—V
D1FZ-7030-D	0.0709-Letter—U
D1FZ-7030-E	0.0719-None
D1FZ-7030-F	0.0728-Color Coded—Blue
D1FZ-7030-G	0.0738-Color Coded—Black
D1FZ-7030-H	0.0748-Color Coded—Brown

7 Slide the synchronizer over the hub and locate an insert in each of three slots in the sleeve. Align etch marks. Lightly oil all parts. Complete assembly of the synchronizer by following directions in previous Step 3.

8 Position second gear and the blocker ring on the output shaft, dog teeth facing rearward. Install the washer and snap-ring. Position third gear on the output shaft, dog teeth forward. Lu-

bricate the gear cones and assemble a blocker ring on third gear cone.

9 Position the third-fourth synchronizer assembly on the output shaft, hub boss facing forward.

10 Install press plates against the boss on the synchronizer hub.

11 Place the entire unit in a press, extension end up, and press the synchronizer assembly onto the output shaft as far as possible.

12 Retain the third-fourth synchronizer assembly to the output shaft with a snap-ring. Pull up on the synchronizer so that the snap-ring is tight in the groove.

13 Lubricate the gear cone. Place the blocker ring on the input shaft gear cone.

14 Using Tool T71P-17271-A, press the speedometer drive gear onto the shaft until the dowels of the tool just contact the bearing outer race.

15 Lubricate the bearing bore of the extension housing. Install the output shaft in the housing. It may be necessary to tap the shaft while holding the synchronizer sleeves firmly. Secure the shaft to the housing with the snap-ring previously installed.

16 Press the bearing on the input shaft. Snap-ring groove must be forward. Use the thickest snap-ring that will fit.

17 Slide the spacer and dummy shaft into the countershaft gear. Position a thin bearing retaining washer on each end of the dummy shaft. Lubricate the roller bearings. Load long bearings in the small end of the gear and short bearings in the long end of the gear. 19 needle bearings are used at either end of the gear on 71 WG and 72 WG series transmissions. 21 needle bearings at either end of the gear on 74 WT series transmissions. Place a thick retaining washer over each end of the dummy shaft. Grease the thrust washers and place one one each end of the

dummy shaft. The tabs must engage the slots in the case when the gear is lowered. Loop a piece of rope around each end of the gear. Carefully install the gear and rope through the rear of the case. Lower the gear in place.

18 Lubricate the reverse idler gear shaft. Position the selector lever relay on the pivot pin. Secure with a spring clip. Hold the gear in the lever, long hub toward the rear of the case, and slide the reverse idler shaft into place. Seat the shaft in the case with a brass hammer.

19 Install a new seal in the input shaft bearing retainer. Install the input shaft in the case with a new bearing retainer O-ring. Tap on the outer race of the bearing to seat the outer snap-ring.

CHILTON CAUTION: *Use a soft hammer. Do not tap on the input shaft itself.*

20 Carefully slide third-fourth synchronizer sleeve into fourth speed position.

21 Place a new gasket on the extension housing.

22 Lubricate and install the input shaft pilot bearing on the shaft. Slide the extension housing and output shaft into place. Don't disturb the fourth speed synchronizer.

23 Align the cutaway in the extension housing flange with the countershaft bore in the rear of the case.

24 Lift the countershaft gear into place. Install the countershaft, making sure that the thrust washers remain in place. The flat on the countershaft should be parallel to the top of the case. Tap the shaft with a brass hammer until the front of the shaft is flush with the case.

25 Rotate the extension housing to align the bolt holes. Loosely install the at-

taching bolts. Make sure that the rail slides freely in its bore. Binding is remedied by slightly rotating the extension housing to free the rail, then pushing the housing into the case. Apply sealer to the attaching bolts and torque to 33–36 ft./lbs. Place the shift forks in the synchronizer sleeves. Install the interlock lever and new retaining pin. Lubricate the shift rail oil seal. Slide the shift rail through the extension housing, case and second and first speed shift forks. Position the selector arm on the rail. Slide the rail through third and fourth speed shift fork. Slide the shift rail through the front of the case until the center detent bore is aligned with the detent plunger bore. Install a new retaining pin in the selector arm.

26 Install the detent plunger, spring and plug with sealer.

27 Install a new access plug in the rear of the case.

28 Position a new oil seal with tension spring and lip facing in the direction of the case.

29 Drive the seal in until it bottoms.

30 Position a new O-ring in the groove in the case. Position the input shaft bearing retainer with the groove in the retainer aligned with the oil passage in the case. Install the retaining bolts finger-tight.

31 Install the flywheel housing. Tighten the retaining bolts and the front bearing retainer attaching bolts. Coat the retainer with grease.

32 Install the clutch release arm and bearing.

33 Install a new extension housing plug, using sealer.

34 Install a new cover gasket and cover, with the vent to the rear. Apply sealer to the left front cover attaching bolt. Torque to 8–10 ft./lbs.

35 Install a new seat belt sensing switch if the old one was removed.

FORD 71WG & 72WG (BRITISH) 71WG-72WG-74WT & 75WT (GERMAN) 4 SPEED

Ford Type 71WG & 72 WG British-Made 4-Speed

Ford Type 71WG, 72 WG, 74 WT & 75 WT German-Made 4-Speed

NOTE: The Ford British-made and German-made Type 71WG and 72WG gearboxes are practically identical in external configuration. However they are NOT the same inside. The basic differences are as follows:

Type 71WG & 72WG (British)

1 Die cast aluminum top cover
2 BB or BC suffix on I.D. tag

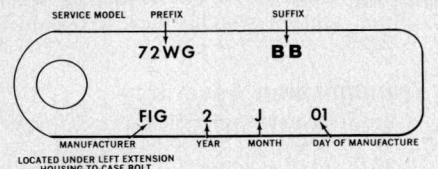

Ford (British) 4–speed: ID tag

Type 71WG & 72WG (German)

1 Pressed steel top cover
2 AE suffix on I.D. tag
3 Metric fasteners

British Design
Transmission Disassembly

1 Remove top cover plate.
2 Pry plug from rear of extension housing.

3 Remove plunger screw from right side of case.

4 From the top cover opening, use a punch to remove the pin securing the shift selector arm to the shift shaft.

5 Pull the shift shaft rearward. Do not drop the shift selector arm and the interlock plate.

6 Move the first-second and third-fourth gear synchronizer hubs toward the input shaft bearing.

7 If necessary, remove the shift shaft plunger spring from the case.

8 Remove the pin from the third-fourth shift fork. Remove the fork.

9 Unbolt extension housing from case. With a plastic hammer, tap the extension housing slightly rearward. Rotate the housing until the countershaft

lines up with the notch in the housing flange.

10 Tap the countershaft rearward with a brass drift until it is just clear of the front of the case. Push the countershaft out with a dummy shaft. Lower the cluster gear to the bottom of the case.

11 Remove extension housing and output shaft assembly. The third-fourth synchronizer sleeve must be pushed forward for clearance.

12 Unbolt front bearing retainer from case. Remove retainer and gasket.

13 Remove input shaft oil seal.

14 Remove the snap ring around the input shaft bearing. Tap the input shaft gear and bearing assembly out of the transmission with a brass drift. Remove the needle roller bearing from the recess in the end of the input shaft gear.

15 Remove the cluster gear, two thrust washers, and the dummy shaft from the case. Remove 20 needle rollers and a retaining washer from each end of the cluster gear.

16 Assemble a nut, a flat washer, and a sleeve on a 5/16 in. × 24 UNF threaded bolt. Screw the bolt into the reverse idler shaft and tighten to pull out the shaft.

17 Remove the low-reverse shift fork from the lever pin inside the case. Do not remove the pin.

Component Disassembly
3RD-4TH SYNCHRONIZER
1 Remove fourth gear blocking ring from input shaft gear side of assembly.
2 Remove synchronizer hub snap-ring

from forward end of output shaft and discard.

3 Support third gear. Press the output shaft out of the third-fourth gear synchronizer and third gear. Do not drop the output shaft.

4 Pull the sleeve off the hub. Remove the inserts and springs.

5 Check all parts for wear. Synchronizer hub and sleeve should be replaced if worn or damaged.

1ST-2ND SYNCHRONIZER
1 Remove plug in extension housing. Remove speedometer driven gear.

2 Remove snap-ring holding output shaft bearing to extension housing. With a plastic hammer, tap output shaft assembly out of housing.

3 Remove snap-ring holding speedometer drive gear. Pull off gear. Remove snap-ring holding output shaft bearing.

4 Support low and reverse sliding gear. Press low and reverse sliding gear, spacer, and output shaft bearing from the output shaft.

5 Remove snap-ring holding first-second synchronizer assembly to output shaft.

6 Support second gear. Press second gear and first-second synchronizer assembly from output shaft.

7 Dismantle synchronizer assembly. Replace synchronizer hub or sleeve if worn or damaged. The output shaft bearing must be replaced.

INPUT SHAFT AND GEAR
1 Remove and discard input shaft snapring.
2 Press off input shaft bearing.

Component Assembly
3RD-4TH SYNCHRONIZER
1 Slide gear over hub. Locate an insert in each slot.

2 Install a synchronizer spring inside the sleeve beneath the inserts. The spring tang should fit into an insert. Install the other spring on the opposite side. Fit the tang into the same insert. When viewed from the edge, the springs should run in opposite directions.

3 Place the third gear on the output shaft with the dog teeth forward. Assemble the blocking ring on the third gear cone.

4 Place the synchronizer assembly on the output shaft with the boss forward.

5 Support the hub. Press the hub on the output shaft and install a new snapring.

1ST-2ND SYNCHRONIZER
1 Install the second gear on the output shaft with the cone and dog teeth to the rear.

2 Slide the synchronizer sleeve over the hub. Place an insert in each of the three slots.

3 Install synchronizer springs as for third-fourth synchronizer assembly.

4 Install a blocking ring to cone on second gear.

5 Install synchronizer assembly on output shaft with the gear teeth on the periphery of the synchronizer sleeve forward. Slide low and reverse sliding gear to the rear of the synchronizer hub.

6 Support the sliding gear. Press synchronizer assembly onto output shaft as far as possible.

7 Secure the synchronizer assembly with snap-ring.

8 Place a blocking ring on first gear side of first-second synchronizer assembly on output shaft. Install first gear, cone side forward.

9 Place the spacer with the larger diameter adjacent to first gear.

10 Select a snap-ring of the proper size to hold the output shaft bearing into the bearing recess with no end float.

11 Position the selected snap-ring loosely on the output shaft next to the spacer.

12 Support the bearing inner race. Press the bearing onto the shaft.

13 Select the thickest snap-ring that fits the groove to hold the bearing to the output shaft.

14 Locate output shaft ball bearing in shaft indent. Push speedometer drive gear onto output shaft. Install new snap-ring.

15 Heat the end of the extension housing. Do not use a torch. A pan of hot water is recommended.

16 Install the output shaft into the extension housing. Install the snap-ring securing the output shaft bearing to the housing.

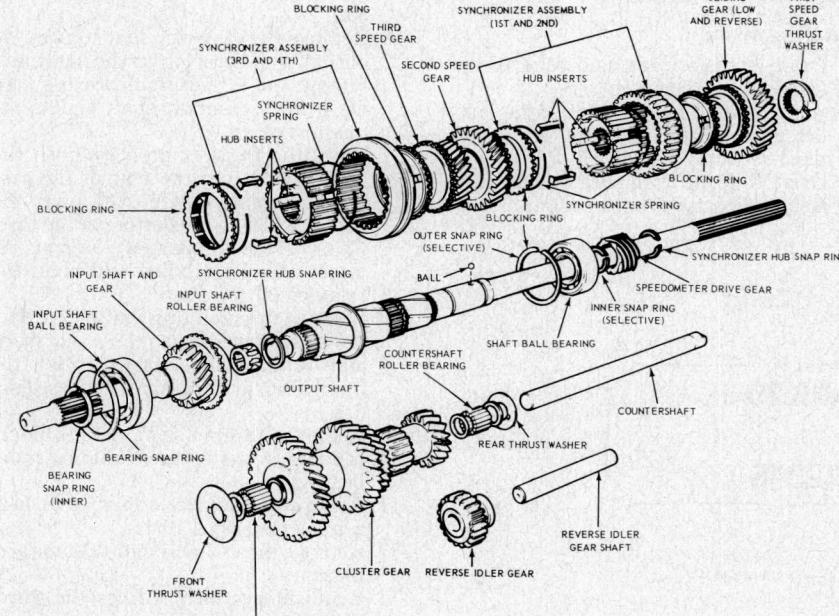

Ford (British) 4–speed: transmission internal component detail

17 Replace the speedometer driven gear. Install a new plug, using sealer.

INPUT SHAFT & GEAR

1 Support the input shaft bearing inner race. Press the bearing onto the shaft.
2 Install the snap-ring securing the bearing to the input shaft.

Transmission Assembly

1 Slide the low-reverse lever onto the lever pin inside the case.
2 Push the idler shaft into the case. Place the reverse idler gear on the shaft. Locate the low-reverse lever in the gear groove. Tap the reverse idler shaft into position with a soft hammer.
3 Slide a dummy shaft into the cluster gear. Push a retainer washer into the gear bore. Grease and install 20 needle rollers and the second retaining washer. Install the washers and rollers at the other end of the gear. Grease and install the thrust washers with their convex side into the gear recess.
4 Place the cluster gear in the bottom of the case. Position the thrust washers with the flat upward.

5 Place the input shaft and gear in the case. Using a brass drift, tap bearing outer race into place. Be careful not to damage the dog teeth on the input shaft gear with the cluster gear. Install the bearing snap-ring.
6 Place the input shaft needle bearing in the input shaft gear recess.
7 Drive a new oil seal into the input shaft retainer. Cover the input shaft splines. Install a new gasket on the transmission front face. Align the retainer oil groove with the oil passage in the case. Coat the bolts with sealer and install them with lock-washers.
8 Locate the fourth gear blocking ring on the input shaft gear cone.
9 Install a new oil seal in with a socket.
10 Install a new sealer coated gasket to the extension housing.
11 Pull the third-fourth synchronizer sleeve forward. Slide the extension housing and output shaft into position. Align the cutaway on the extension housing with the countershaft aperture in the rear face of the case.
12 Using loops of cord, lift the cluster gear into mesh with the output and input shaft gears. Don't drop the countershaft thrust washers.

13 Tap the countershaft into place, driving out the dummy shaft. The lug on the rear of the countershaft fits into the recess on the extension housing flange.
14 Push the extension housing onto the transmission case. Apply sealer to bolts. Torque to 30–35 ft./lbs.
15 Replace both shift forks. Secure third-fourth fork with a new pin.
16 Position shift forks to synchronizer sleeves. Move synchronizer hubs into neutral positions.
17 Grease shift shaft oil seal in rear of case. Slide shift shaft through extension housing. Shift selector and interlock plate locate in cutouts in shift forks. Pass the shift shaft through the shift selector arm and forks until the pin holes are aligned.
18 Replace the plunger ball and spring. Replace the retaining screw, using sealer.
19 Install the pin through the shift selector arm and shift shaft.
20 Apply sealer to plug. Tap plug into rear of extension housing.
21 Install top cover and gasket.
22 Refill transmission with 2.8 pints SAE 80 oil.

FORD 4 SPEED OVERDRIVE

Ford 4 Speed Overdrive Transmission—(SROD) Single Rail Overdrive

Description

The transmission is fully synchronized with all gears except the reverse sliding gear which is in constant mesh. Forward gear changes are accomplished with synchronizer sleeves. All forward gears are helical type. The reverse sliding gear and the external teeth of the first and second speeds synchronizer sleeve are spur type.

The service identification tag is located on the right side of the case at the front. The first line shows the transmission model and service identification code. The second line shows the transmission serial number, and this serial number is also stamped on the top side of the case flange.

Application

FAIRMONT, GRANADA, MONARCH, ZEPHYR

Disassembly

1 Drain the lubricant, and remove the transmission cover.
2 Remove the screw, detent spring and detent plug from the case. A magnetized rod may be needed.
3 Drive roll pin from shifter shaft.
4 Remove back-up light switch assembly, snap ring and dust cover from rear of extension housing. Remove shifter shaft from turret assembly, and unbolt and remove the extension housing.
5 Remove the snap ring securing the speedometer drive gear to the output shaft. Slide the gear off the shaft, and remove the speedometer gear drive ball.
6 Remove the snap ring that secures the output shaft bearing to the shaft and remove the output shaft bearing (slip fit) from the output shaft and transmission case.
7 From the front of the case push the countershaft out the rear of the case with a dummy shaft, and lower the countershaft to the bottom of the case.
8 Remove the input shaft bearing retainer attaching bolts, and slide the retainer off the shaft.
9 Remove the snap ring that secures the input shaft bearing to the input shaft, and remove the bearing from the input shaft and transmission case (slip fit).
10 Remove the input shaft and the blocking ring from the case including roller bearings.
11 Remove the overdrive shaft pawl, gear selector interlock plate.
12 Remove the 1–2 gearshift selector arm plate.
13 Remove the roll pin from the third-/overdrive shift fork.
14 Remove the third/overdrive shift rail

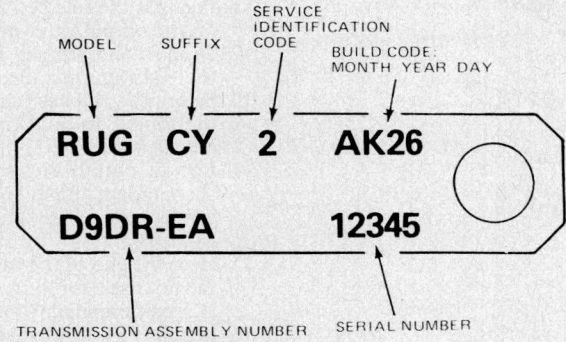

Four speed overdrive transmission service identification tag

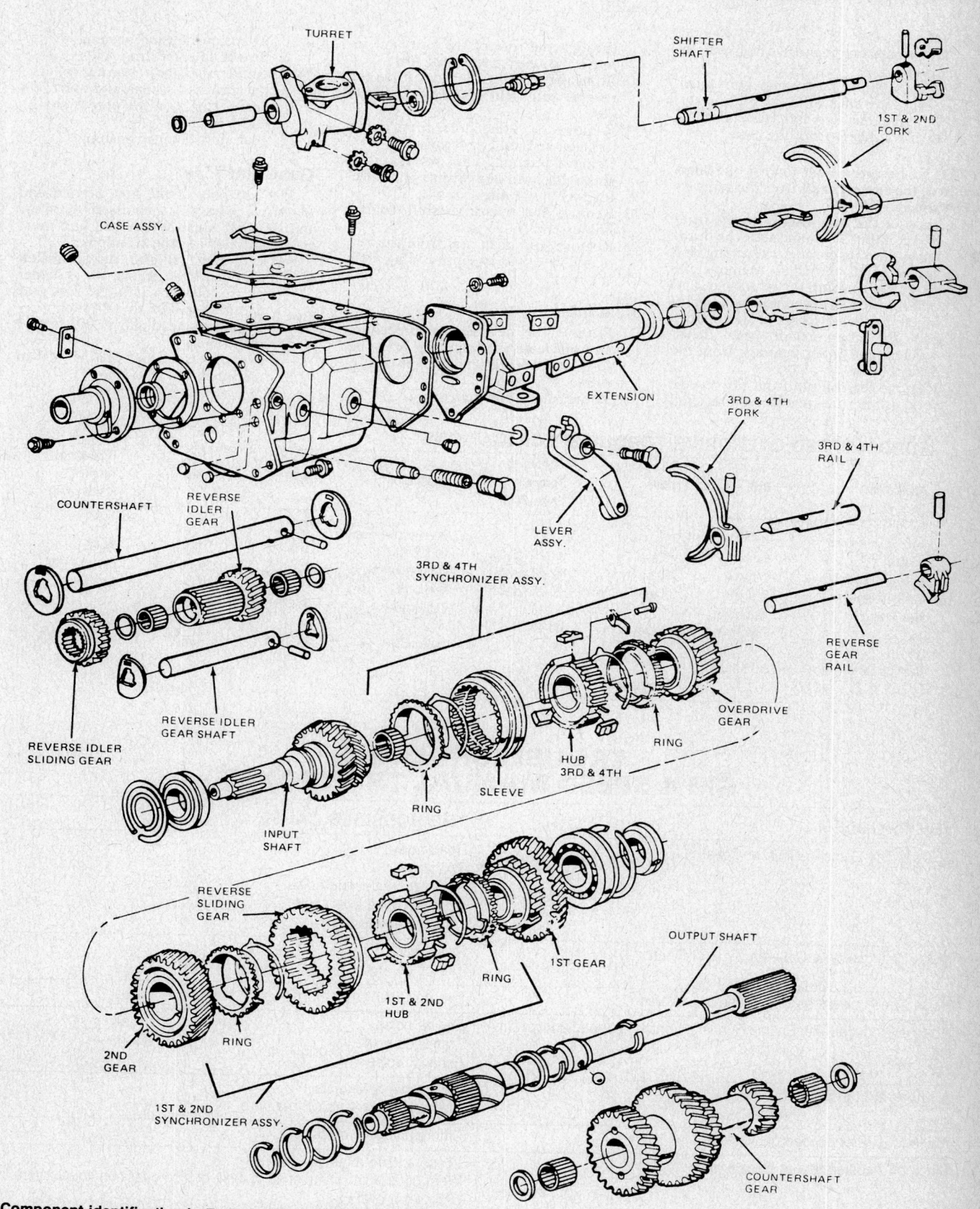

TURRET

SHIFTER SHAFT

1ST & 2ND FORK

CASE ASSY.

EXTENSION

3RD & 4TH FORK

3RD & 4TH RAIL

LEVER ASSY.

COUNTERSHAFT

REVERSE IDLER GEAR

REVERSE IDLER GEAR SHAFT

3RD & 4TH SYNCHRONIZER ASSY.

OVERDRIVE GEAR

RING

REVERSE IDLER SLIDING GEAR

REVERSE GEAR RAIL

HUB 3RD & 4TH

RING

SLEEVE

INPUT SHAFT

REVERSE SLIDING GEAR

OUTPUT SHAFT

RING

1ST GEAR

1ST & 2ND HUB

RING

2ND GEAR

RING

1ST & 2ND SYNCHRONIZER ASSY.

COUNTERSHAFT GEAR

Component identification in Ford four speed overdrive transmission

and expansion plug (drive from rear of case).

15 Remove the first/second and third-/overdrive shift forks.

16 Lift the countershaft gear and the thrust washers from the case.

NOTE: Be careful not to drop the bearings or the dummy shaft from the countershaft gear.

17 Remove the snap ring from the front of the output shaft, and slide the third-/overdrive synchronizer blocking ring and gear off the shaft. Remove the next snap ring and thrust washer, and remove the first speed gear and blocking ring from the rear of the shaft.

18 Lift the countershaft gear thrust washers and roller bearings from the case.

19 Remove the roll pin from the reverse fork, slide the reverse shifter rail through the rear of the case and remove the reverse gearshift fork.

20 From the front of the case, drive the reverse gear shaft out the rear of the case.

21 Remove the reverse idler gear, thrust washers and roller bearings.

22 Remove retaining clip, reverse gearshift relay lever and reverse gear selector fork pivot pin.

23 Remove the overdrive shift control link assembly.

24 Remove shift shaft seal from the rear of the case and expansion plug from the front.

Assembly

1 Reverse the disassembly procedure, and lubricate the following areas before or during assembly with appropriate lubricants:
   a. mainshaft bearing rollers
   b. extension housing bushing
   c. reverse idler bearing rollers
   d. countershaft gear bearing rollers
   e. low gear and second and overdrive gear formals on the output shaft
   f. shifter shaft
   g. gear shift damper bushing

Gear End Play

The end play of the first, second and overdrive gears after their assembly on the output shaft must be checked and must pass the following specifications:
   a. with the first gear thrust washer clamped tight against the shoulder on the output shaft, the first gear end play is .005 to .024 inch
   b. second gear end play is .003 to .021 inch
   c. overdrive gear end play is .009 to .023 inch

FORD 4 SPEED OVERDRIVE TORQUE SPECIFICATIONS

Application	Bolt	Nut	Tightening Torque Ft-Lbs (N·m)	Application	Bolt	Nut	Tightening Torque Ft-Lbs (N·m)
Input Shaft Bearing Retainer	5/16	Case	11–25 (15–33)	Pn—Reverse Gear Fork Pivot	M16–1.5	Case	15–25 (21–33)
Extension Assembly	7/16–14	Case	42–50 (54–67)	Turret Assembly	M8–1.25	Extension	8–12 (11–16)
Case Access Cover	5/16–18	Case	20–25 (28–33)	Service I.D. Tag Screw	#6–32 Self-Tapping	Case	Seat Firmly
Filler Plug	½–14 U.S. Pipe Thread	Case	10–20 (14–27)	Detent Bolt	⅜–16	Case	10–15 (14–20)
Back Up Lamp Switch	9/16–18	Turret Cover Assy.	8–12 (11–16)				

TROUBLESHOOTING
GM 4 SPEED MANUAL TRANSAXLE

THE PROBLEM	THE POSSIBLE CAUSE
Noise is The Same in Drive or Coast	Road noise. Tire noise. Front wheel bearing noise. Incorrect drive axle angle. (Standing Height)
Noise Changes on a Different Type of Road	Road noise. Tire noise.
Noise Tone Lowers as Car Speed is Lowered	Tire noise.
Noise is Produced with Engine Running, Vehicle Stopped and/or Driving	Engine noise. Transaxle noise. Exhaust noise.
A Knock at Low Speeds	Worn drive axle joints. Worn side gear hub counterbore.
Noise Most Pronounced on Turns	Differential gear noise.
Clunk on Acceleration or Deceleration	Loose engine mounts. Worn differential pinion shaft in case or side gear hub counterbore in case worn oversize. Worn or damaged drive axle inboard joints.

TROUBLESHOOTING
GM 4 SPEED MANUAL TRANSAXLE

THE PROBLEM	THE POSSIBLE CAUSE
Clicking Noise in Turns	Worn or damaged outboard joint.
Vibration	Rough wheel bearing. Damaged drive axle shaft. Out of round tires. Tire unbalance. Worn joint in drive axle shaft. Incorrect drive axle angle.
Noisy in Neutral with Engine Running	Damaged input gear bearings.
Noisy in First Only	Damaged or worn first-speed constant mesh gears. Damaged or worn 1–2 synchronizer.
Noisy in Second Only	Damaged or worn second-speed constant mesh gears. Damaged or worn 1–2 synchronizer.
Noisy in Third Only	Damaged or worn third-speed constant mesh gears. Damaged or worn 3–4 synchronizer.
Noisy in High Gear	Damaged 3–4 synchronizer. Damaged 4th speed gear or output gear.
Noisy in Reverse Only	Worn or damaged reverse idler gear or idler bushing. Worn or damaged 1–2 synchronizer sleeve.
Noisy in All Gears	Insufficient lubricant. Damaged or worn bearings. Worn or damaged input gear (shaft) and/or output gear (shaft.)
Slips out of Gear	Worn or improperly adjusted linkage. Transmission loose on engine housing. Shift linkage does not work freely; binds. Bent or damaged cables. Input gear bearing retainer broken or loose. Dirt between clutch cover and engine housing. Stiff shift lever seal.
Leaks Lubricant	Axle shaft seals Excessive amount of lubricant in transmission. Loose or broken input gear (shaft) bearing retainer. Input gear bearing retainer "O" ring and/or lip seal damaged. Lack of sealant between case and clutch cover or loose clutch cover. Shift lever seal leaks.

GM 4 SPEED TRANSAXLE

GM Four Speed Manual Transaxle

Application

Buick—1980 Skylark
Chevrolet—1980 Citation
Oldsmobile—1980 Omega
Pontiac—1980 Phoenix

Description

The four-speed transaxle assembly is a constant mesh design transmission combined with a differential unit; both assembled in a single aluminum case. For shifting, synchronizers with blocker rings controlled by shift forks are used for forward speeds. Reverse uses a sliding idler gear arrangement.

The main components are the transaxle case, clutch cover, input gear (shaft), output gear (shaft) and differential assembly. The input gear, output gear and differential are all supported by preloaded tapered roller bearings. Selective shims are used beneath the right-hand bearing cups to establish the correct preload.

The final output gear (an integral part of the output shaft) turns the ring gear and differential thereby turning the drive axle shafts which are attached to the front wheels.

Case Disassembly

1 Remove the bolts securing the clutch cover to the transaxle case.
2 Use a plastic hammer to carefully tap the clutch cover from the transaxle case. Anaerobic sealant is used be-

tween the case and cover, instead of a gasket.

3 Remove the ring gear/differential assembly.

4 Position the shifter shaft in the neutral position so that shifter moves freely and is not engaged in any drive gear.

5 Bend back tab on lock and remove bolt from shifter shaft. Remove the shifter shaft and the shift fork shaft from the synchronizer forks.

6 Remove the reverse shift fork by disengaging from the guide pin and interlock bracket.

7 Remove the lock bolt securing the reverse idler gear shaft. Remove the gear/shaft/spacer assembly.

8 Remove the detent shift lever and interlock assembly. Leave shift forks engaged with the synchronizers.

9 Grasp the input and output shafts and then lift them as an assembly from the case. Note the position of the shift forks for aid when reinstalling later. Remove the shift forks.

Input Shaft Disassembly

1 Using Tool J-22912-01 in 4th gear groove, press 4th gear and L.H. bearing from input shaft.

2 Remove brass blocker ring. Remove the snap ring from the 3-4 synchronizer.

3 Using support plates behind 3rd gear, press 3rd gear and 3-4 synchronizer from input shaft.

4 Remove R.H. bearing from shaft using J-26946.

Output Shaft Disassembly

1 Using support plates behind 4th gear and J-26943, press on the end of the output shaft to remove 4th gear and the L.H. bearing.

2 Remove the snap ring retaining 3rd gear.

3 Slide the 1-2 synchronizer assembly into first gear position to allow press plates to support 2nd gear. Press 2nd speed gear and 3rd gear from the output shaft. Remove the brass blocker ring.

4 Remove the snap ring retaining the 1-2 synchronizer.

5 Using press plates behind 1st speed gear, press 1st gear and 1-2 synchronizer from the output shaft.

6 Install J-22227-A on the R.H. bearing and remove the bearing by pressing on J-26943 pilot.

Synchronizer Overhaul

1 Carefully pry out both synchronizer key springs from each synchronizer.

2 Separate the hub, sleeve and keys, noting their relative positions. Scribe the hub to the sleeve prior to separation.

3 Clean, inspect and replace parts as necessary

4 Assemble the hub to the sleeve, with the extruded lip on the hub directed

away from the shift fork groove in the sleeve and align previous scribed marks.

5 Carefully install one retaining ring, then carefully pry the ring back and insert keys one at a time, being sure to position the ring so it is "captured" by the keys.

6 Install the ring on the opposite side, with the open segment of the ring "out-of-phase" with the open segment on the other side.

Input Shaft Reassembly

1 Install R.H. bearing onto shaft, using J-28406.

2 Place 3rd gear onto the shaft, oriented toward the 3-4 synchronizer. Install the brass blocker ring onto the gear cone, then install the 3-4 synchronizer, using an appropriate cylinder to contact the hub, near the shaft. Do not press on the sleeve portion. Both synchronizer hubs are a press fit to the shafts.

3 Install snap ring to retain 3-4 synchronizer. Be sure to position snap ring with beveled edges away from synchronizer for later access with snap ring pliers.

4 Install brass blocker ring.

5 Install 4th speed gear onto shaft, oriented toward the 3-4 synchronizer and install L.H. bearing onto the shaft, using J-26942.

Output Shaft Reassembly

1 Install R.H. bearing onto shaft using J-6133-A.

2 Place 1st speed gear onto the shaft, oriented toward the 1-2 synchronizer. Place the brass blocker ring onto the gear cone, then install the 1-2 synchronizer, using an appropriate cylinder to press on the hub, near the shaft. Do not press on the sleeve.

3 Install the snap ring to retain the 1-2 synchronizer. Place the brass blocker ring into position.

4 Place 2nd speed gear onto the shaft, oriented toward the 1-2 synchronizer, then press 3rd gear onto the shaft, with its hub toward 4th gear. Use an appropriate cylinder to contact 3rd gear hub near the shaft.

5 Install snap ring to retain 3rd gear.

6 Press 4th gear onto the shaft, with its hub toward 3rd gear, using support plates and install L.H. bearing cone on the shaft, using J-26942.

Transmission Case Overhaul

1 Remove reverse inhibitor fitting from exterior of case. From inside of case, remove the spring and pilot/spacer.

2 Remove input and output shaft L.H. bearing cups, using J-26941. Turn set screw on J-26941 counter clockwise to insert tool below bearing cup. Turn set screw clockwise to grasp bearing cup. When installing cups, use J-26938.

3 Remove oil slingers.

4 Remove differential side bearing cup, using J-26941. Reinstall cup with J-23423-A.

5 Check two guide pins for interlock bracket and reverse shift fork. Check magnet. Remove sealant from mating surface with J-28410 where the clutch cover contacts the case. Use care not to gouge or damage the aluminum surface or leaks can result.

6 Clean all parts. Thoroughly inspect/replace parts as required.

Clutch Cover Overhaul

1 Using J-26941, remove differential side bearing cup and shim.

2 Using J-26941, remove input shaft and output shaft R.H. bearing cups. Remove the shim from back of input bearing cup and remove oil shield, shim, and retainer from back of output shaft bearing cup.

3 Remove external oil ring, and internal oil seal from sleeve.

4 Remove plastic oil scoop.

5 If necessary to replace the clutch fork shaft or bushing, use J-28412 for removal and installation. Always replace the clutch fork shaft seal after installation of the shaft or bushing.

6 Remove bead of sealant from mating surfaces. Use care not to damage sealing surfaces.

7 Clean and inspect all parts. Replace parts as required.

8 Install plastic oil scoop.

9 Replace external square-cut oil ring on sleeve. Install input bearing retainer, tightening three bolts to specifications.

10 Use J-26936 to install internal oil seal.

Differential Case/Ring Gear Overhaul

1 Separate ring gear from differential case.

2 Remove pinion shaft lock bolt, remove pinion shaft, then roll the gears and thrust washers out through the opening in the case.

3 If differential side bearings are to be replaced, use J-22888 puller and J-22888-20 (puller leg set) to remove the bearings. Use J-22919 cone installer for reinstallation of side bearings.

4 Clean and inspect all parts. Replace parts as required.

5 Install gears and thrust washers into the case; install the pinion shaft and lock bolt. Tighten to correct specifications.

6 Attach the ring gear to the differential case.

NOTE: Selection of the preload shims for reassembly can begin when the input and output shaft assemblies and the differential assembly are reassembled and ready to be installed into the transaxle case.

7 With the (3) L.H. bearing races installed in the case, place the input and output shaft assemblies and the differential assembly into their installed positions. Place the R.H. bearing races onto their respective bearings.

8 Position gauges; J-26935-2 on input bearing and J-26935-4 onto output bearing and J-26935-3 on the differential bearing. Be sure that bearing races fit smoothly into the bores of the gauge tools.

9 On J-26935-4 (output shaft), install metal oil shield retainer into bore on top of tool.

10 Carefully assemble the clutch cover over the gauges and onto the case, using spacers placed evenly around the perimeter. Retain with bolts provided.

11 Draw the cover to the case by tightening alternately and gradually. This will compress all three gauge sleeves.

12 Rotate each gauge to seat the bearings. Rotate the differential case through three revolutions in each direction.

13 With the three gauges compressed, the gap between the outer sleeve and the base pad is the correct thickness for the preload shim at each location. Carefully compare the gap to the available shims. The largest shim that can be placed into the gap and drawn through without binding is the correct shim for reassembly.

14 When each of the three shims has been selected, remove the clutch cover, spacers and gauges.

15 Place the selected shims into their respective bores in the clutch cover, add the metal shield and then install the bearing cups using special Tools J-27936 on input shaft cup and J-23423-A on output shaft cup and J-26938 on the differential side bearing cup.

16 Place input shaft and output shaft together, on a bench. Install the two shift forks.

17 Grasp the shafts as an assembly and carefully lower them into the transaxle case.

18 Place interlock bracket onto guide pin J-28411. Be sure that the bracket engages the fingers on the shift forks. Place detent shift lever into the interlock.

19 Install the shifter shaft through the interlock bracket and the detent shift lever. Do not extend further at this time.

20 Install reverse shift fork onto the guide pin. Be sure the reverse shift fork engages the interlock bracket.

21 Install the reverse idler gear and shaft into position. Be sure the long end of the shaft points upward, and the large chamfered ends of the gear tooth are facing up. Install the spacer onto the shaft. The flat on the reverse idler shaft faces the input gear (shaft).

22 Fully install the shifter shaft through the reverse shift fork, until it pilots

Input and output shafts with shift forks in place.

into the inhibitor spring spacer. Remove dummy shaft. With the shaft in neutral position, install the bolt and lock through the detent shift lever. Bend tab of lock over bolt head.

23 Install fork shaft through the synchronizer forks and into the bore in the case.

24 Carefully install the ring gear-and-differential case assembly.

25 Install magnet.

26 Apply a thin bead of anaerobic sealant to the clutch cover, then carefully install the cover onto the transaxle case, using the dowel pins to guide the cover into position. Tap clutch cover gently with a plastic hammer to insure that the parts are seated.

27 Install the attaching bolts. Torque to correct specifications.

28 Torque idler shaft retaining bolt in case.

29 Shift through the gear ranges to test for freedom of movement of all internal parts.

TORQUE SPECIFICATIONS

Description	Torque (N·m)	Torque Ft. Lbs.
Input Shaft R.H. Bearing Retainer	9	7
Reverse Idler Shaft Lock Bolt	21	16
Reverse Inhibitor Fitting	35	26
Case-to-Cover Bolts	21	16
Ring Gear Bolts	73	54
Pinion Shaft Lock Bolt	9	7

MANUAL TRANSMISSIONS
GM FOUR SPEED TRANSAXLE

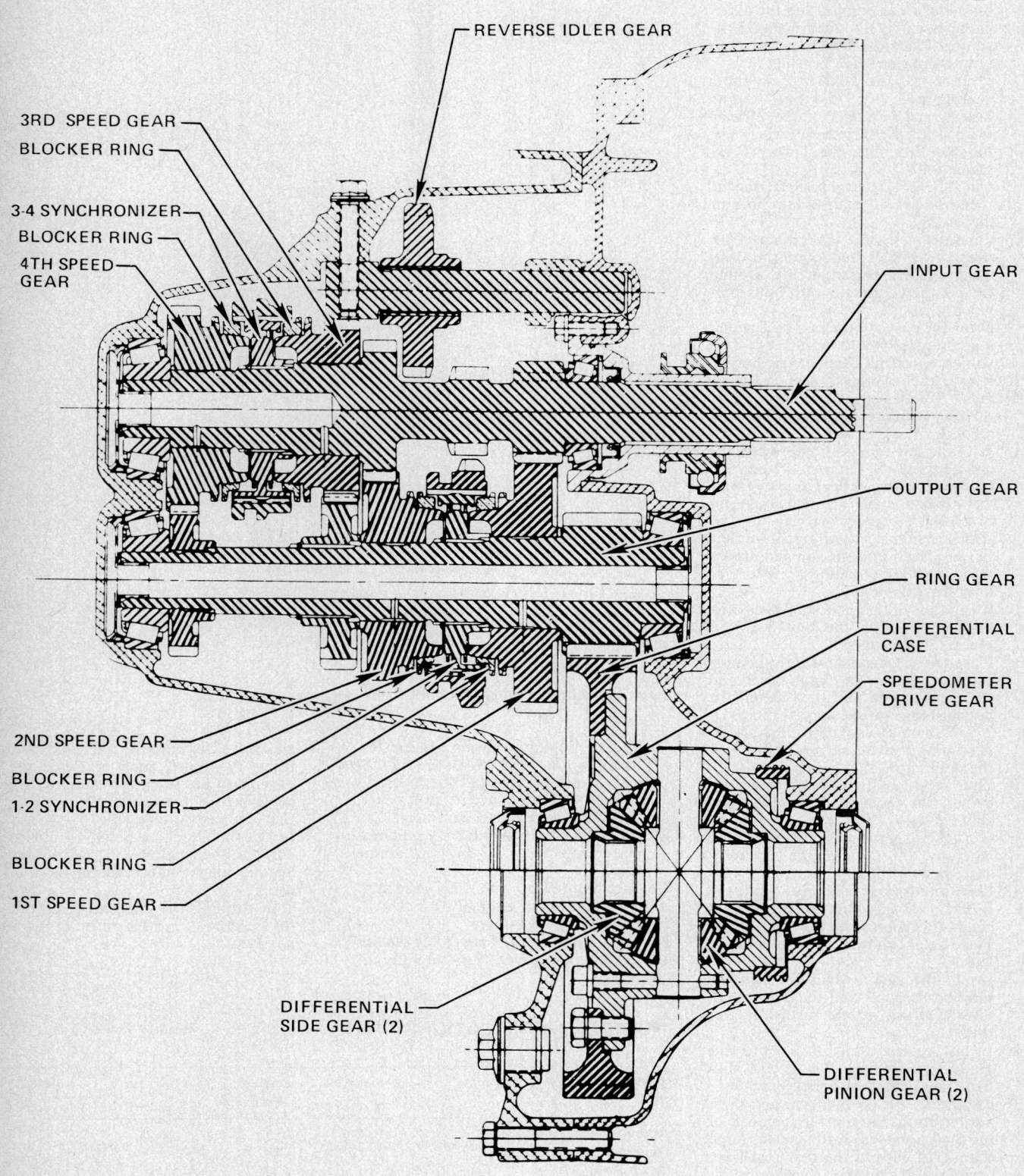

REVERSE IDLER GEAR

3RD SPEED GEAR
BLOCKER RING

3-4 SYNCHRONIZER
BLOCKER RING

4TH SPEED
GEAR

INPUT GEAR

OUTPUT GEAR

RING GEAR

DIFFERENTIAL
CASE

SPEEDOMETER
DRIVE GEAR

2ND SPEED GEAR

BLOCKER RING

1-2 SYNCHRONIZER

BLOCKER RING

1ST SPEED GEAR

DIFFERENTIAL
SIDE GEAR (2)

DIFFERENTIAL
PINION GEAR (2)

Transaxle cross-section and component replacement.

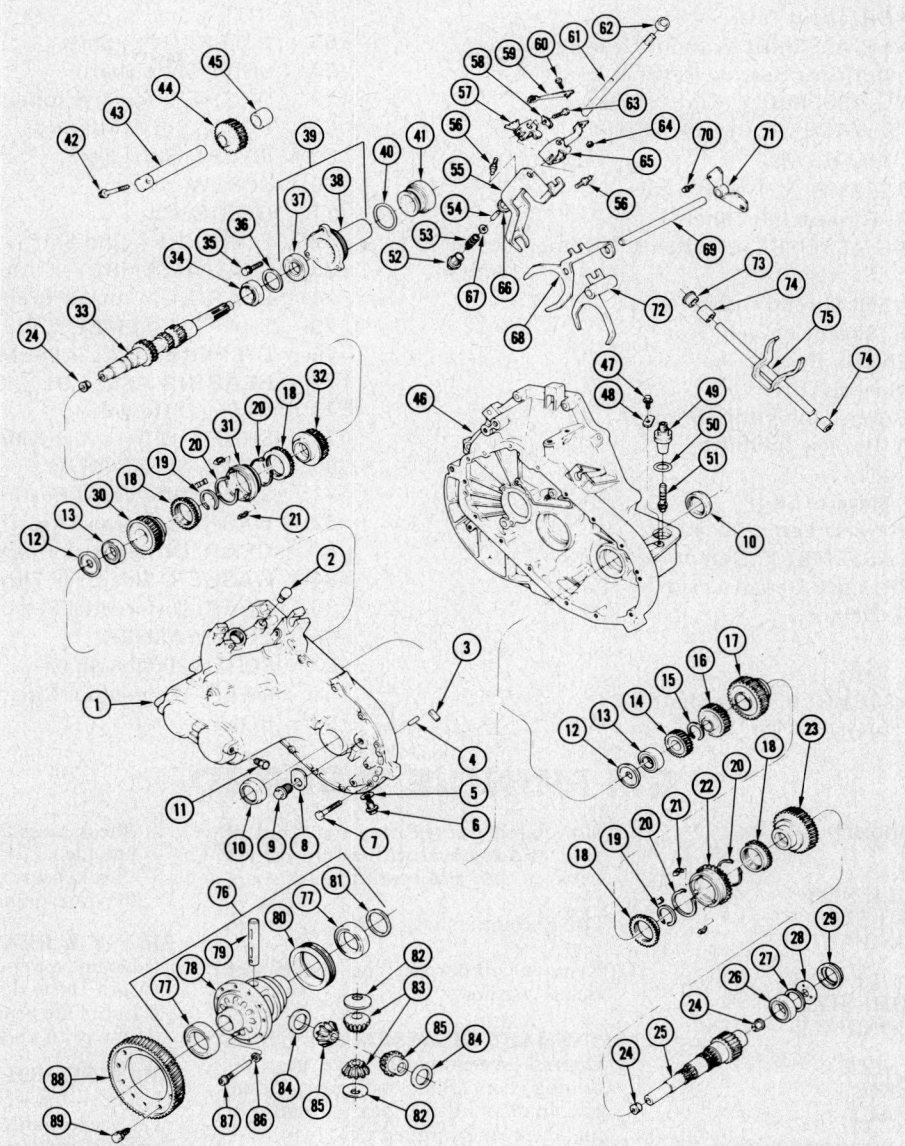

Four-speed manual transaxle components.

1. CASE ASSEMBLY
2. VENT ASSEMBLY
3. MAGNET
4. PIN
5. WASHER, Drain Screw
6. SCREW, Drain
7. BOLT
8. WASHER, Fill Plug
9. PLUG, Fill
10. SEAL ASSEMBLY, Axle Shaft
11. PLUG
12. SHIELD, Oil
13. BEARING ASSEMBLY
14. GEAR, 4th Speed Output
15. RING, 3rd Speed Output Gear Retaining
16. GEAR, 3rd Speed Output
17. GEAR, 2nd Speed Output
18. RING, Synchronizer Blocking

19. RING, Synchronizer Retaining
20. SPRING, Synchronizer Key Retaining
21. KEY, Synchronizer
22. SYNCHRONIZER ASSEMBLY
23. GEAR, 1st Speed Output
24. SLEEVE, Oil Shield
25. GEAR, Output
26. BEARING ASSEMBLY, Output
27. SHIM, Output Gear Bearing Adjustment
28. SHIELD, Output Bearing Oil
29. RETAINER, Output Gear Bearing Oil Shield
30. GEAR, 4th Speed Input
31. SYNCHRONIZER ASSEMBLY
32. GEAR, 3rd Speed Input
33. GEAR, Input Cluster
34. BEARING ASSEMBLY, Input
35. SCREW
36. SHIM, Input Gear Bearing Adjustment
37. SEAL ASSEMBLY, Input Gear

B781

38. RETAINER, Input Gear
39. RETAINER ASSEMBLY, Input Gear Bearing
40. SEAL, Input Gear Bearing Retainer
41. BEARING ASSEMBLY, Clutch Release
42. SCREW & WASHER, Reverse Idler
43. SHAFT, Reverse Idler
44. GEAR ASSEMBLY, Reverse Idler
45. SPACER, Reverse Idler Shaft
46. HOUSING ASSEMBLY, Clutch & Differential
47. SCREW
48. RETAINER, Speedo Gear Fitting
49. SLEEVE, Speedo Driven Gear
50. SEAL, Speedo Gear Sleeve
51. GEAR, Speedo Driven
52. SEAT, Reverse Inhibitor Spring
53. SPRING, Reverse Inhibitor
54. PIN
55. LEVER, Reverse Shift
56. STUD, Reverse Lever Locating
57. LEVER ASSEMBLY, Detent
58. WASHER, Lock Detent Lever
59. SPRING, Detent
60. BOLT
61. SHAFT, Shift
62. SEAL ASSEMBLY, Shift Shaft
63. BOLT

64. NUT
65. INTERLOCK, Shift
66. SHIM, Shift Shaft
67. WASHER, Reverse Inhibitor Spring
68. FORK, 3rd & 4th Shift
69. SHAFT, Shift Fork
70. SCREW
71. GUIDE, Oil
72. FORK, 1st & 2nd Shift
73. SEAL ASSEMBLY, Clutch Fork Shaft
74. BEARING, Clutch Fork Shaft
75. SHAFT ASSEMBLY, Clutch Fork
76. DIFFERENTIAL ASSEMBLY
77. BEARING ASSEMBLY, Differential
78. CASE, Differential
79. SHAFT, Differential Pinion
80. GEAR, Speedo Drive
81. SHIM, Differential Bearing Adjustment
82. WASHER, Pinion Thrust
83. GEAR, Differential Pinion
84. WASHER, Side Gear Thrust
85. GEAR, Differential Side
86. LOCKWASHER
87. SCREW, Pinion Shaft
88. GEAR, Differential Ring
89. BOLT

GM MUNCIE 3 SPEED

GM Muncie 3-Speed
APPLICATION
CHEVROLET FULL SIZE
CHEVROLET MID SIZE
CHEVROLET COMPACT

OLDSMOBILE FULL SIZE
OLDSMOBILE MID SIZE
OLDSMOBILE COMPACT

PONTIAC FULL SIZE
PONTIAC MID SIZE
PONTIAC COMPACT

TRANSMISSION DISASSEMBLY
1 Remove side cover and shift forks.
2 Unbolt extension. Rotate extension to line up groove in extension flange with reverse idler shaft. Drive reverse idler shaft and key out of case with a brass drift.
3 Move second-third synchronizer sleeve forward. Remove extension housing and mainshaft assembly.
4 Remove reverse idler gear from case.
5 Remove third speed blocker ring from clutch gear.
6 Expand snap-ring which retains mainshaft rear bearing. Tap gently on end of mainshaft to remove extension.
7 Remove clutch gear bearing retainer and gasket.
8 Remove snap-ring. Remove clutch gear from inside case by gently tapping on end of clutch gear.
9 Remove oil slinger. Remove 16 mainshaft pilot bearings from clutch gear cavity.

10 Slip clutch gear bearing out front of case. Aid removal with a screwdriver between case and bearing outer snapring.
11 Drive countershaft and key out to rear.
12 Remove countergear and two tanged thrust washers.

MAINSHAFT DISASSEMBLY
1 Depress speedometer drive gear retaining clip. Slide off gear. Some speedometer drive gears, made of metal, must be pulled off.
2 Remove rear bearing snap-ring.
3 Support reverse gear. Press on rear of mainshaft to remove reverse gear, thrust washer, and rear bearing. Be careful not to cock the bearing on the shaft.
4 Remove first and reverse sliding clutch hub snap-ring.
5 Support first gear. Press on rear of mainshaft to remove clutch assembly, blocker ring, and first gear.
6 Remove second and third speed sliding clutch hub snap-ring.
7 Support second gear. Press on front of mainshaft to remove clutch assembly, second speed blocker ring, and second gear from shaft.

INSPECTION
1 Wash all parts in solvent.
2 Air dry.

CASE
1 Check for cracks.

2 Check faces for burrs. Remove with a fine file.
3 Check bearing bores for damage. If they are damaged, replace case.

FRONT & REAR BEARINGS
1 Do not spin bearings with air pressure; turn them slowly by hand.
2 Lubricate bearings with light oil. Turn slowly to check for roughness.

BEARING ROLLERS
1 Check for wear; replace if worn.
2 Check countershaft and reverse idler shaft.
3 Replace all worn washers.

GEARS
1 Check for wear, chips, or cracks.
2 If reverse gear bushing is worn or damaged, replace entire gear.
3 Check that both clutch sleeves slide freely on their hubs.

REVERSE IDLER GEAR BUSHING
This bushing may not be serviced separately. If the bushing requires replacement, replace the gear.

COUNTERGEAR ANTI-LASH PLATE
1 Check the plate teeth for wear or damage.
2 Do not disassemble.

Repair

CLUTCH KEYS & SPRINGS
Keys and springs may be replaced if

GM Muncie 3–speed: exploded view

1 Bearing Retainer
2 Bolt and Lock Washer
3 Gasket
4 Oil Seal
5 Snap Ring (Bearing-to-Main Drive Gear)
6 Main Drive Gear Bearing
7 Snap Ring Bearing
8 Oil Slinger
9 Case
10 Gasket
11 Snap Ring (Rear Bearing-to-Extension)
12 Extension
13 Extension Bushing
14 Oil Seal
15 Thrust Washer
16 Bearing Washer
17 Needle Bearings
18 Countergear
19 Countershaft
20 Woodruff Key
21 Bolt (Extension-to-Case)
22 Reverse Gear
23 Thrust Washer
24 Rear Bearing
25 Snap Ring
26 Speedometer Drive Gear
27 Retainer Clip
28 Reverse Idler Gear
29 Reverse Idler Bushing
30 Reverse Idler Shaft
31 Woodruff Key
32 1st Speed Gear
33 1st Speed Blocker Ring
34 Synchronizer Key Spring
35 Synchronizer Keys
36 1st and Reverse Synchronizer Hub Assembly

37 Snap Ring
38 1st and Reverse Synchronizer Collar
39 Main Drive Gear
40 Pilot Bearings
41 3rd Speed Blocker Ring
42 2nd and 3rd Synchronizer Collar
43 Snap Ring
44 Synchronizer Key Spring
45 Synchronizer Keys

46 2nd and 3rd Synchronizer Hub
47 2nd Speed Blocker Ring
48 2nd Speed Gear
49 Mainshaft
50 Gasket
51 2nd and 3rd Shifter Fork
52 1st and Reverse Shifter Fork
53 2-3 Shifter Shaft Assembly

54 1st and Reverse Shifter Shaft Assembly
55 Spring
56 O-Ring Seal
57 1st and Reverse Detent Cam
58 2nd and 3rd Detent Cam
59 Side Cover
60 Bolt and Lock Washer
61 TCS Switch and Gasket

worn or broken. Hubs and sleeves must be kept together as originally assembled.
1 Mark hub and sleeve for reassembly.
2 Push hub from sleeve. Remove keys and springs.
3 Place three keys and two springs, one on each side of hub, so all three keys are engaged by both springs. The tanged end of the springs should not be installed into the same key.
4 Slide the sleeve onto the hub, aligning the marks.

EXTENSION OIL SEAL & BUSHING
1 Remove seal.
2 Using bushing remover and installer, or other suitable tool, drive bushing into extension housing.
3 Drive new bushing in from rear. Lubricate inside of bushing and seal. Install new oil seal with extension seal installer or suitable tool.

CLUTCH BEARING RETAINER OIL SEAL
1 Pry old seal out.
2 Install new seal using seal installer or suitable tool. Seat seal in bore.

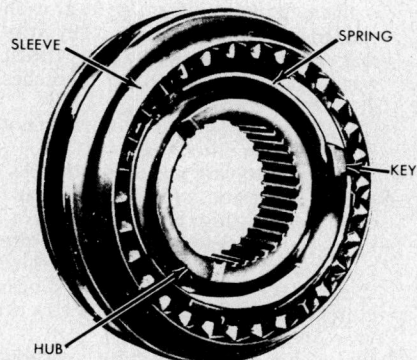

Synchronizer assembly

MAINSHAFT ASSEMBLY
1 Turn front of mainshaft up.
2 Install second gear with clutching teeth up; the rear face of the gear butts against the flange on the mainshaft.
3 Install a blocking ring with clutching teeth downward. All three blocking rings are the same.
4 Install second and third synchronizer assembly with fork slot down. Press it onto mainshaft splines. Both synchronizer assemblies are identical but are assembled differently. The second-third speed hub and sleeve is assembled with the sleeve fork slot toward the thrust face of the hub. The first-reverse hub and sleeve is installed with the fork slot opposite the thrust face. The blocker ring notches align with the synchronizer assembly keys.
5 Install synchronizer snap-ring. Both synchronizer snap-rings are the same.

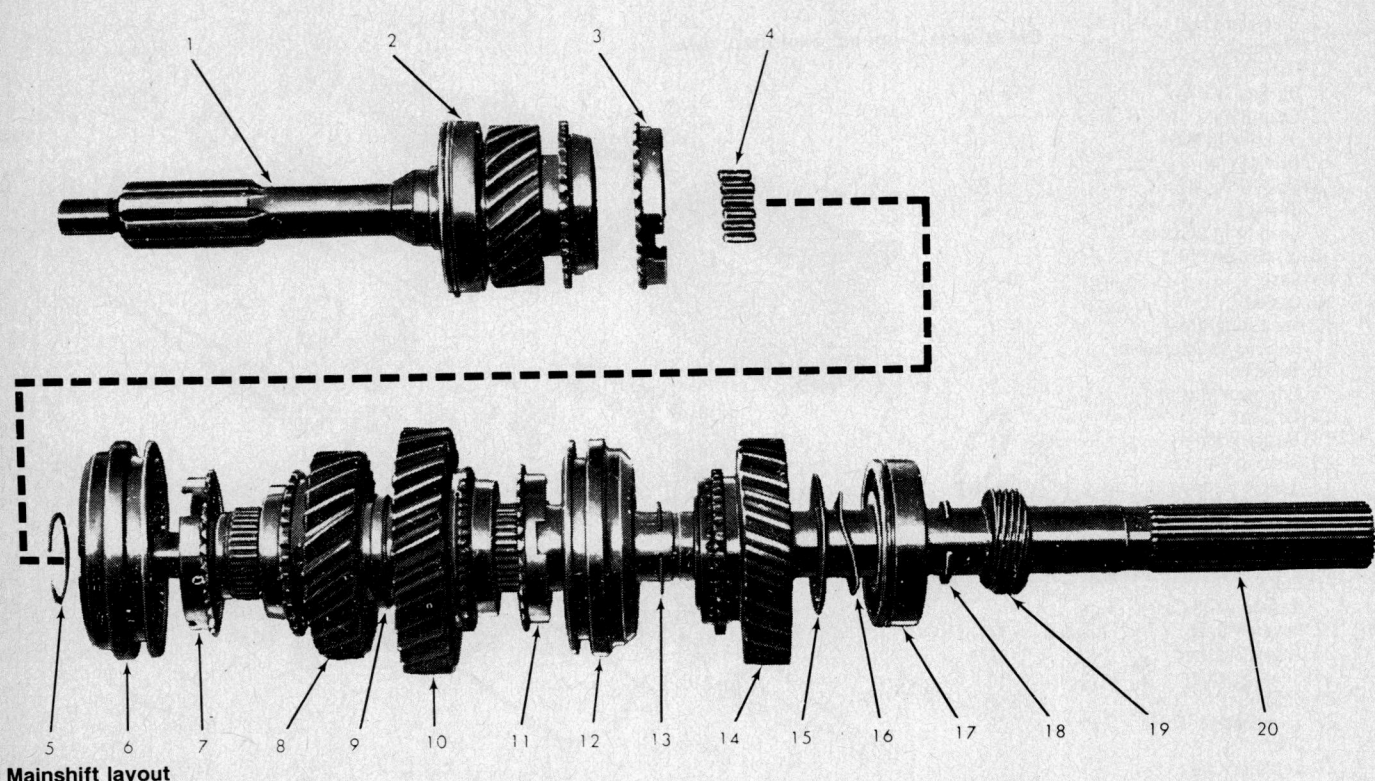

Mainshift layout

1. MAIN DRIVE GEAR
2. MAIN DRIVE GEAR BEARING
3. 3RD SPEED BLOCKER RING
4. MAINSHAFT PILOT BEARINGS (14)
5. SNAP RING
6. 2-3 SYNCHRONIZER ASSEMBLY
7. 2ND SPEED BLOCKER RING
8. 2ND SPEED GEAR
9. SHOULDER (PART OF MAINSHAFT)
10. 1ST SPEED GEAR
11. 1ST SPEED BLOCKER RING
12. 1ST SPEED SYNCHRONIZER ASSEMBLY
13. SNAP RING
14. REVERSE GEAR
15. REVERSE GEAR THRUST WASHER
16. SPRING WASHER
17. REAR BEARING
18. SNAP RING
19. SPEEDO DRIVE GEAR
20. MAINSHAFT

6 Turn rear of shaft up.

7 Install first gear with clutching teeth upward. The front face of the gear butts against the flange on the mainshaft.

8 Install a blocker ring with clutching teeth down.

9 Install first and reverse synchronizer assembly with fork slot up. Press it onto mainshaft splines. Be sure blocker ring notches align with synchronizer assembly keys. Both synchronizer sleeves face front of mainshaft.

10 Install snap-ring.

11 Install reverse gear with clutching teeth down.

12 Install steel reverse gear thrust washer with flats aligned.

13 Press rear ball bearing onto shaft with snap-ring slot down.

14 Install snap-ring.

15 Install speedometer drive gear and retaining clip.

TRANSMISSION ASSEMBLY

1 Assemble the countergear as follows:
   a. 29 Roller bearings
   b. A bearing washer
   c. 29 Roller bearings
   d. A bearing washer

2 Place countergear assembly through rear case opening with a tanged thrust washer, tang away from gear, at each end. Install countershaft and key from rear of case. Be sure that thrust washer tangs are aligned with notches in case.

3 Place reverse idler gear in case. Do not install reverse idler shaft yet.

4 Expand snap-ring in extension. Assemble extension over mainshaft and onto rear bearing. Seat snap-ring.

5 Load 16 mainshaft pilot bearings into clutch gear cavity. Assemble third speed blocker ring onto clutch gear clutching surface with teeth toward gear.

6 Place clutch gear assembly, without front bearing, over front of mainshaft.

Blocker ring notches align with keys in second-third synchronizer assembly.

7 Stick gasket onto extension housing with grease. Assemble clutch gear, mainshaft, and extension-to-case together. Make sure that clutch gear teeth engage teeth of countergear antilash plate.

8 Rotate extension housing. Install reverse idler shaft and key.

9 Torque extension bolts to 45 ft./lbs.

10 Install oil slinger with inner lip facing forward. Install front bearing outer snap-ring to bearing. Slide bearing into case bore.

11 Install snap-ring to clutch gear stem. Install bearing retainer and gasket. Torque bolts to 20 ft./lbs. Retainer oil return hole must be at 6 o'clock.

12 Shift both synchronizer sleeves to neutral positions. Install side cover. Align shifter forks with synchronizer sleeve grooves.

13 Torque side cover bolts to 20 ft./lbs.

GM MUNCIE 4 SPEED

GM Muncie 4-Speed

APPLICATIONS

BUICK FULL SIZE
BUICK MID SIZE
BUICK COMPACTS

CHEVROLET FULL SIZE
CHEVROLET MID SIZE
CHEVROLET COMPACT

OLDSMOBILE FULL SIZE
OLDSMOBILE MID SIZE
OLDSMOBILE COMPACT

PONTIAC FULL SIZE
PONTIAC MID SIZE
PONTIAC COMPACT

DISASSEMBLY

1 Remove side cover and shift controls.
2 Remove front bearing retainer and remove retainer and gasket.
3 Lock up transmission by shifting into two gears and remove main drive gear retaining nut.

NOTE: This nut *may* have left-hand threads.

4 Return gears to neutral and remove lock pin from reverse shifter lever boss. Pull shaft out about ⅛ in. This will disengage reverse shift fork from reverse gear.
5 Remove extension case attaching bolts. Tap extension with soft hammer toward rear. When idler shaft is out as far as it will go, move extension to left so reverse fork clears gear. Remove extension and gasket.
6 Remove reverse idler gear, flat washer, shaft and roll spring pin.
7 Remove speedometer and reverse gears.

NOTE: Slide third-fourth synchronizer clutch sleeve to fourth-speed gear position (forward) before removing mainshaft assembly.

8 Remove rear bearing retainer and mainshaft assembly from case by tapping bearing retainer with soft hammer.
9 Unload bearing rollers from main drive gear. Remove fourth-speed synchronizer blocking ring.
10 Lift front half of reverse idler gear, with tanged thrust washer, from case.
11 Press main drive gear down from bearing.
12 Tap front bearing and snap-ring from case.
13 From front of case, press out countershaft. Remove the countershaft gear and both tanged washers.
14 Remove the rollers (112), six spacers and roller spacer from countergear.
15 Remove mainshaft front snap-ring. Slide third and fourth-speed clutch and third-speed gear and synchronizer ring from front of mainshaft.
16 Spread rear bearing retainer snap-ring and press mainshaft out of retainer.
17 Remove mainshaft snap-ring. Support second-speed gear and press on rear of mainshaft to remove:
a. rear bearing
b. first-speed gear and sleeve
c. first-speed synchronizing ring
d. first-second-speed synchronizer clutch
e. second-speed synchronizer ring
f. second-speed gear

After thoroughly cleaning case and all parts, make thorough inspection. Replace required parts. In checking bearings do not spin at high speeds. Clean and rotate by hand to detect roughness and unevenness. Spinning can damage balls and races.

Assembly

MAINSHAFT

1 From rear of shaft, assemble second-speed gear (hub of gear toward rear of shaft).
2 Install first-second synchronizer clutch assembly onto mainshaft (sleeve taper toward rear, hub to front). Install a synchronizer ring on each side of clutch assembly. Keyways line up with clutch keys.
3 Press first-speed sleeve onto mainshaft. (A 1¾ in. or 1⅝ in. ID pipe cut to convenient length makes a suitable tool).
4 Install first-speed gear (hub toward front) and press onto the rear bearing with snap-ring grooves toward front of transmission. Be sure bearing is firmly seated.
5 Choose selective fit snap-ring (.087, .090. .093 or .096 in.) and install it into groove in mainshaft behind rear bearing. Maximum clearance of snap-ring and rear face should be between zero and .005 in.

NOTE: Always use new snap-ring.

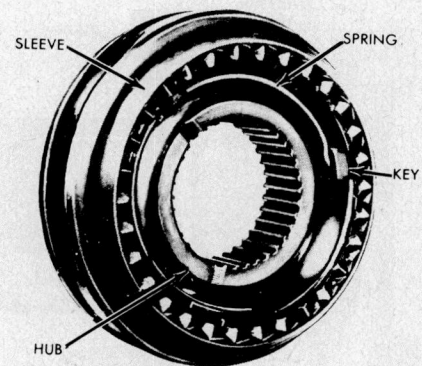

Synchronizer assembly

6 Install third-speed gear (hub to front of transmission) and third-speed gear synchronizing ring (notches to front).
7 Install third and fourth-speed gear clutch assembly. Sleeve taper and hub are toward front.
8 Install snap-ring onto mainshaft in front of third and fourth-speed clutch. Ends of snap-ring seat behind spline teeth.
9 Install rear bearing retainer. Spread snap-ring in plate, to allow ring to drop around rear bearing. Press on the end of mainshaft until snap-ring engages the groove in rear bearing.
10 Install reverse gear (shift collar to rear).
11 Install speedometer drive gear.

COUNTERGEAR

1 Install roller spacer into counter gear.
2 Grease parts for countergear assembly. Install as follows at each end:
a. a spacer
b. 28 roller bearings
c. a spacer
d. 28 roller bearings
e. a spacer
3 Insert dummy shaft into counter gear.

TRANSMISSION

1 Rest case on side with cover opening upward. Install countergear tanged thrust washers in place with heavy grease. Set tangs in proper notches:
2 Set countergear in place. Use care not to disturb tanged washers.
3 Position transmission case so that it rests on front face.
4 Lubricate and insert countershaft in rear. Turn countershaft so flat on end of shaft is horizontal and facing bottom of case.

NOTE: The flat of shaft must mate with rear bearing retainer when installed.

5 Align countergear with shaft in rear and hole in front of case. Push dummy shaft out front of case until flat of shaft is flush with rear of case. Be sure thrust washers remain in place.
6 Check end-play in countergear (dial indicator should be used). If end-play is more than .025 in. install new thrust washer.
7 Install cage and 17 roller bearings into main drive gear. Use heavy grease to hold bearings.
8 Install main drive gear, with bearings, through side opening of case and into position in front bore.
9 Place gasket in position on rear bearing retainer.
10 Install fourth-speed synchronizing ring onto main drive gear (notches toward rear).
11 Position tanged thrust washer for reverse idler on machined face. Position front reverse idler gear next to thrust

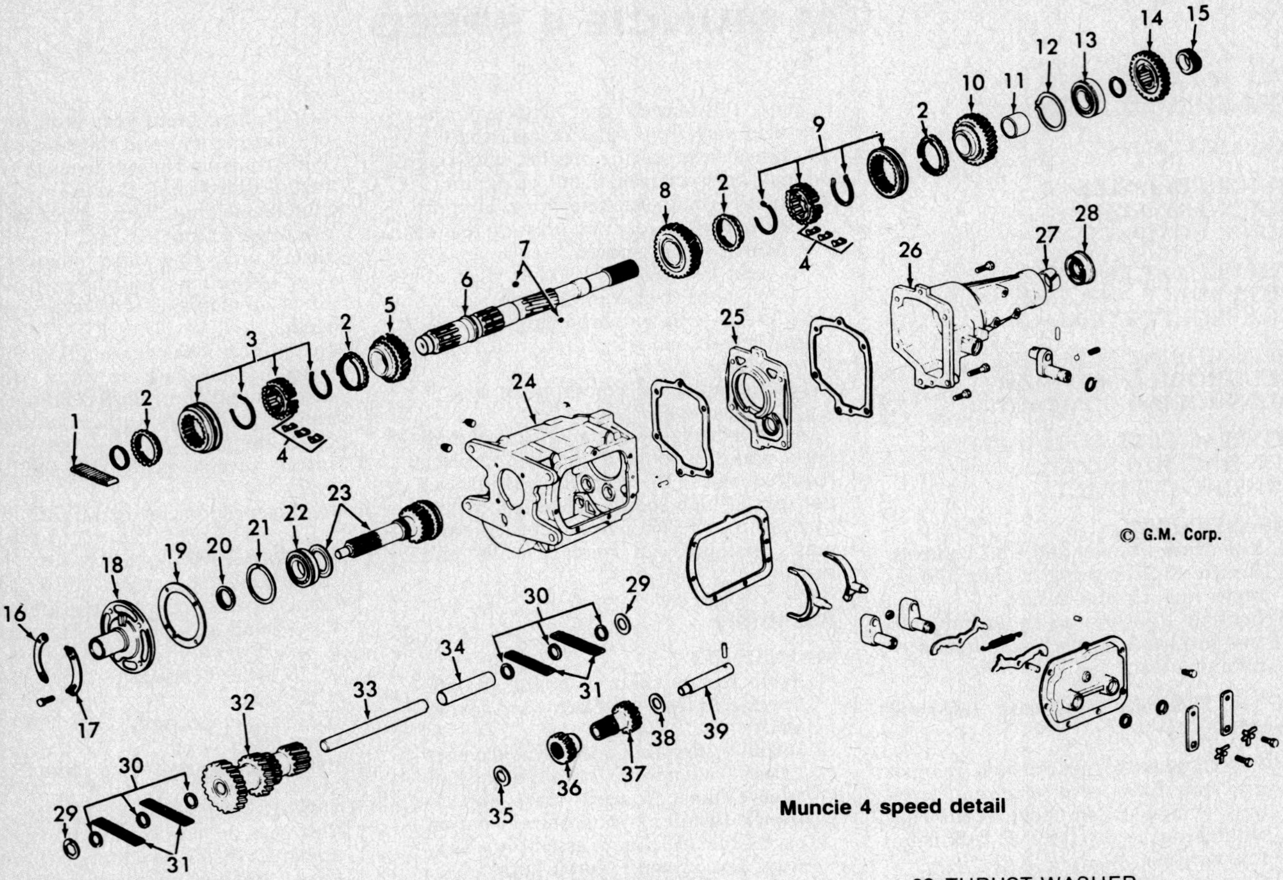

© G.M. Corp.

Muncie 4 speed detail

1. BEARING ASSEMBLY
2. SYNCHRONIZING RING
3. THIRD & FOURTH CLUTCH
4. CLUTCH PLATES
5. THIRD SPEED GEAR
6. MAINSHAFT
7. SPRING
8. SECOND SPEED GEAR
9. FIRST & SECOND CLUTCH
10. FIRST SPEED GEAR
11. SLEEVE
12. RING
13. MAINSHAFT REAR BEARING
14. REVERSE GEAR

15. SPEEDO DRIVE GEAR
16. LOCK-L.H.
17. LOCK-R.H.
18. BEARING RETAINER
19. GASKET
20. NUT
21. SNAP RING
22. MAIN DRIVE GEAR BEARING
23. MAIN DRIVE GEAR
24. CASE ASSEMBLY
25. REAR BEARING RETAINER
26. EXTENSION ASSEMBLY
27. BUSHING
28. SEAL ASSEMBLY

29. THRUST WASHER
30. BEARING WASHER
31. BEARING ROLLERS
32. COUNTERSHAFT GEAR
33. COUNTERSHAFT
34. SPACER UNIT (WITH WASHER)
35. REVERSE IDLER GEAR WASHER (FRONT)
36. REVERSE IDLER GEAR (FRONT)
37. REVERSE IDLER GEAR (REAR)
38. REVERSE IDLER GEAR WASHER (REAR)
39. REVERSE IDLER GEAR SHAFT

washer (hub facing toward rear of case).

CHILTON CAUTION: *Before installing mainshaft to case, slide the third-fourth synchronizer clutch sleeve forward into fourth-speed detent position.*

12 Lower mainshaft assembly into case. Notches on fourth-speed synchronizer ring correspond to keys in clutch assembly.

13 Align guide pin in rear bearing retainer with hole in rear of case. Tap rear bearing retainer into position with soft hammer.

14 From rear of case, insert reverse idler gear, engaging splines with portion of front gear in case.

15 Place gasket in position on rear face of bearing retainer.

16 Install remaining flat washer on reverse idler shaft.

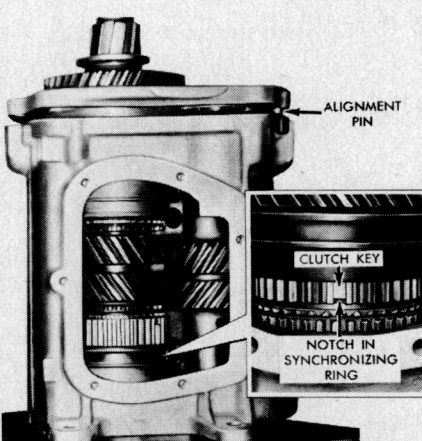

GM Muncie 4–speed: installing mainshaft

17 Install reverse idler shaft, roll pin, and thrust washer into gears and front boss of case. Pick up front tanged thrust washer.

18 Pull reverse shifter shaft to left side of extension and rotate shaft to bring reverse shift fork forward in extension (reverse detent position). Start extension onto transmission case. Slowly push in on shifter shaft to engage the shift fork with the reverse gear shift collar. Pilot the reverse idler shaft into the extension housing, permitting the extension to slide into the transmission case.

19 Install extension and retainer-to-case attaching bolts.

20 Push or pull reverse shifter shaft to line up grooves in the shaft with the holes in the boss. Drive in the lockpin. Install shift lever.

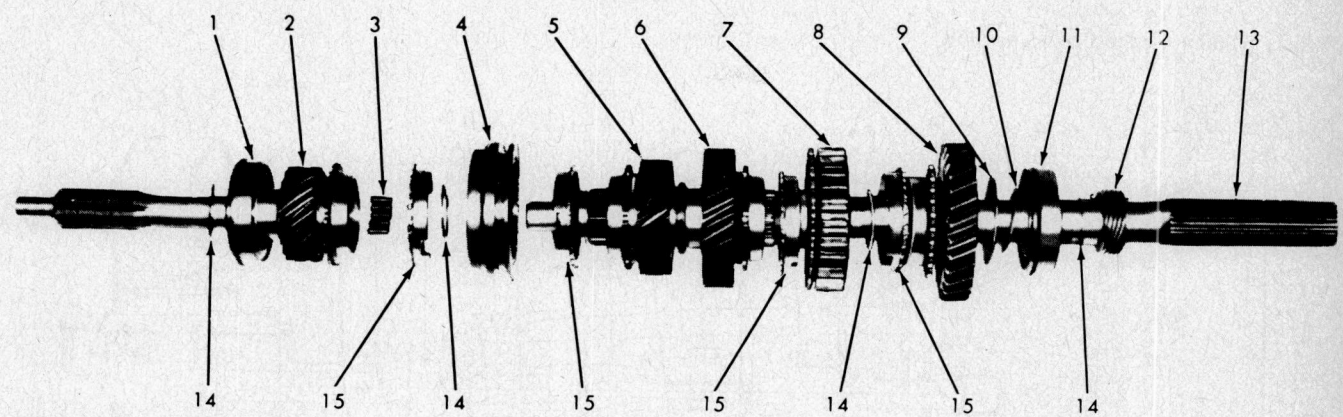

Clutch gears and mainshaft

1. DRIVE GEAR BEARING
2. DRIVE GEAR
3. MAINSHAFT PILOT BEARINGS
4. 3-4 SYNCHRONIZER ASSEMBLY
5. THIRD SPEED GEAR
6. SECOND SPEED GEAR

7. 1-2 SYNCHRONIZER AND REVERSE GEAR ASSEMBLY
8. FIRST SPEED GEAR
9. THRUST WASHER
10. SPRING WASHER
11. REAR BEARING

12. SPEEDO DRIVE GEAR
13. MAINSHAFT
14. SNAP RING
15. SYNCHRONIZING "BLOCKER" RING

21 Press bearing onto main drive gear (snap-ring groove in front), and into case until several main drive gear retaining nut threads are exposed.
22 Lock transmission by shifting into two gears. Install main drive gear retaining nut onto the gear shaft. Draw it up tight. Be sure bearing is completely seated against shoulder. Torque retaining nut to 40 ft./lbs. Lock in place

by staking into main drive gear shaft hole with punch. Do not damage shaft threads.
23 Install main drive gear bearing retainer, gasket attaching bolts and bolt-lock retainers. Use a suitable seal on bolts. Tighten to 20 ft./lbs.
24 Shift mainshaft third-fourth sliding clutch sleeve into neutral position.

Shift first-second sliding clutch into second gear (forward) detent position. Shift side cover third-fourth shift lever into neutral detent. Shift first-second shift lever into second gear detent position.

25 Install side cover, with gasket. Tighten bolts in a rotating pattern. Torque to 20 ft./lbs.

GM MUNCIE (70mm) 4 SPEED

GM Muncie 70mm 4-speed Manual Transmission

The designation derives from the distance measurement between the gearbox shafts—70mm. This gearbox is 100% assembled with metric fasteners.

APPLICATION

CHEVROLET CHEVETTE
CHEVROLET VEGA
CHEVROLET MONZA

PONTIAC ASTRE
PONTIAC SUNBIRD

Transmission Disassembly

With the transmission resting on the front of the bellhousing:
1 Drive the spring pin from the shifter shaft arm assembly and shifter shaft. Remove shifter shaft arm assembly.
2 Remove (5) bolts retaining the extension housing to the case and remove extension.
3 Press down on speedometer gear retainer and remove gear and retainer from mainshaft.
4 Remove snap rings on shifter shaft.
5 Using tool J-25295 with slide hammer 6619-1, remove reverse shifter shaft

cover, shifter shaft detent cap, spring and ball, and interlock lock pin.
6 Pull reverse lever shaft outward to disengage reverse idler. Remove the idler shaft, with gear attached.
7 Remove snap ring on reverse gear and

reverse countershaft gear. Remove gears.
8 Place transmission on its side and remove clutch gear bearing retainer bolts, retainer and gasket.
9 Remove snap ring retaining the clutch

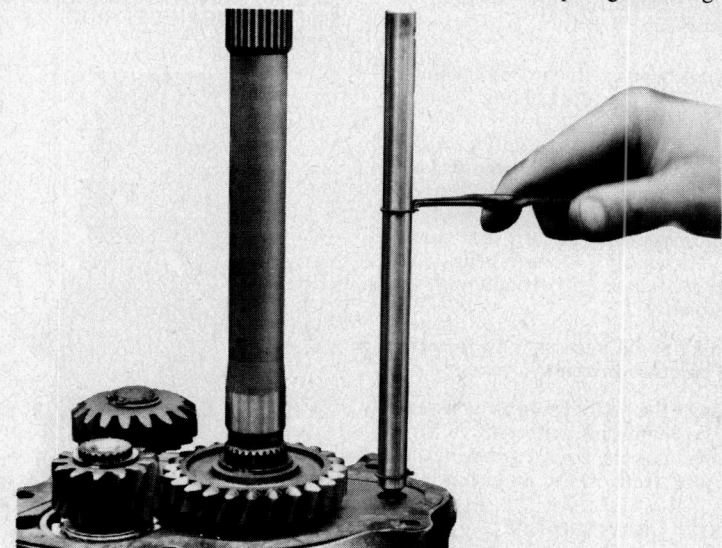

GM 70mm manual 4-speed: removing the shifter shaft

Muncie (70mm) 4 speed cross section

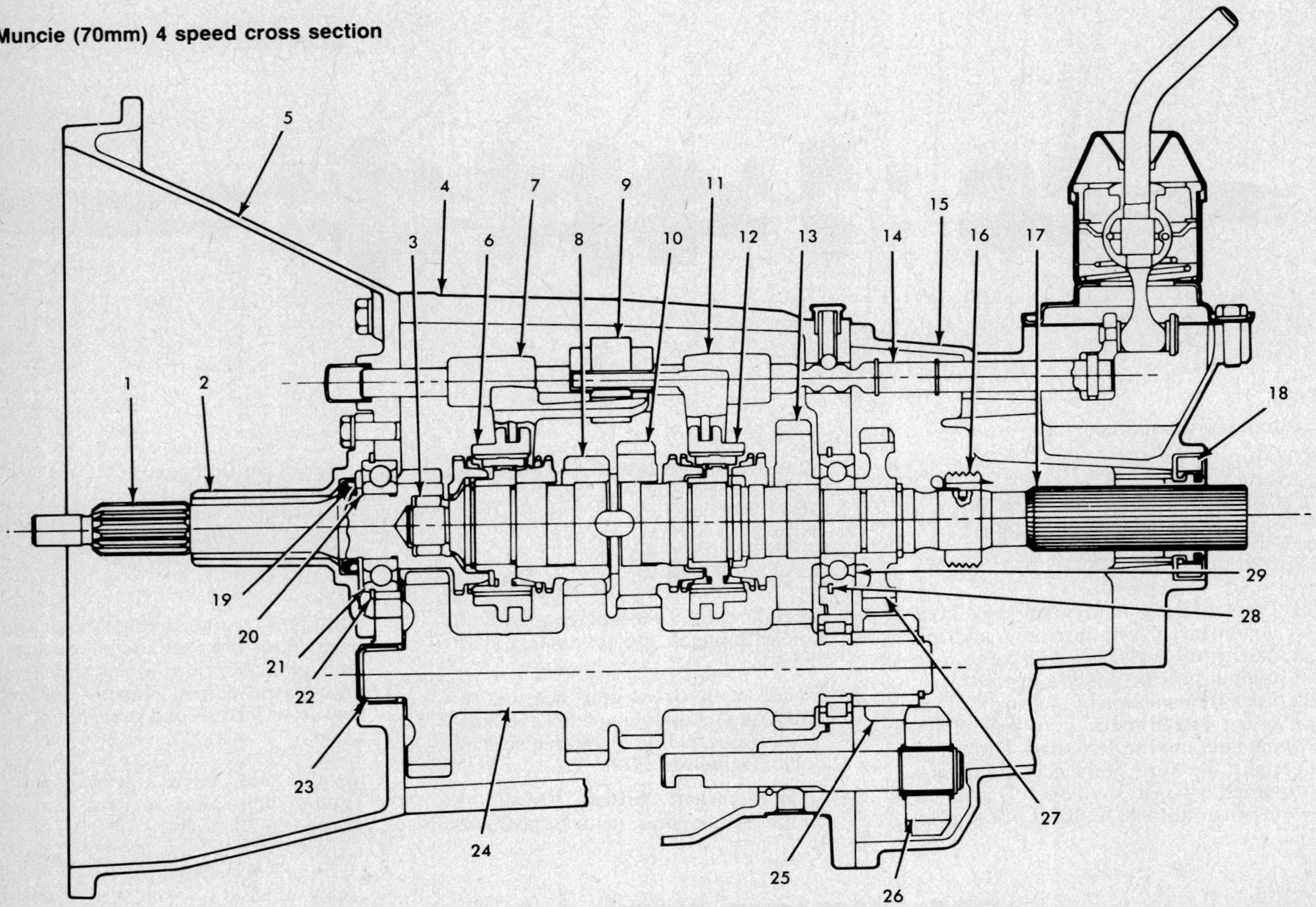

1. DRIVE GEAR
2. BEARING RETAINER
3. PILOT BEARINGS
4. CASE
5. BELLHOUSING
6. 3-4 SYNCHRONIZER ASSEMBLY
7. 3-4 SHIFTER FORK
8. THIRD SPEED GEAR
9. DETENT BUSHING
10. SECOND SPEED GEAR
11. 1-2 SHIFTER FORK

12. 1-2 SYNCHRONIZER ASSEMBLY
13. FIRST SPEED GEAR
14. SHIFTER SHAFT
15. EXTENSION
16. SPEEDOMETER DRIVE GEAR AND CLIP
17. MAINSHAFT
18. REAR OIL SEAL
19. RETAINER OIL SEAL
20. SNAP RING—BEARING TO GEAR
21. DRIVE GEAR BEARING

22. SNAP RING—BEARING TO CASE
23. COUNTERGEAR ROLLER BEARINGS
24. COUNTERGEAR ASSEMBLY
25. COUNTER REVERSE GEAR
26. REVERSE IDLER GEAR
27. REVERSE GEAR
28. SNAP RING—BEARING TO EXTENSION
29. REAR BEARING

gear ball bearing to the bellhousing.

10 Remove the (6) bolts holding the bellhousing to the case.

11 Place transmission so that its again resting on the bellhousing and expand the snap ring in mainshaft bearing opening. Remove the case by lifting it off the mainshaft. Insure that mainshaft assembly, countergear and shifter shaft assembly remain with the bellhousing.

NOTE: It may be necessary to tap with a plastic hammer to remove case.

12 Lift from the bellhousing as an assembly, the mainshaft with shifter forks attached and the countergear meshed with gear teeth in the mainshaft.

Mainshaft Disassembly

1 Separate the shift shaft assembly and countergear from the mainshaft.

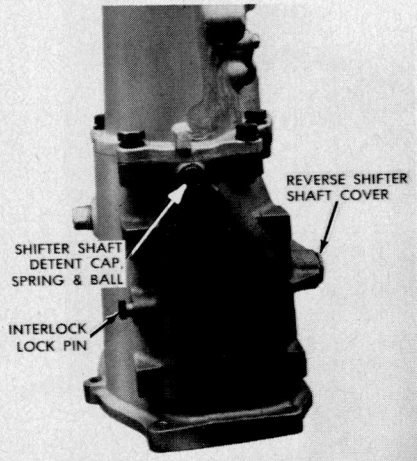

GM 70mm manual 4-speed: removing the cover, cap & interlock pin

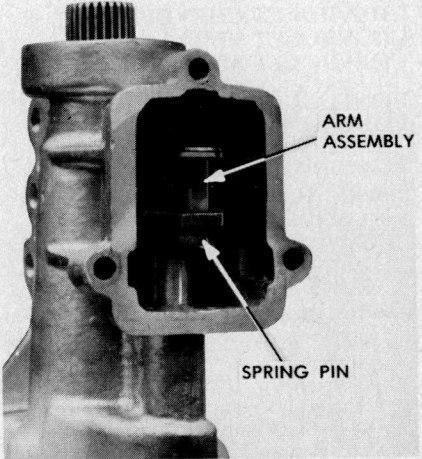

GM 70mm manual 4-speed: removing the spring pin

2 Remove the clutch gear and blocker ring from the mainshaft.

NOTE: The clutch gear as (15) roller bearings. Catch loose roller bearings if they fall out during disassembly so that they can be replaced during assembly.

3 Remove snap ring before 3–4 synchronizer hub and remove synchronizer assembly. Use press if required.
4 Remove blocker ring and 3rd speed gear.
5 Using press plates, remove the ball bearing from the rear of the mainshaft.
6 The remaining components may be removed one at a time from the mainshaft, pressing as required.

Cleaning & Inspection
TRANSMISSION CASE
1 Wash the transmission thoroughly inside and outside with cleaning solvent, then inspect the case for cracks.
2 Check the front and rear faces for burrs, and if present, dress them off with a fine mill file.
3 Make sure bearings are clean, then lubricate with light engine oil and check them for roughness by slowly turning the race by hand.

ROLLER BEARINGS
All countergear bearings should be inspected closely and replaced if they show wear. Inspect countergear and reverse idler shaft at the same time, replace if necessary.

GEARS
1 Inspect all gears for excessive wear, chips or cracks and replace any that are worn or damaged.
2 Inspect reverse idler gear bushing and if worn or damaged replace the entire gear (reverse gear bushing is not serviced separately).
3 Check both clutch sleeves to see that they slide freely on their hubs.

FRONT & REAR BEARINGS
1 Wash the front and rear ball bearings thoroughly in a cleaning solvent.
2 Blow out bearings with compressed air.

CHILTON CAUTION: *Do not allow the bearings to spin. Turn them slowly by hand. Spinning bearings will damage the race and balls.*

Repairs
SYNCHRONIZER KEYS & SPRINGS
REPLACEMENT
The synchronizer hubs and sliding sleeves are a selected assembly and should be kept together as originally assembled, but the keys and two springs may be replaced if worn or broken.

1 If relation of hub and sleeve are not already marked, mark for assembly purposes.
2 Push the hub from the sliding sleeve; the keys will fall free and the springs may be easily removed.
3 Place the two springs in position (one on each side of hub), so all three keys are engaged by both springs.
Place the keys in position and while holding them in place, slide the sleeve onto the hub, aligning the marks made before disassembly.

EXTENSION OIL SEAL &/OR BUSHING REPLACEMENT
1 Pry seal from rear of extension.
2 Remove bushing using Tool J-21424-9. Drive bushing from rear of extension housing.
3 Using a new bushing and Tool J-21424-9 press bushing into extension from rear of extension.
4 Coat I.D. of bushing and seal with transmission lubricant. Install new seal using Tool J-21426.

DRIVE GEAR BEARING RETAINER OIL SEAL REPLACEMENT
1 Pry out old seal.
2 Using a new seal install new seal into retainer using Tool J-23096 until it bottoms in bore. Lubricate I.D. of seal with transmission lubricant.

Mainshaft Assembly
Turn the rear of the mainshaft upward. Install the following components on the mainshaft:
1 Install the 2nd speed gear with clutching teeth upward; the rear face of the gear with butt against the flange on the mainshaft.
2 Install a blocker ring with clutching teeth downward over the synchronizing surface of the second speed gear.

NOTE: All four blocker rings used in this transmission are identical.

3 Install the 1st and 2nd synchronizer assembly with the fork slot downward; press it on the splines on the mainshaft until its bottoms out.

CHILTON CAUTION: *Be sure the notches of the blocker ring align with the keys of the synchronizer assembly.*

4 Install synchronizer hub to mainshaft snap ring.
5 Install a blocker ring with the notches downward so they align with the keys of the 1st and 2nd synchronizer assembly.
6 Install 1st speed gear with clutching teeth downward.
7 Install rear ball bearing with snap ring groove downward; press onto mainshaft.

NOTE: Two ball bearings are used in this transmission. The one used on the

mainshaft is not shielded, but the one used on the clutch gear is and these should not be switched.

Turn the front of the mainshaft upward. Install the following components on the mainshaft:
8 Install the 3rd speed gear with clutching teeth upward; the front face of the gear will butt against the flange on the mainshaft.
9 Install a blocker ring with clutching teeth downward over the synchronizer surface of the 3rd speed gear.
10 Install the 3rd and 4th synchronizer assembly with fork slot downward.

CHILTON CAUTION: *Be sure notches of the blocker ring align with the keys of the synchronizer assembly.*

11 Install a synchronizer hub to mainshaft snap ring.
12 Install a blocker ring with notches downward so they align with the keys of the 3–4 synchronizer assembly.

Transmission Assembly
1 Using an arbor press, install shielded ball bearing to clutch gear shaft with snap ring groove upward.
2 Install snap ring on clutch gear shaft.
3 Load the mainshaft pilot roller bearings (15) into the clutch gear cavity. Use heavy grease or equivalent to hold them in place.
4 Assemble clutch gear to mainshaft.
5 Install detent lever to shift shaft with roll pin, slide 1–2 shifter fork on shaft so it engages detent lever.
6 Assemble 3–4 shifter fork to detent bushing and slide assembly on shift shaft to locate below 1st and 2nd shifter fork arm.
7 Install shifter assembly to synchronizer sleeve grooves on mainshaft.
8 With the front of the bellhousing resting on wooden blocks; place a thrust washer over the hole for the countergear shaft.

NOTE: Locate thrust washer in holes provided in bellhousing.

9 Mesh countershaft gears with mainshaft gears and install to bellhousing as an assembly.

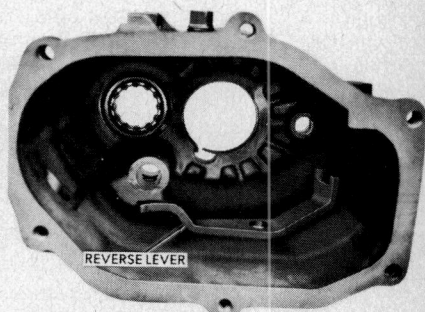

GM 70mm manual 4-speed: reverse lever installed

10. SPRING, Shift Shaft Detent Compression
11. CAP, Shifter Shaft Detent Spring
12. BALL, Shift Detent (5/16″)
13. GASKET, Extension
14. CAP, Reverse Shift Lever
15. RETAINER, Reverse Lever Shift Cap
16. SWITCH, Back-Up Lamp
17. PLUG, Trans.-Magnetic
18. CAP, Shifter Shaft Sealer
19. BOLT, Housing to Case (M 10-1.5 × 35)
20. RING, Clutch Gear Bearing Retaining
21. RING, Main Drive Gear Bearing Locating
22. BEARING ASM., Clutch Gear
23. BEARING ASM., Countershaft Gear-Front
24. BOLT, Housing to Case (M 10-1.5 × 40)
25. GEAR, Main Drive Clutch
26. ROLLER, Main Shaft Bearing
27. FORK, Gearshift-3rd & 4th
28. PIN, Shift Shaft Detent Lock (Part of #9)
29. BUSHING, Shifter Shaft Detent
30. LEVER, Shifter Shaft Detent
31. FORK, Gearshift-1st & 2nd
32. SHAFT, Gearshift
33. PIN, Shift Shaft
34. RING, Shifter Shaft Retaining Lock
35. EXTENSION ASM., Trans. Rear
36. GASKET, Control Lever Housing
37. ARM ASM., Shifter Shaft
38. PIN, Shift Shaft
39. BUSHING, Shifter Shaft Arm
40. SEAL, Rear Extension
41. SHAFT & LEVER ASM., Reverse
42. RING, Reverse Shift Lever Retaining Lock
43. CLIP, Speedo. Drive Gear
44. RING, Synchronizer Retaining
45. SYNCHRONIZER ASM., Trans.-3rd & 4th
46. SHAFT, Trans. Main
47. GEAR, Trans. Second Speed
48. SYNCHRONIZER ASM., Trans. 1st & 2nd
49. RING, Synchronizer Blocking
50. SPRING, Synchronizer
51. KEY, Synchronizer
52. GEAR, Trans. Third Speed
53. GEAR, Trans. First Speed
54. RING, Mainshaft Locating
55. BEARING, Mainshaft Rear
56. GEAR, Trans. Reverse
57. RING, Gear Bearing Retaining
58. GEAR, Speedo. Drive
59. RING, Countershaft Gear Retainer
60. WASHER, Counter Gear Thrust
61. GEAR, Trans. Countershaft
62. RING, Center Gear Bearing Locating
63. RACE, Bearing (Part of #64)
64. BEARING ASM., Countershaft Gear-Rear
65. GEAR, Reverse Countershaft
66. SHAFT, Reverse Idler
67. RING, Retainer (¾″ I.D.)
68. WASHER, Reverse Idler Gear Thrust
69. GEAR, Reverse Idler

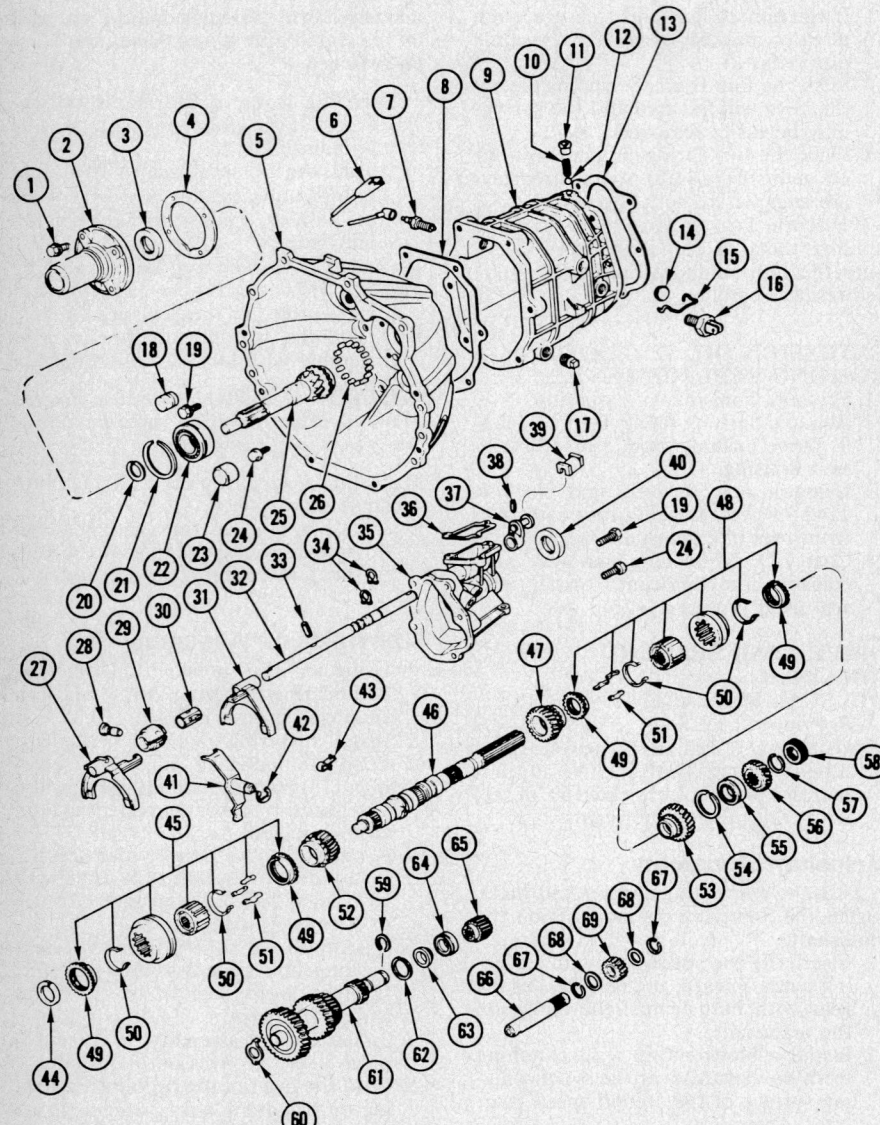

Muncie (70MM) 4 speed transmission

1. BOLT, Bearing Retainer (M8-1.25 × 21)
2. RETAINER, Main Drive Gear Bearing
3. SEAL ASM., Main Drive Gear Bearing
4. GASKET, Main Drive Gear Bearing Retainer
5. HOUSING, Clutch
6. WIRE ASM., Spark Switch (27″ 18 Gauge Wire)
7. SWITCH ASM., Trans. Control Spark
8. GASKET, Clutch Housing
9. CASE ASM., Transmission (Incl. #28)

10 Place bellhousing on its side and install snap ring to ball bearing on clutch gear.

11 Install bearing retainer to bellhousing.

NOTE: Use bolt seal on (4) retaining bolts.

12 Turn bellhousing so it again rests on the wooden block. If removed, install reverse lever to case; use grease or equivalent to hold it in place.

NOTE: When reverse lever is installed the screwdriver slot should be parallel to the front of the case.

13 Install reverse lever snap ring.

14 Install roller bearing to countergear opening with snap ring groove inside of case.

NOTE: Snap ring will be assembled to roller bearing.

15 Install gasket to bellhousing using rubber cement or equivalent to hold it in place.

NOTE: Before installing case, make sure synchronizers are in neutral position, detent bushing slot is facing outward and the reverse lever is flush with the inside wall of the case.

16 Using snap ring pliers expand the snap ring in the mainshaft opening of the

GM 70mm manual 4-speed: countershaft & mainshaft gears positioned for insertion into bellhousing

case and let it pilot over the mainshaft bearing.

NOTE: It may be necessary to tap the case with a plastic hammer to ease assembly.

17 Install interlock lock pin to hold shifter shaft in place.
18 Install idler shaft so it will engage with the reverse inside of case.
19 Install cover over screwdriver arm to hold the reverse lever in place.
20 Install detent ball, spring and cap in case.
21 Install reverse gear with the chamfer on gear teeth upward; push reverse gear onto splines on the mainshaft and secure with a snap ring.
22 Install smaller reverse gear on countergear shaft with the shoulder resting against countergear bearing and secure with a snap ring.
23 If removed, install snap ring, thrust washer and reverse idler gear with chamfer of gear teeth facing downward to idler shaft. Secure with thrust washer and snap ring.
24 Install snap rings on shifter shaft.

25 Engage speedometer gear retainer in hole provided in mainshaft, with retainer loop forward, slide speedometer gear over mainshaft and into position.
26 Place extension housing and gasket on case and install (2) pilot bolts before installing the three remaining bolts (Fig. 28).

NOTE: Pilot bolts are partially threaded and installed in the top right hand corner and bottom left hand corner of the case.

CHILTON CAUTION: *If the pilot bolts are installed in the wrong holes, splitting of the case may occur.*

27 Assemble the shifter shaft arm over shifter shaft to a position aligned with the drilled hole near the end of shaft drive spring pin into shifter shaft arm and shaft to retain these parts.
28 Place transmission on its side; install the (2) pilot bolts before installing the (4) remaining bolts to the bellhouse and case.

NOTE: Pilot bolts are partially threaded and are installed in the right hand top and left hand bottom holes in the bellhousing.

GM SAGINAW 3 SPEED

GM Saginaw 3-Speed

APPLICATIONS:

BUICK FULL SIZE
BUICK MID SIZE
BUICK COMPACT

CHEVROLET FULL SIZE
CHEVROLET MID SIZE
CHEVROLET COMPACT

OLDSMOBILE FULL SIZE
OLDSMOBILE MID SIZE
OLDSMOBILE COMPACT

PONTIAC FULL SIZE
PONTIAC MID SIZE
PONTIAC COMPACT

Transmission Disassembly

1 Remove side cover assembly and shift forks.
2 Remove clutch gear bearing retainer.
3 Remove clutch gear bearing to gear stem snap-ring. Pull clutch gear outward until a screwdriver can be inserted between bearing and case. Remove clutch gear bearing.
4 Remove speedometer driven gear and extension bolts.
5 Remove reverse idler shaft snap-ring. Slide reverse idler gear forward on shaft.
6 Remove mainshaft and extension assembly.
7 Remove clutch gear and third speed blocker ring from inside case. Remove 14 roller bearings from clutch gear.
8 Expand the snap-ring which retains

the mainshaft rear bearing. Remove the extension.
9 Using a dummy shaft, drive the countershaft and key out the rear of the case. Remove the gear, two tanged thrust washers, and dummy shaft. Remove bearing washer and 27 roller bearings from each end of countergear.
10 Use a long drift to drive the reverse idler shaft and key through the rear of the case.
11 Remove reverse idler gear and tanged steel thrust washer.

Mainshaft Disassembly

1 Remove second and third speed sliding clutch hub snap-ring from mainshaft. Remove clutch assembly, second speed blocker ring, and second gear from front of mainshaft.
2 Depress speedometer drive gear retaining clip. Remove gear. Some units have a metal speedometer drive gear which must be pulled off.
3 Remove rear bearing snap-ring.
4 Support reverse gear. Press on rear of mainshaft. Remove reverse gear, thrust washer, spring washer, rear bearing, and snap-ring. Do not cock the bearing on the shaft.
5 Remove first and reverse sliding clutch hub snap-ring. Remove clutch assembly, first speed blocker ring, and first gear.

INSPECTION

1 Wash all parts in solvent.
2 Air dry.

CASE

1 Check for cracks.
2 Check faces for burrs. Remove with a fine file.
3 Check bearing bores for damage. If they are damaged, replace case.

FRONT & REAR BEARINGS

1 Do not spin bearings with air pressure; turn them slowing by hand.
2 Lubricate bearings with light oil. Turn slowly to check for roughness.

BEARING ROLLERS

1 Check for wear; replace if worn.
2 Check countershaft and reverse idler shaft for wear or damage.
3 Replace all worn washers.

GEARS

1 Check for wear, chips, or cracks.
2 If reverse gear bushing is worn or damaged, replace entire gear.
3 Check that both clutch sleeves slide freely on their hubs.

REVERSE IDLER GEAR BUSHING

This bushing may not be serviced separately. If the bushing requires replacement, replace the gear.

COUNTERGEAR ANTI-LASH PLATE

1 Check the plate teeth for wear or damage.
2 Do not disassemble unit.

Repair

CLUTCH KEYS & SPRINGS

Keys and springs may be replaced if

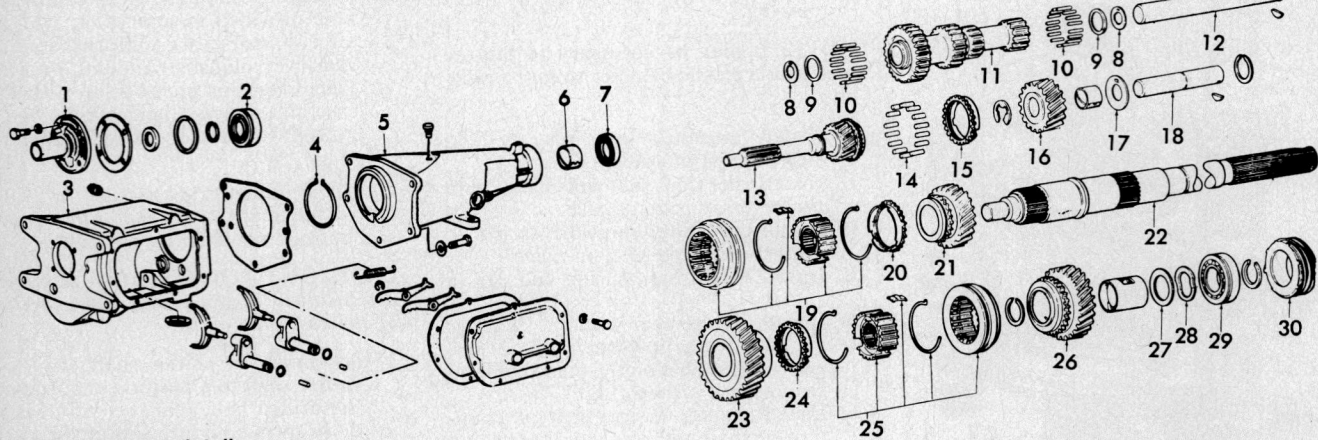

Saginaw 3 speed detail

1. BEARING RETAINER
2. FRONT BEARING
3. TRANSMISSION CASE
4. LOCATING RING
5. CASE EXTENSION
6. BUSHING
7. SEAL
8. THRUST WASHER
9. THRUST WASHER
10. ROLLER BEARING

11. COUNTER GEAR
12. COUNTERSHAFT
13. MAIN DRIVE GEAR
14. ROLLER BEARING
15. SYNCHRO. RING
16. REVERSE IDLER GEAR
17. THRUST WASHER
18. REVERSE IDLER SHAFT
19. SYNCHRO. UNIT
20. SYNCHRO. RING

21. SECOND SPEED GEAR
22. MAINSHAFT
23. FIRST SPEED GEAR
24. SYNCHRO. RING
25. SYNCHRO. UNIT
26. REVERSE GEAR
27. THRUST WASHER
28. WAVE WASHER
29. REAR BEARING
30. SPEEDO. DRIVE GEAR

worn or broken. The hubs and sleeves are matched pairs and must be kept together.
1 Mark hub and sleeve for reassembly.
2 Push hub from sleeve. Remove keys and springs.
3 Place three keys and two springs, one on each side of hub, in position, so all three keys are engaged by both springs. The tanged end of the springs should not be installed into the same key.
4 Slide the sleeve onto the hub, aligning the marks.

NOTE: The groove in the synchronizer hub must be opposite the fork slot in the sleeve.

EXTENSION OIL SEAL & BUSHING
1 Remove seal.
2 Using bushing remover and installer tool, or other suitable tool, drive bushing into extension housing.
3 Drive new bushing in from the rear. Lubricate inside of bushing and seal. Install new oil seal with extension seal installer tool or other suitable tool.

CLUTCH BEARING RETAINER OIL SEAL
1 Pry old seal out.
2 Install new seal using seal installer or suitable tool. Seat seal in bore.

Mainshaft Assembly
1 Turn front of mainshaft up.
2 Install second gear with clutching teeth up. The rear face of the gear butts against the flange on the mainshaft.
3 Install a blocker ring with clutching

teeth down. All three blocker rings are the same.
4 Install second and third speed synchronizer assembly with fork slot down. Press it onto mainshaft splines. Both synchronizer assemblies are the same. Be sure that blocker ring notches align with synchronizer assembly keys.
5 Install synchronizer snap-ring. Both synchronizer snap-rings are the same.
6 Turn rear of shaft up.
7 Install first gear with clutching teeth up. The front face of the gear butts against the flange on the mainshaft.
8 Install a blocker ring with clutching teeth down.
9 Install first and reverse synchronizer assembly with fork slot down. Press it onto mainshaft splines. Be sure blocker ring notches align with synchronizer assembly keys.
10 Install snap-ring.
11 Install reverse gear with clutching teeth down.
12 Install steel reverse gear thrust washer. Install spring washer.
13 Press rear ball bearing onto shaft with snap-ring slot down.
14 Install snap-ring.
15 Install speedometer drive gear and retaining clip. Press on metal speedometer drive gear.

Transmission Assembly
1 Using dummy shaft, load a row of 27 roller bearings and a thrust washer at each end of countergear. Hold in place with grease.
2 Place countergear assembly into case through rear. Place a tanged thrust washer, tang away from gear, at each

end. Install countershaft and key, making sure that tangs align with notches in case.
3 Install reverse idler gear thrust washer, gear, and shaft with key from rear of case. Be sure thrust washer is between gear and rear of case with tang toward notch in case.
4 Expand snap-ring in extension. Assemble extension over rear of mainshaft and onto rear bearing. Seat snap-ring in rear bearing groove.
5 Install 14 mainshaft pilot bearings into clutch gear cavity. Assemble third speed blocker ring onto clutch gear clutching surface with teeth toward gear.
6 Place clutch gear, pilot bearings, and third speed blocker ring assembly over front of mainshaft assembly. Be sure blocker rings align with keys in second-third synchronizer assembly.
7 Stick extension gasket to case with grease. Install clutch gear, mainshaft, and extension together. Be sure clutch gear engages teeth of countergear anti-lash plate. Torque extension bolts to 45 ft./lbs.
8 Place bearing over stem of clutch gear and into front case bore. Install front bearing to clutch gear snap-ring.
9 Install clutch gear bearing retainer and gasket. The retainer oil return hole must be at the bottom. Torque retainer bolts to 10 ft./lbs.
10 Install reverse idler gear shaft E-ring.
11 Shift synchronizer sleeves to neutral positions. Install cover, gasket, and forks. Align forks with synchronizer sleeve grooves. Torque side cover bolts to 10 ft./lbs.
12 Install speedometer drive gear.

GM SAGINAW 4 SPEED

GM Saginaw 4-Speed

APPLICATIONS:

BUICK FULL SIZE
BUICK MID SIZE

CHEV FULL SIZE
CHEV MID SIZE

OLDSMOBILE FULL SIZE
OLDSMOBILE MID SIZE

PONTIAC FULL SIZE
PONTIAC MID SIZE

DISASSEMBLY

1 Remove the side cover and shift forks.
2 Remove the clutch gear bearing retainer. Remove the bearing-to-gear stem snap-ring. Pull out on the clutch gear until a screwdriver can be inserted between the bearing, large snap-ring, and case to pry the bearing off.

NOTE: The clutch gear bearing is a slip-fit on the gear and in the case. Removal of the bearing will provide clearance for clutch gear and mainshaft removal.

3 Remove the clutch gear, mainshaft, and extension as an assembly.
4 Spread the snap-ring which holds the mainshaft rear bearing and remove the extension case.
5 Drive countershaft and its woodruff key out of the rear of the case with a pipe or an old countershaft. Remove the countergear assembly and bearings.
6 Using a long drift, drive the reverse idler shaft and woodruff key through the rear of the case.
7 Expand and remove the third and fourth-speed sliding clutch hub snap-ring from the mainshaft. Remove the clutch assembly, third gear blocker ring, and third-speed gear from the front of the mainshaft.
8 Press in the speedometer gear retaining clip and slide the gear off the mainshaft. Remove the rear bearing snap-ring from its groove in the mainshaft.
9 Support first gear on press plates. Press first gear, thrust washer, spring washer, rear bearing, and snap-ring from the rear of the mainshaft.

CHILTON CAUTION: *Center the gear, washers, bearings, and snap-ring when pressing the rear bearing.*

10 Expand and remove the first and second sliding clutch hub snap-ring from the mainshaft. Remove the clutch assembly, second-speed blocker ring, and second-speed gear from the rear of the mainshaft.

Thoroughly clean all parts and the transmission case. Inspect and replace all damaged or worn parts. When checking the bearings, do not spin them at high speeds. Clean and rotate the bearings by hand to detect roughness and unevenness. Spinning can damage balls and races.

Assembly

MAINSHAFT

Install the following parts with the front of the mainshaft facing up:

1 Install the third-speed gear with the clutching teeth up. The rear face of the gear will abut with the mainshaft flange.
2 Install a blocking ring, clutching teeth down, over the third-speed gear synchronizing surface.

NOTE: All four blocker rings are the same.

3 Press the third and fourth synchronizer assembly, fork slot down, onto the mainshaft splines until it bottoms.

CHILTON CAUTION: *The blocker ring notches must align with the synchronizer assembly keys.*

4 Install the synchronizer hub-to-mainshaft snap-ring. (Both synchronizer snap-rings are the same.)

Install the following parts with the rear of the mainshaft up.

5 The second-speed gear with the clutching teeth up. The front face of the gear will abut with the flange on the mainshaft.
6 A blocking ring, clutching teeth down, over the second-speed gear synchronizing surface.
7 Press the first and second synchronizer assembly, fork slot down, onto the mainshaft.

CHILTON CAUTION: *The blocker ring notches must align with the synchronizer assembly keys.*

8 The synchronizer hub-to-mainshaft snap-ring.
9 A blocker ring with the notches down so they align with the first/second synchronizer assembly keys.
10 First gear with the clutching teeth down. Install the first gear thrust washer and spring washer.
11 Press the rear ball bearing and snap-ring, slot down, onto the mainshaft. Install the snap-ring. Install the speedometer gear and clip.

TRANSMISSION

1 Using a dummy countergear shaft, load a row of roller bearings (27) and bearing thrust washers at each end of the countergear. Grease can be used to hold the bearings in place.
2 Position the countergear assembly into the case through the rear opening. Place a tanged thrust washer at each end of the countergear.
3 Install the countergear shaft and woodruff key from the rear of the case. The shaft engages both thrust washers and the tangs align with their notches in the case.
4 Install the reverse idler gear and shaft and the woodruff key. Install the extension-to-rear bearing snap-ring.
5 Install the 14 mainshaft pilot bearings into the clutch opening. Install the fourth-speed blocker ring onto the clutching surface of the clutch gear

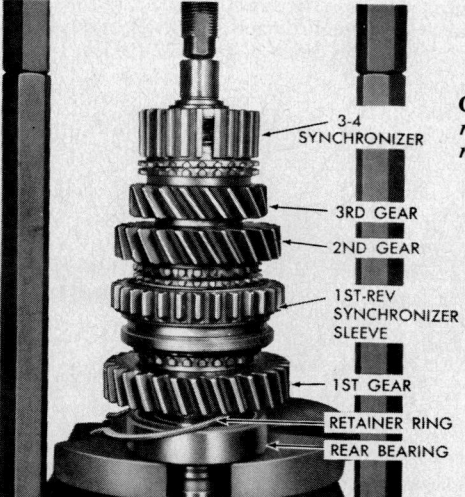

GM Saginaw 4–speed: pressing mainshaft components

- 3-4 SYNCHRONIZER
- 3RD GEAR
- 2ND GEAR
- 1ST-REV SYNCHRONIZER SLEEVE
- 1ST GEAR
- RETAINER RING
- REAR BEARING

GM Saginaw 4–speed: removing clutch gear & mainshaft

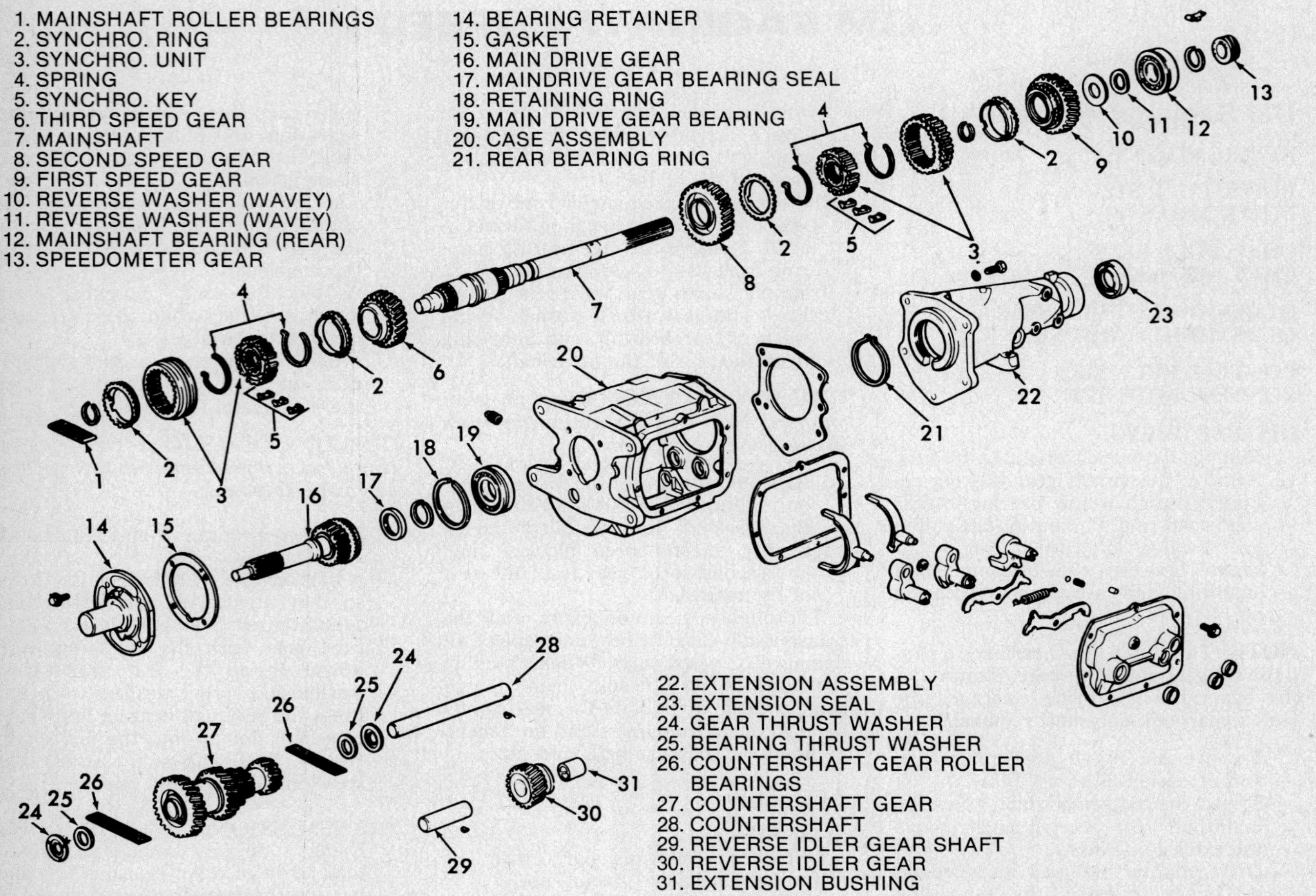

1. MAINSHAFT ROLLER BEARINGS
2. SYNCHRO. RING
3. SYNCHRO. UNIT
4. SPRING
5. SYNCHRO. KEY
6. THIRD SPEED GEAR
7. MAINSHAFT
8. SECOND SPEED GEAR
9. FIRST SPEED GEAR
10. REVERSE WASHER (WAVEY)
11. REVERSE WASHER (WAVEY)
12. MAINSHAFT BEARING (REAR)
13. SPEEDOMETER GEAR
14. BEARING RETAINER
15. GASKET
16. MAIN DRIVE GEAR
17. MAINDRIVE GEAR BEARING SEAL
18. RETAINING RING
19. MAIN DRIVE GEAR BEARING
20. CASE ASSEMBLY
21. REAR BEARING RING

22. EXTENSION ASSEMBLY
23. EXTENSION SEAL
24. GEAR THRUST WASHER
25. BEARING THRUST WASHER
26. COUNTERSHAFT GEAR ROLLER BEARINGS
27. COUNTERSHAFT GEAR
28. COUNTERSHAFT
29. REVERSE IDLER GEAR SHAFT
30. REVERSE IDLER GEAR
31. EXTENSION BUSHING

Saginaw 4 speed detail

(clutching teeth toward the gear.)

6 Assemble the clutch gear, pilot bearings, and fourth-speed blocker ring unit over the front of the mainshaft. Do not assemble the bearing to the gear at this point.

CHILTON CAUTION: *The blocker ring notches line up with third/fourth synchronizer assembly keys.*

7 Install the extension-to-case gasket and secure it with grease. Insert the clutch gear, mainshaft, and extension into the case as a unit. Install the extension-to-case bolts (apply sealer to the bottom bolt). Torque to 45 ft./lbs.

8 Install the outer snap-ring on the front bearing and place the bearing over the stem of the clutch gear and into the case bore.

9 Install the snap-ring to the clutch gear stem. Install the clutch gear bearing retainer and gasket to the case, with the retainer oil return hole at the bottom.

10 Place the synchronizer sleeves into neutral positions. Install the cover, gasket, and fork assemblies to the case. Be sure the forks align with their synchronizer sleeve grooves. Torque the cover bolts to 22 ft./lbs.

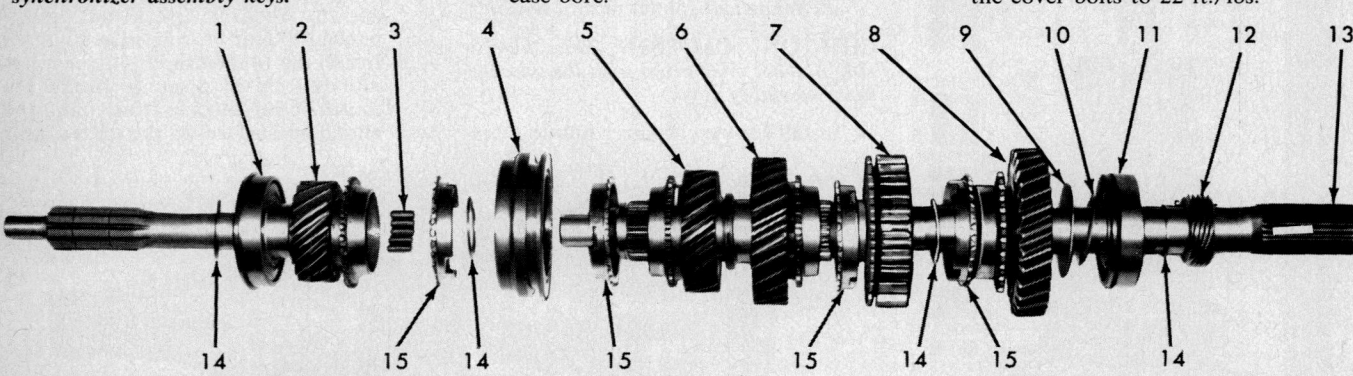

GM Saginaw 4–speed: clutch gear & mainshaft assembly

1 Drive Gear Bearing	4 3-4 Synchronizer Assembly	7 1-2 Synchronizer and Reverse Gear Assembly	10 Spring Washer	14 Snap Ring
2 Drive Gear	5 Third Speed Gear	8 First Speed Gear	11 Rear Bearing	15 Synchronizing "Blocker" Ring
3 Mainshaft Pilot Bearings	6 Second Speed Gear	9 Thrust Washer	12 Speedo Drive Gear	
			13 Mainshaft	

GM BORG-WARNER T 50 5 SPEED

Borg Warner T50 5-Speed

APPLICATION:
CHEVROLET-VEGA, MONZA:
PONTIAC-ASTRE, SUNBIRD,
VENTURA,
OLDSMOBILE-STARFIRE,
OMEGA,
CUTLASS-BUICK-SKYHAWK
NOTE: A wave washer has been added to one end of the cluster gear assembly to take up minor vibration that was apparent on early units in service. This wave washer may not be on some T50 gearboxes, especially those installed on non-air conditioned cars.

DISASSEMBLY

Drain the unit and remove it from the vehicle.

1 Remove selector lever pivot. Remove plug poppet spring and mesh lock plunger.
2 Drive spring pin from shifter head and shift rail.
3 Remove six bolts which retain transmission case and extension housing to center support.
4 Slide case forward from transmission.
5 Disassembly may be completed on a bench; however, a holding fixture will simplify the job by supporting the transmission.
6 Remove extension housing by sliding it rearward. Shifter head, shift rail and selector lever are not fastened to housing and should not be permitted to drop out and be damaged.

NOTE: Needle rollers are not always retained in needle race. Catch loose needles as they fall out during disassembly so that they can be replaced in mating race during assembly.

7 Remove reverse idler gear from idler shaft.
8 Press down on speedometer gear retainer tab and remove gear and retainer from output shaft.
9 Remove snap ring, thrust washer, first

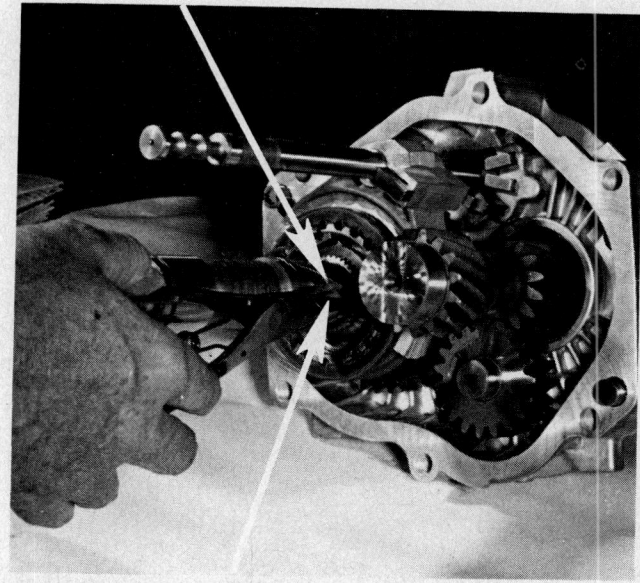

Borg Warner T50: removing the center support

speed gear, and blocking ring from output shaft.
10 Remove snap ring from behind synchronizer hub.
11 Move shift rail to locate pawl to permit removal of first and reverse shift link.
12 Slide first and reverse synchronizer, shift fork, and rail rearward from transmission.
13 Position interlock pawl in a position to permit second and third speed shift link and shift fork to be removed.
14 Position interlock pawl in a position to permit fourth and fifth shift fork and link to be removed.
15 Remove snap ring, thrust washer and slide reverse gear rearward from output shaft.
16 Remove center support from output shaft and cluster gear.
17 Remove needle thrust race and bearing from output shaft.

18 Remove cluster gear from remaining gears.
19 Remove output shaft from input shaft.
20 Remaining components may be removed one at a time from the output shaft.

ASSEMBLY

1 Assemble the 27 tooth third speed gear with coned end up over output shaft and against shaft shoulder.

NOTE: Synchronizer assemblies are similar except hub splines differ. Hub and sleeve are selective fit to obtain a free sliding fit with .002 inch maximum backlash. Keep mated parts together to insure correct sliding fit and backlash.

2 a. Assemble three shift plates in second and third synchronizer hub slots. (35 T. Hub.)
  b. Assemble sleeve over hub and shifter plates. The chamfer on one end of sleeve may be assembled to either end of hub.
  c. Hook an end of one synchronizer spring over one shift plate and wrap spring around inside of hub.
  d. Hook the other synchronizer spring over the other end of the shift plate first spring was hooked over and wrapped inside of hub in a direction opposite to the first spring.
  e. Eight to fifteen pounds force should be required to shift a new sleeve from detent position.
3 Assemble blocker rings with slots aligned with shift plates of synchronizer assembly.
4 Assembly synchronizer and blocker

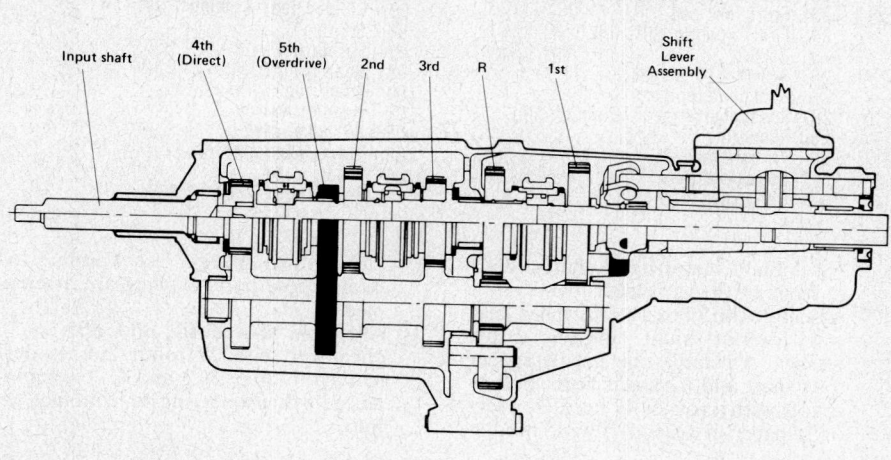

Input shaft | 4th (Direct) | 5th (Overdrive) | 2nd | 3rd | R | 1st | Shift Lever Assembly

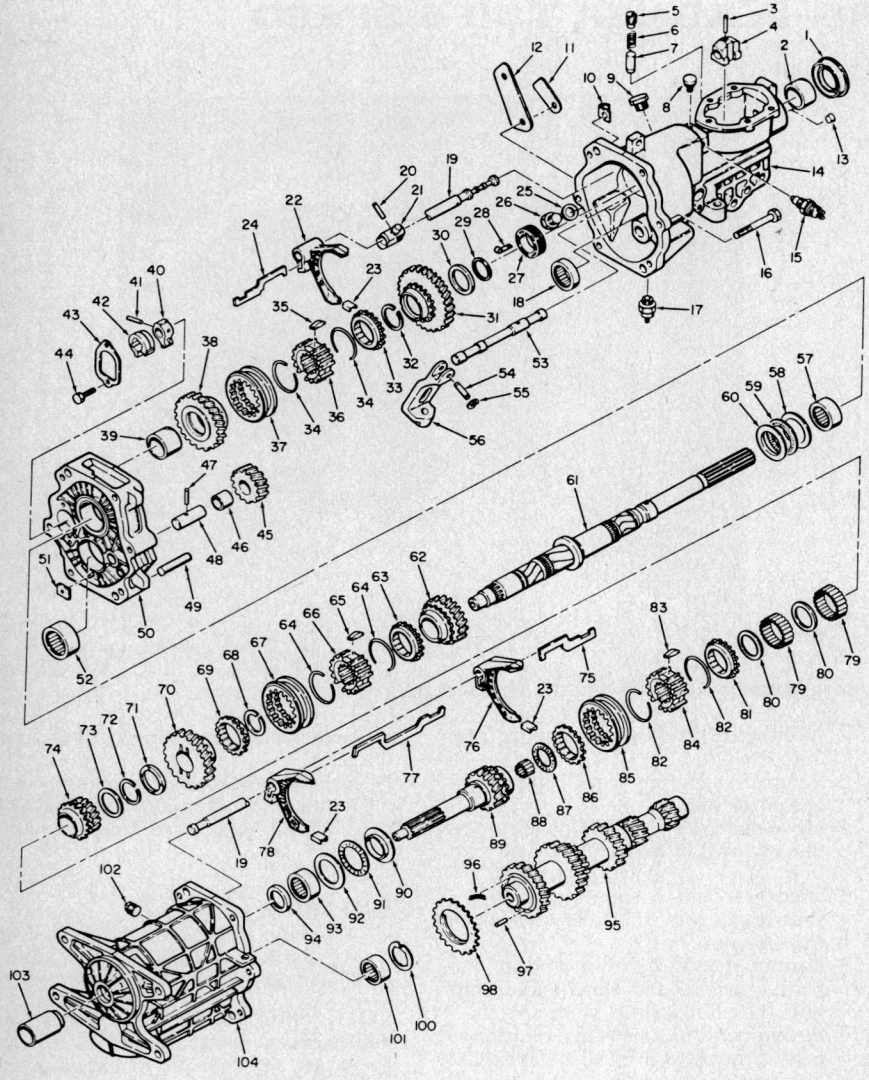

33	Blocking ring
34	Synchronizer spring
35	Shift plate
36	Clutch hub
37	Clutch sleeve
38	Reverse gear & bushing assy.
39	Bushing
40	Selector arm—optional
41	Spring pin
42	Interlock pawl
43	Selector arm retaining plate
44	¼"—20 X ¾" hex. HO, self tapping sch.
45	Reverse idler gear & bushing
46	Bushing
47	Spring pin
48	Reverse idler shaft
49	Dowel pin
50	Center support
51	Magnet
52	Needle bearing
53	Shift rail
54	Pin
55	Retaining clip
56	Selector lever
57	Needle bearing
58	Thrust washer
59	Needle thrust bearing
60	Needle thrust race
61	Output shaft
62	3rd speed gear
63	Blocking ring
64	Synchronizer spring
65	Synchronizer shift plate
66	Clutch hub
67	Clutch sleeve
68	Snap ring
69	Synchronizer blocking ring
70	2nd speed gear
71	Thrust washer
72	Snap ring
73	Spacer
74	5th speed gear
75	2nd & 3rd shift link
76	2nd & 3rd shift fork
77	4th & 5th shift link
78	4th & 5th shift fork
79	Needle rollers
80	Spacer
81	Synchronizer blocking ring
82	Synchronizer spring
83	Shift plate
84	Clutch hub
85	Clutch sleeve
86	Synchronizer blocking ring
87	Needle thrust bearing
88	Bearing rollers
89	Input drive gear
90	Needle thrust race
91	Needle thrust bearing
92	Thrust washer
93	Needle bearing
94	Oil seal
95	Cluster gear & damper assy.
96	Spring
97	Spring pin
98	Gear damper
100	Snap ring
101	Needle bearing
102	½" pipe plug
103	Trans. case sleeve
104	Trans. case
	Trans. case & sleeve assy.

Borg Warner T50 5-speed manual transmission

1	Oil seal	17	Switch
2	Bushing	18	Needle bearing
3	Pin	19	Shift rail
4	Shifter head	20	Spring pin
5	Threaded plug	21	Rail selector end
6	Poppet spring	22	First & reverse shift fork
7	Mesh lock plunger	23	Shift fork pad
8	Breather assy.	24	First reverse shift link
9	Selector lever pivot	25	Gasket
10	Wiring harness clip	26	3/16"—18 plug
11	Name plate	27	Speedometer gear
12	Back-up light bracket	28	Speedometer gear retaining clip
13	Cup plug	29	Snap ring
14	Extension housing with bushing	30	Thrust washer
15	Switch	31	1st speed gear
16	⅜"—16 X 3¼" hex HD bolt	32	Snap ring

rings over output shaft and position on face of third speed gear.

5 Assemble a snap ring in shaft groove ahead of synchronizer hub.

6 Assemble the 34 tooth second speed gear coned end into blocker ring.

7 Assemble a thrust washer on face of second speed gear.

8 Assemble a snap ring in shaft groove in front of thrust washer.

9 Assemble the 22 tooth fifth speed gear over output shaft against thrust washer. Assemble one needle spacer over shaft and into gear bore. Follow spacer with a row or 47 needles, a second spacer, a second row of needles and a third spacer. Use Vaseline to retain these parts as they are assembled.

10 Assemble the fourth and fifth synchronizer with 27 tooth hub as described in Steps 2, 3 and 4. Assemble a needle thrust bearing on front face of hub.

11 Assemble 19 needle rollers into second step of input shaft bore and carefully lower shaft with needles over end of output shaft. Vaseline or low melting point grease should hold needles in position.

12 Mesh cluster gear teeth with teeth of input shaft gear and gears assembled to output shaft as cluster gear. Input shaft and output shaft are positioned to assemble center support.

13 Assemble a needle thrust washer and thrust plate over output shaft against shaft shoulder.

14 Assemble interlock pawl into center support bore. Assemble retaining plate and two $\frac{1}{4} - 20 \times \frac{3}{4}$ hex head self tapping screws.

15 Assemble needle rollers into races in center support. Vaseline or low melting point grease should be used to retain needles during assembly.

NOTE: Some needles are locked in cage and others are not.

16 Assemble center support over output shaft and cluster gear.

17 Assemble the 35 tooth reverse gear and bushing assembly over output shaft and rest on center support.

18 Assemble the 19 tooth reverse idler gear and bushing over reverse idler shaft.

19 Replace worn or damaged shift pads on all shift forks if necessary.

20 Assemble fourth and fifth link into shift fork. Locate interlock pawl to permit shift link to be assembled through right hand slot of center support when transmission is viewed from the rear. Engage shift fork in synchronizer collar.

21 Locate interlock pawl in a position to permit second and third speed shift link to be assembled in the middle slot with shift fork assembled to link and engaged with second and third shift collar.

22 Locate interlock pawl to permit assembling first and reverse shift link in left slot of center support.

23 Assemble first and reverse synchronizer assembly as described in Step 3.

24 Assemble reverse shift link into shift fork.

25 Assemble selector arm over shift rail to a position aligned with the drilled hole near middle of rail. Drive spring pin into arm and rail to retain these parts.

26 Assemble shift rail through shift fork from front to rear with pocket notches located to rear of transmission.

27 Engage shift fork with first and reverse synchronizer sleeve and assemble these parts by sliding synchronizer hub over output shaft as shift rail is assembled through interlock pawl, second and third shift fork and fourth and fifth shift fork.

28 Assemble a blocking ring and the 38 tooth first speed gear over output shaft behind first and reverse synchronizer assembly.

29 Assemble a thrust washer and snap ring over output shaft behind first speed gear.

30 Engage speedometer gear retainer in hole provided in output shaft with retainer looped forward, slide speedometer gear over output shaft and in a position over retainer until retainer end snaps up to lock gear in position.

31 Slide rail selector end with hole located to rear of transmission over end of shift rail. Drive a spring pin into selector and rail to retain these parts.

32 Assemble selector lever to shorter shift rail. Use a pin and two retainer clips to hold these parts together.

33 Press a new oil seal into extension housing.

34 Assemble loose needles in extension housing race, use vaseline or low melting point grease to retain needles.

35 Assemble selector lever and shift rail into hole provided in extension housing. Assemble shifter head onto rail as rail becomes exposed in housing opening. Do not drive spring pin in at this time.

36 Replace oil seal and needle rollers in transmission case.

37 Apply a continuous 1/32 inch bead of Silastic RTV 732 sealer or an approved equivalent to the transmission case and extension housing faces.

38 Extend rail selector end into extension housing to engage rail selector end as extension housing is assembled over output shaft and brought into contact with center support rear face.

39 Assemble lipped thrust race, needle thrust washer and flat thrust race over input shaft, fig. 8. Assemble case to front side of center support. Assemble six $\frac{3}{8} - 16 \times 3\frac{1}{4}$ hex head bolts to retain extension housing and transmission case to center support. Shows seal protection which should be used.

40 Drive spring pin into shifter head and shift rail.

41 Assemble transmission mesh lock plunger, poppet spring and threaded plug.

42 Assemble selector lever pivot, with Loctite #92 applied to threads, into extension housing.

43 Assemble switches into extension housing.

The fluid capacity of the T50 unit is 55 fl. ozs. Use Dexron automatic transmission fluid.

CLUTCH TROUBLE DIAGNOSIS

CLUTCH NOISY WITH ENGINE STOPPED	Pressure plate lugs rubbing against cover. Clutch linkage improperly adjusted or inadequately lubricated.	Clutch assist spring clunking. Release bearing hub burred and dragging on transmission bearing retainer.
CLUTCH NOISY WHEN PEDAL FREE TRAVEL IS TAKEN OUT, ENGINE RUNNING	Release bearing failure due to: Improper travel adjustment. Bearing cocked on hub.	Release lever out of plane. Flywheel housing misalignment. Excessive crankshaft end play.
CLUTCH NOISY WHEN PEDAL IS THREE-QUARTERS TO FULLY DEPRESSED, ENGINE RUNNING	Pressure plate lugs rubbing against window openings in cover.	Release bearing failure. Loose and worn pilot bearing.
CLUTCH SLIPS OR CHATTERS	Incorrect pedal free travel. Grease or oil on clutch facings from: Release bearing.	Release lever. Pilot bearing. Transmission. Pressure plate fingers binding.
CLUTCH VIBRATION	Improper or defective clutch disc. Release bearing out of plane.	Flywheel housing misalignment. Pressure plate fingers binding.
THUD	Excessive engine crankshaft end play.	
GEAR CLASH OR POOR RELEASE	Incorrect pedal free travel. Disc binding on transmission input shaft.	Excessive disc runout. Flywheel housing misalignment. Excessive engine idle speed.
CLUTCH PEDAL SCRUBBING	Release lever cocked. Pedal push rod rubbing on firewall felt and insulator. Release lever pivot knife edge rough. Pedal shaft binding at support bracket.	Pressure plate finger rubbing internally. Burrs on clutch pedal or clutch assist spring retainer. Release bearing hub scrubbing on input shaft bearing retainer.
EXCESSIVE PRESSURE REQUIRED TO DEPRESS CLUTCH PEDAL	Incorrect assist spring over-center adjustment gap. Pedal shaft binding in bushings.	Assist spring not positioned properly.
PEDAL NOT RETURNING TO STOP	Incorrect assist spring over-center adjustment gap.	Assist spring not positioned properly. Clutch Disc Worn.
CLUTCH SQUEAKY	Insufficient lubricant on assist spring seats.	

ENGINE CLUTCH

ENGINE CLUTCH

Clutch Removal

1 Disconnect the drive shaft from the rear U-joint flange. Then slide the drive shaft off the transmission output shaft. Insert the appropriate tool over the output shaft and into the extension housing oil seal.
2 Disconnect the speedometer cable from the extension housing.
3 Disconnect Transmission Shift Levers.
4 Disconnect the first and reverse gear shift rod from the transmission first and reverse lever. Disconnect the second and third speed shift lever from the transmission and the bracket from the frame. If equipped with an overdrive transmission, disconnect the interlock rod from the overdrive.
5 If the car is equipped with overdrive, disconnect the solenoid and governor wires at their connectors, disconnect the overdrive control cable, and then remove the wiring harness and the solenoid from the transmission.
6 Disconnect the parking brake cable, and support the rear of the engine with a transmission jack.
7 Remove the bolts that attach the extension housing to the engine rear support.

8 Remove the bolts that attach the transmission to the flywheel housing.
9 Move the transmission rearward until the input shaft clears the flywheel housing, then remove it from the car.
10 If removing a clutch from a car with an aluminum flywheel housing, re-

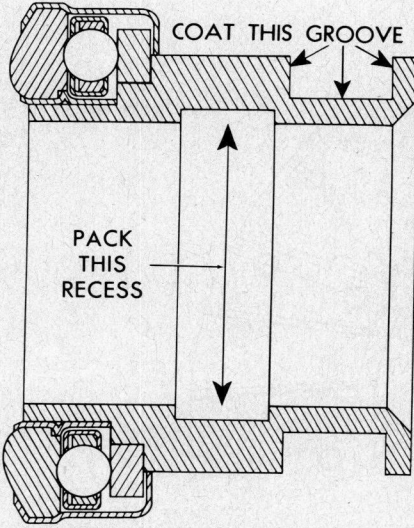

Lubrication points, clutch throwout bearing

move the starter. Remove the bolts that attach the housing to the cylinder block.
11 Remove the complete housing.
12 If the clutch housing is cast iron, Remove the flywheel housing cover (cast iron housings only).
13 Remove the release lever return spring. Then slide the release bearing and hub off the release lever. This applies only to cast iron flywheel housings.
14 Loosen the pressure plate cover attaching bolts evenly to release the spring tension.
15 Remove the pressure plate and the clutch disc from the flywheel. Lower, as a unit, through the opening.

Inspection and Repair

The following procedures apply to all clutch components with exceptions as indicated.

Clutch Release Mechanism

1 Check release fork and ball stud for wear, distortion, cracks or other damage.
2 Check release bearing for roughness or noise by rotating bearing race while

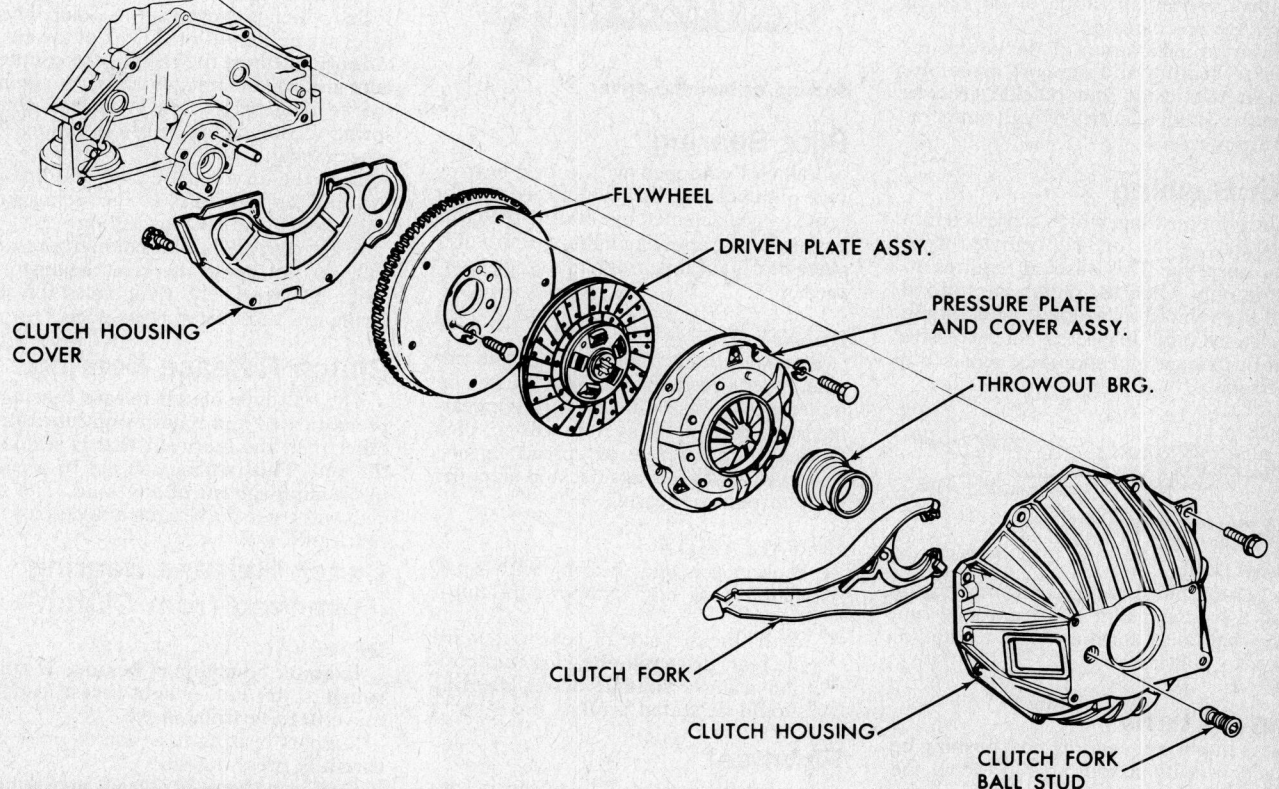

Typical clutch components, aluminum housing

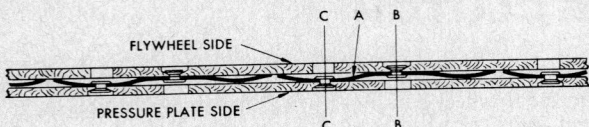

FLYWHEEL SIDE

PRESSURE PLATE SIDE

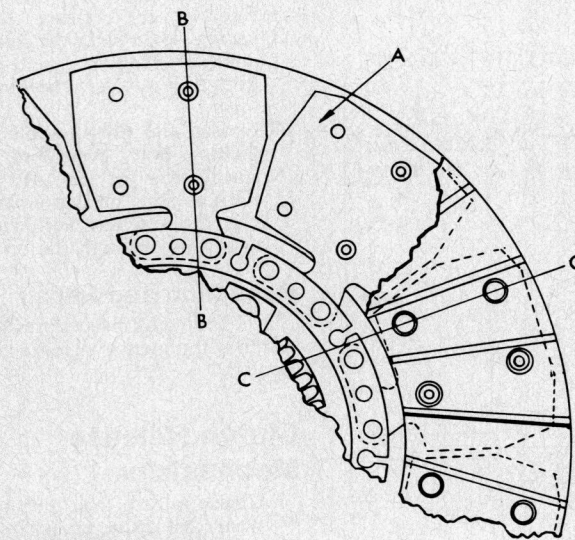

Clutch driven plate

applying light pressure.

3 Replace all components that would affect proper operation of the clutch release mechanism.

4 Prior to installation of the clutch release bearing and support assembly, coat the inside and outside grooves with a small quantity of high temperature grease.

Pilot Bushing

The pilot bushing, which is pressed into crankshaft is an oil impregnated type bronze bearing. This bushing requires attention only when the clutch is removed from the vehicle, at which time it should be cleaned and inspected for excessive wear or damage and should be replaced if necessary.

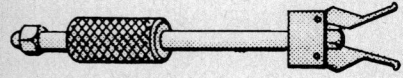

Bearing/bushing puller

REMOVAL

To remove bushing type pilot bearing, install a special puller or a universal type slide hammer knocker with expanding jaws, to pull bushing.

INSTALLATION

It is important that the new bushing be driven in with a tool that protects the bushing during installation. Special driving tools are available.

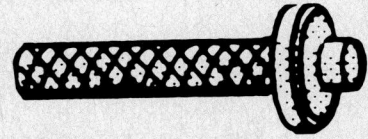

Bearing or bushing driver

Pilot Bearing

Vehicles equipped with a ball bearing type pilot bearing, flywheel. Roughness or noise can be detected by rotating the bearing race while applying light pressure. Replace bearing if it is rough, noisy, or damaged.

REMOVAL

Remove clutch pilot bearing from engine, using slide hammer. With fingers on puller closed, insert fingers through bearing inner race as far as they will go, then tighten thumb screw to spread fingers. Slide weight sharply against stop on puller shaft to remove bearing.

INSTALLATION

1 Pack clutch pilot bearing with small quantity of high temperature lubricant.

2 With shielded side of bearing toward the rear, drive pilot bearing into position using a suitable driver. Bearing should be seated firmly.

Flywheel

Inspect flywheel surface which is contacted by the clutch facing. This surface must be smooth and should not be grooved or show deep heat checks. Replace flywheel if the above conditions are evident.

Driven Disc

Inspect driven disc assembly for worn, loose, and grease or oil-soaked facings. Check for broken springs, loose rivets, or cracks in the driven disc hub. Examine splines in hub for wear and make sure they slide freely on splines of the main drive gear. If any wear or damage is evident, replace with a new driven disc assembly.

If hub and springs are in good condition, but facings are worn or grease or oil-soaked, replace facings.

Driven Plate

RECONDITIONING

No reconditioning of the driven plate other than replacing the friction facings is recommended. Facing replacement requires extreme care and use of proper tools and riveting equipment.

To remove the old facings, drill out the rivets.

CHILTON CAUTION: *Do not punch the rivets out as this will result in damage and distortion to the driven plate.*

To install the friction facing, place the facing on the flywheel side of the driven plate and line up the countersunk holes with the rivet holes in the cushion.

Assemble the facing on the cushion spring which is convex at this point. These holes are in line with the neck of the cushion spring. Insert the rivet in the counterbore and *roll do not split* the rivet against the cushion spring. Rivet each cushion spring to this facing before installing the other facing.

Turn the driven plate over and line up the countersunk holes of the facing with the holes in the cushion spring.

Insert a rivet in the counterbore and roll, do not split, the rivet against the cushion spring. The rivet holes for this facing are those nearer the edge

Clutch Release Bearing

The ball-type clutch release bearing is prelubricated and requires no lubrication other than the lubricant that is sealed in the unit. This bearing can not be washed in cleaning solvent of any kind. The solvent will enter the bearing and destroy the lubricant.

Clutch Release Bearing (Removed from Clutch)

REMOVAL

Examine condition of bearing. If noisy, rough or dry, under light thrust load, remove bearing from sleeve.

Support bearing in a vise or press and carefully press out sleeve.

(3) Clean sleeve in solvent and remove all old lubricant.

INSTALLATION

CHILTON CAUTION: *Exercise care when installing a new clutch release bearing to avoid damaging the bearing race. Never drive the bearing on the sleeve with a hammer. Use either of the following two methods.*

VISE METHOD

1 Position new bearing on sleeve and place old bearing against face of new bearing.
2 Support parts in a vise and carefully press new bearing on sleeve. **Make certain bearing is seated on shoulder of bearing sleeve. Rotate bearings as they are pressed together.**

PRESS METHOD

1 Support sleeve on press bed.
2 Position new bearing on sleeve and place old bearing on new one.
3 Bring press ram into contact with old bearing and apply sufficient pressure to **seat new bearing on shoulder of sleeve. Rotate bearings as they are pressed together.**

Clutch

INSTALLATION

1 Install the clutch release lever if it was removed.
2 Place the clutch disc, and pressure plate assembly in position on the flywheel. Start the cover attaching bolts to hold the pieces in place but do not tighten them. **Avoid dropping the parts or contaminating them with oil or grease.**
3 Align the clutch disc with the alignment tool and torque the pressure plate cover attaching bolts evenly to specification. Then remove the tool.
4 Apply a light film of grease to the outside diameter of the transmission front bearing retainer. Apply a light film of the same type of grease to both sides of the release lever fork where it contacts the release bearing hub and spring clips. Apply a light film of grease to the release bearing surface that contacts the pressure plate release fingers. Care must be exercised to avoid excessive grease from contaminating the clutch disc. Place the release bearing and hub on the release lever.
5 If working on an engine with an aluminum flywheel housing, make sure that the mounting surfaces are clean. Position the felt washer and bushing on the pivot in the flywheel housing. Slip the pivot into the clutch equalizer shaft being careful not to disturb the linkage or trip the assist spring and at the same time position the housing on the dowels in the cylinder block. Install and torque the attaching bolts to specification.
6 Install the starting motor if working on a car with an aluminum flywheel housing.
7 The mounting surfaces of the trans-

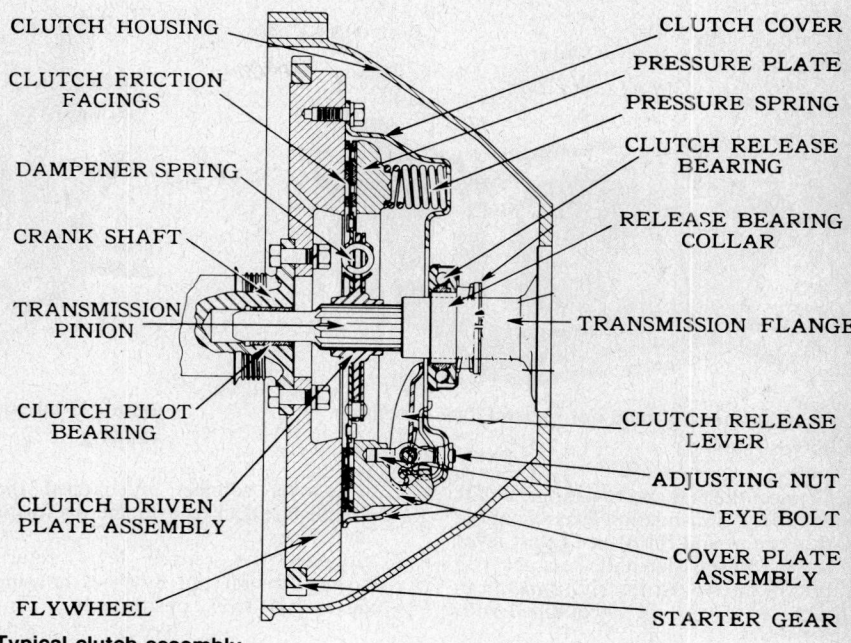
Typical clutch assembly

CLUTCH HOUSING
CLUTCH FRICTION FACINGS
DAMPENER SPRING
CRANK SHAFT
TRANSMISSION PINION
CLUTCH PILOT BEARING
CLUTCH DRIVEN PLATE ASSEMBLY
FLYWHEEL

CLUTCH COVER
PRESSURE PLATE
PRESSURE SPRING
CLUTCH RELEASE BEARING
RELEASE BEARING COLLAR
TRANSMISSION FLANGE
CLUTCH RELEASE LEVER
ADJUSTING NUT
EYE BOLT
COVER PLATE ASSEMBLY
STARTER GEAR

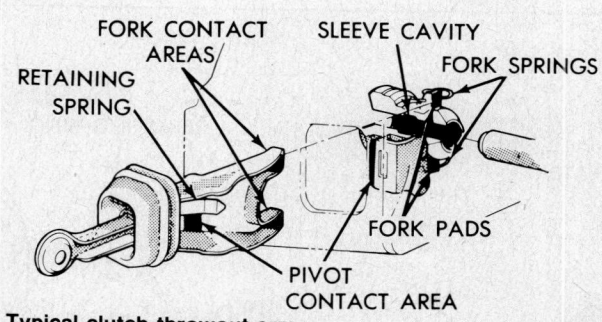
Typical clutch throwout arm

FORK CONTACT AREAS
SLEEVE CAVITY
FORK SPRINGS
RETAINING SPRING
FORK PADS
PIVOT CONTACT AREA

Installing clutch release bearing on sleeve

OLD BEARING
RELEASE BEARING SLEEVE
NEW BEARING
NR134

mission and the flywheel housing must be free of dirt, paint, and burrs. Install two guide pins in the flywheel housing lower mounting bolt holes. Move the transmission forward on the guide pins until it is tightly positioned against the flywheel housing.
8 Install the two upper mounting bolts. Then remove the guide pins and install the two lower mounting bolts. Torque all bolts to specification.

9 Install the bolts that attach the extension housing to the engine rear support.
10 Remove the transmission jack and connect the parking brake cable.
11 If the car is equipped with overdrive, install the solenoid and the wiring harness on the transmission, connect the overdrive control cable, and connect the solenoid and governor wires at their connectors.

ENGINE CLUTCH

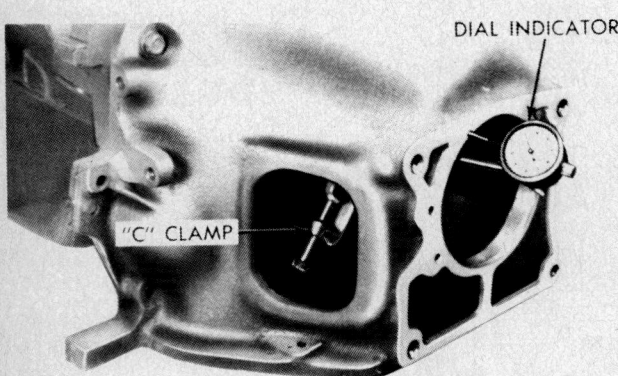

Face squareness should not exceed .006 maximum indicator reading

Bore runout should not exceed .008 inch maximum indicator reading

12 Connect the first and reverse gear shift rod to the transmission lever. Connect the second and third-speed shift lever to the transmission and the bracket to the frame. Adjust the shift linkage as required. If the car is equipped with overdrive, connect and adjust the clutch interlock rod to the overdrive shift lever.

13 Connect the release lever return spring. Install the flywheel housing cover (cast iron housing only).

14 Remove the tool from the transmission output shaft, and install the drive shaft.

15 Check the clutch pedal free travel and the assist spring control gap and adjust as required.

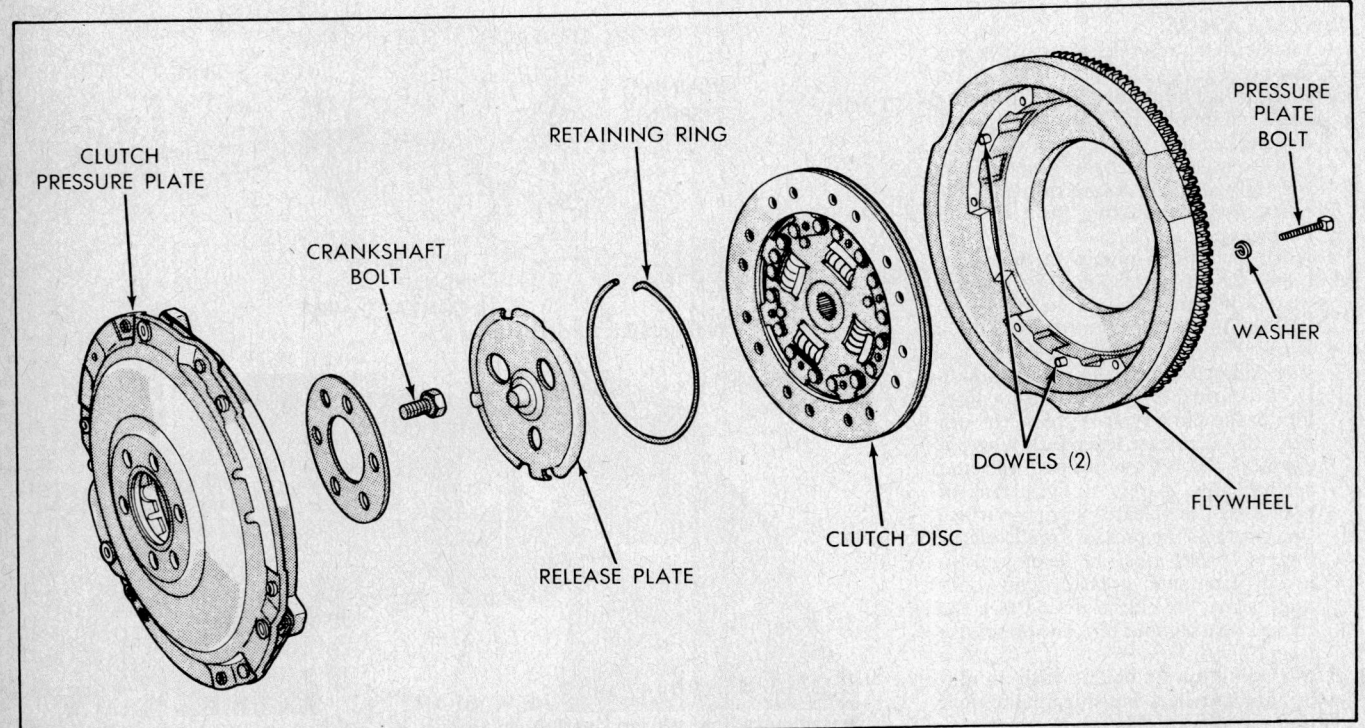

Dodge Omni and Plymouth Horizon

AUTOMATIC TRANSMISSIONS

INDEX

AUTOMATIC TRANSMISSIONS

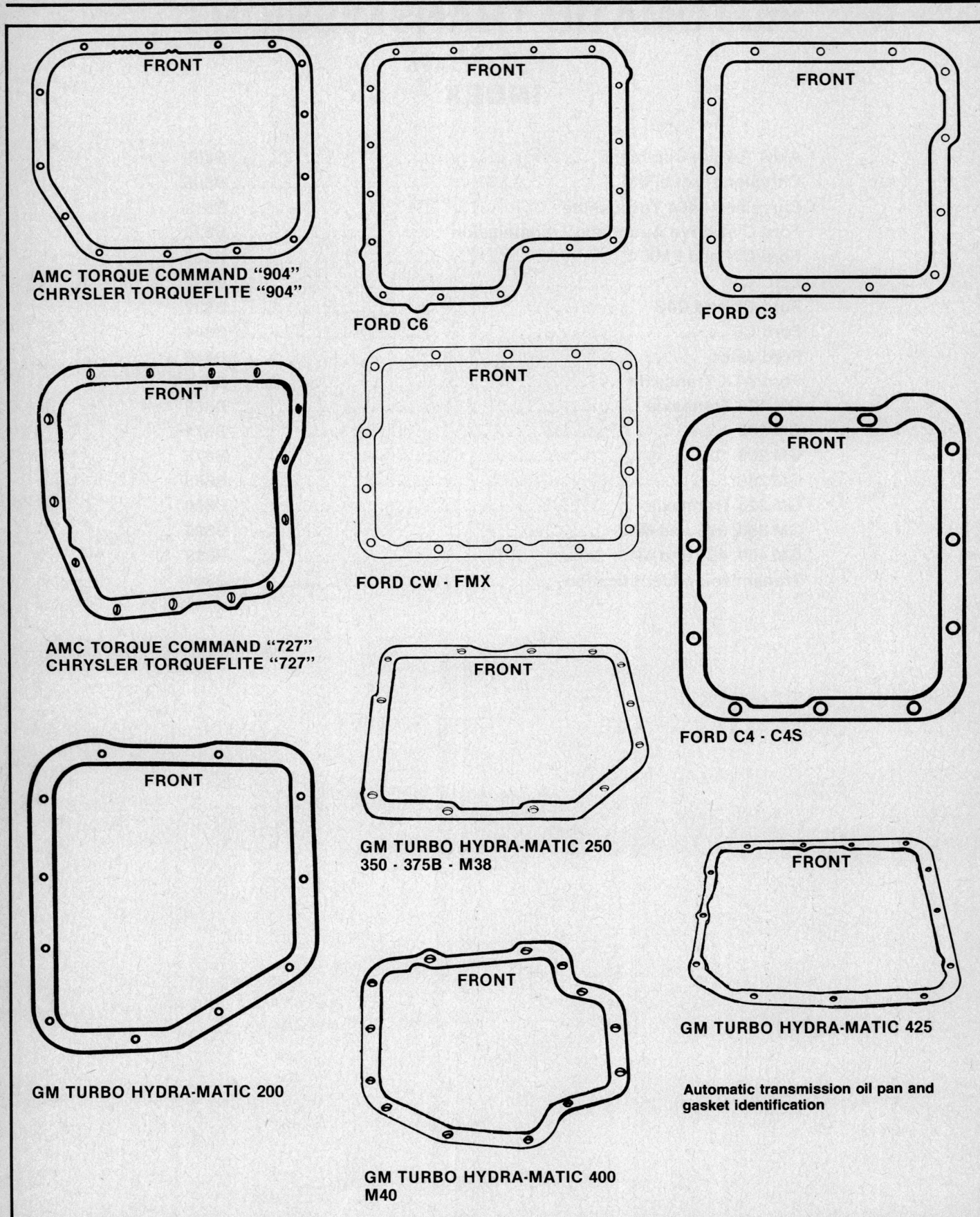

FRONT
AMC TORQUE COMMAND "904"
CHRYSLER TORQUEFLITE "904"

FRONT
FORD C6

FRONT
FORD C3

FRONT
AMC TORQUE COMMAND "727"
CHRYSLER TORQUEFLITE "727"

FRONT
FORD CW · FMX

FRONT
FORD C4 · C4S

FRONT
GM TURBO HYDRA-MATIC 200

FRONT
GM TURBO HYDRA-MATIC 250
350 · 375B · M38

FRONT
GM TURBO HYDRA-MATIC 425

FRONT
GM TURBO HYDRA-MATIC 400
M40

**Automatic transmission oil pan and
gasket identification**

AMC TORQUE COMMAND AND CHRYSLER TORQUEFLITE

Identification

The transmission identification pad is located on the left side of the transmission oil pan flange. The chart below relates the part number shown on this pad to the engine and vehicle application.

In-Car Testing Procedures

AIR PRESSURE TESTS

The front clutch, rear clutch, kickdown servo and low and reverse servo may be checked with air pressure, after the valve body assembly has been removed.

To make air pressure tests, proceed as follows.

CHILTON CAUTION Compressed air must be free of dirt and moisture. Use pressure of 30–100 psi.

FRONT CLUTCH

Apply air pressure to the front clutch apply passage and listen for a dull thud. This will indicate operation of the front clutch. Hold the air pressure at this point for a few seconds and check for excessive oil leaks.

NOTE If a dull thud cannot be heard in the clutch, place finger tips on clutch housing and again apply air pressure. Movement of piston can be felt as clutch is applied.

REAR CLUTCH

Apply air pressure to the rear clutch apply passage. Proceed in an identical manner as that described in the "Front Clutch" procedure.

KICKDOWN SERVO

Air pressure applied to the kickdown servo apply passage should tighten the front band. Spring tension should be sufficient to release the band.

LOW AND REVERSE SERVO

Direct air pressure into the low and reverse servo apply

passage. Response of the servo will result in a tightening of the rear band. Spring tension should be enough to release the band.

If clutches and servos operate properly, no upshift or erratic shift conditions existing, trouble exists in the control valve body assembly.

GOVERNOR

Governor troubles can usually be found during a road or pressure test.

HYDRAULIC CONTROL PRESSURE CHECKS

LINE PRESSURE AND FRONT SERVO RELEASE PRESSURE

NOTE These pressure checks must be made in the Drive position with the rear wheels free to turn. The transmission fluid must be at operating temperature (150°–200°F).

1. Install an engine tachometer. Then, raise the car on a hoist and locate the tachometer so it can be read from under the car.
2. Connect two 0–100 psi pressure gauges to pressure takeoff points at the side of the accumulator and at the front servo release.

Transmission Case Channels

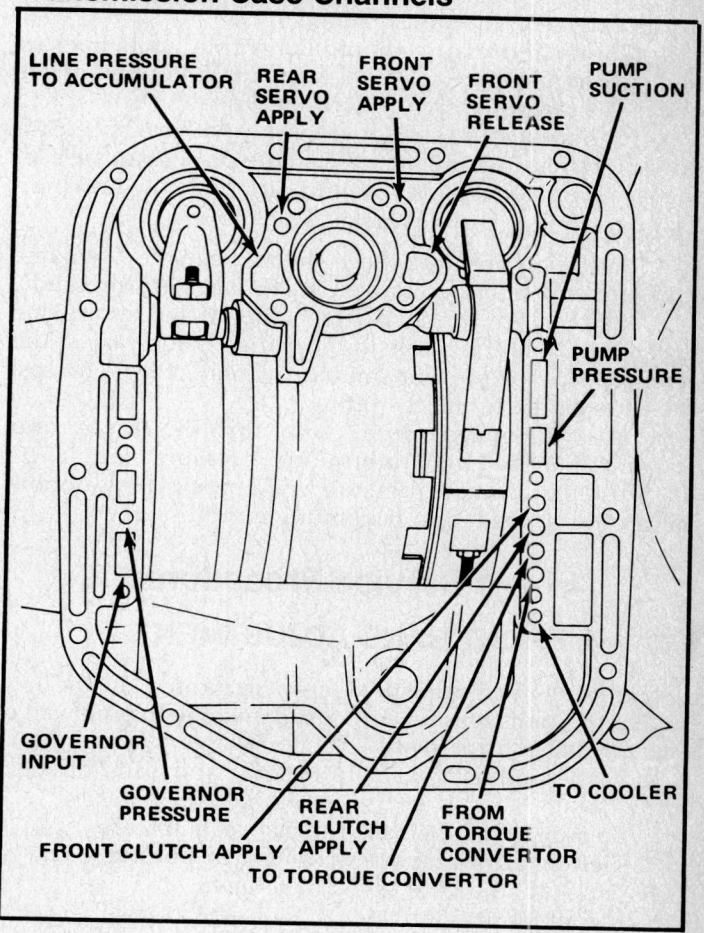

Pressure Test Locations

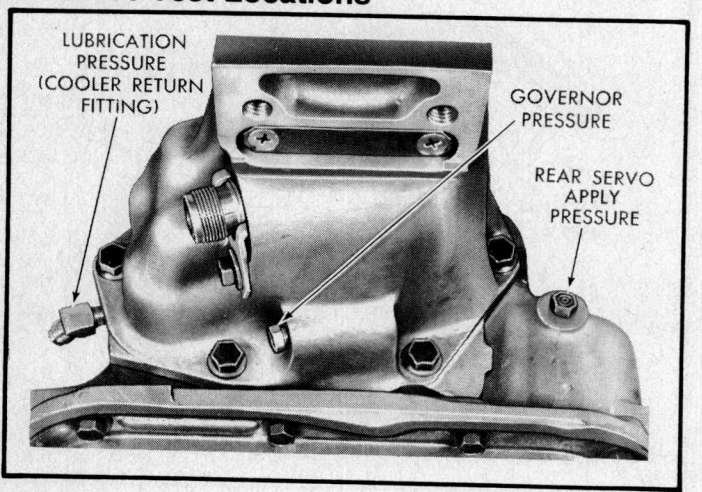

3. With the selector in Drive position, increase engine speed gradually until the transmission shifts into High. Reduce engine speed slowly to 1000 rpm. The line pressure must be 54–60 psi, with front servo release having no more than a 3 psi drop.

4. Disconnect throttle linkage from transmission throttle lever and move throttle lever gradually to full throttle position. Line pressure must rise to a maximum of 90–96 psi just before or at kickdown into low gear. Front servo release pressure must follow line pressure up to kickdown point and should not be more than 3 psi below line pressure. If pressure is not 54–60 psi at 1000 rpm, adjust line pressure.

5. If line prssure is not as above, adjust the pressure as outlined in "Hydraulic Control Pressure Adjustments—Line Pressure." If front servo release pressures are less than specified and line pressures are within limits, there is excessive leakage in the front clutch and/or front servo circuits.

REAR SERVO APPLY PRESSURE

1. Connect a 0–300 psi pressure gauge, to the apply pressure take-off point at the rear servo.

2. With the control in the Reverse position and the engine running at 1600 rpm, the reverse servo apply pressure should be 230–300 psi.

GOVERNOR PRESSURE

1. Connect a 0–100 psi gauge to the governor pressure take-off point. This location is at the lower left rear corner of the extension mounting flange.

2. Governor pressure should fall within limits in chart and should return to 0–1½ psi when car is stopped. If it is above this, transmission will not downshift.

3. Pressure should change smoothly with car speeds. If governor pressures are incorrect at the prescribed speeds, the governor valve and/or weights are probably sticking.

LUBRICATION PRESSURES

A lubrication pressure check should be made when line pressure and front servo release pressures are checked.

1. Install a tee fitting between the cooler return line fitting and the fitting hole in the transmission case at the rear left side of the transmission. Connect a 0–100 psi pressure gauge to the tee fitting.

2. At 1000 engine rpm, with throttle closed and transmission in High, lubrication pressure should be 5–15 psi. Lubrication pressure will aproximately double as throttle is opened to maximum line pressure.

In-Car Service Procedures

FRONT BAND ADJUSTMENT

The front band adjusting screw is located on the left side of the transmission case just above the manual valve and throttle control levers.

1. Loosen adjusting screw locknut and back off five turns.

2. Be sure adjusting screw turns freely in case.

3. Tighten adjusting screw to 72 inch-pounds

4. Back off adjusting screw as follows.

a. Model 904–two turns

Front Band and Linkage

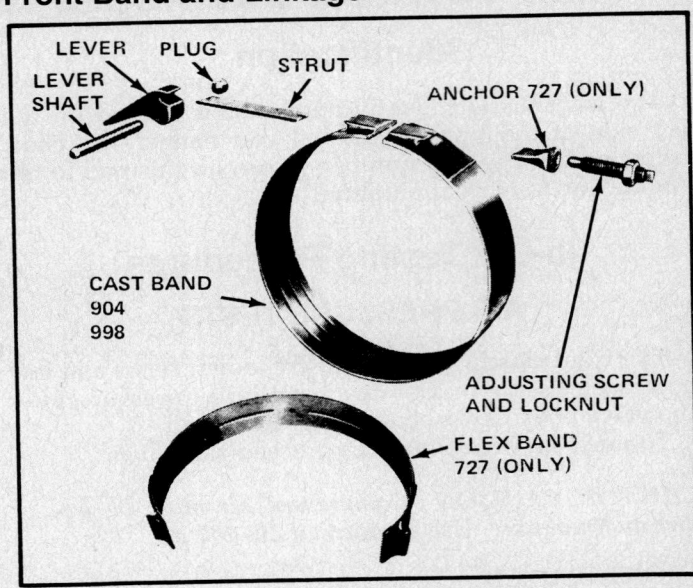

b. Models 998 and 727–two and one-half turns

5. Hold adjusting screw in position and tighten locknut to 35 foot-pounds.

REAR BAND ADJUSTMENT

1. Remove adjusting screw locknut.

2. Tighten adjusting screw to 41 inch-pounds

3. Back off adjusting screw seven turns.

4. Hold adjusting screw in position and install nut.

5. Tighten locknut to 35 foot-pounds torque.

On models 998–727, adjust band as follows.

1. Loosen locknut and back off locknut five turns.

2. Tighten adjusting screw to 72 inch-pounds torque.

3. Back off adjusting screw as follows.

a. Model 998–four turns

Rear Band and Linkage

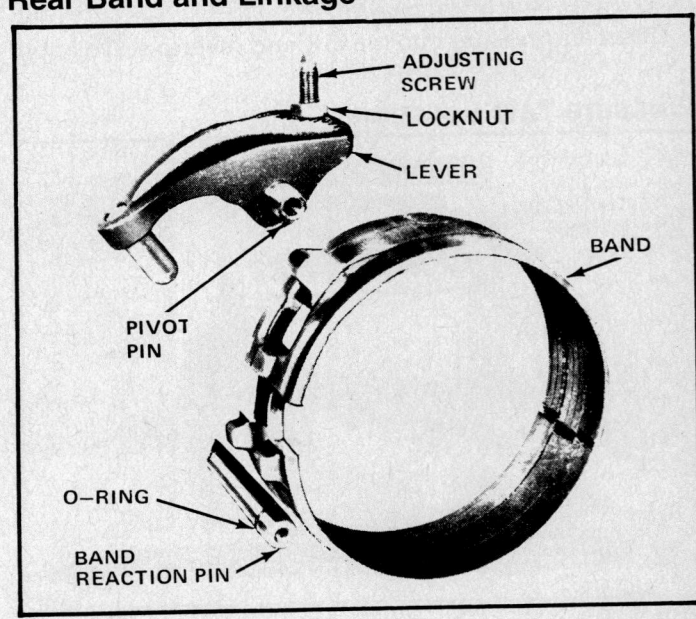

b. Model 727–two turns
4. Hold adjusting screw in position and tighten lock-nut to 35 foot-pounds torque.

FLUID LEAKS

Some leaks that can normally be corrected without transmission removal are as follows:
1. Transmission output shaft oil seal
2. Extension housing gasket
3. Speedometer pinion seal and cable seal
4. Oil filler tube seal
5. Oil pan gasket and drain plug
6. Gearshift control cable seal
7. Throttle shaft seal
8. Neutral starting switch seal
9. Oil cooler line fittings and pressure take-off plugs
Oil found inside the converter housing should be positively identified as transmission oil before diagnosing the need for any major transmission work.

HYDRAULIC CONTROL PRESSURE ADJUSTMENTS

LINE PRESSURE

An incorrect throttle pressure setting will cause incorrect line pressure even though the line pressure adjustment is correct. Always inspect and correct the throttle pressure adjustment before adjusting line pressure.

Line Pressure Adjustment

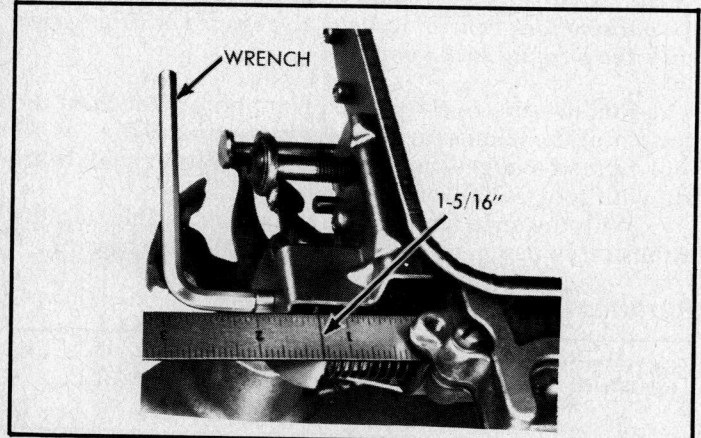

NOTE *Before adjusting line pressure, measure the distance between the manual valve (valve in 1-low position) and line pressure adjusting screw. This measurement must be 1⅞ in. Correct by loosening spring retainer screws and repositioning spring retainer. The regulator valve may cock and hang up in its bore if the spring retainer is out of position.*

If line pressure is not correct, remove the valve body assembly to adjust. The correct adjustment is 1⁵/₁₆ in., measured from the valve body to the inner edge of the adjusting nut. Vary adjustment slightly to obtain specified line pressure.

Throttle Pressure Adjustment

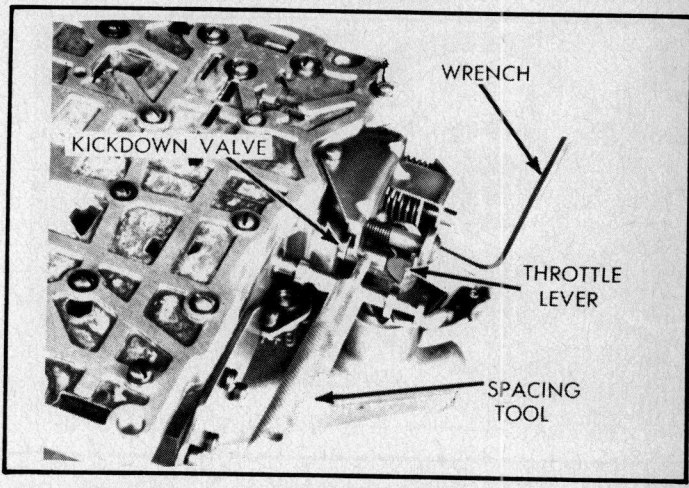

One complete turn of the adjusting screw (Allen head) changes closed throttle line pressure about 1.66 psi. Turning the screw counter–clockwise increases pressure, clockwise decreases pressure.

THROTTLE PRESSURE

Since throttle pressures cannot be checked, exact adjustments should be checked and made correct whenever the valve body is disturbed.
1. Remove the valve body assembly as outlined in the "Valve Body Assembly and Accumulator Piston, R & R" procedure.
2. Loosen the throttle lever stop screw locknut and back off the screw about five turns.
3. Insert the gauge pin between the throttle lever cam and the kickdown valve.
4. Push on the tool and compress the kickdown valve against its spring, so that the throttle valve is completely bottomed inside the valve body.
5. As the spring is being compressed, finger tighten the throttle lever stop screw against the throttle lever tang, with the lever cam touching the tool and the throttle valve bottomed. (Be sure the adjustment is made with the spring fully compressed and the valve bottomed in the valve body.)
6. Remove the tool and secure the stop screw locknut.

SPEEDOMETER PINION R&R

Rear axle gear ratio and tire size determine pinion gear size.
1. Remove the bolt and retainer securing the speedometer pinion adapter in extension housing.
2. With cable housing connected, carefully work the adapter and pinion out of the extension housing.
3. If transmission fluid is found in the cable housing, replace the seal in the adapter. Start seal and retainer ring in adapter, then push them into adapter until tool bottoms.

CHILTON CAUTION *Before installing pinion and adapter assembly make sure the adapter flange and mating area on the extension housing are perfectly clean. Dirt or sand will cause misalignment and speedometer pinion gear noise.*

Speedometer Pinion and Adapter

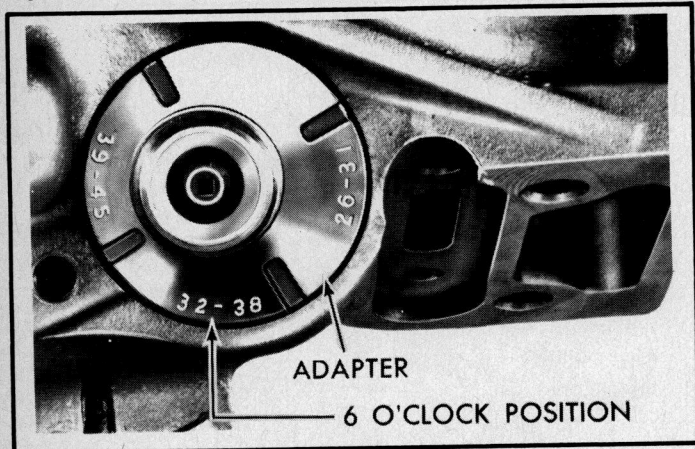

ADAPTER

6 O'CLOCK POSITION

4. Note number of gear teeth and install pinion gear into adapter.

5. Rotate pinion gear and adapter assembly so that the number on the adapter corresponding to the number of teeth on the gear is in the six o'clock position as the assembly is installed.

6. Install the retainer and bolt with retainer tangs in adapter positioning slots. Tap the adapter firmly into the extension housing and tighten the retainer bolt to 100 in. lbs.

Speedometer Drive Components

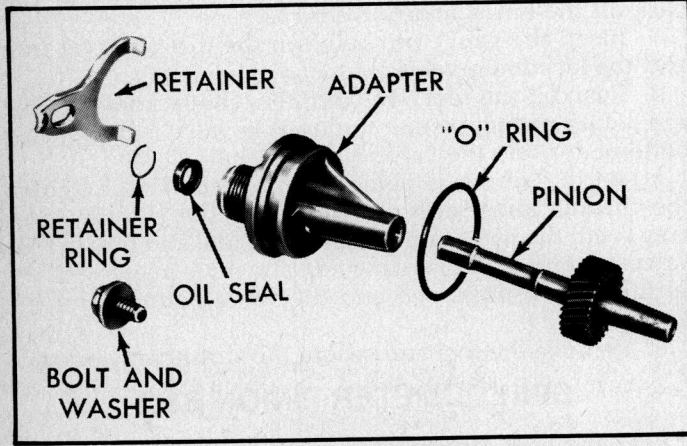

RETAINER   ADAPTER   "O" RING   PINION   RETAINER RING   OIL SEAL   BOLT AND WASHER

OUTPUT SHAFT OIL SEAL R&R

1. Mark parts for reassembly. Disconnect driveshaft at the rear universal joint. Carefully pull the shaft yoke out of the transmission extension housing. Be careful not to scratch or nick ground surface of the sliding spline yoke.

2. Remove the extension housing yoke seal by gently tapping out around circumference of the seal with a slide hammer.

3. To install a new seal, place seal in opening of extension housing and drive it into housing with a suitable drift.

4. Carefully guide the front universal joint yoke into extension housing and onto the mainshaft splines. Align the marks made at removal and connect the driveshaft to the pinion shaft yoke.

EXTENSION HOUSING

REMOVAL

1. Mark parts for reassembly. Disconnect driveshaft at the rear universal joint. Carefully pull the shaft out of the extension housing.

2. Remove the speedometer pinion and adapter assembly. Drain approximately two quarts of fluid from the transmission.

3. Remove bolts securing the extension housing to the crossmember. Raise the transmission slightly with a service jack and remove the center crossmember and support assembly.

4. Remove the extension housing to transmission bolts. On console shifts, remove two bolts securing the gearshift torque shaft lower bracket to the extension housing. Swing the bracket out of way.

Extension Housing Removal and Installation

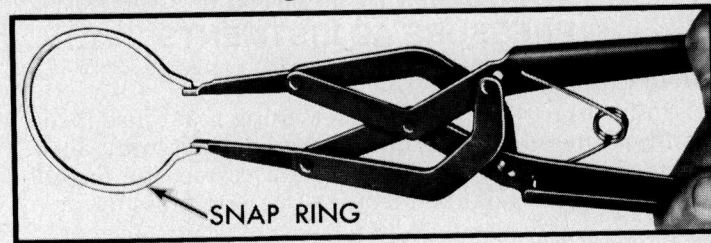

SNAP RING

NOTE *Gearshift lever must be in 1-low position so that the parking lock control rod can be engaged or disengaged with the parking lock sprag.*

5. Remove the two screws, plate and gasket from the bottom of the extension housing mounting pad.

6. Spread a large snap ring from the output shaft bearing with tool C-3301 or equivalent.

7. With the snap ring spread as far as possible, tap the extension housing gently off the output shaft bearing.

Parking Lock Components

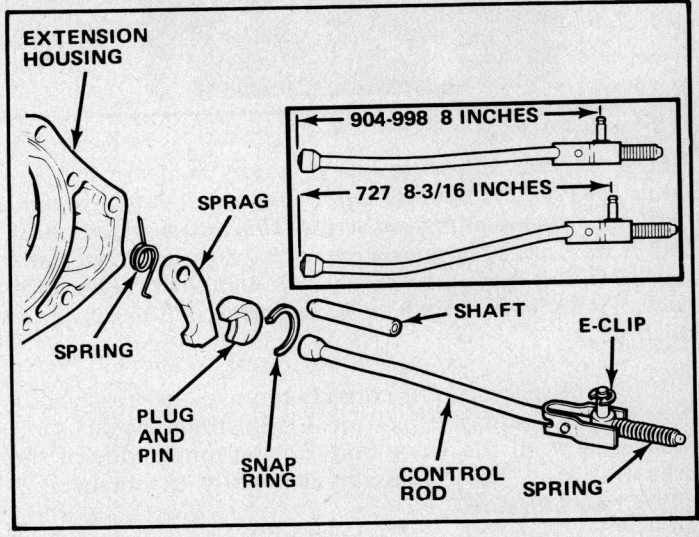

EXTENSION HOUSING   SPRAG   904-998 8 INCHES   727 8-3/16 INCHES   SHAFT   E-CLIP   SPRING   PLUG AND PIN   SNAP RING   CONTROL ROD   SPRING

8. Carefully pull the extension housing rearward to bring parking lock control rod knob past the parking sprag. Remove housing.

INSTALLATION

1. Install the snap ring in front groove on the output shaft.

2. Install the bearing on the shaft with its outer race ring groove toward the front. Press or tap the bearing tight against the front snap ring.

3. Install the rear snap ring. If so equipped, slide the yoke seal front stop ring onto the shaft. Install the seal with lips toward the rear, then install the rear stop ring on the shaft.

4. Place new extension housing gasket on the transmission case.

5. Place output shaft bearing retaining snap ring in the extension housing. Spread the ring as far as possible, then carefully tap the extension housing into place. Make sure snap ring is fully seated in bearing groove.

6. Install and torque the extension housing bolts to specifications.

7. Install the gasket, plate and two screws on the bottom of the extension housing mounting pad.

8. Install the speedometer pinion and adapter assembly.

Governor Assembly

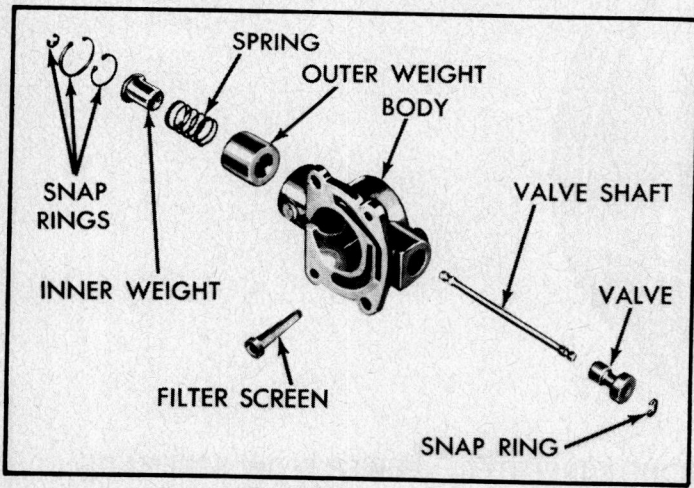

GOVERNOR R&R

1. Remove the extension housing.

NOTE Remove output shaft support bearing, if so equipped.

2. With a screwdriver, carefully pry the snap ring from the weight end of governor valve shaft. Slide the valve and shaft assembly out of the governor housing.

3. Remove the large snap ring from the weight end of the governor housing and lift out the governor weight assembly.

4. Remove the snap ring from the inside governor weight. Remove the inner weight and spring from the outer weight.

Governor Shaft and Weight Snap Rings

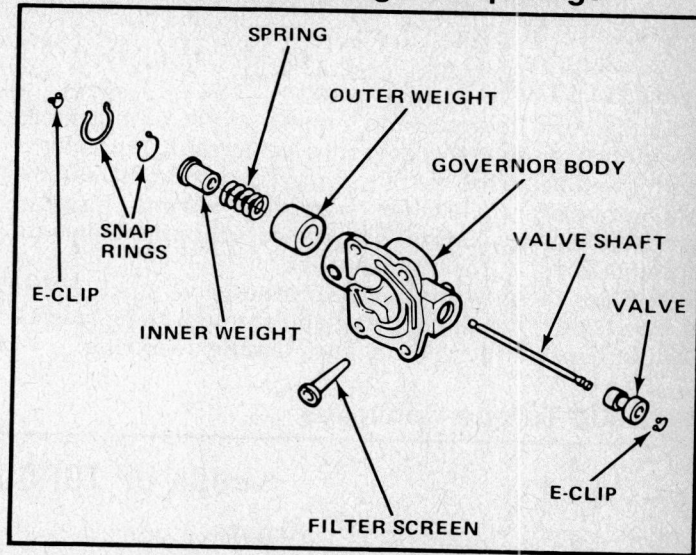

5. Remove the snap ring from behind the governor housing, then slide the governor housing and support assembly from the output shaft. If necessary, remove the four screws and separate the governor housing from the support.

6. The primary cause of governor operating trouble is sticking of the valve or weights, brought about by dirt or rough surfaces. Thoroughly clean and blow dry all of the governor parts. Remove any burrs or rough bearing surfaces with crocus cloth and clean again. If all moving parts are clean and operating freely, the governor may be reassembled.

7. Assemble the governor housing to the support, then finger tighten the screws. Be sure the oil passage of the governor housing aligns with the passage in the support.

8. Align the master spline of the support with the master spline on the output shaft. Slide the assembly into place. Install the snap ring behind the governor housing. Torque bolts to 100 in. lbs.

9. Assemble the governor weights and springs and fasten with a snap ring inside of the large governor weight. Place the weight assembly in the governor housing shafts retaining snap ring. Install output shaft support bearing, if so equipped.

10. Place the governor valve on the valve shaft. Insert the assembly into the housing and through the governor weights. Install the shaft retaining snap ring. Install the output shaft support bearing, if so equipped.

11. Install the extension housing. Connect the driveshaft.

GOVERNOR AND SUPPORT R&R

REMOVAL

1. Remove the snap ring from the weight end of the governor valve shaft. Slide the valve and shaft assembly from the governor housing.

2. Remove the snap ring from behind the governor

housing. Then slide the governor housing and support from the output shaft.

INSTALLATION

1. Place the governor and support on the output shaft. Position it so that the governor valve shaft hole aligns with the hole in the output shaft. Then slide the assembly into place. Install the snap ring behind the governor housing. Torque housing-to-support screws to specifications.

2. Place the governor valve on the valve shaft. Insert the assembly into the housing and through the governor weights. Install the valve shaft retaining snap ring.

VALVE BODY ASSEMBLY & ACCUMULATOR PISTON R&R

REMOVAL

1. Raise the vehicle on a hoist and loosen oil pan bolts. Tap the pan to break it loose, allowing fluid to drain.

2. Remove the pan and gasket.

3. Disconnect the throttle and gearshift linkage from the levers on the transmission. Loosen clamp bolts and remove the levers.

4. Remove the E-clip securing the parking lock rod to the valve body manual lever.

5. Remove the backup light and neutral start switch.

6. Place the drain pan under the transmission. Re-

Lock-Up Torque Converter

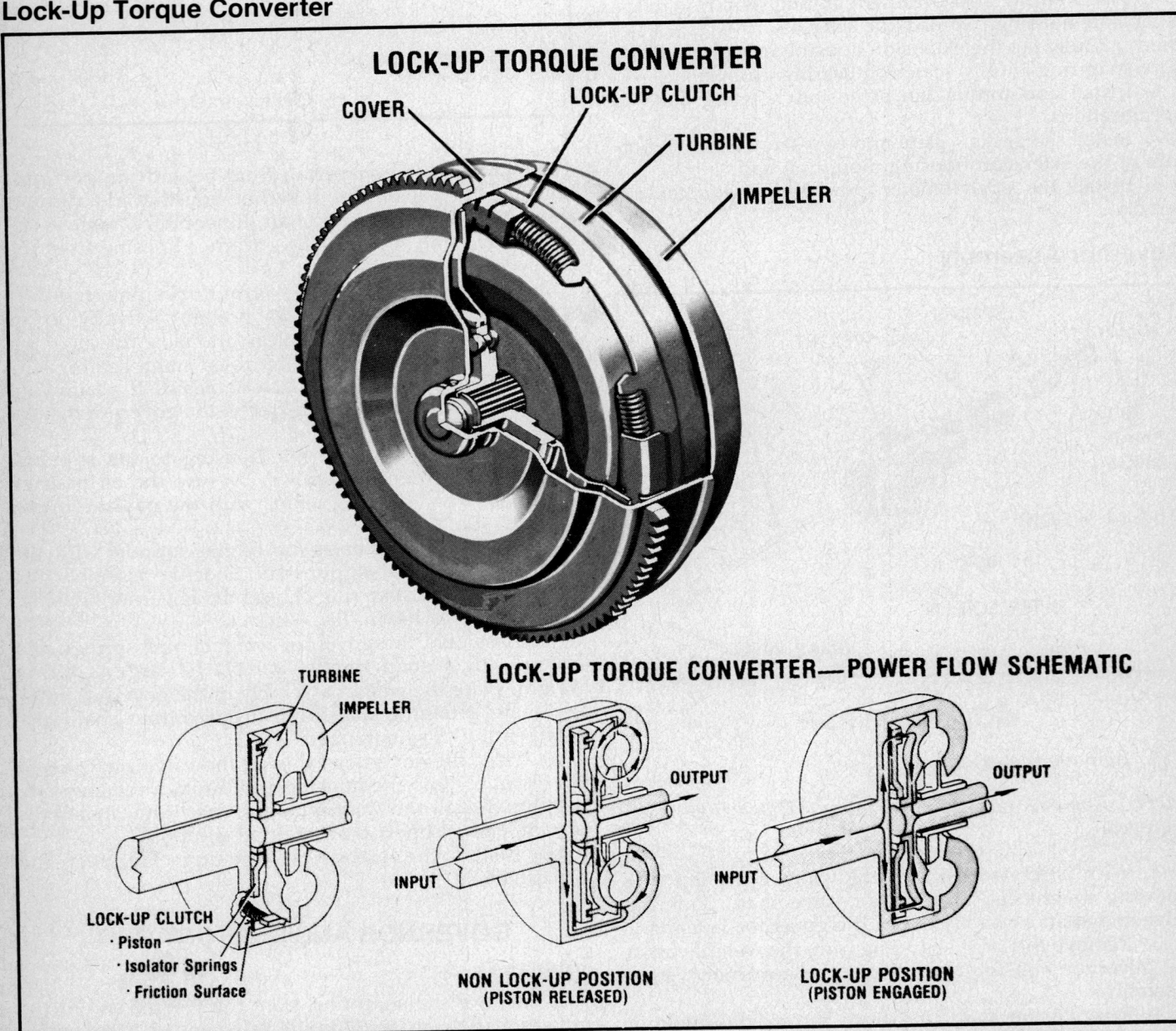

LOCK-UP TORQUE CONVERTER

COVER — LOCK-UP CLUTCH — TURBINE — IMPELLER

LOCK-UP TORQUE CONVERTER—POWER FLOW SCHEMATIC

TURBINE — IMPELLER

LOCK-UP CLUTCH
· Piston
· Isolator Springs
· Friction Surface

OUTPUT / INPUT

NON LOCK-UP POSITION (PISTON RELEASED)

OUTPUT / INPUT

LOCK-UP POSITION (PISTON ENGAGED)

The lock-up clutch type torque converter in some Chrysler Corporation vehicles engages automatically at 28 mph, providing mechanical power transmission

move the ten hex head valve body to transmission case bolts. Hold the valve body in position while removing the bolts.

7. While lowering the valve body down out of the transmission case, disconnect the parking lock rod from the lever. To remove the rod, pull it forward out of the case. If necessary, rotate the driveshaft to align the parking gear and sprag to permit the knob on the end of the control rod to pass the sprag.

8. Withdraw the accumulator piston from the transmission case. Inspect the piston for scoring and the rings for wear or breakage.

9. If the valve body manual lever shaft seal requires replacement, drive it out of the case with a punch.

10. Drive the new seal into the case with 15/16 in. socket and hammer.

INSTALLATION

1. If the parking lock rod was removed, insert it through the opening in the rear of case with the knob positioned against the plug and sprag. Move the front end of the rod toward the center of the transmission while exerting rearward pressure on the rod to force it past the sprag. Rotate the driveshaft if necessary.

2. Install the accumulator piston in the transmission case.

3. Place the accumulator spring on the valve body.

4. Place the valve body manual lever in low position. Lift the valve body into its approximate position. Connect the parking lock rod to the manual lever and secure with an E-clip. Place the valve body in the case. Install the retaining bolts finger tight.

5. With the neutral start switch installed, place the manual lever in Neutral position. Shift the valve body, if necessary, to center the neutral finger over the neutral switch plunger. Snug the bolts down evenly. Torque to 100 in./lbs.

6. Install the gearshift lever and tighten the clamp bolts. Check the lever shaft for binding by moving the lever through all detents. If the lever binds, loosen the valve body bolts and re-align.

7. Make sure the throttle shaft seal is in place. Install the flat washer and lever and tighten the clamp bolt. Connect the throttle and gearshift linkage and adjust as required.

8. Install the oil pan using a new gasket. Add the transmission fluid to the proper level.

TROUBLESHOOTING
AMC Torque Command and Chrysler Torqueflite

Problem	In Car Checks	Out of Car Checks
Harsh Neutral to Drive or Neutral to Reverse shift	Oil pressure. Kickdown band. Low-reverse band. Improper engine idle. Servo linkage. Valve body assembly. Manual valve lever.	Front kickdown clutch. Rear clutch.
Delayed shift Neutral to Drive	Oil level. Oil pressure. Valve body assembly. Accumulator. Air pressure. Manual valve lever.	Front pump and/or sleeve. Front kickdown clutch.
Runaway on upshift and 3-2 kickdown	Oil level. Control linkage. Oil pressure. Kickdown band. Kickdown servo or linkage. Valve body assembly. Accumulator. Air pressure.	Rear clutch.
Harsh upshift and 3-2 kickdown	Control linkage. Oil pressure. Kickdown band. Kickdown servo or linkage. Valve body assembly. Accumulator. Manual valve lever.	Rear clutch.
No upshift	Oil level. Control linkage. Oil pressure. Kickdown band. Kickdown servo or linkage. Valve body assembly. Accumulator. Air pressure. Governor.	Rear clutch.
No kickdown on normal downshift	Oil level. Control linkage. Gear shift cable. Oil pressure. Kickdown band. Kickdown servo or linkage. Valve body assembly. Accumulator. Air pressure. Governor.	Overrunning clutch.
Erratic shifts	Oil level. Control linkage. Gear shift cable. Oil pressure. Improper engine idle. Regulator valve and/or spring. Output shaft bushing. Strainer. Valve body assembly. Air pressure. Governor. Manual valve lever.	Front pump and/or sleeve.
Slips in forward drive positions	Oil level. Oil pressure. Valve body assembly. Accumulator. Air pressure.	Front kickdown. Rear clutch. Overrunning clutch.
Slips in Reverse only	Oil pressure. Low-reverse band. Servo linkage. Valve body assembly. Air pressure.	

TROUBLESHOOTING
AMC Torque Command and Chrysler Torqueflite

Problem	In Car Checks	Out of Car Checks
Slips in all positions	Oil level. Oil pressure. Regulator valve and/or spring. Valve body assembly. Air pressure.	Converter.
No drive in any position	Oil level. Oil pressure. Regulator valve and/or spring. Strainer. Valve body assembly. Air pressure. Manual valve lever.	Front pump and/or sleeve. Front kickdown clutch.
No drive in forward position	Oil pressure. Kickdown band. Regulator valve and/or spring. Kickdown servo or linkage. Valve body assembly. Accumulator. Air pressure.	Front kickdown clutch. Rear clutch. Overrunning clutch.
No drive in Reverse	Oil pressure. Low-reverse band. Servo linkage. Air pressure. Governor. Valve body assembly.	Rear clutch.
Drives in Neutral	Gear shift cable. Valve body assembly. Manual valve lever.	Front kickdown clutch.
Drags or locks	Kickdown band. Low-reverse band. Kickdown servo or linkage. Servo linkage.	Front kickdown clutch. Rear clutch. Planetary. Overrunning clutch.
Noises	Oil level. Regulator valve and/or spring. Converter control valve. Output shaft bushing. Governor. Valve body assembly. Manual valve lever.	Front kickdown clutch.
Hard to fill or fluid blows out	Oil level. Regulator valve and/or spring. Converter control valve. Breather clogged. Cooler or lines. Strainer. Valve body assembly.	
Transmission overheats	Oil level. Kickdown band. Low-reverse band. Regulator valve and/or spring. Converter control valve. Cooler or lines. Governor. Valve body assembly.	Front kickdown clutch. Rear clutch. Converter.

AMC GOVERNOR PRESSURE SPECIFICATIONS

Model	Engine-CID	Axle Gear	15 psi	50 psi	75 psi
Gremlin	6-232	2.73	19–23	46–54	64–73
	6-258	2.73	19–23	46–54	64–73
	V8-304	2.87	17–21	49–57	69–77
Hornet	6-232	2.73	20–24	47–55	66–74
	6-258	2.73	20–24	47–55	66–74
	V8-304	2.87	17–21	49–57	69–77
	V8-360	2.87	17–21	49–57	69–77
Javelin	6-232	3.08	17–21	42–50	59–66
	6-258	3.08	17–21	42–50	59–66
	V8-304	2.87	17–21	49–57	69–78
	V8-360	2.87	17–21	50–58	70–79
	V8-401	2.87	17–21	49–57	69–78
Matador	6-232	3.15	17–21	42–49	58–66
	6-258	3.15	18–22	44–52	62–70
	V8-304	3.15	16–20	45–53	64–72
	V8-360	3.15	17–21	49–57	68–77
	V8-401	3.15	16–20	45–53	64–72
Ambassador	V8-304	3.15	16–20	46–54	65–73
	V8-360	3.15	17–21	49–57	68–77
	V8-401	3.15	16–20	46–54	65–73

GOVERNOR PRESSURE SPECIFICATIONS

Model	Engine-CID	Axle Ratio	Speed (mph)	Pressure Limit (psi)
Chrysler	All	2.76	20–22	15
			48–57	50
			72–79	75
		3.23	17–19	15
			41–49	50
			66–73	75
Dodge Dart and Plymouth Valiant	6–198 and 6–225	2.76	19–20	15
			49–55	50
			72–79	75
Dodge and Plymouth high performance vehicles	8–383 and 8–400	3.23	18–19	15
			53–58	50
			71–77	75
	8–440	3.23	18–19	15
			53–58	50
			71–77	75
All	8–318	2.71	20–22	15
			56–64	50
			80–88	75
	8–340	3.23	17–18	15
			49–53	50
			66–71	75
	8–360	2.71	20–22	15
			54–63	50
			78–86	75
	8–383 and 8–400	2.76	21–22	15
			55–64	50
			80–87	75
	8–440	2.94	20–22	15
			54–62	50
			78–85	75

CHRYSLER A-404 TORQUEFLITE

The transaxle combines a torque converter, fully automatic three speed transmission, final drive gearing and differential into a single assembly. The unit is a metric design.

In-Car Testing Procedures
HYDRAULIC PRESSURE TESTS

NOTE *For hydraulic pressure tests, install a tachometer. Raise the vehicle to allow the front wheels to turn. Disconnect the throttle and shift cable from the transmission levers so they can be controlled from outside the vehicle. Connect 150 psi gauges to required ports. A 300 psi gauge is needed for the reverse pressure test at rear servo.*

TEST ONE

This tests pump output, pressure regulation and the condition of the rear clutch and lubrication hydraulic circuits.

1. Attach gauges to line and rear servo ports. Place selector lever on transaxle all the way forward ("1" position) and operate the engine at 1000 rpm.

2. Read pressures on both gauges as throttle lever on

Transaxle Rear View

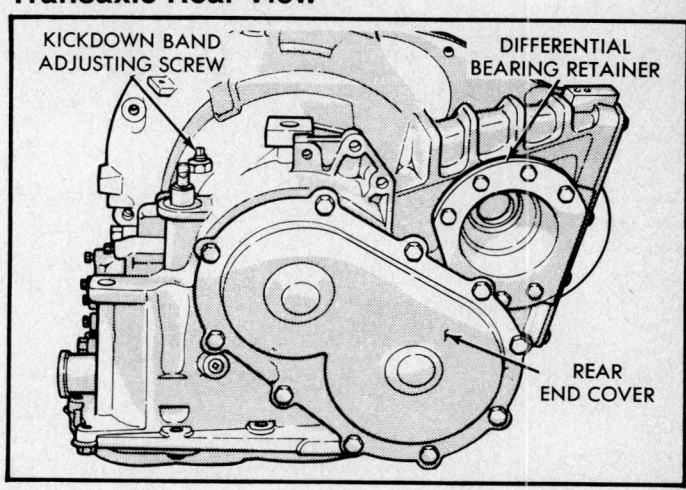

KICKDOWN BAND ADJUSTING SCREW

DIFFERENTIAL BEARING RETAINER

REAR END COVER

Transaxle Right Side

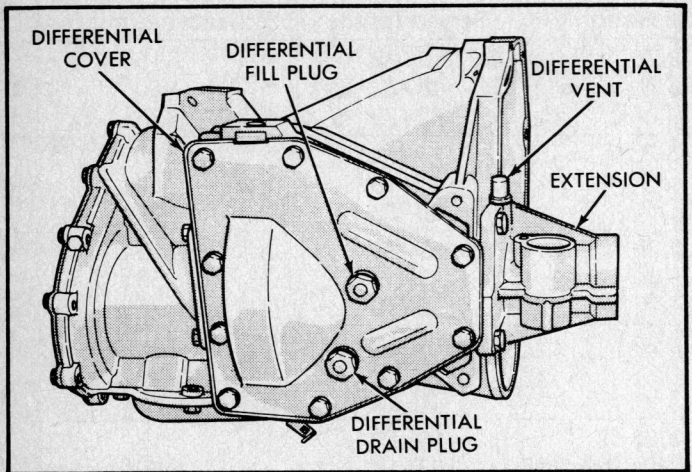

transaxle is moved from full forward to full rearward positions.

3. Line pressure should read 60 to 66 psi with throttle lever forward. It should gradually increase to 97 to 103 psi as lever is moved rearward. Rear servo pressure should be within 3 psi of line pressure.

TEST TWO

This tests pump output, pressure regulation and the condition of the rear clutch and lubrication hydraulic circuits.

1. Connect the gauge to line pressure port, and tee into lower cooler line fitting to read lubrication pressure. Place the transaxle selector lever one detent rearward from full forward ("2" position). Operate engine at 1000 rpm.

2. Read pressures on both gauges as the throttle lever on the transaxle is moved from full forward to full rearward positions.

3. Line pressure should be 60 to 66 psi with throttle lever forward. It should gradually increase to 97 to 103 psi as the lever is moved rearward. Lubrication pressure should be 10 to 25 psi with lever forward and 10 to 35 psi with lever rearward.

TEST THREE

This test pump output, pressure regulation and the condition of rear clutch, front clutch and hydraulic circuits.

1. Connect gauges to line and front servo release ports. Place transaxle selector lever two detents rearward from full forward position (Drive position). Operate engine at 1600 rpm.

2. Read pressure on both gauges as the throttle lever on the transaxle is moved from full forward to full rearward positions.

3. Line pressure should be 60 to 66 psi with throttle lever forward. It should gradually increase as the lever is

Transaxle Left Side

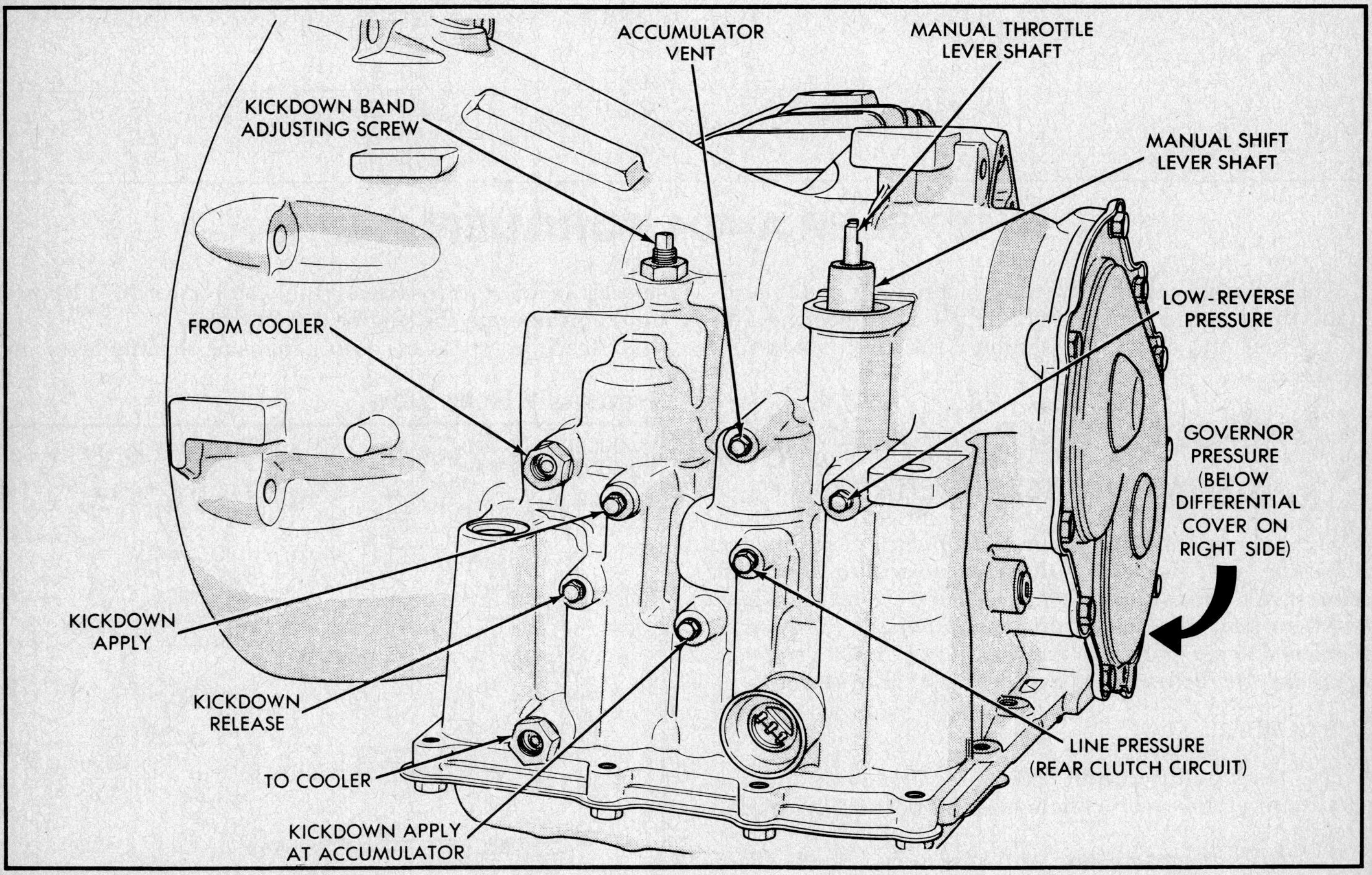

moved rearward. Front servo release is pressurized only in direct drive and should be within 3 psi of line pressure up to the downshift point.

TEST FOUR

This tests pump output, pressure regulation and condition of front clutch and rear servo hydraulic circuits. It also tests for leakage into rear servo due to case porosity.

1. Connect a 300 psi gauge to rear servo apply port. Place transaxle selector lever in Reverse position (four detents rearward from full forward). Operate engine at 1600 rpm.

2. Rear servo pressure should be 176 to 180 psi with the throttle lever forward. It should gradually increase to 270 to 280 psi as the lever is moved rearward. Move the transaxle selector lever to Drive position. Check that the rear servo pressure drops to zero.

TEST RESULT INDICATIONS

1. If proper line pressure, minimum to maximum, is found in any one test, the pump and pressure regulator are working properly.

2. Low pressure in Drive, "1" and "2," but correct pressure in Reverse, indicates rear clutch circuit leakage.

3. Low pressure in Drive and Reverse, but correct pressure in "1," indicates front clutch circuit leakage.

4. Low pressure in Reverse and "1," but correct pressure in "2," indicates rear servo circuit leakage.

5. Low line pressure in all positions indicates a defective pump, clogged filter or stuck pressure regulator valve.

GOVERNOR PRESSURE

Test only if transaxle shifts at the wrong vehicle speeds when the throttle cable is correctly adjusted.

1. Connect a 0–150 psi gauge to governor pressure

Transmission Oil Pan

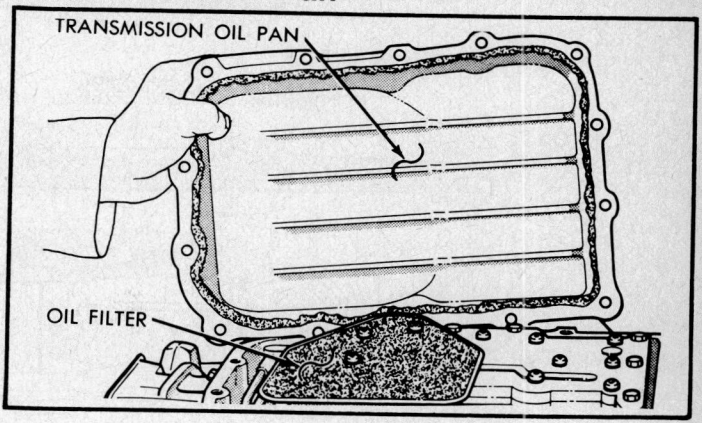

take-off point located at the lower right side of the case below the differential cover.

2. Operate the transaxle in 3rd gear to read the pressure and compare speeds shown in the chart.

3. If governor pressures are incorrect at the given vehicle speeds, the governor valve and/or weights are probably sticking. The governor pressure should respond smoothly to changes in mph and should return to 0 to 3 psi when the vehicle is stopped. Pressure over 3 psi at a standstill will prevent downshifting.

THROTTLE PRESSURE

1. No gauge port is provided for throttle pressure. Incorrect throttle pressure should only be suspected if part throttle upshift speeds are either delayed or occur too early. Engine runaway on upshift or downshift can indicate a too low throttle pressure setting.

2. Verify that the throttle cable adjustment is correct before adjusting the throttle pressure.

AUTOMATIC SHIFT SPEEDS AND GOVERNOR PRESSURE CHART
(Approximate Miles Per Hour)

Carline	Federal MZ	California MZ
Engine (liter)	1.7	1.7
Axle ratio	3.48	3.74
Throttle minimum		
1-2 upshift	8–15	7–14
2-3 upshift	11–21	10–19
3-1 downshift	8–15	7–14
Throttle wide open		
1-2 upshift	32–44	38–44
2-3 upshift	52–65	48–60
Kickdown limit		
3-2 WOT downshift	48–61	44–57
3-2 part throttle downshift	35–50	32–46
3-1 WOT downshift	30–57	28–34
Governor pressure ①		
15 psi	21–23	19–21
40 psi	35–41	32–38
60 psi	50–56	46–52

① Governor pressure should be from zero to 3 psi at stand still or downshift may not occur

NOTE: Changes in tire size will cause shift points to occur at corresponding higher or lower vehicle speeds

Air Pressure Test Ports

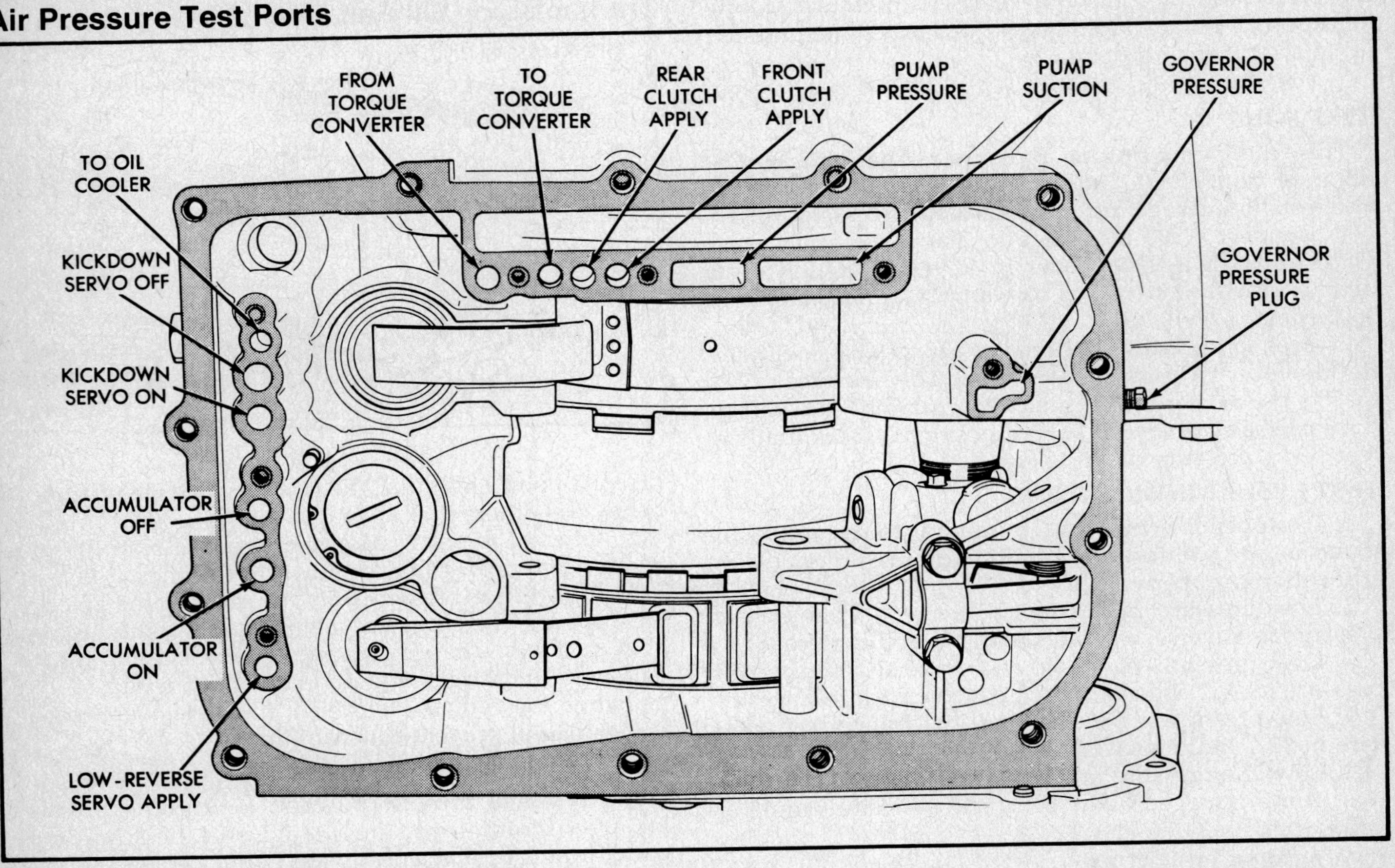

FROM TORQUE CONVERTER • TO TORQUE CONVERTER • REAR CLUTCH APPLY • FRONT CLUTCH APPLY • PUMP PRESSURE • PUMP SUCTION • GOVERNOR PRESSURE • GOVERNOR PRESSURE PLUG • TO OIL COOLER • KICKDOWN SERVO OFF • KICKDOWN SERVO ON • ACCUMULATOR OFF • ACCUMULATOR ON • LOW-REVERSE SERVO APPLY

CLUTCH AND SERVO AIR PRESSURE TESTS

The front and rear clutches, kickdown servo and low-reverse servo may be tested by applying air pressure after the valve body has been removed.

NOTE Compressed air must be free of dirt and moisture. Use a pressure of 30 psi.

CLUTCHES

1. Apply air pressure to each individual clutch apply passage and listen for a dull thud which indicates that the clutch is operating. If the dull thud cannot be heard in the clutches, place finger tips on the clutch housing to feel piston movement.
2. Inspect each clutch system for oil leaks while air pressure is applied.

SERVOS

1. Apply air pressure to each individual servo apply passage. Operation of the kickdown servo is indicated by a tightening of the front band. Operation of the low-reverse servo is indicated by a tightening of the rear band. Spring tension on the servo pistons should release the bands.

In-Car Service and Adjustment Procedures

BAND ADJUSTMENT

KICKDOWN BAND (FRONT)

1. The adjusting screw is located on the left side (top front) of the transmission case. Loosen the lock nut and back off the nut approximately five turns. Test the adjusting screw for free turning in the transmission case.
2. Using wrench, tool C-3380-A with adaptor C-3705, tighten the band adjusting screw 47 to 50 inch-pounds. If the adaptor is not used, tighten the adjusting screw to 72 inch-pounds.

Kickdown Band Adjustment

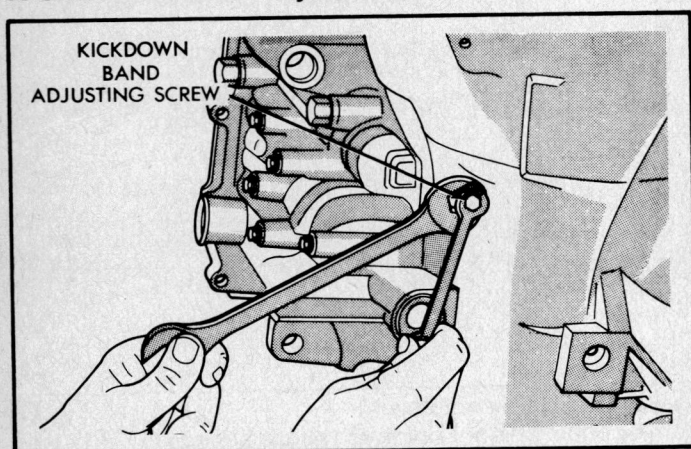

KICKDOWN BAND ADJUSTING SCREW

LOW-REVERSE BAND (REAR)

1. This band is not adjustable, but lining inspection is necessary to determine the need for replacement.

2. The band is within service limits if the grooves in the lining are visible and the groove depth at any point is no less than 0.2 mm. (.080 inch). At the same time, the band end gap as installed on the drum and 100 pounds force applied to the ends must not be less than 0.5 mm.

HYDRAULIC CONTROL PRESSURE ADJUSTMENTS

LINE PRESSURE

An incorrect throttle pressure setting will cause incorrect line pressure readings even though line pressure adjustment is correct. Always inspect and correct the throttle pressure adjustment before adjusting the line pressure.

1. The approximate adjustment is 1 5/16 inches measured from the valve body to the inner edge of the adjusting nut. The adjustment can be varied to obtain specified line pressure.

2. One complete turn of the adjusting screw changes the closed throttle line pressure approximately 1 2/3 psi. Turning counter-clockwise increases the pressure, and clockwise decreases it.

THROTTLE PRESSURE

Throttle pressures cannot be tested accurately. The adjustment should be measured if a malfunction is evident.

1. Insert gauge pin of tool C-3763 between the throttle lever cam and kickdown valve. By pushing in on the tool, compress kickdown valve against its spring so the throttle valve is completely bottomed inside the valve body.

2. As force is being exerted to compress the spring, turn the throttle lever stop screw with adaptor C-4553 with handle until the head of the screw touches the throttle lever cam touching tool and the throttle valve is bottomed. Be sure adjustment is made with the spring fully compressed and the valve bottomed in the valve body.

SPEEDOMETER PINION GEAR

1. Remove the bolt securing the pinion adapter in the extension housing and, with the cable connected, carefully work the adapter and pinion out of the extension housing. Remove the retainer and separate it from the adapter.

2. If the cable housing contains transmission fluid, install a new speedometer pinion and seal assembly. If transmission fluid is found to be leaking between the cable and the adapter, replace the small O-ring on the cable.

3. Before installation, make sure the adapter flange and its mating areas on the extension housing are clean. Dirt will cause misalignment resulting in speedometer pinion gear damage.

TRANSMISSION DIAGNOSIS CHARTS
A404 TorqueFlite

Condition	Cause	Correction
Harsh engagement from Neutral to Drive or Reverse	1. Engine idle speed too high 2. Valve body malfunction 3. Hydraulic pressure too high 4. Worn or faulty rear clutch	1. Adjust to specification 2. Clean or overhaul 3. Adjust to specification 4. Overhaul rear clutch
Delayed engagement from Neutral to Drive or Reverse	1. Hydraulic pressure too low 2. Valve body malfunction 3. Malfunction in low/reverse servo, band or linkage 4. Low fluid level 5. Manual linkage adjustment 6. Oil filter clogged 7. Faulty oil pump 8. Bad input shaft seals 9. Idle speed too low 10. Bad reaction shaft support seals 11. Bad front clutch 12. Bad rear clutch	1. Adjust to specification 2. Clean or overhaul 3. Overhaul 4. Add as required 5. Adjust as required 6. Change filter and fluid 7. Overhaul pump 8. Replace seal rings 9. Adjust to specifications 10. Replace seal rings 11. Overhaul 12. Overhaul
Runaway upshift	1. Hydraulic pressure too low 2. Valve body malfunction 3. Low fluid level 4. Oil filter clogged 5. Aerated fluid 6. Manual linkage adjustment 7. Bad reaction shaft support seals 8. Malfunction in kickdown servo, band or linkage 9. Bad front clutch	1. Adjust to specifications 2. Clean or overhaul 3. Add as required 4. Change filter and fluid 5. Check for overfilling 6. Adjust as required 7. Replace seal rings 8. Overhaul 9. Repair as needed

TRANSMISSION DIAGNOSIS CHARTS
A404 TorqueFlite

Condition	Cause	Correction
No upshift	1. Hydraulic pressure too low 2. Valve body malfunction 3. Low fluid level 4. Manual linkage adjustment 5. Incorrect throttle linkage adjustment 6. Bad seals on governor support 7. Bad reaction shaft support seals 8. Governor malfunction 9. Malfunction in kickdown servo, band or linkage 10. Bad front clutch	1. Adjust to specifications 2. Clean or overhaul 3. Add as required 4. Adjust as required 5. Adjust as required 6. Replace seals 7. Replace seal rings 8. Service or replace unit 9. Overhaul 10. Overhaul
3-2 kickdown runaway	1. Hydraulic pressure too low 2. Valve body malfunction 3. Low fluid level 4. Aerated fluid 5. Incorrect throttle linkage adjustment 6. Kickdown band out of adjustment 7. Bad reaction shaft support seals 8. Malfunction in kickdown servo, band or linkage 9. Bad front clutch	1. Adjust to specifications 2. Clean or overhaul 3. Add as required 4. Check for overfilling 5. Adjust as required 6. Adjust to specifications 7. Replace seal rings 8. Overhaul 9. Overhaul
No kickdown or normal downshift	1. Valve body malfunction 2. Incorrect throttle linkage 3. Governor malfunction 4. Malfunction in kickdown servo, band or linkage	1. Clean or overhaul 2. Adjust as required 3. Service or replace unit 4. Service or replace parts as required
Shifts erratic	1. Hydraulic pressure too low 2. Valve body malfunction 3. Low fluid level 4. Manual linkage adjustment 5. Oil filter clogged 6. Faulty oil pump 7. Aerated fluid 8. Incorrect throttle linkage adjustment 9. Bad seals or governor support 10. Bad reaction shaft support seals 11. Governor malfunction 12. Malfunction in kickdown servo, band or linkage 13. Bad front clutch	1. Adjust to specifications 2. Clean or overhaul 3. Add as required 4. Adjust as required 5. Change filter and fluid 6. Overhaul oil pump 7. Check for overfilling 8. Adjust as required 9. Replace seals 10. Replace seal rings 11. Service or replace unit 12. Overhaul 13. Overhaul
Slips in forward Drive positions	1. Hydraulic pressure too low 2. Valve body malfunction 3. Low fluid level 4. Manual linkage adjustment 5. Oil filter clogged 6. Faulty oil pump 7. Bad input shaft seals 8. Aerated fluid 9. Incorrect throttle linkage adjustment 10. Overrunning clutch not holding 11. Bad rear clutch	1. Adjust to specifications 2. Clean or overhaul 3. Add as required 4. Adjust as required 5. Change filter and fluid 6. Overhaul pump 7. Replace seal rings 8. Check for overfilling 9. Adjust as required 10. Overhaul or replace 11. Overhaul
Slips in Reverse only	1. Hydraulic pressure too low 2. Low/reverse band out of adjustment 3. Valve body malfunction 4. Malfunction in low/reverse servo, band or linkage	1. Adjust as required 2. Adjust to specifications 3. Clean or overhaul 4. Service or replace parts as required

TRANSMISSION DIAGNOSIS CHARTS
A404 TorqueFlite

Condition	Cause	Correction
Slips in Reverse only	5. Low fluid level 6. Manual linkage adjustment 7. Faulty oil pump 8. Aerated fluid 9. Bad reaction shaft support seals 10. Bad front clutch	5. Add as required 6. Adjust as required 7. Overhaul pump 8. Check for overfilling 9. Replace seal rings 10. Overhaul
Slips in all positions	1. Hydraulic pressure too low 2. Valve body malfunction 3. Low fluid level 4. Oil filter clogged 5. Faulty oil pump 6. Bad input shaft seals 7. Aerated fluid	1. Adjust as required 2. Clean or overhaul 3. Add as required 4. Change fluid and filter 5. Overhaul pump 6. Replace seal rings 7. Check for overfilling
No drive in any position	1. Hydraulic pressure too low 2. Valve body malfunction 3. Low fluid level 4. Oil filter clogged 5. Faulty oil pump 6. Planetary gear sets broken or seized	1. Adjust to specifications 2. Clean or overhaul 3. Add as required 4. Change filter and fluid 5. Overhaul pump 6. Replace affected parts
No drive in forward Drive positions	1. Hydraulic pressure too low 2. Valve body malfunction 3. Low fluid level 4. Bad input shaft seals 5. Overrunning clutch not holding 6. Bad rear clutch 7. Planetary gear sets broken or seized	1. Adjust to specifications 2. Clean or overhaul 3. Add as required 4. Replace seal rings 5. Overhaul or replace 6. Overhaul 7. Replace affected parts
No drive in Reverse	1. Hydraulic pressure too low 2. Low/reverse band out of adjustment 3. Valve body malfunction 4. Malfunction in low/reverse servo, band or linkage 5. Manual linkage adjustment 6. Bad input shaft seals 7. Bad front clutch 8. Bad rear clutch 9. Planetary gear sets broken or seized	1. Adjust to specifications 2. Adjust to specifications 3. Clean or overhaul 4. Overhaul 5. Adjust as required 6. Replace seal rings 7. Overhaul 8. Overhaul 9. Replace affected parts
Drives in Neutral	1. Valve body malfunction 2. Manual linkage adjustment 3. Insufficient clutch plate clearance 4. Bad rear clutch 5. Rear clutch dragging	1. Clean or overhaul 2. Adjust as required 3. Overhaul clutch pack 4. Overhaul 5. Overhaul
Drags or locks	1. Stuck lock-up valve 2. Low/reverse band out of adjustment 3. Kickdown band adjustment too tight 4. Planetary gear sets broken or seized 5. Overrunning clutch broken or seized	1. Clean or overhaul 2. Adjust to specifications 3. Adjust to specifications 4. Replace affected parts 5. Overhaul or replace
Grating, scraping or growling noise	1. Low/reverse band out of adjustment 2. Kickdown band out of adjustment 3. Output shaft bearing or bushing bad 4. Planetary gear sets broken or seized 5. Overrunning clutch broken or seized	1. Adjust to specifications 2. Adjust to specifications 3. Replace 4. Replace affected parts 5. Overhaul or replace

AUTOMATIC TRANSMISSIONS

FORD OVERDRIVE

TRANSMISSION DIAGNOSIS CHARTS
A404 TorqueFlite

Condition	Cause	Correction
Buzzing noise	1. Valve body malfunction 2. Low fluid level 3. Aerated fluid 4. Overrunning clutch inner race damaged	1. Clean or overhaul 2. Add as required 3. Check for overfilling 4. Overhaul or replace
Hard to fill, oil blows out filler tube	1. Oil filter clogged 2. Aerated fluid 3. High fluid level 4. Breather clogged	1. Change filter and fluid 2. Check for overfilling 3. Bad converter check valve 4. Clean, change fluid
Transmission overheats	1. Engine idle speed too high 2. Hydraulic pressure too low 3. Low fluid level 4. Manual linkage adjustment 5. Faulty oil pump 6. Kickdown band adjustment too tight 7. Faulty cooling system 8. Insufficient clutch plate clearance	1. Adjust to specifications 2. Adjust to specifications 3. Add as required 4. Adjust as required 5. Overhaul pump 6. Adjust to specifications 7. Service vehicle's cooling system 8. Overhaul clutch pack
Harsh upshift	1. Hydraulic pressure too low 2. Incorrect throttle linkage adjustment 3. Kickdown band out of adjustment 4. Hydraulic pressure too high	1. Adjust to specifications 2. Adjust as required 3. Adjust to specifications 4. Adjust to specifications
Delayed upshift	1. Incorrect throttle linkage adjustment 2. Kickdown band out of adjustment 3. Bad seals on governor support 4. Bad reaction shaft support seals 5. Governor malfunction 6. Malfunction in kickdown servo, band or linkage 7. Bad front clutch	1. Adjust as required 2. Adjust as required 3. Replace seals 4. Replace seal rings 5. Service or replace unit 6. Overhaul 7. Overhaul

FORD OVERDRIVE

Throttle Valve (TV) Control Linkage System

DESCRIPTION

The throttle valve (TV) control linkage system consists of the linkage lever on the carburetor, the transmission control rod assembly and the external TV control lever on the transmission.

The TV control linkage is set to its proper length during initial assembly using the sliding trunnion block at the transmission end of the TV control rod assembly. Under normal circumstances, it should not be necessary to alter this adjustment. Any required adjustment of the TV control linkage can normally be accomplished using the adjustment screw on the linkage lever at the carburetor. Major linkage adjustment (sliding trunnion on rod) may only be required after maintenance involving the removal and/or replacement of the carburetor, TV control rod assembly or the transmission. Minor linkage adjustment (adjustment screw on linkage lever) may be required after

idle speed adjustments greater than 50 rpm and to correct complaints of poor transmission shift quality.

When the linkage is properly adjusted, the TV control lever on the transmission will be at its internal idle stop position (lever up as far as it will travel) when the carburetor is at its hot idle stop with the engine off. There will be a light contact force between the throttle lever and end of the linkage lever adjustment screw. Due to flexibility in the linkage system, the linkage lever adjustment screw would have to be backed out approximately three turns before a gap between the screw and throttle lever could be detected.

At wide open throttle, the TV control lever on the transmission may or may not be at its wide open stop. The wide open throttle position must not be used as the reference point in adjusting the linkage.

LINKAGE ADJUSTMENT AT CARBURETOR

The TV control linkage may be adjusted at the carburetor using the following procedure.

Manual Linkage Gate Stops and Lever Positions

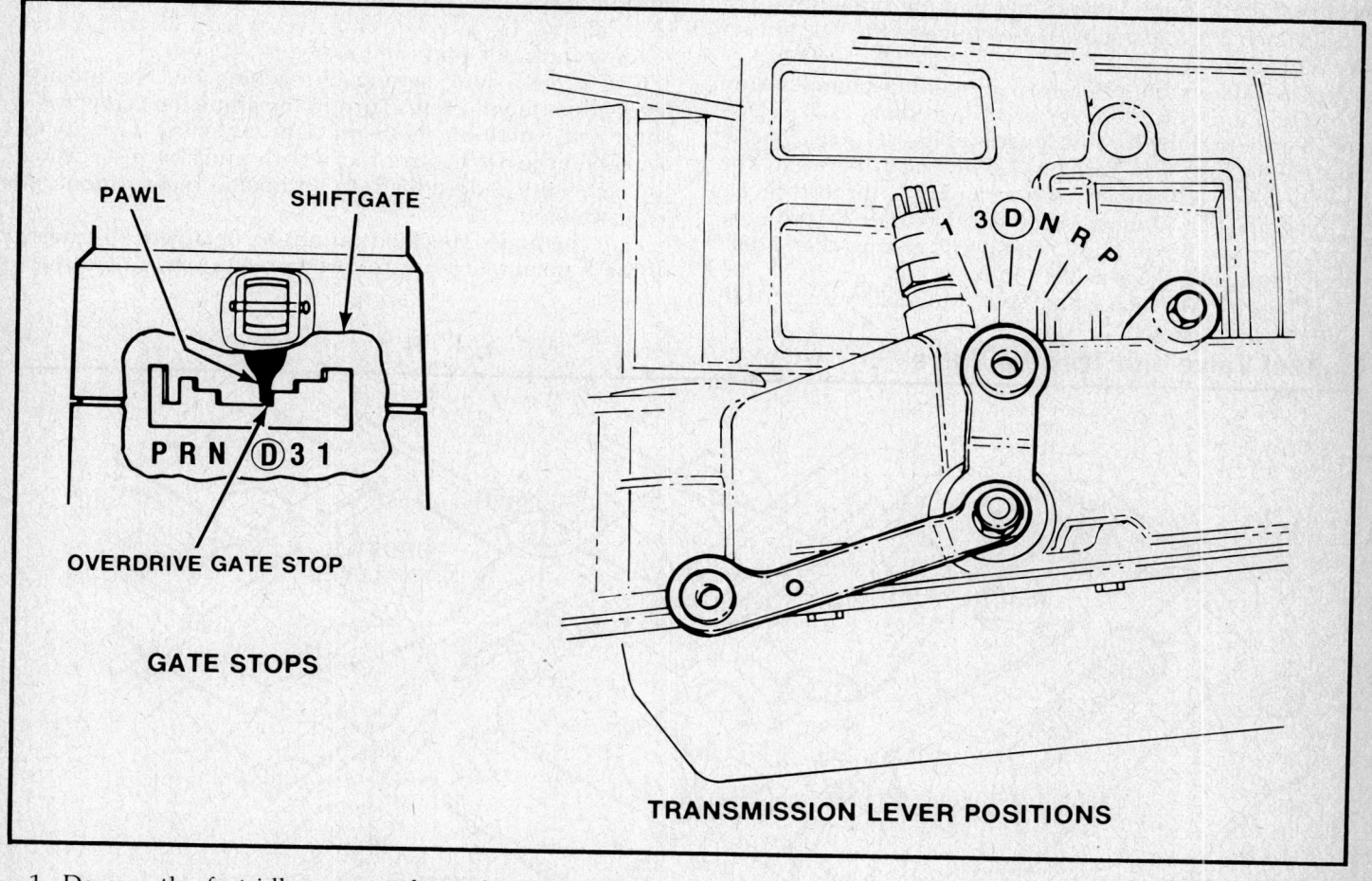

PAWL   SHIFTGATE

P R N D 3 1

OVERDRIVE GATE STOP

GATE STOPS

1 3 D N R P

TRANSMISSION LEVER POSITIONS

1. De-cam the fast idle cam on the carburetor so that the throttle lever is at its idle stop. Place shift lever in Neutral and set parking brake. Engine off.

2. Back out linkage lever adjusting screw all the way (screw end is flush with lever face).

3. Turn in adjusting screw until a thin shim (.005" max.) or piece of writing paper fits snug between end of screw and throttle lever. To eliminate the effect of friction, push the linkage lever forward (tending to close gap). Release it before checking clearance between the end of the screw and the throttle lever. Do not apply any load on the levers with tools or hands while checking gap.

4. Turn in adjusting screw an additional three turns. (Three turns are preferred. One turn minimum is permissible if screw travel is limited.)

5. If it is not possible to turn in adjusting screw at least one additional turn or if there was insufficient screw adjusting capacity to obtain an initial gap in Step Two, refer to "Linkage Adjustment at Transmission."

LINKAGE ADJUSTMENT AT TRANSMISSION

The linkage lever adjustment screw has a limited adjustment capability. If it is not possible to adjust the TV linkage using this screw, the length of the TV control rod assembly must be readjusted using the following procedure. This procedure must also be followed whenever a new TV control rod assembly is installed.

1. Set the engine curb idle speed to specification.

2. With engine off, de-cam the fast idle cam on the carburetor so that the throttle lever is against the idle stop. Place shift lever in Neutral and set parking brake. Engine off.

3. Set the linkage lever adjustment screw at approximately mid-range.

4. If a new TV control rod assembly is being installed, connect the rod to the linkage lever at the carburetor.

5. Loosen the bolt on the sliding trunnion block on the TV control rod assembly. Remove any corrosion from the control rod and free-up the trunnion block so that it slides freely on the control rod.

6. Push up on the lower end of the control rod to insure that the linkage lever at carburetor is firmly against the throttle lever. Release force on rod. Rod must stay up.

7. Push the TV control lever on the transmission up against its internal stop with a firm force (approximately 5 pounds) and tighten the bolt on the trunnion block. Do not relax force on the lever until the bolt is tightened.

LINKAGE ADJUSTMENT USING TV CONTROL PRESSURE

The following procedure may be used to check and/or adjust the TV control linkage using TV control pressure.

AUTOMATIC TRANSMISSIONS

FORD OVERDRIVE

1. Place the shift selector lever in Neutral and disconnect the idle kicker solenoid. Set parking brake.

2. Attach a 0–100 psi pressure gauge to the TV port on the transmission.

3. Operate engine until normal operating temperature is reached and throttle lever is off fast idle.

4. Verify that the throttle lever is at its idle stop. Place a .063 gauge (use 1/16 inch or 1.6mm drill) between the linkage lever adjustment screw and the throttle lever. With engine operating at idle and in Neutral, TV pressure must be below 5 psi. If TV pressure is greater than 5 psi, the TV control linkage is set too long.

5. Place a 0.313 inch gauge (use 5/16 inch or 8mm drill) between the linkage lever adjustment screw and the throttle lever. With the engine operating at idle and in Neutral, the TV pressure must be at least 22 psi. A low reading indicates that the linkage is set short.

6. Correct a long setting by backing out the linkage lever adjustment screw. Turn in the adjusting screw for a short rod condition. If insufficient adjusting capacity is available, the TV control rod length must be reset using the procedure described in ''Linkage Adjustment at Transmission''.

7. If the limits specified cannot be obtained, diagnosis of the transmission control pressure system is required.

Manual Valve and Throttle Valve

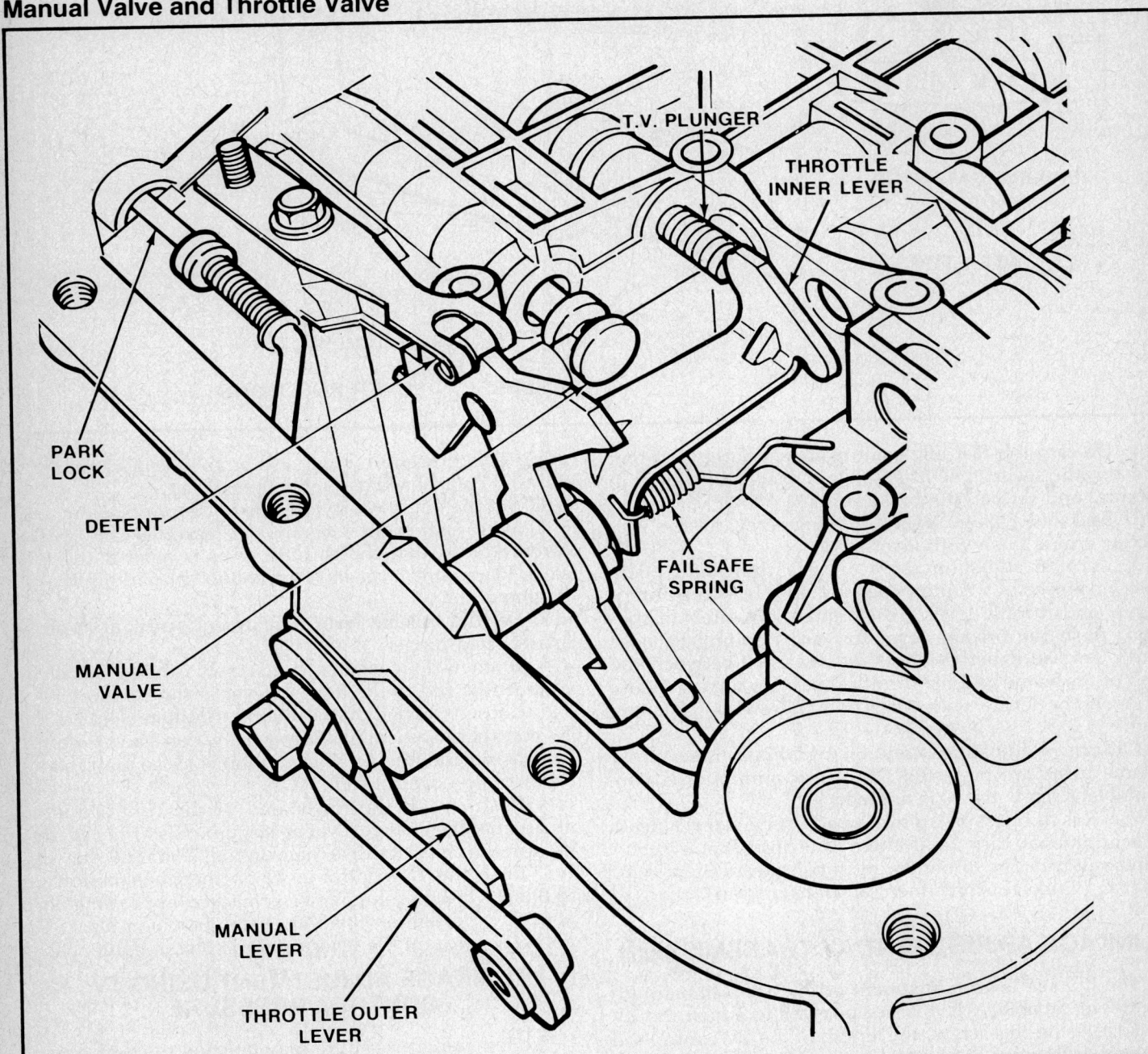

IDLE SPEED ADJUSTMENT

Whenever it is required to adjust idle speed by more than 50 rpm, the adjustment screw on the linkage lever at the carburetor should also be readjusted as shown in following chart.

Idle Speed Change	Turns on Linkage Lever Adjustment Screw
Less than 50 rpm	No change required
50 to 100 rpm increase	1½ turns out
50 to 100 rpm decrease	1½ turns in
100 to 150 rpm increase	2½ turns out
100 to 150 rpm decrease	2½ turns in

After making any idle speed adjustments, always verify the linkage lever and throttle lever are in contact with the throttle lever at its idle stop and the shift lever is in Neutral. If this is not the case, refer to "Shift Trouble Diagnosis."

Component Removal and Installation

MAIN CONTROL VALVE BODY
1. Remove oil pan and screen.
2. Remove the detent spring and attaching bolts.
3. After removing attaching bolts, remove valve body.
4. Installation is the reverse of removal.

OVERDRIVE SERVO ASSEMBLY
1. Remove the main control valve body.
2. Depress overdrive servo piston cover and remove the retaining ring.
3. Apply air pressure to the servo piston release passage in order to remove the overdrive servo piston, cover and spring.
4. Installation is the reverse of removal.

REVERSE SERVO ASSEMBLY
1. Remove the main control valve body.
2. Depress the reverse servo piston cover and remove the retaining ring.
3. Apply air pressure to the servo piston release passage to dislodge the piston.
4. Installation is the reverse of removal.

3-4 ACCUMULATOR PISTON
1. Remove the main control valve body.
2. Depress the 3-4 accumulator cover and remove the retaining ring.
3. Slowly release the tension on the accumulator cover and remove the cover and piston. Also remove the return spring if one is used. Air pressure may be necessary for piston removal.
4. Installation is the reverse of removal. Make certain that the accumulator cover is seated snugly against the retaining ring.

Transmission Case Air Test Pressure Passage Identification

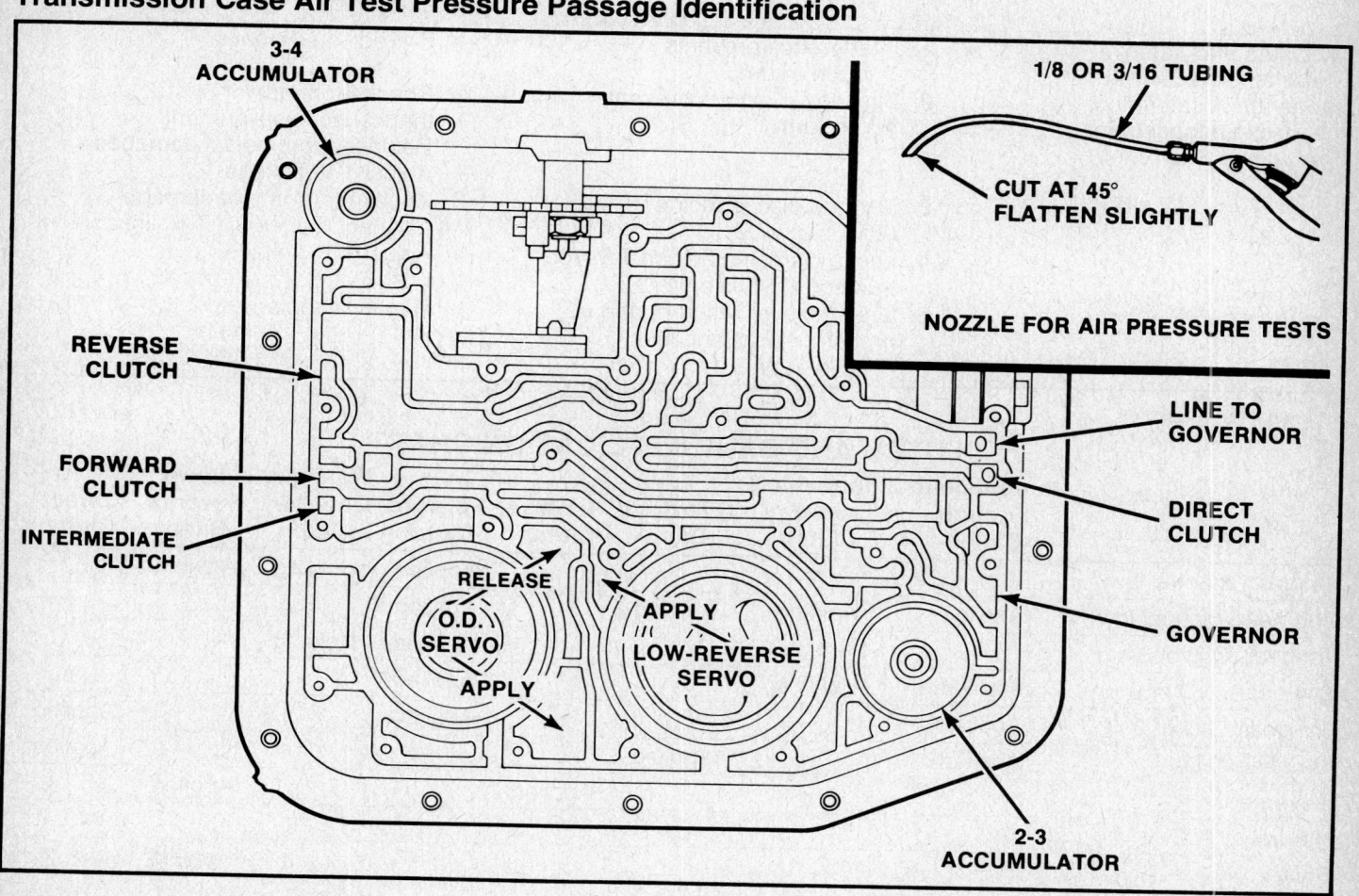

B823

AUTOMATIC TRANSMISSIONS
FORD OVERDRIVE

2-3 ACCUMULATOR PISTON
1. Remove the main control valve body.
2. Depress the 2-3 accumulator piston cover and remove the retaining snap ring.
3. Remove the cover, piston and spring.
4. Installation is the reverse of removal.

EXTENSION HOUSING
1. Remove the driveshaft from the transmission.
2. Disconnect the speedometer cable from the extension housing.
3. Remove the engine rear support-to-extension housing attaching bolts. On Continental, remove the reinforcement plate from under the transmission oil pan.
4. Raise the transmission far enough to remove the weight from the engine rear support and remove the engine rear support.
5. Lower the transmission, remove the extension housing bolts and slide the housing off the output shaft.
6. Installation is the reverse of removal.

GOVERNOR
1. Remove the extension housing.
2. Remove the governor-to-output shaft retaining snap ring.
3. Tap the governor assembly off the output shaft.
4. Installation is the reverse of removal.

SHIFT TROUBLE DIAGNOSIS

Symptoms	Cause	Correction
Early and/or soft upshift, slip-bump feel on light throttle 3-4 or 4-3, no kickdown or wrong kickdown speeds	1. T.V. control linkage is set too short	1. Perform carburetor linkage adjustment If adjusting screw has insufficient travel, perform transmission linkage adjustment
Harsh idle engagement with engine hot (at curb idle), shift clunk in backout shifts, harsh 4-3 coasting shift	1. T.V. control linkage is set too long	1. Perform carburetor linkage adjustment If adjusting screw has insufficient travel or condition is not corrected, perform transmission linkage adjustment
Very late and harsh upshifts, expecially at moderate acceleration, harsh idle engagement	1. Interference prevents T.V. rod return 2. Binding grommets prevent T.V. return 3. T.V. rod disconnected (T.V. is at W.O.T.) 4. Loose clamping bolt on T.V. rod trunnion (T.V. is at W.O.T.) 5. Linkage lever return spring is broken or disconnected (T.V. is at W.O.T.)	1. Correct interference 2. Check for bends or twists that cause misalignment Replace grommets if damaged Adjust T.V. linkage 3. Check for grommet damage Connect rod, adjust T.V. linkage 4. Adjust T.V. linkage 5. Repair or replace spring

CLUTCH AND BAND APPLICATION CHART

	Intermediate Friction Clutch	Intermediate One-Way Clutch	Overdrive Band	Reverse Clutch	Forward Clutch	Planetary One-Way Clutch	Low-Reverse Band	Direct Clutch
1st gear, manual low					Applied	Holding	Applied	
2nd gear, manual low	Applied	Holding	Applied		Applied			
1st gear, O/D or 3					Applied	Holding		
2nd gear, O/D or 3	Applied	Holding			Applied			
3rd gear, O/D or 3	Applied				Applied			Applied
4th gear, O/D	Applied		Applied					Applied
Reverse				Applied			Applied	
Neutral								
Park							Applied	

TORQUE CHART

Application	N·m	In. Lbs.	Ft. Lbs.
Reinforcing plate to valve body	9–11	80–100	
Separator plate to valve body	9–11	80–100	
Valve body to case	9–11	80–100	
Filter to valve body	9–11	80–100	
Oil pan to case	16–22		12–16
Extension to case	22–27		16–20
Governor body to counterweight	9–14	80–120	
Governor body cover to governor body	4–6	34–50	
Inner manual lever to shaft	41–54		30–40
Outer throttle lever to shaft	16–22		12–16
Cooler line to case	14–19		10–14
Converter plug to converter	11–38		8–28
Neutral start switch to case	11–15		8–11
Pressure plug to case	8–16		6–12

FORD CW AND FMX

Identification

The identification tag is located under the left side extension housing bolt. The CW transmission is coded Y on the vehicle certification label. The FMX transmission is coded X. The illustrations below show the transmission identification tags and the code interpretation.

In-Car Testing Procedures

NOTE   The Ford Rotunda ARE-2905 automatic transmission tester is a convenient tool for quick testing. A vacuum gauge, tachometer and 400 psi pressure gauge may be substituted.

CONTROL PRESSURE AT ZERO GOVERNOR RPM
Ford FMX

Transmission Model	Manifold Vacuum In. Hg.	Range	Psi
PHA-F, PHB	12 and above	P, N, D, 2, 1	61–107
		R	90–156
	10	P, N, D, 2, 1	75–20
	Below 1.0 (stall)	R	185–225
		D, 2, 1	154–188

CONTROL PRESSURE CHECK

When the vacuum diaphragm unit operates properly and the downshift linkage is adjusted correctly, all transmission shifts (automatic and kickdown) should occur within the specified road speed limits. If these shifts do not occur within the limits or if the transmission slips during a shift point, perform the following procedure to locate the problem.

1. Connect a Ford Rotunda ARE-2905 automatic transmission tester as follows.
   a. Tachometer cable to engine.
   b. Vacuum gauge hose with a tee fitting between the vacuum hose and vacuum diaphragm.

NOTE   On vehicles equipped with a dual area diaphragm (DAD), check the control pressure at 10 in. of vacuum by removing the exhaust gas recirculation (EGR) control hose from the diaphragm and plugging the hose. Do not plug the EGR port in the diaphragm. This port must be left open to atmospheric pressure. When checking the control pressure at stall and idle, keep the hose connected.

   c. Pressure gauge to the control pressure outlet on the transmission.
2. Apply the parking brake and start the engine. On a car equipped with a vacuum brake release, use the service brakes since the parking brake will release automatically when the transmission is put in any Drive position.
3. Check the transmission diaphragm unit for leaks.
4. Check control pressure in all selector lever positions at specified manifold vacuum (see specifications). Record readings and compare to specifications.

VACUUM DIAPHRAGM UNIT CHECK

1. After disconnecting the vacuum hose, remove the vacuum diaphragm unit from the transmission using a crowfoot wrench.
2. Adjust a vacuum pump until the vacuum gauge shows 18 in. Hg. with the vacuum hose blocked.
3. Connect the vacuum hose to the vacuum diaphragm unit and note the reading on the vacuum gauge. If the reading is 18 inches of vacuum, the vacuum diaphragm unit is good. While removing the vacuum hose from the vacuum diaphragm unit, hold a finger over the end of the control rod. As the vacuum is released, the internal spring of the vacuum diaphragm unit will push the control rod out.

SHIFT POINT CHECKS FOR AUTOMATIC TRANSMISSIONS

To determine if the transmission is shifting at the proper road speeds, use the following procedure.

1. Check the minimum throttle upshifts by placing the transmission selector lever in the Drive position and noting the road speeds at which the transmission shifts from first gear to second to third. All shifts should occur within the specified limits.

2. While driving in third gear, depress the accelerator pedal past the detent (to the floor). Depending on vehicle speed, the transmission should downshift from third gear to second or from second gear to first.

3. Check the closed throttle downshift from third gear to first by coasting down from about 30 mph in third gear. This downshift should occur at the specified road speed.

4. With the transmission in third gear and the car moving at a road speed of 35 mph, the transmission should downshift to second gear when the selector lever is moved from Drive to 2 to 1. This check will determine if the governor pressure and shift control valves are operating properly. If the transmission does not shift within the specified limits or certain gears cannot be obtained, refer to the "Troubleshooting" chart.

AIR PRESSURE CHECKS

If the car will not move in one or more ranges or if it shifts erratically, the items at fault can be determined by using air pressure at the indicated passages.

Drain the transmission. Remove the oil pan and the control valve assembly.

FRONT CLUTCH

Apply sufficient air pressure to the front clutch input passage. A dull thud can be heard when the clutch piston moves.

GOVERNOR

Remove the governor inspection cover from the extension housing. Apply air to the front clutch input passage. Listen for a sharp click and watch to see if the governor valve snaps inward as it should.

REAR CLUTCH

Apply air to the rear clutch passage and listen for the dull thud that will indicate that the rear clutch piston has moved. Listen for leaks.

FRONT SERVO

Apply air pressure to the front servo apply tube and note if the front band tightens. Shift the air to the front servo release tube, which is next to the apply tube, and watch the band release.

REAR SERVO

Apply air pressure to the rear servo apply passage. The rear band should tighten around the drum.

CONCLUSIONS

If the operation of the servos and clutch is normal with air pressure, the "no drive" condition is due to the control valve and pressure regulator valve assemblies. These should be disassembled, cleaned and inspected.

If operation of the clutches is not normal (e.g., both clutches apply from one passage or one fails to move), the aluminum sleeve (bushing) in the output shaft is out of position or badly worn.

Use air pressure to check the passages in the sleeve, shaft and primary sun gear shaft.

If the passages in the two shafts and the sleeve are clean, remove the clutch assemblies. Clean and inspect the parts.

Erratic operation can also be caused by loose valve body screws. When reinstalling the valve body, be careful to tighten all screws and bolts to specifications.

Transmission Case Control Linkage

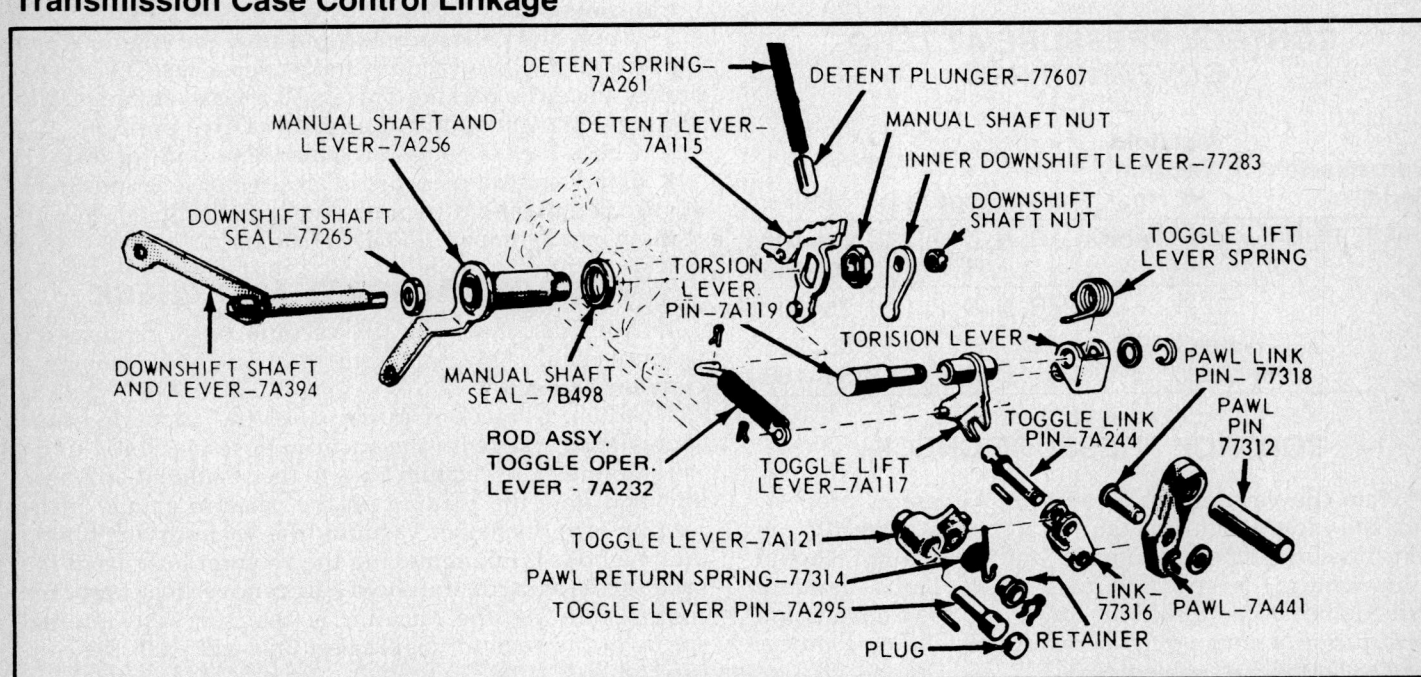

In-Car Service Procedures

SHIFT LINKAGE ADJUSTMENT

Ford Full-Size Cars
Ford Thunderbird
Mercury Full-Size Cars

1. With the engine off, loosen the clamp at the shift lever so the shift rod is free to slide. On models with a shift cable, remove the nut from the transmission manual lever and disconnect the cable from the transmission.
2. Position the lever in Drive position tightly against the D stop.
3. Shift lever at transmission into Drive position.

NOTE Drive position is the third from the rear on all column shift select shift transmissions, fourth from the rear on all console shift select shift transmissions.

4. Tighten clamp and torque nut to 10–20 ft. lbs.

All Ford Mid-Size Cars
With Column Shift

1. Turn the engine off. Loosen the shift rod clamp on the transmission. On cable type units, remove the nuts at the transmission shift rod and at the manual lever stud.
2. Shift the transmission into Drive.
3. Shift the transmission lever into the second detent from the rear.
4. Tighten the shift rod clamp to 10–20 ft. lbs. Position the cable onto the transmission manual lever stud, aligning the flats. Replace the nuts at either end.
5. Check for proper pointer alignment and operation in all positions.

All Ford Mid-Size Cars With
Floor/Console Shift

1. Place shift lever in Drive.
2. Loosen the transmission manual lever retaining nut.
3. Shift the transmission manual lever into the second detent from the rear.
4. Tighten the manual transmission lever nut to 10–20 ft. lbs.
5. Check operation in all positions.

NEUTRAL START SWITCH ADJUSTMENT

All Ford Cars
With Column Shift

Models which are equipped with a column mounted shift lever are not equipped with a neutral start switch. Instead, an ignition lock cylinder-to-shift lever interlock prevents these models from being started in any gear other than Park or Neutral.

THROTTLE LINKAGE ADJUSTMENT

All Ford Cars

1. Disconnect the downshift return spring.
2. Hold the carburetor throttle lever in a wide open position (against stop). Hold the transmission linkage in full downshift position against its internal stop.
3. Turn the carburetor downshift lever adjustment screw to within .010–.080 in. of the contacting pick-up surface of the throttle lever.
4. Connect the return spring.

BAND ADJUSTMENTS

FRONT BAND

When it is necessary to adjust the front band of the transmission, perform the following procedure.
1. Drain the transmission fluid. Remove the oil pan, fluid filter screen and clip.
2. Clean the pan and filter screen. Remove the old gasket.
3. Loosen the front servo adjusting screw locknut.

NOTE Special band adjusting wrenches are recommended to do this operation correctly and quickly.

4. Pull back the actuating rod and insert a ¼ in. spacer bar between the adjusting screw and the servo piston stem. Tighten the adjusting screw to 10 in. lbs. torque. Remove the spacer bar and tighten the adjusting screw an additional ¾ turn, except on CW. Hold the adjusting screw and tighten the locknut securely (20–25 ft. lbs).

CHECKS AND ADJUSTMENTS
Ford FMX

Operation	Specification
Transmission end play check	0.010–0.029 (selective thrust washers available)
Turbine and stator end play check	New or rebuilt 0.023 max., Used 0.050 max.
Front band adjustment (use ¼ inch spacer between adjustment screw and servo piston stem)	Adjust screw to 10 in. lbs. torque. Remove spacer, hold screw and then tighten screw an additional ¾ turn. Torque locknut to 20–25 ft. lb.
Rear band adjustment	Loosen locknut. Adjust screw to 10 ft. lb. torque, then back off exactly 1½ turns. Hold screw and tighten locknut to 35–40 ft. lb.
Primary sun gear shaft ring end gap check	0.002–0.009
Rear clutch selective snap ring thickness	0.060–0.064, 0.074–0.078, 0.088–0.092, 0.102–0.106

AUTOMATIC TRANSMISSIONS
FORD CW & FMX

Front Band Adjustment

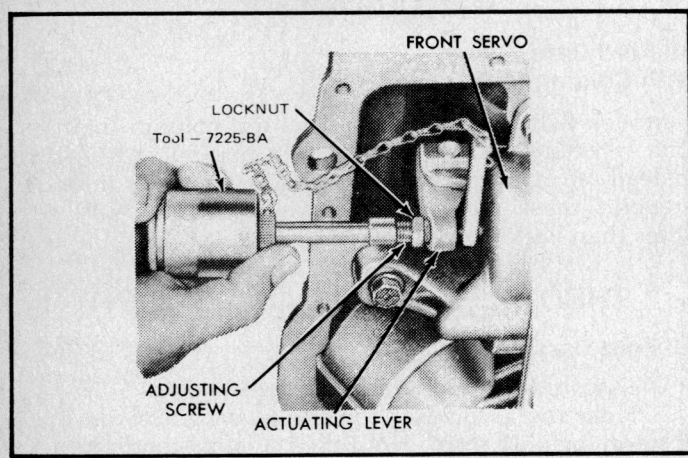

5. Install the transmission fluid filter screen and clip. Install the pan wth a new pan gasket.

6. Refill the transmission to the "FULL" mark on the dipstick. Start the engine and run for a few minutes. Shift the selector lever through all positions. Place it in Park. Recheck the fluid level again and add fluid to the proper level if necessary.

REAR BAND

The rear band of the FMX transmission may be adjusted by any of the following methods. On most cars, the basic external band adjustment is satisfactory. The internal adjustment may be performed in cases where the adjustment required is outside the range of the external adjustment. On certain cars with a console floor shift, the entire console, shift lever and linkage will have to be removed to gain access to the rear band external adjusting screw.

External Adjustment

The procedure for adjusting the rear band externally is as follows.

1. Locate the external rear band adjusting screw on the transmission case. Clean all dirt from the threads and coat the threads with light oil.

Rear Band Adjustment

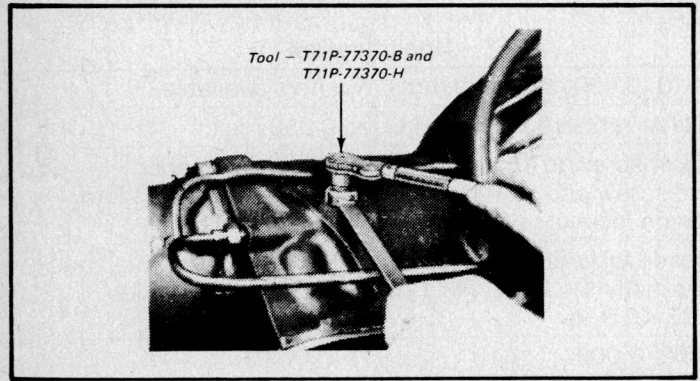

All models except LTD II, Thunderbird and Cougar

Front Band Adjusting Tools

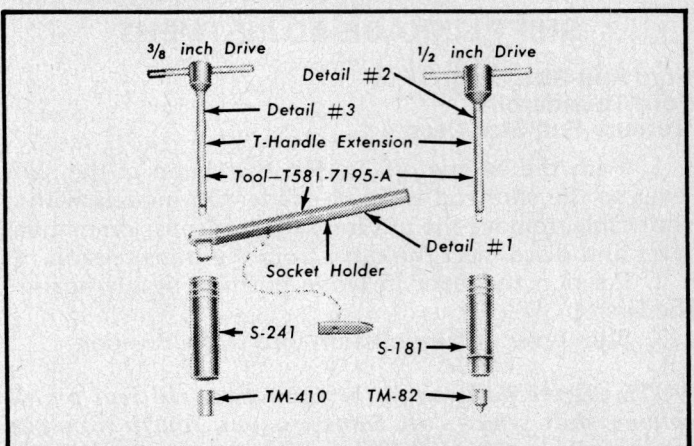

NOTE The adjusting screw is located on the upper right side of the transmission case. Access is often through a hole in the front floor to the right of the center under the carpet.

2. Loosen the locknut on the rear band external adjusting screw.

3. Tighten the adjusting screw to 10 ft. lbs. torque. If the adjusting screw is tighter than 10 ft. lbs. torque, loosen the adjusting screw and retighten to the proper torque.

4. Back off the adjusting screw 1½ (1¼ on CW) turns. Hold the adjusting screw steady while tightening the locknut to the proper torque (35–40 ft. lbs.). Severe damage may result if adjusting screw is not backed off exactly as specified.

Internal Adjustment

The rear band is adjusted internally as follows.

1. Drain the transmission fluid. If it is to be reused, filter it as it drains from the transmission. Reuse the transmission fluid only if it is in good condition.

2. Remove and clean the pan, fluid filter and clip.

3. Loosen the rear servo adjusting locknut.

4. Pull the adjusting screw end of the actuating lever

Rear Band Adjustment

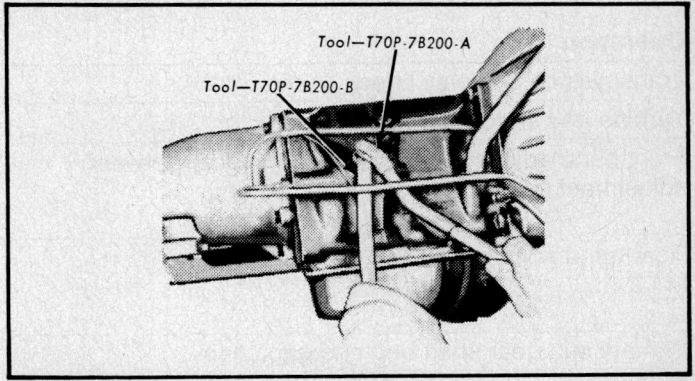

LTD II, Thunderbird and Cougar

away from the servo body and insert the spacer tool between the servo accumulator piston and the adjusting screw. Be sure the flat surfaces of the tool are placed squarely between the adjusting screw and the accumulator piston. The tool must not touch the servo piston and the handle must not touch the servo piston spring retainer.

5. Using a torque wrench with an Allen head socket adapter, tighten the adjusting screw to 24 in. lbs.

6. Back off the adjusting screw exactly 1½ turns. Hold adjusting screw steady and tighten the locknut securely. Remove the spacer tool.

7. Install the fluid filter, clip and pan with a new gasket.

8. Fill the transmission with the correct amount of fluid.

Major Component R&R Procedures

GOVERNOR ASSEMBLY R&R

The extension housing must be removed to remove the governor assembly from the output shaft. It may be necessary to remove the entire transmission from the car.

EXTENSION HOUSING R&R

1. Raise the car high enough for easy access to the extension housing.

2. Drain the transmission.

3. Disconnect the driveshaft from the rear axle. Slide the front yoke from the extension housing.

4. Disconnect the speedometer cable from the extension housing.

5. Remove the rear engine support nuts. Place a transmission jack under the transmission and raise it enough to clear the crossmember.

6. Remove the bolts and nuts securing the crossmember to the side rails of the frame. Move the crossmember out of the way.

7. Remove the attaching bolts holding the engine rear support to the extension housing. Remove the rear support from the extension housing.

8. Remove all the extension housing attaching bolts. Slide the housing off the output shaft and discard the gasket.

9. Installation is the reverse of the removal procedures. Tighten the housing attaching bolts and check that the output shaft rotates freely by hand. If it binds or feels tight, check the needle bearing and race for correct position.

EXTENSION HOUSING BUSHING AND REAR SEAL R&R

1. Disconnect the driveshaft from the extension housing.

2. Carefully remove the rear seal from the housing.

3. Remove the extension housing bushing using a bushing remover tool. Be careful not to damage the spline seal.

4. Install new bushing in the extension housing.

5. Inspect the universal joint yoke sealing surface for scoring or gouges. Replace the yoke if damaged.

6. Inspect the housing counterbore for burrs. If necessary, smooth it with crocus cloth.

7. Install the new rear seal into the end of the extension housing. Check that the seal is firmly seated.

CONTROL VALVE BODY AND OIL PAN R&R

1. Raise the car on a hoist or jackstands. Place a drain pan under the transmission.

2. Drain the transmission.

3. Remove the oil pan, fluid filter screen and clip. Clean them thoroughly. Discard the old pan gasket.

4. Remove the vacuum diaphragm assembly using a crowfoot wrench (Snap-On tool S8696-A or FCO-24). Do not use pliers, pipe wrenches, etc. to remove the vacuum diaphragm unit. Do not let any solvents enter the vacuum diaphragm unit. Remove the push rod, the fluid screen and its retaining clip.

5. Remove the small compensator pressure tube.

6. Disconnect the main pressure oil tube by carefully loosening the end connected to the control valve body. Then remove the tube from the pressure regulator unit.

CHILTON CAUTION   Be sure to remove the tube in this manner. Otherwise, the tube could be kinked or bent, causing improper fluid pressures and possible damage to the transmission.

7. Loosen the front servo attaching bolts about three turns.

8. Remove the three control valve body attaching bolts and carefully lower the valve body, sliding it off the front servo tubes. Do not damage the valve body or the tubes.

9. When installing the control valve body, align the front servo tubes with the holes in the valve body. Shift the manual lever to the 1 detent. Place the inner downshift lever between the downshift lever stop and the downshift valve. Be sure the manual lever engages the actuating pin in the manual detent lever.

10. Loosely install the control valve body attaching bolts. Move the control valve body toward the center of the transmission case until there is a clearance of 0.050 in. between the manual valve and the actuating pin on the manual detent lever.

11. Tighten the attaching bolts to 8–10 ft. lbs. torque. Ensure that the rear fluid filter retaining clip is installed under the valve body.

12. Install the main pressure oil tube, connecting the end to the pressure regulator unit. Then connect the other end to the main control valve assembly by gently tapping it with a soft-faced hammer.

13. Install the compensator pressure tube on the pressure regulator and control valve body.

14. Check the manual lever for free motion in each detent position by rotating it one full turn. If the manual lever binds in any detent position, loosen the valve body attaching bolts and move the valve body away from the center of the transmission case until the binding is relieved. Retighten the attaching bolts according to step 12.

15. Place the pushrod in the bore of the vacuum diaphragm unit and install the vacuum diaphragm unit.

16. Tighten the front servo attaching bolts.

17. Adjust the front band.

18. Install the fluid filter and its retaining clip.

19. Adjust the rear band.

20. Install the oil pan with a new pan gasket.

21. Fill the transmission with fluid. Start and run the engine for a few minutes. Check the fluid level after shifting the transmission through all positions. Do not overfill the transmission.

22. Check the adjustment of the transmission control linkage.

FRONT SERVO R&R

REMOVAL

1. Drain the fluid and remove the pan and screen.

2. Remove the vacuum diaphragm.

3. Loosen the three valve body attaching bolts.

4. Remove the front servo attaching bolts. Hold the strut and remove the screw.

INSTALLATION

1. Position the front band forward with the end of the band facing down.

2. Make sure the front servo anchor pin is in position in the case web. Align the large end of the servo strut with the servo actuating lever. Align the small end with the band lever.

3. Rotate the band, strut and servo to align the anchor end of the band with the anchor in the case. Push the servo body onto the control valve body tubes.

4. Install the bolts and torque to 30–35 ft. lbs.

5. Torque the control valve body attaching bolts to 8–10 ft. lbs.

6. Check the manual valve to manual lever actuating pin clearance (.050'').

7. Adjust the front band.

8. Install the vacuum diaphragm unit and rod.

9. Install the fluid screen and pan. Fill the transmission.

10. Adjust the downshift and manual linkage.

REAR SERVO R&R

REMOVAL

1. Drain the transmission. Remove the pan and screen.

2. Remove the vacuum diaphragm unit.

3. Remove the control valve body and two front servo tubes.

4. Remove the rear servo bolts. Hold the actuating and anchor struts and remove the servo.

PRESSURE REGULATOR R&R

1. Drain the transmission of fluid. Remove the pan, fluid filter screen and its retaining clip. Discard the used pan gasket.

2. Remove the compensator pressure tube from between the control valve body and the pressure regulator.

3. Remove the main pressure oil tube by gently prying off the end connected to the control valve. Then disconnect the other end from the pressure regulator. Be sure to remove the tube in this order to prevent kinking or bending it.

4. Loosen the spring retainer clip and carefully release the spring tension on the pressure springs. Remove the valve springs, retainer and valve stop, and the valves from the pressure regulator body.

5. Remove the pressure regulator attaching bolts and washers. Take the regulator body out of the transmission case.

6. After cleaning, inspection and reassembly, install the pressure regulator unit in the transmission by reversing the removal procedures.

TROUBLESHOOTING
Ford CW and FMX

Problem	In-Car Checks	Out of Car Checks
No drive in L	Manual linkage. Valve body. Air pressure.	Front clutch. Hydraulic system leakage. Fluid distributor sleeve, output shaft.
No drive in Reverse	Rear band. Rear servo. Valve body. Air pressure. Manual linkage.	Rear clutch. Rear pump, no longer used. Fluid distributor sleeve, output shaft.
No drive in any selector position	Fluid level. Manual linkage. Control pressure. Pressure regulator. Valve body. Air pressure.	Hydraulic system leakage. Front pump.
Lockup in D1	Manual linkage. Rear servo. Front servo.	Rear clutch. Parking linkage. Hydraulic system leakage.
Lockup in D2	Manual linkage. Rear band. Rear servo.	Rear clutch. Parking linkage. Hydraulic system leakage. Planetary one-way clutch.
Lockup in L	Front band. Front servo. Valve body.	Rear clutch. Engine rear oil seal. Hydraulic system leakage.
Lockup in Reverse	Front band. Front servo.	Fluid level. Parking linkage. Hydraulic system leakage.
Rough initial engagement in D1 or D2	Engine idle speed. Vacuum modulator or lines. Control pressure. Pressure regulator. Valve body. Front band.	

TROUBLESHOOTING
Ford CW and FMX

Problem	In-Car Checks	Out of Car Checks
1-2 or 2-3 shift points incorrect or erratic	Fluid level. Vacuum modulator or lines. Manual linkage. Governor. Control pressure. Valve body. Downshift linkage.	
Rough 2-3 shifts	Vacuum modulator or lines. Front band. Pressure regulator. Front servo.	
Engine overspeeds on 2-3 shift	Vacuum modulator or lines. Front band. Valve body. Pressure regulator.	Rear clutch piston air bleed valve.
No 1-2 or 2-3 upshift	Governor. Valve body. Manual linkage. Front servo. Front band.	Rear clutch. Hydraulic system leakage. Fluid distributor sleeve, output shaft.
No 3-1 downshift	Engine idle speed. Vacuum diaphragm unit or tubes. Valve body.	
No forced downshift	Downshift linkage. Control pressure. Valve body.	
Runaway engine on forced downshift	Front band. Pressure regulator. Valve body. Front servo. Vacuum diaphragm unit or tubes.	Hydraulic system leakage.
Rough 3-2 or 3-1 shift at closed throttle	Engine idle speed. Vacuum diaphragm unit or tubes. Valve body.	
Creeps excessively	Engine idle speed. Vehicle brakes.	
Slips or chatters in 1st gear, D1	Fluid level. Vacuum modulator or lines. Control pressure. Valve body.	Fluid distributor sleeve, output shaft. Planetary one-way clutch. Front clutch. Hydraulic system leakage.
Slips or chatters in 2nd gear	Fluid level. Vacuum modulator or lines. Front band. Control pressure. Pressure regulator. Valve body. Front servo.	Front clutch. Hydraulic system leakage.
Slips or chatters in Reverse	Fluid level. Rear band. Control pressure. Pressure regulator. Valve body. Rear servo. Vacuum modulator or lines.	Rear clutch. Hydraulic system leakage. Fluid distributor sleeve, output shaft.
No drive in D1	Manual linkage. Valve body.	Planetary one-way clutch.
No drive in D2	Valve body. Perform air pressure checks. Manual linkage.	Front clutch. Hydraulic system leakage. Fluid distributor sleeve, output shaft.
Parking lock binds or does not hold	Manual linkage.	Parking linkage.
Transmission overheats	Fluid level. Oil cooler and/or connections. Pressure regulator. Front band.	Front pump-to-case seal or gasket.
Engine will not push-start	Fluid level. Manual linkage. Pressure regulator. Valve body	Rear pump not used. Hydraulic system leakage.
Maximum speed too low, poor acceleration	Engine performance.	Front pump-to-case seal or gasket
Transmission noisy in Neutral and Park	Pressure regulator.	Front clutch. Front pump.
Noisy transmission during coast 30-20 mph with engine stopped		Rear pump not used.
Transmission noisy in any Drive position	Pressure regulator.	Planetary assembly. Rear clutch. Front clutch. Front pump.
Fluid leaks	Converter drain plug. Oil pan, filler tube and/or seals. Oil cooler and/or connections. Manual or throttle shaft seals. Pipe plug, side of case. Extension housing-to-case gasket or washer. Center support bolt lock. Extension housing rear oil seal. Speedometer drive gear adaptor seal.	Engine rear oil seal. Front oil pump seal. Front pump-to-case seal or gasket.

FORD C3

Identification

The identification tag is located under the left side extension housing bolt. The C3 transmission is coded V on the vehicle certification label.

Band Adjustment

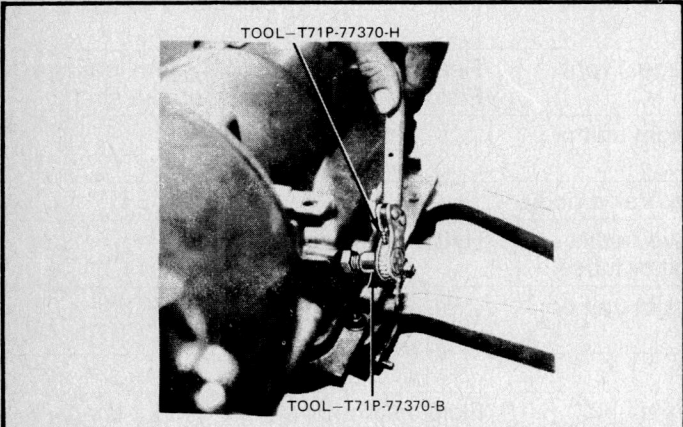

TOOL—T71P-77370-H

TOOL—T71P-77370-B

Front Band Adjustment

1. Remove the downshift rod from the transmission.
2. Clean all dirt from the band adjusting screw. Remove and discard the locknut.
3. Install a new locknut. Tighten the adjusting screw to the present torque with tool kit T71P-77370-A or to 10 ft. lbs. Back off adjusting screw exactly 1½ turns.
4. Torque the locknut to 35–45 ft. lbs.
5. Install the downshift rod.

Governor R&R

1. Remove the small snap ring from the guide rod or connecting pin. Remove the rod and valve.
2. Unscrew the housing from the hub.
3. Move the governor housing toward the rear and the governor hub toward the front of the output shaft to disassemble.

Governor Components

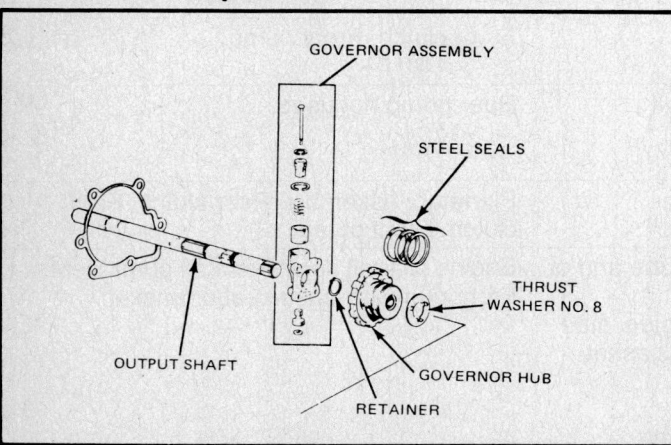

GOVERNOR ASSEMBLY

STEEL SEALS

THRUST WASHER NO. 8

OUTPUT SHAFT

GOVERNOR HUB

RETAINER

4. Remove the snap ring from the housing and remove the weights.
5. Remove the snap ring from the outer weight. Remove the spring and the inner weight.
6. Clean all parts and replace any that are worn or damaged. If necessary, remove the three steel seals and carefully install new ones.
7. Assemble the spring, the inner weight, the outer weight and the snap ring.
8. Secure these in the housing with a snap ring.
9. Assemble the governor housing to the output shaft from the rear, and the hub to the output shaft from the front.
10. Assemble the two together.
11. Install the valve and guide rod or connecting pin. Fasten with the small snap ring.

Governor Housing Disassembled

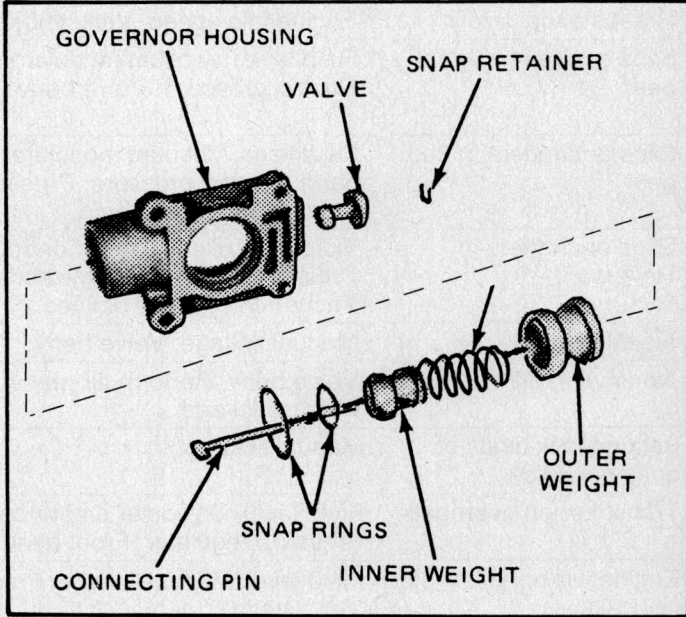

GOVERNOR HOUSING

VALVE

SNAP RETAINER

OUTER WEIGHT

SNAP RINGS

CONNECTING PIN

INNER WEIGHT

Control Valve Body R&R

1. Remove the separator plate bolts and carefully lift off the separator plate.
2. Remove the five ball valves and both relief valves with springs.
3. Remove the retaining plates, dowels, plugs and valves with springs. Do not mix the springs. They can be identified by color.
4. Carefully clean the oil channels and parts by blowing through them with compressed air.
5. Inspect all parts for burring, unevenness and gum deposits. As necessary, replace parts.
6. Lubricate all parts with transmission fluid. Then install the valves, springs, plugs and pins.
7. Using a new gasket, install the separator plate.

Ball Check Valve Installation

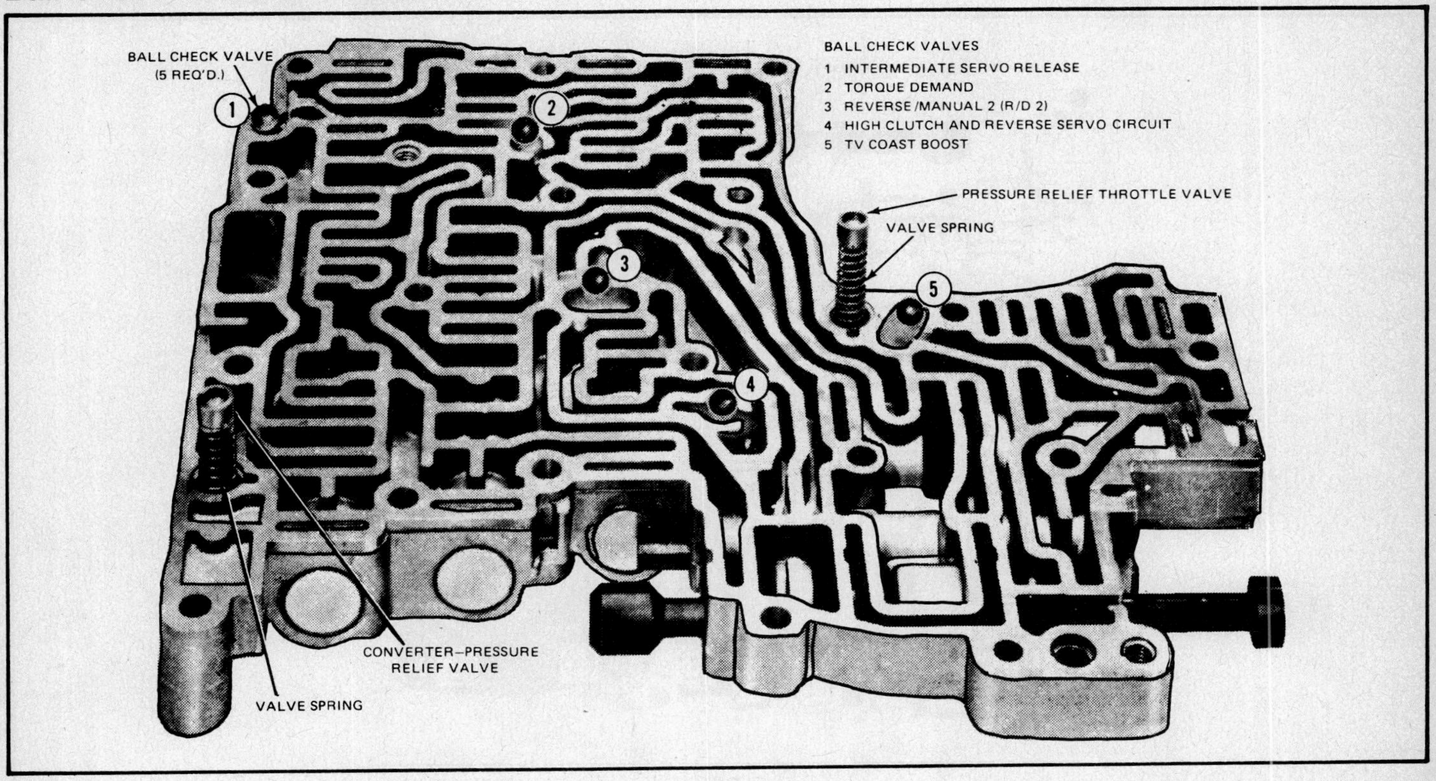

BALL CHECK VALVE
(5 REQ'D.)

BALL CHECK VALVES
1 INTERMEDIATE SERVO RELEASE
2 TORQUE DEMAND
3 REVERSE/MANUAL 2 (R/D 2)
4 HIGH CLUTCH AND REVERSE SERVO CIRCUIT
5 TV COAST BOOST

①
②
③
④
⑤

PRESSURE RELIEF THROTTLE VALVE
VALVE SPRING

CONVERTER—PRESSURE
RELIEF VALVE

VALVE SPRING

Control Valve Body Components

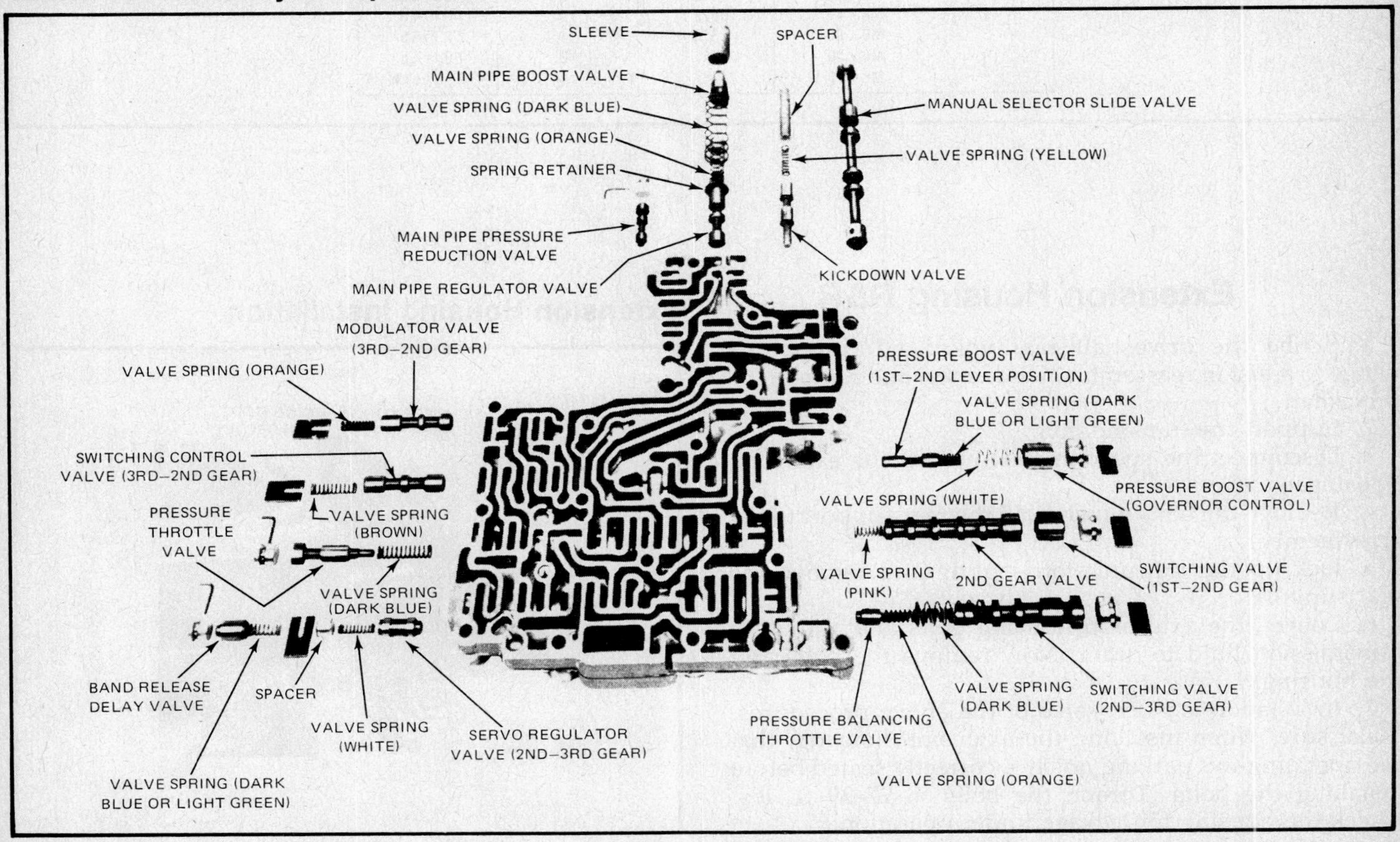

SLEEVE
SPACER
MAIN PIPE BOOST VALVE
VALVE SPRING (DARK BLUE)
MANUAL SELECTOR SLIDE VALVE
VALVE SPRING (ORANGE)
VALVE SPRING (YELLOW)
SPRING RETAINER

MAIN PIPE PRESSURE
REDUCTION VALVE

MAIN PIPE REGULATOR VALVE

KICKDOWN VALVE

MODULATOR VALVE
(3RD—2ND GEAR)

PRESSURE BOOST VALVE
(1ST—2ND LEVER POSITION)

VALVE SPRING (ORANGE)

VALVE SPRING (DARK
BLUE OR LIGHT GREEN)

SWITCHING CONTROL
VALVE (3RD—2ND GEAR)

PRESSURE
THROTTLE
VALVE

VALVE SPRING (WHITE)

PRESSURE BOOST VALVE
(GOVERNOR CONTROL)

VALVE SPRING
(BROWN)

VALVE SPRING
(DARK BLUE)

VALVE SPRING
(PINK)

2ND GEAR VALVE

SWITCHING VALVE
(1ST—2ND GEAR)

BAND RELEASE
DELAY VALVE

SPACER

VALVE SPRING
(WHITE)

SERVO REGULATOR
VALVE (2ND—3RD GEAR)

PRESSURE BALANCING
THROTTLE VALVE

VALVE SPRING
(DARK BLUE)

SWITCHING VALVE
(2ND—3RD GEAR)

VALVE SPRING (DARK
BLUE OR LIGHT GREEN)

VALVE SPRING (ORANGE)

Control Valve Body Specifications

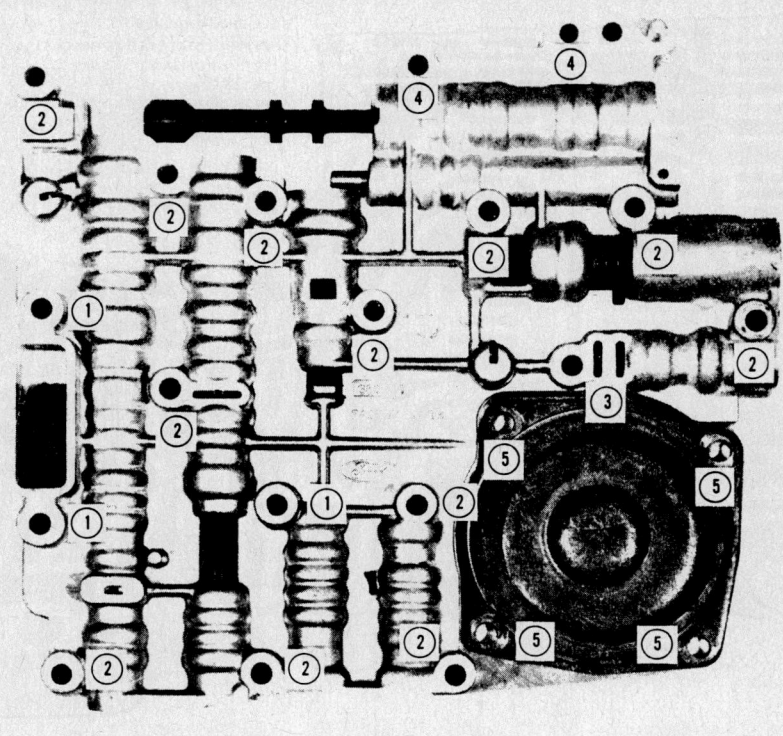

Position	Bolt Size Metric	Length In Inches	Quantity	Torque
1	M6 x 45	1.772	3	7-9 Ft-Lb
2	M6 x 40	1.578	12	7-9 Ft-Lb
3	M6 x 35	1.378	1	7-9 Ft-Lb
4	M6 x 30	1.141	2	7-9 Ft-Lb
5	M6 x 20	.787	4	7-10 Ft-Lb

Extension Housing R&R

1. Scribe the driveshaft rear yoke and companion flange to assist in reassembly. Disconnect and remove the driveshaft.

2. Support the transmission.

3. Disconnect the speedometer cable at the extension housing.

4. Remove the bolts which hold the rear support to the crossmember.

5. Jack up the transmission slightly and remove the rear support.

6. Loosen the extension housing bolts and allow the transmission fluid to drain. Now remove the bolts and the housing.

7. Installation is the reverse of the above procedures. Make sure, when installing the extension housing, that the operating rod parking notch is correctly seated before installing the bolts. Torque the bolts to 27–39 ft. lbs. Check the housing for leakage under operation.

Extension Housing Installation

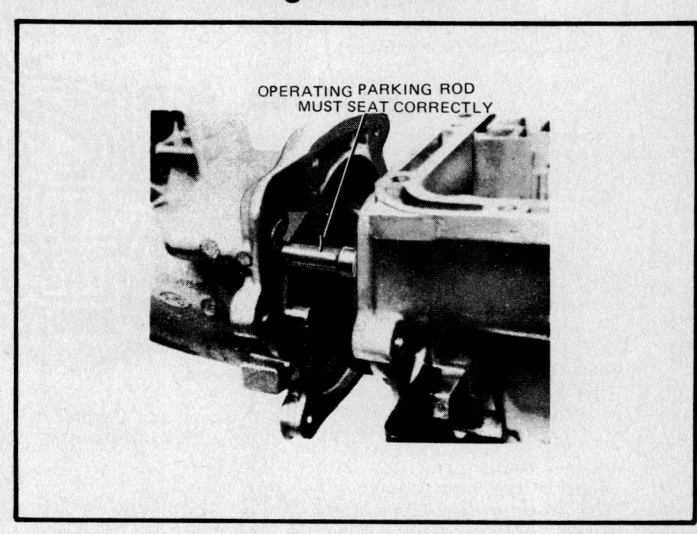

OPERATING PARKING ROD MUST SEAT CORRECTLY

TROUBLESHOOTING
Ford C3

Problem	In-Car Checks	Out of Car Checks
Rough initial engagement In D1 or D2	Engine idle speed. Vacuum modulator or lines. Control pressure. Pressure regulator. Valve body. Intermediate band.	Forward clutch.
1-2 or 2-3 shift points incorrect or erratic	Fluid level. Vacuum modulator or lines. Downshift linkage, inner lever position. Manual linkage. Governor. Control pressure. Valve body. Air pressure.	
Rough 1-2 shifts	Vacuum modulator or lines. Intermediate servo. Make control pressure. Pressure regulator.	
Rough 2-3 shifts	Vacuum modulator or lines. Intermediate band. Control pressure. Pressure regulator. Intermediate band. Valve body. Air pressure.	Reverse, high clutch. Reverse, high clutch piston air bleed valve.
Dragged out 1-2 shifts	Fluid level. Vacuum modulator or lines. Intermediate servo. Control pressure. Intermediate band. Valve body. Pressure regulator. Air pressure.	Hydraulic system leakage.
Engine overspeeds on 2-3 shift	Manual linkage. Fluid level. Vacuum modulator or lines. Intermediate servo. Control pressure. Valve body. Pressure regulator. Intermediate band.	Reverse, high clutch. Reverse, high clutch piston air bleed valve.
No 1-2 or 2-3 upshift	Manual linkage. Downshift linkage, inner lever position. Vacuum modulator or lines. Governor. Control pressure. Valve body. Intermediate band. Intermediate servo.	Reverse, high clutch. Hydraulic system leakage.
No 3-1 shift in D1 or 3-2 shift in D2	Governor. Valve body.	
No forced downshift	Downshift linkage, inner lever position. Valve body. Vacuum modulator or lines.	
Runaway engine on forced downshift	Control pressure. Intermediate servo. Intermediate band. Pressure regulator. Valve body. Vacuum modulator or lines.	Forward clutch.
Rough 3-2 or 3-1 shift at closed throttle	Engine idle speed. Vacuum modulator or lines. Intermediate servo. Valve body. Pressure regulator.	
Shifts 1-3 in D1 & D2	Intermediate band. Intermediate servo. Vacuum modulator or lines. Valve body. Governor. Air pressure.	
No engine braking in 1st gear, manual low	Manual linkage. Reverse servo. Governor. Air pressure.	
Creeps excessively	Engine idle speed. Vehicle brakes.	
Slips or chatters in 1st gear, D1	Fluid level. Vacuum modulator or lines. Control pressure. Pressure regulator. Valve body.	Forward clutch. Hydraulic system leakage. Planetary one-way clutch.
Slips or chatters in 2nd gear	Fluid level. Vacuum modulator or lines. Intermediate servo. Intermediate band. Control pressure. Pressure regulator. Valve body. Air pressure.	Forward clutch. Hydraulic system leakage.

AUTOMATIC TRANSMISSIONS

FORD C3

TROUBLESHOOTING

Ford C3

Problem	In-Car Checks	Out of Car Checks
Slips or chatters in Reverse	Fluid level. Vacuum modulator or lines. Control pressure. Reverse servo. Pressure regulator. Valve body. Air pressure.	Reverse, high clutch. Hydraulic system leakage. Reverse, high clutch piston air bleed valve.
No drive in D1	Fluid level. Manual linkage. Control pressure. Valve body. Air pressure.	Planetary one-way clutch.
No drive in D2	Fluid level. Manual linkage. Control pressure. Intermediate servo. Valve body. Air pressure.	Hydraulic system leakage. Planetary one-way clutch.
No drive in L	Fluid level. Manual linkage. Control pressure. Valve body. Intermediate servo. Air pressure.	Hydraulic system leakage. Planetary one-way clutch.
No drive in Reverse	Fluid level. Manual linkage. Control pressure. Valve body. Intermediate servo. Air pressure.	Reverse, high clutch. Hydraulic system leakage. Reverse, high clutch piston air bleed valve.
No drive in any selector position	Fluid level. Manual linkage. Control pressure. Pressure regulator. Valve body. Air pressure.	Hydraulic system leakage. Front pump.
Lockup in D1		Reverse, high clutch. Parking brake linkage. Hydraulic system leakage.
Lockup in D2	Reverse servo.	Reverse, high clutch. Parking brake linkage. Hydraulic system leakage. Planetary one-way clutch.
Lockup in L	Intermediate band. Intermediate servo.	Reverse, high clutch. Parking brake linkage. Hydraulic system leakage.
Lockup in Reverse	Intermediate band. Intermediate servo.	Forward clutch. Parking brake linkage. Hydraulic system leakage.
Parking lock binds or does not hold	Manual linkage.	Parking brake linkage.
Transmission overheats	Oil cooler and/or connections. Pressure regulator. Vacuum modulator or lines. Control pressure.	Front oil pump seal.
Maximum speed too low, poor acceleration	Engine performance. Vehicle brakes.	Front oil pump seal.
Transmission noisy in Neutral & Park	Fluid level. Pressure regulator.	Front pump. Planetary assembly.
Transmission noisy in any Drive position	Fluid level. Pressure regulator.	Planetary assembly. Forward clutch. Front pump. Planetary one-way clutch.
Fluid leaks	Fluid level. Converter drain plug. Oil pan and/or fillet tube gaskets or seals. Oil cooler and/or connections. Manual or downshift lever shaft seal. Pipe plug, side of case. Extension housing-to-case gasket or washers. Extension housing rear oil seal. Vacuum modulator or lines. Reverse servo. Intermediate servo. Speedometer driven gear adaptor seal.	Engine rear oil seal. Front oil pump seal. Front pump-to-case seal or gasket.
Car moves forward in Neutral	Manual linkage.	Forward clutch.

FORD C4 AND C4S

In-Car Testing Procedures

Prior to performing any tests or adjustments, the engine idle speed and anti-stall dashpot adjustment, the manual linkage adjustment and the transmission fluid level must be checked. If the fluid level is excessively low, check for leakage.

Typical Vacuum Diaphragm and Control Pressure Connecting Point

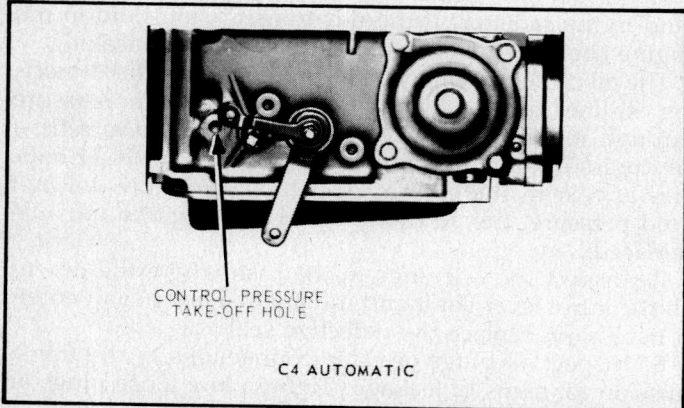

CONTROL PRESSURE
TAKE-OFF HOLE

C4 AUTOMATIC

CHECKS & ADJUSTMENTS
Ford C4 and C4S

Operation	Specification
Transmission end play	0.008–0.042 inch (selective thrust washers available)
Turbine and stator end play	Model PEB, PEG, PEJ. New or rebuilt 0.044 max., used 0.060 max.
	Model PEE, PEA, PEF. New or rebuilt 0.023 max., used 0.040 max.
Intermediate band adjustment	Remove and discard lock nut. Adjust screw to 10 ft. lbs. torque, then back off 1¾ turns. Install new lock nut and torque to specifications.
Low-reverse band adjustment	Remove and discard lock nut. Adjust screw to 10 ft. lbs. torque, then back off 3 turns. Install new lock nut and torque to specifications.

CONTROL PRESSURE CHECK

C4 AUTOMATIC TRANSMISSION

When the vacuum diaphragm unit operates properly and the downshift linkage is adjusted correctly, all transmission shifts (automatic and kickdown) should occur within the specified road speed limits. If these shifts do not occur within the limits or if the transmission slips during a shift point, perform the following procedure to locate the problem.

1. Connect the automatic transmission tester as follows.
   a. Tachometer cable to engine.
   b. Vacuum gauge hose to the transmission vacuum diaphragm unit.
   c. Pressure hose to proper port in transmission.
2. Apply the parking brake and start the engine. On a car equipped with a vacuum brake release, disconnect the vacuum line or use the service brakes since the parking brake will release automatically when the transmission is put in any Drive position.
3. Check the transmission diaphragm unit for leaks.
4. Check control pressure in all selector lever positions at specified manifold vacuum (see specifications). Record readings and compare to specifications.

C4S SEMI-AUTOMATIC TRANSMISSIONS

If the shifts do not occur within the proper road speeds or the transmission slips during a shift point, perform the following procedure to find the possible trouble.

1. Connect the tachometer of the automatic transmission tester to the engine.
2. Attach the pressure gauge to the control pressure outlet at the transmission.
3. Firmly apply the parking brake and start the engine.
4. Check control pressure in all selector lever positions at specified manifold vacuum (see specifications). Record readings and compare to specifications.

VACUUM DIAPHRAGM UNIT CHECK

1. Remove the vacuum diaphragm unit from the transmission after disconnecting the vacuum hose.
2. Adjust a vacuum pump until the vacuum gauge shows 18 in. Hg with the vacuum hose blocked.
3. Connect the vacuum hose to the vacuum diaphragm unit and note the reading on the vacuum gauge. If the reading is 18 in. Hg, the vacuum diaphragm unit is good. While removing the vacuum hose from the vacuum diaphragm unit, hold a finger over the end of the control rod. As the vacuum is released, the internal spring of the vacuum diaphragm unit will push the control rod out.

AIR PRESSURE CHECKS

If the car will not move in one or more ranges or if it shifts erratically, the items at fault can be determined by using air pressure at the indicated passages.

Drain the transmission and remove the oil pan and the control valve assembly.

FRONT CLUTCH

Apply air pressure to the front clutch input passage. A dull thud can be heard when the clutch piston moves.

GOVERNOR

Remove the governor inspection cover from the extension housing. Apply air to the front clutch input passage.

Listen for a sharp click and watch to see if the governor valve snaps inward.

REAR CLUTCH

Apply air to the rear clutch passage and listen for the dull thud that will indicate that the rear clutch piston has moved.

FRONT SERVO

Apply air pressure to the front servo apply tube and note if front band tightens. Shift the air to the front servo release tube, which is next to the apply tube, and watch band release.

REAR SERVO

Apply air pressure to the rear servo apply passage. The rear band should tighten around the drum.

CONCLUSIONS

If the operation of the servos and clutches is normal with air pressure, the "No-drive" condition is due to the control valve and pressure regulator valve assemblies. These should be disassembled, cleaned and inspected.

Operation of the clutches is not normal if both clutches apply from one passage or if one fails to move. When this occurs, the aluminum sleeve (bushing) in the output shaft is out of position or badly worn.

Use air pressure to check the passages in the sleeve and shaft. Also check the passages in the primary sun gear shaft.

If the passages in the two shafts and the sleeve are clean, remove the clutch assemblies. Clean and inspect the parts.

Erratic operation can also be caused by loose valve body screws. When reinstalling the valve body, tighten the control valve body screws to specifications.

TRANSMISSION FLUID LEAKAGE CHECKS

Make the following checks if a leakage is suspected from the transmission case.
1. Clean all dirt and grease from the transmission case.
2. Inspect the speedometer cable connection at the extension housing of the transmission. If fluid is leaking, replace the rubber seal.
3. Inspect the oil pan gasket and attaching bolts for leaks. Torque all bolts and recheck for signs of leakage. If necessary, replace the gasket.
4. Check the filler tube connection at the transmission for signs of leakage. If the tube is leaking, tighten the connection to stop the leak. If necessary, disconnect the filler tube, and replace the O-ring.
5. Inspect all fluid lines between the transmission and the cooler core in the lower radiator tank. Replace any lines or fittings that appear to be worn or damaged. Tighten all fittings to the proper torque.
6. Inspect the engine coolant for signs of transmission fluid in the radiator. If there is transmission fluid in the engine coolant, the oil cooler core is probably leaking.

The oil cooler core may be tested further by disconnecting all lines to it and applying a 50–75 psi air pressure through the fittings. Remove the radiator cap to relieve any pressure buildup outside the cooler core. If air bubbles appear in the coolant or if the cooler core will not hold pressure, the oil cooler core is leaking and must be replaced.
7. Inspect the openings in the case where the downshift control lever shaft and the manual lever shaft enter. If necessary, replace the defective seal.
8. Inspect all plugs or cable connections in the transmission for signs of leakage. Tighten any loose plugs or connectors to the proper torque.
9. Remove the lower cover from the front of the bellhousing and inspect the converter drainplugs for signs of leakage. If there is a leak around the drainplugs, loosen the plug and coat the threads with a sealing compound. Tighten the plug to the proper torque.

NOTE Fluid leaks from around the converter drainplug may be caused by engine oil leaking past the rear main bearing or from the oil gallery plugs. To determine the exact cause of the leak before beginning repair procedures, an oil-soluble aniline or fluorescent dye may be added to the transmission fluid to find the source of the leak if there if one. If a fluorescent dye is used, a black light must be used to detect the dye.

Column Shift Manual Linkage—Full-Size Cars

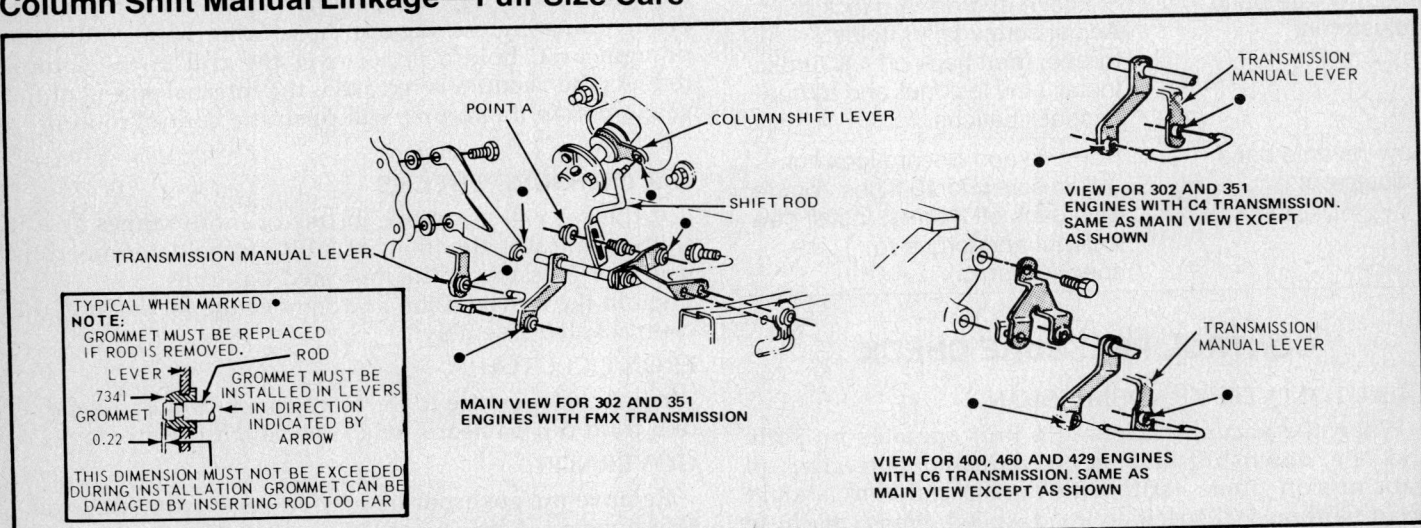

If further converter checks are necessary, remove the transmission from the car and the converter from the transmission. To further check the converter for leaks, assemble and install a converter leak checking tool and fill the converter to 20 psi air pressure. Then, place the converter in a tank of water and watch for air bubbles. If no air bubbles are seen, the converter is not leaking.

In-Car Service Procedures

The following adjustments and repairs may be performed without removing the entire transmission from the car. Some of these procedures will require the use of special tools and instruments.

THROTTLE LINKAGE ADJUSTMENT

All Ford Mid-Size V8

1. Disconnect the downshift return spring.
2. Hold the carburetor throttle lever in wide open position (against stop), and hold the transmission linkage in full downshift position against its internal stop.
3. Turn the carburetor downshift lever adjustment screw to within .010–.080 in. of the contacting pickup surface of the throttle lever.
4. Connect the return spring.

All 6 Cylinder Mid-Size Cars

1. Make sure the idle speed is correct and that the throttle lever is against the hot idle speed adjusting screw when the engine is hot.
2. Disconnect the throttle return spring. Remove the trunnion and cable at the bellcrank.
3. Hold the throttle wide open and hold the transmission in full downshift position.
4. Adjust the trunnion at the bellcrank so the shaft ball stud and cable ball stud receiver are in alignment. Then, give the trunnion one additional turn so as to lengthen it.
5. Reconnect the linkage and throttle return spring.

Ford Pinto, Ford Mustang II and Mercury Bobcat

1. Disconnect the downshift lever return spring.
2. Hold the throttle shaft lever in the wide open position. Hold the downshift rod against the through detent stop. Adjust the downshift screw to obtain 0.050–0.070 in. clearance between the screw tip and the throttle shaft lever tab.
3. Connect the downshift lever return spring.

BAND ADJUSTMENTS

Only the intermediate and low-reverse bands are adjustable.

INTERMEDIATE BAND

1. Clean all dirt from the adjusting screw area. Remove and discard the locknut.
2. Install a new locknut. Tighten the adjusting screw to a torque of 10 ft. lb.

Floor Shift Linkage—Pinto and Mustang

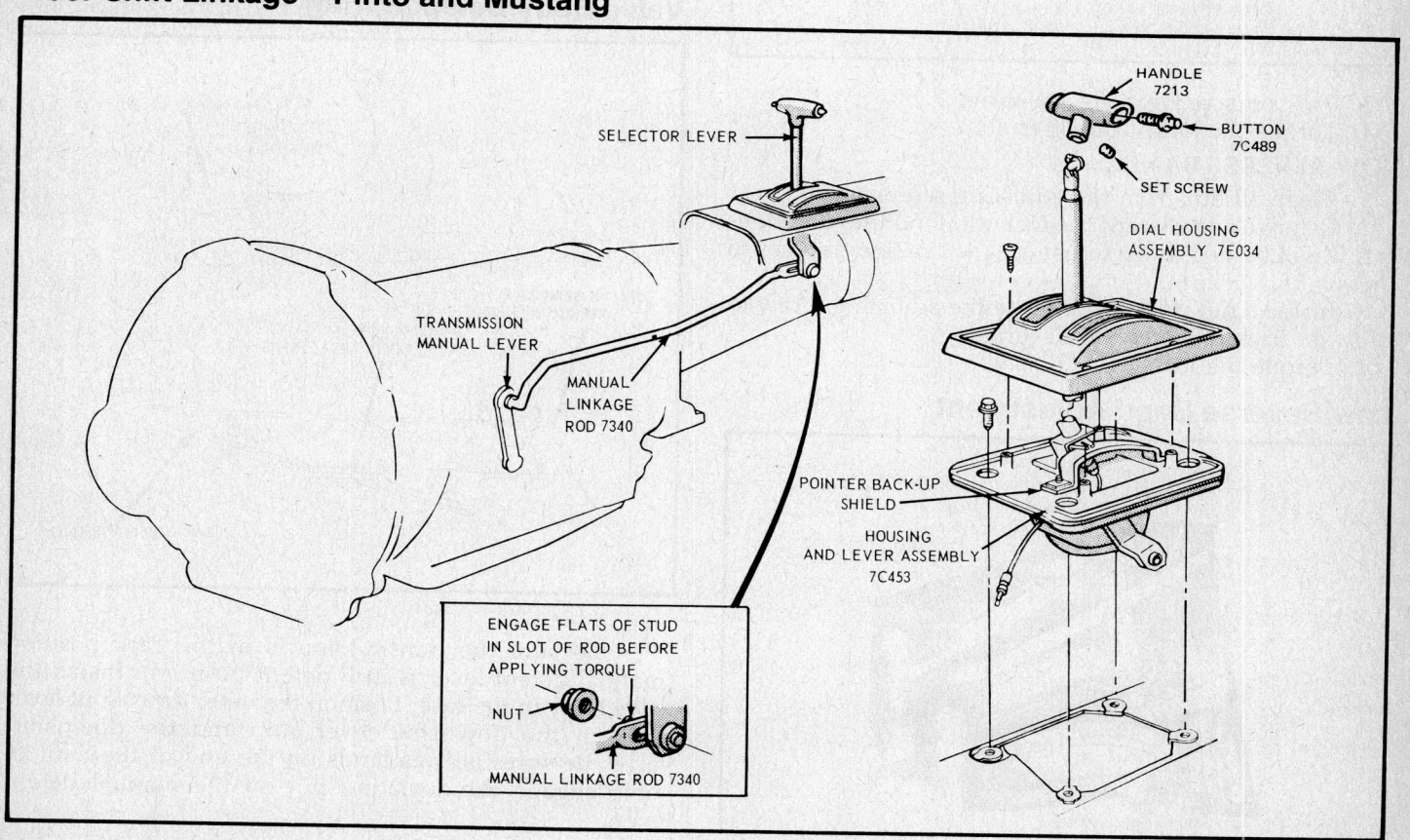

CONTROL PRESSURE AT ZERO OUTPUT SHAFT SPEED
Ford C4 and C4S

Engine Speed	Throttle	Manifold Vacuum In. Hg.	Range	P.S.I.
As required	As required	12 and above	P, N, D	55–86
			2, 1	55–122
			R	55–197
As required	As required	10	P, N, D	98–110
Stall	Through detent	Below 1.0	D, 2, 1	143–164
			R	239–272

Band Adjusting Screws and Nuts

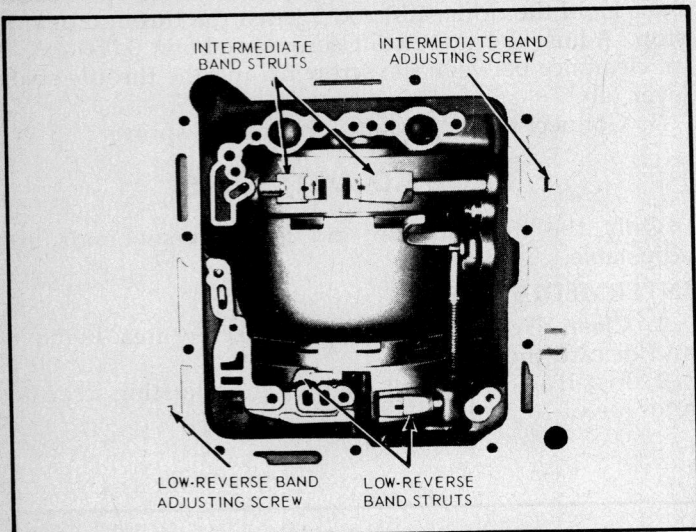

3. Back off screw exactly 1¾ turns.
4. Torque the locknut to 30 ft. lb.

LOW REVERSE BAND

1. Clean all dirt from the adjusting screw area.
2. Remove and discard the locknut. On Pinto and Bobcat, it will be necessary to use a ¾ x 1½" long socket to remove the locknut.
3. Install a new locknut. Torque the adjusting screw to 10 ft. lb. Back off screw 3 full turns.
4. Torque the locknut to 30 ft. lb.

Low Reverse Band Adjustment

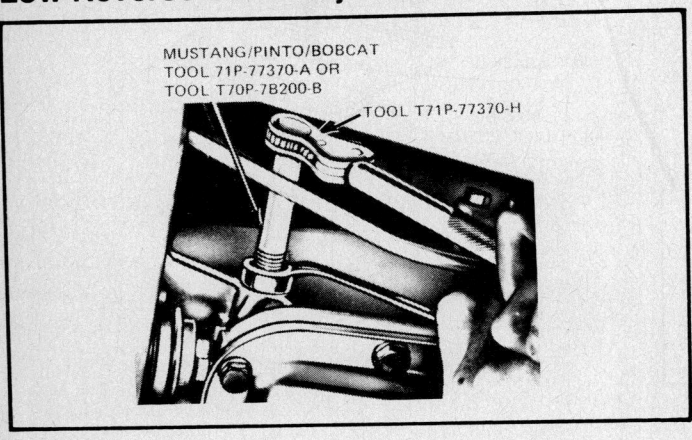

CONTROL VALVE R&R

All Models

1. Make sure throttle linkage and bands are adjusted correctly.
2. Shift the transmission to Park position and remove the two bolts holding the manual detent spring to the control valve body and case.
3. Remove all the valve body-to-case attaching bolts. Hold the manual valve in place and remove the valve body from the case. If the manual valve is not held in place, it could be bent or damaged.
4. Thoroughly clean the old gasket material from the case and remove the nylon shipping plug from the oil filler tube hole. This nylon plug is installed before shipment and should be discarded when the transmission oil pan is removed.

Valve Body Detent Spring

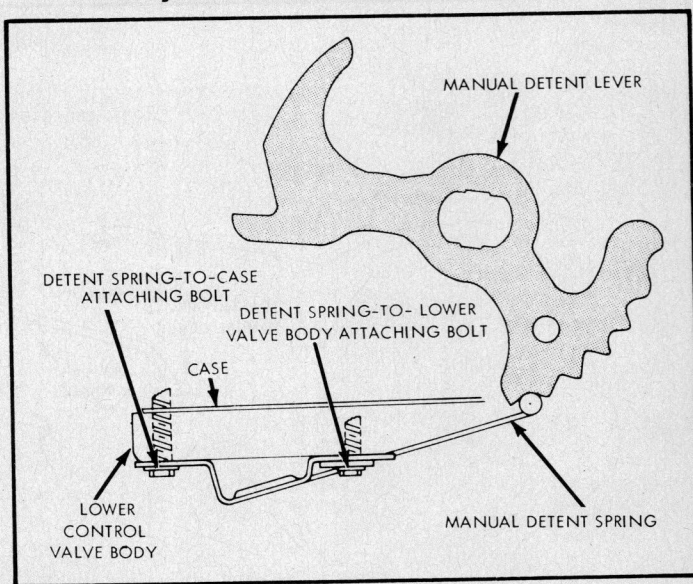

5. Be sure the transmission is in the Park position (manual detent lever is in P detent position). Install the valve body in the case. Position the inner downshift lever between the downshift lever stop and the downshift valve. Be sure the two lands on the end of the manual valve engage the actuating pin on the manual detent lever.

C4 Valve Body-To-Case Attaching Bolts

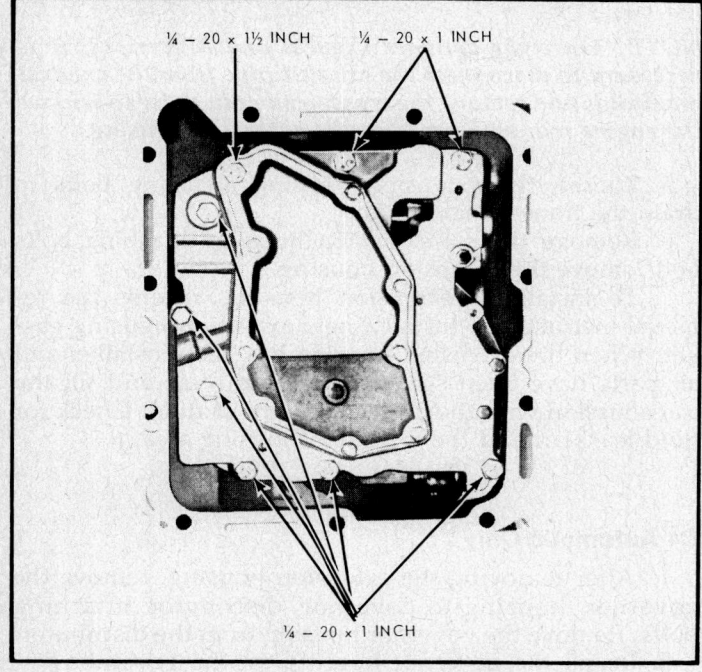

¼ – 20 x 1½ INCH   ¼ – 20 x 1 INCH

¼ – 20 x 1 INCH

6. Install seven valve body attaching bolts, but do not tighten them.

7. Place the detent spring on the lower valve body and install the spring-to-case bolt finger tight.

8. While holding the detent spring roller in the center of the manual detent lever, install the detent spring-to-lower valve body bolt. Tighten it to 80–120 in. lbs. torque.

9. Tighten the remainder of the control valve body attaching bolts to specifications.

10. Put a new gasket on the oil pan. Install pan in place. Install and tighten all the pan attaching bolts to the proper torque.

11. If the filler tube was removed, reinstall it and tighten securely. If necessary, replace the oil seal around the filler tube to prevent leakage.

12. Lower the car and fill the transmission with fluid.

CHILTON CAUTION   Always check the neutral safety switch adjustment after adjusting the shift linkage.

INTERMEDIATE SERVO R&R

1. Raise the car and remove the four servo cover attaching bolts (righthand side of case). Remove the cover and identification tag (do not lose tag).

NOTE   To gain access to the servo on some models, the crossmember must be removed.

2. Remove the gasket, piston and piston return spring.

3. Install the piston return spring in the case. Place a new gasket on the cover. Install new seals on the piston. Lubricate the seals with transmission fluid and install the piston in the servo cover. Install the piston and cover in the transmission case using two 5/16–18 x 1¼ bolts, 180 degrees apart to align the cover against the case.

4. Install the transmission identification tag and two attaching bolts. Remove the two 1¼ bolts and install the other two cover attaching bolts. Tighten all cover attaching bolts to the proper torque.

5. If removed, position the crossmember and install the attaching bolts. Tighten them to the proper torque.

6. Adjust the intermediate band. If the intermediate band cannot be adjusted correctly, remove the control valve body and see that the struts are installed correctly. Adjust the struts and reinstall the control valve body. Install the oil pan with a new gasket.

7. Lower the car and fill the transmission.

Piston Travel Measurement

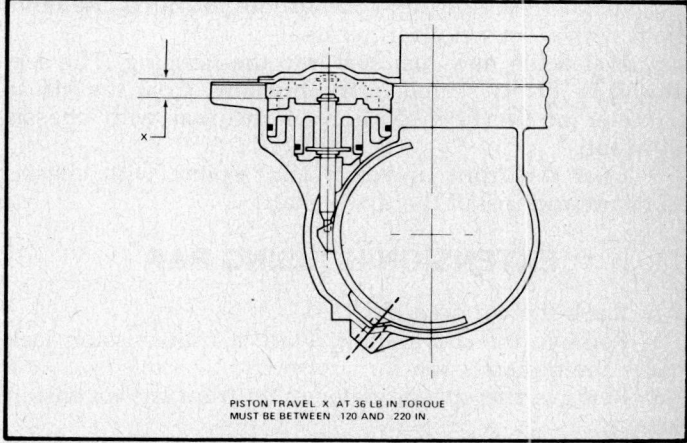

PISTON TRAVEL X AT 36 LB IN TORQUE
MUST BE BETWEEN 120 AND 220 IN.

LOW-REVERSE SERVO PISTON R&R

1. Raise the car on a hoist.

2. Loosen the reverse band adjusting screw locknut and tighten the adjusting screw to 10 ft. lbs. torque. This operation will hold the band strut against the case and prevent it from falling when the reverse servo piston is removed.

3. Remove the four servo cover attaching bolts and remove the servo cover and seal from the case.

4. Remove the servo piston from the case. The piston and piston seal are bonded together and must be replaced together.

NOTE   To remove the piston from the shaft for replacement on a Pinto or Mustang II, insert a small screwdriver through the hole in the shaft to hold the shaft. Remove the retaining nut. Install a new piston and torque the nut to specifications.

5. Install the servo piston assembly into the case. Place a new cover seal on the cover and position it on the case using two 5/16–18 bolts, 1¼ in. long, 180° apart. Install two cover attaching bolts with the identification tag.

6. Remove the two positioning bolts and install the other two cover bolts. Tighten all the cover attaching bolts to the proper torque.

7. Adjust the low-reverse band. If the low-reverse band cannot be adjusted properly, remove the control valve body and check the alignment of the band struts. Reinstall the valve body and the oil pan with a new gasket.

AUTOMATIC TRANSMISSIONS

8. Lower the car and fill the transmission.

EXTENSION HOUSING BUSHING AND REAR SEAL R&R

1. Disconnect the drive shaft from the transmission.
2. If only the rear seal needs replacing, carefully remove it with a tapered chisel or use a slide hammer. Be careful not to damage the spline seal with the bushing remover.
3. Install the new bushing.
4. Before installing a new rear seal, inspect the sealing surface of the universal joint yoke for scores. If the universal joint yoke is scored, replace the yoke.
5. Inspect the housing counterbore for burrs. Remove them with crocus cloth if necessary.
6. Install the new rear seal into the housing. The seal should be firmly seated in the housing. Coat the inside diameter of the fiber portion of the seal with chassis lubricant.
7. Coat the front universal joint spline with chassis lubricant and install the drive shaft.

EXTENSION HOUSING R&R

1. Raise the car on a hoist.
2. Remove the drive shaft. Place a transmission jack under the transmission for support.
3. Remove the speedometer cable from the extension housing.
4. Remove the extension housing-to-crossmember mount attaching bolts. Raise the transmission and remove the mounting pad between the extension housing and the crossmember.

NOTE On eight cylinder Comets and Mavericks, it is necessary to disconnect the exhaust pipe from the exhaust manifolds and remove the crossmember in order to remove the engine rear support from the extension housing.

5. Loosen the extension housing attaching bolts to drain the transmission fluid.
6. Remove the six extension housing attaching bolts and remove the extension housing.
7. To install the extension housing, reverse the removal instructions. Install a new extension housing gasket. When the extension housing has been installed and all parts have been secured, lower the car and fill the transmission with the correct amount of fluid. Check for fluid leaks around the extension housing area.

GOVERNOR R&R

C4 Automatic Only

1. After removing the extension housing, remove the governor housing-to-governor distributor attaching bolts. Remove the governor housing from the distributor.
2. Install the governor housing on the governor distributor. Tighten the attaching bolts to the proper torque.
3. Install the extension housing with a new gasket.
4. When the extension housing has been installed and all bolts have been tightened to the proper torque, lower the car and fill the transmission with fluid to the proper level. Check around the extension housing area for leaks.

TROUBLESHOOTING
Ford C4 and C4S

Problem	In-Car Checks	Out of Car Checks
Rough initial engagement in D1 or D2	Engine idle speed. Vacuum modulator or lines. Control pressure. Pressure regulator. Valve body. Intermediate band.	Forward clutch.
1-2 or 2-3 shift points incorrect or erratic	Fluid level. Vacuum modulator or lines. Manual linkage. Governor. Control pressure. Valve body. Air pressure.	
Rough 1-2 shifts	Vacuum modulator or lines. Intermediate servo. Intermediate band. Control pressure. Valve body. Pressure regulator.	
Rough 2-3 shifts	Vacuum modulator or lines. Intermediate servo. Control pressure. Pressure regulator. Intermediate band. Valve body. Air pressure.	Reverse, high clutch. Reverse, high clutch piston air bleed valve.
Dragged out 1-2 shift	Fluid level. Vacuum modulator or lines. Intermediate servo. Control pressure. Intermediate band. Valve body. Pressure regulator. Air pressure.	Hydraulic system leakage.
Engine overspeeds on 2-3 shift	Manual linkage. Fluid level. Vacuum modulator or lines. Intermediate servo. Control pressure. Valve body. Pressure regulator. Intermediate band.	Reverse, high clutch. Reverse, high clutch piston air bleed valve.

TROUBLESHOOTING
Ford C4 and C4S

Problem	In-Car Checks	Out of Car Checks
No 1-2 or 2-3 upshift	Manual linkage. Downshift linkage, inner lever position. Vacuum modulator or lines. Governor. Control pressure. Valve body. Pressure regulator. Intermediate band. Intermediate servo.	Reverse, high clutch. Hydraulic system leakage.
No 3-1 shift in D1 or 3-2 shift in D2	Governor. Valve body.	
No forced downshift	Downshift linkage, inner lever position. Vacuum modulator or lines.	
Runaway engine or forced downshift	Control pressure. Intermediate servo. Intermediate band. Pressure regulator. Valve body. Vacuum modulator or lines.	Hydraulic system leakage.
Rough 3-2 or 3-1 shift at closed throttle	Engine idle speed. Vacuum modulator or lines. Intermediate servo. Valve body. Pressure regulator.	
Shifts 1-3 in D1 and D2	Intermediate band. Intermediate servo. Vacuum modulator or lines. Valve body. Governor. Air pressure.	
No engine braking in 1st gear, manual low	Manual linkage. Reverse band. Reverse servo. Valve body. Governor. Perform air pressure checks.	
Creeps excessively	Engine idle speed. Vehicle brakes.	
Slips or chatters in 1st gear, D1	Fluid level. Vacuum modulator or lines. Control pressure. Pressure regulator. Valve body.	Forward clutch. Hydraulic system leakage. Planetary one-way clutch.
Slips or chatters in 2nd gear	Fluid level. Vacuum modulator or lines. Intermediate servo. Intermediate band. Control pressure. Pressure regulator. Valve body. Air pressure.	Forward clutch. Hydraulic system leakage.
Slips or chatters in Reverse	Fluid level. Vacuum modulator or lines. Reverse band. Reverse servo. Pressure regulator. Valve body. Intermediate servo.	Reverse, high clutch. Hydraulic system leakage. Reverse, high clutch piston air bleed valve.
No drive in D1	Fluid level. Manual linkage. Control pressure. Valve body. Air pressure.	Planetary one-way clutch.
No drive in D2	Fluid level. Manual linkage. Control pressure. Intermediate servo. Valve body. Air pressure.	Hydraulic system leakage. Planetary one-way clutch.
No drive in L	Fluid level. Manual linkage. Control pressure. Valve body. Reverse servo. Intermediate servo.	Hydraulic system leakage. Planetary one-way clutch.
No drive in Reverse	Fluid level. Manual linkage. Reverse band. Control pressure. Reverse servo. Valve body. Air pressure.	
No drive in any selector position	Fluid level. Manual linkage. Control pressure. Pressure regulator. Valve body. Air pressure.	Hydraulic system leakage. Front pump.
Lockup in D1		Reverse, high clutch. Parking brake linkage. Hydraulic system leakage.
Lockup in D2	Reverse band. Reverse servo.	Reverse, high clutch. Parking brake linkage. Hydraulic system leakage. Planetary one-way clutch.

TROUBLESHOOTING
Ford C4 and C4S

Problem	In-Car Checks	Out of Car Checks
Lockup in L	Intermediate band. Intermediate servo.	Reverse, high clutch. Parking brake linkage. Planetary one-way clutch. Hydraulic system leakage.
Lockup in Reverse	Intermediate band. Intermediate servo.	Forward clutch. Parking brake linkage. Hydraulic system leakage.
Parking lock binds or does not hold	Manual linkage.	Parking brake linkage.
Transmission overheats	Oil cooler and/or connections. Pressure regulator. Vacuum modulator or lines. Control pressure.	Front oil pump seal.
Maximum speed too low, poor acceleration	Engine performance. Vehicle brakes.	Front oil pump seal.
Transmission noisy in Neutral & Park	Fluid level. Pressure regulator.	Front pump. Planetary assembly.
Transmission noisy in any drive position	Fluid level. Pressure regulator.	Planetary assembly. Forward clutch. Front pump. Planetary one-way clutch.
Fluid leaks	Fluid level. Converter drain plug. Oil pan and/or filler tube gaskets/seals. Oil cooler and/or connections. Manual or downshift lever shaft seal. Pipe plug, side of case. Extension housing rear oil seal. Vacuum modulator or lines. Reverse servo. Intermediate servo. Speedometer driven gear adaptor seal.	Engine rear oil seal. Front oil pump seal. Front pump-to-case seal or gasket.
Car moves forward in Neutral	Manual linkage.	Forward clutch.

FORD C6

Identification

The identification tag is located under the left side extension housing bolt. The C6 transmission is coded U on the vehicle certification label. The illustrations below show the transmission identification tag and code interpretation.

In-Car Tests and Adjustments

VACUUM DIAPHRAGM UNIT CHECK ALTITUDE-COMPENSATING TYPE

The vacuum diaphragm unit may be checked for damaged or ruptured bellows as follows.

1. Remove the diaphragm and the throttle valve rod from the transmission.

2. Insert a rod into the diaphragm unit until it is seated in the hole. Make a reference mark on the rod where it enters the diaphragm.

3. Place the diaphragm unit on a scale with the end of the rod resting on the weighing pan and gradually press down on the diaphragm unit.

4. Note the force (in pounds) at which the reference mark on the rod moves into the diaphragm. If the reference mark is still visible at 12 pounds of pressure on the scale, the diaphragm bellows is good. If the reference

CHECKS AND ADJUSTMENTS
Ford C6

Operation	Specification
Transmission end play	0.008–0.044 (selective thrust washers available)
Turbine and stator end play	New or rebuilt 0.021 in. max. Used 0.030 in max. [1]
Intermediate band adjustment	Remove and discard locknut. Adjust screw to 10 ft. lbs. torque, then back off 1 turn. Install new locknut and tighten locknut to specifications. [2]

[1] To check end play, exert force on checking tool to compress turbine to cover thrust washer wear plate. Set indicator at zero.

[2] 1974–77 models: back off adjusting screw 1½ turns.

CONTROL PRESSURE AT ZERO GOVERNOR RPM
Ford C6

Engine Speed	Throttle	Manifold Vacuum In. Hg.	Range	Psi
As required	As required	12 and above	P, N, D	55–86
			2, 1	55–122
			R	55–197
As required	As required	10	D	98–110
Stall	Through detent	Below 1.0	D, 2, 1	143–164
			R	239–272

mark on the rod disappears before four pounds of force, the diaphragm bellows is damaged and the diaphragm unit must be replaced.

VACUUM DIAPHRAGM ADJUSTMENT

A screw is provided in the inlet tube of the vacuum diaphragm assembly to permit small adjustments in control pressure. If control pressure is uniformly high or low in all ranges, it may be brought within specifications by turning this screw. Control pressure may also be varied to alter shift feel, but in no case should it go beyond the specified minimum or maximum.

Control pressure is increased by turning the adjusting screw clockwise, and reduced by turning counterclockwise. One full turn will change control pressure approximately 2–3 psi.

CHILTON CAUTION   Always check the neutral safety switch after linkage adjustments.

Adjusting Intermediate Band

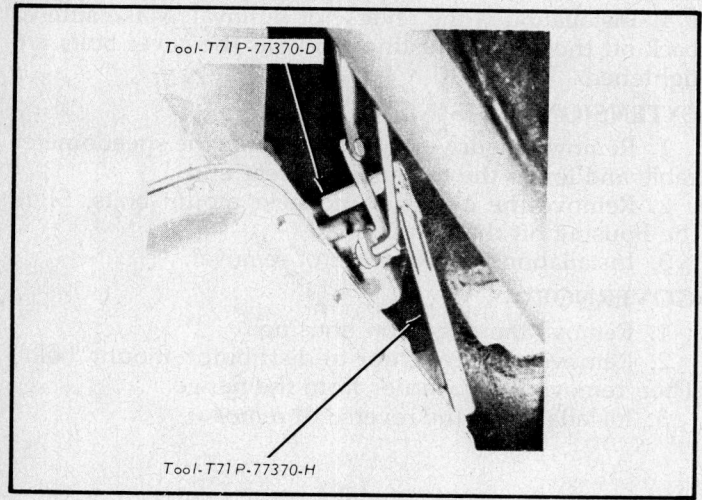

Tool-T71P-77370-D

Tool-T71P-77370-H

INTERMEDIATE BAND

1. Raise the car on a hoist or place it on jack stands.
2. Clean the threads of the intermediate band adjusting screw.
3. Loosen the adjustment screw locknut.
4. Tighten the adjusting screw to 10 ft. lbs., and back the screw off exactly 1½ turns. Tighten the adjusting screw locknut.

THROTTLE LINKAGE ADJUSTMENT

All Ford and Mercury Cars—Except Continental, Mark III, and Mark IV

1. Disconnect the throttle and downshift return spring.
2. Hold the carburetor throttle lever in a wide open position (against the stop). Hold the transmission linkage in a full downshift position against its internal stop.
3. Turn the carburetor downshift lever adjustment screw to within .010–.080 in. of the contacting pick-up surface of the throttle lever.

Downshift and Manual Linkage

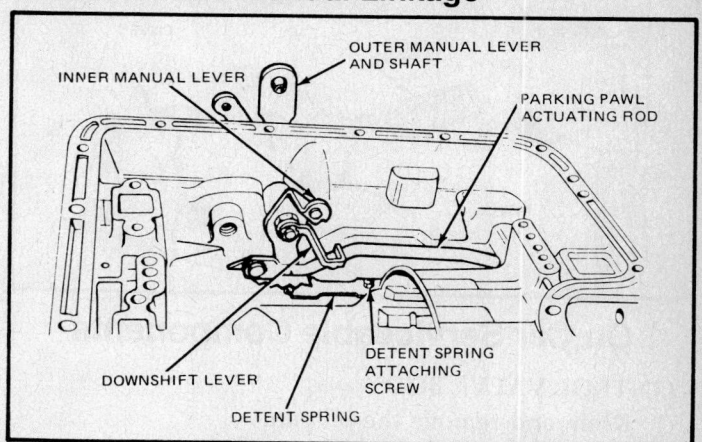

INNER MANUAL LEVER

OUTER MANUAL LEVER AND SHAFT

PARKING PAWL ACTUATING ROD

DOWNSHIFT LEVER

DETENT SPRING ATTACHING SCREW

DETENT SPRING

DOWNSHIFT ROD ADJUSTMENT

Continental, Mark III, Mark IV and Mark V

1. Loosen the locknut on the rod. Disconnect it from the ballstud on the bellcrank by sliding the spring clip off the end of the rod.
2. Pull the rod upward and hold it tightly against the downshift rod against the internal stop. Adjust the length of the rod so the hole in the link is aligned with the stud on the bellcrank assembly.
3. Lengthen the rod one turn and position it on the bellcrank. Slide the spring clip over the end and tighten the locknut.
4. Be sure the outer bracket of the bellcrank is against the stop pin. If not, lengthen the rod one more turn.

TRANSMISSION SHIFT POINTS

Each individual model of transmission has specific limits on transmission shift points for all its possible applications. Since shift point limits are highly specific, the following are general guidelines that apply to transmission shift points.

1. The transmission should shift smoothly and crisply. It should never hunt or shift indecisively.

2. The transmission should be responsive. Full throttle should give a 3-2 or 2-1 downshift, depending on road speed. Greater amounts of acceleration throttle should produce higher upshift speeds.

3. A positive detent at the bottom of the accelerator pedal travel should be felt. Going through detent should greatly increase upshift points. This may also produce downshifts under some conditions.

4. Most transmissions should shift from 3 to 2 range at less than full throttle under 30 mph.

5. Most shift point problems fall into one of the following categories.

a. An improper adjustment or other malfunction of an external mechanical or electrical linkage.

b. An internal transmission problem marked by improper shift feel along with improper shift points.

Intermediate Servo Components

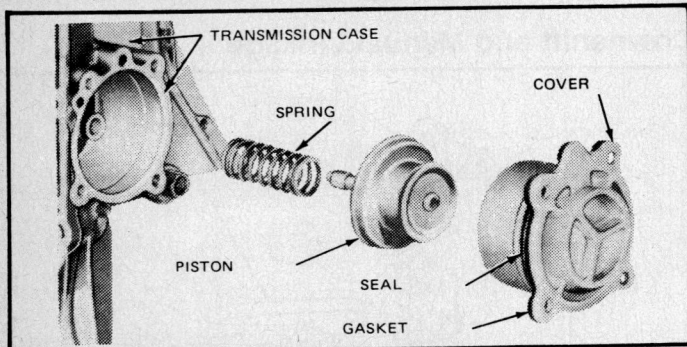

TRANSMISSION CASE
COVER
SPRING
PISTON
SEAL
GASKET

On Car Serviceable Components

CONTROL VALVE BODY

1. Drain and remove the oil pan.

2. Remove the valve body mount bolts. Then remove the valve body from the case.

3. Installation is the reverse of removal. When installing, make sure that the selector and downshift levers are engaged.

INTERMEDIATE SERVO

1. Remove the engine rear support and lower the transmission.

Governor Assembly

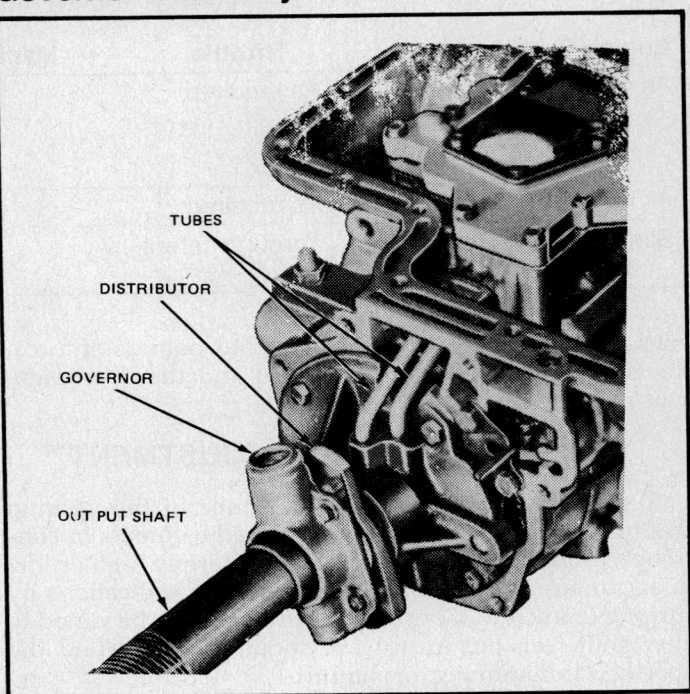

TUBES
DISTRIBUTOR
GOVERNOR
OUT PUT SHAFT

2. Remove the servo cover, piston and spring from the case. Screw the band adjusting screw inward as the piston is removed. This places enough tension on the band to keep the struts properly engaged in the band end notches while the piston is removed.

3. Apply air pressure to the port in the servo rod to remove the piston and rod.

4. Installation is the reverse of removal. Make sure to back off the band adjusting screw as the cover bolts are tightened.

EXTENSION HOUSING

1. Remove the driveshaft, disconnect the speedometer cable and lower the transmission rear end.

2. Remove the extension housing mount bolts. Slide the housing off the output shaft.

3. Installation is the reverse of removal.

GOVERNOR

1. Remove the extension housing.

2. Remove the governor-to-distributor mount bolts. Then remove the governor from the flange.

3. Installation is the reverse of removal.

TROUBLESHOOTING
Ford C6

Problem	In-Car Checks	Out of Car Checks
Slips or chatters in 2nd gear	Fluid level. Vacuum modulator or lines restricted, leaking, adjustment. Intermediate servo. Intermediate band. Control pressure. Pressure regulator. Valve body. Air pressure.	Forward clutch. Leakage in hydraulic system.

TROUBLESHOOTING
Ford C6

Problem	In-Car Checks	Out of Car Checks
Slips or chatters in Reverse	Fluid level. Vacuum modulator or lines restricted, leaking, adjustment. Low-reverse clutch. Control pressure. Pressure regulator. Valve body. Air pressure.	Front pump. Leakage in hydraulic system. Reverse, high clutch piston air bleed valve.
No drive in Drive only	Manual linkage. Control pressure. Valve body.	Planetary one-way clutch.
No drive in 2 only	Fluid level. Manual linkage. Control pressure. Intermediate servo. Valve body. Air pressure.	Leakage in hydraulic system.
No drive in 1 only	Fluid level. Manual linkage. Control pressure. Valve body. Air pressure.	Leakage in hydraulic system.
No drive in Reverse only	Fluid level. Manual linkage. Low-reverse clutch. Control pressure. Valve body. Air pressure.	Reverse, high clutch. Leakage in hydraulic system. Reverse, high clutch piston air bleed valve.
No drive in any selector level position	Fluid level. Manual linkage. Control pressure.	Leakage in hydraulic system. Front pump.
Lockup in Drive only		Parking linkage. Leakage in hydraulic system.
Lockup in 2 only	Low-reverse clutch.	Reverse, high clutch. Parking linkage. Leakage in hydraulic system. Planetary one-way clutch.
Lockup in 1 only		Parking linkage. Leakage in hydraulic system.
Lockup in Reverse only		Forward clutch. Parking linkage. Leakage in hydraulic system.
Parking lock binds or does not hold	Manual linkage.	Parking linkage.
Transmission overheats	Oil cooler and connections. Pressure regulator. Vacuum modulator or lines restricted, leaking, adjustment. Control pressure.	Converter one-way clutch. Converter pressure check valves.
Maximum speed too low, poor acceleration	Engine performance. Vehicle brakes.	Converter one-way clutch.
Transmission noisy in Neutral and Park	Fluid level. Pressure regulator.	Front pump.
Transmission noisy in 1st, 2nd, 3rd, or Reverse gear	Fluid level. Pressure regulator.	Planetary assembly. Forward clutch. Front pump. Planetary one-way clutch.
Fluid leaks	Fluid level. Converter drain plugs. Oil pan gasket, filler tube or seal. Oil cooler and connections. Manual or downshift lever shaft seal ⅛ inch pipe plugs in case. Extension housing-to-case gasket. Extension housing rear oil seal. Speedometer driven gear adapter seal. Vacuum modulator or lines restricted, leaking, adjustment. Intermediate servo.	Engine rear oil seal. Front pump oil seal. Front pump to case gasket or seal.
Car moves forward in Neutral	Manual linkage.	Forward clutch.
No drive in Drive, 2 and 1	Manual linkage. Control pressure. Valve body. Air pressure.	Forward clutch. Leakage in hydraulic system.

B847

AUTOMATIC TRANSMISSIONS

FORD C6

TROUBLESHOOTING
Ford C6

Problem	In-Car Checks	Out of Car Checks
Rough initial engagement in Drive or 2	Engine idle speed. Vacuum modulator or lines restricted, leaking, adjustment. Control pressure. Pressure regulator. Valve body.	Forward clutch.
1-2 or 2-3 shift points incorrect or erratic	Fluid level. Vacuum modulator or lines restricted, leaking, adjustment. Downshift linkage, including inner lever position. Manual linkage. Governor. Control pressure. Valve body. Air pressure.	
Rough 1-2 upshifts	Vacuum modulator or lines restricted, leaking, adjustment. Intermediate servo. Intermediate band. Control pressure. Valve body. Pressure regulator.	
Rough 2-3 shifts	Vacuum modulator or lines restricted, leaking, adjustment. Intermediate servo. Control pressure. Pressure regulator. Intermediate band. Valve body. Air pressure.	Reverse, high clutch. Reverse, high clutch piston air bleed valve
Dragged out 1-2 shift	Fluid level. Vacuum modulator or lines restricted, leaking, adjustment. Intermediate servo. Control pressure. Intermediate band. Valve body. Pressure regulator. Air pressure.	Leakage in hydraulic system.
Engine overspeeds on 2-3 shift	Manual linkage. Fluid level. Vacuum modulator or lines restricted, leaking, adjustment. Intermediate servo. Control pressure. Valve body. Pressure regulator intermediate band.	Reverse, high clutch. Reverse, high clutch piston air bleed valve.
No 1-2 or 2-3 shift	Manual linkage. Downshift linkage, including inner lever position. Vacuum modulator or lines restricted, leaking, adjustment. Governor. Control pressure. Valve body. Intermediate band. Intermediate servo.	Leakage in hydraulic system.
No 3-1 shift in D	Governor. Valve body.	
No forced downshifts	Downshift linkage, including inner lever position. Valve body. Vacuum modulator or lines restricted, leaking, adjustment.	
Runaway engine on forced 3-2 downshift	Control pressure. Intermediate servo. Intermediate band. Pressure regulator. Valve body. Vacuum modulator or lines restricted, leaking, adjustment.	Leakage in hydraulic system.
Rough 3-2 or 3-1 shift at closed throttle	Engine idle speed. Vacuum modulator or lines restricted, leaking, adjustment. Intermediate servo.	
Shifts 1-3 in Drive	Intermediate band. Intermediate servo. Vacuum modulator or lines restricted, leaking, adjustment. Valve body. Governor. Air pressure.	
No engine braking in 1st gear 1 range	Manual linkage. Low-reverse clutch. Valve body. Governor. Air pressure.	
Creeps excessively	Engine idle speed.	
Slips or chatters in 1st gear Drive	Fluid level. Vacuum modulator or lines restricted leaking, adjust. Control pressure. Pressure regulator. Valve body.	Forward clutch. Leakage in hydraulic system. Planetary one-way clutch.

B848

FORD JATCO

Identification

The service identification tag is attached to the right side of the transmission case to the rear of the filler tube. Jatco transmission is identified by the letter "S" on the vehicle certification label.

Adjustments

INTERMEDIATE BAND

1. Raise the vehicle and remove the servo cover.
2. Loosen the intermediate band adjusting screw locknut and tighten the adjusting screw to 10 ft. lbs.
3. Back off the adjusting screw two turns. While holding the adjusting screw stationary, tighten the adjusting screw locknut to 22–29 ft. lbs. (30–39 N.m)
4. Install the servo cover using a new gasket. Lower the vehicle and check the transmission fluid level.

Intermediate Band Adjustment

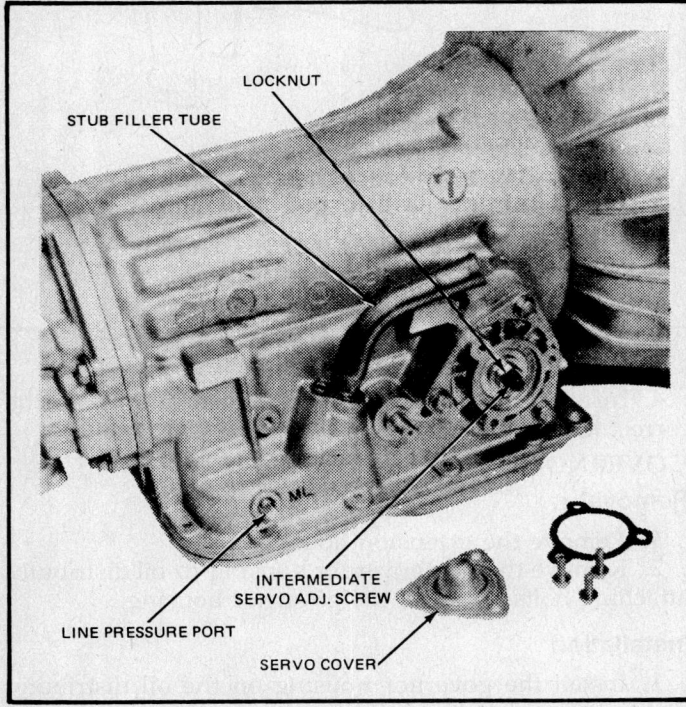

Component Removal and Installation

NOTE These operations can be accomplished without removing the transmission from the vehicle.

CONTROL VALVE BODY
Removal

1. Raise the vehicle. Drain the transmission fluid by removing the transmission oil pan.
2. Remove the downshift solenoid, vacuum diaphragm, vacuum diaphragm rod and O-rings.

3. Remove the valve body-to-case attaching bolts. Hold the manual valve to keep it from sliding out of the valve body and remove the valve body from the case. Failure to hold the manual valve while removing the control assembly could cause the manual valve to become bent or damaged.

Installation

1. Position the valve body to the case and install the attaching bolts.
2. Using a new gasket, secure the transmission oil pan to the case and tighten the bolts to correct specifications.
3. Lower the vehicle and fill the transmission to the correct level with the specified automatic transmission fluid.

SERVO
Removal

1. Raise the vehicle. Drain the transmission fluid by removing the transmission oil pan.
2. Remove the control valve body from the transmission assembly.
3. Remove the servo cover.
4. Remove the three bolts securing the servo retainer to the transmission case. Remove the retainer and servo piston as an assembly. Remove the return spring from the case.
5. Remove the intermediate band apply strut through the bottom of the case.

Installation

1. Install the piston return spring in the case.
2. Install the intermediate band apply strut in the band end.
3. Install the piston and servo retainer into the transmission case and align the piston rod with the band strut. While holding the retainer in place, install the three attaching bolts and tighten the bolts to specifications.
4. Correctly adjust the intermediate band. Install the control valve body.
5. Using a new gasket, install the transmission oil pan and tighten the mounting bolts to the correct specifications.
6. Using a new gasket, install the servo cover and tighten attaching bolts to the correct specifications.
7. Lower the vehicle and refill the transmission to the correct level.

EXTENSION HOUSING REAR SEAL
Removal

1. Remove the drive shaft. Remove the old seal using a sharp chisel.

Installation

1. Install a new seal using tool T61L-7657-A.
2. Install the drive shaft and check the transmission fluid level.

AUTOMATIC TRANSMISSIONS
FORD JATCO

Parking Pawl and Manual Linkage

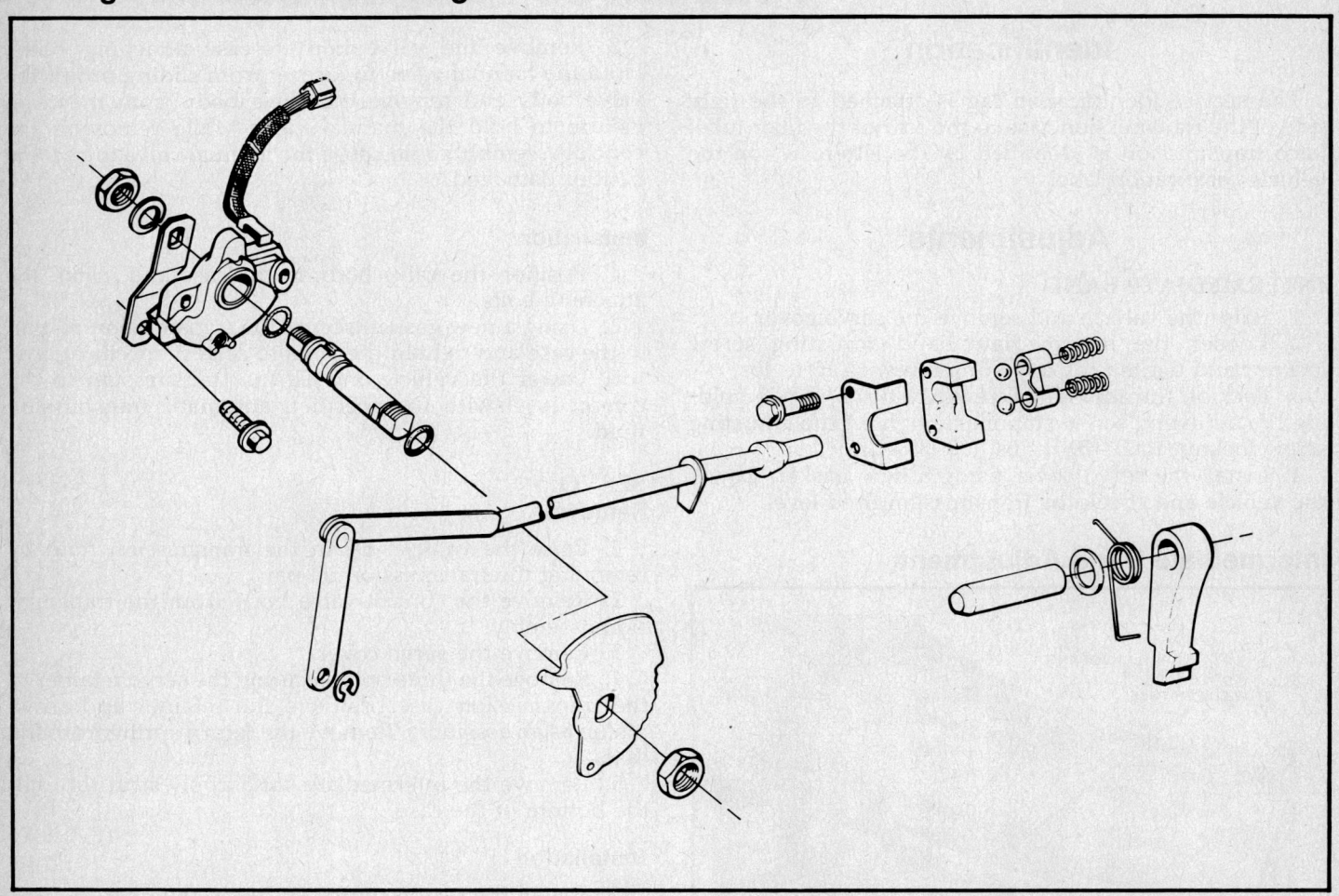

EXTENSION HOUSING
Removal

1. Remove the drive shaft.
2. Disconnect the speedometer cable from the extension housing.
3. Remove the transmission rear support-to-crossmember bolts and nuts.
4. Raise the transmission sufficiently to remove the rear support.
5. Loosen the extension housing attaching bolts to drain the transmission fluid.
6. Remove the eight extension housing-to-case attaching bolts and remove the extension housing.

NOTE   Do not lose the washer from the parking panel shaft.

Installation

1. Using a new gasket, install the extension housing and tighten the attaching bolts to the correct specifications.
2. Install the rear support and lower the transmission.
3. Connect the speedometer cable.

4. Install the drive shaft. Fill the transmission to the correct level with the specified transmission fluid.
GOVERNOR
Removal

1. Remove the extension housing.
2. Remove the four governor housing-to-oil distributor attaching bolts. Remove the governor housing.

Installation

1. Install the governor housing on the oil distributor and tighten the bolts to the correct specifications.
2. Install the extension housing.

GEAR RATIOS

Gear	Ratio
First	2.458:1
Second	1.458:1
Third	1.000:1
Reverse	2.181:1
Stall speed	1750–2000

FORD ATX TRANSAXLE

Description

AUTOMATIC TRANSAXLE

The automatic transaxle (ATX) combines an automatic transmission and differential into a single powertrain component. The ATX uses three friction clutches, one band and a single one-way clutch. These components are applied as necessary to transmit engine torque through a compound planetary gear set. The planetary provides three forward gear ratios and one reverse. The planetary transmits engine torque to the input gear which meshes with the differential idler gear. Meshing with the idler gear is the differential gear which is riveted to the differential case. When powerflow reaches the differential, engine torque flows outward to the wheels through the differential gears.

ATX Transaxle

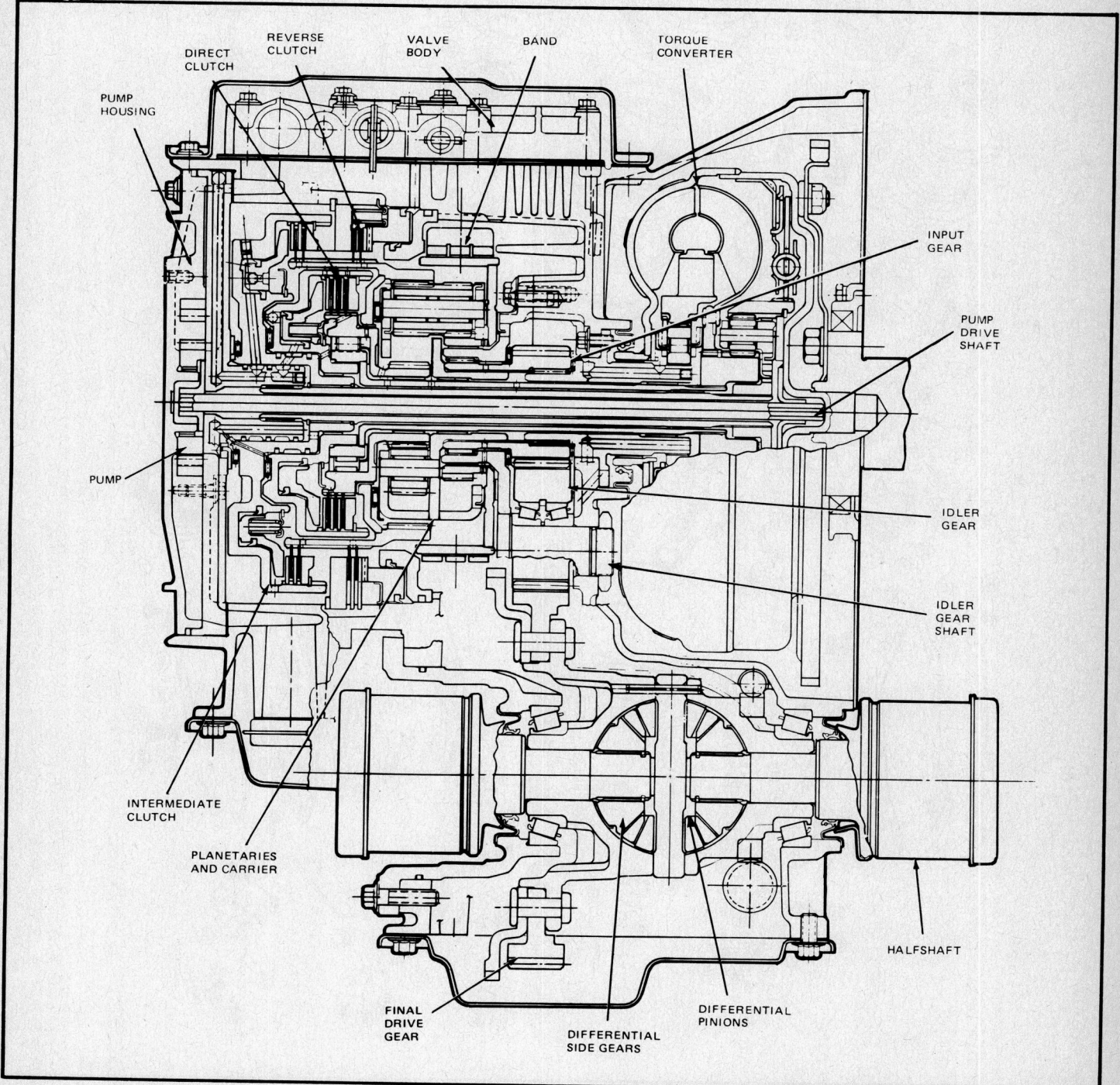

Automatic Transaxle

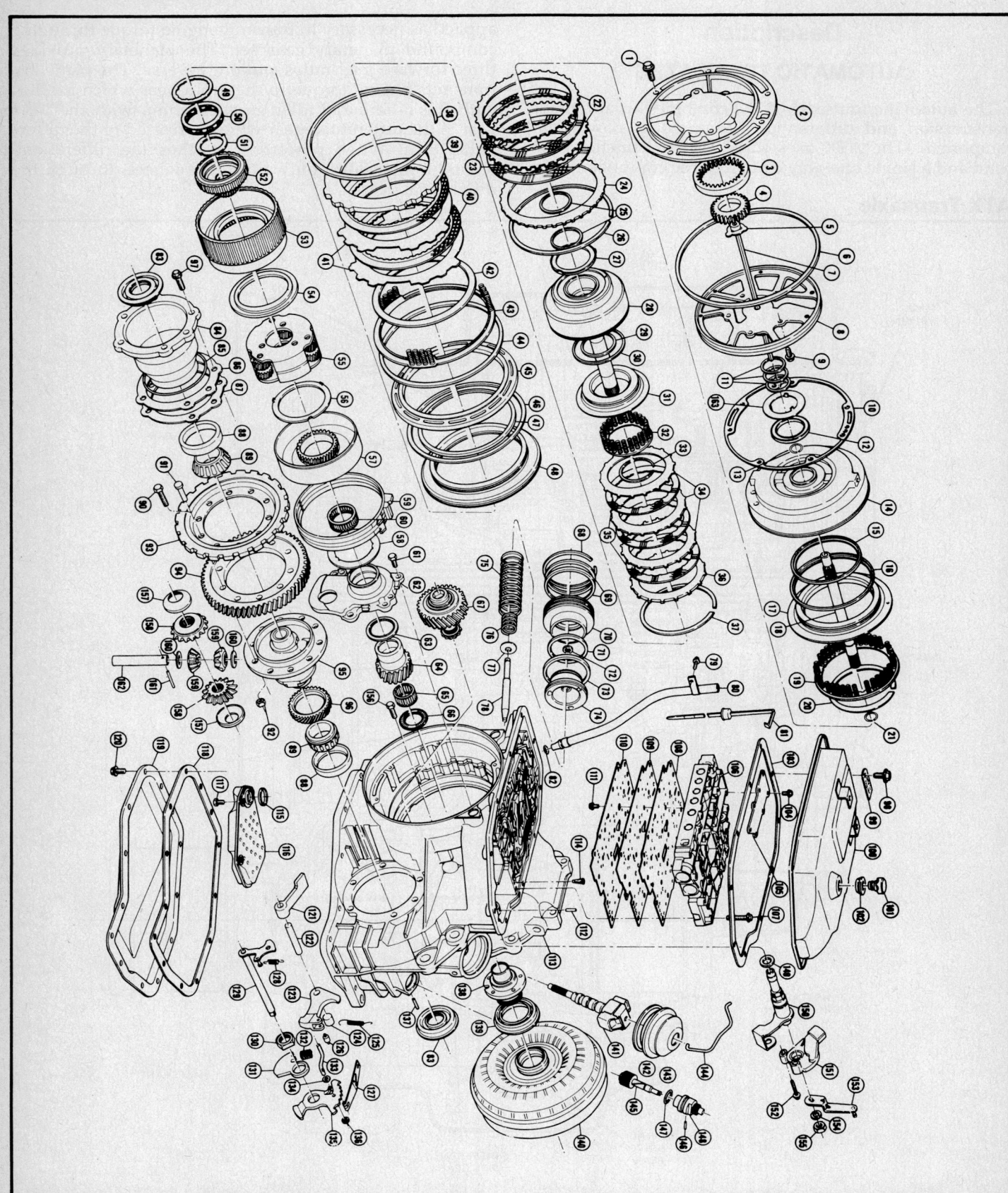

LEGEND:

1. BOLT & WSHR. ASSY (7A103 TO 7005) M6-1 X 40 (7 REQ'D.)
2. BODY & SLEEVE ASSY — OIL PUMP
3. GEAR — OIL PUMP DRIVEN
4. GEAR ASSY — OIL PUMP DRIVE
5. INSERT — OIL PUMP DRIVE GEAR
6. SEAL — OIL PUMP
7. SHAFT — OIL PUMP DRIVE
8. SUPPORT & BSHG. ASSY — OIL PUMP
9. BOLT (7A108 TO 7F370) M6-1 X 16MM LG. (5 REQ'D.)
10. GASKET — OIL PUMP
11. SEAL — INTERM. CLUTCH — REAR (TEFLON)
12. BRG. ASSY — INTERM. CLUTCH DRUM THRUST
13. RING — 17.0 RETAINING RD. WIRE EXTERNAL
14. CYLINDER — INTERM. CLUTCH
15. SEAL — INTERM. CLUTCH PISTON — INNER
16. SEAL — INTERM. CLUTCH PISTON — OUTER
17. PISTON — INTERM. CLUTCH
18. SHAFT — INTERM. CLUTCH
19. RET. & SPRING ASSY — INTERM. CLUTCH
20. RING — 111.76MM RETAINING EXTERNAL
21. RING — 16.4MM RETAINING EXTERNAL
22. PLATE — INTERM. CL. EXT. SPLINE
23. PLATE ASSY — INTERM. CL. INT. SPLINE
24. PLATE — INTERM. CLUTCH PRESSURE
25. SEAL — INTERM. CLUTCH — OUTER (TEFLON)
26. RING — RETAINING INT. (SELECTIVE)
27. BRG. ASSY — DIRECT & INTERM. CLUTCH
28. CYL. SHAFT & RACE ASSY — DIRECT CLUTCH
29. SEAL — DIRECT CL. PISTON — INNER
30. SEAL — DIRECT CL. PISTON OIL — OUTER
31. PISTON — DIRECT CLUTCH
32. RET. & SPRING ASSY — DIRECT CLUTCH
33. RING — 59.5MM RETAINING, EXTERNAL
34. PLATE — DIRECT CLUTCH EXT. SPLINE
35. PLATE ASSY — DIRECT CL. INT. SPLINE
36. PLATE — DIRECT CLUTCH PRESSURE
37. RING — RETAINING INT. (SELECTIVE)
38. RING — RETAINING INT. (SELECTIVE)
39. PLATE — REVERSE CLUTCH PRESSURE
40. PLATE ASSY — REV. CL. INT. SPLINE
41. PLATE — REV. CLUTCH EXT. SPLINE
42. SPRING — REV. CLUTCH CUSHION
43. SPRING & RET. ASSY — REV. CLUTCH
44. SEAL — 196.0MM
45. PISTON — REVERSE CLUTCH
46. SEAL — REV. CL. PISTON — OUTER
47. SEAL — REV. CL. PISTON — INNER
48. CYLINDER — REVERSE CLUTCH
49. BEARING — ONE-WAY CLUTCH
50. SPRING & ROLLER ASSY. — ONE-WAY CLUTCH
51. WASHER — DIRECT CL. CYL. THRUST
52. GEAR ASSY — 1ST-3RD REVERSE SPEED
53. GEAR ASSY — INTER. & REV. CL. RG.
54. RACE & BRG. ASSY — PLANET THRUST REAR
55. PLANET ASSEMBLY
56. WASHER — PLANETARY THRUST — FRONT
57. DRUM & SUN GEAR ASSY — LOW/INTERM.
58. WASHER — INTERM. SUN GR. THRUST
59. BAND ASSY — LOW/INTERM
60. BEARING ASSY — TRANSFER
61. BOLT — M8-1.25 X 25.0 HEX FLANGE HD. (5 REQ'D.)
62. HOUSING — FINAL DRIVE GEAR
63. BRG. ASSY — FINAL DRIVE GEAR THRUST — REAR
64. GEAR — FINAL DRIVE INPUT
65. BRG. ASSY — FINAL DRIVE INPUT GEAR
66. BRG. ASSY — FINAL DRIVE GEAR THRUST — FRONT
67. GEAR & BRG. ASSY — IDLER GEAR
68. RING — 103.5MM RET. FLAT INTERNAL
69. SEAL — LOW & INTERM. BAND SERVO PISTON COVER
70. COVER — LOW/INTERM. BAND SERVO
71. SEAL — LOW/INTERM. SERVO PISTON — SMALL
72. RING — 15.8MM RETAINING EXTERNAL
73. SEAL — LOW/INTERM. SERVO PISTON — LARGE
74. PISTON — LOW & INTERM. SERVO
75. SPRING — LOW/INTERM. SERVO PISTON
76. SPRING — SERVO PISTON CUSHION
77. WASHER — 9.7MM X 30 X 2.5 FLAT STEEL
78. ROD — LOW/INTERM. SERVO PISTON
79. BOLT — M6-1 X 12 HEX. FLANGE HD.
80. TUBE ASSY — OIL FILTER
81. INDICATOR ASSY — OIL LEVEL
82. O'RING (SEAL FILLER TUBE TO CASE)
83. SEAL ASSY — TRANSAXLE — DIFF.
84. RETAINER — DIFF. BEARING
85. SEAL — 106.0 X 2.5 RD. RECT. SECTION
86. SHIM — BEARING RETAINER
87. SHIM — DIFF. BEARING (SELECTIVE)
88. CUP — DIFF. BEARING
89. CONE & ROLLER — DIFF. BEARING
90. BOLT — M10 X 1.5 X 40 HEX. HD. (10 REQ'D.) SERVICE ONLY
91. RIVET — M10 X 38 SOLID FLAT HD. (REF. ONLY — PRODUCTION)
92. NUT — M10 X 1.5 HEX PLT — (10 REQ'D.) SERVICE ONLY
93. GEAR — OUTPUT SHAFT PARK
94. GEAR — FINAL DRIVE OUTPUT
95. DIFF. ASSY. — TRANSAXLE
96. GEAR — SPEEDO DRIVE
97. BOLT — M8-1.25 X 30 HEX FLANGE HD. (6 REQ'D.)
98. BOLT — M6-1 X 14MM LG. (10 REQ'D.)
99. IDENTIFICATION TAG
100. COVER ASSY — MAIN CONTROL
101. VENT ASSY — MAIN CONTROL COVER
102. GROMMET — MAIN CONTROL COVER
103. GASKET — MAIN CONTROL COVER
104. BOLT — M6-1.0 X 45 HEX FLANGE HD. (7 REQ'D.)
105. PLATE — MAIN OIL PRESS. REG. EXH.
106. CONTROL ASSY — MAIN
107. BOLT — M6-1.0 X 40 HEX FLANGE HD. (20 REQ'D.)
108. GASKET — MAIN CONTROL (BET. 7A092 & 7A008)
109. PLATE — CONTROL VALVE BODY SEP.
110. GASKET — MAIN CONTROL (BET. 7A008 & 7006)
111. BOLT — M6-1 X 12 HEX FLANGE HD. (2 REQ'D.)
112. PIN — 3.2MM X 25.65 DOWEL HRDN.
113. CASE & HSG. ASSY
114. SCREEN ASSY — GOV. OIL
115. GASKET — OIL FILTER
116. FILTER ASSY — OIL
117. BOLT — M6-1 X 14MM LG (3 REQ'D.)
118. GASKET — OIL PAN
119. PAN — OIL
120. BOLT — M8-1.25 X 16 HEX FLANGE (13 REQ'D.)
121. STRUT — LOW/INTERM. BAND ANCHOR
122. SHAFT — PARKING PAWL
123. PAWL — PARKING BRAKE
124. PLUG — 11.0MM CUP
125. SPRING — PARK PAWL RETURN
126. PIN — PARKING PAWL ROLLER
127. SPRING ASSY — MANUAL VALVE DETENT
128. SPRING — THROTTLE VLV. CONTROL LEVER
129. SHAFT ASSY. — TV LEVER ACTUATING
130. NUT — M20 X 1.5 HEX
131. LEVER — PARK PAWL ACTUATING
132. SPRING — PARK PAWL RATCHETING
133. ACTUATOR — MANUAL LEVER
134. WASHER
135. LEVER — MANUAL VLV. DETENT — INNER
136. NUT — STAMPED
137. PIN — SPEEDO RETAINING
138. SUPPORT ASSY — CONV. REACTOR
139. SEAL ASSY. — CONV. IMP. HUB
140. CONVERTER ASSEMBLY
141. GOVERNOR ASSEMBLY
142. SEAL — 77.9MM X 3.40 RECT. SECT.
143. COVER — GOVERNOR
144. CLIP — GOV. COVER RETAINING
145. GEAR — SPEEDO DRIVEN
146. PIN — 3MM X 19.9 DOWEL HRDN.
147. SEAL — 25.06MM X 2.6 O'RING
148. RETAINER — SPEEDO DRIVEN GEAR
149. SEAL — MANUAL CONTROL LEVER
150. LEVER ASSY — MANUAL CONTROL
151. SWITCH ASSY — NEUTRAL START
152. BOLT & WSHR — M6 X 1.00 X 35 HEX FLANGE HD. (2 REQ'D.)
153. LEVER ASSY — THROTTLE VLV. — OUTER
154. WASHER — 8MM LOCK
155. NUT — M8 X 1.25 HEX.
156. BOLT — M6-1 X 12 HEX FLANGE HD. (5 REQ'D.)
157. WASHER — TRANSAXLE DIFF. SIDE GR. THRUST
158. GEAR — TRANSAXLE DIFF. SIDE
159. PINION — TRANSAXLE DIFF.
160. WASHER — TRANSAXLE DIFF. PINION THRUST
161. PIN — 4.75MM X 38.1MM
162. SHAFT — TRANSAXLE DIFF. PINION
163. OIL PUMP THRUST WASHER (SELECTIVE)

DIAGNOSIS—AUTOMATIC TRANSAXLE

Condition	Possible Cause	Resolution
Slow initial engagement	• Improper fluid level • Damaged or improperly adjusted manual linkage • Incorrect T.V. linkage adjustment • Contaminated fluid • Improper clutch and band application, or oil control pressure • Dirty valve body	• Add fluid as required • Service or adjust linkage • Change fluid and filter • Perform control pressure test • Clean, repair, or replace valve body
Rough initial engagement in either forward or reverse	• Improper fluid level • High engine idle • Auto. choke on (warm temp) • Looseness in halfshafts, CV joints, or engine mounts • Improper clutch or band application, or oil control pressure • Incorrect T.V. linkage adjustment • Sticky or dirty valve body	• Perform fluid check • Adjust idle to specs. • Disengage choke • Service as required • Perform control pressure test • Service or adjust linkage • Clean, repair, or replace valve body
No drive in any gear	• Improper fluid level • Damaged or improperly adjusted manual linkage • Improper clutch or band application, or oil control pressure • Internal leakage • Valve body loose • Damaged or worn clutches or band • Sticking or dirty valve body	• Perform fluid check • Service or adjust linkage • Perform control pressure test • Check and repair as required • Tighten to specs. • Perform air pressure test • Clean, repair, or replace valve body
No forward drive — reverse OK	• Improper fluid level • Damaged or improperly adjusted manual linkage • Improper one-way clutch, or band application, or oil pressure control system • Damaged or worn band, servo or clutches • Valve body loose • Dirty or sticking valve body	• Perform fluid level check • Service or adjust linkage • Perform control pressure test • Perform air pressure test • Tighten to specs. • Clean, service or replace valve body
No drive, slips, or chatters in reverse — forward OK	• Improper fluid level • Damaged or improperly adjusted manual linkage • Looseness in half-shafts, CV joints, or engine mounts • Improper oil pressure control • Damaged or worn reverse clutch • Valve body loose • Dirty or sticking valve body	• Perform fluid level check • Service or adjust linkage • Service as required • Perform control pressure test • Perform air pressure test • Tighten to specs. • Clean, service, or replace valve body
Car will not start in neutral or park	• Neutral start switch improperly adjusted • Neutral start wire disconnected/damaged • Manual linkage improperly adjusted	• Service or adjust neutral start switch • Replace/repair • Service or adjust linkage
No drive, slips or chatters in first gear in D	• Damaged or worn one-way clutch • Improper fluid level • Damaged or worn band • Incorrect T.V. linkage adjustment	• Service or replace one-way clutch • Perform fluid level check • Service or replace band assembly • Service or adjust linkage
No drive, slips, or chatters in second gear	• Improper fluid level • Incorrect T.V. linkage adjustment • Intermediate friction clutch • Improper clutch application • Internal leakage • Dirty or sticking valve body • Polished, glazed band or drum	• Perform fluid level check • Service or adjust linkage • Service clutch • Perform control pressure test • Perform air pressure test • Clean, service, or replace valve body • Replace or service as required

DIAGNOSIS—AUTOMATIC TRANSAXLE

Condition	Possible Cause	Resolution
Starts up in 2nd or 3rd	• Improper fluid level • Damaged or improperly adjusted manual linkage • Improper band and/or clutch application, or oil pressure control system • Damaged or worn governor • Valve body loose • Dirty or sticking valve body • Cross leaks between valve body and case mating surface	• Perform fluid level check • Service or adjust linkage • Perform control pressure test • Perform governor check. Replace or service governor • Tighten to specs. • Clean, service, or replace valve body • Replace valve body and/or case as required
Shift points incorrect	• Improper fluid level • T.V. Linkage out of adjustment • Improper clutch or band application, or oil pressure system • Damaged or worn governor • Dirty or sticking valve body	• Perform fluid level check • Service or adjust linkage • Perform shift test and control pressure test • Service or replace governor. Clean screen • Clean, service, or replace valve body
No upshift at any speed in D	• Improper fluid level • T.V. Linkage out of adjustment • Improper band or clutch application, or oil pressure control system • Damaged or worn governor • Dirty or sticking valve body	• Perform fluid level check • Service or adjust linkage • Perform control pressure test • Service or replace governor. Clean screen • Clean, service or replace valve body
Shifts 1-3 in D	• Improper fluid level • Intermediate friction clutch • Improper clutch application, or oil pressure control system • Dirty or sticking valve body	• Perform fluid level check • Service • Perform control pressure test • Clean, service or replace valve body
Engine over-speeds on 2-3 shift	• Improper fluid level • Improper band or clutch application, or oil pressure control system • Damaged or worn direct clutch and/or servo • Dirty or sticking valve body	• Perform fluid level check • Perform control pressure test • Perform air pressure test. Service as required • Clean, service, or replace valve body
Mushy 1-2 shift	• Improper fluid level • Incorrect engine performance • Improper T.V. linkage adjustment • Improper intermediate clutch application, or oil pressure control system • Damaged intermediate clutch • Dirty or sticking valve body	• Perform fluid level check • Tune adjust engine idle as required • Service or adjust • Perform control pressure test • Perform air pressure test. Service as required • Clean, service or replace valve body
Rough 1-2 shift	• Improper fluid level • Improper T.V. linkage adjustment • Incorrect engine idle or performance • Improper intermediate clutch application or oil pressure control system • Dirty or sticking valve body	• Perform fluid level check • Service or adjust linkage • Tune and adjust engine idle • Perform control pressure test • Clean, service or replace valve body

DIAGNOSIS—AUTOMATIC TRANSAXLE

Condition	Possible Cause	Resolution
Rough 2-3 shift	• Improper fluid level • Incorrect engine performance • Improper band release or direct clutch application, or oil control pressure system • Damaged or worn servo release and direct clutch piston check ball • Improper T.V. linkage adjustment • Dirty or sticking valve body	• Perform fluid level check • Tune and adjust engine idle • Perform control pressure test • Air pressure test the servo apply and release and the direct clutch piston check ball. Service as required • Service or adjust linkage • Clean, service, or replace valve body
Rough 3-2 shift at closed throttle in D	• Improper fluid level • Incorrect engine idle or performance • Improper T.V. linkage adjustment • Improper band or clutch application, or oil pressure control system • Improper governor operation • Dirty or sticking valve body	• Perform fluid level check • Tune and adjust engine idle • Service or adjust linkage • Perform control pressure test • Perform governor test. Service as required • Clean, service or replace valve body
No forced downshifts	• Improper fluid level • Improper clutch or band application, or oil pressure control system • Damaged internal kickdown linkage • T.V. linkage out of adjustment • Dirty or sticking valve body • Dirty or sticking governor	• Perform fluid level check • Perform control pressure test • Service internal kickdown linkage • Service or adjust T.V. linkage • Clean, service or replace valve body • Clean or replace governor
Runaway engine on 3-2 or 3-1 downshift	• Improper fluid level • T.V. linkage out of adjustment • Band out of adjustment • Improper band or clutch application, or oil pressure control system • Damaged or worn servo • Polished, glazed band or drum • Dirty or sticking valve body	• Perform fluid level check • Service or adjust T.V. linkage • Check and adjust servo rod travel • Perform control pressure test • Air pressure test check the servo. Service servo and/or seals • Service or replace as required • Clean, service or replace valve body
No engine braking in manual first gear	• Improper fluid level • T.V. linkage out of adjustment • Damaged or improperly adjusted manual linkage • Band or clutch out of adjustment • Oil pressure control system • Polished, glazed band or drum • Dirty or sticking valve body	• Perform fluid level check • Service or adjust linkage • Check direct clutch and service as required • Check servo rod travel • Perform control pressure test • Service or replace as required • Clean, service or replace valve body
No engine braking in manual second gear	• Improper fluid level • T.V. linkage out of adjustment • Damaged or improperly adjusted manual linkage • Improper band or clutch application, or oil pressure control system • Servo leaking • Polished, glazed band or drum	• Perform fluid level check • Service or adjust linkage • Perform control pressure test • Perform air pressure test of servo for leakage. Service as required • Service or replace as required

DIAGNOSIS—AUTOMATIC TRANSAXLE

Condition	Possible Cause	Resolution
Transaxle noisy — valve resonance Note: Gauges may aggravate any hydraulic resonance. Remove gauge and check for resonance level.	• Improper fluid level • T.V. linkage out of adjustment • Improper band or clutch application, or oil pressure control system • Cooler lines grounding • Dirty or sticking valve body • Internal leakage or pump cavitation	• Perform fluid level check • Service or adjust T.V. linkage • Perform control pressure test • Free cooler lines • Clean, service or replace valve body • Service as required
Transaxle overheats	• Excessive tow loads • Improper fluid level • Incorrect engine idle or performance • Improper clutch or band application, or oil pressure control system • Restriction in cooler or lines • Seized converter one-way clutch • Dirty or sticking valve body	• Check Owner's Manual for tow restriction • Perform fluid level check • Tune or adjust engine idle • Perform control pressure test • Service restriction • Replace converter • Clean, service or replace valve body

DIAGNOSIS—TRANSAXLE NOISE

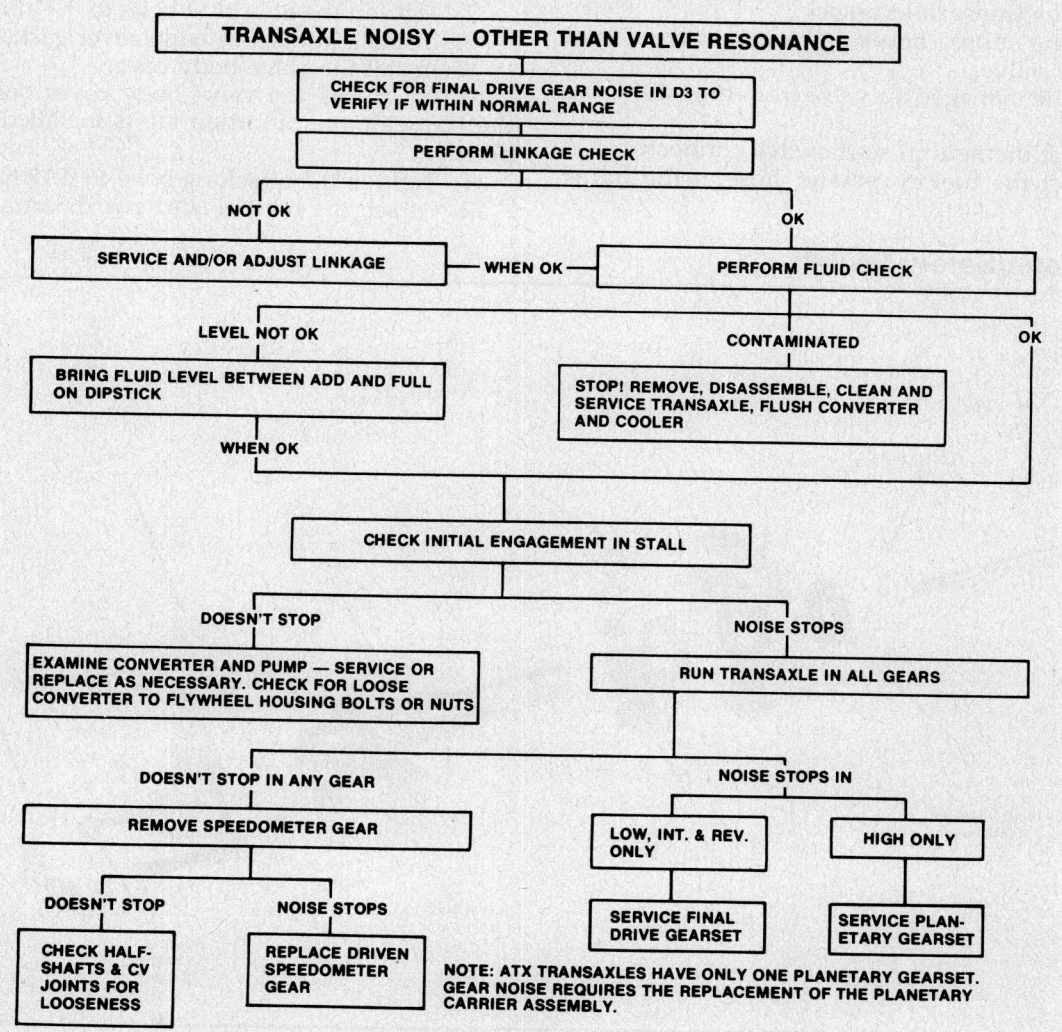

NOTE: ATX TRANSAXLES HAVE ONLY ONE PLANETARY GEARSET. GEAR NOISE REQUIRES THE REPLACEMENT OF THE PLANETARY CARRIER ASSEMBLY.

On-Car Service Procedures

TRANSAXLE FLUID DRAIN AND REFILL

Procedures for partial drain and refill, due to in-vehicle service operation, are as follows.

1. Raise the vehicle on a hoist or jack stands.
2. Place a drain pan under the transaxle.
3. Loosen the pan attaching bolts and drain the fluid from the transaxle.
4. When fluid has drained to the level of the pan flange, remove the rest of the pan bolts. Work from the rear and both sides of the pan to allow it to drop and drain slowly.
5. When all fluid has drained from the transaxle, remove and thoroughly clean the pan. Discard the gasket.
6. Place a new gasket on the pan, and install the pan on the transaxle.
7. Fill the transaxle to the correct level.

VALVE BODY

Removal

1. Remove the battery and battery tray.
2. Remove the ignition coil.
3. Remove the transaxle dip-stick.
4. Remove the supply hoses and vacuum lines from the managed air valve.
5. Remove the managed air valve from the ATX valve body cover.
6. Disconnect the neutral start switch connector.
7. Disconnect the fuel evaporator hose at the frame rail.

8. Disconnect the fan motor and water temperature sending unit wiring.
9. Remove the valve body cover bolts and the valve body cover, with gasket.
10. Remove the valve body bolts and the valve body, with gasket.

Installation

1. Install the two alignment pins (T80L-77100-A or equivalent).
2. Install the valve body to case gasket.
3. Install the valve body. One alignment pin must temporarily be removed to allow the attachment of the manual valve. After the manual valve is attached to its linkage, reinstall the alignment pin.

NOTE Make sure the roller on the end of the throttle valve plunger has engaged the cam on the end of the throttle lever shaft.

4. Connect the throttle valve control spring.
5. Install the 27 valve body retaining bolts, the detent spring and the oil pressure regulator exhaust plate.
6. Remove the alignment pins.
7. Tighten the attaching bolts to 8-11 N•m (6-8 lb-ft).
8. Install a new valve body cover gasket on the case.
9. Install the valve body cover.
10. Install the ten valve body cover bolts. Make sure the transaxle identification tag is installed in its original position.
11. Tighten the attaching bolts to 9-12 N•m (7-9 lb-ft).
12. Attach the neutral start switch connector.

Throttle Linkage/Safety Switch

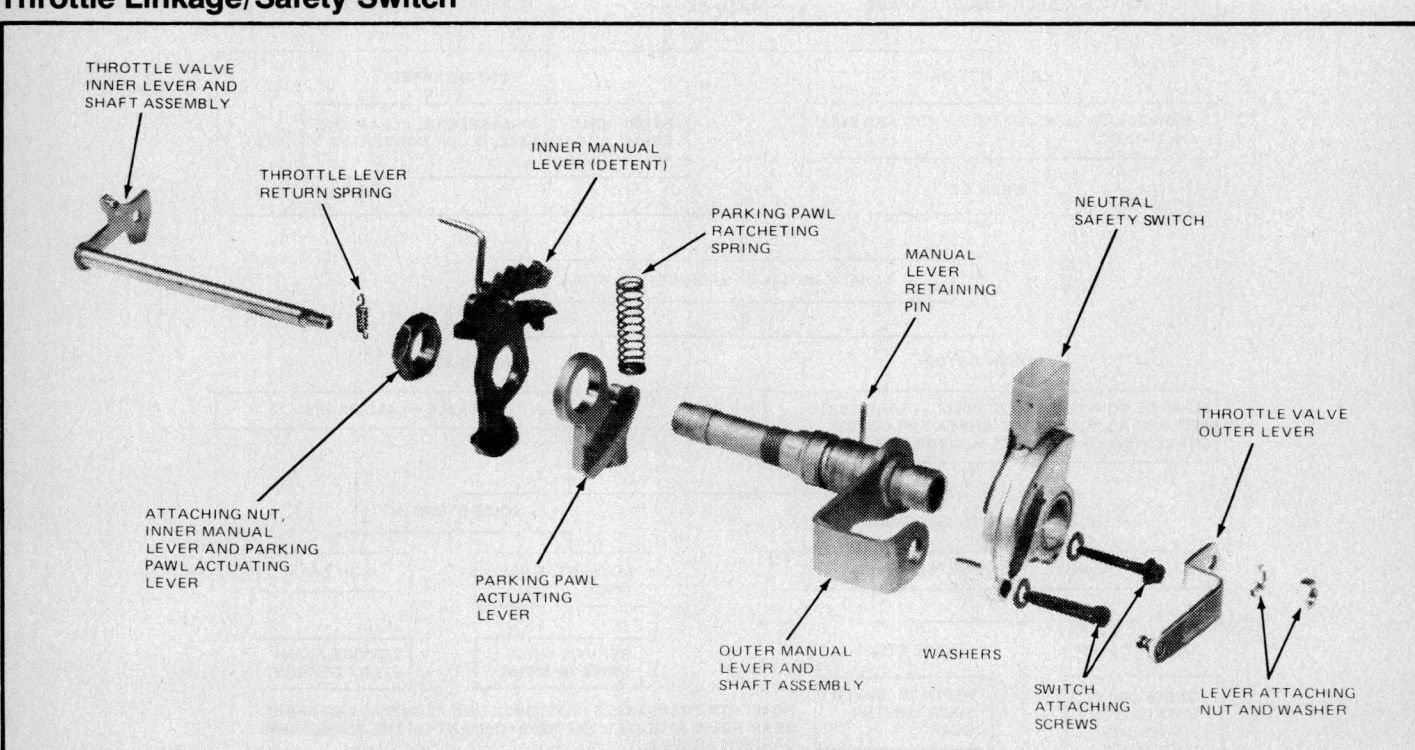

Valve Body Ball Locations

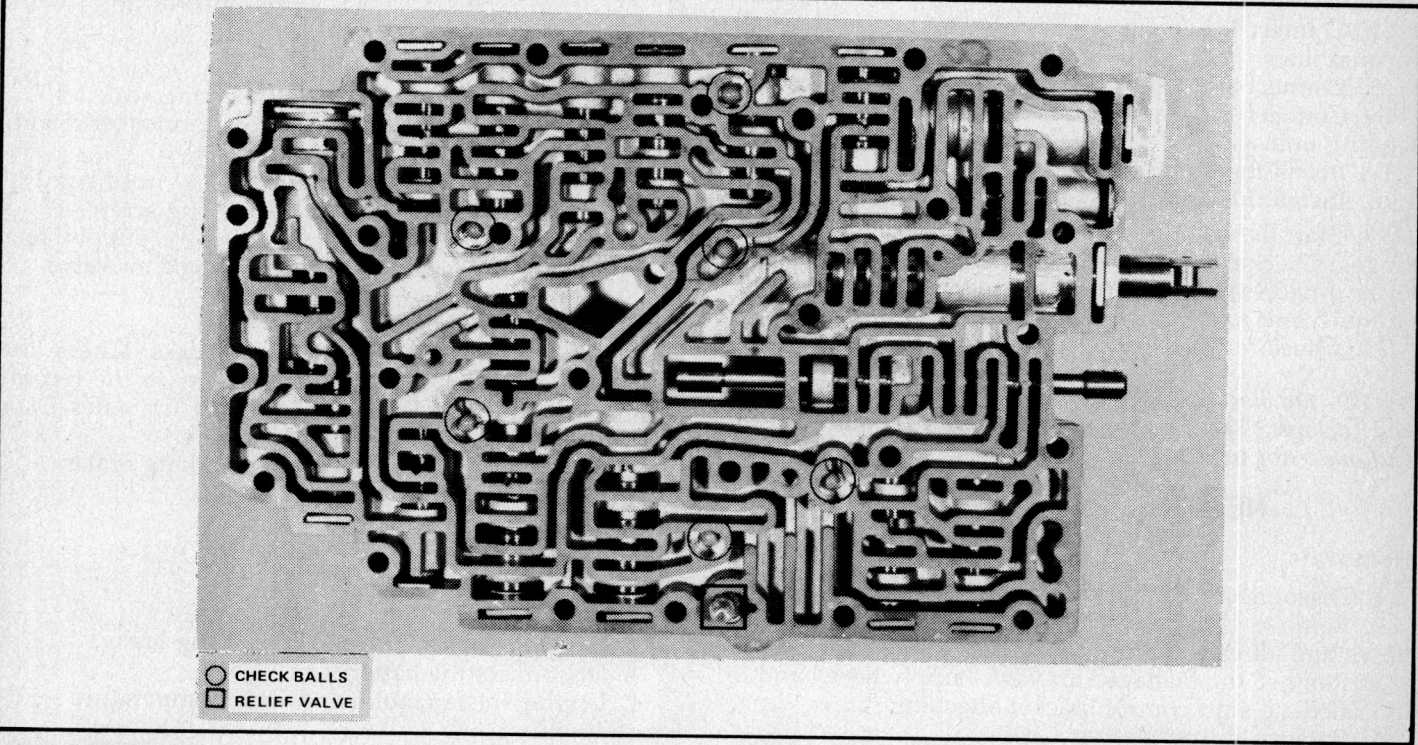

○ CHECK BALLS
□ RELIEF VALVE

Valve Body

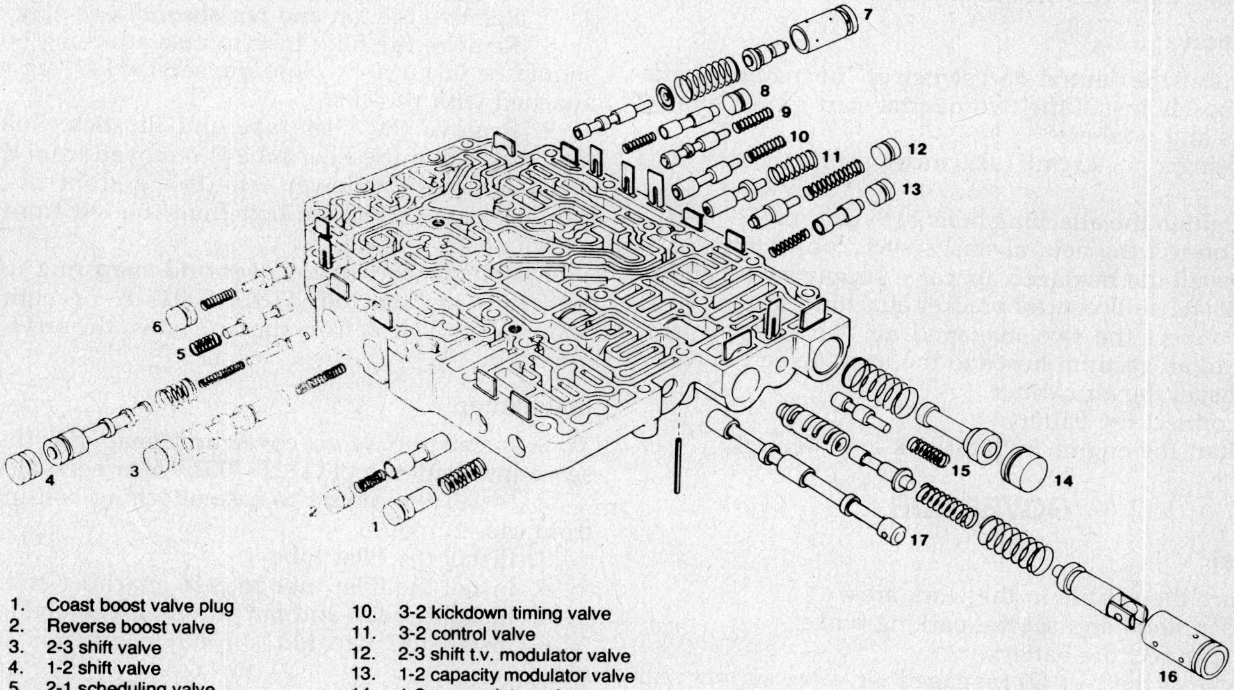

1. Coast boost valve plug
2. Reverse boost valve
3. 2-3 shift valve
4. 1-2 shift valve
5. 2-1 scheduling valve
6. 2-3 backout valve
7. Main oil pressure regulator
8. Manual low downshift modulating valve
9. 3-2 torque demand timing valve
10. 3-2 kickdown timing valve
11. 3-2 control valve
12. 2-3 shift t.v. modulator valve
13. 1-2 capacity modulator valve
14. 1-2 accumulator valve
15. T.v. limit valve
16A. Throttle control assembly
16B. Throttle control assembly
17. Manual control valve

NOTE: Do not turn the throttle valve adjusting screw and lock nut. The adjustment is set during manufacture and must not be altered.

13. Install the managed air valve on the main control cover.

14. Connect the managed air valve supply hoses and vacuum lines.

15. Connect the fuel evaporator hose at the frame rail.

16. Connect the fan motor and water temperature sending unit wiring.

17. Install the ignition coil.

18. Install the battery tray and battery.

19. Start the engine and cycle the transaxle through all ranges. Check the fluid level and fill to the recommended level, if necessary, with Motorcraft Dexron® II, Series D or equivalent transmission fluid.

20. Check for fluid leaks.

NOTE Do not turn the throttle valve adjusting screw and locknut. The adjustment is set during manufacture and must not be altered.

NEUTRAL START SWITCH

Removal

1. Disconnect the battery.

2. Remove the two managed air valve supply rear hoses and all vacuum lines from the managed air valve.

3. Remove the managed air valve supply hose band to intermediate shift control bracket attaching screw.

4. Remove the air cleaner.

5. Disconnect the neutral start switch connect.

6. Remove the two neutral start switch attaching bolts.

7. Remove the neutral start switch.

Installation

1. Install the neutral start switch on the manual shaft.

2. Loosely install the two neutral start switch attaching bolts and washers

3. Using a no. 43 drill (.089 inch), set the neutral start switch.

4. Tighten the attaching bolts to 9-12 N•m (7-9 lb-ft).

5. Connect the neutral start switch connector.

6. Install the managed air valve supply hose band to intermediate shift control bracket attaching screw.

7. Connect the two managed air valve supply rear hoses and all vacuum hoses to the managed air valve.

8. Install the air cleaner.

9. Connect the battery.

10. Start the engine in both Park and Neutral.

GOVERNOR

Removal

1. Place the vehicle in the work area.

2. Open hood and set the parking brake.

3. Disconnect the battery.

4. Remove the two (2) managed air valve supply rear hoses and all vacuum lines from the managed air valve.

5. Remove the managed air valve supply hose band to intermediate shift control bracket attaching screw.

6. Remove the air cleaner.

7. Using a long screwdriver, remove the governor cover retaining clip.

8. Remove the governor cover.

9. Remove the governor.

Installation

1. Install the governor.

2. Install the governor cover with O-ring seal.

3. Using a suitable tool, tap the governor cover retaining clip in place.

4. Install the managed air valve supply hose band to intermediate shift control bracket attaching screw.

5. Connect the two managed air valve supply rear hoses and all vacuum lines to the managed air valve.

6. Install the air cleaner.

7. Connect the battery.

8. Start the engine and check for leaks. Check the transaxle fluid level and fill, if necessary, to the recommended level with Motorcraft Dexron® II, Series D or equivalent transmission fluid.

9. Close the hood and release the parking brake.

SERVO

Removal

1. Place the vehicle in the work area.

2. Open the hood and set the parking brake.

3. Disconnect the battery.

4. Unplug the fan motor and water temperature sending unit wiring.

5. Unplug the FM capacitor wiring, if so equipped.

6. Remove the two fan shroud to radiator attaching nuts.

7. Remove the fan and fan shroud assembly.

8. Remove the filler tube to case attaching bolt. Care should be taken not to lose the service I.D. tag which is attached with this bolt.

9. Remove the filler tube and dipstick. Some fluid may leak when the filler tube is removed from the case.

10. Remove the lower left (facing front of vehicle) mount to case attaching bolt from the left front (no. 1) mount.

11. Remove the servo cover and snap ring using the servo installation tool (T81P-70027-A or equivalent). Some fluid will leak from the case when the servo cover is removed.

Installation

1. Install the servo cover and snap ring using the servo installation tool (T81P-70027-A or equivalent).

2. Install the mount to case attaching bolt in the left front (no. 1) mount.

3. Install the filler tube.

4. Install the filler tube to case attaching bolt.

5. Install the fan and fan shroud assembly.

6. Install the two fan shroud to radiator attaching nuts.

7. Connect the FM capacitor wiring, if so equipped.

8. Connect the fan motor and water temperature sending unit wiring.

9. Connect the battery.

10. Start the engine and cycle the transaxle through all ranges. Check the fluid level and fill if necessary, to the

recommended level with the Motorcraft Dexron® II, Series D or equivalent transmission fluid.

11. Check for fluid leaks.

THROTTLE LINKAGE ADJUSTMENT

The TV control linkage must be adjusted at the TV control rod assembly sliding trunnion block using the following procedure.

1. Set the engine curb idle speed to specification.
2. After the curb idle check, turn the engine off and insure that the carburetor throttle lever is against the hot engine curb idle stop. (The choke must be off.)

NOTE The linkage cannot be properly set if the choke is allowed to cool and the throttle lever allowed to be on the choke fast idle cam.

3. Set the coupling lever adjustment screw at its approximate mid-range. Insure that the TV linkage shaft assembly is fully seated upward into the coupling lever.
4. Loosen the bolt on the sliding trunnion block on the TV control rod assembly one turn minimum.

CHILTON CAUTION The following steps involve working in proximity to the EGR system. Allow the EGR system to cool before proceeding.

5. Free-up the trunnion block so that it slides freely on the control rod.
6. Rotate the transaxle TV control lever up using one finger and a light force, 2.2 Kg (approximately 5 pounds), to insure that the TV control lever is against its internal idle stop. Without relaxing the force on the TV control lever, tighten the bolt on the trunnion block to specification.
7. Verify that the carburetor throttle lever is still against the hot engine curb idle stop.

Using Line Pressure

The following procedure may be used to check and/or adjust the TV control linkage using a line pressure gauge.

1. Place the shift selector lever in the Park position.
2. Apply the emergency brake.
3. Attach a 0-2500 kPa (0-300 psi) pressure gauge to the line press port on the transaxle with sufficient flexible hose to make gauge accessible while operating engine.
4. Operate the engine until normal operating temperature is reached and the throttle lever is against the hot engine curb idle stop (with A/C off, if so equipped).
5. Verify that the coupling lever adjusting screw is in contact with the TV linkage shaft assembly. If not, then the linkage must first be readjusted.
6. Verify that the carburetor throttle lever is against its hot engine curb idle stop. With the engine operating at idle and in Park, line pressure must be 296-406 kPa (43-59 psi). If line pressure is greater than 408 kPa (59 psi), the TV control linkage is set too long.
7. Place a 4mm drill (a $^{5}/_{32}$ inch drill or 0.157 inch gauge pin) between the coupling lever adjustment screw and the TV linkage shaft. With the engine operating at idle and in Park, the line pressure must be 496-606kPa (72-88

Throttle Linkage

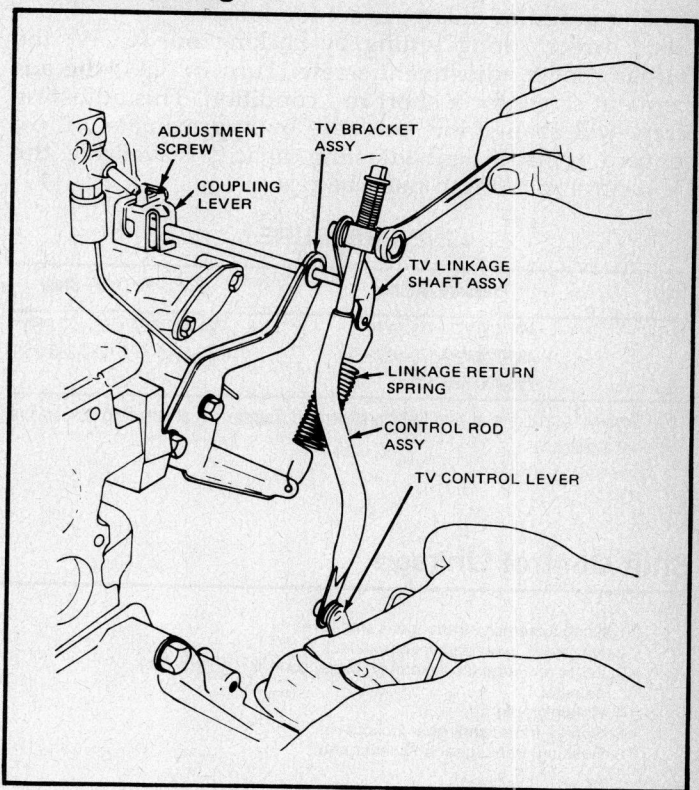

Line Pressure Connection

psi). A low reading indicates linkage is set short. A high reading indicates linkage is set too long.

8. Correct a long setting by backing out (CCW) the coupling lever adjustment screw. Turn in (CW) the adjustment screw for a short rod condition. This adjusting screw will change line pressure by approximately 2 psi per turn. If insufficient adjusting capacity is available, the TV control rod length must be reset.

LINE PRESSURE①

Range	Pressure (At Idle)	Pressure (WOT Stall)
0-2-1	296-400 KPA (43-58 PSI)	724-875 KPA (105-127 PSI)
R	483-724 KPA (70-105 PSI)	1585-1965 KPA (230-285 PSI)
P-N	296-400 KPA (43-58 PSI)	②

① Governor pressure is at zero (vehicle stationary). Transaxle is at operating temperature

② Not available

Adjust Throttle Linkage

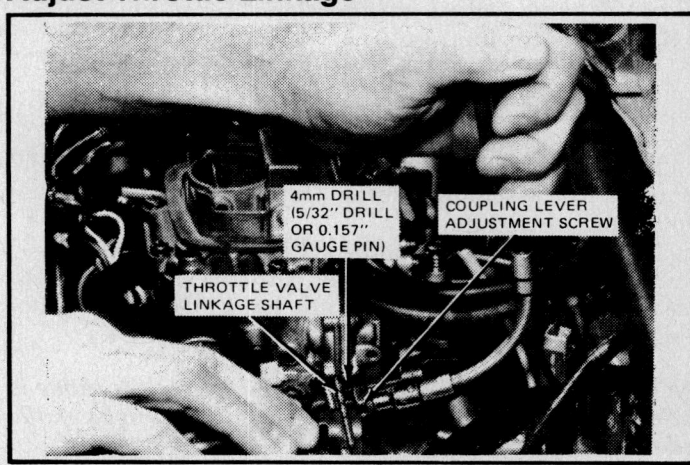

4mm DRILL (5/32'' DRILL OR 0.157'' GAUGE PIN)
COUPLING LEVER ADJUSTMENT SCREW
THROTTLE VALVE LINKAGE SHAFT

Shift Control Linkage

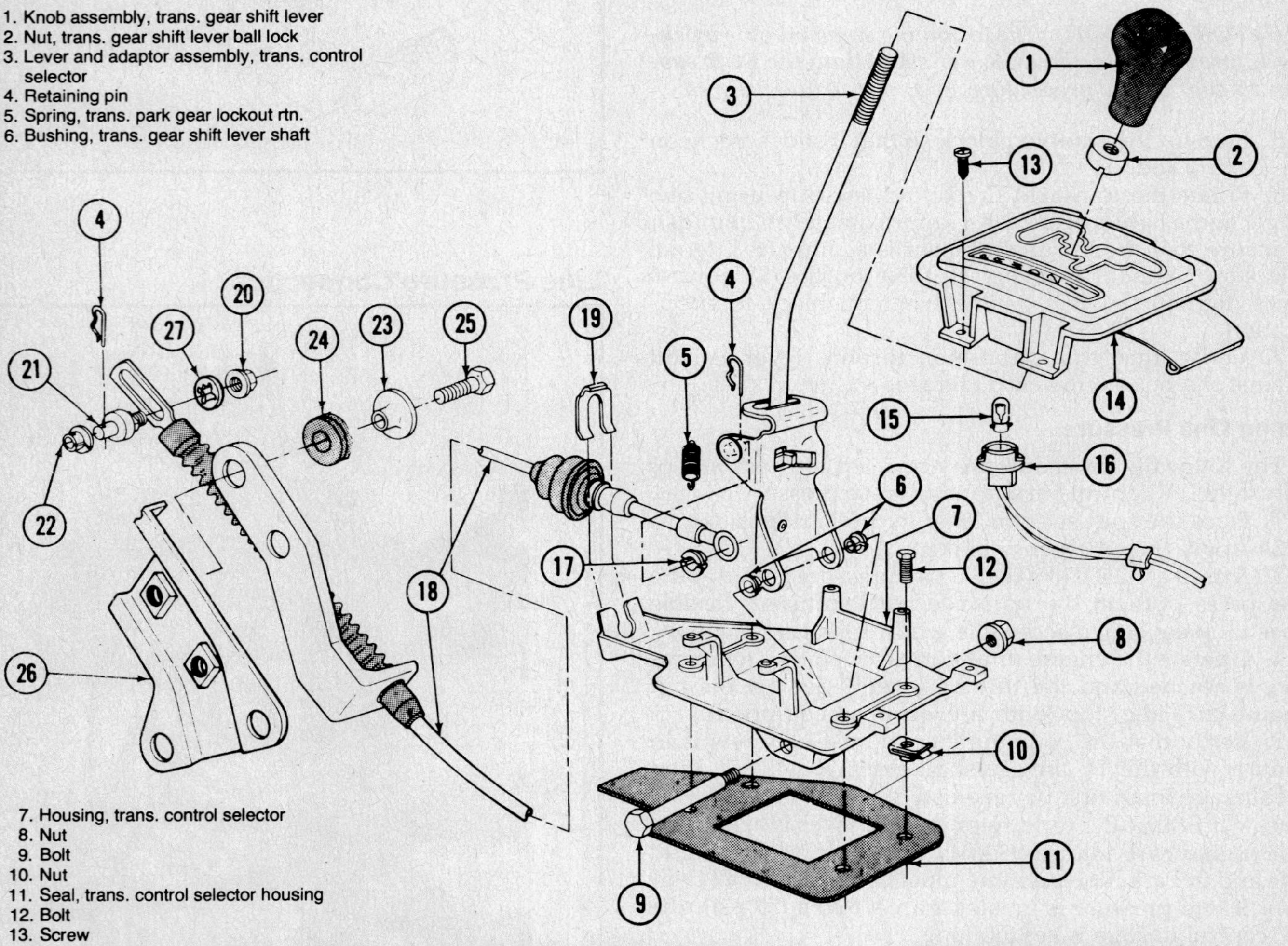

1. Knob assembly, trans. gear shift lever
2. Nut, trans. gear shift lever ball lock
3. Lever and adaptor assembly, trans. control selector
4. Retaining pin
5. Spring, trans. park gear lockout rtn.
6. Bushing, trans. gear shift lever shaft

7. Housing, trans. control selector
8. Nut
9. Bolt
10. Nut
11. Seal, trans. control selector housing
12. Bolt
13. Screw
14. Bezel assembly, trans. control selector dial
15. Bulb
16. Indicator bulb harness
17. Bushing, trans. gear shift lever cable
18. Cable and bracket assembly

19. Clip, hand brake cable spring lock
20. Nut and washer assembly
21. Stud, trans. gear shift connecting rod adjusting
22. Bushing, trans. control shift rod clevis
23. Spacer, trans. control cable bracket

24. Insulator, trans. control cable bracket
25. Bolt
26. Retainer assembly, trans. control cable bracket
27. Nut

GM 125

Description

This unit is fully automatic and consists primarily of a three-element torque converter, compound planetary gear set and dual sprocket and drive link assembly. Additionally, the transaxle incorporates a differential and final drive gear set. Three multiple disc clutches, a roller clutch and a band provide the friction elements required to obtain the desired function of the planetary gear sets. A hydraulic system pressurized by a vane-type pump provides the working pressure required to operate the friction elements and automatic controls.

Approximately four quarts of fluid are required to refill the transaxle after the pan has been drained. The total capacity of the 125 transaxle and converter assembly is approximately nine quarts, but the correct level is determined by the mark on the dipstick.

Trouble Diagnosis

ROAD TEST

1. Position selector lever in Drive range and accelerate the vehicle. A 1-2 shift and 2-3 shift should occur at throttle openings. These shift points will vary with throttle openings.

2. In Drive range, check the part throttle 3-2 downshift at 30 mph by quickly opening the throttle approximately three-fourths. The transaxle should downshift at 50 mph by fully depressing the accelerator.

3. Position the selector lever in Intermediate range and accelerate the vehicle. A 1-2 shift should occur at all throttle openings. The shift point will vary with throttle opening and will be firmer than in Drive range (A 2-3 shift cannot be obtained in this range.)

4. In Intermediate range, check for a detent 2-1 downshift at 20 mph.

5. In Low range, accelerate the vehicle. No shift should occur.

6. In Drive range with vehicle speed at approximately 50 mph, close the throttle and move the selector lever to Intermediate range. The transaxle should downshift to second. Engine speed should increase, and there should be noticeable engine braking.

7. In Intermediate range with vehicle speed at approximately 40 mph, close the throttle and move the selector lever to low. The transaxle should downshift to first between 40 and 25 mph, depending on valve body calibration. This downshift should be accompanied by increased engine speed and noticeable engine braking.

LOW OIL PRESSURE

Insufficient hydraulic pressure can be attributed to one or more of the following.
1. Low oil level
2. TV system (pressure low in Neutral or Drive, low to normal in Intermediate and Reverse)
   a. TV cable misadjusted or sticking
   b. TV linkage binding, incorrect cable, incorrect link
   c. Throttle valve stuck
   d. Shift TV valve stuck
3. Oil screen plugged or O-ring seal damaged
4. Oil screen O-ring seal leaking
5. Control valve assembly bolts loose
6. Pressure regulator stuck or wrong size
7. Control valve assembly check balls 4, 5 or 6 missing or out of location
8. Control valve assembly shift TV valve or reverse boost valve stuck
9. Control valve assembly 1-2 accumulator piston missing or seal cut or leaking
10. Control valve assembly internal leaks
11. Low-reverse clutch housing-to-case seal and cup plug leaking (Reverse only)
12. Pump gears broken
13. Shift TV passage blocked

HIGH OIL PRESSURE

Too high oil pressure can be attributed to one or more of the following.
1. TV system (pressure high in Neutral and Drive, normal to high in Intermediate and Reverse)
   a. TV cable misadjusted or sticking
   b. TV linkage binding, incorrect cable, incorrect link
   c. Throttle valve stuck
   d. Shift TV valve stuck
2. Pressure regulator valve stuck or wrong size
3. Control valve pump assembly
   a. Valves stuck
   b. TV valve and plunger
   c. Shift TV valve
   d. Pump slide stuck
   e. Reverse boost valve
4. Reverse boost orifice in spacer plate plugged (Reverse only)
5. Internal pump or case leaks

DIRECT CLUTCH

A burned direct clutch can be caused by one or more of the following.
1. Driven sprocket support
   a. Leaking (damaged) seal rings on driven sprocket support
   b. Driven sprocket support sleeve loose or mispositioned
2. Numbers 4 or 5 check balls missing or off location in case
3. Low hydraulic pressure
4. Channels blocked or interconnected
5. Accumulator check valve missing
6. Direct clutch assembly
   a. Seals cut, missing or rolled out of groove
   b. Apply ring, release spring, assembly or wrong number of clutch plates
   c. Exhaust ball capsule in housing damaged and not sealing
   d. Piston or housing damaged
7. Intermediate servo assembly
   a. Seals missing or damaged

AUTOMATIC TRANSMISSIONS
GM 125

b. Servo bore scored or damaged
c. Servo orifice bleed plug missing
d. Accumulator check valve not sealing
8. Control valve assembly
a. Control valve assembly-to-case bolts loose
b. Sealing surface on control valve assembly, spacer plate, case and/or gaskets damaged and leaking
c. Porosity in control valve assembly and/or case channels

FORWARD CLUTCH

A burned forward clutch may be caused by one or more of the following.
1. Driven sprocket support
a. Leaking (damaged) seal rings on driven sprocket support
b. Driven sprocket support sleeve loose or mispositioned
2. Numbers 4 or 5 check balls missing or off location in case
3. Low hydraulic pressure
4. Channels blocked or interconnected
5. Forward clutch assembly
a. Seal rings on input shaft damaged or missing
b. Input shaft feed passage or orifice restricted
c. Housing exhaust ball capsule damaged or missing
d. Housing or shaft seal surface damaged
e. Piston seals missing or damaged
f. Apply ring missing, wrong apply ring or wrong number of clutch plates
g. Piston damaged or leaking
6. Control valve pump assembly and case
a. Control valve assembly-to-case bolts loose
b. Sealing surface on control valve assembly, spacer plate, case or gaskets damaged or leaking
c. Porosity between channels in control valve assembly or case

LOW-REVERSE CLUTCH

A burned low-reverse clutch may be caused by one or more of the following.
1. Driven sprocket support
a. Leaking (damaged) seal rings on driven sprocket support
b. Driven sprocket support sleeve loose or mispositioned
2. Low-reverse clutch assembly
a. Housing seal area damaged
b. Piston or seals damaged
c. Apply ring missing, wrong apply ring or wrong number of clutch plates
3. Control valve pump assembly
a. Reverse boost valve sticking
b. Check balls missing or out of location
4. Case assembly
a. Low-reverse clutch housing-to-case cup plug assembly hole restricted, damaged or not correctly seated.
b. Number 4 check ball missing or off location in case
c. Reverse feed passage restricted or leaking
d. Low hydraulic pressure

INTERMEDIATE BAND ASSEMBLY

A burned intermediate band assembly may be caused by one or more of the following.
1. Band anchor pin missing or not engaged in the band
2. Band not properly aligned or apply pin not engaged
3. Intermediate servo assembly
a. Seals missing or damaged
b. Wrong band apply pin
4. Leak in clutch apply stream
5. Control valve assembly
a. 1-2 accumulator piston missing or seal leaking
b. 1-2 accumulator valve sticking
6. Case
a. Accumulator check valve missing or not seating correctly

NOISY TRANSAXLE

Transaxle noise may be caused by one or more of the following.
1. Pump
a. Oil level setting low
b. Cavitation due to plugged screen, porosity intake circuit or water in oil
c. Damaged pump vanes
2. Gears
a. Transaxle grounded to body
b. Roller bearings worn or damaged

THUMPING OR CLUNKING SOUND AT 1-5 MPH IN DRIVE OR INTERMEDIATE RANGE

If the stator roller clutch becomes ineffective, the stator assembly freewheels at all times in both directions. With this condition, the vehicle will accelerate poorly. At speeds above 30–35 mph the vehicle may respond normally.

CONVERTER STATOR LOCKED UP

If the stator assembly remains locked up at all times, engine and vehicle speed will be limited or restricted at high speed. Performance when accelerating from a standstill will be normal. Engine overheating may be noted. Visual inspection of the converter may reveal an overheated blue cover.

On Car Serviceable Components

TV CABLE
Inspection

To check the TV cable for freeness, pull out on the upper end of the cable. The cable should travel a short distance with light spring resistance. This light resistance is due to the small coiled return spring on the TV lever and bracket that returns the lever to the zero TV or closed throttle position. Pulling the cable farther out moves the lever to contact the TV plunger which compresses the TV spring which has more resistance. By releasing the upper end of the TV cable, it should return to the zero TV position. This checks the cable in the housing, the TV lever and bracket, and the TV plunger in its bushing for freeness.

Adjustment

1. Install a line pressure gauge.
2. Check line pressure with the selector lever in Park and engine at 1000 rpm.

3. Check line pressure in Neutral at 1000 rpm. Pressure should be the same to no more than 5 psi higher than in Park.
4. Increase engine rpm to 1200. Line pressure should increase.

TV Cable Mechanism

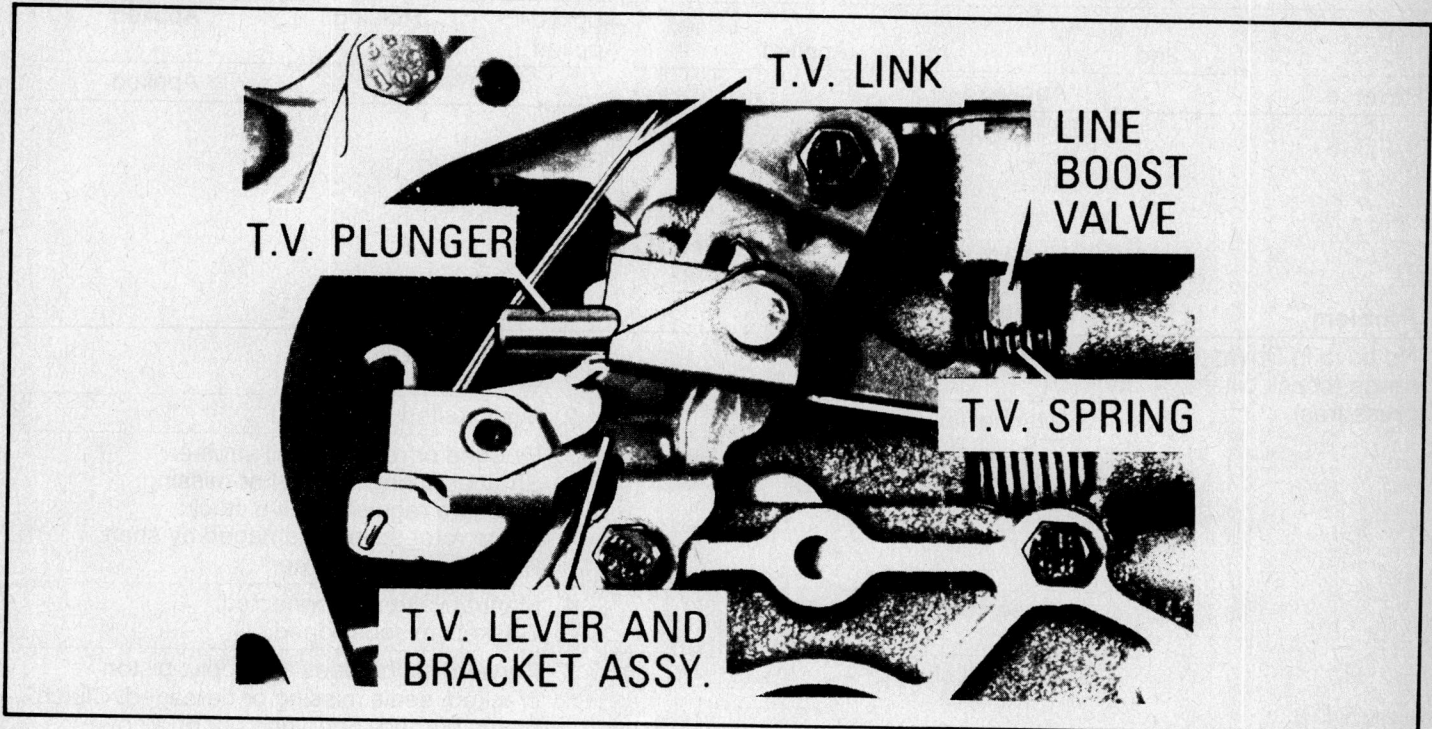

OIL PRESSURE SPECIFICATIONS
GM 125

Range	Normal Oil Pressure at Minimum TV P.S.I.	Normal Oil Pressure at Full TV P.S.I.
Park at 1000 rpm	65–75	No TV pressure in Park, line pressure is same as Park at minimum TV
Reverse at 1000 rpm	120–130 120–130	185–210 185–265
Neutral at 1000 rpm	65–75 65–75	120–130 140–150
Drive at 1000 rpm	65–75 65–75	120–130 140–150
Intermediate at 1000 rpm	115–130	115–130
Low at 1000 rpm	115–103	No TV pressure in Low, line pressure is the same as intermediate at minimum TV

AUTOMATIC TRANSMISSIONS

GM 125

RANGE REFERENCE CHART
GM 125

Range	Gear	Direct Clutch	Intermediate Band	Forward Clutch	Roller Clutch	Low-Reverse Clutch
Park and Neutral	1st			Applied	Holding	
Drive	2nd		Applied	Applied		
	3rd	Applied		Applied		
Intermediate	1st			Applied	Holding	
	2nd		Applied	Applied		
Low	1st			Applied	Holding	Applied
	2nd		Applied	Applied		
Reverse		Applied				Applied

TROUBLESHOOTING
GM 125

Problem	Possible Cause	Possible Condition
No drive in Drive range (check oil pressures)	1. Low oil level	1. Incorrect level. External leaks.
	2. Manual linkage	2. Misadjusted.
	3. Low oil pressure	3. Plugged or restricted oil strainer. Strainer O-ring seal cut or missing. Pressure regulator valve stuck. Pump rotor splines damaged by shaft. Porosity in intake bore.
	4. Case cover	4. Manual valve disconnected. Gaskets mispositioned.
	5. Forward clutch	5. Forward clutch does not apply, piston cracked, seals missing or damaged. Clutch plates burned. Snap ring out of groove. Forward clutch oil seal rings missing or damaged on input shaft. Leak in feed circuits. Clutch housing ball check stuck, missing or damaged. Wrong number of clutch plates. Feed orifice plugged in input shaft.
	6. Roller clutch	6. Springs missing. Rollers galled or missing.
High or low oil pressures	1. Throttle valve cable	1. Misadjusted, binding, unhooked or broken
	2. Throttle lever and bracket assembly	2. Bent, binding, broken, unhooked or mispositioned
	3. Throttle valve or plunger	3. Binding.
	4. Shift TV valve	4. Binding.
	5. Line boost valve	5. Binding. Bore plug installed wrong.
	6. TV boost valve and reverse boost valve	6. Binding. Plugged orifices in bushings.
	7. Pressure regulator valve and spring	7. Binding.
	8. Pressure relief valve	8. Ball missing. Spring damaged.

TROUBLESHOOTING
GM 125

Problem	Possible Cause	Possible Condition
High or low oil pressures	9. Manual valve	9. Unhooked.
	10. Pump	10. Pump slide stuck. Pump slide seal damaged, missing.
1-2 shift, full throttle only	1. Throttle valve cable	1. Binding, unhooked or broken. Misadjusted.
	2. Throttle lever and bracket assembly	2. Binding, unhooked or mispositioned. (Allowing line boost valve to seat causes full TV pressure, regardless of throttle valve position.)
	3. Throttle valve and plunger	3. Binding.
	4. Pump and control valve assembly	4. Gaskets or spacer plate leaking, damaged, incorrectly installed.
	5. Case assembly	5. Porosity.
First speed only, no 1-2 upshift	1. Governor and governor feed passages	1. Plugged governor oil feed in spacer plate. Governor ball or balls missing in assembly. Governor cover rubber O-ring seal missing or leaking. (If governor cover O-ring seal leaks, an external leak will be present, along with no upshifts.) Governor shaft seal missing or damaged. Governor driven gear stripped. Governor weights binding on pin. Governor assembly missing. Governor drive gear loose or missing. Governor springs damaged or missing. Governor oil pipe plugged or mislocated.
	2. 1-2 shift train	2. 1-2 shift valve or 1-2 throttle valve stuck in downshift position.
	3. Case and case cover	3. Porosity in case channels or undrilled 2nd speed feed holes. Excessive leakage between case bore and intermediate band apply pin. Broken or missing band.
	4. Intermediate servo assembly	4. Servo oil seal ring missing or damaged. Porosity in servo cover or piston. Wrong intermediate apply pin.
First and second speeds only, no 2-3 shift	1. Pump and control valve assembly	1. Direct clutch feed orifice in spacer plate plugged. Spacer plate or gaskets leaking, damaged, or incorrectly installed. Check ball #5 missing or mislocated.
	2. 2-3 valve train	2. 2-3 shift valve or 2-3 throttle valve stuck in downshift position.
	3. Case and case cover	3. Porosity in case channels. 3rd oil cup plug missing. Direct clutch accumulator check valve missing. Servo bleed orifice cup plug missing.
	4. Driven sprocket support	4. Oil seals cut, missing or damaged. Feed passages blocked.

TROUBLESHOOTING
GM 125

Problem	Possible Cause	Possible Condition
First and second speeds only, no 2-3 shift	5. Direct clutch	5. Oil seals missing or damaged on piston. Direct clutch piston or housing cracked. Direct clutch plates damaged or missing. Direct clutch backing plate snap ring out of groove.
	6. Intermediate servo assembly	6. Servo oil seal ring broken or missing in piston.
	7. Governor assembly	7. Shaft seal missing or damaged.
Third speed only	1. 2-3 shift valve	1. Stuck in upshift position.
	2. Governor assembly	2. Governor oil pipe plugged or mislocated. Governor feed passages plugged.
Drive in Neutral	1. Manual linkage	1. Misadjusted or disconnected.
	2. Forward clutch	2. Clutch does not release. Exhuast check ball sticking. Plates burned together.
	3. Case and case cover	3. Cross leakage to forward clutch passages.
No drive in Reverse or slips in Reverse (refer to oil pressure checks)	1. Throttle valve cable	1. Binding or misadjusted.
	2. Manual linkage	2. Misadjusted.
	3. Throttle valve	3. Binding.
	4. Shift TV valve	4. Binding.
	5. Reverse boost valve	5. Binding. Bushing orifices blocked.
	6. Low and reverse clutch assembly	6. Piston cracked, broken or missing seals. Clutch plates burned or wrong number.
	7. Case and case cover	7. Porosity in passages. Check ball #4 missing or mislocated. Low and reverse cup plug missing. Reverse oil pipe plugged or mislocated. Reverse oil pipe O-ring seal cut or missing.
	8. Direct clutch	8. Sprocket cover oil seal rings damaged or missing. Piston or housing cracked. Piston seals cut or missing. Housing ball check stuck, leaking or missing. Plates burned. Orifice plugged in spacer plate.
Slips on 1-2 shift	1. Low oil level	1. Oil will aerate, correct oil level.
	2. Spacer plate and gaskets	2. Second speed feed orifice partially blocked. Gaskets damaged or mispositioned.
	3. 1-2 accumulator valve	3. Valve sticking in valve body causing low 1-2 accumulator pressure. Weak or missing spring.
	4. 1-2 accumulator piston	4. Seal leaking, spring broken or missing. Leak between piston and pin.
	5. Intermediate band apply pin	5. Wrong apply pin. Excessive leakage between apply pin and case.
	6. Intermediate servo assembly	6. Porosity in piston. Servo oil seal ring damaged or missing.
	7. Throttle valve cable	7. Not adjusted properly.
	8. Throttle valve	8. Binding, causing low TV pressure.

TROUBLESHOOTING
GM 125

Problem	Possible Cause	Possible Condition
Slips on 1-2 shift	9. Shift TV valve	9. Binding.
	10. Intermediate band	10. Worn or burned.
	11. Case	11. Porosity in passages.
Rough 1-2 shift	1. Throttle valve cable	1. Not adjusted properly. Binding.
	2. Throttle valve and TV plunger	2. Binding.
	3. Shift TV valve	3. Binding.
	4. 1-2 accumulator valve	4. Binding.
	5. 1-2 accumulator	5. Oil ring damaged. Piston stuck. Broken or missing spring. Bore damaged.
	6. Intermediate servo assembly	6. Wrong pin. Servo piston oil seal ring damaged or missing.
Slips 2-3 shift	1. Oil level low	1. Correct oil level.
	2. Throttle valve cable	2. Not adjusted properly.
	3. Throttle valve	3. Binding.
	4. Spacer plates and gaskets	4. Direct clutch orifice partially blocked in spacer plate. Gaskets mispositioned or damaged.
	5. Intermediate servo assembly	5. Servo oil seal ring damaged.
	6. Direct clutch	6. Case porosity in direct clutch feed channels. Driven sprocket channels cross feeding, leaking or restricted. Driven sprocket oil seal rings damaged or missing. Direct clutch piston or housing cracked. Piston seals cut or missing. Direct clutch plates burned. Housing check ball damaged, missing, binding.
Rough 2-3 shift	1. Throttle valve cable	1. Not adjusted properly. Binding.
	2. Throttle valve and plunger	2. Binding.
	3. Shift TV valve	3. Binding.
No engine braking, intermediate range 2nd gear (check oil pressures)	1. Intermediate servo assembly	1. Servo oil seal ring missing or damaged.
	2. Intermediate band	2. Mispositioned. Broken or burned.
No engine braking, Low range 1st gear (check oil pressures)	1. Low reverse clutch assembly	1. No Reverse should also be a complaint with any of the following conditions. Piston seals broken or missing. Porosity in piston or housing. Clutch housing snap ring out of case. Cup plug seal missing or damaged between case and low and reverse clutch housing.

TROUBLESHOOTING
GM 125

Problem	Possible Cause	Possible Condition
No part throttle or detent downshifts (check oil pressures)	1. Throttle plunger bushing	1. Passages not open.
	2. 2-3 throttle valve bushing	2. Passages not open.
	3. Valve body gaskets	3. Mispositioned or damaged.
	4. Spacer plate	4. Hole plugged or undrilled.
	5. Throttle valve cable	5. Misadjusted.
	6. Shift TV valve	6. Binding.
	7. Throttle valve	7. Binding.
Low or high shift points (check oil pressures)	1. Throttle valve cable	1. Binding or disconnected.
	2. Throttle valve	2. Binding.
	3. Shift TV valve	3. Binding.
	4. Line boost valve	4. Missing or binding.
	5. Throttle valve plunger	5. Binding.
	6. 1-2 or 2-3 throttle valve	6. Binding.
	7. Valve body spacer plate or gaskets	7. Damaged or mispositioned.
	8. Throttle lever and bracket assembly	8. Binding, unhooked or loose. Not positioned at the throttle valve plunger bushing pin locator.
	9. Governor shaft seal ring	9. Broken or missing.
	10. Governor cover O-ring	10. Broken or missing. (The ring will leak externally.)
	11. Case	11. Porosity.
Won't hold in Park	1. Manual linkage	1. Misadjusted.
	2. Internal linkage	2. Park pawl binding in case. Actuator rod or plunger damaged. Parking pawl broken. Parking bracket, loose or damaged
	3. Inside detent lever and pin assembly	3. Nut loose. Hole in lever worn or damaged.
	4. Manual detent roller and spring assembly	4. Bolt loose that holds roller assembly to valve body. Pin or roller damaged, mispositioned or missing.
Transmission noisy	1. Pump noise	1. Oil level setting low. Cavitation due to plugged strainer, cut or missing O-ring, porosity in intake circuit or water in oil.
	2. Gear noise	2. Transaxle grounded to body. Roller bearings worn or damaged. If noisy in 3rd gear or on turns only, check differential and final drive unit.

GM 180

On Car Service Procedures

DETENT CABLE ADJUSTMENT

1. Disengage the snap lock, so the cable is free to slide.
2. Position the carburetor lever in wide open throttle position. Push the snap lock flush and return the carburetor lever to the closed position.

VALVE BODY R&R

1. Remove the oil pan and screen.
2. Disconnect the detent cable and remove the throttle lever and bracket. Do not bend the throttle lever link.
3. Remove the manual detent roller and spring assembly.
4. Remove the transfer plate reinforcement and servo cover.
5. After removing the mount bolts, remove the valve body and transfer plate.

NOTE   The two check balls in the case may drop out when removing the valve body.

6. Before installing, position the check balls in the case oil passages.
7. Installation is the reverse of removal.

SERVO R&R

1. Remove the valve body.
2. Using tool J-23075, compress the servo piston.
3. Remove the snap ring. Slowly loosen tool J-23075 to free the servo piston, return spring and apply rod.
4. After installing the servo, adjust the apply rod as follows.
   a. Tighten the bolt to 40 in. lbs.
   b. Back off the bolt exactly five turns.

Valve Body Removal and Installation

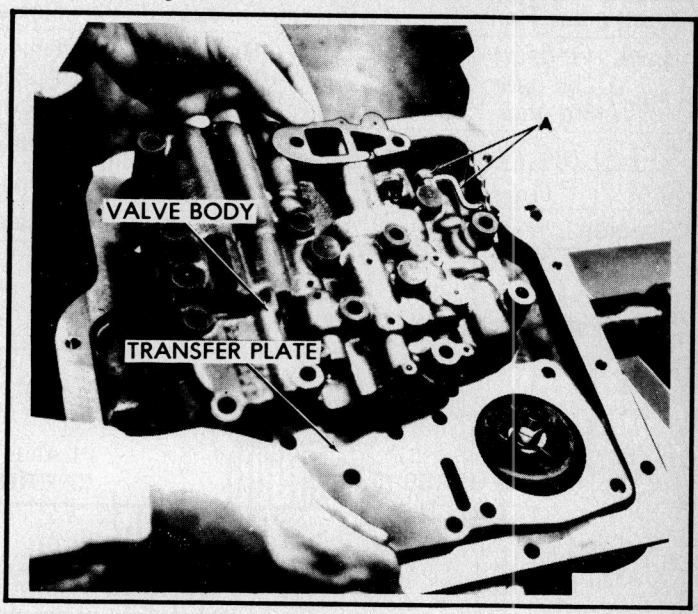

c. Tighten the locknut.

SPEEDOMETER DRIVEN GEAR R&R

1. Remove the driven gear housing retainer and pull the speedometer gear from the housing.
2. Installation is the reverse of removal.

REAR EXTENSION OIL SEAL R&R

1. After removing the drive shaft, pry out the old seal.
2. Coat the lip seal with transmission fluid. Install it using tool J-21426.

Detent Cable Adjustment

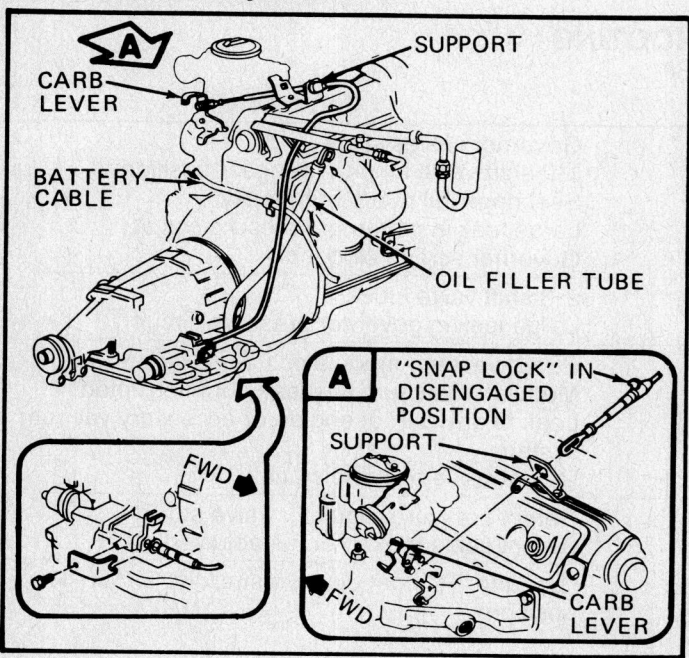

Valve Body Check Body Locations

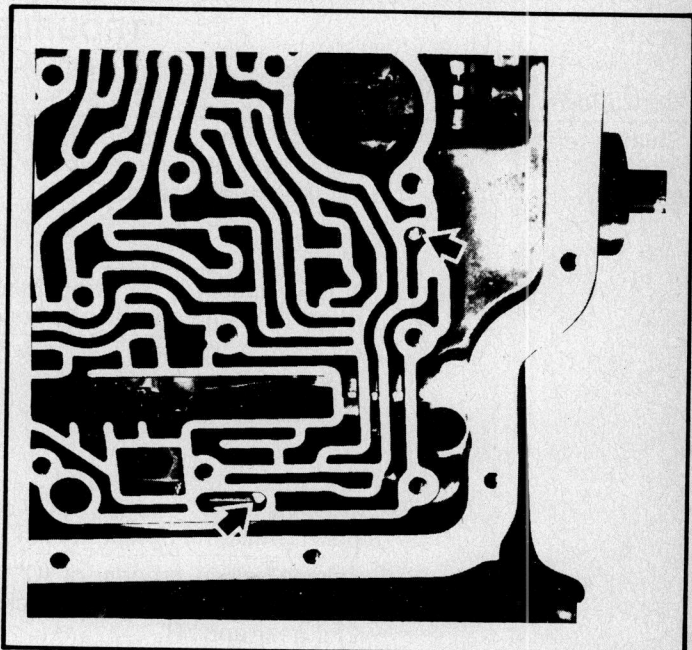

AUTOMATIC TRANSMISSIONS

GM 180

CLUTCH APPLICATION CHART

Range	Reverse Clutch	Second Clutch	Third Clutch	Low Band	Sprag
Neutral and Park	Released	Released	Released	Released	Locked
Drive, 1st gear	Released	Released	Released	Applied	Locked
2nd gear	Released	Applied	Released	Applied	Overrunning
3rd gear	Released	Applied	Applied	Released	Locked
L1	Released	Released	Applied	Applied	Locked
L2	Released	Applied	Released	Applied	Overrunning
Reverse	Applied	Released	Applied	Released	Locked

Clutch Application Chart

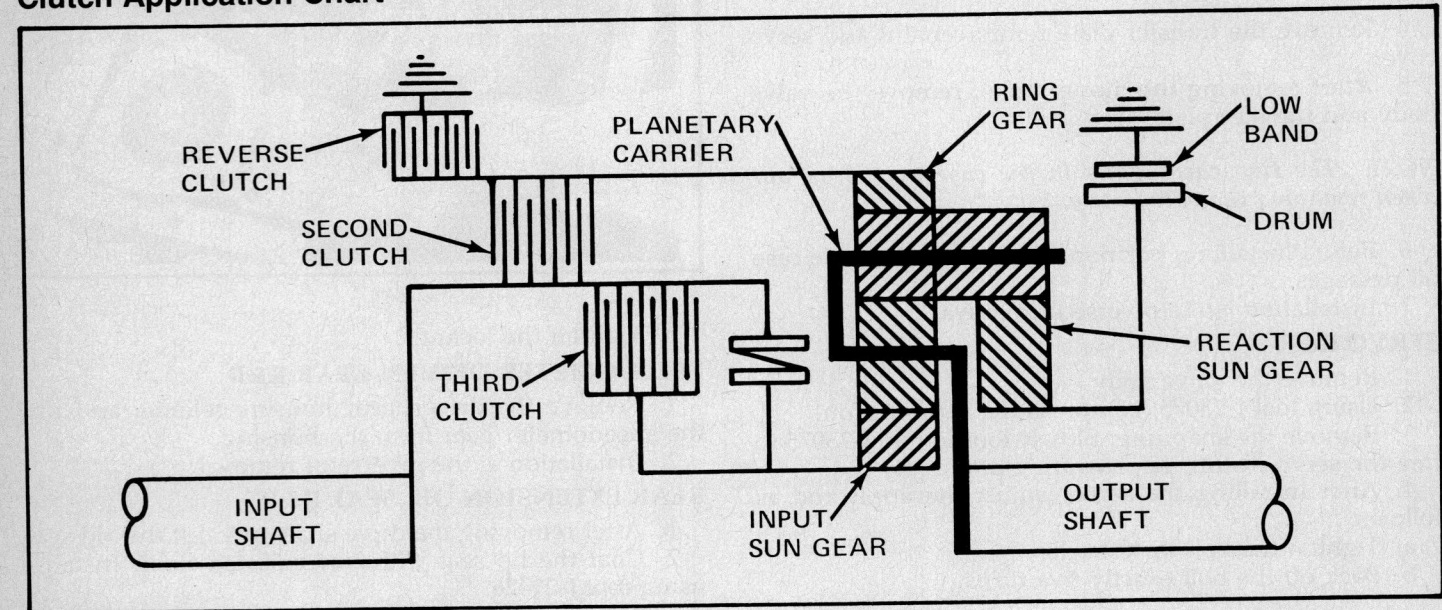

TROUBLESHOOTING
GM 180

Condition	Cause	Correction
Shifting related	No 1-2 upshift in "D" and "L₂", transmission remains in 1st gear at all speeds	Governor valves stuck 1-2 shift valve stuck in 1st gear position Seal rings (oil pump hub) leaky Large leak in governor pressure circuit Governor screen clogged
	No 2-3 upshift in "D" (transmission remains in 2nd gear at all speeds)	2-3 shift valve stuck Large leak in governor pressure circuit
	Upshifts in "D" and "L₂" only at full throttle	Failed vacuum modulator Modulator vacuum line leaky or interrupted Leak in any part of engine or accessory vacuum system Detent valve or cable stuck
	Upshifts in "D" and "L₂" only at part throttle, no detent upshift	Detent pressure regulator valve stuck Detent cable broken or misadjusted
	Driving only in 1st gear of "D" and "L₂" range, transmission blocks in 2nd gear and "R"	"L₁" and "R" control valve stuck in "L₁" or "R" position

B872

TROUBLESHOOTING
GM 180

Condition	Cause	Correction
Shifting related	No part throttle 3-2 downshift at low vehicle speeds	3-2 downshift control valve stuck
	Nor forced downshift	Detent cable broken or improperly adjusted Detent pressure regulator valve stuck
	After full throttle upshifting, transmission shifts immediately into lower gear upon easing off accelerator pedal	Detent valve stuck in open position Detent cable stuck Modulator vacuum line interrupted
	At higher speeds, transmission shifts into lower gear	Retaining pin of selector lever shaft in transmission dropped out Loose connection of selector lever linkage to manual valve Pressure loss at governor
	Hard disengagement of selector lever from "P"	Steel guide bushing of parking pawl actuating rod missing Manual selector lever stuck
	Slipping 1-2 upshifts, engine flares	Low oil pressure Sealing ball in valve body dropped out Second clutch piston seals leaking Second clutch piston centrifugal ball stuck open Second clutch piston cracked or broken Second clutch plates worn Seal rings of oil pump hub leaky
	Slipping 2-3 upshifts, engine flares	Low oil pressure Band adjustment loose Third clutch piston seals leaking Third clutch piston centrifugal ball stuck open Third clutch piston cracked or broken Wear of input shaft bushing Sealing ball in valve body dropped out
	Abrupt 1-2 upshift	High oil pressure 1-2 accumulator valve stuck Spring cushion of second clutch broken Second gear ball valve missing
	Abrupt 2-3 upshift	High oil pressure Incorrect band adjustment
	Abrupt 3-2 detent downshift at high speed	High speed downshift valve stuck open Band adjustment
	Abrupt 3-2 coast downshift, low speed downshift timing valve stuck open	
	Flare on high speed forced downshift	Low oil pressure Band adjustment loose
	Flare on low speed forced downshift	Low oil pressure Band adjustment loose High speed downshift timing valve stuck in closed position Sprag race does not grip on 3-1 down shifting
Starting related	No starting in any drive range	Low oil level Clogged suction screen Manual valve linkage or inner transmission selector level disconnected Input shaft broken Pressure regulator valve stuck in open position Failed oil pump

TROUBLESHOOTING
GM 180

Condition	Cause	Correction
Starting related	No starting in any drive range for a time, driving possible only after repeatedly moving selector lever	Manual valve position does not coincide with valve body channels Selector lever shaft retaining pin dropped out Connecting rod to manual valve shifting Selector lever shaft nut loose
	No starting after shifting lever from "P" to "D", "L₂" or "L₁", inadequate engine acceleration	Parking pawl does not disengage
	Sudden starting only after increase of engine rpm	Band servo piston jamming Low oil level Oil pump defective Oil screen missing Sealing ball in valve body dropped out
	Heavy jerking when starting	Low oil pressure Wrong modulator valve Pressure regulator valve stuck Sealing ball in valve body dropped out
	No starting in "D" or "L₂", but in "L₁" and "R"	Input sprag installed backwards Input sprag failure
	No starting in "D" or "L₂" and "L₁", proper driving in "R"	Band worn, does not grip Band servo piston jamming Excessive leak in band servo Parking pawl does not disengage
	No starting in "R", proper driving in all other ranges	Reverse clutch failure
	Drive in selector lever position "N"	Inadequate selector lever linkage. Planetary gear set broken Improper adjustment of band
Oil related	Low oil level	Oil coming out of filler tube External oil leak Failed vacuum modulator
	Oil coming out of oil filler tube	Oil level too high Coolant in transmission oil External vent clogged with mud Leak in oil pump suction circuit
	External oil leaks in the area of the torque converter housing	Leaking torque converter Converter housing seal Converter housing to case seal Loose attaching bolts on front of transmission
	External oil leaks in the area of transmission case and extension	Shifter shaft seal Extension seal Oil pan gasket Extension to case gasket Vacuum modulator gasket Drain plug gasket Cooler line fittings Oil filler tube seal ring Detent cable seal ring Line pressure gauge connection
	Low oil pressure	Low oil level Clogged suction screen Leak in oil pump suction circuit Leak in oil pressure circuit

TROUBLESHOOTING
GM 180

Condition	Cause	Correction
Oil related		Pressure regulator valve malfunction
	Low oil level	Sealing ball in valve body dropped out
	High oil pressure	Modulator vacuum line leaky or interrupted
		Failed vacuum modulator
		Leak in any part of engine or accessory vacuum system
		Pressure regulator valve malfunction
	Excessive smoke coming from exhaust	Failed vacuum modulator
		Oil from vent valve or leak on hot exhaust pipe
Noise related	Excessive noises in all drive ranges	Too much backlash between sun gear and planetary gears
		Lock plate on planetary carrier loose
		Thrust bearing defective
		Bearing bushings worn
		Excessive transmission axial play
		Unhooked parking pawl spring contacts governor hub
		Converter balancing weights loose
		Converter housing attaching bolt loose and contacting converter
	Screeching noise when starting	Converter failure
	Short vibrating, hissing noise shortly before 1-2 upshift	Dampening cushion of reverse clutch wearing into transmission case
Engine braking	No engine braking in "L_1"	Selector lever linkage improperly adjusted
		Manual low control valve stuck
	No engine braking in "L_2"	Selector lever linkage improperly adjusted
	No Park	Selector lever linkage improperly adjusted
		Parking lock actuator spring
		Parking pawl
		Governor hub

GM 200

Lubrication and Adjustments

IN-CAR THROTTLE VALVE CABLE CHECK

To check the throttle valve (TV) cable for freeness, pull out on the upper end of the cable. The cable should travel a short distance with light spring resistance. This light resistance is due to the small coiled return spring on the TV lever and bracket that returns the lever to the zero TV or closed throttle position. Pulling the cable farther out moves the lever to contact the TV plunger. This compresses the TV spring which has more resistance. By releasing the upper end of the TV cable, it should return to the zero TV position. This checks the cable in the housing, the TV lever and bracket, and the TV plunger in its bushing for freeness.

TRANSMISSION FLUID LEVEL CHECK

Proceed by having vehicle on a level surface with the engine running and the brakes applied. Run lever through all ranges. Then put the transmission in Park.

Now check the oil level. If oil is low, check for possible causes.

The oil level, at room temperature of approximately 21°C (70°F.), should be approximately 6mm (¼'') below the "ADD" mark.

The oil level should be between the "ADD" and "FULL" marks at normal operating temperature, 90°C (200°F.). This temperature is obtained after at least 24 km (15 miles) of expressway driving or equivalent city driving. At this temperature, the oil will heat the gauge end of

Throttle Valve (TV) Cable Adjustment

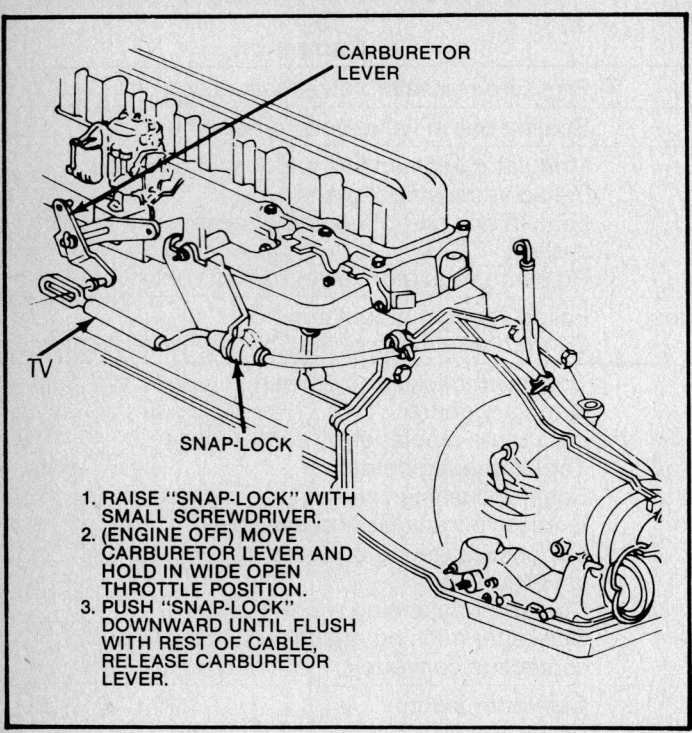

CARBURETOR LEVER

TV

SNAP-LOCK

1. RAISE "SNAP-LOCK" WITH SMALL SCREWDRIVER.
2. (ENGINE OFF) MOVE CARBURETOR LEVER AND HOLD IN WIDE OPEN THROTTLE POSITION.
3. PUSH "SNAP-LOCK" DOWNWARD UNTIL FLUSH WITH REST OF CABLE, RELEASE CARBURETOR LEVER.

the dip stick to a degree where the average person cannot grasp it firmly with his bare hand without discomfort.

CHILTON CAUTION   Do not overfill transmission, as this may cause foaming and loss of oil through the vent pipe.

OUTSIDE MANUAL LINKAGE ADJUSTMENT

The transmission manual linkage must be adjusted so that the indicator quadrant and stops correspond with the transmission detents. If the linkage is not adjusted properly, an internal leak could occur which could cause a clutch or band to slip.

Refer to the car division shop manual for manual linkage adjustment procedure.

NOTE   If a manual linkage adjustment is made, the neutral safety switch should be adjusted, if necessary. The neutral safety switch should be adjusted so that the engine will start only in Park and Neutral positions. With the selector lever in the Park position, the parking pawl should freely engage and prevent the vehicle from rolling.

On Car Service

The following units are serviceable with the transmission in the vehicle.
1. Oil pan
2. Fluid screen
3. Pressure regulator valve
4. Governor assembly

Manual Shaft and Parking Shaft Components

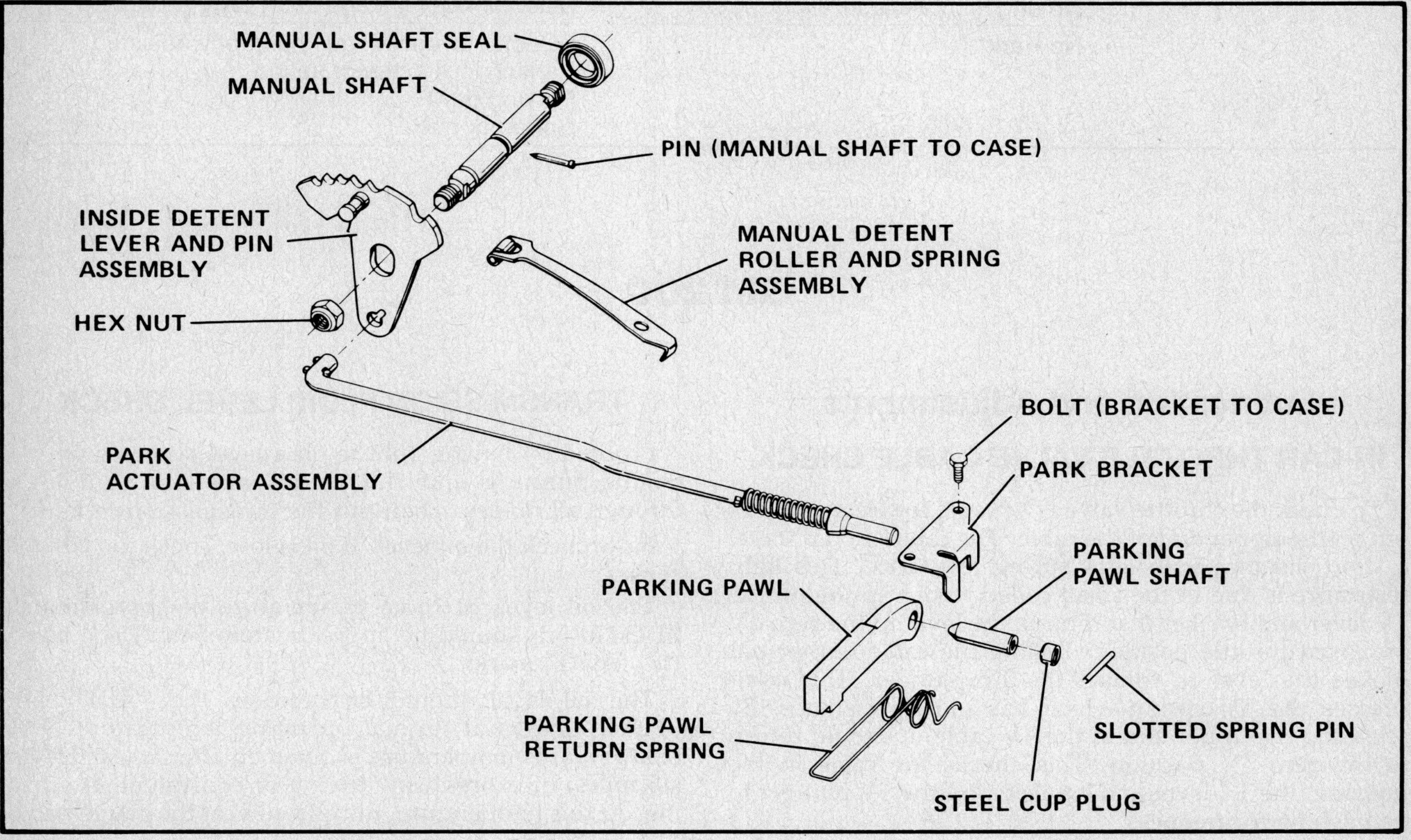

MANUAL SHAFT SEAL

MANUAL SHAFT

PIN (MANUAL SHAFT TO CASE)

INSIDE DETENT LEVER AND PIN ASSEMBLY

MANUAL DETENT ROLLER AND SPRING ASSEMBLY

HEX NUT

BOLT (BRACKET TO CASE)

PARK ACTUATOR ASSEMBLY

PARK BRACKET

PARKING PAWL SHAFT

PARKING PAWL

PARKING PAWL RETURN SPRING

SLOTTED SPRING PIN

STEEL CUP PLUG

5. Valve body
6. Intermediate servo
7. Speedometer driven gear
8. Rear oil seal
9. Inside detent lever and parking brake actuator rod
10. Throttle lever and bracket assembly
11. Detent roller and spring assembly
12. Manual shaft and seal
13. Parking pawl

CONTROL VALVE ASSEMBLY

1. Remove oil pan and screen.
2. Disconnect throttle valve cable.
3. Remove throttle lever and bracket without bending the throttle lever link.
4. Remove the manual detent roller and spring.
5. Support the valve assembly and remove the mounting bolts.
6. Remove valve assembly, spacer plate and gasket together to prevent dropping the four check balls located in the valve body and the fifth located in the case.
7. Installation is the reverse of removal.

PRESSURE REGULATOR VALVE

1. Remove the oil pan and screen.

Valve Body

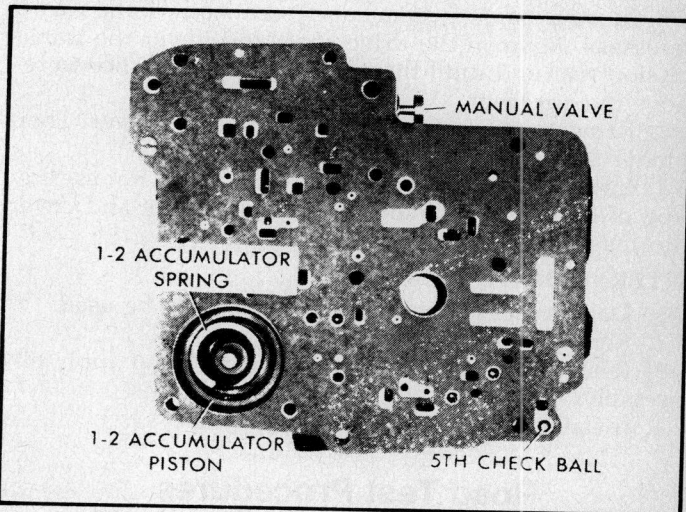

2. Depress the pressure regulator valve bore plug and remove the retaining ring.
3. Remove the bore plug, valve, spring and guide.
4. Installation is the reverse of removal.

Control Valve Assembly

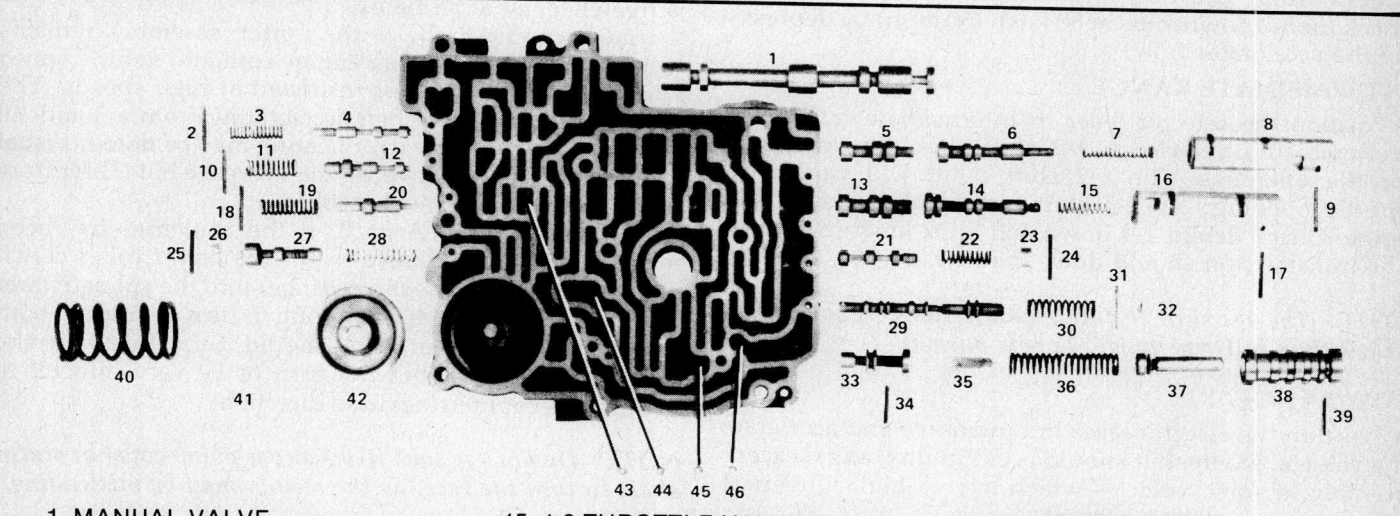

1. MANUAL VALVE
2. ROLL PIN
3. INTERMEDIATE BOOST SPRING
4. INTERMEDIATE BOOST VALVE
5. 2-3 SHIFT VALVE
6. 2-3 THROTTLE VALVE
7. 2-3 THROTTLE SPRING
8. 2-3 THROTTLE VALVE BUSHING
9. ROLL PIN
10. ROLL PIN
11. LOW OVERRUN CLUTCH SPRING
12. LOW OVERRUN CLUTCH VALVE
13. 1-2 SHIFT VALVE
14. 1-2 THROTTLE VALVE
15. 1-2 THROTTLE VALVE SPRING
16. 1-2 THROTTLE VALVE BUSHING
17. ROLL PIN
18. ROLL PIN
19. DIRECT CLUTCH EXHAUST SPRING
20. DIRECT CLUTCH EXHAUST VALVE
21. REVERSE BOOST VALVE
22. REVERSE BOOST SPRING
23. BORE PLUG
24. ROLL PIN
25. ROLL PIN
26. VALVE BORE PLUG
27. 1-2 ACCUMULATOR
28. 1-2 ACCUMULATOR VALVE SPRING
29. SHIFT T.V. VALVE
30. SHIFT T.V. SPRING
31. ROLL PIN
32. SHIFT T.V. PLUG
33. THROTTLE VALVE
34. INNER ROLL PIN
35. THROTTLE VALVE DETENT PIN
36. THROTTLE VALVE SPRING
37. THROTTLE VALVE PLUNGER
38. THROTTLE VALVE BUSHING
39. OUTER ROLL PIN
40. 1-2 ACCUMULATOR SPRING
41. 1-2 ACCUMULATOR SEAL
42. 1-2 ACCUMULATOR PISTON
43. CHECK BALL #4
44. CHECK BALL #3
45. CHECK BALL #2
46. CHECK BALL #1

GOVERNOR

1. Move exhaust system components out of the way if necessary. Remove the drive shaft and lower the transmission rear end until there is sufficient clearance to remove the governor.

2. Remove the governor retainer ring and cover. Then remove the governor from the case.

3. Installation is the reverse of removal. Do not use any type of hammer to install governor assembly and cover into the case or damage could result.

INTERMEDIATE SERVO

1. Depress servo cover. Tool J-28653 may be used.
2. Remove the cover retaining ring.
3. Remove the cover, servo piston and band apply pin assembly.
4. Installation is the reverse of removal.

Road Test Procedures

DRIVE RANGE

Position selector lever in Drive range and accelerate the vehicle. A 1-2 and 2-3 shift should occur at all throttle openings. (The shift points will vary with the throttle openings). Check part throttle 3-2 downshift at 50 km/h (30 mph) by quickly opening throttle approximately three-fourths. The transmission should downshift 3-2. Check for 3-2 downshifts at 80 km/h (50 mph) by depressing the accelerator fully.

INTERMEDIATE RANGE

Position the selector lever in Intermediate range and accelerate the vehicle. A 1-2 shift should occur at all throttle openings. The 1-2 shift point will vary with throttle opening. No 2-3 shift can be obtained in this range. Check detent 2-1 downshift at 32 km/h (20 mph). The transmission should downshift 2-1.

NOTE   The 1-2 shift in Intermediate range is somewhat firmer than in Drive range. This is normal.

LOW RANGE

Position the selector lever in Low range and accelerate the vehicle. No upshift should occur in this range, except possibly in some vehicles which have a high numerical axle ratio and/or engine (rpm).

INTERMEDIATE RANGE OVERRUN BRAKING

Position the selector lever in Drive range. With the vehicle speed at approximately 80 km/h (50 mph) closed or 0 throttle, move the selector lever to Intermediate range. The transmission should downshift to 2nd. An increase in engine rpm and an engine braking effect should be noticed.

LOW RANGE OVERRUN BRAKING

At 64 km/h (40 mph) with throttle closed, move the selector lever to Low. A 2-1 downshift should occur in the speed range of approximately 64 to 40 km/h (40 to 25 mph), depending on axle ratio and valve body calibration. The 2-1 downshift at closed throttle will be accompanied by increased engine rpm and an engine braking effect should be noticed. Stop vehicle.

REVERSE RANGE

Position the selector lever in Reverse position and check for reverse operation.

Diagnosis
CONVERTER STATOR OPERATION

The torque converter stator assembly and its related roller clutch can possibly have one of two different type malfunctions. In condition A, the stator assembly freewheels in both directions. In condition B, the stator assembly remains locked up at all times.

Under condition A, if the stator roller clutch becomes ineffective, the stator assembly freewheels at all times in both directions. With this condition, the vehicle will tend to have poor acceleration from a standstill. At speeds above 30–35 mph, the vehicle may act normal. If poor acceleration problems are noted, it should first be determined that the exhaust system is not blocked, the engine is in good tune and the transmission is in first (1st) gear when starting out.

If the engine will freely accelerate to high rpm in Neutral, it can be assumed that the engine and exhaust system are normal. Driving the vehicle in Reverse and checking for poor performance will help determine if the stator is freewheeling at all times.

Under condition B, if the stator assembly remains locked up at all times, the engine rpm and vehicle speed will tend to be limited or restricted at high speeds. The vehicle performance when accelerating from a standstill will be normal. Engine over heating may be noted. Visual examination of the converter may reveal a blue color from the overheating that will result.

Under conditions A or B, if the converter has been removed from the transmission, the stator roller clutch can be checked by inserting a finger into the splined inner race of the roller clutch and trying to turn the race in both directions. The inner race should turn freely in the clockwise direction, but not turn or be very difficult to turn in the counterclockwise direction.

NOTE   Do not use such items as the pump cover or stator shaft to turn the race, as the results may be misleading.

EXTERNAL OIL LEAKS

Before attempting to correct an oil leak, the actual source of the leak must be determined. In many cases, the source of the leak can be deceiving due to wind flow around the engine and transmission.

The suspected area should be wiped clean of all oil before inspecting for the source of the leak. Red dye is used in the transmission oil at the assembly plant and will indicate if the oil leak is from the transmission.

Oil leaks around the engine and transmission are generally carried toward the rear of the car by the air stream. For example, a transmission oil filler tube to case leak will sometimes appear as a leak at the rear of the transmission. In determining the source of an oil leak, two checks should be made. First, with the engine running, check for

Turbo Hydra-Matic 200 Oil Pressure Checks

OIL PRESSURE
TEST GAUGE
PLUG LOCATION

PRELIMINARY CHECKING PROCEDURE

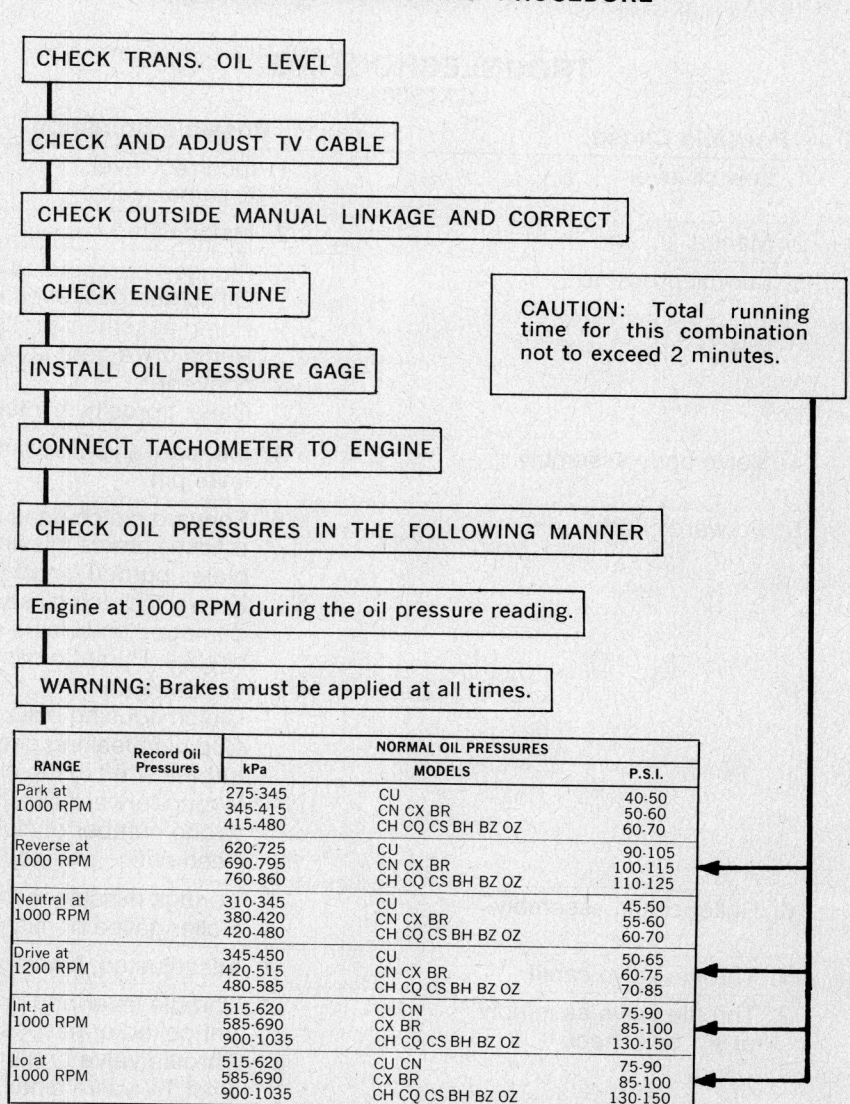

CHECK TRANS. OIL LEVEL

CHECK AND ADJUST TV CABLE

CHECK OUTSIDE MANUAL LINKAGE AND CORRECT

CHECK ENGINE TUNE

INSTALL OIL PRESSURE GAGE

CONNECT TACHOMETER TO ENGINE

CHECK OIL PRESSURES IN THE FOLLOWING MANNER

Engine at 1000 RPM during the oil pressure reading.

WARNING: Brakes must be applied at all times.

CAUTION: Total running time for this combination not to exceed 2 minutes.

RANGE	Record Oil Pressures	NORMAL OIL PRESSURES		
		kPa	MODELS	P.S.I.
Park at 1000 RPM		275-345	CU	40-50
		345-415	CN CX BR	50-60
		415-480	CH CQ CS BH BZ OZ	60-70
Reverse at 1000 RPM		620-725	CU	90-105
		690-795	CN CX BR	100-115
		760-860	CH CQ CS BH BZ OZ	110-125
Neutral at 1000 RPM		310-345	CU	45-50
		380-420	CN CX BR	55-60
		420-480	CH CQ CS BH BZ OZ	60-70
Drive at 1200 RPM		345-450	CU	50-65
		420-515	CN CX BR	60-75
		480-585	CH CQ CS BH BZ OZ	70-85
Int. at 1000 RPM		515-620	CU CN	75-90
		585-690	CX BR	85-100
		900-1035	CH CQ CS BH BZ OZ	130-150
Lo at 1000 RPM		515-620	CU CN	75-90
		585-690	CX BR	85-100
		900-1035	CH CQ CS BH BZ OZ	130-150

external oil pressure leaks. Then with the engine off, check for oil leaks due to the raised oil level caused by drain-back of converter oil into the transmission.

POSSIBLE POINTS OF OIL LEAKS

1. Transmission oil pan leak
a. Attaching bolts not correctly torqued.
b. Improperly installed or damaged pan gasket.
c. Oil pan gasket mounting face not flat.
2. Oil comes out vent pipe
a. Transmission overfilled or underfilled.
b. Water in oil.
c. Screen gasket damaged or improperly assembled, causing oil to foam.
3. Case leak
a. Filler pipe O-ring seal damaged or missing. Misposition of filler pipe bracket to engine, Loading one side of the O-ring.
b. TV cable O-ring seal missing, damaged or improperly installed.
c. Rear seal assembly damaged or improperly installed.
d. Governor cover and O-ring damaged or missing.
e. Speedo gear O-ring damaged.
f. Manual shaft seal damaged or improperly installed.
g. Line pressure tap plug.
h. Porous case.
4. Front end leak
a. Front seal damaged. Check converter neck for nicks, etc. and also for pump bushing moved forward. Garter spring missing.
b. Pump attaching bolts and seals damaged or missing. Bolts loose.
c. Converter leak in weld.
d. Pump O-ring seal damaged. Also check pump oil ring groove and case bore.
e. Porous casting, pump or case.

TROUBLESHOOTING
GM 200

Problem	Possible Cause	Possible Condition
No drive in Drive range (check oil pressure specs.)	1. Low oil level	1. Incorrect level. External leaks.
	2. Manual linkage	2. Maladjusted.
	3. Low oil pressure	3. Plugged or restricted oil screen. Oil screen gasket off location. Pump assembly pressure regulator. Pump drive gear tangs damaged by converter. Case, porosity in intake bore.
	4. Valve body assembly	4. Manual valve disconnected from manual lever pin.
	5. Forward clutch	5. Forward clutch does not apply. Piston cracked, seals missing or damaged, clutch plates burned, snap ring out of groove. Forward clutch oil seal rings missing or damaged on turbine shaft. Leak in feed circuits. Pump to case gasket mispositioned or damaged. Clutch housing ball check stuck or missing. Cup plug leaking or missing in the rear of the turbine shaft in the clutch apply passage. Wrong forward clutch piston assembly or wrong number of clutch plates. Feed orifice plugged in turbine shaft.
	6. Roller clutch assembly	6. Springs missing in the roller clutch. Roller galled or missing.
High or low oil pressures (See specs)	1. Throttle valve cable	1. Misadjusted, binding, unhooked or broken.
	2. Throttle valve assembly or #1 ball check	2. Throttle lever and bracket assembly binding, unhooked or mispositioned. Throttle valve or plunger valve binding. Shift TV valve binding. #1 check ball missing or leaking.

TROUBLESHOOTING
GM 200

Problem	Possible Cause	Possible Condition
High or low oil pressures (See specs)	3. Pressure regulator valve and spring	3. Valve binding. Wrong spring. Oil pressure control orifice in pump cover plugged, causing high oil pressure. Pressure regulator bore plug leaking.
	4. Manual valve	4. Unhooked manual valve.
	5. Intermediate boost valve	5. Valve binding. Pressures will be incorrect in Intermediate and Low ranges only. Orifice in spacer plate at end of valve plugged.
	6. Reverse boost valve	6. Valve binding. Pressures will be incorrect in Reverse only. Orifice in spacer plate at end of valve plugged.
	7. Pump gears and body	7. Low oil pressures.
1-2 shift, full throttle only	1. Throttle valve cable	1. Binding, unhooked or broken. Misadjusted.
	2. Throttle lever and bracket assembly	2. Binding or unhooked.
	3. TV exhaust ball lifter or #5 ball	3. Binding, mispositioned or unhooked. (Allowing #5 ball to seat causes full TV pressure regardless of throttle valve position.)
	4. Throttle valve and plunger	4. Binding.
	5. Control valve assembly	5. Valve body gaskets leaking, damaged or incorrectly installed.
	6. Case assembly	6. Porosity.
1st speed only, no 1-2 upshift	1. Governor and governor feed passages	1. Plugged governor oil feed orifice in spacer plate. Plugged orifice in spacer plate that feeds governor oil to the shift valves. Governor ball or balls missing in governor assembly. Inner governor cover rubber O-ring seal missing or leaking. (If the outer governor cover O-ring seal leaks, an external leak will be present along with no upshifts.) Governor shaft seal missing or damaged. Governor driven gear stripped. Governor weights binding on pin. Governor assembly missing.
	2. Control valve assembly	2. 1-2 shift valve or 1-2 throttle valve stuck in downshift position.
	3. Case	3. Porosity in case channels or undrilled 2nd speed feed holes. Excessive leakage between case bore and intermediate band apply ring. Intermediate band anchor pin missing or unhooked from band. Broken or missing band.
	4. Intermediate servo assembly	4. Servo to cover oil seal ring missing or damaged.

TROUBLESHOOTING
GM 200

Problem	Possible Cause	Possible Condition
1st speed only, no 1-2 upshift	4. Intermediate servo assembly	Porosity in servo cover or piston. Wrong intermediate band apply pin. Incorrect usage of cover and piston.
1st and 2nd speeds only, no 2-3 shift	1. Control valve assembly and spacer plate	1. 2-3 shift valve or 2-3 throttle valve stuck in the downshift position. Direct clutch feed orifice in spacer plate plugged. Valve body gaskets leaking, damaged or incorrectly installed.
	2. Case	2. Porosity in case channels.
	3. Pump	3. Channels in pump plugged or leaking. Pump to case gasket off location. Rear oil seal ring on pump cover leaking or missing.
	4. Direct clutch	4. Oil seals missing or damaged on piston. Direct clutch piston on housing cracked. Direct clutch plates damaged or missing. Direct clutch backing plate snap ring out of groove.
	5. Intermediate servo assembly (direct clutch accumulator oil passages)	5. Servo to case oil seal ring broken or missing on intermediate servo piston. Exhaust hole in case between servo piston seal rings plugged or undrilled.
Drive in Neutral	1. Manual linkage	1. Misadjusted or disconnected.
	2. Forward clutch	2. Clutch does not release.
	3. Pump	3. Cross leakage in pump passages.
	4. Case	4. Cross leakage to forward clutch passages.
No drive in Reverse or slips in Reverse (Refer to oil pressure checks)	1. Throttle valve cable	1. Binding or misadjusted.
	2. Manual linkage	2. Misadjusted.
	3. Throttle valve	3. Throttle valve binding.
	4. Shift TV valve	4. Binding in valve body bore.
	5. Reverse boost valve	5. Binding in valve body bore.
	6. Low overrun clutch valve	6. Binding in valve body bore. (Line pressure readings will be normal.)
	7. Reverse clutch	7. Piston cracked, broken or missing seals. Clutch plates burned. Wrong selective spacer ring.
	8. Direct clutch passages	8. Porosity in case passages. Pump case to pump gasket mispositioned or damaged. Pump channels cross feeding, leaking or restricted. Pump cover oil seal rings damaged or missing. Piston or housing cracked. Piston seals cut or missing. Housing ball check stuck, leaking or missing. Plates burned.

TROUBLESHOOTING
GM 200

Problem	Possible Cause	Possible Condition
No drive in Reverse or slips in Reverse (Refer to oil pressure checks)		8. Incorrect piston. Orifices plugged in spacer plate (see spacer plate). Intermediate servo to case oil seal ring cut or missing.
Slips on 1-2 shift	1. Low oil level	1. Oil will aerate. Correct oil level.
	2. Spacer plate and gaskets	2. Second speed feed orifice partially blocked. Gaskets damaged or mispositioned.
	3. 1-2 accumulator valve	3. Valve sticking in valve body causing low 1-2 accumulator pressure. Weak or missing spring.
	4. 1-2 accumulator piston	4. Seal leaking. Spring broken or missing. Leak between piston and pin.
	5. Intermediate band apply pin	5. Wrong selection pin. Excessive leakage between apply pin and case.
	6. Intermediate servo assembly	6. Porosity in piston. Cover to servo oil seal ring damaged or missing. Incorrect usage of cover and piston.
	7. Throttle valve cable	7. Not adjusted properly.
	8. Throttle valve	8. Binding, causes low TV pressure.
	9. Shift TV valve	9. Binding.
	10. Intermediate band	10. Worn or burned.
	11. Case	11. Porosity in 2nd clutch passages.
Rough 1-2 shift	1. Throttle valve cable	1. Not adjusted properly. Binding.
	2. Throttle valve	2. TV plunger binding. Throttle valve binding.
	3. Shift TV valve	3. Binding
	4. 1-2 accumulator valve	4. Binding.
	5. Intermediate servo assembly	5. Wrong pin. Servo piston to case oil seal ring damaged or missing.
	6. 1-2 accumulator	6. Oil ring damaged. Piston stuck. Broken or missing spring. Bore damaged.
Slips 2-3 shift	1. Oil level low	1. Correct oil level.
	2. Throttle valve cable	2. Not adjusted properly.
	3. Throttle valve	3. Binding.
	4. Spacer plate and gaskets	4. Direct clutch orifice partially blocked in spacer plate. Gaskets mispositioned or damaged.
	5. Intermediate servo assembly	5. Servo to case oil seal ring damaged.
	6. Direct clutch feed	6. Porosity in direct clutch feed channels in case. Pump to case gasket mispositioned or damaged.

B883

TROUBLESHOOTING
GM 200

Problem	Possible Cause	Possible Condition
Slips 2-3 shift	6. Direct clutch feed	Pump channels cross feedings leaking or restricted. Pump cover oil seal rings damaged or missing. Direct clutch piston or housing cracked. Piston seals cut or missing. Direct clutch plates burned.
Rough 2-3 shift	1. Throttle valve cable	1. Not adjusted properly. Binding.
	2. Throttle valve and plunger	2. TV plunger binding. Throttle valve binding.
	3. Shift TV valve	3. Binding.
	4. Intermediate servo assembly	4. Exhaust hole undrilled or plugged between intermediate servo piston seals, not allowing intermediate servo piston to complete its stroke.
	5. Direct clutch exhaust valve ball check #4	5. Missing or mispositioned.
No engine braking in Intermediate range, 2nd gear (check oil pressure specs)	1. Intermediate boost valve	1. Binding in valve body.
	2. Intermediate reverse ball check #3 ball	2. Mispositioned or missing.
	3. Shift TV ball check #1 ball	3. Mispositioned or missing.
	4. Intermediate servo assembly	4. Servo to cover oil seal ring missing or damaged.
	5. Intermediate band	5. Off anchor pin. Broken or burned.
No engine braking in Low range, 1st gear (Check oil pressure specs)	1. Low overrun clutch valve	1. Binding in valve body.
	2. Low-reverse clutch assembly	2. (No Reverse should also be a complaint with any of the following conditions.) Piston seals broken or missing. Porosity in piston or housing. Clutch housing snap ring out of case. Cup plug or rubber seal missing or damaged between case and low reverse clutch housing.
No part throttle or detent downshifts (Check oil pressure specs)	1. Throttle plunger bushing	1. Passages not open.
	2. 2-3 throttle valve bushing	2. Passages not open.
	3. Valve body gaskets	3. Mispositioned or damaged.
	4. Spacer plate	4. Hole plugged or undrilled.
	5. Throttle valve cable	5. Improperly set.
	6. Shift TV valve	6. Binding.
	7. Throttle valve	7. Binding.
Low or high shift points (Check oil pressure specs)	1. Throttle valve cable	1. Binding or disconnected.
	2. Throttle valve	2. Binding.
	3. Shift TV valve	3. Binding.
	4. TV shift ball, #1 ball	4. Missing or mispositioned.
	5. Throttle valve plunger	5. Binding.

TROUBLESHOOTING
GM 200

Problem	Possible Cause	Possible Condition
Low or high shift points (Check oil pressure specs)	6. 1-2 or 2-3 throttle valves	6. Binding in bushings.
	7. Valve body gaskets	7. Mispositioned or damaged.
	8. Pressure regulator valve	8. Binding.
	9. TV exhaust ball #5 and lifter	9. Mispositioned or unhooked. Missing.
	10. Throttle lever and bracket assembly	10. Binding, unhooked or loose at mounting valve body bolt. Not positioned at the throttle valve plunger bushing pin locator.
	11. Governor shaft to cover seal ring	11. Broken or missing.
	12. Governor cover O-rings	12. Broken or missing. (The outer ring will leak externally and the inner ring internally.)
	13. Case	13. Porosity.
Won't hold in Park	1. Manual linkage	1. Misadjusted.
	2. Internal linkage	2. Park pawl binding in case. Actuator rod or plunger damaged. Parking pawl broken. Parking bracket, loose or damaged.
	3. Inside detent lever and pin assembly	3. Nut loose. Hole in lever worn or damaged.
	4. Manual detent roller and spring assembly	4. Bolt loose that holds roller assembly to valve body. Pin or roller damaged, mispositioned or missing.
Transmission noisy	1. Pump noise	1. Oil lever setting low. Cavitation due to plugged screen, porosity in intake circuit, water in oil. Pump gears damaged.
	2. Gear noise	2. Transmission grounded to body. Roller bearings worn or damaged

GM 250

Identification

On all Chevrolet vehicles, see the engine identification chart and check the engine tag for transmission identification.

Intermediate Band Adjustment

1. Raise the vehicle on a lift and put the selector in Neutral.
2. Position special tool J-24367 over the adjusting screw and locknut on the right side of the transmission. Loosen the locknut ¼ turn and hold.
3. Attach a torque wrench onto the special tool and torque the adjusting screw to 30 in. lbs. Back the screw off exactly three turns, using the mark on the tool.
4. Hold the screw in position and torque the locknut to 15 ft. lbs.

On Car Serviceable Components

VALVE BODY
1. Remove the oil pan and strainer.

CAPACITY AND GENERAL SPECIFICATIONS

Fluid capacity (dry)	21½ pints
Cooling	Water (except Vega)
Fluid filter type	Bottom suction screen
Clutches	3
Roller clutches	1
Band adjustment	Intermediate

2. Remove the detent spring and roller assembly from the valve body. Remove the valve body mount bolts.
3. Remove the valve body assembly while disconnect-

Typical Detent Downshift Cable

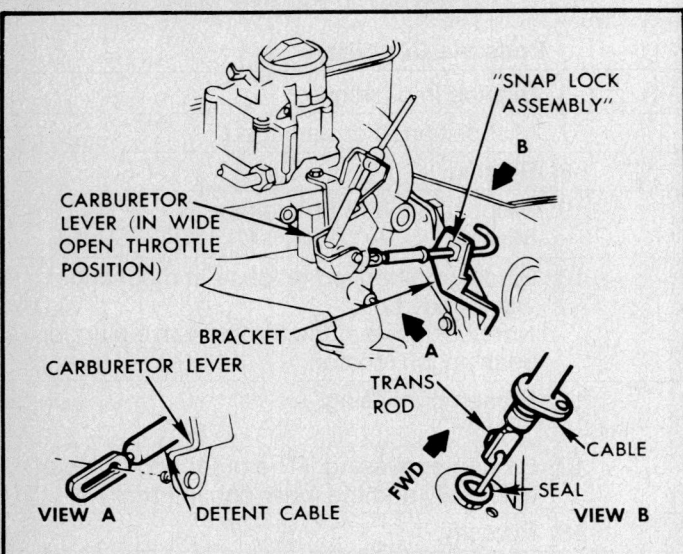

"SNAP LOCK ASSEMBLY"

B

CARBURETOR LEVER (IN WIDE OPEN THROTTLE POSITION)

BRACKET

CARBURETOR LEVER

A

TRANS ROD

CABLE

FWD

SEAL

VIEW A   DETENT CABLE   VIEW B

ing the manual control valve link from the range selector inner lever. Remove the detent control valve link from the detent actuating lever.

4. Installation is the reverse of removal.

Valve Body Check Ball Locations

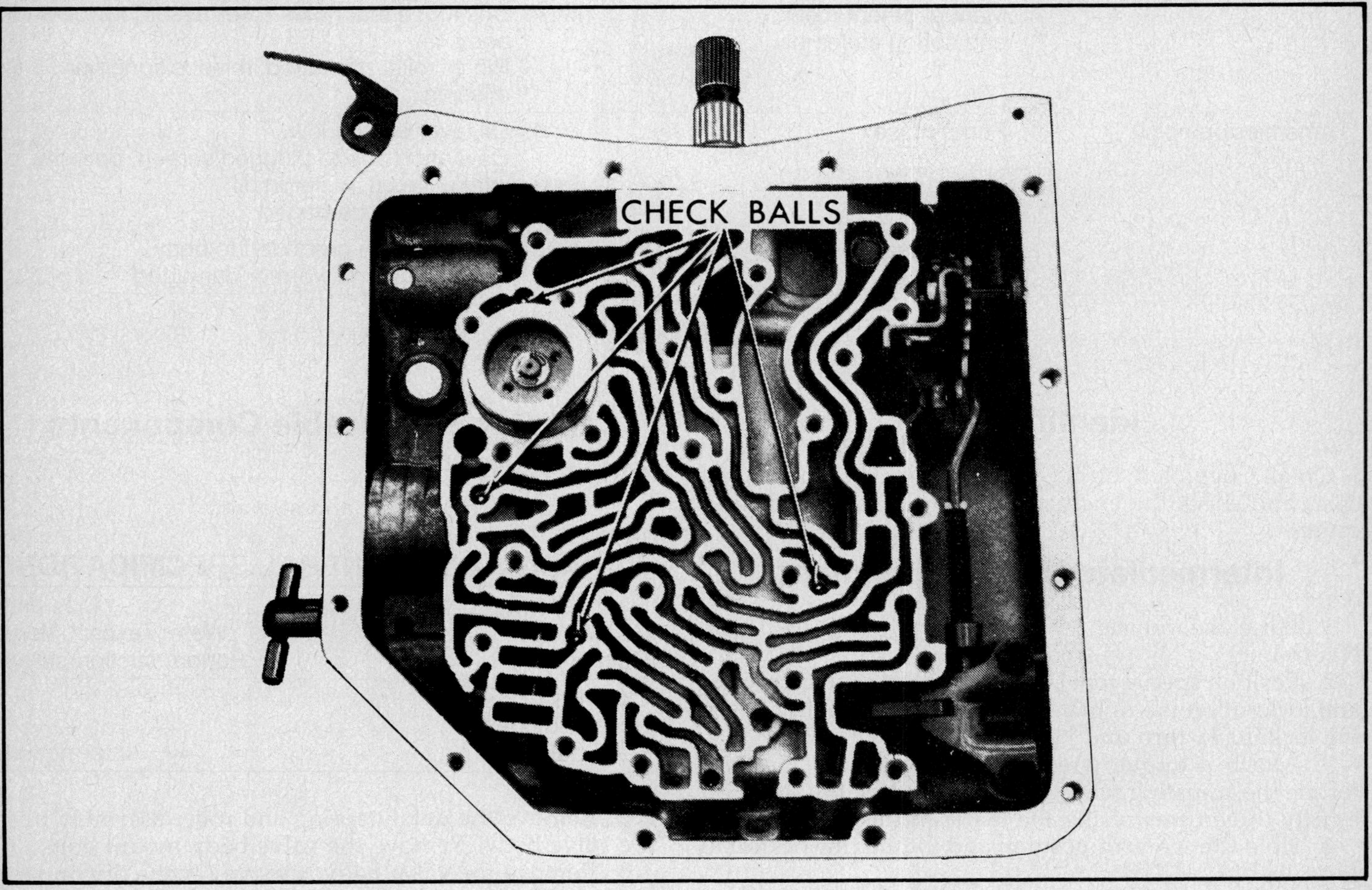

1-2 ACCUMULATOR

1. Using tool J-23069, compress the accumulator cover.
2. After removing the retaining ring, remove the cover, spring and accumulator.
3. Installation is the reverse of removal.

GOVERNOR

1. Disconnect the speedometer cable at the transmission. Remove the governor retainer cover.
2. Remove the governor.
3. During installation, do not distort the governor cover or damage the seal.

SPEEDOMETER DRIVEN GEAR

1. After disconnecting the speedometer cable, remove the retainer, driven gear and O-ring seal.
2. Installation is the reverse of removal.

SPEEDOMETER DRIVE GEAR

1. Support the transmission and remove or disconnect the following.
   a. Drive shaft
   b. Speedometer cable
   c. Crossmember
   d. Extension housing
2. With a puller, remove the speedometer drive gear.
3. Installation is the reverse of removal. Place the speedometer drive gear retaining clip into the hole in the output shaft. Align the slot in the speedometer drive gear with the retaining clip and install.

CHECK BALLS

Governor Assembly Components

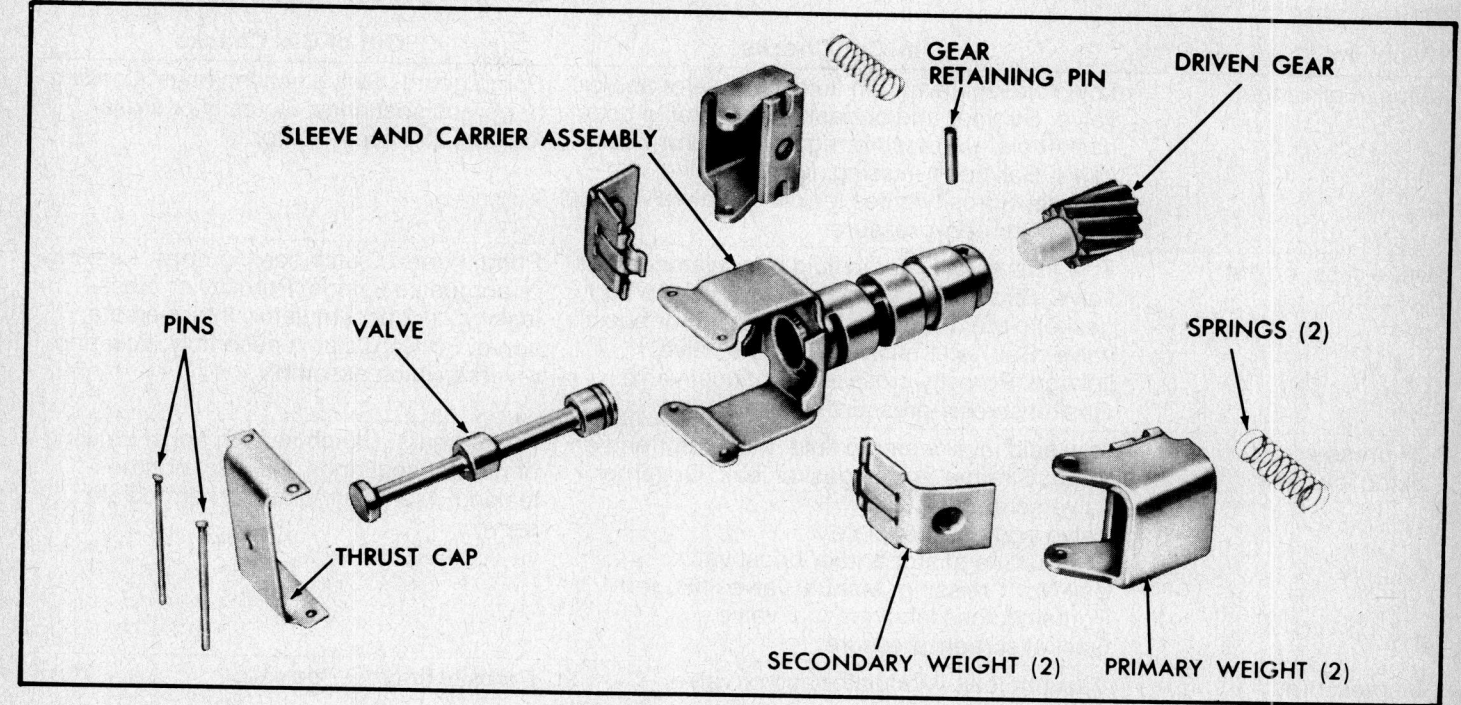

OIL PRESSURE CHECKS WITH VACUUM MODULATOR
GM 250

Model	Altitude (ft.)	Oil Pressure (PSI) in Gear Range [1]		
		D, N, P	L1, L2	R
Vega (L4)	0	55.0	81.9	88.4
	4000	66.9	88.8	107.5
	4000	81.9	97.6	131.5
	6000	95.6	105.6	153.6
	8000	107.9	112.8	173.4
All models (L6)	0	55.0	79.7	83.4
	2000	68.9	89.9	104.4
	4000	86.3	102.8	130.4
	6000	102.4	114.6	155.2
	8000	116.7	125.2	176.9

[1] Made with vehicle stationary, brake on, engine rpm set to maintain 16 in. Hg manifold pressure, oil pressure gauge connected to line pressure tap and vacuum modulator tube connected.

OIL PRESSURE CHECKS WITHOUT VACUUM MODULATOR
GM 250

Model	Oil Pressure (PSI) In Gear Range [1]		
	D	L1, L2	R
Vega (L4)	120.0	120.0	245.2
All models (L6)	168.9	163.6	256.0

[1] Made with vehicle stationary, brake on, 1200 rpm engine speed, oil pressure gauge connected to line pressure tap and vacuum modulator tube disconnected.

TROUBLESHOOTING
GM 250

Problem	In-Car Checks	Out of Car Checks
Slips in all ranges	Low fluid level/water in fluid. Modulator and/or valve. Strainer and/or gasket leak. Valve body gasket/plate. Pressure regulator and/or boost valve. Ball no. 1 missing. Manual valve linkage. Porosity/cross leak, manual valve. Gasket screen-pressure.	Pump gears. Clutch sealing rings. Leaking or porous seal rings. Porosity or cross-leaking. 1-2 accumulator.
Drive slips, no 1st	Low fluid level/water in fluid. Modulator and/or valve. Strainer and/or gasket leak. Valve body gasket/plate. Pressure regulator and/or boost valve. Ball no. 1 missing. Manual valve linkage. Porosity/cross leak, manual valve. Gasket screen-pressure.	Pump gears. Clutch sealing rings. Leaking or porous seal rings. Porosity or cross-leaking. 1-2 accumulator. Intermediate servo. Forward clutch assembly. Low and reverse clutch assembly.
Oil pressure all too low	Low fluid level/water in fluid. Modulator and/or valve. Strainer and/or gasket leak. Governor valve/screen. Valve body gasket/plate. Pressure regulator and/or boost valve. Ball No. 1 missing. Manual valve linkage. Porosity/cross leak, manual valve. Gasket screen-pressure.	Pump gears. Clutch sealing rings. Leaking or porous seal rings. Porosity or cross-leaking. 1-2 accumulator. Intermediate servo.
Oil pressure, all too high	Vacuum leak. Modulator and/or valve. Governor valve/screen. Pressure regulator and/or boost valve. Detent valve and linkage. Porosity/cross leak, manual valve.	Porosity or cross-leaking.
1-2 intermediate	Vacuum leak. Modulator and/or valve. Pressure regulator and/or boost valve. Porosity/cross leak, manual valve.	Porosity or cross-leaking.
1-2 intermediate pressure, low	Low fluid level/water in fluid. Strainer and/or gasket leak. Valve body gasket/plate. Ball no. 1 missing. 1-2 shift valve. 2-3 accumulator. Porosity/cross leak, manual valve.	Pump gears. Clutch sealing rings. Leaking or porous seal rings. Porosity or cross-leaking. 1-2 accumulator. Intermediate servo.
2-3 direct clutch pressure, high	Vacuum leak. Pressure regulator and/or boost valve. Porosity/cross leak, manual valve.	Porosity or cross-leaking.
2-3 circuit clutch pressure, low	Low fluid level/water in fluid. Strainer and/or gasket leak. Valve body gasket/plate. Pressure regulator and/or boost valve. 2-3 shift valve. Porosity cross/leak, manual valve.	Pump gears. Clutch sealing rings. Leaking or porous seal rings. Porosity or cross-leaking. 1-2 accumulator. Forward clutch assembly.
No 1-2 upshift	Vacuum leak. Governor valve/screen. Valve body gasket/plate. Pressure regulator and/or boost valve. 1-2 shift valve.	Clutch sealing rings. Leaking or porous seal rings. Porosity or cross-leaking. 1-2 accumulator. Intermediate band assembly.
1-2 upshift, early or late	Vacuum leak. Governor valve/screen. Valve body gasket/plate. Ball no. 1 missing. 1-2 shift valve. Porosity/cross leak, manual valve.	Porosity or cross-leaking.
1-2 upshift at wide open throttle only	Vacuum leak. 2-3 shift valve. Detent regulator valve and linkage. Porosity/cross leak, manual valve.	Porosity or cross-leaking.
Slips on 1-2 upshift	Low fluid level/water in fluid. Modulator and/or valve. Valve body gasket/plate. Pressure regulator and/or boost valve. Ball no. 1 missing. 1-2 shift valve. 2-3 accumulator. Porosity/cross leak, manual valve.	Pump gears. Clutch sealing rings. Leaking or porous seal rings. Porosity or cross-leaking. 1-2 accumulator. Intermediate servo. Intermediate band assembly.

TROUBLESHOOTING
GM 250

Problem	In-Car Checks	Out of Car Checks
Rough on 1-2 upshift	Vacuum leak. Modulator and/or valve. Pressure regulator and/or boost valve. Porosity/cross leak, manual valve.	Leaking or porous seal rings. Porosity or cross-leaking. 1-2 accumulator.
No 2-3 upshift	Valve body gasket/plate. 2-3 shift valve. Porosity/cross leak, manual valve.	Clutch sealing rings. Leaking or porous seal rings. Porosity or cross-leaking. Direct clutch assembly.
2-3 upshift, early or late	Vacuum leak. Modulator and/or valve. Governor valve/screen. Valve body gasket/plate. Ball no. 1 missing. 2-3 shift valve. Detent valve and linkage.	Porosity or cross-leaking. Direct clutch assembly.
Slips on 2-3 upshift	Low fluid level/water in fluid. Vacuum leak. Valve body gasket/plate. Pressure regulator and/or boost valve. Ball no. 1 missing. 2-3 shift valve. Porosity/cross leak, manual valve.	Pump gears. Clutch sealing rings. Leaking or porous seal rings. Gasket screen-pressure. Porosity or cross leaking. Direct clutch assembly.
2-3 upshift wide open throttle only	Vacuum leak. Detent valve and linkage.	
Rough 2-3 upshift	Vacuum leak. Modulator and/or valve. Governor valve/screen. 2-3 shift valve. 2-3 accumulator. Porosity/cross leak, manual valve.	Porosity or cross-leaking.
No full throttle 1-2 upshift	Vacuum leak. Modulator and/or valve. Governor valve/screen. 2-3 shift valve. 2-3 accumulator. Porosity/cross leak, manual valve.	Porosity or cross-leaking.
No full throttle 1-2 upshift	Detent regulator valve. Porosity/cross leak, manual valve.	Leaking or porous seal rings.
No part throttle downshift	2-3 shift valve. Detent valve and linkage.	
No full throttle downshift	Vacuum leak. Detent valve and linkage.	
Harsh downshift	Ball no. 1 missing	
No engine braking L1 range	Pressure regulator and/or boost valve. 1-2 shift valve. Manual low control valve. Manual valve linkage. Porosity/cross leak, manual valve.	Clutch sealing rings. Porosity or cross-leaking. Forward clutch assembly. Low and reverse clutch assembly.
No engine braking L2 range	Pressure regulator and/or boost valve. manual valve linkage. Porosity/cross leak, manual valve.	Clutch sealing rings.
Car drives in Neutral		Forward clutch assembly.
No Reverse	Pressure regulator and/or boost valve. Ball no. 1 missing. Manual valve linkage. Porosity/cross leak, manual valve. Gasket screen-pressure.	Clutch sealing rings. Leaking or porous seal rings. Porosity or cross-leaking. Forward clutch assembly. Direct clutch assembly. Low and reverse clutch assembly.
Slips in Reverse	Low fluid level/water in fluid. Modulator and/or valve. Strainer and/or gasket leak. Valve body gasket/plate. Pressure regulator and/or boost valve. Ball no. 1 missing. 1-2 shift valve. Manual valve linkage. Porosity/cross leak, manual valve. Gasket screen-pressure.	Clutch sealing rings. Leaking or porous seal rings. Porosity or cross-leaking. Direct clutch assembly. Low and Reverse clutch assembly.
No Park or "ratchets"		Parking pawl/linkage.

TROUBLESHOOTING
GM 250

Problem	In-Car Checks	Out of Car Checks
Noise all ranges	Low fluid level/water in fluid. Strainer and/or gasket leak. Valve body gasket/plate. Gasket screen-pressure.	Pump gears. Converter assembly. Gearset and bearings.
1-2/2-3 shifts noisy	Low fluid level/water in fluid.	Direct clutch assembly. Intermediate band assembly. Gearset and bearings. Converter assembly.
Noisy in Reverse Drive, L1 and L2		Converter assembly.
Spews oil out breather	Low fluid level/water in fluid. Strainer and/or gasket leak.	Leaking or porous seal rings.
Hunts 2-3/3-2	Detent valve and linkage.	

GM 325

On Car Service

PRESSURE REGULATOR VALVE R&R

1. Remove the oil pan and screen.
2. Pushing on the pressure regulator valve, compress the pressure regulator spring with a small screwdriver.
3. Remove retaining ring. Slowly withdraw the screwdriver to release the spring tension. Remove the pressure regulator guide.
4. Installation is the reverse of removal.

CONTROL VALVE

1. Remove the oil pan and screen.
2. Remove the screw and washer securing the cable to the transmission. Disconnect the throttle valve cable.
3. Remove the throttle lever and bracket assembly without bending the throttle lever link.
4. Remove the manual detent roller and spring assembly.
5. After removing the mount bolts, remove the valve assembly spacer plate and gaskets together to prevent dropping the four check balls located in the valve body and the fifth check ball located on the spacer plate.

NOTE After removing the control valve, the intermediate band anchor pin and reverse clutch cup plug may come out.

6. Installation is the reverse of removal. Torque the valve body bolts to 8 ft. lbs. Be sure the intermediate band anchor pin locates on the intermediate band or damage to the transmission will result.

SPEEDOMETER DRIVE AND DRIVEN GEARS R&R

1. Disconnect the cable. Remove the speedometer driven gear attaching bolt and retainer.
2. Remove the speedometer driven gear.
3. After removing the cover, remove the governor and speedometer drive gear assembly.

Governor Assembly

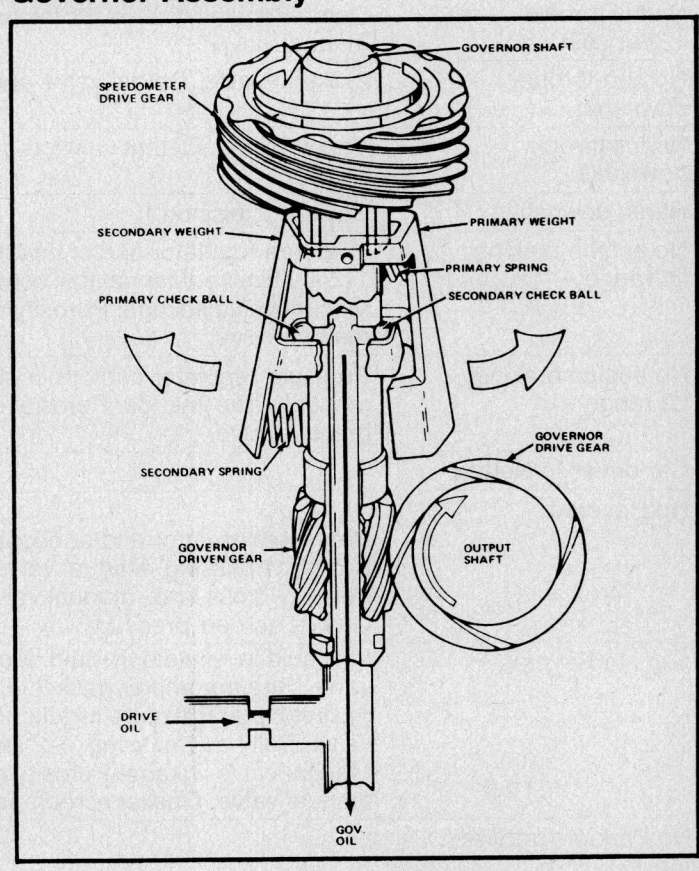

Valve Body Check Balls and Oil Passage Identification

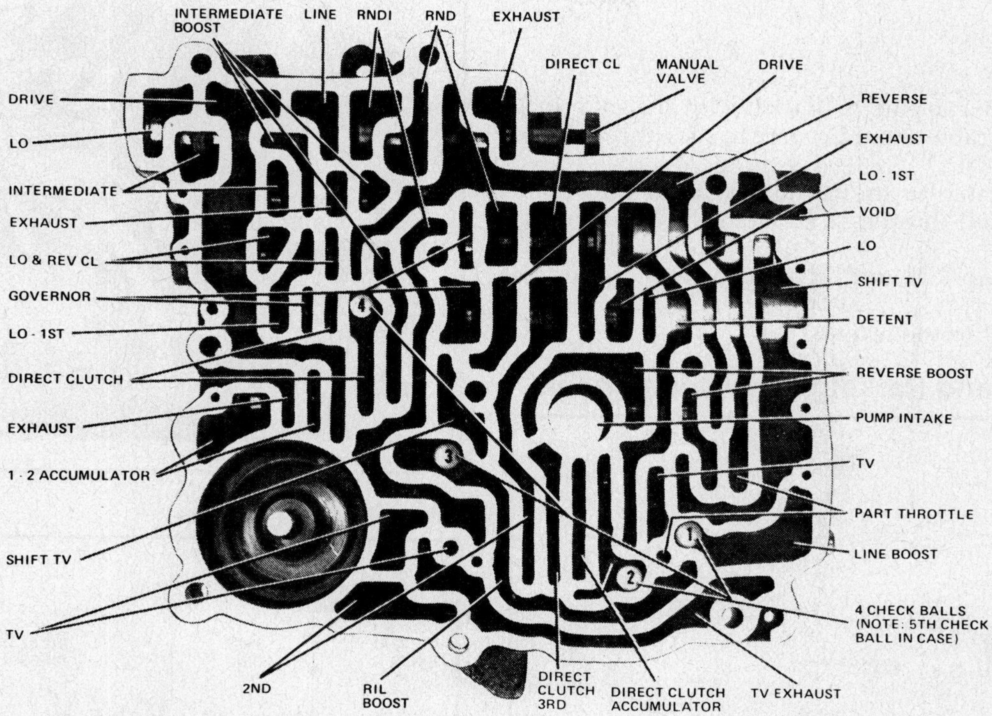

INTERMEDIATE BOOST — LINE — RNDI — RND — EXHAUST

DIRECT CL — MANUAL VALVE — DRIVE

DRIVE
LO
INTERMEDIATE
EXHAUST
LO & REV CL
GOVERNOR
LO - 1ST
DIRECT CLUTCH
EXHAUST
1 - 2 ACCUMULATOR
SHIFT TV
TV

REVERSE
EXHAUST
LO - 1ST
VOID
LO
SHIFT TV
DETENT
REVERSE BOOST
PUMP INTAKE
TV
PART THROTTLE
LINE BOOST
4 CHECK BALLS
(NOTE: 5TH CHECK BALL IN CASE)

2ND — RIL BOOST — DIRECT CLUTCH 3RD — DIRECT CLUTCH ACCUMULATOR — TV EXHAUST

4. Installation is the reverse of removal.

INTERMEDIATE SERVO ASSEMBLY R&R

1. Install tool J-28493 on the case and tighen the bolt to depress the servo cover.
2. Remove the servo cover retaining ring.
3. Remove tool J-28493, the servo cover, servo piston and band apply pin.

Location of Fifth and Sixth Check Balls in Case.

5TH CHECK BALL (T.V. EXHAUST)

6TH CHECK BALL

4. Installation is the reverse of removal.

TV CONTROL CABLE ADJUSTMENT

V-6 Engines

1. Install cable terminal to carburetor lever.
2. Open carburetor lever to full-throttle stop to automatically adjust slider on the cable to the correct setting.

Location of Fifth and Sixth Check Balls on Spacer Plate

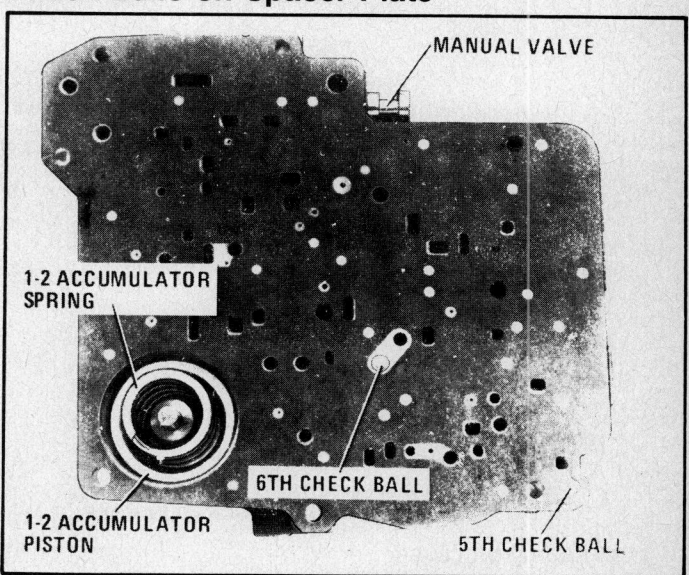

MANUAL VALVE

1-2 ACCUMULATOR SPRING

6TH CHECK BALL

1-2 ACCUMULATOR PISTON

5TH CHECK BALL

AUTOMATIC TRANSMISSIONS

GM 325

3. Release the carburetor lever.

CHILTON CAUTION   Do not depress the lock tab during this operation.

V-8 Engines

1. Install the TV cable in its bracket with the snap-lock disengaged. (The cable should be free to slide through the snap-lock.)

2. Install the cable to the carburetor lever and open the lever to the full-throttle stop. Hold the lever in this position.

3. Push the snap-lock until it is flush with the rest of the TV cable fitting.

4. Release the throttle lever.

Manual Shaft and Parking Pawl Components

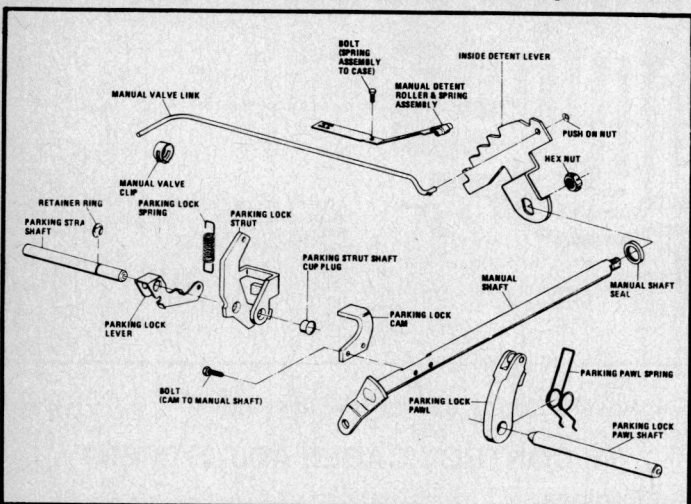

Intermediate Servo Removal

Intermediate Servo

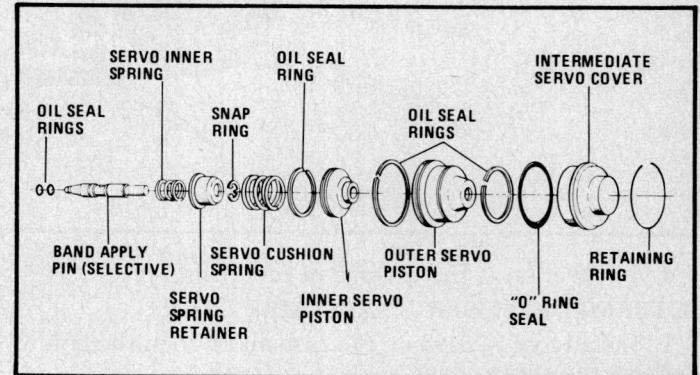

TV Cable Adjustment—V8 Engine

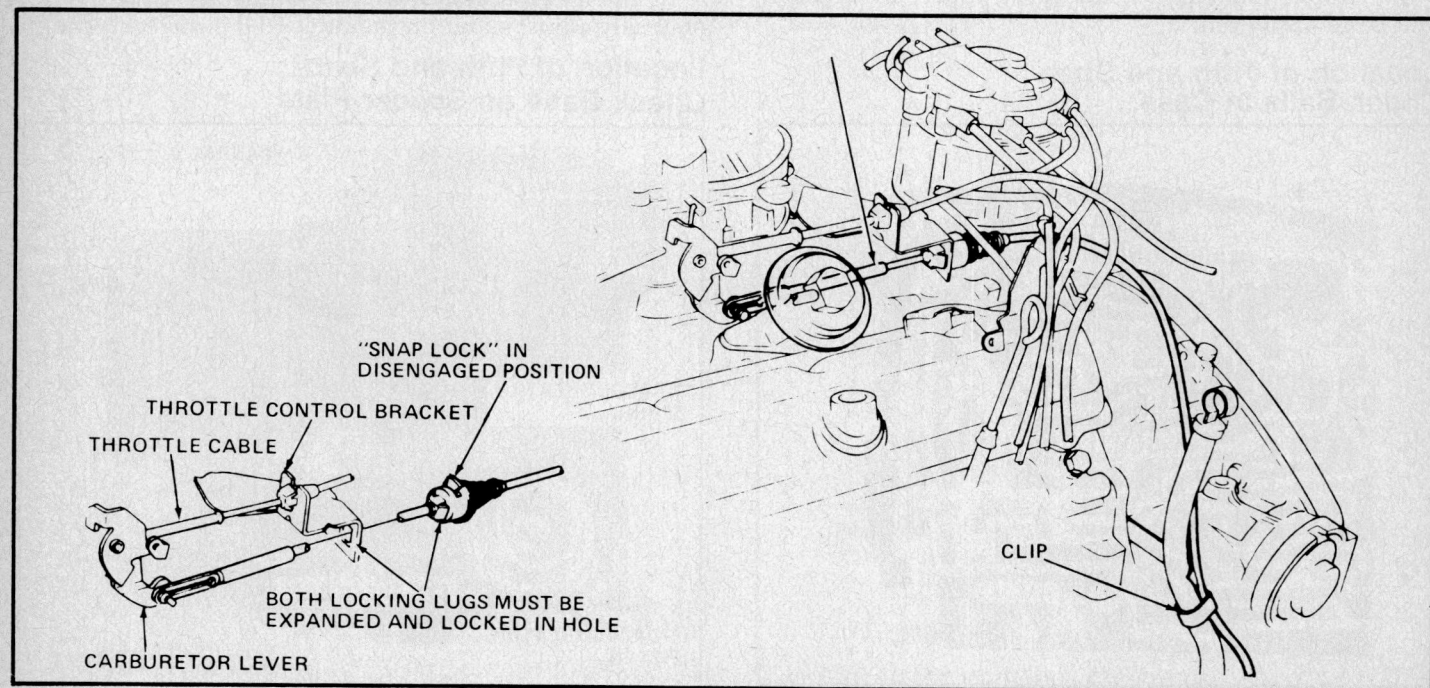

TV Cable Adjustment—V6 Engine

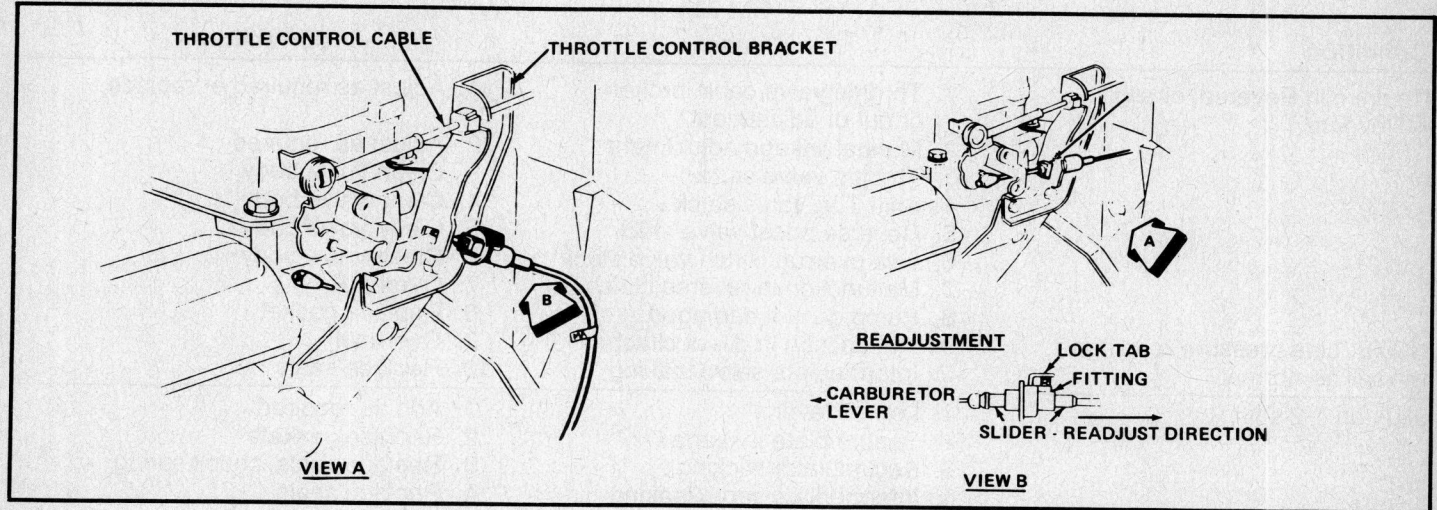

TROUBLESHOOTING
GM 325

Condition	Cause	Correction
No drive in Drive range	1. Low oil level 2. Manual linkage adjustment 3. Low oil pressure 4. Clogged oil filter 5. Manual valve disconnected 6. Bad clutch 7. Malfunction in roller clutch	1. Add as required 2. Adjust as required 3. Clean and check regulator 4. Replace filter and fluid 5. Repair link 6. Overhaul 7. Overhaul or replace
Oil pressure too high or too low NOTE: Pressures will be incorrect in L1 and L2 only NOTE: Pressures will be incorrect in Reverse only	1. Throttle valve cable broken or out of adjustment 2. Shift T.V. valve stuck 3. Throttle valve plunger stuck 4. Pressure regulator valve stuck 5. Manual valve disconnected 6. Intermediate boost valve stuck 7. Reverse boost valve stuck 8. Faulty oil pump	1. Adjust as required or replace 2. Clean valve body 3. Clean valve body 4. Clean regulator parts 5. Repair link 6. Clean valve body 7. Clean valve body 8. Overhaul pump
1-2 shift, full throttle only NOTE: Allowing the #5 check ball to seat causes full T.V. pressure regardless of T.V. position	1. Throttle valve cable 2. T.V. lever and bracket out of place or broken 3. T.V. ball or plunger stuck 4. Valve body malfunction	1. Adjust as required or replace 2. Adjust as required or replace 3. Clean or adjust as required 4. Clean or overhaul, replace gaskets
First speed only, no 1-2 upshift	1. Governor malfunction 2. Valve body malfunction 3. Broken band 4. Band anchor pin unhooked 5. Malfunction in intermediate servo	1. Service or replace unit 2. Clean or overhaul 3. Replace band 4. Replace in proper position 5. Replace seals and/or piston
First and second speeds only, no 2-3 shifts	1. 2-3 shift valve of 2-3 throttle valve stuck 2. Faulty oil pump 3. Malfunction in direct clutch 4. Malfunction in intermediate servo	1. Clean or overhaul valve body 2. Overhaul pump 3. Overhaul 4. Replace seals and/or piston
Drive in Neutral	1. Manual linkage adjustment 2. Forward clutch not releasing 3. Cross leakage in pump or case	1. Adjust as required 2. Overhaul 3. Clean mating surfaces and check for cracks

AUTOMATIC TRANSMISSIONS
GM 325

TROUBLESHOOTING
GM 325

Condition	Cause	Correction
No drive in Reverse, or slips in Reverse	1. Throttle valve cable broken or out of adjustment	1. Adjust as required or replace
	2. Manual linkage adjustment	2. Adjust as required
	3. Throttle valve stuck	3. Clean valve body
	4. Shift T.V. valve stuck	4. Clean valve body
	5. Reverse boost valve stuck	5. Clean valve body
	6. Low overrun clutch valve stuck	6. Clean valve body
	7. Malfunction in reverse clutch	7. Overhaul
	8. Pump gasket damaged	8. Replace gasket
NOTE: Line pressure readings will still be normal	9. Malfunction in direct clutch	9. Overhaul
	10. Intermediate servo leaking	10. Replace seals
Slips on 1-2 shift	1. Low oil level	1. Add as required
	2. Spacer plate leakage	2. Replace gaskets
	3. Accumulator sticking	3. Replace seals, check spring
	4. Intermediate servo leaking	4. Replace seals
	5. Throttle valve cable out of adjustment	5. Adjust as required
	6. Throttle valve sticking	6. Clean valve body
	7. Shift T.V. valve stuck	7. Clean valve body
	8. Intermediate band worn	8. Replace band
Rough 1-2 shift	1. Throttle valve cable out of adjustment	1. Adjust as required
	2. Throttle valve sticking	2. Clean valve body
	3. Shift T.V. valve stuck	3. Clean valve body
	4. Accumulator sticking	4. Replace seals, check spring
	5. Intermediate servo leaking	5. Replace seals
Slips 2-3 shift	1. Low oil level	1. Add as required
	2. Throttle valve cable out of adjustment	2. Adjust as required
	3. Throttle valve sticking	3. Clean valve body
	4. Spacer plate leakage	4. Replace gaskets
	5. Intermediate servo leaking	5. Replace seals
	6. Malfunction indirect clutch	6. Overhaul
Rough 2-3 shift	1. Throttle valve cable out of adjustment	1. Adjust as required
	2. Throttle valve sticking	2. Clean valve body
	3. Shift T.V. valve stuck	3. Clean valve body
	4. Malfunction in intermediate servo	4. Check for plugged exhaust hole between seals
	5. #4 check ball out of place	5. Replace
No engine braking, Intermediate range, 2nd gear (check oil pressures)	1. Intermediate boost valve stuck	1. Clean valve body
	2. #3 check ball out of place	2. Replace
	3. #1 check ball out of place	3. Replace
	4. Intermediate servo leaking	4. Replace seals
	5. Intermediate band worn	5. Replace band
No engine braking in Low range 1st gear (check oil pressures)	1. Low overrun clutch valve stuck	1. Clean valve body
	2. Malfunction in low/reverse clutch (should also have a no reverse complaint)	2. Overhaul and check cup plug between case and clutch housing
No part throttle or detent downshifts (check oil pressures)	1. Throttle plunger bushing passages plugged	1. Clean valve body
	2. 2-3 throttle valve bushing passages plugged	2. Clean valve body
	3. Valve body gaskets leaking	3. Replace gaskets

B894

TROUBLESHOOTING
GM 325

Condition	Cause	Correction
No part throttle or detent downshifts (check oil pressures)	4. Throttle valve cable out of adjustment	4. Adjust as required
	5. Shift T.V. valve stuck	5. Clean valve body
	6. Throttle valve sticking	6. Clean valve body
Low or high shift points (check oil pressures)	1. Throttle valve cable out of adjustment	1. Adjust as required
	2. Throttle valve sticking	2. Clean valve body
	3. Shift T.V. valve stuck	3. Clean valve body
	4. #1 check ball out of place	4. Replace
	5. Throttle valve plunger stuck	5. Clean valve body
	6. 1-2 or 2-3 throttle valves sticking	6. Clean valve body
	7. Valve body gaskets leaking	7. Replace gaskets
	8. Pressure regulator valve sticking	8. Clean regulator valve and bore
	9. #5 check ball out of place	9. Replace
	10. Throttle lever assembly loose or broken	10. Repair or replace
Won't hold in Park	1. Manual linkage adjustment	1. Adjust as required
	2. Internal linkage parts broken	2. Replace affected parts
	3. Detent lever assembly worn	3. Replace
Transmission noisy	1. Low oil level	1. Add as required
	2. Cavication due to plugged screen	2. Replace filter and fluid
	3. Pump gears damaged	3. Overhaul pump
	4. Bearings worn	4. Overhaul unit, replace bearings
	5. Transmission contacting body or frame components	5. Replace defective mounts

GM 350, 375 AND M38

Identification

BUICK
On Buick vehicles, production numbers, transmission model and model year numbers are stamped on the governor cover which is located on the middle rear, left side of the transmission case.

On Car Serviceable Components

VALVE BODY
1. Remove the oil pan and filter.
2. Remove detent roller and spring assembly from the valve body.
3. After removing the mounting bolts, remove the valve body while guiding the manual valve link from range selector inner lever. Remove detent control valve link from detent actuating lever.
4. Installation is the reverse of removal.

GOVERNOR
1. Remove the governor cover. If the cover is damaged in any way, it must be replaced.
2. Withdraw the governor assembly from the case.
3. Installation is the reverse of removal.

SPEEDOMETER DRIVE GEAR
1. Remove the extension housing.
2. Depress the retaining clip and remove the gear from the output shaft.

GENERAL SPECIFICATIONS
GM 350

Cooling	Water
Oil capacity (dry)	20 pints
Oil filter type	Bottom suction screen
Clutches	4
Roller clutches	2
Band (non-adjustable)	1

B895

AUTOMATIC TRANSMISSIONS

GM 350, 375 & M38

Check Ball Locations

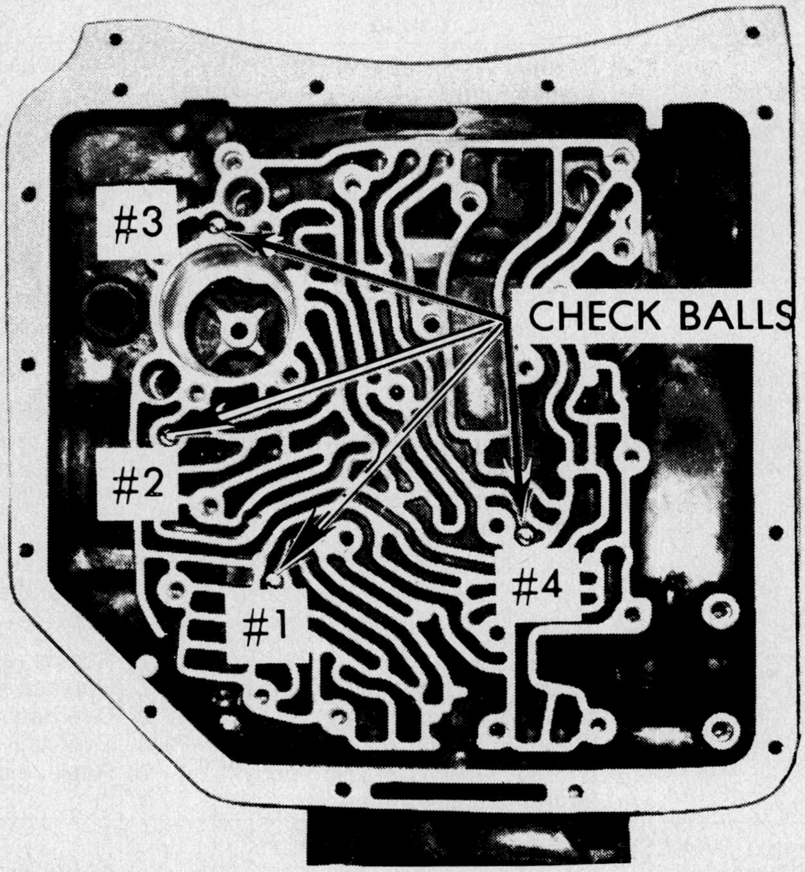

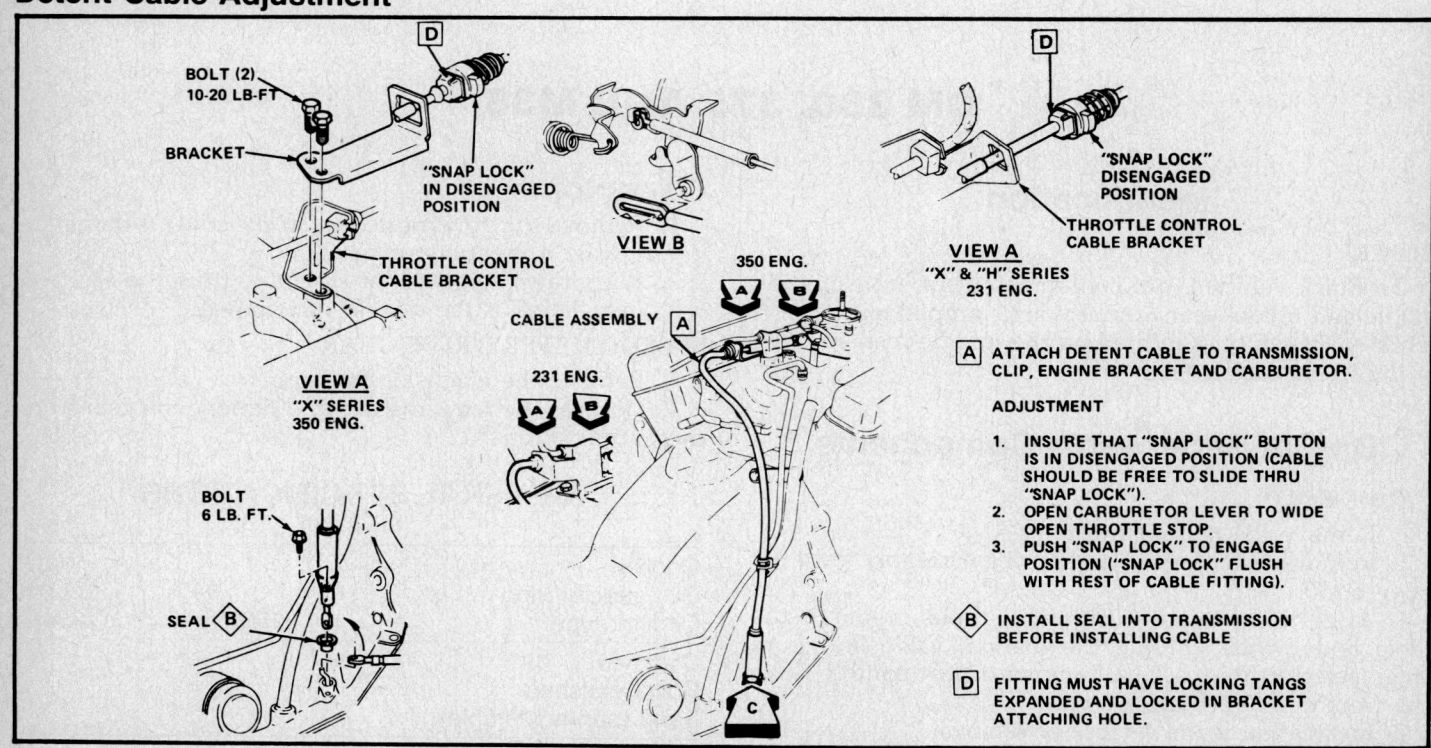

#3

#2

#1

#4

CHECK BALLS

Detent Cable Adjustment

BOLT (2)
10-20 LB-FT

BRACKET

D

"SNAP LOCK"
IN DISENGAGED
POSITION

THROTTLE CONTROL
CABLE BRACKET

VIEW A
"X" SERIES
350 ENG.

BOLT
6 LB. FT.

SEAL B

VIEW B

350 ENG.

A   B

CABLE ASSEMBLY   A

231 ENG.

A   B

D

"SNAP LOCK"
DISENGAGED
POSITION

THROTTLE CONTROL
CABLE BRACKET

VIEW A
"X" & "H" SERIES
231 ENG.

C

A ATTACH DETENT CABLE TO TRANSMISSION,
CLIP, ENGINE BRACKET AND CARBURETOR.

ADJUSTMENT

1. INSURE THAT "SNAP LOCK" BUTTON
IS IN DISENGAGED POSITION (CABLE
SHOULD BE FREE TO SLIDE THRU
"SNAP LOCK").
2. OPEN CARBURETOR LEVER TO WIDE
OPEN THROTTLE STOP.
3. PUSH "SNAP LOCK" TO ENGAGE
POSITION ("SNAP LOCK" FLUSH
WITH REST OF CABLE FITTING).

B INSTALL SEAL INTO TRANSMISSION
BEFORE INSTALLING CABLE

D FITTING MUST HAVE LOCKING TANGS
EXPANDED AND LOCKED IN BRACKET
ATTACHING HOLE.

OIL PRESSURE CHECKS ①
GM 350

Model	Sea Level			2,000 ft.			10,000 ft.		
	D, N, P	S, L	R	D, N, P	S, L	R	D, N, P	S, L	R
Buick, Pontiac	153	153	239	153	153	224	116	125	164
Chevrolet 307	60	87	92	69	93	104	N.A.	N.A.	N.A.
Chevrolet 350	60	87	92	69	93	104	N.A.	N.A.	N.A.

N.A.—Not Available

① Pressures are at 0 output speed, 1200 engine rpm and vacuum line disconnected and plugged. Pressure ± 5 psi.

OIL PRESSURE CHECKS
GM 350–Oldsmobile

Range	Normal Pressure (psi)
Drive—brakes applied, engine @ 1000 rpm	60–90
Super-low—brakes applied, engine @ 1000 rpm	85–110
Reverse—brakes applied, engine @ 1000 rpm	85–150
Neutral—brakes applied, engine @ 1000 rpm	55–70
Drive—idle set to engine specifications	60–85
Drive—30 mph coast (closed throttle) ①	55–70

① Can be performed by running engine on lift at 2000 rpm. Release throttle and read pressure before rpm drops below 1200.

TROUBLESHOOTING
GM 350–375–M38

Problem	In-Car Checks	Out of Car Checks
Slips in all ranges	Low oil level. Water in oil. Modulator and/or valve. Strainer and/or gasket leak. Valve body gasket/plate. Pressure regulator and/or boost valve. Manual valve linkage. Gasket screen-pressure.	Pump gears.
Drive slips, no 1st gear	Low oil level. Water in oil. Modulator and/or valve. Strainer and/or gasket leak. Valve body gasket/plate. Pressure regulator and/or boost valve. Manual valve linkage. Gasket screen-pressure.	Pump gears. Forward clutch assembly. Low and reverse roller clutch.
No 1-2 upshift	Vacuum leak. Governor valve/screen. Valve body gasket/plate. Pressure regulator and/or boost valve. 1-2 shift valve.	Intermediate clutch assembly. Intermediate roller clutch.
1-2 upshift early or late	Vacuum leak. Governor valve/screen. Valve body gasket/plate. 1-2 shift valve.	
1-2 upshift slips	Low oil level. Water in oil Modulator and/or valve. Valve body gasket/plate. Pressure regulator and/or boost valve. 1-2 shift valve. 2-3 accumulator.	Pump gears. Intermediate clutch assembly. Intermediate roller clutch.
Harsh 1-2 upshift	Vacuum leak. Modulator and/or valve. Pressure regulator and/or boost valve.	

AUTOMATIC TRANSMISSIONS

TROUBLESHOOTING
GM 350–375–M38

Problem	In-Car Checks	Out of Car Checks
No 2-3 upshift	Valve body gasket/plate. 2-3 shift valve.	Direct clutch assembly.
2-3 upshift early or late	Vacuum leak. Modulator and/or valve. Governor valve/screen. Valve body gasket/plate. 2-3 shift valve. Detent valve and linkage.	
2-3 upshift slips	Low oil level. Water in oil. Modulator and/or valve. Valve body gasket/plate. Pressure regulator and/or boost valve. 2-3 accumulator.	Pump gears. Direct clutch assembly.
Harsh 2-3 upshift	Vacuum leak. Modulator and/or valve. Pressure regulator and/or boost valve. 2-3 shift valve. 2-3 accumulator.	
No full throttle downshift	Detent valve linkage.	
2-3 upshift, wide open throttle only	Vacuum leak. Detent valve and linkage.	
L1 gear, no engine braking	Pressure regulator and/or boost valve. 1-2 shift valve. Manual low control valve. Manual valve linkage.	Band—intermediate overrun roller clutch. Forward clutch assembly. Intermediate roller clutch.
Car drives in Neutral	Detent valve and linkage.	Forward clutch assembly.
Slips in Reverse	Low oil level. Water in oil. Modulator and/or valve. Strainer and/or gasket leak. Valve body gasket/plate. Pressure regulator and/or boost valve. 1-2 shift valve. Manual valve linkage. Gasket screen-pressure.	Direct clutch assembly. Low and Reverse clutch assembly.
1-2 and 2-3 shift noisy	Low oil level. Water in oil.	Direct clutch assembly. Intermediate clutch assembly. Gear set and bearings.
Noisy in all ranges	Low oil level. Water in oil. Strainer and/or gasket leak. Valve body gasket/plate. Gasket screen-pressure.	Pump gears. Converter assembly. Gear set and bearings. Parking pawl/linkage.
Spews oil out of breather	Low oil level. Water in oil. Strainer and/or gasket leak.	

GM 400, 425, AND M40

Identification

CADILLAC

The Turbo Hydra-Matic 400 transmission unit number is located on a plate located on the right side of the case. This transmission is used in all rear wheel drive applications.

The Turbo Hydra-Matic 425 transmission unit number is located on the left side of the converter housing. This transmission is used with all front wheel drive applications.

CHEVROLET AND OLDSMOBILE

On all Chevrolet vehicles, see the engine identification chart and check engine identification tag for transmission identification.

On Oldsmobile vehicles, the serial plate is located on the right side of the case, except on front wheel drive applications (Turbo Hydra-Matic 425), in which case it is located on the left side of the converter housing.

On Car Serviceable Components

VALVE BODY

1. Remove the oil pan and filter.
2. Remove the valve body mount bolts and detent roller and spring assembly.
3. Remove the valve body without allowing the front servo or manual valve to fall out of it.
4. Installation is the reverse of removal.

Typical External Linkage— 400 Transmission

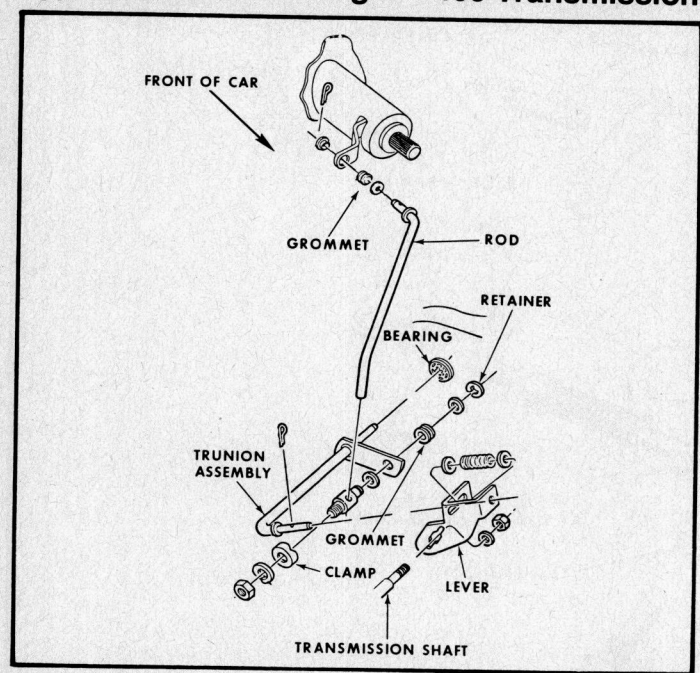

Typical External Linkage— 425 Transmission

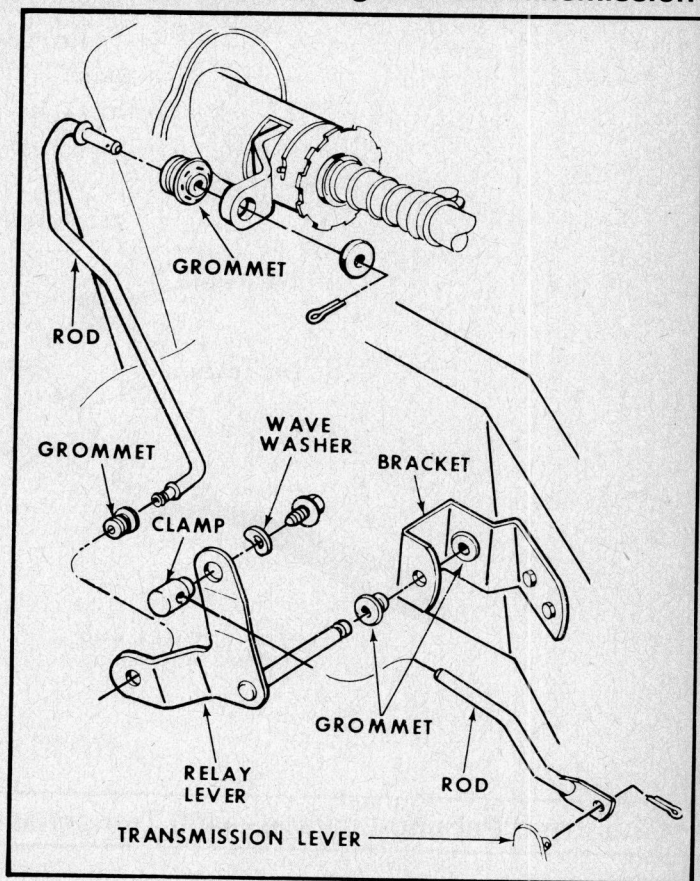

GOVERNOR
1. Remove the governor cover.
2. Withdraw the governor assembly from the case.
3. Installation is the reverse of removal.

SPEEDOMETER DRIVEN GEAR
1. Remove the gear attaching bolt and retainer.
2. Withdraw the gear from the case.
3. Installation is the reverse of removal.

PRESSURE REGULATOR VALVE
1. Remove the oil pan and filter.
2. Compress the regulator boost valve bushing against the pressure regulator spring. Remove the snap ring.

3. Remove the regulator boost valve bushing and valve.
4. Remove the pressure regulator spring.
5. Remove the regulator valve, spring retainer and spacers, if used.
6. Installation is the reverse of removal.

Check Ball Location—400 Transmission

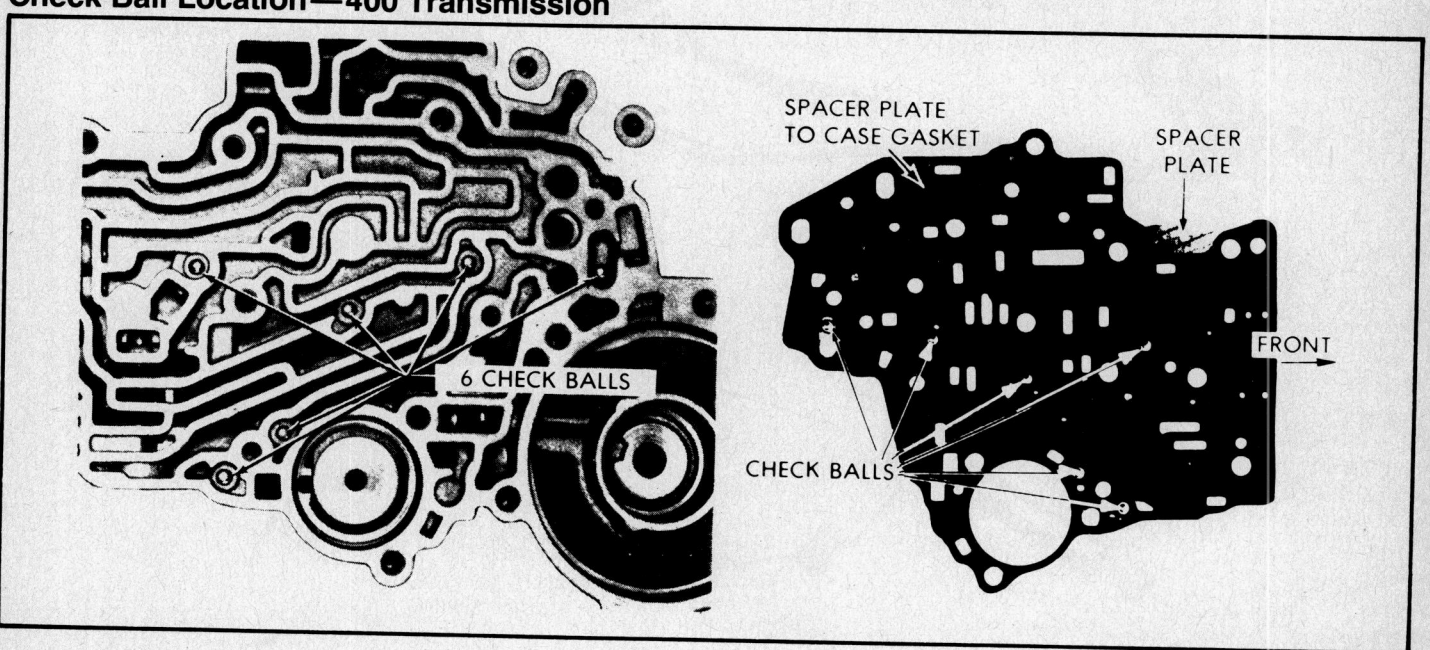

AUTOMATIC TRANSMISSIONS

GM 400, 425 & M40

Manual and Parking Linkage—425 Transmission

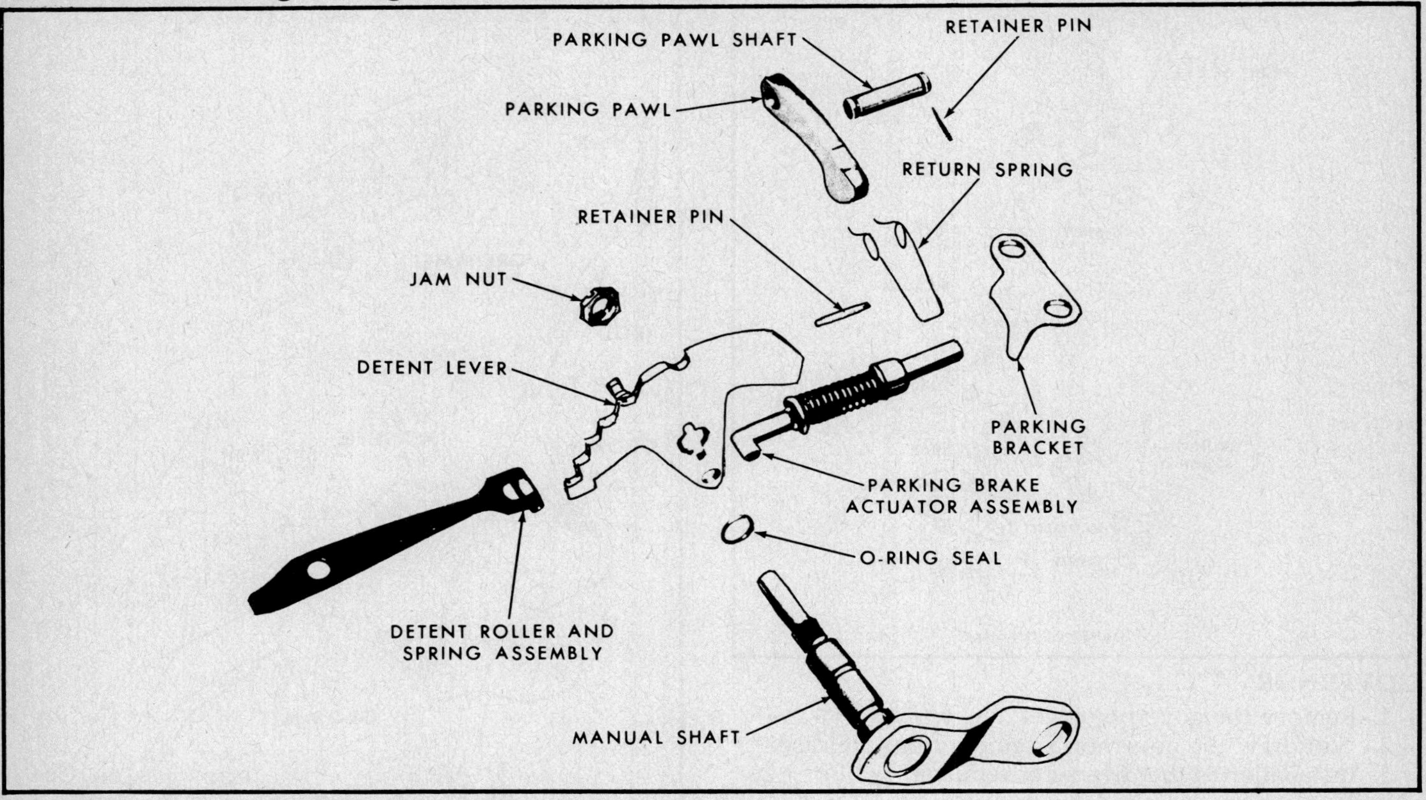

PARKING PAWL SHAFT

RETAINER PIN

PARKING PAWL

RETURN SPRING

RETAINER PIN

JAM NUT

DETENT LEVER

PARKING BRACKET

PARKING BRAKE ACTUATOR ASSEMBLY

O-RING SEAL

DETENT ROLLER AND SPRING ASSEMBLY

MANUAL SHAFT

Manual and Parking Linkage—400 Transmission

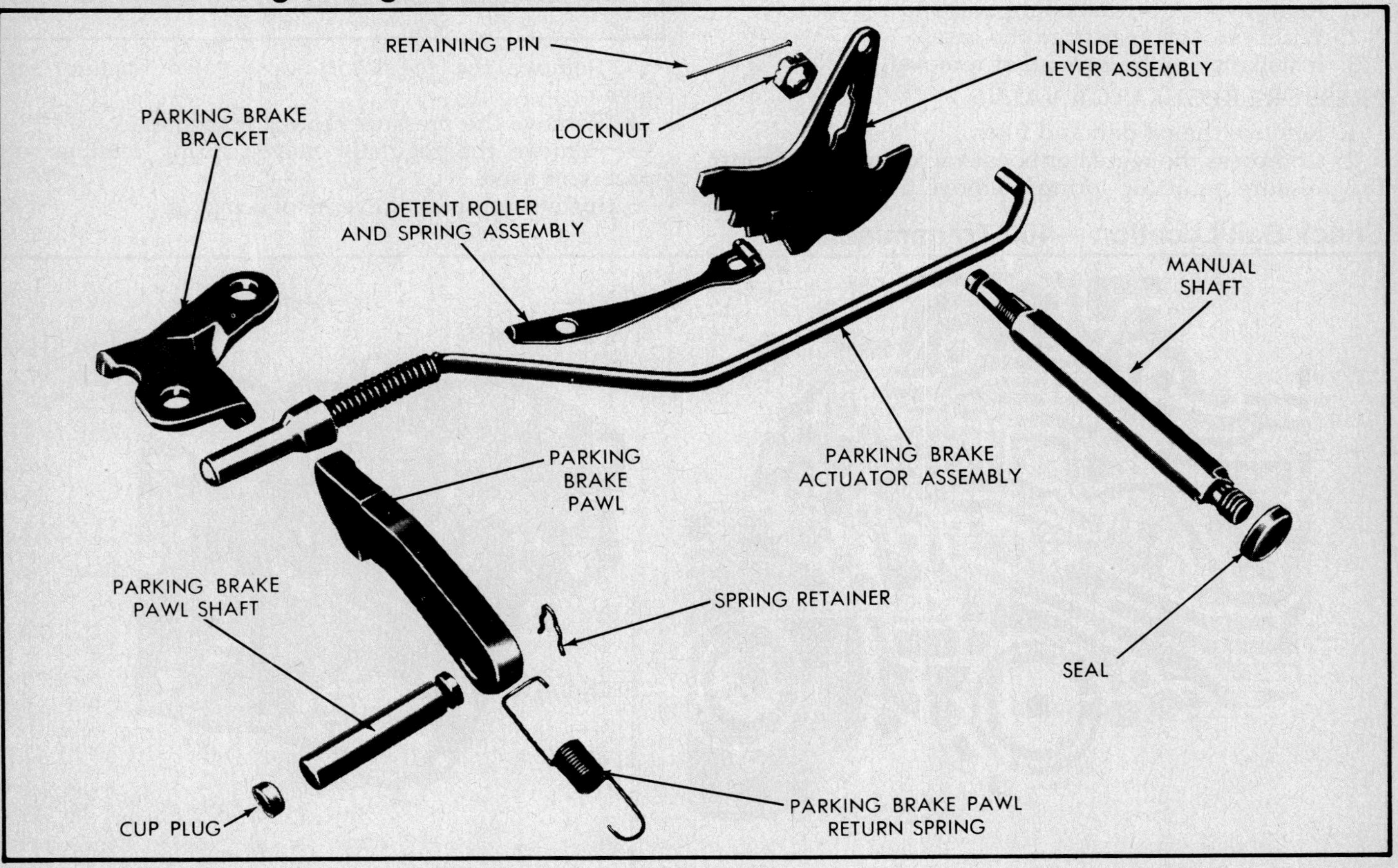

RETAINING PIN

INSIDE DETENT LEVER ASSEMBLY

PARKING BRAKE BRACKET

LOCKNUT

DETENT ROLLER AND SPRING ASSEMBLY

MANUAL SHAFT

PARKING BRAKE PAWL

PARKING BRAKE ACTUATOR ASSEMBLY

PARKING BRAKE PAWL SHAFT

SPRING RETAINER

SEAL

CUP PLUG

PARKING BRAKE PAWL RETURN SPRING

Oil Pan Removed—425 Transmission

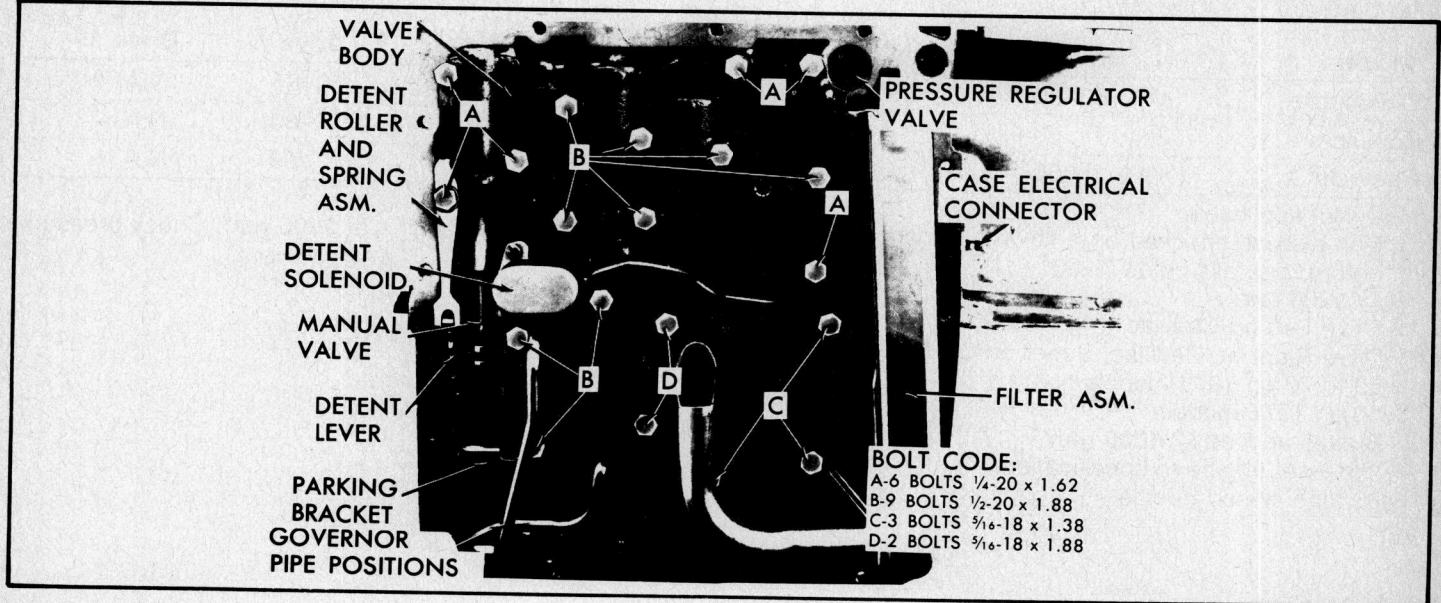

Check Ball Location—425 Transmission

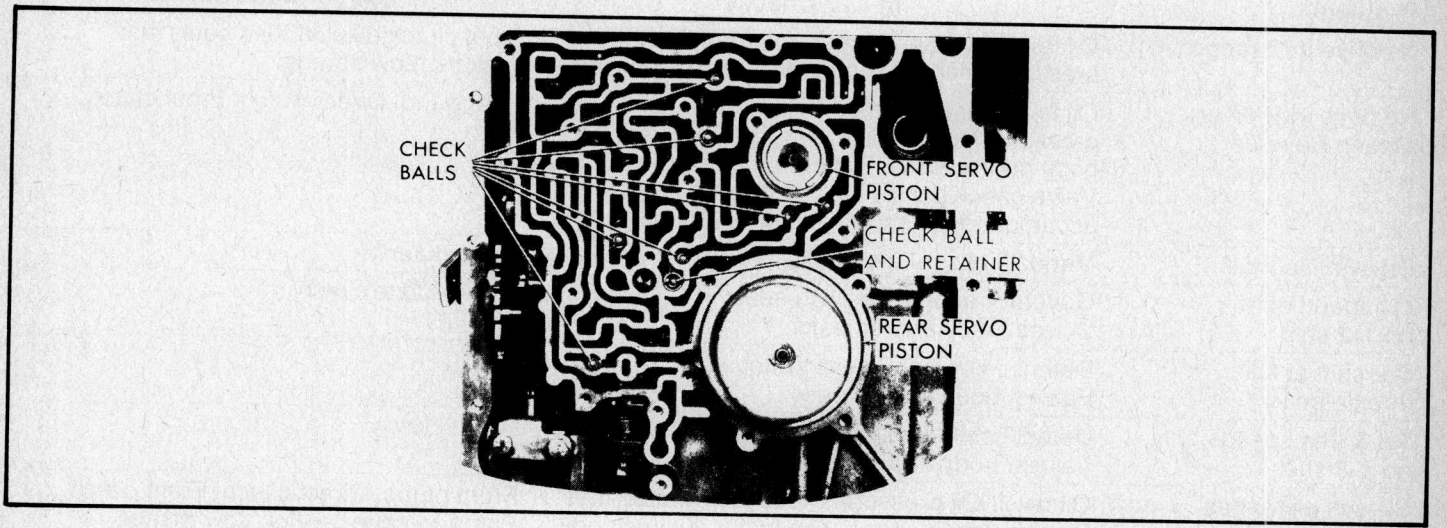

FLUID SPECIFICATIONS
GM 400 and 425

Oil capacity, transmission and converter	22 pints
Capacity between marks on dipstick	1 pint
Drain and refill	24,000 miles
Type of oil	Dexron® automatic transmission fluid type A

CONTROL PRESSURES (PSI) ①
GM 400

Model	Drive ④ ⑧	Super ⑤ ⑧	Reverse ⑧	Neutral ⑧	Drive ⑨	Drive ⑩
Cadillac, Eldorado	60–90	135–160	95–150	55–70	60–85	55–70
Buick ②	60	150	220–260	150	N.A.	60

AUTOMATIC TRANSMISSIONS

GM 400, 425 & M40

CONTROL PRESSURES (PSI) ①
GM 400

Model	Drive ④ ⑧	Super ⑤ ⑧	Reverse ⑧	Neutral ⑧	Drive ⑨	Drive ⑩
Oldsmobile	60–90	135–160	95–150	55–70	60–85	N.A. ⑥
Pontiac ②	60	150	107	60	60	N.A. ⑦
Chevrolet	60	150	107	60	60	N.A.

N.A. Not applicable
① Can also be checked on a lift with transmission in Drive, brakes applied and engine at 2000 rpm. Check pressure before rpm falls below 1200
② @ 1200 rpm
④ Drive Left on Cadillac
⑤ Drive Right on Cadillac, Super on Oldsmobile, D2 on Chevrolet
⑥ 55 to 70 on 1975 models
⑦ 60 on 1975 models
⑧ Brakes applied @ 1000 rpm
⑨ Idle—set engine to specifications
⑩ 30 mph closed throttle

TROUBLESHOOTING
400, 425 and M40

Problem	In-Car Checks	Out of Car Checks
No drive in D range	Oil level. Manual linkage (external). Oil pressure. Manual control disconnected inside.	Front clutch. Clutch feed seals and gaskets. Low sprags.
No drive in R or slips in Reverse	Oil level. Manual linkage (external). Oil pressure. Modulator and/or lines. Valves, body and/or leaks. Reverse feed passages. Valve check balls. Rear servo and accumulator. Pump regulator and boost valve.	Rear band. Direct clutch. Front clutch.
Drive in Neutral	Manual linkage (external).	Front clutch.
1st speed only, no 1-2 shift	Governor and/or feed line seals. Valves, body and/or leaks.	Intermediate clutch.
1-2 shift at full throttle only	Detent solenoid. Detent switch. Valves, body and/or leaks.	
1st & 2nd speeds only, no 2-3 shift	Detent solenoid. Detent switch. Valves, body and/or leaks.	Direct clutch.
Slips in all ranges	Oil level. Oil pressure. Modulator and/or lines. Clogged strainer or intake leaks. Valves body and/or leaks.	Front pump. Direct clutch. Front clutch. Pump-to-case gasket. Low sprags.
Slips on 1-2 shift	Oil level. Oil pressure. Modulator and/or lines. Pump regulator and boost valve. Valves, body and/or leaks. Front servo and accumulator.	Intermediate clutch. Pump-to-case gasket.
Rough 1-2 shift	Oil pressure. Modulator and/or lines. Pump regulator and boost valve. Valves, body and/or leaks. Rear servo accumulator. Front servo and accumulator. Valves, body and/or leaks. Rear servo and accumulator.	Pump-to-case gasket. Intermediate check valve ball in case.
Slips on 2-3 shift	Oil level. Oil pressure. Modulator and/or lines. Pump regulator and boost valve. Valves, body and/or leaks.	Direct clutch. Pump-to-case gasket.
Rough 2-3 shift	Oil pressure. Modulator and/or lines. Pump regulator and boost valve. Front servo and accumulator.	

BRACKES

INDEX

TROUBLESHOOTING DRUM BRAKES

Trouble Symptoms

Possible Causes of Trouble Symptoms	One Brake Drags	All Brakes Drag	Hard Pedal	Spongy Pedal	Car Pulls to One Side	One Wheel Locks	Brakes Chatter	Excessive Pedal Travel	Pedal Gradually Goes to Floor	Brakes Uneven	Shoe Click Release	Noisy or Grabbing Brakes	Brakes Do Not Apply
Mechanical Resistance at Pedal or Shoes Damaged Linkage		X	X										
Brake Line Restricted	X	X	X		X								
Leaks or Insufficient Fluid				X				X	X				X
Improper Tire Pressure					X						X		
Improperly Adjusted or Worn Wheel Bearing	X				X								
Distorted or Improperly Adjusted Brake Shoe	X	X	X		X	X		X				X	
Faulty Retracting Spring	X				X								
Drum Out of Round	X				X		X						
Linings Glazed or Worn			X		X	X	X	X				X	X
Oil or Grease In Lining			X		X	X	X			X		X	X
Loose Carrier Plate	X					X	X						
Loose Lining					X		X						
Scored Drum										X		X	
Dirt on Drum-Lining Surface												X	
Faulty Wheel Cylinder	X				X	X						X	
Dirty Brake Fluid	X	X								X			X
Faulty Master Cylinder		X						X	X				X
Air in Hydraulic System	X			X				X					X
Self Adjusters Not Operating					X			X			X		
Insufficient Shoe-to-Carrier Plate Lubrication	X										X		
Tire Tread Worn						X							
Poor Lining to Drum Contact							X						
Loose Front Suspension							X						
"Threads" Left by Drum Turning Tool Pull Shoes Sideways											X		
Cracked Drum								X					
Sticking Booster Control Valve		X										X	

DRUM BRAKE SERVICE

Drum Brakes

Except for Chevette all drum brakes in this section are self-energizing with automatic adjusters. Utilization of the frictional force to increase the pressure of shoes against the drum is called *self-energizing* action. Utilization of force in one shoe to apply the opposite shoe is called *servo* action.

Brake Lining

Brake lining is made of asbestos impregnated with special compounds to bind the asbestos fibres together. Some linings are woven of asbestos threads and fine copper wire. With a few exceptions the brake lining material is molded asbestos fibers ground up, pressed into shape and either riveted or bonded onto the brake shoe.

PRIMARY SHOE

The primary, sometimes called leading or forward brake shoe, is the shoe that faces toward the front of the car.

SECONDARY SHOE

The secondary, sometimes called the trailing or reverse brake shoe, faces the rear of the car.

Backing Plate

Thorough brake work starts at the brake backing plate. Check the brake area for any indication of lubricant leakage. If the leakage is brake fluid replace or rebuild wheel cyclinder. If it is wheel bearing grease replace the inner bearing seal. It may be necessary to replace the axle bearing or seal. To check the backing plate mounting, tap the plate clockwise and counter-clockwise. If movement occurs in either direction remove the backing plate and check for worn bolts or elongated bolt holes. Replace worn parts. A loose backing plate can usually be detected listening for a "clicking" sound when applying the brakes while the car is moved forward and backward.

Wheel Cylinder

Wheel cylinders should be inspected for leakage. Carefully inspect the boots. If they are torn, cut, heat cracked or show evidence of leakage the wheel cylinder should be replaced or overhauled. Don't gamble. It the cylinder doesn't look healthy, replace or rebuild.

INSPECTION

1 Wash all parts in clean denatured alcohol. If alcohol is not available, use specified brake fluid. Dry with compressed air.
2 Replace scored pistons. Always replace the rubber cups and dust boots.
3 Inspect the cylinder bore for score

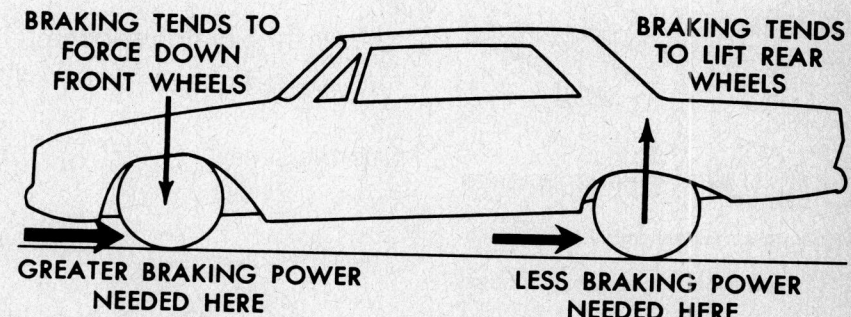

BRAKING TENDS TO FORCE DOWN FRONT WHEELS

BRAKING TENDS TO LIFT REAR WHEELS

GREATER BRAKING POWER NEEDED HERE

LESS BRAKING POWER NEEDED HERE

When a car's brakes are applied, the front of the car dips down and the back of the car rises up. This explains why the major breaking effort is needed at the front of the car.

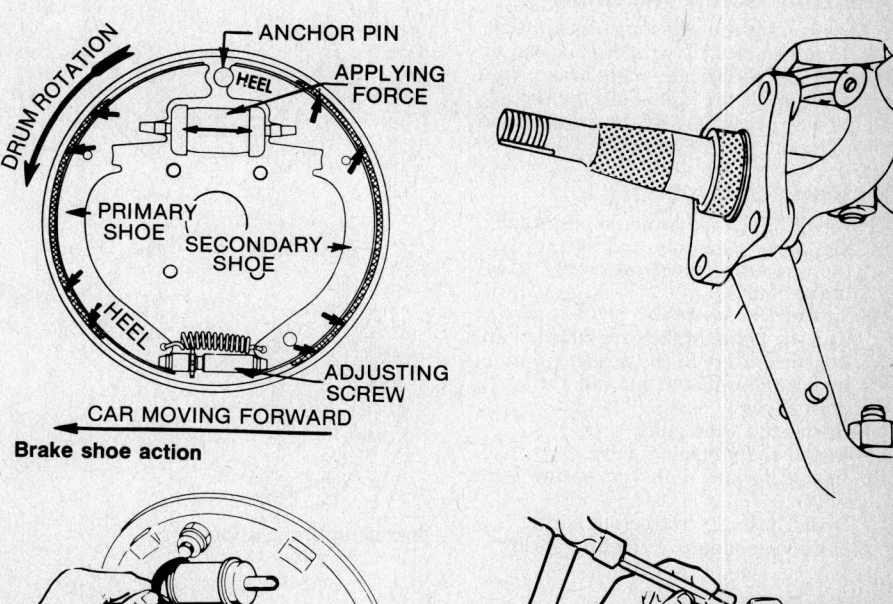

Brake shoe action

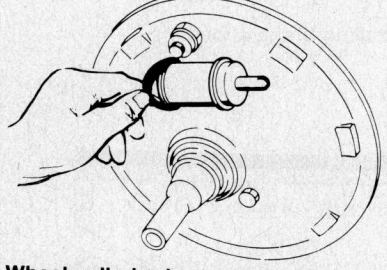

Wheel cylinder inspection

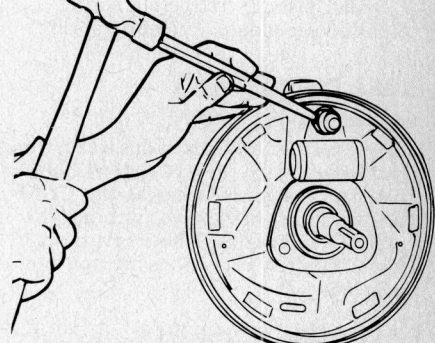

Backing plate mounting

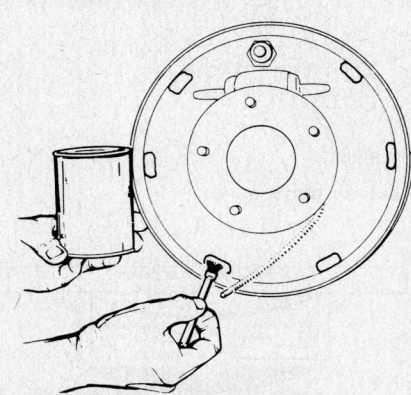

Lubricate paper thin (no globs)

marks or rust. If either condition is present, the cylinder bore must be honed. However, the cylinder should not be honed more than 0.003 inch beyond its original.
4 Check the bleeder hole to be sure that it is open.

ASSEMBLY

1 Apply a coating of heavy-duty brake fluid to all internal parts.
2 Thread the bleeder screw into the cylinder and tighten securely.

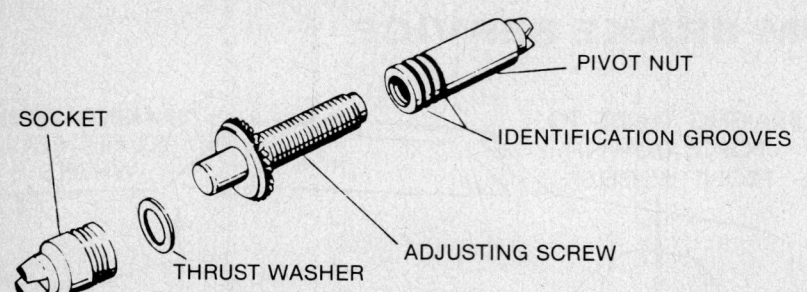

SOCKET

PIVOT NUT

IDENTIFICATION GROOVES

ADJUSTING SCREW

THRUST WASHER

Adjusting screw assembly

3 Insert the return spring, cups, and pistons into their respective positions in the cylinder bore. Place a boot over each end of the cylinder.

Adjusting Screw Assembly

Disassemble the adjusting screw assembly. Using an electric wire brush clean up the threads. Lubricate with brake fluid and reassemble the unit. Turn the threads all the way in by hand. If the threads bind at any point replace the unit.

Installing Brake Shoes

1 Preassemble the brake shoes, adjusting screw assembly and spring, plus the packing lever assembly (rear brakes only).
2 Spread the assembly; place it on the backing plate. Make sure wheel cylinder sockets are in the proper position.
3 Install the retainer pin and spring on both shoes.
4 Install the shoe guide.
5 Install the adjusting cable.
6 Install parking link and spring (rear only).
7 Install primary retracting spring.
8 Install secondary retracting spring.

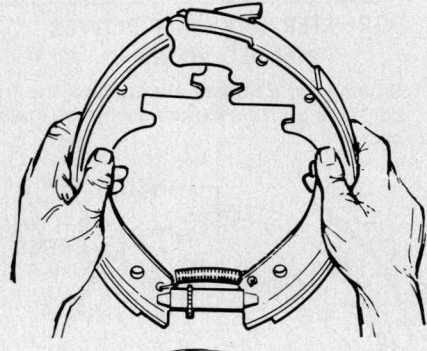

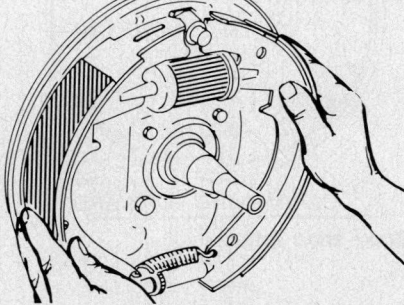

Installing brake shoes

Brake Drums

BRAKE DRUM TYPES

The FULL-CAST drum has a cast iron web (back) of 3/16 to 1/4 inch thickness (passenger car sizes) whereas the COMPOSITE drum has a steel web approximately 1/8 inch thick. These two types of drums, with few exceptions are not interchangeable.

BRAKE DRUM DEPTH

Rest a straight edge across the drum diameter on the open side. The actual drum depth then is the measurement at a right angle from the straight edge to that part of the web which mates against the hub mounting flange.

ALUMINUM DRUMS:

When repaced by other types, aluminum drums must be replaced in pairs.

METALLIC BRAKES

Drums designed for use with standard brake linings should not be used with metallic brakes.

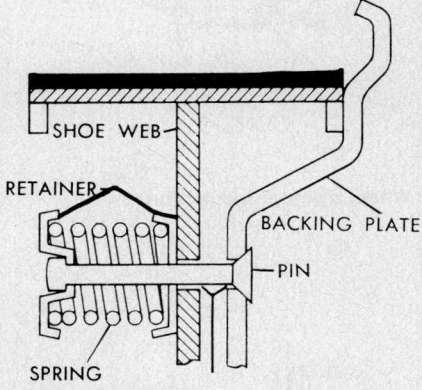

SHOE WEB

RETAINER

BACKING PLATE

PIN

SPRING

Retainer pin & spring

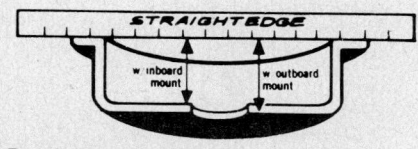

STRAIGHTEDGE

w inboard mount   w outboard mount

Depth measurement

**Web thickness: Full cast-3/16" to 1/4"
Composite-1/8" approximate**

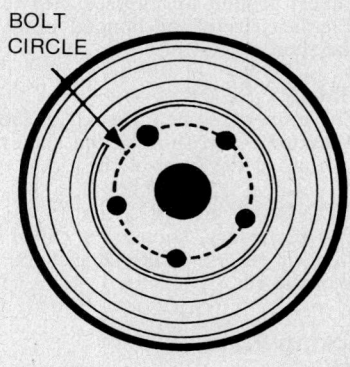

BOLT CIRCLE

BOLT CIRCLE

The circumference on which the centers of the wheel bolt holes are located around the drum-hub center. It is shown as a double number (example: 6-5½). The first digit indicates the number of holes. The second number indicates the bolt circle diameter.

REMOVING TIGHT DRUMS

Difficulty removing a brake drum can be caused by shoes which are expanded beyond the drum's inner ridge, or shoes which have cut into, and ridged the drum. In either case back off the adjuster to obtain sufficent clearance for removal.

BRAKE DRUM INSPECTION

The condition of the brake drum surface is just as important as the surface to the brake lining. All drum surfaces should be clean, smooth, free from hard spots, heat checks, score marks and foreign matter imbedded in the drum surface. They should not be out of round, bell-mouthed or barrel shaped. It is recommended that all drums be first checked with a drum micrometer to see if they are within oversize limits. If drum is within safe limits, even though the surface appears smooth, it should be turned not only to assure a true drum surface but also to remove any possible contamination in the surface from previous brake linings, road dusts, etc. Too much metal removed from a drum is unsafe and may result in:

1 Brake to fade due to the thin drum being unable to absorb the heat generated.
2 Poor and erratic brake due to distortion of drums.
3 Noise due to possible vibration caused by thin drums.
4 A cracked or broken drum on a severe or very hard brake application.

Brake drum run-out should not exceed .005″. Drums turned to more than .060″ oversize are unsafe and should be replaced with new drums, except for some heavy ribbed drums which have an .080″ limit. It is recommended that the diameters of the left and right drums on any one axle be within .010″ of each other. In order to avoid erratic brake action when replacing drums, it is always good to replace the drums on both wheels at the same time.

If the drums are true, smooth up any slight scores by polishing with fine emery cloth. If deep scores or grooves are present, which cannot be removed by this method, then the drum must be turned.

LOOK HERE FOR TURNED DRUM TOOL MARK RIDGE

0.60″

Oversize drum

Adjusting drum brakes

PRELIMINARY ADJUSTMENT

1 Set a brake shoe adjustment gauge at .030 inch less than the brake drum diameter.
2 Center the gauge over the shoes at the greatest lining thickness and run out the adjuster until the new lining touches the gauge.
3 Install the drum.

NOTE: Tight clearance can aggravate normal seating problems. Most service technicians prefer to set the initial brake adjustment with a gauge and then brake the vehicle backward and forward allowing the shoes and drums to seek the correct running clearance. Complete seating normally occurs with 1000 driving miles.

ROUTINE ADJUSTMENT

1 Use a brake adjusting tool to expand the brake shoes agaist the drum. Raising the tool handle turns the star wheel adjuster in the proper direction to expand the shoes. Turn the adjuster until a heavy drag is felt while turning the wheel.

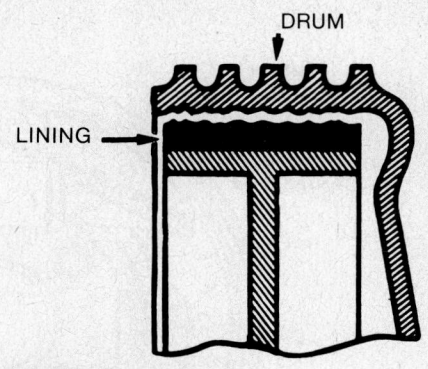

DRUM

LINING

Scored drum surface

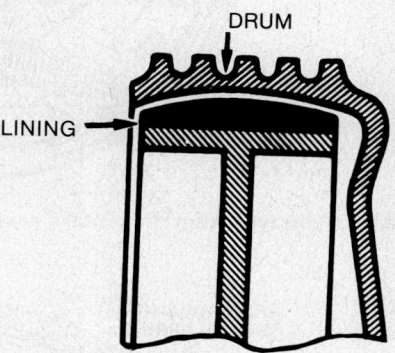

DRUM

LINING

Concave Drum

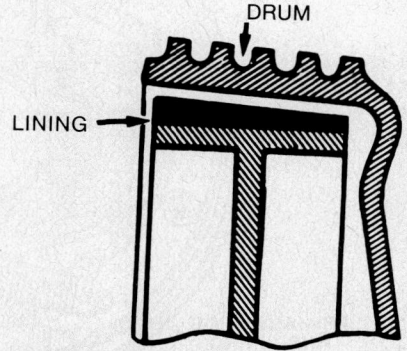

DRUM

LINING

Bellmouth Drum

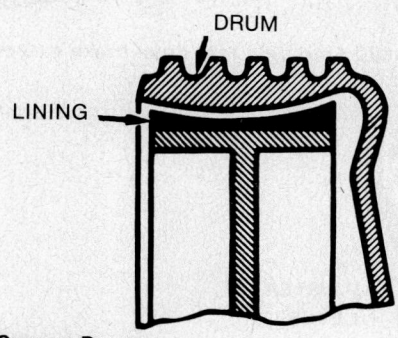

DRUM

LINING

Convex Drum

2 Depress the brake pedal hard several times and recheck wheel drag. Continue to depress brake pedal and recheck drag until a true heavy drag is obtained.

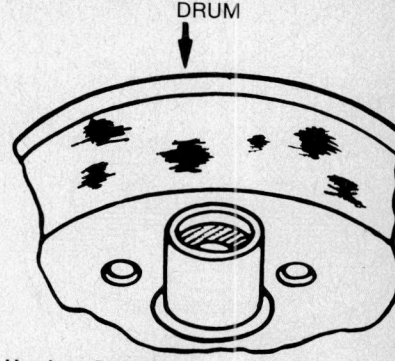

DRUM

Hard or Chill Spots

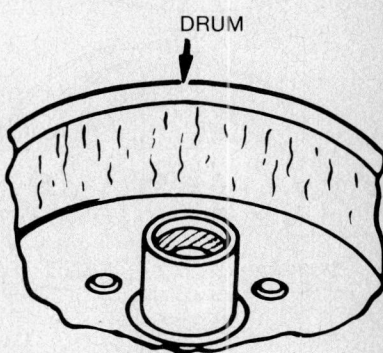

DRUM

Heat checks

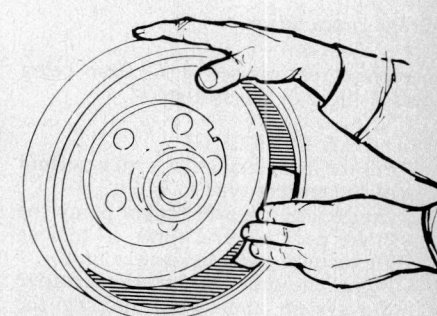

Sanding brake drums

3 Turn the star wheel adjuster in the opposite direction until the wheel turns freely.
4 Drive the car, braking forward and backward allowing the self-adjusters to obtain the best running clearance.

NOTE: Exceptions to the preceding are General Motor's "H" body cars (Astre, Monza, Skyhawk, Starfire, Vega). These brakes are automatically adjusted when the parking brake is applied. After brake service apply and release the parking brake until the brakes are correctly adjusted.

Brake System Bleeding

If the master cylinder has been replaced it is more practical and safe to bleed most of the air out at the master cylinder. This can be done either on or off the car and

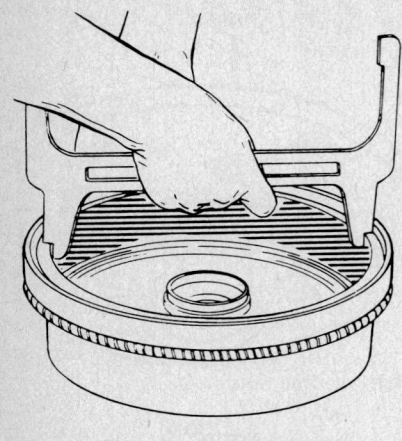

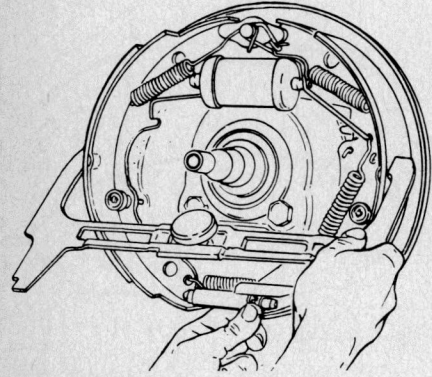

Brake drum guage

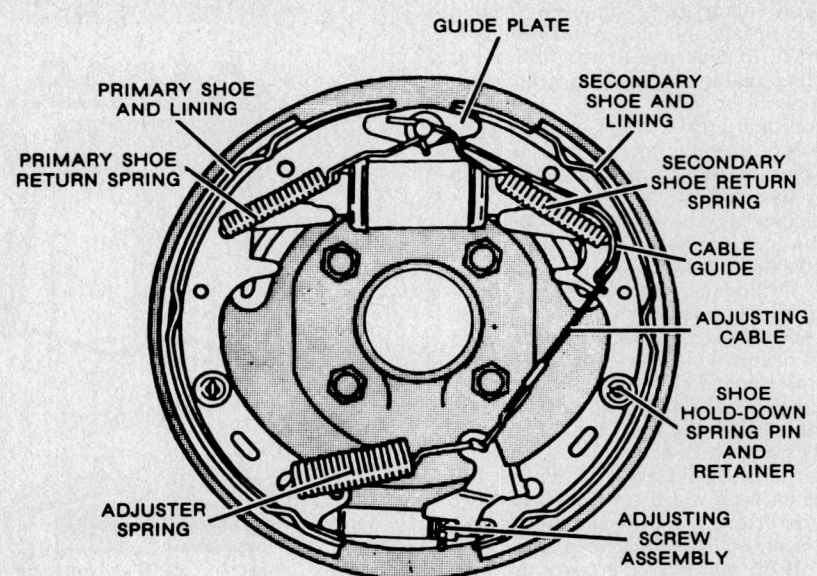

AMC, Ford type front drum brake assembly

prevents great masses of air from being passed through the system.

MANUAL BLEEDING

1 Fill the master cylinder with new fluid of the correct type.
2 On cars with power brakes pump the brake pedal several times to remove all vacuum from the power unit.
3 Pump the brake pedal to pressurize the system and, while holding the pedal down, release the hydraulic pressure at the wheel cylinder bleeder valve. The pedal must be held depressed until the bleeder valve is closed to prevent air from entering the system.

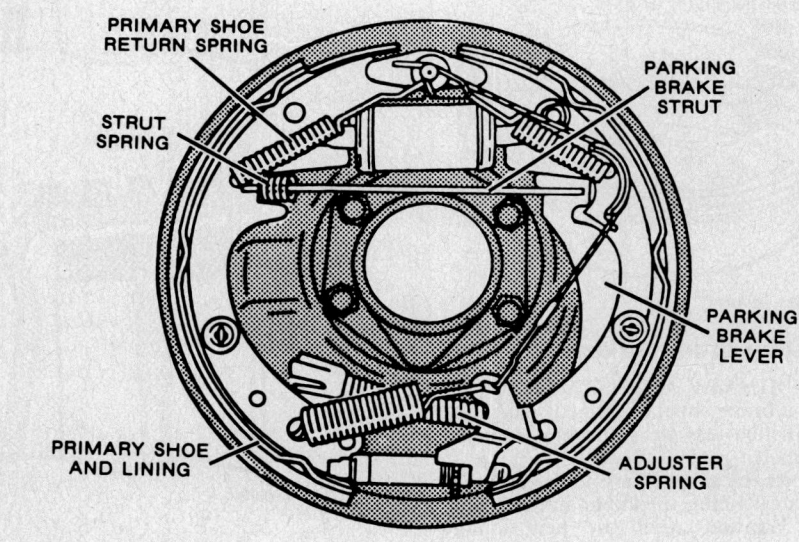

AMC, Ford type rear drum brake assembly

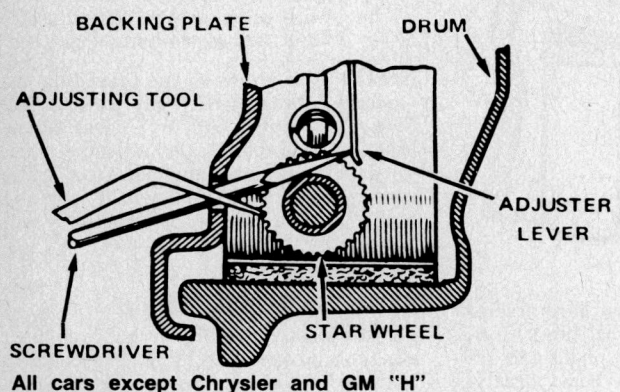

All cars except Chrysler and GM "H" body (Chevette)

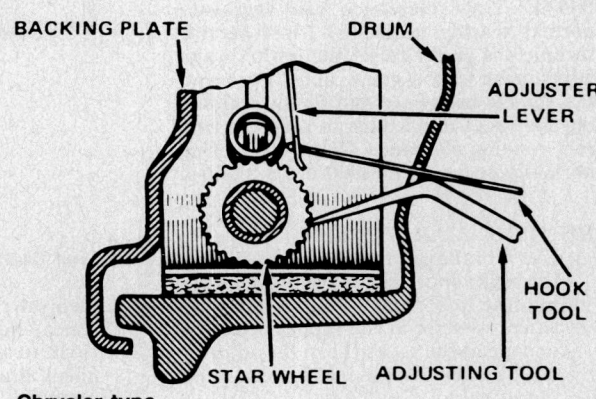

Chrysler type

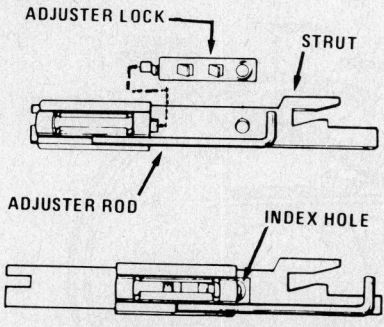

PARKING BRAKE STRUT AND ADJUSTER

G.M. "H" body cars (Chevette)

LEFT REAR   RIGHT REAR

Brake adjustment (as viewed from beneath the car) Up: to retract shoes, Down: to move shoes closer to drum

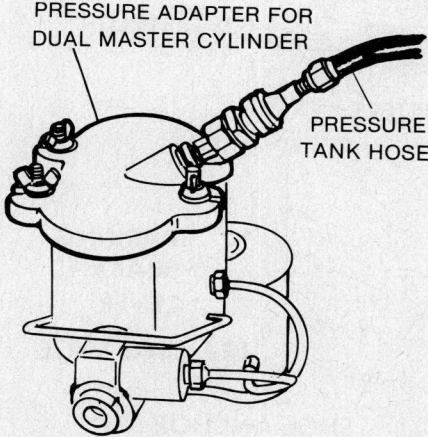

Pressure bleed connection to master cylinder

4 Repeat until a steady, clear (no air bubbles) flow of fluid is seen at the wheel cylinder.

CHILTON CAUTION: *The bleeder valve at the wheel cylinder must be closed at the end of each stroke, and before the brake pedal is released, to insure that no air can enter the system. It is also important that the brake pedal be returned to the full up position so the piston in the master cylinder moves back enough to clear the bypass outlets.*

PRESSURE BLEEDING
Pressure bleeding equipment should be diaphragm type; placing a diaphragm between the pressurized air supply and the

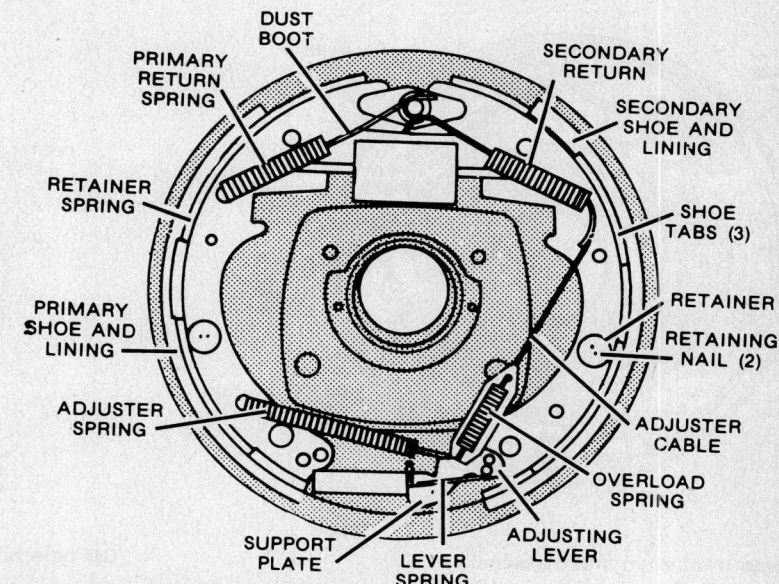

Chrysler type front drum brake assembly

Chrysler type rear drum brake assembly

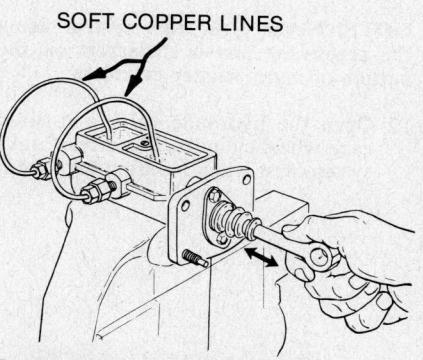

Pre-bleeding the master cylinder

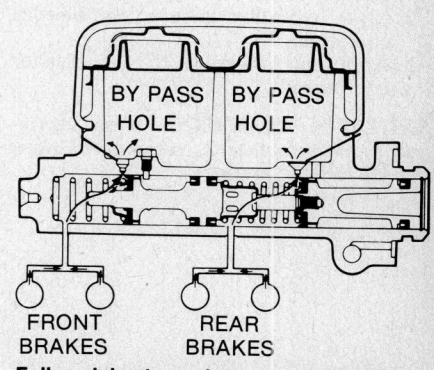

Full pedal return clears bypass holes

BRAKES
DRUM BRAKE SERVICE

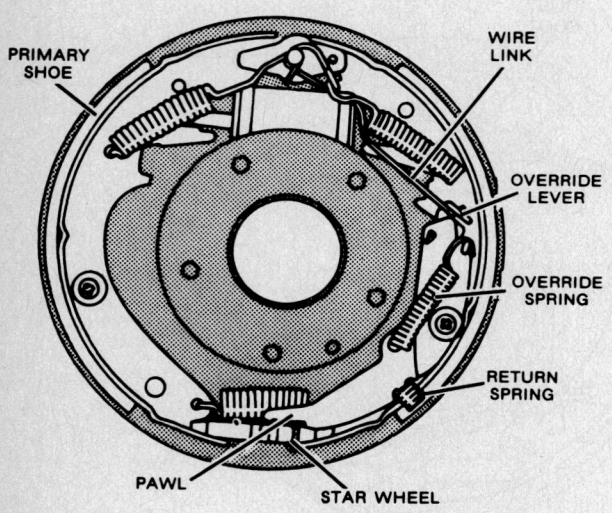

GM type front drum brake assembly

GM type rear drum brake assembly

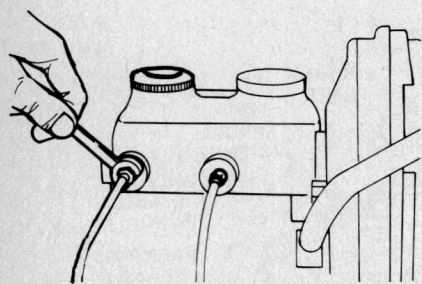

Bleeding the master cylinder after installation

brake fluid. This prevents moisture and other contaminants from entering the hydraulic system.

NOTE: Front disc/rear drum equipped vehicles use a metering valve which closes off pressure to the front brakes under certain conditions. These systems contain manual release actuators which must be engaged to pressure bleed the front brakes.

1 Connect the tank hydraulic hose and adapter to the master cylinder.
2 Close hydraulic valve on the bleeder equipment.
3 Apply air pressure to the bleeder equipment.

CHILTON CAUTION: *Follow equipment manufacturer's recommendations for correct air pressure.*

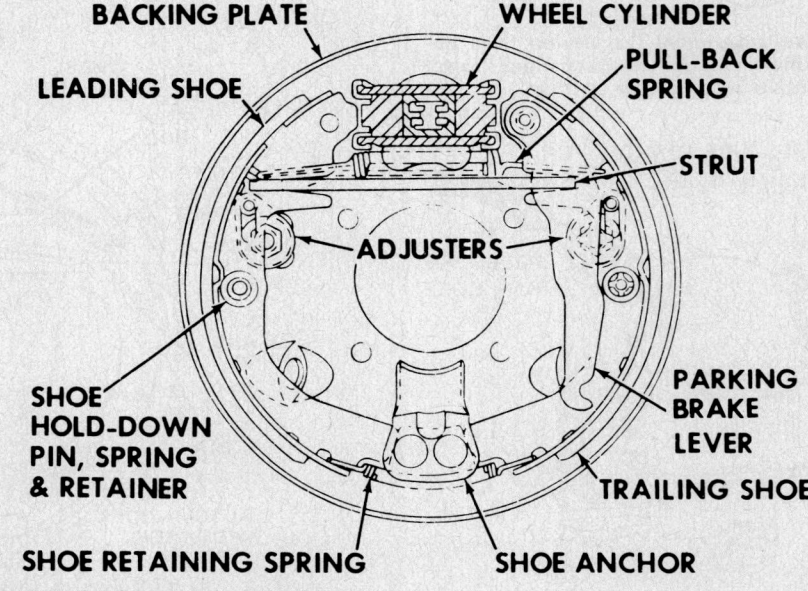

Manual adjusting rear drum brake

1 Open the valve to bleed air out of the pressure hose to the master cylinder.

NOTE: Never bleed this system using the secondary piston stopscrew on the bottom of many master cylinders.

2 Open the hydraulic valve and bleed each wheel cylinder. Bleed rear brake system first when bleeding both front

and rear systems.

FLUSHING HYDRAULIC BRAKE SYSTEMS

Hydraulic brake systems must be totally flushed if the fluid becomes contaminated with water, dirt or other corrosive chemicals. To flush, simply bleed the entire system until *all* fluid has been replaced with the correct type of new fluid.

INSTALLATION PROCEDURE

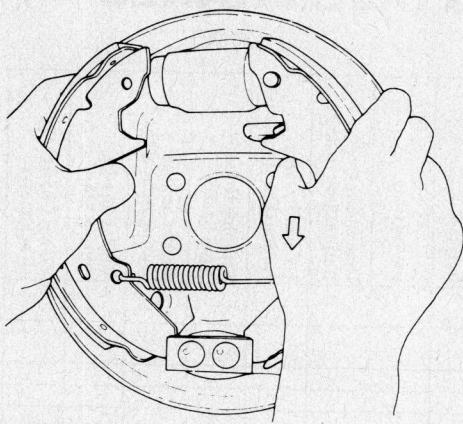

STEP 1

a. Assemble parking brake cable to trailing shoe and parking brake lever.

b. Install lower retracting spring to leading-trailing shoes.

c. Install this assembly to backing plate.

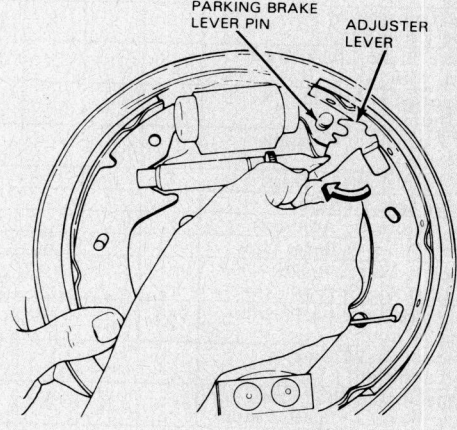

STEP 2

Install adjuster screw assembly.

TRAILING SHOE AND LINING ASSEMBLY

PARKING BRAKE LEVER

DEEP SLOT

NOTE: Socket Blade marked R and L. Install letter in upright position to insure proper slot engagement to parking brake lever.

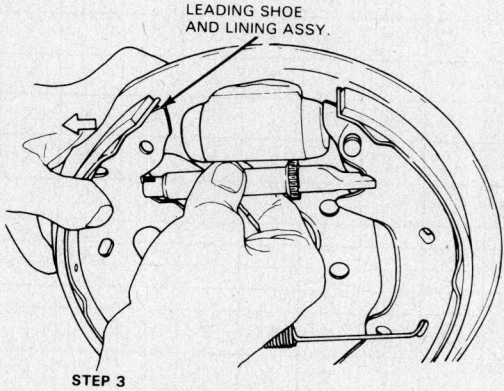

STEP 3

Install adjuster screw to leading shoe and lining assembly.

LEADING SHOE AND LINING ASSY.

PARKING BRAKE LEVER PIN

ADJUSTER LEVER

STEP 4

Install the adjuster lever in groove of parking brake lever pin.

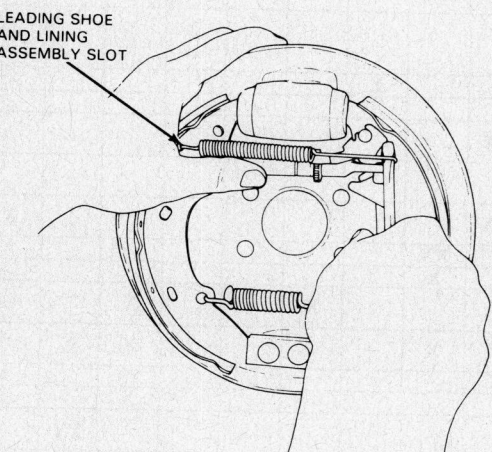

LEADING SHOE AND LINING ASSEMBLY SLOT

STEP 5

a. Install shoe holddown springs and pins.

b. Install upper retracting spring to leading shoe slot— stretch spring to install to trailing shoe. If adjuster lever does not contact star wheel after spring installation check adjuster socket installation.

Rear drum brakes

TROUBLESHOOTING DISC BRAKES

CAUSE	Excessive Brake Pedal Travel	Brake Pedal Travel Gradually Increases	Excessive Brake Pedal Effort	Excessive Braking Action	Brakes Slow to Respond	Brakes Slow to Release	Brakes Drag	Uneven Braking Action (Side to Side)	Uneven Braking Action (Front to Rear)	Scraping Noise from Brakes	Brakes Squeak During Application	Brakes Squeak During Stop	Brakes Chatter (Roughness)	Brakes Groan at End of Stop	Brakes Tell-Tale Glows
Leaking Brake Line or Connection	X	XX	X						X						XX
Leaking Wheel Cylinder or Piston Seal	X	XX	X	X				X							X
Leaking Master Cylinder	X	XX	X												X
Air in Brake System	XX		X						X						XX
Contaminated or Improper Brake Fluid	X				X	X	X								X
Leaking Vacuum System			XX		X										
Restricted Air Passage in Power Head		X	X		XX	X									
Damaged Power Head			X	X	X	X	XX								
Worn Out Brake Lining			X	X				X	X	X	X	X		X	
Uneven Brake Lining Wear - Replace	X		X					X	X	X	X	XX		X	X
Glazed Brake Lining - Sand			XX		X			X	X		X	X			
Incorrect Lining Material - Replace			X	X				X	X		X			X	
Contaminated Brake Lining - Replace				XX				XX	XX	X	X	X		X	
Linings Damaged by Abusive Use - Replace			X	XX				X	X	X	X	X		X	
Excessive Brake Lining Dust - Remove with Air			X	XX				XX	XX		X	XX		X	
Heat Spotted or Scored Brake Drums or Discs				X				X	X		X	X	XX	X	
Out-of-Round or Vibrating Brake Drums													X	XX	
Out-of-Parallel Brake Discs	X												XX		
Excessive Disc Run-Out	X												X		
Faulty Automatic Adjusters	X						X	X	X						X
Incorrect Wheel Cylinder Sizes			X	X				X	X						
Weak or Incorrect Brake Shoe Retention Springs				X		X	XX	X	X	XX	X	XX			
Brake Assembly Attachments - Missing or Loose	X						X	X	X	X		X	X	X	
Insufficient Brake Shoe Guide Lubricant							X	X	X	XX	XX				
Restricted Brake Fluid Passage or Sticking Wheel Cylinder Piston		X	X		X	X	X	X	X						X
Improperly adjusted Stoplight Switch or Cruise Control Vacuum Dump							X								
Faulty Metering Valve	X		X	X	X	X	X		X						X
Faulty Proportioning Valve			X	X	X	X	X		X						
Brake Pedal Linkage Interference or Binding			X		X	XX	XX								
Improperly Adjusted Parking Brake							X								
Improperly Adjusted Master Cylinder Push Rod	X					X	XX								X
Incorrect Front End Alignment								XX							
Incorrect Tire Pressure								X	X						
Incorrect Wheel Bearing Adjustment	X									X			X		
Loose Front Suspension Attachments							X	X		XX			X	X	
Out-of-Balance Wheel Assemblies													XX		
Incorrect Body Mount Torque													X		
Need to Slightly Increase or Decrease Pedal Effort														XX	
Operator Riding Brake Pedal			X				X		X				X		
Sticking Caliper or Wheel Cylinder Pistons							XX								

XX – Indicates more probable cause(s)
X – Indicates other causes

DISC BRAKE APPLICATION CHART

Model/Make	Year	Illustration Type	Fixed Four Piston Caliper	Floating or Sliding Caliper Single Piston
AMERICAN MOTORS				
Some	All	1		
Some	All	5		Bendix
CHRYSLER CORPORATION				Kelsey Hayes
Full Size Models	All	6		
Intermediates	All	6		Kelsey Hayes
Challenger, Barracuda	All	6		Kelsey Hayes
Dart, Valiant	All	6		Kelsey Hayes
FORD MOTOR COMPANY				Kelsey Hayes
All Models Front Drive		12		
All Models Rear Drive	All	1 or 10		Ford
GENERAL MOTORS				Ford
Buick Full Size	All	2		
Buick Special	All	2		Delco
Buick Skyhawk	1976	2		Delco
Cadillac Eldorado	All	2 or 12		Delco
Cadillac	All	2		Delco
Chevrolet Full Size	All	2		Delco
Chevette	All	11		Delco
Corvette	All	4		Delco
Camaro, Chevelle, Nova	All	All		Delco
Vega	All	3		Delco
Monza	1976	2		Delco
Oldsmobile Toronado	All	2		Delco
Oldsmobile 88, 98	All	2		Delco
Oldsmobile F85, Cutlass	All	2		Delco
Oldsmobile Starfire	1976	2		Delco
Pontiac Full Size	All	2		Delco
Tempest, LeMans	All	2		Delco
Firebird, G.P.	All	2		Delco
Ventura	All	2		Delco
Sunbird	All	2		Delco
Astre	All	3		Delco
				Delco

DISC BRAKE SERVICE

Type One:
Bendix Floating Caliper Disc Brakes (Single Piston)

PAD REMOVAL

1. Remove half of the brake fluid from the master cylinder.
2. Remove the retaining screw holding the caliper support key.
3. Use a hammer and drift to drive the caliper retaining key and support spring out of the anchor plate.
4. Lift the caliper off of the rotor.
5. Support caliper so it doesn't hang by the brake hose.
6. Use a large C-clamp to force the piston back into its bore, being careful not to scratch the piston or bore, and being careful not to cut or tear the dust boot.
7. Remove the inboard pad and anti-rattle spring from the caliper.

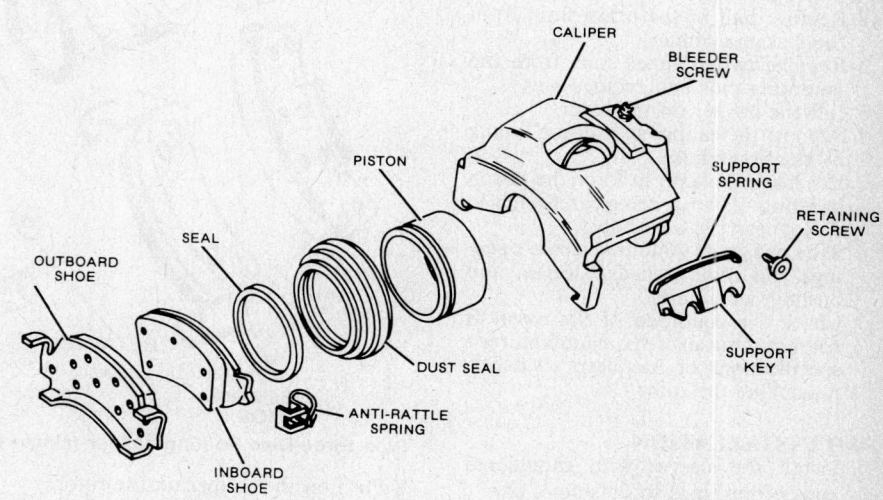

Type one Bendix floating caliper disc brakes (single Piston)

8 Remove the outboard pad from the caliper. Check the condition of the rotor. If rotor run out exceeds manufacturer's specifications or has deep scratches, re-machine the rotor.

PAD INSTALLATION

1 Position the inboard brake pad anti-rattle spring on the inboard pad so that the looped section of the spring is positioned away from the brake rotor.
2 Position the inboard brake pad and anti-rattle spring in the caliper.
3 Position the outboard brake pad in the caliper. Bend ears if necessary to provide slight interference fit in caliper.
4 Position the caliper on the rotor.
5 Position the caliper support spring and support key into the slot and drive them into the opening between the lower end of the caliper and the lower anchor plate abutment.
6 Install and tighten the key retaining screw.
7 Fill the master cylinder with brake fluid.

Type Two:
Delco Floating Caliper
(Single Piston)

PAD REMOVAL

1 Remove half of the brake fluid from the master cylinder.
2 Remove the two caliper mounting bolts, and lift the caliper off of the rotor.
3 Use a large C-clamp to push the piston back into its bore by pushing against the old pad that sits against the piston.
4 Support the caliper so it doesn't hang by the brake hose.
5 Press the outboard pad inward, then lift it out of the caliper.
6 Press the inboard pad outward, then lift it out of the caliper.
7 Check the condition of the rotor. If rotor run out exceeds manufacturer's specifications or has deep scratches, re-machine the rotor.

PAD INSTALLATION

1 Position the inboard pad so the pad contacts the piston and the two support spring ends. Note that the inboard and outboard pads are similar but not interchangeable.
2 Press down on the ears at the top of the inboard pad until the pad lies flat

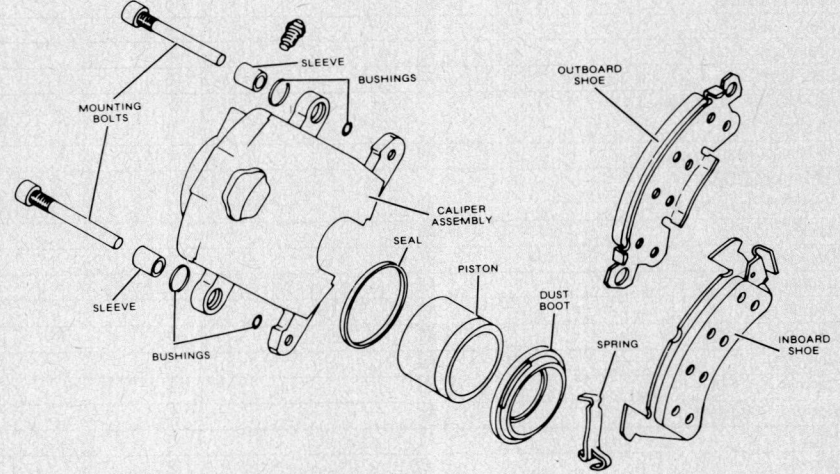

Type two Delco floating disc brakes (single piston)

and the spring ends are just inside the lower edge of the pad.
3 Position the outboard pad with the ears toward the positioning pin holes and the tab on the inner edge of the pad resting in the notch in the edge of the caliper. Bend ears if necessary to provide slight interference fit in caliper.
4 Press the outboard pad tightly into position and use a pair of pliers to clinch the ears of the outboard pad over the outboard caliper half.
5 Position the caliper over the rotor.
6 Install the caliper mounting bolts and tighten to specification.
7 Fill the master cylinder with brake fluid.

Type Three:
Delco Floating Caliper
(Single Piston)

PAD REMOVAL

1 Remove half of the brake fluid from the master cylinder.
2 Remove two stamped nuts from the mounting pins and remove pins.
3 Lift the caliper off the rotor.
4 Support the caliper so it doesn't hang by the brake hose.
5 Use large C-clamp to force the piston back into its bore, being careful not to cut or tear the dust boot.
6 Slide pads past mounting sleeve openings and remove pads, sleeves, and bushing assemblies.
7 Check the condition of the rotor. If rotor run out exceeds manufacturer's specifications or has deep scratches, remachine the rotor.

PAD INSTALLATION

1 Install the sleeves with shouldered ends of bushings to outside of car.
2 Install pads in caliper with ears over sleeve.

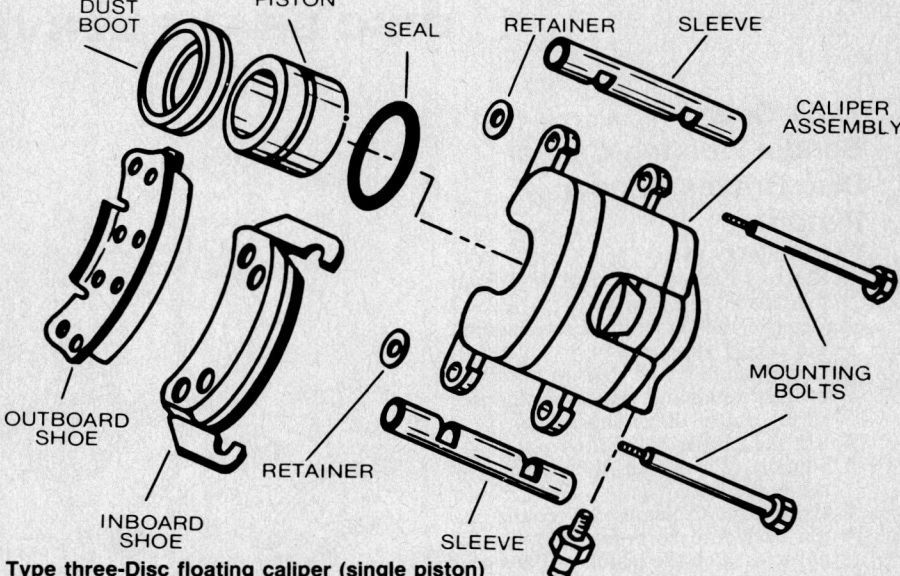

Type three-Disc floating caliper (single piston)

3 Position the caliper on the rotor.
4 Install mounting pins.
5 Install stamped nuts on mounting pins using small socket to press on as far as possible.
6 Fill the master cylinder with fluid.

Type Four:
Delco Fixed Caliper (Four Pistons)

PAD REMOVAL AND INSTALLATION
1 Remove half of the brake fluid from the master cylinder.
2 Remove the brake pad retaining pins.
3 Pry the pistons back into their bores (being careful to pry both pistons at

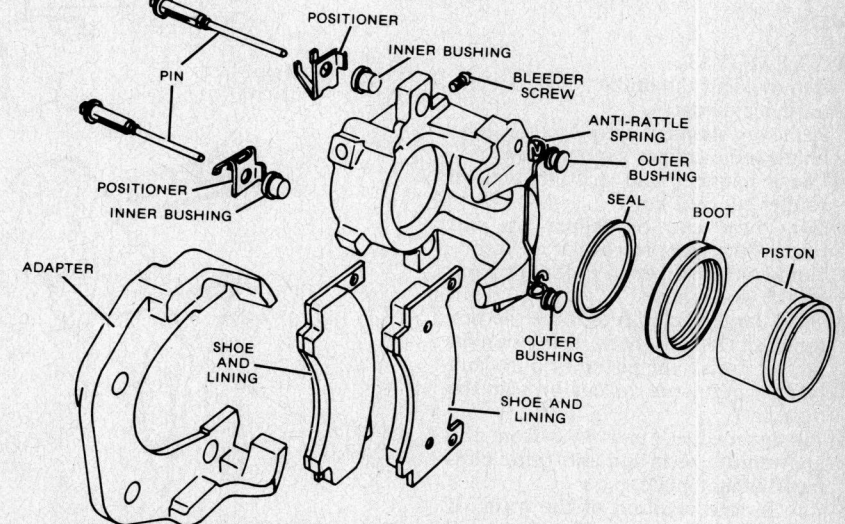

Type four Delco fixed caliper (four pistons)

once so as not to force one out of its bore) and lift out one pad by tipping it down at the rear and up at the front.

4 Hold the rear piston in and slide the rear end of the new pad into place, being careful not to force out the front piston.
5 Check the condition of the rotor. If rotor run out exceeds .003 thousands, or has deep scratches, re-machine the rotor.
6 Now push the front piston back into its bore and slide the front of the new pad into position.
7 Change the other pad in the same manner.
8 Reinstall the retaining pin through the caliper holes and through the holes in the pads.
9 Fill the master cylinder with fresh brake fluid.

Type 5:
Kelsey Hayes Floating Caliper (Single Piston)

PAD REMOVAL
1 Remove half of the brake fluid from the master cylinder.
2 Remove the caliper guide pins and positioners and anti-rattle spring.
3 Lift the caliper off of the rotor.
4 Support the caliper so it doesn't hang by the brake hose.
5 Pry the piston back into its bore, being careful not to scratch the pistons or bores, and being careful not to cut or tear the dust boots.
6 Lift the brake pads out of the caliper.
7 Check the condition of the rotor. If rotor run out exceeds manufacturer's specifications or has deep scratches, re-machine the rotor.

PAD INSTALLATION
1 Clean and lubricate (with light waterproof grease) caliper guide pins and guide surfaces.
2 Position the new pads in the caliper. The inboard and outboard pads are identical and interchangeable.

Type five-Kelsey Hayes floating caliper (single piston)

3 Position the caliper on the rotor.
4 Align the guide pin holes of the adapter and the caliper, and install new positioners over the guide pins, with the open ends facing toward the outside. Tighten the pins to proper specification.
5 Install the anti-rattle spring.
6 Fill the master cylinder with fluid.

Type Six:
Kelsey Hayes Sliding Caliper

PAD REMOVAL

1 Remove half of the brake fluid from the master cylinder.
2 Remove caliper retaining clips and anti-rattle springs.
3 Lift the caliper off of the rotor.
4 Support the caliper so it doesn't hang by the brake hose.
5 Use a large C-clamp to force the piston back into its bore, being careful not to scratch the piston or bore, and being careful not to cut or tear the dust boot.
6 Pry the outboard pad from caliper.
7 Remove inboard pad from the adapter.
8 Check the condition of the rotor. If rotor run out exceeds manufacturer's specifications or has deep scratches, re-machine the rotor.

PAD INSTALLATION

1 Adjust ears of outboard pad to pro-

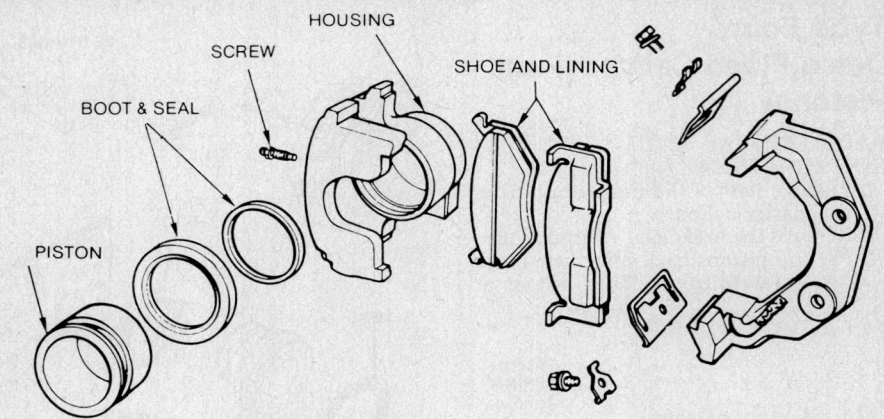

Type six Kelsey Hayes sliding caliper

vide tight fit and install pad in caliper recess.
2 Install inboard pad with flanges inserted in adapter "ways."
3 Position the caliper on the rotor with the caliper egaging the adapter "ways."

4 Install anti-rattle springs and caliper retaining clips and torque retaining screws to 180 inch-pounds (15 ft.-pounds).
5 Fill the master cylinder with brake fluid.

Type Seven:
Ford Center Abutment Type

PAD REMOVAL

1 Remove half the brake fluid from the master cylinder.
2 Remove stainless steel cotter-pins holding the caliper support key.
3 Use a hammer and drift to remove caliper support key.
4 Lift lower end of caliper up and toward the rear, remove from rotor.
5 Support the caliper so it doesn't hang by the brake hose.
6 Use a large C-clamp to force the piston back into its bore, being careful not to scratch the piston or bore, and being careful not to cut or tear the dust boot.
7 Tilt upper edge of pads away from disc and remove pads and anti-rattle clips from anchor plate.
8 Check the condition of the rotor. If rotor run out exceeds manufacturer's specifications or has deep scratches, re-machine the rotor.

PAD INSTALLATION

1 Place pads and anti-rattle clips in the anchor plate.
2 Position caliper on rotor, over pads

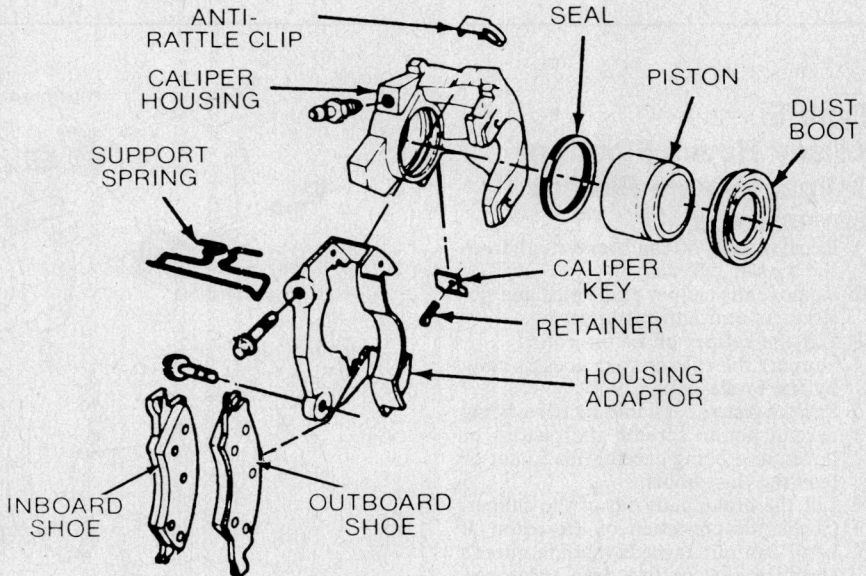

Ford center abutment type

and in anchor plate with upper support spring under caliper projecting ledge.
3 Pry caliper upward and inward, at lower edge, and insert caliper support key between caliper and anchor plate.

Make sure support springs are still in position.
4 Install new stainless steel cotter pins in caliper support key on each side of anchor plate.
5 Fill the master cylinder with fluid.

Type Eight:
Kelsey Hayes Fixed Caliper (Four Pistons)

PAD REMOVAL AND INSTALLATION

1. Remove half of the brake fluid from the master cylinder.
2. Remove the brake pad retainers.
3. Pry the caliper pistons back into their bores, being careful not to scratch the pistons or bores, and being careful to pry both pistons at once so as not to force one out of the caliper bore.
4. Grasp tabs on the outer ends of one of the brake pads with two pairs of pliers and pull the pad straight out of the caliper.
5. Check the condition of the rotor. If rotor run out exceeds manufacturer's specifications or has deep scratches, re-machine the rotor.
6. Slide the new pad into position, mak-

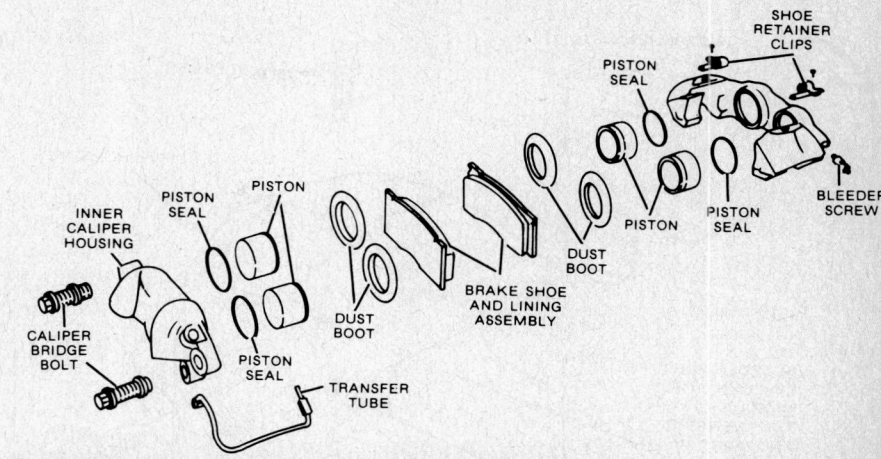

Type eight Kelsey Hayes fixed caliper (four pistons)

ing sure the pad ears rest solidly on the bridges of the caliper.
7. After replacing the first pad, repeat this procedure for the other pad.
8. Reinstall the brake pad retaining hardware.
9. Fill the master cylinder with brake fluid.

Type Nine:
Kelsey Hayes Ford Floating Type

PAD REMOVAL

1. Remove half of the brake fluid from the master cylinder.
2. Remove the lockwire from the two mounting bolts and remove bolts.
3. Lift the caliper off the rotor. A steady twisting motion will cause the piston to be retracted and give clearance for removal.
4. Support the caliper so it doesn't hang by the brake hose.
5. Remove the retaining clips with a screwdriver and remove the outboard pad and retaining pins.
6. Use large C-clamp to push piston back into its bore by pushing against the inboard pad.
7. Remove the inboard pad.
8. Check the condition of the rotor. If rotor run out exceeds manufacturer's specifications or has deep scratches, re-machine the rotor.

PAD INSTALLATION

1. Replace guide pins, stabilizers, or insulators.

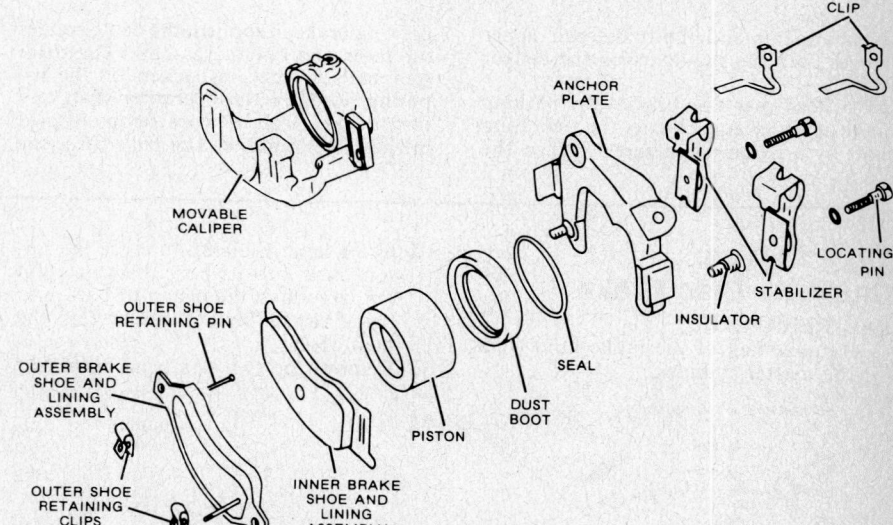

Type nine Kelsey Hayes Ford floating type

2. Position outboard pad on caliper and install two retaining pins and clips.
3. Install inboard pad with ears on top of anchor plate bosses and under pad retaining clips.
4. Spread pads and position the caliper

on the rotor.
5. Install lower bolt finger tight. Install upper bolt and tighten to specifications. Tighten lower bolt to specification. Safety wire both bolts.
6. Fill the master cylinder with fluid.

Type Ten:
Ford Rear Floating Caliper Brake Pad Installation

The recommended procedure for this operation calls for removing the rotor from the car and mounting the caliper in position in the anchor plate with the key only. A special tool is needed to screw the

piston back into its bore. While holding the shaft, rotate the tool handle counterclockwise until the tool is seated firmly against the piston. Now loosen the handle about a quarter turn. While holding the handle, rotate the tool shaft clockwise until the piston is fully bottomed in its bore.

Once the piston is bottomed, remove the caliper from the mounting plate, re-

move the tool from the caliper, and reinstall the rotor. Now the new pads can be installed. Make sure that the brake pad anti-rattle clip is in place in the lower inner brake pad support on the anchor plate, with the loop of the clip toward the inside of the anchor plate. Place the inboard pad on the anchor plate.

Now install the outer brake pad with the lower flange ends against the caliper

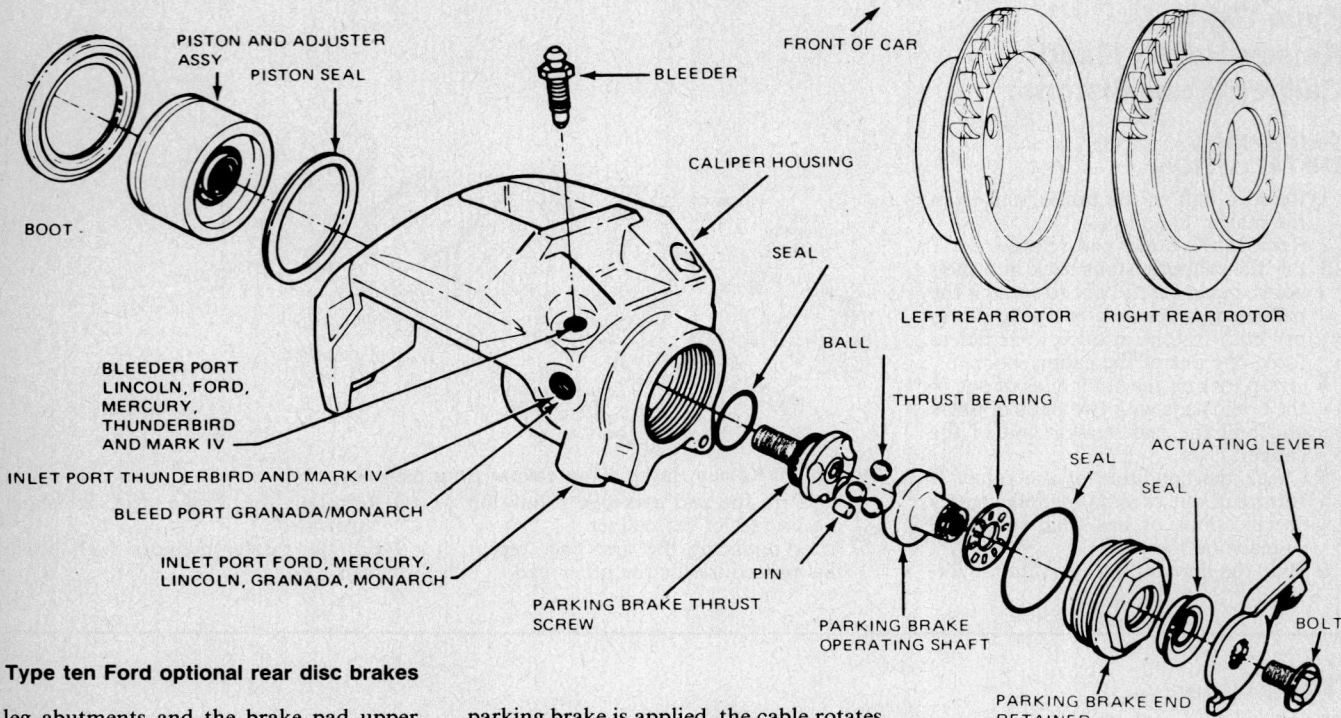

Type ten Ford optional rear disc brakes

leg abutments and the brake pad upper flanges over the shoulders on the caliper legs.

On Ford rear disc brakes, the parking brake lever is attached to the operating shaft by a nylon-patch screw. When the parking brake is applied, the cable rotates the lever and operating shaft. The three steel balls, located in pockets on the opposing heads of the operating shaft and thrust screw, roll between ramps formed in these ball pockets. The balls force the thrust screw away from the operating shaft, driving the piston and pad against the rotor, creating the parking brake force.

Type Eleven:
Chevette Disc Brake
PAD REMOVAL
1 Remove half of the brake fluid from the master cylinder.

2 Use a large C-clamp to force the piston back into its bore, being careful not to scratch the piston or bore, and being careful not to cut or tear the dust boot.
3 Remove the two hex head bolts that attach the caliper mounting bracket to the steering knuckle.
4 Support the caliper so it doesn't hang on the brake hose.

NOTE: Do not remove the socket head retainer bolt.

5 Remove the old shoe and lining assemblies. If the retaining spring does not come out with the inboard shoe, remove the spring from the piston.
6 Check the condition of the rotor. If rotor run out exceeds manufacturer's specifications or has deep scratches, re-machine the rotor.

PAD INSTALLATION
1 Before installing the inboard shoe, make sure that the shoe retaining spring is properly installed. Push the tab on the single-leg end of the spring down into the shoe hole, then snap the other two legs over the edge of the shoe notch.
2 Position the caliper over the rotor, lining up the bracket mounting holes. Install the mounting bolts.
3 Clinch the outboard shoe to the caliper. After clinching, radial and end play of the outboard shoe should be zero to 0.127 nm (zero to 0.005 inch).

Inboard shoe, lining and retainer

Type Twelve:
GM Rear Disc Brake

PAD REMOVAL
NOTE: Calipers must be removed to replace linings.

1 Remove two-thirds of the fluid in the front master cylinder.
2 Remove wheel and tire assembly, and reinstall one wheel mounting nut, flat side toward rotor, to prevent rotor from falling when caliper is removed.
3 Loosen tension on the parking brake cable at equalizer, and remove the cable from the parking brake lever at the caliper.
4 Remove return spring, lock nut, lever, lever seal and anti-friction washer. (Lever must be held in place while removing nut.)
5 Using a "C" clamp with the solid end of the lever stop and the screw end of the back of the outboard lining assembly, tighten clamp until piston bottoms in the caliper.

NOTE: Do not position "C" clamp on actuator screw.

6 Before removing the clamp lube the caliper housing surface (under the lever seal) with silicone.
7 Install new anti-friction washer, new lever seal and lever. Be certain to install lever on hex with arm pointing downward.
8 Rotate lever toward front of car and while holding in this position install nut and torque to 25 Ft./lbs. Rotate lever back to stop.
9 Install lever return spring, and remove "C" clamp. Springs are color coded, red for right side caliper and black for left.
10 Remove brake line from caliper and plug openings to retain fluid and pre-

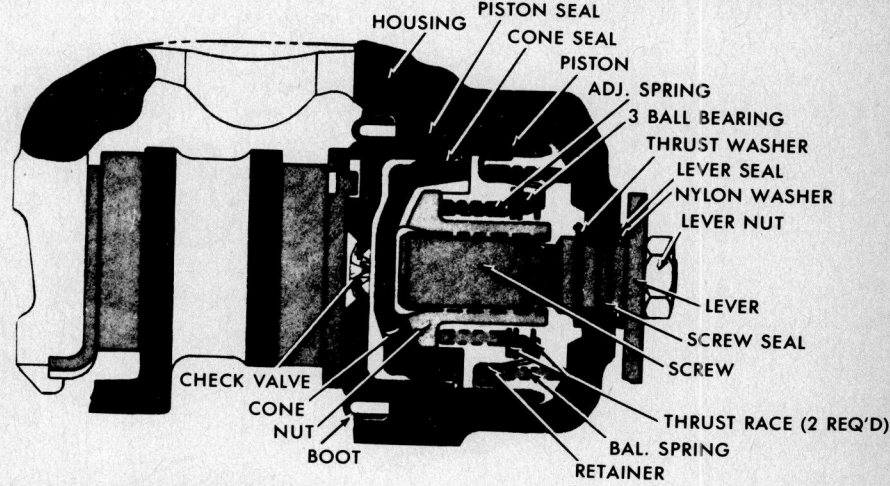

Type twelve GM rear disc brake

vent entrance of dirt.

NOTE: If brake line nut is seized, brass bolt and block on caliper can be removed with brake line attached by removing bolt and block copper washers after removing caliper mounting bolts.

11 Remove caliper mounting bolts and remove caliper and brake shoes.
12 Remove two caliper mounting sleeves and four bushings, and install new parts using a silicone lubricant. (Sleeves are installed in inner bushings.)
13 Position new inboard shoe assembly on piston. D shaped tab must fit in the indentation provided in the piston.
14 Install new outboard shoe assembly.
15 To reinstall caliper replace any corroded caliper mounting bolts with new parts. Wire brushing or sanding will damage the bolt plating.
16 If brass bolt and block was removed

with brass pipe, unplug fittings and install bolt and block using two new copper gaskets. Torque to 30 Ft./lbs. Be sure that all sleeves, bushings and pins are well lubricated with silicone. (Mounting bolt should go under inboard shoe ears.)
17 Install brake line tube nut into caliper and pump brake pedal to seat lining against rotor.
18 Clinch upper ear of outboard shoe by positioning pliers with one jaw on top of upper ear and other jaw in notch or bottom of shoe, opposite upper ear. After clinching there should be no radial clearance between the shoe ears and caliper housing. Repeat clinching procedure if necessary
19 Connect and adjust parking brake cables and bleed rear brake system.
20 Install wheel and tire assembly. Torque sheel mounting nuts to 130 Ft./lbs.

Type 13—Ford Front Drive Disc Brake

Shoe Lining Removal

1. Remove master cylinder cap and check fluid level in reservoirs. Remove brake fluid until each reservoir is half full. Discard the removed fluid.
2. Remove wheel and tire assembly from rotor mounting face. Use care to avoid damage or interference with the caliper splash shield or bleeder screw fitting.
3. Remove brake caliper anti-rattle spring by applying upward pressure to center portion of spring until the spring tabs are free of the caliper holes.
4. Back out the caliper locating pins. Do not remove pins completely unless new bushings are to be installed.

Reinstalling pins after complete removal can be difficult.
5. Lift caliper assembly from integral knuckle and anchor plate and rotor. Remove outer shoe and lining assembly from caliper assembly.
6. Remove inner shoe and lining assembly and inspect both rotor braking surfaces. Minor scoring or build-up of lining material does not require machining or replacement of the rotor.
7. Suspend caliper inside the fender housing. Use care not to damage caliper or stretch the brake hose.

Shoe Lining Installation

1. Use a 4-inch C-clamp and a block of wood 2¾ inch x 1 inch and approximately ¾-inch thick to seat the caliper hydraulic piston in its bore. This must be done to provide clearance for the caliper assembly to fit over the

rotor during installation. Extra care must be taken during this procedure to prevent damage to the aluminum piston. Metal or sharp objects cannot come into direct contact with the piston surface or damage will result.
2. Install the correct inner shoe and lining assembly in caliper piston(s). Do not bend shoe clips during installation in the piston or distortion and rattles can occur.
3. Install the correct outer shoe and lining assembly making sure clips are properly seated. Replace caliper anti-rattle spring. Refill master cylinder to at least ¼-inch from the top in both reservoirs.
4. Install the wheel and tire assembly. Tighten wheel nuts to 109-142 N•m (80-105 ft.lbs.).
5. Pump the brake pedal prior to moving the vehicle to position brake linings.
6. Road test the vehicle.

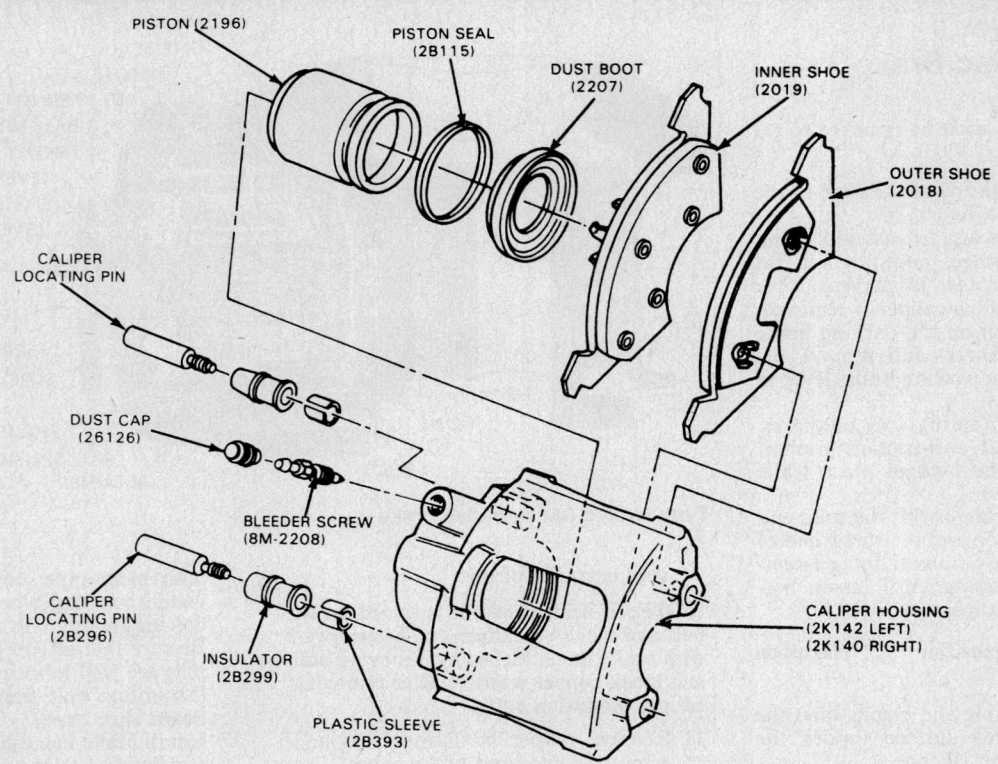

PISTON (2196)
PISTON SEAL (2B115)
DUST BOOT (2207)
INNER SHOE (2019)
OUTER SHOE (2018)
CALIPER LOCATING PIN
DUST CAP (26126)
BLEEDER SCREW (8M-2208)
CALIPER LOCATING PIN (2B296)
INSULATOR (2B299)
PLASTIC SLEEVE (2B393)
CALIPER HOUSING (2K142 LEFT) (2K140 RIGHT)

Disc brakes—sliding caliper

HYDRAULIC BRAKE COMPONENT SERVICE

Hydraulic Brake Component Service

Federal law required cars to be equipped with two separate brake systems, so the if one system should fail, the other will provide enough braking power to safely stop the car. The standard approach has been to use a tandem master cylinder and separate hydraulic circuits for the front and rear brakes. A tandem master cylinder actually uses two piston-and-seal assemblies in-line in a single bore. The dual system includes a red warning lamp on the instrument panel and, to activate it, a "Pressure Differential" valve which is connected to both sides of the system. The valve is sensitive to any loss of hydraulic pressure which results from a braking failure on either side of the system and alerts the driver by switching on the lamp. The lamp is con-

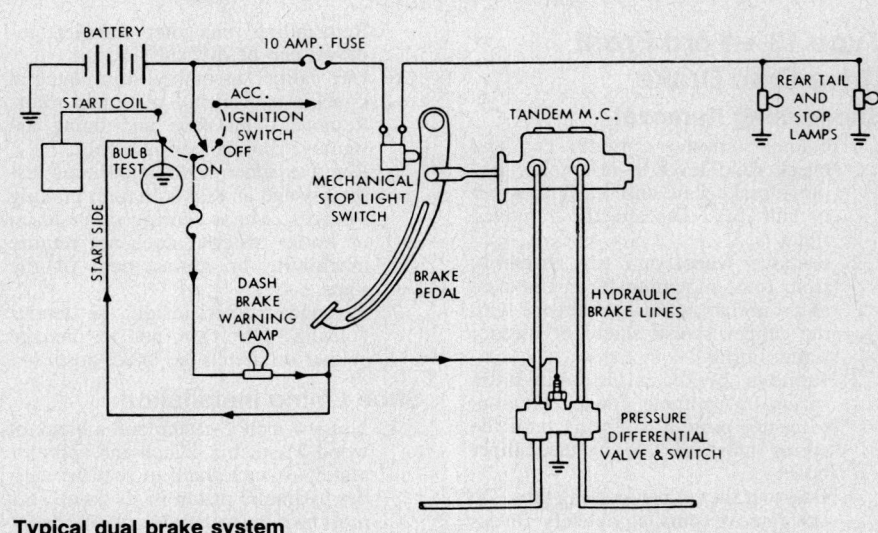

BATTERY
START COIL
10 AMP. FUSE
ACC.
IGNITION SWITCH
OFF
ON
BULB TEST
START SIDE
MECHANICAL STOP LIGHT SWITCH
TANDEM M.C.
REAR TAIL AND STOP LAMPS
DASH BRAKE WARNING LAMP
BRAKE PEDAL
HYDRAULIC BRAKE LINES
PRESSURE DIFFERENTIAL VALVE & SWITCH

Typical dual brake system

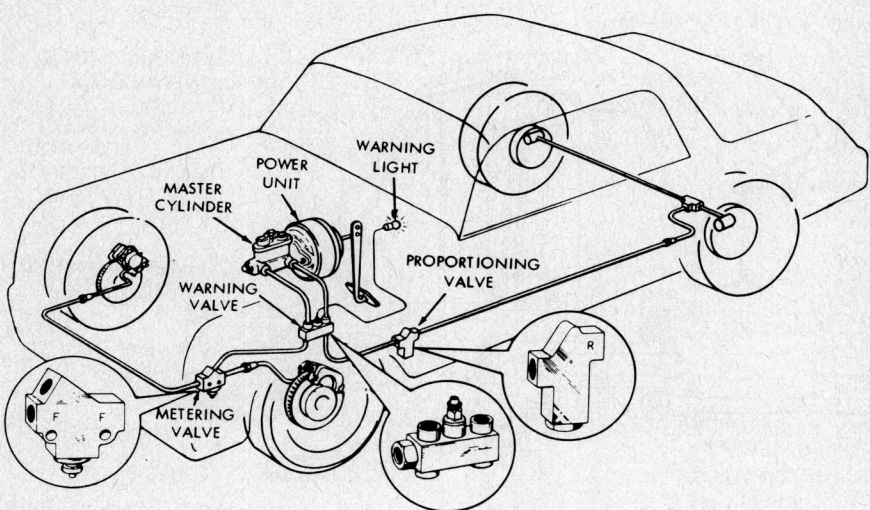

Typical dual system disc brake

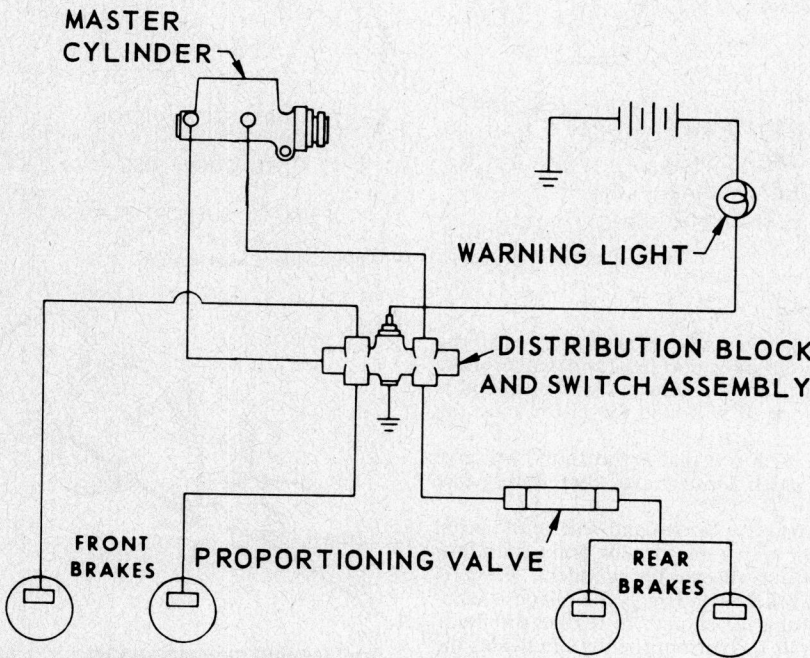

Brake system schematic

CHILTON CAUTION: *All brake valving should be considered as non repairable. Replacement should be an exact duplicate of the unit that was designed for the car.*

The master cylinder is designed so that the front and rear service brakes have separate hydraulic systems. The front section of the master cylinder provides fluid for the front brakes, while the rear section provides fluid for the rear brakes. Should a leak occur in the front hydraulic system, the rear brake system will still function. Likewise, if the rear hydraulic system should develop a leak, then the front system would still function. Increased brake pedal travel and an instrument panel brake light warns the driver that such a condition may have occurred.

The hydraulic unit is sealed from the atmosphere by rubber seals in the master cylinder reservoir. Atmospheric pressure acts on one side of the diaphragm type seal and reservoir fluid pressure on the other side. This arrangement permits the seal to follow the level of the brake fluid and prevents moisture absorption or dust contamination.

CHILTON CAUTION: *The master cylinder unit is a highly calibrated unit specifically designed for the car it is on. Although the cylinders may look alike there are many differences in calibration. If replacement is necessary, make sure the replacement unit is the one specified for the car.*

MASTER CYLINDER
Overhaul Disassambly

1 Remove the secondary piston stop bolt from the bottom or inside the reservoir if so equipped.
2 Depress the primary piston and remove snap ring from retaining groove at the rear of the master cylinder bore.
3 Remove push rod and primary piston assembly from the master cylinder bore. Do not remove the screw that secures the primary return spring retainer, return spring, primary cup and protector on the primary piston. This assembly is factory pre-adjusted and should not be disassembled.
4 Remove the secondary piston assembly. Do not remove the outlet tube seats from the master cylinder body.
5 Inspect the parts for chipping, excessive wear or damage. When using a master cylinder repair kit, install all the parts supplied.
6 Be sure that all recesses, openings and internal passages are open and clean.
7 Inspect the master cylinder bore for signs of etching, pitting, scoring or rust. If necessary to hone the master cylinder bore to repair damage, do not exceed allowable hone specifications, .003 thousands.

Assembly

1 Dip all parts except the master cylinder body in clean brake fluid.

nected to the ignition switch. With the switch in "start" position, the lamp is lit, furnishing a bulb check, but in "running" position, it will light only if a brake failure occurs. Although usual stops occur at moderate hydraulic pressures, during a "panic stop" the master cylinder develops pressure ranging as high as 650-680 psi (pounds per square inch) on drum braked passenger cars, and higher still with disc brakes. Caliper disc brakes, being non-energized, require more applying force than comparable energized-shoe/drum brakes. Caliper pistons, comparatively, are quite large and generally a higher pressure range is provided by power braking. Front disc-rear drum brake vehicles are provided with pressure regulating units not often found when front and rear

brakes are of the same type. Pressure-regulating units refine the braking balance, by changing the ratio of front-to-rear pressure, regulating it for moderate or severe stops as required to lessen skidding and diving. The "pressure metering" valve inhibits pressure to front disc brakes during easy, rolling stops. The "proportioning" valve reduces pressure to rear drum brakes in severe stops. One or both types of valves are found in various systems.

Wheel cylinder sizes influence the proportion of front to rear axle braking balance and various body styles, or other options which change the vehicle weight distribution, often require a corresponding change in the wheel cylinder diameter on one or more axles.

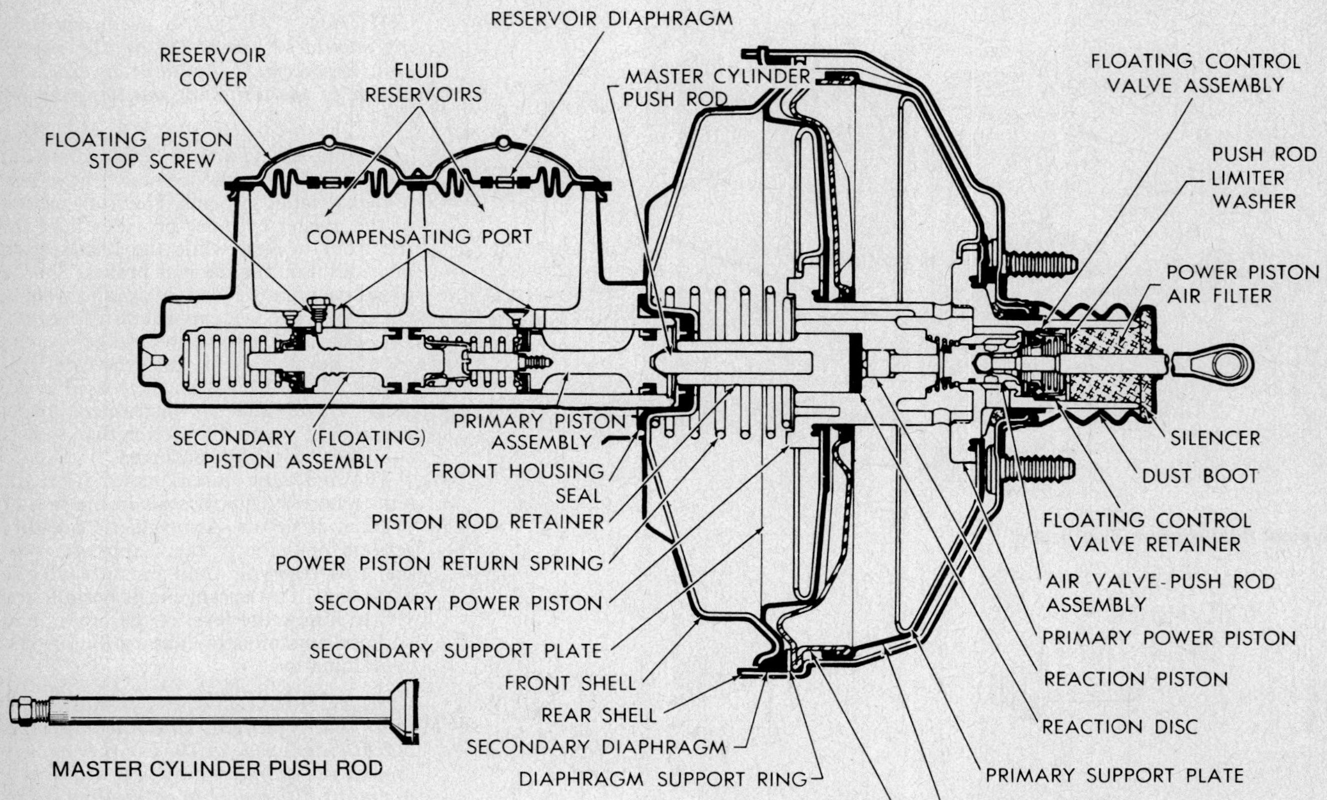

BRAKES

RESERVOIR DIAPHRAGM

RESERVOIR COVER

FLUID RESERVOIRS

MASTER CYLINDER PUSH ROD

FLOATING CONTROL VALVE ASSEMBLY

FLOATING PISTON STOP SCREW

PUSH ROD LIMITER WASHER

COMPENSATING PORT

POWER PISTON AIR FILTER

SECONDARY (FLOATING) PISTON ASSEMBLY

PRIMARY PISTON ASSEMBLY

SILENCER

DUST BOOT

FRONT HOUSING SEAL

FLOATING CONTROL VALVE RETAINER

PISTON ROD RETAINER

AIR VALVE-PUSH ROD ASSEMBLY

POWER PISTON RETURN SPRING

PRIMARY POWER PISTON

SECONDARY POWER PISTON

REACTION PISTON

SECONDARY SUPPORT PLATE

REACTION DISC

FRONT SHELL

REAR SHELL

PRIMARY SUPPORT PLATE

SECONDARY DIAPHRAGM

DIAPHRAGM SUPPORT RING

PRIMARY DIAPHRAGM

HOUSING DIVIDER

MASTER CYLINDER PUSH ROD

Typical dual master cylinder

2 Carefully insert the complete secondary piston and return spring assembly in the master cylinder bore.

3 Install the primary piston assembly in the master cylinder bore.

4 Depress the primary piston and install the snap ring in the cylinder bore groove.

5 Install the push rod, boot and retainer on the push rod, if so equipped. Install the push rod assembly into the primary piston. Make sure the retainer is properly seated and holding the push rod securely.

6 Position the inner end of the push rod boot (if so equipped) in the master cylinder body retaining groove.

7 Install the secondary piston stop bolt, if used, with an O-ring if screw is on bottom outside of master cylinder casting. It's always been a good idea to pre-bleed a master cylinder before reinstalling it in the car. It's far easier to purge air from the master cylinder on the bench than it is to bleed the air out through the entire brake system.

8 Install the cover and gasket on the master cylinder and secure the cover into position with the retainer.

Master Cylinder Push Rod Adjustment

After assembly of the master cylinder to the power section, the piston cup in the hydraulic cylinder should just clear the compensating port hole when the brake pedal if fully released. If the push rod is too long, it will hold the piston over the port.

A push rod that is too short, will give too much loose travel (excessive pedal play).

Apply the brakes and release the pedal all the way observing the brake fluid flow back into the master cylinder.

A full flow indicates the piston is coming back far enough to release the fluid.

A slow return of the fluid indicates the piston is not coming back far enough to clear the ports. The push rod adjustment is too tight, and should be shortened.

Proportioning Valve

The proportioning valve is possibly the most misunderstood valve arrangement on the car.

When the brake pedal is depressed the proportioning valve does all the thinking for the driver, regardless of severity of brake application.

Every car with disc brakes on the front and drum brakes on the rear requires a calibrated (non-repairable) proportioning valve. This controls car deceleration under all braking conditions.

FRONT METERING

The valve restricts pressure to the front disc brakes until pressure at the rear drum

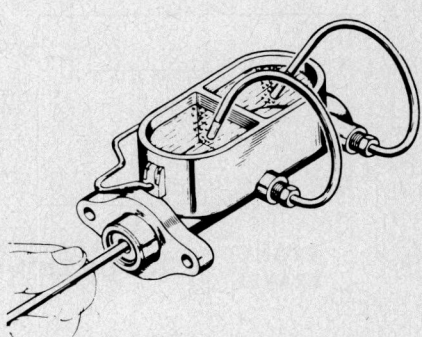

Pre-bleeding master cylinder

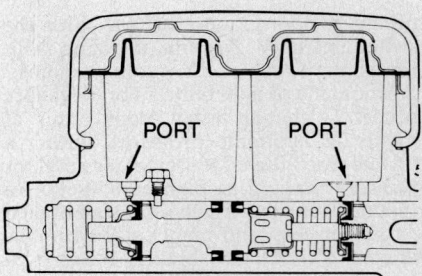

PORT   PORT

Feed and return ports

brakes is sufficient to overcome the force of brake shoe return springs. Above a "cut in" pressure, the valve meters increasing amounts of pressure to the front brakes until, at a "blend" point, metering ceases

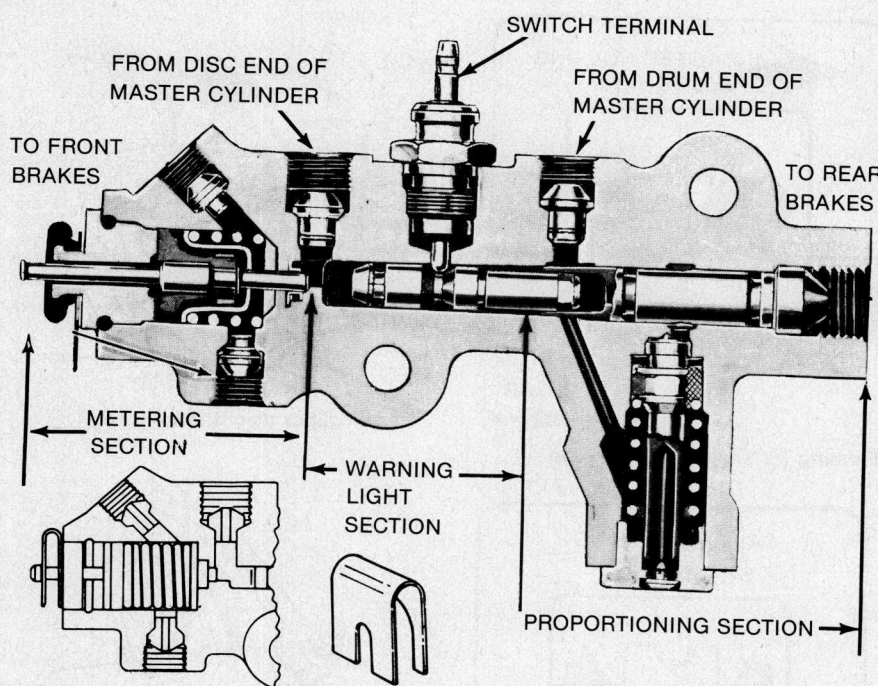

Hold valve out .060 in pressure bleed only-not necessary when using pedal bleed method

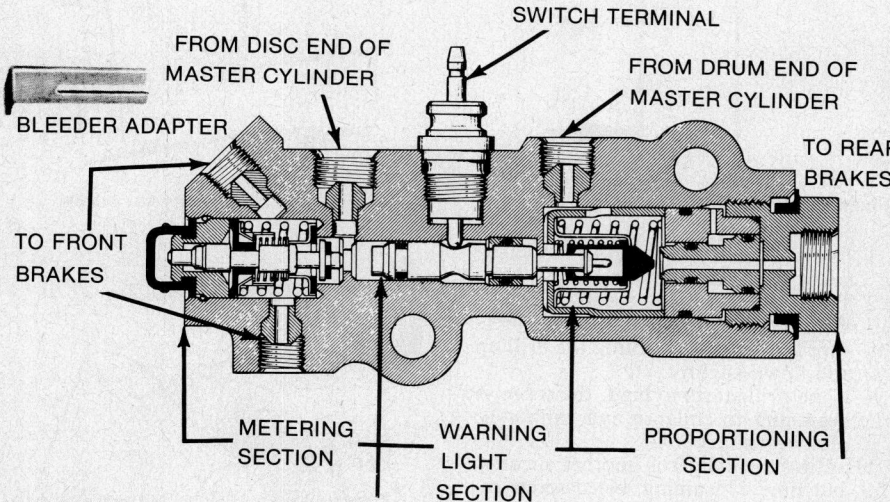

Push valve in when pressure bleeding-not necessary when using pedal bleed method

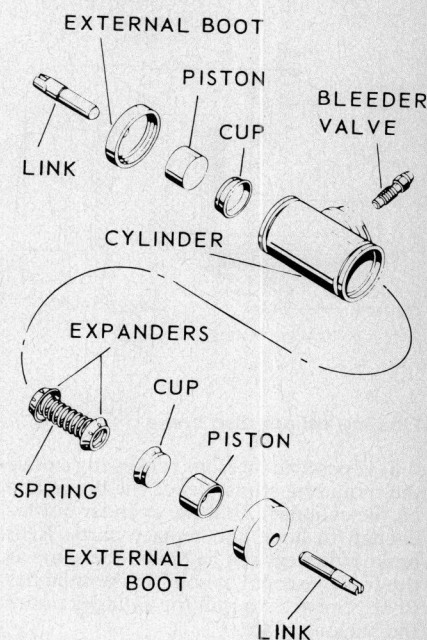

Wheel cylinder components

as the input pressure and front brake pressure become equal.

Without this balancing feature, the front discs would form too much of the work during easy rolling stops. Front brakes would be sensitive to extremely light pedal effort resulting in excessive dive, fast wear and uneven braking.

Dual System Warning Differential (Electrical)

The valve switches on the brake warning lamp, at the instrument panel, should a pressure loss occur in either the front or rear position of the split braking system.

After repairs are made, the lamp should go off, automatically.

If the light does not go out, bleed the brake system that is opposite the failed system. If front brakes failed, bleed the rear brakes, this should force the light control piston toward center.

If this fails, remove the terminal switch. If brake fluid is present in the electrical area, the seals are gone, replace the compete valve assembly.

REAR PROPORTIONING

During easy braking, this valve may remain inactive. Above a predetermined transition pressure point, the valve begins

to ratio input pressure, thus restraining pressure to the rear brakes. Because the vehicle weight transfer is toward the front on hard stops (dive), then a relatively smaller amount of the total braking force is desirable at the rear in order to closely match breaking to the actual axle load. However, should a pressure loss failure occur in the front system, a by-pass prevents proportioning and delivers full pressure to the rear brakes.

Without this balancing feature, excessive rear wheel skid could occur during severe braking actions.

Wheel Cylinders

The front and rear wheel cylinders contain a pair of opposed pistons fitted with rubber cups and compression spring to keep the cups tight against the pistons.

After removing wheel cylinders from brake support plate, remove boots from ends of cylinder. The pistons and cups are forced out of the barrel by the compression spring. Clean all component parts in alcohol or clean brake fluid. If cylinder is scratched or pitted, replace cylinder.

NOTE: Whenever a wheel cylinder is disassembled, replace the cups. Dip all component parts in hydraulic brake fluid upon assembly.

REBUILDING
Wheel Cylinder

Rebuilding can be done on the car, depending on the design of the backing plate. If the backing plate is recessed to the point that it is impossible to get a hone in the cylinder, the cylinder has to be removed from the car.

BRAKES

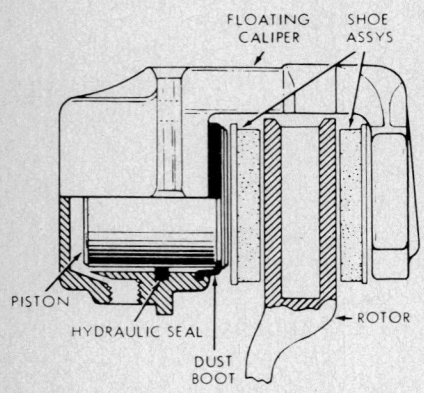

Floating caliper disc brake

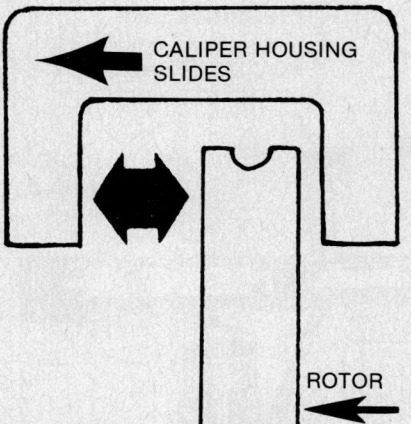

Floating (or sliding) caliper type

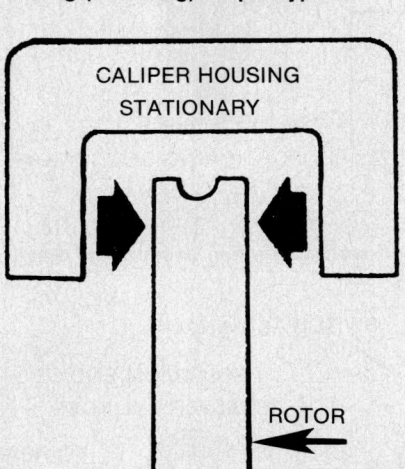

Fixed caliper type

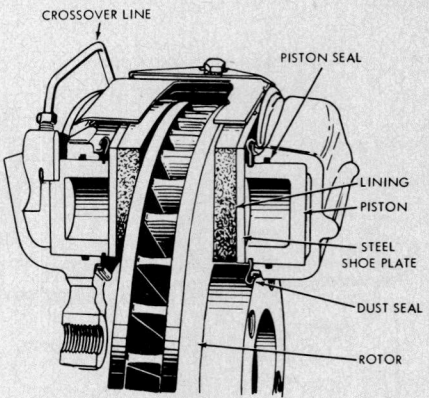

Fixed caliper disc brake

Replacing disc brake bleeder screw

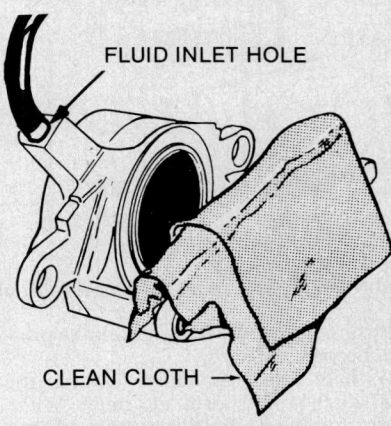

Removing piston hydraulically

It is possible on front brakes to remove the mounting studs, (leave the brake line on the cylinder). Pull the cylinder out far enough to hone and replace parts. Rear brake cylinders can be honed the same as the front, except the solid brake tube has to be removed, to pull the cylinder out of the backing plate.

Disc Brakes

Ther are two kinds of caliper type disc brakes:
1 Floating or sliding type.
2 Fixed caliper type.

The floating caliper straddles the rotor on a mount which permits limited caliper travel at right angle to the rotor. The hydraulic cylinder is located on the inboard side of the caliper housing. The instant the cylinder piston forces the inboard shoe against the inner surface of the rotor, the entire caliper assembly reacts in the opposite direction, thus applying the outboard shoe against the outer rotor surface. Braking force is equalized on both sides automatically by the reciprocal action of the caliper. The fixed caliper is rigidly mounted straddling the rotor. Pistons in two (or more) hydraulic cylinders, located on opposite sides of the caliper housing, press the brake shoes against the rotor.

Disc Brake Calipers

OVERHAUL

Field reports indicate that two factors determine whether to replace or rebuild calipers:
1 Can the piston or pistons be removed?
2 Will the bleed screw break off when removal is attempted? (Rebuilders will not accept a caliper with a broken bleed screw.)

Since there is no way to predict how a bleed screw will react, follow this porcedure to attempt removal.

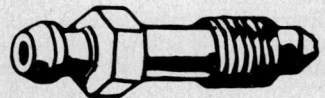

Bleed screw

1 Insert a drill shank into the bleed screw hole (snug fit).
2 Tap the screw on all sides.
3 With a six point wrench apply pressure gently while working the drill up and down slightly.
4 If the drill starts to bind, the screw is beginning to collapse and cannot be removed intact.

Heating the caliper is another successful, but time consuming, bleed screw removal technique.
1 Remove the caliper from the car.
2 Heat the caliper.
3 Shrink the bleed screw by applying dry ice, and attempt removal.

Disc Brake Bleeder Screw

REPLACEMENT

1 Using existing hole in bleed screw for pilot drill ¼ in. hole completely through existing bleeder.
2 Increase hole to $\frac{7}{16}$ in.
3 Tap hole using a ¼ in. (18-national pipe tap) ½ in. deep-(full thread.)
4 Install bleeder repair kit.
5 Test for leaks and full brake pedal pressure.

Frozen Single Piston

REMOVAL (HYDRAULIC METHOD)

1 Remove the caliper assembly from the rotor.
2 Remove brake pads and dust seal.

With brake flexible line connected and bleed screw closed apply enough pedal

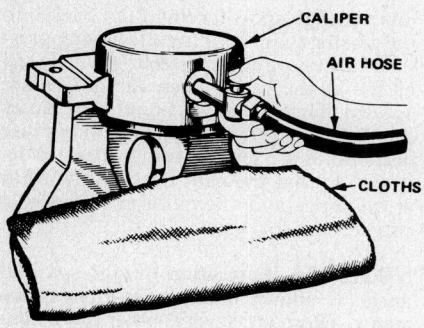

Removing piston pneumatically

pressure to move the piston most of the way out of the bore. (Brake fluid will begin to ooze past the piston inner seal.)

REMOVAL (PNEUMATIC METHOD)
1 Remove the caliper from the car.
2 With the bleed screw closed apply air pressure to force the piston out.

CHILTON CAUTION: *Hydraulic and pneumatic methods of piston removal should be done carefully to prevent personal injury or piston damage.*

Fixed Caliper Pistons
REMOVAL
NOTE: The hydraulic or pneumatic methods which apply to the single piston type caliper will not work on the multiple piston type brake caliper.

1 Remove the caliper from the car with the two halves separated.
2 Mount in a vise and use a piston puller (many types available) to remove the pistons.

Disc Brake Calipers
CLEANING
NOTE: Castings may be cleaned with any type cleaning fluid after all rubber seals have been removed

CHILTON CAUTION: *It is important that all traces of cleaning fluid be completely removed from the caliper casting.*

Honing cylinder bore

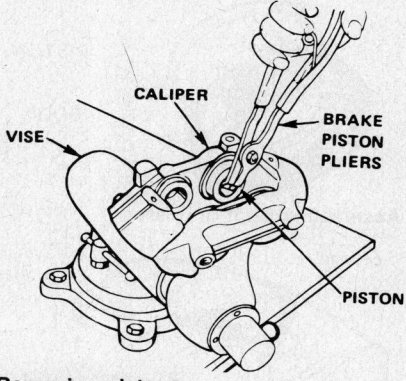

Removing pistons

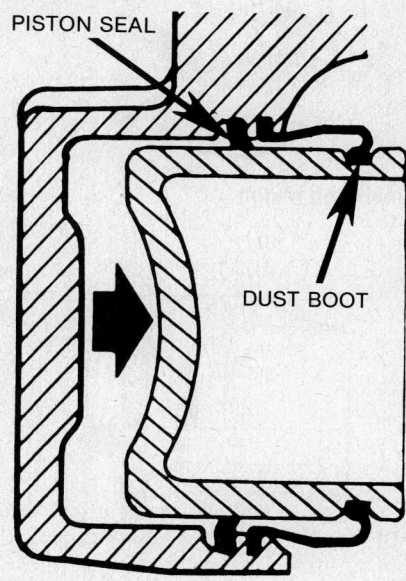

Brake applied

Rubber components are campatable with alcohol and/or brake fluid.

Use a lint free wiping cloth to clean the caliper and parts. Black stains on pistons or walls, caused by the seals, will not do harm; however, extreme cleanliness is essential. Blow out passages with compressed air. A fine grade of crocus cloth

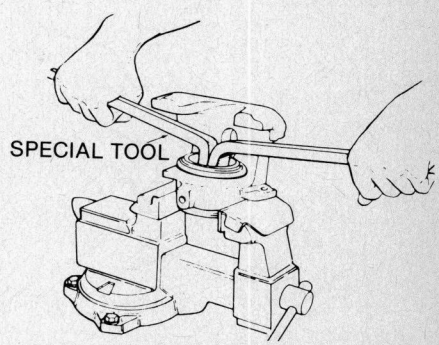

Removing hollow end piston

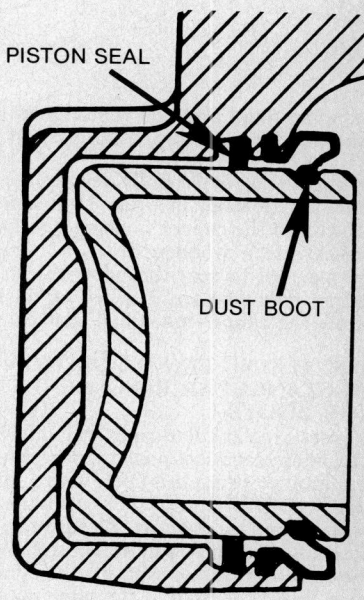

Brake released

may be used to correct minor imperfections in the cylinder bore. Slide crocus cloth with finger pressure in a circular rather than a lengthwise motion. Do not use any form of abrasive on a plated piston. Discard a piston which is pitted or has signs of plating wear.

Disc Brake Calipers
REBUILDING
If a fine stone honing of a caliper bore is necessary it should be done with skill and caution. Some cars can develop 800 p.s.i. hydraulic pressure on severe application so the honing must never exceed .003 in. Also the dust seal groove must be free of rust or nicks so that a perfect mating surface is possible on piston and casting.

INSTALLING STROKING TYPE SEALS AND BOOTS
Stretch boot and seal over piston and seat them in position. The seal lip on Bendix and Delco makes faces toward hydraulic pressure; boot lips face toward the brake shoe. Locate return spring, if used, in the cylinder and carefully start the piston into the cylinder to avoid nicking the seal. Alignment tools are available for in-

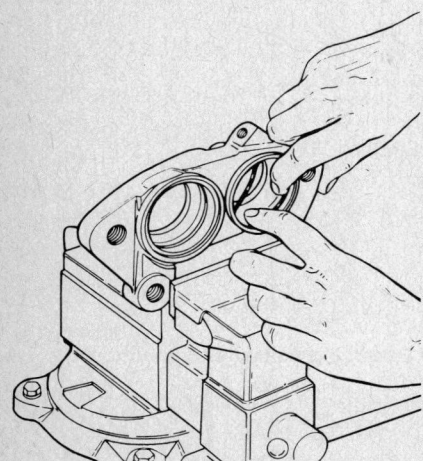

Installing fixed position rectangular ring seal (seal lip toward pressure side)

Assembling boot on piston

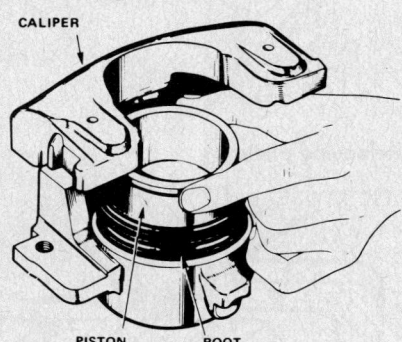

Installing piston

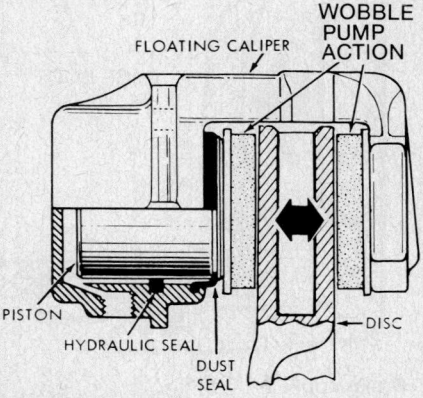

Wobble pump action

serting lip cup seals. Fully depress the piston into the bore in order to fasten the boot lip to the caliper housing. On Delco makes, use a wooden drift or a special seating tool to seat the boot ring in the caliper counter-bore. It must be flush or below the caliper machined surface.

INSTALLING FIXED POSITION (RECTANGULAR RING) SEALS AND BOOTS

Insert rectangular ring seal into bore and, at any location, push the ring into the seal groove. From this area, with a finger, gently work around the bore until the ring is seated in this channel. Be sure the ring does not twist or roll in the groove. When the boot lip is retained inside the cylinder bore, insert the boot in the same manner. Then work the inside of the boot over the pressure end of the piston, stretching the boot with a small plastic tool, and press the piston through the seal, straight in, until it bottoms. The inside of the boot should slide on the piston and come to rest in the boot groove. If the boot lip is retained outside of the cylinder bore, first stretch boot over the piston and seat it in its groove, then press the piston through the seal. Fully depress the piston, 50 to 100 pounds force will be required, in order to fasten the boot lip in place. On Delco-Moraine makes, use a wooden drift or a special seating tool to seat the metal boot ring in the caliper counterbore below the face of the caliper.

INSTALLING FIXED-CALIPER BRIDGE BOLTS

If the caliper contains internal fluid cross-over passages, be sure to install new O-ring seals at joints. Mate the caliper halves and install in-tensile strength bridge bolts. Never replace bridge bolts with ordinary standard hardware bolts. Manufacturers differ widely on permissible runout, but too much can sometimes be felt as a pulsation at the brake pedal. A wobble pump effect is created when a rotor is not perfectly smooth and the pad

hits the high spots forcing fluid back into the master cylinder. This alternating pressure causes a pulsating feeling which can be felt at the pedal when the brakes are applied. This excessive runout also causes the brakes to be out of adjustment because disc brakes are self-adjusting; they are designed so that the pads drag on the rotor at all times and therefore automatically compensate for wear.

NOTE: For illustration purposes a dial guage is shown making rotor measurements. There are several other more convenient types of measurement tools. (Disc illustrations are exaggerated views to more clearly emphasize the conditions.)

To check the actual runout of the rotor, first tighten the wheel spindle nut to a snug bearing adjustment, end-play removed. Fasten a dial indicator on the suspension at a convenient place so that the indicator stylus contacts the rotor face approximately one inch from its outer edge. Set the dial at zero. Check the total indicator reading while turning the rotor one full revolution. If the rotor is warped beyond the runout specification, it is likely that it can be successfully remachined.

"Lateral Runout": A wobbly movement of the rotor from side to side as it rotates. Excessive lateral runout causes the rotor faces to knock back the disc pads and can result in chatter, excessive pedal travel, pumping or fighting pedal and vibration during the breaking action.

"Parallelism" (lack of): Refers to the amount of variation in the thickness of the rotor. Excessive variation can cause pedal vibration or fight, front end vibrations and possible "grab" during the braking action; a condition comparable to an "out-of-round brake drum." Check parallelism

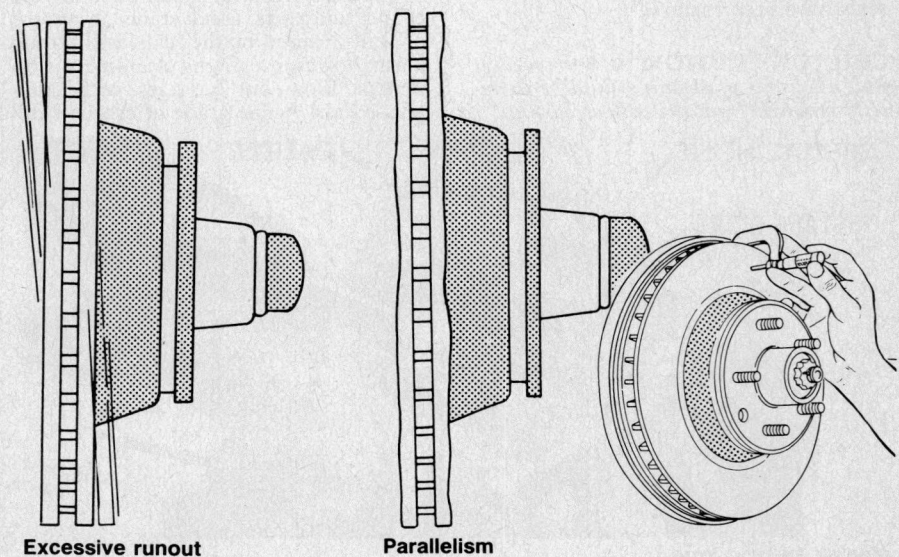

Excessive runout   **Parallelism**

Ideal rotor surface condition

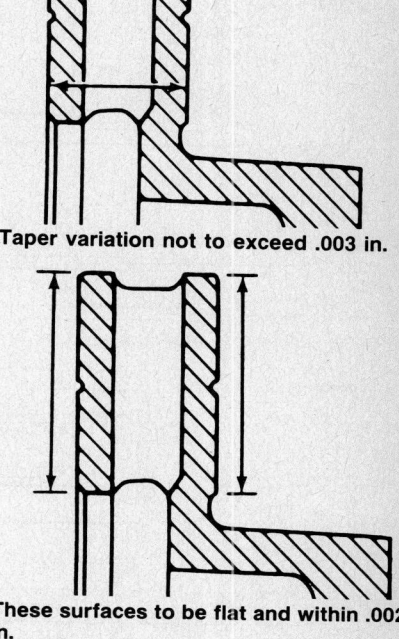

Taper variation not to exceed .003 in.

These surfaces to be flat and within .002 in.

with a micrometer. "Mike" the thickness at eight or more equally spaced points, equally distant from the outer edge of the rotor, preferrably at mid-points of the braking surface. Parallelism then is the amount of variation between maximum and minimum measurements.

"Surface or Micro-inch finish, flatness, smoothness": Different from parallelism, these terms refer to the degree of perfection of the flat surface on each side of the rotor; that is, the minute hills, valleys and swirls inherent in machining the surface. In a visual inspection, the remachined surface should have a fine ground polish with, at most, only a faint trace of non-directional swirls.

Hydro-Boost Hydraulic Brake Booster

ON-CAR TEST

The Hydro-Boost differs from tha vacuum brake boosters not only in the source of power (hydraulic versus vacuum) but in the fact that it is also a part of another major sub-system of the car—the power steering system. Therefore, problems or malfunctions in the steering system may affect the operation of the booster, just as a problem in the booster may effect the steering system. The following noises are

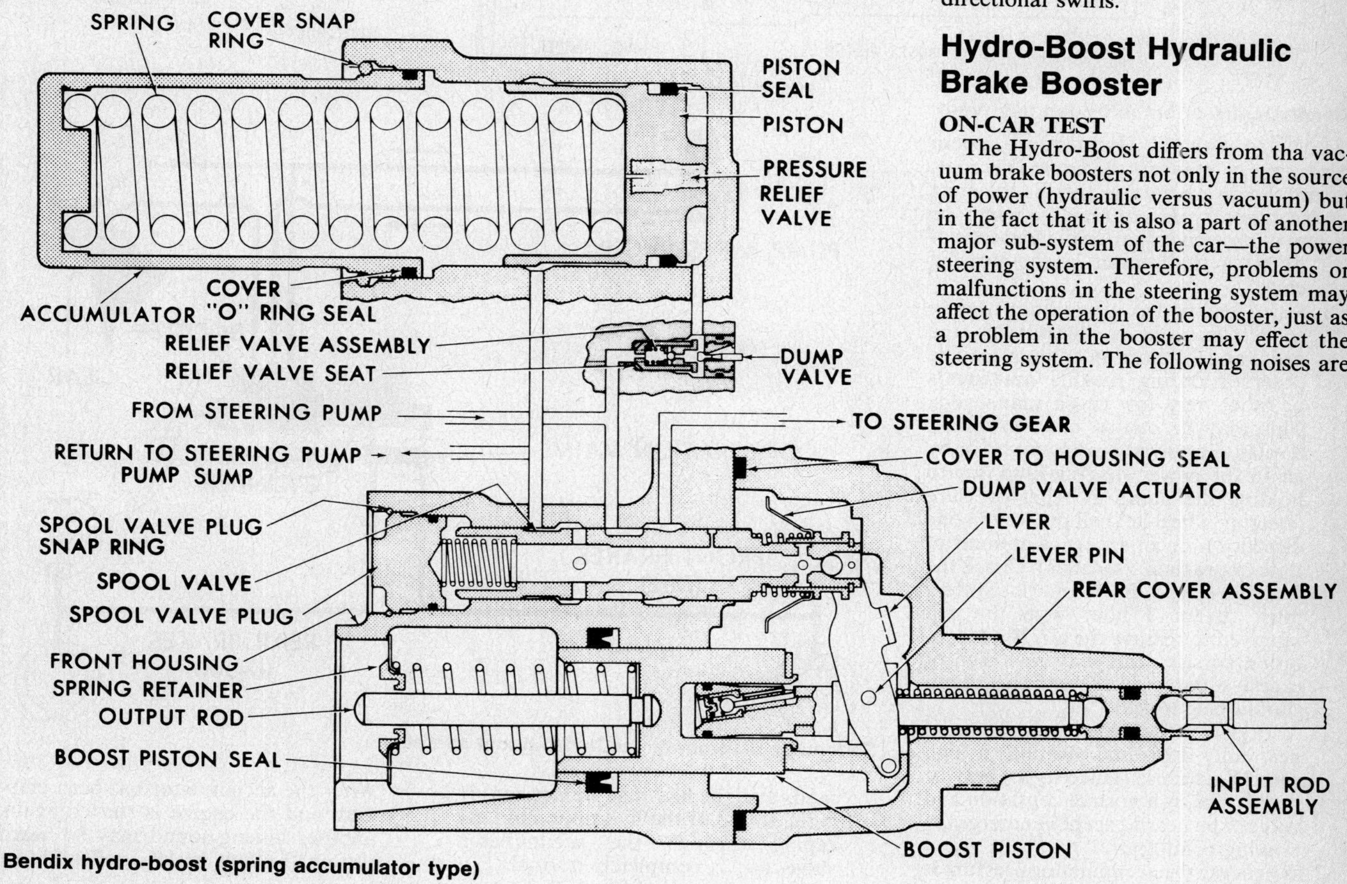

SPRING
COVER SNAP RING
PISTON SEAL
PISTON
PRESSURE RELIEF VALVE
COVER
ACCUMULATOR "O" RING SEAL
RELIEF VALVE ASSEMBLY
RELIEF VALVE SEAT
DUMP VALVE
FROM STEERING PUMP
TO STEERING GEAR
RETURN TO STEERING PUMP PUMP SUMP
COVER TO HOUSING SEAL
DUMP VALVE ACTUATOR
SPOOL VALVE PLUG SNAP RING
LEVER
LEVER PIN
SPOOL VALVE
REAR COVER ASSEMBLY
SPOOL VALVE PLUG
FRONT HOUSING
SPRING RETAINER
OUTPUT ROD
BOOST PISTON SEAL
INPUT ROD ASSEMBLY
BOOST PISTON

Bendix hydro-boost (spring accumulator type)

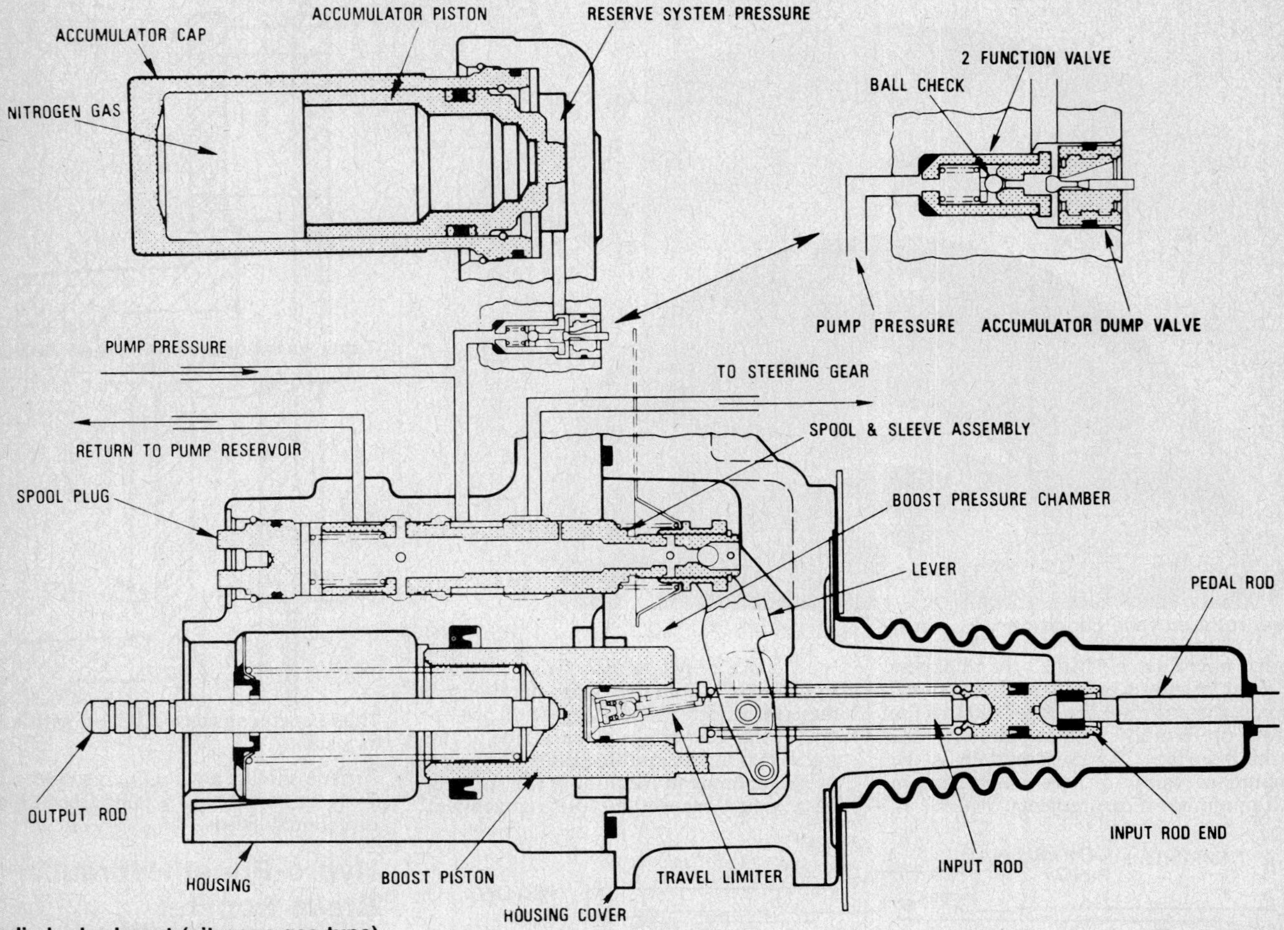

ACCUMULATOR CAP

ACCUMULATOR PISTON

RESERVE SYSTEM PRESSURE

NITROGEN GAS

2 FUNCTION VALVE

BALL CHECK

PUMP PRESSURE   ACCUMULATOR DUMP VALVE

PUMP PRESSURE

RETURN TO PUMP RESERVOIR

TO STEERING GEAR

SPOOL & SLEEVE ASSEMBLY

SPOOL PLUG

BOOST PRESSURE CHAMBER

LEVER

PEDAL ROD

OUTPUT ROD

HOUSING

BOOST PISTON

HOUSING COVER

TRAVEL LIMITER

INPUT ROD

INPUT ROD END

Bendix hydro-boost (nitrogen gas type)

associated with the Hydro-boost system and may or may not be cause for complaint. Some are normal and for the most part temporary in nature. Others may be a sign of excessive wear or the presence of air in either the booster or the steering system.

1 Moan or low frequency hum usually accompanied by a vibration in the pedal and/or steering column may be observed during parking maneuvers or other very low speed maneuvers. This may be caused by a low fluid level in the power steering pump or by air in the power steering fluid due to holding the pump at relief pressure (steering wheel held all the way in one direction) for an excessive amount of time (more than 5 seconds). Check the fluid level and fill to mark. System must sit for 1 hour with the cap removed to remove the air. If the condition persists, this may be a sign of excesive pump wear and the pump should be checked.

2 At or near power runout, (brake pedal near fully depressed position) a high speed fluid noise (faucet type) may be heard. This is a normal condition and will not be heard except in emergency braking conditions.

3 Whenever the accumulator pressure is

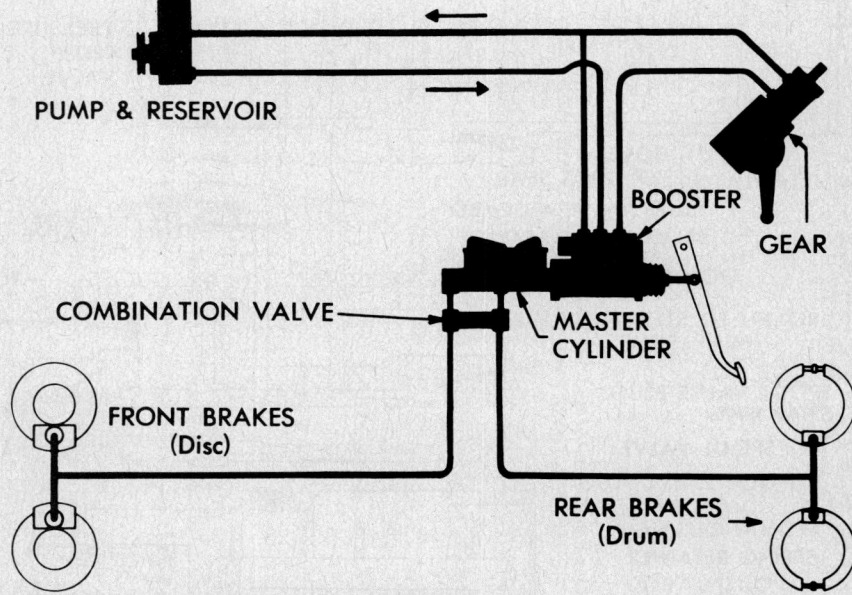

PUMP & RESERVOIR

BOOSTER

GEAR

COMBINATION VALVE

MASTER CYLINDER

FRONT BRAKES (Disc)

REAR BRAKES (Drum)

Schematic diagram of the hydro-boost system

used, a slight hiss may be noticed. It is the sound of the hydraulic fluid escaping through the accumulator valve, and is completely normal.

4 After the accumulator has been emptied, and the engine is started again, another hissing sound may be heard during the first brake application or

the first steering maneuver. This is caused by the fluid rushing through the accumulator charging orifice. It is normal and will only be heard once after the accumulator is emptied. However, if this sound continues, even though no apparent accumulator pressure assist was made, it could be an indication that the accumulator is not holding pressure and should be checked.

BOOSTER FUNCTIONAL TEST

With the engine off apply the brake pedal several times until the accumulator is completely depleted. Depress the service brake pedal (approximately 40 pounds pedal force) and start the engine. The pedal should fall and then push back against driver's foot.

ACCUMULATOR LEAKDOWN TEST

Start engine and charge accumulator by either applying the service break (approximately 100 pounds pedal force) or by turning the steering wheel from stop to stop. Turn off engine and let car sit for one hour. After one hour there should be three power assisted applies with engine stopped.

TROUBLESHOOTING HYDRO-BOOST BRAKE BOOSTER

CONDITION	CAUSE	CORRECTION
Excessive Brake Pedal Effort	Loose or broken power steering pump belt.	Tighten or replace the belt.
	No fluid in power steering reservoir.	Fill reservoir and check for external leaks.
	Leaks in power steering, booster or accumulator hoses.	Replace faulty parts.
	Leaks at tube fittings, power steering, booster or accumulator connections.	Tighten fittings or replace tube seats, if faulty.
	External leakage at accumulator.	Replace "O" ring and retainer.
	Faulty booster piston seal causing leakage at booster flange vent.	Overhaul with new seal kit.
	Faulty booster input rod seal with leakage at input rod end.	Replace booster.
	Faulty booster cover seal with leakage between housing and cover.	Overhaul with new seal kit.
	Faulty booster spool plug seal.	Overhaul with spool plug seal kit.
Slow Brake Pedal Return	Excessive seal friction in booster.	Overhaul with new seal kit.
	Faulty spool action.	Flush steering system while pumping brake pedal.
	Broken piston return spring.	Replace spring.
	Restriction in return line from booster to pump reservoir.	Replace line.
	Broken spool return spring.	Replace spring.
Grabby Brakes	Broken spool return spring.	Replace spring.
	Faulty spool action caused by contamination in system.	Flush steering system while pumping brake pedal.
Booster Chatters — Pedal Vibrates	Power steering pump belt slips.	Tighten belt.
	Low fluid level in power steering pump reservoir.	Fill reservoir and check for external leaks.
	Faulty spool operation caused by contamination in system.	Flush steering system while pumping brake pedal.
Accumulator Leak Down — System does not hold charge	Contamination in steering hydro-boost system	Flush steering system while pumping brake pedal.
	Internal leakage in accumulator system	Overhaul unit using accumulator rebuild kit and seal kit.

INTRODUCTION

Introduction

The rear axle must transmit power through 90°. To accomplish this, straight cut bevel gears or spiral bevel gears were used. This type of gear is satisfactory for differential side gears, but since the centerline of the gears must intersect, they rapidly became unsuited for ring and pinion gears. The lowering of the driveshaft brought about a variation of the bevel gear, which is called the hypoid gear. This type of gear does not require a meeting of the gear centerlines and can therefore be underslung, relative to the centerline of the ring gear.

Gear Ratios

The drive axle of a vehicle is said to have a certain axle ratio. This number (usually a whole number and a decimal fraction) is actually a comparison of the number of gear teeth on the ring gear and the pinion gear. For example, a 4.11 rear means that theoretically, there are 4.11 teeth on the ring gear and one tooth on the pinion. Actually, on a 4.11 rear, there are 37 teeth on the ring gear and nine teeth on the pinion gear. By dividing the number of teeth on the pinion gear into the number of teeth on the ring gear, the numerical axle ratio (4.11) is obtained. This also provides a good method of ascertaining exactly which axle ratio one is dealing with.

Differential Operation

The differential is an arrangement of gears that permits the rear wheels to turn at different speeds when cornering and divides the torque between the axle shafts. The differential gears are mounted on a pinion shaft and the gears are free to rotate on this shaft. The pinion shaft is fitted in a bore in the differential case and is at right angles to the axle shafts.

Power flow through the differential is as follows. The drive pinion, which is turned by the driveshaft, turns the ring gear. The ring gear, which is bolted to the differential case, rotates the case. The differential pinion forces the pinion gears against the side gears. In cases where both wheels have equal traction, the pinion gears do not rotate on the pinion shaft, because the input force of the pinion gear is divided equally between the two side gears. Consequently the pinion gears revolve with the pinion shaft, although they do not revolve on the pinion shaft itself. The side gears, which are splined to the axle shafts, and meshed with the pinion gears, rotate the axle shafts.

When it becomes necessary to turn a corner, the differential becomes effective and allows the axle shafts to rotate at different speeds. As the inner wheel slows down, the side gear splined to the inner

GENERAL DRIVE AXLE DIAGNOSTIC GUIDE
(Also see following text for further differential diagnosis.)

CONDITION	POSSIBLE CAUSE	CORRECTION
Rear Wheel Noise	(a) Loose Wheel.	(a) Tighten loose wheel nuts.
	(b) Spalled wheel bearing cup or cone.	(b) Check rear wheel bearings. If spalled or worn, replace.
	(c) Defective or brinelled wheel bearing.	(c) Defective or brinelled bearings must be replaced. Check rear axle shaft endplay.
	(d) Excessive axle shaft endplay.	(d) Readjust axle shaft endplay.
	(e) Bent or sprung axle shaft flange.	(e) Replace bent or sprung axle shaft.
Scoring of Differential Gears and Pinions	(a) Insufficient lubrication.	(a) Replace scored gears. Scoring marks on the pressure face of gear teeth or in the bore are caused by instantaneous fusing of the mating surfaces. Scored gears should be replaced. Fill rear axle to required capacity with proper lubricant.
	(b) Improper grade of lubricant.	(b) Replace scored gears. Inspect all gears and bearings for possible damage. Clean and refill axle to required capacity with proper lubricant.
	(c) Excessive spinning of one wheel.	(c) Replace scored gears. Inspect all gears, pinion bores and shaft for scoring, or bearings for possible damage.
Tooth Breakage (Ring Gear and Pinion)	(a) Overloading.	(a) Replace gears. Examine other gears and bearings for possible damage. Avoid future overloading.
	(b) Erratic clutch operation.	(b) Replace gears, and examine remaining parts for possible damage. Avoid erratic clutch operation.
	(c) Ice-spotted pavements.	(c) Replace gears. Examine remaining parts for possible damage. Replace parts as required.
	(d) Improper adjustment.	(d) Replace gears. Examine other parts for possible damage. Be sure ring gear and pinion backlash is correct.
Rear Axle Noise	(a) Insufficient lubricant.	(a) Refill rear axle with correct amount of the proper lubricant. Also check for leaks and correct as necessary.
	(b) Improper ring gear and pinion adjustment.	(b) Check ring gear and pinion tooth contact.
	(c) Unmatched ring gear and pinion.	(c) Remove unmatched ring gear and pinion. Replace with a new matched gear and pinion set.
	(d) Worn teeth on ring gear or pinion.	(d) Check teeth on ring gear and pinion for contact. If necessary, replace with new matched set.
	(e) End-play in drive pinion bearings.	(e) Adjust drive pinion bearing preload.
	(f) Side play in differential bearings.	(f) Adjust differential bearing preload.
	(g) Incorrect drive gearlash.	(g) Correct drive gear lash.
	(h) Limited-Slip differential—moan and chatter.	(h) Drain and flush lubricant. Refill with proper lubricant.

GENERAL DRIVE AXLE DIAGNOSTIC GUIDE
(Also see following text for further differential diagnosis.)

CONDITION	POSSIBLE CAUSE	CORRECTION
Loss of Lubricant	(a) Lubricant level too high.	(a) Drain excess lubricant.
	(b) Worn axle shaft oil seals.	(b) Replace worn oil seals with new ones. Prepare new seals before replacement.
	(c) Cracked rear axle housing.	(c) Repair or replace housing as required.
	(d) Worn drive pinion oil seal.	(d) Replace worn drive pinion oil seal with a new one.
	(e) Scored and worn companion flange.	(e) Replace worn or scored companion flange and oil seal.
	(f) Clogged vent.	(f) Remove obstructions.
	(g) Loose carrier housing bolts or housing cover screws.	(g) Tighten bolts or cover screws to specifications and fill to correct level with proper lubricant.
Overheating of Unit	(a) Lubricant level too low.	(a) Refill rear axle.
	(b) Incorrect grade of lubricant.	(b) Drain, flush and refill rear axle with correct amount of the proper lubricant.
	(c) Bearings adjusted too tightly.	(c) Readjust bearings.
	(d) Excessive wear in gears.	(d) Check gears for excessive wear or scoring. Replace as necessary.
	(e) Insufficient ring gear-to-pinion clearance.	(e) Readjust ring gear and pinion backlash and check gears for possible scoring.

wheel axle shaft also slows down. The pinion gears act as balancing levers by maintaining equal tooth loads to both gears while allowing unequal speeds of rotation at the axle shafts. If the vehicle speed remians constant, and the inner wheel slows down to 90 percent of vehicle speed, the outer wheel will speed up to 110 percent.

Limited-Slip Differential Operation

Limited-slip differentials provide driving force to the wheel with the best traction before the other wheel begins to spin. This is accomplished through clutch plates or cones. The clutch plates or cones are located between the side gears and inner wall of the differential case. When they are squeezed together through spring tension and outward force from the side gears, three reactions occur. Resistance on the side gears causes more torque to be exerted on the clutch packs or clutch cones. Rapid one-wheel spin cannot occur, because the side gear is forced to turn at the same speed as the case. Most important, with the side gear and the differential case turning at the same speed, the other wheel is forced to rotate in the same direction and at the same speed as the differential case. Thus driving force is applied to the wheel with the better traction.

NOISE DIAGNOSIS

Noise Diagnosis

The most essential part of rear axle service is proper diagnosis of the problem. Bent or broken axle shafts or broken gears pose little problem, but isolating an axle noise and correctly interpreting the problem can be extremely difficult, even for an experienced mechanic.

Any gear driven unit will produce a certain amount of noise, therefore, a specific dignosis for each individual unit is the best practice. Acceptable or normal noise can be classified as a slight noise heard only at certain speeds or under unusual conditions. This noise tends to reach a peak at 40–60 mph, depending on the road condition, load, gear ratio and tire size. Frequently, other noises are mistakenly diagnosed as coming from the rear axle. Vehicle noises from tires, transmission, driveshaft, U-joints and front and rear wheel bearings will often be mistaken as emanating from the rear axle. Raising the tire pressure to eliminate tire noise (although this will not silence mud or snow treads), listening for noise at varying speeds and road conditions and listening for noise at drive and coast conditions will aid in diagnosing alleged rear axle noises.

External Noise Elimination

It is advisable to make a thorough road test to determine whether the noise originates in the rear axle or whether it originates from the tires, engine, transmission, wheel bearings or road surface. Noise originating from other places cannot be corrected by overhauling the rear axle.

Road Noise

Brick roads or rough surfaced concrete, may cause a noise which can be mistaken as coming from the rear axle. Driving on a different type of road, (smooth asphalt or dirt) will determine whether the road is the cause of the noise. Road noise is usually the same on drive or coast conditions.

Tire Noise

Tire noise can be mistaken as rear axle noises, even though the tires on the front are at fault. Snow tread and mud tread tires or tires worn unevenly will frequently cause vibrations which seem to originate elsewhere; *temporarily, and for test purposes only*, inflate the tires to 40–50 lbs. This will significantly alter the noise produced by the tires, but will not alter noise from the rear axle. Noises from the rear axle will normally cease at speeds below 30 mph on coast, while tire noise will continue at lower tone as car speed is decreased. The rear axle noise will usually change from drive conditions to coast conditions, while tire noise will not. Do

not forget to lower the tire pressure to normal after the test is complete.

Engine and Transmission Noise

Engine and transmission noises also seem to originate in the rear axle. Road test the vehicle and determine at which speed the noise is most pronounced. Stop the car in a quiet place to avoid interfering noises. With the transmission in neutral, run the engine slowly through the engine speeds corresponding to the car speed at which the noise was most noticeable. If a similar noise was produced with the car standing still, the noise is not in the rear axle, but somewhere in the engine or transmission.

Front Wheel Bearing Noise

Front wheel bearing noises, sometimes confused with rear axle noises, will not change when comparing drive and coast conditions. While holding the car speed steady, lightly apply the footbrake. This will often cause the wheel bearing noise to lessen, as some of the weight is taken off the bearing. Front wheel bearings are easily checked by jacking up the wheels and spinning the wheels. Shaking the wheels will also determine if the wheel bearings are excessively loose.

Rear Axle Noises

If a logical test of the vehicle shows that the noise is not caused by external items, it can assumed that the noise originates from the rear axle. The rear axle should be tested on a smooth level road to avoid road noise. It is not advisable to test the axle by jacking up the rear wheels and running the car.

True rear axle noises generally fall into two classes; gear noise and bearing noises, and can be caused by a faulty driveshaft, faulty wheel bearings, worn differential or pinion shaft bearings, U-joint misalignment, worn differential side gears and pinions, or mismatched, improperly adjusted, or scored ring and pinion gears.

REAR WHEEL BEARING NOISE

A rough rear wheel bearing causes a vibration or growl which will continue with the car coasting or in neutral. A brinelled rear wheel bearing will also cause a knock or click approximately every two revolutions of the rear wheel, due to the fact that the bearing rollers do not travel at the same speed as the rear wheel and axle. Jack up the rear wheels and spin the wheel slowly, listening for signs of a rough or brinelled wheel bearing.

DIFFERENTIAL SIDE GEAR AND PINION NOISE

Differential side gears and pinions seldom cause noise, since their movement is relatively slight on straight ahead driving. Noise produced by these gears will be more noticeable on turns.

PINION BEARING NOISE

Pinion bearing failures can be distinguished by their speed of rotation, which is higher than side bearings or axle bearings. Rough or brinelled pinion bearings cause a continuous low pitch whirring or scraping noise beginning at low speeds.

SIDE BEARING NOISE

Side bearings produce a constant rough noise, which is slower than the pinion bearing noise. Side bearing noise may also fluctuate in the above rear wheel bearing test.

GEAR NOISE

Two basic types of gear noise exist. First, is the type produced by bent or broken gear teeth which have been forcibly damaged. The noise from this type of damage is audible over the entire speed

NOISE DIAGNOSIS CHART

PROBLEM	CAUSE
1. Identical noise in Drive or Coast conditions	1. Road noise Tire noise Front wheel bearing noise
2. Noise changes on a different type of road.	2. Road noise Tire noise
3. Noise tone lowers as car speed is lowered	3. Tire noise
4. Similar noise is produced with car standing and driving.	4. Engine noise Transmission noise
5. Vibration	5. Rough rear wheel bearing Unbalanced or damaged driveshaft Unbalanced tire Worn universal joint in driveshaft Misaligned drive shaft at companion flange Excessive companion flange runout
6. A knock or click approximately every two revolutions of rear wheel	6. Brinelled rear wheel bearing
7. Noise most pronounced on turns	7. Differential side gear and pinion wear or damage
8. A continuous low pitch whirring or scraping noise starting at relatively low speed	8. Damaged or worn pinion bearing
9. Drive noise, coast noise or float noise	9. Damaged or worn ring and pinion gear
10. Clunk on acceleration or deceleration	10. Worn differential cross-shaft in case
11. Clunk on stops	11. Insufficient grease in driveshaft slip yoke
12. Groan in Forward or Reverse	12. Improper differential lubricant
13. Chatter on turns	13. Improper differential lubricant Worn clutch plates
14. Clunk or knock during operation on rough roads.	14. Excessive end-play of axle shafts to differential cross-shaft

range. Scoring or damage to the hypoid gear teeth generally results from insufficient lubricant, improper lubricant, improper breakin, insufficient gear backlash, improper ring and pinion gear alignment or loss of torque on the drive pinion nut. If corrected, the scoring will lead to eventual erosion or fracture of the gear teeth. Hypoid gear tooth fracture can also be caused by extended overloading of the gear set (fatigue fracture) or by shock overloading (sudden failure). Differential and side gears rarely give trouble, but common causes of differential failure are shock loading, extended overloading and differential pinion seizure at the cross-shaft, resulting from excessive wheel spin and consequent lubricant breakdown.

The second type of gear noise pertains to the mesh pattern between the ring and pinion gears. This type of abnormal gear noise can be recognized as a cycling pitch or whine audible in either drive, float or coast conditions. Gear noises can be

recognized as they tend to peak out in a narrow speed range and remain constant in pitch, whereas bearing noises tend to vary in pitch with vehicle speeds. Noises produced by the ring and pinion gears will generally follow the pattern below.

A. Drive Noise: Produced under vehicle acceleration.

B. Coast Noise: Produced while the car coasts with a closed throttle.

C. Float Noise: Occurs while maintaining constant car speed (just enough to keep speed constant) on a level road.

D. Drive, Coast and Float Noise: These noises will vary in tone and speed and be very rough or irregular if the differential or pinion shaft bearings are worn.

BEARING DIAGNOSIS

Bearing Diagnosis

This section will help on the diagnosis of bearing failure and the causes. Bearing dignosis can be very helpful in determining the cause of rear axle failure. The illustrations will help to take some of the guess-work out of determining when to

reuse a bearing and when to replace a bearing with a new one.

When disassembly a rear axle, the general condition of all bearings should be noted and classified where possible. Proper recognition of the cause will help in correcting the problem and avoiding a repetition of the failure.

Some of the common causes of bearing failure are:

a. Abuse during assembly or dissambly.
b. Improper assembly methods.
c. Improper or inadequate lubrication.
d. Bearing contact with dirt or water.
e. Wear caused by dirt or metal chips.
f. Corrosion or rust.

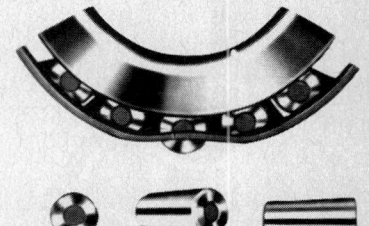

Abrasive Roller Wear
Pattern on races and rollers caused by fine abrasives. Clean all parts and housings, check seals and bearings. Replace bearing if leaking, rough or noisy in operation.

Bent Cage
Cage damage is due to improper handling or careless tool usage. Replace bearing.

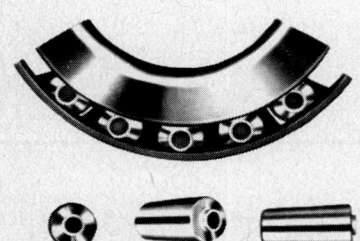

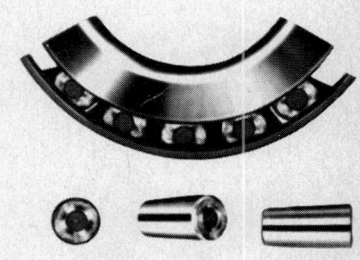

Abrasive Step Wear
Pattern on roller ends is caused by fine abrasives. Clean all parts and housings. Check seals and bearings. Replace bearing if leaking, rough or noisy.

Etching
Bearing surfaces appear gray or grayish black in color. Related etching away of material is usually found at roller spacing gaps. Replace bearing. Check seals for condition and check for proper lubrication.

Galling
Metal smears on roller ends are due to overheating, lubricant failure or chronic overloaded condition. This is especially applicable to station wagons.

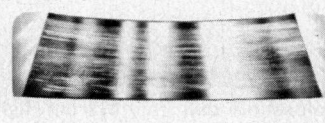

Indentations
Surface depressions on race and rollers are caused by hard particles of foreign material. Clean all parts and housings. Check seals and replace bearing if rough or noisy.

Cage Wear
Wear around outside diameter of cage and roller pockets caused by abrasive material and/or inadequate lubrication. Clean all related parts and housings. Check seals and replace bearing.

Misalignment
Outer race misalignment is due to foreign object. Clean related parts and replace bearing. Make sure races are properly seated.

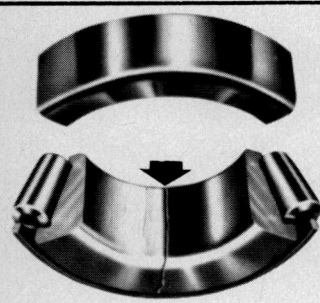

Cracked Inner Race
Race has cracked due to improper fit, cocking or poor bearing seats. Replace bearing and correct bearing seats.

Smears
Smearing of metal is due to slippage. This can be caused by poor fit, improper lubrication, overheating, chronic overloads or handling damage. Replace bearing and clean all related parts. Also check for proper fit and lubrication.

Brinelling
Surface indentations in raceway are caused by rollers that are either under impact loading or vibration while the bearing is not rotating. Replace bearing if rough or noisy.

Frettage
Corrosion set up by the small relative movement of parts which have no lubrication. Replace bearing and clean all related parts. Check seals and ensure proper lubrication.

Stain Discoloration
Discoloration can range from light brown to black. It is caused by incorrect lubricant or moisture. Re-use the bearing if stains can be removed by light polishing, or, if no evidence of overheating can be determined. Check seals and related parts for damage.

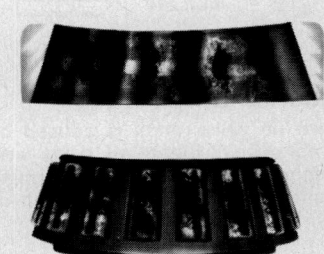

Heat Discoloration
Heat discoloration can range from faint yellow to dark blue. This condition is a result of chronic overloading—particularly in station wagons—or use of improper lubricant. Excessive heat can cause softening of races and rollers.

To check for loss of temper on races or rollers, a simple file test may be made. A file drawn over a part that has suffered loss of temper will grab and cut the metal. A file drawn over a hard part will glide readily with no metal cutting.

Replace bearing if overheating damage is indicated. Check seals and other related parts.

Fatigue Spalling
Flaking of surface metal results from fatigue. Replace bearing and clean all related parts.

g. Seizing to overloading.

h. Overheating.

i. Frettage of the bearing seats.

j. Brinelling from impact or shock loading.

k. Manufacture defects.

l. Pitting due to fatique.

To avoid damage to the bearing from improper handling, it is best to treat a used bearing the same as a new bearing. Always work in a clean area with clean tools. Remove all outside dirt from the housing before exposing a bearing and clean all bearing seats before installing a bearing.

Caution Never spin a bearing, either by hand or with compressed air, as this will lead to almost certain bearing failure.

LIMITED SLIP DIFFERENTIAL DIAGNOSIS

Limited-Slip Differential Dignosis

Lubrication

The use of proper lubricant is very important in limited-slip type drive axles. The forces applied when cornering tend to apply the clutch pack or clutch cones. The use of the wrong lubricant can cause the clutch services to grab and chatter while turning. Always follow the manufacturer's recommendations regarding drive axle lubrication. When chatter is encountered, the differential lubricant should should be drained and refilled with the specified lubricant.

Testing

The clutch operation on all limited-slip type axles can be tested as follows. Refer to the manufacturer in question.

AMERICAN MOTORS "TWIN-GRIP"

1 With the engine off and the transmission in neutral, jack up one rear wheel.

2 Block the other wheel to prevent it from moving.

3 With a socket and a torque wrench on the axle shaft nut, turn the raised wheel foreward.

4 The torque required to move the wheel should be 70–80 ft lbs for 8⅞ in. axles or 80–120 ft lbs for 7-9/16 in. axles.

5 A breakaway torque which is less than the specified figure, indicates a need for repair or replacement.

CADILLAC CONTROLLED DIFFERENTIAL

This unit should not be serviced. If a malfunction exists that cannot be cured by changing the fluid, remove the unit and install a new one.

CHRYSLER CORP. SURE-GRIP

1 Place the vehicle on a hoist with the engine off and the automatic transmission in low gear).

2 Attempt to rotate the wheel by hand, by gripping the tire.

3 If it is extremely difficult, if not impossible, to rotate either wheel the Sure-Grip differential can be assumed to be performing satisfactorily.

4 If it is relatively easy to continously turn either rear wheel, the unit should be removed and replaced.

Caution The Sure-Grip differential is serviced as a unit only. Under no circumstances should the unit be disassembled and reinstalled.

FORD MOTOR COMPANY EQUA-LOK

1 Jack up one rear wheel and remove the wheel cover.

2 Block the other wheel front and rear to prevent the car from moving.

3 Using a 200 ft lbs capacity torque wrench on one of the wheel lug nuts, measure the torque to continuously rotate the wheel. The breakaway torque reading can be disregarded. The minimum torque to continuously rotate the wheel should be as follows.
All types except integral carrier type: 75 ft lbs
Integral carrier type axles: 50 ft lbs

4 If the minimum torque is not as specified, the differential should be checked for improper assembly.

FORD MOTOR COMPANY TRACTION-LOK

1 Follow the procedure for the Ford Motor Company Equa-Lok rear. The minimum torque to continuously rotate the wheel (disregarding the breakaway torque) shoul be at least 40 ft lbs.

GENERAL MOTORS CORP. (EXCEPT CADILLAC) POSITRACTION

1 Place the transmission in neutral.

2 Raise one rear wheel off the floor and block the other rear wheel (front and rear) to prevent the car from moving.

3 Install a torque wrench and extension on the lug nut and note the torque required to continuously rotate one rear wheel. Disregard the breakaway torque figure, as this may be a great deal higher.

4 The minimum torque to continuously rotate the rear wheel should be at least 35 ft lbs. If it is not, the rear axle is in need of service.

General Diagnosis

Improper operation of a limited-slip type rear axle is generally indicated by clutch slippage or grabbing, which will sometimes produce a whirring or chatter sound. Occasionally, this condition is induced by improper lubrication. Check the unit for the wrong type of lubricant or lubricant which has broken down or become contaminated. Replace the lubricant with the type specified by the manufacturer.

During normal operation, i.e., straight-ahead driving, both wheels are rotating at equal speeds, and the driving force is distributed equally between both wheels. When cornering, the inside wheel delivers extra driving force, causing slippage in both clutch packs. Therefore, if the wheel rotation of both rear wheels is not equal, the unit will constantly be functioning as if the car were cornering. This will cause constant slippage and lead to eventual failure of the unit. It is important that there be no excessive differences in wheel and tire size, wear pattern, or tire pressures between both rear wheels. Swerving on acceleration is an indication of one or more of the above conditions. Before attempting an overhaul or replacement operation, check both rear wheels for identical tire sizes, tire pressure, tire tread depth, and wear pattern.

DRIVE AXLES
REPAIR PROCEDURES

REPAIR PROCEDURES INDEX

	R&R Brake Drum	R&R Rear Hub	R&R Pressed-on Bearing From Axle	R&R Axle and Bearing	Install Outer Oil Seal Ⓑ	Install Inner Oil Seal Ⓑ	Axle Shaft Endplay Adj.	Install Pinion Oil Seal	Install Side Gear Seal
AMERICAN MOTORS (AMC & Jeep)									
AMC Passenger Cars & Jeep with tapered rear axle	1	2	9	3	4	5	6	7	None
Jeep Vehicles with flanged rear axle	1	Ⓐ	9	8	13	5	10		
CHRYSLER CORPORATION									
Compact Cars	1	Ⓐ	9	8	13	5	10	7	None
Mid-Size Cars	1	Ⓐ	9	8	13	5	10	7	None
Full-Size Cars	1	Ⓐ	9	8	13	5	10	7	None②
FORD MOTOR COMPANY									
Subcompact Cars	1	Ⓐ	9	8	13	5	10	7	None
Compact Cars	1	Ⓐ	9	8	13	5	10	7	None
Mid-Size Cars	1	Ⓐ	9	8	13	5	10	7	None
Full-Size Cars	1	Ⓐ	9	8	13	5	10	7	None②
GENERAL MOTORS CORPORATION									
Subcompact Cars	1	Ⓐ	9	8	13	5	10	7	None
Compact Cars	1	Ⓐ	9	8	13	5	10	7	None
Buick Mid-Size Cars	1	Ⓐ	9	8	13	5	10	7	None
Buick Full-Size Cars	1	Ⓐ	9	8	13	5	10	7	None
Cadillac (Except Eldorado & Seville)	1	Ⓐ	9	8	13	5	10	7	None
Cadillac Eldorado	1	See car chap.	See car chap.	See car chap.	See car chap.	See car chap.	None	See car chap.	See car chap.
Cadillac Seville	1	Ⓐ	9	8	13	5	10	7	None
Chevrolet Chevette	1	Ⓐ	None	8	None	5	10	12	None
Chevrolet Corvette	1	See car chap.	See car chap.	See car chap.	None	None	None	7	11
Chevrolet Mid-Size Cars	1	Ⓐ	9	8	13	5	10	7	None
Chevrolet Full-Size Cars	1	Ⓐ	9	8	13	5	10	7	None
Oldsmobile Mid-Size Cars	1	Ⓐ	9	8	13	5	10	7	None
Oldsmobile Full-Size Cars	1	Ⓐ	9	8	13	5	10	7	None
Oldsmobile Toronado	1	Ⓐ	9	8	13	5	10	7	None
Pontiac Mid-Size Cars	1	Ⓐ	9	8	13	5	10	7	None
Pontiac Full-Size Cars	1	Ⓐ	9	8	13	5	10	7	None

A. Rear hub is one piece with axle.
B. Procedures No. 5 and No. 13 apply only if the car is
equipped with an inner or outer seal.

REPAIR PROCEDURES

Repair Procedures
Procedure No. 1.
Removing Brake Drum

(ALL CARS)
1 With the weight of the car on the wheels, loosen each lug nut 1/4-turn.
2 Raise the car and support it safely on stands so that the wheels are clear off the floor.
3 Remove the lug nuts. Remove the drum retaining screws or nuts and slide the drum off of the studs. If the drum hangs up on the brake shoes, back off the shoes through the adjustment slot. It may be necessary to punch the metal out of the slot on cars with self-adjusting brakes.

B936

Procedure No. 2.
Removing and Replacing Rear Hub

(AMC ONLY)
REMOVAL

1 With the weight of the car on the wheels, remove the axle shaft nut, and loosen each lug nut 1/4-turn.
2 Raise and safely support the car so the wheels are clear of the floor.
3 Remove the lug nuts, wheel, and brake drum.
4 Attach a hub puller and remove the hub.

CAUTION: *Do not use the type of puller, that screws into the end of the axle and provides a surface for striking. The heavy blows necessary with this type of puller may damage the rear wheel bearings and the differential thrust block. A screw-type or wedge-type puller must be used.*

REPLACEMENT

1 If the same hub is being put back on, reverse the removal procedure and tighten the axle shaft nut to 250 ft. lbs. torque. Install a cotter key if the holes line up. If not, tighten the nut to the next slot and install the cotter key. Do not loosen the nut to align the holes.
2 If a new hub is being installed, it must be pressed onto the axle shaft to form the serrations. The hub is pressed on by using two thrust washers under the nut, greased with chassis grease. With the wheel, hub, and drum installed, the parking break should be firmly applied and the car weight on the wheels. Tighten the nut to the following measurement, from the end of the axle to the end of the hub.

    7-9/16-inch axle   1 3/16 in.
    8-7/8-inch axle   1-5/6 in.

NOTE: The 7-9/16 inch axle is stamped with the letters E, F, G, H, K, R, S, T, U, or V on the side of the differential housing. The 8-7/8 inch axle is stamped with the letters A, B, C, D, N, P, O, or Q.

3 Remove the axle shaft nut and one thrust washer, then reinstall the nut and tighten it to 250 ft. lbs. Install a cotter key if the holes line up. If not, tighten the nut to the next slot and install the cotter key.

Procedure No. 3
Removing Tapered Axle and Bearing

(AMC ONLY)

1 Remove wheel, drum, and hub, referring to correct procedure in this chapter.
2 Disconnect brake line at wheel cylinder.
3 Remove bolts and nuts from housing flange and remove brake backing plate, oil, seal, and retainer. Remove shims if left side shaft is being removed.

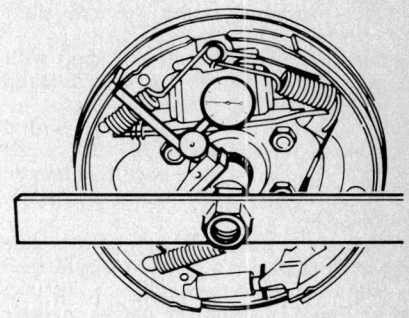

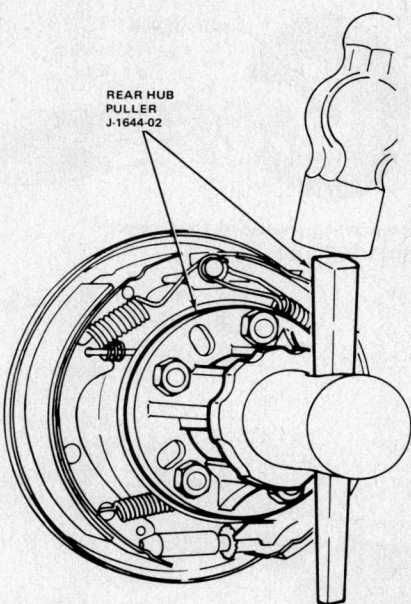

Removing axle hub

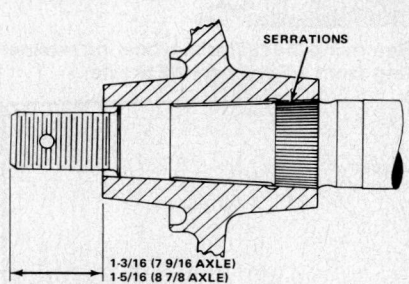

Hub installation measurement

NOTE: Axle shaft end play shims are installed on the left side of the axle only.

4 Use a screw-type puller to pull the axle shaft bearing out of the housing.

CAUTION: *On cars equipped with a self-locking differential, do not rotate the other shaft while one shaft is removed. The side gear splines may misalign if the differential is rotated, preventing insertion of the replacement shaft.*

To install the axle, reverse the removal procedure. On 7-9/16 inch axles, the outer oil seal and retainer is installed between the housing flange and the brake backing plate. On the 8-7/8 inch axle, the outer oil seal and retainer is installed on the hub side of the backing plate.

NOTE: The 7-9/16 inch axle is stamped with the letters E, F, G, H, R, S, T, U, or V on the side of the differential housing. The 8-7/8 inch axle is stamped with the letters A, B, C, D, N, P, O, or Q.

Procedure No. 4
R & R Axle Outer Oil Seal

(AMC ONLY)

1 Remove wheel, drum, and hub, refer-

Checking axle shaft end play

ring to correct procedure in this chapter.
2 Disconnect brake line at wheel cylinder.
3 Remove bolts and nuts from housing flange and remove brake backing plate, oil seal, and retainer. If left side is being removed, make note of any shims next to the backing plate.

To install a new seal, reverse the removal procedure, replacing shims in the original position. On 7-9/16 axles, the outer seal and retainer is installed between the housing flange and the brake backing plate. On the 8-7/8 inch axle, the outer seal and retainer is installed on the hub side of the backing plate.

NOTE: The 7-9/16 inch axle is stamped with the letters E, F, G, H, K, R, S, T, U, or V on the side of the differential housing. The 8-7/8 inch axle is stamped with the letters A, B, C, D, N, P, O, or Q.

Procedure No. 5
R & R Axle Inner Oil Seal

(ALL CARS)
NOTE: Some cars do not use an inner seal.

1 Remove the axle according to the correct procedure.
2 Use a slide hammer puller that will hook onto the seal and pull it out of the axle housing. Or use the end of the axle to pry the seal out, being careful not to gouge or damage the housings. In the same designs, it may be necessary to remove the bearing, also, because the puller will not grab the seal alone. Clean the inside of the housing to remove old sealer.
3 To install a new seal, coat the lip of the seal with rear axle lubricant. Coat the outer metal part of the seal with non-hardening sealer.
4 Use a driver that fits the seal and drive the seal into the axle housing to the same depth as the old seal, with the lip pointing inward.
5 Replace the axle and the other parts, using the correct procedure.

Procedure No. 6
Axle Shaft End Play Adjustment

(AMC ONLY)

1 Remove the drum and hub by the cor-

rect procedure under the axle shaft removal.

2 Strike the end of each axle shaft with a lead hammer to seat the bearing cups against the support plates.

3 Attach a large flat 18 inch bar with a hole in the middle to the end of the axle. The bar will be used as a handle to move the axle in and out while checking end play.

4 Attach a dial indicator to the axle housing backing plate so it will read the in and out movement of the axle.

5 Pull and push on the bar so the axle moves to the limit of its end play. Correct end play is 0.006 inch. Allowable end play is 0.004 to 0.008.

6 Correct the end play with shims on the left side of the axle only. Adding shims will increase end play. Removing shims will decrease end play.

7 The outer oil seal housing acts as a bearing retainer. To be effective, shims must be installed inboard from the oil seal. Any other parts that install inboard from the bearing retainer will affect the end play of the axle. On those axle that the shims inboard from the brake backing plate, the backing plate must be removed to take out the shims.

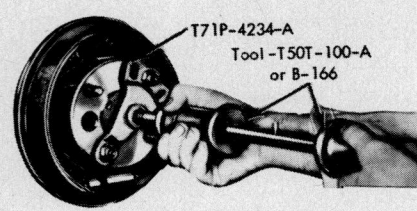

Removing the Ford axle shaft; not WER axle

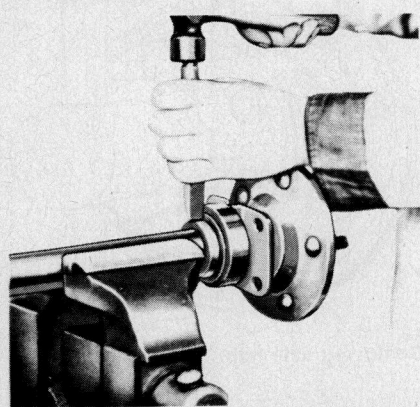

Removing the rear wheel bearing retainer ring from a Ford non-WER axle

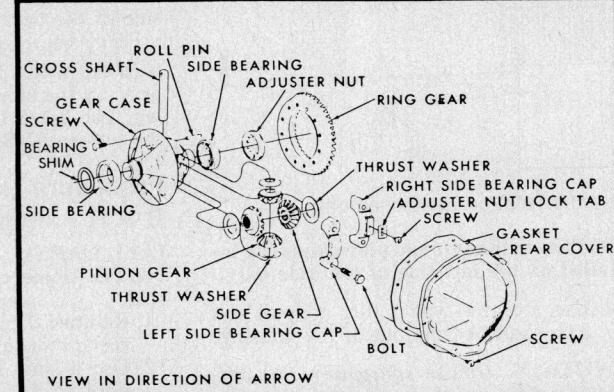

CROSS SHAFT
ROLL PIN
SIDE BEARING
ADJUSTER NUT
GEAR CASE
RING GEAR
SCREW
BEARING SHIM
THRUST WASHER
RIGHT SIDE BEARING CAP
ADJUSTER NUT LOCK TAB SCREW
SIDE BEARING
GASKET
REAR COVER
PINION GEAR
THRUST WASHER
SIDE GEAR
LEFT SIDE BEARING CAP
BOLT
SCREW
VIEW IN DIRECTION OF ARROW

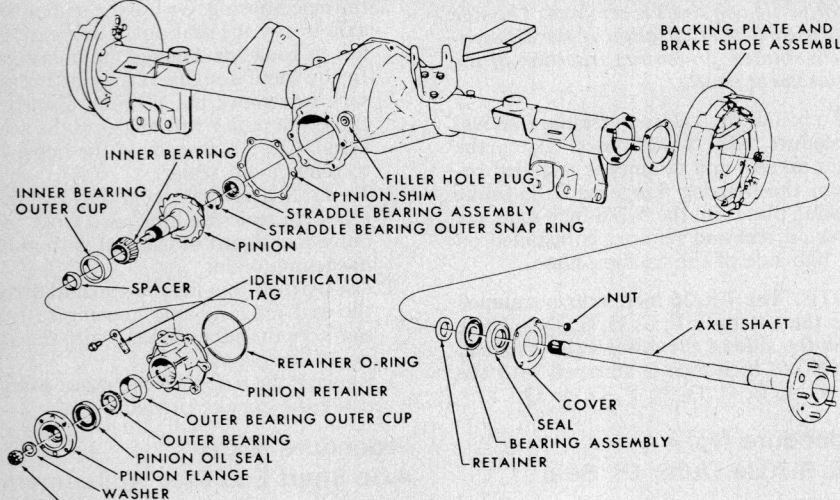

BACKING PLATE AND BRAKE SHOE ASSEMBLY
INNER BEARING
INNER BEARING OUTER CUP
FILLER HOLE PLUG
PINION SHIM
STRADDLE BEARING ASSEMBLY
STRADDLE BEARING OUTER SNAP RING
PINION
SPACER
IDENTIFICATION TAG
NUT
AXLE SHAFT
RETAINER O-RING
PINION RETAINER
OUTER BEARING OUTER CUP
OUTER BEARING
COVER
SEAL
BEARING ASSEMBLY
RETAINER
PINION OIL SEAL
PINION FLANGE
WASHER
PINION NUT

Differential carrier and rear axle assembly

8 Install the hub and drum by the correct procedure under axle shaft removal.

Procedure No. 7
Pinion Oil Seal Replacement

(ALL CARS)

1 Raise and safely support the car. Remove the rear wheels and brake drums.

2 Mark the driveshaft and rear yoke for correct reassembly, then disconnect the driveshaft from the yoke.

3 Rotate the pinion several revolutions, then use an inch-pound torque wrench to measure the amount of inch-pounds required to turn the pinion. If a torque wrench is not available, scribe a line on a nut and pinion shaft, and count the number of exposed threads to establish the position of the nut.

4 Remove the pinion nut. Mark the position of the yoke of the pinion, and remove the yoke. Some lubricant will drain out when the yoke is removed.

5 Check seal surface of yoke. If the surface is damaged or grooved, replace the yoke.

6 Remove the pinion seal using a tool that threads into the inner diameter of the seal, or equivalent.

7 To replace the seal, coat the lip with rear axle lubricant, and drive the seal into position with the lip pointing inward.

8 Install the yoke, aligning the reference marks, and snug the nut, but do not tighten. AMC recommends using a new nut.

9 Use the torque wrench to measure the inch-pounds required to turn the pinion. Turn the pinion several revolutions to insure an accurate reading.

10 Tighten the pinion nut very slightly and measure the rotation torque again. Continue to tighten and measure until the torque is 1 to 5 inch pounds more than it was before disassembly. Do not exceed 5 inch pounds. If a torque wrench is not available, tighten, the nut until the scribe marks line up then tighten 1/16–1/8 inch more.

CAUTION: *Do not overtighten, or loosen and retighten the pinion nut. If the correct torque is exceeded, or the nut is tightened or loosened, the nut and collapsible spacer must be replaced and the pinion bearing preload reset.*

11 Complete the installation by reversing the removal procedure.

Procedure No. 8
R & R Flanged Axle and Bearing

NOTE: Two different axle shaft designs are used. The "C" type axles are retained in the housing by "C" locks at the inner

Bearing replacement using removal box and safety cap.

STEP 1

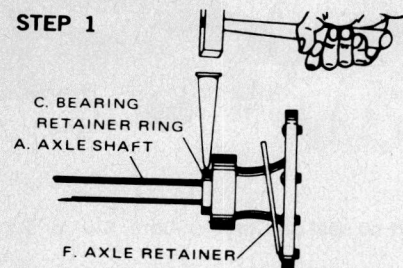

1. Mount axle shaft (A) in vise. Remove the bearing retainer ring (C), using a chisel to split the ring.

STEP 2

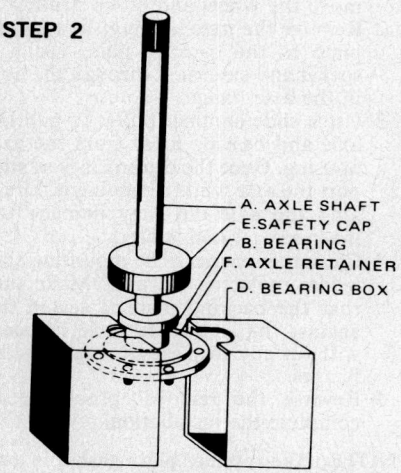

2. At the press table, insert the axle flange and retainer (F) within the removal box (D). Both sections of the box should rest against the axle under the bearing (B). Place safety cap (E) over the shaft on top of the bearing. Press against shaft end to remove bearing. If it does not easily break loose, tap shaft with a ballpean hammer.

STEP 3

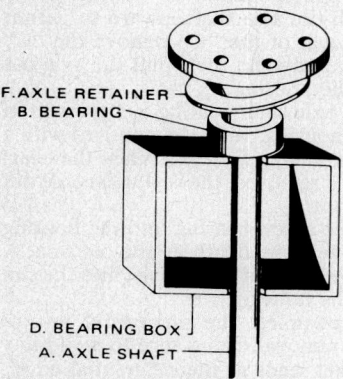

3. Clean shaft and retainer (F) and replace retainer against axle flange. Slip new bearing (B) over the shaft. Be sure a sealed bearing faces the proper direction. Locate axle shaft (A) in the removal box (D) and press the bearing to its seat on the shaft. Also press a new retaining ring (C) against the bearing.

ends. To remove the axles, the differential housing cover must be removed. The other type of axle is retained in the housing by a retainer plate held by the same bolts that hold the brake backing plate. On the retainer plate type, all the work of removing the axle shafts is done at the wheel ends of the axle housing.

The easiest way to find out which type is on any car is to remove a rear wheel and drum. Inspect the area behind the axle

C-lock on a Chrysler 8¼" axle

flange. If the axle is a retainer type, the retainer can be seen. On "C" types, the housing sticks out more, and there is no retainer plate.

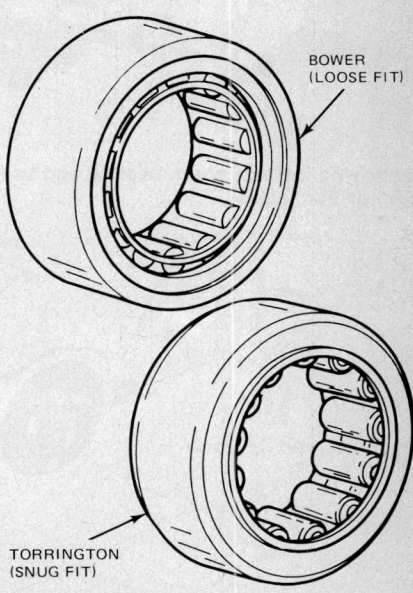

Two types of bearings used on Ford WER axles

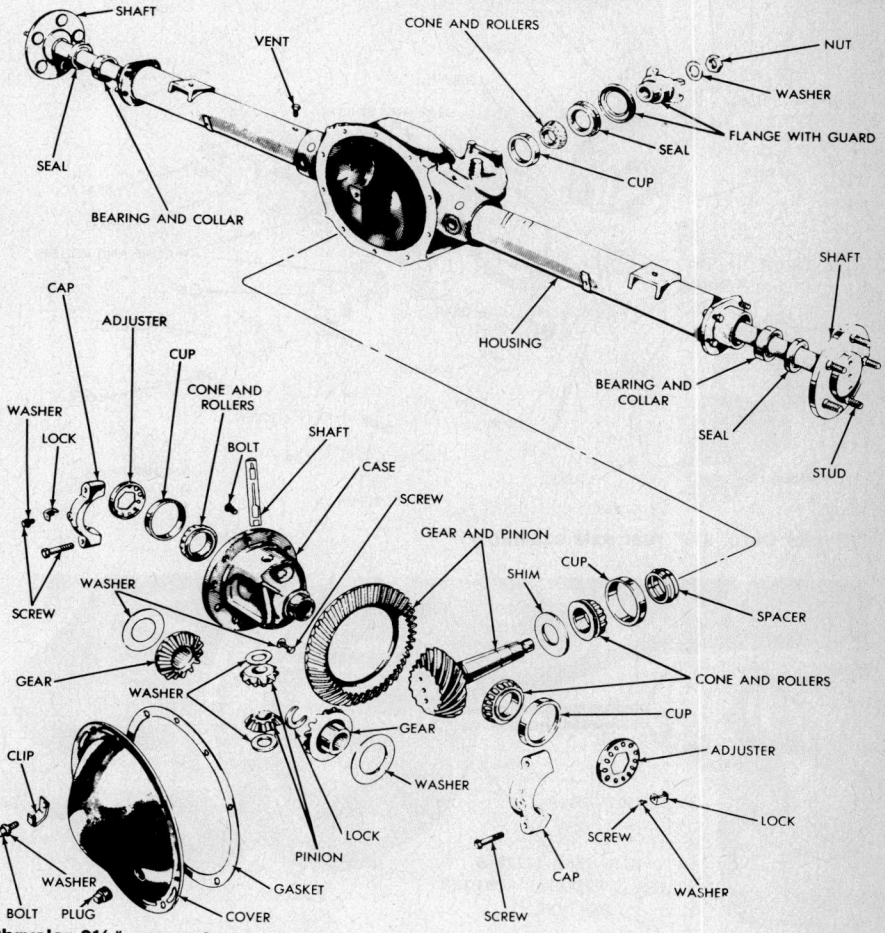

Chrysler 8¼" rear axle assembly

B939

DRIVE AXLES
REPAIR PROCEDURES

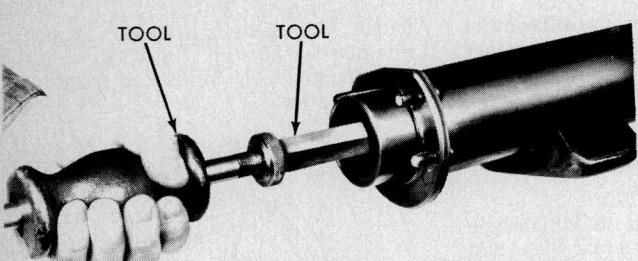

Removing the axle shaft, bearing and seal from Chrysler Corp. 8¼" or 9¼" axles

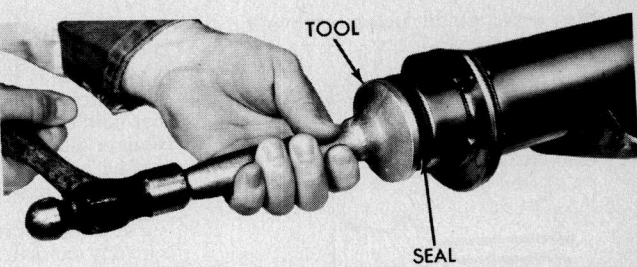

Installing the axle shaft oil seal on Chrysler Corp. 8¼" or 9¼" axles

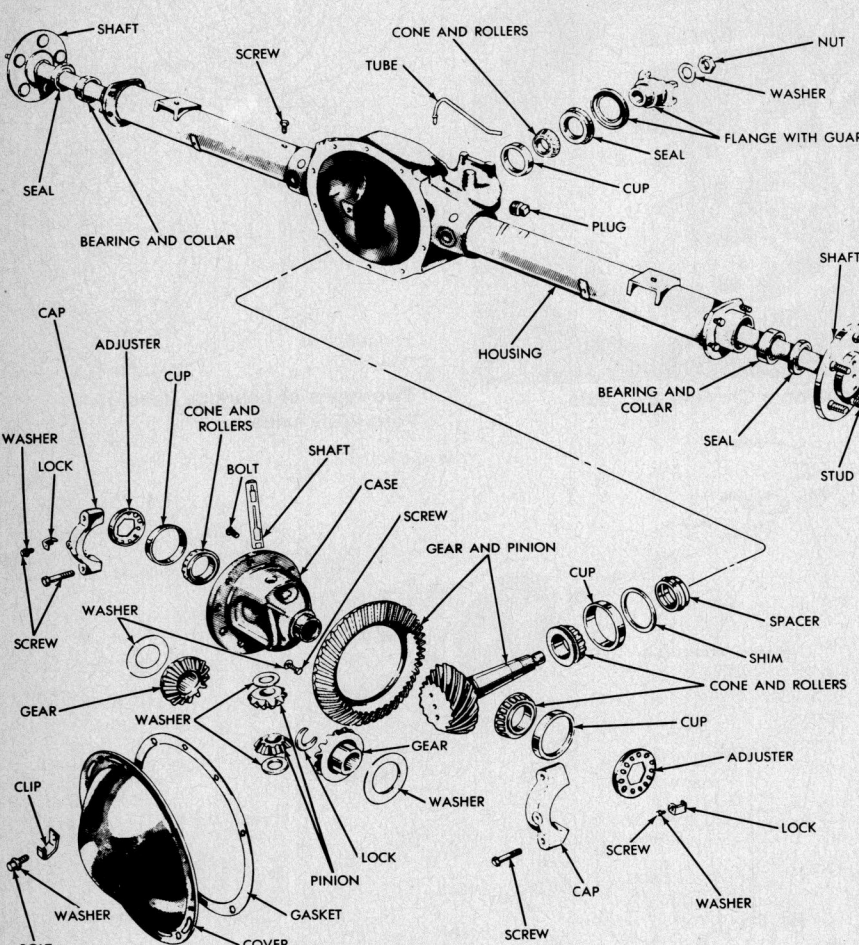

Chrysler Corp. 9¼" rear axle assembly

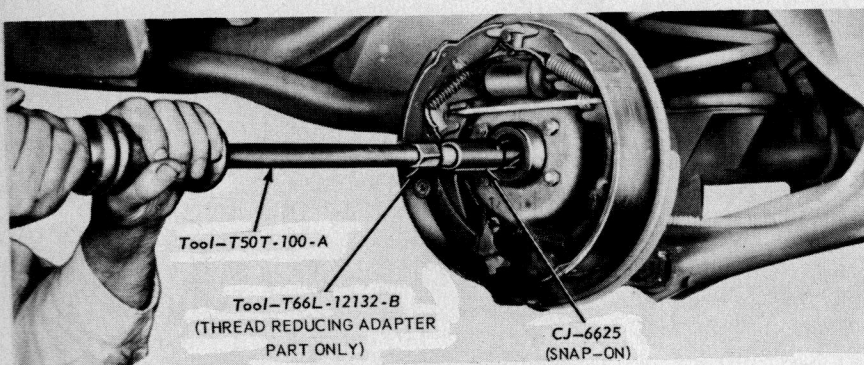

Removing the axle seal or bearing on a Ford WER axle

Tool—T50T-100-A

Tool—T66L-12132-B
(THREAD REDUCING ADAPTER
PART ONLY)

CJ-6625
(SNAP-ON)

RETAINER PLATE TYPE
1 Raise and safely support the car. Remove the wheel and brake drum.
2 Remove the nuts holding the retainer plate to the backing plate, using a socket and extension through the hole in the axle flange.
3 Use a slide hammer puller to pull the axle and bearing loose from the axle housing. Once the bearing is free, support the axle while removing it. Dragging the axle out may damage the inner seal, if one is used.
4 Clean the retainer plate mounting area before replacing the axle. Make sure that the backing plate is seated flat against the end of the axle housing, without any dirt caught between the flanges.
5 Reverse the removal procedure to complete the installation.

NOTE: The retainer plate gasket is usually not available. It is common pratice to replace the plate without a gasket, or to use the old gasket.

"C" TYPE
1 Raise and safely support the car. Remove the wheel and brake drum.
2 Remove the differential cover and catch the lubricant in a pan.
3 Remove the pinion shaft lock bolt and the pinion shaft.
4 Push the axle shaft inward to permit removal of the "C" remove the "C" lock and lock, then/pull the axle out of the housing.
5 The axle shaft bearing is a press fit in the housing. It can be removed with a slide hammer puller. When the bearing is removed, the seal will come out with it.
6 Drive a new bearing into the housing to the same depth as the old one. A new seal should be driven into the end of the housing.
7 To complete the procedure, reverse the removal, being sure to avoid any gasket leads at the differential cover, and refilling the differential with the correct lubricant.

Procedure No. 9
Removing Pressed-On Bearing From Axle
NOTE: A hydraulic or mechanical press

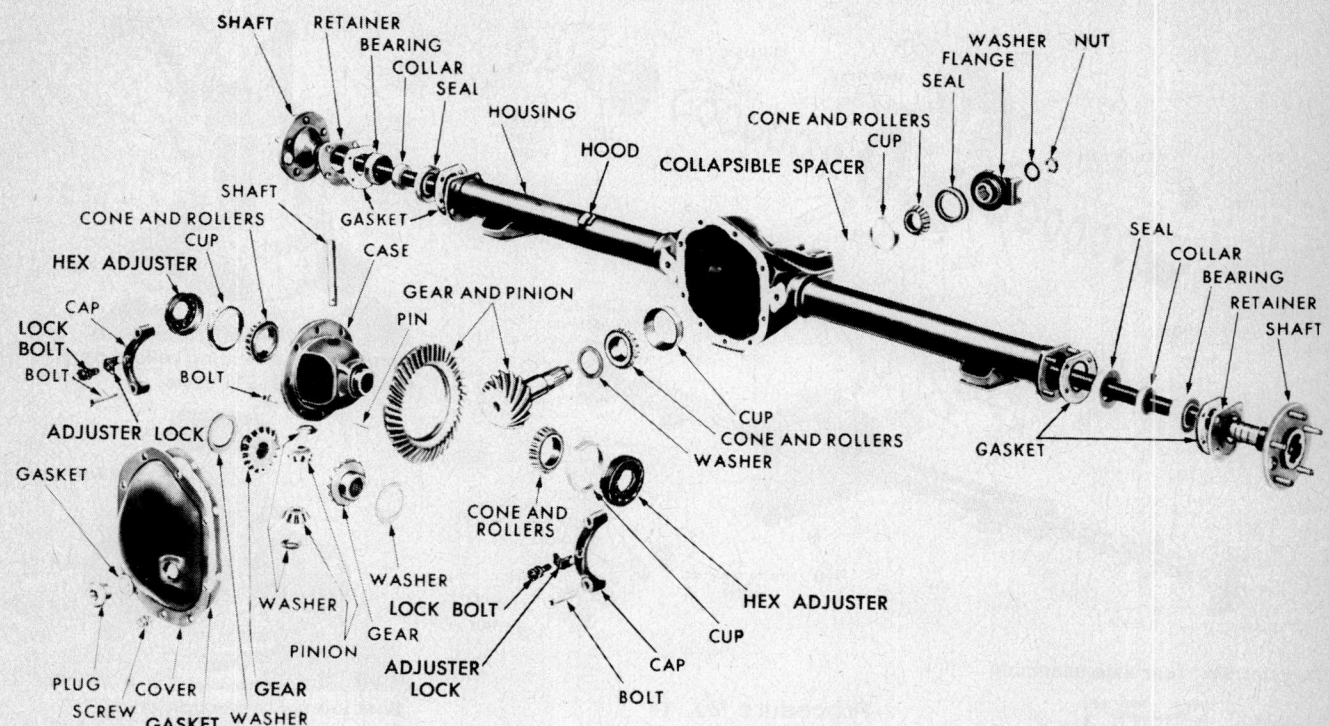

Chrysler 7¼″ rear axle assembly

is necessary. The press should be one that is recommended for axle bearing work.

1 Remove the axle and bearing assembly from the car, following the correct procedure.

2 The retainer ring that is pressed against the bearing (not on AMC with tapered axle) must be V-grooved with a chisel and heavy hammer to relieve the pressure, so it can be slipped off the shaft. Do not attempt to split the ring, because the chisel might damage the shaft. Several deep V-grooves will usually loosen the ring enough that it can be removed by hand.

3 Use a safe press setup, with press blocks that fit the bearing, and a cage or bearing cap that will contain the bearing pieces in case it fractures.

4 Press the bearing from the shaft.

5 Knock the old seal out of the retainer plate (not used on AMC) and install a new seal, with the lip facing in. Slip the retainer plate over the axle, with the seal lip facing in. On some makes, the retainer plate does not contain a seal.

6 Press a new bearing onto the axle, following the same precautions as in removing the old bearing. Then press a new retaining ring up against the bearing.

Procedure No. 10
Adjust Axle End Play

There is no end play adjustment on these axles. If the end play is excessive, it means the bearing is worn, and must be replaced.

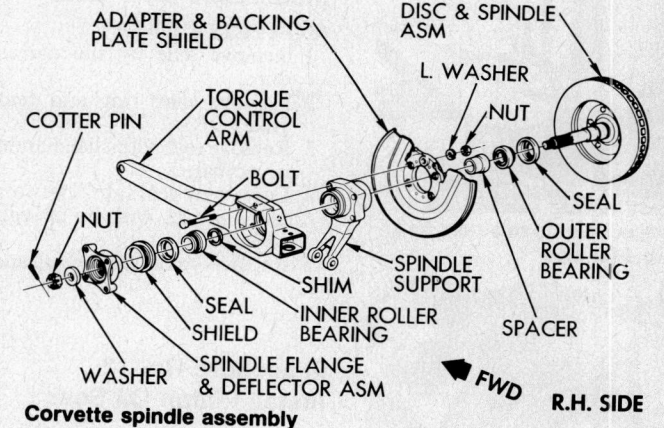

Corvette spindle assembly

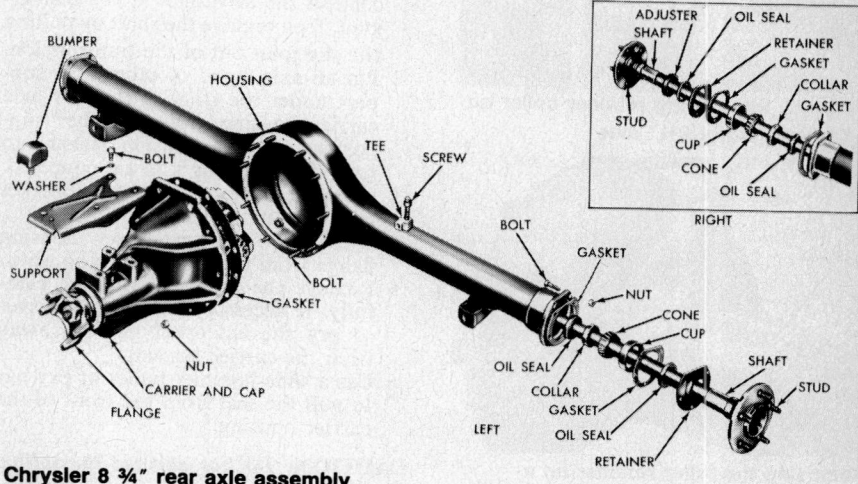

Chrysler 8 ¾″ rear axle assembly

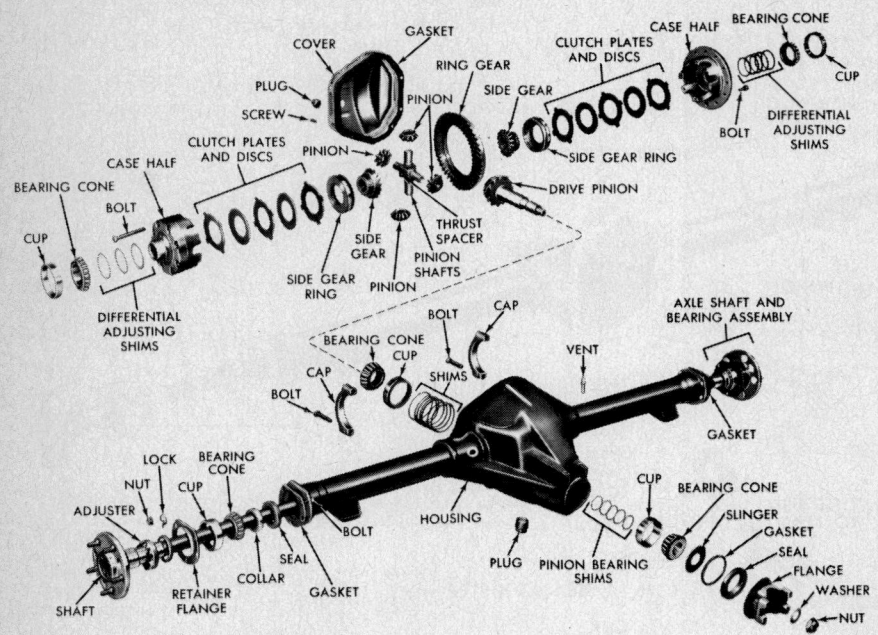

Chrysler 9¾″ rear axle assembly

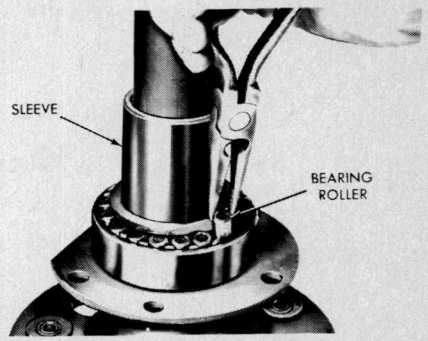

Removing the bearing rollers on a Chrysler Corp. 9¾″ axle

.002 SHIM STOCK

Seat journal protection on a Chrysler 9¾″ axle

Cutting out roller bearing retainers on a Chrysler Corp. 9¾″ axle

Notching the bearing retainer collar on a Chrysler Corp. 9¾″ axle

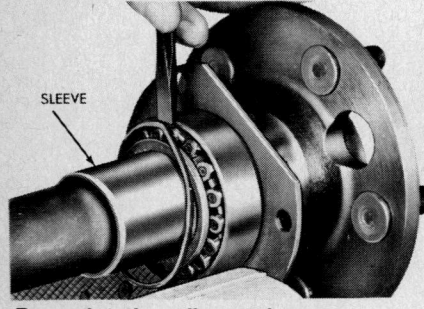

Removing the roller retainer on a Chrysler Corp. 9¾″ axle

Procedure No. 11
Install Side Gear Seal

(CORVETTE ONLY)

1 Remove axle by the correct procedure.
2 Remove snap ring and remove side yoke.
3 Remove seal with slide hammer puller or prybar.
4 Drive new seal into bore to same distance as old, with lip of seal pointing inward.
5 Replace yoke, snap ring, and axle.

Procedure No. 12
Install Pinion Oil Seal

(CHEVETTE)

1 Raise and safely support the car. Disconnect the driveshaft at the rear U-joint, then remove the shaft by pulling the slip joint out of the transmission.
2 Put an axle stand or other firm support under the front of the rear axle carrier housing. Place another support under the extension housing to hold it in place as it is disconnected.
3 Disconnect the center support bracket from the underbody.
4 Disconnect the extension housing flange from the axle carrier housing.
5 Remove the extension housing carefully. If necessary, use a screwdriver to pry the extension housing away from the carrier housing.
6 Use a slide hammer puller or pry bar to pull the seal from the front of the carrier housing.

CAUTION: *Do not damage the splines on the drive coupling.*

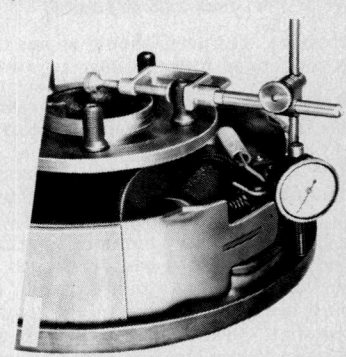

Measuring the axle shaft end play on a Chrysler 9¾″ axle

7 Drive a new seal into the housing to the same depth as the old one, with the lip facing to the rear. Reassemble the extension housing by reversing the removal procedure.

Procedure No. 13.
Installing Outer Oil Seal in Retainer Flange

NOTE: Some cars do not use a seal in the retainer flange.

1 Follow the correct procedure for removing the axle.
2 Follow the correct procedure for removing the pressed-on bearing from the axle.
3 Remove the retainer from the axle and install a new seal in the retainer.
4 Replace the retainer and bearing on the axle, and the axle in the housing, following the correct procedure.

TURN SIGNAL FLASHER AND FUSE BOX LOCATION CHART

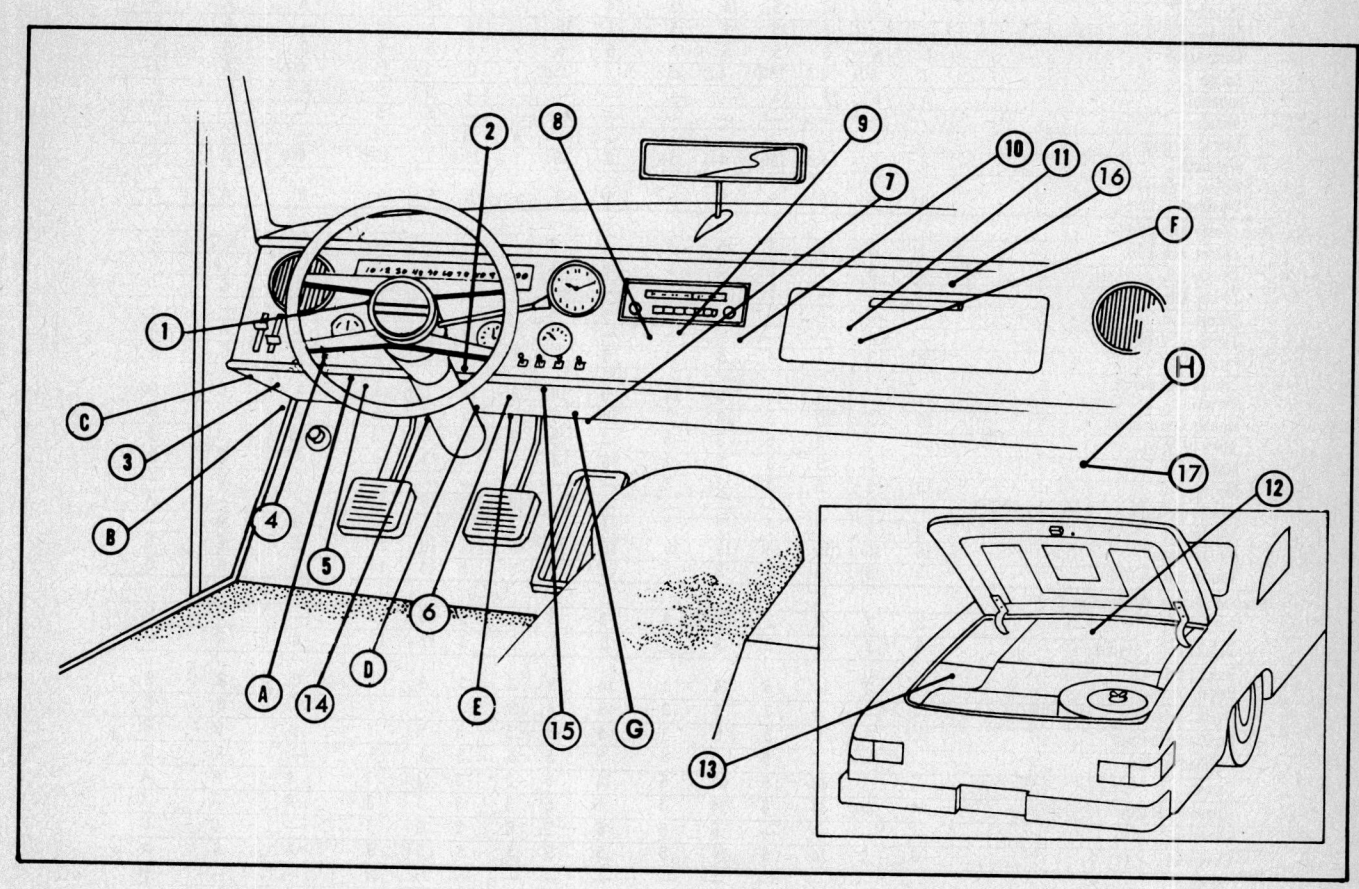

B943

FUSE BOX AND FLASHER LOCATIONS

TURN SIGNAL FLASHER, HAZARD WARNING FLASHER, AND FUSE BLOCK LOCATION

	1974 TSF	1974 HWF	1975 TSF	1975 HWF	1976 TSF	1976 HWF	1977 TSF	1977 HWF	1978-79 TSF	1978-79 HWF	1980-81 TSF	1980-81 HWF	1974 Fuse Block Location	1975-79 Fuse Block Location	1980-81 Fuse Block Location
American Motors															
Ambassador	2	3	—	—	—	—	—	—	—	—	—	—	F	—	—
Concord, Hornet, Gremlin, Spirit, Eagle	3	2	3	2	3	2	3	6	3	6	3	6	C	C	C
Javelin	3	3	—	—	—	—	—	—	—	—	—	—	C	C	—
Matador	2	3	3	1	3	1	3	1	3	1	—	—	F	F	—
Pacer	—	—	3	5	3	5	3	5	3	5	3	5	—	F	F
Chrysler Corporation															
Aires, Reliant	—	—	—	—	—	—	—	—	—	—	5	5	—	—	A
Barracuda, Challenger	6	6	—	—	—	—	—	—	—	—	—	—	C	—	—
Chrysler	5	5	14	5	14	5	14	1	14	1	14	1	A	A	A
Cordoba	—	—	1	15	1	15	1	15	1	15	5	5	—	A	A
Dart, Aspen	8	6	5	5	5	5	5	5	5	5	5	5	D	A	A
Dodge	8	6①	4③	15④	4③	15④	1	15④	1	15④	1	15④	D②	A	A
Imperial	5	5	14	5	—	—	—	—	—	—	5	5	A	A	A
Mirada	—	—	—	—	—	—	—	—	—	—	5	5	—	—	A
Omni, Horizon	—	—	—	—	—	—	—	—	3	3	3	3	—	C	C
Plymouth	8	6①	4③	15④	4③	15④	1	15④	1	15④	1	15④	D②	A	A
Valiant, Volare, Diplomat, LeBaron	8	6	5	5	5	5	5	5	5	5	5	5	D	A	A
Ford Motor Company⑤															
Comet, Maverick	5	5	5	3	5	3	5	3	—	—	—	—	E	E, C	—
Cougar XR-7	3	3	3	3	3	3	5	5	5	5	14	14	C	C, A	D
Torino, Elite	3	3	3	3	3	3	—	—	—	—	—	—	C	C	—
Escort, Lynx	—	—	—	—	—	—	—	—	—	—	5	5	—	—	A
Fairmont, Zephyr	—	—	—	—	—	—	—	—	16	11	16	11	—	A	A
Ford	3	3	3	3	3	3	3	3	3	3	3	3	A	C	B
Granada, Monarch, Versailles, 1981 Cougar	—	—	6	14	6	14	6	14	6	14	6⑥	14⑦	—	C	C⑧
Lincoln Continental	10	5	10	5	10	5	10	5	10	5	3	3	A	A	B
Mark IV, V, VI	3	5	3	5	3	5	3	5	9	5	3	3	A	A	B
Mercury	3	3	3	3	3	3	3	3	3	3	3	3	A	C	B
Montego	3	3	3	3	3	3	—	—	—	—	—	—	C	C	—
Mustang, Capri	—	—	—	—	—	—	—	—	16	11	16	11	—	—	A
Mustang II	7	7	7	7	7	7	7	7	7	7	—	—	G	G	—
Pinto, Bobcat	16	16	16	16	16	16	16	16	16	16	16	16	E	E	E
Thunderbird, LTD II	3	5	3	5	3	5	3	5	5	5	14	14	A	A	D
General Motors Corporation⑤															
Buick	3	3	3	3	3	3	3	3	3	3	3	3	—	B	B
Buick Apollo, Skylark	5	3	3	3	3	3	3	3	3	3	17	17	B	B	H
Buick Skylark, Regal, Century	14	3	14	3	14	3	14	3	3	3	3	3	C	B	B
Buick Skyhawk	—	—	3	3	3	3	3	3	3	3	3	3	C	B	B
Cadillac, Eldorado	14	3	6	3	6	3	5	3	5	3	5	3	B	B	B
Cadillac Seville	—	—	5	5	5	5	5	5	5	5	3	3	—	A	C
Camaro	8	3	14	5	14	5	14	5	3	3	3	3	A	A	A
Chevelle, Malibu	4	3	14	5	14	5	5	5	3	3	3	3	A	A	A
Chevette	—	—	—	—	6	5	6	5	6	5	6	5	—	C	C
Chevrolet	6	3	14	5	14	5	5	5	5	5	5	5	A	A	A
Citation	—	—	—	—	—	—	—	—	—	—	17	17	—	—	H
Nova	10	3	14	5	14	5	6	5	6	5	—	—	A	A	—
Corvette	6	3	14	5	14	5	6	5	6	5	6	5	A	A	A
Monza	—	—	14	3	14	3	14	3	14	3	14	3	—	C	C
Vega	5	3	14	3	14	3	14	3	—	—	—	—	C	C	—
Oldsmobile	5	3	5	5	5	5	5	5	5	5	5	5	C	A	A
Oldsmobile Cutlass	14	3	14	3	14	3	5	5	3	3	3	3	C	C	C
Oldsmobile Omega	6	3	6	5	6	5	3	3	3	3	17	17	C	A	H
Oldsmobile Starfire	—	—	14	3	14	3	3	3	3	3	3	3	—	C	C
Oldsmobile Toronado	5	3	5	5	5	5	5	5	5	5	2	3	C	A	C
Pontiac Astre, Sunbird	—	—	14	3	14	3	3	3	3	3	3	3	—	C	C
Pontiac	3	3	5	3	5	3	3	3	3	3	3	3	C	B	B
Firebird	3	3	5	3	5	3	5	3	3	3	3	3	C	B	B
LeMans, GTO, Grand Am	3	3	5	3	5	3	3	3	3	3	3	3	C	B	B
Ventura, Phoenix	3	3	5	3	5	3	10	3	3	3	17	17	C	B	H

①—5 on full size models
②—A on full size models
TSF—Turn Signal Flasher
HWF—Hazard Warning Flasher
③—14 on full size models
④—5 on full size models
⑤—Most hazard warning flashers and some turn signal flashers are mounted on fuse panel.
⑥—1981:16
⑦—1981:11
⑧—1981:A

AUTOMOBILE YEAR/MAKE/MODEL		ENGINE	BBLs	AC	AUTOLITE	BOSCH
AMERICAN MOTORS						
1978-80	AMX, Concord, Gremlin	L4-121	1 or 2	R42XLSM	922	W9H
1977	AMX, Concord, Gremlin	L4-121	1 or 2	R42XLSM	922	W9H
1980-81	Concord, Eagle, Spirit	L4-151	2	R44TSX	665	HR9BY
1978-80	AMX, Concord, Pacer	L6-232	1 or 2	R44XLSM	925	W9H
1977	Gremlin, Hornet, Matador, Pacer	L6-232	1	R44XLS	65	W9H
1981	Concord, Eagle, Spirit	L6-258	2	—	985	WR9H
1980	Concord, Eagle, Spirit, Pacer	L6-258	2	R44XLSE	—	W9H
1978-79	AMX, Concord, Eagle, Gremlin, Pacer	L6-258	1 or 2	R44XLSM	925	W9H
1977	Gremlin, Hornet	L6-258	1	R44XLS	65	W9H
1977-80	AMC, Concord, Gremlin, Hornet, Matador, Pacer, Spirit	V8-304	2 or 4	R44XLS	55	W9D
1977-78	Concord, Matador	V8-360	2 or 4	R44XLS	55	W9D
BUICK						
1980-81	Skylark	L4-151	2	R44TSX	665	HR9BY
1981	Skylark	V6-173	2	R43TS	24	HR8B
1980	Skylark	V6-173	2	R43TS	25	HR8B
1979	Century, Regal, Wagon	V6-196	2	R45TSX	666	HR10BY
1978	Century, Regal, Wagon	V6-196	2	R46TSX	667	HR10BY
1981	Regal, Century, LeSabre	V6-231	2	R45TS8	966	HR9BY
1979-80	Century, Regal, LeSabre, Skyhawk, Skylark	V6-231	2	R45TSX	666	HR9BY
1977-78	Century, Regal, LeSabre, Skyhawk, Skylark	V6-231	2 or 4	R44TSX	667	HR9BY
1980-81	Century, Regal, LeSabre, Riviera	V6-231(turbo)	4	R45TS	26	HR9B
1979	Century, Regal, LeSabre, Riviera	V6-231(turbo)	4	R44TS	25	HR9BY
1978	Century, Regal, LeSabre, Riviera	V6-231(turbo)	4	R44TSX	665	HR9BY
1981	Electra, Riviera	V6-252	4	R45TS8	966	HR10BY
1980	Electra, Riviera	V6-252	4	R45TSX	666	HR10BY
1980-81	Century, Regal, Wagon	V8-265	2	R45TSX	666	HR9BY
1980-81	Century, Regal, Wagon	V8-301	4	R45TSX	666	HR10BY
1977-79	Century, Regal, LeSabre	V8-301	2	R45TSX	666	HR10BY
1977-79	Century, Regal, LeSabre	V8-301	2	R46TSX	667	HR10BY
1977-79	Century, Regal, LeSabre	V8-301	4	R45TSX	667	HR10BY
1977-81	Century, Regal, LeSabre	V8-305	2 or 4	R45TS	26	HR10BY
1978-79	LeSabre	V8-305 (calif & H.A.)	2	R45TS	26	HR10BX
1981	Riviera	V8-307	4	R46SX	567	WR10FY
1977	Century, Regal	V8-350	4	R45TSX	666	HR10BY
1977	Skylark	V8-350	4	R45TSX	666	HR10BY
1977	Century, Regal	V8-350H	2	R46TSX	667	HR10BY
1977	Century, Regal, Electra, LeSabre, Riviera	V8-350J	4	R46TSX	667	HR10BY
1977-79	Century, Regal	V8-350L	4	R45TS	26	HR10BX
1980	Century, Regal, Electra, LeSabre, Riviera	V8-350R	4	R46SX	847	WR10FY
1977-79	Century, Regal, Electra, LeSabre, Riviera	V8-350R	4	R46SZ	847	WR10FY
1980	Century, Regal, Electra, LeSabre	V8-350X	4	R45TSX	666	HR10BY
1979	Century, Regal, Electra, LeSabre	V8-350X	4	R45TSX	666	HR10BY
1978	Century, Regal, Electra, LeSabre	V8-350X	4	R45TSX	666	HR10BY
1977-79	Century, Regal, Electra, LeSabre	V8-403	4	R46SZ	847	WR10FY
CADILLAC						
1981	Seville, Eldorado, Deville, Brougham	V6-252	4	R45TS8	966	HR10BY
1980	Seville, Eldorado, Deville, Brougham	V6-252	4	R45TSX	666	HR10BY
1980-81	Eldorado, Seville	V8-350	FI	R47SX	847	WR10FY
1977-79	Eldorado, Seville	V8-350	FI	R47SX	847	WR10FY
1980-81	Eldorado, Deville, Brougham, Fleetwood, Seville	V8-368	DFI	R45NSX	646	WR9DY
1977-79	Cadillac	V8-425	4	R45NSX	646	WR9DY
1979	Cadillac, Eldorado	V8-425	FI	R45NSX	646	WR9DY
1977-78	Cadillac, Eldorado	V8-425	FI	R45NSX	646	WR9DY
CHEVROLET						
1977	Chevette	L4-85	2	....	....	....
1979-81	Chevette	L4-98	2	....	....	....
1978	Chevette	L4-98	2	R43TS	25	HR8B
1977	Chevette	L4-98	2	R43TS	23	HR8B
1977	Monza, 2+2, Town Coupe, Vega	L4-140	1 or 2	R43TS	665	HR8B
1981	Citation, Monza	L4-140	2	R44TSX	665	HR9BY
1980-81	Citation, Monza	L4-151	2	R44TSX	665	HR10BY
1979	Citation, Monza	L4-151	2	R44TSX	664	HR10BY
1978	Chevette, Citation, Monza	L4-151	2	R43TSX	664	HR8B
1979	Monza	L4-151 (calif)	2	R44TSX	665	HR10BY
1981	Citation	V6-173	2	R43TS	22	HR8B
1980	Citation	V6-173	2	R43TS	25	HR8B
1979-80	Monza	V6-196	2	R45TSX	666	HR10BY
1978	Monza	V6-196	2	R45TSX	667	HR10BY

*—Original equipment type
**—Autolite recommends 26, however, some early models had the 25 as original equipment. Refer to engine decal for the appropriate spark plug and gap.

[1]—Bosch, Champion, Mighty, Motorcraft, Nippondenso, Prestolite and Valley Forge spark plugs gapped at 0.060
[2]—AC, Champion, Mighty MGK and Nippondenso spark plugs gapped at 0.080

[3]—Mighty, Mopar and Valley Forge spark plugs gapped at 0.035
[4]—Autolite, Champion, Mighty, Prestolite and Valley Forge spark plugs gapped at 0.044, Nippondenso at 0.035

[5]—AC, Bosch, NGK and Nippondenso 1981 spark plugs gapped at 0.044; Champion and Prestolite gapped at 0.035

SPARK PLUG CONVERSION CHART

CHAMPION	MIGHTY	MOPAR	MOTORCRAFT	NKG	NIPPONDENSO	PRESTOLITE	VALLEY FORGE	GAP
N8L	....	....	AGR14	....	....	....	....	0.034
N8L	....	....	AG12*	....	....	....	....	0.060*
RBL13Y6	M4RF426	....	ARF42-6*	BPR5FS-15	T16PR-U15	14RF42 5[14]	124R	0.060
N13L	....	....	AG44*	....	16EXR-U	14GR33	34R	0.035
N12Y	M4GR42	....	AGR42	BPR5ES	16EXR-U	14GR42	34R	0.035
RFN142LY	....	....	AGRP54*	....	....	....	....	0.035
N14LY	....	....	AG54*	BP5ES	....	14GR42	34R	0.035
N13L	....	....	AGR42	....	....	14GR33	34R	0.035
N12Y	M4GR42	....	AGR42	BPR5ES	W16EXR-U	14GR42	34R	0.035
RN12Y	M4GR42	....	AGR42	BPR5ES	W16EXR-U	14GR42	34R	0.035
RN12Y	M4GR42	....	AGR42	BPR5ES	W16EXR-U	14GR42	34R	0.035
RBL13Y6	M4RF426	....	ARF42-6	BPR5FS-15	T16PR-U15	14RF42 5[14]	124R	0.060
RBL11Y	M4RF32	....	ASF32	BPR5S	T20PR-U11	14RF32	23R	0.045
RBL13Y	M4RF42	....	ARF42	BPR4S-20	T20PR-U11	14F42A	24R	0.045
RBL15Y6	M4RF526	....	ARF52-6	BPR4FS-15	T16PR-U15	14RF52A	125R	0.060
RBL17Y6	M4RF626	....	ARF62-6	BPR4FS-15	T14PR-U15	14RF52A	126R	0.060
RBL15Y8	....	....	ARF52-8	BPR4FS-20	T16PR-U15	14RF52 8	25R	0.080
RBL15Y6	M4RF526	....	ARF52-6	BPR4FS-15	T16PR-U15	14RF52A	125R	0.080[1]
RBL17Y6	M4RF626	....	ARF62-6	BPR4FS-15	T14PR-U15	14RF52A	126R	0.080[1]
RBL15Y4	M4RF52	....	ARF52	BPR4FS-11	T16PR-U11	14RF52	25R	0.040
RBL11Y6	M4RF42	....	ARF42	BPR5FS-11	T16PR-U11	14RF42	24R	0.040
RBL11Y6	M4RF426	....	ARF42-6	BPR5FS-15	T16PR-U11	14RF42A	124R	0.040
RBL15Y8	....	....	ARF52-8	BPR4FS-20	T16PR-U15	14RF528	....	0.080[1]
RBL13Y6	M4RF426	....	ARF52-8	BPR4FS-15	T16PR-U15	14RF52A	125R	0.060
RBL15Y6	M4RF526	....	ARF52-6	BPR4FS-15	T16PR-U15	14RF52 5[13]	125R	0.060
RBL17Y6	M4RF526	....	ARF52-6	BPR4FS-15	T16PR-U15	14RF52 5[13]	125R	0.060
RBL17Y	M4RF626	....	ARF52-6	BPR4FS-15	T14PR-U15	14RF52 5[13]	125R	0.060
RBL17Y6	M4RF626	....	ARF62-6	BPR4FS-15	T16PR-U15	14RF52A	126R	0.060
RBL15Y6	....	....	ARF52-6	BPR4FS-15	T16PR-U15	14RF52A	125R	0.060
RBL15Y4	M4RF52	....	ARF52	BPR4FS-11	T16PR-U11	14RF52A[13]	25R	0.045
RBL15Y4	....	....	ARF52	BPR4FS-11	T16PR-U11	14RF52A	....	0.045
RJ18Y8	M4R828	....	AR82-80	BPR4S-20	W9P	14R52 6[13]	148R	0.080
RBL15Y4	M4RF626	....	....	BPR4S-15	T16PR-U15	14RF42A	167R	0.045
RBL15Y4	M4RF626	....	....	BPR4S-15	T16PR-U15	14RF42A	125R	0.045
RBL17Y6	M4RF626	....	ARF62-6	BPR4FS-15	T14PR-U15	14RF52A	126R	0.060
RBL17Y6	M4RF626	....	ARF62-6	BPR4FS-15	T14PR-U15	14RF52A	126R	0.060
RBL15Y4	M4RF52	....	ARF52	BPR4FS-11	T16PR-U11	14RF52A	25R	0.045
RJ18Y8	M4R826	....	AR82-8	BPR4S-20	W9P	14R52A	148R	0.060[2]
RJ18Y6	M4R826	....	AR82-6	BPR4S-15	W9P	14R52A	167R	0.060
RBL15Y6	M4RF526	....	ARF52-6	BPR4FS-15	T16PR-U15	14RF52A	125R	0.060
RBL17Y6	M4RF526	....	ARF52-6	BPR4FS-15	T16PR-U15	14RF52A	125R	0.060
RBL17Y6	M4RF626	....	ARF62-6	BPR4FS-15	T14PR-U15	14RF52A	126R	0.060
RJ18Y6	M4R826	....	AR82-6	BPR4S-15	W9P	14R52A	167R	0.060
RBL15Y8	....	....	ARF52-8	BPR4FS-20	T16PR-U15	14RF528	....	0.080[2]
RBL15Y8	M4RF526	....	....	BPR4FS-15	T16PR-U15	14RF525[13]	125R	0.060
BPL18Y6	M4R826	....	AR82-6	BPR4S-15	W9P	14R52A	167R	0.060
BPL18Y6	M4R826	....	AR82-6	BPR4S-15	W9P	14R52A	167R	0.060
RN14Y6	M4GR526	....	AGR52-6	BPR5ES-15	W14EXR-U11	146R526[13]	155R	0.060
RN14Y6	M4GR526	....	AGR52-6	BPR5ES-15	W14EXR-U11	14GR52A	155R	0.060
RN14Y6	M4GR526	....	AGR52-6	BPR5ES-15	W14EXR-U11	14GR52A	155R	0.060
RN14Y6	MGR526	....	AGR52-6	BPR5ES-11	W14EXR-U11	14GR52A	155R	0.060
....	....	....	....	....	T20PR-U	....	....	0.035
....	....	....	....	....	T20PR-U	....	....	0.035
RBL11Y	M4RF32	....	ARF22	BPR5FS	T20PR-U	14RF32	23R	0.035
RBL11Y	M4RF22	....	ARF22	BPR6FS	T20PR-U	14RF22	23R	0.035
RBL11Y	M4RF32	....	ARF32	BPR5FS	T20PR-U	14RF32	23R	0.035
....	M4RF32	....	ARF42-6	BPR5FS-15	....	14RF42A	124R	0.060
RBL13Y6	M4RF426	....	ARF42-6	BPR5FS-15	T16PR-U15	14RF42A	124R	0.060
RBL13Y6	M4RF426	....	ARF32-6	BPR5FS-15	T16PR-U15	14RF42A	124R	0.060
RBL13Y6	....	....	ARF32-6	BPR5FS-15	T20PR-U15	14RF32A	....	0.060
RBL13Y6	....	....	....	BPR6FS-15	T16PR-U15	14RF32A	124R	0.060
RBL11Y	M4RF32	....	ASF32	BPR6FS-11	T20PR-U11	14RF32	23R	0.045
RBL13Y	M4RF42	....	ARF42	BPR5FS-11	T20PR-U11	14RF42A	24R	0.045
RBL15Y6	M4RF526	....	ARF42-6	BPR4FS-15	T16PR-U15	14RF52A	125R	0.060
RBL17Y6	M4RF626	....	ARF32-6	BPR4FS-15	T14PR-U15	14RF52A	126R	0.060

[6] — Bosch, NGK 1981 spark plugs gapped at 0.044, Motorcraft 0.034 and Prestolite 0.035; for 1979 to 1980 Champion spark plugs gapped at 0.035 and NGK and Nippondenso at 0.034

[7] — Autolite spark plugs gapped at 0.044
[8] — Bosch, Champion, Mopar, NGK and Nippondenso 1981 spark plugs gapped at 0.048
[9] — Champion, Mopar and NGK spark plugs gapped at 0.048

[10] — Champion, Mopar and Nippondenso spark plugs for 1981 gapped at 0.048
[11] — Mighty spark plugs for 1981 gapped at 0.048

[12] — or 14RF42A
[13] — or 14RF52A
[14] — or 14R52A
[15] — Nippondenso spark plugs gapped at 0.045
[16] — Nippondenso spark plugs gapped at 0.030

AUTOMOBILE YEAR/MAKE/MODEL	ENGINE	BBLs	AC	AUTOLITE	BOSCH
Chevrolet continued					
1978-79 Malibu, Monte Carlo	V6-200	2	R45TS	26	HR10BX
1980-81 Caprice, Impala, Camaro, Malibu, Monte Carlo, El Camino	V6-229	2	R45TS	26	HR10BX
1981 Camaro, Chevelle, Malibu, Monte Carlo	V6-231	2	R45TS8	966	....
1979-80 Caprice, Impala, Camaro, Malibu, Monte Carlo, Monza	V6-231	2	R45TSX	666	HR9BY
1978 Malibu, Monte Carlo, Monza	V6-231	2	R45TSX	667	HR9BY
1979-81 Monte Carlo	V6-231 Turbo	4	R45TS	26	HR9B
1977-80 Caprice, Impala, Camaro, Chevelle, Nova	L6-250	4	R46TS	27	HR10B
1977-81 Caprice, Impala, Camaro, Malibu, Monte Carlo	V8-267	2	R45TS	26	HR10BX
1980 Camaro	V8-301	2	....	26	HR9BY
1977-81 Caprice, Impala, Camaro, Chevelle, Corvette, Malibu, Monte Carlo, Monza, Nova	V8-305	2 or 4	R45TS	26	HR10BX
1977-81 Caprice, Impala, Camaro, Chevelle, Corvette, Monte Carlo, Nova	V8-350L	2 or 4	R45TS	26	HR10BX
1978 Caprice, Impala	V8-350X	4	R45TS	26	HR10BX
1978-80 Camaro	V8-350Z28	4	R45TS	26	HR10BX
1977-81 Caprice, Impala, Wagon, Corvette, Malibu Wagon	V8-350	4	R45TS	26	HR10BX
CHRYSLER					
1981 Cordoba, Imperial, Newport, New Yorker	L6-225	1	R45TS	27	HR10B
1978-80 Cordoba, Imperial, Newport, New Yorker	L6-225	1	R45TS	27	HR10B
1981 Imperial	V8-318	EFI	R44XLSE	65	WR9D
1981 Cordoba, LeBaron, Newport, New Yorker	V8-318	EFI	R44XLSE	65	WR9H
1981 Cordoba, Imperial, LeBaron, Newport, New Yorker	V8-318	2 or 4	R44XLSE	65	WR9D
1977-80 Cordoba, Imperial, LeBaron, Newport, New Yorker	V8-318	2 or 4	R44XLS	65	WR9D
1977-80 Cordoba, LeBaron, Newport, New Yorker, Chrysler	V8-360	2 or 4	R44XLS	65	WR9D
1977-78 Cordoba, Chrysler	V8-400	2 or 4	R44S	85	WR10F
1978 Chrysler	V8-440	4	R43S	85	WR10F
1977 Chrysler	V8-440	4	R43S	85	WR10F
DODGE					
1981 Aries, Omni	L4-105	2	R42XLS	65	WR7D
1977-80 Aries, Omni	L4-105	2	R42XLS	65	WR8D
1977-81 Aries, Omni	L4-122	2	....	65	WR9D
1981 Aries, Omni	L4-135	2	R44XLS	....	WR9D
1981 Aries	L4-155.9	2	R44XLS	65	WR9D
1978-81 Cordoba, Diplomat, LeBaron, Mirada, Newport, New Yorker, St. Regis	L6-225	1 or 2	R45TS	27	HR10B
1977 Cordoba, LeBaron, Newport, New Yorker	L6-225	1 or 2	R44TS	26	WR9D
1977-80 Aspen, Charger, Charger SE, Diplomat, Magnum, Magnum XE, Mirada, Monaco, Royal Monaco, St. Regis	V8-318	2	R44XLS	65	WR9D
1977-80 Aspen, Charger, Charger SE, Coronet, Dart, Demon, Diplomat, Magnum, Magnum XE, Mirada, Monaco, Royal Monaco, St. Regis	V8-360	4	R44XLS	65	WR9D
1978 Charger, Magnum, Monaco, Royal Monaco	V8-400	4	R44S	85	WR10F
1977 Charger SE, Coronet, Monaco	V8-400	4	R44S	86	WR10F
1977-80 Monaco, Royal Monaco	V8-440	4	R44S	85	WR10F
1977-78 Coronet, Monaco	V8-440 (H.P.)	4	R43S	84	H8B
1981 Cordoba, Imperial, LeBaron	V8-440 (H.P.)	4	R42TS	85	H8B
1981 Newport, New Yorker	V8-318	4	R44XLS	65	WR9DY
1981 Imperial, New Yorker	V8-318	EF1	R44XLS	65	WR9H
FORD					
1981 Escort	L4-98	2	....	3924	FR8DX
1978-81 Fairmont, Granada, Mustang, Mustang II, Pinto	L4-140	2	R43LTS	765	HR9DX
1977 Mustang II, Pinto	L4-140	2	R43LTS	865	HR9D
1981 Fairmont, Mustang	L4-140 Turbo	2	R43LTS	764	HR9D
1977-80 Fairmont, Mustang	L4-140 Turbo	2	R43LTS	764	HR9D
1977-79 Mustang, Mustang II, Pinto	V6-171	2	R43LTS	765	HR9D
1981 Fairmont	L6-200	1	R85TS	746	DR10B
1978-80 Fairmont	L6-200	1	R85TS	746	DR10B
1981 Mustang, Granada, Thunderbird	L6-200	1	R85TS	747	DR10B
1980 Granada	L6-200	2	R85TS	747	DR10B
1978-80 Fairmont, Granada, Mustang	L6-200	1 or 2	R85TS	746	HR10BX
1977 Granada, Maverick	L6-200	1	R85TS	46	DR10B
1978-80 Fairmont, Granada	L6-250	2	R85TS	746	DR10B
1977 Granada, Maverick	L6-250	2	R85TS	46	DR10B
1981 Fairmont, Granada, Mustang, Thunderbird	V8-255	2	R45TS	726	HR10BX
1980 Fairmont, Granada, Mustang, Thunderbird	V8-255	2	R45TS	726	HR10BX
1979-81 Fairmont, Granada, LTD, LTD II, Mustang, Thunderbird	V8-302	2	R45TS	726	HR10BX

*—Original equipment type

**—Autolite recommends 26, however, some early models had the 25 as original equipment. Refer to engine decal for the appropriate spark plug and gap.

1—Bosch, Champion, Mighty, Motorcraft, Nippondenso, Prestolite and Valley Forge spark plugs gapped at 0.060

2—AC, Champion, Mighty MGK and Nippondenso spark plugs gapped at 0.080

3—Mighty, Mopar and Valley Forge spark plugs gapped at 0.035

4—Autolite, Champion, Mighty, Prestolite and Valley Forge spark plugs gapped at 0.044, Nippondenso at 0.035

5—AC, Bosch, NGK and Nippondenso 1981 spark plugs gapped at 0.044; Champion and Prestolite gapped at 0.035

SPARK PLUG CONVERSION CHART

CHAMPION	MIGHTY	MOPAR	MOTORCRAFT	NKG	NIPPONDENSO	PRESTOLITE	VALLEY FORGE	GAP
RBL17Y	M4RF52	....	ARF52	BPR4FS-11	T16PR-U11	14RF52A	25R —	0.045[4]
RBL15Y4	M4RF52	....	ARF52	BPR4FS-11	T16PR-U11	14RF525[13]	25R	0.045
RBL15Y8	....	....	ARF52-8	....	T16PR-U15	14RF528	....	0.060[2]
RBL15Y6	M4RF526	....	ARF52-8	BPR4FS-15	T16PR-U15	14RF52A	125R	0.080[1]
RBL17Y6	M4RF626	....	ARF62-6	BPR4FS-15	T16PR-U15	14RF52A	126R	0.060
RBL15Y4	M4RF52	....	ARF52-6	BPR4FS-11	T16PR-U11	14RF52	25R	0.040[15]
RBL17Y	M4RF62	....	ARF62	BPR4FS	T14PR-U	14RF52	26R	0.035
RBL15Y4	M4RF52	....	ARF42	BPR4FS-11	T16PR-U11	14RF525[13]	25R	0.045
....	....	....	ARF42	BPR4FS-11	T16PR-U11	14RF52A	25R	0.060
RBL15Y4	M4RF52	....	ARF52	BPR4FS-11	T16PR-U11	14RF525[13]	25R	0.060[15]
RBL15Y4	M4RF52	....	ARF52	BPR4FS-11	W20ESR	14RF525[13]	25R	0.045
RBL15Y4	M4RF52	....	ARF52	BPR4FS-11	....	14RF52A	25R	0.060
RBL15Y4	M4RF52	....	ARF52	BPR4FS-11	T16PR-U11	14RF52A	25R	0.045
RBL15Y4	M4RF52	....	ARF52	BPR4FS-11	T16PR-U11	14RF525[13]	25R	0.045
RBL16Y	M4RF62	P-560PR4	ARF62	BPR4FS-11	....	14RF62	26R	0.048[4]
RBL16Y	M4RF62	P-560PR4	ARF62	BPR4FS	T14PR-U	14RF62	26R	0.035
RN12Y	....	P-68ER	AGR42	....	....	14GR42	34R	0.048[4]
RN14LY	....	P-65PR4	AGR42	....	....	14GR42	34R	0.035
RN12Y	....	P-65PR4	AGR42	BPR5ES-11	....	14GR42	34R	0.035[9]
RN12Y	MGR42	P-65PR4	AGR42	EPR5ES	W16EXR-U	14GR42	34R	0.035
RN12Y	MGR42	P-65PR	AGR42	EPR5ES	W16EXR-U	14GR42	34R	0.035
0J13Y	M4R42	P-35PX	AR42	BPR5S	W14PR-U	14R42	44R	0.035
0J13Y	M4R42	P-35PX	AR42	BPR5S	W14PR-U	14R42	44R	0.035
RJ13Y	M4R42	P-35RR	AR42	BPR5S	W14PR-U	14R42	44R	0.035
RN94	....	P-65PR4	AGR42	BPR5ES-11	W16EXR-U	14GR42	....	0.048[4]
RN9Y	....	P-65PR	AGR42	BPR5ES	W16EXR-U	14GR42	....	0.035
....	....	....	AGR42	....	....	....	....	....
RN12Y	M4GR42	P-65PR	AGR42	BPR5ES	....	14GR42	....	0.035
RN12Y	M4GR42	P-65PR	AGR42	BPR5ES	....	14GR42	....	0.041[4]
RBL16Y	M4RF62[13]	P-560PR4	ARF62	BPR5ES	T14PR-U15	14RF62	26R	0.035
RBL15Y	M4RF52	P-558PR	ARF52	BPR4FS	T16PR-U	14RF52	25R	0.035
RN12Y	M4GR42	P-65PR4	AGR42	BPR5ES	W16EXR-U	14GR42	34R	0.035[10]
RN12Y	M4GR42	P-65PR	AGR42	BPR5ES	W16EX-U	14GR42	34R	0.035
0J13Y	M4R42	P-35PX	AR42	BPR5S	W17P	14R42	44R	0.035
RJ13Y	M4R42	P-35PR	AR42	BPR5S	W14P	14R42	44R	0.035
0J11Y	M4R42	P-35PR	AR42	BPR5S	W17P	....	....	0.035
RJ11Y	M4R42	P-34PX	AR52	BPR5S	W17P	14R32	44R	0.035
RJ11Y	M4R42	P-34P	ARF62	BPR5S	W17P	14R32	44R	0.035
RN12Y	....	P-65PR4	AGR42	BPR5ES-11	W16EX-U11	14GR42	34R	0.048
RN12Y	....	P-65PR4	AGR42	BPR5ES-11	W16EX-U11	14GR42	34R	0.048
....	....	....	AGSP32	....	....	14GRP32	....	0.044
RBN12Y	M4WRF42	....	AWSF42	BPR5EFS	T16EPR-U	14GRF52	175R	0.034[5]
RBN12Y	M4WRF42	....	AWSF42	BPR5EFS	....	14GRF52	175R	0.034[4]
RBN12Y	M4WRF42	....	AWSF32	BPR5EFS	T16EPR-U	14GRF32	....	0.034
RBN12Y	M4WRF42	....	AWSF32	BPR6EFS	T16EPR-U	14GRF32	....	0.034
RBN12Y	M4WRF42	....	AWSF42	BPR5EFS	....	14GRF52	175R	0.034[4]
RF14Y	M8RF82	....	BSF92	APR5FS-15	....	18RF82	18R	0.050
RF14Y	M8RF82	....	BSF82	APR5FS-15	MA14P-U	18RF82T	18R	0.050
RF14Y	....	....	BSF92	APR5FS-15	....	18RF82	18R	0.050
RF14Y	....	....	BSF82	APR5FS-15	MA14P-U	18RF82T	18R	0.050
RF14Y	M8RF82	....	BRF82	APRFS-15	MA14P-U	18RF82T	18R	0.050
RF14Y	M8RF82	....	BRF82	APR5ES-15	MA14P-U	18RF82	18R	0.050[7]
RF14Y	M8RF82	....	BSF82	APR5FS-15	MA14P-U	14RF82	18R	0.050
RF14Y	M8RF82	....	BRF82	APR5FS-15	MA14P-U	18RF82	18R	0.050
RBL17Y6	M4RF52	....	ASF52	BPR4FS-15	T16PR-U15	14RF52 5[13]	25R	0.050
RBL17Y6	M4RF52	....	ASF52	BPR4FS-15	T16PR-U15	14RF52 5[13]	25R	0.050
RBL17Y6	M4RF52	....	ASF52	BPR4FS-15	T16PR-U15	14RF525[12]	25R	0.050

[6]—Bosch, NGK 1981 spark plugs gapped at 0.044, Motorcraft 0.034 and Prestolite 0.035; for 1979 to 1980 Champion spark plugs gapped at 0.035 and NGK and Nippondenso at 0.034

[7]—Autolite spark plugs gapped at 0.044
[8]—Bosch, Champion, Mopar, NGK and Nippondenso spark plugs gapped at 0.048
[9]—Champion, Mopar and NGK spark plugs gapped at 0.048

[10]—Champion, Mopar and Nippondenso spark plugs for 1981 gapped at 0.048
[11]—Mighty spark plugs for 1981 gapped at 0.048

[12]—or 14RF42A
[13]—or 14RF52A
[14]—or 14RF52A
[15]—Nippondenso spark plugs gapped at 0.045
[16]—Nippondenso spark plugs gapped at 0.030

AUTOMOBILE	YEAR/MAKE/MODEL	ENGINE	BBLs	AC	AUTOLITE	BOSCH
	Ford continued					
1978	Fairmont, Granada, LTD, LTD II, Ford, Maverick, Mustang II, Thunderbird	V8-302	2	R45TSX	666	HR10BX
1978-80	Fairmont, Granada, LTD, LTD II, Ford Maverick, Mustang II, Thunderbird	V8-302(calif.)	2	R45TSX	666	HR10BY
1977	Granada, LTD, LTD II, Maverick, Mustang II, Thunderbird	V8-302	2	R45TSX	26	HR10BX
1981	LTD	V8-351	VV	R45TSX	26	HR10BX
1980	LTD	V8-351	2 or 4	R45TSX	726	HR10BX
1978-79	LTD, Thunderbird	V8-351M	2 or 4	R45TSX	726	HR10BX
1977	LTD	V8-351M	2 or 4	R45TSX	26	HR10BX
1979-80	LTD, LTD II, Thunderbird	V8-351W	2	R45TSX	26	HR10BX
1977-78	Granada, LTD, LTD II, Thunderbird	V8-351W	2	R45TSX	26	HR10BX
1978	LTD, LTD II, Thunderbird	V8-400	2 or 4	R45TSX	726	HR10BX
1977	Ford, LTD II, Thunderbird	V8-400	2 or 4	R45TSX	26	HR10BX
1977	LTD, Thunderbird	V8-400	2 or 4	R45TSX	26	HR10BX
1977	LTD, Thunderbird	V8-400(calif.)	2 or 4	R45TSX	666	HR10BX
1977-78	Elite, Ford, LTD	V8-460	4	R45TSX	26	HR10BX
	LINCOLN CONTINENTAL					
1981	Continental, Mark VI, Versailles	V8-302	FI	R45TS	726	HR10BX
1978-80	Continental, Mark VI, Versailles	V8-302	2	R45TSX	726	HR10BX
1977-78	Versailles	V8-302	2	R45TSX	26	HR10BX
1977-79	Versailles	V8-302(calif.)	2	R45TSX	666	HR10BY
1981	Continental, Mark VI, Versailles	V8-351	2	R45TS	726	HR10BX
1980	Continental, Mark VI, Versailles	V8-351	2	R45TS	726	HR10BX
1977	Versailles	V8-351	2	R45TSX	26	HR10BX
1978-79	Continental, Mark V	V8-400	4	R45TSX	726	HR10BX
1977	Continental, Mark V	V8-400	4	R45TSX	26	HR10BX
1977	Continental, Mark V	V8-400(calif.)	4	R45TSX	26	HR10BX
1977-78	Continental, Mark V, Mark IV	V8-460	4	R45TSX	26	HR10BX
	MERCURY					
1981	Lynx	L4-98	2	....	3924	FR8DX
1978-81	Bobcat, Capri, Capri II, Cougar, Zephyr	L4-140	2	R43LTS	765	HR9DX
1977	Bobcat, Capri II	L4-140	2	R43LTS	865	HR9D
1979-81	Capri, Zephyr	L4-140 Turbo	2	R43LTS	764	HR9D
1977-79	Bobcat, Capri, Capri II	V6-171	2	R43LTS	765	HR9D
1981	Capri, Cougar, XR-7, Zephyr	L6-200	1	....	747	DR10B
1977-80	Capri, Monarch, Zephyr	L6-200	1	R85TS	746	DR10B
1977	Comet, Monarch	L6-200	1	R85TS	46	DR10B
1978-80	Monarch, Zephyr	L6-250	1 or 2	R85TS	746	DR10B
1977	Comet, Monarch	L6-250	1 or 2	R85TS	46	DR10B
1981	Capri, Cougar, XR-7, Marquis, Zephyr	V8-255	2	R45TS	726	HR10BX
1980	Capri, Monarch, XR-7, Zephyr	V8-255	2	R44TSX	746	HR10BX
1981	XR-7, Marquis, Cougar	V8-302	2	R45TS	726	HR10BX
1979-80	Capri, Cougar, XR-7, Marquis, Monarch, Zephyr	V8-302	2	R45TS	726	HR10BX
1979	Marquis, Cougar, XR-7, Zephyr	V8-302 (calif)	2	R45TSX	3606	HR10BY
1977-79	Comet, Cougar, XR-7, Monarch, Zephyr	V8-302 (calif)	2	R45TSX	666	HR10BY
1979-80	Marquis, Mercury, Monterey	V8-351	2	R45TSX	726	HR10BX
1980	Marquis, Mercury, Monterey	V8-351 (calif)	2 or 4	R45TSX	726	HR10BY
1981	Marquis	V8-351	VV	R45TS	726	HR10BX
1978-80	Cougar, XR-7, Marquis	V8-351M	2	R45TSX	726	HR10BX
1977	Cougar, XR-7, Marquis, Mercury, Montego, Monterey	V8-351M	2	R45TSX	26	HR10BX
1979-80	Cougar, XR-7, Marquis	V8-351W	2	R45TSX	726	HR10BX
1977-78	Cougar, XR-7, Monarch, Montego	V8-351W	2	R45TSX	26	HR10BX
1978	Cougar, XR-7, Marquis	V8-400	4	R45TSX	726	HR10BX
1977	Cougar, XR-7, Marquis, Mercury, Monterey	V8-400	4	R45TSX	26	HR10BX
1977	Cougar, XR-7, Marquis, Mercury, Monterey	V8-400 (calif)	4	R45TSX	26	HR10BY
1977-78	Marquis, Mercury, Monterey	V8-460	4	R45TSX	26	HR10BX
	OLDSMOBILE					
1977	Starfire	L4-140	2	R43TS	24	HR88
1980-81	Omega, Starfire	L4-151	2	R44TSX	665	HR9BY
1979	Starfire	L4-151	2	R44TSX	665	HR9BY
1978	Starfire	L4-151	2	R43TSX	664	HR10BY
1981	Omega	V6-173	2	R43TS	24	HR8B
1980	Omega	V6-173	2	R43TS	25	HR9B
1981	Cutlass, 88	V6-231	2	R45TS8	966	HR9BY
1980	Cutlass, 88, Omega, Starfire	V6-231	2	R45TSX	666	HR8BY
1979	F85, Cutlass, Starfire	V6-231	2	R45TSX	666	HR9BY
1977-78	Cutlass, 88, Omega	....	....	....	....	....
1981	Starfire, 98	V6-231	2	R46TSX	667	HR9BY
1981	Cutlass, 88	V6-231 turbo	4	R45TS	966	HR9BY

*—Original equipment type

**—Autolite recommends 26, however, some early models had the 25 as original equipment. Refer to engine decal for the appropriate spark plug and gap.

1—Bosch, Champion, Mighty, Motorcraft, Nippondenso, Prestolite and Valley Forge spark plugs gapped at 0.060
2—AC, Champion, Mighty MGK and Nippondenso spark plugs gapped at 0.080

3—Mighty, Mopar and Valley Forge spark plugs gapped at 0.035
4—Autolite, Champion, Mighty, Prestolite and Valley Forge spark plugs gapped at 0.044, Nippondenso at 0.035

5—AC, Bosch, NGK and Nippondenso 1981 spark plugs gapped at 0.044; Champion and Prestolite gapped at 0.035

SPARK PLUG CONVERSION CHART

CHAMPION	MIGHTY	MOPAR	MOTORCRAFT	NKG	NIPPONDENSO	PRESTOLITE	VALLEY FORGE	GAP
RBL17Y6	M4RF52	....	ARF52	BPR4FS-15	T16PR-U15	14RF52A	25R	0.050
RBL17Y6	M4RF526	....	ASF52-6	BPR4FS-15	T16PR-U15	14RF52A	125R	0.060
RBL17Y6	M4RF52	....	ARF52	BPR4FS-15	T16PR-U15	14RF52A	25R	0.050
RBL17Y6	M4RF52	....	ASF52	BPR4FS-15	T16PR-U15	14RF52 5[13]	24R	0.060**
RBL17Y6	M4RF52	....	ASF42	BPR4FS-15	T16PR-U15	14RF52A	25R	0.050
RBL17Y6	M4RF52	....	ASF52	BPR4FS-15	T16PR-U15	14RF52A	25A	0.050
RBL17Y6	M4RF52	....	ASF52-6	BPR4FS-15	T16PR-U15	14RF52A	25A	0.050**
RBL17Y6	M4RF52	....	ASF42	BPR4FS-15	....	14RF52A	25R	0.050
RBL17Y6	M4RF52	....	ARF52	BPR4FS-15	T16PR-U15	14RF52A	25R	0.050**
RBL17Y6	M4RF52	....	ASF52	BPR4FS-15	T16PR-U15	14RF52A	25R	0.050
RBL17Y6	M4RF52	....	ASF52-6	BPR4FS-15	T16PR-U15	14RF52A	25R	0.050*
RBL17Y6	M4RF52	....	ARF52	BPR4FS-15	T16PR-U15	14RF52A	25R	0.050**
RBL17Y6	M4RF526	....	ARF52-6	BPR4FS-15	T16PR-U15	14RF52A	....	0.060
RBL17Y6	M4RF52	....	ARF52	BPR4FS-15	T16PR-U15	14RF52A	25R	0.050
....	M4RF52	....	ASF52	....	T16PR-U15	14RF52 5[13]	25R	0.050
RBL17Y6	M4RF52	....	ASF52	BPR4FS-15	T16PR-U15	14RF52A	25R	0.050
RBL17Y6	M4RF52	....	ARF52	BPR4FS-15	T16PR-U15	14RF52A	25R	0.050
RBL17Y6	M4RF52	....	ARF52-6	BPR4FS-15	T16PR-U15	14RF52A	125R	0.060
RBL17Y6	M4RF52	....	ASF52	BPR4FS-15	T16PR-U15	14RF52 5[13]	25R	0.050
RBL17Y6	M4RF52	....	ASF52	BPR4FS-15	T16PR-U15	14RF52A	25R	0.050
RBL17Y6	M4RF52	....	ARF52	BPR4FS-15	T16PR-U15	14RF52A	25R	0.050
RBL17Y6	M4RF52	....	ASF52	BPR4FS-15	T16PR-U15	14RF52A	25R	0.050
RBL17Y6	M4RF52	....	ARF52	BPR4FS-15	T16PR-U15	14RF52A	25R	0.050
RBL17T6	M4RF526	....	ARF52-6	BPR4FS-15	T16PR-U15	14RF52A	125R	0.060
RBL17Y6	M4RF52	....	ARF52	BPR4FS-15	T16PR-U15	14RF52A	25R	0.050
....	....	....	AGSP32	....	W20EXR-U	14GRP32	175R	0.044[16]
RBN12Y	M4WRF42	....	AWSF42	BPR5EFS	T16EPR-U	14GRF52	175R	0.050[5]
RBN12Y	M4WRF42	....	AWRF42	BPR5EFS	T16EPR-U	14GRF52	175R	0.034*
RBN12Y	M4WRF42	....	AWSF42	BPR5EFS	T16EPR-U	14GFR32	....	0.034[4]
RBN12Y	M4WRF42	....	AWSF42	BPR5EFS	W16EX-U	14GRF-52	175R	0.034[4]
RF14Y	....	....	BSF92	APR5FS-15	MA9PR-U	18RF82	....	0.050
RF14Y	M8RF82	....	BSF82	APR5FS-15	MA9PR-U	18RF82	18R	0.050
RF14Y	M8RF82	....	BRF82	APR5FS-15	MA14P-U	18RF82	18R	0.050
RF14Y	M8RF82	....	BSF82	APR5FS-15	MA14P-U	18RF82	18R	0.050
RF14Y	M8R82	....	BRF82	APR5FS-15	MA14P-U	18RF82	18R	0.050
RBL17Y6	M4RF52	....	ASF52	BPR4FS-15	T16PR-U15	14RF52 5[13]	25R	0.050
RBL17Y6	M4RF42	....	BPRF82	APR5FS-15	T16PR-U15	14RF42A	24R	0.050
RBL17Y6	M4RF52	....	ASF52	BPR4FS-15	T16PR-U15	14RF52 5[13]	25R	0.050
RBL17Y6	M4RF52	....	ASF52	BPR4FS-15	T16PR-U15	14RF52A	25R	0.050
RBL17Y6	M4RF526	....	ASF52-6	BPR4FS-15	T16PR-U15	14RF52A	125R	0.060
RBL17Y6	M4RF526	....	ARF52-6	BPR5FS-15	T16PR-U15	14RF52A	125R	0.060
RBL17Y6	M4RF52	....	ASF52	BPR4FS-15	T16PR-U15	14RF52A	125R	0.050
RBL17Y6	M4RF526	....	ARF52-6	BPR4FS-15	T16PR-U15	14RF52A	125R	0.060
RBL17Y6	M4RF52	....	ASF52-6	BPR4FS-15	T16PR-U15	14RF52 5[13]	....	0.050
RBL17Y6	M4RF52	....	ASF52	BPR4FS-15	T16PR-U15	14RF52A	25R	0.044**
RBL17Y6	M4RF52	....	ARF52	BPR4FS-15	T16PR-U15	14RF52A	25R	0.050
RBL17Y6	M4RF52	....	ASF52	BPR4FS-15	T16PR-U15	14RF52A	25R	0.050**
RBL17Y6	M4RF52	....	ARF52	BPR4FS-15	T16PR-U15	14RF52A	25R	0.050
RBL17Y6	M4RF52	....	ASF52	BPR4FS-15	T16PR-U15	14RF52A	25R	0.050
RBL17Y6	M4RF52	....	AFR52-6	BPR4FS-15	T16PR-U15	14RF52A	125R	0.060
RBL17Y6	M4RF52	....	ARF52	BPR4FS-15	T16PR-U15	14RF52A	25R	0.060
RBL11Y	M4RF32	....	ARF32	BPR5FS	T20PR-U	14RF32	23R	0.035
RBL13Y6	M4RF426	....	ARF42-6	BPR5FS-15	T16PR-U15	14RF42 5[12]	124R	0.060
RBL13Y6	M4RF426	....	ARF42-6	BPR6FS-15	T20PR-U15	14RF32A	124R	0.060
RBL13Y6	....	....	ARF32-6	BPR6FS-15	T20PR-U15	14RF32A	124R	0.060
RBL11Y	M4RF32	....	ASF32	BPR6FS	T20PR-U11	14RF32	24R	0.045[4]
RBL13Y	M4RF42	....	ARF42-6	BPR5FS-11	T16PR-U11	14RF42A	24R	0.045
RBL15Y8	....	....	ARF52-8	BPR4FS-20	T16PR-U15	14RF52 8	....	0.080
RBL15Y6	M4RF526	....	ASF52-6	BPR4FS-15	T16PR-U15	14RF52A	125R	0.060
RBL15Y6	M4RF526	....	ARF52-6	BPR4ES	T16PR-U15	14RF52A	125R	0.060
RBL17Y6	M4RF626	....	ARF62-6	BPR4FS-15	T16PR-U15	14RF52A	126R	0.060
RBL15Y4	....	....	ARF52	BPR4FS-11	....	14RF52	....	0.040

*—Bosch, NGK 1981 spark plugs gapped at 0.044, Motorcraft 0.034 and Prestolite 0.035; for 1979 to 1980 Champion spark plugs gapped at 0.035 and NGK and Nippondenso at 0.034

[7]—Autolite spark plugs gapped at 0.044
[8]—Bosch, Champion, Mopar, NGK and Nippondenso 1981 spark plugs gapped at 0.048
[9]—Champion, Mopar and NGK spark plugs gapped at 0.048

[10]—Champion, Mopar and Nippondenso spark plugs for 1981 gapped at 0.048
[11]—Mighty spark plugs for 1981 gapped at 0.048

[12]—or 14RF42A
[13]—or 14RF52A
[14]—or 14R52A
[15]—Nippondenso spark plugs gapped at 0.045
[16]—Nippondenso spark plugs gapped at 0.030

SPARK PLUG CONVERSION CHART

AUTOMOBILE YEAR/MAKE/MODEL	ENGINE	BBLs	AC	AUTOLITE	BOSCH
Oldsmobile continued					
1981 Toronado, 98	V6-252	4	R45TS8	966	HR9BY
1981 Cutlass, 88	V8-260	2	R46SX	567	WR10FY
1980 Cutlass, 88	V8-260	2	R46SX	567	WR10FY
1977-79 Cutlass, 88, Omega, 98, Toronado	V8-260	2	R46SZ	847	WR10FY
1980-81 88	V8-265	2	R45TSX	666	HR9BY
1980 88	V8-301	2	R46TSX	667	HR9BY
1979 88	V8-301	2	R46TSX	667	HR10BY
1977-80 Cutlass, Omega, Starfire	V8-305	2	R45TS	26	HR10BX
1981 Cutlass	V8-305	4	R45TS	....	HR10BX
1977-80 Cutlass	V8-305	4	R45TS	26	HR10BX
1980-81 Cutlass, 88, 98, Toronado	V8-307	4	R46SX	567	WR10FY
1977 Cutlass, Delta 88, 98, Omega	V8-350	2 or 4	R46SZ	847	WR10FY
1977-79 Cutlass, Omega, Delta 88, 98	V8-350L	4	R45TS	26	HR10BX
1980-81 Cutlass, Supreme, 88, 98, Toronado	V8-350R	4	R46SX	567	WR10FY
1977-79 Delta, 88, 98, Omega	V8-350R	2 or 4	R46SZ	847	WR10FY
1978 Oldsmobile	V8-350X	4	R46SZ	667	....
1977-79 88, 98, Toronado	V8-403	4	R46SZ	847	WR10FY
PLYMOUTH					
1981 Horizon, TC-3	L4-105	2	R42XLS	65	WR8D
1977-80 Horizon, TC-3	L4-105	2	R42XLS	65	WR8D
1981 Horizon, TC-3, Reliant K	L4-122	2	R44XLS	65	WR9D
1981 Horizon, TC-3, Reliant K	L4-135	2	R44XLS	....	WR9D
1981 Reliant K	L4-158.6	2	R44XLS	65	WR9D
1981 Duster, Fury, Gran Fury, Volare	L6-225	1	R45TS	27	HR10BX
1978-80 Duster, Fury, Gran Fury, Volare	L6-225	1	R45TS	27	HR10BX
1977 Duster, Fury, Scamp, Valiant, Volare	L6-225	1 or 2	R44TS	26	HR9B
1981 Duster, Fury, Scamp, Valiant, Volare	V8-318	2 or 4	R44XLS	65	WR9D
1977-80 Duster, Fury, Scamp, Valiant, Volare	V8-318	2 or 4	R44XLS	65	WR9D
1981 Grand Fury	V8-318	4	R44XLS	65	WR9DY
1978 Fury, Grand Fury	V8-400	4	R44S	85	WR10F
1977 Fury, Grand Fury	V8-400	4	R44S	85	WR10F
1978 Fury	V8-440	4	R44S	84	
1977 Fury, Grand Fury	V8-440	4	R44S	85	WR10F
1978 Grand Fury	V8-440HP	4	R43S	85	....
1977 Grand Fury	V8-440HP	4	R43S	85	WR10F
PONTIAC					
1977 Astre, Sunbird	L4-140	1 or 2	R43TS	24	HR8B
1981 Phoenix, Sunbird	L4-151	2	R44TSX	665	HR9BY
1977-80 Astre, Phoenix, Sunbird, Ventura	L4-151	2	R43TSX	664	HR10BY
1977 Astre, Phoenix, Sunbird, Ventura	L4-151	2	R44TSX	665	HR10BY
1981 Phoenix	V6-173	2	R43TS	24	HR8B
1980 Phoenix	V6-173	2	R44TS	25	HR8B
1980-81 Grand Am, LeMans	V6-229	2	R45TS	....	
1981 Catalina, Bonneville, LeMans	V6-231	2	R45TS8	966	HR9BY
1979-80 Bonneville, Catalina, Firebird, Grand Prix, LeMans, Phoenix, Sunbird, Trans Am	V6-231	2	R45TSX	666	HR9BY
1977-78 Bonneville, Catalina, Firebird, Grand Am, Grand Prix, LeMans, Phoenix, Sunbird, Trans Am	V6-231	2	R46TSX	667	HR9BY
1980-81 Bonneville, Catalina, Firebird, Grand Am, Grand Prix, LeMans, Trans Am, Formula, Espirit	V8-265	2	R45TSX	666	HR9BY
1981 Bonneville, Catalina, Wagon	V8-267	2	R45TS	....	HR10BX
1978-79 Bonneville, Catalina, Firebird, Grand Am, Grand Prix, LeMans, Phoenix, Trans Am, Ventura	V8-301	2	R46TSX	667	HR9BY
1978-81 Bonneville, Catalina, Firebird, Grand Am, Grand Prix, LeMans, Trans Am	V8-301	4	R45TSX	666	HR10BY
1979-81 Firebird, Trans Am	V8-301 Turbo	4	R45TSX	4	HR9BY
1977-81 Firebird, Grand Am, Grand Prix, LeMans, Phoenix, Sunbird, Trans Am, Ventura	V8-305	2 or 4	R45TS	26	HR10BX
1981 Bonneville, Wagon, Catalina, Formula	V8-307	4	R46SX	567	WR10FY
1977-79 Firebird, Grand Am, LeMans, Phoenix, Trans Am, Ventura	V8-350L	4	R45TS	26	HR10BX
1977 ..Bonneville, Catalina, Firebird, Grand Prix, LeMans	V8-350P	4	R45TSX	666	HR10BY
1980 Bonneville, Catalina	V8-350R	4	R46SX	567	WR10FY
1977-79 Bonneville, Catalina, Firebird, Grand Prix, LeMans, Phoenix, Ventura	V8-350R	4	R46SZ	847	WR10FY
1980 Bonneville, Catalina	V8-350X	4	R45TSX	666	WR10FY
1979 Bonneville, Catalina	V8-350X	4	R45TSX	666	HR10BY
1978 Bonneville, Catalina	V8-350X	4	R45TSX	667	HR10BY
1977-79 Bonneville, Catalina, Firebird, Grand Prix, LeMans, Trans Am	V8-400	4	R45TSX	666	HR10BY
1977-79 Bonneville, Catalina, Firebird, Grand Prix, LeMans, Trans Am	V8-403	4	R46SZ	847	WR10FY

*—Original equipment type
**—Autolite recommends 26, however, some early models had the 25 as original equipment. Refer to engine decal for the appropriate spark plug and gap.

[1]—Bosch, Champion, Mighty, Motorcraft, Nippondenso, Prestolite and Valley Forge spark plugs gapped at 0.060
[2]—AC, Champion, Mighty MGK and Nippondenso spark plugs gapped at 0.080

[3]—Mighty, Mopar and Valley Forge spark plugs gapped at 0.035
[4]—Autolite, Champion, Mighty, Prestolite and Valley Forge spark plugs gapped at 0.044, Nippondenso at 0.035

[5]—AC, Bosch, NGK and Nippondenso 1981 spark plugs gapped at 0.044; Champion and Prestolite gapped at 0.035

SPARK PLUG CONVERSION CHART

CHAMPION	MIGHTY	MOPAR	MOTORCRAFT	NKG	NIPPONDENSO	PRESTOLITE	VALLEY FORGE	GAP
RBL15Y8	....	....	....	BPR4FS-20	T16PR-U15	14RF528	....	0.080
RJ18Y8	M4R828	....	AR82-8	BPR4S-20	....	14R526[14]	148R	0.080
RJ18Y8	M4R828	....	ARF52-6	BPR4S-20	W14P	14RS52A	148R	0.080
RJ18Y6	M4R826	....	AR82-8	BPR4S-15	W14P	14RS52A	167R	0.060
RBL15Y6	M4RF526	....	....	BPR4FS-15	T16PR-U15	14RF525[13]	125R	0.060
RBL17Y6	....	....	....	BPR4FS-15	T16PR-U15	14RF52A	....	0.060
RBL17Y6	....	....	....	BPR4FS-15	T16PR-U15	14RF52A	....	0.060
RBL15Y4	....	....	ARF52	BPR4FS-11	T16PR-U15	14RF52A	25R	0.045
RBL15Y4	M4RF52	....	ARF52-6	BPR4FS-11	T16PR-U11	14RF525[15]	25R	0.045
RBL15Y4	M4RF52	....	ARF62-6	BPR4FS-11	T16PR-U15	14RF52A	25R	0.060
RJ18Y8	M4R828	....	ARF52-6	BPR4S-20	W9P	14R526[14]	148R	0.080
RBL15Y4	M4R828	....	ARF62-6	ARF52	T16PR-U15	....	148R	0.045
RBL15Y4	M4RF52	....	ARF52	BPR4FS-11	T16PR-U11	14RF52A	25R	0.045
RJ18Y8	M4R828	....	AR82-8	BPR4S-20	W9P	14R525[14]	148R	0.080
RJ18Y6	M4R828	....	AR82-6	BPR4S-15	W14P	14R52A	167R	0.060
....	M4RF626	....	ARF62-6	BPR4FS-15	T16PR-U15	....	126R	0.060
RJ18Y6	M4R826	....	AR82-6	BPR4S-15	W14P	14R52A	167R	0.060
RN12Y	M4GR42	P65PR4	AGR42	BPR5ES-11	W16EXR-U11	14GR42	34R	0.035
RN12Y	M4GR42	P-65PR4	AGR42	BPR5ES	W16EXR-U	14GR42	34R	0.035[10]
....	M4GR42	....	AGR42	....	W16EXR-U	14GR22	34R	0.035
RN12Y	....	P-65PR	AGR42	BPR5ES	....	14GR42	....	0.035
RN12Y	M4GR42	P-65PR	AGR22	BPR5ES-11	W16EXR-U11	14GR42	34R	0.044
RBL16Y	M4RF62	P-560PR4	....	BPR4FS-11[4]	T14PR-U11	14RF62	26R	0.035[10]
RBL16Y	M4RF62	P-560PR	ARF62	BPR4FS	T14PR-U	14RF62	26R	0.035
RBL15Y	M4RF52	P-558PR	ARF52	BPR4FS	T16PR-U	14RF52	25R	0.035
RN12Y	M4GR42	P-65PR4	AGR42	BPR5ES-11	W16EX-U11	14GR42	34R	0.035[16]
RN12Y	M4GR42	P-65PR4	AGR42	BPR5ES	W16EXR-U	14GR42	34R	0.035
RN12Y	M46R42	P-65PR4	AGR42	BPR5ES-11	W16EXR-U11	14GR42	34R	0.048
OJ13Y	M4R42	P-35PX	AR42	BPR5S	W16EX-U	14R42	125R	0.035
OJ13Y	M4R42	P-35PX	AR42	BPR5S	W14P	14R42	125R	0.035
RJ11Y	M4R42	P-35PR	AR42	BPR5S	W14P	14R42	44R	0.035
RJ13Y	....	P-35PR	AR42	BPR5S	W17P	14R42	44R	0.035
RJ11Y	....	P-34PX	AG42	BPR5S	W17P	14R32	44R	0.035
RJ11Y	....	P-34P	AR42	BPR5S	W17P	14R32	44R	0.035
RBL11Y	M4RF32	....	ARF32	BPR5FS	T20PR-U	14RF32	23R	0.035
RBL13Y6	M4RF426	....	ARF52-8	BPR5FS-15	T20PR-U	14RF425[12]	124R	0.060[2]
RBL13Y6	M4RF426	....	ARF42-6	BPR6FS-15	T20PR-U15	14RF-42A	124R	0.060
RBL13YL	M4RF426	....	ARF42-6	BPR6FS-15	T16PR-U15	14RF-42A	124R	0.060
RBL11Y	M4RF32	....	ASF32	BPR6FS	T20PR-U11	14RF32	23R	0.045
RBL13Y	M4RF42	....	ARF42	BPR5FS-11	T16PR-U11	14RF32	24R	0.045
RBL15Y4	....	....	ARF52	....	T16PR-U11	14RF525[15]	....	0.045
RBL15Y8	....	....	ARF52-8	BPR4FS-20	T16PR-U15	14RF528[15]	....	0.080
RBL15Y6	M4RF526	....	ARF52-6	BPR4FS-15	T16PR-U15	14RF525[13]	....	0.060
RBL17Y6	M4RF627	....	ARF52-6	BPR4FS-15	T16PR-U15	14RF52A	126R	0.060
RBL15Y6	M4RF526	....	ARF52-6	BPR4FS-15	T16PR-U15	14RF525[13]	125R	0.060
RBL15Y4	....	....	ARF52	....	T16PR-U11	....	....	0.045
RBL17Y6	M4RF626	....	ARF52-6	BPR4FS-15	T16PR-U15	14RF626[15]	126R	0.060
RBL15Y6	M4RF526	....	ARF52-6	BPR4FS-15	T16PR-U15	14RF525[13]	125R	0.060
RBL17Y6	M4RF526	....	ARF52-6	BPR4FS-15	T16PR-U15	14RF525[13]	125R	0.060
RBL15Y4	M4RF52	....	ARF52	BPR4FS-11	T16PR-U11	14RF525[13]	25R	0.045
RJ18Y8	M4R826	....	AR82-8	BPR4S-20	W9P	14R526[14]	148R	0.080[1]
RBL15Y4	M4RF52	....	ARF52	BPR4FS-11	T16PR-U11	14RF52A	25R	0.045
RBL17Y6	M4RF526	....	ARF52-6	BPR4FS-15	T16PR-U15	14RF52A	125R	0.060
RJ18Y8	M4R828	....	AR82-8	BPR4S-20	W14P	14R52A	148R	0.080
RJ18Y6	M4R826	....	AR82-6	BPR4S-15	W14P	14R52A	167R	0.060
RBL15Y6	M4RF52	....	ARF52	BPR4FS-15	T16PR-U15	14RF52A	125R	0.060
RBL17Y6	M4RF526	....	ARF52-6	BPR4FS-15	T16PR-U15	14RF52A	125R	0.060
RBL17Y6	M4RF626	....	ARF62-6	BPR4FS-15	T16PR-U15	14RF52A	126R	0.060
RBL17Y6	M4RF526	....	ARF52-6	BPR4FS-15	T16PR-U15	14RF52A	125R	0.060
RJ18Y6	M4R826	....	AR82-6	BPR4S-15	W14P	14R52A	167R	0.060

—Bosch, NGK 1981 spark plugs gapped at 0.044, Motorcraft 0.034 and Prestolite 0.035; for 1979 to 1980 Champion spark plugs gapped at 0.035 and NGK and Nippondenso at 0.034.

[7]—Autolite spark plugs gapped at 0.044

[8]—Bosch, Champion, Mopar, NGK and Nippondenso 1981 spark plugs gapped at 0.048

[9]—Champion, Mopar and NGK spark plugs gapped at 0.048

[10]—Champion, Mopar and Nippondenso spark plugs for 1981 gapped at 0.048

[11]—Mighty spark plugs for 1981 gapped at 0.048

[12]—or 14RF42A

[13]—or 14RF52A

[14]—or 14R52A

[15]—Nippondenso spark plugs gapped at 0.045

[16]—Nippondenso spark plugs gapped at 0.030

ENGLISH TO METRIC CONVERSION: TORQUE   FT./LBS.

Torque is expressed as either foot-pounds (ft./lbs.) or inch-pounds (in./lbs.). The metric measurement unit for torque is the Newton-meter (Nm). This unit—the Nm—will be used for all SI metric torque references, both the present ft./lbs. and in./lbs.

To convert foot-pounds (ft./lbs.) to Newton-meters: multiply ft./lbs. by 1.3
To convert inch-pounds (in./lbs.) to Newton-meters: multiply in./lbs. by .11

ft./lbs.	N-m	ft./lbs	N-m	ft./lbs.	N-m	ft./lbs.	N-m
0.1	0.1	33	44.7	74	100.3	115	155.9
0.2	0.3	34	46.1	75	101.7	116	157.3
0.3	0.4	35	47.4	76	103.0	117	158.6
0.4	0.5	36	48.8	77	104.4	118	160.0
0.5	0.7	37	50.7	78	105.8	119	161.3
0.6	0.8	38	51.5	79	107.1	120	162.7
0.7	1.0	39	52.9	80	108.5	121	164.0
0.8	1.1	40	54.2	81	109.8	122	165.4
0.9	1.2	41	55.6	82	111.2	123	166.8
1	1.3	42	56.9	83	112.5	124	168.1
2	2.7	43	58.3	84	113.9	125	169.5
3	4.1	44	59.7	85	115.2	126	170.8
4	5.4	45	61.0	86	116.6	127	172.2
5	6.8	46	62.4	87	118.0	128	173.5
6	8.1	47	63.7	88	119.3	129	174.9
7	9.5	48	65.1	89	120.7	130	176.2
8	10.8	49	66.4	90	122.0	131	177.6
9	12.2	50	67.8	91	123.4	132	179.0
10	13.6	51	69.2	92	124.7	133	180.3
11	14.9	52	70.5	93	126.1	134	181.7
12	16.3	53	71.9	94	127.4	135	183.0
13	17.6	54	73.2	95	128.8	136	184.4
14	18.9	55	74.6	96	130.2	137	185.7
15	20.3	56	75.9	97	131.5	138	187.1
16	21.7	57	77.3	98	132.9	139	188.5
17	23.0	58	78.6	99	134.2	140	189.8
18	24.4	59	80.0	100	135.6	141	191.2
19	25.8	60	81.4	101	136.9	142	192.5
20	27.1	61	82.7	102	138.3	143	193.9
21	28.5	62	84.1	103	139.6	144	195.2
22	29.8	63	85.4	104	141.0	145	196.6
23	31.2	64	86.8	105	142.4	146	198.0
24	32.5	65	88.1	106	143.7	147	199.3
25	33.9	66	89.5	107	145.1	148	200.7
26	35.2	67	90.8	108	146.4	149	202.0
27	36.6	68	92.2	109	147.8	150	203.4
28	38.0	69	93.6	110	149.1	151	204.7
29	39.3	70	94.9	111	150.5	152	206.1
30	40.7	71	96.3	112	151.8	153	207.4
31	42.0	72	97.6	113	153.2	154	208.8
32	43.4	73	99.0	114	154.6	155	210.2

METRIC TABLES

GENERAL CONVERSION TABLE

Multiply By	To Convert	To	—
Length			
2.54	Inches	Centimeters	.3937
25.4	Inches	Millimeters	.03937
30.48	Feet	Centimeters	.0328
.304	Feet	Meters	3.28
.914	Yards	Meters	1.094
1.609	Miles	Kilometers	.621
Volume			
.473	Pints	Liters	2.11
.946	Quarts	Liters	1.06
3.785	Gallons	Liters	.264
.016	Cubic inches	Liters	61.02
16.39	Cubic inches	Cubic cms.	.061
28.3	Cubic feet	Liters	.0353
Mass (Weight)			
28.35	Ounces	Grams	.035
.4536	Pounds	Kilograms	2.20
Area			
.645	Square inches	Square cms.	.155
.836	Square yds.	Square meters	1.196
Force			
4.448	Pounds	Newtons	.225
.138	Ft./lbs.	Kilogram/meters	7.23
1.36	Ft./lbs.	Newton-meters	.737
.112	In./lbs.	Newton-meters	8.844
Pressure			
.068	Psi	Atmospheres	14.7
6.89	Psi	Kilopascals	.145
Other			
1.104	Horsepower (DIN)	Horsepower (SAE)	.9861
.746	Horsepower (SAE)	Kilowatts (KW)	1.34
1.60	Mph	Km/h	.625
.425	Mpg	Km/1	2.35
—	To obtain	From	Multiply by

TAP DRILL SIZES

NATIONAL COARSE OR U.S.S.						NATIONAL FINE OR S.A.E.					
Screw & Tap Size	Threads Per Inch	Use Drill Number	Screw & Tap Size	Threads Per Inch	Use Drill Number	Screw & Tap Size	Threads Per Inch	Use Drill Number	Screw & Tap Size	Threads Per Inch	Use Drill Number
No. 5	40	39	1/2	13	27/64	No. 5	44	37	1/2	20	29/64
No. 6	32	36	9/16	12	31/64	No. 6	40	33	9/16	18	33/64
No. 8	32	29	5/8	11	17/32	No. 8	36	29	5/8	18	37/64
No. 10	24	25	3/4	10	21/32	No. 10	32	21	3/4	16	11/16
No. 12	24	17	7/8	9	49/64	No. 12	28	15	7/8	14	13/16
1/4	20	8	1	8	7/8	1/4	28	3	1 1/8	12	1 3/64
5/16	18	F	1 1/8	7	63/64	5/16	24	1	1 1/4	12	1 11/64
3/8	16	5/16	1 1/4	7	1 7/64	3/8	24	Q	1 1/2	12	1 27/64
7/16	14	U	1 1/2	6	1 11/32	7/16	20	W			